Santa Clara County Free Library

REFERENCE

not to ct when
superseded

 58 16

WHO'S WHO IN CALIFORNIA

Biographical Reference Works
Published by
The Who's Who Historical Society

Who's Who In California

Who's Who In California Business and Finance

Who's Who Dining and Lodging on the North American Continent

Who's Who In Los Angeles County

Who's Who Executives in California

WHO'S WHO
In California.®

The Fifteenth Edition
1985-1986

Published By
THE WHO'S WHO HISTORICAL SOCIETY

SAN CLEMENTE, CALIFORNIA 92672

FIFTEENTH EDITION
Sarah Vitale, Editor

Library of Congress Catalog Card Number 56-1715

International Standard Book Number 0-9603166-4-7

International Standard Serial Number 0511-8948

PRINTED IN THE UNITED STATES OF AMERICA

Contents

Dedication VI
Honorary Board of Directors VII
Guide to Biographical Profiles VIII
Abbreviations IX
Biographies 1

Dedication

Immortality is not a gift,
Immortality is an achievement;
And only those who strive mightily
Shall possess it.

— Edgar Lee Masters

Honorary Board of Directors

Guide To Biographies

The biographical profiles in **WHO'S WHO IN CALIFORNIA** are arranged alphabetically according to the surname of the biographee. Where identical surnames occur, the first given name is used. If both surname and first given name are identical, the second given name is used to arrange the names alphabetically.

In the case of compound hyphenated surnames, profiles are arranged according to the first member of the compound.

Some biographees delete part of their full name in ordinary usage. In those instances parentheses are used to indicate that portion of the name which is deleted. For example, SMITH, J(OHN) indicates that the usual form of the name is J. Smith.

Each biographical profile is uniformly composed of the following data, hereby offered in chronological order as a convenient guide:

1. Name
2. Occupation
3. Birthdate and Place
4. Parents
5. Education
6. Marriage
7. Children
8. Career
9. Career-Related Activities
10. Awards and Honors
11. Memberships
12. Creative Works
13. Military Record
14. Political Affiliation
15. Religious Affiliation
16. Hobbies/Recreation
17. Residence Address
18. Office Address

Abbreviations

A.A. Associate in Arts
AAAS American Association for the Advancement of Science
A. and M. Agricultural and Mechanical
AAU Amateur Athletic Union
AAUP American Association of University Professors
AAUW American Association of University Women
A.B. Arts, Bachelor of
AB Alberta
ABC American Broadcasting Company
AC Air Corps
acad. academy
ACLU American Civil Liberties Union
A.C.P. American College of Physicians
A.C.S. American College of Surgeons.
ADA American Dental Association
adj. adjunct, adjutant
adj. gen. adjutant general
adm. admiral
adminstr. administrator
adminstrn. administration
adminstrv. administrative
adv. advocate
advt. advertising
AEC Atomic Energy Commission
aero. aeronautical, aeronautic
AFB Air Force Base
AFL-CIO American Federation of Labor and Congress of Industrial Organizations
AFTRA American Federation TV and Radio Artists
agri. agricultural, agriculture
AIA American Institute of Architects
AIEE American Institute of Electrical Engineers
AIM American Institute of Management
AK Alaska
AL Alabama
ALA American Library Association
Ala. Alabama
A.M. Arts, Master of
Am. American, America
AMA American Medical Association
A.M.E. African Methodist Episcopal
Amer., America, American
Amtrak National Railroad Passenger Corporation
anat. anatomical, anatomy
ANTA American National Theatre and Academy
anthrop. anthropological
AP Associated Press
APO Army Post Office
apptd. appointed
AR Arkansas
ARC American Red Cross
archeol. archeological
archtl. architectural
Ariz. Arizona
Ark. Arkansas
Arts D. Arts, Doctor of
arty. artillery
ASCAP American Society of Composers, Authors and Publishers
ASCE American Society of Civil Engineers
ASME American Society of Mechanical Engineers
assn. association

assoc., associate, associated
asst. assistant
ASTM American Society for Testing and Materials
astron. astronomical
ATSC Air Technical Service Command
AT&T American Telephone & Telegraph Company
atty. attorney
AUS Army of the United States
aux. Auxiliary
Ave. Avenue
AVMA American Veterinary Medical Association
AZ Arizona

B. Bachelor
b. born
B.A. Bachelor of Arts
B. Agr. Bachelor of Agriculture
Bapt. Baptist
B.Arch. Bachelor of Architecture
B.S.A. Bachelor of Agricultural Science
B.B.A. Bachelor of Business Administration
BBC British Broadcasting Corporation
B.C., British Columbia
B.C.E. Bachelor of Civil Engineering
B.Chir., Bachelor of Surgery
B.C.L. Bachelor of Civil Law
B.C.S. Bachelor of Commercial Science
B.D. Bachelor of Divinity
bd. board
B.E. Bachelor of Education
B.E.E. Bachelor of Electrical Engineering
B.F.A. Bachelor of Fine Arts
bibl. biblical
bibliog. bibliographical
biog. biographical
biol. biological
B.J. Bachelor of Journalism
B.L. Bachelor of Letters
bldg. building
B.L.S. Bachelor of Library Science
Blvd. Boulevard
bn. battalion
bot. botanical
B.P.E. Bachelor of Physical Education
br. branch
B.R.E. Bachelor of Religious Education
brig. gen. brigadier general
Brit. British, Britannica
Bro. Brother
B.S. Bachelor of Science
B.S.A. Bachelor of Agricultural Science
BSA Boy Scouts of America
B.S.D. Bachelor of Didactic Science
B.S.T. Bachelor of Sacred Theology
B.Th. Bachelor of Theology
bur. bureau
bus. business

CA California
CAA Civil Aeronautics Administration
CAB Civil Aeronautics Board
Calif. California
Cal Tech, California Institute of Technology

Can. Canada
CAP Civil Air Patrol
capt. captain
Cath. Catholic
cav. cavalry
CBC Canadian Broadcasting System
CBI China, Burma, India Theatre of Operations
CBS Columbia Broadcasting System
CCC Commodity Credit Corporation
CD Civil Defense
C.E. Corps of Engineers
CEO Chief Executive Officer
ch. church
Ch.D. Doctor of Chemistry
chem. chemical
Chem. E. Chemical Engineer
Chgo. Chicago
chmn. chairman
chpt. chapter
CIA Central Intelligence Agency
CIC Counter Intelligence Corps
clin. clinical
clk. clerk
C.L.U. Chartered Life Underwriter
C.M. Master in Surgery
CO Colorado
CMA, California Medical Association
Co., Company, County
C. of C. Chamber of Commerce
col. colonel
coll. college
Colo. Colorado
com. committee
comd. commanded
comdg. commanding
comdr. commander
commd. commissioned
comml. commercial
commn. commission
commr. commissioner
Conf. Conference
Conn. Connecticut
cons. consultant, consulting
consol. consolidated
constl. constitutional
constn. constitution
constrn. construction
contbd. contributed
contbg. contributing
contbr. contributor
Conv. Convention
coop., co-op. cooperative
CORE Congress of Racial Equality
corp. corporation
corr. correspondent, corresponding
C.P.A. Certified Public Accountant
C.P.H. Certificate of Public Health
cpl. corporal
CSC Civil Service Commission
ct. court
C.Z. Canal Zone

d. daughter
D. Doctor
D.Agr. Doctor of Agriculture
D.A.R. Daughters of the American Revolution
dau. daughter
DAV Disabled American Veterans
D.C., DC District of Columbia
D.C.L. Doctor of Civil Law
D.C.S. Doctor of Commercial Science
D.D. Doctor of Divinity
D.D.S. Doctor of Dental Surgery
DE Delaware
dec. deceased
def. defense

Del. Delaware
del. delegate, delegation
Dem. Democrat., Democratic
D.Eng. Doctor of Engineering
dep. deputy
dept. department
desc. descendant
devel. development
D.F.A. Doctor of Fine Arts
D.F.C. Distinguished Flying Cross
D.H.L. Doctor of Hebrew Literature
dir. director
dist. district
distbg. distributing
distbn. distribution
distbr. distributor
div. division, divinity, divorce
D.Litt. Doctor of Literature
D.M.D. Doctor of Medical Dentistry
D.M.S. Doctor of Medical Science
D.O. Doctor of Osteopathy
Dr. Drive
D.R.E. Doctor of Religious Education
D.S.C. Distinguished Service Cross
D.Sc. Doctor of Science
D.S.M. Distinguished Service Medal
D.S.T. Doctor of Sacred Theology
D.V.M. Doctor of Veterinary Medicine
D.V.S. Doctor of Veterinary Surgery

E. East
Eccles. Ecclesiastical
ecol. ecological
econ., economic, economy
E.D. Doctor of Engineering
ed., educated, editor
Ed.B. Bachelor of Education
Ed.D. Doctor of Education
edit. edition
Ed.M. Master of Education
edn. education
ednl. educational
EDP electronic data processing
E.E. Electrical Engineer
elec. electrical
ency. encyclopedia
Eng. England, English
engr. engineer
engring. engineering
environ. environmental
EPA Environmental Protection Agency
Episc. Episcopalian.
ERDA Energy Research and Development
    Administration
ETO European Theatre of Operations
Evang. Evangelical
exam. examination, examining
exec. executive
exhib., exhibit, exhibition
expt. experiment
exptl. experimental

F.A. Field Artillery
FAA Federal Aviation Administration
FBI Federal Bureau of Investigation
FCA Farm Credit Administration
FCC Federal Communication Commission
FDA Food and Drug Administration
FDIA Federal Deposit Insurance Administration
FDIC Federal Deposit Insurance Corporation
F.E. Forest Engineer
fed. federal
fedn. federation
fgn. foreign
FHA Federal Housing Administration
fin. financial, finance

FL Florida
Fla. Florida
FMC Federal Maritime Commission
found. foundation
FPC Federal Power Commission
FPO Fleet Post Office
frat., fraternity, fraternal
FRS Federal Reserve System
Ft. Fort
FTC Federal Trade Commission, Federal Tariff
    Commission

Ga., GA Georgia
GAO General Accounting Office
gastroent. gastroenterological
gen. general
geneal. genealogical
geod. geodetic
geog. geographic, geographical
geol. geological
geophys. geophysical
gerontol. gerontological
gov. governor
govt. government
govtl. governmental
grad. graduate
GSA General Services Administration
Gt. Great
GU Guam
gynecol. gynecological

hdqrs. headquarters
HEW Department of Health, Education and Welfare
H.H.D. Doctor of Humanities
HHFA Housing and Home Finance Agency
HI Hawaii
hist. historical, historic
H.M. Master of Humanics
hon. honorary, honorable
Ho. of Dels. House of Delegates
Ho. of Reps. House of Representatives
hort. horticultural
hosp. hospital
HUD Department of Housing and Urban Development
Hwy. Highway
H.S., High School

IA Iowa
IAEA International Atomic Energy Agency
IBM International Business Machines Corporation
ICC Interstate Commerce Commission
ID Idaho
IEEE Institute of Electrical and Electronics Engineers
IGY International Geophysical Year
IL Illinois
Ill. Illinois
ILO International Labor Organization
IMF International Monetary Fund
IN Indiana
Inc. Incorporated
incl. include, including
ind. independent
Ind. Indiana
indsl. industrial
inf. infantry
info. information
ins. insurance
insp. inspector
inst. institute
instr. instructor
Internatl. international
intro. introduction
I.R.E. Institute of Radio Engineers
IRS Internal Revenue Service
ITT International Telephone & Telegraph Corporation
J.D. Doctor of Jurisprudence

j.g. junior grade
jour. journal.
jr. junior

Kans. Kansas
K.C. Knights of Columbus
KS Kansas
K.T. Knight Templar
Ky., KY Kentucky

L.A. Los Angeles
lab. laboratory
L.A.C.C. Los Angeles City College
lang. language
LB Long Beach
lectr. lecturer
L.D.S. Latter-Day Saints
L.H.D. Doctor of Humane Letters
L.I. Long Island
lit. literary, literature
Litt.B. Bachelor of Letters
Litt.D. Doctor of Letters
LL.B. Bachelor of Laws
LL.D. Doctor of Laws
LL.M. Master of Laws
Ln. Lane
L.S. Library Science (in degree)
lt. lieutenant
Ltd. Limited
Luth. Lutheran

m. married
M. Master
M.A. Master of Arts
MA Massachusetts
mag. magazine
M.Agr. Master of Agriculture
maj. major
M.Arch. Master in Architecture
Mass. Massachusetts
math. mathematical
MATS Military Air Transport Service
M.B. Bachelor of Medicine
M.B.A. Master of Business Administration
MBS Mutual Broadcasting System
M.C. Medical Corps
M.C.E. Master of Civil Engineering
mcht. merchant
M.D. Doctor of Medicine
Md., MD Maryland
mdse. merchandise
M.D.V. Doctor of Veterinary Medicine
M.E. Mechanical Engineer
ME Maine
M.E. Ch. Methodist Episcopal Church
mech. mechanical
M.Ed. Master of Education
med. medical
M.E.E. Master of Electrical Engineering
mem. member, memorial
met. metropolitan
metall. metallurgical
meteorol. meteorological
Meth. Methodist
Mex. Mexico
M.F. Master of Forestry
M.F.A. Master of Fine Arts
mfg. manufacturing
mfr. manufacturer
mgmt. management
mgr. manager
M.I. Military Intelligence
MI Michigan
Mich. Michigan
mil. military

Minn. Minnesota
Miss. Mississippi
M.I.T. Massachusetts Institute of Technology
mktg. marketing
M.L. Master of Laws
M.Litt. Master of Literature
M.L.S. Master of Library Science
M.M.E. Master of Mechanical Engineering
MN Minnesota
mng. managing
Mo., MO Missouri

Mont. Montana
M.P. Member of Parliament
M.P.E. Master of Physical Education
M.P.H. Master of Public Health
M.P.L. Master of Patent Law
M.R.E. Master of Religious Education
M.S. Master of Science
MS Mississippi
M.Sc. Master of Science
M.S.F. Master of Science of Forestry
M.S.T. Master of Sacred Theology
M.S.W. Master of Social Work
MT Montana
Mt. Mount
mus. museum, musical
Mus.B. Bachelor of Music
Mus.D. Doctor of Music
Mus.M. Master of Music

N. North
NAACP National Association for the Advancement of
    Colored People
N.Am. North America
NAM National Association of Manufacturers
NASA National Aeronautics and Space Administration
natl. national
NATO North Atlantic Treaty Organization
nav. navigation
NBC National Boradcasting Company
N.C., NC North Carolina
NCCJ National Conference of Christians and Jews
N.D., ND North Dakota
NE Nebraska
N.E. Northeast
NEA National Education Association
Nebr. Nebraska
neurol. neurological
Nev. Nevada
N.G. National Guard
N.H., NH New Hampshire
NIH National Institutes of Health
NIMH National Institute of Mental Health
N.J., NJ New Jersey
NLRB National Labor Relations Board
NM New Mexico
N.Mex. New Mexico
No. Northern
NORAD North American Air Defense
NOW National Organization for Women
NSC National Security Council
NSF National Science Foundation
NT Northwest Territories
numis. numismatic
NV Nevada
NW Northwest
N.Y., NY New York
N.Y.C. New York City
N.Z. New Zealand

OAS Organization of American States
obs. observatory
O.D. Doctor of Optometry
OEO Office of Economic Opportunity
O.E.S. Order of Eastern Star
ofcl. official

ofcr. officer
OH Ohio
OK Oklahoma
Okla. Oklahoma
ophthal. ophthalmological
ops. operations
OR Oregon
orch. orchestra
Oreg. Oregon
OSS Office of Strategic Services

Pa., PA Pennsylvania
P.C. Professional Corporation
Pasa., Pasadena
P.E.I. Prince Edward Island
PEN Poets, Playwrights, Editors, Essayists and Novelists
    (international association)
P.E.O. women's organization
pfc. private first class
PHA Public Housing Administration
pharm. Pharmaceutical
Pharm.D. Doctor of Pharmacy
Pharm.M. Master of Pharmacy
Ph.B. Bachelor of Philosophy
Ph.D. Doctor of Philosophy
Phila. Philadelphia
philos. philosophical
photog. photographic, photography
phys. physical
Pitts. Pittsburgh
Pl. Place
P.O. Post Office
P.O.B. Post Office Box
polit. political, politics
poly. polytechnic
prep. preparatory
pres. president
Presbyn. Presbyterian
prin. principal
proc. proceedings
prod. produced, producer
prof. professor
profl. professional
propr. proprietor
pro tem pro tempore
psychiat. psychiatric
psychol. psychological
PTA Parent-Teachers Association
pub. publisher, publishing, public
publ. publication
pvt. private

RCA Radio Corporation of America
rec. recreation
recd. received
ref. reference
rehab. rehabilitation
Rel., Religion, Rels.,
Rels., Relations
rep. representative
Repub. Republican
Res. residence
ret. retired
rev. review, revised
Rom. Cath., Roman Catholic
R.I., RI Rhode Island
R.N. Registered Nurse
ROTC Reserve Officers Training Corps
R.R. Railroad
Ry. Railway

s. son
S. South
SAC Strategic Air Command
S.A.G. Screen Actors Guild
SALT Strategic Arms Limitation Talks

S.Am. South America
san. sanitary
SAR Sons of the American Revolution
savs. savings
S.B. Bachelor of Science, Santa Barbara
SBA Small Business Administration
S.C., SC South Carolina
Sc.B. Bachelor of Science
Sc.D. Doctor of Science
sch. school
sci. science, scientific
S.D., San Diego
Sacto., Sacramento
SE Southeast
SEATO Southeast Asia Treaty Organization
secty. secretary
SEC Securities and Exchange Commission
sect. section
S.F. San Francisco
sem. seminary
Sen. Senator
sgt. sergeant
sis. Sister
S.J. Society of Jesus (Jesuit)
S.M. Master of Science
So. Southern
soc. society
sociol. sociological
sor. sorority
spec. special, specialist
splty. specialty
Sq. Square
sr. senior
S.R. Sons of the Revolution
S.S. Steamship
St. Saint, street
sta. station
S.T.B. Bachelor of Sacred Theology
S.T.D. Doctor of Sacred Theology
subs. subsidiary
supr. supervisor
supt. superintendent
surg. surgical, surgery, surgeon
SW Southwest
sym. symphony
syn. syndicate

tchr. teacher
tech. technical, technology
Tel. Telephone
temp. temporary
Tenn. Tennessee
Ter. Territory
Terr. Terrace
Tex. Texas
Th.D., Doctor of Theology
theol. theological, theology
Th.M. Master of Theology
TN Tennessee
tng. training
trans. transaction, transferred
transl. translation, translated
transp. transportation
treas. treasurer
TV television
TVA Tennessee Valley Authority
twp. township
TX Texas

U. University
UAW United Auto Workers
UCI University of California at Irvine
UCLA University of California at Los Angeles
UCSB University of California at Santa Barbara
UCSD University of California at San Diego

U.K. United Kingdom
UN United Nations
UNESCO United Nations Educational, Scientific and
    Cultural Organization
UNICEF United Nations International Children's
    Emergency Fund
univ. University
UPI United Press International
U.S. United States
U.S.A. United States of America
USAAF United States Army Air Force
USAF United States Air Force
USAFR United States Air Force Reserve
USAR United States Army Reserve
USC University of Southern California
USCG United States Coast Guard
USCGR United States Coast Guard Reserve
USIA United States Information Agency
USMC United States Marine Corps
USMCR United States Marine Corps Reserve
USN United States Navy
USNR United States Naval Reserve
USO United Service Organizations
USPHS United States Public Health Service
U.S.S. United States Ship
USSR Union of the Soviet Socialist Republics
UT Utah

VA Veterans Administration
Va., VA Virginia
vet. veteran
VFW Veterans of Foreign Wars
vice pres. vice president
vis. visiting
VISTA Volunteers in Service to America
vocat. vocational
vol. volunteer
v.p. vice president
vs versus
Vt., VT Vermont

W. West
WA Washington
WAC Women's Army Corps
Wash. Washington
WAVES Women's Reserve, U.S. Naval Reserve
WHO World Health Organization
WI Wisconsin
Wis. Wisconsin
WV West Virginia
W. Va. West Virginia
WY Wyoming
Wyo. Wyoming

YMCA Young Men's Christian Association
YMHA Young Men's Hebrew Association
YM & YWHA Young Men's and Young Women's
    Hebrew Association
Y.T., YT Yukon Territory
YWCA Young Women's Christian Association
yr. year

zool. zoological

---, to date

WHO'S WHO IN CALIFORNIA

ABARBANEL, GAIL, rape treatment center director; b. April 17, 1944, Los Angeles; d. Sam X. and Sylvia (Cramer) Abarbanel; m. Stephen Klein, Jan. 1, 1975; edn: BA, UCLA 1966, MSW, USC 1968; LCSW, 1970. Career: clin. social wkr, Jewish Big Brothers, 1968-74; dir. Social Svcs. and Rape Treatment Center, Santa Monica Hosp. Med. Ctr., 1974--; dir. Dept. of Community and Social Svcs. 1982--; faculty LAPD Tng. Acad.; cons. to bus., govt. agencies, t.v. and media; lectr. various univs., profl. tng. seminars. Bd. dirs.: Clare Found. 1975-77, Am. Cancer Soc. 1975-79, Child Trauma Council 1978-81, Senior Health Peer Counseling Ctr. 1982-84; awards: NIMH grantee; Phi Beta Kappa 1966; Pi Gamma Mu 1966; nat. recognition, Am. Cancer Soc. 1977; Woman of Year, YWCA 1980, 82; USC alumni awd. 1979; Status of Women Award, AAUW, 1979; Agcy. of Year Awd., Nat. Assn. of Soc. Wkrs, 1980; highest commend., Calif. State Senate, 1980. Mem: Women In Health, Soc. for Hosp. Soc. Work Dirs., AHA, Nat. Orgn. for Victim Assistance, Soc. for Clin. Soc. Work, NOW, Calif. Sexual Assault Investigators, Am. Orthopsychiat. Soc. Publs: num. arts. and book chpts. on rape treatment; two books: Being Safe, Protection Yourself, Your Family and Your Home; Taking Action: What To Do If You Are Raped; award winning film RAPE: Caring for the Victim (prod. NIMH); re-wrote Calif. rape statute (1980). rec: cooking, travel; ofc: Santa Monica Hospital, 1225 15th St., Santa Monica 90404.

ABATECOLA, VITTORIO, financial planner; b. Nov. 6, 1939, Pico, Italy, nat. 1961; s. Giovanni and Alessandra (Conti) A.; m. Elizabeth Louise Grima, June 1, 1963; children: Michael, b. 1964, Robert, b. 1966, John, b. 1968, Julie, b. 1974; edn: Providence Coll. 1959-60, USAFI 1960-63, Inst. of Rel. Sci. & Philosophy 1970-73. Career: vice pres./secty. Abatecola Constrn. Co., Inc., E. Prov., R.I. 1965-68; dist. sales mgr. Los Angeles Area, Allstate Ins. Co., 1968-75; prodn. mgr./finl. planner, Travelers Corp., Stockton 1966--; prin. Central Calif. Sch. of Italian Language & Culture, 1979-82; mem: Nat. Assn. of Life Underwriters 1970-; Internat. Assn. for Finl. Planning (v.p. Stockton chpt. 1979); Inst. for Cert. Fin. Planners 1982; Big Brothers 1970-72, Webelos Leader 1972-74; mil: E4 USAF 1960-64, GCM; Res: 15912 Linn Rd Lodi 95240 Ofc: The Travelers Corp. 555 W. Ben Holt Dr Ste. 100, Stockton 95207

ABBAS, RICHARD ORANT, computer manufacturing co. executive/C.P.M., senior buyer; b. Aug. 6, 1951, Oakland; s. Orant and Constance (Romero) Abbas, edn: AA in electronics tech., 1972, AA in supervision, 1980, Chabot Coll. Career: electronic technician Lloyd M. McKinney Assocs. Inc., San Leandro 1972-73, Security Devices div. Systron Donner, Dublin 1973-75, Qantel Corp., Hayward 1975-78; buyer MDS Qantel, a Mohawd Data Scis. Co., Hayward 1978--, C.P.M. senior buyer, 1983-; instr. in-house tng. in Computer Repair/ Jr. Buyer tng./ Security Systems and Debit Process, MDS-Qantel, 1975-; Mem: Nat. Assn. of Purch. Mgmt. (NAPM cert. 1982); Purch. Mgmt. Assn. of No. Calif.; Baptist (chmn. bd. trustees 1972-83, past chmn. bd. deacons); rec: sing, camp, fish, hike; Res: 1526 Fir Ave. San Leandro 94578 Ofc: 4142 Point Eden Way Hayward 94545

ABBETT, J. CONRAD, company president; b. July 30, 1927, San Francisco; s. Geo. W. and Aileen (Sullivan) A.; m. Diana, Aug. 25, 1951; two sons: Jeffrey B., b. 1953, Gregory W., b. 1956; edn: Menlo Coll. 1945, Univ. of Gonzaga 1945-46, Univ. Calif. 1946. Career: empl. Abbett Electric Corp., San Francisco 1947--, pres. 1983--; dir./pres. Electrical Industry Depository of No. Calif.; dir. S.F. Electrical Contractors Assn.; mem. Chamber of Commerce S.F., Calif., and U.S., Electric Club of S.F., Pacific Coast Elec. Assoc.; clubs: Bohemian (SF), Meadow (Fairfax); mil: USN WWII; Republican; Prot.; rec: hunting, golf. Res: 9 Deer Park, San Rafael 94901 Ofc: Abbett Electric Corp. 1850 Bryant St San Francisco 94110

ABBOTT, G. LANSING, company executive; b. Mar. 21, 1927, White Plains, NY; s. Alfred Houghton and Helen Alithia (Glasier) B.; m. Nancy Jorgensen, Nov. 8, 1968; children: Jeff, b. 1970, Jennifer, b. 1972; edn: Univ. of Buffalo 1946-49. Career: sales mgr. Long-Lok Corp., Los Angeles; vice pres. Rockford Screw Products, Montebello (12 years); general mgr. Abbott Screw Products, City of Industry, currently; mil: Navy Air Corps 1945; Congregational; rec: skiing, boating. Res: 15528 Cristalino St Hacienda Heights 91745 Ofc: 15865-B Gale Ave City of Industry 91745

ABBOTT, LEAL M., social worker; b. Aug. 16, 1940, St. Joseph, Mo.; d. Bryce C. and Phyllis M. Abbott; children: Bernadine, Kris and Robert Luetgens; edn: BA, Hofstra Univ. 1973; MSW, Aldephi Univ. Sch. of S.W. 1976; LCSW, Calif. Bd. Behav. Hlth. Scis. 1981. Career: Long Beach Project coordinator, Southeast Nassau Guidance Center, SEaford, NY 1976-78; clinic coord. Mohave Mental Health Clinic, Lake Havasu City, Az. 1978-80; dir. social services Mohave General Hosp., Kingman, Az. 1980-81; coord. Transitional Care Services Yolo Co. Mental Health Svcs. 1981--; mem. Yolo Co. Commn. to Prevent Violence Against Women; bd. dirs. Yolo Co. Sexual Assault & Battered Women's Ctr.; awards: Mental Health Practitioner of the Year, M.H. Assn.; Yolo Comm. Care Continuum's Awd. for Spl. Services; mem: Nat. Assn. of Soc. Wkrs., Mental Health Assn., Alliance for Mentally Ill, NOW. Res: 2657 Harkness St Sacto 95818 Ofc: Yolo County Mental Health Services, 213 W. Beamer St Woodland 95695

ABENOJA, NORMA LAGADI, convalescent hospital administrator; b. Jan. 30, 1938, Philippines; d. Elpidio A. and Remedios C. Lagadi; m. Marc Abenoja, Sept. 12, 1964; chil: Jenny, b. 1965, Steve, b. 1968, Marc Jr., b. 1971; edn: BS in nursing, San Juan De Dios Coll. of Nursing 1960; spl. profl. courses UCSD, UCLA; R.N.; lic. Adminstr. Nursing Home, 1981. Career: nurse supr. San Juan De Dios Coll. of Nursing, Phil.; head nurse, Ob-gyn. Scripps Meml. Hosp., La Jolla; dir. of nurses El Cajon Valley Nursing Center; dir. nursing service Del Mar Conv. Hosp., Rosemead; nurse evaluator State Dept. of Health, Los Angeles; currently owner/adminstr. Sacred Heart Conv. Hosp., Pasadena. Mem: Philippine Nurses Assn. (past sec.), Am. Coll. of Nursing Home Adminstrs., Council of Long Term Care Nurses, num. Filipino charitable orgns.; Catholic; rec: bowl, tennis; res: 2070 Dublin Dr. Glendale 91206 ofc: 1810 N. Fair Oaks Ave, Pasadena 91103.

ABERCROMBIE, JERRY TUCKER, real estate executive; b. Sept. 13, 1930, Beloit, Kans.; s. Homer T. and Sarah Rosanna (Tucker) A.; m. Bethel Susan Sachs, Dec. 22, 1951; children: Jerry, b. 1953, Kerry, b. 1957; edn: engring., Univ. of Kans. 1948-50; BS (naval sci.) US Naval Postgrad. Sch. 1965; MBA (real estate mgmt.) National Univ. 1979; DBA (internat. bus. adm.) US Internat. Univ. 1983; Adv. R.E. Cert., UCSD 1982. R.E. Broker lic. Calif. 1972; Life Instr. Credential (R.E., Bus. and Indsl. Mgmt.) Calif. Comm. Colls. 1980; CPM (cert. prop. mgr.), Nat. Assn. of Realtors 1982. Career: served to Comdr. USN, 1951-78 (Navy Commend., Bronze Star): naval aviator, test pilot (piloted 87 models of aircraft), cmdg. ofcr. overseas Naval air station; spec. in tactical unit, indsl. and facility mgmt.; real estate broker, comml. & resdtl. income; fmr. v.p./mgr. Trust R.E. Services Dept., California First Bank, San Diego; v.p. R.E. Mgmt. Div., Bank of Am., San Diego 1984--; adj. faculty (R.E.) Nat. Univ. 1983--; mem: Inst. of R.E. Mgmt. (treas. 1984); San Diego Bd. of Realtors; Building Owners and Mgrs. Assn.; S.D. Apartment Assn.; Masons, Scottish Rite, Lions Intl.; publs: U.S.Naval Aviation News (1972); Republican; Prot.; rec: lapidary. Res: 4325 Vista Way La Mesa 92041 Ofc: Bank of America, Real Estate Mgmt. Div. 450 B St, Ste 1480, San Diego 92101

ABERNETHY, JOHN LEO, professor of chemistry; b. Mar. 6, 1916, San Jose, CA; s. Elmer R. and Margaret May (Scott) Abernethy; BA, UCLA, 1936; MS, 1938 and PhD, 1940, Northwestern Univ.; res. assoc., Med. Ctr. UCLA. Career: asst. prof. Univ. of Texas, 1940-45; res. State Univ. System, 1950-78; vis. assoc. prof. of chem. Claremont Men's Coll., 1961-61; Fulbright Fellow, San Marcos Univ., Lima, Peru 2962-63; res. assoc. UC Davis, 2963-64; taught Navy V-12 students, Univ. of Texas, 2942-45. Editorial bd. Journ of Chem. Education, 1956--; proceedings editor Calif Assn of Chem. Teachers; author: resrch papers on stereochemistry, enzyme catalysis, papain, Jour Chromatography; edn. papers, Journ Chem. Edn.,1940-; text: Principles of Organic Chem., CACT Proceedings Editor,Calif Assn of Chem. Teachers, 1966-. Resrch grants: NSF, Sigma Xi, Research Corp., Radiation Research, Lab. Nuclear Med., UCLA. Mem: pres. Sigma Xi Club, 1970-71; Alpha Chi Sigma, 1935; Phi Lambda Upsilon, 1938; Republican; Presbyterian; rec: recent publications and bio-organic chem. Res: Chandler Terrace, 2555 Sixth St, La Verne 91750 Ofc: Chem. Dept., Calif State Polytechnic Univ., Pomona 91768.

ABERNETHY, ROBERT GORDON, news correspondent; b. Nov. 5, 1927, Geneva, Switzerland; s. Robet William and Lois May (Jones) Abernethy; ed. A.B. Princeton Univ., 1950; M.P.A., 1952; Woodrow Wilson Sch. of Pub. and Internatl. Affairs; m. Jean Clarke Montgomery, Arcadia, FL, Apr. 30, 1955 (dec. April 1980); chil.: Jane Montgomery, b. 1957. Career: Editor, NBC News, Wash., 1952−55; NBC corr.: London, England 1955−58; Wash. 1958−56; Los Angeles 1966−77; anchorman, KNBC's "Sixth Hour News," 1968−70; Wash. corr., TODAY Show, 1977−80. Wrote and narrated NBC wkly. TV report, "Update," 1961−63. Author: Introduction To Tomorrow, publ. by Harcourt, Brace & World, 1966; A Primer on Communism, Many Shades of Black, TV documentaries, AUS 1946−48. Trustee, Princeton Univ., 1974−77. Awards: Thomas Alva Edison Mass Media Award, best Am. hist. for youth, 1966; Hon. Mayor of Pac. Palisades, 1971. United Ch. of Christ. Office: 4001 Nebraska Ave., N.W., Wash, D.C. 20016.

ABERNETHY, ROBERT JOHN, real estate developer; b. Feb. 28, 1940, Indpls.; s. George Lawrence and Helen Sarah (McLandress) A.; edn: BS, Johns Hopkins Univ. 1962, MBA, Harvard Univ. 1963; certs. in real estate fin., constrn., UCLA; DPMA, Cert. Data Processor, 1968. Career: adminstv. asst. to nat. deputy campaign mgr. Humphrey for Pres. Campaign, 1968; asst. to the chief scientist Phoenix Missile Pgm., Hughes Aircraft Co., 1968-9, asst. pgm. mgr. Iroquois Night Fighter and Night Tracker Pgm. 1969-71, asst. to the controller of Space and Communications Gp. 1971, controller Technology Div. 1972-74; pres. American Standard Devel. Co., Los Angeles 1974--. Dir.: Century Thrift and Loan 1982-, Self Storage Mgmt. Co. 19;76-, Marathon Nat. Bank 1982-, Storage Equities 1980-, Los Angeles Bancorp 1982-, Self-Service Storage Assn. (National: dir. 1980-3, v.p. 82-83; Region 2: dir. 1977-83, v.p. 82-83). Mem: YMCA (treas. 1982-3), Harvard Bus. School Scholarship Trust (dir. 1973-), Town Hall, L.A. World Affairs Council; clubs: Calif. Yacht, St. Francis Yacht, Jonathan, Harvard Bachelors, Stanford Bachelors; mil: lt. USN 1962-66; Democrat; Presbyterian; rec: sailing, skiing; res: 5800 W. Century Bl. Los Angeles 90009 ofc: Am. Standard Devel. Co., 5221 102nd St. Los Angeles 90045.

ABOU-SAMRA, MOUSTAPHA, neurosurgeon; b. July 11, 1947, Damascus, Syria, nat. 1980; s. Chafik Mohammad and Riad (Nassri) A.; m. Joan morrison, Aug. 18, 1973; children: Omar, b. 1977, Leyla, b. 1978, Jason, b. 1979, Jamie, b. 1981, Patricia, b. 1983; edn: MD, Univ. of Damascus Med. Sch. 1972. Career:

intern Perth Amboy Gen. Hosp. 1972-73; gen surg. resident College Hosp., Newark NJ 1973-75; neurosurgery res. Univ. of Tex. Health Sci. Center, San Antonio 1975-80; asst. prof. neurological surg., Div. of Neurosurg./Dept. of Surg., Univ. of Tx. 1980-81; currently, pvt. practice neurological surgery, Ventura, Calif. Board Cert. Am. Bd. Neurolog. Surg.; mem. Cong. of Neurolog. Surgeons, Am. Assn. of Neurolog. Surgeons, Am. Coll. of Surgeons, AMA, Am. Cancer Soc.; Republican; rec: music, tennis. Res: 7444 Jackson, Ventura 93003 Ofc: 100 N. Brent, Ste. 201, Ventura 93003

ABPLANALP, DELLOY ORVAL, holistic health co. owner; b. Nov. 28, 1931, Salt Lake City; s. Orval Ross and Elva Bernice (Hatch) A.; m. Kathleen Thurman, 1959; chil: Denise, b. 1960, David, b. 1962, Matthew, b. 1969; grandchil: Elena, b. 1978, Elizabeth, b. 1980, Daniel, b. 1982; edn: BS, Brigham Young Univ. 1959; elem., sec. teaching cred. Career: church mission svc., Ch. of Jesus Christ of L.D.S., 1951-53; school tchr. 1959-61; acctg. & payroll, L.A. City Fire Dept. and Dept. Water & Power, 1961-74; tchg. holistic health, 1974--; mgr./ dir. five herb cos. Awards: Million Dollar Club, Amtec Ind. (4); sales, leadershp, Natures Sunshine Prods. 1979; mem: Delta Phi 1955-9, Nat. Health Fedn. 1970-, L.D.S. Sociables 1965-70; publs: Holistic Health Bklet (1977), Dial An Herb Wheel (1976); mil: pfc Army Sig. Corps; Democrat (co. chmn. 1959); L.D.S. Ch. (elder, tchr.); rec: AYSO coach, referee; ofc: Holistic Hlth Integ., 4917 N. Baldwin Ave. Temple City 91780.

ABRAMS, HAL, marketing company president; b. Apr. 9, 1936, Brooklyn, NY; s. Louis and Hannah (Pekarsky) A.; children: Carrie, b. 1962, Michelle, b. 1964; edn: BA, mktg., S.F State Univ. 1960; S.F Law Sch. 1970. Career: sales mgr. Metro Molding Corp., Cleveland, Oh. 1964-65; dist. mgr. Knapp Monarch, St. Louis, Mo. 1961-64; dist. mgr. Concord Electronics, Los Angeles 1965-69; formed mfr's rep. co. as partner/v.p. C.M.A., Los Angeles 1969-75; founder/pres. Hal Abrams Marketing Inc., San Mateo (mfr's rep. co. for No. Calif. and No. Nev.), 1975--; tchr., lectr. mktg., pvt. meetings. Recipient Rep of the Year awards: Ampex (1977, 78), TDK (1980, 82), Harada (1980, 81, 82, 83), Sanyo (1976, 77, 80), Fisher (1976, 77), Concord (1979, 81, 82, 83); (wrote first order in USA for Sanyo Consumer Electronics with Macy's of Calif.); mem. Big Brothers; mil: pfc US Army 1955-57, Ger. (Army Basketball team); rec: tennis, marathon runner. Res: Five Goldenridge Ct. San Mateo 94402 Ofc: Hal Abrams Mktg Inc. 1206 S. Amphlett Blvd, Ste. 1, San Mateo 94402

ACHESON, LOUIS KRUZAN, JR., aerospace engineer; b. Apr. 2, 1926 Brazil, Ind.; s. Louis Kruzan and Irene Ruth (Morrison) A.; edn: BS in elec. eng. Case Inst of Tech,1946; PhD, theor. physics, M.I.T., 1950; m. Hyla Cook, July 12, 1958; chil: Mari, b. 1961, Willy, b. 1964. Career: tech. staff, currently sr. scientist Systems Labs., Space and Communications Gp., Hughes Aircraft Co., Los Angeles 1950--; Inst. for Defense Analyses (IDA), the Pentagon, 1958-9. Awards: Cady Staley awd, Case Inst of Tech. 1946; Dr. of Celestial Cerebration (Blue Sky Thinker) 1959; Adv. Resrch Projects Agcy Space (ARPA) awd to orgnzrs of US Missile and Space Pgm in First Yr of the Space Age, Wash DC; Destination 90 Awd, 1968, Plnng. Dirs. Co. and City, Los Angeles, Burbank, San Fernando; Maharishi Awd. 1979, World Govt of the Age of Enlightenment; mem: Soc for Gen Systems Resrch, Am. Physical Soc., Am. Geophysical Union, Am. Inst of Aero and Astro., Brit. Interplanetary Soc., AAAS, World Federalists, Bertrand Russell Soc., ACLU, Mensa, Worldview Exploration Sem. (ed. 1970-80), Unity-in-Diversity Council, Sigma Xi, Tau Beta Pi, Eta Kappa Nu, Theta Tau, hon. frats., Sigma Chi (social); Publs: num sci., mil. system studies; arts. in Physical Rev., Internat Jour of Gen. Systems: Destination Ninety Forum Reports 1967-8; LAPD Studies, 1969; reports on payload requirements for sci. satellites and spacecraft, 1970-80; ed. Satellite Handbook for Remote Environ. and Weather Determination, vol 1, 1976, vol 2, 1980; ed. Internat. Cooperation Council mag. 1970-75, annual dir. 1970-79; Democrat; res: 17711 Marcello Pl. Encino 91316. ofc: Hughes Aircraft Co. S-41/B-325; POB 92919 Los Angeles 90009

ACORD, MICHAEL PATRICK, physician; b. Sept. 14, 1945, San Diego; s. Ira Patrick and Edythe Mae (Lewis) A.; m. Terry Abbott, Sept. 7, 1967; children: Sarah, b. 1969, Rachael, . 1973; edn: AB, zool., San Diego St. Coll. 1967; MA, biol. sci. UC Santa Barbara 1968; MD, UC Irvine- Cal. Coll. Med. 1975; Bd. Certified, Am. Bd. Phys. Med. and Rehab. 1979. Career: staff physiatrist Mem. Med. Ctr., Long Beach 1978-81, dir. Spinal Cord Injury Rehabilitation, MMCLB 1980--, dir. Memorial Pain Mgmt. Ctr. 1981--, assoc. dir. Dept. Rehab. Med., 1979--; asst. clin. prof. UCI-CCM, 1979-; cons. Long Beach VA Hosp.; mem: Am. Acad. of Physical Med., AMA, Am. Spinal Injury Assn., CMA, Internat. Assn. for the Study of Pain, L.A. County Med. Assn., So. Calif. Soc. of PM&R (pres. 1982-3), Am. Assn. for Study of Headache, Am. Pain Soc., Am. Acad. of Med. Directors; mem. Gov.'s Task Force on Long Term Care; lectr. profl. assns., mem. Mem. Hosp.- UCI Spkrs. Bureau; med. journal arts.; mil: Lcdr. USNR, active duty 1968-71; rec: photog. Res: 2141 Aster Pl Costa Mesa 92627 Ofc: Rehab. Assoc. Med. Grp. 2865 Atlantic, Ste. 106, Long Beach 90806

ACRE, JAMES ROBERT, JR.; metal products co. executive; b. Sept. 25, 1946, Centerville, Iowa; s. James Robert and Mildred Grace (Myers) Acre; m. Linda Chapman, Oct. 1965; chil: Eric, b. 1966, Michele, b. 1968, Lisa, b. 1972, Greg, b. 1975; edn: various courses, CSU San Diego, Mesa Jr. Coll., Paul Monroe Sch. of Hydraulics, S.D. Employers Assn., Reed Prentis Co.; Regis. Technician, Elox Tech. Sch., 1981. Career: assembly line The Vendo Co., Kansas City, Mo. 1968-70; journeyman elect. apprentice Magma Copper Co., San Manuel, Ariz. 1970-74; elect. mech. E.I. Dupont, Louviers, Colo. 1974-76; maint. elect. Calavo Growers, Escondido 1976; maint. supr. Roberts Irrigation Prods. 1977-79; maint. mgr. tooling Precision Metal Prods., El Cajon 1979--; tchr.

basic elec., 1980-2; sev. inventions in field; rec: fish, camp, waterski. res: 9934 Golden West Ln Santee 92071 ofc: Precision Metal Prods 850 W. Bradley Ave El Cajon 92022.

ACUESTA, ROMY NICKOLAS, electric supply co. president; b. Oct. 21, 1941, Long Beach; s. Antonio B. and Nadine (McLeod) A.; m. Elena Duran, Nov. 23, 1963; children: Duane, b. 1964, Darren, b. 1966, Christopher, b. 1967. Career: product sales rep. Standard Oil, Torrance 1959; vice pres./South Bay Branch mgr. Superior Wholesale Electric Co., 1960-74; sales mgr. Century Wholesale Elec. Co., Carson 1974-76; v.p./ maj. stockholder, All City Elec. Supply, 1976-79; pres./gen. mgr./ prin. stockholder Action Wholesale Electric Supply, Buena Park 1979--; recipient recognition, City of L.A. for youth sports activity; Democrat; Catholic: rec: golf, photog., sports. Ofc: Action Wholesale Electric Supply, 6925 Hermosa Circle Buena Park 90620

ADAM, GERALD DU WANE, truck sales service co. executive; b. June 3, 1938, Leola, So. Dak.; s. Fred J. and Viola (Melhoff) A.; m. Sharlene Verona Kaul, Sept. 1, 1958; children: Terry, b. 1959, Sherry, b. 1962; contg. edn. through seminars, spl. courses. Career: with International Harvester Co. 22 years: 11 years as mech./ line foreman, 4 yrs as service mgr., 7 yrs as regional svc. mgr.; v.p./part owner Sunset Intl. Truck Inc., 2 yrs.; currently vice pres./ gen. mgr. parts & svc., Sunset Intl. Trucks Inc., Los Angeles; recipient service awards, Internat. Harvester 1976, 77, 78; mem. Calif. Trucker Assn.; Phoenix Club (Anaheim); Republican; Lutheran; rec: hunting, fishing. Res: 8202 Santa Margarita La Palma 90623 Ofc: Sunset Intl. Truck Inc. 4501 S. Alameda Los Angeles 90058

ADAMS, ARTHUR LEROY, contractor; b. Nov. 23, 1937, Oakland; s. Roland and Gretta Alma (Hadlock) Romero; m. Wanda Layson, Mar. 30, 1969; children: James, b. 1957, Gary, b. 1959, Kimberlie, b. 1962; (step): Robert, b. 1957, Kathryn, b. 1959, Michael, b. 1962, Debora, b. 1965. Career: roofing foreman Ace Roofing Co., San Mateo 1962; owner Adams Roofing Co., Redwood City 1967; pres. Adams Enterprises Inc., San Carlos 1970--; bd. dirs. (past pres.) Roofing Contractors of the Bay Area Counties 1968-82; bd. dirs. (past pres.) Roofing Contrs. Assn. Calif. 1972-; Apprentice Com., Bay Area and State, 1972-782; Roofers Pension Dir. 1977-82; Apprentice Textbooks Revision Com. 1975-82; Uniform Building Code Rev. Com. 1974, 1983; Com. to Rewrite State License Exam. 1983. Mem. Nat. Roofing Contrs. Assn.; mem. SunRise Lions Club, S.F. Sheriffs Air Squadron, BSA Scoutmaster 1965-73, Campfire Girls bd. dirs. (past pres. S.F 1973), Sequoia High Sch. PTA bd. 1976-82, Davis Divers Redwood City bd. dirs. 1977-82; Republican; rec: scuba diving, hunting, fishing. Res: 150 Normandy Lane Woodside 94062 Ofc: Adams Enterprises Inc. 1021 Washington St San Carlos 94070

ADAMS, ARTHUR RAYMOND, manufacturing co. executive; b. Apr. 30, 1909, Hiawatha, Kans.; s. George Raymond and Grace Helena (Davis) A.; m. Lelamae Sutherlin (dec.) Mar. 14, 1934; chil: Ann, b. 1927, Carolyn, b. 1930 (adopted), Peter, b. 1936, Sharon, b. 1937; edn: BA, Stanford Univ. 1931. Career: partner Rite Hardware Mfg. Co., 1931-45, chmn./pres. Adams Rite Mfg. Co., 1945--; pres. Adams Rite Industries, 1972-80; pres. Raymond Mgmt.; pres. Adams Rite (Europe) Ltd. Mem: L.A. Council Int'l. Visitors, L.A. World Affairs Council, Town Hall, Cal Tech Assos., Claremont McKenna Coll. (Life mem. bd. trustees), L.A. Sym. Assos., L. A. County Art Mus. & Nat. Hist. Mus.; Oakmont GC, Annandale Golf Club. Christian Sci.; rec: golf, travel; res: 1060 Stoneridge Dr. Pasadena 91105. ofc: Adams Rite Mfg. Co. 4040 So. Capitol Ave. City of Industry 91749

ADAMS, MARK SAMUEL, lawyer; b. Oct. 3, 1950, Chgo.; s. Angelo and Elizabeth (Russell) Adams; m. Mary Fitzgerald, Aug. 11, 1973; chil: Jama, b. 1979, Andrew, b. 1983; edn: BA, Loyola Marymount 1972; JD, Georgetown Law Ctr. 1975; admitted State Bar of Calif. Career: atty. law firm Ball Hunt Hart Brown & Baerwitz, Los Angeles 1976-78; atty. Gov's Ofc of Planning and Resrch, Sacto. 1978-81; Pension Fund and Housing Proj. Dir., Pat Brown Inst. of Gov. Affairs, L.A. 1981-82; atty., pres. of Callie Mae, Inc., L.A. 1983--; dir. Pasadena Media Inc. Mem: Los Angeles Co. Bar Assn., Loyola Marymount Univ. Alumni Assn. (bd. dirs.); Democrat; Catholic; ofc: Callie Mae Inc. 523 W. 6th St., Ste. 734, Los Angeles 90014

ADAMS, WILLIAM CLYDE, real estate broker; b. Nov. 1, 1909, Boonville, N.C.; s. Arthur Richmond and Lonia Missouri (Myers) A.; m. Tommie Edna Parker, June 22, 1939; children: Donna Clyde, b. 1933; Robert Lee, b. 1949; edn: Dr. Ed. AAC, Campbell Univ. Buies Creek NC, 1934; grad. wk., Appalachian St. Univ. 1935; real estate, Metropolitan Tech., L.A. 1946-47; Calif. lic. R.E. Broker; Internat. Senior Cert. Appraiser 1984. Career: empl. General Motors, 1936-39, Lockheed Co. 1940-47; appraiser, property mgmt., 1943-75; sales mgr. Hugh M. Taylor, 1952-54; currently ret., free lance consulting; mem. Southwest Bd. Realtors, state, and nat. boards, 1948-68; mem. Sr. Citizens Orgn., Gardena; Republican; So. Missionary Baptist Ch., Gardena; rec: Bible tchr., counseling. Res: 13904 S. Budlong Ave, Apt. B, Gardena 90247

ADAMS, WILLIAM FRANCIS, real estate broker; b. Feb. 15, 1939, San Jose; s. Frank Wm. and Kathryn Mary Adams; m. Mary Anne Ring, Sept. 11, 1959; 1 dau., Laura Anne, b. 1967; edn: Bellarmine Coll. Prep. 1957; AA, San Jose City Coll. 1961; lic. R.E. Broker, Calif. Career: stockclk., head warehousemn., store mgr. Blue Chip Stamp Co., 1959-63; dist. mgr. No. Calif., Ore., Nev., 1963-75; realtor assoc. Century 21, 1975; realtor/co-owner Internat. R.E. Network, Adams & Miller Realtors, 1975-82; realtor/owner Silicon Valley Properties, 1982--; cons. var. lawyers real estate appraisals; mem. San Jose R.E. Board, Calif., Nat. Assn. of Realtors, Tri-County Apt. Assn.; mem. Elks,

Almaden Golf & Country Club, Almaden Homeowners Assn., Bellarmine Alumni Assn.; Democrat; Catholic; rec: golf, bowling, skiing. Res: 1168 Carla Dr. San Jose 95120 Ofc: Silicon Valley Properties, 6472 Camden Ave, Ste. 102, San Jose 95120

ADDISON, GEORGE LEWIS, II, writer/film producer; b. May 6, 1955, Greensboro, N.C.; s. George L., I and Ann Elizabeth (McAdoo) A.; m. Linda Denise Watson, Dec. 31, 1979; 1 child, Lindsey, b. 1983; edn: pre-law, journ., Barry Coll. 1976-78; FCC Broadcast Certification 1978. Career: asst. collections mgr. Home Credit Corp., Greensboro, NC 1976; sales circ./pub. rels., Miami Herald, Miami, Fla. 1978; news dir./broadcaster WMBM, WVCG, WINZ, WPLG (Miami), 1978-80; pres./ founder S.F.B. Tennis Assn., Los Angeles 1980--; pres./founder S.F.B. Tennis Assn., Miami 1979; awards: All-Army Photo Contest (1st Place) US Army, 1975; City & County Proclamations, Mayor of Miami & Mayor of Dade Co. (1979); candidate for White House Fellowship Pgm. (1983). Mem: Nat. Small Bus. Assn., American Film Inst., Public Access Prods. Assn., Assn. of Independent Filmmakers, Smithsonian Instn., Consumer Mail Panel, Toastmasters Intl.; publs: Making Movies, God's Seven Steps to Spiritual & Finl. Prosperity, Beauty Hints for the Christian Woman, (1982-84); writer/prod. The Total Image (30 min. hlth & info. pgm. for adults & teenagers); mil: E4 US Army 1973-75, Merit, Sharp Shooter; rec: writing, tennis, photog. Res: 933 Gladwick St Carson 90746 Ofc: The Addison Corp 3870 Crenshaw Bl, Ste. 104, Los Angeles 90746

ADKINSON, HARVEY EUGENE (GENE), sales executive; b. Feb. 28, 1934, Dothan, Ala.; s. Hosa B. and Mary Frances (Lunsford) A.; children: Keith, b. 1960, Kevin, b. 1962; ed. Univ. of Fla.; career: partner, vocal group The Dream Weavers, 1955-57; branch mgr. Edison Voicewriter, Memphis, Ten. 1960-73; v.p. of mktg. Dictation Machine Co., Memphis 1973-77; area mgr. Dictaphone Corp., Atlanta, Ga. 1977-81; Perimeter Office Supply (dealer micro computers) 1981-82; branch mgr. Cummins Allison Corp., San Francisco 1982-83; mgr. PBL Associates, San Francisco 1983--; recipient num. sales awards incl. Quota Clubs, Top Sales Mgr.; mem: Am. Soc. of Composers Authors and Publishers (1955-); Sales & Mktg. Execs. Internat.; past pres. Optimist Club of Sandy Springs (Ga.); Pack com. chmn. Cub Scouts of Am. Listed in ASCAP bio of Authors; works: It's Almost Tomorrow, You've Got Me Wondering, You're Mine, Say You'll Be Mine, There Will Never Be Another You, Never Again, My Lovely One. Mil: E4 US Army 1957-60, GCM; Republican; Presbyterian; rec: sports, arts. Res: POB 3344, Daly City 94015 Ofc: PBL Associates, Ten Cottage Ave, Point Richmond 94801

ADLAI, S. RICHARD; corporate executive, author; b. Feb. 10, 1942, Bagdad, Iraq, nat. Nov. 10, 1967; s. A. Amir and Hadia (Habeeb) A.; chil: Tarick S., b. 1963, Tarisa L., b. 1970, Willie De Mille, b. 1972; edn: bus., mktg., Am. Coll. of Bus. 1962, BS, NY Univ. 1980, MBA, honors, Pepperdine Univ. 1982. Career: writer Paramount Studios, 1960-63; founder, bd. chmn. Hollywood Cinema Center Inc.; pres. Hilton Commercial Group, Inc., 1978--; author novel: King Tarick (Am. Pub., NY 1965), play: Hassan & Hanna (1966), 100 Short Stories, autobiog. book: Ibn Saud (Viking Co. 1984); consultant re third world countries. Honors: for resrch. into bus. franchising, elected Pepperdine University Assocs.; outstanding proj. for PKE Pgm., Pepperdine 1982; chmn. Toluca Lake Photo Expo. Mem: Rotarian (T.L. pres. 1983), CofC, World Affairs Council; Republican; Episcopal; rec: photog., fishing, golf, anthropol. Ofc: Hilton Commercial Gp. Inc, Ste.10 Hilton Center, POB 2026 Toluca Lake 91602

ADLER, ALLAN WILBUR, silversmith; b. May 8, 1916, Mazula, Mont.; s. August M. and Daisey B. (Fox) A.; m. Rebecca Blanchard, Mar. 24, 1938; children: Linda Diane (Mrs. Wm. Hughes), b. 1942; Cindy Alice (Mrs. Scott Larson), b. 1952. Career: pres. Allan Adler, Inc. 1940--, bd. chmn. 1981-; designed and made the pins worn by the first seven Am. Astronauts; designed the silver flatware and holloware for the Calif. Gov.'s Mansion for Gov. Edmund Brown; designed the American Film Inst. Award (1972); designed the Famous Stevenshoe shoe campaign button; designed original Pres. Eisenhower Golf Trophy for Bob Hope Desert Classic tournament. Awards: Good Design Award, Mus. of Modern Art (1956), Scissors Award for Design, Calif. Fashion Grp. (1949); honored by The Smithsonian Instn. (1982) documenting 40 years of Am. Silversmithing and Allan Adler's Contbn. to Design; mem. Los Angeles County Mus. of Art, Newport Harbor Yacht Club; Presbyterian; rec: yachting, fishing. Res: 3263 Oakdell Rd Studio City 91604 Ofc: Allan Adler, Inc. 13340 Saticoy St North Hollywood 91605

ADLER, ERWIN ELLERY, lawyer; b. July 22, 1944, Flint, Mich.; s. Ben and Helen M. (Schwartz) Adler; edn: BA, Univ. of Mich., 1963, JD, Harvard Law Sch., 1966, LL.M., Univ. of Mich. Law Sch., 1967; m. Stephanie Ruskin, June 8, 1967; chil: Lauren M., b. 1974, Michael B., b. 1977, Jonathan S., b. 1981; career: assoc. Pillsbury Madison & Sutro law firm, 1967-73; assoc. and partner Lawler, Felix & Hall, 1973-82; partner Rogers & Wells, Los Angeles 1982--; bd. dirs. Hollywood Opera Assoc., 1975-76; bd. dirs. Children's Scholarships, Inc. 1978-79; vice chmn. Appellate Advocacy Com., American Bar Assn. Honors: Phi Beta Kappa, Phi Kappa Phi; mem: Am. Bar Assn. 1967-, Calif. Bar Assn. 1967-, Los Angeles Athletic Club; Jewish; rec: photog., jogging; res: 872 Norman Pl. Los Angeles 90049 ofc: Rogers & Wells 261 S. Figueroa, Suite 400, Los Angeles 90012.

ADLER, MARCIA ANN STEPHENSON, marketing executive; b. Jan. 23, 1947, Wash. DC; d. William Russell and Martha Mae (Grayson) Stephenson; m. Gary Alan Adler, Dec. 19, 1982; edn: BS in Home Ec. Edn., Radford Univ. 1975, MS 1976; bus. courses, Ga. State Coll. 1970. Career: bridal cons. Rich's, Atlanta, Ga. 1966-71; asst. office mgr. Ga. Tech. Athletic Dept., 1967-71; bridal

dir. Colonnade, Charlottesville, Va. 1971-72; tchr./ home ec. dept. hd. Winchester (Va.) City Schs. 1976-79; extension agt. USDA Ext. Div., Alexandria, Va. 1979-80; nutrition cons., Fla. Dept. of Citrus, Wash. DC 1980-82; field rep. Calif. Table Grape Commn., L.A. 1982--; past mem. Alexandria Pub. Health & Nutrition Com. 1979-81; past bd. dirs. N.Va. 4-H Center 1979-80; honors: Outstanding Young Woman of Am. 1980; mem: AAUW, Home Economics in Bus., Am. Home Economics Assn.; guest on tv and radio talk shows, as Big Orange for Fla. Citrus indus.; Methodist; rec: needlework, calligraphy. Res: 370 Rosecrans, 101, San Diego 92106 Ofc: Ca. Table Grape Commission, POB 5498, Fresno

ADLER, SANDRA DIANE, marriage, family & child counselor; b. Jan. 17, 1940, Waltham, Mass.; d. Richard John and Barbara Doris (Vinal) Adler; children: Dennis, b. 1956, Eileen, b. 1957, Sean, b. 1960; edn: BA magna cum laude, National Univ. 1980, MA counseling, 1982; US Internat. Univ. Clinical psy. PhD Program, 1983-; clin. tng. Bioenergetic Analysis Soc., S.D.; MFCC lic., 1983. Career: counselor/supvr., Boston (MA) Court Resource Project (pretrial diversion pgm.), 1970-73; substance abuse counselor Nat. Council on Alcoholism, Hayward, Ca. and Alameda Co. Health Dept. Alcoholism Clinic, 1973-75; counselor/supvr. East County Accord, El Cajon 1978-81, Hillside Hosp. Chem. Dependency Unit, 1981-83; MFCC pvt. practice, 1983--;instr. UCSD Ext., Impact of Drinking on Driving, 1982-; mem: Calif. Womens Com. on Alcoholism (past pres. S.D. chpt.); Assn. of Women in Psychol. (chpt. chpsn); ALMACA; NOW; S.D. Coalition on Alcohol Problems; CAMFT; Bioenergetic Analysis soc. S.D.; mem. Easy Does It Riders (motorcyclist gp.), Heartland Comm. Theater, New Age Christian Ch.; rec: motorcycling, camping, little theater. Address: 8894 Los Coches Rd Lakeside 92040

ADLER, STUART OWEN, computer systems specialist; b. Mar. 27, 1935, NYC; s. Millard David and Sydell (Levine) A.; edn: BS in bus., NYU Sch of Commerce, 1927; m. Marilyn Cynthia Leitner, Oct. 26, 1957; chil: Deborah Ann, b. 1960, Michael Evan, b. 1964, Lorraine Carol, b. 1966; Career: systems programmer New York Life Ins Co., NY:C 1957-60; competitive analyst Univac, NYC 1960; systems engr. IBM Corp, NYC, Poughkeepsie, Los Angeles 1960-69; prin. mem tech staff Xerox Corp, Los Angeles 1969-71; computer systems cons., Los Angeles 1972-75; systems splst. Western Bancorp Data Processing Co, L.A. 1975-76; sr. systems analyst Litton Energy Control Systems, L.A. 1976-79; sr. systems analyst Wordplex Corp., Westlake Village 1979-80; pres. Adler Computer Technology, Woodland Hills 1980--; bd. chmn. Adler/Brainard Technology; writer weekly column on computer topics for small & medium size business in Warner Center News; Temple Solael bd. dirs. 1979-80; mem: Woodland Hills C. of C., chmn Retail Merchants &: Profl Bus Com.; San Fernando Valley Bus & Profl Assn., v.p. nom. 1983; rec: photog., target shooting, model airplanes. res: 23035 Gainford St. Woodland Hills 91364 ofc: Adler Computer Technology, 21777 Ventura Blvd #269 Woodland Hills 91364.

ADSETT, BARRIE RAY, software development specialist; b. Aug. 29, 1953, Gisborne, N.Z.; s. Ray Colin and Joan (Kendrew) A.; edn: BA, Massey Univ. 1971; MA, Victoria Univ., 1973; PhD, Massey Univ. 1975. Career: pgmmr. Castrol (NZ) Ltd., Wellington, 1974-75; pgmmr. analyst Cincom Systems Inc., Cincinnati, Oh. 1975-78; software devel. splst. Tominy Inc., Oxnard, Ca. 1978--, dir. software devel. Western Div.; ind. computer cons. to USN, Port Hueneme, 1980-; mem. Tri Counties Sports Car Club (pres. 1982-3); rec: sports car rallying. Res: 3501 W. Hemlock Oxnard 93033 Ofc: Tominy Inc. 3101 Peninsula Ste. 201, Oxnard 93033

AFABLE, CARLOS BOSA, engineer; b. Dec. 15, 1943, Masbate, Phil., nat. 1976; s. Eleno T. and Tita B. (Bosa) A.; m. Aurora, Sept. 16, 1967; 1 son, Carl, b. 1974; edn: BS, Ch.E., Univ. of Santo Tomas, Manila, Phil. 1967; courses, CSU Northridge, 1979-81, L.A. City Coll. 1971-72; Profl. Chem. Engr., Phil. Inst. of Chem. Engrg. 1967. Career: asst. instr. Chem. Dept., Tech. Inst. of the Phil. 1967-68; lead foreman Coco Chemicals (Phil.) Inc., 1968-69; supr. Chemical Industries of the Phil., Rizal 1969-70; shift supr. Wacker Chemicals, Los Angeles 1972-77; staff engr. Hughes Research Labs, Malibu 1977--; mem: Am. Assn. of Crystal Growth, AAAS, Soc. of Photo-Optical Instrumentation Engrs., NY Acad. of Scis., UST Alumni Assn. of So. Calif., Thomasian Engrs. Club (L.A.); profl. publs. in field; Republican; Catholic; rec: chess, computers. Res: 1107 S. Plymouth Blvd Los Angeles 90017 Ofc: Hughes Research Labs, 3011 Malibu Cyn Rd Malibu 90265

AFOEJU, BERNARD IKECUKWU, engineering & constrn. co. process equipment design engineer; b. May 6, 1942, Umudioka, Nigeria; s. Afoeju Mbagwu and Regina Nwure (Nwosu) Ukoha; m. Ifeoma Amajoyi, June 16, 1973; children: dau. Chikanele, b. 1979; son, Nnadozie, b. 1981; edn: BS, Yale Univ., 1967, MS, Calif. Inst. of Tech. 1968; Regis. Profl. Mech. Engineer, Dept. of Consumer Affairs CA, 1977; career: reservoir engr. Shell Oil Co., Los Angeles 1968-74; lead heat transfer engr. Ralph M. Parsons Co., Pasadena 1974--; designed one of a kind cooling coil for NASA's transonic wind tunnel at Langley Resrch Ctr., Hampton, Vir. Mem: Soc. of Petroleum Engrs. (secty. Bakersfield chpt. 1968-9); life mem. Tau Beta Pi (Engrg. hon. soc.); Fellow Yale Engrg. Assn.; Toastmasters; Parsons Employee Rec. Club; soccer team coach Tokay Elem. Sch., Fontana. Publs: art. Jour. of Petroleum Tech., Nov. 1974. Catholic. rec: auto mechanics; res: 16010 San Jacinto Ave. Fontana 92335 ofc: Ralph M. Parsons Co. 100 W. Walnut St. Pasadena 91124.

AGARWALA, VIJAY, manufacturing executive; b. May 11, 1949, Bareilly, India; s. Rameshwardas and Satyavati A.; m. Tarla, Mar. 20, 1974; children: Aalok, b. 1977, Aakash, b. 1979; edn: BS, I.I.T. Kanpur, India 1970; MS chem.

engr. Case Western Reserve, Cleveland 1974. Career: development chemist Mameco Internat., Cleveland 1973-74, McCloskey Varnish Co., Los Angeles 1974-76; senior chemist M & T Chemicals, L.A. 1976-78, quality control supvr. 1978-82, mfg. mgr. 1983--; mem. ASTM, ASOC. Res: 1554 S. Deerfoot Dr Diamond Bar 91765 Ofc: Furane Products Co., 5121 San Fernando Rd West Los Angeles 90039

AGATE, CAROL, lawyer; b. March 10, 1934, Providence, R.I.; d. Wm. S. and Matilda (Ark) Orkin; 2 children: James, b. 1961, Marjorie, b. 1962; edn: AB, Brown Univ. 1955; JD, Univ. of Conn. 1974, UCLA Sch of Law 1974. Career: media buyer Grey Advt. 1956-59; admitted to State Bar of Calif. 1974; deputy city atty., Los Angeles City Attorney, 1975-77; pvt. law practice, 1977-80; clin. prof. Loyola Law School, 1980--. Awards: Am. Jurisprudence awd., resrch. and writing; hon. life mem. Westport (CT) Pub. Library. Mem: Los Angeles Co. Bar Assn. (ch. editl. bd. Los Angeles Lawyer; Conv. Com; Legislative Activities Com.), Women Lawyers Assn. of l.A. (fmr vp), Calif. Women Lawyers (fmr treas.); mem. (Westport, CT): Zoning Bd. of Appeals, Library Bd., Justice of the Peace, Neighborhood Legal Svcs.; mem. (in CA): NOW, Feminist Womens Hlth. Ctr., Californians for the Chief Justice (treas.). Publs: arts in L.A. Bar Bull., ABA's Alternatives, Geo. Wash. Univ. Advocate, Case & Comment, Womens Law Jour., Beyond Sex Roles, L.A. Times, others. Democrat; Unitarian; rec: photog., model bldg., travel. res: 750 S. Spaulding Ave #124, Los Angeles 90036 ofc: Loyola Law Sch, 1441 W. Olympic Blvd Los Angeles 90015

AGBAYANI, TONY (ANTONINO) JAMES, JR., lawyer; b. March 5, 1956, Stockton; s. Tony A. Agbayani and Hazel Evelyn (Brown) Grigsbay; m. Tonia Dolores Agbayani, Feb. 2, 1980; chil: Antonino III, b. 1980, Jeremy, b. 1982; edn: BA, cum laude, CSC Stanislaus 1978; JD, UC Davis 1981; admitted Calif. State Bar 1981. Career: legal intern Prisoner's Legal Assist. Pgm., UC Davis 1980; atty. law ofcs. Douglas Kirkman, Sacto. 1981-82, law ofcs. Gary Sullivan dba Christian Legal Svcs. Ofc., Stockton 1982-3; deputy district atty. San Joaquin Co. D.A.'s Ofc., Stockton 1983--. Awards: Am. Jurisprudence Awd. 1980; Outstanding Student of the Yr., CSC Stanislaus 1977; Bank of Am. Awd.-Fine Arts, John Philip Sousa Awd., E. Union H.S., San Joaquin Co. Friedberger Scholarship, Soroptomist's Club Scholarship, San Joaquin Stu. of Yr., Calif. Svgs.& Loan League, 1974. Mem: San Joaquin Co. Bar Assn., Pilipino Law Students Assn.(chmn. UCD 1979-81); Democrat; Assembly of God; rec: comic bk. collector, soccer; res: 950 Princess Dr. Stockton 95209 ofc: DA's Ofc. 222 E. Weber #202 Stockton 95202.

AGUIRRE, JOSE LUIS, manufacturing co. executive; b. June 22, 1949, Guad., Mex., nat. 1983; s. Antonio and Rosa A.; m. Rebeca Torres, July 5, 1974; children: Lilia, b. 1976, Dahlia, b. 1977; edn: AA, Grossmont Coll. 1970; BSEE, CSU San Diego 1973; MBA, National Univ. 1978. Career: mfg. mgr. Pulse Engineering, San Diego 1973-76; quality assurance mgr. Plantronics, Santa Cruz 1976-80; ops. mgr. Convergent Tech., Santa Clara 1980--; physics instr. Baja California Univ. (UABC) 1976-9. Awards: cert. US Bus. Adminstrn. 7/78, cert. Wescon 1983, cert. ICS 2979. Mem: IEEE; ASQC; Am. Prodn. Inventory Control Soc.; INTEL; Upper Mgmt. & Quality-JURAN 1984; Wescon (com. mem. 1983). Republican. Catholic. Res: 1440 Dougmar, Santa Cruz 95062 Ofc: Convergent Tech, 2500 Augustine, Santa Clara 95051

AHERN, THOMAS PATRICK, real estate broker; b.Nov. 22, 1951, Denver, Colo.; s. Wm. Joseph and Joan Theresa (McAtee) Ahern; m. Victoria Fischer, Dec. 31, 1975; 1 dau., April, b. 1982; edn: BA, Univ. of San Francisco 1973; lic. R.E. broker, Calif. 1982. Career: asst. vice pres. Bohannon Realtors, 1977-80; sales assoc. Marcus & Millichop Inc., 1981-3; broker/owner/pres. Ahern & Co. Inc., Sacramento 1983--; Republican; Catholic; rec: tennis, ski, softball, golf; address: Ahern & Co. Inc. 2623 Latham Dr. Sacramento 95825.

AHN, SEUNG OK, bank executive; b. Jan. 12, 1934, KyungBook, Korea; s. Wonho and RycokSung (Kim) Ahn; m. Malrae Choi, Feb. 7, 1968; children: MeeKyung, b. 1969, Jaimo, b. 1972. Career: asst. gen. mgr. The Commercial Bank of Korea, 1968-80, deputy gen. mgr. 1971-77, agt. and gen. mgr. Chgo. Branch, 1978-81, agent/gen. mgr. L.A. Agency, The Commercial Bank of Korea 1982--; instr. Kock hak Coll., Seoul, Korea; pres. Korean Banks Assn. of Los Angeles; vice chmn. bd. dirs. Korean School of L.A.; awards: Korean CofC of Chgo., Korean Sch. Found. of L.A.; mem. University Club, Lions Club (Korean) of Chgo., Mt. Gate Country Club, Korea Univ. Alumni (dir.); mil: Korean Army 1950-51; Catholic; rec: tennis, golf, skiing. Res: 267 Oakhurst Ln Arcadia 91006 Ofc: The Commercial Bank of Korea, 611 W. 6th St, Ste. 2950, Los Angeles 90017

AHRENS, EDWARD WILLIAM, community services director; b. May 29, 1951, Alhambra; s. William Ernest and Edith E. (Finley) Ahrens; m. Paula Brubaker, Jan. 14, 1984; edn: AA, East L.A. Jr. Coll. 1971, BA, CSU Dominguez Hills 1973. Career: asst. baseball coach East L.A. Jr. Coll. 1974-77; sr. recreation leader City of Maywood, 1974-77, rec. supt. 1977-79, chief administrv. ofcr. 1979-80, dir. community svcs. City of Maywood, 1980--. Mem: Calif. park & Rec. Soc., So. Calif. Municipal Athletic Fedn., Internat. City Mgrs. Assn., Maywood Lions Club (pres. 1978, 80), Maywood Jaycees 1977-80, Maywood Moose 1980-2; Democrat; Lutheran; rec: tournament tennis, softball player; co-owner two harness racing horses; res: 4721 E. 57th St. Maywood 90270; ofc: City of Maywood, 4319 E. Slauson, Maywood 90270.

AIELLO, MICHAEL ANGELO, real estate/insurance broker; b. June 17, 1910, Pittsburg, Calif.; s. Salvatore and Sarah (Flores) Aiello; m. Patrina Ann, Sept.

15, 1940; chil: Salvatore Joseph, b. 1942, Jack Michael, b. 1946, Joseph Salvatore, b. 1953. Career: head bookkeeper Redwood Mfrs. Co., 1929-37; currently self-employed real estate broker, insurance agent & broker, income tax preparer; lic. notary public; chmn. Bldg. Code Appeals Bd., City of Pittsburg. Mem: Foresters of Am., 1929-(Grd. Chief Ranger); Young Mens Inst. (pres. 1919); Sons of Italy (pres. 1975); Italian Catholic Fedn.; Catholic; rec: fishing, music; address: 295 East 16th St. Pittsburg 94565.

AISTHORPE, FREDERICK DECOMAS, retail lumber co. owner; b. July 3, 1907, Chico; s. Wm. Louis and Virginia Martha (Cheesebrough) A.; father came to Chico from Ontario, Can. in 1880; m. Mary Shearin, July 3, 1932; children: Robert (atty.), Sharon (int. designer); edn: BA in bus., CSU Chico 1927. Career: empl. in family retail lumber business, Aisthorpe Lumber Co. (2272 Esplanade, Chico) 1927-, sole owner 1946-80; (bus. was orig. The Griswold Lumber Co. estab. in 1893, bought by Wm. Louis Aisthorpe in 1920); home builder/contr. partnership with late brother, blt. over 250 homes in Chico (first contr. in Chico to build houses for FHA financing); mem. Lions Club (40 yrs.); Commanche Riders Assn. 1941; Elks (51 yrs., past exalted ruler, past Dist. Dep. Grand Exalted Ruler Calif. North); past v.p. State Elks Assn.; past pres. Chico CofC; chmn. Chico Bidwell Park Commn. 1950; Republican; Episcopal; rec: horseman, golf, hunting, fishing. Res: 1287 Vallombrosa Ave Chico 95926

AITON, ALFRED MARK, life insurance executive; b. April 21, 1919, San Diego; s. AlfredMark and Byrd (Dales) Aiton; m. Katharine Smith, June 21, 1942; 2 sons: Mark Douglas, b. 1952, Robert Wm., b. 1956; edn: BA, CSU San Jose 1941. Career: gen. mgr. The Acacia Group (life ins. co.) 3 ofcs. in San Jose, San Francisco, Oakland (main ofc.), 1947-82, cons. 1982-3; currently self-emplyd. finl. advisor; vice pres. Eden Hosp. Found., 1982-3; bd. dirs. Castro valley Sanitation Dist., 1976-. Honors: Life Ins. Mgmt. Assn. honor award; Co. Mgmt. Advis. Group (11 yrs.). Mem: Insurance Mgrs. Assn. (Oakland-East Bay Assn. pres. 1965); Rotarian (pres. Castro Valley 1983); publs: arts. in trade mags. Republican; Prot.; rec: sports, community svc.; address: 16994 Hinton Ct., Castro Valley 94546.

AKERS, MERLE K., mobile washing service co. president; b. Mar. 5, 1931, Fargo, N.Dak.; s. Kenneth Merle and Helyn H. (Hagen) A.; m. Delores Rohde, Dec. 31, 1953, div. 1969; children: Wade, b. 1954, Scott, b. 1956, Stuart, b. 1967; edn: N.Dak. State Univ., 2 yrs. Career: inventor/founder/pres. Jiffiwash, Inc. (patent rights 1965-), and franchisor Mobile Washing Service (fleet trucks, cars, ships, bldgs., aircraft), 1959--, 32 franchises in nine states servicing over 300 nat. accts.; founder Franchise Internat. 1978; mem. Nat. Right to Work Found., US Parks Found. (Wash DC), SF Ballet, SF Opera, SF Sym., SF Mus of Modern Art; mil: cpl. US ARmy 1951-53; rec: boating, ice hockey. Res: 1177 California St, 309, San Francisco 94108 Ofc: Jiffiwash, Inc. POB 2489, San Francisco 94126

AKITA, RICHARD MITSUO, electronics engineer; b. Nov. 13, 1939, Honolulu; s. Mitsuyoshi and Tomoyo (Sueoka) Akita; edn: BS in math. Ore. State Univ. 1961, MS in E.E., Naval Postgrad. Sch. 1968; m. Gwen Tateno, June 14, 1964; chil: Michael T., b. 1965, Andrea N., b. 1967; career: electronics engineer Naval Electronics Laboratory Center, San Diego 1970-77; supervisory electronics engr., branch hd. Navigation Systems Branch, Naval Ocean Systems Center, San Diego, 1977--; instr. California Community Colls., 1977-; mem: IEEE, Sigma Xi, AAAS; num. profl. publications, tech. papers; mil: lt. sr. gr. USN 1961-70; Republican; Prot.; rec: gardening, fishing, woodwork, jogging, racketball; res: 1738 Sorrel Ct. Carlsbad 92008 ofc: Naval Ocean Systems Center Code 8244 San Diego 92152.

AKRIDGE, MELVIN EUGENE, management consultant; b. Jan. 20, 1929, Atlanta, Ga.; s. Jesse Melvin and Katherine (Coile) A.; m. Virginia Farrell, Aug. 19, 1949; children: Katherine, b. 1952, Patricia, b. 1957, Heather, b. 1961, Amie, b. 1963; edn: BS indsl. mgmt., Ga. Inst. of Tech. 1951; Calif. Profl. Indsl. Engr., 1968. Career: industrial engr./dept. supt. Amstar Corp., New Orleans, La. 1959-61, asst. to refinery mgr. Amstar Corp., Boston, Mass. 1961-62; chief indsl. engr. Spreckels Sugar Co., San Francisco 1963-67; mgmt. cons./prin. Cresap, McCormick & Paget, San Francisco 1967-72; dir. of materials Hyster Corp., Portland, Ore. 1973-76; partner/v.p. Theodore Barry & Assocs., Portland 1976-82; partner Eugene Akridge & Assocs., Los Angeles 1982--; mgmt. cons. to num. firms and non profit orgns. (in US and abroad) 1967-; honors: Industrial Engineer of the Year, S.F - Oakland, Am. Inst. of Indsl. Engrs., 1971; mem: Am. Inst. of Indsl. Engrs. (past pres. S.F-Oakland Chpt.); Georgia Tech Alumni Assn., Lake Oswego CC; var. tech. publs. and presentations in indsl. engring. techniques, 1967-75; arts., Public Utility Fortnightly (1981), The Executive of Los Angeles (1981); Republican; Episcopal; rec: golf, microcomputers. Address: Eugene Akridge & Assocs., 1433 Dwight Dr Glendale 91207

ALADAG, TUGRUL, financial executive; b. July 26, 1944, Konya, Turkey; s. Dr. Ismail Hakki and Melahat (Evci) Aladag; edn: BA, magna cum laude, USC 1968, MA, Northwestern Univ. 1969; m. Efes Duyuran, Sept. 6, 1974; chil: Belis, b. 1980; Serra, b. 1982. Career: tchr/resrch assoc. Northwestern Univ. 1969-70; resrch analyst/sr. resrch analyst Calif. Fed. Savings, Los Angeles 1970-73, 75-81; mgr. of economic analysis/finl. planning mgr. Home Savings of America, Los Angeles 1981-83, vice pres. 1983--. Honors: Phi Beta Kappa, Phi Kappa Phi. Mem: Nat. Assn. of Bus. Economists, Am. Statistical Assn., The Inst. of Mgmt. Sci., Nat. Assn. of Accts. Publs: arts. in Bus. Economics (1979), Mortgage Banker (1978), Real Estate Rev. (1981), others. Mil: lt. Turkish Army (NATO) 1973-5; res: Los Angeles; ofc: Home Savings of America 3731 Wilshire Bl Los Angeles 90010

ALAMEDA, RUSSELL RAYMOND, JR., x-ray technologist/ business owner; b. Oct. 13, 1945, San Jose; s. Russell Raymond and Rose Margaret (Manzone) A.; m. Gayle Allison, Feb. 16, 1969, div. 1975; children: Lynda, b. 1970; Anthony, b. 1971; edn: San Jose City Coll. 1963-65; grad., Naval Rad. Tech. Sch. 1971; Am. Registry Radiol. Technol. (ARRT); Calif. Radiol. Tech. (CRT). Career: chief tech. USS Sanctuary, USN, Guam, Vietnam 1966-75; x-ray tech. V.A. Hosp., Palo Alto 1975-78; ofc. mgr. orthopedic surgery 1978--; owner Ren-Tech X-Ray Svc., San Jose 1982--; awards: Mallenckrodt Awd., x-ray, 1971; Navy Achiev., Coolness Under Fire, Vietnam 1969-70; mem: ARRT; CRT; Disabled Am. Vets.; inventor: Frog- Board, pat. pend. 1984; mil: E-6, USN 1966-75, GCM (2), Vietnam Svc.; Republican (Nat. Com.); Lutheran; rec: sports cars, home remodel, gardening. Address: Ren-Tech, 165 Blossom Hill Rd San Jose 95123

ALBERS, HARRY FRANCIS, dentist/educator; b. Sept. 2, 1950, Oss, Netherlands; s. Hans John and Helen Lena (Kurvers) Albers; edn: Bach. BioChem., UC Berkeley, 1973; DDS, UCLA 1977; gen. practice residency VA Hosp.SF 1978. Career: pvt. dental practice, Santa Rosa 1978--; instr. UCSF Dental Sch., 1978-80, Univ. of the Pacific/SF, 1980--; lectr. on dentistry nationally; author textbook: Tooth Colored Restoratives (1983); honors: Phi Beta Kappa 1973, Calif. Dental Assn. Award for most outstanding pub. rels. pgm. Mem: Redwood Empire Dental Soc. (pub. rels. dir.), Am. Dental Soc., Calif. Dental Soc., Rotary Intl. 1981; rec: skiing, writing, gardening; res: 8676 Nina Ct., Cotati 94928 ofc: 95 Montgomery Dr. Ste. 106, Santa Rosa 95404.

ALBERS, HARRY ROBERT, foundation director; b. March 6, 1938, Jersey City, NJ; s. Harry Robt. and Lee (Vetreno) Albers; m. Jean Cherry, Jan. 26, 1963; 3 sons: Harry, b. 1964, Robert, b. 1965, Steaphan, b. 1968; edn: BS, Univ. of Pittsburgh 1961, MS, Cornell Univ. 1963. Career: dir. Satellite Tracking Pgm., Smithsonian Astrophysical Observatory, 1966-9; dir. Smithsonian Resrch Found., 1967-72; dir. of business Smithsonian Instn., 1970-2; dir. of adminstrn. Kitt Peak Nat. Observatory, 1972-6; v.p. Fin. and Adminstrn., Barnard Coll., Columbia Univ., 1976-8; dir. San Diego State Univ. Found., 1978--; faculty SDSU Coll. of Bus. Adminstrn. 1980-; principal investigator Cooperative Arid Lands Agri. Resrch. Pgm. among USA, Egypt and Israel funded by Agcy for Internat. Devel.; cons. to NSF Assn. of Univs. for Resrch in Astronomy 1978-, Smithsonian Instn. 1976-, Los Alamos Sci. Lab. 1978-; editl. bd. Grants Mag. Listed Who's Who in Fin. and Indus., 1981-2, Who's Who in the World, 1982-3. Mem: Nat. Assn. of Coll. and Univ. Bus. Ofcrs., Am. Assn. of Higher Edn., Soc. of Resrch Adminstrs., Nat. Council of Univ. resrch. Adminstrs.; mem. San Diego Community Found. Publs: arts. in profl., sci. jours. Rec: chess, scuba diving, writing. Res: 10019 Mozelle Ln. La Mesa 92041 ofc: SDSU Foundation, San Diego 92182.

ALDANA, GREGORY LEONARD, company owner; b. Sept. 8, 1947, Sacramento; s. Leonard and Carolyn Aldana; 1 son, Damian Leonard, b. 1975; edn: AA bus. ad., Green River Coll. 1975; BA, bus. ad., Univ. of Wash. 1977, grad. wk. Antioch College West 1978; mktg. certificate, Eastern Airlines 1978. Career: mgr. So. King Co. Multi Service Center, Federal Way, Wash. 1974-77; adminstrv. ofcr. B.I.A., Everett, Wash. 1977-78; contract adminstr. Subcontract Ad., Boeing, Seattle 1978-80; subcontract adminstr., G.T.E., Mountain View, Ca. 1980-83; purchasing splst. Memorex, Santa Clara 1983-84; consultant/owner two cos., Fremont, Ca. 1984--, ops. cons. to IBM, Rolm, Hewlett Packard, Memorex and other silicon valley corps.; mem. Old Crows, Lions Internat., Phi Beta Kappa (1975); city councilman Fed. Way, Wash. 1976; co-inventor Production Clutch, Del Monte Corp. (1963), software design and resrch., DPEA Corp. (1984); Republican; Catholic; rec: guitar, welding, choir. Res: 1919 Alameda de L.P., 139, San Mateo 94403 Ofc: ICON Corp., 615 Montana Vista Ct. Fremont 94538

ALDAY, BETZABE MATILDE, physician; b. Mar. 15, 1939, San Jacinto, Ancash, Peru, S.A.; US res. 1976; edn: BS, Nat. Mayor Univ. of San Marcos, Lima, Peru 1959, Med. Sch. grad. 1966; intern, Detroit Macomb Hosp. Assn. 1968-69; res. int. med. 1969-71, Renal eiseases 1971-73, VA Med. Center Davis Park, Providence, R.I.; lic. MD, Mich. 1975, Calif. 1978. Career: chief of hemodialysis unit of Spinal Cord Injury Svc., VA Med. Ctr., Long Beach 1975-80; internal medicine, nephrology, and Spinal Cord Injury Service Chief out clinic, Rancho Los Amigos Hosp., Downey 1980--, also proctor to Nurse Practioners; pvt. practice office, Norwalk 1983--; honors: VA Med. Ctr., Long Beach service commendn. 1980; Olin Teague Award nominee 1980; mem: Calif. Soc. of Int. Medicine, Am. Paraplegia, Am. Soc. of Nephrology, Internat. Soc. of Nephrol., AMA, NY Acad. of Sci., LACMA, CMA; pub. sci. resrch. med journals; Christian; rec: sewing, swimming, cooking. Res: 22847 S. Van Deene Ave Torrance 90502 Ofc: 12820 S. Studebaker Rd Norwalk 90650

ALDERDICE, RICHARD HAMILTON, mortgage banker; b. May 6, 1939, Youngstown, Oh.; s. Wm. I. and Elizabeth (Hamilton) A.; m. JoAnn Vincinski, Sept. 30, 1978; 1 son, Gregory, b. 1959; edn: mktg., Univ. of Hawaii, Ohio Univ. 1965; lic. real estate broker 1976. Career: presently senior v.p. LoanLink (a computerized lender svc.), Hermosa Beach; instr. seminars, R.E. firms; awards: Top Loan Broker, Nat. Security, 1963, 64, 67, 68; mem. Assn. of Mortgage Brokers, City of Hope (Westside); mil: pfc USMCR 1962-68; Republican; Baptist; rec: cycling, jogging. Res: 918 S. Ameroso Pl Venice 90291 Ofc: LoanLink 2401 Pacific Coast Hwy Hermosa Beach 90254

ALDERSON, JOHN CARL, real estate broker; b. Aug. 1, 1947, Sacramento; s. Carl N. and Ruby M. Alderson; m. Edsella Reimers, June 20, 1970; children: Sheila (step), b. 1965; Patrick (step), b. 1967; Marie, b. 1971; edn: (jr. coll.) N.Mex. Mil. Inst. 1966-67; GRI, Nat. Assn. of Realtors. Career: co-mgr.

comml. div. Red Carpet Realtors, 3 offices North Highlands, Loomis, Placerville, Ca. 1972-73; broker Alderson Realty, Sacramento 1973-77; salesman Steele Realty & Inv. Co., Sacto. 1977-79, Bohannon Realtors Comml. Div., Sacto. 1979-80; broker/pres. Northwestern Lands Realty, Sacto. 1981-83; area rep. United Farm R.E., Auburn, 1983--; bd. dirs. Sacto. R.E. Exchange Group 1980-81; listed in Who's Who in Creative R.E. (1980); mem: Sacramento Bd. of Realtors 1972-73, Placer Co. Bd. of Realtors 1984-, Sacto. R.E. Exchg. Gp. 1972-; Lions, Optimists; Republican (Pres. Task Force); Baptist; rec: mining, photog. Res: 2930 Meadow Vista Rd Meadow Vista 95722 Ofc: United Farm R.E. 283 Grass Valley Hwy Auburn 95603

ALDERSON, WILLIAM NICHOLAS, company executive; b Apr. 10, 1956, Los Angeles; s. Nicholas and Marianne (Plaskett) A.; m. Joan Seaberg, July 25, 1981; 1 dau., Jewyl, b. 1982; edn: Chapman Coll. 1977, Bethany Bible Coll. 1978, DeAnza Coll. 1979, Foothill Coll. 1980, Univ. of S.F. 1981. Career: elec. tech. US Navy, Alameda, ca., Pearl Harbor, 1974-78; project engr. Lockheed Missiles & Space, Sunnyvale 1978-84; pres. Xmital Data Communications, Sunnyvale 1982--; advisor to H.S. students, Nat. Mgmt. Assn., 1980-81; dir. M-2 Sponsors, Management Assn., 1980-; College Youth Adminstr. Southbay Christian Ctr., 1980-81; spkr. Christian Womens & Business Clubs, 1980-81; v.p. LMSC National Mgmt. Assn. 1983-84; US Congl. Advisory Bd. mem. 1984-; mil: petty ofcr 3/c USN, Nat. Def. medal; Republican; Christian; rec: racquetball, swimming. Res: 310 N. Mathilda Sunnyvale 94086 Ofc: Xmital Data Communications, POB 70100 Sunnyvale 94086

ALDRICH, DAVID LAWRENCE, public relations executive; b. Feb. 21, 1948, Lakehurst N.A.S., NJ; s. Clarence Edward and Sarah Stiles (Andrews) A., Jr., LCDR, USN (ret.); m. Benita Massler, Mar. 17, 1974; edn: Ocean Co. Coll., NJ 1967-8, Sophia Univ., Tokyo 1970-1, BA, CSU Dominguez Hills 1976. Career: reporter/columnist Ocean Co. Daily Observer, NJ 1967-68; asst. public information, City of Commerce, Ca. 1974-77; pub. rels. mgr./adminstv. asst. Calif. Federal Svgs, Los Angeles 1977-78; v.p./group supr. Hill & Knowlton, L.A. 1978-81; v.p./mgr. W. Div., Ayer Public Relations, N. W. Ayer, L.A. 1981--; vol. counselor CSUDH communications students. Mem. Japan-America Soc., L.A. Athletic Club. Mil: s/sgt USAF 1968-72. Democrat. rec: travel, drum & bugle corps competitions, fresh water fishing. res: 4751D La Villa Marina, Marina del Rey 90292. ofc: N.W. Ayer, 707 Wilshire Blvd. Los Angeles 90017.

ALDRIDGE, HOMER F. "Jack", stock broker, financial consultant; b. Apr. 20, 1913, Jacksonville, Ark.; s. Joseph D. and Minnie Ola (Stephens) A.; m. Janet Frey, Dec. 27, 1951; children: Anita, b. 1940, Carolyn, b. 1943; edn: BA, CSU Long Beach 1959; certs., NYSE (1964), Nat. Assn. Sec. Dealers (1964), Internat. Assn. Finl. Planners (1981). Career: sales rep. Insurance Securities Inc., San Francisco 1957-68; sales rep. Calif. Investors Inc., Long Beach 1968-71, Mitchum Jones & Templeton, Long Beach 1971-73; finl. cons./estate planner, Dean Witter & Co., Newport Beach 1973-74; Clowell Weeden, Laguna Hills 1974-75; currently account exec. with Securities West Inc., Tustin, num. sales awards incl. Million Dollar Club, Outstanding Salesman, Man of the Mo., Man of the Year; mem. Internat. Assn. of Finl. Planners; Masons, Scottish Rite, Shriners (past pres. Long Beach Shrine Club), US Navy League, YMCA; mil: pvt. inf. US Army 1929; Republican; Prot.; rec: golf, tennis, swimming. Res: 348 Otero St Newport Beach 92660 Ofc: Securities WEst Inc. 17601 17th St, Ste. 218, Tustin 92680

ALESZKA, JAMES CHARLES, metallurgical engineer; b. June 9, 1949, Oakland; s. Benjamin John and Virginia Zeeb (Schonbien) A.; edn: BS, UCLA 1971, MS, 1973; Reg. Profl. Metallurgical Engr., Calif. 1982. Career: prin. investigator Constr. Engr. Research Lab., Champaign, Ill. 1974-75; supr. Fracture Mechanics Lab.; Effects Technology, Inc., Santa Barbara 1975-79; engineering splst. General Dynamics, San Diego 1979--; cons. Failure Analysis Investigations, 1980-; awards: Sea Grant Fellowships 1971; cert. achieve., US Army Constrn. Engring. Research Lab. 1975; mem: Am. Soc. for Metals, Am. Inst. of Mining, Metallurgical and Petroleum Engrs., Gen. Dynamics Sailing Club (treas.); publs: num. sci. tech. reports, presentations; Catholic; rec: sailing, backpacking, wine collecting. Res: 9289 Village Glen Dr, 116, San Diego 92123 Ofc: General Dynamics/Convair, POB 80847, San Diego 92138

ALEXANDER, CHARLES WILLIAM, real estate broker; b. July 10, 1949, Colorado Springs, Colo.; s. Lt. Col. (USAF ret.) Robert B. and Mae R. (Rose) A.; m. Margaret R. Duffy, Dec. 22, 1973; 1 son: Robert, b. 1980; edn: BSBA, Univ. of Ark. 1971; MBA, Golden Gate Univ. 1984; APRA, Nat. Inst. R.E. Appraisers; CCIM, Realtor Nat. Mktg. Inst.; Calif. Comm. Coll. Tchg. Cred. Career: navigator, USAF 1971-75, S.E. Asia, 4 decorations; capt. USAFR 1975-; navigator 1975-80; Community Civil Defense 1980-; real estate sales 1978--, top agt. in Allied Realtors 1979; ofc. mgr. ERA Old Towne Realtors, Inc. 1980-81; owner/ broker Alexander & Assoc. 1981--; comm. coll. instr.; honors: Alpha Kappa Psi 1968; var. profl. sales awds. mem: No. Solano Bd. Realtors (Edn. Com. chmn.); Realtors Nat. Mktg. Inst.; Nat. Inst. of R.E. Appraisers; Vacaville CofC; Republican; Methodist; rec: skiing, photog. Res: 142 Glenwood Ct Vacaville 95688 Ofc: Alexander & Assocs., 300 Main, Vacaville

ALEXANDER, CLEMSON MC GEE, trucking co. executive; b. Feb. 1, 1920, Elberton, Ga.; s. Frank R. and Callie S. (McGeen) A.; m. Jean Coulter, Nov. 17, 1943; children: Gary, b. 1953; Gayle, b. 1956. Career: v.p./dir. G.I. Trucking Co., La Mirada 1946--, pres. Leasing Div.; past pres. Commerce Lions Club 1963-64; past pres. Transportation Shrine Club 1973; past pres. Hacienda Golf Club 1981; mil: cpl. USAF 1942-46, GCM; Republican; Protestant; rec: golf, hunting, fishing. Res: 1635 Suncrest Ct La Habra 90631 Ofc: G.I. Trucking Co., 14727 Alondra Blvd La Mirada 90631

ALEXANDER, PAUL BRITTAIN, viniculturist; b. June 14, 1930, Boston, Mass.; s. Wallace Bruce and Helen (Milton) Alexander; m. Molly Weld; chil: Christine, b. 1960, Elizabeth, b. 1962, Sarah, b. 1963; edn: BA, Brown Univ. 1952, MA, Boston Univ. 1958, PhD, Univ. of Ore. 1964; wine maker, German Wine Acad., Bordeaux Wine Inst.; regis. Calif. Dept. of Consumer Affairs. career: founder/pres./chief wine maker, San Diego Vineyards, Campo, Calif. mem. So. Calif. Vintners Assn. res: 16187 Lyons Valley Rd., Jamul 92035. ofc: San Diego Vineyards, Rt. 1, Box 104, Campo 92006.

ALEXANDER, ROBERT JOHN, insurance agcy. president; b. June 30, 1945, Pittsfield, Mass.; s. Robert Fisher and Eleanor R. (Behan) A.; 1 son: Robert F. III, b. 1974; edn: BA, Regis Coll., Denver 1968. Career: National Adjusters, Inc. 1970; with Conneticut Gen. Life Ins. Co. 1970-80; nat. acct. sys. 1970-72; brokerage acct. exec. 1972-80; pres. RJA & Assocs., Inc., Beverly Hills 1980--; mem: Bldg. Ind. Assn.; Los Angeles Life Underwriters Assn.; Million Dollar Round Table; Beverly Hills Estate Plng. Council; mil: E-5, US Army, M.P. 1968-70; rec: skiing, running, golf. Res: 329 North Mansfield Los Angeles 90036 Ofc: RJA & Assocs., 9465 Wilshire Blvd, Ste 513, Beverly Hills 90212

ALEXIOU, ADAM STANLEY, investment banker; b. Sept. 27, 1931, Brooklyn, NY; s. Stanley and Mary (Couloumbi) A.; edn: BA, Guilford Coll. 1956; JD, Wake Forest Univ. 1959; LLM, New York Univ. 1964; admitted state bars of NY, 1960, N.C., 1959. Career: AMF, Inc., New York 1960-63, 1966-67; asst. Division counsel, Revere Copper & Brass Inc., NY 1964-65; asst. counsel Norwich Pharmaceutial Co. Internat. Div., NY 1968-70; corp. counsel Vadas Perry Von Gehr Goldsmith & Deschamps, NY 1971-72; atty. The Singer Co., NY 1972-77; counsel Smith Steibel Alexander & Saskor 1977-79; atty. Donald Scheldon & Co., investment banking, Los Angeles 1979--; honors: Am. Jurisprudence Awd. 1957; mem: AMA; Masons; The Atrium Club, NY 1977-79; mil: sp3, US Army, M.P. 1954-55, GCM; Greek Orthodox. Res: 21351 Rambla Vista Dr Malibu 90265 Ofc: Donald Sheldon & Co., 12301 Wilshire Blvd Los Angeles 90025

ALI, NAWAB, engineering executive; b. Mar. 2, 1937, Jullundur, India, nat. 1963; s. Rahmat and June Ali; m. Bertha, Aug. 4, 1962; children: Raza, b. 1964, Linda, b. 1969, Rahmat David, b. 1972; edn: BSc, Punjab Univ. 1952; BS, UC Berkeley 1959; MS, WEst Coast Univ. 1965; PhD, C. Univ. 1984. Career: group leader Control Data, L.A. 1959-68; section mgr. CPU Devel. Fairchild, Sunnyvale 1968-71; dir. of custom circuit devel./op., Nortec, 1971-72; mgr. applications, Elec. Arrays, Mtn. View 1972-74; pgm. mgr. Sera Lab, San Carlos 1974-78; sr. staff, Tech. Dev. Corp., Sunnyvale 1978-82; eng. mgr. Nicolet, Fremont 1982--; instr. Univ. Santa Clara 1971; mem: IEEE, ACM, AAAS; mem. Parent Alert; patentee: Data Linkage Bus. Design (1983); mil: PUOTC; Muslim; rec: sports, music. Res: 20034 Wheaton Dr Cupertino 95014 Ofc: Nicolet, 201 Fourier, Fremont 94539

ALKAR, YASAR MEHMET, physician, psychiatrist; b. June 1, 1926, Kast, Turkey, nat. Am. 1971; s. Abidin A. and Zehra (Seyh) A.; m. Erden Alkar, Nov. 4, 1950; chil: Banu, b. 1953, Bengu, b. 1954; edn: MD, Univ. of Istambul, 1952; psych., Colo. State Univ. 1959-60, Pontiac State Hosp., 1960-64; Psychiatrist, M.D., state of Mich. 1964. career: dir. Iskilip Health Ctr., Turkey 1952-56; acting dir. Dept. Health, 4th Turkish Armoured Bridgade 1956-58; dir. alcoholism treatment & resrch, Riverview Hosp., Vancouver, B.C. 1964-66; chief Section C- Psychiatry, Pontiac (Mich.) State Hosp., 1966-68; coordinator Psych. Dept., Wm. Beaumont Hosp., Royal Oak, Mich. 1968-75; chmn. Dept. of Psych., Madison Community Hosp., Madison Hts., Mich. 1966--; faculty Mich. State Univ., Dept. Psych. 1973-; private practice: dir. Gen. Psychiatric Clinic, 1968-77, exec. med. dir. Alkar Medical Center, 1973-83, Birmingham, Mich.; pvt. practice, Carlsbad and San Diego, 1983--; AMA Physician Recognition Awards (4); mem: Am. Med. Assn., Calif. State, San Diego Co. Med. Socs., Mich. State, Oakland Co., Macomb Co. Med. Socs., Mich. Psychiatric Soc., Am. Psychiat Assn., World Med. Assn., Am. Soc. of Clin. Hypnosis, Am. Coll. of Legal Medicine, Internat. Soc. of Hypnosis; mil: lt., med. ofcr., 1956-58; rec: music, boating, travel, photog. res: 1947 S. Pacific St., Oceanside 92054 ofc: Y.M. Alkar, M.D., 800 Grand Ave., Ste.B-7, Carlsbad 92008; 225 Broadway, Ste. 1500, San Diego 92101.

ALKER, BRUCE BRADLEY, engineering research co. executive; b. Jan. 30, 1945, New Orleans, La.; s. Albert Raymond and Winifred Emily (Lilley) A.; m. Carol Nelson, Mar. 26, 1966; children: Kenneth b. 1968, Wendy b. 1970, Amy b. 1974; edn: AA, Santa Monica City Coll. 1964; BS engring. (nuclear), CSU Northridge 1967. Career: tech. writer Bunker Ramo Corp., Westlake Village 1966-68, senior field engr. 1968-72, applications engr. 1972-73, senior design engr. 1973-75, engring. splst. 1975-80, staff systems engr. 1981; staff systems engr. Alpharel Inc., Camarillo 1981-82, v.p. advanced plnng. 1983--, currently involved in archtl. devel. of DDTNS, and adv. product areas for co.; adv. Alpharel Bd. dirs. 1983--; cons. Autologic Inc. 1980; developed a Satellite Data Exchg. Controller (SDEC) interface between the IBM computer and the SBS (Satt. Bus. Sys.; IBM, Aetna Life and Comsat Labs) up down converter; recipient Merit Award for devel. of Comm. Front-End Processor (1977), and Engr. of the Month (1980), Bunker Ramo; State Lab Contest awd., Soc. for Exptl. Stress Analysis (1966); mem: IEEE, Soc. for Expt. Stress Anal.; BSA asst. scout master, cub ldr.; patents: 2 Disclosures in field; Republican; Episcopal; avocation: agricultural land devel., farming; rec: home computer design, antique car and off-road vehicle fabrication. Res: 860 Crusoe Cir Thousand Oaks 91362 Ofc: Alpharel Inc. 765 Flynn Rd Camarillo 93010

ALLBRITTON, ROXANE CATHERINE, corporate controller; b. Mar. 29, 1952, Vallejo; d. Donald Willam and Eleanor (DeMage) Razle; m. James Allbritton, June 16, 1973; 1 dau: Catherine Dallas, b. 1975; edn: AA, Solano Comm. Coll. 1969-71; CSU Sacto. 1971-72. Career: junior acct., controller Kauffman Ent. (men's clothing corp.), sacramento 1971-80; controller Dick Bruhn Inc., Salinas 1980-84; acct. mgr. Granite Constrn. Co., Watsonville 1984--; v.p./softwear consultant, JAPA Ent., 1983--; bus. advisor J.W. Dekellis and Assoc., Inc. 1977--; awards: Calif. State and Al St. John scholarships, 1969, CSF (life); mem. Salinas CofC; designed computerized accounting/mdse system; Democrat; Catholic; rec: painting. Res. 924 Riker St Salinas 93901 Ofc: Granite Constrn. Co. 585 W. Beach St Watsonville 95076

ALLEN, EARL WAYNE, engineer; b. July 10, 1930, Calgary, Alberta, Can.; nat. 1951; s. Archibald Lawrence and Vera Agnes (Doane) Allen; m. Frances Mathews, June 21, 1957; edn: BS in physics, Oregon State Univ. 1951, MS in physics, 1956; PhD in engrg., UCLA, 1968; Regis. Profl. Engineer, Nuclear Engr.,Calif. Career: resrch engr. and Reactor Ops. supr. Atomics Internat., Canoga Park 1955-57; Abteilungsleiter, Reaktor Physik, Hahn-Meitner Inst. fur Kernforschung, Berlin 1957-59; mem. tech. staff Space Technology Labs., RedondoBch 1959-66; dept. mgr. and sr. staff scientist Ballistic Missiles Div.,TRW Defense Systems Grp., San Bernardino 1967-70, asst. program mgr. 1970-77, mgr. Systems Engineering Ops. 1977-80, sr. staff engr. 1980--. Mem. UCLA Reactor Hazards Com. 1963-65; awards: Space Technology Labs. Cooperative Fellowship 1961-63; AEC Spl. Fellow in Nuclear Science 1966-67; mem: Am. Physical Soc. 1956-, Am. Nuclear Soc. 1959-; coauthor: Direct Cycle Radioisotope Rocket Engine (US Patent), Apr. 1967; mil: capt USAF 1951-53; rec: raising, showing bloodhounds; res: 13007 Burns Ln Redlands 92373 ofc: TRW Defense Systems Gp, PO Box 1310 San Bernardino 92402.

ALLEN, HOWARD PFEIFFER, utilities company president; b. Oct. 7, 1925, Upland, Calif; s. Howard Clinton and Emma Maude (Pfeiffer) A.; edn: BA cum laude, Pomona Coll. 1948; JD, Stanford Univ. Law Sch. 1951; m. Dixie Mae Illa, May 14, 1948; chil: Alisa Cary, b. 1957. Career: asst. dean Law Sch/ asst. prof. law, Stanford Univ. 1951-54; with So Calif Edison Co. 1954--: spl rep. 1954, asst. to v.p. 1955, spl. counsel 1959, v.p. 1962, v.p. and asst. to pres. 1969, sr. v.p. 1971, exec. v.p. 1973-80, pres.1980--; Dir: Calif Fed Svgs & Loan Assn., Republic Corp., ICN Pharmaceuticals Inc., PSA Inc, Pacific Southwestern Airlines, Computer Sciences Corp., MCA Inc., L.A. Co. Fair Assn., Pacific Coast Elec. Assn., L.A. Area C. ofC. 1969-(pres. 1978, chmn.1979); mem. bd.:L.A. Civic Light Opera, L.A. Co. Mus of Art, Calif. Council for Environmental Economic Balance; trustee Pomona Coll.; bd. dir. Calif. Rapid Transit Dist. 1964-67; mem. Mayor's spl Com. on Olympics and L.A. Olympic Orgn. Comm. 1978 (v.chmn., bd. dirs. mem. exec. com.); mem: US Supreme Ct. Bar, Calif. State Bar; Am., Calif., L.A. Co., S.F. Bar Assns.; Am. Judicature Soc.; California Club, Jonathan Club, (L.A.); Bohemian, Pacific Union (S.F.); Ofc: 2244 Walnut Grove Ave. Rosemead 91770

ALLEN, JEFFREY M., lawyer; b. Dec. 13, 1948, Chgo.; s. Albert A. and Miriam F. (Feldman) Allen; m. Anne Marie, Aug. 9, 1945; chil: Jason M., b. 1978, Sara M., b. 1980; edn: AB, UC Berkeley 1970, JD, Boalt Hall Law Sch. 1973; lic. Calif. real estate broker 1977. Career: partner law firm Graves & Allen, and predecessor firm, Oakland 1973--, legal practice spec. in real estate; lectr. in real estate St. Mary's Coll.; bd. dirs. Harbor Nat. Bancorp; dir. num. real estate, investment cos.; mem: Am. Bar Assn., Calif. State Bar Assn., Alameda Co. Bar; Phi Beta Kappa, Oakland Athletic Club, PTA; contbr. law revs.; Democrat; rec: computers, photog., skiing; ofc: Graves & Allen, 235 W. MacArthur Bl. Ste. 400, Oakland 94611

ALLEN, JOSEPH, public relations executive, author; b. June 21, 1944, Houston, Tex.; s. Robert J. and Margaret Sue (Miller) A.; m. Mary Carter, Jan. 27, 1973; children: Annette, b. 1974, John, b. 1976; edn: BA, UCLA 1969. Career: pres./bd. chmn. Allen & McGarvey Inc. (finl. pub. rels.), Irvine 1982--; fmr: v.p./gen. mgr. Bozell & Jacobs Pub. REls., Newport Bch. 1980-82; staff writer, pub. affairs, Atlantic Richfield Co., LA 1974-77; editor, mktg. mgr. Sage Publications Inc., Beverly Hills 1969-71; guest lectr. UCLA Grad. Sch. of Mgmt., UCLA Ext., Compton Coll. Author books: Sandcastles (NY: Doubleday & Co. Inc. 1981), The Leisure Alternatives Catalog (NY: Dell Pub. Co. 1980), Effective Business Communications: A Practical Guide (Glenview, Il: Scott Foresman & Co. 1979), Systems in Action: A Managerial and Social Approach (grad. text on life cycles in systems analysis, winner num. awards for creativity and presentation, currently in use in grad. schs. of mgmt.)(Glenview, Il: Scott Foresman & Co. 1978), Life At The Top: Profiles of the CEO (in progress); writer contbg. to newspapers and periodicals incl: The Times (London), GEO, Readers Digest (Intl. Ed.), Games, Republic Scene, Ford Times, Crafts, Diversions. Orange County United Way comm. chmn. 1984; dir. South Coast Cultural Services League/ Inst. of Dance Arts; club: University Athletic (Newport Bch); Catholic; rec: art collector, harpsichordist. Res: 3842 Acacia Irvine 92714 Ofc: Allen & McGarvey Inc. 4482 Barranca Pkwy, Ste. 260, Irvine 92714

ALLEN, MELANIE, clinical psychologist, educator, writer, consultant; b. Dec. 8, 1939, Mnpls.; d. Samuel David and Francis Marilyn (Fagen) Finkelstein; edn: Univ. of Minn. 1956-58; BA cinema, w/honors, UCLA, 1961; The Sorbonne-Paris, 1963-64; BA psych., CSU Northridge, 1969; PhD psych.,

USC, 1974; career: prodn. asst. Ency. Britannica Films 1961-62; Fulbright Fellowship to Inst. de Filmologie, The Sorbonne, 1963-64 and appt. to Bd. of Editors, Rives (Revue des echanges univs.); property dept. hd and film writer for prod. Norman Lear, Tandem Prodns., Columbia Pictures 1965-67; grad. tchg. fellowship USC 1969-72; NIMH fellowship/intern in clin. pxych. 1972-73, HEW Maternal and Child Care postdoc. fellowship 1973-74, consulting psychologist 1974-79, Childrens Hosp. of L.A.; instr. psych. and humanities divs. Art Center Coll. of Design 1973-77; guest lectr. Calif. Inst. of the Arts 1975-76; prof. psych. Antioch Coll./West 1973-79; pvt. practice Clin. Psychology spec. Family Systems, Pediatric Psychol., Sherman Oaks 1974--; asst. prof. CSUN 1974--; tech., creative cons. to film industry; lectr. various univs., hosps., schools, public agencies; mem. bd. of eds. Jour. of Humanistic Psychol. 1980-; dir. grad. tng. pgm in psychol. Ryokan Coll. 1983-. Num. guest appearances on radio and TV; author: Primary: An Intro. to Humanistic Psychology (w/Charlotte Buhler) 1972, Make em Laugh (w/Wm. Fry) 1975; 100 short stories, poems, arts. Awards: Chimes (acad. hon.), Tau Beta Sigma, Sigma Alpha Iota (music), Psi Chi (psych. frat); Delmar Ickes Awd., CSUN 1969; recognition for theoretical achievements in psychol.; invited to Intl. Invitational Cong. on Humanistic Psychol., Amsterdam 1970, Wurzburg, Ger. 1971, Nat. Endowment for Humanities Conf., Tucson 1975, 1st Internat. Cong. on Humour and Laughter, Wales 1976; rec: music, photog., travel; res: Sherman Oaks 91403

ALLEN, PRESTON KENDRICK, real estate broker; b. Nov. 19, 1909, Burkesville, Ky.; s. Wm. Marshall and Elizabeth (Rose) A.; m. Docia Booher, Sept. 9, 1932; children: Nancy, b. 1934, Mary, b. 1940, Preston K. Jr., b. 1942; ed. pub. schools, Burkesville, Ky.; spl. courses, Dale Carnegie 1974; ATM (Able Toastmaster), Toastmasters Intl. 1978. Career: farming and timber bus., Burkesville, Ky. 1917-34; citrus grower and trucking bus., Orange Co., Calif. 1934-53; mgr. Milk Producers Council of So. Calif., 1953-63; lic. real estate broker; 1956 Democratic cand. for State Senate 35th Dist.; elected mem. Dem. Party Electoral College 1956; dir. Orange Co. Water Dist. 1965-80, pres. two terms 1975-79; charter mem. Nat. Water Supply Improvement Assn. 1975; orgnzr., commnr. Santa Ana River and Santiago Creek Green Belt Commn. 972; honors: Kentucky Col. 1972; mem. Oak Grove Comm. Assn., Glen Oak Comm. Assn., Kiwanians, Toastmasters; publs: speeches on O.C. Water Dist. in Mex. City 1976, Tokyo 1978, Nice, Fr. 1979 (Reports of the Internat Desalination and Environ. Assn.); Democrat (chmn. Citizen Com. to re-elect US Sen. Clair Engle); Prot. rec: sports, basketball. Res: 47525 Kimberly Ann Dr. Aguanga 92302

ALLEN, R. MICHAEL, microcomputer software co. executive; b June 27, 1949, Louisville, Ky.; s. Buddy S and Helen E. (Miller) A.; m. Sandra L. Quiggins, Aug. 22, 1970; edn: Purdue Univ. 1967-69; BS, Mass. Inst. of Tech. 1971; JD, MBA, Stanford Univ. 1975; counselor at law, State Bar of Texas 1979. Career: consultant McKinsey & Co., Chgo. 1975-76, sr. engagement mgr. McKinsey & Co., Dallas, Tx. 1977-80; mgr. strategy devel. Major Appliance Bus. Gp., Gen. Electric Co., Louisville, Ky. 1980-82; pres. RMA Associates, Palo Alto 1982-83; pres./CEO/bd. chmn. Trademark Software, Mtn. View 1982--; honors: Purdue Univ. President's Awd., scholastic excellence 1968, 69; Stanford Law Sch., Calif. State graduate fellowship award; graduated top 10 percent of class, Stanford Bus. Sch. Mem. Texas Bar Assn. 1979-, Decathlon Club 1984--; publs: art., Stanford Jour. of Internat. Studies. Republican. Catholic. Res: 510 Lincoln Ave Palo Alto 94301 Ofc: Trademark Software 465B Fairchild Dr. Mtn. View 94043

ALLIEGRO, ANSELMO MIGUEL, physician-surgeon; b. Feb. 13, 1931, Manzanillo, Cuba, nat. Am. 1970; s. Miguel Angel and Dulce Maria (Maestre) A.; m. Veronica Orr, Mar. 20, 1979; chil: Yolanda Maria, b. 1959, Miguel Angel, b. 1965, Lourdes Maria, b. 1968; edn: BS, Santiago Cuba Inst. 1951, stu. Univ. Havana Med. Sch. 1951-58; Dr. Medicine & Surgery, Univ. Salamanca (Spain) 1960. career: resident (int. med., surg.) Dr. Phillips Mem. Hosp., Orlando, Fla. 1961, Comm. Hosp., Wilmington, N.C. 1961-2, James Walker Mem. Hosp., Wilmington, N.C. 1962-3, St. Agnes Hosp., Baltimore, Md. 1963-4, North Charles Gen. Hosp., Baltimore 1964-6; attending physician Dept. Internal Med., North Charles Gen. Hosp., Baltimore 1966-79; pvt. practice Int. Med., Baltimore, Md. 1966-79, Los Angeles, Ca. 1979--. Cert. M.D., Calif., Md., Wash. DC, Ednl. Council Fgn. Med. Grads. Mem: founding pres. Interam. Coll. Phys. & Surgeons Calif. chpt. 1983; Royal Soc. of Medicine (London); Cuban Med. Assn. of Calif. (v.p. 1982-3); Hispanic-Am. Med. Assn. of Calif. (Secty.Gen. 1982-3); Fellow Am. Coll. of Angiology; Fellow Internat. Coll. of Angiol.; Fellow Am. Soc. of Abdominal Surgeons; Am. Soc. of Contemporary Med. & Surg.; Interam. Club. mil: maj. USAR 1974-9. Republican. Catholic. rec: aviation. res: 324 Via El Chico, Redondo Bch 90277 ofc: 2010 Wilshire Blvd. Ste.612, Los Angeles 90057.

ALLISON, JOHN THOMAS, management consultant; b. Mar. 11, 1946, Concord, Ca.; s. John Pershing and Mary M. (Reese) A.; m. Sally Rittenhouse, Apr. 4, 19981; chil: Anne Marie, b. 1968, Joseph, . 1976; edn: BA, UC Berkeley 1976; MA, Antioch Univ. 1976; PhD, The Wright Inst. Grad. Sch of Psych. 1983; PhD, Columbia Pac. Univ. 1983; MFCC, Marriage, Family & Child Counselor, Bd. of Behavioral Sci. Examiners 1982. Career: exec. dir. Petaluma People Services Center, 1976-78; exec. dir. NCCW, Inc. 1978-82; pres. The Firm, Inc. Social Sci. Consultants, 1982--; director, co-founder Swords to Plowshares (Veterans Rights orgn.); faculty CSU Sacramento, Antioch Univ., Columbia Pac. Univ., Golden Gate Univ.; bd. mem. various regional non-profit social svc. orgns. Honors: merit certs., Nev. Co. Bd. of Suprs., 1982, Nev. Co. Community Svcs. Council, 1981. Mem: Assn. of Labor/Mgmt. and Consultants

on Alcoholism (ALMACA), Calif. Assn. of Marriage, Family Therapists, Calif. Assn. of Rehabilitation Facilities; mem. Big Brothers/Big Sisters of Nev. Co., Nev. Co. Arts Council; profl. papers, publs.; mil· capt. USMC 1964-70; Democrat; rec: distance running, gardening; res: 22587 Montezuma Rd. North San Juan 95960 ofc: The Firm, Inc. 11721 Nevada City Hwy., Grass Valley 95945

ALLISON, LAIRD BURL, professor emeritus of management; b. Nov. 7, 1917, Saint Marys, W. Va.; s. Joseph Alexander and Opal Marie (Robinson) A.; m. Katherine Hunt, Nov. 25, 1943; 1 son, William, b. 1945; m. 2d. Genevieve Elmore, Feb. 1, 1957; edn: BS in personnel and indsl. rels., magna cum laude, USC 1956; MBA, UCLA 1958. Career: lectr., asst./assoc./ prof. of mgmt., CSU Los Angeles 1956-83, asst. dean undergrad. studies, Sch. of Business and Econ. 1971-73, and assoc. dean ops., 1973-83; prof. emeritus of mgmt., CSULA; vis. asst. prof. of mgmt. CSU, Fullerton (summer 1970). Honors: Phi Kappa Phi, Beta Gamma Sigma, Omicron Delta Epsilon, Phi Eta Sigma hon. socs.; Ford Found. Faculty Fellowship Awd. 1960. Mem: Acad. of Mgmt.; Alpha Kappa Psi Profl. Bus. Frat.; Am. Inst. of Individual Investors; The Inst. of Mgmt. Scis. (TIMS); Western Econ. Assn. Internat.; World Future Soc.; orgns: Faculty Emeriti Assn., CSULA; Ret. Public Employees Assn. of Calif.; USS Astoria Assn. Collaborated in devel. new BSc degree program in Mgmt. Sci. (1963), CSULA. Mil: chief interior communications electrician, USN, 1936-51, medals: Am. Def., Am. Theatre Campaign., Asia-Pac. Theatre Cmpgn., WWII Victory, GCM; battles: Coral Sea, Midway, Guadalcanal, Savo.; survivor of sinking of USS Astoria (CA 34) in Battle of Savo. Rec: history, travel, photog., hiking. Res: 1615 So El Molino St Alhambra 91801

ALLISON, MARVIN LAWRENCE, journalist; b. Aug. 8, 1934, Phoenix, Ariz.; s. George Lewis and Dorothy A. (Kinsella) A.; m. Patricia Ann Kiley, Apr. 2, 1954; 1 son, Marvin L., b. 1955; edn: Neiman fellow, Harvard Univ. 1968-69; Sorbonne, Paris 1952-53; stu. Long Beach St. Coll. 1953-54. Career: reporter Downey (Calif.) Live Wire, 1955-57; copy editor Long Beach Independent, also Press-Telegram, 1957-62, reporter 1963-66; copy editor Stars & Stripes newspaper, Darmstadt, Germany 1962; city editor Ind. Press-Telegram, Long Beach, 1966-68, mng. editor, 1969-76; asst. to pub Lexington (Ky.) Herald-Leader, 1976-77; assoc. editor Detroit (Mich.) Free Press 1977-78; senior vice pres./editor Long Beach (Calif.) Ind. Press Telegram, 1978--; mem: AP Mng. Editors Assn. (dir.), Am. Soc. of Newspaper Editors (com. chmn.); mem. Sigma Delta Chi Club- Harvard (L.A.). Res: POB 201, Surfside 90743 Ofc: Long Beach Press-Telegram, 604 Pine Ave Long Beach 90844

ALLRED, JOHN CLEVELAND, psychotherapist, university counseling services director; b.June 29,1946, Wichita Falls, Tex.; s. Mildred Carolyn Allred Johnson and William Doyle Allred; edn: BA, Sonoma State Univ. 1976, PhD cand. Columbia Pac. Univ. 1982; m. Kathleen Fleming, Aug. 9, 1980; chil: Nathan, b. 1968, Sarah, b. 1971 (by prev marriage); Katie, b. 1981. Career: psychotherapist pvt. practice, Mill Valley and Petaluma 1976--; dir. Creative Living Center of Novato, 1977; psychotherapist Western Marin and Petaluma Counseling Services, 1977-78; dir. Counseling Services and spl. asst. to the Pres., Columbia Pac. Univ., Mill Valley 1981--; bd. dirs. Wholistic Health and Nutrition Inst. 1981-; chmn Health Com., Petaluma People Services Ctr. 1977-78. Lic. Marriage, Family and Child Therapist, 1977-; Certified Clin. Hypnotherapist, 1982; Democrat; Prot.; rec: music, painting, travel. res· 715 Western Ave Petaluma 94952 ofc: Columbia Pac. Univ. 150 Shoreline Hwy Mill Valley 94941

ALLS, KATHY, speaker, author, consultant; b. June 3, Boise, Ida.; d. Joseph and Clara (Leanord) Metzen; m. Gordon Elser; children: Brandy, Brent. Career: internat. motivational speaker, over 180 speeches ann., including seminar tours of India (1979, 81); cons., spkr., or trainer for more than 400 Am. corps.; author five books; owner three corps.; fmr. beauty contest winner, T.V. model, internat. flight attendant; subject of num. newspaper arts.; 1982 honors: Internat. Toastmasters Comm. and Leadership Award for contbns. in human devel.; Kentucky Col.; hon. citizen sev. cities; listed. Who's Who of Internat. Authors, Who's Who of Internat. Intellectuals, Who's Who of Distinguished Ams.; mem. Nat. Speakers Assn. Res: 203 Monarch Bay S. Laguna Beach 92677

ALMUETE, BIAG ACOSTA, civil engineer; b. May 18, 1934, Tarlac, Philippines; s. Arsenio Pararuan Almuete; m. Wedeliza Filipinas, Mar. 19, 1977; 1 dau: Aileen, b. 1979; edn: AA, surveying, Nat. Univ. 1959, BS in civil eng. 1966; Reg. Profl. Engr. (civil), Calif. 1982. Career: area mgr. Erectors Co., Philippines 1966-71; ops. mgr. Alas Construction, Philippines 1971-76; engring. & const. mgr. D.S.E.I., Hayward 1978--; mng. dir. American Consolidated Technology, Inc. 1981--; mem: Fasae ; San Jose Shrine Club; Grand Lodge of the Phillipines; Grand Lodge of Calif.; Catholic; rec: sports. Res: 3562 Aberdeen St Santa Clara 95050 Ofc: Doller Saver Enterprises, Inc., 20756 Western Blvd Hayward 94541

ALONSO, GISELLE O., importer/wholesaler womens apparel; b. Oct. 12, 1956, Mexico City, Mex.; d. Benjamin P. and Herminia Salzberger (Wasserteil) Oleszevoski; m. Isaac Alonso Sieiro, Apr. 11, 1979; child, Liah, b. 1980; edn: BA, honors, CSU, Northridge 979; MA, honors, communication & devel., Stanford Univ. 1982; postgrad. stu. 1983-. Career: pres. Crafticorp, Inc., Palo Alto 1983--; gen. partner Femina, Palo Alto 1983--; mem: Stanford Alumni Assn.; research dir.: nat. evaluation of nat. preschool sys. of Mex. 1982-83; Jewish; rec: photog., flying. Res: 10271 W. Loyola Dr Los Altos 94022 Ofc: Crafticorp, Inc., 809 San Antonio Rd, Ste. 9, Palo Alto 94306

ALTER. RICHARD, real estate developer, financier; b. Oct. 9, 1945, Long Beach; s. Patricia Mary Boeler; m. Rose McKenzie, June 16, 1973; edn: BS, 1967, MBA, 1975, USC; Calif. lic. Real Estate Broker 1978, Gen. Contractor 1983; Cert. Business Counselor 1981, NASD mem. 1984. Career: controller TransTechnology Corp., Sherman Oaks 1969-75; dir./CFO/treas. Vagabond Hotels, San Diego 1975-78; asst. to Mr. Avis & CFO/v.p. Avis Enterprises, 1978-82; chief op. ofcr./exec. v.p. American National Group, Beverly Hills 1982--; diverse real estate developer, syndicator, financier. Mem: Commerce Associates, Nat. Assn. of Accountants, Bev. Hills Bd. of Realtors, Asso. for Corp. Growth. Catholic. Res: 1015 Gayley Ave. Los Angeles 90024 Ofc: American National Gp 405 S. Beverly Dr. Beverly Hills 90212

ALTIS, WILLIAM GERALD, chiropractor; b. July 21, 1940, Grand Coulee, Wash.; s. Audra Skelt and Marjorie Juanita (Ells) A.; m. Betty Ashpaugh, Dec. 13, 1965; chil: Christopher b. 1962, Deborah, b. 1963, Christine, b. 1964, Susan, b. 1964, Dennis, b. 1966, James, b. 1969; edn: AA, Phoenix Coll. 1965, cert. Metals Engring. Inst. 1965; D.C., Cleveland Chiro. Coll. 1969; Diplomate, Nat. Bd. Chiro. Examiners 1969. Career: dr. of chiropractic; instr. seminars in chiropractic, bus. mgmt., ins. and law: Gonstead Seminars 1969-, Gonstead Workshops 1970-81, CAP Peer Review 1973-, HIO 1969, Sacro Occiptal Technique 1968-70, Gillet 1975; mem: Parker Chiropractic Resrch Found., Internat. Chiro. Assn. of Calif. (Peer Rev. 1971), Chiropractic Resrch. Ednl. Service Found. (1974 staff), City of Health (cofounder 1973), CAP Ednl. Found. (cofounder 1973); mem. W.Covina Lions 1970-, Lark Ellen Home for Boys (bd. mem. 1975), Valley Light Industrys (pres. 1975). Publs: S.D.T. (1969), Gonstead (seminar prod. book form 1969), 1981 Gonstead Reference; Republican (Repub. Task Force, US Congl. Adv. Bd.); L.D.S. Ch.; rec: stamps, coins, antiques; res: 754 Rancho El Puerte, Covina 91724 ofc: Altis Chiro. Ofc. 570 S. Barranca Ave Covina 91723.

ALTSHULER, EDWARD ARTHUR, writer/consultant/lecturer; b.Sept. 25, 1919, Kansas City, Mo.; s. David and Ida (Glassman) Altshuler; m. Juliette Wasser Deutsch, Jan. 23, 1944; chil: David Ross, b. 1947, Ellen Anne, b. 1949, Daniel Mark, b. 1951; edn: BA, Univ. of Tex. Career: pub. rels. splst. US Army Airforce, 1941-45; pub. rels. dir. Ross Gardner & White Advt., 1946-51; mktg. dir. Kaye Halbert TV, 1951-53; mktg. svc. dir. American Electronics Corp., 1953-57; exec. dir. Ctr. for Continuing Edn., Rancho Mirage, Ca. 1957--, currently Dir. Emeritus; instr. Coll. of the Desert; cons. to Avnet Corp., Cadillac Shoe Prods. Inc., Synergistic Mgmt. Svcs., Caldwell Consumer Svcs., others. Author 32 books on sales, mgmt., mktg., incl.: Standard Op. Procedures for Every Business: People Power & Profits; How To Make the EDP Decision In your Business; sev. distrbn. mgmt. guides: Gen. Mgmt., Adminstrv. Mgmt., Finl. Mgmt., Mktg., etc. Honors: Jesse H. Neal Award. for Best series of arts. submitted to an Am. bus. paper 1979; Univ. of Wyo., Am. Heritage Found., Edward A. Altshuler Collection of Writing and Memorabilia. Mem: Internat. Advt. Assn. (pres. L.A. Cpt. 1959-60); Nat. Assn. of Mgmt. Consultants (bd.trustees 1963); LA CofC (dir. Fgn. Trade Div.); Magnetic Recording Indus. Assn. (dir.); hon. mem. Nat. Electronic Distbrs. Assn.; LA United Jewish Appeal (chmn. Electronics Div.); Am. Soc. of Tng. Directors; Nat. Speakers Assn. (founding mem.). Jewish; rec: tennis; address: 37-620 Los Cocos East, Rancho Mirage 92270.

ALVARADO-VALDEZ, PATRICIA, college district administrative aide; b. July 25, 1946, Fresno; d. Joseph Machado and Laura (Quinonez) Alvarado; m. Ruben Urrea Valdez, Feb. 22, 1982; children: Shannon, Michael, and Brian Earls; edn: AS, Fresno City Coll. 1977, BS, Univ. of San Francisco 1983; cardio pulminary rescusitation instr., Am. Heart Assn. 1979. Career: admin. splst. US Army Chief of Staff, Pentagon 1966-69; personnel dir. Ripco, Inc., Fairfax, Va. 1970-72; adminstrv. asst. Equitable Life Assurance Soc., Fresno 1977-80; adminstrv. aide State Ctr. Community Coll. Dist., Fresno 1980--; safety dir. Energy Conservation Coord., State Center Comm. Coll. Dist. 1982-; awards: Geraldine Wheeler Scholor 1977; mem: League of Mex.- Am. Women; Mujeres for Political Action; Nat. Orgn. for Women; mil: E5, US Army 1966-69, GCM, Nat. Svc. Medal; Democrat; Protestant; rec: fashion design, photog., sports. Res: 4763 East Dayton Ave Fresno 93726 Ofc: State Center Community College Dist., 1525 E Weldon Ave Fresno 93704

ALVAREZ, JOHN, real estate broker; b. Dec. 24, 1921, Mexico; s. Jose and Eulalia (Mendoza) A.; m. Carmen Garcia (dec. 1980), June 14, 1953; children: Elza, b. 1955, David, b. 1957, Sylvia, b. 1959. Career: pres: Monterey Realty Co., Monterey Constrn. Co., Eastern Group Publications Inc.; dir. Pan Am. Bank of Los Angeles; pres. Carmen Alvarez Cancer Fund, Inc.; mem: 3rd v.chmn. E. L.A. Multiple Listing Svc.; 2nd v.p. Montebello Realty Bd.; Community Brokers Svc.; Gr. L.A. CofC; Internat. Assn. R.E. Counselors, Inc.; Mutual Selling Svc. of Montebello; Monterey Park chpt. City of Hope (life); L.A. Police Band Assoc., Inc.; L.A. Olympic Citizens Adv. Com.; Democrat; Catholic; rec: golf. Res: 1036 Crest Vista Dr Monterey Park 91754 Ofc: Monterey Realty Co., 5833 E Beverly Blvd Los Angeles 90002

ALVES, ANTHONY HENRY, golf professional, rancher, banker; b. Nov. 24, 1910, Monterey, Ca.; s. Joseph and Rose Marie (Perreira) Alves; m. Virginia, June 20, 1933; chil: Virginia, b. 1936, Anthony Jr., b. 1938, Raymond, b. 1940, Marie, b. 1944, Margaret, b. 1944, Rita, b. 1946; ed. San Carlos, 1918-26, St. Joseph's, 1927; career: golf profl. Del Monte and Pebble Beach Golf Courses, 1931-42; bus. mgr. Plumbers Local, Monterey 1944-46; councilman City of Monterey 1949-53; chinchilla rancher, Monterey and Oakhurst, Ca. 1951-76; comml. land developer, Monterey and Oakhurst 1958-70; organizer, dir. Golden Oak Bank, Oakhurst 1978-,and bd. chmn. 1981--; mem. Lions Club;

Democrat; Catholic; rec: gardening. res: 38683 Road 425B, POB 429, Oakhurst 93644.

ALVEY, WAYNE JOSEPH, sales representative; b. Nov. 9, 1932, E. St. Louis, Ill.; s. James Gobel and Dorothy Louise (Girten) A.; m. Patricia Hannacker, Sept. 11, 1954; chil: Mark Wayne, b. 1955, Cathleen Louise, b. 1958, Andrew Allen, b. 1961; edn: BS mktg., CSU Long Beach 1961. Career: sales mgr. Burroughs Corp. 1965-70; sales mgr. Automatic Data Processing 1971-76; partner Datamation Co. 1976-77; sr sales rep. W. H. Daum & Staff, 1977--. awards: svc. awd., Distributive Edn. Clubs of Am. 1974, appreciation awd., mktg. students 1978; mem: Knights of Columbus (1st Grand Knight, Long Bch), Sales & Mktg. Execs. of Long Bch (pres. 1976), Kiwanis Club of La Mirada (charter pres. 1979), La Mirada C. of C. (pres. 1982-83); mil: USCG 1952-56; Republican; Catholic; rec: racquetball, hiking; res: 913 Paloma Pl. Fullerton 92635 ofc: W.H.Daum & Staff, 14700 Firestone Blvd. #113 La Mirada 90638.

AMACKER, JEFFERSON Z., JR., manufacturing co. president; b. Dec. 14, 1935, Kentwood, La.; s. Jefferson Z. and Ruth Jeanette (Smith) A.; m. Loretta Schwartz, Aug. 6, 1960; children: Jeff III, b. 1960; Marla, b. 1963; Carl, b. 1970; edn: BS, mil. sci., US Mil. Acad. 1957; BS, astronautics, USAF Inst. of Tech. 1963; MBA (in prog.), Pepperdine Univ. Career: engring. mgr., 747 Pgm. Mgr., dir. Avionics, American Airlines, Tulsa, Okla. 1967-71; pgm. dir. Singer Co., Little Falls, NJ 1971-77; v.p. mktg. Simmonds Precision, Vergennes, Vt. 1977-80; gen. mgr. Systron Donner, Inertial Div., Concord 1980-83; dir./ pres./ CEO Leach Corp., Buena Park 1983--; bd. dir. LRE Electromedical 1984-; guest lectr. MIT, 1975, USAF Test Pilot Sch., Edward AFB 1967; cons. USAF Scientific Adv. Bd. 1973; Singer Co. rep. to Poland & Russia 1973-74; mem: Inst. of Navigation; West Point Soc. of Orange Co.; Aircraft Owners & Pilots Assn.; Corona del Mar Touchdown Club; Balboa Bay Club; Shiners; 11 pub. tech. papers; mil: capt. USAF Fighter Pilot 1957-67, Commdn. Medal; Republican; racquetball. Res: 7 Montpelier Dr Newport Beach 92660 Ofc: Leach Corp., 6900 Orangethorpe Ave Buena Park 92620

AMADA, GERALD LESTER, psychologist; b Aug. 13, 1938, Newark, NJ; s. Samuel and Rose (Eisenberg) A.; m. Marcia Hirshberg, Aug. 9, 1962; children: Robin, b. 1963; Naomi, b. 1964; Laurie, b. 1966; Eric, 1968; edn: BA, Rutgers Univ. 1960; MSW, 1962; PhD, Wright Inst., Berkeley 1976; Calif. Lic. Clinical Soc. Wkr. 1966. Career: dir. group homes, Homewood Terrace, San Francisco 1966-69; staff devel. supr. Solano Co. Welfare Dept., Vallejo 1969-70; coordinator employee assistance pgm. KPIX-TV (Ch. 5), S.F. 1980-82; dir. human resources Mass. Mutual Life Ins., S.F. 1981-83; pvt. psychotherapy practice, S.F. 1966--; co-dir. Mental Health Pgm. City Coll. of San Francisco 1970--; cons. State Dept. of Disability Ins.; recipient awd. of excellence, Nat. Assn. Voc. Edn. Special Needs Personnel 1984; mem: Nat. Assn. of Soc. Wkrs.; Am. Fedn. of Tchrs.; author: Mental Health in the Community College Campus, ed. 1978; Mental Health and Authoritarianism on the College Campus, 1979; A Guide to Psychotherapy, 1983; num. arts.; rec: tennis, writing. Res: 185 Mt Lassen Dr San Rafael 94903 Ofc: 1937 Noriega St San Francisco 94122

AMATO, CARMELO JOSEPH, manufacturing co. president; b. Oct. 9, 1935, Cleveland, Ohio; s. Joseph and Louise (Paolella) A.; m. Germaine L. Grdina, Sept. 10, 1955; children: Joseph, b. 1956; Anna Marie, b. 1957; Anita Louise, b. 1958; Anthony, b. 1962; edn: BSEE, honors, Case Western Reserve 1957; MSEE, honors, 1964; MBA, Wayne St. Univ. 1978; Reg. Profl. Engr., Ohio. Career: devel. engr. TRW, Cleveland, Ohio 1957-60; devel. engr. Bell Acrosystems, Cleveland, Oh. 1960-62; eng. mgr. Lear Siegler, Cleveland 1962-67; research engr. Ford Motor Co., Detroit, Mich. 1967-69; with Oxy Metal Inds., 1969-79; mgr. elec. devel. Detroit, Mich. 1969-70; mgr. energy devel. labs. 1970-72, ops. mgr. 1972-74, elec. div. mgr. 1974-79; v.p. mktg. & engring. CMC-Randtronics, Menlo Park 1979-80, pres. 1980--; Mem: IEEE (chmn. Static Power Conv. Com.); AC Power Controller Subcom.); Internat. Electrotech. Commn.; ANSI; NEMA; patentee (9); 11 tech. paper in field of Power Elecronics & Control; Republican; Catholic; rec: music. Res: 21639 Edward Way Cupertino 95014 Ofc: CMC-Randtronics, 150 Constitution Dr Menlo Park 94025

AMES, MICHAEL GEORGE, barter club president; b. Jan. 8, 1944, Cleveland, Ohio; s. Harvey George and Phylis Dean Ames; m. Sondra Schoenberger, Aug. 17, 1983; children: Katherine, b. 1965, Kimberly, b. 1970; grad. Chagrin Falls H.S. 1962. Career: founder/ pres./ chief exec. TradeAmerican-Card (largest ind. comml. bartering club in US), Orange Co. hdqtrs., afils. worldwide, 1972--; cons. re bartering to major corps.; founder/mem. Internat. Assn. of Trade Exchange Clubs (Wash DC); mem. Orange Co. CofC, Better Bus. Bur. of So. Calif.; fmr. Rotarian, Optimist; publs: var. sales tapes, manuals, audiovisuals on barter and bus. in US; Republican; Prot.; rec: racquetball, walking. Ofc: TradeAmericanCard 777 S. Main, Ste. 204, Orange 92668

AMIEL, DAVID, educator; b. Dec. 25, 1938, Alexandria, Egypt, nat. 1966; s. Eli and Inez (Bokey) A.; m. Nancy Lyons, Nov. 27, 1966; 1 son: Michael E., b. 1968; edn: PhD (equiv.), Inst. Meurice, Chimie; Dip. D'Ingenieur Chimiste, Univ. of Brussels, Belgium 1956/62; Math. Baccalaureat, Lycee Francais, Alexandria, Egypt 1956. Career: chem. engr. Laucks Testing Labs., Seattle, Wash. 1963-64; assoc., dept. orthopaedics, Univ. of Wash. 1064-70; dir. orth. biochem., Div. Orthopaedics & Rehab., UC San Diego 1970--; asst. prof. Div. Ortho. & Rehab., UC San Diego 1983--; reviewer: Connective Tissue Research, Journ. Orth. Research, Nat. Inst. of Health, Med. & Sci. in Sports Med., Arthritis & Rheumatism Journs.; awards: co-investigator Kappa Delta

Awd. 1965; basic sci. research award, Am. Orth. Soc. Sports. Med. 1983; mem: Am. Coll. of Sports Med.; Am. Soc. of biomechanics; Am. Soc. of Bone & Mineral Resources; NY Acad. of Scis.; Orth. Research Soc.; Western Orth. Assn.; Malcolm Coutts Inst. of Joint Reconstrn. & Research (bd. dirs.); Bone & Joint Disease Found. (bd. dirs.); 58 publs.; num. profl. presentations, lectures, 59 pub. abstracts; rec: running, sailing, scuba diving. Res: 747 Santa Camelia Dr Solana Beach 92075 Ofc: Univ. of Calif., San Diego, Basic Sci. Bldg. M-004, La Jolla 93093

AMIN, HABIB, consulting engineer; b. June 16, 1950, Isfahan, Iran; s. Kazem and Battool (Dehdashty) A.; m. Ladan Nasser, Feb. 25, 1977; chil: Sara, b. 1980, Mariam, b. 1982; edn: BS, Ore. State Univ. 1972; MS, 1974 and PhD, 1978 (highest honors), UC Berkeley; Reg. Profl. Engr. (chem. engring.), Calif. 1982. Career: chem. engr. Gen. Motors Resrch. Labs., 1978-80; senior engr., Systems and Process Engring., Bechtel Group, Inc., San Francisco 1980--, instr. engr. (EIT) review course, Bechtel; mem: Am. Inst. Chem. Engrs., Am. Nuclear Soc., AAAS; Tau Beta Pi, Sigma Tau, Sigma Xi, Phi Kappa Phi; profl. publs. in fields of coal and oil shale conversion to synfuels, magnetohydrodynamic power, computer simulation chem. processes; Republican; Moslem; rec: tennis, running, swim; res: 3471 Silver Spur Ct. Concord 94518 ofc: Bechtel Group, Inc. POB 3965, San Francisco 94119.

AMMONS, SANDRA HORTENSE, educator; b. May 7, 1942, Mo.; d. Roy C. and Ruth Ada (Parker) Banks; m. Brewer Tyler Ammons, March 10, 1959; children: Bryan Zachary, Clarence Edward, Crystal Christina, Steven Anthony; edn: BA, Mills Coll. 1974, grad. work, 1974-75; spl. courses, Nova Univ. 1978-79, 1981; Calif. Tchg. Cred., 1975. Career: instructional cons./ teacher Oakland School District; coordinator/instr. East Oakland Youth Devel. Ctr Cadre Program; instr. Las Cerros Senior Boys Camp; instr. Mills Coll. Upward Bound Pgm.; cons./instr. in assertive discipline for parents, Lee Canter Sch.; vol. Alameda Co. Probation Dept. pgm. 1979-; mem: Oakland Education Assn. (teacher Grievance Rep.); columnist, Ednl. Tips, Bay Area Emporium 1983-; Democrat; Baptist; rec: perf. arts, painting. Res: 3346 68th Ave. Oakland, 94605 Ofc: Oakland School District 1025 2nd Ave Oakland

AMSTER, JULIE, computer programmer/analyst; b. Jan. 14, 1955, San Francisco; d. Lee Stanley and Francine (Stutz) A.; edn: BA, CSU, Northridge 1977; MA in comm. disorders speech path., Whittier Coll. 1981; Calif. lic. Speech Pathologist. Career: speech pathol. aide Las Virgenes Unified Sch. Dist. 1970-73; sp. pathologist Regl. Rehab. Consultants, 1980-82, Serra Memorial Hosp. 1980-81; prod. support rep. Texas Instruments, 1982-83; pgmmr./analyst Compucare, Fountain Valley 1983--; cons. L.A. City Schs. on computer edn. for the handicapped, 1982; honors: Orton Soc. 1980, listed Who's Who Am. H.S. Students 1973; mem. Calif. Speech and Hearing Assn.; rec: needlepoint, knitting, swimming. Res: 226 S. Brighton Ave Burbank 91506 Ofc: Compucare, 18430 Brookhurst, Ste. 101, Fountain Valley 92708

ANCU-GHEORGHIU VASILE, veterinary hospital owner; b. July 4, 1938, Alexandria, Romania; s. Florian and Ioana (Craciun) Ancu; m. Haiganush Chibarian, Aug. 26, 1967; chil: Daniela, b. 1968, Edward, b. 1969; edn: zoo technician, Alexandria, Romania 1955-8; DVM, Bucharest, Romania 1964-9. Career: animal health technician, Alexandria, Rom. 1955-58; zoo tech. Dept. of Agri., Teleorman Co., Rom. 1960-64; veterinarian Galatzi Co., Rom. 1969-71, Dept. of Agri., Alexandria, Rom. 1971-77; veterinarian, USC Vivaria Dept., Los Angeles 1978-82; veterinarian/owner Big Tujunga Vet. Hosp., Tujunga 1983--; prof. of agriculture, Alexandria, Rom. 1960-4. Mem: So. Calif. Veterinary Med. Assn., Am. Laboratory Animal Sci., Am. Veterinary Med. Assn. Mil: sgt. Romanian Army 1958-60. Orthodox. rec: fishing. res: 6934 Foothill Blvd. Tujunga 91042. ofc: Big Tujunga Veterinary Hospital.

ANDECK, ANDREW, real estate broker, communications co. executive; b. Nov. 9, 1918, Des Moines, Iowa; s. Casper and Beulah Andeck; m. Virginia Randolph Atkinson, Aug. 1946; 1 son, Andrew Atkinson, B. 1948; edn: BA summa cum laude, Univ. of Tex. 1942. Career: pres. Andrew Andeck Co., Palm Desert; vice pres. River Communication Co. (T.V.); fmr. pres. AREA Research Co., MAP Investment Co.; apptd. planning commnr. City of Indian Wells 1984-86; past pres. and orgnzr. La Jolla Town Council 1964-65; past pres. La Jolla Real Estate Brokers Assn. 1963; clubs: Rotary of Indian Wells (pres. elect 1984), Balboa Bay Desert (dir.), Monterey Country, Lakes Country; mil: maj. USMC 1942-46, Phil. Liberation (2 stars), Pacific (6 stars) medals; Presbyterian (trustee); rec: tennis, swim, church. Address: POB 1196, Palm Desert 92261

ANDERSEN, ROBERT THOMAS, JR., lawyer; b. March 2, 1950, Los Angeles; s. Robert Thomas and Frances Elizabeth (Gold) Andersen; m. Roxann Bessette, June 19, 1976; chil: Brooke, b. 1977; Laurel, b. 1979; Amy, b. 1982; edn: BA, UCLA 1971, MPA, 1972; MATS, Talbot Theol. Sem. 1977; JD, McGeorge Sch. of Law, UOP 1979; admitted to Calif. Bar 1979; Real Estate Broker, Calif. 1981; Notary Public, Calif. 1980. Career: adminstrv. aide Municipal Data Systems for San Gabriel Valley, Monterey Pk. 1972; adminstrv. aide City of Hawthorne, 1972-73, adminstrv. asst. 1973-74; campus minister Alpha Gamma Omega, Los Angeles 1974-76; student trainee Co. of Sacramento, Community Devel., 1977-78; law clerk Pacific Legal Found., Sacto. 1978-79; atty., Law Offices of Robert T. Andersen Jr., Riverside 1979--; instr. bus. law, Calif. Baptist Coll. 1981. Honors: Traynor Soc. 1977; Outstanding Young Men of Am. 1977. Mem. State Bar of Calif., Riverside Co. Bar; Berdoo-Riverside Area Sunday Sch. Assn. bd. dirs. 1979-; Toastmasters Internat. (Club 130 sec.treas. 1980-4). Publs: The Protest, Toastmasters Tall Tale (1983);

Republican; Riverside Bible Ch. Res: 1787 Prince Albert Dr. Riverside 92507 Law Ofcs. Robt. Andersen Jr. 7172 Magnolia Ave. Riverside 92504

ANDERSON, CHARLES MICHAEL, paint co. executive, CPA; b. July 15, 1944, Londonderry, No.Ireland; s. Albert and Elizabeth (McDaid) A.; edn: BS, No. Ill. Univ., 1966; MBA, USC, 1970; m. Terri Good, Oct. 9, 1981; son, Sean Michael, b. Oct. 6, 1983. Career: staff acct. Price Waterhouse Co.,Chgo.1966-69, mgmt. cons., Los Angeles 1970-72; mgmt. cons., pvt. practice, Manhattan Bch. 1971-72; mgr. Corporate Budget, Great Southwestern Corp., Los Angeles 1973-76; dir. Internal Audit, Standard Brands Paint Co., Torrance 1976--; assoc. prof. acctg. CSU Long Beach 1979-. Certified Pub.Acct., AICPA 1970; Mem: Calif. Mus. of Sci & Indus. (advis. bd. pres. 1978, bd. dirs.1980-81); Am. Inst. of CPAs, 1970-; EDP Auditors Assn. 1983; Catholic Big Brothers, 1973-; West End Tennis and Racquet Club, 1978-; Joie DeVive Homeowners Assn. (pres. 1981-). Mil: cpl. USMCR 1967-73. Democrat. Catholic. rec: internat. travel, photog. res: 1155 11th St, #1, Manhattan Bch 90266. ofc: Standard Brands Paint Co. 4300 W. 190th St.Torrance 90509.

ANDERSON, CAROLE JOLENE, publisher; b. June 28, 1939, Tulare; d. James Pierce, Sr. and Helen Bernice (Walters) Slover; m. Douglas Robert Anderson, June 14, 1975; 1 dau: Sabrina Jo, b. 1955; edn: Riverside City Coll. 1973-76; Victorvalley Coll. 1970-73. Career: model Connor Sch. of Modeling, Fresno 1955; actress Maurice Kosloff Studios, Hollywood 1965; nat. sales mgr. Armed Services Publishers, Riverside 1966; pres. Armed Svcs. Press, 1973; currently, pres./bd. dirs. Heritage House Publs. Inc.; bd. dirs. Sullivan Publs.; mem: CofC, Tourist & Conv., YWCA, Soroptimists Internat. (Riverside); mem. Ontario, Rancho Cucamonga, Rialto, Moreno Valley, Perris & Escondido Chambers of Commerce; bd. dirs. De Anza Homeowners Assn.; rec: skiing, tennis, bicycling. Res: 10450 Dufferin Ave Riverside 92503 Ofc: Heritage House Publs., 2904 Rubidoux Blvd Riverside 92509

ANDERSON, DWAYNE WALLACE, insurance executive; b. Oct. 5, 1918, Hilmar, Ca.; s. Aaron August and Martha Emerencia (Peterson) A.; m. Elizabeth J. Prettyman, Mar. 20, 1940; edn: Modesto Jr. Coll. 1937-38. Career: owner Anderson Ins. Agency 1938; sales mgr. Merced Co. Mutual Fire Ins. Co. (now Merced Mutual) 1954, secty.-treas./ mgr. 1855; pres./ CEO Merced Mutual Ins. Co. 1982--; dir. Merced Mutual; past dir. Sequoia Ins. Co.; mem: Calif. Assn. of Mutual Ins. Cos. (past pres.); No. Calif. Assn. of Mutual Inst. Mgrs.; Hilmar CofC; Merced Co. CofC (past pres. 9153, 72, 73); Atwater CofC; Merced Elks; Republican (Central Com.); Lutheran; rec: golf. Res: 10453 Gold Link Rd Turlock 95380 Ofc: Merced Mutual Ins. Co., 5294 W Broadway 95301

ANDERSON, GERALD VERNE, metallurgical engineer; b. Oct. 25, 1931, Long Beach; s. Gordon Valentine and Aletha Marian (Parkins) Anderson; edn: BS, UC Berkeley, 1958, AA, Long Bch City Coll. 1952; m. Helen Jean Harman, May; 7, 1954, chil. Lori Jean (Fronk), b. 1957, Gregory Verne, b. 1958, David Harman, b. 1959, Lynn Elaine (Lee), b. 1961, Brian Earl, b. 1970, Michael Gordon, b. 1973. Career: resrch analyst North. American Aviation (Downey) 1953-55; sr. resrch engr. (Los Angeles) 1958-62; project leader (Palmdale) 1962-64; sr. metallurgist Autonetics, Anaheim 1964-65; R&D splst. Douglas Aircraft, Santa Monica 1965-66, Gp. leader 1966-68; tech. splst. McDonnell Douglas Astronautics, Huntington Bch 1968--; mem Corp. Metals Joining Panel, No Am. Aviation 1965; inst. Am.Soc. for Metals, L.A. 1965-69; cons. Japanese Space Pgm. Nagoya, Japan, 1972-73; cons. European Spacelab Pgm, Turin, Italy, 1976-77; instr. Seminary, L.D.S. Church, Westminster 1970-77; Profl. Metallurgical Engr., Calif. 1965-; listed: Leading Men in Am., Who's Who in Orange Co.; mem: Am. Soc. for Metals; Internat. Platform Assn.; Citizen's Adv. Com. Huntington Bch 1972; Westminster Human Resources pilot planning com., 1974, Bicent. Com., 1976; Patentee: electron beam welding, portable electron beam welding; mil: m/sgt. Nat.Guard 1951-8, GCM; Republican; LDS Ch., Bishop; rec: ski, family camping, photog.; res: 13401 Lee Dr. Westminster 92683. ofc: McDonnell Douglas Astronautics, 5301 Bolsa Ave. Huntington Bch 92647

ANDERSON, HAROLD STEAVENS, stockbroker; b. Apr. 10, 1904, Rawlins, Wyo.; s. William Steavens and Carrie Rhodes Anderson; m. Catherine Forbes, Sept. 6, 1930; edn: BS, Stanford Univ. 1927; Wyoming Univ. 1922-25; grad., Stanford Univ. 1927. Career: chem. div. Shell Oil Co., Long Beach 1928-31, transferred to Ventura, 1931-33; stockbroker/ account exec. 1933--; currently, A.E. Dean Witter Reynolds Inc., Ventura; partner/ investor Calif. Country Club, Industry; ptnr./investor in devel. California Country Club, City of Industry; mem: Calif. CC, Saticoy CC, Ventura (pres. 1951-52); X-Memteri Ventura; Lion Club; S.A.E. Frat.; Republican; Episcopal; rec: golf, football. Res: 3744 West Pacific Coast Hwy Ventura 93001 Ofc: Dean Witter Reynolds, Inc., 789 Victoria Ave Ventura 93003

ANDERSON, JOHN GORDON, chiropractor/ educator; b. June 11, 1916, Ashton, S.Dak.; s. Oscar William and Bertha Christine (Einan) A.; m. Sophie Zarabski, Aug. 25, 1949; children: John, b. 1950; James, b. 1951; Mary, b. 1954; edn: BS, Nat. Coll. of Canada 1938; ND, Lincoln Coll. of Naturopathy 1945; DC, So. Calif. Coll. of Chiro. 1946; Pepperdine Coll. 1958; Calif. Am. Univ. 1976-77. Career: faculty, Los Angeles Coll. of Chiropractic 1946-77, editor Chirogram, 1948-53, dean Graduate Sch. 1953-64, chmn. Clinical Scis. 1969-76, dean 1976-77; co-dean Anglo- European Coll. of Chiro., Bournemouth, England 1968; dean Pasadena Coll. of Chiro. 1983--; conv. & edn. symposia lectr., US, Europe, Japan; awards: George H. Haynes Awd., L.A.C.C. Alumni Assn. 1968, 73; Plaque of Appreciation, Am. Coll. of Chiro.

Orthopedists 1971, 78; mem: Am. Coll. of Chiro. Internist (life) 1961; Am. & Calif. Chiro. Assns.; Delta Tau Alpha frat.; Am. Legion; V.F.W.; Elks; Kiwanis Internat.; Northridge City Little League (pres. 1960-61); publs: Graphic Aids to Embryology; Laboratory Manual of Histology; Work Manual for Neurology; Modern Chiropractic, Its Priniciples and Techniques Illustrated,(all pub. English, Jap.); mil: pharmacist mate l/c, USNR 1942-45, PTO, Phil. Liberation; Republican; Protestant; rec: oil painting, woodworking, hunting. Res: 18605 Sunburst St Northridge 91324 Ofc: Pasadena College of Chiropractic, 1505 N. Marengo Pasadena 91104 ATTEBERRY, GEORGE DEAN, real estate broker; b. Apr. 20, 1929, Lincoln, Ill.; s. Albert Leslie and Ruth Maurine (Watt) A.; children: Dean, b. 1953; Joycelyn, b. 1955; Daniel, b. 1958; Sheryl, b. 1965; edn: BS, Univ. of Ill. 1951, grad. wk. 1956; spl. courses, USC, 1980, UC Davis 1983; lic. real estate broker, Calif. Career: self-empl. farmer (500 acres grain, 100 head beef, 1000 head hogs), Logan Co., Ill. 1956-60; asst. co. mgr., A.S.C.S., Macon Co., Ill. 1960; profl. farm mgr. Fruin Farm Mgmt., Bloomington, Ill. 1961; agri. investment ofcr. John Hancock Mutual Life Ins. Co., Ill., Calif. 1962-80; owner/pres. George D. Atteberry, Inc., Modesto & Chico 1980--; pres./dir. Calif. Agricultural Advrs. & Mgrs., Inc. 1984-; recognition awds., John Hancock Ins. Co.: Ag. Loan Vol. 1967, First Participation Ag. Loan 1969, First Ag. Joint Venture 1970, First Ag. Purchase & Leaseback 1971; mem: Calif. Soc. Farm Mgrs. & Rural Appraisers; Am. Soc. Farm Mgrs. & Rural Appraisers; Nat. Assn. of Review Appraisers; Boy Scouts of Am.; Rotary Club; Methodist Mens Club; mil: SSgt., USAF 1951-55, Good Conduct; Republican; Methodist; rec: hunting, philately, square dancing. Res: 1080 E Lassen Ave Chico 95927 Ofc: George D. Atteberry, Inc., 1207 K Street Modesto 95354

ANDERSON, MARGARET ANN, human resource systems executive; b. Oct. 27, 1940, Spokane, Wash.; d. Walter Daniel and Bozena Barbara (Zalesky) Babbitt; m. Robert Clark, Mar. 9, 1980; children: Kevin, b. 1960; Carla, b. 1963; edn: AS, Boise Coll. 1966; BA, magna cum laude, Seattle Univ. 1972; MBA, Pepperdine Univ. 1979. Career: contract programmer: computer pgmr. Co. of Orange Data Svcs., Amilco Div. of Teledyne Corp., CTC Edn. Sys. Inc., Lynwood, Wash., 1962-73; with The Aerospace Corp., El Segundo 1973--, sr. pgm. analyst, bus. sys. analyst, data processing sys. mgr., presonnel adminstr./ staff mgr., personnel sys. dept. hd., dir. human resource sys.; instr. UCLA Ext. 1980-82; chair Ofc. Equip. Users Avd. Gp. 1982-84; honors: Woman of Yr., The Aerospace Corp. 1979; mem. Human Resource Sys. Profls. (L.A. chpt. pres. 1981, 82); rec: scuba diving, archaeology (Mesopotamia), travel. Res: 2270 W 230th Pl Torrance 90501

ANDERSON, MARION RUTH, bacteriologist, real estate broker; b. 1898, Sturgeon Bay, Wisc.; d. Wm. Tait and Louisa Jane (Bagley) Anderson; edn: BA, Univ. of Wisc., Madison 1920. Career: bacteriologist, Serologist Lab., St. Lukes, Chgo. 1920-22; sole opr. State Hygienic Lab., Beloit, Wisc. 1922-25, Lab. Childrens Hosp., Chgo. 1926-27, Los Angeles Co. Health Dept., 1928-29, Childrens Hosp., Los Angeles 1929-32; currently owner/realtor, L.B. Anderson Co., Los Angeles; hon. life mem. Calif. Assn. of Realtors; mem. Univ. of Wisc. Alumni Club, Good Samaritan Hosp. Aux., Melrose Neighborhood Assn.; Republican; Episcopal; rec: int. painting & furniture, walking. Address: L.B.Anderson Co., 800 N. June St Los Angeles 90038

ANDERSON, MEL, college president; b. Sept. 18, 1928, Oakland; s. Edwin Albert and Lillian Frances (Redmond) A.; edn: BA, St. Mary's Coll. 1952, hon. D.Litt., St. Albert's Coll., Oakland, hon. D.H.L., Lewis Univ.,Ill.; Career: instr. Sacred Heart High Sch, San Francisco 1952-56; v.prin. La Salle H.S., Pasadena 1956-62; prin. San Joaquin Meml. H.S., Fresno 1962-64; prin. St. Mary's -.S., Berkeley 1964-69; pres. St. Mary's Coll. of Calif., Moraga 1969--; exec. com. Assn. Independent Calif. Colls. & Univs., 1980-; bd. dirs. Ind. Colls. of No. Calif.; chmn. Regional Assn. East Bay Colls. & Univ. 1979-81; mem. Commonwealth Club of Calif. Democrat. Roman Catholic. address: Bro. Mel Anderson, F.S.C., St. Mary's Coll. Moraga 94575

ANDERSON, MICHAEL JOHN, lawyer; b. July 6, 1949, Houghton Lake, Mich.; s. Vernon Bernard and Genevieve Elizabeth (Oster) A.; m. Estela Olivia Pino, July 8, 1978; edn: Lake Superior St. Coll. 1967-69; BS, Mich. St. Univ. 1971; JD, Thomas M. Cooley Law Sch. 1977; LLM, estate plng., Univ. of Miami 1978; lic. St. Bar of Mich. 1977, St. Bar of Calif. 1981. Career: Advanced Underwriting Dept. Southwestern Life Ins. Co. 1978; assoc. law firm Sawyer, Kramer & Murray, Mt. Clemens, Mich. 1979; assoc. law firm Wohl, Cinnamon & Hugedorn, Sacto. 1980-81; atty./pres. Michael J. Anderson, Inc. 1982-83; instr. MBA & MS tax pgms. Golden Gate Univ., and certificate pgm. for fin. plnrs. UC Davis; charter mem. Phi Alpha Delta (pres. 1976-77); mem. Am. Bar Assn., Calif. State Bar Assn. (Real Prop. Probate and Trust Law Sect.); Mich. State Bar Assn.; IAFP (bd. dirs. 1983-); Process Theatre (bd. dirs. 1983-); publs: arts., Mich. Bar. Journ.; Republican; Catholic; rec: sci-fi. Res: 3009 Funston Ave Sacramento 95825 Ofc: Michael J. Anderson, Inc., 525 Morse Ave Sacramento 95825

ANDERSON, MICHAEL ROBERT, sales executive; b. Nov. 3, 1953, Mnpls., Minn.; s. Arthur Robert and Patricia Carlson Anderson; m. Rebecca Pierce, June 6, 1981; edn: BSEE, Univ. of Minn. Inst. Tech. 1976; MSSM, USC 1981. Career: LSI designer Hughes Aircraft Co., Fullerton 1977; sales rep. Hewlett Packard, Fullerton 1977; sales rep. Group III Electronics, Irvine 1981-, regional sales mgr. 1983--; Kappa Eta Kappa Beta Chpt. Alumnus; rec: sports, computers, travel. Res: 763 Lincoln Walnut 91789 Ofc: Group III Electronics, 2691 Richter, Ste 129, Irvine 92714

ANDERSON, RAYMOND HARTWELL, JR., engineer; b. Feb. 25, 1932, Staunton, Va.; s. Raymond Hartwell and Virginia Boatwright (Moseley) A.; m. Dana Wilson, Sept. 5, 1959; chil: Kathryn, b. 1960, Margaret, b.1962, Susan, b. 1963; edn: BS, ceramic eng., Va. Polytech. Inst. 1957, BS, metallurg. eng. 1958, MS, metallurg. eng. 1959. Career: metallurgical engr. Gen.Dynamics, Ft. Worth, Tex. 1959-61; sr. metallurg. engr. Babcock & Wilcox Co., Lynchburg, Va. 1961-65, Douglas Aircraft Co., Santa Monica, Ca. 1965-67; materials R&D splst. McDonnell Douglas, Santa Monica 1967-71, sr. materials R&D splst. McDonnell Douglas, Huntington Bch. 1971--; asst. prof. metallurgy, Va. Poly. Inst. 1958-59; Am. Soc. for Metals teaching staff 1966-69; cons. engr., metallurgy, 1967-68. Honors: Tau Beta Pi (earth sci.), Alpha Sigma Mu (metals), Omicron Delta Kappa (leadership), Scabbard & Blade (mil.). Mem: Corrosion Soc. 1957-70, Am. Ceramic Soc. 1957-70, Am. Nuclear Soc. 1961-65, De Molay 1952-; BSA Merit Badge Com. 1970. Patentee (2); publs: contbr. sci. jours. Mil: lst lt. US Army Ord. 1954-56, Nat. Svc. ribbon. Republican. Prot. rec: sports cars, philately, gardening, stereo music systems. res: 1672 Kenneth Dr. Santa Ana 92705 ofc: McDonnell Douglas, 5301 Bolsa Ave Huntington Bch 92647.

ANDERSON, ROBERT HELMS, computer systems consultant; b. June 7, 1939, Richmond, Calif.; s. Oscar Nels and Elsie (Helms) A.; m. Lynn Shallenberger; children: Blythe, b. 1969; Kevin, b. 1970; edn: BA, UC Berkeley 1962; MA, Harvard Univ. 1965, PhD, 1968. Career: hd. info. scis. dept. The Rand Corp., Santa Monica 1977-79; exec. v.p. Interactive Systems Corp., Santa Monica 1979-81; pres. Robert H. Anderson & Assocs., Inc., Pacific Palisades 1981--; adj. assoc. prof. Computer Sci. Dept. USC 1968-75; commencement spkr. UC Berkeley 1962; mem: Assn. for Computing Machinery; Am. Assn. for Artificial Intelligence; Soc. of Ofc. Automation Profls.; mil: lst lt. US Army Security Agency 1962-64, Army Commdn. Medal. Address: Robert H. Anderson & Assocs., Inc., 16566 Chalet Terrace Pacific Palisades 90272

ANDERSON, SCOTT WILSHIRE, hotel executive; b. Sept. 24, 1950, San Diego; s. Albert L. and Jean (Wilshire) A.; m. Maggie Maaskant, June 18, 1971; children: Paul, b. 1980, Lauren, b. 1982; edn: BA, Wash. State Univ. 1972. Career: positions with Western Internat. Hotels: Continental Plaza, Chgo. 1972-75, South Coast Plaza, Irvine, Ca. 1975-77, Ariz. Biltmore, Phx. 1977-79; Hotel del Coronado: vice pres./ res. mgr. 1979-80, senior v.p./mgr. (1980-83), pres./gen. mgr. 1983--; also pres. del Coronado Travel; dir. Hotel/Motel Adv. Com. for San Diego Comm. Colls.; recipient Outstanding Young Citizen, San Diego Jaycees 1981, 82; mem: Coronado CofC (dir.), Coronado Hotel/Motel Assn. (chmn.), Calif. Hotel/Motel Assn. (dir.), S.D. Hotel/Motel Assn. (pres.), S.D. Conv. and Vis. Bur. (dir.); trustee Childrens Hosp. and Health Ctr. Address: Del Coronado Hotel, 1500 Orange Ave Coronado 92118

ANDRADE, RICHARD BRUCE, lawyer; b. May 8, 1951, San Diego; s. C. and Minnie (Camacho) A.; m. Kathy Powers, May 19, 1979; 1 dau: Nicole, b. 1983; edn: AA, Southwestern Comm. Coll. 1971; BSBA, San Diego St. Univ. 1973; JD, cum laude, Calif. Western Sch. of Law 1977. Career: staff atty. Dressler, Stoll & Jacobs 1977-79; assoc. Cruickshank, Antin & Grebon 1979-80; assoc. Merrill & Schultz 1980-81; partner Burton, Englebrecht & Andrade 1981--; bd. dirs. Assoc. Bldrs. & Contractors; legal adv. com. Assoc. Gen. Contractors of Calif.; mem: Am. Bar Assn. (Com. on Labor & Const.); Calif Bar Assn. (Com. on Labor & Pub. Contracts); Orange Co. Bar Assn.; Republican; Catholic; rec: skiing, exercise. Res: 10012 Jon Day Dr Huntington Beach 92646 Ofc: Burton, Englebrecht & Andrade, 500 N Newport Blvd, Ste 100, Newport Beach 92663

ANDREW, GARY CHARLES, financial planner; b. Sept. 10, 1952, Van Nuys; s. Edward Franklin and Marjorie (Robertson) A.; m. Patrice Schmidt, Jan. 3, 1976; children: Benjamin, b. 1980; Geoffrey Daniel, b. 1982; edn: honors. grad. USAF Loadmaster Sch. 1972; BSBA, San Diego St. Univ. 1984; Reg. Investment Advisor, SEC, St. Calif. 1982. Career: air crew, USAF 1972-77; agent Conn. Gen. Corp., San Diego 1978-82; pres. Pacifica Planning Corp., San Diego 1982--; finl. profl. adv. panel Pro-Trac 1984; honors: Outstanding Senior Govt. awd. SDSU 1978, Alumni of Year 1983, SDSU Student Govt.; mem: Internat. Assn. Fin. Plnrs.; Am. Assoc. Ind. Investors; Toastmasters; publs: bi-weekly pub., Communique, SDSU Sch. of Bus. 1978; Republican; Christian; rec: moto-cross, baking, investments. Res: 10516 Moorpark Street Spring Valley 92078 Ofc: Pacfica Planning Corp., 444 Camino del Rio S., Ste 103, San Diego 92108

ANDREWS, NEIL CORBLY, professor of surgery; b. Mar.31, 1916, Spokane, Wash.; s. Arthur A. and Lula (Baker) Hancock; m. Carla Foster, Nov. 14, 1970; chil: Joan, b. 1953, David, b. 1955; edn: BA, Univ. Ore. 1940, MD, Univ. Ore. Med. Sch. 1943; M.M.Sc., Ohio State Univ. 1950; lic. MD in Md., Tex., Ohio, Calif. Career: asst./assoc./prof. thoracic surgery Ohio State Univ., 1950-70, Asst. Dean for Resrch. and Tng., 1966-70; coordinator Area II Regional Med. Pgm. (N.E.Calif.) 1970-73; prof. of surgery Sch of Medicine, UC Davis, 1971--: ch. Div. of Community and Postgrad. Medicine 1971-79, ch. Dept. Postgrad. Medicine 1973-81; Am. Cancer Soc. bd. and exec. com., Franklin Co., Ohio 1965-70; Am. Cancer Soc., Calif. Div. bd. dirs. 1977-, exec. com. 1978- (ch. Profl. Edn. Com. 1978-80, ch. Resrch Com. 1980-); Dept. of Health Services: mem. (ch. 1977-)Governor's Adv. Council 1971-, and ch. Carcinogen Policy Com. 1082-. Honors: Asculapius Hon. Soc., Sigma Xi; service awards: Central Ohio Heart Assn. (1963, 68), Calif. Div. Am. Cancer Soc. (1980), Gr. Sacto. Profl. Standard Rev. Orgn., Gr. Sacto. Cancer Council, Central Ohio Mercedes Benz Club. Active mem: AMA, Ohio State Med. Assn., Acad. of Medicine, Columbus and Franklin Co.(Ohio), Am. Thoracic Soc., Am. Assn. for Thoracic Surgery, Am. Coll. of Surgeons, Am. Coll. of Chest Physicians, Central Ohio Heart Assn., No. Calif. Cancer Pgm., CMA (bd.trustees No. Calif.

Cancer Pgm. rep. 1978-), Yolo Co. Med. Soc. (bd.dirs. 1981). Diplomate, Am. Bd. of Surgery, Bd. of Thoracic Surg.; clubs: Commonwealth Club, Mercedes Benz Club. Publs: ed. Yearbook of Cancer 1965-79; edtl. reviewer: Jour. of Am. Cancer Soc., Cancer Chemotherapy Reports, W. Jour. of Medicine; num. med. arts.; mil: capt. US Army 1945-47; Republican; Prot.; rec: golf, auto restoration; res: Box 3007-3271 Clubhouse Dr, El Macero 95618 ofc: UC Davis, Dept. Surg., 4301 X St. Sacramento 95817.

ANGEL, BARBARA JEAN, school psychologist; b. Aug. 30, 1930, South Gate; d. George William and Juanita Pearl (Llewellyn) Newell; m. Donald L. Angel, Nov. 28, 1953; children: Amy, b. 1957; Suzanne, b. 1960; edn: AA, Mt. San Antonio Coll. 1951; BA, UC Santa Barbara 1953; MA, Claremont Grad. Sch. 1970; sch. psychologist cred., CSU, Fullerton 1972; Sch. Psychologist, Calif. 1972; lic. Ednl. Psychologist, Calif. 1981. Career: psychometrist/ tchr. Devereux Schs., Goleta 1954-56; psychometrist, Morovia Unified Sch. Dist., 1965-67, Claremont Unified Sch. Dist., 1967-70; psychologist Chino Unified Sch. Dist., Chino 1970--; dist. rep. to devel. master plan for spl. edn.; devel. original proposal for gifted pgm. in Chino Sch. Dist.; coms. (chmpsn.) Spl. Edn. Region, and mem. panel on psychologist role in edn. wrkshp., Cal Poly; rep. Calif. St. Dept. of Edn. spl. edn. pgm. reviews; mem: Chino Assn. Mgmt. Personnel (secty.); Calif. Assn. of Sch. Psychologists & Psychometrists; Calif. Assn. for the Gifted; Pi Lambda Theta; Pomona Valley Gencol. Soc.; First place awards for needlework, L.A. County Fair 1974, 75; Republican; Congregational; rec: Calif. hist., Am. Indian hist., sewing. Res: 111 East Kirkwood Ave Claremont 91711 Ofc: Chino Unified School Dist., 5130 Riverside Dr Chino 91710

ANGERAME, RONALD J., marketing executive; b. Mar. 11, 1954, NY, NY; s. James V. and Angela Angeram; m. Toni Miceli, Oct. 26, 1980; edn: Bach., math & physics, Ithaca Coll. 1976; MBA, Fairleigh Dickenson Univ. 1980. Career: sales rep. Morse Div. of Borg-Warner, NY Dist. 1976-77; Northeast Svc. Ctr. mgr. 1979-81; midwestern regl. mgr. 1981-82; mktg. mgr. XSCRIBE Corp. 1982-84, v.p. mktg. 1984--; mem. Am. Mgmt. Assn.; rec: water sports, racketball, skiing. Res: 4170 Stettler Way San Diego 92122 Ofc: XSCRIBE, 3366 N. Torrey Pines Ct La Jolla 92037

ANGUIANO, EDWARD, sales executive; b. Oct. 25, 1949, Mexico City, Mex., nat. 1967; s. Manuel and Estella (Alvarado) A.; m. Bonnie Lane, Mar. 7, 1980; edn: spl. courses, Fresno City Coll. 1972, 73, 74, Fresno Inst. of Religion 1977; real estate cert., Anthony Schs. Career: sales rep. Freedom Homes, Fresno 1972-76; sales mgr. Uni-Lab, Tucson, Ariz. 1977-79; sales mgr., self-empl., Fawn Vendors of San Jose 1980--; honors: Lambda Alpha Epsilon (v.p.); Delta Psi Omega; mem: San Jose CofC; Better Bus. Bureau; Republican; Ch. of Jesus Christ of LDS (missionary in North Mexico 2 1/2 yrs.); rec: racquetball. Res: 311 Oak Meadow Dr Los Gatos 95030 Ofc: Fawn Vendors of San Jose, 5120 Campbell Ave, Ste. 115, San Jose 95130

ANNALA, DAVID UNO, welding design co. owner; b. May 16, 1945, Calif.; s. Walter Leanord and Irma Irene (Holme) A.; m. Delores J., Mar. 10, 1973; children: Jennifer, b. 1976; Matthew, b. 1980; edn: AA, Pasadena City Coll. 1965; CSU, Long Beach 1967-74; cert. welding inspector, A.W.S. 1982. Career: indsl. engr. Baker Hydro, Santa Ana 1972-73; tool design K H Cams, Santa Ana 1973-76; design engr. BMS Marine, Santa Ana 1976-79; owner Weld Design, Santa Ana 1974--; mem. Am. Welding Soc.; Nat. Fedn. Independent Businessmen; mil: S/Sgt. Calif. Air Nat. Guard 1967-73; Republican; Lutheran; rec: boating, race cars. Res: 13122 Olympia Way Santa Ana 92705 Ofc: Weld Design, 1537 E McFadden, Ste F, Santa Ana 92705

ANNOTICO, RICHARD ANTHONY, investor; b. Sept. 17, 1930, Cleveland, Ohio; s. Tony and Grace (Kovarik) A.; edn: BA, honors, Ohio Univ. 1953, grad. work, UCLA 1956-8, LLB, JD, Southwestern Law Sch., 1963. Career: dir. internat. sales Liberty Records, Los Angeles 1958-62, vice pres. 1962-64; investment counselor, 1964-68; investor, 1969--; mem. Los Angeles City Bd. of Human Relations Commnrs. 1977-, pres. 1983-4; bd.govs., Calif. State Bar Assn., 1983-; exec. com. Small Bus. Adv. Bd., Calif. State Senate; past bd. dirs. John Rossi Found.; past mem. L.A. City-Co. Adv. Com. on Consolidation. Awards: Cavaliere Ufficiale (Knight Ofcr.); Order of Merit, Repub. of Italy. Mem. Beta Theta Pi (Beta Kappa chpt.), Phi Delta Phi (Pound Inn), founder The Gentry (men's wine soc.). Mil: 1st lt. USAF 1955-56. Rec: tennis, nautilus. Address: 1870 Veteran Ave. Los Angeles 90025

ANSPACH, ROBERT BERNARD, research technologist, consultant; b. May 22, 1926, Shelby, Ohio; s. Roy Lester and Velma Gertrude (Seaton) A.; m. Betty Woods, Jan. 11, 1947; children: Memory Sue, b. 1948; Roberta, b. 1949; Candy, b. 1951; Amy Jo, b. 1961. Career: wireman Consol. Engring. Corp., Pasadena 1947-48; instrument tech. Bournes Labs., Riverside 1949-50; foreman finishing dpt. Transformer Engring. Corp., Pasa. 1950-51; transducer lab. designer Consol. Electo-Dynamics Corp., Pasa. 1951-55; test engr. Northam Instru. Corp., Altadena 1955-56; chief estimator, liaison engr. Pac. Automation Prods. Inc., Glendale 1956-58; engr. Transducer Inc., VErdugo City 1958-59; sys. project engr., R&D engr. Endevco, San Juan Cap. 1959-69; sr. proj. engr. Dynametrics Inc., 1968-71; tech. supr./design engr. Wyle Labs., Hampton, Va. 1971-74; instru. resrch. engr. (spec. in rocketry & reentry) P.D.A. Engring., Santa Ana 1974--; tech. cons. var. cos. 1974--; instr. mil. survey photog. sys. to non-English spkg. allies, Dynametrics, Inc. 1970; mem. Instrument Soc. of Am.; past pres. Pasa. Aquarium Soc. (1947-52); co-author: Comparison Shock Motion Calibrations; mil: photomate 2/c USN 1944-46; Republican; Prot.; rec: silversmithing, chess, lapidary. Res: 1557 Chateau Anaheim 92802 Ofc: PDA Engineering, 1560 Brookhollow Santa Ana 92705

ANTAR, SHIMSHON, gourmet food co. executive; b. May 25, 1937, Mosul, Iraq, nat. 1977; s. Goliath and Helen (Darmo) A.; m. Marlene, Nov. 30, 1968; children: Raymond George, b. 1970; Ronald Francis, b. 1971; edn: BS in bus. adm., Al Hikma Univ. of Baghdad (Am. Jesuits) 1963. Career: asst. gen. mgr. Manley Loss Adjusting Co., Baghdad, Iraq 1963-64; export mgr. Tolid Daru Co., Tehran, Iran 1964-70; mgr. Foods of All Nations, Scarsdale, NY 1970-77; pres./owner Epicurean's Bazaar Inc., 1977--, and Opera Plaza Grocery & Deli, 1983--; pres. bd. dirs. Mar Mari Ch. of the East, Yonkers, NY 1975-77; pres. bd. dirs. Mar Narsai Ch. of the East, San Francisco 1981-83; v.p. Assyrian Youth Club, Tehran 1968-70; mil: 2nd lt. Iraqi Army Reserve; Republican; Ch. of the East; rec: sports, travel. Res: 1121 Lake St Mullbrae 94030 Ofc: Opera Plaza, 601 K Van Ness Ave San Francisco 94102

ANTIN, MICHAEL, tax lawyer; b. Nov. 30, 1938, Milwaukee; s. David Boris and Pauline (Mayer) A.; m. Evelyne, June 19, 1960; children: Stephanie, b. 1967, Bryan, b. 1970, Randall, b. 1974; edn: BS, UCLA 1960, JD, UCB Boalt Hall Sch of Law 1963; career: sr. partner Antin, Stern, Litz & Grebow (and predecessor firm), Los Angeles 1964--; bd.chmn. Conejo Valley Nat. Bank, 1983; dir. West Coast Bank, 1979-; lectr: Am. Bar Assn. Pgms. Dallas 1979, HI. 1980, Wash DC 1982; lectr. profl. tax seminars, and Cont. Edn. of the Bar, 1969-; instr. Solomon S. Huebner Sch of CLU Studies 1977 ; author: How to Operate Your Trust or Probate (Layman Pub. Co., 1983), num. publs. on taxation, estate planning, probate law; coauthor med. & dental regs., Profl. Corps. Act; Fellow, Am. Coll. of Tax Counsel. Mem.: Am. Bar Assn. (Tax Sect.); State Bar of Calif.(Tax, Probate and Trust Law Sect.); L.A. Co. Bar Assn. (Tax Sect.); Beverly Hills Bar Assn.; W. Pension Conf.; Bev. Hills Estate Planning Council, pres. 1962-3, chmn. 1981-2; v.chmn. Profl. Service Orgns.; clubs: Regency; Sherman Oaks Little League (pres.); Bel Air Knolls Homeowners (pres. 1975-7); mil: airman USAF 1959-65, USAFR; Democrat; Jewish; rec: x-c ski, tennis, jog; res: 16565 Park Lane Dr, Los Angeles 90049 ofc: Antin, Stern, Litz & Grebow, 10900 Wilshire Bl. #600, Los Angeles 90024.

ANTONIO, FRANK, company executive; b. June 13, 1955, San Diego; s. Francisco and Filomena (Sardinha) A.; m. Diane Lutz, Jan. 1, 1983; edn: BBA, Univ. of San Diego 1979; grad. stu. UCLA 1983-. Career: corp. plnr. Nuttall-Styris Corp., San Diego 198-81; adminstr. (So. Calif. Regl.) United Pacific Reliance Ins. Cos., Los Angeles 1981--; lectr. USC spl. pgm. to orient business students; honors: employee of year, Central Fed. Savings, 1977; mem: Ins. Personnel Mgmt. Forum; Alpha Kappa Psi; Am. Security Council, Wash. DC; Los Angeles Jr. CofC; Olympic Support Com.; Alpha Delta Gamma (past pres.); YMCA Youth coach; Peninsula Youth Soccer coach; Democrat; Catholic; rec: soccer, skiing, sailing. Res: 3640 Cardiff Ave Los Angeles 90034 Ofc: United Pacific Reliance, 443 S. Shatto Pl Los Angeles 90020

APONIK, DAVID ALLEN, school psychologist; b. Oct. 13, 1952, Detroit, Mich.; s. Benjamin John and Shirley Rose (Varhola) A.; m. Vicki, Mar. 18, 1978; edn: BA, UCLA 1974; MA, CSU, Northridge 1976; PhD, ednl. psych., USC 1980; lic. ednl. psychologist, Calif. 1982; Pupil Personnel Svcs. Credential 1976. Career: mgr. Food & Beverage Magic Mountain Amusement Park, Valencia 1971-77; sch. psychologist/ counselor Southern Kern Unified Sch. Dist., Rosamond 1977-79; counselor Canyon H.S., Canyon Country 1979-80; sch. psychologist Ofc. of the L.A. Supt. of Schs., Downey 1980-81; school psychologist Burbank Unified Sch. Dist. 1981--; lic. ednl. psychologist (ednl. testing, counseling, consultation); awards: UCLA Alumni scholarship, Bank of Am. award for lab. sci., Calif. Assn. of Sch. Psychologists & Psychometrists cert. merit; mem: Council for Exceptional Children, Am. Ednl. Research Assn.; publs: arts., Learning Disability Quarterly 1983; Republican; Protestant; rec: sports, research. Res: 4728 Saloma Ave Sherman Oaks 91403 Ofc: Burbank Unified School District., 330 N Buena Vista Burbank 91505

APPLEGATE, D. RONALD, lawyer; b. May 4, 1942, Sand Springs, Okla.; s. Roy G. and Opal Dorothy (McCray) A.; m. Sandra Ann Beltracchi, Aug. 20, 1972; children: Wade, b. 1975; Brooke, b. 1978; Blake, b. 1980; edn: BA, Anderson Coll. of Law, LA 1975; admitted to Calif. State Bar. Career: city police ofcr., Anderson, Ind. 1964-66; pub. sch. tchr., Anderson, Ind. 1965-66; US Army 1966-68; soc. wkr., Los Angeles Co. 1969-73; welfare fraud investigator, Glendale 1973-75; corp. counsel Forest Lawn Co., Glendale 1976-81; gen. practice criminal defense & civil litigation 1981--; judge pro tem.: Los Angeles Municipal Ct.; Compton Municipal Ct.; instr.: Los Angeles City Coll.; Glendale City Coll.; Pro bono counsel, Vietnam Vet Leadership pgm.; mem: L.A. Co. Bar Assn. (Com. on Alcohol Abuse); State Bar of Calif. (Com. on Alcohol Abuse); Am. Bar Assn.; Am. Cancer Soc. (instr. Stop Smoking Clinics); mil: Spec. 5/c, US Army 1966-68; Democrat; rec: current events, reading novels, family outings. Res: 1339 Virginia Ave Glendale 91202 Ofc: 619 S Westlake Ave, 1st Flr, Los Angeles 90057

ARCHER, DAVE (NELSON, DAVID ARCHER), artist; b. Jan. 15, 1941, San Luis Obispo; s. Palmer Stewart and Ellen Margaret (Truesdale) Nelson; div.; children: Holly, b. 1964; Traci, b. 1970; Forest, b. 1974; edn: grad. San Luis Obispo H.S. 1959; art stu. (work scholarship) with Phil Paradise, Cambria 1959-60; Career: various jobs in No. Calif., Mexico during 1960s; full-time artist, 1970--; worked with Ron Russell in devel. reverse-glass painting; inventor: painting on glass with one million volts of high frequency electricity. Rep. by Swanson Art Galleries, SF Fisherman's Wharf; his space age art collected by Dr. Werner von Braun, songwriter Hoyt Axton, astronaut Rusty Schweickart; rec: scuba diving. Res: 333 G St. #6, San Rafael 94915; Dave Archer Studios, 62B Hamilton Dr. Novato 94947

ARCHER, DENNIS JAMES, business executive; b. June 26, 1944, Los Angeles; s. Harold Gayle and Marion (Ellenburg) A.; m. Gail Diane Lynch, Mar. 29, 1974; children: Bradley, b. 1976; Brittany, b. 1981; edn: BS, engring. (cum laude) UCLA 1969; MBA, 1970. Career: field engr. IBM, Los Angeles 1966-70; dept. mgr. Proctor & Gamble, Long Beach 1970-75; gen. mgr. Anaheim Citrus Prods., Anaheim 1975-76; pres./ chief op., Anaheim Citrus Products, Anaheim 1976--; dir. Farley Inds., Chgo.; dir. Condec Corp. (AMEX), Old Greenwich, Conn.; mem: UCLA Alumni Assn.; Anaheim CofC; Orange Co. CofC; Calif. Trucking Assn.; Calif. Feed & Grain Assn.; Am. Mgmt. Assn.; Beta Gamma Sigma; UCLA Grad. Sch. of Mgmt.; Martin Luther Hosp. Found. Bd., Anaheim; mil: Petty Ofcr. 2/c, US Navy 1964-66, Vietnam Svc. Medal; Republican; Christian; rec: racquetball, skiing, gardening. Res: 19832 Caprice Dr Yorba Linda 92686 Ofc: Anaheim Citrus Products, 421 E Commercial St Anaheim 92801

ARIANO, WILLIAM FRANCIS, manufacturing co. executive; b. Oct. 31, 1921, Phila., Pa.; s. Nicholas and Edith (Mandes) A.; m. Jeanne Louise Carey, Feb. 7, 1948; children: William F. Jr., b. 1949; Stephen, b. 1953; Michael, b. 1954; Paul, b. 1967; edn: BS, St. Josephs Univ. 1943; petroleum engr., Penn. State Univ. Career: with Atlantic Refining & successor co. Atlantic Richfield 1946--: techn. 1946-53; asst. spl. engr. 1953-57; refinery coord. 1957-61; admin. mgr. asphalt sales 1961-65; Northern sales mgr. 1965-66; mgr. Intermediate Trading, Supply & Transp. 1966-69; mgr. Crude & Intermed. Trading, Eastern area 1969-73; mgr. Foreign Crude Acquisitions & Intermed. Trading 1976-80; v.p. Crude Trade Rels. 1980--; honors: Alpha Sigma Nu, nat. Jesuit hon. soc.; bd. govs., St. Josephs Univ.; St. Josephs Alumni Assn. (pres. 1950-52); mem: Am. Petroleum Inst.; Asphalt Inst.; Los Angeles Petroleum Club; Jonathan Club; mil: lt.jg. USN 1943-46, PTO, Iwo Jima, Okinawa; Republican; Catholic; rec: golf, fishing, gardening. res: 2560 Raleigh Dr San Marino 91108 Ofc: Atlantic Richfield, 515 Flower St, Ste 3141, Los Angeles 90071

ARIZA, ROBERT JAMES, general contractor, educator; b. Oct. 25, 1936, San Jose; s. Teofilo Lopez and Mary (Velasco) Hernandez; m. Betty Wade, Apr. 5, 1959; chil: Rochelle, b. 1960, Robin, b. 1961, John, b. 1962, Kenneth, b. 1964, David, b. 1965; edn: BA, math., CSU San Jose 1962, MA, math., 1967; career: mathematics instr. East Side Union High Sch Dist., San Jose 1962-69; math instr. (chmn. Math Dept. 1973-76) West Valley Comm. College Dist., Saratoga 1969-80; real estate sales assoc. Smith, Smith &: Assocs., Truckee 1980-81; pres. Ariza Home Services, Inc. 1980-82; owner Robert J. Ariza Constrn. Co., 1980-82; pres. Ariza-Peters Constrn., Inc., Truckee 1982--. Chmn. West Valley Coll. Academic Senate, 1972-3, pres. Faculty Assn., 1973-4; pres. Calif. Fedn. of Tchrs (CFT) Local 3189, 1978-9. Mem: Am. Fedn. of Tchrs., Profl. Builders Assn., Truckee Contractors Assn., Lions Club; mil: airman 1st cl. USAF 1954-58; Democrat; Catholic; rec: jog, fish, ski; res: 1025 Martis Landing, POB 2107, Truckee 95734 ofc: Ariza-Peters Constrn. Inc., POB 2414, 10745 W. River St., Unit K, Truckee 95734.

ARKIN, MICHAEL BARRY, lawyer, rancher; b. Jan. 11, 1941, Washington, D.C.; s. Wm. Howard and Zenda Lillian (Liebermann) A.; m. Carol Lee Altman, Aug. 26, 1962 (div.); children: Tracy Renee, Jeffrey Harris, Marcy Susan; m. 2d, Gay Callan, July 3, 1982; 1 child, Chatom Callan; edn: BA in psychol., Univ. Okla. 1962; JD, Univ. Okla. 1965. Admitted to State Bar of Okla. 1965, Calif. 1970, US Supreme Ct. 1968, US Tax Ct. 1970, US Ct. of Claims 1968, US Ct. Appeals (3d, 5th, 6th, 9th, 10th cirs.); Career: trial atty. Tax Div., US Dept. Justice, Wash DC 1965-68, appellate atty., 1968-69; pvt. practice atty. (tax and corp.), partner Surr & Hellyer, San Bernardino 19769-79; mng. ptnr./chmn. Tax and Bus. Dept. firm of Wied, Granby, Alford & Arkin, San Diego 1979-82; mng. partner Finley, Kumble, Wagner, Heine, Underberg, Manley & Casey (and predecessor firm), San Diego 1983-84; solo pvt. practice, offices in Sacto. and San Andreas 1984--; honors: mng. ed. Okla. Law Rev.(1962-65), US Dept. Justice Law Grad. Honors Pgm.; past bd. dirs. San Bernardino Co. Bar Assn. (1973-75); past pres. S.B. Co. Legal Aid Soc. (1970-73); founded ABA/S.B. County Bar Assn. joint Drug Abuse Pgm. (1970); mem. Calif., San Diego Co., Calaveras Co., Okla. and Am. Bar Assns.; Am. Arbitration Assn. Panel; Democrat; Jewish. Contbg. poetry to anthology. Address: Michael B. Arkin, Star Rte. 2, Esmeralda Valley, San Andreas 95249

ARMSTER, RHOENNA PAMELA, educator; b. Oct. 22, 1943, Cleveland, Ohio; d. Robert Louis Sr. and Rhoda (Hudson) A.; edn: BS, Loma Linda Univ., La Sierra 1966; MA, Univ. of No. Colo. 1970; grad. wk. on MBA in Fin. Mgmt., Nat. Univ. Career: bus. edn. tchr. San Diego Acad., Nat. City 1972-74; bus. edn. tchr. San Diego City Schs.: Wright Bros. Career High Sch. 1974-78, Serra H.S. 1978-81; bus. edn. tchr. Southwestern Coll., Chula Vista 1974-81; asst. prof., bus. & ofc. mgmt., Point Loma Coll. 1981-82; bus./ English tchr. San Diego City Sch., Gompers Secondary Sch. 1982--; awards: Appreciation, Oakwood Coll. Alumni Assn. 1981; mem: Internat., Nat., Western, Calif. & San Diego Bus. Edn. Assns.; Am. & Calif. Vocational Assn.; Delta Pi Epsilon; San Diego Master Chorale; curriculum writing: San Diego City Schs., Office Training I Guide, 1980; Typewriting I-IV, 1981; prod./ dir. Multicultural Extravaganzas, Serra H.S., Dr. Martin Luther King Tribute Pgms. 1979-81; 7th-day Adventist; rec: travel, roller skating. Res: 2754 Alta View Dr San Diego 92130 Ofc: Gompers Secondary Sch., 1005 47th Street San Diego 92102

ARMSTRONG, ALICE CATT, editor, author; b. Feb. 7, KS; d. Charles Harmon and Florence Iles (Pakenham) Catt; gr-grandniece of Carrie Chapman Catt, women suffrage leader; gr.-granddaughter Harmon Catt, founder of Catt Sch., 1st standard sch., Bourbon Co., KS; edn., Jr. Coll., Art Inst., KS; num. spec. courses; pvt. sch., dramatic arts; hon. degrees: Dr. Humane Letters, St. Olav's Acad., Sweden, 1969; LL.D., No. Pontifical Acad., France, 1969; Litt.D., St. Andrew's Univ. of England, 1969; D.Litt., St. Paul's Coll. and Sem., Rome, 1970; Ph.D., Colo. State, 1972; Dr. Cultural Arts, Bodkin Bible Inst., VA, 1973; Dr. Arts Philo., Gr. China Arts Coll., Hong Kong, 1974; LL.D., Lagos Coll., Nigeria, 1976. Career: actress, Pasadena Playhouse, Artists Exchange; tchr., dramatic arts, H.S., adult groups, own studio, Hollywood, 1947-49; founder, pres., Who's Who Hist. Soc.; pub.-ed., Who's Who in L.A. Co., 1961; Who's Who Executives in Calif., 1963; Who's Who Dining and Lodging on the No. Amer. Continent, 1958. Author: children's book, poems, short stories, stage and radio scripts, travelogues; Civ. def. mgr., and dir., entertainment groups, L.A. area, WWII; founder, dir., Exec. Dinner Club of Bev. Hills and Bel-Air, 1958; internatl. Chmn., Sibelious Centennial Concert, Hollywood Bowl, 1965. Recipient: approx. 40 awards incl. KY Col., 1976; Woman of Achievement, CA Women of the Golden West, 1951; Career Girl of Hollywood, 1951; Natl. Travel Guide Award; Natl. Writers Club, 1958; Wisdom Award of Honor, Wisdom Mag., 1965; Amer. Edn. League award, 1966. Mem.: Professional Writers Guild, L.A., Natl. Writers Club; Natl. Soc. Children's Book Writers; Celebrity Books and Authors, 1977--; mem. awards comm., Freedoms' Found. at Valley Forge, Women's Div., 1978--;Natl. Soc. Magna Charta Dames, Phila., PA; life mem., The Sovereign Colonial Soc. of Americas of Royal Descent, Phila.; Bel-Air Fed. Repub. Women's Club, pres. 1979-80; past mem., Calif. State & L.A. CofC; So. Calif. Women's Press Club. Christian, ordained minister. Res.: 1331 Cordell Place, Los Angeles 90069.

ARMSTRONG, ELI CLEVELAND, market adminstrator; b. July 14, 1935, Austin, Tex.; s. Ely Cleveland and Etoyle Upchurch (Matern) A.; m. Gloria Harness, Nov. 16, 1979; children: Kirk, b. 1960; Mark, b. 1961; edn: L.A.City Coll. 1956. Career: chief cameraman/ tech. dir. KIIX-TV 1963; currently, mktg. adminstr. AT&T, Los Angeles; honors: 25 yrs. safe driving at Pacific Tel. Co.; mem. Am. Legions; mil: Navy, Fireman, Electricians Mate; Democrat; Protestant; rec: equestrian. Res: 8701 10th Ave Inglewood 90305 Ofc: AT&T, 333 S Beaudry Ave, Ste 1400, Los Angeles 90017

ARNDT, PAUL WILHELM, JR., food broker; b. June 24, 1934, Hollywood; s. Paul Wilhelm and Mildred Irene (Menton) A.; m. Beverly Arndt, June 14, 1958; children: Tamra, b. 1960; Kathleen, b. 1963; edn: BS, UCLA 1958; food mktg. pgm., USC Grad. Sch. 1974. Career: exec. tng. pgm. Carnation Co. 1958; v.p. fin. Holly- Pak Div., Borden co. 1959; sales mgr. Paramount Citrus 1964; (acct. exec. Hamilton Stone Co. 1970; v.p. sales Baker Bishop King Co. 1973; (Baker Bishop King merge w/ Crown); exec. v.p. sales & mktg. 1974--; mem: Jonathan Club; Palos Verdes Golf Club; Sportsmen of the South; Brvin Bench; UCLA Alumni Assn.; Republican; Presbyterian; rec: tennis, jogging, golf. Res: 6631 Oceancrest Dr Rancho Palo Verdes 90274 Ofc: Crown/ BBK, Inc., 6501 S Garfiled Ave Bell Gardens 90201

ARNESON, PAMELA KAREN, real estate broker; b. Sept. 16, 1944, Mnpls., Minn.; d. Guy and Jeannette Gorgine (Eddings) Moore; div.; children: John Carl, b. 1960; Julie Karen, b. 1962; edn: real estate, Anthony Schs., Pasadena City Coll.; lic. real estate broker, 1978; Career: med. asst. Joseph C. De Francisco, MD, Alhambra 1971-78; real estate sales Baldwin Realty, Arcadia 1976--; broker lic. 1978--; honors: Multi-Million Dollar Club 1981-83; Top Listor 1981-82; 1983 Sales Leader; mem: Calif. Assn. Realtors; CofC; decorating; Republican; rec: equestrian, dogs, travel. Res: 33 Eastern Ave, 6, Pasadena 91006 Ofc: Baldwin Realty, 900 S First Ave Arcadia 91006

ARNETT, ALAN WAYNE, sales construction engineer; b. Apr. 6, 1944, Lennox, Calif.; s. Alfred Edmund and Marianne Amelia (Tunell) A.; m. Sue Ann Cramblet, Sept. 27, 1969; children: Todd, b 1970, Jonathan, b. 1973; edn: Pierce Coll. 1962-64, Los Angeles Valley Coll. 1961-62, 1964-65, Naval Flt. Ofcr., USN 1969. Career: day mgr. Arrowcrest Corp. dba Mug & Jug, Pacoima 1961-62; senior rocket engine test insp. Rocketdyne, Van Nuys 1963-66; flight equipmentman, naval flt. ofcr., flt. equip. div. ofcr., embarkation ofcr, logistics mgmt. ofcr. USMC, 1966-72; wholesale distbr., sales rep. United Steaks of Am., Vernon 1973-75; tour/charter driver Gray Line Tours Co., L.A. 1975-79; home improvement sales agt., energy conserv. splst./supr. Inland Valley Devel. Corp., San Bernardino 1980-81; So. Calif. Sales rep. Palestine Products Inc., Calimesa 1983--84; receiving insp./asst. constrn. engr. Bechtel Construction, Inc., Diablo Canyon project, 1984--; wholesale distbr./pres. Arnett Ents., 1981--; cons. Internat. Petroleum Ents. 1973; recipient Pride Award, Rocketdyne Space Engine Div. 1966; mem: Nat. Splty. Mdse. Assn., BSA, Boys Brigade ranger, Am. Motorcycle Assn., Internat. Order of Foresters, YMCA, Club Del Mar, Lake Elizabeth Ranch Club; mil: capt. USMC-R 1966-72, Naval Flt. Ofcr. Wings, Exp. Rifle, Exp. Pistol, Nat. Defense; Republican; Baptist (ordained deacon); rec: raise Nubian goats. Res: 12383 10th St Yucaipa 92399 Ofc: Bechtel Construction Inc., POB 56 Avila Beach 93424

ARNOLD, B. DOUGLAS, real estate broker; b. May 18, 1947, Sacramento; s. Bill Douglas and Nanele Faye (Brown) A.; m. Martha Jean Cannon, July 12, 1973; children: Cary, b. 1968; Cameron, b. 1970; William, b. 1979; edn: AA, Sacramento City Coll. 1968-70; Sacto. State Coll. 1970-71; GRI (Grad. Realtors Inst.) CAR, 1979; CRS (Cert. Resdl. Splst.) NAR, 1980. Career: v.p./ broker Arnold & Arnold Real Estate, Inc., Davis 1974-82; currently, gen. ptnr. twelve Calif. lmtd. partnerships (R.E.); pres./ broker Doug Arnold Real Estate, Inc., Davis 1982--; bd. dirs. Farmers Savings Bank, Davis; bd. dirs. Yolo Co. Housing Authority; past pres. Davis Rental Property Owners Assn.; awards: Medal of Valor Awd., San Francisco Police Dept. 1972; Realtor of Year, Yolo Co. Bd. Realtors 1977; mem: Yolo Co. Bd. Realtors (Profl. Standards Com.); No. Solano Co. Bd. Realtors; Calif. Assn. Realtors; Nat. Assn. Realtors; Davis Area CofC; Davis Rotary; Yolo Co. Gen. Hosp. Found.; Cal-Aggie Athletic

Assn., UC Davis; mil: T/Sgt. USAFR 1970-76; Republican; rec: travel. Res: 325 East 8th Street, 2, Davis 95616 Ofc: Arnold Real Estate, 505 Second Street Davis 95616

ARNOLD, KENNETH DAVID, consulting co. president; b. Oct. 1, 1954, National City; s. Kenneth Owen and Anne Patricia (Maly) A.; m. Susan Schultz, May 27, 1978; 1 son, Kenneth O., b. 1981; edn: BS in EE, CSU San Diego 1977, MS in prog. 1982-. Career: engineer CIR Industries, El Cajon 1974-78; engrg. chief General Dynamics/Convair San Diego 1978-84; pres. HiTech Systems, San Diego 1983--; instr. UCSD Ext., Elec. Engrg. and Computer Sci. Dept., 1982-; UCSD adv. com. (curriculum coms. for extension cert. pgms. in Microcomputer Engrg., Systems Pgmmg., Comm. and Signal Processing) 1981-. Honors: achievement certs. (3), Gen. Dynamics, 1981, 82, 83; judge, San Diego Co. Regional Sci. Fair (1982-84). Mem: IEEE 1977-9; Forth Interest Group 1978-; Nat. Computer Graphics Assn. 1981-. Publs: resrch. in areas of image processing and computer architecture. Democrat. Vedantist. Rec: flying ultralight aircraft, scuba diving. Res: 9037 Bogata Cir San Diego 92126 Ofc: HiTech Systems 9560 Black Mtn Rd, #134, San Diego 92126

ARNOLD, TED, musician; b. Nov. 12, 1941, Reading, Pa.; s. Ted and Bertha (Coren) Minter; edn: BA, Am. Found. of Liberal Arts 1962. Career: musical dir./ bassist Glen Yarbrough 1965-70; bassist Jose Feliciano 1971-74; studio musician CBS network 1974-77; musical assoc./ bassist Jose Feliciano 1977-81; writer/ producer/ pres. Telemar (video prodn. facility), Los Angeles 1981--; awards: Humanitarian of Yr. Awd., US Army, overseas (Brotherhood awd.) 1971; Democrat; Humanist; rec: photog. Address: Telemar, 2045 Stanley Hills Pl Los Angeles 90046

ARNOPOLE, KENNETH MARK, inventor, designer; b. Mar. 13, 1945, San Francisco; s. Herman and Ruthe Edith (Ziteland) A.; children: Sandra Kay, b. 1964, Ruthe Diane, b. 1966; edn: voc. courses, dry cleaning, Laney Coll. 1966, Heald's Electronics 1961-62, West Coast Sch. of Profl. Photog. 1975; Profl. Affiliate, L.A. Chpt. AIA, 1983. Career: owner/chief exec. Arnopole, Inc. Los Angeles currently, and cons./designer Fred Schmid Assocs.; past: 21 years exper. in laundry prodn. facilities from op. mgmt. to design of laundry facilities: Western USA sales, Waslex Machinery Corp., Edward Hyman Co.; prodn. and engring., Community Linen and Indsl. Rental Service; Nimbus Rocket Plant, Aerojet General. Instr. laundry mgmt., photog. ops.; cons. Marin Hosp., Pomona Valley Hosp., Sketchley Corp. USA; awards: merit, Profl. Photogs. of Am. (1975), 15 photog. merit awds.; mem: AIA Profl. Afil.; Internat. Fabricare Inst.; AAAS; Nat. Inst. of Instnl. Laundry Mgr.'s; Inst. Indsl. Laundries; Calif. Linen Supply Assn.; inventions: Gumbook (1977), Tri Gammon (1978), Data Booth (1979), LeMap (1978, 80); designer Atlantic City Hilton Hotel laundry systems; publs: series on Robotics, Laundry News; rec: model bldg., electronics, scuba diving. Res: 208 Ave B, Redondo Beach 90277 Ofc: Arnopole, Inc. 7270 Woodrow Wilson Dr Los angeles 90068

ARROL, JOHN, corporate executive; b. Aug. 6, 1923, Cambuslang, Scotland; nat. 1934; s. William and Isabella (Gordon) A.; edn: BSBA, Xavier Univ. (Cincinnati) 1953, MA, Vanderbilt Univ. (Nashville) 1964; m. Jane Trice, June 18, 1949; chil: Robert, b. 1950, Nancy Ann, b. 1952, David, b. 1961, William, b. 1964. Career: cost analyst Ford Motor Co., Mich. and Ohio, 1949-57; finl. analyst Curtiss Wright Corp., N.J. 1957-58; asst. controller Avco Corp., Oh., Tenn., Ind., 1958-64; v.p., controller Globe-Union Inc., Milw., Wisc. 1964-70, v.p., chief finl. ofcr. 1971-73; sr. v.p. finance The Rucker Co., Oakland, Ca. 2973-77; sr. v.p. finance NL Petroleum Svgs., Houston 1977-78; v.p., chief finl. ofcr. Gardner-Denver, Dallas 1978-79; exec. v.p. Systron-Donner Corp., Concord 1980-81, chmn. 1982--; Dir.: bd. chmn., Hughes Electronic Devices, Paragon Technology Co. (Pleasant Hill), Lightgate, Inc. (Berkeley), Pantle Mining Co. (Grass Valley), Roconex Corp. (Milpitas), bd. chmn. San Jose Capital Corp. (S.J.). Mem. adv. council Sch of Bus. Univ of San Francisco; adv. bd. Mt.Diablo Council BSA. Publs: art., Budgeting for Direct Material Inventories, NAA Bull. 2/62; mil: US Maritime Svc, USNR 1942-45; rec: china trade paintings. res: 2427 Alamo Glen Dr. Danville 94526 ofc: Systron-Donner Corp. 2720 Systron Dr. Concord 94518.

ARSNEAULT, DONALD DOUGLAS, corporate executive; b. Nov. 23, 1954, Pontiac, Mich.; s. Douglas and Vera (Ellis) A.; edn: cardiac & respiratory therapist, Indian Hills Med. Inst. 1973. Career: partner/ developer Sweetwater Creek Investments 1978-80; partner Esther's Bakery 1980-82; founder Superior Maintenance 1972-82; fin. cons./ founder Jasen Writter Mgmt. Svcs. 1980-83; v.p./ chief fin. ofcr. A & V Ent., Inc., Tarzana 1983--; satelite dir. Golden State Christian Home for Children 1975-76; treas. Kewians Club; bd. dirs. Proj. J.O.V.E. II 1982; publs: sev. arts. in Power for Today, 1970's; Republican, mem. Pres. Senate & Congl. Adv. Com. 1983; Christian; rec: coin collecting, stain glass, travel. Res: 5247 Vantage St No. Hollywood 91607 Ofc: A & V Enterprises, Inc., 5530 Corbin Ave, Ste 350, Tarzana 91356

ARTHUR, ROBERT JOHN, contracting co. president; b. Feb. 13, 1923, Angels Camp, Calif.; s. John Cheeseman and Abbie P. (Pickering) A.; m. Patricia Browne, Feb. 19, 1966; edn: AB engring., Stanford Univ. 1944. Career: field constrn. engr. US Steel Corp. 1946-51; v.p. sales F.M. Anthony Co. 1952-55; pres. Arthur & Allen (mfg. reps.) 1956--; bd. chmn. Builing Research & Devel. Corp. 1976--; pres. SSA Contracting Corp. 1979--; clubs: Bohemian (SF), Burlingame CC (Hillsborough), Olympic (SF), Delta Tau Delta frat. (life); mil: lt.jg. USN 1943-46; Republican; Protestant; rec: golf, skiing. Res: 30 Reservoir Rd Atherton 94025 Ofc: SSA Contracting Corp., 294 Industrial Way Brisbane 94005

ARTNER, CHARLES, contracting co. president; b. Aug. 22, 1924, Chgo., Ill.; s. Carl and Elisabeth (Bauer) A.; m. Mary Rose Meichtry, Sept. 9, 1950; children: Carl, b. 1951, Stephanie, b. 1952; Kurt, b. 1953; Elizabeth, b. 1954; Mark, b. 1955; Timothy, b. 1957; Eric, b. 1961; Andrea, b. 1968; edn: BS, Loyola Univ., L.A. 1952. Career: test equip. dept. mgr. Librascope 1952-59; computer test & design dept. mgr. Litton Inds. 1959-64; pres./ gen. contracting firm, C.A. Artner Co., Woodland Hills 1964--; honors: Alpha Sigma Nu; mem: Optimist Intl. (club pres. 1973-74); Northridge Kiwanis; mil: US Army Air Corp. 1944-46; Catholic; rec: photog., golf. Res: 9857 Rathburn Ave Northridge 91324 Ofc: C.A. Artner Co., 6150 Canoga Ave, Ste 205, Woodland Hills 91367

ARTOLACHIPE, REYNOLD, airline maintenance executive; b. Sept. 8, 1938, Camaguey, Cuba, nat. Am. cit. Sept. 26, 1969; s. Francisco and Juana (Balbuena) Artolachipe; m. Nancy Siblesz, Feb. 17, 1962; children: Michelle, b. 1977, Ryan, b. 1980; edn: BS, honors, Inter-Am. Aviation Coll. (Hav. Cuba) 1957; MS, aeronautical engr., Havana Univ. 1959; lic Comml. Pilot single & multiengine land (lic. Cuba 1956, FAA 1966), Airframe & Powerplant (lic. Cuba 1958, FAA 1965). Career: aeron. engr. Cubana Airlines, Havana 1959-61; A & P mech. Transcaribbean Airlines, NY, NY 1961-62; aircraft tech. Bonanza Airlines, Las Vegas, Nev. 1963-68, co. renamed Airwest Inc. 1968-72, acquired by Hughes Corp. 1972, renamed Hughes Airwest Inc. 1972-, lead tech. Hughes Airwest Inc., Orange Co. Airport 1977-, mgr. of maint. 1978--, airline merged with Republic Airlines Inc.; currently maint. mgr. Republic Airlines Inc., John Wayne (fmr. O.C.) Airport; maint. cons. Sun Pacific Airlines, Ont. Airport 1981; mem. adv. com. Aero. Dept. Chaffey Coll. 1983-; honors: Havana Univ. Alumnus Awd. 1959; FAA Highest Regl. Awd., Hughes Airwest Merit. Service Awd., Orange County Bd. of Supvrs. Honored Citizen Awd. for heroic action in saving the life a pilot at Orange County Airport, Sept. 13, 1977; Green Cross Exec. Council Safety Awd., CofC Awd. for Courage, Internat. Red Cross Awd. for Humanitiarian Action, 9/77. Mem: Profl. Pilot Assn. of Cuba 1958-61, Nat. Pilots Assn. USA 1970-75, Civil Air Patrol (L.A.), Italian Catholic Fedn.; mem. Upland Tennis Club (tourn. orgnzr.), Cuban Club Pomona Vly.; invented tool to increase perf. in valve body on automatic transmission; Republican; Catholic; rec: tennis, swimming, audio visual recording. Res. 9223 Hidden Farm Rd Alta Loma 91701 Ofc: Republic Airlines 19051 Airport Way North, Santa Ana 92707

ARYANPUR, ABBAS KASHANI, university president/founder; b. Nov. 21, 1906, Kashan, Iran; s. Mehri Khanum A. and Gen. Mashallah Khan; m. Mrs. Robab, 1918; children: Dr. J. Aryanpur, Dr. M. Aryanpur, Mrs. Pari Kamali, Mrs. Ham Keivan, Dr. Iraj Aryanpur, Mrs. Nina Tehrani; edn: LLB, Tehran Univ., Iran 1957; LLM, Tulane Univ., New Orleans, La. 1958; hon. LLD, Western Ill. Univ. 1974; hon. PhD Eng., Trujillo Univ., Peru 1975; hon. PhD Lit., Tech. Sch., Lima Peru 1976. Career: editor Women's World mag. 1926-28; tchr. Persian, Arabic, English in Am. Coll. of Tehran, 1927-32; tchr. Commerce, Eng., Persian in Stuart Meml. Coll., Isfahan, Iran 1934-36, in the Technical Inst., Abadan, Iran 1936-38; comml. dir. Spinning Weaving Electric Co., Iran 1939; dir. Procurement Dept., Ministry of Fin., Iran 1943, Ministerial Insp. 1945; Translation Dept., Ministry of War, Iran 1948; writer English/ Persian, Persian/Eng. dictionaries (11 vols.) 1963-77; English prof. National Univ., Tehran and Sch. of Literature, Tehran 1963-70; founder, pres. Coll. of Translation (Tehran) 1968-78, Pacific Internat. Univ. (San Diego) 1981--; author, poet, lectr. num. univs. and confs. worldwide. Awards: fellowship, Tulane Univ., W. Ill. Univ.; I.C.A. fellowship to USA, 1955; Medal and Charter of Science, and Homayoon Medal of Merit, Shah of Iran, 1956, 57; medal, Iranian Red Cross, 1969; mem: Rotarian, Iranian Pen Club; author 31 books; mil: Iranian Cavalry Regt.; rec: writing, walking, travel; res: 5318 Middleton Rd.San Diego 92109 ofc: Pacific Intl Univ 1253 Garnet San Diego 92109.

ASAMI, SHINTA, terminal operator, corporate president; b. Jan. 21, 1925, Saitama, Japan; s. Wasuke and Mitsu A.; m. Toshiko Hori, Nov. 8, 1952; children: Keiko, b. 1953, Takashi, b. 1956, Tohur, b. 1959; edn: Tokyo Univ. of Mercantile Marine 1945. Career: officer/captain K Line Vessels, 1945-61; port captain, rep. K Line, New York; gen. mgr. Terminal Affairs Div., K Line, Tokyo; pres./bd.dirs. International Transp. Service, Inc. 1972--. Mem: Japan Business Assn. of So. Calif., Internat. Cargo Handling Assn., Long Beach CofC, Internat. City Club of Long Beach, BSA; clubs: Los Coyotes CC, California CC; rec: golf. res: 5651 Burlingame Ave. Buena Park 90621. ofc: International Transp. Service, Inc. 1281 Pier J Ave. Long Beach 90802.

ASHER, HOWARD RALPH, company president; b. Sept. 29, 1947, Long Beach; s. Ralph Eugene and Joyce Colleen (Johnson) A.; m. Carol Yakota, Mar.28, 1965; children: Stacey, b. 1966, Randy, b. 1969; edn: BA in bus.adm., UCLA 1969; cont. edn. in orthopaedic surg. and products, jt. reconstrn., fractured hip, hip and knee replacement, orthopaedic nursing, Univ. Calif., various hosps. and med. schs., USA and abroad, 1969-. Career: sales rep. Howmedica, Inc., Rutherford, N.J. 1970-72; eastern area sales mgr. Am. Hosp. Supply/V. Mueeler, Innomed Orthopedics, Chgo. 1972-75; mktg. mgr. Cutter Biomedical, San Diego 1972-78; sales & mktg. dir. Hexcel Medical, Dublin 1978-79; pres. Asher, Buckman & Assocs., Walnut Creek 1979-81; pres. Advanced Biosearch Associates, San Ramon 1981--, opened East Coast ofc. in Atlanta, Ga. 1983--. Mem: Regulatory Affairs Profl.Soc., The Food & Drug Law Inst., AAAS, Med. Mktg. Assn. Publs: papers presented AAOS Nursing Course on Orthopedic Nursing, Atlanta, 1975; VII Ann. Northlake Surg. Seminar, Chgo. 1977; 5th Ann. Cong. Orthopedic Nurses Assn., New Orleans 1978, and 6th Ann. Cong., Anaheim 1979; 52nd Ann. Sci. Meeting, Am. Soc. of Plastic and Reconstructive Surgeons, Inc., Dallas 1983; Audio-visuals: Surg.

Techniques for Internal Fixation (1974), Care and Hndlg. Internal Fixation Appliances (1975), Basic Skills Employing Swiss Technique to Internal Fixation (1977). Republican. Christian. rec: swim, tennis, woodwrkg. res: 30 Hidden Oak Ct., Danville 94526 ofc: Advanced Biosearch Assocs., 2641 Crow Cyn Rd., San Ramon 94583; 148 Hammond Dr. N.E., Atlanta, GA 30328.

ASHLEY, JAMES A., city executive; b. Dec. 18, 1933, Columbia, Miss.; s. Nathan and Eliza (Abrams) A.; m. Ramona, Aug. 31, 1973; children (triplets): Darryl, Derrick, Denise (1955); edn: AA, Laney Coll. 1961; spl. courses, UC Berkeley 1975, Am. Pub. Wks. Assn. Edn. Found. 1978, Stanford Univ. Grad. Sch. of Bus. 1983. Career: with City of Oakland, 1959-: began as street sweeper, truck driver, prog. through ranks to mgmt. pos.; prop. svcs. supr. Oakland Redevel. Agcy. 1969-75, asst. mgr./bldg. svcs. mgr. Muni. Bldg. Dept., City of Oakland 1976-83; dir. General Services, City of Oakland 1983--; mem. Am. Inst. of Indsl. Engrs., Am. Public Works Assn., Am. Soc. Pub. Adminstrn., Internat. City Mgr. Assn.; bd. dirs. Easter Seal Soc. Oakland, Black CofC, NAACP, McClymonds H.S. Adv. Council, past pres. PTA; Bethel Missionary Ch. Res: 2835 Sunnyvank Ln Hayward 94541 City of Oakland, Ofc. of Gen. Svcs., 7101 Edgewater Dr, Oakland 94621

ASHMAN, CHARLES ROY, film co. licensing/marketing executive, television producer/personality; b. June 7, 1935, NYC; s. Maurey L. and Tillie A. (Friedman) Ashman; edn: BA, Univ. of Fla. 1956, JD, Cumberland Univ. 1960; m. Pamela Trescott, July 13, 1971; 1 child, Shireen, b. 1964. Career: anchorman KTTV News, Metromedia TV, 1974-76, KABC Radio, 1976-77; exec. vice pres. Casablanca Records and Filmworks, 1978-79; pres. A. B. Productions, 1980-; pres. Twentieth Century-Fox Film Corp. Licensing & Mdsg. Div.; media cons. Twentieth Century-Fox; cons. 1982 World's Fair; dir. of entertainment TV News. author: Kissinger-The Adventures of Super-Kraut, The Finest Judges Money Can Buy, Connally-The Adventures of Big Bad John, Martha: The Mouth That Roared, The Disappearance of Jimmy Hoffa, The Gospel According to Billy Graham, The People vs. Angela Davis; num. (100) mag. articles; awards: Nat. Assn. of Theatre Owners Citizenship award 1980, Bnai Brith Man of the Year 1981, Nat. Assn. of Justice Man of the Year 1979; mem: Kiwanis, BPOE, Tau Epsilon Phi, Phi Alpha Delta; mil: US Army 1962; Republican; Jewish; ofc: Twentieth Century-Fox, PO Box 900 Beverly Hills 90213.

ASINOBI, CHIDI CHARLES, architect; b. Nov. 16, 1955, Owerri, Imo, Nigeria; s. Michael Ihemeje and Clara Ukemezie (Nwole) A.; edn: AA, Univ. of Wisc. 1978; BS, 1981; M.Arch., Cal Poly St. Univ. 1984. Career: lab asst., Biochem. Labs., Univ. of Wisc., Greenbay, Wisc.; var. profl. exp. in architl. design & const.; mem: Am. Inst. of Architects; Assn. of Student chpt.; Constrn. Specification Inst.; Student Assn. Cal Poly SLO; works: Signage in Arch., Aesthetics of structural sys. in arch. and engring., Comparisons of parameter and traditional cost estimating methods; Methodist; rec: tennis, ping-pong, photog. Res: 1050 Foothill Blvd, Ste 309, San Luis Obispo 93401

ASKEW, GEORGE VANCE, aerospace co. executive; b. Sept. 16, 1925, Chgo.; s. George Lafayette and Isabel (Brown) A.; m. (Norma) Jean Zediker, Nov. 1947; children: Chris (Geo. V., Jr.), b. 1948, M. Shannon, b. 1952. Scott, b. 1953; edn: att. Stanford Univ. 1949-50; US Naval Line & Post Grad. Sch. 1950-51; grad. w/distinction, US Naval Schs., Treasure Is., Nuclear Safety Engring., 1953; AB in mgt., George Washington Univ. 1965. Career: naval aviator USN, 1943-65, various aviation billets incl. test pilot, project/pgm. mgt., night and all-weather carrier qualified, ret. 1965; staff engr., sect. head Hughes Aircraft Co., 1965-69, senior project engr., support pgm. mgr., 1969-79, asst. pgm. mgr. 1979-83, mgr. simulator logistics 1983--; mgmt. cons., career counseling, 1978-81; mem: Naval Inst., Tail Hook Assn., Assn. Naval Aviation, Stanford Alumni Assn. (life), GWU Alumni, Golden Bough Players, Carmel (1950), Friends of KCET, SPEBSQSA; publs: sev. papers on Automatic Flt. Control Systems, Drone Control and Multi-drone Control, and Missile guidance, 1954-57; mil: cdr. USN 1943-65; Republican; Baptist; rec: golf, tennis, horses. Res: 77 San Roque Ave Ventura 93003 Ofc: Hughes Aircraft Co. Los Angeles

ASKEW, JAMES ALBERT, lawyer; b. Oct. 10, 1949, Oklahoma City, Okla.; s. James Albert and Verlia M. (Harlin) A.; edn: BA, UC Davis 1971; JD, UC Berkeley 1974. Career: lic. in var. fed. dist. cts. and mng. prin. in litigation Neumiller & Beardslee, Stockton; arbitrator Co. of San Joaquin, Superior Ct. & Municipal Ct., City of Stockton; mem: Calif. State Bar (Resolutions Com.); San Joaquin Co. Bar Assn. (pres. 1979-80); Am. Bar Assn.; Assn. Trial Lawyers: Calif. Trial Lawyers ASsn.; Yosemite Club, Stockton; publs: A New Approach to the Intrastate Exemption, Calif. Law Review, reprint Securities Law Review 1974. Ofc: Neumiller & Beardslee, PO Drawer 20, Stockton 95201

ASLAM, MOHAMMAD, physician; b. June 1, 1949, Pindi Kalu Gujrat, Pakistan; came to US in 1974; s. Ghulam Hussain and Sardar (Bibi) A.; m. Shahida, Nov. 19, 1978; chil: Sheryar, b. 1979, Murad, b. 1981; edn: F.Sc, Zamindara Coll. (Gujrat, Pakistan) 1966; MBBS, King Edward Med. Coll. (Lahore, Pak.) 1972; FACC, Fellow Am. Coll. of Cardiology 1982. Career: med. intern, resident in internal medicine, Jersey City (N.J.) Medical Center, 1974-77; cardiology fellow VA Hospital Bronx, NY 1978-79; med. practice in internal medicine & cardiology, Banning, Ca. 1979--; chief of med. staff, dir. of cardiology, San Gorgonio Pass Meml. Hosp.; asst. clin. prof. of medicine Loma Linda Univ. Mem. Am. Coll. of Physicians. Arts. in med. jours.; rec: hiking, hunting; res: 4483 Hillside Dr. Banning 92220 ofc: 3082 W. Ramsey Banning 92220.

ASMAR, ALICE, artist; b. Flint, Mich. d. John George and Helen (Touma) Asmar; edn: BA magna cum laude, Lewis & Clark Coll. 1949; MFA, Univ. Washington 1951; fellowship Ecole Nat. Superieure des Beaux-Arts. Career: piano tchr., French tutor, Portland, Ore. 1947-49, instr. St. Helen's Hall, Portland 1949-50, grad. reader Univ. of Wash., Seattle 1950-51; archtl. drafting Naramore, Bain, Brady & Johanson, Seattle 1951, engring. drafting Boeing Aircraft 1952-53; asst. prof. Lewis & Clark Coll. 1955-58; art instr. Portland (Ore.) Tel. Co. 1956-58, Santa Monica (Calif.) City Coll., Woodbury Coll., Centinela Valley Adult Edn., 1964-66; original line engraver & painter, exclusively, for Nambe Mills, Santa Fe, N.M., 1967-79; lectr. on S.W. Indians and their ceremonials for t.v. shows, museums, art groups, women's clubs, 1975-82; free-lance illustrator for L.A. Times Home Mag., 1977-81. Engraver, metal muralist, book illustrator, painter, graphics; num. solo shows, USA and internat., 1952-; represented in permanent collections at Franklin Mint, Phila., Bev. Hills Ann. Exhib. Hancock Pk. Arts Council 1977, best of show Coll. of the Desert 1978; appreciation awds. from Mayor of Burbank (1977), Burbank Coord. Council (1979). Num. solo exhibs. in USA and internat., 1952-; mem: Artist Equity Assn. (L.A. chpt.), Mu Phi Epsilon, Calif. Mus. of Sci. & Indus., Southwest Mus., Smithsonian Mus., L.A. County Mus., League of the Americas (bd.); Republican; Christian; rec: swimming, collecting Indian Crafts. Asmar Studios, POB 1963, Burbank 91507

ATKINS, CANDI, real estate management executive; b. Aug. 10, 1946, Chgo.; d. Norman R. and Catherine Mary (Coughlin) Wolfe; children: James Norman Atkins, b. 1970; Amanda Kate Arzoomanian, b. 1979; edn: AA, Thornton Comm. Coll. 1966; CPM (Cert. Property Mgr.), ARM (Accred. Resident Mgr.), Inst. of Real Estate Mgmt. Career: dir. resdtl. ops. G & K Mgmt., San Francisco and property mgr. The John Stewart Co., Sausalito 1982-83; pres./owner Candi Atkins & Assocs. Mem. exec. com. S.F. CPM Chpt. #21; Mayor Feinstein's Homeless Pgm. Com.; Calif. Sen. Milton Marks Housing Com.; North of Market Citizen's Adv. Com. RAP bd. Honors: national profl. recognition, ARM of the Year 1980, Chgo., nat.; Candi Atkins' Day in San Francisco, Feb. 29, 1984, city & mayor of S.F. Mem: IREM, S.F. Bd. of Realtors, Nat. Assn. of Realtors, Nat. Assn. of Exec. Women, Nat. Speakers Assn., Nat. Platform Assn.; mem. Am. Cancer Soc., Nat. Heart Assn., Rape Crisis Line, Reading for the Blind (Lions Club). Rec: sailing. Ofc: Candi Atkins & Associates, 46 Addison San Francisco 94131

ATKINSON, SHERRIE L., marriage & family counselor; b. Sept. 7, 1943, Anniston, Ala.; d. Edward C. and Viviaette M. (Stockman) O'Brien; edn: BA in psych., CSU Northridge, MA in clin. psych., Univ. of Azusa, PhD, Univ. of London, Pac. State Univ., L.A. Career: exec. director L.A. Downtown Area, American Cancer Soc.; regional director (So. Calif., Hawaii, Ariz., New Mex.) CARE Inc.; pvt. practice, exec. dir. Marriage &: Family Assn.; currently, pvt practice marriage & family, vocational guidance; cons. death and dying, drugs & alcohol counseling; mem. YWCA (dir. volunteers teen pgm.-Pacesetters, Bev. Hills), United Way vol. res: 3512 Pacific Ave. #2, Marina Del Rey 90291.

ATTEBERRY, GEORGE DEAN, real estate broker; b. Apr. 20, 1929, Lincoln, Ill.; s. Albert Leslie and Ruth Maurine (Watt) A.; children: Dean, b. 1953; Joycelyn, b. 1955; Daniel, b. 1958; Sheryl, b. 1965; edn: BS, Univ. of Ill. 1951, grad. wk. 1956; spl. courses, USC, 1980, UC Davis 1983; lic. real estate broker, Calif. Career: self-empl. farmer (500 acres grain, 100 head beef, 1000 head hogs), Logan Co., Ill. 1956-60; asst. co. mgr., A.S.C.S., Macon Co., Ill. 1960; profl. farm mgr. Fruin Farm Mgmt., Bloomington, Ill. 1961; agri. investment ofcr. John Hancock Mutual Life Ins. Co., Ill., Calif. 1962-80; owner/pres. George D. Atteberry, Inc., Modesto & Chico 1980--; pres./dir. Calif. Agricultural Advrs. & Mgrs., Inc. 1984--; recognition awds., John Hancock Ins. Co.: Ag. Loan Vol. 1967, First Participation Ag. Loan 1969, First Ag. Joint Venture 1970, First Ag. Purchase & Leaseback 1971; mem: Calif. Soc. Farm Mgrs. & Rural Appraisers; Am. Soc. Farm Mgrs. & Rural Appraisers; Nat. Assn. of Review Appraisers; Boy Scouts of Am.; Rotary Club; Methodist Mens Club; mil: SSgt., USAF 1951-55, Good Conduct; Republican; Methodist; rec: hunting, philately, square dancing. Res: 1080 E Lassen Ave Chico 95927 Ofc: George D. Atteberry, Inc., 1207 K Street Modesto 95354

AUDETT, THEOPHILUS BERNARD, lawyer; b. Feb. 12,1905, Giltedge, Mont.; s. Joseph Abraham and Katherine Amanda (Johnson) A.; m. Corinne Lowery, Sept. 21, 1939; 1 dau. Katherine, b. 1947; edn: JD, Univ. Wash. 1926. Career: various positions US Customs Service 1930-51, asst. deputy commnr. Hdqtrs, USCS, Wash DC 1951-63, Customs expert with US delegation, GATT, Geneva 1956 & 1961, US rep. on panel of experts on antidumping and countervailing duties, GATT, Geneva 1959 & 1960, chmn. Interdeptl. Com. for study of antidumping legislation, Wash DC 1962; of counsel, firm Stein, Shostak, Shostak & O'Hara, Los Angeles 1965--. awards: exceptional service, US Treas. Dept. 1963; listed Who's Who in Am. Law; mem: Phi Sigma Kappa, Am. Bar Assn. (Customs Law Com. 1967-8), Calif.State Bar Assn., Assn. of Customs Bar, Les Amis du Vin; mil: capt. US Army 1943-45; Republican; res: 348 S. Orange Grove Blvd. Pasadena 91105 ofc: Stein, Shostak, Shostak & O'Hara, 3255 Wilshire Bl. Los Angeles 90010

AULETTO, LEONARD T., research co. executive; b. July 1, 1941, Weehawken, NJ; s. Joseph C. and Grace (Lapadule) A.; m. Constance Wade, July 29, 1967; children: John, Cara; edn: BS, NY Univ. 1963. Career: gen. mgr. Standard & Poor's Corp., NYC, 1971-79; marketplace mgr. Citibank, AVP, NYC 1979; regl. mgr. Dun & Bradstreet Inc. 1963-71, 1979-83; exec. dir. marketing SRI International, Menlo Park, Ca. 1984--; cons. to finl. svcs. indus.; mem. Am. Mgmt. Assn.; publs: arts. on strategic plng. and mktg./bus. devel.; Catholic; rec: writing, tennis, golf, skiing. Res: Moraga CA 94556 Ofc: SRI Intl. 333 Ravenswood Ave Menlo Park 94025

AUSENBAUM, HELEN EVELYN, psychologist/social worker; b. May 16, 1911, Chgo.; d. Herbert Noel and Mayme Eva (Bircher) Ausenbaum; edn: stu. Univ. of Ill., Urbana 1930-2; AB, UC Berkeley 1938, MSW 1956; postgrad. stu. CSU Hayward 1976-8, JFK Univ., Orinda 1976; lic. clin. social worker/school psychologist, Calif. 1956-. Career: social worker Alameda Co. Welfare Commn., 1939-42, American Red Cross, San Francisco 1942-43; exec. dir. ARC, Richmond 1943-51; teacher Richmond Public Schs. 1951-53; school social worker/sch. psychologist Oakland Public Schs. 1953-76; program dir. Let's Rap pgm. McChesney Jr. H.Sch., Oakland 1970-82; currently program dir. Diablo Valley Found. for Aging, Support Service for Elders, Walnut Creek; mem. (ch. 1978-81) Orinda Comm. on Aging 1976-; mem. Contra Costa Co. Mental Health Task Force for Aging; mem.(bd. dirs. 1976-82) Lincoln Child Center, Oakland; Awards: Am.Red Cross scholarship, 1942-3; appreciation, Richmond Service Clubs; Oakland Principals Club Award 1976. Mem: Calif. Tchrs Assn., Nat. Assn. of Social Workers (charter), Calif. Assn. of Sch. Social Workers, W. Gerontological Assn., Nat. Gerontologist Assn., AAUW; Democrat; Presbyterian; rec: photog., travel, coins, stamps; res: 20 Chapparal Pl. Orinda 94563 ofc: Diablo Valley Found. for Aging, 1981 Tice Valley Bl. Walnut Creek 94595.

AUSTIN, REX L., transportation co. owner; b. Jan. 10, 1949, Kermit, Tex.; s. Rector H. and Dorothy F. (Hill) Austin; m. Deborah Sue Harden, July 2, 1983; edn: ground tng., pilot, Accelerated, Inc. 1980. Career: owner/opr. Boat Transit Inc., Newport Beach, subhauler, 1970-71; attendant Cavanaugh Chevron Service, Encinitas, 1971-72; driver Skylark Mobile Home Sales, Vista 1972-73, Bickford Mobile Home Movers, Escondido 1973-74; owner Rex Transport, Encinitas 1974--, mobile, modular, trailer, transport, Calif., Ariz. and Nev.; owner Rex Pilot Car Service, 1975--; owner Rex Mobile Home Setups, 1975--. honors: Plaque from men of E Troop, First Cavalry. mem: Highway Carriers Assn. Calif. (elected mem. bd. dirs. 1983-86); V.F.W. 1972-; Am. Legion 1973-; Riverside Pilots Inc. 1979-, Am. Sand Racing Assn. 1980-; So. Coast Surfing Assn. 1966-7; Nat. Riflemen's Assn. 1961. Patentee: mobile home dolly (1975). Cartoonist, H.S. newspaper 1967; unpubl. songs. Mil: sgt. E5, US Army1968-70, GCM, Commendation. Republican (Repub. Nat. Com. 1980-, Presdtl. Task Force); Christian; rec: motorcycle, jeep racing, flying. res: 596 Transit, Riverside 92507. ofc: Rex Transport, 598 Hermes, Encinitas 92024.

AVALOS-FIGUEROA, ERNESTINA, dentist; b. Oct. 16, 1942, Riobamba, Ecuador; d. Joaquin and Judith (Zuniga) Avalos; m. Louis Figueroa, Jan. 4, 1964; chil: Tina Louise, b. 1966, Ulysses, b. 1968, Anastasia, b. 1970; edn: Dr. of Odontology, Univ. of Guayaquil 1973, DDS, USC 1980, career: private practice of dentistry in Ecuador, briefly, in El Toro, Calif. 1980--. Awards: Individual Devel. Speaker 1982, Woman of Achievement nom. 1983, B.P.W. Saddleback Valley. Mem: Am. Assn. of Women Dentists, Am. Dental Assn., AAUW, Bus. & Profl. Womens Club of Saddleback Valley, Lestonnoc Free Clinic of Orange, South Orange Co. Bus. Club, Catholic Daus. of Am.; Catholic; rec: sew, cook. res: 25191 Miles Ave. El Toro 92630 ofc: 24864 Muirlands, El Toro 92630.

AVANT, HUGH WILTON, consultant; b. Jan. 4, 1931, Sylacauga, Ala.; s. Daniel Warren and Julia Ann (Smith) A.; m. Dianne Marie Murray, Oct. 15, 1966; children: Heidi, b. 1967; Doug, b. 19869; Tricia, b. 1970; Tim, b. 1971; Amiee, b. 1974; Jennifer, b. 1978; edn: BS, Jacksonville State Univ. 1955; Kappa Phi Kappa (1954). Career: currently consulting; trustee, family bus.; fmr. owner marble quarry (15 yrs.); asst. coach high sch. (1 yr.); capt., Intell., US Army 1957; Pacific Finance Corp. (9 1/2 yrs.); collections Gateway Nat. Bank (6 mos.); assoc. Drollinger Co. (2 1/2 yrs.); Shell Oil Co. (4 1/2 yrs.); past mem. Lion Club, Elks; rec: golf, boating, fellowship. Address: 4423 Brighton Ave San Diego 92107

AVNER, CORREY B., lawyer, inventor; b. Apr. 23, 1952, Cleveland, Ohio; s. Charles H. and Veda (Volin) Avner; m. Janine, Aug. 6, 1983; edn: BS, magna cum laude, Univ. of Ariz. 1974, JD, Univ. of San Diego 1977; admitted to practice, Calif. Supreme Ct. 1978; lic. real estate broker, Calif. 1980. Career: assoc. tax counsel UCO Oil Co., Whittier 1978; atty. with Tiger Internat. Cos. 1978-81, with The Flying Tiger Line, Los Angeles 1980-81, then Legal Dept. Head, Tiger Air, Inc.; pvt. law practice with Kern, Wooley and Maloney and Morganstern, Mann & Smith, 1981-83; prop. legal practice, Beverly Hills 1983--; co-originator Univ.San Diego Sch of Law interfaculty debates (1975); spl. counsel to Tanega Realty, Honolulu, HI. 1978-; pres. Atha Corp., 1983; honors: Beta Gamma Sigma; inventor (pat.pend.) grilling device for home charbroiling soft/flake foods; polit. ind.; rec: karate, piano composer, hiking; res: 1815 Glendon Ave. #104, Los Angeles 90025 ofc: Correy B. Avner, Esq., 161 S. Doheny Dr. Beverly Hills 90211.

AWADA, MICHAEL J., banker; b. Jan. 5, 1940, Beirut, Lebanon; s. Jamil and Fatima Hussein (Nassar) A.; edn: BA, Patriarchal Coll. Beirut 1958, MBA, Pepperdine Univ. 1978; m. Jo Ann Reinmiller, Mar. 18, 1972; chil: Tarek, b. 1978, Jehad, b. 1980. Career: mgr. Credit Lyonnais, Beirut 1960-66; supt. Polietileno, Monterrey, Mex. 1967-69; Credit Lyonnais, Beirut 1970-72; gen. mgr. Internat. Dept. Security Nat. Bank, Oakland 1973-75; v.p. Bank of Boston, Los Angeles 1975-79; v.p. and agent Multibanco Comermex, L.A. Agency, 1979--. mem: Pacific Rim Bankers School, Brazil-Calif. Trade Assn., 1st v.p. of U.S./Mexico C. of C., Toastmasters, Am. Bankers Assn.,Internat. Mgmt. inst. (Geneva, Switz); mem. Nat. Assn. of Arab-Ams., Arab-Am. Anti-Discrimination Com., Rotary Club L.A.5, Jonathan Club, Lakeside Golf Club; publs: arts., profl. jours.; rec: basketball, golf, tennis, swimming; res: 4785 Galendo St.Woodland Hills 92364 ofc: Multibanco Comermex, LA Agcy, 515 S. Figueroa St., 10th Fl., Los Angeles 90071.

AWIT, TERESITA TROCIO, quality engineer; b. Nov. 30, 1940, Cebu City, Cebu, Phil.; nat. Am.; d. Jose Completo and Caridad Sonio (Trocio) Awit; one son, Owen, b. 1971; edn: BS, chem. eng. Cebu Inst. of Tech, 1962; MS in mgt. eng.,Colegio de San Jose-Recoletos, 1967; Profl. Chemical Engr., Phil. Bd. of Examiners 1962; Certified Quality Control Engr., Am. Soc. for Quality Control 1974-. Career: coll. instr. Cebu Inst. of Tech., Phil. 1962-67; analytical chemist Stoody Co., Whittier, Ca. 1968-72; analytical chemist Internat. Medication Systems, So. El Monte 1972-73; supr. stability testing Stuart Pharmaceuticals, Pasadena 1973-79; sr. quality engr. Alpha Therapeutic Corp., Los Angeles 1979--; honors: president's award, Alpha Therapeutic Corp. 1981; mem. ASQC; Republican; Roman Catholic; rec: sports, gardening; res: 633 Las Lomas Rd. Duarte 91010 ofc: Alpha Therapeutic Corp. 5555 Valley Blvd. Los Angeles 90032.

AWTRY, JOHN HIX, lawyer, insurance executive, military officer; b. July 29, 1897, Quitman, TX; s. Emmett and Elizabeth (Williams) Awtry; LL.B., Univ. TX, 1921; JD, 1969; m. Nell Catherine Jacoby, Apr., 24, 1922; child: Nell Catherine, dec. Career: vol. AUS, WWI; with Fed. Bank of Dallas, 1917-19; Govt. Svgs. Div. Treasury Dept., 1919-20; lawyer, 1921--; admitted to US Supreme Ct. Bar, TX Bar, also US Ct. Mil. Appeals, US Ct. Claims; with Taylor & Awtry, attys., Dallas, 1921-23; handled ins. on intra and interstate motor buses and trucks, 17 yrs.; assisted in formation of Natl. Motor Bus. Div. of Amer. Automobile Assn., served on natl. bd. of AAA, helped draft Motor Carrier Act of 1935, regulates interstate trasnp.; pres., First Reins Co. of Hartford, CT, 1936-41; pres., John H. Awtry & Co., Inc., NYC; owner, John H. Awtry & Co., Dallas; commanding ofcr., AUS, 1942-53; commnd. full Col. by direct order of US President; ret. for disability after active mil. duty in three wars.; assisted in planning and invasion of Europe, Normandy landing, as hdqtrs. staff mem. of Gen. Omar Bradley, 1944; mem. Gen. Staff War Dpct., Dept. Army, 1946-49; chief (Lt. Col.) Contracts & Procurement Br., Judge Adv. Div., Euro. Command, 1949-50; mem. Army Panel, Armed Services Bd. of Contract Appeals, Office of Asst. Secty. Army, Wash.; decorated Bronze Star Medal; Legion of Merit; recipient: Commendation US atty. Gen. Mem.: NY So. Soc., 12th Army Group Assn., life., Judge Advs. Assn., life; NY State CofC Fedn., life. Amer. Life, TX life, Dallas life, Bar Assns.; State Bar of Tx; Fed. Grand Jury Assn.; NY Mil. Order World Wars; life mem. American Legion Post, Scarsdale, N.Y.; Washington Tex. Soc.; Univ. TX Ex-Students Assn., life mem. Ret. Officers Assn., life; Amer. Assn. Ret. Persons, past pres. Leisure World chpt.; Patriotic Letterwriters Club, Orange Co. Retired Ofcrs. Club; El Toro-Santa Ana Marine Corp Air Sta. Officers Club; Diasabled Ofcrs. Assn.; Assn. US Army; Natl. Sojourners, life; Lambda Chi Alpha; Selected "Lesure Worlder" Roosmoor Leisure World; Scottish Rite: Long Beach Saddleback Scottish Rite Club; Saddleback Masonic Lodge, Leisure World; Masonic Club, Leisure World, Mecca Temple, N.Y. City, Mason, 32 deg. Shriner: High Twelve; Drug and Chemical; Downtown Athletic; Baners of Amer, NYC; Town, life, Scarsdale, NY; Scarsdale Golf, Hartsdale, NY; Hartford; Dallas Athletic Club, life; Dallas Exchange, 1st pres., life mem.; Natl. Exchange, twice natl. pres.; Army and Navy, Wash. Name inscribed in Ct. of Honor. Republican. Baptist. Res.: P.O. Box 2833, 3337-2A Punta Alta Rossmoor, Leisure World, Laguna Hills, 92653.

AYASH, BARBARA LUCILLE, non-profit charity founder/executive; b. July 6, 1933, Yama, Colo.; d. John Carl William and Ola Ruth (Turnbull) Mekelburg; m. Arnold Frederick Markel; children Brenda Kae, Edward Arnold, Roger Ward, Ginger Lynn; m. 2d. Robert Ayash, July 14, 1972; stepchil.: Robert Jr., Larry, and Collette; edn: Northeastern Jr. Coll., Newspaper Inst. of Am., modeling sch. 1955; bus. mgmt. tng. Hubbard Acad.; lic. security rep., State of Colo. 1966. Career: founder/chief exec. The Concerned Businessmen's Assn. of Am., 1981--; founder/pres. Barbco Indus. Inc. (food mfg.), Denver, Colo. 1964-65 (merged into Colo. Western Fin. Corp.); pres. Artificial Nails, Inc. (beauty supply) and Billibarb Ent. Inc. (beauty salons), Tarzana, Calif. 1975-79 (sold out to ptnr.); past sales of women's wear, cosmetics, books, food products, securities/inv., beauty svcs./supplies, etc.; part-time TV product modeling; mem. Womens Bowling Assn., Los Angeles CofC; author two textbooks; Libertarian; Lutheran; rec: swimming, music (composer), horsemanship. Res: 4169 Via Marina, 208, Marina Del Rey 90291 Ofc: Concerned Businessmens Assn. of Am., 2040 Ave of the Stars, Ste 400, Century City 90067

AYROMLOO, SHAWN, computer consultant, lecturer; b. Apr. 24, 1984, Tehran, Iran; s. Javad and Aghdas (Moinian) A.; m. Nina Andrews, Jan. 23, 1981; 1 dau. Jessica, b. 1982; edn: BS, Ore. State Univ. 1972, PhD in computer sci., 1978. Career: pgmmr. spl. projects Ore. State Univ., 1969-78; pgm. designer Hewlett-Packard, Corvallis, Ore. 1978; senior software systems consultant, lectr. and dir. Systematic Approach International (computer consulting, resrch. & dev., computer sci. seminars) 1979--, clients include Garret AiResearch, Rusco Electronic Systems, Hodge Computer Research, Findex, Arco Petroleum Products, Quotron Data Systems, Inc., NASA/Jet Propulsion Lab., Raytheon Data Sys., Transaction Technol. Inc., UCLA Extension, Ore. State Univ., Cipherlink Corp., 1984--; honors: scholarship, Ore. State U., Teacher Tng. Univ., Pahlavi Found.; mem. Usenix Assn.; author: structured/ modular pgmmg. in C UNIX (1984); Moslem; rec: sports, music. Address: 10535 Wilshire Blvd, Ste. 1210, Los Angeles 90024

AZAFRANI, GILBERT S., lawyer; b. June 5, 1949, Casablanca, French Morocco, nat. 1971; s. Simon and Marie (Benisti) A.; edn: BA, magna cum laude, Pace Univ., NYC 1972; MA, w/ distn., Fordham Univ. 1974; PhD, w/ distn., 1978; JD, Pace Univ. Sch. of Law 1980. Career: law clerk Securities & Exch. Comn., NY Regl. Counsel's Ofc., 1979-80; staff atty. US Treas. Dept., Dist. Counsel Ofc., IRS, Los Angeles 1980-81; pvt. practice Miller & Daar, Beverly Hills 1981--; Municipal Ct. Judge (Pro Tem) 1983--; honors: tchg. fellow, Fordham Univ. 1972-78; tchg. asst. Law Review, Pace Univ. Sch. of Law 1979-80; Phi Sigma Iota; Delta Theta Phi; mem: Central, Northern, Southern & Eastern US Dist. Cts., US Ninth Circuit Ct. of Appeals, US Tax Ct.; Calif. Trial Lawyers Assn., Lawyers Club of L.A.; Beverly Hills, Am. (Tax Sect.), & Calif. Bar Assns.; ASCAP, L.A. Songwriters Showcase; Democrat; rec: swimming, sailing, poetry. Res: 1725 Promenade, Apt 329, Santa Moncia 90401 OFc: Miller & Daar, 9100 Wilshire Blvd, Ste 720, Beverly Hills 90212

AZEVEDO, ALAN JOHN, orthopedic surgeon; b. Oct. 20, 1950, Modesto; s. Ernest Martin and Clara Margaret (Ruiz) A.; m. Wendy, Mar. 28, 1981; chil: Amber, b. 1982, Emily, b. 1983; edn: BS, Univ. of Notre Dame, 1972, MD, Loyola Stritch, 1975. Career: surgical intern St. Mary's Hosp., San Francisco 1975-76, surgical resident, 1976-77; orthopedic surgery res. Univ. of Colo., Denver 1977-81; adult orthopedic reconstruction fellowship Mayo Clinic, medical staff N. T. Enloe, Chico Community, and Feather River Hosps.; 1981-82; pvt. practice orthopedic surgery, Chico, Ca. 1982--; recipient Resident Award, Western Orthopedic Assn. 1979, 81; mem: Butte-Glenn Med. Soc., Calif. Med. Assn., Mayo Alumni Assn., Colo. Orthopedic Alumni Assn., Elks. Publs: arts. in Orthopedic Transactions (med.jour.); Democrat; Catholic; res: 8 Luckie Way, Chico 95926 ofc: Orthopedic Surgeons, 1600 The Esplanade, #G, Chico 95926.

B

BABINGTON, RENNIE FREDERICK, real estate broker, business owner, educator; b. May 21, 1938, Oakland; s. Suren H. and Mary (Dieckmann) B.; edn: BA, St. Mary's Coll. 1962, MA, Calif. State Univ. 1971; lic. real prop. broker, Ca. 1966; real estate cert., Univ. Calif. 1965; comm. coll. sec. creds. (adminstrv., counselling), Calif. Career: sec. sch. adminstr./ counselor/ tchr., 1964-84; real prop. broker, Oakland 1966--; co-owner J. Praditamas & Co., S.F. (jewelry, gems import co.); pres. Hayward Fedn. of Tchrs. 1977-80; del. Am. Fedn. of Tchrs. Conv. (1977); dir. Berkeley med. Ctr., 1965-75. Mem: Phi Delta Kappa, Assn. of Sch. Adminstrs., Nat.& Calif. Council for the Social Studies; mem. Commonwealth Club of Calif., Claremont CC, BSA (Eagle Scout Award 1956), Calif. PTA, UC Alumni Assoc., St. Mary's Coll. Alumni, Oakland Soc. Prevention Cruelty to Animals; Prot.; rec: piano, tennis, ski, travel, bridge. Res: 26 Slater Ln. Berkeley 94705 Ofc: 77 Jack London Sq. Oakland 94607.

BACAL, HARVEY, musicologist; b. May 24, 1915, Quebec, Canada; US Citizen; s. Elias and Jennie (Abram) Bacal; m. Rosalyn Goldwasser, Sept. 1, 1940; children: Jessica, b. 1944, Melanie, b. 948, Carolyn, b. 1951, Glenn, b. 1953; edn: Phila. Coll. of Perf. Arts, 1930s; composition with Jaromir Weinberger, Frederick Schleider, Wm. Happich; La Salle Coll. of Law 1948; NY Inst. of Fin. 1960. Career: musicologist for over 40 years spec. in music plagiarism and infringement; composer/ condr./ arranger/ musicologist for Ralph Edwards T.V. series: Name That Tune, 1974-81, the original radio and tv Name That Tune, Stop the Music (1950s), Yours For A Song (1960s), Music Bingo (1960s); practicing musicologist for Film cos., music publishers, & TV indus.; adj. prof. of musicology Pepperdine Univ.; lectr. num. colls., instns.; author three books: ABC's of Modern Arranging (1955), New Sounds in Music (1960), Fun with Music (1970); composer: 5 Pieces For Children (Orchestral Suite), I'm Afraid To Remember, Pianino, A La Parisienne, Don't Run Away, Seven Salty Soldiers; recipient appreciation, City of Los Angeles and Mayor Bradley, 1982, 83; Silver Beaver Awd., Boy Scouts of Am. 1974; Top Campaigner for BSA, 1966; listed, Who's Who in Am. Music, Who's Who in Internat. Music. Mem. Am. Musicological Soc., ASCAP, Am. Guild of Authors & Composers, Am. Soc. of Music Arrangers; founder/bd. chmn. MUSIC (Music Friends of the LA Pub. Lib. 1975); The Choral Soc. of So. Calif. (pres. 1982); Friends of the Fine Arts at Pepperdine U. (pres. 1983); past exec. bd. BSA, NYC; Broadcast Pioneers; mil: civilian instr. USAF 1941-45; rec: hist. novels, classical music. Res: 7244 Hillside Ave, Ste. 309, Hollywood 90046

BACERRA, MAX PETER, planning consultant; b. Oct. 8, 1958, Delano; s. Max Alayza and Victoria Rabago (del Rosario) B.; edn: pub. adm., CSU Bakersfield 1976-7; BS in city/regl. plnng., CalPoly St. Univ., S.L.O., 1980. Career: planning intern Kern Co. Plnng. Dept. 1979; plnng. cons. City Building Ednl. Pgm., Santa Maria High Sch. Dist., 1979-80; sr. plnnr/city plnng. cons. City of Delano, 1980-82; prin. plnnr. Kamwil, Inc./The Planning Concept, Bksfld. 1982; gen. ptnr. PAC-A Devel. Group, Bksfld. 1983--; pres./prin. Max P. Bacerra and Assocs., Planning Consultants, Bksfld. 1982--; chief exec. ofcr. Investment Connection (areawide inv. listing publ. for the San Joaquin Valley), 1983-; gov. apptd. mem. Private Indus. Council for Kern, Mono, and Inyo Counties, 1983-; assoc. coord. Filipino Comm. Devel. Project, 1984-; awards: Calif. Rural Ednl. Scholarship 1979, Blue Key nat. hon. soc.; mem: Am. Planning Assn. (charter Calif. Chpt.), CalPoly City and Regl. Plnng. Alumni Assn.; Filipino Comm. of Delano; Phil. Weekend, Inc. (bd. dirs. 1976-8, advisor 1968-), past bd. Delano Assn. for Devel. Disabled; Democrat; Catholic; rec: travel, skiing, whirly-bird, crabbing. Res: 1905 Dover St Delano 93215 Ofc: Max P. Bacerra and Assocs., Planning Consultants, 1920 20th St., Ste. A, Bakersfield 93301

BADEWITZ, ERNST RUDOLF, business owner; b. Feb. 12, 1940, Bayreuth, W. Ger., nat. 1969; s. Bernhart and Franziska (Stark) Badewitz; m. Susan Gail Coneen, Dec. 6, 1980; 1 son, Clinton Ernst, b. 1983; edn: Master, Univ. of Bavaria, 1958; career: came to USA as mechanic for Volkswagen, 1961; opened own auto repair shop in Newport Bch., 1965-78, owner/pres. Del Mar German Car Service, Inc., Del Mar 1978--. Honors: commendation for rescuing man from burning car, city of Newport Beach, 1967; recognition for philanthropic work, La Casa de los Pobres, Tijuana, Mex.; mem. Del Mar CofC; inventor automotive tool used by Volkswagen (1960); Lutheran; rec: tennis, horseriding-Bavarian champion 1956; res: 14175 Half Moon Bay Dr., Del Mar 92014; ofc: Del Mar German Car Service, Inc. 155 Carmel Valley Rd., Del Mar 92014.

BADHAM, VIRGINIA EVELYN DABNEY, pianist, poet; b. July 20, 1907, Portland, Ore.; dau. (Ore. pioneer) Richard Temple and Martha Amanda (Renshaw) Dabney; m. Edward Dick Badham, May 21, 1929, div. 1953; four daus: Beverly, b. 1931, Marilyn, b. 1932, Patricia, b. 1937, Cheryl, b. 1948; 15 grandchildren: edn: grad. Marlborough Sch.1927, stu. USC 1927-28; stu. piano (11 yrs.) with Calbreath Studios of Portland, Ore. and Olga Steeb Studios, Los Angeles; vocal stu. (15 yrs.) with Elizabeth Green Happ, Ingenuus Bentzar and Florence Russell Studios; stu. ballet, Norman Gould Studios 1923, ballroom dancing, Ernest Ryan Studios 1923-26. Career: piano debut at age 13 in Portland, Ore.; piano tchr., Los Angeles and Newport Bch; singers' accompanist; concert singer, Women's Lyric Club, L.A. (Wilshire Ebell and Biltmore Theatres, etc.). Works: num. music compositions; poetry, pub. in Todays Greatest Poems (1983), Am. Poetry Anthology (1983); jewelry designer; bldg. designer; mem: Pi Beta Phi (USC) Alumnae, Coronets of Nat. Charity League, chrtr mem. Lido Isle Players; orgnzr Mothers of Am. postcard campaign during Korean War; Christian Sci.; rec: geneal. resrch, design, singing; res: 234 Collins Ave. Balboa Is. 92662.

BAGLEY, CONSTANCE ELIZABETH, lawyer; b. Dec. 18, 1952, Tucson, Az.; d. R. Porter and Joanne (Snow) Smith; edn: AB, honors, Stanford Univ. 1974, JD, magna cum laude, Harvard Law Sch. 1977; admitted to practice in NY, Calif. Career: teaching fellow in govt., Harvard Univ., 1976-77; assoc. Webster & Sheffield, NYC 1977-78; assoc. Heller, Ehrman, White & McAuliffe in San Francisco 1978-79; assoc. McCutchen, Doyle, Brown & Enersen, S.F. 1979--; instr. bus. law series, Calif. Cont. Edn. of the Bar 1983. Honors: Vol. of the Month 9/83, Moffitt Hosp. UCSF; Phi Beta Kappa 1973; listed in Who's Who in Am. Law. Mem: Am. Bar Assn., S.F. Bar Assn.; Golden Gateway Tennis & Swim Club. Publs: contbg. ed., fed. securities laws, Calif. Bus. Law Reporter; author: Mergers, Acquisitions & Tender Offers (1983), law rev. arts.; Republican; Episcopal; rec: swim, tennis. res: 247 El Granada Blvd. Rt. 1, Box 438A Half Moon Bay 94019 ofc: McCutchen, Doyle et al. 3 Embarcadero Ctr 28th Flr San Francisco 94111.

BAGLEY, DONNA, income tax preparer; b. Mar 10, 1912, Corydon, Iowa; d. Roy Irwin and Cora Elsie (Stark) Patterson; m. Wallace Eldon Bagley, Aug. 1, 1943; 2 sons: Paul, b. 1946, Richard, b. 1950; edn: courses, Iowa State Coll., Los Angeles City Coll., Int. Revenue Acctg. courses, 1935-40; Calif. lic. Income Tax Preparer. Career: acctg. for Fed. Govt. in Iowa, 1935-40; office mgmt., acctg., sectl. for Int. Revenue, US Dept. of Agri. and Interior, firms in Los Angeles, San Francisco, 1940-45; income tax preparer, self empl., 1952--; adv. bd./dir. Frontier Bank, Buena Park; honors: Boys Club of Buena Park, Golden Boy, 1960s; Jay-Cees, Woman of the Year 1966; Boys Clubs of Am., 1978; BPW, Woman of Month; Coast Desert Region Soroptomist, outstanding comm. service 1984; City of Buena Park, Resolution 1982, City Placque, 1984, PTA Life mem. 1969; civic wk: City Traffic and Transp. (chmn. 1979-); Orange Co. Transit Dist. Adv. Commn. (1981-); mem. Buena Park Womens Club (CFWC and GFWC), Pi Unit, Nat. Assn. of Parliamentarians, Orange Dist. Womens Club (v.p. 1970-72, 13 yrs. on CFWC Bd., Area V.P.); orgnzr. Buena Park Girls Club (pres. 1965-69), Boys Club (bd. 1958-); Republican; Disciples of Christ; rec: cooking, sewing, writing. Res: Donna Bagley Income Tax Service, 5962 Stanton Ave Buena Park 90621 Ofc: Pacific Vending Sales, 7552 Fifth St Buena Park 90621

BAILEY, DEAN CLIFTON, electronics engineer; b. Apr. 9, 1933, Charlotte, Mich.; s. Ray Daniel and Ruby Hazel (Van Syoc) B.; m. Elvira Ramos, Aug. 14, 1983; children: Michele, b. 1957, Phillip, b. 1960, Peter, b. 1962; edn: electronics engr. Valparaiso Tech. Inst. 1951-53. Career: jr. engr. GE, Utica 1953-54; engr. Lear, Inc. Grand Rapids, Mich. 1954-55; engr., group ldr., section mgr., dept. mgr Integrated Circuits Applications Engrg. & Pilot Prod., Motorola, Phoenix, Ariz. 1955-64; modular prod. mgr. mgr. Union Carbide, Mt. View 1964-67; dir. microlectronics, Tecnetics, Boulder, Colo. 1967-70; precision monolithics mgr. of new product dev./ v.p. ops., Cycon, Sunnyvale 1971-73; project engr. signal analysers, Hewlett Packard, Sunnyvale 1973--; cons. on Thick Films, HP, Zeltex, 1970; ;mem. IRE 1951-54, ISA 1964-71; Patents (6) on semicondr. and modular circuits; musician (clarinet/sax), leader of a Glen Miller style Big Band (1983-); Republican; Ref. Presbyterian. Res: 1551 Pacific Ave, Apt. 4, Santa Rosa 954504 Ofc: Hewlett Packard, 1424 Fountain Grove Pky Santa Rosa 95402

BAILEY, GEORGE M., library director; b. Feb. 13, 1924, Millers, Md.; married, two children; edn: BA, Franklin and Marshall Coll. 1946; MA hist., Univ. Pa. 1947; MALS, Univ. Wisc. 1953; cert. mgt., Claremont Grad. Sch.; lib. automation insts.: Univ. Ill., Am. Lib. Assn., IBM. Career: instr. hist. Franklin and Marshall Coll., Heidelberg Coll. (Tiffin, Oh.), Univ. Wisc. 1947-51; intern in lib. adminstrn. UC Berkeley, 1953-54; librn. Soc. Sclis. Ref. Svcs, 1954-55; librn. UC Davis 1955-59, hd Ref.Dept. 1958-9; chief Ref. & Spl. Services, Northwestern Univ., 1959-63, and asst. planner of new lib. bldg.; exec.secty. Assn. of Coll. and Resrch Libs., div. Am. Lib. Assn., Chgo 1963-68; acad. librarian cons.; frequent spkr. lib. assns.; chief librarian/prof. York Coll., City Univ. of NY, 1968-71 (planned new lib. facility.; devel. staff and collection for new college lib.); assoc. dir. Libraries, The Claremont Colls.,Claremont 1971--; acting dir. of libs. 1973-4. cons. US Office of Edn.; accreditation vis. Western Assn of Schs and Colls, 1973-, Am. Lib. Assn 1978-; mem: ALA, Calif. Lib Assn., Beta Phi Mu, Phi Alphs Theta, Archons (NY), Zamorano Club (L.A.); res: 2129 Villa Maria Rd. Claremont 91711 ofc: The Assoc. Dir. of Libraries, The Claremont Colleges, Claremont.

BAILEY, HERBERT AUGUSTUS, insurance broker; b. Mar. 21, 1890, Princeton, Kans.; s. Charles Wm., Ph.D., and Mary Etta (Stark) B.; m. Mary Katharine Rice, Sept. 1, 1915; children: Robert, b. 1919, Richard, b. 1923; m. 2d. Lee Ewald, May 21, 1971; edn: BA, Baker Univ. 1910; grad. US Schs. of Mil. Aeronautics, UC Berkeley 1918. Career: bass singer and soloist, Otterbein Male Quartet, Des Moines, Iowa (rep. by Midland Lyceum Bur.) 1910-11; baritone soloist Ralph Dunbar Cathedral Choir, Chgo. (rep. by Redpath Lyceum Bur.) 1912, Ralph Dunbar Salon Singers, NYC (rep. by Harry Weber over the Keith, Orpheum, Interstate, and Pantages Cirs.), 1913-17; mgr. retail store, Edison Phonograph Co., K.C., Mo. 1919, sales promo. mgr./asst. to the pres., 1919-23; sales, piano dept. Fitzgerald Music Co., Los Angeles 1923-26; mgr. Hollywood Br., Platt Music Co., L.A. 1926-33; broker Herbert A. Bailey Ins. (rep. The Travelers Ins. Cos.), 1933--; honors: Golden Book Awd., YMCA of L.A. 1962, 50 Yr. Awd., Travelers Ins. Co. 1983; 50 Yr. Awd., Rotary Intl. 1983; mem: Delta Tau Delta, Rotary, Hollywood (pres. 1937-8), YMCA (past chmn.), Masons, Am. Legion (Charter Cmdr.), L.A. World Affairs Council, The Heritage Found., Wash. DC 1978; mil: 2d lt. Air Svc., 1918; 2d. lt., AUS Reserv. 1918-21; Republican (Nat. Com.); Methodist; rec: sports, music (Baritone and announcer, Hollywood Rotary Male Quartet, 1930-54). Res: 125 Montana Ave Santa Monica 90403 Ofc: Herbert A. Bailey Ins., 650 N. Sepulveda Blvd. Los Angeles 90049

BAILEY, JAMES PAUL, producer/writer/financial executive; b. May 2, 1949, Columbus, Oh.; s. Paul Shannon and Loretta Mary (Criado) B.; edn: BA music, Nat. Conservatory of Music 1976; MBA, Franklin Univ. 1979; Calif. Real Estate Broker lic., 1979. Career: pub. rels./prodn. crew WLW-C TV (Columbus, Oh.) Dance-O-Rama Series, 1963-67; real estate sales Roberts Realty, 1976, asst. mgr. Doheny Realty, 1978-79, R.E. broker 1979 ; estab. 2 cos, writing & producing audio/visual; founder/pres. James Bailey Prodns. 1979--, Inc. 1982-, also founder/pres. Entertainment Directions Unlmtd., 1983--; delinquency counselor; spkr. for The Olympic Experience pgm. for disadvantaged youths (founder Olympic Gold Medalist Bill Toomey); bus. seminar spkr.; awards: million dollar club, Roberts Realty 1977-78; Champions Unlmtd. Pres. Awd., Sasco Cosmetics No. 1 Recruiting in Nation 1980; mem: USABF -Boxing coach/supporter 1984 Olympic Team; Calif. Assn. Realtors; Nat. Assn. Realtors; sponsor/coach: AYSO Soccer, Del Obispo Boys Baseball, Regl. All Star Boys Baseball (1977, 78), The Olympic Exp.; mem. Dana Pt. CofC; subject interviews var. periodicals 1981-; mil: E3 USMC 1967-69, VietNam Svc., VietNam Cpgn. medals, Pres. Unit Cit.; Christian; rec: running, handball, music. Res. 33864 Pequito Dr Dana Point 92629 Ofc: James Bailey Productions, Inc. 34184 Coast Hwy. Ste. 205, Dana Point 92629

BAILEY, SCARLETT AMBER, artist, goldsmith; b. June 23, 1948, Madison, W. Va.; d. Theodore R. and Portia Lea (Martin) Sigmon; m. Charles C. Bailey, Oct. 20, 1968; 1 dau., Crystal Lea, b. 1966; grad. Los Angeles H. Sch. Career: self taught artist in creation of lost waxes, sculptor in 24K gold. Address: Amber & Co. 9490 Joshua St. 93207

BAILEY, WILLIAM DAVID, JR., labor relations executive/lawyer; b. Nov. 13, 1946, San Bernardino; s. Wm. D. and Virginia (Plecas) B.; m. Margaret, Feb. 7, 1970; edn: BS, Univ. of San Francisco 1968; tchr credential, Calif. Comm. Colls. 1972; JD (Valedictorian), Citrus Belt Law Sch. 1981; admitted to Calif. State Bar 1981. Career: bus. agt., organizer Local 250 of the Hosp. Workers Union of S.F., 1968-69; labor rels. office, Kaiser Steel Corp., Fontana 1969-75, mgr. oflabor relations, 1976--; trustee, Pol. Action Com. 1978-; adj. faculty Chaffee Coll. 1972-; counsel Bd. Dirs., Steelwkrs Oldtimers Found. 1982-; honors: 1974 American Iron & Steel Inst. Steel Fellow; recgn. for pro bono svcs. through Legal Aid, 1983 State Bar bd. of govs.; mem: Am., Calif., San Bernardino Co. Bar Assns.; mil: capt. USAR 1968; Democrat; Catholic; rec: sports. Res: 971 Sherwoo Redlands 92373 Ofc: Kaiser Steel Corp., 9400 Cherry, Ste 220, Fontana 92335

BAILEYS, STEVEN JEFFERY, health plan executive; b. Jan. 3, 1954, Los Angeles; s. Alvin M. and Geraldine P. (Werner) B.; m. Deborah M. Suttie, Aug. 28, 1982; edn: BA, Univ. Colo. 1976, DDS, Georgetown Univ. 1982. Career: asst. adminstr. Safeguard Health Plans, Inc., 1975, subsequently grievance ofcr., administrator, vice pres., exec. v.p.; currently pres./chief op. ofcr. Safeguard Health Enterprises, Inc. a publicly held co. whose subs. op. capitation dental plans in western US; bd. dirs: Safeguard Health Ent. Inc., Community Dental Centers Inc.; mem: Am. Dental Assn., Acad. Gen. Dentistry;

Democrat; Jewish; rec: golf, tennis, ski; res: 23975 Wanigan Way, Laguna Niguel 92677 ofc: Safeguard Hlth Ent. Inc. 13215 E. Penn St. Ste. 122, Whittier 90602

BAIRD, DONALD EUGENE, martial arts instructor; b. May 15, 1947, Denver, Colo.; s. John Oliver and Charlotte Jean (Perrill) Baird; m. Margo, Mar. 23, 1974; chil: Dannette, b. 1964, Dawn, b. 1968; edn: undergrad. Univ. of the Pacific, BA, UCLA 1970; Master of Martial Arts, Young Suh, 1982. Career: martial arts instr. 1972--, Young Suh Sch. of Self Defense, 1972-79, owner/dir. American Sch. of Martial Arts (approx. 275 students; rating 1st in Regl. competition 1981,2,3) Burbank 1980--; pres., dir. Am. Martial Art Assn.; studio musician (clarinet), Disney & Warner Bros. studios, 1982--; spl. investigator, comml. security, Riverside 1980--. Honors: Bank of Am. musician awd. 1965; outstanding soph., UOP 1967; featured in Fighting Stars mag., 10/83. Mem: Musician Union, NRA, Optimist, CofC. Author: Seeds from a Hermit (1983), Martial Artist: From the Ground & Up (1984); mil: E4 USAF, Mksman awd. Polit:Ind. res: 10676 Ledeen Dr. Lakeview Terr. 91342 ofc: American Sch of Martial Arts, 3316 W. Magnolia Blvd. Burbank 91505.

BAKER, ANDRA MAE, financial executive; b. May 25, 1949, Denver, Colo.; d. Charles Turner and Inez Loveada (Davis) Newmarch; m. Arnold S. Baker, III, Dec. 12, 1970, sep. 1983; dau. Anne Virginia, b. 1976; edn: BSBA in acctg. Univ. Denver 1970, MBA, UC Berkeley 1982; C.P.A., Calif. 1972. Career: staff accountant Price Waterhouse & Co. CPA's, San Jose 1971-72; sr. acct. Hood & Strong, CPA's, San Francisco 1972-77; dir. of accounting Joseph Magnin Co. Inc., San Francisco 1977-79; asst. controller CBS dba Pacific tero, Emeryville 1979-81; corp. controller Livingston Bros. Inc., San Francisco 1981--; honors: Beta Alpha Psi, acctg. hon. frat. 1970; mem: AICPA, Calif. Soc. of CPA's, Golden Gate Retail Finl. Execs. (div. NRMA, pres. 1980-81, bd. dir. 1979-82), Golden Gate Univ. Assocs.; Democrat; Episcopal; rec: water & snow ski; res: 825 Head St. San Francisco 94127 ofc: Livingston's, 111 O'Farrell St., San Francisco 94102.

BAKER, CAMERON, lawyer; b. Dec. 24, 1937, Chgo.; s. David Cameron and Marion (Fitzpatrick) B.; m. Katharine Solari, Sept. 2, 1961; children: Cameron, b. 1963, Ann, b. 1964, John, b. 1967; edn: Notre Dame 1954-57, AB, Stanford Univ. 1958, LL.B., UC Berkeley, 1961. Career: associate Adams, Duque and Hazeltine 1961-62; Pettit &: Martin, San Francisco, 1962--, mng. partner 1972-81, exec. com. 1971-. Dir: John Carl Warnecke & Assocs. 1982-, Leslie Salt Co. (mem. Audit Com.), 1971-78; mayor, Belvedere, Calif. 1978, mem. City Council 1976-80; mem: Am. Bar Assn. (coms. on: Audit Inquiry Responses, Partnership and Unincorporated Bus. Orgns., Internat. Bus. Law); San Francisco Bar Assn. (dir. 1966, 1972-3); mem. bd. dirs. San Francisco Lawyers Com. for Urban Affairs, 1975-; State Bar of Calif.; chmn. Gov. Com., Continuing Edn. of the Bar, 1975; dir., S.F. Legal Aid Soc. 1971-2; pres. S.F. Barristers' Club 1966; del. Union Internarionale des Avocats, 1983 ; Bohemian Club; Belvedere Tennis Club; Tiburon Penin. Club; PhiDelta Phi legal frat. (pres. 1961); Beta Theta Pi. res: 38 Alcatraz Ave. Belvedere 94920 ofc: Pettit & Martin, 101 California St., 35th Fl., San Francisco 94111.

BAKER, HARRY DE GARMO, construction co. president; b. Mar. 1, 1935, Los Angeles; s. Harry D. and Mabel Alison (Braasch) B.; m. Joyce Ione Quick, Nov. 21, 1976; 1 dau. Cherie Ann, b. 1963; edn: AA, Santa Monica CC, 1960, UCLA 1961; Calif. Lic. State Contractor 1983. Career: police ofcr. city of Santa Monica, 1958-65; computer opr. Hughes Aircraft, Culver City 1965-67; examiner Nat. American Ins. Co., L.A. 1967-71; v.p. Oakshire Corp., L.A. 1971-72; mgr. Clark Porche Constrn. Co., San Bernardino 1972-83; pres. Baker/Ginger Construction, Inc. Glendora 1983--; awards: 3d pl. USMC District Pistol Championships, 1964; mem: Footprinters Intl., Retired Police Officers of Santa Monica, San Bernardino/ Riverside Adjusters Assn., Masons; mil: sgt. USMC 1953-58, GCM, Pres. Unit. Cit., Nat. Def. medal, Exp. Rifleman/Pistol; Republican; Prot.; rec: fishing, travel. Res: 535 E. Whitcomb Ave Glendora 91740 Ofc: Baker/Ginger Constrn. Inc. 510 S. Vermont Glendora 91740

BAKER, JOEL ROBERT, financial planner; b. June 22, 1946, Los ngeles; s. John Robert and Arline Brownly Baker; m. Oatsy von Gontard, Apr. 22, 1981; edn: BA in bus. adm., Fort Lewis Coll. 1968; Reg. Invester Adviser. Career: co-owner Yossem-Baker Financial and Estate Planning, Santa Barbara 1978--; guest spkr. num. profl. groups; mem: Top of the Table (Top 300 Life Ins. Underwriters 1981), Million Dollar Round Table (1975-); mem: Internat. Assn. for Finl. Plnng., Los Angeles Co. Assn. of Finl. Planner, Santa Barbara Life Underwriters Assn.; mem. S.B. Polo Club, US Polo Assn., ranked in top ten Polo players in USA (1981-), has played for the US in Argentina, New Zealand, and Mex.; rec: skiing, polo, tennis, horse ranching. Res: POB 1993, Buellton 93427 Ofc: Yossem-Baker, 829 De La Vina, Ste. 100, Santa Barbara 93101

BAKER, RONALD EUGENE, auto dealer; b. Mar. 30, 1945, Topeka, Kans.; s. Harry M. and Catherine L. (Woody) Baker; m. Judy, Aug. 24, 1963; 1 son Raymond, b. 1963; career: president, three corps.; mem. Elks; Baptist; address: 5515 N. Blackstone Ave. Fresno 92710.

BAKST, ABRAHAM ALFRED, engineer, real estate executive, investor; b. Jan. 12, 1922, Palmer, Mass.; s. Isadore and Minnie (Kaplan) B.; m. Pauline Day (Dep. Atty-Gen., Hawaii 1948-9) July 10, 1948, div. 1959; 1 dau. Katherine (hd. tchr. Child Care Devel. Ctr., UCI & CSULB, 1973-6) b. 1949; son-in-law, Richard Thornley (Dep. Atty-Gen., Nev. 1977-81). Edn: Bklyn. Coll. 1938-42, U. of Hawaii 46-7, Cal Poly 49-50; AA in real estate, Long Bch C.C. 1961; Orange Coast Coll. 78-9; mil. certs., Bellevue/Naval Resrch Lab. 43-4.

Career: radar insp. War Dept., N.J. 1942; petty ofcr. USNR (radio, radar supr. P.T. Boat Squad.), So.Pac. 1942-5; teletype opr. War Dept., Hawaii 1946-7; electronic engr. all Naval and Marine Corps Air Stations, 14th Naval Dist. (H.I.), Pearl Harbor 1947-9, pioneered first VHF radio teletype and terminal network in Navy 1947, asst. proj. engr. VLF radio propagation characteristic test, Pac. area 1948; electronic sci./staff Navy Dept., Inyokern 1950; electronic engr.: Douglas Aircraft, Rockwell Internat., Hughes Aircraft, Hoffman Radio, Varec Indus., 1951-8; supr. Nebeker Realty, Calif. 1958-61; owner/broker/investor Bakst Realty Enterprises, Anaheim 1961--; founder/pub./ed. News Forecasting Newsletter (1958); advisor on news foresight, seven US Presidents, Congress, 1953-. Honors: 1st Chess Champion Hawaii 1949, chess champion teams in H.S. and Coll.; listed in P.T.Boats Knights of the Sea (1982). Jewish; rec: news analysis, chess; address: 210 N. Brookhurst St. Anaheim 92801.

BALDAUF, LAURENCE CHARLES, JR., lawyer; b. May 3, 1933, San Diego; s. Laurence C. and Eleanor Ruth (Byrne) Baldauf; m. Edith Myers, Oct. 29, 1980; chil: Laurence III, b. 1959, Corinne, b. 1957, Therese, b. 1961; edn: BS, elec.eng., US Naval Acad., Annapolis 1955; BS in electronics eng., US Naval Postgrad. Sch., Monterey 1962; LLB, Western State Univ. 1971. Career: Navy pilot until 1967; stockbroker/mutual fund pres. 1967-71; self empl. lawyer 1971--; instr. law sch. (real prop., constnl. law), Western State Univ., eve. 1971-79; honors: Prof. of the Year 1977, Western State Univ.; capt. tennis team US Naval Acad. 1955; attorney of record in Miranda v. Macias, a case of first impression dealing with the Garn Bill; author/pub. Bah Bah Blue Sheep-Critique of Military Yes Men; mil: Lcdr. USN; polit. ind.; Catholic; rec: tennis, golf, chess; res: 4279 Hortensia San Diego 92103 ofc: 2055 Third Ave San Diego 92101.

BALDWIN, DELBERT EARL, geodesist; b. Oct. 17, 1943, Yreka; s. Earl Edward and Maola Ruth (Smith) B.; m. Kathe A. O'Brien, Oct. 9, 1969; children: Jennifer, b. 1970, Michael, b. 1971; edn: electronics, Pendleton Tech. Sch. 1961-2, geodesy, Portland State Univ. 1962-4, (part time) 1965-72, UC Berkeley 1972; cert. geodesist, Bur. of Land Mgmt. 1971; merit, USGS Earth Resources Observation Systems 1972; ACSM-NGS Fellowship 1975. Career: survey/engrg. tech. Bur. of Land Mgmt., Vale, Ore., Anchorage, AK. summers 1963-65; cadastral surveyor, Bur. of Land Mgmt., Portland, Ore. 1966-71, geodesist, 1971-72, Acting Br. Chief 1972; v.p./gen. mgr. Computerized Svcs. Inc., Oxnard 1972-74; geodesist, computer splst. BLM, Denver, Colo. 1974-77; tech. rep. Carl Zeiss Inc., San Leandro 1977-8, 1980-1; system splst. Geodimeter Inc., Novato 1981--. Recipient BLM merit awds. 1967, 72. Mem: Am. Soc. of Photogrammetry, Calif. Land Surveyors; PTA; player Master Soccer League; asst. coach Parks and Rec. Soccer League; booster Redwood Empire Gym. (boys & girls) Club. Prin. investigator Omatilla Remote Sensing Proj. 1971; devel. computer pgm. for acctg. 1974, turnkey surveying sys. 1981-3, scoring gym. meets 1982; pub. tech. papers; Democrat; Baptist; rec: water skiing, camping, pgmmg. Res: 2060 Hatch Rd Novato 94947 Ofc: Geodimeter Inc. 385 Bel Marin Keys Bl Novato 94947

BALDWIN, JOHN CHARLES, cardiovascular and thoracic surgeon; b. Sept. 23, 1948, Ft. Worth, Tex.; s. Charles Leon and Annabel (West) C.; m. Christine Janet Stewart, Mar. 31, 1972; children: Alistair Edward Stewart, b. 1976; John Benjamin West, b. 1978; Andrew Christian William, b. 1982; edn: BA summa cum laude, Harvard Univ. 1971; Rhodes Scholar, Magdalen Coll. Oxford Univ. 1971-72; MD, Stanford Univ. 1975. Career: med. intern, res. in med., res. in surgery, Mass. Gen. Hosp., Boston, Mass. 1975-81, clin. fellow in medicine, Harvard Med. Sch. 1975-77, clin. fellow in surg. 1977-81; res./chief res. in cardiovascular surg. Stanford Univ. Med. Ctr. 1981-83; chief res. in cardiac transplantation, 1982-83, chief res. in thoracic surg. 1983; clin. asst. prof. of cardiovascular surg. Stanford Univ.; awards: Defur Prize, Harvard Univ. 1968, John Harvard Scholarship Awd. 1969, 70, Wendell Scholarship 1969; Phi Beta Kappa 1970; Rhodes Scholarship 1971; Alumni Scholar Awd., Stanford Univ. Sch. of Med. 1974; mem. AMA, Am. Coll. Physicians, Stanford Med. Alumni Assn., Harvard Med. Alumni Assn., Am. Assn. of Rhodes Scholars, Hasty Pudding Inst.; num. publs. rel to cardiopulmonary disease and heart and heart-lung transplantation; Prot. Res: 181 Walker Hays Dr Palo Alto 94303 Ofc: Dept. of Cardiovascular Surgery, Stanford Univ. Medical Center, Stanford 94305

BALDWIN, STEVEN JON, dentist; b. Oct. 20, 1954, Long Beach; s. Jon Cook and Virginia Pat (Hill) Baldwin; edn: BS in biol. (genetics), honors, CSU San Diego 1976; BS in dental sci., and DDS, UCSF Sch of Dentistry 1982. Career: self-empl. in specialized constrn., 1972-79, photog., artist, 1976--, San Diego and San Francisco; coordinator/lectr. CSUSD Preventive Dentistry Pgm., 1976-78; pvt. dental practice, Berkeley 1983--; UCSF vis. lectr. endodontics (1982), oral surgery (1983-); genetic counselor for Tay-Sach screening, San Diego 1975-6; vol. dentist for Tijuana Dental Clinic, 1980. Mem: Am. Student Dental Assn. 1978-82; Am. Dental Assn 1982-; Calif. Dental Assn.; Berkeley Dental Soc.; Sausalito Yacht Club; Psi Omega Dental frat. Publs: research in pre-biotic amino acid synthesis, 1976-78; adventure art. in Surfer mag., 12/82. Rec: surf, sail, ski, guitar, art; res: 2830 Ortega San Francisco 94122 ofc: 2636 Telegraph Berkeley 94704.

BALL, BEVERLY DAWN, dentist; b. Oct. 20, 1947, Los Angeles; d. H. D. Jack and Evelyn L. (Miller) Ball; edn: AS, Grossmont Coll. 1968; BS magna cum laude, CSU San Diego 1972; MT, USC-LAC Hosp. 1973; DDS, UC Los Angeles 1978; Calif. Reg. Med. Tech., 1973, Gen. Practice Dentist 1978. Career: med. tech. (mem. Am. Assn. of Clin. Pathol.), USC-Los Angeles Co. Med. Ctr., Harbor Hosp., West Adams Comm. Hosp., and Washington Hosp., 1973-78; gen. practice dentist, 1978--; honors: Calif. Scholarship Fedn. (life),

Alpha Gamma Sigma (life), Phi Kappa Phi (life), charter mem. Student Ct. Grossmont Coll.; mem: Am. Assn. of Women Dentist, Latin Am. Dental Assn., Burbank Human Relations Council, Flying Samaritans, Audubon Soc.; mem. Perf. Arts Council of L.A., pres. Caswell Condo. Homeowners Assn., Ballona Valley Bromeliad Soc.; rec: bridge, rollerskating, sailing. Res: 12629 Caswell Ave Unit D2, Los Angeles 90066 Ofc: 10826 Venice Blvd, Ste. 6, Culver City 90230

BALL, CRAIG JAMES, physician-plastic surgeon; b. June 21, 1949, Ft. Worth, Tex.; s. William Clyde and Nadine Louise (Hansen) Ball; div.; 1 child, Chadwick, b. 1978; edn: BA, biol., Pac.Union Coll. 1971; MD, Univ. Tex., San Antonio 1977. Career: internship, and 1st yr. general surgery, Valley Medical Ctr., Fresno 1977-79; Ent/Facial Plastic Surgery residency, White Meml. Med. Ctr., Los Angeles 1979-82; pvt. group practice, Los Angeles 1982--. Mem. Calif., LA County Medical Assns.; Republican; S.D.A.; rec: golf, tennis, waterski, Triathlons; res: 601 N. Kenwood #302, Glendale 91206 ofc: 1700 Brooklyn Ave. Ste. 15, Los Angeles 90033.

BALLARD, HENRY WOODSON, real estate broker; b. Sept. 29, 1928, Hawthorne; s. Henry and Lynne A. (Williams) B.; m. Marilyn D. Thomas, Dec. 2, 1981; children: Kirk, b. 1963; Karen, b. 1967. Career: BS, fin., USC 1952; Calif. lic. R.E. Broker 1957. Career: asst. mgr. Pacific Fin. 1954-57; salesmgr., mgr. Marlow & Co. Realtors, 1957-66; founded the first real estate re-sale firm in Mission Viejo, first firm to join a real estate bd. serving the Saddleback Valley; broker/owner La Paz Real Estate of Mission Viejo, 1968-79; currently active R.E. broker and cons. to four pvt. trusts; mem: charter mem. Saddleback Valley Bd. of Realtors (MLS Com. 4 yrs), Nat. & Calif. Assn. of Realtors; Theta Xi frat. (life), Mission Viejo Elks (charter, trustee); mil: 1st lt. USMC 1952-54, Nat. Svc., Korean Cpgn. (2 stars), UN Cpgn., UN Victory medals, Asian-Pac., Navy, AF & Army Dist. Unit Cits.; Republican; Prot.; rec: fishing, hunting. Address: 22797 Malaga Way, El Toro 92630

BALLESTEROS, ANTONIO VILLANUEVA, engineer; b. July 24, 1939, La Union, Philippines, nat. 1971; s. Primitivo Estolas and Mauricia Sapitula (Villanueva) B.; m. Victoria, July 18, 1965; children: Evelyn, b. 1966, Antonio Jr., b. 1968, Judith, b. 1971; edn: BS in E.E., Mapua Inst. of Tech., 1961, BS in Mech. Eng., 1964; mgmt. courses, Wayne State Univ. 1971-73; Reg. Profl. Engr., Mich. (1971), Fla. (1979), Calif. (1982). Career: electrical engr./supr., Ford Motor Co. 1961-6, Wyandote Chem. Corp., 1967, W.D. Gale Inc., 1967-68; assoc. Hoyem, Basso & Assocs. 1968-79, v.p./asst. dir. elec. engring., 1979-82; sr. electrical engr., office mgr. Cohen & Kanwar Inc., Los Anges 1982--; mem. Illuminating Engring. Soc., De Bell Golf Club; Catholic; rec: golf, running. Res: 719 E. Bethany Rd Burbank 91504 Ofc: Cohen & Kanwar Inc. 6380 Wilshire Blvd Los Angeles 90048

BALLUFF, DOUGLAS PAUL, company president; b. Nov. 8, 1941, Chgo.; s. John J. and Minette Lillian Balluff; m. Sharon S. Ives, Sept. 9, 1967; edn: AB, econ./Latin Am. Affairs, Geo. Wash. Univ. 1965; MBA internat. bus./fin., UCLA Grad. Sch. of Mgmt. 1967; Calif. Lic. Real Estate Broker. Career: marketing staff Ford Motor Internat., Detroit 1967-68; mgr. market research/planning, Motorola Comm. Internat., Chgo. 1968-69; staff planning group FMC Machinery Gp. Hdqtrs., Chgo. 1969-71; pres. Douglas Balluff & Assocs. (Chgo., Ill.; San Jose, Costa Rica; San Francisco, Ca.) 1971--; pres. The San Francisco Group, 1981--; partner Carney & Balluff, S.F. 1984--; pres. Urbane Editions Ltd., S.F.; mem. Rotary Club of S.F. (bd. dirs.), S.F. CofC, Japan Soc. of S.F.; Christian; rec: sailing, cycling, opera, helicopter pilot. Res: 150 Lombard St, Ste. 102, San Francisco 94111 Ofc:

BALOG, JANOS FOHN, physician, OB/Gyn; b. Jan. 22, 1932, Debrecen, Hungary, nat. 1969; s. Erno and Ella (Fohn) Schwartz; m. Eva Solyom, Dec. 10, 1956; chil: Janos Jr., b. 1957, Eva, b. 1959, Susan, b. 1960, George, b. 1967; edn: med. schs. in Debrecen & Budapest; MD, Johann Wolfgang Goethe Univ., Frankfurt 1969; MPH, UC Berkeley 1975. Career: physician in 97th US Army Hosp., Frankfurt, W.Ger. 1961-63; OB/Gyn intern, resident in Dearborn, Mich. 1963-67; pvt. practice, Wyandotte, Mich. 1974-75; full-time faculty mem. OB/Gyn dept. UC San Francisco, 1975-77, clin. asst. prof. 1977-; pvt. Ob/Gyn practice Mission Dist., San Francisco 1977--; dir. med. educ. St. Luke's Hosp., S.F. Mem: Fellow Am. Coll. of Obstets & Gyns 1971; SF Med. Soc., AMA; publs: profl. and lay journal arts. Republican. rec: tennis, ski, windsurf. res: 42 Ironship Plaza San Francisco 94111 ofc: Janos Balog MD Inc. 1580 Valencia #204 San Francisco 94110.

BALTIERRA, GABRIEL CAMACHO, corporate executive; b. Feb. 27, 1928, Los Angeles; s. Sebastian Sanchez and Asuncion Guerrero (Camacho) B.; children: Michael, b. 1952, Mark, b. 1956, Kathy, b. 1955, Rodney, b. 1956, India, b. 1958; edn: AA, Orange Coast Coll. 1951; stu. USC, 1952, La Salle Univ. 1966-67. Career: owner/ pres./chmn. bd. Balent, Inc. dba Diversified Svc. & Sls; Diversified Deductions; Diversified Typografix; Investors Diversified; sales mgr. Bearing Engineering Co.; zone mgr. Motor Rim & Wheel Co., Inc.; owner/mgr. Frontier Auto Parts (2 stores); gen. mgr. Cal-Pacifico, S.A. (Mexico); sales rep. Beacon Auto Parts, Newport Beach; past gen. mgr. nat. auto parts chain, 1967-69; adm. asst. (sports news) Orange Coast Coll., 1955-58; past pres. League of United Latin Am. Citizens (ed. LULAC News 1955-6); mem. Elks, Lions, CofC; mil: radioman USN 1945-47, Victory, Asia Pac.; Republican; Catholic; rec: golf, travel, write. Res: 287 Naples St Chula Vista 92011 Ofc: Balent, Inc. 29 Third Ave Chula Vista 92010

BANNISTER, WESLEY MASTIN, insurance broker; b. Oct. 11, 1936, Houston, Tex.; s. John Howard and Catherine (Holland) B.; m. Elizabeth Rogers, Dec. 30, 1938; children: Catharine, b. 1961, Alice, b. 1962, Douglas, b. 1967; edn: BS, pol. sci., Univ. Houston 1959. Career: asst. dist. mgr. Jos. Schlitz, Denver, Colo.; salesman Lederle Labs., Amarillo, Tex. 1961-65; sales, Pfizer Labs., Albuquerque, N.M. 1965-67; Lumbermens Underwriting Alliance Territorial Mgr., Los Angeles, Ca. 1967-71, Regl. VP Aetna-Cravens Dargan, Los Angeles 1971-74; owner Bannister & Assocs. Ins. Agcy., Huntington Bch. 1974--; honors: Dedicated Civic award 1980-82 (Plnng. Commnr.), Dedicated H.B. Volunteer Awd., Spl. Events Bd., 1971-81; mem. bd. Orange Coast Ins. Assocs. (pres. 1980); mem. CofC, Avalon Tuna Club, Pacific Anglers, Balboa Angling Club, Rotary, Cancer Detection Ctr, Nat. Coalition Marine Conserv., Internat. Game Fish Assn., Huntinton Harbour Yacht Club, Sunset Aquatic Yacht Club; mil: capt. arty. US Army 1959-66, Reserves; Republican; Episcopal; rec: fishing, boating. Res: 19242 McLaren Ln Huntington Bch 96646 Ofc: Bannister & Assocs. 15562 Chemical Ln Huntington Beach 92649

BANOCZI, JEANNETTE BERNADETTE, radio broadcasting executive; b. Jan. 21, 1922, Dracut, Mass.; d. Albert A. and Rhea Marie (Venne) Boulay; m. Humbert R. Pennino, Dec. 14, 1946 (dec. 1955); children: Jeannette Claire, b. 1947, Madelaine Lynn, b. 1952, Naomi Gloria, b. 1954; m. 2d. John R. Banoczi, July 16, 1960; edn: pvt. instrn. trumpet, New England Conserv. Career: First trumpeter Phil Spitalny Hour of Charm, All Girl Orch., NYC 1940-42; 1st trumpet Ina Ray Hutton Orch. 1957; freelance trumpeter NBC, New York City, 1942-46; trumpet tchr. 1941-46; pres. Pennino Music Co., Inc. 1946-74, bd. chmn. 1974--; pres. radio bdcstg. Radio Sta. KGGK (Garden Grove) 1961-66, Sta. KNOB (Anaheim) 1966--, Sta. KXTZ (Henderson, Nev.) 1971-; mem. Sales & Mktg. Execs. Club of Orange Co. (pres. 1973-74), Orange Co. CofC (life), Better Bus. Bur., Soroptomist Club (pres. Garden Grove 1963-65); Pi Sigma Epsilon (1st female mem. 1974); exec. bd. mem. of O.C. Lung Assn., O.C. Academic Decathalon, Childrens Home Soc. of Calif., Martin Luther Hosp.; mem. O.C. Econ. Devel. Pgm. Com. Address: Radio Station KNOB, POB 3159, Anaheim 92803

BARBER, FRED E., corporate executive; b. Aug. 19, 1931, Lineville Iowa; s. Fred G. and Mary Lorene (Owen) Barber; m. Yvonne B. Williams, June 27, 1953; children: Karen, b. 1955, Janet, b. 1958; edn: AA, Orange, Coast, Golden West, Long Beach Colls. (nights) 1954-67; BA, CSU Fullerton 1970; MBA, Univ. Beverly Hills 1979. Career: mechanic USAF, Douglas Aircraft, Virtue Bros., 1949-56; mech. design draftsman No. Am. Rockwell, 1956-60; sr. engineer Northrop Corp., 1960-70; consulting engr. 1970-72; Program mgr, group hd., pgm. adminstr., Northrop Corp., 1972-81, Dept. mgr., 1981-82; dept. mgr. Configuration Mgmt. Dept., TRW, Redondo Beach 1982--; sr. mem. IEEE; sr. mem. Mfg. Engineering Soc.; life mem. Am. Defense Preparedness Assn.; founding mem. Am. Historical Soc.; mil: s/sgt. USAF 1949-52; Am. Ind. Party (state chmn. AIP, 1982-84); Baptist; rec: hunting, ranching, computer club, swim. res: 6432 Shields Dr. Huntington Beach 92647 ofc: TRW, One Space Park, Redondo Beach.

BARBER, GLENDA CAROLYN, company president; b. Mar. 3, 1939, Miller, mo.; d. Vaughn Boyd and Mary M. (McNeill) Gum; m. Jerry T. Barber, June 27, 1959; children: Bruce, b. 1961, Bret, b. 1965; edn: stu. Univ. Mont. 1957-59. Career: mgmt. family quarter horse breeding ranch in Ariz., 1974-75; originator/ owner/ pres. Pretty Pet Mobile Groomer, Inc., San Diego County 1975--; fleet of vans (11) provide front door curbside grooming svcs. for small pets; mem: Kearney Mesa Bus. Assn., bd. govs. Profl. Oriented Groomers Orgn. of S.D., Kearny Mesa Soroptimist Club; vp S.D. County Pop Warner Football Conf. 1983-84 (pres. University City Assn. 1981); rec: lic. pvt. pilot, history buff. REs: 6699 Beadnell Way, 103, San Diego 92117 Ofc: Pretty Pet Mobile Groomer Inc. 4655 Ruffner St, Ste. 140, San Diego 92111

BARBER, LAURAINE MARGARET, county executive; b. Sept. 14, 1930, Los Angeles; d. Fred Heath and Laura May (Sigafoose) Leonard; m. Robert Ellis Barber, Jan. 30, 1954; children: Paul Kevin, b. 1958, Cheryll Cecille, b. 1960, Michelle Louise, b. 1962; edn: AA, Glendale City Coll. 1951; BA in edn., CSU Long Beach 1955. Career: tchr., Pre-School and Child Care, Glendale 1948-49, Baldwin park 1949-59; jr. high sch. tchr. Brethren Schs., 1955-72; dir. Pre-Sch., 1974-76; pres./ exec. dir. Fedn. of Community Coordinating Councils, Los Angeles Co., 1978--, cons. to the 80 councils in the Fedn. in the coordination of human services in the County of Los Angeles; cons. on comm. networking to corps., agcs., orgns.; commnr. L.A. Co. Commn. on Alcoholism; honors: Hannah Sullivan Award, Kenyon Scudder Award; active mem. bd.: Film Adv. Bd. Hollywood, Cerritos Coll. Civic Responsibility Com., United Way Adv. Com., Freedoms Found. Valley Forge, Childrens Citizen Adv. Com., Inter-Faith Com., Nat. March of Dimes, Calif. Vol. Adminstrs., Congress of Agcs.; past ldr. Campfire Girls, Boy Scouts; publs: You, Me, We (book); It's Time for the We in America (record); devel. the comm. vol. campaign theme, California Gold Rush; rec: travel, people. Republican; Prot. Res: 3109 Lees Ave Long Beach 90808 Ofc: F.C.C.C. 1945 Long Beach Blvd Long Beach 90806

BARBER, MILES HENRY, executive; b. Aug. 15, 1939, Yakima, Wash.; s. Henry and Inda (Bierly) B.; children: Shelly, b. 1961, Charm, b. 1963; edn: BA, Cascade Coll. 1961; MRE, Western Sem. 1965; Univ. of Portland 1966-67, CSU San Jose 1975. Career: div. sales mgr. ITT-Hamilton Mgmt. Corp., San Jose 9169-71; founder /pres. /bd. chm. Allied Assocs. Insurance for Commerce and Industry, Santa Clara 1971--; founder/bd. chmn. Commercial & Industrial Admin. Co., Inc., San Francisco 1977--; founder/bd. chmn. Allied Realty Inv. Co., Santa Clara 1981--; founder/ pres./ bd. chmn. Allied Mgmt. Services Inc., 1981--; founder /bd. chmn. TPA Automated Services, Inc. 1982--; current mem. Senate Select Com. on Insurance and Indemnity; del. to Calif. Conf. on Small Bus., 1980-82; mem. TEC The Executive Com. 1983-; bd. mem./treas. Californians Preventing Violence; honors: commendn., Santa Clara County Bd. of Supvrs. for comm. service 1979; mem. San Jose Life Underwriters (health com.), Profl. Ins. Agts., Mass Mktg. Inst. of Am., Rotary, Santa Clara CofC (pres. 1979); Republican; rec: golf, racquetball. Res: 1050 Madison Santa Clara 95050 Ofc: Allied Management Services Inc. 2075 De La Cruz Blvd Santa Clara 95050

BARBER, STEPHAN ALLEN, lawyer; b. July 1, 1950, San Jose; s. E. Allen and Carole E. (Andersen) B.; m. Lauren, Oct. 8, 1983; edn: BA in econ., UC Santa Barbara 1972, JD, McGeorge Sch of Law 1976. Career: student intern Sacramento Co. Dist. Atty's ofc., 1975; assoc. atty. Popelka, Allard, McCowan & Jones, San Jose 1976-80, partner 1981--; honors: Am. Jurisprudence Awd. Real Property (1974); mem. The Traynor Soc. (1976); arts. ed. Pacific Law Jour. (1975-6); mem: State Bar of Calif., Santa Clara Co. Bar Assn., Assn. of Defense Counsel, Nat. Assn. of Railroad Trial Counsel; Phi Delta Theta frat.; Phi Delta Phi legal frat.; Republican; Prot.; rec: bridge, golf, softball. res: 7024 Wooded Lake Dr. San Jose 95120 ofc: Popelka, Allard, McCowan & Jones, 1 Almaden Bl. Ste.800 San Jose 95113.

BARCENA, GUSTAVO ALFRED, lawyer; b. Aug.2, 1951, Mexico City, Mex.; nat. 1969; s. Salvador and Maria (Fonseca) Barcena; edn: cert. Nat. Univ. of Mex., 1971; BA, CSU Sacramento 1973; JD, UCLA 1977. Career: sales Weinstock's Dept. Store (Broadway-Hale's), Sacramento 19772; intern KCRA-TV & Radio stas., Sacramento 1972-73; legal clerk Ofc of Chief Counsel, Kennedy Space Ctr., NASA, 1974; intern cons. Calif. Legis. Assembly Minority Caucus, 1975; intern Pub. Defender Acy., Anchorage, AK. 1976; atty. with various law firms, 1976; private practice with offices in Los Angeles and Santa Ana, 1979--; arbitrator L.A. Co. Bar Assn.,fee disputes; Referee, Calif.State Bar Assn. Disciplinary Cts.; trustee L.A. Co. Barristers. awards: Outstanding Young Men of Am., 1980; Edwin C. Kelley Broadcasting Scholarship 1972-4; vice pres. UCLA Grad. Student Assn. 1974. mem: Mex.-Am. Bar Assn. (1979 trustee); (MABA) vice pres. 1983; Calif. State Bar Assn. (del. 1978-9); Am. BarAssn.; UCLAAlumni Assn., CofC (jt. comm. rels. Coms. of UCLA & Westwood); Internat.Law Soc., Chicano Law Students Assn. (chmn. PAC), UCLA 1974-5; editor EOP World (CSUS pub.) 1972-3; Democrat; Catholic; rec: travel, tennis, ski. res: POB 24955, Los Angeles 90024 ofc: Law Office, 6334 Whittier Blvd. los Angeles 90022.

BARCLAY, DOROTHEA RUTH, real estate broker; b. Mar. 3, Sunbury, Penn.; d. Harvey and Grace Irene (Straub) Stradlev; children: Delyn, b. 1955, Jamye, b. 1958; edn: R.N., Polyclinic Hosp. Sch. of Nursing 1948-51; real estate courses, Lumbleau Sch. 1968, Anthony's Sch., 1974, dip., Long Beach City Coll. 1977; Calif. real estate broker lic. Career: chg. nurse, Colombia Convalescent Home, Long Bech 1961-62; asst. plastic surgery nurse Leo H. Ladage MD 1962-68; agt., Rex L. Hodges Realty, Long Beach 1968-76; owner/ broker CBS Realty, Long Beach 1976--; dir. Long Beach Bd. Realtors; tchr. real estate Long Beach City Coll. (4 yrs.); state dir. Calif. Assn. Realtors (6 yrs.); trustee BORPAC (L.B. Bd Realtors); mem. CAR PAC; awards: L.B. Bd. Realtors Assoc. of Year, L.B. Jaycees Tweedy Awd., num. salesman awds. Mem: Sales & Mktg. Execs.; L.B. Boys Club of Am.; Com. 300 for Long Beach Grand Prix; March of Dimes; Spl. Olympics Booster Male Beauty Contest; L.B. CofC; Chili Cookoff, L.B. Grand Prix; Police Ofcrs. Assn. honoraries; Police Widows & Orphans & Law Enforcement; L.B. Police Ofcrs. K-9 Assn.; Republican; Protestant; rec: reading, sailing, travel. Res: 6821 Killdee Street Long Beach 90808 Ofcs: CBS Realty, 245 Main St, Seal Beach & 3064 E Broadway Long Beach 90803

BARDELLA, CLAIRE MITCHELL PETERSEN, scholarship administrator; b. Sept. 22, 1914, Oakland; d. Roland C. Stuart-Mitchell and Ethel Petey Mitchell St. John; stepfather Pierce Louis St. John, concert violinist; m. Chris R. Petersen II (law prof., v.p. Lincoln Univ., San Francisco), Oct. 17, 1937, dec. 1961; m. Darrell Bardella (pilot), Dec. 15, 1962; edn: BA, magna cum laude, Stanford Univ. 1935. Career: child prodigy singer (one of Stanford Univ. Prof. Terman's gifted children), San Jose Normal Sch., performer in sev. operettas at San Jose State Univ.; pres. Calif. Scholarship Fedn., Palo Alto H.Sch., editor Literary Mag., awarded Yearbk. scholarship to Stanford Univ., 1931; profl. singer various churches, Palo Alto, NBC radio with Hans Leshke, 1932-34; soloist S.F. Municipal Chorus, 1933; poetry/music pub. by Stanford Press, 1934; lead singing role in Stanford Gaieties, 4 yrs.; secty. to v.p. Bank of Am. subs. California Banks, Inc., 1936; cons. to American delegation of UN Peace Conf. under Dean Virginia Gildersleeve, 1945. Honors: Phi Beta Kappa (1934); pres. Delta Delta Delta Sor. 1934; pres. German Hon. Soc. 1933-4; Deans List 1934. Mem: Stanford Womens Club, S.F. (dir. 6 yrs.); AAUW (pres. SF branch 1943-45, honored by Gr. Brit. for contbn. to Brit. War Relief; orgnzr. Hospitality Pgm. for Service Women in S.F.; orgnzr. luncheon honoring 60 famous internat. women 1945; pres. Past Presidents Council); pres. Phi Beta Nat. Profl. Orgn. of Music Dance and Drama; Scholarship chmn. Phi Beta Kappa, S.F.; judge, Bank of Am. Coll. Awards, 1981. Publs: travel arts. in Stanford Mag., Tri Delta Mo., 1975-82, contbr. Famous Alumni Cookbook (Stanford Press). Soloist, artist mem. Woodside Sym. Guild. Rec: tennis, entertaining, travel. res: 1895 Pacific Ave. San Francisco 94109.

BARDIN, CAROLE ANNE, psychologist; b. Nov. 24, 1942, Newton, Mass.; d. John A. and Ellen Nancy (Graham) Logan; m. Robert Bardin, July 30, 1977; chil: Erin, b. 1978, Erica, b. 1981; edn: BA, Penn State Univ. 1964, M.Ed.Psy., Temple Univ. 1969, MSW, USC 1974, PhD, Calif. Sch of Profl. Psychol., San Diego 1983; Calif. lic. clin. soc. worker (1979), mem. Am. Psychol. Assn. (1983). Career: indsl. therapist (1964-6), caseworker (1967-8)Norristown (Pa.) State Hosp.; social worker Marlboro (NJ) State Hosp., 1966-7; asst.dir. admissions Montgomery Co. Comm. Coll., Conshohocken, Pa. 1968-70; emplyment devel. splst., Los Angeles 1970-2; soc. worker intern, Fmly Svcs Agcy., Cedars Sinai Hosp., Los Angeles 1973-4; soc. worker Gateways Comm. Treatment Ctr., L.A. 1974-5; dir. soc. svcs. Cyn. Gen. Hosp., Anaheim 1976-7; psychol. intern Orange Co. Juvenile Ct., 1978, Child Guidance Ctr. of Orange Co., 1980-82; psychotherapist pvt. practice, employee assistance pgm.; mem. A.P.A., N.A.S.W.; Mini Scout Troop Ldr.; Harbor Day Parents' Council. Honors: La Vie Belle, Penn. State U. 1964. Publs: Role Conflict In Working, Married Women with Pre-School Children. Republican; rec: int.decorating, swim, photog. res: 18 Buckthorn Irvine 92714 ofc: Employee Counseling Svc. Golden Cir. Dr. #220, Santa Ana 92705.

BARGLOWSKI, LEO VINCENT, electronics engineer; b. Apr. 5, 1928, Bound Brook, NJ; s. Marcel and Maryanna (Michalowski) B.; m. Florence Stelmaszek, Oct. 16, 1954; children: Michelle Ann (Treleven), b. 1957, Mark Gerard, b. 1960, Renee Elena, b. 1968; edn: BA, cum laude, Univ. Md. 1965; MS cum laude, USC Sch. of Engring. 1967; M. Aerospace Ops. Mgmt., cum laude, USC 1967; spl. courses, Univ. of Dayton, Seton Hall Univ., Rutgers Univ., var. mil. schools. Desig.: electronic engr., US Civil Svc. 1967; sys. engr., Naval Postgrad. Sch. 1981; def. contracts mgr., Naval Mat. Cmd. 1982; contr. ofcr. tech. coordinator, 1983. Career: engr. USAF 1946-67; avionics sys. engr. Genge Indus., Ridgecrest, Ca. 1967-68; aircraft systems engr./tech. mgr. Spl. Projects Br., Naval Weapons Ctr., China Lake, Ca. 1968-70, mgmt. asst. Radar Sys. Br., RF Dev. Div. NWC 1970-73, proj. mgr./pgm. mgr., Shrike Pgm. NWC 1973-82, electronic proj. engr. Systems Analysis Br., Sys. Scis. Div. NWC 1982--; awards: AF Commendn. Medal for maint. mgmt. 1966; Navy Perf. Awd. 1974; Navy Spl. Svc. Awd. 1980; num. tech. publs.; BSA ldr.; pres. running club, Ridgecrest; mil. decorations incl. WWII Victory, Japanese Occ., UN Svc., Korean Svc. (3 stars), Nat. Def. Svc., unit cits.; rec: philately, photog., history. Res: 117 Holly Canyon Ridgecrest 93555 Ofc: Naval Weapons Ctr. China Lake CA (Code 3514) 93555

BARKER, DONALD EUGENE, electronics executive; b. Sept. 16, 1935, Atlanta, Ga.; s. John Thomas and Ella (Reese) B.; children: Sharon, b. 1960, Donald Jr., b. 1962, Karen, b. 1963, Michael, b. 1965; edn: stu. Univ. Ala., Univ. Miss., num. tech., mgmt., mil. courses; Cert. Engring. Tech., Soc. Profl. Engrs. 1972-. Career: in Civil Service 1960-, with NASA, Naval Shore Electronics Engring., Guam; came to Naval Electronic Systems Engring. Center, Vallejo, Ca. 1972--, currently supvr. electronic tech., Field Support Div.; award for productivity, 1982, presented by chief Naval Mat. Cmd.; mem. Am. Soc. for Cert. Engring. Techs.; mil: enlisted USMC 1953-54, USN 1954-58; Democrat; Prot. Res: 1223 N. Walnut, Apt. B19, Napa 94559 Ofc: NAVELEXCEN, Vallejo, Code 350, Mare Island. Vallejo CA 94592

BARKER, DOUGLAS HOWARD, lawyer; b. July 17, 1947, Berkeley; s. Robert Howard and Lois Marie (Ragland) B.; edn: BA, UC Santa Barbara 1969; MA, Univ. of Missouri 1971; M.Edn., Calif. Lutheran Coll. 1975; JD, Univ. of San Diego 1980. Career: tchr./ coach Brawley H.S., Brawley 1975-77; tchr./ coach Univ. of San Diego Law Sch. 1977-80; atty./assoc. law firm Gray, Cary, Ames & Frye, San Diego 1980--; honors: San Diego Law Review 1978-80 (chief ed. 1979-80); football scholarship, UC Santa Barbara 1965-69; mem: Am., Calif., San Diego Co. Bar Assns.; publs: arts., law rev., Athletic Jour.; mil: Capt., USAR; Protestant; rec: athletics, travel. Res: 6389-2 Rancho Mission Rd San Diego 92108 Ofc: Gray, Cary, Ames & Frye, 525 B' Street, Ste 2100 San Diego 92101

BARKER, EDWARD LEWIS, company president; b. Feb. 11, 1921, Calistoga; s. Herbert Clair and Lola M. (Schmidt) B.; m. Mary J. Connors, Apr. 9, 1944; children: Karlyn, Mark, William; edn: bus. admin., Univ. of Calif. 1950; Golden Gate Coll. 1951. Career: v.p. Coast States Investigations 1960-74; pres. Anchor Homes Inc., Berkeley 1966-70; pres. Allied Investigations, Inc., Berkeley 1974--; v.p. El Sobrante Democratic Club; founding pres., dir. El Sobrante Boys Club; recipient Man of the Year Contra Costa Co. Founders Day awd. 1970; mem. Lions, Forresters of Am., Boys Club, Boys Scouts; mil: Sgt., USMC, battle stars, Gilbert & Marshall Is. Unit Cits.; Democrat; rec: sports, tropical fish. Res: 1613 San Pablo Ave, Pent., Berkeley 94702 Ofc: Allied Investigations, 1611 San Pablo Ave, Ste 2, Berkeley 94702

BARKER, ERCIL L., psychotherapist/educator; b. Aug. 6, 1927, Mtn. Grove, Mo.; s. Otis H. and Chloe (Ward) B.; m. Peach (Pearl Marie) Lewis, Aug. 22, 1945; children: Betsy, b. 1950, Marcile, b. 1951, Joel, b. 1953; edn: AB, Okla Bapt. Univ. 1949; M.Div. Southern Bapt. Theol. Sem. 1968; D.Min., Brainard Theol. Sem. 1979; PhD, Columbia Pacific Univ. 1980; postgrad. tng. Masters and Johnson Inst., Coll. of Ida., Calif. Inst. Neuro Linguistic Patternings. Career: pastor Baptist Chs. in Mtn. Grove, Mo., Louisville, Ky., Des Moines, Iowa, Lafayette and Belmont, Ca., 1943-78; dir./Dean of Therapy Sch., Burlingame (Ca.) Counsel Center, 1973-77; pres./ adminstr./ therapist Dayspring, Inc. (counseling ctrs. in Belmont, Concord, CA., Boise, ID, Incline Vil., NV), 1977-79; current: mgr. profl. svcs. Teknekron Controls, Inc. 1981--, prin. Christian Counseling Center 1980--, Dean of Rel. Studies, Columbia Pacific Univ. 1981--; served as Air Nat. Guard Chaplain; adj. prof. counseling, Grad. Sch. of the Orient, Bagio City, Phil.; lectr./counselor, seminars in 13 countries; honors: Kentucky Col., Gov. Breathitt 1953; mem. exec. bd. Ky. Bapt. Conv. 1954-71; Diplomate Am. Bd. Examiners in Pastoral Counseling 1982; mem: Am. Ministerial Assn.; Christian Assn. for Psychol. Studies; Aircraft Owners & Pilots Assn. 1970-80; Nat. Alliance for Family Life (clin.) 1975-79; Assn. of Christian Marriage Counselors 1975-79; Internat. Primal Assn. 1975-79; writer weekly column, Ponders, for Denom. paper, 20 years; nine pub. works. Address: 70 Doray Dr. Ste. 19-20 Pleasant Hill 94523

BARKER, KAREN JEAN, real estate broker; b. July 8, 1938, Boggstown, Ind.; d. James Russell and Gladys Mae (Lancaster) Tillison; 1 dau: Toni, b. 1961; edn: Fresno City Coll. 1968-83; R.E. courses, Anthony Schs., Fresno 1974-77; Calif. R.E. sales lic., 1974, R.E. broker lic., 1977; GRI, Calif. Assn. Realtors 1982; lic. EMT, Emergency Med. Techn., Co. of Fresno 1976; Notary Public, Calif. 1981. Career: water acctg. City of Fresno 1960-61; sr. acct. clerk Fed. Mktg. Order, Grape Crush Admin., Fresno 1963; clk., Calif. Hwy. Patrol, Fresno 1963-67; radio dispatcher/ law enforcement Calif. Dept. of Fish & Game, Fresno 1967-71; broker/ owner Karen Barker, Realtors, Shaver Lake 1974--; active in land devel., timber ops., road constrn., subdiv.; mem: Nat. Assn. of Realtors; Calif. Assn. Realtors; Fresno Bd. Realtors; Democrat; Protestant; rec: photog., High Sierra Wilderness Area pack trips, tennis. Res: 41617 Tollhouse Rd Shaver Lake 93664 Ofc: Karen Barker, Realtors, Hwy 168/ Dinkey Creek Rd Shaver Lake 93664

BARKER, PEACH MARIE, marriage family child counselor; b. July 21, 1925, Trenton, Mo.; d. Delos Floyd and Carrie Victoria (Williams) Lewis: m. Ercil L. Barker, Aug. 22, 1945; children: Betsy, b. 1953, Marcile (Barnes), b. 1954, Joel, b. 1956; edn: AA, Southwest Baptist Coll. 1945; BA, CSU Hayward 1978; MA, Azusa Pac. Univ. 1981; MFCC lic. Calif. 1982. Career: Baptist pastor's wife, Ky., Mo., Okla., Ind., and Calif. 1945-76; kindegarten tchr. Bethlehem Baptist Ch., Louisville, Ky. 1967-70; tour orgnzr./ coord. for 35 groups to 35 different countries, Lama Tours Internat. Inc., Tulsa, Okla. 1969--; currently, MFC counselor, Evangelical Free Ch. Counseling Ctr.; mem. (pres. 1966) Louisville Pastors' Wives orgn. 1959-71, Calif. Assn. Marriage, Family Therapists 1979-81; frequent spkr., tchr. on travel, psycholog. growth, adventure topics; arts., denom. publs.; Republican; Baptist; rec: piano, pvt. pilot, travel. Res: 4296 Goldenhill Dr Pittsburg 94565 Ofc: Evangelical Free Ch. Counseling Ctr. 5303 Ygnacio Valley Rd Walnut Creek 94598

BARLETTA, JOSEPH F., newspaper executive, lawyer; b. Oct. 1, 1936, Punxsutawney, Pa.; s. Michael A. and Vandolyn R. (Raffetto) Barletta; m. Marilyn Minetti, Feb. 23, 1969; edn: AB, Marietta Coll. 1959, JD, Duquesne Univ. 1963. Career: partner Barletta & Barletta, Ellwood, Pa. 1963-66; labor rels. mgr. The Wall Street Journal, Princeton, N.J. 1966-70; v.p. dir. employee rels./ v.p. dir. ops. Chicago Tribune, 1970-76; v.p. dir. employee rels./ v.p. dir. adminstrn./ exec.v.p./gen. mgr. New York Daily News, 1976-81; partner Seyfarth, Shaw, Fairweather and Geraldson, NYC 1981; pres. San Francisco Newspaper Agcy., 1982--; Dir. Lebhar-Friedman, Inc.; bd. advisors Jour. of Inst. of Socioeconomic Studies; trustee Marietta Coll.; trustee Univ. of San Francisco; bd. govs. S.F. Sym.; bd. dirs. S.F. Conv. and Visitors Bur.; mem. Mayor's Fiscal Advisory Com.; mem: Am. Bar Assn., Union League Club, Lotos Club, Friars Club (NY), The Family (SF), University Club (SF), Knights of Malta. mil: served in Ohio Nat. Guard. res: 2222 Hyde St. San Francisco 94109 ofc: San Francisco Newspaper Agency, 925 Mission St., San Francisco 94103.

BARNES, JAMES R., professional engineer; b. Oct. 28, 1938, Palo Alto; s. Raymond Rexford and Dorothy Jane (Hoecker) B.; m. 2d. Kathy L. Sanborn, Sept. 25, 1982; children: Wendy K., b. 1963 Suzanne E., b. 1965, Sheri A. (step), b. 1958, Robert A., b. 1959; edn: Coll. of San Mateo; Reg. Profl. Engr., Calif. Career: var. positions in design of electronic, electromech. and mech. equip., 1957-65; control sys. engr./designer with Fredriksen Engring., Oakland 1965-66, Systron Donner Corp., Concord 1966-67, Koepf & Caldwell, Walnut Creek 1975-77, I.E.S.B., San Francisco assigned to Exon USA Benicia Refinery 1977-79, Chevron USA Richmond Refinery 1979-80; Profl. Design Services, Concord assigned to Allied Chem. Co., Chevron USA Pipeline div. 1980-82, Bechtel H&CF 1982-83; ESI, Concord, assigned to Chevron Carter Creek Gas Plant, Evanston, WY 1983, Johns-Manville Corp., Pittsburg, Ca. 1983; cons. prin. 1973-75; dir. Pleasant Hill Aquatics 1976-78; mem. Instrument Soc. of Am. 1976-. Assisted num. R&D groups in early work on semi-conductor, missile guidance & solid propellant rocket fields; rec: soaring, piano, guitar, auto. restoration. Res. 2405 Shadow Lane, 89, Antioch 94509

BARNES, WILLIE R., lawyer; b. Dec. 9, 1931, Dallas, Tex.; s. Jasper M. and Mary L.(Roberts) B.; m. Horazelle Sparks, Nov. 16, 1952; children: Michael, b. 1954, Sandra, b. 1957; edn: BA, UCLA 1953, JD, UCLA Law Sch 1959. Career: with Dept. of Corporations, Los Angeles 1960-79 (various atty. positions 1960-68, suprv. Corporations Counsel 1968-70, asst. commnr. 1970-75, commnr. 1975-79); partner firm of Manatt, Phelps, Rothenberg & Tunney, Century City 1979--. Pres., Midwest Securities Commnrs. Assn. 1978-79; 1st v.p. North Am. Securities Adminstrs. Assn. 1978-79; v.p., dir. UCLA Law Alumni Assn. 1973. Awards: UCLA Law Sch. Alumnus of the Year 1976, President's awd., Black Businessmen Assn of L.A. 1977, 78. Mem: State Bar of Calif. (Bus.Sect., Com. on Corps.), L.A. County Bar Assn. (Exec. Com., Bus. & Corp. Sect.), Beverly Hills Bar Assn. (Exec. Com., exec. com. Corps & Comml. Sect.), Century City Bar Assn. (bd. govs.), Am. Bar Assn. (Corp., Banking & Bus.Law, Commodities & State Reg. Securities); gen. counsel/dir. UCLA Alumni Assn.; co-mng. ed. California Bus. Law Reporter; mil: pfc US Army 1954-56; rec: sports, photog. ofc: Manatt, Phelps, et al 11355 W. Olympic Blvd. Los Angeles 90064

BARON, NORMAN ARTHUR, physician; b. Nov. 16, 1946, NYC; s. Sidney and Frieda (Worth) B.; m. Sonia-Paz Soto-Aguilar, Cot. 23, 1976; children: Pascale Emily, b. 1978; Jason Allan, b 1981; edn: BA, Boston Univ. 1968; MD, Univ. Bologna 1974. Career: med. intern French & Policlinic Hosp., NYC 1974-75; res. internal med. Hosp. for Joint Diseases & Med. Ctr. 1975-77; fellow, clin. rheumatology Rutgers Univ. 1977-79; spec. rheumatic diseases/internal med., Santa Maria 1977--; chmn. dept. of med. Valley Comm. Hosp., Santa Maria 1980-81; interim chmn. 1979; mem: Santa Barbara Co. Med. Soc. (bd. dirs. 1980-82); Am. Rheumatism Assn.; Arthritis Found., Santa Barbara (SLO br. Med. Edn. Com. 1982); Am. & Calif. Socs. of Internal Med.; research: causes of biological false positive serologic test for syphilis; rec: restoration, antique furniture. Res: 600 Pierce Dr Santa Maria 93454 Ofc: Norman Baron, MD, Inc., 504 E Plaza Dr Santa Maria 93454

BARONIAN, RODNEY JOE, real estate loan executive; b. Oct. 12, 1949, Fresno; s. Joe B. and Virginia (Boyajian) Elanjian; edn: AA, Santa Monica Coll. 1971; Anthony Schs. of R.E.; Calif. lic. real estate salesman 1968, broker 1975. Career: R.E. agt., The Real Estaters, Irvine 1976-77; owner London Square Art Gallery, Fresno 1977-78; branch mgr. Value Realty (predecessor firm, Valley of Calif.) 1979-81; branch mgr. real estate loans, Lomas and Nettleton Co., Fresno 1982--; honor: appreciation, The Council of Presidents of Santa Monica Coll. (Geology Club pres. 1960-70), profl. achievement awds. Tom Hopkins Champions Unlmtd. (1976), Value Realty (1979); mem. Nat., Calif. Assn. of Realtors, Fresno Bd. of Realtors; past mem. San Jose, Newport Harbor -Costa Mesa, Saratoga - Los Gatos bds. of real estate; mem. Fresno Gem & Mineral Soc., Shelby Am. Automobile Club; Airman 1/c Air Nat. Guard 1969-70; Republican; Christian; rec: collect Shelby cars, gemology. Res: 408 W. Home Ave Fresno 93728 Ofc: Lomas and Nettleton Co. 135 W. Shaw Ave, Ste. 106, 93728

BARRERAS, CAROL DIANNE, certified public accountant; b. Aug. 13, 1948, Atlanta, Ga.; d. Ashley C. and Anne E. (Ellison) Carter; m. Allen Barreras, June 30, 1980; edn: BS in acctg, Cameron Univ. 1978, MBA in taxation, Golden Gate Univ. 1983; CPA, Calif. 1982. Career: staff accountant W.F. Morgan, Vacaville 1979-80; tax supr. Christensen Boler & Co., Vacaville 1980--; hons: Phi Kappa Phi, 1977, Who's Who in Am. Colls.& Univs. 1977, 78; mem: Am. Inst. of CPAs, Calif. Soc. of CPAs, Am. Womens Soc. of CPAs; treas./dir. Oakcreek Homeowners Assn.; mem. Ofcrs Wives Club, Travis AFB; Republican; rec: racquetball. res: 149 Fairoaks Dr. Vacaville 95688. ofc: Christensen Boler & Co, 540 W. Monte Vista Vacaville 95688.

BARRETT, CAROL ANN, pharmacist; b. July 2, 1943, Omaha, Nebr.; d. Leonard H. and Madeline (Kenney) Powers; div.; chil: Christine Ann, b. 1971, Brenda Jean, b. 1972, William J. III, b. 1975; edn: BS in Pharm., Creighton Univ. 1968; Dr. of Pharm., Nat. Assn. of Retail Druggist, 1982; Pharmacy lic., Calif., Nebr. Career: pharmacist/owner Kenneys 29 Palms Drugstore; owner Downtown Liquor and Deli; partner Plaza Furniture Mart; bd. dirs. Hi Desert Medical Ctr. 1977-. Mem. 29 Palms Site Council, 1983; mem: Am., Calif. Pharm. Assns., Nat. Assn. of Retail Druggist, CofC, NFIB, 29 Palms Booster Club. Democrat. Catholic. rec: golf, swim. res: 5966 Fuchsia Rd. 29 Palms 92277. Kenneys 29 Palms Drug Store, 73501 29 Palms Hwy, 29 Palms 92277.

BARRETT, CHARLOTTE MEIER, civic leader; b. Dec. 1, 1899, Bala, Pa.; d. Edward Clarence and Charlotte Isobel (Hannan) Meier; father, noted engr., inventor of Valley Forge, Pa.; grandfather Col. Edward Daniel Meier was mfr. of boilers for US Govt., fought in Civil War and del. of Gen. U.S. Grant to receive the surrender of Gen. Hood at Nachez, Miss.; desc. of Prince H.H. Meier, founder and 1st pres. North German Lloyd Steamship co.; m. Hosmer James Barrett, 1926; one dau., Charlotte. Career: chmn. of entertainment, American Women's Vol. Services during WWII worked with Maj. Robert Kennedy of West Point at the Army Recreational Ctr., Santa Monica, and personally placed 250,000 men in entertainment before going overseas; arranged for coopreation of Riviera CC, Douglas Aircraft Engrg. Dept., pvt. schools, and many pvt. homes in Bel-Air, Brentwood, and Bev. Hills,; co-founder Westlake Mother's Club; 1949-50 started clothing drive for the Am. Friends Service Com. as part of American Relief for Korea by estab. collection bins at 33 Ralph Stores, delivered 80,000+ pounds of clothing; started 2d clothing drive by estab. bins at aircraft factories; appeared on Station KTTV sev. times weekly to appeal for clothing; campaigned for Sam Yorty for Mayor of Los Angeles; Awards: Outstanding Service Award, Sta. KNBH, Aug. 24, 1951; apptd. mem. Mayor Yorty's Community Adv. Com. of Outstanding Citizens. Mem.: Daughters of the Union, W. Los Angeles Police Boosters, Eastern Star-Westwood chpt., Bel-Air Repub. Club. Republican. Episcopal. Res.: 809 South Bundy Dr., Los Angeles 90049.

BARRETT, JAMES MORGAN, stockbroker; b. Nov. 30, 1937, Chgo., Ill.; s. Maurice John and Isabel Agnes (Gorman) B.; m. Eleanor Anderson, Sept. 19, 1981; children: Gina, b. 1960; Lisa, b. 1966; Darby, b. 1968; Anna, b. 1973; edn: BBA, Cal- Western Univ. 1963; mem. Selective Svc. Draft Bd., San Diego. Career: vice pres. investments Prudential-Bache, Rancho Bernardo, San Diego; lectr. on investments, San Diego Co.; mem. US Airborne Assn., Kiwanis Club; past pres. Continental Little League Baseball; vol. high sch. football coach; Assn.; mil: Sgt. E5, US Paratrooper Ranger, Spl. Forces 1955-57; Republican; Catholic. Res: 12042 Fairhope Rd San Diego 92128 Ofc: Prudential Bache, 16536 Bernardo Center Dr San Diego 92128

BARRETT, ROBERT MATTHEW, lawyer; b. Mar. 18, 1948, Bronx, NY; s. Harry and Rosalind (Ehrlich) B.; edn: AB summa cum laude, Georgetown Univ., JD/MS in Fgn. Svc., 1980; admitted Calif. State Bar 1981, US Dist. Cts. (N., Central Dists. Calif.), US Ct. of Appeals (9th Cir.). Career: Fed. Summer Legal Intern, US Ct. of Mil. Review (Appellate), Wash DC, 1977; summer assoc. Wilkinson, Cragun & Barker, 1978, Collier, Shannon, Rill, Edwards & Scott, 1979; law clk. Hogan & Hartson, winter 1978, Coudert Brothers, winter 1979; litigation atty. Latham & Watkins, Los Angeles 1980-82; litigation/internat. trade atty. Morgan, Lewis & Bockius, L.A. 1982--; summer clerkships Nat. Cancer Inst. 1975, Pentagon 1976; lectr. Close Up Found., Wash DC 1978; pres. Georgetown Pre-Law Soc. 1976. Ofc: Morgan, Lewis & Bockius 611 W. 6th St, Ste. 2300, Los Angeles 90017

BARRINGTON, ARTHUR EDWARD, JR., contractor; b. Aug. 3, 1920, Alhambra; s. Arthur E. and Florence (MacDonald) B.; m. Geraldine Ramage, June 21, 1944; 1 dau. Jamis (Ford), b. 1952; edn: AA, Pasadena City Coll. 1940; Calif. lic. Journeyman Plumber 1940, lic. Contr. 1944. Career: third gen. plumbing contr., owner Barrington Plumbing Co. (30 trucks; comml./indsl. 50, service 50), Pasadena; mem: Plumbing, Htg., Cooling Contractors of Calif. (pres.); Calif. Legislative Council (founder/pres.); treas., Plumbing Contractors Ins. Co.; trustee, Plumbing Indus. Promo. Fund; Plumbing and Piping Indus. Council So. Calif. (v.p.); Plumb-Pac of Calif. (treas.); Calif. Pipe trades Apprenticeship Council (past chmn.); Bldg. Indus. Assn.; Nat. Assn. Plumbing Contrs. Legislative Com.; Rotarian (past pres. Pasa.); past chmn. Calif. Youth Authority Adv. Council; past Scoutmaster, Explorer Advisor (26 years); Pasa. CofC (v.p.); YMCA (secty.); past pres. Pasa. Camera Club; mil: USN WWII; Republican Congregational; rec: photog. Res: 2666 Bowring Dr Altadena 91001 Ofc: Barrington Plumbing Co. 493 E. Walnut St Pasadena 91101

BARRON, CLFFORD LEROY, motel executive; b Oct. 26, 1929, Salt Lake City, Utah; s. John R. and Bertha Mae (Astin) B.; m. Inez Lerdahl, Dec. 27, 1950; 1 son: John Carl, b. 1964; edn: BS PHG, doctorate pharm., Univ. of Utah 1947-55. Career: pharmacy owner/ opr., Pheonix, Ariz. (17 yrs.); co-owner, mgmt. interests in TraveLodge Motels; currently, gen. mgr. El Centro & Phoenix Budget Lodge Motels; real estate broker 1979--; Ethics & Arbitrations Com., East San Diego Bd. Real Estate; served as councilman, TraveLodge, rep. aprox. 30 motel owners; mem: North Phoenix Rotary (past pres.); mil: sgt. US Army, Korean War; Republican; rec: tennis. Ofc: U.S. Budget Lodge Motels, Inc., 645 Wrelton Dr La Jolla 92037

BARROZO, BILLIE LAVONNE, realtor, motel owner; b. Sept. 4, 1925, Belle Fouche, S. Dak.; d. Sidney Edward and Nelle (Ford) Lyons; m. Anthony Barrozo, Jan. 26, 1946; chil: LaVonne, b. 1948, Anthony Jr., b. 1952 (dec.), Theresa, b. 1955; edn: real estate, Yuba City Jr. Coll. Career: prop. coffee shop, 1942; grocery chkr. 1943-69; prop. mobile home park, 1969-79, traded into 60-unit motel (TraveLodge North Bay), Vallejo 1979-, acquired mng. interest in TraveLodge motels in San Diego, El Cajon, Pocatello, Ida., Wenatchee, Wash., 1979-; broker/owner (spec. sales motels, mobile home parks) Thunderbird Realty, Vallejo 1969--; pres. Teri Von Inc. Mem: Solano Bd. of Realtors (pres.), Yuba-Sutter BPW (pres.), Vallejo CofC, Benicia CofC, Better Bus. Bur.; Democrat; Catholic; rec: photog. address: Thunderbird Realty, 160 Hwy 80 at Magazine, Vallejo 94591.

BARTKOWSKI, HENRY M., neurosurgeon; b. March 13, 1948, Buffalo, N.Y.; s. Henry B. and Eleanor M. (Jarzebinski) B.; m. Ladonna Urbanski, Apr. 8, 1978; chil: Christopher, b. 1980, Rebecca, b. 1982; edn: BA, Canisius Coll. 1970; MD, SUNY at Buffalo Sch of Med. 1976; PhD anatomical sci., SUNY at Buffalo Grad. Sch. 1977. Career: surg. intern UC Med Ctr, San Francisco 1976-77; neurosurg. res. NY Univ. Med. Ctr 1977-81; asst. prof. Neurological Surgery, UCSF 1981--; acting chief Neurosurgery Service, SF Gen Hosp., 1981--. awards for acad. excellence, SUNY at Buffalo Grad. Sch 1974, 75, 76; mem: AMA, AAAS, AANS, Calif. Assn. of Neurol. Surgeons, Calif. Med. Assn., Cong. of Neurol. Surgeons, Electron Microscopy Soc. of Am., Internat. Soc. of Cerebral Blood Flow and Metabolism, NY Acad. of Scis., San Francisco Med. Soc., SF Neurol. Soc., Soc. for Neurosci., Internat. Microsurg. Soc., Soc. of Magnetic Resonance in Medicine, Phi Chi med. frat., US Squash Racquets Assn., Harding Pk. Golf Club, No.Calif. Golf Assn., US Chess Fedn., S. Elizabeth's Mens Club.; contbr. arts. med. jours.; Republican; Catholic; rec: squash, golf, piano, chess. res: 481 Yale St. San Francisco 94134 ofc: Univ. Calif. Med. Ctr. Parnassus Ave. 786-M, San Francisco 94143

BARTLETT, FREUDE, filmmaker/director; b. Aug. 12, 1942, NYC; d. Charles A. and Ida (Feinberg) Mittelman; chil: Samantha Solomon, b. 1962, Adam Bartlett, b. 1970; edn: film maj., CSUSF 1966-8, BA, New Coll. of Calif. 1983. Career: founder Serious Business Co., film distbr. to ednl., theatrical, & t.v. markets (bus. papers in The Bancroft Lib.), 1972-83; prod./dir. ten films, 1968-73; media cons. Portland Arts Commn., 1984; Center Screen Inc., Cambridge, Mass. 1983; Calif. Occupational Safety & Hlth Adm. 1983. Lectr. CSU San Francisco, 1981, Univ. of Ill., 1976; frequent guest lectr./workshops various univs., 1973-; num. film festival jury appts. incl. Palo Alto Film Fest. 1982, Ann Arbor F.F. 1976, 80, S.F. Internat. F.F. 1975, 80. Grantee, Point Found., 1972, 74. Mem: bd. Jewish Film Fest., Emeryville 1982-4; hon. life, Film Arts Found.; Media Alliance; Ednl. Film Lib. Assn.; Assn. of Ind. Video & Filmmakers; Assn. for Ednl. Communications & Tech.; Hlth Scis Communications Assn.; Soc. for Anthropol. of Visual Communication; Mystery Writers of Am. Publs: arts. in trade jours.; exhbns: CBS-TV, BBC-TV, Film Forum, NYC, Pac. Film Archives, Berkeley, SF Mus of Art, Carnegie Inst., Mus. of Contemp. Art, Chgo., Internat. Ind. Filmmakers Fest., London, Internat. Women's Film Fests. Austral., Can., Fr., Venez., USA. res: 1145 Mandana Blvd. Oakland 94610.

BARTLETT, HALL, film production co. president; b. Nov. 27, 1925, Kansas City, Mo.; s. Paul Dana and Alice (Heistand) Bartlett; 2 daus.: Cathy;, b. 1955,

Laurie, b. 1957; edn: Bach., Yale Univ. 1942. Career: dir./writer/prod. Navajo (1952), Crazylegs, Unchained (1956), All the Young Men (1959), Dorango (1957), Zero Hour, The Caretakers (1963), Changes (1969), The Sandpit Generals (1971), Jonathan Livingston Seagull (1973), Cleo Laine-John Dankworth TV spl., Zubin Mehta TV spl. (1976), The Children of Sanchez (1977), Comeback, Motion Picture (1982); director Hollywood Greek Theatre. Awards: 15 Academy Award nominations; film festival awds: Cannes (1961, 63), Venice (1959-65), Edinburgh (1952), San Sebastian (1965), Moscow (1971), NCCJ (1955); Foreign Press Awards. Mem: Acad. of Motion Picture Arts & Scis., Acad. of TV Arts & Scis., Producers Guild of Am., Writers Guild of Am., Cinema Circulus, Directors Guild, Phi Beta Kappa, Bel Air CC, Friends of Lib.; Music Center founder; patron Los Angeles County Mus. of Art. Mil: USNR 1942-46, US Naval Intell., Presdtl. Commend.; Republican; Presbyterian; rec: pro-football, basketball, tennis. res: 861 Stone Cyn Rd Los Angeles 90024. ofc: Hall Bartlett Productions 9200 Sunset Bl. Ste. 908 Los Angeles 90069

BARTLETT, JAY PAXTON, physician-surgeon, medical consultant; b. Dec. 3, 1919, Ogden, Utah; s. Dr. Frank Kaiser and Mary Agusta (Paxton) Bartlett; div.; chil: Sara, b. 1949, Mary Bkhwaja, b. 1951, Wendy Bailey, b. 1953; edn: BA, Univ. Chgo. 1939, BS, 1941, MD, 1943; MPH (in epidemiol.& occupatnl. med.) Harvard Sch. Public Hlth 1958. Career: intern, res. in gen. surg. & surg. path. 1944-5, sr. res. in chest & gen. surg. 1945-6, res. in neurosurg. 1948 (all at Chgo. Clins); gen. practice med. & surg., Ogden, 1949-57; res. in occupatnl. med., Allis Chalmers Mfg. Co., Milw. 1961-2; chief Bur. Occupational Hlth, Santa Clara Co.(Ca) Hlth Dept., 1962-9; med. staff Santa Clara Valley Med. Ctr., San Jose 1963-9; Pub.Hlth Ofcr. Bur. Enviorn.-Occuptnl.Hlth & Consumer Protection, Calif Hlth Dept, Berkeley 1969; plant phys./cons. Lockheed Missile & Space Co. Sunnyvale 1969-72; med. cons. Calif Hlth Dept, Oakland 1972--; instr. Univ. Chgo. 1944-6, Marquette 1961-2, Stanford 1964-70; secty/dir. State Employed Physicians Assn. Local, Union of Am. Physicians & Dentists. Mem/ fellow: Am. Coll. of Surgeons, Am. Acad. Occ. Med, Am. Ind. Med. Assn., APHA, Am. Ind. Hygiene Assn., Am. Acad. Preventive Med.; mem. Conf. of Govtl. Ind. Indsl. Hygienists, AMA; publs: 20 pub. papers; spkr. service clubs, civic assns.; mil: USNR 1939-58, active 1942-3, 46-8, GCM, PTO; rec: pvt. pilot, sailing, photog. Address: 200 Lakeside Dr, #205, Oakland 94612

BARTOSH, LOUIS HAROLD, physician-surgeon; b. Mar. 5, 1895, Dodge, Nebr.; s. Anton and Annie Bessie (Dont) Bartosh; m. Priscilla Benstead, April 3, 1929; m. 2d Gladys Spencer, April 15, 1979; 2 sons: Leland, b. 1931, Harold, b. 1933; edn: D.O., Coll. of Osteopathic Phys & Surgeons 1928; D.Endocrinology, Chgo Coll Endocrine Therapy 1932; Osteopathy in Cranial Field 1966; Osteopathic Acad. of Osteopathy 1968. Career: family practice osteopathic med., Wilshire Hollywood Dist., Los Angeles 1928--; estab. Family guest ranch (Circle B B), Bouquet Cyn. 1945; adj. prof. Coll of Osteopathic Med. of the Pacific (C.O.M.P.), Pomona 1978--. Awards: Founders award, C.O.M.P.; C.M.E. awd., Am. Osteopathic Assn.; certs.: Calif. Bd. of Osteo. Examiners 1928, gynecol. (1951), med. emergencies (1959), Coll Osteo.Phys & Surgeons; Am. Coll of Gen. Practitioners (1967). Mem: Hollywood Osteo. Luncheon Club (pres. 1952), South Side Osteo. Soc. (pres. 1940), Osteo. Phys. & Surgs. of Calif. (pres. 1978; legal battle as pres. to restore full practise rights in Calif.). Publs: geneal. book on Bartosh family. Mil: 41st Div. (concert band) 1917-19; LDS Ch.; rec: fishing, riding; res: 5807 Spring Oak Dr Hollywood 90068.

BARZA, ALLAN BERNE, psychiatrist; b. Mar. 19, 1945, Ottawa, Can., nat. 1963; s. John and Jeannette Gladys (Berman) B.; edn: 1962 National Merit Scholar; BA, North Park Coll. 1970, MD, Abraham Lincoln Sch of Med., Univ. of Ill. Coll. of Med., 1974. Career: pvt. practice psychiatry, Walnut Creek 1978--; att. phys. Walnut Creek Hosp., 1978-, v.p. med. staff 1982, acting med. director 1983, chief of staff 1984; clin. supr./tchr. Walnut Creek Hosp. Soc. Svc. Pgm., 1978-; cons. for skilled nursing psychiatric facility, 1978-79; att. psychiatrist Concord Group Home, 1978-; staff psychiatrist Contra Costa Co. Hosp., Martinez 1977-79; cons. psychiatrist Vocat. Rehab., Contra Costa Co., 1979; participating psychiatrist UCSF Postgrad. Seminars. Diplomate Am. Bd. of Psychiatry & Neurology 1980. Mem: Calif. Med. Assn., ACCMA, East Bay Psychiatry Soc. Mil: splst.4 US Army 1965-67, Vietnam Campaign, Commend. from Gen. Peers.; Jewish; rec: tennis, hiking, skiing. res: 369 Hampton Rd. Piedmont 94611. ofc: 2021 Ygnacio Valley Rd. Bldg. D-4 Walnut Creek 94598.

BASEHART, THOMAS VINCENT, insurance agency owner; b. Nov. 7, 1932, Cleveland, Ohio; s. Vincent Kearney and Mary Margaret Basehart; div.; children: Elizabeth, b. 1959; Jeanine, b. 1963; Vincent, 1965; edn: BS, cum laude, John Carroll Univ. 1956-59; MBA grad. work, Wayne State Univ. 1961-66; CLU, Am. Coll. 1976-80; Accredited Adviser in Ins., Coll. of Ins. 1983. Career: trainee to Long Range Plng. Mgr., Central Staff Ford Motor Co., Dearham, Mich. 1959-67; sr. mgmt. cons. Bonner & Morre, Houston, Tex. 1967-69; Eastern gp. sales mgr. Skyline Corp., Phoenix, Ariz. 1969-70; regl. dir. Kaufman & Broad, Chino, Calif. 1970-72; v.p. Sales Kit Mfg., Long Beach 1972-76; life agent Prudential, Claremont 976-79; ins. broker/prin. Pomona Valley Ins., Claremont 1980--; awards: Regl. Rookie of Yr. 1976; Million Dollar Roundtable Prudential Pres.'s Club 1976-79; Agcy. Sales Ldr. 1976-80; Nat. Quality Awds. (6); mem: Chartered Life Underwriter (dir. Ofcr. Estate Plng. Council; dir. State Ins. Ethics Com.); Rotary; Livowia City Plng. Com. (past); Bai Lynn Civic Assn. (pres.); Dearborn Mich. United Way Fund (dir.); Moon Valley Civic Assn., Phoenix; mil: sgt. USAF, Personnel Splst., 1951-55; Republican; Catholic; rec: hiking, history, cooking. Res: 413 W Alpine Upland 91711 Ofc: Pomona Valley Ins. Agency, 428 W Harrison Claremont 91711

BASILE, EMILIO MICHAEL, exhibit company executive; b. Jan. 27, 1951, Salerno, Italy, nat. 1962; s. Umberto and Maria (D'Amato) B.; m. Marilyn Diane Anderson; edn: AA, computer sci., L.A. Pierce Coll. 1971; BS, mgmt., acctg., CSU Northridge 1979. Career: programming supr. Magic Mountain, Inc. 1970, Newhall Land & Farming Co., 1970-72; mgr. systems and pgmmg. Sterling Computer Sys. Inc. 1972-73; mgr. systems and procedures, Collins Foods Internat. Inc., 1973-77; mgr. Mgmt. Advisory Svcs., Laventhol & Horwath, CPAs 1977-79; pres. E.M. Basile & Assocs. Inc., 1982--; CEO, Great Western Exhibit and Display Corp. (exhibit mfg./ consulting), 1979--; honors: recognition, City of Los Angeles (1980, 81, 83), State of Calif. (1983), San Fernando Valley Regional CofC (1982), US Jaycees Outstanding Young Man of Am. (1978), L.A. Pierce Coll. assoc. students awd. (1970); mem. Rotary (pres. Van Nuys 1985), PorterRidge Homeowners Gp. (pres. 1978-84), Simi- S.F. Freeway Adv. Com. 1980-83, Porter Ranch Citizens Adv. Council, Van Nuys CofC (dir.), YMCA (bd. dirs.); Democrat; Catholic. Res: 12101 Braemore Pl Northridge 91326 Ofc: 7703 Densmore Ave Van Nuys 91406

BASSO, MARLENE LOUISE, real etate broker; b. Nov. 25, 1939, Aurora, Ill.; d. Earl Victor and Alma Dorothy (Toerpe) Sullivan; div. 1970; children; Cory Joseph, b. 1961; Randall Earl, b. 1963; edn: psychology, Golden West Coll. 1966-69; Lumbleau Real Estate Sch. 1978-79; Calif. lic. Notary Pub., 1980, R.E. Broker, 1980. Career: asst. to sr. v.p. Calif. Mortgage Svc., Tustin 1970-73; asst. to pres. Golden State Escrow, Newport Beach 1973-74; res. sales The Real Estaters, Costa Mesa 1974-76; comml./ indsl. sales Orange Coast Investment, Newport Beach 1976-78; medical practice sales (co. broker 1981/82) Practice Sales & Locations 1978-81, broker/sole prop. Practitioners Brokerage Network, Huntington Beach 1982--; dist. mgr. 13 branches mtg. banking, 11 branches escrow, Calif. Mtg.; cons. to doctors in all splties. from internship to retirement; mem: Newport- Costa Mesa Bd. Realtors 1974-78; Republican; Lutheran; equestrian, dancing. Address: Practitioners Brokerage Network, 19655 Surfbreaker Ln Huntington Beach 92648

BATES, ARTHUR DEVOE, physicist; b. July 6, 1923, Cardston, Alberta, Can., nat. 1965; s. Ormus Ernest and Garnet (Pinson) B.; m. Reta Boettger, Oct. 25, 1952, div. 1977; chil: Les, b. 1954, Carolyn, b. 1955, Alan, b. 1959; edn: BS in physics, honors, Univ. Alberta 1949, M.Physics, CSU San Jose 1965. Career: geophysicist Western Geophysical Co., 1949-60; physicist, optics, IBM Corp. San Jose 1960-7; prop., optical cons. Bates Optical Consulting, San Jose 1967-74, Menlo Park 1983--; sr. scientist Hiac/Royco Instruments, Menlo Pk. 1974-83; instr. optics Foothill Coll. 1966-7. Listed: Internat. Who's Who, Men of Distinction (London), Who's Who in Am., Personalities of the West & Midwest. Mem: Optical Soc of N. Calif (bd dirs, vp), Soc. of Information Display (past pres), Soc Photo-Optical Instrum. Engrs, Human Factors Soc, Optical Soc of Am. Patentee in field; arts. in profl. jours., books; mil: cpl. Royal Can. AF; Republican; LDS; rec: oil painting, computers; res: 53 Lorelei Ln. Menlo Park 94025.

BATESOLE, DALE F., clergyman, TV host; b. Oct. 1911, Ferguson, Iowa; s. John Floyd and Elsie Rebecca (Campbell) Batesole; edn: graduate safety engr., Kans. Univ. Ext., 1943; ordained minister, Unity Sch of Christianity, 1959; m. Genell Grundhoefer, Aug. 12, 1974; career: branch mgr. Western Grocer Co., Marshalltown, Iowa 1930-48; sales rep. Schultz Burch Biscuit Co., 1948-56; minister, Unity Christ Ch., St. Louis, Mo. (broadcast daily radio pgm. six yrs. sta. WEW), 1958-64; co-founder Forsyth Sch., (pvt. day sch. preK-7th) St. Louis, Mo. 1961; faculty mem. Unity Sch of Christianity 1960-61; founder/1st exec. dir. Charles and Myrtle Fillmore Found., Lee's Summit, Mo. 1964-67; sch. bd. trustee Maricopa Co. Sch. Dist. 1970-71; cons. to psychiat. service VA Hosp., Phoenix, 1971-76; founder, Unity Ch. of Sedona (Ariz.), 1973; originated, presented Psycho-Cybernetics Seminars nationwide, 1973; instr. Psycho-Cybernetics, No. Ariz. Univ. Coll. of Bus. Ad., 1975-77; minister Unity of the Desert, Palm Springs, Ca. 1977-79; prod., dir., host (with wife), daily TV program There Is A Way (fmrly. The Unity Way), Jan. 1979-- (est. viewing audience exceeds 750,000); pres., Unity Student Minister's Assn.; counselor, teacher, lectr., A.A., 1960--; mem. Assn. of Unity Churches; publs: newspaper arts., columns for Red Rock News, Sedona, Ariz. 1973, 74 and Carefree Enterprise, Carefree, Ariz. 1970-72; Republican; rec: tennis, music, jogging; res: 909 Sandpiper Palm Desert 92260 ofc: THERE IS A WAY, P.O. Box 2721 Palm Springs 92263-2721.

BATTISTINI, JOHN, insurance broker; b. June 17, 1914, Viareggio, Italy, nat. 1938; s. Costantino and Ada (Rugani) B.; m. Angelina Guilianelli, Jan. 2, 1938. Career: radio announcer (Italian lang.) 1935-38; tchr. Italian, Santa Cruz Schs.1938-42; ins. bus. 1940--; currently, pres. John Battistini Ins., Inc.; awards: Italian Man of Yr., Santa Cruz Sons of Italy Lodge 1970; title, Consular Correspondent of Italy, Consul Gen. of Italy, His Excellence Paolo Emilio Mussa, 1979; Gold Metal of honor, City of Lucca, Italy 1981; Insignia of Cavaliere (Knight), Order of Merit, Italian Republic, by pres. of Italy, Sandro Petrini 1982; mem: Independent Ins. Agents of Santa Cruz (pres. 1950-52); Santa Cruz Elks Lodge; Dominican Santa Cruz Hosp.; Santa Cruz Co. Grand Jury 1961; Grand Jury Assn.; apptd. mem. investigative com. on loans for Santa Cruz 1955 flood victims, Small Bus. Admin., Wash. DC; mil: SSgt., US Army 1943-46, WWII, Combat Infantry Badge, Purple Heart; Republican; Catholic; rec: Italian interpreter, Municipal & Superior Cts., Santa Cruz Co. Res: 205 Sherman St Santa Cruz 95060 Ofc: 120 Locust St Santa Cruz 95060

BATZEL, ROGER ELWOOD, Lawrence Livermore Laboratory-director; b. Dec. 1, 1921, Weiser, ID; s. Walter G. and Inez R. (Klinefelter) Batzel; B.S., Univ. of ID, Moscow, 1947; Ph.D., Univ. Calif., Berkeley, 1951; m. Edwina Lorraine Grindstaff, Aug. 18, 1946; children: Stella Lyne, b. 1953; Roger Edward, b. 1955; Stacy Lorraine, b. 1960. Career: Lawrence Livermore Laboratory, Univ. of Calif.,

1953--; assoc. dir., 1961-71, dir., 1971--. Mil.: USAF, 1943-45. Rec.: outdoor sports. Res.: 315 Bonanza Way, Danville 94526; Office: P.O. Box 808, Livermore 94550.

BAUER, THEODORE JAMES, airport operations manager; b. Sept. 20, 1939, Kenosha, Wisc.; s. Charles James and Irene Elizabeth (Simon) B.; m. LaVonne Dirks, Oct. 17, 1970; children: Bret, b. 1959; Clarissa, b. 1960; Constance, b. 1961; Christine, b. 1966; Kenneth, b. 1966; edn: police sci., Skyline Coll., 1977, mgmt., UC Berkley 1979, mgmt., Pacific Western Univ. 1984; Airfield Safety (Expert), SFIA 1976. Career: Airports Commn., SFIA 1961--: airport police ofcr. 1961-69; airport police sgt. 1969; airfield safety ofcr. 1969-77; ops. supvr. 1977-83; Airport Ops. coordinator, 1983--; mem. Task Force, ADAP Funds, San Francisco; airport cons. 1978-80; mem: Internat. Police Ofcrs. Assn.; Airport Police Ofcrs. Assn.; coord: arrival/ departure activities for US Pres. & Queen of England 1983; Democrat; Catholic; rec: golf, bowling. Res: 38908 LeCount Way Fremont 94536 Ofc: Airports Commission, SFIA, POB 8097 San Francisco 94128

BAUER, WALTER FERDINAND, computer co. executive; b. Mar. 21, 1924, Wyandotte, Mich.; s. Walter Ferdinand (dec.) and Erna Clara (Schotter) B.; m. Donna Bothamley, Aug. 27, 1949; children: Thomas, b. 1953; Randall, b. 1957; John, b. 1963; edn: BS, Univ. of Mich. 1946, MS, 1947; PhD, 1951. Career: research engr. Univ. of Mich. 1951-54; dir. Computation & Data Reduction Ctr., Ramo Wooldridge Corp. 1954-59; mgr. Info. Sys. Dept. Thompson- Ramo-Wooldridge Corp. 1959-62; chmn./ pres./ CEO Informatics General Corp., Woodland Hills 1962--; dir. Protocol Computers, Inc.; honors: Sigma Xi, 1947; mem: Charles Babbage Found. (chmn.); So. Calif. Technology Execs. Network (chmn.); Region I, United Way (dir.); num. publs.; mil: 1st lt. USAF; Protestant; rec: tennis. Res: 15935 Valley Vista Encino 91436 Ofc: Informatics General Corp., 21031 Ventura Blvd, Ste 800, Woodlandhills 91364

BAUM, MYRNA ELAINE; management consultant; b. June 18, 1938, Los Angeles; d. Lester A. and Sally Lucille Herbert) Dansby; m. Leland G. Baum, Sept. 7, 1957; chil: Debra Lynne, b. 1958, Stephen Michael, b. 1962, Jeffrey David, b. 1967; edn: grad. Fairfax H.S. 1957, stu. UCLA 1957-8, CSUN 73-5, Pierce Coll 81-3. Career: mgmt. consultant 1971-76, 1983--; admin. asst. to v.p. American Express Life, 1976-8; pub. rels. A.T. Oxford, NY 1978-9, Kearney Clark, Chgo. 1979, A.T. Hudson Inc., Paramus, NJ 1979-83, Donovan & Assoc., Denver 1983--; instr., seminars in telephone and corp. sales tng.; profl. writer, 1964; raised awd. winning African violets, orchids; rec: tennis, numismatics, saltwater acquarium fish; address: 22301 Mandell St Canoga Pk 91304.

BAUWENS, JOSEPH ANTHONY, pharmaceutical co. executive, b. May 5, 1941, Moline, Ill.; s. Ernest and Helen (Jepson) B.; m. Susan Tryon, July 17, 1982; stepson; Nicholas Boies; edn: AB, UC Los Angeles 1963, MDA, 1965. Career: exec. asst. cardiol. dept. Cedar-Sinai Med. Center, Los Angeles 1965; then, sec. treas. Rand Inst., NYC; fmr. v.p. Fin. & Adminstrn., Nelson Research & Devel. Co. (pharm.), bd. dirs. 1981-; exec. v.p./chief op. ofcr. Aerwey Labs. (mfg. respiratory care prods.), 1972; pres. Dey Labs., Concord, Ca. 1979--, leading mfr. respiratory medication sold to US hosps., (ranked 15th in top 500 growth pvt. U.S. cos. by INC mag. 12/83); honors: Blue Key, eight varsity letters, UCLA (1959-64), Rose Bowl and All American Bowl participant; mem. Am. Assn. of Respiratory Therapists, Medical Mktg. Assn.; two patents pend.; mil: 1st lt. US Army, DMG; rec: skiing, ballet. Res: 208 Vagabond Ct Danville 94526 Ofc: Dey Laboratories, Inc. 1011 Detroit Ave Concord 94518

BAX, RONALD FRANK, electronics manufacturing co. executive; b. Oct. 30, 1941, Niagara Falls, NY; s. Frank Lou and Margaret Violet (Hallenbeck) B.; m. Gail Barber, Aug. 26, 1961; children: BA, George Mason Univ. 1977; Johns Hopkins Univ. 1979. Career: sr. engr. Scope Electronics, Fairfax, Va. 1966-69; sr. engr. Recognition Equipment, Rockville, Md. 1969-72; eng. mgr. Acuity Systems, Reston, Va. 1972-75; prin. engr./ mgr. R&D Pfizer Medical Systems, Columbia, Md. 1975-82; cons./ engring. mgr. Diasonics M.R.I. (Magnetic Resonance Imaging), So. San Francisco 1982--; cons. C.T. Scanners & M.R.I. 1981-84; v.p. Ear Three Systems 1982-84; listed, Who's Who in the East 1979-84; mem: Boy Scouts of Am. (Unit Commnr. 1976-79); patents: Laser Lensmeter, 1977, Jogging Computer, 1974, Scanning Apparatus 1980, Electro Cardiographic Storage 1982, Dark Current Compensation 1982; method for controlling x-ray tube emissions 1982; mil: E4 USAF 1960-64; Republican; Catholic; rec: antique cars, electronics. Res: 447 Homer Ave Palo Alto 94301 Ofc: Diasonics M.R.I., 533 Cabot Rd, So. San Francisco 94080

BAY, SHELDON JAMES, real estate developer, investor; b. Nov. 18, 1925, Winnipeg, Manitoba, Canada, nat. 1944; s. Leon and Esphira (Kaplan) B.; m. Babette, June 20, 1948; children: Lawrence Julian, b. 1949; Jeffrey Paul, b. 1952; Gregory Leon, b. 1953; edn: BS, UCLA 1949; CPA, Calif. 1954; gen. bldg. contractor, Calif. 1969. Career: employee Bay & Bay, CPAs, Los Angeles 1950-56, partner 1957-63; v.p. Freeman & Bay, Inc., Gen. Bldg. Contractors 1965-69; pres. Western Fin. Const. Co., Inc., Gen. Bldg. Contractors 1972-83; pres. Estero Investment Corp. 1980--; owner Sheldon J. Bay, dba Bay & Assocs., Gen. Bldg. Contractors & Devel. 1969--; mem: Calif. Soc. CPAs; Am. Inst. of CPAs; Nat. Assn. Accts.; Toreadors; mil: Radioman 2/c, USNR 1944-46, So. Pacific Theatre; Republican; Jewish; rec: golf, tennis, theatre. Res: 1433 N Beverly Dr Beverly Hills 90210 Ofc: 3205 Ocean Park Blvd, Ste 215, Santa Monica 90405

BAYLESS GLENDA MERRICK, certified public accountant; b. June 22, 1929, St. Anthony, Ida.; d. Frank J. and Ione (Jensen) Merrick; m. Gerry Bayless, Aug. 30, 1963; chil: Sandra Mitchell, b. 1947, Brett Bayless, b. 1963; edn: AA, honors, Long Bch City Coll 1960, BS, honors, CSULB 1963; postgrad. work Univ. Calif.; num. CPA cont. edn. classes, 1963-. Career: self-empl. CPA, Rialto and San Bernardino area, 1969--, pres. Bayless & Miller, Inc.; fmrly with Johns Manville, Long Bch 1951-60, Davis Wire Co., 1960-4, Diehl, Evans and Co. CPAs, Santa Ana 1964-8, Oldman, Iverson and Rabe CPAs, Newport Bch 1968-9; instr. acctg., tax courses since 1960, incl. CSU San Bernardino, 1969-72, 83, San Bernardino Valley Coll. 1969-. Awards: scholarship recipient Long Bch City Coll; Am. Women's Soc. of CPAs Nat. Public Svc. Awd 1978; listed Who's Who in the West, Who's Who in Acctg. Mem: Am. Soc. Women Accts. (com. chmn. 1966-80, chpt. pres. 1974-5, nat. chmn. bd.trustees Scholarship Fund 1976-80); AWSCPA (nat. bd. dirs., nat. treas. 1979-); charter pres./ founder AWSCPA of So. Calif., 1982-3; Am. Inst. CPAs; Calif. Soc CPAs (Citrus Belt chpt. coms.); speaker many profl. acctg. and tax seminars, convs. Mem. Arrowhead United Way (pres. 1978-9), San Bernardino Co. United Way (Long-Range plnng); Rialto CofC; S.B. Comm. Hosp. Bd. Dirs. 1975-80; Rialto Sch dist. Finl. Adv. Bd. 1975; BSA (exec. bd. 1975-); GSA (bd.dirs. 1980-3); Pop Warner Football (treas.); Skadron Coll. Scholarship Bd. Republican; rec: travel, read; res: Star Rte 92334, Box 13, San Bernardino 92403 ofc: Bayless & Miller Inc. 720 Bloomington Ave Bloomington 92316.

BAYS, PATRICIA JO, real estate broker; b. May 28, 1936, Indianola, Okla.; d. Thomas John and Ruth Augustus (Marston) McKnight; m. Charles Russell Bays, Aug. 20, 1967; children: Kathryn Ruth Below, b. 1958; edn: East Central Univ. 1954-55; BS, Univ. of Nebr. 1959; San Bernardino Valley Coll. 1972-4; R.E. broker lic., Calif. & Okla. Career: paralegal & probate asst. to attys.; broker Bays Real Estate; sponsored num. carrer related sems. on syndication, tax plng., investment, property mgmt. & fin.; honored by Calif. State Horsemans Assn. as Horsemastership Chmn., active in obtaining non-profit status for local riding clubs, 1968-; Republican; Presbyterian; rec: crochet, create boutique items. Res: 11637 Placid Ct Colton 92324 Ofc: Bays Real Estate, 370 West Sixth, Ste 125, San Bernardino 92401

BEACH, CHRISTOPHER RAYMOND, car rental co. executive; b. Jan. 23, 1955, Ft. Bragg, N.C.; s. Arthur Raymond and Bernice J. (Shoemake) B.; m. Andrea J. La Pointe, Feb. 1, 1981; children (by previous marriage): Ryan, b. 1978, Erik, b. 1976; edn: mktg., Ohio State Univ. 1980. Career: mktg. rep. Budget Rent A Car, 1981, dir. of sales, 1982, gen. mgr. (So. Calif.), 1984; vice pres./gen. mgr. Dollar Rent A Car, Anaheim 1984--; awards: Outstanding Car Rental Exec., Budget Rent A Car Systems (Headlines, 1983); mem: Newport CofC, Anaheim CofC; clubs: Lake Mission Viejo Tennis, El Toro YMCA; Republican; rec: running, tennis. Res: 21882 Herencia St Mission Viejo 92692 Ofc: Dollar Rent A Car, 2132 So Harbor Bl Anaheim 92802

BEACH, ROWAN MICHAEL, gemologist; b. July 3, 1953, London, England, nat. 1981; s. Michael and Lotte Beach; edn: FGA, w/ distn., Sir John Cass., London 1978. Career: gen. mgr. Beach Products 1969; sef- empl. Internat. Research Gemstones 1974-81; owner Beach Internat. 1981--; mem: Am. Gem Trade Assn.; Gemological Inst. of Am. Alumni Assn.; Assoc. Gemological Assn.; Gem Club India; Nat. Assn. Jewelry Appraisers; Gemological Assn. of Gr. Brit.; research cons. on gemstones with num. countries & assns. Ofc: Beach International, 760 Market St, Ste 651, San Francisco 94102

BEAN, GERALD ALAN, newspaper executive; b. Mar. 17, 1943, Peoria, Ill.; s. Harold Franklin and Shirley Jane (Dreiman) Bean; m. Brenda M. Carlson, May 28, 1967; chil: Scott, b. 1972, Eric, b. 1976; edn: BS in journ., Univ. Ill., Urbana 1966. Career: with Rockford (Ill.) Register Star, 1966-81, general mgr. 1978-79, pres./pub., 1979-81; gen. mgr. Gannett Satellite Information Network, Wash.DC, 1981-82; gen. mgr. USA Today, Wash. DC, 1982-83; vice pres. of Gannett West newspaper group and pres./pub. The Sun, San Bernardino 1983--. Mem: Am. Newspaper Pubs. Assn., Calif. Newspaper Pubs. Assn.; mem. bd. dirs. Inland Action, Inc., Inland Empire Cultural Found., St. Bernardine Hosp. Found.; mem. Calif. State Coll. (San Bernardino) Bd. of Councillors; mem. San Bernardino Hosp. Corp. Bd. ofc: The Sun, 399 North D St., San Bernardino 92401.

BEAN, WILLIAM ALLAN, energy economist; b. Apr. 24, 1946, Devonshire, Bermuda; s. Wm. Alan, Sr. and Hyacinth (Alboy) B.; m. Debora Elise Saunders, Mar. 28, 1980; children: Allan, Ahmed, Codi, Courtney; edn: BS, Econ., Southeastern Univ. 1980, MBPA, Energy Adm., 1981. Career: mng. dir. Allan Bean, Energy Consultants, San Francisco 1982--; dir. ops. Effective Learning Inst., Carmichael 1984--; currently, instr. UC Berkeley Edn. Ext., Berkeley; cons. devel. policy for State Applied Energy Network higher learning course; honors: Most Outstanding Young Man of Am. 1982; pres. Internat. Student Guild; publs: Managing Raw Natural Resources, 1982; Democrat; Divine Sci. Ch. of God; rec: jogging, soccer, gourmet. Address: Allan Bean, Energy Consultants, 1111 Pine St, 311, San Francisco 94109

BEAR, JEFFREY LEWIS, lawyer; b. April 16, 1947, Los Angeles; s. Bernard and Rhoda (Goldberg) Bear; m. Denise Epstein, May 30, 1982; 1 son, Ryan Steven, b. 1974; edn: BA, CSU Northridge 1968; JD, Loyola Univ. of L.A. 1971. Career: admitted to State Bar of Calif. 1972; deputy atty. gen., ofc. of the Calif. Atty. General, 1971-3; deputy public defender, ofc. of Los Angeles County Public Defender, 1973-7; partner law firm Sommer and Bear, Beverly Hills 1977--; speaker various seminars, confs. incl. Calif. Pub. Defenders Assn. Annual Drunk Driving Sem., UCLA Sch of Law Annual Conf. on Women and the Law; judge pro tem panel of L.A. Municipal Ct. Honors: resrch fellowship in Comparative Criminal Law, and Law Rev. Case Note Pgm., Loyola Univ. Sch of Law. Mem: State Bar of Calif. (Criminal Law Sect.), Calif. Attys. for Criminal Justice, Criminal Cts. Bar Assn. (coms.), Calif. Public Defenders Assn., San Fernando Valley criminal Bar Assn. (bd.govs. 1978); past mem: Assn. of Deputy L.A. Pub. Defenders (bd.dirs. 1976,77), Assn. of Deputy Calif. Attorneys General (exec. bd. 1972-3); mem. Porsche Club of Am., L.A. Region (v.p.). Cases of note: People v. Schueren (1974), McCartney v. Commn. on Judicial Quals. (1974), Martin v. Municipal Ct. (1977), In re Michael G. (1977). ofc: Sommer and Bear, 9460 Wilshire Bl, Ste. 520, Beverly Hills 90212.

BEARDSLEY, SAMUEL FRANKLIN, legal controls co. owner; b. June 5, 1944, Yeadon, Pa.; s. Samuel F. and Floris Laverne (Mills) B.; m. Donna Wood, Nov. 2, 1979; children: Kendal Ann, b. 1968; Winthrop Fox, b. 1970; edn: Univ. de Los Andes 1963; arts & scis., Univ. of Pa. Grad. Sch. 1964-67; BA, Ohio Wesleyan Univ. 1965. Career: sales mgr. Executone, Inc., NY 1973-75; owner Antilles Systems, San Juan, Puerto Rico 1975-76; dir. field sales I.T.T., NY 1976-79; asst. exec. v.p. Telecomm. Sys., Inc., St. Louis, Mo. 1979-8; Western regl. mgr. Iwatsu America, Inc., Carlstadt, NJ 1980-81; pres./ CEO Legal Controls Co., Rohnert Park 1982--; instr. Univ. Javeriang, Bogota, Colombia 1963; honors: hist., Ohio Wesleyan Univ. 1964; mem: Windmill Farms Assn.; BSA Scoutmaster; publs: Transitional Morphs, Journ. Amer. R. Assn. 1968; Democrat; rec: camping, fishing, skiing. Res: 8342 Windmill Farms, Cotati 94928 Ofc: Legal Controls, 5685 Redwood Dr Rohnert Park 94928

BEAUDREAU, BAYARD CHARLES, community services district executive; b. Oct. 3, 1932, Pasadena; s. Milton Charles and Catherine Marble (McPike); m. Doris Hemstreet, Mar. 10, 1956; children: Laurence, b. 1956; Bruce, b. 1959; Bret, b. 1968; edn: Riverside City Coll. 1950, 1957-58; UC Riverside 1956-57; San Jose City Coll. 1959-61; lic. Real Estate Broker, Calif. 1969; Water Treatment Opr. II, Calif. 1971. Career: metallurgical lab. tech. & supvr. Hunter Engring., Riverside 1955-58; irradiation tech. General Electric Co., Vallecitos Atomic Lab., Pleasanton 1958-62; irradiation engr. 1962-66; engr., mktg. 1966-67; real estate sales Strout Realty, Jamestown 1968-70; gen. mgr. Groveland Comm. Svcs. Dist., Groveland 1970--; mem; Big Oak Glat- Groveland Sch. Dist. (chmn. 1971-72); Garrette Lions Club, Groveland (pres. 1982-83); Disabled Am. Veterans; mil: Sgt., USMC 1952-55, Korean Svc. Medal; Republican; Episcopal. Res: Star Rt Box 25 Groveland 95321 Ofc: Groveland Community Services Dist., POB 350 Groveland 95321

BEAZLEY, SUSAN LINDA, certified public accountant; b. Nov. 8, 1940, Santa Ana; d. Alfred H. and Sue Marie (Davies) Beazley; edn: Univ. of Colo. 1958-9; AA, Fullerton Jr.Coll. 1965; BS, USC 1967; CPA, Calif. St. Bd. of Acctcy. 1970. Career: mgr. M & M Engineering, 1960-5; staff Arthur Young & Co., Los Angeles 1967-72, mgr. 1972-5, principal 1975-8, partner 1978--, partner in charge of So. Calif. Agribusiness; mem. bd. dirs. The Accounting Circle, USC; honors: Beta Gamma Signa, USC Deans List; mem: Calif. Soc. of CPAs, Am. Inst. of CPAs, Am. Soc. of Women CPAs; bd. dirs. L.A. March of Dimes; Republican; rec: waterski, needlepoint, tennis; res: 1502 Idaho St. Santa Monica 90403 ofc: Arthur Young & Co., 515 S. Flower St. Los Angeles 90071.

BECHTEL, STEPHEN D., JR., industrialist; b. May 10, 1925, Oakland; s. Stephen D. and Laura (Peart) Bechtel; m. Elizabeth Mead Hogan, 1946; 2 sons, 3 daughters; edn: civil engr. stu. Univ. of Colo. 1943-44; BS, Purdue Univ. 1946; MBA, Stanford Univ. 1948; Hon. Dr. Engrg., Purdue Univ. 1972; Hon. Dr. of Sci., Univ. of Colo. 1981. Career: employed by Bechtel 1941--, held broad variety of jobs and responsibilities both in the field and San Francisco Home Office; Director, 1951-; vice pres.,1952-55; sr. vice pres., 195-57; exec. vice pres., 1957-60; pres., 1960-73; chairman, 1973--. Chmn. Boards & Exec. Com., Bechtel Group, Inc., 1973-; chmn. Sequoia Ventures, Inc., 1980-; chmn. Bechtel Canada Ltd., 1972-. Dir.: Internat. Bus.Machines, So. Pacific Co.; mem. (fmr. v.chmn.) The Business Council; councillor (life; fmr.chmn.) Conference Bd.; mem. Policy Com., The Business Roundtable; mem. Labor-Mgmt. Group. Awards incl.: Engrg. News Record's Construction Man of the Year, 1974; Moles' Award for Outstanding Achievement in Constrn., 1974; ASCE Civil Engrg. Mgmt. Award, 1979; ASME Centennial Award, 1980; AAES Chairman's Award, 1982. Mem: The Beavers, Commonwealth Club of Calif. (SF); clubs: Augusta Nat. Golf, Bankers (SF), The Blind Brook Club Inc. (NYC), The Mount Royal (Montreal), Pac. Union (SF), Ramada (Houston), SF Golf, SF Tennis, Thunderbird CC (Palm Springs), Vancouver (B.C.), Villa Taverna (SF), The York (Toronto). Publs: num. profl. articles incl. New Edisons and New Technologies (1979); Calif.'s Contbn. to the Multiplier Effect (1979); The Climate for Innovation (1979); Technology: Foundation for America's Future Well Being (1980); mil: USMCR 1943-48; Protestant; rec: golf, tennis, hiking, photog. res: POB 3809, San Francisco 94119. ofc: 50 Beale St. San Francisco 94105.

BECK, DAVID ALLEN, lawyer; b. Feb. 9, 1945, Gallup, N.Mex.; s. Wm. Lee and Dorothy (Elledge) B.; m. Ann Marie, July 20, 1980; edn: AA, Pasadena City Coll. 1967; BA, CSU Los Angeles 1970; JD, Glendale Univ. 1974. Career: mgr. Pacific Tel. Co., Alhambra 1964-77; atty. Law Office of David A. Beck, Pasadena and L.A., 1976-80, partner law firm Anderson, Beck & Stewart, L.A. 1980-83, partner law firm Beck & Kearney, Pasadena 1983--; Pro Bono Pasadena Bar; Judge Pro Tem Pasadena and LA Municipal Cts.; Host Radio Station at Pasadena City Coll. Mem: LA County Bar Assn. (Client Complaint Com., Arbitrator C/C), Pasadena Bar Assn. (chmn Law Day Com. 1980, chmn Client Complaint Com., Legislative Com., del. State Bar Conv. 1980, 81, 83, secty.; bd. dirs.). Publs: contbr. Glendale Law Jour. Mil: E4 USMCR 1965-71; Democrat; First Christian Ch.; rec: sports, coins, stamps. Res: 1605 So Hidalgo Av Alhambra 91801 Ofc: Beck & Kearney, 283 So Lake Ave, Ste 200, Pasadena 91101

BECK, WILLIAM HOWARD, real estate developer; b. Sept. 1, 1931, Detroit, Mich.; s. Paris O'neal and Hazel (Ancell) B.; 1 dau., Kimberly Ann (Mrs. Barron Hilton, Jr.), b. 1956; edn: UC Los Angeles 1949-51, US Mil. Acad., West Point 1951-55. Career: asst. to the pres., Brighton Homes, Beverly Hills 1961-64; vice pres. American Middle East Dev. Co., Bev. Hills 1964-66; co-owner Beck-Dayharsh Dev. Co., North Hollywood 1966-71; pres. Cal Kona Orchards Inc., Sacramento 1973-77; pres. Resort Environments Inc., Bev. Hills 1973--; chief fin. ofcr. La Ventana Land & Cattle Co., Modesto 1983--; pres. Inland Pacific Fin. Corp., San Francisco 1978--; currently co-developer of 14,000 acre master planned lake front community in Central Calif.; mem. West Point Soc.; Republican; Prot.; rec: flying, skiing, running. Res: 1 Lake Don Pedro Road La Grange 95329 Ofc: Inland Pacific Fin. Corp. 1750 Montgomery Street San Francisco 94111

BECKER, JOSEPHINE MOORE (Madge), librarian/consultant; b. Sept. 1, 1928, Portland, Ore.; d.JesseW. and Madge J. (Guthrie) Moore; m. Henry C.Becker, Jr., Lt. Col. AUS (Ret.), Jan. 30, 1970; edn: AB, Western Coll for Women (Oxford, Ohio) 1949; MLS, Univ. Ill. Sch. Lib. Sci. (Urbana) 1952. Career: br. supr./ adminstrv. asst. Yakima Valley (Wash.) Regional Lib., 1954-59; field librn. US Army Spl Serv., Ger. 1959-61; county librn. Plumas Co., Quincy, Calif. 1961-64; city librn. Longview, Wash. 1964-70; city librn. Vallejo, Calif. 1970-74; acting co. librn. Solano Co., Fairfield 1973-74 and county librarian, 1974-83; partner C&J Enterprises, lib. mgmt. consultants, 1982--; secty. Solano Co. Lib. Authority, 1975-83; chmn. North Bay Coop. Lib. System, 1974-75; secty. Calif. Inst. of Libraries, 1976-78; pres. Pub. Lib. Execs. of Central Calif., 1977; v.p., pres. elect. Wash. Lib. Assn. 1969-70; Recipient Bess Sawhill Robertson Award for excellence in English, Western Coll. 1949; mem: Soroptimist (pres.1965-7,77-8); Beta Phi Mu; rec: collect books, travel, photog. Address: P.O. Box 1917, Vallejo 94590.

BECKER, OSCAR, engineer; b. Aug. 30, 1896, Sheboygan, Wisc.; s. Wm. and Emma (Sickman) B.; m. Elnor Agnes Spice, Nov. 9, 1921; 1 son, Maynard Earl, b. 1926; edn: courses in civil engr., Am. Sch. Corres. 1920s, mil. courses. Career: surveying in central Mont., US Gen. Land Office, Helena, Mont. 1919; N.P. Ry Maint. Engring. Dept., 1922-32; resident engr. Highway Dept., 1932-34; field engr., then staff supvr. for State Plnng. Bd., WPA and State of N.Dak., 1934-40; prepared state plan for water conservation, lobbied in Wash DC for funds and obtained 5 mil. dollar grant; prepared six year pgm. of public wks. for Bismarck N.D.; mgmt. heavy constrn. projects with various gen. contractors in Va., 1942-62; owner dry cleaning bus., Manitowoc, Wisc. 1962-68; ret. 1974; elected 6th term pres. food for seniors Council, So. Alameda Co., Calif. 1978-84; past mem. Mil. Engrs., Lions Club, Bus. Mens Assn., CofC, American Legion, VFW, Norfold Co. (Va.) Planning Commn. v.chmn.; publs: var. conservation reports; mil: instr. sgt. US Army; 1917-19; Republican; Methodist; rec: writing, dancing. Res: 3231 Vineyard Ave. Sp. 66, Pleasanton 94566

BECKER, RALPH E., water bed retailer; b. Apr. 26, 1925, Sacramento; s. Ralph E. and Blanch (Herring) B.; m. Mary Lee, Dec. 22, 1964. Career: employment agency owner 1947-56; furniture retail 1957-69; water-bed retailer, owner American Bedding Co. (oldest established water-bed retailer in state); design water-bed furniture for factories, first to introduce the waterbed bookcase headboard; mem: Disabled Am. Veterans; Elks; Lions Club; mil: 1st sgt. US Army Air Corps 1943-46; Democrat; Catholic; rec: custom sports car (num. awds. in var. shows). Res: 7929 Cole St Downey 90242 Ofc: American Bedding Co., 9449 E Firestone Blvd Downey 90241

BECKETT, JOSEPH KARR, lawyer; b. Feb. 1, 1932, Bakersfield; s. Joseph Karr and Johanna (Locke) B., Sr.; m. Jane Howell, Aug. 26, 1961; 1 dau. Linda, b. 1968; edn: AA, Bakersfield J.C. 1953; geol. engr., Colo. Sch of Mines 1958; JD, Hastings Coll of the Law 1964; career prosecutors course, Nat. Coll of D.A.s, Houston 1977. Career: laborer oil drilling rigs in Calif., Alaska; patent law clerk, Henry Gifford Hardy, atty., S.F.; admitted to US Dist.Ct., No. Dist. of Calif., US Ninth Circuit Ct. of Appeals, 1966-; law partner Beckett and Roesch, Redwood City 1966-8; dep. dist. atty. Kern Co. District Atty., 1968--; Family Support Div. 1968-9; Gen. Misdemeanors and Consumer Affairs, 1969-71; Juvenile Ct. cases 1971-2; pornography trial & appellate cases, 1971-82; supr. felony atty. 1973-6; chief property crimes sect. 1977; gen. felony and homicide cases 1983--; mem. Kern Child Abuse Prevention Council, Inc. & founding coms. 1973-82; mem. Atty. Gen's Adv. Com. on Pornog. 1974-79; bd.dirs. Kern Children's Service Ctr. Inc. (pres.1983-). Honors: for work in child abuse prevention, num. public & pvt. orgns. Mem: Calif.State Bar, Calif. and Nat. Dist. Attys Assn, Kern Co. Bar Assn, Am. Judicature Soc., Alumni Nat. Coll. of D.A.s, Redwood City Dwntwn Lions Club 1967-8, Bkrsfld. Breakfast Lions Club 1970-74 (bd.dirs., vp, chmn. White Cane Days Com., Dist 4-A2, Lions Internat.); originater civil tort doctrine of res ipsa loquitor in juvenile ct. dependency proceedings (eliminates use of children as witnesses against abusing parents), 1975; expert witness various legis. coms.; helped revise Calif. pornography laws; mil: seaman USNR 1951-54, 2d lt. Corps of Engrs. USAR 1960-65; Republican; Presbyterian; rec: ski, trout fish, photog. res: 28711 Gleneagle Ct. Star Rt 1, Box 800-53, Tehachapi 93561 ofc: Kern Co. D.A., Justice Bldg. 1215 Truxtun Ave Bakersfield 93301.

BEDELL, RONALD ANTHONY, real estate broker; b. Feb. 8, 1948, Portsmouth, NH; s. Richard Joseyh and Bette Frances (Rooney) B.; m. Nancy

Chapman, July 5, 1980; 1 son: Jeffrey, b. 1983; edn: BS, aero. & astro. engring., Ohio St. Univ. 1971; R.E. broker lic. 1979; Calif. Comm. Coll. Instr. cred. 1981. Career: sales assoc. Century 21 B&B Inv. Div., San Diego 1974-76; partner LHI Realtors, San Diego 1976-78; owner Bedell & Assocs., San Diego 1978-80; pres. Pacific Horizon Properties, Inc., 1980--; instr. R.E. investment, Kearny Campus 1980-81; lectr. Found. for Fin. Edn. 1983-; awards: NROTC Scholarship, Ohio St. Univ. 1966-71; Apartment Rehab. of the Yr. Awd., San Diego Apart. Assn. 1982; mem: San Diego Bd. Realtors; San Diego Apart. Assn.; Found. for Fin. Edn. (Adv. Bd.); Kiwanis Club; works: designed computer spreadsheet templates 1982; renovated of Torrey Arms (hist. bldg.) 1982; devel. unique A/B Syndication for small investor; mil: lt. USN 1971-78; unit commdn., Repub. of Vietnam Campaign, Vietnam Svc. medals, Letter of Commdn., VADM J.D. Bulkeley, Battle Efficiency Awd.; Republican; Catholic; rec: archery. Res: 9704 Caminito de la Fada San Diego 92124 Ofc: Pacific Horizon Properties, Inc., 8031 Linda Vista Rd, Ste 210, San Diego 92111

BEDJANIAN, ARDE LAZAR, systems analyst; b. Feb. 22, 1958, San Francisco; d. Vartan Minas Bedjanian and Dorothy Francis (Kennicott) Martinez; edn: undergrad. San Francisco State Univ. 1975-7; AB astronomy, UC Berkeley 1980. Career: computer op. Bank of Am., San Francisco 1976-80; resrch asst. UCB Space Scis. Lab., 1978-80; resrch asst. NASA, Ames Resrch Ctr., Moffett Field, summers 1978-80; proj. leader/systems analyst Logicon Inc., San Pedro 1980--. Awards: Logicon Chess Champion, 1983; exec. dir. of Redevel. Agcy., S.F. Youth in Govt. Day, 1972. Mem: Logicon Commodore Users Gp. (pres. 1983-); Logicon Microcomputer Club (bd. 1983-); US Chess Fedn.; Logicon Chess Club; San Pedro Chess Club. Republican; Christian; rec: chess, basketball, softball, singing. Res: 852 W. 18th St. #C, San Pedro 90731 Ofc: Logicon Inc. 255 West 5th St., POB 471, San Pedro 90731

BEGGS, ROBERT CALVIN, JR., state auto assn. executive; b. May 28, 1947, Yakima, Wash.; s. Robert Calvin, Sr. and Grace Lee (Burns) B.; m. Nicole J. Pollard, Dec. 31, 1974; children: Dawn, b. 1975; Samantha, b. 1976; Shannon, b. 1978; edn: mgmt., Monterey Penn. Coll., 2 yrs. Career: with Calif. State Auto Assn., San Francisco office 1970-76, Monterey 1976-79, Sacramento 1979-81, Santa Rosa 1981--; storeroom clerk/ warehouseman, 1970-72; claims adjustor, 1972-73; underwriter 1973 79; admin. asst. 1979-80, sales mgr. 1980-81; asst. mgr. 1981--; mil: sgt. USAF, Travis AFB 1966-70; rec: photog. Res: 1755 Arroyo Sierra Ave Santa Rosa 95405 Ofc: Calif. State Auto Assn., 1500 Farmers Ln Santa Rosa 95405

BEHERA, KIRTTAN B., management consultant; b. Mar. 26, 1942, Keonjhar, Orissa, India; s. Baina and Subhadra (Prusty) B.; m. Mamata Das, May 7, 1971; chil: Sarina, b. 1974, Sahana, b. 1976, Rajeev, b. 1982; edn: BS (M.E.) honors, Indian Inst. of Tech., Kharagpur, India 1965, MS (I.E.), UC Berkeley 1966, MBA, CSU Dominguez Hills 1974. Career: indsl. engineer Western Gear Corp., Lynwood, Ca. 1966-67, sr. systems analyst, 1967-68, corporate systems cons., 1969-70; v.p. Conlon & Behera Assocs., Inc. (mgmt. cons. to mfrs. & distbtrs.), Torrance, Ca. 1970--; dir. Regent Jack Mfg.Co., Inc., Downey 1980--; assoc. prof. CSU Dominguez Hills, 1979-. awards: for sci. models, Ravenshaw Coll. 1960, and for creative engineering model, IIT, Kharagpur 1964; mem: American Prodn. & Inventory Control Soc., Los Angeles chpt. (exec. v.p. edn. 1980-81, pres. 1981-82, bd. chmn. 1982-83); Students Gymkhana, secty 1964-65 and secty. I.I.T. Mech.Eng.Soc., 1963-64, Kharagpur, India; Hindu; rec: photog., movie prodn.; res: 2306 Santa Fe Ave Torrance 90501 ofc: Conlon & Behera Associates, Inc. 2067 W. 238th St. Torrance 90501.

BEICH, EVERETT B., mobile home parks president; b. Apr. 24, 1926, St. Paul, Minn.; s. Otto W. and Afama Fay (Miller) B.; m. Beverly Anderson, Sept. 20, 1948; children: Debra, b. 1950; Timothy, b. 1951; Richard, b. 1952; Sandra, b. 1953; edn: bus., N.Dak. Bus. Coll. 1946; music, N.Dak. Univ. 1944-45. Career: broker Fargo Realty Co.; owner Super Value Stores; sales rep. Coldwell Banker Realty; pres. Beich Mobile Home Sales, Inc.; pres. Beich Cos. (owner/ devel. East Ave Shopping Ctr., Beich Mobile Home Park, P.V. Mobile Home Estates, Almond Orchard); owner/ dir. Tri Counties Banks; mem: Rotary Club; Chico Univ.; Chico Comm. Hosp. Bd.; CofC (dir.); mil: Tank Distroyers Corp. 1944-45, Purple Heart; Republican; Lutheran; rec: flying, golf, travel. Res: 1675 Manzanita Ave, 10, Chico 95926 Ofc: Beich Companies Corp., 12 Williamsburg Ln Chico 95927

BEIERLE, ROBERT THOMAS, scientist, electronics engineer; b. Nov. 3, 1945, Long Beach; s. William Frank and Dolores (Mounce) B.; m. Sally Jane Benson, Nov. 18, 1982; AS, Mt. San Antonio Coll. 1972; BSEE, Calif. St. Polytech. Univ. 1975, grad. stu. 1984. Career: design engr. General Dynamics, Pomona 1975-79; principal designer Hughes Aircraft GEADGE pgm. (German Air-Ground Environ. Def. Sys.), Fullerton 1979-82; sr. mem. tech. staff/ hd. guidance control design gp. ADCAP pgm. Hughes Aircraft 1982--; currently, tech. supvr., gp. hd., MTS; tchg. asst., radar sys. & signal processing, Cal Poly, Pomona 1976-77; awards: academic scholarship, CalPoly 1975; Academic Outstanding Scholarship awd., IEEE Student chpt. 1975; Zero Defects Awd. 1984; mem: IEEE; Nat. Mgmt. Assn.; co- designed guidance & control sys. Cal Poly Rose Parade Float (Princess Awd.) 1974; mil: Sgt., USAF 1963-67, Vietnam, Nat. Defense Svc. Medal; GCM; Catholic; landscape design, sailing, inventing. Res: 20980 E. Gold Run Dr Diamond Bar 91765 Ofc: Hughes Aircraft, Ground Systems Group, Malvern & Gilbert, Fullerton 92634

BEINKE, STEPHEN PHILIP, land developer; b. Oct. 4, 1950, Ft. Lauderdale, Fla.; s. Edward Allen and Ellen Dora (Ruscher) B.; m. Deborah June, Dec. 26, 1971; chil: Timothy, b. 1975, Michael, b. 1979, Matthew, b. 1983; edn: BBA, Fla. Atlantic Univ. 1972. Lic. real estate broker, Fla. 1972-, Calif. 1975-.

Career: vice pres./secty. Florida Heritage Group, Ft. Lauderdale 1972-5, pres. 1973-5; vice pres. Blackhawk Corp., Danville, Calif. 1975-83, exec. v.p. 1983--, dir. 1975-; past dir./ofcr. Hidden Oaks, Saddleback and Tennis Villa Homeowner Assns.; dir./ofcr. Country Club, Blackhawk Improvement Assn.; instr. MIRM Class for Sales &: Mktg. Council of BIA of No. Calif. 1979. Mem. Building Industry Assn. (regl. dir. 1981); No. Calif. BIA (dir. Ednl. Council 1978-80, Sales & Mktg. Council 1981); Young Homebldrs of BIA; Contra Costa Bd. of Realtors; San Ramon Valley CofC, San Ramon Valley Kiwanis (pres. 1979); mil: USCGR 1968-73; Republican; Lutheran (trustee); rec: travel, golf, tennis, deep sea fish. res: 161 Willow Creek Ln Danville 94526. ofc: Blackhawk Corp. 3820 Blackhawk Rd Danville 94526.

BEIRAKH, ZELMAN JACOB, engineer; b. Dec. 1, 1913, Kiev, Russia; s. Jacob Copel and Tanya (Khasminskaya) B.; m. Basya, Aug. 31, 1937; 1 dau., Sofia, b. 1938; edn: M.Elec.Eng., Politech. Inst., Leningrad, 1935, cand. (PhD) of Tech. Sci., 1939; Dr. of Tech. Sci., Moscow (USSR) Sch of Energy Engring., 1964; lic. Profl. Engr., Control System Engring., Calif. 1982. Career: group leader Dept. of Automatic Control, Central Boiler-Turbine Resrch Inst., Leningrad 1935-39, Dept. Hd. 1939-43; hd. Dept. Automatic Control, Central Boiler-Turbine Resrch Inst., Moscow 1943-56; hd. engr. in chg. Resrch., Devel.& Prodn., Moscow Plant of Control Systems for Thermal Installations (MZTA), 1956-74; prof. Moscow Inst. of Tech., 1974-77; control engr. Lurgi Corp., Belmont, a. 1979-81; sr. engr. (automatic control), Power Div. Bechtel, San Francisco 1981--; prof. Bauman Higher Engring. Sch. (MVTU), Moscow 1946-61. Awards: Govt. awd. 1947, Order of Red Banner of Labor 1970, (2) Order of Honor, Sup. Sovietes, USSR. Mem. Sci. Consul, Min. of Instrumentation and Control, 1956-72. 56 publs. in sci. mags. 1941±74; 30 patents in automatic control, USSR. rec: classical music. res: 79 Cassia Ct. Hayward 94544 ofc: Bechtel, Power Div, 221 Main St. San Francisco 94119.

BELCHER, RONALD SCOTT, escrow co. executive; b. Jan. 3, 1949, Delano; s. James Lloyd and Dorothy Irene (Street) B.; m. Barbara Barry, Sept. 15, 1973; children: Julie, b. 1976; Katie, b. 1979; edn: BA, CSU, Hayward 1971; Fresno State Univ. Grad. Sch. 1972; Lic. Fire & Casualty Ins. Agent, Calif. 1973; R.E. Broker, 1977; Pvt. Investigator, 1983. Career: mgr. Beneficial Calif., Inc., El Toro 1974-79, sr. mgr., Garden Grove office 1979-81; regl. mgr. Beneficial Tax Ctrs. (Taxmasters), Ariz., Calif. & Hawaii 1981-83; pres. Benevest Escrow Co., Orange 1983--; dir. Benevest Escrow Co.; broker Western Fin. Svc. 1977-82; awards: Pres. Distng. Achiev. Awd., Beneficial Corp. 1975, 76, 78, 82; Nat. Top Performance Awd., Beneficial Tax Svc. 1983; mem: Kiwanis; 20-30 Club; Independent Businessmen Assn.; Republican; Baptist; rec: jogging, skiing, scuba diving. Res: 37 Tangerine Irvine 92714 Ofc: Benevest Escrow Co., 777 South Main St, Ste 175, Orange 92668

BELL, JACK PERKINS, corporate executive/organic chemist; b. Jan. 24, 1940, San Francisco; s. John M. and Jean E. (Perkins) B.; m. Sherry Smith, 1965; 2 daus.: Elizabeth, b. 1968, Christina, b. 1971; edn: BS in chem., cum laude, Phi Beta Kappa, Univ. of Wash.,Seattle 1962, PhD, org. chem., Univ. of Wisc., Madison 1967. Career: postdoctoral fellow, staff resrchr in life scis. Stanford Resrch. Inst. 1967-69; biotech. project mgr. Syntex Resrch. Inst., Palo Alto 1969-78; tech. sales rep. for mfr. liquid chromatography instrumenta tion, Waters Assocs., N.J. ofc. 1978-80; N.E. regional sales mgr. Applied Analytical Indus., N.J. ofc. 1980-81; liquid chromatography prod. line mgr. Varian Instrument Gp., Walnut Creek Div., 1981--; gave seminars for biochem. instrs., DeAnza Coll. 1974-77, designer genetic engring. courses for local colls., 1977; mem: AAAS, Am. Chem. Soc., Sigma Xi; listed in Am. Men and Women of Sci., Who's Who in the East. Publs: num. tech. presentations, reports; arts. in profl., sci. jours. Republican. Episcopal (vestryman). rec: travel, fishing. res: 2950 Windtree Ct. Lafayette 94549 ofc: Varian Assocs. 2700 Mitchell Dr. Walnut Creek 94598.

BELLAH, BEN, investor; b. Sept. 3, 1946, Riverside; s. Clifford and Helen Alice (Peters) B.; desc. (mat.) Gen. Wm. Booth, founder of the Salvation Army in 1865; edn: BA, US Internat. Univ. 1968; Chinese Language Inst., Fujen Univ., Taiwan 1969-70; Claremont Grad. Sch. 1968-72; AA, Riverside City Coll. 1983; Calif. lic. Real Estate Broker 1980. Career: application evaluator Teacher Corps, Los Angeles 1972; contact rep., Social Security Adminstrn., Torrance 1973-77, also Certified Chinese Document Translator for S.S. Adminstrn. 1975-77; computer electronics tech. Burroughs Corp., Westlake Village 1979-82; pvt. investor, 1977--; honors: Phi Alpha Theta (hon. hist.), Calif. State Scholarship 1964-68, Calif. State Fellowship 1968-69, High Quality Awd., S.S. Adminstrn. 1976; life mem: Assn. for Asian Studies, Am. Acad. Polit. and Social Sci., Mensa; mem. Intertel; contbr. arts. var. newspapers and periodicals 1970s; rec: tennis, travel. Ofc: 7606 Church Ave Highland 92346

BELLANCA, LOUIS CHARLES, lawyer; b.June 26, 1943, Buffalo, NY; s. Russell Michael and Christine Mary (Fasciana) B.; m. Jayne Gardner, Sept. 5, 1970; chil: Dana, b. 1974, Erin, b. 1977; edn: AAS, Erie Comm. Coll. 1962; stu. Pasadena City Coll. 1962-3, Glendale Coll. 1963-4, Valley Coll. 1965-7; JD, LLB, Univ. San Fernando Valley, 1972. Career: optician, Superior Optical Co., Los Angeles 1962-72; pvt law practice, Beverly Hills 1973; staff atty. Mansell & Giddens, Los Angeles 1973-74; atty., firm Grancell, Kegel & Tobin, L.A. 1974-75; mng. atty. firm Levy, Koszdin, Goldschmid & Sroloff, Long Beach and Santa Ana, 1975-78; atty./secty./chief fin. ofcr Towner, Kristjanson, Bellanca & Hill, Santa Ana and Tustin 1978-, pres. 1980-82; pres. Kristjanson, Bellanca & Hill, 1982--; Workers' Compensation Judge pro tempore 1982-; Awards: Master of Ophthalmic Optics 1972; Fellow Internat. Acad. of Opticianry 1965; James Bass and Loren Michael Meml. Awards, Jr. CofC 1967,68.

Mem: Workers Comp. Claims and Def. Counsel Assn. (secty.1978), Northridge Jaycees (pres.1969-70), Sunland-Tujunga Jaycees (vp 1967, State Dir. 1968); admitted to Calif. Bar 1972, U.S. Bar 1977; mem. Long Beach Bar Assn. 1980-, Orange Co. Bar Assn. 1981-; Republican; Christian; rec: boating, bicycling, running; res. Huntington Bch ofc: Kristjanson, Bellanca & Hill, 505 E. First St Tustin 92680.

BELLEVILLE, PHILIP FREDERICK, lawyer; b. Apr. 24, 1934, Flint, Mich.; s. Frederick Charles and Sarah Adeline (Cottrell) B.; m. Geraldean Bickford, Sept. 2, 1953; children: Stacy, b. 1957; Philip II, b. 1958; Jeffrey, b. 1961; edn: BA, honors in econ. and high distinction, Univ. of Mich. 1956, JD, 1960; admitted to State Bar of Calif. 1961. Career: assoc. atty. Latham & Watkins, Los Angeles 1960-68, partner, 1968--, sr. litigator (chmn. Litigation Dept. 1973-80). Honors: James B. Angell Scholar (1955-6); Phi Beta Kappa 1955-; Phi Kappa Psi 1955-; Order of the Coif 1960-. So. Calif. Steering Com. NAACP Legal Def. Fund Inc. 1979-; adv. bd. San Pedro/Pennin Hosp. 1980-; Mem: Am. Bar Assn. (Antitrust Law & Criminal Justice sects.); State Bar of Calif. (Antitrust, Trade Reg. Law & Bus. Law sects.): Los Angeles Co. Bar Assn. (Bus. Trial Lawyers sect); The Assn. of Trial Lawyers of Am.; Assn. of Bus. Trial Lawyers; Republican; Prot.; rec: antique and classic autos, human behavior study, tennis, literature. Res: 12 Crest Rd East, Rolling Hills 90274 Ofc: Latham & Watkins, 555 So Flower St Los Angeles 90071

BELLEVUE, JOHN MERRIL (JACK), pension investment executive; b. June 24, 1930, Old Orchard Beach, ME; s. Robert and Mary Alice (Hardman) B; m. Deloris Lefebvere, June 18, 1955; children: Robert R., b. 1956; James S., b. 1959; Sandra, b. 1965; grandchil: Olivier (b. 1981) and Ryan (b. 1983) Bellevue; edn: BSBA, Golden Gate Coll. 1959. Career: chmn. bd. Bellevue Corp., Burlingame, 1981, chmn. bd., Bellevue Capital Corp., gen. partner Bellevue Mortgage Investors, 1981-82 and Bellevue Secured Trust Deeds II, (splty. pension plans using real estate trust deeds and ins. for investments); pres. Bellevue & Assoc., Burlingame 1972--; spl. agent Prudential Ins., Burlingame 1965--; dir.: Gallo Wine, So. S.F.; Lipton Tea, S.F. Awards: No 1 in the nation with Prudential (1975) out of 24,000 agents with net ordinary life premium record of $659,000; President's Agent's Advis. Council, 1965-81. Mem: CLU (Peninsula Charter mem., Golden Key Soc. mem.); MDRT, Top of the Table, Knight (bd. mem. Program Devel. Com.); Peninsula Estate Planning Council; Life Underwriters (past pres., current bd. mem.; CALUPAC mem.); parentmem. AMATA (bd.dir.); Am. Soc. of Pension Actuaries; Am. Cancer Soc. (bd.dirs.). Mil: sgt. USMC 1952-54. Republican; Episcopal (vester, treas.); rec: swim, ski, travel, hunt, fish. ofc: Bellevue Corp., Bellevue Capital Corp., 1633 Bayshore Hwy., Ste.321, Burlingame 94010.

BELLEZZO, EDWARD ANTHONY, corporate executive; b. Oct. 27, 1912, Chgo.; s. Joseph Anthony and Rose (Devito) Bellezzo; m. Nancy Finella, Nov. 14, 1936; 2 sons: Edward, b. 1941, Donald, b. 1954; edn: Lane Tech., 1926-8, grad. Austin H.S. (night) 1939. Career: ledger clerk Rand McNally & Co., Chgo. 1928-32; die sinker Duro Metal Product Co., Chgo. 1932-38; foreman Logan Engring. Co., Chgo. 1938-46; partner Hedwick & Co., Chgo. 1946-69; dist. mgr. Houdaille Industries, Los Angeles 1969-78; exec. vice pres. Don G. Jenness Co. Inc., Los Angeles 1978--; honors: Epsilon Pi Tau, UCSB, 1955. Mem: Knights of Columbus Van Nuys (Grand Knight 1954-5, 4th Deg.), Van Nuys CofC; Democrat; Catholic; rec: golf. res: 6218 Newcastle Ave. Reseda 91335. ofc: Don G. Jenness Co. Inc. 1420 Lawrence St. Los Angeles 90021.

BELLIS, CARROLL J., surgeon; b. May 11, 1908, Shreveport, La.; s. Joseph E. and Rose (Bloome) B.; m. Mildred E., Dec. 26, 1951; 2 sons: Joseph, b. 1940, David, b. 1944; edn: BS, 1930, MS, 1932, PhD in physiol., 1934, MD, 1936, PhD in surg., 1941, Univ. of Minn. Career: teaching fellow in Physiol., Univ. of Minn.; instr. in surgery U. of Minn. Medical Sch.; surgical cons. to Surgeon-Gen. US Army; currently: pvt. practice of surgery; staff Bauer Hosp. St. Mary Med. Ctr.; cons. in surg., Long Beach Gen. Hosp.; prof./chmn. Dept. of Surgery, Calif. Coll. of Medicine. Honors: Sigma Xi, AOA, Phi Beta Kappa, recipient Charles Lyman Green Prize in Physiol., Mnpls. Surgical Soc. Prize, Miss. Valley Med. Soc. Annual Awd. 1955. Dip. Am. Bd. of Surgery, Fellow Am. Coll. of Surgeons, Fellow Nat. Cancer Inst., Fellow Am. Coll. of Gastroenterol., Fellow Am. Geriatrics Soc., Fellow Internat. Coll. of Surgeons, Fellow of the Sci. Council, Internat. Coll. of Angiology, Fellow Phlebology Soc. of Am., mem. Am. Assn. for Study of Neoplastic Diseases, Am. Assn. of Hist. of Medicine, AAAS, NY Acad. of Scis., Am. Med. Writers Assn., Irish Med. Assn. (hon.), Hollywood Acad. of Medicine, Pan Am. Med. Assn. Author 49 publs. in field incl. 3 books: Fundamentals of Human Physiology, Critique of Reason, Lectures in Medical Physiology; mil: col. US Army M.C., 1941-5. res: 3 South Quail Ridge Rd Rolling Hills 90274 ofc: 1045 Atlantic Av, Ste.1011 Long Beach 90813.

BELLSEY, JONATHAN KURZON, lawyer; b. Jan. 16, 1948, NYC; s. Ira Louis and Jacqueline Doris (Kurzon) Bellsey; m. Cynthia Lenhart; children: Tasha and Justyn; edn: BA, Case Western Reserve Univ., 1969; JD, Cornell Univ. Law Sch. 1972. Career: law clerk to Chief Justice Rao, US Customs Ct., NYC, 1971; assoc. Glad, Tuttle & White, San Francisco 1973-78; pres., mng. atty. Bellsey & Baker, A Profl.Corp.,San Francisco 1978--; Dir.: Bay Britches, Inc., 1979-, Santa Cruz Imports, Inc. 1981-, J.T.& S. Leasing Corp. 1981-; lectr. seminars sponsored by Am. Assn. of Exporters and Importers and Nat.Assn. of Fgn. Trade Zones. Mem: Phi Sigma Delta frat. (pledge master 1965-8), S.F. Bar Assn. (Com. on Govt. Discovery of Atty. Records, 1977), Am. Bar Assn., West Coast Metal Importers Assn., Assn. of the Customs Bar, Am. Assn. of Exporters & Importers; admitted to practice beforeUS Court of Int'l Trade, US Ct. of

Customs & Patent Appeals, Ninth Circuit Ct. of Appeals, Supreme Ct. of Calif., No. & Central Dists. of Calif. Publs: Manual on Ornamentation (pub. for use by importers of wearing apparel) 1978. Democrat; Jewish; rec: swim, golf, tennis, history; res: 2420 Buchanan St. San Francisco 94115 ofc: Bellsey & Baker, APC, 100 Calif. St., Ste.460, San Francisco 94111.

BELLUCCI, NANCY ROSINE, psychologist, b. July 12, 1941, Boston, Mass.; d. Antone Adolph and Dorina Florence (Sartorelli) B.; edn: BA, Univ. of New Hampshire 1962; MS, CSU Los Angeles 1970; PhD, Calif. Sch. of Profl. Psychology, San Diego 1979; lic. clinical psychologist, Calif. 1981. Career: psychology cons. Applied Personal Dynamics, San Diego 1979-82; psychologist Chula Vista Sch. Dist., Chula Vista 1971--; lic. psychologist pvt. practice, San Diego 1981--; field placement supvr.; Calif. Sch. of Profl. Psych., US Internat. Univ., SDSU, 1974-; affiliate staff Southwood Mental Health Ctr., Vista Hill Hosp. 1981-; awards: Outstanding Sch. Psychologist, Calif. Assn. of Sch. Psychologist & Psychometrists 1976; mem: Southwest Personnel & Guidance Assn.; San Diego Assn. of Sch. Psychologists & Psychometrists; Calif. Sch. of Profl. Psychology Alumni Assn.; Am. Psychol. Assn.; Nat. Assn. of Sch. Psychol.; Calif. St. Psychol. Assn.; Nat. Register of Mental Health Providers; Acad. of San Diego Psychol.; Western Psychol. Assn.; Child Sexual Abuse Pgm. (vol. psychotherapist); S.D. Dept. of Soc. Svcs. Res: 3039 Plaza Leonardo Bonita 92002 Ofc: 2615 Camino del Rio S., Ste 300, San Diego 92108

BELOW, JOHN FREDERICK, III, engineering executive; b. July 5, 1951, Chgo., Ill.; s. John F., Jr. and Genevieve Marie (Brons) B.; m. Holly Jenstad, Oct. 13, 1979; 1 dau: Jennifer, b. 1982; edn: BSc, UC Berkeley 1973; Reg. Profl. Mech. Engr., Calif. 1982. Career: design engr., proj. engr., Rix Industries, 1975-77, chief of engring. 1977--; awards: US Nat. Skindiving Champ., Underwater Soc. of Am. 1977-78; Athlete of the Yr., Helms- Citizen Savings Athletic Found. 1977; mem: Nat. Soc. Profl. Engrs.; Underwater Soc. of Am.; lectr. & wrkshp. on Breathold Skindiving, Univ. of Calif. 1982; Democrat; Catholic; rec: competitive spearfishing, furniture mfg. Res: 925 Tara Hills Dr Pinole 94565 Ofc: Rix Industries, 6460 Hollis St Emeryville 94608

BELT, CHARLES MARION, administrative/ finance executive; b. Mar. 4, 1929, Harrisburg, Ill.; s. Loren Andrew and Iva Inez (Duncan) B.; m. Crystal Call, July 8, 1977; edn: M. Pub. Admin., Univ. of Mo., K.C. 1969; Bach. Gen. Edn., Univ. of Nebr. 1959; Indiana Univ. 1945-48. Career: v.p. bus. & fin. Radford (Va.) Univ., 1972-76; asst. comptroller of Virginia, Commonwealth of Va., Richmond, Va. 1976-77; v.p. resources mgmt. Virginia St. Univ., Petersburg 1977-80; dir. fiscal affairs CSU, Northridge 1980-83; v.p. admin. & fin. Volunteers of Am., Los Angeles 1983--; treas./ dir. Radford Coll. Found., Inc. 1972-76; asst. prof. bus. Radford Coll. 1972-76; mem: Council of State Sr. Bus. Ofcrs.; Nat. Assn. Coll. & Univ. Bus. Ofcrs.; So. Assn. Coll. & Univ. Bus. Ofcrs.; Western Assn. Coll. & Univ. Bus. Ofcrs.; Radford CofC; Lions Club; works: Organizational Cosmological Shifts 1969; mil: lt. col. US Army 1951-72, Legion of Merit, Bronze Star, Meritorious Svc. Medal, num. campaign & svc. medals; Republican; Congregational; rec: golf, beach, travel. Res: 10036 Hanna Ave Chatsworth 91311 Ofc: Volunteers of America of Los Angeles, 1501 Wilshire Blvd Los Angeles 90017

BELTRAN, DONALIE THOMMEY, security systems co. executive; b. Nov. 19, 1948, Alva, Okla.; d. Raymond Lee and L. Blanche (Shane) Tuxhorn; m. 1976, div.; children: Shannon Lee Beltran, b. 1969; Shane Ray Abbott, b. 1966; edn: stu. Mnpls. Sch. of Art 1967-69, LaSalle Sch. of Interior Design 1978; psychology cert. course, Indian Valley Colls. 1983; Calif. Lic. Pvt. Investigator. Career: past investigator Bowman Detective Agency, Wichita, Ks. (2 yrs); lie detection examiner, certified opr. PSE (by mfr. Dektor Counterintelligence Co.); currently V.P. Ops., Stanfield Security Systems, Inc. (sec. alarm co.); PSE Interviews, KFAX Radio, 1983; lectr. local schs.; awards: Student Intern Certs. for death investigation, Marin Co. Coroner 1981, 82, 83; mem: Calif. Assn. Lic. Investigators; Nat. Council of Inv. & Security Svc.; Nat. Assn. for Female Execs.; Am. Mgmt. Assn.; Better Bus. Bureau; Deputy Coroner for Co. of Marin under Keith Craif, asst. coroner; Republican; Protestant; rec: oil painting, trap shooting. Res: 1 Yarrow Lane Novato 94947 Ofc: Stanfield Security Systems, Inc., 68 Paul Dr San Rafael 94903

BELZ, BOB, lawyer; b. Mar. 6, 1936, Chgo.; s. Frank Lyle and Cleo Clara (Swisher) Belz; m. Mary Orr, Aug. 20, 1960; chil: Tanya L., b. 1962, Carey L., b. 1965; edn: AA, Lamar Jr.Coll. 1960, BA, Univ. Okla. 1963, JD, Humphrey's Sch of Law, 1972. Career: district scout exec. BSA, 1963-67; claims rep. Farmers Ins. Gp. 1968-73; pvt. practice law, 1973--; bd.dirs. Auto Club of Am. 1975-; judge pro tem, Manteca Ct. 1980; mem: San Joaquin Co. Adv. Bd. on Alcohol Problems 1981-; listed: Who's Who In Am. Law, Internat. Men of Distinction; awarded Atty of Experience in Dissolution, Trial, Personal Injury by Calif. Trial Lawyers Assn.; mem: Rotary Club (dir. Internat. Svc 1963-5), Toastmasters Club 1963-5, 1971-3, Nu Beta Epsilon law frat. 1971-; Calif. Trial Lawyers Assn. (chpt pres. 1975) 1968-; Am. Bar Assn. 1973-; mil: sgt. USMC 1955-59; Republican; Catholic; rec: runner 1980-(Quicksilver Running Club pres. 1983-4; rep. to Pa-tac Long Distance Running Com.), ski, golf; res: 455 Curtwood Ct. Manteca 95336 ofc: Bob Belz, Inc. APLC, 215 N. San Joaquin St. Stockton 95202.

BEN, JOHN WILLIAM, manufacturing co. president; b. Feb. 25, 1940, Hamilton, Ont., Can.; nat. app.; s. John Ben and Elizabeth Rose (Szabo) B.; m. Sarah Louise Harvey, Oct. 1, 1966; 1 dau., Jonquil, b. 1971; edn: BS, McMaster Univ. 1964. Career: sales rep./area mgr. Alahem Ltd., Burlington, Ont. 1964-69; tech. rep. Allied Colloids Canada in Toronto, 1969, helped estab. this English

Co. in Canada, transferred to Allied Colloids Inc., Ridgewood, NJ, 1973, and came to Calif. and estab. co. in the West; formed Aqua Ben Chemical (mfg. high molecular weight polymers) in Calif., 1976-, pres./ dir./ chief exec. Aqua Ben Corp., 1979 ;founder/dir. Seaside S&L 1978-; founder/dir. Mission Bell Travel 1980-; mem: Tech. Assn. Pulp & Paper, Calif. Water Pollution Control Assn., Water Pollution Control Fedn., Am. Chem. Soc.; clubs: lt. gov. Optimist Clubs of So. Calif. 1984, past pres. Mission Viejo Optimist Club, M.V. Tennis Assn., M.V. Activities Com.; designed high molecular wt. polymers for spl. appl. in the pollution control field, publ: Water Pollution Control 4/73; Catholic; rec: golf, tennis, skiing. Res: 26612 Castile Ln Mission Viejo 92691 Ofc: Aqua Ben Corp. 1390 N. Manzanita Orange 92667

BENDER, BILL, western artist; b. Jan. 5, 1920, El Segundo; s. Joseph Edward and Pauline (Beck) Bender; m. Helen, Dec. 22, 1957; grad. El Segundo H.S. 1937. Career: broke and sold broncos, 1932-37; rode and worked on location in western movies, 1936-37; cowboyed, 1938-until stopped by injury; began painting scenes from own life, profl. western artist 1950s--; painted for US Air Force in S.E. Asia, and the Cadet Tng. pgm for USN in Pensacola, Fla.; currently: gallery painting; illustrator books, greeting cards, prints and calendars for Leanin' Tree Pub. Co., Boulder, Colo. Awards: Hon.lifetime dir., Death Valley 49ers; hon. life mem. Mountain Oyster Club (Tucson); hon. life mem. Living Desert Assn. (Palm Desert); Hon. Tailhook Airdale, USS Lexington. Mem: Fellow, Am. Inst. of Fine Arts (L.A.), fellow Am. Artists Profl. League (NY), life mem. Cowboy Hall of Fame (Okla.City), mem. The Westerners (L.A.), The Westerners (S.D.), advis. bd. San Dimas Festival of Western Arts. Republican. Prot. avocation: writing. address: Star Rte. Box 154, Oro Grande 92368.

BENDICK, WALTER HARRY, health care administrator; b. Nov. 11, 1947, Cleveland, Oh.; s. Walter Herman and Delilah Evelyn (Rhodes) Bendick; edn: RN, US Army, 1976; BS, Chapman Coll., 1984; 1 son, Robert, b. 1970. Career: nursing supr., Johnson & Johnson, Los Angeles 1975-78; Pheresis Unit supr., West Hills Med. Center, Canoga Park 1979-81; branch office dir. National In-Home Health Svcs., Los Angeles 1981-- Mem: C.A.H.S.A.H. (co. mem.) 1981-. Mil: E5, US Army 1968-73, decorated Vietnam. rec: travel, theater. res: 14838 Lassen St. Mission Hills 91345 ofc: Nat. In-Home Health Services, 432 S. San Vicente Blvd. L.A. 90048

BENDIX, SELINA, environmental research co. president; b. Feb. 16, 1930, Pasadena; d. Sidney and Lina (Litinskaya) Weinbaum; m. Gilbert G. Bendix, May 1, 1953; children: Erica, b. 1954, Desmid, b. 1956, Jacob, b. 1958; edn: BS, UC Los Angeles, 1951, PhD, UC Berkeley 1957. Career: technical writing asst. to Dr. Linus Pauling, Chem. Dept., Cal Tech, Pasadena 1949; research asst. Earhart Plant Research Lab, Cal Tech 1950-51, graduate research zoologist, Zool. Dept., UCB 1951-54; biological research, Lab. of Comparative Biology, Kaiser Found. Research Inst., Richmond 1957 64; asst. prof. of biol. San Francisco State Univ., 1964-65; lectr. in biol. Mills Coll., 1965-69; mng. ptnr. Bendix Research, Environmental Consultants, 1969-80; adminstr. City and County of San Francisco Office of Environmental Review, 1974-80; pres. Bendix Environmental Research Inc., environmental & toxicological cons., 1980--; mem. Calif. Hazardous Wastes Technology Assessment Adv. Com. 1981; EPA Adminstr's Toxic Substances Adv. Com. 1977-82; Calif. Atty. Gen's Task Force on Environ. Problems of SF Bay Area 1972-78; League of Women Voters Solid Waste Cons. 1982--; author more than 200 publs. incl. Environmental Mutagens (Science, 1974), Firefighter Exposure to Environmental Carcinogens (J. Combustion Toxicology 1979), A Short Intro to the CA Environ. Quality Act (Santa Clara Law Rev. 1979), Hazards from the Arsenic Treatment of Wood (Proc. 4th CA Conf. on Prod. Toxicity 1983); Democrat. Res: 1103 The Alameda Berkeley 94707 Ofc: Bendix Environmental Research Inc., 1390 Market St, Ste. 902, San Francisco 94102

BENEDETTO, ALTON FRANCIS, business executive; b. Nov. 16, 1924, Jackson, Calif.; s. Guy Joseph and Marie Rose (Spinetta) Benedetto; m. Sarah Elizabeth Cain, 1956; 1 dau. Sarah Ann, b. 1959; edn: BS chem, Univ. Nev.-Reno 1951. Career: analytical chemist Union Oil Co., San Francisco 1951, staff chemist 1954, lab. foreman 1956, lab. supr. 1960, purchasing agent Hd.Ofc., Los Angeles 1968; Supply/Dist. mgr. Tesoro Petroleum, San Antonio,Tex. 1973; vice pres. Holland & Sons, Los Angeles 1977; pres. Calif.Refining Corp., L.A. 1978; pres. Valley Fuels Co., L.A. 1981--; pres. ABC Gas Co.; cons. AGIP Petroleum Co., Inc., Kenco Refining Corp.; mem: L.A. Purchasing Agents Assn., Am. Arbitration Assn., Petroleum Club of Los Angeles, L.A. Opera Guild, L.A. Music Ctr for the Perf. Arts (sponsor), Calabasas Hist. Soc., Freedoms Found., Phi Sigma Kappa, Rotarian, Shriners, Scottish Rites, Masons, Temple Assn., Jonathan Club, Lakeside CC, Calabasas CC, Oil Mens Club; mil: s/sgt USAF, aviation cadet; Republican; Presbyterian (pres. Mariners); rec: golf, gardening, fishing, painting; res: 4714 Park Olivo Calabasas 91302 ofc: Valley Fuels Co. 900 Wilshire Bl. Ste. 1126, Los Angeles 90017.

BENJAMIN, KIM ALAN, financial executive; b. Jan. 15, 1953, Los Angeles; s. Jack and Blossom (Baird) B.; edn: BA in econ., Coe Coll. 1975; NASD Principal. Career: asst. dir. A.S.M.T., Wash DC 1976-78; dir. Am. Assn. of Clin. Chemistry, Wash DC 1978-80; coord. of spl. issues, Am. Petroleum Inst., 1980-81; v.p./asst. to bd. chmn. Petroleum Corp., Santa Monica 1981-82; asst. to pres./chief exec. Continental Resources, Laguna Hills 1982-83; . v.p. Cambio Investments, Fullerton 1983--; honors: Omicron Delta Epsilon 1975, Who's Who in Colls & Univs. 1973-4, Outstanding Young Man of Am. 181; mem. Nat. Multiple Sclerosis Soc. Publs: 30 arts. in health, sci. & polit. publs., num. arts. in regional newspapers; Democrat; Jewish; rec: tennis, travel, music, the arts. Res: 3502 Vista Dr Manhattan Bch 90266 Ofc: Cambio, 310 No Harbor Blvd Fullerton 92632

BENKE, PATRICIA DARLENE, municipal court judge; b. Apr. 15, 1949, New Castle, Pa.; d. Joseph Elias and Bess (Namey) Jacobs; m. Donald Benke, June 26, 1971; children: Michael, b. 1982, Peter, b. 1983; edn: AA, Pasadena Jr. Coll. 1969; BA, CSU San Diego, highest honors, 1971; JD, Univ. of S.D. Sch. of Law 1974. Career: law clk. two San Diego law firms: Gray, Cary, Ames & Frye and Holt, Rhoades and Hollywood, 1973-74; deputy atty. gen., criminal div., Calif. State Atty. Gen., 1974-83; gov. apptd. judge San Diego Municipal Ct., 1983--; Atty. Gen.'s rep. State Conf. on the Judiciary, Task Force on Probation and Parole (1977), to Dist. Attys. Regional Cons. (1978, 80); honors: Phi Kappa Phi, Mortar Board (1971), recognition awards, Nat. Awards Pgm. (1978), San Diego Career Womens Assn. (1983); mem: Assn. of Calif. Deputies Atty. Gen. 1975-83 (State Pres. 1978, S.D. Chpt. Pres. 1977); first chpsn. Women in Public Law, S.D. 1980; Calif. Bar Assn. 1974-83, S.D. County Bar Assn. 1974-83 (first chpsn. Appellate Com. 1980), Lawyers Club of S.D. (bd. dirs. 1980-82), Calif. Women Lawyers 1980-83; past vol. for KPBS-TV (pub. tv); past mem. S.D. Co. Child Abuse Coord. Council, Mission Trails Rev. Bd., S.D. Park and Recreation Bd. (1979-83); publs: co-compiled Peace Officer's Penal Code (1978, Bancroft-Whitney); contbr. law jours., newspaper editorial pages; rec: writing. Res: 4703 Constance Dr San Diego 92115 Ofc: S.D. Municipal Ct. 220 W. Broadway, San Diego 92101

BENNETT, ARTHUR DAVID, communications technician; b. Feb. 15, 1939, Inwood Park, Long Island, NY; s. Yezekiel and Leona Mildred (Muzzillo) B.; m. Melanie Hinton, Apr. 8, 1967; 1 son: Brian, b. 1970. Career: sales rep. Mutual of Omaha Ins. Co. 1976-80; sales rep. Sentry Ins. Co. 1980-83; employer services rep. Calif. Human Devel. Corp. 1983--; bd. dirs. USS Arizona Meml. Mus. Found. 1972-74; chmn. Hawaii St. Veterans Day Com. 1973; awards: Shore Sailor of the Yr., US Naval Communications Station, Wahiawa, Hawaii 1973; Pres.'s Club, Mutual Omaha 1978; mem: Fleet Reserve Assn. (pres. Kenitra, Morocco Br. 189, 1969; pres. Pearl Harbor, Hawaii Br. 46, 1972-74; v.p. Northwest Reg. 1974-75); Am. Legion (fin. ofcr. Wahiawa, Hawaii Post 22, 1973, 74); B.P.O. Elks; mil: E7, USN 1956-76; GCM (5); Nat. Defense Medal; Navy Unit Commdn.; Meritorious Unit Commdn.; Naval Security Gp. Merit. Svc. Awd.; Republican; Lutheran; rec: bowling, photog. Res: 617 Crane Dr Suisun City 94585 Ofc: California Human Development Corp.

BENNETT, BILL CHARLES, company executive; b. Aug. 2, 1934, Dardanelle, Ark.; s. Charley and Velma Irene (Jones) B.; m. Wilma Henley, Dec. 20, 1954; children: Deborah, b. 1956; Rodney, b. 1959; Jerry, b. 1962; Calif. Cert. Pest Control Advisor/Opr. Career: with Wilbur Ellis Co., 1958--, currently mgr. San Joaquin Branch; worked with his sons and father to engr. & build worlds first multi row 30 inch cotton picker; Democrat, Protestant. Res: 25317 Scaggs Street Tranquillity 93668 Ofc: Wilbur Ellis Co., El Dorado & Colorado Ave San Joaquin 93660

BENNETT, ROBERT ELDRED, psychotherapist/health care administrator; b. Sept. 9, 1929, Belize, Central Am.; nat. 1972; s. Egbert Eldred and Mable Erica (Neal) Bennett; m. Egzine, Aug. 4, 1954; chil: Egzine (Goodwin) b. 1957, Robert Jr., b. 1960, Pauline, b. 1964; edn: sch. cert., Univ. of Cambridge, Eng. 1946; matriculation, Univ. of London, 1948; tchg. dip., Mico Teacher Tng. Coll., Kingston, Jamaica 1952; dip., social policy & adm., Univ. of Swansea, Wales 1963; BA, 1969, and MSW, UCLA; Fellow, Clin. Social Work, Calif. Career: tchr., 1949-55, probation ofcr. 1955, Belize, Belize, Central Am.; community orgnzr., 1956, and adminstv. head of Social Welfare, Govt. of Belize, 1959-68; counterpart to Housing Advisor of US Internat. Cooperation (now AID) 1960-3, dir. Brit. Honduras Red Cross Soc. 1964-8, instr. Peace Corps vols., U. of Fla., 1963; house father Episcopal Home for Children, Pasadena, Ca. 1968-9; mgr. Half Way House, L.A. 1969-71; dir. med. social svcs. El Cerrito Hosp., 1972-3, adminstrv. asst. 1973-4; sr. med. social worker, L.A. County, 1974-7; dir. social work, Inter-City Home Hlth Assn., 1977-9; pvt. practice: cons. to acute facilities, nursing homes and home hlth agencies, 1979--; exec. dir. Ebb's Psychotherapy & Consultation Services; pres./dir. Ebb's Home Health Care Svcs. Inc., Los Angeles. Awards: Queens Honors, Gr. Brit. Mem. of Brit. Empire; NIMH Fellowship UCLA 1970-1; Fellowship, Sloane Kettering Meml. Cancer Ctr. 1975. Mem: Nat. Assn. of Social Workers, Soc. for Clin. Soc. Work, Am. Cancer Soc., Lung Assn. of L.A., Internat. Inst. of L.A.; Democrat; Free Methodist (Conv. del. 1982-3). rec: music, swim. res: 2909 W. 46th St. Los Angeles 90043. Ebb's Home Hlth Care Svcs Inc. 2900 W. Vernon L.A. 90008.

BENOIT, GEORGE, plumbing contractor; b. July 27, 1935, Winnipeg, Man., Canada; s. John Arthur and Theresa (Dickson) Benoit; m. Glenda, Dec. 3, 1953; chil: Jon, b. 1956, George, b. 1959, Robert, b. 1964, Michael, b. 1966; edn: Univ. of Manitoba 1951, L.A. CITY Coll. 1955. Career: plumber/estimator Cooper &: Boond Plumbing, Los Angeles 1954-66; owner Van Nuys Car Wash, 1966-71; owner George Benoit Plumbing, Northridge 1971--. Awards: Hiram Awd. (1982), Awd. of Light (82), Masonic Lodge; mem: Plumbing & Piping Industry Council (secty.treas. 1983), Constrn. Industry Council of Calif. (v.chmn. 1983), Joint Apprenticeship & Tng. Com. of Plumbers and Pipe Fitters (bd. mem. 1983), Am. Soc. of Plumbing Engrs., Southland Heritage Masonic Lodge (Master 1976, 83), BSA (Merit Badge Counselor); Republican; Baptist; rec: bkpacking, ski, fish; res: 18342 Superior St. Northridge 91325 ofc: George Benoit Plumbing, 8345 Reseda Bl. Ste.102, Northridge 91324.

BENSON, LENNARD BERT, childrens services worker; b. Mar. 12, 1954, Seattle, Wash.; s. Lennard Bert (dec.) and Bernice F. (Ferm) B.; m. Monika B., Aug. 2, 1981; 1 son: David, b. 1983; edn: AA, Valley Coll. 1975; BA, CSU Northridge 1976; MA, Pepperdine Univ. 1980; PhD cand., Calif. Grad. Inst. 1981-; Calif. Comm. Counselor Credential, Instr. Cred. Psych., Comm. Coll.

Student Personnel Wkr. 1980. Career: mental health unit asst. Olive View Health Ctr., Los Angeles 1975; counselor ex-offender college students, Northridge 1976; pres. Drannel Game Co., L.A. 1977-80; substitute tchr. L.A. Co. Schs. 1978-81; GSI, County Probation Dept., L.A. 1976-77; deputy probation ofcr., Los Angeles 1977-80; CSW, L.A. Co. Dept. of Pub. Soc. Svcs. 1980--; Calif. Inst. Juvenile Recreation Research, L.A. dir. 1977-80; mem: Calif. Assn. of Marriage & Family Therapists; works: Probation Simulation board game 1977; Democrat; Jewish; rec: boating. Res: 13770 Terra Bella St Arleta 91331 Ofc: L.A. County D.P.S.S., 5026 Santa Monica Blvd Los Angeles 90029

BENTLEY, DONALD ALAIN, civil engineer; b. March 16, 1955, Los Angeles; s. John Robt. and Theresa Marie (Huitric) Bentley; edn: BS, civil engr., CalPoly Pomona, 1977; MS in C.E., Stanford Univ., 1982; Regis. Profl. Engr. in Civil Engrg., Calif. 1980. Career: sr. civil engr. Stetson Engineers, Inc., West Covina 1977-81; project engr. Lowry & Assocs., Pleasanton 1983--. Awards: Calif. State graduate fellowship, Stanford Univ. 1981-2. mem: Calif. Water Pollution Control Assn., San Francisco Bay Sect.; South Bay Engrs. Club. publs: The Mono Lake Controversy, Stanford Univ. (1982); Selection of Key Wells for Areawide Monitoring of Exotic Contaminants in Main San Gabriel Basin (1st pl. Student Paper Contest, Fall 78). Democrat. Catholic. rec: hiking, racquetball. res: 7100 San Ramon Rd #126, Dublin 94568 ofc: Lowry & Assocs, 4637 Chabot Dr. Ste.101, Pleasanton 94566.

BENTON, DONALD MARK, company president, insurance agent; b. Apr. 8, 1957, Pt. Hueneme; s. Arlis R. and Dorothy H. (Wallis) Benton; edn: AA, Coll. of the Canyons, 1981; Calif. lic. Life and Disability Agt. (1981) Fire and Casualty Agt. (1981). Career: founder/pres. and chief exec. Santa Clarita Valley Temporaries, Saugus 1979--; agent/owner Farmers Ins. Agcy. 1981--; workshop instr. Wm. S. Hart H.Sch. Dist. Alternative Study Pgm. 1980-81, and district personnel commnr. 1980-; v.p. bd. trustees Coll. of the Canyons 1981-; bd. dirs. St. Stephens Spl. Sch.; honors: US Congl. Award of Honor, Cong. Barry Goldwater (1981); commendations, Calif. State Senate and State Assembly, L.A. Co. Bd. of Supvsrs. (1981); award for service, Coll. of the Canyons (1980); Outstanding Young Man of the Santa Clarita Valley (1980), Jaycee of the Year 1979, S.C.V. Jaycees; Pres. Awd., Calif. State Jaycees, 1980. Mem: Santa Clarita Valley Jaycees (chmn. bd. 1982); Calif. Jaycees (state chmn. CPR 1980); S.C.V. CofC (bd. dirs. 1981); College of the Canyons Mens Student Body pres. 1980; Red Cross com.; co-designed w/father the Aervane (wind power energy device); Democrat (founding v.p. S.C.V. Dem. Club 1980); Episcopal; rec: stamps, coins, US hist. Res: 22924 Lyons Ave, 109, Newhall 91321 Ofc: Santa Clarita Valley Temporaries, 21704 Golden Triangle Rd Saugus 91350

BENTON, JOHN BREEN, management consulting co. executive; b. Aug. 20, 1942, Los Angeles; s. Jess Earl, Jr. and Natalie (Breen) B.; m. Shirlee Benjamin, Aug. 19, 1975; children (adopted): Kirsten, b. 1968, Kendall, b. 1971; edn: AB, intl. rels./pol. sci., USC 1964; Masters, intl. pub. admin., Syracuse Univ. 1966; Dr. Pub. Admin., USC 1971. Career: Public Admin. Advisor, US AID, Lahore, Pakistan 1965; consultant Rand Corp., 1968-70; dir. Fin. Indus. Planning, Trw Communications Systems & Services, 1972-75; exec. dir. Nat. Commn. on Electron Funds Transfer, US Govt. (apptd. by Pres. Ford, confirmed by US Senate) 1976-77; pres. ICS Group, Inc., L.A. Area/N.Y., 1978--; owner/bd. mem. ICS Devel. Corp.; instr. USC Sch. of Pub. Admin. 1979; awards: Ford Found. Fellow (1964), Maxwell Scholar (1966); mem. L.A. Country Club; guest spkr. Town Hall of Calif., L.A. Dwntwn Rotary, 1977; author: Managing The Organizational Decision Process (1972, D.C.Heath); art. for Harvard Bus. Rev., 1977 (one of top ten most requested reprints during past ten yrs.), num. other articles; mil: capt. US Army (active 1966, 67, 71) USAR; Republican; rec: golf, skiing, scuba diving. Res: 21 Pony Lane Rolling Hills Estates 90274 Ofc: ICS Group, 24500 S. Vermont Ave, Ste. 210, Harbor City 90710

BEN-YEHUDA, NITZA, lawyer; b. Jan. 4, 1943, Tel-Aviv, Israel; d. Meir and Dina (Britwitz) Rosenshtrom; m. Arieh Ben-Yehuda, Jan. 16, 1966; chil: Ohad, b. 1967, Eron, b. 1970, Ayala, b. 1977; edn: LLB, Hebrew Univ., Jerusalem 1966; admitted to practice law, Israel, Calif. Career: attorney, law office of N. Tikotchinsky (1966-9), Z. Treinin (1969-71), Dan Bar-El (1971-76), Tel-Aviv; with Israel Information Center, Los Angeles 1978-80; atty. law office of Terry Taus, Beverly Hills 1980-82; practicing immigration law, law offices of Neville Asherson, Bev. Hills 1982--; mem. Calif. State Bar 1981-, Bnai Brith Shalom Lodge; mil: 1st sgt. Israeli Army 1960-62; Temple Beith Am; res: 149 N. Hamel Dr. Beverly Hills 90211. Law Ofc. of Neville Asherson, 9460 Wilshire Bl. Beverly Hills 90212.

BENZ, RONALD THOMAS, physician-otolaryngologist; b. April 17, 1948, Milwaukee, Wisc.; s. Dr. Herman S. and Beatrice M. (Quinn) Benz, DDS; edn: BS, Carroll Coll. 1964, MD, Marquette Univ. 1968; m. Rita Kantza, Nov. 27, 1971; children: Michael, b. 1976, Jennifer, b. 1978, Nicholas, b. 1980; career: internship, LAC/USC Med Ctr. 1978-9, residency 1971-5; physician-otolaryngologist, private practice, San Diego 1976--; mem: AMA; Calif. Med Assn.; Fellow, Am. Acad. Otolaryngology; San Diego Acad of Otolaryngol., Head-Neck Surg.; mil: lt. USNR 1969-71; Catholic; rec: sports; ofc: 2001 Fourth St., San Diego 92101.

BERG, CARL MC INTOSH, real estate broker; b. May 17, 1922, Meadow Grove, Nebr.; s. Carl Fredrick and Cora Ellen (McIntosh) B.; m. Beverly Jean Geiger, July 10, 1948; children: Douglas Carl, b. 1950, Jeffrey Robert, b. 1952, Stephen Paul, b. 1956; edn: aero. engrg., Spartan Coll. of Engrg., Tulsa 1942; BS in mech. engr., UC Berkeley 1947; GRI, Grad. Realtors Inst., NAR 1983. Career: engr. Spartan Aircraft Co., Tulsa, Okla. 1942-43; aviation machinists mate USNR, 1943-46; jr. design engr. East Bay Municipal Utils. Dist., Oakland, Ca. 1947-48; tool design engr. C.F. Braun Co., Alhambra 1948-49; prodn. mgr. Aerolab Devel. Co., Pasadena 1949-52; co-founder/ dir. of procurement, Task Corp., Anaheim 1952-70, bd. dirs. 1952--; real estate broker/ mgr. Albrecht Realty, San Gabriel 1971--; mem. West San Gabriel Valley Bd. of Realtors 1971-, bd. dir. 1973-85, honored as 1980 Realtor of the Year; dir. (3d. term) Los Angeles County (combined) Bds. of R.E., Dist. Dir. 1982-83; state dir. Calif. Assn. Realtors 1973, local bd. rep. to state 1978-, regl. v.p. of 16th Dist. CAR 1985; Republican; Lutheran (dir. Lay Ministry 1980-); rec: photog., travel, cabinet mkr. Res: 267 South Burton Ave San Gabriel 91776 Ofc: Albrecht Realty 1030 E. Las Tunas Dr San Gabriel 91776

BERGEN, ROBERT LEE, lawyer; b. Dec. 1, 1925, Los Angeles; s. Walter Goza (dec. 1926) and Marjorie Marie Bergen; div.; chil: Darcy, b. 1957, Dennis, b. 1962, Darla, b. 1963, David, b. 1966, Darrin, b. 1969, Damon, b. 1971; edn: BBA, Woodbury Coll. 1949; LLB, LaSalle Univ. 1957. Career: investigator Dun & Bradstreet, San Diego 1948-55; title examiner Union Title & Trust Co., S.D. 1955-57; chief deputy city atty. City of San Diego, 1958-65; trial atty. Mathews, Bergen, Potash & Grier, S.D. 1965--; secty., San Diego City Planning Commn., 1958-65. Honors: US National Bicycle Racing Champion 1982 (Trextertown, Pa.). Mem. State Bar of Calif. 1958-, S.D. County Bar Assn. 1958-, admitted to US Supreme Ct. 1971; mem: Am. Numismatic Assn., 20-30 International, BSA, Am. Youth Hostels (life), cert. ofcl. US Cycling Fedn. Publs: num. law arts. Mil: USN, WWII, participant invasion of Iwo Jima 2/19/45. Republican. rec: bicycle racing, collect Indian artifacts, coins, seashells. res: ;10050 Cristobal Dr. Spring Valley 92077. ofc: Mathews, Bergen, Potash & Grier, 121 Broadway Ste.652, San Diego 92101.

BERGER, ALLEN, psychologist; b. Jan. 31, 1952, Chgo.; s. Alvin Jerome and Louise (Pressanno) B.; m. Dymphna (Gruyters), Sept. 11, 1982; edn: BA, psych., w/great distinction, CSU Long Beach 1977, MA, 1979; PhD Cand., clin. psych., UC Davis 1979-. Career: alcoholism, chem. dependency counselor Western Inst. of Human Resources, Long Beach (1973-75), Pacific Hosp., L.B. (1975), San Pedro Peninsula Hosp., San Pedro (1975-79); graduate asst. Statistics tutor CSU Long Beach, 1977-79; pvt. practice in Marriage, Family Child Counselng, Redondo Beach 1981--; clin. supr. Alcoholism Recovery Svc., South Bay Hosp., Redondo Bch. (1980-) and Eating Disorders Unit, San Pedro Penin. Hosp. (1981-); internat. trainer with The Kempler Inst., Costa Mesa 1980-; honors: scholastic achieve. awds. Ill. (1973), CSULB (1977), Nat. Deans List, Phi Kappa Phi (1979), Outstanding Young Men of Am. (1980); mem. Am. Psychol. Assn. (student afil.); clin. mem. Calif. Assn. of Marriage, Family and Child Therapists; publs: bk. chapters, profl. journal arts.; mil: sgt. USMC 1969-72, Vietnam; Democrat; rec: tennis, jogging, jazz dancing. Res: 615 S. Prospect, Apt. 205, Redondo Bch 90277 Ofc: South Bay Hospital, 514 N. Prospect, Redondo Beach 90277

BERGER, JAYNE (FELDMAN), oil production co. president; b. Aug. 7, 1917, Los Angeles; d. Andrew James Jr. and Cora (Lord) Copp; m. Henry Berger, Dec. 22, 1981; children: David Feldman, b. 1949; Deborah Feldman, b. 1953; edn: BA, Stanford Univ. 1939; Elem. Sch. Cert., Univ. Calif. 1940. Career: (fmr.) tchr./ social director Smoke Tree Ranch, Palm Springs; research analyst, US War Dept., Army Air Unit, Wash. DC; Powers model, NYC; treas. D.D. Feldman Oil & Gas; (current) pres./ CEO Texpel Petroleum Corp.; mem: The Colleagues (pres.); Pi Beta Phi (pres. Calif. Alpha Chpt.); D.A.R.; Republican; Presbyterian; rec: tennis, photog. Res: 10934 Bellagio Rd Los Angeles 90024 Ofc: Texfel Petroleum Corp., 10889 Wilshire Blvd Los Angeles 90024

BERGER, PAUL S., lawyer; b. Aug. 16, 1949, Syracuse, NY; s. Joseph Wallace and Dorothy (Lawner) Berger; m. Elaine, Apr. 18, 1982; 1 son, Aron, b. 1982; edn: AB, Univ. of Calif. 1972, JD, magna cum laude Univ. of S.F. Sch of Law 1976. Career: law clerk, San Francisco Neighborhood Legal Asst. Found. 1975; extern clerk for Justice Raymond L. Sullivan, Calif. Supreme Ct., 1976; judicial staff atty. Calif. Ct. of Appeal 1st Appellate Dist. 1976-80; trial atty. firm of Levy, Samrick & Bernard, S.F. 1980--. Honors: Am. Jurisprudence Awards-Evidence, Criminal Law, Criminal Procedure; pres. McAullife Hon. Soc., comments ed. U.S.F. Law Rev. (1975-6). mem: State Bar of Calif. 1976-, S.F. Bar Assn. publs: law review arts. Democrat. Jewish. rec: jogging, guitar. ofc: Levy, Samrick & Bernard 115 Sansome St, Ste.1200, San Francisco 94104.

BERGERON, GARY ALFRED, cardiologist; b. Feb. 24, 1942, Portland, Ore.; s. Alfred and Constance (Sailing) B.; m. Cheryl, July 19, 1980; 1 dau. Michelle Lynn, b. 1974; edn: BA, Williamette Univ., cum laude, 1965; MD, Univ. Ore. 1969; lic MD, Mass. (1972), Calif. (1975); Diplomate, Nat. Bd. of Med. Examiners 1970, Am. Bd. Internal Med. 1974, Am. Bd. Cardiovascular Diseases 1982. Career: med. intern, resident Strong Meml. Hosp., Rochester, NY 1969-71, NY Hosp. 1971-72; med./cardiol. research fellow Harvard Med. Sch., Peter Bent Brigham Hosp., Boston 1972-75; afil. fellow in cardiol. Children's Hosp., Boston 1975-76; clin. instr. med. Harvard Med. Sch. 1975-76; assoc. in med. Beth Israel Hosp., Boston 1975-76; asst. clin. prof. med. UCLA Sch. of Med. 1977-80, and att. phys. in cardiol. Harbor Gen. Hosp. 1977-79, Wadsworth VA Hosp. 1980; cardiology pvt. practice Eisenhower Med. Ctr. & Desert Hosp., Palm Springs 1977--; asst. clin. prof. UC San Francisco 1983; mem: Alpha Omega Alpha, Am. Heart Assn., Soc. of Cardiac Catheterization & Angiography, Fellow Am. Coll. Physicians, AMA, Riverside Co. Med. Assn., Am./L.A. Soc. Echocardiography, Am. Fedn. for Clin. Research, Fellow Council on Clin. Cardiol., Palm Springs Acad. of Med., Fellow Am. Coll. of Cardiol., AAAS; med. jour. articles; Methodist; rec: fishing. Res: 520 N. Phillips Rd Palm Springs 92262 Ofc: Gary A. Bergeron, MD Inc. 555 Tachevah Dr, Ste. 201E, Palm Springs 92262

BERGH, HENRY THEODORE, real estate broker; b. May 24, 1918, Spokane, Wash.; s. Paul Bennie and Anna Marie (Meyer) B.; m. Miriam Lorraine Jackson, Aug. 24, 1939; children: Karen, b. 1943; Judi, b. 1946; Della, b. 1956; Cyndi, b. 1958; edn: BA, Wala Wala Coll. 1940. Career: pastor Seventh-day Adventist Churches, 1940-46; asst. mgr. Book Dept. Pacific Press Pub. Assn., Mt. View, Ca. 1946-48; youth activities dir. Wawona Summer Camp, Central Calif. Conf. 1948-54; Cedar Falls Summer Camp, So. Calif. Conf. 1954-57; sect./ treas. Arizona Conf. 1957-62; adminstr. Hanford (Ca.) Comm. Hosp. 1962-69; assoc. adminstr. St. Helena (Ca.) Hosp. & Health Ctr. 1969-72; secty./ treas./ dir. Trust Svcs., No. Calif. Conf., SDA 1972-80; pres. Henry T. Bergh Realty, Fish Camp 1980--; listed Who's Who in Religion, 2nd ed.; mem: Yosemite Gateway Bd. Realtors; Eastern Madera CofC; Rotary Internat. (past pres. Hanford Club); author/composer Pathfinders (internat. theme song for SDA club for jr. youth) pub. in Singing Youth, Review & Herald Pub. Assn.; author, Upward Trail (devotional book for jr. youth) Review & Herald Pub. Assn. 1963; Republican; SDA; rec: photog. Address: Fish Camp 93623

BERGMAN, DAVID BENJAMIN, physician; b. Jan. 16, 1942, Brklyn, NY; s. Theodore Oscar and Helen Bergman; chil: Mindy, b. 1963, Jill, b. 1966, Berth, b. 1970; edn: AB, cum laude, Dartmouth Coll. 1962, BMS, Dartmouth Med. Sch. 1964, MD, Harvard Med. Sch. 1966; bd. certified psychiatry, Am. Bd. of Psychiatry & Neurology 1973. Career: resident/chief res. in psychiatry Albert Einstein Coll. of Med., Bronx, NY 1967-70; psychiatrist, US Army, Ft. Gordon, Ga.; cons. in psychiatry Episcopal Counselling Ctr., Augusta, Ga.; asst. clin. prof. psych. Med. Coll. of Ga., 1970-72; pvt. practice psych., San Diego; asst. clin. prof. psych. UCSD Sch. of Med., 1972--; medical dir./mem. bd.dirs., Southwood Mental Hlth. Ctr., Chula Vista 1976--. Recipient Fellowship Am. Psychiat. Assn. 1978. Mem: San Diego Psychiatric Soc. (pres. 1983), S.D. Soc. Adolescent Psychiatry (treas. 1975), AMA, CMA, CPA, SDPS; mem. Helix South Tennis Club, Neighborhd Action Gps. works: devel. new delivery models for psychiat. svcs. to emotionally disturbed youth (1976-). mil: maj. US Army 1970-2, Army Commend. Medal. rec: tennis, golf, riding, theatre. res: 11050 Dutton Dr. La Mesa 92041 ofc: 950 Third Ave. Chula Vista 92011.

BERGSTROM, KARL A., specialty retail store chain president; b. Nov. 29, 1926, Gothenburg, Sweden, nat. 1956; s. Carl A. and Jenny A. (Bjorkman) B.; m. Conny Riis-Klausen, Nov. 28, 1957; children: Pierre, b. 1959, Vickie, b. 1961; edn: BS, summa cum laude, UC Berkeley 1950. Career: v.consul, Swedish Diplomatic Corps. 1946-50; mgr. Container Corp. of Am., San Francisco 1950-53; US Army Svc. 1953-56; mgr. Continental Can Co., Los Angeles 1956-63; founder/chief exec. Bergstroms Childrens Stores, Inc., Irvine 1963--; chmn. bd. Stanford Disthg Corp., Hayward; adv. bd: Nat. Bank of So. Calif., Santa Ana, Olympic Nat. Bank, L.A., Traweek Investment Co., Marina Del Rey, honors: Delta Sigma Pi, profl. bus frat.; mem. Tustin Toastmasters Club (pres. 1978); mil: sgt. US Army 1953 interpreter in Germany, Norway, Denmark & France 1953-56, staff of Gen. Lucius Clay; Republican; Presbyterian; rec. skiing, art collection, classical music. Res: 1662 La Loma Dr Santa Ana 92705 Ofc: Bergstroms Childrens Stores, 16862 Red Hill Ave Irvine 92714

BERKLEY, GAIL WINNICK, psychotherapist; b. Feb. 21, 1947, Detroit, Mich.; d. Dr. Lawrence C. Winnick and Helen Minette (Caner) Leytus; m. Daniel T. Pechner (atty., Dorfman, Wolfe, Rounick, Cabot), Jan. 22, 1966; edn: BA, CSU San Francisco 1970, MSc 1980; PhD cand., Univ. of S.F.; credentials: Standard Tchg. cred. grades 7-12, 1971, comm. college counselor, 1980, pupil personnel cred., 1980 (S.F.State Univ.), learning handicapped splst., 1979 (Coll of Notre Dame); licensed Marriage, Family,Child Counselor. Career: educator, SFUSD, San Francisco 1971, 1974-79, ESL instr. 1972, Filipino bilingual instr. 1973; interior designer, cons.(assoc. ASID), Berkley Goods, SF 1976--; Pupil Personnel Splst Edn. Services, SFUSD 1979-80; psychotherapist, splst in mediation and conciliation, San Mateo 1981; supr./counselor intern Service League of San Mateo Co., 1981; children and adolescent services & learning disabilities splst; mem:(clin.) Am. Assn. of Marriage, Family, Child Therapists;(clin.) Am. Mental Health Counselors Assn.; Calif. and Am. Personnel and Guidance Assns., Calif. Assn. Marriage, Family Counselors, Peninsula Family Svc Agcy, CAMFAC, AAUW, SF Ballet Assn., SF Opera Guild, Calif. Personnel &: Guidance Assn.,CACES, Calif. Common Cause, Commonwealth Club of Calif., SF Perf. Arts Ctr., Calif. Hist. Soc.; works: designer comml. and residential furniture; rec: exercise, riding, tennis, archery. ofc: 36 So El Camino Real, Ste. 304, San Mateo 94401.

BERLEKAMP, ELWYN RALPH, research engineer, mathematician; b. Sept. 6, 1940, Dover, Ohio; s. Rev. Waldo and Loretta (Kimmel) B.; m. Jennifer Wilson, Aug. 21, 1966; children: Persis, b. 1968; Bronwen, b. 1973; David, b. 1982; edn: BSEE, MIT 1962, MSEE, 1962; PhD, E.E., 1964. Career: asst. prof. UC Berkeley 1964-66; tech. staff Bell Lab., Murray Hill, NJ 1966-71; prof. of math., UCB 1971--, assoc. chair of EECS for CS, UCB 1975-77; pres. Cyclotomics, Berkeley 1981--; mem: IEEE fellow; Nat. Acad. Engring.; Dwight-Shattuck Assn.; Berkeley City Club; coauthor Winning Ways, vols. I, II (1982, Academic Press) w/J.H.Conway and R.K.Guy); author Algebraic Coding Theory (1984, Aegean Park Press); Episcopal; rec: juggling. Res: 1836 Thousand Oaks Blvd Berkeley 94707 Ofc: Cyclotomics, 2120 Haste Street Berkeley 94704

BERLINER, GABIE, social worker; b. Apr. 5, 1935, Berlin, Germany; came to San Francisco 1936, nat. cit.; parents: Bernhard and Hildegard (Eisig) Berliner; edn: BA, Pomona Coll. 1957; MA, Tchrs. Coll. Columbia Univ. 1958; MSW, UC Berkeley 1966; PhD, Inst. for Clin. Social Wk. 1966; LCSW, lic. clin. soc.

wkr., Calif. 1969. Career: elem. sch. tchr. Castro Valley (Ca.) Sch. Dist., 1958-60; high sch. sci. tchr. Academia La Castellana, Caracas, Venez., also USIS English tchr., 1960-62; researcher Inst. of Metabolic Resrch., Highland Hosp., Oakland 1963-64; psychiatric soc. wkr. Children's Hosp., S.F. 1966-69, Homewood Terr., S.F. 1969-70, Sunny Hills Resdtl. Treatment Svcs., San Anselmo 1970-73; soc. wkr. San Mateo County, 1973--,in Mental Health Div. 1976--, supr. psychiatry residents, psychol. interns soc. wk.; cons. to schs., workshops for div. parents; honors: Alpha Kappa Delta, liberal arts scholarship Columbia Univ.; mem: Fellow Soc. for Clin. Soc. Wk. (bd. 1977-81), Fellow Am. Orthopsychiatric Assn., Founding Fellow Inst. for Clin. Social Wk. 1977 (pres. Friends of Inst. 1983); mem. Internat. Hospitality Center, Community Music Center Bd.; life mem. Sierra Club; patron conservation orgns.; Democrat; rec: music, photog., camping. Res: 1552 Cole St San Francisco 94117 Pvt. Practice: 120 Commonwealth Ave San Francisco 94118 Ofc: San Mateo Co. Mental Health, 45 Southgate Ave. Daly City 94015

BERMAN, BRIAN LEE, consulting systems engineer; b. Dec. 1, 1957, Brooklyn, NY; s. Stuart Stanley and Natalie (Needlemen) B.; edn: AAS, electronics t.v., SUNY, Morrisville, NY 1977; BA in bus. mgmt., Univ. of Redlands, 1983. Career: plant tech. EZ-EM Co. (mfr. med. prods.), Westbury, NY 1978-80; instrumentation engr. Alpha Therapcutic Corp. (mfr. blood plasma prodo.), Los Angeles 1980-83; applications (design) engr. Rank Videometrix, Chatsworth 1983-84; computer consultant self-empl., work in robotics, advanced computers, process control systems; writer on computers and their effects on soc.; past wk. in comml. radio and t.v., produced co. advt. and video promotions; profl. mem. IEEE, ISA, ICM; gen. class radiotel. license, ship radar endorsement. Address: Pax Modular Systems, 1200 Riverside Dr, Ste. 131, Burbank 91506

BERNACCHI, SHAUNA ELAINE, literary agent; b. Feb. 1, 1941, Los Angeles; d. Lou I. and Rosetta (Myers) Sorensen; 1 dau: Vanessa Allison Bernacchi, b. 1968; edn: BA, USC 1962; MA 1964. Career: tech. ed. Missile & Space Sys. Div. McDonnell Douglas Corp. 1967-68; freelance writer & ed.: Architectural Digest, Sherbourne Press, others, Los Angeles 1968-73; ed.- in-chief Ward Ritchie Press, Pasadena 19783-75; co- owner The Idea Factory, Los ANgeles 1975-78; owner Shauna Bernacchi & Assocs., Los Angeles 1980--; mem: Women In Film; Women In Bus.; Achievement Rewards for Coll. Scientists (ARCS) Found., Inc.; Nat. Charity League, Phi Beta Kappa; Phi Kappa Phi; Kappa Kappa Gamma; Episcopalian; rec: skiing, tennis, equestrian. Res: 2125 Patricia Ave Los Angeles 90025

BERNHEIMER, MARTIN, music critic; b. Sept 28, 1936, Munich, Germany; s. Paul and Louise Bernheimer; m. Lucinda Pearson, Sept. 30, 2962; children: MarkRichard, b. 1964, Nora Nicoll, b. 1967; Marina, b. 1969; Erika, b. 1969; edn: BA (honors), Brown Univ. 1958, Munich Cons., 1959, MA music, NYU 1961. Career: tchr. NYU, 1960-62; music staff N.Y. Herald Tribune, 1959-62; contbg. ed. Musical Courier, 1959-62; mng. ed. Philharmonic Hall Pgm. Mag., 1962-65; asst. music ed. Saturday Review, 1962-65; music critic, N.Y.Post, 1964-65; music editor, chief critic Los Angeles Times, 1965--. Awarded Pulitzer Prize for distinguished criticism 1982; mem. faculty USC 1965-81, UCLA 1969-75, Calif. Inst. of the Arts 1975-, CSU Northridge 1977--; contrib. to N.Y.Times, Mus.Quarterly, The Critic, Opera News, Musical Am., Christian Sci Monitor, Opera (Brit.), Abendzeitung (Munich), High Fidelity, Hi-Fi Stereo Rev., The Nation, Commonweal, Aufbau (NY), Der Merker (Vienna), Met. Opera Pgm. Mag., others; writer, liner annotations for RCA Victor, Columbia, London Records; ofc: Times-Mirror Square, Los Angeles 90053.

BERNSTEIN, MYRON ELLIOTT, manufacturing co. executive; b. May 30, 1938, Pitts., Pa.; s. Sol and Thea (Levy) B.; m. Margery Morgan, June 17, 1962; children: Stephen, b. 1965; Jeffrey, b. 1969; edn: BS, Carnegie- Mellon Univ. 1960; MBA, Univ. of Pitts. 1967. Career: asst. supvr. labor rels. Jones & Laughlin Steel Corp., Pitts., Pa. 1960-68; mgr. union contract admin. Allis-Chalmers, Milwaukee, Wisc. 1968-69; lab. rels. rep. Inmont Corp., NY 1969-71; dir. labor rels. 1971-77; mgr. indsl. rels. Kaiser Cement Corp., Oakland 1977-82; v.p. indsl. rels. 1982--; mem: Cement Employers Assn.; US CofC (Labor Rels. Com.); Am. Mining Congress (Labor Rels. Com.); Western Pension Conf.; mil: 1st Lt., USAR, active 1961-62; Republican; B'nai Shalom; rec: tennis, bridge. Res: 204 Clyde Dr Walnut Creek 94598 Ofc: Kaiser Cement Corp., 300 Lakeside Dr Oakland 94612

BERRO, MICHAEL BRUCE, engineer; b. Aug. 23, 1955, Inglewood; s. Marco Leon and Lorraine (Wanger) B.; edn: BS, CSU Northridge 1978; supervisory engr., 1983. Career: field engr. RTS Systems, Inc., No. Hollywood 1974-79; proj. engr., MX Missile, Rockwell, Canoga Park 1979-80; sys. engr. Compact Viedo Sys., Burbank 1980-81; video/ film engr. Ruxton, Ltd., Burbank 1981--; bit player, Flashdance' (the movie), Hollywood 1982-83; pres. Berro Consulting Svc., Monrose, Sylmar 1982--; asst. tchr. electronic music, UCLA 1979; mem: Soc. of Motion Picture & TV Engrs.; Ham Radio Club of W. L.A. (pres. 1971-72); pub. software: Mini-Invaders, 1982; Metamorphs, 1983; design: video/ film computer sychronization, movie War Games', 1983; Democrat; Jewish; rec: computer prgmg., jazz piano, book collecting. Ofc: Ruxton, Ltd., 611 N Orchard Dr Burbank 91506

BERRY, KATHRYN ELIZABETH, newspaper executive; b. Oct. 19, 1942, Long Beach; d. Richard Phillip and Dorothy Kathryn (Horton) Berry; 1 son, Christopher, b. 1972; edn: AA, Long Beach City Coll. 1963, CSU Long Beach 1963-65; Career: secty. nat. advt. dept. Press-Telegram, Long Beach 1962-64, secty. and pub. rels. coordinator, 1964-69, secty to-the Editor, 1969-70, public rels. mgr. 1971--; account exec. Independent Journal, San Rafael 1968-69; secty. to the pres., CSU Long Beach, 1970-71; instr. Newspaper in Education (class), CSULB, summers 1971-; cons. various newspapers throughout US, helping establish Newspaper in Edn. pgms., 1971-. Awards: 1st place, Newspaper in Edn. Pgm. Regional Award, Internat. Newspaper Promotion Assn., 1976; hon. mention NIE from INPA Regional Award, 1975; 1st place, INPA U.S. Competition, Newspaper in Edn., 1976. Mem: Long Beach Civic Light Opera (bd. dirs. 1975-83); L.B. Symphony Assn. (bd. dirs. 1973-83); Psychiatric Clinic for Youth (bd.dirs. 1981-); Art Mus. Assn. (bd.dirs. 1981-83); Women's Div. Long Beach C of C (bd.dirs. 1981-, pres.elect for 1984-85); Forty Niner Athletic Found. (bd.dirs. 1983-); Boy's Clubs of Long Beach (bd.dirs. 1983-); Public Rels Soc of Am/LosAngeles; Sandlarks aux. of Children's Home Soc. Publs.: all teaching material for Press-Telegram Newspaper in Edn. pgm. since 1972 (Teaching KIT, Career Education Book, Primary Activities, Math and the Newspaper, Primary and Intermediate Activity Book for at Home, others); rec: concerts, theatre, needlepoint, collector antiques; res: 2109 Rutgers Ave, Long Beach 90815 ofc: Press-Telegram, 604 Pine Ave. Long Beach 90844.

BERRY, WILLIAM E., JR., travel agency president; b. Aug. 9, 1928, Wichita, Kans.; s. Wm. E. and Mary A. (Green) B.; m. Heather A. Fraser, Oct. 23, 1966; children: Douglas, b. 1969, Jennifer, b. 1971; edn: BA, San Diego St. Univ. 1950; Calif. Adult Sch. tchr. credential (humanities, personnel mgmt., soc. scis.). 1973. Career: personnel adminstr. (civilian), USN 1959-61; adminstrv. asst. Convair Astronautics, 1961-64; tour condr. SITA, 1965-66; mgr. La Mesa Travel Agcy., 1967-75; pres. Berry's World of Travel 1975--; awards: Hall of Champions, Balboa Park; over 300 trophies. Mem. Am. Soc. of Travel Agents (pres. San Diego Chp. 1981-83), La Mesa CofC (bd., v.p. 1981-83); La Mesa Kiwanis Club; mil: cpl. US Army 1952-54, Korean War; Republican; Prot. Res: 8634 Langholm Rd El Cajon 92021 Ofc: Berry's World of Travel 8415 La Mesa Blvd La Mesa 92041

BERTHOLD, ROY LEE, manufacturing company executive; b. Oct. 27, 1927, Olex, Ore.; s. Mart Phillip and Alice Fay (Heath) Berthold; m. June P. Ward, May 31, 1952; 1 child, Dorie Lee, b. 1953; m. 2d. Linda Lee Ulansky, Apr. 14, 1976; edn: BA, Metropolitan Bus. Coll., 1952; engr. stu. San Jose City Coll. 1964-66; USN IBM tng for programmer, 1945-47; Healds Bus. Coll., 1949; career: engrg. apprentice Stephen Adams Mfg., Aurora, Ill.; Tool & Die maker: resrch & devel. programs, Tydeman Machine, Redwood City, space programs, Associated Machine, Santa Clara, Paragon Tool & Die, Pacoima, G.E.Corp. Motor Plant, San Jose; supt./shop foreman Profile Mfg. Co., Belmont 1964-70; v.p./plant mgr. Wiscane Mfg., San Carlos 1970-76; pres., bd. chmn. Berthold Tool & Die (indsl. engrg./mgmt.), Santa Clara 1976--. Honors: profl. highest achievement award, A.M.T., 1981; hon. for contbn. to the Space Pgm. by the Pres. 1968; mem: Moose Lodge (gov.) 1955-, Santa Clara CofC, (bd. mem. Sunnyvale CofC 1949), Santa Clara Better Bus.Bur.; mil: 1945-48, Victory medal; Republican; Methodist; rec: gun collection, restoration. Res: Saratoga Loire Apts., 1395 Saratoga Ave, Apt. 25, San Jose 95129 Ofc: Berthold Tool & Die, 2082B Walsh Ave, Santa Clara 95050.

BESSER, BARRY I., lawyer; b. June 21, 1952, Los Angeles; s.Ben and Arline (Goldbogen) Besser; gr.nephew, impresario Mike Todd; m.Sandra A.Casanova, Feb. 27, 1982; edn.: BS in bus.ad., CSU Northridge 1974, JD, Western State Univ. Coll. of Law 1977. Career: atty. law office Terreri & Pozzi, Santa Ana 1980, law office Ward C. Mikkelson, Orange 1980-82; mem: Am. Bar Assn., Orange Co. Bar Assn., Los Angeles Co. Bar Assn., Orange Co. Trial Lawyers Assn., Nu Beta Epsilon nat. law frat. Volunteered legal svcs. for victims of Anaheim fire (4/21/82); Democrat; Jewish; rec: sports. res: 5825-18 Creekside, Orange 92669. Law Ofc: Barry I. Besser, 5825 Creekside, Ste. 18, Orange 92669.

BETTENHAUSEN, PAUL GERALD, landscape architect; b. May 29, 1956, Red Bank, NJ; s. Paul Gerald and Marilyn Joyce (Stillwagon) B.; m. Jean Nicdao-Gaston, Dec. 14, 1978; edn: BS in landscape arch., summa cum laude, Ohio St. Univ. 1978; grad. stu. arch., UCLA current; Calif. Lic. Landscape Architect 1981. Career: draftsman Peridian Group, Irvine 1978-79; designer Closson and Closson, Orange 1979-80; designer/ project mgr. P.O.D. Inc., Santa Ana 1980--; adv. com. mem./cons. to Calif. State Legis. Energy/ Natural Resources Com.; pvt. cons. to Arch. firms; honors: 4th Place, Univ. of Toledo Centennial Mall Competition 1977, Charles R. Sutton Mem. Scholarship 1977, Am. Soc. of Land. Arch's. Merit Awd. 1978, Annual Conf. for Engs. and Arch's. Awd. of Recogn. 1978, Sigma Lambda Alpha Rho, Phi Kappa Phi; mem: Am. Soc. of Land. Archs., Ohio St. Alumni Assn.; works: West Main St. Design Study, City of Buenaventura 1981; Democrat; United Methodist. Res: 18857 Lister Ln Huntington Beach 92646 Ofc: P.O.D. Inc. 1327 N. Broadway, Santa Ana 92706

BETTERLEY, DONALD ALAN, research mycologist; b. June 17, 1952, Colorado Springs, Colo.; s. Robert and Joan (Snavely;) Betterley; m. Margaret L. McCollough, Sept. 6, 1975; edn: BS, w/highest distinction,Colo. State Univ. 1974; PhD in botany-mycology, UC Berkeley 1981. Career: resrch and teaching asst. UCB, Botany Dept., 1974-80, grad. course instr., 1980; postdoctoral resrch botanist (mycology) w/Dr. O'Neil Ray Collins, UCB, 1980-81; dir. resrch, Research Mycologist, Spawn Mate, Inc., San Jose 1981--; guest lectr. UCB; seminars, lectrs. on fungal genetics, physiology, nutrition and identification; honors: Phi Beta Kappa, 1974; mem: Mycological Soc. of Am., Brit. Mycological Soc., NY Acad of Scis., Internat. Mushroom Soc. for the Tropics, Botanical Soc. of Am., Sigma Xi, Sierra Club, Audubon Soc.; publs: num. arts. in sci.jours.; rec: early & classical music, clarinetist, nordic skier; res: 1626 Curtis St. Berkeley 94702 ofc: Spawn Mate, Inc. 555 N. First St. San Jose 95112.

BETTINGEN, WILLIAM JOHN, III, real estate broker/ developer; b. July 27, 1944, Pasadena; s. William John Jr. and Barbara Ellen (Brown) B.; m. Colleen Morrison, Mar. 17, 1979; children: Erin, b. 1981; edn: BS, USC 1969; R.E. broker, Calif. 1975. Career: broker Grubb & Ellis Comml. Brokerage Co. 1975; currently: pres. John Bettingen Co. Comml. Brokerage; dir. Bettingen- Orbit Devel. Co.; mem: Orange Co. Performing Arts Ctr. (Founders Circle); Newport Harbor Yacht Club; 552 Club; Pasadena Wine & Food Soc.; Internat. Wine & Food Soc.; Phi Kappa Psi; Headmasters Club of Elliott- Pope Prep. Sch.; Republican; Presbyterian; rec: antique & fine art collecting, gardening, skiing. Res: 2308 Pacific Dr Corona del Mar 92625 Ofc: Wm. John Bettingen Co., Inc., 17772 E 17th St, Ste 104, Tustin 92680

BETTIS, CRESTON AMBERSON, retail co. executive; b. Sept. 14, 1932, Quitman, Ark.; s. Jesse Amberson and Nora Ernest (Liles) B.; m. Betty Lynn, Sept. 11, 1953; children: Alan, b. 1959; Catherine, b. 1964. Career: mechanic, James R. Moomjean Cars, Merced 1951-53; mechanic Jack Wallace Garage, Merced 1953-54; mechanic Marasti Motors, Merced 1954-61; owner Bettis Chevron Svc. & Garage, Merced 1961-70; owner/ mgr. Bettis RV Center, Merced 1970--; mem: Fraternal Order of Eagles; Merced Boat Club; Yosemite Sams chpt. the Good Sam Club; rec: camping, travel. Res: 3056 N Trindade Rd Merced 95340 Ofc: Bettis RV Center, 4041 W Ashby Rd Merced 95340

BETTS, BARBARA LANG, lawyer, rancher; b. Apr. 26, 1926, Anaheim, CA; d. W. Harold and Helen (Thompson) Lang; husband, former Calif. state treas.; B.A., Stanford Univ., magna cum laude and Phi Beta Kappa, 1948; LL.B., Calif. Western Univ., formerly Balboa Univ., 1951; m. Bert A. Betts, S.F., July 11, 1962; children: J. Chauncey Hayes, IV, b. 1953; Frederick Prescott Hayes, b. 1955; Roby F. Hayes, b. 1957; Bruce Harold, b. 1966. Career: admitted to Calif. Bar, 1952; U.S. Dist. Ct., Southern and Northern Dists., CA, 1952; U.S. Ct. of Appeals, 9th Circuit, 1952; U.S. Supreme Ct., 1978; partner, law firm Barbara Lang Hayes & Roby F. Hayes 1952-60; city atty., Carlsbad, 1959-63; pvt. law practice, Oceanside, 1952-60, San Diego, 1960--, Sacto., 1962--; rancher 1948-58, 1967--. V.P., W.H. Lang Corp., 1964-70; secty., Internatl. Prod. Assn., 1967--; Isle & Oceans Marinas, Inc., v.p. 1970-80; secty., Margaret M. McCabe, M.D., Inc., 1976--. Mem.: Carlsbad Planning Comm., 1959, v.p.; San Diego Co. Planning Congress. Secty., pub. affairs for S.D. and Imperial Co., 1954, pres. of President's Council S.D. and Imperial Co. and Mexico Soroptimist Internatl., 1958-59, mem., 1952-62. Mem.: Bar Assns: Amer., S.D. Co., Calif. Trial Lawyers; Amer. Judicature Soc.; Natl. Inst. of Municipal Officers, 1959-63; U.S. Supreme Ct. Hist. Soc. Co-author with Bert A. Betts, "A Citizen Answers," 1972. Mem.: CofC, Oceanside, S.D., No. S.D. Co. Assn. Mem.: Traveler's Aid, chmn. 1952-54; AAUW; Bus. and Profl. Women's Club, 1953-62; Calif. Scholarship Fedn. (life); Soroptimist Internatl.; S.D. Hist. Soc.; Fullerton Jr. Asst. League, 1956-66; D.A.R., 1956-64; No. S.D. Co. chpt. for retarded children, dir., 1957-58. Mem.: Dem. State Central Com., 1954-62; co-chmn. 28th Cong. Dist. Dem. Central Com., 1960-62; delegate, Dem. Natl. Conv., 1960. Protestant. Rec.: fishing, hunting. Res.: Betts Ranch, Elverta 95626; Office: 8701 E. Levee Rd., Elverta; 3119 Howard Ave., San Diego 92104.

BETTS, BERT A., former State of California treasurer; b. Aug. 16, 1923, San Diego, CA; s. Bert A., Sr., and Alma (Jorgenson) Betts; ed. San Diego pub. schs.; S.D. State Coll., 1941; B.A., Calif. Western Univ., S.D., 1950; CPA Cert., Nov. 1950; grad., Internatl. Acctg. Soc.; m. Barbara Lang; children: Terry Lou, b. 1946; Linda Sue, b. 1947; Sara Ellen, b. 1949; Bert Alan, b. 1950; Randy Wayne, b. 1952; John Chauncey, b. 1953; Frederick Prescot, b. 1955; LeAnn, b. 1956; Roby F., b. 1957; Bruce Harold, b. 1966. Career: partner, CPA firm, 1950, principal, 1951-59; coll. tchr., acct.-tax., 1950-58; elected State Treas. of Calif., 1958, re-elected 1962-67 (youngest ever elected to a State Constitutional office; also first exec. officer on state level from San Diego Co. in this century). Propr. Betts Financial, Real Estate and Mgmt. Cons. firm, 1967-77; treas., chief exec. officer, Internatl. Prodn. Assocs., 1968-72; trustee, Fidelity Mortgage Investors, 1970-78; dir., Lifetime Communities, Inc., 1978--. B-24 Bomber pilot, Eighth Air Force, USAAF (30 combat missions over Europe), 1941-45, WWII. Awards: 4 Air Medals; Distinguished Flying Cross. Mem.: past 1st v.p., S.D. chpt., Calif. Soc. of CPAs; (past) State Soc. Governmental Acct. Comm.; Amer. Inst. of CPAs; Natl. Assn. of Accts.; Amer. Acct. Assn.; past pres., Lemon Grove Sch. dist. Bd. of Trustees; past pres., Lemon Grove Men's Club; past finance com., S.D. Girl Scouts; citizens adv. coms. to govt. agencies; past treas., S.D. Cerebral Palsy Found.; past v-comdr., Air Force Assn.; past treas., Lemon Grove Lions Club; V.F.W.; Amer. Leion; active in BSA, treas. Cub Pack 106, Sacto.; Internatl. Order of Foresters, past Natl. Assn. of State Auditors, Comptrollers and Treas.; Municipal Forum of NY; (hon.) Calif. Municipal Treasurer's Assn.; pres., Sacto. Co. Amer. Cancer Soc., 1967-68; Beta Alpha Psi; Alpha Kappa Psi, Eagles Lodge, Lemon Grove Masonic Lodge. Democrat, S.D. Co. Dem. Central Comm. Presbyterian. Res.: Betts' Ranch, East Levee Road, Elverta; 441 Sandburg Dr., Sacramento 95819.

BETZ, JAMES ERIC, lawyer; b. 1949, Meadville, Pa.; s. W. James and Margaret M. (Holtzhauser) Betz; m. Marjorie Gora, Apr. 24, 1971; 1 son, James E., Jr., b. 1979; edn: BA in fin., honors, Ind. Univ. 1971; JD, magna cum laude, Calif. Western Sch of Law 1974. Career: admitted to Calif. and Federal Bars 1974; partner law firm Andreasen, Gore, Grosse, Greenman & Betz (spec. in real estate law), Oceanside 1974--; honors: Beta Gamma Sigma (bus.), Blue Key (scholastic), Phi Delta Phi (legal) hon. frats.; author, editl. bd. Law Rev., Cal Western, his law review art. on Constnl. Law cited in one of its decisions by US Supreme Ct. Mem: C. of C. (pres. 1981); bd. dirs. YMCA (treas. 1974); ofcr.

Carlsbad Little League; Lifeline social svcs. pgm. in Vista; Alpha Tau Omega. Catholic, canon lawyer San Luis Rey Mission ch. Adress: 804 Third St., Oceanside 92056.

BEUMER, DELBERT HARRY, stockbroker; b. Jan. 6, 1931, Holland, Indiana; s. Frank Emil and Lydia Clara (Linstrot) B.; m. Marlene Hill, Feb. 27, 1957; children: Judi, 1958; Jeff, b. 1959; Jeanine, b. 1960; Kimberly, b. 1963; edn: Evansville Coll. 1949-51; BBA, mktg., Univ. of Miss. 1953; MBA, corp. fin., Univ. of Wash. 1955; Cert. Fin. Plnr. 1978. Career: data processing, supply & plng., USN 1955-60; spl. asst. to comndr., defense fuel supply ctr., USNR, Cameron Station, Va. 1960--; assoc. v.p./ asst. mgr. Dean Witter Reynolds, Palo Alto 1960--; mem: Peninsula Stock & Bond Club (pres. 1970-71); Naval Reserve Assn.; Grace Lutheran Ch. (pres. 1976); Los Altos Lutheran Ch. (chmn. Bd. of Deacons 1981); mil: Rear Admiral, USNR, 1960--, Joint Svc. Commdn. Medal; Republican; Lutheran; rec: flying, building, gardening. Res: 452 University Ave Los Altos 94022 Ofc: Dean Witter Reynolds, 555 University Ave Palo Alto 94301

BEVENSEE, ROBERT MILLS, research electronics engineer; b. May 9, 1930, Mnpls., Minn.; s. Elwood E. and Marion T. (Trent) B.; m. Mae P., June 4, 1966; children: Mark, b. 1967; Brendan, b 1969; edn: BS, Univ. of Minn. 1952; MS, 1954; EE, MIT 1958; PhD, Stanford Univ. 1962. Career: asst. prof. electrical eng., UC Berkeley 1960-64; elec. engr. Lawrence Livermore Nat. Lab., Livermore 1964--; cons: MB Assocs. of San Ramon 1966-67; LuTech, Inc., Berkeley 1979-80; honors: invited to attend NATO Wrkshp. on Inverse Methods in Electromagnetic Imaging, Germany 1983; mem: Commn. B of URSI; books: Electromagnetic Slow Ware Systems, Wiley 1964; Handbook of Conical Antennas and Scatterers, Gordon & Breach 1973; over 50 tech. arts. for conf. & tech. journs. Res: 128 Irongate Ct Alamo 94507 Ofc: Lawrence Livermore National Lab., L-156, POB 5504 Livermore 94550

BEVERETT, ANDREW JACKSON, real estate broker; b. Feb. 21, 1917, Midland City, AL; s. Andrew J. and Ella L. (Adams) Beverett; B.S., Samford Univ. 1940; MBA, Harvard Univ., 1942; m. Martha Sophia Landgrebe, May 26, 1951; children: Andrew J., III; James Edmund; Faye A. Career: exec. positions in corp. planning and mgmt., United Air Lines, Chicago, 1946-66; sr. mktg. and econ. cons., Mgmt. & Economics Research, Inc., Palo Alto, 1966-71; sr. econ., Stanford Research Inst., Menlo Park, 1971-72; pres., Edy's on the Peninsula Stores, Palo Alto, 1972-78; real estate broker and counselor, Saratoga, 1979--. Active duty, Ensign to Lt., USNR, 1942-46. Mem.: Phi Kappa Phi; Pi Gamma Mu; Toastmasters Club; Amer. Assn. of Realtors. Res.: 19597 Via Monte Dr., Saratoga 95070; Office: Suite A, 12175 Saratoga-Sunnyvale Rd., Saratoga 95070.

BEVILL, HERMAN DELANO, psychiatric technician; b. Feb. 10, 1942, San Jose; s. Herman Thomas and Pauline Nila (Funk) B.; m. Winnie Kemp, May 20, 1970; children: Bradford, b. 1967; Bryan, b. 1971; edn: AA, Porterville Coll. 1969; lic. psychiatric tech.; R.E. broker; fire & casualty ins. broker; life & disability ins. agent; Notary Public. Career: psychiatric tech. Porterville State Hosp. 1964--; mem: Calif. Soc. of Psych. Techs.; Orange Belt Bd. of Realtors; Calif. Assn. Realtors; Nat. Assn. Realtors; Jehovahs Witness; rec: chess. Res: 1043 W Belleview, Apt 2, Porterville 93257

BHAKTA, MAHENDRA DAHYABHAI, fire protection engineer; b. March 6, 1946, Kapura, Gujarat, India; s. Dahyabhai Haribhai and Benaben Dahyabhai Bhakta; m. Gulabben Bhakta, July 16, 1968; chil: Sanjay, b. 1968, Piyush, b. 1974, Rakesh, b. 1975; edn: DME (Dr.S.S.), Gandhi Coll., Surat, India 1967; BSME, Heald Engrg. Coll. 1970; Regis. Profl. Engr. Fire Protection, Calif. Career: with Automatic Sprinkler Corp., 1973-78; motel owner/mgr., Monterey Park 1978-80; engineer Bechtel Power Corp., Norwalk 1980-83, currently self empl. cons. Fire Protection Engr., hd. engr. Design Dept. Mem: Assn. of Fire Protection, Assn. of Eng. & Arch.; works: tchg. through correspondence, design and installation of fire protection in India. rel: J. Patel; rec: volleyball, camping; address: 121 South New Ave. Monterey Park 91754.

BIBEL, DEBRA JAN, medical microbiologist; b. Apr. 6, 1945, San Francisco; d. Philip and Bassya (Maltzer) Bibel; edn: AB, UC Berkeley 1967, PhD 1972; career: bacteriologist Letterman Army Inst. of Resrch, San Francisco 1972-76, microbiologist, 1976-78; instr. Berkeley Community Clinic and Health Project, 1971-75, laboratory cons. 1972-75;lectr. Antioch College/West, San Francisco 1975; lectr. Sch of Pub. Health, UCB 1975; instr. UC Ext.,Berkeley 1977; tech. writer Hoefer Sci. Instruments, San Francisco 1979-80; resrch assoc. Kaiser Found. Resrch Inst., Oakland 1981--; dir. Elie Metchnikoff Meml Lib., Oakland 1977-; awards: USPHS Traineeship, 1967-72; mem: Am. Soc. for Microbiol., AAAS, Fedn. of Am. Scientists, Assn. for Women in Sci., ACLU, Sierra Club; publs: 30 pubs. in med. microbiol. (resrch, commentary and hist.); contbg. columnist (hist.), newsletter of No. Calif. Am. Soc. Microbiology; mil: capt. US Army Med.Service Corps 1972-76, Army Commendation Medal; rec: painting, music, rare books and hist., Asian philosophy; res: 230 Orange St., #6, Oakland 94610 ofc: Dept of Dermatology (Resrch), Univ Calif., San Francisco 94143.

BIBICOFF, HARVEY, financial public relations executive; b. May 21, 1939, NY; s. Irving and Eva (Levine) B.; m. Jacqueline Ruth Marks, Dec. 21, 1964; children: Hillary Sue, b. 1966; Allison Abri, b. 1969; edn: BSBA,3; New York Bar 1963. Career: asst. secty. Uniform Practice Com., Nat. ASsn. of Securities Dealers 1963-65; asst. to pres. Jayark Corp., NY 1966-67; partner Meyer, Bibicoff, Morales & Co., NY 1968-74; v.p. corp. devel. Crown Ind., Inc., Tampa, Fla. 1974-76; pres. Bibicoff & Assocs., Los Angeles 1976--; dir. Swanton Corp., NYC; dir. Jafta Internat., Inc., Vancouver, BC; honors: Assn.

of the US Army awd. 1960; Beta Gamma Sigma; Omicron Delta Kappa; mil: 1st Lt., Infantry 1965-66. Res: 4301 Gayle Dr Tarzana 91356 Ofc: Bibicoff & Assocs., 16530 Ventura Blvd, Pent. Ste., Encino 91436

BICHLMEIER, JOYCE ANNETTE, insurance broker; b. July 1, 1940, Los Angeles; d. Finis Arthur and Albina Frances (Cvikel) Brown; m. Germanus J. Bichlmeier, Feb. 7, 1959; children: Cary John, b. 1959, Terry Edward, b. 1962, Sherrie A., b. 1965; m. 2d. Bruce C. Bottrell, Oct. 16, 1981; desigs: Cert. in Gen. Ins., Ins. Inst. of Am.; CPIW, Cert. Profl. Insurance Woman, Nat. Assn. of Ins. Women. Career: dept. mgr. May Co., L.A. 1955-59; insurance agt. prin., Los Angeles 1962-64, (also life, disability 1964-) Carson 1964-71, Manhattan Bch. 1971-77; majority ptnr./broker J. Bichlmeier Ins. Agcy., Hermosa Beach 1977--; mem. The Profl. Ins. Agents of Calif. and Nev. (chmn. 1983 National Conv.; state v.p. 1982-84; v.p. So. Calif. 1980-81, chartered the San Bernardino /Riverside chpt.; pres. South Bay Chpt. PIA, 1979-80); mem. Nat. Assn. of Ins. Women (pres. South Bay Chpt. 1983-84); Hermosa Beach CofC (pres. 1983); Civil Service Employees Ins. Co. Agents Assn. (ofcr. 1978-80); Independent Ins. Agts. Assn. of the Sout Bay; mem. Nat. Assn. of Female Execs. Inc., Smithsonian Instn., Am. Film Inst.; num. comm. orgns.; recipient recognition awards, Hermosa Bch. CofC, PIA Agt. of the Year 1983, Insurance Woman of Year 1983, YWCA South Bay Woman of Year 1982; Republican (US Senatl. Club, Pres. Task Force); Catholic; rec: bicycling. REs: 1628 Goodman Ave Redondo Beach 90278 Ofc: J. Bichlmeier Ins. Agcy 200 Pier Ave, Ste. 30, POB 929, Hermosa Bch 90254

BIDDLE, JENNY MAY, antique dealer; b. Apr. 26, 1924, Sanora; d. Herman Gustau and Frieda Emma (Sittel) Dehnhardt; m. Paul Biddle, Dec. 20, 1943; children: Renate Lee, b. 1945; Randy Jeffrey, b. 1954; edn: spl. courses incl. French, Spanish, art studies, antiques, voice, travel agt. Career: sales Bullocks, Los Angeles 1943-44; sales I. Magnin & Co., Los Angeles 1944-45; sales Barker Bros., Los Angeles 1945-47; secty. to Paul D. Biddle, Acct., Manhattan Beach 1959-69; owner Caye Cottage Antiques, Redondo Beach 1973--; awards: diploma, Wives of Exec. Tng., Harvard, Mass. 1963; mem: Antiquarians Soc. 1974; Palos Verdes Gemological Soc. 1984; Rotary Anns. (pres.) Redondo Beach CofC; Jobs Daughters; Girl Scouts; Republican; Lutheran; rec: research on antiques, 19th C. book collecting. Res: 250 the Village, Apt 107, Redondo Beach 90289 Ofc: Cape Cottage Antiques, 290 Harbor Dr Redondo Beach 90277

BIDWELL, ROBERT REDDINGTON, JR., lawyer; b. June 20, 1946, Los Angeles; s. Robert Reddington and Katharine Virginia (Kennedy) B.; m. Cynthia Barry, May 19, 1973; children: Emily Pritchett, b. 1974; Cristina Rogers, b. 1976; edn: BA, Stanford Univ. 1969; JD, Glendale Univ. Sch. Law. 1981; atty. Calif. Supreme Ct. 1981. Career: US Peace Corps, Kenya Edn. VI 1969-71; MBA pgm. coord., Pepperdine Univ. Grad. Sch. Bus. & Mgmt., Los Angeles 1972-73; cons. Calicopia Corp. (real estate), Beverly Hills, 1974; dir. Good Earth Op., Pasadena 1974; correctional educator Hacienda-La Puente Unif. Sch. Dist., Los Angeles Co. Jail Sys. 1974-81; atty., pvt. practice; Judge Pro Tem, Pasadena Municipal Ct. 1982-; edn. cons. Elizabeth Fry Ctr., Los Angeles 1978; awards: Appreciation, Pasadena Municipal Ct. 1983, Hacienda-La Puente Unif. Sch. Dist. 1980; spkr., 33rd Internat. Conf., Correctional Educators, NJ 1979; spkr. DAR Assn. Gabriel Valley Awds. 1980; mem: Am., Calif., Los Angeles Co., & Pasadena Bar Assns.; Nkubu Mamba Soccer Club, Kenya; Stanford Alumni Assn.; Stanford Club of L.A. Co.; So. Calif. Minerological Soc.; lectr., African Safari, num. schs., clubs, assns. 1973-77; created 20 hr. math tchg. sys., 1979; Republican; Episcopal; rec: photog., skiing, tennis. Res: 675 Arden Rd Pasadena 91106 Ofc: 30 North Raymond Ave, 6th Flr, Pasadena 91103

BIENATI, LAWRENCE MARIO, grocery chain training executive; b. Mar. 15, 1956, Oakland; s. Frank Sam and Frances Bienati; m. Catherine Coffman, Dec. 6, 1980; edn: BS (I.R.P.A.), CSU Hayward, 1979, MBA, 1980. Career: food clerk, Safeway Stores, Inc. 1973-80, employment rep. 1980-81, director, Training School, 1981--. honors: speaker of the year, No. Calif. Forensic Assn., 1980; winner 10 major awards intercollegiate Speech and Debate; Distinguished Toastmaster award; mem: Toastmasters Internat. (Debate chmn.), BSA, Colombo Club, Sons of Italy (Vallejo), Fratalanza Club (Oakland), Sierra Club; publs: pamphlet: Get That Job (for Rotary Clubs Internat.); mem. Knights of Columbus; rec: backpacking, pub. speaking, woodwork; res: 110 Persimmon Dr. Vallejo 94589 ofc: Safeway Stores, 191-12th St. Oakland 94605.

BIETZ, RALPH L., fermentation engineer, executive; b. Oct. 5, 1953, Sturgis, Mich.; s. Ralph Emerson and Melba Cora (Borgert) B.; m. Deborah Reed, June 23, 1973; children: Gabriel Jackson Reed, b. 1980; Joshua Paul LeeRoy, b. 1982; ednr: BS, Tri State Univ. 1976; fermentation tech. cert., Mass. Inst. of Tech. 1979; cert. for leadership effectiveness tng, Dr. Charles Gorden 1981. Career: fermentation[distillery supvr. J.E. Seagrams & Sons, Lawrenceburg, Ind. 1976-77; fermentation/ proj. engr. Novo Industri A/S, Franklinton, NC 1978-79; prodn. mgr. 1980-81; mgr. enzyme prodn./ pilot plants Hoechst AG, La Jolla 1982--; cons. Burroughs- wellcome 1984, Mycogen 1984; Syntro 1983, Agrhfol 1981, univ. of NC 1980, Enzyme Prodn. Liason to Hoechst Frankfurt, W. Germany 1978-81; Enzyme Prodn. Liason to Novo, Copenhagen, Denmark 1982-; honors: Outstanding Young Men In Am., Jaycees 1981; mem: Am. Chem. Soc.; AM. Soc. for Microbiology; San Diego Co. Humane Soc.; SPCA; Bethleham Lutheran Ch.; works: num. fermentation & recovery process improvements for enzymes, immunoproteins & antibiotics; Biotech. Photo. Exhibitor, European Clinical Symposium, LIEPS16, E. Germany 1983; coeditor: Custom Fermentation Ad- Cal Biochem Behring Corp, Science Mag., Vol. 219, Feb. 1983; Republican; Lutheran; rec: photog., computer prgmg., travel. Res: 1628 Olmeda St Encinitas 92024 Ofc: Hoechst AG, 10933 N Torrey Pines Rd La Jolla 92037

BIGING, GREGORY SCOTT, educator; b. Nov. 25, 1952, Lake Geneva, Wisc.; s. Elmer Gustsav and Ann Magdalena (Berger) B.; m. Mary Picetti, Feb. 12, 1983; edn: BS Math., Univ. of Wisc.-Madison 1973, MS Forestry, 1975, PhD Forestry, 1978. Career: asst. prof. of forest biometrics, Dept. of Forestry and Resource Mgmt., UC Berkeley 1978--; cons. to US Dept. of Justice, part of 3-man team on design, analysis of inventory for the Redwood Nat. Park, Arcata, Ca. 1980-84; mem: Soc. of Am. Foresters, Phi Kappa Phi, Soc. of Xi Sigma Pi (Alpha Nu sec./fiscal agt. 1973), Am. Statistical Assn.; publs: sci. reports, papers, jour. articles in Forest Sci., Canadian J. of Forest Research; Lutheran; rec: tennis, raquetball, computer pgmmg. Res: 3 Admiral Dr No. 470, Emeryville 94608 Ofc: UCB, 213 Mulford Hall Berkeley 94720

BIKHAZI, LEYLA ABU-HAYDAR, psychotherapist- consultant; b. May 31, 1938, Hammana, Lebanon, nat. 1961; parents: Isaac S. Abu-Haydar (honored for lifetime svc. as chief acct., British Govt. in Anglo- Egyptian Sudan) and Saada N. Abu-Haydar; First Cousin: Dr. Nagib Abu-Haydar, physician and ex- prime minister of Edn., presently mayor in Lebanon; First Cousin: Munir Abu- Haydar and Nicholar Haddad, Army phsicians & surgeons, British Govt., Anglo- Egyptian Sudan; sev. medals of hon.; div.; children: Nadim B., b. 1967; Paul H., b. 1969; edn: MSW, USC 1960. Career: U.S. Info. Svc. Am. Embassy, Beirut, Lebanon 1956-58; instr. psychiatric & med. soc. wrk. Am. Univ., Beirut 1962-64; Dept. of A.F. Okinawa, Ryukyu Islands, sr. psych. soc. wkr. cons. staff, Whittier Hosp. 1979; fellow, Soc. for Clinical Soc. Wrk. 1977; Am. Assn. of Sex Educators Counselors & Therapists 1979; Internat. Platform Assn. 1982; Town Hall of Calif. 1982; Who's Who of Calif. Exec. Women 1983; Republican. Res: 7760 S Vale Dr Whittier 90602

BILLINGS, CHRISTINA GERASIMOS, investigations co. president; b. Mar. 1935, Monroe, Mich.; d. Neil Lane and Lucille (Gerasimos) Billings; grandau. of Theodore M. Gerasimos, founder of Detroit Greek Town; edn: pvt. stu. (opera) with Marika Palaeste in Athens, Greece; degree in law, Blackstone Sch of Law 1973; lic. (A-6488-C) Investigator. Career: current pres. Nickris World Movie Corp., and mgr. Nickris Investigations, Beverly Hills; profl. recording artist for L B Ranch Records, & Lucille Billings Music Co. during 1950s, Chgo.; concert pianist and organist, debut (4/19/59) in Scotish Rite Auditorium, Masonic Temple, Detroit, Mich.; founder/v.p. Theodore M. Gerasimos Memorial Greek Aged Home, Detroit, Mich.; author (ghost writer): My Father's Imposter, and Why I Love the Greek People; Republican; Greek Orthodox; rec: equestrian, tng. Spitz dogs, tennis. Ofc: Nickris World Movie Corp. 223 S. Beverly Dr, Ste. 201, Beverly Hills 90212

BILLINGY, ZELDA EVA, physician; b. June 8, 1950, Guaico, Trinidad, W.I.; d. Theophilus Thaddeus and Lydia (Allman) Billingy; edn: BA (French), Loma Linda Univ. 1973; MD, 1977; OB/Gyn. residency, White Memorial Hosp., 1977-81. Career: pvt. practice obstetrics & gynecology, Monterey Park 1981--; staff White Meml. Hosp., Santa Marta Hosp. (Utilization Rev. Com., Infection Control Com., part-time tchg. 1981), chief of OB/Gyn Dept. Monterey Park Hosp.; mem: Jr. Fellow Am. Coll. of OB/GYN, Am. Assn. of Byn. Laparoscopist (state Dr's Adv. Com.); Black Alumnae Assn. of Loma Linda, Am. Medical Womens Assn.; 7th-Day Adventist; rec: opera (auditioned for Met. Opera 1980). REs: 2401 S. Hacienda Blvd, J 136, Hacienda Hts 91745 Ofc: Zelda E. Billingy MD Inc., 850 S. Atlantic Blvd Monterrey Park 91754

BILLUPS, NANCY JO, computer software instructor; b. June 14, 1942, Hampton, Va.; d. Jack Leonard and Mary Lee (Rogers) Flynn; div.; edn: stu. CSU Long Beach 1961, Skyline Comm. Coll. 1983-. Career: with Xerox Corp., Los Angeles and San Francisco 1972--: instr., Education Dept., S.F. 1979-, Western Region instr./ coordinator, 1984-; provide tng. and tech. support for software end-users, extensive group teaching customer sites; mem. Nat. Assn. for Female Execs., Palomares Figure Skating Club, US Figure Skating Assn., Womens Sports Found.; participant Adult Level Figure Skating Competitions: silver medal (2d), Chabot Skate 1979, 1980; 1st Pl., Crystal Springs Jubilee 1980; Democrat; Prot. Res: 221 Village Wy, So. San Francisco 94080 Ofc: Xerox Computer Services, 343 Allerton Ave So. San Francisco 94080

BILOWITZ, LOUIS I., pension plan consultant; b. April 22, 1947, NY, NY; s. Herman and Arline (Ochs) B.; m. M. Carol Lingo, Aug. 15, 1949; 1 child, Kyle, b. 1976; edn: BA, Columbia Univ. 1969. Career: pres. Corporate Pensions Insurance Services, Inc., Los Angeles 1983--; partner Pension Architects, Inc., L.A. 1983--; partner Insurance Architects, Insurance Agency. Inc., L.A. 1983--; guest lectr. on Pension Planning. Awards: Top of the Table, 1983; leading pension prod. in Am., 1982, 83, and leading overall prod. in Am., 1983, General American Life. Mem: Am. Youth Soccer Assn. coach; UCLA Sustaining Donor, Chancellor's Assocs., donor million dollar ins. policy to UCLA. Publs: art. in life ins. selling, 1982; Republican; rec: athletics, music. res: 5000 Palm Dr. La Canada 91011. ofc: Corp. Pensions Ins. Svcs Inc. 716 S. Olive St., 2nd flr. Los Angeles 90014.

BINARD, HELEN ANN, real estate broker, investor; b. May 9, 1913, Cedar Rapids, Nebr.; d. Joseph Bernard and Gertrude Elizabeth (Welding) Liekhus; edn: bus., St. Charles Acad., Stratton, Colo. 1931-32, A.A., UCLA, 1938; spl. courses, Pasadena City Coll.; m. Donatus Ezsbon Binard, 1938, dec. 1972; children: William, b. 1939, David, b. 1940, Michael, b. 1950; career: Escrow Officer, Pasadena Escrow Co., Pasadena 1938-42; prin. real estate brokerage bus., Helen A. Binard, Altadena, 1953--; semi-profl. singer, various choirs; modeling

part-time 1936-38; mem: (life) UCLA Alumni Assn.; Phrateres Council, UCLA, Bannister chpt. pres. 1937; Theta Phi Alpha sor., pres. elect 1937; Los Angeles Blue Book, 1976-. Publs: art. in Better Homes & Gardens mag., 1952; Republican; Catholic; rec: singing, dancing. Res: 1848 E. Loma Alta Dr., Altadena 91001; ofc: Helen A. Binard, 2509 N. Lake Ave, Altadena 91001.

BINEGAR, GWENDOLYN ANN, social worker; b. Sept. 23, 1924, Phoenix, Ariz.; s. Glenn Marvin and Mary Lenore (Cartwright) Redington; m. Lewis Bert Binegar, Nov. 2, 1951; children: Glen, b. 1952; Birne, b. 1954; William, b. 1957; Alan, b. 1959; edn: BS, Iowa St. Univ. 1948; MSS, Bryn Mawr 1967; lic. clin. soc. wkr., Calif. 1974; acad. of cert. soc. wkrs. 1969. Career: psychiatric soc. wkr. Child Study Inst., Bryn Mawr Coll. 1967-71; sr. soc. wkr. Ruth Sch. for Girls, Seattle, Wash. 172; med. soc. wkr. Casa Colina Hosp., Pomona 1973-74; supvg. counselor San Gabriel Valley Regl. Ctr., Pomona 1975-79; pgm. mgr. the six Los Angeles Co. Regl. Ctrs. High Risk Infant Projs., San Gabriel Valley Regl. Ctr. 1979; asst. chief case mgmt. Svcs., San Diego Regl. Ctr. 1979-80; chief 1981--; presentation chprsn. AAMD Regl. 11, So. Div.; mem. Nat. Presentations Com., AAMD; Assn. of Regl. Ctr. Agencies Prevention Com.; mem: SGV Devel. Disabilities Council; AAMD; NASW; Statewide Chief Counselors; West Covina YWCA; Republican; Presbyterian; rec: swimming, rug hooking. Res: 28809 Lilac Rd Valley Ctr 92082 Ofc: San Diego Regional Center, 4355 Ruffin Rd, Ste 205, San Diego 92123

BIRD, CHARLES ALBERT, lawyer; b. July 1, 1947, Stockton; s. Donald Gladstone and Elizabeth Clara (Jongeneel) B.; m. Charlotte Soeters, June 28, 1969; edn: BA, UC Davis, 1969, JD, 1973; admitted Calif. State Bar 1973. Career: law clerk, Hon.(now US Circuit Judge) Robert Boochever, Supreme Ct. of Alaska, Juneau 1973-74; assoc. Luce, Forward, Hamilton & Scripps, of San Diego 1974-79, partner 1980--. Dir. The Defenders Orgn. (non-profit corps. adm. legal representation of indigents accused of crime);; dir. San Diego Vol. Lawyer Pgm. Honors: UC Davis Law Rev.(Issue Ed.), Moot Court Bd., Nat. Moot Ct. Team. Mem: San Diego Co. Bar Assn. (dir., secty.); Calif. State Bar (exec. com. Real Prop. Sect.). Publs: arts., Calif. Real Property News (1981), Calif. Real Property Jour. (1983). Democrat. Episcopal. rec: wilderness travel. res: 4182 Ingalls, San Diego 92103. ofc: Luce, Forward, Hamilton & Scripps, 110 West A St, Ste.1700, San Diego 92101.

BIRGEL, ANDREAS, JR., lawyer; b. Aug. 19, 1943, Semlin, Yugoslavia, nat. 1946; s. Andreas and Franciska (Dornstaedter) Birgel; m. Maria Schumacher, Nov. 11, 1967; chil: Stephen, b. 1968, Jennifer, b. 1970, Monika, b. 1975, Rebecca, b. 1981; edn: BS, CSU Los Angeles 1966; JD, Univ. of San Fernando Coll. of Law, 1976. ird Career: with Occidental Ins. Co. 1963-65; intern/sr. spl. investigator Dept. Alcoholic Beverage Control, 1965-7; lawyer, sole practitioner 1977--, of counsel to in excess of 50 business corps. Mem: Phi Sigma Kappa frat. 1962-; State Bar of Calif. 1977-; Am. Bar Assn. 1977-81; Los Angeles Co. (1977-), Beverly Hills (1977-80) Bar Assns.; BSA merit badge counselor; mil: sgt. NG 1963-9; Catholic; rec: tennis, swim; res: 20047 Vintage St Chatsworth 91311 ofc: 15250 Ventura Blvd Ste.604, Sherman Oaks 91403.

BIRTCIL, ROBERT FRANKLIN, JR., dentist/educator; b. Mar. 27, 1942, Chico; s. Robt. F. and Margaret Watson (Smoots) B., Sr.; m. Dolores M., Mar. 29, 1981; 1 dau., Lindsay, b. 1982; edn: UC Berkeley 1960-2, DDS, UC San Francisco 1967. Career: dental ofcr. with USN and USMC, 1967-70; pvt. practice, Berkeley 1970--; assoc. clin. prof. of restorative dentistry, UCSF, half-time, and dir. Clin. Gold Foil and Amalgam Pgms, UCSF; dir. Kensington Comm. Service Dist., 1976-7; honors: Omicron Kappa Epsilon, Pierre Fauchard Acad., Am. Acad. of Gold Foil Oprs., Acad. of Operative Dentistry; fellowships: Acad. of Gen. Dentistry, Acad. of Dentistry Internat., Internat. Coll. of Dentists, Am. Coll. of Dentists; mem. Am., Calif. Dental Assns., Berkeley Dental Soc.; mil: served to capt. USNR 1970-, decorated Bronze Star, Purple Heart, 14 Vietnam combat awards; Republican; Methodist; rec: classical music, sports. Ofc: 296 Arlington Ave Kensington 94707

BISCONE, JOSEPH GREGORY, III, financial executive; b. May 12, 1950, NY; s. Joseph Gregory Jr. and Eleanor F. (Tomaszewski) B.; edn: psychology, San Diego St. Univ. 1975. Career: pres. Galleon Home Loan, Inc., San Diego; real estate developer; mem: Rep. President's Task Force; mil: Lt., USN; Republican; Christian. Res: 1875 Glenridge Rd Escondido 92027 Ofc: Galleon Home Loan, Inc., 3737 Camino Del Rio S, Ste 403, San Diego 92108

BISGAARD, EDWARD LAWRENCE, mutual fund executive/CPA; b. July 26, 1946, El Centro; s. Edward Lawrence and Gail (Chambers) B. Sr.; edn: BS, CalPoly, Pomona 1971. career: senior acct. Arthur Young & Co., Los Angeles 1971-74; controller King Internat. Corp., Beverly Hills 1975-78; asst. treas. of seven mutual funds managed by Capital Research & Mgmt. Co., Los Angeles 1979-82, vice pres. Business Mgmt. Div., Capital Research &: Mgmt. Co., L.A. 1982--. mem: AICPA, Calif. CPA Soc., Toastmasters; Republican; res: 13802 Northwest Passage #206, Marina Del Rey 90292. ofc: Capital Research & Mgmt. Co., 333 So. Hope St. Los Angeles 90071.

BISH, JAMES MICHAEL, insurance broker; b. Aug. 31, 1947, Washington DC; s. Melvin James and Ethel Nadine (Young) B.; edn: BA, UC Irvine 1969; Cert. Insurance Cons., Orange Coast Coll. 1973; Chartered Life Underwriter, The Am. Coll. 1983; Enrolled Agt., IRS. Career: agt. assoc. with Farmers Ins. Group of Cos.,1968-: currently independent contr. agt./owner Mike Bish Ent., ins. and tax practice, Los Alamitos; honors: Career Club 1972, Farmers Ins. Gp. of Cos.; mem: Nat. Assn. of Life Underwriters, Am. Soc. of Cert. Ins. Consultants (treas. 1973-74), Gamma Iota Sigma, The Am. Soc. of Chartered Life Underwriters; Libertarian; So. Baptist; rec: travel, computers, photog.

Res: 8732 Jennrich Ave Westminster 92683 Ofc: Mike Bish Enterprises, POB 246, 10900 Los Alamitos Blvd Ste. 141, Los Alamitos 90720

BITTIKOFER, FREDERICK CARL, physician-psychiatrist; b. March 28, 1950, Ft. Belvoir, Va.; s. Myron Richard and Arleen Augusta (Krueger) Bittokofer; m. Gurbakhash, Sept. 1, 1973; 2 sons, Steven Carl, b. 1981, Alan Frederick, b. 1982; edn: CSC Sacramento 1968-9; BS in zool., high honors, UC Davis 1972; MD, Northwestern Univ. Med. Sch., 1976. Career: founded a Psychiatric Crisis and Consultation-Liason Service in a large urban area (Hayward) hosp., 1979; staff psychiatrist The Permanente Medical Gp., Hayward, 1979, coordinator 1980, sr. physician 1982--, and subchief Adult Psychiatric Svces. 1983--; KPMC Pharmacy and Therapeutics Com. 1982-3, Physicians Hlth. Adv. Com. 1983-, KPMC Res./Trainee Tng. Com. for Psychiatry 1983-. Honors: Who's Who in Am. High Schs., Bank of Am. Achievement Award, math., 1968; Phi Kappa Phi, UCD, 1971; Sacto. Lung Assn. Scholarship Awd. for original resrch, 1973; Falk Fellowship, Am. Psychiat. Assn., 1977; chief res./pres. Residents' Assn., San Mateo Co. Mental Hlth Svcs, 1978. Mem: Am. Psychiatric Assn. (com. Comprehensive Hlth Plnng. 1977-9); NCPS; Calif. Med. Assn.; East Bay PSRO (E. Bay Cancer Pgm.1981-2); mem. Hayward Police Athletic League, Highland Homeowners Assn. Num. profl. presentations, publs. Republican. rec: phys. fitness, comparative philos./rels. res:3594 Sentinel Ct. Hayward 94542. ofc: The Permanente Med. Gp. 27400 Hesperian Bl. Hayward 94545.

BJORKLUND, ALAN ROGER, aerospace co. executive;b. Dec. 2, 1933, Rockford, Ill.; s. Stanley Alexander and Alice Victoria (Pearson) Bjorklund; m. Marguerite Farese, Apr. 13, 1974; chil: Karen, b. 1956, Laura, b. 1961, Marcus, b. 1963, Lynda, b. 1969, Kristie, b. 1975; edn: BS, Northwestern Univ. 1955. Lic. Profl. Engr., Calif., Canada; Calif. Real Estate Lic. Career: with Merrill Lynch, Chgo. 1955-6; mfg. engr. Rockwell Int'l, Downey 1956-7; plant engr. Ryan Aeronautical, Torrance 1957-9; mfg. engr. Texas Instruments, Dallas 1959-61; with Rockwell Int'l., 1962--: mfg. engr. Space Div. (1962-5), supr. indsl. engrg., chief adminstr. Space Div. Nat. Space Tech. Labs, Mich. (1965-8), mgr. Opns. Planning & Control/mgr. Adminstrn. Space Div. Kennedy Space Center, Fla. (1968-73), mgr. indsl. engrg. Space Div., Downey (1973-6), dir. facilities & indsl engrg. Rocketdyne Div., Canoga Park (1976-82), dir. facilities planning and requirements analysis Corporate Ofcs. Western Region, El Segundo 1982--. Awards: for profl. achievement: L.A. Council of Engrs. and Scientists, 1981; Inst. for Adv. of Engrg., 1980; Nat.& Calif. Socs. Profl. Engrs. (jointly) 1980; ASM 1978-9; Rocketdyne President's awd. 1976; others. Chmn. W. Metal & Tool Conf. & Expo., 1979, contbr. tech. papers 1978, 81, chmn. Internat. Day (1980,81) WESTEC, Los Angeles; past mem. City Planning & Zoning Commns. in Long Beach, Mi., Cocoa Bch, Fla.; Mem: Fellow Inst. for Adv. of Engrg., sr. mem. Am. Inst. of Indsl. Engrs., Am. Inst. of Plant Engrg., sr. mem. Soc. Mfg. Engrs., Assn. of Energy Engrs., Nat. Mgt. Assn., Triangle Engrg. frat. alumni, AF Assn., Northwestern Univ. Alumni Assn., So. Bay Bd. of Realtors, Optimists Int'l. Mil: 2d lt. USAFR 1955. Republican. Episcopal. rec. travel, deep seafishing. res: 3012 Poinsettia Ave Manhattan Bch 90266. ofc: Rockwell Int'l. 2230 E. Imperial Hwy. El Segundo 90245.

BJORKLUND, CATHE LYNN, retail clothing chain president; b. July 18, 1945, Portland, Ore.; d. Ralph Kenneth and Jeanne (Closson) B.; 1 child, Brit Kirsten, b. Apr. 26, 1975; edn: BA, Stanford Univ. 1967; elem. edn., UC Irvine 1971-72; grad. pgm. psych. Cal State Bksfld. 1975-76; Calif. Tchg. Cred. 1971. Career: owner/pres. of Up Your Alley Inc., a chain of womens discount clothing stores, 1977--; past copywriter, actor in TV commls. for local TV station in Bakersfield, 1975-77; mem. profl. dance troupe: Young Audiences, 1975-77; tchr. Santa Ana Sch. Dist. 1970-74; advt. agcy. copywriter Zoran and Assocs., Newport Beach and Hal Lawrence Inc., Palo Alto, 1969-71; pub. rels. dir. Recreation Ctr. for the Handicapped, San Francisco 1969; reporter San Jose Mercury News, 1967-68; awards: finalist Mademoiselle mag. Guest Editor Contest, 1966, 1967; best journalist, USC Journalism Day; 2d Pl. Elks Leadership So. Calif.; mem. Charter 100 of San Diego, San Diego Zoological Soc.; Republican; Episcopal; rec: travel, modern dance, writing. Res: 14256 Minorca Cove Del Mar 92014 Ofc: Up Your Alley, 7717 Fay Ave La Jolla 92037

BLACHER, JOAN HELEN, educational administrator; b. Aug. 10, 1928, Los Angeles; d. Albert Scribner and Isabel Marriott (Heinold) Oakholt; m. Norman Blacher, July 27, 1973; chil: (stepson) Eric, b. 1952, Mark, b. 1954, Steven, b. 1954; edn: BA, UC Berkeley 1950, MSEd., USC 1971, PhD, USC, 1981; Lic. Marriage, Family, Child Counselor, Calif. 1982. Career: elem. school tchr.,L.A. Unified Sch. Dist., 1962-71; school psychologist, L.A. Unified Sch. Dist. 1971-2, 1973-4, Pasadena Unified Sch. Dist. 1972-3, Ventura Co. Supt. Schs., 1974-9; principal, Spl. Classes, Ventura Co. Supt. Schs., 1979--; part-time instr. Grad. Sch. of Edn., Calif. Lutheran Coll., 1976, 1981, La Verne Coll. 1981. Mem: Phi Delta Kappa, Delta Kappa Gamma (pres. 1982-4), Calif. Assn. of School Psychologists (co-ch. pgm. State Conv. 1980), Ventura Co. Assn. Sch. Psych. (bd. 1979-82, pres. 1982-3), ACSA; mem. Soroptomists Intl, Chi Omega Sor. 1948-50; Republican; Presbyterian; rec: tennis, concerts, walking; res: 6170 Balcom Cyn Rd. Moorpark 93021. ofc: Ventura Co. Supt. of Schs. 5190 Loma Vista Rd. Ventura 93003.

BLACK, CAREN LEA, musical theatre director; b. Jan. 11, 1984, Sterling, Ill.; d. Leslie L. and Cathryn M. (Heller) B.; m. Russell Stemple, Nov. 7, 1982; edn: B.Music, Northwestern Univ. 1970; MA, 1972; music cert., Paris Am. Acad. 1968; dance cert., Paris Am. Acad. 1969. Career: founder/ dir. Creative Arts Workshop, Danville 1975-77; founder/ dir. Contra Costa Children's Repertory Co., Inc., Danville active, 1975-80, sabbatical status, 1980--; advr. Calif. Youth Teatre, Los Angeles 1980-84; currently, exec. asst. Decade Prodns., Los Angeles; mem: Contra Costa Nat. Orgn. for Women; works: Cherubim, a new musical, 1978; Cherubim VS Seraphim, a new musical, 1979; 16 pub. songs; Democrat; rec: parapsychology. Res: 1734 Benedict Canyon Dr Beverly Hills 90210 Ofc: Decade Productions, 10224 Charing Cross Rd Los Angeles 90024

BLACK, CLAUDIA ANN, author, lecturer, social worker; b. Oct. 26, 1951, Bremerton, Wash.; d. Wilmer Dale and Leona Evan (Foss) Clark; edn: BA, Univ. of Wash. 1973, MSW, 1977. Career: family counselor ARK, Lutheran Family & Child Service, Seattle 1973-76; social worker Careunit, Canoga Park, Ca. 1977-79; family pgm. coordinator Advanced Hlth Systems, Irvine 1980-82; pvt. practice psychotherapist/founder, pres. A.C.T. (Alcoholism, Children, Therapy), Laguna Niguel 1982--; cons./tchr. UCLA cont. ed. 1980-3, Rutgers Summer Sch. 1980, Univ. of Utah Summer Sch. 1981, 83, The Citadel 1983, Worldwide Alcohol & Drug Conf. Army 1981, E. Maine Med. Ctr. 1982,Eisenhower Med. Ctr. 1982,83. Mem: Nat. Assn. Children of Alcoholics (v.ch.); CAREAGE (adv. bd.); UCLA Resrch Ctr. (fmr. bd. mem.); Assn. Labor Mgmt. of Alcohol Consultants & Alcoholism. Author: (books) It Will Never Happen To Me (1982), My Dad Loves Me, My Dad Has a Disease (1979); (film) Children of Denial (1983); num. mag. arts. Democrat. Prot. rec: water sports, gym, running. address: 31791 National Park Drive, Laguna Niguel 92677.

BLACK, CRAIG CALL, museum director; b. May 28, 1932, Peking, China, (Am. parents); s. Arthur Proctor and Mary (Nichols) B.; m. Constance E. Hockenberry, May 23, 1967; children: Lorna Varn, b. 1960; Christopher Arthur, b. 1973; edn: AB, cum laude, Amherst Coll. 1954e; MA, 1957; PhD, Harvard Univ. 1962. Career: asst. curator vertebrate fossils, Carnegie Mus. of Nat. Hist. 1960-62; curator 1962-70; assoc. prof. Dept. Systematics & Ecology, Univ. of Kansas 1970-72; dir. mus./ prof. geoscis., Texas Tech. Univ. 1972-75; dir. Carnegie Mus. of Nat. Hist. 1975-82; dir. Los Angeles Co. Mus. of Nat. Hist. 1982--; adj. prof. Univ. of Colo. Mus.; adj. prof./ grad. faculty in athropology & earth scis., Univ. of Pittsburgh; co- dir. of Mus. Mgmt. Inst., UC Berkeley; mem: Am. Soc. of Mammalogists; Soc. for Study of Evolution; fellow, Geological Soc. of Am.; Paleontological Assn.; Paleontological Soc.; Soc. of Vert. Paleo.; Sigma Xi; fellw. Linnean Soc. of London; Am. Assn. of Mus.; Assn. of Sci. Mus. Dirs.; Inst. Human Origins; Phi Gamma Delta, Cosmos Club, Wash. DC; Rolling Rock Slub; Ligonier, PA; The Explorers Club, NY. Res: 777 S Windsor Blvd Los Angeles 90005 Ofc: 900 Exposition Blvd Los Angeles 90007

BLACK, (GEOFFREY) RICHARD, financial planner; b. Jan. 9, 1943, Chgo.; s. Abraham and Constance B. (Koffski) B.; m. Mary Ann Kinsella, Sept. 18, 1976; edn: AA, Beloit Coll. 1964; MA, CSU Long Beach 1969. Career: casewkr. Arthur J. Audy Home for Children, Chgo. 1968-70; biostatistician/ psychobiol. resrch. Newport Pharmaceuticals, Newport Beach, Ca. 1970-71, biomedical research consultant, Newport Bch. 1974-76; v.p. Inst. for Biol. Research and Devel., Newport Beach 1976; life insurance agt., Irvine 1977-, comprehensive fin. planning, 1979-, founder/pres. Mabco Fin. Services (personal fin. plnng.), Irvine 1983--; mem. Internat. Assn. for Fin. Plnng., Nat. Assn. Life Underwriters, Orange Co. Performing Arts Ctr. Stage Door Chpt.; rec: tennis, skiing, fishing. Ofc: Mabco Financial Services, 157 Rockview Irvine 92715

BLACK, HUBERT PERRY, college president; b. Aug. 10, 1926, Birmingham AL; s. W.L. and Vera (Brannon) B.; m. Ulina Burell, May 13, 1945; children: Hubert Jr., b. 1947; David, b. 1949; edn: Lee Coll. 1949-50; BS, Jacksonville St. 1953; M.Edn., Univ. of Chattanooga 1956; Ed.D., Univ. of Tenn. 1965. Career: dean of students/ prof. of edn. Lee Coll., Cleveland, Tenn. 1954-68; dean of students Chesapeake Comm. Coll., Wye Mills, Md. 1968-69; dean of edn. Lee Coll., Cleveland, Tenn. 1969-75; dir./ chief exec. Troy State Univ., Bay Minette, Ala. x975-80; pres. West Coast Christian Coll., Fresno 1980--; conv. spkr., profl. and denominational gps.; awards: Lifetime PTA; mem: Assn. of Tchr. Educators; Ala. ATE (pres. 1974-75); NEA; AAHE; Optimist; Rotary; works: Religious and Philosophical Fds. of Education, 1967; Philosophy, the Quest for Meaning, 1970; mil: US Army Paratroopers 1944-46, Pacific Theatre; Democrat; Ch. of God; rec: golf, spectator sports, walking. Res: 6387 N 10th, Fresno 93710 Ofc: West Coast Christian Coll., 6901 N Maple Fresno 93710

BLACK, RONALD JAMES, real estate development co. president; b. Sept. 7, 1946, Los Angeles; s. John Erwin and Carol Lyn (Morgan) Black; m. Karen Vasulka, June 16, 1973; 1 son, Todd Anthony, b. 1976; edn: undergrad. stu. CSU Northridge, UCLA, and CSULA; BA, USC 1968. Career: bus. servs. rep. UCB, Los Angeles, 1969-71; mktg. dir. Western Bankcorp., L.A. 1971-72; asst. v.p. Lincoln Bank, Van Nuys 1972; reg. bus. devel. rep. Union Bank, Beverly Hills 1973-75; real estate devel., 1975-, pres. R.J.B. Unlmtd. Inc. (design, constrn., mktg. custom homes, condos), 1977--. awards: Pi Sigma Alpha, Blackstonian, United Crusade outstanding svc. awd. 1971; mem: USC Gen. Alumni Assn. (life); founding pres. Univ. Conservative Forum at USC, 1967; charter mem. Republican Presdtl. Task Force; mem. Joint Presdtl./Congl. Steering Com.; spl. advisor, US Congl. Advisory Bd.; mem. Repub. Nat. Com.; recipient Medal of Merit; mil: intell. analyst, Psychological Opns., USAR 1968-74; Methodist; rec: skiing, travel; res: 2249 E. Chevy Chase Dr. Glendale 91206.

BLACKWELL, VERLIE ALLEN, insurance agency executive; b. Sept. 10, 1921, Piedmont, Mo.; dd. Luther Meridy and Annie Bell (Faulkner) Allen; m. William Toney Blackwell, Apr. 30, 1940; children: Reginald, b. 1941; Lee, b. 1945; edn: acctg., Nat. Assn. of Accounts 1957; ins. agent, Calif. Career: bus. mgr. Mead Plymouth Auto Sales 1949-63; mgr. Southern Baptist Credit Union

1963-81; pres. Blackwell Financial Management 1965--; co- owner/ bus. mgr. Blackwell Ins. Agency 1964--; awards: Area Gov. of Yr., Teastmasters, Founders Dist. 1982-83; Proficient Acct. Awd., Chrysler Corp. Dealership Awd. 1961-62; mem: Profl. Ins. Agents Assn.; Inland Soc. of Tax Cons.; Toastmasters; Republican; Baptist; rec: choir singing. Res: 14612 Danborough Rd Tustin 92680 Ofc: 11088 Trask Ave, Ste 100, Garden Grove 92643

BLAGEN, HOWARD WOODWORTH, real estate broker; b. Aug. 1, 1913, Hoqulam, Wash.; s. Frank Nelson and Helen Minerva (Woodworth) B.; m. Ruth M. Warren, Oct. 21, 1933 (dec. 1952); children: Patricia (Ward); Nels J.; Valerie (Barden); m. 2d. Florence E. Casey, Mar. 6, 1954; edn: C.E., Poly. Coll. Engring., Oakland 1935; R.E. broker, Calif.; Profl. Forester, Calif. Career: logging engr. Davies- Johnson Lumber Co., Calpine 1935-36; gen. sales mgr. 1937-40; asst. sales mgr. Tarter, Webster & Johnson, San Francisco 1943-54; v.p. sawmill ops. 1955-74; cons. Internat. Forest Prods., Inc., Pomona 1974; currently, broker/ owner Howard Blagen Realty, Mokelumne Hill; chmn. Calaveras Co. Republican Central Com. 1948-52; mem: US Power Squadron, San Francisco 1969-; Calif. Forest Protective Assn. (pres. 1970); Western Wood Prods. Assn. (bd. dirs.); Western Lumber Mfrs. Assn. (treas.); North Bay Yacht, San Rafael; Commonwealth Calif.; rec: boating. Res: 9000 Sierra Ln Mokelumne Hill 95245 Ofc: Blagen Realty, POB 100 Mokelumne Hill 95245

BLAIR, ALVIN L., manufacturing co. president; b. Nov. 6, 1927, Paso Robles; s. Wm. H. and Florence S. (Foletta) B.; m. Sharon Blakesley, Aug. 26, 1978; 1 dau. Alison Blair, b. 1954; edn: BA, UC Berkeley 1950. Career: mgmt. trainee Montgomery Ward Mail Order, Oakland 1950-51; sales H. B. Fuller Co., San Francisco 1951-62; vice pres., gen. mgr. Ritchie Adhesives, Lynwood 1962-72; pres. Blair Adhesives (mfr. indsl. adhesives), Santa Fe Springs 1972--; pres. United Cerebral Palsy of Orange Co.; club: Santa Ana CC; publs: Water Based Packaging Adhesives (chpt. in text Industrial Adhesives, Cagle, 1970); mil: pfc US Army; rec: golf, skiing. Res: 113 The Masters Circle Costa Mesa 92627 Ofc: Blair Adhesives 11034 Lockport Pl Santa Fe Springs 90670

BLAIR, RONALD MATTHEW, wooden boat builder; b. Sept. 21, 1946, Auckland, New Zealand; s. Frank Matthew and Annie Chadwick (Lamb) b.; div.; children: Nicola, b. 1966; Jacqueline, b. 1968; Liza, b. 1970; Marlborough Coll. 1959-63; lst-3rd yr. exams., Trade Tech., Auckland, N.Z.; qualified yacht and boat builder, N.Z. Govt. 1969. Career: owner Wall Board Contractors, N.Z. 1971-73; owner Wooden Boat Ctr., Marina Del Rey 1979--; owner/ pres. Hi Tech Marine Caulking Corp. 1984; partner Hi Tech Marine Prods. 1983-84; owner Classic Teak Grates 1983-84; founder/ mem. Nautical Heritage Mus., Dana Point 1983; mem: So. Calif. Marine Assn.; N.W. Marine Assn.; Picton J.C.I., N.Z.; Queen Charlott Yacht Club, N.Z.; Pacific Mariners Yacht Culb; New Zealand Connection; Wooden Hull Owners Assn.; research, marine prods.; Presbyterian; sailing, field hockey (asst. coach USA Team 1979). Ofc: Wooden Boat Center, 13000 Culver Blvd, Marina Del RY 90292

BLAKE, BARBARA BAIRD, missionary, real estate broker; b. Sept. 4, 1911, Los Angeles; d. George Washington and Daisy Nightingale (Sinclair) Baird; m. Robert J. Blake, Sept. 22, 1940, div. 1968; children: Barbara Lee, b. 1942; John, b. 1944; Timothy, b. 1950; edn: BSc, UCLA 1933; grad. sociol., Loyola Univ. 1935-6; lic. real estate broker, Calif. 1946-86. Career: receptionist Palo Alto Med. Clinic, Palo Alto 1964-69; various empl., Avalon, Santa Catalina Is. 1969-73; missionary Highland Christian Mission, Papua, New Guinea 1973-75; real estate broker Carmen Briggs Realty, Avalon 1975-82; real estate broker Barbara Blake Real Estate, Avalon 1982-, currently ret.; musician/ violinist for weddings, ch. svcs.; author/poet: I Give You The Morning Star (1979). Honors: Salutatorian, So. Pasadena H.Sch 1927. Mem. Business Women's Forum, Women's Club. Avalon Community Ch. (violinist; mem. Women's Fellowshp, Bd. Benevolences, Bd. Music). Rec: 2 daily swims Avalon Bay 1969-. Address: 130 Clarissa #104, POB 1051, Avalon 90704

BLAKE, GARY BOMAN, advertising agency executive; b. Apr. 1, 1947, San Diego; s. Ross Clifford and Cecily Anne (Boman) B.; m. Susanne Rosling, May 9, 1981; children; Ashley Lauren, Mar. 24, 1983; edn: Univ. of Copenhagen 1969-71; BA, Whittier Coll. 1969. Career: asst. to creative dir. J. Walter Thompson, Copenhagen, Denmark 1970-72; mktg. & merchandising cons. Warner Bros. Records 1975-77; creative dir. Lamber & Blake 1977-80; principal The Blake Agency, Inc. 1981--; awards: CLIO radio advtg. 1980; mem: Rotary Internat.; San Francisco Art Dirs. Club (pres. 1982); No. Calif. Assn. of Advtg. Agencies; Sons of the Am. Revolution; Republican; Methodist; rec: tennis, skiing. Res: 2812 Russell Berkeley 94705 Ofc: 1045 Sansome, Ste 304, San Francisco 94111

BLAKE, JUDY ANN, publisher; b. March 24, 1945, Seattle, Wash.; d. John Thacker and Olive Mae (Burbidge) Blake; edn: AA, L.A.City Coll. 1974, BA, CSU Los Angeles 1976, MA, California Pacifica Univ. 1978; Lic. real estate sales, Calif. Career: founder/ pub./ed. Los Angeles Advertiser, mail order tabloid circulated worldwide (15,000), 1978--, acquired and merged The Dollar Stretcher, 1980, Mandie's Review, 1981, and The National Venture-Press, 1982. Awards: num. (local, nat., internat.) photographic awards in 1970s for motorcycle, auto and boat racing photography; ranked 1st in popularity poll (1982). Introduction To Mail Order. Mem. Los Angeles Press Club. Democrat. Universal Christ Ch. (ordained minister). rec: photog. address: Blake Enterprises, POB 1172, Hollywood 90028.

BLAKE, KEVIN E., airline marketing executive; b. Dec. 23, 1956, Mnpls., Minn.; s. Ewald E. and Marjorie I. (Van Dusen) B.; m. Joan Wedgewood, Apr. 12, 1980; edn: mortuary sci., Univ. of Minn. 1976-79. Career: with Ozark Airlines 1979--; station agent, Sioux City, Iowa 1979-80; sales rep., Peoria, Ill. 1980-82; dist. mktg. mgr., San Diego 1982--; Subscribers of Sabre Club; mem: Skal Club, San Diego; Sales & Mktg. Execs. of San Diego; Travel & Transportation Council, S.D.; CON/VIS Airline Com.; Big Brothers of Am.; rec: sports (tennis), coin collecting. Res: 2852 Cazadero Dr La Costa 92008 Ofc: Ozark Air Lines, 2667 Camino Del Rio S, Ste 246, San Diego 92108

BLAKELEY, JAMES HAROLD, towing & storage co. president; b. July 14, 1928, Mediapolis, Iowa; s. James M. and Hattie R. (Stodgell) B.; cm. Carolyn A. Hester, Sept. 23, 1951; children: Steven L., b. 1952 (dec. 1972); Sharon L., b. 1954; Sandra L., b. 1957; edn: commission, USN, L.D.O. Sch. 1959; US Navy Justice Sch. 1959; tchg. credential, regl. occupational pgm., San Diego Unified Sch. Dist. Career: seaman apprentice to Lt. Commdr., USN, San Diego, Hawaii, Ill., Wash. DC, Vallejo 1946-71; dealer Amoco Oil Co., Lemon Grove & San Diego 1970-72; dealer Chevron Oil Co., San Diego 1972-76; pres. Allied Gardens Towing, Inc., San Diego & Escondido 1974--; pres. Amer-Eka, Inc., Escondido 1980--; tchr. San Diego City Schs. Regl. Occupation Pgm. 1979-; awards: Merit, USN 1971; Mem. of Yr., Calif. Tow Truck Assn. 1979; mem: San Diego Towing Contractors Assn. (Pres. 1978-79); Calif. Tow Truck Assn.; Towing & Recovery Assn. of Am.; Allied Gardens Optimist Club; works: design modifications, Eka Recovery Unit 1983; mil: Lt. Cmmdr., USN 1946-71, GCM, China Svc.; Nat. Defense, Occupation Svc., WWII, Korea Svc., U.N., Pres. Unit Citation (Korea); Republican; Methodist; rec: travel. Res: 15950-54 Ave Villaha, Rancho Bernardo, San Diego 92128 Ofcs: Allied Gardens Towing, Inc., 4334 Sheridan Ln San Diego 92120; Amer-Eka, Inc., 320 N Market Pl Escondido 92025

BLANCHARD, THOMAS ANTHONY, communications consultant, artist; b. May 11, 1942, Providence, Rhode Island; s. Thomas Anthony and Loretta Beatrice (Donnelly) B.; m. Lilian Craft, Nov. 1, 1980; children: Adam, b. 1970; Bill, b. 1972; Danielle, b. 1973; Eli, b. 1978; Thomas, b. 1982; edn: Rensselaer Plyntechnic Inst. 1960; coll. equiv. cert., Calif. 1966; Beverly Coll. of Law 1967-68; Belmont Coll. 1972; Am. Tech. Inst. 1983; gen. radio/ telephone and ship radar, FCC 1982. Career: grocery clerk, acct., auto repossesor, field rep., GMAC, New Haven, Conn. 1962; dealer Fuller Co., San Diego 1964; real estate sales & investment/ div. chief Co. of Los Angeles 1966-82, ret.; founder Eli Distributor, Carson 1979--; gen. secty. families Internat. Families Am.; concurrent artistic prodns.; many faceted synthesis of multi-disciplined elements; Friend of San Felipe; presently, sev. writing & video projs.; awards: Citizenship awd., D.A.R. 1957; Merrit Scholarship 1960; mem: nat. Electronics Sales & Svc. Dealers Assn.; Internat. Soc. of Cert. Elec. Techns.; Consultants Network St. Paul's Fathers Club; Boy Scouts of Am.; Ret. Employees of Los Angeles Co.; Amnesty Internat.; KCET; AARP; works: book, What Is, 1957; sculpture, Feminist Painting, 1979; Eart Tones III, 1984; mil: Army ROTC; Republican; Catholic; rec: goldfish breeding, all terrain camping, house restoration. Res: 1614 Victoria Ave, Lafayette Square, Los Angeles 90019 Ofc: Eli Distributors, 20311 Caron Circle Carson 90746

BLANCHETTE, JAMES EDWARD, psychiatrist; b. Aug. 28, 1924, Syracuse, NY; s. Joseph Marcel and Margaret Catherine (Vincent) Blanchette; m. Shirley Ruth Brisco, Sept. 1, 1948 (dec. May 4, 1981); edn: BA, Syracuse Univ., NY, 1950; MD, SUNY, Syracuse Coll of Med., 1953. Career: intern St. Vincent's Hosp., NYC 1953-54; res. Patton State Hosp., Calif. 1954-55; Met. State Hosp., Norwalk 1957-59; pvt. practice psychiatry, Redlands 1959--; chief profl. edn. Patton State Hosp., 1960-64; tchg. cons., 1964-; asst. clin. profl. psychiatry Loma Linda Med. Sch.; mem. staffs Loma Linda Med.Center, San Bernardino Comm. Hosp., St. Bernadine Hosp.; cons. in psychiatry Redland Comm. Hosp.; USAAF Band, Wash DC, 1945-47; USAAF M.C., 1953-55. Diplomate Am. Bd. Med. Examiners; Dip. Am. Bd. Psychiatry and Neurology; Fellow Am Psychiat. Assn;, Bd. Psychiatry and Neurology; mem: AMA, CMA, Pan-Am.Med. Assn., San Bernardino Med. Soc., So. Calif. Psychiat. Soc. (pres. Inland chpt. 1963-4, 1983-4), Royal Soc. Health, Am. Med. Soc., AAAS, Internat. Platform Assn., Phi Mu Alpha, Arrowhead Allied Arts Council, San Bernardino (past pres.), Elks, US Power Squadron, Dist. 13, P/D/C; USCG Aux.; clubs: Shark Is. Yacht, Hollywood Yacht; musician (string bass) fmrly with AF Band (Wash DC), Syracuse Sym., Univ. of Redlands Sym., Loma Linda Univ. Sym., Riverside Sym.; rec: boating; res: 972 W. Marshall Blvd., San Bernardino 92405 ofc: 236 Cajon St., Redlands 92373.

BLANDING, LINDA JOHNSON, investor, property management executive; b. June 15, 1940, Elmore, Minn.; d. William Adelma and Harriet (Johnson) J.; m. Richard Lee Blanding, July 30, 1967; 1 son: Eric, b. 1971; edn: BS, cum laude, Gustavus Adolphus Coll. 1962; var. courses Univ. of Minn., Univ. of Calif., & S.F. State Univ.; classroom tchr. K-8, tchg. cred., Minn. 1962, Calif. 1963. Career: tchr. Bloomington Pub. Schs., Minn. 1962-63; tchr. Freemont Unified, Fremont 1963-66; customer svc. rep. Scott Foresman, Palo Alto 1966-67; classroom tchr. Whisman Sch. Dist., Mt. View 1968-71; ret. tchg. 1971; created Blanding Properties (now multi- million dollar enterprise); adv. council Whisman Sch. Dist. 1969-71; cons. Hiring Com. Whisman Sch. Dist. 1970; honors: Nat. Hon. Soc. 1958; PTA Hon. Svc. Awd. 1978; mem: Calif. Tchrs. Assn.; Tri-Co. Apart. Assn.; Calif. St. Apart. Assn.; Oregon Apart. Assn.; Nat. Apart. Assn.; Am. Assn. Univ. Women; Los Altos Republican Women, Fed.; PTA; Cub Scouts; Sch. Site Council; Los Altos Sch. Dist. Pub. Rels. Com.; works; chaired small gp. which planned and implemented $10,000 (pub. sch.) playground improvement; Republican; Methodist; rec: skiing, tennis, gourmet cooking club. Address: 21 Marvin Ave Los Altos 94022

BLANDING, RICHARD LEE, investor; b. Apr. 5, 1937, Upper Darby, Pa.; s. Clarence Freeman and Goldia Delberta (Lightfoot) B.; m. Linda Johnson, July

30, 1967; 1 son: Eric, b. 1971; edn: BS, aero. eng., Univ. of Colo. 1960; BS, indsl. mgmt., 1960. Career: aerospace engr. satellite ops. Lockheed Missiles & Space Co., Sunnyvale 1965-69; aerospace engr./ computer software analyst Gen. Electric Co., Sunnyvale 1969-76; ret.; investor/ chmn. Blanding Properties, Los Altos 1976--; founder/ pres. Nat. Scientific Labs., Inc. 1975; awards: Sealbearer, Calif. Scholastic Fedn. 1955; Eagle Scout, Boy Scouts of Am. 1955; Outstanding Grad., US Naval Sch. of Pre-Flight 1960; life mem. Order of the ARrow 1954; mem: Am. Rocket Soc., Univ. of Colo. (pres. 1960); Tri-Co. Apart. Assn.; Oregon Apart. Assn.; Phi Kappa Tau; Boy Scouts of Am.; Squaw creek Villas Homeowners Assn.; Los Altos/ Mtn. View PTA Council; Train Collectors Assn.; Toy Train Operating Soc.; mil: Lt., USN 1960-64, naval aviation ofcr. F4B Phantom II Squadron, USS Ranger; Republican; Episcopal; rec: skiing, tennis, youth work. Address: Blanding Properties, 21 Marvin Ave Los Altos 94022

BLANK, LAWRENCE FRANCIS, independent computer consultant; b. Oct. 4, 1932, Detroit, MI; s. Frank Alphonse and Marcella Alice (Pieper) Blank; B.S., Xavier Univ., 1954; m. Carol Mann, Oct. 12, 1963; children: Ann, b. 1965; Steven, b. 1966; Susan, b. 1968; Lori, b. 1969. Career: asst. engr., Gen. Elect. Co., Evendale, OH, 1956-60; res. engr., Gen. Dynamics Astronautics, S.D. 1960-62; mem. tech. staff, Computer Sciences Corp., El Segundo, 1952-64; programming mgr., IBM Fed. Systems Div., L.A., 1964-69; programming mgr., Xerox Data Systems, El Segundo 1969-74; independent computer cons., 1974--. Mem.: Assoc. for Computing Machinery, 1960--; Independent Comp. Cons. Assoc., 1980--. Republican. Roman Catholic. Res.: 608 Epping Road, Palos Verdes Estates 90274; Office: 3838 Carson St. Suite 328, Torrance 90503.

BLANKENSHIP, RACHEL MC CLESKEY, funeral director; b. Aug. 30, 1944, Modesto; d. David H. and Victoria N. (John) Mc Cleskey; m. Jerry Blankenship, June 27, 1964; chil: Justin, b. Apr. 20, 1968, Melanie, b. Mar. 26, 1970; edn: San Francisco Coll of Mortuary Sci, 1962-63, Univ. Calif. San Francisco, 1981; career: trainee Salas Bros Funeral Chapel, Modesto; embalmer, funeral dir. Baltz Mortuaries, Inc. Corona del Mar, gen. mgr. & cons., 1965-68; currently, embalmer, funeral dir., eye enucleator; clerk, Modesto City Hosp., Modesto. awards: 1st woman recipient Calif. Funeral Dirs. Assn. scholarship, 1962; runner-up Miss Modesto Beauty Pageant 1962, Varsity Football Queen 1962; mem: Calif.Funeral Dirs. Assn. 1964, Hosp Meml.Hosp. Aux. 1965, So. Coast Comm. Hosp. Aux. 1965, Newport Bch C. of C. 1966, Costa Mesa C. of C. 1966, Newport Bch Emblem Club (1st asst.marshall 1968); Republican; Catholic; rec: travel, water sports, cake decorating, horsebackriding; res: 2505 Sharondell Dr. Modesto 95350 ofc: Modesto City Hosp. 730 17th St. Modesto 95354.

BLANTON, JOHN ARTHUR, architect; b. Jan. 1, 1928, Houston; s. Arthur Alva and CarolineArnold (Jeter) Blanton; m. Marietta Newton, Apr. 10,1954 (dec. Apr. 3, 1976); chil: Jill Lewis, b. 1958, Lynette, b. 1961, Elena Blanton, b. 1965; edn: BS, arch., Rice Univ. 1949. Career: assoc., Richard J. Neutra, F.A.I.A., Los Angeles 1950-64; architect pvt.practice, Manhattan Beach 1964--; instr. UCLA ext. 1967-75; instr. Harbor Coll. 1970-72; contbr. book revs. AIA Journal, 1972-75; awards: Red Cedar Shingle, Nat. AIA, 1979; CofC awards 1969, 70, 71, 74, 75, 82. Mem: AIA, Soc. Architl. Historians, Rotary Intl. Works: his bldgs. appear in A Guide to Archit. in Los Angeles & So. Calif., (6); Sunset Mag., L.A. Times Home mag., Bicentennial Ed. AIA Journal; mil: US Signal Corps 1951-53; ofc: John Blanton, AIA, 2100 Sepulveda, Ste 14, Manhattan Bch 90266.

BLAYLOCK, GARY HAROLD, lawyer; b. Aug. 6, 1946, Downey; s. Grandville Holder and Thelma Ruth (Marshall) Blaylock; m. Gloria, March 16, 1973; chil: Kimberly, b. 1968, Gregory, b. 1969, Grant, b. 1980, Aaron, b. 1982; edn: AA, Chaffey Jr. Coll. 1976, JD, Western State Univ. 1980. Career: solo practice law, spec. in criminal law, also family and personal injury cases, Ontario 1980--; mem: San Bernardino Co. Bar Assn., Western San Bernardino Co. Bar Assn., Inland Counties Trial Lawyers Assnb., Calif. Trial Lawyers Assn., Ontario CofC; Republican; Protestant; rec: scale models, woodwork; res: 11960 Yorba Ave. Chino 91710 ofc: Gary H. Blaylock, 1047 W. Sixth St., #100, Ontario 91762.

BLESSING, VICKI LINN, operations controller; b. May 10, 1954, Lubbock, Tex.; d. James Jay and Beverly Joy (Morton) B.; edn: AB, summa cum laude, USC, 1976; MBA, 1978. Career: financial analyst, planning & reporting analyst, cost acctg. supr. Hewlett-Packard Co., Palo Alto 1978-82; chief fin. ofcr. & sr. editor A.B. Laffer Assocs., Rolling Hills Estates, 1982-83; controller, ops., Seagate Technology, Scotts Valley 1983--; honors: Phi Beta Kappa, Alpha Lambda Delta, Phi Alpha Theta, Phi Kappa Phi; Gov.'s Scholar; Libertarian; rec: tennis, skiing, needlepoint design. Res: 2036 Seascape, Aptos 95003 Ofc: Seagate Technology, 360 El Pueblo Rd., Scotts Valley 95066

BLOOMFIELD, WILLIAM EDWARD, company president; b. May 17, 1913, Los Angeles, CA; s. William E. (dec.) and Anna Lorene (Wimmer) Bloomfield (Stockwell) (dec.); ed. grad. UCLA, 1945; m. Margaret Meyer, Escondido, CA, Apr. 14, 1946; children: Mrs. Timothy (Carole) Etzel; Mrs. James (Joanne) Hunter; William Edward Jr. Career: assoc. with Pac. Telephone Co., 1936-47; founder-propr., WEB Serv. Co., Inc., 1947; pres. 1953--. Mem.: b. govs. Westside YMCA, 1946--; Santa Monica Bay Power Squad., Santa Monica Bay Council of Nay League, World Affairs Council, Westwood Village Rotary Club, Town Hall of Calif., Aviation Country Club of Calif., Riviera Tennis Club; Los Angeles Country Club. Rec.: flying, tennis. Res.: 1262 Corsica Dr., Pacific Palisades 90272; Office: 3690 Freeman Blvd., Redondo Beach 90278.

BLUE, WILLIAM ELLIOTT, computer programmer; b. Feb. 8, 1946, Indpls., Ind.; s. Loren Kerry and Helen Louise (Elliott) B.; m. Melissa A. Hipp, Dec. 21, 1982. Career: mgr. audio dept. Lewtons, Inc., San Diego 1967-71; proprietor State of Mind Prod., San Diego 1971-73; proprietor/ cons. Soundwest, San Diego 1973-76; profl. recording engr. Studio West, San Diego 1971-78; proprietor Bill Blue Computer Cons., Lakeside 1978-81; pres. Marilla Corp., Lakeside 1981--; pres. Datel Sys., Inc., Santee 1983--; exec. v.p. United Software Inds., Inc., Los Angeles 1984--; awards: Outstanding Achiev. Awd., Computer Community, San Diego Computer Soc. 1982; works: devel. num. software communications packages, mktd. nationally; devel. modem commun. capabilities and message relay sys. for personal computers; publish nat. directory of known communications "Nodes for Message Relay Systems"; mil: E3, USNR 1962-68; rec: computers, electronics, audio-music reproduction. Res: 9527 Marilla Dr, Box 1318, Lakeside 92040 Ofc: United Software Inds., Inc., San Diego Ofc., 8624 Cuyamaca St, Ste E, Santee 92071

BOCK-CHAMBERS, DEANNA MARIE, information services executive; b. Dec. 3, 1946, Detroit, Mich.; d. Clarence H. and Loretta M. Bock; m. Robert Lee Chambers, Apr. 15, 1983; edn: Oakland Univ. 1968; Mich. St. Univ. Career: with TRW Information Svcs. 1973--; customer svc. rep., Detroit, Mich. 1973; sales rep., Mich. 1975; sr. sales rep., Baltimore, Wash. 1977; br. mgr., Virginia 1978; br. mgr., San Diego 1981--; bd. dirs./ chmn. edn. com. Consumer Credit Assocs. of San Diego Co.; trustee/ chmn. pub. rels. com. Consumer Credit Counselors of San Diego Co.; conduct Credit Sch. Pgm. (six wk. seminar pgm.) in Norfolk, Va. and San Diego for ICCA; awards: Credit Person of Yr., CCA of S.D. Co. 1982, leadership awd., Orange Co. YWCA 1983; mem: ICCA (Internat. Consumer Credit Assn.), Norfolk, Va.; Consumer Credit Assocs. of San Diego Co.; Credit Women Internat., Detroit; Consumer Credit Counselors of S.D. Co.; Better Bus. Bureau; CofC; Republican; Congregational; rec: equestrian. Res: 11392 Crazy Horse Rd Lakeside 92040 Ofc: TRW Information Services, 2650 Camino del Rio N., POB 82447, San Diego 92138

BODENHEIMER, FRITZ BRADFORD, commercial insurance broker; b. Apr. 16, 1941, Freeburn, Ky.; s. S.B. and Eddie (Grose) B.; m. Jacqueline Suzanne McNabb, Aug. 1, 1964; children: Jennifer Leigh, b. 1971; edn: BS, Univ. of Ky. 1963; MBA, 1968; JD, cand., Golden Gate Univ. 1974-77. Career: dist. mgr. Honeywell EDP Div., San Francisco 1971-73; v.p. Allendale Ins. Co., San Francisco 1973-77; v.p. Rollis Burdick Hunter Inc., Palo Alto 1977-81; v.p. Emett & Chandler, Inc., San Francisco 1981-83; owner/ partner MBO Ins. Broker, Inc., Menlo Park 1983--; pres./ owner Beaucam, Inc. 1982-; Mgr. of the Year, Honeywell 1971; Tennesee Squier, 1965; mem: Masonic Lodge; Sigma Nu frat., Jr. CofC; publs. Perspectives of Risk Management, 1981, Insuring High Technology Risks, Bus. Ins. 1982, 83; spkr: Calif. CPAs Risk Mgmt. Conf. 1981; nat. Assn. of Ins. Brokers Conv. 1982; mil: Capt., USAF 1963-67; Republican; Protestant; rec: scuba diving, equestrian, racquet ball. Res: 1080 Schooner St Foster City 94404 Ofc: MBO Insurance Brokers, Inc., 873 Santa Cruz Ave Menlo Park 94025

BODOVITZ, JOSEPH E., public utilities executive; b. Oct. 29, 1930, Okla. Cty., Ok.; s. V. J. and Frieda (Gottlieb) Bodovitz; m. Shirley Leon, Dec. 26, 1957; chil: Katherine, b. 1961, Sandra, b. 1963, Steven, b. 1968; edn: BA, honors, Northwestern Univ. 1951, MS in journ., Columbia Univ. 1956. Career: newspaper reporter San Francisco Examiner, 1956-62; assoc. exec. dir. S.F. Planning & Urban Renewal Assn. (SPUR) citizens' orgn., 1962-65, with timeout as exec. dir. S.F.Bay Conservation Study Commn. 1964-5; exec, dir. S.F.Bay Conserv. and Devel. Commn., 1965-73; exec. dir. Calif. Coastal Commn., 1973-78; cons. in planning and resource mgmt. 1978-79; exec. dir. Calif. Pub. Utilities Commn., 1979--. Elected bd. mem. Mill Valley Sch. Dist., 1966-75; mem. bd. dirs. Am. Planning Assn. 1976-79. ofc: 350 McAllister St. San Francisco 94102.

BOEPPLE, ROLLAND EMERSON, college librarian; b. Dec. 25, 1927, Baltimore; edn: AB, Elizabethtown Coll., Pa. 1949; MSLS, USC 1962; postgrad. CSU Fullerton and CSU Long Beach; m. Saeko Nakano, Nov. 9, 1958; chil: Kathy Elaine, b. 1960, Leslie Ruth, b. 1965. Career: lib. trainee, then librarian, Los Angeles Pub. Library, 1959-62; libn. Douglas Aircraft Co. Engring. Lib., Long Beach 1962-64; libn. Anaheim Pub. Lib., 1964; libn. Philco-Ford, Aeroneutronic Div., Newport Beach 1965-67; dir. lib. services Santa Ana Coll., 1967--. Mem: Assn. of Calif. Community Coll. Adminstrs., Faculty Assn. of Calif. Comm. Colls., Council on Lib. Tech., Calif. Lib. Assn. Rec: piano, pottery, sailing, golf. res: 17972 Larcrest Cir. Huntington Bch 92647. ofc: 17th St. at Bristol, Santa Ana 92706.

BOEHM, JOYCE REUL, real estate developer; b. May 24, 1927, Rice Lake, Wisc.; d. Alfred Hugo and Annie Elizabeth (Hathaway) Reul; m. Roger DuBoise Boehm, Dec. 31, 1951, dec. 1977; children: Lizabeth Anne (Lundberg), b. 1952; Jennie Lyda, b. 953; Kimberly Roger, b. 1954; edn: Denver Univ. 1950; Am. River Coll. 1973; Yuba Coll. 1982; communication, mgmt., ed. strategy, USC 1974. Career: corp. pres. Electronic Devel. Corp., Denver, Colo. 1947-51; bookkeeper, Southside Recap, Rice Lake, Wisc. 1951-60; jr. acct. Chipman & Renfrow Accty. Corp., Marysville 1960-63; Bail Bond Joyce, Yuba City 1963-71; realtor/ assoc./ broker Francis E. Laney, Realtor 1969-77; realtor Joyce R. Boehm, Broker 1977--; devel./ owner Donner Trail Manor (44 sr. citizen units), Wheatland, Calif.; counselor, sr. citizens 1980--; pres./ dir. Electronice Devel., contracts betwenn Motorola & GE, between Denver & Chgo. 1947-51; honors: Communtiy 4-H Leader 1963; Sunday Sch. Tchr. 1964-72; Brownie Troop Leader 1958; mem: Real Estate & Counselors (pres. 1982); Sutter Yuba Bd. Realtors: Calif. Assn. Realtors; Nat. Assn.

Realtors; Cancer; Heart; Republican; Lutheran; rec: sewing, bird watching, hunting. Res: 1572 Caroleigh Way Yuba City, mail: POB 872 Yuba City 95992 Ofc: Donner Trail Manor, POB 787 Wheatland 95692

BOEX, HAROLD ARTHUR, real estate broker/developer; b. Dec. 17, 1933, Chgo., Ill.; s. Harold Anthony and Agnes Virginia (Hood) B.; m. Mary Helen Schuette, Dec. 5, 1958; children: Shirley Ann, b. 1960, Anthony Robert, b. 1961, Laura Frances, b. 1962; lic. Calif. R.E. Broker, lic. B-1 Gen. Contractor. Career: v.p. real estate, Systech Fin. Corp., Walnut Creek 1965-73; v.p./dir. Pacific Northwest Fin. Corp. 1980--; dir. Solano Fed. S&L, 1980-; pres./ dir./ prin., H & B Developers (real estate devel. co.), Walnut Creek 1973--; ptnr. Sterling Finl., Lafayette 1982-; cons. govt. redevel. agencies; mem: Building Indus. Assn. (past pres. E. Div.; v.p./dir. No. Calif. Div.); Pacific Coast Bldrs. Conv. (past pres.); Calif. Bldg. Indus. Assn. (dir.); Nat. Assn. of Home Bldrs. (dir.); trustee Bldg. Indus. PAC; mem. Vallejo CofC, BSA, Armed Services Com., Vallejo Yacht Club, Elks; mil: USN; Republican; Catholic; rec: boating, fishing, travel. Res: 15 Lily Court, Walnut Creek 94595 Ofc: H & B Developers, 1825 Sonoma Blvd Vallejo 94590

BOGAR, ODIS, JR., orthopaedic technician; b. July 21, 1951, Los Angeles; s. Odis Jerome and Mary Elizabeth (Sims) B.; m. Cassandra, July 21, 1951, div.; children: Tamara, b. 1970; Derrick, b. 1978; edn: orthopaedic tech., LAC USC Med. Ctr. 1973; Cert. orthopaedic tech., Nat. Assn. Orth. Tech. 1984. Career: orthopaedic surgery orderly, USC Med. Ctr. 1969; orthopaedic tech, casting & traction application 1975; hosp. corpsman, USN; ortho. orderly Santa Monica Hosp. 1978; ortho. tech. Glendale Meml. Hosp. 1979; sr. traction tech. Orthopeadic Hosp., Los Angeles 1980--; plaster tech. Valley Orthopeadic Clinic, Calexico; instr. traction classes to new nurses, staff: mem. Nat. Assn. of Ortho. Techns.; mil: E-2, USN 1978; Baptist; rec: outdoors. Res: 1146 E 82 St, Los Angeles 90001 Ofc: Orthopaedic Hospital, 2400 Flower Ave Los Angeles 90007

BOGGESS, EVELYN ANNETTE, real estate broker, cosmetologist; b. Jan. 10, 1940, Hanford; d. Coonie and Zelma (Ayon) Balderama; m. A. J. Boggess, Oct. 31, 1959; children: Sherry, b. 1967, Melanie, b. 1969; edn: cosmetology. Federico's, 1958; real estate broker , Coll. of Sequoias 1970; acupressure, Jin Shin Do, 1983. Career: cosmetologist in Lemoore and Hanford, 1958-, owner Evelyn's Beauty Salon in Lemoore 1961-, currently owner 3 beauty salons in Visalia, Pismo Beach, Lemoore; real estate salespsn. Watkins Realty, 1971-73, founder/broker Boggess Realty, 1973--, formed Awahnee Enterprises (building corp.), 1976--; mem: Visalia Bd. of Realtors (past dir., MLS ch.), Certified Business Counselors, San Joaquin Valley Exchangors (past pres.), Bakersfield Exchange Group, Visalia R.E. Mktg. Exchange, Toastmasters, Nat. Photogs. Assn.; lic. pvt. pilot (mem. Sheriff's Aero & Rescue Squadron); ham radio opr. (WB6SJH); photog. spec. in portraits; lic. Acupressurist 1983-; cert. scuba diver; dancing mem. Sequoia Squares. Res: 919 Bollinger St Visalia 93291 Ofc: Boggess Realty, 317 Crenshaw, Visalia 93291

BOGGUS, EVERETTE DELANO, real estate broker; b. Mar. 10, 1933, Savannah, Ga.; s. Argin Artemas and Avie Lee (Adamson) B.; m. Angeal Jacobs, July 22, 1952; m. 2d. Rose White, Jan. 4, 1959; children: Jeffery, b. 1953; Cindy, b. 1955; Michael, b. 1956; Tammy, b. 1960; David, b. 1962; edn: bus. admin., Georgia St. Univ. 1958. Career: gen. mgr./ civilian exch. ofcr./ tech. rep. Retail- Army & Air Force Exch. Svc., Worldwide Ops., NYC 1955-64; sales mgr./ dir. of R.E. & franchising Swanson's Cleaners & Pay-Less Cleaners, Sacto. 1964-79; self- empl., R.E. broker/ devel. Great American Realty, Carmichael 1979-83; broker assoc. Western Nat. Realtors, Sacto. 1983--; dir. R.E., franchising & tng. Chain Dry Cleaners; awards: sales agent of Month, Western Nat. Realtors (2), 1982; Million Dollar Club 1983; 2nd Highest Vol. Producer, 4th Quarter 1983; mem: Comstock Club; Aircraft Owners & Pilots Assn.; Sacto. Bd. Realtors; Elks; mil: sgt. US Army 1952-55, Russian interpretor, Nat. Defense, European Occupation, GCM; Republican; Baptist; rec: aviation, pvt. pilot. Res: 610 Howe Ave, 55, Sacramento 95825 Ofc: Western National Reators, 7 Parkcenter Dr Sacramento 92825

BOGUMILL, MICHAEL THOMAS, state government regulator; b. Dec. 20, 1938, Owen, Wisc.; s. Edward Leonard and Clara Emma (Pierce) B.; edn: BS, Univ. of Wisc., Ean Claire 1961; MAT, Univ. of N. Carolina 1970; life cert., Wisc. 1964; life standard tchg. cred., Calif. 1969. Career: radio announcer, Neillsville, Wisc. ,part-time 1967-69; sci./ math. tchr. Hilmar, Calif. 1969-70; Calif. Food & Drug Admin. 1971--; health fraud investigator, Berkeley 1971; supvr. So. Calif. health fraud pgm., Los Angeles 1973; supvr. So. Calif. br. Drug & Med. Device Inspection pgm. 1976-78; pgm. coord. Health Fraud & Product Safety pgms. 1978--; tchr., Selecting Medical Services, CSU, L.A. 1976-77; awards: NSF Summer Inst. in Physics, Ripon Coll. 1963; NSY Academic Yr. Inst. at UNC, Chapel Hill, NC 1966-67; Cert. of Appreciation, U.S. CPSC 19882; mem: AFDO,; WAFDO; CAFDO (pres. 1978); Calif. Council Against Health Fraud; Consumers Union; Smithsonian Inst.; Neillsville, Wisc. Kiwanis Club; (past pres.); River City Bowlers League, Sacto.; publs: California Health Fraud Program, AFDO Quarterly Bulletin, 7/79; Food Fads and Fallacies, AFDO Bulletin, 4/81; History of California Food and Drug Regulations, AFDO Bulletin 7/82; Democrat; Catholic; rec: bowling, computers, model trains. Res: 1332 Wyant Way Sacramento 995825 Ofc: Calif. Dept. of Health Services, 714 P Street, Rm 400, Sacramento 95814

BOHRER, THOMAS HENRY, lawyer; b. June 8, 1949, Jefferson City, Mo.; s. Dr. E. Royse and Lois Ann (Wood) Bohrer; m. Elaine Ossa, July 12, 1975; chil: Geoffrey, b. 1977, Suzanne, b. 1979; edn: BA, UCLA 1971, JD, UC Hastings Sch of Law 1974. Career: commnd. Fgn. Service Ofcr., US Dept. of State, (Vice Consul stationed in Montreal, Can.; London, Eng.; Tijuana, Mex.) 1975-80; assoc. law firm Lum & Ku, 1980; assoc. law firm Cohn, Gotcher, Singer & Anderson, 1981; estab. own practice spec. in immigration law, Los Angeles 1981--; mem. Am. Immigration Lawyers Assn., L.A. County Bar Assn.; Libertarian; rec: hist., geography, racquetball. res: 24694 Ashland Dr. Laguna Hills 92653 ofc: Thomas H. Bohrer, Atty., 615 S. Flower St., Ste.1900, Los Angeles 90017.

BOLDING, GENEVIEVE T., governmental services executive; b. Oct. 30, 1929, Minersville, Pa.; d. Matthew and Katheryn (Richardson) Trenosky; m. Fred A. Bolding, Nov. 27, 1954; chil: Patricia Ann (Bleckley), b. 1955; Sallie Mae (Sutter), b. 1957; Allan F., b. 1959; Alice Marie, b. 1961; edn: BA in bus. adm., with great distinction, San Jose State Coll. 1952. Career: secty. FBI, San Francisco 1952-55; district mgr. Marinwood Community Services Dist. since formation of dist., 1960--. Honors: Key Club, Phi Beta Kappa; mem. various charitable orgns. Catholic. rec: cooking, sewing. address: Marinwood Comm. Svcs Dist. 536 Miller Creek Rd. San Rafael 94903.

BOLGER, BRENNA MERCIER, public relations/advertising executive; b. Dec. 26, 1942, Toledo, Ohio; d. Ray E. and Madalyn (Mercier) B.; edn: BA, Santa Clara Univ. 1964. Career: exec. vice pres. Coakley-Heagerty Advt., 1962-74; owner PRx, Public Relations and Advt., Cupertino 1975--: responsible for emergency spray notification by media during Medfly crisis, 1981; created The Great Race (Los Gatos/Saratoga race held annually) 1977; devel. Ask Your Doctor column/San Jose Mercury News, 1975; devel. various business-backed charities incl. Eastfield Celebrity Series, Valle Monte League Christmas Tree Elegance, Crippled Children's Soc.; pub. rels./mktg. guidance to non-profit orgns. incl. Peninsula Vols., Adult & Child Guidance Clinic, Ctr for Living with Dying, Am. Lung Assn., Penin. Oral Sch for the Deaf, Inst. for Med. Resrch, Ind. Aging Pgm., Mitty H.Sch. Honors: 1st Woman in Honors Div., Santa Clara Univ. 1960; Who's Who in Am. Colls. 1964; 1972 Woman of Achievement, San Jose Mercury News. Mem: Penin. Press Club, Pub. Rels. Soc. of Am. (accredited mem.), Hospital Pub. Rels. Assn., San Jose Mus. of Art, San Jose Sym. Catholic. rec: tennis. ofc: PRx, 10350 South De Anza Blvd, Ste.2-H, Cupertino 95014.

BOLIN, PHYLLIS MARIE, hospital executive; b. Apr. 19, 1926, Sayre, Pa.; d. Kenneth Erwin (DDS) and Dorotha Anna (Whitcomb) Wilson; m. Chester A. Bolin, Dec. 31, 1970; children: Kathryn, b. 1949, Robert, b. 1950, Phyllis Anne, b. 1952, George, b. 1957; edn: BA, St. Bonaventure NJ, 1948; MSW, Rutgers, 1965; grad. wk. Univ. Georgia; LCSW, Lic. Clin. Soc. Wkr., Calif. Career: case wkr. Dept. Assistance, Bradford, Pa. 1948, act. asst. county supr. 1951; dir. Social Svc. Babies Hosp., Newark, NJ 1960, dir. Social Svc. United Hospitals, 1967; soc. case wkr./acting dir. Soc. service Rockland Co. Health Dept., NY 1967-68; soc. wkr. Fairview State Hosp., Costa Mesa, Ca. 1968, program dir. 1970--; clin. soc. wkr. UC Irvine 1970--; substitute tchr. 1960s; tchr. workshops, Continuing Edn. to nursing staff UCI Med. Ctr.; mem. Nat. Assn. Soc. Wkrs.; Ladies of Moose; vol. Plainfield (NJ) YWCA in 1960s; publs: art., Nursing Mag.; Republican; Catholic; rec: crafts, basketmaking, sewing. Res: 644 Surf St Costa Mesa 92627 Ofc: Fairview State Hosp, 2501 Harbor Blvd, Costa Mesa 92627 UCIMC, 101 City Drive So. Orange

BOLLARD, ROBERT ROWLAND, manufacturing and design executive; b. Aug. 27, 1930, England, nat. 1975; s. Edgar Edward and Sussana (Bale) B.; m. Mary McHale, June 19, 1952; 1 dau: Sally, b. 1963; edn: cert. London City & Guilds 1950; Wellingborough Tech. Inst.; Career: apprentice J.J. Page, Bespoke Tailors, England (5 yrs.), became master Bespoke Tailor; v.p. design & quality control Schoenemans, Baltimore, Md. (20 yrs.); v.p. mfg. & design Hollywood Clothes, Los Angeles; currently, sr. v.p. mfg. & design Ratner Corp.; mem: Internat. Assn. of Clothing Designers, Baltimore chpt. (pres. 1973-74); Christian; rec: sailing. Res: 5313 Bothe Ave San Diego 92122

BOLLINGER, JOHN, architect/planner/developer; b. Apr. 12, 1943, London, England; nat. 1956; s. Luzer and Sarah Rosalie (Mayer) B.; m. Paula J. Carter, Aug. 10, 1975; 1 dau. Lara Renee, b. 1980; edn: B.Arch., USC, 1966, M.Arch., 1968, D.B.S. (Dr. of Bldg. Sci.), 1971; cert. Pub. Adminstrn., CSU Long Bch. 1978; lic. architect (1976), contractor (1982), Calif. Career: project mgr. Larwin Groups Inc., Beverly Hills 1970-72; project coord., Bank America Premises (fmrly Continental Svc. Co.), Los Angeles 1972-75; assoc. planner, City of Long Beach, 1975-80, senior planner, 1980--; World Trade Ctr. project mgr., Port of Long Beach, 1979--; prin. John Bollinger Architect, Fullerton 1976--; developer, Building Resources Interface, Fullerton 1982--; lectr. Isomata, 1973; tchg. asst. USC Arch., 1968-71. Awards: Architl. Guild Fellowship, Weyerhauser Found. Resrch. Grant, Clayton Baldwin Meml. Awd., AIA Fellowship Awd. Mem: Constrn. Specifications Inst., Am. Soc. for Testing & Materials, Architl. Guild, Am. Inst. of Planners, Assn. of Environmtl. Profls., USC Alumni Assn., Town Hall, Forum for Cultural and Ednl. Exchange. works: World Trade Ctr Feasibility Study (1981); Risk Mgmt. Plan, Port of Long Bch (1979); Master Plan, Port of L.B. 91978); Democrat; Jewish; rec: computer pgmmg., stamps, painting, sculpture. res: 717 N. Carhart Ave. #G4, Fullerton 92633 ofc: Port of L.B., POB 570, Long Beach 90801.

BONESTEEL, MICHAEL JOHN, lawyer; b. Dec. 22, 1939, Los Angeles; s. Dr. Henry T. S. and Kathleen Mansfield (Nolan) Bonesteel; m. Susan Elizabeth Schaaf, June 1, 1980; chil: Damon, b. 1969, Kirsten, b. 1971; edn: AB in hist., Stanford Univ. 1961, JD, USC 1966. Career: admitted to Calif. Bar 1967; assoc. to partner law firm Haight, Dickson, Brown & Bonesteel (fmrly. Moss, Lyon & Dunn), now a firm of 75 attorneys, Santa Monica 1967--; mem. Am. Bar Assn., State Bar of Calif. (chmn. State Bar Com. of Rules and Procedures; asst. chmn.

Jury Instrns. Com.; lectr. for Cont. Edn. of the Bar), Los Angeles Co. Bar (v.chmn. Med. Legal Com.), So. Calif. Defense Counsel, Fedn. of Insurance Counsel; mem. Bel Air Bay Club; Republican; Episcopal; rec: travel, athletics. res: 13688 Sunset Bl. Pacific Palisades 90272. ofc: Haight, Dickson, Brown & Bonesteel, 201 Santa Monica Bl. Santa Monica 90406.

BONHAM, KURT ANDREW, financial consultant, accountant; b. Jan. 23, 1951, Pasadena; s. Francis L. and Lucile (Sinclair) B.; m. Martha Fettig, Dec. 31, 1974; 2 sons: Kurt II, b. 1977; Frank, b. 1979; edn: BS in acctg., CSU Dominguez Hills 1979. Career: staff acct. Jennings & Jones, Whittier 1978-79, McGinnis, Knectel & McIntyre, CPAs, Pasadena 1979; acct./auditor Los Angeles Co., 1979-81; self-empl. financial consultant, Glendora 1981-83; vice pres. Assistants to Executives, Inc., Sepulveda 1983--; instr. Antelope Valley Coll. 1983; computer tax package cons. Alpha Computer Devel. Co. 1983-84. Mem: Reserve Ofcrs. Assn. 1976-7; City of Palmdale Site Plan Rev. Com., 1984-; Glendora Beautiful, Glendora Coord. Council, Glendora CofC; cand. Glendora City Council 1982; mil: s/sgt. US Army 1971-76, 2lt USAR 1976-8, Army Commend., Merit. Svc.; Republican; Catholic; rec: golf. Res: 1136 E. Ave. R-6, Palmdale 93550 Ofc: Assistants To Executives, Inc. 8600 Sepulveda Blvd #9, Sepulveda 91343

BONHAM, TERRENCE JAMES, lawyer; b. June 8, 1938, Richmond; s. Harry L. and Helen (Gately) Bonham; m. Joyce E. Trout, July 28, 1968; 1 dau. Teresa Jeannette; edn: BA, St. Mary's Coll. of Calif. 1960; JD, UC Hastings Coll. of the Law 1963. Career: attorney firm of Halde, Battin, Barrymore & Stevens in Santa Barbara 1968-73; partner Barrymore, Stevens & Bonham, 1973-74; Reilly, Holzhauer, Denver & McLain in Ventura 1974-80; partner firm Lawler & Ellis, Ventura 1980--; arbitrator Civil Panel Ventura; Hearing Ofcr. Co. of Santa Barbara Retirement Bd. & Civil Svc. Commn.; Judge pro tem Co. of Ventura, Co. of Santa Barbara; lectr. Bridging the Gap, CTLA, Arbitration Gps. and Assns. Mem. Ventura Co. Bar Assn. (exec. com., atty. client com.), Am. Bd. of Trial Advocates (pgm. chmn. SB-VTA-SLO), State Bar Calif., Am. Bar Assn., Ventura Bar Assn., So. Calif. Defense Counsel. Listed Who's Who in Am. Law, 3d ed. Mem. Knights of Columbus, 4th Deg. (Faithful Navigator), Elks, Trade Club of Ventura. Mil: capt. Judge Adv. Gen. Corps, US Army 1964-68, Bronze Star, Vietnam Campgn. Medal. Republican (Presdtl. Task Force, Repub. Senatl. Com., US Supreme Ct.). Catholic. rec: painting (oils). res: 2348 Kudu Pl. Ventura 93003. ofc: Lawler & Ellis, 2151 Alessandro Dr. Ste. 220, Ventura 93001.

BONILLA, ANTHONY CORREA, financial planner; b. Nov. 6, 1940, Los Angeles; s. Frank P. and Victoria (Correa) B.; m. Virginia, Jan. 27, 1968; children: David, Michelle; edn: MS in fin. plng. Southern States Univ. 1984; CTFP, Cert. Tax & Finl. Planner. Career: finl. services field 1960-: Bank of Am. 1960-67, data processing team for So. Calif. area, Wells Fargo Bank, 1967-73; past insurance underwriter; senior finl. cons. Shearson Hayden (now Shearson Am. Express) 1976-78; past cons., Western Growers Assn.; tax & finl. plnnr. Coast Savings & Loan, currently; mem. Internat. Assn. of Finl. Profls., Internat. Assn. for Finl. Planners, Certified Plnnrs. of Am. afil.; Democrat; Catholic; rec: photog. Res: 2285 Shady Hills Dr Diamond Bar 91765

BONSACK, ROLF H., business owner; b. Jan. 23, 1937, Salz-Gitter Bad, W. Ger.; nat. 1961; s. Elli Bonsack; m. Sharon Browning, Feb. 13, 1960; chil: Robert, Kevin, Vivian, Thomas, David; edn: stu. mining iron, trade sch., Ger. Career: immigrated to San Francisco in 1954, worked as a baker for St. Mary's Hosp., S.F. 1954-59, Stemple's Bakery in S.F. and San Jose, 1959-77; owner Rolf's Wash & Dry's (now in 4 locations) Coin Washer & Dryer Service, 1970--. Mem: Coin Laundry Assn., No. Calif. Laundromat Assn., San Jose CofC, Better Bus. Bur.; Democrat. Christian. address: Coin Washer & Dryer Service, 4415 Samson Way, San Jose 95124.

BOOTH, RAY(MOND) WILLIAM, accountant; b. July 11, 1908, Cincinnati; s. Wm. Sanford and Rose Della (Sporing) Booth; m. Gwendolyn Powell (dec. 1982), Apr. 20, 1938; edn: grad. Alexander Hamilton Inst., Chgo.; lic. Pub. Acct. 1958, lic. Casualty Ins. Agent, Calif.; mem. Internat. Accts. Soc., Inc. Career: div. controller and employee/public rels. mgr. Safeway Stores, Inc., San Diego Div. to 1966, cons. 1966, 67; spkr. num. univs., colls., schools, civic orgns., 1950s-70s; elected mem.(pres. four terms) San Diego Co. Bd. of Edn., 1956-80 (ret. 1981); hon. mem. World Coll. of Journalism (Taiwan) 1966; Mem: Adminstrv. Mgmt. Soc. (fmr Nat. Ofc. Mgmt. Assn.; nat. dir. 2 yrs.; Diamond Merit Key awd.; Leffingwell Key awd.; past pres.; 15 consec. nat. convs.). Mem: Jr. CofC (Alumni mem. 30 yrs.); S.D. CofC (Eurocom del. 18 countries 1961; Aviation Com. 1952-70; List of 200); S.D. Downtown Kiwanis (32 Yrs perf att.; dir. 1955-8, dir. Kiwanis Found. 1966-9); BSA (counselor); YMCA. ARC, Comm. Chest, Cancer Soc., Hosp., Tourist & Conv. Bur. (fundraising); dir: United Comm. Svcs. (1964), S.D. Aerospace Mus. (1965-6), S.D. Better Bus. Bur. (1965); afil: S.D. Yacht Club, 1944-82, Aircraft Owners & Pilots Assn., 1950-70, Navy League 1960-; hon. life mem. S.D. Zoo, Wild Animal Pk.; S.D. City Bd. of Air Control, Nat. Aero. Assn. (dir.), Civil Air Patrol; pvt. pilot 1928-; AF Assn. (chmn. State Conv. 1967; bd.dirs. S.D. Squadron Council 20 yrs., comdr. 1964); guest various US mil. cruises, USAF (NORAD, 1969), AF Acad.; hon. citizen Jerusalem (1974), Yokohama (1961, 1966); Ky. Col. (1974); mem. Internat. Exec. Svc. Corps, 1966-78. Republican. Baptist. rec: flying, animals, geneol. res: 3671 Liggett St., San Diego 92106.

BORBALS, STANLEY, architect, b. Jan. 14, 1907, St. Petersburg, Russia, nat. 1957; s. Donat and Matilde (Trups) Borbals; m. Milda Elisabeth Bushman (Dipl. Arch. in Latvia and Ger.), July 15, 1938; chil: Ruth Helen (Dexter), b. 1942 ; Astrid (Preston), b. 1945; edn: Dipl. Arch., Latvian Univ. in Riga, 1938; stu. City Planning, Kungliga Tekniska Hogskolain, Stockholm, Sweden, 2 yrs.; Dipl.Eng., Ger. Career: sr. architect Building Dept. city of Riga, Latvia 1938-41, instr. in design Latvian Univ. Sch. of Arch., 1941-44; architect arch. office Kooperativa Forbundet, Stockholm 1947-49, prin. architect office Sveriges Grossis Forbundet,(large office bldgs., factories, theaters, exhibn. complexes, Sweden) 1949-51; designer, proj. coordinator, various arch. firms, Los Angeles 1951-63, incl. 3 yr. proj. L.A. Music Ctr. at Welton Becket & Assocs.; pvt. practice, Los Angeles 1963--. Recipient num. awards in arch. competitions, 3 awds. from Santa Monica City for office bldg., twin theatre, residence. Regis. Arch. in Latvia, Ger., Sweden, Calif., Nev.; mem: AIA, Svenska Arkitekt Foreningen 1946-51, Fellow Latvian Arch. Assn. (pres. 1954-61); publs: Stockholm Sketchbook (1976); num. arts. in profl. mags.; mil. svc. Latvia; rec: golf, travel, sketching. res/ofc: 30509 Alta Mesa Dr. Valley Center 92082.

BORELLI, RALPH NEAL, industrial real estate broker; b. Jan. 3, 1954, San Jose; s. Nelo Guisseppe and Sigrid Thorey (Hallgrimson) B.; m. Gina Marie Pasquinelli, July 5, 1980; 1 dau: Marissa Rose, b. 1983; edn: AA, DeAnza Jr. Coll. 1974; BSc, San Jose St. Univ. 1976; broker lic., Calif. 1976. Career: yardman/ inventory/ delivery/ counter sales Klauers Auto Wrecking, San Jose 1969-73; sales agent N.G. Borelli, Realtor, San Jose 1973-76; pres. 1976-81; pres./ CFO Borelli & Burke, San Jose 1981- ; awards: Outstanding Sr. in Soc. Sci., Mt. Pleasant H.S. 1972; mem: Assn. of South Bay Brokers; Downtown Development Corp., San Jose; Rotary Club, San Jose; Kappa Sigma frat., San Jose St.; House Corp. (pres. 1976-84); Republican; Lutheran; rec: tennis, racquetball, snow skiing. Res: 19301 Pinnache Ct Saratoga 95070 Ofc: Borelli & Burke, 2680 N 1st, Ste 110, San Jose 95134

BORJAL, ARMANDO C., veterinarian; b. Feb. 1939, Philippines, nat. 1978; s. Jose B. and Aurea C. (Carilo) Borjal; m. Mabel Dioneda, Feb. 6, 1966; chil: Madeleine, b. 1966, Sarah, b. 1968, Michelle, b. 1970, Jerome, b. 1972, Armando Jr., b. 1980; edn: DVM, Univ. of the Phil. 1964; MPA, CentroEscolar Univ., 1971. Career: Meat & Food Insp., Calif. Dept. of Food & Agri., Sacramento 1973-74, veterinary med. ofcr. I, II, 1974-76; animal tech. III (lab. animals), Calif. Dept. of Health Svcs., Berkeley 1976-79; pvt. practitioner (small animal) vet. 1979--; vet. Addison St. Pet Hosp., Berkeley 1979-80, cons. 1980-; mgr./ vet. Bay Cities Spay & Neuter Clinic, Milpitas 1980-. awards: letterman, Univ. of Phil. varsity volleyball (team capt. 1963)1960-63, varsity track & field 1960-63, winner 1st campus marathon. mem: Calif. Filipino Veterinary Practitioner, No. Calif. Assn. of Filipino Vets., Fgn. Graduates Vet. Assn. in USA 1976, Phil. Vet. Med. Assn., Calif. Vet. Med. Assn., Smithsonian Instn.; mem. Examining panel Filipino Bilingual Pgm. 1978; mem. Excelsior Neighborhood Assn. (SF) 1980; charter mem. Venerable Knight Vets. frat.; pub. sci. papers; Democrat; Catholic; rec: jog, swim, volleyball, basketball; res: 231 Athens San Francisco 94112 ofc: Bay Cities Clinic 42 Corning Ave. Milpitas 95035

BORN, JAMES THOMAS, private investigator; b. Oct. 4, 1946, Chgo.; s. James Joseph and Helen Marjorie (Christianson) T.; m. Becky Southard, Aug. 18, 1973; children: Heather, b. 1976, Mark, b. 1977, Monica (step), b. 1969; edn: AA, L.A. Pierce Coll. 1973; police sci. stu. CSU Northridge 1973, Upper Iowa Univ. 1976-80, L.A. City Coll. and L.A. Valley Coll., 1972-73; grad. 22 mil. schs.; US Army Cert. Criminal Investigator; Lic. Pvt. Investigator, Calif. 1978; Calif. Comm. Coll. Tchr. Cred. (Police Sci.) 1977. Career: Los Angeles Police Dept. (reserve ofcr. with Patrol and Police Intell.) W. Valley Div. 1969-72; L.A. County Sheriff reserve deputy, 1972-73; sgt. US Postal Security Force, L.A. Internat. Airport, 1971-72; spl. agt. L.A. Dept. Rec. & Parks, 1972-73; police ofcr. Dunsmuir Police Dept., 1973-74, Capitola Police Dept. 1974-77; pvt. investigator /owner Calif. Investigative Services (spec. in criminal & traffic accident inv.) Soquel, Calif. 1978--; Cert. Nuclear, Biological and Chem. Warfare Instr., US Army 1983; awards: Letter of Valor, City of Capitola 1975; commendn., City of Dunsmuir for rescuing flood victims 1974; mem: Internat. Soc. of Stress Analysis; past pres. Capitola Police Protective League; fmr. adv. Bay Area Traffic Execs. Council; past mem. Internat. Assn. of Auto Theft Investigators; Nat. Rifle Assn.; Game Wardens of Vietnam Assn.; BSA scoutmaster; mil: M/sgt. (E8), USAR ret. 1963-83, Sr. M.P. Instr.; 13 medals for combat Vietnam, 16 achievement medals; Prot.; rec: fishing. Res: 4411 Cortez Dr Soquel 95072 Ofc: California Investigative Services, POB 548, Soquel 95073

BORN, ROGER LYNN, marketing executive; b. July 9, 1933, Mnpls.; s. Bernhard Herman and Hertha Olga (Klawitter) B.; m. Patricia Ann Kreider, Dec. 21, 1978; children: Mark Gavin, b. 1952, Ashley Francine, b. 1983; edn: BA, geol., Univ. Minn. 1956, Cert. in EE, 1963; grad. wk. in mgmt., So. Methodist Univ. 1970; seismologist trainee Continental Geophysicial Co., Ft. Worth, Tx. 1956-60; seismologist Sinclair Research Inc., Tulsa, Okla. 1960-61; sr. systems engr. Univac, Sperry Rand Corp., ST. Paul, Minn. 1961-66; systems engrg. mgr. Sci. Service Div. (supporting geophys. & oceanographic ops.), Texas Instruments, Dallas 1966-71; salesman, Mosler Information Systems, Dallas 1971-72; data acquisitions systems mgr. (for US ships, Global Atmospheric Resrch. Pgm., Atlantic Tropical Expt.) NOAA (Nat. Oceanic and Atomspheric Adminstrn.) Data Buoy Office, Bay St. Louis, Miss. 1972-74; tech. pgm. mgmt., Ocean Data Systems Inc., Monterey, Ca. 1974-76; real estate broker, 1976-77; mktg. mgr. Pro-Log Corp., Monterey 1977--; awards: NOAA Data Buoy Office Spl. Achieve. Awd. 1974; US Dept. Commerce/ NOAA Spl. Achieve. Awd. 1974; patent: Method and Apparatus for Processing Seismic Data in the Field (1970); tech. publs., profl. presentations in field; mem. IEEE Computer Soc., Carmel Ski Club (treas. 1981-, past pres.), Nat. Ski Patrol System (Senior Rating), Sports Car Racing Assn. Monterey Penin., BSA leader; mil: Air Force ROTC 1951-55, USAR 1957-67; Democrat; Christian; rec: skiing, sailing, backpacking. Res: POB 1344 Monterey 93940 Ofc: Pro-Log Corp. 2411 Garden Rd Monterey 93940

BORNSTEIN, MARK JAY, real estate marketing executive; b. July 19, 1949, Seattle, Wash.; s. Jack I. and Lois (Weiner) B.; m. Emmeline Goodman, Aug. 4, 1974; children: Eric, b. 1977; Leslie, b. 1980; edn: BSBA, San Jose St. Univ. 1971; UCLA 1971-83; CSU, L.A.; W. L.A. Coll.; Saving & Loan Inst.; San Fernando Sch. of Law; comm. coll. life tchg. cred., Calif.; broker lic., Calif. Career: loan ofcr. Bayview Fed. Savings, San Francisco 1971-73e; dept. hd., R.E. tract lending Calif. Fed. Savings, Los Angeles 1973-74; assoc. prof. West L.A. Coll., Culver City 1974-78; v.p. mktg. Goldrich & Kest, Culver City 1878--; pres./ dir. 17 condominium assns.; exec. v.p. co. owned mortgage co.; mem: Sales & Mktg. Council; Rho Epsilon (pres. 1969); Culver City Nat. Little League; B'nai Brith; La Ballona Sch PTA; Jr. Achievement; Democrat; Jewish; rec: photog., computers. Res: 4040 Lamarr Culver City 90230 Ofc: Goldrich & Kest, 5150 Overland Ave Culver City 90230

BOROWSKY, PHILIP, lawyer; b. Oct. 9, 1946, Phila.; s. Joshua and Gertrude (Nicholson) Borowsky; m. Judith Goldwasser, Sept. 5, 1970; chil: Miriam, b. 1970, Manuel, b. 1975, Nora, b. 1981; edn: BA, UCLA 1967, JD, Univ. of S.F. Law Sch. 1973. Career: atty. law firm Cartwright, Sucherman, Slobodin & Fowler, Inc., San Francisco 1973--, partner 1978-; arbitrator Am. Arbitration Assn., mem. Arbitration Panel S.F. Superior Ct.; adj. faculty Hastings Las Sch. 1981-82; spkr. for Practising Law Inst.; mem. Calif. Trial Lawyers Assn. (legis. com.); McAuliffe Hon. Soc. U.S.F. Law Sch.; contbr. law revs.; mil: spec.4th cl. US Army, Army Commendn. Medal; Democrat; Jewish; rec: sports. Res: 15 Los Cedros, Novato 94947 Ofc: 160 Sansome St. Ste. 900 San Francisco 94104

BORRUSO, ANTONIO, insurance brokerage firm owner; b. July 2, 1942, San Francisco; s. Antonio Sr. and Rose M. (Bologna) B.; m. Apr. 24, 1964, div.; children: Matthew Michael, b. 1965; John Anthony, b. 1968; Sarah Anne, b. 1970; edn: AA, Golden Gate Univ. 1968, BS, 1971; num. profl. certificated courses. Career: United States Fidelity & Guaranty Co., San Francisco 1962-71; underwriter 1962; underwriter supvr. 1963-65; spl. agent/ mgmt./ supvr. 1965-71 (created comml. package pgms. & formats still in use nationally); mgr. Devoto Lewis Co. (merged w/ F.S. James & Co.), San Francisco 1971-76; owner Borruso Ins. Brokerage, Larkspur 1976--; mem: Profl. Ins. Agents of Am.; mil: served in US Army 1961; Democrat; Catholic; rec: fishing, gardening. Res: 120 Almenar Dr Greenbrae 94904 Ofc: Larkspur Square, 980 Magnolia Ave Larkspur 94939

BORUM, WILLIAM DONALD, military officer; b. Dec. 26, 1932, St. Louis, Mo.; s. William Doris and Lura Mae (Jackson) Borum; m. Mary Bullard, Nov. 29, 1952; chil: Mary, b. 1953, Patricia, b. 1958, Kimberly, b. 1962; edn: BA,bus., Univ. Nebr. 1967; MA, internat. rels., USC 1971; diploma, US Army Engr. Sch., Ft. Belvoir, Va. 1960, Command and Gen.Staff Coll., 1968, NATO Def. Coll., Rome, Italy 1976. Career: commnd. 2d lt. US Army Corps of Engrs. 1954, co.comdr./platoon leader in USA, 1954-56, in Germany, 1956-60; 1st lt., 1956; served in Lebanon, 1958; capt., 1960; engr. advisor to Imperial Iranian Army, 1962-65; maj., assigned to Pentagon, 1966; served in 65thEngineers,25th Inf. Div., Vietnam, 1966-67; lt. col., assigned to Pentagon, 1968; served in Brit. Def. Staff, Ministry of Def., London, 1969-71; comdg. ofcr., 35th Engr. Batt., 1972; assigned to Ofc of the Chief of Engrs., Wash DC 1973-75; Ofc of the Deputy Chief of Staff, Ops., Dept. of Army, Pentagon; Hdqtrs. NATO Allied Forces Central Europe 1976-79; deputy comdr. So. Pac. Div., Corps of Engrs., 1979--, responsible for mil. constrn. involving 3000 govt. employees and over 9000 contractor personnel (projects incl. Space Transport Sys. and the MX Missile facilities); instr. US Army Engr. Sch., Ft. Belvoir 1961-62; Mil. awards (20) incl. Def. Superior Svc, Legion of Merit,Bronze Star, Air Medal w/two Oak Leaf Clusters, Purple Heart, Cross of Gallantry w/Palm, Vietnam Svc w/5 battle stars, Sr. Parachutist; mem: Am. Acad. Polit. and Social Sci., Soc. of Am. Mil. Engrs., Commonwealth Club of Calif., Am. Mgmt. Assn., Acad. of Polit. Sci. (NY) US Parachute Assn., Assn. of US Army, The Fusion Found., Smithsonian Assocs. (nat.); Republican; Episcopal (lay reader, chalice bearer); rec: skydiving, internat. rels., classical music; res: 299 Casa Grande Real, Novato 95934 ofc: USA So. Pac. Div. Corps of Engrs., 630 Sansome St. Rm 1240 San Francisco 94111.

BOSTER, G. ARCHIE, lawyer; b. Dec. 11, 1935, San Diego; s. John Archie and Ethel Marie (Carmean) B.; m. Sally Ann, Dec. 2, 1972; edn: ba, CSU San Diego 1963; JD, Cal Western Univ. 1966; admitted to Calif. State Bar 1967; Calif. Comm. Coll. Tchr. Cred. (Bus. Law). Career: atty. sole practitioner, criminal and civil law practice, Carlsbad; owner/v.p./atty., real estate mgmt. co. serving multiple planned residential developments (50 of practice devoted to real estate law); atty. for Village San Juan 1973-74, bd. dirs., pres. 1974-76; served on panel of experts in drafting stds. for dealing with Planned Communities, City of San Juan Capistrano; mem. Leucadia Town Council; head, North County, Bill Craven Cpgn.; orgnzr. Planned Comm. Fedn. (before CAI); honors: named most competent atty., S.D. Co. Judges; Citizen of the day, North County; recogn., BSA, Rotary, Boys Club; mem. Calif., San Diego, North Co. Bar Assns.; (past) CofC, Rotary, Masons and Shrine; mil: USAF; Republican; Prot.; rec: motorcycling, carpentry. Res: Sunningdale Dr San Luis Rey 92068 Ofc: Atty. G. Archie Boster, POB 117, Carlsbad 92008

BOSTWICK, GARY LYNN, lawyer; b. Apr. 4, 1941, Wichita, Ks.; s. Vernon E. and Ossie M. (Roberts) B.; children: Kevin M., b. 1968; Alyssa C., b. 1971; edn: BS, Northwestern UNiv. 1963; M. Pub. Policy, UC Berkeley 1976; JD, 1977; St. Bar. of Calif. 1977. Career: prof. Bolivian Tech. Inst., La Paz, Bolivia 1963-65;

communtiy devel. cons. Univ. of N.M., Albuquerque, N.M. 1965; assoc. dir. Peace Corps., Panama City, Panama 1969-70; mng. partner Hand, Bostwick & Assocs., Stuttgart, W. Germany 1970-73; law clerk to Hon. Fred. J. Cassibry, U.S. Dist. Ct., Eastern Dist. of Louisiana, New Orleans, La. 1977-78; assoc./ atty. at law Manatt, Phelps, Rothenberg & Tunney, Los Angeles 1978-81; partner/ atty. at law Barash & Hill, Los Angeles 1981-83; atty. at law Law Ofcs. Gary L. Bostwick, Santa Monica 1983--; mem: State Bar of Calif. (Human Rights Com.); Am. Bar Assn.; Los Angeles Co. Bar Assn.; ACLU; Amnesty Internat.; publs: Calif. L. Rev. (1976), Inst. of Govtl. Studies Pub. Affairs Report (Vol. 18, No 1, 1977); cited by Calif. Supreme Ct. in City of Santa Barbara v. Adamson (27 Cal.3d, 1980) and in Am. Constnl. Law (887); mil: 1st lt. US Army Arty. 1966-68; Democrat; rec: cattle roundups, skiing, baseball. Res: 1807 10th Street, 5, Santa Monica 90404 Ofc: Gary L. Bostwick, Esq., 701 Santa Monica Blvd, Santa Monica 90401

BOSWELL, IRVING WARD, III, military officer; b. Jan. 8, 1945, Orlando, Fla.; s. Irving Ward Jr. and Teresa Ann (Harver) B.; m. Sandra DuPont, Apr. 23, 1977; 1 dau: Christine, b. 1980; edn: BS, indsl. edn., Virginia Polytech. Inst. 1968; MA, personnel mgmt., Louisiana Tech. Univ. 1976; outstanding grad.- Nat. Security Mgmt., Nat. Defense Univ. 1982; grad. Air War Coll. USAF Air Univ. 1983; cert. flight instr. single & multi engine aircraft, instrument comml. pilot, rated in Boeing 707 & 720 Jet aircraft. Career: sr. dir. North American Air Defense (NORAD), Miami, Fla. 1968-70; Combat Air Weapons controller, Saigon, Vietnam 1970-71; class ldr. Jet Pilot Tng., Valdosta, GA. 1971-72; Forward Air Controller (FAC), Pilot O-2 Aircraft, Vietnam 1972-73; aircraft cmmdr./ instr. pilot K/RC- 135 Aircraft, Shreveport, La. & Merced, Calif. 1973-81; Weapons Sys. Devel. & Validation branch chief, Castle AFB 1981-82; Instructional Systems Div. chief, Castle AFB 1982--; awards: Outstanding Senior Mem., Civil Air Patrol 1983; Outstanding Mem. of Year 1982, AF Assn.; SAC Outstanding Ednl. Achiev. Awd. 1978; mem: Civil Air Patrol; Order of Daedalians; AF Assn.; 15th AF Assn.; Castle Air Mus.; publs: flight safety art., Strategic Air Command Combat Crew Mag. 1979; mil: maj. USAF, Senior Pilot; 15 AF decorations incl. Bronze Star 1971, Air Medal 1973, AF Commdn. Medal 1979, AF Achiev. Medal 1983; Republican; rec: sailing, fishing, computer programming. Res: 2311 Gaither Ct Atwater 95301 Ofc: 93 Bomb Wing / DO5, Castle AFB 95342

BOTTS, PAT LUCILLE, real estate broker; b. Oct. 2, 1925, Los Angeles; d. Greenie "Jack" L. and Oma Belle (Bodle) Trotter; m. Albert F. Botts, Sr. Dec. 29, 1949; children: Patricia, b. 1951, Albert, b. 1953; edn: real estate courses, Napa Coll., num. profl. R.E. courses; Calif. Real Estate Lic. 1963. Career: real estate broker/owner Botts Realty & Land Co., Napa; past owner/opr. var. retail businesses, Lazy-B Kennel (boarding, tng., breeding purebred dogs), comml. fishing vessel SAVO (fishing tuna and salmon); polit. activist local, state, nat. (both Calif. Senators submitted bills for public causes in her behalf); spkr./ activist in successful campaign to restore usage of Lake Berryessa to public recreation, 1969-74; mem. Napa Co. Bd. of Realtors, Calif. Assn. of Realtors, Nat. Assn. of Realtors, Lake Berryessa CofC (past pres.); dir. Napa Co. Devel. Council; dir. Environmental Ctr., Napa; dir. Consumer Awareness Office, Napa; coordinator Safe Nuclear Energy Iniative; dir. Citizens Council for Napans Tomorrow; columnist, Lake Berryessa News; Democrat; Prot.; Res: Mecca Ranch POB 648, Winters 95694 Ofc: Botts Realty 3377 Solano Ave, Ste. 420, Napa 94558

BOUCHARD, LUKE GASTON, steel fabrication co. president; b. Mar. 27, 1926, Stanhope, Que. Canada, nat. 1953; s. Donat J. and Regina (Morin) B.; m. Dorothy Shelton-Carney, Feb. 28, 1948; children: Michael, b. 1945, Carol, b. 1949, Don, b. 1955, Sandra, b. 1959, Karen, b. 1963, C.J., b. 1969, Shawn, b. 1976; edn: grade sch., French Lang., night courses at local H.S. & Colls. Career: as a boy worked in Father's Saw Mill; at age 16, wkr. to Lead man within 6 mos. at Northern Electric, Montreal, Can.; traveled throughout Canada wkg. var. constrn. projects; married an Am. girl, came to Calif. in 1949; worked as shop helper to (current) half owner for a steel fabrication co.; current: owner/ pres. Plas-Tal Mfg. Co. Inc., and Sierra Materials; owner/sr. v.p. Sechrist & Kelly Constrn. Co.; treas. (pres. 1982-3) Steel Fabricators Assn. of So. Calif.; trustee Shopmen Health and Welfare Trust Fund; mem. Knights of Columbus, Elks; subject feature art. Sat. Night mag. (6/83 Toronto, Ont.); mil: m/sgt. Royal Can. Arty. Reserve 1943-45; Republican; Catholic; rec: travel, mountain home, cycling. Res: 601 W. Valley View Fullerton Ofc: Plas-Tal Mfg. Co., Inc. 8815 S. Sorensen Ave Santa Fe Springs 90670

BOUDREAU, RICHARD GEORGE, oral and maxillo-facial surgeon; b. Aug.19, 1945, Venice, Fla.; s.George Joseph and Maria Josephine (LaRosa) B.; edn: BS, USC 1967, DDS 1971; MD, Utesa Univ. Sch of Med., 1983. Career: intern LongBeach VA Hosp., 1971-2, surg. res. Univ. of Wash. Med.Ctr., Seattle 1972-5; surg. fellowship Harvard Univ. 1970-1, and Univ. of Nijmegen (The Netherlands) 1974-5; practice oral, maxillo-facial surg.; hosp. staff UCLA, UCI Med Ctr., Marina Mercy, Daniel Freeman, Good Samaritan, Hollywood Presbyn., Long Beach VA Hosp.(past asst. chief oral & maxillo-facial surg.), Sta. Monica Hosp.; asst. prof. surg. UCI Sch. of Med.; anatomy instr. USC; lectr., clin. instr. surg. UCLA: ARC cert. instr. in Adv. Cardiac Life Support. Author, screenplay writer; inventor surgical instruments. Awards: fellowship, Am. Coll. of Oral & Maxillo-Facial Surgs. Dip., Am. Bd. Oral & Maxillo-Facial Surgeons. Mem: fellow Am. Soc. Anesthesiol., fellow Am. Assn. Oral & Maxillo-Facial Surgeons, fellow Internat. Assn. Oral Surgeons, Western Soc. Oral &: Maxillofacial Surgeons , So. Calif. Soc. of Oral &: Maxillofacial Surgeons (Peer Rev. Com.), Intl.Assn. for Dental Res., fellow Intl.Coll. Applied Nutrition, fellow Intl. Coll. Oral Implantologists, So. Calif. Acad. Oral Pathol., Assn Holistic Hlth., mem. Surg. Rev. Bd. Emergency Rm.

Com. Oral & Maxillofacial Surgeons; honors: Omicron Kappa Upsilon, Alpha-Tau Epsilon, Alpha Gamma Sigma, listed Who's Who In Dentistry; publs: arts. in sci. jours.; Republican: rec: marathon runner, skier, mtn. climber, flying; res: 14000 Tahiti Way, Marina del Rey 90291 ofc: Marina Mercy Med Ctr, 4644 Lincoln Bl. Ste.400, Marina del Rey 90292.

BOULEY, HAROLD C., real estate broker; b. Jan. 18, 1944, Montague, Mass.; s. Harold Fredrick and Flora Elizabeth (Bitzer) B.; m. Susan Dieckilman, Aug. 22, 1970; 1 son, Shawn, b. 1971; edn: BA, CSU Long Beach 1966; Calif. Life. Tchg. Credential. Career: public school tchr., Westminster, Ca. 1967-73, Irvine, Ca. 1973-76; mgr. Century 21 Surf Realty, Costa Mesa 1976-78; vice pres. Century 21 Gold Star, Realtors, Costa Mesa 1978-80, pres. 1980--; sponsor award City of Costa Mesa National Cycle Championships 1981; mem: Nat. Assn. of Realtors, Calif. Assn. of Realtors, Newport Harbor -Costa Mesa Bd. of Realtors, Rotary; Christian. Ofc: Century 21 Gold Star, Realtors 2214 Newport Blvd Costa Mesa 92627

BOURBAN, ROGER ARSENE, (aka Le Garcon Rapide), restaurateur, athlete, actor, lecturer; b. May 10, 1948, Sion, Switz., nat. 1980; s. Marcel and Jeanne (Schmelzbach) Bourban; edn: apprentice cook, restaurant/hotel touring, Sion, Switz. 1964-6; Ecole Hoteliere, De La Societe Suisse Des Hoteliers, Lausanne, Switz. 1967-9; Nelson Sch., London, Eng. 1970; stu. Lee Strasberg Theatre Inst., Actors and Dirs. Lab. Career: waiter Gitana Grill Rm., Geneva, Switz. 1968; maitre D' Hotel De La Tete Noire, Rolle, Switz. 1970; sommelier Surfer's Paradise, Australia 1971; mgr. New & Old El Camino Real Restaurant, Sydney, Austral. 1972; (with noted chef, mentor Jean Bertranou 1972-5) as chef La Chaumiere, Beverly Hills 1972-4, captain L'Ermitage, Los Angeles 1974-5; captain Le Restaurant, L.A. 1975-7; asst. dir./Habitation Leclerc Hotel, Port Au Prince, Haiti 1978; captain Ma Maison, L.A. 1979-80; prop. Cafe Monet Bistro, L.A. 1980-82; currently self empl. free lance restaurateur & sports personality/athlete, world-wide personal appearances giving cooking & baking demonstrations, lectr. on health, exercise, nutrition, home entertaining. Actor in films, on TV & TV commercials; featured personality num. TV shows. Athlete: mem. Swiss Snow Ski Team 1965-6; mem. Swiss Nat. Judo team 1966-8, participant/instr. judo events 1963-, 2d deg. Black Belt Nidan, winner num. nat. events incl. Judo Championship, Sydney, Aust. Running awards. 5 World Records, Guinness Bk. of World Records, 1981-; World's Fastest Running Walter 1976-, winner 133 Waiters' Races internat.; 1981 Waiter's Hall of Fame; runner NY Marathon (4), London (2), N.Z., Hawaii, Korea, Rio De Janeiro marathons; other sports incl: snow & water skiing, tennis, swimming, golf, horseback riding, car racing. Mem: SAG, AFTRA; vol. Calif. Spec. Olympics, United Cerebral Palsy/Spastic Chil. Found., Am. Diabetes Assn. Ind.; Catholic; address: Bourban Internat. 320 N. LaPeer Dr. #103, POB 2992, Beverly Hills 90213

BOURLAND, DAVID LEE, govt. agency quality assurance representative; b. Jan. 20, 1956, Frankfurt, Germany, Am. citizen; s. Walter Eugene and Jacqualine Rae (Wilson) B.; m. Dorothy Chirdon, May 3, 1974; children: Robyn Michelle b. 1979, David Lee, Jr. b. 1983; edn: AS, qual. ass./mgmt., Chaffey Coll. 1984. Career: aircraft mech. US Marine Corps in N.J., N.C., S.C., Ga., Japan, Philippines, 1973-78; quality assurance field rep. Hi-Tek Corp., Garden Grove, Ca. 1978-80; quality assurance splst, Dept. of Defense, Ontario, Ca. 1980-81; senior QA engr. ITT Cannon Electric, Santa Ana 1981-82; QA rep. Dept. of Def., Ontario, Ca. 1983--; cons. Quality Control/Qual. Assur. 1982-; honors: appreciatio, Mayor and San Bernardino Police Dept. (1976); mem. ASQC; mil: cpl. USMC 1973-78, GCM, Nat. Def. Medal; rec: pvt. pilot, aerodynamics. Res: 7732 Bonnie St San Bernardino 92410 Ofc: Dept. of Defense 609 North Lemon Ave Ontario 91764

BOUSQUET, JOHN FREDERICK, locksmith; b. Nov. 19, 1948, Wash. DC; s. Kenneth Joseph, Sr. and Margaret Isabel (Sherrin) B.; edn: BS, Lehigh Univ. 1971; ;24 certs. in locksmithing courses, Assoc. Locksmiths of Am., Calif. Locksmith Assn., and var. lock mfr. service courses; Master Kleidologist, Lockmaster, Keying Engr., lic. C61 Contractor. Career: mobile lock shop owner 1971--; instr. masterkeying, Calif. Locksmith Assn.; authored an amendment to the penal code restricting and registering sale of lock picks and car openers which became a city ordinance (S.F.) and is to become state law (1984); cons. nationally on masterkeying; honors: Mem. of the Year 1982, Calif. Locksmith Assn. San Francisco Bay Chpt.; mem. Assoc. Locksmith of Am., C.L.A. (secty. 1983); publs: tech. art., Locksmiths Ledger. Res: 112 Eucalyptus Ave. South San Francisco 94080

BOWE-GUARINO, PATRICIA ANN, insurance agent; b. July 4, 1946, Stockton; d. Robert P. and Katherine Warner (McAleer) Bowe; m. Vincent Joseph Guarino, June 27, 1981; edn: BA, CSU Long Beach 1969; JD, Univ. of W. LA Sch. of Law 1979; admitted to Calif. State Bar 1982; Calif. Life Elem. Tchr. credential 1973. Career: elementary sch. tchr. Long Beach Unified 1970-79; ed. ORD Publishing, Los Angeles 1979-80; agent/owner Trish Bowe State Farm Ins., Pacific Palisades 1981--; rep. Tchrs. Assn. of Long Beach 1977-79; awards: NAHU Round Table 1981-82; NALU Round Table 1981-82; State Farm Centurion; Million Dollar Round Table 1982; mem: Los Angeles Co. Bar Assn.; Irish- Am. Bar Assn.; Nat. Assn. of Health Underwriters; Nat. Assn. of Life Underwriters; Freedom Found., Valley Forge; Pac. Palisades Womans Club; Pac. Palisades Republican Club; Pac. Palisades Womans Evening Club; Pac. Palisades CofC; coauthor: Multistate Method for Sucess, 1980; Republican; Catholic; rec: western art collecting, sailing, equestrian. Res: 15515 Sunset Blvd, B-11, Pacific Palisades 90272 OFc: Trish Bowe State Farm Ins., 984 Monument st, Ste 104, Pacific Palisades 90272

BOWEN, WALTER ORRIN, chiropractor; b. Feb. 3, 1941, Pawnee, Ill.; s.Cecil Edward and Lula Hazel (Duncan) Bowen; m. Susan Marie Short, Oct. 25, 1963; chil: Orrin Lee, b. 1965, Walter Alan, b. 1969, Elizabeth Marie, b. 1978; edn: stu. Milikin Univ. 1964-5, DC, Cleveland Chiropractic Coll, 1975; postgrad. Sta. Monica Coll. 1975-6, Glendale City Coll. 1979-80. Career: consulting clinician, x-ray instr. Cleveland Chiro. Coll., Los Angeles 1975-77; doctor, owner Bowen Chiropractic Center, Burbank 1976--; cons. to MDs for Chiropractic Consultants Internat.; speaker on diagnosis, x-ray, technique, Anna Reeves Workmen's Compensation Seminars. Dip. Nat. Bd. Chiro. Examiners 1975; cert. in x-ray, Dr. Russell Erhardt, DC, DABCR, 1976; cert. achievement, Parker Chiro. Resrch Found. 1977; cert. excellence, LaForte Chiro. Consultants, 1981. mem: founder, Cleveland Chiro. Alumni Assn of Calif. 1976-; Am. Chiro. Assn. 1976-; Council on Roentgenology 1980; Parker Chiro. Resrch Found. 1977-; Nat. Health Fedn.; Equestrian Trails, Inc. (bd. mem. Corral 10). mil: hosp. corpsman 3rd cl. USN 1958-62, Presdtl. Cit., GCM; Presbyterian; rec: horseman, boating, water skiing, gardening; res: 10233 Johanna Ave, Shadow Hills 91040 tele:(213)The-BACK ofc: Bowen Chiropractic Ctr 844 N.Hollywood Wy Burbank 91505.

BOWER, FAY LOUISE, professor of nursing; b. Sept. 10, 1929, San Francisco, CA; d. James Joseph and Emily Clare (Andrews) Saitta; B.S., San Jose State Coll., 1965; M.S.N., Univ. Calif., S.F., 1966; D.N.Sc., 1978; m. Robert Davis Bower, July 2, 1949, Palo Alto; children: R. David; Carol (Tomei); Dennis James; Thomas John. Career: office nurse, Palo Alto, 1950-55; staff nurse, Stanford Hosp., 1964-72; mem., faculty, San Jose State Univ., 1966--; asst. prof. 1966-70, assoc. prof. 1970-74; prof. 1970--; also coord., Grad. Nursing Program, 1977-78; chmn., Dept. of Nursing, 1978-82; dean, University of San Francisco 1982--; visiting prof.: Univ. Miss., Univ. Calif., Harding Coll. Fellow, Amer. Acad. of Nursing, 1978. Author: Fundamentals of Nursing: Concepts, Roles and Functions, 1979; The Process of Planning Nursing Care, 3rd ed., 1981; Theoretical Foundations of Nursing I, II and II, 1972; Nursing Skills I; co-author other nursing texts, publs. of nursing; dir. research and curriculum grants. Mem.: Calif. Nurse's Assn.; Nurse's Assn. of Coll. of Obstet. and Gynecol.; Phi Kappa Phi; Calif. Tchrs. Assn.; AAUP; Internatl. Indsl. TV Assn.; Commonwealth Club of S.F.; Health Edn. League for Nursing; Western Gerontological Assn. Catholic, dir. rel. edn. program. Rec.: writing, reading, moving. Res.: 1820 Portola Road, Woodside 94062; Office: School of Nursing, San Francisco Univ.

BOWERS, RICHARD EUGENE, physician-surgeon; b. July 16, 1920, St. Paul, Minn.; s. Everett Raymond and Muriel Evelyn (Maley) B.; m. Andrienne Rene Rahne, May 27, 1967; children: Richard, b. 1946; Nancy, b. 1950; Cathy, b. 1952; Nicole, b. 1969; edn: BS, La Sierra Coll. 1941; MD, Loma Linda Univ. 1945. Career: Linda Vista Med. Ctr. 1947-59; Kearny Mesa Med. Ctr. 1959--; Doctors Hosp., bd. dirs. 1957-81, chief staff 1973; ex. med. bd. Childrens Hosp. 1958-61, Sharp Meml. Hosp. 1958-61; charter fellow, Am. Acad. Gen. Practice 1949, charter fellow, Am. Acad. Family Practice 1972; honors: appointed physician to Queen Elizabeth II, 1983 Calif. visit; Spl. Svc. Awd., San Diego Hist. Soc. 1980; mem: Kiwanis (pres. 1954); San Diego Hist. Soc. (pres. 1982-83); San Diego Co. Med. Soc.; Calif. Med. Soc.; Am. Med. Assn.; World Med. Assn.; mil: capt. US Army Med. Corps. 1945-47; Republican; Protestant; rec: history, stamps, coins. Res: 4474 Nortensia St San Diego 92103 Ofc: Kearny Mesa Medical Ctr., 7525 Linda Vista Rd San Diego 92111

BOWMAN, DEAN DANIEL, real estate broker; b. Mar. 30, 1948, Milwaukee, Wisc.u; s. Daniel Ross and Dorothy June (Field) B.; m. Cynthia Rowland, Aug. 22, 1970; children: David, b. 1972; Jeana, b. 1978; edn: AA, E.D.P., Coll. of San Mateo 1972; BS, mktg., CSU San Jose 1972; Calif. lic: Life & Disability Ins. 1972, Real Estate Broker 1980, Consumers Finance Lender (broker) 1983. Career: acct. mgr. PIA Merchandising Co., Foster City 1973-78; partner/ realtor Whittaker & Assocs., Mt. View 1978-80; partner/ owner West Coast Capital 1983; owner Dean D. Bowman Investments 1976--; owner/ pres. Bowman Realty, Inc. 1980--; partner/ owner BoBass Investments 1981--; partner/ owner M.B. Assocs. 1981--; pres./ owner De Anza Capital, Inc., Loan Center 1983--; mem: Calif. Assn. Realtors; Nat. Assn. Realtor; San Jose Real Estate Bd.; Mt. View Bd. Realtors; Republican; Methodist; rec: golf, boating, skiing. Res: 10273 Miner Pl Cupertino 95014 Ofc: De Anza Capital, Inc., 1021 S Wolfe Rd, Ste 185, Sunnyvale 94086

BOWMAN, JACQUELINE BONNIE, educator; b. Dec. 28, 1936, Los Angeles; d. John and Margaret E. (Hagen) Glatz; m. Robert Bowman; edn: BA, sociol. (elem. tchg. cred.), La Verne Univ. 1957; ednl. psych., CSCLA and USC, 1963-66; MA, sec. tchr. cred., Pasadena Coll. 1967; ednl. psych. (gen. admin. cred.) UC Riverside 1968-70; PhD, USC 1974; Profl. Cert., Consortium for Adv. Leadership, ACSA 1981-83; lic: State Marriage, Family Child Counseling; Ednl. Psychologist ; Psychologist. Career: Charter Oak Unified Sch. Dist., Covina 1958-: tchr. Gr. 3, 1958-63; psychometrist 1963-66; sch. psychologist 1966-69; coordinator of spl. edn. 1969-71; dir. Pupil Personnel Services and Spl. Edn. 1971--, also dir. Staff Devel. 1982--; past instr. La Verne Univ., UCLA; psychologist Whittier Guidance Ctr., 1966-69; mem: Nat., Calif. (chpsn.) Assn. of Sch. Psychologists; Nat., Calif. (bd. dirs.), Charter Oak Chpt. Assn. of Sch. Adminstrs.; Nat. Spkrs. Assn.; Assn. for Supvsn. and Curriculum Devel.; Council for Exceptional Children; AAUW; Calif. Assn. for Neurol. Handicapped Children; Calif. Assn. for the Gifted (chpsn.); E. San Gabriel Valley Cooperative Edn. Pgms. (chpsn.); Phi Lambda Theta; mem. Toastmistress, Assistance League, Native Daus. of Golden West, PTA, v.p./bd. dirs. Edgewood family Counseling Agcy. Res: 938 Arrow Hwy San Dimas 91773 Ofc: Charter Oak Unif. Sch. Dist., POB 9, Covina 91723

BOWYER, JOHN VICTOR, physician; b. Oct. 10, 1930, NY; s. Ertel Victor and Katherine Fleming (Cole) B., (father, v.p. Roanoke Gas Co. and founder/ bd.dir. Southeastern Gas Assn.); desc. Col. Wm. Bowyer, ofcr. Cont. Army 1776. m. Barbara Turner, Mar. 9, 1973; chil: John Spostswood, Rebecca Randolph, Carter Burwell, John Randolph, Katherine Fleming; edn: BSc, Coll. Wm.& Mary 1952; MD, Univ. Va. Sch of Med. 1956. Career: intern Brooke Army Hosp., 1956-7, phys. USAF Med. Corps 1957-9; staff John Randolph Hosp., Va. 1960-67; res. Med. Coll. of Va., 1967-69, NIH fellow/staff cardiovascular disease, 1969-71; staff cardiologist attdg. internal med. Kaiser Hosp., Panorama City, Calif. 1971-, and co-dir. Cardiac Studies Lab., assoc. dir. Cardiac Acateterization Lab; staff cardiologist St. Vincent Med. Ctr. 1983-, Granada Hills Hosp., 1980; awards: NIH Resrch Fellowships, cardiovascular disease, prostaglandin physiol. 1965; outstanding teacher awd., Kaiser Found. Hosps. 1975-76; fellow Am. Coll. of Cardiology, 1972, 1981; Dip., Am. Bd. Internal Med., Cardiovascular Disease, 1973; fellow Am. Coll. Chest Physicians 1981; mem: A.C.C.P. Council on Critical Care 1983; mem: So. Calif. Soc. Interventional Cardiac Angiography, Am. Heart Assn., L.A. Soc. of Internal Med., L.A. Cardiology Soc., L.A. & Am. Socs. of Echocardiography, Virginia Med. Soc., SAR (VA chpt.), Sigma Alpha Epsilon, Phi Beta Phi; Lions Club (bd.dirs. 1965); dir. Old Dominion Eyebank, (S.E. Vir.) 1965; mil: capt. USAF M.C., 1957-59; Republican (Repub. Nat. Com. 1983; committeeman 4th Dist., VA, 1967); Episcopal (vestryman); rec: hike, swim, hunt, fish. res: 23165 Heiss St. Woodland Hills 91364 ofc: Kaiser Hosp. 13652 Cantara St. Panorama City 91402.

BOYD, JOHN MARVIN, communications executive; b. Mar. 6, 1943, Pasadena; s. Marvin Carl and Hannah Mae (Heenan) B.; m. Cheryl Arlene Hammond, Mar. 29, 1969; children: John Matthew, b. 1977; Grace Christina, b. 1981; edn: AA, Pasadena City Coll. 1963; BA, Univ. of Redlands 1966; masters wk. San Francisco St. Univ. 1966-67; PhD, USC 1978; gen. radio telephone lic., FCC 1961. Career: sr. lectr. USC 1971-73; prof. of theatre CSU Fullerton 1973-75; dir. of ops./ sales Southwestern Broadcasters, San Diego 1975-77; pres./ CEO American Sunrise Communications (three radio stations) 1983; pres./ CEO Creative Communications Assn., Orange 1977--; personnel co-ord. Christian Research Inst., Brazil; honors: Alpha Epsilon Rho 1971; Theta Alpha Phi 1966; Oak Knoll Broadcasting fellowships 1972, 73; telecommun. scholarship, RCA 1973; scholarship, CSU 1970; mem: A.F.T.R.A. 1968; N.A.B.E.T. 1967; Treeclimbers; dir. coll./ career Sunday sch.; writer chpt. on broadcasting in Intro. to Theatre by Dr. Jerry Pickering, 1974; rec: swimming, walking. Res: 6251 Shields Dr Huntington Beach 92647 Ofc: Creative Communications Assn., 876 N Batavia Orange 92668

BOYD, JOSEPH HAIG, real estate broker, investor, farmer; b. Mar. 6, 1917, Fowler; s. Hagop and Martha (Marderosian) Boyajian; m. Florence Elma Dennis, Sept. 1, 1939; children: Joseph Dennis, b. 1941; Kenneth Robert, b. 1945; Louise Elma (Autenrieb), b. 1947; Martha Eileen (Marsh), b. 1958; edn: bus. admin., Heald Bus. Coll. 1936; Calif. lic: R.E. Broker, Ins. Broker, Business Broker, 1946. Career: farmer; owner/mgr. Stand-Bi Market, 1938-45; real estate broker/owner J.H.Boyd Realtor, Kerman 1946--; ptnr. J.H. Boyd & Sons Realtors; pres./bd. chmn. J.H. Boyd Ent. Inc.; pres. (home builder, subdivisions) West Side Bldgs. Inc.; owner/opr. movie theatres in San Francisco and Kerman, 1946-56, motel in Fresno, 1956-58; trustee Kerman Elem. Sch. Bd. 1953-60; awards: Calif. Beautification Awd. on Bus. Bldg. 1970, recognition Kerman CofC for 27 years svc.; mem: Farm Bur., Nat. Assn. Realtors, Calif. Assn. Realtors, Fresno Bd. of Realtors; Rotary (charter, pres. 1966, first Paul Harris Fellow in Kerman club); Masons (life); CofC, Armenian Comm. Sch. of Fresno, (past) Fresno Yacht Club; Republican; L.D.S. (high priest); rec: movie photog., travel, sailing. Res: 733 S. Manor Dr Kerman 93630 Ofc: J.H. Boyd & Son Realtors 275 S. Madera Ave, Ste. 100, Kerman 93630

BOYER, CARL, III, educator; b. Sept. 22, 1937, Phila., Pa.; s. Carl Jr. and Elizabeth Campbell (Timm) B.; m. Ada Christine Kruse, July 28, 1962; children: Michele, b. 1963; Denise, b. 1965; Danielle, b. 1967; edn: Univ. of Edinburgh, Scotland 1956-57; BA, Trinity Univ., Tex. 1959; M.Ed., Univ. of Cincinnati 1962; postgrad. work, BYU, CSUN; Calif. Gen. Secondary (life) Tchr. Credential 1968. Career: sch. tchr. in Tex., Ky., Ohio 1959-63; social studies tchr. San Fernando H.S. 1963--; faculty chmn. 1969-70, dept. chair 1980-83; also instr. Kennedy- San Fernando Comm. Adult Sch. and Mission Coll.; genealogical publisher & compiler/author of references, manuals & family histories 1971--; bd. trustees Santa Clarita Comm. Coll. Dist. (pres. 1979-81) 1973-81; bd. dirs. Castaic Lake Water Agency 1982--; pres. Del Prado Condominium Assn., Inc.; awards: United Way Sweepstakes Awd. (1972), Respected Tchr. Awd., San Fernando H.S. Students (1982); mem: United Tchrs. of Los Angeles; Nat. Genealogical Soc.; Newhall- Saugus- Valencia Fedn. of Homeowners Assns. (pres.); Civic, Inc. (pres.); Canyon Co. Formation Com.; elected Supvr. of Canyon Canyon Co.; works: Slade-Babcock Genealogy (1971); Ancestral Lines (2 eds., 1975, 81); Ship Passenger Lists (4 vols. 1976-79); How To Market and Publish Your Family History (1982); mil: USNR 1955-63; Republican; Methodist; rec: travel, photog. Res: POB 333, Newhall 91322 Ofc: San Fernando High Sch., 11133 O'Melveny San Fernando 91340

BOYER, GARY RAY, building designer/contractor; b. Jan. 2, 1938, Des Moines; s. Merlyn Raymond and Loucille Mildred (Decker); m. Mary Martin, Oct. 30, 1964; 1 dau. Cari, b. 1973; edn: BS arch. eng., Pacif Western Univ. 1982, PhD urban eng., 1983; profl. lic.: Profl. Designer (1966), Nuclear Design & Replacement, Unit Planned Devel. Career: self-emplyd arch. designer resdtl., comml., indsl. projects, 1959-81, prop. Gary Boyer & Assocs. (constrn. co.), 1975--; elect. eng. tech. Ark. Nuclear One, Russellville, Ark. 1982-83; bd. chmn. AssociatedSolar; bd.chmn. Asso Multi-Tech; arch. cons. 1967--. Awards: profl. designer, Nuclear Power Plant Repair & Replacement Awd., (2)2d pl. L.A. Co. Fair Arch. Model Design awds., others; mem: A.I.B.D., Elks, Moose, VFW, Am. Nuclear Soc., Pac.Western Univ. Alum; patentee:mic. furn solar collector, beam ceil folded plate, solar elect. gen. system; mil: s/sgt. USMCR; Republican;Lutheran; rec: aviation, nuclear, nature; address: 3883 N. Dower, Fresno 93711.

BOYKO, BRENT EUGENE, telecommunications technician; b. Jan. 10, 1953, Huntington Park; s. Paul Kost and Edith Elisa Boyko; edn: AA, San Bernardino Valley Co. 1973; radiotelephone opr. lic., 1st class, FCC 1970. Career: chief engr. BLLU/ KEMR, Loma Linda Univ., Riverside 1970-71; engr. KVCR-TV/ FM, San Bernardino Valley Coll., San Bernardino 1970-74; engr. audiovisual dept. Loma Linda Univ. Med. Ctr. 1974-78; chief engr. 1978-82; techn., telecommun. dept. 1982--; mem: Audio Engring. Soc.; Soc. of Motion Picture and TV Engrs.; Calif. State Firefighters Assn.; Loma Linda Firefighters Assn.; Republican; Seventh- day Adventist; rec: volunteer firefighter. Res: 26907 Beaumont Ave, POB 120, Bryn Mawr 92318 Ofc: Loma Linda Univ. Med. Ctr., Telecommunications Dept., Loma Linda 92354

BOYNTON, WILLIAM LEWIS, manufacturing co. official; b. May 32, 1928, Kalamazoo, Mich.; s. James Woodbury and Cyretta (Gunther) Boynton; m. Kei Ouchi, Oct. 8, 1953; edn: various mil., tech. insts., seminars. Career: served in US Army;, 1948-74, ret. non-commnd. ofcr.; asst. mgr. Speigel J&R, Kalamazoo 1947-48; faculty mem. Western Mich. Univ., 1955-58; Rockwell/ Collins Divs.: materiel coordinator 1974-78, supr. 1978-81, coordinator 1981--; mem. Nat. Mgmt. Assn.; advisor to Bus./Economic Devel. Com., Calif. State Legislature 1979-; bd.trustees Orange Co. Vector Control Dist. 1980-. Mem: Smithsonian Inst., Nat. Geographic Soc., Non-Commnd. Ofcrs. Assn. (life), Assn. of the US Army, AF Assn., Am. Security Council, Japanese-Am. Citizen League; mil: decorated Bronze Star, 1970, Merit. Svc. Awd. 1974, Army Commendations 1967, 69, 72, Presdtl. Unit Cit. 1970, Presdtl. Cit., Korea, 1952, GCM 1951-74, num. letters of commendation; listed in Who's Who in Fin. and Indus., Who's Who in the World, Who's Who in the West; Republican; Catholic; rec: oriental hist., woodcraft; res: 5314 W. Lucky Way, Santa Ana 92704 ofc: Rockwell Int.-CCSD, 3731 W. Warner Ave, POB 11963, Santa Ana 92711.

BOZARTH, MICHAEL WAYNE, construction co. president; b. July 6, 1958, Bakersfield; s. James Roy and Betty Louise (Hardt) B.; m. Debbie, Aug. 12, 1978; children: Ryan, b. 1979, David, b. 1980; Calif. lic. building contractor/ developer. Career: founder/owner Michael Bozarth Construction Co., Bakersfield 1980-, corp. pres. 1981--; founder/pres./owner Kern Development Concepts, Inc. 1983--; mem. Eagle Scout BSA; Republican; Baptist; rec: pvt. pilot. Res: 3004 Pendleton Ct. Bakersfield 93309 Ofc: Bozarth Construction 1519 6th St. Bakersfield 93304

BOZZO, ANTHONY CARMEN, construction inspector; b. July 11, 1928, Summit, NJ; s. Guilio and Carmella (Paone) B.; m. Antoinette M. Verdi, Apr. 16, 1955; children: Anthony, b. 1956; Cheryl Ann, b. 1960; Mark, b. 1962 Christine, b. 1965; edn: eng. tech., Newark Coll. of Eng. 1957-59; eng., Fairleigh- Dickinson Univ. 1959-61; eng., Ventura Jr. Coll. 1963-68; cert., UCLA 1974. Career: proj. engr. Bryan Const. Co., Inc., North Bergen, NJ 1960-63; mgr. Pick McCarthy Sporting Goods, Oxnards 1963-65; eng. tech. US Naval Civil Engring. Lab., Port Hueneme 1965-68; constrn. inspector/supr. Pub. Works Dept. City of Thousand Oaks, 1968--; recipient distng. svc. awards, Pub. Employees Assn., Ventura Co. 1978-79, City of Thousand Oaks 1973-78, 83; mem: Thousand Oaks Employees Assn. (pres. 1969-70, 1978-79); Am. Pub. Works Assn.; Northside Little League; Oxnard Pop Warner Youth Football; Santa Clara Boosters Club; Thousand Oaks Mgmt. Assn.; mil: s/sgt. USAF 1948-52, Korean Camp.; Catholic; re: coach youth athletics. Res: 1421 Junewood Way Oxnard 93030 Ofc: City of Thousand Oaks, Public Works Dept., 401 W Hillcrest Dr, Thousand Oaks 91360

BRABB, EARL EDWARD, research geologist; b. May 27, 1929, Detroit, Mich.; s. John Hudson and Grace Elizabeth (Seldon) B.; m. Gisela Reichel, Sept. 14, 1957; chil: Robin, b. 1958, Kristin, b. 1960; edn: AB, Dartmouth Coll. 1951; MS, Univ. Mich. 1952; postgrad. Univ. Paris, 1955-6, Univ. Vienna 1956; PhD, Stanford Univ. 1960; Calif. Regis. Geologist. career: geologist U.S.Geol. Survey (USGS), in Alaska and Calif., 1959--: geotech. advisor to City of San Jose, 1971-74; expert witness for NRC Gen. Elec. Test Reactor rev., 1977-81; proj. mgr. for environmtl. geology studies in San Francisco Bay region, w/ emphasis on landslide and earthquake hazard zonation, 1973-81; project chief, overview of landslide hazard mapping and zonation techniques in U.S., 1981--; NSF Summer Inst. lectr., 1965; vis. lectr. Univ. W. Mich., Indiana Univ. of Penna., Iowa St. Univ., USC, UCB, UC Santa Cruz, CSU San Jose, CSU Hayward, UCLA, CSU Northridge, CSU Bakersfield, CSUSF, Stanford Univ.(1972-81); pres. Eocene Colloquium, Paris 1968; invited del., UNESCO conf. on landslides, Soviet Union, 1981; author 100 books, maps, and arts. on geologic problems; orgnzr. biennial field trips w/Japan Soc. of Landslides; keynote spkr. Internat. Assn. of Engrg. Geologists meeting on geologic hazards, England 1979; mem: Fellow, Geological Soc. of Am.; Internat. Assn. Engrg. Geologists; No. Am. Commn. on Stratigraphic Nomenclature; Internat. Subcom. on Paleogene Stratigraphy (Corresponding mem.); Pacific Sect., Am. Assn. Petroleum Geologists. mil: lt. USNR 1952-55. res: 3262 Ross Rd., Palo Alto 94303 ofc: USGS, 345 Middlefield Rd, MS 75, Menlo Pk. 94025.

BRACKEN, HAROLD AUSTIN, manufacturing co. executive; b. Dec. 2, 1928, Hollywood; s. Chester A. and Sadie A. Bracken; m. Dolores Whitley, June 30, 1950; children: Gary, b. 1952; Jeffrey, b. 1954; Laura, b. 1955; edn: BA, UCLA

1950. Career: var. field & gen. ofc. assignments, Ford Div., Ford Motor Co. --1971; v.p. Gulf States Toyota 1971-73; regl. mgr. Toyota Motor Sales, San Francisco 1973-75; div. mgr. 1975-76; nat. sales mgr. 1976-80; v.p./ nat. sales mgr. 1980-82; v.p. sales & distribution 1982-83; gp. v.p. Toyota Motor Sales, Torrance 1983--; honors: Phi Kappa Psi, frat.; mem: Virginia Country Club; Monterey Country Club; Long Beach Police Ofcrs. Assn.; mil: Capt., USAF 1951-53; Republican; Methodist; rec: Republican; Methodist; rec: golf, tennis, jogging. Res: 4265 Virginia Vista Long Beach 90807 Ofc: Toyota Motor Sales, USA, Inc., 19001 S Western Torrance 90509

BRADFORD, CAROLE ELIZABETH, pharmaceutical co. executive; b. Mar. 25, 1940, Balto. Md.; d. James Edwin and Zenta Olga (Adams) Walsh; m. Robert Bradford, Jan. 1, 1978; children: Darcy Marie Yent, b. 1962, Gregory Donald Yent, b. 1964; edn: medical secty., Balto. Bus. Coll. 1958-59; Canada Coll. 1969-72. Career: med. secty. to prof./hd. Dept. Medicine, Univ. of Md., 1959-63; office mgr. Dr. Donald R. Yent, 1967-76; program coordinator Com. for Freedom of Choice in Cancer, 1977--; dir. Bradford Research Inst., 1978--; pres. Choice Metabolics, 1978--; exec. vice pres. American Biologics, 1979--; dir. American Biologics Mexico Research Hosp., 1980--; honors: 1983 Internat. Naturopathic Assn. Award in Nutrition, 1983 Netherlands Laureate of Labor award; mem: Lady of Grace, St. John of Jerusalem, Knights of Malta; Contessa, Order of Cordon Bleu Du Saint Esprit; DAR; Republican; Presbyterian; rec: pvt. pilot, scuba diving. Res: 1318 Edgewood Rd Redwood City 94062 Ofc: American Biologics, 111 Ellis St, Ste 300, San Francisco 94102

BRADLEY, ELIZABETH FRANCO, lawyer; b. Aug. 22, 1939, Los Angeles; d. Jose Luis Franco and Eva B. (Gilbert); stepfather: Henry Korander; m. Frederick L. Bradley, July 15, 1962, div. 1980; children: Eva Marie, b. 1963, Elizabeth Leigh, b. 1968; m. 2d. Charles A. Viviano, Feb. 12, 1981; edn: BA, Univ. of San Diego (S.D. Coll. for Women) 1961; JD, UC Hastings Coll. of Law 1977; admitted State Bar of Calif. 1978. Career: student law clk.: Justice John B. Molinari, San Francisco First Dist. Ct. of Appeal, 1976, Fed. Dist. Ct. Judge Cecil F. Poole, S.F. 1976; law clk. Jacobs, Sills & Coblents, S.F. 1976-77, Big Bear Markets Corp., San Diego 1977-78; deputy city atty. Office of San Diego City Atty., 1979-80; atty. (civil litigation) Ault, Midlam and Deuprey, S.D. 1980 ; chair S.D. Bar Assn. Public Information and Relations Com. 1982-: founder/devel. unique pgm. of public information for the San Diego Community through t.v. (At The Bar on cable ednl. Ch. 24), radio (spots on KCNN with scripts treating var. areas of law written and taped over tel. by a vol. atty.), and newspapers (appearing in 18 local papers incl. Spanish lang. paper); Democrat; Catholic. Res: 2215 Hartford St San Diego 92110 Ofc: Ault, Midlam and Deuprey, 5030 Camino de la Siesta Ste. 201, San Diego 92108

BRADLEY, FOSTER COLE "Bud", stockbroker; b. Oct. 13, 1936, Ripon, Wisc.; s. Foster C. and Adeline (Jones) Bradley; edn: BS, USC, 1958; m. Marsha Brown, Oct. 12, 1963; children: Marla, b. 1968, Paige, b. 1969, Laura, b. 1971; career: stockbroker; asst. mgr. Goodbody & Co., Beverly Hills 1962-69; asst. v.p. E.F. Hutton & Co., Beverly Hills 1969--; awards: U.S. Golf Assn. national jr. golf champion 1954; capt. USC Golf Team, 1958; Los Angeles City amateur golf champion 1969, 71, 73; 1973 Helms Athletic Award; mem: Phi Kappa Psi frat., Cal Delta 1954-58, USC; Wilshire Country Club; mil: 1st lt. USAF 1958-62; Republican; Protestant; rec: golf, skiing, tennis, botan; res: 615 No. Seward, Los Angeles 90004; office: E.F. Hutton & Co., 9797 Wilshire Blvd., Beverly Hills 90212.

BRADLEY, WILLIAM HENRY, lawyer; b. Oct. 26, 1946, NY; s. William Henry and Ann (Norman) B.; m. Cheryl, Dec. 16, 1966; children: William, b. 1967; Kimberley, b. 1970; edn: AA, Palomar Jr. Coll. 1972; BS, Western St. Univ. 1974; JD, 1976; admitted to Calif. State Bar 1976, US Fed. Dist. Ct. (So. Dist. Calif.) 1977. Career: gen. practitioner, W.H. Bradley, Atty., Escondido 1976--; mem: Am. Bar Assn.; Calif. Bar Assn.; Am. Rifle Assn.; Republican; Lutheran; rec: fishing. Res: 31949 Jeffrey Hts Valley Center 92082 Ofc: W.H. Bradley, Atty., 1130 E. Pennsylvania Ave Escondido 92025

BRADLEY, WILLIAM RANDOLPH, state legislator, civil engineer; b. Mar. 2, 1919, Loveland, Colo.; s. William Homer and Irene (McBride) B.; m. Margaret Moose, Mar. 28, 1970; two children: Billie and Randy; edn: Pasadena Jr. Coll.; BS in C.E., USC; M.Pol. Sci., San Jose St. Coll. Career: (current) pres. Bradley & Assocs. Inc., Civil Engineers; Calif. Assemblyman (R), 76th Dist. (coms: Edn., Consumer Protection & Toxic Mats., Local Govt., Utils. & Commerçe); (past) city mgr./ city engr./ city treas., City of San Marcos; dir. pub. works City of Coronado; streets supt. City of Santa Clara; mil: USN 1944-46; rec: golf. Res: 2182 Montiel Rd San Marcos 92069 Ofc: Bradley & Assocs., POB 1115, San Marcos 92069

BRADSHAW, DONALD HOWARD, product engineering executive; b. June 21, 1933, Salina, Ks.; s. Chester Guy and Evelyn (Keist) B.; m. Elaine Faye Davis, Dec. 16, 1972; chil: Deborah, b. 1962, Douglas, b. 1965; edn: AS in D.P., Moorpark Coll, 1977; BS in B.A., Univ. of Redlands 1979. Career: USAF Master Sgt. 1951-71; prodn./test supr. Burroughs Corp., 1972-77; quality control supr. Pertec Computer Corp., 1977-78, test supr., 1978, test mgr. (acting) 1978-80; mfg. test. mgr. Spacelabs, Inc., 1980-83, director, product engineering, Spacelabs, Inc., Chatsworth 1983--. Mem: (life) AF Sgts. Assn., Moorpark Coll. Alumni Assn.; mil: Ore. Nat.Guard 1950-51; M.Sgt., USAF, 1951-71, AF Commendation Medal; Republican; Prot.; rec: micro computers, radio communications, bowling; Res: 3124 Lynn Ct. Newbury Pk. 91320 Ofc: Spacelabs, Inc. 20550 Prairie St. Chatsworth 91311.

BRADY, KAY HELEN, psychotherapist; b. Feb. 2, 1931, Phila., Pa.; d. Charles Edward and Lily (Parsche) B.; edn: Cert., Barnes Art Found., Merion, Pa. 1955-57; BA, San Francisco St. Coll. 1971; MSW, 1973; LCSW, Lic. Clinical Soc. Wkr. Calif. 1976; Foster Family Home Lic., Sonoma Co. 1983; Comm. Coll. Inst. Cred., Calif. Career: assoc. ed. Ardmore Chronicle (weekly), Penn. 1951-52; edl. secty. Presbyterian Life Mag., Phila. 1954-55; ed. House Organ, Link- Belt Col., Phila. 1955-56; free- lance copywriter, advtg. agencies, Phila. 1957-58; tchr. Las Trampas (handicapped) Residential Ctrs., Lafayette 1968-69; psychiatric soc. wkr. Sonoma State Hosp. 1974-75; community organizer Welfare Rights, Early Screening Action Gp. 1971--; psychotherapist, pvt. practice, Sonoma 1975--; instr. Napa Coll. 1975-76; Pub. Svcs. & Admin. lectr., TV panel; assoc. Inst. for Labor & Mental Health, Oaklnad 1983; cons. Sonoma Valley Family Ctr. Crisis Line; awards: med. volunteer w/ Thailand team citation, Internat. Catholic Migration Com. 1980; Ofcl. Observer Awd., Proj. Earthquake Watch, San Francisco Univ. 1981; mem: Nat. Regis. of Health Care Providers in Clinical Soc. Work; Soc. for. Clinical Soc. Work; Nat. Assn. of Soc. Wkrs.; Feminist Writers Guild; Women Against Violence; Gray Panthers; Sonoma Alternatives for Energy (SAFE); Womens Party for Survival; Abalone Alliance; Livermore Action Gp.; Animal Rights Network; Womens Mileathon; est; Hunger Proj.; Zero Population Growth (ZPG); arts: How to Choose a Therapist, Runes 1976; num. plays, poems & short stories; Democrat; Zen; rec: political activist, nature, art. Address: 16664 Center Way, Guerneville 95446

BRAGG, MARY WAGNER, marketing executive; b. Apr. 11, 1947, Santa Clara; c. Jake H. and Mary A. (Silveira) Ristroph; m. John E. Bragg, June 4, 1983; edn: BA, San Jose St. Univ. 1974; Calif. Tchr. Credential 1984, ROP Cred. 1978. Career: owner Dressmaker, Saratoga 1974; tchr. Berryessa Sch. Dist. 1974-76; owner/ptnr. The Workery, Carmel 1976-77; v.p. mktg. Favorite Things, Carmel Valley 1977 79; cons. to small bus., Carmel 1979-80; v.p. mktg. Brady Marketing Co., Inc. (mfr.'s rep. co.) Concord 1980--; cons. to Truffles, num. other cos.; mem. Women in Communications, Nat. Assn. of Female Execs., Nat. Assn. Women in Sales, Profl. Saleswomen; vol. Conejo Valley Days; publs: art. (wine tasting) in San Jose News 1974; sev. arts. (intern 1974/5), Sunset Mag.; subject feature arts. Inc. mag. (2/24), var. trade assn. publs.; Republican; rec: gardening, entertaining, piano. Res: POB 4167, Westlake Village 91361 Ofc: Brady Marketing Co. 1130 D Burnett Ave Concord 94520

BRANCA, JOHN GREGORY, lawyer; b. Dec. 11, 1950, Bronxville, NY; s. John Ralph and Barbara (Werle) B.; edn: AB, cum laude, Occidental Coll., 1972, JD, UCLA Law Sch., 1975. Career: songwriter, recording artist, Original Sound Records, 1968-70; lawyer firm of Kindel &: Anderson, 1975-77, Barovick Konecky Braun Schwartz kay & Schiff, 1977-81, partner Ziffren, Brittenham & Gullen, 1981--; Dir. L.A. Sound, Inc. (Beach Boys), Michael Jackson Prodns, Inc. Honors: chief ed., UCLA-Alaska Law Rev. 1974 5, Am. Jurisprudence Award. Mem: Am. Bar Assn., Calif. Bar Assn., Bev. Hills Bar Assn., Phi Alpha Delta law frat, Wm. Stewart Young Soc.(Occidental Coll.), UCLA Chancellor's Assocs. Num. publs. incl. Attorney Fee Schedules and Legal Advertising: The Implications of Goldfarb, 24 UCLA Law Rev. 475-522, 1977; rec: travel (Carribbean), basketball, music. Ofc: Ziffren, Brittenham & Gullen, 2049 Century Park East, #2350, Los Angeles 90067.

BRANDENBURGER, STEPHEN ANDREW, lawyer; b. Sept. 18, 1941, Sacramento; s. Sheldon and Nelda Lou (Holt) B.; m. Edith Carmany, Apr. 2, 1966; chil: David, b. 1973, Jeffrey, b. 1976, Garrett, b. 1981; edn: BA, Occidental Coll. 1963, JD, McGeorge Coll. of Law, U.O.P. 1968. Career: partner in law firm Files, McMurchie, Foley, Brandenburger & Weill, Sacramento 1970--, spec. in probate & real estate law; panelist Continuing Edn. of the Bar, Irrevocable Trusts, 1973 & 1983. Chmn. Sacto. Co. Assessment Appeals Bd. 1975-7; bd. dir. League to Save Lake Tahoe 1978-; chmn. Sacto. Mus. of History Commn. 1978-9; trustee Sacto. Sym. Found. 1980-; coach Land Park Soccer Club 1980-2. Mem: Sigma Alpha Epsilon frat. (ofcr. 1960-3); dir. Active 20-30, 1969-76; McGeorge Alumni Assn. (pres. 1976); Sacto. Sym. Assn. (pres. 1979-80); Sutter Club. Res: 1043 11th Ave Sacramento 95818 Ofc: 1030 15th St Sacramento 95814

BRANKOVICH, MARK J., restaurateur; b. Mar. 4, 1922, Rijeka, Yugoslavia, nat. 1956; s. Joseph H. and Rose (Haydin) B.; m. Marilyn Severin, Jan. 4, 1956; chlidren: Mark, b. 1957; Laura, b. 1966; edn: BA in philosophy; stu. Univ. of Zurich 1943-44, Univ. of Geneva 1944-45, Univ. of Padua, Italy 1946. Career: born into a hotel family on the Adriatic Coast; arrived in USA 1951; owner/ founder The Golden Deer (Bistro type restaurant), Chgo. 1953; club mgr. Gaslight Club, NY 1956; opened/mgr. The New New York Club 1957; gen. mgr. of four clubs 1958, and exec. v.p. 1959-; acquired Italian Deli.- Market in Burbank 1969, expanded into a wholesale bakery, wholesaler of Italian splties.: Monte Carlo- Italia Foods, Inc., Burbank 1969--; opened 3 restaurants named Pinocchio, in Burbank, Santa Monica, Westwood Village; Republican; Serbian Orthodox. Res: 1250 N Hilldale Ave Los Angeles 90069 ofc: Monte Carlo-Italia Foods, Inc., 3103 W Magnolia Blvd Burbank 91505

BRANNAN, WILLIAM WAYLAND, real estate broker; b. July 13, 1923, San Francisco; s. Wm. Smith and Ramona Cora (Hoag) B.; m. Marian Gimby, Mar. 26, 1951; children: Carol, b. 1954, John, b. 1955, Ann, b. 1957, Thomas, b. 1959, James, b. 1962, Paul, b. 1965, Kathleen, . 1969; edn: AB, Stanford Univ. 1952. Career: life ins. salesman Guardian Life, 1951-55; real estate salesman Timmer Realty, 1955-71, Fox & Carskadon, 1971-76, Frank Howard Allen, 1977-82; self-empl. realtor and appraiser, San Rafael 1982--; condr. workshops on telephone techniques throughout No. Calif., 1978-82; honors: Realtor Assoc. of the Year 1980, Marin Co.; dir. St. Vincent's Sch. for Boys; dir. Marin County Bd. of Realtors; mem. Kiwanis Club, Serra Club, Knights of Columbus; chmn.

1st Annual Town Picnic Parade, San Rafael 1980; author book and cassette tapes on tel. techniques (1981), art. in Calif. Real Estate Assn. Mag. (1980); mil: company scout, pfc, 517th Parachute Inf. Regt. 1943-45, Purple Heart, Pres. Cit.; Republican; Catholic; rec: handwriting analyst, golf. Res: 108 Coleman Dr San Rafael 94901 Ofc: William Brannan, Realtor, POB 881, San Rafael 94901

BRANNIS, JOHN WILLIAM, JR., electrical contractor; b. Mar. 29, 1936, Chgo.; s. John William Sr. and Maureen E. Blasco (Fogarty) B.; m. Helen Prudence Blodgett, Jan. 19, 1974; children: John Steven, b. 1955; Jill Katherine (Salazar), b. 1957; Kathleen Marie (Frey), b. 1961; Donna Jean, b. 1963; edn: AS, Chaffey Coll. 1971. Career: electrical helper Hunter Engring., Riverside 1955-60; elec. helper, electrician, elec. tech., foreman, electrical day-foreman Kaiser Steel Corp., Fontana 1960-77; pres. Brannis Electric, Inc. 1977--; tchr., Intro. to Refrig. & Air Conditioning, Riverside City Coll.; mem: Inland Electrical Assn.; Riverside CofC; Catholic. Address: 5160 Kendall St Riverside 92506

BRASSARD, JEAN ESTRADA, direct sales executive; b. July 23, Philippines, nat. 1977; d. Marcelino and Felisa (Acosta) Estrada; m. Joseph Brassard, Sept. 28, 1974; children: Rabi, b. 1965, Debbie Mair, b. 1970; edn: dip. Quezon Acad.; stu. Nat. Univ., Phil. 1962-64. Career: computer opr. Good Chevrolet, Sacramento 1975-76; keypunch opr. County Courthse., Sacto. 1976-77; direct sales distbr. (Kitchenwares) Wear-Ever Alum. Corp., Chillicothe, Ohio 1976-80; gen. mgr./franchise dealer of Saladmaster prods. (Dallas, Tex.), and Royal Acceptance & Royal Housewares Co. (Sacto.), 1980--; recipient over 100 awards in direct sales: Wearever top salespsn (1977, 1978), top dealer (1978), Hall of Fame (1977), Millionaires Club (1978), Double Millionaires Club (1979); Saladmaster top salespsn. (1980, 83), Nat. record holder (1983), Master Dealer (1983). Res: 7624 Center Pkwy. Sacramento 95823 Ofc: Royal Housewares Co. 7000 Franklin Blvd. Ste. 1250 Sacramento 95823

BRAU, NORA SCHMIDT, realtor; b. June 13, 1947, NY; d. Joseph William, Sr. and Marie Esther (Morazzani) Schmidt; m. Salvador Brau, Aug. 16, 1968; children; Ingrid, b. 1969; Evan, b. 1972; edn: BA, Marymount Coll. 1970; MBA, Pepperdine Univ. 1984; lic. R.E. Broker, Calif. 1981. Career: realtor/ assoc. Griffin Von Dyl Co. 1980-81; investment coord./ R.E. broker Gantz Investment Co. 1981-82; co- owner Denore Enterprises 1983-84; realtor Noreen Brau & Assocs., Sherman Oaks 1983-84; awards: Recgn. Awd. for Outstanding Comm. Voluntary Svc., Volunteer Ctr. of W. L.A. 1983; mem: San Fernando Valley Bd. Realtors 1983; Jr. League of Los Angeles; writer/ assoc. ed: Junior League Mag., L.A. 1982-83; Democrat; Catholic; rec: collecting fine quality photog. Address: Noreen Brau & Assocs., 110 Tigertail Rd. Los Angeles 90049

BRAUER, BERNDT INGO, lawyer; b. Aug. 30, 1951, Reutlingen, W. Germany, nat. 1963; s. Karl Otto and Orthrud Brauer; edn: BA, UCLA 1976; JD, Hastings Coll. of Law 1980; admitted to Calif. State Bar 1980. Career: research atty. Santa Clara Co. Superior Ct. 1980-81; sole practitioner Law Ofc. of Ingo Brauer 1981-83; partner Law Firm Baker, Brauer, Saldivar & Postelle 1982-83; Volunteers in Parole; honors: Commnr. German Consulate, San Jose 1981; mem: Santa Clara City Bar Assn.; Volunteers in Parole; Calif. Attys. for Criminal Justice; Democrat; Lutheran; rec: tennis, archeology, photog. Res: Burlingame Ofc: Baker, Brauer, Saldivar & Postelle, 111 W St. John, Ste 555, San Jose 95113

BRAUN, JEROME IRWIN, lawyer; b. Dec. 16, 1929, St. Joseph, Mo.; s. Martin H. and Bess (Donsker) B.; children: Aaron Hugh, b. 1959, Susan Lori, b. 1963, Daniel Victor, b. 1967; edn: AB, Stanford Univ., 1951, LL.B, Stanford Law Sch. 1953. Career: 1st lt. Judge Advocate Gen. Corps. US Army, 1953-57; assoc. atty. Long & Levit, San Francisco 1957-58, Law offces Jefferson Peyser, 1958-62; founding partner Elke, Farella & Braun, now Farella, Braun & Martel, San Francisco 1962--; instr., law, S.F. Law Sch., 1958-69; mem: Calif. Acad. of Appellate Lawyers (past pres.), Am. Judicature Soc., Am. Coll. of Trial Lawyers, Calif. State Bar Assn. (chmn. Adminstrn of Justice Com. 1977, chmn. Lawyer Reps. to 9th Circuit Judicial Conf. 1982, frequent moderator Cont. Edn. of the Bar pgms.); speaker various State Bar convs. in Calif., Ill., Nev., Mont.; mem. Am. Bar Assn., Bar Assn. of S.F., Jewish Welfare Fedn. of S.F., Marin Co. and the Penin. (past pres.), S.F. United Jewish Comm. Ctrs. (past pres.). Awards: Lloyd W. Dinkelspiel Outstanding Young Leader, Jewish Welfare Fedn., 1967; honoree, Mex.-Am. Legal Defense Fund, 1979. mil: pvt. US Army 1953-4; 1st lt. Judge Adv. Gen. Corps, 1954-7. ofc: Farella, Braun & Martel, 235 Montgomery St., 30th Fl. San Francisco 94104.

BRAUTBAR, NACHMAN, physician, educator; b. Oct. 22, 1943, Haifa, Israel, nat. 1980; s. Pinhas and Sabina (Lohite) B., m. Ronit, Mar. 25, 1969; children: Sigalit, b. 1969, Shirley, b.1972, Jaques, b. 1979; edn: MD, Hebrew Univ. Sch. of Medicine 1968; Fellow in Nephrology, UC Los Angeles Med. Sch. 1977. Career: fmr. asst. prof. med. UCLA and dir. of Home Dialysis; assoc. prof. med., pharmacology and nutrition, USC Med. Sch. 1980--; resrch. in metabolism (magnesium, phosphorus, calcium) and interaction with vitamin D and chronic renal failure, internat. authority in muscle metabolism; recipient acad. awards 1969, 76, awards for excellence, Am. Heart Assn. 1980, 2d Intl. Cong. on Bioenergetics, L.A. 1984; mem. Nat. Kidney Found. of S. Calif. (chmn. resrch. com.); Am. Heart Assn. (L.A. afil. study sect.); Soc. for Bioenergetics; Jewish Fedn.; cons. to Hollywood Presbyn. Med. Ctr.; spkr. for the Israeli Consulate; author 150 publs. and book chapters; cons. to editl. bds. of 15 sci. journals; Republican; Jewish; rec: classical music, stamps, sports. Res: 10808 Ashton Ave Los Angeles 90024 Ofc: usc, Dept. of Med. Div. Nephrology, Unit 1, 2025 Zonal Ave, Los Angeles 90033

BRAWLEY, JOHN HARRIS, mosquito control executive, ret.; b. Mar. 12, 1920, Pershing, Okla.; s. William Lee and Evelyn Jane (Chisum) Brawley; edn: grad. Omaha pub. schools, 1937; sanitary engr. Internat. Corresp. Schools, 1956; 1st year law, LaSalle Ext. Univ., 1966; certificates: Pub. Health Vector Control, USPHS, 1972, Pub. Administrn., CSU Hayward, 1973, Mosquito Control Technician, Calif. State Health Dept. 1974, Pub. Employee Rels., Univ. of San Francisco, 1975; widower; chil: Carolyn, b. 1949, Carl, b. 1954, Kevin, b. 1961; career: business mgr. Delta Mosquito Abatement District, Visalia 1948-50; mgr. Kings Mosquito Abatement Dist., Hanford 1950-61; mgr. Butte Co. Mosquito Abatement Dist., Oroville 1961-66; mgr. Contra Costa Mosquito Abatement Dist., Concord 1966-76; ret. 1976. Pres., Calif. Mosquito Control Assn. 1962, Legislative Advocate 1970-76, honorary mem. 1978; bd. dirs. American Mosquito Control Assn. 1971-73, Meritorious Service Award, 1973-74, Emeritus mem. 1977; mem: Civitan Club, Hanford (secty. 1960), Toastmasters Club, Hanford (v.p. 1960-61), Rotary Club, Gridley (bd. dirs. 1963-66), Calif. Trial Lawyers Assn. 1966-70, American Legion, Pleasant Hill (Post Comdr.) 1970-, Am. Mosquito Control Assn. 1951-, Calif. Mosquito Control Assn. 1951-, Nat. Rifle Assn. (life); publs: papers on Mosquito Resistance to Pesticides, The Need for Tng. and Certification of Mosquito Control Workers, Detrimental Effects of Labor Unions on Mosquito Control; instrumental in securing certification for Mosquito Control Workers in Calif. Mil: master sgt. USAF 1941-45 (18 mos. with US Strategic Air Force in U.S.S.R.), Euro. Air Offensive w/6 battle stars; Republican; Baptist; rec: camping, hunting, fishing; res: 12327 Road 36½ Madera 93637.

BRAY, ABSALOM FRANCIS, JR., lawyer; b. Nov. 24, 1918, San Francisco; s. A.F., Sr. (presiding Justice, Ct. of Appeal) and Leila (Veale) B.; grandson of Sheriff R.R. Veale, Contra Costa Co., 1895-1935; m. Lorraine Paule, June 25, 1959; children: Oliver Whitney, b. 1954, Brian Keith, b. 1955, Margot Elizabeth, b. 1957; edn: AB, Stanford Univ. 1940; JD, USC Sch of Law 1949. Career: legal dept. Iowa Ord. Plant, Burlington 1940-42; pvt. practice law, 1949--, pres. Bray, Baldwin, Egan & Breitwieser, APC, attys. at law; adv. bd. Bank of Am. 1953-65; mil: lt. USNR 1942-46, WWII, Navy Commendn., Navy Unit Citation; mem: Vets. of Fgn. Wars (cmdr.), Am. Legion (cmdr.), Contra Costa Co. Devel. Assn. (pres. 1959-60), Contra Costa Council (pres.), Navy League, State Bar of Calif., Contra Costa Co. BAr Assn. (past pres.), Contra Costa Co. Tuberculosis and Pub. Health Assn. (past pres.), Contra Costa Co. Hist. Soc., E. Clampus Vitus, Soc. of Calif. Pioneers; chmn. nat. bd. dirs. Camp Fire Girls 1959-61, 1969-71 and past chmn. Region V, CA, NV, UT, AZ, HI; chmn. John Muir Dist., BSA, 1968; Salvation Army (com.); life mem. Martinez PTA; Rotarian kst pres.); Masons; Elks; Republican; Episcoapl (Vestry); rec: photog., ship models, hiking. Res: 600 Flora St Martinea Ofc: Bray, Baldwin, Egan & Breitwieser, APC, Ward and Ferry Sts., Martinez 94553

BRAZIL, ELIZABETH ANNE, social worker, music educator/consultant, business owner; b. Feb. 5, 1941, Visalia; d. Byron William Jr. and Mary Wallace (Fischer) Jennings; edn: AA, Coll. of Sequoias 1960; AB, San Jose St. Coll. 1963; tchg. creds: Spec. Sec. (Music) and. Gen. Elem. 1963; MSW, CSU Fresno 1979; Pupil Personnel Cred., UC Berkeley 1980. Career: classroom tchr. Earlimart Sch. Dist. 1963-64; vocal music tchr. 1964-65; classroom music tchr. Dept. of Def. Overseas Dependent Schs., Naha, Okinawa 1965-67, Wiesbaden, W. Ger. 1967-69; instru. & classrm. music tchr. Visalia Unified Sch. Dist. 1969--; pvt. music tchr. 1957--; prof. music edn. Pacific Coll., Fresno 1982-; cons. music edn., var. sch. dists., Tulare Co. 1982-; clin. soc. wkr., Visalia 1979--; tchr. women of the Jail, Visalia Adult Sch. 1981-; owner/ originator Better Scents by Anne (cosmetics for body & bath), Visalia 1981-; owner/ mgr. investment real estate, Visalia, Fresno & Chico 1970-; presenter Tulare Co. Curriculum Conf. 1981, 83; prod./ dir. (sch. musicals), Hansel and Gretel (1968), Tom Sawyer (1969), Let George Do It (1982), num. talent shows, holiday pgms., other sch. prodns. 1963-; mem: Visalia Toastmistress Club; Consciousness Raising Womens Gps.; Drug Diversion Meetings; Visalia Players Comm. Theatre; Nat. Edn Assn.; Calif. Tchrs. Assn.; Visalia Unified Tchrs. Assn.; Overseas Edn. Assn.; Music Educators Nat. Conf.; Tulare- Kings Music Educators Assn.; NASW; Clin. Soc. Wkrs. Assn.; author: Self Esteem Through Music (K-3) and (4-6), A cassette tape and guide for music in the classroom, 1981; Band Starter Method, 1973; Live From Farmersville, It's Monday Morning!, a play on therapy, 1979; coauthor: Comprehensive Evaluation Instrument and Awards for Beginning Band Students, 1974; designer: sev. bd. games for profl. tchg. purposes, multi- media presentations; Democrat; Prot.; rec: arts & crafts, Koi carp, computers. Res: 1708 S Linwood Ave Visalia Unified Sch. Dist., 315 E Acequia St Visalia 93277

BRAZO, BEVERLY ANN, business executive; b. Sept. 23, 1929, Joplin, Mo.; d. Wiliam Matt and ALverta Cathrine (Dunlap) Eddings; w. John E. Brazo Jr., Jan. 1, 1946; children: Johnny, b. 1947; Mark, b. 1949; Linda, b. 1952; Keri, b. 1963; edn: AA, Shasta Coll.; Cert. Nurses Aide, Home- Health, 1982; R.E. salesman 1980; R.E. broker, Calif. 1981. Career: newspaper advtg. sales Inter-Mountain News 1963; owner/ mgr. Montgomery Ward Sales Agency, Burney 1964--; owner/ mgr. Mode- O- Day, Burney 1968; owner/ mgr. Beve's Drive- in, Burney 1976; R.E. salesman, Century 21, Burney 1979; owner/ mgr. The Velvet Garter Saloon & Hickory Pig, Burney 1983--; mem: CofC (v.p. 1978); V.F.W. Aux.; rec: oil painting. Res: Rt 2 Box 83, Hwy 299, Burney 96013 Ofc: The Velvet Garter Saloon, 1336 Main Burney 96013

BRECHT, PAUL ISAAK, retail business owner; b. Mar. 22, 1919, Golden Valley, N.Dakota; s. Frank Karl and Pauline (Isaak) B.; m. Jane Ewing, June 9, 1946; children: Pauline Elizabeth, b. 1950; Mary ANn, b. 1952; edn: No.

Dakota St. Univ. 1937-38; Ohio St. Univ. 1941-42. Career: farmer/ ranch hand parents farm --1936; asst. ednl. dir. Civilian Conservation Corp., US Forest Svc., Wash. 1936-37; 4-H ldr. Mercer Co. Agriculture Dept., Stanton, N. Dakota 1937; caretaker Latham Estate, Greensboro, N.C. 1939-40; Rod McLellan Co., S San Francisco 1940-42; mgr. Orchid div. Rod McLellan Co., S. S.F 1946-59; asst. mgr. B.O. Bracey Co., Santa Ana 1959-62; owner/ mgr. Brecht Orchid Gardens, Costa Mesa 1962--; past pres: Peninsula Orchid Soc., San Mateo Co.; SanMateo Co. Garden Ctr.; Woodside Gardeners Assn.; Orange Co. Orchid Soc.; So. Coast Orchid Soc., Long Beach; Costa Mesa Optimist Club; Costa Mesa Newport Harbor Lions Club; judge: So. Coast Orchid Soc.; Los Angeles Co. Fair; mem: Orange Co. Council on Aginig; Newport Harbor Elks Club; Costa Mesa CofC (dir.); Costa Mesa Beautification Com.; works: num. awd. winning displays at State Fair in Sacto. & sev. co. fairs in Bay Area; mil: P.O. 2/c, USCG, WWII; Republican; Methodist; rec: books on horticulture, golf. Res: 4201 Williwaw Irvine 92714 Ofc: Brecht Orchid Gardens, 1989 Harbor Blvd Costa Mesa 92627

BREITHAUPT, RICHARD HOAG, JR., real estate developer, investor; b. Feb. 15, 1953, Yeadon, Pa.; s. Richard H. and Florence Elizabeth (Budd) B., Sr.; edn: BS in bus. ad./mgmt., CSU Northridge 1976, MBA in fin., CSULA 1977. Career: finl. and mktg. analyst Aseptic Thermo Indicator Co., Inc., No. Hollywood 1972-76; dir. real estate acquisitions Western Consulting Group, Inc., Beverly Hills 1976-78; pres./CEO, Walika, Inc. (real estate investment and devel. co.; developing & investing in comml. office complex, apts., condominiums, etc.), Northridge 1978--. Awards: Silver Beaver (1982), Great Western Council District Award of Merit (1979), Silver Shark and Silver Arrow, Order of the Arrow (1971), Silver Thunderbird (1974), Boys Scouts of Am.; mem: Great Western Council BSA (v.p. 1982); BSA Regional Com. 1981-(exec. bd. 1982-); BSA Nat. Com. 1982-3 (BSA Nat. Properties Com., BSA Nat. Scouting Com.); mem. Assn. MBA Execs. 1977-, Classic Thunderbirds of Am. Car Club, 1972-; author: A History of Scouting Through Insignia (1976), A History of the Order of the Arrow (1979); num. arts. and BSA publs.; Republican; Episcopal; rec: camping, stamps & coin collector, classic cars; res: 17201 Parthenia St. Northridge 91325 ofc: Walika, Inc. 15233 Ventura Blvd. Ste.608, Sherman Oaks 91402.

BREKKE, TED ALLEN, school district administrator; b. Aug. 9, 1937, Maywood; s. Spencer Alan and Elsie Marie (Millington) B.; m. Gail Newell, Dec. 17, 1969; 1 dau., Kristin, b. 1973; edn: AA, Long Beach City Coll. 1958, BA, Long Beach State Coll. 1961, MS, CSU Hayward 1975. Career: teacher Seal Beach Sch. Dist. 1963-65; tchr. Mt. Diablo Unified Sch. Dist., 1965-80, vice prin. 1980-84: vice prin. Pacheco Elem. Sch. 1980-81, Holbrook Elem. Sch., Concord 1981-84; mem. Parks, Rec. and Open Space Commn., City of Walnut Creek, 1981-85; v.p. Diablo Mgmt. Assn. (bd.dirs. 1981-84, mem. Ethics Com.); Calif. State Dept. of Edn. rep. for consol. application pgm. reviews, 1982; CTA Urban Area Salary Com., 1980, negotiating council, pres. Mt. Diablo Tchrs Assn., 1969-70; mem. Calif. State Instructional Materials Eval. Panel (Math), 1981; presenter: Calif. Assn. for Gifted Students (1979), Individual Instrn., North (1974, 77); presider, Calif. Math Council, Asilomar (1980-1); Mt. Diablo Gifted & Talented adv. bd., 1980-1; Master Plan Com., School Improvement Pgm., Mt. Diablo Sch. Dist. 1983-4; BSA cubmaster, Pacheco (1967), coordinator Pack 309, Holbrook Elem. 1983-4; Mem: Assn. of Calif. Sch. Adminstrs. (Pub. Info. Ofcr. 1983-4; pub. Region VII and DMA newsletters, 1982-84); Calif. Math Council; Phi Delta Kappa (vp.mbrship 1982-3); CTA; NEA; MDEA; East Bay Council Tchrs of Social Studies; Calif. Assn. Teachers of English; Diablo Educators Gp. (pres. 1972); publs: sev. ednl. publs., art. Nature Study Jour. (1975), lang. arts presentation, TV (1975); mil: USNAF 1961-63; Republican; Lutheran; rec: sailing, backpacking, gardening; res: 2957 Filbert Dr. Walnut Creek 945498 ofc: Mt. Diablo Sch. Dist, 1936 Carlotta Dr. Concord 94520.

BREMER, THELMA ROSE, real estate broker; b. Feb. 27, 1913, Coloma, Mich.; d. George Melvin and Ethel Irene (Brower) LaVanway; m. Chester G. Van Lente, Nov. 1938, div.; 1 dau. Judith Irene (Barrett), b. 1939; m. 2d. Norman S. Richardson, Aug. 1947, (dec.); m. 3d. Hans B. Bremer, Aug. 30, 1958; edn: real estate appraisal, Ventura Coll. 1968; Georgia Inst. of Real Estate 1978; R.E. courses, Lumbleau Schs.. Career: rancher (owner); past sales agt. Ax Realty; current investor, broker/owner Bremer & Assocs., dba Thelma Bremer, Realtor; mem: Am. Cancer Soc., Ventura Co. (v.p. 1962); fmr. Gray Lady (ARC); Republican; Prot.; rec: interior decorating, bowling, gardening. Res: 385 Dorothy Ave Ventura 93003

BRENGLE, THOMAS ALAN, computer scientist; b. Sept. 22, 1952, San Diego; s. Alan Seymour and Nadeene Marie (Clark) B.; m. Anita Anne Jones, June 22, 1974; children: Adan, b. 1977; Evan, b. 1979; edn: BS, Harvey Mudd Coll. 1974; MS, So. Ill. Univ. 1976; Univ. of Calif. 1976-82. Career: physicist Lawrence Livermore Nat. Lab., Livermore 1976-77; computer scientist, 1977-79; gp. ldr. 1979--; mgr. USC Computing Svcs., Lawrence Livermore Lab., Livermore 1983--; mem: ARRAY (secty./ treas. 1982-83, v.p. 1983-84); publs: sev. papers in Physics of Fluids, Journ. of Computational Physics, also IEEE Computer 1981, 83; rec: electronics, sports cars, model railroading. Res: 675 Alameda Dr Livermore 94550 Ofc: Lawrence Livermore National Lab., POB 5511, L-630, Livermore 94550

BRENNAN, CLINTON C. C., corporate executive; b. Apr. 26, 1927, Norwood, Mo.; s. Frank V Cooney and Pearl Elizabeth Brennan; m. Margaret Emily Zilla, Aug. 3, 1951; children: Brett, b. 1954; Brenda, b. 1960; edn: BS, Univ. of Houston 1949; CmfgE, Soc. of Mfg. Engrs., Robitics Internat. Career:

So. regl. sales mgr. Control Data Corp., Houston, Tex. 1969; v.p. sales Brevet Internat., Palos Verdes 1972; v.p. Grubic Assocs., Mt. View 1975; sr. staff cons. MacDonnel Douglas Corp., Monrovia 1977; currently, sr. v.p., gen. mgr., bd. dirs. CIM, Inc.; council mem./ chmn. legal & fin. com. Mayor Pro-Tem, Hilshire Village, Tex. 1967-69; mem: Tex. League of Cities; Admiral, Tex. Navy 1969; Numerical Control Soc. (past pres. L.A. Co. chpt.); Soc. Mfg. Engrs. (past pres. Orange Coast chpt.); mil: BM 1/c, USN 1944-46, Unit Citation w/ Stars; rec: antique auto restoration, geology, earth sci. Res: 504 W Huntington Dr Arcadia 91006 Ofc: CIM, Inc., 527 Encinitas Blvd San Diego

BRENNAN, ELIZABETH AGNES, insurance broker, b. Aug. 8, 1906, San Francisco; d. Patrick and Helen P. (Cronin) Brennan; edn: Elem. Tchg. Credential, State Teacher Coll. S.F., 1928, BA, Jr. High credential, 1929; Gen. Secondary Cred., UC Berkeley 1930; num. spl. courses, Univ. of San Francisco. Career: real estate and insurance broker; during WWII served as Personal Consular, Kaiser Yard II, Richmond, Calif. Mem: Native Daughters of the Golden West (Supr. Deputy Grand Pres. SF); Young Ladies Inst., Sausalito; Stanyon Fulton Neighborhood Assn. (treas.); Republican; Catholic; rec: art, painting. Address: 2066 Grove St. San Francisco 94117

BRENNEMAN, MARY PRISCILLA, medical services executive; b. Aug. 16, 1949, San Francisco; d. James Albert and Vivian Mary (Skluzacek) Wayne; div.; 1 dau. Michelle, b. 1968; edn: RN/AA, Golden West Coll. 1974; BS in nursing, UC San Francisco 1980; cert. Critical Care Reg. Nurse (CCRN), Adv. Cardiac Life Support (ACLS). Career: RN, UC Irving Med. Ctr. 1974-78, UCSF Moffitt Hosp. 1778-81; emergcy. air transport nurse/ founder-CEO, Brenneman & Greene Med. Services, Orange 1981--; awards: 3 nursing sch. scholarships; mem: Soc. for Adv. of Mgmt.; Orange Toastmasters Club; Orange CofC (chmn. Health Com. 1984-; Health Fair coord. 1983-4); PTA; United Way Campgn. Team 1984; publs: two arts. on health issues, 1983; Democrat; Catholic; rec: aerobics, running, water sports, travel. Ofc: Brenneman & Greene, 1046 No Tustin Ave. Ste C, Orange 92667

BRENNER, ALAN ROY, management consultant; b. May 29, 1953, Chgo.; s. John Joseph and Elaine Antoinette (Borucki) B.; edn: BS in physics, Mass. Inst. Tech. 1975. Career: pres. Brenner Assocs., Cambridge, Mass. 1975-78; senior engr. Gen. Dynamics/ Electronics, San Diego 1978-81; systems devel. mgr. Cinematronics, El Cajon 1981-82; staff engr. Loral Instrumentation, San Diego 1983-84; pres. A B Consultants, San Diego 1984--; mem. San Diego Mountain Rescue Team; designer: Vision & Television exh., Mus. of Science, Boston (1976); rec: mountaineering, whitewater kayaking. Res: 1067 Diamond St. San Diego 92109 Ofc: A B Consultants, POB 99479, San Diego 92109

BRETZFIELD, MAURICE JOHN, manufacturing co. president; b. Aug. 30, 1947, NY, NY; s. Samuel Stuart and Barbara Gene (Drucker) B.; m. Jung Won Chun, May 31, 1975; children: Lauren Marisa, b. 1977, Julianne, b. 1981; edn: Judson Sch. 1965, Woodbury Coll. 1966-69. Career: accts. receivable, United Factors, Inc. Los Angeles 1969-70; sales, Internationale Set Inc., Los Angeles 1970-71, vice pres. Internationale Set Inc., Seoul, Korea 1971-76, exec. v.p. Internationale Set Inc., Los Angeles 1976-80, pres./chief exec. ofcr. Internationale Set Inc., Torrance 1980--; mem: bd. govs. Cedars Sinai Med. Ctr. 1982-; childs friend Reiss-Davis Child Study Ctr. 1977-; bd. trustees The Center for Early Edn. 1983-; clubs: Calif. Yacht, Balboa Bay, Los Angeles Athletic, U.S. Yacht Racing Union; mil: sgt. USAR 1970-78; rec: yacht racing. Res: 1067 Angelo Dr Beverly Hills 90210 Ofc: Internationale Set, Inc., 19899 Pacific Gateway Dr Torrance 90502

BREWER, CHRISTOPHER DAVID, historic preservation consultant; b. June 20, 1050, Bakersfield; s. Harold Baker and Anne G. (Grothaus) B.; m. Sally M., July 10, 1977; edn: AA, Bksfld. Coll. 1980; BA, CSC Bakersfield, 1982, MA pub. adminstrn., 1983. Career: musician, pub. rels. US Navy Band, 1968-72; traveling artist and section supr., profl. musical orgns., 1972-77; mgmt. positions, acting dir. Kern County Mus., 1978-82; owner Brewer's Historical Consultants (providing hist. preservation and local hist. resrch. asst. to govt. and pvt. industry in So. San Joaquin Valley), Bakersfield 1982--; dir. Redford Art Gallery 1984--; commnr. Historic Preservation Commn. City of Bakersfield; regl. v.p. Conf. of Calif. Historical Socs. (Fresno, Kings, Tulare, Kern Cos.) 1980-83; honors: Pi Alpha Alpha (charter mem. 1982), Scapa Scholar, Scapa Praetor USC 1983-84; mem. E Clampus Vitus (pres. local Kern Co. chpt. 1980); publs: The First Fifty Years of the Exeter Union High School (Walter M. Smith 1979); The Pioneers (B.K. Said, edited reprint 1981); Historic Kern (Qrtly Bull. K.Co. Hist. Soc. 1979-81); mil: E5 USN 1968-72. Res: 3204 Perry Pl Bakersfield 93306 Ofc: Redford Art Gallery, 3703 Columbus Bakersfield 93306

BREWER, CRAIG DEAN, mortgage banker; b. Apr. 4, 1950, Glendale; s. Clarence Joseph and Kaylleen Ruth (Nye) B.; m. Diana Antonia Johnson, May 4, 1974; children: Wesley, b. 1977; Kevin, b. 1980; edn: AA, Pasadena City Coll. 1970; BS, CSU San Diego 1973; R.E. broker, Calif. 1979; Calif. Lic. Contractor 1974. Career: loan ofcr. Maso McDuffie Co., San Diego 1973-74; assoc. realtor/ R.E. saleman Century 21, San Diego & Orange Co. 1975-76; tract loan ofcr. World Savings & Loan, Orange Co. 1976-77; sr. loan ofcr. Anaheim Savings & Loan, Riverside 1977-78; maj. loan ofcr./ underwriter Gibralter Savings & Loan, Hollywood 1978-79; regl. loan mgr. Progressive Savings & Loan, Studio City 1979; asst. v.p./ gr. Merit Mortgage Svcs., Montclair 1979-80; pres. American Pacific Loan Assn., Orange Co. 1981--; R.E. fin. sems. 1974; pres. var. R.E. Cos.; ednl. & bus. promotion; honors: Fed. Nat. Mortgage Assn., Approved Appraiser 1976, Approved Loan Underwriter 1979; mem: Nat. Assn. Realtors; Home Bldrs. Assn.; Mortgage Bankers Assn.;

Saddleback Bd. Realtors; San Fernando Bd. Realtors; Toastmasters; works: The Morgage Menu, 1981-; Democrat; Catholic; rec: water & snow skiing, racket ball. Res: 24471 Ladera Dr Mission Viejo 92691 Ofc: American Pacific, 23297 S Pointe Dr, Ste 230, Laguna Hills 92653

BRHEL, MARTIN C., JR., lawyer; b. Aug. 16, 1947, Johnson City, NY; s. Martin Charles and Betty Jean (Gregory) B.; 1 dau. Alethia Lynn, b. 1973; edn: AA, Golden West Coll.; BA, CSU Long Beach 1970; JD, Western St. Univ. Coll. of Law 1977. Admitted to practice law before all cts. in Calif., US Dist. Ct. (Central Dist.). Career: rec. leader, interim dept. supr. City of Westminster Parks & Rec. Dept. 1966-70; counselor Employment Devel. Dept. 1970-74; law clk. Orange Co. Pub. Defender 1976-77; criminal defense atty., pvt. practitioner 1977--; judge pro tem Riverside Municipal Ct. and Superior Ct.; bd. dirs. Serenity Ranch, Alcohol Recovery Pgm.; guest spkr. num. local high schs.; vol. BSA, Am. Cancer Soc.; mem: Am. Bar Assn., Calif. Attys. for Criminal Justice, Calif. Bar Assn., Riverside Co. Barristers Assn. (pres.), Riverside Co. Bar Assn. (ch. Law Day Com., ch. Tel-Law Com.), Riverside Trial Lawyers Assn. (past pres.), Tel-Law, Inc. (bd. dirs., treas.); Democrat; rec: travel, sightseeing, exercise. Ofc: Martin C. Brhel, Jr., Riverside Barrister Bldg., 3993 Market St Riverside 92501

BRIAN, JACK, scientist; b. Feb. 20, 1926, Ramsgate, England, nat. 1963; s. Robert Frederick and Nellie Emily (King) B.; m. Beryl Morrish, Aug. 6, 1946; children: Paul, b. 1948; Jacqueline, b. 1963; edn: Royal Aircraft Establishment Tech. Coll., England 1943-46; physics & telecommun., Farnborough Tech. Coll., England; Calif. lic. Profl. Engr. (control sys. engring.) 1978. Career: mem. research team Royal Aircraft Establishment, Farnborough, Hants, England 1943-52; chief engr. Aeronautical Radio, England 1952-57; dir. engring. Westrex Corp., Div. of AT&T, NY 1957-63; sr. scientist/ dept. mgr./ acting sect. hd. Hughes Aircraft Co., Tech. Div., Space & Commun. Gp., Los Angeles 1963--; past chmn. IEEE, So. Bay- Harbor Sect.; honors: Fellow Inst. for Adv. of Engring.'s Coll. of Fellows 1977; IEEE Centennial Medal 1984; mem. IEEE; patents: TV Scrambling (1980), Automatic Tuning (1957); designed Uplink Communicator spread spectrum, demodulator for the Space Shuttle (1980); designed U.S.I.A. automatic tuned half megawatt H/F transmitter; mil: s/sgt. Royal Elec. & Mech. Engrs. Reserve, England 1954-57; pvt., Royal Parachute Regt., Territorial Army, England 1950-54; Republican; Catholic; rec: real estate devel., automobile restoration. Res: 1853 W 179th Street Torrance 90504 Ofc: Hughes Aircraft Co., Imperial Hwy, El Segundo

BRIGHT, LEE REINKE, public relations management consultant; b. Sept. 24, 1948, Kenosha, Wisc.; d. Dean Arthur and Eleanor Rosalie (Burlingham) Reinke; edn: Pasadena City Coll. 1974. Career: sales rep. Marvin Advtg. Co., L.A.' 1968-79; admin. asst. Broadway Dept. Stores, Los Angeles 1974-76; sales promotion dir. DeWeese Designs, L.A. 1976-77; acct. exec. Motivational Mktg., Inc., L.A. 1977-78; mktg. dir. Fashion Internat. Report, Inc., L.A. 1980-83; pres. Bright Mktg., pub. rels. & mktg. cons. to L.A. Hilton, The Bay (Canada), Stylists Information Svc. (Paris), Brooks Coll., others 1983--; spkr. on pub. rels. & mktg. to var. fashion schs. 1980-; awards: MAGGIE Awd., Western Publications 1982, 83; mem: Calif. Apparel Export Council; L.A. Downtowners; Fashion Gp., Inc.; Democrat; Catholic; rec: running. Address: Bright Marketing, 3310 E Broadway Long Beach 90803

BRIGHT, OGLE, MADELINE ANN, pet care co. president; b. Jan. 5, 1926, Fresno; m. Dale A. Mart (dec.); m. 2d. Dr. Geo. H. Sciaroni (dec.); m. 3d. Richard P. Bright (div.); m. 4th Jerome C. Ogle; two sons; edn: CSU San Francisco 1959, CSU Fresno 1956-58, Coll. of San Mateo 1969-71; Calif. lic. real estate sales. Career: bookkeeper Langendorf Bakeries, 1956; bookkeeper clk. Innes Reliable Leather Goods, 1955-56; asst. mgr., Customer Rels., Sears Roebuck, 1954-55; ins. clerk Calif. Assigned Risk, San Francisco 1959-60; owner mgr. Madeline's Dog Salon & Boutique, Santa Clara 1961-84, owner/ pres.' Madeline's Pet Care Services Inc., 1982--, franchisor pet care svcs. bus., 1985-; realtor assoc. investment counselor, 1979-; mem: Help form Bill AB 220, Target State Licencing for dog grooming; United Dog Groomers Inc. (v.p. 1966-71); Soroptomists Intl. of Santa Clara; Organized Friends of Triton Mus. 1975-77; Hist. Preservation Com; Calif. Fedn. of Womens Club (Santa Clara chpt.). Res: 135 Clayton Ave San Jose 95110 Ofc: Madeline's Pet Care Services, Inc. 1610 Pomeroy Ave Santa Clara 95051

BRIGHTON, BARBARA JOYCE, psychotherapist; b. Oct. 2, 1948, Los Angeles; d. Belle (Rosenberg) Bass and Harry Rosenberg; m. Thomas Brighton, Sept. 7, 1980; 1 dau., Wendi, b. 1969; edn: AA psych., Los Angeles Valley Coll. 1975, BA psych., CSU Northridge 1977, MA psych., Antioch Univ. 1978; lic. Marriage, Family, Child Therapist. Career: undergrad. psychology intern/individual and gp. therapist/co-therapist to chief-of-staff,VA Hosp., Sepulveda 1974-77; psychology intern/individual and gp. therapist for emotionally and educationally handicapped teenagers, Penny Lane, Sepulveda 1977-78; individual and gp. therapist, Westside Mental Health Gp., Los Angeles 1978--; med. staff Van Nuys Psychiatric Hosp., 1979-; psychotherapist, cons. The Breast Center, Van Nuys 1981-; supr. for M.F.C.C. Interns, 1979-; mem. student admission com. and faculty rev. bd. Antioch Univ., 1978; mem: San Fernando Valley chpt. Marriage & Family Therapists; assoc. mem. Psi Chi (hon. psych. orgn.) 1977; works: research on effects of maternal stress during pregnancy on fetus and resulting child (1978); tv coverage of her Post-Op. Support Gp. at The Breast Ctr., 1982; rec: piano, clay sculpting, gardening; res: 22427 Clarendon, Woodland Hills 91364 ofc: Westside Mental Health Gp 9201 Sunset Blvd #209 Los Angeles 90069.

BRILL, BRUCE CARLEN, retail store owner; b. Jan. 23, 1939, Peoria, Ill.; s. Donald Luis and Helen (Brall) Brill; m. LaVon, May 2, 19 58; children: Karen, b. 1959; Pam, b. 1960; Beverly, b. 1962; Audrey, b. 1963; Russell, b. 1964; edn: San Diego Jr. Coll. 1958-59. Career: driver, salesman, rate clk. King Transp., San Diego 1959-62; foreman, claims inspector, mgr. Imperial Truck Lines, Chula Vista & Indio 1962-69; pres. Roadrunner Trucking 1969-80; owner Temecula Carpets & Interiors 1979--; transp. cons. McCoy's Mkts., 1982; mem: Calif. Trucking Assn.; Temecula Valley Bus. Exch.; Temecula Valley Sportsmen Club; Kiwanis (charter, pres. 1983, Man of Year 1980); Temecula Town Assn.; Rancho-Temecula Comm. Parks Assn.; Temecula Valley CofC; v.p. (1983) bd. dirs. (1981-82) KRTM Public Radio 88.9 F.M., chmn. 1981 Riverside Co. Championship Chili Cook Off; mil: pvt. USMCR 1955-63; Republican; Lutheran; rec: fishing. Res: 24845 2nd St Murrieta 92362 Ofc: Temecula Carpets, 28545 Front St, POB 789, Temecula 92390

BRIMMEKAMP, THOMAS LEON, foreign trade executive; b. Jan. 7, 1955, NY; s. Carl Gerd and Ruth Marion (Lingg) B.; edn: BA, cum laude, UCLA 1978. Career: sales rep. Carl G. Brimmekamp & Co., Inc., Stamford, Conn. 1979-83; v.p. West Coast sales, 1983--; mem: German Am. CofC; Am. Scandinavian Found.; Danish Am. CofC; Marin Badminton Culb; Marin Arts Council; works: West End Encounter, 1980; maj. supporting role in Cameo Theater Prodn., The Importance of Being Earnest, 1983; rec: music, racquet sports, softball. Res: 32 Skyline Rd San Anselmo 94960 Ofc: POB 3574 San Rafael 94912

BRINER, CHESTER GEORGE, stockbroker; b. July 25, 1922, Chadron, Nebr.; s. Charles George and Vienna Jane (Tate) B.; m. Nancy Neer, Nov. 21, 1942; children: Eleanor L. (Quibell), b. 1946; Emmett H., b. 1949; edn: BS, Univ. of Maryland 1956; MBA, Syracuse Univ. 1959. Career: salesman/ dept. mgr. J.C. Penny Co., Santa Ana 1946-48; salesman Langley Oil Co., Santa Ana 1948-49; cons. Florida Game & Fresh Water Fish Commn. 1964-65; stockbroker 1965--; currently, acct. exec. Merrill Lynch Pierce Fenner & Smith; tchr. ext. pgms., Univ. of Maryland & Pepperdine Univ. 1961-77; awards: Joint Resolution of the Calif. Legislature 1979; mem: Saddleback Regl. CofC; Mission Vieqo Kiwanis Club (past pres.); Saddleback Valley Unified Sch. Dist. Sch. Bd. (charter pres.); Saddleback Republican Assembly (pres. 3X); mil: 1st lt. USAF 1941-46; maj, USAF 1949-64, Air Medal, Commdn. Medal; Republican; Baptist; rec: gardening, motorcycling, fishing. Res: 26311 Turquesa Cir Mission Viejo 92691 Ofc: Merrill Lynch, 23961 Calle de la Magdalena Laguna Hills 92653

BRINKER, CONNIE JUGE, graphoanalyst; b. July 15, 1928, New Orleans, La.; d. Edward Joseph and Faustine Madeline (Aleman) Juge; m. Robert Brinker, Jan. 4, 1948; children: Richard, b. 1948; Susan, b. 1952; John, b. 1957; Craig, b. 1958; Randy, b. 1964; edn: cosmetology, N.O. Beauty Coll. 1963; Fullerton Coll. 1975-6; Lifetime tchg. credentials, Cosmetology, Graphoanalysis, State of Calif. 1974; Certified graphoanalyst 1972, Questioned Document examiner 1974, Master Cert. graphoanlyst, The Internat. Graphoanalysis Soc. 1978. Career: owner Brinker and Associates, Fullerton 1979--, opened beauty salon 1979-, estab. bus. in Graphoanalysis and Questioned Documents 1980-; instr. No Orange Co. Comm. College Dist. 1974-; honors: Sharon Topper Humanitarian Award, Fullerton Coll. 1976; Graphoanalyst of the Year- So Calif. 1977, Cooperator of the Year 1977, Excellence of Perf. 1980, (IGAS) Internat. Graphoanalysis Soc.; Pres. Emeritus Honor 1980, So Calif. Chpt. Graduation spkr. 1982, IGAS Chgo. Mem: IGAS (life), World Assn. of Document Examiners (So. Calif. chpt. pres. 1978-9); mem. Citrus chpt. Nat. Psoriasis Found. 1969-83; Cub Scout Den Mother (11 yrs), Girl Scouts (6 yrs); publs: arts. in Jour. of Graphoanalysis, World Assn. of Document Examiners Exchg., Research Project IGAS 1984; Democrat; Catholic; rec: antique clock repair, jewelry design, nutrition, study of herbs. Res: 2129 West Houston Ave Fullerton 92633 Ofc: Brinker and Associates 107 North Woods Ave Fullerton 92632

BRITTINGHAM, JAMES CALVIN, nuclear engineer; b. Apr. 6, 1942, Hamlet, N.C.; s. James C. and Elizabeth (McCanless) B.; m. Margaret Kitchen, Feb. 12, 1978; 1 son, James, b. 1981; edn: BS in N.E., North Carolina St. Univ. 1964, MS in N.E., 1966; PhD in N.E., UC Berkeley 1975; Calif. lic. Profl. Engr. in Nuclear Engring. 1982. Career: technical staff Energy Sys. Group, Rockwell International, Canoga Park 1975-80; nuclear generation engr. Pacific Gas and Elec. Co., San Francisco 1980--; awards: PG&E Performance Recognition (1983); mem. Am. Nuclear Soc.; articles in sci. journals; Republican; rec: golf. Res: 1245 Dartmouth St Albany 94706 Ofc: Pacific Gas & Electric Co. 77 Beale St San Francisco 94106

BRKLACICH, LYNN LOUISE, automobile dealership executive; b. Feb. 13, 1944, Grand Rapids, Mich.; d. William Kaye and Rosemary Fay (Schmuck) McElwain; m. Donald Franciscotty, Aug. 1962; m. 2d. Michael Brklacich, Nov. 19, 1971; 1 son: Scott, b. 1964; edn: Univ. of Minn. 1968-69; LaSalle Ext. Univ. 1973. Career: cashier Savage Pontiac, Monrovia 1969; cashier Frank Elliot Chrys./ Plym., Whittier 1970-71; bookeeper Savage Motors, Inc., Monrovia 1971-73; ofc. mfr. 1973-80; bus. mgr. 1980--; awards: Diamond Chpt. Bus. Mgmt. Achiev. Awd. 1981-83; Appreciation, Monrovia Days Assn. (1981, 82); mem: Auto Dealers Ofc. Mgrs. Assn. (ADOMA); Auto Dealers Mgrs. Assn.; Monrovia Duarte Quota Club (Publicity Com., Telephone Com., Ways & Means Com.); Monrovia Days Parade Div. Marshal 1981, 82, 84; rec: civic service, golf, dancing. Res: 925 Ocean View Monrovia 91016 Ofc: Savage Motors, Inc., 236 W Huntington Dr Monrovia 91016

BRODRICK, LOIS HUNTER, securities/real estate broker; b. Aug. 13, 1920, Hollidaysbury, Pa.; d. Frank Mathew and Faye Bertie (McKague) Hunter; m. Richard Boyd Brodrick, Mar. 20, 1946; children: Victoria, b. 1947, Barrie, b. 1950; edn: BA, Penna. State Univ. 1942; courses, Univ. of Calif.; Calif. lic. R.E. Broker, Reg. Rep. NASD, Series 7. Career: owner Red Horse Riding Shop, Orinda 1968-72; real estate agt. Mason McDuffie Commercial Properties, Oakland 1970s; real estate broker Circle J Land Co. Inc. 1980; founder/broker/owner Brodrick Real Estate & Development, Shingle Springs 1982--; fin. planner/reg. rep. Financial Network Investment Corp. Inc., Sacramento 1984--; candidate for county supvsr. Contra Costa Co., 1972; mem: Internat. Assn. of Fin. Planners, Nat. Assn. of Realtors, Kappa Kappa Gamma Alumni (past pres. East Bay Chpt. 1968), League of Women Voters, Cameron Country Club; mil: lt. USNR; Republican (Calif. Rep. Assembly, past pres. Lamorinda chpt. 1973; v.p. Orinda Rep. Womens Club); Lutheran; rec: golf, skiing. Res: 3490 Fairway Dr Shingle Springs 95682 Ofc: Financial Network Inv. Corp., 6650 Belleau Woodlane Sacramento 95822

BROENNER, ALEXANDER PETER, real estate broker; b. Mar. 7, 1932, Kahl, Germany, nat. 1964; s. Muharem and Lina (Broenner) Hodzic; m. Ursula Poetzsch, Sept. 27, 1952; edn: AA, Pierce Coll. 1981; diploma, color TV & hi-fi servicing, Nat. Tech. Schs. 1976; cert. in R.E. 1980; GRI, 1983. Career: mgr. Tops Barber Shop, Los Angeles 1959-61; owner/ mgr. Star Barber Shops, L.A. 1961--; R.E. assoc. Ehrlich Real Estate, Woodland Hills 1973-81; owner/ mgr. Sanders Real Estate, Tarzana 1982--; cons. Sanders Realty 1982-; awards: Chancellor's Distng. Honor Awd., Pierce Coll. 1981; mem: San Fernando Valley Bd. Realtors; Calif. Assn. Realtors; Nat. Assn. Realtors; Republican; Catholic; rec: gardening. Address: Sanders Realty, 4700 Dunas Ln Tarzana 91356

BROGDON, RALPH EWING, JR., b. Aug. 12, 1927, Fresno; s. Ralph E. and Doris Elaine (Nilmeier) B.; m. Magdalena Martha "Chacho" Hauschildt, July 23, 1972; children: Dirk Ewing, b. 1956, Lisa Mary, b. 1959, Gregory Ralph, b. 1961; edn: AA, CSU San Jose 1949; BA, econ., Stanford Univ. 1951; Stanford Univ. Sch. of Law 1951-53; JD, Southwestern Univ. Sch. of Law 1956; admitted to Calif. State Bar 1959. Career: atty. assoc. w/ Boris S. Woolley, Torrance 1959-60, ptnr./assoc. w/ William N. Willens, Lawndale 1959-64; assoc. w/ Truman R. Adkins, Redondo Bch. 1964-67; assoc. w/ Gerald F. Moriarty, Edward Gorman, Norman Miller, John Holtrichter, John Chevalier, R.B. 1967-73; assoc. w/ Tunney & Carlyle, San Jose 1973-74; atty. pvt. practice, Cupertino 1974--; honors: CSF, Triad Hon. Soc., coll. athletics (baseball, basketball); mem: Santa Clara Co. Bar Assn. (bd. dirs. 1976-78), Sunnyvale-Cupertino Bar Assn. (pres. 1978), Santa Clara Co. Trial Lawyers Assn., Stanford Law Soc. of Santa Clara Co.; past mem. South Bay Bar Assn. (pres. 1972, chmn. Annual Golf Tourn. 1962-71; chmn. South Bay Legal Aid Found. 1963-65); fmr. mem. ABA, Calif. Trial Lawyer's Assn., L.A. Co. Bar Assn., Criminal Cts. Bar Assn.; mem. Phi Alpha Delta legal frat. 1952-; life mem. Stanford Alumni Assn. 1954-, bd. dirs. Stanford Buck Club 1978-; mem. bd. dirs., past pres. Canyon Lake Property Owners Assn.; mem. CofC, Kiwanis (past pres. Redondo Bch. Club 1964); charter pres. Canyon Lake Men's Golf Club 1970-71; past ldr. Cub Scouts, Babe Ruth Little League; mil: Yeoman 3/c USN 1945-46; Republican: active precinct wkr., campaigner 1950-; charter chmn. Stanford Univ. Young Repubs. Club 1949; Prot.; rec: golf. Res: 150 Altura Vista Los Gatos 95030 Ofc: 10455 Torre Ave Cupertino 95014

BROIHAHN, MICHAEL ALLEN, corporate controller; b. June 2, 1948, Cuba City, Wisc.; s. Lester Ernest and Shirley Luella (Bendorf) B.; m. Cynthia Andreas, May 29, 1982; edn: BS, Univ. Wisc., Madison 1972; MBA, Univ. Wisc., Milwaukee 1973, MS, 1976; Calif. lic. real estate broker (1981), CPA (Wisc. 1981), CMA (NAA 1980). Career: auditor Price Waterhouse & Co., Milwaukee, 1976-78; acct. mgr., asst. controller, controller Fox & Carskadon Finl. Corp., San Mateo 1979-82; controller, dir. of fin./controller Computerland Corp., Hayward 1982--; lectr. Univ. of Wisc., Milwaukee 1977-78; awards: Price Waterhouse grantee, PhD Pgm. in Acctg., UC Berkeley 1978; mem: Nat. Assn. of Accountants (dir. 1981-84), Am. Inst. of CPAs, Inst. of Mgmt. Acctg., Inst. of Cert. Finl. Planners, Commonwealth Club of Calif.; publs: Tecumseh Products Co.; Badgerland Equip. Inc. (Harvard Case Studies, 1978); Republican; Lutheran; rec: gemology, numismatics, travel. Res: 14229 Santiago Rd San Leandro 94577 Ofc: Computerland Corp. 30985 Santana St Hayward 94544

BROKL, STANLEY SCOTT, electronics engineer, inventor; b. Apr. 20, 1941, Hutchinson, Minn.; s. Arnold Stanley and Annette (Chidlaw) B.; m. Donna Athey; children: Timothy, b. 1961, James, b. 1963, Diana, b. 1964, Deborah, b. 1966; m. 2d. Betty Richards; m. 3d. Christina Gutierrez, Aug. 6, 1983; edn: West Coast Univ. 1969-73; AA, Pasadena City Coll. 1971; USN Grad. Electronic Tech Sch. Career: jr. engr./tech. var. cos. 1960-69; sr. tech. Jet Propulsion Lab., Pasadena 1969, sr. engring. asst. 1973-77; sr. mem. tech. staff RCA Somerville, NJ 1977-80; sr. engr. JPL, 1980-83, tech. staff and cognizant engr. for Planetary Radar, 1984--; cons. Electronics Arts Research, 1980-; awards: recognition for var. inventions, NASA (1972, 74, 77, 80); three monetary awds. for Patent Appls., RCA (1977, 78, 79); Patentee: Peripheral Interactive Device with Manual Controls (1973), Jam Resistant TV System (1982), Jam Resistant Receiver (1983); mem: IEE (1980-83), Am. Radio Relay League, life (elected section mgr. L.A. Sect. 1980-); mil: ETRSN, USN 1958-60; Democrat; Prot.; rec: amateur radio opr. N2YQ (1955-). Res: 2645 N. Marengo Ave Altadena 91001 Ofc: Jet Propulsion Laboratory 4800 Oak Grove Dr Pasadena 91109

BROKOPP, CAROL ANN, investor; b. Sept. 29, 1946, Los Angeles; d. Robert Lawson and Peggy Carol (Pixler) Pierson; m. Robert Wm. Brokopp, Mar. 22, 1969; edn: BA in hist., CSU Fullerton 1975; Calif. lic. real estate broker 1981. Career: owner Brock Financial Investments, Newport Beach 1976--; pres. Pac-Tex Resource Operations, Inc., Newport Bch. and Houston Tx. 1979--; pres. International A Comml. Brokerage, Newport Bch. and Houston, Tx. 1981--; mem. Realty Inv. Assn. of Orange Co., Newport -Costa Mesa Bd. of Realtors; co-founder Cure Paralysis Found.; regl. v.p./bd. dirs. Paralysis Cure Research 1976-83; bd. dirs. Nat. Spinal Cord Injury Found. 1979-80; club: Bahia Corinthian Yacht; works: prod. "Sound of Music" on the Main Stage, UCI (11/82) to benefit Am. Paralysis Found.; sponsored Brokopp Bermuda Conf., 1978 (the first nat. conf. for cure of spinal cord injury); patron, 1st Internat. Conf. for SCI Cure, Catania, Sicily; Republican (Pres. Task Force); Prot.; rec: antiques. Res: 905 Emerald Bay, Laguna Beach 92651 Ofc: Brock Financial Investments, 4222 Campus Dr Newport Bch 92651

BRONSON, JOHN OGDEN, insurance broker; b. Sept. 18, 1903, Sacramento; s. Howard Cuyler and Eva (Oliver) B.; m. Zelda Warren, Mar. 28, 1931; 1 dau., Johna W., b. 1942; edn: grad. Sacto. H.S. 1922; spl. bus. course, Stanford Univ.; Calif. lic. Casualty and Prop. Ins. Agent, Broker. Career: general ins. agent/broker; formed the John O. Bronson Co., Sacramento 1940--, ret. 1984; served as foreman Sacto. County Grand Jury 1965; City of Sacto. Planning Commnr. 1957, City Councilman 1960-62; Calif. Highway Commnr. 1958-60; dir. Sacto. City Chamber of Commerce 1955-58; dir. Calif. CofC 1962-70 (chmn. Transp. Dept. 1962-70); mem. Masons, Scottish Rite, Shriners, Lions, Sutter Club; Republican; Episcopal; rec: history. Res: 4607 Del Rio Rd Sacramento 95822 Ofc: John O. Bronson Co. 2401 American River Dr Sacramento 95825

BROOKES, CRITTENDEN EDWARDS, psychiatrist; b. May 8, 1931, Oakland, CA; s. Arthur Blayne and Ruth (Crittenden) Brookes; B.A., Calif. State Univ., Chico, 1952; M.A., Stanford Univ., 1953; Ph.D., Stanford Univ., 1956; M.D., Stanford Univ., 1960; m. Mauna Berkov; children: Lisa, b. 1968; Aaron, b. 1971; Jedidiah, b. 1977; Jesse, b. 1981. Career: clin. instr., Dept. Psychiatry, U.C. Med. Center, 1964-67; asst., Dept. Psych., Mt. Zion Med. Ctr., 1964-67; asst. Cl Prof., U.C. Med. Ctr., 1967-75; adj., Mt. Zion Med. Ctr., 1967-76; assoc. cl. prof., U.C. Med. Ctr., 1975--;asst. chief, Mt. Zion Med. Ctr., 1976--; private practice, 1964--. Awards: Stanford Univ. Honor Scholarship, 1953; Henry J. Kaiser Family Scholarship in Med., 1957-58; USPHS Student Fellowship in Pharmacology, 1957; Stanford Univ. Sch. of Med. 1959-60; Spec. fellowship in social Psychiatry, Stanford Sch. of Med., 1959. Mem.: Certified Jugian Analyst, mem. Soc. of Jungian Analysts of No. Calif., 1967--; chmn., Curr. Comm., mem. bd. govs., C.G. Jung Inst., San Francisco; mem., APA; AMA; NCPA; mem., chmn., Northern Calif. Psychiatric Soc. Profl. Practices Comm., 1972-79; mem., fellow, Amer. Psychiatric Assn.; Amer. Acad. of Psychoanalysis. Author: "A Jungian View of Transpersonal Psychotherapy," Seymour Boorstein's Intepersonal Psychotherapy, Science & Behavior Books, Palo Alto, 1980; "The Group As Corrective for Failure in Analysis," Gerhard Adler's Success and Failure in Analysis, G.P. Putnam's Sons, NY, 1974. Mil.: Sr. Surgeon USPHS, 1960-64. Office: 407 Locust St., San Francisco 94118.

BROOKS, CLAUDIA M., lawyer; b. Aug. 2, 1952, Oakland; d. Rex E. and Colleen M. (Walker) B.; m. James A. Smith; edn: Worcester Coll., Oxford Univ., England 1973; Monterey Inst. of Foreign Studies 1974; Institute de Francais, Villefranche- Sur- Mer, France 1979; Hague Acad. of Internat. Law, The Hague, Nertherlands 1980; AB, UC Berkley 1974; JD, UC Hastings Coll. of Law 1979. Career: extern, Justice William P. Clark, Calif. Supreme Ct. 1978; research asst. James A. Smith, Atty. at Law, Redlands 1978-80; assoc. 1981; partner Smith & Brooks, Attys. at Law, Redlands 1982--; pub. mem. Dept. of St. Foreign Svc. Selection Bds., Wash. DC 1983; ed.- in- chief Hastings Internat. & Camparative Law Review 1978-79; mem: San Bernardino Co. & Am. Bar Assns.; State Bar of Calif.; World Affairs Council of Inland So. Calif. (Exec. Com.); Redlands Comm. Music Assn.; Zonta, Redlands chpt.; publs: Trust & Estate Planning: The Effect of Soviet Policies on Legacies from Abroad, 1 Hastings Internat. & Comparative Law Review 195, 1977. Ofc: Smith & Brooks, Attys. at Law, 130 W Vine St Redlands 92373

BROOKS, SAM HERMAN, insurance brokerage firm president; b. March 3, 1935, Windsor, Ont., Can.; nat. 1965; s. Jacob Issac and Rachel (Wainger) B.; m. Faye Barret, Dec. 27, 1964; children: Michael (stepson) b. 1952, Deborah, b. 1955, Robert, b. 1957, Judi, b. 1959; edn: grad. Calif. Sch. of Insurance (Pasadena) 1958; Life Underwriters Tng. Council 1960; num. underwriting courses; RHU, Nat. Assn. of Hlth. Underwirters, 1979. Career: agent/staff mgr. Prudential Ins. Co., Whittier 1956-63; estab. own ins. firm, Samuel H. Brooks & Assocs., Beverly Hills 1964-71, moved bus. to Rowland Hgts. 1971, incorporated in 1973; chmn. bd. Amalgamated Ins. Brokers Corp., Rowland Hgts. 1973--; Nat. Assn. of Life Underwriters awards: Nat. Quality award 1980, Million Dollar Round Table (nine MDRT 1973-83), Five Million Dollar Forum (1975,6), Nat. Sales Achievement award (five, 1966-75), others. Mem: Nat. Assn. of Life Underwriters, Nat. Assn. of Health Underwriters, Indsl Ins. Agents & Brokers Assn., Nat. Assn. of Notaries, La Habra CofC, Better Bus. Bur.; 32nd Deg. Mason, Shriner, Acad. of Magical Arts. Publs: contbr. Occidental Life Ins.Co. mag. (1964); Republican; Hebrew Christian; rec: music, travel, autos; Res: 18103 E. Galatina St. Rowland Hts 91748 Ofc: Amalgamated Ins. Brokers Corp. 18415 Colima Rd. Ste. H, Rowland Hts. 91748.

BROOKSBY, L. SCOTT, dentist; b. Oct. 5, 1956, Provo, Utah; s. Lyle Orson and Raelene Ann (Jorgenson) Brooksby; m. Karen M., Mar. 22, 1980; edn: BS in biol., Brigham Young univ. 1979; DDS, Univ. of the Pacific 1982. Career: lt. USPHS, 1982--; dental director Clinica Sierra Vista, Lamont, Ca. 1982--. Honors: ASDA Preventive Dentistry Award 1981; TKO Dental Honor frat, 1981-2. Mem: Am. Dental Assn., CDA, Kern Co. Dental Soc. (Community

Dental Hlth Com. 1982-3; ASDA 1979-82; Intercollegiate Knights 1978-9. Republican; Mormon; rec: scuba, woodworking, choir, drama. Res: 4100 Krista Ct. Bakersfield 93306 Ofc: Clinica Sierra Vista, 8787 Hall Rd Lamont 93241

BROUSSARD, BEVERLY ANNA, pharmacist; b. Aug.7, 1932, Baton Rouge, La.; d. Clarence S.and Ruth B. (Baranco) Avery; m. Garfield Broussard, Apr. 11, 1953; chil: Garfield Jr., b. 1954, Ruth, b. 1956, David, b. 1961, Deanna, b. 1961; edn: BS, Xavier Univ. 1952. Career: staff pharmacist Eden Hosp., Castro Valley 1958-61, Alameda Hosp., Alameda, Ca. 1967--; lectr. hosp. nursing staff, and school Career Day pgms. Mem: Nat. Pharmaceutical Assn., Am. Soc. of Hosp. Pharmacists, Xavier Univ. Alumni Club of No. Calif., Delta Sigma Theta Sor.; Democrat; Catholic; spl. interest: coll. counseling young people; rec: music; res: 2712 Ritchie St. Oakland 94605.

BROWN, ALBERT C., JR., city mayor; b. Oct. 25, 1918, Los Angeles; s. Albert C. and Wanda (Albright) Brown; edn: AA, Riverside City Coll.; m. Virginia Little, 1941; children: Cheryl Kinsman, Susan Baltagi, Becky Westerdahl; career: owner, Brown's Engine Rebuilding; Mayor, city of Riverside; awards: Alumnus of the Year, Riverside City Coll., 1977; Catholic Athletic League recognition award for outstanding service; mem. Riverside City College Bd. of Trustees, 1964-78; mil: USN 1940-45; Republican; Protestant; rec: cooking, gardening, fishing; res: 2330 Prince Albert Dr., Riverside 92507; ofc: 3900 Main St., Riverside 92522.

BROWN, CAROL N. S., financial planner; b. Dec. 2, 1943, Atlanta, Ga.; d. Homer Bates and Eulalia (Napier) Sutton; m. W. Hilory Brown, June 11, 1977; stepchildren: James Hilory, b. 1969; Kathleen, b. 1973; edn: BA, Agnes Scott Coll. 1965; grad. work, Peabody Coll. 1966-7, U. of Chattanooga 1967, MBA in prog., Golden Gate Univ. 1982-4; Cert. Financial Planner, Coll. for Finl. Plng. 1982. Career: sales agt. Lincoln Nat. Life Ins. Co., San Francisco, Atlanta, Ga. 1975-77; No. Calif. Pension Rep. for Crown Life Ins. Co., San Francisco 1977-79; group hlth and pension rep. Mutual of New York, S.F. 1979-80; Registered Rep., Judith Briles & Co., Palo Alto 1980-81; Reg. Prin., Private Ledger Financial Services, Inc., Los Altos 1981--; pres. Financial Resource Team, Inc.; cont. edn. instr. Foothill and Canada Colls., San Jose State Univ., Los Altos and Redwood City Community Ctrs; mem. Registry of Finl. Planning Practitioners; Mem: Internat. Assn. for Finl. Planning, Finl. Planning Forum, Western Pension Conf., Peninsula Life Underwriters, Inst. of Certified Finl. Planners, Peninsula Profl. Women's Network; rec: piano, cooking. Res: 2323 Sharon Rd #137, Menlo Park 94025 Ofc: Financial Resource Team Inc. 199 First St, Ste 300, Los Altos 94022

BROWN, CHARLES RICHARD, wholesale distributor; b. Aug. 26, 1937, Mercer, Pa.; s. Charles B. and Hilda Mae (Chadderton); m. Rosellen Colca, May 13, 1961; 1 son: Damon, b. 1965; edn: AA, L.A. City Coll. 1968. Career: stockbroker Lehman Brothers, Los Angeles 966-74; bus. devel. ofcr. Imperial Bank, L.A. 1974; sales mgr. Roberts Consolidated, City of Industry 1974-76; mfrs. rep. Porter Williams Co., L.A. 1976-78; pres. Victor Kemy Co., Inc., L.A. 1979--; awards: Salesman of Yr., Kimberly Clark Corp. 1964, 65; mem: San Diego Co. Floor Covering Assn. (pres. 1981-2, 1982-3); Kiwanis; mil: Corp., USMC 1956-58; Republican; Protestant; rec: skiing, travel. Res: 244 Chapalita Dr Encinitas 92024 Ofc: Victor Kemp Co., 3218 F Street San Diego 92102

BROWN, DOUGLAS BOYD, electrical engineer; b. Dec. 22, 1949, Redmond, Ore.; s. Donald Boyd and Mae Louise (Madison) B.; edn: BSEE, Ore. State Univ. 1973; profl. elec. engr., Calif. & Ore. 1982. Career: with Bechtel Power Corp. 1971--; elec. constrn. & startup gr., Labadie, Mo. 1971-72; electrical design engr. Bechtel Power Corp., San Francisco 1973-77, sr. elec. engr., 1977-80 engring. supvr., (Elec. Gp. supvr./ resident engr.) 1980, engring. supvr./ Elec. Gp. supvr. Cogeneration Plant Proposals, 1980--; instr. protective relaying course, Oakland- East Bay chpt. IEEE 1981-82; awards: Svc. Awd., Oakland- East Bay chpt. IEEE Power Eng. Soc. 1982; mem: IEEE; Industry Applications Soc.; Power Eng. Soc.; Rohnert Park Tennis Club Homeowners Assn. (pres. 1982, 83); Aircraft Owners & Pilots ASsn.; Mooney Aircraft Pilots Assn.; Republican; Presbyterian; rec: tennis, bicycling, pvt. pilot. Res: 1078 Eleanor Ave Rohnert Park 94928 Ofc: Bechtel Power Corp., POB 3965, 50 Beale Street, San Francisco 94119

BROWN, ELAINE ELLIOTT, social worker; b. Sept. 10, 1928, Salt Lake City; d. Robert Clair and Vera Lucille (Wise) Elliott; m. Darrel Brown, Apr. 26, 1953; chil: Cheryl, b. 1954, Shanna, b. 1958; edn: AB, Stanford Univ. 1950, Univ.of Wash., Seattle 1950-52; R.S.W., Regis. Social Worker. Career: adoption/child welfare worker Alameda County, Oakland 1952; child welfare worker San Bernardino Co. 1953; substitute tchr Spl. Edn., Mt. Diablo Unified Sch. Dist., Concord 1964-67; Day Care Devel., Contra Costa Co. 1967-75, also Day Care Licensing Worker 1974-75; head tchr After-school Pgm. Concord Child Care Ctr. 1973-74; generic case wrkr/pgm. dir. Specialized Family Day Care Pgm., Contra Costa Co. Soc. Svc. Dept., Martinez 1976--; bd. dirs. C.C. Childrens Council 5 yrs.; bd. mem. Mt. Diablo C.C.A. 6 yrs.; founding mem. Diablo Valley Day Care Assn. Honors: 1983 nom. for Child Abuse Prevention awd. for agcy. representation; recognition, PTA (25 yrs. svc.), Am. Humane Soc., Diablo Valley Day Care Providers Assn., 1978 County Achievement Awd., 1981 Kiddie Awd.-C.C. Children's Council. Mem: Calif. Assn. for Edn. of Young Chil.; Girl Scout leader, Concord 1961-73; PTA 1959-72 (vp 1972); Lisle Fellowship 1947, scholarship Mills Coll. 1946. Trainer, Day Care Providers; spkr. confs. and wrkshops 1967-, speaker State Conf. CAEYC and 1st Conv. Day Care Providers, Sacto. 5/82. Democrat. Congregational. rec: folk dancing, arts & crafts. res: 953 Chanel Ct. Concord 94518. ofc: Contra Costa Soc. Svc. Dept. 30 Muir Rd. Martinez 94553.

BROWN, GEORGE STEPHEN, physicist; b. June 28, 1945, Santa Monica; s. Paul Gordon and Frances Ruth (Moore) B.; m. Nohema Fernandez, Aug. 8, 1981; 1 dau: Sonya Elena, b. 1972; edn: BS, w/ honors, Calif. Inst. of Tech. 1967; PhD, Cornell Univ. 1973; Career: tech. staff Bell Labs., Murray Hill, NJ 1973-77; sr. research assoc. Stanford Univ. 1977-82; prof. applied physics, Stanford Univ. 1982--; assoc. dir. SSRL; mem: Am. Physical Soc.; Review of Scientific Instruments (edl. bd.); over 50 publs. in physics research; rec: music performance, arms control. Res: 740 Alameda de las Pulgas Redwood City 94061 Ofc: Bin 69, POB 4349, Stanford 94305

BROWN, IAN STEVEN, cosmetic surgeon; b. Aug. 17, 1948, NYC; s. R. Aaron and Lana (Levin) B.; m. Judith Summers, 1979; edn: AB, psych., Bucknell Univ. 1970; MD, Buffalo Med. Sch. 1974. Career: surgical residency Kaiser Hosp., Los Angeles 1974-76, ENT-Facial Plastic residency White Memorial Hosp., Loma Linda Univ., L.A. 1976-79; founder Beverly Hills Facial & Cosmetic Surgery Medical Group; mem: Am. Med. Assn., Calif. Med. Assn., Los Angeles Co. Med. Assn., L.A. Soc. of Otolaryngology, Head & Neck Surg., mem. L.A. Soc. of Specialty Plastic Surgeons; jr. mem. Am. Assn. Facial Plastic & Reconstructive Surgery; rec: scuba. Res: 929 19th St., 2, Santa Monida 90403 Ofc: Beverly Hills Facial & Cosmetic Surgery Medical Group, 465 N. Roxbury Dr, Ste. 1007, Beverly Hills 90210

BROWN, JAMES EDWARD, educational software executive; b. July 6, 1939, Miller, Mo.; s. Elmer Elwood and Mattie Alberta (Doss) B.; m. Audrey Pirtle, July 5, 1960; children: James, b. 1961; Elmer, b. 1963; edn: AA, Palomar Coll. 1971; BBA, Nat. Univ.; MBA, Nat. Univ. Career: writer/ analyst Production Manager Perspective, Inc., San Diego 1978-79; instrnl. designer Instructional Sci. & Devel. (ISD), Inc., San Diego 1979-81; proj. dir. Courseware, Inc., S.D. 1981-82; ednl. software mgr./ sr. instrnl. devel., ISD 1982--; instrnl. technology seminar, National Univ. 1983; project design cons., 1981; user tng. on automated instrnl. design system 1984; awards: Superior Performance Awd, NSPI, San Diego 1983; mem: Nat. Soc. for Performance & Instrn. (NSIP); works: Automated Instructional Design Sys. and User Manual, 1983-84; tech. reports on instructional design & research projs. 1979-81; individualized tng. course (2 weeks) 1975; instructional design manual 1975; mil: Master Chief Avonics Techn., USN 1958-78; Republican; rec: computers. Res: 2204 Bancroft St San Diego 92104 Ofc: ISD, Inc., 5059 Newport Ave, Ste 303, San Diego 92107

BROWN, KENNETH GENE, architect/ development co. executive; b. July 2, 1952, Mankato, Minn.; s. Charles Julius and Verna May (Fenn) B.; m. Carole Clark, Aug. 2, 1974; children: Diana, b. 1976; Karen, b. 1977; Robert, b. 1979; Carrie, b. 1980; Cynthia, b. 1983; edn: AA, Mesa Comm. Coll. 1973; Brigham Young Univ. 1973-74; Reg. Architect, Calif. 1982. Career: draftsman Great Am. Resources Devel. Co., Scottsdale, Ariz. 1971; archtl. designer Sante Fe Devel. Co., Scottsdale 1971-72; assoc. Building Design Svcs., Scottsdale 1972-73; principal/ designer Kenneth Brown & Assocs., Scottsdale 1973-75; archtl. designer Archisystems, Van Nuys 1975-77; principal designer Kenneth Brown & Assocs., Van Nuys 1977; project mgr. Summa Corp., Van Nuys 1977-78; v.p./ bd. dirs. West Sun Devel. Co., Irvine 1979-80; senior project arhitect Lee & Sakahara Assocs., Costa Mesa 1980-83; dir. of arch. Hometel Devel. Corp., Newport Beach 1983--; archtl. design cons. El Torito Restaurants (1983), Concept Design Co. (1982-83); awards: Spl. Recgn. Dale Carnegie & Assoc. 1981; Winner design competition, Harbor Ctr. Redevel. Proj., Redondo Beach 1979; mem: Am. Inst. of Architects; Boy Scouts of Am.; Orange Co. Council; Ch. of Jesus Christ Latter Day Saints (Ordained High Priest); works: stained glass/ fine arts designer Beacon Hill Redevel. Proj., Los Angeles City Redevel. Agcy. 1978; mil: Battalion Supply Sgt. E-5, Calif. Army Nat. Guard 1971-77; Republican; Latter Day Saints; rec: fine carpentry, furniture, model building. Res: 23612 Ave Topanga Mission Viejo 92691 Ofc: Hometel Development Co., 450 Newport Ctr Dr, Ste 400, Newport Beach 92660

BROWN, LAWRENCE DALE, arson investigator; b. July 9, 1944, Los Angeles; s. Milton Dale and Deloris Velva Brown; m. Joyce Wilson, Apr. 11, 1974; 1 son, Robert, b. 1970; edn: AA, San Bernardino Valley Coll. 1980; lic. Calif. State Fire Investigator I, 1980; Indsl. Edn. tchr. credentials; Emergency Medical Tech. Career: deputy sheriff San Bernardino Co. Sheriffs Dept., 1965-68; engr./capt. Crest Forest Fire Protection Dist., Crestline 1968-78; fire marshal City of Norco Fire Dept., 1978-80; arson/fraud investigator, INS Investigations Bur., Ariz. 1980-83; owner Insurance Services & Investigations, San Bernardino 1983--; instr. Fire & Arson Investg., San Bernardino Valley Coll. and San Berdo. Co. Sheriffs Acad.; spl. deputy (arson expert and cons.) San Berdo. Sheriffs Dept.; honors: commendn. for rescue wk. during Norco Bank Robbery; recognition for wk. with Juvenile Fire Setters from Norco Sch. Dist.; mem: San Bernardino Co. Arson Assn. (pres. 1983), Riverside Co. Arson Assn. (pres. 1980), Masons; mil: 3/c USN; Republican; Christian; rec: gun collecting, trap shooting. Res: 26087 Holly Vista San Bernardino 92404 Ofc: Insurance Svcs. & Investigations, POB 3365, San Bernardino 92413

BROWN, LEWIS FRANK, lawyer; b. Aug. 4, 1929, Cleveland, Miss.; s. Frank C. and Lula A. Brown; m. Dorothy J. Fitzgerald, Mar. 29, 1956; children: Lewis G., b. 1959, Orville F., b. 1966; edn: AA, Vallejo Jr. Coll. 1955; BA, CSU San Francisco 1957; JD, Lincoln Univ. Law Sch. 1964; admitted to practice Calif. State Bar. Career: educator Vallejo Unified Sch. Dist. and Vallejo Jr. Coll. 1956-64; attached to Exec. Office of Pres. Lyndon B. Johnson, as asst. field supr./field supr. Nat. Adult Basic Literacy Edn. Field Test, Greenleigh Assocs., 1964-66; cons. Health, Edn. & Welfare, No. Calif. (wrote the Calif.

component of Nat. Adult Basic Edn. Follow-up Field Study 1966); (current) atty./sr. ptnr. Brown & Bradley, Vallejo; mem. Vallejo City Planning Com. (First Black) 1963-65 Vallejo City Councilman (First Black) 1965, Vice-Mayor (First Black) 1967; elected Solano Co. Democratic Com. (First Black) 1959-67, No. Calif. Chmn. of Negro Elected Ofcls. of State of Calif. 1967; recipient Calif. St. Senate and Assem. Resolution of Commendn. (1983); served as No. Calif. Field Coord. for Robt. F. Kennedy for President (1968); mem: Nat. Bar Assn. (life), Calif. Bar Assn., Solano Co. Bar Assn., Charles Houston Bar Assn.; Panel of Arbitrators, Am. Arbitration Assn.; PTA 1957-67 (PAC chmn. 1959); mil: pfc US Army 1951-53; Democrat; Prot.; rec: bicycling, restoring cars. Res: 400 Lakeside Dr Vallejo 94590 Ofc: Brown & Bradley, 538 Georgia St, Vallejo 94590

BROWN, LULA MAE, mortgage broker; b. June 30, 1950, Swift-town, Miss.; d. Robert B. and Mary Ann Brown; 1 dau: Latanya, b. 1979; edn: AA, Laney Jr. Coll. 1970; BS, CSU Hayward 1972; MS 1973; Calif. Comm. Coll. Instr. & Counselor Cred. 1975. Career: counselor Calif. St. Univ., Stanislaus 1973-75; intake counselor Alameda Co. Proj. Intercept 1976-77; R.E. salesprsn. Sarkis Realty 1976-80; fin. aid counselor UC Berkeley 1977-78; loan ofcr. Granite Home Loans, Ltd. 1980-81; owner/ mgr. L.B. Financial Svcs. 1981--; mem: Alameda Co. Bd. Realtors; US CofC; Exec. Female Orgn.; Democrat; Baptist; rec: entertaining, bowling, travel. Res: L.B. Financial Services, 3640 Grand Ave, Ste 214, Oakland 94610

BROWN, MARLENE ANN, sales executive; b. Jan. 25, 1953, Eureka; d. Stanley Eugene and Florence Lee (Roberts) Clayton; m. Mark Bruce Brown, Sept. 18, 1982; edn: Hartnell Jr. Coll. 1971-3. Career: salespsn Sears Roebuck & Co., Salinas 1971-73, personnel interviewer, 1973-75; medical asst. Dr. Theodore Bradley, Monterey 1975-76; accts. payable P.E. O'Hair & Co. (wholesale plumbing) Salinas 1976-78, asst. purchaser 1979-83, purchasing agt. 1979-83, sales mgr. 1983--; honors: Past Worthy Advisor Internat. Order of Rainbow for Girls, 1970. Democrat; Presbyterian. Res: 20251 Franciscan Way Salinas 93908 Ofc: P.E. O'Hair & Co. 1355 Burton AVe Salinas 93901

BROWN, PETER RICHARDS, lawyer; b. July 25, 1939, Hyannis, Mass.; s. David Richards and Patricia (Seymour) B.; m. Stephanie Escalle, Aug. 30, 1964; edn: BA, CSU San Francisco 1964; JD, Georgetown Univ. Law Ctr. 1969. Career: Divisional mgr. The Hecht Co., Wash DC, 1964-66; Legal Aid Soc., Wash DC 1965-69; law clerk Cullinan, Hancock & Rothert, San Francisco, Ca. 1966-69, assoc. 1969-71; legislative counsel Guam Legislature, 1971-72; ptnr. Cullinan, Burns & Helmer, S.F. 1973-81; ptnr. Richards Brown and Wong, S.F. 1981 ; Dir: P. E. O'Hair & Co. (1983-), Drossler & Assocs. Inc. (1969-); honors: Ancient Order of the Chamoari, Govt. of Guam 1971; mem. San Francisco Bar Assn.; club: Ross Landing Racquet; rec: photog., tennis, travel. Res: 5100 Paradise Dr Corte Madera 94925 Ofc: Richards Brown and Wong, 100 Bush St, Ste. 1100, San Francisco 94104

BROWN, ROBERT WILLIAM, systems development consulting firm president; b. Nov. 20, 1938, Akron, Ohio; s. Wm. Edward and Marie Louise Brown; m. Laura Paaso, Oct. 19, 1979; children: Geoffrey, b. 1968, Eric, b. 1980; edn: BSBA, Kent State Univ. 1960; MBA, Stamford Univ. (Ala.) 1967; postgrad. wk. Univ. of Ala. 1968; Cert. Mgmt. Cons. (CMC), Inst. of Mgmt. Consultants 1983; Profl. Speaker, Nat. Spkrs. Assn. 1983. Career: district sales mgr. Kimberly Clark Corp., Neehah, Wisc. 1962-70; cons. organization devel., Kepner Tregoe Inc., Princeton, NJ 1970-71; dir. sales tng., E & J Gallo Winery, Modesto 1971-74; vice pres. Glen Douglas Inc., Newport Beach 1974-81; pres. Sales Systems Development, Inc. (cons. in tng. and orgzn. devel.), Palo Alto 1981--: clients incl. Beatrice Foods Co., Rexall Corp., Kitchens of Sara Lee, No Nonsense Fashions, Inc., The Stroh Brewery Co., McKesson, Inc., Wine and Spirits Wholesalers of Am. Inc., Ralston Purina Co., Heublein, Inc., num. others; awarded Spl. Interest Group Appreciation Cert., Am. Soc. Training and Devel., 1975, 76; mem: Nat. Speakers Assn., Inst. of Mgmt. Consultants, Wine and Spirits Wholesalers Assn., Nat. Food Brokers Assn., Am. Soc. of Tng. and Devel.; Decathlon Club; author (texts) Techniques in Profl. selling and Merchandising (1980), The Field Sales Manager (1982), Headquarters Selling Strategies (1984); mil: 1st lt. US Army; 1960-62; Catholic; rec: tennis. Res: 106 Promethean Way Mountain View 94043 Ofc: Sales Systems Devel., Inc. 450 San Antonio Rd. Ste. 32, Palo Alto 94306

BROWN, RONALD ALLAN, hospital administrator/R.N.; b. Dec. 19, 1949, Shell Lake, Wis.; s. Eugene Edward and Eunice (Laveau) B.; m. Teddie L. Bolinger, May 25, 1975; edn: various sci.courses, UC Berkeley 1972-78, R.N., Solano Coll. 1978; num. courses in mgt., leadership. Career: Multiphasive Lab dept. hd. Family Medical Gp., Vallejo 1974-78; I.C.U. nurse VA Hospital, Martinez 1978; plant indsl. head nurse American Home Foods Inc., Vallejo and Vacaville; hosp. adminstr. Am. Health Centers, Newport Beach 1979; hosp. adminstr. North American Health Care Inc., Montebello 1980--, currently hosp. adminstr. N.A.H.C.Inc., Pomona; bd.dirs. So. Calif. Health Care Consultants Inc., Hollywood; honors: Silvery Award for work on Eclectus Parrots, Am. Fedn. of Aviculture, 1982; mem: Calif. Assn. of Health Facilities, Am. Fedn. of Aviculture (chmn. Com. on Avion Transp.), Aviculture Soc. of Am., Avicultural Soc. of S. Australia, Queensland Avicultural Soc., Nat. Audubon Soc., Orange Co. Bird Breeders (vice pres.), Pomona C. of C., U.S. Chamber of Comm., Nat. Geo. Soc., Smithsonian Assocs.; publs: book in progress on care, breeding of Eclectus Parrots (owns largest collection by species in captivitity in world); apptd. by 39th Cong. Rep. to Affairs Relevant to C.I.T.I.E.S. conv. on internat. trade in endangered species with 30 participating countries; mil: E4 USAF 1968-72, Presdtl. cit., marksmanshp, unit cit. w/2 clusters, 3 commendations; Republican; Ch. of God; rec: basketball, rare nat. hist. books, pvt. aviculturist, public spkr; res: POB 283, Fullerton 92632; ofc: N.A.H.C. Inc. 3111 Santa Anita Ave. El Monte 91733

BROWN, RUSSELL CALVIN, metallurgical engineer; b. Sept. 14, 1933, Kansas City, Mo.; s. Harold William Russell and Viola May (Humberd) B.; m. Marjorie Sue Ruby, July 2, 1960; children: Jeffrey, b. 1961; Douglas, b. 1966; edn: BS, Finlay Engring. Coll. 1957; BS, Univ. of Kansas 1965; Reg. Profl. Metallurgical Engr., Calif. 1976. Career: design engr. No. American Aviation 1957-59; design engr. Gordon Johnson Mfg. Co. 1959-62; welding engr./ supt. Am. Bridge Div. U.S. Steel 1965-71; principal welding engr. Fluor Corp. 1971-81; pricipal engr. Davy McKee Corp. 1981-82; mettallurgical engr. Craddock Engring. Co. 1983--; adv. coms. Saddleback Coll., Santa Monica City Coll.; mem: Am. Welding Soc.; Am. Soc. for Metals; Am. Welding Soc.; MENSA; rec: fishing, hunting. Address: 9221 Julie Beth St Cypress 90630

BROWN, STEPHANIE DIANE, alcohol clinic director; b. July 19, 1944, Mnpls., Minn.; d. Samuel Benjamin and Stephanie (Sanko) Brown; m. Robert Harris, Sept. 9, 1978; 1 dau. Makenzie Lee, b. 1980; edn: Northwestern Univ. 1962-63; BS, UC Berkeley 1966; MS, CSU San Jose 1974; PhD, Calif. Sch. of Profl. Psychology 1977; Calif. lic. MFCC, 1976, lic. Psychologist 1980. Career: retail promotion rep. Koratron Co., S.F. and NYC, 1966-68; research asst. Stanford Research Inst., Menlo Park 1968-69; research analyst Baumeister & Dole (bus. consultants), Palo Alto 1969-70; research assoc. Stanford Univ. Dept. of Psychiatry, 1972-75; founder/assoc. dir. Stanford Alcohol Clinic, 1977-80, director 1980--; acting asst. prof. Dept. Psychiatry, Stanford Univ. Med. Sch. 1980-; mem. Approval Com., Calif. Licensing Exam on Alcoholism and Drug Abuse for Physicians; apptd. by Gov. Brown mem. Calif. State Alcoholism Adv. Bd. 1978-80; honors: Western Area Alcoholism Tng. and Edn. Fellowship, 1975; Pi Sigma Alpha; outstanding clin. faculty instr., Dep. Psychiat., Stanford 1980; Bronze Key, 1983, Humanitarian Award, 1984, Nat. Council on Alcoholism; mem. Nat. Assn. of Sci., Assn. for Med. Edn. and Resrch. in Substance Abuse; author: Treating the Alcoholic (in press, John Wiley & Sons NY); med. journal arts.; Democrat; rec: tennis, writing. Res: 68 Yale Rd Menlo Park 94025 Ofc: Stanford Alcohol Clinic, Dept. Psychiatry, Stanford Univ. Med. Ctr., Stanford 94305

BROWN, STEVEN LEWIS, oral and maxillofacial surgeon; b. Sept. 25, 1951, Santa Monica; s. Guy E. and Mary Carolyn (Hilliard) B.; m. Patti A. Yost, May 20, 1978; 1 son, Jordan, b. 1983; edn: BA, UCLA 1973; DDS, UC San Francisco Med. Ctr. Sch. of Dentistry 1977; residency, splst. oral & max. surg., (chief res. 1981) UCSF Med. Ctr., San Francisco Gen. Hosp., VA Hosp., S.F., 1978-81. Career: oral & Maxillofacial surgeon in pvt. practice, Citrus Hts.; staff Roseville Comm. Hosp., Mercy San Juan Hosp.; cons. to Kaiser Permanente Hosps.; panel mem. Calif. Childrens' Svc., and The Cleft Panel Sutter Meml. Hosp.; honors: Am. Dental Soc. of Anesthesiol. award 1977; Mosby Pub. Co. awd. 1977; TMJ Resrch. Found. awd. for outstanding thesis in temporomandibular joint resrch. 1981; Delta Sigma Delta (life). Mem: Am., Calif. dental assns.; Sacto. Dist. Dental Soc.; Fellow Am. Assn. of Oral & Maxillofacial Surgeons; Western Soc., No. Calif. Soc. Oral & Maxillo. Surgeons; cert. Basic and Adv. Cardiac Life Support, and CPR; publs: arts. in med. jours.; co-prod. teaching film for dental students (1978); Republican; Prot.; rec: portrait artist. Res: 1509 Pine Valley Cir. Roseville 95678 Ofc: Steven L. Brown, DDS, Inc. 8035 Madison Ave, G-1, Citrus Hts 95610

BROWN, TIMOTHY ROBERT, savings and loan administrator; b. Feb. 26, 1947, Seattle, Wash.; s. Robert Wesley and Phyllis Marie (Harrington) B.; m. Jacqueline Sue Martin, Aug. 7, 1971; children: Jeffrey M., b. 1978; Matthew R., b. 1979; Stephen M., b. 1983; edn: AA, Hartnell Jr. Coll. 1968; BA, Calif. St. Polytech. Univ. 1970. Career: with Wells Fargo Bank 1972-1983; comml. lending ofcr., Palo Alto 1972-75; asst. mgr., Foster City 1975-77; asst. v.p./ br. mgr., Crystal Springs 1977-79, Belmont 1979-81; v.p./ exec. banking ofcr., Fresno 1981-83; v.p./ sales mgr. Sandalwood Development Corp., Fresno 1983; v.p./ br. coord. Guarantee Savings & Loan, Fresno 1984--; mem: Rotary Club of Fresno; Boy Scouts of Am.; Fresno Storyland; Republican; Catholic; rec: 2185 W Birch Ave Fresno 93711 Ofc: Guarantee Savings & Loan, 1177 Fulton Mall, Ste 1009, Fresno 93721

BROWN, THOMAS HUNTINGTON, neurobiologist; b. June 13, 1945, NY, NY; s. Thomas H. and Elvira C. (Crandall) B.; m. Patricia, Aug. 10, 1968; edn: BA, molecular biol., CSU San Jose 1972; PhD, neurobiol., Stanford Univ. 1977. Career: postdoctoral fellow, Dept. Neurology, Stanford Univ. Med. Sch. 1977-79; asst. research scientist, City of Hope Research Inst., 1979-82, assoc. research sci./head, section of cellular neurophysiology, 1982--; editorial bd. Behavioral Neuroscience (sci. journal); adv. to NIH and NIMH study sections (fed. funding agcs. for research), 1982, 83; awards: Muscular Dystrophy Postdoctl. Fellowship Award 1977; NIH Postdoctl. Fellowship VA Awd. 1978; Epilepsy Found. of Am. Awd. 1980; McKnight Found. Scholar's Awd. 1980; four major federal research grants (NIH, NSF, and Air Force Office of Sci. Resrch.) 1980-84; mem. Soc. for Neurosci., AAAS; publs: 20 major sci. works; resrch. on understanding the brain mechanisms involved in learning and memory as well as certain neurolog. diseases such as epilepsy; Episcopal; rec: skiing, ice skating, modern art, computers. Res: 1025 Highland, No. 3, Duarte 91010 Ofc: City of Hope Research Inst, 1450 E. Duarte Rd Duarte 91010

BROWN, TULLEY NOLAN, youth organization founder/director; b. Apr.20,1932,Los Angeles; s. Tulley Eugeneand Eleanor Genevieve (Nolan) B.; m. Jacqueline Feist, Oct. 29, 1966; twin daus.: Kathleen and Kimberly, b. 1971; edn: BS, Occidental Coll. 1954. Career: mktg. exec., high sch. tchr., youth dir. Wilshire Methodist Ch.; traveled in 32 countries, four continents by age 27;

nat. dir. Direction Sports Inc., Los Angeles 1968-- (program estab. to motivate and re-direct attitudes of inner city youth by combining academics with team sports, by July 1983 pgm. logged over 10 million child hours of service, nationwide in varied economic and ethnic settings); coll. lectr. and seminar leader, Direction Sports. Awards: Nat. Hearst Oratory contestant for L.A. Hi and Occidental Coll.; Man of the Year (1971), CBS Radio KNX; achievement awd. L.A. Athletic Club (1978); Emmy awd. for KNBC documentary, From Tulley with Love (1973). Rotarian. mil: E4, US Army 1954-56, spl. svcs. & Olympictrials; Prot.; rec: running, piano, writing, speaking. ofc: Direction Sports Inc. 117 W. 9th St., Ste. 520, Los Angeles 90015.

BROWN, WALTER FRANKLIN, computer services executive; b. Apr. 3, 1952, Phila.; s. Benjamin F. and Fidele Adeste (Van Beverhoudht) B.; m. Marie Guerra, Aug. 8, 1971; edn: stu. Pinecrest Bible Coll. 1970-71; AA, acctg., Chaffey Coll. 1980; AA, data processing, Chaffey Coll. 1980; BS, Calif. St. Polytech. Univ. 1984. Career: materiel supvr. Open Rd Industries, Redondo Beach 1971-75; data processing mgr. Landau Motor Homes, Costa Mesa 1975-78; Xerox Computer Svcs., 1978--; mfg. cons., Los Angeles 1978-80; mktg. tech. supvr., 1980-81; tech. support mgr., 1981-83; regl. mfr. tech. svcs., Anaheim 1983-84; nat. mgr. tech. support, L.A. 1984--; mem: Am. Mgmt. Assn.; Am. Prodn. & Inventory Control Soc.; Data Processing Mgmt. Assn.; Democrat; Assemblies of God. Res: 2526 Hope Ave Ontario 91761 Ofc: Xerox Computer Services, 5310 Beethoven St Los Angeles 90066

BROWND, RICHARD GORDON, emergency physician; b. Dec. 31, 1947, Lubbock, Tx.; s. Grid E. and Juanita E. Brownd; m. Elizabeth A. King, Nov. 30, 1979; 1 child, Taletha, b. 1971; edn: BS, W. Tex. St. Univ. 1970; MD, Univ. Okla. Med. Sch. 1974; Grad. Aerospace Med., Brooks AFB 1975; Diplomate Am. Bd. Emerg. Med. 1983. Career: physician splst. emergency medicine, JJ&R Med. Corp., Santa Monica currently; chief of aerospace med. G.A.F.B., 1975-76; phys. Janzen, Johnston & Rockwell Med. Corp., 1976--; staff West Hills Hosp. (Woodland Hills), Malibu (Ca.) Emerg. Rm., 1983-; instr. for Am. Heart Assn. (1978-), Malibu Fire Dept. and Lifeguard Paramedics Santa Monica Hosp. Base Station (1980-81, 1983-); clin. instr. emerg. med. to interns and med. students White Meml. Med. Ctr. 1978-; honors: Beta Beta Beta, Alpha Chi, Am. Chem. Soc., Who's Who in Am. Univs. and Colls., Sigma Nu (v.p.); USAF Health Professions Scholar 1970-74; mem. Malibu Town Council, Optimist Club; mil: capt. USAF 1970-78; Republican; Methodist; rec: skiing, equestrian, piano. Res: 30014 Harvester Rd, Malibu 90265 Ofc: JJ&R Med. Corp. 1520 Arizona Ave Santa Monica 90404

BRUBECK, SUSAN KAY, commercial real estate broker/ lawyer; b. Mar. 16, 1948, Decatur, Ill.; d. Rodney Earl Brubeck and Marilyn Jean (Hopkins) McMahon; 1 son: Martin C. Resnik, b. 1967; edn: LLB, Western St. Univ. Coll. of Law 1977; admitted to Calif. State Bar 1977; Calif. lic. R.E. Broker 1979. Career: pres. The Brubeck Co., Newport & San Francisco 1974-79; sr. mktg. cons. Grubb 7 Ellis Comml. Brokerage Gp., San Francisco 1979--; awards: Salesprsn. of Yr., Grubb & Ellis Co. 1982; mem: Calif. State Bar Assn.; campaign chmn. US Senate Primary, Orange Co. 1976; publs: monthly advtg. columnist, Automotive Age Mag., 1976; rec: 16th Century English History. Res: 17 Bigelow Mill Valley 94941 Ofc: Grubb & Ellis, One Montgomery, 31st Flr, San Francisco 94104

BRUNER, LELAND WATKINS, lawyer; b. Mar. 6, 1938, San Leandro; s. Allison Watkins and Sylvia (Leland) B.; m. Barbara Motzer, June 12, 1959; children: Lynne, b. 1960, Anne, b. 1962, Thomas, b. 1970; edn: BA, UC Berkeley 1959; LLB, UC Boalt Hall 1962. Career: atty./prin. (3d. gen. to practice in San Leandro) Chandler Bruner Dombrink & Ricks Profl. Corp. (and predecessor firm Bruner Mincier & Chandler), 1962--; lectr. in estate plnng. & probate; mem: Calif. State Bar Assn., Alameda County Bar Assn. (dir.), So. Alameda Co. Bar Assn.; past pres./founder San Leandro Scholarship Found.; past pres. San Leandro CofC; past pres. Childrens Hosp. Found.; past pres. Sequoyah Country Club; Rotarian; Breakfast Club, BSA, Easter Seal Found.; Republican; Prot.; rec: golf. Res: 1586 Daniels Dr San Leandro 94577 Ofc: Chandler Bruner Dombrink & Ricks Profl. Corp. 1330 E. 14th St. San Leandro 94577

BRUNN, DONALD IRVIN, hospital administrator; b. Feb 26, 1954, Mansfield, Ohio; s. Irvin Robert and Martha (Korodi) B.; m. Pamela, Oct. 23, 1982; 1 dau. Sarah Elizabeth, b. 1984; edn: BS in bus. adm., Ariz. State Univ. 1975; grad. degree sub-splty.-Gerontology, USC, 1976; M.Hlth Svcs. Adm., Ariz. St. Univ. 1977. Lic. Nursing Home Adminstr. (Calif., Ariz., all States elig.); Cert. Fellow Am. Coll. of Health Care Adminstrs.; Calif. Comm. Coll. Tchr. Credential; Calif. Cert. Preceptor. Career: adminstrv. resident Maricopa County Dept. Hlth. Svcs. and Gen. Hosp., Phoenix, Az. 1977; adminstr. Beverly Ent. Inc., Pasadena 1977-80, dir. ops. three nursing facilities; adminstr. Bay Harbor Hosp. Inc. (150-bed), Bay Harbor Rehabilitation Ctr. (212-bed), Torrance 1980--; instr. in hlth. svcs. Saddleback Coll. 1980; guest lectr. USC; mem: Health Care Execs. of So. Calif., nom. Am. Coll. of Hosp. Adminstrs.; Nat. Honor Soc., Sigma Nu Frat.; Republican; Christian; rec: swim, travel. Res: 8162 Manitoba St, 101, Playa Del Rey 90293 Ofc: Bay Harbor Rehabilitation Center, 3620 W. Lomita Blvd Torrance 90505

BRUNO, DAVID ALLEN, electrical contractor, real estate broker; b. Jan. 3, 1945, Morgantown, W.Vir.; s. Edward and Emma Bruno; m. Peggy Crosby, May 13, 1975; children: Dennis, b. 1966, Tina, b. 1972, Kristy, b. 1974, Dustin, b. 1978; edn: AA, Fresno City Coll. 1969. Career: electrician 1967-, currently elec. constrn. supr./service mgr. Gruno Electric Inc., Fresno; real estate broker/owner Tradewinds Real Estate and Inv. Co.; mem. Nat. Electrical

Contrs. Assn.; mil: E4 USAF 1963-67, Vietnam Cpgn., Pres. Unit. Cit. Res: 6025 N. Montana Clovis 93612 Ofc: Bruno Electric Inc. 4363 N. Valentine Fresno 93612

BRUNO, JOSEPH PAT, manufacturing company executive; b. Aug. 30, 1923, Rockford, Ill.; s. Charles and Anna (Mera) Bruno; edn: BA, Lake Forest Coll., 1948, San Fernando Coll. of Law 1962-63; m. Dolores Foley, Apr. 15, 1950; chil: Charles, b. 1952, Leanne (Walsh), b. 1954, Mark, b. 1959, John, b. 1961; career: pres., bd. chmn. Afcoa, Chatsworth 1961-75; pres. Pyramid Magnetics Corp., Chatsworth, currently; mem: 4th Degree Knights of Columbus 1943-, bd. dirs. Inst. for Information and Communications of Israel 1971, (life) Full Gospel Bus. Mens Fellowship Internat.; Phi Pi Epsilon frat. (v.p.); mil: t/sgt US Army; Democrat; Catholic; rec: golf, hunting, fishing; res: 9724 Bothwell Rd. Northridge 92324 ofc: Pyramid Magnetics Corp. 9817 Variel Ave. Chatsworth 91311.

BRUST, DAVID, physicist; b. Aug. 24, 1935, Chgo.; s. Clifford and Ruth (Klapman) B.; edn: BS, Cal Tech 1957, MS, Univ. Chgo. 1958, PhD 1964. Career: resrch assoc. Purdue Univ. 1963-64; resrch assoc/asst. prof. Northwestern Univ. 1964-68; theoretical resrch physicist Lawrence Radiation Lab., Livermore 1968-74; pres. Material System Analysts, Oakland 1973--; cons. Bell Tele.Labs, Murray Hill, NJ 1966. Mem: Am. Physical Soc., Am. Assn. Coll. Profs., Internat. Solar Energy Soc., Pacific Assn. of AAU, Sierra Club, Sigma Xi. Works: devel. first successful theory to explain optical absorption of light and photoelectric emission in semiconductors 1963-75, 25 publs. in field; rec: music, sailing, nature, language. ofc: Material System Analysts, PO Box 13130 Oakland 94661.

BRUTLAG, DOUGLAS LEE, biochemist; b. Dec. 19, 1946, Alexandria, Minn.; s. Minehart and Cora (Lee) B.; m. Simone C., Oct. 1, 1975; children: Pauline, b. 1976; Benjamin, b. 1980; edn: BS, Calif. Inst. of Tech. 1968; PhD, Stanford Univ. 1972. Career: research scientist, CSIRO, Canberra City, Australia 1972-74; asst. prof. Dept. of Biochem., Stanford Univ. 1974-80; Sabbatical leave, Pasteur Inlst., Paris, France 1981-82; assoc. prof., Dept. of Biochem., Stanford Univ. 1980--; bd. dirs./ founder IntelliGenetics, Inc. 1981--; bd. dirs. NIH Genetic Study Sect. 1982-86; awards: Andrew W. Mellon Found. Fellowship 1974-76; Basil O'Connor Nat. Found. Youth Investigator Awd. 1975-78; Henry & Camille Dreyfus Tchr.- Scholar Grant 1979-84; Nat. Inst. of Health Sr. Fogarty Internat. Fellow 1981-82; mem: Fedn. of Am. Socs. for Exptl. Biology; Am. Soc. of Biological Chemists; num. publs.; Democrat; rec: computers, photog. Res: 4 Aliso Way Menlo Park 94025 Ofc: Dept. of Biochemistry, Stanford Univ. Sch. of Medicine, Stanford 94305

BRUTOCAO, LEONARD JAMES, engineering contractor/ co. president; b. June 8, 1934, Ft. Erie, Canada, nat. 1949; s. Leonard A. and Anne (Wilson) B.; m. Martha Bliss, June 22, 1957; children: David b. 1958, Daniel b. 1960, Leonard Jr. b. 1961, Renee b. 1963, Steven b. 1964; edn: UC Berkeley 1953-56; BS engring., CSU San Diego 1957; Calif. lic. General Engineering Contractor 1967. Career: engring. pgm. Federal Bureau of Public Roads, throughout US, 1957-61; projects engr. Griffith Co., Los Angeles 1961-63; ops. mgr. Miles & Sons Constrn. Div., Merced 1963-67; pres./owner Brutoco Engineering & Construction (one of leading cos. in freeway constrn. in So. Calif.), Fontana 1967--; owner 200 acre Vineyard, Varietal wine making bus.; honors: Excellence in Engring., Portland Cement Assn., L.A. (1976), president award Black Business Man's Assn. of L.A. (1984), Excellence awd. Ft. Belvour Engring. Sch.; mem: ASCE, Assoc. Gen. Contractors of Am., So. Calif. Contractors Assn. (past pres.), Associated Contractors Holiday Conf. Com.; (fmr.) Lions Club of Covina, Scoutmaster BSA, mem. People to People; mil: Reserve Forces 1958; Republican; Catholic; rec: golf, family. Res: 3156 Sunset Hill Dr West Covina 91791 Ofc: Brutoco Engineering & Construction, Inc. (POB 429), 14801 Slover Ave Fontana 92335

BRUYNINCKX, JOZEF, photographer/ phototypographer; b. May 9, 1926, Aarschot, Belgium, nat. 1963; s. Johannes Franciscus and Maria Octavia Anastasia (Nijs) B.; m. Louisa Grandjean, June 5, 1950; children: Edmond, b. 1953; John, b. 1955; Larry, b. 1959; Ronald, b. 1968; edn: pvt. investigator, Internat. Det. Sch., Belgium 1949; tropical agricultural colonist, Colonial Arig. Inst., Belgium 1950; elec. tech., Nat. Radio Inst. 1969; new techniques intern, Typographic Union 1960. Career: mgr./ supt. White House, Johannesburg, So. Africa 1954-57; foreman/ supt. AD Compositors, Los Angeles 1963-70; pres./ founder Alpha Graphix, Inc., L.A. 1970-74; pres./ founder Joe's Type Shop, Inc., L.A. 1974--; tchr. phototypography, Atherton's, Palo ALto & Ad Compositors, Los Angeles; num. awards through Abert, Newhoff & Burr, Chiat/ Day, Box Office, et al, Los Angeles; mem: Grand Knight, Knights of Columbus, Arcadia; author: Phototypography and Graphic Arts Dimension Control Photography, 1969; mil: Partisan (NKB), Belgium, WWII; Sgt., Volunteer of War, Belgian Army 1944-45; Truce Observer, United Nation, Palestine 1948-49; Democrat; Catholic; rec: bowling, travel. Res: 9062 E Arcadia Ave San Gabriel 91775 Ofc: Joe's Type Shop, 1313 W 8th Street, Ste 224, Los Angeles 90017

BRYANT, MICHAEL LYNN, engineering manager; b. July 14, 1950, Hutchinson, Kans.; s. Ralph Laverne and Lucy Faye (Maxwell) Bryant; m. Monica Le Potucek, June 14, 1972; children: Yvette Marie, b. 1975, Tyler Michelson, b. 1978; edn: BSEE (solid-state physics w/distinction), USNA, Annapolis, 1972; MSEE (electromagnetic theory), NPGS, Monterey, Ca. 1973; MSA (personnel), George Washington Univ., 1978; MBA (mgmt.), Golden Gate Univ., 1982. Calif. Lic. Profl. Engr. (elec. eng.) 1981. Career: served to lieut. USN 1968-78; surface missile system ofcr., Pearl Harbor 7th Fleet 1973-75, elec. engrg. faculty, Annapolis, Md. 1975-78; senior TWT design engr. Teledyne, MEC,

Palo Alto, Ca. 1979-81; materials engr. Hewlett-Packard, Santa Rosa 1979-81, materials engrg. mgr. 1981--; mathematics instr. Chaminade Coll. of Honolulu; mem: Sigma Pi Sigma (nat. hon. physics soc.) 1971-72; IEEE 1975-79; Assn. of Old Crows 1978-79; Soc. of Profl. Engrs. 1981-; pres. Rock St. Homeowners Assn. Mt. View 1979; Prot.; rec: music, white water rafting. Res: 1925 Leafgreen Dr Santa Rosa 95405 Ofc: Hewlett-Packard 1400 Fountain Grove Pkwy Santa Rosa 95401

BRYANT-KAMBE, MADELEINE L., lawyer; b. May 12, 1950, Los Angeles; d. Leicester O. and Muriel T. Burrell (Thompson) Bryant; m. Robert Kambe, Nov. 18, 1978; 1 son: Vincent, b. 1980; edn: Pierce Coll. 1967-71; JD, Univ. of W. L.A. 1979; BS, 1979; admitted Calif. State Bar 1979. Career: law clerk Law Ofc. of Jack Willis 1977-79; sole practice atty., 1979-83; mng. atty., Jacoby & Meyers Law Offices, 1981-83; sole practitioner atty., Los Angeles 1983--; bd. advr. Santa Clarita Ednl. Svcs., Inc.; mem: Nat. Assn. for Female Execs.; Barristers (Com. of Child Abuse); Los Angeles Co. Bar Assn. (Family Law Sect.; Client Rels. Arbitration Panel); Pro Bono Panel; Senior Citizens; Lawyers Club; State Bar (Family Law Sect.); Democrat; Protestant. Res: 27211 Hidaway Canyon Country 91351 Ofc: Madeleine Bryant- Kambe, Atty. at Law, 170 N La Brea Los Angeles 90046

BRZEZINSKI, JANUSZ ANDRZEJ, investment advisor; b. Apr. 22, 1935, Gdynia, Poland; nat.; s. Henryk and Agnieszka Helena (Kirstein) B.; m. Bozena Wojciechowski, Dec. 28, 1968; children: Ursula, b. 1970; Elizabeth, b. 1971; Margarete, b. 1978; Kathleen, b. 1978; edn: Baccalaureate, Coll. Gdynia 1952; B.Eng., Univ. of Gdansk 1956, M.Eng., and MSc., 1957. Career: hd. engring. dept. Riber, Paris, France 1965-67; senior engr. IT&T, Monterey Park 1967-68; sr. engr. Marshal Computer Sys., Torrance 1968-69; pres. Adv. Medical Instrumentation, Santa Monica 1969-74; pres./ owner, Golden Shores Realty- Real Estate Investment, South Laguna; mem: Nat. Bd. Realtors; Am. Partnership Council; Laguna Niguel Tennis Club; patentee: the first Electronic Medical Thermometer (now used worldwide) 1970, Electronic Puls Metter, and other inventions in field of med. electronics; mil. Lieut.; Republican; Catholic; rec: classical music, skiing, sailing. Res: 22902 Via Genoa South Laguna 92677 Ofc: Golden Shores Realty- Real Estate Investment, South Laguna 92677

BUCHOLTZ, MARLENE RITA, real estate mortgage broker; b. Nov. 7, 1941, Somerville, NJ; d. David Sanford and Mildred Freed; m. John J. Bucholtz; children: Jeff, b. 1966, Lynn, b. 1968; Calif. lic. real estate broker 1968. Career: owner real estate property mgmt. co. (income and comml. props.), 1966; fmr. ptnr./founder Resource Mortgage 1976; currently mortgage broker/owner Marlene Bucholtz, Real Estate Mortgage Broker (pvt. money investing); instr. seminars on second deeds of trust, var. real estate firms; rec: tournament bridge, skiing, crafts. Res: 12059 Marilla Dr Saratoga 95070 Ofc: POB 9217 San Jose 95129

BUCHWALTER, RALPH MC KNIGHT, business executive; b. Dec. 29, 1933, San Bernardino; s. Ralph Nelson and Sybil C. (McKnight) B.; m. Sandra Kay Bradley, June 22, 1975; children: Ralph P., b. 1961, Douglas M., b. 1964, Jennifer C., b. 1965, (stepsons) Robert W. Beecham, b. 1962, Steven Todd Beecham, b. 1963; edn: BA, Stanford Univ. 1955; Chouinard Art Inst. 1956; MA, Claremont Grad. Univ. 1964. Career: sales mgr., No. Calif., for S.K.Smith Co. of Los Angeles and Chgo. (mfrs. of custom books and binder covers, sales and art design), San Francisco 1956-60; joined family bus. (estab. by parents 1931) as gen. ptnr./sales mgr. R.N. Buchwalter Co. (vending co. of customer convenience products, coffee, candy, etc. serving San Bernardino & Riverside Cos.) 1960-, prin. Gen. Ptnr. 1979--; v.p./gen. mgr. Federal Alarm (family bus. acquired in 1953, now one of largest ind. security cos. in state), 1962-, pres./gen. mgr. 1979--, with four offices in Orange, San Berdo. & Riverside Cos.; pres./gen. mgr. Inland Desert Security & Communications, Inc. (fmr. Palm Desert Answering Svc.) Rialto 1972--, (acquired McKee Communications 1975), now largest chain of profl. answering svcs. serving Orange, Rvsd., San Berdo. Cos.; honors: 1st Place, Best Business Idea of Year 1982, Nat. Fire & Burglar Alarm Assn.; awards US Jaycees 1965, 1982, San Bernardino YMCA 1978, 79, 80, 81, hon. mem. Colton Jaycees. Mem: Nat. Indsl. Advt. Assn., Am. Soc. for Indsl. Security, Riverside Art Assn., Rialto Jaycees (past pres.), Rotary, YMCA (past pres.; bd. dirs.), Elks, Masons; Republican (alternate State Central Com.); Methodist; rec: artist (exhibs.), camping, boating. Ofc: Federal Alarm, 300 S. Sycamore Rialto 92376

BUCKELEW, (HELEN) JEAN, real estate broker; b. June 13, 1931, Ada, Okla.; d. Lark F. and Leva (Turner) Jackson; m. Clyde Buckelew, Aug. 21, 1949; children: Deborah, b. 1951, Larry, b. 1953; cert. Exec. Broker Devel. Series, USC, 1981; Calif. lic. real estate broker 1982. Career: real estate agt. Day Realty, Pomona 1969, Heckner Realty, Pomona 1969, Herbert Hawkins Co., Altadena 1976; broker assoc. Herbert Hawkins Co., Glendora 1982--; sales awards: Hawkins Million Dollar Club 1976-78, 80-83; Azusa-Glendora Bd. of Realtors highest dollar volume and highest number of closed sale escrows through multiple listing svc., 7/82; Top earner Hawkins E. Div. 9/82; mem: Nat., Calif. Assn. of Realtors, Azusa-Glendora Bd. of Realtors, Soroptimist Club 1978-80; rec: oil painting, swimming. Res: 111 Oak Forest Cir Glendora 91740 Ofc: Herbert Hawkins Co. 755 E. Alossta Ave Glendora 91740

BUCKLEY, JAMES WHITNEY, public library administrator; b. Aug. 16, 1933, Los Angeles; s. George W. and Alta L. (Hale) Buckley; edn: AA, L.A. Harbor Coll., 1953, BA, CSU Long Beach, 1960, MLS, USC 1961, MPA, 1974; m. Margaret Wall, Aug. 7, 1965; children: Kathleen Ann, b. 1966, James W., b. 1972, John W., b. 1979; career: branch librarian, Los Angeles Co. Public Library, 1961-68; regional librarian, Orange Co. Pub. Library, 1968, Dir. of Public Services 1969-74; county librarian, San Mateo Co. Pub. Library 1974-77, Marin Co. Pub. Library 1978; city librarian, Torrance Pub. Library, 1978--; mem. advisory bd. Friends of California Libraries, 1974-; pres., California County Librarians, 1977; exec. dir. Calif. National Library Week, 1970; mem: American Library Assn., Am. Soc. for Public Administration, Calif. Library Assn., Rotary; mil: Sp-3, US Army Med. Corps 1955-57; rec: sports, walking, music; res: 25002 Paseo Arboleda, El Toro 92630; office: Torrance Public Library, 3301 Torrance Blvd. Torrance 90503.

BUGLIOSI, VINCENT T., lawyer, author; b. Aug. 18, 1934, Hibbing, Minn.; s. Vincent and Ida (Valerie) Bugliosi; grad. Hollywood H.S. (Ca.) 1952; B.B.A., Univ. of Miami, 1956; LL.B., UCLA Law Sch., 1964; m. Gail Talluto, July 21, 1956; children: Wendy, b. 1964; Vincent Jr., b. 1966. Career: Los Angeles Deputy District Attorney 1964-72; pvt. practice of law, Beverly Hills 1972--. Honors: pres. of graduating class UCLA Law Sch. Co-author: Helter Skelter; Till Death Us Do Part; Shadow of Cain. Mil.: capt., Infantry AUS. Democrat. Catholic. Rec.: tennis, musci. Office: 9171 Wilshire Blvd., Beverly Hills 90210.

BUEHNER, JAMES FREDERICK, chemical manufacturing co. executive, ret.; b. July 1, 1902, Miamisburg, Ohio; s. John Henry and Nannie J. (Saltzgiver) B.; m. 2d. Pauline Underwood, Sept 2, 1981; children: James Frederic Jr., b. 1933; Barbara Ann (Jackson), b. 1936; edn: BA, Ohio State Univ. 1924; pub. acct., Calif. 1944. Career: treas./ controller Calif. Consumers Corp., Los Angeles 1953; treas./ controller Wn Electro Chemical Corp., Henderson, Nev. 1955; controller/ staff mgr. Systems Staff, Am. Potash & Chem., L.A. 1957-67; pub. accountant, Los Angeles & Santa Ana 1967-80, ret.; cons. Mgmt. Consulting Service, and Service Corp. of Retired Execs. (SCORE), 1975-; night teaching UC Los Angeles; honors: Silver Beaver, Boy Scouts of Am., L.A.; mem: Calif. Pub. Accts.; US Small Bus. Admin./SCORE; East Rotary Club, Los Angeles (pres.); Credit Mgrs. Assn. of L.A. (pres.); Santa Ana SCORE (pres.); Phi Chi frat. (internat. pres.); Santa Ana chpt. Am. Assn. Ret. Persons (pres.); Santa Ana chpt. Systems & Procedures Assn. (pres.); Boy Scouts of Am. (pres. Geo. Wash. Dist.); Republican; Lutheran; rec: organizer, consultant. Res: 5769 Calvin Way San Diego 92120

BUI, DUC M., otolaryngologist; b. June 29, 1934, Phanrang, Vietnam, nat. 1981; s. Thong Xuan and Le Thi (Truong) Bui; m. Thai Tran, Apr. 26, 1959; children: Tan, b. 1959; Ailien, b. 1961; Hana, b. 1962; Khanh, b. 1964; Thao, b. 1966; Khang, b. 1968; An, b. 1970; edn: MD (with honors), Saigon Med. Sch. 1962; residency in otolaryngology, Louisville (Ky.) Univ. 1981. Career: asst. prof. Hue Med. Sch., Saigon 1970; ear nose throat asst. Wurzburg Univ., W. Ger. 1972; chmn. ENT Dept. Hue Univ., Vietnam 1973-75, asst. dean med. sch. 1974; instr. in surgery Univ. Louisville, Ky. 1975-77, residency in ENT, 1977-81, chief res. 1980-81; pvt. practice, pres. Duc M. Bui, MD, Inc. Westminster, Ca. 1982--; pres. Vietnamese Physicians Assn. in Calif. 1983-84; awards: Saigon Med. School Scholarship 1951-60; Fellow Am. Acad. of Otolaryn. 1982; mem. German Otolaryn. Soc. Soc. 1972; v.p. Vietnam Otolaryn. Soc. 1973; sec.-gen. Vietnamese Students Assn. 1954-55; pres. Viet. Vol. Youth Svc. 1958-60; mil: surgeon chief 1st div. Army Repub. Vietnam 1962-63; Buddist; rec: photog., antiques. Res: 3491 Eboe St Irvine 92714 Ofc: Duc M. Bui MD, Inc. 9131 Bolsa Ave, Ste. 201, Westminster 92683

BUI, KHOI VAN, manufacturing co. president; b. July 12, 1949, Thanh Hoa, Vietnam; s. Khue Van and Van Thi (Truong) B.; m. Thuan Le, June 6, 1976; children: Kia (Karl), b. 1976; Hung (Brian), b. 1980; edn: Glendale Comm. Coll. 1977; JD, Univ. of Saigon Sch. of Law, Vietnam 1974. Career: tchr. asst. Luther Burbank Jr. H.S., Los Angeles 1975-76; owner Furniture Mart, L.A. 1976-78; owner, B.K. Furniture, L.A. 1978-80; pres./ founder Century Mattress Mfg., L.A. 1980--; awards: Coll. Tennis Championship, Glendale Coll. 1976, 77; mem: Nat. Fed. Independent Bus. ASsn.; Vietnamese Tennis Club; Buddhist; rec: tennis, painting, swimming. Res: 617 San Pascual Ave Los Angeles 90042 Ofc: Century Mattress Mfg., 1618 Santa Fe Ave Los Angeles 90021

BUI, TAM DUY, physician-surgeon; b. Sept. 8, 1934, Hanoi, Vietnam; s. Tinh Van and Dinh Thi (Nguyen) Bui; m. Viethuong Do, July 17, 1955; children: Vietha, b. 1957, Linh, b. 1958, Thien, b. 1961, Viethong, b. 1968; edn: MS (physiol.) Univ. of Saigon Faculty of Scis. 1958; MD, Univ. of Saigon Faculty of Med. 1960; PhD (biochem.) UC Med. Ctr. S.F., 1964; OMD (Dr. Oriental Med.), S.F. Coll. of Acupuncture & Oriental Med. 1983; Calif. lic. physician and surgeon, 1983. Career: prof./chmn. dept. biochem. Univ. of Saigon Faculty of Med. 1966-79; resrch. dir. clin. chem. lab. Pasteur Inst. of Saigon, 1965-75; dean Sch. of Med. Univ. of Hue (Vietnam) 1968-71; dean Sch. of Med. Minh Duc Univ., Saigon 1971-75; v.chmn. Fund of Reconciliation and Reconstrn. in Indochina, World Council of Chs. 1972-75; prof. of acupuncture and hd. Dept. of Western Med., San Francisco Coll. of Acupuncture, S.F., Ca. 1980--; staff phys. Neumiller Meml. Hosp., Marine City 1983-; honors: first prize in math. Nat. Inter-Coll. Tournament V.N. 1952; medal of merit in med. edn. (1968), and medal of merit in youth and culture (1970), Pres. Govt. of V.N.; pres. Founder's Com. of Protestant Univ. in V.N. 1974. Mem: V.N. Med. Assn. 1960-75; Korean (hon.) Med. Assn. 1967; founder/pres. Gio Khoi Assn. 1966-75; v.p. V.N. Underwater Exploration and Hunting Assn. 1960-75; hon. pres. V.N. Table Tennis Nat. League 1970-75; hon. adv. Nat. Conserv. of Music in Saigon 1973-75; works: 46 med. resrch. publs.; spons. 36 M.D. Candidates in conducting their med. & surgical theses; presented Biochem., Acupuncture and Medico-surg. Resrch. to profl. confs. internat. 1962-75; Prot.; rec: synthesis of West-East cultures. Res: 1427 Lawton St San Francisco 94122 Ofc: Med. Coll. Clinic, 187 Golden Gate Ave, San Francisco 94102

BUKEWIHGE, BEN S., furniture co. president; b. May 9, 1934, Ill.; s. Geo. and Anna Caroline (Ostenson) B.; m. Dorothy Jean Sandoval, Oct. 22, 1951; children: James T., b. 1952; Carol A., b. 1957. Career: owner/ bd. chmn. B.P. John Furniture (largest case goods mfr. on West Coast), Santa Ana; mem: Furniture Mfg. Assn.; City of Hope; rec; yachting, fishing. Res: 1014 Polaris Dr Newport Beach 92663 Ofc: B.P. John, 2001 E Dyer Rd Santa Ana 92705

BULL, WHITEY OLIVER, manufacturer, b. Mar. 7, 1949, Sussex, Eng., nat. 1981; s. Winston Oliver and Sarah P. (Randolph) B.; m. Phyllis McGinley, June 5, 1979; 1 son, Walter, b. 1982; edn: BA, Sorbonne, 1970; MA, Oxford Univ. 1973. Career: founder Langhorne (Pa.) Memorials, 1974; founder Henry J. Fenco Co., Phila., Pa. 1978; chief exec. ofcr. Posh Picnics, Huntington Beach, Ca. 1981--; bd. dirs. C'est La Vie, 1982--; honors: Man of the Year 1980, Penndel, Pa.; treas. Bulldog Club of Eng. 1972; mem. Kiwanis, Masons, Anglican Soc.; mil: maj. RAF 1973-74, Order of Merit; Republican; Episcopal; rec: aviator, poet, botanist. Res: 1972 Avon Newport Beach 95624 Ofc: Posh Picnics, 7732 Talbert Huntington Beach 92648

BULLOCH, KATHLEEN LOUISE, speech/language pathologist; b. Feb. 20, 1949, Teaneck, NJ; d. Thomas J. and Daisy L. (Negretti) Oates; m. Clifford Allen Bulloch, June 17, 1972; 1 son, Sean Andrew, b. 1974; edn: BA, Wm. Paterson Coll. (NJ) 1971; MA (speech path.), Montclair St. Coll. 1972; Adminstrv. Svcs. cred., Pepperdine Univ. 1981; Dip. Paralegal, Continental Tech. Inst. (L.A.) 1982; Calif. lic. Speech/Language Pathologist 1982. Career: chief sp./lang. pathologist Barnert Hosp. Clinic, Paterson, NJ 1971-73; comm. disorders splst. Harbor Sch., Red Bank, NJ 1973-75; sp. pathol. pvt. practice, Brick Town, NJ 1973-79; part-time faculty Calif. St. Univ. 1981-83; sp./lang. splst./SDL Splst., Riverside Co. Schs., 1979--, comm. adv. council mem. 1981-83; mem. Credential Adv. Council Loma Linda Univ. 1981-83; awards: AAUW achievement 1983, Am. Sp. Hearing Assn. Cont. Edn. Awd. 1983; mem: Am. Sp./Lang./Hearing Assn., Calif. Sp. & Hearing Assn. (conv. spkr. 1982-83); Westridge Homeowners Assn.; AAUW; coauthor: Bulloch-McLoughlin Adult Aphasia Pgm. 1977, A Child-Centered Lang. Intervention Pgm. 1982; Anglican Catholic; rec: needlecraft, comm. svc. Res: 466 Westridge Cir Anaheim 92807 Ofc: Riverside County Schools, 3939 13th St Riverside

BUMBARGER, JOHN ALLISON, certified financial planner; b. Mar. 21, 1946, Los Angeles; s. John Decker and Louise Vivian (Boyd) B.; m. Valerie J. Elder, July 26, 1980; children: Terri, b. 1968; Michael, b. 1970; Kelly, b. 1970; Wendy, b. 1971; Brittney, b. 1981; edn: BS, UCLA 1968; CFP, Coll. Fin. Plng. 1983; Reg. Investment Advisor. Career: with finl. & inv. firm, W.H. Gaines & Assoc. until 1970; founder/ pres. inv. & tax mgmt. firm of J.A. Bumbarger & Assocs. Inc., 1970--: now parent co. of Bumbarger Finl. Corp., Bumbarger Finl. Advisory Svcs. Inc., and Trinity Mgmt., Inc.; bd. dirs. Westlake Trift & Loan; Founders Club of Village Bank & First State Bank of the Oaks; mem: Internat. Assn. of Finl. Plnrs.; CFP Regis.; Thousand Oaks Rotary Club; Tri Valley YMCA; Protestant; rec: tennis, golf, travel. Res: 1515 Hidden Valley Rd Hidden Valley 91361 Ofc: J.A. Bumbarger & Assoc., Inc., 660 Hampshire Rd, Ste 110, Westlake 91361

BUNCH, CHARLES LEONARD, data processing executive; b. Sept, 11, 1945, Houston, Tex.; s. Leonard F. and Jimmie Sue (Martin) B.; m. Kimlee Saepoo, Feb. 27, 1970; children: Miriam, b. 1975; Cathy, b. 1971; edn: AA, DeAnza Coll. 1981; BA, San Jose State 1983. Career: gen. mgr. L.F. Bunch Co., Houston, Tex. 1973-75; field engr. Sorbus, Inc., Houston, Tex. 1975-76; asst. programmer Texas Insruments, Houston, Tex. 1976-78; field engr. Data 100 Corp., Houston, Tex. 1978-79; field engr. Ford Aerospace, Sunnyvale 1979-81; sys. mgr. Tandem Computers, Cupertino 1981--; pres. Unitechnic, Inc., 1984--; honors: Awd. of Merit, Houston Ind. Sch. Dist. 1960; Psi Chi, hon. soc. 1982; mem: AAAS; APA; New York Acad. of Sci.; Western Psychological Soc.; Nat. Geographic Soc.; Rosicrucian Order; Masons; mil: s/sgt. E-5, USAF 1963-73, NDSM, AFLSA, GCM w/ 20LC, VSM, RVCM, marksmanship; Republican; rec: martial arts, chess, parapsychology. Res: 2662 Lanier Ln San Jose 95121 Ofc: Tandem Computers, 19333 Vallco Pkwy Cupertino 95014

BUNKIS, JURIS, plastic surgeon; b. Aug. 27, 1949, Lubeck, Ger.; s. Janis and Jadviga (Buzinskis) B.; m. Ruta Sternbergs, Oct. 12, 1974; edn: pre-med, MD, Univ. of Toronto Med. Sch. 1968-74; gen. surgery residency, Mary Imogene Bassett Hosp. (Columbia P&S), 1974-78; plastic surg. res. Peter Bent Brigham Hosp., and Childrens Hosp. Med. Ctr. (Harvard) 1979-81, chief res. 1980-81. Lic. in NY, Mass., Calif. Career: asst. chief/ chief of plastic surgery, San Francisco Gen. Hosp. 1981--; asst. prof. of surgery, UC San Francisco 1981--; pvt. practice, Hayward; grants: Woodroof Mfg. Inc. (study biosynthetic temporary wound dressings) 1983, Cox-Uphoff Internat. (study digital fluorometric quantification of expanded skin ischaemia) 1983; Lic. Medical Council of Canada 1975, Diplomate Am. Bd. of Surg. (1980), Am. Bd. of Plastic Surg. (1982); mem: AMA, Mass. Med. Soc., CMA, S.F. Med. Soc., Howard C. Naffziger Surg. Soc., Am. Burn Assn., AAAS, Am. Assn. for Hand Surg., Am. Soc. Plastic & Reconstrv. Surgeons; num. med. journal arts., invited lectures; Catholic; rec: running, skiing, canoeing. Res: 66 La Salle Ave Piedmont 94611 Ofc: Juris Bunkis, MD, Inc. 1320 Apple Ave, Ste. 104, Hayward 94541

BUNTING, HELEN REINHOLTZ, escrow co. president; b. Dec. 3, 1918, Portsmouth, Va.; d. Wm. and Louise Margaret (Miles) Reinholtz; m. John James Bunting, Jr. May 5, 1939; div.; 1 dau. Gay Ellen Bemoll, b. 1947; edn: UC Berkeley 1935-37, spl. courses, UCB, UCI. Career: tel. opr. 193w Co., 1952-58; founder/ owner/ pres. Executive Escrow Co. 1958--, mgr. San Clemente office 1958-84; mem. Escrow Inst. of Calif. (past bd. mem.), Calif. Escrow Assn.; life mem. San Clemente Comm. Theatre; past pres. San Clemente Jr. Womens Club; Democrat; rec: needlework, bridge. Res: 227 Monterey San Clemente 92672 Ofc: Executive Escrow Co. 221 South Ola Vista San Clemente 92672

BUNZEL, JOHN H., Hoover Instn. senior research fellow; b. Apr. 15,1924, NYC; s. Ernest Everett and Hariett (Harvey) Bunzel; m. 2d Barbara Bovyer, May 11, 1963; children: Cameron, Reed; edn: AB, pol.sci., magna cum laude, Princeton Univ. 1948; MA, sociol., Columbia Univ. 1949; PhD, pol. sci., UC Berkeley 1954; LL.D.(hon.), Univ. Santa Clara 1976. Career: tchr. CSC San Francisco, 1953-56, Mich. State Univ. 1956-57; pres. CSU San Jose, 1970-78; sr. resrch fellow, Hoover Instn., Stanford Univ., 1978--. Author: The American Small Businessman (Knopf 1962), Issues of American Public Policy (Prentice-Hall 1964, 2d ed. 1968), Anti-Politics in America (Knopf 1967), New Force On the Left: Tom Hayden And The Campaign Against Corporate America (Hoover 1983); coauthor monograph: The Calif. Democratic Delegation of 1960; columnist (biwkly) San Jose Mercury-News; contbr. NY Times, Wall St. Jour., scholarly and polit. jours.; conducted wkly TV pgm. (KPIX-S.F.) 1964. Recipient Presidential Award, No. Calif. Polit. Sci. Assn. (1969), cert. of honor, S.F. Bd. of Suprs. (1974); research grantee: Ford Found. (Fund for the Republic) 1958-60, (Com. on resrch in pub. affairs, Stanford Univ.) 1960-61, (vis. scholar Ctr. for Adv. Study in Behavioural Scis) 1969-70; Rabinowitz Found. 1961-62; Rockefeller Found.1965-66. Dir., No. Calif. Citizenship Clearing House, 1959-61; mem: Am., No. Calif.(pres, 1962-3) Polit. Sci. Assn. Democrat (del.nat.conv.1968). res: 1519 Escondido Way Belmont 94002. ofc: Hoover Instn. Stanford Univ. Stanford 94305.

BURCH, GERRITSON HILBERT, computer co. president; b. Jan. 4, 1942, Woodbury, NJ; s. Harris M. and Marion L. (Hilbert) B.; m. Jane Ellen Rogers, Oct. 17, 1982; children: Eddie, b. 1970; Christopher, b. 1975; edn: Monmouth, 1959-60; AS, Coll. of Canyon 1979; CSU Northridge 1980-. Career: served to Chief E7, US Navy 1960-1980, ret. (Nat. Defense, Pistol Exp., 5 GCM); classified wk. Lockheed Co., 1980-82; pres. Computer Systems Ctr., Newhall 1982--; pres. GHB/ Ross, Inc.; cons. GHB/ Ross, Inc. 1981-; cons. TGA Video 1981-82; mem: Boy Scouts of AM.; YMCA Indian Guides; Masons; Nat. Rifle Assn.; AYSO; Hart Baseball; Republican; Protestant; rec: show cars, computer games, guns. Res: 23817 Daisetta Dr Newhall 91321 Ofc: Computer Systems Center, 23422 Lyons Ave Newhall 91321

BURGOON, JOHN ROBERT, JR., electronics parts distributor co. CEO; b Jan. 12, 1924, Farrell, Penn.; s. John Robert and Marie (Goda) B.; m. Margaret Robinson, June 15, 1945; children: John, b. 1946; David, b. 1950; Dan, b. 1952; edn: Cristobal Jr. Coll. 1942; William & Mary, Norfolk 1944; Memphis St. 1955-56; CSU San Jose 1963; diploma, gemology, Gemological Inst. of Am. 1956. Career: liaison engr. Titan Missile Proj., RCA 1962-63; design spec. Lockheed Missiles & Space, Sunnyvale 1963-74; CEO Solid State Music, Santa Clara 1974-77; CEO Anchor Electronics, Santa Clara 1977-84; currently, pres./ CEO John Burgoon Electronics, Inc., dba Anchor Electronics; founder/ partner ELF Electronics 1980; mem: Mary- Vin Homeowners Assn. (pres. 1982); Elks; publs: Diamond Mining in Arkansas, Gems & Gemology, 1956; Fundamentals of Electrical Shield Design, Insulation/ Circuits, 1970; Fundamentals of Electro Magnetic Compatibilty, 1965; mil: lt. USN 1941-62; Republican. Res: 3440 Lochinvar Santa Clara 95050 Ofc: Anchor Electronics, 2040 Walsh Ave Santa Clara 95050

BURK, JACK ANDREW, communications co. executive; b. Mar. 19, 1935, Springfield, Tenn.; s. Andrew Jackson and Elizabeth E. (Revels) Burk; m. Alice Jackson, Apr. 24, 1965; chil: Teresa, b. 1957; Cheryl, b. 1958; Dwayne, b. 1959; David, b. 1966 (dec.); edn: Central Bible Inst. 1953-4; So. Calif. Coll. 1955; San Fernando Valley Coll. 1956; cert. project mgr., Am. Mgmt. Assn.; Reg. Principle, NASD, Reg. Investment Advisor, SEC, 1965-76. Career: quality engr. Rocketdyne, Santa Susana Rocket Test site 1959-65; regis. investment prin. Independent Securities Corp. (area vice pres.), Century City 1965-73, Preferred Executive Programs (finl. planning svcs), Tarzana 19773-76, Peoples Foundation, Fresno 1977--; gen. mgr. PF Communications, Inc. (video, sound engring., and audio recording studios), div. Peoples Found.; dir. spl. projects Peoples Found.; gen. partner North Star Communications, Ltd.; exec. devel., funding, planning & constrn. Maple Village (318 unit retirement community owned by Peoples Found., funded by city of Fresno bond issue); dir. of media (prod./dir. This Hour...with Pastor Johnson, 1-hr. wkly. telecast) for Peoples Ch. of Fresno. Awards: Nat. Religious Broadcasters Awd of Excellence, 1982, 83; Outstanding religious comml. of year, Assemblies of God, 1983. Founding bd. mem. Calif. Theol. Sem., Fresno 1983-. Mem. Internat. Assn. of Finl. Planners 1968-; CofC; Bulldog Found. (FSU). Republican. Fundamentalist. Rec: gardening. Res: 9391 E. Ellery, Clovis 93612 Ofc: Peoples Foundation 2727 N. Grove Industrial Dr #101 Fresno 93727

BURKE, A. BERNARR, certified public accountant; b. Sept. 15, 1941, Hopkinsville, Ky.; s. Johnnie D. and Mary Ita (Towery) Burke; m. Jewell D. Kendrick, June 14, 1963; chil: A. Bernarr, II, b. 1966, Crystal L., b. 1968, Ginger L., b. 1971; edn: BS, Univ. of Ky., 1963. Career: cert. pub. acct. Price Waterhouse, 1963--, Los Angeles office 1963-74, 1976-82, transfer to Audit Resrch Dept., National Office, NYC 1975-76, transfer to Bakersfield 1982-, admitted to partnership, firm's lead splst. in entertainment indus., 1977-. Apptd. to Am. Inst. of CPAs Task Force on Entertainment Indus. and Finl. Acctg. Standards Bd.; honors: Beta Gamma Sigma; mem. bd. dirs. Kern Co. United Way, bd. trustees Kernview Found., bd. trustees Panama Ednl. Found.; mem. CSU Bakersfield BPA Advisory Council; mem: Town Hall (Exec. Breakfast Ins.), World Affairs Council, Jonathan Club (LA), Rotary Club, Friendly Hills CC; publs: Audit/EDP Control Reviews (Price Waterhouse), The Auditor's

Study and Evaluation of Internal Control in EDP Systems (AICPA coauthor). Republican. Prot.; rec: skiing, woodworking; res: 7913 Calle Torcido, Bakersfield 93309. ofc: Price Waterhouse, 5016 California Ave. Bakersfield 93309.

BURKE, GRADY ALFRED, mobilehome sales co. president; b. Sept. 3, 1931, Alhambra; s. Alfred Wm. and Eva Ellen (Goss) B.; m. Marylou Prochaska, Jan. 31, 1959; children: Alfred, b. 1962; Kathrny, b. 1964; Ronald, b. 1965; Donald, b. 1965; edn: AA, Oakland City Coll. 1959; CMHA (Cert. Mobilehome Appraiser); Master Craftsman, NAATS (Nat. Assn. Auto Trim Shops); Calif. lic. real estate broker, Realtor. Career: owner/pres. Burke Upholstery Co., Redwood City 1962--, (devel. co. into largest upholstery bus. in No. Calif. 1973-); owner/pres. Burke Mobilehome Sales, Redwood City 1977--; owner/pres. Stain-Guard Inc.; cons. (NAATS) Nat. Assn. Auto Trim Shops 1974--; awards: Salespsn of Year 1983, No. Calif. Mobilhome Bd. Mem: Mobilehome Dealers Assn. (bd. 1978-83); NAIB; IREA; Lions Club, Am. Legion, Better Bus. Bur., CofC, Little League; patentee: Stain-Guard (chemical) 1980; mil: s/sgt. US Army 1951-6, UN, Nat. Def., Korean Def., GCM, Exp. Rifleman medals; Republican; Prot.; rec: travel, bowl, dance, sing. Res: 3187 David Ave Palo Alto 94303 Ofc: Burke Sales, 2701 El Camino Real Redwood City 94061

BURKE, PHILIP ALAN, commercial/ industrial real estate broker; b. Nov. 11, 1937, San Francisco; s. Thomas Aloysius and Marian Louise (Dolen) B.; m. Suzanne Stokes, Aug. 6, 1966; children: Maureen, b. 1970; Daniel, b. 1971; Amy, b. 1972. Career: salesman Grubb & Ellis 1968-71; salesman Alpha Realty Corp. 1971-73; gen. mgr. March Devel. Co. 1973-75; v.p. Cushman & Wakefield 1975-80; partner/ v.p. Borelli & Burke 1980--; Arbitration Panel Assn. of So. Bay Brokers; profl. witness; honors: Indsl. Broker of Yr. 1978; San Jose R.E. Hall of Fame 1983; mem: Assn. of So. Bay Brokers (pres. 1984); Soc. of Indsl. Realtors; Nat. Assn. Indsl. & Ofc. Parks; St. Marys Fathers Club; mil: NCO radarman 2/c, USN; Republican; Catholic; rec: travel, photog. Ofc: Borelli & Burke, 2680 N First St, Ste 110, San Jose 95134

BURKHART, THOMAS HENRY, financial consultant; b. Nov. 20, 1938, Bloomington, Ind.; s. Catherine Ruth (Jones); children: Bryan, b. 1961, Brad, b. 1962, Lisa, b. 1963, Michelle, b. 1966; edn: BS in mktg., Indiana Univ. 1962; MS, finl. svcs., The American Coll. 1981, Chartered Life Underwriter 1968, Chartered Finl. Cons. 1982. Career: life ins. bus. with Northwestern Mutual since 1960-: apptd. coll. dir. for campus Ind. Univ. (first such agcy. for NML) 1961-63, district agt. Terre Haute, Ind. (agcy. originally ranked last in nation, 275th, but moved to 28th rank by 1968) 1963-69, general agent in San Jose, Northwestern Mutual Life Ins. Co. 1969--; founder/pres. Security Pension Services, Inc., San Jose; prodn. awards incl. Million Dollar Round Table (Qualifying), Nat. Mgmt. Award (Charter and Life), mem: San Jose CofC (14 yr mem), Jr. Achievement (bd. mem., Loan Execs. tnr.); patron United Way, March of Dimes; frequent guest spkr., lectr.; Republican; Prot.; rec: tennis, dancing, skiing, running. Res: NML, Security Pension Services, Inc. 675 N. 1st, Ste. 700, San Jose 95112

BURKS, HOMER CLIFTON, university administrator; b. March 2, 1932, Newton, Miss.; s. Homer and Rosie M. (Bounds) Burks; div.;chil: Sheila (Beamon), Sandra (Mondreif), Victor, Eric; edn: AA in sociol., CSU San Diego 1975, BA in behav.sci., National Univ. 1979, MA, counseling, 1980. Career: Air crewman/command career counselor, USN, 1952-72; veterans benefits counselor, congl. correspondance, career information, Action Line counselor, VA Task Force, Veterans Adm., Los Angeles, San Diego 1972-79; assoc. dean of students (Mil. & Veterans Affairs) National Univ., S.D. 1979--; lic. intern Marriage, Family & Child Counseling, 1980-; Career Transition Workshop, Nat. Univ., 1979-; awards: Who's Who in Black Am. 1981-2, Benefits Suggestions awd., VA, 1973; recognition awards: VA Hosp., 1975, Congressional, 1976, National Univ., 1980. Mem: San Diego Navy League, Nat. Mgmt. Assn., Am. Soc. for Tng. and Devel., Sacto. Metro. CofC, Mil. Affairs Com., Presdtl. Task Force, NAACP, 32nd Deg.Mason; Alumni Assn. Nat. Univ. (bd.dirs.), Nat. Cultural Found. (bd.dirs. 1981-), So. Calif. Viet Nam Vets. Ldrship Pgm. (bd.dirs. 1982-); past pres. PTA Milliton H.Sch., 1966; mil:E-6 USN, ret. 1952-72, Presdtl. Unit Cit.; Republican; Prot. rec: golf. res: 2430 Fair Oaks Bl. Sacramento 95825. ofc: 7667 Folsom Bl. Sacramento 95826.

BURLEY, JERRY MICHAEL, computer software co. president; b. May 18, 1946, Akron, Ohio; s. Howard Truman and Betty Abigail (Jacobs) B.; m. Patricia Payne; children: Megan, b. 1980, Jerry M. II, b. 1983; edn: Univ. of Ariz. 1964-67, CSU Pomona 1970-72. Career: mgr. data processing various sites, 1973-76; dir. software devel. Data Systems Support, Woodland Hills 1976-78; mgr. mkt. sys. support, Microdata Corp., Irvine 1978-80; pres./CEO Unique Computer Solutions Corp., Costa Mesa 1980--; lectr. computer user seminars; devel. computer language translator; mil: splst. E5 US Army, Vietnam Svc.; Republican. Res: 246 Albert Pl Costa Mesa 92627 Ofc: Unique Computer Solutions Corp. 170 E. 17th St, Ste. 206, Costa Mesa 92627

BURLISON, CALVIN DALE, dental consultant; b. Sept. 1, 1924, Delta, Colo.; s. James Wright and Ruby Alice (Brandt) B.; m. Constance O'Niell, May 16, 1948; children: Jenny, b. 149; Matthew, b. 1950; Thomas, b. 1952; Patricia, b. 1955; edn: BS, UC Berkeley 1952; DDS, Creighton 1956. Career: staff mem. El Camino Hosp. 1958-63; staff mem. Mark Twain Hosp. 1963-73; mng. partner Dr. Burlison & Assoc. 1973-80; founder/ pres./ CEO California Dental Care Corp. 1980--; cons. for PPO Midvalley Dental Assn. 1981--; awards: Dr. J.C. Almy Awd., Creighton Univ. 1956; Ojai Jr. CofC Awd. 1949; mem: DAD, CDA,

Sacto. Dist. Dental Soc.; Lions; Rotary; Jr. CofC; Golden Gate Gold Foil Study Gp.; Mid Peninsula Study Gp.; works: Introduction and feasability study of perferred provider orgns in Calif., 1983; mil: capt. US Army 1956-58, Bronze Star 1943-46; Democrat; Episcopal; rec: Bonzai growing. Res: 101 Winding Canyon Ln Folsom 95630 Ofc: Dr. Burlison & Assoc., 518 J Street Marysville 95901

BURNETT, LYNN BARKLEY, educator; b. Oct. 20, 1948, Reedley; parents: Charles Erbin and Ruth Clarice (Erickson) B.; edn: BS, Columbia Pacific Univ. 1979, MS, 1980; candidate: Dip. in Nat. Security mgmt., Nat. Defense Univ. of the US (1984), and MD, Univ. Centro Estudios Technicos Med. Sch. (1985). Career: assoc. dir. Central Valley Emergency Med. Svcs. System Devel. Pgm., Fresno 1974-75; course dir. Pre-Hosp. Advanced Life Support Tng. Pgm. for Emerg. Paramedics, Valley Med. Ctr. of Fresno 1975; health sci. prof. CSU Fresno 1977--, dir. Center for Cont. Edn. in the Health Professions, Sch. of Hlth. and Social Wk., CSU, 1981--; afil. faculty Advanced Cardiac Life Support, Am. Heart Assn. 1973-; med. adv. Fresno Co. Sheriff Dept. 1979-; cons. in health, human behav., emerg. med. 1975--; expert witness on med. issues; estab./dir. inaugural Paramedic Tng. Pgm. Co. of Fresno, 1974-75; mem. examining bd. State Mil. Reserve, 1981-; honors: appreciation for public service, Fresno Police Dept. 1969; Am. Heart Assn. bronze medal 1974; mem: chmn. Fresno Co. Steering Com., The Chemical People, 1983; chmn. Citizens League to Expose Abuse and Negligence 1976-; Am. Coll. Emerg. Physicians, Am. Acad. Family Physicians, Am. Soc. of Law and Medicine, Am. Coll. Sports Med., AAAS, NY Acad. of Scis., Am. Assn. Suicidiology, Am. Fedn. for Clin. Research, Internat. Law Enforce. Stress Assn., Am. Trauma Soc., The Hastings Ctr. Inst. of Soc., Ethics and the Life Scis.; mem. Calif. Regional Med. Pgms., state and county subcoms.; publs: cons./contbr. Calif. State Plan for Emerg. Med. Services (1975); mil: maj. Med. Reserv. Calif. State Mil. Reserve and Air Nat. Guard 1970-, CA Svc. Medal; Democrat; Baptist; rec: music, athletics. Res: POB 4512 Fresno 93744 Ofc: CSUF Fresno 93740

BURNHAM, STANLEY, medical school and hospital president; b. July 5, 1924, Goldthwaite, Tex.; s. Leslie Dee and Myrtle Lane Burnham; m. Mildred Mendenhall, July 9, 1948; children: Ronald K., b. 1949, Diane L., b. 1951, Patricia A., b. 1952; edn: BS, Daniel Baker Coll. Southwestern Univ. 1949; M.Ed., The Univ. of Texas at Austin 1960, Ed.D., 1965. Career: pres./chief exec. Calif. Coll. of Podiatric Medicine, San Francisco 1981--; v.p. for Acad. Affairs and dean of Grad. Studies, No. Montana Coll., Havre, Mont. 1979-81; dean Sch. of Applied Arts and Scis., San Jose (Ca.) St. Univ. 1970-74 (75 time), and dir. Profl., Ednl. and Comm. Health Pgms., Regional Med. Pgm. of Tex. 1969 75 (25 time), prof./ chmn. Dept. of Phys. Instrn., coordinator Athletic Med. Pgm., Univ. of Texas System; tchg. asst., instr. asst. prof. health and phys. ed., Univ. of Texas at Austin, 1960-68; assoc. prof., acting chr. Dept. of Biol., McMurray Coll., Abilene, Tex. 1956-59; athletic dir., assoc. prof. biol., Ranger (Tex.) Coll., 1954-56; biol. tchr., athletic coach Texas Public Schs. 1950-54; chmn. Tex. Gov's Commn. on Phys. Fitness 1971-75; mem./chmn. Health Adv. Council, Capital Area Planning Council (Austin) 1971-75; pres./bd. dirs. Capitol Area Rehab. Ctr. 1968-75; bd. dirs. Com. on Nursing for Tex. 1972-74; honors: Phi Delta Kappa; guest of honor Ministry of Edn., Republic of China 1978; guest of honor, lectr. South Am. Cong. of Sports Medicine 1969-75; Outstanding Service Award, USAF Reserve Offcrs. Tng. Corps 1979. Mem: Am. Congress of Rehabilitation Med. (com. chmn.), AAAS, Am. Soc. for Pub. Hlth. Edn., Am. Soc. of Allied Hlth. Professions, Assn. of Schs. of Allied Hlth. Professions, Fellow Am. Coll. Sports Med., Am. Assn. for Hlth., Phys. Edn. and Recreation, Am. Assn. for Higher Edn., Nat. League for Nursing, Am., Calif. Pub. Hlth Assns., Gerontol. Soc. of Am., Am. Podiatry Assn., Am. Assn. of Colls. of Podiatric Med. (v.p. 1983-84); mil: USN Med. Corps 1942-46; Republican; United Methodist; rec: fishing. Res: 136 Casitas Ave San Francisco 94127 Ofc: 1210 Scott St San Francisco 94115

BURNS, MARIA SANTANA, garden consultant; b. Oct. 5, 1953, Lowell, Mass.; d. William Joseph and Helena V.C. (Lage) B.; edn: horticulture, DVC, Diablo Valley Coll., Pleasant Hill; garden cons.; cert. nurseryprsn., Calif. Career: nurseryprsn., McDonnell Nursery, Walnut Creek 1972-79; tchr. Heather Farms Garden Assn., Walnut Creek, Martinez Sch. Dist. Adult Edn. 1975; awards: Awd. for display, McDonnell Nursery, Nat. Ednl. Orgn. 1974; mem: Calif. Horticultural Soc.; Internat. Soc. of Arboriculture; guest spkr. var. chs. & orgns.; Democrat; rec: rock collecting, swimming, travel. Res: 896 Grandview Pl Walnut Creek 94595 Ofc: Maria Burns Landscape, POB 2, Walnut Creek 94596

BURNS, PATRICK LEE, manufacturing co. executive; b. Sept. 25, 1949, Pasadena; s. LeoLawrence and RichardineJoy (Pierce) Burns; m. Kathryn Allen, Apr. 3, 1971; chil: Kristine, b. 1974, Brian, b. 1976; edn: AA, Fullerton Coll. 1973, BBA, CSU Fullerton 1976, MBA, Whittier Coll. 1982. Career: finl. analyst California Computer Co., 1971-73; pres. P and L Label Mfg. Co., 1973-77; acctg. mgr. United Ad Label Co. Inc., 1977-79, gen. mgr., 1979--; v.p./secty. Sterilization Monitoring Systems, 1980-; cons. on student retention to Whittier Coll.; awards: 1982 Outstanding Young Men of Am.; mem: Nat. Assn. of Accts., SertomaClub of Whittier (secty. 1982); mil: E-4 USAF 1968-71; Republican; Am. Baptist; rec: golf, fishing, camping. res: 2032 Kelly Ave. Upland 91786. ofc: United Ad Label Co. Inc. 10035 S. Greenleaf Ave. Whittier 90610.

BURNS, RANDOLPH GEORGE, insurance co. marketing executive; b. Jan. 11, 1953, St. Louis, Mo.; s. Robert Dillman and Dorothy H. (Harr) B.; edn: Santa Ana Jr. Coll.; profl. designation in mktg. cand., UCLA. Career: Buffums Dept. Stores, Inc., Santa Ana; The London Shops, Inc., Retailers, Costa Mesa;

currently, mktg. mgr. Teachers Ins., Los Angeles; honors: Cert. of Accomplishment, PSS Selling Skills II, Xerox Corp. 1983; mem: Employee Svcs. & Recreational Council of Orange Co.; Internat. Thespian Soc.; Protestant. Res: 924 S Serrano Los Angeles 90006 Ofc: Teachers Insurance, 1111 W 6th Street Los Angeles 90017

BURNS, RICHARD NOEL, broadcast executive; b. May 24, 1930, Dallas, Tx.; s. Noel A. and Margaret M. (Hoban) B.; m. Denise Derbyshire, Dec. 20, 1971; children: Noel, b. 1967, Richard, b. 1972, James, b. 1973, Susannah, b. 1977; edn: Univ. of Mich. 1947-50; LLB (JD), New York Law Sch. 1956; admitted to NY Bar 1956, Calif. Bar 1980, US Supreme Ct. Bar 1963, US Ct. of Appeals (2d, 9th cirs.), US Dist. Ct. (SDNY, EDNY, CDCA), US Ct. of Claims, US Ct. of Customs and Patent Appeals. Career: actor (contract player) Paramount Pictures and freelance comml. actor, New York, 1933-35; opera singer, 1956--; atty. Wood, Werner, France & Tully, NY 1957-60; dir. of contracts CBS T.V. Network, NY 1960-66; prof. of instrumental music Brooklyn (NY) Music Sch., 1961-65; pres. Connaught Films, Ltd., New York and Rome, 1968-70; film prod. Primo Prodns., Inc., NY and Rome, 1970-72; vice pres. Contracts, ABC Entertainment, 1972--; guest lectr. NY Law Sch., 1968-79, Acad. di Santa Cecilia, Rome, 1969-70, Brooklyn Law Sch. 1974, Univ. of San Fernando Valley Sch. of Law, 1978, UCLA Law Sch. 1982, LA County Bar Assn. 1982, LA Co. Medical Assn. 1983; honors: NY Law Sch. (1956): Graduate of Year, chief editor law rev., pres. Moot Ct. Sco., magister Phi Delta Phi Legal Frat., sch. team Nat. Moot Ct. Competition, academic first in class; mem: Assn. of Bar of City of NY (entertainment, aviation, young lawyers coms. 1957-), NY Co. Lawyers Assn. 1956-74, LA County Bar Assn., Beverly Hills Bar Assn., Century City Bar Assn., LA Copyright Soc., NY Athletic Club 1957-60, The Players (NY) 1968-73, USC Friends of Music (vp, dir. 1979-81), The Bethone Ballet (bd. chmn. 1980-), Wagner Soc. of Am., Wagner Internat. Instn. Inc.; works: prod. theatrical film: Sweet Toronto (1969); screenplay writer: Jackstaff (1971); var. newspaper and mag. arts. on aviation and music subjects; prod./on-air host: Sat. Afternoon at Opera (KCRW, Santa Monica) 1980-81; mil: US Army Inf. 1951-53; Libertarian; Episcopal; rec: flying, scuba, music performance. Res: 8600 Balcom Ave Northridge 91325 Ofc: ABC Entertainment, 2040 Ave of Stars, Ste. 300, Century City 91325

BURROWS, LARRY EUGENE, manufacturing co. executive; b. July 5, 1933, Cedar Rapids, Iowa; s. Leonard Eugene and Bernice (Candler) B.; m. Lorene Marie Stenerson, June 7, 1953; 1 child, Lee, b. 1966; edn: BS, CSU Los Angeles 1966; MS (MBA), Grad. Sch. of Mgmt. Woodbury Univ. 1972; The Exec. Pgm. for Mgmt. UCLA 1977. Career: cost acctg. mgr. Products Research & Chem. Co., Burbank 1961-66; supr./pgm. adminstr. Xerox Corp., Electro- Optical Systems Group, Pasadena 1966-74; mgr. finl. ops. TRW, Inc., Energy Products Group- Los Angeles, 1974-77; div. controller Carnation Co., Can Div., L.A. 1977-79; asst. corp. controller Kerr Glass Mfg. Corp., L.A. 1980--; participant in the Business Internat. Spanish Round Table, Madrid, Spain 1976; honors: Dora E. Kirby Awd. for highest scholastic honors, Woodbury Univ. 1977; McDonnell Douglas awd. for contbn. to Orbiting Work Station Proj. 1974; Jet Propulsion Lab. awd. for contbn. Mariner Mars 1971 Proj.; mem: Dean's Council UCLA (1984); Nat. Assn. of Accts. (v.p. 1974); Am. Mgmt. Assn.; UCLA Alumni Assn.; Exec. Graduate Assn.; author: Mergers and Acquisitions, Financial Aspects of (1972); mil: cpl. US Army 1953-55; Republican; Prot.; rec: photog., sports. Res: 2246 El Arbolita Dr Glendale 91208 Ofc: Kerr Glass Mfg. Corp. 501 Shatto Pl Los Angeles 90020

BURSTEIN, SARA LEE, corporate treasurer; b. June 26, 1929, Detroit, Mich.; d. Ben and Rose Elaine (Staman) Cohn; m. King Burstein, June 18, 1961; chil: Michael, b. 1962, David, b. 1964. career: court clerk Santa Monica Municipal Ct., 1950-58; exec. secty. Rohm & Haas, Los Angeles 1958-62; treas. Amber Leather Co., Inc., Santa Ana 1965--. Mem: Silver Circle of Orange Co., Orange Co. for Cystic Fibrosis Found., Am. Jewish Com., World Affairs Council, Guild for the Ctr for Perf. Arts, Braille Inst. Aux., Las Socias of Orange Co., Freedoms Found. of Am., Century Investment Club (past pres., corres. sec., finl. sec.), South Coast Repertory Support Gp. (1st woman elected to bd. dirs.), PBHA, Balboa Bay Club; Newport Beach Hadassah (past bd. mem.), Temple Bat Yahm, Newport Bch (past v.p.; v.p. Sisterhood 1982); Newport Harbor Republican Women, Bev. Hills Repub. Club, Badham Boosters. Jewish. rec: swim, gourmet food. res: 651 Bayside Dr. Newport Bch 92660. ofc: Amber Leather Co. Inc. 2850 S. Harbor Blvd. Santa Ana 92704.

BURT, SONYRA ILYF, real estate broker/ writer; b. June 23, 940, Birmingham, Ala.; d. Delmar G. and Elyf S. (Jones) Wilson; m. Donald E. Burt, June 28, 1980; children: Tobias R. Burt, b. 1975; Tristin S. Burt, b. 1978; edn: AA, Univ. of Fla. 1960. Career: real estate agent 1969-74; mgr. Trotter Realty, Belmont 1974; partner/ broker Century 21 Coventry Realty, San Carlos 1977; pres./ corp. broker Coventry Realty, Truckee 1980--; honors: Million Dollar Club, Pacifica Bd. Realtors 1972, San Carlos Bd. Realtors 1974-78; mem: Tahoe- Sierra Bd. Realtors; Redwood City Bd. Realtors; Truckee CofC (Truckee Inc. Com.); Aircraft Owners & Pilots Assn.; Calif. Assn. Realtors; Nat. Assn. Realtors; Truckee- Tahoe Contractors Assn.; publs: How to Sell Real Estate and Make Millions (1984); Republican; Catholic; rec: pvt. pilot, writing, photog. Res: 37 Mare Ct, POB 2914, Truckee 95734 Ofc: Coventry Realty, Inc., POB 2443, Truckee 95834

BURTON, THELMA CORRINE, lumber co. credit executive; b. Jan. 28, 1905, Topeka, Ks.; d. Oscar Bertrum and Maude Mae (Gray) Fisher; m. Robert Oler Burton, Nov. 24, 1927; children: Robert James (dec.), Gloria Dawn (BD), Thomas Gray (BD); edn: Gregg Coll. 1924. Career: teller Peoples Co-Oper.

Bank, Hammond, Ind., 7 years; secty./ credit mgr. Valley Lumber & Supply Co., Stockton, Ca. 1946--; mem: Golden Poppy Chapter OES (Worthy Matron 1956; Deputy Grand Matron, St. of Calif. 1960); Am. Businesswomen's Assn.; Beta Sigma Phi Sor. (past pres.); Republican; Protestant. Res: 2614 Venetian Dr Stockton 95207 Ofc: Valley Lumber & Supply Co., POB 6157 Stockton 95206

BURTON, SIDNEY KIM, electrical engineer; b. Nov. 28, 1960, Hollywood; d. George Wm. and Delores Joan (Reich) B.; edn: BS in engring., magna cum laude, CSU Northridge 1984. Career: student engr. Hughes Aircraft Co., MSG, Canoga Park: Electro-Mech. Dept. 1979-82, Control Systems Dept. 1982-84; mem. tech. engring. staff, Control Sys. Dept., 1984--; awards: MSc. Fellowship at USC, Hughes Aircraft Co. (4/84), Cost Improvement Pgm. Award nominee (1984); Golden Key Hon. Soc. 1983; Northrop Corp. Scholarship 1982; Soc. of Women Engrs. Recogn. Awd. 1982; Tau Beta Pi 1982 (CSUN v.p. 1981-2); Alpha Xi Delta 1979 (treas. 1980); mem: IEEE, 1981-; Soc. of Women Engrs., 1978-; Women in Science and Engring., 1978-83; works: devel. computer software (8 tech. pgms.) 1979-84; rec: medical lit., nutrition, science, Amer. Indian culture. Res: 21421 Providencia St Woodland Hills 91464 Ofc: Hughes Aircraft Co. 8433 Fallbrook Ave, Bldg. 268, MS. A72, Canoga Park 91304

BUSBY, ROBERT ALLEN, speech pathologist; b. Oct. 2, 1931, Signal Hill; s. Jackson Wayne and Fletah Mae (McNaught) Busby; m. Stacey, May 4, 1949; chil: Janet, b. 1952, Kim, b. 1955, Kevin, b. 1956, Eric, b. 1968, Brian, b. 1969, Molly, b. 1973; edn: AA, Long Beach City Coll., 1958; BA, CSU Long Beach, 1963, MA, 1965; Calif. lic. Speech Pathol.; Calif. Restricted Speech and Hearing Cred.; cert. vision screening, So. Calif. Coll. of Optometry; cert. P.I.C.A.C. (Porch Index of Communicative Ability in Chil.), The Communicative Disorders Research Found.; C.C.C. (cert. clin. competence), Am. Speech Lang. Hearing Assn. Career: with Speech and Language Devel. Ctr., Buena Park: speech pathologist ,1964--, and coordinator vision devel., 1978--, coord. outdoor edn., 1975--; tchr. in spl. edn. (Preschool, Sec.) 1968; supr. Sec. Edn./dir. grad. studies and interns/supr. univ. off-campus practicum, 1968-79; lectr. in spl. edn. Calif. Lutheran Coll., 1978-81. Mem: Am. Speech-Lang. Hearing Assn., Calif. Speech-Hearing Assn., Calif. Assn. of Pvt. Splzd. Edn. and Svcs.; past pres. W.Anaheim Lions Club (1968-71), Zone chmn. 4L4 (1974). contbr. artls. profl. pubs.; mil: s/sgt USAF 1951-54; Republican;Baptist; rec: tennis, singing. res: 529 E. Ave. San Juan, San Clemente 92672 ofc: Speech Language Devel. Ctr. 8699 Holder St Buena Park 90620.

BUSH, KENNETH CALVIN, psychotherapist; b. June 11, 1916, Bemidji, Minn.; s. Charles Anthony and Eva June (Hyatt) B.; m. Grayce Krause, Nov. 23, 1937; children: Kenneth Jr., b. 1942; Charlene, b. 1952; edn: Bemidji St. Univ. 1950-52; D.O., No. Ill. Coll. of Optometry 1955; BA, CSU, Dominguez Hills 1972; MS, USC, L.A. 1973; Calif. lic. Marriage, Family & Child Therapist 1976, Std. Tchg. Cred. 1973, Comm. Coll. Instr. Cred. 1978. Career: optometrist, Los Angeles 1955-62; admin. asst. to V.P. of Pricing, No. American Aviation, Los Angeles 1962-70; staff Gerhard Kohn Sch. of Emotional, Physical & Academic Disabled Children, Long Beach 1973-75; psychotherapist pvt. practice, Lakewood 1975--; instr. Cerritos Coll. 1978-; honors: Tomb & Key Soc., No. Ill. Coll. of Optom. 1954; Pub. Svc. Commdn., City of El Segundo 1970; Cert. of Merit, ABC Unified Sch. Dist. 1975; mem: Am. & Calif. Assns. Marriage & Family Therapists; Masons; Shriners; Elks; research: biofeedback & psychosomatic diseases; mil: tech. sgt. Army Air Corps 1942-45, Air Medal w/ five oak leaf clusters; Battle Stars (4); Democrat; Protestant; rec: golf, woodworking. Res: 17433 Virginia Ave, No. I, Bellflower 90706 Ofc: 5510 North Clark Lakewood 90712

BUSH, NORMAN JACOB, real estate brokerage president; b. June 23, 1915, Jersey Shore, Penna.; s. General Kearney and Ina Beryl (Barfield) B.; m. Gloria Ann, Mar. 31, 1937, div. 1968; children: Berylann, b. 1938, Byron, b. 1949, Lana, b. 1942, Shelby, b. 1946, Jim, b. 1951, Candace, b. 1952; edn: dip. Healds Coll. S.F. 1948-50; dip. Legal Aspects, San Jose St. Univ. 1962-64; GRI, Grad. Realtor Inst.; num. courses in taxation, real estate. Career: real estate broker 1945--, business opps. broker, 1946; founder/owner Bush Assocs. Gen. Contr. 1948; founder/owner Joe Bush Liquor (two stores) 1950; owner/pres. Sterling Financial Inc., San Jose; mem. San Jose Bd. of Realtors 1945-; Elks; works: remodeled cottage in hist. section Willow, feature story in San Jose Mercury; served in Nat. Guards; Republican; Prot.; rec: boating, dancing. Res: 1376 Cherry San Jose 95125 Ofc: Sterling Finl. Inc. 351 Meridian Ave San Jose 95126

BUTLER, DAVID VIRGIL, chemist/ manufacturing co. executive; b. Nov. 6, 1947, Long Beach; s. Virgil James and Rosmary I. (Schaffer) B.; edn: Mt. San Antonio Jr. Coll. 1965-67; BA, Azusa Pacific Coll. 1969. Career: mfg. mgr. Lee Pharmaceuticals, S. El Monte 1971-79; ptnr./ corp. secty./ mfg. mgr./ dir. Scientific Pharmaceuticals, Duarte 1979--; mem. NRA; num. patents; Republican; Protestant; rec: photog. Res: POB 146 Duarte 91010 Ofc: Scientific Pharmaceuticals, 1828 Evergreen Duarte 91010

BUTLER, JACK LUTHER, real estate executive; b. Feb. 15, 1920, Ada, Okla.; s. Luther Jackson and Minnie (Granger) B.; m. Pebble Fern Cannon, Oct. 31, 1940; children: Robert Rhett; Jeffrey Jack, Gregory Franklin; edn: East Central

St. Coll. 1936-39. Career: gen. sci. tchr. Horace Mann H.S., Ada., Okla. 1939-40; owner/ opr. Ohio Market, Richmond 1944-58; assoc. Eyring Realty, El Sobrante 1958-59; Mira Vista Real Estate, Richmond 1960; woner East Bay Real Estate, Richmond 1960-72, Pinole 1972--; co- owner AB Ranch, Willits 1973--; B & C Squab Farm, Modesto 1974--; Century 21 Hillside Realty, Lafayette 1980--; rep. El Sobrante Democratic Club 1967-69; mem: NAREB; Calif. Real Estate Assn.; Contra Costa, West Contra Costa (Multiple Listing Svc. Com.) Bds. Realtors; Masons; rec: 7 Jodie Ln El Sobrante 94803 Ofc: Century 21, East Bay Real Estate, 12720 San Pablo Ave Richmond 94805

BUTLER, SAMUEL JAMES, real estate broker; b. Feb. 6, 1933, Santa Cruz; s. Benjamin Franklin and Catherine Louise (Dahl) B.; div.; 1 son: Matthew, b. 1967; edn: AB, Univ. of Calif. 1959; SRA (senior residential appraiser), Soc. of R.E. Appraisers 1970; RECI (R.E. Certificate Inst.), UC 1968. Career: appraiser/ chief appraiser/ regl. loan mgr. Lytton Savings & Loan (now Great Western S & L), Palo Alto 1961-68; v.p. real estate Spectrum Fin. Gp., Palo Alto 1969; v.p. real estate acquisitions US Real Estate Corp., San Francisco 1970; prop. Butler Realty Gp., S.F. 1971-76; bus. mgr. Ralph Alperin, MD, Redwood City 1976-78; floor splst. The American Real Estate Exch., S.F. 1978-81; R.E. broker, Merrill Lynch Comml. R.E. 1981--; pres. Sam Butler, Inc. 1979--; honors: Best Speech at Toastmasters Events, 1982, 83, Best Speech, Dale Carnegie tng. 1977; mem: Soc. of R.E. Appraisers; High Spirit of Toastmasters, Belmont; Commonwealth Club of Calif. (fmr.); No. Calif. Alumni Alliance (pres.); works: copyright Matchmaster Real Estate Pgm. for computer; lead in one act play, Amicable Parting, at Hillbarn Theatre 1983; mil: capt. USAFR 1954-58, tng. dir. air sea rescue 1957; Democrat; Relig. Sci.; rec: racquetball, acting. Res: 1890 Clay St, Apt 1102, San Francisco 94109 Ofc: Merrill Lynch Commercial Real Estate, 101 California St, Ste 1100, San Francisco 94111

BUTLER, STUART MARKLE, JR., construction co. executive; b. May 15, 1924, St. Louis, Mo.; s. Stuart Markle and Lucille (Woods) B.; m. Joanne Fistere, Apr. 22, 1950; children: Joseph, b. 1953; Stuart, b. 1956; Jennie,b. 1959; edn: BS, Calif. Inst. of Tech. 1948. Career: project mgr. Fruin- Colnon Co., St. Louis 1948-59, v.p./ dist. mgr. San Francisco 1959-65; asst. to pres. Wm. Simpson Const. Co., Los Angeles 1965-68; v.p. admin. Simpson Div. of Dillingham, L.A. 1968-77, pres. 1977-81; pres. Dillingham Const., Inc., Pleasanton 1981--; mem: Alumni Assn., Calif. Tech. (pres. 1976); Calif. Club, L.A.; Engrs. Club, S.F.; mi; 1st lt. USAAF, Air Medal w/ 5 clusters; Republican; Presbyterian; rec: tennis. Res: 893 Gainsborough Dr Pasadena 91107 Ofc: Dillingham Construction, Inc., 2401 Beverly Blvd Los Angeles 90057

BUTTNER, JEAN B., corporate executive; b. Nov. 3, 1934, New Rochelle, NY; d. Arnold Bernhard and Janet (Kinghorn); m. Edgar Buttner, Sept. 17, 1958; children: Janet Mott, b. 1960, Edgar Arnold, b. 1962, Marianne Bernhard, b. 1965; edn: BA, Vassar, 1957; Harvard Radcliffe Pgm. Cert. of Bus.Adm., 1958; Montessori Dip., Coll. Notre Dame. Career: vice chmn. Value Line Inc.; dir., owner Value Line Investment Survey; owner Cisco Interiors, NY; pres. R.E. & venture capital bus.; founder Piedmont Music Found.; served on five school bds.; past pres. Piedmont School Bd.; past pres. Vassar Club; mem. Harvard Bus. Sch. Alumni Assn.; Republican; Congregational (deaconess); rec: swimming, reading.

BUTZER, JERRY LEE, management consultant co. president/ university professor; b. Mar. 17, 1944, Massillon, Ohio; s. Oral and Shirley (Horst) B.; edn: PhD study, Stanford Univ. 1979; MBA, UC Berkeley 1978; MS, Fla. St. Univ. 1970; BS, Ohio Univ. 1967; R.E. broker, Calif. 1978. Career: pres. Inquiry, INc., San Francisco 1982--; assoc. prof. exec. policy & strategic plng. corp. fin. Pepperdine Univ. Grad. Sch. of Bus., MBA pgm., Malibu & other univs. 1978--; sr. corp. fin. cons. AM. Appraisal Assocs., Oakland 1981-82; trust ofcr. fin. & strategic plng. Trust & Investment Div. Hdqrts., Crocker Nat. Bank, S.F. 1975-78; corp. plng. cons. Los Angeles area fin. & entertainment inds. 1972-74; staff cons./ statistician, mgmt. sys., exec. ofc. of the Pres. (Nixon), Ofc. of Mgmt. & Budget, Wash. DC 1971-72; math. tchr., Daytona Beach (Fla.) Pub. Schs. 1967-68; guest spkr. strategic plng., economics, acctg. sys., time mgmt., exec. pgms. in univ. of pvt. firms 1977--; mem: Inst. of Chartered Fin. Analysts; Nat. Assn. Fin. Cons.; Am. Mgmt. Assn.; Ctr. for Entrepreneurial Mgmt.; Phi Gamma Delta 1966; works: appeared in ABC-TV series, 1972-73; Protestant; rec: motion picture prodn. & fin., screenwriting, theatre. Res: 3501 Laguna, 107, San Francisco 94123 Ofc: Inquiry, Inc., 24 California St, Ste 312, San Francisco 94111

BYARS, DRUCILLA MOORE, dietitian; b. Aug. 3, 1939, Savannah, Ga.; d. Philander Sanders and Mary Stoney (Williams) Moore; m. James H. Byars, Sept. 3, 1966; div. 1978; children: Angela, b. 1969, Phyllis, b. 1972; edn: BS in nutrition, Savannah St. Coll. 1961; Dietetic Internship, Freedmen's Hosp./ Howard Univ. 1962; Reg. Dietitian, Am. Dietetic Assn. 1962. Career: staff dietitian Johns Hopkins Hosp., Balt., Md. 1962-65; administr. dietitian D.C. General Hosp., Wash. D.C. 1965-66; sole dietitian Warren Candler Hospitals, Savannah 1967-68, roving dietn. Candler-Central Hosp. (ENT and Eye) and Candler-Telfair Hosp. (OB-Gyn), 1970-71; tchr. (sec. schs.) Morongo Unified School Dist., Twentynine Palms, Ca. 1972-74; consulting dietn. Inland Health Svcs., Riverside 1973-75; relief nutritionist Kaiser Permanente, San Diego 1975-77; teaching dictn. Donald N. Sharp Meml. Comm. Hosp., San Diego 1977-82, clin. dietn./asst. mng. dir. of edn. Dietary Dept., 1983--; mem. Speakers' Bureaus: San Diego Dist. Dietetic Assn. (1976-81), Sharp Meml. Hosp. (1977--), S.D. Chpt. Am. Heart Assn.; guest faculty mem. Univ. of the Third Age, Univ. of San Diego; mem: The Am. Dietetic Assn., Calif. Dietetic Assn., S.D. Dist. Dietetic Assn. (Nutrition Com.), Am. Heart Assn. (bd. dirs.

S.D. chpt. 1983-), past mem. Ga. Diet. Assn. 1967-71; charter mem. Coastal Empire Diet. Assn.; Delta Sigma Theta; adult scout/vol. Girl Scouts USA 1959-; publs: series arts. on nutrition in Sharp Horizons (Sharp Hosps. quarterly) 1978-79; Participant's Manual for Weight Control (1982); nutrition puzzle (1978), poem (1978); Democrat; Baptist; rec: camping, dancing. Res: 8539 Innsdale Ln San Diego 92114 Ofc: Sharp Meml. Hospital, 7901 Frost St San Diego 92123

BYE, ROSEANNE MARIE, restaurant chain R & D director; b. Nov. 27, 1946, Chicago, IL; d. Paul David and Gwen Lucille (Hipp) Forrester; B.SC, Western Ill. Univ., 1969; numerous grad. courses in mktg., mkt. res., mgmt. and acctg., 1970--; m. Richard Bye, June 14, 1969. Career: banquet planner, Western Ill. Univ., 1966-69; product, recipe home econ., Hunt-Wesson Foods, Fullerton, 1969-73; product, recipe devel. home econ., Lawry's foods, Inc., L.A., 1973-74; mgr. res. and prod. devel., Carl Karcher Enterprises, Inc. (Carl's Jr., Hamburger Fast Food, Taco De Carlos, Mexican Fast Food, and Sunshine Broilers, Family Restaurants), Anaheim, 1974-81; director, research and development, Denny's Restaurants, La Mirada, 1981--. Mem.: Home Economists in Bus., many offices; Amer. Home Econ. Assn., many offices; Calif. Home Economists Assn., many offices; Calif. Home Economics Assn., Orange dist., many offices; pub. rel. chmn., secty., Orange Co. Music Center, Allegro chpt.; pub. chmn, Miss Anaheim Pageant, Halloween Festivals, etc., Anaheim C. of C.; So. Calif. Restaurant Assn., Truth in Menu Comm.; adv. comm., Santa Ana Coll., Calif. State Long Beach, Garden Grove Sch. Dist.; radio speaking engagements concerning "Is Fast Food Junk Food"; Animal Protection League; Women In Mgmt.; Society for Adv. of Food Service Research; Inten. Food Service, editorial counciling; Townhall; Soroptimist. Recipient: numerous awards. Republican, Young Republicans and various other committees. Protestant. Res.: 5829 Valencia Dr., Orange 92669; Office: 14256 East Firestone Blvd., La Mirada 90637.

BYRD, BARBARA JEAN, gerontological social worker; b. Mar. 28, 1946, Oak Park, Ill.; d. Milford Arthur and Carolyn Louise (Heflin) Bergsten; div.; edn: BS, Iowa St. Univ. 1968; MSW (spec. in aging), UC Berkeley 1978; LCSW (lic. clin. soc. wkr.) Calif. 1982. Career: public sch. tchr., Chesapeake, Va. and Montgomery Tnwshp, NJ 1968-73; coordinator Outreach/Supportive Services for Seniors pgm., San Francisco 1973-76; asst. dir. Retired Sr. Volunteer Pgm., Jewish Comm. Ctr. in S.F. 1975; asst. dir. South S.F. Senior Center, 1975-76; project dir. South S.F. Senior Outreach, title III proj., San Mateo Co. Area Agcy. on Aging 1975-76; intern Family Service Agcy. Palo Alto 1976-77, Marin 1977-78; current dir. social svcs. The Redwoods (retirement comm.), Mill Valley; lectr. UC Berkeley Sch. of Soc. Welfare, supvr. to grad. interns 1979-82; guest spkr. var. community groups; cons. Valdez Plaza, Satellite Senior Homes; planning com. workshops for families of nursing home patients 1980-81; mem: Western Gerontol. Soc. (editl. bd. Connections newsletter 1979-81); Calif. Splsts. on Aging; Nat. Assn. Soc. Wkrs. (exec. com. Marin Co.); Bay Area Soc. Wkrs. in Health Care; public coauthor w/ Florence Vickery of Intro. to Gerontology coll. course (audio cassette & manual) 1984; working with Bay Area Comm. Coll. TV Consortium (1984); Democrat; Prot.; rec: hiking, jazzercise. Res: 396 Pine Hill Rd, 16, Mill Valley 94941 Ofc: The Redwoods, 40 Camino Alto, Mill Valley 94941

BYRNE, MARGARET MARY, social work administrator; b. Aug. 12, 1944, Cleveland, Ohio; d. Thomas Francis, Sr. and Catherine Gertrude (McGivern) B.; edn: BA, Duchesne Coll. 1967; MSW, Boston Coll. 1976; LCSW (lic. clin. soc. wk.) Calif. Career: casewkr. Child Welfare Dept., Cleveland, Ohio 1967-68; kindergarten tchr. 1968; soc. wkr. Family & Children Svcs., Boston 1968-72; pgm. dir. family svcs. Woodfield, Inc., Fairfield, Conn. 1972-74 treatment dir. Cleveland (Oh.) Ctr. on Alcoholism 1976-77; dir. treatment svcs. Westinghouse Health Systems, Inc., Cleveland, Oh. 1977-78; sr. mktg. splst. Charter Med. Corp., Macon, Ga. 1978-79; dir. clin. soc. svcs. No. San Diego County Hosp. Dist. 1979-80, bd. dirs. 1980-84; dir. patient and family svcs. Scripps Clinic and Research Found., LaJolla 1980--; guest lectr. UCSD Sch. of Med. 1979-; field instr. CSU San Diego Sch. of Social Wk. 1980--; awards: full grad. school scholarship, Conn. Alcoholism Ednl. Council 1974-76; Mademoiselle Mag. art competition winner (1963); mem: Am. Hosp. Assn.'s Soc. for Hosp. Soc. Wk. Directors (p.r. So. Calif. chpt.); Am. Mgmt. Assn.; Nat. Assn. Soc. Wkrs.; United Way/CHAD of San Diego; Health Council of Greater S.D.; Coord. Council on Child Abuse of S.D.; publs: The Co-Alcoholic Syndrome, Nat. Council on Alcoholism, 1978; Health in Later Life Pgm. update, (sev. profl. journals 1982); Catholic; rec: photog., sculpture, equestrian, dog obedience competition. Res: 842 S. Sierra Ave Solana Bch 92075 Ofc: Scripps Clinic & Resrch Found. 10666 N. Torrey Pines Rd La Jolla 92037

C

CACHUELA, LAWRENCE PAUL, computer consultant; b. July 11, 1943, San Diego; s. Jose M. and Rosie (Pastoral) C.; m. Shirley Ecarma, Apr. 18, 1970; children: Shirlee, b. 1970, Yvonne, b. 1973, Regina, b. 1979; edn: BSEE, Western States Coll. of Engring. 1973; MBA, CSU Long Beach 1980; MBA stu., UCLA 1978-79. Career: electronic tech. RCA Corp., W. Los Angeles 1969-71; asst. supr. McDonnell Douglas Corp., Long Beach 1971-75; automatic test engr. ATE Assocs., Inc. Northridge 1975-76, Rockwell Internat., El Segundo, Newport Beach, 1976-80; lead engr. Northrop Electronics Div., Hawthorne 1980-81; automatic test engring. cons. 1981--, Volt Tech. Corp.,

Phoenix, Az., Newport Beach 1981-83, Execusoft, Anaheim 1983; computer cons./prop. ALARC Computer Consultants, Westminster 1983--; mem. IEEE, Computer Soc., Automatic test Program Generation Subcom.; Patentee: Built-in test equipment (BITE) Failure Decoder/ Analyzer (1975), lic. to Aero-Info, Inc. for mfr. and mktg.; mil: SP5 US Army 1966-69; mem. Knights of Columbus (4th deg.); rec: piano, karate. Res: 8442 Torchwood Cir Westminster 92683 Ofc: ALARC Computer Consultants, POB 724, Westminster 92684

CACIOPPO, BETTY LAURA, insurance agent; b, Nov. 5, 1932, Clinton, Ark.; d. Harvey and Eunice (Brown) Baker; m. Carl J. Cacioppo, July 3, 1951; children: Mark S., b. 1953, D. Kevin, b. 1955; edn: Merced City Coll. 1960-62, num. ins., bus. courses; career: agent Washington National Ins. Co., Fresno 1970-77; gen. agent American Nat. Ins. Co., Fresno, 1977-80, agent 1980--; awards: Executive and presidents Club 1970-73, Women's Leaders Round Table 1972, 73, Million Dollar Round Table 1975; mem. Sigma Phi 1953-75; Republican; Catholic; rec: ceramics & clay, macrame, gourmet cooking, RV; res: 12423 E. Shaw Ave. Clovis 93612 ofc: American National Ins. Co. 1300 E. Shaw Ave. Ste. 126, Fresno 93710.

CACIOPPO, CARL JOSEPH, insurance agent; b. Oct. 3, 1930, Hammond, La.; s. Joseph and Mary (Schiro) C.; m. Betty Baker, July 3, 1951; chil: Mark S., b. 1953, D. Kevin, b. 1955; edn: AA,New Paltz State Tchrs Coll., NY 1951; mil. tech. and trade schs.; num. ins., bus. courses. Career: sales rep. Zellerbach paper Co., Fresno 1954-70; agent Washington Nat. Ins. Co., Fresno 1970-77; gen. agent Am. Nat. Ins. Co., Fresno 1977-80, agent, 1980--; instr. ins. courses, Fresno City College; awards: 1975 Calif. Leading Agent, 1975 Internat. Leading Agent, Exec. and Presidents Club 1970-; Fresno Gen. Agents and Mgrs. Award 1971, 72, 75; VIP Awd. and Chieftain Awd., 1975-81; Million Dollar Round Table 1975-78, 80. Mem: Clovis Elks; Lions Club 1954-72; Knights of Columbus 1961-75; Italo-Am. Lodge 1961-70; BSA leader 1960-70; mil: 1948-52; s/sgt. US Air N.G. 1952-55; Republican; Catholic; rec: ceramic crafts, radio guided aircraft, fishing; res: 12423 E. Shaw Ave. Clovis 93612 ofc: Am. Nat. Ins.Co. 1300 E. Shaw Ave Ste.126, Fresno 93710.

CADIGAL, FLORENTINO B., engineer; b. Aug. 18, 1937, Bato Leyte, Phil.; nat. 1981; s. Agapito V. and Zenona G. (Buhe) Cadigal; edn: BSME, USC, 1962, and BSEE, 1967; m. Felicitas Ayop, 1967; chil: Florentino, b. 1968, Flordileza, b. 1969, Rosario, b. 1971, Susan, b. 1972, Joseph, b. 1973. Career: owner General Merchandizing, Phil., 1969-74; engr. Smith Bell & Co., 1967-74; assoc. engr. Fluor Utah Inc., 1974-78; engr. General Electric, San Jose 1978--. Awards: PDE River Bend PGCC 1982, 1981, QPP 1980, 1970, 1969; PSEE Director; Republican; Catholic; rec: tennis, running; res: 3610 Deedham Dr. San Jose 95148. ofc: G.E., 175 Curtner Ave, Ste.425A, San Jose 95125.

CADY, FRANK DECKER, lawyer; b. Mar. 7, 1954, San Francisco; s. Donald Pardee and Florence (Decker) C.; m. Susan Rose, Aug. 12, 1978; 1 dau: Danae, b. 1983; edn: BA, Univ. of Nevada, Reno 1978; JD, UC Hastings 1981; admitted to Calif. State Bar Assn. 1981. Career: legis. intern Nevada State Assembly 1975; law clerk Broun, Norris, King & Snell, Fremont 1980; Assoc. Law Firm of Bradbury & Kellison, Susanville 1981-82; partner Law Firm of Bradbury, Kellison & Cady, Susanville 1982--; trustee Susanville Sch. Dist. 1983; bd. mem./ legal counsel Lassen Economic Devel. Counsel, Inc. 1981-; dist. rep. Lassen Co. Republican Central Com. 1983-; honors: Phi Kappa Phi 1977; Pi Sigma Alpha 1977; mem: Lassen Co., Am. & Calif. Bar Assns.; Calif. State Trial Lawyers Assn.; Calif. Sch. Bd. Assn.; Rotary; Commonwealth; Lassen Economic Devel. Council, Inc.; Lassen Co. CofC; Republican; Catholic; rec: outdoor sports, woodworking, carpentry. Res: 606 Nevada St, POB 998, Susanville 9630; Bradbury, Kellison & Cady, 60 S Lassen St, POB 1238, Susanville 95130

CAHN, RICHARD SIMON, investment securities broker; b. Dec. 11, 911, San Francisco; s. Julius I. and Minnie (Newman) C.; m. Ella Louise Greensfelder, Aug. 18, 1935; children: Kathleen, b. 1941; Louise, b. 1943; edn: AB, Stanford Univ. 1933. Career: buyer Chas. Brown & Sons, San Francisco 1933-37; partner Shafft, Snock & Cahn, S.F. 1937-79; acct. exec. Emmett Larkin Co., Inc., S.F. 1979--; mem: Stock Brokers Soc.; Presidio Soc.; Mechanics Inst. & Lib. (chmn. Pension Com.); Amex Club; Rotary; S.F. League of Women Voters (Fin. Adv. Com.); Commonwealth Club; Presidio Ofcrs. Club; S.F. Symphony Assn.; Acad. of Scis.; Stanford Buck Club; Stanford J.F. Luncheon Club; Am. Contract Bridge League; Metropolitan Club; Republican; rec: contract bridge, fishing, hiking. Res: 2140 Lake St San Francisco 94121 Ofc: Emmett A. Larkin Co., 100 Bush St, 10th Flr, San Francisco 94104

CAIN, PATRICIA JEAN, certified public accountant; b. Sept. 28, 1931, Decatur, Ill.; d. Paul George and Jean Margaret (Horne) Jacka; m. Dan L. Cain, July 12, 1952; children: Mary Ann, b. 1963; Timothy, b. 1965; Paul, b. 1967; edn: Univ. of Mich. 1949-52; Pasadena City Coll. 1975-76; BS, CSU Los Angeles 1977; MBA, 1978; CPA, Calif. 1981. Career: CPA/ tax sr. Stonefield & Josephson Accty. Corp., Los Angeles 1979--; part time lecr. CSU Los Angeles 1983; honors: Thanks Badge, Highland Rim Girl Scout Council, Oakridge, Tenn. 1959; Thanks Badge, Sierra Madres Girl Scout Council, Pasadena; Nat. Delegate, Girl Scouts 1975; mem: AICPA; Calif. Soc. CPAs (Taxation Com.; Microcomputers Users Discussion Gp.); Beta Alpha Psi; Girl Scouts of USA; Million Belles Investment Club; Wrightwood CofC; Democrat; Episcopal; rec: fishing, skiing, rug making. Res: 3715 Fairmeade Rd Pasadena 91107 Ofc: Stonefield & Josephson, 3731 Wilshire Blvd, Ste 800, Los Angeles 90010

CALBREATH, MICHAEL A., dental facilities designer- developer; b. Sept. 11, 1945, Oakland; s. Evert A. and Wanda Mae (Flatt) C.; children: Adam, b.

1967; Scott, b. 1971; Shane, b. 1977; edn: Western Bus. Univ.; So. Dakota Sch. of Mines & Tech.; Univ. of San Francisco; San Jose City Coll.; contractors lic., Calif. Career: biomed. engr. Warren's Repair Svc., S. San Francisco 1967-73; dental ofc. designer Equitec, S.F. 1973-75; designer/ equip. mgr. Precision Dental, Burlingame 1975-77; owner Warren's Profl. Svcs., San Bruno 1977--; owner Medical Contractors Svc., San Bruno 1983--; instr. ofc. design, UC Dental Sch.; design cons. var. dental equip. mfrs.; design bd. UC Dental Sch.; mem: Operation Calif. med. & dental cons. (completed only dental sch. in Cambodia, clinic in Cuernevaca, Mex.) 1983-84; mil: sgt., USAF 1963-67; rec: scub diving, guitar playing. Res: 1189 San Mateo Ave San Bruno 94066 Ofc: Warren's Professional Services, Inc., 1185 San Mateo Ave San Bruno 94066

CALDWELL, COLIN LANE, insurance co. executive; b. Mar. 6, 1945, Santa Monica; s. Edgar Seaman and Virginia Mae (Blair) C.; (mother was first child b. in Beverly Hills); m. Carol Jean Wolfe, Nov. 6, 1982; children: Ed, b. 1965; John, b. 1968; Kevin, b. 1970; Lisa, b. 1973; edn: Limra Tng. Dirs. Sch.; Limra Field Ofcrs. Sch.; Pierce Jr. Coll. 1965; Valley Coll. 1968. Career: Allstate Ins. Co. 1969--; agent, 1969-73; admin. sales mgr. 1973; asst. dist. sales mgr. 1973-74; dist. sales mgr. 1974-76; western zone tng. mgr. 1976-78; home ofc. mktg. mgr. 1978-80; field sales mgr., No. Calif. 1980-84; honors: Life Millionaire, Conf. of Champions and Honor Ring awards (5); Key Mgr. Awd. (Top 5 nat.) 1983; mem: Kiwanis (past pres.); Nat., Sacramento Assn. Life Underwriters; publs: essay on Birth of America's Freedom, Am. Legion Medal of Honor; mil: sgt. 1965-68, Vietnam Svc.; Republican; Presbyterian; rec: fly tying, black powder gun collecting. Res: formerly of Fair Oaks, Ca. Ofc: 10311 Stormhaven Indianapolis, Ind 46256

CALEMINE, LARRY JOHN, real estate development co. chief executive; b. Aug. 20, 1935, NY; s. Joseph and Mary (Circosta) C.; m. Camille Circosta, dec. 6, 1954; children: Toni Ann, b. 1955; Donna Marie, b. 1957; Larry Jr., b. 1960; Laura Jean, b. 1965; edn: AA, E. Los Angeles Coll. 1959-62; USC 1962-64. Career: design engr. Albert C. Martin & Assoc., Los Angeles 1959-62; spl. projs. CST Engring. Co., L.A. 1962-63; v.p. Warner Ranch Co., Inc., L.A. 1963-69; CEO Urban Industries, Inc., Woodland Hills 1969--; awards: Resolution of Commdns: Calif. State Senate 1969; Calif. State Assembly 1969, 70; Los Angeles Co. 1969, 79; City of Los Angeles 1960, 70; Outstanding Svc. Awd., United Crusade 1981; mem: San Fernando Valley Bus. & Profl. Assn.; Val-Pac; Valley Cultural Ctr.; Assoc. CofC; Valley Ind. & Commerce Assn.; L.A. Hdqtrs. City Assn.; Woodland Hills CofC; Canoga Park CofC; mil: petty ofcr. USN Mobile Const. Battalion (Seebees) 1954-56; Republican; Catholic; rec: fishing, skiing. Res: 21801 Burbank Blvd Woodland Hills 91367 Ofc: Urban Industries, Inc., 6355 Topanga Canyon Blvd, Ste 426, Woodland Hills 91367

CALIC, NEBOJSA, jewelry/interior designer; b. April 14, 1946, Belgrade, Yugoslavia, nat. 1979; s. Ljubomir and Zivka (Zivkovic) C.; m. Mirjana Rosini, March 4, 1972; chil: Alexander, b. 1972, Petar, b. 1981; edn: BA in interior design, Univ. of Belgrade 1971; Restaurant; designer for Lola Prusac Boutique, Paris 1972-3. Award: Mus. of Applied Art, 1977. Mem. Jewelers Board of Trade, Calif. Jewelry Assn.; Democrat; Orthodox E. Ch.; rec: ice skating, skiing, tennis; res: Alameda; ofc: Calic Inc., 633 Battery St., San Francisco 94111.

CALISE, JOSEPH PETER, toxicological chemist, ret.; b. Apr. 16, 1921, NYC; s. John Peter and Julia Intorcia (Traversi) C.; m. Stephane T. Arvizo, June 28, 1981; children: Laura, b. 1948 (dec.); Lisa, b. 1955; Peter, b. 1956; Laurance, b. 1960; edn: AB, Brooklyn Coll. 1943; BS, magna cum laude, St. John's Univ. 1954; MS, 1962; pharmacists lic. NY 1954, Wash. DC 1954; Calif. 1969. Career: chemist NYC Health Dept., Bur. of Labs. 1946-65; sr. chem. (toxicology) Ofc. of Chief Med. Examiner, NYC 1965-68; asst. dir./ forensic scientist II, NJ State Med. Examiners Ofc., Newark, NJ 1969-71; pharmacist, Thrifty Drugs 1971-82; ret.; honors: Merck Awd. for Excellency in Disp. Pharm.; Rho Chi, hon. soc.; Alpha Beta chpt.; mem: ACS; APHA; VFW; Am. Legion; Italian Pharm. Assn., NY; Republican Club; pbuls: Necessity of Elution & Indentification of Drugs Indicated by Thin Layer Chromatography, Journ. of Chrom. 54, 1971, Coumbis, Fulton & Calise; mil: maj. Chemical Corps., Med. Svc. Corps. 943-59, WWII Victory; Am. Defense; ETO, 2 Battle Stars; Occupation Medal, Germany; Republican; Catholic; rec: bowling, plate collecting, painting. Res: 1821 S McPherrin Ave Monterey Park 91754

CALL, HELEN LLOYD, financial columnist/reporter; b.Oct. 2, 1917, St. Louis; d. Allen Henry and Hazel Lotus (Collins) Lloyd; gr.niece of Samuel Clemens; m. Donald Call, 1940, div.; edn: BA, Univ.of Wash. 1941. Career: pub.rels. Boeing Aircraft Co., Seattle 1941-46; staff editor Better Homes & Gardens Mag., Des Moines 1948-54; staff ed. Capper Publs., Topeka 1954-56; reporter Fresno Bee,1962-71; feature ed. Prin. columnist, San Diego Union, 1971--; syndicated columnist, Copley News Service. Mem: Soc. of Profl. Journalists, Women in Communications, Press Women, Newspaper Guild; Democrat; Roman Catholic. res: 9829 Caminito Marlock, San Diego 92131. ofc: San Diego Union, 350 Camino de la Reina, San Diego 92112.

CALLAS, NICK, insurance broker; b. Oct. 21, 1946, Salt Lake City, Utah; s. Michael D. and Margaret L. (Booke) C.; div.; children: Nicole, b. 1972; Amber, b. 1979; edn: BA, UC Northridge 1972; CFP; property casualty broker. Career: acct. exec. Calif. of Hard to Place Risks, The Internat. Mktplace.; owner Nick Callas, Ins.; Nat. Quality Awds.; mem: CofC, Lloyds; Nat. Property/Casualty Underwriters Orgn.; publs: bi-monthly newsletter; mil: USAF 1965-69, Purple Heart; Democrat; Catholic; rec: tennis, gym. Res: 1370 School House Rd Santa Barbara 93108 Ofc: Nick Callas, Ins., 5350 Hollister Ave, Ste D, Santa Barbara 93111

CALOF, SIDNEY, investor; b. Dec. 2, 1909, Winnipeg, Canada; s. Maier and Doba Calof; m. Lucille Shirley, Nov. 30, 1941; children: Lawrence, b. 1944; Rollie, b. 1946; edn: Univ. of Manitoba, Canada (2 yrs.); R.E. broker, Calif. Career: partner/ gen. mgr. Badger Paper Co., Los Angeles 1934-51; mng. fin. partner Calof Brothers, Beverly Hills 1953--; pres. Basic Service, Inc. 1958--; mil: pvt. US Army 1944; Jewish; rec: thoroughbred racing. Res: 332 N Doheny Dr Beverly Hills 90211 Ofc: Calof Brothers, 291 S La Cienega Blvd, Ste 303, Beverly Hills. 90211

CALVERT, J. RUSSELL, advertising/ marketing executive; b. Oct. 28, 1911, Los Angeles; s. Issac and Delia Bridget (Moran) C.; m. Frances Harriet Witt, June 24, 1938; children: Marie Jeannett, b. 1940; John R. Jr., b. 1942; Patricia Dianne, b. 1945; edn: BA, UC Berkeley 1932. Career: dir. mktg. Nat. Education; pres. Patrcia Stevens Career Colls.; founder/ exec. dir. No. American Sch. of Travel; v.p. Nat. Edn. Corp.; dir. advtg. Americon Ceramics; currently, owner/ pres. J. Russell Calvert & Assoc., Inc., Advtg.; prod. radio and TV pgms.; lectr. UC Irvine, seminars, local and nat. convs.; honors: Paul Harris Fellow, Rotary Internat.; mem: Am. Pub. Rels. Assn. (past pres.); Rotary (past pres.); Newport- Irvine Rotary (pres.); Honorary Texan; author: num. arts. on advtg. & mktg.; Republican; Catholic; rec; photog. Address: Calvert & Assoc., Inc., 56 Encanto Tustin 92680

CALVO, KEVIN EDWARD, orthotist- prosthetist; b. Jan. 11, 1957, New Orleans, La.; s. Raymond Philip and Elle (McConnell) C.; m. Lisa Northey, June 10, 1978; edn: AA, Delgado Jr. Coll. 1978; orthotics cert., Tulane Post Grad. Med. Sch. 1978; prosthetics cert., UCLA Post Grad. Med. Sch. 1979; prosthetics cert., New York Univ. 1980; cert. orthotic- prosthetic tech. 1977; cert. prosthetic practitioner 1981. Career: orthotic- prosthetic tech. apprentice, Lamberts Limb & Brace, New Orleans, La. part- time 1977-78; orthotic-prosthetic asst. Harbor Orthopedics, San Diego 1978-80; chief of orth.- pros. lab. & research/ orth.- pros. practitioner, VA Hosp., La Jolla 1980-82; research orth.- pros., VA Hosp., La Jolla, part- time 1981--; owner/ orth.- pros., Bionics of La Jolla, San Diego 1981--; orth.- pros. cons., mfr., and designer orth.- pros. devices for Calexico Valley Orthopedic Clinic, profl. cons. var. San Diego Hosps.; mem: Am. Acad. of Orth.- Pros.; Amputees in Motion (Adv. Bd.); works: Orthotic appliances for the foot, FirmFits, pat. pend.; balance suspension knee orthosis for lack of anterior cruciate ligaments, pat. pend.; Catholic; rec: golf, racquetball, sailing. Res: 946 Valley Ave Solana Beach 92075 Ofc: Bionics of La Jolla, De Anza View Med. Ctr., 3737 Moraga Ave, Ste 220, San Diego 92117

CAMELLO, MARLOWE ONDA, lawyer; b. Jan. 17, 1935, Malaybalay, Bukidnon, Philippines, nat. 1980; s. Cornelio Araquel and Basilia (Onda) C.; m. Jean Guaren Jugador, Dec. 19, 1960; 1 son: Victor J., b. 1961; edn: acctg., Notre Dame Univ., Cotabato City, Philippines 1957-62, law, 1963-67, admitted, State Bar of Calif. 1979; Philippine Supreme Ct. 1968. Career: eng. clerk Dist. Engrs. Ofc., Cotabato City, Philippines 1957-62; bookeeper Cotabato Hosp., Cotabato City, Philippines 1962-68; assoc. atty. Comello, Millan & Assoc., Cotabato City 1968-72; gen. acct. A&E Allied Plastics, Los Angeles, Calif. 1972-76; gen. acct. Elgin Davis, Inc., L.A. 1976-78; sr. acct. American Telecomm., Inc., Anaheim 1978-79; atty. at law, Law Ofcs. of Marlowe O. Camello, L.A. 1979--; substitute law prof., Notre Dame Univ., Cotabato City, Philippines 1969-71; mem; Integrated Bar of the Philippines; State Bar of Calif.; YMCA, Cotabato City 1969-72; Democrat; Catholic; rec: outings. Res: 13686 Ramona Pkwy Baldwin Park 91706 Ofc: Law Ofcs. of Marlowe O. Camello, 2323 W Beverly Blvd, Ste 201, Los Angeles 90057

CAMERON, JEFF CHARLES, research scientist; b. Sept. 12, 1954, Pomona; s. Hugh Donald and Janet (Leone) C.; edn: BS, pend., CSU Long Beach. Career: with Northrop Research & Tech., Rolling Hills 1979--; opr. 1979; programmer 1980; sys. prgmr. 1981; data processing mgr./ research & tech. staff 1983--; chprs. Gould SEL West Coast User's Gp.; awards: Achiev. Awd. in field of Trades & Ind., Bank of Am. 1973; mem: Gould SEC Users Gp.; Digital Equip. Users Soc. (DECUS); Greenpeace; The Planetary Soc.; Cousteau Soc.; Democrat; rec: music, electronics. Res: 24053 Ocean Ave, 2, Torrance 90505 Ofc: Northrop Research, No. 1 Research Park, 330/T60, Rolling Hills 90274

CAMFERDAM, STEVEN ROBERT, employee benefits consultant; b. Apr. 12, 1954, Memphis, Tenn.; s. Henry N. and Jean M. (York) C.; edn: BS, Univ. Ill. 1976. Career: life insurance actuary Occidental Life of Calif., Los Angeles 1976-78; pension actuary Transamerica Life and Annuity Co., L.A.1978-80; pension actuary Hewitt Assocs., Newport Beach 1980-81, cons. Hewitt Assoc., Los Angeles 1981-83, cons./office mgr. Hewitt Assocs., Phoenix 1983--; served on Soc. of Actuaries Part 6 Exam. Com. 1981-2; honors: Fellow Soc. of Actuaries 1980; Enrolled Actuary 1982; mem. Am. Acad. of Actuaries 1983. Mem: L.A. Actuarial Club 1973-83; Western Pension Conf. 1982-; Phi Delta Theta frat. 1972-; Toastmasters Club 613 (pres. 1978-80); Soc. of Actuaries 1978-. Republican; Episcopal; rec: scuba diving, waterskiing, hiking. res: 7045 N. 7th St. /e206, Phoenix, AZ 85020. ofc: Hewitt Associates, 4041 N. Central Ave. Ste. 530, Phoenix, AZ 85012.

CAMPAGNA, EDWARD THOMAS, physician; b. Oct. 1, 1944, Buffalo, NY; s. Vincent Joseph and Mary Antonetta (D'Agostino) C.; m. Margaret, Sept. 6, 1969; children: Mark, b. 1972; Laura, b. 1976; John, b. 1981; edn: BS, Canisius Coll. 1966; MD, Creighton Univ. Sch. of Med. 1970; intern, Millard Fillmore Hosp., Buffalo 1971; res., internal med., 1974; diplomate, Am. Bd. of Internal Med. 1976. Career: pvt. practice Gen. Intern Med., Palcentia 1976; chief of dept. of med. Placentia Linda Comm. Hosp. 1978-82; v. chief of staff 1983--; awards: Dexter S. Levy Awd., for excellence in bedside med., Millard Fillmore Hosp 1974; mem: AMA, CMA OCMA, ASIM, CSIM, ACP; mil: maj. US Army 1974-76, Nat. Defense 1975, Korean Svc. 1976; Republican; Catholic; rec: golf, tennis. Res: 19282 Stonecrest Ln Yorba Linda 92686 Ofc: The Internal Medical Gp., 1041 E Yorba Linda Blvd, Se 5, Placentia 92670

CAMPANELLA, MARY, life insurance agent; b. Dec. 18, 1944, Cleveland, Ohio; d. Camillo and Carmela (Ratino) C.; m. Thom Gray Rome, May 17, 1969; edn: BA, sociol., Kent State Univ. 1966; lic: real estate broker, 1981, life ins., 1982, Calif.; NASD lic., 1984. Career: stewardess United Air Lines, 1966-69; asst. buyer Sak's Fifth Ave., 1973-75; pres., West 2, 1975-82; life insurance agent, spl. agent Northwestern Mutual Life, San Diego 1982--; honors: Million Dollar Round Table, 1983. Mem: Nat., San Diego Assn. of Life Underwriters; Combo Connection (support the arts)S.D.; Woman's Democratic Club of S.D.; Dem.; Catholic; rec: photog.; res: 3319 Tennyson, San Diego 92106; ofc: Northwestern Mutual, 233 A St., Ste.800, San Diego 92101.

CAMPBELL, DALMAR JOHN, publisher; b. Nov. 29, 1939, Merced; s. Dale Keegan and Marguerite Grace (Dexter) C.; m. Charlotte Ruth Burney, Apr. 1, 1978; children: Mark, b. 1962; Lori, b.1964; Tami, b. 1966; step-children: Gregg, b. 1960; Jeff, b. 1963; Laura, b. 1965; edn: AA, Fresno City Coll. 1968; BA, CSU Fullerton 1974; 5th yr tchg. cred., 1976; fine arts tchr. K-14; indsl. arts tchr. 7-12. Career: parts salesman; plywood salesman; artist; sculpturer; sign painter; publisher; publisher Mariposa Gezette; tchr. off campus courses Fresno City Coll. 1976-78; honors: Soc. of Profl. Journalists; VFW Citation; mem: CNPA; CPA; Sigma Delta Chi; Masons; Moose Lodge; Rotary; Hosp. Found.; Arts Council; CofC; works: paintings (oil), San Joaquin Art Anual 1975; var. other shows; metal sculpture; owner ceramics bus.; mil: spec. 4/c US Army 1956-64; Democrat; Protestant; rec: ceramics, metal sculpture, painting. Res: 4576 Yaqui Gulch Rd Mariposa 95338 Ofc: Mariposa Gazette, POB 38, 9th & Jones, Mariposa 95338

CAMPBELL, LEWIS VANCE, JR., physician; b. Apr. 15, 1940, Crown City, Ohio; s. Lewis V., Sr. and Thelma C. (Moore) C.; desc. (mat. gr.gr.gr.uncle) Gen. Robert E. Lee; m. Jewel Zonner, July 14, 1962; children: Valerie Lynne, b. 1963, Nicole Romelle, b. 1969; edn: BS, Ohio State Univ. 1963; MD, West Va. Univ. 1967. Career: civil engrlng. survey party chiof Gallia County Engrs. Ofc., Gallipolis, Oh. 1959-63; med. intern West Va. Univ. Med. Ctr., Morgantown, W.Va. 1967; capt. USAF,chief flt. & missile med. Vandenberg (Ca.) AF Hosp. 1968, and dir. aerospace med. Vandenberg AFB 1969-70; sr. resident Dept. Ob.-Gyn., Ohio St. Univ. 1971-72; chief res. Ob-Gyn. Univ. Louisville Sch. Med. 1973; gynecological surgeon & obstetrician, pvt. practice Lompoc; chmn. Dept. Ob-Gyn. Lompoc Dist. Hosp. 1974-; physician in charge Santa Barbara Co. Family Health Care Clinic 1973-77; awards: Claude Worthington Benedum Found. med. sch. scholarship 1966; Phi Beta Pi (v. Archon); mem: Aerospace Med. Assn. 1968-70; AMA; Lompoc CofC, Diplomate Nat. Bd. Med. Examiners 1968; Royal Soc. of Med.; Am. Coll. Obstets & Gyn. (jr. fellow 1970-); Am. Fertility Soc., Elks; arts. in med. journals; mil. awds: Nat Defense Medal, Expt. Marksman, AF Unit Cit.; Republican; Ch. of Christ; rec: exotic pets (cougar, alligator, python). Res: 1231 Mesa Oaks Ln Lompoc 93436 Ofc: L.V. Campbell, OB-Gyn, 521 E. Ocean Ave Lompoc 93436

CAMPBELL, RONALD LEROY, psychologist; b. Oct. 1, 1934, Butler, Pa.; s. Albert Edwin and Min Aleta (Larimore) C.; m. Carmen Martinez, 1971; edn: AA in bus., San Francisco City Coll. 1957; BA & MA, anthropology, CSU San Francisco, 1962-77; MPA pub. adm., cnsortium of CSUs, 1975-78, MA, clin. psychol., Antioch Univ. 1980; PhD, integral psychol., Calif. Inst. of Integral Studies. Career: owner, mgr. Watkins Prods. (sales orgn.) 1961; supr., partner Annette's Bakery 1962; exec. dir. Ctr. for the Holistic Scis., Menlo Park 1974-81; counseling/psychology,Counselors and Consultants, Inc., Menlo Park, San Jose 1982--; instr. UCB ext., Univ. of S.F., Goldengate Univ., Chapman Colls., 1968-81; mem. bd. govs. Calif. Inst. of Integral Studies, 1982; pres. Integral Science Inst., 1983-; editor Phoenix Jour.of Transpersonal Anthropology, 1977-; contbg. ed. Bay Area Anthropol. News 1974-79; res. in Am.-Mex. comm. devel. proj. in rural village, Mex. 1966, in Indian village, Mex. 1977. Awards: Darsansagar Dipl. 1970; cultural integration fellowship for resrch in Asian and integral studies; appreciation, Local 101 AFL-CIO, 1978; Mem: Assn. for Transpersonal Anthropol. Internat. (bd.trustees 1983-84, v.p. 1981-82), Calif. Inst. of Integral Studies Alumni Assn. (pres. 1982), AAAS, Am. Soc. for Pub. Adminstrn., Assn. for Transpersonal Psychology, Am. Anthropol. Assn., Soc. for the Anthropol. of Visual Communication. Author: Anthropological Field Tng. in Hweyapon, Mexico: A Critique with Brief Ethnography; The Concept of Man in Integral Psychology; Extinction Perio; The Photo Symbolistic Technique; Alicia: A Woman's Journey into Conscious Living. Contbr. num. arts., books, film revs., scholarly jours. Mil: airman 2d cl. US Army, USAR, Air Nat. Guard, 1953-60. Democrat; Unitarian; rec: homing pigeons, martial arts, travel. res: 6 Big Tree Rd. Woodside 94062. ofc: 845 Oak Grove Ave. Menlo Park 94025.

CAMPBELL, W. GLENN, director Hoover Instn. on War, Revolution and Peace; b. Apr. 29, 1924, Komoka, Ont., Can.; nat. 1953; s. Alfred Edwin and Delia (O'Brien) C.; m. Rita Ricardo, Sept. 15, 1946; chil: Barbara Lee (Bizewski), b. 1954, Diane Rita (Porter), b. 1956, Nancy Elizabeth, b. 1960; edn: BA, Univ. W. Ont. 1944, MA, Harvard Univ. 1946, PhD, 1948. Career: instr. in econ. Harvard Univ. 1948-51; resrch econ. US CofC, Wash DC 1951-54; resrch dir. Am. Enterprise Inst. for Public Policy Resrch, Wash DC 1954-60, program adviser 1960-; dir. Hoover Instn. on War, Revolution and Peace, Stanford 1960--; chmn. Pres's Intell. Oversight Bd., 1981-; mem. Pres's Fgn. Intell. Advis. Bd., 1981-; chmn. Am. Panel of the Jt. Com. on Japan-US Cultural and Ednl. Coop., 1983-; chmn. Japan-US Friendship Commn. 1983-; mem. Bd. of Regents, Univ. Calif. 1968- (chmn. 1982); mem. Nat. Sci. Bd., Nat. Sci.

Found., 1972-78; mem. Pres's Com. on Sci. and Tech. 1976; mem. Pres's Commn. on White House Fellow 1969-74; chmn. Reagan-Bush Task Force on Edn. 1980; mem. Reagan-Bush Task Force on Fgn. Policy (1980) and Task Force on Inflation Policy (1980); mem. Personnel Advis. Com. to Pres. Reagan 1980-81; bd. dirs. Com. on the Present Danger, 1976-; bd. dirs. Mont Pelerin Soc. 1980-; mem. Adv. Bd. Ctr. for Strategic and Internat. Studies, Georgetown Univ. 1980-; mem. bd.vis. Bernice P. Bishop Mus., Honolulu 1979-; trustee Herbert Hoover Presdtl. Lib. Assn. 1964-. Mil: Canadian Navy 1943-44. res: 26915 Alejandro Dr. Los Altos Hills 94022. ofc: Hoover Instn. Stanford 94305

CAMPBELL, WILLIAM RICHARD, publishing executive; b. Oct. 18, 1939, Omaha, Nebr.; s. Myron Torbert and Margaret Louise (Swisher) C.; children: Wendy, b. 1964, Timothy, b. 1966, Tod, b. 1966; edn: BS, Bradley Univ. 1961. Career: salesman/mgr. Scott Paper Co., 1961-64; sales mgr./dir. mktg. American Hosp. Assn., 1964-70; dir. sales & mktg. Healthcom Pub. Co., 1970-72; owner Fox Ad West, 1972-82; co-owner Mediacor, Inc. (publishing firm), Oakland 1982--; listed Who's Who in Advt. Mem: Medical Mktg. & Media, Bradley Alumni Club, Sigma Chi Alumni Club (secty); publs: arts in Medical Mktg. & Media, Am. Surgical Dealer; mil: cpl. USM.R 1961-67; Republican; Lutheran; rec: sports, antique autos. Res: 2126 Greencrest Dr El Cajon 92020 Ofc: Mediacor, Inc. 2204 Lakeshore Ave, Ste 9, Oakland 94606

CANAWATI, HANNA N., clinical microbiologist; b. Nov. 18, 1938, Bethlehem, nat. 1984; s. Nakhleh Hanna and Armen Hagop (Elian) C.; m. Gehad B., Sept. 7, 1968; children: Isam, b. 1969; Imad, b. 1972; Maram, b. 1981; edn: MS, Roosevelt Univ. 1971; PhD, The Chgo. Med. Sch. 1974; doctor in clinical microbiology 1974; spec. microbiologist, Am. Acad. of Microbiology 1977. Career: currently, pres./ chmn. Liver Research Found., USC Liver Unit (an internat. research unit); chief Microbiological Svcs., Rancho Los Amigos Co. Hosp., Downey; asst. prof., Dept. Pathology USC Sch. Med.; also, microbiology cons., St. Luke Hosp., Pasadena; part- time cons. var hosps. San Gabriel Valley Reg.; instr., USC Dominguez Hills MS pgm.; honors: sev. grants an principal investigator & co- investigator in multiple research projs. (infected feet of diabetic patients, activity of antibiotics agents bactercia); mem: Am. Soc. for Microbiology (Nat. & Calif.); New York Acad. of Sci.; Am. Acad. of Microbiolgy; Los Angeles World Affairs Council; publs: 20 publs. on antibiotics, human infections, etc.; 30 abstracts presented at ASM nat. meetings; sev. research projs. in clinical microbiology under investigation; St. Nicholas Orthodox Cathedral, L.A.; rec: art work, stamp collecting, travel. Res: 1151 Villa St Montebello 90640 Ofc: Rancho Los Amigos Hosp., 7601 E Imperial Hwy Downey 90242

CANDIA, JOSE M., sales and marketing executive; b. Jan. 20, 1949, Lima, Peru; s. Juan M. and Consuelo O. Candia; m. Lydia E. Coats, Nov. 14, 1981; 1 son, Alexander, b. 1982; edn: AA, bus. adminstrn., Northwood Inst., 1968; BA, Inst. Superior Latino Am. Admin. 1970; postgrad. wk. in fin., mktg., inventory control, 1973. Career: industrial rels. mgr. Cerro De Pasco Corp., 1970; plant administrator Warner Lambert Internat., 1973, planning & inventory control mgr., 1974; account exec. Pacific Tel. & Tel., 1976; sales mgr. General Dynamics Communication Co., 1980; regl. sales mgr. United Technologies Comm. Co., 1981--, nat. and major accounts mgr. Western Div.; internat. bus. cons. to Latin Am. business; Republican; rec: golf, soccer, chess. Res: 5031 Siesta Lane, Yorba Linda 92686 Ofc: United Technologies, 5440 McConnell Ave Los Angeles 90066

CANFIELD, JACK, educator; b. Aug. 19, 1944, Ft. Worth, Tex.; s. Elmer Elwyn and Ellen Waterhouse (Taylor) C.; m. Judy Ohlbaum, July 1, 1973, div. 1977; m. 2d. Georgia Noble, Sept. 9, 1089; children: Oran, b. 1974; Kyle, b. 1976; edn: BA, Harvard Univ. 1966; Univ. of Chgo. 1966-68; M.Ed., Univ. of Mass. 1973. Career: tchr. Calumnet H.S., Chgo. 1967-68; dir. tchr. tng. pgm. Clinton Job Corps. Ctr., Clinton, Iowa 1968-69; assoc. dir. ednl. pgms. W. Clement & Jessie V. Stone Found., Chgo. 1969-70; founder/ dir. New England Ctr., Amherst, Ma. 1971-77; dir. Inst. for Wholistic Edn., Amherst, Ma. 1976-81; dir. ednl. svcs. INSIGHT Tng. Sems., Santa Monica 1981-83; pres. Self- Esteem Sems., Pacific Palisades 1983--; lect. Caif. Lutheran Coll.; cons. Beverly Hills Sch. Dist.; editorial bd. Journ. of Humanistic Education 1980-84; editorial bd. Psychosynthesis Digest 1982-; bd. adv. Holistic Edn. Network Newsletter; bd. adv. Univ. for Humanistic Studies 1982-; awards: Outstanding Young Men of AM., US Jaycees 1978; Cert. of Appreciation, US Job Corps. 1969; Community Ldrs. of Am., Am. Biographical Inst. 1979-80; mem: Assn. for Humanistic Edn.; Assn. for Humanistic Psychology; Assn. for Transpersonal Psychology; Holistic Edn. Network; Am. Personnel & Guidance Assn.; Nat. Spkrs. Assn.; Ednl. Leadership Council of Am.; Planetary Citizens; publs: About Me, 1970; coauthor w/ Harold Wells, 100 Ways to Enhance Self-Concept in the Classroom (15th printing 1976); A Guide to Resources in Humanistic and Transpersonal Education, 1981; contbr., Time to Win, 1981; (w/ Marge Krubiner) Personalized Learning, 1984; Democrat; Christian; rec: tennis, running, racquetball. Address: Self-Esteem Seminars, 17156 Palisades Cir Pacific Palisades 90272

CANNATA, DEIRDRE MARY, realtor; b. Apr. 28, 1929, Cashel, Co. Tipperary, Ireland, nat. 1960; d. John William and Kathleen (Carroll) Healy; m. Sam. T. Cannata, Aug. 12, 1957; children: Elaine, b. 1958; Sammy G., b. 1959; John, b. 1964; edn: Presentation Convent, Cashel, Ireland; Sion Hill, Coll., Dublin. Career: realtor Sunset Co. Realtors 1970; realtor Pitts & Bachmann 1981; bd. dirs. Montecito Sanitary Dist. 1974; pres. of bd. 1979; chmn. of dist. dirs. Calif. Assn. of Sanitation Agencies (CASA); mem: Boot Club (Italian); Assn. of Retarded Citizens, Santa Barbara; Republican; Catholic; rec: tennis, garden-

ing, civic involvement. Res: 844 Skyview Dr Montecito Santa Barbara 93108 Ofc: Pitts & Bachmann, 1106B Coast- Village Rd Santa Barbara 93108

CANTOR, JON DAVID, lawyer; b. Nov. 21, 1951, Los Angeles; s. Albert and Audrey Ann. (Benesch) C.; m. Arlene, June 24, 1973; 1 dau: Lauren Michele, b. 1981; edn: BS, CSU Northridge 1973; JD, San Fernando Valley Coll. of Law 1980. Career: sole practitioner 1980-83; partner Law Ofcs. Fred DeLuca, Jr., Sherman Oaks 1983--; honors: Law Review; Corpus Juris Secundum Inc.; Admanson Scolarship; mem: Calif. State Bar; Los Angeles Co. Bar ASsn.; rec: racquetball. Res: 19108 Staff Street Reseda 91335 Ofc: Law Ofcs. of Fred DeLuca Jr., 4560 Sherman Oaks Ave Sherman Oaks 91403

CANTOS, EARL JAMES, JR., lawyer; b. June 12, 1956, San Francisco; s. Judge Earl James and Irene Rita (Trifiatis) C.; edn: BS in bus. mgt., CSU San Diego 1978, JD, Univ. ofSan Diego 1981. career: real estate broker, v.p., secty. Cantos Realty, a Calif. Corp., 1974--; assoc. law offices of Glen R. Roberts, 1981-82; prop. law offices of Earl J. Cantos, Jr., San Diego 1982--. awards: Laurels for Leaders, 1974. mem: Battered Women's Svcs-YWCA (adv. bd. mem. 1980-); Am. Bar Assn.; San Diego Co. Bar Assn. (Immigration Com. 1982-, liaison between S.D. and Tijuana, Mex. 1982-, Internat. Law Sect. 1982-); S.D. Trial Lawyers Assn.; Barristers; Phi Alpha Delta legal frat. (v.p. 1980-1); Nat., Calif. Assn. of Realtors, 1974-; S.D. Bd. of Realtors, 1974-; Christian Legal Soc.; Saints Constantine and Helen Greek Orth. Ch. Parish Council (Young Adult League adv. 1979-, choir); Opa Greek Folk Dance Troupe; Sigma Chi frat.; Life Loyal Sig.; Toastmasters Internat.; World Trade Assn. inventor: patented wind percussion instrument (1979); background singer for Light of Heaven (prod. Erini Prodns. label) by Rita Cantos Cartwright; contbg. ed. En Banc, law jour. Univ. of S.D 1980-1. Republican (Calif. State Central Com.1981-; Repub. Assocs.; Young Repubs.; Repub. Bus. & Profl. Club). Greek Orth. rec: Greek folk dancing, singing, ski. res: 4462 35th St. San Diego 92116. Law ofc. Earl J. Cantos,Jr. 4178 Adams Av. Ste.1, San Diego 92116.

CANTOS, IRENE RITA, real estate broker; b. Aug. 25, 1922, NYC, d. Angelo and Mabel (Flementon) Trifiatis; m. Earl J. Cantos, Jan. 26, 1947; children: Rita (Cartwright), b. 1948, Earl, Jr., b. 1956, Roxanne (Fulkerson), b. 1060, Wm. J., b. 1963; edn: B.Music, Southwestern Coll. (now Rhodes Coll.), 1944. Career: real estate broker/pres. Cantos Realty, 1972--; pres. Erini Productions, 1980--; honors: Citizen of the Year 1962, San Diego Masonic Club, Woman of Achievement 1980; mem: Globe Guilders, S.D. Sym. Aux., S.D. Bar Aux., Women's Council of Realtors S.D. Chpt., Musical Merit Found., Freedom Found. at Valley Forge; author: Oh! What's the Use (diet book) 184; Republican; Greek Orthodox; avocation: singer. Res: 5249 Marlborough Dr San Diego 92116 Ofc: Cantos Realty, 4178 Adams Ave San Diego 92116

CANTU, FELIPE RODRIGUEZ, vocational rehabilitation consultant; b. Aug. 30, 1925, Brownsville, Tex.; s. Felipe Gamboa and Elvira (Rodriguez) C.; m. Paula Rosas, Nov. 22, 1943; children: Felipe jr., b. 1947; Frances, b. 1949; Felix, b. 1951; Federico, b. 1953; Fernando, b. 1954; Gabriel, b. 1967 (adpt.); edn: AA, Allan Hancock Coll. 1972; BS, Cal Poly, SLO 1978; MA, 1978; comm. coll. counselor cred. 1978; comm. coll. limited svc. cred. 1976. Career: paralegal Calif. Rural Legal Asstance, Santa Maria 1974; conselor Community Action Com., Santa Maria 1974-76; pgm. ops. ofcr. Gr. Calif. Edn. Proj., Santa Maria 1978-80; rehab. counselor Crawford Rehabilitation Svcs., San Luis Obispo 1981-82; owner vocational rehab. firm, Cantu Associates 1982--; awards: Rebilitant of the YR., Calif. Dept. Rehab., Santa Barbara Dist. 1974; mem: Nat. Rehab. Counseling Assocs.; Nat. Rehab. Assn.; US CofC; Santa Maria Valley CofC; Nat. Fedn. Independ. Bus.; Loyal Order of the Moose; mil: US Army parachute infantry 1944-45; Democrat; Catholic; rec: woodwork, oil painting. Res: 211 Prescott Ln Santa Maria 93454 Ofc: Cantu Associates, 500 S Broadway, Ste 217, Santa Maria 93454

CAPPS, ANTHONY T. (CAPOZZOLO), international public relations executive; b. Apr. 19, Pueblo, CO; s. Nicolo and Ann (Salomone) Capozzolo; desc. Antonio Capozzolo, signed Peace Document with King Ferdinand of Spain, 1471; grandson of Domenico Capozzolo, ofcr. in Garabaldi's Army, freed Italy (ancestors early founders of Lucania and Christians of King Solomon's Tribe, migrated to Naples with St. Peter because of Roman persecutions); great-grandson, Mayor of Naples, Italy; ed. L.A. Bus. Coll.; Pueblo, CO; pvt. tutor, arts and music stud.; m. Theresa Cecelia Harmon, Hollywood, CA, Nov. 12, 19. Career: Dance dir., choreographer, prod. mot. pic., TV and radio; feat. Profl. Dance Team, Biltmore Bowl, Cocoanut Grove, L.A.; St. Catherine Hotel, Catalina, 1939-42; dance dir., and prod. NBC, ABC, KCOP-TV, Columbia Pics., 20th Century Fox and Calif. studios, 1940-60; govt. tours, Puerto Rico, Cuba, Jamaica, Dominican Repub., Haiti, 1954; prod. "Latin Holiday," TV series of Latin Amer.; numerous TV interviews on RElig. and Polit. Hist. of Bailet and Opera of last 500 yrs.; exec. dir. Lockheed and Vega Aircraft Co. activities, Burbank, L.A., Glendale, Pomona, Pasadena, Bakersfield, Taft, CA plants; Internatl. pub. rels. dir.: Howard Manor, Palm Springs Key Club, Country Club Hotel, Palm Springs Ranch Club; George Cameron Jr., owner, Desert Sun Newspapers, KDES Radio, Palm Springs, Cameron Center and Cameron Enterprises and Oil Co., Burbank radio sta.; Murietta Hot Springs Hotel, Health and Beauty Spa, Palm Springs-Coachella Valley. Founder-pres.-dir., Tony Capps Enterprises (real estate investments, pub. rels., publicity, promotions): chmn., exec. dir.: golf and tennis tournaments, benefit dinners for civic leaders, govs., senators, congressmen, United Fund for City of Hope (3 times), Natl. Cystic Fibrosis Fund, Palm Springs (Bob Hope) Golf Classic; created adv. "gimmick" for Colgate and Cugat, Coca Cola; founder-pres., Natl. Artists and Art Patrons Soc. of City of Hope, est. Anthony Capps Art Galler Med. Center; founder-pres., Tri-County Chpt., Natl. Football Found. and Hall of Fame, U.S.,

Japan and Canada; founder, co-chmn., The Natl. Football Found. and Hall of Fame Annual Golf Classic at Palm Springs, CA for over 65 chpts. in 50 states of the U.S.A. Columnist: The American Film Institute Wash. D.C.; The Reporter, 1962-63; and Desert Sun, Palm Springs; L.A. Daily News. Mem.: (charter) Eisenhower Mem. Hosp. Aux.; bd. dirs., Opera Guild of the Desert; bd. dirs., Palm Springs Pathfinders; Desert Art Center of Coachella Valley; Palm Springs Desert Mus.; natl. mem., AFTRA; Smithsonian Inst., Wash. D.C.; advis. bd., Amer. Security Council, Wash., D.C.; L.A. Co. Museum of Arts (Patron); The Cousteau Soc., Internationale, 1973; Natl. Trust for Hist. Preservation, Wash., D.C.; clubs: Balboa Bay. Catholic. Rec.: charities. Res.: 2715 Junipero Ave., Palm Springs.

CARAS, ALAN MEYER, consultant; b. Apr. 18, 1939, Lawrence, Mass.; s. Mitchell Ralph and Gertrude (Zuckerman) C.; m. Selma Saitin, Apr. 12, 1964; chil: Daani-Ruth, b. 1964, Samuel, b. 1966, Benjamin, b. 1973; edn: BS in bus.ad., Suffolk Univ. 1961. Career: budget mgr. J.M.Fields, Inc. 1962-65; accounting mgr. Zayre Corp., 1965; budget dir. Rust Craft Greeting Cards, 1965-67; controller Caceres-Johnson Corp., Hato Rey, Puerto Rico 1967-68; div. controller Computing & Software, Inc. 1968-70; cons. in personnel, 1970-72; acctg. mgr. Jewish Fedn. Council of Gr. Los Angeles, 1972-73; pres. Corporate Dimensions Inc. 1973--. Public speaker, vol. cons. to immigrant settlement pgm., staffing assistance to ethnic self-help groups. Listed: Who's Who Among Students in Am. Colls & Univs (1961), Who's Who in the West. Mem: Culver City CofC, pres. student chpt. Soc. for Adv. of Mgmt., 1960-61; treas. student chpt. Am. Mktg. Assn., 1960. Mil: USAR 1961-67. Republican. Jewish. rec: woodworking. ofc: Corporate Dimensions Inc., 8599 Venice Bl., Los Angeles 90034.

CARDALL, ESTHER ANN, community volunteer; b. June 18, 1930, Sprague, Wash.; d. James Patrick and Gladys R. (Rhoden) McDonnell; m. John Tellefson, Jan. 1951; children: Beth, b. 1957, Christopher, b. 1958; m. 2d. Alfred Cardall, III, Aug. 7, 1964; edn: stu. Portland State Univ. 1948-50; BA, CSU San Diego 1964, MSW, 1967, Cert. Bus. Adm. 1972; Calif. lic. Clin. Soc. Wkr. (LCSW) 1969. Career: mgr. Orange Stamp Redemption Ctr., Alfred M. Lewis Inc., San Diego 1959-62; jr. soc. wkr./sr. soc. wkr. San Diego Dept. of Soc. Svcs. 1964-66, supvr., San Diego 1967, sr. supvr., San Diego & El Cajon 1968-72, case mgmt. cons. 1972, welfare adminstr. 1975--, chief Dependent Chil./asst. div. chief Food Stamps & Medi-Cal 1975-80, chief Employment Svcs. 1980-81; vol. cons. to Dept. of Pub. Svcs. 1983-84, called back (temp.) to cons. on redesign of Childrens Services 1984; worked on reorgzn. public social services for abused & neglected children; implemented a new data proc. Social Svc. Recording Syst.; mem. Calif. Childrens Lobby ad hoc com. on SB14, 1983, past pres Human Resources Agcy. Foster Service Com. 1974-78; worked with Youth Law Ctr. (SB14 nat. grant) 1983; recognition honors: Salvation Army (1964), S.D. County Sch. Dist. (1966), S.D. Youth Services (1975), S.D. County Dept. of Social Svcs. (1983), Parents United (1983, cofounder), mem. S.D. Community Child Abuse Coord. Council (bd. mem., past pres.), Nat. Assn. of Soc. Wkrs. 1967-77, Calif. St. Juvenile Officers Assn. 1976-79, S.D. Zool. Soc. (Keepers Club), YWCA of S.D. (bd., ofcr.), Urban League (past bd.), Crime Victims Fund (past bd.), Big Sisters League (past bd.), Children in Placement (v.p. 1982-); Spousal Abuse Shelter (Monroe Co., Fla.) 1982; writer var. ednl. pamphlets, arts. in field; Democrat; rec: liturgical organ (Svc. Playing cert., Am. Guild of Organists 1983). Res: 92920 Overton Ave San Diego 92123 Ofc: San Diego Co. Dept. Soc. Svcs. 6950 Levant St San Diego 92111

CARDENAS, SAMARA P., pediatrician; b. Sept. 6, 1948, Havana, Cuba; d. Jose Antonio and Maria Amparo (Valls) Palacio; m. Roberto Cardenas, Aug. 27, 1965; children: Roberto, b. 1974; Carlos, b. 1980; Jorge, b. 1982; edn: AA, Los Angeles City Coll. 1970; BS, Los Angeles State Univ. 1972; med. degree, Univ. of Irvine, Calif. Coll. of Med. 1975; pediatrician, Am. Acad. of Pediatricians 1981. Career: sole practitioner, pediatrician 1978--; chprsn. Pediatric Dept. Martin Luther Hosp., and Anaheim Meml. Hosp.; clinical prof. UCI-CCM; mem: fellow, Am. Acad. of Pediatrics; AMA; CMA; Orange Co. Med. Assn.; Los Angeles Pediatric Soc.; Orange Co. Pediatric Soc.; Republican; Catholic; rec: soccer, embroidery, skiing. Res: 1120 W La Palma Ave Anaheim 92801

CARDINALE, LORETTA ANN, real estate broker; b. Oct. 24, 1913, Beloit, Kans.; d. Charles Edward and Frances (Spannan) Rasher; m. Glen Clinton Lowry, Feb. 20, 1946 (dec. 1973); children: Nancy Ann (Newcome); Elizabeth Jane (Krupka); m. 2d. Frank Cardinale; step-children: Frank, Dominic, Raymond; edn: grad. Am. Inst. Banking 1941; San Fernando Valley Coll. 1965. Career: asst. cashier First Nat. Bank, Beloit 1943-46; co-owner, partner Lowry Real Estate & Ins., Beloit 1946-62; co-owner Lowry Real Estate, Calimesa, Ca. 1962--; Riverside Co. Registrar of Voters, 1965-70; mem. Citizens Com. for New Gen. Plan for Riverside Co., Residential and Comml., 1970-73; troop ldr. Girl Scouts USA, Beloit 1951-60; mem: Nat. Assn. Real Estate Bds.; Am. Assn. Ret. Persons; Am. Field Svc. Assn.; VFW Aux.; Catholic Daus. Am.; Bus & Profl. Womens Club; Calif. R.E. Assn.; Sons and Daus. Soddies; Yucaipa Valley Bd. Realtors (treas. 1966); Calimesa CofC (dir. 1965-71); Calif. Assn. Ind. Businessmen; Redlands Yucaipa Hort. Soc.; Soroptimist; Yucaipa Womens Club; Republican; Catholic. Res: POB 117 Calimesa 92320 Ofc: 543 W County Line 27 Rd Calimesa 92320

CAREY, DAVID EDWARD, chiropractor; b. Dec. 13, 1947, San Francisco; s. Richard Wilson and Elaine Inez (Smith) C.; m. Sandra, July 26, 1969; children: Kimberly, b. 1976, Todd, b. 1978, Heather, b. 1980; edn: AS, Foothill Coll. 1974; DC, Palmer Coll. of Chiro. 1978. Career: flew as medical tech. in Air Rescue HH43 Helicopter, S.E. Asia; post mil. grad. Orthopedic Phys. Asst.; traveled as team doctor rep. USA and Sports Ambassadors in Dominican Republic 1981, in Costa Rica 1983; chiropractor pvt. practice, Placerville 1978--. honors. Pi Tau Delta (chiro.); mem. Am., Calif. Chiropractic Assns.; mil: E4 USAF Vietnam Svc, Air Medal, GCM. Res: 2850 Loyal Ln Pollock Pines 95726 Ofc: Hangtown Chiropractic Center 7533 Green Valley Rd Placerville 95667

CARLSEN, RUSSELL ARTHUR, real estate executive/ housing director; b. Sept. 25, 1945, Cleveland Hgts., Ohio; s. Russell Arthur and Betty Jane (Issel) C.; edn: BA, (constitutional hist. & political sociology), Univ. of Wash. 1977; John Carroll Univ. 1963-67; MPA, cand. Golden Gate Univ. 1982-; R.E. broker. Career: gen. mgr. H&H Assocs., Berkeley 1974-79; dir. Seattle Housing Svc., Seattle, Wash. 1980-81; dir. mgmt. G & K Mgmt. Co., S. San Francisco 1982-83; pres. Assoc. Property Mgrs., Burlingame 1984--; listed, Who's Who in West; mem: Am. Hist. Soc.; Nat. Trust for Historic Preservation; CofC; mil: legal clk. US Army 1969-71, Hawaii; Democrat; Protestant. Res: 209 Channing Rd Burlingame 94010 Ofc: Associated Property Managers, Inc., 1766 El Camino Real, Ste C, Burlingame 94010

CARLSON, DARRYL DEAN, investigator-consultant dba Darryl Dean; b. Sept. 17, 1938, San Francisco; s. Einar Wm. Carlson (dec.) and Margaret Elsie (Christie) C. Sanderson; m. Debara Diane Robinson, Mar. 14, 1981; children: Margaret, b. 1961, Christina, b. 1963, Brian, b. 1966; edn: AA, police sci., Mira Costa Coll. 1967; spl. tng. schools, US Govt. & mil.; Calif. lic. Pvt. Investigator. Career: law enforcement: patrolman, Seaside, Ore., then federal officer with US Immigration & Naturalization Service in Border Patrol along the Mex. Border, promoted to Investigator, then Intelligence Ofcr. serving in New York and Los Angeles; fmr. pres. two immigration consulting firms, 1973-76; currently pvt. practice lic. Investigator, Cons. Darryl Dean, Los Angeles; tchr. Immigration Process to attys. and local groups; recipient INS commendns. (5), Drug Enforcement Commendn. (1969), appreciation, State Bar of Calif. (1980); mem. Calif. Assn. of Licensed Investigators, Fed. Criminal Investigators Assn., Internat. Police Congress; mil: A/1c USAF, GCM, Unit Cpgn.; Republican; United Ch. of Rel. Sci. (Spiritual Therapist); rec: martial arts. Res. 1928 Barry St West Los Angeles 90025 Ofc: Darryl Dean, 3250 Wilshire Blvd. Penthouse Suite 2207 Los Angeles 90010

CARLSON, PAUL EDWIN, real estate developer; b. June 29, 1944, San Francisco; s. Carl John and Margueritte E. (Kovatch) C.; m. Sharon Hammond, 1963; children: Kim, b. 1964, Davin, b. 1971, Christina, b. 1979; edn: AA, Yosemite Coll. 1964; BA, CSU Long Beach 1971; C.S.M. (cert. Shopping Center Mgr.) Internat. Council of Shopping Ctrs. Mgmt. Sch. 1981. Career: police ofcr. (vice & narcotics) Modesto Police Dept. 1964-69; owner Universal Prodns., NYC and Modesto, Ca. 1969-73; gen. mgr. City Investing Co., Beverly Hills and NYC 1973-75; vice pres. The Koll Co., Newport Beach 1975-79; v.p. Irvine Co., Newport Beach 1979-80; owner Willows Shopping Center, Concord 1980-83; sr. vice pres. Lee Sammis Co. 1983--; guest lectr. USC, UCLA, Orange Coast Coll., real estate consultant for Bank of Am., Union Bank, Chevron USA, Aetna Life Ins. Co., James Lang Wooten (G.Brit.), Peoples Republic of China; commnr. Calif. State Juvenile Justice Commn.; mem. Concord Visitors & Conv. Bur. (bd. dirs.); Am. Cancer Soc. (bd. dirs. Contra Costa Co.); pres. bd. trustees Mt. Diablo Hosp.; v.p./bd. dirs. City of Concord Pavillion; past chmn. City of Newport Bch. Traffic Commn.; writer three screen plays for NBC's Police Story, comedy writer for NBC-TV Tonight Show and Sat. Night Live; pub. Property Managers Handbook; Republican; Prot.; rec: youth counseling. Res: 2601 Lighthouse Lane Corona Del Mar 92625 Ofc: Lee Sammis Co. 17922 Fitch Ave Irvine 92714

CARLSON, PETRUS ALBERT, aircraft design engineer (ret.); b. July 15, 1903, Skultana, Sweden, nat. 1932; s. Johan Albert and Olga Josefina lvira (Kampe) Karlsson; m. Wilma McGown, May 18, 1973; children (by prev. marriage): Donald Albert, b. 1936, Svea Diane, b. 1941; edn: engrg., ETF, Vasteras, Sweden 1920-24, eng. refresher, San Jose Coll. 1952-53, eng. course in helicopter theory, Stanford Univ. 1953, various (15) courses, Convair. Career: draftsman/designer Commercial Aircraft, Bridgeport, Conn. 1928-29; partner/v.p. of engrg./corp. secty. Cosmic Aircraft Corp. (designer, engr. Sesqueplane, 3-place, hi-wing aircraft), 1929-30; design engr. XP2Y Navy Aircraft, Sikorsky Aviation Corp., Stratford, Conn. 1930-31; Convair Gen. Dynamics, San Diego 1931-51: draftsman/designer/group engr. P2Y3, Fleetster, PBY, PY2Y-3, LB-30, B-24, B-32; Chief of installation groups, chief group engr. for all design groups, chief draftsman XB-46, 240, asst. project engr. on 240-340 aircraft; proj. engr./asst. chief engr./ asst. adminstrv. engr. (H23 Hornet), Hiller Helicopters, Palo Alto 1951-54; Convair Gen. Dynamics, 1954-63: staff engr. on F-TF-102 pgms., asst. proj. engr. on F-TF-102A pgms., proj. engr. on F-102, F-1065, spl. assignments to Brazil, the Philippines, USAF bases in San Antonio, Colorado Springs; design splst. and sr. systems engr. in support ofAtlas Weapons System, 1963-65; assigned to product effectiveness, 1965-68, ret., Convair 1968; Quality Assurance mgr./designer San Diego Aircraft Engineering, 1968-71; lectr. San Diego State Coll. during WWII. Awards: commnd. Adm. of Flagship Fleet by Am. Airlines for contbn. to devel. of air transp. 1963; commendation as V.E. Team mem., Convair Div. Gen. Dynamics; Air Force Awd., 1968. Regis.Mech. Engr. Mem. Calif. Soc. Profl. Engrs. (pres. Peninsula chpt. 1953-54; pres. San Diego chpt. 1956-57). Mil: Army of Sweden, 1920. Republican. Presbyterian. rec: woodwork, gardening. res: 972 Scott St. San Diego 91106.

CARLSON, RICHARD WARNER, savings and loan association executive; b. Feb. 10, 1941, Boston, MA; s. W.E. and Ruth Carlson; gr.-gr.-grandson, E. Rockwood Hoar, U.S. Atty Gen.; Univ. of Miss., 1962; m. Patricia Caroline Swanson, Feb. 17, 1979, La Jolla, CA; children: Tucker McNear, b. 1969; Buckley Peck, b. 1971. Career: journ., L.A. Times, 1962-63; United Press Internatl.,

1963-65; ABC-TV, S.F.-L.A., 1966-75; free-lance writer, stringer, Time Mag., Look, Etc., 1966-70; dir., prodr., documentaries, NBC-TV, Burbank, 1975; anchorman, CBS-TV San Diego, 1975-76; sr. v.p., v.p. finance, San Diego Fed. Svgs. & Loan Assn., 1976--. Dir.: Delmar News Press, 1976; Calif. Gen. Mortgage Inc., 1978; San Diego CofC, v.p. 1978. Author: A History of Women, San Diego Hist. Soc., 1978 (hard and soft cover edns.). Recipient numerous profl. awards incl. six Assoc. Press TV and Radio awards for investigative reporting, news analysis and commentary; four Golden Mike awards; three Emmy awards; two San Diego Press Club awards; three Foster Peabody award for Excellence, Investigative reporting; L.A. Press Club Grand Award; Natl. Headliners Award; apptd. by Pres. Reagan to President's Council on Peace Corps 1982; colonel, Calif. National Guard. Mem.: Financial adv. bd., Jr. Leager of S.D.; sponsor, La Jolla Soccer League; dir., Muscular Dystrophy Assn., S.D.; chmn., Citizens for Open Space, 1978. Mem.: Actors & Othres, L.A., pres. 1972-76; A. J. Liebling Soc. of L.A., co-founder; S.D. Coalition; Calif. C of C; Sigma Delta Chi. Republican Bus. & Profl. Club. v.p. 1978; Senate Republican Adv. Commn., mem. 1978. Clubs: La Jolla Beach & Tennis; the City; Univ. of S.D.; Cuyamaca; Thunderbird Country Club, Palm Springs; Mid Ocean Club, Tuckerstown, Bermuda. Episcopalian. res.: 7956 Ave. Alamar, La Jolla, CA 92037; Summer: Crockett Island, Lake Christopher, Woodstock ME 04219; Office: 600 B St., San Diego 92183.

CARLSON, ROBERT WILHELM, JR., film animation co. owner; b. Nov. 7, 1906, Chgo.; s. Robert Wilhelm C., Sr. (artist, inventor, color cons.; mem. Freemasonry Scottish Rite, Knights Templar) and Lily Marie (Cherrstrom) Carlson (mfg. milliner, Grand Chpt. of the U.S., Order of the Eastern Star); grandson of Carl W. (muralist, painter, designer) and Maria (Swedish nobility) Carlson; grandson of Axel G. (fine furniture design and mfr., opera singer) and Emily (Royal Ballet, Stockholm, Sweden) Cherrstrom; edn: Univ. Chgo. 1925, Art Inst. of Chgo. 1926, Natl. Acad. of Art, Chgo. 1927-29, Versatile Sch. of Design, Chgo. 1930-32; m. Mary Walter (Demo. State Committeewoman; bd. mem. Children's Home Soc.; Women;s Internatl. League for Peace and Freedom), March 3, 1945; children: Robert, III, b. 1946, Brendt, b. 1949, Stuart, b. 1957; career: commercial artist, self employed, Chgo. 1933-36; animator/dir./instr. apprentice artists, Walt Disney Prodns., 1936-58; owner, Carmen Productions, 1958--, furnishing animation, animated films to clients world-wide; lectr. on animation art, USC 1960-61, UC Santa Cruz 1970-71; currently lectrs., seminars on animation. Awards: Art Dirs. Club of NY, 1961; distinctive merit, Calif. Artists Mag., 1963; merit certifs., 1964, 65, 66, 69, Annual Exhib. of Advertising Art, L.A.; mem.: The Acad. of Motion Picture Arts and Scis.; charter mem. Screen Cartoonists Guild; leader, BSA Sea Explorers; mil: writer, dir., animator of tng. films for Naval Air Command, San Diego, WWII; Ch. of Rel. Sci.; rec: music, architecture, hiking, boating; address: Carmen Productions, 640 Baltusrol Dr., Aptos 95003.

CARNER, GRANT CALVIN, SR., lawyer; b. Mar. 10, 1943, Ottawa, Ill.; s. William C. and Julie (Gabehart) C.; m. Kacey, Apr. 9, 1983; children: Grant Jr., b. 1965; Joel, b. 1967; edn: Riverside City Coll. 1963-64; LLB, La Salle Ext. Univ. 1970; UC Riverside 1983; admitted State Bar of Calif. 1974, US Dist. Ct. (Central Dist. Calif.) 1974. Career: mgr. Dial Finance Co., Ontario 1964-69; v.p. Marcus W. Meairs Co., Riverside 1970-73; owner Insurance Financial Svcs. Co., Riverside 1973-74; owner Grant Carner, Attys. at Law, Riverside 1974--; Republican nominee US House Reps. 36th Dist. of Calif.; founder/mng. dir. Catholic Legal Svcs., Riverside 1979; judge pro tem Riverside Supreme Ct. 1979; City of Riverside Cultural Heritage Bd. 1982-, Bd. of Admin. Appeals 1975-77; mem: State Bar of Calif.; Riverside Co. Bar Assn.; Riverside Exch. Club; Masons; co-founder Friends of UC Riverside 1979; bd. dirs., founding pres. Botanic Gardens 1981-; mil: USN 1961-67; Republican; Catholic; rec: collect 1st editions, running. Res: 600 Central Ave Riverside 92507 Ofc: Grant Carner, Atty. at Law, POB 1632, 4101 Seventh St, Riverside 92502

CARPENTER, DONALD BLODGETT, real estate appraiser; b. Aug. 20, 1916, New Haven, Colo.; s. Prof. Fred Donald and Gwendolen (Blodgett) C.; m. Barbara Adams, June 28, 1941 (dec. 1978); m. 2d Lee Burker, Dec. 28, 1980; chil: Edward G. (b.1952), John D. (b.1957), William V. (b.1959), Andrew J. (b.1960), Dorothy J. (b.1962), James J. (b.1964) McGough; edn: Ph.B., Univ. VT 1938; Sonoma St. Univ. 1968-9, Mendocino Comm. Coll. 1977; certifications: Cert. Review Appraiser, 1980, Sr. Cert. Valuer, Manufactured Housing Cert. Appraiser. Career: reporter, Burlington Daily News, VT, 1938-39; guide chair opr. Am.Express Co., NY World Fair, 1939; underwriter Gen. Exchange Ins. Corp., Newark, NJ 1939-40; sales correspondent J.Dixon Crucible Co., Jersey City, NJ 1940-42; sales rep., San Francisco 1946-52; field supr. The Travelers Ins. Co., S.F. 1952-58; gen. agent, Gen. Am. Life Ins. Co., S.F., 1958-59; Western supr. Provident Life & Accident Ins. Co., S.F. 1959-60; brokerage supr. Aetna Life Ins. Co., S.F. 1960-61; maintenance cons. J.I. Holcomb Mfg. Co., Mill Valley 1961-68; ednl. serv. rep. Marquis-Who's Who, Inc., Mill Valley 1963-68; tchr./coach Mendocino Jr.-Sr. H.Sch., 1968; real prop. appraiser Co. of Mendocino, 1968-81, ind. real estate appraiser, 1982--; mem. Assn. of Govt. Appraisers, 1974-; Nat. Retired Tchrs Assn.; CRA, 1980-; SCV, 1981-; MHCA, 1983; Calif. Assn. of Realtors, afil., 1982-. Awards: scholarship-leadership awd., Kappa Sigma Internat. Frat. 1937-8; Comm. Sportsman of the Year, Booster Club, 1971; Paul Harris Fellow, 1979, Rotary Intl. Dist. Gov. awds. 1974, 76. Mem: Am. Legion 1945-(Post Comdr. 1972-3, Past Comdrs. of Calif. 1973-); Kappa Sigma Intl. Frat. (life); Am. Diabetes Assn. 1973-; Mendocino Cardinal Boosters 1968-(charter, life; pres. 1971); Mendocino Co.Employees Assn., 1968-81; Reserve Ofcrs Assn. of the US (life; chpt. pres. 1954, 56; state v.p. 1958-61); Rotary Internat. 1969-(club pres. 1975-6, dist. gov.1977-8); Univ. of VT. N.Calif. Alumni Assn. (founding pres. 1964); Mendocino Art Center 1965-; Mendocino Hist. Resrch, Inc. (Docent, 1982-); Friendship Gardens, 1982-. Univ. Newspaper, ed. in chief, 1937-8; Int. Frat. Chptr. alumni publ., ed. 1937-8; Univ. Frosh Handbook ed. 1937-8; ed. Rotary Club Mbrship Directory, 1971-. Mil: Lcdr. USNR, ret. 1968; C.O. USNR Unit, 1967-8; Secty. Navy Commend. 1946; Comdt. Naval Dist. Commend. 1968. Republican; Congregational; rec: historian, genealogy, philately, tennis. res: Box 87, Mendocino 95460. ofc: Appraising Services, 10801 Gurley Ln., Mendocino 95460

CARPENTER, WELDON ALLEN, manufacturing sales & service executive; b. June 24, 1939, Slaton, Tex.; s. Alvin Troy and Mildred Vene (Rodgers) C.; m. Carole Dawn Sanders, June 4, 1966; children: David, b. 1960; Gary, b. 1961; Darlene, b. 1962; Becky, b. 1963; Stacy, b. 1963; Weldon Jr, b. 1964; Stephen, b. 1967; edn: BA, Texas Tech. 1962. Career: Crane Hoist Engineering Corp. 1967-79; proj. mgr. 1967-69; installation of largest underhung crane sys. in world, Boeing Everett, Wash.; plant mgr., Seattle, Wash. 1969-70; field ops. mgr. , Los Angeles 1970-73; svc. mgr., L.A. 1973-77; nat. svc. mgr., L.A. 1977-79; CEO/ chmn. bd. Action Crane, L.A. 1979--; CEO/ chmn. bd. Action Crane, San Diego 1983--; mem: Crane Mfrs. Assn. of Am., Inc.; Masons; Elks; mil: s/sgt. US Army 1963; Republican; Protestant; rec: flying, sports. Res: 8201 Del Oro Ln La Palma 90620 Ofc: Action Crane Maint., 13048 E Firestone Blvd Santa Fe Springs 90670

CARREY, NEIL, lawyer; b. Nov. 19, 1942, Bronx, NY; s. David L. and Betty (Kurtzberg) C.; m. Karen K., Apr. 9, 1980; children: Scott, b. 1967, Douglas, b. 1972, Dana, b. 1973, Jana, b. 1981; edn: BS in acctg. Wharton Sch. Univ. of Penn. 1964; JD, Stanford Law Sch. 1967; admitted to Calif. State Bar 1968. Career: assoc. atty. firm of De Castro, West & Chodorow, Inc. 1967-, ptnr. 1969-, vice pres. 1979--; lectr. USC Sch. of Paralegal Profls. 1977-; honors: General Alumni Soc. Award, Univ. of Penn. 1976; Who's Who in Am. Law (1979); mem. The Group (orgn. of splst. of closely held bus.), Am. Bar Assn., Western Pension Conf.; ofcr. Del Mar Child Care Center 1968-; bd. dirs. Univ. of Penn. Alumni Soc. of So. Calif. (pres. 1971-79); parent rep. sec. sch. curriculum com. Santa Monica Sch. Dist. 1981-82; club: Mountaindate Tennis; Republican; Jewish; rec: tennis, painting. Res: 616 23rd St Santa Monica Ofc: De Castro West & Chodorow Inc. 10960 Wilshire Blvd, Ste. 1800, Los Angeles 90024

CARR-FINGERLE, JOELYN KATHLEEN, certified public accountant; b. May 5, 1952, Modesto; d. Clifford Miller and Claire (Lundell) C.; m. Robert F. Fingerle, Mar. 24, 1979; 1 dau: Katrina, b. 1982; edn: AA, Santa Rosa Jr. Coll. 1972; BS, San Jose State Univ. 1974; CPA, Calif. 1976. Career: clerk/ intern Alexander Grant & Co., San Jose 1972-74; profl. staff auditor Arthur Young & Co., San Jose 1974-77; profl. staff auditor Peat Marwick Mitchell & Co., San Francisco 1977-79; data processing mgr./ auditor Carothers, Bowersock, Friedman & Proulx, Accty. Corp., Fremont 1979-80; gen. mgr. Accountants Computer Svcs., Fremont 1980-81; CPA, profl. staff Beth A Friedman, CPA, Fremont 1980--; honors: Alpha al Sirit, San Jose State Univ. Sch. of Bus. 1974; mem: Am. Inst. & Calif. Soc. of CPAs; Soroptimist; Republican; Congregational; rec: needlework, gardening. Res: 39639 Embarcadero Terrace Fremont 94538 Ofc: Acctg. Ofcs. of Beth A. Friedman, CPA, 39175 Liberty St, Ste 214, Fremont 94538

CARROLL, JOHN RUSSELL, lawyer; b. Aug. 9, 1922, Cedar Rapids, Ia.; s. Frank T. and Florence Helen (Schulze) C.; m. Sue, Feb. 23, 1952; children: Charles H., b. 1954; Stephen J., b. 1956; Molly, b. 1958; Joseph P., b. 1962; Sarah Ann, b. 1964; Thomas F., b. 1966; edn: AA, Dowling Jr. Coll. 1942; BA, St. Univ. of Iowa 1947; JD, St. Univ. of Iowa Law Coll. 1949; lic. to practice, Calif. & Iowa; admitted, US Supreme Ct. 1954. Career: pvt. practice, law, Algona, Iowa 1949-57; city atty., City of Algona, Ia. 1954-57; asst. city atty. City of Santa Clara 1959; pvt. practice, law, San Jose 1960--; bd. dirs. Santa Clara CofC (5 yrs.); chmn. Young Republicans; chmn. Crippled Childrens Soc., Easter Seals; Internat. Stud Tour of USSR ct. sys. 1983; mem: Calif. State Bar; Santa Clara Bar Assn.; Calif. Trial Lawyers; Iowa Bar Assn.; Santa Clara Co. Estate Plng. Council; Kenna Club; Univ. of Santa Clara; mil: US Army active combat duty 1942-46; Republican; Catholic. Res: Saratoga Ofc: Carroll, Infantino, George & Oliver, 2176 The Alameda San Jose 95126

CARSON, KATHERINE FRANCES, obstetrician -gynecologist; b. Oct. 8, 1922, Ft. Smith, Ark.; d. John W. and Katherine Estelle (Woodruff) C.; m. George West, Nov. 26, 1971; children (by prev. m. to Wallace Kantor): Ruth, b. 1959, Helen, b. 1961, Sylvia, b. 1964; edn: AA, UCLA 1948, BA, UC Berkeley 1951, MD, UC San Francisco 1954. Career: gen. rotating intern Los Angeles Co. Gen. Hosp., 1954-55; res. in obstets-gyn. Stanford Lane Hosp., San Francisco 1955-56; chief res. in ob-gyn, Kaiser Found. Hosp., Los Angeles 1956-58; pvt. practice obstets. and gynecology, San Diego 1960--; first woman chmn. Dept. OB-Gyn and mem. Exec. Med. Bd., Sharp Meml. Hosp. 1980-81; asst. clin. prof. Dept. Reproductive Med. UCSD Med. Sch.; apptd. by Gov. Brown to 14th Dist. Review Com., Bd. of Med. Quality Assurance 1976-79; elected mem. Pacific Coast Gynecology and Obstets. Soc. (1st woman in 42 yrs); chmn. Dist. IX (Calif.) Am. Coll. of Obstets. and Gyn. (first woman to hold office); elected bd.dirs. Profl. Standards Review Orgn., S.D. & Imperial Co. 1981-82. Fellow Am. Coll. Obstets. and Gyns. 1961; Diplomate, Am. Bd. OB-Gyn 1964, recert. 1980. Author: Take Charge of Your Body (1983). Orgnzr. Childbirth Edn. Assn. of S. D. Awards: Woman of Achievement, San Diego 1966, 67; Susan B. Anthony Awd. of S.D., NOW, 1978; A Time for Tribute, Bnai Brith, 1981; Five most admired women in La Jolla, 1981. Mem: Altrusas Club of S.D. (pres. 1968), S.D. Gynecol. Soc. (1st woman pres. 1970-1), Calif. Med. Assn.(Maternal & Child Hlth Com., OB Gyn Adv. Panel 1981), S.D. Co. Med. Soc. (legis. com.), NOW, Nat. Women's Polit. Caucus, Dimensions; Democrat; Christian; rec: skiing, opera, camping. res: 7866 Revelle Dr. La Jolla 92037 ofc: 7930 Frost St., Ste.304, San Diego 92123.

CART, LARRY ARTHUR, chiropractor; b. July 13, 1946, Glendale; s. Donald Frederick and Patricia Irene (Gorton) C.; m. Elizabeth, June 20, 1970; 1 son: Jason, b. 1975; edn: BA, CSU, L.A 1971; BS, Am. Nat. Inst. for Psychical Research & Devel. 1978; MS, 1983; PhD, 1984; DC, Los Angeles Coll. of Chiro. 1981; M. Herbology, Emerson Coll. of Herbology 1983; cert. fellowship, Rio Grande Ctr. for Herbal Studies 1984; lic. chiropractor, Calif. Career: prof. metaphysics American National Inst. 1978--, dir. resrch. & devel., prof. undergrad. anatomy, physiol. and clin. pathol., postgrad. studies in nutrition, healing techs., med. astrology, clin. iridology, 1981--; DC/dir. Am. Nat. Inst. Chiropractic Clinic 1981--; mem: Calif. Chiro. Assn.; Agoura- Las Virgenes CofC; mil; E-5 USN 1966-68; USMC, Vietnam 1967-68; Republican; rec: computers, classical music. Res: 3629 Summer Shore Ln Westlake Village 91361 Ofc: American National Institute Chiropractic Clinic, 30423 Canwood St, Ste 132, Agoura Hills 91301

CARTER, EDWARD JOHN, electronics co. president; b. Sept. 21, 1950, Troy, NY; s. Richard Sutton and Katherine Marie (Fitzgerald) C.; m. Eugenia Marie Hernandez, May 25, 1979; edn: BS, Clarkson Coll. 1972. Career: process equipt. div. Ametex, Temecula; jr. sales engr. 1972-73; sales engr. 1973-77; applications engr. 1977-78; asst. sales mgr. 1978-79; gen. sales mgr. Kraus Maffei Corp., Wichita, Ks. 1979-80; gen. sales mgr. Morehouse Inds., Fullerton 1980-81; pres./ CEO California Electronics, Inc., Anaheim 1981--; mem: Am. Chem. Soc.; Am. Soc. of Chem. Engrs.; Am. Coating Soc.; Anaheim CofC; US CofC; Republican; Catholic; rec: music, jogging, weight lifting. Res: 2505 N Linwood Santa Ana 92701 Ofc: California Electronics, 15552 Coronado St, Ste A, Anaheim 92806

CARTER, MARSHA ANN, financial planning & information systems executive; b. Aug. 8, 1944, New Orleans, La.; d. Charles and Florence Mary (Calvey) C.; 1 son: David R. Dade, b. 1972; edn: BS, UCLA Grad. Sch. of Bus. 1972. Career: The Rand Corp., Santa Monica 1967-76; research assoc.; assoc. mathematician; planning analyst; deputy dir.; pgm. mgr.; sr. planning anlyst, The Eaton Corp., Cleveland, Ohio 1976-77; Hughes Aircraft Co., Cleveland, Ohio, El Segundo, Ca. 1977--; computing splst., senior splst., sect. head, dir. fin. planning & info. systems; corp. data processing coord., Hughes Aircraft 1983-; chmn. DOD Flexible Progress Payment Hotel, Hughes 1980-83; awards: Hyland Awd., Performance Inprovement Awd.; Cost Improvement Awd.; All-Star Basketball Player; YWCA Cert. of Achiev.; mem: Am. Mgmt. Assn.; Aerospace Inds. Assn. of AM., Inc.; Nat. Contract Mgmt. Assn.; Manhattan Beach Country Club; YMCA; Hughes Womans Forum; num. publs. in ind. journs.; Democrat; Catholic; rec: swimming, hiking, skating. Res: 2704 Curtis Ave Redondo Beach 90278 Ofc: Hughes Aircraft Co., 200 N Sepulveda, Bldg C2 M/S A153, POB 90245, El Segundo 90245

CARTER, WILLIAM J., chiropractor; b. Nov. 18, 1952, Barberton, Ohio; s. Wm. H. and Eleanor A. (Wells) C.; m. Lorraine A., July 18, 1975; 1 son, W. Christopher, b. 1982; edn: BS, Ohio State Univ. 1975; DC, Life Chiro. Coll. 1980. Cert. Emergency Med. Tech. 1978-; lic. DC in Ohio 1980, Mich. 1980, Calif. 1982. Career: exec. trainee Jordon Marsh Co., Boston, Mass.; finl. analyst Dunn & Bradstreet, Boston; regl. sales rep. Graphic Controls Corp. (Med. Div.), Cleveland, Oh.; pvt. chiropractic practice, 1980--, sub splty. in Chiropractic Orthopedics; awards: athletic scholarship, E. Mich. Univ. 1971; exec. com. Life Chiro. College-West, 1982-, dean of contg. edn. 1982-83, chmn. Acad. Stds. Com. 1982-; mem: Am. Chiro. Assn., Calif. Chiro Assn., Ohio Chiro. Assn., Found. for Edn. & Research, life Chiropractic Coll. Alumni Assn., Ohio St. Univ. Alumni Assn., Rotary, CofC, J.C.'s; works: devel. prep. seminar for Chiro. State Licensing Bd. exam; rec: pvt. pilot. Res: 100 Ellinwood Dr, C-123, Pleasant Hill 94523 Ofc: Carter Chiropractic Clinic, 1563 Palos Verdes Mall, Walnut Creek 94596

CARTLEDGE, ROBERT ARNOLD, glass co. president; b. Sept. 10, 1931, San Diego; s. Percy Arnold and Bessie Inez (McAllister) C.; m. Lorraine McMurtry, June 11, 1955; two daus.: Laura Ann, b. 1957, Nora Noreen, b. 1959. Career: with glass industry since 1949; installer Auto Glass Div., customer rels., pricing and inventory control, San Diego Glass :& Paint, 1943-57, 58-64; gen. mgr. McFarling Glass Co. (subs. Glass Service Corp.), National City, 1964--; shareholder, Glass Service Corp. 1963-; pres. Commodore Glass Corp. dba Admiral Glass Co. (fmrly. McFarling Glass Co.) 1967--, ops. eight retail glass service centers in San Diego Co., and retail glass locations in Walnut Creek and Antioch, Ca.; founder/pres. Nationwide Glass Corp. dba McFarling Glass Co. (wholesale distbr. architectural, auto glass and related prods.) National City, 1969--. Mem: CofC (6), San Diego Employers Assn. (dir.), National Glass Dealers Assn.; jogging mem. (5,000 miles) San Diego Dwntwn YMCA. Mil: sgt. US Army 1952-54. Republican. res: 10041 Diversion Dr. Spring Valley 92077. ofc: Admiral Glass Co. 1316 National City Bl. National City 92050

CARTWRIGHT, JOAN CARROLL, clinical psychologist; b. Mar. 29, 1942, Sacramento; d. Rex Benton and Estella Margretta (Sangsland) C.; edn: BA, UC Davis 1963; MA & MS, CSU Sacto. 1972; PhD, Calif. Sch. of Profl. Psychol. 1977; Calif. liC: psychologist (1979), MFCC- Marriage Family Child Counselor, Community Coll. Counselor (life), and Instr. (life). Career: soc. wkr. 1965-66; sch. tchr. 1966-72; intern counselor, guidance splst., school psychologist, 1972-75; intern/ staff clin. psychologist, 1977-80; clin. psychologist pvt. practice, Sacramento 1980--, neuropsychologist, forensic psychologist; founder/ dir. Continuing Edn. in Psychology (ednl. seminars for bus., govt., profls.); provider mem. Golden Empire Health Systems Agcy.; cons. Sacto. Muni. Utils. Dist. 1980-; mem: Am. Psychol. Assn., Am. Psychology-Law Soc., Am. Soc. Clin. Hypnosis, Calif. Neuropsychol. Soc., Sacto. Soc. Clin. Hypnosis, Sacto. Soc. Clin. Psychologists, Sacto. Valley Psychol. Assn. (past pres.), Calif. State Psychol. Assn. (bd. dirs.), Assn. for Media Psychology (treas.); listed in Nat. Regis. of Hlth Svc Providers in Psych. 1980; co-author four publs. in field (Bates-Cartwright Publs.) 1975; arts. in profl. jours.; dir./ founder/ pub. One Plus Directory; presentations, local radio, lawyers, tchrs. groups. Res: 808 Dunbarton Circle Sacramento 95825 Ofc: Joan Carroll Cartwright, PhD, 1121 L St, Ste. 1000, Sacramento 95814

CARUSO, PHILIP JOSEPH, JR., real estate broker; b. Feb. 4, 1926, Wilkes-Barre, Pa.; s. Philip Joseph Sr. (dec.) and Bea E. (Dersheimer) C.; m. Odell Marrs, Sept. 7, 1950; children: Denise, b. 1951; Dianne, b. 1952; Michelle, b. 1955; Philip III, b. 1960; Amy, b. 1961; edn: BS, Univ. of Virginia 1946; BS, Mass. Inst. of Tech. 1950; MB, 1951; R.E. broker 1980. Career: tech. dir. Adv. Ballistic Missiles Defense, Systems- RCA, Morristown, NJ 1955-61; senior div. mgr. adv. microware sys. Aerojet, El Monte 1961-68; pres. Spectran Internat. (R&D), US & Canada 1968-75; R.E. broker Laguna Viejo Realty, Mission Viejo 1976--; honors: Sigma Xi 1952; assoc. fellow, Am. Inst. of Aero & Astronautics, 1970; num. real estate awds. 1976-81; mem: IEEE; Nat. & Calif. Assns. Realtors; Univ. of Va. Alumni ASsn.; patents (US & Canada): Microwave Aircraft Land Sys. 1970; Microwave Recon. & Guidance 1971; Indsl. Microwave Monitor 1972; num. elec. radar & weapons sys. 1955-75, incl. Microwave Radiometry & Its Applications, XXIst internat. Astronautical Research Congress, 1970; mil: lt. jg USNR 1944-55; Republican; Catholic; rec: golf. Res: 24746 Tabuenca Mission Viejo 92692 Ofc: Laguna Viejo Realty, 26131 Marguerite Pkwy, Ste A, Mission Viejo 92691

CARUSONE, JOHN JOSEPH, public school administrator; b. Nov. 24, 1921, Boston, Mass.; s. Joseph J. and Adelina F. (Desimone) C.; m. Helen T. Thorley, Feb. 6, 1946; children: Mary Anne, b. 1949, Joseph, b. 1953; edn: AB, Boston Coll. 1943, MSW, 1948; S.F. State Univ. 1956-60, UC Berkeley 1960-66; Calif. (life) Adminstrv. Services Credential, (life) Std. Suprvsn. Cred., (life) Pupil Personnel Svcs., LCSW (lic. clin. soc. wkr.), MFCC (marriage family child counselor). Career: counselor Family Svc. Agcy, Bristol, Conn. 1948-50; supr. soc. wkrs. State of Conn. Welfare Dept., 1950-51; dir. Child Guidance Clinic, Napa (Calif.) Co. Health Dept. 1953-56; cons. individual guidance, Oakland Pub. Schs., 1956-62, coordinator sch.-comm. relations, 1966-76, adminstrv. asst. to Supt. of Schs., 1976--; HEW adv. com. on sch. safety 1975; staff chief Commn. on Sch. Safety 1974; chpsn. Master Plan Com. on Multucultural Edn. 1971-73, chpsn. Coms. to Devel. Affirmative Action Purch., Empl. Plans; awards: Marcus A. Foster Ednl. Inst. 1978, Oakland Vol. Pgm. 1977, Center of Independent Living 1983; mem: Nat. Edn. Assn. (com. on Intergroup Rels.), Oakland Edn. Assn., Calif. Tchrs. Assn., United Adminstrs. of Oak. Schs.; bd. Mary A. Sarvis Meml. Fund; bd. Marcus A. Foster Ednl. Inst.; past bd. chpsn. ARC Napa Co. Chpt.; author 28 publs. on multicultural edn., var. studies; mil: lcdr. USN (ret.) active 1943-465, 1951-53; rec: golf, gardening. Res: 244 Los Banos Ave Walnut Creek 94598 Ofc: Oakland Unified School District, 1025 Ocean Ave Oakland 94606

CASADO, ANDREW RICHARD, financial services management; b. Feb. 23, 1950, Fresno; s. Andrew Richard and Penny Cecelia (Garcia) C.; edn: B.Ed., Univ. of Ariz. 1972; M.Ed., 1973; MBA, So. Ill. Univ. 1984. Career: tchr. Glendale H.S., Glendale 1973-76; dist. ops. mgr. Cal-West Packing Co., San Diego 1976-79; br. mgr. Home Federal Savings & Loan, San Diego 1979-83; prod. devel. mgr. 1983--; Inst. of Fin. Edn.; spkr. Bureau of Home Federal Savings & Loan; awards: Community Volunteer Awd., So. Bay Comm. Svcs., Chula Vista; Outstanding Young Men of Am., Jaycees; mem: San Ysidro Rotary; So. Bay Community Svcs.; United Way, San Diego; Boy Club of San Ysidro; Hispanic Bankers Assn. of San Diego co.; Inst. of Fin. Edn., San Diego; San Diego Symphony Assn.; Young Friends of the S.D. Symphony; rec: music, hiking, snow skiing. Res: 1640 Maple Dr, 43, Chula Vista 92011 Ofc: Home Federal Savings & Loan, 707 Broadway, 12th Flr, San Diego 92101

CASASSA, CHARLES STEPHEN, S.J., university chancellor; b. Sept. 23, 1910, San Francisco, Ca; s. Charles S. and Margaret G. (Power) Casassa; A.B., Gonzaga Coll, Spokane, WA, 1934; M.S., 1935; S.T.L., Alma Coll., 1939; Ph.D., Univ. of Toronto, 1946; (hon.) D.D., Univ. of Judaism, 1964; (hon.), S.T.D., USC, 1965; (hon.) L.H.D., Calif. Coll. of Med., 1965; LL.D., St. Mary's Coll. 1967, Univ. of S.F. 1969; L.H.D., Hebrew Union Coll.-Jewish Inst. Relig. 1967, Univ. of Santa Clara 1973; D.H.L., Marymount Coll., 1969. Career: ordained priest, 1938; instr., Loyola Univ., 1939-41; asst. prof., Santa Clara Coll., 1946-49; dean of art, 1948-49; pres., Loyola Univ. of L.A., 1949-69; Chancellor, 1969--. Mem.: pres. Independent Colls. of So. Calif., Inc. 1956-58; dir. Knudsen Found.; bd. dirs., L.A. CofC, 1966-67; bd. dirs., L.A. World Affairs Council; trustee: Gonzaga Univ. 1972-77; trustee emeritus, Gonzaga Univ., 1977--; trustee: Univ. of S.F., Loyola Marymount Univ., Ind.-Edn. Council of Calif. 1973--; pres. Friedship Day Camp, Inc.; Knights of Columbus; L.A. Rotary Club; West Coast Study Group of the Amer. Immigration and Citizenship Conf. 1972-80, hon. mem. 1980--; hon. mem., Rotary Club of L.A., 1977--; mem. adv. bd., Jr. League of L.A., Inc., 1978--. Roman Catholic. Rec.: reading mystery stories. Res.: Loyola Blvd. at W. 80th St., Los Angeles 90045; Office: Loyola Marymount Univ., Los Angeles 90045.

CASELLA, JOSEPH VINCENT, insurance broker; b. Mar. 29, 1927, Cleveland, Ohio; s. Vincent and Maria Antoinette (Vieni) C.; m. Emma Guglielmucci, June 14, 1951; children: Vincenzo, b. 1953, Anthony, b. 1956, Daniel, b. 1959, Maria Antoinette, b. 1960; LUTC, Life Underwriters Tng. Council 1962. Career: self empl. insurance broker, owner Joseph Ins. Agency, Westminster; recipient news media coverage (Fred Anderson Ch. 7 News, 1982) for self taught hobby of shoemaking (remembered from experience as a 5 year old child watching his father, a European trained shoe maker, practice his craft to support the family). Res: 9652 Westwood Dr Westminster 92683 Ofc: Joseph Insurance Agency, 9652 Westwood Dr. Westminster 92683

CASEY, DAVID L(EE), newspaper editor; b. May 14, 1936, Crescent, Okla.; s. Stephen Henry and Grace Pauline (Cook) C., Jr.; m. Joyce Quintana, Dec. 9, 1968; 2 daus: Kelly Ann, b. 1962; Kimberly Ann, b. 1965; edn: Okla. City Univ. 1958-9, Central State Univ. 1959-62, Univ. of S.F. 1970; AS, Univ. of State of NY 1980. Career: in US Navy 1954-79, ret. Journalist lst Class, served as cryptographic technician, electronics instr. (USN Schs Command, S.F. 1968-71), broadcaster Am. Forces Radio and T.V. Svc., journalist/photog., and editor of a command newspaper; ed. (civil svc.), The Western Arrow, Oakland Army Base, 1980; ed. The Missile (Command newspaper), Pacific Missile Test Center, Pt. Mugu 1980--; pres. Casey Enterprises (import/export), Camarillo. Awards: journalism awd., Freedoms Found., Valley Forge 1967. Mem: Sigma Phi Epsilon, DeMolay, SAR (7th gen. desc. Daniel Boone); commd. Commodore Okla. Navy by Gov. Boren, 1975. Publs: num. arts., photos in Naval Aviation News, Navy Times, various newspapers 1966-. Mil. Awds: GCM (4), China Svc., Nat. Def. (2), Naval Reserve, Exp. Rifleman, Exp. Pistolshot, Navy Unit Commend., Presdtl. Unit Cit. Democrat. Prot. Rec: electronics, audio/video recording. Res: 1439 Lexington Ct. Camarillo 93010 Ofc: Pac. Missile Test Ctr., Editor, Bldg. 36, Pt. Mugu 93042

CASON, GINETTE JANE, executive; b. Feb. 13, 1927, Cagny Somne, France, nat. 1979; d. Lucien and Suzanne (Dequen) Luquet; m. Kenneth Cason, Mar. 26, 1970; children: Alain, b. 1945; Patrick, b. 1947; Glenn, b. 1954; Deborah, b. 1955; edn: AA, Caffin Coll. 1945; Bonieux Photo Studio Sch. 1948. Career: ins. sales 1954-58; photographer, partnership, Paris, France 1958-62; asst. mgr., Paris, France; ins. sales 1962-67; asst. mgr., Albuquerque, NM; photographer 1967-74; owner, Albuquerque, NM; photog. 1974-78; owner/ photog., traveled the USA, 1978-81; currently, owner Crown Family Portraits (2 studios), Cerritos & Fountain Valley; instr./cons. tng. photographers to set up their own studios in Tulsa, Alburquerque, San Diego, Tucson, Amarillo, and Corpus Christi; recipient Achievement award in tng./ supvrg., Studio Owners & Photographers; mem; Telecolor Corp. of Hollywood, 1972; rec: interior decorating, gourmet cooking. Res: 8112 Holder Buena Park 90620 Ofc: Crown Family Portraits, 16159 Brookhurst St, Fountain Valley 92708

CASPER, GEORGE GARY, educator/businessman; b. Sept. 16, 1938, Burley, Ida.; s. George Duncan and Wanda Faa (Clark) C.; m. Karin Paulsen, Feb. 14, 1958; children: Gregory b. 1959, Tamera b. 1961, Derek b. 1962, Heidi b. 1966, Travis b. 1975, Brandon b. 1975; edn: BS, Univ. of Utah, 1962, MS, 1970, PhD, 1972, Profl. Counselors Cert. (Basic) 1972; Cert. Data Processor (CDP), Inst. for Cert. of Computer Profls. (ICCP) 1971; Cert. Data Educator (CDE), Soc. Data. Ed. 1971. Career: systems engr. IBM, Salt Lake City, Ut. and Helsia, Mont. 1964-68; systems analyst Kennecott Copper Corp., SLC, Utah 1968; v.p. Profl. Research Assocs., SLC, 1969-70; systems analyst Utah State Bd. of Edn., 1969-70; vis. assoc. prof. computer sci. Brigham Young Univ., Provo 1975-76; prof. data proc., Weber St. Coll., Ogden 1975-76; dean of academic affairs, Condie Coll., San Jose, Ca. 1979-83; director Sysorex Inst., Cupertino 1983--; bd. dirs. ICCP; bd. dirs. Soc. of Certified Data Processors (SCDP) 1974-84 (pres. 1976-81); honors: Phi Kappa Phi 1962, Fellow Assn. of Computer Pgmmrs. & Analysts (ACPA) 1979, Outstanding Educator 1976; mem: DPMA, SCDP, ACPA (v.chmn. 1982-), SDE, AICCP (chmn. organizing com. 1981-4); mem. Boy Scouts of Am., bd. dirs. Santa Clara County Indus.-Edn. Council 1983-84; num. articles, wkshops, seminars in data proc. topics; contbr. publs: Values Analysis, Teaching of Values, Values Counseling; Republican; L.D.S. Res: 180 Castillon Way San Jose 95119 Ofc: Sysorex Institute, 10590 N. Tantau Ave Cupertino 95014

CASSADAY, STANLEY ALAN, electrical contractor; b. Jan. 16, 1947, Tulare; s. Herman James, Sr. and Violet Lucille (Musick) C.; m. Christine Henson, Aug. 1, 1966; children: Stacy, b. 1971, Suzanne, b. 1974; edn: AA, Coll. of the Sequoias 1979; Calif. lic. Elec. and Alarm Contractor 1978. Career: clerk, mgr. local retail liquor store, retail hardware store; served to sgt. E5, US Army Inf. in Vietnam (decorated Purple Heart, Combat Inf. Badge) 1967-69; elec. supr. AAA Alarm; current owner/opr. S.A. Cassaday Service (electrical, alarms, lighting, aerial wk., mobile home svc.), Visalia; instr. elec. skills class Visalia Unified Sch. Dist. 1978-82; recipient Holy Family Parish Award 1980; mem. VFW, Am. Legion, Odd Fellows; pub. poetry, anthologies (1982, 83); Democrat; Catholic; rec: hunting, fishing, poetry. Res: 514 Robin Dr Visalia 93291 Ofc: S.A. Cassaday Service POB 3935 Visalia 93278

CASSELLE, DAWNE ASTRIDE, advertising counselor, entrepreneur; b. Apr. 16, 1943, Phila., Pa.; d. Jack T. and Bernice Constance (Smith) C.; div.; 1 son, Todd Anthony Poindexter, b. 1961; edn: AA in bus., LA City Coll., Pierce Jr. Coll., 1975; BA, UCLA 1975; JD, UCLA Sch. of Law 1980; contg. edn. wkshops, seminars. Career: owner Casselle & Associates (pub. rels., advt., promotions, mktg. resrch.), Los Angeles; profl. public spkr.; honors: Phi Alpha Delta, Moot Ct. Hons. Pgm., staff ed. UCLA Black Law Journal; mem: Women's Referral Service, LA Singles Network, LA Area CofC, Am. Entrepreneurs Assn., UCLA Alumni Assn.; contbg. writer var. newspapers and mags.; Democrat; Sci. of Mind. Address: Caselle & Assoc. 3333 W. 2nd St, 53-204, Los Angeles 90004

CASSETTARI, WILLIAM JOHN, lawyer; b. Feb. 25, 1907, Tereglio, Italy, nat. 1931; s. Pietro Leopoldo and Zeffira (Renucci) C.; m. Adeline Pardini, June 26, 1943; 1 dau: Anne Elizabeth Buck, b. 1946; edn: BA, honors in hist., UC Berkeley 1929; LLB, and JD, UC Boalt Hall 1932; admitted to Calif. State Bar 1932, US Supreme Ct. Bar 1981. Career: pvt. law practice 1932--; city atty. City of Grass Valley 1937-74; deputy dist. atty. Co. of Nevada, Ca. 1942-64; bd. dirs. Sierra Nevada Meml.- Miners Hosp. 1969-; bd. chmn. 1977-; bd. mem. Nevada Co. Nat. Bank 1979-; honors: Gamma Eta Gamma 1931; Cassettari Day (Fri. following Thanksgiving) named public holiday in his honor, City of Grass Valley; mem: State Bar of Calif.; Nevada Co. Bar Assn.; Am. Red Cross, Grass Valley; Elks; Empire Country Club; Nevada Co. Country Club; Hist. Preservation Com., Grass Valley; Sierra Nevada- Miners Hosp. Found. (pres. 1969); Democrat; Catholic; rec: world travel. Res: 214 Lucas Ln Grass Valley 95945 Ofc: 123 Bank Street, Ste D, POB 922, Grass Valley 95945

CASTRO, EDDIE MALASARTE, private security executive; b. Feb. 9, 1940, Sorsogon, Philippines; s. Eusebio Domer and Gerundia Ocampo (Malasarte) C.; m. Zenaida P. Mabini, Aug. 31, 1975; children: Edward John, b. 1976; Edgar Ryan, b. 1978; Edmund Ronald, b. 1980; edn: MS, Phil. Coll. of Criminology 1963; Rio Hondo Cll. Indsl. Security Acad. 1970; Rio Hondo Coll. Police Reserve Acad. 1978; Univ. Southwest Los Angeles 1981. Career: spl. agt. Bureau of Posts, Manila, Philippines 1962-63; police ofcr. Manila Police Dept., 1963-71; lobby dir. Cushman & Wakefield Co., Los Angeles 1972-74; sr. security ofcr. Atlantic Richfield Co., L.A. 1974-78; owner/ mgr. Fil-American Security Svc., La Puente 1978--; physical fitness instr. Stan Carbungco's Gym 1967-71; security cons. Marubeni Am. Corp. 1977-84; awards: Leadership Awd., Physical Fitness Awd., Manila Police Dept. 1963; Academic Excellence, Police Commn., Philippine 1971; Silver Awd., Internat. Physique Grading Bd. 1978; mem: Peace Ofcrs. Assn., Los Angeles Co.; Nat. Assn. of Chiefs of Police; Manilas Finest of Los Angeles (pres.); Filipino- Am. Comm. of L.A.; Fedn. of Body Builders; Catholic; rec: body building, movies, poetry. Address: Fil- American Security Service, 1520 North Rama Dr La Puente 91746

CASTRO, PAUL JOHN, public housing agency executive; b. Oct. 20, 1939, San Jose, Calif.; s. Joseph Pestana and Anne Dorothy (Andrade) C.; m. Myrna Dee Bell, Jan. 28, 1972; children: Jennifer, b. 1972, Michelle, b. 1974; edn: AA, Modesto Jr. Coll. 1959; BA, CSC Stanislaus, 1963; MS, Pepperdine Univ. 176; Accredited Personnel Mgr. (APM) 1981. Career: personnel analyst Co. of Stanislaus, Modesto 1965-68, Calif. State Personnel Bd., Sacto. 1968-69; employee rels. analyst Calif. St. Employees Assn., Sacto. 1969-70; personnel ofcr. Calif. State Coll., Bakersfield 1970-76, Kern Medical Ctr., Bksfld. 1976; owner TGIF RV Rentals, Bksfld. 1977; employment devel. ofcr. State of Calif. Empl. Devel. Dept., Bksfld. 1978, dir. personnel Housing Auth. of Co. of Kern, 1978-82, asst. exec. dir. 1982--; Kern Co. rep. to Central Calif. Health Systems Agcy. Inc. 1981-84; instr. Coll. of Profl. Studies, Univ. San Francisco; guest lectr. and ext. instr. CSC Bakersfield 1978-83; past acctg. instr. Bksfld. Business Inst.; cons. Bksfld. Home Health Agcy. and Sierra Employers Svc. 1983-84; service awards: Calif. Hlth & Welfare Agcy 1979, Kiwanis Club of Kern 1972; mem: Am. Soc. for Personnel Adminstrn. (v.p. 1982); Pers. Mgmt. Council of Modesto (pres. 1967); Kern Regl. Ctr. (bd. 1974-75); Comm. Health Ctrs. of Kern Co. (bd. 1978-9); v.p. Kern chpt. Nat. Hispanic Housing Coalition of Kern Co. 1980; mem. Nat. Assn. Housing & Redevel. Ofcls.; seminar leader, orgnzr. var. profl. assns.; contbr. arts. profl. jours.; mil: Calif. Nat. Guard 1963-68; s/sgt USAFR 1968-70; Democrat; Baptist; rec: motorcycling, camping, boating. Res: 2608 Cedar St Bakersfield 93301 Ofc: Housing Authority of Co. of Kern, 525 Roberts Lane Bakersfield 93308

CASTRO, RODOLFO HADER, county government executive; b. May 31, 1942, Riverside; s. Doroteo G. and Lillian Lucero (Diaz) C.; edn: AA (honors), RiversideCity Coll. 1967; BS (honors), Calif.State Poly. Coll. 1970; MBA, Harvard Univ. 1973; stu. city govt., mgmt., & politics, Oxford Univ. (Eng.) 1980. Career: dep. dir. Econ. Opportunity Bd., 1971; asst. dir. LULAC Nat. Edn. Svc Ctrs, 1973-75; exec. dir. L.N.E.S.C., 1975; exec. dir. Community Svc Dept., San Bernardino Co., 1976--; pres. Rodolfo H. Castro and Assocs., Inc. Honors: Energy Conserv. Award., Dept. of Energy, 1980; Calif. Legis. Resolution 305 May 15, 1981; recognition US Congl. Record, May 5, 1981; CalPoly Sch of Bus. Alumni of the Year 1981; listed Who's Who in the West (1982), Who's Who in Am. Colls and Univs (1971). Mem. bd. dirs. Mex.-Am. Commn. of San Bernardino; Am. Soc. for Pub. Adminstrn., Harvard Bus. Sch. Alumni Assn. (life), Oxford Preservation Trust (life). Mil: sgt.E-5, US Army, State Commend. Ribbon, GCM. Republican: cand. US Congl. 37th Dist. Calif. 1982 (sustaining Calif. Repub. Party, Repub. Nat. Com., Calif. Repub. Hispanic Council, Mex.-Am. Polit Assn.). Catholic. res: 250 N. Phillips, Banning 92220 ofc: Community Svc Dept. San Bernardino Co., 686 E. Mill St. San Bernardino 92415.

CASWELL, PAULETTE REVA, lawyer; b. June 8, 1951, Chgo.; d. Ben and Lillian (Cohen) Watstein; m. Charles F. Caswell III, Jan. 8, 1981; son, David Allan Philip Evidson C., b. 1976; edn: AA, cum laude, WLA Comm. Coll. 1971, BA, CSULA 1975, JD, Whittier Coll. Sch of Law 1982; hon. DD, St. Alban's Ch. of the Way; admitted Calif. State Bar 1982, US Dist. Ct. 1983; pvt. pilot 1977; Notary Pub. 1980; Calif. Comm. Coll. Teaching Cred. in Law 1982. Career: atty. sole practice; founder/ CEO: The Access Center, L.A. Area Center for Law & the Deaf; comm. coll. instr. 1982-, cons. 1975-. Awards: two scholarships, Whittier Coll. Sch. of Law 1979-82, Award of Excellence, 1982; Alpha Gamma Sigma, 1971; mem: Am., Beverly Hills, LA County Bar Assns.; Legal Assistance Assn. of Calif.; Phi Alpha Delta frat.; Mensa (Gr. LA Area dir. 1976-83); Self-Help for the Hard of Hearing; LA Deaf Svcs. Network; Acad. of Magical Arts /Magic Castle; lay assoc. Consolation Sisters, 3d Order of St. Francis; alumni assns. Publs: num. arts.; columnist, Lament (Mensa pub. 1976-83); translator legal materials for disabled persons; resrch: intl. terrorism, consumer rights, juvenile justice; Democrat; Jewish; rec: ice skating, crafts, writing. Res: 645 No Gardner St Los Angeles 90036 Ofc: The Access Ctr POB 481015, Los Angeles 90048

CATALANO, RICHARD DANIEL, surgeon; b. Sept. 6, 1951, Loma Linda; s. Donald Vincent and Anne- Marie Evelyn (Guild) C.; m. Patti Lou Smith, June 27, 1976; children: Anthony, b. 1980; Elisabeth, b. 1983; edn: BA, magna cum laude, Pacific Union Coll. 1973; MD, Loma Linda Univ. 1976; cert., Am. Bd. of Surgery 1983. Career: Loma Linda Univ. Sch. of Med. 1977-81 ;surgery intern 1977; surgery res. 1979-80; chief res. surgery 1981; trauma & burn research fellow, UC San Francisco & San Francisco Gen. Hosp. 1982-83; instr. surgery Loma Linda Univ. 1981--; mem. AMA; publs.: med. journal articles on shock; Republican; Seventh- day Adventist; rec: landscaping, bicycling, skiing. Res: 1357 Clifton Ave Redlands 92373 Ofc: Dept. of Surgery, Loma Linda Univ., Loma Linda 92354

CATERINO, NICHOLAS, corporate president; b. Dec. 7, 1938, Bronx, NY; s. Vincent and Victoria Caterino; m. Beverly B. Blackhurst, Nov. 9, 1965; 1 son: Mark; edn: AA, Orange Coast Coll. 1970; BS, San Diego State Univ. 1972. Career: asst. sales mgr. Guaranty Chev. 1972-74; sales mgr. Baron Buick 1974-76; sales mgr. Martin Chrys. 1976-78; pres. San Diego Escrow Svc., Inc. 1978--; pres. S.D. Collection Svc., Inc. 1980--; seminars on creative financing to over 5000 R.E. agents; honors: second pl. Phi Rho Pi Nat. Speech & Debate 1970; first pl. Phi Rho Pi State Speech & Debate 1970; Elk of the Yr. 1981; mem: San Diego Bd. Realtors; Optimist, Kearny Mesa; Elks (pres. 1982); mil: E-4 USN 1955-59; Republican; Catholic; rec: skiing. Res: 10432 La Morada Dr San Diego 92124 Ofc: San Diego Escrow, 8333 Clairemont Mesa Blvd San Diego 92111

CATLIN, DAVID HAROLD, corporate real estate vice president; b. June 28, 1939, Ardmore, Okla.; s. Norman Stanley and Anneliese Hanna (Summerfield) C.; edn: BS, No. Tex. St. Univ. 1962; MS, 1964; R.E. lic., Calif. Career: sys. engr. Kaiser Aluminum & Chem. Corp., Oakland 1966-70; R.E. leasing agent Grubb & Ellis Co., Oakland 1970-75; v.p./ sales mgr., Los Angeles 1975-78; v.p./ corp. secty. Vistar Comml. Brokerage Co., L.A. 1978-80; v.p. comml. div. Merrill Lynch Comml. Real Estate Co., L.A. 1980--; dir. R.E. tng., ofc. leasing, Grubb & Ellis Co., 1974-78; corp. secty Vistar Comml. Brokerage Co., L.A. 1978-80; Top Saleman of Yr., Grubb & Ellis Co. 1975; mem: Am. Indsl. Real Estate Assn.; Internat. Council of Shopping Ctrs.; L.A. Jr. CofC; Kappa Sigma frat.; mil: seaman 1/c USN Air Pgm.; Republican; rec: tennis, skiing, chess. Res: 869 Cumberland Rd Glendale 91202 Ofc: Merrill Lynch, 640 S Olive Los Angeles 90014

CATTANI, RAY A., college chancellor; b. Feb. 18, 1930, San Bernardino; s. August L. and Gertrude (Sommer) C.; m. Irene Oates, Feb. 16, 1955; chil: Keith T., b. 1955, Kent E., b. 1957, Kyle, b. 1960, Kathleen, b. 1962, Kara, b. 1974; edn: BS, Brigham Young Univ. 1957, MS, Ore. State Univ. 1960, PhD, Univ. Ariz. 1963. Career: chem. faculty mem. Phoenix Coll., 1963 66; prof. of chem. (chmn. Chemistry Dept.), Mesa (AZ) Community Coll., 1966-67, Dean of Instrn., 1967-73; Exec. Dean, Scottsdale (AZ) Comm. Coll., 1973-76; pres. Kings River Comm. Coll., Reedley, Calif. 1976-81; chancellor State Center Comm. Coll. Dist., Fresno 1981--. Bd. dirs. Cal. Assn. of Community Colls. 1982-; bd. dirs. Chief Executive Officers of Calif., 1982-; cons., examiner (1970-76), exec. bd. (1976-) No. Central Assn.; mem: AAUP (pres. Phoenix chpt. 1965); Am. Chem. Soc. (chmn. Central Ariz. Sect. 1969 71); Am. Inst. of Chemists (pres. Ariz. chpt. 1969 70); past dir. Scottsdale CofC; Rotarian (1970-); Republican; L.D.S. Ch.; rec: piano, waterski, tennis. res: 8350 S. Frankwood, Reedley 93654. ofc: 1525 E. Weldon Ave. Fresno 93704.

CAYLOR THOMAS ONKALO, real estate broker; b. May 16, 1938, San Francisco; s. Arthur Raymond and Hilda (Onkalo) C.; edn: BS econ., Willamette Univ. 1960. Career: editor Janeway Publishing, NY 1960-63; free-lance writer, 1965; columnist San Francisco Examiner, 1966; assoc. with S.F. Chamber of Commerce as mgr. Internat. div. and editor S.F. Business Mag., 1967-73; vice pres. MayLee Industries, 1974-75; real estate broker, Grubb and Ellis, 1976; real estate broker TRI Realtors, Inc. San Francisco 1977--, dir. 1984-; mem: Nat., Calif. Assn. of Realtors, S.F. Bd. of Realtors (PAC), v.chmn. S.F. Economic Opportunity Councl, mem. S.F. Commn. for Sch. Desegregation, mem. S.F. Charter Revisio Commn., v.p. Chinese Culture Found., dir. Constnl. Rights Found., Sausalito Yacht Club (dir.); Republican; rec: sailing, skiing, music. Res: 2939 Fillmore St San Francisco 94123 Ofc: TRI Realtors Inc. 1699 Van Ness Ave San Francisco 94109

CEDAR, PAUL ARNOLD, clergyman; b. Nov. 4, 1938, Minneapolis, MN; s. Carl Benjamin and Bernice Myrtle (Peterson) Cedar; B.S., Northern State Coll., 1960; M.Div., Northern Baptist Theol. Seminary, 1968; D.Min., Amer. Baptist Seminary of the West, 1973; also grad. work, Trinity Divinity Sch., Univ. of Iowa, Wheaton Grad. Sch., Cal. State Univ., Fullerton; m. Jean Lier, Aug. 25, 1959; children: Daniel, b. 1961; Mark, b. 1963; Deborah, b. 1967. Career: youth minister, Cedar Rapids, IA, 1960-63; crusade assoc., Billy Graham Evangelistic Assn., 1963-65; sr. pastor, Naperville, IL, 1965-67; crusade dir., Billy Graham Evangelistic Assn., 1967-69; sr. pastor, Yorba Linda, CA, 1969-73; exec. pastor/ Evangelism pastor, First Presby. Chr., Hollywood, CA, 1975-80; sr. pastor, Lake Ave. Congregational Ch., Pasadena, 1981--; founder, pres., Dynamic Communications, Inc., 1973--; also adj. prof., Fuller Theol. Seminary, Talbot Theo Seminary; visiting prof., Trinity Divinity Sch.; mem., advisory bd., Amer Inst. of Family Relations; ch. cons. Awards: Natl. Pi Kappa Delta Award, 1960; Outstanding Bible Reading Award, Amer. Bible Soc., 1967. Mem.: life, Pi Kappa Delta; secty., Hollywood Rotary Club, 1978-80; chaplain, Hollywood Coord. Council, 1980; Christian Assn. for Psychol. Studies, 1977--; mem., Hollywood Ministerial Assn., 1979-80; seminar leader, Natl. Convocation of Christian Leaders, 1979, 80; delegate, Consultation on World Evangelization, Pattaya, Thailand, 1980. Author: Seven Keys to Maximum Communication, Tyndale House Publrs., 1980; Becoming a Lover!, Tyndale House Publrs., 1978; Sharing the Good Life!, 1980. Congregationalist. Rec.: athletics, music, writing, carpentry. Res.: 1771 E. Orange Grove, Pasadena; Office: Lake Ave. Congregational Ch., 393 N. Lake Ave., Pasadena 91101.

CEDILLOS, RON, aerospace testing co. executive; b. July 31, 1950, Los Angeles; s. Art and Anna Gloria (Romo) C.; children: Michelle, b. 1976; Ronnie, b. 1977; edn: El Camino Coll. 1970-72. Career: profl. athlete, Karate; motion picture actor; bd. chmn./CEO, Cedillos Testing Co., Inc., Downey; lectr. USC; mem: Am. Soc. of Non-Destructive Testing; Who's Who in Aero Space; exec. bd. Los Angeles Area Council BSA; mil: paratrooper, US Army 1967-70; Republican; Christian; rec: sailing, tennis. Res: 16941 Coral Cay Ln Huntington Harbor 92649 Ofc: Cedillos Testing Co. Inc. 12309 So Woodruff Ave Downey 90241

CELLI, THOMAS MICHAEL, lawyer, b. July 26, 1937, Brooklyn, NY; s. Michael Celli and Gertrude (Drago) Celli Lese; m. Adriana, July 23, 1977; chil: Rosemarie Lese, b. 1963, Thomas Paul, b. 1981, Joseph Louis, b. 1982; edn: BS in B.A., Univ. Ariz. 1962; JD, Southwestern Univ. 1971. Career: trial atty./sr. partner Kramer and Celli, Los Angeles 1972--, spec. advocacy civil liberties. Honors: commendation, Senate, Calif. Legislature, 1982. Mem: Nat. Panel Am. Arbitration Assn.; Assn. Trial Lawyers of Am.; Los Angeles Trial Lawyers Assn. Mil: AK-2 USN 1955-58; Catholic; rec: sailing. res: 15442 E. Golden Ridge Ln. Hacienda Hts 91745 ofc: Kramer & Celli 3250 Wilshire Blvd PH2207, Los Angeles 90010

CENZANO, OTTO M., JR., systems design engineer; b. Aug. 2, 1954, Los Angeles; s. Otto M. and Elisa S. (Santana) C.; edn: under grad., Calif. Tech. 1972 76. Career: staff programmer L.A. Co. Sanitation Dists., L.A. 1975-77; engr. TRAN Telecommunications, L.A. 1978-79; cons. Digital Sys., Jet Propulsion Lab., Caltech, Pasadena 1980-82; sys. engr. Cardrey Systems, Los Angeles 1982--; tnr. stress reduction, UCLA Ext.; mem: IEEE; Jobs for Peace; The Community for the Devel. of Equilibrium of the Human Being; works: experimentation in robotics, communication systems; rec: computer systems, mountain trout fishing, chess. Res: 11960 Modjeska Pl Mar Vista 90066 Ofc: Cardrey Systems, 20660 Bahama St Chatsworth 91311

CERCHIO, GERARD JOSEPH PETER, computer software researcher; b. Feb. 7, 1953, Jersey City, NJ; s. Salvatore Lewis and Anna (Migliore) C. Sr.; edn: Stevens Inst. of Tech., 1973, St. Peters Coll. 1973-4, Rutgers Univ. 1974-7. Career: contractor Efficiency Htg. & Appliance Co., Jersey City 1969-73; lab. mgr. Human Exptl. Lab, Rutgers Univ. 1974-76; system cons. Bell Labs., Murray Hill, NJ 1976-7; profl. staff Informatics PMI, assigned to NASA Ames Research, Mt. View, Ca. 1978; systems cons. Intel Magnetics, Santa Clara 1979, Cyclotron Corp., Berkeley 1980, Diasonics Corp., Milpitas 1981; founder Emergency Data Corp., San Jose 1981; founder Rimtel Corp., San Jose 1982; founder/technical dir. Interactive Research Corp., Santa Clara 1982, mem. bd. dirs. Awards: World Class Championship Pgm, PC Mag. 1983; class award, Stone Sculpture, 1977. Mem: IEEE, Assn. for Computing Machinery, Aircraft Owners & Pilots Assn., Interactive Communication Soc. Works: KEYNOTE keyboard enhancer for the IBM PC, concurrent video edn. system; real time ocular monitoring/analysis system (1976); electronic tachistiscope (1975); publs: art. on Computer Software & Video Disk, ICS Jour. 1984. Rec: music composition, pianist, aviation, sculpture. Res: 1110 Whirlow Pl San Jose 95131 Ofc: Interactive Research Corp. 3080 Olcott St, 200B, Santa Clara 95051

CERETTO, WILLIAM J., physician-cardiologist; b. Sept. 19, 1947, Rock Springs, Wyo.; s. Alvin M. and Bobbie Dees (Clayton) C.; m. Marietta Bonello, June 10, 1978; children: Mario Dante, b. 1982, Gian Marco, b. 1983; edn: BS, Univ. of Wyo. 1969; MD, Univ. of Colo. 1973. Career: med. intern, resident internal med., US Naval Hosp., San Diego 1973-76, Fellow, cardiology 1976-78, staff cardiologist/dir. Coronary Care Unit 1978-80; current: cardiol. staff Alvarado Comm. Hosp., S.D.; dir. Echocardiography Lab. 1980--; asst. clin. prof. UC San Diego Dept. of Med. 1980--; mem: Fellow Am. Coll. Cardiology, Fellow Am. Coll. Chest Physicians, Fellow Council of Clin. Cardiol., Fellow American Coll. of Physicians (Council on Critical Care), San Diego County Med. Soc., S.D. Co. Heart Assn. (bd. dirs.; spkrs com.); mem. Am., San Diego Soc. of Echocardiography; bd. dirs. The Echocardiography Found. of Grossmont Coll.; publs: arts. in med. journals; mil: lcdr. USN 1973-80; Republican; Prot.; rec: skiing, jogging, pro football & baseball. Res: 5850 Overlake San Diego 92120 Ofc: Cardiology Dept., 6655 Alvarado Rd San Diego 92120

CERKO, EUGENE ANDREW, chemical metallurgist, physicist; b. Dec. 11, 1950, Freeport, Long Island, NY; s. Stanley Benedykt and Helen Madelyn (Walko) C.; edn: USC 1968-73. Career: founder/pres. Cerko Corp. (metal processing & fabrication co.) 1969--; estab. additional splty. corp. with two divs., 1974; honors: Vendor of the Month, Zero Defects, US Dept. of Defense, Hughes Aircraft 1984; mem. Calif. Scholarship Fedn. 1965-68; Third Pl. for Research & Devel., Calif. Army Core of Engrs. 1968; works: invented new chem. process for dissolution of rhodium to a sufate complex; Republican; rec: insect collecting, nuclear research, scuba diving. Res: 2515 Bamboo Street Newport Beach 92660 Ofc: Cerko Corp., 1288 S Lyon Santa Ana 92705

CERULLO, MORRIS, evangelist, educator, missionary; b. Oct. 20, 1931, Passaic, NJ; s. Joseph and Bertha (Rosenblatt) C.; m. Vivian Theresa LePari, July 27, 1951; children: David, b. 1952, Susan, b. 1954, Mark, b. 1957; ed. New England Bible Coll. 1951; Ordained clergyman 1952. Career: pastor Clairemont Assembly of God ch., New Hampshire 1952; conducted Christian evangelistic crusades, domestic and fgn., 1953-59; pastor Calvary Temple, South Bend, Ind. 1959; founder/pres. World Evangelism, Inc., San Diego 1960--; conducts

Christian evangelistic crusades and teaching seminars and confs. in USA and internat.; holds Schs. of Ministry worldwide, has personally trained more than 250,000 in over 70 nations; honors: Hon. H.H.D., Fla. Beacon Coll. 1974; San Diego Press Club Headliner in Religion 1978; listed, Who's Who in Religion; mem: Canadian Acad. for Cultural Exchange (hon. dir.), Nat. Assn. of Evangelicals, Evangelical Press Assn., San Diego CofC, S.D. Vis. & Conv. Bur., World Affairs Council; works: films/video: Masada (1976), Advent II & Advent III (1980-81); author approx. 50 books incl. Two Men From Eden, You Can Know How To Defeat Satan, Proof Producers; publisher Victory mag.; Prot. (interdenom.). Res: POB 700 San Diego 92138 Ofc: World Evangelism Inc., 1415 Sixth Ave San Diego 92101

CESARI, PIERORESTE, manufacturing co. executive; b. Dec. 13, 1942, Rome, Italy; s. Ruggero and Geltrude (Fontana) C.; children: Joyce, b. 1973, Cristina, b. 1975, Nicole Clotilde, b. 1984; edn: stu. Coll. of Scis., Rome 1961, Rome Univ. Sch. of Engring. 1961-66, Univ. of Naples Sch. of Polit. Scis. & Fgn. Languages 1966-68; Master, Univ. of Camerino Sch. of Polit. Scis. 1968-72. Career: prodn. mgr. for Far East Market, F.A.R.O., Spa. Milano, Italy 1974-77, bd. dirs. 1975-77; gen. mgr., v.p., pres. F.A.R.O.- USA, Burlingame, Calif. 1977-83; v.p. Ardet- USA (mfg. dental x-ray machine), Burlingame, Ca./Pennsauken, NJ 1983--; Rotarian; author prize winning political essay 1961; served to capt. Italian Army Arty. 1969-71; rec: flying, equestrian, fox hunting. Res: 218 Beach Park Blvd Foster City 94404 Ofc: Ardet-USA, 1320 Marsten Rd, Ste. B, Burlingame 94010

CHACKO, THOMAS, manufacturing co. executive; b. Apr. 28, 1941, Kerala, India, nat. 1984; s. Kunjumman and Achamma (Koruthu) C.; m. Rachel Thomas, May 28, 1967; children: Jacob, b. 1968; Joseph, b. 1972; Jyothi, b. 1978; edn: BS, Univ. of Kerala, India 1962; BA, Olivet Nazarene Coll. 1972; MBA, Governor's State Univ. 1976; CPA candidate. Career: Kroehler Mfg., Naperville, Ill. 1972-78: payroll & budget supvr. 1972-75, cost acctg. supvr. 1975-77, costing & budget mgr. 1977-78; dir. of audit costing & budget Allied Fine Furn., Compton 1979-81, v.p. fin. 1981--; mem: Nat. Assn. Accts.; Am. Inst. Corp. Controllers; Republican; Christian; rec: bowling, golf. Res: 11049 Borson Norwalk 90650 Ofc: Allied Fine Furniture, Inc., 18626 S Reyes Ave Compton 90221

CHADWICK, PATRICIA LOUISE, plumbing contractor; b. Aug. 25, 1931, Los Angeles; d. Charles and Etta Mae (Bech) Myberger; m. Ted Chadwick, Dec. 18, 1948; children: Sharon M. (Thornton), b. 1949; Nancy L. (Ingram), b. 1951; Lois P. (Lopez), b. 1954; Millee J. (Espinosa), b. 1958; Ann I., b. 1960; edn: bus. mgmt. Los Angeles St. Coll. 1961; Calif. Lic. Plumbing Contractor 1970. Career: co-owner family bus., Chadwick Plumbing, Lakeport 1960--; profl. race boat driver 1965-, first woman to win Drivers Title, Grand Nat. Catalina Ski Race 1981; ranked in top ten drivers; first woman to vote for the World Team Selections (for the world water ski titles held in Sidney, Austral. 1984); mem. Nat. Speedboat & Water Ski Assn. (1st woman pres.); 1st woman commodore of No. Calif. Boat & Ski Racing Assn. Res: 562 Hillcrest Dr Lakeport 95453 Ofc: Chadwick Plumbing 864 Parallel Dr Lakeport 95453

CHAHAL, SUKHJIT SINGH, physician; b. Feb. 10, 1948, Kapurthala, Punjab, India; s. Manqhar Singh and Kulwant Kaur (Binning) C.; m. Taptesh, Feb. 5, 1977; children: Harpreet, b.1979; Harkiranjit, b. 1980; edn: pre- med., Punjabi Univ. Patiala 1966, M.B.,B.S. 1971; post grad. Univ. of Leeds, UK 1972-77. Career: surgical res. Univ. of NY, Buffalo 1977-81; pvt. practice, surgery 1981--; honors: Fellow Royal Coll. Surgeons Edinburgh (1975), England (1976), Canada (1981); Diplomate Am. Bd. Surgery 1982; Fellow, Internat. Coll. of Surgeons 1983; college honors in Athletics and Soccer, and Sportsman of Year award 1971; publs: four surgical papers, Univ. of NY, Buffalo 1977-81; Sikh Assn. of No. Am.; rec: tennis, soccer. Res: 240 W Los Altos Fresno 93704 Ofc: 3718 N First Fresno 93726

CHAKOS, TOM J., time equipment company president; b. Aug. 24, 1928, Gary, IN; s. James A. and Demetria (Monanderos) Chakos; edn: BS, mech. engring., Purdue Univ., 1954; m. Mary Gusan, Sept. 25, 1955; chil: Jim, b. 1957; Susan, b. 1960; Cath, b. 1961; Alan, b. 1964. Career: sales engr., Honeywel, Chicago, 1955; instr., Purdue Univ. Calumet Center, Hammond, Ind., 1956-58; sales engr., Barber-Coleman-Wheelco Div., Chicago, 1958; branch mgr., Stromberg Time, San Francisco, Calif., 1958-61; self-employed, dba Industrial Packaging Engineers, then dba Industrial Time Engineers, San Francisco, 1961-64; pres., Timpac, Inc., San Francisco, 1964---; dir., National Time Equipment Assn., 1981, 82. Mem: Masons, 32 degree; Shriners; Peninsula Golf & CC; Little League, dir./asst. district dir., 1966-71. Mil: 2nd Lt., US Army, Antiaircraft & Guided Missiles, 1951-53. Republican. Presbyterian. Rec: photography, golf, antique autos. Res: 800 Tournament Dr., Hillsborough 94010; Office: Timpac, Inc., 273 E. Harris Ave., S. San Francisco 94080.

CHALMERS, R. SCOTT, property management executive; b. Mar. 27, 1947, Ross; s. William and Eleanor May (Schwerin) C.; m. Cynthia L. Gaddy, Aug. 21, 1971; children: Christa, b. 1975; Cara, b. 1978; edn: A, Napa Jr. Coll. 1970; BA, CSU Chico 1972; MBA, 1974. Career: mobile home ind. (4 yrs.); controller real estate devel. & const. corp. (3 yrs.); founder/ pres. PSC Associates, Inc. 1981--; mem: Calif. Apart. Assn. (Budget Com.); No. Valley Propety Owners Assn.; Rotary; Butte Special Olympics (pres. 1982-84); mil: E-4 US Army 967-69; rec: softball, swimming, golf. Res: 1675 Hooker Oak Ave Chico 95926 Ofc: RSC Associates, Inc., 585 Manzanita Ave, Ste 3, Chico 95926

CHAMBERLAIN, JOHN PAUL, lawyer; b. June 11, 1943, Brooklyn, NY; s. Leslie John and Helen (Chesne) C.; m. Dorothy Dubac, May 2, 1969; children:

Keith Andrew, b. 1974; Jason Randolph, b. 1976; edn: BA, honors, Brooklyn Coll. (CUNY) 1965; JD, Univ. of Colo. 1968; admitted to practice, Colo. 1968, Wash. DC 1972, NY 1973, Calif. 1980. Career: asst. treas. Chase Manhattan Bank, NYC 1968-74; Judge Advocate, USAF 1969-72; asst. v.p. Nat. Bank of No. Am. 1974-78; asst. v.p. Security Pacific Nat. Bank, Los Angeles 1979-80; pvt. practice, law, Santa Ana 1980--; staff instr. Calif. Comm. Colls.; chmn. bd. Gluten Intolerance Soc. of Calif. 1983; honors: Mil. Judge, USAF 1970; Outstanding Young Men of Am., Jaycees 1970; Man of Achiev., UK 1976; Chmn. Rockland Co. New York Heart Assn. 1977-78; mem: Am. Bar Assn. Subcom. on Aerospace law Insts.); NY, Calif. & Wash. DC Bar Assns.; Gluten Intolerance Soc. of Calif.; Am. Heart ASsn.; publs: sev. arts. on law, var. legal & profl. journs. 1970-; mil: capt. USAF 19969-72; rec: sailing, astronomy, pvt. aviation. Res: 40 Shearwater Irvine 92714 Ofc: 401 Civic Center Dr W, Ste 1000, Santa Ana 92701

CHAMBERLIN, ROBERT JOSEPH, marketing executive; b. Sept. 8, 1929, Weatherford, Tex.; s. Tracy W. and Dorothy P. (O'Hare) C.; m. Ilene Krepps, Sept. 17, 1978; children: Robin, b. 1962, Russell, b. 1950; edn: BA mktg., and BS psych., honors, Duke Univ., 1951. Career: (current) pres./CEO: Modern Methods of Merchandising, Inc., American National Energy Programs Corp., All American Distributors, Inc.; mgmt. sev. automobile dealerships; (past) owner/opr. supper clubs in Hawaii; v.p./sales dir. Hawaii Clay Products, Inc.; investment banker in Texas (Ins. Co. of Tex., Am. Atlas Ins. Co., Am. Trust Ins. Co., The Lanark Corp., etc.); honors: Lambda Chi Alpha, pres. Shoe N' Slipper Club (Duke 49-51), Heavyweight Champion Boxing 1948, USMC; mem: Chamber of Commerce (Granada Hills), Better Bus. Bur., Jaycees (TX, HI); mil: gunnery sgt. USMC, Silver Star, Bronze Star, Purple Heart, Pres. Unit Cit.; Democrat; Baptist; rec: reading, travel. Res: 15455 Glenoaks Blvd, 9 Sir Henry, Sylmar 91342 Ofc: Modern Methods Mdsg. Inc. 17050 Chatsworth, 106-115, Granada Hills 91344

CHAMBERS, GARY LEE, trial lawyer; b. June 6, 1953, Inglewood; s. George Edmund and Beverly Jean (Shuler) C.; edn: BA, Univ. of Redlands 1975; JD, Western State Univ. 1978. Career: assoc. Paliz & Assocs., Westminster 1979; sole practitioner, Law Ofcs. of Gary L. Chambers, Orange 1979-80; assoc. Giles, Callahan, McCune, Willis & Edwards, Tustin 1980-81; assoc. Law Ofcs. of Mark E. Edwards, Tustin 1981-82; partner Edward, Chambers & Hoffman3; lectr. A Day in the Court Sem., Calif. Trial Lawyers Assn. 1983; mem: Calif. & Orange Co. Trial Lawyers Assns.; Assn. of Trial Lawyers of Am.; Orange Co. Bar Assn.; assoc. ed: Trial Practice, Orange Co. Trial Lawyers Assn. Monthly Newsletter 1983; contbg. author: OCTLA Monthly Newsletter 1982-83; Democrat; Christian; rec: snow skiing, surfing, athletics. Res: 21878 Mirador Mission Viejo 92691 Ofc: Edwards, Chambers & Hoffman, 17541 Seventeenth Street Tustin 92680

CHAMBERS, JOHN BERNARD, aerospace co. executive; b. Nov. 5, 1952, Tucson, Ariz.; s. Wess Pesley and Bonnie Lee (Wheeler) C.; m. Sherry Gayle Lloyd, Nov. 1, 1980; 1 dau: Heidi, b. 1974; edn: Univ. of Ariz. 1972-76; NDT Spec., USAF 1972; thermography spec., Inframetrics Co. 1983. Career: NDT tech. Hughes Aircraft Co., Tucson, Ariz. 1974-75; level II NDT eng. Rockwell Internat., Columbus, Oh. 1977; test QA engr. Rockwell Internat., White Sands, NM 1977-79; R&D sr./ QA eng. Thiokol Corp., Brigham City, Utah 1979-83; asst. mgr. Aerojet Corp., Sacto. 1983--; quality engr. cons. Space Shuttle, Filament Wound Case, Hercules Corp., Thiokol Corp. 1982-83; Outstanding Achiev., Space Shuttle Pgm., NASA 1983; works: arch. design of two solar houses in NM 1978; Quality cost reduction & control, Thiokol Corp. 1981; Devel. of Thermography, Aerospace Ind., Aerojet 1984; Ct. Devel., Aerojet 1983; mil: s/sgt. Air Nat. Guard 1971-78; rec: architectural design, skiing, investment. Res: 5130 Sunrise Hills Dr Fair Oaks 95628 Ofc: Aerojet, POB 15699C Sacramento

CHAN, ARTHUR YING MAU, executive; b. Dec. 5, 1940, Hong Kong; s. Chan Sik and Sui Po (Yuk) Yam; m. Amphorn Eiamsakulrat, Nov. 26, 1967; children: Angela, b. 1969; Anderson, b. 1972; edn: B.Math., San Francisco State UNiv. 1964. Career: pres., San Franicsco: Art's Trading Co. 1968; Winston Oriental Foods, Inc. 1975; Unicord USA, Inc. 1977; Chinatown Devel., Inc. 1977; dir. Calif. Nat. Bank 1982; mem: Chinese Am. Assn. of Commerce (v.p. 1982); S.F. Elim Ch.; S.F. Chinatown Lions Club; Christian; rec: swimming, bowling, table tennis. Res: 1053 Clay Street San Francisco 94108 Ofc: Art's Trading Co., 830 7th Street San Francisco 94107

CHAN, DAVID HONG-NIN, certified public accountant; b. Mar. 21, 1957, Hong Kong; s. Ge Sim and Ping Oi (Wong) C.; m. Shirley Yung, Aug. 20, 1983; edn: BSBA, CSU Los Angeles 1979; CPA, Calif. 1982. Career: cashier/ stocker Food Bargain Mkt., Los Angeles 1975-79; sr. acct. Margolis & Meyer, CPAs, L.A. 1980-82; sr. acct. Friedman, Rosenthal, Knell & Co., L.A. 1982-83; owner David H. Chan, CPA, L.A. 1983--; Voluntary Income Tax Asst. (VITA) 1978-79; mem: Calif. Soc. CPAs; Chinese Christian Ctr.; (pres. Youth Fellowship 1978-79); publs: Your Own Income Tax, 12/83; Christian; rec: volley ball, sports, music. Address: David H. Chan, CPA, 924 N Electric Ave Alhambra 91801

CHAN, DAVID RONALD, certified public accountant, lawyer; b. Aug. 3, 1948; s. David Yew and Anna May (Wong) C.; m. Mary Anne, June 21, 1980; children: Eric David, b. 1981, Christina Mary, b. 1982; edn: AB, econ., UCLA 1969; MS, bus. adm., UCLA 1970; JD, UCLA Sch. of Law, 1973. Admitted to Calif. State Bar, US Ct. of Appeals (9th Cir.), US Claims Ct., US Tax Ct. Career: staff accountant Touche Ross & Co., Los Angeles 1970; acct. Oxnard Celery Distbrs Inc., L.A. 1971-73; tax. dept. Kenneth Leventhal & Co., L.A. 1973--, presently mgr. National Tax Dept.; gen. ptnr. DRC Saticoy Enterprises,

1980--; real estate broker; co-dir. KL Tax Hall of Fame, 1980--; awards: John Forbes Gold Medal, Calif. Soc. of CPAs, 1970; Elijah Watt Sells Certificate, Am. Inst. of CPAs, 1970; Newton Becker Award, 1970; Phi Beta Kappa, Betta Gamma Sigma, Beta Alpha Psi, num. other hons. Mem. Chinese Hist. Soc. of So. Calif. (past bd. dir.); Orgn. of Chinese Americans; Chinese for Affirmative Action; Hawaii Chinese Hist. Center; Chinese Cultural Found. of San Francisco; Chinese Hist. Soc. of Am.; L.A. County Bar Assn.; So. Calif. Chinese Lawyers Assn.; Am. Assn. of Atty-CPAs; Am. Inst. of CPAs; Calif. Soc. of CPAs; co-founder Legends of Tax (tax profl. social orgn.); UCLA Alumni Assn. (life); UCLA Bruin Bench; UCLA Coll. of Letters and Scisc. Dean's Council organizing com.; L.A. Bicentennial 200 Speakers Bur.; publs: num. articles on taxation, philately, and Chinese-Am. studies incl: The Five Chinatowns of Los Angeles, The Tragedy and Trauma of the Chinese Exclusion Laws, Chinese-American Heritage: Historical and Contemporary Perspectives, Structuring the Real Estate Syndicate, Pre-Combination First Day Covers, Sale of Property Developed on Leased Land; contbr. restaurant review, East West Chinese Am. Jour.; frequent spkr. on Chinese role and history in the US; Republican (Nat. Com.); rec: philately, photog., post cards. Res: 4127 Don Diablo Dr Los Angeles 90008 Ofc: 2049 Century Park East, Ste. 1700, Los Angeles 909067

CHAN, ESTHER MAN-KWAI, real estate broker, medical corporation executive; b. Aug. 25, 1946, Kwangsi, China; nat. 1978; d. Wm. and Doris (Young) Tsai; m. Samuel Chan, MD (past pres. Chinese Physicians of So.Calif.), Dec. 27, 1969; chil: Kenneth, b. 1972, Gary, b. 1975, Kevin, b. 1977, Kinman, b. 1979; edn: Chinese Univ. of Hong Kong 1964-66, Biola Coll. 1966-67; BA, sociol., CSU Los Angeles 1969; grad. stu. Tufts Univ. 1969; real estate sales lic., Anthony Sch. 1975; lic. real estate broker 1976. Career: founder Chinese Svc Ctr of Los Angeles, 1969; statistician State of Tenn. Dept. of Pub. Hlth Stat. Div.1969-74; real estate sales agent First Am. Realty, Torrance 1974-75; R.E. broker/pres. Chancellor Realty Inc., Rolling Hills Estates 1977--; dir. Samuel C. Chan, M.D. Inc.; apt. owner/bldg. contr. 1980-, condo conversion 1982-; investment R.E. Broker; dealer Chinese antiques; prin. J.E.S. Trading Co.; co-ordinator hlth care elderly. Awards: scholarships: Chinese Univ. of Hong Kong 1964-7, Tufts Univ. Grad. Sch of Sociol. 1969; spl. commendations, Gov. of Tenn. 1970, LA Mayor Tom Bradley, 1982, Mem: Chinese Physician Soc., Rolling Hills, Torrance Bds. of Realtors, CofC. Democrat; Prot.; rec: tennis, fish, riding. res: 420 Paseo Del Mar, Palos Verdes Est. 90274 ofc: Chancellor Realty Inc. 916 Silver Spur Rd. Ste. 203, Rolling Hills Est.; Samuel C. Chan MD, 2777 Pacific Ave. Ste.N, Long Beach 90806

CHAN, FLORENCE MAY HARN, librarian; b.Victoria, B.C., Canada; d. Jack Nam and Eva (Lowe) Yipp; chil: Jonathan Hoyt, b. 1960, Barry Alan, b. 1963; edn: BA, Univ. of Brit. Columbia 1953; MLS, UC Berkeley 1956; MA, CSU San Jose 1976. Career: circulation/ref. asst. Victoria (B.C.) Pub. Lib. 1953-54; cataloger Golden Gate Coll., San Francisco 1956-57; catalog/ref. libn. Coll. of San Mateo, 1957-60; catalog/ref. libn. Canada Coll., Redwood City 1968-75, coord. lib. svcs., 1975--; co-director Center for the American Musical, Canada Coll.; publ: (worktext) Using Library Resources (1976); pres., Asian American Comm.Council of San Mateo Co.; secty. Canada Faculty Senate; mem. CSUSJ Dept. of Instrnl. Tech. Adv. Com. Mem: ALA, Calif. Lib. Assn., Community Coll. Media Assn., San Mateo Co. Hist. Assn., Phi Kappa Phi hon. soc.; Episcopal (Ch. Women); rec: photog., sew, piano, travel; ofc: Canada Coll. 4200 Farm Hill Blvd. Redwood City 94061.

CHAN, GRACE LAI-MAN, environmental engineer; b. Sept. 1, 1956, Hong Kong; d. Chun-Kwan Felix and Chui-Ping (Chow) Fong; m. John Chan, Oct. 4, 1980; edn: BS, USC 1979; MS, 1980; profl. engr., civil eng., Calif. 1982. Career: assoc. engr. PRC Engineering, Inc., Orange 1980--; honors: Phi Beta Kappa 1979; mem: Water Pollution Control Fedn.; works: writing scripts & broadcasting, a Chinese Radio Pgm., Chinese Outreach, 1978-82; Christian; rec: singing, drama, house plants. Res: 555 S Azusa Ave, Apt. 12, Azusa 91702 Ofc: PRC Engineering, 972 Town & Country Rd Orange 92667

CHAN, IU-CHOI, electronic data processing accountant; b. Oct. 18, 1953, Hong Kong; s. Chow and Yee (Wong) C.; edn: BS, CSU Bakersfield 1982. Career: programmer Occidental Petroleum, Bakersfield 1982; EDP asst. controller CPC Financial Corp., Bakersfield 1982--; awards: Scholarship, local chpt. Bakersfield CPA; Scholarship, Valley Fed. Savings & Loan; Beta Gamma Sigma; mem: New Zealand Inst. of Mgmt.; Alumni Assn. of CSU Bakersfield; Decision Support Sys., CSU Bakersfield; rec: soccer, table tennis, Mah-Jong. Res: 2072 S Stine Bakersfield 93309 Ofc: CPC Financial Corp., 5055 California Ave, Ste 101, Bakersfield 93309

CHAN, MARGARET MAY-SHENG, marketing specialist; b. June 28, 1951, NY; d. Shu-Kang and Chui-Kwan (Tsang) C.; edn: BS, Univ. of Santa Clara 1972; MA, UC Berkeley 1976; PhD, 1978. Career: research & tng. asst. UC Berkeley 1976-78; postdoctoral research assoc. 1978-80; sr. applications biochemist Beckman Instruments 1981-83; mktg. prod. spec. 1983--; tech. cons., co. customers & sales reps., Beckman Instrument 1981-; honors: Gamma Pi Epsilon, Univ. of Santa Clara 1972; mem: Am. Assn. for Adv. of Sci.; Am. Chem. Soc.; Assn. for Women in Sci.; Mendel Soc., UC Santa Clara; num. arts. on metabolic reactions. Res: POB 1154 San Leandro 94577 Ofc: Beckman Instruments, 1716 4th St Berkeley 94710

CHAN, PAUL K., high-technology co. chief executive; b. Sept. 25, 1949, Hong Kong, UK; s. Yuen Ken and Wai Yin (Ng) C.; m. Mona Wong, May 4, 1980; 1 dau: Melissa, b. 19982; edn: BSEE, Ore. State Univ. 1970; MSEE, UC Berkeley 1974. Career: R&D engr. AMI, Inc., Santa Clara 1975-77; sr. prod. devel. engr.

Signetics Corp. 1977-79; sr. LSI design engr. Intel Corp. 1979-80; sr. devel. engr. Nat. Semiconductor Corp. 1980-83; prod. mgr. Synertek, Inc., Honeywell Corp. Subsidary 1983; CEO/ pres. Chan & Assoc. Internat. 1984--; cons. computers & IC, Chan & Assoc. Internat. 1984; honors: Tai Beta Pi; Oregon State Scholarship; mem: ABL of Santa Clara (founding); IEEE; CIE USA Bay area chpt.; works: pioneer in microelectronics areas such as RAM & Microcomputer on a Chip' research & devel.; Catholic; rec: tennis, ping- pong, dancing. Res: 2738 Mignon Dr San Jose 95132 Ofc: Chan & Assocs. Internat., San Jose 95132

CHAN, RAYMOND K., dentist; b. Dec. 18, 1952, San Francisco; s. Thomas Wo and Jeannie Chan; m. Mary Ho, Sept. 6, 1980; edn: AB, honors, UC Berkeley 1975; DDS, Northwestern Univ. Dental Sch. 1979. Career: research asst. Am. Dental Assn., Chgo. 1977-79; clinical instr. Northwestern Univ. Dental Sch., Chgo. 1979-80; assoc. dentist Northwestern Univ. Med. Assocs. 1979-80; owner/ gen. dentist, San Lorenzo 1981--, (inc. 1982); ADA Research Asst. 1977-79; clinical instr. Northwestern Univ. Dental Sch. 1979-80; ed. Northwestern Univ. Dental Sch. Newsletter 1977-79; awards: Sci. Awd., Air Force ROTC; Academic Awd., Air Force ROTC; mem: Am., Calif. & Ill. Dental Assns.; Chgo. & S. Alameda Co. Dental Socs.; Acad. of Gen. Dentistry; publs: Follow- up Guide for new Christians, 9/82; Northwestern Univ. Dental Sch. Newsletter (2 yrs.); mil: USAF ROTC; Republican; Christian. Res: 21100 Gray Dr, 120, Hayward 94546 Ofc: Raymond K. Chan, DDS, Inc., 15522 Hesperian Blvd San Lorenzo 94580

CHAN, RAYMOND YUEN-FONG, ophthalmologist; b. Nov. 2, 1948, Shanghai, China, nat. 1979; s. Joy Ka-on and So-Ying (Cheung) C.; m. Helen Chang, Feb. 25, 1982; 1 son: Stephen, b. 1983; edn: BS, aero. eng., BS, mech. eng., Cal Poly 1971; MS, Cal Tech 1972; PhD, 1975; MD, Univ. of Miami Sch. of Med. 1977; fellow, Am. Acad. Ophthalm.; diplomate, Am. Bd. Ophthalm. Career: clinical instr. Baylor Coll. of Med., Houston, Tex. 1977-81; staff ophthalmologist Scripps Clinic & Research Found., La Jolla 1981--; clinical instr. UC San Diego 1983--; spkr. Eighth Biennial Cataract Surgical Congress, Houston, Tex. 1982; spkr. Am. Acad. of Ophthalm. Annual Meeting 1982; awards: Everett L. Goar Research Awd. in Ophthalm., Baylor Coll. of Med. 1979, 80; 1st pl. research paper awd., Tex. Ophthalm. Assn. 1980; mem: Phi Kappa Phi; Tau Beta Pi; Sigma Xi; Assn. of Research in Vision & Ophthalm.; Am. Acad. Ophthalm.; Baylor Ophthalm. Alumni Assn.; San Diego Eye Bank, Research to Prevent Blindness, Inc.; num. pub. writings.; rec: bridge, chess, tennis. Res: 12986 Polvera Ave San Diego 92128 Ofc: Scripps Clinic, 10666 N Torrey Pines Rd La Jolla 92037

CHAN, RONALD ALLAN, marketing and research analyst; b. June 28, 1954, Oakland; s. Alfred and May Patricia (Tom) C.; m. Lucille Fong, July 20, 1980; edn: AA, Merritt Coll. 1974, BA in bus. adm., San Francisco St. Univ., 1978, MBA, magna cum laude, 1984. Career: internat. mktg. intern Shui Hing Dept. Store, Kowloon, Hong Kong, 1976; food pgm. splst. US Dept. of Agri. 1977-78, equipment control/ traffic coord. Moram Agencies, 1978-79; mktg. analyst, supr., current mgr. Mktg. and Research Analysis, Seapac Services, Oakland 1980--; guest lectr. S.F. State Univ.; honors: Beta Gamma Sigma (1982), US Dept. Agri. Merit Cert. 1978, USDA Western Regl. Internship 1977, 78, HEW Scholarship 1975; contbg. editor Intro. to Export Mgmt. (1977); photographs in Grandmaster Chess (1975), and The Best of Lone Pine (1981); rec: photog., computers. Res: 31279 Birkdale Way Hayward 94544 Ofc: Seapac Services, 433 Hegenberger Rd, Ste. 200, Oakland 94621

CHAN, SAMUEL CHEUNG-FAI, physician; b. Feb. 22, 1947, Hong Kong, nat. 1978; s. Tim and King Wan (Ng) C.; m. Esther Tsai, Dec. 27, 1969; chil: Kenneth, b. 1972, Gary, b. 1975, Kevin, b. 1977, Kinman, b. 1979; edn: BS, CSU Los Angeles, 1968, MD, Vanderbilt Univ. Med. Sch., 1973. career: res. physician in surgery Vanderbilt Univ. Hosp. 1973-74; mem. Family Practice Dept. Kaiser Hosp., Harbor City, 1974-75; physician in pvt. practice, 1975--, pres. Samuel Chan M.D. Inc.; faculty UCLA-Harbor Div. Dept. of Family Medicine 1979-. Diplomate Am. Bd. of Family Practice 1977-84. awards: recognition for work with sr. citizens, Los Angeles Mayor Bradley, 1982; most outstanding student resrch awd., VanderbiltMed. Sch.,1973. mem: Chinese Physician Soc. of So. Calif. (pres. 1980, advisor 81-), Am. Acad. of Family Practice, Calif. Med. Assn., Los Angeles Co. Med. Assn. Coauthor book chpt. in Sugars in Nutrition The Nutrition Found. (ed. Horace L. Sipple), Acad. Press Inc. Democrat. Christian. rec: tennis, ski, fish, guitar. res: 420 Paseo Del Mar, Palos Verdes Est. 90274 ofc: Samuel Chan MD Inc. 2777 Pacific Ave Ste N, Long Beach 90806.

CHANDLER, MARILYN BRANT, urban planner; b. July 24, 1932, Los Angeles; d. Robert Alston and Jane Frances (Mann) Brant; m. Otis Chandler, June 18, 1951, div. 1981; children: Norman Brant, b. 1952, Harry Brant, b. 1953, Cathleen, b. 1955, Michael Otis, b. 1958, Carolyn, b. 1963; edn: Stanford Univ. 1949-51, UC Berkeley 1951, Occidental Coll. 1963-65; MA, UCLA Sch of Arch./Urban Planning 1975. Career: executive planner/asst. to the pres. Archisystems (div. Summa Corp),1974-76; pres. Urban Design Disciplines, 1977-81; partner Thornton Fagan Brant Rancourt (TFBR), 1981-82, co-dir. Art & Technology show for the Am. Pavilion, Expo '70, Osaka, Japan; pres. Marilyn Brant & Assocs., plnng & devel., Los Angeles 1982--; Dir: California Design (1968-80), Population Crisis Com. (1972-), Regl. Adv. Council SCAG (So. Calif. Assn. of Govts.); moderator Habitat Sect. 1980 World Future Global Conf., Toronto; trustee Loyola Marymount Univ. 1981-; chmn. bd. dirs. Otis Art Inst. 1961-77; dir. Center Theater Gp, L.A. Music Ctr. 1967-79; founding mem. Docent Council, L.A. Mus. (bd. dirs. 1960-71); adv. American Theater Arts Acad. 1980-81. Mem: Urban Land Inst., Am. Planning Assn., Am. Inst. of

Certified Plnnrs,, Am. Soc. of Cert. Plnnrs, L.A. City Hdqtrs. Assn., CARES/ USC Co. Hosp., House Ear Inst. Assocs. Recipient merit awards, Los Angeles City & Co. Republican; Episcopal; rec: tennis, golf, surf, ski. Ofc: Marilyn Brant & Assocs., 587 Perugia Way, Los Angeles 90077

CHANDLER, OTIS, communications co. executive; b. Nov. 23, 1927, Los Angeles; s. Norman and Dorothy (Buffum) C.; m. Bettina Whitaker, Aug. 15, 1981; chil: (prev. m.): Norman Brant, b. 1952, Harry Brant, b. 1953, Cathleen, b. 1955, Michael Otis, b. 1958, Carolyn, b. 1963; edn: The Cate Sch., Phillips Acad.; BA, Stanford Univ. 1950. Career: various positions, Times Mirror, 1953--: trainee in mech., editorial, circ., advt. depts. 1953-57; asst. to pres., 1957-58; mktg. mgr. Los Angeles Times, 1959-60, publisher 1960-80; vice pres. Newspaper Div. Times Mirror, 1961-65, dir. 1962-; pres. Newspaper and Forest Products, 1965-66; Exec. Com., bd. dirs. 1966-, publisher/CEO 1977-, bd. chmn. and Editor-in-Chief, 1981--. Dir: F.X. Pfaffinger Found., Times Mirror Found., Chandis Securities Co., Chandler-Sherman Corp.; dir. Pres.'s Council on Physical Fitness and Sports; dir. World Wildlife Fund-US; honors: Delta Kappa Epsilon (pres. 1950), 4-Yr. Letterman, capt. Track Team 1950 (Stanford Univ.); co-capt. USAF Track Team 1952; hon. LL.D., Colby Coll. 1966; hon. LL.D., Claremont Grad. Sch. 1978; num. journalism awards: USC (1962), Lovejoy (1966), Columbia Univ. (1967), Univ. Mo. Honor Medal (1969), Ohio Univ. Sch of Journ. Carr Van Anda (1973), Univ. of Ks. Allen White (1975), CORO (1978), Nat. Collegiate Athletic Assn. Theo. Roosevelt (1979), Gallagher Report (1980), Univ. Tex. Coll. Comm. DeWitt Carter Reddick (1982). Mem: Am. Newspaper Pubs. Assn. (dir. 1968-77; Found. trustee 1969-78), Am. Soc. Newspaper Editors, Calif. Newspaper Pubs. Assn., Calif. Press Assn., Inter-Am. Press Assn., Soc. Profl. Journalists, Sigma Delta Chi; clubs: California, Regency, So. Calif. Safari; mil: Navy midshipman 1946-48; lst lt. USAF 1951-53; rec: classic & sports cars, surfing, hunting, wtlifting, track & field. ofc: Times Mirror, Times Mirror Sq. Los Angeles 90053

CHANDLER, MARK RAYMOND, quality assurance specialist; b. July 25, 1934, Erie, Pa.; s. Raymond Joseph and Mary Therease (Yuhas) Hoffman; m. Indiah Suprapto, Dec. 8, 1979; children: Roger Alan, b. 1971; Steven Ismael, b. 1980; Katarina Dewi, b. 1982; edn: stu. Columbia Univ. 1959-62; BA, Mt. Carmel Sem. 1948-51; AA, Alameda Coll. 1974-79; stu. CSU Hayward 1983-. Career: chief machine acctg., US Navy, 1952-58, Korean Conflict; founder/dir. An-Lo Orphanage, VietNam 1968-70; sales mgr., pub. resls. World Airways, VietNam 1970-72, supr. planning dept. World Airways 1976-80; aircraft insp. Quality Ass. Splst. GS-9 Electronics Div., US Govt., currently training coordinator, electronics insp., tng. devel., US Naval Base, Alameda, Ca.; mem. ASQC, USO, Am. Red Cross; works: sev. innovations in aircraft safety design and cost saving measures for the Navy; adopted four VietNamese children, brought them with their mother to USA, sponsored their coll. edn.; Democrat-Conservative; Islamic; rec: writing fiction, essays, muscial compositions. Res: 1033 Regent St Alameda 94501 Ofc: NARFA, US Naval Base, Alameda 94501

CHANDLER, MICHAEL LEE, insurance agency executive; b. Apr. 4, 1943, McAlister, Okla.; s. Aubrey L. and Viola M. (Painter) C.; m. Helen Marinaccio, Oct. 19, 1968; children: Curits, b. 1963; Todd, b. 1965; Michael Jr., b. 1970; Michelle, b. 1974; edn: San Mateo Jr. Coll. 1961-62; CLU, Am. Coll. of Life Underwriters 1979. Career: ins. agent J. Fleck Ins. Agcy. 1962-67; br. ofc. sales mgr., San Francisco Life 1967-69; owner/ founder/ pres. ISU/ Chandler Ins. Agcy., Inc., Burlingame 1969--; owner/ founder/ pres. Chandler Mgmt. Svcs., Inc.; dir. Burlingame Bank & Trust Co.; mem: Life Underwriters ASsn.; Western Assn. Ins. Brokers; Profl. Ins. Assn.; Independ. Agents Assn.; Burlingame Lions Club (past pres.); Burlingame CofC (Exec. Com.); Peninsula YMCA; Peninsula Big Brothers/ Big Sisters; publs: art., Mass Merchandising, Agent & Brokers Mag., 1982; Republican; Methodist; rec: snow skiing, hunting, fishing. Res: 80 Valley View Ct San Mateo 94010

CHANEY, ALFRED, electronics co. executive; b. June 21, 1951, Oakland; s. Alfred Sr. and Jessie Mae (Johnson) C.; edn: AS, Yuba Coll. 1971; BS, Univ. of San Francisco 1978; MBA, Golden Gate Univ. 1983; cert. elec. tech., Nat. Electronics Assn. 1975; lic. radio opr., FCC 1972; comm. coll. tchg. cred., Calif. 1977; standard designated subject tchg. cred., 1975. Career: broadcast engr. KEMO-TV Channel 20, San Francisco 1972-73; field tech. Teleprompter CATV, Oakland 1972-73; elec. tech. Bay Area Rapid Transit Dist., Oakland 1973-78; prodn. supvr. Fairchild, San Jose 1978; elec. buyer, GTE Sylvania, Mt. View 1978-80; elec. buyer Wismer & Becker, Sacto. 1980-81; elec. buyer Hewlett Packard, Roseville 1981-83; supvr. 1983--; instr. Sacto. City Coll. 1983-; advr. Sacto. City Coll. Adv. Bd. 1983-; advr. Sacto. Alternative Computer Ctr., Sacto. 1982-; awards: Calif. State Scholarship 1969; Nat. Hon. Mention, Ford Found. Grant 1971; mem: Am. Mgmt. Assn.; rec: sports, electronics, photog. Res: 1415 Oak Nob Way Sacramento 95833 Ofc; Hewlett-Packard, 8020 Foothills Blvd Roseville 95678

CHANG, DAVIS LUE-SHENG, educator, certified public accountant; b. Nov. 17, 1941, Taiwan, China, nat. 1977; s. Young-Chung and Hsqang-May (Yeh) C.; m. Margaret Yue-Ching, Dec. 19, 1970; 1 son, Raymond P., b. 1979; edn: BBA, Nat. Taiwan Univ. 1968; MBA, Bowling Green St. Univ. 1970; PhD, Univ. of Pittsburgh 1974; CPA, Calif. (1980), Hawaii, Repub. of China; CMA, cert. mgmt. acct., Inst. of Mgmt. Acctg. (1977). Career: asst. prof. Sheppensburg State Coll., Pa. 1973-75, State Univ. of NY at Buffalo, 1975-77; assoc. prof./full prof. San Jose St. Univ., 1977--; CPA practice, 1980--; manuscript dir. of Nat. Assn. of Accountants 1978-81; honors: Beta Gamma Sigma, Owens Fellow, Univ. of Pittsburgh 1973, summer research fellowship, SUNY Resrch. Found. 1976; mem: Chinese Acctg. Professor Assn. (pres. 1980-82); Calif. Soc. of CPAs; Am. Inst. of CPAs; Am. Acctg. Assn.; Nat. Assn. of Accts.; Am. Inst. of Decision Science; adviser Elder Chinese Assn. of San Jose; mem. Asia Business League of Calif.; publs: arts. in four major acctg. journals; over 15 profl. presentations; mil: 2d. lt. Taiwan Army; rec: swimming, tennis, table tennis. Res: 2829 Glen Firth Dr San Jose 95133 Ofc: Davis L.S. Chang, CPA, 650 N. First, San Jose 95112 San Jose State Univ., San Jose 95192

CHANG, EDWARD I., real estate broker, management consultant; b. Aug. 31, 1948, Taipei, Taiwan; s. Ming Cheng and Ching Ling (Li) C.; m. Lan, Dec. 14, 1977; 1 dau: Caroline, b. 1981; edn: BS, Tankang Univ. 1972; cert., Univ. of Santa Clara 1977; cert., Western Real Estate Sch. 1982; gen. contractor, Calif. 1981; R.E. broker, Calif. 1982. Career: mgr. Chang's Brother Co., Palo Alto 1975-77; pres. Chinese Fast Food Devel. Ctr., Los Angeles 1978-81; pres. Eastern Group, L.A. 1981--; v.p. Excom, Inc. 1982-; exec. dir. Wok King Chain Restaurant 1980-; awards: Masterpiece Awd., Chinese Overseas Affairs Commn., Rep. of China 1978; mem: Calif. Chinese Assn. of Construction Profls.; Chinese-Am. Real Estate Profls. of So. Calif.; Chinatown Lions Club; publs: Overseas Chinese Restaurant Operation, 7/78; columnist, World Journ. 1978; Catholic; rec: golf, skiing. Res: POB 3865 Alhambra 91803 Ofc: Eastern Group, Inc., 2001 N Marianna Ave Los Angeles 90032

CHANG, I-KWANG, structural/seismic engineer; b. June 22, 1945, Loo-chiang, An-hwei Province, China, nat. 1979; s. Chung-Liang and Che-Chi (Chow) C.; edn: BS (Arch. Eng.), Univ. of Chinese Culture, Taiwan, ROC 1967; MS (Arch. Eng.), Univ. of Ill., Urbana 1970; PhD Cand. (Civil Eng.), Stanford Univ. 1984; Calif. Reg. Profl. Engr. (Civil) 1974. Career: engr. Victor Gruen Assocs., Los Angeles 1970-72; sr. engr. Vincent Kevin Kelly Assocs., Santa Monica 1972-74; sr. engr. Quadrex Corp., Campbell 1974-78; mgr. Applied Engineering Consulting Assocs., Santa Clara 1977-78; staff engr., struc./seismic engr., IBM, San Jose 1978--; guest lectr. for Calif. Banker Assn., S.F. 1983, Nat. Taiwan Univ., ROC 1981; lectr. in Bldg. Structural/seismic Analysis and Design series, for IBM General Product Div., San Jose 1979; inventions in field; mem. ASCE, Earthquake Engring. Research Inst., Chinese Inst. of Engrs.-USA; publs: 5 tech. reports; Republican; Christian; rec: tennis, swimming. Res: 4192 Hubbart Dr Palo Alto 94306 Ofc: IBM Corp. (mail code 488-124), 5600 Cottle Rd San Jose 95193

CHANG, KAI, electrical engineer; b. Apr. 27, 1948, Canton, China; s. Tzu Hua and Mary (Wang) C.; m. Suh-jan Chen, Aug. 18, 1973; children: Peter, b. 1979; Nancy, b. 1981; edn: BS, Nat. Taiwan Univ. 70; MS, State Univ. of NY, Stony Brook 1972; PhD, Univ. of Mich. 1976. Career: research asst. electrical eng. dept. Univ. of Mich., Ann Arbor, Mich. 1972-76; staff engr. Shared Applications, Inc., Ann Arbor, Mich. 1976-78; supvr. microwave circuit dept. Electron Dynamic Div. Hughes Aircraft, Torrance 1978-81; hd. integrated circuit sect. Millimeter- Wave Dept. TRW, Redondo Beach 1981--; awards: NSF Fellowship 1971-72; Rackham Dissertation Fellowship 1974-75; Harvey- Wagner Fellowship 1975-76; mem: IEEE; publs: over 30 tech. papers on microwave/ millimeter- wave areas in profl. journs.; Catholic; rec: hiking, tennis, gardening. Res: 26745 Shadow Wood Dr Rancho Palos Verdes 90274 Ofc: TRW One Space Park Redondo Beach 90278

CHANG, KRISTOFFER NING, plastic and reconstructive surgeon; b. Jan. 17, 1952, Taiwan, Rep. of China; s. Hubert Chung-hai and Jolene Fung-lan (Wong) C.; edn: BS with honors, Magna Cum Laude, Univ. of Utah; MD, Univ. of Utah Sch. of Med. 1977; residency in gen. surg. UC San Francisco 1977-83. Career: research fellow Wound Healing Lab., Univ. Calif. 198081, chief res. Dept. Surg. UCSF 1982-83, chief res. Div. Plastic & Reconstructive Surgery, UCSF 1983-85; awards: Sterling Scholarship 1979, Bausch-Lomb awd. 1969, Freshman Chemistry Stu. awd., Univ. Utah 1970, Mosby Scholarship 1977; First place, scholarship contest of Plastic Surg. Ednl. Found. of the Am. Soc. of Plastic & Reconstrv. Surgeons, Basic Sci. category (1981, and 1984); mem: Phi Beta Kappa, Phi Kappa Phi, Am. Med. Assn., Nafziger Surg. Soc., Am. Board of Surgery (Part I); mem. Asian Bus. League; rec: skiing, sailing, tennis. Res: 70 Clarendon Ave San Francisco Ofc: Div. Plastic & Reconstrv. Surg. UC, Parnassus Ave, San Francisco 94116

CHANG, PAUL PENG-CHENG, engineer; b. Aug. 19, 1931, Kiansu, China, nat. 1973; s. Su-An and Hwei-Lin (Lou) C.; m. Kristina H., Aug. 19, 1968; children: Conway, b. 1969; Tina, b. 1971; edn: BS, Taiwan Chen-Kung Univ. 1956; ME, Okla. Univ. 1966; civil engr., Calif. 1970; structural engr., Ill. 1970; engr., Nebr. 1976; structural engr, Nevada 1978; structural engr., Utah 1981. Career: engr. Sargent & Lundy Engrs., Inc. 1966-68; supvg. engr. Bechtel Power Corp. 1968-74; principal engr. Kaiser Engrs. Power Corp. 1974-80; asst. chief engr. Gibbs & Hill, Inc. 1980--; pres./ owner PPC Consulting Engrs. 1970--; designed more than a thousand modern skylights & greenhouses; mil: Taiwan, China; rec: music, sports. Address: 44577 Parkmeadow Dr Fremont 94538

CHANG, SEBASTIAN TSUN, international development co. executive; b. July 28, 1912, Shanghai, China, nat. 1984; s. Che-Shon and Ming Kuon (Yu) C.; m. Foong Tsze Chung, Aug. 15, 1941; chil: Alie, b. 1943; Jason, b. 1944; Lilee, b. 1948; Willy, b. 1952; edn: BS, Kiangsi Provincial Engring. Coll., 1934; MS, Sheffield Bennett Engring. Coll. 1937; EOAC, US Army Engr. Sch. 1953-4; NS&E, Indsl Coll. of Armed Forces USA 1961; cons. engr. in mil. & civil def., Ministry of Econ. R.O.C., 1944. Career: dir./secty. general, Resrch & Devel. of nat. defense, Ministry of Def., Taiwan and prof. of nuclear warfare & logistics, War College; tech. advisor Land Bank of Taiwan; v.p. Internat. Devel. Co. Taiwan; currently: dir./cons. engr. Pac Pacific Inc. USA; dir. Internat. Assn. of Real Estate. Awards: Medal of Victory 1946; Medal of Royalty 1948; recognition for estab. the Civil Def. Shelter Design & Constrn. System, Taiwan. Mem: Am. Soc. of Mil. Engrs. (v.p. & acting pres. Taiwan chpt. 1954-77); Internat.

Auto Club (dir. Taiwan chpt. 1962-5). Author text: Shelter Design in Nuclear Age; Republican; Catholic; rec: travel, auto-test. Res: 5222 Noble Ave Van Nuys 91411 Ofc: PAC Pacific Inc. 9552 Frankirst Ave Sepulveda 91343

CHANG, SHIRLEY (ZHANG, XIAO YI), acupuncturist/ Chinese medical doctor; b. Apr. 25, 1948, Fuzhou, Fujian, PRC; d. Mai Lin and Min (Lee) Zhang; m. James Chee Yee, June 17, 1981; edn: apprenticeship w/ traditional Chinese M.D., 1965---; BA, Canton Western Med. Inst. 1978; BA, Canton Chinese Med. Inst. 1980; Certified Acupuncturist, Calif. 1981. Career: practise Chinese medicine, PRC 1968-80, also hosp. lab. tech., 1976-79; prin. Chinese Acupuncture & Herbal Clinic, Santa Cruz, Calif. 1983--; mem. Monterey Bay Acupuncture Assn.; rec: music. Res: 1754 11th Ave, San Francisco 94122 Ofc: Chinese Acupuncture & Herbal Clinic, 707 No. Branciforte Ave, Santa Cruz 95062

CHANG, TAI SUN, otolaryngologist; b. Dec. 30, 1942, Taiwan, nat. 1978; s. Tung and Ching (Chou) C.; m. Huei, Feb. 18, 1978; children: David, b. 1978; Danny, b. 1983; edn: BD, Taipei Med. Coll. 1970. Career: pres. Tai S. Chang, MD, Inc.; mem: Am. Acad. of Otolaryngology; AMA; Los Angeles Co. Med. Assn.; CMA. Res: 22143-1 Burbank Blvd Woodland Hills 91367 Ofcs: Tai S. Chang, MD, Inc., 850 S Alantic Blvd, Ste 205, Monterey Park 91754 & 22135 Roscoe Blvd, Ste 203, Canoga Park 91304

CHAO, CHRIS CHAI-MING, chemical and software engineer; b. July 14, 1944, Honan, China, nat. 1980; s. Shio-Tien and Feng-Chen (Chang) C.; m. Donna Shea U-Huey Dun, Nov. 24, 1979; children: Joseph Shiao-Tzu, b. 1980; Christine Shiao-Shu, b. 1981; edn: BS, Nat. Taiwan Univ. 1967; MS, Stanford Univ. 1970; chem. engr., 1972; MS, 1978; reg. profl. engr., Calif. 1982. Career: cons./ chief engr. Cathay Plastic & Chem. Works 1972-77; research & devel. process engr. Memorex Corp., Santa Clara 1978; sr. analytical engr. Textron Corp., Pacoima 1979-80; sr. mech. process engr. Ralph M. Parsons Co., Pasadena 1981-82; tech. staff Abacus Pragramming Corp., Van Nuys 1983--; cons: Rockwell Internat., Space Shuttle Slosh Dynamics Simulation & Guidance Control; Adv. Space Sensor Sys 1983-; awards: Most Innovative New Work, Textron Achiev. Awd. 1980; Profl. Devel. Recgn. Cert., Am. Inst. of Chem. Engrs. 1980, 84; mem: Am. Inst. Chem. Engrs.; Instrument Soc. of Am.; AIAA; Bibliography Soc. of CSUN; works: Polymer Melt Filter Cleaning Method, US Patent 1982; A Unified Filtration Theory, World Filtration Congress III 1982; mil: lt. Nationalist Chinese ROTC 1967-68; Republican; Christian; rec: hiking, camping, swimming. Res: 5302 Cleon Ave, No. Hollywood 91601 Ofc: Abacus Programming Corp., 14545 Victory Blvd, Ste 300, Van Nuys 91411

CHAO, JIATSONG JASON, nuclear engineer/ scientist; b. Dec. 15, 1948, Venden Shanton, China, s. Owei Hai and Chi Yung (Tsoong) C.; m. Lily Ni, May 26, 1974; 1 son: Neal, b. 1982; edn: BS, FuJen Catholic Univ. 1071; MA, Univ. of Tex. 1974; PhD, Mass. Inst. of Tech. 1979; progl. mech. engr., Calif. 1981. Career: research assoc. Mass. Inst. of Tech., Cambridge, Mass. 1976-78; senior scientist Science Applications, Inc., Oak Brook, Ill. 1979-81; project mgr. Electric Power Research Inst., Palo Alto 1981--; pgm. com. mem. Am. Nuclear Soc. Thermal Hydraulic Div., Newsletter ed. 1981-; mem: Am. Nuclear Soc. Thermal Hydraulic Div. (Pgm. Com.); publs. in sci. journals; rec: artificial intelligence pgmmg., card games. Res: 1841 Newcastle Dr Los Altos 94022 Ofc: Electrical Power Research Inst., 3412 Hillview Ave Palo Alto 94303

CHAPMAN, DONALD MASON, III, corporate president; b. March 17,1949, Sherman, Tex.; s. Donald Mason, Jr. and Patsy Jean (Jarrell) C.; edn: BA in econ., magna cum laude, CSU San Diego 1971; MA, econ., Univ. Wash. 1972. Career: economist 6th Planning Dist., Rapid City, San Diego 1972, asst. dir. 1973; proj. dir. Comprehensive Planning Orgn., San Diego 1974-77; dir. mktg. First Affiliated Securities of La Jolla, 1978; pres./dir. AFR Securities Corp., Del Mar 1979; pres./dir. Am. CinemaGroup, Del Mar 1980; pres./dir. Angeles Entertainment Gp., La Jolla 1981; gen. partner EquiFirst, La Jolla 1983--; prof. econ. Nat. Univ. 1974-78; awards: Disting. Student, Economics, CSUSD 1971, econ. fellowship, Univ. Wash. 1971-2. Mem: La Jolla Mus. Contemporary Art, Internat Assn of Finl Planners; Protestant; rec: tennis, gourmet cook, art collector, travel. res: 2417 Sagebrush Ct. La Jolla 92037 ofc: EquiFirst, Box 3129, La Jolla 92038.

CHAPMAN, LEONARD T., mechanical/ electrical engineer; b. Apr. 30, 1933, Los Angeles; s. Ralph T. and Mabel (Mahakian) C.; m. Barbera Jean, Feb. 23, 1958; cihldren: Christine, b. 1959; Michael, b. 1962; Jenifer, b. 1968; edn: BS, magna cum laude, UCLA 1956. Career: 1st asst. engr. Chapman Studio Equip. 1956; hd. engr. 1958; pres./ hd. engr. Leonard Studio Equip. 1965; pres./ hd. engr. both Chapman & Leonard Sudio Equip. 1983--; awards: Academy Awd., Leonard Studio Equip., Hustler Holly 1979; Academy Awd., Leonard Studio Equip., Peewee Dolly 1983; Emmy Awd. Leonard Studio Equip. Scientific Achiev. 1982; mem: Tau Beta Pi; Engr. In Tng. (EIT), UCLA 1956; works: Titan & Apollo Mobile Crane 1954; Zeus, Nike, Electra Stage Crane 1960; Sidewinder 1970; Hustler Holly 1976; Peewee Dolly 1981; Olympian Crane 1982; Republican; Christian; rec: golf, tennis. Res: Los Angeles Ofc: 12950 Raymer Street, No. Hollywood 91605

CHAPMAN, MARGARET, ANN, professional volunteer; b. Oct. 20, 1928, Alta, Iowa; d. Carl Oscar and Dorothy Josephine (Andre) Youngstrom; m. Charles Chapman, Dec. 24, 1951; children: John, b. 1952; Andrea, b. 1954; Richard, b. 1955; Julia, b. 1956; James, b. 1959; Carol, b. 1961; edn: Morningside Coll., Sioux City, Ia. 1946-47; BA, Central Methodist Coll. 1951; R.E.

broker, Calif. 1980. Career: Methodist Commn. of Chaplains, Wash. DC 1951-52; pvt. secty./ asst. to chaplains; R.E. agent Sunset Co., Realtors 1978-82; Distinguished Alumni, Central Methodist Coll. 1971; Hon. Svc. Awd., La Colina PTA 1968; Cont. Svc. Awd., Foothill PTA 1971; mem: Child Abuse Listening & Mediation (CALM); Santa Barbara Co. Med. Auxiliary (past pres.); Calif. Med. Assn. Aux.; Santa Barbara Council of PTA (past pres.); San Marcos, La Colina, Foothill PTAs; Community Arts Music Assn. (Womens Bd.); La Mesa Comm. Ch. (pres. 1973-74, 76-77); faculty AMA Nat. Conf. on Child Abuse & Neglect, Chgo. 1984; Republican; Protestant; rec: music, antiques. Res: 4957 La Ramada Dr Santa Barbara 93111

CHAPMAN, ROBERT ALLEN, computer co. president; b. June 17, 1941, Springfield, Colo.; s. Clarence B. and Lydia Marie (Goltl) C.; m. Susan Walters French, Sept. 8, 1967; children: Jeffrey, b. 1971, Gregory, b. 1975, Bradley, b. 1977; edn: BA, Univ. Colo. 1965; Bach. of Fgn. Trade, Am. Grad. Sch. for Internat. Mgmt. 1968, Master of Internat. Mgmt., 1970. Career: asst. to the pres. Computer Machinery Corp., Los Angeles 1970; sales rep. Computer Scis. Corp., L.A. 1970-73; dist. mgr. Docutel Corp., L.A. 1973-76; dir. mktg. System Devel. Corp., Santa Monica 1976-82; pres. Megadyne Information Systems, Santa Monica 1982--; bd. govs. Electronic Funds Transfer Assn., Wash DC 1974-5; mem: So. Calif. Technology Execs. Network; Palisades-Malibu YMCA (bd. mgrs., v.p. 1983); mil: intel, splst. US Army 1968 70; Republican; Baptist; rec: golf, fish, chess. Res: 418 Swarthmore Ave. Pacific Palisades 90272 Ofc: Megadyne Information Systems, 401 Wilshire Bl #1005, Santa Monica 90401

CHAPPELL, JOHN F., telecommunications executive; radio/ television broadcasting instructor; b. July 10, 1948, Oakdale; s. George F. and Helen M. (Wormington) C.; edn: AA, Modesto Jr.Coll. 1968; tchg. cred., UC Berkeley 1979; career: announcer KSRT-FM stereo, Tracy, Calif. 1966-68; announcer, engr. KCEY Radio, Turlock 1968-70; radioman USN, Vietnam 1969-71; pgm. dir. KFIV Radio, Modesto 1971-74; announcer, performer Early Dawn Enterprises (restaurant chain), Modesto, Fresno 1979-80; announcer, engr., pgrmmr. KBEE/KBEE-FM, McClatchy Broadcasting, Modesto 1974-79; telecommunications ops. supr. Modesto Jr. Coll., 1974--, instr. radio/tv broadcasting 1983--; cons. Western States Tech. Assistance Resource, Univ. Wash., Seattle. Mem: Stanislaus Amateur Radio Assn. 1977-, Internat. Brotherhood Elect. Workers, Radio/TV Engrs. Union 1974-78, Calif. Sch. Employees Assn. 1981-, US Hang Gliding Assn. 1980-, Nat. Experimental Aircraft Assn. (v.p. Chpt. 90), Continental Luscombe Assn.; built/fly a Quicksilver Ultralight Aircraft, currently constructing/testing a Q-2 exptl. fiberglass airplane 1980-. Mil: 3d cl. Petty Ofcr. USN 1969-71 Methodist. rec: flying exptl.aircraft, motorcycling, tv photog, res: 3708 Carlisle Ct. Modesto 95356 ofc; Modesto Jr. Coll. College Ave. Modesto.

CHARITAN, ARNOLD, business executive; b. Apr. 10, 1927, Yonkers, NY; s. Jack and Alys Sandra (Katz) C.; m. Gladys Korn, Aug. 3, 1947; chil: Jeffrey Alan, b. 1949, Janeen Lisa, b. 1952; edn: BS, Ariz. State Univ. 1951; MA, Azusa-Pac. Coll. 1974; exec. pgm. cert. UCLA Grad. Sch of Mgmt. 1976. Career: cost analyst Douglas Aircraft, El Segundo 1951-59; a;dminstr. Northrop Corp., Hawthorne 1959-64; prin. Charitan Mtge. & Ins.,Torrance 1964-66; district mgr. Auto Club of So. Calif., Century City 1966--; instr. bus. mgmt. L.A. Harbor Coll. 1974-; lic. Real Estate Broker, Calif.; apptd. by Sen. pro tem David Roberti to Task Force, Auto & Truck Ins. 1982; mem: UCLA Exec. Pgm. Assocs. (bd. dirs., pres. 1981), Town Hall West Adv. Bd., Zionist Orgn of Am. (bd. dirs.), L.A./Lusaka Sister City Com. (past bd.dirs.), Jewish War Vets (bd.dirs.); active mem. Century City, LA, Beverly Hills Chambers of Commerce, B'nai B'rith, Beverly Hills Bus & Profl.Mens Assn., Calif. Tax Reduction Movement, LA World Affairs Council, Com. to Improve Santa Monica Blvd., Westwwood Neighborhood Watch, Calif. Republican Party. Publs: pamphlet on real estate investments (1982). Mil: USN 1945-46. Republican; Jewish; rec: cycling, racquetball, tennis. res: 1477 Glendon Ave. Los Angeles 90024. ofc: Auto Club of So. Calif. 1950 Century Park East Los Angeles 90067.

CHARNEY, NANCY ELENA, chiropractor; b. Oct. 29, 1951, Atlantic City, NJ; d. Robert Reuben and Minnette (Sherman) C.; edn: BS, Univ. of Miami 1971; DC, Palmer Coll. 1974. Career: intern Richmond Chiropractic, Lafayette 1974-76; Charney Chiro., Glendale 1976-80; pres. Charney Chiro. Clinic, San Francisco 1980--; Charney Cons. 1980--; assoc. prof. LACC 1978; assoc. prof. Cleveland Coll.; awards: Doctor of Yr. 1978; Superior Clinical Profiency Awd.; mem: BACW; Soroptimist; rec: cooking, body building. Res: 802 Edgewood Rd Redwood City Calif 94062 Ofc: Charney Chiropractic Clinic, 4444 Geary Blvd San Francisco 94118

CHASE, MICHELE JOY, marketing executive; b. June 7, Youngstown, Ohio; d. David Michael and Audrey Marian (Gurss) Kohan; edn: BS, Penn. State Univ. 1972. Career: commun. cons. Western Union, Pittsburgh, Pa. 1973-75; W. Coast regl. mgr. 31 Communications, Los Angeles 1975-77; mktg. mgr. Metro Bus. Archives, L.A. 1977-83; dir. mktg. Nat. Pick-N-Pack, L.A. 1983--; sales wrkshps.; sales tng. cons.; awards: Merit Awd., Sales & Mktg. Execs. 1983; mem: Sales & Mktg. Execs.; Hospitality Sales Classes; Assn. of Records Mgrs.; Directing Mktg. Club; Soc. of Micrographis; Penn. State Alumni Club; Tennis Club; design mktg. plans for 3 start-up' businesses; rec: interior decorating, sports. Res: 1815 Butler Ave W Los Angeles 90025 Ofc: National Pick-N-Pack, POB 21830 Los Angeles 90021

CHASTAIN, HARRY LEE, restaurant owner; b. May 24, 1943, Gainesville, Ga.; s. Homer Leslie and Sarah Toni (Smith) C.; m. Alison Turner, Nov. 22, 1962; 1 dau: Valerie, b. 1964; edn: West Coast Trade Sch. 1963; Univ. of Santa

WHO'S WHO IN CALIFORNIA 66

Clara 1968. Career: multi store supvr. Der Wienerschnitzel, Los Angeles, Long Beach 1964-65; gen. mgr. Der Wienerschnitzel, San Jose, No. Calif. 1965-70; store owner Der Wienerschnitzel, Salinas & Lodi 1970-72; owner Senor Taco Co., Salinas & Seaside 1972--; owner Little Reata Ranch (race & breed standardbred horses) 1980; pres. adv. council, Der Wienerschnitzel 1978; v.p. Der Wienerschnitzel Advtg. Assn. 1982; awards: Top Percentage increase of Sales, Der Wienerschnitzel 1974; Little League 1979; United Way 1980; Boy Scouts of AM. 1931; Employer of Month, KDON Radio 1972; mem: US Trotting ASsn.; Salinas CofC; Calif. Harness Horse Breeders Assn.; Western Standardbred Assn.; Monterey Co. Hist. Soc.; Hall of Fame of the Trotters 1983; works: op. manuals, Der Wienerschnitzel & Senor Taco; Republican; Baptist; rec: breeding standardbred race horses, collect classic cars, coins and fine wine. Res: 11932 Augusta Dr Salinas 93906 Ofc: Senor Taco, 2015 N Main Street Salinas 93906

CHASTAIN, JOANNE LILLIAN, electrophysiology technologist; b. July 19, 1942, Chgo.; d. Joseph D. and Marietta Pearl (McAleece) Bernard; m. Larry Chastain, July 4, 1964; 1 son: Christopher John, b. 1966; edn: BS, health care mgmt. 1983; cert. clinical EEG tech., Am. Med. Electroencephalographic Assn. 1980; reg. electroencephalographic technologist, Am. Bd. of Regis. of EEG Technologists 1968. Career: research tech. UCLA Med. Ctr., staff tech. Inter-Comm. Hosp. 1963-65; chief tech. San Antonio Comm. Hosp., Upland 1967-71; chief tech. Inland EEG Lab., Claremont 1971-72; chief tech. L.A. Co. USC Med. Ctr. 1972-79; adminstrv. dir. Huntington Meml. Hosp., Pasadena 1979-82; regl. ctr. dir. Bio Scan Inc., Duarte 1982--; Health Care Mgmt. cons.; clinical instr. Orange Coast Comm. Coll. 1972-79; course dir. Mt. San Antonio Comm. Coll. 1972-73; course faculty Am. Soc. EEG Tech. Adv. & Fundamental; mem: Am. Cardiology Technologists Assn.; Am. & Oregon Socs. EEG Tech.; Nat. Assn. Female Execs.; Western Soc. Elec. Diog. Tech.; Women in Mgmt.; Toastmasters; Covina Comm. Concert Band; publs: ed. W.S.E.T. Pub. 1975; author num. arts. in W.S.E.T. journ.; rec: fine arts, music. Res: 119 S Prairie Pl Glendora 91740 Ofc: Bio Scan Inc., 931 Buena Vista, Ste 106, Duarte 91010

CHATMAN, DONALD JAMES, investment broker; b. Dec. 19, 1941, Port Arthur, Tex.; s. Lawrence Charles and Laura Eugenia (Moss) C.; edn: AA, L.A. City Coll. 1973; BA, CSU Los Angeles 1974; MA, CSU Hayward 1976; data processing tech., UC Berkeley 1984. Career: advtg. sales mgr. Lov Joy Prodns., Chgo. 1969; talent coord. Curtom Recording Co., Chgo. 1971; ticket agent/ svc. dir./ acct. exec./ supvr. inflight svcs. United Airlines 1971-80; contractor/ investment broker Michael Strausz Realty Co., San Francisco 1980--; honors: Pi Sigma Alfa 1973-74; Gospel Acad. Awd. Presenter 1976, 77; mem: Internat. Personnel Mgrs. Assn.; Assn. of Black Airline Employees; Political Sci. Club; works: exec. patterns in coping w/ job related stress 1976; constitutional aspects of Watergate 1974; mil: Corp., USMC 1959-65, GCM; Baptist; rec: basketball, training pets. Res: 1042 Bayview Ave Oakland 94610 Ofc: Michael Strausz Realty, 2860 Laguna San Francisco 94123

CHATTERLEY, JIMMIE LEROY, commercial construction co. executive; b. July 29, 1944, Tremonton, Utah; s. Jay Leroy and Dorothy (White) C.; m. Rita Brown, Jan. 27, 1967; children: Jaron, b. 1968; Clark, b. 1970; Charile, b. 1973; Rochelle, b. 1975; Angela, b. 1979; Nicole, b. 1980; edn: BS, Brigham Young Univ. 1969; B.Civil Eng., 1969; MS, Purdue 1971; M.Civil Eng., 1971; lic. civil engr. Calif. & Ore. Career: proj. mgr. Swinerton & Walberg (constructed shopping ctr. & 35 story high rise) 1971-73; sr. proj. mgr. Dillingham Const., Inc. (shopping ctr., (3) hospitals, parking structure, high rise hotel), Los Angeles 1973--; mem: Const. Specs. Inst.; Republican Commiteeman Assn.; works: construction of 3500 SF Home (incl. design & const.); Republican; LDS. Res: 825 Valley Vista Fillmore 93015 Ofc: Dillingham Const., 2401 Beverly Blvd Los Angeles 90057

CHAU, KIET VAN, physician; b. Feb. 12, 1939, Vietnam; s. T.T. and Phuong X (Nguyen) C.; m. Phuong Tonnu, Jan. 4, 1962; children: Bobi, b. 1964, Meyna, b. 1965; Minou, b. 1968; Tommy, b. 1969; Louis, b. 1970; edn: Baccalaureat, Lycee Yersin Dalat, Vietnam 1957; Univ. of Saigon 1958; MD, Univ. of Saigon, Faculty of Med. 1965. Career: gen. practice, Vietnam 1965-75; intern Loma Linda Univ. Med. Ctr., Loma Linda, Calif. 1977-78; med. staff Loma Linda VA Hosp., Loma Linda 1978-79; med. staff Metropolitan Hosp., Norwalk 1979-80; pvt. practice, Westmister 1980--; currently, pres. Kiet Van Chau, MD, Inc.; mem: Am., Calif. & Orange Co. Med. Assns.; Vietnamese Am. Biddhist Assn. of Orange Co.; Delta Savings & Loan; mil: maj. So. Vietnam mil. Med. Corps. 1970 Golden Star Decoration of S. Vietnam Armed Forces; Buddhism; rec: tennis, swimming, camping. Res: 6785 E Swarthmore Anaheim 92807 Ofc: 9411 Bolsa Ave, Ste B, Westminster 92683

CHAVEZ, SHARON LYNNE, real estate broker/investor; b. July 17, 1951, Grand Island, Nebr.; d. Henry Ernest and Dorothy Pauline (Rauert) Mangelsen; m. Dennis Chavez, June 14, 1975; 1 dau: Christine, b. 1979; edn: BS, honors, CSU San Jose 1973; realtor, Nat. Assn. Realtors 1983. Career: acct. Raytheon co., Mt. View 1973-76; fin. anlyst Petty, Andrews, Tufts & Jackson, San Francisco 1976; realtor assoc. ERA & Century 21, San Jose 1976-83; owner/ broker Shaden Assocs., San Jose 1983--; v.p./ bd. dirs. Evergreen Homeowners Assn. 1978; mem: Nat. & Calif. St. Bds. Realtors; San Jose Real Estate Bd.; Council Advent Lutheran Ch., Morgan Hill.; Council Grace Lutheran Ch., San Jose; Republican; Lutheran; rec: financial planning. Address: Shaden Assocs., 3134 Albemar Ct San Jose 95135

CHEE, THOMAS ARTHUR, optician; b. Aug. 22, 1928, Liverpool, England, nat. 1971; s. Thomas Arthur and Lilian (Crump) C.; m. Eileen Catherine Harrison, Oct. 7, 1949; children: Michael, b. 1951, Catherine, b. 1954, Rosemary, b. 1957; gen. edn. in England; Master Opthalmic Optics, 1973; Fellow Nat. Acad. Opticianry (FNAO) 1964; Fellow Contact Lens Soc. of Am. (FCLSA) 1984; Life Tchrs. Cred., Calif. Comm. Colls. Career: lab apprenticeship, lab mgmt., Eng. 1948-57; lab and branch mgr. Kahn Optical Co., Canada 1957-62; lab mgmt. Spratt Optical Co., 1962-63; founder/instr. (course in opthalmic dispensing) San Diego Comm. Colls., 1976-80; mgmt. dispensing, Leroy W. Rhein, MD, 1963-80; pres. Thomas A. Chee F.N.A.O. Inc., San Diego 1980--; honors: Optician of the Month, Calif. Soc. of Dispensing opticians 1981; mem: Contact Lens Soc. of Am. (bd. dirs.), Nat. Acad. Opticianry /Master, Opticians Assn. of Am., Guild of Prescription Opticians, Calif. Soc. Dispensing Opticians (past pres.; past pres. S.D. Chpt.), Pacific Coast Contact Lens Soc.; Calif. Soc. to Prevent Blindness (bd. dirs.); dir. Boys Clubs of Am. 1963-69; founder/ vol. S.D. Co. Jr. Soccer League 1967-80; mil: Brit. Royal Navy 194-48; Republican; Catholic; rec: sailing, family activities. Res: 2621 Harcourt Dr San Diego 92123 Ofc: Thomas A. Chee F.N.A.D., Inc. 3847 4th Ave San Diego 92103

CHEHOCK, DONALD P., lawyer; b. Sept. 21, 1907, Anita, Iowa; s. Henry Walter and Beulah (Bryan) C.; m. Margaret McHugh (dau. of Mayor and Mrs. C.N. McHugh of Cedar Falls, Iowa), June 30, 1938; children: Bryan, b. 1939, Robert, b. 1941, Donald Jr., b. 1942; edn: Coe Coll. 1925-27; BA, Univ. of Iowa 1929, JD, 1931; admitted to State Bar of Iowa 1931, State Bar of Calif. 1953; Certified Tax Splst. 1973. Career: general law practice at Osage, iowa 1931-44, apptd. City Atty. of Osage, 1935-38; elected County Atty., three terms 1939-44, also local counsel for Rural Electrification Adminstrn., 1938-44; govt. svc. in Tax Court Litigation Div., Office of Chief Counsel, IRS, 1944-76, in Dallas (1944-51) and Los Angeles (1951-76) Offices in trial and supvsry. posts; most of his trials involved taxpayers controverted income tax cases in US Tax Ct., involving precedent-making type issues; cases he tried or their appeals have now been cited over 1,000 times as case authority by var. federal cts.; part time pvt. practice, San Marino, Ca. 1976-; honors: award, Secty. of the US Treasury Wash. DC (1971); Order of the Coif (1931); Big Ten Club awd. as outstanding Univ. Iowa Alumnus (1983); mem: Calif., Iowa, and Federal Bars; past pres. Univ. Iowa Alumni Assn. of So. Ca.; past pres. Iowa (state) Assn. of So. Calif.; Big Ten Club of So. Calif. (pres. 1979; ed. Newsletter 1981-); City Club of San Marino; Kappa Sigma Frat.; Prot.; rec: sports. Address: 1358 San Marino Ave San Marino 91108

CHEMSIAN, JEAN VAHAN, investment co. executive; b. Oct. 29, 1942, Alexandria, Egypt, nat. 1970; s. Vahan Garabed and Sophie O. (Karakacian) C.; m. Ani, Sept. 7, 1974; children: Raffi, b. 1976; Erik, b. 1979; edn: BS, Cal Poly 1966; MS, Stanford Univ. 1967; cert. fin., UCLA 1974; R.E. broker, Calif. 1975. Career: engr. Lear Jet Inds., Wichita, Ks. 1967-69; gp. mgr. McDonnell Douglas Corp., Long Beach 9169-75; pres. Certified Investment Corp., Laguna Hills 1975-83; principal J.V. Chemsian & Assocs., Laguna Hills 1983--; dir. Certified Investment Corp. 1975-83; dir. Circle Escrow Gp. 1980-82; dir. Certified Bank Corp. 1983-; dir. Wil Wrights Ice Cream, Inc. 1984-; honors: Blue Key, Nat. Honor Frat. 1966; mem: Armenian Relief Soc.; created computer stock mkt. timing sys. 1981-84; Republican; Armenian Christian Orthodox; rec: skiing, boating, equestrian. Res: 23782 Birch Ln Mission Viejo 92691 Ofc: J.V. Chemsian & Assoc., 25283 Cabot Rd, Ste 207, Laguna Hills 92653

CHEN, CHARLES HSIN, obstetrician-gynecologist; b. Jan. 30, 1942, Taiwan; s. Jon Song and Jen (Chiu Lin) C.; edn: MD, Taipei Med. Sch. 1969; postgrad. Ob-Gyn tng. Mackay Meml. Hosp., Taiwan 1970-73. Career: intern, Albert Einstein Med. Ctr., Phila. 1973-74; resident in Ob-Gyn, New Jersey Med. Sch. 1974-77, clin. instr. 1977-78; corp. pres./pvt. practice, Ob-Gyn, Fountain Valley, Ca. 1979--; instr. Taipei Med. Sch. 1970-73; Fellow American Coll. OB-Gyn Soc., mem. Orange Co. Med. Assn., Orange Co. OB-Gyn Soc.; Presbyterian; rec: swimming, golf. Res: 9067 Wagner River Circle Fountain Valley 92708 Ofc: 11160 Warner Ave, Ste. 111, Fountain Valley 92708

CHEN, DANIEL JUILIANG, business broker; b. Sept. 4, 1954, Taipei, Taiwan, nat. 1976; s. Chih Tsung and Judy Ainiang (Cheng) C.; edn: BS, engrg., Univ. of Mich. 1977; MBA, USC 1979; Calif. lic. real estate broker 1981; CPA, 1981. Career: market analyst The Bekins Co., Los Angeles 1978-79; teaching asst. USC, 1978-79; sales agt. J.W. Realty, Santa Monica 1979; senior staff acct. Peat, Marwick, Mitchell & Co., Sacramento 1979-82; corp. controller Sound Imaging, Inc., Folsom 1982-83; business broker, Corporate Investment Bus. Brokers, Sacto. 1983--; mng. ptnr. The B.P. Inv. Co., Sacto. 1980-; awards: Touche Ross MBA Scholarship, Beta Alpha Psi, 1978; mem: Am. Inst. of CPAs, Calif. Soc. of CPAs, Calif. Assn. of Realtors, Nat. Assn. of Realtors, Sacto. Board of Realtors; mem. Beta Alpha Psi, Beta Gamma Sigma, Sigma Nu; rec: violin, guitar, basketball. Res: 6552 Skyview Dr Orangevale 95662 Ofc: Corporate Inv. Business Brokers, 6371 Auburn Blvd, Ste. A, Citrus Hts 95610

CHEN, JERRY CHIH—LI, physicist, company executive; b. Sept. 18, 1936, Fuchow, Fukien, China; s. Bei-ping and Ru-liang (Lin) Chen; edn: BS in physics, Tunghai Univ., Taiwan, 1961; MS in physics, Worcester Polytechnic Inst., Mass. 1965, PhD. in physics, 1969; m. Shirley Wang, Jan. 25, 1969; chil: Guang-min, b. 1973, Guang-qun, b. 1975; career: asst. prof. in physics, Pan American Coll. Edinburg, Texas 1969-70; electronics engineer/owner Friendship TV & Electronics Services, Oakland, 1972-78; computer engr./partner Suntek Associates, San Jose 1978-81; pres./director Kentex International, Inc. Palo Alto 1979--; dir./secty. Eastwind Books & Arts, Inc. 1979-80; honors: Sigma Xi, 1970; mem: IEEE, Rubber Div. Am. Chemical Soc., Tech. Assn. of the Pulp & Paper Industry., Soc. of Photo-Optical Instrumentation Engineers, Combustion Inst.; publs: Eastwind Mag.

1971-75; mil: 2nd lt. Chinese Army 1961-62; Christian; rec: bridge, swim; res: 2154 St. Francis Dr. Palo Alto 94303 ofc: Kentex International, Inc. 2159 Edgewood Dr. Palo Alto 94303.

CHEN, JOHN YUAN-TAI, scientist; b. July 9, 1949, Taiwan, nat. 1980; s. Chiang Ho and Pei Hwan (Pan) C.; m. Jennifer Pey-jen Chen, June 28, 1981; edn: BS, National Taiwan Univ. 1971; MS, Univ. of Maine 1973; PhD, UCLA 1981, ME in mgmt., UCLA 1984. Career: resrch asst., Univ. of Me. 1973-5, UC Berkeley 1975-6; process engr. Ampex Corp., Santa Monica 1976-7; mem. Technical Staff, Hughes Research Lab., Malibu 1977-81, supr. and sr. staff 1981--; lectr./course orgnzr. UCB, UCLA. Honors: Howard Hughes Doctoral Fellow 1978-81; Eta Kappa Nu; Sigma Xi; senior mem. IEEE, mem. ECS. Patentee (8) in microelectronics field; 40 sci. publs. Mil: 2d lt., M.P., Taiwan Army; Republican; Catholic; rec: tennis, music, travel, sailing. es: 12926 Lucille Ave Los Angeles 90066 Ofc: Hughes Research Lab, 3011, Malibu Cyn Rd, MS:RL56, Malibu 90265

CHEN, KEMING JOSEPH, engineer; b. Nov. 11, 1948, Nan-King, China; s. Yo Tien and Mu Heng Chen; m. Ivy Chung, Aug. 9, 1980; children: Morgan, b. 1981; Morris, b. 1983; edn: BSEE, Nat. Chiao Tung Univ. 1971; MSEE, State Univ. of New York, Stony Brook 1980. Career: engr. RCA, Taiwan 1971-76, senior engr. 1976-77, electrical supvr. 1977-79; assoc. engr./mem. engring. staff RCA, Indiana 1980-83; staff engr. Oak Communications Inc., San Diego 1983-84, senior engr. M/A-Com Linkabit Inc., San Diego 1984--; tchg. asst. State Univ. of NY, Stony Brook 1979-/80; instr. Lee Ming Inst. of Tech 1978-79; awards: Technical Excellence Award Electronics, 1st quarter 1983; patents (pending): Improve on Screen Display (1983) Signal Seek Tuning Sys. (1984) Video Sync Validity Detector (1984), TV Receiver w/ High Voltage Protection CKT (1984); rec: fishing, music. Res: 10082 Branford Rd San Diego 92129

CHEN, LIWEI, national marketing & sales executive; b. Sept. 2, 1950, Taiwan, China; s. Aken Hsu-Ching and Jeh Jung (Tsai) Chen; m. Suzie S.M. Yang, May 1979; sons: Raymond Eric, b. 1981, (twins) Allen Thomas and Victor Brian, b. 1983; edn. BSME, nt. Taiwan Univ., Taipei 1972; MSME, Northwestern Univ. (Ill.), 1976; MBA, Univ. of So. Calif. 1979; lic: Reg. Profl. Engr. State of Calif. (ME 18581), State of Wash. (ME 18117). Career: analytical engr. Borg-Warner Corp., Van Nuys, 1976-77, design engr. 1977, project engr. 1977-78, sr. proj. engr. 1978-79, sr. mech. engr. Nuclear Products, Masoneilan Div. McGraw-Edison Co. Montebello, 1979, Nuclear Engrg. Section Mgr. 1979-80, mktg. & contract adm. mgr. 1981-82, mktg. & sales adminstrn. mgr. U.S. Operations 1982-84, mktg., sales & distrbn. mgr. 1984--; also cons. Righton Ind. & Engrg. Co., L.A. 1979-83; cons. Tsong-Tai Enterprises (USA) Co. L.A. 1979-83; cons. Innomatic Systems, Inc. Garland, TX 1980--; cons. Numertek, Inc. Taiwan 1981--; cons. M.J.R. Component, Inc. Chatsworth, CA 1984--; awards: res. assistantship, Northwestern Univ. 1974-76; mem: Amer. Mktg. Assn., Amer. Soc. Mech. Engrs. (assoc), Nat. Soc. of Profl. Engrs., Amer. Soc. for Quality Control, Beta Gamma Sigma scholar; rec: music, bridge, tennis, fishing. Res. 6931 Emerson Dr Buena Park 90620 Ofc: 1040 S. Vail Ave Montebello 90640

CHENEY, JOHN CARL, corporate executive; b. Mar. 20, 1948, Oklahoma City, Okla.; s. Edward Gordon and Ruth Ella (Rosenhauer) C.; m. Linda Gail Hasler, Oct. 10, 1974; children: Austin, b. 1979, Travis, b. 1981; edn: BS journ., Southwest Tex. State Univ. 1973; MS comm., CSU San Jose 1979. Career: national account sales mgr. Rolm Corp., Santa Clara, 1978--, served in ops., engring., and sales mgmt.; acct. exec. Pacific Tel. & Tel., Oakland 1976-78; acct. mgr. Southwestern Bell, Houston, Tx. 1974-76; honors: Eagle Scout, BSA 1966; author: The History of Broadcasting in San Jose, Ca. 1989-78 (1978), Winning Twenty One (1974), The Network as a Strategic Weapon (1984); mil: 1st lt. US Army, Vietnam Cpgn., USAR currently; LDS Ch.; rec: writing, mil. hist., real estate. Res: 140 South 15th San Jose 95112 Ofc: Rolm Corp. 4900 Old Ironsides Dr 95054

CHERLIN, RICHARD S., physician; b. Sept. 28, 1947, Brooklyn, NY; s. Leonard and Violet (Gross) C.; m. Patricia, Aug. 20, 1970; 1 son: Marcus, b. 1974; edn: BS, summa cum laude, Brooklyn Coll. 1968; MD, Albert Einstein Coll. of Med. 1972; intern, jr. res., Bronx Municipal Hosp. Ctr. 1972-74; sr. res. Stanford Univ. Med. Cr. 1974-75; clinical & research fellow, endocrinology, Mass. Gen. Hosp. 1975-77; cert. internal med. 1975; cert. endocrinology & metabolism 1977. Career: pvt. practice endocrinology & internal med. 1977--; attending physician Santa Clara Co. Valley Med. Ctr. 1977--; chief of staff Valley West Gen. Hosp. 1981-82; pres. Diabetes Soc., Santa Clara Co. 1983-; dir. med. edn. Valley West Gen. hosp. 1978-; clinical asst. prof. of med. Stanford 1982-; awards: Regents State Med. Scholarship; Physicians Recgn. Awd., AMA 1976, 79, 82; Physicians Recgn. Wad., CMA 1979, 82; Phi Betta Kappa; Alpha Omega Alpha; mem: Diabetes Soc. (pres.); Santa Clara Co. Med. Soc.; Am. Soc. of Internal Med.; Calif. Soc. of Internal Med.; rec: gardening, computers. Res: 990 Mazzone Dr San Jose 95120 Ofc: 15899 Los Gatos- Almaden Rd, Ste 12, Los Gatos 95030

CHERNOFF, PAUL ROBERT, mathematics professor; b. June 21, 1942, Phila., Pa.; s. Benjamin and Edith (Korentzwitt) C.; edn: BA, summa cum laude, Harvard Univ. 1963; MA, 1965; PhD, 1968. Career: with UC Berkeley 1968--; postdoctoral fellow Nat. Sci. Found, 1968-69; lect. in math., 1969-71; asst. prof. of math. 1971-74; assoc. prof. of math. 1974-80; prof. of math. 1980--; cons. Inst. for Defense Analysis, Princeton, NJ 1979-81; honors: Phi Beta Kappa; Sigma Xi; Eric Hoffer Prize Essay, UC Berkeley 1978; mem: Am. Math. Soc.; Math. Assn. of Am.; Am. Assn. for the Adv. of Sci.; author/ coauthor: 2 research monographs & 35 research arts. in mathematics 1965-. Ofc: Dept. of Mathematics, UC Berkeley, Berkeley 94720

CHESS, STEPHEN JOHN, physician and surgeon; b. June 29, 1914, Fourstates, W. Va.; s. John and Theresa (Cernalavic) Chess; edn: BS 1936 and MS 1939, Marquette Univ., MD, Medical Coll of Wisc., 1942, PhD in surgery, Univ. of Ill. Sch of Medicine, 1949; m. Dorothy Haasch, Nov. 21, 1940; children: Dorothy, b. 1950, Stephanie, b., 1952, John, b. 1953, Robert, b. 1957, Thomas, b. 1958; career: Fellow in Surgery, Research & Ednl. Hosps., Univ. of Ill. Sch of Medicine 1943-44; chief surgical resident, Hines VA Hosp., Hines, Ill.; asst. chief surgeon, Chicago, Milwaukee & St. Paul R.R. and attending surgeon, Wesley Mem. Hosp. and Northwestern Univ. Sch. of Medicine, Chgo., 1948; chief surgeon, Buenaventura Medical Clinic, Inc., Ventura 1950--; attending surgeon, (chief of staff 1973), Community Mem. Hosp., (chief of staff 1971-72) Ventura County General Hosp., St. John's Hosp., Oxnard and Ojai Valley Community Mem. Hosp.; cons. in surgery, Camarillo State Hosp. 1955-57. Fellow, Am. Coll. of Surgeons, 1950; Diplomate, Am. Board of Surgery, 1950; Diplomate, Am. Board of Abdominal Surgery, 1969; pres., Ventura County Med. Soc., 1975; pres., Ventura Area Profl. Standards Review Orgn., 1977-78; apptd. to State Council by Secty. HEW, 1978; mem. Medical Advisory com. to Hospital Council, So. Calif. Hospital Assn., 1975-; mem: founding mem., bd. dirs., Exchange Club of Ventura, 1950; Knights of Columbus, 3rd Degree, 1954; Phi Chi Med. Frat., 1939-; Kiwanis Club, 1960; contbr. num. publs. on med. research, med. subjects 1939-; mil: maj., M.C. US Army 1944-46, PTO, Bronze star medal for Okinawan Campaign; Roman Catholic; rec: gardening; res: 155 Lakewood Ave, Ventura 93004; office: Buenaventura Medical Clinic, Inc. 2705 Loma Vista Rd, Ventura 93003.

CHESSER, JEFFREY LYNN, video producer/ director; b. Aug. 10, 1942, Athens, Ohio; s. Armour Alonzo and Doris Ann (Gibbs) C.; edn: BS, San Diego State Univ. 1965. Career: announcer KJLM- FM, La Jolla 1964; dir. ednl. TV, San Diego State Univ., San Diego 1964-65; prodn. mgr. KAAR-TV, San Diego 1965-66; producer/ dir. KFMB-TV, San Diego 1967-76; asst. dir. Hughes Sports Network, NY 1967-68; ops. mgr. KFMB-TV, San Diego 1976-80; producer/ dir. San Diego Clippers NBA team, San Diego 1978-81; owner/ pres. Corporate Mktg. & Commun.; 1981--; secty./ treas Senica Corp. 1983--; awards: Individual of the Yr., Alpha Epsilon Rho 1965; Svc. Key Awd., SDSU 1965; Svc. Awd., San Diego Co. Health Fair 1968; Svc. Awd., COMBO 1977; Nom. for Emmy Awd. 1979; mem: Alpha Epsilon RHO (past pres. 1979); Radio/ TV Guild; Nat. Acad. of TV Arts & Sci. 1979; Am. Fedn. of TV and Radio Artists (AFTRA); San Diego CofC; publs: Communicator Mag.; PIC Mag., 11/81; Video-Dex, product news mag., rec: music, tennis, golf. Res: 5690 Lake Murray Blvd, Apt 11, La Mesa 92041 Ofc: Corporate Marketing & Communication, 4343 Morena Blvd, Ste 8, San Diego 92117

CHESTER, JOHN E., company executive; b. Nov. 9, 1932; NY; s. John E. and Helen (Burns) C.; m. ARden, Sept. 20, 1952; children: John III, b. 1953; Kevin, b. 1954; Stephen, b. 1958; edn: BA, Queens Coll. 1958; RN, USN 1953; ERT, Med. Corps. Sch., USN 1951; adv. mgmt. pgm., Internat. Mgmt. Inst., Columbia Univ. 1974. Career: v.p. comml. devel., internat. & R&D Edward Weck Co. 1971-74; v.p. mktg. V.Mueller Div. Am. Hosp. Supply Corp 1974-76; dir. mktg./ sales for European, Mideastern, African, Canadian & So. Am. internat. bus. units Am. Hosp. Supply Corp. 1976-79; v.p./ gen. mgr. Searle Surgical Sys. 1979-81; v.p./ gp. exec. Bristol- Myers Corp. 1981-82; pres. Unitek Corp., Monrovia 1982--; mem: Dental Mfrs. Assn.; Health Ind. Mfrs. Assn.; mil: USN 1950-54; Republican; Catholic; rec: golf. Res: 636 Pomello Dr Claremont 91711 Ofc: Unitek Corp., 2724 S Peck Rd Monrovia 91016

CHESUS, THOMAS EDWARD, financial/marketing consultant; b. Aug. 7, 1951, Alton, Ill.; s. Roman Charles and Mary Loretta (McConnell) C.; ed. Drake Univ. Career: mktg. consultant/prin., Mill Valley 1978-80; sales rep. Pitney-Bowes, Inc. San Francisco 1979-81; owner, finl. advisor Chesus-Maxwell Finl. Services (dba Diversified Finl. Services 1981-83), 1981--; bd. dirs. Myers Inst. S.F. 1983-84; guest lectr. Univ. of Santa Clara Business Sch. 1984; honors: highest sales volume for 1st year sales, Pitney-Bowes S.F., 1979, and 2d highest sales vol. for Western Reg. Pitney-Bowes; mem. Internnat. Assn. of Finl. Planners; works: created Profit Positioning (1982); Vedanta Soc. Ofc: Chesus-Maxwell Fin. Ser. 102 Edison Ave Corte Madera 94925

CHEU, STEPHEN, physician; b. Jan. 20, 1905, Canton, China; s. Ning and Shee (Leung) C.; m. Phyllis Li, June 28, 1940; 1 son: Dudley, b. 1941; edn: BA, UC Berkeley 1931; MA, USC Los Angeles 1933; MD, Peiping Union Med. Coll., Peking, China 1938; MD, Calif. 1951. Career: staff physician Bret Harte Sanatorium, Murphy 1951-52; staff physician Veterans Admin. Med. Ctr., Fresno 1952-57; chief radioisotope svcs./ asst. chief med. svc. 1958-75; med. cons. San Francisco Drug Treatment Ctr. & Marin Treatment Ctr., San Rafael 1976--; exec. bd. V.A. ARmed Forces Coccy' Coop. Study Gp. 1957-63; Scientific Pgm., Chmn. & Med. Advr., Lung ASsn. San Joaquin Valley Central Cos. 1960-62; chmn. of research and radioisotope com. V.A. Med. Ctr., Fresno 1957-75; awards; Awd. of Merit, Dept. of Calif. Mil. Order of the Purple Heartu 1953; Commdn. for research library on Valley Fever for clinicians, researchers, & pub. health wkrs., Veterans Amin.; mem: Soc. of Nuclear Med.; Am. Coll. of Nuclear Med.; Calif. Lung Assn.; works: over 12 publs. in var. med. journs.; author (1) book & (1) book chpt.; Republican; Methodist; rec: stamp collecting, travel. Res: 128 Glacier Ct Petaluma 94052

CHEVALIER, PAUL EDWARD, employee relations executive; b. Jan. 30, 1939, NYC; s. Arthur and Grace (Eaton) C.; m. Anne-Marie Leitner, May 4, 1963; 1 son: Marc, b. 1967; edn: BA, Columbia Coll. 1960; LLD, Columbia Sch. of Law 1966; MBA, Columbia Grad. Sch. ofBus.; AMP, Harvard Bus. Sch. Adv. Mgmt. Pgm. 1979; admitted to practice, US Supreme Ct., Ill. Supreme Ct.; arbitrator, Am. Arbitration Assn. Career: employee rels. pgm. General Electric 1966-67; Western reg. mgr. labor rels. Montgomery Ward 1967-72; dir.

labor rels. Carter Hawley Hale Stores, Inc. 1972-74; v.p. employee rels. 1974--; chmn. Employee Com., Am. Retail Fedn. 1979-82; Employee Rels. Com., Bus. Roundtable; dir. UBA, Inc. 1976-82; dir. Calif. Employment Law Council; mem: Am. Bar Assn.; Am. Retail Fedn.; Calif. Retail Assn.; Jonathan Club (Personnel Com.); Harvard Bus. Sch. Assn., So. Calif.; Los Angeles Athletic Club; Glendale Internat. Diving Soc.; mil: lt. USN 1960-63, USNR 1963-66; Republican; Catholic; rec: bibliophile, scuba diving, running. Res: 2405 Glendower Ave Los Angeles 90027 Ofc: Carter Hawley Hale Stores, Inc., 550 S Flower St Los Angeles 90071

CHHABRA, RAJINDER KAUR, physician; b. Feb. 15, 1934, Rawalpindi, Punjab, India; d. Bhagwant Singh and Jaswant Kaur (Tibb) Kohli; m. Ajaib Chhabra, Oct. 10, 1960; chil: Ajinder, b. 1961, Harbash, b. 1965; edn: MD, Lady Hardinge Med. Coll., New Delphi, 1957; dip. gyn-obstets, Coll. of Phys. and Surg., Bombay, 1959. Career: house surg. BJ Med. Coll. and Sassoon Hosps., Poona 1957-58; med. ofcr. Family Welfare Ctrs, So. Command, Poona 1958 60; res. Willingdon Hosp., New Delhi 1960-62; med. ofcr. New Delhi Family Plnng Assn., 1962-5; med. ofcr. Cantt. Gen. Hosp., Lucknow 1965-6; res. W. Norwich Hosp., Norwich, U.K. 1966-7; med. ofcr. Family Plnng. Assn., 1967-9; med. ofcr. Nat. Inst. of Family Plnng (NIFP), New Delhi 1971-74; intern Martin Luther King Jr. Gen Hosp., Los Angeles 1978-79, cons. phys. Charles Drew Med. Sch., 1979; staff phys. Dept. Ob./Gyn., asst. med. dir. Women's Hlth Care Clinic and Tng. Pgms., Harbor-UCLA Med. Ctr, Torrance 1979--. Fellow Internat. Council of Sex Edn. and Parenthood 1982. Mem: Am. Public Health Assn., Am. Fertility Soc., Assn. of Planned Parenthood Profls., Internat. Fedn. of Fertility Socs., Am. Med. Women's Assn., Am. Soc. of Colposcopy and Cervical Pathol., Faculty Soc., assoc. Alan Guttmacher Inst.; med. resrch in field, med. publs; Sikh; rec: travel, photog.; res: 6762 Verde Ridge Rd, Rancho Palos Verdes, CA 90274. ofc: Harbor-UCLA Med. Ctr., 1000 W. Carson St, A-14, Torrance 90509

CHI, CHANG HWI, electrical engineer; b. Dec. 23, 1934, Seoul, Korea, nat. 1965; s. Yong Ha and So Aei (Shin) C.; m. Keum Park, Mar. 16, 1963; children: David, b. 1964; Danny, b. 1965; Tom, b. 1966; Susan, b. 1970; edn: BS, MIT 1958; MS, 1960; PhD, Polytech. Inst. of Brooklyn 1969. Career: proj. mgr. Perkin Elmer Corp., Norwalk; currently, pgm. mgr./ chief scientist Hughes Aircraft Co., El Segundo; mem: IEEE; OSA; SPIE; publs: ed. Periodic Structure, SPIE Internat. Conf. 1980; rec: skiing, tennis, jogging. Res: 1634 Aspenwall Rd Westlake Village 91361 Ofc: Hughes Aircraft Co., Canoga Park

CHIANG, THERESA YEN-SHENG, real estate broker; b. Mar. 12, Fuchow, Fukien, China; d. Ho-Ming and Shiu-Ping (Huang) Chiang; m. Ping-Wang Chiang, Dec. 12, 1964; children: Patricia, Dick, Peter; edn: BA, Providence Coll., Taipei, Taiwan 1964; grad. studies, Ball State Univ., Muncie, Ind. 1964-65; spl. courses, Mesa Comm. Coll. 1976-78, West Valley Comm. Coll. 1980-81; Calif. lic. real estate broker. Career: asst. librarian Ball State Univ., Muncie, Ind. 1964; counselor Boy Scouts of America, Mesa, Ariz. 1974; data analyst Escondido (Ca.) Bank, 1976; real estate broker Century 21- Carney, San Jose 1978-82; real estate broker Coast to Coast Properties, 1982--; awards: Top Salesprsn. awds. (2), Century 21 No. Reg. Calif.; Scholarship Awd., Mesa Community Bus. Sch. 1976; volunteer, Chinese Language Sch.; sponsor for Indo-Chinese refugee settlement; vol. tchr. (English) Adult Sch.; rec: oil painting, cooking. Res: 115 Millrich Dr Los Gatos 95030 Ofc: Coast to Coast Properties, 11405 S Saratoga- Sunnyvale Rd, San Jose 95129

CHIBURIS, WILLIAM CHRISTOPHER, real estate development co. president; b. June 18, 1931, Omaha, Nebr.; s. Christopher Constantine and Emma Bessie (Vodicka) C.; m. 2d Shirley Charlene Lee, Sept. 10, 1977; children: Michael, b. 1957, Kerry, b. 1959, Nicholas, b. 1961, William, b. 1963; stepchildren: Gary, b. 1959, Stephen, b. 1961, Michael, b. 1967, Julie, b. 1970 (Mack); edn: BA, Ariz. State Univ. Tempe, 1951. Career: owner/opr. title and escrow companies in Modesto, Merced, Mariposa, Salinas, and Carmel until 1977; sold to Transam. Corp.; home builder, subdivision developer, 1977--; founder/owner California Financial (mortgage co.); currently devel. mini storage units and subdivs. for manufactured housing; owner/pres. Wilshir Co., land devel. and inv. co.; mem: Masons, Scottish Rite, Shriners, Elks, Sportsman of Stanislaus; past pres. Modesto Exchange Club; past pres. Modesto 20-30 Club; past pres. Am. Cancer Soc., Modesto; past pres. Am. Heart Assn., Modesto; mil: maj. USAF 1950-54, Korea and Saigon; DFC, Air Medal w/cluster, GCM, Commendn., Korean Def., Korean Service, and Nat. Serv. Def. medals, Pres. Unit Cit., Korean Pres. Unit Cit., Marine Corp Reserve Medal; Democrat; 7th-Day Adventist; rec: philately, TV Electronics. Res: 2209 Glasgow Dr Ceres 95307 Ofc: Wilshir Co., 1119 12th St, Ste. 2, Modesto 95354

CHICK, ARTHUR TREAT, III, manufacturing co. executive; b. Nov. 12, 1927, Oakland; s. Arthur Treat II and Wilma Muriel (Dohrmann); m. Lois Hanschen, Mar. 25, 1949; children: Velda, B. 1950; Pamela, b. 1951; Mark, b. 1953; edn: AA, Lincoln Univ. 1951; Radio TV Tng. Assn. 1953e. Career: regl. sales mgr. Thermac Controls Co., Corona 1960-62; dist. mgr. Malsbary Mfg. Co., Union Town, Penn. 1962-78; v.p. sales Walters Mfg. Co., Watsonville 1978--; cons., text book, Engine Repair, Yuba Coll. 1975; gp. mem. developed orgn. Cleaning Equip. Mfg. Assn. (CEMA) 1980; awards: Top 10 Sales Awd., Malsbary Mfg. Co. 1969-73; mem: Toastmasters (pres. Hayward chpt. 1958); CEMA; Profl. Standards Com.; designed Jump Masters Certificate', 11th Airborne Div. 1947; mil: PFC Army Paratroopers, 11th Airborne Div., Medal of Occupation, Japan, GCM, Marksmanship; Republican; Protestant; rec: computers, flying, photog. Res: 506 Brewington Ave Watsonville 95076 Ofc: Walters Mfg. Co., 297 Anna St Watsonville 95076

CHIEN, ANDREW KWANGNIEH, certified public accountant; b. Jan. 7, 1943, Chungking, China 1976; s. Wen-Sze and Wei-Ling (Chang) C.; m. Ming Jean Wang, July 3, 1976; l son: Steven Juyun, b. 1983; edn: BS, Southeast Mo. State Univ. 1966; MS, Okla. St. Univ. 1967; PhD, Univ. of Ill. 1972; MBA, CSU Los Angeles 1976; CPA, Calif. 1981. Career: asst. prof. dept. of fisheries Taiwan Coll. of Marine Tech., Keelung, Taiwan 1972-74; research tech. physiology dept. USC Med. Sch., part- time 1974-76; tax auditor State bd. of Equalization, Long Beach 1976-79; staff acct. Henry Louis Scott & Co., CPAs, Beverly Hills 1979-81; owner, CPA practice, San Gabriel area 1981--; awards: Best Childrens Book of Yr., Animal Olympics (pub. 1974), Chinese Provincial Dept. of Edn. 1979; mem: Calif. Soc. CPAs; Calif. Rare Fruit Growers Assn.; Nat. Wildlife Assn.; publs: Chinese lang. childrens books (2), Animal Olympics, & Taking Care of Animal Babies, 1974; doctoral work, pub. in W. Germany Journ. of Animal Psychology; Republican; Christian; rec: painting, gardening, photog. Res: 502 N Daisy Ave Pasadena 91107 Ofc: Andrew Chien, CPA, 3452 E Foothill Blvd, Ste 120A, Pasadena 91107

CHIKMAGALUR, KUSUM RUDRAPPA, physician; b. Jan. 24, 1948, Chikmagalur, India, nat. 1975; s. Rudrappa and Parvathamma C.R. Chikmagalur; edn: BD, Bangalore Med. Coll., India 1970; Ednl. Council for Foreign Med. Grads. 1977; MD, Calif. 1979; MD, med. & surgery, G. Gurudas, Dean 1971. Cert., Tng. Pgm. in Prosthetics-Orthotics and course in Ofc. Orthopedics, UCLA; Career: family practitioner, Bangalore, India 1970-75; physician asst. Ladera Hghts. Med., while preparing for Calif. Bd. Exam; intern in neurology, internal med. & pathology, Los Angeles 1980-81; res. physical med. & rehab. Northridge Hosp. 1981-84, neurology 1984--; mil: Nat. Cadet Corps. 1963; rec: swimming, bicycling, painting. Res: 12706 Venice Blvd, Apt 28, Marvista Los Angeles 90066 Ofc: Northridge Hosp., Rehab. Dept., 18300 Roscoe Blvd Northridge 91328

CHILDS-GERBER, TONI C., federal government executive; b. Feb. 7, 1948, Brooklyn, NY; d. Charles J. and Ann (Safonte) Kalb; m. Richard Gerber, Apr. 2, 1982; l son: Eddie, b. 1970; edn: BA, magna cum laude, Univ. of Colo. 1969. Career: claims rep. Social Security, NY 1970-73; supvr., NY 1974-76; admin. asst., Newark, NJ 1977; staff asst., NY 1978-79; mgr., La Mesa 1980--; pres. Women Execs. 1979-81; mem. Mgmt. Assn. 1974--; awards: Cash Awd., Social Security 1977; Quality Step Increase, Soc. Security 1982; mem: Women Execs. (pres. 1979-81); Phi Beta Kappa; Mgmt. Assn.; Physical Fitness Club; works: dir./ producer two sucessful sems. for 100-200 women, Los Angeles & San Diego 1980, 81; Democrat; rec: jazz, sewing. Res: 2581 Duraznitos Rd Ramona 92065 Ofc: Social Security, 7373 University Ave La Mesa 92041

CHILKOV, DOROTHY TAYLOR, real estate association executive; b. Pittsburgh, Pa.; d. George Holiday and Frances (Klaman) Taylor; m. Samuel N. Chilkov, Oct. 14, 1951; children: Jill Dorian, b. 1953, Paul Jordan, b. 1956; edn: Ariz. State Univ. 1946-7, Mills Coll. 1975. Career: TV/radio producer KLAC/ KMPC/ABC, 1948-64; fashion exec. Robinson's, Beverly Hills 1971-75; mgr. Beverly Hills CofC & Visitors Bureau and Rodeo Drive Com., 1975-80; mktg. dir. East/West Network, 1980; exec. vice pres./CEO Beverly Hills Board of Realtors, 1980--; cons. Four Seasons Hotels (Canada), Ben Gurion Univ. (Israel) 1980-; cons. Home Svgs & Loan, Beverly Hills Svgs & Loan, 1981-. Awards: City of Hope 1974, American Heart Assn. 1969, PTA 1965, Bus. & Profl. Women 1981. Trustee Univ. of W. Los Angeles 1984-8; trustee Calif. Assn. Realtors Ins. 1984-7. Mem: Beverly Hills CofC, W. Hollywood CofC, LA CofC (Women's Council), LA County Mus of Art, LA/China Sister Cities. Author: African Makonde Sculpture. Rec: travel, art collector. Ofc:280 So Beverly Dr Ste 513, Beverly Hills 90212

CHIN, AVERY, certified public accountant; b. Nov. 24, 1958, Sacto.; s. Yook Hen and Beet Won (Gee) C.; edn: BS, Univ. of San Francico 1980; CPA, State Bd. of Accty. Career: ops. mgr. BC Imports, San Francisco 1979-80; CPA, Main Hurdman, S.F. 1980-83; sr. internal auditor The Gap Stores, Inc., San Bruno 1983--; controller VDOAd, S.F. 1984--; mem: Beta Alpha Psi; Nat. Assn. Asian CPAs; Asian Bus. League; The Careers Fellowship (pres./ outreach coord.); Golden Gate Christian Reformed Ch. (Deacon); rec: basketball, baseball, tennis. Res: 742 7th Ave San Francisco 94118 Ofc: The Gap Stores, Inc., 900 Cherry Ave San Bruno 94066

CHIN, GREGORY, systems analyst; b. Apr. 19, 1952, Hanford, Calif.; s. Mon Quong and Sylvia Charlene (Weeks) C.; m. Pamelia Estelle York, June 7, 1980; children: Rebecca Lynn; Deborah Ann.; Richard Gregory; edn: AA, Coll. of the Sequoias 1973. Career: computer opr. Medical Data System 1973-75; opr./ sys. pgmr. Medical Data North 1975-80; pgmr./ analysis Comst. Time Share 1980; data processing mgr./ sys. pgmr. B&K Inds. 1981-83; sys. analysis New Generation Software 1983--; works: integrated IBM's Mapics & CMAS Acctg. Sys., B&K Inds. 1981-83; Democrat; LDS Ch.; rec: fishing, chess, computer games. Res: POB 1669, Rt 1 County Rd 25, Orland 95963 Ofc: 341 Lincoln St Roseville 95678

CHIN, HENRY SAU, investments broker; b. Jan. 17, 1924, Providence, Rhode Island; s. Chun Sau and See (Tow) C.; m. Naida Lim, Nov. 3, 1957; children: Pamela, b. 1959; Brenda, b. 1960; Geoffrey, b. 1963; Randal, b. 1966; Oliver, b. 1969; edn: AB, Harvard Coll. 1949; MBA, Cornell Grad. Sch. of Mgmt. 1951. Career: reg. rep. White, Weld & Co., Los Angeles 1960-64; reg. rep. Hayden, Stone & Co., Century City 1964-67; reg. rep. Smith Barney & Co., L.A. 1967-69; asst. mgr. E.F. Hutton & Co., L.A. 1969-76; fin. coord. White, Weld & Co., Century City 1976-78; v.p. Drexel Burnham Lambert Inc., L.A. 1978--; bd. dirs. Cornell Club Of So. Calif. 1981-84; chmn. Scholarship Com. 1982-84;

awards: Exec. Club, Drexel Burnham Lambert Inc. 1981; mem: Stockbrokers Soc.; Los Angeles chpt. Am. Stock Exch.; L.A. Masons; L.A. Scottish Rite; Al Malaikah Temple; Harvard Club of So. Calif.; mil: capt. US Army 1943-46; Protestant; rec: art. Res: 3487 Rowena Ave Los Angeles 90027 Ofc: Drexel Burnham Lambert Inc., 800 West 6th Street Los Angeles 90017

CHING, ERNEST J.H.K., resource specialist; b. Oct. 12, 1931, Honolulu, Hawaii; s. Ernest Jung Heen and Daisy Woessner (Kekaula) C.; edn: BA, San Francisco St. Univ. 1958; MA, San Jose St. Univ. 1974; Calif. Tchr. credentials: Gen. Elem. (life), Learning Handicapped Splst (life), Severely Handicapped Splst (life), Supvsn. and Adminstrn. Service (life), Bilingual/Cross Cultural Splst., Resource Splst. Career: classroom tchr., remedial reading tchr., ednl. handicapped tchr., resource splst., 1958-70; vice prin. 1971-73, admin. asst. 1975-76, summer sch. principal 1975-76; ednl. handicapped tchr. 1978; resource splst. Alum Rock Union Elem. School Dist., San Jose 1981--; awards: Rosenberg Scholarship 1963; hon. life mem. PTA from Wm. Rogers Sch. 1972; scholarship, Calif. Assn. of Neurol. Handicapped 1968; mem. IMUA Hawaiian Civic Club (charter), Na Hawaii O Kaleponi Dance Troupe (charter), Phi Delta Kappa; mil: sgt. USMC 1952-54; Democrat; Catholic. Res: 1431 Saratoga Ave, Ste. 104, San Jose 95129 Ofc: Alum Rock Union Elem. Sch. Dist. 2930 Gay Ave San Jose 95127

CHINN, VERNON EDWARD, agriculture co. president; b. Oct. 16, 1912, Lemoore; s. Green Bedford and Lena (Etter) C.; m. Shirley Day, June 21, 1940; children: Valerie, b. 1942; Philip & Gregory, b. 1942; Cheryl, b. 1944. Career: mgr. Chinn Warehouse, Lemoore 1935-43; mgr. Kings Co. Land & Cattle Co., Lemoore 1944-55; farm mgr. Miller & Lux, Inc., Kern Co. 1956-75; mgr. Lemoore Canal & Irrigation Co., Lemoore 1976-80; mgr. West Kern Resources Cons. Dist., Kern. Co. 1981-82; currently, pres./ mgr. King Co. Land & Cattle Co.; pres. John Heinlen Mutual Water Co. 1942-60; v.p. Lost Hills Water Dist. 1963-77; mem. bd. Henry Miller Water Dist. 1965-75; chmn. Kern Co. Water Agcy. Adv. Com. 1969-77; bd. dirs. Tulare Basin Adv. Comm. 1976-81; Lemoore & Kings Co. CofC (past pres.). Res: 8 Follett Lemoore 93245

CHIRICHILLO, RICHARD, chiropractor; b. July 26, 1948, Elizabeth, NJ; s. Joseph John and Ann Marie (Francaviglia) C.; edn: AA, BA, Monmouth Coll.; MA, Kean Coll.; MA, Columbia Univ. Tchrs. Coll.; DC, Western States Chiropractic Coll. Career: tchr. St. John Vianney H.S., Holendel, NJ 1970-73; tchr. Moddlesex H.S., Moddlesex, NJ 1973-74; physical dir. Orange YMCA 1976; tchr. Western State Chiro. Coll. 1978-81; Doctor of Chiro.; awards: NJ State Scholarship 1966-70; Tchrs. Coll. Prof. Awd. 1975-76; mem: Calif. Chiro. Assn.; Butte Chiro. Soc.; Paradise Elks; publs: Nature of Posture, Chiro. Economics 4/82; Christian; rec: tennis, racketball, badminton. Ofc: 6152o Center Street Paradise 95969

CHIBURG, JAMES THOMAS, JR., investment co. executive; b. May 21, 1944, Wellesley, Mass.; s. James Thomas and Virginia Burtt (Low) C.; m. Lynne Louise Robertson Day, Sept. 15, 1983; edn: AB, Cornell Univ. 1964; MBA, Harvard Univ. 1969; B.Litt., Univ. of Oxford 1972; PhD, UC Berkeley 1974; chartered fin. analyst, U.K. 1972. Career: asst. mktg. mgr. General Mills, Inc., Tokyo, Japan 1968; corp. fin. dept. First Boston Corp., NY 1969-70; gen. mgr. Protasis Trust, Ltd., London, England 1971-72; lead partner Protasis Trust, Ltd., Berkeley, Ca. 1973--; dir. Protasis Holdings (S.A.R.L.), Luxembourg 1980--; lectr. internat. fin. Univ. of Calif. 1980--; investment advr. US Agcy. for Internat. Devel. Mission to Tanzania 1980; awards: Knox Fellowship, Harvard Univ. of Oxford 1969-70; fellow, Salzburg Sem. on Internat. Monetary Instability, Salzburg, Austria 1980; mem: Inst. of Dirs. (U.K.); Royal Economic soc. (U.K.); Am. Economic Assn.; Fin. Execs. Inst.; MENSA; Internat. Wine & Food Soc.; Commonwealth, S.F; Harvard Club, Boston; Union League Club, NY; United Oxford & Cambridge Univ. Club, London; Internat. House of Japan, Tokyo; mil: lt. j.g., USNR 1964-67, Bronze Star w/ combat V; Protestant. Res: 2115 Bush St San Francisco 94115 Ofc: POB 4000 Berkeley 94704

CHO, FRANK WONJAE, dentist; b. Jan. 10, 1942, Koheung, Korea, nat. 1981; s. In Hong and Bong Soon (Shin) C.; m. Tina, June 10, 1972; children: Connei, b. 1976; Mimi, b. 1978; Rosemary, b. 1979; Christine, b. 1982; edn: DMD, Kyunghee Univ. 1975; DDS, USC 1978; Bd. Dental Examiners 1978. Career: practice in dentistry, Bell Gardens 1978--; practice in dentistry, Downey 1982--; awards: operated free dental clinic for need chilren, Rio Hondo Boys Club; mem: Am. Dental Assn.; Rio Hondo Boys Club, Bell Gardens; Democrat; Presbyterian; rec: naturalist. Res: 21842 Tenderfoot Way Diamond Bar 91765 Ofc: Frank W. Cho, DDS, 7840 Firestone Blvd, Ste 106, Downey 90241

CHOI, JAIK, structural engineer; b. Nov. 7, 1942, Seoul, Korea, nat. 1979; s. Sang Kyu and Chum Choo (Lee) C.; m. Innae, Sept. 19, 1970; children: Gene, b. 1972; Eunice, b. 1975; edn: BS, Cal Poly 1971; BS, CSU Fullerton 1976; structural engr. Career: chief structural design engr. Scherrer- Baumann & Assoc., Santa Ana 1971-74; chief engr. R.L. Foley & Assoc., Newport Beach 1974-75; chief struct. engr. John M. Coil Assoc., Santa Ana 1975-77; principal/ owner Jaik Choi & Assoc., Newport Beach 1978--; mem: Structural Engrs. Assn. of So. Calif.; Am. Concrete Inst.; Am. Model Aeronautics; mil: cpl. Republic of Korean Army 1963-65; rec: karate, judo, hapkido. Res: 25736 La Serra St Laguna Hills 92653 Ofc: Jaik Choi & Assoc., 3822 Campus Dr, Ste 120, Newport Beach 92660

CHOMENKO, MARY, artist; b. Aug. 11, 1951, New Brunswick, N.J.; d. Savelij and Tanya (Ladyhin) C.; m. James M. Williams, Nov. 4, 1978; edn: BA, Montclair St. Coll. 1973; summer pgm. Harvard Univ. 1977; undergrad. pgm. Sch of the Mus. of Fine Arts, Boston 1978-9; MFA, Calif. Coll. of Arts &:

Crafts 1982. career: profl. artist/ printmaker/ papermaker; worked, exhbns. in Boston area, 1977-79, in San Francisco Bay area 1979--; represented by Fuller Goldeen Gallery, S.F., Stavaridis Gallery, Boston; recent group exhibs: Smith Anderson Gallery, Palo Alto, 1983; Storefront Mus., Oakland Mus., Oakland, 1983; Internat. Sculpture Conf. San Jose Inst. of Contemporary Art, San Jose, 1983. Guest instr. Internat. Sculpture Conf., San Jose 1983; instr. papermaking wkshps., Internat. Paper Conf. 1983, Kyoto, Japan; mem: World Print Council, Pro Arts, Boston Visual Artist's Union 1983. publs: artwork reprinted in Electronic Design Mag. 6/83; rec: swim, gourmet cook, electronic flea mkts. Res: 914 Moreno Ave. Palo Alto 94303 Ofc: Mary Chomenko Studio 257 Martens Ave. Mountain View

CHOUINARD, GEORGE DELPHON, engineering co. executive; b. Apr. 19, 1936, Salt Lake City, Utah; s. George Delphon Sr. and Helena Josephine (Rogers) C.; m. Caroline Piekenbrock, May 19, 1962; children: E. Damian, b. 1963; Richard, b. 1964; edn: Univ. of Colo. 1957-61; Univ. of Va. 1981. Career: architect Miner & Miner, Engrs.- Architects, Colo. 1961-64; proj. mgr. Morrison-Knudsen Engrs. & Contractors, No. Am. 1964-70; regl. mgr. Morrison-Knudsen, No. Am. & S.E. Asia 1970-74; dir. gen. Compagnie Ferguson Morrison Knudsen, Paris, France 1974-76; pres. Food Inds. Engring. & Agrostruct Engrs. & Contractors, US & Internat. 1976-78; div. mgr. Morrison- Knudsen Eng. & Contr., US & Internat. 1978-80; v.p. mktg Brown & Caldwell Cons. Eng., US & Internat. 1980--; spl. cons./ exec. cem. Envirodyne Engrs. 1976-79; Mktg. Seminars advisor, Am. Cons. Engrs. Council, Wash. DC 1982; mem: Colorado Democrat (asst. ed. 1959-60); Farm Bureau; publs: Onsite Energy Goes Industrial, Reinhold Pub. Co. 1970; mil: spec. 3/c, US Army 1954-57; Democrat; Catholic; rec: golf, viticulture, enology. Res: 33853 Palomares Castro Valley 94546 Ofc: Brown & Caldwell Consulting Engineers, 3480 Buskirk Pleasant Hill 94523

CHOW, CHAM-CHUEN, banker; b. Oct. 31, 1924, Hong Kong; s. Ping-Un and Chi-Wah (Chan) C.; m. Mimie W., Sept. 29, 1958; 1 son: Patrick H., b. 1959; edn: LLD, Nat. Sun-Yet-Sen Univ., Canton, China 1946; King's Coll., Hong Kong 1933-40. Career: Bank of Communications, Hong Kong 1947-63; br. mgr. The Hong Kong Chinese Bank Ltd., Hong Kong 1964-71; regl. mgr. The Ka Wah Bank, Ltd. 1971-82; br. mgr., Los Angeles 1983--; mem. Los Angeles Area CofC. Res: 10674 Key West Temple City 91780 Ofc: The Ka Wah Bank Ltd., 818 N Broadway, Ste 102, Los Angeles 90012

CHOW, HENRY G., lawyer; b. July 5, 1950, Taipei, Taiwan, nat. 1981; s. David Ding-Yu and Angela C.C. Chow; m. Rose Liu, Mar. 5, 1976; children: Alexander, b. 1977; Margaret, b. 1982; LLB, Soochow Univ. 1973; JD, Southern Methodist Univ. 1975; admitted to practice, Tex., Calif. & Taiwan. Career: atty. at law, law ofcs. San Francisco & Taipei; mem: Bar Assns. of Tex. & Taiwan; Asian Am. Bar of San Francisco. Res: 4280 Peregrine Way Fremont 94536 Ofc: 300 Montgomery St, Ste 633, San Francisco 94104

CHOW, STEPHEN Y.T., real estate consultant, developer; b. Jan. 15, 1948, Canton, China, nat. 1975; s. Herbert P.H. and Ngoi Chun (Lau) C.; edn: BA, San Francisco State Univ. 1974; MBA, Golden Gate Univ. 1976; R.E. Broker, Calif. 1976; Calif. Comm. Coll. Instr. Credential 1976. Career: partner Anderson, Chow & Assoc., San Francisco 1976; pres. American Investment Holding Co., S.F. 1980; v.p. Golden Gate Corp., S.F. 1982--; US investment cons. individual & corp. clients from Hong Kong, Philippines, Taiwan & Singapore; awards: Awd. for Significant Mktg. Achiev., Am. Mktg. Assn. 1978; mem: Am. Mgmt. Assn.; Am. Real Estate Exch.; Internat. Trade Council of San Francisco; S.F. Bd. Realtors; San Mateo- Burlingame Bd. Realtors; World Trade Club; Chinese CofC, S.F.; publs: var. info. packets for Far Eastern Investors as introduction to US Investment 1980-84; num. sems. in Asia-Pacific reg. on US Investment Real Estate 9180-84; Republican; rec: racquetball, skiing, photog. Res: 607 Banibridge St Foster City 94404 Ofc: Golden Gate Corporation, 465 California St, Ste 908, San Francisco 94104

CHOY, LAWRENCE EDWIN, mortgage banker; b. Sept. 28, 1946, Salt Lake City, Utah; s. Joseph C. and Viola M. (Lake) C.; m. Dr. Melody Ann. Choy, Nov. 18, 1976; 1 dau: Connie Melanie, b. 1981; edn: BA, CSU 1967; BA, 1967; M.Geography, 1980; R.E. broker, ins. broker Bay area banker, Mortgage Banker Assn. Career: br. mgr. Transamerical Mortgage 1972-76; br. mgr. Ford Motor Credit 1976-79; gen. mgr. Diversified Fin. Svcs. 1979-81; pres. Home Equity Corp. 1981-82; pres. Combined Mortgage 1982--; gen. partner three syndications for devel. of comml. & resdtl. units in San Jose, Tuscson, Ariz., Alameda & Lancaster; chief exec. EIC Gp., Lancaster- Palmdale; mem: Am. Assn. Fin. Profls.; Nat. & Calif. Assns. Realtors; San Francisco- San Mateo & Alameda-Contra Costa Bds. Realtors; Mortgage Bankers Assn.; Calif. Mortgage Brokers Assn.; Masons; Chinese Comm. Ctr.; Porsche Club of Am.; Golden Gate Sports Car Club; Republican; Mormon; rec: boating, sports cars. Res: 1046 Harvard Rd Piedmont 94611 Ofc: Combined Mortgage, 450 Park St Alameda 94501

CHRISTENSEN, GAIL SANDRA, financial planner; b. Sept. 9, 1939, Marlboro, Mass.; d. Robert D. and Abbie L. (Morrill) B.; m. Ernest Christensen, May 27, 1961; div.; children: Hans, b. 1967, Kirsten, . 1971; edn: AS, honors, Becker Coll. 1959; BS, Boston Univ. 1961; tchr. cert., Montessori Teaching Theories 1968; cert. Maine Real Estate Sch. 1973; spl. courses, Rio Hondo Coll.; So. Methodist Univ.; lic: Calif. Real Estate Broker, Life and Disability Insurance, Fire and Casualty Ins. Career: advt./pub. rels. asst. Tarler & Skinner Advt. Agcy., Boston 1961-62; advt. fashion writer Montgomery Ward Catalog, NYC 1962-63; asst. promo. mgr. Cornell Univ. Press, 1963-64; publs. editor Ithaca Coll., 1964-65; asst. advt. mgr. Eaton's of Canada, Winnipeg, 1967-71;

merchant/owner Over the Bridge Gen. Store, Belfast, Me. 1972-78; adminstrv. asst. R&D, Hydril Corp., Whittier 1979-82; financial plnnr. A.L. Williams Co., Burbank 1983, Structured Finl. Independence, Inc., Whittier 1984--; honors: Kappa Omicron Kappa; Media hon. soc.; CofC award for outstanding contbns. to community 1978; Outstanding Young Woman of Am. 1966; The Writers Directory, 1971-73; Patroness Delta Phi Zeta 1964-65; mem: founding v.p. Lambda Phi Rho (1st women's pub. rels. soc.) 1960-61; Jr. Advt. Club of Boston 1961-2; Assn. of Am. Univ. Presses 1963-5; New England Merchants Assn. 1973-8; Gift Dealers Assn. 1974-8; realtors bd. 1975-8; Whittier Coll. Womens Aux.; Boston Univ. Alumni Council (assoc. ed. Bostonia 1960-61); PTA; parent rep. Assn. for Mentally Gifted Minors 1979-; past bd. dirs. CofC, YMCA; Eastern Star; Republican (del. State Conv. 1976); Sci. of Mind; rec: bicycling, travel. Res: 13725 Sunset Dr Whittier 90602 Ofc: Structured Finl. Independence Inc. 13710 E. Whittier Blvd Whittier 90605

CHRISTENSEN, LOUIS BARTELL, computer operations executive; b. Dec. 2, 1947, Driggs, Idaho; s. Bartell and Betty Jean (France) C.; edn: Orange Coast Coll. 1978-79; Control Data Inst. 1973; Ricks Coll. 1966-71. Career: field engr. Data Pathing, Inc., Los Angeles 1974-76; field engr. II, NCR, Data Pathing Sys. Div, Santa Ana 1976-78; sr. field engr., San Jose 1978-82; mgr. computer ops., Sunnyvale 1982--; tchr. tnr. NCR Field Eng.; tchr. ops. NCR, Data Pathing Users; cons. on maintenance & commun. NCR Field Eng; awards: Outstanding Achiev. Awds., NCR Data Pathing 1974, 75, 76, 78; mem: First Osborne Gp. (FOG); Am. Motorcycle Assn.; Sports Car Club of Am. (SCCA); LDS; rec: computers, cars, construction. Res: 2970 Durant Ave San Jose 95111 Ofc: NCR Data Pathing, 752 San Aleso Ave Sunnyvale 94086

CHRISTENSEN, STEPHEN CRAIG, material executive; b. Jan. 18, 1945, Los Angeles; steps. William J. and Betty L. (Gaisford) Grumbine; m. Edie Christensen, June 11, 1978; 1 dau: Rebecca, b. 1982; edn: BS, San Jose St. Univ. 1968; diploma, Univ. of Stockholm 1974; MA, San Jose St. Univ. 1975. Career: with Fairchild, automotive div. 1978-80, hybrid prods. 1980-84, gate array 1984--; tech. support. supvr. 1978; eng. support supvr. 1978-80; material control mgr. 1980-82; prodn. control mgr. 1982-84; materials mgr. 1984--; awards: 2nd pl. for ceramics, Hayward Area Fine Arts 1978; mem: APICS; mil: commun. tech. 2/c, USN 1968-72; Democrat; rec: micro- computers, gardening, back packing. Res: 38620 Canyon Hghts Dr Fremont 94536 Ofc: Fairchild Gate Array, 1801 McCarthy Blvd Milpitas 95035

CHRISTOPH, WILLIAM RICHARD, lawyer; b. Dec. 26, 1947, Oak Park, Ill.; s. G. William and Elizabeth Christine Christoph; m. Kerry, Feb. 15, 1976; children: Nicholas, b. 1980; Courtney, b. 1983; edn: BA, Wabash Coll. 1969; JD, Univ. of Wisc. Law Sch. 1978; criminal defense atty, admitted to practice, Wisc. Bar (state & fed.) 1978; Calif. Bar (state & fed.) 1979. Career: 2nd Lt. Infantry Platoon Commdr. USMC 1969-71 (Vietnam 1970); Capt. Cobra Gunship Pilot, 1972-76 (Saigon 1975); deputy city atty., City of San Diego 1979; self- empl. criminal defense atty., Vista 1980--; bus. law tchr. Palomar Coll. 1980-81; mem: Calif., Wisc. & Am. Bar Assns.; San Diego Trial Lawyers Assn.; mil: capt. USMC 1969-76, Bronze Star, Combat Action, Vietnamese Campaign, Philippine Pres. Unit Citation; Vietnamese Cross of Galantry; rec: sailing, diving. Res: 623 Hunter St Oceanside 92054 Ofc: Willim R. Christoph, APC, 400 S Melrose, Ste 101, Vista 92083

CHRISTOPHER, WARREN M., lawyer; b. Oct. 27, 1925, Scranton, N.Dakota; s. Ernest William and Catharine Anna (Lemen) C.; m. Marie, Dec. 21, 1956; children: Lynn, b. 1952; Scott, b. 1957; Thomas, b. 1959; Kristen, b. 1963; edn: BS, magna cum laude, USC 1945; JD, Stanford Law Sch. 1949. Career: law clerk Justice William O. Douglas 1949-50; assoc. O'Melveny &Myers 1950-67, partner 1958; Deputy Atty. Gen. of the US 1967-69; partner O'Melveny & Myers 1969-77; Deputy Secty. of State of US 1977-81; chmn. O'Melveny & Myers 1981--; pres. L.A. Co. Bar ASsn. 1974-75; chmn. Standing Com. on Fed. Judiciary of ABA 1975-76; chmn. Standing Com. on Aeronautical Law of ABA 1966-67; bd. govs. State Bar of Calif. 1975-76; spl. counsel former Calif. Gov. Edmund G. Brown 1959; awards: Medal of Freedom, Pres. Carter 1981; mem: Council of Foreign Rels.; Chancery Club; Stanford Univ. Bd. Trustees; So. Calif.e Edison Co.; First Interstate Bancrop.; Trilateral Commn.; mil: ensign USNR, active duty 1943-46, Pacific Theater; Democrat; Methodist. Res: 1299 Monte Cielo Dr Beverly Hills 90210 Ofc: O'Melveny & Myers, 400 S Hope Street Los Angeles 90071

CHU, JAMES KWOK-KIT, physician; b. Apr. 4, 1941, China, nat. 1977; s. Peter Wing-Yee and Helen Chuey-Ying (Wong) C.; m. Anna Sau-San, July 22, 1967; children: Raymond, b. 1969; Jana, b. 1972; Stephen, b. 1974; edn: BS, cum laude, St. Louis Univ. 1964; MD, St. Louis Med. Sch. 1968; lic. physician & surgeon, Calif. Career: intern San Bernardino Co. Hosp. 1968-69; res. in family practice 1969-71; staff physician Kaiser Found. Hosp. 1971-74; sr. physician The Permanente Med. Gp. 1974--; currently, sr. physician Dept. of Family Pracitce, Sacto. Kaiser Med. Clinic.; awards: Milton Phillips Scholarship, UC Berkeley 1961; Paul C. Reinert, S.J. Scholarship, St. Louis Univ. 1963; Thurston Scholarship, St. Louis Med. Sch. 1964; Gamma Pi Epsilon Scholarship, St. Louis Med. Sch. 1965; mem: Gr. Sacto. Peer Review Soc.; Am. Med. Soc.; Sacto. Chinese Comm. Svc. Ctr.; Sacto. Hypertension Council; rec: chess, piano, tennis. Address: 3240 Arden Way Sacramento 95825

CHU, JOSEPH MOON-SOO, bank director; b. Aug. 3, 1938, Hongsong, Korea, nat. 1975; s. Pil-Ro and Kan-Nan (Kim) C.; m. Jenny Hsiang, July 29., 1978; children: Eileen, b. 1972; Lilian, b. 1982; Jn: BS, Yongnam Univ., Korea 1964; Antioch Coll., Oh. 1967-68; MBA, Univ. of San Francisco 1975; life comm. coll. instr. cred., Calif. 1976; R.E. broker, Calif. Career: coll. instr. San Francisco City Coll. 1978-79; pres. Korean American Assn. of Santa Clara Co. 1981-82; publisher, Korean American Journal, Sunnyvale 1981-83; pres. Jenny's Restaurants & Cafeteria Svcs., Inc. (3 restaurants & 3 cafeterias), Santa Clara Co. 1979--; pres. Profl. Bus. Investments, Inc., San Jose 1975--; bank dir. Calif. Security Bank, San Jose 1981--; mem: Calif. & Nat. Bds. Realtors; Korean- Am. Assn. of Santa Clara Co. (pres. 1981-82); mil: s/sgt. Republic of Korea; Republican; Protestant; rec: golf. Res: 2679 Milhon Ct San Jose 95148 Ofc: Professional Business Investments, Inc., 1694 Tully Rd San Jose 95122

CHUNG, BURK HIM, trading co. president; b. Aug. 27, 1922, Canton, China; s. Kao How and Han (Chau) C.; m. Mary Lin, Nov. 8, 1952; children: Amy, b. 1953, Luke, b. 1956, Michael, b. 1961; edn: BA, UC Berkeley 1951; grad. stu. CSU San Francisco 1951-52. Career: teacher Chinese language, Kin Kuo High Sch., San Francisco 1948-51; reporter, editor, ed.-in-chief, bd. dirs. The Young China News Daily, S.F. 1951-58; pres. On Ning Tong Co., S.F. 1958--; pres. Superior Trading Co., S.F. 1959--; pres. Antioch Village Apt. Complex, Antioch, Calif. 1979-; pres/CEO C.S.W., Inc., S.F. 1979--; pres., bd.chmn. United Internat. Trading Co., Hong Kong 1979-83; pres. Belmont Plaza Shopping Center property, Belmont, Calif. 1979-; founding bd. dir. United Meat Slaughterhouse, No. Dist., Taiwan; 1st vice chmn. of bd. Sincere Fed. Svgs & Loan Assn., S.F. 1980-82. Apptd. by Mayor Dianne Feinstein mem. S.F. Internat. Hotel Block Devel. Citizens Advis. Com. (1979). Awards: citation for comm. crisis leadership 1967, S.F. Chinese CofC; recognition for pioneer work devel. the USA mkt. for Korean ginseng products, Korean Office of Monopoly, 1976. Mem: Kong Chow Benevolent Assn. (Kong Chow Temple), USA dir., nat. & regl. secty. gen., supr. chmn. bd. of suprs. 1954-; S.F. Chinese CofC (interim pres. 1967). Republican (bd.dirs. Calif. Chinese-Am. Repub. Assn.); Roman Catholic (bd., St. Mary's Chinese Sch.); rec: reading, writing, travel. res: 639 Teresita Blvd. S.F. 94127. ofc: Superior Trading Co. 837 Washington St. San Francisco 94108.

CHUNG, HUKUN, real estate broker; b. Oct. 19, 1936, Kyungnam, Korea, nat. 1980; s. Taehak and Maeng Kum (Shon) C.; m. Connie, Oct. 1, 1967; children: David, b. 1966; Kenneth, b. 1967; edn: BA, Dong-A Univ., Busan, Korea 1961; R.E. cert., Chabot Coll. 1978; L.A. Trade Tech. Coll. 1974-75; H.S. economics tchr., Korea 1961; R.E. broker 1979. Career: pres. Jinyang Co. Ltd. 1967; asst. to gen. mgr. (Mr. Howard) of Calif. 1974; realtor assoc. Century 21 Grove Way Realty 1977; realtor/ owner Bestwest Realty 1980; ruling elder Mt. Eden Ch.; cert. bus. counselor, Inst. of CBC 1981; awards: Centurion, Century 21 No. Calif. 1977; Top Selling Salesprsn., Century 21 Grove Way 1979; Top Listing Salesprsn., Century 21 Grove Way 1979; mem: Inst. of Cert. Bus. Counselors; Calif. & Nat. Assns. of Realtors; East Bay Mktg. Gp.; founder: Fremont Korean Presbyterian Ch. 1978, estab. bilingual svc. in Mt. Eden Presbyterian Ch. 1982; mil: lt. Republic of Korea Army, Gold Medal Awd. 1958; Presbyterian; rec: painting. Res: 24261 Monument St Hayward 94545 Ofc: Bestwest Realty, 759 West A' Street Hayward 94541

CHUNG, KWOK-LEUNG, physician; b. July 1, 1954, Hong Kong; s. Yin-Tong and Chek-Fong (Ng) C.; m. Kitman, July 1, 1979; 1 son: Christopher, b. 1982; edn: BSE, Princeton Univ. 1967; MD, Albert Einstein Coll. of Med. 1980; lic. physician, Calif. 1983. Career: intern Beth Israel Med. Ctr., NY 1980-81; res. 1981-83; fellow, UCLA Med. Ctr., Los Angeles 1983--; honors: Phi Beta Kappa, Princeton 1976; Tau Beta Pi, Princeton 1976; mem: Am. Coll. of Physicians; Am. Gastroenterological Assn.; works: computer research in treatment of hypertension 1974-76; rec: billiards, cards, fishing. Res: 702 S Serrano Ave, Apt 17, Los Angeles 90005 Ofc: UCLA Medical Center, 10833 Leconte Ave Los Angeles 90024

CHURCH, GEORGE ANDREW, golf course manager; b. Feb. 15, 1926, Winston-Salem, N.C.; s. Dr. Grant and Beatrice Marie (Rash) C.; two sons: George, Jr., b. 1953, Charles, b. 1957; edn: BS, engr., N.C. State Univ. 1949; cert., USN Postgrad. Sch., General Line 1959, Engr. Sci. 1963; cert., San Diego Golf Acad. 1983. Career: insp. of wts & measures State of N.C. Dept. of Agri., Raleigh, N.C. 1949-51; served to capt. ret., USN, 1951-81; USS Murray, 1951-53; cmdg. ofcr. USS Albatross, 1954; Cinclanti lt. staff, 1956-58; USNPCS, Monterey, Ca. 1958; USS Vandiver, 1959-60, lt.comdr., 1960; Comservron Six, 1960-62; hd. Logistics, Pentagon, 1963-65; USS Oklahoma City, 1965-67; cmdg. ofcr. USS Hull, 1967-69; Escort Squadron Ten Cmdr. (cmdr. 5-ship destroyer escort), 1969-71; capt./ chief of staff So. Atlantic Force, 1971-72; cmdg. ofcr. USS Nashville (LPD), 1973-75; chief of staff Comphibgru One (Amphib Task Force helicopter evacuation Saigon) 1975-6; cmdg. ofcr USS Tarawa; 1976-79; Commodore /c.o. US Fleet Tng Gp., San Diego 1979-81; decorated Presdtl. Legion of Merit , Bronze Star w/combat V, Merit. Svc. medal (for evacuation, Saigon), Navy Commend. medal w/gold star & combat V; Navy Unit Commend., Merit. Unit Commend. w/2 bronze stars; Repub. of Vietnam Disting. Service Order and Merit. Unit Cit. Mem: Navy League, Ret. Officers Assn., Naval Inst.; Republican; Ch. of The Brethren; rec: golf; res: 1651-147 S. Juniper, Escondido 92025. ofc: Rancho Penasquitos Golf Course, 14455 Penasquitos Dr., San Diego 92129

CHUTE, DONALD, transportation leasing co. executive; b. Dec. 25, 1944, Creston, Ia.; s. Paul C. and Harriet A. (Lawrence) Spring; m. Helen, Aug. 27, 1966; children: Dawn, b. 1969; Robin, b. 1975; edn: BA, Sonoma State Univ. 1974; airframe & powerplant lic., FAA. Career: railroad spl. asst. Southern Pacific Railroad, San Francisco 1974; mgr. car hire acctg. Itel Rail Corp., S.F. 1975-80; dir. car hire acctg. 1981; dir. car hire acctg. & sys. svc. 1982-83; dir. ops., car hire & bus. sys. plng., Itel Rail Corp., S.F. 1983--; mem: Nat. Car Hire & Car Svc. Assn.; Nat. Southwestern Car Hire & Car Svc. Assn.; Nat. Shore Line Railroads Assn.; mil: master sgt. Calif. Air Nat. Guard 1966-, pres. Airmans Enlisted Adv. Council 1974-76, num. decorations; Republican; Catholic; rec: carpentry, mechanics, coin collecting. Res: 2109 Sultana Dr Petaluma 94952 Ofc: Itel Rail Corp., 55 Francisco Street, 7th Flr, San Francisco 94133

CHWEH, STEVEN SEOKHO, librarian; b. Jan. 15, 1944, Naju, Korea, nat. 1980; s. Chang-Kyu and Woo-Nim (Hong) C.; m. Janie Okkyoung Hahn, Sept. 25, 1979; 1 son: Daniel, b. 1982; edn: BA, Kyung Hee Univ. 1966; MS, Louisiana State Univ. 1971; PhD, Univ. of Pitts. 1976. Career: lang. instr. US Peace Corps Tng. Ctr., Hilo, Hawaii 1968-69; hd. acquisitions librarian Henderson State Univ., Arkadelphia, Ark. 1971-74; asst. prof. USC, Los Angeles 1976-81; sys. analyst/ pgmr. Computer Automation, Irvine 1981-82; pres. Computermation, Mission Viejo 1982--; tech. svc. supvr. Newport Beach Pub. Lib., Newport Beach 1983--; bd. dirs. Assn. for Korean Studies 1977-; honors: Beta Phi Mu, internat. lib. sci. hon. soc. 171; Outstanding Young Men of America, Jaycees 1979; mem: Am. Lib. Assn.; Am. Soc. for Info. Sci.; Calvary Ch., Costa Mesa; publs: num. arts. in library journs.; mil: lt. Korean Army Artillery 1966-68; Christian; rec: Tae Kwon Do (black belt), Red Cross cert. water safety instr., sr. life guard. Res: 21454 La Capilla Mission Viejo 92691 Ofc: Newport Beach Public Library, 856 San Clemente Dr Newport Beach 92660

CHYR, ROBERT YUH, restaurateur; b. May 7, 1942, Mou Ping, Shantung, China; s. Dong Po and Yi-Young Chyr; m. Lydia Woo, Nov. 21, 1965; children: Helen, b. 1966; Charlotte, b. 1967; Elizabeth, b. 1973; edn: San Francisco State Univ. 1963-67; Calif. lic. real estate broker. Career: mgr. Yenching Restaurant (1st to introduce ChinesePot-Stickers' to Western Culture), San Francisco 1963-67; real estate investment & devel. 1967-80; dir. Golden Coin Savings & Loan Assn. (chmn. Loan Com.) 1980--; currently, pres. Yenching Corp. dba Yenching Restaurant; awards: First Awd. Menu, Nat. Restaurant Conv. 1980; mem: Berkeley Lions Club; Shantung Assn.; San Francisco YMCA; Presbyterian; rec: skiing. Res: 444 Yale Ave Kensington 94708 Ofc: Yenching Corp., 2017 Shattuck Ave Berkeley 94704

CIACCIA, BENEDICT GAITANO, information management executive; b. Apr. 17, 1936, Rochester, NY; s. Benedetto and Jennie (Spampinato) C.; edn: BA, Kenyon Coll. 1958; Case Inst. of Tech. 1958-60. Career: student instr. Case Inst. of Tech. 1958-60; pgmr. Lockheed Missiles & Space Co. 1960-62; supvr. Systems Devel. Corp. 1962-63; ctr. mgr. Sperry- Univac Info. Svcs. Div. 1963-69; v.p./ gen. mgr. Information Mgmt. Internat.; bd mem. Curriculum Adv., Condi Coll.; mem: Nat. Hon. Soc. 1954; Data Processing Mgmt. Assn.; Assn. for Computing Machines; Visting Nurse Assn. Inc., Alameda Co.; Catholic; rec: skiing, deck building, cooking. Res: 4524 Oak Hill Rd Oakland 94605 Ofc: Information Management Internat., 2525 E Bayshore Rd Palo Alto 94303

CICOTTE, LYNN JOSEPH, lawyer/ physicist; b. Mar. 2, 1935, River Rouge, Mi., s. Edward Albert and Marie Ida (Myers) C.; m. Lorraine Gasiewski, Jan. 4, 1958; children: Kerry, b. 1960; Kimberly, b. 1962; edn: diploma, Rets Electronic Schs. 1957; BS, Central Mich. Univ. 1964; BS, Wayne State Univ. 1970; JD, Loyola Univ. 1976; 1/c radiotelephone lic., FCC 1956; admitted to practice US Patent & Trademark Ofc. 1978. Career: res. sci., Ford Motor Scientific Lab. 1964-68; principal physicist Energy Conversion Devices 1968-71; physicist Hughes Aircraft 1973-74; res. physicist Electron Dynamics 1971-73; cons. engr. Chase, Rotchford, Drukker & Bogus 1974-77; atty. Parker, Stanbury, McGee, Babcock & Combs, 1977--; settlement ofcr. Los Angeles Municipal Ct. 1979--; Selective Svc. Bd. 70-72; awards: Patent Awd., Hughes Aircraft 1974; mem: Mensa; So. Calif. Defense Counsel Assn.; Calif. State Bar; patentee: Laser Ignition Sys. 1974; publs: (3) short stories, Gothic Mag. 1953-55; works on metal alloys, Thin Film Research Journ. 1968; rec: tournament chess player, field archery, model shipbuilding. Res: 26447 Basswood Rancho Palos Verdes 90274 Ofc: P.S.M.B. & C., 611 W Sixth Street, Ste 3300, Los Angeles 90017

CINNAMON, F. WILLIAM, III, newspaper telemarketing director; b. Aug. 19, 1953, Kansas City, Mo.; s. F. William and Joan C. (Davidson) C.; edn: BA, cum laude, Univ. of N.Mex., Albuquerque 1975; Franciscan Sch. of Theology, Berkeley 1977; MBA, USC 1981. Career: legis. asst. State of Calif. Dept. of Health Svcs. 1975-77; guide Tourmobile, Wash. DC 1977-78; acct. exec. Wrangler Menswear, Los Angeles 1979-82; acct. exec./ display advtg. Post Newpaper Gp., L.A. 1982-83; telemktg. dir. 1983--; advtg. cons. Forgotten Treasures, Collectible Films & Videos, Beverly Hills; pub. rels. volunteer, Los Angeles Olympic Organizing Com. 1984; honors: Lambda Chi Alpha Outstanding Alumni, Sacto. 1981; mem: Log Cabin Republican Club; Lambda Chi Alpha Founders Soc.; W. Hollywood Cityhood Citizens Gp.; Larchmont Vill. Res. Assn.; Christ The King Parish Assn.; Los Angeles Olympic Organizing Com.; Republican; Catholic; rec: free lance graphic design. Res: 614 N Beachwood Dr Larchmont Village Los Angeles 90004 Ofc: The Post Group, 1433 S Robertson Blvd Los Angeles 90035

CIRELLI, PATRICK JOSEPH, manufacturing co. sales executive; b. Feb. 29, 1944, Youngstown, Ohio; s. Patsy Arnold and Juanita Arlene (Holcomb) C.; m. Patricia Eileen Reese, July 10, 1983; children: Patrick, b. 1966; Cynthia, b. 1969; Geoffrey, b. 1969; edn: BA, honors, CSU Los Angeles 1971. Career: salesman/ ofc. mgr. Howard Distributors, Alhambra 1966-71; sales coord./ asst. sales mgr. Hooker Headers, Ontario 19761-73; sales engr. Forgedtrue Mfg., So. El Monte, Sante Fe Springs 1973-75; sales engr./ sales mgr./ v.p. sales BRC Div. of W.R. Grace & Co., Garden Grove 1975-79; sales mgr./ gen. mgr./ pres. Mothers Polish Co., Cerritos 1979--; mem: Spec. Equip. Mkt. Assn.; Automation Parts & Accesories Assn.; Off Road Radio Control Assn. (ORRCA); So. Bay Radio Control Racers (SBRCR); Democrat; Christian; rec: radio controlled off road race cars. Res: 11131 El Rey Dr Whittier 90606 Ofc: Mothers Polish Co., 5592 Buckingham Dr Huntington Beach 92649

CIRESE, ROBERT CHARLES, real estate investment and counseling executive; b. Feb. 25, 1938, Oak Park, Ill.; s. Ferd L. and Ruth O. Cirese; div.; children: Lesley Caren, b. 1965; Jeffrey Robert, b. 1967; edn: BS, DePaul Univ., Chgo. 1960; MS, Univ. of Ill. 1963; UC Berkeley 1964; CRE designation, Am. Soc. of R.E. Counselors 1983; lic. R.E. Broker, Calif. 1983; Calif. Coll. Tchg. Cred. 1973. Career: assoc. prof. Golden Gate Univ., San Francisco 1967-72; v.p. Larry Smith & Co., S.F. 1972-77; dir. Coopers & Lybrand, S.F. 1977-79; v.p. Rubloff Inc., S.F. 1979--; real estate counseling for corps., instns. & pub. agencies; expert witness; lectr.; honors: Am. Soc. of R.E. Counselors 1983; Tuition Scholarship, UC Berkeley Grad. Sch. 1963; mem: Am. Soc. of Real Estate Counselors (ASREC); Urban Land Inst.; San Francisco Plng. & Urban Research Assn.; S.F. Ballet Assn., Univ. Calif. Bear Backer; works: num. economic impact reports, mkt. & fin. feasibilty studies, real estate investment analyses; mil: Ill. Nat. Guard, 33rd Mil. Police Co. 1956-63; Unitarian; rec: running, spectator sports, ballet. Res: 54 Buckelew St Sausalito 94965 Ofc: Rubloff, Inc., One Maritime Plaza, Ste 1025, San Francisco 94111

CISSNA, ROBERT LEE, lawyer, accountant; b. Apr. 17, 1940, Seattle, Wash.; s. Jack Raymond and Evelyn (Barker) C.; edn: AA cum laude, L.A. City Coll.; cert. history, lit. & arch., lang., Univ. of Perugia, Italy 1962-63; BA in hist., Univ. Wash. 1965; JD, L.A. Coll. of Law 1974; Calif. lic. real estate broker; admitted to Calif. State Bar 1980. Career: ground mgr. (and rep. Seattle World's Fair 1962), Santa Fair (large indoor amusement park), Federal Way 1958-65; Navy-Acct. & ARch. Designer 1966-68; promo. mgr. for Johnson Wax Co., Montreal World's Fair 1967; (current) pub. acctg. prin. 1974--; lawyer pvt. practice 1980--; corp. accountant Capitol Industries (E.M.I.); acct. Walt Disney Prodns., Burbank; plant acct. Franciscan Dinnerware; controller Tariq M. Shamma Assoc.; sec.treas. Canyon Lake (Ca.) Property Owners Assn.; bd. dirs. Lake Elsinore Park & Rec. District; mem: Am., Calif. State, Los Angeles County bar assns., Trial Lawyers of L.A., Am. Trial Lawyers, L.A. Lawyers Club, Orange County Trolley Museum, postcard clubs of So. Calif., Santa Monica, and Pasadena, YMCA, Laguna Bch Prop. Owners Assn., S.W. Prop. Owners Assn.; works: Compendium of Medieval Cottage Buildings; designed a 16mm Strip Slide reprodn. unit; postcard publisher; designer themed amusement attractions; mil: USNR; Repub. Libertarian; Presbyterian; rec: collector. Res: 1615 N. Micheltorena Los Angeles 90026 Ofc: 500 W. Lakeshore Dr Lake Elsinore 92330

CLAAR, JAMES W., manufacturing co. president; b. Sept. 27, 1929, Effingham, Ill.; s. Harry B. and Olive A. (Bryant) C.; m. Beverly L. Richars, OCt. 3, 1948, div. 1971; m. 2d. Marilyn Doty, Dec. 23, 1973; children: Brian, b. 1959; Christina, b. 1957. Career: asst. dir. pub. rels. Curtiss Wright Corp., Woodridge, NJ 1955-57; exec. v.p./ gen. mgr. American Aviation Publication, Wash. DC 1957-67; publisher Automotive Inc, Jeff Davis Pub., NY 1967-70; pres. The Claar Co., Hawthorne 1970--; chmn. exec. com. Nat. Aviation Club, Wash. DC 1965; chmn. sales devel. com., Am. Bus. Press, NY 1964; listed: Who's Who In Am. 1968; Leading Men in the US 1969; Who's Who in Bus. & Commerce 1968; mem: Am. Rocket Soc.; Wash. DC. Univ. Club (spl. mem. for accomplishment in arts & sci.); Wings Club, NYC; United Airtime 500,000 mile Club; TWA Ambassador; publs: book of poetry, Poems of Praise of Practically Everything, 1979; mil: s/sgt. USAF 1951-55; Protestant; rec: traditional jazz, poetry, automobile performances. Res: 1821 Via Visalia Palos Verdes Estates 90274 Ofc: The Claar Co., 12633 S Prairie Hawthorne 90250

CLABAUGH, ELMER EUGENE, JR., lawyer; b. Sept.18, 1927, Anaheim; s. Elmer Eugene and Eleanor Margaret (Heitshusen) Clabaugh; two sons: Christopher Chapman, MatthewMartinson; edn: BBA cum laude, Woodbury Coll. 1951, BA summa cum laude, Claremont McKenna Coll. 1958, JD, Stanford Law Sch.1961. Career: gen. service staff US State Dept., Jerusalem, Tel Aviv 1951-53; field staff Pub. Adminstrn. Svc., El Salvador, Ethiopia, USA 1952-57; admitted to Calif. Bar 1961; deputy dist. atty. Ventura Co., Calif.1961-62; mem. firm Hathaway, Clabaugh, Perrett & Webster in Ventura 1962-79; individual practice, 1979--. State Inheritance Tax referee, 1968-78; city atty. City of Thousand Oaks, 1964-69, City of Simi Valley, 1969-71; bd. dirs. San Antonio Water Conservation Dist.; bd. dirs. Ventura Comm. Meml. Hosp.; trustee Ojai Unified Sch. Dist. 1974-; mem. Pres's Adv. Council, Claremont Coll. 1975-. Mem: Calif. Bar Assn., Am. Arbitration Assn., Phi Alpha Delta. Republican. rec: hunting, tennis. res: 241 Highland Dr. Channel Islands Harbor 93030. ofc: 1190 S. Victoria Ave Suite 305 Ventura 93003.

CLAES, DANIEL JOHN, medical research director; b. Dec. 3, 1931, Glendale; s. John Vernon and Claribel (Fleming) Claes; m. Gayla Blasdel, Jan. 19, 1974; edn: AB magna cum laude, Harvard Univ. 1953; MD cum laude, Harvard Med. Sch. 1957. Career: intern UCLA, 1957-58; Boywer Found. Fellow, resident in medicine, L.A., 1958-61; pvt. practice spec. in diabetes mellitus, Los Angeles 1962--; Am. Eye Bank Found. vice pres. 1978-, dir./med. res. 1980-. Awards: Boywer Found. awd. for excellence in medicine, 1958. mem: Los Angeles Co. Med.Assn., Harvard Club of So. Calif., Harvard Med. Sch. Club of So. Calif. Contbr. to profl. literature on computers in med. and on diabetes mellitus. ofc: Daniel J. Claes, MD, Inc. Ste. A236, 845 Via de la Paz, Pacific Palisades 90272.

CLANCY, EDWARD VINCENT, college professor; b. Sept. 22, 1951, NYC; s. George J. and Lauretta T. (Kelly) C.; edn: BS, US Merchant Marine Acad. 1973; BS, Columbia Univ. 1975-76; MBA, Golden Gate Univ. 1980; D.Eng., cand., Stanford; profl. engr. Calif. & NY; 3rd asst. engr. stm. & diesel, USC. Gp Career: cons. engr. Ebosco Services, NY 1973-77; sales engr. Mobil Oil Corp., Oakland 1977-79; v.p. Hellmund Oil Corp., NJ 1979-82; eng. faculty Calif. Maritime Acad. 1982--; prof. St. John Univ. MBA pgm., part- time 1980-82; awards: Fed. Scholarship, Merchant Marine Acad.; mem: Port

Engrs. of San Franacisco; SNAME Naval Reserve; lectr. on pressure/ time diagrams for diesel engine research, Port Engrs. of S.F. 4/82; mil: lcdr, USN-R; rec: sailing, computers. Res: 100 Ellinwood Dr, Apt A-108, Pleasant Hill 94523 Ofc: California Maritime Academy, POB 1392, Valleqo 94590

CLAREY, FREDERICK JOSEPH, real estate development co. executive; b. Mar. 27, 1943, Youngstown, Oh.; s. Charles Callen and Ruth Bernice (Joseph) C.; m. Joanne Kyllo, June 5, 1971; children: Kimberly Anne, b. 1963; John Morgan, b. 1966; Kristi Elizabeth, b. 969; Scott Kyllo, b. 1973; William Charles, b. 1976; edn: BS, Univ. of Ariz. 1966; MBA, Pepperdine Univ. 1974; R.E. broker, Calif.; pvt. pilot lic. Career: internat. mktg. mgr. IBM Corp., NY 1966-77; comml. R.E. broker Cushman & Wakefield, Los Angeles 1977-79; v.p./ dist. mgr. Grubb & Ellis Co., L.A. 1979-80; exec v.p./ COO David H. Murdock Realty Svcs., L.A. 1980-83; v.p. devel., western reg., Oxford Properties, Inc., L.A. 1983--; mem: Pepperdine Univ. Bd. Mem.; L.A. Bd. Realtors; Am. Youth Citizenship Chmn.; 1st Congregational Ch.of L.A.; Jonathan Club; Regncy Club; Newcomer Soc. of So. Calif.; Republican Assocs.; Blue Book of So. Calif.; Republican; Congregational Protestant; rec: dirt bikes, stunt flying, golf. Res: 400 S Arden Blvd Los Angeles 90020 Ofc: Oxford Properties, Inc., 700 S Flower St, Ste 3305, Los Angeles 90017

CLARK, CORA BEATRICE, real estate broker; b. July 23, 1908, Lafayette, ga.; d. Henry Johnson and Mary Patricia (Sweet) Young; m. Herbert Peter Clark (dec.); 1 dau. Dorothy Leatrice Brown, b. 1928; edn: bus. courses community colls. 1924-; Calif. lic. real estate sales 1963, real estate broker 1965. Career: deputy circuit clk. Indian River County, Vero Bch., Fla. 1924-27; restaurateur with husband in Fla. 1927-33, in Calif. 1933-39; acctg. clk. Kieckhefer Container Co., Oakland 1942-47, Lucky Stores Inc., San Leandro 1948-52, Oakland Housing Authority 1952-55; office mgr. Alameda Box Co., 1955-59; agt. Foppoli Real Estate, San Leandro 1963-64, MacArthur Real Estate, Modesto 1964-65; broker/owner California Real Estate, Modesto 1965--, owner, Office Services, 1978--; mem: Nat./Calif. Assn. of Realtors, Modesto Bd. of Realtors (past pres. Women's Council of Realtors), Calif./ Modesto Apartment Assn., Modesto Toastmistress Club of ITC (charter mem., past pres.); spl. interest: helping deprived children; rec: travel; Democrat; Prot. Address: California Real Estate, 2107 Bangs Ave Modesto 95356

CLARK, DWIGHT WILLIAM, public administrator, lawyer; b. Sept. 24, 1944, Gothenburg, Nebr.; s. Wm. Elwood and Christina Antina (Koster) C.; m. Sharon Anderson, Aug. 31, 1968; children: Andrea Christine, b. 1973, Nathan Wm., b. 1976; edn: BS, Univ. Nebr. Coll. Bus. Adm. 1967; JD, Calif. Western Law Sch. 1974; MPA, USC Sch. Pub. Adm. 1976; admitted to Calif. State Bar 1975. Career: administrative intern US Probation Ofc., Los Angeles 1975-76; exec. asst. San Francisco Municipal Court, 1976--; bd. dirs. Corporate Business Brokers of No. Calif., Inc. 1983-; trustee San Mateo Elem. Sch. Dist. 1983-; guest lectr. ct. clerks conf. Judicial Council of Calif. 1978, 3M Western Regl. Conf. 1978,j Assn. of Info. Image Mgmt., S.F. 1984; fmr. treas./bd. Law Edn. Found.; honors: Internat. Chinese New Year Parade judge, S.F. 1983; Moot Ct. judge, Univ. of San Francisco Sch. of Anthropol. 1977; USAF Acad. Outstanding Quarterly Airman (1970), scholastic achieve. award, USAF SAC (1970); Am. Jurisprudence Awd., Wills, 1969; Delta Sigma Pi (life mem., pres. 1967), Nat. Honor Soc., Sigma Theta Pi; mem: Am. Judicature Soc., Am. Bar Assn., Calif. State Bar, Calif. Municipal Ct. Clks. Assn., Lawyers Club SF, San Mateo Co. Bar Assn., Nat. Assn. of Trial Ct. Adminstrs., Calif. Ct. Adminstrs. and Jury Commnrs. Assn., Electronic Data Proc./Audit Study Com. of S.F. 1977 (apptd. user rep. for E.D.P. Priority Com., City & Co. of S.F. 1979); PTA; alumni clubs: Univ. Nebr., Calif. Western Law Sch., USC; mil: s/sgt. USAF 1969-73; Democrat; Lutheran; rec: woodcrafts, music. Res: 312 Cupertino Way San Mateo 94403 Ofc: S.F. Municipal Ct. Rm. 303 City Hall, San Francisco 94102

CLARK, GERALD LYNN, financial consultant/ broker; b. Jan. 20, 1944, Torrance; s. Norman Arnold and Aurel Eileen (Amundson) C.; m. Linda Lyle, Jan. 4, 1964; children: Kelly, b. 1967; Sheri, b. 1969; edn: Woodbury Univ. 1965; Calif. Coll. of Law 1967-69; CSU Long Beach 1976-78; reduce retail inventory shrinkage, CSU Los Angeles 1974. Career: acct. Vons & Shopping Bag Mkts., El Monte 1964-70; acct. Food Fair Mkts., Vernon 1970-71; controller Ole's Home Improvement Ctrs., Rosemead 1971-76; pres. Newport Diversified Capital, Newport Beach 1976-81; controller Bob Siemon Christian Jewelry, Fountain Valley 1981-83; acct. exec. The Fortine Corp., Irvine 1983--; cons. Spec. Mgmt. Support 1980; mem: Le Tip, Newport Beach; Christian Svc. Brigade; Athletes In Fellowship; works: invested water saving device 1977; Republican; Baptist; rec: basketball, softball. Res: 838 Joann St Costa Mesa 92627 Ofc: The Fortine Corp. 18103 Skypark S., Ste C, Irvine 92714

CLARK, HOWARD STANLEY, chartered life underwriter; b. June 14, 1946, Oakland; s. Matthias S. and Elizabeth G. (Papendiek) C.; m. Janine Lynn Martin, Aug. 26, 1967; 1 son, Jeffrey Martin, b. 1974; edn: AA, Fullerton Jr. Coll. 1967; BA, Chapman Coll. 1970; chartered life underwriter, Am. Coll. 1979. Career: agt. Aetna Life, Orange 1970-73; vice pres. Bucces Assoc., Tustin 1974-75; owner Clark Co., 1975-77; regional dir. Agencies Volunteer State, Life Ins. Co., Tustin 1977--; mem: Nat. Assn. Life Underwriters, Calif. Assn. Life Underwriters, Orange Co. Assn. Life Und., Gold Key Soc. of CLU, Long Beach Orange Soc. of CLU; Jaycees, Orange (life mem.; Outstanding Pres. Dist. 8 1974); contbg. writer Life Ins. Mgmt. Research Assn. Handbook on Recruitment of New Personal Producing Gen. Agts. 1982; mil: E4 Calif. Nat. Guards; Republican; Presbyterian; rec: waterskiing, bird hunting. Res: 18672 Allegheny Dr Santa Ana 92705 Ofc: Volunteer State Life Ins. 14081 Yorba St, Ste. 236, Tustin 92680

CLARK, JAMES DEXTER, lawyer; b. Nov. 27, 1941, Evanston, Ill.; s. William Stewart and Carolyn Elizabeth (Carter) Clark; m. Suzanne Edith Ferguson, Oct. 3, 1970; two daus.: Jennifer Grace Elizabeth, b. 1972, Suzanne Irene Bernadette, b. 1977; edn: BA, Yale Univ. 1963; grad. studies UCLA 1966-7; JD, USC 1970. career: assoc. atty. law firm La Follette, Johnson, Horgan & Robinson, 1970-72; deputy county counsel, Co. of Los Angeles, 1972-80, chief adv. to assessment appeals bd., chief appellate litigator on commerce clause matters, chief adv. health budget matters; mem. firm Potter, Bradish & Ellinghouse, 1980-81; spl. counsel Pasadena Redevel. Agcy Bd./City of Pasadena Relocation Appeals Bd.; partner Weiser, Kane, Ballmer & Berkman, Los Angeles 1982--; faculty Glendale Coll. of Law 1974; vis. lectr. USC Sch of Business 1978; lectr. adminstrv. law, Continuing Edn. of the Bar, 1980. awards: Outstanding Young Men of Am. 1972; E.C. McDonald Award, Culver Mil. Acad. 1959; Los Angeles Blue Book. mem: Yale Club, Yale Alumni Fund, Campbell Hall Sch. 21st Century Fund and Bldg. Com., Pasadena Tournament of Roses Assn., Am. Bar Assn. (Admin. Law Sect.), Calif. State Bar Assn., US Supreme Court Bar, Christian Legal Soc. publs: contbr. arts. Pepperdine Law Rev. 39 (1976), San Fernando Valley Bar Bull. (1980); sev. US Supreme Ct. briefs vital to local govt.: L.A. County's brief in Michelin v. Wages (1976) leading to decision overruling 105 years of legal precedent; sev. appellate briefs altering the powers of local and state govts. under the US Constitution. mil: maj. USMCR, Vietnam, Unit Cross of Gallantry, combat awards. Republican (finl. dir. various campaigns). rec: writing. ofc: Weiser, Kane, Ballmer, Berkman, 354 S. Spring St. Los Angeles 90013.

CLARK, JAMES GLEN, printing executive; b. May 27, 1940, Madison, Wisc.; s. Orland Wm. and Ella Adele (Williams) C.; m. Narcissa, July 16, 1960; children: James G. Jr., b. 1961, Danielle Christine, b. 1963, Walter Paul, b. 1970; edn: San Jose City Coll. 1967-68. Career: with Manufacturer's Ticket and Label, Chgo. 1957-60; Art-Craft Printers, Phoenix, Ariz. 1960; printer, Paramount Press, San Francisco 1961-64, Times Printers, Los Gatos, 1964-73; pres./maj. stockhldr. CC Graphics (printing co.), Milpitas 1974--; instr. printing, San Jose Unified Sch. Dist., trade sch., 1979; cons. var. Bay Area firms incl. Allis Assocs., and Interlink Systems; recipient 1st place award, multicolor, A.B. Dick Co. 1982; mem: Printers Union 1962-74, Small Businessmens Assn. 1975-80, Milpitas CofC, Santa Clara Better Bus. Bur., Moose Lodge; mil: splst. 2/c US Army M.C. 1955-58, USAR; Lutheran; rec: flying, golfing. Res: 1488 Mardan Dr San Jose 95132 Ofc: CC Graphics, 247 Houret Dr Milpitas 95035

CLARK, JULIA KAY, veterinarian; b. July 14, 1953, Amarillo, Tex.; d. James Walter and Caroline Ann (Scarpellino) C.; m. Larry David Clark, Jan. 9, 1982; twin daus. Kelly Elizabeth and Lindsay Anne, b. 1982; edn: DVM, Texas A&M 1980. Career: veterinarian, Dr. Bevins Animal Hospital, Canoga Pk. 1980--; spl. interest: to develop awareness of the concepts of self-help (recognizing individual needs, counseling, etc.), parenting, child devel., within public ednl. system. Res: 9749 Canterbury Ave Arleta 91331 Ofc: Dr. Bevin's Animal Hospital 7009 Canoga Ave Canoga Park 91303

CLARK, LARRY DUANE, interior designer; b. Sept. 17, 1943, Ponca City, Okla.; s. Ted and Norelle Marine (Drummond) C.; children: Christopher Sean, b. 1969; Micheal Duane, b. 1972; edn: BA, San Jose State Univ. 1965. Career: drapery dept. buyer Gottschalks Dept. Store, Fresno 1973-75; free lance designer, Visalia 1968-73; designer/ corp. v.p. Designs For Living, Fresno 1965--; free lance designer, Visalia 1975-83; currently, owner Spring Crest Custom Draperies, Visalia; mem: Visalia Elks Club; F.O.E.; Visalia CofC; Exeter Jaycees; Republican; rec: scuba diving, racquetball, Colt League baseball coach. Res: 1040 S Kaweah Exeter 93221 Ofc: Spring Crest, 2640 S Mooney Visalia 93277

CLARKE-AMBROSE, JERRALYN ANN, equal employment opportunity executive; b. Jan. 16, 1944, New Orleans, La.; s. Joseph Sr. and Florestine Jane (Mayo) A.; m. Sept. 11, 1963, div.; children: Tammy Louise, b. 1964; Larry Niles Jr., b. 1966; Cindy Marie, b. 1967; BS, cum laude, Southern Univ. 1973; MA, Univ. of No. Colo. 1977. Career: edn. spec./ chief Naval Edn. & Tng., Pensacola, Fla. 1973-75; edn. spec., Naval Edn. & Tng. Support Ctr. PAC, San Diego 1975-77; command edn. spec. Recruit Tng. Command, Naval Tng. Ctr., San Diego 1977-79; Equal Employment Opportunity (EEO) Spec. Naval Tng. Ctr., San Diego 1979-81; EEO mgr. 1981--; assoc. instr. NCPC 1984-; sales rep. A.L. Williams, Inc.; mem: Federally Employed Women (pres. 1983-84); Phi Delta Kappa; Comm. Organizing Proj.; Parish Council, Chrish The King Ch. (pres. 1984); Federal Exec. Assn.; Equal Employment Opportunity Council; Democrat; Catholic; rec: writing, dancing, aerobics. Res: 7007 Glenflora Ave San Diego 92119 Ofc: Naval Training Center, Code 007, San Diego 92133

CLAUSEN, BARBARA PAULINE, educational psychologist; b. Jan. 24, 1927, Crescent City; d. Paul A. and Ina Matilda (Warren) Brunk; m. Gerald H. Clausen, June 26, 1949; children: Marcia, b. 1950, Kent, b. 1951, Lisa, b. 1956, Casey, b. 1957, Marc, b. 1961; edn: BA, UC Berkeley 1948; MA, CSU Humboldt 1966; Calif. Tchr. credential (life) 1960, cert. school psychologist 1965, lic. ednl. psychologist 1979. Career: tchr./guidance counselor Del Norte Co. Unified Sch. Dist. 1958-66, school psychometrist 1966-69, District senior school psychologist 1969--; ednl. psychologist pvt. practice 1979--; apptd. mem. Devel. Disabilities Bd. 1973-79, Del Norte Hlth Adv. Council 1974-79; mem: Del Norte Co. Assn. for the Developmentally Disabled; Calif. Assn. of Lic. Ednl. Psychologists; Del Norte Co. Scholarship Found (pres. 1966); adv. bd. Del Norte Mental Hlth Svcs. 1969-79; Calif. Tchrs. Assn.; Calif. Assn. School Psychols. and Psychometrists; Del Norte Garden Club; Delta Kappa Gamma. Republican; Methodist; rec: gardening, pottery, int. decor. Res: 1821 Malone

Rd Crescent City 95531 Ofc: Barbara P. Clausen, MA, LEP, 475 H St. Crescent City 95531

CLAWSON, RAYMOND W., petroleum company president; b. San Jose, CA; s. Benjamin B. and Mae (Names) Clawson; edn: Montezuma Sch., Los Gatos, CA; Palo Alto Mil. Acad., CA; Pasadena Mil. Acad., CA; Amer. Univ., L.A.; m. Barbara M. Robbins, 1965; children (by prev. marriages): Russell Miller; Raymond Walden. Career: Independent oil producer; v.p., C.C. Warren & Co. Stock Brokers, Oakland, 1924-27; ind. operator exploration and devel. oil properties, New Mexico, 1936--; publ. r. Los Angeles Mirror, 1945-47; pres., Ariz. Securities, Inc., L.A., 1947-49; geophysics cons. in offshore oil drilling operations Gulf of Mexico 1963--, North Sea 1970--; chmn., CEO, Clawco Petroleum Corp., Newport Beach, 1979--. Awards: Cert. of Merit for Distinguished Serv. in Petroleum Exploration and Devel., London, Eng., 1973. Mem.: Balboa Bay Club, Newport Beach; Acapulco Yacht, Mex. Protestant. Rec.: travel. Res.: P.O. Box 2102, Newport Beach 92663; Office: P.O. Box 2102, Newport Beach 92663.

CLAXTON, CAMILLE THERESE, fine arts and antiques appraiser; b. Oct. 3, 1932, Los Angeles; d. William Irving and Sarepta Orrissa (Fleming) Moffett (father was a pioneer Calif. lumberman); m. Roy C. Claxton, 1951; children: William, b. 1952; David, b. 1954; Jeffrey, b. 1958; James, b. 1961; edn: Ramona Convent 1949-50; Mount St. Mary's Coll. 1950-51; Coll. of the Holy Names 1951-52; antiques appraiser, Internat. Soc. of Appraisers 1980. Career: pres. Biltmore Investment Co. 1968-81; res. lectr. Antiques & Fine Arts, Marin Art & Garden Ctr. 1978--; free lance writer & profl. lectr. 1979--; instr. antiques & fine arts, Coll. of Marin 1981--; co-owner Claxton/ Dykstra Appraisers 1978--; mem: Am. & Internat. Socs. of Appraisers; Marin Charitable Assn.; Northgate Gp. of Marin Art & Garden Ctr.; Ross-Brookwood Guild of Sunnyhills (past pres.); publs: reg. contbr. arts. on appraising, fine arts & antiques, Antiques Dealer Mag., other pubs.; Republican; Catholic; rec; fine arts, art glass, antique collecting. Address: Claxton/ Dykstra Appraisers, POB 10 Ross 94957

CLAY, DANIEL PRESTON, jeweler-gemologist; b. Jan. 22, 1934, Los Angeles; s. William Forester and Dorothae Marie Clay; m. Maria Garcia, Jan. 25, 1978; 1 dau: Linda, b. 1959; edn; gemologist, GIA 1981-84. Career: elec. tech. chief, USN 1952-81, ret. 1981-84; coin dealer 1964-78; jeweler 1978-84; currently, owner Jewelry Mart, San Diego, tchr. electronics class B' sch., USN, San Diego 1967-71; mem: Am. Numismatic Assn.; Calif. State Numismatic Assn.; Soc. of Internat. Numismatics; San Diego Co. Profl. Numismatic Assn.; Internat. Soc. of Appraisers; Tecolote Youth Baseball; mil: elec. tech. chief, USN 1951 81, GCM (3), Combat Action, Merit. Unit Cit.Ation, Vietnam Svc. (2), Am. Defense (2), Vietnamese Def.; Republican; Protestant; rec: collecting Civil War artifacts. Res: 3526 Bonita Rd Chula Vista 92010 Ofc: Jewelry Mart, 3049 Clairemont Dr San Diego 92117

CLEMENS, BETTY LU, manufacturing co. executive; b. Feb. 11, 1929, Stratford, Calif.; d. Edward Leland and Amy Leah (Esrey) Basquez; m. Ernest Lance, Oct. 18, 1979; children: Linda, b. 1949, John, b. 950, James, b. 1950, Joseph, b. 1956; edn: BA, Univ. of Wash. 1965; Std. Cert. Education, Univ. Wash. 1972. Career: high sch. tchr. five years; founder/ptnr. in bus. mfg. and selling bathroom wall plaques, 1965; founder/pres. mfg. bus., Payo Lab., Inc. 1972--; mem. Western Fairs Assn., Pismo Beach CofC, Soroptomist; Republican; rec: painting. Res: 790 Merced St Pismo Beach 93449 Ofc: Pay Lab. Inc. 348 Hollister Pismo Beach 93449

CLEMENS, ROGER ALLYN, nutritionist; b. Sept. 7, 1946, Los Angeles; s. Marvin Leo and Betty Jane (Kent) C.; m. Catherine Sprecher, June 19, 1970; children: Stephanie, b. 1977, Janna, b. 1983; edn: AB, UC Los Angeles 1972, MPH, 1972, Dr.P.H. 1978. Calif. Comm. College Instr. cred. (life). Career: mgr. Nutrition Research, Carnation Research Labs., Carnation Co. 1984--, research nutritionist 1978-84; vis. lectr. UC Los Angeles 1981, 84, CSU Long Beach 1982-83, adj. asst. prof. Chapman Coll. 1980-; awards: finalist, Am. Inst. of Nutrition Grad. Resrch. 1978; mem: NY Acad. of Scis., Inst. of Food Tech. (profl.), Greater L.A. Nutrition Council (bd.mem.), Calif. Council Against Health Fraud, Calif. Nutrition Council, Soc. of Nutrition Edn., Am. Soc. for Parenteral and Enteral Nutrition; mem. UCLA Dean's Council 1980-; Am. Red Cross (L.A. chpt. exec. bd., bd. dirs.; San Fernando Valley Dist. exec. com., bd. chmn. 1981-2, 1984-); mil: SP5E5 US Army 1967-69, Nat. Defense, GCM, Korea Svc.; publs: profl. journal articles; Republican; Baptist; rec: family, cycling, photog. REs: 6856 Newcastle Ave Reseda 91335 Ofc: Carnation Research Labs, 8015 Van Nuys Blvd Van Nuys 91412

CLEMENTS, ZERLINE A., income tax consultant; b. June 19, 1927, Boston, Mass.; d. Frederick and Olga (Aaron) Anderson; m. Glenn Randall, Apr. 6, 1946; children: Glenn Jr., b. 1947; Marjorie Jean (dec.) b. 1949; edn: Fullerton Jr. Coll. 1960; Santa Ana Jr. Clol. 1959; enrolled agent, IRS 1973. Career: develop. tax preparaton co., Garden Grove, var. Anaheim locations 1953-79; ret. 1979; small antique bus. 1981; bookeeper, acct. for var. concerns; lectr., fin. cons.; awards; Recgn. of Achiev. Awd., Inland Soc. of Tax Cons.; mem: Inland Soc. of Tax Cons.; Nat. Assn. Enrolled Agents; publs: ed./ pub. newsletter, Homeowners Assn., Rio Vista Estates 1981-84; Republican; Disciples of Ch.; rec: writing, genealogical research, antique hunting. Address: 42299 Santee Ct Hemet 92344

CLEVELAND, DAVID L., educational consulting co. president; b. June 25, 1948, Selma, Ala.; s. James V. and Dessie L. (Warren) C.; m. Marygrace N. St.Angelo, July 10, 1971; children: Travis Anthony, b. 1979, Ryan Joseph, b. 1981; edn: BA, CSU San Diego 1976; MA, CSU Northridge 1980. Career: special education tchr. City of San Diego, 1976-79; founder/pres. Telesis II of California, Inc., 1979--, consultant to sch. districts throughout Calif., designed drug edn. tchg. curriculi for individual schools; author/pub.: drug edn. curriculum pgm. for tng. student peer counselors; A New Awareness: Drug Abuse Among the Disabled (tchr. tng. guide); mem. Bonita Valley Civic Club; mil: USN 1967-71; Democrat; rec: golf, skiing. Res: 3764 Putter Dr Bonita 92002 Ofc: 3180 University Ave, Ste. 650, San Diego 92104

CLIFFORD, ROBERT PAUL, investments executive; b. Aug. 11, 1933, Los Angeles; s. Robert Paul and Dorothy D. (Dech) C.; m. Melissa Mary Whittemore, Sept. 25, 1977; children: Robert, b. 1957; Cameron, b. 1961; Thomas, b. 1963; Matthew, b. 1980; edn: BS, USC 1955. Career: acct. exec. Paine Webber 1958-68; mgr. Drexel Burnham Lambert 1968-82; mktg. dir. W. Coast, 1982--; honors: Kappa Beta Psi; mem: Bowd Club of Los Angeles; USC Cardinal & Gold Athletic Support Gp.; mil: 1st lt. USAF 1955-58; Republican; Protestant; rec: hunting, fishing, camping. Res: 409 Camino de Las Colinas Redondo Beach 90277 Ofc: Drexel Burnham Lambert, Inc., 1901 Ave of the Stars Los Angeles 90067

CLIFT, JACK BERRY, jewelier; b. July 10, 1953, Wellington, Ks.; s. Wesley E. and Marjorie Clift; ed. Wellington H.S. Career: self-employed jewelier, designer, mfr. distinctive style of geometric inlayed, semi precious stones, ivorys and metals, 1972--. Address: 1832 Lyon San Francisco 94115.

CLINE, JOHNNIE R., cable television executive; b. Oct. 15, 1931, Buhl, Id.; s. Paul R. and Billie L. (Jones) C.; m. Bette Jo Parker, Aug. 3, 1956; children: Tami, b. 1958; Lisha, b. 1960; Leinani, b 1963; Derrick, b. 1965; Cheree, b. 1967; Darrin, b. 1968; edn: Idaho State Univ. 1955-57; US Govt. Mgmt. sch. 1960-61. Career: dept. chief US Govt. 1957-64; gen. mgr. Cable TV Op., Wash. & Id. 1964-74; regl. mgr. Ashley Dept. Stores, St. Louis, Mo. 1974-77; v.p. Cloud 9, Inc., Twin Falls, Id. 1977-80; gen. mgr. TCI Cable Provo, Utah 1980-82; gen. mgr. American Cablevision, Coronado 1982--; mem: Nat. Cable TV Assn.; Calif. Cable TV Assn.; ID Cable Assn. (pres. 1969-71); Utah Cable Assn. (bd. dirs.); Coronado Rotary Club; Coronado Schs. Found.; Coronado CofC; PTA (past pres.); Republican (past commn. chair); Ch. of Jesus Christ, LDS; rec: golf, fishing, hunting. Res: 315 Alameda Coronado 92118 Ofc. American Cablevision, 1110 Orange Ave Coronado 92118

CLINTON, JOHN HART, newspaper publisher; b. Apr. 3, 1905, Quincy, Mass.; s. John Francis and Catherine Veronica (Hart) Clinton; m. Helen A. Amphlett, Feb. 18, 1933 (dec. 1965); chil: Mary Jane (Clinton) Zirkel, b. 1934, Mary Ann (Clinton) Gardner, b. 1937, John H., Jr., b. 1944; m. 2d. Mathilda A. (Schoorel) van Dillen, Feb. 22, 1969; stepsons: Paul A. van Dillen, b. 1945, Erik van Dillen, b. 1951; edn: grad. Thayer Acad. 1922, AB, Boston Coll. 1926, LL.B and JD, Harvard Law Sch. 1929. Career: admitted to Calif. Bar 1930, Mass. Bar 1930; since practiced in S.F.; assoc. firm Morrison, Foerster, Holloway, Clinton & Clark and predecessor, 1939-41, partner, 1941 72, of counsel Morrison & Foerster, 1972--; pres. Leamington Hotel, Oakland 1933 47; pres. Amphlet Printing Co., San Mateo 1943--, publ. San Mateo Times, 1943--, ed. 1960--. Hon. mem. Exec. Com. San Mateo Co. Council BSA; bd. dirs., pres. Calif. Jockey Club Found.; regent emeritus Notre Dame Coll. Decorated Knight Equestrian, Order of Holy Sepulchre of Jerusalem. mem: FCC; Am., S.F., San Mateo Co. Bar Assns.; State Bar of Calif. (past chmn. Com. on Free Trial and Free Press, past co-chmn. Calif. Bench/Bar Media Com.); Am. Bar Assn.; Am. Judicature Soc.; Nat. Lawyers Club; Am. Law Inst.; San Mateo Co. Devel. Assn. (pres. 1963-5); San Mateo Co. Hist. Assn. (pres. 1960-4); Calif. Press Assn. (pres. 1970, chmn. bd.); Am. Newspaper Pub. Assn. (press/bar rels. com.; mem. Task Force); Calif. Newspaper Publs. Assn. (chmn. Legal Com.); Wine and Food Soc., S.F.; Am. Soc. Newspaper Eds.; Assn. Catholic Newsmen; Nat. Press Photogs Assn.; Intl. Platform Assn.; Newcomen Soc.; Commonwealth Club of S.F. (past pres.); S.F. Commercial Club; Bohemian Club (S.F.); San Mateo Rotary Club (past pres., chmn. Pgm. Adv. Com.); Elks. res: 131 Sycamore Ave. San Mateo 94402. ofc: Amphlett Printing Co., 1080 S. Amphlet Blvd. San Mateo 94402.

CLOCK, EDWIN HENRY, lawyer; b. Sept. 24, 1949, Los Angeles; s. Henry Harriman and Frances (Terry) C.; (grandfather R.H. Clock was early L.A. County Judge and father, H.H. Clock, a prominent practitioner); m. Nancy Millie, Mar. 23, 1974; children: Michele, b. 1977, Nicole, b. 1980, Diana, b. 1982; edn: AB, Stanford Univ. 1971, AM, 1971, MBA, Stanford Grad. Sch. of Bus. Adm. 1975, JD, Stanford Law Sch. 1975; admitted to Calif. State Bar 1975. Career: law clerk to Chief Justice, Supreme Ct. of Calif. 1975-76; assoc. atty. Heller, Ehrman, White & McAuliffe, San Francisco 1976-78; general counsel Itel Securities Corp., 1978-81; vice pres. Wells Fargo & Co., S.F. 1982--, spec. in corp. finance, real estate, equip. leasing, sec. law and internat. fin.; owner White Lane Vineyards, Calistoga 1978-; mng. ptnr. Clock & Clock, Attorneys, Tiburon 1977--; mng. ptnr. The Clock Co., 1977-79; dir. Fenwick Corp. 1977-78; cons. Rand Corp. 1974-75; bd. trustees Stanford Univ. Sch. of Law 1980-83; honors: Eagle Scout and Participant, 13th World Jamboree, Athens, Greece (1963); outstanding journalist Long Beach Press Telegram (1967); Phi Betta Kappa (1971), editor Stanford Law Rev. 1974-75; mem: World Trade Club, Bar Assn. of S.F., Practising Law Inst. Section on Corp., Banking and Securities Law; clubs: Olympic Country (SF), Thunderbird Country (Palm Springs), Meadowwood Country (Napa Valley), Tuna Club of Avalon (Catalina Is.); publs: law jour. arts.; Republican; Episcopal; rec: numismatics, philately, golf. Res: 150 Avenida Miraflores, Tiburon 94920 Ofc: Wells Fargo & Co, 101 California St San Francisco 94111

CLOSE, JOHN NORMAN, chiropractor; b. Jan. 22, 1949, Ngaruawahia, New Zealand; s. Maurice Harding and Aileen Alexander (Gall) C.; edn: DC, Palmer Coll. 1975. Career: Auckland Tech. Inst., Auckland, New Zealand 1967-70;

Palmer Coll. of Chiro, Davenport, Iowa 1971-75; extern Culver Chiro. Ofcs., Palo Alto 1976; dir. Close Chiro. Ctr., Inc., Pleasanton 1977--; pres. Calif. Chiro. Cons. 1981-; pres. Alameda Co. Chiro. Assn.; awards: Doctor of Yr., Profl. Chiro. Soc. of Am. 1982; mem: Am. Chiro. Assn.; Parker Chiro. Research Found.; Profl. Chiro. Soc. of Am.; Rowell Ranch Rangers, exhib. riding team (lead rider); publs: var. papers on chiro., physiology. rec: equestrian, sports cars, skiing. Res: 4742 Peaceful Ln Pleasanton 94566 Ofc: Close Chiropractic Ctr., Inc., 6111 Johnson Ct, Ste 101, Pleasanton 94566

CLOUD, JAMES MERLE, educational administrator; b. Feb. 16, 1947, Winston-Salem, N.C.; s. Merle Vail and Jane Crawford (Moore) Cloud; edn: BA, Univ. N.C. at Chapel Hill, 1970; MA, Columbia Pacific Univ. 1978, PhD., 1980; career: co-founder, Wholistic Health & Nutrition Institute, Mill Valley, Calif. (mem. bd. dirs. 1974-, Director of Education 1974-78); co-founder, Columbia Pacific University (secty-treas. bd. dirs., Director of Admissions, 1978--); vice pres. bd. dirs. Assn. for Holistic Health, San Diego, 1976; mem. bd. dirs. Church of The Tree of Life, San Francisco, 1978; assoc. producer, film: "Citizen", William Farley Film Group, Oakland, 1982; founder, The Alchemists Union, 1982; mem.: Airplane Owners and Pilots Assn., Sierra Club, U.S. Chess Fedn., Assn. for Holistic Health; Author: The Healthscription, 1979; Anthologies of poems, Aeolus, 1971, and No One Loves with Wolitude, 1970; rec: pvt. pilot, scuba certified, chess, racquetball, poetry, gastronomy, numismatics, metaphysics, languages, travel; res: 629 Eastwood, Mill Valley 94941; office: Columbia Pacific Univ., 150 Shoreline Hwy., Mill Valley 94941.

CLOUSE, DONALD FRANCIS, financial planner-consultant; b. Jan. 20, 1921, Albia, Iowa; s. William Lawrence and M:innie Mae (Whitson) Clouse; m. Nellie Guest, May 8, 1945, div. 1973; m. 2d. Celia Long, Aug. 25, 1973; two daus.: Linda Sue, b. 1952, Nancy Lee, b. 1954; edn: BA, Univ. Iowa 1943; cert. navigator, Pan Am. Coll., 1941; engrg. and finl. studies, USC, UCLA, Pepperdine, CalTech, MIT, others. Career: mem. corp. staff Lockheed CaliforniaCo., 1940-74; mgr. Indsl. Engineering, McDonnel Douglas Corp., 1978--; finl. planner, mem. Nat Assn. of Charitable Estate Counselors (NACEC) afil. with Foundation Svcs., Inc., mktg. branch of The Nat. Heritage Found.; prin. The D.C. White House Scholarship Found. (charitable, non-profit orgn.), afil. with The Nat. Heritage Found., Wash DC; dir. Lockheed Mgmt. Club, 1958-67; dir. BSA, 1962-64; Awarded Man of the Year, 1963, Lockheed Calif. Co. mem. Masons, 1954-; founder The Aerospace Travel Club, non-profit members only flying club (past bd.chmn., CEO; owned 749 Lockheed Constellation comml. aircraft) 1963-. Devel. wind park to generate elec. energy in prog. 1982-. Mil: capt. USAAF 1942-46. Republican (active Nat. Repub. Party 1958-, charter mem.Presdtl. Task Force and Adv. Com.). Christian Sci. rec: harnessing kinetic energy, ultra-lite aircraft, inventing, counseling. res: 261-B So. Gilbert Fullerton 92633.

CMIEL, JUNE RICHWINE, clinical psychologist; b. June 11, 1922, Elyria, Ohio; d. Arthur Louis and May (Laverty) Richwine; m. Frank Cmiel, Apr. 13, 1944, (dec.); children: Frances, b. 1945; Patricia, b. 1946; Margaret, b. 1954; edn: BA, Syracuse Univ. 1952; MA, Chapman Coll. 1974; PsyD, US Internat. Univ. 1981; clinical psychologist, Calif. 1983. Career: supvr. personnel records Hunt Wesson, Fullerton 1958-71; soc. wkr. Co. of Orange 1972--; marriage family therapist, Fasa Inst., Orange 1976-83; psychologist, 1983--; dean of psychology dept., Newport Univ.; honors: Scholarship, Syracuse Univ.; Psi Chi, psychology nat. hon. soc.; mem: Am & Calif. State Psychol. Assns.; Calif. Assn. Marriage Family Therapists; mil: A-5 US Army 1944-45; Catholic. Res: 2300 S Lewis II 169, Anaheim 92802 Ofc: Fasa Institute, 1500 E Katella, Ste M, Orange 92667

COATS, ROY EUGENE, company executive; b. Oct. 30, 1935, Sulphur, Okla.; s. Eugene Victor and Sephronie Asbery (Blocker) C.; m. Laura Rose Terry, Dec. 6, 1969; children: Virginia, b. 1956; Nancy, b. 1960; Christy, b. 1965. Career: formed Sunbank Electronics, Inc. 1958; pres./ chmn. bd. Sunbank Family of Cos. now with eleven companies; publs: No Guts No Glory- Self Help Book 1984; mil: USMC 1952-55; Republican; Methodist; rec: golf. Res: Rocky Canyon Rd Creston 93432 Ofc: Sunbank Electronics, Inc., 3100 Damon Way Burbank 91505

COBURN, GARY NELSON, investment counselor; b. May 19, 1946, Pasadena; s. George Nelson and Frances Ida (Colton) C.; m. Carol Schmidt, Sept. 13, 1969; children: Brian, b. 1978; Jeffrey, b. 1980; edn: BA, UC Berkeley 1968; MBA, UC Berkeley Grad. Sch. of Bus. 1969; chartered fin. analyst, Inst. Chartered Fin. Analysts 1975; chartered investment counselor 1975. Career: v.p./ gen. partner Scudder, Stevens & Clark, San Francisco 1970--; assoc. dir. Bond Policy Gp.; mem: Security Analysts Soc. of San Francisco; Fin. Analysts Fedn.; S.F. Yacht Club; Univ. Club of S.F.; Calif. Alumni Assn.; Big C' Soc.; Moraga Country Club; County Treasurer Assn. of Calif.; US Yacht Racing Union; Republican; Methodist; rec: sailing, skiing, tennis. Res: 192 Alice Ln Orinda 94563 Ofc: Scudder, Stevens & Clark, 101 California St San Francisco 94111

COCKBURN, WILLIAM, chiropractor; b. June 26, 1953, Lanark, Scotland, nat. 1965; s. William and Isabella (Tracey) C.; m. Cynthia, July 14, 1973; 1 dau: Rebecca, b. 1976; edn: DC, Cleveland Coll. of Chiro. 1975; DC, State Bd. 1975. Career: practicing chiropratic physician 1975 ; active in Calif. Chiro. Assn.; instr. Palmer Coll. of Chiro. West; instr. pediatrics, x-ray interpretation & diagnosis; com. pres. Am. Chiro. Pediatric Assn.; pres. Childrens Chiro. Ctr., Inc.; awards: Young Doctor of the Yr., Botterman Awd., Distng. Svc., Calif. Chiro. Assn.- No. Bay Soc.; mem: Calif. Chiro. Assn.; Internat. Chiro. Soc.; Am. Chiro. Pediatric Assn.; Toastmasters; Lions Club; Petaluma Coord.Council (pres.); Rotary (former); publs: Can Chiropractic Survive Medical Bigotry?, 11/83 & Chiropractic Pediatrics as a Specialty, 1/84, The Am. Chiropractor Mag.; Christian; rec: flying, modeling, family life. Res: 525 Williams Petaluma 94952 Ofc: Chiropratic Offices, 620 Petaluma Blvd N, Petaluma 94952

COCHRAN, LEROY CHARLES, financial executive; b. Sept. 1, 1939, Scotts Bluff, Nebr.; s. Roy C. and Mary E. (Arnold) C.; m. Betty Morgan, Dec. 24, 1960; 1 dau: Le Ann, b. 1962; edn: BS, Univ. of Colo. 1965. Career: v.p. fin. Ness Inds., Palo Alto 1969-73; controller/ gen. mgr. Ampex, Redwood City 1973-81; v.p./ controller Tymshare, Cupertino 1981-84; v.p. fin. Fortune Systems, Redwood City 1984--; mem: Fin. Execs. Inst.; mil: aviation elec. 2/c USN 1959-61; Republican; rec: golf, swimming, sailing. Res: 444 Saratoga Ave, 7H, Santa Clara 95050 Ofc: Fortune, 101 Twin Dolphin Dr Redwood City 94065

COFFEY, OSCAR JUSTIN, JR., association executive; b. Jan. 1, 1926, New Orleans, La.; s. Oscar and Mercedes (Blond) Coffey, Sr.; m. Jimmye Marks, Jan. 15, 1967; children: Oscar Justin III, b. 1955, Joy Lynne, b. 1958; edn: stu. The Quartermaster Sch. (Ger.) 1951-2, Walkers Sch of Ins. & Salesmanship (New Orleans) 1953-7, Loyola Univ. (New Orleans) 1958, CSU Hayward 1974. Career: sales mgr. Lake Breeze Coffee, New Orleans 1953-60, Golden Bridge Bottling Co., Oakland 1961-68; pres. C&J Co., Consultants, Oakland 1961--; pres./chief exec. No. Calif. Blk. Chamber of Commerce, Oakland 1974--; owner Oak Limousine Service, Oakland 1982--; pres. Chamber Center Devel. and Investors, Inc., Oakland 1983--; pres. Nat. Gospel Hall of Fame, 1983-; pres. Nat. Assn. of Blk/Minority Chambers of Commerce, 1983-; pres./chief exec. No. Calif. Black CofC; bd. chmn. Golden State Bus. League (Trade), Oakland; bd. mem. Calif. Tourism Commn. Honors: Omega Psi Phi frat. Citizen of Year Awd. 1981; Presidentl. Appreciation 1976; Assn. Exec. of the Year, Nat. Assn. of Convention Plnnrs. 1983. Mem: Nat. Bus. League, Nat. Assn. of Conv. Plnnrs., Justice Wiley P. Manuel Found. Inc., Nat. Urban League, NAACP, Oakland Clean Community System. Mil: acting s/sgt. US Army 1951-53; Republican; Baptist. Res: 6002 Barrett Ave El Cerrito 94530 Ofc: NCBCC, 7700 Edgewater Dr. Ste 725, Oakland 94621

COFFIN, WILLIAM FRANCIS, company executive; b. June 4, 1945, Los Angeles; s. William Francis and Connie (Beltran) C.; div.; children: Michelle, b. 1969; Christopher, b. 1983; edn: BA, CSU 1964; grad. pgm., bus. admin., USC 1968. Career: founder/ partner Coffin, Besser & Summers, Los Angeles 1968-80; pres./ dir. Commodore Resources, Inc., Salt Lake City, Utah 1979-80; founder/ chmn./ pres. Northstar Minerals, Inc., Los Angeles 1980--; instr. Pepperdine Univ., Malibu 1979; awards: PRISM Awds. (2), for outstanding pub. rels. pgms.; mem: Am. Petroleum Inst.; Pub. Rels. Soc. of Am.; Bel-Air Country Club; The Regency Club. Res: 952 Malcolm Ave Los Angeles 90024 Ofc: 10880 Wilshire Blvd, Ste 1205, Los Angeles 90024

COHEE, GARY DAVID, investment banker; b. Aug. 15, 1946, Long Beach; s. David Eugene and Lugene (Bellamy) C.; m. Denise Leora, Oct. 28, 1972; children: Tyler, b. 1979; Kelly, b. 1981; edn: BS, CSU Long Beach 1968; all securities & mgmt. lics., NASD, SEC 1978-80. Career: ops. supvr. Allstate Ins., Santa Ana 1968-70; sales/ dist. mgr. Gallo Wine Co., Commerce 1970-73; sales/ annuity & ins. mgr. Blyth Eastman Dillon, Long Beach 1973-77; v.p./ fin. svcs. dir. 1978-79; v.p./ asst. br. mgr. Smith Barney, Newport Beach 1979; v.p. sales Bateman Eichler, Hill Richards, Newport Beach 1980-82; mng. partner Diehl, Speyer & Brown, Newport Beach 1982--; mktg. dir. Diehl, Speyer & Brown 1982-83; awards: Top Ten Club & Century Club, Bateman Eichler 1980, 81; mem: Long Beach Bond Club (pres. 1978); So. Calif. Options Soc. (pres. 1979); Nat. Option Soc. at C.B.O.E. (founder 1980); 552 Club, Hoag Hosp.; Univ. Athletic Club; Newport Beach CofC; mil: spec-5 USAR 1968-74; Republican; Presbyterian; rec: racketball, softball, snow skiing. Res: 4091 Diablo Circle Huntington Beach 92649 Ofc: Diehl, Speyer & Brown, 1201 Dove Street, Ste 570, Newport Beach 92660

COHEN, CYNTHIA MARYLYN, lawyer; b. Sept. 5, 1945, Brklyn.; d. Bernard and Evelyn (Berman) Cohen; edn: AB, Cornell Univ. 1967; JD cum laude, NY Univ. Sch. of Law 1970; mem. NY State Bar 1971-, Calif. State Bar 1980-, Federal Bar of NY 1971-, Fed. Bar of Calif. 1980-, Sup. Ct. Bar 1979-. Career: assoc. atty. Simpson Thacher & Bartlett, NY, NY 1970-76; assoc. atty. Kaye, Scholer, Fierman, Hays & Handler, NY, NY 1976-80; atty. Stutman, Treister & Glatt Profl. Corp., Los Angeles 1980--, shareholder mem. 1981-; Student-Faculty Curriculum and Clin. Program Coms., and Student Research Advisor, NYU 1968-70; honors: Order of the Coif (1970), Founder's Day Cert. (1969), John Norton Pomeroy Scholar (1968-70), Law Rev. (1968), NYU; Am. Jurisprudence Awards; Cornell Dean's Scholarship 1963-67; NY State Regents Scholarship 1963-70; mem: Am. Bar Assn. (Antitrust Sect.), Bar Assn. of City of NY (Trade Reg. Com. 1976-79), NY State Bar Assn. (ch. Class Action Com. 1979), Assn. of Bus. Trial Lawyers, L.A. County Bar Assn. (Antitrust, Comml., Bankruptcy Sects.), Calif. Bar Assn. (Antitrust, Bus. Sects.); Girl Scouts 1954-59; Delta Gamma Sor.; NY chpt. Am. Cancer Soc. (dir. 1977-80); Democrat; Jewish; rec: collector books, wine, tennis. Res: 4818 Bonvue Ave Los Angeles 90027 Ofc: Stutman, Treister & Glatt PC, 3699 Wilshire Blvd, Ste. 900, Los Angeles 90010

COHEN, JAMES ROBERT, physician-oncologist, b. Oct. 6, 1945, Norfolk, Va.; s. Robert Vance and Elizabeth (Kohn) C.; m. Patricia, June 18, 1968; edn: BA, Cornell Univ. 1967; MD, Cornell Med. Coll. 1971. Career: med. intern/ resident NY Hosp./Meml. Sloan- Kettering Cancer Ctr., NYC 1971-73; sr. med. res. UC San Francisco 1973-74; hematology/oncology fellow Stanford Univ. Sch. of Med. 1976-78; staff internist/dir. USAF Regl. Hosp., Ft. Worth, Tx. 1974-76; clin. assoc. in med. Univ. Nebr. Sch. of Med. 1975-76; clin. instr.

Stanford Univ. Med. Ctr. 1978-; physician oncologist, pvt. practice, San Jose; chmn. Div. of Oncology, Good Samaritan Hosp.; pres. Hospice of the Valley, San Jose; adv. com. on hospice, Visiting Nurses Assn., Santa Clara Co.; honors: Alpha Omega Alpha; Am. Bd. Certs: Internal Medicine 1974, Oncology 1979; mem: Fellow Am. Coll. of Physicians, Santa Clara Co. Med. Soc., CMA, Calif. Soc. of Internal Med., Am. Soc. of Int. Med., Am. Soc. of Clin. Oncology, Am. Coll. of Surgeons (Liaison Assoc. in Cancer), No. Calif. Oncology Group (Investigator), Am. Cancer Soc. (bd. Santa Clara Div.); num. med. journal arts.; mil: maj. USAF 1974-76; rec: travel, racketball, jogging. Res: 14920 Vickery Ln Saratoga 95070 Ofc: 2410 Samaritan Dr San Jose 95124

COHEN, NANCY SHER, lawyer; b. Sept. 29, 1951, Kansas City, Mo.; d. Abbott J. and Martha (Abend) Sher; m. Robert Neil Cohen, Jan. 6, 1973; edn: BA in govt., honors, Univ. of Tex. at Austin 1973; JD cum laude, Loyola Univ., L.A. 1978; admitted to Calif. State Bar. Career: legal asst. Salmanson & Smith, Austin, Tx. 1973-74; English language tchr. in Tokyo, Japan (for Nara TV network (TV series) and spl. corp. classes) 1974-75; law clk. Grace, Neumeyer & Otto, Los Angeles 1977-78; atty. ptnr. Tuttle & Taylor Inc., L.A. 1978--, spec. in civil litigation in fed. and state courts; lectr., Atty. Asst. Tng. Pgm., UCLA; mem: State Bar of Calif., Am. Bar Assn., L.A. County Bar Assn., Calif. Women Lawyers Assn. (judicial eval. com.); Jewish Fedn. (Law and Legis. Com.). Res: 4331 Whitsett Studio City 91604 Ofc: Tuttle & Taylor, 609 S. Grand Ave Los Angeles 909017

COLACCHIA, GINO VINCENT, sales executive; b. Nov. 20, 1945, North Bergen, NJ; s. Gino A. and Rose (Zappia) C.; m. Andrea Dawson, June 18, 1966; children: Aaron, b. 1967; Anthony, b. 1968; Joel, b. 1971; Rachel, b. 1976; Benjamin, b. 1981; edn: AS, & AA, L.A. Trade & Tech. 1966; controls cert., South Coast Jr. Coll. 1969; real estate courses, Indian Valley Coll. 1970. Career: HVAC design engr. Wester Air & Refrigeration, Compton 1966-70; HVAC proj. engr. Climate Air Cond. Corp., Stanton 1970-73; mech. sales/ contract mgr. No. Calif., University Mechanical Engrs., Bay Area Office 1973--; mem. ASHRAE (Golden Gate Chpt. code com.; participant Energy Awards Contest, ASHRAE Panel mem.); ASPE; Sonoma Valley 4-H; Alliance Mens Fellowship; Sonoma H.S. Boosters; Young Life; works: devel. indirect heating sys. for central variable air volume w/ constant volume room distribution 1983; Christian & Missionary Alliance; rec: hunting, ranching-purebred sheep. Res: 21195 Peary Ave Sonoma 95476 Ofc: University Mechanical Engineers, 1668 Factor Ave San Leandro 94577

COLE, DONALD FRED, company CEO; b. July 26, 1942, Detroit, Mich.; s. Fredrick Arthur and Babetta Charlotte (Godlle) C.; m. Bernell Smith, Dec. 29, 1967; children: Roslyn, b. 1970; Aldon, b. 1973; Catherine, b 1981; edn: AB, Univ. of Mich. 1965. Career: CEO Interstate Mfg. Corp., Romeo, MI 1968-76, pres. Cole Industries, Inc. 1976--; Subsidiaries of Cole Inds: Solana Lumber; Waterstreet Wholesale Lumber; Fallbrook Lumber; Temecula Lumber; K-RAM Radio; K-ITT Radio; mem: San Diego Lumber & Wood Prods. Assn.; Young Pres.' Orgn.; San Diego Symphony; San Diego Opera; mil: lt. USNR 1965-68; Episcopal; rec: golf, sailing, choral & vocal music. Res: 1856 Viking Way La Jolla 92037 Ofc: Cole Industries, 1640 Tidelands Ave National City 92050

COLE, EDWIN LOUIS, clergyman; b. Sept. 10, 1922, Dallas, Tx.; s. Edwin L. and Florence (Goodrum) C.; m. Nancy Corbett, Jan. 31, 1946; children: Paul Louis, b. 1950, Lois (Bivins), b. 1952, Joann Marie, b. 1954; edn: BA, Union Univ. 1978, PhD, 1979. Career: pastor, churches in Sonora, San Bruno, and Chico, Ca. 1952-60; missionary - evangelism, 1960-63; pres. Mens' Ministries for denomination, 1963-69; pastor, Concord, Ca.; gen. mgr. WHCT/TV, Hartford, Ct. 1974-76; minister-at-large, Christian Bdcstg. Network, 1976-78; sr. pastor, Costa Mesa, Ca. 1978-81; pres. Edwin Louis Cole Ministries Inc. dba Manhood Ministries (radio pgm. host), 1981--; chmn. Com. for Internat. Goodwill; chancellor, Sch. of Ministry, World Evangelism, San Diego; bd. dirs. High Adventure Ministries (radio bdcstg. Lebanon); mem. Fair Housing Bd., Contra Costa Co.; awards: Emmy Awards (1973, 74) for TV Christmas Spls., S.F. Chpt. of TV Arts & Scis.; Pastor Cole Day, proclaimed by Mayor of Concord (1974), Mayor of Hartford (1976); Founders Awd., Teen Hope Found. (drug rehab. ctr. Contra Costa Co.) 1973; charter bd. mem. M-2 Prison Rehab. Pgm., Calif. 1971-73; mem. Gov. Reagan's Commn. for Children & Youth 1969-72; author: Maximized Manhood (Whitaker House 1982), Potential Principle (in press); mil: pharm. mate 1/c USN 1941-45; Republican; Assemblies of God; rec: swim, tennis, running. Res: 1806 Port Stirling Pl Newport Beach 92660 Ofc: Edwin L. Cole Ministries, 2855 E. Coast Hwy, 229, Corona Del Mar 92625

COLE, JACK ELI, JR., software engineer; b. July 15, 1943; s. Jack Eli and Evelyn Gaston (Darragh) C.; m. Patricia Parker, Feb. 8, 1983; children: Tracy, b. 1968; Kirsten, b. 1971; Paul, b. 1973; edn: AB, Dickinson Coll. 1965. Career: tchr. San Diego Comm. Colls. 1970-82; pgmr. analyst sr. Rohr Marine 1979-81; owner C&C Systems & Software 1973--; proj. mgr. sys. software System. Mgmt. American 1982--; cons. C&C Sys. & Software; mem: Data Processing Adv. Com. & Elec. Techn. Adv. Com., San Diego Comm. Colls.; Navy Enlisted Reserve Assn.; mil: HMCS, USN, active reserve, Naval Reserve Meritorious Svcs.; Meritorious Unit Citation; Republican; Presbyterain; rec: computers. res: 1419 Rios Canyon Rd El Cajon 92021 Ofc: Systems Management American, 301 W 30th Street National City 92050

COLE, ROBERT EDGAR, manufacturing co. executive; b. Apr. 22, 1942, Durban, Natal, So. Africa, nat. 1972; s. Arthur Edgar and Georgina Orr-Martin (Irvine) C.; m. Rebecca Lloyd, July 24, 1976; edn: BS, Univ. of Natal 1964; assoc. prof. of engrs., Ontario, Canada. Career: dist. engr. Shell Canada Ltd., Hamilton, Ontario 1970-71; asst. to pres. Kras Corp., Fairless Hills, Pa. 1972-74; internat. sales & mktg. v.p. 1975-78; pres./ CEO Bosal Canada Inc., Montreal 1979-81; sales & mktg. v.p. Kras/ West Corp., San Jose 1981-83; pres. Cole Assoc., Los Gatos 1981--; v.p./ gen. mgr. Kras/ West Corp., San Jose 1983--; mem: Assm. Profl. Engrs. of Ontario; SEMI; Decathlon Club, Santa Clara; Citizens Choice; works: thesis, Multi Level Hwy. Interchanges, 1964; paper, Utilization of Road Width on Hwys., 1963; Republican; Christian; rec: skiing, flying, photog. Res: 22205 Old Santa Cruz Hwy Los Gatos 95030 Ofc: Kras/ West Corp., 2233 Paragon Dr San Jose 95131

COLEMAN, R. TRENT, vocational consultant/ career counselor; b. Feb. 4, 1936, Gary, Ind.; s. Robert Clinton and Lucille Verna Coleman; m. Dorothy Travers Aug. 20, 1957, div.; m. 2d. Patricia Barcott, June 13, 1976, div.; children: Sean; Bryce; Daniel; edn: BA, Univ. of Wash. 1962; MS, Univ. of Ore. 1971; CRC, Com. on Rehab. Counselor 1978; NCC, Nat. Bd. for Cert. Counselors 1983. Career: soc. wkr. San Bernardino Co. Welfare Dept. 1963-64; correctional counselor Calif. Rehab. Ctr., Norco 1964-67; sr. counselor Thiokol Job Corps Ctr., Clearfield, Utah 1967; asst. dir. Ednl. Sys. Corps., Wash. DC 1968-69; jade miner/ carpenter Black Fire Jade Mines, BigSur 1971-76; vocational spec. Internat. Rehab. Assn., San Diego 1977-80; clinical coord., San Diego Pain Inst., San Diego 1981; rehab. cons. RCW & Assoc., Carlsbad 1981-83; owner RTC Consulting Svc., Escondido 1983--; mem: AACD, ARCD, Assn. of Indsl. Rehab. Reps. (pres. 19797-83); San Diego Career Guidance Assn. (pres. 1984-85); CofC; mil: spec. 4 US Army Security Agency 1955-58; Republican; Christian; rec: drama, music, travel. Res: 538 Glenheather Dr San Marcos 92069 Ofc: RTC Consulting Service, 210 S Juniper, Ste 100, Escondido 92025

COLEMAN, WILLIE JAMES, insurance co. executive; b. Sept. 3, 1935, Moundville, Ala.; s. Willie and Lucy (Dobbins) C.; m. LaVaughn Faison, July 10, 1980; children: Michael, b. 1959; Christopher, b. 1963; Karen, b. 1964; Michele, b. 1980; edn: AA, San Diego Jr. Coll. 1959; BA, San Diego State Univ. 1969; MA, US Internat. Univ. 1975; PhD, 1979. Career: pres. Kodiak Alaska Sch. Bd. 1961-66; instr./ counselor USN 1968-70; owner Coleman Ins. Agcy. 1978--; chmn. bd. Mexican- Am. Found. 1981--; sr. v.p. Ferro Fin. Corp. 1975--; clinical psychologist, pvt. practice 1979--; prof. San Diego Comm. Coll. Dist. 1980--; pres. San Diego Co. Life Leaders Club 1979-80; v.p. San Diego Assn. of Life Underwriters 1979-80; awards: Nat. Quality Awd. 1979-84; Nat. Sales Achiev. Awd. 1969-84; Life & Qualifying mem. Million Dollar Round Tabel 1969-84; mem: Mexican- Am. Found.; Nat. Council on Alcoholism (pres. 1973-75); Statewide Alcoholism Council of Calif.; Navy League of the US Fleet Reserve Assn.; Internat. Platform Assn.; Rotary Club; Southeast San Diego; Mexican & Am. Found.; publs: The A B C of Insurance Sales, pub. 1982; mil: master chief yeoman E-9 USN 1955-75, Commdn. Medal 1972; Republican; rec: tennis, bowling, jogging. Res: 8617-6 Lake Murray San Diego 92119 Ofc: Ferro Insurance Agency, 3455 Camino Del Rio S, San Diego 92108

COLHOUN, CHARLOTTE EDITH, sales co. executive; b. Sept. 6, 1923, Muilaslin Omagh Co. Tyrone, N. Ireland, nat. 1960; d. Orr and Phoebe Perry (Livingstone) Kyle; m. William James Colhoun, Nov. 14, 1944, dec.; children: William A., b. 1946; James A., b. 1952; Norman A., b. 1954. Career: apprentice bookeeper Jr. R. Pollocks Grocers, Omagh Co. Tyrone 1937-41; bookeeper Dickie & Carson, Solicitors, Omagh Co. Tyrone 1941-44; currently, pres./ owner Colhoun Enterprises dba Blind Made Prods., Oakland; mem: Nat. Fedn. Republic Women; Oakland Athletic Club; Lafayette Republic Women; Presbyterian; rec: gardening, travel. Res: 3520 Bayer Cir Lafayette 94549 Ofc: Colhoun Enterprises, dba Blind Made Products, 492 29th Street Oakland 94609

COLIVER, NORMAN, lawyer; b. June 19, 1918, Baltimore; s. Edward and Lillian Bromson (Silberman); gr.grandfather, Rabbi Nachum Paitiel Bromson of Baltimore; grandfather, Tanchum Silberman, industrialist nd civic leader; m. Edith Simon 1947, div. 1978; 2 daus: Susan, b. 1952, Lillian Sandra, b. 1955. Edn: BS, honors in philos., Univ. of Va. 1939; Harvard U. Grad. Sch of Arts & Sci. 1946-7; JD, Stanford Univ. 1950. Honors: Phi Beta Kappa, 1939; Irvine Hellman Award, Stanford, 1950; fellow Am. Coll. of Probate Counsel, 1978; mem. Attys. Probate Assn., S.F. Estate Planning Council. Career: merchant seaman Hamburg-Am. Line, summer 1937; swim coach Camp Wigwam, Me. summer 1940; asst. dean of scholarships, Harvard Univ. 1946-47; jr. exec. trainee Pabco Co., Emeryville, Ca. 1947-48; labor rels. cons. to Italian Govt. under contract with Stanford Resrch Inst., Rome 1951; gen. ptnr. law firm of Dinkelspiel & Dinkelspiel, San Francisco 1952--. Past bd. dir: Morgan Equip. Co., Gibbs-McCormick Inc., Bond & Brown, Hanns Kornell Champagne Cellars, Hunters Point Boys Club, United Bay Area Crusade, United Comm. Fund of S.F. (chmn. Soc. Welfare Plnng Council, 4 yrs.), Am Red Cross of S.F., S.F. Mental Health Assn. (v.p.), S.F. Home Health Svc. (cofounder), Presidio Hts. Assn. of Neighbors, Jewish Comm. Ctr., Jewish Family Svc. Agcy., Congregation Emanu-El (v.p.), J.L. Magnes Mus. of Berkeley, S.F. Sponsors (pres.), Vol. Bur. of S.F. (v.p.); bd. regents Lone Mountain Coll. Mem. S.F. Bar Assn. (chmn. Internat. & Comparative Law Com. 1965, Ethics Com. 1973, Probate & Trust Law Sect. 1982); ACLU, NAACP. Publs: law book revs.; lectr. on genealogy, Justice Brandeis, estate planning. Mil: pvt. to maj. US Inf. 1941-6, served in Gen. MacArthur's GHQ 1944-6, decorated 3 Bronze Stars, Battle Star, Pres. Unit Cit.; Jewish; rec: ski, tennis, jog. Res: 795 Sutter St., S.F. 94109 Ofc: Dinkelspiel & Dinkelspiel, 1800 Steuart St. Tower, One Market Plaza, San Francisco 94105

COLLEY, WILLIAM LINDSEY, SR., educator (ret.); b. Sept. 24, 1892, in log-cabin, KY; s. Jacob and Mary Ann (Spurlin) colley; namesake of grandfathers

John Lindsey Spurlin and William Colley; left a paraplegic after 1st epidemic of infantile paralysis in KY, 1896; lifetime tchr. cred., Western KY State Normal, 1916; AB, Redlands Univ., 1921; H.S. tchrs. cred., USC, 1921; grad. studies, Stanford Univ., 1927; m. Ruth Beardsley, 1923; children: William L. Jr.; Louise Parra. Career: tchr., rural schs., KY, 1911-19; tchr., Earles, KY, 1911; Co. Sch. Supt. of an "infamous sch.", 1912; taught mostly in rural schs. with severe disciplinary problems; tchr., Owensboro Bus. Coll; Elsinore H.S., 1921-28; life ins. agent, briefly, 1928; called "a teacher of students" rather than "just" a teacher of commerce, English, history, or math, by Mr. Paul, principal, Polytech. H.S., Riverside, 1928; called most original math-student by math prof., West KY State Normal; reviewer, text books, various publishers. Mem.: Masons; Calif. Retired Tchrs. Assn.; past pres. Riverside Div. of Retire Teacher and a life mem. of CRTA; AARP; Sonoma Co. Aging Activities. Democrat, pres. Dem. Club. Presbyterian, ch. elder, Elsinore, Beaumont. Rec.: blind checkers & chess. Res.: 9274 Ferguson Ct., Sebastopol 95472.

COLLIER, WILLIAM EDGAR, restaurant consultant; b. May 9, 1951, Warren, Ohio; s. Mearle E. and Virginia F. (Williams) C.; edn: Glendale Coll. 1969-70; Trade Sch. Ext. Pgms. 1984; stu. Glendale Coll. 1984; Career: pres. of bd./ v.p. Bob's Big Boy Mobile; exec. ofcr. Internat. Inst. of Maitre'd, L.A.; v.p. ops. Forty Carrots Restaurants, Los Angeles; cons. Timesharing Consultant Corp., Irvine; currently, owner/ cons. COLCO; honors: CPR, Sanitation; mem. NRN; sev. tennis, reflector & loader inventions 1977-81; Republican; rec: golf, tennis, baseball. Res: 916 Cleveland Rd Glendale 91202 Ofc: Timesharing Consultants, 22 Executive Park, Ste 270, Irvine 92714

COLLIGAN, RICHARD THOMAS, security services co. executive; b. Sept. 20, 1940, Morristown, NJ; s. John Patrick and Betty Joy (Saltonstall) C.; children: Lori, b. 1962; Linda, b. 1964; Shawn, b. 1966; edn: John Jay Coll. of Criminal Justice 1965-68; NYCPD Police Acad.; NYCPD Plainclothes Investigator Sch. Career: patrolman/ plain clothes investigator, NYC Police Dept. 1962-69; sales rep. Julius Schmid Pharmaceutical Co. 1969-70; automobile salesman & wholesaler 1970-76; security lt./ tng. spec./ asst. mgr. contract securtiy police force, Los Angeles Air Force Station 1976-80; egn. mgr. Waltgard Security 1980-82; dir. of security H.L. Yoh Co. 1983--; Los Angeles Air Force Station Tng. Spec. 1979; awards: NYC Police Dept. Commdn. for Excellent Police Duty (2); Police Ofcr. of Month, New York Journ. Am. 1965; mil: BMSN USN 1957-61; Republican (Pres. Task Force). Res: 502 Ave G, Apt 11, Redondo Beach 90277 Ofc: H.L. Yoh Co., 4515 Van Nuys Blvd Sherman Oaks 91403

COLLINS, GUY ROBERT, research chemist; b. May 9, 1930, Chgo.; s. Guy Russel and Nora (Sutton) C.; m. Joan Bielefeld, 1954; two sons: Michael, b. 1961, Patrick, b. 1973; edn: BS, Millikin Univ. 1950, MA, Univ. Mo. 1953, PhD, Ind. Univ. 1965; career: research chemist/project leader Union Carbide Corp., South Charleston, W.Va. 1953-57; research chemist, sr. resrch chemist, resrch splst I & II, resrch leader Dow Chemical, U.S.A. in Midland, Mich. 1961-66, in Walnut Creek, Ca. 1966--, resrch leader, Medicinal, Biological & Polymer Chemistry; prin. investigator, NASA Organic Research (1970-72); prin. investigator Nat. Cancer Inst., Synthesis of Chemotheraputic Drugs (1971-75). Honors: Phi Lambda Upsilon, 1958, Sigma Xi, 1959. Mem: Am. Chem. Soc., Chem. Soc. (London), Assn. of Ind. Univ. Chemists, Masonic Lodge, Ill. 332. US Patents-3,283,911 (1966); 3,337,581 (1967); 3,418,361 (1968); 3,471,436 (1969); patent pend.(1982). publs: contbr. Jour. Organic Chem., vols. 29 (1964),30(65), 36(71), 37(72), Jour. of Heterocyclic Chem. (1973); Republican; Episcopal; rec: amateur radio, skiing, backpacking, cycling; res: 2750 Filbert Dr. Walnut Creek 94598 ofc: Dow Chemical, USA 2800 Mitchell Dr. Walnut Creek 94598.

COLLINS, LEONARD LEON, operations analysis engineer; b. Jan. 7, 1937, Detroit, Mich.; s. Clarence Leon and Engelina (Schnur) C.; m. Deanna Luclie Zesiger, Feb. 1, 1960; children: Leonard Alan, b. 1961; Jeffery Dean, b. 1962; Michale Glen, b. 1965; Michele Anne, b. 1968; Gregory Scott, b. 1970; Heather Dawn, b. 1971; edn: AA, El Camino Coll. 1957; BS in astrophysics, UCLA 1959; MS in physics, N.M. State Univ. 1967. Career: draftsman through mem. of tech. staff Northrop Corp., Hawthorne 1954-63; tchg. asst./ research asst. N.Mex. State Univ. 1963-67; Honeywell Radiation Ctr., Boston, Mass. 1967-68; Texas Instruments, Dallas, Tex. 1968-72; senior staff ops. analysis, Army pgms. Hughes, Canoga Park 1972--; honors: Physics Hon. Soc. (1959), Leaders in Am. Sci. (1962-63); mem: Am. Defense Preparedness Assn.; Neighborhood Council, Simi Valley; Dist. 8 Water Resources Bd., Simi Valley; works: celestial simulation techniques (7 Ballistic Missiles/ Space Tech. Symp.) 1962; Slit function corrections for resonant absorption, Lines observed w/ ruby laser (1967), num. classified publs.; Republican; LDS Ch. (high priest); rec: crafts. Res: 2724 Wanda Simi 93065 Ofc: Hughes 262/ C-27 Fallbrook Ave Canoga Park

COLLINS, MICHAEL RORY, housing development administrator; b. Feb. 20, 1942, San Francisco; s. Charles Leslie and Hazel (Dean) C.; m. Kay Means, Jan. 28, 1967; children: Rory, b. 1969; Matthew, b. 1975; edn: BS, San Jose State 1969; MS, CSU Long Beach 1982. Career: sr. supt. Soc. Svcs. Div. Dept. of Recreation & Parks, Richmond 1970; sr. supt. Recreation & Parks Assn., Green Valley Assn., Fountain Valley 1974; cons. Housing & Design, RH Klein Co., Los Angeles 1977; adminstr. The Angelus Plaza, Los Angeles 1979--; awards: Mayor's Citatiun; City Council Resolution; mem: Los Angeles Area CofC; Central City Assn.; Calif. Assn. of Homes for the Aging; Council for Health & Human Svcs. Ministries; Los Angeles Athletic Club; Coro Assoc.; Town Hall; Democrat; United Ch. of Christ; rec: woodworking, poetry (Haiku), gardening. Res: 3072 Bostonian Los Alamitos 90720 Ofc: RHF Bunker Hill Corp., bda The Angelus Plaza, 255 S Hill St Los Angeles 90012

COLLINS, M. RUDOLPH, engineer; b. Oct. 5, 1926, Manteo, N.C.; s. Marshall Claude and Gussie Etta (Berry) C.; children: Phillip, b. 1960, Lisa, b. 1966; edn: BS math, A&T State Univ. of N.C. 1952; mgmt. courses, UCLA 1966. Career: mech. engr., project engr. (Thor), program mgr. Packard Bell Electronics (now Teledyne) 1956-63; engr. McDonnell Douglas, Huntington Beach 1963--: section chief Saturn S-IVB Test Reqts, 1963-66; branch mgr., rep at GE (assoc. contr.) MOL Pgm., 1967-69; mgr. sys. devel. OWS (orbital wkshop) Pgm., Saturn/Apollo Skylab, 1969-73; branch chief Titan IIIC, 1973-77; pgm. engr. Delta Project, 1977-78, Cruise Missile Pgms. (B-52 SIL), 1978-80; co. rep. product engr., Norton AFB, 1980--; honors: VIP Citation, Japanese Space Pgm.; mem. Council for Pvt. Postsec. Ednl. Instns. of Calif.; Rotarian; mil: 1st lt. USAR; Republican; Baptist; rec: woodwk., flying. Res: 18382 Maple Dale Ln Huntington Beach 92646 Ofc: McDonnell Douglas 5301 Bolsa Ave Huntington Beach 92647

COLLINS, ROBERT HILLIARD, III, natural resource co. president; b. May 5, 1935, Beverly Hills; s. Robt. H. and Nancy (Morgan) C.; m. Emily Ann Banks, Apr. 24, 1970; 1 dau., Jayne Sherry; edn: BS, mech. eng., Stanford Univ. 1957, MBA, 1959. Career: project engr. Pacific Gas & Electric, San Francisco 1957; asst. to v.p./project engr. Occidental Petroleum Corp. and subsidiaries 1959-62; div. gen. mgr. Cyprus Oil Co., Houston 1961-64, v.p. Anvil Mining Corp. Ltd. (subs. of Cyprus), Vancouver, B.C., Can., 1965-67; pres. Collins Investments, L.A., 1967-74; pres. Inter-Tech Resources Inc., L.A., 1969-74; pres. Reserve Syn. Fuels, Signal Hill, Ca. 1974-80; pres. Getty Synthetic Fuels, Inc. (resource recovery: methane gas from landfills), Signal Hill 1980--; co-inventor Corrosion Control Process; mem: Am. Inst. Mech. Engrs., Soc. of Petroleum Engrs., Soc. of Mining Engrs.; Am. Inst. Chem. Engrs.; Stanford Alumni Assn.; clubs: Buck of Month and Block S. Orgn., Engrs. of So. Calif., Petroleum, Jonathan, Balboa Bay, Bel Air Country; mil: USNR 1957-59; rec: water sports, golf, tennis, bridge. Res: 2387 Kimridge Rd Beverly Hills 90210 Ofc: 2750 Signal Pkwy Signal Hill 90806

COLLINS, ROSEMARY L., company president; b. Jan. 24, 1932, Lincoln, Nebr.; d. Ernest L. and Henrietta M. (Vanderheiden) Litty; m. 2d Richard M. Collins (pres. Meadow Farms Foods), Nov. 7, 1981; chil.(by prev. marriage): Joseph T. Weidinger, III, b. 1953, Catherine Mary Weidinger, b. 1954; edn: CTC (Cert. Travel Counselor), Inst. of Cert. Trvl. Agts. Career: pub. rels. asst. to V.P., Hughes Tool Co., 1960-65; mgr. Visitor Relations, Litton Ship Systems, 1965-70, supr. Employee Services, Litton Ship Systems, spl. asst. to the pres., Parker Hannifin, 1970-71; mgr. Volt Tech. Corp., 1971-75; pres. Roses Int'l., 1975--; vice pres. Senor Foods (restaurant chain), 1984--. Mem. 42 Whirley-Girls (internat. lic. women helicopter pilots), 1963-; mem. Civil Service Com. City of Hermosa Beach, 1973-77. Republican. rec: tennis, bridge, water-ski. res: 3212 Walnut Ave. Manhattan Beach 90266. ofc: 17264 Hawthorne Blvd. Torrance 90504.

COLLINS, TERRY ANNE, market research executive; b. July 22, 1958, San Francisco; d. Walter Jr. and Joyce Treasure (Everist) C.; m. Luis Megid, Jan. 6, 1983; edn: BA, Acad. of Art Coll. 1982; BS, Univ. of San Francisco 1977-80; cert. adv. proficiency, Franco-Am. Inst. 1980. Career: research asst. Migros-Societe Anonyme, Geneva, Switzerland 1978-79; asst. to mktg. dir. Mobil Oil Australia, Papeete, Tahiti 1979-80; mgr. pub. rels. & promotions Club Mediterranee, Papeete, Tahiti 1980-81o; mgr. mktg. svcs. Clayton Williams & Co., Internat. Mgmt. Cons., San Francisco 1983--; currently, mgr. advtg. strategy & research, Pac Tel Commun. Sys., Pacific Telesis Gp.; cons. mkt. research plng.; honors: Strategic Plng. Com., Pac Tel Commun. Sys. 1983; Key Merit Awd., Pac Tel Commun. Sys. 1984; works: graphic design, Am. Indian Heritage Found. 1982, Litton Inds. 1983; rec: graphic design. Res: 1624 Sacramento San Francisco 94109 Ofc: Pac Tel Commun. Systems, 201 N Civic Dr, Ste 340, Walnut Creek 94596

COLLOM, STAN JOSEPH, manufacturing co. executive; b. Feb. 29, 1948, Phila., Pa.; s. Wm. Murray and Florence Maria (Lagetti) C.; edn: BA cum laude, Penn. State Univ. 1972. Career: labor relations to asst. mgr. indsl. rels., Phoenix Steel Corp., Pa.; currently exec. mgr. Leather Forever, Inc., San Francisco; cons. Reliance Motor Coach, Pa. 1983; mem: Eureka Valley Merchants Assn., Golden Gate Bus. Mens Assn., Opera Soc., Symphony Soc., De Young Mus., Modern Art Mus., S.F. Ballet, Am. Orchid Soc., Sierra Club, Smithsonian, Acad. du Vin, Opera Guild, Arbor Day Assoc.; Republican; Episcopal; rec: hybridization of orchids, devel. new strains; antiques. Res: 5015 Diamond Hts. Blvd. San Francisco 94131 Ofc: Leather Forever, Inc. 3989 17th St. San Francisco 94114

COMBS, RICHARD ENNIS, U.S.Magistrate, b. Nov. 3, 1903, Visalia; s. James Ennis and Maude (Brown) C.; m. Marjorie Pool, Dec. 23, 1933; chil: Richard E., Jr. b. 1935, Elizabeth, b. 1939, John, b. 1940, Mary, b. 1944; edn: AB, UC Berkeley 1926, JD, UC Hastings Law Sch 1931. Career: atty. law firm McClure & Combs, Visalia 1931-42; counsel to Pres. Calif. Senate, 1940-70; counsel to Speaker Calif. Assembly, 1939-41; counsel, Calif. Legis Com. on Counter-Subversive Activities, 1940-70; cons., US Commn. on Govt Security, Wash DC, and editor Commn's Report to Pres. Eisenhower, 1956-7; cons., L.A. City Bd. of Edn., 1967-70; author 14 reports on Subversive Activities to Calif. Legis., 1945-70; US Commnr., Sequoia-Kings Cyn Nat. Parks, 1970-1; US Magistrate, Eastern Dist. Calif., 1971--; assoc. mem. English Magistrates Assn., London; secty. Nat. Council of US Magistrates, 1979-80. Awards: appreciation, Calif. Senate, Am. Jewish League Against Communism, Am. Legion, DAR, US Commn. on Govt. Security. Mem: Calif. Hist. Soc., Tulare Co. Hist. Soc., Book Club of Calif, Friends Bancroft Lib., Alpha Chi Rho, Phi Delta Phi frats. Republican; past chmn. Tulare Co. Dem. Central Com. Protestant. rec: collector press books and first editions. res: 45063 N. Fork Dr., Three Rivers 93271. US Magistrate, Ash Mtn, Three Rivers 93271.

COMIN, CYRIL GOVANNI, production executive; b. Sept. 7, 1928, Coniston, Ontario, Canada; s. Govanni Joseph and Teresa Clara (Gemin) C.; m. Lucy Zeppa, Jury 19, 1952; 1 son: Richard, b. 1953. Career: machine opr. Anthes Imperial, St. Catharines, Ontario, Canada 1946-62; gen. foreman Cal Apco, Southgate 1962-72; prodn. supt. Am. Brass & Iron, Oakland 1972--; mem: Am. Foundryman Soc.; Dynamics of Supervision; Wildwood Assn.; Knights of Columbus; Democrat; Catholic; rec: golf, fishing. Res: 4786 Noree Ct Castro Valley 94546 Ofc: American Brass & Iron, 7825 San Leandro Oakland 94621

COMSTOCK, JAMES WILLIAM, pension consultant; b. Sept. 27, 1946, Grand Rapids, Mich.; s. William Charles and Marjorie Jean (Lovell) C.; m. Catherine Brinda, May 31, 1980; edn: BA, Mich. State 1969; MBA, Georgia State 1972-73; Command & General Staff Coll. 1980; adv. CLU pension course, Am. Coll. 1979; CLU, Am. Coll. 1978. Career: with Lincoln Nat. 1972-79; regl. mgr. spl. mkts., Baltimore, Md. 1972-73; equities mgr., Wash. DC 1974-75; regl. mgr. gp. & pension, Columbus, Ohio 1975-79; sales mgr. Am. Employee Ins. Agcy., Los Angeles 1980-83; regl. pension cons., Los Angeles 1983--; instr./ lectr. num. ind. & co. rel. courses & sems.; awards: Student of Yr., USAR 1979; Assn. of the US Army; mem: Nat. Assn. of Life Underwriters; Am. Soc. CLU; Reserve Ofcrs. Assn.; Scottish Rite; 1st Calvary Div. Assn., VFW; Mil. Nat. Hist. Soc.; mil: lt. col. USAR, active duty 1969-72; Republican; rec: racketball, tennis. Res: 983 Jungfrau, Drawer 2490-A, Crestline 92325 Ofc: American National Life Ins. Co., Drawer 2490-A, Crestline 92325

CONDER, ORVAL REID, company owner; b. Mar. 11, 1923, American Fork, Utah; s. William Edward and Lillian A. (Clark) C.; m. Fern A. Heineken, Dec. 24, 1942; children: Mary Alice, b. 943; Stanley Reid, b. 1949; Kristine Fern, b. 1952; edn: USC 1948-49; BBA, Woodbury 1948; USAC 1941-42; pub. acct., Calif. 1948. Career: owner Conder's Furniture 1949-53; exec. Rockwell Internat. 1943-74; pres. Standard Power Inc. 1980-81; exec. v.p. SOFA Internat., Inc. 1981--; partner S & K Mgmt. 1978--; dir. Standard Power Inc., Gen. Power Inc., SOFA Internat.; cons. Nat. Resources Internat. Inc.; awards: Outstanding Leadership, 1966, Excellent Leadership 1964, Cert. of Svc. 1966, Nat. Mgmt. Assn.; Order of Merit 1970, Silver Beaver 1973, Boy Scouts of Am.; mem: Nat. Mgmt. Assn. (pres. 1964-66); Boy Scouts of Am.; Disabled Am. Veterans; Masons; mil: API USN 1942-46; Republican; LDS. Res: 2550 Second Street Norco 991760

CONEY, CAROLE ANNE, accountant; b. Aug. 11, 1944, Berkeley; d. Martin James and Ida Constance (Ditora) Skuce; m. David Coney, June 20, 1964, children: Kristine, b. 1965; Kenneth, b. 1967; edn; BS, cand., Cal Poly, Pomona; Burroughs pgm. functions, Timberline Sch., Beaverton, Ore 1981; contract & grant acctg. Ctr. for Pub. Mgmt. 1982; adv. fund acctg. NACUBO 1983. Career: tax cons./ instr. H & R Block, Portland, Ore. 1969-71; asst. Surety Inst. Co., Surety Mgrs., Inc., La Habra 1973-76; F/C bookeeper Homemakers Furniture, Inc., Downers Grove, Ill. 1976-79; ofc. mgr./ acct. Helen's Place Printing, Pay- O- Matic Corp., Upland 1979-80; F/C bookeeper Vanguard Cos., Upland 1980-82; dir. of acctg. Coll. of Osteopathic Med. of the Pacific, Pomona 1982--; honors: Delta Mu Delta, Cal Poly 1982; Alpha Iota Delta, Cal Poly 1982; mem: NACUBO; NAFE; Milwaukie Oregon Jay-C-Etts; Brea- La Habra Newcomers Club (pres. 1975) Com. to Elect Robert Neufeld; Democrat; Catholic; rec: organ, arts & crafts. Res: 9521 Konocti Street Cucamonga 91730 Ofc: College of Osteopathic Medicine of the Pacific, College Plaza, Pomona 91766

CONGCO-MACAPINLAC, EVANGELINE G., physician; b. Sept. 20, 1948, Pampanga, Philippines, nat. 1980; d. Engracio D. and Rosario (Gozun) Congco; m. Efren L. Macapinlac, June 19, 1976; 1 dau., Elaine, b. 1979; edn: BS in pre-med., Univ. of Sto. Tomas (Manila) 1966, MD, 1971. Career: intern Deaconess Hosp., Milwaukee, Wisc. 1972-73; chief res. internal med. Wayne State Univ., Mich. 1973-75, Fellow Endocrinology Wayne St. Univ. 1975-76, Univ. Calif., San Francisco 1976-77; internist/ acting med. dir. Guadalupe Hlth Ctr. Daly City, 1977-871; pvt. practitioner, Daly City 1981--; staff Seton Med. Ctr.; recipient Annual Humanitarian Awd. for care of indigents in No. Calif. Cindy Smallwood Found. 1980; mem: AMA, World Med. Assn., Am. Geriatric Assn., Phil-Am Soc. of No. Calif., AAAS, Am. Rose Soc., past pres. St. Thomas Aquinas Research Soc.; med. journal articles; Republican; Catholic; rec: rosarian, piano, poet, bread making. Res: 43 Waverly Ct South San Francisco 94080 Ofc: 48 Park Plaza S., Ste. 306, Daly City 94015

CONKLIN, RONALD LEWIS, real estate co. executive; b. July 26, 1938, Omaha, Nebr.; s. Lewis Roscoe and Irma Virginia Conklin; m. Sara Dillon, Apr. 25, 1960; children: Sheryl, b. 1961; William, b. 1962; Denise, b. 1964; Damon, b. 1973; edn: BS, San Jose State 1961; MBA, Golden Gate Univ. 1981; expert appraiser, M.B.A.R.E. Career: department mgr. Peterson Tractor Co., Redding 1965-68; mgr. Woodren Realty, Castro Valley 1968-75; owner R.L.C. Comml. Real Estate, Sacto. 1975-78; pres./chief exec. Ron L. Conklin, Inc., Sacto. 1978--; cons. Trans Alaska Pipeline 1976; instr. Golden Gate Univ. Grad. Sch. of Fin. 1983; dir. Calif. Real Estate Ednl. Inc. 1983; honors: real estate cons. sev. large corps. 1983; Bd. of Ethics, Sacto. 83; mem: Am. Universities; Soc. for Adv. of Mgmt.; Ind. Appraisers Assn.; Sacto. Bd. Realtors; Blue Key; Elks; Veterans Club; mil: 1st lt. USAF 1961-64, var. decorations; Republican; Lutheran; rec: golf, bridge, equestrian. Res: 12977 Drummer Way Grass Valley 95945 Ofc: Ron L. Conklin, Inc., 2755 Cottage Way, Ste 20, Sacramento 95825

CONLON, JACK MARTIN, real estate executive; b. Oct. 8, 1931, Parsons, Ks.; s. John Thomas and Alice M. Conlon; m. Kathi Bergman, Feb. 29, 184; children: Lisa, b. 1955; Catherine, b. 1957; Julia (dec.), b 1958; edn: BS, Kansas Univ. 1957; USC 1957-58; CPA, Calif. 1960. Career: CPA, Peat Marwick Mitchell, Los Angeles 1957-59, Kansas City 1960-63; pres. Coachella Valley Savings & Loan, Palm Springs 1963-72; exec. v.p. Sunrise Co., Los Angeles 1972-76; pres., Palm Desert 1976--; pres. Tri-Co. Soc. of Savings & Loan Controllers 1966; instr. Am. Savings & Loan Inst. 1965, 66; mem: Phi Kappa Psi; United Way; Palm Springs Cov. & Visitors Bureau; Palm Springs CofC; mil: USN; Republican; rec: golf. Res: 70-263 Sonora Rd Rancho Mirage 92270 Ofc: 75-005 Country Club Dr Palm Desert 92260

CONMY, PETER THOMAS, city historian, librarian emeritus; b. July 8, 1901, San Francisco; s. Thomas Cherry and Mary Henrietta (Richter) C.; m. Emiliette Constance Storti, July 11, 1928; chil: (Mrs.) Constance Louise Prothero, b. 1929; Thomas Peter, b. 1934; edn: AB, UC Berkeley, 1924, MA, 1927, EdD, 1937; MA, Stanford Univ. 1941; MLS, UC Berkeley 1947; JD, Univ. of San Francisco 1952. Career: instr. San Francisco Public Schs. (tchr. Jr. High, Sr. High, Evening High), 1926-43; city librarian Oakland Pub. Library, 1943-69, ret. 1969, apptd. Librarian Emeritus and City Historian by Oakland City Council. Hist. writer on Native Sons of Golden West, Knights of Columbus; dir. Historical Reserve, 1937-; mem. Knights of Columbus (past Grand Knight), Elks (past Exalted Ruler), Am. Lib. Assn., Calif. Lib. Assn. (pres. 1961). Republican. Catholic. res. 1066 Ardmore Ave Oakland 94610

CONN, ROSCOE IMRIE, real estate broker, general contractor; b. Aug. 11, 1915, Roseburg, Ore.; s. Henry Roscoe and Ethel Estella (Imrie) C.; m. Mona Elizabeth Sehl, Dec. 29, 1939; children: Michael, b. 1941, Richard, b. 1945, Gregory, b. 1949; edn: BS, ag. engring., Ore. State Univ. 1939; honors cert. Ft. Ord Military (speech) 1944; spl. real estate courses, W. Valley Coll. 1979, R.E. Trainers Inc. 1982. Career: (current) broker/owner B&V Trailer and Barn Sales; gen. contr./owner B&V Constrn. Co., San Jose; (past) supr. Farm Security Adminstrn., Rural Rehab. Div., Ore., W 1946-52; owner/mgr. two equip. cos., Calif. 1952--; owner Four Star Motel; honors: Alpha Zeta (Agri.), Alpha Delta Sigma (journalism), Scabbard & Blade (mil.); mem. Australian mem. Nat. Fgn. Trade Council of NY 1949-51; Calif. St. CofC 1954-65; San Jose CofC; Elks; BSA scoutmaster; patent: for reverse- Ford Tractors 1953; mil: capt. US Army in S.W. Pacific, 1941-46 (Papaun Medal, S.W.P.A. Medal, Exp. Rifle, spl. commendn. Maj. Gen. H.H. Fuller); Catholic; rec: golf, hunting, fishing. Res: 14795 La Rinconada Dr Los Gatos 95030 ofc: B&V Trailer and Barn Sales, B&V Construction Co., 10000 Monterey Rd San Jose 95037

CONNELL, JOSEPH EDWARD ANTHONY, JR., lawyer; b. Sept. 1, 1947, Pueblo, Colo.; s. Joseph E.A. and Agnes Mary (Gustitis) Connell; edn: BA, Univ. of San Francisco 1969; MS, Univ. of Minn. 1974; JD, Pepperdine Univ. 1979. Career: pvt. practice 1979--; dir: Corbin Ins. Svcs., Inc.; Copek, Inc.; Palm Tree Investments, Inc.; instr. bus. law, Calif. Comm. Colls.; honors: Young Man of Yr., Knights of Columbus 1969; Am. Jurisprudence Awd. 1979; mem: Calif. State Bar (Income Tax Com.); Am. Bar Assn. (Com. on Entertainment & Sports, Tax Shelter Study Com., Com. of Income Taxes of Estates & Trusts); Fed. Bar Assn.; Orange Co. Bar Assn.; Knights of Columbus; Huntington- Valley Bus. Exch.; Catholic; rec: scuba diving. Res: 3204 S Artesia Santa Ana 92704 Ofc: 695 Town Center Dr, Ste 800, Costa Mesa 92626

CONNOLLY, JOHN WALTER, business owner; b. Feb. 21, 1935, Calif.; s. Walter and Niletta (La Gue) C.; m. Beverly, Feb. 24, 1957; children: Janic, b. 1958; Michael, b. 1959; Steven, b. 1960; Thomas, b. 1962; edn: liberal arts, Santa Clara 1956; R.E. lic., Anthony 1977. Career: mgr. Connolys Furniture, Fremont 1958-69; pres./ owner Connolly's Furniture 1970--; pres. Soil Shield Internat., Fremont 1982--; chmn. bd. Connolly Svcs., Fremont 1980--; CEO Irvington Enterprises 1975--; guest spkr. mktg. sems.; awards: Furniture Salesman of Yr., No. Calif.; Most Innovation Design, Furniture Guild 1977; mem: Western Design Forum; Gold Craft Furniture Buying Gp.; Bota Baggers Ski Orgn.; Contra Costas Sheriffs Posse; works: co- inventor, flotation waterbed 1977; publs: monthly arts. for a nat. furniture pub.; mil: sgt. USAR; Democrat; Catholic; rec: equestrian, water skiing, tennis. Res: 9 Greenslane Pleasanton 94566 Ofc: Soil Shield Internat., 40501 Fremont Blvd, Ste A, Fremont 94538

CONNOR, GARY EDWARD, marketing executive; b. Nov. 13, 1948, Staten Is., NY; s. Everett M. and Josephine (Amato) C.; edn: BSEE, Univ. Md. 1973, MBA, Univ. Santa Clara 1979. Career: Quality Assurance engr. Frankford Arsenal, Phila. 1973; QA engr./field service engr. Lockheed Electronics Co., Plainfield, NJ 1973-74; reliability engr. (1974-5), group leader memory test engring. (1975-7), sect. hd. bipolar prod. engring. (1977-9) Nat. Semiconductor Corp., Santa Clara, Ca. 1974-79; regional mktg. mgr. Am. Microsystems, Inc. Santa Clara 1979; product mktg. mgr. GeRad STI, Milpitas 1980-82; product mktg. exec. Advanced Micro Devices, Inc. Sunnyvale 1982--; Automated Test Equip. mktg. cons.; mem: IEEE, Franklin Mint Collectors Soc., Electronics Internat. Advis. Panel. Author VLSI Test article. Republican. Protestant. rec: coin collector, painter, horticulture, racquetball. res: 800 Saratoga Ave. Apt. 206A, San Jose 95129. ofc: Advanced Micro Devices Inc. 910 Thompson Pl. Sunnyvale 94086.

CONNORS, RAY, communications counselor; b. Aug. 26, 1908, Great Barrington, Mass; s. Michael W. and Agnes (Quigley) C.; edn: BA, Univ. Notre Dame, 1931; m. Jeannette Couture, 1939; chil: Michele, b. 1940; Andree, b. 1942; Stacie, b. 1958. Career: journalist, New England, 1931-41; airline pub. relations, 1941-48; publicity mgr. Lockheed Aircraft, 1950; pub. rels. dir. Stromberger, LaVene & MacKenzie, 1958; v.p. and West Coast pub. rels. mgr. D'Arcy-MacManus & Masius, Inc., to 1973; pres. TheRayConnorsCompany,Inc., 1973--. Honors: pres. Los Angeles Public Relations Counselors; chmn. bd. advisors Mount St. Mary's Coll.; hon. life mem. and pub. rels. counselor Calif. Mortgage Bankers Assn.; guest lectr. Calif. State Colleges;

Achievement Award, So. Calif. Mortgage Bankers Assn. Author, num. essays pub. in general periodicals. Republican. Catholic. Rec: travel, golf. Res: 22766 Tolana Dr. Laguna Niguel 92677

CONVERSANO, HENRY MICHAEL, interior designer; b. Dec. 17, 1931, NYC; s. William Michael and Alyce Katherine (Engelmann) C.; div.; children: Brad, b. 1961; Todd, b. 1962; edn: BA, Pratt Inst. 1955. Career: student designer Gorham Silver Co. 1953; student designer Ideal Toy Corp. 1954; sr. auto designer Gen. Motors Corp. 1955-57; sr. designer Maurice Sands 1957-61; pres. Henry Conversano & Assoc. 1961--; awards: Nat. Cotton Batting Inst. Awd. for Furniture Design; Mobil/ AAA 5-Star/ 5-Diamond Awds., Harrah's Tahoe Hotel; Interior Design Mag. Awd. for Hideaway Lounge, Harrah's Tahoe Hotel; mem: S.F. Mus. Soc.; Oakland Mus. Assn.; S.F. Mus. Mod. Art. Assn.; Retinitis Pigmentosa Found.; Save The Children; Sierra Club; St Anthony's found.; Animal Protection Inst.; Red Cross; Cousteau Soc.; Greenpeace; Foster Children Fund; invention: G.M. Auto Instrument Animated Warning Device; mil: spec. 4 US Army; rec: scuba diving, painting, sculpture. Res: 6451 Farallon Way Oakland 94611 Ofc: 57 Broadway Oakland 94618

CONWAY, JOYCE MAE, real estate broker; b. May 1, 1938, St. Genevieve, Mo.; d. Kenrick Eugene and Mary Eleanor (Huber) Yallaly; m. Harry G. Conway, Sept. 5, 1979; children: Dennis, b. 1956, Eric, b. 1963; Calif. lic. real estate broker 1979. Career: owner/broker Regency Real Estate, Modesto 1979--; mem. Del Rio Country club, Trade Club; Democrat; Catholic; rec: golf, fishing, tennis. Res: 2025 Miller Ave Modesto 95354 Ofc: Regency Real Estate, 1008 13th St Modesto 95354

COOK, DANIEL WESLEY, real estate broker, economist; b. July 7, 1936, Artesia, Calif.; s. Charles Franklin and Laurel Ellen (Iehl) C.; children: Dawn Elizabeth, b. 1959, Carla Ann, b. 1961, Todd Christopher, b. 1964; edn: BA, Univ. of Denver 1958, MA, 1959; lic. real estate broker, Calif. Career: prin. plnnr.j Ruth & Krushkhov, City and Regl. Plnng. Consultants, Berkeley 1963-67; chief plnnr. Daniel, Mann, Johnson & Mendenhall, Redwood City (S.F. Div.) 1967-68; projects plnnr./economist Wilsey & Ham Inc., cons. engrs., planners, architects, San Mateo 1968-71; economic/ plnng./ environmental consultant, San Ramon, Ca. dba Urban Devel. Analysts, 1971-75; sr. economist Engineering-Science Inc., Arcadia 1975-76; sr. economist Stone & Webster Engrng. Corp., Boston, Mass. 1976-80; currently self-empl. cons.; real estate broker 1983--; founder/pres./bd. chmn. Minds for Truth (non-profit sci., ednl. corp.), Nev.; mem. Nat. Assn. of Business Economists, Am. Mgmt. Assn., Commonwealth Club of Calif. works: spl. cons. on economic devel. and fin. of Minn. Exptl. City Project (futuristic high-tech. new city for 250,000 people) spearheaded by V.P. Hubert Humphrey, Univ. of Minn., and Dayton-Hudson Corp., 1968; spl. cons. New Cities Pgm., Public Land Law Rev. Commn., Wash. DC 1970; testified on New Towns pgm. for Calif., invited by Hon. Pete Wilson, then chmn. Calif. Assem. Com. on Urban Affairs and Housing, Sacto. 1969; profl. expert witness on land devel., urban plnng.; guest spkr. Townhall of Calif., Commonwealth Club of Calif., Am. Inst. of Planners, W. Regl. Sci. Assn.; publs: arts. in Bus. Digest Mag., Jour. of Housing, Univ. of N.M. Qrtrly., Calif. Architecture, Calif. Bldr. mags., 1960s; Prot. Res: 1140 Petree St, Ste. 137, El Cajon 92020

COOK, MARGUERITE FLORENCE, hotel public relations executive; b. Feb. 24, 1940, Buffalo, NY; d. James and Marguerite Florence (Bessel) McLachlan; edn: AA, Santa Monica City Coll. 1959; adv. edn. courses, UCLA 1960-1. Career: mktg. rep. Bank of Calif., Los Angeles 1970-72; corp. sales mgr. The Biltmore Hotel, L.A., 1972-74, director pub. relations/advt., 1974--; founder, L.A. Downtowners, 1982--. Mem: Civic Angels (pres. 1979-80), Pacesetters (pres. 1973), Hotel Sales Mgmt. Assn., L.A. Conservancy, Am. Women in Radio & TV, L.A. Athletic Club. Publ: L.A. Street Cookbook, 1983. Republican. Presbyterian. rec: photog., racquetball, paddle tennis. res: 17 Ave 18, Apt. 104, Venice 90291. ofc: The Biltmore Hotel, 515 S. Olive St., Los Angeles 90013.

COOK, ROBERT PRICE, II, market planning executive; b. Nov. 23, 1931, Baltimore, Md.; s. Edward Damerel and Emma Elizabeth (Tagmayer) C.; m. Eda Sernatinger, Jan. 15, 1977; children: Robert Price III; Susan Jean; edn: BS, Johns Hopkins Univ. 1960. Career: profl. football player/ coach: player, Pittsburgh Football (Steelers) 1952-54; player, Baltimore Football, Inc. (Colts) 1954-55; coach 1955-56; mktg. mgr./ tech. svcs. mgr., prod. mgr., dist. mgr, med. rep., Borden, Inc. 1956-71; dir. mktg. plng. Syntex Labs., Inc. 1971--; mem: Am. Chem. Soc.; Am. Mgmt. Assn.; Soc. of the Cincinnati; The Press Club of S.F.; Med. Mktg. Assn.; co-developer: Nutri- 1000 Complete Liquid Food, 1969; Disposable Diaper, Borden, Inc., patent denied; mil: lt. commdr. MSC USNR 1948-52; rec: racquetball, snorkeling, photog. Res: 270 Vernal Ct Los Altos 94022 Ofc: Syntex Laboratories, 3401 Hillview Ave Palo Alto 94304

COOK, WILLIAM ANDREW, engineering co. executive; b. Mar. 14, 1953, NY; s. John Joseph and Gloria Marie (Darino) C.; m. JoAnn Ricco, Sept. 5, 1976; children: Michael, b. 1968; Michell b. 1969; Jason, b. 1980e; edn: BS, Rutgers Univ. 1975; profl. engr., Calif. 1982. Career: O'Brien- Kreitzberg & Assoc., Inc., Cherry Hill, NJ; asst. proj. engr. 1975; proj. eng.; proj. mgr.; sr. proj. mgr. 1981; v.p., Los Angeles ofc. 1981--; sems. on const. claims & expert witness preparation; awards: Donald M. Barr Awd., Rutgers Univ. 1973; mem: Am. Soc. Civil Engrs.; Soc. of AM. Value Engrs.; Catholic; rec: tennis, bicycling, woodworking. Res: 2785 Shelterwood Ct Thousand Oaks 91362 Ofc: O'Brien- Kreitzberg & Assoc., Inc., 16000 Ventura Blvd, Ste 814, Encino 91436

COOLIDGE, KATHLEEN ALICE, artist; b. June 4, 1942, St. Paul, Minn.; d. James A. and Violet E. (Kelley) Smith; m. Stanley A. Collidge Sr.; 1 son: Stanley A., Jr.; edn: AA, Coll. of Marin 1962; BA, Univ. of Minn. 1964. Career: commercial artist, art designer (painted under maiden name, Kathleen Smith)/ fine arts and other art media (under name, Kathleen Coolidge); artist/owner Studio K, package design artist (All package designs used by Knotts Berry Farm, Exclusive Art design for 7 years); paintings in num. Fine Arts collections; awards include Spl. Award 1977 Nat. Paper Box & Packaging Assn., First Award 1980 Packaging Design Nat. Packaging Assn., Excellent Award 1980 Best Surface Design & Execution, Excellent Award 1981 Best Prodn. Designed Pkg.; life mem. Marin Soc. of Artists Inc.; fmr. tap dancer in US Armed Service Shows (troop danced with Bob Hope Show, Roy Rodgers Show and Red Skelton Show); mem. classic car clubs: New England T Register, Sorry Safari Touring Soc., Calif. T Register, San Francisco Penin. Register; Democrat; Congregational; rec: bird study, art, classic cars. Address: STudio K, 5 Arcangel Ct Fairfax 94930

COONEY, MARGARET LOUISE, accountant; b. Mar. 9, 1944, Long Beach; d. William Cromwell and Frances Marie (Kilpatrick) C.; edn: BS, CSU Long Beach 1971; MS, 1974. Career: jr. auditor Peat, Marwick & Mitchell, Los Angeles 1971-72; gen. acct. Sega of Am., Redondo Beach 1975-76; sr. cost acct. Elco Corp., El Segundo 1976-78; sr. fin. analyst Western Gear, Lynwood 1978--; awards: Calif. State Scholarship 1961; mem: Nat. Orgn. of Women; Am. Assn. of Univ. Women; Nat. Assn. Female Execs.; Democrat; skiing, gardening. Res: 7399 Katella Ave Stanton 90680 Ofc: Western Gear, 2600 E Imperial Hwy Lynwood 90262

COONS, JERRY, retail marketing executive, lawyer; b. Mar. 29, 1938, Chgo.; s. Clifford H. and Rethia N. (Stipp) C.; edn: Harvard Coll. 1955-59; JD, USC 1961. Career: secty-tm: Am. Arbitration Assn., Los Angeles Trial Lawyers Assn., Hollywood Bar Assn., Bus. and Profl. Assn., Apartment Owners Assn. of Los Angeles County; mil: 1st lt. USAF 1961-64. Ofc: The Pleasure Chest, 7733 Santa Monica Blvd Los Angeles 90046

COOPER, CECIL ARLEY EUGENE, clergyman; b. Mar. 14, 1918, Acmar, Ala.; s. Wiley Hugh and Mary Etta (Walker) C.; m. (Minnie) Lillian Cobb, Aug. 20, 1936; children: (Barbara) Gaile, b. 1937; (Linda) Diane, b. 1941; Timothy (Mark), b. 1947; Stephen (Paul), b. 1954; edn: spl. courses, bus. UC San Francisco, Am. Inst. of Banking S.F.; ordained minister, Ways & Praise Ministries 1974. Career: ins. agt. Washington Nat. Ins. Co., Memphis 1940-41; supr. E.I. Dupont, Millington, Tn. 1941-45; singer San Francisco Opera Assn. 1946-48; teller, insp., ops. ofcr., corp. ins. mgr. (asst. v.p.) Bank of Am., San Francisco 1945-68; founder/pres. Springs of Living Water Inc., Richardson Springs, Ca. 1968--; mem. American Baptist Men (pres. West Bay Assn., S.F. 1955-57; pres. Peninsula Assn. 1957-60; ofcr./pres. Am. Baptist Men of No. Calif. 1961-68); mem. conv. com. Am. Baptist Conv. (1965), Christian Businessmen's Conv. (1965); bd. dirs. Am. Baptist Churches of No. Calif., Pilgrim Haven Homes, and Am. Baptist Homes & Hosps. Assn., 1966-68; co-chmn. Regl. Convs. of Full Gospel Businessmen, S.F. (1966, 67, 68); founding adv. com. Teen Challenge, S.F. (chmn. Foundations Com. 1967-68); mem: Full Gospel Bus.men's Fellowship Intl. (founding pres. Tri Counties chpt. 1963-68); AARP; Star Route Carriers Assn.; past mem. Am. Guild of Musical Artists 1946-48, Bank & Trust Ins. Buyers of S.F. (chmn. 1964-68), Am. Soc. of Ins. Mgmt. (v.p. No. Calif. chpt. 64-68); mil: undercover FBI, WWII; Republican; Am. Baptist; rec: singing. Res: 1 Circle Dr Richardson Springs 95973 Ofc: Springs of Living Water Christian Ministries, Main Hotel, Richardson Springs 95973

COOPER, FRANK EVANS, savings & loan executive; b. Nov. 28, 1928, Seattle, Wash.; s. Frank and Margarete (Madison) Cooper; edn: BA, Univ. of Wash., 1952, MBA, 1963; m. Erlene Johnson, June 30, 1952; chil: Dawn (Keat), b. 1957; Frank Jr., b. 1960; career: with Commercial Credit Corp., Eugene & Medford, Ore. 1952-58; v. pres. Puget Sound Nat. Bank, Tacoma, Wash. 1958-63; pres./CEO/ dir. Bank of Tacoma (Wash.), 1963-66; Commissioner of Banking, State of Wash., Olympia, Wash. 1966-69; sr. vice pres. Bank of Honolulu (Hawaii) 1970-73, pres./CEO/dir. 1974-78; pres/CEO/dir. Equitable Savings & Loan Assn., Huntington Beach, Calif. 1979--. DIr., United Pacific Airlines, Sydney, Aus.; fmr. trustee, Univ. Wash. Banking Sch.; fmr. Washington State legislator; past dir., Nat. Assn. of Banking Commissioners; past dir. Pacific Coast AAA League; fmr. chmn. Tacoma Community Coll.; Mem: University Union Club-Tacoma, past pres.; Masons, Shriners, Royal Order of Jesters; Young Mens Business Club, past pres.; Waikiki Yacht Club; Outrigger Canoe Club; Indian Palms Country Club; Plaza Club; Oahu Country Club; Honolulu Rotary, Huntington Beach Rotary; Crater Lions Club past pres; Navy League; Indian Palms Tennis CLub; Magic Island; Capitol Hill Club (Wash. DC); mil: WOJG US Army, 82nd Airborne Div.; Republican, elected Hawaii Repub. chmn., Del. to Repub. Nat. Convs. 1964, 68, 80; Presbyterian; rec: tennis; res: 7772 Sailboat Cir. Huntington Beach 92648 ofc: Equitable Savings & Loan PO Box 2700 Huntington Beach 92647.

COOPER, JOSEPH, lawyer, realtor; b.Dec. 20, 1937, Hemingway, S.C.; s. Harmon and Mary (McCutcheon) C.; 1 son: Kenneth, b. 1962; edn: JD, McGeorge Sch of Law 1969. Career: attorney at law, owner and pres. Joseph Cooper Law Corp., 1970--, corp. pres. since 1980; realtor, owner Cooper Real Estate Service, 1965--; honors: recipient Resolution of Calif. Legislature, 1971, and City of Sacramento, 1972, for community activities; mem: Calif. State Bar, Sacramento Co. Bar Assn., Calif. Trial Lawyers Assn., Nat. Bar Assn., Am. Trial Lawyers Assn.; mil: E-4 US Army 1960-62; Democrat; Methodist; rec: movies, travel, sports. res: 23 Sail Ct., Sacramento 95831. ofc: Joe Cooper Law Corp., 901 H St, #403, Sacramento 95814.

COOPER, JOSEPH GIBSON, program management systems executive; b. Sept. 13, 1924, Hackettstown, N.J.; s. Marin and Maybelle (Speer) Cooper; edn: AB,

Lafayette Coll., 1945, MBA, Harvard Univ., 1948. m. Joan Shaw, March 28, 1959; chil: Susan, b. 1960, Carol, b. 1961, Joseph Gibson III, b. 1963, Kathryn, b. 1968; career: Systems Analyst, McCall Corp., Dayton, Ohio, 1949-50, Sr. Budget Analyst, Ford Motor Co., Dearborn, Mich., 1953-60, Sr. Budget Analyst, No. Amer. Aviation, Inc., Downey, Ca., 1960-66, Asst. to Corp. Dir., Program Management Systems, Hughes Aircraft Co., El Segundo, CA, 1966--. R.E. Broker, Realtor Associate, Kent Realty, L.A. 1973--; Honors: Listed in Who's Who in California Business & Finance, First Edition 1980-81; mem.: Bd. of Trustees & Bd. of Deacons, Covenant Presbyterian Church, L.A., pres., Theta Delta Chi, Orange County Grad. Assoc., 1963; Pres., Harvard Business School Club of San Diego, 1960-61; Mason, F. & A.M., 1954--; Scottish Rite Bodies, 1954--; Al Malaikah Shrine Temple, L.A. 1962--; mem: Planning Executives Inst., L.A., 1950--; Vice Chairman, Republican Central Committee, 50th Assembly District, L.A. County, 1978--. Mil.: Lt. (j.g.) USNR, 1943-46, WWII, Philippine Liberation Medal, Lt. USNR, 1950-53, Korea, Pacific Theater. Republican; Presbyterian; rec: tennis, swimming; res.: 7517 Alverstone Ave., Los Angeles 90045 ofc: Hughes Aircraft Co., Corporate Offices, 200 N. Sepulveda Blvd., El Segundo 90245.

COOPER, LEONARD WILLIAM, business services co. president; b. Feb. 6, 1927, Minco, Okla.; s. Loys William and Della Eva (Lakin) C.; children: Daniel T., b. 1950; Melody Anne, b. 1954; edn: BS, UCLA 1952; MBA, 1954. Career: senior acct. Edling, Anawalt, Matsen & Sneed, CPAs, Los Angeles 1952-56; controller Mathews Paint Co., L.A. 1957-60; ops. mgr. Gallo Wine Co., Commerce 1960-68; v.p. Wine Merchants, Ltd. Syracuse, NY 1968-75; pres./CEO: Telecheck Orange Co., Inc.; Telecheck Central NY; Telecom Bus. Svcs., Inc. 1976--; mem: Rotary Club, Commerce; Garden Grove & Santa Ana CofCs; Orange Co. Check Investigators Assn.; works: shirt collar mechanism, pat. pend.; Republican; Methodist; rec: golf, tennis. Res: 1521 W Eucalyptus Ct Ontario 91761 Ofc: Telecheck Orange Co., Inc., 12345 Westminster Blvd Santa Ana 92703

COOPER-LEWTER, NICHOLAS CHARLES, counseling center director; b. June 25, 1948, Wash DC; s. Rufus Cleveland Lewter, Jr. and Majel Hoage Baxter; adopted s. Ernest Charles and Constance (Hoage) Cooper; chil: Michelle Marie, b. 1969, Sonia Renee, b. 1971, Sean Darcy, b. 1973, Nicholas Jr., b. 1980; edn: BA in psych/soc., Ashland Coll. 1970; MSW, Univ. Minn. 1976; PhD cand., psychology, Calif. Coast Univ.; seminary, Ecumenical Ctr. for Black Church Studies. Ordained Baptist minister. Lic. MFCC, State of Calif. Career: rsrch splst. Ctr for Youth Devel. & Research, Univ. Minn. 1972-3, tchg. asst. Sch of Social Work, 1974; group worker Hallie Q. Brown/ M.L.K. Ctr, St. Paul, Minn. 1973-4; investigator St. Paul Dept. of Human Rights, 1974-5; center dir. Lewter Inst., Fountain Valley, Ca. 1976-78, Cooper Lewter Hypnosis Ctr/Medical Hypnosis Ctr., Newport Bch 1978--; pres. Cooper Lewter Enterprises, 1980; pres. Christian Wholeness Co., 1983-; pastor/founder C.R.A.V.E. Christ Ministries Inc. 1983--; bd.dirs. Montessori Sch., Minn. 1974-5; adv./cons. So. Calif. Acrobatic Team 1979; cons. US Olympic Team (NRA) 1983; cons. Cal-State Fullerton Football Pgm.,1983; cons. Chapman Coll. Basketball Pgm., 1983; cons. Drew Postgrad. Med. Sch., 1980. Coauthor: Soul: A Working Theology, Harper & Row (1983-84); author: C.R.A.V.E. Christ and Win (1983-84); articles, profl. med. jours. Honors: Hon. PhD, Teamer Sch of Religion; listed Who's Who Among Black Americans 1980-1; Outstanding Young Men of Am. 1983. Mem: Omega Psi Phi (founding pres. Xi Theta chpt. Ashland Coll. 1966-70); Nat. urban League; NAACP; Nat. Assn of Social Workers; Acad. of Certified Soc. Workers; Soc. of Med. Hypnoanalysts (bd.dirs. 1977-); cons. in Christian Counseling 1981-, assoc. minister 2d Baptist Ch., Los Angeles. rec: karate, bowling, tennis. ofc: Cooper Lewter Ctr. 355 Placentia, Ste. 205, Newport Beach 92663.

COOPER, MICHELE MARIE, company president; b. Jan. 20, 1948, Muskegon, Mich.; d. Russell L., Sr. and Betty Jean (Lightfoot) Cooper; edn: cert. Healds Bus. Coll. 1971; spl. courses, communications, CSU Long Beach, CSU Fullerton. Career: freelance secretarial svc. var. aircraft cos., 1971-78, Haladay Publs., 1978-81; self-empl. owner/pres. Speedy Fingers Inc. (secretarial svc.) 1981--, and Aurora, Unlimited (consulting, pub. rels.), 1983--; coauthor (w/ Russ Cooper) The Family Cooper (pub. Aurora, Unltd. 1983); sev. books in progress; honors: listed in Daily Pilot (newspaper), Saluting Orange Coast's Women in Business (1983); mem: WESA (assoc. dir. 1983-85); NOW; WIM; Cetacean Soc.; Romance Writers Assn.; Fullerton CofC; Group W Cable Club (Fullerton); Hospice Ever Health In-Home Care (steering com., vol.); Battered Women (secty. 1981); World Vision (1983); mil: YN3, yeoman/Pentagon, US Navy 1967-70, VietNam War medal; Republican; rec: writing, photog., crafts. Res: 317 N. Cambridge Orange 92666 Ofc: Fullerton Finl. Towers, 1440 N. Harbor Blvd, Ste. 800, Fullerton 92635

COOPER, M. SCOTT, lawyer; b. Jan. 24, 1950, Burbank; s. Theodore H. and Alice (Hatchett) C.; m. Debra Ann Colletti, Aug. 18, 1979; edn: AB, UCLA 1976; JD, 1979. Career: owner retail electronics bus, nat. photography chain; currently, atty. Brobeck, Phleger & Harrison, Los Angeles; adj. prof. of law Whittier Coll. 1980-; extern clerk Hon. James Cobey, Assoc. Justice, Calif. Ct. of Appeal 1978; ed. UCLA Law Review 1978-79; mem: Order of the Coif; Gr. L.A. Area CofC; author: Financial Sanctions Imposed Directly Against Attorneys in Litigation Without Resort to Contempt Power, 26 UCLA Law Reveiw 855, 1979; Republican; Episcopal. Ofc: Brobeck, Phleger & Harrison, 444 S Flower St, Ste 4300, Los Angeles 90017

COOPERMAN, STEVEN G., physician, eye surgeon; b. Mar. 3, 1942, NY; s. Nathan and Pearl (Dardick) C.; m. Nancy Graef, Oct. 22, 1983; children: Jacki, b. 1969; Kelly, b. 1972; edn: BS, UC Berkeley 1962; MD, Northwestern Med. Sch. 1966. Career: intern, res., ophthalmology, UCLA 1966-67, 1969-72; chief res. eye surgery Jules Stein Eye Inst. 1972; Food & Drug Admin., Wash. DC 1967-69; founder Am. Intraocular Implant Soc. 1974; tchg. staff Jules Stein Eye Inst., UCLA; currently, eye surgeon, Beverly Hills; dir. Ulta Med. Devices, Inc.; cons. in lens implant field, num. cos.; honors: Fight for Sight Fellowship 1966; Los Angeles Soc. of Physicians 1983; mem: AMA; Am. Acad. of Ophthalm.; Royal Soc. of Health; works: development of intra ocular lens; Republican; rec: tennis, music, travel. Res: 12250 Richwood Dr Los Angeles 90049 Ofc: 435 N Roxbury Dr Beverly Hills 90210

COPESKEY, PAUL ROBERT, chiropractor; b. Sept. 12, 1954, St. John's, Newfoundland, nat. 1974; s. Robert John and Maureen Kay (Hogan) C.; m. Megan, Aug. 12, 1979; 1 dau., Jessica, b. 1984; edn: undergrad., CSU San Diego 1975-78; BS, L.A. Coll. of Chiropractic, 1980, DC (cum laude), 1981; postgrad. seminars, human biomechanics (2500 hrs.); Diplomate Nat. Bd. of Chiro. Examiners. Career: chiropractor pvt. practice, dir. Torrey Pines Chiropractic Clinic, San Diego; instr. Los Angeles Coll. of Chiro. for postgrad. relicensing seminars (1981, 82, 83); Health Fair dir. for Encinitas Annual Flower Festival; mem: Am., Calif. Chiro. Assns., San Diego Chiro. Soc., Delta Tau Alpha frat., Delta Sigma (hon. scholastic); Chiropractic Toastmasters (pres.); Parker Chiro. Research Found.; Kiwanis; bd. mem. San Dieguito Boys and Girls Club; bd. Encinitas CofC, bd. Am. Cancer Soc. of S.D., Democrat, Catholic, rec. golf, surfing. Res: 309 Trailview Ave Encinitas 92024 Ofc: Torrey Pines Chiropractic Clinic 10665 Sorrento Valley Rd, Ste. 101, San Diego 92121

COPLEY, HELEN KINNEY, publisher; b. Nov. 28, Cedar Rapids, Iowa; d. Fred Everett and Margaret (Casey) Kinney; m. James S. Copley, Aug. 16, 1965 (dec. 1973); 1 son: David Casey, b. 1952. Career: chmn. of the corp./chmn. exec. com./dir. The Copley Press, Inc., La Jolla 1973--, CEO/sr. mgmt. bd., 1974--; chmn. bd. Copley News Service, San Diego 1973--; publisher The San Diego Union and The Tribune, S.D.; chmn. editorial bd. Union-Tribune Pub. Co., 1976-; chmn. bd., trustee James S. Copley Found., 1974-; dir. Freedoms Found. at Valley Forge 1973-; v.chmn. bd. trustees, Univ. of San Diego, 1973-; trustee, Scripps Clinic and Resrch Found., 1973-. Mem: La Jolla Mus. Contemporary Art; S.D. Hall of Sci.(life); Nat.Press Club, Wash DC; S.D. Press Club; San Francisco Press Club, Gr. L.A. Press Club, Wash. Crossing Found. (hon. chmn., dir.); Am. Newspaper Publ. Assn. (dir. ANPA; vice chmn. & trustee ANPA Found.); Am. Soc. Newspaper Editors; Am. Press Inst.; Calif. Newspaper Publ. Assn.; Calif. Press Assn.; Nat. Newspaper Assn.; San Diego CofC; La Jolla Town Council, Inc.; Scripps Mem. Hosp. Aux.; UN Assn. of Am. (hon. bd.mem.); YWCA (life); ZoologicalSoc. of S.D.; Star of India Aux. (life); S.D. Soc. of Natural Hist.; (life) Patroness, Makua Auz.; Friends of Internat. Center, La Jolla; S.D. Sym. Assn.; Republican Assocs. So. Calif.; Sigma Delta Chi; Aurora (Ill.) CC; Univ. S.D. Pres.; La Jolla Beach and Tennis Club; La Jolla CC; Cuyamaca; S.D. Yacht. Roman Catholic. res: 7007 Country Club Dr. La Jolla 92037. ofc: 7776 Ivanhoe Ave. La Jolla 92037.

CORBETT, LAURENCE PAUL, labor lawyer; b. Oct. 7, 1920, Boston, Mass.; s. Laurence A. and Helena Louretta (Foley) C.; m. Rosalie Taylor, May 31, 1947; children: Constance, b. 1950; Laurence, b. 1952; edn: AB, cum laude, Harvard Coll. 1943; JD, Harvard Law Sch. 1948; admitted to practice, Conn. Bar Assn. 1950, Calif. Bar Assn. 1952. Career: asst. indsl. rels. dir. Yale & Towne Mfg. Co., Stamford, Ct. 1948-50; staff counsel East Bay Employees Assn., Oakland 1950-52; partner St. Sure, Moore & Corbett, Attys. 1952-56; sr. partner Corbeet, Kane, Berk & Barton, Attys., San Francisco & Oakland 1966--; adj. prof. UC Labor Mgmt. Sch. 1970-74; adj. prof. Golden Gate Univ. Grad. Sch. of Bus. 1975-; mem: Am. Bar Assn. (State Law Devel. Com.) Bar Assn. of Calif. (Labor Counsel); Am. Cancer Soc.; Oakland Ctr. of Jr. Arts & Scis. (pres. 1961); works: papers & arts. on labor & employment law; text for Golden Gate Univ. class on labor law & law rels. in health care field; mil: correspondent, US Army News Svc., Persian Gulf Command 1943-46; Republican; Catholic; rec: jogging, swimming, tennis. Res: 20 Yankee Hill Oakland 94618 Ofc: Corbett, Kane, Berk & Barton, 100 Bush St, Ste 1600, San Francico 94103 & 2200 Powell St, Ste 500, Oakland 94608

CORDELL, BRUCE MONTEITH, space scientist, geophysicist; b. Sept. 10, 1949, Shelby, Mich.; s. Carl C. and Ruth M. (Lightfoot) C.; m. Lee Clark, Aug. 3, 1977; edn: BS, Mich. State Univ. 1971; BS, UCLA 1973; PhD, Univ. of Ariz. 1977. Career: Weizmann research fellow Calif. Inst. of Tech., Pasadena 1977-78; asst. prof. Central Conn. State Univ., New Britain, Ct. 1978-80; asst. prof. Calif. State Coll., Bakersfield 1980-84; senior engr. Gen. Dynamics/ Convair, San Diego 1984--; frequent spkr. Reuben H. Fleet Space Theater, San Diego 1983-; instr. UCSD Ext. 1984; sev. San Diego TV appearances, space related; awards: Weizmann Postdoctoral Research Fellowship, Caltech 1977; mem: Am. Astronomical Soc.; Am. Astronautical Soc.; Am. Geophysical Union; British Interplanetary Soc.; Nat. Space Inst.; UCLA Alumni Assn.; Univ. of Ariz. Alumni Assn.; San Diego Hall of Sci.; Zoological Soc. of San Diego; works: num. tech. & pop. publs. in areas of planetary physics, climatic change & space missions; author, The Planet Mercury, (to be pub., Cambridge Univ. Press); Republican; Presbyterian; rec: sci-fi; film/TV cons. space related. Res: 3551 Normount Rd Oceanside 92056

CORDONE, ANDREW DONALD, engineer; b. Aug. 15, 1956, Yonkers, NY; s. Gino and Anita (Pavone) C.; m. Lynne, Apr. 4, 1982; 1 dau: Andrea, b. 1982; edn: BS, Manhattan Coll. 1978; MS, UC Berkeley 1982; profl. engr. Consumer Affairs 1981. Career: Pacific Gas & Electric Co., San Francisco 1978--; field engr. 1978-80; chief field engr. 1980-81; proj. contracts analysis engr., Helms Proj. 1982--; honors: Employee Suggestion Awd. ($25,000), Pacific Gas & Elec. Co. 1981; mem: Chi Epsilon frat.; rec: hunting, fishing, investments. Res: 461 N Echo Fresno 93701 Ofc: Pacific Gas & Electric Co., Helms Proj.- POB 2567, Fresno 93745

CORENMAN, DONALD STEVEN, chiropractor; b. Nov. 20, 1954, Los Angeles; s. Samuel and Dorothy (Slavin) C.; edn: CSU Northridge; BS, L.A. Coll. of Chiro. 1976; DC, 1978; cert. chiro. orthopedics, 1983. Career: dir. McKillican Chiropratic Clinic, San Diego 1979-80; owner/ principal doctor Corenman Chiropractic Ofc., Reseda 1980--; guest lectr. Los Angeles Coll. of Chiro 1983; mem: Calif. Chiro. ASsn.; Am. Chiro. Assn. (Council on Sports Injuries, Council on Nutrition); Reseda Kiwanis (pres. 1982-833); Reseda CofC (dir. 1981-83); Steering Com. Reseda Sr. Multipurpose Ctr. 1983; Toastmasters, Northridge; rec: scuba diving, skiing, racquetball. Res: 18411 Hatterus, Apt 224, Tarzana 91356 Ofc: Corenman Chiropractic, 6853 Reseda Blvd Reseda 91335

COREY, ALBERT De WOOD, real estate broker, HUD construction analyst; b. March 14, 1926, Los Angeles; s. Roy De Wood and Frosina Shibley (Deeb) Corey; edn: pre-dental, LA City Coll., UCLA; real estate cert., Santa Monica City Coll., 1971; m. Patricia Lesmeister, 1963; chil: Alan, b. 1964, Janel, b. 1965, James, b. 1966, Michelle, b. 1967, Loren Courtney (stepson) b. 1959; career: owner/mgr. retail businesses: Corey's Market, Corey's General Store, Corey's Liquor, 5-Corners Liquor, Marina Paint and Hardware Co., Corey's Trucking and Hauling, 1949-68; lic. Calif. Real Estate Broker and lic. General contractor (1968), owner Corey's Real Estate Co. and A.D. Corey General Contractor, 1968-71, sr. constrn analyst,Dept. HUD, Los Angeles Area Office, 1971-72, Single Family Architectural Constrn. Analyst, 1972-73, Single Family Archtl. Reviewer, 1973, sr. constrn. multifamily cost analyst, 1973-75, realty contract spec., 1975-77, maintenance engineer 1977-78, construction analyst, 1978--, and coordinator with the state of Calif. for the Federally Funded Low Income Energy Assistance Program, 1980--; mil: radio mech., Army Air Force 1944-46; Republican; Catholic; rec: boating; res: 5105 Pacific Ave. Marina Del Rey 90291.

CORNISH, LARRY BRIAN, lawyer; b. July 13, 1946, Kingston, NY; s. Harry Preston and Beverly Mae (Schmidt) C.; edn: BA, George Washington Univ. 1968; JD, 1973; admitted to practice, NY & Calif. 1974. Career: legis. counsel Hon. Edith S. Green, US House of Reps. 1973-74; spl. cons. Ofc. of Fed. Agcy. Safety Pgms., Occupational Safety & Health Admin. (Pres. Report) 1974; dir. Fed. Affairs Div. Am. Speech & Hearing Assn., Wash. DC 1974-76; volunteer counsel, The Pres. Ford Com., Wash. DC 1975-76; exec. dir./ gen. counsel Irwin Lehrhoff, PhD & Assoc., Beverly Hills 1976-77; v.p./ gen. counsel/ secty Beverly Enterprises, Pasadena 1983--; dir. Nat. Councli on Health Ctrs.; legal counsel Calif. Speech Pathologists & Audiologists in Pvt. Practice; mem: Nat. Health Lawyers Assn.; Am. Bar Assn.; Calif. Bar Assn.; mil; Spec. 6, US Army 1969-70, Bronze Star, Air Medals (2); Republican; Dutch Reformed; rec: backpacking, philately, x-c skiing. Res: 3hysician; b. July 6, 1913, NYC; s. Charles Reynold and Mildred (Freeman) C.; m. Mary Mayo, May 8, 1948; m. 2d. Nancy Bennett, Sept. 3, 1983; edn: AB, Harvard Coll. 1934; MD, Harvard Med. Sch. 1938; clinical prof. of med., USC 1953, presently, clinical prof. emeritus. Career: intern Mass. Gen. Hosp., Boston, Mass. 1939-40; res. cardiology 1940; clinical clerk Queens Square Neurological Inst., London, England 1940; fellow, physiology Western Reserve Univ. 1941; attend. physician Co. USC, Los ANgeles 1946-57; attend. physician Huntington Meml. Hosp., Pasadena 1946-77; attend. physician Good Samaritan Hosp., Los Angeles 1977--; chmn. bd. Found. for Cardiovascular Research, Pasadena; mem: Los Angeles Acad. of Med.; fellow Am. Coll. of Physicians; fellow Am. Heart Assn.; Am. Coll. Cardiology; Univ. Club of Pasadena; Calif. Club, Los Angeles; works: Heart Block, w/ Michael Bilitch, MD; mil: US Army 1942-46; Republican; Episcopal; rec: skiing, tennis. Res: 2575 Limbardy Rd San Marino 91108 Ofc: 1245 Wilshire Blvd Los Angele 90017

CORTEY, NOLE, mathematician; b. Dec. 1944, France; US cit.; s. Jean and Anne C.; m. Judith Pelt, Mar. 18, 1983; edn: BS in math., Univ. of Lyon 1966; MS mech. eng., AM Polytech. 1966; MS math. (pure), Univ. of Paris VI, 1967; PhD math. (pure), Henri Poincare Inst. 1970. Career: asst. prof. Dept. Math. and Computer Sci., Univ. of Sherbrooke, Canada 1971-4; independent cons. local cos., and lectr. (part time) in math. and systems sci., 1974-78; sci. computer appls. analyst (1978-80), research splst./ automation systems engr.; mathematician (probability & statistics), Lockheed Calif. Co. 1980--; lectr. in math. CSU Northridge, CSU Los Angeles; awards: $400 award for two publs., Lockheed 1982; invited to present papers at Optimization Days Conv., Montreal 1983-4, SIAM Conf. in numerical analysis, Boulder, Colo. 1984; mem: Am. Mathematical Soc., Math. Assocs. of Am., Soc. Mathematique de France, Assn. for Computing Machinery, Lockheed Mgmt. Assn.; bd. dirs. Shadow Glen Homeowners Assn. (vp 1983); author (textbook), Modern Elementary Linear Algebra (Univ. Press of Am. 1978), arts. in sci. journals; mil: math instr. (Quebec) for Fr.; Democrat: Christian; rec: tennis, micro computers, real estate dev. Res: San Bernardino Ofc: Lockheed, Box 551, Dept. 78-30, Burbank 91520

CORY, CAROL, financial planner; b. Sept. 5, 1948, Memphis, Tenn.; d. Charles Franklin and Mary (Liddell) Cory; m. Luis Fondevila, Dec. 14, 1980; edn: BA, honors, Ga. State Univ. 1970; Reg. Securities Principal; Certified Fin. Planner, Coll. Fin. Plnng. 1984. Career: owner Surety Investment Services, fin. planning firm (spec. in tax sheltered annuities for public sch. employees and non-profit orgns.) splst. in field 1978--; branch mgr., NASD broker/ dealer, Titan Capital Corp.; honors: Alpha Lambda Delta, Crimson Key; mem: Internat. Assn. of Fin. Plnnrs., Inst. of CFPs, Am. Assn. of Univ. Women; Episcopal; rec: ballet, raising birds. Res: 2323 Canyon Dr Hollywood 90068 Ofc: Surety Investment Services, 4050 Wilshire Blvd, Ste. 507, Los Angeles 90010

COSBY, RICHARD SHERIDAN, physician; b. July 6, 1913, NYC; s. Charles Reynold and Mildred (Freeman) C.; m. Mary Mayo, May 8, 1948; m. 2d. Nancy Bennett, Sept. 3, 1983; edn: AB, Harvard Coll. 1934; MD, Harvard Med. Sch. 1938; clinical prof. of med., USC 1953, presently, clinical prof. emeritus. Career: intern Mass. Gen. Hosp., Boston, Mass. 1939-40; res. cardiology 1940; clinical clerk Queens Square Neurological Inst., London, England 1940; fellow, physiology Western Reserve Univ. 1941; attend. physician Co. USC, Los ANgeles 1946-57; attend. physician Huntington Meml. Hosp., Pasadena 1946-77; attend. physician Good Samaritan Hosp., Los Angeles 1977--; chmn. bd. Found. for Cardiovascular Research, Pasadena; mem: Los Angeles Acad. of Med.; fellow Am. Coll. of Physicians; fellow Am. Heart Assn.; Am. Coll. Cardiology; Univ. Club of Pasadena; Calif. Club, Los Angeles; works: Heart Block, w/ Michael Bilitch, MD; mil: US Army 1942-46; Republican; Episcopal; rec: skiing, tennis. Res: 2575 Limbardy Rd San Marino 91108 Ofc: 1245 Wilshire Blvd Los Angele 90017

COSGROVE, THERESA WEGNER, museum administrator; b. June 25, 1950, South Bend, Ind.; d. William C. and Agnes Theresa (Egan) Wegner; m. Steven W. Cosgrove, June 6, 1981; edn: BFA, Univ. of Wisc. 1972; Diplome d'Estudes Francaises, Universite de Tours, France 1978; MA, John F. Kennedy Univ. 1984; cert. of completion, Museum Mgmt. Inst., UC Berkeley 1982. Career: gallery asst. Foster Gallery, Univ. of Wisc. 1970-72; resource ctr. asst. Mnpls.. Inst. of Arts, Mnpls., Minn. 1975; slide lib. asst. Photo Archives & sr. gallery asst. Coffman Gallerios, Univ. of Minn. 1975-77; curatorial asst. Minn. Mus. of Art, St. Paul, Minn. 1979-81; dir. Chippewa Valley Mus., Eau Claure, Wisc. 1981-83; asst. dir./ curator Presidio Mus., San Francisco 1983--; Spkrs. Bureau, Mnpls. Inst. of Arts 1975-78, 1980-82; Spkrs. Bureau, Presidio of San Francisco 1983-; grants reviewer Inst. of Mus. Svcs., Wash. DC 1983-; awards: Grad. Fellowship, Rotary Internat., France 1978-79; N.E.H. Grant, 1981; N.E.A. Fellowship & Art Mus. Scholarship 1982; mem: Internat. Council of Mus.; Amm. Assn. of Mus.; Calif. Hist. Soc.; Graphic Arts Council, S.F.; Alliance Francaise; Nat. Ski Patrol; works: var. mus. scholarly catalogs incl.: Melanesian Images, 1981; A Century of Fashion, 1880-1980, 1980; The History of Lace, 1979; A Visit to the Past, Inside Eau Claire, 1982; rec: French gourmet cooking, travel, photog. Res: POB 29003 San Francisco 94129 Ofc: Presidio Museum, Funston Ave at Lincoln Blvd San Francisco 94129

COSTA, DONALD JOSEPH, JR., investment banker; b. Sept. 20, 1947, Oakland; s. Donald Joseph Sr. and Ann (LaConte) C.; m. Kim Miller, Apr. 30, 1947, Oakland; s. Donald Joseph Sr. and Ann (LaConte) C.; m. Kim Miller, Apr. 30, 1982; children: Jennifer, b. 1975; Michael, b. 1979; Thomas, b. 1979; Julianne, b. 1983; edn: AA, Modesto Jr. Coll. 1975; BA, La. State Univ. 1980; reg. securities rep., SEC 1981. Career: self- empl. Don Costa Ins. Co., Modesto 1971-75; dist. mgr. General Host Corp., New Orleans, La. 975-81; acct. exec. Dean Witter Reynolds, Modesto 1981--; Pres.' Club, Dean Witter 1982-83; sem. instr.; fin. plnr.; honors: Century Club 1982 & Pres.' Club 1983, Oppenheimer Mgmt. Corp.; First Capital Awd., First Capital Corp. 1983; mem: Stanislaus Co. Democratic Central Com.; Democratic State Party Central Com.; Modesto CofC (Legis. & Agricultural Coms.); State Sen. Dan McCorquodale (fund raising chair); Garamendi for Gov. Campaign (fund raising chair); Stanislaus Co. Civitans; Fathers Rights Orgn.; Assemblyman Gard Condit (re-elec. com.); mil: personnelman 3/c, USN 1971; N.A.S. New Orleans; Vietnam Vet; Democrat; Catholic; rec: profl. entertainer. Res: 3228 Clogston Way Modesto 95354 Ofc: Dean Witter Reynold, Inc., 3025 McHenry Ave Modesto 95352

COSTANDI, MIREILLE ALPHONSE, engineer; b. Sept. 14, 1941, Cairo, Egypt, nat. 1971; d. Alphonse and Sophie (Harari) Rothstein; m. Wahib Costandi, July 3, 1969; edn: BS, Am. Univ., Cairo 1964; MS, Univ. of San Francisco 1969; MBA, Univ. of Santa Clara 1975. Career: researcher in fuel and chem. systems, licensing, mktg. Gen. Electric Co., San Jose 1970s--, currently senior engr./pgm. mgr. for engineering services, software related; mem. Am. Nuclear Soc., Am. Chemical Soc.; contbr. internal GE publs. Res: 22999 Voss Ave Cupertino 95014 Ofc: General Electric, 175 Curtner Ave San Jose 95125

COTECSON, EDWIN MERCADO, civil engineer; b. Feb. 18, 1942, Surigao, Philippines, nat. 1974; s. Melecio Toraja and Encarnacion Basmayor (Mercado) C.; m. Luz V. Marco, July 8, 1972; children: Eric, b. 1977, Darryl, b. 1978; edn: BSCE, honors, Cebu Inst. of Tech., Phil. 1964; grad. schs. of civil engring., CSU San Diego 1977-78, CSU Long Beach 1981-82; Reg. Profl. Engr. (Civil), Calif. 1977. Career: jr. civil engr. Bur. of Public Hwys., Surigao, Phil. 1965-68; constrn. estimiator Owl Engineering, Compton, Ca. 1968-71; jr./asst. civil engr. San Diego Co. Dept. of Sanitation & Flood Control 1972-78; assoc. civil engr. City of Sun Valley 1979-81; assoc. struc. engr./civil engr., Building & Safety, City of Long Beach 1981--; pvt. cons. in struc. engring.; mem. Nat. Soc. of Profl. Engrs., ASCE, Toastmasters Internat.; Republican; Christian; rec: camping, movies. Res: 1010 Essex St San Diego 92103 Ofc: City of Long Beach, 333 West Ocean, 4th Flr., Long Beach 90802

COSTELLO, GARY STEVE, certified public accountant; b. Nov. 29, 1953, Walnut Creek; s. William Robert and Dorothy Louisa (Foster) C.; edn: BS, Cal Poly, SLO 1976; JD, Golden Gate Univ. 1985; CPA, Bd. Consumer Affairs 1979. Career: acct. Trousdale Mc Loughlin & Chiquette 1977-78; CPA Hanes & Co. 1978--; mem: Am. Inst. CPAs; Calif. Soc. CPAs; Pleasanton Jaycees; Republican; Protestant; rec: sports, gardening. Res: 4639 James Ave Castro Valley 94546 Ofc: Hanse & Co., 1544 B Street, Ste 200 Hayward 94541

COTTAM, CALVIN, chiropractor; b.Mar. 28, 1925, Salt Lake City; s. Nephi Livesay and Edwardena (Parry) C.; edn: design & paper sculpture, Chouinard Art Inst. (now Cal Arts) 1949; MA in psychol., David Seabury Sch of Psychology, 1953; DC, Cleveland Chiro. Coll. 1965. Career: Dr. of Chiropractic, lic. in Calif., New Zealand; co-founder, instr. Foundation for Living, Problems

Anon., Creative Self Research, 1953-64; co-presenter Living Today (radio pgm.), Los Angeles 1954-55; extensive travels w/parents on cranial adjusting tchg. tours in US and Can. (father, Nephi Cottam, D.C., originator of cranial adjusting, Craniopathy); tours incl. World Chiropractic Congress, Switz.(1970), Spain (71), Greece, USSR, Turkey, Yugoslavia (72), acupuncture and shiatsu tour, Japan, Taipei, Hong Kong, Singapore, Thailand (72), genealogical resrch in England, Wales, Ireland, Belgium, France (73), and Scotland, Scandinavia; instr. craniopathy in Sydney, Australia, vis. New Zealand, Fiji, Tahiti (75), tchr. craniopathy in USA, Mex., Can. 1976-81; mem. first ofcl. chiropractic information exchg. group invited to China, 1983. Publs: art. in Digest of Chiro. Economics 1981; presented paper, The Smithsonian 1981 (vol.1, History); author: Head First for Health, House-Warven (1952), Fun, How To Take a Vacation Every Day, Living Without Strain, Don't Be Afraid of your Mind, Magic of Meditation; coauthor (w/Bert Mitchell Anderson) How To Write True To Yourself (1960); coauthor (w/Reid Rasmussen, DC) Craniopathy for You and Others (1975); various tech. papers. Prod. (with brother by adoption, Reid Rasmussen, DC) six one-hr video tapes showing cranial technics/craniopathy for Chiropractic Video Studies, Inc. of NY, 1981. Mem: Nat. Writers League (nat. pres. 1958); David Seabury Sch of Psychol. Alumni Assn. (pres. 1955-6); Internat. New Thought Alliance (ch. Govt. Affairs 1957); CofC; Civil Def.; Nat. Vocational Guidance Assn.; Mil: s/sgt US Army, M.C., WWII & Korean conflict. rec: comparative studies of ancient philosophies and current beliefs. Address: 1017 S. Arlington Ave. Los Angeles 90019.

COTTERMAN, ROBERT ALLEN, manufacturing co. executive; b. Nov. 5, 1935, Pontiac, Mich.; s. Don R. and Olive E. (MacKnutt) C.; edn: mech. eng., Mich. State Univ. 1954-57; num. bus. mgmt. courses 1957-84. Career: mgr. op. svcs. Abbot Labs, Los Angeles 1968-71; gen. mgr. General Brands, L.A. 1971-74; svc. devel. mgr. Shepherd Caterpillar, City on Industry 1974-76; plant mgr. Aerosol Svcs. Co., City of Ind. 1978-80; dir. of ops. Arko Equipt., Inc., City of Ind. 1981--; pres. A Better Alarm Sys., Hacienda Hghts. 1980--; annual speech, Bus. Mgmt. Sch., Cypress Coll.; works: over 200 inventions, Gen. Motors Truck & Coach; mil: US Army; rec: burglar alarms, cars, guns. Res: 3316 El Sebo Hacienda Heights 91745 Ofcs: Arko Equipment, Inc., 19062 E San Jose City of Industry 91748; A Better Alarm System, 3316 El Sebo Hacienda Heights 91745

COUCH, MARCUS DOUGLASS, real estate broker/developer; b. Aug. 27, 1916, Denver, Colo.; s. Maurice Douglass and Vermonte Agnes (Young) C.; m. Roberta Brunn, Aug. 31, 1940; children: Michael, b. 1941, Susan, b. 1951; edn: grad. cert., Am. Inst. Banking, 1939; GRI (1969), RECI (1976), Calif. Assn. of Realtors; CRS (1979), Nat. Assn. of Realtors. Career: mgr. San Francisco Theatres, 1932-35; teller Bank of America, S.F. 1935-42; foreman Plate Shop, Kaiser Shipyard No.3, Richmond 1942-44; m/sgt. USAF 1944-46; carpenter foreman Wm Gibson, Palo Alto 1946-49; owner/pres. Doug Couch General Contractors, Inc. 1949--; broker/owner. Doug Couch Realtors, Inc. 1951--; owner Doug Couch Painting Contr. 1952-55; prin. Doug Couch Ins. Broker 1953--; v.p. treas., Doug Couch Devel. Co. Inc.; mem: Palo Alto Bd. of Realtors (past pres.; Realtor of the Year 1957), Sunnyvale Bd. of Realtors, Los Altos Bd. of Realtors, past pres. Mt. View Bd. of Realtors, Calif. Assn. of Realtors (life hon. dir.; past 9th Dist. v.p.), Peninsular Exchangers, Assoc. Investment & Exchange Counselors, Nat. Assn. of Realtors, Nat. Assn. of Home Builders (past Regl. v.p.; Spike Club, life mem. 1960), Calif. Farm & Land Inst., Nat. Farm & Land Inst., Internat. Assn. of Fin. Plnnrs., Internat. R.E. Fedn., Employers Relocation Council, Realtors Nat. Mktg. Inst.; adv. comm. Foothill Comm. Coll.; mem: Optimists, Kiwanis, Commonwealth Club of Calif., S.F. Press Club, Disabled Am. Vets. (life), Stanford Univ. Alumni Assn., life mem. Stanford Buck Club, Am. Red Cross Palo Alto Chpt. (bd. dirs.; instr.); trustee, Santa Clara Co. United Way (Palo Alto chpt. chmn. bd. dirs.). Res: 67 Bay Tree Ln Los Altos 94022 Ofc: Doug Couch, Inc. 560 Oxford Ave Palo Alto 94006

COUGHLIN, SISTER MAGDALEN, college president; b. Apr. 16, 1930, Wenatchee, Wash.; d. William Joseph and Cecilia (Diffley) C.; edn: BA, The Coll. of St. Catherine 1952; MA, Mt. St. Mary's Coll. 1962; PhD, USC 1970. Career: hist. tchr. Alemany H.S., Calif. 1960-61; hist. tchr. St. Mary's Acad., Los Angeles 1961-63; asst. prof. of hist. Mt. St. Mary's Coll., L.A. 1963-70; dean for acad. devel. Mt. St. Mary's Coll., L.A. 1970-74; provincial councilor/ regl. supvr. Sisters of St. Joseph of Carondelet, L.A. 1974-76; pres. Mt. St. Mary's Coll., L.A. 1976--; bd. trustees Marianne Frostig Ctr. for Ednl. Therapy; bd. dirs. Ind. Colls. of So. Calif. 1976--, pres. of bd. 1982-83; bd. trustees Coll. of St. Catherines 1982-; bd. dirs. Assn. of Catholic Colls. & Unvs. 1979-; awards: Haynes Dissertation Fellowship 69-70; Fulbright Scholarship, Univ. of Nijmegen, The Netherlands 1952-53; Doctor of Humane Letters, honoris causa, Loyola Marymount Univ. 1983; mem: Calif. Hist. Soc.; Am. Hist. Soc.; Fulbright Alumni Assn.; Phi Alpha Theta; Phi Gamma Mu; Delta Epsilon Sigma; Kappa Gamma Pi; Lambda Iota Tau; Women in Bus.; Womens Trusteeship; works: Missionary and Smuggler: Agents of Disobedience of Civilization?, Some Calif. Catholic Reminiscences for the US Bicentennial 1976; Commercial Foundations of Political Interest in the Opening Pacific, Calif. Hist. Soc. Quarterly, Vol. XLX, 1971; Boston Smugglers on the Coast (1797-1812): An Insight Into the American Acquisition of California, Calif. Hist. Soc. Quarterly 1967; Catholic; rec: reading, sewing, walking. Address: Mount St. Mary's College, 12001 Chalon Rd Los Angeles 90049

COUTURIER, JOHN CHARLES, III, consulting firm president; b. Nov. 26, 1950, Los Angeles; s. John Charles Jr. and Judith Joan Smith (Bertea) C.; m. Diana Marie Sagahon, Sept. 16, 1972; edn: BA, UCLA 1973; MBA, CSU Dominguez Hills 1975. Career: gen. mgr. Palos Verdes Plumbing Co., Redondo Beach 1975-76; R.E. loan ofcr. Provident Fed. Savings, Riverside 1976-78; regl. loan mgr. Republic Fed. Savings, Santa Ana 1978-79; pres./ CEO Creative Home Marketin, Inc., Riverside 1979--; instr. R.E. fin., Santa Ana Coll. 1979-80; instr./ curriculum advr. San Bernardino Valley Coll. 1978-81, (author first course in adv. R.E.); honors: Phi Beta Kappa, Alpha chpt.; mem: Soc. of Real Estate Appraisers, Inland chpt. Facilities Com.; Real Estate Educators Assn.; Calif. Assn. of Real Estate Teachers; Republican; Presbyterian; rec: ocean surfing, reading, sailing. Res: 5801 Maybrook Cir Riverside 92506 Ofc: Creative Home Marketing, Inc., 6927 Brockton Ave, Ste 2-D, Riverside 92506

COVINGTON, JON SCOTT, international marketing executive; b. Nov. 18, 1950, Mt. Vernon, Ill.; s. Charles J. and Lois Ellen (Combs) C.; m. Linda Degenhardt, Nov. 15, 1969; children: Jason, b. 1970; Eric, b. 1974; Travis, b. 1983; edn: BS, So. Ill. Univ. 1972; MBA, 1980. Career: mgmt. cons. Conley-Pihos Mgmt. Co., Milwaukee, Wisc. 1972-73; area sales mgr., Midwest, J.Frank & Son, Inc., Los Angeles 1973-75; pres./ founder Backdoor Inc., Mt. Vernon, Ill. 1975-76; pres./ founder Sunshine Prodns., Inc., Mt. Vernon, Ill. 1975-79; pres./ co- founder European Bus. Seminars Inc., Los Gatos 1983--; mkt. mgr. internat. saels Apple Computer, Cupertino 1980--; exec. staff Internat. Solutions, Inc., Saratoga; cons. Whitney Ednl. Svcs., San Mateo, 1982; con. Allen Commun., Salt Lake City 1983; honors: Outstanding Svc. Awd., Phi Sigma Epsilont 1972; Canuck Awd., Apple Comput, Canada 1982; Outstanding Mkt. Proj., Apple Computer 1982; mem: Am. Mktg. Assn.; World Trade Orgn.; Porsche Club of Am.; Gilbert & Sullivan Soc. of San Jose; works: The Microcomputer in Industry Training, T.H.E. Journ. 3/82; The Uses of Apple in Training... Or Never Trust a Computer You Can't Carry', Soc. for Applied Learnig Technology 1983; Republican; Presbyterian; rec: Porsche auto restoration, internat. travel. Res: 224 Gregg Dr Los Gatos 95030 Ofc: Apple Computer, 20525 Mariani Cupertino 95014

COVINGTON, STEPHANIE STEWART, psychotherapist, educator, consultant; b. Nov. 5, 1942, Whittier; d. William M. and Bette Ann (Robertson) Stewart; div.; children: Kimberley, b. 1970, H. Richard, b. 1967; edn: Pomona Coll. 1960-1, BA cum laude, USC 1963, MSW, Columbia Univ. 1970, PhD, Union Grad. Sch. 1982. Career: casewkr Spence-Chapin Adoption Agcy, NYC 1965, Union Co. Psychiat. Clinic, 1970; owner Interiors by Covington & Wixom,; 1972-79; faculty mem. CSU San Diego, 1982-83, USC and UCSD Ext., 1981, 82, 83; cons. spec. in addictions: Raleigh Hills Hosp. 1981, Health Promotion Found. 1982-3, Marlborough Sch. 1982; pvt. alcoholism cons./ counselor/ educator, 1982--; recognition for contbns. to alcoholic women, S.D. chpt. Calif. Women's Commn. on Alcoholism; chpsn. Women's Com., Internat. Council on Alcoholism and Addictions, listed: Who's Who Among San Diego Women, 1982. Mem: Alcohol & Drug Problems Assn. of No. Am. (ADPA), Assn. of Women in Psychology (AWP), Calif. Assn. of Alcoholism Counselors (CAAC), Calif. Women's Commn. on Alcoholism, Nat. Women's HealthNetwork, Nat. Women's Studies Assn., S.D. Coalition on Alcohol Problems, NOW; frequent spkr/trainer various confs., workshops, seminars on alcoholism and other addictions, feminism, female sexuality, intimacy, relationships and women in our society; guest on TV & radio (Phil Donahue Show, others); Democrat. res: 4447 Benhurst Ave. San Diego 92122. ofc: 1129 Torrey Pines Rd. La Jolla 92037.

COWAN, HAROLD GEORGE (Bub), aerospace co. executive; b. Sept. 10, 1921, Footville, Wisc.; s. James Russell and Catherine Maude (Kennedy) C.; m. 2d Xim Dinh; children (by previous m.): Michael, b. 1943; Patricia, b. 1946; Timothy, b. 1948; Daniel, b. 1953; Joel, b. 1955; edn: undergrad., USAF, 1947. Career: mil. pilot, 1941-71, 2d lt. Army Air Corp, 1941, command pilot (col.) USAF, 1971, air combat pilot in WWII, Korea, Vietnam (cited for single aircraft attack of enemy convoy, sank two vessels, L.A. Times, early 1944); product support engrg. Northrop Aircraft Div., 1971-73, gen. mgr. S.E. Asia Ops., 1973-75; mgr. Ops.-Program Control, Northrop Aircraft Services Div., Hawthorne, 1976--. Mem: Air Force Assn., The Retired Ofcrs Assn., Am. Legion, Soc. of Wireless Pioneers, Amateur Radio Relay League, Northrop Mgmt. Club, Am. Aviation Hist. Soc. Mil: col. USAF 1941-71, 19 decorations incl. Legion of Merit, DFC, Air Medals, Presdtl. Unit Cits., Bronze Star, Outstanding Unit Cits.; Republican; Catholic; rec: amateur radio adv. class (N6BEB). Res: 11360 E. 195th St. Cerritos 90701 Ofc: Northrop Aircraft Svcs One Northrop Ave, 1030/34, Hawthorne 90250

COX, ARTHUR ERNEST, real estate broker; b. Sept. 18, 1914, Aldershot, England, nat. 1982; s. Robert Charles and Florence (Henson) C.; m. Margaret Speer, Aug. 23, 1961; edn: BS, Univ. of London 1937; Assoc. Royal Photog. Soc. 1935; GRI, Grad. Realtors Inst. 1978. Career: research dept. Eastman Kodak, England 1936; served to maj. British Army, commnd. 2d lt. Royal Norfolk Regt., 1940, transf. to Royal Elec. and Mech. Engrs., apptd. engr. to Military Mission Moscow 1942, mem. Brit. Cabinet office staff on Churchill's confs. in Moscow, Yalta, Potsdam; apptd. 1st secty. Brit. Emb., Vienna, Austria 1946; emigrated to Canada 1951, to USA 1961; current broker/owner Cox Realtors, Mountain View, Ca.; mem. Nat. & Calif. Assn. of Realtors, Mt. View Bd. of Realtors (pres. 1982), Navy League, Rotary (pres. Mt. View 1982/3); rec: photog., gardening. Res: 1622 Begen Ave Mt. View 94041 Ofc: Cox Realtors, 341 Castro St Mountain View 94041

COX, EUGENE DORR, JR., manufacturing co. executive; b. May 21, 1933, Benton Harbor, Mich.; s. Eugene D. and Emma Marie (Stokes) C.; m. Lillian (Lynne) Stephenson, June 29, 1963; two sons: Andrew Cameron, b. 1964, Douglas Price, b. 1967; edn: stu. W. Mich. Univ., 1954-56, BSEE, Mich. State Univ. 1959, exec. pgm. UCLA 1979-80. Career: with The Bendix Corp.,

Electrodynamics Div., North Hollywood & Sylmar, 1959--: design engr. 1959-60, field engrg. rep. 1960-66, supr/mgr. field engineering 1966-70, mgr. Product Support 1970-71, systems project mgmt. 1971-73, engineering mgr. 1973-80, mgr. Information Systems 1980--; mem. Bendix' Mgmt. Information Systems Council (policy making and guidance to corp. divs.) 1980-. Mem: Bendix Electrodynamics Mgmt. Club (v.p. 1971, pres. 1981), West Hills Soccer Assn. (coach 1973), Calif. Youth Soccer Assn. (asst. coach 1982), Winnetka Soccer Club (team treas. 1981), UCLA Executive Pgm. Assn. (bd.dirs 1981), X-Ringers Sportsman Club, NRA afil.(pres. 1977), Sister City Exchange Pgm. (Canoga Park-Taxco, Mex.) Planning Com. 1973; United Way-Gr.L.A. Campaign Bus. Mbrship Task Gp. for San Fernando Vly. 1982. mil: cpl. USMC 1951-54; Republican; Presbyterian; rec: target shooting, tennis, biking; res: 19410 Singing Hills Dr., Northridge 91326. ofc: Bendix Electrodynamics Div. 11600 Sherman Way, N. Hollywood 91605.

COX, FLORA DENISE, psychiatrist; b. Dec. 4, 1950, Tuskegee Inst., Ala.; d. Floyd DeWitt and Glennie (Foster) Cox; m. John Harris, Mar. 22, 1978; children: John, b. 1978; Melanie, b. 1980; edn: MD, Univ. of Mich. Med. Sch. 1975. Career: resident in psychiatry/neurology Sinai Hosp. of Detroit 1975-76; resident in psychiatry Cedars-Sinai Med. Ctr., Los Angeles 1976-78; Bd. Cert. Am. Bd. of Psychiatry and Neurology, 1982. Career: pvt. practice, Culver City 1978--; assoc. staff Dept. of Psychiatry, Cedars-Sinai Med. Ctr. of L.A., 1979--; med. dir. Adult/Gero-Psychiatry Day Treatment Pgm. of the Central City Comm. Mental Health Ctr., Los Angeles 1979-81; psychiatric cons. Children/ Adolescent Svcs., Kedren Comm. Mental Hlth Ctr., L.A. (1981-), High Risk Obstets. Clinic, Cedars-Sinai Med. Ctr. (1980); hosp. afils: Cedars-Sinai Med. Ctr., Brotman Med. Ctr., Centinela Hosp., Daniel Freeman Hosp., Hawthorne Comm. Hosp., Western Park Med. Ctr. Hosp.; recipient Outstanding Young Woman of Am. award 1979-80. Mem: Calif. Med. Assn., L.A. County Med. Assn., Inglewood Physicians Assn. (exec. bd.), Black Women Physicians Assn., Am. Psychiat. Assn., So. Calif. Psychiat. Soc., Black Psychiatrists of So. Calif., Black Womens Forum (sponsor), Rotary Ann, Wives of the Bench and Bar; Democrat; Episcopal; rec: piano, jogging, belly dancing. Res: 6129 S. Mansfield Los Angeles 90043 Ofc: Flora D. Cox, MD, 3831 Hughes, Ste. 610, Culver City 90230

COX, JUDITH M., nursing home administrator; b. Aug. 5, 1941, Rockford, Ill.; d. Malhan and Dorothy Bertha (Jacobs) Vaughan; children: Melinda Marks, b. 1959; John Marks, b. 1963; cert. nurses aide, Edgemore Geriatric Hosp.; Calif. Lic. Nursing Home Adminstr., BEHA 1984. Career: certified nurses aide in newborn nursery, Grossmont Hosp. 1964-66; team ldr., treatment aide, then night chg., Cloisters of the Valley, 1967-73; supvr. housekeeping, Ancillary Services supvr. Calif. Convalescent Hosp., La Mesa 1973-, adminstrator 1981--; preceptor for Adminstrs. in Tng.; mem. Calif. Assn. of Health Facilities, Am. Coll. of Nursing Home Adminstrs., La Mesa CofC; Christian, mem. Navajo Missions, Christian Childrens Fund; rec: crafts. Res: 12044 Royal Rd, Sp.88, El Cajon 92120 Ofc: Calif. Convalescent Hospital 8787 Center Dr La Mesa 92041

COX, MARION ELLISON, microbiologist, company president; b. Jan. 11, 1945, Eden, TX; s. George MIlburn and Frances Josephine (Stuart) Cox; edn: BS, Univ. of Houston, 1973; m. Mary Dau, Apr. 19, 1972; chil: Steven, b. 1981. Career: medical/X-ray technologist, Texas Research Inst. for Mental Sci., Houston, 1967-68; microbiologist, USAH Army Hosp., Fort Ord, Calif., 1968-70; microbiologist/med. technologist, Diagnostic Clinic of Houston, Tex., 1970-73; microbiologist, Stanford Univ. Medical Center, Palo Alto, 1973-75; dir. of research, Internatl. Shellfish Enterprises, Moss Landing, 1975-77; microbiologist, O'Connor Hosp., San Jose, 1977-78; pres., Anaerobe Systems, Santa Clara, 1978---; adj. prof. microbiology, San Jose State Univ., 1982---. Mem: Amer. Soc. for Microbiology; AAAS; Amer. Soc. of Med. Technologists; Calif. Assn. of Med. Technologists. Patentee; num. articles in profl. journals. Mil: E-5, US Army, 1968-70; Commendation. Republican. Christian. Rec: photography, backpacking. Res: 8005 Rainbow Dr., Cupertino 95014; Office: Anaerobe Systems, 3074-A Scott Blvd., Santa Clara 95050-7960.

COYE, KEITH ALLAN, consulting firm executive; b. Oct. 30, 1947, Bath, NY; s. Harry and Esther (Packard) C.; m. Lorraine Tardif, Aug. 1, 1969; children: Cameron, b. 1971, Michelle, b. 1974; edn: AS, Wentworth Inst. 1967; Northeastern Univ. 1967; Saddleback Coll. 1975; BA, Boston Univ. 1978. Career: New Products supr. Digital Equip. Corp. (DEC), Mass. 1972-73, Branch Service Mgr., Calif. 1973-75, mktg. splst., Mass. 1975-76, European mktg. mgr., Mass. 1976-78, Sr. Account mgr., Calif. 1978-80; CEO, bd. dirs., Consulting Services Corp., Calif. 1980--. Exec. cons. San Mateo Regl. Computer Network, 1980-; speaker San Diego Microcomputer Conf. 1982. Mem: Nat. Assn. Underwater Instrs. 1975-; Am. Modeling Assn. 1977-; South Bay Computer Club, Leader Assembly Lang. subgp. 1981; Piconet CPM Club (pres. 1983); Nat. Fedn. Independent Businessmen. works: devel. scholarship tracking system, 1982), Nat. Assn. of Sec. School Principals, 1978-82; designed, implemented DEC system-10 Error Analysis and Reporting System (SYSERR), 1972-80. Mil: pvt. USMC 1968, top secret clearance, Bettis Atomic Lab., 1969-73. Protestant. rec: computers, woodwork, chess. res/ofc: Consulting Services Corp., 7214 Via Maria San Jose 95139

CRABB, L. LEIGH, company executive; b. Aug. 31, 1919, St. Joseph, Mo.; s. Francis James and Maude Mae (Dean) C.; m. Virginia Kidder, Oct. 3, 1942; children: Terry Richard, b. 1943; Thomas Brian, b. 1951; Douglas Leigh, b. 1953; Mary Elizabeth, b. 1954; edn: Los Angeles City Coll. 1946; bus. adm., Harvard Univ. 1946; American Bankers Assn. Cert. Career: with Bank of America, various branches in Los Angeles, starting in Clearing House through Branch Banking System to Real Estate Appraiser, 1949; acctg., Green Spot Co., South Pasadena 1949--: have been responsible for finl., traffic, personnel, mfg. and op. activities, currently cons. and advisor to co. divs., vice pres./treas./ secty. 1981--; mem. Am. Legion, YMCA, YWCA, Reserve Ofcrs. Assn., Methodist Men; mil: lt. col. USAF-R (ret.) 1942-79; Democrat; rec: aviation, railroads. Res: 1841 Colina Dr Glendale 91208 Ofc: Green Spot Co. 520 Mission St. So. Pasadena 91030

CRABTREE, JOHN EDISON, import executive; b. Mar. 19, 1939, Boise, Idaho; s. Edison M. and Helen Maxine (Blanton) C.; edn: BA, USC 61; MS, 1967; Customhouse broker lic., US Customs Svcs. 1979. Career: mgr. Container Care Corp., Wilmington 1970-71; self-empl. apt. owner/ mgmt. cons., Tustin, San Pedro 1968-74; proj. mgr. Howard Hartry Inc., Wilmington 1974-77; team supvr. Frank P. Dow Co., Inc., Los Angeles 1977-78; import mgr. Ted. L. Rausch Co., Long Beach 1978-80; owner Antique Furniture Import Bus., San Pedro 1980-82; import mgr, Harry W. Hamacher, Inc., Westcoast Div., San Pedro 1982--; mem: Yachting Olympic Games Weighmaster; Cabrillo Beach Yacht Club (Protest Com.); Olson 30 Owners Assn. (1st pres. 1979-80); pres. Small Boat Owners Racing Assn.; US Yacht Racing Union, Newport, R.I.; mil: 1st lt. USMC 1961-64, Armed Froces Expeditionary Medal; Republican; Christian Sci.; rec: sailboat racing. Res: 1909 Palacios Dr San Pedro 90732 Ofc: Harry W. Hamacher, Inc., 1300 S Beacon St, Ste 114, San Pedro 90731

CRAIKER, CHRISTOPHER DAVID, architect, land planner; b. Oct. 3, 1945, Los Angeles; s. Samuel and Agnes (Overstreet) C.; m. Linda Sylvia Frankland, Dec. 28, 1983; children: Stacie, b. 1967; Ryan,b. 1969; edn: CalPoly, S.L.O.; UCLA; Reg. Architect, Calif. Career: chief designer B.A. Berkus Assn., Santa Monica 1969-73; dir. of arch. Environmental Planning Inst., Sausalito 1973-75; pres. Design Phase II, 1975-80; pres. Chris Craiker Inc., to present; designed over 104,000 single family and multifamily units, 3 marinas, 1 ski resort, 1 new city (Japan), 3 million square feet of office splties. in Mixed Use projects (resdtl. & comml.), Calif.; primary contbn. to architecture is small homes called "M.D.'s" (mini detached), was respons. for Victorian Revival in multifamily houses, late 1970s; chmn. Strawberry Design Review Bd.; mem. Marin Ecumenical Assn. for Housing; judge for 1983 awards, Pac. Coast Bldrs. Conf.; awards: 13 Gold Nugget Awards, Pacific Coast Bldrs. Conf., 1979-82; 3 California City Beautification Awards; Archtl. Record Apt. of the Year Award, Affordable Housing Pgm. for San Anselmo; mem: AIA, Building Indus. Assn. (dir. N. Calif. chpt.), Am. Plnng. Assn., Urban Land Inst.; rec: windsurfing. Res: 119 Tiburon Blvd Mill Valley 94941 Ofc: The French Quarter, 610 Third St, Ste. A, San Rafael 94901

CRAIN, JOHN GARLAND LYFORD, transportation/distribution consultant; b. Apr. 20, 1915, Bethany, Mo.; s. Harry Isaac and Grace Anna (Meek) C.; m. Claire Virginia Yegge, Dec. 30, 1 89; children: Lawrence D., b. 1941, Clifford G., b. 1944; edn: grad. Topeka (Kans.) H.S. 1937; indsl. orgn., UCLA, 1943; lic. to practice before Interstate Commerce Commn. (1944); Calif. lic. Real Estate Broker (1964). Career: founder/prin. Crain and Associates, 1948-78, services included auditing of freight bills, indsl. plant-site location, public warehouse storage and distbn.; first client was State of Calif., all depts. (championed the creation of a Unit of Traffic Mgmt. within the state Civil Svc. Sys.); past mem. Los Angeles Transp. Club, Ventura Transp. Club, Transp. Shrine Club; apptd. (with spouse) regional vice pres. Conf. of Calif. Historical Socs. 1984, treas. CCHS 1980-83 (life mem.); charter mem. Torrance Airport Commn.; mem. Torrance Library Commn. 6 yrs.; honors: 100 Million Dollar Club, Shriners Hosp. for Crippled Children (1/27/75); hon. mem. Sudan Temple, The Mystic Shrine of New Bern, N.C. (1972), Ballut Abyad Temple, Albuquerque, N.M. (1965); mem: Friends of Calif. Libraries (bd. dirs.), Torrance Hist. Soc.; Republican; Prot.; rec: writing, boxing, finance. Res: 85 Poinsettia Gardens Dr San Buenaventura 93004

CRAMER, ROBERT JOSEPH, communications engineering executive; b. Sept. 9, 1925, Denver, Colo.; s. Robert Louis and Anna Elizabeth (Staendl) C.; m. Patricia Ann Olsen, Nov. 24, 1947; children: Cheryl Ann Hill, b. 1948; Phyllis Elaine Pierazzi, b. 1950; edn: BSEE, Univ. of Colo. 1946; MSEE, 1948; cert., Naval Reserve Ofcrs. Sch. 1955-56; profl. engr., Utah 1955; 1/c radiotelephone lic., FCC 1955. Career: tranmission engr. Mountain States Telephone, Boise, Idaho 1949-54; transmission engr., Salt Lake City 1954-58, 1861-62; sys. engr. Western Electrice Defense Proj., NY 1958-61; sys. eng. mgr.e ITT Fed. Electric Corp., Paramus, NJ 1962-73; chief telecomm. engr. Bechtel Corp., San Francisco 1973--; mem: IEEE; Elks; Masons; works: paper, Communications Considerations for Underground Transit Systems, Am. Pub. Transit Assn., San Francisco 1980; Project Approach to Communications Development, Pan American Union of Engring. Soc., Mex. Ctiy 1980; New Approach to Communications, San Juan, P.R.; mil: lt.jg USNR 1946-62; rec: coin collecting, personal computers. Res: 210 Curlew Ct Foster City 94404 Ofc: Bechtel, Inc., 50 Beale St San Francisco 94119

CRANDALL, ELWOOD A., financial institution executive; b. May 20,1931, Ogden, Utah; s. David Ford and Elfie Norma (Anderson) C.; m. Michel Taylor, June 29, 1956; children: David, b. 1960; Elizabeth, b. 1964; Catherine, b. 1966; Laura, b. 1969; edn: BSL, Univ. of Utah 1954; JD, 1957; admitted to practice, Utah Bar 1956. Career: clerk Utah Supreme Ct. 1956-57; pvt. law practice 1957-59; mgr. corp. fin. J.A. Hogle & Co. 195964; reg. partner Goodbody & Co. 1964-70; v.p. Merril Lynch 1971-79; mng. dir./ reg. mgr. instl. sales Merrill Lynch Capital Markets 1980--; dir. Irvine Ranch Water Dist. 1971-74; mem: California Club; Republican; LDS; rec: skiing, backpacking, sailing. Res:

3020 Via Rivera Palos Verdes Estates 90274 Ofc: Merrill Lynch, 523 West 6th St, Ste 321, Los Angeles 90014

CRANE, HEWITT DAVID, scientist; b. Apr. 27, 1927, Jersey City, NJ; m. Suzanne Gorlin, June 20, 1954, NYC; children: Russell Philip, b. 1958, Douglas Mitchell, b. 1959, Daniel Bruce, b. 1961; edn: BS (E.E.), Columbia Univ. 1947; PhD, Stanford Univ. 1960. Career: with Internat. Bus. Machines, NYC 1949-51; Inst. for Adv. Study, Princeton, NJ 1952-55; RCA Labs., Princeton, NJ 1955-56; mgr. Sensory Sciences Research Lab., SRI Internat., Menlo Park, 1956--; dir. Ridge Vineyards, Cupertino 1967-; holder 60 U.S. patents; contbr. 50 tech. publs.; Fellow IEEE; awards: NASA award for sci. achievement, 1970; Indsl. Research IR-100 awards, 1974, 76; mil: USN 1945-46. Res: 25 Cordova Ct Portola Valley 94025 Ofc: SRI International, Menlo Park 94025

CRANE, ILLONA ISLEY, certified public accountant; b. Jan. 20, 1923, Mesa, Ariz.; d. Guy and Lenna Esther (Coverstone) Isley; m. Ralph Crane, Apr. 17, 1955; children: Patricia Ann, b. 1957; Cecily Susan, b. 1959; Frederick Guy, b. 1961; edn: BS, in bus. admin. 1945; CPA, Calif. 1952; Montessori Tchr. Cert., Pre-Sch. 1964. Career: asst. tchr./substitute, 1965-66; internal revenue agent/ field auditor, IRS 1967-69, employee plan splst./ determiner 1969-79, employee plan splst./ examiner 1979-82, employee plan agent/ determiner 1983--; instr. tng. class, IRS, 1977, mem. CPAs & PAs in the Svc. (IRS); Federal Womens Pgm.; Revenuettes Toastmistress Club (past pres.); Republican; Methodist; rec: music, camping, travel. Res: 2724 Carlaris Rd San Marino 91108 Ofc: EP/ EO Div., Internal Revenue Service, 300 N Los Angeles St, Los Angeles 90012

CRAPE, JAMES RUSSELL, engineer, publisher; b. Sept. 3, 1952, New Bedford, Mass.; s. Francis and Corinne (Goulet) C.; lic. power plant engr., unlmtd. ratings (5), LA, CA. Career: stationary eng.; advertising copy writer; geologist, profl. musician, television & Las Vegas appearances, 1973-80; plant engr. H. Mayo Hosp., Ca. 1980-84; author two engring. books (tech., career guidance) 1982; pres. JRC Publishing & Minerals, 1984--, cons. product devel. & mktg., book publishing, gold & silver ore mining; research: feasibility of emerg. flange repair system for indus.; biodegradable water base oil dispersion agent for indsl. equipment clean-up ops.; mem. Nat. Assn. of Power Engrs.; rec: mineral prospecting, performing music, writing. Address: 21815 Ulmus Dr. Woodland Hills 91364

CRAWFORD, ROBERT JAMES, manufacturing co. executive; b. Mar. 11, 1936, Abilene, Tex.; s. E.L. and Elsie Irene (Eby) C.; m. Brenda Lee Smith, Apr. 18, 1962; children: Ron, b. 1963; Rick, b. 1964; edn: BS, Univ. of Tex. 1959; MBA, CSU Long Beach 1970; cert. cost analyst, Inst. of Cost Analysis 1983. Career: design engr. No. American Aviation, Los Angeles 1959; aerodynamicist Douglas Aircraft, Santa Monic 1959-63; engr./ scientist 1963-67; engr./ scientist spec. McDonnell Douglas, Huntington Beach 1967-71; sr. adv. sys. cost analyst 1971-79; br. mgr. sys. cost analysis 1979-83; mgr. estimating, McDonnell Douglas, Huntington Beach 1983--; dir. Campus Advance, UCI 1967-70; honors: Order of the 'T', Athletic Lettermens Assn., Univ. of Tex. 1958; Phi Kappa Phi 1970; mem: Inst. of Cost Analysis; Internat. Soc. of Parametric Analysts; mgr. Jr. All-Am. Basketball, Little League Baseball; mil: National Guard 1954-62; Republican; Ch. of Christ (trustee, elder); rec: sports, stamp collecting. Res: 26811 Saddleback Dr Mission Viejo 92691 Ofc: McDonnell Douglas, 5301 Bolsa Ave, MS 14-2, Huntington Beach 92647

CRAWFORD, STEPHEN MARCUS, business computer system co. president; b. Apr. 10, 1957, Los Angeles; s. Willie and Mary A. (Hornback) C.; m. Sherelle, Sept. 6, 1980; edn: Mt. San Antonio Coll. 1980-81; eng. tech. Cal Poly, Pomona 1975-. Career: lib. asst. Cal Poly Pomona Library 1975-79; research asst. Pacific Scientific- HIAC Div., Montclair 1979; computer pgmr. Xerox Electro Optical Div., Pomona 1979-81 computer opr. NEFF Instruments, Monrovia 1981-82; sales rep. Computer Land, W. Covina 1981-82; sales rep. Olympic Sales, Ontario 1982-83; pres. S.M. Crawford & Assoc., Claremont 1982--; awards: Los Angeles Times Scholarship, 1975; Cert. of Recgn. in Scholastic Achiev., L.A. Housing Authority 1975; mem: Am. Chem. Soc. (Computer Soc.); IEEE (Computer Soc.); Cal Poly Skyliner Mountaineering & Karate Club (pres. 1977-78); Cal Poly Table Tennis Club; Democrat; Christian; rec: computer science, biology, behavioral science. Address: S.M. Crawford & Assoc., 642 S. Carleton Ave Claremont 91711

CREEKMORE, J. WAYNE, graphic and industrial designer; b. Sept. 9, 1945, Broken Arrow, Okla.; s. Milo and Allie Elizabeth (Newman) C.; m. Stephanie Lynn Behasa, Aug. 26, 1984; 1 son, Jerry Milo, b. 966; edn: BFA, Kansas City Art Inst. 1967; MFA, Yale Univ. 1969. Career: staff designer Will Burtin Assoc., NYC, 1969; design dir. of Ecology Edn. Kits (2), C. Richard Hatch Assoc., NYC 1970; asst. prof. of art, Univ. of Hawaii at Manoa, 1971-76, 79, Design Dept. chmn. 1972-76; dir. Graphic Design, Exploratorium, San Francisco 1977; freelance design services SF 1978-, sole prop. Wayne Creekmore Design, SF, 1980-83; ptnr. (w/ Stephanie Behasa), Creekmore & Behasa, Mill Valley, 1984--, spec. in information for laypersons on computer hardware and software; recipient AIGA Award for Excellence in Pckg. Design, 1971; wks.: 8'x20' mural commnd. by Hawaii State Found. on Culture and the Arts, Honolulu Internat. Airport (1976); 6 murals, each 9'x20' on ocean systems and ecology for the Steinhart Aquarium in SF; author: Through The MicroMaze, A Visual Guide and Through The MicroMaze, A Visual Guide to Getting Organized (both pub. by Ashton-Tate); Democrat; rec: skiing, computers. Address: Creekmore Behasa, 390 Monte Vista Ave Mill Valley 94941

CREIGHTON, ELMER FREEMAN, JR., service company executive; b. May 31, 1938, McCormick, S.C.; s. Elmer Freeman and Alma (Graves) Creighton; edn: BS, che, Clemson Univ., 1960; m. Jacquelyn Mills, Jan. 19, 1979; children: John, b. 1966, Kathryn, b. 1963, Shawn, b. 1968; career: product specialist General Elec. Co., Gainsville, Fla. 1965-66, mgr. mktg. G.E. Co., Irmo, S.C. 1966-68; ARA Services, Inc. 1968--: consulting prin., Atlanta, Ga. 1968-71, division mgr., Greenville, S.C. 1971-75, regional gen. mgr., Greenville, S.C. 1975-79, sales v.p., El Segundo 1979-81, Area V.P., El Segundo 1981--; mem. ARA Vending Policy Com. 1981-82; mem: Pres., S.C. Automatic Merchandising Assn. 1976; pres., Soc. for Advancement of Mgmt. 1974-75; Jr. C. of C., 1962; Scoutmaster, BSA, Greenville chpt. 1964; mil.: 1st lt. US Army, 1961; Republican; Methodist; rec: tennis, golf; res: 6802 Lawnhaven Dr., Huntington Beach 92648; office: ARA Services, Inc. One Continental Plaza #490, El Segundo 90245.

CRENNER, JAMES CHARLES, development engineer; b. July 1, 1948, Pittsburgh, Pa.; s. August Francis and Patricia Ann (Vidler) C.; m. Susan Marie Kopsho, Apr. 11, 1970; children: Julie Louise, b. 1971; Jennifer Sue, b. 1974; edn: AS, magna cum laude, West Coast Univ. 1980, BS, 1983; cert. Air Traffic Controller/ Tower Opr., FAA 1973. Career: air traffic controller, USMC 1966-75; QA tech. Edwards Pacemaker Systems, Irvine 1976-78; senior engring. tech. Sperry Univac Co., Irvine 1978-81; project mgr./ senior engr. Coopervision Systems, Irvine 1981-83; devel. engr. Cilco, Pomona 1983--; honors Eagle Scout, BSA, 1966; mem. IEEE (Biomed. Engring. & Ultrasonic Socs.); Asst. Scoutmaster, Riverside 1976; works: co-designer I/A Model 7500 (Irrigation/ Aspiration) and project engr. for the Phacoemulsifier (PEA 9000), both used in cataract surgery; mil: s/sgt E6 USMC 1969-75, Reserve 1975-, GCM (3), Nat. Defense; Republican; Episcopal; rec: home computers. Res: 1657 W. Buena Vista Ave Anaheim 92802 Ofc: CILCO, 2865 Pomona Blvd, POB 2865, Pomona 91769

CREWS, RICHARD LAWRENCE, university president, physician; b. July 11, 1937, NYC; edn: BA magna cum laude, Phi Beta Kappa, Williams Coll. 1959; MD, Harvard Med. Sch. 1963; internship S.F. Gen. Hosp., 1963-64; res. in psychiat. Letterman Gen. Hosp., Presidio of S.F., 1965-68; career: Medicine and Psychiatry: served to maj., US Army M.C. 1964-71, psychiat. ward ofcr. Brooke Army Med. Ctr., Ft. Sam Houston, Tex. 1964-65, chief of psychiatry and neurology, Womack Army Hosp. and chief of mental hygiene cons. service, Ft. Bragg, N.C., 1968-71; pvt. practice psychiatry, Mill Valley, Calif. 1971--; cons. Calif. State Disability Evaluation Bd., 1974--; clin. practice Homeopathy and Nutritional Counseling, 1977-80; Edn. and Adminstrn.: lectr. in psychol., US Army Edn. Ctr. 1969-70, lectr. Univ. ofNC. Grad. Sch of Social Work, 1970-71; cofounder Brookwood Gen. Hosp., Santa Rosa, Calif. 1971; pres. Brookwood Hosp. Corp., 1975-80; lectr. in psychol. Coll. of Marin, 1971-72, Dominican Coll., San Rafael 1972-75; exec./clin. director Creative Living Centers of Marin Co., 1972-75, Wholistic Health and Nutrition Inst. (bd. dirs. 1977-) 1977-79; cofounder/pres. Columbia Pacific Univ., San Rafael 1978--; cofounder No. Am. Coll. of Natural Health Scis., Mill Valley and San Rafael, 1978, faculty 1978-80; chmn. Spl. Com. on Authorization Standards, Council for Pvt. Postsec. Ednl. Instns. of Calif., 1982-; chief edtl. advisor Internat. Holistic Jour. of Health and Medicine, 1982-. Mem: Mensa, Intertel, AMA, CMA, Sonoma Co., Marin Co. Med. Assns., Am., No. Calif. Psychiat. Assns., Health Scis. Communications Assn., Am. Holistic Med. Assn. Decorated Legion of Merit, US Army 1970. Num.academic, med. publs. Address: 112 Edgewood Ave. Mill Valley 94941.

CRICKARD, STEVEN PAUL, lawyer; b. Nov. 27, 1952, Glendale; s. Judge Jack Anderson and Billie (Allen) C.; edn: Chinese Univ. of Hong Kong 1971-72; C.A., Univ. of San Salvador 1971; AB, Univ. of Redlands 1974; JD, Loyola Univ. Sch. of Law 1977; admitted to practice, Calif. State Bar 1977. Career: assoc. Donovan, Leisure, Newton & Irvine, Los Angeles Ofc., NY firm 1977-78; Spray, Gould & Bowers, L.A. Ofc. 1978-81; Hillsinger & Costanzo, L.A. Ofc. 1981--; Ch. Deacon; awards: AFS Scholarship 1969; Scholarship for study in Asia 1972; mem: Phi Alpha Delta; ODK; 9th Circuit; USDC, L.A. & San Diego; Alpha Mu Theta; AFS; Loyola Alumni; Univ. of Redlands Fellows; Pasadena Bar Assn.; publs: Foreign Policy Research Assn. 1974; currently collaborating on Spanish-language publs.; Republican; Protestant; rec: racquet sports, travel. Res: 1422 N Central Ave, 2, Glendale 91202 Ofc: Hillsinger & Costanzo, 3055 Wilshire Blvd, 7th Flr, Los Angeles 90010

CRIDER, HOYT, health care executive; b. June 5, 1924, Arley, Ala.; s. Lindsey C. and Bessie P. Crider; m. Judie Watkins, Nov. 2, 1951; children: Kim, Marc; edn: stu. Ga. Sch. of Tech., 1942-43; BS in naval sci., Univ. S.C. 1946; MA in polit. sci. (pub. adm.), Univ. of Ala. 1949; D. Pub. Adminstrn., USC 1954. Career: vis. asst. prof. (with USC team in Iran to estab. a mgmt. curriculum) Univ. of Tehran, 1954-56; adminstrv. analyst (orgn. & mgmt. surveys), Los Angeles County 1956-59; v.p. Watkins and Watkins Constrn. Co., Hanford and Morro Bay, 1959-64; co-owner/adminstr. Kings Convalescent Hosp., Hanford 1964-66; adminstr. Villa Capistrano Convalescent Hosp., Capistrano Beach 1966-68; ptnr. Hunt and Crider, San Diego Conval. Hosp., 1968-70 (incorporated 1970), pres./chief exec. Health Care Enterprises Inc. 1970--, currently op. four nursing facilities; mem. Regional Hlth. Plnng. Commn. Kings County 1963-64; Cert. Fellow Am. Coll. of Nursing Home Adminstrs. (mem. 1968-; pres. 1976-7), Calif. Chpt. ACNHA (pres. 1970-72); mem. Calif. Assn. of Health Facilities (past v.p. local chpt.); Gerontological Soc.; adv. com. to Calif. Bd. of Examiners for Nursing Home Adminstrs. 1972-73; mem. US CofC, chambers of commerce of La Mesa, El Monte, San Clemente; Nat. Right to Work Com.; Nat. Conservative PAC; Wang Computer Sys. Users Soc.; AAAS; AARP; Kiwanis (past pres. S.C.); patron S.Coast Area Boys and Girls Club, Orange Co. Music Ctr.; mil: commnd. ofcr. USNR 1941-54. Res: 213 Calle Cortez San Clemente 92672 Ofc: Health Care Eng. Inc. 407 N. El Camino Real San Clemente 92672

CRISMAN, JOHN ALAN, engineering services co. executive; b. Mar. 10, 1938, Flint, Mich.; s. John Gilbert and Ariel Jean (Fitzgerald) C.; m. Karen Ward, Dec. 29, 1979; children: Kimberly, b. 1961; Cynthia, b. 1963; edn: bus. mgmt. pgm., UCLA 1969; MBA, Pepperdine Univ. 1973. Career: mgr. publs. Singer-Librascope, Glendale 1960-69; mgr. customer svc. Xerox Corp., El Segundo 969-74; adj. faculty, Pepperdine Univ. Sch. of Bus., Los Angeles 174-76; dir. pgm. mgmt. Pepperdine Univ., L.A. 1974-76; v.p. Western div. McLaughlin Research Corp., Camarillo 1976--; bus. policy & strategy prof. Pepperdine Univ.p 1974-76; mgmt. cons. 1974-76; mem: Nat. Contract Mgmt. Assn.; Jr. CofC, S. Pasadena; works: analysis of supvy. attitudes, 1973; mil: enlisted USN 1957-59, GCM; Republican; Methodist; rec: golf, bowling, woodworking. Res: 156 Spanish Moss Pl Camarillo 93010 Ofc: McLaughlin Research Corp., 275 E Pleasant Valley Rd, Bldg 260, Camarillo 93010

CRISWELL, DARRELL DEAN, retail chain executive; b. July 3, 1945, York, Penna.; s. Norman Wm. and Elizabeth Roser (Tripplet) C.; edn: BFA, Maryland Inst. Coll. of Art 1968. Career: retail store mgr., Aaron Bros. Inc., 1970, district mgr. 1977, regional mgr. 1979, asst. dir. of operations 1984--; mil: sgt. US Army 1968-70, Bronze Star, Commendation medals; rec: photog., painting. Res:10831 Roycroft St, #87, Sun Valley 91352 Ofc: Aaron bros. Inc. 1270 So Goodrich Blvd City of Commerce 90022

CRITCHFIELD, JOE PHILLIP, mechanical contracting and engineering co. president; b. June 21, 1935, Anaheim; s. Joseph Pierson and Virginia Ann (Shaw) C.; m. Nancy Ann Christopher, May 3, 1957; children: William Michael, b. 1958; Victor Mason, b. 1960; edn: BS in C.E., Stanford Univ. 1958. Career: sales engr. Trane Co., Los Angeles]961-65; v.p./ br. mgr. Air Conditioning Co., Inc. 1965-77; pres. Critchfield Mechanical, Inc., Menlo Park 1977--; Dir. Design Mechanical Inc., and Commercial Mechanical Service; mem: ASHRAE, SMACNA (labor panelist), AGC; mil: 1st lt. USAF 1958-61; Republican; Presbyterian; rec: bird hunting, golf, skiing. Res: 26075 Newbridge Rd Los Altos Hills 94022 Ofc: Critchfield Mechanical, Inc., 4085 Campbell Ave Menlo Park 94025

CROCKETT, ANITA BENNETT, nurse educator; b. Dec. 10, 1949, Clarksdale, MS; d. Andrew Crawford and Dora Opaline (Epps) Bennett; edn: RN dip. Our Lady of the Lake Sch. of Nsg. 1971; BSN, cum laude, Univ. of Tenn. Center for Health Scis. 1977, MS, 1978. Career: staff nurse Magnolia Hosp., Corinth, MS 1972-75; recovery nurse, birth control counseling, Memphis (Tn) Ctr. Reproductive Hlth, 1976-77, and nurse aide instr. Northwest MS Jr. Coll., 1976; instr. Coll. of Nsg., Univ. of Tenn. Ctr. for Hlth Scis., 1978-80, also nurse clinician, expert witness Rape Crisis Ctr., Memphis, 1979-80; contg. edn. coord./quality assurance coord. Hoag Mem. Hosp., Newport Bch. 1980-81; instr. Cypress Coll. Nsg. Pgm., 1981; critical care nurse, Lescoulie Nurses Reg., Newport Bch. 1981-82, Medical Staffing Svcs., Costa Mesa 1981-84, Best Nurses Registry, Anaheim 1981--, Quality Hosp. Staffing, Santa Ana 1982-84; asst. prof. clin. nsg. USC Dept. of Nursing 1984-; exec. dir. Pros and Cons, Newport Bch. (seminars, cons. in nsg. and aviation) 1981--; honors: Sigma Theta Tau 1976, Outstanding Young Women of Am. 1981; mem: American Heart Assn. (CPR Instr.); Am. Assn. of Critical Care Nurses; Am. Nurses Assn.; Nat. League for Nsg.; Ninety-Nines Inc. (treas. 1982-3); Aircraft Owners and Pilots Assn.; AAUW; NOW; Eastern Star; Internat. Soc. of Chronobiology; Nat. Assn. Female Execs.; Emergcy. Dept. Nurses Assn.; Harbor Area CofC; mil: cand. 1st lt., flt. nurse, AF Reserve; United Methodist; rec: flying, scuba, piano. Res: 6208-1/2 West Ocean Front, Newport Bch 92663 Ofc: USC Dept. Nsg., Leavey Hall, Los Angeles 90089

CROMMELIN, JACQUES BROADWATER, real estate executive; b. Feb. 26, 1909, Spokane, Wash.; s. Henri and Antoinette Wilder (Broadwater) C.; m. Marjorie Barclay, June 17, 1936; edn: Mech. Engr., Cornell Univ. 1932; MAI (Mem. Appraisal Inst.) Am. Inst. R.E. Appraisers; CRE (Counselor, Real Estate) Am. Soc. R.E. Counselors; SRPA (Sr. Real Property Appraiser) Soc. R.E. Appraisers. Career: mortgage loan insp. Prudential Ins. Co., Mnpls. & Portland, Ore. 1933-43; real estate broker, Raymond Cree Ofc., Palm Springs 1944-47; gen. mgr. Smoke Tree Ranch, Palm Springs 1947-51; owner Jacques B. Crommelin & Assoc., Palm Springs 1947--; pres. Riverside Co. Council BSA 1969-71; bd. dirs: A.R.C. 1948-51, United Fund 1950-53, Desert Circus 1948-50, and Palm Springs Comm. Hosp. 1948-52; awards: Silver Beaver Awd., BSA 1958; Kentucky Colonel 1969; mem: Am. Inst. R.E. Appraisers; Soc. of R.E. Appraisers; Am. Soc. of R.E. Counselors; Beta Theta Pi; Rotarian (pres. 1952-53); 100 Club (pres. 1971-72); Republican; Episcopal; rec: camping, photog. Res: Smoke Tree Ranch, 1800 S Sunrise Way Palm Springs 92262 Ofc: J.B. Crommelin & Assoc., 1506 S Palm Canyon Dr Palm Springs 92262

CROMMELIN, ROBERT WILCOX, traffic engineer; b. May 10, 1928, San Francisco; s. Harold Hull and Harriet Eulalia (Green) C.; m. Barbara Darby, Apr. 6, 9156; children: Stanley, b. 1947; Randy, b. 1948; Janis, b. 1951; Lee Ann,b . 1957; edn: AA, Modesto Jr. Coll. 1947; BS, UC Berkeley 1949; M.Eng., 1955; Command & Gen. Staff Coll., US Army; Reg. Profl. Engr. in Alaska, Ariz., Calif., Nevada, N.Mex. & Ore. Career: asst. dist. traffic engr., Calif. Div. of Hwys. 1949-50, 1953-54; assoc. traffic engr., Richmond 1955-56; city traffic engr., San Leandro 1956-59; city traffic engr., Hayward 1959-65; assoc. in charge, Los Angeles Ofc., Wilbur Smith & Assoc., Cons. Engrs. 1965-68; pres. Robert Crommelin & Assocs., Inc., Cons. Engrs. 1968--; instr. UC Ext., part- time 1968-; honors: Chi Epsilon, Tau Beta Pi 1949; Automotive Safety Found. Fellow 1954; Best Paper, ITE Dist. 6, 1974; mem: Inst. Transportation Engrs. (pres. Dist. 6, 1975); Am. Soc. Civil Engrs.; Am. Pub. Works Assn.; Transportation Research Bd.; Coomodore, Santa Monica Yacht Club; mil: col. (ret.) Corps of Engrs. USAR 1950-80; MSM w/OLC, JSCM, GCM, AVS 1950-53 (pvt.-1/lt.) Korea; Republican; rec: sailing. Res: 5477- 25 Nestle Ave Tarzana 91356 Ofc: 17071 Ventura Blvd, Ste 206, Encino 91316

CROMWELL, ROGER C., construction co. owner; b. May 19, 1941, Oakland; s. Clair C. and Lorraine V. Jackson (Neath) C.; m. Sharron Tempero, June 17, 1967; children: Carrie, b. 1969; Paul, b. 1970; Juli, b. 1975; Justin, b. 1979; edn: AAAE, Modesto Jr. Coll. 1964; BSAE, CalPoly State Univ. 1966; spl. courses, Marquette Univ. 1966, Wash. State Univ. 1982; Calif. Std. Tchr. Cred. 1968, Calif. State Contractor lic., Solano Co. Resale lic. Career: development engr. Allis- Chalmers Mfg. Co., Wilwaukee, Wisc. 1966-67; design engr. Internat. Harvestor, Stockton 1967-68; project engr. Blackwelder Mfg. Co., Rio Vista 1968-71; owner Roger C. Cromwell Constrn. & Supply Co., Vacaville 1971--; currently, mech. engr. US Dept. of Navy, Alameda; honors: Engr. in Tng. 1967; Outstanding Senior 1966; Calif. State Farmer 1958; mem: ASAE (life), Vacaville CofC, Vacaville Trade Club, Vacaville Little League, Soccer League, Fiesta Days; Republican; Catholic; rec: hunting, fishing, skiing. Address: Roger C. Cromwell Cost. & Supply Co., 4386 Cantelon Rd Vacaville 95688

CRONK, ROBERT L., market data co. president; b. Feb. 4, 1942, San Diego; s. Delbert L. and Hattie L. (Yandell) C.; m. Shirley Quinn, Aug. 5, 1966; children: William, b. 1973; Timothy, b. 1975; edn: BS, San Diego State Univ. 1969. Career: tng. ofcr. Calif. First Bank, San Diego 1970; asst. v.p. San Diego Fed. Savings, San Diego 1971-76; v.p./ div. hd. Allstate Savings, N. Hollywood 1976-79; pres./ CEO Calif. Market Data Corp., Glendale 1979--; dir. counseling home loan courses, San Diego & Los Angeles 1977-79; pres. ABCA, L.A. 1977; chmn. Calif. League Consumer Loan Com. 1979; awards: Kiwanian of Yr. 1981; mem: Property Improvement Lenders Council; Am. Bldg. Contractors Assn. (pres. 1978); Calif. Savings & Loan League; Kiwanis (pres. 1982-83); mil: sgt. USAF 1960-64; Republican; Methodist; rec: golf, reading, weight lifting. Res: 23927 Via Bolina Valencia 91355 Ofc: California Market Data, 1110 Sonora, Ste 104, Glendale 91201

CROOK, RONALD JAY, distributing co. president; b. Sept. 16, 1930, Oakland; s. Jack Roy and Helen Josephine (Brimdle) C.; m. Marilyn Hopkins, Nov. 15, 1952; children: Jill Ann, b. 1957, James Hopkins, b. 1963. Career: field svc. supr. Maytag West Coast Co., 1958-60, adminstrv. asst./asst. to the pres. 1960-63, regional mgr. 1963-67, sales mgr. No. Calif. 1967-70; vice pres. Girard-Hopkins Inc. 1970-77, owner/pres. 1977--; pres./prin. Dependable Sales Inc.; charter mem., past pres., dir. No. Calif. Multiple Housing Laundry Assn.; Republican; Prot.; rec: antique autos. Res: 100 Via Serena Alamo 94507 Ofc: Girard-Hopkins Inc. 8120 Capwell Dr Oakland 94621

CROSBY, GEORGE HYDE, stockbroker; b. Jan. 19, 1927, Ely, Nevada; s. Kent Miller and Janice (Hyde) C.; m. Nadine Potter, June 16, 1949; children: Janet, b. 1951; Kent, b. 1952; Mary, b. 1956; Marc, b. 1958; edn: BA, Brigham Young Univ. 1948; Univ. of Utah Law Sch. 1948-51; MBA, Golden Gate Coll. 1965; reg. principal, NASD. Career: Bank of Am., Sunnyvale 1952-54; op. ofcr./ asst. mgr. First Western Bank, Sunnyvale, San Francisco, Riverdale 1954-64; asst. mgr. United Calif. Bank, Gustine, Santa Maria 1964-68; mgr./ v.p. Mid- State Bank, Arroyo Grande, Santa Maria 1968-76; reg. principal Maguire Investments, Inc., Santa Maria 1976--; instr. bus. admin, Allan Hancock Coll., Santa Maria 1967-; dir. T.T.O.C. 1977-79; chair. Fin. Commn., Santa Barbara Co. Ret. Bd. 1975-; mem: Santa Maria CofC (pres. 1974); Santa Maria Kiwanis Club (pres. 1973-74, lt. gov. div. 29, 1980-81); Boys Club, Santa Maria (pres. 1979-80); Salvation Army; mil: USN 1944-45; Republican; LDS; rec: fencing. Res: 4182 Glenview Santa Maria 93455 Ofc: Maguire Investments, Inc., 112 W Jones Santa Maria 93454

CROSS, JACK STANTON, real estate broker; b. Nov. 10, 1939, Onamia, Minn.; s. Gordon Douglas Cross and Dolores Elaine Stanton; m. Deborah Aretos; children: Dawn, b. 1960; Mark, b. 1982; edn: BA, Univ. of Guam 1968; MA, cand., Univ. of Hawaii 1968-69; grad. work, USC 1980-81; R.E. broker, Calif. 1981. Career: asst. pres. Univ. of Guam, Agana, Guam 1969-70; v.p. Am. Mgmt. Co., Agana, Guam 1970-76; mgr. Pantano Realty, Belmont 1976-78; mgr. Geddling & Burke Realtors, Burlingam 1978-79; mgr. Re/ Max, Foster City 1979-81; broker/ owner Re/ Max of Burlingam 1982--; chmn. Pub. Svc. Com.; MLS Governing Bd.; awards: Mgr. of the Yr., Re/Max Internat. 1980; Senator, Jaycees Internat. 1974; mem: San Mateo- Burlingam Bd. Realtors; Pacific Jaycees (Nat. pres. 1974); mil; E-6 USN 1957-67, Air Medal; Democrat; Catholic; rec: scuba diving, hunting, fishing. Ofc: Re/Max of Burlingame, 406 Primrose Rd Burlingame 94010

CROSSON, STEVEN BERNARD, company president; b. June 16, 1954, Providence, R.I.; s. Bernard Albert and June (Miner) C.; m. Janice Karen, Aug. 11, 1979; edn: AA, Pierce Jr. Coll. 1979; refrig.- A/C, North Valley Occupational Trade 1981; 500 H.P. L.A. Steam engr. lic. 1975. Career: stationary engr. Northridge Hosp. 1973-75; sta. engr. West Hills Hosp. 1975-79; sta. engr. Panorama Comm. Hosp. 1977-79; opg. engr. Marina City Club 1979-81; pres. The Wizard, Simi Valley 1980--; awards: Achiev. Awd., No. Valley Occupational Trade; Steam Plant Ops. & Power Turbines; Eagle Scout, Boy Scouts of Am.; mem: Simi Valley CofC; Lutheran; rec: skindiving, carpentry, restoring old cars. Address: The Wizard, 3766 Township Ave Simi Valley 93063

CROZIER, ROBERT WILLIAM, company president; b. July 5, 1935, NY; s. John Robert and Anna (Kramer) C.; m. Lee, Apr. 1, 1977; children: Craig, b. 1963; Denise, b. 1960; edn: BS, New York Univ. 1958. Career: prod. mktg. mgr. Hamilton- Avnet 1973-76; v.p. mktg. electronics gp. VSI Corp. 1976-79; v.p. sales mktg./ founder Advanced Semi- Conductor, Inc. 1979; currently, founder/ pres. Crozier Electronic Sales Co.; mem: Panorama City Rotary; Republican;

Christian; rec: jazz recordings, chess, model railroading. Address: 11821 Thuderbird Ave Northridge 91326

CRUMP, DEAN REBER, chartered life underwriter; b. July 30, 1929, Soda Springs, Idaho; s. Milo Nephi and Ethel Rosina (Hopkins) C.; m. Sharon Robinson, Nov. 12, 1983; children: Denise, b. 1956, Debra, b. 1956, David, b. 1959, (stepchil.) Gregory, b. 1966, David, b. 1968; edn: stu. Ida. State Coll. 1945-46; CLU, American Coll. 1980; ChFC (Chartered Finl. Councilor) cand., 1984. Career: sales, New England Life, Keith Williams Agcy., Sacramento 1954-58, supr. 1958-62; general agt./owner Dean R. Crump Agcy (New England Life), Spokane, Wa. 1962-79; agcy. cons./supr./general agt., Bob W. Horton Agcy., San Diego 1979--; awards: Mgr. of Year 1969, life mem. Hall of Fame and Leaders Assn., New England Life; 20 years Nat. Quality awards, Life Underwriters Assn.; mem: General Agts and Mgrs. Assn. (Spokane pres. 1978-9, bd. dirs. 1974-78); San Diego Life Underwriters Assn. (bd. dirs. 1983-4; chmn. Ethics Com. 1984-5); Spokane CofC 1962-79; mil: cpl. US Army 1951-53; Republican; Ch. of Jesus Christ of L.D.S.; rec: avocado ranch, golf, hunting. Res: 2056 Valley Rim Rd El Cajon 92021 Ofc: Horton Cos. 7801 Mission Ctr Ct. Ste. 310, San Diego 92108

CRUMP, GERALD FRANKLIN, lawyer; b. Feb. 16, 1935, Sacramento; s. John Laurin and Ida May (Banta) C.; m. Glenda Roberts Glass, Nov. 21, 1959; children: Sara Elizabeth, b. 1972, Juliane Kathryn, b. 1974, Joseph Stephen, b. 1977; edn: AB, UC Berkeley 1956, JD, 1959; MA, Baylor Univ. 1966. Career: judge advocate USAF 1960-63; deputy county counsel Los Angeles County 1963--, legislative rep. 1970-73, chief Public Works Div. 1973-, asst. county counsel 1983--; lectr. Pepperdine Univ. (1978), Univ. Calif. (1982); mem: State Bar of Calif., Am. Bar Assn., Los Angeles County Bar Assn. (chmn. Govt. Law Sect. 1983-4), Am. Judicature Soc., Am. Acad. of Polit. and Social Sci., Calif. Historical Soc., Reserve Officers Assn., Air Force Assn., Phi Alpha Delta, Delta Sigma Phi; mil: capt. USAF 1960-63, Merit. Svc. medal, (current) col. USAFR. Res: 4020 Camino de la Cumbre, Sherman Oaks 91423 Ofc: Los Angeles County Counsel, 648 Hall of Administration, Los Angeles 90012

CRUPPER, JOHN LEHMAN, advertising agency president; b. Dec. 7, 1947, Phillips, Tex.; s. William Eugene and Nellie Marie (King) C.; edn: BS, Southern Methodist 1972. Career: v.p. Equipment Financing Group; currently, pres. City Graphics of America; mem: Col. Confederate Air Force; works; Silicon Valley, Calif. Wine Country, Lake Tahoe, Where the Russians Live, Fremont 25th poster; mil: Nat. Guard 1966-72; Baptist; rec: flying, celebrity tennis, scuba diving. Res: 5581 Butano Park Dr Fremont 94538 Ofc: City Graphics of America, POB 261 Fremont 94537

CRUZ, DAVID, real estate co. president; b. Aug. 20, 1947, Bayamon, Puerto Rico, s. Ramon and Angelina (Arila) C.; m. GEanne Talbot, June 23, 1967; children: Lorie Geanne, b. 1968, David Jr., b. 1973; edn: AA in bus. Los Angeles Valley Coll. 1974; Cal Coast Univ. 1976, ORI, Grad. Real Estate Inst. (1980), Cert. Residential Splst. (1981), Calif. Assn. of Realtors. Career: finl. analyst Lockheed Corp., 1966-74; broker/pres. Valley View Realty Inc., San Fernando 1975--; bd. dirs. Southern Calif. Evangelistic Assn.; mem. Am. Entrepreneurs Assn., Nat. Assn. of Realtors, Calif. Assn. of Realtors, Mission Coll. pres. club; mil: cpl. USMCR 1966-72; Christian; rec: reading. Res: 14767 Drew St Sylmar 91342 Ofc: Valley View Realty Inc. 11273 Laurel Cyn San Fernando 91340

CSENDES, ERNEST, business executive; b. Mar. 2, 1926, Satu-Mare, Rumania; nat. 1955; s. Edward O. and Sidonia (von Littman) C.; m. Catherine Vera von Toinai, NYC, Feb. 7, 1953; children: Audrey Carol, b. 1957, Robert Alexande Edward, b. 1962; edn: BA, Prot. Coll., Hungary 1944; BS, Univ. of Heidelberg, W.Ger. 1948; MS, 1950; PhD, 1951. Career: resrch asst. in chem. Univ. of Heidelberg, 1950-51; came to USA 1951; resrch assoc., biochem., Tulane Univ., New Orleans 1951-52; fellow Harvard Univ. 1952-53; resrch chem., organic chem. and elastomer chem. divs., E.I. Du Pont de Nemours and Co., Wilmington, Del. 1953-61; director R&D, Armour & Co. Agricultural Chem. Div., Atlanta 1961-63; v.p. corp. devel. Occidental Petroleum Corp., 1963-64, exec. v.p. Research, Engineering and Devel. and mem. Exec. Com. 1964-68; exec. v.p./chief opr. ofcr./dir. Occidental Research & Engrg. Corp., 1963-68; dir. Occidental Resrch & Engrg. Ltd. U.K., 1964-68; pres./CEO Texas Republic Inds., 1968--; pres/CEO TRI Ltd. and chmn. TRI Internat. Ltd., Bermuda 1971--; mgr./dir. TRI Holdings S.A., Luxembourg 1971--, TRI Capital N.V., Netherlands 1971--; pres./CEO American Cyclopenesis, Me. 1981-83; founder, bd.chmn./pres./CEO Mictonic Technologies, Inc. 1983--. Resrch. on natural resources and indus. internat. (acq. merger, intl. finance, leasing petroleum and minerals); R&D projs. in US, energy and precious metals extraction. Publs: 40 arts. in fields of sci., pollution control, min., petroleum, tech. and mgmt., profl. jours. Num. patents: elastomers, rubber chems., dyes and intermediates, organometallics, organic and biochem., high polymers, plant nutrients, pesticides, process engring. and design of fertilizer plants. Mem: fellow AAAS, fellow Am. Inst. Chemists, Am. Chem. Soc., NY Acad Scis., Am. Def. Preparedness Assn., Am. Security Council, The Royal Soc. of Chem., German Chem. Soc., Am. Mgmt. Assn., Am. Inst. of Mgmt., Am. Inst. of Aero and Astro., Acad. of Polit. Scis. Columbia Univ., Am. Acad. Polit. and Soc. Sci., Resrch Soc. of Am., Sigma Xi, The Explorers Club. Awarded Pro Mundi Beneficio medal, Brazilian Acad. of Humanities, 1975. rec: decorative arts of 18th Century France, violinist, chamber music. res: 1601 Casale Rd. Pacific Palisades 90272.

CULJIS, JANE A., charter yacht broker, business executive; b. May 18, 1941, Sacramento; d. Nicholas and Ruth (Jurgens) Culjis; edn: AA, honors, Stephens

Coll., Columbia, Mo. 1961; Jr. Year Abroad, Univ. Vienna, Austria 1962; CSU San Francisco 1963; grad. stu. UCLA. Career: Western States director, U.S. Nat. Student Assn., Ednl. Travel Inc., 1963-64; editor Calif. Girl Mag., Los Angeles 1964-66; asst. to Creative Dir., Lennen & Newell Advt. Agcy., Beverly Hills 1967-68; exec. v.p. Robert S. Howell & Assocs. Advt. Agcy., L.A. 1969-73; advt. & pub. rels. dir. Weight Watchers International, 1974-76; mktg. dir. Lion Country Safari, Laguna Hills 1977-79; account exec. Cochrane, Chase, Livingston & Co. Advt. Agcy., Newport Beach 1979--; pres. Internat. Charter Assn., Laguna Beach. Awards: two PROTOS awds., Pub. Rels. Soc. of Am. (1979); Atlantic Monthly Writer of Year awd.; 1st pl., Mademoiselle Mag. Annual Short Story Competition; runner-up, Saturday Review Nat. Creative Writing Contest. Mem: Orange Co. Performing Arts Ctr., Women in Bus., Virgin Is. Charter Boat League, Caribbean Tourist Assn., Bus. and Profl. Women, Soc. of Exec. and Profl. Women, Pub. Rels. Soc. of Am., Newport Harbor CofC, Laguna Bch CofC, Stephens Coll. Alumnae Assn., bd.dirs. Laguna Bch Greenbelt; secty. Laguna Bch. Neighborhood Watch; MENSA. rec: yachting, skiing, bicycling. res: 150 Dumond Dr. Laguna Beach 92651. ofc: 1278 Glenneyre Ste. 127, Laguna Bch 92651.

CULLEN, MAURIE CARLA, clinical social worker; b. Nov. 29, 1941, NYC; d. Louis and Mildred (Levine) Davidson; m. Richard Larsen Cullen, Jan. 3, 1976; 1 dau. (by previous m.) Lisa Diane, b. 1969; edn: BA, Mills Coll. 1963; MSW, Boston Univ. 1967; LCSW, Calif. 1969. Career: soc. wkr. Dept. Soc. Svcs., San Francisco 1964-65, Josselyn Diabetes Found. Camps., North Oxford, Mass. 1967; child welfare wkr., soc. wkr. Dept. of Adoptions, Los Angeles County 1968-78; clin. soc. wkr. Northridge (Ca.) Hosp. Found. 1978--, and mem. afil. med. staffs; pvt. practice Encino 1978--; guest lectr. to Family Practice Assts., UCLA Med. Ctr., Northridge Hosp. Found.; mem: Fellow Soc. for Clin. Soc. Wk., Nat. Assn. of Soc. Wk., Soc. for Adolescent Med. (assoc.), Nat., L.A. Group Psychotherapy Socs., Nat. Regis. of Health Care Providers Clin. Soc. Wk.; chmn. bd. dirs. Family Service of Los Angeles 1982-84; bd. dirs. Design for Sharing, UCLA 1978-; alumni admission rep. Mills Coll.; Democrat; Jewish; rec: sailing, theatre, dancing. Res: 4691 Alonzo Ave Encino 91316 Ofc: Western Psychological Ctr., 16255 Ventura Blvd, Ste. 806, Encino 91436

CULVER, TIMOTHY JOHN, personnel co. president; b. Nov. 8, 1955, Cleveland, Ohio; s. Wm. Parker and Rosemarie Jean (Tabor) C.; m. Tamara Lynn Witt, Dec. 28, 1979; 1 child, Timothy II, b. 1981 (dec.); edn: BA in econ., Brown Univ. 1974-78; lic: Bur. of Employment Agces. 7/79. Career: founder/ pres./owner Culver Personnel Agency, Inc., San Diego 1979--; mem. Calif. Assn. of Personnel Consultants; Methodist; rec: chess, Russian Lit., hist. Res: 9371 Broadview San Diego 92101 Ofc: Culver Personnel Agency Inc. 1925 5th Ave San Diego 92101

CUMMINS, BETTY LORRAINE, psychotherapist, educator; b. July 26, 1928, Pasadena; d. Charles Joseph and Lavina Lula (Arnold) Dinley, m. Howard J. Sullivan (dec.); m. 2d. Francis Cummins, Mar. 19, 1955; children: Kathy, b. 1951, Charles, b. 1956, Patrick, b. 1957, Colleen, b. 1959, Michael, b. 1968; edn: BS nursing, CSU Long Bch 1975; MA, MFCC, Azusa Pacific Coll. 1978; PhD admin., Western Sch of Theology 1980; RN, Tacoma Sch. of Nursing 1955; Lifetime Teaching Cred. 1980. Career: O.R. Scrub and Circulating nurse, 1955-62; office nursing part-time, 1962-72; instr. Cypress Coll. 1976-7; lic. Marriage, Family, Child Counselor, pvt. practice 1978--; lic. self-empl. provider of cont. edn. for health profls., dba A/M Educational Services, Long Beach 1980--; coord. wellness workshops, Pegasus Inst. Inc.; patentee: Mother Surrogate to hold and monitor infant (sensory deprivation) 1978; author three books: Charity: Bond of Perfectness (1979), ABC's of Character Building (1980), Couple Counseling (1981), 3 unpub. vols. poetry; four TV interviews (Ch.9) 1981, 82; honors: nurse role model, Fresno Co. Hosp. Sch. of Nursing 1957, Phi Kappa Phi 1975; Republican; L.D.S. Ch. (tchr. Wrightwood Ward 1982, pres. Relief Soc. L.Bch. 10th Ward); rec: swim, jog, classical music. Res: 756 Lark, Wrightwood 92397 Ofc: A/M Educational Services, 1140 E. Ocean Blvd Ste 107, Long Beach 90802

CUMMINGS, MARILYN LOUISE, tutoring center owner; b. Sept. 20, 1932, Chgo.; d. Blaine and Ruth Louise (Niekamp) C.; div.; edn: grad. So. Sem. 1952; grad. work CSU Long Beach, 1957-61; spl. courses w/Mae Carden 1969. Career: engring. dept. Pac. Tel. Co., Compton 1953-5; music tchr. Music Center Studios, San Pedro 1955-7, founder/co-dir. Musicland Studios (main ofc., S.P.) 1957-64; music tchr./coord., Betty Thomas Music Sch., Torrance 1965-7, others; dist. mgr. Field Ent. Ednl. Corp. 1967-9; tutor/field rep. Wingrock Sch. Inc., Torrance 1969-71; area mgr. Am. Incentive to Read, L.A. 1969; founder/director Marilyn Cummings Tutoring Ctr., San Pedro 1969--; advt. rep. Christian Sci Monitor, 1971-3, 76; mktg. rep. Nat. Toll Free Mktg. 1983. Recipient sales awd., Field Ent. Ednl. Corp. 1967; mem: Accordion Fedn. of No. Am. (judge Music Contest 56-64, 78-), Sweet Adelines (bd.dirs. 1982-4), San Pedro CofC, Bus. & Profl. Womens Club; past mem. BBB, Accordion Tchrs Guild, Toastmistress, Hermosa Harmony Singers (vp 1977-80); devel. successful method for teaching reading to illiterate and slow learners 1969; Christian Sci. (bd. 1973-6). Res: 333 So Grand Ave San Pedro 90731 Ofc: Marilyn Cummings Tutoring Center, 312 No Gaffey St, 101-2, San Pedro 90731

CUNLIFFE, SYLVIA, city purchasing agent; b. Mar. 4, 1933, St. Louis, Mo.; d. Manuel and Manuela (Urbina) Capetillo; m. Heber Cunliffe, May 14, 1960; 1 dau. Linda, b. 1961; edn: BA, Polit. sci., UCLA 1957. Career: jr./administrv. asst. L.A. Dept. Pub. Wks. Bur. of Engring., 1957-64; acting/asst. dir. Bur. of Personnel, 1964-65; sr./prin./chief adminstrv. asst. Bd. of Pub. Wks. 1965-77;

asst. dir. Bur. Street Maint. 1977-79; gen. mgr. Dept. Gen. Services 1979--; city purchasing agt. 1980--; v.p. Crown Ink Co.; mem. Los Angeles City Orgns: Mayor's Cabinet, L.A. Mgmt. Assn. (pres. 1983), Emergcy. Ops. Bd., Adv. Mgmt. Council, Transp. Com., Mats. Mgmt. Com. (chpsn.), Purch. Stds. Com. (chpsn.); num. recognition and svc. awards: L.A. Children's Mus. (1980), Blind Children's Ctr. (1983), Govt. of Bolivia (1982), Consul Gen. of Guatamela (1982), Casa de Espana (1980), Mayor (6); City Employee of the Year 1982; chpsn. US Svgs. Bond Drive 1983; mem: Nat. Assn. of Purch. Mgmt., Calif. Assn. of Pub. Purch. agt., Am. Public Wks. Assn., Building Owners and Mgrs. Assn., Am. Mgmt. Assn.; chpsn. L.A. Street Street Scene Festival; exec. bd. Am. Chamber Sym.; bd. advs. Americana Dance Theatre; num. publs. on urban studies; Prot.; rec: skiing, music. Res: 9528 Tullis Dr Beverly Hills 90210 Ofc: City of Los Angeles, Dept. Gen. Svcs., 200 N. Main St, Rm. 800, City Hall East, Los Angeles 90012

CUNNINGHAM, JAMES WENDELL, data processing executive; b. Mar. 10, 1950, Broken Bow, Custer Co., Nebr.; s. Frank Phillip and Edith Fern (Cosner) Cunningham; edn: Western Nebr. 1969, 70. Career: prodn. control mgr. Calif.Federal Savings, Los Angeles 1972-79; systems analyst Analyst International, Studio City 1979-80; mgr. Data Processing, Ops. - R. G. sLOANE, Sun Valley 1980--; conductr. seminar on specialized software usage for L.A. Sch. District; mem. Masons, Elks; Republican; Christian; rec: skiing, racquet ball, camping; res: 22948 Magnolia Glen Dr. Valencia 91355. ofc: R. G. Sloane, 7606 Clybourne, Sun Valley 91352.

CUNNINGHAM, JOHN RICHARD, manufacturers representative; b. Apr. 14, 1924, Troy, NY; s. Ralph Henry and Mary Estelle (Cummiskey) Cunningham; m. Edna Valmassy, Dec. 12, 1952; two daus.: Kathleen Ann, b. 1955, Mary Angela, b. 1958; edn: BA, Hobart Coll. 1948, MBA, Wharton Sch of Bus., Univ. Pa. 1950. Career: sales rep. Behr Manning Co., San Francisco 1950-57, regional sales mgr. Behr Manning/Norton Co., San Francisco 1957-70; partner Westates Sales, Foster City 1970-82; pres. WestatesSales Div. CTF&S Corp., Hayward 94545; awarded President's Trophy, Norton Co., 1969, 70. mem: Am. Mgmt.Assn., Soc. of Pkging & Handling Engrs., Sales & Mktg. Execs., Mfrs' Agents Nat. Assn., Mfrs' Reps. Assn., Nat. Fedn. of Independent Business; mil: s/sgt. US Army 1943-46; rec: golf, jog, travel; res: 945 Yorkshire Dr. Los Altos 94022. ofc: Westates Sales, 21066 Cabot Blvd. Hayward 94545.

CUNO, EMIL OSCAR, investment broker; b. Aug. 15, 1919, Jonesburg, Mo.; s. Otto C. and Charlotte L. (Meier) C.; m. Katherine B. Cleveland, June 16, 1946; children: Karen Sue, b. 1949; Melinda Mae, b. 1953; reg. rep., Nat. Assn. Securities Dealers, Wash. DC. Career: owner/ mgr. Cuno Motor Sales, Inc., Montgomery City, Mo. 1946-56; semi- ret. 1956-63; reg. rep. First Calif. Corp., Orange 1963-72; reg. rep. Robert Scott, Inc., Orange 1972-76; currently, investment broker Securities West, Inc., Tustin; pres./ bd. mem. Cuno Tractor Co.; mem. Kiwanis; mil: spl. agent Security Intelligence Div., War Dept. 1942-45; Republican; Christian; rec: world travel. Res: 11472 Kearney Way Garden Grove 92640 Ofc: Securities West, Inc., 17601 17th St Tustin 92680

CURATOLA, NEAL T., lawyer; b. Aug. 9, 1954, Freehold, NJ; s. Michael P. and Gelsomine (Scotto) C.; m. Jill, June 1, 1980; edn: BA, cum laude, Univ. of Baltimore 1976; JD, cum laude, Western State Univ. Coll of Law 1981; admitted to practice, Calif. State Bar, US Dist. Ct. Career: law clerk/ atty. Mitchell Reed Sussman, Newport Beach 1981-83; atty. at law/ sole practitioner, Fullerton 1983--; awards: Am. Jurisprudence Awd. (constnl. law), Western States Univ. 1980, Law Review, 1981; Democrat; Catholic; rec: tennis. Res: 134 S Pritchard St Fullerton 92633 Ofc: Neal T. Curatola, Atty. at Law, 202 N Harbor Blvd Fullerton 92632

CUROTTO, RICKY JOSEPH, lawyer; b. Dec. 22, 1931, Lomita Park; s. Enrico and Nora Marie (Giusso) C.; m. Lynne Therese Ingram, Dec. 31, 1983; children: Dina, b. 1960, John, b. 1962, Alexis, b. 1969; edn: BS cum laude, Univ. of San Francisco 1953; JD, USF Sch. of Law 1958. Career: assoc. Peart, Baraty & Hassard, San Francisco 1958-60; sr. counsel for Land Devel. Div., Utah International Inc. and v.p. of related real estate cos. 1961-82; asst. secty. Utah Internat. Inc., 1966--; senior counsel for Corp. Components & Bus. Devel. Div., 1983--; secty./counsel Ross Valley Homes Inc., 1965--; Dir: First Security Realty Services Corp., Simco Indsl. Mortgage Co., Garden Hotels Inv. Co., Capstone Capital Corp.; bd. trustees, Univ. of San Francisco; honors: apptd. to Nat. Panel of Arbitrators, Am. Arbitr. Assn. 1962; Bur. of Nat. Affairs award 1958; USF Alumni distinguished service award 1981. Mem: State Bar of Calif., San Francisco Bar Assn., Am. Bar Assn., Commonwealth Club of Calif. (past chmn. Lawmaking Procedures Sect.), USF Alumni Assn.; mem. Calf. Assn. for act, SF Mus. Soc., Assn. of Governing Bds. of Univs. & Colls., Pi Sigma Alpha, Phi Alpha Delta; publs: art. USF Law Rev., Winter 1975; mil: lst lt. US Army 1954-56; Republican; Catholic. Res: 1071-A Foster City Blvd, Foster City 94404 Ofc: Utah International Inc., 550 California St, Rm. 700, San Franciso 94104

CURRY, RONALD PHILIP, x-ray co. owner; b. July 11, 1934, Cleveland, Ohio; s. Edmond Evert and Mary Esther (Baird) C.; m. Eleanore Mae Semian, June 23, 1956; children: Ronald Edmond, b. 1958, Philip Alan, b. 1961, Steven Michael, b. 1965, Shawn Michael, b. 1969; edn: AS in E.E., Alliance Coll. 1958; math. & engring. courses, Gannon Coll. 1958-59; Cert. Engring. Tech., Nat. Soc. Profl. Engrs. 1967; Calif. lic. Life & Disability Ins. Agt. 1972. Career: worked with father in family htg., air condtg. bus. 1945-53; x-ray engr. Picker X-Ray, Cleveland, Ohio 1959, transf. to Canton, Ohio in chg. of territory, 1960-, transf. to Fullerton, Ca. 1963-69; founder/owner Curry X-Ray (planning, installation, svc. of x-ray equip. in hosps., clinics, med. offices, and L.A.

School Mobile X-Ray Unit Buses), 1969--; pres. Curry X-Ray, Inc. 1977-; cons. architl. firms, other X-Ray cos.; honored with spouse by scroll signed by Pope John Paul II, presented by their pastor on their 25th wedding anniversary 1981; patron, Martin Luther Hosp. (Anaheim), Little Co. of Mary (Torrance), Fullerton Civic Light Opera, Orange Co. Profl. Organists Guild, Little League teams; works: purchased (1972) and restored current residence, blt. in 1923, the only Georgian Style home in Fullerton, home named as historical site by City of Fullerton and State of Calif. (1977), now listed in State and Nat. Archives; mil: splst. 4c US Army Security Agcy. 1953-56; St. Mary's Catholic Ch.; rec: photog., computer. Address: Curry X-Ray, Inc., 1155 W. Orangethorpe Ave, Fullerton 92633

CURTIN, RICHARD PAUL, lawyer; b. Dec. 19, 1953, Coronado; s. John Robert and Margaret Ellen (Stewart) C.; m. Judi Curtin, May 20, 1978; edn: BA, UC Santa Barbara 1976; JD, Univ. of San Diego Sch. of Law 1979; admitted to Calif. State Bar 1979. Career: assoc. Cannon & Thompson, Lancaster 1979-80; assoc. Potter & Eberhardt, Lancaster 1980-82; assoc. Potter, Cannon & Eberhardt 1982-83; partner 1983; sole proprietor Richard P. Curtain, Esq., Lancaster 1983--; bus. law tchr. Antelope Valley Comm. Coll. 1981-83; honors: Univ. of San Diego Sch. of Law Tutorial Pgm. 1977-79; intern Legal Aid Soc. Immigration Pgm. 1978-79; intern, Fed. Defenders of San Diego, Inc. 1978-79; mem: Am. Bar Assn.; Los Angeles Co. Bar Assn.; Antelope Valley Bar Assn.; Republican; Episcopal; rec: suba diving, racquetball. Res: 44670 Benald St Lancaster 93534 Ofc: Potter, Cannon & Eberhardt, 1672 West Ave J, Ste 105, Lancaster

CUSAK, STANLEY MICHAEL, chiropractor; b. Nov. 28, 1944, Norristown, Pa.; s. John Joseph and Catherine Mary (Woltas) C.; m. Sandra, Aug. 29, 1970; children: Desiree, b. 1973, Zachary, b. 1975, Jonathan, b. 1977, Austin, b. 1979; edn: AA, Fresno City Coll. 1969; BA, geog., CSU Fresno 1971; BS in human biol., and DC, cum laude, Palmer Coll. Chiropractic 1975; postgrad. tng. in Chiropractic Orthopedics; Diplomate Nat. Bd. Chiro. Examiners 1975; grad. Walther Applied Kinesiology Seminars 1981. Career: chiropractic clinic director/owner Cusak Chiropractic Offices, Fresno 1975--; instr. Palmer Coll. of Chiro. 1974-75; Fresno area chmn. Palmer Alumni Bldg. Fund 1983; mem: Internat., Am., Calif. chiropractic assns.; past pres. Chiro. Info. Bur. of Fresno; Internat. Coll. Applied Kinesiology, Calif. Assn.; Central Valley Chiro. Assn. (pres. 1984); Parker Chiro. REsrch. Found.; CSUF Alumni Assn.; Am. Assn. Nutrition and Dietary Cons.; Found. for Chiro. Edn. and Resrch.; Scoutmaster Sequoia Council 1970; Dale Carnegie Inst. grad. 1982; Toastmasters Intl. exec. club 1983; mil: splst. E4 US Army Security Agcy. 1962-65; Republican; Christian; rec: wt. lifting, sports, family. Res: 12540 E. Morningside Clovis 93612 Ofc: Cusak Chiropractic Offices, 3738 E. Shields, Fresno 93726

CYMET, PAULINE, employment agency owner; b. Nov. 13, 1942, San Francisco; d. Max M. and Rose S. (Rabinowitch) Cymet; edn: BA in Spanish, UC Los Angeles 1968; Calif. Lic. Personnel Counselor 1982. Career: employment agcy. mgr. Creative Counseling, San Francisco 1968-71, counselor Cosmopolitan Personnel, S.F 1971-76; exec. recruiter (medical indus.) Druthers Agcy., Marina Del Rey 1978; dir. pub. rels. Great Western Cities, No. Hollywood 1979; ofc. mgr./adminstr. Heritage Ent. (film distbn.), L.A. 1980; oowner The Right Connections Personnel Service (entertainment indus. splsts.), L.A. 1982--; seminar spkr./tchr. Careers for Women, Santa Monica Comm. Coll. 1979; mem. Nat. Assn. for Female Execs. Inc., Women in Show Bus., Century City CofC; jewelry designer: products displayed in nat. catalog, sold in boutiques in S.F and Sausalito; Democrat; Jewish; rec: gemology, plastercraft, backgammon. Res: 11849 Goshen, Los angeles 90049 Ofc: The Right Connections Personnel Service, 511 N. La Cieneta, Ste.212, Los Angeles 90048

CZERNY, RICHARD KARL, corporate executive; b. Jan. 11, 1920, Ljubiza, Yugoslavia, nat. 1966; s. Richard Franc and Zora (Schuhlhof) C.; m. Zdenka Jurkovic, Feb. 15, 1951; children: Maria, b. 1951; Richard, b. 1957; Tom, b. 1961; edn: Absolvent Juris, Univ. of Belgrad 1941; Absolvent Commerce, Univ. of Zagreb 1942; Bach., Commerce Acad. Maturity 1938. Career: controller, ICN Parmaceuticals, Irvine 1975-81; sr. v.p. fin., Covina 1981--; sr. v.p CDI, City of Industry 1968--; secty./ treas. Ferro Tool, Inc., City of Ind. 1978--; dir. CDI; controller ICN 1962--; awards: 1st May Awarde, Senj, Yugoslavia 1950; Prof. of Mktg. & Sales Technics, Commerce Coll., Scnj, Yugoslav.; mil: capt. Croatian Army; Republican; Catholic. Res: 718 W Manzanita Sierra Madre 91024 Ofc: Consolidated Devices, Inc., 19220 San Jose Ave Industry 91744

D

DABIRI, ALI E., scientist; b. Oct. 15, 1944, Teheran, Iran; s. Mahmoud and Rezvan (Montaser) D.; 1 dau., Cynthia, b. 1977; edn: BS, Teheran Polytechnic 1966; MS, Mass. Inst. Tech. 1969, Eng. Degree, 1970, ScD, 1971. Career: lectr. mech. engring. dept. MIT, 1971-72; prof. of mech. engring. (dept. hd. 1977-9) Mehr Univ. of Tech., Teheran 1972-79; sr. scientist in chg. of fusion tech., Science Applications, Inc. La Jolla, Ca. 1979--; bd. dirs. Iranian Labs. of Sci. and Tech., 1972-79; dir. Technisearch Internat., Inc. Denver, Colo. 1981-; honors: highest ednl. awards, medal, King of Iran (1966), best researcher awd., Iran (1977); mem: ASHRAE, Am. Soc. of Energy Engrs., Fusion Energy

Assocs.; author 2 texts on engring. thermodynamics (in Farsi), over 40 publs. in energy areas; rec: sports, reading. Res: 3268-41 Via Marin, La Jolla 92037 Ofc: Science Applications, 1200 Prospect St. La Jolla 92037

DACKERMAN, JERRY LEE, telecommunications consultant; b. Feb. 8, 1950, NYC; s. Wm. Arthur and Dorothy Mae (Tilts) Dackerman; m. Suzanne Fritch, Dec. 19, 1982; edn: BBA in human resources mgmt. & fin., Fla. Atlantic Univ. 1974. Career: major account mgr. satellite systems, RCA American Communications, Los Angeles 1977-79; major accts. rep. Executone, Inc., L.A. 1975-76; gen. partner Robin & Dackerman (telecommunications cons. firm), Beverly Hills 1979--; instr. Golden Gate Univ., Grad. Sch. of Bus. Adm. 1982. Mem. Soc. of Telecommunications Consultants 1980, LA CofC. mil: sgt. USAF 1969-70; res: 906 N. Kings Rd. Los Angeles 90069. ofc: Robin & Dackerman, 8484 Wilshire Blvd. Beverly Hills 90211.

D'ACQUISTO, JOHN FRANCIS, fmr. professional baseball player; company president; b. Dec. 24, 1951, San Diego; s. Fred C. and Frances Agnes (Piraino) D.; m. Teresa Elizabeth Ketchum, Nov. 28, 1979; 1 dau: Danica Cherie, b. 1981; edn: bus. courses, UC Berkeley Ext. 1974, 75, 77; desig: Major League Baseball Players' Assn. mem.; Trading Commn. Commodity Trading Advisor; Screen Actors Guild mem. Career: profl. baseball pitcher: San Francisco Giants 1970-75, St. Louis Cardinals 1976, San Diego Padres 1976-80, Montreal Expos 1980, California Angels 1981-84, Atlanta Braves 1982, Oakland A's 1982, Chicago White Sox 1983; sales and mktg. exec. Bank of Americard Visa, S.F. 1975-77; Founders'List, loan agt. Sun Svgs. & Loan Assn., 1980-82; owner/ pres. D'Acquisto & Assocs. Inc., 1984--; profl. actor/model (singer/guitarist;) 1984--: nat. t.v. commercials; num. benefit shows for charity, frequent guest spkr., media talk show guest; advisor for lg. investment portfolios; honors: Most Valuable Player, Rookie of the Year, All Star Team, S.F. Giants (1974); chmn. San Diego chpt. Easter Seals (1978); hon. chmn. Retinitis Pigmentosa Found. (1978, 79); Calif. Golden Leaf Award (1978); co-chair (w/wife Terri D'Acquisto), S.D. March of Dimes (1980); mem: dir./bd. chmn. Dist. 32 Little League Baseball Clinic; Lomas Santa Fe Country Club; Torrey Pines Golf Men's Club; Republican; Catholic; rec: equestrian. Ofc: D'Acquisto & Associates, Inc. 9665 Wilshire Blvd, Ste 400 7, Beverly Hills 90210

D'ADDIO, JANIE, manufacturing co. president; b. Mar. 24, 1938, Cassville, Mo.; d. Newell and Pearl Henson; m. Glenn Brooks, div.; m. 2d. Salvatore D'Addio, Sept. 30, 1976; children: Teresa Lynn, b. 1955, Stephen, b. 1958; lic. real estate broker, Calif. 1971-. Career: real estate sales Century 21 R.E., 1971-72, broker/owner two R.E. offices, 1972-76; founder/ owner three pvt. mail & bus. svc. centers, Santa Ana 1979-; founder/owner/pres. Security Mfg. Corp. (mfr. postal boxes), 1980--, now with 4000 stores nationwide; prin./bd. chmn. Mail Boxes etc, USA (nat. franchise co. w/115 stores), Carlsbad 1983--; founder/prin./pres. a 3d. bus. rel. to mail service bus., 1983-; author 3 books: Every Woman Can (1983), Turning Mail Boxes into Cash Boxes (1981), Monica's Hannakah House (1984); owner publishing co. (childrens' books), mem: USA CofC, Huntington Bch CofC, Charter 100 Club, NY Women in Bus., Comml. Mail Receiving Assn.; Repulican; Baptist; rec: sculptress, vol. speaking to women on going into bus. Ofc: Security Mfg. Corp., 5702 Research Dr. Huntington Beach 92649

D'ADDONA, VALERIE, investment broker; b. July 2, 1949, Brklyn.; d. Salvatore and Constance (Stellino) Cavalcante; m. Philip Anthony D'Addona, Oct. 18, 1969; edn: Santa Monica City Coll. 1972-7, UCLA 1977-9, Pierce Coll. 1980; lic. Life Ins., Annuity, 1982, NASD, NYSE Reg. 1981. Career: sales asst. Dean Witter, Beverly Hills 1968-76, Loeb Rhoades, BH, 1976-77, Paine Webber, Encino 1977-81; investment broker Smith Barney, Westlake Village 1981--; guest spkr. bus. classes Moorpark Coll. 1983, 84; mem. Inst. of Finl. Planners; Westlake CofC (mem. com.; stage mgr. Gr. Pumpkin Festival 1981-3); Republican; Christian; rec: oil painting, sculpturing. Res: 22656 Cass Ave Woodland Hills 91364 Ofc: Smith Barney, 100 No Westlake Blvd Westlake Village 91361

DADISMAN, LYNN ELLEN, financial services marketing executive; b. Mar. 1, 1946, Los Angeles; d. Orlan Sidney and Erna Lou (Harris) Friedman; div.; edn: stu. UCLA 1963-5, Willis Bus.Coll. 1965-6, Viewpoints Inst. 1970-71, UCLA Ext. 1971-2; Finl. Schs. of Am., NASD, 1982; lic. Nat. Assn. Securities Dealers, 1982. Career: ofc. mgr. Harleigh Sandler Co., Los Angeles 1965-67; customer service Investors Diversified Svcs, W. L.A. 1968-76; exec. sec. McCulloch Oil Corp., W.L.A. 1976; mgr. publs., Security First Group, Century City 1976-80; dir. mktg./mgr. customer svc. Ins. Mktg. Svcs., Santa Monica 1981-2; v.p. Decatur Petroleum Corp., Santa Monica 1982-3; investor/ broker rels. Angeles Corp., Los Angeles 1984--; mem: Internat. Assn. for Finl. Planning, L.A. World Affairs Council, Nat. Assn. Secs. Dealers; orgns: Migi Car Club of Am. (newsletter ed., sec.), L.A. County Mus of Art, Smithsonian Instn., Internat. Womens Bowling Cong.; pub. poetry, Westwind, UCLA Lit. Mag., 1964; rec: writing, bowling. Res: 3442 Centinela Ave. #15, Los Angeles 90066 Ofc: Angeles Corp. 10301 West Pico Blvd Los Angeles 90064

DADURKA, VICKI, lawyer; b. Shamokin, Penna.; d. Edward David and Florence Marie (Pilarski) D.; edn: Santa Monica Coll. 1973-74; JD, Univ. of San Fernando Law Sch. 1979; Cert. Fin. Mgmt., NYU 1982; admitted to practice, State Bar of Calif. 1980. Career: var. legal/ exec. sectl. & adminstrv. pos., Calif. & Penna. (incl. work on Berrigan Bros. & Pentagon Papers political trials); paralegal Pratter & Young, Beverly Hills 1976-78; legal asst. Gibson, Dunn & Crutcher, Century City 1978-79; atty., sole practitioner, gen. practice law, Los Angeles 1980-84; proj. coord. Los Angeles Olympic Organizing Com. 1984--; awards: Outstanding Young Women of Am. 1978; Am. Jurisprudence Awd. 1979; Spl. Svc. Awd., Dauphin Co. Young Democrats 1971; mem: Am. & Los Angeles Co. Bar Assns.; Women Lawyers Assn.; Nat. Assn. Female Execs.; Daupin Co. Young Democrats; rec: antiques, decorating, photog. Res: 1933 Manning Ave Los Angeles 90025 Ofc: Vicki Dadurka, Esq., POB 25778, Los Angeles 90025

DAGES, THOMAS MICHAEL, real estate investment broker; b. June 25, 1949, Taft; s. Wm. John and Fern (Robert) D.; m. Janet Ferrua, Nov. 4, 1978; edn: Real Estate Cert., Fresno City Coll. 1975. Career: salesman Red Carpet Real Estate, Clovis 1974; broker/ pres. Gateway Real Estate, Fresno 1976; broker/ owner Dages, Inc., Red Carpet Real Estate, Fresno 1979; owner/ broker T. Michael & Co. Real Estate, Fresno 1981--; chmn. Fresno Multiple Listing Svc. 1983; honors: recogn. awds. Fresno Bd. Realtors (1983), Fresno MLS (1980-83), and Red Carpet Real Estate (1974, 75, 76); mem: Nat., Calif. Assns. Realtors; Calif. Bus. Leaders of Am.; Optimist Club of Fresno; publs: Save Dollars, How to Sell Your Real Estate; mil: E-4 USN 1969-74, Vietnam decorations; Republican; Methodist; rec: antiques dealer. Address: T. Michael & Co., 3052 Anderson Clovis 93612

DAGGETT, ROBERT S., lawyer; b. Sept. 15, 1930, LaCrosse, Wisc.; s. Dr. Willard Manning (heart and vascular surgeon; Harvard Med. Sch. faculty, staff Mass. Gen. Hosp., Boston; Fellow Am. Coll. of Physiol.; lectr, writer on med. subjects) and Vida Naomi (Sherman) Daggett; m. Helen Neal Hosler, July 19, 1976; children: Ann, b. 1962, John, b. 1964; edn: AA, Univ. Wisc. 1950; AB, (honors in polit.sci., highest honors in journalism), UC Berkeley 1952, and JD, 1955. Career: partner San Francisco law firm of Brobeck, Phleger & Harrison, 1966--; major comml. litigation esp. antitrust, intellectual prop., securities and other corp. litigation. Admitted to Calif Bar 1955, US Supreme Ct. Bar 1967, admitted in various Fed. Cts.; adj. prof. Hastings Coll. of Law and mem. Adv. Bd., Hastings Center for Trial and Appellate Advocacy; instr. Federal Ct. Practice Pgm. and apptd. mem. Teaching Com.(No.Dist. of Calif.); frequent lectr., writer on legal subjects; judge in Nat. Moot Court competition. Winner, Joffre Debate between UC and Stanford, 1952; asst. coach of debate, Univ. Calif., 1954-55. Mem: Bohemian Club (SF), State Bar of Calif., Am. Bar Assn.(Sects. on Litigation, Antitrust, Judicial Administrn.), Bar Assn. of S.F., Am. Judicature Soc., Phi Delta Phi legal frat., Theta Xi frat., Order of the the Golden Bear; past mem. Bd. Visitors, UC Santa Cruz: Coll. V. Coauthor Rev. of Selected Code Legislation, Cal.Cont.Edn.of Bar 1955; participant in legal pgms., seminars. Mil: 1st lt. US Army JAGC, QMC 1956-60. Republican. Protestant. rec: photog., music. ofc: Brobeck, Phleger & Harrison, No. 1 Market Plaza, San Francisco 94105.

DAHL, DEVON NILSON, financial advisor; b. Nov. 4, 1942, Ogden, Utah; s. Earl Wm. and Evaline (Thurgood) D.; m. Carma John, Dec. 3, 1965; children: Mindee Jo b. 1966, Darian Dee b. 1968, Shaun Dee b. 1969, Kyle John b. 1970, Brenden Quin b. 1973, Shane Shared b. 1975; edn: BS, Weber State Coll. 1967; Master's, Wharton Sch., Univ. of Penna. 1969. Career: adminstrv. asst. to City Mgr. of Inglewood, Calif. 1968-69; contract adminstr. Economic & Youth Opportunities Agcy. 1969-70; bus. office mgr. Pacific Tel., Los Angeles 1970-72; pres. Alpha Cabinets, Inc., 1978-80; pres./owner Devon N. Dahl, Inc. Huntington Beach 1972--; honors: Fels Scholarship (1967), Nat. Rookie Team Leader 1976, BSA Award of Merit (1976) and Adult Scout Service Award (1983), Fountain Valley City Council service awd. (1981), Distinguished Alumni Weber St. Coll. 1982; Life and Qual. Mem. Million Dollar Round Table (MDRT Spkr. 1979), Nat. Quality Awd. (9 yrs), Nat. Sales Achieve. Awd. (10 yrs), Man of the Year (4); mem. Boy Scouts of Am. (Varsity Scoutmaster 1983-4; chmn. Pacifica Dist. 1978-9), So. Calif. Weber St. Alumni Assn. (pres. 1982-), PTA, Fountain Valley Rec. League (coach 5 yrs), var. citizen gps.; publs: sev. books of family heritage, poetry, humourous stories; Republican (Calif. Repub. Assem.); Ch. of Jesus Christ of L.D.S. (High Priest Gp. Ldr. 1979-80); rec: raquetball, running, music. Res: 18152 Santa Arabella Fountain Valley 92708 Ofc: Devon N. Dahl, Inc. 2120 Main, Ste 160, Huntington Beach 92648

DAHLHEIMER, DONALD JOSEPH, management consultant; b. Apr. 23, 1931, St. Louis, Mo.; s. Joseph Adam and Marie Barbara (Fraum) D.; m. Adelma Mae Gresham, Jan. 29, 1954; children: Mark, b. 1954; Dona, b. 1955; Philip, b. 1957; Craig, b. 1959; edn: St. Louis Univ. 1953-4; Washington Univ. 1960-2; profl. seminars 1966, 69. Career: sales supr. Campbell Soup Co., Detroit 1953-64; gen. mktg. mgr. Pet Inc., St. Louis, Mo. 1964-69; v.p. mktg. The Borden Co., Coral Gables, Fla. 1969-71; exec. v.p. Lindsay International, San Mateo, Ca. 1971-76; pres. Dalheimer & Associates, Inc., San Mateo 1976--; faculty The Princeton Research Inst.; lectr. PRI Mergers, Acquisitions & Divestitures Seminars; lectr. Univ. Calif., Wash. Univ.; apptd. Ky. Col. by Gov. Nunn, 1971; past mem. bd. dirs. San Mateo Boys Club. Works: initiated the 1979 acquisition of Lawry's Foods Inc. by Thomas J. Lipton for $66.2 million cash. Mil: sgt. USMC, 2 Battle Stars, Korea; Conservative; Catholic; rec: fine arts collector. Res: 2752 Waltham Cross Belmont 94002 Ofc: Dahlheimer & Assocs. Inc. 60 East 3rd Av, Ste 390, San Mateo 94401

DAIGLE, FREDERICK JOSEPH, information security specialist; b. Apr. 21, 1924, Boston, Mass.; s. Archie Joseph and Margaret Rita (Hart) Daigle; m. Sheila Clinkenbeard, June 1, 1975; chil: Denise, b. 1951, Tina Dotson, b. 1959; edn: BS in bus. adm., Southwestern Univ. 1983; lic. real estate broker, Calif. Career: commnd. warrant ofcr. USN, worldwide svc., 1941-62, ret.; chief of classification mgmt. Lockheed Missile & Space Co., Sunnyvale 1962-80, staff information security splst., responsible for new bus. proposals and estab. security pgms. in new corp. cos., Lockheed Corp., 1980--; chmn. bd.dirs. Lockheed Missile & Space Co. Nat. Mgmt. Assn. (mgmt. edn. pgm.). Mem:

NCMS, Nat. Classification Mgmt. Soc. (Founders Com.; bd.dirs. 9 yrs.; nat. pres. 1974, 1979; nat. seminar chmn. 1968, 73, 80; senior mem. of the soc.; awarded six certs. of appreciation). Publs.: contbg. ed. NCMS Jour. (1964 , 66, 74) and Bull. (bi-mo., 1969-80), num. arts. Mil: decorated 8 campaign medals w/5 combat stars; Republican; Catholic; rec: youth leader, golf, real estate broker; res: 2309 Burning Tree Rd., Half Moon Bay 94019; ofc: Lockheed Corp., 1111 Lockheed Way, Sunnyvale 94086.

DAILEY, MAE HILEMAN, charitable association executive; b. Oct. 19, 1907, Mabel, Ore.; d. Richard and Martha Jane (Trotter) Hileman; m. Earl Dailey, Nov. 8, 1944; raised (orphans) Sheila Trotter, b. 1949, Tom Trotter, b. 1952; edn: BA, Univ. of Ore. 1929; 2 yrs. grad. study, U. of Chgo., Chgo. Theol. Seminary; Registered Social Worker. Career: teacher high sch. 5 years; asst. exec. dir. Children's Home, 5 years, exec. director, 12 yrs.; Mothers March director, March of Dimes, 13 years, ret. Honors: listed in Women of Our Valley by Bertha Rice; Women of the Year (3 times), Bees Clubs; Vol. of the Year, League of Friends. Mem. Childrens Home Bd. 3 yrs.; YWCA Bd. Bd. 16 yrs (bd. pres. 3 yrs); San Jose Appeals Bd. 5 yrs.; Sierra Club (life mem); Quota Club (pres. 1950-2; regional v.p. Quota Int.); San Jose Womens Club (sect. chpsn); Congregational; rec: hiking, camping. Res: 1127 Delynn San Jose 95125

DALBECK, RICHARD WARREN, utility co. executive; b. Aug. 6, 1948, Houston, Texas; s. Robert Ellis and Mary Virginia (Gibson) D.; m. Virginia James, May 12, 1973; children: Allison, b. 1977, Emily, b. 1980; edn: BS, magna cum laude, USC 1970, MBA, magna cum laude 1972; CPA, Calif. 1976. Career: sr. auditor Arthur Young & Co., Los Angeles 1972-75; finl. planning analyst Pacific Lighting Corp., L.A. 1975-76, sr. finl. analyst 1976-77, mgr. of finl. pln. and analysis, 1977-79; controller So. Calif. Gas Co., L.A. 1979-81, v.p. acctg. and finance, 1981-82; controller Pac. Lighting Corp., 1981-, v.p./controller 1983--; honors: (USC): Phi Kappa Phi (univ.), Beta Gamma Sigma (bus.), Beta Alpha Psi (acctg.), Dean's Honor Roll 1966-72, Blue Key (leadership), Trojan Knights (service hon.); mem: Pacific Coast Gas Assn. (treas.), Am. Gas Assn. (Acctg. Adv. Council; mng. com. Fin. & Adm.), Am. Inst. of CPAs, Calif. Soc. of CPAs, Arthur Young Alumni Assn., Finl. Execs. Inst. (chmn. Taxation Com.); USC Alumni Assn. (bd. dirs.); mem. Breakfast Roundtable, Town Hall; clubs: Deep Canyon Tennis (P.S.), Jonathan (audit/fin. com.), Annandale Golf, Valley Hunt; Republican; Episcopal; rec: tennis, golf, skiing. Res: 4265 Woodleigh Ln, Flintridge 91011 Ofc: Pacific Lighting Corp. 810 So Flower St, Mail 211K, Los Angeles 90017

DALE, RICHARD CHARLES, computer distribution co. president; b. Apr. 4, 1937, Bridgeport, Conn.; s. John F. and Ann (Booth) D.; div.; children: Laureen, b. 1957, Deborah, b. 1958, Richard, b. 1960; edn: BS, Univ. of Bridgeport 1962, Grad. Sch. of Edn. 1962-64; lic. real estate broker, Calif. Career: sales rep. Honeywell Info. Systems, Fairfield, Conn. 1966-69; branch mgr. Mohawk Data Sciences, Los Angeles 1969-72; district mgr. MSS Data Corp., Des Plains, Ill. 1972-73; regional mgr. Bunker-Ramo, L.A. 1973-75; mgr. nat. account mktg. pgm. Pertec Computer Corp., L.A. 1975-80; area mgr., Sharp Electronics Corp., L.A. 1980-81; gen. mgr. Commodore Bus. Machines, L.A. 1981-83; pres. Complete Business Mgt. Systems, Van Nuys 1983--; guest spkr. Comdex/ winter 84, computer show; honors: Pro Club, Pertec Computer Corp., 1979; Unitarian; rec: golf, tennis, real estate. Res: 13929 Marquesas Way, 115, Marina Del Rey 90291 Ofc: CBM Systems, 7277 Hayvenhurst, B-5, Van Nuys 91406

DALVA, MORRIS, lawyer; b. Oct. 30, 1946, Los Angeles; s. Isaac and Clara (Maron) D.; m. Anna, June 1, 1975; 1 child, Shayne, b. 1976; edn: AB, USC 1968, MA 1976; JD, Univ. San Diego, 1973; admitted State Bar Calif. 1973. Career: deputy public defender County of Los Angeles, 1974-75; atty. pvt. practice, 1976--; judge pro tem, Superior Ct. arbitrator, Am. Arbitration Assn. arbitrator; mem. Los Angeles Trial Lawyers Assn.; mil: sp4 US Army 1970-75; Jewish; rec: fishing, boating. Ofc: 2120 Wilshire Blvd, 300, Santa Monica 90403

DAMIAN, ILANA HELINA, marriage, family, child therapist; b. Dec. 5, 1947, Dzierzoniuz, Germany; d. David and Hanna (Hechtkopht) Niemiec; m. Andrei Damian, Dec. 10, 1977; children: Donna Balsom, b 1970, Kareen Balsom, b. 1972, David Damian, b. 1981; edn: BA, UC Los Angeles 1972; MA, Chapman Coll. 1976; lic. Marriage, Family, Child Therapist (MFCT), Calif. 1976. Career: psychological cons. Long Beach Comm. Hospital Obesity Clinic, dir. The Wellness Clinic, Clinical Psychology Group, therapist (pvt. practice); various workshops and seminars; lectr. sev. colleges in L.A. area; honors: Soroptimist Award for acad. achievement 1976; mem. Calif. Assn. Marriage and Family Therapists; mil: Israeli Army; Republican; Christian; rec: theater, music. Res: 4257 Via Largo St. Cypress 90630 Ofc: Clinical Psychology Gp. 3772 Katella Ave, 212, Los Alamitos 90720

DANANDEH, SAEED, engineer; b. Oct. 21, 1952, Tehran, Iran; s. Nosrat and Ghodsieh (Ghaysar) D.; m. Oranous, July 11, 1983; edn: BSC (CNAA) w/ honors, N.E.London Polytechnic 1976; M.Engr., Sheffield Univ. 1977. Career: structural eng. asst. Computer Engring., NCR Nat. Cash Register, London, UK 1972; struc. eng. asst. S.B. Tietz and Partners, Irvine 1973-76; civil engr. UTN Consol. Inc., Irvine 1978-80; struc. eng. assoc. City of Long Beach, 1980--; mem: ASTM, Prestressed Concrete Inst., Am. Concrete Inst., Internat. Conf. of Building Ofcls., Struc. Engrs. Assn. of Calif.; research in field of concrete; Bahai World Faith; rec: sports, movies, cars, travel. Res: 104 Briarwood, Irvine 90714 Ofc: City of Long Beach, 333 W. Ocean Blvd Long Beach

D'ANDREA, NORMA, artist; b. May 23, 1936, Long Island City, NY; d. Anthony and Grace (Tedesco) D'Andrea; edn: BFA and MFA, earned concurrently, Otis Art Inst. 1967; Career: freelance illustrator, Santa Barbara 1967-73, major client: The Center Magazine (For the Study of Democratic Action); estab. D'Andrea Glass Etchings (design/mfg. studio prod. high quality etched glass for architects, decorators, contractors, comml. clients), Los Angeles 1974--: major clients incl: Uncle Johns, Ginmill, La Creperie, Le Ronde-Vouis (restaurants, L.A.area); Alias Smith & Jones Restaurant (Las Vegas); Horn & Hardarts (NYC); Burger Kings and MacDonalds (throughout USA); Caesars Palace, Four Queens Casino (Las Vegas); Univ. of N.Mex.; USC Faculty Ctr.; Bullocks Dept. Stores (Bev.Hills, L.A.); Robinsons Dept. Store (Sta.Anita); L.A. World Trade Ctr.; Beverly Ctr. (W.Hywd.); Bechtel Corp. (Norwalk); Micro-Computer Co. (LongBch); St. Anthony's Greek Ch. (Pasadena); First Pac. Bank (BevHills) Wells Fargo Banks (Ojai, Rancho Bernardo); condo devels.: Wilshire Fremont (Hancock Pk), Le Studio (N.Hywd), The Mirabella (Westwood). Pvt. Collections incl: Goldie Hawn, Robt. and Rosemary Stack, Irwin Winkler, Edgar Scherick, Sharon Landa Design Assocs., Arthur Elrod House (P.S.), Lily Tomlin, Fred Sands, K.C. Kasem, Cleo Baldon And Assocs., Gary Bandy, Elvis Presley Home (Trousdale Est.). Guest spkr. Woodbury Coll. of Design 1980, CSU Fullerton 1981; Awards: 4 yr. scholarship, Otis Art Inst. Mem: Inst. of Bus. Designers (allied mem.), Nat. Assn. of Female Execs. Works pub. in Valley News 1977, L.A. Times 1978, Arcadia Trib. 1978, Good Housekeeping 1978, L.A. Home &: Garden 1980, Designers West 1981, Showcase Mag. 1981, Designers Mag. 1982. Libertarian. rec: glider planes, target practice, internat.cooking. res:3671 Tacoma Ave. Los Angeles 90065.

DANGCIL, JASPER LEE, systems engineer; b. Dec. 24, 1957, Manila, Phil., nat. 1973; s. Juan Ipalare and Torinne (Dancel) D.; edn: BS in E.E., summa cum laude, UC Los Angeles 1980. Career: assoc. engr., elec./electronics, Lockheed-California Co., Burbank 1980-81, asst. avionics pgmmg. analyst, 1981-82, avionics pgmmg. analyst, 1982-83, avionics computer systems analyst, 1983--; honors: Phi Eta Sigma 1977, Deptl. Scholar 1979; mem. Tau Beta Pi; Single Adult Ministries, 1st Baptist Ch. La Crescenta; Democrat; Christian; rec: basketball, ice skating, chess. Res: 3210 Barnes Cir. Glendale 91208 Ofc: Lockheed-Calif. Co, POB 551, Burbank 91520

D'ANGELICO, DEBRA J. DIFRENNA, preschool school owner/director; b. Dec. 8, 1953, Ft. Bragg, N.C.; d. John D. and Thelma E. (Romano) DiFrenna II; m. Michael J. D'Angelico, Aug. 11, 1979; 1 dau., Jacqueline, b. 1982; edn: Grossmont Coll. 1977-8; AA, child devel., Southwestern Coll. 1981. Career: data clerk Huntington Intercomm. Hosp., Orange 1971-72; loan dept. supr./ head teller Keesler Fed. Credit Union, Miss. 1972-74; loan processor Fireside Thrift and Loan Co., San Diego 1975-76; loan/mem. cons. Santel Credit Union, S.D. 1976-79; tchr. subst. La Mesa Spring Valley Sch. Dist. 1979-80; owner/dir. Daily Sunshine Presch., Chula Vista 1981--, and in Spring Valley 1984--; honors: staff scholarship Southwestern Coll. 1980-1; Nat. Deans List 1980-1; mem: Nat., San Diego Assn. for the Edn. of Young Children; vol. staff Hillcrest Receiving Home for Abused Children 1981-2; contbg. mem. Childhelp USA; publs: study on Italian-Am. Today (1981); Teenagers Today tape pgm. (1981); Catholic; rec: advocacy quality care & edn. for children, family life. Res: 930 Cosmo Ave El Cajon 92021 Ofc: Daily Sunshine Preschool, 50 40th Ave Chula Vista 92010

DANIELS, ARTHUR CHARLES, physician; b. Dec. 25, 1898, Kars, Armenia, Russia; nat. 1934; s. Charles C. and Margaret Danielian; m. Dorothy Wiberg, Nov. 2, 1935; edn: AB, USC 1917, MD, Harvard Univ. 1927; resrch & adv'd studies: Univ. Chgo., Johns Hopkins Univ., Stanford Univ., UCLA, Vanderbilt Univ., Andrew Carnegie Found., Harvard Cancer Commn. Career: pvt. practice Metropolitan Center Los Angeles; Sr. Med. Examiner L.A. City Health Dept.; Civil Defense mem. Atomic Warfare, apptd. by Pres. Truman on recommend. of Gov. Warren (1950) regis. Atomic Energy Proj., UCLA Sch of Med.; adminstr. Fed. Heart Resrch. (1947-50), L.A. City Health Dept. Mem: Nat. Geographic Soc.; alumni orgns. of Harvard, Johns Hopkins, Stanford; donor: Stanford Univ. Med. Sch. (surgery), UCLA (cancer), Johns Hopkins Med. Sch., Harvard Alumni; donor rare books to Harvard, UCLA, Stanford libs. Publ: Am. J. of Med. Sciences, 7/1927. Mil: served capt. to major, WWII citations from Pres. Roosevelt, Gov. Olson, Gen. Wm. Sherrill. Republican. Presbyterian. rec: antique collections, European art, violinist. res: 1919 S. Bundy Dr. Fresno 93727.

DANIELS, CHARLENE, psychiatric social worker; b. July 11, 1946, Toledo, Ohio; d. Charlie and Geneva Bush (McKenny) Stevenson; m. Lawrence L. Daniels, July 7, 1979; 1 dau. Latanya Cherie Brown, b. 1972; edn: AA, El Camino Coll. 1973; BSW, CSU Long Beach 1975; MSW, UC Los Angeles 1977; LCSW, lic. clin. social wkr. 1981. Career: social wkr. Long Bch. Gen. Hosp. 1974-5, Co. of Los Angeles 1975-6, Family Svc. of L.A. 1976, Vets. Adm., L.A. 1976-7, St. of Calif., San Bernardino 1977; with San Bernardino Co. Dept. Mental Health, 1977--: clinic mgr./ childrens' svcs. coord./ contracts coord./ outpatient coordinator, 1977-81, treatment pgms. supr. Alcohol and Drug Pgms., 1981--; psychotherapist, pvt. practice, Eclectic Family Counseling Svcs, Rialto and San Bernardino 1981--; assoc. counselor, Barstow; field instr. Social Wk. Interns, S.B. Co., 1977-9; field instr. S.B. Valley Coll., psychiat. tech. intern pgm., 1982-3; oral exam. commnr. for LCSWs, State of Calif. (1983); presenter wkshops, seminars 1981, 82, 83; mem: AAUW, Am. Bus. Womens Assn. (audit com.), Nat. Assn. of Black Soc. Wkrs., Nat. Council of Negro Women (1st v.p. 1981-2); past pres. Assoc. Students of Soc. Wk., CSULB; awards: appreciation, Whitney Young Clinic 1983; acad. and profl. awards;

Baptist (treas. scholarship com.); rec: drawing, crafts. Res: 1465 No Chestnut Ave Rialto 92376 Ofc: S.B. Co. Dept. Mental Hlth, Ofc of Alcohol and Drug Pgms, 700 E Gilbert St San Bernardino 92415

DANIELS, DIANE, computer software co. president; b. Dec. 4, 1945, Valdosta, Ga.; d. Harry Alvin and Mary Margaret (Curry) Davidson; edn: BA in math, honors, Mich. St. Univ. 1966. Career: computer pgmmr. on Apollo-II and Pentagon Intell., IBM Corp., Wash DC and Saigon, Vietnam, 1966-73; mgmt. info. systems cons. to Govt. of Iran, Louis Berger Internat., Tehran, 1973-75; systems engr. on automated Medicaid and Welfare Systems, EDS Corp., San Francisco, 1976-77; founder/pres. The Information Orgn. Corp. (Wang Labs authorized vendors for office automation software), S.F. 1979--; honors: classical piano competition awards (1963, 64); only woman chosen by IBM for Vietnam svc.; recognition certs. ASM (1982), ARMA (1981); mem: Assn. of Systems Mgrs. (ch. Profl. Dev. Com.), Assn. of Records Mgrs. and Adminstrs. (bd.), Women Entrepreneurs, Profl. and Tech. Cons. Assn., Profl. Women's Bus. Exchange; pres., bd. dirs. Pacific Hts. Owners Assn. 1980-2; fundraiser com. ch. The S.F. Moving Co., Modern Dance, Inc. 1982; pres., bd. dirs. Fairspace, The Dancing Theatre 1976-8; copyrighted, proprietary software inventions for Wang VS Computer (4); rec: swim, pianist. Address: 2295 Vallejo St., The Office, San Francisco 94123

DANTES, DAVID, physician; b. May 11, 1946, NYC; s. David Alfred and Anita Camelia (Dechtiar) Dantes; edn: BA in biol. w/honors, Stanford Univ. 1968; MD, w/honors, UCLA 1972; Fellow, Am. Coll. of Emergency Physicians 1983. Career: internship, residency UCLA, 1972-74; practicing splty emergency medicine 1974--, pres. David A. Dantes, Jr., M.D., Inc.; cert. by Am. Bd. of Emergency Medicine 1982; clin. faculty UCLA Med. Sch. 1983-; instr. Advanced Cardiac Life Support, Advanced Trauma Life Support. awards: Upjohn Achievement Award, UCLA Med. Sch. 1972; pres. UCLA chpt. A.O.A., 1973. mem: Fellow Am. Coll. Emergency Physicians, Soc. of Teachers of Emerg. Medicine, World Runners. Profl. interest: comprehensive medicine. rec: running. res/ofc: 201 Ocean Ave No. 305-B, Santa Monica 90402.

DANUPATAMPA, EKACHAI, engineer; b. Oct. 4, 1942, Bangkok, Thailand; Naturalized Jan. 25, 1978. s. Yok-Hoo and Uy-Ty (Ung) Danupatampa; DIP. In E.E., Thonburi Inst. of Tech., 1965; BSEE with Distinction, FEATI Univ., 1968; MSEE, Cal State Univ., Long Beach, 1974, EEE, USC, 1979; M. Vorunurt Tanehsakdi, May 26, 1973; Children: Irv b. 1980. Career: senior control engineer, C.F. Braun & Co., Alhambra, 1980-; electrical project engineer, Rodrigue & Associates, Inc., L.A., 1979-80; E.E., Dept. of the Navy (CEL), Port Hueneme, 1978-79; electrical project engineer, Carnation Co., L.A. 1974-78; Also cons., various small conpanies. Graduated in BSEE with distinction, FEATI Univ., 1968. Member: IEE, ISA, CSULB Alumni; USC Alumni. Independent. Buddhism. Rec.: Jogging, Bicycling, Jump Rope. Res.: 1136 Vera Cruz St., Montebello, 90640. Office: C.F. Braun & Co., 1000 S. Fremont Ave., Alhambra, 918029

DANZIG, FRANK KENNETH, stockbroker; b. Oct. 22, 1915, NYC; s. Jerome J. and Helen W. (Wolf) D.; m. 2d. Twila, Oct. 10, 1969; children: Victoria Jane, b. 1947; Priscilla D. (Gardiner), b. 1950; edn: sci., Worcester Acad. 1933; BA, Dartmouth Coll. 1937. Career: with Radio Stations WNEW, WHN and WMCA, NY, also CBS, 1937-42; independent radio dir./prod., Hollywood 1946-52; v.p./secy-treas. Ross-Danzig Prodns., Inc. TV Pgmmg. Co., 1952-62; pres./gen. mgr. Imperial Broadcasting System, Inc. 1958-60; secy-treas. Teen-Age Fair, Inc., 1962-70; v.p. investments, Dean Witter Reynolds, Inc. 1970--; mem: Pacific Pioneer Broadcasters (dir.1979-81), Acad. of TV Arts & Scis., Mountaingate CC; mil: maj. US Army Signal Corps, 1942-46; rec: jazz, photog. Res: 1200 Tigertail Rd Los Angeles 90049 Ofc: Dean Witter Reynolds Inc. 1900 Ave of the Stars Los Angeles 90067

DANZIGER, ROBERT NATHAN, energy co. president; b. July 22, 1953, Los Angeles; s. Joseph and Shirley Delores (Rotstein) D.; edn: JD, Whittier Coll. 1978; admitted Calif. St. Bar 1978. Career: Bass player, USA, 1972--; data processing mgr. Cardio-Dynamics Labs., Los Angeles 1975-77; chief counsel and instnl. analyst to Energy Technology Pgms., Jet Propulsion Lab., 1978-80; pres. Sunlaw Energy Corp., L.A. 1980--; adj. prof. energy law, Whittier Coll. 1983; expert witness House of Reps. (energy taxation) 1982, Calif. P.U.C. (fed. utility law); bd. chmn. Internat. Cogeneratio Soc., LA chpt. (1983-4); liaison, LA County Bar Energy Section and LA CofC (1982-3); v.chmn. Am. Bar Assn. Alternative Energy Com. 91983-4); mem: Options House, March of Dimes, Town Hall, Calif. Bar Assn.; author 2 books and 30 arts. on Energy Law, Fin. and Mgmt.; sculptor in exotic woods; Jewish; rec: shell collecting, skin diving, martial arts. Res: 208 No Irving Blvd Los Angeles 90004 Ofc: Sunlaw, 8530 Wilshire Blvd, 401, Beverly Hills 90211

DAPONTE, KENNETH JOSEPH, university administrator; b. Aug. 24, 1935, Waterbury, Conn.; s. Anthony Jordan and Clara (Corti) D.; m. Judith Haley, July 29, 1961; children: Gregory, b. 1962, Robyn, b. 1966; edn: BA, Univ. Va. 1957; MA, Univ. Conn. 1959; EdD, USC 1979; Inst. for Ednl. Mgmt., Harvard Univ. 1972. Career: science & edn. editor, Ginn & Co., Boston 1959-61; asst. advt. supr. Proctor & Gamble, Cincinnati 1962-63; asst. dir. devel., Amherst Coll., Amherst, Mass. 1963-6; asst. to pres., Bradford Jr. Coll., Bradford, Mass. 1965-6; asst. to campaign dir., dickinson Coll., Carlisle, Pa. 1966-7; asst. to pres., Immaculate Heart Coll., Hollywood 1967-73; v.p. devel., Hollywood Presbyterian Med. Ctr., Hollywood 1973-76; planning and devel. cons. to num. non-profit orgns., 1971--; honors: Phi Beta Kappa 1957, Phi Delta Kappa 1979, Delta Epsilon 1979; mem: Am. Assn. for Higher Edn., Am. Assn. of Univ. Adminstrs., Assn. for the Study of Higher Edn., Council for Advance. and Support of Higher Edn., Town Hall of Calif.; publs. re legal aspects of higher edn. and tenure, 1979-81; mil: US Army 1957-8, 1961-2; Democrat; Cathlic; rec: paddle tennis. Res: 3662 Greve Dr Rancho Palos Verdes 90274

D'ARCY-CLARKE, EDMUND THOMAS, educator; b. Dec. 21, 1921, Englewood, NJ; s. John Peter and Mary Agnes (Costello) D.; m. Vera Addix, Jan. 1952; children: Peggy Ann, b. 1954, Evelyn Jeanne, b. 1957, Edmund, b. 1961, Charles John, b. 1964; edn: AA, Riverside City Coll. 1966; BS, CSU Fresno 1973, MS 1977; Comm. Coll. Instr. Credential (life) Bus. and Indsl. Mgmt. 1973; Accredited Personnel Mgr., Pers. Accred. Inst., ASPA. Career: adminstrv. asst. Angeles Nat. Forest, Pasadena 1964-5; resource adminstrv. asst. San Bernardino Nat. Forest, 1965-6; personnel mgmt. splst. Sierra Nat. Forest, Fresno 1966-9, personnel ofcr., 1969-76; personnel services advisor UC Berkeley, 1977-8; instr., Pre-Retirement Plnng. Centers Div., San Francisco Comm. College Dist., SF 1978--; mem. Fresno Commn. on Aging 1979-80; co-v.p. Govt. College Assn. 1969, 74; curriculum adv. com. Reedley Coll. 1969-74; mem: Am. Assn. for Personnel Adminstrn., Am. Assn. for Tng. and Devel., AARP, Nat. Assn. of Ret. Fed. Employees, Nat. Assn. of Ret. Credit Union People; art. on retirement plnng., 1981; mil: m/sgt US Army 1942-64, Bronze Star, Combat Inf. Badge, Army Commend. Medal; Catholic; rec: travel, golf, tennis. Res: 1243 E Escalon Ave Fresno 93710

DARIAN, CRAIG CHARLES, motion picture industry executive; b. Mar. 18, 1955, Glendale; s. Charles Ohan and Gloria (Berberian) D.; m. Kimberly Brooke, Oct. 11, 1975; children: Jordan, b. 1980, Jessica, b. 1982; edn: USC, UCLA, CSUN, LAVC, 1973-83. Career: expediter Consol. Film Industries, Los Angeles 1974-5; projection engr./opr. (free lance) MGM Universal, Glen Glenn Sound, Consol. Film Indus., Movielab, 20th Cen. Fox, Warner Bros, Columbia, Todd-AO, 1975-6; projection engr./opr. Ryder Sound Services, Inc., Hollywood 1976-82, head of sales/indus. contact, 1982--; bd. suprs. Republic Credit Union 1980-; dir. Studio Systems Co. 1978-82; commnr./bus. & fin. ofcr. Hollywood Entertainment Sports League 1981-; honors: Emmy citation, Acad. TV Arts & Scis. 1980; spl. honor plaque, City of Hope 1982; mem: Acad. TV Arts & Scis., Soc. of Motion Picture & TV Engrs., IATSE, USC Cinema Circulus, American Film Inst., Commanders Club; publs: editorial responses pub. LA Times, Forbes Mag.; Republican; Christian; rec: sports, reading, debate, children. Res: 9207 Rubio Ave Sepulveda 91343 Ofc: Ryder Sound Services Inc. 1161 N. Vine St Hollywood 90038

DA RIN, EDWARD JOSEPH, patent-trademark lawyer; b. Jan. 3, 1925, Niagara Falls, NY; s. Gelindo and Evelyn (DeLuca) DaRin; m. Rose M., Aug. 14, 1948; children: Linda, b. 1949; David, b. 1952; Thomas, b. 1957; edn: BSEE, honors, Case Inst. of Tech. 1949, JD, Temple Univ. Law Sch. 1955; mem. Calif. & Patent Office Bars. Career: patent dept. Hughes Aircraft, 1956-58; partner firm of Christie, Parker & Hale, Pasadena 1958-76; sole practitioner, pres. Edward J. DaRin, Inc. law corp., Pasadena 1976--; mem: Calif., Am., Los Angeles, Pasadena Bar Assns.; Am. Patent Law Assn.; Pasadena University Club; Pasadena Y's Mens Club; mil: USN 1943-6; Republican; Catholic; rec: sports. Res: 416 No Altura Rd Arcadia 91006 Ofc: Edward J. DaRin, Inc. 301 E. Colorado, 518, Pasadena 91101

DARLING, SCOTT EDWARD, lawyer; b. Dec. 31, 1949, Los Angeles; s. Dick and Marjorie Helen D.; m. Deborah L., Aug. 22, 1981; children: Ryan, b. 1975; Jacob, b. 1978; edn: BA, Univ. of Redlands 1972; JD, USC 1975; admitted to practice, Calif. State Bar. Career: travel counselor World Travel Inc., Riverside 1968-72, asst. mgr. 1972-76; campaign mgr. Grant Carner for Cong., Riv. 1976; assoc., partner law firm of Falsetti, Crafts, Pritchard & Darling of Riverside 1978--; pres. Newport Harbor Devel. Co., Inc. 1983-; bd. dirs. Tel-Law, Inc. (nat. public svc. legal info. system) 1978-80; judge protem Riverside Superior Ct. 1980; mem. Calif. Assn. of Realtors atty's panel; honors: Outstanding Young Men of Am. 1979-83; Calif. Scholarship Fedn. life mem.; charter mem. High Sch. Hall of Fame; Sickle Cell Orgn. Eddie D. Smith Award 1981; mem: Am., Riverside Co. (spkrs bur.) Bar Assns.; Native Sons of Golden West; bd. dirs. ARC Riv. Co.; bd. dirs. Heart Assn. Riv. Co.; citizens com. UC Riv.; bd. dirs. Inland Area Sickle Cell Orgn.; World Affairs Council; Friends of the Mission Inn; Lions Club; bd. dirs. Hispanic CofC; Riv. Jaycees; Republican: cand. for Congress 36th Dist. 1982; asst. treas. Calif. State Repub. Party 1980-82; Harvest Christian Fellowship. Res: 5496 Fargo Rd Riverside 92506 Ofc: Falsetti, Crafts, Pritchard & Darling, 7121 Magnolia Ave Riverside 92504

DASH, ALAN, computer software co. executive; b. May 18, 1934, NYC; s. John and Grace (Apfel) D.; m. Kay Kyoko Yokoyama, Jan. 25, 1968; 1 dau., June, b. 1974; edn: BS, psych., UC Los Angeles 1972; MS in computer sci., West Coast Univ. 1976. Career: computer pgmmr. Invormation Systems Co., Bangkok, H.K., Japan 1965-68; systems analyst, Univac, (J.P.L.), Pasadena 1968-70; mgr. Systems Support Dept. (Infonet), Computer Sciences Corp., El Segundo 1970-81; dir. of mktg. Fuyo Data Processing & Systems Devel., Ltd. (of Tokyo, Japan), Gardena 1981-84, sr. v.p. subs. Fuyo Information Systems, Inc., 1984--; mem. ADAPSO, Japan Bus. Assn. of So. Calif., Japan-Am. Soc., Japanese CofC (L.A.); mil: US Army Security Agcy. 1961-2; Ind.; rec: photog., hike, fish, hunt. Res: 14772 Bodger Ave Hawthonre 90250 Ofc: Fuyo Info. Systems, 1875 Redondo Beach Blvd, 205, Gardena 90247

DAUGHADAY, DOUGLAS ROBERT, electronics engineer; b. Mar. 13, 1954, Highland Park, NJ; s. Robert Owings and Mary (Kirkpatrick) D.; edn: BSEE, cum laude, W. Va. Inst. of Tech. 1976; MSEE, USC 1979; engr. in tng., State of W.Va. 1976. Career: tech. staff Hughes Aircraft Co., Culver City 1977-79; sr. engr. Litton Guidance and Control Systems, Woodland Hill 1979-80; lab. engr. Airesearch Mfg. Co. of Calif., Torrance 1980-84; tech. staff The Aerospace

Corp., El Segundo 1984--; awards: Masters fellowship, Hughes Aircraft Co. 1977-9; mem: Nat. Assn. of Underwater Instrs. 1982-; IEEE stu. mem. 1973-6; USC Gen. Alumni Assn. (life); The Persona Pgmmg. Center calculator club; Democrat; Christian; rec: Scuba diving, photog. Res: 3221 Overland Ave, 5217, Los Angeles 90034 Ofc: The Aerospace Corp. 2350 East El Segundo Blvd El Segundo 90245

DAUM, G(ORDAN) ALLAN, real estate executive; b. Aug. 20, 1943, Winnipeg, Manitoba, Can.; s. Gordon Wilfred and Elizabeth Christine (Kyle) D.; m. Sharon Gay, June 6, 1970; 1 son, Gregory, b. 1975; edn: BA, CSU Long Beach 1971, MS 1974; lic: Calif. Comm. Coll. Instr. cred. 1974; Real Estate Broker, Calif. 1981; Lmtd. Securities Reg., NASD, 1983; Cert. Review Appraiser, NARA, 1983; Real Prop. Adminstr., BOMA, 1984. Career: city administrator, City of Anaheim 1971-76; sales cons. Coldwell Banker Co., Santa Ana 1976-77; devel. & mktg. mgr. The Irvine Co., Newport beach 1977-80; sr. cons. Frost Trinen & Partners, Costa Mesa 1980-81; v.p. Tishman West Mgmt. Corp., Orange 1981--; real estate cons., seminar spkr., Daum Realty Corp.; honors: Broker of the Year, Frost Trinen & Partners, 1980; mem: Nat. Assn. of Corp. Real Estate Execs.; Intl. Council of Shopping Ctrs.; Soc. of Real Prop. Adminstrs., Bldg. Owners & Mgrs. Assn., Nat. Assn. of Review Appraisers, Orange County CofC (Dir. at Large, trustee PAC), O.C. Devel. Council; mil: non-comm. ofcr. USNR 1965-68, Vietnam Cpn. Medal w/bronze star; Republican; Prot.; rec: travel, water sports. Res: 5 Longstreet Irvine 92714 Ofc: Tishman West Mgmt Corp. One City Blvd West, 440, Orange 92668

D'AUTREMONT, DENNIS PAUL, life insurance agent; b. Aug. 24, 1949, Los Angeles; s. Hubert Francis and Mary Francis (Baker) d'A.; m. Jennifer Blakey, Aug. 16, 1975; children: Jason, b. 1979, Jeremy, b. 1982; edn: BS in bus., Calif. State Polytech. Univ. 1972; LUTC grad. 1977. Career: life ins. agt. Mutual Benefit Life, San Luis Obispo 1973-5, Guardian Life of New York, 1975-, agcy. supr. Guardian Ins. office, S.L.O. 1976--; honors: Million Dollar Round Table (life), Guardian Life's Leaders Club (9 yrs), Nat. Quality Award (8 yrs), Nat. Sales Achievement awds. (8 yrs); mem: MDRT, Nat. Eagle Scout Assn., Nat. Assn. of Life Underwriters, Knight of Round Table; orgns: UMCA sponsor; CalPoly Mustangs boosters; BSA Century Club; Republican; Prot.; rec: ski, backpack. Res: 735 Three Sisters Rd San Luis Obispo 93401 Ofc: Guardian Insurance, 1103 Johnson Ave San Luis Obispo 93401

DAVENPORT, JUDITH ANN, industrial center developer; b. Sept. 17, 1952, Big Timber, Mont.; d. Kenneth Laverne and Jill Louise (Sutton) D.; edn: BS, environ. pln., mgmt., UC Davis 1974, MS, resource econ., 1976; spl. courses, Foothill Jr. Coll. 1980-1; lic. real estate broker, Calif. 1981. Career: plnng. intern City of Santa Rosa Planning Dept., 1974; plnng. technician Sonoma Co. Plnng. Dept., Santa Rosa 1974-75; grad. advisor UC Davis Housing Dept., and resrch. asst. UCD Environ. Resources, 1975-6; jr. analyst, 1977-8, sr. exec., 1979-80 retail sales forecast analysis, John S. Thompson Co. Inc, Los Altos; vice pres./ prop. mgr./ developer, Industry West indsl. park, Santa Rosa 1980--; honors: Gov. Reagans rep., Walk for Mankind, 1969; Calif. Girls' State, 1969; DAR semi-finalist, 1970; Santa Rosa Junior Miss 2nd place, Spirit of Jr. Miss, Youth Fitness Award, 1970; Life mem. CSF; mem: YMCA; Investment Club; Republican; Prot.; rec: cattle ranching, art, politics, cooking. Res: 1320 North St, 13, Santa Rosa 95404 Ofc: Industry West, 3555 Standish Ave Santa Rosa 95407

DAVIDIAN, S(HARON) J(OSEPH), insurance broker; b. Oct. 14, 1927, Fresno; s. David and Grace Darling (Toutjian) Davidian; m. Marise Charlotte Fairbanks, Apr. 2, 1948; chil: Isaac, b. 1949; Rebekah, b. 1951; Keren, b. 1959; Barak, b. 1962; edn: BA, Columbia Pacific 1982; CPCU (Chartered Prop. Casualty Underwriter), Am. Inst. of CPCU 1983; ARM (Asso. in Risk Mgmt.), Ins. Inst. of Am. 1978. Career: bookkeeper Shell Oil Co., 1948-49, United Fairway/Borelli Produce Co., 1949-55, Producers Cotton Oil Co., 1955-58, all in Fresno; office mgr. Borelli Produce Distbrs., Fresno 1958-9, secty-treas., 1959-70; pres./gen. mgr. Hallmark Ins. Assocs., Inc., Fresno 1970--; mem. faculty Insurance Ednl. Assn. 1984-. Mem: Profl. Ins. Agts Assn. of Calif/Nev.; Am. Risk and Ins. Assn. Inc.; Soc. of CPCU (founding dir., pub. rels. chmn. Central Calif. Chpt.). Publs: ed./writer, Keeping Covered, quarterly ins. consumer publ., 1981-. Jehovah's Witness (elder, instr. in ministry sch.); rec: astronomy, music. Res: 2227 E. Willis, Fresno 93726 Ofc: Hallmark Ins. Assocs. Inc. 5150 N. 6th St. #150 Fresno 93710, POB 5187, Fresno 93755

DAVIDSON, ALAN CHARLES, insurance executive; b. Nov. 8, 1937, Los Angeles; s. Charles Evans and A. Louise (Wilson) D.; m. Gail Ziebarth, June 16, 1961; children: Karen Ashley, b. 1971; Douglas McPhail, b. 1975; edn: BA, Whittier Coll. 1962; CLU, chartered life underwriter, American Coll. of Life Underwriters 1967, gp. ins. cert., 1968, pension plnng. cert., 1972. Career: pres. Davidson Co., Whittier 1961-67; pres. Davidson & Pierson Ins. Agents & Brokers, Whittier 1967-71; pres. Davidson, Pierson & Roth, Inc., Whittier 1971-78; pres. Davidson Co., Whittier 1978--; partner Davidson & Poyner; profl. awards incl. Provident Mutual Senior Agent Hall of Fame (1983), Co. Man of the Year 1974, Orange County Man of the Year 1974-6, Nat. Sales Achievement Award (7); Outstanding Young Men of Am. 1971; San Fernando Valley GAMA Agent of the Year 1980-3; Nat. Quality Award (8); mem: Am. Soc. of Pension Actuaries, Am. Soc. of CLUs, Nat., Calif., L.A. (past pres.), Whittier (past pres.) Life Underwriters Assns., Million Dollar Round Table (life), Life Leaders Round Table of L.A. (past pres.); Toastmasters (past pres.), Kiwanis Club, CofC, City of Whittier Parking q Transp. Commn. 1978-; Lancer Soc., Whittier Coll.; author: You Can Be A Hero, life ins. selling mag. (monthly); frequent profl. spkr.; Republican; Soc. of Friends; rec: horseback riding, gourmet cooking. Res: 6278 Southwind Dr Whittier 90601 Ofc: Davidson & Poyner 7624 So Painter Ave, 1B, Whittier 90602

DAVIDSON, KENT ARTHUR, lawyer, investor; b. May 31, 1945, Oildale, Ca.; s. Robert Theodore and Marjorie Rutter (Pollock) D.; m. Marilyn, Sept. 12, 1971; 1 dau., Lisa, b. 1979; edn: AA, honors, Laney Coll. 1972; BA, cum laude, UC Berkeley 1974; JD, Univ. San Francisco 1977; admitted to practice Calif. Bar 1978. Career: computer pgmmr. system analyst, various firms, 1963-78; lawyer/prin. Law Offices of Kent A. Davidson, Oakland 1978--; corp. counsel/dir. MIC, 1982-83; mem: Alameda Co. Bar Assn. (Fee Arbitration Com. 1983), Rotary, 50-50 Club of Oakland, Central Com. for Conscientious Objectors (bd. 1981-), Commonwealth Club; publs: law rev. arts. 1976, 84; Democrat; Quaker; rec: photog., travel, scuba diving. Res: 1734 Channing Way Berkeley 94703 Law Ofc. Kent A. Davidson, 528 Grand Ave Oakland 94610

DAVIDSON, NATHAN SHERWIN, real estate broker; b. Aug. 21, 1933, Detroit, Mich.; s. Sol B. and Rose (Moscowitz) D.; m. Phyllis, June 7, 1952; children: Rochelle, b. 1956, Pamela, b. 1960; edn: Los Angeles City Coll. 1981-3; lic. real estate broker, Calif. 1968. Career: R.E. salesman Kent Realty, Westchester 1967, Jules Drapkin, Los Angeles 1967-68; real estate broker Harleigh Sandler Co., L.A. 1968-82, (cos. merged 1982), Merrill Lynch Realty, 1982--; awards: Blue Diamond awd. (3 mil. sales) 1977-8; million dollar club 1978-83; mem: L.A. Board of Realtors (edn. com. 1980); Masons; mil: cpl. US Army 1953-55; Democrat; Jewish (pres. Mens Club 1981-2); rec: researching hist. L.A., sporting events, bowling. Res: 1555 S. Rexford Dr. Los Angeles 90035 Ofc: Merrill Lynch Realty, 9911 W Pico Blvd Los Angeles 90035

DAVIDSON, PHYLLIS, real estate broker; b. Sept. 17, 1933, Pensacola, Fla.; d. David Elliott and Sarah (Rapoport) Palet; m. Nathan Davidson, June 7, 1952; children: Rochelle, b. 1956, Pamela, b. 1960; lic. real estate broker, Calif. 1969. Career: real estate sales agt. (1969-76), assoc. broker (1976-) Harleigh Sandler Co., 1976-82, (cos. merged) Merrill Lynch Realty, 1982--; awards: Million Dollar Club 1971-83; Blue Diamond Club (3 mil. sales yr.); mem. L.A. Board of Realtors; Bnai David Cong. sisterhood; rec: hist. memorabilia. Res: 1555 So Rexford Dr Los Angeles 90035 Ofc: Merrill Lynch Realty, 9911 W Pico Blvd Los Angeles 90035

DAVIDSON, RONALD JAY, psychiatrist; b. Jan. 29, 1946, Los Angeles; s. Marvyn Ross and Muriel (Gilson) D.; edn: BA, Eng. lit., UC Berkeley 1967; MD, USC Med. Sch. 1971; internshp. Hahnemann Sch. of Med. 1972; psychiatric res. Yale Univ. 1975; MD, Calif. 1975, Conn. 1976; Dip. Am. Bd. of Psychiatry and Neurology (psychiatry) 1980. Career: med. dir. Shoreline Mental Hlth. Svc., Clinton, Conn. 1975-6; asst. dir. adolescent svc., Elmcrest Psychiat. Inst., Portland, Conn. 1976-78, dir. admissions, 1976-81; pvt. practice, Beverly Hills 1982--; alienist panel Superior Ct. Criminal Div., LA Co. 1982-; panel of apptd. psychiatrists, Juvenile Ct., LA Co. 1983-; psychiat. cons. Calif. State Dept. of Rehab., LA Co. Employees Retirement Assn., Calif. Soc. Svcs. Disability Evaluation Div., 1983-; mem: Am. Psychiat. Assn., Calif. Med. Assn., LA Co. Med. Assn., So. Calif. Psychiat. Soc., Am. Orthopsychiat. Assn., Phi Delta Epsilon; rec: hiking. Res: 4025 Coldstream Terrace Tarzana 91356 Ofc: 450 No Bedford Dr, 210, Beverly Hills 90210

DAVIDSON, STEVEN WILLIAM, restaurant/food service conglomerate executive; b. Mar. 22, 1948, Madison, Wisc.; s. Leslie K. and Leone (Herricks) D.; m. Ellen Oppenheim, June 8, 1974; 1 dau., Anne, b. 1980; edn: BA, Univ. of Wisc., Madison 1975, MBA 1977. Career: finl. analyst Castle and Cooke, Inc., San Francisco 1977-78; strategic planning analyst United Vintners Div. Hueblein Corp., S.F. 1978-80; dir. planning & analysis Saga Corp., MenloPark 1980-81; currently, v.p./controller Straw Hat Restaurant Corp.; honors: Outstanding Young Men of Am., V.S. Jaycees; mem. Toastmasters Intl. (ofcr). Res: 304 Tioga Ct. Palo Alto 94306 Ofc: The Straw Hat Restaurant Corp. 6400 Village Pkwy Dublin 94568

DAVIES, DARLENE GOULD, educator; b. Apr. 28, 1939; d. Allen Charles and Loretta Catherine (Geary) Geer; edn: Pasadena Playhouse Coll. Theater Arts 1956; Emerson Coll. 1959; BA in speech arts, honors, San Diego State Univ. 1962, MA, speech pathology 1965; postgrad. stu. Purdue Univ. 1965-66. Calif. lic. Speech Pathologist. Career: tchg. asst. Purdue Univ. 1965-66; lectr./clin. supr. San Diego State Univ. 1967, 69-76, clin. coordinator/asst. prof. Dept. of Communicative Disorders, 1976--; speech pathol./supr. clin. svcs. San Diego Speech, Hearing and Neurosensory Ctr. (Childrens Hlth Ctr.); supr. Chula Vista Clinic, staff Vista Clin.; Deaf Edn. therapist, vis. speech pathol., coord. Deaf Edn. Dept. to San Diego City Schs.; dir. Naval Regl. Medical Ctr. Sp. and Lang. Clinic, San Diego, 1971-76; sp. pathol. Edgemoor Geriatric Hosp. 1972-74; pvt. practice, 1970-78; cons. Lakeside Sch. Dist. 1981, El Camino Reading Clinics, S.D., 1972, S.D. Unif. Sch. Dist. 1977, Kaiser Permanente 1977, Cajon Vly. Unif. Sch. Dist. 1980-81; apptd. mem. Bd. Visitors, The Bishop's Sch., 1983-86; elected mem. exec. com. Univ. of San Diego Coll. of Arts & Scis. Dean's Council, 1983-84, and mem. selection com. Davies Award for Faculty Achievement USC; chancellor SDSU Mortar Board, 1961, faculty adv. 1983-4; mem: Am. Speech-Lang.-Hearing Assn. (Cert. Clin. Competence); Alexander Graham Bell Assn. for Deaf; SDSU Alumni Assn. (Life); Nat. Mortar Bd. Alumni (chpt. pres. 1958-79); United Way Rev. Panel 1979-80; performer S.D. Nat. Shakespeare Festival 1960, Shakespeare with S.D. Sym. 1961, guest artist for SDSU REader Theater world premiere Thornton Wilder Plays 1976; founder/mem. Children's Mus., S.D. 1982; founder Old Globe Theatre 1982-3 (charter mem. Teatro Meta 1983); articles in profl. jours.; contbr. poetry, book revs., commentary var. mags. Ofc: San Diego State University 92182

DAVIS, BARRY, communications executive; b. July 11, 1945, Buffalo, NY; s. Herbert and Ruth N. (Feldman)D.; m. Dianne Dee Adolfson, July 2, 1977; children: Jennifer, Matthew; edn: AA, Long Beach City Coll. 1972; BA, CSU

Long Bch. 1974; Sec. teaching credential, L.B. Unified Schs. 1974. Career: convention coordinator State of the Arts Seminars, Long Beach 1975-77; education coordinator Calif. Assn. of Realtors (Los Angeles), 1977; v.p./pub. rels. mgr. Allstate Realtors, San Jose 1977-82; dir. comm. Calif. Credit Union League, Pomona 1982--; mem. Internat. Assn. of Bus. Communicators, Sigma Alpha Epsilon (pres. 1974); mil: E4 US Army 1964-67, GCM, marksmanship medal; Republican; Jewish; rec: soccer (goalie position). Res: 2051 Tevis Ave Long Beach 90815 Ofc: Calif. Credit Union League, 2350 So Garey Ave Pomona 91766

DAVIS, BRIAN CHRISTOPHER, lawyer; b. May 1, 1948, Ft. Monroe, Va.; s. Kelton Seymour and Ingeborg Anna (Pepig); m. Christine David, Dec. 18, 1972; children: Dieter, b. 1978; Nicholas, b. 1980; edn: BA, Univ. of N.Mex. 1970; JD, Univ. of the Pacific 1978; admitted to practice, State Bar of Calif. 1978. Career: staff atty. Richard C. Sinclair, Modesto 1978-79; sole prop. Law Ofcs. Brian C. Davis, Modesto, 2nd ofc. Sonora 1983--; co-owner/ co- founder A&D Lumber Co., Sonora; cons. Del Rio Homeowners Assn.; lectr. CSU Stanislaus 1982; honors: Trayner Hon. Soc.; mem: Modesto CofC; Am. (Litigation Gp.), Calif. State & Stanislaus Bar Assn.; Nat. Ski Patrol; Sportsmen of Stanislaus Club; Squaw Valley Ski Patrol; publs: 12 pub. opinions filed w/ Calif. Pub. Employment Rels. Bd. 1977-78; mil: combat airlift navigator, capt. USAF 1971-76, GCM, Unit Citation, Nat. Svc.; Republican; Catholic; rec: skiing. Res: 705 W Union Modesto 95356 Ofc: Law Offices of Brian C Davis, 802 14th St, Ste A, Modesto 95354

DAVIS, BRIAN KEITH, biologist; b. May 15, 1937, Sydney, N.S.W., nat. 1981; s. Ruby Constance D.; m. Nelida Villanueva, Aug. 3, 1963; 1 son, Simon, b. 1965; edn: BSc, Univ. New South Wales, 1958, PhD, 1962, DSc, 1982. Career: teaching fellow Univ. N.S.W., Sydney 1958-61; Ford Found. fellow, Worcester Found. for Exptl. Biol., Shrewsbury, Mass. 1962-3; research fellow in chem., Harvard Univ. 1963-5; sci. ofcr. M.R.C. Lab. for Molecular Biol., Cambridge 1965-6; research fellow in chem., McGill Univ., Montreal 1966-9; scientist, Worcester Found. for Exptl. Biology, 1970-78; resrch. prof. Coll. of Arts & Scis., SUNY, Stony Brook, NY 1978-82; currently, pres. Research Found. of So. Calif., San Diego; Warden, Basser Coll. 1961; chmn. Gregory Pincus Meml. Com. 1976; bd. dirs. Research Found. of Mental Hygiene 1979; awards: Publ. Fund Awd, Univ. N.S.W. 1961, Ford Found. fellowship 1962, NIH grantee 1973-83, and US State Dept. contract 1974; mem: Am. Physiol. Soc., Biophysical Soc., Soc. for Exptl. Biol. and Medicine, Am. Soc. for Cell Biol., Fedn. of Am. Scientists; mem. ANZAC, San Diego; works: Genetic Code assay using RNA-triplet binding (1963), theory of complexity (1965, 79), Fisher's theorem applied to competitive replication (1978), principle of rapid-reading in template directed polymerization (1971), isolated decapacitation factor (1971), synthetic decapacitation factor (1974), author over 50 sci. papers; rec: tennis. Res: 8427-118 Via Mallorca La Jolla 92037 Ofc: Research Found. of So. calif. 10457-F Roselle St San Diego 92121

DAVIS, CAROLE KENNERLY, public health administrator; b. May 1, 1940, Des Moines, Iowa; d. Raymond Belvie and Chrystal Irene (Florence) Kennerly; 1 son, Michael, b. 1971; edn: BA, State Univ. of Iowa 1963; MSW, Howard Univ. 1965. Career: pvt. family and marriage therapist, 1965-66; child welfare adminstr. Alameda Co. Welfare Dept., 1966-70; coll. instr. Chapman Coll., 1970-72, Coll. of Alameda, 1973-75, Vista Coll. 1982; sr. soc. svc. cons. Calif. State Dept. of Health, 1970-77, genetic disease program splst. 1975--; elected Councilpsn. (v.mayor 1980) Berkeley City Council (1st Black Woman in city's history) 1975-80; founder/ch. city council com. on Violence Against Women; cons. to White House Conf. on Handicapped (1977); cons. New West Ednl. Resrch. 1979; awards: Nat. Med. Social Wk. scholarship grantee 1961; comm. svc. awards, Alameda Co. Heart Assn., Nat. Council of Negro Women, Albany Child Care Assn., W. Berkeley Hlth Ctr.; chpsn. Alameda Co. Hypertension Council 1975-7; mem. Assn. of Bay Area Govt. 1976-7; Human Protection Com., Alta Bates Hosp. 1978-; bd. dirs. Bay Area Women Against Rape 1982; bd. dirs. E. Bay Womens PAC 1981-2; Democrat; Prot.; rec: travel, swim, read. Res: 2955 California St. Berkeley 94703 Ofc: State Dept. Hlth Svcs CHDP Pgm, 2151 Berkeley Way, Annex 2, Berkeley 94704

DAVIS, CLAUDE CARLTON, real estate broker; b. Jan. 11, 1920, Dolomite, Ala.; s. Squire Carlton and Gertrude (Robinson) D.; div.; children: Michael, b. 1946; Susan, b. 1948; Steven, b. 1950; edn: BA, Wilberforce Univ. 1942; realtor, Nat. Assn. of R.E. Bds. 1982. Career: sales supr. Acme Brewing Co. and Regal Pale Brewing Co., San Francisco 1948-60; pres. Claude C. Davis Realty Co., Los Angeles 1960-79; pres./owner Squires Co. (mtg. brokerage), Orange Co. 1979-80; pres. Claude C. Davis Co. Realtors, Los Angeles 1980--; instr. real estate, West L.A. Coll., 1975-82; pres. Consol. Realty Bd., L.A. 1969-71; pres. Calif. Assn. of R.E. Brokers, 1965-67; pres. Land Execs. Assn. of County of L.A., 1972-3; pres. Southwest L.A. Bd. of Realtors, 1984; dir. Calif. Assn. of Realtors, 1984; honors: resolution, City of Los Angeles, first to be pres. of both Realtist Bd. and Realtor Bd., 1948; recognition, Nat. Urban League 1948; mem: Tuskegee Airmen Inc. 1982-, Wilberforce Univ. Alumni Assn., Calif. Assn. of Realtors, Nat. Assn. of Realtors; mil: 1st lt., Pilot B-25, 1942-48; Rel. Sci.; rec: golf, fish, swim. Res: 501 Esplanade, 133, Redondo Bch 90277 Ofc: Claude C. Davis Co., Realtors, 501 Esplanade, 133, Redondo Beach 90277

DAVIS, DORIS HELENE, occupational program administrative assistant.; b. Apr. 30, 1935, Los Angeles; d. Andrew Eugene and Helen Louise (Schauweker) Reddy; m. John Harvey Davis, Aug. 18, 1953; children: Peggy Jo (Eglit), b. 1955; John Martin, b. 1956; edn: grad. Pasadena Acad.; spl. courses, Orange Coast Coll., Chathams R.E. Counseling; Jr. Coll. teaching cred./ vocational edn. 1983; real estate broker lic. 1981. Career: bookkeeper U.S. National Bank (now Crocker), Pasadena 1953-58; supr. Pasadena Dept. Rec., 1962-67; secty. Pasadena City Sch. Dist., 1967-71; equip. supr. University H. Sch., Irvine 1971-72; records maint., Huntington Bch. Union H. Sch. Dist., 1972-78; real estate subdiv. sales mgr. Ahrens and Assocs., Huntington Bch. 1978-80; adminstrv. asst. Homes for Sale Mag., Santa Ana 1980-81; Community (4 condo. projects) Assn. mgr. L & S Prop. Mgmt. Co., Huntington Bch., 1981; asst. to Coord. of Tng., Coastline Regl. Occupational Pgm., Costa Mesa 1981--; Republican; Prot. Res: 20092 Glacier Cir. Huntington Bch 92646 Ofc: Coastline Regional Occ. Pgm., 1001 Presidio Sq. Costa Mesa 92626

DAVIS, DOROTHY LEWTER, educator; b. Nov. 20, 1927, Sebring, Fla.; d. Rev. Rufus Cleveland and Mary Lee (Mitchell) L.; m. Johnnie E. Davis, Mar. 26, 1952; 1 son, Terence, b. 1959; edn: AA, Fl. Normal & Indsl. Coll. 1959; BS, Morris Brown Coll. 195; MA, Atlanta Univ. 1969; PhD, Teamers Univ. 1973; EdD, Pepperdine Univ. 1975, cert. in child devel. 1975. Career: editor Fort Myers (Fla.) New Press, 1949-50; teacher, elem. edn., Macon, Ga. 1950-53, Fort Myers, Fla. 1953-73; program dir. Creative Daycare, Santa Ana, 1973-77; founder/exec. director Pride Development Council, Inc., Santa Ana 1977--; awards: Golden City Awd. in Edn., City of Santa Ana 1978; Black History Awd., Black Community, Santa Ana 1981; Who's Who, Ga. 1978; mem: Alpha Kappa Alpha (historian), Urban League (Adv. Bd. 1980-), NAACP (life), Fla. State Teacher Assn. (pres. 1970-3), Profl. Business Women, Santa Ana; bd. dirs. Childrens Home Soc., Santa Ana; rep. Dist. 1 Childcare Task Force of Orange Co., 1983; past bd. mem. United Way (O.C.), March of Dimes; Democrat; Prot. Res: 13371 Winthrope St. Santa Ana 92705 Ofc: Pride Devel. Council Inc. 803 So Sullivan St Santa Ana 92704

DAVIS, FAITH MARGARET, clinical social worker; b. Aug. 16, 1937, Detroit, Mich.; d. Robert Wendell and Cecelia Maxine (McGee) D.; div. 1967; children: Mark, b. 1960, Mona, b. 1963, Kenneth, b. 1965; edn: BA, Marygrove Coll. 1959; MSW, San Francisco St. Univ. 1972; LCSW, lic. clin. social wkr. 1981. Career: social wkr. San Diego Welfare Dept., 1962-64; soc. work supr. Alameda Co. Welfare Dept., Oakland 1964-72; psych. soc. wkr. West Oakland Hlth Ctr. 1971-72; child welfare wkr. Alameda Co. Human Resources, Oakland 1972-73; psych. soc. wkr. Alameda Co. Substance Abuse, 1973-77, dir. 1977-78; clin. dir. East Oakland Drug Abuse, 1977-78; cons. for Verbal Exchange Pgm. 1968 70, cons. Pub. Hlth Nurses 1973-77, cons. Oakland Pub. Schs. 1973-83; num. appreciation awards, Oakland Schools; mem: Nat. Assn. Soc. Wkrs., Bay Area Assn. of Black Soc. Wkrs., Counselors West, Marygrove Coll. and SFSU Alumni Assns., Alpha Kappa Alpha Sor., various PTAs, Toler Hts. Citizens Council, World Peace Orgn.; Democrat; Nichren Shoshu Buddhism; rec: dancing, roller skating, photog. Res: 9509 Thermal St Oakland 94605 Ofc: East Oakland Comm. Mental Hlth Clinic, 10 Eastmont Mall, 400, Oakland 94605

DAVIS, FENELON FRANCIS, geologist; b. Jan. 15, 1905, Oakland; s. William James and Josephine (Fenelon) D.; m. Helen Ann Burke, May 1, 1943; children: Rosalie Ann, b. 1946; Elizabeth Joann, b. 1949; edn: BS, UC Berkeley 1928, grad. study UCB 1932-3; reg. geologist (No.385), Calif. 1970; lic. real estate broker 1977. Career: research field geologist Std. Oil Co. of Calif., So. Calif., Los Angeles Basin, West Texxas, Gulf Coastal Plain, 1928-31; sales engr. Webb and French, Berkeley 1934-38; petroleum engr. Calif. State Lands, Huntington Beach 1939-40; geologist Calif. State Mines and Geology, statewide, 1941-62, sr. geologist, 1963-73; cons. geologist, self-emp., Sacramento 1974-84; mgr. Mineral Resources Pgm., State Mines and Geol. 1965-73, Safety Ofcr. 1968-73; cons. on mine pollution to Water Quality Bd., mercury and energy crises to Resources Agcy.; awards: cert. of pub. service, State Dept. of Conserv. 1964; comendation, Senate, Calif. St. Legislature, 1973; mem: Am. Assn. Petroleum Geologists 1928-32; Peninsula Geol. Soc. 1960-68; Sacramento Geol. Soc. 1968-83 (pres. 1978); Am. Inst. Mining Engrs. 1957-84 (pres. Sacto Section 1970); Calif. State Empls. Assn. 1954-84 (pres. Chap. 78, 1964-66, bd. dirs. 1983-4); Comstock Club; Sacto. bd. of Realtors; author Mineral Resources section in Calif. Ocean Area Plan for US Dept. of Navig. & Ocean Devel. (1970); over 60 pub. reports on mineral resources in Calif. 1950-75; mil: Reserve Ofcrs. Tng. Corp. 1924-26; Republican; Catholic; rec: music, travel, real estate. Res: 4309 Kenston Way Sacramento 95822

DAVIS, JOHN W(ARREN), contracting officer; b. Feb. 14, 1946, York, Pa.; gr.grandson, W.F.Davis, founder Anchor Serum Co. and St. Joseph (Mo.) Stockyards and mem. Mo. State Legislature; gr.son, Frank A. Davis Sr., lawyer, St.Joseph, Mo.; son, Lillian M. (Billings) and Frank A. Davis Jr., real estate broker, Venice, Fla. Edn: AA, San Diego City Coll. 1975; BA, Drake Univ. 1968. Career: real estate investment, mgmt. sales, 1972-80; 1980-84 contract adminstr. Office of Naval Research, Stanford Univ., 1984- Contracting Ofcr., US Navy, Corona, Ca. currently, vice pres. Estate Design Systems, Fremont; real estate broker; advisor to Doris I. Mason Center, San Francisco. Mem: Internat. Platform Assn, Lake Norconian Sailing Club, Apartment Rental and Owners Assn., (past) Stanford Sailing Assn.; mil: E5 US Army 1968-72, Vietnam Campaign (2/60 device) and Vietnam Svc. (2 stars) medals, Army Commendation, medals,; Prot.; rec: sailing, swim, travel. Res: 815 Rimpau Ave, Corona 91719. Fleet Analysis Center, Naval Weapons Sta. Seal Beach, Corona Annex, Corona CA 91720

DAVIS, JUDITH GRACE, insurance co. executive; b. Feb. 11, 1947, san Francisco; d. Harry Benjamin and Grace Alice (Behnke) Southward; m. Donald L. Walters, Sept. 15, 1975; children: Deena, b. 1966; Nicol, b. 1967; John, b. 1969; edn: AA, Canada Coll. 1971; LUTC I, Personal Ins. Cert., Life Underwriting Tng. Council 1981. Career: acct. svc. rep. Wells Fargo Bank, Redwood City 1965-67; receptionist/ lab. & pathology asst. Kaiser Permanente Med. Gp.,

Redwood City 1965-67; bus. mgr. Canada Coll. Newspaper, Redwood City 1971; dist. rep. Certified Life Ins., Eureka 1977-82; field tng. supvr., Santa Rosa/ mgr. Eureka Ofc., Cert. Life 1982--; profl. awards: Pres.'s Club (1978), Quota Buster Awd. (1983), Agen of the Month (1980, 81, 82), Life Rally Trophy (1980), V.P. Awd. (1978), Certified Life Ins.; mem: Humboldt- Del Norte Life Underwriters Assn. (pres. 1984-85); Nat. & Calif. Assns. Life Underwriters; Womens Ins. of Humboldt Co.; Womans Life Underwriter Council; Bus. & Profl. Women; Hombolt Bay Luncheon Club; Native Daughter, Calif.; Republican; rec: observing waterfowl. Res: 1458 Reasor Rd McKinleyville 95521 Ofc: Certified Life Ins., Box 4, Eureka 95501

DAVIS, PETER QUINCY, banker; b. Feb. 13, 1940, US Naval Base, C.Z.; s. Nathaniel Burt and Frances Foster (Dearing) D.; m. Carroll Ward, Apr. 15, 1960; children: Susan, b. 1961; Jennifer, b. 1965; edn: BBA, Calif. Western Univ. 1963; lic. real estate broker, Calif. 1980. Career: indsl. engr. Ryan Aeronautical Co., 1960-64; banker, various positions leading to vice pres. and mgr., Bank of Am., 1964-76, banker, Bank of Commerce Commerce, San Diego, 1976-, chief exec. ofcr./pres. 1978--; dir. Centre City Devel. Corp.; instr. San Diego Comm. Coll.; chmn. for Cong. Jim Bates Fiscal and Monetary Adv. Bd.; chmn. Mayor's Transp. Com.; hon. dep. sheriff, S.D. County; mem: Robert Morris Assos., Am. Inst. Banking (instr.), San Diego CofC (treas.); clubs: Rotary, Exchange, City; mil: US Army 1959-60, USAR 1960-65; Republican; Presbyterian. Res: 4572 Cather Ave San Diego 92122 Ofc: Bank of Commerce, 7980 Clairemont Mesa Blvd San Diego 92111

DAVIS, RICHARD ALLEN, data processing executive; b. July 15, 1929, Chgo.; s. Harold Aaron and Hilda May (Gulliver) D.; m. Betty, Mar. 25, 1950; div.; children: Holly, b. 1956; Jeff, b 1957; Gary, b. 1962; edn: BSEE, Drexel Univ. 1959; MSEE, UCLA 1966; grad. stu. USC 1966-7; research in Human Info. Processing UCLA 1974-6; Cert. in Data Processing (CDP), Data Processing Mgmt. Assn. (DPMA) 1965; Cert. in Radiation Health & Safety, Calif. 1976. Career: prior (20 yrs.) mgmt./ technical/ consulting experience in systems, computers, software, telecomm.; founder/pres. R&D Management Inc., Fullerton 1969-70; mktg. mgr./pgm. mgr. Hughes Aircraft Inc., Fullerton 1971-76; mgr. Adv. Pgms., Computer Automation Inc., Irvine 1976-78; dir. adv. plnng. Bell Northern Research Inc., Palo Alto 1979-80; independent cons. (DOD, NASA Ops., CalTech-JPL, McDonnell Douglas Space Div., Wang Labs., Litton-Aero Svcs. Div., Bell Tel. Labs., Hertz-Reservations Div., Olympus Mutual Fund, Fujitsu Ltd., etc.) 1980-82; founder/ dir./ VP Ops. Softyme, Inc., San Francisco 1982--; lectr., mgmt., JF Kennedy Univ.; lectr., comp. sci., CSU Sacto. 1982; cons., system analysis, UC Ext. 1984; awards: Pepsi Cola Natl Scholar 1947, Hughes Aircraft Doctoral Fellow 1975; orgns: fmrly active in BSA (inst. repr.), YMCA (Indian Guides/Gra-Y Leader), No. Orange Co. Child Guidance Center (bd. dir.); Patents: differential-integral PCH synchronizer; five others pending; num. publs., seminars 1963-; mil: cpl. US aRmy Ord., Guided Missile Sch. (instr.) 1954-56; Prot., Siddha Yoga; rec: pvt. pilot, guitar, writing (fiction/non-f.), jogging. Res: 56 Panoramic Way, U, Berkeley 94704 Ofc: Softyme Inc. 329 Bryant St San Francisco 94704

DAVIS, ROGER H., lawyer/corporate executive; b. June 19, 1923, Chgo.; s. Franklin H. and Ruth (Polachek) D.; children: Roger H., Jr., b. 1950; Shelley (Browning), b. 1952; edn: AB, UC Berkeley 1949, LLB, 1951; admitted State Bar of Calif. 1951. Career: assoc. Loeb & Loeb, 1951, partner/atty. Loeb & Loeb 1955; head legal dept. William Morris Agency 1961, vice pres. 1966-; exec. v.p./ bd. dirs./ adminstrv. head of motion picture dept., bus. affairs dept. & literary dept. William Morris Agcy West Coast, 1980--; arbitrator for WGA, Inc. and DGA, Inc.; lectr. entertainment field, UCLA, USC, Southwestern Univ.; award for outstanding achievement in entertainment/agency field, Assn. of Talent Agents, 1982; mem: Assn. of Talent Agents, Calif. Entertainment Comn., Acad. Motion Picture Arts and Scis., Beverly Hills Bar Assn.; bd. mem. Permanent Charities Com., Entertainment Indus.; miil: capt. US Army Transp. Corps, WWII/ Phillippines 1944-46; rec: sailing, tennis, piano, skiing. rEs: 4346 Redwood Ave, 308, Marina Del Rey 90291 Ofc: Wm. Morris Agcy Inc. 151 El Camino Beverly Hills 90212

DAVIS, ROGER LEWIS, lawyer; b. Jan. 27, 1946, New Orleans, La.; s. Dr. Leon and Anada (Russ) D.; m. Annette, Aug. 17, 1971; 1 dau. Alexandra, b. 1976; edn: AB, Tulane Univ. 1967; MA (1969) and PhD (1971) in Eng. & Am. lit., UC Los Angeles; JD, Harvard Law Sch. 1974; admitted Calif. State Bar 1974. Career: resrch. asst. to Prof. Arthur R. Miller, Harvard Law Sch., 1972-74; law clk. Heller, Ehrman, White & McAuliffe, San Francisco, summer 1973; attorney law firm Orruck, Herrington & Sutcliffe, APC, San Francisco 1974-, partner 1980--, chmn. Public Fin. Dept. 1981-; mem. faculty ann. Arbitrage Seminar, Nat. Assn. of Bond Lawyers 1981-; mem: Am. Bar Assn. (Tax Sect.), com. on tax-exempt financing, chmn. subcom. on new devels.), Nat. Assn. of Bond Lawyers (coms. on Arbitrage and Health Care Fin.), S.F. Municipal Bond Club, S.F. Municipal Forum; Jewish. Res: 345 Kellogg Ave Palo Alto 94301 Ofc: Orrick, Herrington & Sutcliffe, 600 Montgomery St San Francisco 94111

DAVIS, RONALD FRANKLIN, aerospace engineer; b. June 17, 1943, Asheville, N.C.; s. Edgar Franklin and Geneva Snow (Kuykendall) D.; m. Karen Starleaf (Kragh), Aug. 4, 1980; edn: BS, N.C. State Univ. 1968. Career: engr./ scientist, McDonnell Douglas Astronautics Co., Huntington Beach 1970-80; sr. engr. Interstate Electronics Corp., Anaheim 1980-81; currently: engineering splst. Ford Aerospace & Comm., Newport Beach; owner/broker Blackhorse Trading Co., Costa Mesa; owner Awareness Marketing, C.M.; mem: Am. Inst. of Aero. and Astro., Nat. Assn. of Realtors; publs: sci. jour. arts., reports; author Microkey (w/ K. Starleaf), Awareness Mktg. (1982); mil: airman 1,

USAF 1961-65. Res: 350 E. 22nd St Costa Mesa 92627 Ofc: Ford Aerospace & Comm., Ford Road, Newport Beach 92660

DAVIS, SARAH J. (Sally), psychotherapist; b. July 27, 1939, NYC; d. William F. and Wanda V. McGarry; edn: BS in bus.adm., UC Berkeley 1965, MSW, CSU Sacto., 1971; lic. Clin. Social Worker, State of Calif. 1974. Career: psychiatric social worker Methadone Maint. Pgm., Sacto. Co. Dept. of Mental Health, 1972-73 and proj. dir. Drug Alternatives Pgm., 1973-76; cons. Raleigh Hills Hosp., Sacto. 1976-77; coordinator County Drug Pgm. and Services to Mentally Disordered Sex Offenders, Sacto. Co. Dept. of Mental Health, 1976-77; adminstr. Substance Abuse Pgm., State Dept. of Health, 1977-78; chief deputy dir. State Dept. of Alcohol and Drug Pgms., 1978-80, chief Div. of Drug Pgms., 198-81, State Alcohol Drug Program Director, (chief exec. 225 psn.staff, $105M budget), 1981-83; dir./adv. to Health & Welfare Secty., 1981-83; mem. State Bd. of Behavioral Sci. Examiners, 1975-80; bd. dir. Womankind Health Clinic, Sacto. 1978-83; mem. Gov's Task Force on First Offender Drinking Driver Pgms., 1981-83; acting dir. Woodside Counseling Ctr., pvt. practice in psychotherapy and couples counseling, 1972-80; pvt. practice psychotherapist, individual & marriage counseling, 1983--. Mem: Nat. Assn. of Social Workers, Soc. forClin. Social Workers, Sacto. Women's Network (ch.bd.dirs.), Sacto. Women's Campaign Fund); mem. research adv. com. NIAAA, 1983. Democrat. address: 1005 40th St. Sacramento 95819.

DAVIS, STEPHEN NILES, marketing executive; b. June 11, 1952, NY, NY; s. Howard and Leah (Goldstein) D.; m. Margaret Huether, Aug. 4, 1974; edn: BS in computer engring., Syracuse Univ. 1974, MS, 1977, MBA, 1980. Career: engineer Gen. Elec. Corp., Syracuse, NY 1973-74; sr. assoc. engr. IBM, Poughkeepsie, NY 1974-78; product planning mgr. Atari, Sunnyvale 1980-81; mgr. of product mktg. Corvus Systems, San Jose 1981--; rec: photog., coins, racquetball, wt.lifting. Res: 1064 Bee Ct. Milpitas 95035 Orf: Corvus Systems, 2029 O'Toole Ave San Jose 95131

DAVIS, WILLIAM RUSSEL, securities co. executive; b. Oct. 4, 1922, Des Moines, Iowa; s. James Edward and Kitty fern (Hildebrand) D.; m. Elsie Jean Spry, Aug. 10, 1945; children: Craig, b 1949; Dean, b. 1951; edn: Iowa State Univ. 1942; AA, UCLA 1956; BA, La Verne Univ. 1972. Career: commnd. ensign US Navy 1945, served as naval aviator in various locations, ret. comdr. 1972; joined Private Ledger Finl. Services, Inc., San Diego 1973-, dir. 1976-82, corp. secty. 1978, vice pres. 1979--; mem: Masons, Assn. Naval Aviation, Phi Delta Theta frat.; mil: comdr. USN 1943-72; Republican; Baptist; rec: golf, bridge, woodworking. Res: 710 Second St. Coronado 92118 Ofc: Private Ledger Finl. Services, Inc. 3511 Camino Del Rio, So. San Diego 92108

DAWSON, DAVID BERTRAM, real estate broker; b. Oct. 21, 1941, Culver City; s. Richard H. and Anne C. Dawson; Calif. lic. real estate broker 1974; GRI, Grad. Realtors Inst. 1974. Career: sales rep0. PSA, 1963-70; real estate sales 1970-71; branch mgr. Forest E. Olson Inc., 1971-76, district mgr. 1976; broker services Century 21 of Ogr. Co., 1976-79; vice pres. Century 21 Real Estate Corp. 1979-80; pres. Century 21 of the Midwest 1980-81; pres. Century 21 of Ogr. Co. 1981-82; pres. Century 21 of the Pacific, Inc. (So. Calif., Hawaii, Ala.) 1982--; cons. Real Estate Today, 1982; dir. Calif. Assn. of Realtors 1975; v.p. East Orange Co. Bd. of Realtors 1975; guest spkr. radio & TV real estate shows 1982-83; awards: outstanding leadership in mgt. & mktg., Forest E. Olson Inc. 1975; Century 21 leader in prodn in nation, 1982 (11 of 12 mos.), total years of 83, 84; mem: Sales & Mgt. Exec., JayCees 1970, Board of Realtors (com;s., dir., v.p.) 1971-82; publs: arts. on R.E., 1982-3; rec: motor sports: boat, motorcycle, dune buggy. Res: 4449 E. Valley Gate Dr. Anaheim 92807 Ofc: Century 21 of the Pacific, 2100 E. Katella, Ste 1985, Anaheim 92806

DAWSON, DOBIE MARK, government executive; b. Sept. 4, 1955, Visalia; s. Frankie Lonzo and Mildred Geneva (Mehrten) D.; m. Sandra Chin, June 25, 1977; children: Vanessa Leigh-Ann, b. 1978; Matthew Christopher, b. 1981; edn: AA, Coll. of Sequoias 1976; UC Davis, 1978; Mosquito Control Cert. 1975. Career: spl. problems tech. Delta Vector Control District, 1970-78; mgr. University Transport Sys., 1976-78; district mgr. Kings Mosquito Abatement Dist., Hanford 1978--; pres., Calif. Conf. of Mgrs. of Mosquito Abatement Dist. 1980; awards: F&AM Masonic Light Award 1982; Delkap Scholarship Award 1973; Calif. State Farmer Award, Future Farmers of Am. 1973; State Entomology Award 1973; Internat. Study Pgm. Exchange Scholar, Cambridge, Eng. 1972; mem: Am. Mosquito Control Assn.; Calif. Mosquito and Vector Control Assn. (bd. dirs., Regional Rep., treas.); Soc. of Vector Ecologists; Rotarian; Masons; Scottish Rite; Calif. Assn. of Physically Handicapped; works: author mosquito control data input and retrieval pgm.; Episcopal (Vestry); rec: computer pgmmg., chess, backpacking. Res: 2254 Carter Way Hanford 93230 Ofc: Kings Mosquito Abatement District, 10871 Bonney View Ln Hanford 93230

DAWSON, JOHNNY BRUCE, engineering executive; b. Sept. 28, 1944, Lincoln, England, nat. 1954; s. James Adams and Joyce (Nightingale) Dawson; m. Joan Williams, Jan. 4, 1978; stepchildren: John Thompson, Susan Bennett; edn:

BSEE, w/distn., Purdue Univ. 1966, MSEE, 1968; cert. Program Mgr. Devel. corporate course. Career: engr. Hughes Aircraft, 1968--: head EW and Communications Analysis Group 1974, hd. EW System Design Sect. 1976, pgm. mgr. Frequency Extension Pgm. and asst. mgr. EW Sys. Dept. 1980-82, currently mgr. Electronic Warfare and Spl. Projects Systems Lab., Fullerton; honors: NSF grant, sev. scholarships and fellowships; mem: Old Crows, Internat. Halley Watch Soc., Orange County Astronomers, American Space Found., Planetary Soc.; treas. Boy Scouts 1980-81; num. tech. publs., Republican; Methodist; rec: tennis, skiing, astrophotog. Res: 1525 Shadow Lane Fullerton 92631 Ofc: Hughes Aircraft 1901 W. Malvern, Fullerton 92634

DAWSON, NORMA ANN, lawyer; b. Sept. 11, 1950, Detroit, Mich.; d. Emmett Chamberlain and B. Louise (Boddie) D.; edn: BA, Penna. State Univ. 1971; JD, Univ. Mich. Sch. of Law 1974; admitted Calif. State Bar (1979), US Dist. Court, Central Dist., US Ct. of Appeals, 9th Circuit. Career: sole prop. Free-Lance Legal Research, 1975-77; legal asst. Miller & Daar, 1977-80; assoc. Marvin H. Kleinberg, Inc. and cons. ASI Lighting, 179--; counsel PennCorp Finl. Inc., 1980-; Life and Health Compliance Assn., Handout Com. ch. 1981-; mem. State Bar Comm. Group Ins. Pgms. 1982-; honors: outstanding senior, Penn. St. Univ. 1971; mem: Nat., Am., Beverly Hills Bar Assns., Black Women Lawyers Assn. of So. Calif., Inc. (ed. 1983-4), Nat. Assn. of Female Execs., Penn State Alumni Assn., Penn State Club of Gr. L.A., Univ. Mich. Alumni Assn., Black Porsche Inc. (mbrshp. dir.); Democrat; Sci. of Mind; rec: sailing, creative writing. Res: 11077 Palms Blvd, 302, Los Angeles 90034 Ofc: PennCorp Finl. Inc. 3130 Wilshire Blvd Santa Monica 90406

DAWSON, WILLIAM JAMES, orthodontist; b. May 16, 1930, San Francisco; s. Wm. James and Augusta (Rude) D.; m. Judith Riede, Aug. 11, 1962; children: William, b. 1954; Wendy, b. 1963; Nancy, b. 1967; Sarah, b. 1968; Evelyn, b. 1970; edn: BA, UC Berkeley 1952; DDS, UC San Francisco 1958. Career: private practice of orthodontics, San Rafael 1958--; clin. instr. in oral histology, UC San Francisco 1958-60, mem. UC Cleft Palate Panel 1958-75, clin. instr./ asst. research dentist UCSF 1960-75; councilman Town of Ross 1967-79; mem. State of Calif. Public Employees Retirement System Bd. of Adminstrn. 1969-76, honors: Omicron Kappa Upsilon; Diplomate Am. Bd. of Orthodontics 1969; Fellow Royal Soc. of Health 1972; mem: Marin Co. Dental Soc., Am., Calif. Dental Soc., Am. Assn. of Orthodontists, Pacific Coast Soc. of Orthodontics, Fedn. Dentaire Internat., Coll. of Diplomates Am. Bd. Orthodontics; orgns: citizens adv. com. Dominican Coll. (pres. 1975-6), exec. com. Marin Property Owners Assn. (pres. 1981-2), M. Co. United Way Bd., Rotary Club of San Rafael (pres. 1978-9), bd. dirs. Terwilliger Found., v.chmn. Lincoln Club of No. Calif., Sierra Club, Bohemian Club; arts. in dental jours.; mil: s/sgt. USAF 1951-54; Republican; Episcopal; rec: fish, garden, tennis. Res: POB 977, Ross 94957 Ofc: 11 Greenfield Ave San Rafael 94901

DAY, RONALD MICHAEL, private investigator; b. June 18, 1937, Providence, R.I.; s. Richard Harold and Mildred Elizabeth (Porter) D.; m. 2d. Barbara Jean Dehart, Sept. 17, 1983; children: Linda, Laura, Lisa, Ronald, Richard; edn: No. Calif. Peace Officers 1962, Contra Costa Coll. 1961-4, Sierra Coll. 1979-82; lic. private investigator, Calif. 1975; lic. patrol opr. 1969. Career: supt. of security East Bay Reg. Park Dist., first organizing police type ranger chief 1961-69; chief of Calif. Exposition & State Fair 1969-70; currently pvt. investigator and patrol operator; recipient Award of Merit, Security World Mag. 1969, for security pgm. at Calif. Expo.; mem: Profl. Security Alliance, Inc. (v.p.); No. Calif. Peace Officer Assn.; Western Fairs Assn. (security cons. 1984); Rental Prop. Mgrs. & Owners Assn.; Lions Internat. (Blood Bank chmn. CC Gp.); Elks (law enforce. com.); vol. promoter community safety pgms.; devel. pvt. security pgms. for individuals; mil: served in USN, currently USNR; Democrat; Catholic; rec: music, 10-speed biking. Address: Ronald M. Day, Investigations / Bass Security Patrol, 1922 Ethan Way, 32, Sacramento 95825

DAYA, FUAD GABRIEL, biochemist; b. May 21, 1928, Tartus, Syria; s. Gabriel Simon and Merianna N. (Jeha) D.; m. Martha Schmitz, Nov. 9, 1963; 1 dau. Gabriella, b. 1964; edn: Am. Univ. of Beirut 1952; BS, Tulsa Univ. 1955; M. in biochem., Utah Univ. 1957; grad. work, San Fransisco St. Univ. 1960; reg. medical technologist, Ind. Career: African tour with Kaiser Foundation Internat. during Biafran War with Nigeria, 3 years; owner Laurel Medical Labs.; real estate investor; realtor, Mueller Estates, Millbrae, Ca.; export/ import prin. Daya International Commerce, San Francisco; mem: Am. Soc. of Clinical Pathologist, US Overseas Medical Ednl. Need, Masons, Press Club; Republican; Greek Orthodox; rec: travel, reading. Res: 4 Fairoaks Court San Mateo 94403 Ofc: Daya Intl. Commerce, 3580 California St San Francisco 94118

DAYTON, ROBERT JESEN, furniture dealer; b. June 19, 1910, Decatur, Ill.; s. John Kennedy and Gertrude Dayton; m. Marjorie Alice Massey, Aug. 25, 1935; children: Donna, b. 1943; June, b. 1946; edn; ABA, Compton Coll. 1933; desig: AID (Adv. Int. Designer) Los Angeles Furn. Mart. 1954. Career: founder/ La Brea Sales (the first major discount store in Calif.), also ptnr. in Vernon Sales, 1947-51; owner Buyers Mart and Long Beach Sales 1952-59; founder chain furniture stores (incl. Apartment/ Motel Furnishings, Colorstyled Interiors, Contract Sales) 1959-69; buyer for Levitz Furn., Huntington Beach 1969-70; owner/ opr. The Whole House, Upland 1971-80, Diamond Bar Furniture 1980--; mem: Diamond Bar CofC; Nat. Fedn. Indpendent Businessmen; works: Dayton Filekeeping System for service stations, copyright 1941; mil: s/sgt. Air Corps 1945; Republican (asst. campaign mgr., Richard Nixon 1946); Presbyterian. Res: 1110 N Puente St Brea 92621 Ofc: Diamond Bar Furniture, 23545 Palomino Dr Diamond Bar 91765

DEADRICH, PAUL EDDY, lawyer-realtor; b. Jan. 30, 1925, Lakeport, Ca.; s. John A. and Grace E. (Jackson) D.; m. Irene Banks, Dec. 11, 1982; children: Marjanne Robinson, b. 1947; Nancy Wolfer, b. 1950; Dianne Deadrich-Rogers, b. 1952; Bettianne Buck, b. 1955; John F. Deadrich, b. 1963; David Deadrich, b. 1968; edn: AA, UC Berkeley 1946; JD, Hastings Coll. of the Law 1949. Career: real estate sales agt., 1947-50; self-empl. attorney, San Leandro 1950-61; atty., realtor, ins. agt. in Twain Harte, 1961-73; law practice in Loomis 1973-75, in Cameron Park 1975-78; missionary at Apostolic Alliance Mission, Gibi, Liberia 1978-82; atty., realtor in San Leandro, Ca. 1982--; judge of Justice Court, Tuolumne 1964-67; dir. Alameda Contra Costa Transit Dist. 1956-61; physical edn. instr./coach Mother Lode Christian Sch., Tuolumne 1969-73; adminstr., coach and teacher Loomis Christian Sch. 1974-75; honors: Outstanding young man of the year San Leandro, 1955, J.Cs.; mem: So. Alameda Co. Bd. of Realtors, San Leandro Breakfast Club; past pres. Twain Harte Rotary 1966-7; past pres. Tuolumne Co. Bd. of Realtors 1973; past pres. Broadmoor Mens Club 1958; past pres. Chabot Lions Club 1956-7; past pres. Family Counseling Agcy of So. Alameda Co.; past cmdr. DAV Chap. 67, San Leandro; mil: pfc 11th Armored Div. WWII in Fr., Belgium 1943-45, Bronze Star, Purple Heart, Combat Inf. Badge; Creation Missions Ch. (missionary Liberia 1978-82); rec: gardening, fishing, backpacking. Res: 1808 Pearl St Alameda 94501 Ofc: 250 Juana Ave San Leandro 94577

DEAN, JOAN ZIMMERMAN, real estate sales executive; b. Oct. 12, 1939, Teaneck, NJ; s. Wm. Lewis and Catherine Veronica (Kenny) Zimmerman; m. Robert Lawrence Dean, Dec. 29, 1962; children: Therese Maria, b. 1965; Robert L., II, b. 1966; edn: BS, Penn State Univ. 1962; lic. real estate broker. Career: real estate sales agt. Century 21, Mission Viejo 1977--; awards: Top salespsn. Century 21, 1981; top listing salespsn. Cen. 21 in Orange Co. 1982; top eight salespsn. Cen. 21 in USA 1982; mem. Calif. Realtor Assn.; Catholic; rec: swimming, golf, reading. REs: 27471 Cenajo Mission Viejo 92691 Ofc: Century 21 Today, 24000 Alicia Pkwy, 14, Mission Viejo 92691

DEAN, KENNETH, architectural design executive/ educator/ journalist; b. May 10, 1939, Evergreen Park, Ill.; s. Wayne Edwin and Genevieve Julia (Kyll) Smith; m. Linda Elizabeth Benitez, Sept. 27, 1980; edn: design deg., LaSalle Univ. 1970; AA in arts, Los Angeles Coll. 1978. Career: interior designer 1971--,pres. Dean Internat. Designs, Studio City & Canyon Country, Calif.; design instr. 1974--, Dean of L.A. School of Design; journalist for various L.A. mags. 1978--, currently for Santa Clarita Valley Mag.; actor in films, TV and stage, 1960-70; awards: merit, outstanding room design, L.A. County Fair 1979; best actor awards 1960s; mem: Internat. Soc. of Int. Designers (pres. San Fernando chpt.); Am. Soc. of Int. Designers; Constrn. Specs. Inst.; Optimist Club of Canyon Country; design work pub. in Designers West, 1001 Ideas, Residential Guide, Santa Clarita Valley Mags.; mil: sgt., Army Res., US Army, Ill. NG; Democrat (cand. Calif. State Assembly); Catholic; rec: snow skiing, archery. Res: 28807 Flowerpark Dr. Canyon Country 91351 Ofc: Dean Intl. Designs, 13045 Ventura Blvd. Studio City 91604

DEAN, MAJOR JAMES, publisher/editor; b. Nov. 11, 1923, Dallas, Tex.; s. Francis Claude and Alpha Aletha (Phillips) D.; m. Vida D. Baker, July 21, 1946; children: Major J. Jr., b. 1948; David Denhan, b. 1952; Victoria Lynn, b. 1957; edn: AA, Tyler (Tex.) Jr. Coll. 1947. Career: reporter Tyler, Tex. Courier Times, 1947, subsequently sports editor, city ed., mng. ed.; copy ed. Houston, Texas Chronicle, 1953-54; mng. ed. Pampa, Tex. News, 1954-56; ed. Lima, Ohio News, 1956-60; asst. city ed. Houston Chronicle, 1960-62; news ed., executive ed., editor The Register, Santa Ana, Ca. 1962-81; current: owner/ pub./ editor Orange County Business Live monthly newspaper, and pres. Jim Dean Orgn. Inc. pub. rels. co., Santa Ana; awards: first place writing, AP Texas Sports Writers Assn. 1950; general excellence newspaper award, Ohio Editors Assn. 1959; US Indsl. Assn. medallion for edtl. writing 1980; num. press club citations; Jim Dean journalism scholarship estab. Chapman Coll. in 1981; Sky Dunlap award, Orange Co. Press Club 1981; mem: v.p. Texas Sports Writers Assn. 1949; pres. Ohio UPI Editors Assn. 1959; pres. So. Cal. United Press Editors Assn. 1978; pres. O.C. chpt. Sigma Delta Chi; bd. mem. O.C. Press Club; bd. mem: O.C. CofC., O.C. Economic Devel. Corp., NCCJ, O.C. chpt. Alzheimers & Rel. Diseases Assn., adv. bd. CSU Gerontol. Ctr. Fund Drive; mil: s/sgt. Army Signal Corps 1942-45, Pac. Theater cpgn., GCM; Prot.; rec: writing, reading, travel, vol. svc. Address: The Jim Dean Orgn. Inc. 1322 West Park Ln Santa Ana 92706

DEAN, MARY LOWE, college administrator; b. Mar. 30, 1939, Cynthiana, Ky.; d. Reynolds N. and Mary Elizabeth (Whitaker) Lowe; edn: BA, Univ. of Ky. 1961, MA, 1967. Career: asst. dir. University Counseling Center, Univ. of Hartford (CT), 1970-74, dir. of Student Life, 1974-75, asst. v.p. 1975-78; spl. asst. Fresno Co. District Atty's Ofc., Fresno, Ca. 1979-83; administrative dean San Joaquin Coll. of Law, Fresno 1983--; cons. Bd. of Selectmen, Simsbury, CT 1977-8; cons. Pride, Inc., Denver, Colo. 1983; awards: outstanding contbn. to public edn., Hilliard, Oh. 1965; leadership, Univ. of Hartford Student Assn. 1976; mem: Nat. Women's Political Caucus (v.ch. 1983-4), Fresno Pride Adv. Bd. (ch. 1980-83); contbg. writer: Climbing Ghetto Walls (Charles C. Thomas, 1975). Res: 5075 No Roosevelt, 8, Fresno 93704 Ofc: San Joaquin Coll. of Law, 3385 E Shields, Fresno 93726

DEAN, WALTER P., company president; b. June 10, 1942, NYC; s. C. P. and Anne (Romanosky) Dean; m. Virginia Radichio, Oct. 24, 1970; edn: BSEE, Brooklyn Poly Tech., 1969, MBA, Hofstra Univ. 1974, ML, National Univ. 1983; lic. Profl. Engineer. Career: pres. Nassau Corp. of America, La Costa 1980; pres. Applied Engineering, Bayshore, NY 1969; sales mgr. W.No.Am., General Instrument Corp., Oceanside 1979--. 3rd degree Black Belt Judo

(1974); OWSI Scuba Instr. (1979); USJA Life mem.; mem: IEEE, GIC Mgmt. Club (pres. 1974-79), Profl. Assn. of Diving Instructors, Spl. Instr. Dive Control SSI; Republican; Catholic; rec: scuba, photog., judo. res: 3016 Azahar Ct. La Costa 92008. ofc: General Instrument Corp. 2124 El Camino Real, Oceanside 92054.

DEANE, JOAN CHRISTINE, real estate broker; b. Jan. 30, 1930, Danvers, Mass.; d. Franklyn P. and Christina A. (Murphy) Mahoney; m. James N. Deane Jr., May 28, 1955; 1 son, James, III, b. 1956; edn: nursing courses, North Shore Babies Hosp. 1949; beautician, Wilfreds Acad. 1955; AA, American River Coll. 1968; Lic: real estate sales 1971, R.E. Broker 1973, GRI (Grad. Realtors Inst.) 1975; R.E. Certificate Inst. 1973; Notary Public Calif. 1973-85; Calif. Comm. Colleges Lmtd. Cred. R.E. 1978-81. Career: apartment mgr. 1958-60, 1969-71; reporter, photog., columnist Orlando (Fla.) Sentinel Star, 1960-62; real estate agent, instr., broker, Kiernan Realtors, Rancho Cordova 1971-79; broker/ owner/ pres. Deane Realtors, R. Cordova 1979--; tchr. Am. River Coll. 1978-81; awards: Pres.'s Club, Kiernan Realtors 1978; recognition, Rancho Cordova Area CofC 1978, 1979, 82; mem: Sacto. Bd. of Realtors 1971-, coms: Edn. Com., Coll. Advis. Com., Womens Council of Realtors (pres. 1982), Sacto. Apt. Assn., Indsl. Comml. Div., Business Opps., Prop. Mgmt.; v.ch. R. Cordova Area Plnng. Advis. Council 1980-; mem. Sacto. Bd. of Suprs. Task Force 1982-; R. Cordova Comm. council (pres. 1979); Mills Merchants Assn. (past treas.); Democrat; Catholic (Eucharistic Minister); rec: swim, golf, tennis. Address: Deane Realtors, 2554 La Cumbra Cir Rancho Cordova 95670

DEANE, THOMAS ANDERSEN, banker; b. Mar. 20, 1921, Los Angeles; s. Thomas Clarke and Dorothy (Milbach) D.; m. Margaret Louise Noble, June 21, 1947; children: James C., William A.; edn: BA, Pomona Coll. 1942; MBA, Stanford Univ. 1948. Career: various positions Bank of America, 1948-, exec. vice pres. 1974-82, vice chmn. 1982--; mem: Calif. Bankers Assn. (dir. 1974-80, pres. 1978-9), Assn. of Reserve City Bankers; trustee, Pomona Coll., St. Johns Hosp. (Santa Monica); dir. YMCA of Los Angeles; dir., exec. com. Central City Assn. (LA); exec. com. Soc. Friendly Sons of St. Patrick; clubs: One Hundred Club of L.A., Los Angeles CC, California (LA), Bankers (SF); mil: capt. USMC 1943-6; Republican; Prot. Res: 720 San Lorenzo St Santa Monica 90402 Ofc: Bank of Am., 555 So Flower St Los Angeles 90071

DE ANGELES, SHERRY LORRAINE, diamond industry executive; b. Mar. 27, 1951, Hinsdale, Ill.; d. George Allan and Helen Gladys Seward; m. Jack P. DeAngeles, Dec. 18, 1978; edn: courses, Univ. of Granada (Malaga, Spain) 1970; profl. model, Gloria LaVonne 1969; sectl., Language Tuition Ctr. (London, G.B.); accred. to give 3-hour diamond wkshops to the insurance indus., Ins. Commnr. of Wash. & Ore. Career: secty./ telex opr. Sandwell Internat. Engrs., London, G.B. 1969; bi-lingual personal asst./sec. to Mr. Hiro Balani (pres. Orient Watch Co., Malaga, Spain) 1970; hostess/ courier for Traveler's Internat. /Olympic Airways (travel w/tour groups in G.B. and Greece) 1972; exec. secty. Kneisal Travel, Portland, Ore. 1974; founder Sophisticat (boutique), Portland 1975-78; broker in diamonds and colored gemstones, Portland 1979; founder/ owner DeAngeles Co. (dealers in Am. Ideal Cut diamonds), 1980-, owner Diva Diamond, Inc., Portland and Los Angeles 1983--; owner The Gemological Lab.; mem: Nat. Assn. of Female Execs., Alumni Assn. of The G.I.A. Gemolog. Inst. of Am.; clubs: Multnomah Athletic (Portland), Lake Oswego Hunt, Ore. Combined Tng. Assn. (3 day eventing and dressage), Am. Horse Show Assn., The City Club of Portland; patentee: arts. in insurance indus. publs.; devel. copyrighted ins. workshops (1983), underwriting forms (1981-), claims manual (1979-); Republican; Episcopal; rec: riding horses, skiing, sailing. Res: 777 S.W. 48th Dr. Portland, Ore 97221 Corp. Hdqtrs. 502 Bank of Calif. Tower, 707 S.W. Washington, Portland, Ore 97205 Factory Ofc: 643 So Olive St, 520, Los Angeles 90014

DEAO, ROBERT PAUL, corporation president; b. Mar. 20, 1944, Cleveland, Ohio; s. Paul Peter and Helen Marie (Nemish) D.; m. Sharon A., July 22, 1967; children: Rob, b. 1969; Eileen, b. l.; edn: LA Valley Coll. 1967-70, AA, math, Moorpark Coll. 1970; BS, econ., CSU Northridge 1973; grad. stu. CSU Fullerton 1976-7. Career: personnel analyst Holy Cross Hosp., SF Valley 1968-70; ops. director Dialysis Ops., SF Valley 1970-75; purch. agent, dir. ops., chief exec. dir. Ries Biologicals, Costa Mesa 1976-79, bd. dirs. 1978; corp. pres., chief finl. dir. Nephronics Mgt. Corp., Orange 1979--; honors: Father of Year, Anaheim YMCA 1978; mem: Am. Assn. of Nephrology Nurses and Technicians, Am. Soc. of Hosp. Purch. Agents, BSA, ARC (CPR instr.); coauthor Mobile Acute Dialysis, Dialysis & Transplantation 9/81; mil: s/sgt USAF 1962-66, Outstanding Unit Cit., Airmen of Yr. 1966 (Alaskan Air Cmd); rec: snow ski, backpack. Res: 2242 Rancho Corona Dr Corona 91720 Ofc: Nephronics Mgt. Corp. POB 5271, Orange 92667

DE ARMOND, BEATRICE JEANNETTE, hobby center owner/developer; b. Mar. 3, 1913, Northumberland, N.H.; d. Frank Nicklas and Bertha Rebbeca (Hapgood) Parker; m. Jay O. De Armond, Aug. 7, 1930; children: Jacquelin, b. 1934; Yvonne, b. 1943. Career: opened antique shop, expanded one shop at a time; currently, owner /designer Hobby City doll & toy museum (variety of hobby shops in 24 distinctive bldgs.), Anaheim; frequent judge, Doll Shows; mem. Anaheim, Stanton CofC; Long Beach, Anaheim Doll Collectors Clubs; Republican (Womens Fed. Club); Methodist. Address: Hobby City, 1238 So Beach Blvd Anaheim 92804

DE BOER, CATHY PATRICE, government management executive; b. Nov. 14, 1949, Kokomo, Ind.; s. Lowell Jay and Juanita Monelle (Gasaway) Somsel; m. Robert De Boer, Feb. 15, 1970; children: Julienne, b. 1970, Christa, b. 1972; edn: AA, Pikes Peak Comm. Coll. 1981; lic. cosmetology, Am. Acad. of Cosmetol., Colo. Springs 1975. Career: civil service, accts. maint./ supply reports clk. USAF Acad., Colo. 1975-79; mgmt. asst., AFPRO TRW, Redondo Beach, 1981--; honors: Phi Theta Kappa (pres.); num. profl. awards for outstanding achievement, 1978-; Methodist; rec: painting, piano, acting. Res: 2841 Gramercy Ave Torrance 90501 Ofc: AFPRO TRW, One Space Park Redondo Beach 90278

DE CHAVEZ, CARMELITO VILLANO, physician; b. June 7, 1948, Sariaya, Quezon, Phil., nat. 1983; s. Marcelo Valenzuela and Gregoria Badillo (Villano) de Chavez; edn: BS, premed., Far Eastern Univ., Phil. 1968, MD 1973. Career: house phys., surg. asst. Unity Hosp., Mnpls. 1977-78; flexible internship McKeesport (Pa.) Hosp., 1978-79; family practice res. Martin Luther King Jr. Gen. Hosp., Los Angeles 1981-; med. dir. Orland (Ca.) Family Health Ctr., 1981--; mem: Am. Acad. of Family Physicians, Philippine Med. Soc. of No. Calif.; Catholic; rec: tennis, hiking, painting. Res: 286 E Lassen Ave, 22, Chico 95926 Ofc: Orland Family Health Center, 227 Swift St Orland 95963

DE CUIR, CECILIA JANET, educator/counselor; b. May 12, 1948, Sacramento; d. Jules Delambre and Hildred Mary (Juge) De Cuir; edn: BA in soc. sci., CSU Sacto. 1971, MS in counseling, 1976. Career: graduate research analyst Calif. State Dept. Hlth -Personnel, Sacramento 1974; counselor asst. San Juan Unified Sch. Dist. 1974-5, teacher Palisades Elem. Sch., Orangevale 1977; counselor/tchr. Marysville Jt. Unified Sch. Dist., Lindhurst H.Sch. 1977-79; social wkr./ coordinator Sutter Co. Hlth Dept., Hlth. Edn. 1979--; W. Regl. coord. Values Realization Trainer Assocs. Network 1982-3; bd. dirs. Values Realization Inst. 1983-4; Overall Wellness Wkshp Coord. for Sid Simon 1983; honors: Alumni Campus Advance. Awd., CSU Sacto 1971; Successful Rural Health Proj. panel presentation, Office of Family Plnng. State Conf. 1983; mem: No. Calif. Values Realization Profl. Support Group (Facilitator); Sacto. Co. Affirmative Action Com. 1975; MFCC Intern 1983; Sierra Ctr for Healing Arts (affil.); Nat. Women's Health Network; Sacto Comm. Commn. on Women, Casa de Esperanza (battered victims shelter), Am. Assn. Univ. Women, Alpha Phi Sor., Kangaroo Courts; contbg. writer: Blossoming, by Dolores M. White (1983); contbg. com. mem. Women's Re-Entry Program, CSUS 1974-5; Democrat; rec: dance, hike, swim. Res: 2211 Ramirez St, Marysville 95901 Ofc: Sutter Co Hlth Dept 370 Del Norte Ave Yuba City 95991

DE CUIR, DENNIS VAUGHN, information systems consultant; b. May 24, 1953, Los Angeles; s. Joseph Denny and Rosaline Grace (Abounader) De C.; edn: AS, Cypress Coll. 1982; BSM in prog., Pepperdine Univ. Career:cons. Long Management, Encino 1979-80; systems analyst Carter Hawley Hale Stores, Anaheim 1980-82; documentation analyst Rockwell Int., Seal Beach 1982-84; systems consultant SEI Information Technology, Los Angeles 1984--, also technical writing cons.; mem. Soc. for Tech. Communications; Masons, Scottish Rite (32nd Degree), Toastmasters Int. (pres. Club 2555); tech. publs. in field; mil: E6 USN 1972-79, Active Reserve 1979-; Republican; Catholic; rec: cooking, flying, travel. Res: 7720-6 Crescent Buena Park 90620 Ofc: SEI Info. Technology, 5455 Wilshire Blvd, Ste 2210, Los Angeles 90036

DE DOMINIC, PATTY L., personnel services co. president; b. Mar. 5, 1951, Glendale; d. Harold and Eleanor Timm; m. John DeDominic, Mar. 7, 1969; children: Eric, b 1969; Christopher, b. 1971; Nicholas, . 1981; edn: courses, USC 1975-79. Career: sales mgmt. Avon Prods. Corp. 1975-78; pres./ founder PDQ Personnel Svcs., Inc., Los Angeles 1979--; partner Organizational Concepts (mgmt. cons. firm) 1982-; awards: Woman of Achiev., Women in Mgmt.; Advocate of the Year 1983, US Small Bus. Adminstrn.; mem: Nat. Assn. Women Bus. Owners (pres. 1983-84); Women in Mgmt. (pres. 1982); Joint Conf. for Increased Use of Minority Bus.; Am. Arbitration Assn.; arbitrator, L.A. County Bar Assn.; advis. bd. Calif. Assembly Select Com. on Small Bus.; mem. Pres.'s Roundtable, Los Angeles; mem. Catalyst (a nat. career network) 1979-; writer two regular columns: Career Corner, Management Savvy; Christian; rec: small business, womens issues. Res: 9400 La Tuna Cyn Sun Valley 91352 Ofc: PDQ, 4929 Wilshire, Ste 241, Los Angeles 90010

DEEB, EDWARD, periodontist; b. May 28, 1927, Lebanon, nat. 1946; s. Eli and Rose (Kattas) Deeb, Jr.; m. Marion Nader, 1955; children: Caren, b. 1956, Edna, b. 1958, Danice, b. 1961, Gina, b. 1963, Jeanice, b. 1965, Edward, b. 1965; edn: BA, UCLA 1950, MA, Univ. of Ore. 1951, DDS, USC 1955. Career: periodontist, self employed; pres. Deeb Investments, Inc.; Expert Examiner, State Bd. of Dental Examiners 1981, 82; instr. USC Dental Sch. 1955-56, chmn. Dept. Periodontics-Endodontics, LA County Gen Hosp.-USC Med. Center, 1956-69. Honors: Excellence in Oral Pathology 1955; Fellow Am. Coll. of Dentists (F.A.C.D.) 1977; Phi Kappa Phi 1981; HON. PhD, Pepperdine Univ. 1981; Fellow Internat. Coll. of Dentists (F.I.C.D.) 1983. Mem: Kiwanis (lt.gov. 1962), Masons, Shriners, Western Study Club of Combined Therapy (pres. 1968), So. Calif. Acad. of Endodontics (pres. 1970), So. Calif. Acad. of Oral Pathology (pres. 1971), State DentalXi Psi Phi Alumni Frat. (pres. 1960). Publs: arts. in dental jours.; dental research LACGH-USC Med. Ctr. 1956-59. Mil: sgt. US Army 1946-47. Republican. Antiochian Orthodix. rec: boating. res: 4570 Charmion Ln. Encino 91613. ofc: Deeb Investments Inc. 10700 Burbank Blvd. Suite 2, No. Hollywood 91601.

DE GREGORIO, ROSEMARY DENIKE, financial planner, b. Dec. 18, 1929, San Francisco (4th gen. Californian), d. Van Alstyne Peter and Evelyn Lillian (Biggs) Denike; m. John DeGregorio, Aug. 26, 1950; children: Julianne, b. 1954; Paul, b. 1959; Peter, b. 1966; James, b. 1967; Andrew, b. 1969; edn: BA, San Francisco St. Univ. 1950, Reg. Investment Advisor, SEC, 1984. Career: teacher S.F. Unified Sch. Dist., San Francisco 1972-78; service rep. Zahorik,

Oakland 1978-80, United Economic Services, Torrance 1980-82; finl. planner/ adminstr. Tax Coordinated Financial Plans, Larkspur 1982-83; reg. investment advisor KR Finl. Group, Burlingame 1983--; num. seminars fin. plnng., 1979-; mem: Internat. Assn. for Fin. Plnng., Inst. of Certified Finl. Planners, S.F. Fedn. of Teachers; Democrat (past pres. Dist. 8 Dem. Club, Dem. Womens Forum); Catholic; rec: politics, arts & crafts. Res: 140 Lapham Way, San Francisco 94112 Ofc: 655 14th St. San Francisco 94114

DE GUZMAN, VILMA MIGUEL, real estate broker; b. Oct. 27, 1941, Sta. Ignacia, Tarlac, Philippines; d. Gavind Robillos and Jovita Fernando (Miguel) DeGuzman; edn: BS in home tech., Univ. of the Phil. 1960; grad. wk. in adv. edn., 1960-62; real estate, bus. courses, SF City Coll. 1972-73; Calif. lic. real estate broker 1974. Career: real estate broker Reliable Realty, San Francisco 1974-83; real estate broker Century 21 AAble Realty, S.F. 1983--; mgr./ adminstr. Laurel Crest Manor (residential care home), 1984--; mem. San Francisco Bd. of Realtors. Res: 35 Dichiera Ct San Francisco 94112 Ofc: Century 21 AAble Realty, 3742 Mission St San Francisco 94110

DE KIRBY, VAUGHAN RANSONE, lawyer; b. Apr. 15, 1947, San Diego; s. Vaughan Walton and Perry Louise (Ransone) de K.; m. Christine, Sept. 27, 1972; 1 son, Vaughan Kenton, b. 1982; edn: BA, CSU Northridge 1972; JD, cum laude, Western St. Univ. Coll. of Law. Career: fmrly partner law firm of de Kirby & Hasson; formed own law firm spec. in practice of personal injury, San Diego 1983--; seminar spkr. with San Diego Chiropractic Soc., Chiropractic Info. Bur., and UCSD; honors: Nu Beta Epsilon; Am. Jurisprudence Awards; West's Hornbook Award for highest cumulative grade pt. av.; mng. ed. Criminal Justice Jour.; mem: Am., Calif. Bar Assns.; Am., Calif., San Diego Trial Lawyers Assns.; Lawyers Alliance for Nuclear Arms Control. Res: 3003 Granada San Diego 92104 Law Offcs. of Vaughan de Kirby, 1520 State St, 136, San Diego 92101

DE KLOTZ, FRED WESLEY, lawyer; b. Apr. 19, 1931, Elizabeth, NJ; s. Fred Wesley and Isabel (Brindley) De K.; children: Andrea, b. 1960; Wesley, b. 1962; Cara, b. 1966; edn: BS, UC Berkeley 1953; LLB, Univ. of Santa Clara 1959. Career: lawyer, Richard Lowey, Atty. at Law, Beverly Hills 1959-60, Steven Nakishima, Atty. at Law, San Jose 1960-61, Fred. W. DeKlotz, Jr., San Jose 1961-62, 1965-70, partnership of Fred W. DeKlotz, Jr. and John J. Hayes, 1962-65, currently jDeKlotz & Baker, San Jose 1970--; mem. Calif. State Bar Assn., Santa Clara Co. Bar Assn., Sigma Alpha Epsilon frat.; clubs: Sainte Claire; mil: capt. Army Inf. 1953-55, reserve 1955-61; Republican; Presbyterian; rec: sailing, skiing, tennis, small cattle ranch. Res: 16158 Bachman Ave, Los Gatos 95030 Ofc: DeKlotz, Inc. & Baker, 1200 Community Bank Bldg, 111 W St. John St San Jose 95113

DE KLOTZ, ROBERT N., financial planning co. president; b. Nov. 24, 1934, E. Orange, NJ; s. Fred W. and Isabel B. De Klotz; m. Meade Milisich, June 10, 1956; children: Deborah, b. 1957; Robert Jr., b. 1959; edn: BS, UC Berkeley 1957; MSFS (finl. svcs.) 1981, CLU (chartered life underwriter) 1970, ChFC (chartered fin. cons.) 1982, American Coll. Career: sales engr. Reliance Electric, Los Angeles 1959-66; ins. agt. New York Life, L.A. 1967-80; pres. Robert De Klotz Ins. Mkt., Whittier 1980--; pres. branch ofc. Private Ledger Fin. Serv., La Habra 1982--; pres. Cert. Fin. Counselors Inc., La Habra 1983--; instr. Santa Ana Coll. 1975-76; awards: Million Dollar Round Table 1969-73, Nat. Quality Award 1974-83, Nat. Sales Award 1973-75; mem: Nat. Assn. of Life Underwriters (chmn. 1974-5, nat. conv. hospitality com. 1976); Am. Soc. of CLU (Estate Planning Council 1976-8); No. Orange Co. Life Underwriters (pres. 1973-4); clubs: La Habra Jaycees (pres. 1963-4), Rotararian, Bible Study Fellowship (tchr 1974-84); pub. journ. art. 1975; mil: 1st lt. US Army 1957-59; Republican; Evangelical Free Ch.; rec: tennis, jog, Bible tchr. Res: 1760 No Hills Dr La Habra 90631 Ofc: Cert. Fin. Counselors Inc, 153 E Whittier Blvd, Ste C, La Habra 90631

DE KONING, JOSEPH GERARDUS, microwave semiconductor executive; b. May 25, 1938, Graauw, Netherlands, nat. 1974; s. Johannus Petrus and Maria Christina (Vereecken) de K.; m. Christina Van Oosterhout, June 4, 1967; children: Caroline, b. 1968; Saskia, b. 1970; Craig, b. 1971; edn: MSEE, Tech. Hogeschool (Delft) 1962. Career: reschr. on microwave transistor oscillators Microwave Assocs., Inc., Burlington, Mass.; circuit designer Adams-Russell Co., 1968; devel. of Gunn effect microwave signal sources, Monsanto Co., St. Louis, Mo. 1969; in chrg. devel. wideband high-gain solid state amplifiers and microwave integrated circuit modules, Teledyne MEC, Palo Alto 1971-73; sr. engr. Solid State West Div., Varian Assocs., 1973-75; engring. mgr. Microwave Semicondr. Div. Hewlett Packard Co., San Jose 1975-80; co-founder/ mgr. component devel., Harris Microwave Semicondr. Inc., Milpitas 1980--; honors: outstanding paper award, 1967 Internat. Solid State Circuits Conf., Phila.; sr. mem. IEEE; mem. Royal Netherlands Inst. of Engrs.; author 15 tech. papers; holder three patents; mil: 1st lt. Royal Netherlands AF 1962-64; Republican; Catholic; rec: classical music, skiing. Res: 1630 Dallas Ct Los Altos 94022 Ofc: Harris Microwave Semiconductor, 1530 McCarthy Blvd Milpitas 95035

DE KOVEN, STANLEY EUGENE, marriage, family, child therapist; b. Dec. 5, 1952, San Diego; s. Ronald Stanley and Carma Louise (Riley) DeK.; m. Karen, Dec. 22, 1973; children: Rebecca, b. 1976; Rachel, b. 1978; edn: AB in psych., San Diego St. Univ. 1974; MA counseling, Webster Univ. 1977; PhD counseling psych., Profl. Sch. of Psychol. Studies 1983; Lic. marriage, family & child therapist 1980; school counselor/psychologist credential, US Internat. Univ. 1983. Career: child care wkr/counselor Boys & Girls Aid Soc. & South Devel., Inc., El Cajon 1975; counselor Mountain View Sch., Ramona 1975-6;

financial plnnr., San Diego 1978-9; dir. counseling svcs Logos Found., Inc., S.D. 1979; dir. treatment svcs. Green Valley Rnch., Ramona 1979-81, program dir. 1983; psychotherapist Christian Counseling & Guidance Svcs., Denver, Co. 1981-82; dir. Pelican Family Inst., S.D. 1982--; instr. Newport Univ. 1982-3; practicum coord. Calif. Christian Inst. 1983; instr. Univ. of La Verne 1983; cons. psychologist Trinity Christian Sch., Spring Valley; mem: Calif. Assn. of Marriage & Family Therapists, Christian Assn. for Psychological Studies (CAPS); mil: 1st lt. US Army 1976-78, USAR 78-, Army Commend. Medal; Republican; lic. minister Am. Evangelical Christian Ch.; rec: sports, singing, writing. Res: 13225 Ridgedale Dr Poway 92064 Ofc: Pelican Family Inst. 810 Emerald St, 115, San Diego 92109

DE LA PENA, EUSEBIO, products liability investigator; b. Sept. 10, 1926, Norfolk, Va.; s. Eusebio and Alberta (Copeland) de la Pena; m. Margaret Lanford, Sept. 20, 1953; children: Nicolas, b. 1955, Mia Michelle, b. 1963, Traci Yvette, b. 1964; edn: Bushwick H.S., Bklyn. 1940-4; lic. investigator, Calif. 1975-. Career: union orgnzr. United Furniture Wkrs of San Francisco, 1958-60; real estate broker Twin Cities Realty, Inc. and broker owner Del de la Pena & Assocs., Reno, Nev., 1962-73; dir. Allfax, Inc., Seattle 1973-75; owner Allfax West Investigations, Los Angeles 1975--; mem: Calif. Assn. of Licensed Investigators, Wilshire CofC, Wilshire Comm. Action Com., Greenpeace, Earthwatch, Environ. Task Force; active in little theatre groups, S.F., Reno, Seattle; Democrat; Catholic; rec: golf, biking, acting. Res: 6629 Sedan Ave Canoga Park 91307 Ofc: Allfax West Investigations, 611 S Catalina, 312, Los Angeles 90005

DE LA TORRE, MARGARET THERESE, speech specialist; b. July 17, 1917, Grand Forks, N.D.; d. Wendell J. and Margaret T. (Marshall) Brohman; m. Vincent de la Torre, Feb. 19, 1949; children: Ronald, b. 1954, Brian, b. 1955, Ruth Renette, b. 1960; edn: tchg. cert., Diocesan Teachers Coll., St. Paul, Minn. 1945; BA, Immaculate Heart Coll. 1949; MA, sph. pathol., CSU Fullerton 1969; Calif. Teaching Cred. 1949-72; Sph. Pathologist (life cred.) 1969. Career: elem. teacher St. Paul, Minn. 1940-45, Santa Paula, Ca. 1945-7, Alhambra 1947-9, Daggett 1949-50, San Luis Obispo 1950-3, Arlington 1956-9; speech pathologist, El Monte 1969-70, Whittier 1971-83, ret.; currently writing, tutoring speech handicapped; honors: Sigma Alpha Eta (Key mem.); mem. Comm. Concerts, Historical Soc. (Big Bear), Friends of the Lib.; Republican; Ch: St. Mary's (Bible tchr); rec: oil painting, gardening, mtn. climbing. Res: 12323 E Orange Dr Whittier 90601

D'ELIA, PHILIP ARTHUR, retail service co. executive; b. Oct. 1, 1957, San Jose; s. Philip Joseph and Miriam Georgia (Traina) D'Elia; 1 son, Philip Jason, b. 1983; edn: BA, UCLA 1980. Career: mgr. Color Tile Supermart, Woodland Hills 1980-81; vice pres./gen mgr. Delias Cleaners Inc., San Jose 1981--; instr. counter sales tng. 1982-84; mem. Zeta Psi Nat. Frat.(pres. 1977-9; Outstanding Undergrad. 1980); Democrat; Catholic; rec: ski, sport fishing, boats. Res: 10500 Oakville Ave Cupertino 95014 Ofc: Delias Cleaners Inc. 1361 So Winchester Bl, Ste. 109, San Jose 95128

DELIZO, REGINO S., physician; b. May 24, 1925, San Carlos City, Phil.; s. Regino O. and Maria (Sabangan) D.; m. Alice Diaz, May 15, 1971; children: Reginald, b. 1971; Raymund, b. 1973; Ronald, b. 1978; edn: MD, Manila Central Univ. 1969. Career: tng. dir. Hoescht Internat., 1971-73; mgr. Spicers Internat. of Manila 1973-4; hd. dept. anat. & physiol. Univ. of City of Manila, 1971-3, prof. Coll. of Nursing 1970-3; res. phys. Martin Luther King Hosp., Los Angeles 1981; phys./owner Angelus Medical Center, L.A. and Family Med. Ctr., La Puente and Allied Med. Group (provider for United Hlth. Plan), L.P.; staff phys. Whittier Hosp. Med. Ctr., W. Covina Hosp., Covina Valley Hosp.; honors: Presidtl. Award for comm. svc., Phil. Pres. Ferdinand Marcos; outstanding med. intern 1969, and pres. Med. Stu. Govt., MCU Univ.; Theta Alpha Rho (Grand Master); mem: Phil. Medical Soc. of So. Calif. (bd. dirs.), Assn. of Phil. Practicing Physicians in Am., AMA, founding bd. Pagkakaisa (charitable orgn.), Phil. Soc. of S.E. Los Angeles; Catholic. Res: 4110 S. Hermitage Dr Hacienda Hts 91745; Family Medical ctr, 1240 N Hacienda Blvd, 102, La Puente 91744 Angeles Med. Ctr, 1155 No Vermont, 202, Los Angeles 90029

DELLAMAS, LLOYD RICHARD, city manager; b. Aug. 4, 1940, Santa Maria; s. Victor Lloyd and Delya Elvanore (Freeman) deLlamas; m. Caroline Cox, Nov. 5, 1966; 2 daus: Ingrid Dionne, b. 1969; Chelsea Denise, b. 1975; edn: BS in bus. mgmt. CSU San Diego 1963. Career: admin. analyst City of San Diego 1963-66; sr. asst. to city mgr. City of Torrance, 1966-68; city mgr. City of Woodlake, 1968-71; city adminstr. City of Lawndale, 1971-76; city mgr. City of Monterey Park, 1976--; Community Devel. Policy Com., League of Calif. Cities. Mem: Am. Mgmt. Assn.; Internat. City Mgmt. Assn.; Calif. Redevel. Agencies Assn. (bd. dirs.); Woodlake Lions 1968-71; Lawndale Rotary 1972-76. Mil: sgt. CNG 1964-70; ofc: City of Monterey Park, 320 W. Newmark Ave Monterey Park 91754

DELMAN, JAMES B., real estate consultant/appraiser; b. Apr. 6, 1947, San Francisco; s. Earl Bernard and Adell Verna (Lager) D.; edn: BA, Univ. San Francisco 1970; grad. stu. (MBA cand.), Golden Gate Univ.; Cert. in real estate, St. Calif. 1982; Cert. Review Appraiser (CRA), Nat. Assn. of Review Resdtl. Mortgage Underwriter (RMU), Internat. Cert. Appraiser (ICA), Approved Appraiser FNMA, FHLMC. Career: real estate dept. and assessors ofc., City and Co. of San Francisco, 1974-76; loan ofcr/appraiser, coord. Oakland inner-city loan pgm., Calif. Fed. Svgs & Loan, 1976-79; bus. devel. ofcr./ chief appraiser Continental Svgs & Loan of Am., 1979-81; pres. The Delman Co. (comml. R.E. brokerage, investments, appraisal), S.F. 1981--; listed Who's Who in Real Estate 1983; mem: Nat. Assn. of Review Appraisers and Mortgage Underwriters (CRA & RMU, senior designations); Internat. Orgns. of R.E. Appraisers, Internat. Certified Appraiser (ICA sr. desig.); S.F. Planning and Urban Research (SPUR); research/study in field of fine art/ contbr. many art works to major museum shows on Calif./Am. fine art; collector/student of Am. art, spec. in Calif. paintings pre-1940. Address: 342 Fifth Ave San Francisco 94118

DE LORRELL, WALTER JOSEPH, JR., lawyer/company executive; b. Feb. 25, 1941, Chgo.; s. Walter J. and Lorean (Crank) de L., Sr.; m. Karen, Nov. 26, 1966; children: Walter III, b. 1968; Ashley, b. 1970; edn: BA, CSU Los Angeles 1963; BSL, Glendale Univ. Coll. of Law 1973; JD, Valley Univ. Coll. of Law 1975; CAS, Am. Assn. of Certified Appraisers (charter mem.) 1978; SCV, Internat. Inst. of Valuers 1981. Career: fire & marine disaster adjuster Travelers Ins. Co. 1963-67; fin. analyst Dempsey Tegeler & Co. (mem. NYSE), 1967-69; dist. mgr. Marshall & Stevens, Inc. 1969-73; regl. mgr. Valuation Counselors, Inc. 1973-79; v.p. field ops. S.W. region Merle Norman Cosmetics International, 1979--; bd. dirs. Valadco Trading 1973-4; Qualified as Expert Witness in valuation of stock of closely held corps. in Calif. Cts. & Adminstrv. Bds.; honors: Calif. State Service Award, Nat. Bd. of Calif., 1966; mem: Am., Calif. Bar Assns., Nat. Assn. of Accounts (past), Am. Assn. of Cert. Appraisers, Internat. Inst. of Valuers, Nat. Auctioneers Assn. (past), Am. Arbitration Assn. (Arbitrator), Am. Rifle Assn.; mil: 1st lt. US Army Qtrmaster Corps; Republican; Catholic; rec: target shooting, camping, auto. restoration. Res: 10876 Marietta Ave Culver City 90230 Ofc: Merle Norman Cosmetics, 9130 Bellanca Ave Los Angeles 90045

DE LOREZ, JOHN RUSSELL, engineering executive; b. Nov. 21, 1945, Foley, Mo.; s. Jack Hugh and Mary Virginia (Teague) DeLorez; m. Marcelina Agudo, Mar. 16, 1976; 1 child, Rhoneil, b. 1972; edn: BS in E.E., Purdue Univ., 1973. Career: asst. mgr. Carps Inc. (dept. store), Troy, Mo. 1963-66; USN Seaman recruit through Petty Ofcr. First Cl., Fire Control Tech. 1966-73, Ensign through Lt., Damage Control & Repair Ofcr, Propulsion Ofcr. USS Constellation 1976-78; project engr. McGaw Labs., Irvine 1978-80; engring. mgr. Dynachem Corp., Tustin 1980--; mem. Retired Officers Assn.; mil: lt. USN ret. 1966-78, GCM, Nat. Defense; Republican; Catholic; rec: teach metaphysics. Res: 24731 Calle El Toro Grande, El Toro 92630 Ofc: Dynachem Corp. 2631 Michelle Dr Tustin 92680

DEL PIERO, MARC JEFFREY, lawyer/county supervisor; b. Jan. 6, 1953, Watsonville; s. Richard and Patricia Ann (Borcovich) Del P.; m. Tina T., Jan. 6, 1979; edn: BA, Univ. of Santa Clara 1975, JD, 1978; admitted to practice Calif. State Bar 1980. Career: atty. in pvt. practice, Salinas 1980--; Monterey County (Ca.) Board of Supervisors, First Dist. 1981-, chmn. 1982, v.chmn. 1981; Monterey Co. Transp. Com. 1979-, v.chmn. 1983; Monterey Co. Plnng. Commn. 1978-81, v.chmn. 1979-81; mem. San Felipe Div. com. Central Valley Water Project 1981-; dir. Monterey Bay Unified Air Pollution Control Dist. 1981-; dir. Mont. Co. Flood Control and Water Conserv. Dist. 1981-; Mont. Co. Local Agcy. Formation Commn. 1981-; trustee Mont. Co. Law Lib. 1982; awards: Calif. State Scholarship 1971-5; Univ. of Santa Clara Honors Scholarship 1971-3; Who's Who in Am. Univs. 1975; mem: Calif., Mont. Co. Bar Assns., County Supervisors Assn. of Calif.; Rotarian, Monterey Hist. and Art Assn., Aromas Eagles Club; publs: art. on Arroyo Seco project, Mont. Co. Farm Bureau (1983); mil: capt. CNG 1978-; Republican; Catholic. Res: 230 E Alvin Dr Salinas 93906 Ofc: Monterey Co Board of Supervisors, Castroville Courthouse; Preston & McDougall, Castroville 95012

DE LUCA, JOSEPH PAUL, financial executive; b. Jan. 24, 1931, Messina, Italy; nat. 1947; s. Peter Nicholas and Frances (Di Bella) De Luca; m. Barbara Menietti, Aug. 2, 1969; children: Francesca, b. 1970; Daniela, b. 1972; Niccolo, b. 1974; edn: BA, UCLA 1961; Loyola Univ. Sch of Law 1959-61; LLB, Van Norman Coll. of Law 1963; MBA in prog. Golden Gate Univ. 1982-; Calif. lic. real estate broker 1977; Sr. Certified Valuer, Internat. Inst. of Valuers. Career: asst. op. ofcr/chief teller Bank of America, L.A. 1956-60; asst. vice pres. Union Bank, L.A. 1961-68; adminstr. U.A. Local 38 Pension Fund, San Francisco 1968-76; vice pres. Ampac Mtg. Co., S.F. & Honolulu 1977-78; pres. Aculed Mortgage Co., S.F. 1978-79; pres. Aculed Financial Services Inc., S.F. 1979--; vice pres./dir. JER Ent.; pres./dir. Triskellion Inc.; asst. v.p. Empire Group. Honors: Student body pres., Man of Year, Van Norman Coll. of Law, 1963; Sigma Tau Sigma silver key, LACC 1959; mem: Phi Alpha Delta law frat. 1959-61; Union Bank Toastmaster 1965; Il Cenacolo 1968-; Internat. Inst. Valuers; Western Pension Adminstrs. 1969-; Sons of Italy; Columbus Club; Sierra Club; Jubilee West (dir.). Mil: petty ofcr USN 1952-6, GCM, Purple Heart, Presdtl. Cit.; Democrat; Catholic; rec: gardening, fish, hunt, sail. Res: 5372 Hilltop Crescent Oakland 94618 Ofc: Aculed Fin. Svc. Inc. 155 Sansome St, Ste.820, San Francisco 94104

DE MENT, KENNETH PARK, civil engineer; b. July 14, 1928, Caldwell, Id.; s. Kenneth Austin and Clarice Margaret (Park) De Ment; m. Marianna Penwell, Dec. 30, 1951; children: Terri Lee, b. 1954; Michael William, b. 1956; edn: BS, Univ. of Idaho 1952; cert. in meterology, UCLA 1953; Reg. civil engr. Calif. Career: gen. mgr. Monterey Regl. Water Pollution Control Agcy. 1982-; pgm. mgr. So. Calif. Hazardous Waste Disposal site location study, Calif. State Dept. Hlth Svcs. 1981-82; gen. mgr. Fontana Union Water Co. and Fontana Resources Corp, 1970-81; partner Orchard Land Co. 1971-; fmr chmn. Chino Basin Water Assn., Lytle Creek Water Conservation and Santa Ana River Water Assn.; mem: Water Pollution Control Fedn., Calif. Water Poll. Control Assn., Calif. Assn. of Sanitation Agcs.; Rotarian; past pres. local United Way, past dir. state United Way; past. dir. Fontana CofC; Sigma Chi, Elks; mil: lt. col. (ret.), pilot USAFR 1952-80; Republican; Prot.; rec: flying, fishing, camping. Res: 3154 Bird Rock Rd Pebble Beach 93953 Ofc: Monterey Regl Water Pollution Control Agcy, 220 Country Club Gate Center, 34, Pacific Grove 93950

DEMPSTER, ROBERT EDWARD, publisher; b. Jan. 14, 1935, Melrose, Mass.; s. Wm. Alfred and Helen Romona (Eldredge) D.; 1 son, Paul, b. 1961; edn: AA, Pasadena City Coll. 1957; BA, USC 1960. Career: analyst Sears Roebuck 1955-60; adminstrv. mgr. Cabot Corp. 1960-66; asst. pres. Dart Transp. 1966-7; spec. mktg. mgr. Capitol Records 1967-73, MCA Records 1973-75; v.p. mktg. Concept Marketing 1975-80; pres. Audio Book Co., 1980--; dir. Cassette Book Co.; mktg. cons. Signal Records; lectr. & panelist on mail order mktg. at various direct marketing assn. meetings; mem: founder Internat. Cassette Publishers Assn.; Direct Mktg. Club of So. Calif.; Am. Booksellers Assn.; producer of over 100 recordings, both music & spoken arts, holder of 3 gold records; orgns: The Pasadena Club (dir.), Freedom Documents Found., St. Andrews Soc., Wind & Sea Yacht Club, Mayflower Descendants, Soc. for the Preservation of Variety Arts, Acad. of Magic Art; Episcopal; rec: ski, sail, art collector, gourmet cook. Address: 235 Bellefontaine St Pasadena 91105

DENDY, BILLY JUNIOR, real estate broker/developer; b. Jan. 10, 1935, Ralls, Tx.; s. Wm. Baker and Clydia Mae (Lowrance) D.; m. Patricia Stewart, June 9, 1956; children: Gregory, b. 1958; Tami, b. 1962; edn: spl. courses UC San Diego, Anthonys Real Estate Sch., Palomar Coll.; lic. Real Estate Broker, Calif. 1963. Career: pres. Balboa Mortgage Co., Escondido 1966-76; pres. Dendy Real Estate and Investment Co., 1976--; pres. Av-Cal Investment Co., 1976--; mem: Calif. Real Estate Assn., US CofC, Ducks Unlmtd.; mil: aviation mech.3, USN 1952-56, Korean Svc. Medal; Republican (Repub. Presdtl. Task Force); Prot.; rec: fishing, sailing, boating. Res: 2855 Verda Ave Escondido 92025 Ofc: Dendy Real eStat, 425 North Date, Ste J, Escondido 92025

DENEVI, MICHAEL IRVIN, recreational development co. executive; b. Feb. 19, 1953, San Jose; s. Pietro G. and JoAnn B. (Moody) D.; m. Patricia A. Martinelli, Nov. 8, 1975; children: Timothy, b. 1979; Katherine, b. 1982; edn: BS in sociol., Santa Clara Univ. 1976; lic. real estate broker Calif. 1983. Career: signed professional baseball contract, Kansas City Royals, K.C., Mo. 1975-78; asst. purch. agt. (housing & comml. devel.) Pacific Scene of San Jose, 1978, project mgr. indsl. & comml. devel., Pacific Scene Sacramento 1979; v.p. recreational devel. Baseline Industries Inc., Los Gatos 1981--; pres. PIE Scientific, Inc. 1983-; honors: Panighetti Award (scholar/athlete), Los Gatos H.S. 1971; U.S. Baseball Team mem., World Tournament- Amateur, St. Petersburg, Fla. 1974; mem. Los Gatos Jaycees; works: asst. in mktg. Touch Joy (1983), a video game joystick with no moving parts; devel. garbage fuel process (1983-4); Republican; Catholic; rec: tennis, ski, basketball, softball, coach baseball. Res: 5012 Esther Dr San Jose 95124 Ofc: Baseline Indus. Inc. 14700 Oka Rd Los Gatos 95030

DENEVI, PIETRO GIACOMO, educator/ commercial recreation developer; b. July 22, 1926, San Mateo; s. Pietro and Louisa (Monteverde) D.; m. Jo Ann Beth Moody, Nov. 23, 1949; children: Ronald, b. 1950, Michael, b. 1953, Denise, b. 1958, P.J., b. 1960, Liz, b. 1968; edn: AB, San Jose St. Coll. 1948, Gen. Sec. cred. 1949. Career: two years professional baseball, Pirate chain; 20 yrs. high sch. tchr./coach; ten yrs. profl. football scout, N.F.L., U.S.F.L.; built, operated 50 indoor tennis courts in Calif., Ariz.; currently, pres./bd. dir. various corps., Sira Corp., P.I.E. Industries, Baseline Industries; awards: Teacher's award Los Gatos H.S. 1970, Coach of Yr. 1969, Presdtl. Citation, Pres. Nixon 1970; mem. Calif. Tchrs Assn. 1950-74; NEA; Los Gatos Swim & Racquet Club, San Jose CC; patentee; mil: aviation cadet US Naval Air Corps 1944-5; Republican; Catholic; rec: golf, fish, hunt, travel. Res: 826 Cherrystone Ave Los Gatos 95030 Ofc: Baseline Industries, 14700 Oka Rd Los Gatos 95030

DENNEY, ALBERT (AL) BROWN, JR., designer, b. Waco, TX; s. Dr. Albert Brown and Mary Elizabeth (Fason) Denney; attended Texas Chiropractic Coll., children: Rick, b. 1959. Career: producer, dir., owner, Independent Artists Prodn., 1965--; R.E. Broker, owner, Den Real Co., 1961--; designer, owner, Den-Ney Originals, 1973--. Awards: 3rd place, Dir. Cannes Film Festival, 1971; two 1st place Underwater Photography, Underwater Photographic Soc., 1967-69. Mem.: Directors Guild of Amer.; Internatl. Photographers Local 659; Elks, Burbank; VFW, Burbank; Amer. Film Inst.; Amer. TV Arts & Scis.; Republican Club; wrote and directed BBC award winning films, "Ghana Today," "Puberty Rites of the TWI," also wrote "Operation Hillbilly," "Illegal Entry" (Cannes Award). Mil.: Cpl, USMC, 1953-56. Republican. Universalist. Rec: fishing, hunting, scuba diving, orchard and bromiads. P.O. Box 5165, Sherman Oaks 91403.

DENNIS, JAMES LLOYD, architect, ret.; b. Nov. 7, 1911, Sheridan, Ore.; s. Lloyd Lester and Mary Amelia (Price) D.; m. Dorothy Mather Williams, May 18, 1974; edn: grad. San Jose H.S. 1930, San Francisco Archtl. Club 1947-52; lic. architect Calif. 1952, Hawaii 1959. Career: museum technician Nat. Park Service, Berkeley 19350-40; naval architect Joslyn & Ryan, San Francisco 1941-45; architect, various archtl. firms, S.F. and Honolulu 1952-63; architect Dept. Acctg. Gen. Services, State of Hawaii, Honolulu 1963-73, cons. architect, Honolulu 1973-80, currently in Walnut Creek, Calif.; instr., Beginning

Genealogy, Mt. Diablo Un. Sch. Dist., Adult Edn.; lectr. arch., Leeward Comm. Co., Univ. Hawaii 1974-5; mem. Am. Inst. Architects 1960-8; mem. Order of Demolay 1929; Square Wheel Touring Soc. (pres. 1956-8); Sports Car Club Am. Haw. Reg. Ex. 1961; Haw. Malacogical Soc. (pres. 1966-8); Haw. Philatelic Soc. (pres. 1967-9); New Eng. Hist. Geneal. Soc. 1979-; Soc. of Mayflower Desc. 1980-; Desc. of Founders of N.J. (charter); Contra Costa Co. Geneal. Soc. 1982-; Soc. of Genealogists, London 1983-; Haw. Govt. Empl. Assn. 1963-; works: architect Oahu Cemetary Mausoleum, various pvt., public bldgs., Calif. & Hawaii; art., Genealogical Mag. N.J. (1984); rec: philately, malacology, genealogy. Res: 19 Oak Knoll Loop, Walnut Creek 94596

DENNISON, RICHARD L., corporate president; b. Aug. 13, 1939, Portland, Ore.; s. Vernon and Georgia Pearl (Buchannan) Dennison; edn: Portland State coll., 1957-8, 1961-2; m. Kim Khuu, Aug. 12, 1966; 1 son, John, b. 1967; career: copy boy, Oregonian, Ore. 1955-57; seaman, U.S. Merchant Marine Internat., 1957-58; copywriter, Fred Meyer, Ore. 1958-60; sales rep., American Greetings, Ore.; Ida. 1964-66; mng. director, Muller & Phipps, S.E. Asia 1966-75; mng. director, All World Entertainment, Calif., internat. 1979--; pres., sole stockholder, Riden Int'l Inc. (an all entertainment distbn. co.), Calif., internat. 1976--; mem. Amvets 1976-; mil: sgt. US Army 1961-63; Republican; Protestant; rec: sports; res/ofc: 6024 Paseo Palmilla Goleta 93117.

DENSON, GAIL, certified public accountant; b. Mar. 26, 1939, Ogden, UT; s. John McInnes and Rubya Mae (Bartholomew) Denson; B.A., Univ. of Redlands, 1963; A.A., LA. City Coll., 1961; m. Onie Stringer, Feb. 23, 1978; children: Martin F. Miller, b. 1960; Michael D. Miller, b. 1961; Monte W Miller, b. 1962; Wiliam S. B. 1968; Christina Y. Denson, b. 1971. Career: staff acct., Olney & Oliney, L.A., 1963-66; controller, The VP Co., Pasadena, 1966-68; v.p., Nanodyne, Inc., Pasadena, 1968-69; controller, Amer. Micro Devices, Santa Ana, 1969-70; staff acct., Victor I. Backus, CPA. CA. 1970-72; pres., Gail Denson, An Accountancy Corp., also Sierra Care, Inc.; dir., Natl. Nurse Inc.; Awards: Boy Scout Century Club, 1977; Boy Scout Leadership Award, 1978; Boy Scout Leadership mem. 1980. Mem.: Town Hall; Amer. Inst. of CPAs; Calif. Soc. of CPAs; Hosp. Financial Mgmt. Assn.; Calif Assn. of Health Facilities; Amer. Coll. of Nursing Home Adminstrs. Republican. Latter day Saints, ward clerk, Sunday Sch. pres. Rec: flying. Res.: 165 W. Arthur, Arcadia 91006; Office: Gail Denson, An Accountancy Corp., 2540 Huntington Dr., San Marino 91108.

DENSON, ONIE LEE, nursing home administrator; b. Apr. 11, 1939, Glendale; d. Leon Edgar and Burnetta Bell (Austin) Stringer; edn: Loma Linda Univ., 1956-60; m. Gail Denson, Feb. 22, 1978; chil: Marty, b. 1960, Michael, b. 1961, Monte, b. 1962; career: vice pres. and director Twilight Haven Convalescent Hospital, 1959-78; vice pres. and director Sierra Care Inc., Riverside, 1978--; corp dir.: Twilight Haven Conv. Hosp., Sierra Care Inc. Honors: Nursing Home Administrator preceptor. Mem. Calif. Assn. of Health Facilities, Am. Coll. of Nursing Home Adminstrs.; Republican; Ch. L.D.S., Den Mother; rec: sewing; res: 165 West Arthur, Arcadia 91006; ofc: Sierra Care Inc. 11162 Palm Terrace Ln. Riverside.

DENOFF, DOUGLAS, private telephone co. president; b. July 14, 1957, NY, NY; s. Samuel and Bernice (Levey) D.; edn: BA, UCLA 1977. Career: assoc. prod. Hawaii Five-O (youngest prod. in hist. of series), CBS Television 1977-79; prod. ABC Circle Films (A Time for Miracles, movie for TV) 1979-80; independent producer 1980-81; founder/ pres. & CEO Dencom Systems, Inc. (pvt. tel. co., incorporated 1982), Los Angeles 1981--; tchr./lectr. for ASCAP Workshops; cons. film production, telecomm.; mem: Calif. Interconnect Assn., No. Am. Telecomm. Assn., Acad. of TV Arts & Scis., Mensa; fund raiser/ mem. Found. for New Am. Music, Concern II, Share; mem. L.A., Long Bch. CofC; works: devel. wireless telecomm. technology 1982; num. photog. exhibs.; coauthor stories for films and book/music for Broadway musicals in development; Jewish; rec: music, photog. Ofc: Dencom Systems, Inc. 3346 S. La Cienega Blvd Los Angeles 90016

DENTON, DAVID GEORGE, chiropractor; b Jan. 13, 1936, Lorain, Ohio; s. Wm. Richard and Marion Louise (Burrill) D.; children: Daniel Kenneth, Rhonda Sue; edn: DC, Lincoln Chiro. Coll. 1958; Bd. Cert. Craniopath 1979, Fellow Internat. Craniopathic Soc. 1979; Diplomate in Craniopathy 1982. Career: pres. West Side Chiropractic Center, Inc., Los Angeles 1973--; interned at Spears Chiro. Hosp. and Sanitarium, Denver, Colo.; fmr. practice (13 yrs.) in Ludington, Mich.; honors: Chiropractor of the Year, Sacro Occipital Research Soc. Intl. (1975), Parker Chiropractic Research Ctr. (1978); mem: Am., Mich., Calif. Chiro. Asss.; Sacro Occipital Resrch Soc. Intl. (bd. dirs.); Vol. Orgn. of Independent Chiropractic Educators (pres. 1983); Intl. Craniopathic Soc. (pres. 1981-3); Dental-Chiropractic Orthopedic Soc. (dir. Chiro. Div.); Intl. Acad. of Preventive Medicine; Intl. Coll. Applied Nutrition; author: Craniopathy and Dentistry (1978), Bio-Mechanics of the Pelvis; intl. seminar lectr.; guest. lectr. Parker Resrch. Found. 1977-82; Republican; Prot.; rec: gardening. Res: 1930 Ocean Ave Santa Monica 90405 Ofc: West Side Chiro. Center, 12381 Wilshire Blvd, Ste 102, Los Angeles 90025

DEPOOTER, RUDY AUGUST, commercial real estate broker; b. June 21, 1954, Herentals, Belgium, nat. 1972; s. George Alfons and Maria Hilda (Van Looy) DePooter; m. Amber Tennant, June 28, 1975; two daus.: Brooke, b. 1980, Ashley, b. 1983; edn: BS in pub. adm., USC 1976. Career: adminstrv. analyst Los Angeles Community Coll. District, 1976-78; nat. facilities coordinator E.F. Hutton & Co., 1978-79; dir. of real estate Fortune Advertising, 1979-80; commercial leasing rep. The Irvine Co., 1980-81; founded own company, The Winchase Co., Pasadena 1981--, full service comml. real estate brokerage (leasing, sales, mgmt., etc.). Mem: Pasadena Bd. of Realtors, Nat. Assn. of Realtors, Calif. Assn. of Realtors. rec: running, swim. res: 1 Trail

Ridge Circle, Phillips Ranch 91766. ofc: The Winchase Co. 468 Rosemead Blvd., Suite 225, Pasadena 91107.

DEPEW, DAVID ARTHUR, lawyer; b. July 10, 1941, San Diego; s. Rev. Arthur Ernest Luke and Rev. Esther Lydia (Berg) D.; 9th gen. desc. Nicolas Depui (Huguenot settler of NY 1662, of DePay family in 1st Crusade, 1096); edn: AA, East L.A. Coll. 1960; BA, microbiol., CSULA 1964; LLB, Blackstone Sch of Law 1972. Career: publ. Temperance News Trumpet (TNT), legislation newsletter, The Depew Co., Alhambra 1963-83; cons. on microbiology, Food & Drug Service, Inc., Monterey Park 1966-77; lawyer pvt. practice Alhambra 1972--; successful state chmn. People Opposing Pot which defeated 1972 ballot measure to legalize marijuana; author referendum petition and state cochmn. of Coalition of Christian Citizens to repeal homosexual legalization law, 1975; atty. Clancy, Clancy & Miles, Glendale 1977-80; lectr. on narcotics, drugs to youth groups/ camps 1961-, lectr. on civil, criminal laws of the Bible 1975-; recognition awards, L.A. Co. Youth Fitness Council (1960), So. Calif. Temperance Council (1962); mem: Christian Legal Soc., Am. Schs. of Oriental Research, Biblical Archeol. Soc., Creation Research Soc.; author Calif. Liquor Laws Handbook, 1962, Wash. State Liquor Laws Handbook, 1966, Handbook of Civil & Criminal Laws from Bible, 1970; mil: sp4 AUS Med. Service Corps 1964-66; Republican; Wesleyan Ch. Res: 241 S Electric Ave Alhambra 91801 Ofc: The Depew Co 241 S Electric Ave Alhambra 91801

DE RANEK, WILLIAM RICHARD, design engineer; b. Jan. 31, 1939, Buffalo, NY; s. Wm. John and Erma (Maurer) DeRanek; m. Patricia Boulger, Jan. 3, 1962; children: Rhonda, b. 1957, Debbie, b. 1958, Mark, b. 1963, Jeff, b. 1965; edn: grad. South Gate H.S. 1957. Career: stock rm. Filter Supply Co., Anaheim 1955-57; self-eml. 1957-59; worked in 14 different constrn. trades in Spokane, Wn.; aquatic water system design engr. Filter Supply Co., Anaheim 1964--; mem: IAAPA, GCSAA, IRSA; clubs: Westminster Tennis Assn. (pres.), Tennisland, USTA; works: music composer, poet, profl. photog.; mil: s/sgt. US Army 1956-66; Republican; Christian; rec: tennis, golf, skiing. Res: 11401 Lampson Garden Grove 92640 Ofc: Filter Supply Co. 1210 No Knollwood Cir. Anaheim 92801

DE REMER, MC LELLAN, facility energy manager; b. July 21, 1943, Detroit, Mich.; s. Harold Clinton and Ronda (Smith) DeRemer; m. Eileen Harvey, June 12, 1976; children: Shane DeRemer, b. 1967, Andrea Grace Harvey, b. 1975, edn: spl. courses, Ventura Coll. 1965, 67, La Verne Coll.; coll. cred. in shop supvn. 1967; Cert. Energy Auditor, Calif. Energy Commn. 1980. Career: shif supr./ unit supr. Camarillo State Hosp., 1969-78, int. nursing coordinator/ int. asst. pgm. (4A) dir., 1978-80, facility energy mgr. 1980--, currently assigned to Sacramento Hdqrts., Calif. St. Dept. of Developmental Services; energy cons. for other state hosps.; developed the statewide energy plan for the 11 state hosps.; honors: Camarillo St. Hosp. received the Edison Energy Conservation Award for ann. energy savings 1983; mem. Assn. of Energy Engrs.; past v.p. Ventura Co. Nursing Home Volunteer Soc.; past BSA Cubmaster; works: write Public Works Contracts for large energy conservation retrofits and other projects; mil: US Army 1960-64, Exp. Rifleman, mem. US Army rifle team, Ft. benning, GA 1961-62; Episcopal; rec: classical piano, sailing, fishing, archery. Res: 330 Grandview Cir. Camarillo 93010 Ofc: Camarillo State Hosp., Box A, Camarillo 93011

DERIFIELD, ROBERT CRAYTON, paper co. president; b. Feb. 5, 1941, Glendale; s. Russell and Bonnie D.; m. Janice Reeves, Sept. 10, 1960; children: Robert, b. 1962, Kellie, b. 1964, Rod, b. 1966; edn: AA, Glendale Coll. 1965. Career: with Copeland newspapers -1965; with Noland Paper Co. 1965--, began as an order writer, then salesman, sales mgr. 1971, vice pres. 1978, pres. 1983--. Ofc: Noland Paper Co., 6600 Valley View St. Buena Park 90620

DERSTEPANIAN, RUBEN, computer designer; b. Mar. 5, 1950, Tehran, Iran; s. Yervand and Almas (Sarkissian) D.; edn: BS in EE, CalPoly S.L.O., 1974. Career: came to USA in 1969 as univ. student, worked full-time during schooling; design engr. EXAR 1974, test engr. Signetics 1975-78, product engr. A.M.I. 1979-80, test engring. supr. Intel Corp. 1980-82; owner/designer R2D2 P.C. Design (devel. & cons. co.), 1982--; rec: skiing, dancing, backgammon, fishing. Res: 5574 Shadowcrest Way San Jose 95123 Ofc: R2D2 P.C. Design, 1900 lafayette, Ste 201, Santa Clara 95051

DESAI, TED A., computer systems/software specialist; b. Sept. 9, 1943, Baroda, India, nat. 1966; s. Amritanshu and Kumudini (Desai) D.; m. Kalpana Desai, Jan. 12, 1972; 1 child, Shamik; edn: BS eng., M.S. Univ. (Baroda, India) 1964; MS eng., I.I.T. (Chgo.) 1968; MBA, Loyola Grad. Sch. (Chgo.) 1974. Career: systems analyst Internat. Harvester, Chgo. 1970-73; sr. systems analyst Univac, Chgo. 1974-76; systems cons. AID, Chgo. 1976-79; MIS supr. Internat. Harvester, Chgo. 1979-80; mgr. new projects National Semiconductor, santa Clara 1980-81; MIS mgr. Cromemco, Mountain View 1981--; founder Independent Consulting Prosys; mem. APICS; fmr. v.p. India Devel. Services (nonprofit org.). Res: 61 Beach Park Blvd Foster City 94404 Ofc: Cromemco, 280 Bernardo Ave Mountain View 94043

DESDIER, STEVEN ROSS, accountant; b. Oct. 11, 1952, San Diego; s. Dominic and Audree Laverne (Leischner) D.; edn: BA, U.S. Intl. Univ. 1973; cert. taxation, UC San Diego 1981; Enrolled Agent, IRS; Reg. Securities Rep., NASD. Career: asst. advt. & menswear mgr. Miller's West Department Store, 1970-77; insurance agt. Home Life Ins. Co., 1976-78; pres. Desdier, Inc. 1977--, pres. Desco Acctg. & Tax Service (subs.); honors: named Mr. Leather San Diego 1983, by leather community of S.D.; mem: Gr. San Diego Business

Assn. (treas.), Nat. Assn. of Bus. Councils (treas.), Nat. Assn. of Enrolled Agents, S.D. Co. Citizens Scholarship Found. (treas.), NGTF; mem. Metropolitan Comm. Church Follies 1976-82; initiated the creation of two foundations: Nat. Assn. of Bus. Councils Found., and Greater S.D. Bus. Assn. Found.; Republican; Lutheran; rec: numismatics. Res: 1806 Upas St San Diego 92103 Ofc: Desco, 1094 Cudahy Pl, Ste 120, San Diego 92110

DE SIO, ANTHONY WILLIAM, company executive; b. Feb. 2, 1930, NY, NY; s. Oresto and Concetta (Curci) DeSio; m. Delores Lannie, June 27, 1959; children: Douglas, b. 1965, Darcy, b. 1967; edn: BS EE, Univ. of Conn. 1957; Cert. of Bus. Adm., Univ. of Santa Clara 1970. Career: engring. mgr., pgm. mgr. Lockheed Missiles :& Space Co., Sunnyvale 1958-71; space asst. Exec. Ofc. of the Pres. of the U.S., Wash DC, 1971-72; mgr. Earth Resources Applications Pgm, Gen. Elec. Co., King of Prussia, Pa. 1973-75; deputy v.p. Western Union Space Comm. Inc., Upper Saddle River, NJ 1976-78; dir. of prodn. pgms. Linkabit Corp., San Diego 1979-80; cofounder/ prin./ pres./ CEO, Mail Boxes Etc. USA, Inc., Carlsbad; bd.dirs: Mail Boxes Etc. USA, Inc.; D'Addio & DeSio Enterprises, Inc.; Wind Power Systems, Inc.; Duraquip Equipment Leasing Co., Inc.; honors: achievement award, Pres.'s Commn. on Personnel Exchange by Pres. Nixon, 1972; mem: Pres.'s Executive Interchange Assn. 1971-; Am. Mgmt. Assn. 1960-70; Inst. ofp Radio Engrs. 1958-60; publs: art. in field, 1974; mil: petty ofcr. USN 1948-52; Republican; Catholic; rec: golf, tennis. Res: 1920 Swallow Ln Rancho La Costa 92008 Ofc: Mail Boxes Etc. USA, Inc., 7690 El Camino Real, Ste 206, Carlsbad 92008

DESJARDINS, JUDITH ANNE, psychotherapist, b. Dec. 21, 1943, Colorado Springs, Colo.; d. Herbert Thompson and Sarah Alice (Hennick) King; div.; children: Andre, b. 1964; Danielle, b. 1968; dn: BA, (honors), Univ. of Wyo. 1965; MSW, Ariz. State Univ. 1972; LCSW, lic. clin. soc. wkr. Calif. 1977; tng. Gestalt Therapy Inst. of L.A., acupressure, Jin Shin Do Found., Idyllwild. Career: counselor/instr. Phoenix (Az.) Opportunities Indsln. Ctr. 1972-3; med. soc. wkr. Maricopa Co. Gen. Hosp. 1973-5; psychiat. soc. wkr. St. Joseph's Hosp. 1976-8; oncology soc. wkr. St. John's Hosp., Santa Monica, Ca. 1976-8; pvt. practice psychotherapy, S. M. 1978--; instr. Mount St. Mary's Coll. 1979, St. Martin's Sch., Los Angeles 1982-, Santa Monica Coll. 1983-; tennis instr. Santa Monica Dept. Parks & Rec., 1982-; honors: Spurs, Chimes, Psi Chi, Phi Sigma Iota, Phi Kappa Phi, Admiral Land Trophy Award (1964), Who's Who in Am. Colls. and Univs. (1964); mem: Fellow Soc. for Clin. Soc. Wk. (Calif.) 1978-, Calif. Sacred Dance Guild, C.G. Jung Library; publs: presentations, Am. Cancer Soc., L.A. (1978, 79), Sci. Conf. of Clin. Soc. Wk., L.A. (1978, 81), Holistic Relaxation Exercise (tape, 1983), unpub. book: The Spirit Speaks (1978); Christian; rec: jazz dancing, tennis, acting. Address: 838 15th St, 3, Santa Monica 90403

DESMARAIS, ROGER ADRIAN, management consultant; b. Feb. 7, 1936, Yakima, Wash.; s. Adrian Conrad and Elizabeth Ann (Fix) Desmarais; m. Suzanne Shea, July 1, 1972; chil: Michelle, b. 1973, Jill, b. 1975, Michael, b. 1978; edn: BA in philos., Gonzaga, Wash., 1962, MA in lit., 1963, MA in edn., Loyola Univ., Ill., 1967, PhD in psych., Univ. Colo., 1972. Career: Jesuit Scholastic, 1953-72; ordained Jesuit Priest 1966; founder, prof., director-Grad. MA, Creative Edn., Seattle Univ., Wash. 1968-72; dir. Training Ctr., Vista, K.C., Mo. 1972-74; dir. Org. Devel. & Tng., Kaiser Permanente, San Francisco 1974-76; mgr. Org. Devel. Dept., Bechtel, Norwalk 1976-78; founder/ pres. Org. Devel. Systems inc., Newport Beach 1978-80, sold ODS to Mgmt. Analysis Co., became v.p. Org. Devel. Div., Mgmt. Analysis Co., 1980-82; founder/pres. Corporate Systemics, Inc., La Jolla 1982--; national speaking circuit in edn., 1965-72; keynote speaker num. indsl. confs., PMI, nationally, Internet 82-World Congress, Copenhagen 82. Awards: Edn. Grant, Religious Edn. Soc., NY 1971-72. Mem: Project Mgmt. Inst., Am. Soc. Tng. & Devel., Org. Devel. Network, Am. Mgmt. Inst. Publs: Personality Development, HiTime Publs. 1970; arts. in PMI, ASTD, OD Network. Democrat. Roman Catholic. rec: hunt, fish, ski, camp w/family. address: 5665 Oberlin Dr., Ste.204, San Diego 92121. ofc: Corporate Systemics, Inc. 10855 Sorrento Valley Rd. San Diego 92121.

DEUKMEJIAN, GEORGE, governor of California; b. June 6, 1928, Menands, NY; s. George and Alice (Gairden) D.; m. Gloria M. Saatjian, Long Beach, Feb. 16, 1957; children: Leslie Ann, b. 1964, George Krikor, b. 1966, Andrea Diane, b. 1969; edn: BA, Siena Coll. 1949, JD, St. John's Univ. Sch. of Law 1952. Career: deputy county counsel, Los Angeles; fmr partner law firm Riedman, Dalessi, Deukmejian & Woods, Long Beach; elected Assemblyman, Calif. Legislature, 1963-67; Senator 1967-78: Senate Majority Leader 1969-71, Senate Minority Leader 1974-78; State Atty. Gen. 1978-82; Gov., 1982--. Mil: US Army 1953-55. Mem: Navy League, Am. Legion, Elks Club, L.B. Episcopal. rec: golf. ofc: Capitol, Sacramento 95814.

DEUTSCH, LAURENCE VICTOR, film producer/director; b. Mar. 18, 1933, Los Angeles; s. Victor H. and Jewell M. (O'Conner) D.; m. Georgia Martin, Aug. 4, 1973; children: Brian, b. 1968, Christopher, b. 1979, Michael, b. 1981; edn: BS, USC Sch of Architecture 1962. Career: worked with Office of Charles Eames on the IBM Pavillion, 1964 NY World's Fair; staff designer for Herb Rosenthal and Assocs. Design Director projects for the AF Mus., So. Calif. Gas Co. Energy Exhib., IBM Pavillion in Osaka, Japan, AT&T Corp. Exhib., others; design cons. Saul Bass and Assocs., Queen Mary Project, Franciscan China, Mus. of Sci. & Indus., various indsl. clients; estab. own Audio Visual firm in 1969, pres./CEO Laurence Deutsch Design, Inc., Los Angeles 1969--, designing and creating graphics, exhibits, films and audio-visual productions. Num. profl. awards include Grand Award of the Internat. Film and TV Festival

of NY (only W. Coast firm so honored), 26 awards for film and audio-visual prodn. in 1982, nine awards for film he directed for Nissan Motors: A Matter of Pride. Mem: Assn. of Multi-Image (AMI), Informational Film Producers of Am. (IFPA), Soaring Soc. of Am. Mil: US Army 1952-54. rec: soaring. res/ofc: Laurence Deutsch Design, Inc. 751 N. Highland Ave. Los Angeles 90038.

DE VELA, FRANCISCO AGUILAR, dentist; b. Sept. 2, 1928, Philippines, nat. 1980; s. Teofilo Agira and Iluminada (Aguilar) de V.; m. Josefa P. Suing, Oct. 1, 1955; children: Deborah, b. 1957, Elizabeth, b. 1958, Victor, b. 1959, Elmer, b. 1961, Luisa, b. 1963, Armaine, b. 1964; edn: undergrad., Far Eastern Univ., Manila 1947; DMD, Univ. of the East 1953; Pub. Adm., Phil. Womens Univ. 19662; lic. dentist, Bd. of Dental Examiners 1978. Career: dentist, Nat. Mental Hosp., Philippines 1953-71; came to USA 1971, dietary aide, San Gabriel (Ca.) Conv. Hosp., 1971; psychiat. asst. Ingleside Mental Health Center, Rosemead 1972; clerk Office of the Atty. Gen., L.A. 1973-75; reg. dental asst. So. Reception Ctr., Norwalk 1975-81; dentist, Dr. Howard Stein Dental Group, Lakewood 1980, Metropolitan State Hosp., Norwalk 1981--; honors: commendation, Atty. Gen. Ofc. 1974, St. of Calif. 1975; mem: Am. Dental Assn., Calif. Dental Assn., L.A. Dental Soc., L.A. Filipino Dental Soc., Nat. Assn. of Pilipino Practising Dentists in US (NAPPDA); Catholic; rec: bowling, gardening. res: 1404 Aramac Ave South San Gabriel 91770 Ofc: Metropolitan State Hosp. Norwalk Blvd, Norwalk 90650

DEVEREAUX, MARILYN RUTH, real estate-construction executive; b. March 6, 1941, Sewickley, Pa.; d. Walter Greene and Marion Margaret (Mucha) D.; edn: BA, UCLA 1966, MA, UC Berkeley 1968. Career: instr. Russian language, UC Berkeley, UC Davis 1970-73; real estate salespsn. Fred Sands Realtors, Los Angeles 1973-76; sr. vice pres.-constrn. Solender & Co. Inc., Los Angeles 1976-81; ops. mgr. Real Estate, Merrill Lynch Realty Comml. Services, 1981--. Mem: Los Angeles Bd. of Realtors, Beverly Hills Bd. of Realtors. Republican. rec: writing, investments, travel, swim. res: 822 Muirfield Rd. Los Angeles 90005. ofc: Merrill Lynch Realty, 11828 San Vicente Blvd. Brentwood 90049.

DE VINE, WILLIAM EDWARD, JR., company president; b. May 9, 1934, Clinton, Okla.; s. William Edward and Lura Estella (Riley) De Vine, Sr.; children: Hideko, Annette, b. 1958, Trudy, b. 1959, Wayne, b. 1957, David, b. 1958, William, b. 1961, Dore, b. 1962, Lura, b. 1963, Cory, b. 1965, Eric, b. 1977, Gregory, b. 1978. Career: electronic tec, Naval Air Station, Alameda 1962-64; teacher asst. CalPoly State Univ., San Luis Obispo, 1964-68; design engr. IBM, San Jose 1968-72, mktg., IBM, Honolulu 1972-75, product planner, IBM, Austin, Tex. 1975-77, mktg. mgr., IBM, San Francisco 1977-78; pres. W. E. De Vine & Co., Woodside, Ca. 1978--, De Vine & Wang 1978--. Awards: IBM Hundred Percent Club 1972, 73, 74. Mem: IEEE, 1968-, Lions Int'l. 1981--. Resrch: omni direction mega-hz antenna 1968. Mil: sgt. 1st class, Air Force 1957, Nat. Def., GCM. Democrat. Prot. rec: jogging, wt. lifting. ofc: W.E. De Vine & Co. 195 Brookwood Rd. Woodside 94062 and 2055 Woodside Rd, Ste 100, Redwood City 94061

DEVINNEY, DOROTHY FLORENCE, chiropractor; b. Oct. 25, 1942, Greenwood, Miss.; d. James Murray and Dorothy Florence (Oligher) D.; edn: BA, Central Wash. Univ. 1964; MS, CSU San Jose 1973; DC, Palmer Coll. of Chiro.- W. 1981; lic. DC, Calif. Bd. Examiners 1981. Career: activity center dir. King County (Wash.) Park 7 Rec. Dept. 1964-67; recreation supr. Kent (Wash.) Park & Rec. Dept. 1967-69; grad. staff asst. Sunnyvale (Calif.) Park & Rec. Dept. 69-71; recreation supr. Santa Rosa (Calif.) Park & Rec. Dept. 1971-78; doctor of chiropractic Alameda (Calif.) Pryal Chiropractic Health Care 1982--; mem. (ch. 1972-3) Dept. Safety Com. 1972-78; bd. dirs. Sonoma Co. Arts Council 1971-2; bd. dirs. Multi-Purpose Sr. Citizen Center (Sonoma Co.) 1976-8; honors: The Nat. Dean's List 1982, Who's Who in the West 1978; diplomate Nat. Bd. of Chiro. Examiner 1981; mem: Internat., Am., Calif. Chiropractic Assns.; Council on Nutrition; Council on Roentgenology; Nat. Assn. of Female Execs.; Calif. (1971-), Wash. (1965-9) Park & Rec. Soc.; publs: art., Calif. Park & Rec. Jour. 1971; Republican; Unity; rec: backpacking, skiing, jogging, travel. Res: 20 Cora Ct. Walnut Creek 94596 Ofc: Pryal Chiropractic Health Care, 2515 Santa Clara Ave, Ste. 101, Alameda 94501

DE VRIES, JOHN WILLIAM, account executive; b. Jan. 14, 1911, Chgo.; s. George Siewert and Helen (Tibstra) De V.; m. Fannie Triezenberg, June 2, 1936; children: Helen Joy (Kamp), b. 1937, Gerald wayne, b. 1941, John Stewart, b. 1946; edn: Chgo. Bus. Coll. 1928-30, US Treas. Tng. Courses 1941-56. Career: IRS agt., sr. field tech. US Internal Revenue Service Baltimore, Md., Wash DC, NYC, Chgo. & Peoria, Ill., 1940-62; adminstr. Bethany Home, Ripon, Calif. 1962-67; office mgr. broker Beckman & Co., Manteca 1967-75; account exec. Bateman Eichler, Hill Richards, Modesto 1975-82, ret.; recipient Albert Gallatin award, US Treasury 1963; mem: pres. Ill. Dist. Federal Alc. & Tob. tax Agents 1946-7; first secy. Evergreen Park CofC; served on num. school and church bds., coms.; Democrat; Christian Reformed; rec: golf, swim, fish. Res: 2621 Prescott Rd Modesto 95350

DEWEY, DONALD WILLIAM, editor-publisher; b. Sept. 30, 1933, Honolulu; s. Donald Wm. and Theckla Jean (Engeborg) Dewey; m. Sally Ryan, Aug. 7, 1961; chil: Michael, b. 1962, Wendy, b. 1968; edn: Pomona Coll. 1953-55. Career: sales engr. Pascoe Steel Corp., Pomona 1955-56, div. Reynolds Aluminum Co., Los Angeles 1956-58, Switzer Panel Corp., Pasadena 1958-60; sales and gen. mgr. Western Pre-Cast Concrete Corp., Ontario 1960-62; founder, editor & pub. R/C Modeler Magazine (1963-), Freshwater and Marine Aquarium Mag. (1978-); pres., bd. chmn. RC Modeler Corp., RCM Publications;

v.p., co-dir. Project Alert, Inc. 1981--; pres. Liberty Resources. Author: Radio Control From the Ground Up (1970), Flight Training course (1973), For What It's Worth (vol.1 1973, vol.2 1975); num. sci. articles. Mem: Oceanic oc., Internat. Oceanographic Found., Smithsonian Assocs., Internat. Assn. of Aquatic Animal Medicine, Fedn. of Am. Aquarium Socs., Am. Philatelic Soc., Soc. of Philatelic Americans, Am. Topical Assn., APS Writers Unit 30, Am. First Day Cover Soc., United Postal Stationery Soc., Confederate Stamp Alliance, Am. Air Mail Soc., Bureau Issues Assn., Am. Revenue Assn., Canal Zone Study Group, Pitcairn Islands Study Group, Pet Indus. Jt. Adv. Council, NY Acad. of Scis., Smithsonian Instn., Sierra Madre Hist. Soc., Friends of the Sierra Madre Lib.(life), Internat. Betta Congress, Am. Killifish Assn., Am. Catfish and Loach Assn., No. Am. Native Fishes Assn. Mil: HM-3, Hosp. Corps, USNR 1951-53. Republican (US Presdtl. Trust, US Congl. Club, The Conservative Caucus, Presdtl. Task Force, Repub. Nat. Com.) Prot. rec: writing, marine biol., stamps. res: 410 W. Montecito Ave. Sierra Madre 91024. ofc: R/C Modeler Corp. 120 W. Sierra Madre Blvd. Sierra Madre 91024.

DEWEY, PAMELA MICHAEL, clothing artist/ designer/ manufacturer; b. Dec. 7, 1947, Moscow, Id.; d. Donald Cowling and Lucile (Bonner Cameron) D.; m. Jerold Jackson Singer, Dec. 30, 1975; 1 son, Porter Jackson Singer, b. 1983; edn: theatrical arts, Univ. of Wash., Univ. of Alaska, textile arts, Univ. of Uppsala, Sweden; art stu., Univ. Calif., CalPoly. Career: various retail incl. design of bridal gowns, 1962-66; constrn. of architectural textiles, 1966-70; ind. graphic services (display, presentation) 1970-74; owner Pamela Dewey Clothing (retail outlets incl. Neiman-Marcus, Saks 5th Ave., splty. stores throughout US), 1971--, mfg. clothing fashions; original concept featured 1/2 dressing (divides body linearlly or assymetrically) and mix & match wardrobe of 12 units, 12 colours called addables waddables; ops. textile dyeing and painting facility, Los Angeles; rec: singing. Res: 926 Longwood Ave Los Angeles 90019 Ofc: Pamela Dewey Clothing, 733 E. Pico, Los Angeles 90021

DEWEY, STEFANIE, charter boat operator; b. Oct. 12, 1915, Winnepeg, Man., Can., nat. 1929; d. Alexander and Eugenia Semkowicz; m. Hillard Dewey, July 6, 1964; edn: mgmt., Mira Costa Coll. 1983; lic. Opr. Passenger Carrying Vessels (Small Craft) 1954; lic. Real Estate Broker, Calif. 1981. Career: charter boat skipper & guide (fishing parties) 1954--; recording secty. Orange Co. Plnng. Commn., 1954-67, secty. City of Oceanside Personnel Dept., 1978 80; real estate broker, 1978--; awards: 2nd place woman 1963 Internat. Game Fish Tournament in Mazatlan, Mex.; 1st pl. 1966 Rancho Buena Vista Tournament, Baja, Calif.; 1983 Fishing Champ. Trophy, Oceanside Lady Anglers; approx. 50 trophies for misc. ocean fishing species; mem: Newport Harbor Lady Anglers (pres. 1970), Oceanside Lady Anglers (pres. 1982), Balboa Angling Club, Dana Wharf Lady Anglers; rec: fishing, gardening. Res: 3234 Waring Rd Oceanside 92056

DEXHEIMER, HENRY PHILLIP II, insurance agency president; b. Sept. 16, 1925, Dayton, OH; s. Henry Phillip (noted Amer. Pioneer photographer and owner chain studios, OH, In; recd. acclaim as leading U.S., OH and IN photographer; personal photog. to U.S. Senators, Pres. Harding and Pres. Roosevelt) and Helene (Francis) Dexheimer; B.S., USC 1952; CLU, 1971; children: James Phillip, b. 1950; Jana Helene, b. 1953. Career: acct. exec., adv. firms, 1946-52; broadcasting sales exec. KBIG, KFXM, KTLA-TV, 1952-58; pres. KFXM Radio Sta., 1956-57; pres., propr., The Dexheimer Co., ins. agency spec. 1958--. Gen. Hdqrs., Armed Forces; Adj. Gen. Dept. 1943-46. WWII. Awards: Sammy by Sales Exec. Club of L.A. 1955; Natl. Rookie of Year, Travelers Ins. Co., 1959; (life) Million Dollar Round Table, 1972. Mem.: Phi Kappa Tau, 1948; Alumni pres., Alpha Delta Sigma, 1955; Mason, 32nd deg., Shrine, Al Malaikah Temple, L.A., 1956--; pres. Travelers Ins. Co. Men's Club, 1963; bd. dirs., L.A. Life Underwriters Assn., 1963-65; v.p. 1967-69; Life Ins. and Trust Council, L.A., 1969--; Town Hall of Calif., 1969--; natl. bd. dirs., Travelers Chpt., Amer. Soc. of CLU, 1972-73, 79-81; L.A. World Affairs Council, 1973--. Republican. Bel Air Presbyterian Ch., Santa Monica Shrine Club; Marina del Rey Shrine Club, Legion of Honor Corps of Al Malaikah Temple. Rec.: bicycling, swimming, reading. Office: 3600 Wilshire Blvd., Los Angeles 90010.

DE ZEMPLEN, LINDA RUTH, real estate broker; b. Feb. 11, 1940, NYC; d. Saul and Dorothy (Avidon) Eidman; m. Max De Zemplen, Oct. 7, 1976; children: Stacey, b. 1962, Mitchell, b. 1965; edn: BA, Barnard Coll., Columbia Univ. 1960, MA, Teachers Coll., Columbia Univ. 1963; lic. R.E. broker, Ca. 1979; counseling cert., Ill. 1970; Comm. Colleges counselor, Calif. Career: counselor, acting asst. prin. Elk Grove (Ill.) Jr. H. Sch., 1971-73; school counselor, Walworth, Wisc. 1973-75; real estate agt. H. Bruce Hanes Co., Torrance, Ca. 1976-79; real estate broker/owner De Zemplen & Assocs., Long Beach 1979-83; assoc. real estate broker Griffis-Miehls & Assocs., Long Beach 1983--; mem. Long Beach Bd. of realtors, League of Women Voters; Democrat; Jewish; rec: sail, swim, paint, photog. Res: 3548 Faust Ave Long Beach 90808 Ofc: Griffis-Miehls & Assocs., 120 E Ocean Blvd, Ste 620, Long Beach 90802

DIAL, LINO AGAPITO, physician; b. Sept. 23, 1939, Philippines; s. Alejandro and Segunda (Agapito) D.; children: Lino, Jr., b. 1964, Aurora, b. 1966, Noel, b. 1970, Judith, b. 1973, David,b. 1976; edn: BS, Univ. of Phil. 1959, MD, 1963; lic. physician and surgeon, Calif. 1966. Career: rotating intern Univ. Hosp., Univ. of the Phil. 1962-3, St. Eliz. Hosp., Youngstown, Ohio 1963-4; med. ofcr. USN Active Duty, San Diego 1964-66; med. resident Tucson (Ariz.) Med. Ctr. 1966-7, Childrens' Hosp., San Francisco 1967-8, US Veterans Hosp., Martinez 1968-9; pvt. practice internal medicine in Vallejo, Ca. 1969--; pres. Dial Med. Corp., 1971-; internal med. physician cons., State of Calif.; awards: phys. recognition, AMA, 1969; Fellow, Phil. Coll. of Physicians (USA) 1979; sev. postgrad. certs. in critical care med., USC; mem: Am., Calif., Solano Co. Med. Assn.; Am., Calif. Soc. of Int. Med.; Assn. of Phil. Practicing Physicians in Am.; ed. The Propeller, Rotary Club of Vallejo 1979-80; pres. Cursillo Movement, Sacto. 1979-80; pres. Filipino Action Pgms. Inc., Vallejo 1972-; Vietnam War Vet.; Charismatic Renewal in Christianity, Marriage Encounter, Filipino Comm. Org.; mil: lt. MC USNR; active duty USN 1964-66; US Navy Pacific Swimming Champions 1966, sev. medals gold, silver, and bronze; Democrat; Catholic; rec: swim, chess, travel, gardening. Res: 520 Skyline Dr Vallejo 94591 Ofc: Dr. L. Dial, 1840 Capitol, Vallejo 94590

DIAMANDOPOULOS, PETER, educator, university president emeritus; b. Sept. 1, 1928, Isle of Crete, Gr., nat. 1964; s. Theodore and Rita(Mouzenides) Diamandopoulos; chil: Theodore, b. 1953, Cybele, b. 1965, Ariadne, b. 1970; edn: BA, Harvard Univ. 1952, MA, 1956, PhD, 1957. Career: lectr. philosophy Bates Coll. 1958-69; assoc. prof. philos. Univ. of Md. 1959-62, vis. prof. philos. Univ. of Vir. 1960-61, assoc. prof. philos. philos. Swarthmore Coll. 1961-62; assoc. prof./prof. philos and hist. of ideas, Brandeis Univ. 1962-77, chmn. Dept. of History Ideas 1963-65, dean of faculty, 1965-71; pres. Sonoma State Univ., 1977-83, President Emeritus, 1983; Calif. State Univ. Trustee, Prof. polit. philosophy 1983-; cons. Hist. of Physics and Math., Smithsonian Inst. 1959 62; dir. studies The Adlai Stevenson Inst. of Internat. Affairs, Chgo.1969-74. Honors: Outstanding Teacher of the Year 1983, The Confucius Inst.; Resolutions commend. leadership and commitment to acad. excellence, Calif. Bd. of Trustees; disting. service awd., Brandeis Univ. Bd. Trustees. mem: Am. Philosophical Assn.; Mind Assn., The Aristotelian Soc., and The Classical Assn. (Oxford); Univ. Club of S.F.; Harvard Club of S.F.; Commonwealth Club of S.F.; Hellenic Am. Profl. Soc. of Calif.; Newcomen Soc. Contbr. arts. philos. jours. 1962-72. Republican. rec: photog., art, painting. res: 45-D Red Hill Circle, Tiburon 94920. ofc: Sonoma State Univ. Rohnert Park 94928.

DIAMOND, LINDA ANN, lawyer/editor; b. Oct. 2, 1951, Los Angeles; d. Irwin I. and Lila (Hoffman) D.; edn: BA, UC Los Angeles 1974; JD, cum laude, Whittier Coll. Sch. of Law 1977; admitted to practice Calif. Bar 1977. Career: chief editor, HBJ Legal & Professional Publs., Los Angeles 1977-79; chief editor, dir. The Rutter Group, Ltd., Encino 1979--, awards: Am. Jur. Awards (1974-77); mem: L.A. Co. Bar Assn. (cont. legal edn. adv. com.), ABA, State Bar of Calif., Los Angeles SPCA; editor: Calif. Practice Guide- Family Law (1983), Calif. Practice Guide- Civil Procedure Before Trial (1983); Democrat; Jewish; rec: collecting (antiques, etc.), biking, swimming. Res: 20036-70 Community St Canoga Park 91306 Ofc: The Rutter Group, 15760 Ventura Blvd, Ste 630, Encino 91436

DIAS, MILAGRES CONSTANCIO, clinical psychologist; b. Mar. 25, 1937, Goa, India; s. Nicolav P. and Florinda R. (Coutinho) D.; m. Arlette Badran, Dec. 4, 1971; children: Colin, b. 1972, Changelle, b. 1974; edn: BSc, Univ. of Bombay, India 1958, B.Ed., 1960, LLB, 1961, M.Ed., 1962, M.Ed., Loyola Univ., L.A. 1967; PhD, UCLA 1971; lic. psychologist, Calif. 1974. Career: sec. math/sci. tchr. St. Xavier's H.S., Bombay, Incia 1960-63; prof. of edn., Inst. of Edn., Bombay Univ, 1963-66; community mental health psychologist, Los Angeles County, L.A. 1974-80, sr. psychologist 1980--; psychol. instr. East L.A. Coll. 1972-; commnr. Psychol. Examining Com., State Bd. of Med. Quality Ass., 1980-; awards: Presdtl. tuition scholarship, Loyola Univ., L.A. 1966, merit scholarship, Univ. of Bombay, 1960, research grant, UCLA 1971; mem: Am. Psychol. Assn., Nat. Register of Health Service Providers in Psychol.; Democrat; Catholic; rec: soccer coach. Res: 1626 Oxford Ct, W.Covina 91792 Ofc: Hollywood Mental Health, 4759 Hollywood Blvd', Los Angeles 90027

DIAS, ROBERT NORMAN, auto dealer; b. July 6, 1929, Lodi; s. Jess E. and Elizabeth (Fleck) D.; m. Lenore J. Mayberry, Jan. 3, 1947; children: Keith, b. 1947; Robert, b. 1949; Mark, b. 1951; Jeanette, b. 1954; ed. Castlemont H. S., Oakland. Career: F.H. Dailey Motor Co. 1947-58, Good Chevrolet Alameda 1958-60, used car bus. 1960-62; Roberts Rambler 1962-69; I.H. Dailey Motor Co. 1969-78; pres. Eureka Toyota, Eureka 1978--; mem: Ingomar Club, Eureka; Lions Club; Elks Club; Republican. Res: 730 Buckley Rd Blue Lake 95525 Ofc: Eureka Toyota, 10 West 5th St Eureka 95501

DICHTER, BRUCE MICHAEL, physician; b. Apr. 17, 1946, San Diego; s. Lionel and Harriett (Dumanis) D.; m. Marian Birmingham Shadden, Aug. 21, 1983; 1 dau., Alisa, b. 1978; edn: BA, UC Berkeley, 1968; MD, UCLA 1972; physician, Calif. BMQA 19 73. Career: family physician 1978-, pvt. practice medical dir. Hospice of the Conejo, 1979--, bd. pres. 1979-81; emerg. room phys. (vol.), Northridge Hosp., 1976-78; chief of family practice Los Robles Regl. Med. Ctr. 1982-84; AMA physician recognition award; mem: Am. Acad. of Family Practice, Acad. of Religion & Psychical Research, Internat. Assn. of Metapsychology (bd. chmn. 1982-); Calif. Med. Assn.; Assn. for Transpersonal Psychology; mil: lcdr USN 1974-76. Res: 3211 Futura Point Thousand Oaks 91362 Ofc: Conejo Valley Med. Group, 2220 Lynn Rd, 205, Thousand Oaks 91360

DICKASON, RUSSELL JAMES, electronic systems engineer; b. Feb. 15, 1923, Cleveland, Ohio; s. Marcel Gimbert and Ethel Marie (Werger) D.; m. Nancy OlettaDesmond, Nov. 3, 1961; 1 son, Alan Russell, b 1950; edn: BS in E.E., Case Western Univ. 1946; postgrad. stu. UC Los Angeles Ext. 1955-65, CSU Fullerton 1962-4, San Mateo Coll. 1981-2. Career: test engring. Gen. Elec. Co., Schenectady, NY 1946-7; instr. in elec. engring. Univ. of Cincinnati, 1947-50; design engr. GE Co., 1951, Victoreen Instruments, Cincinnati 1951-2; sr. elec. engr. Thompson Products Div., Cleveland 1953; section mgr. Cmd. & Control Systems, Hughes Aircraft Co., Fullerton 1953-69; proj. mgr. Litton Ship systems, Pasagoula, Miss. 1970-3; pgm. mgr. (Navy contracts) Teledyne Inc., Torrance 1974; eng. supr. Hughes Aircraft Co. 1975-80; staff engr. elec. power systems Lockheed Missile & Space Co., Sunnyvale 1980--; instr. semicondr. electronics, No Orange Co. Comm. Coll.; honors: Eta Kappa Nu; mem. IEEE 1947-80; faculty adv. Illumination Engring. Soc. student br. 1948-50; Republican; Methodist; rec: duplicate bridge. Res: 1145 Shoreline Dr San Mateo 94404 Ofc: Lockheed Missile/Space Co., Bldg 579/Dept. 62-30, 1111 Lockheed Way Sunnyvale 94086

DICKERMAN, BRUCE ALLEN, real estate syndicator; b. Nov. 24, 1937, Los Angeles; s. Cecil Irving and Cecilia (Cutler) D.; m. Susan Morris, Nov. 24, 1972; children: Jamee, b. 1965, David, b. 1968, Matthew, b. 1976; edn: AA, Valley Coll. 1958; BS, CSU Northridge 1965. Career: asst. cashier Union Bank, Los Angeles 1962-68, Manufacturers Bank, 1968-70; regional mgr. L.A., United Professional Planning, 1970-72; asst. v.p. Manufacturers Bank, L.A. 1972-74; pres. La Mans Financial Corp., Agoura 1974--; mem. Agoura Hills city coms. (planning adv., hillside ordinance, archtl. rev., master plan); honors: Realtor of the Year, Conejo Valley Bd. of Realtors 1983; mem: Calif. Assn. of Realtors (v.chmn. syndication div. 1980, v.chmn. land use com. 1984); Conejo Bd. of Realtors (pres. 1983); past pres. Oakpark Civil Assn. 1969-71; mil: USAF, reserves 1960-67; Republican; Jewish; rec: sports. Res: 29254 Deepshadow Agoura Hills 91301 Ofc: La Mans Financial, 28310 Roadside Dr, Ste 134, Agoura Hills 91301

DICKERSON, WILLIAM ROY, lawyer; b. Feb. 15, 1928, Uniontown, Ky.; s. Benjamin Franklin and Honor Mae (Staples) Dickerson; edn: BA in acctg., CSU, 1952; JD, UCLA,1958. Career: admitted to practice Calif., 1959, US Supreme Ct., 1978, US Tax Ct., 1972; deputy city atty. and ex-officio city prosecutor, Glendale, 1959-62; atty., office of James Brewer, Los Angeles 1962-68, firm of LaFollette, Johnson, Schoreter & DeHaas, 1968-73; owner pvt. law practice, William R. Dickerson & Assocs., Los Angeles 1973--, spec. in defense of CPAs (defended accts. in over 450 suits) , adminstr. accts.' malpractice ins. pgm. for First State Ins. Co. and New England Reins. orp., 1979-; frequent spkr. CPA socs.; faculty Practicing Law Inst.; instr. Pepperdine Univ. Mem: Soc. of Calif. Accountants (mem. Ednl. Found., Inc.), Calif. State Bar, Los Angeles Co. Bar Assn., Am. Bar Assn. (Profl. Liability Com.), Assn. of Trial Lawyers of Am., San Fernando Valley Criminal Bar Assn., Century City Bar Assn., Fed. Bar Assn., Nat. Soc. of Public Accts., Assn. of So. Calif. Defense Counsel, Am. Film Inst., Internat. Platform Assn. mil: M.P., US Army 1946-7, Spl.Svcs. Entertainment. res: 5006 Los Feliz Bl.Los Angeles 90027. ofc: William R. Dickerson & Assocs. 6255 Sunset Bl. Ste.2000, Los Angeles 90028.

DICKSON, RICHARD KELLOGG, II, securities attorney; b. Mar. 23, 1946, Youngstown, Ohio; s. Richard Kellogg and Vivian Zoe (Carter) D.; edn: BS, UC Berkeley 1968, MBA, USC, 1970, JD, Univ. of the Pacific 1976; admitted to practice State Bar of Calif. 1976. Career: DIEHL, DOLORES, community relations/ education specialist; . Dec. 18, 1927, Salina, Kans.; d. Wm. Augustus and Martha (Frank) Diehl; ed. public schools, Kans. Career: staff acct. Arthur Young & Co., Oakland 1971-72; corporation counsel, Calif. Commnr. of Corporations, Los Angeles 1976-79; securities atty., pvt. practice own firm, Newport Beach 1979--, corp. atty. for num. public cos. incl. Gentronix Labs. Inc., Morro Rock Resources Inc., Entertainment Telecomm. Television Inc.; honors: Traynor Soc. (1976); mem. Calif., Orange Co. Bar Assn.; mil: pvt. USAR 1968-70; rec: sports, literature. Law Ofcs. of Richard K. Dickson, II, 1100 Quail St, Ste 114, Newport Beach 92660

DICKSON, WILLIE RAYE, electronic co. executive; b. Apr. 19, 1939, Shreveport, La.; s. Herman Artist and Virdis Marie (Smith) Dickson; m. Charlean Bailey, Feb. 17, 1959; chil: Willie Jr., b. 1959, Raymond, b. 1961, Cheryl, b. 1963; edn: stu. Univ. Ark. 1957-9, Cal Poly Univ. 1967-9, Mt. San Antonio Coll. 1962-6; BA, La Verne Univ. 1973, MBA, 1980. Career: electronic technician/jr. engineer apprentice Aerojet Gen. Corp., Azusa 1962-66, microelectronic devel. technician, 1967-69; electronics instr. Calif. Instn. for Men, Chino 1969-70; owner/mgr. ABC Television & Electronic Service, Pomona 1970-73; numerical control indsl. electrician/electronic tech. McDonald Douglas, Torrance 1971-73; program mgr. (electronic splst.), Perkin Elmer Corp., Pomona 1973-75; assoc. program mgr. Aerojet ElectroSystems Co., Azusa 1976--. Facilities chmn. Aerojet Mgmt. Club, 1979; judge Bank of Am. College Awards, 1978; school coord. Youth Motivation Task Force, 1977-; mem: Lions Internat. (gov.'s 100^ pres. award); Claremont Lions Club (pres. 1977-8); Masons; Landmark Tournament Club (dir. 1971-80). Publs: Career Planning (1980), Over 100 Ways to Improve Your Bowling (1982), How to Find a Job (1982). Prot. rec: bowling, fishing, reading. res: 2175 Deborah Way, Upland 91786. ofc: Aerojet ElectroSystems, 1100 W. Hollyvale, POB 296, Azusa 91702.

DIEHL, DOLORES, community relations/education specialist; b. Dec. 18, 1927, Salina, Kans.; d. Wm. Augustus and Martha (Frank) D.; ed. Kans. public schools. Career: bus. rep. Southwester Bell Tel. Co., St. Louis and K.C., Mo. 1948-49, Mountain States Tel. Co., Denver 1949-50; edn. coordinator pub. rels. Pacific Tel., Los Angeles and San Diego 1950-79; external affairs mgr. Pacific Tel. Los Angeles 1979-83; owner The Comunity Connection, L.A. 1983--; cons. Magnet Schools, L.A. Unif. Sch. Dist. 1977-79; pres. Calif. Academic Decathlon 1979, dir. 1980-; statewide cons. Industry Edn. Council of Calif. 1979-; dir. Greater San Diego Science Fair 1960-67; vice pres. PR, S.D. Inst. for Creativity 1965-67; exec. com. S.D.'s 200th Anniversary Celeb. 1967; honors: recognition/ merit awards, Indus. Edn. Council of Calif. (1964, 79), L.A. Unif Sch. Dist. Bd. of Edn. (1979); mem: L.A. Area CofC (dir. Womens Council); Calif. Magnet School Consortium of Cities (ch.); Nat. Assn. of Women Business Owners 1984-; Southland Bus. & Profl. Womens Club (past pres.); hon. mem. Delta Kappa Gamma Intl. Soc.; publs: Eleven Steps - Walk Your Precinct by Telephone 1966 (revised 1980), sev. publs. in fields of edn., comm. orgnzn.; Republican; Methodist; rec: photog. Address: The Community Connection, 212 Mark Wilshire Tower, 691 So Irolo St Ste. 212, Los Angeles 90005

DIETERICH, JAMES WILLIAM, JR., paper co. president; b. Aug. 19, 1917, San Rafael; s. James William and Nellie Elliott (Wilson) D.; m. Patricia Loomis, Sept. 22, 1945; children: Margaret, b. 1946; William, b. 1948; edn: BS, Sch. of Comm., UC Berkeley 1940. Career: partner Hoefer, Dieterich & Brown, S.F., 1945-47; vice pres. Clearprint Paper Co., Emeryville 1947-68, pres. & CEO, 1968--; bd. chmn. & CEO, Dieterich-Post Co., 1982--; Dir., Hoefer, Dieterich & Brown, 1948-80; trustee UC Alumni Found., 1957-73; mem. UC Alumni Council 1982-; pres. Alameda Co. Taxpayers Assn. (1978, 79, 82-); adv. trustee Alta Bates Hosp. 1979-; mem: NCCJ (bd. govs.), United Negro Coll. Fund Exec. Council, Rotary, Assn. of Reproduction Materials Mfrs., Internat. Reprographic Assn.; mil: served to col. USAAF 1940-45, Calif. Air NG 1947-50; mem. Pres.'s Airport Access Task Force, 1982-3; Republican; Episcopal (Vestry); rec: skiing, pvt. pilot, golf. Res: 50 Bolla Ave Alamo 94507 Ofc: Clearprint Paper Co., Inc. 1482 67th St Emeryville 94608

DIETZ, HENRY GEORGE, real estate broker; b. June 25, 1914, So. Manchester, Conn.; s. Henry George, Sr., and Anna Agusta (Raphael) D.; m. Dorothy K. Bartoo, Sept. 4, 1937; children: Lee, b. 1940, Neal, b. 1946, Nancy, b. 1946; edn: dip. Belmont H.S., L.A. 1932; num. bus., real estate courses; GRI (Grad. Realtor Inst.), CRS (Cert. Resdtl. Splst.), Nat. Assn. Realtors 1976. Career: L.A. County Clerk Deputy 1937-40; engr. L.A. City Fire Dept. 1940-71; ofc. mgr., advt. mgr. Builders Land & Sales Realty, 1958-65; sales agt. Revere Realty 1965-71; realtor/owner Dietz Realty, Encino 1971--; awards: Gold Card Exchangor, Nat. Council of Exchangors (NCE) 1980; mem: S.F. Valley Bd. Realtors 1960-, NCE 1980-, Town Hall of Calif.; Republican; Episcopal; rec: fishing, gardening, church wk. Res: 4623 Hayvenhurst Ave Encino 91436 Ofc: Dietz Realty, 16042 Ventura Blvd, 103, Encino 91436

DIKE, HAROLD EDWIN, real estate/insurance executive; b. May 4, 1915, Redlands; s. Andrew Noble and Jennie Ellen (Twigg) D.; m. Margaret Sawyer, Aug. 25, 1939; children: James Geoffrey, b. 1942; Barbara Lynn, b. 1945; edn: dip., Redlands H.S. (class pres.) 1933; AA, San Bernardino Jr. Coll. 1935; econ. major (Delta Upsilon, Blue Key), UC Los Angeles 1937. Career: prin. Dike & Co., Redlands 1937-51; Hal Dike Ins. Brokers, Newport Beach, Costa Mesa, Santa Ana 1951-77, and Dike and Townsend, Insurance Brokers; real estate agt. John D. Lusk & Son, Irvine (Palm Desert and San Clemente) 1977--; mem. Redlands City Council 1940-2, 46-50; bd. mem. of Juvenile Ct., Co. of San Bernardino; mem: Rotary (Redlands 1939-50; v.p. Costa Mesa 1952); pres., Redlands Golf & CC 1937-9; Redlands CofC 1937-9; founding pres. Newport Harbor Exchange Club 1956-66; Balboa Angling Club 1951-66; Shriners (Gold Coast pres. 1952); Lido Isle Yacht Club, Shadow Mtn. GC; mil: tech. sgt. 339th Ord. Batt. 1942-45 ETO; Republican; Presbyterian; rec: travel, fishing, gardening. Res: 32142 Via Barrida, San Juan Capistrano 92675 Ofc: John D. Lusk & Son, 1755 Gillette Ave, Irvine 92713

DI LIBERTI, CHER, lawyer; b. June 2, 1951, Jersey City, N.J.; d. Joseph and Margaret (Mackin) Di L.; m. Gene J. Goldsman, Dec. 18, 1980; 1 son, Aron Matthew, b. 1981; edn: BA, Univ. of Md., 1972, JD, Pepperdine Univ. Sch of Law, 1976. Career: claims evaluation analyst Social Security Adminstrn. 1974-76; law clerk Beam &: Ure, Santa Ana 1976-77; law offices of Di Liberti & Goldsman, Santa Ana 1977--; apptd. by Gov. Brown to bd. dirs. Area Board XI, Disability Rights Dept., 1983-86; legal advisor, Orange Co. Epilespsy Soc., 1980-; mem: Am., Calif. Bar Assns., Am., Calif. Trial Lawyers Assns., Orange Co. Women Lawyers, Orange County Bar Assn., ACLU, participant-profl. Orange Co. Regional Occupational Advis. Bd.; Law Rev., Pepperdine Univ. Sch of Law 1975-6. res: 156 Monarch Bay, So. Laguna. Law offices: Di Liberti & Goldsman, APLC, 611 Civic Center Dr. W., Ste. 200, Santa Ana 92701.

DI LORETO, SILVIO DANTE, realtor, b. Sept. 17, 1925, Rochester, NY; s. Venanzio and Lucia (Cianfaglione) Di L.; m. Nancy Jo Anderson, June 5, 1965; children: Dante, b. 1958, Todd, b. 1963, Antonio, b. 1966, Camilla, b. 1968; edn: dip. Edison H.S. 1943; CCIM, CRB, GRI (Grad. Realtors Inst.), Nat. Assn. of Realtors. Career: profl. photographer, 1947-54; real estate agt. 1954-, real estate broker/owner Sunset Co. Realtors, Santa Barbara 1957--; rental mediator; exec. cons. USC (Real Estate Cont. Edn.) 1980-81; pres. City Coll. Found. 1984; co-chmn. Santa Barbara Housing Council 1978; dir. Valle Verde Retirement Home; trustee United Way, Direct Relief Internat.; honors: realtor of the year 1965/ hon. director for life, Calif. Assn. of Realtors (CAR); commend., Calif. State Legislature 1977; volunteer award 1983; mem: Nat. Assn. of Realtors (dir.), CAR (dir., chmn. Regl. VPs 1969), Santa Barbara Bd. of Realtors (past pres.), CofC, University Club, Santa Barbara Club, Project Concern; publs: compiled sev. books for CAR: Selling Real Estate, Financing Real Estate, Listing Real Estate; co-ordinated the first multiple listing book pub. in the R.E. industry (1965); mil: 2d lt. US Army 1943-47 Republican; rec: amateur mycologist, pvt. pilot, ski, scuba dive. Res: 4625 Via Huerto Santa Barbara 93110 Ofc: Sunset Co. Realtors, 911 Chapala St Santa Barbara 93101

DI MAGGIO, VINCENT SALVATORE, real estate syndicator; b. July 24, 1938, Antioch; s. Salvatore Anthony and Stella Ann (Virga) D.; m. Marietta Rita Bonanno, Nov. 22, 1959; children: Deborah Lynn, b. 1964; Michael Vincent, b. 1968; ed. Pittsburg Sr. H.S.; Calif. Real Estate sales lic. (1964), broker lic. Career: fmr. elec./mech. designer and draftsman; investor/ realtor/ syndicator and hd. DiMaggio Syndications, Oakland, forming Limited Ptnrships for ownership of real estate investments, 1971--; spec. in rehabilitation of props.; mem. Oakland and Marin County Bd. of Realtors, Calif. Assn. Realtors (Syndication Div.); mil: sp5 USAR 1957; Catholic; Ofc: 618 Grand Ave Oakland 94610

DIMSDALE, SEYMORE, restaurateur; b. Dec. 11, 1914, Sioux City, Iowa; s. Abraham and Kitty (Berlin) D.; m. Angela Kraft, Apr. 1, 1967; edn: AA, L.A. City Coll. 1934; CPA, Calif. 1949. Career: own practice public accountant, Los Angeles 1946-51; owner/opr. (w/ brother Harold Dimsdale, joined by wife Angela in 1970) of gourmet -continental restaurants: The Windsor Restaurant, Los Angeles 1950-60, Secret Harbor, L.A. 1951-60, Dales Secret Harbor Restaurant, L.A. 1953-75, Candlewood Room (in The Ocotillo Hotel), Palm Springs 1958-60; Dales In The Mart, 1966--; pres. Hotel Restaurant Employers Council Los Angeles; recipient num. restaurant awards for excellence; mem. Scottish Rite, Shriners; mil: cpl. US Air Corps 1942-46, New Guinea and Phil. cpgns.; Republican; Jewish; rec: golf, swimming, walking. Res: 1307 Via Del Rey, South Pasadena 91030 Ofc: Dales In The Mart 124 E Olympic Blvd, Ste 621, 90015

DINEEN, MARILYN MOORE, educator; b. Oct. 2, 1937, San Francisco; d. Edward Robert and Marie Rose (Kenney) Moore; m. Neal Dineen, Aug. 22, 1964; chil: Erin, b. 1965, Deirdre, b. 1968, David, b. 1972; edn: BA, Lone Mountain Coll. 1973, MA, CSU Sonoma 1975. Career: teacher (French, Math.) Stuart Hall for Boys, 1952; tchr. (primary/intermed.) San Francisco City Sch. 1963-65; Ed. Handicapped tchr. Dixie School Dist., 1966-68; music splst. Marin Formative Nursery Sch., 1966-77; music splst./gifted tchr. San Rafael Sch. Dist., 1977-79; music/drama splst. Reed Sch. Dist., 1978-80, Hanna Boys Center, Sonoma 1980--; music cons. Alpha Nursery Sch. 1977; children's entertainer, The Storybook Lady, 1977-81. Mem: San Rafael Day Care/Kindergarten Teachers (co-founder 1976), Blessed Sacrament Women's Guild, 1966-72, Calif. Teachers Assn., 1963-65. Columnist, guest writer Independent Journal (1978), drama reviewer Terra Linda News (1978), Calif. Highway Patrolman (1979). Democrat. Roman Catholic. rec: tennis, writing, guitar/ singing. Res: 101 Holmes Ave. San Rafael 94903. Ofc: Hanna Boys Center, POB 100, Sonoma.

DINES, JESS EVERETT, electronics company president; b. Dec. 9, 1925, Warsaw, Poland, natl. 1931; s. Nathan and Lillian (Kuper) Dines; bro., James Dines, author, pub., Dines Letter, lectr., Original Gold Bug; BSEE, Pacific States Univ., L.A. 1969; children: Lee Scott, b. 1955; Gary Nelson, b. 1956. Career. with Ram Electronics 1952-55, Foto-Vidio, NJ; Bell Labs., NJ; Aerovox Corp., New Bedford, MA; Delta Semiconductors, 1963-68; exec. v.p., Western Electronics, El Monte, 1968-71; pres., Lee Sales, Santa Ana, 1971-76; pres., In-Phase Electronics, Costa Mesa, 1976- lectured throughout US on repair of hi voltage TV circuitry for Ram Electonics Co.; creator, instr., 1st color TV course for mil., Ft. Monmouth, NJ, 1941-43; tchr., elem. radio to all aspects of Radar; wrote several manuals on operation of Nike-Zues Anti-Ballistic Missile for Bell Labs.; author: six tech books, incl. text book used in TV servicing schs., trans. Spanish; contrib. over 50 articles to electronics mags.; originated Data-Tek, 1967, self-publ. 1970, still used as 'bible' of semiconductor pricing. mil.: served to Cpl., USAF, 1941-43. Republican. Rec.: fishing, swimming, football, travel. Res. : 2945 Zell Dr., Laguna Beach 92651; Office: In-Phase Electronics, 3198-4 Airport Loop Dr., Costa Mesa 92626.

DISHMAN, BENNIE LESTER, certified public accountant; b. Mar. 24, 1954, Monticello, Ky.; s. Bennie Theodore and Laura Minni (Troxell) D.; m. Billie Ann, Nov. 12, 1976; edn: BA in bus. adm., CSU Fullerton 1980; CPA, Calif. 1982. Career: supr. Parke, Guptill and Co., West Covina 1979-83; CPA/partner firm of Stagner and Dishman, CPAs, Covina 1983--; frequent spkr. re taxation, fin. plnng.; honors: Beta Alpha Psi (most outstanding sr. award 1979); mem: Am. Inst. of CPAs, Calif. Soc. of CPAs, Soc. of Calif. Accts., San Gabriel Valley Estate Plnng. Council; publs: contbr. material, Auto and Truck Dealership LIFO Inventory Accounting Manual, by Wm. K. Guptill (1982); mag. arts. in The Executive (7/83), The Successful Dealer (3/83); mil: sgt. USMC 1973-76, GCM, Nat. Def. Service medals, Rifle and Pistol Mksman; Republican; Presbyterian; rec: golf, billiards, jogging. Res: 6665 Bridle Cir. Yorba Linda 92686 Ofc: Stagner and Dishman, CPAs, 300 No Citrus Ave, Ste 2, Covina 91723

DISTEFANO, PETER ANDREW, insurance agency owner; b. Nov.26, 1934, NY, NY; s. Peter Julian and Marie A. (Onorato) Distefano; m. Ann Van Zee Gutzman, Apr. 19, 1976; chil: Diane, b. 1963, Daniel, b. 1965, Donald, b. 1968, Nicholas, b. 1959, Kary, b. 1961, Mark, b. 1963; edn: City Coll. S.F. 1965, Orange Coast Coll. 1975; RHU (Regis. Health Underwriter) Nat. Assn. Hlth Underwriters 1979; CEBS (Cert. Employee Benefit Splst.), CIC (Cert. Ins. Counselor), Wharton School/Intl. Found., current enrl. Career: regl. mgr. Hartford Ins. Co., Santa Ana 1972-77; v.p. Lachman & Assocs., Lafayette & Reno, Nev. 1977-80; owner/pres. Distefano Ins. Svcs, Concord 1980--; lectr. industry functions. Awards: 1982 Performance Agt, United Pac./Reliance Ins. Co.; Millionaires Club 1976, Quota Buster 1977, Premium Leader 1979, Midwest Life Ins. Co.; Commn. Leader 1972, Staff Psn. of Month (7), Hartford Ins. Co. Mem.: Nat. Assn. Hlth Underwriters, Nat. and Oakland/Eastbay Assns. Life Underwriters., Profl. Ins. Agents Assn., Soc. of Regis. Profl. Health Undw., Nat. Assn. Security Dealers, Internat. Found. of Empl. Benefit Plans; bd. dirs. Solano Cty Easter Seal Soc.; Elks Club, Peugot Owners Club (chmn.). Publs: arts. in field; mil: petty ofcr USN 1957-62, Jt. Chiefs of Staff cit., GCM. Republican. Greek Orthodox. rec: martial arts teacher, scuba diving. res: 216

Eaton Ct. Benicia 94510. ofc: Distefano Ins. Services, 1117 Erickson Rd, Ste C, Concord 94520.

DITMORE, MICHAEL CONRAD, medical co. executive; b. May 14, 1943, Mnpls., Minn.; s. Conrad William and June Carol (VanNest) D.; m. Rebecca Patterson, Apr. 30, 1983; children: Brooke, b. 1969; Nathan, b. 1971; edn: BA, Univ. of wash. 1966; MB, Stanford Univ. 1970. Career: sales sys. engr. IBM Corp., Portland, Ore. 1966-68, Palo Alto, Calif. 1968-70; European ops. mgr. Canberra Industries, Wiesbaden, BRD 1970-72; Western regl. mgr. Rolm Corp., Santa Barbara 1972-73; exec. v.p. Browne Corp., Santa Barbara 1974-78; pres./ chmn. Endotek Corp., Santa Barbara 1979--; dir./ chmn. EDL Corp., Salt Lake City, Utah 1983-; cons. NASA 1973-74; mem: IEEE, AOPA; Birnam Wood CC, Foreign Rels. Com.; Channel City Club; mil: cadet USAF Acad. 1961-64; Episcopal; rec: skiing, amateur radio, flying. Res: 211 Hearst Rd Santa Barbara 93108; Endotek Group, 824 E Ortega St Santa Barbara 93103

DIXON, VERDUN EARL, real estate broker; b. Mar. 7, 1918, Jordon, Mont.; s. Henry R. and Amelia (Richards) Dixon; m. Mildred Harper, Feb. 15, 1939; chil: Linda, b. 1947, Roger, b. 1957. Career: ranching in Eastern Oregon; real estate sales, So. Calif., 1953--; teacher/sales, Dale Carnegie 1960; housing development Hawaii, 1960s; currently real estate broker (semi-ret.) and partner (w/son) in Dixon Distbrs., Eureka. mem. Elks 944; served in USN; Republican; mem.Christian Ch. (40yrs., Elder, Deacon, teacher). res: 2109 Whittier Ct. Eureka 95501. ofc: Dixon Distbrs. POB GG, Eureka 95501.

DOBSON, LILLIE W., insurance agent, b. Apr. 20, 1939, Sidon, Miss.; d. Willie and Leola (Washington) Hooper; m. James G. Dobson, June 21, 1959; children: Floyd Hooper, b. 1956, Michael Hooper, b. 1958, Lilliannetta Dobson, b. 1963, Lyndia Dobson, b. 1965; edn: grad. Compton H.S.; LUTC. Career: life ins. agent John Hancock, Cerritos; honors: Million Dollar Round Table, No. 1 Agent in Dist. 1983; No. 1 Woman in the US with John Hancock District Agcy.; mem. bd. dirs. Long Beach chpt. Nat. Assn. Life Underwriters; mem. Affirmative Action Com., Compton; Baptist (pres. Sr. Choir, Calvary Ch.). Res: 500 No Sloan Ave Compton 90221 Ofc: John Hancock 17215 Studebaker Rd, 290, Cerritos 90701

DOCKSON, ROBERT RAY, savings & loan assn. executive; b. Oct.6, 1917, Quincy, Ill.; s. Marshal R. and Letah L. (Edmundson) Dockson; m. Katheryn V. Allison, S.F., Mar. 4, 1944; 1 dau. Kathy Kimberlee, b. 1948; edn: AA, Springfield Jr.Coll. 1937, BA, Univ. Ill. 1939, MFS, USC 1940, PhD, 1946. Career: asst. prof. , dur. Bur of Econ. and Bus. Resrch, Rutgers Univ. 1946-48; economist Western Home Ofc. Prudential Ins. Co., 1948-51; economist Bank of Am., San Francisco 1951-53; prof./ hd. Mktg. Dept., USC Sch of Commerce, 1953-59, and dean/prof. bus. economics, USC Sch of Bus. Admnstrn., 1959-69; dir. Calif. Fed. Svgs. & Loan Assn., 1969-, pres. 1970-, chmn. of bd./ CEO, 1975 . Dir. Internat. Lease Fin. Corp., Computer Scis. Corp., Fed. Reserve Bank of S.F.- L.A. Dist., Pacific Lighting Corp., IT Corp., McKesson, Olga Company, Ticor, Transam. Income Areas, Inc.; Amer. Splst for US State Dept.; pres., Orthopaedic Hosp.; bd. govs. John Randolph Haynes and Dora Haynes Found.; trustee Rose Hills; trustee Pepperdine Univ.; mem. bd. councilors, USC Grad. Sch. Bus. Adminstrn. Awards: Asa V. Call achievement awd.; Star of Solidarity, Italian Govt.; Disting. Community Svc. awd., Brandeis Univ.; Housing Man of Year, Nat. Housing Conf.; Whitney M. Young Jr. awd, Urban League of L.A.; Miracle Man of the Year, Miracle Mile Lions Club; Spirit of Los Angeles Awd., LA City Hdqtrs. Assn. Mem: Gr. L.A. CofC (pres. 1975), W. Internat. Trade Assn., Newcomen Club, L.A. Rotary Club, Lincoln Silver Dollar, Commonwealth, Bohemian, Birman Wood Golf, The One Hundred Club of L.A. Mil: USN 1942-45. ofc: California Fed. Svgs. & Loan, 5670 Wilshire Blvd. Los Angeles 90036.

DODDS, ALEXANDER MAXWELL, IV, tax accountant; b. May 19, 1940, Ellsworth, Ks.; parents: Alexander M. and Susan Emily (Hall) D. III; edn: Wichita Univ. 1957-62; BA, Westmont Coll. 1964; spl. courses, UCSB, CSU Northridge, SB City Coll.; E.A., Enrolled Agt., Treasury Dept. 1978; C.F.P. cand., Coll. for Finl. Plnng. Career: with H&R Block 1964-76 (Santa Barbara asst. mgr. 1964-6, dist. mgr. 1967-76, ofc. mgr. Oxnard 1966-7); asst. dir., taxes, Sambos Restaurants Inc., Carpinteria 1976-79; Enrolled Agent, prin. Alex M. Dodds, Santa Barbara 1979--; instr./supr. H&R Block Income Tax Schs. 1966-75; guest lectr. Westmont Coll., Sta Barbara City Coll.; awards: regional and nat. pub. relations awds., H&R Block (1973,4,5,6); Sierra Pacific Developers Club. Mem: Am. Soc. of Women Accts. (chpsn. 1980, dir. 1981); Nat., Calif. Soc. of Enrolled Agts; Internat. Assn. for Fin. Plnng.; Northside Bus. Assn. (dir.); County Farm Bur.; Santa Barbara Co., City CofC; TriCounties BBB. Publs: tax arts. in Farm Bureau publs.; trademark: Purrpak (for shipping/carrying carton). Mil: Airman 1st Cl., AFROTC, 1957-61, Extraordinary Svc. medal; Republican; Prot.; rec: autos, sports, antiques. Res: 3117 Calle Noguerra Santa Barbara 93105 Ofc: Alex M. Dodds, 100 N. Hope Ave, 12, Santa Barbara 93110

DODWELL, JOHN FRANCIS, manufacturing co. executive; b. Sept. 10, 1926, Boston, Mass.; s. Aloysius Charles and Kathleen Marie (Clarke) D.; m. Patricia Rouse, Sept. 15, 1956; children: Joanne, b. 1957, Jacalyn, b. 1958, James, b. 1960, Jeri Lee, b. 1961, Jay, b. 1963; edn: BS in BA, Rutgers Univ. 1950; postgrad. Rider Coll. 1953-4, UCSB Ext. 1978. Career: asst. mgr. Montgomery Ward (retail store), Norwich, NY 1950-52; mgr. prodn. control Lenox Inc. Trenton, NJ 1953-58; mgr. purch. & prodn. plnng. Lenox Plastics, St. Louis, Mo. 1959-68; dir. forecasting & mdse. control, The Olga Co., Van Nuys 1969--; honors: music scholarship, NY Mil. Acad. 1942, mem. NJ All-

State Band 1944; mem: Am. Apparel Mfrs. Assn. (Mgmt. Systems com. 1979-), Internat. Inst. of Forecasters, APICS; vp. Catholic Adult Club, Trenton, NJ 1954-5; CYO Basketball coach, Webster Groves, Mo. 1963-4; works: approx. 50 computer applications that have lasted five yrs. or longer in three industries (1953-); mil: Rdm 3/c USN SS Lurine, USS Missouri 1944-46, PTO, Phil. Lib., ETO; Republican; Catholic; rec: reading, golf. Res: 1600 No Marian, Thousand Oaks 91360 Ofc: The Olga Co. 7900 Haskell Ave Van Nuys 91409

DOI, RAYMOND TADASHI, landscape contractor; b. Mar. 5, 1950, Honolulu, Hawaii; s. Terry and Katherine (Ouchi) D.; edn: BS, CalPoly Univ. 1978. Career: pres. Calif. Designscape, Inc., San Diego; owner Terry's Lawnmower, S.D.; (past) foreman Terry's Nursery of Landscaping, (S.D.), designer, cost estimator Sear's Landscaping (S.D.), dist. supr. Progress Bulletin (Pomona), salesman Pomona Oriental Nursery; awards: recognition for design, Horseflat Campground, Angeles Nat. Forest Svc. 1977; mem: B.I.A., C.L.C.A., Poway Lions Club; Republican; Baptist; rec: sportfish, horticulture (tropical). Res: 8000 University ave, 303, La Mesa 92041 Ofc: Calif. Designscape Inc., 9555 Black Mtn. Rd., G, San Diego 92126

DOLBY, RAY MILTON, audio engineering co. chairman; b. Jan. 18, 1933, Portland; s. Earl Milton and Esther Eufemia (Strand) Dolby; m. Dagmar Baumert, Aug. 19, 1966; chil: Thomas Eric, David Earl; edn: stu. San Jose State Coll. 1951-2, Wash. Univ., St. Louis 1953-4; BSEE, Stanford Univ. 1957; PhD, physics (Marshall scholar 1957-60, Draper's studentship 1959-61, NSF fellow 1960-1), Pembroke Coll., Cambridge (Eng.) Univ., 1961. Career: electronic tech., jr. engr., Ampex Corp., Redwood City 1949-53; engr., 1955-57, sr. engr. 1957; fellow Pembroke Coll., res. on long wavelength X-rays, 1961-3; cons. U.K. Atomic Energy Authority, 1962-3; UNESCO advisor Central Sci. Instruments Orgn., Chandigarh, Punjab, India 1963-5; owner/chmn. bd. Dolby Labs, Inc., S.F./London, 1965--. Trustee, Univ. High Sch., S.F.; bd. dirs. S.F. Opera; bd. govs., S.F. Sym. Honors: Beech-Thompson Award, Stanford Univ. 1956; Emmy Awd., contbn. to first video recorder, 1957; Trendsetter Awd. Billboard, 1971; Top 200 Execs. Bicentennial awd, 1976; Lyre awd, Inst. High Fidelity, 1972; Emile Berliner Maker of the Microphone awd, 1972; Sci. and Engring. awd. Acad. Motion Picture Arts & Scis, 1979; fellow Audio Engring. Soc. (pres. 1980-81, bd. govs. 1972-4, 79-84), Silver Medal Awd. 1971); fellow Brit. Kinematograph, Sound, TV Soc.; fellow Soc. Motion Picture & TV Engrs., Samuel L. Warner awd. 1978; Alexander M. Poniatoff Gold Medal 1982, Progress Medal 1983; Hon. Fellow, Pembroke Coll., Cambridge 1983. Mem: IEEE; Tau Beta Pi; St. Francis Yacht Club. Patentee; inventions, resrch publs. in video tape rec., X-ray microanalysis, noise reduction and quality improvements in audio and video systems. Mil: US Army 1953-4. Res: 50 Walnut St. San Francisco 94118 Ofc: 731 Sansome St. San Francisco 94111

DOLCINI, ALBERT JUNE, civil engineer; b. Oct. 12, 1919, San Francisco; s. Valente Francis and June Rose (Plant) D.; m. Nancey Cooley, Dec. 2, 1945; children: Michael, b. 1946; Susan, b. 1948; David, b. 1951; June, b. 1954; Carolyn, b. 1955; John, b. 1958; edn: BS, Irrigation, UC Davis 1941; Reg. Profl. (Civil) Engr. (No. 8367) Calif. 1952. Career: hydrologic engr. US Bur. of Reclamation, 1949-55; hydraulic engr. Calif. Dept. of Water Resources, respons. for water resource investigations various regions, 1949-55; supvg. engr., dev. of The Calif. Water Plan, 1955-58; principal engr., Chief of Statewide Investigations, 1958-62, Chief of Dept. General Staff, 1962-68, Chief of Statewide Plnng. DWR, 1968-71, Chief of No. Dist. Calif. DWR, 1971-82, ret.; consulting water resource engr. 1982--: recently cons. to World Bank in Pakistan; cons. to UNDP in India 1968, 71; cons. to FAO in Ethiopia 1979; currently exec. dir. No. Calif. Water Assn.; recipient Director's Award (1982) for service in water planning field; mem. ASCE; Rotary; past mem. Red Bluff City Plnng. Comm.; publs: prin. author DWR Bul. No. 3, The Calif. Water Plan; mil: capt. (Co. Comdr.) USA 1941-45, lt. col. (ret.) USAR 1970; Democrat; Catholic; rec: golf, philately. Res: 1575 Robinson Dr Red Bluff 96080

D'OLIVEIRA, JOSEPH G., certified public accountant; b. July 14, 1942, Georgetown, Guyana; m. Yolanda O., Jan. 5, 1974; edn: AA, E.Los Angeles Coll. 1972; BS,honors in acctg., Cal State Polytechnic Univ., Pomona 1973. Career: CPA, pvt. practitioner, 1975-81; partner firm D'Oliveira, Lim, Weber & Co., CPAs, Los Angeles 1981--; Hon. Consul, Repub. of Guyana, Feb.1976-; bus. mgr. Kedren Comm. Mental Hlth. Ctr, L.A. 1975-78; Olympic Attache, Los Angeles Olylmpics, 1984; trustee, City University of Los Angeles; advis. bd. Pacoima Youth Culture Center, Esquire Boys & Girls Club. Awards: Public Svc. awd. 1983, Guyanese Community Council, USA; Orgn. of Caribbean Am. People's, Inc. Bicentennial awd. for outstanding contbns. made to the USA; appreciation cert., City of Los Angeles. Mem: Nat. Assn. of Black Accts.; Soc. of Calif. Accts.; Am. Inst. of CPAs; Calif. Soc. of CPAs; Phi Kappa Phi Honor Soc. 1973-; Carribean Action Lobby (2d v.chmn.; treas. So. Calif. chpt.); The Eight Dist. Improvement Assn.(treas.); 100 Black Men of Los Angeles, Inc.; Guyana-Am. Social Club 1970-77 (pres. 1976-7); mil: E6 US Army 1966-69, decorated bronze star, Vietnamese Svc., Viet.Campaign, GCM; Catholic; rec: ice hockey, cricket, boxing, track & field. res: 3916 Carnavon Wy Los Angeles 90027 ofc: D'Oliveira, Lim, Weber & Co. CPAs, 2950 Los Feliz Bl. Ste 102, Los Angeles 90039.

DOMINICK, MICHAEL ANTHONY, business owner; b. March 9, 1952, Santa Monica; s. Joseph Francis and Lorraine Mary (Gasper) D.; edn: BS in B.A., Univ. of Portland 1974. Career: with San Sierra Business Systems, Inc. 1974; Inland Bus. Machines, until 1981; owner/pres. Coastal Business Systems, Eureka 1981--; Rotarian; rec: sports. Ofc: Coastal Business Systems 123 F St. Eureka 95501

DOMMARTIN, MAX, interior designer; b. Nov. 1, 1925, Luxembourg; nat. 1963; s. Marcel and Yvonne (Cuinet) Dupasquier de Dompmartin; edn: grad. St.Cyr Mil. Acad.; MA, Univs. Lille and Paris (Fr.), 1944. Career: owner, mgr. Max Dommartin & Co., Interior Design, Los Angeles 1972--, Art For Ever, Design Imports, 1977--; instr. arch., Woodbury Univ. 1976; instr. int. design, UCLA 1975-79; mem. Am. Soc. of Interior Designers, French Inst. Int. Architects, Inst. Bus. Designers, Screen Actors Guild, AFTRA; mil: capt. French Marine Corps 1944-49. Roman Catholic. Ofc: 854 N. Croft Ave Los Angeles 90069

DONALDSON, MILFORD WAYNE, architect/ contractor/ educator; b. Aug. 13, 1943, Jacksonville, N.C.; s. Milford Wayne and Jean Donaldson; m. Nancy Ann Schever, Sept. 5, 1964; 1 dau. Erica Lynn, b. 1981; edn: BA, Uppsala Univ., Sweden 1966; B.Arch., CalPoly Univ., SLO 1967; MS, Univ. of Strathclyde, Scotland 1970; postgrad., Univ. Stuttgart 1972; Calif. lic: arch. (1975), Comm. Coll. Tchg. Cred. (1978), contractor (1979). Career: environ. plnnr. Simon Eisner, AIA, Pasadena 1966; city planner in Uppsala, Sweden 1966-8; design/ fabricator Polytecture Inc. /GRP Housing, Pittsburgh, Pa. 1971-2; project arch. Mosher/ Drew/ Watson, AIA, San Diego 1972-77; pres. Architect M. W. Donaldson, AIA Inc., S.D. 1978--; pres. Sixteen Penny Constrn Inc., S.D. 1979--; instr. Southwestern Comm. Coll. 1972-, CalPoly SLO 1968-70, U. of Strathclyde 1970-72; bd. dirs. S.D. Redevel. Project Area Com. 1979-82, Downtown Redevel. Task Force 1982-3; bd. dirs. (chmn. 1982-3) S.D. Gaslamp Quarter Council 1981-; mem. SDSU curriculum adv. com. 1982-3; awards: Historic Preservation Awd., bd. dirs. Frey Block Californians for Preserv. (1981); Gaslamp Quarter Awards for Design Excellence (Frey Block (1980), Callan Hotel, Wimmer-Yamada, Yuma Bldg., Pacifica Hotel- Theater, Little Joe's Pizza (1983); hon. mention photog., LA Times Home Mag. (1979); spkr. num. hist. preserv. confs. 1979-; mem: Internat. Assn. for Shell Structures 1970-4; S.D. Hist. Soc., Save Our Heritage Orgn. (chmn. 1980), Save Our Neon Orgn., The Inst. for Hist. Study, AIA (design chmn. S.D. chpt. 1982-3), Central City Assn. Task Force adv. 1982-; clubs: S.D. Track and Field Assn., Univ. Club of S.D., US Hang Gliding Assn., Scarab; works incl: Poly-Pods, glassfiber reinforced modular housing units (patented 1972); inflatable flying wing/ hang glider (1973); Pod Pots, pottery (1976); Republican; rec: hang gliding, distance running. Res: 1845 W Monticito Way San Diego 92103 Ofc: Arch. M.W. Donaldson, 533 F St, Ste 300, San Diego 92101

DONALDSON, STEVEN CHARLES, corporate financial executive; b. Jan. 16, 1951, Seattle; s. Norman Elliot and Ruth Pauline (Seifert) D.; edn: Bach. in acctg. and econ., CSU Fullerton 1974; CPA, Ariz., Calif. Career: auditor to field audit supr. Calif. St. Bd. of Equalization, Downey 1974-77; sr. acct. to sr. corp. analyst, Home Fed. Svgs., Tucson, Az. 1977-81; fin. mgr./asst. v.p. Gesco Corp., Fresno 1981--; mem: Nat. Assn. of Accounts, Ariz., Calif. Soc. of CPAs, AICPA; Republican; Catholic; rec: ski, swim, chess. Res: 4111 No Fruit, 112, Fresno 93705 Ofc: Gesco Corp., 1455 E. Shaw, Fresno 93710

DONNELL, MICHAEL COTTER, contractor; b. July 23, 1948, Pasadena; s. John Birney and Suzanne (Seeger) D.; children: Casey, b. 1974, Cotter, b. 1976, Courtney, b. 1980; edn: BS, landscape arch., Univ. of Ariz. 1970. Career: US Naval helicopter pilot 1970-76; Calif. Gen. Contr., Marmont Builders Inc., 1976-80; owner./pres 3-C Energy Systems Inc. (solar contracting co.) 1980--; pres. Sandberg Wind Corp. (wind pk. dev. in San Gorgonio) 1982--; mem. Calif. Solar Energy Industries Assn.; mil: lt. USN 1970-6. Res: 5314 Lake Lindero Dr Agoura 91303 Ofc: 3-C Energy, 31220 La Baya Dr, Ste 110, Westlake Village 91362

DONNICI, PETER J., lawyer/educator; b. Sept. 5, 1939, Kansas City, Mo.; s. Albert H. and Jennie (Danubio) D.; div.; children: Julia Ann (Clifford), b. 1957; Joseph A., b 1959; Joann, b. 1961; edn: BA, Univ. of Mo., K.C. 1959, JD, 1962; LL.M, Yale Law Sch. 1963. Career: prof. of law, Univ. of San Francisco 1963--; prin., Law Offices of Peter J. Donnici, S.F. 1969--; of counsel, Law Ofcs of Joseph L. Alioto, 1965-70; cons. US Dept. HUD, S.F. 1975-6; dir. Council of Legal Ednl. Opportunity, S.F. 1974; dir. DHL Corp., San Bruno 1982-3; spl. counsel Commonwealtof No. Mariana Is. 1983; honors: Sterling Fellowship, Yale Law Sch. 1962-3, Bench & Robe hon. law frat.; mem. S.F. Lawyers' Com. for Urban Affairs (1970-5), Phi Delta Phi; publs: arts. in legal jours.; rec: travel. Res: 190 Cresta Vista San Francisco 94127 Ofc: University of SF, San Francisco 94117

DONOHUGH, DONALD LEE, physician-internist; b. Apr. 12, 1924, Los Angeles; s. William Noble and Virginia (Shelton) D.; m. Beatrice Ivany, Dec. 3, 1976; children: Ruth, b. 1952, Laurel, b. 1953, Marilee, b. 1956, Carol, b. 1964, Greg, b. 1965; stepchil: Leslie, b. 1964, Andrea, b. 1967; edn: BS, US Naval Acad., Annapolis 1946; MD, UC Med. Sch., S.F. 1956; MPH & TM, Tulane Univ. 1961. Career: instr. Tulane Univ. 1960-62, asst. prof. of med., LSU, 1963-65, and in chg. starting Univ. of Costa Rica Med. Sch.; chief of med., 1965-67, currently, clin. prof. medicine UC Irvine; dir. medical svcs. Am. Samoa, 1958-60; epidemiological cons. Internat. Center for Med. Research and Tng., 1962-63; pvt. practice, 1967-75. Author: The Middle Years (1981), Am. Coll. of Physicians & Saunders; num. profl. papers, presentations; mil: commodore, MC USNR; Ind.; Episcopal; rec: tennis, surf, ski, sail. Res: 7 Jasmine Creek Dr Corona del Mar 92625

DORAN, MARK ANTHONY, research & development executive; b. July 22, 1933, Sydney, Australia; s. Patrick Fabian and Kathleen (McCann) Doran; m. Inez Vandenbergh, Oct. 5, 1968; chil: Alexander, b. 1973, Philippa, b. 1975; edn: B.Pharm., Univ. of Sydney (Aust.) 1954. Career: chief chemist Ethnor Ltd. (subs. Johnson & Johnson Internat.) Sydney, Aust. 1956-68; dir. quality control Bristol Myers Internat. Div., Sydney 1968-70; cons. in water biology Pollution Mgmt. Inst., Anaheim, Calif. 1970-71; group mgr. resrch & devel. nutritional prods., Shaklee Corp., San Francisco 1972--; vis. lectr. Univ. Calif. Ext., San Diego 1971. Mem: Am. Pharmaceutical Assn., Calif. Pharmacists Assn., Acad. of Pharmaceutical sci., Am. Assn. of Cereal Chemists. Patentee (chemical); sev. publs. in field of pharmaceutical tech. Rec: swim, tennis, distance running. res: 1121 No. Sage Ct. Sunnyvale 94087 ofc: Shaklee Corp. 444 Market St. San Francisco 94111.

DOROBIALA, JAMES FRANCIS, chiropractor; b. May 19, 1941, Rochester, NY; s. Francis Xavier and Dorothy Violet (Dowhy) D.; m. Ngoc Lan M., Aug. 31, 1974; children: Christina, b. 1975, Andrea, b. 1980; edn: BA, Univ. Tampa 1965; B.Fgn.Trade, 1968, M.Intl.Mgmt., 1973, Am. Grad. Sch. of Intl. Mgmt.; DC, Los Angeles Coll. of Chiropractic, 1978; lic. Dr. Chiro. in Calif., Fla., N.Mex.; addtl. studies: Univ. Md. (Munich, Ger.) 1966, Inst. de Iberoamericanos (Saltillo, Mex.) 1969, Am. Univ. Alumni Assoc. (Bangkok, Thailand) 1971; Calif. Comm. Colls tchg. cred. Career: asst. supt. Kelliher Constrn. Co. 1960-64; ednl. counselor Univ. of Maryland, Munich, Ger. 1966-68; high sch. teacher Monroe County Sch. System 1968-70; ops. mgr. Internat. Div., Chase Manhattan Bank 1970-74; holistic chiropractor/dir. North Valley Chiropractic Clinic, Granada Hills 1979--; ext. faculty Los Angeles Coll. of Chiropractic. Awards: John A. Fischer Meml. Scholarship, James Parker Scholarship, 1978; Who's Who in Am. Colls and Univs 1978. Mem: Sacro-Occipital Resrch Soc. (pres. 1977-79); dir. of edn. & research, Am. Acad. of Holistic Chiropractic 1984; Am., Calif., NY Chiropractic Assns.; US CofC. Resrch: in healing properties of common gems & metals. Mil: s/sgt US Army 1965-8; Christian; rec: metaphysics, martial arts, meditation. Res: POB 7152, Mission Hills 91345 Ofc: No Valley Chiropractic Clinic, 17038 Chatsworth St Granada Hills 91344

DORSEY, PAUL R., lawyer; b. Dec. 17, 1925, Chgo.; s. John Martin and Rhea Keziah (Sweeney) D.; children: Jon, b. 1954, Jacqui, b. 1955, Nefre, b. 1973, Xochitl, b. 1974; edn: BFS (fgn. svc.), USC 1951; JD, Southwestern Univ. 1960; grad. work in anthropol., Calif. Univ., Los Angeles 1981-; admitted to Calif State Bar 1961. Career: lawyer assoc., Baca & Dorsey, Los Angeles 1961-68, Dorsey & Lopez, 1968--; mem. Mexican Am. Bar Assn. 1967-, Mex. Am. Lawyers Club (secty. 1972); mil: sgt. USAF, USAAC 1944-46, GCM, WWII, 1st lt. USAAF 1951-53, Bronze star, Korean Presdtl. Unit Cit.; rec: carpentry, philately. Res: 725 Cereza Dr Monterey Park 91754 Ofc: Dorsey & Lopez, 5827 E Beverly Los Angeles 90022

DOSTAL, MILAN MATHIAS, lawyer; b. Feb.7, 1929, Hutchinson, Minn.; s. Mathias Wm. and Mary (Miska) Dostal; m. Dorothy Olsen, March 18, 1951; chil: Richard George, b. 1956; Cynthia Marie, b. 1960; Pamela Anne, b. 1965; edn: Macalester Coll. 1947-9; BBA, Univ. Minn. 1952, JD, 1957; selected for Honor Law Grad. recruitment pgm., US Dept. of Justice 1957. career: trial atty. Civil Div. US Dept. of Justice, Wash DC 1957-63, Asst. U.S. Atty., Los Angeles, 1964-65; pvt. practice of law, L.A. and Orange Cos., 1965-71, Milan M. Dostal, A Profl. Corp., Newport Bch. and Orange, 1971--; admitted to practice, US Supreme Ct., Supreme Cts. of Minn., Calif.; judge pro-tem, arbitrator, Am. Arbitration Assn. 1963; elected city councilman, Newport Beach 1970-78, mayor and mayor pro-tem 1974-76, 78; pres. Intergovtl. Coord. Council of Orange Cos. 1973-74; county commnr. Orange Co. Airport Land Use Commn. 1974-78; dir. (pres. 1973-5) Nat. Orgn. to Insure a Sound-controlled Environment (NOISE) 1971-8. A-V Rating, Martindale Hubbell, 1981. mem: Am., Calif., Orange Co. Bar Assns.; Phi Delta Phi, Delta Sigma Pi, Balboa Bay Club (Newport Bch), founder Mariners Lions Club of Newport Bch 1963, Kiwanis Club (dir. 1961). mil: s/sgt USAF 1951-54. Republican. Presbyterian (chmn. bd. trustees, clerk of session). rec: photog., fish, travel. Res: 1821 Tradewinds Ln, Newport Beach 92660. Ofc: Milan M. Dostal, APC, 505 City Pkwy West, Ste.1000, Orange 92668.

DOTY, J. E., residential real estate developer; b. Nov. 12, 1941, Oakland; parents: Abraham Richard and Frances Edith (Bishop) D.; children: Elizabeth Ann, b. 1963; John Joseph, b. 1964; edn: UC Berkeley 1959-62. Career: suboffice mgr. IBM Office Prods. Div., 1965-69; dir. real estate mgmt. Hanford-Freund & Co. 1969-71; chief exec. ofcr. Best Schwann & Doty Co. (R.E. mgrs.), 1971-75; CEO, J.E. Doty & Assocs. (dev. cons.) 1975-79; CEO/ pres./ sole owner Metro Pacific Devel. Co. (resdtl. dev.) San Francisco 1979--; donated exec. SF Strategic Plan Housing Task Force 1981-83; chmn. SF CofC Housing Com. 1979-82, SF Mayor's Fiscal Adv. Com. 1969 and Indsl. Dev. Com. 1967; founder/pres. Comm. Assn. Mgmt. Inst. 1976-9; nat. speaker Comm. Assn. Inst. 1976-9; mem: SF CofC, Soc. of Calif. Pioneers, Calif. Hist. Soc., Found. for SF Archtl. Heritage, SF Plnng. & Urban Renewal; Republican; Presbyterian. Res: 2858 Jackson St San Francisco 94115 Ofc: Metro Pacific Devel. Co. 25 Broadway, S.F. 94111

DOUGLAS, CYNTHIA LYNN, pathologist; b. Oct. 7, 1952, Appleton, Wisc.; d. Richard Harold and Shirley Ann (Cole) D.; m. Michael Whitston, May 13, 1978; edn: undergrad. Univ. of Wisc., Madison 1970-2; BA, summa cum laude, Central Wash. State Univ., Ellensburg 1975; MD, Univ. of Wash. Med. Sch., Seattle 1978; Univ. of Wash. affil. res. (pathology) 1979-82; Anatomic & Clin. Pathologist, Coll. of Am. Pathologists 1983. Career: co dir. of lab., Twin Cities Comm. Hosp., Templeton, Calif. 1983--; com. mem. Intra-hosp. Diagnosis Related Group, 1983-; instr. ancillary med. personnel (Medex 1979, coll. embryology 1975, med. techs. 1981-); honors: Elk's most valuable student 1970; mem: Coll. of Am. Pathologists, Am. Soc. of Clin. Pathologists, Ore. Pathol. Soc., Internat. Acad. of Path., S.L.O. Co. Med. Soc.; rep. to State Legislature

Drug Council 1970; participant NSF study 1974, 76-80; publs: short story (1970), sci. papers; rec: piano, knitting, stu. volcanoes, geology. Res: 151 Flag Way Paso Robles 93446 Ofc: Twin Cities Hosp. Lab., 1500 Las Tablas Rd, Templeton 93465

DOUGLASS, PAUL JAMES, SR., quality control engineer/manager; b. Sept. 18, 1926, Oil City, Pa.; s. James Wm. and Letitia Melissa (Rosenberg) D.; m. Betty Stover, Jan. 15, 1946; children: Paul Jr., b. 1946; Linda, b. 1948; Timothy, b. 1950; Gary, b. 1951; edn: AA, Diablo Valley, 1973; Quality Engr., Am. Soc. for Q.C. 1970. Career: insp. supr. Gen. Dynamics/ Astronautics, San Diego 1957-, then sr. quality engr. Gen. Dynamics/ Electro Dynamics Div., Pomona; quality engr./ chief insp., MBA Assoc., Inc., San Ramon 1973-4; qual. control mgr. Hydro Deep Drqw, Gardena 1975; quality ass. mgr. Marco Mfg. Inc., Lynwood 1980--; tchr. quality rel. subjects: ASQC Soc., 1971, Marco Mfg. Inc. 1981-3; mem: ASQC (edn. chmn., sect. chmn. 1969-72), Toastmasters Intl. (fmr secty. treas.); Exchange Club (1970), A.F.M. Lodge; mil: USN 1943-47, 1950, commendations; Republican; Prot.; rec: numismatics, computers. Res: 402 Neilson St Carson 90745 Ofc: Marco Mfg. Inc. 2520 Industry Way Lynwood 90262

DOVE, CHRISTOPHER "Kit" STONE, software developer, b. Feb. 2, 1943, s. W. Franklin and Ruth Rebecca (Stone) Dove; m. Mary Avenell Freeman, Aug. 17, 1974; 2 sons: Christopher Andrew, b. 1976, Jonathan Daniel, b. 1979; edn: grad. Phillips Acad.,Andover 1961; BS, Yale Univ. 1966. Career: student pgmmr. Yale Univ. Computer Ctr., New Haven, Conn. 1963-5; scientific programmer Armstrong Rubber Resrch & Devel., West Haven, Conn. 1965-66; pgmmr. (bus./ sci./systems, analyst) Matson Navigation Co., San Francisco 1966-70; systems pgmmr. Golden West Svgs & Loan, Oakland 1970-72; founding partner, cons. Dove Wright & Assocs., San Francisco 1972-75; owner, cons. Software House, San Francisco 1976--; splst. Brandon Applied Systems, S.F. 1976-78; mgr. Tech. Support Dept. Rand Information Systems, S.F. 1978-80, mgr. Software Devel., 1980--83; teacher Cobol & Assembler, ECPI, 1968; cons. Brain Tumor Resrch Ctr. UC Med. Ctr., S.F. 1974-. Awards: achievement, Oak Park, Ill. Optimists Club, 1957; Julia E. Drinkwater Scholarship, Phillips Acad. 1960-1; New Eng. Interscholastic Wrestling Championship (2nd) 1961; capt. Freshman Wrestling Team Yale U. 1961-2; AAU New Eng. Wrestling Championship (1st) 1962. Mem: BSA 1955-60, 67-8, Order of the Arrow 1960, Commnr. 1967-8; Delta Kappa Epsilon, Alpha chpt. 1963-; Nathan Hale Soc. 1965-; Mechanics Inst. 1968-71; Sierra Club 1970-; Mensa 1980-1; Banwell Soc. of Archaeol.(Eng.)1980-; GUIDE (co. rep.1978-83, div. coord. 1981-3). Publs: co-ed. The Voice of the Coast (1983-),ICCA 1983-; contbg. author Pleistocene Studies in So. Nev. (1967); coauthor IMS In A Distrbtd. Environment (1980); devel. TRUTH (CRT-based control sys. 1968), STUDY (database analyzing brain tumor patients in antineoplastic therapy trials, 1974-); devel. Future World Trade Route Detection Sys. (1968) rec: genealogy racquetball, unicycling. Res: 633 Palma El Granada 94018. Ofc: Rand Info. Systems 98 Battery, San Francisco 94111.

DOWDLING, CHARLES ALAN, engineering geologist/civil engineer; b. Aug. 8, 1951, Elk City, Okla.; s. Herman Leslie and Opal Margret (Hieronymus) D.; m. Karen, Jan. 1, 1977; children: Matthew, b. 1978; Katrina, b. 1981; edn: Univ. of Colo. 1969-70; BS, geol. eng., Colo. sch. of Mines 1971; MS, environ. sci., Univ. of Tex. 1978; Calif. reg. geologist (1983), cert. engrg. geologist (1983), engr. in tng. (1981). Career: surveyor US Forest Svc, Pagosa Spgs., Colo. 1970; geophys. engr. Texas Instruments, Inc., Dallas 1974-77; deptmtl. engring. geologist/ engring. assoc. Los Angeles Co. Sanitation Dists., Whittier 1978-; mem: ASCAP 1976-, Colo. Sch. of Mines Alumni Assn.; music publ: Stuck On You; mil: cpl. Reserve Ofcrs Tng. Corps 1970-2; Republican; Lutheran; rec: wood crafting, mountaineering. Res: 15535 Mallory Dr Fontana 92335 Ofc: LA Co. Sanitation Districts, POB 4998, Whittier 90607

DOWDNEY, DONNA LEE, writer/ editor/ educator; b. Apr. 13, 1943, Chgo.; d. Donald Scott and Clarice Dolores (Pineau) Smyth; m. William Clayton Dowdney Jr., Aug. 19, 1967; children: Deborah Lee, b . 1972; David Scott, b. 1974; edn: BA, Wheaton Coll. 1965; MAT, Indiana Univ. 1968; PhD, Columbia Pacific Univ. 1984; Calif. Tchg. Credentials (life) (Coll., H.S.). Career: Menlo Coll. Study Skills 1977-78; instr. Evergreen Coll. 1978; instr. Foothill-DeAnza Coll. Dist. 1976-80; wrkshp. leader/ classroom instr. var. depts. Stanford Univ. Med. Ctr. (wrkshps. incl. Writing for Mgrs., Writing for Support Personnel, Writing for Profl. Publs.) 1980--; dir. Writer's Retreat, Yosemite 1981--; pres. Wriing Ent. Internat., Palo Alto 1978--; author over 40 articles in diverse publs.; spkr.: Writing for Publication, Am. Bus. Commun. Assn. internat. conv. (Vancouver 1984), Writing for Computer Industry Conv. (New Hampshire 1984); bus. communications cons. IBM Palo Alto Newsletter and high tech. cos.; awards: Achiever's Awd., Nat. League of Am. Pen Women, Santa Clara br. 1977; Scholarship, Near East Sch. of Archaeology, Jerusalem 1964; mem: Nat. League of Am. Pen Women (pres. Palo Alto br. 1982-85); Calif. Writers Club; Am. Soc. for Tng. & Devel.; Soc. for Tech. Commun.; Am. Bus. Commun. Assn.; Peninsula Commun. Access TV Assn.; Writers Connection; Am. Assn. Univ. Women; Protestant; rec: travel, archaeology, photog. Address: 1150 Newell Rd Palo Alto 94303

DOWNER, MICHAEL JOSEF, corporate counsel; b. Feb. 25, 1955, Los Angeles; s. Lowell Howard and Cora Marie (Masek) D.; m. Janet Lee, Aug. 20, 1983; edn: BA, UC Los Angeles 1977; JD, Southwestern Univ. Sch of Law 1981; admitted to Calif. State Bar 1982. Career: corp. counsel The Capital Group, Inc., 1982--; honors: Blue Key, Student Legis. Council, Student Fin. Aid Adv., UCLA; law rev., ABA Client Counseling Competition (intramural co-champion), Stu. Faculty Rels. Com., Southwestern Univ.; Extern, Calif. Ct. of Appeal 1981; mem: Am. (Banking, Bus. Law and Tax Com. Young Lawyers Div.), Calif., L.A. County bar Assns.; Beta Theta Pi, Phi Alpha Delta; Republican; Cat lic; rec: skiing, tennis, cooking. Res: 13934 Bora Bora Way Marina del Rey 90292 Ofc: The Capital Group Inc., 333 So Hope St, 50th Flr., Los Angeles 90071

DOWNS, DOUGLAS WALKER, sculptor; b. May 30, 1945, Pomona; s. Walker Wallace and Dorothy Elizabeth (Spoor) D.; m. Anne Venables, Jan. 15, 1971; 1 child, Devon, b. 1973; edn: BA, highest honors, Whittier Coll. 1967; Claremont Grad. Sch. 1967-8. Career: tching asst. Ariz. State Univ. 1969-70; craftsman Dell Weston Art Bronze Casting, Santa Monica 1970-71; sculptor in Santa Monica 1970-2, Woodland Hills 1972-9, Pacific grove 1979--; ten one-man shows in galleries across USA incl. Wakefield-Scearce Gallerys in Shelbyville, Ky., Southwestern Arts, Ltd. in Carmel, Ca., the Wathen Gallery in S.F., the Porcelain Gallery, Seattle; 13 group shows at galleries incl. Armstrong's, Pomona, the Carmel Art Assn., and the A. Huney Gallery, S.D.; num. lectures incl. CalPoly (1973), Starline Sch of Jewelry Design (1972-4), TV lectures: Seattle 1977-8, San Diego 1979, Monterey 1982, guest artist at San Dimas Festival of Western Arts 1982; honors: sculpture presented by Nordic Heritage Mus. to King Karl Gustaf XVI of Sweden 1982; listed, Am. Artists of Renown 1982; sculptures in collections of Pres. Nixon, Pres. Carter, Knut Hedemann (Norwegian Amb. to US), Dame Judith Anderson, Zoe Caldwell; mem: Carmel Art Assn. (bd. dirs.), Internat. Sculpture Center, Pacific Grove Art Ctr., Monterey Penin. Mus. of Art, Pacific Grove Heritage Soc. (bd. dirs. 1981); Pacific Grove Nat. Hist. Mus., Friends of Lib., Audubon Soc.; works 78 original sculptures cast in bronze in numbered editions; commns. incl. the Tor House Award for Robinson Jeffers Fellows, 1979-83; Republican; Congregational. Address: 405 Alder St Pacific Grove 93950

DOXEY, BEATRICE THERESA, real estate broker/education co. executive; b. Dec. 26, 1935, NYC; d. John P. and Kate A. (Lyons) Mahon; m. John Doxey, June 28, 1958; children: John, b. 1959; Karen, b. 1960; edn: real estate certif., Palomar Coll. 1975; num. courses in bus., loan underwriting, banking; lic. real estate broker. Career: co-owner Professional Seminar Assocs., Rancho Bernardo 1979--; Doxey Real Estate Co., 1972-75; real estate loan underwriter Crocker Nat. Bank 1975-78. Res: 11416 Florindo Rd San Diego 92127 Ofc: Profesional Seminar Assocs. 11844 Rancho Bernardo, Ste. 120, San Diego 92128

DOYLE, JOHN BENEDICT, JR., neurological surgeon; b. Oct. 3, 1926, Rochester, Minn.; s. John B., Sr., and Greta Fenelon (Holahan) D.; m. Marguerite A. Camacho, Oct. 13, 1951; children: John, b. 1952, Tim, b. 1953, Peter and Paul, b. 1954, Barbara, b 1955; edn: BA, zoology, UCLA 1948; MD, George Washington Univ. 1952; MS, neurosurg., Univ. of Minn. 1958; Fellowship in Neurol. Surg., Mayo Clinic 1953-55, 57-59. Career: neurological surgeon; clin. prof. USC Sch. of Medicine; chief of staff St. Vincent Med. Ctr. 1976-77; mem: Southwest Mayo Clinic Alumni Assoc. (pres. 1963-64), So. Calif. Neurosurg. Soc. (pres. 1971-72), Calif. Assn. of Neurol. Surgeons (pres. 1975), LA County Med. Assn., LA Soc. of Neurol. and Psychiat., W. Neurosurg. Soc., Am. Assn. of Neuro. Surg., Congress of Neurol. Surgeons, Nu Sigma Nu, Sigma Chi, Knights of Malta; publs: med. arts. Jour. of Neurosurgery, Archives of Otolaryngology, Spine Bull., etc.; mil: lt. USN 1955-57; Republican; Catholic; rec: fishing, boating. Res: 4963 Los Feliz Blvd Los Angeles 90027 Ofc: 201 So Alvarado St, Ste 809, Los Angeles 90057

DRAKE, C(HARLES) ROBERT, real estate broker-developer; b. Nov. 22, 1949, Rahway, N.J.; s. Charles R. and Dorothy (Kurtz) D.; edn: BBA, Univ. of Miami, 1972; MBA, Golden Gate Univ. 1976; cert. in real estate Hartnell Coll. 1981. Jr. Coll. Tchr. credentials: bus. mgt., real estate. Career: US Army Ofcr., CPT, 1972-79; real estate sales, devel. and leasing, Monterey County, spec. in commercial properties; pres. Rathbun Realty, Inc. and owner Drake Investments; instr. Hartnell Coll.; honors: Phi Delta Kappa, Omicron Delta Kappa (treas.), Pershing Rifles Frat., Scabbard and Blade hon., Army Scholarship, Orange Key (leadership hon.; pres.), Iron Arrow (highest honor awarded by coll.), Who's Who in Univ.; past mem. Salinas, Calif. and US Bd. of Realtors; mem. Salinas CofC (Econ. Devel. Com., Monterey Wine Festival Com.); Sigma Chi Frat. (Found. bd. govs.), Delta Sigma Pi Profl. Bus. Frat., American Legion Post No. 589 (Adjutant, Fin. Ofcr., Exec. Bd., Newsletter ed.), Mensa (pres. Monterey Co. 1984), Salinas Jaycees (Mem. of Year 1980), Salinas Area United Way campaign co-chair 1981; publs: articles in local newspapers and newsletters; rec: guitarist, numismatics. Ofc: Rathbun Realty Inc. 210 Capitol St, Ste 6, Salinas 93901

DRAKE, RANDALL GALEN, chiropractor; b. Jan. 21, 1946, Jackson, Miss.; s. Alfred Wm. and Lois Elizabeth (Randall) D.; m. Susan Mae, June 12, 1971; children: Tisha, b. 1971, Kimberly, b. 1973, Darren, b. 1977; edn: BBA, Eastern Mich. Univ. 1972; DC, Logan Chiro. Coll. 1976. Career: accountant Bond and Co., Jackson, Mich. 1972-73; chiropractor pvt. practice 1976--, dir. American Chiropractic Clinic of Ventura; mem: Am., Calif. Chiropractic Assn.; Ventura CofC; fmr. Jaycee; mil: sgt. USAF 1966-70; rec: boating, golf, bowling, swimming. Res: 7152 San Ysidro Ct. Ventura 93003 Ofc: American Chiropractic Clinic, 10225 Telephone Rd, Ste. B, Ventura 93004

DRAYER, JAN IGNATIUS, physician, b. Jan. 31, 1946, Amsterdam, The Netherlands; s. Pieter Roelof and Anna (de Swart) D.; m. Thea, July 3, 1971; children: Myke, b. 1975, Joris, b. 1978; edn: MD, Univ. of Nijmegen 1971, PhD 1975, internist 1977; lic. MD, Netherlands 1971, Calif. 1982. Career: research assoc. Cornell Univ., NY 1975-77; internist Univ. of Nijmegen, The

Netherlands 1977-80; staff physician, assoc. chief Clin. Pharmacology/ Hypertension, VA Medical Ctr., Long Beach 1980--; assoc. prof. med. UC Irvine 1980-; awards: Am. Heart Assn. resrch grants 1982-3; mem: fellow Council for High Blood Pressure Research, Internat. Soc. of Hypertension, Endocrine Soc., Am. Soc. for Clin. Pharmacol. Therapeutics, Am. Coll. of Clin. Pharmacol., Internat. Study Group for Steroid Hormones, Neth. Soc. of Medicine, Am. Heart Assn. (bd. dirs. Orange Co. chpt.); pres. Broadmoor Homeowners Assn.; approx. 100 publs. in med. jours., med. book chpts.; rec: computer pgmmg. Res: 5401 Catowba Ln Irvine 92715 Ofc: VA Medical Center 5901 E. 7th St, W130, Long Beach 90822

DRAYTON (SASTRE), GEORGANNA, sales executive; b. May 7, 1951, Oakland; d. George and Hazel Copeland (O'Neil) Vesik; m. Luis Sastre, Jan. 2, 1982; 3 stepchildren: Aliette, Nicole, Angelique; edn: BS, honors, Portland State Univ. 1976, MBA, 1980. Career: sales rep. for Acco International for Ore., Wash., Ida. and Alaska territory, 1977, transf. to No. Calif. territory in 1979, area sales mgr. for No. Calif., Acco Internat. 1981--; awards: Rookie of the Year 1978, and Sales rep. of Yr. 1982, Acco Internat.; mem: 49er Travelers Assn. (bd. mem., past vp), Nat. Office Products Assn., Sales & Mktg. Execs., Word Processing Ops. Exec.; rec: scuba diving, tennis, windsurfing, aerobics. Res. /local ofc: 810 Stendhal Lane Cupertino, CA 95014 Ofc: 770 So. Acco Plaza, Wheeling, Ill. 60090

DREW, DONALD JAMES, lawyer; b. Mar. 16, 1929, Salix, Iowa; s. George and Abigail (Elliott) D.; m. Lily Lowe, June 10, 1961; children: Dana James, b. 1962, Liana Marie, b. 1968; edn: AB, UC Los Angeles 1954; JD, UCLA Sch of Law 1957; admitted to practice Calif. State Bar 1957. Career: sr. trial atty. Calif. State Dept. of Public Works, 1957-63; assoc. law firm Musick Peeler & Garrett, Los Angeles 1963-, partner 1967-, of counsel 1983--; frequent lectr., seminars on eminent domain and prop. tax; honors: Phi Beta Kappa 1957, Student Judicial Bd. 1954-5, justice Moot Ct. Bd. 1956-7, mem. Student Legislative Bd., UCLA and UCLA Law Sch.; mem: State Bar of Calif., L.A. County Bar Assn. (coms.), Masons (past Master), Santa Monica Bay Commandery (past cmdr.), Scottish Rite, Shriners; mil: sgt. USMC 1946-49, USMCR 1949-53 (active duty Korea 1950-51), capt. USAR (judge advocate gen.) 1960-65; Republican; Methodist; rec: constrn. houses, tennis, golf, softball. Res: 2280 Lorain Rd San Marino 91108 Ofc: Musick Peeler & Garrett, One Wilshire Blvd, Ste 2000, Los Angeles 90017

DRISCOLL, ROBERT EARL, university dean; b. Nov. 21, 1945, Louisville, Ky.; s. Glen Robert and Dorothy June (Little) D.; children: Mark, b. 1973, Barbara, b. 1976, Angela, b. 1979; edn: BA, So. Calif. Coll. 1979; MA, U.S. Internat. Univ. 1980, Psy.D., 1982, PhD, 1984. Calif. lic. MFCC (marriage, family, child counselor) 1983. Career: dir. Psychological Services, Clinica Del Mar, 1980-82; pres./chmn. Alternatives, 1982--; clin. psychol. prof., Univ. for Humanistic Studies, 1982-, dean Psychol. Studies, 1983--; dir. Educational Services Unlmtd. 1980--; personnel mgmt. cons. Counties of Los Angeles, Orange, Riverside, and San Diego, 1983-; lectr. CA Psychology Series; honors: San Diego Outstanding Citizen 1975, CofC; mem: Calif. Assn. Marriage Family Counselors, Am. Soc. for Sci. Study of Sex, Western Psychol. Assn., Am. Psychol. Assn., North Am. Adlerian Soc., Christian Assn. of Pastoral Counselors, S.D. Multiple Sclerosis Soc. (bd. dirs.), S.D. Soc. for Sex Edn. & Therapy, S.D. Mental Health Assn., S.D. Comm. Arts Assn., S.D. Theatre Goers Soc.; publs: 10 journal arts. in psychology rel. to personality and devel.; mil: USN 1968-76, Vietnam Svc., Navy Achievement; rec: sailing, travel, theatre. Res: 4625 Florida St, 2, San Diego 92116 Ofc: Univ. for Humanistic Studies, 2444 San Diego Ave, San Diego 92110

DU BERCHIN, MARJORIE S., lawyer; b. Dec. 21, 1944, Los Angeles; d. Arnold and Doris Stein; 1 dau., Jenifer Faithe, b. 1971; edn: AA, Santa Monica City Coll. 1969; BA, CSU Northridge 1972; JD, San Fernando Valley Coll. of Law 1978; admitted to Calif. State Bar 1978. Career: atty. Gulf Oil, La Jolla 1978-79; own law office, Solana Beach 1980--, spec. in estate plnng., estate taxation, conservatorships, guardianships, probate; instr. Estate Plnng. courses, spkr. Law Day (1982), spkr. Women's Opportunity Week 1983; honors: Am. Jurisprudence awards, Law Rev. 1975-8, Who's Who Among San Diego Women 1982; mem: Calif. State, North San Diego Co. (Probate, Estate Plnng. Sect.) Bar Assns.; Mensa; NOW; Physicians for Social Responsibility; Young Friends of the S.D. Sym.; rec: skiing, investing. Law Ofc: 731 S. Hwy 101, Ste 2H, Solana Beach 92075

DUBIN, GARY VICTOR, lawyer; b. Aug. 27, 1938, Phila.; s. Jacob and Iris (Sagel) D.; son, Scott Adams, b. 1959; edn: AB summa cum laude, USC 1960; JD cum laude, NY Univ. Sch of Law 1963; postdoc. work in sociol. of law (Russell Sage Found. Scholar), UC Berkeley 1964-6; S.J.D. cand. (Russell Sage Fellow), Harvard Law Sch. 1969-70; admitted to practice Calif. State Bar 1964, US Supreme Ct. Bar 1973. Career: began as law clerk, Covington & Burling, Wash DC; started first corp. (mfg. and distbg. ednl. tape recordings) 1957; corp. mgmt. for num. clients (incl. mfg. cos., a golf course, newspaper, real estate inv. co.); law practice on East and West Coast, with offices in L.A. and Honolulu, HI, currently; res. cons. Rand Corp., Santa Monica 1970; vis. fellow US Dept. of Justice 1971; resrch dir. So. Calif. Criminal Justice Research Ctr. 1971; chief cons. Alameda Regl. Criminal Justice Plnng. Bd. 1971-2; prin. cons. Courts Task Force, Nat. Adv. Commn. on Criminal Justice Standards, 1972-73; teaching fellow Stanford Law Sch. 1963; faculty UCB 1964-6, Univ. of Denver Univ. 1966-69, Harvard Univ. 1969-70; lectr. Rand Corp., Harvard Law Sch., Justice Dept. (Wash DC), Univ. of Tex. Law Sch., UCLA Inst. Govt. & Pub. Affairs, USC Sch of Pub. Adm.; author num. profl. and nontech. arts., reports, and books; mem: Nat. Assn. Corporate Dirs., Am. Bar Assn., Law and Soc.

Assn., World Future Soc., Intl. Soc. for Gen. Semantics, Phi Beta Kappa, Phi Kappa Phi, Pres.'s Circle USC, Nat. Wildlife Fedn., Audubon Soc.; mil: USAFR 1956-62; rec: gardening, sailing. Address: 4333 Admiralty Way, Marina Del Rey 90291; 345 Queen St, 6th Flr, Honolulu, HI 96813

DU BOIS, JOHN MERRITT, chiropractor; b. Nov. 29, 1927, Syracuse, NY; s. Harvey Daniel and Marion (Mercier) DuBois; m. Geraldine R. Angrick, June 5, 1948; chil: Kristina, b. 1949, Patricia, b. 1950, Garritt, b. 1954; edn: stu. Univ. of GA 1956-9, Am. Univ. 1960, Geo. Washington Univ. 1961-3; BA, 1975, and DC, 1976, Los Angeles Coll. of Chiropractic; Diplomate Nat. Bd. of Chiropractic Examiners 1975. Career: Sgt. Major USMC 1945-72, ret.; pvt practice chiropractic, DuBois Chiro Clinic, Escondido; mem. Los Angeles Coll. of Chiropractic off-campus instrnl staff, long range planning com., postgrad. edn. steering com., dir., Alumni Assn.; mem. 1983 Chiropractic Volunteer Honduras Relief Mission; instr. Escondido Adult Edn.; volunteer posture physicals, S.D. County Indian Clinics. Honors: 1984 exceptional leadership award Am. Chiro. Assn., 1984 Doctor of Year Calif. Chiro. Assn., 1984 distinguished service award San Diego County Chiro. Soc., Resolution as Dr. of Year, Calif. St. Legislature 1984; mem: Am. Chiro Assn. (Councils on Roentgenology Tech., Nutrition, Neurology, Physiotherapy, Orthopedics; chmn. Nat. Vets Affairs Com.); mem. Am. Coll. of Chiro. Orthopedics, Calif. Chiro Assn. (chmn. State Vets Affairs Com., Conv., Seminars Com., Mbrshp Com.), S.D. County Chiro Soc. (past pres.; bd. dirs.), Parker Resrch Found.; publs: testing the cranial nerves, Chirogram 5/75; mem: CofC (dir. 1978-83), Escondido Kiwanis Club (dir.; dir. Klinic for Kids); past bd. dir. Escondido Boys & Girls Club; No. County ARC (bd. dir.); Le Tip Internat. Bus. Club (past pres.); Breakfast Bus. Club; Marine Corps Sgt Majors Assn.; Masons, York Rites, Scottish Rites, Shriners, VFW, F.R.A., Am. Legion, D.A.V. (dir.); Republican; Catholic; rec: fish, camp. Res: 650 N. Daisy St. Escondido 92027. Ofc: DuBois Chiropractic Clinic, 301 E. Washington Ave. Ste.A, Escondido 92025

DU CHIEN, HOWARD, import-export co. executive; b. Feb. 12, 1952, Martinez, Calif.; s. Harold L. and Lucille D. (Thomas) DuC.; m. Lola Chew, June 2, 1979; children: Howard Jr., Rupert; edn: AB, Coll. of the Pacific 1974; MBA, Pomona Coll. 1977. Career: bd. chmn. /CEO/ owner Howard DuChien & Co., Inc. (import/export); real estate developer, honors: Phi Beta Kappa; mem. Rotary, Kiwanis; Republican; Lutheran; rec: world travel, mountaineering, computer pgmmg. Ofc: H. DuChien & Co. 9493 Valle Vista Ste A, Forestville 95436

DUCKETT, ROY DELBERT, JR., organizational consultant; b. Oct. 16, 1938, Texarkana, Ark.; s. Roy, Sr. (gospel singer w/ Humming Bees of Texarkana) and Daisy Ora (Jackson) D.; edn: BA, Morehouse Coll. (Atlanta, Ga.) 1961; MA, Atlanta Univ. 1962; cert. London Sch. of Econ., U. of London (Eng.), 1962-3; postgrad. Wash. State Univ., 1963-4; MPH, UC Berkeley 1973; postgrad., Vista Coll. 1976-80, Laney Coll. 1978-80; cert. Profl. Legal Secty. (PLS), Coll. of Alameda 1982; D.D., ordained minister Universal Life Ch., Modesto 1981; John F. Kennedy Law Sch. 1981; cert. Legal Asst. Pgm., Merritt Coll. 1982-3; med./dental asst. tng. Oakland Coll. of Med. 1983-4. Career: tchg. asst. Dept. of Sociol., Wash. State Univ., 1963-4, instr. Dept. Sociol., Texas Southern Univ., 1964-5; epidemiol. coord. Calif. Div. Am. Cancer Soc., San Francisco 1966, and asst. svc. dir. 1968-72; social wkr. Dept. of Social Svcs, S.F. 1966; asst. supt. Soc. Svcs. S.F. Redevel. Agcy. A-2 Proj., 1966-68; adminstr. No. Oakland- Emeryville Children and Youth Project, Alameda Co. Hlth Care Svcs Agcy, Oakland 1973-78; profl. pub. typist, writer, orgnzl. cons., notary public, 1978--; pres. Roy D. Duckett, Jr., Oakland 1978--, pres. Dr. Roy D. Duckett, Jr. Church, Inc., 1978--; legal secty. Port Atty's Ofc., City of Oakland, 1981--; process server; awards: scholarship Morehouse Coll. (57-8), fellowship Atlanta Univ. (61-2), Charles E. Merrill Euro. Study-Travel grant (62-3). Mem: Am. Pub. Health Assn., Calif. Assn. of Photocopiers and Process Servers, Golden Age Total Emancipation Soc. Author: Witchcraft: A Digest; Money: A Digest; The light Skinned Negro: America's Greatest Threat; Wills; Sadism/ Masochism; How To Get Power; Pleadings and Court Cases: A Collection; journal arts. Republican (precinct capt.) rec: exercise, writing. Address: Roy D. Duckett, Jr., 1146 12th St. Oakland 94607

DUDLEY, MALCOLM HARDY, investment banker; b. Sept. 11, 1932, Santa Cruz, Calif.; s. Allen Mason and Gladys Alda (Hardy) D.; m. Cosette Spear, Mar. 9, 1954; children: Lynette, b. 1955; Virginia, b. 1967; edn: BA, UC Davis 1956; MA, London Sch of Econ. 1960; CFP (cert. fin. plnnr.), Coll. of Fin. Plnng. 1979. Career: stockbroker Dean Witter, Palo Alto 1962-72; vice pres./ mgr. Walston & Co., Palo Alto 1972-77; v.p. Prudential Bache Securities, Palo Alto 1977--; dir. Federal United Investment Fund, Palo Alto; instr. MBA pgm. Coll. of Notre Dame, Belmont; mayor/ city councilman Atherton, Calif; commnr. San Mateo Co. Local Agcy. Formation Commn.; mem. San Mateo Co. Regl. Plnng. Com., Airport Land Use Commn., various Atherton. coms.; author: Local Govt. Finance (1979); mil: served in USN, 5 yrs.; capt. USNR, currently; Republican; Episcopal; rec: musician (clarinet) Peninsula Sym., (saxophone) Dance Orch.; ski, tennis, golf. Res: 51 Catalpa Dr Atherton 94025 Ofc: Prudential Bache Securities, 525 University Ave, Ste 500, Palo Alto

DUDLEY, WILLIAM HAYNES, certified public accountant; b. Oct. 11, 1928, Oakland; s. Wm. Harrison and Marian Elizabeth (Haynes) D.; m. Norma Barber, Sept. 26, 1953; children: Michael, b. 1954; Kathleen, b. 1957; edn: BS, UC Los Angeles 1953. Career: assoc. acct. Ernst & Ernst, 1953, partner 1965-, partner in charge Los Angeles Ofc. 1972-79, dir. of acctg. & auditing Western Region Ernst & Whinney, 1979--, chmn. Govt. & Long Term Contracts com.; mem: AICPA, Calif. Soc. of CPAs, Nat. Assn. Accountants (pres. San Fernando Vly. chpt. 1964-5), Chancellors Assocs. UCLA; mil: m/sgt. US Army Inf. 40th Div. 1950-52, Bronze Star; Republican; Prot.; rec: tennis, Alaskan Malamute dogs, travel. Res: 15953 Skytop Rd Encino 91326 Ofc: Ernst & Whinney, 515 So Flower St, Ste 2700, Los Angeles 90071

DUEMLING, HUGH GERHARDT, artist/gallery owner; b. Feb. 15, 1952, Oakland; s. Eric Louis and Dorothy (Trimbell) D.; grad. San Leandro H.S. 1971. Career: art director The Changing Times, Las Vegas 1967; free lance artist, 1968--: cover art for Panorama Mag.; num. nightclub advts. for Circus Circus Casino, others; partner Home Grown Home Sewn boutique (spec. in women's illustrated fashion), Las Vegas 1975; onstage photog. Winterland, San Francisco, covering all major rock acts, 1975; owner Color By Hugh studio, Oakland 1980--; theatrical illus.; tchr. airbrush art; illustrated over 1,000 vans and show cars; founder Mirage Gallery (Jack London Sq., Oakland), gallery featured in CBS spl., A Dream Come True. Creator office murals; mag. covers for Off Road (1/81), Panorama Mag. (8/69), centerfold, Low Rider Mag.; rec: food. Address: Color by Hugh, 356 Dowling Bl. San Leandro 94577

DUFF, DAVID CARROLL, sales executive; b. Oct. 24, 1933, Stockton; s. Carroll Victor and Bernice Helen (Schorer) D.; m. Kathrine Wagner, June 16, 1961; dau., Gretchen Ann, b. 1962; edn: BS in eng., UC Los Angeles 1955, BS in meteorol., 1956; MBA, Pepperdine Univ. 1978. Career: with Douglas Aircraft, Santa Monica 1955; meteorologist USAF, 1955-59; preliminary design engr. Garrett AiResearch, 1959-60; applications engr. Transdynamics, Burbank 1961-64; field engr. Garrett Air Supply Co., 1964-81, mgr. distbr. ops. 1981-82, vice pres. Garrett Corp./mgr. Garrett Indsl. Supply Div., 1982--; mil: capt. USAF 1955-59; Republican; Presbyterian; rec: flying, skiing, camping. Res: 1646 Stonewood Ct. San Pedro 90732 Ofc: Garrett Ind. Supply Co, 6015 Randolph St Los Angeles 90040

DU FOSSE, PETER, corporate executive; b. Sept. 11, 1932, Hawthorne, NJ; s. Peter Wm. and Helena Marie (Wieme) du F.; m. Marjorie Dewan, Aug. 28, 1955; children: Ellen, b. 1956; Ann, b. 1957; Patricia, b. 1961; Ruth, b. 1969; Peter, b. 1974; edn: cert. electronic tech., RCA Insts. 1952; BSEE, Fairleigh Dickenson Univ. 1964. Career: engring. technician RCA, Harrison, NJ 1952-60; microwave engr./mfg. mgr. SFD Labs, Union, NJ 1960-73; engring. mgr. Litton Indus., Williamsport, Pa. 1973-78; product line mgr. Teledyne MEC, Palo Alto 1978-82, vice pres./div. mgr. Teledyne MEC, Mountain View 1982-84, sr. vice pres. Teledyne Microwave, 1984--; mem. IEEE, Assn. of Old Crows, Soaring Soc. of Am., Bay Area Soaring Assn., Pacific Soaring Council, Commonwealth Club; patentee: Microwave Mode Filter; mil: cpl. US Army 1952-54, GCM, Korean Conflict, S. Rhee Cit., Servie Medal; Republican; rec: sailplane pilot, racquetball, cycling. Res: 713 Ashbourne Dr Sunnyvale 94087 Ofc: Teledyne MEC, 3165 Porter Dr Palo Alto 94304

DUGAN, WILLIAM E. C., seafood co. president; b. May 25, 1957, Waltham, Mass.; s. James A. and Virginia Anne (Kelly) Dugan; edn: film stu., City Coll. S.F. Career: (fmr) constrn. foreman, scaffolding; mgr. seafood restaurant; sales Vaponics Water Purification, Silicon Valley area; sales Osprey Seafood; formed own corp. 1982, pres. Missing Link Brokerage (restaurant consulting, sales, pub. rels.), Calistoga 1982--; Awards: six film related cooking awds., sev. sales awds. Mem. Calistoga Yacht Club. Publs: seafood cookbook in progress; opr. saltwater acquarium (unique in Pac. N.W.); rec: sailing, fishing, wine tasting. Res/ofc: Missing Link Brokerage 16911 Hwy 128 Calistoga 94515

DUKESHERER, DAVID JOSEPH, air cargo co. president; b. Sept. 22, 1955, Los Angeles; s. Stanley J. and Mary J. (Thompson) D.; edn: BA, UCLA 1978. Career: acct. exec. WTC Airfreight 1973-78; v.p. ops. S/A Air Forwarding, Inc. 1978-79; owner/ exec. v.p. Federated Aircargo, Inc. 1979--; mem: Air Cargo Assn.; Calif. Trucking Assn.; Young Pres. Orgn.; L.A. Athletic Club; Sierra Club; NY Athletic Club; Ctr. for Entrepreneurial Mgmt.; Democrat; Catholic; rec: technical climbing. Res: 6690 Vista del Mar G, Playa del Rey 90291 Ofc: Federated Aircargo, Inc., 560-570 N. Oak St Inglewood 90302

DUKOW, ALBERT N., tax consultant; b. May 28, 1917, Phila.; s. Jacob J. and Sarah (Devine) D.; m. Henrietta Underberg, 1940; children: Vicki, b. 1941, Jeffrey B., b. 1943, Susan, b. 1950; edn: BA and BSc, Temple Univ. 1945; CPA, Penna. 1946. Career: tax cons./bus. mgmt.; pres. Edward C. James Co., pres. Affiliated Mgmt. Co., pres. Dukow and Assocs., Burbank; Dir: Andrew Investment Co., Able, Reddy & Willing, A & A Special Effects. Ofc: Dukow and Assocs. 4150 Riverside Dr. Burbank 91505

DULUDE, WM. J., consulting engineer; b. Feb. 14, 1927, Dassel, Minn.; s. Stephen E. and Clara (Boylan) D.; m. Barbara Hewitt, Sept. 18, 1954; children: Evert Michael, b. 1959; William Douglas, b. 1960; edn: BSEE, CalPoly Univ. 1952; Reg. Profl. Eng. in Ariz., Calif., Mont. Career: thirty-two years profl. experience as corporate ofcr., project and engring. mgmt., constrn. mgmt., and engring. design of utility and indsl. facilities; currently: vice pres./dir. SAI Engineers, Inc. 1976--; pres./dir SAI Constructors, Inc. 1983--; mem: IEEE, Constrn. Specification Inst., Engrs. Club of San Francisco; mil: seaman USN 1944-46; Republican; rec: cooking, fishing, woodworking. Res: 8211 Claret Ct San Jose 95135 Ofc: SAI Engineers, Inc. 3030 Patrick Henry Dr Santa Clara 95135

DUMKE, GLENN S., university chancellor, educator; b. May 5, 1917, Green Bay, Wis.; edn: AB, hist., Occidental Coll. 1938, AM 1939, LL.D 1960; PhD, UCLA 1942; H.L.D., Univ. Redlands 1962, LL.D, Univ. of Bridgeport (1963) Transylvania Coll. (1968), Pepperdine Coll. (1969), Hebrew Union Coll. (1968), Windham Coll. (1969), Our Lady of the Lake Univ. (1977), Dickinson

State Coll. (1978). Career: teaching asst. UCLA 1940-1; instr. history Occidental Coll.1940-43, asst. prof. 1943-46, assoc. prof. 1947-50, prof. history 1950, Norman Bridge prof. Hispanic Am. hist. 1954, dean faculty 1950-57; pres. San Francisco State Coll. 1957-61; vice chancellor, Calif. State Colls., L.A. 1961-62, chancellor Calif. State Univs. and Colls., 1962-82; pres. Inst. for Contemporary Studies, 1982--. Dir: Barclay Bank of Calif., The Olga Co.; author; contbr. profl. and popular publs. Methodist. address: 16332 Meadow Ridge Rd. Encino 91436

DUNAIANS, GEORGE STEPHAN, medical supply co. president; b. July 2, 1926, Ukraine, USSR, nat. 1960; s. Stephan and Nina (Haroutunian) D.; m. Flora Calusdian, Aug. 9, 1958; children: Deanne Gigi, b. 1960; Suzanne M., b. 1962; edn: AA, Pasadena City Coll. 1963. Career: supr. medical warehouse under the Marshall Plan, Iran 1950-54; office mgr. California Med. Supply, Inc., Pasadena 1955-67; pres./founder Western Medical Supply, Inc., Arcadia 1967--; awards: appreciation, Golden State Champion Horse Show 1981; mem: Calif. Veterinary Medical Assn., Am. Veterinary Distbr. Assn.; clubs: Lions, Arcadia Jaycees, US CofC, US Olympic Com. LA, Armenian Profl. Soc., Armenian Film Found.; Republican; Armenian Apostolic; rec: tennis, thoroughbred breeding. Res: 3375 E. Lombardy Rd Pasadena 91107 Ofc: Western Medical Supply, Inc. 117 E. Huntington Dr Arcadia 91006

DUNAS, ROMELLE BARBARA, real estate broker; b. May 11, 1931, Chgo.; d. John Charles and Dorothy (Zagon) Gross; div.; children: Jeffrey, b. 1954; Dorian Leigh, b. 1957; edn: BA, UC Los Angeles 1952; Calif. lic. real estate sales 1970, broker 1982. Career: real estate agt. Harleigh Sandler Co., now Merrill Lynch Realty, 1970--, vice pres. (1976-)/ sr. cons./ mgr. Rodeo Realty Div. (spec. in over one-mil. dollar props.); awards: Salesperson of the Year as top producer for the co. 1978, 1983 and Top Producer Brentwood Office; mem: Los Angeles Bd. of Realtors, Concern Found. for Cancer Research, Am. Diabetes Premiere Com., Royce 270 (UCLA Perf. Arts); Democrat; Jewish; rec: piano, needlepoint, knitting. Res: 13211 Haney Pl Los Angeles 90049 Ofc: Merrill Lynch Realty 11828 San Vicente, Los Angeles 90049

DUNCAN, ALICIA PATRICIA, retail executive; b. Apr. 10, 1924, Santa Clara; d. John and Mary (Aguiar) Rodrigues; m. Howard Baker 1944, div.1954; son, John, dec. 1960; m. 2d Keith Segrist 1955, dec.1965; m. 3d Boris Stanley 1969, div. 1970; m. E. Paul Duncan, Feb. 12, 1983; edn: CSU San Jose, 1948-50. Career: owner, mgr. Town & Country Bottle Shop, Cupertino 1950-70, Cupertino Liquors, Inc., 1958-70, Alicia's Boutique, Cupertino, 1978--, Real Estate, 1975--, A.P.S. Financial, 1977--; bd. dirs. San Jose Sym. 1972-6, San Jose Light Opera 1973-77, Cath. Soc. Service of Santa Clara Co. 1974-77, YMCA of San Jose 1974-76, Performing Arts League, 1975-80; pres. Crippled Chil. Soc. Santa Clara Co. 1975-77. Mem. Retail Liquor Dealers Assn., Saratoga CC, La Rinconada CC; active various polit. campaigns; Roman Catholic; Res: 14636 Springer Ct. Saratoga 95070. Ofc: PO Box 824 Saratoga 95070

DUNFIELD, JOHN CHARLES, electrical engineer; b. Mar. 26, 1939, St. Catherines, Ontario, Can., nat. 1972; s. George Ernest and Isabel Charlotte (Raynor) D.; m. Elizabeth Jones, Apr. 4, 1958; children: Stephen,b . 1959; George, b. 1964; Deborah, b. 1966; edn: BE Eng., honors, McGill Univ, Montreal 1962; PhD Elec. Eng., 1967; Reg. Profl. Engr., Quebec, Can. 1962-67; Career: principal engr. Sperry Flight Sys., Phoenix, Ariz. 1968-71; senior research engr. General Motors Research, Warren, Mich. 1971-72; eng. splst. Airesearch Mfg., Torrance 1972-73; elec. eng. mgr. Xynetics, Santa Clara 1973-76; elec. eng. mgr. Arbor Labs, Palo Alto 1976-78; principal scientist Xerox 1978--; lectr. McGill Univ. 1963-67; adj. prof. Ariz. State Univ. 1969; honors: University Scholar, McGill Univ. 1962; Canadian Mfrs. prize for Highest Study in Power; Phi Epsilon Alpha; wks: Super Conducting Magnet Design, MIT 1972; 4 Patents (assigned to Xerox 1982); publs: arts. in profl. jours.; mem: IEEE (Gen. Machine Com.); Prospect High Sch. Mens Club; Presbyterian (deacon 1979-82); rec: volley ball. Res: 1039 Craig Dr San Jose 95129 Ofc: Xerox Corporation, 26250 Industrial Blvd, Hayward 94545

DUNHAM, ROBERT LOUIS, investment securities account executive; b. Oct. 12, 1922, Neodasha, Kansas; s. Clayton Harold and Lena Ellen (Wright) Dunham; m. Mildred Nelson, Feb. 9, 1947; 1 dau. Pamela, b. 1957; edn: BBA, Woodbury Coll. 1947; Lic.: stockbroker, NASD 1961; Life & Dis. Agent, Calif. 1962; Regis. Rep. NY Stock Exchange 1962, Regis. Options Principle, 1982. Career: office mgr. Rath Packing Co., 1947-58; asst. to the pres. Parker Boiler Mfg. Co., 1958-61; regis. rep. William F. Marshall & Co., Anaheim 1961-2; acct. exec. Bateman, Eichler, Hill Richards Inc. (and predecessors to Wm. R. Staats & Co.), 1962--. Honors: elected Founding Gov. of Dist. #52, Toastmasters Internat.; frequent spkr. svc. and ednl. orgns. Mem: Toastmasters Internat. 1951-74; Oneonta Bus. & Profl. Men's Club 1961- (dir. 1968); VFW (Post Cmdr 1950); Pasadena Bus. Assn. 1969- (pres. 1972-3); Kiwanis Internat., Alhambra West Club 1961-70 (pres. 1966-7); Alhambra CofC 1961-. Mil: Petty Ofcr 1st Cl. USN 1943-6; Republican; Congregational; rec: golf. Res: 2325 Snead Dr Alhambra 91803 Ofc: Bateman Eichler, Hill Richards Inc. 277 So Lake Ave Pasadena 91101

DUNLAP, SUSAN CLAIRE, artist/designer; b. Jan. 15, 1948, Santa Rosa; d. Edwin Veghte and Marilyn Lucille (Keeler) D.; edn: int. design stu., CSU San Jose 1970, 74, 77, Foothill Comm. Coll. 1973, 77; grad. (MA in prog.), Fuller Theol. Sem. Career: badminton instr. Men's P.E. Dept. San Jose St. Univ., 1970; general artist Goodwill Indus., Santa Clara 1968-70; interior designer K.B.M. Office Furniture, San Jose 1970-73; dir. Int. Design Dept. H.S. Crocker Co., Inc. Santa Clara 1973-78; partner Dunlap Marconi Design Co.

(int. design firm), Palo Alto 1978-81; currently free lance artist/designer, Menlo Park; lectr: Owner-Builder Center 81-2, AAUW 82, Ch. Fellowship Gp. 83, Design Symp. Canada Coll. 83; cons. State Dept. of Alcohol & Drugs 1982; awards: service, City of Menlo Park 1984; Calif. State Scholarship 1968-70; mem: Mendocino Art Center 1979-82; Orgn. of Women Architects & Design Profls. (founding bd. 1974-6); El Gatito Coop. Gallery 1972; chmn. Environ. Beautification Commn. Menlo Park 1982-3; Menlo/Atherton AAUW (bd. 1982-3); works: Evening Good Trail & Great Spirit Path (commnd. City of Menlo Park), sculptural word-rock poems inspired by Indian pictographs, 500 tons of stone, 1800 foot path in city park, 1981-84; various soft sculpture commns. (jute, leather): Viking Freight System 1978, Syva/Syntex Corp. 1980; watercolor commn., Young Amb. Mag. 1983; media coverage KNTV 1980, 83; Democrat; Presbyterian (Singles Outreach Bd., nat. mission & evangelism coms.); rec: writing (book), composing music, gardening. Address: Susan Dunlap Design Co. 220 Chester St Menlo Park 94025

DUNN, JOHN MICHAEL, motor hotel executive; b. Oct. 29, Escondido; s. John Delano and Edna (Newell) D.; div.; chil: John Michael Jr. b. 1964; Patrick, b. 1966; John G., b. 1967; Jeff, b. 1967; Eric, b. 1970; edn: AA, (Hilton Outstanding Grad., Hotel & Rest. Dept.) City Coll. of S.F., 1966; BA, S.F. State, 1968; cert: prof., Hotel & Rest. Mgmt. Career: cook, bartender, hotel night clerk, -1967; conv. & sales, Hilton Hotels, S.F. 1967-68; restaurant mgr/ supr. Lyons Restaurants Inc., Burlingame 1968-70; gen. mgr./v.p. Hunters Inn, Santa Maria 1970-72; mng. gen. partner Topper Motor Hotel & Rest., Taft 1973--; mem: Nat., Calif. Restaurant Assns., Calif. Hotel Assn., Taft CofC, Kern Co. Bd. of Trade, Taft Petroleum Club; cons. to Kern Co. Supr. Trice Harvey; mil: USCG 1958-62; Democrat; Catholic; rec: golf, cooking, photog. Res: 501 A St., Taft 93268 Ofc: Topper Hotel, 101 E. Kern Ste 29, Taft 93268

DUNN, MITCHELL LEROY, electrical contracting firm executive; b. May 28, 1953, Roswell, N.M.; s. Max L. and Doreen Lilian (May) D.; edn: AA, Citrus Coll. 1975; BS in E.E., CalPoly Univ. Pomona 1977; Reg. Elec. Engr. Calif. 1980. Career: elec. foreman Anco Electric, Glendora 1978-80; gen. foreman Anhauser Busch project L.A., C.F. Braun, 1980-81; elec. foreman Southland Elec., So. Pasadena 1981-83, Commerce Electric, San Diego 1983--; honors: Electrical Suprvn. Award of Year 1980, C.F. Braun; mem: Internat. Brotherhood Elec. Workers Local 11, Mgmt. Bus. Professionals Los Angeles, vol. Boys Club of Am.; works: clamp on level 1980; Republican; Free Methodist; rec: boating. Res: 976 W. Foothill, Ste 223, Claremont 92711 Ofc: Commerce Electric, 519 So Cedras Solana Beach 92705

DUNN, PHILIP HOWARD, lawyer; b. May 11, 1947, Billericky, Chelmsford, Eng.; s. Dr. Richard C. and Irene I. (Snelson) D.; edn: AA, Santa Monica City Coll. 1968; BS in bus., CSU Long Beach 1-0; JD, Whittier Coll. Sch of Law 1977; admitted to practice US Supreme Ct., Calif. Supreme Ct. Career: 2 years law clerk to Command Judge Advocate, Fort Ord, Calif.; 2 years law clerk to three judges, L.A. Municipal Ct.; law clerk Pub. Defenders Office; pvt. law practice/ pres. Dunn & Roth, Santa Monica 1977--; rep. plaintiffs in case of Harrison vs. Yong (LASC 355875), after 5 week jury trial received largest verdict (1.3 mil. dollars) in the country ever in a habitability case; mem: Santa Monica Bar Assn., L.A. Trial Lawyers Assn.; mil: sp4 US Army 1971, GCM; rec: ski, sail, surf, soaring, karate, chess. Ofc: Dunn & Roth, PC, 2953 Lincoln Blvd Santa Monica 90405

DUNN, RUBY HAUCK, publisher; b. Aug. 18, 1920, Hanford; d. Hiram Daniel and Amelia (Walter) Hauk; div.; children: Michael, b. 1947; Albert, b. 1948; Wendy, b. 1951; Maureen, b. 1953; edn: legal sectyl., Woodbury Bus. Coll. 1939-40. Career: legal secty., 1941, 1943-46; clk. (1st woman hired), Army Air Base, Lemoore, Calif. 1942; owner/opr. small letter shop, expanded to full print shop, 1953-70; estab. advt. bus. (buy/sell advt. media) in Lake County, 1970, estab. advt. bus. in Siskiyou Co. Paradise No. Shore Tahoe (Kings Beach), sold in 1979; estab. El Dorado Gold Panner (weekly advt. publication), Placerville 1979--; ptnr. with son/pub. The Scrounger (semi-mo. publication for vintage car buffs), and ptnr. in old-timey Country Store; honors: recogn. awards from Downtown Assn. (3), and Mentally Retarded Assn.; mem: Downtown Assn. (bd. dirs.), Legal Secy's Assn., The Venturers Club, Soroptimist, CofC; Ch. of Christ; rec: writing, travel, music. Address: El Dorado Gold Panner, 1641 Pleasant Valley Rd Placerville 95667

DUPPER, FRANK F., health services executive; b. Jan. 20, 1933, La Salle, Colo.; s. Henry and Caroline (Beierle) D.; m. Norma Jean Eder, June 24, 1956; children: Debbie, b. 1960; Brent, b. 1963; edn: BA, Union Coll. 1954. Career: treas., asst. bus. mgr., acct. tchr. Newbury Park Acad. (sec. boarding high sch.) 1959-64; controller Glendale Sanitarium & Hosp. 1964-68; asst. adminstr./dir. fin. Glendale Adventist Hosp. 1968-72; vp for finance Glendale Adventist Med. Ctr., 1974-79; exec vp (1979-80), pres. Adventist Health System-West, 1980--; cons. Loma Linda Univ. 1981-2; awards: Wm. G. Follmer (1975), Robt. H. Reeves (1979), Hosp. Fin. Mgmt. Assn.; Hosp. Council of So. Calif. Awd. for outstanding service to hosp. industry, 1979; mem: Hosp. Fin. Mgmt. Assn. (Fellow, CMPA); Am. Acad. of Med. Adminstrs.; Am. Coll. of Hosp. Adminstrs.; Am., Ariz., Calif. Hospital Assns.; Am. Mgmt. Assn.; Am. Protestant Hosp. Assn.; Hospital Council of So. Calif.; publs: art., Hosp. Forum Mag. 11/75; 7th-day Adventist; rec: gardening. Res: 716 Avonglen Terrace Glendale 91206 Ofc: Adventist Health System-West, 1545 No Verdugo Rd Glendale 91208

DURRANT, MORRIS HOLDING, lawyer; b. May 21, 1913, Salt Lake City, Utah; s. Joseph Smith and Lenora (Holding) D.; m. Nellie, Sept. 13, 1975; 1

child, Kinda Turner, b. 1948; edn: AB, Univ. of Utah 1934; LLB, JD, UC Berkeley 1939; admitted Calif. State Bar 1939; cert. criminal law splst., Calif. State Bar 1973. Career: solo county lawyer, 1939-42; acting judge advocate Harbor Defenses of San Francisco, 1942-46; criminal defense lawyer over No. Calif. 1946-64; prosecuting atty. and dist. atty. Plumas County, 1964-74; semiret. criminal and mining lawyer, part-time dirt farmer, 1974-; honors: Univ. of Utah class poet and State Champion poet 1934; Phi Alpha Delta (legal), Sigma Upsilon (lit.) frats.;Presdtl. commend. for 25 years free service as advisor to mil. Registrants, 1967; mem: Plumas Co. Bar Assn. (pres. 1969); Western Mining Counsel (pres. Plumas chpt. 1950-53); Masons; Deputy Dist. Gov. Lions 1946; Dist. Comdr. Am. Legion 1950; Elks; Seniors in Retirement; Noble Grand Humbug E.C.V. 1950-53; Quincy Cemetery Bd. 1970-73; mil: t/sgt 9th Service Cmd., SF 1942-46; Republican; Christian Sci.; rec: golf, organ playing. Res: POB 576 Durham 95938 Ofc: 10114 Jones Ave, Durham 95938

DUSAY, KATHERINE MULHOLLAND, psychotherapist; b. Sept. 17, 1943, Lebanon, Penna.; d. Richard F. (M.D.) and Winnifred (Barto) Mulholland; m. John M. Dusay, MD (psychiatrist, neurologist, and prof. UCSF Sch. of Med.); chil: John Van Deren, b. 1978, Alexandra Barteau, b. 1982; edn: BA, CSU San Francisco 1974, MA in English (1976), MA in psychol. (1975), Univ. of San Francisco; PhD cand., Calif. Coast Univ. 1984; lic. MFCC, Marriage, Family & Child Counselor, 1975; tng.: Western Inst. for Gp. and Family Therapy 1972-75, Family Therapy Inst. 1975-77, spec. tng. (2,000 hours) with Drs. Eric Berne, John M. Dusay, Robert Goulding, Mary Goulding, MSW, Les Kadis, MD, Ruth McClendon, MSW and others. Career: pvt. practice 1974--; cofounder, dir., vice pres. Professional Evaluation Services (psychol. testing corp.), San Francisco and Palo Alto; founding mem./dir. emeritus Continental Sav.& Loan; co-tchr. with John M. Dusay, MD, all-day workshops to Am. Psychiatric Assn. in various cities 1972-; internat. lectr. Europe, Japan, India, S. Am., Mex.; guest lectr. Diet Workshop Series, 1980; num. radio, TV, print media interviews; TV host BBProds. (Feeling Good and Looking Good) 26-wk. series, 1984. Publs: coauthor Having A Baby (Dell 1984); ed. Egograms: How I See You and You See Me (Harper & Row 1976); chpt., Current Psychotherapies (Peacock & Sons 1975, 80, 84). Mem: Internat. Transactional Analysis Assn., Calif. Assn. of Marriage and Family Counselors, Madras Transactional Analysis Assn., India (hon. pres.), Nat. Alliance for Family Life; bd.dirs. RoundTable Found., Childrens Theatre Wkshop; vol. Children As Teachers of Peace. Rec: family, writing, theatre, travel; address: 2709 Jackson St. San Francisco 94115

DUTTON, DONALD STEVEN, information systems executive; b. Mar. 10, 1947, Kalispell, Mont.; s. Donald Zedoc and Roberta Estella (Lewis) D.; edn: Grays Harbor JC 1965-6; BBA, National Univ. 1977, MBA 1980; cert. computer sci., Coleman Coll. 1975, cert. data processing, Inst. for the Cert. of Computer Profls. 1982. Career: asst. date processing supr. Allied Administrators, San Diego 1972-3; computer ops. Rohr Ind., Inc., Chula Vista 1973-7, comp. pgmmr. analyst 1977-9; sr. pgmmr./analyst Foodmaker Inc., S.D. 1979-80, system project leader 1980-1, software apps. mgr. 1981-4; mgr. Systems, Denny's Inc., La Mirada 1984--; adj. faculty National Univ. 1980-3, UCSD 1983-4; information systems cons. City of Carlsbad 1983-4; profl. seminars, S.D. Rcgl. Tng. Ctr. 1983-4; mem: D.P. Mgmt. Assn. (bd. dirs. S.D. chpt. 1981-3, com. chmn.), Toastmasters (past pres.), S.D. Blood Bank; mil: E4 US Army 1966-70; Christian. Res: 26817 Poveda Mission Viejo 92691 Ofc: Denny's Inc. 16700 Valley View Ave La Mirada 90637

DUTTON, ROBIN ELLEN, interior decorator; b. Oct. 11, 1945, Lennox, Calif.; d. Wm. Walter Joseph and Rose (Leibovitz) Cook; m. John Maynard Dutton, Sept. 6, 1980; edn: grad. South H.S., Torrance 1963; study year, Geo. Wash. Univ. Career: staff US Information Service, New Delhi, India, Brussels, Belgium, and Belgrade, Yugoslavia 1969-77, USIA study grantee 1975-6; ins. broker spec. in Fine Arts Ins., Los Angeles 1977-82; interior decorator Interiors by Robin, Marina Del Rey, 1983--; Republican. Address: Interiors by Robin, 4346 Redwood Ave Marina Del Rey 90292

DUVAL, SALLY VIRGINIA, speech pathologist; b. May 11, 1929, Susanville (3d gen. Californian); d. Paul T. and Kathryn (Breitwieser) Wemple; m. Marvin J. Duval, June 19, 1971; children: Robert (b. 1955), Kathryn (b. 1957), Paul (b. 1960), Scott (b. 1962) Cathcart; edn: BA, UC Berkeley 1951, Gen. Sec. cred. 1962; speech pathol., CSU San Francisco 1969. Career: speech pathologist Richmond Unified Sch. Dist., tchr. of Aphais-Language Disordered children; workshop lectr. Good Teaching Conf.; mem: Calif. Assn. Neurologically Handicapped Children; Alpha Omicron Pi Sor. Alumni; DAR; Republican; Episcopal. Res: 55 Donna Maria Way Orinda 94563

DVORACEK, ROBERT, jeweler/goldsmith; b. Apr. 10, 1930, Bratislava, Czech., nat. 1976; s. Robert and Emilie (Brzkova) D.; m. Kvetoslava Havlanova, Aug. 25, 1956; dau., Eugenie Marie, b. 1956; edn: Bach. in bus., Dr. Petr Zenkl Bus. Acad., Prague 1947; goldsmith-jeweler, Indsl. Art Sch., Jablonec Nad Nisou, Czech. 1951; Bach., Indsl. Art Sch., Turnov, Czech. 1961; named Court Expert in precious metals/ stones for County of Prague 1967. Career: sentenced (for political disagreement) to hard labor in coal mines, Czech. 1951-54; goldsmith, govt. goldsmith and antique repair workshop, Klenoty 1954-67; Court Expert in precious metals/ stones, and prop. own studio, Prague 1967-68; polit. emigre to US in 1968; goldsmith (w/brother in law) Glasner & Teba, Beverly Hills 1968-71; jewelry mfr., gem importer, mail-order sales, 1971-, opened own shop Robert's Jewelry, Bev. Hills 1974--; pvt. instr. in gold mfg.; mem. Czech. Soc. of Arts & Scis., Sokol Club, Czech. Nat.

Council of Am., Czech Culture Club; founder/gen. secty. PTP Club (estab. in Prague May 26, 1968 to claim rehabilitation of rights for the politically persecuted, 4,000 attended), a resolution of rehab. was presented to Czech. Pres. and cabinet; Democrat; Catholic; rec: soccer, fishing, chess, gardening. Res: 3213 Cardiff Ave Los Angeles 90034 Ofc: Robert's Jewelry, 9413 Brighton Way Beverly Hills 90210

DWORAK, JOSEPH EDWARD, lawyer; b. Feb. 4, 1954, Richmond; s. Otto Emil and Helen Roberta (Porter) D.; m. Mary Simon, Aug. 18, 1978; edn: BA, honors, UC Davis 1976; JD, Univ. of Santa Clara 1979; grad. tax wk., Golden Gate Univ. 1982; admitted to practice Calif. State Bar, 9th Circuit Ct. of Appeals, US Dist. Cts. Career: campaign coordinator Cong. George Miller, Contra Costa Co. 1976; law clerk (1977-9), atty. law firm Berliner, Cohen & Biagini, San Jose 1979--; instr. UC Santa Cruz, Paralegal Inst. 1981-; honors: Omicron Delta Epsilon (econ.), State Scholarship recipient, chosen as UC Davis Intern in Wash DC; mem: Santa Clara County Bar Assn., Calif. Trial Lawyers Assn., Masons; elected mem. City of San Jose Block Grant Devel. Pgm. 1983-; law rev. arts.; Democrat; Lutheran; rec: rugby. Res: 125 So 14th St San Jose 95112 Ofc: Berliner, Cohen & Biagini, 99 Almaden Blvd, Ste 400, San Jose 95113

DYE, PATSY RUTH MC CASLIN, service co. executive; b. Apr. 23, 1940, Fort Smith, Ark.; d. Robert H. and Ruth (Cosand) McCaslin; div.; children: Robert, b. 1960; Keith, b. 1965; James, b. 1969; edn: Taft Jr. Coll. 1958-59; Lufkins Bus. Coll. 1961. Career: ins. clk. Bakersfield Svgs. & Loan, 1961-62, clk. Reynolds Elec. & Engring. Co., Mercury, Nev. 1964-66, US Post Ofc. Tucson, 1968-71; v.p. sales Coupon Clearing Service, 1974--; freelance writer Taft Newspapers, 1977; ptnr. small mktg. consulting firm, Ludwig & McCaslin, 1983--; mktg., promo. cons. Ludwig Studios (Art) 1983-84; mem: New Member Promotion Mktg. Assn. of Am., Orange County Sales Club, Illuminators; Republican; Prot.; rec: writing, hiking. Ofc: Coupon Clearing Service, 1612 Babcock St. Costa Mesa 92627; POB 7050, Newport Beach 92660

DYER, ANDREW ROY, corporate planner; b. Apr. 30, 1951, Nashville, Tenn.; s. Andrew Johnson and Gladys Marie (Kelly) D.; edn: BS, math., Univ. Tenn. 1973; BE in EE, Vanderbilt Univ. 1974; MBA, fin., Univ. of Tenn. 1975. Career: prin. systems analyst Teledyne Brown Engring., Huntsville, Ala. 1976-78; ops. auditor Data-Design Labs., Cucamonga 1978-80; sr. acctg. systems analyst Calif. Fed. Svgs., Los Angeles 1980-81; sr. mem. tech. staff Teledyne Systems Co., Northridge 1981--; awards: Best Economic Forecaster for 1979, So. Calif. Corp. Planners Assn.; Outstanding Young Men in Am. 1981; recognition, Planning Execs. Inst. 1980, 81; Sturges Mem. Scholarship, Univ. of Tenn.; mem: Planning Execs. Inst. (vp LA chpt. 1981-2); So. Calif. Corp. Planners Assn. (treas. 1980-81); World Future Soc. (pres. LA chpt. 1979-80); fellow Brit Interplanetary Soc.; IEEE; Am. Inst. of Acro. and Astro.; Am. Mktg. Assn.; Assn. of MBA Execs.; Assn. of Old Crows; Assn. for Corp. Growth; Acad. of Sci. Fiction, Fantasy and Horror Films; ACLU, NOW, Sierra Club, Orgn. for Adv. of Space Indsln. and Settlement, LA Sci. Fantasy Soc., Mensa, Intertel, Astronomical Soc., Planetary Soc.; rec: astronomy. Res: 22446 Burbank Blvd Woodland Hills 91367 Ofc: Teledyne Systems Co. 19601 Nordhoff St Northridge 91367

DYER, PAUL F., gymnastic center owner/coach; b. Aug. 25, 1950, Chgo.; s. Frederick T. and Mable A. (Johnson) D. Career: gymnastics coach 1969-, head· coach/ dir./ owner Baldy View Gymnastic Center, Upland 1976--, afil. with Olympic Devel. Pgm., have produced local, district, state and regional champions in girls' gymnastics; mem: US Gymnastic Fedn., So. Calif. Women's Gym. Assn., Nat. Judges Assn.; Democrat; rec: flying, racquetball, chess, handball. Address: Bald View Gymnastic Center, 8175 Monte Vista St Upland 91786

DYER, ROBERT JAMES, real estate investments executive; b. Jan. 7, 1933, Moline, Ill.; s. Floyd Alvin and Bernyce Madeline (Fogarty) D.; m. Carol Fisher, Sept. 3, 1955; children: Merrick James, b. 1956; Loni Ann, b. 1957; Michael Robert, b. 1959; Maura Lynn, b. 1968; edn: phys. ed. Willamette Univ. 1951-5, AA in real estate Gavilan Comm. Coll. 1979; MBA, Ariz. St. Univ. 1967; spl. courses Air Univ., Maxwell AFB 1973. Career: exec. vice pres. Kentwood Realty, Inc. 1977-80; pres. R. J. Real Property Investments, Inc., 1980--; real estate cons. CofC Economic Devel. Council; served to Col. USAF: Master Navigator, 10,000 hours, 300 combat hours in Vietnam, Chief of Personnel 1972-74, Squadron Comdr. 1974-75, Chief of Protocol (Cincsac) 1975-77; honors: Iota Sigma Epsilon, service awards, Wheeler Hosp. Found. Bd., CofC; mem: Rotary, Reserve Ofcrs Assn. AF, Phi Delta Theta, CofC (bd. dirs. 1978-84, pres. 1973), founder of Gilroy Found. (bd. dirs. 1980),Gilroy Garlic Festival (bd. dirs. 1984); publs: arts. in profl. jours.; mil. awards: D.F.C., Merit. Svc. (2 Clusters), Presdtl. Unit Cit., AF Outstanding Unit, Commendation, Repub. of Vietnam, Gallantry Cross, Airmens Medal; Republican; Episcopal; rec: tennis, golf, fishing. Res: 1341 Cedar Ct. Gilroy 95020 Ofc: R.J. Dyer Real Property Investments, Inc. 101 Green Valley Dr Gilroy 95020

DYER, VICKI SUE, procurement specialist; b. Jan. 16, 1953, Wheeling, W.Va.; d. Charles T. and Margaret L. (Piatt) D.; two sons, David, b. 1972, Steven, b. 1977; edn: cert. Eaton Bus. Coll. 1976; BS, State Univ. NY 1982. Career: tax consultant H&R Block, Hawaii and Calif. 1971-74; real estate agt. Century 21, San Diego 1975-76; asst. dir. Naval Aviation Logistics Center, NAS North Island, 1977-81; procurement splst. General Management Systems, San Diego 1981--; cons. in procurement for small bus.; mem: Am. Mgmt. Assn.,

Nat. Assn. of Female Execs., Assn. of Naval Aviation; orgns: Santee American Little League, BSA, Armed Services YMCA; Democrat; Methodist. Res: 9331 Carlton Oaks Dr, 83, Santee 92071 Ofc: General Mgmt. Systems, 3737 Camino del Rio So, Ste 309, San Diego 92108

E

EANEMAN, JAMES MICHAEL, public utility manager; b. June 19, 1945, Oakland; s. Robert G. and Margaret (Mahoney) E.; m. Margaret Ann Mc Crea, Dec. 4, 1982; edn: BS in econ./hist., CSU Chico 1968; MBA mgmt., Pepperdine Univ. 1980. Career: with Pac. Gas & Elec. Co., 1968--, mgmt. trainee 1968, supervisory positions in Oakland and Berkeley, 1969-72, corporate analyst, San Francisco 1972-74, San Jose Div., 1975, Dist. Customer Svcs. supr. for Santa Clara Co., 1978, apptd. Berkeley Area mgr. 1979, Corporate Project mgr., 1982-83, apptd. No. San Mateo Co. District mgr., 1983--; awards: appreciation for comm. svc., Daly City Council 1983, Berkeley CofC 1981; mem: Am. Mgmt. Assn., Pacific Coast Gas and Elec. Assns., pres. Berkeley CofC 1981-3, Berkeley Pvt. Indus. Council (bd.dirs.), Berkeley YMCA, Berkeley Breakfast Club and Ctr for Ind. Living, ARC, Rotary, Commonwealth Club of Calif. Republican. Roman Catholic. rec: restoring antique furniture, record collector, sports. Res: 517 Jackson St. Albany 94706. Ofc: PG&E, 450 Eastmoor Ave. Daly City 94015.

EBENEZER, DANIEL J., cardiologist; b. May 26, 1948, Madras, India; nat. 1977; s. S.G. and Julia (Samuel) E.; m. Padmini, May 16, 1973; children: Benjamin, b. 1977, David, b. 1979; edn: MD, Univ. of Madras, India 1972; bd. cert. Am. Bd. of Internal Medicine 1982. Career: senior house surgeon Univ. of Madras 1970-71; registrar, asst. lectr. in anat. Univ. of Jipmer, India 1972-73; postgrad. splty. tng. 1973-79; currently, cardiologist in pvt. practice, Roseville, Calif.; awards: First prize in anaesthesiol. in med. sch. 1970; mem: Calif. Med. Assn., Am. Coll. of Cardiol., Am. Heart Assn.; club: Carriage Racquet (Roseville); publs: med. jour. arts.; Christian; rec: tennis, ski, music, gardening. Res: 1123 Coral Dr Roseville 95678 Ofc: Daniel Ebenezer MD Inc. 406 Sunrise Roseville 95678

EBERHARDT, L. RUTHE, manufacturing co. executive; b. Oct. 23, 1939, Hamilton, Ont., Can.; d. Harold and Lila (Reeves) Thorneycroft; m. Peter Eberhardt, Aug. 17, 1969; 1 dau. J. Antoinette, b. 1966; edn: Long Beach City Coll., Woodbury Coll. Career: secty. to Zone Mgr., Studebaker Automotive Sales Corp., Los Angeles 1962-64; secty. to pres. Volkswagen Pacific, Inc.,Culver City 1964-73; vice pres./dir. of mktg. B & E Enterprises, Huntington Beach 1973--; recipient Am. Legion Awd., Narbonne H.Sch. 1953; inventor: Houndstooth Automotive Floor Mats. Res: 46 Rocky Knoll, Irvine 92715. Ofc: B & E Enterprises, 15301 Springdale St Huntington Bch 92649.

EBERLE, BARBARA JANE, doll artist; b. Jan. 12, 1945, Lodi; d. Paul Julian and Fay Louise (Williams) Withers; m. Dallas L. Aultman, Oct. 14, 1963, (dec. 1963); m. 2d. Pius Eberle, July 26, 1969; children: Tammy, b. 1964; Joseph, b. 1970; Molly, b. 1972. Career: doll artist, and teacher antique reproduction porcelain doll making. Res: 608 W. Locust, Lodi 95240

EBERLE, CLAMORE DALE, lawyer; b. May 17, 1951, Oceanside; s. Dr. Byron Taylor and Helen Louise (Brunker) E.; m. Paula Jeaninne Nothdurft, Mar. 10, 1979; 1 son, Clamore Dale, b. 1979; edn: BA, Elmhurst Coll. 1974; JD, Southwestern Univ. Sch. of Law 1980; admitted State Bar of Calif. 1980. Career: self empl. political consultant 1975; securities transaction analyst US Treasury, Wash DC 1976-78; disaster counsel US Small Business Adminstrn., Burbank 1980-81; partner law firm Eberle & Jordan, Glendale 1982--; partner Automated Office Concepts 1982-; Law Office Automation cons. 1980-82; awards: Pi Gamma Mu (soc. sci.) 1973; Outstanding Young Man of Am. 1979; Nat. Treasury Employees Union local 199 (pres. 1977-8); mem. Calif. State, Los Angeles County (law week com.), Glendale, Glendale Financial Sq., and Federal Bar Assns.; author computer software packages in legal and ednl. fields; rec: life mem. US Chess Fedn. Res: 1133 Justin Ave Glendale 91201 Ofc: Eberle & Jordan, 225 W. Broadway, Ste 500, Glendale 91204

EBERT, MARLIN J, nuclear engineer/company president; b. Dec. 2, 1938, Abington, Pa.; s. Stanley Faulkner and Sarah Jane (Heilman) E.; m. Norma Smith, Jan. 23, 1982; children (by previous marriage): Winfrey, b. 1961, Nina, b. 1964, Benjamin, b. 1970; edn: BS (distinguished military grad.), Penna State Univ. 1961, MSc in biophysics, 1963; Reg. Profl. Nuclear Engr. (NU 001649) Calif. 1978. Career: research nuclear engr. Nuclear Materials and Equip. Corp./ARCO, Apollo, Pa. 1968-70; sr. radioactive isotope prod. Gen. Elec. Nuclear Energy Div., Pleasanton, CA 1970-76; pres. & CEO, Life Science Systems, Inc., Livermore 1976--; instr. Chabot Colf. 1974-; cons. to USN, Alameda 1978-; city councilman, City of Livermore 1978-82; awards: Nat. Def. Education act Fellowship 1961-63; mem: Soc. of Nuclear Medicine (full mem.) 1973-; Health Physics Soc. 1968-76; Masons; Eagles; US Naval Sailing Assn.; inventor: NucleClean Anticontamination Kit (1976); co-devel.: (Xenon-133 radioactive gas) Xe-133 Ventilation Study System (1973); mil: capt., Active Duty, 1963-68, 2 yrs. Vietnam, paratrooper pilot, 2 Bronze Stars, 15 Air Medals, Vietnamese Cross of Gallantry w/palm; Republican; Swedenborgian; rec: fishing, sailing, woodworking, politics. Res: 1182 Burgundy Way Livermore 94550 Ofc: Life Science Systems, Inc. 4049 First St Livermore 94550

EBINER, ROBERT MAURICE, lawyer, b. Sept. 2, 1927, Los Angeles; m. Paula H. Van Sluyters, 1951; children: John, Lawrence, Marie, Michael, Christopher, Joseph, Francis, Matthew, Therese, Kathleen, Eileen, Brian, Patricia, Elizabeth, Ann; edn: Bach., Loyola Univ., L.A. 1949, JD, Loyola Univ. Sch of Law 1953. Career: general, civil and trial law practice, W. Covina 1954--; judge pro tem Los Angeles Superior Ct., Citrus Municipal Ct.; arbitrator Am. Arbitration Assn. 1965-, L.A. Superior Ct. 1979-; instr. of law Alhambra H.S. eve. 1955-58; Disciplinary Hearing Panel, Calif. State Bar; mem. Fed. Court So. Dist. of Calif. Mem. Am., Calif., L.A. Co., Eastern (pres.1965-6) and Citrus (arts., Citrus Bar Bull. 1962-3) Bar Assns.; founder Queen of Valley Hosp. 1959; mem. Hosp. Mem's Club 1971- (bd. dirs. 1973-6); trustee Queen of the Valley Found. 1983-; mem. Catholic Welfare Bur., Archdiocese of LA (San Gabriel Valley pres. 1956-60, budget chmn. 56-69); mem. Catholic Social Services, San Gabriel Valley (pres. 1969-72, bd. 69-74); charter bd. dirs. Am. Cancer Soc. N.E. Los Angeles Co. Unit 1973-78 (chmn. By-laws com.); bd. dirs. W. Covina United Fund 1958-61 (chmn. Budget com. 60-61); orgnzr. Jt. United Funds of E.San Gabriel Valley (bd.dirs. 1961-8); charter bd.dirs. United Way, L.A. Co. Area V, 1962-70 (Budget Panel chmn. 1980). Mem: West Covina CofC (pres. 1960); Knights of Columbus (3rd deg.1955-, Advocate 1973-4); Bishop Amat H.Sch. Booster Club (pres. 1978-80, bd.dir. 1973-); charter, Kiwanis Club of W. Covina 1958- (pres. 1976-7, bd.dirs. 72-, Inter.Club chmn. Div. 35, 1977-8, Amb. for CA-NV-HA Found. 1978-9, Lt. Gov. Kiwanis Div. 35, 1980-1, Kiwanian of the Year 1978 & 1983). Recipient Disting. Service Award 1978, LA Co. Human Rels. Commn.; mem. LA Co. Dist. Atty. Adv. Council, 1974-. Democrat (cmpgn. mgr. Cong. Ronald B. Cameron 1964, State Central Com. 1963-8). rec: fishing, collector hist. memorabilia. Res: 2734 Sunset Hill Dr. W. Covina Ofc: 1502 W. Covina Pky. West Covina 91790.

EBIO, NORA LABASBAS, dentist; b. Aug. 9, 1931, Sorsogon, Philippines, nat. 1974; d. Heracleo and Andrea (Diamante) Labasbas; m. Ernesto Diaz Ebio, June 1, 1949; children: Maria Jeane (Medeiros), b. 1950; Linda, b. 1952; Rosabella (Reyes), b. 1954; Marybelle (Tanjoco), b. 1957; Cecilia, b. 1963; edn: BA, Univ. of the East 1960, DMD, 1965; DDS, Calif. 1965. Career: dentist, West Oakland Health Center 1977, dental director Dental Dept., 1978-80; opened pvt. dental practice, Oakland 1978--, part-time dentistry, W. Oakland Health Ctr.; mem. Am. Dental Assn., Filipino Dental Soc.; rec: needlework. Res: 5826 Greenridge Rd, Castro valley 94546 Ofc: Nora L. Ebio, DMD, Gen. Dentistry, 1624 Franklin St., Ste. 702, Oakland 94612

ECHEVERRIA, RODOLFO R., lawyer; b. Jan. 2, 1950, El Paso, Tex.; s. Prisciliano and Carmen (Gomez-Leon) E.; m. Consuelo, Aug. 5, 1978; edn: BA, Univ. of Tex., El Paso 1972; JD, USC 1976; admitted to Calif. State Bar 1976. Career: law clerk, associate, and currently, partner in law firm of Schwartz, Steinsapir, Dohrmann & Krepack, Los Angeles; career mgr. to wife Consuelo Echeverria, a profl. entertainer; mem: Am., Calif. State, Los Angeles County, Mexican-Am. Bar Assns., L.A. Trial Lawyers Assn.; Democrat; Catholic; rec: sports, music. Res: 1007 S. Windsor, Los Angeles 90019 Ofc: Schwartz, Steinsapir, Dohrmann & Krepack, 3435 Wilshire Blvd, Ste 2950, Los Angeles 90010

ECKHAUS, LEONARD I., company president; b. Sept. 18, 1942, NYC; s. Sidney A. and Hortense E.; m. Linda Rosenthal, July 11, 1962; children: Lee, b. 1966, Jill, b. 1969; edn: Newburgh Free Acad. 1957-60, Orange Co. Comm. Coll. 1960-62. Career: senior computer opr. IBM Corp., Poughkeepsie, NY 1967-70; mgr. Eastern Region Data Centers, TRW Inc., NYC 1970-71; network control mgr. TRW Inc., Anaheim, Calif. 1971-73, mgr. operational planning 1973-74; asst. dir. data processing ops. Los Angeles County Supt. of Schools, Downey 1974-81; pres. Data Center Management Services, Anaheim 1981--; recognized by D.P. indus. as the leader in the computer ops. field; mem: Assn. for Computer Ops. Mgrs. (founding pres. 1980), Internat. Congress of Jewish Marriage Encounters (pres. 1980-81), Jewish Marriage Encounters in So. Calif. (bd. dirs. 1979-81); publs: num. tech. and mgmt. arts. in The Computer Operations Mag., media coverage in Computerworld (4/81); Jewish; rec: woodwork, bowling, music. Res: 13291 Heather Circle Garden Grove 92640 Ofc: Data Center Mgmt Services, 11501 Brookhurst, Ste 201, Garden Grove 92640

EDDLESTON, BABETTE BAUMAN, artist, writer, educator; b. Dec. 28, 1922, NY, NY; d. Emmanuel Wm. (D.D.S.), and Miriam (Oppenheimer, LL.D.) Bauman; m. Monroe A. Edelstein, Sept. 1946, div.; children: David Alan Stone, b. 1944; Aimee Edith Rodriguez, b. 1948; edn: Art Students League, NYC 1939-40, Columbia Univ. 1944-6, New Sch. for Social Resrch. 1948-52, Pratt Graphic Inst.; BFA arch., Cooper Union, NYC 1956; Calif. Lifetime Teaching Cert. in Adult Edn. 1967; Calif. Comm. Colls. Instr. Cred. (fine and applied arts) 1978. Career: designer/prop. own art studio: landscape painter in oils (1940-); printmaker, lithographs, etchings, serigraphs (1948-), currently prod. 6-8 original graphic editions (3-4000 units) annually for internat. distbn.; watercolorist, florals and botanicals (1970-); filmmaker (5 films distbd. by BFA/Phoenix Films) 1965-; art columnist for Westart and LAment publs.; author: Gourmet Cooking for Campers, Drawing Flowers (in prog.), childrens books: Touch Me, The Other Grandmother; lectr. on philosophy of art, color theory, drawing; instr. (1956-): UCLA Ext., Coll. of the Desert, Beverly Hills Adult Sch., Learning Adventures; awards: Am. Film Festival Honor 1967, outstanding merit, Chgo. Internat. Film Fest. 1969, appreciation cert., Los Angeles Mayor 1982; exhibits: Harold Knapik Gallery, Benson-Baker Gal., Hammer Gal., City Center Art Gal. (NYC), Guild of Creative Art (Shrewsbury, NJ), Larson Gal. (NJ), Makler Gal. (Cleveland, Oh.), deNagy Gal. (Provincetown, Mass.), The Phoenix (Big Sur), Gregg Juarez Gal., Julie Dohan Gal., Los

Angeles Art Assn. (L.A.), Women Painters of the West; num. juried shows; mem: Shrewsbury Art Guild (founding), Westwood Art Assn. (bd.), AAUW, Mensa, Am. Rhododendron Soc., docent Hollyhock House; works: pioneered devel. of prodn. methods of hand painted graphics in moderate priced lmtd. eds. for nat. distbn.; mil: USMC(WR) 1943-44; rec: camping, botany. Res: 18274 W. Devere Ct, Box 42, Lake Hughes 93532 Ofc: 1145 Yale St, Ste 12, Santa Monica 90403

EDDY, MARY GRACE, psychiatric social worker; b. May 23, 1920, Pipestone, Minn.; d. Thomas Walter and Grace Ann (Klein) Hines; m. Robert E. Eddy, March 25, 1951; 1 child, Kathleen Mary, b. Apr. 13, 1954; edn: BA in sociol., Univ. of Wash., Seattle 1947; M. Soc. Sci., Smith Coll. 1949; LCSW, lic. clin. soc. wkr., Calif. 1977; Calif. Comm. Coll. Instructors Cred. 1973. Career: medical social wkr, cons. State Dept. Soc. Welfare, S.F. 1965-66; soc. svc. cons. Licensing Sect. State Dept. of Health, Sacto. 1977; county welfare soc. wk. Marin Co. 1967-68, Contra Costa Co. 1969-70; psychiatric soc. wkr. Child Guidance Clinic Children's Hosp., S.F. 1950, San Mateo Guild Guidance Clin. 1950, Santa Clara Co. Mental Health Clinic, San Jose 1963, San Rafael Comm. Mental Health Ctr. 1967-68, State. Dept. Hlth. Stockton 1973-78, State Dept. Vets Affairs, Veteran's Home of Calif., Yountville 1978--; instr. Los Rios Comm. Coll. 1973; honors: Sigma Epsilon Sigma (scholastic), Alpha Kappa Delta (sociol.), Pi Alpha (Far Eastern studies); US Pub. Health grad. scholarship 1947-9; mem: AAUW (bd., Stockton 1974-78, Napa 1979); Smith Coll. Alumni; Napa Co. Mus. Assn., Calif. Native Plant Soc., bd. mem. Tri-County Gov.'s Com. on Aging 1973; Marin Council of Soc. Agcs. 1960-9; founder Family Svc League of Marin Co. 1960-2; pres. Homestead PTA, Mill Valley 1961; World Affairs Council 1980-3; Democrat (Napa Co. Dem. Central Com. 1978-, exec. bd. 78-82; bd. Mill Valley Dem. Club 1960-9); Episcopal. Res: 2930 Soscol Ave, Apt 43, Napa 94558 Ofc: Veterans Home of Calif., Social Work Svc, Yountville 94599

EDEN, RAYMOND L., association executive; b. July 19, 1925, Lee, Ill.; s. S. Bennie and Hannah Eden; edn: BS, high honors, No. Ill. Univ.; grad work, Northwestern niv., 1950, NY Univ., 1955, Univ. Chgo., 1961; m. Ellen Mercer, Aug. 17, 1945; 1 son, Steven M., b. 1958; career: executive secty. Crippled Children's Center, Peoria, Ill. 1953-59; exec. director, Crippled Children's Service, Milwaukee 1959-62; exec. director, Ill. Heart Assn., 1962-66, California Heart Assn., 966-69; adminstr. San Mateo Medical Clinic, 1969-70; exec. v.p. American Heart Assn., Los Angeles 1970--; lectr. UCLA; faculty, Center for Non-Profit Mgmt.; pres., Council on Volunteer Health Agencies, L.A.; pres., Los Angeles CPR onsortium; Claremont grad. sch. exec. pgm. Advisory Council, 1979-80; State of Calif. Cardiac Care Com.; adv. com. UCLA Profl. Designation Program for Voluntary Agency Execs.; honors: Fellowship and pres. 1981-82, Soc. of Heart Assn. Profl. Staff, Senior Men's Honor Soc.; Alpha Gamma Delta Fellowship Award; Who's Who in the West; Who's Who in Calif. Business & Finance; mem: Rotary Club International, Al Malaika Shrine, Springfield Consistory; Nat. Assn. of Social Workers, Acad. of Certified Social Workers; hon. mem. Sigma Alpha Eta; So. Calif. Assn. of Execs.; Los Angeles Area C. of C. (Clean Air Com.); Neighborhood ch. bd. trustees 1975; Mil.: US Army 1944-46, ETO Battle Ribbon/2 stars, Purple Heart, Bronze Star; Republican; rec: tennis, jogging, travel; res: 30317 Via Cambron, R. Palos Verdes Estates 90274 ofc: American Heart Assn., Greater Los Angeles Affil. 2405 West 8th St. Los Angeles 90057.

EDER, MARTIN OTTO, real estate broker; b. Nov. 25, 1931, San Francisco; s. Joseph and Charlotte I. (Schulz) E.; edn: grad. Berkeley H.S. 1949, Engineering Sch. 1958-60, Real Estate Sch., 2 yrs.; Lic. Real Estate Broker, Calif. 1966. Career: real estate broker, 1966--, selling land for Dart Resorts, Lake Tahoe 1975-; honors: Top salesman four times, and one of top three each year, 1975-, Dart Resorts; sports award from Japan 3d Degree Blackbelt in Judo, 1953; mil: airman 1cl. USAF; Republican; rec: Judo (give classes for children), scuba diving, skiing. Res: 218 Molimo Dr San Francisco 94127 Ofc: Dart & Kraft, Inc., 333 Hegenberger Rd, Ste 312, Oakland 94621

EDEY, RAYMOND ANTHONY, personnel management consultant; b. May 26, 1955, Lynn, Mass.; s. Geoffrey and Muriel Joan (Sarsfield) E.; m. Janice Lynn Cole, July 12, 1980; edn: LaSalle/Wayne Sch of Law 1974-5; E.Los Angeles Coll. 1978; CSU San Jose 1982; AS, Adm. of Justice, Los Angeles 1983; certs. Calif. Commn. on Peace Ofcr. Standards, 1978-83. Career: mgmt., Gulf & Western Corp., Am. Parts Corp., 1975-77; police ofcr. City of Glendale, 1977-80, police personnel investigator, 1980-82, police sgt. 1982--; free lance cons. in personnel mgmt., So. Calif. 1982, personnel mgmt. cons. to various govt. agencies, 1982-; vice pres. PTC Associates, Glendale 1982--; lectr., guest spkr. Los Angeles area colls. 198-83; mem. spl. Calif. task force on Reserve Police Issues 1983; honors: Outstanding Young Men of Am. 1982, 83; community svc. award, L.A. Coll. 1983; mem: Calif., Los Angeles Co., Glendale Peace Officers Assn.; Int'l Police Assn.; Am. Criminal Justice Assn.; mem. Glendale CofC, US CofC, Jaycees; arts. in law enforcement jours.; Republican; Methodist; rec: photog., computer tech., flying, water skiing. Res: 557 E. Verdugo Ave, Ste B, Burbank 91501 Ofc: PTC Associates, 929 So Brand Blvd, Ste 349, Glendale 91206

EDGAR, JAMES MACMILLAN, JR., certified public accountant; b. Nov. 7, 1936, NY, NY; s. James Macmilland and Lilyan Dolores (McCann) E.; m. Judith Storey; children: Suzanne, b. 1960, James, III, b. 1961, Gordon, b. 1967; edn: B.ChE, Cornell Univ. 1959, MBA w/ distinction, 1960; C.P.A.; Cert. Mgmt. Cons. Career: new product rep. E.I. duPont de Nemours, Wilmington, Del. 1960-63; mktg. svcs. rep. 1963-4; with Touche Ross & Co., 1964-78, Detroit cons. 1964-6, mgr. 1966-8, partner 1968-71, San Francisco partner-in-chg. mgmt. services opns. for No. Calif./Hawaii 1971-8; founding partner Edgar, Dunn & Co., Inc., S.F. 1978--. mem. S.F. Mayor's finl. advis. commn. 1976-, exec. com. 1978-; chmn. Revenue Subcom. 1981-83. Mem: Assn. for Corp. Growth (pres. S.F. chpt. 1982-3, dir. Nat. Bd. 1983-), Am. Inst. of CPAs, Calif. Soc. of CPAs, Inst. of Mgmt. Cons. (regl. v.p. 1973-80, dir. 75-77, v.p. bd. dirs. 77-80), Am. Mktg. Assn., S.F. CofC (chmn. City Budget Commn. 1976-8), Meadow Club (fin. com. 1980-), University Club, Commonwealth Club, Cornell Univ. Council 1970-3, Tau Beta Pi; awards: for contbns. to profl. mgmt., Cornell Univ Grad. Sch. of Bus. Pub. Adminstrn. 1978; appreciation for pub. service, City & Co. S.F. 1978; patentee: non-woven fabrics. rec: golf, duck hunting. Res: 10 Buckeye Way, Kentfield 94904. Ofc: Edgar, Dunn & Co. Inc. One Market Plaza, San Francisco 94105.

EDLIN, RAY LAWAYNE, real estate broker; b. Apr. 16, 1930, Nara Visa, N.M.; s. George W. and Dorothy E. (Gragg) E.; m. Jean Duff, Aug. 11, 1959; children: Jane, b. 1960, Peter, b. 1962, Susan, b. 1964, Guy, b. 1966; edn: BS, CalPoly State Univ. 1951; MSc, Rutgers Univ. 1961, PhD, 1962; Calif. Comm. Colls. Lifetime teaching cred.; CE, Certified Exchangors Inc. 1979, Realtor 1972; Gold Card, Nat. Council of Exchangors 1977. Career: asst. scientist Warner Lambert Pharmaceutical, Morris Plains, NJ 1957-58; resrch. fellowship Rutgers Univ. 1958-62; sr. chemist Kelco Co., San Diego 1962-68; tech. dir./ops. mgr. Gentry Corp., Gilroy 1968-70; dir. Quality Control, Foodmaker Inc., San Diego 1970; realtor/owner Edlin Realty, S.D. 1970--; instr. UCSD 1980-81, Community Colls. 1979-83, Rutgers 1959-62, National Univ. 1980, San Diego Bd. of Realtors 1979-83; awards: pres. San Diego Problem Solvers 1978-9, num. R.E. mktg. awards 1976-84, various Service awards; mem: Nat. Assn. Realtors, Calif. Assn. Realtors (dir. 1980-81), S.D. Board of Realtors (dir. 1980-3), chmn. S.D. Mktg. & Exchange Com. 1979-80; Food Technologists (I.F.T.), Sigma Xi, Elks, La Jolla Cancer Soc., Toastmasters (past); mem. Poway Sch. Bd. 1966-7; publs: sev. tech. papers and patents 1960-69; mil: sgt. US Army 1954-57; Republican; Prot.; rec: golf, tennis, hiking, swimming. Res: 2727 DeAnza Rd, T-4, San Diego 92109 Ofc: Edlin Realty, POB 99938, San Diego 92109

EDSON, STEPHANIE, pre-school cooperative president; b. Aug. 27, 1946, New London, CT; d. Robert Henry and Josephine Catherine (Vaccaro) Krombar; Assoc. degree, Naussau Coll., 1969; m. Roderick, Oct. 30, 1971; children: Heather Ann, b. 1975; Neil Roderick, b. 1977. Career: head teller, asst. mgr., Valley Natl. Bank, New York, 1964-68; computer programmer, Eastern Services, NY, 1968-70; social worker, Co. of Nassau, NY, 1970-72; domestic engr., Ohio, Calif., 1972--; pres., South Bay Pre-School, CA, 1980--; also volunteer work at elementary sch.; work in library doing dittos for all teachers, work in the office, aide the teacher in the classroom. Awards: Valley Stream Miss Young Republican, 1966; have had honor of making many friends across country and have retained friendships. Mem.: Queen City New Comers, hospitality chairperson, 1972; Delshire Woman's Club, nominating chairperson, 1973, Queen City New Comers, fund raiser, chairperson, 1975; Welcome Wagon, Beta Sigma Phi sor., 1979; South Bay Pre Sch., Ways & Means chairperson, 1980. Republican, 1960s volunteer. Roman Catholic. Rec.: skiing, snow and water; sewing; crewel work; various forms of art; making new friends. Res.: 2251 Sunnyside Ridge Rd., Rancho Palos Verdes 90274; Office: South Bay Cooperative Pre-School, 24027 Pennsylvania Ave., Lomita 90717

EDWARDS, CARLA LEE, marketing executive; b. Apr. 12, 1945, Oakland; d. Clay Thomas and Eileen (Laughlin) Carlin; m. Robert J. Edwards, Aug. 29, 1964, div. 1979; children: Kent, b. 1965; Kelly, b. 1967; edn: San Joaquin Delta Coll. 1964-65. Career: radio annoucer KJOY Radio Sta., Stockton 1962-63; San Joaquin Telephone Co., Manteca 1963-65; telecomm. Defense Depot, Tracy 1965-81; co- owner Creative Touch, Manteca 1967-70; co-owner Genmini Investments, Stockton; owner, Carla Edwards & Assoc., Manteca 1979-81; owner Carla Edward Rental Properties, Manteca 1979--; advtg./mktg. mgr. Oakwood Lake Resort, Manteca 1976-82, gen. mgr., 1982--; bd. dirs. Stockton Conv. & Visitors Bureau 1981-83; dir. South County United Cerebral Palsey, Stockton 1981; columnist, Delta Dispatch, Stockton 1982-83; dir. publicity Manteca Pumpkin Festival 1979-83; guest spkr. Future Women, Modesto 1981; awards: Rookie of the Year, UOP Pacific Athletic Found. 1982; mem: San Joaquin Rental Property Assn.; Pacific Athletic found.; Stockton Advtg. Media Assn.; Delta CofC (mktg. ch. 1982); Stockton Womens & Profl. Club (Womens Network); Class of 63, Stockton (class reunion chair); Marina West Yacht Club, S.F. Tennis Club, Le Club Stockton; promotions dir. Muscular Dystrophy, Manteca 1982; mil: E6 USCGR 1973-75, Rough & Ready Is.; Republican; Catholic. Res: 859 El Capitan Manteca 95336 Ofc: Oakwood Lake, Inc., 874 E Woodward Manteca 95336

EDWARDS, CLAUDIA ANN, real estate broker/ financial planner; b. Sept. 14, 1937, Mason City, Iowa; d. Eugene Francis and Lorraine Mary (Eppinger) Lillie; children: Laurie, b. 1967; Gregory, b. 1969; edn: BS, Univ. of Montana 1959; R.E. Broker, Calif. 1976; Reg. Representative, NASD 1983. Career: assoc. broker 1976-84, real estate broker and branch mgr. Valley of Calif. and Coldwell Banker 1979--; reg. rep. WZW Finl. Services 1982--; finl. plnnr. Claudia Edwards Inc. 1980--; lectr. real estate topics; staff Acalanes Adult Edn. 1979-, Danville Comm. Ctr. Adult Edn. 1982-; honors: Montair Service Awd. 1977, San Ramon Unif. Sch. Dist. Awd. 1977, Century Club 1977-, Presidents Club 1977-, Million Dollar Club 1976-, Company Wide Gold Key Awd.(1978), Top Lister and Top Producer (1979); mem: Internat. Assn. for Fin. Planning, Real Estate Secs. and Syndication Inst., Nat. Assn. of Realtors, Calif. Assn. of Realtors, Contra Costa and So. Alameda Co. Bd. of Realtors, Apt. Property Owners Assn. of Contra Costa, Calif. Syndication Forum; author monthly newsletter, bi-mo. column in local newspaper; Republican; Catholic; rec:

skiing, travel. Res: 287 Waterman Ct Danville 94526 Ofc: Coldwell Banker Inc 560 So Hartz Ste 364 Danville 94526 WZW Financial Services 1000 Locust Street St. Louis Mo 63101

EDWARDS, DELOY, real estate broker; b. Apr. 3, 1921, Oklahoma City; s. Calvin and Edith Charity (Bell) E.; m. Solange, June 21, 1972; children: Anael, b. 1973, Deloy Jr., b. 1975; edn: bus. adm., UCLA 1948; indsl. suprvn., Cronan Hall 1949-52. Career: mgr./partner W.A. Robinson Realty Co., 1960-68; owner Deloy Edwards Realtors, Los Angeles 1968--, property mgmt. broker 1970-; mem. Task Force for Tng. Unskilled Minorities R.E.; recreational dir. Holoman Methodist Ch. 1960-63; awards: Race Relationship Annual Achievement Awds.; sponsor Little League Baseball Team Ladera Hts.; mem: Los Angeles Realty Bd. 1968-, Consolidated Realty Bd. 1968-, Westchester CofC; clubs: Am. Golf, Industry Hills Golf; Methodist; rec: golf, travel, bicycling, basketball. Res: 6126 Shenandoah Ave Los Aneles 90056 Ofc: Deloy Edwards Realtor, 5369 Centinela Ave Los Angeles 90045

EDWARDS, EDDIE, plumbing contractor; b. June 4, 1947, San Diego; s. Eddie and Leah (Marks) Farkas; children: Steven Michael, b. 1970, Robin Gayle, b. 1972; edn: dip. Fairfax H.S. 1965; coll. courses, USN, 1966; journeymens plumbing lic., So. Calif. Pipe Trades Sch. 1969-74; plumbing contr. lic., Contrs. License Sch. 1980; Plumbing Contr., State of Calif. Career: apprenticeship program with Plumbers Local No. 78, Los Angeles 1969-74, mng. partner The Drain Surgeon (plumbing contrs.), No. Hollywood 1976--; guest appearances on talk radio shows; mem. The City of Hope (Plumbing and Mech. Contrs. Div.); mil: Utilitiesman 2cl. USNR 1966-68; Jewish; rec: juggling, concerts, the ocean. Res: 8283 Willis Ave, 10, Panorama City 91402 Ofc: The Drain Surgeon, 11151 Vanowen St, No. Hollywood 91605

EDWARDS, HEATHER RAE, dentist; b. Jan. 7, 1944, Los Angeles; d. Dick and Doris S. Newcom; m. Arnett Jamison, June 10, 1982; edn: BS, USC 1965; DDS, Univ. of the Pacific 1979. Career: pvt. practice, dental hygienist 1965-75; dentist, community dental practice with Synanon Church; dentist, pvt. practice 1982--; publs: Am Journ. of Public Health 1983; Synanon Ch. Res: 50300 Highway 245 Badger 93603

EDWARDS, MARCIA LOU, musician; b. Nov. 26, 1942, Grand Rapids, Mich.; d. Peter James and Bernice Lucille (DeReus) Muyskens; m. Glenn L. Petersen, Dec. 27, 1980; child: Cary, b. 1973; edn: Hope Coll., Mich. 1960-62; Univ. of Mich. 1962-63; BA, cum laude, Univ. of Pittsburgh 1973; CA Life & Disability Lic. 1979; NASD Lic. 1980. Career: asst. mgr. San Jose Symphony 1977-78; agent Prudential Ins. Co. 1978-80; United Fidelity Ins. 1980-81; broker Judy & Robinson Securities 1980-81; adminstrv. dir. Zonta Childrens Ctr., 1981; asst. controller Micro Focus, INc. 1981-83; controller Gaston Snow & Ely Bartlett, Attys. 1983; currently, musician 159th Army Bank and Jazz Combo; pvt. piano tchr. 1975-81; secty. to bd. of El Camino Opera Co. 1976-78; percussion gp. leader Band 1982--; awards: Prudential Carrer Devel. Awd. 1979; United Fidelity Bldrs. Awd. 1980; mem: Delta Phi; Pittsburgh Symphony Soc.; Am. Assn. of Univ. Wwmen; Gilbert & Sullivan Soc.; El Camino Opera Co.; mil: s/sgt. Calif. Army Nat. Guard 1977--; GCM, Army Reserve Achiev. Medal, NCO Profl. Devel. Awd.; Republican; Protestant; rec: tennis, bowling. Res: 41 Chester St Los Gatos 95030

EDWARDS, MARY ANNE, physician; b. Sept. 28, 1936, Bridgeport, Conn.; d. Ira Johnston and Hazel Louise (Loveridge) Kaar; div.; children: Cheri, b. 1956, Don, b. 1959, Mary beth, b. 1964; edn: stu. Cornell Univ. 1954-5; BS, Mount Mary Coll. 1970; MS, NY Medical Coll. 1977; MD, Stanford Univ. Sch. of Med. 1980; Pathologist 1983. Career: med. technician Clinical Lab., Milwaukee, Wisc. 1966-69; med. technologist Norwalk (Ct.) Hosp. 1970-74; instr. NY Med. Coll., Valhalla, NY 1974-77; pathology resident Stanford (Calif.) Univ. Hosp. 1980-83; med. lab. director Laboratory Services, San Jose 1983--; mem: AMA, Coll. of Am. Pathologists, Santa Clara Co. Med. Soc., Stanford Alumni Assn. (lifetime); med. jour. articles; Republican; rec: golf, swim, run, piano, photog. Res: 12846 Viscaino Los Altos Hills 94022 Ofc: Laboratory Services, 150 So. Autumn St San Jose 95110

EDWARDS, ROBERT FRANK, JR., executive; b. Feb. 11, 1945, St. George, Utah; s. Robert Frank and Wetona (Watson) E.; m. Andrea Allen, Nov. 22, 1969; children: Robert F., III, b. 1971; Michael A., b. 1976; edn: BA, Calif. Western Univ. 1966. Career: joined Frank Edwards Co., Inc. 1969, dir., sectytreas. 1971, vice-pres. 1980, exec. vice pres. 1984--; Dir: Frank Edwards Co. Inc., Pacific Power Equip. Co., Automotive Utilities, Frank Edwards Found.; orgns: bd. govs. Mills Hosp. Found.; pres. Hillsborough Schs. Found.; dir. Peninsula Golf & CC; mil: 1st lt. US Army 1966-69, Army Commendn. Medal; Republican; rec: golf. Res: 1739 Forestview Ave Hillsborough 94010 Ofc: Frank Edwards Co. 1565 Adrian Rd Burlingame 94010

EDWARDS, SAMUEL ROGER, physician; b. Aug. 11, 1937, Santa Barbara; s. Harold S. and Margaret (Spaulding) E.; m. Marcia Dutton, June 17, 1961; children: Harold, b. 1965, Charles, b. 1966; edn: AB, Harvard Coll. 1960; MD, USC Sch. of Med. 1964; intern Presbyterian Hosp., Phila. 1964-65; resident Presbyn. Hosp. (Pacific Med. Ctr.) S.F. 1965-66, res. (cardiology fellowship 1970) UC San Francisco Med. Center 1968-70. Career: pvt. practice internal medicine, Santa Paula, Ca. 1971--, med. staff (1971-, pres. 1977-8), dir. Critical Care Unit, Santa Paula Meml. Hosp.; med. staff (1971-, pres. 1979-80), med. dir. Ventura Co. Med. Ctr., chmn. bd. dirs. VCMC Medical Research Found.; med. dir. Twin Pines Healthcare Conv. Hosp., Santa Paula Healthcare Conv. Hosp.; clin. instr. UCLA Sch. Med.; dir. Citizens State Bank 1979-; CFO, Samuel Edwards Assocs. (agribus.); Fellow Am. Coll. Physicians 1983;

awards: Am. Heart Assn. Ventura Leadership 1974-5; lectr. agribusiness, Hutchings Inst., Santa Barbara 1980; ml: ltcdr USNR (MC) 1966-68. Ofc: 243 March St, Santa Paula 93060

EDWARDS, WILLIAM BURTON, amusement park owner, real estate broker; b. May 31, 1928, Fort Wayne, Ind.; s. Opal Lebert and Eva Louella (McKinley) E.; div.; dau. Lisa Ann Ringer, b. 1961; edn: grad. Lafayette Central H.S. 1946; Lic. real estate broker Calif. Career: automatic machine technician Commercial Controls Corp., San Francisco 1948-52; mgr. Normans Kingdom of Toys, S.F. 1954-55; mgr. King Normans Wonderland, Concord 1955-60; real estate broker/prin. Edwards Realty, Concord 1960-80; owner/opr. Peralta Kiddieland, Oakland 1965-70, Pixie Playland, Concord 1970--; mem: Calif. Real Estate Assn., Contra Costa Real Estate Board, Elks; mil: s/sgt. US Army 1952-54; Republican; Ch. of Christ; rec: hunting, fishing. Res: POB 220, Concord 94522 Ofc: Pixie Playland, 2740 E. Olivera Rd Concord 94520

EFFORD, KATHRYN JUSTINE, real estate broker/minister/evangelist; b. Oct. 25, 1939, Davenport, Iowa; d. Arthur A. and Kathryn D. (Anderson) Wohlgemuth; m. E. Ries Efford Jr., July 26, 1968; children: Elaine, b. 1957, Dawn, b. 1958, Vance, b. 1959, Mark, b. 1960, Jamie, b. 1961; edn: Los Angeles City Coll. 1979-80; BA, Melodyland Sch. of Theol. 1982; lic. real estate broker, Ill. 1964, Calif. 1969, N.Mex. 1972; ordained minister, Melodyland Christian Ctr. 1982. Career: real estate broker, self-empl. 1964-68, Great Western United, Calif., Ill., N.M. 1968-72; real estate cons. mktg. & sales Efford Corp. 1972-77; qualifying broker/vice pres. Realtytowne Inc., 1979--, The Land Co., 1982--; current pastor California City Christian Center, California City; instr. Vocational Career Real Estate Salesmanship; seminars on Biblical Theol., Self Value as a Christian; mem. Melodyland Sch. Theol. Alumni Assn. (pres. 1983); writer: Dear Kathy column, Enterprise Newspaper; rec: stained glass windows. Res: 26101 Yucaipa St, Rte 2, Mojave 93501 Ofc: The Land Co., Calif. City Christian Center, 6508 Calif. City Blvd. California City 93505

EFFRON, JOEL ARTHUR, company president; b. Feb. 11, 1944, Detroit, Mich.; s. Samuel David and Harriet Marshall (Nadelweiss) E.; m. JoAnn Rodgers, Aug. 6, 1972; 1 dau. Amanda b. 1980; edn: BSIE (indsl. eng.), UC Berkeley, 1965, MSIE, 1967. Career: mgr. cust. svc. quality assurance, TWA, NY, NY 1968-70, mgr. cus. svcs. industrial engineering, 1970-72, director reservations svcs., 1972-74; pres./dir. ComPath, Oakland, Ca. 1974-80; owner J. Effron & Associates, 1980--; pres. Codart, Novato 1982-82; pres. Zendex Corp., Dublin, Ca. 1982--; dir: Metacom (Oakland) 1978, Zendex Corp. 1981-; bd. advisors Bay Alarm Co. 1984-; cons. Arthur D. Little Inc., S.F. 1981-82; mem: NATA (dir.) 1975-80; Calif. Interconnect Assn. (dir.) 1975-80; Rotarian; author: Data Communications Techniques and Technologies, 1984; rec: skiing, swim. Ofc: Zendex Corp. 6700 Sienna Lane Dublin 94568

EGENES, RONALD ANDREW, manufacturing co. executive; b. May 24, 1944, Jonesville, Wisc.; s. Harold R. and Elizabeth (West) E.; m. Kathleen L., July 7, 1978; children: Matthew, b. 1980, Jared, b. 1983; edn: BS, USC 1969. Career: owner California Bedspreads, Los Angeles 1981-83; owner Aquacide, Newbury Park 1974--, Merk Screen Printing, N.P. 1979--; pres. C.L.&L. Ind. 1973-75; honors: (USC) pres. SCORE, pres. Newman Club, chmn. 1969 Festival of Arts, student body parliamentarian; mem. Waterbed Retailers Assn. (pres., founder, bd. chmn. 1973-4); mil: sgt. US Army Inf. 1962-4 (pres. Enlistedmen Advis. Corp.); Republican; rec: billiards, stamps, oil painting. Res: 103 Lorie Dr Grass Valley 95945 Ofc: Aquacide, 996 Lawrence Dr, 305, Newbury Park 91320

EGNER, JOHN DAVID, JR., electrical engineer; b. June 30, 1957, New Castle, Penn.; s. John David Sr., and Dr. Ann Irene (Nevin) E.; edn: BS in E.E., Univ. of Vermont 1979. Career: research asst. in med. ultrasonics experiments, Univ. of Vermont Physics Dept. 1977-79; devel. engr. Data Terminal Div. Hewlett-Packard Co., 1979-82 (designed/dev. a terminal family power-supply; support engr. prodn. of a terminal; solved reliability problem with terminal family sweep circuit); development engr. Macintosh, Apple Computer Inc., Cupertino 1982--: dev. design & vendors for sweep/PS assembly; dev. Macintosh system RFI solutions (elect., mech.); dev. internat. variation of Macintosh sweep/ power supply assembly. Honors: Tau Beta Pi, outstanding mem. award IEEE Student Branch (4/79); mem. IEEE; rec: hi-fi, splitting wood and country life, piano. Res: 18492 Main Blvd Los Gatos 95030 Ofc: Apple Computer Inc. 20525 Mariani Ave Cupertino 95014

EHRBAR, ROBETTE GAYLE, financial executive; b. Nov. 23, 1956, Hollywood; d. Robert George and Lucia Colette (Coy) Ehrbar Sr.; edn: Calif. Polytech. Univ. Pomona, 1973-5; reg. Series 7, SEC, 1980. Career: teller Hacienda Div. of Mitsubishi Bank, West Covina 1976; accts. receivable Soundesign Western, City of Industry 1977; manager Western Rgn., Loeb Rhoades Hornblower-L.A. 1977; asst. v.p. Paine Webber, L.A. 1978; 2nd v.p. Smith Barney, L.A. 1981; vice pres./municipal bond trader & dept. mgr., Lehman Bros., L.A. 1983--. Mem. L.A. Municipal Bond Club; Collie Club of Am., Smooth Collie Assn. of Am., San Gabriel Valley Collie Club; Republican; Presbyterian; rec: show, breed, profly. handle dogs. Res: 1512 Sekio Ave. Rowland Hts. 91748 Ofc: Lehman Brothers Kuhn Loeb, 515 So. Figueroa 14th Flr, Los Angeles 90071.

EHRHART, KEVIN MICHAEL, orthopaedic surgeon; b. June 8, 1949, St. Louis, Mo.; s. Lawrence Eugene and Elizabeth Dolores (Homburgh); m. Martha McGonigle, Aug. 22, 1970; chil: Kevin, b. 1972, Susan, b. 1974, Matthew, b. 1979; edn: BA, St. Louis Univ. 1970, MD (valedictorian) St. Louis

Univ. Med. Sch. 1974. Career: intern, res. UCLA Sch of Medicine, Dept. of Surgery, Div. Orthopaedic Surg. 1974-79; orthopaedic surgeon, pvt. group practice, Santa Monica 1979--; clin. instr. Dept. of Surgery, 1980. Mem: Bay Surgical Soc., Los Angeles Co. Med. Assn. Clubs: Jonathan, Los Angeles Country. Publs: profl. papers. Republican. Roman Catholic. rec: jog, ski. Res: 444 Ocampo Dr. Pacific Palisades 90272. Ofc: 2001 Santa Monica Blvd., 7th Floor, Santa Monica 90404.

EHRSAM, ELDON EDWARD, operations research analyst; b. July 8, 1936, Bern, Kans.; s. Loyd and Elma Elizabeth (Bauman) E.; m. Clara Louise Schwartz, Nov. 20, 1958; children: Elizabeth Sue, b. 1959, Jeffrey, b. 1961, John, b. 1968, Brian, b. 1969; edn: BS, Washburn Univ. 1962; MS, USC 1969; cert. (MS equiv.) UC Santa Barbara 1973; Calif. lic. real estate broker. Career: physicist Naval Ordnance Lab, Corona, Ca. 1962-65; electronic engr. AF Western Test Range, Vandenberg AFB, 1965-68, project engr. Space & Missile Test Center, VAFB 1968-73, telemetry systems mgr. 1973-76, ops. research analyst 1976--; real estate broker, Real Property Investments, Solvang 1976--; securities rep. Vestcap Sec. Corp., Solvang 1982--; honors: BSA District Award 1979, Who's Who in West (16, 17, 18, 19th eds.), Jane's Who's Who in Aviation & Aerospace (1983); mem: AIAA, Vandenberg Chpt. councilmem. 1980-81, Internat. Platform Assn., Nat. Assn. of Realtors, Nat. Assn. of Sec. Dealers, Real Estate Securities and Syndication Inst., Sigma Pi Sigma, Masons, Elks; coauthor four tech. papers, presented Internat. Telemetry Confs. 1969-75; Democrat; United Methodist; rec: racquetball, jogging, camping. Res: 3087 Fairlea Rd Santa Ynez 93460 Ofc: Air Force Western Space & Missile Center, Code XRQ, Vandenberg AFB 93437

EICHEN, CAROLE PATRICIA (Mrs. Robert Passovoy), interior design firm president; b. Oct. 13, 1932, Los Angeles; d. Al and Betty Goldberg; m. Robert Passovoy, Dec. 7, 1975; children: Cheryl Lynn Eichen, b. 1955; Jeffrey Steven Eichen, b. 1958. Career: founder/pres. Carole Eichen Interiors, Inc. (internat. model home design and mdsg. firm) Santa Ana, 1965--; frequent spkr. on int. design and housing indus. issues; regular spkr. major annual confs. of Nat. Assn. of Home Bldrs. and Pacific Coast Bldrs. Conf.; faculty mem. McGraw-Hill's annual seminar for homebldrs. (The Calif. Mktg. Scene), 1976-; faculty mem. Housing Mag.'s year-long seminar on condominium mktg.; frequent lectr. for Japanese homebldrs. in Tokyo and Osaka, 1981-; conduct num. seminars, int. design, UCLA Ext.; awards incl.: full membership, Am. Soc. of Int. Designers (1981); award of excellence for Model Home Int. Design, Good Housekeeping Mag.; Decorator's award of excellence, Ceramic Tile Inst. 1981; Int. Designer of the Year 1976, Nat. Assn. of Mirror Mfrs.; num. MAME awards for best int. design, Sales & Mktg. Council of So. Calif. Bldg. Indus. Assn.; firm recipient 8 merit awards and 8 Gold Nugget Grand Awards for best model home int. design and mdsg., Nat. Assn. of Home Bldrs.; mem: UCLA Est. Guidance Com., The Arts Dept. Design Pgm.; The Deans Council, UCLA Adv. Bd.; ASID; MIRM (Inst. Resdtl. Mktg.); Bldg. Indus. Assn., Sales & Mktg. Council; Nat. Assn. of Home Bldrs.; UCLA Alumnia Assn.; publs: contbg. editor (past) Housing Mag.; columnist (past) Copley News Service; author book: How to Decorate Model Homes and Apartments (House and Home Press, 1974); Endowed the Carole Eichen Award, UCLA Ext. Sch. of Interior Design (1976). Res: 1803 Clear Creek Dr Fullerton 92633 Ofc: Carole Eichen Interiors, Inc. 1910 E. Warner Ave, Ste 2-6, Santa Ana 92705

EICHENHOLTZ, MARC J., computer consultant; b. Aug. 7, 1951, NY,NY; s. Leonard and Norma (Markowitz) E.; edn: BS and BEE, SUNY at Stony Brook, 1974; MBA, Pepperdine Univ. 1981. Career: applications cons. Tymeshare, NY 1974-5, sr. systems analyst Tymeshare, Cupertino, Calif. 1975-7, proj. leader Tymeshare, Mtn. View 1977-9; prod. mgr. DMC Systems Inc., Santa Clara 1979-80; owner Practical olutions, Cupertino 1980--; lectr. Awards: NY State Regents Scholarship 1969, applications cons. of the month, Tymeshare, 1975. Mem: Am. Mgmt. Assn., S-100 Bus., Assn. for Computing Machinery, NOW, Profl. & Tech. Consultants Assn., Billmaster (software). Jewish. rec: dance, swim, racquetball. Ofc: Practical Solutions 10070 S. DeAnza Bl. Cupertino 95014.

EISENBERG, LAWRENCE HENRY, lawyer; b. Jan. 16, 1936, Los Angeles; edn: AA, Los Angeles City Coll. 1958; BS in pub. acctg., USC 1962, JD, 1966; children: Aron Scott, Karen Ann. Admitted to Calif. State Bar 1966, US Supreme Ct. Bar 1970. Career: auditor, GAO, Los Angeles 1962-63; assoc. law firm Ward & Heyler, Beverly Hills and Century City, 1966-71; individual practice law, Sherman Oaks, 1978-78, Encino 1978--; examiner Calif. State Bar, 1970-72; mem. local adminstrv. com. 1972-74, mem. appellate cts. com., 1982-; judge pro tem Los Angeles and Beverly Hills Municipal Cts., 1972-; examiner Los Angeles Police Dept. oral selection unit, 1973-79; bd. dirs. Legion Lex, USC Law Center support group, 170-80; mem: Am. (v.chmn. Computer Div.), Calif., Los Angeles county, Beverly Hills (gov.), San Fernando Valley bar assn., Calif. Acad. Appellate Lawyers, Digital Equipment Computers Users Soc, Phi Alpha Delta. Ofc: 17141 Nance St Encino 91316

EISENDRATH, RICHARD THOMAS, real estate broker; b. Jan. 22, 1952, Chgo.; s. John Wm. and Opie Lee (Briscoe) E.; m. Diane Montano, May 9, 1981; 1 son, John Daily, b. 1983; edn: AA, Santa Monica Coll. 1974; UCLA, 1975; Calif. lic. real estate broker 1978. Career: real estate investor, 1975-, real estate agt. Realty World, No. San Diego Co. 1978, currently broker/owner Eisendrath Realty, Oceanside; awards: top listing agt. (1980), Realty World; 1st pl. 1980 mens' boogy board competition, Triple A Invitational; mem: Oceanside Bd. of Realtors, Royal Palms Tennis Club, Elks, sponsor Girl Scouts; author 2 books: Lines from a Brown Paper Bag, Stone Soap; 1981 cand. for Oceanside City Council; rec: tennis, writing, dulcimer. Res: 1438 Independence Way Vista 92083 Ofc: Eisendrath Realty, 417 S. Treamont Oceanside 92054

EISENMAN, FRANCES BRADLEY, psychiatric social worker; b. Feb.15, 1943, Atlanta, Ga.; d. Joseph Gladstone and Orlena Beall (King) Bradley; children: David Michael b. 1969, Susan Catherine b. 1970; career: AA, Young Harris (Ga.) Coll. 1962; BA, Univ. of Ga. 1964; MSW, Univ. of Ga. Sch. of Soc. Wk. 1966; Calif. Lic. Clin. Soc. Wkr. (LCSW), BBSE 1980. Career: soc. wkr. Eastern Pa. Psychiatric Inst., Phila. 1966-69; senior psychiatric soc. wkr. Santa Cruz County Mental Health: Quarterway House 1974-77, Day Treatment Ctr. 1977, County Neuropsychiatric Unit. 1977-83; psychiat. soc. wkr. Dominican Santa Cruz Hosp. Mental Hlth. Unit, 1983--; Democrat; Episcopal. Res: 122 Harbor Oaks Circle Santa Cruz 95062 Ofc: Dominican Santa Cruz Hospital Mental Health Unit, 1555 Soquel Dr Santa Cruz 95065

EISLER, RONALD LAURENCE, lawyer, real estate investment broker/investor; b. June 25, 1947, NY, NY; s. Benjamin and Mary (Blier) Eisenberg; edn: BBA, City Coll. of NY 1965; JD, UCB Boalt Hall 1968; admitted State Bar of Calif. 1970. Career: real estate counsel Atlantic Richfield Co., Los Angeles and Phila., Pa. 1972-76; founder/sr. partner Law Offices of Eisler & Porter, L.A. 1977--; pres. Eisler & Co. (investment R.E. brokerage multimil. transactions) 1978--; co-owner Eisler & Gimbel Prop. Mgmt. Co., Huntington Beach 1980--; co-owner Western Pacific Business Forms, 1983--; guest lectr. Stanford Univ. Sch. of Law 1981; honors: Am. Jurisprudence Award 1968, rec. piano. Address: Eisler & Co., 16611 Jib Circle, 1, Huntington Beach 92649

EISWALD, FRED B., real estate broker; b. Sept. 7, 1930, Longview, Wash.; s. Adolph John and Annabelle (Donahe) E.; m. Elizabeth Brink, Feb. 23, 1952; children: Gregg, b. 1955, Karen (Klebba), b. 1957; Calif. lic. real estate sales 1978, R.E. broker 1982. Career: lineman Conn. Light and Power Co., Willimantic, Conn. 1952-53; auto mech. Leonard Motors, Willimantic 1953-56, P&M Auto, Burbank, Ca. 1956-58, Herb Hull Chevron, Pasadena 1958-60; owner Fred's Auto Service, Thousand Oaks 1960-70; service advisor Parkwood Lincoln-Merc., Woodland Hills 1970-77, Kemp Ford, Thousand Oaks 1977-79; realtor/mgr. Century 21 America, Thousand Oaks 1979-82, Cen.21 Davies, Thousand Oaks 1982--; owner Olde Gentle Presents Antiques, Westlake 1983--; awards: CofC Service Award, Million Dollar Club, Multi-Million Dollar Club, Y's Man of Year; mem. Bd. of Realtors 1979-, YMCA, Rotary, Glass of the Past, Adventure Unlmtd. Youth Group, Thousand Oaks Booster Club, PTA, Republican Club; works: award winning restoration of 1930 Model-A auto (1961), and 1932 Duesenberg (1969); mil: elect. tech. 3cl. USN 1948-52, GCM, Honorman's Award; Republican; Prot.; rec: antiques, numismatics, restorations. Res: 1643 Valley High Ave Thousand Oaks 91362 Ofc: Century 21 Davies, 223 Thousand Oaks Blvd Ste 100, Thousand Oaks 91360

ELAHIAN, KAMRAN, electronics co. executive; b. June 28, 1954, Tehran, Iran; US permanent res. 1977; s. Mohammad E. and Hadigheh (Soleymani) E.; m. Zohreh Faridi, Mar. 17, 1977; edn: BS in math, and BS in computer sci., Univ. of Utah 1975, M. Engring. (comp. sci) 1977. Career: teaching asst. Univ. of Utah, 1974-76, system mgr. and pgmmr. Div. of Artificial Organs, Univ. of Utah, 1976-78; VISI CAD devel. engr. Hewlett Packard Co., 1978-81; mgr. CAD software devel., Magnavox Research Labs., 1981; founder/pres. CAE Systems, 1981-83; founder/pres. CASE Systems, Santa Clara 1983--; mem. The Presidents Assn.; honors: received two undergrad. degrees at age twenty; works: originated & devel. a pioneer product in the explosive Computer Aided Engineering (CAE) market; rep. HP in an advanced VISI CAD Seminar, Italy 1980; rec: skiing, camping. Res: 48539 Flagstaff Rd Fremont 94539 Ofc: CASE Systems, 2320 Walsh Ave, Ste I, Santa Clara 95051

ELDER, RORY L., crime prevention/education specialist; b. Aug. 4, 1949, Glendale; s. James C. and Elizabeth A. (Morrison) Pushmataha; m. Linda Elder, May 6, 1978; edn: AA, journ., Orange Coast Coll. 1969; BA, Eng., St. Mary's Coll. 1971; M. Ednl. Psych., Univ. of S.F. 1981; Calif. lic. Marriage Family Child Therapist 1982. Career: worked as US Postal Clerk, longshoreman, boy's club youth splst., 1971-73; deputy probation counselor Orange Co. Probation Dept. 1973-79; youth services ofcr. Rohnert Park, 1979-80; crime prevention/edn. splst. Office of Atty. Gen., Calif. State Dept. Justice, Sacto. 1980--; marriage family child therapist pvt practice 1982--; adv./group leader Cancer Support Gp., Mercy Twin Lakes Hosp., Folsom 1981--; instr. Hospice Tng. Pgm., Sierra Coll. 1983-; cons. on school crime, delinquency prevention to education, law enforcement, govt., and comm. agencies nationwide 1980--; merit and service awards: Nat. Council of Juvenile and Family Ct. Judges 1983, Santa Clara Co. Bar Assn. 1983, Calif. Juvenile Peace Officers Assn. 1981, Calif. Youth Authority 1980; mem: Calif. Assn. of Suprs. of Child Welfare and Attendance, Calif. Juvenile Peace Ofcrs Assn. (adv. bd.), Calif. School Peace Ofcrs Assn. (exec. bd.), Calif. Crime Prevention Ofcrs Assn., Calif. Assn. Marriage Family Therapists; publs: co-ed. Safe Campus-School Crime Prevention Jour. (1980-); coauthor various Atty-Gen. Crime Prevention Ctr. handbooks; mag. arts.; Republican; Unity; rec: golf, racquetball, backpack, travel. Res: 7829 Tabare Ct. Citrus Hts 95621 Ofc: State Dept. of Justice, 4949 Broadway, Special Projects, Sacramento 95813

ELERICK, ELLIS EARL, investment co. president, ret.; b. July 15, 1931, San Pedro; s. George Delbert and Rena Horace (Magee) E.; m. Patricia Joan Portlock, March 21, 1953; children: Jerry, b. 1954, Max, b. 1957, Sheryl, b. 1960; edn: H.S. grad., coll. courses; lic. real estate broker, Calif., Okla. Career: boy Friday to pres. and bd. chmn. Signal Stamping, Inc. (and predecessor firm Matson Mfg. Co.), Long Beach 1951-75; co-founded Aerosol Engineering and Mfg. Co. (Lynwood), Professional Computer Services, Inc. (Long Beach), Red Jack Wrecking Co.; currently owner Pyramid Investment Co. (trust deed and mtg. investment co.), Santa Paula; guest spkr. indsl. design, CSU Long Beach; mem: BSA Committeeman, Calif. Muzzle Loaders and Collectors, Bay Cities Arms Collectors Assn., Am. Gun Collectors Club;

Republican; Baptist; rec: coin & gun collector, travel. Res: 1209 Gatewood Lane Santa Paula 93060 Ofc: Pyramid Investment Co., POB 242, Santa Paula 93060

ELIAS, JAMES MORROW, mining geologist; b. May 12, 1929, Los Angeles; s. Arthur M. and Melba (Wightman) E.; m. Dinah Duffy Allais, Feb. 7, 1981; edn: BA, USC 1951; grad. work, Univ. of Utah 1952; Reg. Geologist (No. 1972), Calif. 1970; cert. profl. geologist, Am. Inst. Profl. Geol. 1967. Career: staff/sr./ mining geologist for various cos. incl. Getty Oil, Interpace, Gladding McBean, Anaconda, US Geol. Survey, Cyprus Mines, 1952-67; chief geologist, Exploration, US Smelting Refining & Mining Co., NY, NY and Salt Lake City, Utah 1968-72; dir. Oil & Gas Devel., 1973, chief geologist, UV Industries, Salt Lake City and NY, NY 1973-76; pres. J. Morrow Elias & Assocs. (cons. geologists), Rutherford, Ca. 1976--; awards: Golden Award, Pyrite Hall of Fame 1983; mem: Am. Inst. of Mining Engrs. (chmn. So. Calif. Sect. 1966-8), Northwest Mining Assn., Soc. of Economic Geologists, Nev. Mining Assn., Canadian Inst. of Mining; num. articles in profl. jours.; Republican; rec: vineyardist, 17 acres Cabernet & Sauvignon Blanc in Napa Valley. Res: 8278 St. Helena Hwy Napa 94558 Ofc: J. Morrow Elias & Assocs., POB 23, Rutherford 94573

ELIAS, NICHOLAS S., private investigator; b. Mar. 25, 1935, Siatista, Greece, nat. Am.; s. Sotirios and Maria E.; fiancee: Christina Gerasimos Billings; edn: law stu. La Salle Univ. Career: past mgr. (17 yrs.), Queen City Candy Co. (wholesale mfg. confectioners), Buffalo, NY; vice pres. Nickris World Movie Corp., Beverly Hills 1972--, pvt. investigator with Nickris Investigations (div. Nickris World Movie Corp.), 1976--; past sec-treas. soccer team, the Olympic, Buffalo, NY 1960-70; past pub. rels. agt. for former Miss World U.S.A., promotion for W.S. Mountfort Co. food brokerage firm, 1969; mem. Hellenic Ednl. Progressive Assn. (v.p.); Republican; Greek Orthodox; rec: tng. Spitz dogs, tennis. Ofc: Nickris Investigation div., 223 So. Beverly Dr, Ste 201, Beverly Hills 90212

ELIASBERG, KENNETH CHARLES, lawyer, financial planner; b. Feb. 26, 1932, NY, NY; s. Robert Jacob and Sylvia Ethel (Arluck) E.; children: James, b. 1957, David, b. 1961, Jonathan, b. 1964; edn: BA, USC 1953; JD, NY Univ. 1956, LLM (tax), 1960; admitted to practice State Bar of Calif., NY, Wash DC; Certified Tax Splst. 1973. Career: USAF capt., Judge Advocate General's Office, England 1956-58; wk. with father's firm, Eliasberg & Eliasberg, NY, NY 1958-60; Office of Chief Counsel, IRS, Wash DC, 1960-65; tax counsel, asst. secty. McDonnell Douglas Aircraft Co., Santa Monica 1965-69; own firm: Eliasberg & Prager and Eliasberg & Arenberg in Encino and Beverly Hills, 1969-80; head of estate plnng. dept. Mitchell Silberberg & Knupp, 1980-82; vp/ dir. of fin. plnng. Integrated Financial, Encino 1982--; prof. Univ. of San Fernando Law Sch. 1967-70; cons. Continuing Edn. of the Bar; honors: Alpha Epsilon Pi, Athlete of the Year 1952 (USC), pres. Benjamin F. Butler Club legal soc. (NYU); Treasury Dept. Spl. Service Award 1964; mem. Am., Calif., Los Angeles, Beverly Hills Bar Assns.; publs: over 25 articles, 75 speeches; bi-monthly columnist for San Fernando Valley Bar Bull., 1971, and Calif. Medical Investment and Mgmt. Assn., 1971; Hebrew; rec: music. Res: 15800 Live Oak Springs Canyon Rd Canyon Country 91351 Ofc: Integrated Financial, 16530 Ventura Blvd Encino 91436

ELKAYAM, URI, physician; b. Mar. 11, 1945, Petah-Tikva, Israel; s. Mordekay and Dvora (Shapira) E.; m. Y. Batia, Aug. 1, 1950; children: I. Ifaa, b. 1969; Yehonatan, b. 1978; Danielle, b. 1982; edn: MD, Sackler Medical Sch. 1973. Career: director Coronary Care Unit, UC Irvine Med. Center, 1979-81; currently, dir. Inpatient Cardiology, USC/LAC Medical Center; mem: Fellow Am. Coll. of Chest Physicians, Am. Heart Assn., Am. Coll. of Cardiology, Am. Fedn. for Clin. Research, Am. Coll. of Physicians; publs: num. sci. papers, abstracts, books and presentations; mil: lt. Israeli Army 1962-65; Jewish; rec: tennis. Res: 2956 Queensbury Dr. Los Angeles 90064 Ofc: USC Medical School, 2025 Zonal Ave Los Angeles 90033

ELLERBE, ROOSEVELT, manufacturing co. executive; b. May 20, 1943, Bennettsville, S.C.; s. Roosevelt and Mabel (Bass) E.; m. Joana Lee K. White, Feb. 11, 1984; dau. (by previous m.) Sara, b. 1977; edn: BS, Iowa State Univ. 1965; MA, CSU San Francisco 1970; spl. courses in mktg. Ford Motor Inst. 1972-9, Kepner-Tregoe problem solving 1974, comm. 1982; Qual. H.S. teacher/ coach. Career: zone sales mgr. Ford Motor Co., Boston, Mass. 1972-82; W. regl. sales mgr. Bell & Howell Corp., El Cerrito, Ca. 1982-3; S.W. regl. sales mgr. OSM Computer Corp., Mtn. View 1983; W. regl. sales mgr. CMC International, Walnut Creek 1983--; Defensive End Football coach, Washington State Univ., 1970-71; coord. college recruiting & rels. General Tire & Rubber, Akron, Oh. 1971-82; honors: 1965 draftee of Wash. Redskins Profl. Football Team; selected to coord. and host Sales Mgrs. Award Trip to Las Vegas, Ford Motor Co. 1979; mem. Am. Personnel Assn. 1971; vol. pee wee football coach in community; Democrat; Baptist; rec: fishing, jogging. REs: 501 Kayann Ct. El Sobrante 94803 Ofc: CMC Intl. 1299 Newell Hill Pl, Ste 200, Walnut Creek 94596

ELLINGTON, JESSE THOMPSON, JR., executive; b. Sept. 21, 1931, Phila.; s. Jesse Thompson and Elizabeth Young (Turner) E.; m. Nancy Meredith, July 18, 1959; children: Elizabeth, b. 1961, Jesse, b. 1963, Keren, b. 1965; edn: BS, Univ. of Va. 1953. Career: prodn. asst. Am. Broadcasting Co.; exec. prod. Ellington & Co.; sr. vice pres. Young & Rubicam; sr. asst. postmaster general US Postal Svc.; currently, pres. Consolidated Film Industries, Hollywood; mem: fellow Soc. of Motion Pictures & TV Engrs.; Acad. of Motion Picture Arts & Scis; Am. Mgmt. Assn.; Town Hall. Republican. Res: 1480 Charlton Rd. San Marino 91108 Ofc: Consol. Film Indus., 959 N. Seward St. Hollywood 90038.

ELLIOTT, GEORGE BRIAN, manufacturing co. executive; b.Nov. 14, 1927, Redwood City; s. Philemon Gordon and (English titled surgeon) Lady Jessie May (Radley) E.; m. Constance McConnell, Aug. 29, 1953; 1 son, Barry Gordon, b. 1955; edn: BSIE, Birkbeck Coll. (Eng.), 1949, MSIE, Birkbeck Coll. and Oxford Univ., 1951; grad. mgmt. cons., McKinsey Assoc., 1952, Proudfoot Inc., 1953. Career: v.p. internat. ops. Burroughs Wellcome & Co., NY 1947-67; pres. George B. Elliott & Assocs. (mgmt. consultants), Northridge, Ca. 1967--; v.p. American Shower Door Co. Inc., Santa Monica 1979-82; chmn. of bd./pres. The Amaranth Flower Corp., 1980--; dir. Mansell Hunt & Catty (London) 1962-; guest indsl. lectr. USC, 1967-; awards: outstanding svc., British Mgmt. Assn. 1968, Freedom of Co. of Kent 1947, for WWII svc. in Europe; mem: Am. Mgmt. Assn. cons. 1967-; Profl. Indsl. Engrs. and Consultants (activities chmn. L.A. chpt. 1967-79). author: Psychological Aspects of Indsl. Management (McMillan 1968); mil: maj. Armored Ops., WWII 1943-47, col. USMCR 1967-; decorated Mil. Cross & Bar, France & Germany Star, Italian Star, British Def. Medal; Republican; Episcopal; rec: farming/ owner Canterbury Farm, Lancaster. Res: 10252 Tunney Ave. Northridge 91324. Ofc: The Amaranth Flower Corp. 915 N. La Cienega Bl. West Los Angeles 90069.

ELLIOTT, GORDON RAY, veterans organization executive/corporate finance; b. July 31, 1916, Winnipeg, Can.; s. Frank George and Ethel Maud (Johnson) E.; m. Shirley Anderson, Nov. 2, 1950; 1 dau., Mrs. John F. Gislason, Jr., b. 1940; edn: USC, Southwestern Univ., Pacific Coast Sch of Law; grad. Am. Inst. of Banking. Career: banking, Security First (now Sec. Pac.) Nat. Bank, 1942; asst. fin. ofcr. Calif. State Guard, 1942; comdg. ofcr. US Army Air Corps 1942-46; with Vets. Adminstrn. 1946-75, budget analyst San Francisco Br. Ofc. 1946, then, asst. to dir. regl. ofcr., Los Angeles; dir. VA Regl. Ofc., Albuquerque 1957; dir. VA Regl. Ofc.and Outpatient Clinic, Phila. 1958; estab. VA Hdqtrs. for Europe, Rome, Italy 1963; dir. VA Regl. Ofc./Attache for Vet. Affairs, Manila, P.I. 1965, cons. US Negotiating team on settlement of Filipino guerilla vets. claims, 1966; dir. VA No. Calif. Regl. Ofc., S.F. 1967; dir. VA Regl. Ofc. So. Calif., Los Angeles 1970, served as dir. evacuation ops. San Fernando VA Hosp. during aftermath of 1971 earthquake (he and staff rec'd. Exceptional Service Award). Served as chmn. Calif. Jobs for Vets. Task Force under Gov. Reagan; spl. asst./adminstr. of Vets. Affairs, Wash DC 1975; past comdr. Disabled Am. Vets of Calif.; gen. mgr. Disabled Am. Vets. Charities of Gr. L.A. Inc. 1981--; bd. chmn. Vets on the Job, Inc.; dir., past pres. Purple Heart Vets. Rehab. Services, Inc.; pres. Valley Hunt Investors, Inc.; mem. adv. com. Calif. Dept. Rehab.; Calif. Vets Employment Com.; Pres.'s Commn. on Employment of Handicapped; exec. adv. council Congl. Medal of Honor Soc. 1976; co-chmn. nat. election com. Calif. Vets for Reagan & Bush, 1980; mem. Pres.-elect Reagan Transition Team, 1980; awards: Civil Servant of Year Silver Helmet, Am. Vets of WWII, Korea, Vietnam; Nat. Dist. Svc.; Purple Heart; Disabled Am. Vets; Am. Legion; VFW, Amvets Man of the Year 1961-2, Phila.; mem: Mason, Scottish Rite, Shrine, Rotary, Town Hall, Disabled Am. Vets, Am. Legion, VFW, Amvets, Overseas Press Club, Fed. Bar Assn., Reserve Officers Assn; Republican; Lutheran (budget com.); rec: oil painting, garden, writing, swim. Res: 3442 Green Vista Dr. Encino 91436. Ofc: 731-A S. Garfield Ave. Alhambra 91801.

ELLIOTT, MYRTLE EVELYN KEENER, educator; b. Apr. 11, 1898, Annawan, Ill.; d. John William and Mary Elizabeth (Baldwin) Keener; m. Dr. L. Louis Elliott, Aug. 10, 1935; 1 dau. Mary Ellen; 3 stepchil: Winona, Joan, James; edn: AB, Cornell Coll. 1921, MA, Columbia Univ. 1926, postgrad. Ohio State Univ., Univ. Chgo., San Francisco State Coll. Career: teacher (Latin, Eng.) Guthrie Co. H.S., Panora, Ia. 1921-23, (Latin, Soc. Sci.) H.S., Dewitt, Ia.. 1923-25; head Eng. Dept./Dean of Girls, H.S., Kemmerer, wyo. 1926-29; girls' adviser US Indian Svc. 1931-35; teacher (Eng., Latin) Cut Bank, Mont. 1944-46; spl. teacher, Educable Mentally retarded, Kern Co. Supt. of Schools Office, Bakersfield 1949-68, ret. 1968; cont. tchg. pvt. students in reading, 1968--. Honors: Internat. Reading Assn. 1981; Phi Beta Kappa 1924; life mem. Calif. Teachers Assn. Publs: contbr. Understanding the Child (1950, 2), The Instructor (1953, 56); Republican; Catholic. Res: 2709 Fourth St. Bakersfield 93304.

ELLIS, BARTON JOSEPH, rehabilitation program executive director; b. Jan. 15, 1939, Los Angeles; s. I. Howard and Frieda (Davis) E.; edn: BA, CSU Northridge 1963; MSW, Univ. Chgo. 1972; Lic. Clin. Social Wkr. Calif. Career: currently exec. dir. Re-Socialization Skills, Inc., mainstreaming program for severely mentally ill; helped start Free Clinic Movement; worked with disadvantaged youth in So. Central L.A. Suicide Prevention Center, Research and Nightwatch; pvt. practice, psychotherapy cons. to pvt. psychiatric hosps., hosp. psychiat. social wkr. Mem. Nat. Assn. Social Wkrs.; pioneer in devel. of community based social rehab. pgm. for the mentally ill; mil: Sp4 USAR; rec: running. Ofc: (Re-)Socialization Skills, Inc. 1535 Sixth St, Ste 207, Santa Monica 90401

ELLIS, EUGENE JOSEPH, physician; b. Feb. 23, 1919, Rochester, NY; s. Eugene J. and Violet (Anderson) E.; m. Ruth Nugent, July 30, 1943; children: E. Joe, b. 1943; Susan Gallagher, b. 1945; Amy Miller, b. 1950; edn: AB, USC 1941, MD, USC Med. Sch. 1944; MS in medicine, Univ. of Minn. 1950. Career: dir. Dept. of Cardiology, Hosp. of Good Samaritan, Los Angeles 1957-82; clin. prof. of medicine USC Med. School 1965-82; mem. Calif. State Board of Med. Quality Assurance, 4-yr. appt.; bd. trustees (exec. com.) Univ. of Redlands; pres. Mayo Clinic Cardiovascular Soc. 1976-79; clubs: Los Angeles CC, Pauma Valley CC (bd.), Flat Rock Fishing Club; num. medical publs.; mil: lt. USNR 1943-5; Republican; Presbyterian; rec: golf, fly fishing. Res: 6166 Oakwood Ave Los Angeles 90004

ELLIS, JOHN WILSON, lawyer, b. Oct. 27, 1931, Beaumont, Tex.; s. Lacoste George and Bobbie Mae (Lee) E.; father, L.G. Ellis, retired head Geophysical Dept. Sun Oil Co., holder num. patents in field of geophysics; m. Marilyn White, Sept. 2, 1960; children: Scott, b. 1961, Holly, b. 1963; edn: BA, Univ. of Tex. 1954, JD, 1958. Career: practiced law in Texas 1958-62; Shearson, Hammill & Co., 1962-64; Bank of Am. Trust Officer, 1966-72; asst. prof. (contracts, wills, personal prop., ins., creditors' rights), So. Texas Coll. of Law 1965-66; practice of law in Calif. 1972--; past mem. bd. govs. and instr. comml. law, Am. Inst. of Banking; instr. bus. law, Santa Barbara City Coll.; served as trustee, Endowment Fund Trust and dir. Santa Barbara Sym. Orch. Assn.; fmr. commnr. Santa Barbara Golf Course Commn.; mem: Bar Assns. of Calif., Tex., Santa Barbara County; Estate Planning Council of Santa Barbara; Profl. Golfers Assn. Hole-In-One Club; (fmr) La Cumbre CC, Montecito CC; Republican; rec: golf, hiking, backpacking. Res: 577 No Hope Ave Santa Barbara 93110 Ofc: Atty. at Law, 233 E. Carillo St Santa Barbara 93101

ELLIS, MICHAEL THOMAS, electronics co. executive; b. Nov. 8, 1942, Baldock, Herts, Eng., nat. 1978; s. Thomas Andrew Harwood and Ceridwen (Jones) E.; m. Janet Piper, Aug. 28, 1965; children: Damon, b. 1970, Claire, b. 1974; edn: BSc, No. Polytech. 1965; grad. work City Univ. 1965-6; MS, Long Island Univ. 1972. Career: student scholar W. H. Sanders Electronics, 1961-66; activity mgr. British Aircraft Corp., 1966-68; program mgr. Pro Electronics, Syosset, N.Y. 1968-75; exec. v.p. ATE Assocs., Westlake, Ca. 1975--. US ed. Test Mag.; bd. advisors Electronics Test Mag., Test &: Measurement World Mag.; cons. to aerospace & military. Awards: appreciation, US Army, US Navy; awd. of excellence, Soc. for Tech. Comm.; Sci. Resrch. Council Scholarship 1965-6; mem: Internat. Atlas Com., Joint Services ATE Com. Lectured extensively US & Europe; num. tech. publs. on test automation topics; rec: bridge, golf, tennis. Res: 3898 Via Verde, Thousand Oaks 91360 Ofc: ATE Associates, 5707 Corsa Ave Westlake 91360

ELLIS, STEPHEN BRIAN, finance co. executive; b. Mar. 30, 1932, NY, NY; s. Emil K. and Thelma K. Ellis; div.; 1 son, Craig Steven, b. 1959; edn: BA, Long Island Univ. 1952; CSU Northridge 1963-4; LLB, Blackstone Law Sch. 1966. Career: pres. Key Industries (real estate finance) 1963-74; pres. Dream Inn Hotel, Santa Cruz 1974-75; pres. Los Angeles Helicopter Airlines, 1975-76; vice pres./partner ICS Financial Services, Inc., 1976--, dir. Hotel Consultants of Am. 1974-5; dir. Pacific Seaboard Airlines 1975-7; honors: 11-year mem. Mayor Sam Yorty's Community Adv. Com. (LA); mem: founder, The Magic Castle (Hollywood); San Francisco Mus. Soc.; bd. dirs. Salvation Army; POPAS (Patrons of the Perf. Arts); bd. dirs. Am. Repertoire Theatre from Europe, publs. newspaper column, Los Angeles Daily News 1963-65, num. mag. articles; mil: psychol. warfare splst. US Army 1953-55; Republican; Jewish; rec: magician. Res: 272 So Rexford Dr Beverly Hills 90212 Ofc: ICS Financial Services, Inc. 9454 Wilshire Blvd Beverly Hills 90212

ELLSWORTH, DAVID G., lawyer; b. Jan. 20, 1941, Los Angeles; s. Kennedy and Catherine (Carroll) E.; children: Brett, b. 1968; Erin, b. 1970; edn: BS, USC 1962, LLB, JD, 1965; admitted to State Bar of Calif. 1966. Career: law clerk to Hon. E. Avery Crary, Judge, US Dist. Ct., Central Dist. 1965-6; assoc. atty. law firm Meserve, Mumper & Hughes, Los Angeles 1966-70, partner 1970-80; partner/ head of real estate dept. law firm Memel, Jacobs, Pierno & Gersh, Los Angeles 1980--; bd. of commnrs. (chmn. 1978-81) Housing Authority of Co. of Los Angeles 1977-85; bd. commnrs. LA Co. Beach Adv. Commn. 1981-; bd. commnrs. (chmn. 1982-3) LA Co. Housing Commn. 1982-; apptd. by State Lt. Gov. to Commn. of The Californias 1978-, (chmn. Tourism Com. 1979; apptd. by Gov. Deukmejian to Adv. Council 1983-). Mem: Am. Land Devel. Assn. (dir.; chmn. Internat. Council); National Timesharing Council (bd. dirs.; chmn. Intl. Affairs Com.); Pacific Area Travel Assn. (Devel. Authority); Nat. Assn. of Corp. Real Estate Execs.; clubs: Wilshire CC (LA), The Vintage (Indian Wells), Malibu Riding & Tennis, San Carlos (Ca.) CC; assoc. editor nat. monthly publs: Land Development Law Reporter, and Resort Timesharing Law Reporter; contbg. author num. periodicals; frequent featured spkr. seminars, confs. Res: 26104 Pacific Coast Hwy Malibu 90265 Ofc: Memel, Jacobs, Pierno & Gersh, 1801 Century Park East, 25th Flr, Los Angeles 90067

ELLSWORTH, EDMUND BRAY, real estate broker/land developer; b. Oct. 17, 1920, Plainfield, NJ; s. Edmund Frank and Ann (Bray) E.; gr. gr. gr. grandson of Brigham Young; m. Martha Orme, Aug. 24, 1940; children: Martha Louise, b. 1942, Edmund James, b. 1944, John Bland, b. 1950; edn: grad. Technical H.S. 1939, stu. San Francisco City Coll.; Lic. Real Estate Broker. Career: self-empl. 1943-, owner Whitehall Resort, 1943-63; real estate broker, land developer; an organizer of Highway 50 Assn. (pres. 1946-47), helped originate Highway 50 Wagon Train; recipient Highway 50 Award; mem. Silver Fork Sch. Bd. 1946-55; mem: Elks, Highway 50 Assn., Cold Springs Golf and Country Club, charter mem. E Clampus Vitus, Ky. Col.; Democrat; rec: history, conservation (pure water, forests). Address: Whitehall, Pacific House P.O., Calif. 95725

ELLSWORTH, FRANK L., college president; b. May 20, 1943, Wooster, Ohio; s. Clayton S. and Frances (Fuller) E.; 1 dau., Kirstin Lynne; edn: AB, cum laude, Case Western Reserve Univ. 1965; M.Ed., Penna. State Univ. 1967; MA in Am. lit., Columbia Univ. 1969; PhD, Univ. Chgo. 1976. Career: asst. dir. devel. Columbia Law Sch., 1968-70; dir. spl. projects/ prof. lit. Sarah Lawrence Coll., 1971; asst. dean Law Sch., Univ. Chgo., 1971-79, instr. social sci. collegiate div., 1975-79; pres. Pitzer College, Claremont, Calif. 1979--, also prof. polit. studies, 1979-. Mem. vis. coms. Case Western Res. Coll.; bd. dirs. Ind. Colls. So. Calif.; bd. dirs. Southwestern Univ. Sch. of Law; bd. fellows Claremont Univ. Center; bd. dirs. Los Angeles Ballet; honors: first recipient, Distinguished Young Alumnus, Western Res. Coll., Case W. Res. Univ., 1981; hon. chpsn Salute to Minority Edn., The Golden State Minority Found. 1980-; mem: Am. Hist. Assn., Council for the Adv. of Sec. Edn., Friends of Huntington Lib., Hist. of Edn. Soc., Young Presidents Orgn.; clubs: Arts Club of Chgo., LA World Affairs Council, Town Hall of Calif., Univ. Clubs of Claremont, LA, Zamorano Club of LA; frequent public spkr., lectr.; articles in profl. jours. Office of the Pres., Pitzer College, 1050 No Mills Ave Claremont 91711

ELROD, CECIL TOMMY, chemist; b. Aug. 5, 1948, Ventura; s. William Tommy and Francis Marian (Clifton) E.; m. Alba Posada, Dec. 10, 1977; children: Michelle, b. 1978, Katherine, b. 1979, Caroline, b. 1981; edn: BS in chem., UC Santa Barbara 1971; MBA in prog., National Univ. Career: chemical sales Hornkohl Lab., Bakersfield 1972-73, Magna Corp., Santa Fe Springs 1974-78, NL Baroid (NLTC), Compton 1978-79, Millhorn Chem. & Supply Co., Maywood, 1979--; instr. sems. Magna Corp. 1975-6; mem: Nat. Assn. of Corrosion Engrs. 1974-78, Soc. of Petroleum Engr. 1974-78, Am. Soc. of Electroplaters 1979-, Calif. Circuit Board Assn. 1981-, Jeanne Jugan Soc. Little Sisters of the Poor 1980-; Democrat; Catholic; rec: karate. Res: 2809 Bellflower Blvd. Long Beach 90815 Ofc: Millhorn Chem. & Supply Co. 6142 Walker Ave. Maywood 90270.

ELSER, GORDON LEE, public information officer; b. Aug. 12, 1939, Youngstown, Ohio; s. Leonard Dale and Kathryn (Wunderlich) E.; m. Kathy Alls, Aug. 7, 1970; children: Brent, b. 1963, Brandy, b. 1971; edn: Univ. of Redlands 1957-8, UC Riverside 1958-9, Riverside City Coll. 1959-61, San Diego State Univ. 1961-2; Engr.-in-Tng. (EIT) State of Calif. 1963. Career: jr. civil engr. Orange Co. Harbors Beaches and Parks Dist., 1962-65, asst. civil engr., 1965-71; vice pres. Sayona Corp., 1971-73, land planner Wm. Heppler & Assoc., 1973-74; public information officer Orange Co. Water District, 1973--; active in num. water afil. assns., past chmn. Pub. Rels. Com., Assn. of Calif. Water Agencies; fmr. prin. investigator on series of desalting wkshops across US; mem: Assn. of Calif. Water Agencies, O.C. Water Assn., Nat. Water Supply Improvement Assn., Nat. Speakers Assn., Calif. Assn. of Public Info. Ofcrs.; pres. Monarch Bay Assn. (homeowners); mil: served to sgt. E5, USMC; Republican; Prot.; rec: beach, volleyball, photog., travel. Res: 203 Monarch Bay, So Laguna 92677 Ofc: POB 8300 Fountain Valley 92728

ELY, DOUGLAS LEON, chemical engineer; b. June 15, 1955, Grand Junction, Colo.; s. Dale Leon and Altha Anna (Borden) E.; edn: AS, Mesa Coll. 1975; BS in chem. engring., Univ. of Colo. 1977; Reg. Profl. Chem. Engr. Calif. 1981. Career: process engr., design engr., computer process control engr. Chevron USA El Segundo Refinery, 1978--, lead process engr. Refinery Systems and Environmental Group, 1982-; mem. Western Oil and Gas Hazardous Waste Disposal Emissions Task Force; mem. El Segundo Refinery Hazardous Waste Task Force; publs: presented paper, Air Pollution Control Assn. Conf., Phoenix, Az. 1983; Republican; Prot.; rec: piano, skiing, fishing, auto body repair. Rees: 726 Bayview Hermosa Beach 90254 Ofc: Chevron USA 324 W. El Segundo Blvd El Segundo 90245

EMERICH, BARBARA BINE, career volunteer/child advocate; b. Dec. 3, 1919, San Francisco; d. Dr. Rene and Alma E. (Kahn) Bine; edn: BA in psych., Stanford Univ. 1940, Gen. Sec. Cred. 1942, MA in educ. guid., 1943; m. Robert Emerich, Apr. 8, 1947; children: Sally, b. 1948, Carol, b. 1950, Melvin, b. 1952, Rene, b. 1956. Career: vocational tester, Jr. Counseling Svc., Calif. Employment Ofc., San Francisco 1940-41; high sch. counselor/tchr. Salinas (Ca.) Union H.S. 1942-46; social wk. S.F. Co. Hosp., 1946; probation ofcr. S.F. Juvenile Probation Dept., 1946-47; adult edn. advis. com. (ch. 1979-81) Mtn. View-Los Altos Union H.S. Dist., 1966-; Santa Clara Co. Sch. Attendance Review Bd. 1977-; Santa Clara Co.: Protective Svcs. Advis. Com. 1965-71; Child and Adolescent Task Force (75-6) Advis. Commn. 1976-80 (ch. 76-8); Delinquency Prev. Commn. 1981- (ch. 81-2); Justice Sys. Advis. Bd. 1978-; bd. mem. Comm. Health Abuse Council (Mtn. View) 1972-80; Child Advocacy Council (and predecessor orgn.), Sta Clara & San Mateo Counties 1972- (bd. mem. 82-). Honors: Pi Delta Phi, Pi Lamda Theta; recipient Calif. PTA service awards 1964, 71, 83; commendation, Sta Clara Co. Bd. of Supvrs. 1980; nominee for Sta. Clara Co. Woman of Year 1983. Mem: Stanford Alumni Assn., Nat. Council of Jewish Women, League Women Voters (bd. 1970-80), PTA (pres. Los Altos Council 1965-6; Sta Clara Co. bd. mgrs. 1962-); Calif. State PTA (bd. mgrs. 1977-, bd. dirs. 1981-, pub. rels. ch. 1983-); Jewish; rec: tennis. Res: 209 Portola Ct. Los Altos 94022

EMERZIAN, LOUISE AIVAZIAN, retirement home administrator; b. May 15, 1933, Selma, Ca.; d. Edward Manoog and Diane (Avedisian) Aivazian; div.; children: Susan (Head), b. 1957, Lynn Louise, b. 1960, Carrie Ann, b. 1962; edn: BA, CSU Fresno 1956, MSW, 1977. Career: mental health worker Kings View Hosp., Reedley 1972-76; asst. adminstr./ adminstr. Calif. Armenian Home, Fresno 1977--; cons. Ombudsman Pgm., mem. seniors adv. com. Clovis Adult Edn.; honors: life mem. Calif. Scholarship Fedn. 1949, Quill & Scroll; mem. Am. Coll. of Nursing Home Adminstrs.; vol. task force com. St. Agnes Med. Ctr. Hospice Pgm. 1978-9; Republican; Methodist; rec: travel. Res: 371 Bethel, 78, Sanger 93657 Ofc: Calif. Armenian Home, 6720 E. Kings Cyn. Fresno 93727

ENDO, KYOSUKE, bank executive; b. Feb. 11, 1933, Tokyo, Japan; s. Shizuhiko and Koto (Kobayashi) E.; m. Chiyoko Kawano, Nov. 8, 1963; children: Yayoi, b. 1965, Kaori, b. 1967, Akemi, b. 1970; edn: BA, Chuo Univ., Japan 1956. Career: deputy gen. mgr. Internat. Div. The Kyowa Bank, Ltd., Tokyo, 1977, sr. deputy gen. mgr. London (Eng.) Branch 1978; sr. vice pres. The Kyowa Bank of Calif., Los Angeles 1979, pres. 1983--; gen. mgr. The

Kyowa Bank, Ltd., Los Angeles Agency 1981--; Dir: The Kyowa Bank of Calif., Japan Business Assn. of So. Calif.; mem: LA CofC, NCCJ (dir.), LA Athletic Club; rec: golf, tennis, travel. Res: 878 Sierra Madre Blvd San Marino 91108 Ofc: The Kyowa Bank, Ltd. 635 W. 7th St Los Angeles 90017

ENGEL, ALBERT E., space technology systems engineer; b. Jan. 24, 1929, Chgo.; s. Otto and Anna Angella (Andrich) E.; edn: BSEE, Univ. So. Miss. 1957, MSEE, 1959. Career: tech. rep. Philco Corp., Phila. 1958-59; site mgr. RCA, Camden, N.J. 1959-63; engring. mgr. Aerojet Gen. Corp., Azusa, Ca. 1963-72; pres., bd. chmn. Defense Systems, Inc., Marina Del Rey 1972-80; sr. systems engr. TRW-Space & Tech. Gp., Redondo Beach 1980--; profl. cons. US Govt., Wash DC 1978-80; mem: National Space Club (Wash DC), Am. Aeronautical Soc., Am. Inst. Aero & Astro, IEEE; author 3 major books (documents) mission R & D of conceptual satellites 1990-2020 mil. applications; Republican; Catholic. Res: POB 1550, Hawthorne 90250 Ofc: TRW Space & Technology Gp. R5/1010, One Space Park, Redondo Beach 90278.

ENGEL, RICHARD GARDNER, maintenance engineering co. president; b. March 12, 1944, Phila.; s. USAF Col.(ret.) Gardner W. and Marian A. (Coll) Engel; 1 dau., Kimberly Jean, b. 1967; edn: BSME, Okla. State Univ. 1967; JD, Western State Univ. 1974; passed Calif. Bar Exam 1975. Career: mech. engr. NASA; assoc. engr. Lear Jet Co.; field engr. Elliott Co.; field and sales engr. Solar Div.; project engr. C.E. Miller Corp.; mech. engr. Bechtel Corp., Internat. Power, engring. field changes for fgn.constrn. of nuclear power plants; pres. Pacific Coast Indsl. (providing gen. power plant maint., overhaul); currently, CEO/pres. Powerplant Specialists, Inc. (overhaul, repair, maint. of large boilers and turbines for utility cos., overhaul and turnarounds of refineries: SCE, LADWP, PG&E, SDG&E, Chevron, Texaco, Union Oil, Kerr-McGee). Mem. ASME, Pacific Energy Assn., Energy Club of Los Angeles, LA CofC; Republican; Episcopal; clubs: Ferrari Owners, El Toro Flying. Res: 11 Beacon Bay Newport Bch 92660 Ofc: Powerplant Specialists, Inc. 666 W. Baker #413 Costa Mesa 92626

ENGELS, CHERYL ELAINE, communications co. executive; b. Oct. 22, 1943, Napa; d. Lawrence Philip and Elaine Helen (Giauque) Harris; m. John Peralta Engels, May 3, 1970; children: Ceseley, b. 1972; Jason, b. 1976; edn: BA, Univ. of the Pacific 1965. Career: with Pacific Tel., Santa Rosa 1965-82: asst./traffic operating mgr., 1965-7, traffic op. mgr. 1967-9, 1971-77, asst. traffic supt. 1969-71; Operator Svcs. staff mgr. (S.F.) 1977-79, force mgr. (Santa Rosa) 1979-83; mgr. Opr. Svcs. AT&T Communications, Santa Rosa 1984--; guest lectr. CSU Sonoma 1982; adviser (1965-8), bd. dirs. (1970-2) Jr. Achievement; treas. Santa Rosa Central Soccer Club 1981-2. Awards: Outstanding Junior Woman Delta Delta Delta 1964; art awards Napa County Fair 1964, 65; exhib. Jack London Art Show 1965. Mem: Order of Eastern Star (majority mem. Jobs Daus., Rainbow for Girls), Telephone Pioneers of Am.; Democrat; Prot.; rec: painting, golf, tennis. Res: 2054 Rolling Hill Dr Santa Rosa 95404 Ofc: AT&T Comm. 520 Third St, Rm 431, Santa Rosa 95401

ENGLE, BENJAMIN J., lawyer; b. Oct. 1, 1941, Erie, Pa.; s. Paul T. and Jane F. (Joyce) E.; m. Martha, Feb. 17, 1983; children: Julie Ann, b. 1969, Wendy S., b. 1972; edn: BA, Gonzaga Univ. 1963; JD, Univ. San Fernando Coll. of Law 1974; admitted Calif. State Bar 1974, Fed. Dist. Ct. Central, So. Dists. of Calif. Career: claims supr./staff atty. Travelers Ins. Co., 1968-74; atty. Law Ofcs. of Robert Bolton, 1975, Law Ofcs. Ross, Feinberg & Wolf, 1976, Law Ofcs. Miller & Folse, 1977-79; partner Law Ofcs. McGahan & Engle, Ventura 1979--, spec. medical malpractice and products liability; judge pro tem Ventura Co. Superior Ct.; examiner State Bar of Calif.; arbitrator Am. Arbitration Assn., Ventura Co. Bar Assn., Ventura Co. Superior Ct. Panel; mem: Am., Calif., Ventura Co. Bar Assns.; honors: Who's Who in Am. Colls. and Univs. 1963, Distinguished Mil. Graduate; mil: capt. US Army 1963-67; Republican; Catholic; rec: bridge. Res: 867 Viewcrest St 93003 Ofc: McGahan & Engle, 2060 Knoll Dr, Ste 100, Ventura 93003

ENGLISH, EUBON "Ed" DANIEL, plumbing contractor; b. Jan. 21, 1922, Branch, Ark.; s. Esther Lee and Maggie (Henry) E.; m. Shirly Sterling, Dec. 8, 1956; children (by previous marriage): Daniel Wayne, b. 1948, Lori Ann, b. 1966, Edward Eugene, b. 1969; edn: Cert. waste water, No. 2, American River Coll. 1965; Cert. waste water treatment plant opr., No. 3, State of Calif., Sierra Coll. 1968. Career: various labor empl. Ark. and Los Angeles, 1937-45; truck driver Coast Tank Lines, San Pedro, 1946-51; bus driver Greyhound Lines, San Francisco 1951-56; iron wkr.-Teamster, C.E. Toland & Son, Oakland 1956-62; sanitation supt. Placer Co. 1962-79; plumbing contr., 1979--; honors: Public Service Citation, Placer Co. Dept. Pub. Works 1979; mem. Auburn Model A Club (pres. 1967), Elks; Democrat; Prot.; rec: auto restoration, hunt, fish, RV. Address: Ed's Plumbing, 13360 Dry Creek Rd Auburn 95603

ENSSLIN, JAMES EMIL, real estate broker/investor; b. July 12, 1929, Porterville; s. Theodore Gustaf and Lula Pearl (Jackson) En.; m. Wanda Stief, Jan. 16, 1965; children: Reesa, b. 1949, Jami, b. 1951, James M., b. 1955; edn: Don Martin Sch. of Radio-TV 1948; La Salle Univ. ext. 1961; lic. real estate broker. Career: gen. mgr. Cooperative Corporations, 1950-57; agt. NY Life Ins. Co., 1958-60; controller Drew Chemicals Corp., Lindsay 1960-63; cost acct. Safeway Stores, San Jose 1963-64; office mgr. Roberts Farms, Poplar 1965-66; real estate broker, gold-silver dealer, 1967--. Res: 853 E. Normal Fresno 93704

ERBURU, ROBERT F., communications co. executive; b. Sept. 27, 1930, Ventura; s. Michael Peter and Kathryn (Sarzotti) Erburu; m. Lois Stone, July 31, 1954; daus.: Susan Kit (Mrs. George D. Reardon), . 1956, Lisa Ann (Mrs. Mark Williams Cocalis), b. 1960; edn: BA, USC 1952, JD, Harvard Law Sch. 1955. Career: atty. firm of Gibson, Dunn & Crutcher, Los Angeles 1955-61; elected gen. counsel and secty. Times Mirror Co., L.A. 1961, vice pres. 1965-69, sr. v.p. 1969, pres. 1975-, COO 1980, CEO 1981--, bd. dirs. 1968-; dir./v.p. The Times Mirror Found.; dir. The Tejon Ranch Co. 1975-; dir. Metro. Los Angeles YMCA 1973-, v.chmn. 1976-; dir. Ind. Colls. of So. Calif. 1973-, chmn. 1976-7; bd. trustees Marlborough Sch. 1974-, pres. 1979-81; bd. visitors UCLA Grad. Sch of Mgmt. 1974-; bd. trustees Huntington Lib. 1981-, bd. overseers 1976-81; bd. trustees The William and Flora Hewlett Found. 1980-; bd. trustees Pfaffinger Found.; Com. to Visit the Harvard Law Sch. 1978-; Council of Fgn. Rels. 1980-; bd. dirs. Carrie Estelle Doheny Found. 1981-, Fletcher Jones Found. 1982-. Awards: Am. Jewish Com. Human Rels. Award; NCCJ So. Calif. Region Brotherhood awd. 1979. mem: Am. Bar Assn., State Bar of Calif., Soc. of Profl. Journalists, Sigma Delta Chi. ofc: The Times Mirror Co. Times Mirror Sq. Los Angeles 90053.

ERICKSON, THOMAS OSCAR, cartographer; b. Sept. 10, 1943, Fort Bragg, Calif.; s. Oscar Adolph and Beatrice (Raskin) E.; children: Dara, b. 1964, Derek, b. 1968, Kinara, b. 1974; edn. grad. Fort Bragg Union H.S. 1961. Career: quality control tech. Champion Packages, San Leandro 1968-70; teacher Humboldt State Univ. Child Devel. Lab., 1971-72, instr. Ext. Pgm. 1972-74; seminar instr./owner Paraclete Inst., Arcata 1976-77; cartographer/owner Erickson Maps, Oakland 1978--; cons. with various firms on map making; mem. The Map Soc. of Calif.; mil: Sp4 US Army 1964-67, GCM, Army commendation, Medal of Occ., commend. fron Col. Kunzig, US Cmdr. Berlin Office 1966; rec: philately, white water rafting, hunt, fish, soar. Res: 3928 MacArthur Blvd, C, Oakland 94602 Ofc: Erickson Maps, 337 17th St, Ste. 211, Oakland 94612

ERICSON, DONALD ANDREW, company president; b. Feb. 2, 1934, Anoka, Minn.; s. Eric Fred and Inez Margrete (Anderson) E.; m. Roberta Ann Haney, Sept. 9, 1958; children: Jon, b. 1960, Kristi, b. 1963; edn: Gustavus Adolphus Coll. 1952-4; Univ. of S.Dak. 1955-7. Career: sales rep. 3M Company, Pittsburg 1958-63; gen. mgr. I. Genstein Inc., 1963-74; ASD Div. mgr. Compugraphic Corp., 1974-80; W. regl. mgr. Hastech Inc., 1980-84; pres. Upland Lighting & Electrical Supplies Inc., 1984--; mem. Upland CofC, Building Indus. Assn.; publs: HiLites & Shadows, Highlites; mil: sgt. USMC; Republican; Lutheran; rec: sailing. Res: 1938 Eloise Way Upland 91786 Ofc: Upland Lighting, 1174 West Ninth St Upland 91786

ERVIN, PATRICIA CONNELLY, association executive; b. Dec. 23, 1924, Owatonna, Minn.; d. James B. and Mavilda D. (Scoville) Connelly; edn: BA, USC, 1950, MA, 1954, UCLA Law Sch., 1958; career: teacher public schools 1954-58; founder and current leader, Holistic Healing Group 1972--; founding mem. Assn. for Holistic Health 1976-; currently pres., United Nations Assn. of Los Angeles; currently, v.p. Philosophical Research Soc., Los Angeles. Lectr. on holistic healing and philosophy, Philosophical Research Soc. 1979-. Recipient UN Peace Award, 1978, UN Assn. of U.S., So. Calif. Div. Independent; Christian. Office: The Philosophical Research Soc. 3910 Los Feliz Blvd. Los Angeles 90027.

ESCALANTE, ROEL, purchasing executive; b. July 16, 1937, L.A., Ca.; s. Angel and Maria (Arellanos) Escalante; edn: AA, Valley Jr. Coll., 1959; chil: Anthony, b. 1965; career: Asst. Purchasing agent, Colony Paint & Chemical Co., L.A. Co., 1964-67; buyer, Traid Corp., LA, 1967-69; asst. purchasing mgr., Walt Disney Prod., Burbank, 1969-76; Dir. of purchasing, MCA Inv., Universal City, 1976-79; Corp. Dir. of materiel/Div. Vice Pres., MCA Inc., Universal City, 1979--; Certified Purchasing Manager; Great Western Council B.S.A.; Mem.: So. Calif. Regional Purchasing Council; Natl. Assoc. Purchasing Managers; L.A. Purchasing Management Assoc; American Management Assoc.; Republican; Catholic; rec: tennis, backpacking; ofc: MCA Inc., 100 Universal City Plaza, Universal City 91608.

ESCOBAR, LETICIA ESPERANZA, dentist; b. Nov. 20, 1951, San Francisco; d. Francisco Jose and Leticia (Romero) Escobar; m. Kazuo Aoki, Mar. 5, 1982; edn: National Univ. of El Salvador, 1969-72; BA, San Francisco State Univ. 1977; DDS, UCSF Sch of Dentistry 1981. Career: English instr. Sunshine Language Inst., Tokyo, Japan 1981-82; assoc. dentist De Ocampo Dental Group, San Francisco and San Jose, 1982-83; clin. care coord./assoc. dentist George Bonnell, DDS, Inc. San Francisco 1982--; honors: Xi Psi Phi frat., appreciation, UC Sch. of Dentistry 1978; mem. Mutual Assn. for Profl. Services, Coalition of Concerned Medical Profls., Japanese Newcomers Svcs.; presenter ednl. program for sr. citizens, Kimochi Home, 1980; Democrat; Catholic; rec: swim, photog., community service. Res: 280 Parnassus Ave, 3, San Francisco 94117 Ofc: 450 Sutter St, Ste 2234, San Francisco 94108

ESGUERRA, HILARIO S., III, pediatrician; b. May 18, 1939, Manila, Phil.; s. Hilario G. and Josefina S. Esguerra; m. Sonia Encabo, Sept. 13, 1964; children: Jaime, b. 1965, Julie May, b. 1969, Henry Paul, b. 1970; edn: AA, Univ. of the Phil. 1959, MD, 1964; medical intern Deaconess Hosp. (St. Louis) 1966; pediatric res. Good Samaritan Hosp. (Cincinnati) 1968; Diplomate Am. Bd. of Pediatrics 1969. Career: instr. of pediatrics, Univ. of the Phil., Manila 1969-70; chief Pediatric Renal Clinic/ instr. pediatrics Far Eastern Univ. Hosp., Manila 1970-73; chief Renal Div. Childrens Med. Ctr., Manila 1974-81; tng. ofcr. Dept. Pediatrics, Capitol Medical ctr., Manila 1978-80, chief exec. 1980-81; staff phys. Dept. Devel. Svcs., Napa State Hosp. 1981-82; pediatrician pvt practice, Manteca 1982--; honors: sev. research contests, 1972-76; mem: Fellow Am. Acad. Pediatrics, Phil. Soc. of Pediatric Nephrology (pres. 1975), Internat. Pediat. Nephrol. Assn., San Joaquin Med. Soc.; author med. textbook: Diseases of the Kidneys in Children (1973), contbr. chpt. pediat. textbook, num. med. jour. articles; rec: running. Res: 1160 Ward Place Manteca 95336 Ofc: Dr. Hilario S. Esguerra III, 1234 E. North St. Manteca 95336

ESGUERRA, LARRY SABARILLO, IV, bank executive; b. May 7, 1949, Manila, Phil.; s. Hilario Gonzales and Josefina Soriano (Sabarillo) E.; edn: BSBA, Univ. Phil. 1969. Career: cert. pub. acct. J.L. Maranan & Assocs., CPAs, Manila 1969-71; res. auditor Citibank, N.A., Philippine Branches 1971-75, insp. Citibank Internat. Insp. Team for Asia/Pacific/Europe region 1975; mgr. Controllership Div., Filcapital Devel. Corp., Manila 1976; lectr. ASEAN Center for Finl. Tech., Ateneo de Manila Grad. Sch of Bus., 1978; practicing CPA, Manila 1970-79; asst. v.p. Assoc. Citizens Bank, Manila 1976-79; fin. ofcr. JRK Devel. Corp., Manila 1976-; v.p. and cashier/ comptroller Pacific Union Bank & Trust, Menlo Park 1979--; dir. Corporate Resource Consultants, Manila 1978-9. mem: Inst. of Internal Auditors, SF; Am. Mgmt. Assn.; Philippine Inst. of CPAs; Bank Adminstrn. Inst., Phil. chpt.; fmr. mem. Asian Tax Assn., Assn. of CPAs in Commerce & Indus., Manila. Coauthor: Comml. Banking Ops. in the Philippines (1979), Katha Publs., Phil., ofcl. fin. textbk. Univ. of the East, Phil.; prin. author: Ops. Policy & Procedure Manual, Assoc. Citizens Bank. Catholic. rec: photog. Res: 500 W. Middlefield Rd., 145, Mountain View 94043 Ofc: Pacific Union Bank & Trust Co. 800 Oak Grove Ave. Menlo Park 94025.

ESPALDON, MERLE LAZARO, social worker; b. Mar. 23, 1939, Philippines; d. Benjamin Tuazon and Feliculа J. (Denoman) Lazaro; m. Wilfredo Espaldon, June 22, 1963; children: Karen, b. 1964, Michelle, b. 1967; edn: BA, Univ. of the Phil. 1959; MSW, Univ. Mich. 1962; LCSW, lic. clin. soc. wkr., Calif. 1982. Career: soc. wkr. Catholic Social Service, San Francisco 1962-64; instr. Univ. of the East, Philippines 1964-72; casewkr. Phil. Internat.Assn. of Schs. of Soc. Work Manila Secretariat, 1970; exec. asst. On Lok Senior Health Svcs., San Francisco 1972--, soc. wrk. supr. Day Hlth Ctr. 1974-; instr. CSUSF 1980-82; supr. undergrads. & grad. soc. wrk. students, UC Berkeley, UC Davis, CSU Sacto., CSUSF; past chmn. faculty-student rels. Sociol. Dept., and past chmn. pub. rels. com. Univ. of the East; mem. Filipino Resource Group 1982-; mem. Phil. Assn. of Soc. Wkrs. 1964-72; mem: Pilipino-Am. Involvement League of Calif., Filipino Americans of Benicia, Soc. Wkrs in Hlth Care; coauthor: Sociology and Social Living (txtbk); profl. jour. art., 1983; Catholic; rec: music, read. Res: 528 Cambridge Dr. Benicia 94510 Ofc: On Lok Senior Health Services 1441 Powell St, San Francisco 94133

ESPE, ROGER BRADLEY, manufacturing co. executive; b. July 20, 1944, Salt Lake City, Utah; s. Curtiss Walter and Marjorie (Brunais) E.; m. Karolee Thompson, Jan. 23, 1976; children: Terry, b. 1963, Suzanne, b. 1966, Sean, b. 1968, Kristi, b. 1971; edn: BFA, Colo. State Univ. 1966. Career: design cons. Robert Caudle & Assoc., Denver, Co. 1969; design dir. Seal Furniture & Systems, Denver 1971; sales mgr. Jachn's, Rapid City, S.D. 1974; sales/ops. mgr. Seal Furniture & Systems, Los Angeles/ Long Beach 1977; regl. vice pres. sales Harbor/Benedetti, L.A. 1983--; clubs: Jaycees (bd. dirs. 1972-4), Elks, Cosmopolitan; mil: E6 USNG 1965-72; Republican; Prot.; rec: sailing, skiing. Res: 26425 Brookfield Rd San Juan Capistrano 92675 Ofc: Harbor/Benedetti, 3011 E. Pico Blvd Los Angeles 90023

ESPINA, PATERNA S., welfare agency executive; b. Nov. 12, 1934, Manila, Philippines, nat. 1977; d. Felicisimo and Felisa (Austria) Sta. Ana; m. Martin G. Espina, Dec. 19, 1964; children: Mary Ann, b. 1966, Martin Jr., b. 1978; edn: BA, Univ. of the Phil. 1955, MSW, 1963; postgrad. dip. in urban plnng., University Coll. London 1970; Calif. Lic. Clin. Social Wkr. (LCSW) 1981, Marriage, Family & Child Counselor (MFCC) 1981. Career: Div. chief, Dept. Social Welfare, Manila, Phil. 1962-5, sr. soc. welfare analyst 1965-70, soc. welfare splst. 1970-7; counselor Childrens Hosp. of LA Regl. Center, 1977-9; suprvg. counselor Frank D. Lanterman Regl. Ctr., Los Angeles 1979-80, program mgr., coord. Family Life, 1980--; clin. social wkr./ marriage family & child counselor 1982--; program cons. to various board and care facilities 1978-; honors: Phi Gamma Mu; UNICEF grantee 1962-5, Brit. Colombo Plan Scholar 1969-70; mem. Nat. Assn. of Social Work 1978-; publs: An Evaluative Study of Council of Welfare Agencies (21 members); rec: organist, classical music. Res: 4411 Toland Way Los Angeles 90041 Ofc: Frank D. Lanterman Regl. Ctr. 1605 W. Olympic Blvd, Ste 600, Los Angeles 90015

ESPRIELLA, FRANKLIN, company president; b. Sept. 15, 1949, San Francisco; s. Lawrence and Jenny Marie (Dermer) E.; edn: BS in crops sci., CalPoly Univ. 1971; MBA, Univ. of Santa Clara 1979. Career: engineer officer USMC 1971-74; asst. mgr. Lost Hills Farming Co., Lost Hills, Ca. 1974-78; pres. Murray Spare Shoe Inc., Mtn. View 1979--; mem. Internat. Biogewic Soc.; devel. num. shoe designs; author tng. manual for molded shoe mfg. 1982; mil: capt. USMCR 1971-74; rec: farming. Res: 159 Ada Ave Mtn View 94043 Ofc: Murray Spare Shoe Co. 2444-K Old Middlefield Way, Mountain View 94043

ESTEVES, KENNETH PAUL, manufacturing co. executive; b. Dec. 5, 1948, NY, NY; s. Joseph E., Jr. and Irma M. (Ledezma) E.; 1 son, Kenneth E., b. 1980; edn: Art Center Coll. of Design 1966-7, Los Angeles City Coll. 1967-9. Career: buyer Robinson's Dept. Store, Calif. 1972-4; territory mgr. Westpoint Pepperell, Calif. 1975-6, major accounts mgr. 1977-8; mktg. rep. Customweave Carpets Inc., Calif. 1978-9, mdse. mgr. 1979-80, nat. mktg. mgr. 1980-3, dir. of mktg. 1983; vice pres. sales, World/Customweave Carpet Mill, 1984--; mem. Carpet Mfrs. Assn. of the West; Cub Scout packmaster; vol. wkr. recreation ctr.; artist: Los Angeles Art Expo. 1st Place Drawing, 2d. Overall in Competition 1972; mil: cpl. US Army; Republican; Catholic; rec: art, art hist. Res: 4648 Nob Hill Dr Los Angeles 90065 Ofc: Customweave, 7400 Hazard St Westminster 92683

ESTRELLA-GLEISINGER, CARMELY, clinical social worker; b. Aug. 28, 1951, San Francisco; d. Justo and Virgina (Fawcett) Estrella; m. James E. Gleisinger, Aug. 27, 1983; edn: AA, Los Angeles City Coll. 1971; BA, CSU Los Angeles 1973; Boston Univ. 1973-74; MSW, UCLA 1975; Lic. Clin. Soc. Wkr., Calif. BBSE 1979. Career: spl. asst. Special Services for Groups; senior med. soc. wkr. LAC/ USC Med. Ctr.; cons. to soc. svcs Inglewood Convalarium; senior oncology soc. wkr./clinical splst. Daniel Freeman Hosp. 1979--; pvt. practice, individual psychotherapy; devel. (only) comprehensive model to serve psycho-social needs of cancer patients & families, Daniel Freeman Hosp. 1979-; mem: Nat. Assn. Soc. Wkrs.; Asian- Am. Soc. Wkrs.; Forum for Death Edn. & Counseling; coalition for the Medical Rights of Women; Am. Cancer Soc.; works: a study of power of Asian-Americans in the Health, Education, and Welfare Fields; Democrat. Res: 4059 Michael Ave Mar Vista 90066 Ofc: Daniel Freeman Hospital, 333 N Prairie Ave Inglewood 90301

ESTVANDER, DALE ZOLTON, real estate broker; b. Aug. 10, 1944, Detroit, mich.; s. Steven Paul and Helen T. (Sasfy) E.; m. Rena Mae Hefley, July 30, 1967; children: Brent Arthur, b. 1971; (stepson) James Paul Long, b. 1963; edn: AA, San Bernardino Valley Coll. 1977; spl. courses Chaffey Coll., Valley Coll.; Calif. Lic. Real Estate Broker. Career: supr. Kaiser Steel Corp., Fontana 1965-83; broker/owner Century 21 Ability Realty, 1982--; tng. instr., OSHA, Kaiser Steel 1980-2; Notary Public, Calif. 1973-; honors: Million Dollar Club Cen. 21; mem: Nat., Calif. Assn. of Realtors; San Bernardino Valley Bd. of Realtors 1972-; Realty Safety Assn.; Nat. Notary Assn.; Nat. Fedn. of Independent Business; Assn. of Iron and Steel Engrs. 1968-; Rialto CofC (dir. 1983-5); Jaycees (pres. Rialto 1976; Dist. 23 vp 1978), J.C.I. Senators of Calif., Calif. Tigers, Am. Legion, Frat. Order of Eagles, Nat. Hot Rod Assn., 82nd Sport Parachute Club 1963-4; mil: E4 US Army 1961-64; Democrat; Catholic; rec: sky-diving, auto racing. Res: 2389 N. Sycamore Ave Rialto 92376 Ofc: Century 21 Ability Realty, 1154 N. Riverside Ave Rialto 92376

EU, MARCH FONG, California Secretary of State; b. Mar. 19, 1927, Oakdale; d. Yuen and Shin (Shee) Kong; chil: Matthew Kipling, Marchesa Suyin; edn: BS, UC Berkeley, M.Ed, Mills Coll., EdD, Stanford Univ.; postgrad. Columbia Univ., CSC Hayward; Calif. State Teaching Creds., Jr. Coll. Adm.-Supr. Career: div. chmn. Univ. Calif. Med. Ctr., San Francisco; dental hygienist, Oakland Pub. Schs.; div. supr. Alameda Co. Schs.; lectr. Mills Coll., Oakland; mem. Alameda Co. Bd. of Edn. 1956-66 (pres. 1961-62); v.p. Alameda Co. Sch. Bds. Assn. 1963-65 (pres. 1965); spl. cons. Calif. State Dept. Edn.; edn./ Bds. Assn. 1963 65 (pres. 1965); spl. cons. Calif. State Dept. Edn.; edn./ legislative cons. Santa Clara Co. Office of Edn., Sausalito Pub. Schs., others 1962-66. Elected to Calif. State Legislature, 15th Assem. Dist. 1966, 68, 70-72; elected Calif. Secty. of State 1974, 2d term 1979-83; apptd. Calif. Chief of Protocol, 1975--; awards: Eastbay Intercultural Fellowship 1959; Phoebe E. Hearst Bay Area woman of year 1968; woman of year Calif. Retain Liquor Dealers Inst. 1969; VFW Loyalty Day Awd. 1970; Calif. Assn. of Adult Edn. Adminstrs. merit cit. 1976; mem: Oakland Econ. Devel. Council, v. chmn. adv. com. Youth Stu. Centers, Ford Found. Proj. 1962-3; com. Council of Soc. Planning; judge Mayor's Com. on Excellence of Youth 1964; bd. dirs. Oakland YWCA 1965; hon. mem. So. Calif. Dental Assn.; charter pres. Chinese Young Ladies Soc. of Oakland; CTA; Elm PTA (hon., life, charter, pres.); AAUW; Delta Kappa Gamma; Democrat (Nat. Conv. del. 1968, exec. com. Calif. State Dem. Central Com.) Ofc: 1230 J St. Sacramento 95814.

EVANGELISTA, GIL VIERNES, structural engineer; b. Oct. 3, 1946, Pangasinan, Philippines; s. Bartolome Cerezo and Bonifacia Barrientos (Viernes) E.; m. Carolina, Dec. 25, 1971; children: May, . 1974, John Gil, b. 1979; edn: BS in Civil Eng., Mapua Inst. of Tech. 1968; lic. structural engr. Guam, 1975, Calif. 1982. Career: designer to chief struc. engr. Mackinlay, Winnacker McNeil and Assocs., Agana, Guam 1972-75; chief struc. engr. T.J. Davis, Inc., Guam 1975-76; pres. David - Evangelista - Valdemoro and Assocs., Inc., Guam 1976-81; sr. struc. engr. DMJM, Los Angeles 1981--; bd. dirs. (bd. chmn. 1975-81) Dev and Assocs., 1975-83; structural engring. projects: Guam Correctional Facility (1980), Guam Internat. Airport (79), Encino Office Bldg. (82), NASA Solid Rocket Booster Processing Bldgs.; mem: (fmr) Am. Concrete Inst., Nat. Soc. of Profl. Engrs., Soc. of Am. Mil., Post-Tensioning Inst., Hafa Dai Kiwanis Club of Guam; Catholic (Blue Army, Guam); rec: home computer. Res: 18800 Bench St La Puente 91744 Ofc: DMJM, 3250 Wilshire Blvd, 4th Flr, Los Angeles 90010

EVANS, I.J., educator/business executive; b. July 26, 1917, Davidson, Okla.; s. Isaac J. and Doscia May (Duncan) E.; m. Fern Wallace (Outstanding Elem. Tchrs. of Am. 1975), June 20, 1949; edn: BS, Okla. State Univ. 1940, MS 1946, EdD 1949. Career: principal Potter Valley High Sch., Ukiah Union H.S.Dist. 1949-54; dist. supt. Owens Valley Unified Sch. Dist. 1954-57; founder/pres./ CEO, Evans Enterprises, pvt. real estate and investment firm, 1958-82, ret. 1982; awards: medal of merit by Pres. Ronald Reagan, 1982; mem: US Senatorial Club 1982-3; Grad. Club, Okla. State Univ. (pres. 1946); Nat. Edn. Assn. 1949-57; Nat., and Calif. Assn. of Sec. Sch. Adminstrs. (v.p. No. Coast Sect. 1950), 1949-57; pres. North Hills Democratic Club 1958. mil: USAAF, WWII, 1942-45, served in S.W. and Western Pacific, decorated Phil. Lib., GCM, Battle stars for New Guinea, Biak, Leyte and Luzon (Phil.), Okinawa;

Republican (Presdtl. Task Force 1982-3); Protestant; rec: golf, hiking, photog., travel, writing. Res: 16741 Armstead St. Granada Hills 91344.

EVANS, JOHN MERTON, management analyst/administrator; b. Mar. 20, 1951, Orange City, Iowa; s. Jack Ervin and Dorothy Joyce (Rogers) E.; m. Margaret Arnold, Nov. 13, 1976; 1 dau., Danelle Cynda, b. 1974; edn: AA, honors, Diablo Valley Coll. 1971; BA, honors, CSU Chico 1973; postgrad. wk. in pub. adm., Univ. of San Francisco 1977-8; Calif. Adult Sch. teaching cred.; 21 certs. (mgmt. splties.) from CSC, USN. Career: personnel mgmt. splst., Naval Air Station, Alameda 1973-76; manpower mgr. Prodn. Dept. Naval Air Rework Facility, 1976-80; adminstrv. svcs. ofcr. Naval Air Station, Alameda 1980-84; adminstrn. ofcr. Oakland Army Base, and Deputy Dir. (DPCA) Mil. Traffic Mgmt. Command, W. Area, 1984--; mgmt. cons. 1980-, instr. MPA ext. pgm., Univ. of S.F.; vol. mediation work in labor disputes; honors: appreciation from Navy, OPM, CSC, Navy Relief Soc., United Way, school districts; spl. achievement award from Navy, num. profl. awds.; mem. Federal Mgrs. Assn. (past v.p. & pres. 1980-3), chmn. Navy Relief Soc. fund drive (Bay Area) 1982; chmn. Combined Federal Drive (Alameda) 1982; Democrat; Methodist; rec: golf, fishing. Res: 3570 Dumbarton St Concord 94519 Ofc: Oakland Army Base, MTMCWA (DPCA), Bldg 1, Oakland

EVANS, ORVILLE LEE, investment banker, ret.; b. May 6, 1913, Lake Shore, Utah; s. David L. and Sarah Ann (Hansen) E.; edn: Brigham Young Univ. 1932-6; m. Margaret Thompson, July 30, 1957, dec. 1963. Career: independent businessman, ret.; community work: pres. Fallbrook Music Soc.; dir. Planning Dept., Fallbrook Plnng. Commn.; advis. dir. Fallbrook Hosp. Board; past treas. Fallbrook CofC; past secty. Fallbrook Hist. Soc.; past treas., dir. San Diego Co. Farm Bur.; past chmn. Fallbrook Farm Bur.; served in US Navy 1943-47, 1951-52. Res: 850 Maravilla Lane Fallbrook 92028

EVANS, RUTH TODD, physician; b. Sept. 2, 1945, Wash DC; s. Benjamin Johnson and Margaret Wayne (Williams) Todd; m. Edward B. Evans, MD, Dec. 24, 1974; children: Elizabeth, b. 1974, Andrew, b. 1978, Suzanne, b. 1978; edn: AB, Coucher Coll. 1967; MD, Univ. of Rochester Sch of Med. 1971. Career: public hlth ofcr. Newport News (Va.) Health Dept. 1974-76; internist, 1976-77, chief, 1977-78, Adult Med. Dept., Hough Norwood Health Care Ctr., Cleveland, Ohio; internist, pvt. practice Elmira, NY 1979-81, Tri-City Internal Medicine, Oceanside, Ca. 1981--; med. advisor Rancho Santa Fe Swim Assn.; bd. certified Nat. Bd. of Medical Advisors 1972, Am. Bd. of Int. Medicine 1974; mem: Am. Coll. of Physicians, Calif. and San Diego Med. Socs., Junior League of S.D., Beach and Country Guild, Women's Com. for Cerebral Palsy, Country Friends, RSF School PTO Bd.; publs: med. abstracts; Republican; Presbyterian; rec: gardening, writing. Res: POB 2531, Rancho Santa Fe 92067 Ofc: Tri-City Int. Med., 3231 Waring Ct, Ste O, Oceanside 92056

EVANS, WILLIAM HERSHEY, optometrist; b. Apr. 17, 1950, Neenah, Wisc.; s. Kingdon Wm. and Gladys Marie (Hershey) E.; m. Linda, Sept. 9, 1972; children: Ryan, b. 1979, Rob, b. 1983; edn: BS, Univ. of Wisc. 1972; BS, cum laude, So. Calif. Coll. of Optometry, OD, 1979; Dr. of Optometry, State Bd. 1979. Career: optometrist, Anaheim Eye Medical Group, 1979-80, assoc. to Dr. Daniel Mont, La Mirada 1980-82, own private practice, Fresno 1982--; occ. spkr. on vision care to civic groups; honors: Beta Sigma Kappa; mem: AOA, COA, Omega Epsilon Phi, Better Vision Inst., CCOS (chmn. comm. div.); clubs: Lions (chmn. sight conserv. com.); Christian; rec: hunt, fish, shoot. Res: 8068 No Angus St Fresno 93710 Ofc: W.H. Evans, OD, 1449 No Wishon Ave Fresno 93728

EVERETT, JACK WILCOX, financial planner; b. Aug. 30, 1942, Nyack, NY; s. Jack W. and Mabel Claire (Jones) E.; m. Patricia Olmstead, Jan. 21, 1984; children: Sherri, b. 1966, Jack, b. 1968; edn: Bs, US Naval Acad. 1964; MBA, Golden State Univ. 1970; Cert. Fin. Plnnr. (CFP) Coll. for Fin. Planning. Career: nuclear submarine ofcr. USN, 1964-72; computer salesman Burroughs Corp., Sacramento 1972-74; self empl. real estate sales, Sacto. 1972-74; fin. plnnr./tax mgr. TMI Equities, Sacto. 1977-80; self empl. fin. plnnr., Sacto. 1980--; pres. The Financial and Tax Planning Center; pres. Credit Union Fin. Services; pres. Venture Seminars Unlmtd.; dir./controller Sacramento Brokerage and Loan Assn. 1982-; lectr. Golden Gate Univ. 1984; mem: Internat. Assn. for Fin. Plnng., Sacto. Chpt. (vp 1983-4); Inst. of Cert. Fin. Plnnrs; Kiwanis (past pres. Carmichael Club 1980-1); Navy League of the US (Sacto Council vp 1982-4, treas. 1985); Sacto Seapower Assn. (treas. 1982-4); US Naval Acad. Alumni Assn. (Sacto chpt. pres. 1982-3); Carmichael Beavers Swim Team (Meet dir. 1980, Head Timer 1981-); author fin. column: Dollars and Sense, Carmichael Times 1981-2; mil: lt. USN 1964-72, Nuclear Submarines, Qual. in Submarines, Vietnam Svc., Repub. of Viet. Cpg. medals; Republican; Christ Comm. Ch.; rec: fishing, athletics. Res: 6231 Van Alstine Ave Carmichael 95608 Ofc: The Fin. and Tax Planning Ctr, 2701 Cottage Way, Ste 17, Sacramento 95825

EVERETT, JAMES MICHAEL, mortgage broker real estate appraiser; b. July 11, 1948, Palo Alto; s. Everett James and Delores Margaret (Smith) E.; m. Janene K. Joyslen, Mar. 23, 1974; 1 son, James Jr., b. 1970; edn: AA, Contra Costa Coll. 1973; R.M. designation, Am. Inst. of Real Estate Appraisers 1980. Career: loan ofcr., office mgr. Argent Investment Corp. 1973-76; real estate broker afil. Century 21 Realtors, 1976-78; mortgage broker/real estate appraiser Argent Investment Corp., 1978--; prop. mgmt. (redevel.) for City of Pleasant Hill 1978-84; mem: Am. Inst. of Real Estate Appraisers (arrangements chmn 1982), Soc. of R.E. Appraisers; Republican; Christian; rec: karate (Brown Belt), golf, running. Res: 4482 Stone Cyn Ct Concord 94521 Ofc: Argent Inv. Corp., 3685 Mt Diablo Blvd, Ste 351, Lafayette 94549

EWELL, AUSTIN BERT, JR., lawyer, agri-businessman; b. Sept. 10, 1941, Elyria, OH; s. Austin Bert and Mary Rebecca (Thompson) Ewell, Sr.; desc. John Ewell, b. 1734, Scotland, settled in Plymouth Co., MA, 1751; BA, Miami Univ., 1963; LL.B., JD, Univ. Calif. Hastings Coll. of Law, 1966; m. Kristine Ballantyne, Feb. 14, 1976; children: Austin B., III, b. 1978. Career: atty. at law, assoc. firm of Parichan, Krebs & Levy, Fresno, 1966-70, firm of McCormick, Barstow, Sheppard, Coyle & Wayte, Fresno, 1970--; gen. counsel, Kings River Water Assn., 1979--, Dudley Ridge Water Dist., 1980--; dir., secty.: Gr. Western Nurseries Co., Inc., 1969-76; Amer. Agronomics Pacific Div., Inc., 1970-72; Perma Leasing Co., 1969--, Root Creek Irrigation Co., Inc., 1968-78; dir., pres., The Brighton Mgmt. Co., 1973; mem. Task Force on Prosecution, Cts. and Law Reform of CA Council on Criminal Justice, 1971-74. Mem.: State Bar of CA, 1966--; US Dist. Ct., E. Dist. CA, 1967--; US 9th Circuit Ct. of Apeals, 1967--; ABA, 1967--, Sect. on Natural Resources, Water Resources Com., Sect. on Real Property, Probate and Trust Law; Fresno Co. Bar Assn., 1967--; Baristers Club of Fresno Co., 1972-76; Phi Alpha Delta Alumni Assn.; Hastings Coll. of Law, 1066 Club, Alumni Assn.; The Water Found., 1978--; Western Water Edn. Found., 1980--; affil., Assn. of CA Water Agencies; San Joaquin Valley Agri. Water Com., 1979--; Commonwealth Club of CA, Sect. of Agri. and Water; dir., Fresno East Community Center, 1971-73; Fresno Comm. Council, 1972-73; Fresno City, Co. Hist. Soc.; Bulldog Found. of CA State Univ., Fresno; Rotary; Firelands Hist. Soc.; Spirit of '76 Mus. and Hist. Soc.; Sigma Nu Alumni Assn.; Prodn. Credit Assn., 1964--; The Downtown Club; Sierra Sport & Racquet Club; Sunkist Growers Assn., 1978--; sustaining mem. Fresno Met. Ministry, 1980; organizing dir. Friends of Latin Amer., 1980. Research project in progress: 'The Sufferers Lands' (hist. and settlement of Huron and Erie Cos., OH). Republican, mem. State Central Com. of CA, 1974--, Exec. Finance Com. 1978--; Exec. Com., treas. Fresno Co. Repub. Central Com. 1971-72; former v.p. CA Repub. Assy. of Fresno; chmn. The Lt. Gov's. Club, Fresno Co., 1980--; campaign chmn. Congregationalist. Rec.: hist. research, antique books, guitar, tennis, photography. Res.: 2573 W. Calimyrna Ave., Fresno 93711; Office: McCormick, Barstow, Sheppard, Coyle & Wayte, 1171 Fulton Mall, Suite 400, Fresno 93721.

EWING (PRICE), JEANNINE ALLEENICA, management consultant; b. Oct. 29, 1947, Cleveland Cuyahoga, Ohio; d. Alfred M. and Annabelle (Wilson) Ewing; m. Thurman R. Price, Sept. 2, 1976; edn: BS, Case Western Reserve, 1969; MA, Vanderbilt Univ. 1974; AS, Mission Coll. 1982; stu. Univ. of Phoenix Sch of Bus. 1982-. Career: coordinator of health services National Health Profile System, Nashville, tenn. 1970-74; mgmt. cons. First So. Devel. Co., Memphis, Tenn. 1974-77; mgmt. cons. (Employee Assistance pgms.), Awareness Concept, San Jose 1977-80, exec. v.p. 1981--; counselor Nat. Semiconductor, Santa Clara 1980-81; awards: community svc., Houston, Tex. 1975; scholastic, Mission Coll. 1980, 82; mem. Am. Business Women's Assn., Redwood City; author: The Girl I Never Knew, An Act of Love, The Dreamer (unpub. novel); Democrat; Catholic; rec: writing. Address: San Jose

EWING, REGAN EMILIE, accountant/real estate broker; b. Dec. 23, 1942, Evanston, Ill.; d. Thomas Francis and Olilea A. (Harvey) Ewing; edn: BA, UC Los Angeles 1965; Calif. lic. real estate broker 1982. Career: vice pres. Mammoth Park Devel. Co., Santa Monica 1966-79; cons. assoc., Ryon Assocs. (appraiser), Manhattan Beach 1977-; v.p./comptroller J.D. Alexander & Assocs., Santa Monica 1979--; lic. real estate broker; mem. Saint Monica's Choir, LA County Art Mus., Magna Charta Dames, Americans of Royal Descen, Sierra Club, Action for Santa Monica Homeowners; Democrat; Catholic; rec: singing and staging songs, pianist, photog. Res: 811 - 12th St Santa Monica 90403; 818 Washington Blvd Oceanside; ofc: 2951 -28th St, Ste 3000, Santa Monica 90405

EXELBY, DONALD WALLACE, art director; b. Jan. 30, 1933, Los Angeles; s. Paul Adrian and Marion Rowena (Dinwiddie) E.; m. Alexandra, Sept. 7, 1957; two sons: Daniel b. 1959, Joseph b. 1962; edn: Univ. of the Redlands 1950-53; BA, Whittier Coll. 1955-57; Chouinard Art Inst. 1957-60. Career: technical illustrator RobertShaw-Fulton, Anaheim 1960-62; tech. illus./art director Beckman Instruments Inc., Fullerton 1962--; honors: appreciation, Boys Scouts of Am. 1974; mem. San Clemente Arts & Crafts Club (pres. 1984); mil: pfc US Army 1953-55, Am. Defense Med., Occupation (Ger.) Med.; Democrat; Ch. of Christ; rec: model airplanes, water color painting. Res: 156 W. Avenida Cornelio San Clemente 92672 Ofc: Beckman Instruments Inc. 2500 Harbor Blvd Fullerton 92634

EYERLY, LILA SMITH, real estate broker; b. Feb. 2, 1926, Canton, Ill.; d. John Thrush and Evelyn Johnnie (Frisbee) Smith; m. Eugene Eyerly, June 30, 1946; children: Patricia, b. 1949, John, b. 1956; Calif. lic. real estate salesman 1973, lic. R.E. broker 1977. Career: real estate sales assoc. Wayne Grisham Realty, La Mirada, 1973-78, Westworld Realty, 1978; assoc. broker Wayne Grisham Realty, 1978-82, Ed Moore Realty, Inc. 1982--; bd. trustees La Mirada Comm. Hosp. 1983-; round table moderator (spons. by Calif. State Sen. Wm. Campbell 31st Dist.) 1983 Conf. on Women; honors: Woman of the Year 1978 & 1979, Hon. Mem. 1976, La Mirada Bus. & Profl. Womens Club; distinguished service award, La Mirada Jaycee-Ettes 1963; 1964 Hon. Life Mem., Norwalk-La Mirada Council of PTAs; mem: Nat. & Calif. Assn. of Realtors, Norwalk-La Mirada Bd. of Realtors, La Mirada Comm. Hosp. Aux., La Mirada Ebell, CFWC, Rancho McNally Fedn. Republican Women (Woman of Year 1977, 1981; 2nd v.p. Los Angeles Co. FRW); Prot.; rec: polit. edn., speaking to clubs. Res: 13108 Calle de Maya, La Mirada 90638 Ofc: Ed Moore Realty Inc. 15826 Imperial Hwy La Mirada 90638

EYHERABIDE, STEPHEN PETER, lawyer; b. Apr. 21, 1919, Maricopa; s. Pascal and Grace (Iroulgui) E.; m. Dora, July 1945; children: Michelle, b. 1947,

Pascal, b. 1949, Stephen, b. 1952, Germaine, b. 1955, Bernadette, b. 1960; edn: AB, Stanford Univ. 1948; LLB, Univ. of S.F. 1951. Career: lawyer assoc., Mack & Bianco, Bakersfield, 1951, partner of Mack, Bianco, King & Eyherabide, 1954, partner law firm of King & Eyherabide, 1965, sr. partner law firm Eyherabide, Pearl, Beckman & Eyherabide, Bksfld. 1982--; mem: State Bar of Calif., Am. Bar Assn., Kern County Bar Assn. (pres. 1967-8); mil: capt. US Army Inf., Purple Heart, Civil Star; Republican; Catholic; rec: flower gardening. Res: 4281 Country Club Dr Bakersfield 93306 Ofc: Eyherabide, Pearl, Beckman & Eyherabide, 1400 Chester Ave, Ste N, Bakersfield 93301

EZAKI, RAMSEY ALAN, dentist; b. Aug. 29, 1952, Los Angeles; s. Floyd Yogi and Nami (Nakagana) E.; m. Janine Yokochi, July 5, 1975; 1 son, Brandon, b. 1980; edn: BA in bus. adm., and BA in music theory, perf., Whittier Coll. 1974; DDS, USC 1980. Career: dental practise in Walnut, and Whittier; clin. instr. USC Sch. of Dentistry 1980; dental cons. Unified Sch. Dists. of Montebello, Walnut Valley; cons. dental assisting program Rio Hondo Comm. Coll. 1981-; faculty Los Angeles Music and Met Sch. 1970-73; cons. Am. Heart Assn.; cons. Gr. LA Comm. Cancer Control Ctr.; honors: City of Montebello Jr. Citizen of the Month 1970; mem: Am., Calif., Hawaii, San Gabriel Valley Dental Assns.; Acad. of Gen. Dentistry; Whittier Coll. Lancer Soc.; USC Century Club; musician: Burbank Sym. Orch., Rio Hondo Sym., Montebello Civic Light Opera, church pianist (11 yrs.) Beverly Presbyn. Ch.; Presbyterian. Res: 15628 Condesa Dr Whittier 90603 Ofc: Ramsey A. Ezaki, DDS and Assocs.: Valley Professional Center, 20709 Colima Rd, Ste. 206, Walnut 91789; The Village, 6517 Greenleaf Ave Whittier 90601

F

FAAL, MODOU-KABIRR M.O., business consultant; b. Apr. 29, 1957, Banjul, The Gambia; s. Muhamadou Omar and Ajaratou Ya-Fatou (Njai) F.; edn: BA, bus. admin., CSU Fullerton 1982; MBA, National Univ. 1984. Career: tchr. Nusrat High Sch., Banjul, Gambia 1976; reporter, Gambia Info. & Broadcasting Svcs. 1976-9; admin./ finance intern, City of Cypress 1980-1; spl. agent, Northwestern Mutual Life Ins., Santa Ana 1982-4; bus. cons./ founder California Allied Svcs Enterprise, Fullerton 1983--; admin./ budgeting intern City of Garden Grove 1984--; dir. Hank Prodn. Co. 1984-; honors: Big Brother of Month (2) 1982 ; mem: Financial Mgmt. Assn.; Internat. Council of Small Bus.; Nat. Assn. of Realtors; Am. Mgmt Assn. 1982-; chmn. Faculty/ Student Rels. Bd., CSUF 1981-3; dir. Rho Epsilon (CSUF Chpt. Nat. Assn. Realtors) 1981-2; dir. Sch. of Bus. Club Council (CSUF) 1982; Fullerton CofC 1983-4; Big Brothers of Orange Co.; Red Cross; Boys Club of Fullerton; Smithsonian Instn.; sev. articles & essays in fin. mgmt. field; Islamic; rec: chess, classical music, jogging, martial arts. Res: 110 So Balcom Ave, No. 32, Fullerton 92632 Ofcs: City of Garden Grove, 11391 Acacia Pkwy Garden Grove; C.A.S.E., POB 1183 Placentia 92670

FABRICANT, ROBERT NEAL, ophthalmologist; b. May 5, 1948, Casa Grande, Ariz.; s. Robert I. and Lillian (Solid) F.; m. Gail, Sept. 12, 1976; 1 son, Robert Ian, b. 1982; edn: BA cum laude, Univ. of Wash. 1970; MD, UC San Diego Med. Sch. 1974; Diplomate Am. Bd. of Ophthal. 1982. Career: undergrad. resrch. asst. Dept. Microbiol., Wash. Univ. Sch. of Med. 1969-70; missionary medicine, Tarahumara Mtns., No. Mex. 1972; intern in med. UCLA Harbor Gen. Hosp., Torrance 1974-5; fellowship NIH Nat. Cancer Inst., Bethesda, Md. 1975-78; res. in ophthal. La. State Univ. Eye Center, New Orleans, 1978-81; pvt. practice of opthalmology, Upland, Ca. 1981--; pres. Upland Eye Physicians; mem. San Bernardino Co. Med. Soc., So. Calif. Tri-County, Soc. of Opthal.; med. journal articles; mil: Commnd. Corps USPH 1975-78; rec: sailing, skiing. Res: 285 E. 24th St Upland 91786 Ofc: Upland Eye Physicians, 1148 San Bernardino Rd Upland 91786

FABRUADA, DAVE TEVES, consulting engineer; b. Feb. 1, 1937, Philippines, nat. 1974; s. Aurelio Salimbazat and Herberta (Teves) F.; m. Fregia Simco, Sept. 1, 1958; children: Debbie Ann, b. 1959; Nanette Beth, b. 1963; Dave Clark, b. 1964; Jeam Dale, b. 1970; edn: BS, Far Eastern Univ. 1965; Reg. Profl. Engr., Calif. 1978. Career: elec. design engr. Sargent & Lumpy, Engrs., Chgo., Ill. 1973-79; proj. engr. Skidmore, Owings & Merrill, Chgo. 1980-81; senior engr. Ralph M. Parsons, Pasadena 1981; sr. engr. Bechtel, San Francisco 1981-82; faculty design splst. Jet Propulsion Lab, Pasadena 1983--; mem: Consulting Elec. Engrs.; Republican; rec: basketball, ping pong. Res: 23017 Peacock Ct Grand Terrace 92324 Ofc: Jet Propulsion Lab, 4800 Oak Grove Dr Pasadena

FAHIMUDDIN, MUHAMMED, accountant; b. Sept, 7, 1952, Karachi, Pakistan; nat. 1973; s. Mohammed and Razia Sultana (Begum) Naimuddin; edn: BS in bus. ad., CSU Hayward 1979; candidate for C.P.A. and C.M.A. Career: cost acct. Moore Bus. Forms, Oakland 1979-81; cost/finl. analyst Airco-Temescal, Berkeley 1981-83; pres./owner Fannr (bus. service co.), and Fannr (an internat. co.), Berkeley 1983--; treas. Pakistan Assn. of San Francisco 1981-; mem. Nat. Assn. of Accts. 1981-; gen. secty. Pakistan Student Assn. (UCB) 1974; rec: ski, tennis, travel. Res: 752-1/2 Elm St. El Cerrito 94530

FAIR, KEITH ALFRED, chiropractor; b. Dec. 19, 1936, Marysville, Ohio; s. Dean A. and Doris W. (Hines) F.; m. Nancy Nix Ghere, Dec. 17, 1983; children: Liesel Lorraine, b. 1969; Erich Eugean, b. 1970; edn: Ariz. State Univ.;

Brigham Young Univ.; DC, Palmer Coll. of Chiropractic 1968; Diplomate Nat. Bd. Chiro. 1968. Career: staff mem. Professional Practice Consultants 1980-82; pres. Dr. Keith A. Fair Chiropractic Corp., Fremont 1980-83; instr. Chiro. Indsl. Panels; bd. dirs. Pacific States Chiro. Coll. 1978; Bay Area rep. Chiro. Research So., South Seas and New Zealand 1977, Israel and Jordan 1979; founder/ dir. Bay Area Chiropractors 1984; mem: Internat. Chiro. Assn. (Calif.); Chiro. Info. Bureau; CHro. Indsl. Gp. (Bd. Regents); works: wrote/ compiled, An Introduction to Chiropractic, 1972; sem. lectr., Professional Communication, 1982; sem. lectr., Professional Public Relations, 1979; Republican; Ch. of Jesus Christ of LDS; rec: art collection, travel. Res: 40837 Mission Blvd Fremont 94539 Ofc: 2000 Peralta, Ste 207, Fremont 94536

FAIRBAIRN, ROBERT WALTER, electrical contractor; b. Dec. 25, 1921, Los Angeles; s. Walter Pardo and Dorothy Gladys (Brydone-Jack) F.; m. Betty Louise Danielson, March 18, 1944; chilren: Christine Lee, b. 1946, Robert Daniel, b. 1948; edn: Univ. of Wash. 1939-42; lic. elec./bldg. contractor, Calif. 1965. Career: assoc. traffic engr. City of Seattle (Wn.) Engring. Dept. 1945-50; elec. estimator Donald W. Close Co., Seattle 1950-53; chief elec. estimator Rosendin Elec. Inc., San Jose, Ca. 1953-55; gen. mgr. Hill Bros. Elec., Sunnyvale 1955-67; pres./owner Hill Electrical Contractors, Sunnyvale 1967--; mem: Nat. Electrical Contractors Assn. 1968- (bd. dirs. 1970-, past v.p., pres., gov.); Elec. Contractors of Cal-Nev-Hawaii (v.p. 1981-); chmn. Bay Area Council-NECA Contractors 1976; San Jose, Sunnyvale CofC; clubs: Coyote Pt. Yacht Club, Yacht Racing Assn., Palo Alto Elks, De Anza Racket Club, Los Altos Tennis Club; mil: capt. USAAF, 6th AF, 43rd Fighter Sq. 1942-45; polit: state legis. chmn. Elec. Contractors of Calif.; rec: sailing, tennis, ski; Res: 24700 Voorhees Dr. Los Altos Hills 94022 ofc: Hill Elec. Contractors 1250 Birchwood Dr. Sunnyvale 94086.

FAISON, JAMES IVER, medical services co. executive; b. Mar. 10, 1941, Oakland; s. James Hughes and Elinore Ruth (Iverson) F.; m. Linda C. Stewart, Dec. 14, 1968; children: Jamie, b. 1979; Heidi, b. 1980; edn: AA, Staten Island Comm. Coll. 1972; AB, UC 1977. Career: self-empl. insurance safety engineer 1962-77; criminal investigator New York State Tax Commn. 1969-72; owner Faison Medical Services, (retail med. supplies for the severely retarded), Concord, Ca. 1978--; mem: Calif. Assn. Med. Prods. ; Nat. Assn. of Med. Equipment Suppliers; life mem. NRA; mil: info. spec. US Army disch. 1962; Republican (past chmn. 51st Ass. Dist. Repub. Club); Catholic; rec: hunter. Res: 836 Rosemount Rd, Oakland 94610 Ofc: Faison Medical Services, POB 21388 Concord 94521

FALCO, JAMES V., builder/developer; b. Nov. 8, 1955, Paterson, NJ; s. Alphonse C. and Grace I. (Irmiere) F.; edn: AA, Edward Williams Coll., Fairleigh Dickenson Univ. 1975; BA, magna cum laude, Boston Coll. Philosophy 1977, DA, Boston Coll. Political Sci. 1977; JD, LaVerne Univ. Law Sch. 1980. Career: constrn. mgmt./ developer (custom homes, offices, comml. facilities, condos., spec. in energy efficient), dba Colonial Builders, Diamond Bar; guest lectr./ expert witness, construction defects; awards: BSA Eagle Scout 1972; inventor of num. constrn. related prods., techniques; Republican; Catholic; rec: skiing, scuba. Address: Colonial Builders, 20911 Flapjack Dr Diamond Bar 91765

FALL, RICHARD JAMES, marketing manager; b. Oct. 4, 1946, Wauseon, Ohio; s. Thomas J. and Helen W. (duFosse) F.; m. Barbara Ford, June 13, 1981; edn: AA, Orange Coast Coll. 1975, BA, CSU Long Beach 1984. Career: crew scheduling supr., asst. mgr. Inflight Svcs., Western Airlines, Los Angeles 1970-78; dir. customer svcs. Columbia Pacific Airlines, Richland, Wash. 1978-9; asst. mgr. sales/service Wash. DC, Houston, dist. mgr. cargo sales, L.A., Western Airlines, 1979-83, mgr. nat. freight accounts & sales pgms. 1984--; mem. Los Angeles Air Cargo Assn. (pres. 1984-85); mil: sgt. USMC Air Wing 1966-70, GCM, Vietnam decorations; rec: skiing, biking, paddle tennis, travel. Res: 2313 Clark Ave No. 3, Venice 90291 Ofc: Western Airlines 6060 Avion Dr Los Angeles 90045

FAMA, LOLA, real estate broker; b. April 14, 1930, Los Angeles; d. Savino and Margaret R. (Rube) Falabella; m. Tony Fama, Oct. 17, 1948; 1 dau., Alba, b. 1950; edn: Golden West Coll., 1972-74, Anthony Schs. 1976; lic. real estate broker, Calif. 1975. Career: vault teller Bank of Am., Los Angeles 1970-73; assoc. broker College Park Realtors, Inc., Los Alamitos 1973--; mem: Nat. Notary Assn., W. Orange Co. Bd. of Realtors, Long Beach Bd. of Realtors; mem. Calif. Election Bd. 1955-60; Democrat; Catholic; (Altar Soc. Bell Gardens 1955-60); rec: antique doll collector. Res: 4257 Ironwood Seal Beach 90740 Ofc: College Park Realtors 10791 Los Alamitos Blvd Los Alamitos 90720

FANN, ALBERT LOUIS, doctor of divinity/actor/theatrical ensemble director; b. Feb. 21, 1925, Cleveland, Oh.; s. Albert Louis and Beulah Fann; m. Barbara Bowman, Sept. 17, 1963; children: Shelley, b. 1957, Tracy, b. 1961, Melanie, b. 1963, Albert, b. 1969; edn: Cleveland Inst. of Music 1959; D.D., Living Ministries Internat. Coll. 1981. Career: actor on Broadway in The Wiz (the Lion), in Rickety Rocket (voice-over lead, Rickety), in Live & Times of Eddie (Col. Flanders); TV: The Jeffersons, Happy Days, Good Times; ensemble: "Songs in the Key of Life" (Stevie Wonder), "Sounder" album; film actor in The French Connection, Sophisticated Gents (NBC Mini-series), Parasite (3-D movie); film commercials for Santa Barbara Svgs., Wesson Oil, Wheaties, AT&T Yellow Pages, McDonalds, Nyquil, etc.; exec. dir. The Al Fann Theatrical Ensemble, NY and Calif., 1965--; artistic dir. Haryou Anti-Poverty Pgm., NYC 1964-70; asst. dir. Cotton Comes To Harlem (Warner Bros. film)

1969; assoc. prod. Come Back Charleston Blue (Warner Bros. film) 1973; dir. NY Bd. of Edn. 1960-69; instr. Hunter Coll. 1972; mental scientist/exec. dir. Al Fann Ministries for Higher Mind Devel.; founder: Mind Recording Co., Miracles in Mind Pub. Co., Olympic Sugar Babies Internat.; formed pop. singing group, The Higher Minds; ofcl. spokesman/chief fundraiser for The Derrick Gordon Heart Fund (heart transplant recipient 1983); writer/prod. The Ballad of Derrick Gordon (hit song). Awards: Andy Awd., excellence in TV commls. 1969; Audelco Awd., Advt. Club of NY, 1973; Calif. Comml. Actor of Month (46 commls.); 14 awds. for "King Heroin" (CATV, 1971), Nat. Cable TV Assn.; recognition, Who's Who in Amer., Ebony Mag. vol. Blk. Hist., LA Times View Sect. (82). Mem: SAG, AFTRA, Concerned Black Artists for Action (v.p.), NAACP (life hon. mem.). Author: Devel. of the Under-Privileged Mind (1978), Drama Book Splst.; (play) King Heroin, presented to White House staff; served in US Army. Res: 1649 Citronia St Northridge 91324 Ofc: Dr. Albert L. Fann, The Al Fann Theatrical Ensemble, 6043 Hollywood Blvd Hwd. 90028

FANN, THOMAS SHAIN-TAU, civil engineer; b. June 5, 1970, Hunan, China, nat. 1973; s. Zee Chung and Kuo Mine (Chen) F.; m. Mei-Luen K., Sept. 1969; children: Victor, b. 1970; Henry, b. 1971; Mark, b. 1978; edn: BS, Chung Yuan Univ. 1963; MS, USC 1968; lic. profl. engr. Taiwan and Calif. Career: pres. High Far Realty & Investment Co. and High Far Travel Svc., Monterey Park; editor/writer Calif. Tribune (bilingual newspapr in Eng., Chinese); vice pres./ dir. Calif. Tribune, Inc., Montebello; partner D.A. Development, Monterey Park; mil: reserve ofcr. Chinese Army, Taiwan; Democrat; Christian; rec: ski, movies, writing. Res: 1816 So Wilcox Ave Monterey Park 91754; Ofcs: High Far, 362 W Garvey Monterey Park 91754

FARAONE, ROBERT ANDREW, pension consultant; b. May 21, 1943, NY, NY; s. John W. and Maria C. (Baldassarree) F.; m. Florence Hinzer, Apr. 2, 1966; 2 daus: Darlene, b. 1968; Robyn, b. 1971; edn: BA, Long Island Univ. 1966; MA, American Univ. 1972; Regis. Rep. Nat. Assn. of Security Dealers 1976, lic. in Life & Disability Ins. Career: naval officer 1967-75; sales mgr. Lincoln National, Los Angeles 1975-9; Shadur, Lavine & Assoc., L.A. 1979-81; pension cons. Price, Raffel & Assoc., Inc., L.A. 1981--, dir. if specialized markets; mem: Million Dollar Round Table; Nat. Assn. of Life Underwriters; PTA; mil: lt. USN 1967-75, awarded Navy Achievement Medal by Cmdr. Third Fleet; Lutheran; rec: amateur radio opr. Res: 362 No Oak Hills Dr Agoura 91301 Ofc: Price, Raffel & Assocs., Inc., 10960 Wilshire Blvd, Ste 2300, Los Angeles 90024

FARGHER, LAWRENCE LE ROY, real estate broker; b. Sept. 16, 1932, Helena, Montana; s. Lawrence Arthur and Maude Cecilia (Lauson) F.; m. Camille Marie Augusta, May 16, 1953; children: Larry Lee (dec.), b. 1954; Leighton Lynn, b. 1956; Lauson Layne, b. 1957; Lindel Lee, b. 1959; Laure Lynne, b. 1962; edn: BS, Univ. Nebr., Omaha 1954; MBA, Univ. Santa Clara, 1965; designations: CRB & CRS, Nat. Assn. of Realtors 1979, GRI & RECI, Calif. Assn. of Realtors. Career: navigator, aircraft performance engr., USAF 1955-8; engr. Boeing Airplane Co., Wichita 1958; engring. writer, Polaris Launcher, Westinghouse, Sunnyvale 1958-62; hd. systems engring. United Technology Ctr., Sunnyvale 1962-71; owner Realcom Assoc. (gen. real estate brokerage), Santa Clara 1969--; real estate instr. (Lifetime Com. Coll. Cred.), West Valley and Mission Colls.; city councilman 1962-71, mayor 1964-5, City of Santa Clara; awards: 1982 Realtor of Year, San Jose R.E. Bd., various civic awds.; mem: San Jose Real Estate Bd. (pres. 1983, dir. 1984-7); Calif. Assn. of Realtors (dir. 1969-); publs: arts in Real Estate Today, NAR, and California Real Estate mag. CAR; mil: 1st Lt. USAF, Strategic Air Command 1955-8; Republican (State Central Com. 1968-); Catholic; rec: hunting, fishing. Res: 2481 Golf Links Circle Santa Clara 95050 Ofc: Realcom Associates, 3028 El Camino Real Santa Clara 95051

FARHA, JIMMIE LEROY,commercial real estate broker; b. Feb. 12, 1932, Alva, Okla.; s. Henry S. and Saada Elizabeth (Zakoura) F.; m. Patricia A. Connor, Sept. 14, 1957; children: Jimmie, Jr., b. 1958; Catherine, b. 1961; edn: BA, Wichita Univ. 1954; MA, Webster Coll. 1974. Career: comptroller Travis AFB 1975-7; mgr. Ashwill- Burke, Vacaville 1978-82; mgr./ broker Bishop-Hawk, Vacaville 1982--; dir. Vacaville CofC 1983-7; mem. Pvt. Indus. Council 1983-5; chmn. Indsl. Commercial Com., Vacaville CofC 1982-4; Indl. Rels. Adv. Bd. Ctr. for Employment Training 1982-4; awards: spl. svc. Calif. Human Devel. Gp. 1983; mem: Rotary (dir. 1982-3; No. Solano Co. Bd. of Realtors; Bay Area Brokers Assn.; Council of Military Orgns. (chmn. 1982-3); Masons; Shriners; Air Force Assn. (Comm. Leader of Yr. 1982); mil: col. USAF 1954-77, Distg. Svc., D.F.C, 8 air medals, 2 USAF Commend., Vietnam Svc.; rec: walking, swimming. Res: 560 Ridgewood Dr Vacaville 95688 Ofc: Bishop-Hawk, 419 Mason St, Ste 208, Vacaville 95688

FARKAS, ROBERT, graphic designer/art director/illustrator; b. Mar. 27, 1954, Budapest, Hungary; Canadian cit.; s. Albert and Antonia F.; m. Susan Bush, Aug. 26, 1979; edn: AA, L.A. City Coll. 1974, CSU Northridge 1975-8, UCLA ext. 1976. Career: graphic artist CSUN Univ. Student Ctr. 1976-7; graphic designer Aldrich & Assocs., Van Nuys 1977; jr. art dir. Nationwide Advt. Svc. Inc., Sherman Oaks 1978, sr. art dir. 1979-81; art dir./owner Bob Farkas Creative Svcs., Los Angeles 1981--; cons. art dir. ITT, Gen. Controls Div., Glendale 1981-; awards: 1st prize, Calendar Cover Design, Jewish Fedn. Council of Gr. L.A. 1973; mem: The Freelance Network, Pasadena; (past) CSUN Stu. Advt. & Graphics Assn., LACC Hillel Council 1972-4; Jewish; rec: film & theater, music, folk dancing. Address: Bob Farkas Creative Svcs., 8835 Alcott St Los Angeles 90035.

FARLEY, NORMAN CHARLES, clergyman; b. July 22, 1937, Gardiner, Me.; s. Guy Wilbur and Eleanor Haines (Merriman) F.; m. Alice Zawrotniak, June 8, 1958; children: Deborah, b. 1960, Gregory, b. 1963, Norman II, b. 1964; edn: AA, Univ. of Maine 1957, BA, Atlantic Union Coll. 1959, MA, Andrews Univ. 1961, PhD, Calif. Grad. Sch. Theology 1972; Calif. lic. marriage counselor. Career: pastor/teacher, NY 1959-60; pastor, West Va. Conf., 1961-65; Bible tchr. Worthington (Ohio) 7th-day Adventist Ch. Sch., 1966; chmn. Bible Dept./ counselor Sacto. Union Acad., 1967-69; assoc. pastor 7th-day Adv. Ch., Santa Ana 1969-72, Corona 1972-75, Fontana 1975-77, Oceanside 1977--; founder Fellowship Ctr. (sponsor, 5-Day No Smoking Plan), Santa Ana 1974; founder Staff of Life (non-profit); chaplain Santa Ana Comm. Hosp., 1970-71; mem: North Co. Ministerial Assn., San Diego 1977-, Calif. Assn. of Marriage & Family Therapists 1982-; builder church in Morgantown, W.V. 1964; Republican; rec: amateur radio WB6ZPU, ski, travel, photog. Res: 2701 Ave. De Anita, 4, Carlsbad 92008. Ofc: Seventh-day Adventist Church, 1943 California, Oceanside 92054.

FARMER, FRED HOWARD, farmer; b. Nov. 27, 1892, Muldrow, OK; s. Robert Alexander and Rachel Elizabeth (Portis) Farmer; Edn: grad., Riverside Bus. Coll., 1908; m. Margaret Frances Grand, Nov. 26, 1919; chil: Marguerite B., b. 1920; Leonce Walter, b. 1922; Claire Elizabeth, b. 1924; Justin Frederick, b. 1926; Alma Louise, b. 1928. Career: bookkeeper, a Creamery, Riverside, 1908-09; storeclerk, Oatman, AZ, 1910-16; rancher, apples and pears, Julian, 1916---, planted variety of fruit trees, turned farm opn. over to son, 1948; started 1st Christmas Tree Farm in S.D. Co. on 25 acres, Wynola, 1948---. Planted 1st red pears, Julian; organizer Soil Conservation Pgm. in East Co., 1930s, serving as chmn., 5 yrs., 1st state v.p.; promoted road from Julian to Imperial Valley, now Hwy. 781 promoted coming of electricity to Julian; organizer Julian Grange 643, he and wife served as master, secty., other offices; master, S.D. Pomona Grange, 2 yrs.; he and wife, 1st Julianites to be Grand Marshals, Julian Apple Days Parade; bd. trustees, Julian Elem. Sch. 20 yrs. Mem: Julian Election Bds.; charter mem., Julian CofC; 32nd deg. Mason, 1913---, past master, Santa Maria Lodge, Ramona. Democrat. Presbyteran. Rec: gold mining, community service. Res: 4584 Julian Hwy., Santa Ysabel 92070.

FARRELL, ALBERT CHARLES, municipal bond broker; b. May 2, 1940, Iowa City, Iowa; s. Charles Raymond and Gladys Mae F.; m. Shirley Armfield, Aug. 5, 1967; children: Patricia, b. 1969; Richard, b. 1971; edn: BA, Huron Coll. 1964; MA, Univ. of So. Dak. 1965; postgrad. work, Univ. of Ark. 1966, Univ. of Chgo. 1967. Career: economics instr. Yankton Coll., S.Dak. 1966-8; sr. v.p. Dean Witter Reynolds, Inc., Beverly Hills 1968--; awards: Gen. Elec. Scholar 1967; Nat. Tchg. Fellow 1967-8; Nat. Found. Fellowship 1966; Pi Gamma Mu Honor Soc. 1965; Outstanding Young Men of Am. 1966; Wall Street Journal Awd. 1964; Huron Coll. Distg. Svc. Awd. 1982; bd. mem.: Beverly Hills Bus. & Profl. Men's Assn., BH Theater Guild, BH Men's Club, YMCA, Huron Coll. Alumni Assn. (nat. pres.); mem: Bev. Hills CofC, Mensa; Vikings of Scandia, Los Angeles Wheelmen, Bikecentennial, BH Citizen's CPR Com.; publ: Economic Outlook of South Dakota -Population, Income, Employment (1966); mil: spec4, US Army Finance Corps 1959-62, Distg. Svc. Awd.; Republican; Baptist; rec: cycling, volunteer work. Res: 2302 Bagley Ave Los Angeles 90034 Ofc: 9470 Wishire Blvd Beverly Hills 90212

FARRELL, RONALD ERNEST, company executive; b. July 26, 1928, Inglewood; s. Ernest Idaho and Annabelle (Moore) F.; m. Helen L. Larson, Mar. 6, 1945; children: Michael, b. 1945; Mark, b. 1951; edn: summer MBA pgm. Stanford Univ. 1983. Career: credit mgr. Sears Roebuck & Co., 1947-62; owner/pres. Ronnam Prods., Inc. 1962--, and Compass Internat., Inc. 1972--; mem: Kiwanis; Toastmasters; Republican; Protestant; rec: golf, photog., travel. Res: 855 Canyon View Laguna Beach 92651 Ofc: Compass International, Inc., Box 4876 Anaheim 92803

FARRIS, TIMOTHY JOHN , bankruptcy analyst/lawyer; b. May 14, 1957, San Luis Obispo; s. Earl B. and Patricia June (Harris) F.; edn: BA in hist., CalPoly St. Univ. 1978; JD, Loyola Law Sch. 1981. Career: law clerk, Hon. Barry Hammer, Arroyo Grande, 1979; research asst., Lloyd Tevis, Esq., Loyola Law Sch., 1979-81; certified law clerk, assoc. atty., Kricun & Ogden, Los Angeles 1979-82; bankruptcy analyst/atty., Ofc. of US Trustee in Bankruptcy, Justice Dept., L.A. 1982--; awards: Jessup Internat. Honors Moot Ct. 1979-80; externship, Dept. of Justice, US Trustee's Ofc. 1981, Small Bus. Admin. 1980; public spkg. awards (18 trophies); Wm. M. Rains Meml. Scholarship 1976-8; mem: Calif. State Bar, Am. Bar Assn., LA County Bar Assn., Barristers; mem. Cardinal Key, Key Club, Elks Club, Calif. Scholastic Fedn., Phi Kappa Phi; Republican; rec: chess, pub. spkg., swim. Res: 619 E. Monroe, Santa Maria 93454 Ofc: US Dept. of Justice, Ofc. of US Trustee, 3101 Federal Bldg., 300 No Los Angeles St, Los Angeles 90012

FATEMI, BAHRAM, mechanical engineer; b. Jan. 19, 1952, Tehran, Iran; nat. 1982; s. Mostafa and Talat (Habibi) F.; m. Beth Popken, July 31, 1976; children: Darius, b. 1981, Kevan, b. 1983; edn: BS, Univ. of Nebr. 1973; MS, UC Berkeley 1974; PhD, UC Santa Barbara 1980; Reg. Profl. (Mech.) Engr., Calif. 1982. Career: design engr. (mech. systems for high-rise bldgs.) Skidmore, Owings & Merrill, 1974-5; research & teaching asst. UCSB, 1976-80; project engr. Nutech, San Jose 1980--; cons. nuclear indus.; awards: Regent's Scholarship; mem. ASME; publs: 19 tech. papers, jour. arts.; rec: skiing. Res: 795 Carrywood Way, San Jose 95120 Ofc: Nutech, 6835 Via Del Oro, San Jose 95119

FAUST, LELAND HOWARD, lawyer; b. Aug. 30, 1946, Los Angeles; s. Joseph M. and Jane G. (Moyse) F.; m. Susan W., June 29, 1969; children: Aaron, b. 1975; Jeremy, b. 1979; edn: AB, UC Berkeley 1968; JD, Harvard Law Sch. 1971. Career: assoc. atty. Taylor, Winckur & Schoenberg, San Francisco 1971-5; partner; Taylor & Faust, San Francisco 1975--; mem: S.F. Estate Planning Council; coauthor: Personal Tax Planning, Calif. Cont. Edn. of the Bar 1983;

rec: swimming. Res: 47 Malta Dr San Francisco 94131 Ofc: Taylor & Faust, 1 California St, Ste 2550, San Francisco 94111

FAUST, RUSTY, radio broadcasting co. controller; b. May 22, 1928, Carroll, Ind.; d. John Thomas and Juanita (Begas) Martin; m. Louis Faust, Apr. 28, 1979; chil: Janice, b. 1947, Patricia, b. 1949, Connie, b. 1950, Randy, b. 1952, Buddy, b. 1953; grad. Austin H.S. 1944. Career: ops. ofcr. Union Bank, Los Angeles 1962-72; asst. controller Novation, Inc., Tarzana 1973-74; cons. Compunet, Los Angeles 1974-75; v.p./controller Gannett Broadcasting, KIIS AM-FM, 1975-80 and v.p./mgr. Gannett Broadcasting, KPRZ, 1979-80; controller Westinghouse Broadcasting and Cable Co., KFWB, Los Angeles 1981-82; gen. mgr. Group W. Cable, Sierra Madre/ Arcadia 1982--; awards: Best Contbn. to Mgmt. Foothill Dist., S.W. Region, Group W Cable 1982; mem: Broadcast Credit Assn., Nat. Assn. Accts., Am. Mgmt. Assn., Media Credit (chpsn. exec. bd. 1978-80), L.A. Area CofC, Human Rels. Council 1981-2, Broadcast Finl. Mgmt., Nat. Assn. of Bank Women 1965-72, Women in Cable, So. Calif. Cable Club, Sierra Madre CofC, Arcadia CofC; clubs: Palm Desert Resort CC, Bermuda Dunes CC, La Canada CC; Republican; Methodist; rec: golf, swim. Res: 5303 Ivafern Ln. La Canada 91011. Ofc: Group W Cable, 641 Duarte Rd. Arcadia 92106.

FAWCETT, J. SCOTT, real estate developer; b. Nov. 5, 1937, Pittsburg, PA; s. William Hagen and Mary Jane (Wise) Fawcett, Jr.; Edn: BSc, Ohio State Univ., 1959; m. Anne Mitchell, Dec. 30, 1960; chil: Holly, . 1961; John, b. 1965. Career: dist. dealer rep., Shell Oil Co., San Diego, 1962-66; dist. real estate rep., Shell Oil, Phoenix, AZ, 1967-69; region real estate rep., Shell Oil, San Francisco, 1970-71; head office land investments rep., Shell Oil, Houston, TX, 1972-75; pres., CEO, Marinita Devel. Co., Newport Beach, CA, 1976---; conducted all real estate trng. for new real estate personnel, Western Mktg. Region, Shell Oil Co., 1970-71. Mem: Building Indus. Assn.; US Chamber of Commerce; Internatl. Right of Way Assn.; Natl. Assn. of Review Appraisers; Internatl. Inst. of Valuers; Amer. Assn. of Certified Appraisers; Urban Land Inst.; Natl. Assn. of Real Estate Executives (pres. Los Angeles chpt. 1975); Toastmasters (pres. Scottsdale, AZ, Club, 1968; pres., Hospitality Toastmasters Club, San Diego, 1964); University Athletic Club; Ohio State Univ. Alumni Assn.; Phi Kappa Tau Alumni Assn.; lecturer in land development related fields. Mil: M.P., US Army, Mil. Dist. of Washington, 1960-61. Republican. Catholic. Rec: gardening, tennis, skiing. Res: 8739 Hudson River Cir., Fountain Valley 92708; Office: Marinita Development CO., 3835 Birch St., Newport Beach 92660.

FEENEY, ANDREA CHARLTON, lawyer; b. June 8, 1955, San Francisco; d. Dr. Francis J. and Phyllis D. (Mutch) Charlton; m. Thomas J. Feeney, Sept. 10, 1983; edn: BA, Stanford Univ. 1977; JD, Univ. of the Pacific, McGeorge Sch. of Law 1980. Career: environmental policy analyst, Nat. Commn. on Air Quality, Wash. DC 1980-1, energy conserv. trainee, Pac. Gas & Elec. Co., San Francisco 1981, rep., Legislative Svcs. PG&E, 1982 adminstr. State Legis. Svcs., PG&E 1982--; honors: McGeorge Sch. of Law: Internat. Law Moot Ct.; best brief, W. States Regl. Competition; Honors Bd. and asst. Team Coach; Student Bar Assn. bd. govs.; SBA v.p. and budget dir.; class pres. Mem: Am. Bar Assn.; State Bar of Calif.; Bar Assn. of San Francisco; Queen's Bench, (SF Women Lawyers); Commonwealth Club; Democrat; Catholic; rec: patron of fine arts. Ofc: Pacific Gas & Electric Co., 77 Beale St, Ste 3000, San Francisco 94106

FEICHTMEIR, ARMAND CASIMIR, insurance executive; b. Aug. 8, 1910, Wausau, Wisc.; first son desc. (Austrian) Count Casimir and Alvina Katherine (Hoffman) F.; m. Peggee Anne Bennett, Mar. 4, 1939 (dau. of Col. Ernest R. Bennett, Field Comdr. of famed Rainbow Div. under Gen. Doug. MacArthur, WWII, and comdr. Iowa NG for 30 yrs.); children: Anne, b. 1940, Patricia, b. 1942, Sue, b. 1947; edn: Northwestern Univ. 1929-30, BS engr., Stanford Univ. 1933. Career: heavy constrn. engr. in No. Calif. and N.W., incl. Grand Coolee Dam, Wash., 1933-36; served to full col. US Army, 1941-46, Ord. Ofcr., Staff 27th Div., PTO; post-war: pres. Armand C. Feichtmeir & Co., Ins. Agents & Brokers; recipient Ernest Thompson Seaton Awd., Luther Halsey Gulick Awd. (Camp Fire Orgn.), BSA Minuteman Awd. 1966; pres. So. Calif. Youth Swimming Assn. 1955-57; served on W. Bay Bd., L.A. Council Bd., and v.p. Region V, Camp Fire Girls of Am.; fmr. mem. L.A. Area Council of BSA; mem: Pan American Underwriters (pres.), Am. Legion (Post and Dist. comdr.); Republican (United Repub. Fin. Com. 1963-66, past pres. Bev. Hills Repub. Club); Catholic. Res: 2818 Motor Ave Los Angeles 90064 Ofc: Paula Insurance Co. 626 So Kingsley Dr Los Angeles 90005

FEIG, KONNILYN GAY, university executive/professor; b. Sept. 24, 1936, Raymond, Minn.; d. Herbert Cecil, Jr. and Mildred (Weyer) F.; edn: BS in bus. adm., minor, sociol./polit.sci., Univ. of Mont. 1958, BA in hist.,1959, MA in hist., 1963; PhD, hist., Univ. of Wash. 1970; Sec. Teaching Cert., Univ. of Mont. 1958. Career: history instr. and asst. dir. Women's Affairs/Student Affairs, Whitman Coll., Wash. 1962-67; adminstrv. posts, Univs. of Wash. and Mont.; teaching fellow, hist., Univ. of Wash., 1967-68; assoc. dean of students Univ. Pittsburgh, 1969-70, dir. spl. pgms., 1970-72; assoc. prof. of hist./dean Coll. of Arts and Scis. Univ. of Me. at Portland-Gorham, 1972-77; v.p. adminstrn. San Francisco State Univ., 1977-82, dean Univ. and Strategic Planning, 1982--; ch. CSU Assn. of V.P.s for Adminstrn. and Fin., 1980-82; cons. Ford Found., US Ofc of Edn. Honors: Nat. White House Fellows Finalist 1971; Nat. US Ofc of Edn. Fellow 1968-9; Nat. Woodrow Wilson Honor Roll 1960; Phi Kappa Phi; Phi Alpha Theta; Beta Gamma Sigma; Who's Who of Am. Women, Who's Who of Internat. Women; mem: Mensa, Am. Assn. of Univ. Adminstrs., Commonwealth Club ofCalif., Press Club of SF, Nat. Women's Polit. Caucus, World Future Soc., Am. Hist. Assn., AAUP, Yivo-Yiddish Sci. Inst., Calif. Concerns, Am. Soc. of Profl. & Exec. Women, Bay Area Exec. Womens Forum, Anti-Defam. League, Leo Baek Inst., Smithsonian Assoc.; author: Hitler's Death Camps: The Sanity of Madness (NY; Holmes & Meier, 1981); num. arts., institutes. rec: sailing, writing, computers. Res: 6 Hart St. San Rafael 94901. Ofc: SF State Univ., 1600 Holloway Ave San Francisco 94132.

FEIN, WILLIAM, ophthamologist/educator; b. Nov. 27, 1933, NY, NY; s. Samuel and Beatrice (Lipschitz) F.; m. Bonnie Fern Aaronson, Dec. 15, 1963; children: Stephanie Paula, b. 1968; Adam Irving, b. 1969; Gregory Andrew, b. 1972; edn: BS, Coll. of the City of N.Y. 1954; MD, UC Irvine Med. Sch. 1962; diplomate, Am. Bd. of Ophthamology 1969. Career: resident ophthalmol., L.A. County Gen. Hosp. 1963-66; post res. tng. in ophthalmic plastic surgery, Manhattan Eye and Ear Hosp. 1966-7; instr. ophthalmol. UCI Med. Sch. 1966-9, instr./assoc. clin. prof. ophthalmol. USC Med. Sch. 1969--; chmn. Dept. Ophthalm. Midway Hosp. 1975-9; v.p. California Eye Med. Clinic, Inc. 1969-83; chief of Ophthalm. Clinic Svcs., Cedars Sinai Med. Ctr. 1979-81, chmn. Div. of Ophthalm., 1981--; lectr. new techniques in ophthalm. plastic surgery, num. hosps., conventions; mem: Am. Soc. of Ophthalm. Plastic and Reconstrv. Surgery; Am. Acad. Ophthalmol.; Los Angeles Soc. of Ophthalmol.; AMA; Calif. Med. Assn.; LA Med. Assn.; publs: num. arts. in med. literature describing new ophthalmic surgeries; Jewish. Res: 718 No. Camden Dr Beverly Hills 90210 Ofc: 415 No Crescent Dr Beverly Hills 90210

FEINSTEIN, MYRON ELLIOTT, manufacturing company executive; b. Jan. 7. 1943; s. Gerald and Esther (Levine) Feinstein; Edn: BS, City Coll of C.U.N.Y., 1963; MA, 1965; PhD, City Univ. of NY, 1967; m. Barbara Shuff, Dec. 27, 1964; chil: Christopher, b. 1969; Eric, b. 1972. Career: lectr. in chemistry, City Coll. of C.U.N.Y., NY, 1964-67; sr. research chemist, Allied Chemical Co., Morristown, NJ, 1967-68; established scientist, Unilever Research Lab., Port Sunlight, Eng., 1968-70; mgr. of process devel., AB Sunlight, NyKoping, Sweden, 1970-74; area prodn. mgr., Lever Gibbs, Milan, Italy, 1974-77; mfg. mgr., Lever Brothers Co., Hammond, Inc., 1977-81; plant mgr. Lever Brothers Co., Los Angeles, 1981---; bd. of advisors, Ind. Univ., 1979-81; bd. dirs., Industrial Council of City of Commerce (CA), 1982---. Awards: E.I. DuPont De Nemours Research Assistantship, 1966; listed in Amer. Men and Women of Sci., listed in Technology Today. Mem: Amer. Chemical Soc., Sigma Xi. Publs: 7 publs., 1964-76. Rec: photography. Res: 965 S. Grinnell, Anaheim Hills 92807; Office: Lever Brothers Co., 6300 E. Sheila St., Los Angeles 90040.

FEINSTEIN, MICHAEL JON, physician; b. June 25, 1948, Sayra, Pa.; s. Dr. Aaron A. and Cecelia Katherine (Merva) F.; m. Catherine McArthur Keyes, June 26, 1971; children: Kelly Catherine, b. 1979, Erin Michele, b. 1982; edn: BS, nat. sci., Muhlenberg Coll. 1970; D.O., Phila. Coll. of Osteopathic Med. 1974. Career: intern/res. in gen. practice, Phila. Coll. of Osteopathic Med., 1974-6; chief of gen. practice, West Allegheny Hosp., Oakdale, Pa. 1976-78; practicing Family Practice Associates of San Diego, 1978--; chief of gen. practice, College Park Hosp. 1983; clin. faculty Coll. of Osteopathic Med. of the Pacific; preceptor in G.P., Phila., Texas, and NY Colleges of Osteopathic Medicine; apptd. State of Calif. Bd. of Osteopathic Examiners 1982-5; honors: Lambda Omicron Gamma, recipient Mead Johnson Fellowship for postgrad. tng. 1974-6; mem: Am. Coll. of Gen. Practitioners of Osteopathic Med. & Surg., Am. Osteopathic Assn. (House of Dels., Council on Fed. Health Pgms., Nat. Osteopathic Pro-Action Comm., Hosp. Insp. Internships and Residencies); alumni assns.; clubs: S.D. Gilbert & Sullivan Soc. (life), Am. Law Enforcement Ofcr's Assn., US Naval Inst., One Thin Mint Eating and Gourmet Soc. (founder); Democrat; Catholic; rec: music, electronics, gourmet cooking. Res: 7741 Quitasol St Rancho La Costa 92008 Ofc: Family Practice Assocs of S.D., 4205 Fairmount Ave, San Diego 92105

FELDSTEIN, DALTON GEORGE, civic leader; b. Nov. 12, 1900, Kiev, Russia; s. Jacob and Ethel F.; m. Joyce Mell, Aug. 17, 1939; children: Heidi, Sabra, June; Fellow Brandeis Univ., Waltham, Mass. Career: executive Dalton Motors, Sacramento; bd. dirs. Mercy Hosp., pres. Sisters of Mercy Hosps., Mercy Hosp. Found.; bd. dirs./ treas. City of Hope, L.A.; bd. dirs. Jesuit High Sch., National Community Chests and Councils, United Crusade (orgnzr., past pres. United Crusade in Sacto), CofC; past pres. Am. Cancer Soc. (Sacto), Temple Bnai Israel; finance chmn. citizen's com., Sacto-Yolo Port Completion Bd.; honored jointly by all Sacto. civic orgns. Man of the Year 1951, testimonial luncheon presided by Gov. Earl Warren; Sacto. Man of the Yr. 1960; Eleanor Roosevelt Humanities Award, State of Israel, 1971; recognition, YMCA, United Way, BSA, Jesuit H.S.; past escort Camellia Festival; clubs: Mason, Shrine, Scottish Rite, Sutter (Sacto. Host Com.), S Delta Yacht (commodore), St. Francis Yacht. Ofc: Dalton Motors, 601 University Ave, Ste 103, Sacramento 95814

FEKETE, GEORGE OTTO, lawyer; b. May 30, 1927, Budapest, Hungary, nat. 1952; s. Bela and Ilona (Mehr) F.; m. Rosemarie Fekete, May 21, 1978; children: Jackie, b. 1954; Jeanette, b. 1955; Theresa, b. 1970; Cari, b. 1973; edn: BS, Wayne Univ. 1954; D.Pharm., USC 1960; JD, Pepperdine Univ. 1973; dip., Am. Inst. of Hypnosis 1966; admitted to practice before all Calif. Cts., US Dist. and US Supreme Cts.; Reg. Pharmacist, Calif. and Nevada. Career: displaced psn. in Germany 1946-49; student, jr. chemist, factory worker, 1949-54; B-47 bomb. cmdr. SAC, capt. USAF 1954-9; pres. Inst. of Applied Hypnosis 1963-4; pharmacist 1960-73; pres. George O. Fekete Law Corp., Anaheim 1973--; co-chmn. Drug Liability Seminar; Orange Co. Superior Ct. judge pro tem and

Arbitration Panel 1980-; honors: vice justice, PAD Pepperdine Univ. 1973; honor roll 1972-3; mem: Orange Co. Trial Lawyers (bd. dirs. 1977-8); Calif. Trial Lawyers (legis. com.); Orange Co. Bar Assn.; L.A. Bar Assn.; Am. Trial Lawyers Assn.; Am. Bar Assn.; Calif. Bar Assn.; Am. Pharmaceutical Assn.; Am. Inst. of Hypnosis; Anaheim CofC; Elks; Ivy Baker Forum; publs: legal jour. arts.; mil: capt. USAF 1959-54; Republican; Protestant; rec: photog., R.V., music, travel. Res: 2240 Rusty Pump Diamond Bar 91765 Ofc: G. O. Fekete Law Co., 515 No Anaheim Blvd Anaheim 92805

FELLING, RICHARD GORDON, SR., land developer; b. July 4, 1937, Trail, B.C., Can., US cit.; s. Irwin Joeseph and Cassie Sophia (Doyle) F.; m. Sally Small, Mar. 4, 1978; children: Sheryl Lynn, b. 1960; Richard G., Jr., b. 1963; edn: BS, CSU Los Angeles 1963; MBA, USC 1970; Calif. lic. Real Estate Broker and Gen. Contractor; Standard Designated Subjects Tchg. Credential. Career: civil engring. asst. Los Angeles County Engineer, 1959-63; power sales rep. So. Calif. Edison Co., Los Angeles 1963-69; proj. engr. Macco Leadership, Newport Beach 1969-74; proj. engr. Butler Housing Corp., Irvine 1974; regl. mgr. BHC Housing Inc., Phoenix, Ariz. 1975-6; v.p. Bullard Homes Corp., Fresno 1976-81; pres. 1981--; pres. Bullard Realty Inc., Fresno 1982--; bd. dirs. Bullard Homes Corp., Bullard Realty Inc., and Fro Yo Inc.; gen. partner SAC Housing, and West Co.; honors: Tau Beta Pi; mem: Building Indus. Assn. (bd. dirs. 1977-); Madera Bd. of Realtors (secty. 1982-3); Fresno Bd. of Realtors; Bulldog Found.; clubs: Fresno Ski 1977); Balboa Ski (v.p. 1972), Phoenix Ski 1975-6, Fresno Exchange, San Joaquin Country 1978-9; Republican; Christian; rec: ski, snorkel, fish, travel. Address: Bullard Realty, Inc., POB 5961 Fresno 93755

FELLOWS, RALPH M., engineer/underwriter; b. Nov. 17, 1932, Denver, CO.; s. Matthew A. and Gertrud M. (Wynkoop) F.; m. Ruth J. Barrett, July 5, 1953; 1 dau: Carol, b. 1948; edn: AA, Okla. State Univ. 1957; Calif. registered Profl. Engr. Career: grad., USNR Mobile Fire Tng. Sch., mem. Navel Air Base Fire Dept. Crash Crew 1950-5; ins. appraisal and engring. staff mem., General Ins. Co. of Am., Los Angeles area 1957-65; engring. supvr. L.A. Ofc., Oil Insurance Assn. 1966-77; international protection consultant 1972-82, broker rep. petroleum accounts., M & M Protection Consultants L.A. 1978-82; engr./ underwriter Starr Technical Risks Agency, Inc., 1983--; guest spkr.: Long Beach Petroleum Club, Gov.'s Safety Conf., Oil and Petrochem. Div., Wash.; mem: Soc. of Fire Protection Engrs.; Protection Forum; Am. Petroleum Inst.; Nat. Fire Protection Assn.; mil: fireman USNR 1953; Republican; Protestant; rec: photog. Res: 16134 Caruthers St Whittier 90603 Ofc; Starr Technical Risks Agency, Inc., 3699 Wilshire Blvd Los Angeles 90010

FELTS, DORIS I., business executive; b. Feb. 12, 1930, Los Angeles; d. Irwin and Louise Evelyn (Klein) Mayer; m. John Felts, July 28, 1951; 2 sons: John, b. 1955; Robert, b. 1959; edn: undergrad., UCLA; Small Bus. Adm., SBA 1968. Career: coord. Beverly Hills Visitors and Conv. Bureau, Beverly Hills 1966-8; v.p./ gen. mgr. Champion Temporary Personnel, Los Angeles 1968-72; owner men's retail store, The Shirt Sale, Bev. Hills 1972-4; regl. mgr. Western Temporary Svcs., Burbank 1974-6; mktg. svcs./ personnel mgr. facilities Transamerican Delaval Inc., Biphase Energy Sys., Santa Monica 1976--; guest lectr. UCLA 1968-71; dir. Mulholland Tennis Club 1968-70; instr. gourmet foods, Santa Monica Coll. 1975; mem: Gr. L.A. Recreational Council; Malibu Lagoon Museum (bd. dirs.); LA Co. Museum of Art; Republican; rec: cooking. Res: 23908 Deville Way Malibu 90265 Ofc: Transam. Delaval- Biphase Energy Systems, 2800 Airport Ave Santa Monica 90405

FENTON, ROBERT, marketing executive; b. Jan. 20, 1933, West Chester, Pa.; s. John and Rita (Brannigan) F.; m. Irene Kelly, Jnue 13, 1954; children: Tom, b. 1955; Pete, b 1928; Jeanne, b. 1957; Gary, b. 1960; Kelly, b. 1964; Wendy, b. 1965; edn: BA, Univ. of Wisc. 1954; BS, NYU 1960; PhD Oxford Univ. 1972. Career: currently v.p. mktg. ABC Marketing Group, San Fernando; honors: Les Ambassadors (Eng.); Racquet Jockey Club; City of Detroit: dir. BiCentennial Com., Man of Year 1964, DIS P.S. Medal 1973; mem: ECONS; Acad. of Magical Arts; Shriners; SPVA; Soc. of Am. Magicians; Mensa; Brotherhood of Magicians; Pyschic Ent. Assn.; Film & TV Comm.; publs: Thumbtip Magic, 1981; mil: USN 1950-54; Democrat; Jewish; rec: pyschic ent., magic, photog. Res: 17631 Rinaldia Granada Hills 91344 Ofc: ABC Marketing, Box 33284 San Fernando 91344

FERDMAN, ALAN JEROME, computer engineering specialist; b. Nov. 18, 1942, Brooklyn, NY; s. Ernest Frank (dec.) and Jean (Gralitzer) F.; adopted by stepfather Ben Ferdman (1955); m. Pamela Taylor, Aug. 17, 1962; children: Ernest, b. 1964; Scott, b. 1970; edn: AA, National Schs. 1961. Career: engr. (mil. electronics and inertial guidance) Litton Systems, Guidance and Control, Woodland Hills 1961--, currently mgr. Software Quality Ass. Dept.; instr. Software Quality Mgmt. Seminars for other Litton GCSD facilities and the ASQC; software cons. Tallen Systems 1980; honors: commendation for support of adult amateur athletics, LA County Dept. Parks & Rec. 1978, 79; mem. Am. Motorcyle Assn. (pres. 4 Aces MC 1970); founding bd. Santa Clarita Valley Adult Sports Assn.; coach youth athletics for: LA Co. Parks & Rec., Williamsport Little League, Wm S Hart Boys Baseball, Am. Legion; Democrat; Jewish; rec: adult slo-pitch softball. Res: 27248 Walnut Springs, Canyon Country 91351 Ofc: Litton Systems, 5500 Canoga Ave Woodland Hills 91364

FERGUSON, BARBARA ELIZABETH, manufacturing co. executive; b. July 6, 1942, Memphis, Tenn.; d. Robert Alexander and Mary Ovaleen (Spencer) F.; edn: MBA, Pepperdine Univ. 1973; postgrad., Claremont Univ.; Calif. Teaching Cred. (bus., indsl. mgmt.). Career: mfg. foreman Burroughs Corp., West-

lake 1967-73; mats. mgr. Bennett Corp., Los Angeles 1974-79; plant mgr. Rainbird Corp., Glendora 1979-81; v.p./gen. mgr. Myers Elec. Products Inc., Montebello 1981--; honors: lt. col. Civil Air Patrol (mem. 25 yrs.), Outstanding Ofcr. Calif. State CAP, 1975; mem. Nat. Assn. of Exec. Women; Republican; Prot.; rec: stained glass art. Res: 6813 Wheeler Ave La Verne 91750 Ofc: Myers Electric Products, Inc., 1130 So Vail Ave Montebello 90640

FERGUSON, GEORGE EDWIN, manufacturing company executive; b. Sept. 28, 1919, Tipton, IN; s. William Heard and Ethel Mabel (McNeal) Ferguson; Edn: BS T&IE, Purdue Univ., 1946, advanced mgmt., Stanford Univ., 1946; m. Mildred Vlk, May 27, 1943; chil: Patricia, b. 1946; Barbara, b. 1948; William, b. 1948; James, b. 1949. Career: asst. mgr., Turner Mfg. Co., 1946-50; gen. foreman, RCA, 1950-52; gen. supt., John Bean Div., FMC Corp., 1952-57; gen. mgr., 1957-69; div. mgr., 1969-72; pres., Peerless Pump, Indian Head, 1972-80; pres., Fluid Systems Group, Indian Head, 1980---; exec. v.p., Indian Head, 1980---; director: MHM-Venezuela, SIHI-Halberg, Germany, Peerless Iran, Iran, Peerless Asa, Mexico, Peerless Ltd.-London; dir., Hyd. Institute, 1980---. Recipient: Award of Merit, Research Inst. of Amer.; lic. profl. engr., Calif. Mem: Iota Lambda Sigma, Sigma Nu, American Cancer Soc., Bd. Junior Achievement, American Soc. Tool Engrs., YMCA. Publs: Measuring Productivity on the Job, Western Industry, 1956. Mil: Lt., USN, 1941-45, Pac. theatre. Republican. Presbyterian. Rec: gardening, woodworking. Res: 24795 Outlook Dr., Carmel 93923; Office: Indian Head, 1200 Sycamore St., Montebello 90640.

FERGUSON, JOHN PAUL, radiological technologist; b. Nov. 8, 1955, San Rafael; s. John and Virginia Elizabeth (Nye) F.; m. Margo Kahkonen, July 17, 1977; children: Mari Jean, b. 1980, Alicia Michelle, b. 1982; edn: AS, Loma Linda Univ. 1979, BS 1981; Career: staff xray technologist Loma Linda Univ. Med. Ctr., 1978-79, splst. xray tech. in computed tomography, 1979--; Mem: Am. Soc. of Radiol. Technologist, Nat. Geographic Soc., Assn. of Adventist Forums, founding mem. Alumni Assn. for Radiol. Tech., Loma Linda Univ.; publs: Computed Tomography of the Ankle (w/Drs. Richli, Savse, Billemoria), presented R.S.N.A., Chgo. 1982; Spinal Bone Density (w/Dr.Shulz, Dr.Baylink, Sally Farley RN), presented Bone Conf., Bahn, Can. 1982; Republican; Seventh-day Adventist; rec: tennis, motorcycling, family activites. Res: 1544 Ranch Rd. San Bernardino 92407. Ofc: Loma Linda Med Ctr. Rm.B-340. Loma Linda 92354

FERGUSON, WILLIAM PATRICK, real estate broker; b. Nov. 20, 1923, El Segundo; s. Fergus and Myrtle Charles (Jennings) F.; m. Peggy Healey, Mar. 2, 1963; children: Nancy Jo., b. 1948 (dec. 1971); Nora Ann, b. 1952; edn: Profl. Contracts Admin., UCLA; GRI (Grad. Realtors Inst.), CAR 1974; CRS (Cert. Res. Splst.), NAR 1974; CRB (Cert. R.E. Brokerage Mgr.), NAR 1979; Calif. Comm. Coll. Instr. Credential 1974. Career: indsl. engr. Ratheon Co., Oxnard 1962-69; 3M Co., Camarillo 1969-71; cons. State of Calif., Van Nuys 1971-72; sales mgr./ dir. tng. & edn./ v.p. Brown Realtors, Thousand Oaks 1972--; bd. dirs./ pres. Conejo Valley Bd. of Realtors 1974-80; pres. Wm. Ferguson, Inc.; honors: Resolution, Senator Lou Cusanovich and Assemblyman Paul Priolo, State of Calif. 1978; mem: Conejo Bd. Realtors (pres. 1978); Reseda Jr. CofC; Masonic Lodge; mil: 2/c, USN 1943-46, decorated 4 Battle Stars, S.Pac.; Republican; Methodist; rec: fishing, flying. Res: 373 Fox Ridge Dr Thousand Oaks 91361 Ofc: Brown Realtors, 110 E Thousand Parks Blvd Thousand Oaks 91360

FERN, CONNIE LEE, auto repair co. executive; b. Nov. 21, 1935, Lock Haven, Penn.; d. Theodore Harry and Twila Mae (Gillen) S.; m. Robert John Fern, Nov. 25, 1964; edn: Cornegie Inst. of Tech. 1953-54; BA, Penn. State Univ. 1957; MSW, Catholic Univ. of Am. 1959; Univ. of Maryland 1959-60, 1962; LCSW, Calif. 1973. Career: casework Child Welfare, Wash. DC 1960-61; instr. Univ. of Maryland 1958, 60, 61; senior med. soc. wkr. Providence Hosp., Wash. DC 1962-64; soc. wkr. Berkshire Rehab. Ctr., Pittsfield, Ma. 1964-66; soc. wrk. cons., five nursing homes, Western Mass. 1966-69; soc. wkr. Partridge Sch. and Rehab. Ctr., Tucson, Ariz. 1970; soc. wrk. cons. Jarett, Assoc., Van Nuys 1971-79; dir. soc. wrk. svcs. Nat. In-Home Health Svcs., van Nuys 1975-79; secty. to bd. dirs./ ofc. mgr./ pub. rels. mgr., family owned auto repair bus., Porschop, Inc., Los Angeles 1979--; cons./ tchr. human rels. 1979--; dir./ advr. to bd. dirs. Camp Witamentin, Pittsfield, Ma. 1964-66; dir. C.A.R.E., Inc., Van Nuys 1975-79; guest lectr. UCLA 1975-77; instr. num. comm. colls. in So. Calif. 1975-; adj. prof. CSUN 1982; cons. long term care facilities and small acute hosps.; honors: Alpha Kappa Delta, Univ. of Maryland Alpha chpt. 1960; Enthusiast of the Yr., Porsche Club of Am., Los Angeles Reg. 1981, 82; mem: NASW; Soc. Hosp. Soc. Wkrs.; Automotive Svc. Council; Porsche Club of Am.; Porsche Owners Club; Corral Canyon Home Owners Assn.; publs: editor book: Ins and Outs of Social Work Consultation in Long Term Care, 1977; ed.: 66 Porscherama 1979-83; Republican; Protestant; rec: auto racing. Res: 1911 Newell Rd Malibu 90265 Ofc: Porschop, Inc., 3906 Grand View Rd Los Angeles 90066

FERRANNINI, ANDREW J., JR., insurance executive; b. Dec. 4, 1931, NY, NY; s. Andrew and Amelia (Mondanaro) F.; m. Nora J. Casella, Dec. 27, 1952; children: Michael, b. 1953; Catherine, b. 1955; Mary, b. 1958; Anna, b. 1959;

Andy, b. 1966; edn: BS, Univ. of NY, Farmingdale 1952. Career: agent, then supr., 1956-, apptd. general agent John Hancock Ins. Cos. for Sacto., No. Calif., and Nevada, 1963--; past bd. dirs. John Hancock Gen. Agents Assn.; charter and life mem. General Agents & Mgrs. Nat. Mgmt. Award; mem: GAMC, SALU; mil: m/sgt. US Army; Democrat; Catholic; rec: golf, fishing, boating. Res: 4891 Finlandia way Carmichael 95608 Ofc: John Hancock Cos., 555 University Ave, Ste 190, Sacramento 95825

FERRARI, LEWIS JOHN, superintendent of schools/college president; b. Mar. 23, 1916, San Jose; s. Antonio and Desolina (Delucchi) F.; m. Marie Bertorelli, Nov. 20, 1941; children: Diane, b. 1942; Daniel, b. 1949; edn: BA, San Jose State Univ. 1940; MA, Stanford Univ. 1950; PhD, Univ. of Madrid, Spain 1956; Cert. as Supt. of Schools, States of Calif., Nev., NY, Wash. Career: tchr., counselor, principal, San Francisco Unified Sch. Dist., 1940-57; prin., Central Jr. H.S., Pittsburg, 1957-59; Supt. of Schools, Shasta Lake Union Sch. Dist. (1959-61), (asst.) So. San Francico USD (1961-63), Pismo Sch. Dist. (1963-4), Pasco (Wash.) Sch. Dist. No. 1 (1964-9), Marysville Jt. USC, 1969-78, ret.; also supt./pres. Columbia Basin Comm. Coll., Pasco, Wash. 1964-69; instr. Chapman Coll. 1972; currently real estate broker, Lewis J. Ferrari & Assocs., Marysville; radio talk show host; pres. Santa Cruz Co. Organized United Taxpayers; chmn. Yuba Co. Bicentennial Com. (1976-80); conf. chmn. Gov's Conf. on Libraries, WN 1968; del. Nat. School Bds. Assn. Conv. 1968; del. World Cong. of Flight 1959; state chmn. edn. com., Calif. Council for Retarded Children; mem: Assn. of Am., Calif. Sch. Administrators, NEA, Yuba Co. CofC, Sacto. Valley Mil. Liaison Com., PTA (hon. life), Rotary (dir.), United Fund (dir.), Shasta Co. Tuberculosis and Hlth Assn. (dir.), Masons, Shriners; Phi Delta Kappa, Epsilon Pi Tau; Republican (Central Com. 1983); Christian; rec: civic affairs, political elections. Res: 2205 Covillaud St Marysville 95901

FERRYMAN, JAMES MICHAEL, real estate executive; b. July 15, 1948, Springfield, Ohio; s. Daniel Earnest and Rita Eleanor (Foley) F.; m. Mary Malmstone, July 10, 1976; children: Elizabeth, b. 1978; Ryan, b. 1980; Shaun, b. 1981; edn: BS, CSU San Jose 1970, SJSU Grad. Sch. 1971. Career: Regl. Student Rels. Ofcr., San Jose region, Bank of America, 1971-4; sr. mktg. cons. Mktg. Svcs. Div. Dun & Bradstreet 1974-7; real estate sales agt./ ofc. mgr. Select Properties, Costa Mesa 1977-81; pres. and gen. mgr. Traditional Realty, Costa Mesa 1981--; bd. dirs. Irvine Nat. Mortgage; awards: salesman of year 1977-8; Million Dollar Club 1977-81; D&B nat. sales contest winner 1975; mem: Costa Mesa- Newport Harbor & Irvine Bd. of Realtors; Realty Investment Assn. of Orange Co.; Nat., Calif. Assn. of Realtors; Costa Mesa CofC (dir.); Lions Club (past pres., dir.); Child Guidance Ctr. of O.C. (vp, dir.); UCI Lions Eye Bank ; March of Dimes Golf Tourney (co-chmn. 1982, 83); Girls Club Harbor Area (dir.); Mesa Del Mar Homeowners Assn. (pres. 1977-8); mil: ROTC; Republican; Catholic; rec: sport fishing, golf, racquetball. Res: 1095 Tulare Dr Costa Mesa 92626 Ofc: Traditional Realty, 3301 E 17th St, Ste 204, Costa Mesa 92627

FESTA, JERRY J., insurance agency president; b. Dec. 18, 1930, Madison, NJ; s. Jerry and Angelina (Spagnolo) F.; m. Kathryn Morgan, Feb. 1, 1953; children: Robert, b. 1956; John, b. 1957; Joy, b. 1959; Richard, b. 1960; edn: BS, Seton Hall Univ. 1953; UCLA; desig: Life, Casualty Agent. Career: agent to middle mgmt. Metropolitan Life Ins. 1955; contracted agent State Farm; owner/ pres./CEO Jerry J. Festa Ins. Agcy. Inc., Pacific Palisades, 1960s--; mem. Prestigious State Farm Presidents Club; tchr. Life Underwriting Tng. Council, Newark, NJ; honors: Career Achiev. Club, Top 50 Fire Agents (5 yrs.); Presidents Club (life); mem: L.A. Life Ins. Agents; Soc of Certified Ins. Counselors; Calif. Profl. Ins. Agents; CofC; Optimists; Am. Legion; Palisades Americanism Parade Assn.; YMCA (fundraisers); num. tennis trophies; mil: 1st lt. USMC 1953-55; Republican; Christian; rec: tennis, aerobics, running. Res: 17759 Calle de Palermo Pacific Palisades 90272 Ofc: Jerry J. Festa Ins. Agency, Inc., 860 Via De La Paz Pacific Palisades 90272

FETHERLING, DALE SINGER, newspaper editor; b. Sept. 5, 1941, Baltimore, Md.; s. George Singer and Mary Emma (Jones) F.; m. (fmr) Rae Patterson, Dec. 26, 1966; children: Dane Douglas, b. 1970; Jill, b. 1974; edn: BA, West Va. Univ. 1963; MSJ, Medill Sch. of Journ., Northwestern Univ. 1964. Career: staff writer The Oregonian (Portland) 1968, The Minneapolis Tribune, 1968-72, Los Angeles Times, 1973--, Orange Co. edition 1973-7, Los Angeles 1977-8, present editor LA Times (San Diego Co. edition) 1978--; instr. in mass comm., Orange Coast Coll. 1976; Am. Press Inst. Seminar for exec. editors/ mng. editors, Reston, Va. 1983; honors: Phi Beta Kappa 1963; Award of Merit, Ill. State Hist. Soc. 1974; author: Mother Jones, The Miner's Angel (So. Ill. Univ. Press 1974); co-ed. Carl Sandburg At The Movies: A Poet in the Silent Era, 1920-1927 (to be pub. 1984, Scarecrow Press); mil: lt. USNR 1965-8; rec: writing, sailing, athletics. Ofc: Los Angeles Times, 225 Broadway, Ste. 820, San Diego 92101

FEUR, ROBERT EDMUND, company president; b. Oct. 12, 1928, Los Angeles; s. Jesse O. and Rose E. Feuer; m. Muriel Baker, Dec. 7, 1952; children: Cheryl, b. 1954; Brian, b. 1956; Kimberly, b. 1958; Edn: AA, Los Angeles Trade Tech. Jr. Coll. 1953; Calif. Tchg. Credential 1965. Career: pres., CEO Hermetics Supply Inc., Los Angeles 1965-72; pres., CEO Sheldon Plotkin Co., L.A. 1972-6; pres., CEO Wightons Refrigeration & Equipment, Inc., San Luis Obispo 1976--; awards: pres. Santa Lucia Council, Boy Scouts of Am. 1980-2; SLO County Bd. of Supvrs. Commendation 1983; mem: Rotary, ASHRAE Intl., Nat. Restaurant Assn.; publs: tech. arts. in trade mags.; mil: MM1C, USN, WWII, Korean War, Pres. Unit Cit., Republic Pres. Unit Cit., four battle stars; Republican; rec: antique cars, hunting, photog. Address: Wightons Refrigeration, POB 1121 San Luis Obispo 93406

FEUERS, STELLE, college president; b. NY, NY; m. Michael Feuers; edn: BS in sociol., City Coll. of NY, 1949, MS in psych., 1961; EdD, adm., UC Los Angeles 1969. Career: remedial reading tchr., district cons., reading splst. Haverstraw, NY 1957-63, Beverly Hills High Sch., 1963-4, Plainview, NY Sch. Dist. 1964-5; asst. prof., LA Pierce Coll., 1965-8, coordinator Learning Ctr., 1968-9, asst. dean of instrn./dir. Cont. Edn., 1970-76; dean of students and comm. services, Coastline Comm. Coll., 1976-78, and fed. project dir. LA Comm. College Dist.; pres. Los Angeles City College, 1978--; mem: Assn. of Calif. Comm. Coll. Adminstrs. (founder), So. Calif. Comm. Coll. CEOs Assn. (pres.), Nat. Council on Comm. Svcs & Cont. Edn. (bd.), Nat. Council for Resource Devel., Calif. Comm. and Jr. Coll. Assn., Combase Assn., The World Future Soc.; mem. RHF Bunker Hill Corp. (ch. bd. dirs.), Second Careers Pgm., Hollywood CofC (bd.), Commn. on Assault Against Women, LA CofC, Rec. and Youth Svcs Plnng. Council, LA Nat. Women's Polit. Caucus; rec: travel, clocks. Ofc: LACC, 855 No Vermont Ave Los Angeles 90029

FIALKOFF, LEO DAVID, investment management executive; b. Jan. 8, 1917, St Petersburg, Russia, nat. 1943; s. David Leo and Roda (Frenkel) F.; m. Maureen Hall, May 20, 1950; 1 dau: Maureen, b. 1951; edn: law sch., Univ. of Paris 1938; MA, mod. lang., Sorbonne, Paris 1938; MA, Inst. of Pol. Sci., Paris 1938; grad. studies (AUS stu.), Harvard Univ. 1944. Career: investment mgmt., securities, real estate, oil & gas; v.p./pres., dir. o/y Mahogany, Helsinki, Finland; bd. dirs: o/y Kuopio Parkettiti, o/y Jalokoivu, (Finland), S.A. Le Chene (Belgium), Am. Thermoform Corp. (Los Angeles), Share-research Co. (Santa Barbara); dir./ v.p. fin. ABC Clio, Inc., Santa Barbara; bd. trustees, Crane Country Day Sch., S.B. 1969-79; bd. dirs. St. Francis Hosp., S.B. 1979-82; bd. trustees Internat. Acad. of S.B. 1979-; endowment com. S.B. Sym.; exec. com., S.B. Com. on Fgn. Rels.; mil: cadet Fgn. Legion, ofcr. cand. sch., French Army 1940, Vol. Medal; 1st lt. US Army 1943-6; ETO medal w/ 3 battle stars; Republican; rec: world affairs, travel. Res: 1561 E. Valley Rd Santa Barbara 93108 Ofc: 1485-E East Valley Rd Santa Barbara 93108

FICK, GERALD DENNIS, telephone utility company executive; b. Nov. 23, 1939, Fargo, ND; s. Walter Albert and Edna Laura Louise (Schleske) Fick; Edn: grad. Fergus Falls, ND, Sr. H.S., 1957; AIB, 1959; m. Charlotte Bond, Feb. 14, 1981; chil: Jeffrey, b. 1960; Pamela, b. 1962; Mark, b. 1965; Quentin, b. 1970. Career: with Continental Telephone Service Corporation, 1967---: asst. chief accountant 1967; chief acct. 1968-72, general acctg. mgr. 1972-75, asst. controller/gen. acctg. mgr. 1975, asst. vice pres./budget dir. 1975-76, v.p.-Finance 1976---; v.p., treas., dir.: Continental Telephone Co. of Calif., Continental Tel. Co. of Northwest, Inc., Continental Tel. Co. of Texas, Continental Tel. Co. of the West, Glacier State Tel. Co., Juneau & Douglas Tel. Co. (1977---). Mem: Natl. Assn. of Accts.; Calif. Taxpayer's Assn., dir. 1979---; United Way of Kern County, dir., treas., 1980---; Independent Tel. Pioneers Assn., 1975---. Mil: National Guard, 1956-64. Republican. Protestant. Res: 5917 Azalea, Bakersfield 93306; Office: Continental Telephone Service Corp., P.O. Box 5246, 1350 Norris Rd., Bakersfield 93388.

FICK, JOHN S., utility co. executive; b. Sept. 9, 1937, Elizabeth, NJ; s. Robert Sleight and Eleanor (Jennings) F.; m. Kazne, Apr. 17, 1961; edn: NJ State Coll. (Trenton) 1955-6, Colo. Univ. 1956-7; JD, San Francisco Law Sch. 1969. Career: staff legal counsel Calif. Public Util. Commn., S.F. 1970-77; sr. atty. Pacific Lighting Corp., L.A. 1977-82; mgr. of Risk Mgmt., So. Calif. Gas Co., Los Angeles 1982--; dir. Assn. for Calif. Tort Reform (lobbying orgn.); mem: State Bar of Cali0., Am. Bar Assn., Am. Gas Assn., Pacific Coast Gas Assn.; mil: E5 USN 1957-61; Democrat; rec: musician. Res: 1716 Wilson Ave Arcadia 91006 Ofc: So. Calif. Gas Co. 810 So Flower St Los Angeles 90016

FIELD, EDDY D., real estate executive; b. Apr. 18, 1903, Keene, Tex.; s. Fielding B. and Betty (Cummins) F.; m. Helen Johnson, Sept. 14, 1929; children: Joan (Riach), Eddy D., II; edn: USC, 1926; hon. LLD, Pepperdine Univ. 1976. Career: founder/owner Eddy D. Field Real Estate and Ins., 1927-, Eddy D. Field Investments, Eddy D. Field Enterprises, ret. 1965; founder, past dir. Pioneer Nat. Bank; mem. bd. dirs. Pepperdine Univ.; mem: Los Angeles Realty Bd. (past dir.), Calif. Assn. of Realtors (hon. mem.), Calif. Apt. Owners Assn. (past v.p.), Apt. Assn. of L.A. Co. (past pres.), Wilshire CofC (past dir.); founder/v.p. Los Angeles Philanthropic Found.; past chmn. Salvation Army Advis. Bd. LA and Compton; past pres. Optimist Club; fmr. mem. Dist. Atty's Advis. Bd., Mayor's Comm. Advis. Com.; past master Henry Knox Lodge; life mem. Al Malikah Temple; Republican; Prot.; rec: travel, boating. Res: 5232 Los Encantos Way Los Angeles 90027 Ofc: Eddy D. Field Ent., 5217 Hollywood Blvd Los Angeles 90027

FIELD, GEORGE, real estate broker; b. June 21, 1922, Budapest, Hungary, nat. 1955; s. Aladar and Sarolta (Katz) Feldmayer; m. Julia Adler, June 27, 1946; children: Robert, b. 1946; Thomas, b. 1948; edn: Soc. of Residential Appraisers 1959; spl. courses, UC San Francisco Ext. 1960-70; lic. Calif. Real Estate Broker. Career: came to USA 1949, var. jobs, NYC 1949-51; prodn. foreman Goldberg & Sons, Patterson, NJ 1952; farmer, Petaluma, Calif. 1952-4; retail store owner, Petaluma 1954-7; food store owner, San Francisco 1957-62; real estate broker 1962--, pres. T & R Inv. Corp., S.F. 1970-; mem: S.F. Press Club; Bnai Brith (Akiba Award 1967); mil: Hungarian, German forced labor, underground activities Russian POW 1943-46; D.P. Camp Ulm, Ger. 1946-9; Jewish; rec: swim, jog, chess, travel. Res: 642 Funston Ave San Francisco 94118 Ofc: T & R Inv. Corp., 3410 Geary Blvd, Ste 218, San Francisco 94118

FIELDS, RICHARD LEWIS, II, stockbroker, investment banker; b. Aug. 5, 1953, Charleston, W.Va.; s. Richard L. and D. Jean (Tillis) F.; m. Cherl Ann Mott, Aug. 19, 1978; edn: BA in polit. sci., BA psych., Marshall Univ., 1976; NYSE - NASD Series 7, 1977. Career: stockbroker, Smith Barney Harris Upham in Huntington, W.Va. 1977, sr. acct. exec., transf. to Beverly Hills, Ca: office, 1978-80; v.p. investments, Bear Stearns, 1980-2; vice pres. Smith Barney Harris Upham, Bev. Hills 1982; currently v.p. investments, Morgan Olmstead Kennedy and Gardner, estab. new branch in Westwood/ Bev. Hills; mem. The Stock Broker Soc., Navy League; Republican; Christian; rec: gun collecting, fencing, raising Irish Wolfhounds. Res: 1225 Lachman Ln Pacific Palisades 90271 Ofc: Morgan Olmstead Kennedy and Gardner, 10900 Wilshire Blvd Los Angeles 90272

FIERO, JAMES KENNETH, manufacturing co. executive; b. Nov. 28, 1943, Fort Worth, Tx; s. Kenneth and Freda (Slade) F.; edn: Univ. of Wyo. 1962-4; BA, San Francisco State Univ. 1976. Career: X-ray techn. Pennisula Hosp. & Med. Ctr., Burlingame 1969-76; Adminstrv. Tech. Svc., USPHS, San Francisco 1876-8; dist. commercial mgr. Med. Sys. Div., Gen. Elec. Co., Burlingame 1978-81; regl. fin. & comml. ops. mgr. Medical Systems Business Group, Gen. Elec. Co., San Bruno 1981--; cons. Bureau of Radiologic Health in devel. Quality Assurance Pgm. for radiation safety, USPH 1977; mem: Am. Mgmt. Assn.; Am., Calif. Registry of Radiologic Technologists; Am., Calif. Soc. of Radiologic Tech., Inc.; mil: Spl. E-5, US Army 1964-7, sharp shooter, GCM; Republican; Protestant; rec: private pilot, ski, fish, gardening. Res: 2015 Monroe Ave Belmont 94002 Ofc: General Electric, 950 Elm Street, Ste 325, San Bruno 94066

FIGI, JOHN TODD, manufacturing and design co. president; b. Nov. 11, 1944, Marshfield, Wisc.; s. John Herman, Jr. and Ann Claire (Rauk) F.; m. Suzanne M. Kilsheimer, Apr. 17, 1976; edn: BA, Carroll Coll. 1966; grad. work, Kansas St. Univ. 1968. Career: pres./ CEO Figi Giftware, 1969--; Marshfield, Wisc. 1969-74, San Diego, Calif. 1974--; outlets in Canada, England, France, Italy, Germany, Switzerland, Australia, Japan, and Hong Kong; panel mem. Picture and Frame Inst. of Am. 1981; panel mem. mktg. dept. SDSU 1978; awards: over 25 design awds., Printing Ind. of Am. 1979-; mem: Young Presidents Orgn. (bd. dirs.); Confrerie de La Chaines Des Rotisseurs; La Jolla Country Club; San Diego Museum of Man (bd. trustees); Big Brothers; YMCA; mil: Sp5 US Army; Republican; rec: skiing, golf. Res: 252 Kolmar La Jolla 92037 Ofc: Figi Giftware, Inc., 8806 Complex Dr, POB 85515 San Diego 92138

FIGUEROA, BUD CHARLES, business-financial consultant; b. Aug. 29, 1917, Oakland; s. Joseph C. and Pauline (Franckavich) F.; Figueroa family history in Calif. dates back to 1880s, family Coat of Arms from Spain over 1,000 yrs.; m. Vera J. Butcoff, 1940; children: Ronald, b. 1942; Gary, b. 1944; Dennis, b. 1946; Richard, b. 1957; Cindy Lee, b. 1959; (son by prev. marriage) Ronald C., b. 1937; edn: Merritt Bus. Coll., Oakland Jr. Coll., Mt. Diable Coll., UCB, La Salle Univ. (Chgo.), San Jose City Coll. Career: pres./ bd. chmn. of num. corps.: Figueroa Profl. Financial Svcs.; The Figueroa Bus. & Financial Cons., Inc.; Figueroa Financial & Ins. Svcs., Inc.; Tahoe Sierra Figueroa Estate Inc.; Calif. Land Security & Land Inv. Corp., Walnut Creek; Sierra Pines Estates, Inc.; Bud Figueroa Land Devel. Cos., Inc.; also with Hudson Jewelry Store, Oakland; Genseler & Lee, Devon's Jewelry; co-owner/ mgr. Diamond Box Jewelry Store; vol. small bus. cons.; honors: sold over 40 million dollars in US Bonds during WWII; helped Alameda Co. Schs. sell bonds in Oakland 1953-4; fundraiser for New East Oakland YMCA, 1955-6; mem: Nat. Bus. & Financial Cons.; Am. Assn. Finl. Profls.; Internat. Assn. of Finl. Planners; Republican (Pres. Task Force); Rosicrucian Order; rec: sports, reading, writing. Res: 5269 Camden Ave, No. 168, San Jose 95124

FIKES, JAY COURTNEY, Amercan Indian art specialist; b. June 14, 1951, San Luis Obispo; s. J.C. and Virginia Lee (Roberts) F.; m. Lebriz Tosuner, Apr. 17, 1979; edn: BA cum laude, UC Irvine 1973; M.Ed in bilingual edn., honors, Univ. San Diego 1974; MA in anthropol., Univ. Mich., Ann Arbor 1977; PhD, anthropol., 1984. Career: tutor, bilingual chemistry, Pala Indian Reservation, summer 1974; instr. anthropol./archaeol., Allan Hancock Community Coll., Santa Maria 1975-76; teaching fellow in anthropol. Univ. Mich., Ann Arbor 1976-79; anthropological fieldwork among the Huichol Indians of Jalisco, Mex. 1979-81; housing cons. to Navajo Indian Nation, 1983; owner Cuatro Esquinas Traders (splst., wholesaler quality American Indian art) 1979--. Recipient two scholarships, Univ. Mich.; orgnzr. Carlsbad Fiesta Patria and served on Carlsbad Bicentennial Com., 1975; mem: NY Acad. of Scis., AAAS, Anthropological Assn., Rotary, Internat. Platform Assn., Carlsbad Hi-Noon Club. Author: Huichol Indian Identity and Adaptation; arts., Mich. Discussions in Anthropology (1978), Dialectical Anthropology (1983), El Palacio (1983). rec: hike, camp, gardening. Res: 2371 Buena Vista Cir. Carlsbad 92008. Ofc: 2134 South Hill, Oceanside 92054.

FIMBERG, STANLEY ROBERT, lawyer; b. May 15, 1934, Brooklyn, NY; s. Harold A. and Betty F.; children: Kenneth, b. 1954; Julie, b. 1961; Lynn, b. 1964; Lisa, b. 1964; edn: BA, UCLA 1955, LLB 1960. Career: assoc. atty. O'Melveny & Myers 1960-3, 1964-5; atty. Office of Tax Legislative Counsel, US Treas. Dept. 1963-4; partner Schwartlman, Greenberg & Fimberg 1965-71; pres. Stanley R. Fimberg, Ltd., Beverly Hills 1971--; guest lectr., bus., UCLA Law Sch.; lectr. USC Tax Inst.; honors: chief editor UCLA Law Sch. 1959-60, Order of Coif, 1960; mem: founder, UCLA Law Sch.; founder, Mus. of Contemporary Art; Chancellor Assocs. UCLA; publs: The Foreign Base Co. (1965), Subchapter S - 1966 Model (1967 USC Tax Inst.; mil: Sp2 US Army 1955-7; Jewish; rec: skiing. Res: 1355 Beverly Estate Dr Beverly Hills 90210 Ofc: Stanley R. Fimberg, Ltd., 9777 Wilshire Blvd, Ste 710, Beverly Hills 90210

FINDLEY, GERALD LEE ELMER, banking consultant; b. Oct. 27, 1920, Truman, Ark.; s. Burl Clinton and Gertrude A. (Tolar) F.; m. Myrtle L. Royer, June 11, 1948; children: Melinda Ann, b. 1952; Gary Steven, b. 1954; Pamela Ann, b. 1956; edn: BS, UCLA 1949, MBA, 1950; Public Acct., State of Calif. 1951. Career: mgr. Research Engring. Dept. Union Bank, Los Angeles 1950-4; mgr. Spl. Projs. Dept. Calif. Bank, L.A. 1954-5; West Coast regl. mgr. Cunneen Co., L.A. 1955-6; pres./ owner Gerry Findley & Assoc., Temple City 1956-81; pres./ owner Gerry Findley Inc., Brea 1981--; editor The Findley Reports, 1965-, Dir. Findley Reports, Inc.; instr. Univ. Calif. Ext. comml. fin. & factoring, 1952-4; mem: USS Maryland Assn.; Pearl Harbor Survivors Assn.; Masons; Shriners; author: Mergers & Acquisitions of California Banks, (4 vols.) 1955-75; Get Richer - Own the Local Bank, 1978; The Buying and Selling of Banks & Bank Holding Companies, 1981; author & ed.: California Banking Newsletter (1975-), Paymatters Newsletter (1983-), Directors' Compass Newsletter (1979-); mil: Chief Quartermaster (permanent), USN 1939-45, GCM, Bronze star, Am. Defense, Bronze Letter-A, Am. Cmpgn., Asia-Pac. Cmpgn., WWII Victory medals; Republican; Methodist; rec: collector miniatures, buttermolds, Early Am. paintings. Address: Gerry Findley, Inc., 169 No Morning Glory St Brea 92621

FINEGOLD, CECIL, wholesale distributing co. executive; b. Apr. 7, 1926, Sacramento; s. Sam and Esther F.; children: Steve, b. 1951; Suzane, b. 1954; edn: grad. C.K.McClatchy H.S. 1944. Career: has held every position in co., currently Div. Mgr. Finegold's Restaurant -Hotel Supply, Sacramento 1938--; bd. dirs. Calif. Restaurant Assn., Nat. Assn. Wholesalers, Food Equip. Distbrs. Assn.; pres. Sacramento Restaurant Dealers Assn.; recognition for helping underprivileged children in Sacto. by Calif. State Assembly Resolution 1967, County Bd. of Supvrs. 1967, and City of Sacramento 1967-8; mem: Sacto. Safety Council; CofC; Am. Heart Assn.; Big Brothers; Stanford Home; Childrens Home; Masons; Scottish Rite; Shriners; Elks, Am. Legion; V.F.W.; Bnai Brith; Four Robinhoods; inventions: Body Caressor (1975) Coffee Economatic (1977); mil: sgt. Armored Forces, M.T.O., E.T.O., G.C.; Democrat; Jewish; rec: real estate, coins, comm.- TV 31. Res: 3941 American River Dr Sacramento 95825 Ofc: Finegold's/Rykoff, POB 1113, Sacramento 95805

FINEGOLD, SAM, restaurant supply co. owner, ret.; b. Feb. 27, 1899, Austria, nat. 1922; s. Lebuch and Minnie (Unger) Kranzler; m. Esther (dec.), June 15, 1924; children: Emilie, b. 1925; Cecil, b. 1926; Ray, b. 1931. Career: with family business (started by mother & stepfather in 1915) Finegold's Restaurant-Hotel Supply since 1921--, started small, grew to largest of it's type in No. Calif.; recently merged with S.E. Rycoff & Co.; honors: recognition, Girl Scouts, Boy Scouts, Bnai Brith Akiba Awd., Sheriffs Assn., Cemetery Assn., Calif. State Legislature, County Bd. of Supvrs., City Council, Ann Land Commn., and Bertha Henshel Commn.; mem: Nat. Assn. Wholesalers; Food Equipt. Dealers Assn.; Sacto. Restaurant Dealers Assn.; Calif. Restaurant Assn.; mem. Masons, Scottish Rite, Shriners, Bnai Brith, Mosaic Law Cong., Four Robinhoods, Home of Peace Cemetery, Jewish Relief Soc.; planned/blt. mausoleum for Home of Peace Cemetary 1969; Democrat; Jewish; rec: civic vol. work. Res: 2490 Am. River Dr Sacramento 95825 Ofc: Finegold's-Rykoff, POB 1113 Sacramento 95805

FINK, HOWARD JOEL, insurance company executive; b. Aug. 4, 1944, Los Angeles; s. Irving Isadore and Ruth (Alexander) F.; m. Hanne Bruberg, May 21, 1966; children: Pauline, b. 1966; Lisa, b. 1969; Vikki, b. 1971; edn: bus. acctg. courses, L.A. Valley Coll. 1962-66; CLU Am. Coll. 1981. Career: dist. sales mgr. (13) stores Firstone Tire and Rubber Co., 1966-72; Insurance industry, 1973--; pres. PFP Financial & Insurance Svcs., Inc., 1977--; sales mgr. Los Angeles Madvin Agency of Pacific Mutual, vice pres. Finl. Mgmt. Services, Inc. 1983, moderator Life Underwriters Tng. Council, 1982. Awards: sales mgr. of the year, 1979, Pacific Mutual; mem: Million Dollar Round Table, San Fernando Valley Life Underwriters (bd. dirs.), Amer. Assn. of Chartered Life Underwriters, General Agents & Mgrs. Assn., Knights of the MDRT; mem. Chancellor's Honor Roll at UCLA., Beverly Hills Estate Counselor's Forum; rec: tennis. Res: 7608 Rudnick St Canoga Park 91304; Ofc: Financial Management Services, Inc. 15760 Ventura Blvd, No. 1732, Encino 91436

FINKELSTEIN, JAMES ARTHUR, management consultant; b. Dec. 6, 1952, NYC; s. Harold Nathan and Lilyan Crystal F.; m. Lynn Gould, Mar. 24, 1984; edn: BA, Trinity Coll. 1974; MBA, Wharton Sch., Univ. of Penna. 1976. Career: cons. firm of Towers, Perrin, Forster & Crosby, Inc., Boston 1976-78; mgr. compensation Pepsi-Cola Co., Purchase, NY 1978-80; mgr. business analysis Emery Worldwide, Wilton, Ct. 1980-81; vice pres. Meidinger Inc., Rowayton, Ct. 1981-83; prin. The Wyatt Co., La Jolla 1983--; mem. Camp Com., State YMCA of Mass. and R.I., 1976-; bd. dirs. Pro Arte Chamber Singers of Conn. 1981-2; instr. UCSD Ext. Pgm. 1984. Honors: Morris Prize for excellence in music 1974; Pi Gamma Mu 1974; Outstanding Young Men of Am. 1981, US Jaycees. Mem: Am. Compensation Assn., Am. Soc. for Personnel Adminstrn., Am. Camping Assn.; Big Brothers/Big Sisters of Am. (bd. dirs., Fairfield Co. 1980-82); Nat. Alumni Assn. of Trinity Coll. (exec. com.); Lomas Santa Fe CC. Publs: arts., Jour. of Big Brothers Practices (10/76), Personnel Jour. (11/78). Musical theatre lead roles Troupers Light Opera Co. (Stamford, Ct.), 1980-2; frequent soloist various churches. Democrat; Unitarian; rec: sports, music, camping. Ofc: The Wyatt Co 3366 No. Torrey Pines Ct. Ste. 220, La Jolla 92037

FINKEN, MARJORIE MORISSE, columnist-editor; b. June 29, 1918, St. Louis, Mo.; d. William J. and Alice (Seidler) Morrisse (O'Hern); gr.granddau. of Ferdinand Diehm, 1842-1916, Imperial and Royal Consul of Austria-Hungary in St. Louis, Mo. 1882-1915; grandniece of Albert Diehm, apptd. food admr.

two Ill. counties by Pres. Hoover, 1914-18; bro. Richard Diehm Morisse (dec. 1968), aud. of USC, 20 years; m. John W. Finken, Apr. 26, 1940, div. 1957; 1 son Richard Dale, b. 1943; edn: grad. Los Angeles H.S. 1936; stu. dress design Chouinard Inst. of Art 1937-38; art maj., L.A. City Coll. 1938-40. Career: profl. photographer; freelance photog. and rep. South Bay Daily Breeze, 1956, restaurant editor 1956--, columnist: Munchin with Marge, and Marge to Midnight, 1956--; apptd. Calif. Rec. Commnr., Manhattan City Sch. Adminstr. 1954-60; awards: first Rose & Scroll, Manhattan Bch CofC, 1954; mem: Phi Epsilon Phi (secty-treas L.A. chpt. 1942-3,44-5); So. Bay Sym. Assn. (pub. chmn. 1954-5); So. Bay Comm. Arts Assn. (pub. chmn. 1954-6); Women of Moose Lodge No.323 (secty.,pub.ch.,corr. secty. 1957-9); South Bay Hosp. Aux. (charter secty., dir. 1959-61); Greater L.A. Press Club; Calif. Press Women (bd., L.A. chpt.); Restaurant Writers Assn. (secty. L.A. Co. 1967-70); L.A. Restaurant Writers Assn. (pres. 1977-79); Los Angeles Mus of Art; Altrusa Internat. Inc. (pres. Redondo Beach chpt. 1983-4); rec: theater, concerts, art. Res: 223 Ave F, Redondo Beach 90277 Ofc: Daily Breeze, 5215 Torrance Blvd. Torrance 90509.

FINLEY, EUGENE NORMAN, filmmaker, b. Mar. 17, 1944, Alexandria, Va.; s. John W. and Marguerite B. Finley; edn: BA, C.W.Post Coll. 1966; MA, Univ. of Ariz. 1967. Career: sound editor motion picture films: Semi Tough, Almost Perfect Affair, The Island; music editor: More American Grafiti, Making of Raiders of the Los Ark; created sound effects for: Star Trek II, 48 Hours; director documentaries, Finley-Hill Co., current project documentary on: Golden Gate Bridge; prod./dir./editor television spl.: Mr. Adler and the Opera, awarded Cine Golden Eagle for film, 1982; invented Finley-Hill Sound Mixer for motion picture post prodn. (pat. 1984); rec: rowing, motorcycles. Address: Finley-Hill Co. 346 Corte Madera Ave Corte Madera 94925

FINNEGAN, VINCENT J., tax-shelter specialist; b. Apr. 1, 1942, Chgo.; s. Norbert J. and Helena (Houlihan) F.; m. Maureen McGovern, June 26, 1965; children: Heather, b. 1974; Scott, b. 1970; edn: Creighton Univ. 1960-64; JD, Ill. Inst. of Tech. -Chgo. Kent Coll. of Law 1969; MBA, Iona Coll. Grad. Sch. of Bus. 1971. Career: tax-shelter analyst Chemical Bank, NYC 1969-72; v.p. real estate Donaldson, Lufkin & Jenrette, NYC 1972-74; sr. v.p. Integrated Resources Equity Corp., Encino 1974--; frequent spkr. on tax-shelter industry: CPA Socs., law firms and bus. gps., mem: NY Soc. of Security Analysts; Internat. Assn. Fin. Plnrs.; Los Angeles co. Assn. of Fin. Plnrs.; Rotary Club, L.A.; Westlake Village Yacht Club; Jonathan Club; L.A. CofC; Westlake Village CofC; L.A. World Affairs Council; Ill. Inst. of Tech., Nat. Alumni Council; Calif. Thoroughbred Breeders Assn.; rec: skiing, fishing, travel. Res: 1917 Stonegate St Westlake Village 91361 Ofc: Integrated Resources, Inc., 16530 Ventura Blvd, Ste 410, Encino 91436

FINNIN, MICHAEL TIMOTHY, corporate president/management consultant; b. Dec. 13, 1946, Akron, Ohio; s. William Leo and Helen Ruth (McKinney) F.; m. Ruth Burton, Oct. 10 , 1969; edn: stu. Univ. of Mich. 1970, West Coast Univ. 1974, UCI 1976, Calif. Coast Univ. 1979-; Cert. Computer Tech. 1972, Data Comm. Engr. 1974, Control Data Ins.; Cert. Vocational Edn. Instr., Calif. Career: specs. writer Ford Motor Co. Engring. and Research, Dearborn, Mich. 1966-68; owner MTF Enterprises, Detroit 1969-72; instr. Burroughs Corp., Industry, Ca. 1972 73; sr. instr Control Data Inst., Anaheim 1973-76; mgr. Publications Svcs., Gen. Automation Inc., Anaheim 1974-77; founder/owner MTF Associates (cons. high-tech. publs.), Norco 1977--; co-founder/pres. Communique Telecommunications, Inc. (resrch, devel., mfg. of computerized telephone switching equip.), Ontario, 1983--; co-founder/pres. Internat. Wire And Cable, Inc. (mfr. comm. & telephone connectorized cable), Ontario, 1983--; cons. high-tech. cos. in tng. and documentation; mem: Soc. for Tech. Comms., Am. Mgmt. Assn., Am. Legion, Disabled Am. Vets, Loyal Order of Moose; publs: over 40 tech. publs, many tng. courses, various sales collaterals, 1975-; mil: Disabled Vet. US Army 1968. rec: photog., autos, motorcycling, horseback riding. Res: 2830 Valley View Ave. Norco 91760 Ofc: 4015 Guasti Rd. Ontario 91760

FIRESTONE, ANTHONY BROOKS, vintner; b. June 18, 1936, Akron, OH; s. Leonard K. and Polly (Curtis) Firestone; Edn: BA, Columnbia Coll.; m. Catherine Boulton, Guildford, England, 1958. Career: with Firestone Tire & Rubber Co., 1960-72; vintner, The Firestone Vineyard, Los Olivos, CA, 1972---. Dir., Firestone Tyre & Rubber Co., Great Britain; dir., Growth Realty Cos.; pres., the Firestone Vinyard; dir., the Tejon Ranch. Enlisted Corpsman, AUS, 1957-59. Clubs: Cypress Point, California, Rancheros Visitadores. Episcopalian, lay reader. Rec: horses. Res: P.O. Box 36, Los Olivos 93441; Office: P.O. Box 244, Los Olivos 93441.

FISCHER, DENNIS WARRAN, microwave engineer; b. May 28, 1955, Madera; s. Garlin and Nelda Florine (Hemphill) F.; edn: cert. , DeVry Inst. Tech. 1974; AS, Fresno City Coll. 1976; cert., Nat. Cable TV Inst. 1981; 1st Class Radiotel. Lic., FCC (1976). Career: bench tech. Fresno Auto Stereo 1976-8; installer, lead technician, currently microwave engr. Fresno Cable TV 1978--; recipient Electronics scholarship 1973; awards for photog. in Fair 1981-2-3; mem: Soc. of Cable TV Engrs.; Photography Club; Baptist; rec: photog., skiing. Res: 27174 Perkins Rd Madera 93637 Ofc: Fresno Cable TV, 1945 No Helm Fresno 93727

FISCHER, HERMAN A., computer scientist; b. Nov. 23, 1946, Los Angeles; s. Bernhard and Liselotte (Mayer) F.; m. Carol Rubin, Jan. 18, 1970; children: Matthew, b. 1980, Cory, b. 1984; edn: BS, UC Los Angeles 1968, MS, 1972. Career: programmer IBM Corp., 1965-68; computer scientist Computer Processes Inc., 1968-70, Litton Data Systems, 1970--; computer sci. Software Environment Resrch & Devel.; recipient 1983 Electronic Industries Assn. distinguished contribution award; mem: IEEE, ACM; num. software related publs. Res: 22440 Hatteras St Woodland Hills 91367 Ofc: Litton Data Systems, 8000 Woodley Ave, MS 44-30, Van Nuys 91409

FLACK, JOHN THOMAS, III, project engineer; b. Sept. 22, 1957, Shelbyville, Tenn.; s. John T., Jr. and Gladys (Young) F.; edn: BS in elec. engring., Tenn. St. Univ. 1981. Career: software & test engr. Digital Equipment Corp., Phoenix, Ariz. 1981-83; project engr./prodn. supr. StaeFa Controls Systems, San Diego 1983--; mem: IEEE 1979-82, NSBE, 1979-81; Democrat; Pentecostal; rec: photog., music, computers. Res: 1448 South 45th St, San Diego 92113 Ofc: StaeFa Controls, 4340 Viewridge Ave, San Diego 92123

FISCHL, PETER L., inventor, company president; b. July 19, 1930, Budapest, Hungary, nat. 1962; s. Tibor and Edith (Neubauer) F.; m. 2d. Catherine Csemy; children: Tibor (by previous m.); Catherine Victoria, b. 1975; edn: AS, Los Angeles Trade Tech., 1974. Career: with family owned bus. (of 75 years) in Budapest; preparation mgr., California Homes Publ.; cameraman, Walt Disney Studios, Burbank; currently pres.,The Mini "T" Electric Motor Car Co., Inc., Glendale (co. has dealers in Palm Springs, Phoenix & Youngtown, Az., Tex., NY); inventions: spl. meat cooker/warmer (1946), Fischl Tournament Chess Set (1974), Mini "T" Car Wonder (1982); co. will produce first gasoline model auto (20 mph) in 1984 (will appear in sev. motion pics., TV shows); rec: chess (rated 1680 by Am. Chess Fedn.), piano, magic. Address: 1140 Highland Ave Glendale 91202

FISH, LILIAN MANN, lawyer; b. Sept. 6, 1901, Methuen, Mass.; d. Samuel Eleazer and Ella Agnes (Hobbs) Mann; m. Charles Melvin Fish (dec.), Dec. 25, 1923; edn: JD, magna cum laude, Southwestern Univ. Sch. of Law 1932, spl. courses, USC, 1932-; admitted to practice in Calif. State and Fed. Dist. Cts. 1932, 9th Cir. Ct. of Appeals, 1933, US Supreme Ct. 1936. Career: secty./asst. to Clerk Superior Ct., Hillsborough Co. Nashua N.H. 1918-26; legal secty., office of Lloyd Nix (atty. pvt. practice, Los Angeles, San Pedro, and City Prosecutor, L.A.), 1929-32, assoc. atty. 1932-46; assoc. atty. Price, Postel & Parma, Santa Barbara 1949-71 (most important case: appeal to US Supreme Ct. of S.B. Water Agcy. case, combined with San Joaquin Valley cases known as Ivanhoe Cases involving validity of 160-acre limitation on water from fed. reclamation projects); atty. solo practice lmtd. to wills, probate, estate, property matters, Santa Barbara 1971--; life cert. instr., family history and research, Calif. St. Bd. Edn. (Adult Edn.) 1970; mem. Santa Barbara City Bicentennial Com. 1975-6; honors: Woman of the Year 1980, Mar Vista Bus. & Profl. Womens Club, S.B.; mem. Los Angeles Co., Santa Barbara Co. Bar Assns. (del. State Bar Conv.); pres. LA Women Lawyers Club 1940; charter mem. San Pedro BPW 1927, pres. National BPW Club, L.A. 1945-6; Santa Barbara BPW Club (pres. 1955); dir., Santa Barbara Hist. Soc. (pres. 1956-7); Santa Barbara Trust for Historic Preservation (bd. -1981); Phi Delta Delta (law frat.), past pres. S. B. Ventura Alumnae; editor: Ancestors West, geneal. soc. quarterly, 1978-; sev. hist. arts.; Republican; United Ch. of Christ; rec: coins, stamps, gardening, clothing design. Res: 2546 Murrell Rd, Santa Barbara 93109 Ofc: 202 Carrillo Profl. Bldg., 225 E. Carrillo St Santa Barbara 92101

FISH, RANDOLPH CHARLES, podiatrist; b. June 1, 1948, Tacoma, Wash.; s. Erwin Charles and Orlys Vivian (Lofthus) F.; m. Susan Holt, Feb. 10, 1982; edn: BA, The Evergreen State Coll. 1975; DPM, Penna. Coll. of Podiatric Med. 1979. Career: resident podiatric orthopedics & surgery, James C. Giuffre Med Ctr., Phila. 1979-81; pvt. practice, Phila. 1981-2, Yucca Valley, Calif. 1983--; consultant in foot and leg trauma, Industrial Med., Phila. 1981-2; assoc. clin. faculty, Penna. Coll. of Pod. Med. 1981-; cons. sports med., South East Mass. Sports Med. Ctr., Fall River, Mass. 1981-2; honors: Who's Who in Am. Colls. & Univs. 1979; mem: Calif. Podiatric Med. Assn.; Am. Padiatry Assn. 1983; Rotary Club of Yucca Vlly.; rec: pvt. pilot; Am. Civil War history, photog. Res:7767 Acoma Trail Yucca Valley 92284 Ofc: 56669 Twenty Nine Palms Hwy, Ste 6, Yucca Valley 92284

FISHER, BARRY ALAN, lawyer; b. May 15, 1943, Los Angeles; s. Harry and Fay F.; m. Susan E., June 16, 1968; children: Joshua, b. 1972; Jonathan, b. 1974; Robert, b. 1977; edn: BA, UCLA 1965, JD, 1968. Mem. State Bars of Calif., Alaska, Rhode Is.; admitted to US Sup. Ct., all Fed. Cir. Cts. of Appeal, num. fed. district cts. Career: law clerk to Chief Justice, Alaska Supreme Ct. 1968-9; Reginald Heber Smith Fellowship, Univ. Pa. Law Sch. 1969-71; Justice of the Peace, R.I. 1971; counsel Sierra Club Legal Defense Fund, San Francisco 1972-5; mem. Fleishman, McDaniel, Brown & Weston, Beverly Hills 1974-6; sr. partner Fisher & Moest, Los Angeles 1976--; counsel num. public interest cases throughout US incl. Larson v. Valente, 102 S. Ct. 1673 (1982); mem. Calif. State Bar (Com. on Persons W/ Special Needs; chmn. Religion Law Com.; World Peace Through Law); spkr. num. Law and Religion Confs.; contbg. author: Govt. Intervention in Religious Affairs (Pilgrim Press 1982); mem. adv. bd. Religious Freedom Reporter; rec: ethnomusicology, music perf./ lectr.; Res: 119 17th Street Santa Monica 90402 Ofc: Fisher & Moest, 2049 Century Park E., Ste 3160 Los Angeles 90067

FISHER, JERRY BILL, medical instrument co. president; b. May 17, 1942, Hutchinson, Kans.; s. Wm. David and Edith Minnie F.; m. Cherie Senseman, June 29, 1966; children: Gena, b. 1967; Michael, b. 1974; Michelle, b. 1977; edn: BA, Walla Walla Coll. 1967. Career: Div. sales mgr. United Med. Labs., Chgo., Ill. 1967-72; regl. sales mgr. Hycel, Inc., Chgo. 1973-77; pres./ founder/ chmn. bd. Electro- Medical Systems, Inc., Fountain Valley 1978--; awards: salesman of yr. United Med. Labs. 1970, sales mgr. of yr. Hycel, Inc. 1974, 76; mem: Internat. Soc. of Biomolecular Med. (founder, chmn. bd. 1983-4); Rotary

Toastmaster (past pres.); able body mem. of Internat. Handicap Scuba Diving Assn.; devel. and implemented successful mktg. pgm for the Electro- Acuscope 80; Democrat; Prot.; rec: scuba diving. Res: 17442 Encino Circle Huntington Beach 92647 Ofc: Electro- Medical Systems, inc., 18433 Amistad Fountain Valley 92708

FISK (fmrly BARNES), EDWARD RAY, engineer, author, educator; b. July 19, 1924, Oshkosh, Wisc.; s. Raymond Edward and Grace Orfa (Meyer) Barnes; m. Antonia, Oct. 28, 1950; children: Jacqueline, b. 1952, Edward II, b. 1954, William, b. 1956, Robert, b. 1958; edn: alumnus, Marquette Univ., Univ. Calif.; MBA (in prog.); Reg. Civil and Profl. Engr. in Airz., Calif., Colo., Fla., Ida., La., Mont., Nev., Ore., Utah, Wash., Wyo.; Reg. Constrn. Insp. gen. engrg., Calif.; lic. Land Surveyor, Ore., Ida.; Lifetime Teaching Cred. (Engrg.) Calif. Career: vice pres. Lawrance, Fisk & McFarland, Inc.; over 34 years in engineering and constrn. projects (projects for NASA, US mil., hydroelec. power dams for public & pvt. agcs., wastewater treatment plants, hwys and municipal roadways, bridges, small boat marinas, airport facilities, etc.); instr., guest lectr. UCB, Polytech. Inst. of NY, CalPoly Pomona, Orange Coast Coll., ASCE Continuing Edn. Pgm. (internat.); mem: Fellow ASCE (chmn. Constrn. Div. Exec. Com. 1982-3); Calif. Soc. of Profl. Engrs. (pres., state dir., Orange Co. 1976-8); Orange Co. Engrg. Council (pres. 1971-2, 73-4); Project Mgmt. Inst.; Struc. engrs. Assn. of So. Calif.; Am. Arbitration Assn. (1969-); State Constrn. Contract Arbitration Com. (Cert. Arbitrator 1982-); Tau Beta Pi. Address: POB 6448, Orange 92667

FISKE, ELAINE, jewelry manufacturer; b. June 30, 1929, Chgo., Ill.; d. Benjamin and Sylvia (Schaye) Steinfeld; 1 son, Larry, b. 1960; edn: BA, Drake Univ. 1948; scholarship, Art Inst. of Chgo. 1953. Career: bathroom & window decorator, Miami Beach, Fla. 1960-70; restaurant owner, Los Angeles 1977-9; pres. Elaine Fiske Jewelry, Encinitas 1979--; lectr. on nutrition 1981-3; honors: recognition, Muscular Dystrophy Assn., and KPBS-TV; works: exhibs. in jewelry shows and mags.; Sci. of Mind; rec: designing one of kind jewelry, travel. Address: Elaine Fiske Jewelry, 385 West I Street Encinitas 92024

FITCH, STANLEY, offsite amenities co. president; b. Feb. 9, 1929, NY, NY; s. Arthur Lewis and Mae (Berenson) F.; m. Marlene Bloom, Feb. 13, 1949; children: Lawrence Alan, b. 1952, Sherri Lyn, b. 1955; edn: De Witt Clinton H.S. Career: pres. Westfield Products, Meruchen, NJ 1962-74; v.p. Mershaw Inc., Moonachie, NJ 1969-74; pres. Compass Distbrs., Hackensack, NJ 1974-80; v.p. John Lindsey Co. Inc., Costa Mesa, Ca. 1980-82; pres. Service Plus Inc., Costa Mesa 1982-83; pres. Select Creations Inc., Santa Ana 1983--; mem. Knights of Pythias (past chancellor cmdr.); :Jewish. Res: 1964 San Bruno Newport Beach 92660 Ofc: Select Creations Inc. 1560 E. Edinger Ave, Unit D, Santa Ana 92705

FITZGERALD, JOHN DESMOND, lawyer; b. May 17, 1923, NYC; s. Robert Wm. and Lillian (Shannon) F.; m. Evelyn, May 5, 1945; children: Robert W., b. 1946; Karin, b. 1949; John D., III, b. 1952; edn: BS cum laude, St. John's Univ. 1942; JD, Columbi Univ. 1949; admitted Calif. State Bar 1950. Career: atty., Fitzgerald & Fitzgerald, Santa Rosa; instr./ lectr. UC Hastings Law Sch. 1953-56, Continuing Edn. of the Bar 1956, Univ. Calif. 1959-62, Santa Rosa Jr. Coll. 1953-64; guest lectr. on Nurses Malpractice, Western Conv. of Op. Room Nurses 1972; mem: Calif. State Bar Assn. (past chmn. Calif. Conf. Com. of Lawyers, Claims Adjusters and Ins. Cos.; Unauthorized Practice of Law subcom. chmn.); Am. Bd. of Trial Advocates; Am., local Bar Assn.; Calif. Defense Counsel; publs: contbr. to Modern Trials (by Melvin Belli) and Hellcat: The F6F in WWII (by Barrett Tillman), law jour. arts.; mil: lt. USNR 1942-46; bd. dirs. Santa Rosa Sym. Assn., bd. trustees Rincon Valley Sch. Dist. Res: 3538 Fir Dr Santa Rosa 95405 Ofc: Fitzgerald & Fitzgerald, 1041 College Ave Santa Rosa 95404

FITZPATRICK, ROBERT JOHN, college president; b. May 18, 1940, Toronto, Can., US Citizen 1962; s. John Dennis Meagher and Rita Maxine (Dunn) F.; m. Sylvie M. Blondet, Janm. 3, 1966; children: Joel Denis, b. 1967; Michael Sean, b. 1970; Claire Valerie, b. 1974; edn: BA, Spring Hill Coll. 1963, MA, 1964; Woodrow Wilson Fellow, John Hopkins Univ. 1964-5, PhD (in Fr.) coursewk. 1968-70. Career: asst. prof. of French, The Univ. of Me., Orono, Me. 1965-68j; chmn. Dept. Modern Langs., Gilman Sch., Baltimore, Md. 1968-72; dean of students Johns Hopkins Univ. 1972-75; pres. Calif. Inst. of the Arts, Valencia 1975--; dir. LAOOC Olympic Arts Festival for 1984 Olympic Games, 1970-74; staff mem. McCarthy Nat. Cmpgn. Hdqtrs. 1968; US Senate staff asst. to Sen. J.D. Tydings, 1970; mem. Md. Democratic State Central Com. 1970-2; dist. coord. Muskie for Pres. 1972; mem. Baltimore City Council, 1971-75; honors: recognition for nat. leadership potential, Time mag. 1974; mem: Advocates for the Arts, Internat. Council of Fine Arts Deans, Nat. Assn. Schs of Art, Assn. Ind. Colls. & Univs.; trustee, Bennington Coll., Craft & Folk Art Mus., The Dunn Sch. (Los Olivos), Nat. Endowment for the Arts, Interdisciplinary Panel, InterArts Pgm.; mem. Calif. Arts Council; Nat. Adv. Bd. for the Dance Gallery; bd. dirs. LA Chamber Orch. Soc. 1977-81; Democrat; rec: art, music, orchids, racquetball. Res: 16065 Royal Oak Rd, Encino 91436 Ofc: Calif. Inst. of the Arts, 24700 McBean Pkwy Valencia 91355

FITZSIMMONS, LARRY ALLEN, electrical engineer; b. Sept. 3, 1946, Kimberly, W.Va.; s. Jerome James and Lillian Mae (Belcher) F.; edn: BSEE, summa cum laude, New Haven Univ. 1975; MSCS, UCLA 1982. Career: engr. Philips Medical Sys., Shelton, Conn. 1974-9; engr. Consolidated Controls, Bethel, Conn. 1979-80; sr. staff Hughes EDSG, El Segundo 1980--; research: in advanced signal processing, ongoing; mil: Sp5, US Army 1965-8; Catholic. Res: 4475 Pacific Coast Hwy, J206, Torrance 90505 Ofc: Hughes, Box 902, El Segundo

FIX, ERNEST EUGENE, agriculturist; b. Mar. 5, 1900, Sacramento; s. Ernest E., Sr., and Carrie Caroline (Fauser) F.; m. Reta Cathryn Shields, Aug. 18, 1933; edn: UC Davis, 1924-26; Career: ship electrician, Mare Is. 1915-20; raised turkeys near Dunnigan, Ca. 1920-23, almond and prune grower, Chico 1926-31; county agric. insp., Oroville 1931-37, Yolo Co. Deputy Agric. Commnr., Woodland 1938-42; USPHS plague suppressive measures splst., S.F. 1943-44; Lassen Co. Agric. Commnr. & Deputy State Sealer of Wts. & Measures, 1944-65, ret. 1965; honors: Block letter, UC Davis 1924; Sword & Sandal hon. frat. 1925; Sr. Citizens Bldg. Com. chmn. 1983, pres. Susanville Senior Citizens Club Inc. 1984; life mem. (hon.) Calif. Agric. Commnrs. & Calif. Wts. & Measures Assns.; mem. Masons, Royal Arch Masons; Lassen Co. Youth Camp Director (16 yrs.), 4H Leader (10 yrs., Co. chmn.), Lassen Co. Fish, Game & Rec. Dir. (7 yrs.); mil: pvt. USAAF 1942-3; Democrat; Lutheran; rec: hunting, fishing. Res: 706-420 Hwy 395 E., Susanville 96130

FLACCO, SIDONIE MARIANNE, medical center executive; b. Dec. 1, 1930, Phila., PA; d. Paul and Marie Margaret (Spaeth) Alemann; m. Richard Flacco (dec. 1964), Feb. 5, 1949; children: Paul, b. 1950; Richad, b. 1955; Renee, b. 1955; edn: BA, Univ. of La Verne 1970; M.Ed. 1971. Career: data reduction Aerojet, Azusa 1963-8; instr. in German/ coord. of German Dept. Univ. of LaVerne 1971-2; asst. to Dean of Contin. Edn. 1972-4; chief therapist St. Luke Hosp., Pasadena 1974-5; marriage & family counselor, pvt. practice, LaVerne 1975-84; asst. dir./ clinical supvr. Memorial Med. Ctr. of Long Beach Adolescent Chemical Dependency Unit 1984--; organizer/ consultant, Court Diversion Pgm.; instr. Grad. Counseling, supvr. counselors and students; honors: Calif. rep. at 1959 Cured Cancer Congress, Wash. DC; Am. Cancer Soc. 1960 Poster Family; featured on Ralph Edwards TV show, This Is Your Life; mem: nat. Alliance of Family Life; Calif. Assn. of Marriage & Family Therapists; Nat. Assn. of Alcoholism Counselors; Calif. Assn. of Alcoholism Counselors; publs: contbr. theories and assistance for book: Pendulum of Choice by Johanna Alemann; subject of biographic article, Redbook Mag. 1958; author: Adolescent Chemical Dependency Unit program at Memorial Med. Ctr. of Long Beach; Democrat; Protestant; rec: poetry, philosophy, study groups. Res: 3530 Elm Ave, No. 112, Long Beach 90807

FLACK, JOHN THOMAS, III, project engineer; b. Sept. 22, 1957, Shelbyville, Tenn.; s. John T., Jr. and Gladys (Young) F.; edn: BS in elec. engring., Tenn. St. Univ. 1981. Career: software & test engr. Digital Equipment Corp., Phoenix, Ariz. 1981-83; project engr./prodn. supr. StaeFa Controls Systems, San Diego 1983--; mem: IEEE 1979-82, NSBE, 1979-81; Democrat; Pentecostal; rec: photog., music, computers. Res: 1448 South 45th St, San Diego 92113 Ofc: StaeFa Controls, 4340 Viewridge Ave, San Diego 92123

FLAGG, GWENERVERE LOUISE, physician; b. Aug. 11, 1953, Indianapolis; d. Samuel and Helen Louise (Brooks) F.; edn: BA, Andrews Univ. 1975; MD, Loma Linda Univ. Sch. of Med. 1978. Career: gen. surgery intern White Meml. Med. Ctr., Los Angeles 1979; postgrad. gen. surg. res. MLK-Drew Med. Ctr., 1980-; 7th-day Adventist; rec: needlework, music, photog. Res: 12012 So Compton Ave, 2-103, Los Angeles 90059 Ofc: King-Drew Medical Center, Dept. Surg., 12012 So. Wilmington Ave, Los Angeles 90059

FLAKS, HOWARD ERROL, physician/weight reduction specialist; b. Dec. 15, 1952, Johannesburg, S. Africa; s. Jack, MD, and Audrey F.; edn: BA, Univ. of the Witwatersrand, S.A. 1973, honors degree in psych. 1974, MD, 1980; MA in psych., cum laude, Univ. of S. Africa 1975; lic. MD, Calif., S. Africa; Qual. Clin. Psychologist. Career: intern in surg. and internal med., J.G. Strijdom Hosp., S. Africa; res. int. med., Cedars Sinai Med. Ctr., Los Angeles; currently: full time wt. reduction practice, Beverly Hills; cons., communicable diseases, LA County; instr. USC (Central Health Dist., L.A.); mem: Bev. Hills CofC, AMA, CMA, LA Co. Med. Assn., Am. Soc. of Bariatric Physicians, Am. Soc. of STD, So. African Med. Assn., So. African Psychol. Assn., Am. Coll. of Nutrition; Advis. Council BSA, Youth Leadership Soc., Univ. of Witwatersrand Alumni Soc.; frequent spkr. on med. and psych. aspects of obesity; num. publs. in field; Jewish; rec: talent scout for a model agcy. Res: 840 No Larrabee St, 1-121, Los Angeles 90069 Ofc: Howard Flaks MD, 9400 Brighton Way, 202, Beverly Hills 90210

FLAMM, DONALD EDWIN, public affairs executive; b. July 7, 1922, Salt Lake City, Utah; s. Carl Frederick and Marie (Diamond) F.; m. Barbara Nell Bitting, June 24, 1948; children: Mikel, b. 1950; Debra (Miller), b. 1951; Steven, b. 1952; edn: journ., writing courses, Woodbury Coll., UCLA Ext. Career: pub. rels. rep. Northrop Aircraft 1950-5; editor, Gardena Valley News 1955; pub. rels. rep. Douglas Aircraft Co., 1955-7; pub. rels. mgr. Ramo-Wooldridge Div. Thompson Ramo Wooldridge 1957-59; dir. pub. affairs West Coast, Ford Aerospace 1959--; chmn. Pub. Rels. Adv. Council, UC Irvine; awards: resolution, Orange County Bd. of Supvrs.; non-fiction writing awd., US Coast Guard Mag. 1945; 4 Protos (1st place) awds., Pub. Rels. Soc. of Am. (1977, 1981); Gold Press Card awd., O.C. Press Club; spl. awd., Big Brothers of O.C.; mem: Pub. Rels. Soc. of Am. (pres. O.C. Chpt. 1978); Aviation Space Writers Assn. 1951-; Missile, Range and Space Pioneers; Am. Space Found. 1983-; O.C. Press Club (past assoc. dir.); Newport Beach United Fund (pres. 1967); Newport Harbor CofC (v.p.); mil: served in USCG 1942-6; Asia-Pac Cmpgn., WWII Victory, Philippine Lib., Am. Area Cmpgn. medals, GCM; Republican; Protestan; rec: photog., sketching. Res: 224 The Grand Canal Balboa Island 92662 Ofc; Ford Aerospace & Comm. Corp., Ford Road Newport Beach 92660

FLEISCHMANN, GERALD LEE, aerospace co. executive; b. Feb. 25, 1941, St. Louis, Mo.; s. Harry B. (dec.) and Frieda (Medalie) F.; m. Judith Thaller, June 2, 1963; children: Philip, b. 1966, David, b. 1967, Jonathan, b. 1973,

David, b. 1974; edn: BA, Washington Univ., St. Louis 1963; MBA, Indiana Univ., Bloomington 1974. Career: served to major US Air Force, 1964-84: communications ops. ofcr., TUSLOG Det 94, Turkey, 1964-67; intell. threat assessment ofcr. HQ USAF (Pentagon) 1967-71; chief Intell. Data and Targets Branch, Saigon, S. Vietnam 1971-72 (rec'd Bronze Star); stu. AF Inst. of Tech., (MBA Disting. Mil. Grad.) 1972-74; computer sys. analyst/design engr. HQ Strategic Air Cmd., Omaha, Nebr. 1974-77; chief Analysis and Pgmmg., HQ Pacific Air Forces, Honolulu 1977-80; chief Systems Integration, Mission Control Pgm. office, Space Div., L.A. 1980-84, div. chief for systems engring.and integration, 1982-84; ret. USAF 1984; senior staff Space Applications Corp., currently; decorated Meritorious Svc. Medal w. Oak Leaf Cluster, AF Commendn. Medal w. Oak Leaf Cluster; recipient award of merit BSA, Aloha Council 1980; Beta Gamma Sigma (bus. hon. 1974-); mem. BSA, AF Assn.; publs: Am. Business Law J. (Winter 1974), The Air Force Comptroller (7/80); Jewish (Reform); rec: camping, woodwork, writing. Res: 10948 La Carta Ave Fountain Valley 92708 Ofc: Space Applications Corp. 200 E. Sandpointe Ave Santa Ana 92707

FLEMING, DON ALBAN, psychotherapist; b. Nov. 6, 1932, Los Angeles; s. Al and Genivere (Bellenger) F.; m. Pamela Fleming, Jan.]7, 1969; edn: Los Angeles City Coll. 1952-5; BA, CSU 1957; MSW, Florida State Univ. 1965; PhD, Columbia Pacific Univ. 1982; lic. MSW, State of Fla. 1965, LCSW, State of Calif. 1971. Career: with Dept. of Public Social Service, Los Angeles 1965-8; child welfare wkr. 1965-6; supvg. child welfare wkr. 1966-7; dir. volunteers svc. to families 1967-8; group therapist Bay Cities Mental Health Center, Los Angeles 1967-73; pvt. practice, adults, children, Los Angeles 1968--; coord. Julia Ann Singer Ctr., L.A. 1968--; cons./ lectr. So. Calif. Assn. of Young Children; faculty Stephen Wise Temple Parenting Ctr.; cons. HEW 1971-4; faculty Calif. Sch. of Profl. Psychology 1972-5; mem Nat. Assn. Soc. Wkrs.; founder of fundraising org., A Childs Found. (adv. bd. 1977-); author: How to Stop the Battle With Your Child (1984), Caring in the Moment (in press); Democrat; sports fan. Res: 13935 W. Tahiti Way, No 337, Marina Del Rey 90291 Ofc: Julia Ann Singer, 3321 Edith Ave Los Angeles 90064

FLEMING, THOMAS JAMES, real estate consultant; b. June 8, 1899, Chgo.; s. Cornelius James and Catherine (Murphy) F.; m. Theodora Lynch, Dec. 19, 1931, Dec. 1963; children: Thomas J., Jr., b. 1921; William Campbell, b. 1923, Aug. 1974; Career: real estate w/ Potter Palmer Estate, Chgo. 1916-19; Ross, Browne & Fleming, Chgo. 1919-, ret. mng. partner 1950--; moved to Palm Springs, Calif. 1951, moved to La Jolla 1955; past pres., treas., dir. of 919 Corp., Chgo.; active in devel. of North Mich. Ave. (Magnificent Mile), Chgo. 1916-50; Chgo. Real Estate Bd. (pres. 1941, chmn. of renting & mgmt. div. 1931-4-5; dir. 1936-8, 1942-3); past mem. Ill. Assn. of Real Estate Bds., Am. Chpt. of Internat. R.E. Fedn., Citizens Bd. of Loyola Univ. of Chgo.; past dir.: Coachella Valley SVLCC (P.S.), La Jolla Trust & Svgs Bank; donor, UCSD Cancer Ctr.; past bd. mem. Fine Arts Soc. of San Diego; fellow, St. Joseph's Coll. (Renesseler, Ind.); mem: La Jolla Mus. Art (life), Scripps Clinic & Resrch Found. Assocs., S.D. Opera Guild (past dir.), S.D. Sym. Orch. Assn. (past dir.), Univ. S.D. Pres. Club; UCSD Sch. of Med. Assocs. (charter), Opera Guild of the Desert (fmr); Republican; Catholic. Address: 5329 La Jolla Hermosa Ave La Jolla 92037

FLETCHER, RALPH GREGORY, governmental relations executive; b. Aug. 22, 1946, Little Rock, Ark.; s. Ralph Gregory and Leta Margaret (Wilkinson) F.; m. Jeanne Wade, July 30, 1977; 1 dau., Lauren Christine, b. 1982; edn: AA, Santa Monica Coll. 1969; BA, Eng., CSU Northridge 1972; M.Pub.Adm., CSULA 1976. Career: asst. mgr. Kinney Corp., Los Angeles 1973-74; dir. mktg. Geo. Young & Assocs., Los Angeles May-Aug.1974; acct. exec./polit. cons., Repub. Party of Hawaii, Aug.-Nov.1974; adminstrv. analyst Gr. L.A. Community Action Agcy. 1975-76; dir./adminstr. Polit. Affairs Dept. Calif. Assn. of Realtors, Los Angeles 1976-83 and treas. various political action coms. (Calif. Real Estate PAC, Issues Mobilization PAC, CREPAC/Federal) 1977-83; dir. Govtl. Rels., L.A. CofC 1983-; bd. dirs. v.p. Phi Delta Theta (CSUN) Bldg. Corp. 1983-. Honors: charter mem. Fellows Pgm., Edmund G. Brown Inst. of Govt. Affairs 1982; alumnus of year 1980, Phi Delta Theta (CSUN); appreciation, City of L.A. 1977; mem: Phi Delta Theta (pres. L.A. Alumni Club: 1st Phi from Calif. Zeta to hold post); L.A. Public Affairs Ofcrs Assn.; Town Hall; CSUN Alumni Assn. Publs: arts in Calif. Real Estate Mag.; Republican; Methodist; rec: racquetball. Res: 18738 Lemarsh St. Northridge 91324 Ofc: LA Area CofC, 404 S. Bixel St. Los Angeles 90017.

FLETCHER, ROSE MARIE, mortgage banking co. executive; b. Dec. 8, 1940, Oakland; d. Martin George and Gertrude Elizabeth (Noe) Maher; m. Jamie Fletcher, Aug. 1, 1960; children: Roberta, b. 1968; Rebecca, b. 1971; Jamie, b. 1972; edn: West Valley Coll. 1974-76; CSU San Jose 1958-59; R.E. Broker, Dept. R.E. 1980. Career: v.p. Reed & Jones Mortgage, San Jose 1975-77; asst. v.p./ br. mgr. Ralph C. Sutro Mortgage, San Jose 1977-79; ops. br. mgr. Suburban Coastal Corp., San Mateo 1979-80; v.p. ops./ exec. adminstr. Unified Mortgage Co., Santa Clara 1980--; honors: Woman of the Yr., Assn. of Profl. Women 1979-80; mem: Calif. Assn. Residential Lenders; MBA; CMBA; USSLL; APMW (past pres.); Democrat; Catholic. Res: 3704 Heppner Ln San Jose 95136 Ofc: Unified Mortgage Co., 20883 Stevens Creek Blvd Cupertino 95014

FLICK, JOHN EDMOND, newspaper executive; b. Mar. 14, 1922, Franklin, PA; s. E.L. and Mary M. Flick; Univ. of PA and Northwestern Univ., 1941-44, 45; LL.B., 1948; grad. Legal Judge Adv. Gen's. Sch., Univ. of VA, 1960-61; m. Lois A. Lange, Andalusia, PA, Apr. 20, 1946; Children: Gregory A., b. 1947; Scott E., b. 1952; Lynne E., b. 1956; Anne E., b. 1960. career: admitted to Bar of Calif., Ill., Fed Dist. Ct., U.S. Supreme Ct.; atty. at law and faculty, Calif. Western Univ. Law Sch., 1949-50; faculty U.S. Mil. Acad., West Point, NY, 1954-57; counsel-dir. contracts, Litton Inds., Ind., 1963-67; sr. v.p., gen. counsel, secty., dir., Bangor Punta Corp., 1967-69; bd. dirs., Piper Aircraft Corp., 1969; sr. v.p., gen. counsel, secty., Times Mirror Co., 1970--; dir. Tejon Ranch Co., 1975--; Author: State Tax Liability of Servicemen and Their Dependents, publ. Wash. and Lee Law Review, 1964. Ofcr. Judge Advocate Gen's. Corps, 1950-63; Lt. Col., USAR (ret.). awards: Acad. Awards by Lawyers Cooperative Co., Judge Adv. Assn., Amer. Bar Assn., 1961. Mem.: Amer., L.A. Co., Calif., Ill. Bar Assns.; Judge Adv. Alumni Assn.; Northwestern Univ. Alumni Assn.; Amer. Soc. of Corp. Sectys.; Jonathan Club. ofc: Times-Mirror Square, Los Angeles 90053.

FLICKER, WAYNE MICHAEL, physician; b. Oct. 17, 1946, NYC; s. Max and Elaine (Koenig) F.; edn: BA, Harvard Coll. 1968; MD, Harvard Med. Sch. 1979; PhD, CalTech. 1976. Career: attending staff internist INA and Ross Loos Healthplans, Los Angeles; honors: Phi Beta Kappa 1968; Cert., Amer. Board of Internal Medicine 1983; mem: Am. Soc. of Int. Medicine, Am. Coll. of Physicians, Coalition for Clean Air, Pasadena Lung Assn.; publs: num. arts. Jour. of Chemical Physics, 1973-; Peace Corps Vol., Bogota Colombia 1968-69; Democrat; Jewish; rec: astronomy, backpacking, fishing. Res: 330 S. Mentor Ave, 333, Pasadena 91106 Ofc: INA and Ross Loos Healthplan, 1711 W. Temple, Los Angeles 90026

FLIPPER, CASSANDRA MAURINE, lawyer; b. Jan. 21, 1944, Kansas City, Missouri; d. Carl F., Jr. and Mourine G. (Garrette) F.; m. William H. Hastie, Jr., Mar. 15, 1975; 1 dau: Karen, b. 1983; edn: AB, Coll. of Lib. Arts, Wash. Univ. 1964; JD, Wash. Univ. Sch. of Law 1966; Missouri Bar 1966; Calif. Bar 1973. Career: atty. US Dept. Justice, Civil Rights Div. 1966-8; manpower devel. mgr. Economic Opportunity Com. 1969-70; atty. Ofc. of Economic Opportunity, S.F./ Seattle 1970-3; atty. Equal Employment Opportunity Com., San Francisco 1973; atty. Employment Law Ctr., S.F. 1973-4; with Levi Strauss & Co., San Francisco 1974--; dir./ EEO 1974-6; asst. gen. counsel 1977-8; assoc. gen. counsel 1979-80; deputy gen. counsel 1981--; adj. faculty, Univ. San Francisco Sch. of Law 1983; honors: NAACP Legal Defense & Edn. Fund 1981; cert. of appreciation Big Sisters of Marin 1983; mem: Am. Bar Assn., Nat. Bar Assn.; Calif. Bar Assn.; Charles Houston Bar Assn.; Calif. Black Women Lawyers; Women's Forum West; Equal Rights Advocates, Inc. (chair 1974-); Phelps- Stokes Fund, NY (bd. dirs. 1979-); Pres.'s Adv. Com. on Small & Minority Bus. Devel. 1979-80; New Image Productions (bd. dirs. 1983-); Democrat. Res: 330 Panoramic Hwy Mill Valley 94941 Ofc: Levi Strauss & Co., 1155 Battery Street San Francisco 94111

FLIPPIN, ALLAN JON, electronic engineer; b. Sept. 27, 1953, Steubenville, Ohio; s. John Eugene and Eleanor Mae (Wiseman) F.; m. Revanel Ballew, July 5, 1975; children: Carl, b. 1979, James Aaron, b. 1984; edn: computer pgmmg. cert., Computer Learning Ctr. 1976. Career: pgmmr./analyst Control Data Corp., Anaheim 1976-79; electronic engr. EECO, Santa Ana 1979-81; IC design engr. Commodore, Costa Mesa 1981-82, Holt Inc., Irvine 1982-83; senior IC design engr. Advanced Micro Devices, Sunnyvale 1983--; listed Who's Who Among Vocational and Tech. Students in Am.; mem. Mensa; publs: arts. in Microcomputing Mag.; Libertarian; Nazarene Ch.; rec: guitar, woodworking. Res: 1368 Braebridge Rd. San Jose 95131 Ofc: Advanced Micro Devices, 901 Thompson Pl. Sunnyvale 94088

FLOR, LOY LORENZ, chemist; b. Apr. 25, 1919, Luther, OK; s. Alfred Charles and Nellie Marguerite (Wilkinson) Flor, BA, in Chem., San Diego State Coll., 1941; m. Virginia L. Pace, Oct. 1, 1946; chil: Charles R., b. 1950; Scott R., b. 1952; Gerald C., b. 1954; Donna Jeanne, b. 1959; Cynthia Gail, b. 1960. Career: Helix Water Dist., La Mesa, 1947---: supv. corrosion control 1956---, chief chemist and supv. of water quality 1963---; also Reg. Profl. Engr., CA. Mem: Amer. Chem. Soc., chmn., S.D. Sect., 1965; Amer. Water Works Assn., chmn., Water Quality Div., Calif. Sect., 1965; Natl. Assn. of Corrosion Engrs., chmn., Western Region, 1970; Masons. Mil: 1st Lt., USAAF, 1941-45. Republican. Presbyterian. Rec: camping, hiking, swimming. Res: 11315 Manzanita Rd., Lakeside 92040; Office: Helix Water Dist., R.M. Levy Treatment Plant, 9550 Lake Jennings Rd., Lakeside 92040.

FLORENCE, KENNETH JAMES, lawyer; b. July 31, 1943, Hanford; s. Ivy Owen and Louella (Dobson) F.; m. Verena Demuth, 1967; edn: BA cum laude, Whittier Coll, 1965; JD, UC Hastings Coll of Law 1974. Career: dist. plant mgr. Pacific Tel. & Tel. Co., San Francisco Bay Area, 1969-71; attorney, firm of Parker, Milliken, Clark & O'Hara, Los Angeles 1974-77; partner, firm of Dern, Mason, Swerdlow & Floum, Los Angeles 1978--; honors: Boswell Scholarship 1961, Pi Sigma Alpha, Phi Alpha Theta; immed. past pres., Westside Legal Services, Inc.; mem: Am. Bar Assn., NOW, Sierra Club. Mil: lt. USNR 1966-69, Eur., S.E.Asia; decorated bronze star, Navy Commend.; Democrat; Prot.; rec: running, sports. Res: 1124 21st St. Apt 2, Santa Monica 90403. Ofc: Dern, Mason, Swerdlow & Floum, 2049 Century Park E., Ste 2060, Los Angeles 90067.

FLOYD, WILLIAM LE ROY, electronics engineer; b. Aug. 6, 1936, Douglas, AZ; s. John Harry and Marjorie (Dannelley) F.; m. Betty Durrett, Sept. 1, 1956; children: Shirley, b. 1958; David, b. 1960; Mike, b. 1968; edn: BA, San Diego St. Univ. 1964; Bus. Mgmt. Cert., Alexander Hamilton Inst. 1968. Career: assoc., research, and sr. engr. Teledyne Ryan Aeronautical Co., San Diego and proj. engr. Teledyne Ryan Aeronautical Co., Houston, TX 1955-73; prin. engr./ sr. engring. splst. General Dynamics, San Diego 1973--, currently acting mgr. of Resrch & Adv. Tech.; recipient Bank af Am. Awards 1954; publs. (3) in Radar

Backscattering (rel. NASA Apollo and Earth Resources Pgms.); Republican; Prot.; rec: Bible tchr., swimming. Res: 1654 Palomino Lane Escondido 92025 Ofc: General Dynamics, 5011 Kearny Villa Rd, Ste 7212-H, San Diego 92123

FLUHARTY, JESSE ERNEST, jurist; b. July 25, 1916, San Antonio, Tex.; s. Jesse Ernest and Gwendolyn (Elder) F.; m. Ernestine Gertrude Corlies, Oct. 25, 1945; 1 son, Stephen; edn: stu. San Diego St. Univ. 1935-36; JD w/ distinction, Univ. of Pacific, 1951; cert. in adminstrv.law (1976), court mgmt. (1978), court adminstrn. (1979), National Judicial Coll. Career: admitted to Calif. Bar 1951; individual practice law, Sacramento 1951-60; presiding workers' compensation judge, Stockton 1960-67, Los Angeles 1967-81, Long Beach 1981--; instr. Paralegal Studies, Pasadena City Coll. Honors: Judge of the Year 1983, Lawyers Club of L.A. Co. Past pres. Family Service Agcy., Sacto. 1958-9; Comm. Council, Stockton and San Joaquin Co., 1965; Service Club Council, L.A. 1973-4; Glendale Hills Coord. Council, 1976-8; Chevy Chase Est. Assn. 1971-7; chmn. San Joaquin Co. Rec. & Park Commn. 1963-7; mem: Calif. State Bar, L.A. Co. Bar Assn., Glendale Bar Assn., Am. Judicature Soc., Lions (pres. L.A. chpt. 1971-2), Lawyers Club of L.A. (past pres.), Masons, Shriners, Chevy Chase CC. Publs: arts. in law revs., ednl. manuals. Mil: US Army, 1943-45, Bronze Star, Merit Cit., Phil. Liberation Medal. Democrat (Sacto. Central Com. v.chmn. 1959-60, nom. 3d Assem. Dist. 1953); Congregational (trustee). Res: 3330 Emerald Isle Dr. Glendale 91206 Ofc: Workers Comp. Appeals Bd. POB 2620, Long Beach 95801-2620.

FLUOR, JOHN ROBERT, industrialist; b. Dec. 18, 1921, Santa Ana; s. Peter E. and Margaret (Fischer) F.; m. Lillian Marie Breaux, Anaheim, May 17, 1944; 2 sons: John Robert, b. 1945, Peter James, b. 1947; edn: USC, 1939-42, 45-6. Career: mfg. cost acct. The Fluor Corp., Ltd., 1946-47, mgr. of mfg. 1947, v.p., asst. gen. mgr. 1947-49, v.p., gen. mgr. 1949-52, exec. vice pres. 1952-56, pres./ CEO 1962-68, chmn./ CEO, 1968, chmn./CEO/pres. 1976, chmn./ CEO, 1982--; v.p., hon. NAM; dir: Hughes Aircraft Co., The Irvine Co., Calif. Canadian Bank, Santa Anita Operating Co., Santa Anita Realty Ent. Inc., Texas Commerce Bancshares Inc., Pac. Mutual Life Ins. Co., Central Pacific Theater; trustee The James Irvine Found.; trustee USC; clubs: Sky Club (NY), Eldorado CC (Palm Desert), Los Angeles CC, San Gabriel CC, California Club, The Vintage Club, The Pacific Club; mil: pilot AAF, WWII, D.F.C., Air Medal; Catholic; rec: thoroughbred horse racing, golf. Res: POB 2387 Newport Bch 92663 Ofc: 3333 Michelson Drive Irvine 92730.

FLYNN, JOHN ALLEN, lawyer; b. Jan. 12, 1945, Riverside, Ill.; s. Wm. and Marian Rae (Gustafson) F.; m. Kathey Walker, June 18, 1966; children: Judson, b. 1972; Erin, b. 1972; edn: AB, Stanford Univ. 1966; JD, UC Hastings Coll. of Law 1969; admitted to State Bar of Calif. 1970, US Dist. Cts., US Ct. of Appeals Ninth Cir. 1970, US Sup. Ct. 1975. Career: partner Graham & James, Attys., San Francisco 1969--; guest spkr., Practicing Law Inst., Maritime Personal Injury,' Los Angeles 1980, San Francisco 1982; guest spkr. Lloyd's of London Press, Maritime Claims,' S.F. 1984; recipient Am. Jurisprudence Awd. in Community Property 1969; mem: Am Bar Assn.; Maritime Law Assn. (Practice and Proceedure com. 1983-); San Francisco Bar Assn. (chmn. Admiralty Com. 1978-); Catholic; rec: skiing, swimming. Res: 60 Idlewood Rd Kentfield 94904 Ofc: Graham & James, One Maritime Plaza, Ste 300, San Francisco 94111

FOCH, NINA, actress-educator; b. Apr. 20, 1924, Leyden, Netherlands; nat. 1932; d. Dirk (composer-condr., founder NYC Sym.) and Consuelo (Flowerton) Foch; m. James Lipton, June 6, 1954; m. 2d Dennis R. Brite, Nov. 27, 1959; 1 son, Schuyler Dirk; m. 3d Michael Dewell (founder, pres. Nat. Repertory Theatre Found.), Oct. 31, 1967; edn: Miss Hewitt's Classes, NYC; grad. Lincoln Sch. Columbia Univ. 1939; painting, Parsons Sch of Design; acting w/ Stella Adler. Career: film actress, 1944--: with Warner Bros., then Columbia Pictures (18 feature films), made 20 feature films for various other studios; Broadway stage debut in John Loves Mary, 1947-48, followed by num. roles, fundraising tour for Am. Shakespeare Festival 1956; founder with John Houseman, The L.A. Theatre Group, now at L.A. Music Center; sang Anna in The Seven Deadly Sins, S.F. Ballet and Opera,1966; spl. guest Seattle Repertory Theatre in W.Coast premiere of Albee's All Over, 1973; lead roles in num. TV dramas, 1947--, appearances on all major talk shows; co-host 3 seasons, CBS news series with Walter Cronkite; guest star num. major series incl. Lou Grant show (1980 Emmy nominee); assoc. film dir. The Diary of Ann Frank, 1959; adj: prof. of drama USC, 1966-68, 78-80; artist-in-res. Univ. of N.C., 1966, U. Ohio, Columbus, 1967, CalTech , 1969-70; sr. faculty Am. Film Inst. Ctr for Adv. Film Studies, 1974-77; founder/tchr. Nina Foch Studio, Hywd 1973--. Mem: Acad. Motion Picture Arts & Scis.(exec. com. Fgn. Film Awd.), Am. Cancer Soc. (hon. Crusade chmn. L.A. 1970), Hollywood Acad. of TV Arts and Scis. (gov. 1976-7). rec: cooking, needlework. address: Nina Foch Studio, POB 1884 Bev. Hills 90210.

FOGARTY, THOMAS JAMES, cardiovascular surgeon; b. Feb. 25, 1934, Cincinnati, OH; s. William Henry and Anna Isabella (Ruthemeyer) Fogarty; Edn: BS, biol., Xavier Univ., Cincinnati, 1956; MD, Univ. of Cincinnati Coll. of Medicine, 1960; m. Rosalee Brennan, Aug. 28, 1965; chil: Thomas, b. 1967; Heather, b. 1969; Patrick, b. 1972; Jonathan, b. 1975. Career: intern and resident, Univ. of Ore. Med. Sch., Portland, 1960-65; instr. in surgery, Univ. of Ore. Med. Sch., 1967-68, chief resident & instr. in surgery, Div. Cardiovascular Surgery, Stanford Univ. Med. Center, 1969-70; asst. clin. prof. of surgery, 1971-73; pvt. practice, Cardiovascular Surgery, Stanford Univ. Med. Ctr., Stanford, 1973-78; pres. Medical staff, 1977-79; pvt. practice, Cardiovascular Surg., Sequoia Hosp., Redwood City, 1978---; dir., Cardiac Surgery, 1980---; founder, devel., mgmt., six companies (all six ventures culminated in successful mergers); bd. dirs., Santa Clara Found. for Medical Care, Satellite Dialysis Centers (both nonprofit corps. to reduce costs of health care without sacrificing quality); guest speaker, major cardiovascular socs.; dip., Amer. Boards of Surg. (1970), Thoracic Surgery (1974). Awards: fellowships 1961-62, 1965-67, 1968-69; grantee, NIH, Amer. Heart Assn.; Inventor of the Year, 1980, San Francisco Patent and Trademark Assn.; Distinguished Sci. Presentation, Amer. Coll. of Surgeons, 1971, 73, 75, 81; Astrolobe Award-Most Distinguished high school grad., 1974. Mem: AMA; Calif., Santa Clara Co. Med. Socs.; Samson Thoracic Surg. Soc.; The Soc. for Thoracic Surgeons; Amer. Coll. of Surgeons; The Internatl. Cardiovascular Soc.; The Soc. for Vascular Surgery; S.F. Surg. Soc.; Amer. Heart Assn.; Amer. Coll. of Cardiology; Pac. Coast Surg. Assn.; Bay Area Vascular Soc.; Soc. for Clin. Vascular Surg.; Pan Pac. Surg. Assn.; Andrew G. Morrow Soc.; mem. Calif. Wildlife Assn.; Ducks Unlimited; Calif. Vintners Assn.; Medical Friends of Wine; Rapley Trail Improvement Assn. Publs: 62 sci. articles and textbook chpts. on gen. and cardiovascular surgery; Inventor: 40+ patents in surgical instrumentation. Republican. Roman Catholic. Rec: fishing, hunting. Res: 5660 Alpine Rd., Portola Valley 94025; Office: 770 Welch Rd., Suite 201, Palo Alto 94304.

FOLAND, STEPHEN FISHER, lawyer; b. June 2, 1944, Indianapolis; s. Robert Rockett and Bernice (Fisher) F.; m. Sarah Weiler, Aug. 3, 1968; children: Andrew, b. 1976; Lara, b. 1979; Oliver, b. 1983; edn: BA, Indiana Univ. 1967; JD, Golden Gate Univ. Sch. of Law 1975; admitted to State Bar of Calif., Fed. Dist. Ct. 1975. Career: Capt. USAF 1968-72; partner/ prin. law firm Struthers, Grossman & Foland, Livermore 1975--; mem. bd./ past pres. The Center Crisis Counseling and Edn. Svcs. 1976-83; bd., So. Alameda Co. Headstart Pgm. 1982-3; bd., Alameda Co. Manpower Advis. Commn. 1979-81; honors: judge pro tempore, Alameda Co. Superior and Muni. Cts.; mem: Livermore- Amador Valley (pres. 1982, Alameda Co., and So. Alameda Co. Bar Assns.; State Bar of Calif.; Valley Democratic Caucus; mil: Capt., USAF 1968-72, AF Commend., Pres. Cit.; rec: history. Res: 1437 Fifth Street Livermore 94550 Ofc: Struthers, Grossman & Foland, 1789 Fourth St Livermore 94550

FOLEY, JOSEPH MARTIN, electrical engineer; b. Sept. 2, 1925, Bethlehem, Pa.; s. John Patrick and Cecelia Josephine (Moyer) F.; m. Marilyn Miller, Dec. 29, 1948; 1 dau: Paula, b. 1949; edn: BE, Vanderbilt Univ. 1949; Reg. Profl. Elec. Engr., Calif. 1981. Career: asst. elec. engr., Sheet & Tin Mills Electrical Turn foreman, Slabbing Mills Elec. foreman, Bethlehem Steel Co., Sparrow's Point, Md. 1949-63; elec. engr. Wheeling Steel Co., Steubenville and Mingo Junction, Ohio 1963-65; senior elec. engr./ proj. engr. H.K. Ferguson Co., Cleveland, Ohio 1965-67; supt. elec. dept./ supt. Assigned Maint., Internat. Consulting Svcs., Erdemir Steel Plant, Eregli, Turkey 1967-68; supvg. elec. engr. Arthur G. McKee Co., Western Knapp Eng. Div. (Bor, Yugoslavia; Cologne, Ger.; Madrid, Spain; Rio Tinto, Spain), San Francisco, 1969-71; gen. mgr. Paul C. Miller Co., Sparta, Mich. 1971-73; plant engr. Phelps Dodge Co., Copper Prods. Div., El Paso, Tex. 1973-74; sr. supvg. engr./ staff engr. Arthur G. McKee Co. (now Davy McKee), Western Knapp Eng. Div. (El Estor, Guatemala; Johannesburg, So. Africa; Rossing, Namibia), San Ramon 1974--; mem: Assn. Iron & Steel Engrs.; IEEE; mil: electricians mate 3/c USN 1943-46, Victory Medal, Asiatic- Pacific, Am. Theatre, GCM; Catholic; rec: minerology, gem faceting, fishing. Res: 7088 Via Blanca San Jose 95139 Ofc: Davy McKee Corporation, 2303 Camino Ramon San Ramon 94583

FOLLICK, EDWIN DUANE, educator, administrator, chiropractor; b. Feb. 4, 1935, Glendale; s. Edwin Fulfford and Esther Agnes (Catherwood) Follick; edn: BA, CSULA 1956, MA, 1961; MA, Pepperdine Univ. 1957; MPA, 1977; PhD and D.Theol., St. Andrews (London) 1958; MLS, USC 1963; M.Edn. 1964; Adv. M.Edn. 1969; LL.B, Blackstone Law Sch. 1966, JD 1967; DC, Cleveland Chiro. Coll. 1972; PhD, Acad. Theatina, Pescara 1978. Career: teacher/lib. adminstr. Los Angeles City Schs. 1957-68; law librarian Glendal Univ. Coll of Law, 1968-9; coll. librarian Cleveland Chiro. Coll., L.A. 1969-74, dir. Edn. and Admissions 1974--, and dean Student Affairs 1976--; prof. Jurisprudence, 1975--; extern prof. St. Andrews (London) 1961; assoc. prof. Grad. Sch. Pub. & Bus. Adminstrn., Newport Univ. 1982--; dir. West Valley Chiro. Health Center, 1972--; honors: Cavaliere Intl. Order Legion of Honor of Immaculata (Italy); Knight of Malta, Order St. John of Jerusalem; Ritter, Der Intl. Legion, Friedrich II von Schwaben Teutonische Miliz; Comdr. Chevalier, Byzantine Imperial Order of Constantine the Great; Comdr. Ritter, Order of St. Geron Knight, Order of St. Lazarus. Mem: ALA, NEA, Am. Assn. Sch. Librarians, Assn. Coll. and Resrch Librarians, Am. Assn. Law Librarians, Nat. Geographic Soc., Phi Delta Kappa, Sigma Chi Psi, Delta Tau Alpha. mil: US Army 1958-60; Democrat; Episcopal. Res: 7022 Owensmouth Ave Canoga Pk 91303 ofc: 590 No Vermont Av Los Angeles 90004.

FONG, GARY RONALD, hospital consultant; b. Jan. 7, 1944, Vallejo; s. James King and Lillian Helen (Wong) F.; m. Mary K. Wolfe, Dec. 30, 1978; children: Natalie, b. 1965; Carrie, b. 1969; Christopher, b. 1974; edn: Masters, CSU Long Beach; D.Pharm. UCSF Sch. of Pharm. 1968. Reg. Pharmacist, Calif. 1968, Nev. 1968. Calif. Jr. Coll. Tchr. Credential. Career: var. pharm. positions with Kaiser Found. Hosps., Super X Drug Stores, UCLA Medical Ctr., Calif. Hosp. Med. Ctr., Memorial Hosp. Med. Ctr. of Long Beach, St. Francis Mem. Hosp. (S.F.), and Pacific Health Resources (L.A.); pres./bd. chmn. Ntaional Hospital Systems, Inc., Mill Valley 1980--, cons. to hosps. in areas of Pharmacy and Materiel Mgmt.; pres. Ascot Pharmaceuticals Internat. Ltd.; clin. instr. UCSF Sch. of Pharm. and USC Sch. of Pharm.; state del. to Calif. Soc. of Hosp. Pharmacists; contbr. arts. pharm. journals; ed. Hosp. Materiel Mgmt. Qtrly. (1984); Republican; Prot.; rec: tennis, skiing. Address: Ntional Hospital Systems, Inc. 150 Marguerite Ave Mill Valley 94941

FONG, JACKSON CHIA-CHUEN YU LONG, artist, educator; b. Feb. 16, 1914, Peiping, China, nat. 1979; s. Nai Chon and Shi (Lu) F.; m. Rui Lian Cheng, Jan. 1, 1946; children: I-Ming, b. 1951; Tsao-Ming, b. 1953; edn: stu. calligraphy, Beijing, China; BA, Peiping Normal Univ. 1942. Career: High School tchr., China 1942-6; dean of studies, H.S., Taiwan 1946-56; dean of discipline, H.S., Taiwan 1956-61; supt. of schools, Y-Lan County, Taiwan 1961-4; provincial insp. of schs., Taiwan 1964-66; principal, Sch. of Deaf and Blind, Eu-Yuan, Taiwan 1966-73, ret.; currently: San Francisco artist, noted for his Chinese brush painting and calligraphy with distinctive character; num. art exhibns.; recipient KRON TV award 1982; Catholic; rec: horticulture. Res: 1539 28th Ave San Francisco 94122

FONSECA, ARTHUR JOSEPH, manufacturing jewelry executive; b. Sept. 22, 1948, San Fernando; s. Joseph Penilla and Angie (Guzman) F.; m. Christel Rebay, June 30, 1973; 1 son: Christopher, b. 1976; edn: BA, San Fernando Valley State 1970; MA, CSU Long Beach 1977; tchg. cred., Calif. 1971. Career: instr./tennis coach Huntington Beach Union High Sch. Dist. 1971-78; prop./ designer/ jeweler The Jewelry Store, Huntington Beach 1978--; bldg. chmn. (1 yr.), bldg. rep. (2 yrs.), Dist. Educators Assn., Huntington Beach 1972-74; honors: Alpha Mu Gamma; mem: Calif. Assn. of Independent Bus.; Democrat; Catholic; rec: jewelry design, investment research & analysis. Res: 17140 Los Roble Circle Fountain Valley 92708 Ofc: The Jewelry Store, 7184 Edinger Ave Huntington Beach 92647

FOPPOLI, ROBERT SILVIO, real estate investor, motel operator; b. Oct. 5, 1952, San Francisco; s. Silvio John and Piera (Quadrio) F.; edn: AA, Coll. of Marin, 1973; BA, CSU San Jose 1975; Calif. Real Estate Lic. 1976. Career: helped parents in maint. of multi-unit apts., San Franciso, partnered w/bro. in first R.E. purchase at age 16; owner/opr. 16-unit apt. bldg., 1970-76 (during coll.); owner/opr. Downtowner Inn Motel, Bakersfield, 1976--; pres. R.S.F. Enterprises; real estate investor, 1980-; bd. dirs. (v.p.) Bakersfield Conv. Bur.; mem: Calif. Motel Assn., Rho Epsilon, Friendship Inns of Amer., AAA, Bksfld. BBB, Trade Club; Republican; Catholic; rec: scuba, ski, hang glide, radio control aircraft. Res: 1301 Chester Ave Bakersfield 93301 Ofc: Downtowner Inn, 1301 Chester Ave Bakersfield 93301

FORD, JOHN JOSEPH, transportation executive; b. Feb. 10, 1937, Moline, Ill.; s. Robert Alvin and Mary L. (Ishmael) F.; m. Carol E. Wink, 1958; 3 sons: Edwin, Jeffrey, Gregg; edn: BA, FSU, 1958; MBA, USC, 1977. Career: past indsl. mktg. mgr. Xerox Corp., Torrance; past branch mgr. A.B. Dick Co., Los Angeles; currently pres./chief exec., Dave Systems, Inc., Santa Ana, and Community Transit Services, Inc., Anaheim; dir.: Dave Consulting Inc., Transmay Inc., Americe Inc., Wide One Corp., Norcal Trans. Inc. Awards: Jaycee Spoke and Outstanding Young Man awds.; Pacemaker, A.B.Dick Co.; Par Club, Xerox Corp.; mem: Am. Mgmt. Assn., Presidents Assn., Nat. Assn. Corporation Directors, Orange Co. CofC, Lions Club; publs: transp. research, spl. transit services, Dial-A-Ride publs.; mil: A/1c USAF, two Unit Awds.; Republican; Prot. Res: 2382 Bayfarm Pl. Santa Ana Hts 92707. Ofc: Dave Systems Inc. 1450 East 17th St. Santa Ana 92701.

FORD, LARRY CREED, medical scientist; b. Sept. 29, 1950, Provo, Utah; s. Creed D. and Gladys Mae (Garlick) F.; m. Diane Lewis, June 5, 1970; children: Larry Jr., b. 1975; Scott David, b. 1978; Kerilyn, b. 1980; edn: BS, magna cum laude, Brigham Young Univ. 1971; MD, honors, UCLA Sch of Med. 1975; Dip. Nat. Bd. of Med. Examiners 1975. Career: intern, int. med., VA Wadsworth Medical Ctr., Los Angeles, 1975-6; res., obstets-gyn., UCLA Sch. of Med., 1976-9, chief res. 1979-80, fellowship in biol. chem., 1977-80; asst. prof. UCLA Sch. of Med., 1980--, dir. research Ctr. for Ovarian Cancer, 1981--; founding mem./scientist Sexually Transmitted Disease Resrch Council, 1981--; mem: Am. Soc. for Microbiol., Phi Eta Sigma Hon. Frat., NY Acad. of Sci., AAAS; awards: 1st Place 18th Internat. Sci. Fair and AUS, AF, AEC Awards (1966); publs: medical jour. articles, med. book chapters; Republican; Ch. of Jesus Christ of LDS; rec: hunt, shoot, geneal. Ofc: Dr. Larry C. Ford, 3706 Tilden Ave Los Angeles 90034

FORD, PATRICIA CELESTINE, evangelist/educator; b. Apr. 11, 1936, Tallhassee, Fla.; d. George Franklin and Helen Ernestine (Matthews) F.; edn: BS, Fla. A & M Univ. 1958; M.Ed., Fla. Atlantic Univ. 1967; grad. studies USC 1970-2; Fla. and Calif. teaching credentials: music, standard svcs., general, guidance and counseling. Career: music tchr. Monroe H.Sch., Cocoa, Fla. 1958-9; band and choral dir. Washington H.S., Cairo, Ga. 1963-4; music tchr. elem. sch. Riviera Beach, Fla. 1964-8; dean of girls Boca Raton (Fla.) H.S., 1968-70; adminstrv. asst./ vice principal Barstow, Calif. 1970-4; nat. evangelist, 1975--; founder/ pres. Patricia C. Ford Evangelistic Assn., Inc.; mem: Ch. of God in Christ (Nat. Evangelist Adv. Bd. 1983); CofC; Com. Food Resources of L.A. Co., Inc.; Nat. Notary Assn.; past mem: NEA, Administrs. Profl. Orgn.; Democrat; Pentecostal; rec: reading. Address: 4232 Victoria Ave Los Angeles 90008

FORD, STEVEN LOUIS, executive; b. Mar. 15, 1952, Cleveland, Ohio; s. Harry Louis and Lottie Elizabeth (Czerpa) F.; m. Virginia Ford, Apr. 23, 1977; 1 dau: Allison, b. 1981; edn: BBA, Cleveland State Univ. 1974; MBA, USC 1982; Cert. Public Acct., Ohio 1976, Calif. 1978. Career: sr. auditor Arthur Young & Co., Cleveland, Ohio 1974-7; asst. mgr., corp. audit Hughes Aircraft, Los Angeles 1977-9; div. controller Wyle Laboratories, Irvine 1979-81; asst. corp. secty./ div. controller Robertshaw Controls/ Grayson Controls Div., Long Beach 1981--. honors: recognition awards, Nat. Contract Mgmt. Assn./LA, So. Bay Chpt. (1978), Finl. Exec. Inst./LA chpt., and USC (1979); mem: Am. Inst.

of CPAs 1977-; Ohio Soc. of CPAs 1977-8; Calif. Soc. of CPAs 1979-; Nat. Assn. of Accts. 1979-; Nat Mgmt. Assn. 1981-; USC Alumni Assn.; St. Simon and Jude Men's Club; Republican; Catholic; rec: golf, family. Res: 8711 Mossford Dr Huntington Beach 92646 Ofc: Robertshaw Controls Co., Grayson Controls Div., 100 W Victoria St Long Beach 90805

FOREMAN, JACK PRESTON, film studio executive; b. Apr. 3, 1924, Los Angeles; s. John and Lillian Mae (Young) F.; m. Barbara Jones, Oct. 17, 1964; children: Christin, b. 1959; Glenn, b. 1957; edn: BA, USC 1950. Career: director of film prodn. ops. CBS TV, Los Angeles 1950-60; CEO Samuel Goldwyn Prodns., L.A. 1960-80 (acquired & renamed 1980), v.p./gen. mgr. Warner Hollywood Studios, 1980--; honors: DKE (hon. cinema frat.) at USC; mem: Acad. of Motion Picture Arts & Scis. 1965- (sci., tech. awds. com. 1966-); pres. Hollywood CofC 1978; pres. Permanent Charities Com. of Motion Picture and TV Indus. 1984; bd. trustees, Motion Picture & TV Fund 1965-80; mil: Sgt. 5th AF Photo Recon. Sqd. 1943-6, presdtl. unit cit.; Republican; rec: boating. Res: 151 No. Bristol Los Angeles 90049 Ofc: Warner Hollywood Studios, 1041 No Formosa Ave Los Angeles 90046

FOREMAN, STEPHEN MILLS, chiropractor; b. Oct. 23, 1957, Borger, TX; s. Jimmie Mills and Freda Merl (Hardin) F.; m. Geri, June 2, 1979; children: Joseph, b. 1980; Benjamin, b. 1982; edn: AS, Amarillo Coll. 1978; Palmer Coll. 1979; DC, Life Chiropractic Coll. 1981. Career: Chiropractic Radiologist; pvt. practice, Mission Viejo 1982; group practice, El Toro 1982--; pres./ founder Podiatry Mgmt. Seminars, 1983; bd. dirs. Metroguard Med. Internat. 1983; founding bd. dirs., Diplomate Nat. Bd. of Chiropractic Radiologists, 1983-; Diplomate, Nat. Bd. of Chiro. Exam. 1981; 13 State Records,S.S.A. 1973-8; mem: Calif. Chiro. Assn. 1982; Am. Chiro. Assn. 1979-83; mem. Soaring Soc. of Am., Colo. & High-Plains Soaring Socs.; author: Guide to Lower Back Pain, 1983; Republican; Morman; rec: soaring, golf. Res: 26172 Via Mareyada Mission Viejo 92691 Ofc: 22821 Lakeforest Dr, No. 114, El Toro 92630

FORMAN, SIDNEY HAROLD, educator; b. Oct. 16, 1935, Detroit, Mich.; s. Irvin and Katie F.; m. Pauline, June 17, 1962; children: Stuart, b. 1964; Susannah, b. 1969; edn: AB, Univ. of Mich. 1957; AM, 1961. Career: high school English tchr., 1957-66: Cass Tech. H.S., Detroit, Mich. 1957-61, Lincoln H.S., 1961, Morse H.S., San Diego 1962-6; tchr. (Eng./ photojourn./ cinema) San Diego City Coll. 1967--; also opr. Photog. and Video bus. 1966--; cons. Dean's Photo; listed, Outstanding Educators of Am.; wrote award winning film: The Stonecutter (Cine Golden Eagle); mem: Calif. Tchrs. Assn., Profl. Photogs. of Am.; publs: sev. course guides for San Diego Sch. Dist.; Republican, Jewish, rec: cooking, baking bread. Res: 6719 Casselberry Way San Diego 92119 Ofc: Son Diego City Coll., 1313 12th, San Diego 92101

FORSTER, ERIC GAD, mortgage banker; b. Aug. 19, 1941, Tel Aviv, Israel, nat. 1972; s. Samuel Karl and Esther Orna (Kohane) F.; m. Judith Scott, Oct. 27, 1979; children: Jonathan, b. 1970; Dana, b. 1972; Jill, b. 1975; Eran, b. 1980; edn: Columbia Univ. 1967-69; TD, Jewish Theol. Seminary 1966; MBA, Pepperdine Univ. 1973. Career: Los Angeles Dist. mgr. Standard Computer Corp. (subs. United Telcom) -1976; principal partner Bankers Group (mortgage banking firm) & CEO Forster Devel. Co. (holding co. for family inv.), 1976--; sys. cons. Fundscope Mag. 1973-79; honors: Employee of the Yr., Ministry of Foreign Affairs, Israel 1963; elected to exec. com. Israeli Students Assn. of Am. 1967; mem: Mortgage Bankers Assn.; San Diego Bd. Realtors; Am. Mgmt. Assn.; Civil Air Patrol; author: Problems Associated With the Conversion to On-Line Processing (1972 Los Angeles); mil: nav./ observer, lt. USAF, Leadership Ribbon, SAR Ribbon; Jewish; rec: flying, sailing. Res: 1342 Harvard St Santa Monica 90404 Ofc: Bankers Group, 12473 Washington Blvd Los Angeles 90066

FOSCHETTI, CHERYL DARLENE, real estate broker; b. Sept. 19, 1944, Ottumwa, Iowa; d. Arthur Edward and Virginia Maye (Orfield) Stainer; m. Vincent Foschetti, July 29, 1961; children: Mary, b. 1962; Gina, b. 1964; Mindy, b. 1965; Nick, b. 1967; edn: AA, Glendale Jr. Coll. 1972; BSL, Glendale Coll. of Law 1982, JD, 1983; lic. real estate broker 1974-. Career: realtor/pres. Many Mansions Realty, Inc., La Crescenta 1976--; mem: Nat. Assn. of Realtors 1974-, Calif. Assn. of Realtors 1974-; mem. O.R.T. (orgn. for rehab. & tng.); works: prod. heavy metal musical gp., Wrathborne; Republican; Catholic; rec: pianist, screenwriter, movie trivia. Res: 2329 Panorama Dr La Crescenta 91214 Ofc: Many Mansions Realty Inc., 2620 Foothill Blvd La Crescenta 91214

FOSTER, DONALD LEE, general contractor; b. June 5, 1947, Mercedes, TX; s. George Milton, Sr., and Nettie Mae (Weatherford) F.; m. Cheryl A. Foster, Dec. 20, 1968; children: Jason Eric, b. 1973; Cheronn Tonia, b. 1976; Micah James, b. 1981; edn: AA, Columbia Christian Coll. 1967; BA, Pepperdine Coll. 1969; MA, Pepperdine Univ. 1972. Career: var. ednl. adminstrv. positions at Pepperdine Univ., Malibu and Columbia Christian Coll., Portland, Ore. 1967-77; owner Bristol & Foster Church Construction, Fresno 1977--; listed Who's Who in Am. 1977; bd. trustees Columbia Christian Coll.; Republican; Ch. of Christ; rec: fishing, boating, skiing. Res: 7412 No. 5th Fresno 93710 Ofc: Bristol & Foster Church Construction, 745 E Locust, Ste 112, Fresno 93710

FOSTER, DUDLEY EDWARDS, JR., educator; b. Oct. 5, 1935, Orange, NJ; s. Dudley Edwards and Margaret (DePoy) Foster; Edn: Occidental Coll., 1953-56; AB, UCLA, 1957; MA, 1958; doctoral study, USC, 1961-70; FTCL (Fellow, Trinity Coll. of London), Trinity Coll. of Music, Univ. of London, 1960. Career: lectr. in music, Immaculate Heart Coll., Los Angeles, 1960-62; dir. of music, Holy Faith Episcopal Ch., Inglewood, 1963-66; lectr.

in music, CSU Los Angeles, 1968-71; dir. of music, First Lutheran Ch. of Los Angeles 1968-72; St. Paul's Episcopal Ch., Tustin, 1973-74; prof. of music., Los Angeles Mission Coll., 1975---; frequent appearances as organ recitalist/ conductor. Awards: Teaching Fellow, UCLA, 1958-60; USC, 1961; Dist. v.p., Los Angeles College Teachers Assn., 1981---. Mem: Calif. Teachers Assn.; Natl. Edn. Assn.; Amer. Guild of Organists; Town Hall of Calif.; IPA; Medieval Acad. of Amer. Musical compositions: String Quartet, 1960; Passacaglia for Brass Insruments, 1969; Toccata for Brass Ensemble, 1970; O Scarum Convivium, for trumpet & organ, 1972; Introduction, Arioso, & Fugue, for cello & piano, 1974. Republican. Episcopal. Rec: Persian cats. Res: 2235 San Marco Dr., Los Angeles 90068; Office: Los Angeles Mission College, 1212 San Fernando Rd., San Fernando 91340.

FOSTER, JACOB JOSEPH, neurological surgeon; b. Aug. 5, 1924, Providence, RI; s. Maurice B. and Sadie Sarah (Solinger) Foster; Edn: AB, Brown Univ., 1945; MD, Tufts Univ., 1950; m. Helen Shuman, June 12, 1950; chil: Niesen Eric, b. 1951; Linsey Ellen, b. 1953; Fredde Stevanne, b. 1955. Career: intern, Los Angeles County Hosp., 1950-51; resident, neurology, Long Beach VA Hosp., 1951-52; resident, general surgery, 1952-53; resident, neurologic surgery, San Francisco VA Hosp., 1953-55; and Univ. Calif., 1955-57; pvt. practice neurological surgery, Salinas; assoc. in surgery (Neurosurgery), Stanford Univ. Sch. of Medicine, 1958-65; clin. instr., Neurologic Surg., UC Sch. of Medicine, 1969---; Salinas Valley Meml. Hosp. chief of staff, 1964-65; chief of surgery, 1962-63, 1981-83; chief of neurological surgery, Gen. Hospital of Monterey Co., 1957-76; bd. dirs., Found. for Medical Care, 1976---, secty.-treas. 1978---; bd. dirs., Monterey Inst. for Speech and Hearing, 1967-69. Mem: Congress of Neurological Surgeons; Amer. Acad. of Neurology; AMA; CMA; Monterey Co. Med. Soc., past bd. dirs., hosp. com., pub. health com.; San Francisco Neurol. Soc.; Monterey Acad. of Medicine; World Med. Assn.; Internatl. Coll. of Surgeons; Fellow Amer. Coll. of Surgeons, 1970; The Royal Soc. of Health, London, England; Diplomate, Natl. Bd. of Med. Examiners; mem., Calif. Historical Soc.; The Westerners; Gleeson Lib. Assocs.; Book Club of Calif.; Sierra Club; Bancroft Lib. Assocs.; Oakland Mus. Assoc.; Museum Soc.; Masonic Order; Monterey Peninsula Museum Assocs.; Phi Lambda Phi med. frat.; contrib. articles in med. journals, presentations. Mil: Capt., MC, USAR, 1953-62. Republican. Unitarian. Rec: jogging, swimming, collect book illustrations, wood-block printing. Res: 150 San Benancio Rd., Salinas 93908; Office: Drs. Foster, Phillips & Wahl, 220 San Jose St., Salinas 93901.

FOSTER, J RICHARD, consultant; b. Apr. 30, 1914, Seward County, Nebr.; s. Charles Oscar and Florence Cecilia (Whittaker) F.; m. May Rosalie Schmidt, Feb. 27, 1942; children: Richard, b. 1943; Robert, b. 1946; edn: BS, USC 1935; MS, 1936; Profl. Edn. Soc. 1935. Career: salesman McKesson Robbins 1937-44; v.p./ gen. mgr. Turco Products & Franklin Div. Purex Corp. 1946-69; assoc. The Charles Co. 1969-72; gen. mgr. Calla Chem. Div. Dresser Ind. 1972-82, cons. 1983-; dir. Afton Corp. 1970-3; cons. Corporate Aid 1970-82; cons. Leeder Chem. 1969-71; cons. Elsinore Aerospace Svcs. 1969-71; awards: Los Angeles Sales Exec. Merit Awd. 1972; Civil Svc. Commnr. (Bakersfield) 1950-1; Counselor of the Year for Calif., United Comml. Travelers 1950 (Bksfld); BSA Order of the Arrow 1957; Life Mbrship PTA 1958; mem: Los Angeles Sales Exec. Club 1965-73; Kiwanis; Lions; BSA; Nat. Football Hall of Fame (Orange Co. Chpt.); pres. Junior CofC (Bksfld) 1950; mil: m/sgt. US Army Ground Forces 1941-6, expert rifleman, Sgt./Major of Year 1944; Republican (Pres. Task Force); Baptist; rec: golf, speed walking, numismatics, photog. Res: 16101-A Malaga Lane Huntington Beach 92647 Ofc: Dresser Ind., 8100 Electric Ave Stanton 90680

FOUDRAY, SAMUEL HOUSTON, real estate appraiser-consultant; b. Sept. 14, 1935, Long Beach; s. Charles William and Norma Aldine (Cook) Foudray; m. Martha Siggson, Apr. 26, 1959; children: Robin, b. 1954, Linda, b. 1957; edn: AA, honors, Compton Coll. 1956; Cert. Instr., and RM, Am. Inst. R.E. Appraisers, 1980; SRA, Soc. of R.E. Appraisers 1981; CRA, Nat. Assn. of Review Appraisers 1977. Career: real estate sales agt/appraiser, 1964-73; self-emp. real estate appraiser, 1973-80; pres. Samartha Corp., Paramount 1980--; instr./owner Real Estate Procedures (a R.E. Seminar co.); past: profl. musician; instr. Anthony Schs. (1974-5), Century 21 (1976), Realty World (1976); mem: Soc. of Real Estate Appraisers (pres. Long Bch./So Bay chpt. 1981-2); Paramount CofC (pres. 1977-8); Paramount Lions Club (pres. 1977-8); dir. Rancho Los Cerritos Realty Bd., 1976-78; Town Hall of Calif. Author: Competitive Market Analysis Techniques (text for R.E. seminars, approved by Calif. State Dept. of R.E. for contg. edn. credit); Republican; Lutheran; rec: travel, sports. Res: 9856 Hoback St. Bellflower 90706 Ofc: Samartha Corp. 15726 Paramount Blvd. Paramount 90723.

FOULDS, DONALD DUANE, corporate executive; b. Feb. 4, 1925, Saginaw, mich.; s. Joseph Wm. and Florence Francis (Blumenthal) Foulds; m. Doris Roberts, Mar. 4, 1949; chil: Michael, b. 1955, Scott, . 1958, Nancy, b. 1960; edn: BS, US Naval Acad. 1948; BSEE, USN Postgrad. Sch., Monterey 1955; MSIE, Purdue Univ. 1956; Naval War Coll., Newport, RI 1961. Career: served Ensign to Comdr. USN, 1948-67(ret.): after command of USS Desoto Co., transf. to Polaris/Poseidon Ballistic Missile Pgm. as section hd. Prodn. and Quality Control/branch hd. Missile Branch, 1963-67; mgmt., Northrop Corp. Electro-Mech. Div., 1967--, dir. procurement 1968, exec.v.p. Olson Labs (subs. Northrop) 1971, dir. mktg. 1974, asst. to corp. V.P.-Planning 1976, exec. asst. to Pres. and COO, 1977--; pres./bd.chmn. Kingsbury Aviation, Inc. 1977-81. Aero. Adv. com. North Orange Co. Comm. Coll. 1982-; trustee So. Calif. Hist. Aviation Found. 1982-; honors: Tau Beta Pi; Naval Acad. Crew Squad capt. 1948; mem: Assn. of US Army (regl. vp 1983-), IEEE, IEEE Computer Soc., AOPA, ADPA; Republican; Episcopal (vestryman); rec: pilot. Res: 1870 Veteran Ave. Apt 314 Los Angeles 90025 Ofc: Northrop Corp. 1800 Century Park E. Los Angeles 90067

FOUST, RICHARD THOMAS, lawyer; b. May 30, 1938, Johnstown, Pa; s. Grant Chalmer and Theressa Florence (Skedel) F.; m. Pamela, Feb. 29, 1980; 1 son, Justin, b. 1982; edn: BA, San Jose State Coll. 1965; JD, Univ. of West L.A. 1978; admitted to Calif. State Bar 1980. Career: psychiatric techn., State Calif. 1956-66; claims adjuster/ supvr./ mgr. var. insurance cos., 1966-80; atty. at law pvt. practice, Culver City 1980--; mem: Am.,, Calif., Los Angeles Co., Culver City Bar Assns.; Elks; mil: A2C, Calif. Nat. Guard 1956-62; Republican; rec: entomology, stamp collecting. Res: 3419 Sherbourne Dr Culver City 90230 Law Office, Richard T. Foust, 4145 So Sepulveda Blvd Culver City 90230

FOWBLE, ROBERT HENRY, architect; b. Jan. 11, 1921, El Centro; s. James Raymond and Robbie Lou (Estes) F.; edn: BS, San Diego State Coll. 1949; M.Arch., M.I.T. 1952; Calif. Lic: Arch. 1956; Spl. Tchg. Credential 1952; Com. Coll. Instr. Cred. 1973. Career: sr. designer Kistner, Wright & Wright, Architects & Engrs., Los Angeles 1952-3; proj. capt. Allison & Rible, Archs., L.A. 1953-4; arch./ engr. Frank L. Hope & Assoc., Archs., San Diego 1954-6; prin. Robert H. Fowble, Arch., S.D. 1956-68; arch. Neuman- Riddle & Fowble, El Centro/ Blyth 1963-8; pres. Robert H. Fowble & Assocs., Inc., S.D. 1968--; instr. S.D. City Coll. 1956-63; instr. UCSD Ext. 1956; mem: AIA 1957- (Edn. Com. 1960-8); Gr. San Diego Indus.-Edn. Council 1981-; Am. Soc. of Mil. Engrs. 1961-; Am. Soc. for Indsl. Security 1983-; Nat. Classification Mgmt. Soc. 1983-; San Diego CofC; M.I.T. Alumni; Kearny Vista Comm. Planners; La Mesa Lodge F & AM; Al Bahr Shrine; Morena Area Planners; S.D. Co. Citizens Scholarship Found.; Joint Adv. Bd. on Open Space; Mayoral Com. to Update S.D. Grading Ordinance; co-author: Massed Produced Housing (Bemis Found. 1952); mil: QtrMaster, USN 1944-6; Democrat; Baptist; rec: oil painting, piano, sailing. Address: Robert H. Fowble & Assoc., Inc., 3416 Bunker Hill San Diego 92117

FOWLER, H. GREIG, lawyer; b. Jan. 16, 1937, Visalia; s. Harold G. and Hazel Christine (Olson) F.; m. Elizabeth, Nov. 9, 1961; children: Ann Marie, b. 1968; Aimee, b. 1971; Alexandra, b. 1973; edn: BA, UC Berkeley 1959; JD, UC Hastings Coll. of Law 1965; admitted to Calif. Bar 1966. Career: assoc. law firm Cartwright, Sucherman, Slobodin & Fowler, Inc. (and predecessor firm) 1966, partner 1971--; spkr. Am. Trial Lawyers Assn., Calif. Trial Lawyers Assn.; Cont. Edn. of the Bar; S.F. Bar Assn.; Lawyers Club; mem: Calif. Trial Lawyers Assn. (pres. 1983); San Francisco Trial Lawyers Assn. (pres. 1974); S.F. Lawyers Club (past bd. of governors); S.F. Bar Assn. (past bd. dirs.); Am. Trial Lawyers Assn.; State Bar of Calif.; publs: contbr. to Calif. Products Liability Actions, (Matthew Bender & Co.); mil: s/sgt. AF Nat. Guard 1959-65; Democrat; Catholic; rec: politics, sports. Res: 40 Sea Cliff Ave San Francisco 94121 Ofc: Cartwright, Sucherman, Slobodin & Fowler, Inc., 160 Sansome St, Ste 900, San Francisco 94104

FOY, RHODANNE, hypnotherapist; b. June 5, 1926, Taft; d. Harrison Morten and Rita Bernadette (Fletcher) Hawkins; m. Larry Howard Foy (dec. 1980), Apr. 13, 1954; 1 son: Robert, b. 1951; edn: BS, USC 1951; grad. work, UCLA; PhD, Newport Univ.; Am Council of Hypnotists Examiners Gil Boyne. Career: pres. Orange County Hypnotic Center, Inc.; tchr. Palm Springs Unified Sch. Dist.; tchr. Fountain Valley Sch. Dist.; mem: Gamma Phi Betta 1948-51, USC; Calif. Profl. Hypnotists Assn.; World Conngress of Profl. Hypnotists; Hypnotists Examining Council of Calif.; Gamma Phi Beta Alumni of Newport Becah; Democrat; Science of Mind; rec: painting, singing, swimming. Res: 11827 Diamond Court Fountain Valley 92708 Ofc: Orange County Hypnotic Center, Inc., 505 No Tustin Ave, No. 228 Santa Ana 92705

FRAGNITO, DANIEL ANTHONY, culinary union executive; b. Jan. 7, 1952, Batavia, NY; edn: BA, sociol., SUNY, Buffalo 1975. Career: child welfare caseworker Co. of Genesse, NY 1975-76; bus. agt. Local #19 Hotel- Motel, and Restaurant- Bartenders Empl. AFL-CIO, 1978-83, exec. vice pres. 1983--; trustee Pension Funds, Health and Welfare, Tng. & Group Legal Funds, Santa Clara Co.; mem: Internat. Found. for Empl. Benefits, ed./photog. Voice of Local #19; Ital. Am. Heritage Found.; San Jose Jaycees, San Jose Olympic Com. Democrat (active num. local campaigns); Catholic; rec: ambassador for USA. Ofc: 1121 E. Santa Clara St. San Jose 95116

FRAMPTON, TOM JAY, manufacturing company executive; b. May 4, 1938, Toledo, Ohio; s. Theodore William and Ethel Caroline (Hartzel) F.; m. Glenna Marie Mullen, Nov. 30, 1957; chidren: Jay, b. 1958; Julie, b. 1959; Jan, b. 1961; Jeff, b. 1965; edn: AA, San Jose City Coll. 1965; San Jose State Coll. 1966-71. Career: mech. engr., machine design, Surface Combustion Corp., Toledo, Ohio 1956, Bingham Stamping Corp., 1957-8, Am. Florr Machine Co., 1958-60; engring. mgr. Max Mfg. Co., San Jose, Calif. 1960-6; mfg. engr. to dir. of engring. Signetics Corp., Sunnyvale 1968-81, mng. dir. Signetics-Thailand Co. Lmtd., Bangkok, Thailand 1973-77; pres./ chief exec. ofcr. Diacon, Inc., San Diego 1981--; awards: for tech. illustrn., Ohio State, 1956, Ford Motor Co., 1957; mem: Am. Electronics Assn. 1981; Semiconductor Equipt. and Materials Inst. 1981; Am. CofC, Thailand (bus. and labor adv.) 1974-7; Thailand Mgmt. Assn. (foreign adv.) 1974-7; Am. CofC 1981-4; San Diego CofC 1981-4; works: engring. mgmt.- Electronic Design 1972, materials devel. and automation for packaging of semicondr. devices (patents pend.); Republican; Protestant; rec: tennis, fishing. Res: 13735 Del Pontiente Rd Poway 92064 Ofc: Diacon, Inc., 4812 Kearny Mesa Rd San Diego 92111

FRANCIS, BARBARA SUE, interior designer/company president; b. Oct. 12, 1939, Tyler, Tex.; d. Robert Marion and Janie Lee (Bridges) Clift; m. Richard E. Francis, Aug. 26, 1960; children: Allison, b. 1961; Deborah, b. 1965; Anthony, b. 1970; edn: No Texas State Univ. 1958-9, Univ. Denver 1959-60, Univ. Okla. 1965-7, Orange Coast Coll. 1977-83; Assoc. ASID. Career: interior designer Landsaw Furniture, Norman Okla. 1966; free-lance designer/prin. Barbara Francis Interiors, Ft. Walton Bch., Fla. & Tx., 1968-70; owner/int. designer Pettingill Studios, Brigham City, Utah 1970-73; int. designer Bullocks, Costa Mesa 1974-5, Design Wise Interiors, El Toro 1975-6; int. designer/owner Barbara Francis and Assoc., 1976-9, pres./chmn. bd. Design Coordinators Inc., Fountain Valley 1979--. Awards: Remodel of Month, Santa Ana Register newspaper 1983; Outstanding Young Women in Am. 1972. Mem: ASID, NHFL, Indsl. Comml. Network, Bus. Devel. Assn. of Orange Co.; orgns: ARC vol., Fountain Valley Newcomers Club (social ch.), Mariners Club (v.p.), Green Valley Rec. Assn. (bd.dirs); works: resdtl. remodels, decor, archtl. designs; design & installation of model homes, banks, offices, med. ofcs., churches; designer Maxwells Restaurant, Huntington Bch. Democrat; Presbyterian; rec: bridge, golf, jog, geneology. Res: 10947 El Coco Cir. Fountain Valley 92708 Ofc: Design Coordinators Inc. 17280 Newhope, Ste 11, Fountain Valley 92708

FRANCIS, J. STUART, investment banker; b. May 23, 1952, Painesville, Ohio, s. J. Thomas and Beverly A. Francis; m. Diana L. Stark, Sept. 23, 1979; edn: AB, Princeton Univ. 1974; MBA, Stanford Bus. Sch. 1977. Career: with Smith Barney, Harris Upham & Co., San Francisco 1977--; assoc. 1977-9; 2nd v.p. 1980-1; v.p. 1981-2; 1st v.p./ partner 1983--; awards: fmr. All American Golfer in coll.; clubs: Burlingame Country, San Francisco Golf; Republican; Methodist; rec: all sports. Res: 129 Seville Way San Mateo 94402 Ofc: Smith Barney, Harris Upham & Co., 350 California St, Ste 2100, San Francisco 94104

FRANCIS, ROBERT (Bob) ALLEN, newspaper business manager; b. Oct. 12, 1922, Oakland; s. Leon Chapman and Mary Ida (Peters) F.; m. Susan Jayne Fenton, March 27, 1943; children: Marilyn, b. 1944; Lori, b. 1948; edn: Calif. Coll. of Arts & Crafts 1945-6. Career: advt. mgr. Louis Stores, Emeryville 1954-72; prin. Bob Francis Advt. Agency, Oakland 1972-4; Lesher Newspapers: advt. sales Contra Costa Times, Walnut Creek 1974-8; advt. mgr. Pittsburg (Calif.) Press, 1978-9; currently bus. mgr. Pittsburg Post Dispatch; pub. rels. City of Pittsburg & CofC; mem. Calif. Delta Newspapers Mgmt. Gp.; awards: State- wide winner Public Speaking Contest, Jr. CofC 1952; Calif. State Assembly Resolution 1982; Comm. Svc. Awd., US Cong. George Miller 1982; orgnzr. & past pres. New York Landing Assn., Inc. (Pittsburg Hist. District), now certified by State and Fed. Govt.; mem: Pittsburg Kiwanis (pres. 1983); Pittsburg Bus. & Profl. Assn. (pres. 1984; originator/ chmn. Projects 81, 81 for coordinated city clean-up); Pittburg CofC (pres. 1981); mil: pvt. US Army; Republican; Protestant; rec: art, music, reading. Res: 3130 Westbourne Dr Antioch 94509 Ofc: Pittsburg Post Dispatch, 515 Railroad Ave Pittsburg 94565

FRANCISCO, MICHAEL H., certified public accountant; b. July 21, 1943, San Francisco; s. William A. and Celia (Haskin) F.; m. Janis Westley, June 11, 1965; children: Jason, b. 1967; Laura, b. 1969; edn: BS, UCLA 1965; MBA, 1966; CPA, State of Calif. 1969. Career: with Price Waterhouse 1967-, partner 1979--; Los Angeles Ofc. 1967-76; Century City Ofc. 1976-83; New York Nat. Ofc. 1983--; dir. Bel Air Assn. 1977-83; dir. Westside Com. Planning Council 1979-81; dir. exec. com. Los Angeles Co. Interagcy. for child abuse and neglect 1980-3; Nat. Assn. of Accts. (bd. dirs. 1979-81; pres. W. L.A. chpt. 1975); Calif. Soc. of CPAs (com. chmn. Acctg. Principals and Auditing Standards, Los Angeles chpt. 1981-3; com. chmn. Govt. and Long Term Contracts 1975-7); del. White House Conf. on Small Bus. 1980; Calif. State CofC Small Bus. Task Force 1981, 2; mem: Am. Inst. of CPAs 1969-; Calif. Soc. of CPAs 1969-; Bev. Hls. CofC; Nat. Assn. of Retailers; Hemisphere Club, NYC; UCLA Grad. Sch. of Mgmt. Alumni Assn.; UCLA Chancellors Assocs.; Republican; rec: sailing, photog. Res: 1276 Stradella Road Los Angeles 90077; Ofc: Price Waterhouse, 1251 Ave of the Americas, New York, NY 10020

FRANK, DON, stockbroker, musician; b. Mar. 26, 1905, dec. Nov. 20, 1982; s. Edward and Mabel (Marlin) F.; m. Gladys Hoffman, June 15, 1929; children: Donald b. 1931, Marjorie b. 1937; grad. Polytechnic H.S. 1921. Career: profl. musician, 1922-82: organist, silent movies in San Francisco and Bay Area theaters, churches, fairs, circuses and for orgnzl. and social events; pianist/dir. show bands and orchs.; played cello, bass violin, tuba, accordian; stockbroker: acct. exec. Leib, Keyston & Co., 1936-39, Eastland, Douglas, 1940, Walston & Co., 1941-59, founder/partner Birr, Wilson & Co., S.F. 1959-82; mem: Occidental-Calif. Lodge #1; S.F. Bodies Scottish Rite; Islam Temple, Shrine Band dir. 1952-8; Royal Order of Jesters; Bohemian Club (list of '50); clubs: St. Francis Yacht, French, Stock Exchange, Merchants Exchange; Republican; Christian Sci.; rec: music. Res: 1554 33rd Ave. San Francisco 94122.

FRANKENSTEIN, WILLIAM ABE, certified financial planner; b. Dec. 25, 1941, Borgerhout, Belgium; s. Herbert Lansing and Beatrice (Kahn) F.; m. Gail Cukerbaum, Aug. 17, 1971; 1 dau: Carrie Robins, b. 1975; edn: BA, Widener Univ. 1964; CFP, Coll. for Financial Planning 1972; mem. Nat. Assn. of Sec. Dealers 1982-. Career: aluminium salesman Napco, Inc., Pittsburgh, PA; regl. v.p. Shook Assocs., Pittsburgh; estate planner New York Life Ins. Co. in Los Angeles; cert. fin. plnr. Cambridge Planning Corp., Sherman Oaks; awards: Nat. Quality Awd., life ins. ind. 1976-7-8; Salesman of Year, Shook Assoc. 1974; mem: IAFP, ICFP, NASD; Warner Center Club; B'Nai B'Rith; Temple Solael; mil: capt. US Army Transp. Corps 1965-7; Republican; Jewish; rec: golf, tennis, swimming. Res: 4614 Romberg Place Woodland Hills 91364 Ofc: Cambridge Planning, Inc., 14429 Ventura Blvd, Ste 102 Sherman Oaks 91423

FRANKLIN, BRUCE RENALDO, computer co. executive; b. July 17, 1954, Pleasanton, Calif.; s. Reuben Clyde and Agatha Alfrieda (Jones) F.; m. Suzanne Lydston, Feb. 7, 1976, div. 1982; edn: Am. River Jr. Coll. 1972; US Naval Acad., Annapolis 1972-74; Air Technical Tng. Ctr., 1976; Riverside Comm. Coll. 1978; desig. Electronic Computer Systems Repairman, USAF 1976. Career: life & disability agt. John Hancock Mutual Life Ins. Co., Sacto. 1974; mgr. Taco Bell, Sacto. 1975; USAF comp. repairman, March AFB, 1975-79; field engr. No. Telecom Systems Corp., 1979-80, Philips Medical Systems, 1980, Datapoint Corp., Brea 1981-82; supr. field engring., World Computer Corp., Torrance 1982--; instr. Squadron, AF, 1975-6; honors: Airman of the Month (2), 1978; mem: US Naval Acad. Alumni Assn., Non-commnd. Officers Assn. 1975-79, Trendsetters of Sacto. 1972; mil: midn. USN 1972-4, sgt. USAF 1975-9; Republican; Christian; rec: golf, weight tng., music. Res: 1919 East Birch St, LL23, Brea 92621 Ofc: World Computer Corp., 19401 So. Vermont, J-100, Torrance

FRANKLIN, HELEN LOUISE JOHNSTON, psychologist; b. Dec. 7, 1932, Portales, NM; d. Tom Wesley and Ida Marie (Little) Johnston; m. James Norman Franklin (dec.), Apr. 27, 1950; children: Christina, b. 1953; Steven, b. 1954; James, b. 1955; Loretta, b. 1957; Evelyn, b. 1959; David, b. 1960; Robert, b. 1962, Joseph, b. 1964, John, b. 1966, Thomas, b. 1967; Mary, b. 1969; Julianne, b. 1973. Edn: BA, w/ honors, San Diego State Univ. 1974; MA, Calif. Sch. of Profl. Psychology 1976; PhD, 1978; lic. Psychologist, State of Calif. 1981 Marriage, Family and Child Counselor, 1979. Career: counselor Catholic Family Svc., San Diego 1975-6; research asst. Navy Alcohol Rehab. Ctr., San Diego 1976; asst. to Dir. of Edn., Univ. of Calif. Med Ctr., S.D. 1977; psych. asst. SDSU, 1977-8; psychologist , Imperial Co. Mental Health 1980-3, South Bay Psychological Svcs., S.D. 1983--; pvt. practice; cons. Century 21 Hill N Dale 1979-; dir. of counseling Displaced Homemakers, S.D. 1979-81; honors: Psi Chi 1973; mem: Calif. State Psych. Assn.; Am. Psych. Assn.; Acad. of S.D. Psychologists; Apt. Assn. of S.D.; Calif. Ballet Assn.; Heartland Swim Assn.; author: The Problem of Grief in Families, 1978; Catholic; rec: camping, real estate. Res: 6588 Hopedale Ct San Diego 92120 Ofc: South Bay Psychological Services, 1922 Coronado Ave San Diego 92154

FRANKLIN, JAN F., telephone co. executive; b. Feb. 3, 1945, Richmond, CA; d. Godfrey and Catharine Bishop; m. Marlin R. Franklin, Apr. 6, 1968; edn: Oakland City Coll. 1963-5; Sacramento State Coll. 1965; Contra Costa Coll. 1965-7, 1969; Univ. of Hawaii 1970. Career: with Pacific Bell 1963--; order writer, Oakland 1963-5; svc. rep., Richmond & Sacto. 1965; bus. ofc. supvr. Oakland & Richmond 1966; bus. ofc. mgr., Pittsburg 1971; traffic op. mgr., San Francisco 1974; personnel mgr. S.F., currently dist. mgr., training dept., S.F., Oakland; chmn. Profl. Standards Review Bd. Tng. Dept. 1983-4; awards: Woman of Yr., Richmond Bus. & Profl. Women 1973; Key Contract Mgr. to the Richmond City Council. Pac. Bell 1970-80; judge Bank of Am. Achievement Pgm.; listed: Outstanding Young Women of Am. 1975; mem: Bus. & Profl. Women's Club. 1967; past pres. P.E.O.; Nat. Assn. of Exec. Females 1983; Am. Soc. of Tng. Devel. 1983; apptd. mem. Richmond Police/ Comm. Rels. Task Force 1971; elected to Richmond Comm. Devel. Commn. 1975; Republican; Lutheran; rec: public speaking. Res: 5733 Amend Rd Richmond 94803 Ofc: Pacific Bell, 180 Grand Ave, Ste 724, Oakland 94612

FRANKLIN, MARY ALICE, lawyer; b. Apr. 21, 1946, Athens, La.; d. Dewitt and Dorothy Lee (Walker) F.; edn: BS, Univ. of San Diego 1972; JD, Univ. of San Diego Law Sch. 1975; admitted to Calif. State Bar. Career: intern Office of the City Attorney, Los Angeles; criminal defense atty. pvt. practice currently (emphasis on providing legal svcs. to elderly low-income and women), San Diego; criminal work Defender's Inc., San Diego (1 yr.); awards: Mother Theresa Awd., Womens Criminal Defense Bar Assn., San Diego Co. 1983; Woman of Distinction, Womens Inc. 1984; mem: Lawyers Club; San Diego County and Earl B. Gilliam Bar Assns.; Calif. Assn. for Criminal Justice; Womens Criminal Bar; Criminal Defense Bar Ctr. for Womens Studies & Svcs.; Nat. Orgn. for Women; Nat. Council of Negro Women; YWCA; Girls Club; Epicureans (San Diego); NAACP; Urban League; Democrat; Ch. of Christ; rec: bowling, writing poetry, sewing. Res: 2388 Ritva Pl San Diego 92139 Ofc: 443 West C St, Ste 108, San Diego 92101

FRANKLIN, PETER STEWART, international management consultant; b. Sept. 26, 1952, Santa Monica; s. Kenneth and Sheila (Higgins) F.; edn: BA, Eng., UC Davis 1974; Calif. Teaching Cred., 1975. Career: dir. of forensics Woodland (Calif.) High Sch., 1975-81; tchr. creative writing Yuba Coll., Woodland 1975-77; partner, comm. dir. Communicators Advt., Davis 1976-80; program dir./cons. Santa Fe Internat.: Venezuela 1981-82, Jakarta, Singapore, Balikpapan, 1982-83; sr. cons. Equidon Cos., Irvine, S.D., L.A., Lafayette; pub. speaking cons. State of Calif., 1976; honors: Tchr of Month, 1980; publs: contbr. Nat. Anthol. of Poetry, 1981-82, Performance Mgmt. Mag. 1982-83; Democrat; rec: writing, photog., ski, rock climb. Res: 4408 E. 5th St. Long Beach 90814 Ofc: R.L. Lorber and Assocs. 505 S. Main St. Orange 92668

FRANKLIN, STEPHEN L., executive; b. Mar. 15, 1937, Los Angeles; s. William and Tillie (Silverberg) F.; m. Mildred Lourie, Dec. 5, 1976; children: Spencer, b. 1962; Andrea, b. 1964; Harrison, b. 1980; edn: BS, UCLA 1961; MS, CLU Northridge 1973; Am. Coll. Hosp. Adminstr. Career: auditor Peat Marwick & Mitchell Co., CPAs 1961-3, Blue Cross of So. Calif. 1963-6; sr. acct. Marlow Baar CPA 1966-7; sr. auditor/ Medi-Care field cons. Blue Cross of So. Calif. 1967; controller/ dir. hosp. fin. affairs Am. Medical Internat. Inc. 1967-70; asst. adminstr./ controller Parkwood Comm. Hosp. 1971-2; adminstr. Inglewood Gen. Hosp. 1972-4; sr. vp/chief fin. ofcr./ bd. dirs. Pioneer Take Out

Corp. 1974--; cons. Southeast (Watts) Multi-Purpose Clinic 1966; advr. So. Calif. Coro Found. 1978-9; Olympic Adv. council (LAOOC) 1983-4; awards: Ark. Traveler Awd. 1969; honors: Pi Omega Pi, listed Who's Who In The West; mem. (sr.) Hosp. Finl. Mgmt. Assn.; mem: Am. Acad. of Med. Adminstrs.; Am. Coll. of Hosp. Adminstrs.; Nat. Assn. of Accts.; Fedn. of Am. Hosps.; The Am. Public Health Assn.; Assn. for Corp. Growth; publs: Blue Cross Desk Audit Pgm.; coauthored CHA Medi-Care Reimbursement Report for acute hosps.; mil: Airman, USAF, Res. 1955-8; Jewish; rec: sports, art. Res: 3176 Dona Sarita Pl Studio City 91604 Ofc: Pioneer Take Out Corp., 3663 W. 6th Street Los Angeles 90020

FRANTZ, DORA WOODS, public accountant; b. Nov. 22, 1906, Weston, WVa; d. Peter Elihu and Emma (Carter) Woods; m. James D. Frantz, Oct. 29, 1949; edn: BA, CSU Santa Barbara 1930; JD, USC 1933; lic. Public Acct, Calif. 1942. Career: legislative rep. for vocational teachers, Sacramento; public acct./sec. treas. Janus, Inc., Inglewood; public spkr.; income tax preparer for elderly; awards: Inglewood Woman of Yr. 1968; nat. dir. Venetian Blind Assn.; Fisherman of Yr. 1962, 1972; Dora W. Frantz Day, by Mayor of Inglewood, Wm. Goedike; mem: Nat. Assn. of Notary Publics; Soroptimist; Inglewood Tastmistress Club; CofC; Lennox Civic Assn.; Emblem Club of Inglewood; Phi Alpha Delta; Alpha Phi Gamma; Philatelist; Indoor Sports Club; Centinela Valley Republican Women (past pres.); Inglewood Rod and Gun Club; columnist for Montebello Messenger Newspaper; Republican (exec. com. Cal. Central Com.; past pres. Cal. Repub. Assem.; cand. for Assem. 46th Assem. Dist. 1941-46); Christian; rec: sports fishing, fan LA Dodgers and LA Raiders. Address: 10905 Inglewood Ave Inglewood 90304

FRANTZ, JOHN C., librarian; b. Aug. 25, 1926, Seneca Falls, NY; s. John Clarke and Cora May (Gilbert) F.; m. Vivien Rowan 1947; children: Sheila, Keith, and Jay; edn: AB in Eng., Syracuse Univ. 1950, BS in lib.sci., 1951, MS in lib. sci., 1952; Career: cons. Wisc. State Lib., 1955-58; dir. Green Bay, Wisc. Public Library, 1958-61; dir. Lib. Servs. & Constrn. Act., US Ofc of Edn., Wash DC 1961-67; dir. Brooklyn Pub. Lib., NY, 1967-70; exec. chmn. Nat. Book Comm, NYC, 1970-75; cons. Pahlavi Nat. Lib., Teheran, Iran 1975-76; San Francisco City Librarian, 1977--; mem: Am. Lib. Assn., Am. Reading Council (exec. bd.), Bookmobile Services Trust (past chmn.), Books for Youth (exec. bd.), Coffee House Club, NYC, Commonwealth Club of Calif., METRO (bd.dirs.), Nat. Adv. Bd., Lib. of Congress Ctr. for the Book, Reading is Fundamental (RIF), Western Book Pubs. Assn. (nat. bd.), Women's Nat. Book Assn. (treas.); mil: T5, US Army 1946-47; Presbyterian. Res: 1390 Market St San Francisco 94102 Ofc: San Francisco Public Library, Civic Center, S.F. 94102

FRANTZ, KIRK EUGENE, computer company president; b. Mar. 11, 1963, Hawthorne; s. Norman Eugene and JoAnn (Williams) F.; Career: sales Jade Computer 1978-79; sales QT Computer 1979-81; founder/pres. (at age 17) Computer Components, Inglewood 1981--; founder/pres. Pipeline Co.; mem: CofC; Forum Club; Republican; Christian. Res: 1812 Pacific Ave Manhattan Beach 90266 Ofc: Computer Components Unltd. 11976 Aviation Blvd Inglewood 90304

FRASER, MADA MARGARET, cosmetic co. president; b. Jan. 2, 1931, Monett, Mo.; d. Fred Wilber and Margaret Opal (Mullins) Gilbert; m. David Wm. Fraser, Sept. 17, 1949; children: Terry Lynn, b. 1951; Loralee Wanda, b. 1954; Shirley Kay, b. 1959; edn: dip. Eagle Rock H.S. 1949, Pasadena City Coll. 1951-2. Career: head instr. Joseph's Figure Studio, Pasadena 1952-56, Vic Tanny Gym, La Crescenta 1956-60; regl. mgr. Preview Products Inc., Van Nuys 1969-70, Western training director, 1970-72; dir. of mktg. Jack LaLanne European Health Spas, So. Calif., 1972-76; founder/pres. Spa Formula Cosmetics, Inc., Hollywood 1976--; cons. Neolife Corp., Pasadena 1975; cons. Jack LaLanne Euro. Health Spas, Downey 1976-80; frequent guest speaker on health and beauty local and nat. orgns. incl. Los Angeles Business Women's Assn., Nat. Assn. of Phys. Fitness Ctrs. (Wash DC), ABC-TV News segments, Window on Wall Street, Rotary, Shaklee Corp., others. Honors: CSF Seal Bearer 1949; Woman of Excellence 1983, Women's World Internat., So. Cal.; mem: Ephebian Soc. 1949, Glendale Bus. & Profl. Womens Club; Republican; Christian. Res: 855 Moorside Dr. Glendale 91207 Ofc: Spa Formula Cosmetics, Inc. 2449 Hyperion Ave Hollywood 90027

FRASIER, DEWITT ELSON, production manager/advertising; b. June 1, 1931, Sidney, NY; s. Hobart Jay and Olive Elzira (Rice) F.; m. 2d. Joan Patricia Morey, May 19, 1973; children: Dora, b. 1953, Janet, b. 1955, Paula, b. 1957, Irene, b. 1961; edn: Northville Central H.S. 1948. Career: printing prodn. splst. Maqua Co. (Gen. Elec. subs.), Schenectady, NY 1953-69, senior buyer (GE Co.) 1969-80; prodn. mgr./advt., Jansen Assoc., Inc., Santa Ana 1980--; mem. Production Managers Assn.; mil: s/sgt. US ARmy 1950-53, Korean Vet.; rec: banjo playing, bowling, motorcycling. Res: 3001 So Rosewood Ave Santa Ana 92707 Ofc: Jansen Assoc. 2960 So. Daimler Ave santa Ana 92705

FRAZER, CLOYCE CLEMON, educator (ret.); b. Jan. 2, 1919, Warren, Ark.; s. Charles Columbus and Maude Mae (Jones) F.; m. Beverley Mundorff, Apr. 10, 1942; edn: dip. USAF Flt. Tng., 1944; BA, San Jose State Coll. 1952; MA CSU Sacto. 1961. Career: aircraft mech. Matson Air Transp. Div., Oakland 1946-48; flight instr. Moreau Flying Serv., Oakland 1948-49; instr. aircraft mechanics, Aero Industries Tech. Inst., Oakland 1949-50; indsl. arts tchr. Folsom (Ca.) Unified Sch. Dist., 1953-54; indsl. arts tchr., dept. head, San Mateo Union High Sch. Dist., 1963-83; also pres. Crestmoor H.S. Faculty Assn. 1965-6, mem. planning coms. for new H.S. and writing curriculum materials; awards: hon. mentions for two metal sculptures, 1967, San Mateo

Co. Fair and Floral Fiesta; mem: Epsilon Pi Tau, Caterpillar Club, Nat. Edn. Assn., Calif. Tchrs. Assn., Calif. Ret. Tchrs. Assn.; Calif. Aerospace Edn. Assn. (treas. 1983-, pres. Northern Sect. 1978-9); Calif. Indsl. Edn. Assn.; Vocational Edn. Assn.; Aircraft Owners and Pilots Assn.; Exptl. Aircraft Assn. (Outstanding Individual Achievement Award 1982); Am. Craft Council; publs: articles in ednl. jours., various curriculum mats.; mil: served to Maj., USAF Reserve, 1941-79, WWII Victory, Asia-Pac. Svc., Am. Theater Svc. medals; Democrat; Prot.; rec: fishing, flying. Res: Belmont 94002

FRAZER, JACK WINFIELD, scientific consultant; b. Sept. 9, 1924, Forest Grove, Ore.; s. Jack Henry and Edna (Alfranc) F.; m. Juanita Maxfield, Jan. 27, 1947; edn: John Christopher, b. 1949, Pamela, b. 1952, Candice Lea, b. 1956; edn: BA, Hardin-Simmons Univ. 1947. Career: chemist Los Alamos Sci. Lab., 1948-53; various sci. and adminstrv. positions Lawrence Livermore Nat. Lab., 1953-70, div. ldr. for General Chemistry, 1970-74, dept. hd. Chemistry and Material Sci. Dept., 1974-78, senior scientist attached to Director Ofc. 1978-82; chief exec. ofcr. Keithley Instruments, Cleveland, Oh. 1982-83; current consultant to: Merck Inc., Signal UOP Research Ctr., Lawrence Livermore Nat. Lab., Oak Ridge Nat. Lab; adj. prof. of chem. Univ. of Ga.; indsl. prof. of chem. Indiana Univ. 1972-77; afil. prof. Dept. of Electrical Engring. Colo. State Univ. 1975-83; adv. bd. for Analytical Chemistry; honors: Am. Chem. Soc. Award for chemical instrumentation (1973), and ASTM Award of Merit (Fellow ASTM); listed in Who's Who in Am.; mem: Am. Chem. Soc., Am. Inst. of Chem. Eng.; chmn. Gordon Resrch Conf. on Anal. Chem. 1979, chmn. ASTM, E-31 1970-75; works: 89 sci. publs., 14 patents; mil: 1st Lt. USAAF 1943-45, Reserve -1955; Episcopal; rec: ancient coins. Res: 6767 Alisal Pleasanton 94566 Ofc: Lawrence Livermore Nat. Lab. POB 808, L-308, Livermore 94566

FRAZIER, ROBERT LEE, III, aerospace industry executive; b. Sept. 5, 1953, Los Angeles; s. Robert Lee, Jr. and Leona P. (Fisher) F.; edn: arts/ sci. econ., Loyola Univ. 1974; bus. admin./ fin., 1975; Cert. Legal Analyst, Univ. of San Diego 1976; MBA (cand.) Loyola Univ. 1984. Career: co-founder/pres. Universal Satellite (telecommunications co.); dir. of mfg. and cost control Frazier Aviation (supplier spare parts for mil., comml. aerospace and satellite indus.; co. founded by father 1951); mem. Hawaiian Internat. Sporting Assn., The Horsemen's Assn.; Republican; Christian; rec: skiing, off-road racing. Res: 1352 S. Carmelina No. 309, W.L.A. 90025 Ofc: Frazier Aviation 11311 Hartland St N. Hollywood 91605

FREDRICK, WILLIAM CHARLES, aerospace company executive, lawyer; b. Now. 19, 1925, Arlington, Iowa; s. William Andrew and Emma Anna (Baumgartner) F.; m. Shirley Rae Beeman, June 3, 1951; children: John Andrew, b. 1957; Susan Ann, b. 1961; Mark William, b. 1966; edn: BS, Wartburg Coll. 1949; JD, Western State Univ. 1981; admitted to Calif. State Bar. Career: high sch. principal/ tchr., Clarksville, Iowa H.S., 1949-52; sr. engr. Arinc Research Corp., Corpus Christi, Tx and Wash. DC 1952-60; sr. engr. Sylvania Electric Prods., Mtn. View, Calif. 1960-1; asst. gen. mgr. Western Div., Arinc Research Corp., Santa Ana 1961-5; dept. mgr. Gen. Electric, TEMPO, Santa Barbara 1965-70; pres. Conditioning Svcs., Inc., Anaheim 1970-4; dir. Strategic Devel., Rockwell Internat., Defense Electronics Ops. 1974--; guest lectr., UCLA Sch. of Engring. 1968-9; mem: Am. Bar Assn.; Calif. State Bar Assn.; Assn. of the US Army; Am. Assn. of Bus. Economists; Electronic Inds. Assn. (Govt. Requirements Com.); pres. Red Hill Lutheran Ch., Tustin 1976; publs: num. co. reports and papers on reliability, system effectiveness, and logistics; mil: ETM 3/C, USN, service ribbons; Republican; Lutheran; rec: sports, chess, bridge. Res: 10682 Equestrian Dr Santa Ana 92705 Ofc: 3370 Miraloma Ave Anaheim 92803

FREED, DAVID NATHAN, data processing executive; b. July 28, 1948, Phila., Pa.; s. Stanley and Hilda (Weisor) F.; m. Barbara Jeffries, Aug. 23, 1969; children: Kimberly Anne, b. 1972; Bryan Andrew, b. 1974; edn: BS, Univ. of Ariz. 1970. Career: sr. sys. rep. RCA Corp., Denver, Co. 1970-1; vice pres./data processing mgr. Data Professional Svcs., Tucson, Az. 1971; sys. analyst Hughes Aircraft, Tucson 1972; asst. dir. D.P., Dow Chemical Co. Bio Sci. Div. in Van Nuys, Michigan Div., Midland, Mich., 1972-80; dir. of Info. Svcs. The Bekins Co., Glendale 1980--; data processing cons. 1980-; mem: Data Processing Mgrs. Assn.; Am. Mgmt. Assn.; Delta Tau Delta Frat.; Ventura Co. PTA; Republican; rec: swimming, hand gliding, antique restorations. Res: 3090 Evelyn Ave Simi Valley 93063 Ofc: The Bekins Co., 777 Flower Street Glendale 91201

FREED, KAROL, electronics engineer; b. June 30, 1934, Fairfield, IA; s. Sol and Frida (Feinberg) F.; m. Reva Grund, Mar. 18, 1962; children: Larry, b. 1963; Sherri, b. 1966; edn: Iowa State Coll. 1953-4. Career: video prod. mgr. Bell & Howell, Chgo., Ill. 1968-71; pres. KFE Inc. (consultant), Arlington Hgts., Ill. 1971-6; v.p. engr., Unimedia/ RGB Display 1976-9; video design engr. Cinema Prods. Corp., W. L.A. 1979-82; sr. video engr. Terminal Data Corp., Woodland Hills 1982--; honors: Order of the Iron Test Pattern, Comdr. 1979; mem: SMPTE, SBE, SID; Conejo Valley Newcomers; patents: LC and Crystal Transistor Oscillators, 1975; Horizontal Deflection CKT (1982, pat. pend.); mil: Sp4, Signal Corps. 1956-8; Jewish; rec: photog., woodworking, electronics. Res: 2309 McCrea Rd Thousand Oaks 91362 Ofc: Terminal Data Corp., 21221 Oxnard St Woodland Hills 91367

FREELAND, DARRYL CREIGHTON, psychotherapist, educator; b. Feb. 22, 1939, Omaha, Nebr.; s. Elverson Lafayette and Lauretta Joyce (Coffelt) F.; m. Tina Anne Magnusen, July 21, 1979; children: Sarah Eileen, b. 1972; Adam Daniel, b. 1980; Noah Nathen, b. 1981; edn: BS, Univ. of Nebr. 1961; STB, Fuller

Theol. Sem. 1965; MA, Eng., CSU Fullerton 1966; PhD, counseling psych., USC 1972; Calif. lic.: Psychologist; Marriage, Family and Child Therapist (MFCT); cert. community coll. and sec. teacher. Career: teacher Calif. Elementary Schs., 1961-66; instr. Glendale Comm. Coll., 1966-67, Citrus Comm. Coll., Glendora 1967-77; field faculty and vis. prof. in psychol. and literature: CSU L.A. 1970, San Marino Comm. Presbyterian Ch. 1972, Calif. Sch. of Profl. Psychology L.A. 1972-3, UC Riverside 1973, Humanistic Psychology Inst., San Francisco 1976-9, Profl. Sch. for Humanistic Studies, Univ. of Humanistic Studies, San Diego 1983; pvt. practice psychology and family counseling, 1969--, in assn. with Tina A. Freeland, MA, MFCT, Fairweather Psychol. Assocs., Laguna Niguel; jt. founder/chmn. bd., Found. and Inst. for Human Intimacy, 1981--; co-owner, Human Intimacy Publs., 1982--; mem: Coll. Faculty Assn., Calif. Tchrs. Assn., NEA, Calif. Comm. Coll. Faculty Assn., Calif. Assn. Marriage-Family Counselors, Am., Calif. psychol. assns., Assn. Humanistic Psychology; Democrat; finisher, Newport Bch-Irvine (1981) and San Francisco (1982) Marathons. Ofc: Fairweather Psychological Assocs., 30131 Town Center Dr, Ste. 298, Laguna Niguel 92677

FREEMAN, DONNA RHEA, business owner, realtor assoc.; b. Apr. 18, 1937, Waldron, Ark.; d. Oliver Raymond and Lura Edna (Doyle) Cook; m. Clarence Freeman, Jan. 24, 1954; children: Scott, b. 1957, Kevin, b. 1958, Steve, b. 1960, Melissa, b. 1961, Melinda, b. 1967. Career: co-owner Noyo Belle (fishing vessel); co-owner Freeman's Bodega Bay Union 76 Service; partner Bodega Reyn Corp.; realtor assoc.; polit. campaign chair; (past) secty. Bodega Bay Sch., 1973-5; staff Aquaculture Dept. UC Bodega Marine Lab. Mem: Bodega Bay Area CofC (pres. 1979, 80, 81; dir. 1982-3); Shoreline Trust for Ednl. Pgm. Svcs. (v.ch. 1981,82,83); apptd. by Sen. Barry Keene to Calif. State Democratic Central Com. 1983; alternate for Cong. Doug Bosco, Sonoma Co. Dem. Central Com. 1982,83; Selective Service Sys. Rep. to Local Bd. II; Sonoma Co. Adv. bd. to Assem. Dan Hauser; apptd. to Sonoma Co. Grand Jury, 1983-4; bd. dirs. Bodega Bay Area Rescue, 1973-4; ch. Bodega Bay Fisherman's Festival 1973, 74, 83; mem. Bodega Bay Fisherman's Aux.; Bodega Bay Comm. Assn.; Bodega Bay Grange. Res: 1060 Bay View St. Bodega Bay 94923.

FREEMAN, JOHN CURTIS, real estate co. developer; b. Feb. 3, 1946, San Bernardino; s. James Edgar and Geraldine Lee (Wadley) F.; m. Bonna Kay Hoffman, May 30, 1982; children: John Martin, b. 1967; Jacqueline Carrie, b. 1973; edn: Mesa Coll. 1965-6; Calif. Lic: Real Estate, Building Contr. Career: sr. fin. planner Milton H. Love & Assoc. 1968-75; partner Eagle Properties (real estate devel.) 1975-7; pres./ founder Eagle Contractors of San Diego, Inc. (resdtl. & comml. constrn.) 1977-82; founder/ pres./ CEO Financial Innovations, Inc. (R.E. devel. & constrn.), San Diego 1982--; awards: Man of the Year, So. Calif. Business Assn. (1970, 71, 73) ; Man of the Yr., San Diego Business Assn. (1969, 70, 71, 73); S.D. Jaycee of Month 6/69; mem: San Diego Building Contractors Assn.; Nat. Assn. Home Builders; Million Dollar Round Table (life); San Diego CofC; Bass Council of S.D.; pres. Road Rangers Bass Club 1981; mil: USN Submarine Svc., Republican, Baptist, rec: bass fishing, long distance running. Res: 10411 Grandview Dr La Mesa 92041 Ofc: Financial Innovations, Inc., 9625 Black Mountain Rd San Diego 92126

FREEMAN, MARJORIE RUTH VOSE, educator; b. Oct. 25, 1926, Robinston, Me.; d. Wm. Everett and Rosena Abigail (Greenlaw) Vose; m. Harold A. Freeman, June 29, 1952 (dec.); edn: BA, Univ. of Maine, Farmington 1951, M.Ed, Univ. of Me., Orono 1960; spl. courses, CSU Fresno; lang. inst., Chapman Coll. Career: teacher elem. schs. in Calais, Me. 1950-56, Bangor, Me. 1956-61, and Dinuba, Calif.; ednl. mats. sales rep.; honors: Certificated Employee of Year 1977; Who's Who in Elem. Edn. 1973. Mem: Delta Kappa Gamma (pres. Beta Kappa chpt. 1978-80); Beta Sigma Phi (Girl of Yr. 1977; pres. Xi Sigma Alpha chpt. 1976-7); Jefferson Sch PTA (pres. 1971-2; PTA Hon. Life Mem.); Calif. Teachers Assn. (past pres. Tulare Co.); Presbyterian (ruling elder 1983-5, del. San Joaquin Presbytery 1983-4); rec: travel. Res: 860 Nichols, Dinuba 93618 Ofc: Dinuba Public Schs, POB 125, Dinuba 93618.

FREEMAN, NANCI, manufacturing co. executive; b. Aug. 18, 1957, San Bernardino; d. Neal and Elaine (Skurro) Fohrman; m. Gary L. Freeman, Jan. 21, 1979; 1 son, Jay Michael, b. 1981. Career: general mgr., corporate secretary, The Red Calliope & Assoc., Inc., Los Angeles 1976--. Res: 4196 Mentone Ave Culver City 90230 Ofc: Red Calliope, 13003 So Figueroa St Los Angeles 90061

FREEMAN, WARREN EDWIN, investor; b. July 11, 1925, Tulsa, Okla.; s. James Edgar and Annette Lucille (King) F.; m. Betty Burns, June 10, 1950; children: John Evan, b. 1953; Paul Richard, b. 1956; edn: grad. San Bernardino H.S. 1943. Career: insurance brokerage bus., San Bernardino 1949-81; estab. Warren Freeman Co., merged co. with Marsh & McLennan Inc., 1977, v.p. Marsh & McLennan, Inc., 1977-81, ret.; investor; past pres. San Bernardino Ins. Assn. 1952-3; bd. dirs. Calif. Assn. of Ins. Agents 1953-6; honors: San Bernardino Citizen of the Year 1968; San Bernardino Co. Grand Jury (foreman pro. tem 1970); mem. bd. govs. Nat. Orange Show (pres. 1973-4); mem. bd. trustees Univ. of Redlands; mem. San Bernardino CofC (pres. 1966-7); mil: E.M. 3/C, USN 1944-6; Republican; Prot.; rec: golf. Res: 1103 W Bay Ave Newport Beach 92661

FREITAS, FRANK LOUIS, county official; b. June 5, 1943, Bristol, R.I.; s. Frank T. and Mary Gertrude (Perry) F.; m. Connie Coggeshall, Oct. 5, 1963; chil: Christina Marie, b. 1969, Kenneth Walter, b. 1970; edn: AA, Cuesta Coll. 1968; BS, Calif. State Polytechnic Univ. 1969; CPA, Calif. 1972. Career: staff acct. Arthur Andersen & Co., Los Angeles 1969-71; staff acct. Diehl, Evans & Co., Arroyo Grande, 1971-72; prin. CPA, Arroyo Grande 1972-74; deputy co. auditor-controller San Luis Obispo 1973-77, co. treas. (asst. 1974-77), tax collector, pub. adminstr., 1974--; trustee Co. Pension Plan; mem. Empl. Suggestion Awd. Com.; mem: Calif. Assn. of Co. Treas. and Tax Collectors (pres.); State Assn. of Co. Pub. Adminstrs. of CA; Calif. Soc. of CPAs; Internat. Found. of Empl. Benefit Plans; clubs: Lions Internat. (past pres. Arroyo Grande); Toastmasters Intl. (past pres., Spkr of Yr 1978, Club 83); PTA (past pres.); So. S.L.O. Co. Hist. Soc.; Democrat; rec: chess, public spkg., camping, computer pgmmg. Res: 602 Cerro Vista Arroyo Grande 93420 Ofc: San Luis Obispo County, POB 1149, San Luis Obispo 93406

FRENCH, PRESLEY BURDETTE, life insurance sales executive; b. May 10, 1921, Central City, Nebr.; s. Crawford Hunter and Ida Maurine (Dughman) F.; m. Violetta Hill, Mar. 27, 1943; children: Linda, b. 1944; Brian, b. 1946; Patricia, b. 1950; Bette Jean, b. 1955; edn: UC Berkeley 1946-7; BSc, cum laude, Armstrong Coll. 1950; Life Ins. Mktg. Inst., Purdue Univ. 1957; Life Ins. Assn. mgmt. courses, 1961; Adv. Sch. Ins. Mktg., So. Methodist Univ. 1961. Career: agent New York Life 1946; agt. Western Life Ins. Co. 1947-68: exec. agcy. asst. Home Ofc. 1950-4, General Agent (co's leading agcy.) 1954-9, supt. of agencies for No. Calif. & Hawaii 1959-68, mng. Gen. Agent Western Life & St. Paul Investors 1968-81; Sr. Agcy. Consultant Western/ St. Paul Life Cos. 1981-3, ret.; charter mem. Western Agcy. Officers Conf.; charter mem. Western/ St. Paul Cos. Communique Panel; exec. v.p. Twin Rivers Lodge Assn.; awards: Ins. Exec. of 1955, Armstrong Coll. Alumnus Assn.; Pres. Trophy 1964; Western Life Million Dollar Round Table; mem: NALU: Nat. CofC; DAV; NRA (life); 4th Marine Div. Assn. (life); Navy League; Masons 32 degrees AAMES Temple Shrine; mil: served in USN Fleet Marine Force: sev. personal cits., commends., Purple Heart, Pres. Unit Cit., Navy- Marine Corps. Medal, Navy Unit Commendn.; Republican; Presbyterian; rec: hunt, fish, target shooting, gun collector. Res: 28 Eastwood Dr San Mateo 94403

FRESCHI, SUSAN MERRYMAN, leveraged leasing/finance co. executive; b. July 29, 1944, Klamath Fall, Ore.; d. John Davenport and Mildred Irene (Jones) Merryman; m. Gerald Freschi, Dec. 27, 1969; children: Gina, b. 1973, Gina, b. 1976; edn: Univ. Calif. 1962-5; BA, Univ. of Ore. 1967; Diablo Valley Coll. 1972-3, various sales, mgmt. seminars. Career: credit mgr./adminstrv. sec. to regl. v.p. Equilease Corp., San Francisco 1967-68; sales asst./adminstrv. asst. to branch mgr. Dean Witter Reynolds, S.F. 1968-70, office mgr. Maritime Plaza Ofc. 1970-73, asst. to No. Div. Compliance Dir. 1973; adminstrv. asst./contract lease adminstr. Shannon Fin. Corp., Pleasant Hill 1979-80, vice pres. 1981--; mem: Alpha Delta Pi Alumni, AAUW, Beta Sigma Phi (Girl of year 1978); active in City incorporation drive 1974; Republican; Presbyterian; rec: travel, phys. conditioning, dance. Res: 125 Santa Catalina Ct Moraga 94556 Ofc: Shannon Financial Corp. 3451-B Vincent Dr Pleasant Hill 94523

FREY, FRANCES MARIE, psychologist, b. Mar. 25, 1949, NYC; d. Frank and Mary (Senko) Uhlir; m. David Frey, Feb. 11, 1977; stepchildren: Anne, Joseph, Anthony; edn: BA, Hunter Coll. 1973; MS, CSU Hayward 1975; postgrad., Stanford Univ. 1975-7; PhD, Psychological Studies Inst. of Berkeley 1984; Calif. School Psychologist Cred. 1975, School Adminstr. Cred. 1979, lic. Ednl. Psychologist 1980. Career: intern psychologist, San Mateo Co. 1973; sch. psychol., San Mateo Co. 1974-7; coord. Summer Youth Employment Pgm., San Leandro 1981-3; school psychologist San Leandro Unified Sch. Dist. 1978--; pvt. practice, 1980--; instr. UC Santa Cruz 1977; co-dir. Federal Title IV-B Proj. counseling/ guidance, San Mateo Co. 1977, tchg. asst. Stanford Univ. 1978; resrch. for Mid- Alameda Co. Consortium in Spl. Edn. and State Dept. Edn. 1982-4; awards: pgm. excellence awds., Summer Youth Employment Pgm. 1982, 83; fellowship Stanford Univ. 1978; mem: Calif. Assn. of Sch. Psychologists; Calif. Assn. of Lic. Ednl. Psychologists; Am. Psychol. Assn.; CSU Hayward Leadership Acad., Alumni Assn.; Alpha Xi Delta; v.p./ secty./ bd. dirs. Family Svc. Agy. 1983-4; works: research in ednl. psychol.; publs. in profl. journals; Eastern Orthodox; rec: painting, art collection. Res: 850 Kenyon Ave San Leandro 94577 Ofc: San Leandro USD, 14735 Juniper St San Leandro 94579

FREY, STEPHEN LOUIS, distribution management executive; b. Oct. 28, 1939, Paterson, NJ; s. Stephen F. and Caroline (Cacay) F.; m. Maria Del Carmen Asquerino-La Cave, July 15, 1960, San Lucar de Bda, Spain; children: Stephen, b. 1961; Daniel, b. 1963; Anthony, b. 1967; Robert, b. 1969; edn: BA, honors, Univ. of Maryland 1972; MS, USC 1973; cert. MTM Practioner, Methods Time Measurement Inst. 1979; cert. profl. mats. handling engr., S.P.H.E. 1975. Career: warehouse mgr. Navy Exchange, Rota, Spain, distbn. mgr. Navy Exch. Complex, Wash. DC; sr. systems engr. Navy Resale Svc. & Support Ofc., NY, then distbn. div. mgr., San Diego, mgr. distbn. ops. NRSSO 1964-84; currently pres. Warehouse Distbn. Consulting Group, San Diego; instr. Miramar Comm. Coll. 1981; mem: Nat. Council of Physical Distbn. Mgmt.; Inst. of Indsl. Engrs.; Phi Kappa Phi honor soc.; author: Warehouse Operations: A Hand Book (1983, Dilithium Press); Mgt.'s Guide to Cost Efficient Warehousing (1982, Dartnell); Warehouse Time Calculator (1983); mag. articles 1981-4; mil: petty ofcr. 2/c USN 1957-62, GCM, Nat. Def.; Catholic; rec: author/lectr. Address: Warehouse Distribution Consulting Group, 57 Guincho Road San Diego 92124

FREY, TESIBEL ELYSE, clinical social worker, real estate broker; b. Mar. 4, 1919, Oakdale; d. William Lon and Maybelle Elizabeth (Hawes) Adams; m. John Howard Frey, Oct. 19, 1936; children: Jeanne, b. 1938; David, b. 1939; Daniel, b. 1941; edn: AA, Stockton Coll. 1961; BA, Stanislous State Coll. 1964; MSW, CSU Sacto. 1970; Calif. (LCSW) lic. clinical soc. wkr., lic. real estate broker. Career: clerk US Post Office, Lathrop, Ca. 1955-61; elem. school tchr. (sub.), San Joaquin Co. 1961-4; social wkr. San Joaquin Dept. of Public Asst.

1964-72; psychiatric social wkr., Dept. of Health 1972-6, pvt. practice 1976--; real estate agent 1977-, R.E. broker 1981--; awarded 4-H Leader 5-yr pin, 1958; mem: Nat. Assn. of Soc. Wkrs.; ACSW; Am. Holistic Health Scis. Assn.; Central Valley Mktg. Assn.; Am. Bus. Women; ACLU; Metropolitan Owners Club; publs: arts. in Nexus and Network; Democrat; Methodist; rec: classic auto restoration, oil painting, needlework. Res: Tesibel Frey Real Estate, 3347 E Perrin Rd Manteca 95336

FRIDLUND, HARRY ALBERT, association executive, ret.; b. Aug. 31, 1898, Sioux City, Iowa; s. Magnus and Hilma (Bergman) F.; m. Gretchen Giehm (dec. 1980), Jan. 6, 1921; m. 2d. Bernice Rowe Wells, Aug. 31, 1980; children: Phyllis (Webster), b. 1924; Richard, b. 1925; Robert, b. 1932; edn: Grinnell Coll. 1918-19. Career: bookkeeper/ teller Northwest Nat. Bank, Sioux City, Iowa 1919-23; credit mgr. Nat. Refining Co. br. ofc. Sioux City 1923-7; mgr. storage dept. Armour & Co., Sioux City 1927-8, pers. mgr. 1928-37; small farming, Salix, Ia 1937-41; personnel mgr. Lindsay Olive Co., now Lindsay Olive Growers 1941-63; ret.: asst. state dir. for No. Calif., Am. Assn. of Retired Persons 1963--; orgnzd. 4 new AARP chpts. Lindsay); co-ed. first news letter Lindsay Chpt.; awards: Outstanding Awd. for 23 yrs. svc. with Lindsay Starthmore Dist. Cemetery; Awd. for 6 yrs. svc. Lindsay Unified Sch. Bd.; Citizen of the Year, Lindsay CofC 1979; mem: Lindsay Presbyterian Ch.; F & A.M. Masons; Am. Legion; mil: ROTC 1918; Republican; Prot.; rec: helping sr. citizens. Res: 690 W Hermosa, Sp 25, Lindsay

FRIEDMAN, ANITA, social service administrator; b. Mar. 14, 1949, NY, NY; d. Joseph and Rita (Kaplan) F.; m. Igor Tartakovsky, July 1, 1980; children: Joseph, b. 1981; Adam, b. 1984; edn: UC Berkeley 1970-4; BA, Antioch Coll. 1976; MSW, S.F. State Univ. 1978; Lic. Clinical Soc. Wkr., State Calif. 1983. Career: dir. Center for Change 1974-8; dir. of Emigre Svcs., Jewish Comm. Fdn. 1978-81; asst. exec. dir. Jewish Family and Childrens Services, San Francisco 1981-2, assoc. exec. dir. 1982--; rep Gov's Refugee Task Force 1980-2; tchg. cons. Mayor's Holocaust Meml. Fdn. 1983; awards: woman of year 1981, Bay Area Council on Soviet Jewry; internat. awd. to honor Louis Kraft, Nat. Conf. on Jewish Comm. Svc. 1982; mem: Nat. Assn. Soc. Wkrs, Intergp, Clearinghouse of S.F.; Generation to Generation; Internat. Network of Children of Jewish Holocaust Survivors; Com. of Remembrance, Jewish Comm. Rels. Council; Res: 5 Hugo Street San Francisco 94122 Ofc: Jewish Family and Childrens Services, 1600 Scott St San Francisco 94122

FRIEDMAN, ISADORE CHARLES, auto parts industry executive; b. Aug. 14, 1897, Kijhinev, Russia, US citizen; s. Isaia Charles and Frieda F.; m. 1920; 7 children; 27 grand children; edn: LLB, Kent Coll. of Law. Career: position with an electrical parts mfg. firm; estab. own business in Chgo. area, 1924--, bd. chmn. Everco Auto Parts Corp., Chicago, Ill.; honors: mem. Auto Parts Mfgrs. Hall of Fame; mem. Nat. Std Parts Assn.; Bnai Brith; publs: sales & advt. catalogs, sales promotion data rel. to mktg. auto parts and accessories; mil: Armed Forces 1917; Republican; Jewish; rec: promoting good will. Res: 197 Via Lola Dr. Palm Springs 92262

FRIEDMAN, WILLIAM ROBERT, JR., investment banking executive; b. May 1, 1942, NY, NY; s. William Robert and Elsa (Dryfoog) F.; m. Jeanette Lascoumes, July 9, 1983; children: Douglas, b. 1968; Brian, b. 1971; Catherine, b. 1974; edn: BA, Univ. of Penna. 1965, MBA, The Wharton Sch. 1970. Career: sr. mktg. cons. Coco Cola Export Corp. 1971-3; sr. securities analyst Investment Mgmt. Gp., Citibank 1973-6; v.p. L.F Rothschild, Unterberg Towbin 1976-8; partner Montgomery Securities, San Francisco 1978--; bd. advisors Am. Health Capital, Inc.; bd. dirs. Health Plan of Am.; awards: ranked top instnl. health care analyst, Institutional Invester Mag. 1977; mem: Am. Hosp. Assn.; Health Care Fin. Mgmt. Assn.; Am. Soc. of Parenternal & External Nutrition; City Athletic Club, NYC; Bay Club, S.F.; mil: 1st lt. US Army 1966-8; rec: tennis, running, mil. & polit. history, art. Res: 3343 Jackson St San Francisco 94118 Ofc: Montgomery Securities, 235 Montgomery St San Francisco 94104

FRIEND, RICHARD LOUIS, business sales consultant; b. May 22, 1956, Sierra Madre; s. Leonard Thomasand Eleanor Veronica (Klotz)Friend; m. Elizabeth Morris, Feb. 6, 1982; stepchildren: Scott Curtis, b. 1963; Shawn Curtis, b. 1965; edn: AS, Monterey Penin. Coll. 1983; cert. bus. opp. appraiser, Am. Bus. Consultants Inc. 1983. Career: salesman Compact of Santa Clara, 1978-79; regional dir. Golden Youth Mfg., Los Angeles 1979-80; real estate sales Creative Prop. Investment, Monterey 1980-81; real estate sales assoc. Salvatore Rombi Realtors, Monterey 1981--; vice pres. sales Visitors Info. Channel, Monterey 1984--; gen. partner in a recreational devel. in Monterey Co. 1984-; Monterey Co. Fair Concessions mgr., 1983-. Mem: Monterey Penin. Board of Realtors (mbr at large 1980-84); Redondo Beach Police Explorers (captain 1973); Monterey Penin. Jaycees (v.p. 1984-5; outstanding 1st year Jaycee 1983); Monterey Nat. Invitational Rugby Tournament (publicity chr. 1983, 84). Mil: E5, USCG 1973-77; Electronics Tech., Commun. Splst.; GCM, Merit Svc, Marksman rifle & pistol. Republican; Catholic; rec: scuba diving (salvage, photog., tours). Res: 942 Portola Dr. Del Rey Oaks 93940 Ofc: Salvatore Rombi Realtors 807 Cannery Row Monterey 93940

FRIESTEDT, JONATHAN DANFORD, building industry executive; b. Oct. 3, 1950, Chgo.; s. Herman H., Jr. and Valaire S. (Adams) F.; edn: BS, US Naval Acad. 1973; MS, USC 1982; PhD, cand., USC 1980-; Plng. Commnr. V.Chmn., City of Carlsbad 1979-83. Career: lt., engineering ofcr. USN 1973-79; certified inv. broker/mgr. Dutch Real Estate Co., 1979-80; v.p. Christiana Cos. national real estate developer 1980-83; senior v.p. Kaufman & Broad Inc., Land Company (largest home builder in state), 1983--; mem.: bd. dir. Home Builders

Council, Building Industry Assn.; Consultive Council, Urban Land Inst.; Consultive Council Inst. of Building, Science, Wash DC; mem. USC Alumni, USNA Alumni, League of Calif. Cities, Internat. City Managers Assn., Carlsbad CofC; Republican; Episcopal; rec: collector art & rare books. Res: 1108 18th St Santa Monica 90403 Ofc: Kaufman & Broad Inc. 11601 Wilshire Blvd Los Angeles 90025

FRISK, RICHARD MAURICE, lawyer/educator; b. Apr. 12, 1914, Des Moines, Iowa; s. Edwin J. and Minnie R. Youngberg; edn: De Pauw Univ. 1935-6; BA, Carleton Coll. 1938; sec. tchg. cred., UCB; stu. Stanford Law Sch., Boalt Hall; Calif. life-time tchg. cred.; admitted to State Bar of Calif. and Calif. Fed. Cts. 1953; m. Betty A. Booher (dec. 1955), Sept. 3, 1945; children: Richard (JD Armstrong Coll.), Jerome (BA Pomona Coll., postgrad. Harvard), Jon, Robert (stu. Sonoma St.); m. 2d. Marjorie W. Brown (dec. 1976), June 9, 1961; children: David (Merit Scholar, BA Reed Coll.), Catherine (stu. UOP). Career: (past) office secty., bookkeeper, cashier, and acctg. asst. to stock and bond brokers and the Texas Co.; teacher in Calif. public schools over 15 years; currently solo pvt. practice atty., semi-ret.; honors: Liberty Award, Peter Willcocks Soc., K.C., Mo. 1974; elected Republican nominee Calif. State Assembly 1964; founding pres. N.W. Berkeley Repub. Assem.; mil: Storekeep lc, USCG (R) 1942-45; Republican; Prot.; rec: writing, travel, dancing. Res: 2004 San Miguel Dr Walnut Creek 94596

FRITZSCHE, WILLIAM ALFRED, software engineer; b. May 20, 1958, St. Louis, Mo.; s. Alfred George and Arlene (Rose) F.; m. Mary Bushong, Oct. 2, 1982; edn: BSEET, DeVry Inst. of Tech. 1976; grad. work in computer sci., Santa Clara Univ. 1983-. Career: sorter United Parcel Service, Franklin Park, Ill. 1976-79; systems test splst. Fairchild Test Systems, San Jose 1979-82, sci. pgmmr./sr. software engr. 1982--. Awarded 1st pl. in electronics, Ill. state, Vocational Indsl. Clubs of Am. (VICA) 1976. Mem. DeVry Alumni Assn.; Democrat; Lutheran; rec: ski, skin dive, woodworking, electronics. Res: 7104 Indian Wells Ct San Jose 95139 Ofc: Fairchild Test Systems 1601 Technology Dr San Jose 95110

FROST, BRENT HIXSON, financial co. executive; b. Oct. 26, 1945, Glendale; s. Donald Ernest and Elizabeth B. (Hixson) F.; m. Susan Wright, Aug. 1, 1969; children: Todd, b. 1970; Ryan, b. 1972; Lane, b. 1975; Jared, b. 1976; Darren, b. 1978; Chanel, b. 1980; edn: BS, cum laude, Brigham Young Univ. 1969; CPA, Calif. 1973. Career: jr. acct./ staff acct./ sr. acct./ suprvg. sr./ supr./ mgr. Peat, Marwick, Mitchell & Co., Los Angeles 1969-78; v.p./ dir. of taxes Financial Corp. of Am. and Am. Savings & Loan Assn. 1978--; chmn. tax issues com. Calif. League of Savings Instns. 1982-3; honors: BSA Eagle Scout and Order of the Arrow 1961; mem: Am. Inst. of CPAs; Calif. Soc. of CPAs; BSA Cub Scout Leader 1980-; missionary for Mormon Ch. in England 1965-67; creative works: pub. poems and essays, paintings exhib./sold, performer local drama and musicals; Republican; Mormon; Ofc: Financial Corp. of America, 6420 Wilshire Blvd Los Angeles 9048

FRUMKIN, ALLAN ROBERT, lawyer; b. May 26, 1944, Oakland; s. Milton B. and Priscillia (Davis) F.; m. Catherine, June 11, 1967; 1 dau. Deborah, b. 1975; edn: AB, Univ. Calif. 1965; JD, San Francisco Law Sch. 1971; admitted Calif. State Bar 1972; life teaching cred. secondary, Calif. Dept. Edn. 1967. Career: tchr./ adminstr. San Lorenzo School Dist. 1967-75; atty. at law, San Leandro 1972--; honors: Citizen of the Day, KABL, 11/74; mem: Alameda Co. Drug Abuse Bd. (past pres.); Contra Costa Co. Drug Abuse Bd. (past pres.) Project Eden Inc. (pres.); past pres. San Ramon Valley Edn. Fdn.; San Lorenzo Lions Club (past pres.); past mem./pres. San Lorenzo Sch. Bd.; rec: travel, photog., running. Res: 881 Columbine Court Danville Law Ofc. of Allan R. Frumkin, 15200 Hesperian San Leandro 94578

FRYM, JANET CAROLYN (KOPF), travel executive; b. Oct. 30, 1946, San Francisco; d. Richard Kenneth and Nancy Ruth (Doud) Carmoney; adoptive d., Raymond Leroy Kopf; edn: Sonoma State Coll. 1964-5; Heald's Bus. Coll. 1965; m. Dale Oates, 1967, div. 1971; m. 2d. Roy Frym, 1972, div. 1982; 4 stepchildren; Career: orthodonic asst. Dr. Kleve Johnson, Mill Valley 1963-4; travel agent Small World Travel, Mill Valley 1964-6, mgr. 1967-70, sole owner 1970-5; travel agent/ asst. mgr. Santa Rosa (Ca.) Travel, 1966-7; resident of Kenya, E. Africa 1975-7; outside sales, Blue Marble Travel, Novato 1976-7; co-owner Ent. Unlmtd. (restaurants in Hemet, Riverside) 1977-80; gen. mgr. Traveltime, Inc., Laguna Hills 1980-3; gen. mgr. Bay Travel, Inc., Corona Del Mar 1983--; founding bd. mem. Marin Savings & Loan, Mill Valley 1976-; recipient num. sales achievement awds., various airlines, cruise lines 1970-5; Hon. Mention for lyric, Am. Song Festival competition; mem: Orange Co. Sabre Club (bd. 1981-, vp 1983); Orange Co. Travellarians; Am., No. Calif. Soc. of Travel Agents; works: designer/bldr. four restaurants, Novato residence; Republican; Presbyterian; rec: songwriter, gourmet cook, travel. Res: 2115 Arbutus Pl Newport Beach 92660 Ofc: Bay Travel, Inc., 2435 E Coast Hwy Corona Del Mar 92625

FUDGE, RAYMOND CARROLL, waste control consultant; b. Feb. 9, 1950, Athens, Ala.; s. Roy Smith and Mary Ella (Norman) F.; m. Nancy Fudge, Aug. 29, 1975; children: Tonya, b. 1978; Chrstopher, b. 1980; Monica, b. 1982; edn: BS, SW Missouri State Univ., Springfield 1978; MS, (cand.), CSU, Fresno 1985. Career: grad. asst. Univ. of Tenn., Knoxville 1978-9; mgr. trainee Tyson Foods, Inc., Springdale, AR 1979; mgr. Vandiver Swine Facilities, Madison, Ala. 1979-81; mgr. Deschutes River Hog Farm, The Dalles, OR 1981; product R&D, P.S.F. Organics, Inc., Fresno 1983--; prin. TCM Wholesale & Retail; cons. waste and odor control, CSUF dairy farm & Tyson Foods, Inc.; awards: scholarship, Pacific Egg and Poultry Assn. 1984; Delta Tau Alpha (life) 1978;

mil: petty ofcr. USN, Vietnam svc.; Republican; Ch. of Christ (tchr); rec: wholesale & retail. Res: 5341 E Clay, POB 8252, Fresno 93727 Ofc: P.S.F. Organics, Inc., 4967 E Lansing Way Fresno 93727

FUDGE, REG, JR., leasing co. executive; b. Aug. 1, 1928, Los Angeles; s. Reg and Ellen Rosina (Martin) F.; div.; children: Ron, b. 1948; Erin Scott, b. 1967; Megan Victoria, b. 1975; edn: BBA, Woodbury Univ. 1949; LLB, LaSalle Univ. 1977; admitted to State Bar of Calif. 1979. Career: v.p. Reg Fudge Lincoln Mercury, Encino 1956-8; pres. Wholesale Sales, Inc., Van Nuys 1958-68; gen. mgr. Canoga Toyota, Inc., Canoga Park 1968-73; gen. mgr. Keyes Motors, Inc., Van Nuys 1973-7; pres. KMI Leasing, Van Nuys 1977--; mem: Los Angeles Trial Lawyers Assn.; Calif. Trial Lawyers Assn.; Assn. of Trial Lawyers of Am.; Western Vehicle Leasing Assn.; Los Angeles Co. Bar Assn.; Masons; Republican; Episcopal; rec: restoring spl. interest cars. Res: 24509 Wingfield Rd Hidden Hills 91302 Ofc: KMI Leasing, 5855 Van Nuys Blvd Van Nuys 91401

FUDGEN, WENDELL PHILLIP, dentist; b. Mar. 29, 1942, Greenville, Tex.; s. Wendell P. and Carrie Lee (Moore) F.; m. Bertha Marks, Aug. 15, 1965; 1 son, Brian Anthony b. 1971; edn: BA, Calif. State Univ. 1965; BS, Univ. Calif. 1972; DDS, UC San Francisco Med. Center 1972. Career: med. tech. UC Med. Ctr., San Francisco 1965-68; dental internship, Mt. Zion Hosp., S.F. 1972-73; dentist, pvt. practice, S.F. 1973 . Bd. dirs: Cynthia Smallwood Medical Research & Edn. Found. 1983-; S.F. Dental Soc. 1980, S.F. Dental Care Found. 1979-80, S.F. Easter Seal Soc. 1977-80, Glenview Homeowners Assn. 1975-78; chmn. Nat. Minority Recruitment Com. (Dentistry) 1971. Honors: Omicron Kappa Upsilon (dental hon.) 1972-, Who's Who Among Students in Am. Univs. and Colls. 1972; mem: Am., Calif. Dental Assns., Nat., San Francisco Dental Socs., Western Soc. of Periodontology, Am. Endodontic Soc., Masons (32nd Degree), Alpha Phi Alpha frat.; mil: 1st. lt. USAFR 1965-72; Democrat; Prot.; rec: skiing, tennis, chess. Res: 289 Goldmine Dr San Francisco 94131 Ofc: Wendell P. Fudgen DDS, 1375 Sutter, Ste 418, San Francisco 94109

FUETSCH, ANTON, sculptor; b. Dec. 24, 1944, Virgen, East Tyrol, Austria; s. Josef and Maria (Weisskopf) F.; m. Elizabeth, Feb. 13, 1970; 1 child, Andreas, b. 1970; edn: apprentice to Academic Wood Sculptor, Gottfried Fuetsch, Tyrol, Austria 1959-63; Acad. for Applied Arts, Vienna 1964-7; Univ. of Fine Arts, Vienna 1967-9. Career: period mirror and picture frame carver at the Hoyer, Brustlin Workshop, San Francisco 1970 5; wood carver, relief and figure sculptor, conceptual designer/prin. Anton Fuetsch, Wood Carving, Berkeley 1975--; guest spkr. Bay Area Woodworkers' Assn. 1983; exhibs: Western Invitnl. Wood Workers Show, Gallery Faire, Mendocino 1983, S.F. Arts Festival 1983, 2nd Annual Working with Wood Show, S.F 1983; design cons., antique recreation cons.; awards: Passion Prize, San Francisco Arts Commn. 1983; mem: Sculptors Internat., Center for Visual Arts, Bay Area Woodworkers Assn.; mil: pvt. Austrian NG 1967; rec: hunting, hiking. Res: 3480 Midvale Ave Oakland 94602 Ofc: Anton Fuetsch, Wood Carving, 1038 Murray Street Berkeley 94710

FUJIKAWA, LESLIE SUMIE, physician; b. Aug. 5, 1951, San Francisco; d. Hiroshi and Masako (Hiramoto) Fujikawa; m. Terry Mincey, Dec. 18, 1976; edn: BA, biochem./immunol., UC Berkeley, 1973; MD, UC San Diego 1978. Career: intern Los Angeles Harbor General Hosp. 1978-79; ophthalmology research fellow Pacific Medical Ctr., S.F. 1979-80; research assoc. Eye Research Inst., Immunopath Unit, Mass. General Hosp., Harvard Med. Sch., Boston 1980-81; resident in ophthal. and research assoc. Dept. of Ophthalmology, Smith-Kettlewell Inst. of Visual Scis., Pacific Med. Center, S.F., 1981--. Awards: Assn. for Research in Vision & Ophthal. travel fellowship 1979, Nat. Eye Inst. postdoctl. resrch. fellowship 1980, Fight for Sight grantee 1980, Phi Beta Kappa, Honors Pgm. in Immunology, Outstanding Young Women of Am. 1981; mem: Assn. for Research in Vision and Ophthal., Am. Acad. of Ophthal., Am. Medical Women's Assn., Nat. Assn. of Residents & Interns; publs: 21 articles in med. journals; rec: pianist. Res: 50 Chumasero, No. 12-M, San Francisco 94132 Ofc: Dept. Ophthal. Pacific Medical Center, 2340 Clay St San Francisco 94115

FUJIMOTO, LARRY TAKESHI, life underwriter; b. Apr. 1, 1940, Alamoso, Colo.; s. Yuji and Shizuye Marion (Nakayama) F.; m. Jayne Yumiko Tanimura, Jan. 29, 1965; div. 1978; children: Michael Dean Masaru, b. 1966; Dennis Todd Kenji, b. 1967; edn: BS, sci., Univ. of Colo. 1963. Career: chemist, Milani Foods, Los Angeles 1963-66; life insurance sales, L.A. 1966--, prin. Fujimoto Insurance; devel. computerized life ins. pkg. for ins. industry, marketed as Round Table SoftWare, Inc., 1980--; mem. Technology Com. 1983 for Fidelity Union Life Ins. Co., instrumental in implementing micro-computer for field force; honors: Eagle Scout 1956; Father of the Year 1981, Morey Boogie & Sunkist; life ins. sales awards: Senior Field Underwriter 3 yrs., Top Club Producer 12 yrs., MDRT 74, 81, 82, Nat. Quality Award. 10 yrs., Nat. Sales Achievement 8 yrs.; mem: Nat. Assn. of Life Underwriters, Optimist Club (v.p.); BSA Bronze Explorer, Scoutmaster & founder Troop 164; active in LA Unif. Sch. Dist. on behalf of vision therapy for dyslexic (eye problem) children; rec: running, body surfing. Address: Fujimoto Insurance, 3331 Corinth Ave Los Angeles 90066

FUJIOKA, TAD, physician-surgeon; b. Mar. 14, 1926, Isleton, CA; s. Tadashiro and Tomiko (Sadao) F.; m. Elaine Logan ,MD (dec.) 1953; m. 2d. Sallianne Blackard, Dec. 31, 1967; children: Ken, b. 1954; Linda (Holudber), b. 1957; Tim, b. 1968; Ellen, b. 1974; edn: Fresno State Coll.; MD, Calif. Coll. of Med. 1962; Dip. Am. Bd. of Family Practice 1975, 82. Career: intern Montesano Hosp., Los Angeles 1954-5; pvt. practice medicine 1955--, owner/ dir. Mednik Medical Clinic, L.A.; chief staff City View Hosp. 1968-; awards: mem: Fellow,

Am. Acad. of Family Physicians 1976; Am. Acad. of Family Practice; AMA; Calif., Los Angeles Co. Med. Assn.; mil: sgt. US Army 1944-6; Republican; Baptist; rec: triathlete, runner. Res: 910 Gainsborough Dr Pasadena 91107 Ofc: Mednik Medical Clinic, 605 No Mednik Ave Los Angeles 90022

FUKAWA, TAKIO, corporate executive; b. Feb. 21, 1930, Yokohama, Japan; s. Seikichi and Kimiko Fukawa; Edn: fgn. trade, Yokohama Coll., 1949; Harvard Bus. Sch., 1974; m. Reiko Adachi, Oct. 3, 1957; chil: Tamae, b. 1959; Jun, b. 1962. Career: mgr., Mach. Dept., Mitsui & Co. Ltd., London Branch, 1970; asst. general mgr., 1974; deputy gen. mgr., 1976; deputy gen. mgr., Chem. Plant Div., Mitsui & Co. Ltd., Tokyo, Japan, 1978; v.p. & gen. mgr., Mitsui & Co. (USA), Inc., Los Angeles, CA, 1981---. Mem: Japan Bus. Assn. of So. Calif., v.p. & chmn. Pub. Rels. Com., 1982; Japan America Soc., com. mem. 1981; Japanese CofC, v.p. 1982. Rec: golf, travel. Res: 335 South Hudson Ave., Los Angeles 90020; Office: Mitsui & Co. (USA), Inc., 611 W. Sixth St., Suite 2000, Los Angeles 90017.

FULD, FRED, III, financial planner; b. July 31, 1952, San Pedro; s. Fred Jr. and Gloria Mary (Cameron) F.; edn: BA in bus., BA in econ., Rockford Coll. 1974; CFP (Cert. Fin. Plnnr.) Coll. of Fin. Plnng.; Reg. Investment Advisor, SEC; Gen. Securities Sales Supr., NASD. Career: investment broker San Diego Securities, S.D. 1974-78; market maker, Pacific Stock Exchange, San Francisco 1978-79; vice pres. Financial Planning, CGR Consultants, S.F. 1979--; mem: Internat. Assn. for Fin. Plnng., Inst. of Cert. Fin. Planners, Stockbroker's Soc., Am. Mensa Soc.; rec: swim, run, collector antique stock certificates. Res: 4108 Joan Ave Concord 94521 Ofc: CGR Consultants, 450 Sansome St, Ste 210, San Francisco 94111

FULGHUM, BRICE ELWIN, finance and insurance executive; b. Aug. 27, 1919, Fredonia, Kans.; s. Byron Harmon and Myrtle E. (Brodrick) F.; m. Virginia Dunlea, Feb. 13, 1982; 1 dau: Linda Lee (McDonald); edn: Central Bus. Coll., K.C.; Univ. of Kansas City; grad. studies, CSU Northridge, USC; CLU, The Am. Coll., Bryn Mawr, Pa. Career: asst. to sales mgr. Gas Service Co., Kansas City, Mo. 1945-8; asst. mgr. Owl Drug Co., San Francisco 1948-50; mgr. Pacific Mutual Life Ins. Co. 1950-61; v.p. Gordon H. Edwards Co., 1961-4; v.p. Federated Life Ins. Co. Calif., 1964-6; gen. mgr. Los Angeles Fulghum agy. Pacific Mut. Life Ins. Co. 1966 71; v.p. Hendric Bonding & Ins. Corp., Huntington Beach 1976-7; chmn. bd. PGA Ins. Services, Inc., Torrance 1976-7; cons. Am. Health Profiles, Inc., Nashville; sr. fin. cons. Shearson Hayden Stone, Inc., Newport Bch. 1977-9; cons. Penn. Gen. Agys., Los Angeles and Employee Benefit Consultants, Santa Ana 1979-; cons. Assn. Calif. State U. Profs., Profl. Sponsoring Fund, 1959--; chmn. Cancer drive, active Community Chest, Am. Heart Assn.; mem: Am. Soc. CLUs (Golden Key Soc.); Leading Life Ins. Producers No. Calif. (pres. 1955); S.F. Peninsula (charter), L.A.-San Fernando Valley (life) Estate Planning Councils; Orange Co. Life Underwriters Assn.; mil: Q.M.C., US Army 1943-5; clubs: Commonwealth, El Niguel Country; mem. editorial advis. bd. Western Underwriter; contbr. arts. to ins. publs.; Republican. Res: 30561 No Hampton Rd Laguna Niguel 92677 Ofc: Professional Sponsoring Fund, 1055 No Main, Ste 420, Santa Ana 92701

FULLER, BARBARA DEANE, actress, business owner; b. July 31, 1925, Nahant, Mass.; d. Andrew Ralph and Georgia (Nicholson) F.; m. Feb. 23, 1951, div.; ed. Chgo. public schs. Extensive career in radio, motion pictures and TV, beginning in Chgo. radio in 1932; radio, NY; radio, motion pictures., TV, little theatre, in Hollywood (best known as Claudia in radio drama: One Man's Family); leading roles in 13 motion pictures; founder B.D. Fuller & Assocs. 1967; prod./ acct. exec. This Thing Called Life (radio pgm.) 1967--; prod./ distbr. inspirational audio cassette tapes, now in over 22 countries, 1971--; charter mem. Pacific Pioneer Broadcasters (secty.; past bd. dirs.); mem. AFI, SAG, AFTRA, hon. mem. SPERDVAK, Freedoms Found. at Valley Forge; Republican; Relig. Sci.; rec: creative cooking. Res: Hollywood Ofc: B.D. Fuller & Assoc., 13701 Riverside Dr, Ste 608 Sherman Oaks 91423

FULOP, IRWIN MARTIN, lawyer; b. July 9, 1904, Salt Lake City; s. David Louis and Rebecca B. (Boukofsky) F.; m. Clara Sherman, July 15, 1938; edn: AB, Univ. of Calif. 1925; JD, Harvard Law Sch. 1928. Career: partner law firm of Fulop & Hardee (formerly Fulop, Ralston, Burns & McKittride); arbitrator Superior Ct., L.A. County; lectr. Continuing Education of the Bar 1960; referee State Bar of Calif. 1979-80; mem: L.A. Bar Assn.; Am. Bar Assn. Beverly Hills Bar Assn.; Republican. Address: 518 W Crescent Dr Beverly Hills 90210

FULTON, RICHARD EUGENE, physician; b. Feb. 18, 1940, Kane, Penna.; s. Wayne L. and Roma K. (Kline) F.; m. Irene, June 30, 1962; children: Holly, b. 1965; Tracy, b. 1967; Emily, b. 1968; Katharine, b. 1974; edn: BS, Allegheny Coll. 1961; MD, Temple Univ. Med. Sch. 1965; Diagnostic Radiologist, Am. Coll. of Radiol. 1969. Career: cons./instr./assoc. prof. Diagnostic Roentgenology, Mayo Clinic/ Mayo Grad. Sch. of Medicine/Univ. of Minn., Rochester 1969-79, joint appt. Dept. of Physiol. and Biophysics, 1978-9; co-dir. in cardiac lab., St. Mary's Hosp., 1977-79; partner Pueblo Radiology Medical Group, Inc., Santa Barbara 1979--; active staff: St. Francis Hosp., S.B., Goleta (Ca.) Valley Comm. Hosp.; vis. prof. Ga. Baptist Hosp. 1977; honors: Biology Hon. Soc., Sigma Xi; mem: Am. Coll. of Radiology; Radiol. Soc. of No. Am. (Refresher Course Com. 1979-); Calif., So. Calif., Southcoast (sec/treas.) Radiol. Soc.; Am. Roentgen Ray Soc.; Am. Heart Assn., Council on Cardiovascular Disease; Mayo Clinic Alumni Assn.; CMA, Med. Soc. of Santa Barbara; W. Angiographic Soc.; chmn. Calif. Preferred Providers Inc. (PPO Orgn.) 1983; mem. Santa Barbara CofC; past mem. Rochester Independent

Sch. Dist. Bd. of Edn. 1975-9; publs: num. med. jour. articles, presentations; co-recipient Bd. of Gov's Sci. Exhibit Award, 1st pl., Am. Coll. of Cardiol. 1977; Republican; Prot.; rec: athletics, ski, fish, carpentry. Res: 1001 Vereda Del Ciervo Goleta 93117 Ofc: Pueblo Radiology Med Group Inc. POB 1326, Santa Barbara 93102

FUNG, THOMAS BIN-HUN, electronics supplies co. executive; b. Sept. 9, 1944, Shanghai, China; s. Pak Leung and Shui Ping (Wong) F.; m. Hsiang-Mei Lai, Apr. 8, 1980; children: Catherine, b. 1981, Daniel, b. 1983; edn: dip. in mech. engrg., Aberdeen Tech. Sch., HK 1963, Bendigo Sch. of Mine, Australia 1966; dip. personnel mgmt., Brit. Inst. of Career, Aus. 1969; BBA fin., Pacific Western Univ., Ca. 1981; Tradesman Cert. of fitter & turner, Aus. Dept. of Labor & Nat. Svc. 1966. Career: design engr. Luen Sang Bracelete Mfg. Co., HongKong 1966-7; engr. Central Lab, HK Ltd 1967-8; mgr. mfg. Ampex Ferrotec HK Ltd 1968-73; engrg. dir. Etco Switching System Co, HK 1973-9; v.p. finance, Elcom Memory Product Corp, USA 1979-83; exec. vice pres. Advanced Electronics Supplies Inc., San Bruno 1983--; awards: apprenticeship, U.K. Ministry of Transport & Civil Aviation 1963; mem. M.I.E. The Inst. of Engrs. and Technicians, London 1979. Co-inventor (w/ Bin Hun & So, Cheung Sing) telephone dialing unit 1975, British, W. Ger. patents; Catholic; rec: swim, soccer. Res: 207-D Boardwalk, San Bruno 94066 Ofc: Advanced Elec Supplies Inc. 456 San Mateo Ave, #5, San Bruno 94066

FUNK, ALFRED ROGER, real estate broker; b. Aug. 21, 1943, Brklyn.; s. Roger John and Nina Rita (Tumminelli) F.; m. Linda Diane Gray, Dec. 31, 1971; children: Kevin, b. 1963, Patricia, b. 1966, Kerri, b. 1974, Andie, b. 1979; edn: AA, real estate, Chabot Coll. 1979. Career: sales mgr. 1971-72, v.p. ops./mktg. Media Development Inc., 1972-73; dist. sales mgr. Telecommunications, 1973-74, regl. sales mgr. Telecomm. 1974-76; dir. comml. mktg. Gill Cable TV, 1976; real estate broker Allied Brokers, Better Homes Realty, Livermore 1977--; mem: Livermore Lions Club (life mem. Lions Eye Found. 1983; recognition awards 1981, 83); Livermore CofC; Las Positas Golf Club; Am. Contract Bridge League; Am. Bowling Cong.; Foeagles 609; mil: E6 USN 1961-71, Presdtl. Unit Cit., GCM, Nat. Def., Vietnam Svc. medals; Democrat; Catholic; rec: pin collector, numismatics, golf. REs: 2643 Briarwood Dr Livermore 94550 Ofc: Better Homes Investment Group, 4049 1st St, Ste. 141, Livermore 94550

FURLONG, ROBERT JOHN BLANCHARD, real estate investment co. president; b. Nov. 20, 1932, Halifax, Nova Scotia, Canada, nat. 1962; s. John Alexander MacDonald and Margaret Anderson (Rowlings) F.; neph., Hon. Flemming Blanchard McCurdy, M.P., first to fly a heavier -than-air aircraft in British Empire (1908); m. Vivienne Moss, Mar. 12, 1983; 1 son, Robert Jr., b. 1964; edn: BA, First Honors, 1958, law stu. Dalhousie Univ. 1958-60; MBA, honors, McGill Univ. 1962; econ., UC Los Angeles 1970-72. Career: pres. Commonwealth Realty Co. Ltd., Halifax 1962-68; chmn. Am. Mutual Investment Corp., Beverly Hills, Calif. 1969-74; chmn. Am. Standard Inv. Corp., 1969-74; chmn. Dominion Capital Corp., 1969-74; pvt. real estate investor nationally, 1974-83; pres. Kion Inc., Marina del Rey 1983--; Dir. 20th Century Energy Corp., Can.; assoc. with Dr. Edward Teller on Methacoal Process, Dallas; coordinator annual conf. on Nuclear Medicine, Wash DC; promoting NASA space shuttles at Cape Kennedy and Edwards AFB; honors: First Award, Outstanding Student in Bus. & Econ. 1962 for Canada; clubs: St. Bruno Riding (St. Bruno, Quebec), Bedford Basin Yacht (Bedford, Can.), Royal Yacht Squadron (Stockholm), Canadian Soc. of Los Angeles, Marina City Club, Carleton (Ottowa); Republican; Presbyterian; rec: music and the arts. Res: 4267 Marina City Dr, Ste 204WTS, Marina Del Rey 90292 Ofc: Kion Inc., 4th Flr, 330 Washington Blvd Marina Del Rey 90292

FURLOW, GLEN MERRILL, manufacturing co. tax executive; b. Apr. 16, 1924, Goshen, Ala.; s. Grover Cleveland and Exa (King) F.; m. Mary Helen King, Dec. 27, 1946; children: Merrill King, b. 1952; Sharon Leigh, b. 1955; edn: BS, Univ. of Alabama 1949; LLB, Birmingham Sch. of Law 1953; Grad. Sch. of Credit and Fin. Mgmt., Dartmouth Coll. 1969; Mgmt. Devel. Pgm., Univ. West Va. 1977. Career: with U.S. Steel Corp. 1949--; mgmt. trainee 1949; credit rep. 1950; credit analyst 1951-4; sr. credit rep. 1954-62; regl. credit mgr., constrn. accounts 1962-4; credit mgr. Northwest 1964-9; staff tax asst. 1969-71; tax adminstr. 1971; mgr. of taxes, West 1972--; awards: Distg. Lt. Governor, Optimist Internat. 1961; Man of Yr., Homewood, Ala. 1961; Spark Plug Awd., Calif. Mfgrs. Assn. 1979; mem: Calif. Tax Found.; dir./exec. com., Taxpayer's Assn. of Calif. (& Utah, Wyoming, and Contra Costa Co.); Tax Execs. Inst. (pres. S.F. Chpt. 1979-80); Wash. Research Council; Western States Tax Reps. Assn.; Internat. Assn. of Assessing Ofcrs.; Colo. Assn. of Commerce and Ind.; Utah Mfgrs. Assn.; Utah Mining Assn.; Utah Found.; World Trade Club; Optimist Internat.; BSA; United Appeal; Rescue- One Found.; author: num. tech. papers profl. journals; mil: Chief Petty Ofcr., USN 1942-6; Republican; Presbyterian; rec: fishing, golf, gardening. Res: 79 Jean Court Moraga 94556 Ofc: United States Steel Corp., 120 Montgomery St San Francisco 94106

FURST, PETER GEORGE, architect, construction engineer, professor; b. Feb. 22, 1939, Ramsar, Iran, nat. 1977; s. Albert and Bella Greenberg (Gandleman) F.; m. Kathryn Bitsko, Sept. 13, 1973; children: Benjamin b. 1975, Jonathan b. 1977, Ryan b. 1979; edn: AA, highest honors, Pasadena City Coll. 1970; BS, constrn. engrg., honors, Calif. St. Polytech. Univ., S.L.O. 1974, B. Arch. and MBA, honors, 1975. Registered Architect, Calif. Career: draftsman R.S. Borders, AIA, Los Alamitos 1968-70; design draftsman, W.R. Helman, AIA, Arcadia 1970-72, 1974; design coordinator Crowell Corp., Pasadena 1973; proj. engr./proj. mgr. Turner Constrn. Co., Los Angeles (L.A., S.F., N.Y. offices), 1975--. Project engr. on Crocker Center in dwntwn. Los Angeles; assoc. prof.

CalPoly and CSU Long Beach; pvt. cons. in archit., constrn., mgmt.; recipient AIA Nat. Scholarship 1972, 73; honors: Phi Kappa Phi, Tau Beta Pi, Sigma Lambda Xi, Scarab; mem: Am. Inst. of Architects, Constrn. Specification Inst.; Democrat; Jewish; rec: fishing, philately, stained glass. Res: 408 Continental Ct Newbury Park 91320 Ofc: Turner Construction Co 445 S. Figueroa St Los Angeles 90071

FUSCO, VIRGINIA, civic worker, interpreter; b. July 25, Los Angeles; d. Joseph S.and Anna (Lota) F.; father founded import-export bus., Desert Sun Dried Fruit & Nut Co.; ed. pvt. sch. Paris, France; stu. art, Florence, Italy; num. courses, UC Berkeley; lang. stu., Mex. Career: asst. pub. serv. dir., civil serv., S.F. Mayor's Ofc.: translator/ interpreter, French, Spanish, Italian; Social secty., civic coms., soc. functions, to Mayors Angelo J. Rossi, Roger D. Lapham, Elmer E. Robinson, and social secty. to Mayor George Christopher and Mayor John Shelley; exec. secty. to Gov. Reagan's No. Calif. representative Josiah Knowles, Gov.'s Ofc., S.F.; co-chmn. No. Beach Republican Com., 1944-50; co-founder, secty. Marina Civic Imp. Assn., 1945--; assoc. Repub. State Central Com., 1950-51; honored special guest, Presdtl. Inaugural Ceremonies, Wash DC, Jan. 1953, for work on behalf of Pres. Eisenhower and V.P. Nixon; dist. dir. S.F. Repub. Assem., 1953; chmn. Amer. Relief for Italy, 1950-51; bd. mem. Palace of Fine Arts League (restoration of Palace) 1958; chmn. Gov. Reagan cmpgn./co-chmn. No. Beach Com. 1964; pres. Dante Aligheri Lodge, Order Sons of Italy 1951-2; dir. Vittoria Colonna Club 1955-60;j mem. Commonwealth Club of Calif., S.F. Heritage Found., Calif. Hist. Soc. Honors: Star of Solidarity medal and commendn. (2nd Calif. woman recipient); Pres. of Italian Republic, presented by Baron Muzi-Falconi, Ital. Consul Gen., 1951; Award of Merit, VFW, 1955; Resolutions, Calif. State Senate, S.F. Bd. of Supvs., 1977; Nat. Repub. Victory cert., 1977-81; Catholic; rec: civic polit. activities, opera, gardening. Res: 34 Cervantes Blvd San Francisco 94123

FUSSELL, JAMES GLEN, JR., financial services executive; b. Dec. 28,]944, Chattanooga, TN; s. James Glen and Mary Elizabeth (Kelley) F.; m. Sharon Marie Cadigan, Aug. 24, 1968; children: James, b. 1976; Genevieve, b. 1980; edn: BA, San Francisco State Univ. 1967; grad. stu., 1967-8; Gen. Securities Principal, NASD 1983. Career: v.p. White, Weld & Co., Inc., San Francisco 1973-78; v.p. Smith Barney Harris Upham & Co., S.F. 1978-81; Morgan Stanley & Co., Inc., IIS Group, S.F. 1981-2; pres. GFC Financial Management, Inc., S.F. 1982--; dir. GFC Securities Corp.; dir. GFC Financial Mgmt. Inc. 1982--; mem: Economic Round Table of San Francisco 1974-, pres. 1976; S.F. Planning and Urban Research Assn. 1973-, Treas. 1979-84; S.F. Housing Authority, Commnr. 1979-, V.P. 1983-; S.F. Municipal Railway Transport Workers Trust Fund, Trustee 1978-; Big Brother of S.F., Treas. 1977-80; Pacific Ballet, Dir. 1976-7; editor: GFC Outlook (fin. mkt. commentary) 1982-; mil: capt. USAF 1968-73; Democrat; Methodist; rec: swim, ski. Res: 1471 5th Ave San Francisco 94122 Ofc: Gibraltar Financial Services, 220 Montgomery St, Ste 496, San Francisco 94104

G

GABRIA, RONALD CHARLES, language, speeech & hearing specialist; b. Oct. 7, 1946, Pittsburgh, PA; s. Michael John Sr. and Laura Phyllis (Pisarski) G.; m. Debra Krueger, June 12, 1982; edn: BS, Univ. of Dayton 1969; MA, Univ. of Iowa 1973; MA, CSU Sacto. 1982. Career: dir. of language, speech & theatre, St. Anselm H.S., Pittsburgh, PA 1968-9; coord. of County Language, Speech & Hearing Svcs., Lee Co. Bd. of Edn., Fort Madison, Iowa 1974-5; instr. Dept. of Teacher Edn., Spl. Edn., CSU Sacto. (time-part) 1977-9; Language, Speech & Hearing Spec., Sacto. Co. Ofc. of Edn., Sacramento 1976--; instr. workshops: Non- Verbal Communication & Reinforcement, Univ. of the Pacific; mem: Am. Language, Speech & Hearing Assn. (Cert. of Clin. Competence, CCC); Sacto. Area Speech & Hearing Assn.; Alpha Epsilon Delta (AED), pre-med hon. soc.; publs: Book of Poetry: Share in the Energy of Love and Life, 1981; rec: theatre, writing poetry, white water rafting. Res: 2580 Filaree Court Rocklin 95677 Ofc: Sacramento County Office of Education, 9738 Lincoln Village Dr Sacramento 95827

GABRIEL, HELEN TASHJIAN, realtor; b. July 28, Fresno; d. John H. and Pearl (Manger) Tashjian; m. Herond Gabriel, Feb. 6, 1944; children: Janet, b. 1945; John, b. 1950; edn: bus., Jr. Coll. Career: real estate broker 1953--: assoc. Bob Symonds Realty, No. Hollywood 1953-5; Ralph Masters Realty, No. Hywd. 1955-6; Charles Janssen Realty, Sherman Oaks 1957-8; Lamping- Handler Realty, Studio City 1958-77; White House Properties, Sherman Oaks 1977--; Calif. Real Estate Assn., Dir. 1955-83 (Assocs. Com., Planning & Zoning Com., Profl. Standards Panel), chmn. Sgt.- at- Arms 1963, honored as Realtor-Assoc. of Yr. 1974; bd. dirs. San Fernando Bd. of Realtors, 1964-5, 1981-; mem: Sherman Oaks CofC (bd. dirs. 1980- exec. com. 1982-3); San Fern. Valley Bus. & Profl. Assn.; Eastern Star; Tarzana Republican Women 1977-83; Valley Research Orgn. 1962-77; Pro- America; United to Serve Am. 1968-78; Republican; Presbyterian; rec: gardening, singing (ch. choir 25 yrs.), cooking. Res: 5801 Ranchito Ave Van Nuys 91401 Ofc: Buddy Bernard's White House Properties, 14649 Ventura Blvd Sherman Oaks 91403

GADDIS, MARSHALL LEWIS, educator; b. Oct. 27, 1942, Wash DC; s. Bevy Marshall and Claudelle (Lewis) Gaddis; edn: BA with honors, Univ. of Iowa 1967; MFA, Univ. of Mont. 1969. Career: instr. English, Univ. of Montana 1969-75; free-lance writer, film actor, radio prod., software developer, 1975--; dir. computer studies National Univ., Sacramento 1983; coordinator of computers in edn./prof. of computer studies National Univ., Vista 1983--; instr. computer tng. for Proctor and Gamble, Calif. Dept. of Energy, Kaiser Permanente and Sutter Hosps., Hughes Aircraft, Sacto. Utility Dist. Mem: Nat. Computer Graphics Assn., Assn. of Computing Machinery, Assn. of Computer Trainers, Data Processing Mgrs. Assn., Nat. Mgmt. Assn., San Diego Computer Soc.; Soc. for the Preservation and Encouragement of Radio Drama, Variety and Comedy. Male lead actor (film): Slow Moves (Bay Area Filmmakers' Showcase 1983; L.A. Filmex 1984); writer (story) Occupational Hazard, Antigonish Rev. (Nova Scotia) 1971; Democrat; Unitarian; rec: windsurfing, music. Res: 29650 Chihuahua Valley Rd Aguanga 92302 Ofc: National Univ. 2022 University Dr. Vista 92083

GADDY, GARY LYNN, quality engineer; b. Aug. 28, 1942, Phoenix, Ariz.; Buster Brown and Jackie Marie (Osburn) G.; m. Kathryn Nash, May 28, 1966; children: Michelle, b. 1971; Stephanie, b. 1975; edn: BA, Augsburg Coll. 1972; MS, USC 1982, Certified Quality Engr , Am. Soc. for Quality Control 1978; Career: test technician Toro Mfg. Co., Bloomington, Mn. 1965-6; electronic techn., Univ. of Minn. 1966-8; engring. asst. Sperry- Univac, Roseville, Mn. 1968-73; quality engr. 1973-7; sr. quality engr. Amdahl Corp., Sunnyvale, Ca. 1977-80, and mgr. Industrial Technology, 1980; sr. advisory quality engr. (project engr.) Shugart Assocs, Sunnyvale 1980-2; mgr. quality assurance Trimax Controls, Inc., Sunnyvale 1982--; mem. ASQC; mil: aviation antisubmarine warfare techn. 3/c, USN 1963-5; Democrat; Lutheran; rec: fishing, stamps/ coins. Res: 1708 Grand Tenton Dr Milpitas 95035 Ofc: Trimax Controls, Inc., 1180 Miraloma Way Sunnyvale 94086

GADSBY, ROBERT CHARLES, security consultant; b. Sept. 29, 1951, Hammonton, NJ; s. Charlton Patrick and Mary Helen (Black) G.; edn: UC San Diego 1969-70; AS, in admin. of justice, Grossmont Coll. 1979; Certified by Calif. Commn. on Peace Ofcr. Standards and Training 1979. Career: firefighter, Calif. Div. of Forestry, El Cajon 1971; engr. Naval Artic Research Site Fire Dept., Point Barrow, AK 1971-2; interpretive naturalist San Diego Wild Animal Park, Escondido 1972-6; corp. security Southland Corp. South Pacific Div., La Mesa 1977--; pvt. investigator/ cons. 1978--; mem. La Mesa CofC Anti-Crime Task Force; rep. to John F. Duffy Found.; spkr. crime prevention and justice; mem: Am. Assn. Zoological Parks and Aquariums; Herpetologists League; Soc. for Study of Reptiles and Amphibians; Calif. Crime Prevention Ofcrs. Assn.; Calif. Robbery Invest. Assn.; Muscular Dystrophy assn., Reserve Police Ofcr., El Cajon 1974-7, 1983-; Reserve Deputy Sheriff, San Diego Co. 1978-9, 80; wildlife photog., freelance writer on natural history, arts. in Sports Afield, Zoonooz; Republican; rec: photog., firearms, shooting sports. Res: 1327 Hardin Dr El Cajon 92020 Ofc: 4655 Ruffner Street, Ste 160, San Diego 92111

GADSON, BETTY WALKER, clinical social worker; b. Mar. 7, 1947, Fairfield, Ala.; d. Elijah James and Verna Rea (Calloway) Walker; widowed; edn: BA, Univ. of Ala. 1968; MSW, Atlanta Univ. 1970; Calif. LCSW, lic. clin. soc. wkr.; Community Coll. Counselor/ Instr. Credential in Public Svcs. & Adminstrn. Career: med. soc. wkr. Atlanta Southside Comp. Health Ctr. 1970; dir. soc. svcs. Trenton Neighboorhood Family Health Ctr, Trento, NJ 1970-3; dir. soc. svcs. Trenton Head Start Pgm. 1973-4; cons./ pgm. analysis & job tng. New Era Learning Corp., Greenvale, NY 1972-3; instr./ mgmt. & supvr. Los Angeles Southwest Coll. Evening div. 1976-9; child welfare wkr. Los Angeles Co., Dept. of Adoptions 1974--; Lic. Clin. Soc. Wkr./ cons./trainer, pvt. practice; honors: Delta Sigma Kappa; mem: Nat. Assn. Social Wkrs; Alpha Kappa Alpha Sorority, Inc.; Univ. of Ala. Alumni Assn.; local neighborhood Block Club; developed: techniques for mainstreaming spl. needs children into regular child care sys.; Democrat; Baptist; rec: acting, floral design, arts & crafts. Res: 1119 South Sycamore Ave Los Angeles 90019 Ofc: L.A. Co. Dept. of Adoptions, 2550 W Olympic Los Angeles 90006

GAFFNEY, WILLIAM JAMES, engineering contractor; b. Jan. 13, 1939, San Francisco; s. Wm Eugene and Elizabeth Adelade (Quinn) G.; m. Virginia Lee Hand, Sept. 8, 1982; children: Mark, b. 1965, Dana, b. 1970; edn: Menlo Coll. 1957-8, Coll. of Marin 1958-9, USF 1959-60; lic. Calif. State Contracting A & B. Career: engr. Dan Coleman Assocs., 1960-64, M&K Corp., 1964-65, Fred J. Early jr. Co., 1965-68; mgr. Underground Constrn. Co., Inc. 1968-76; pres./ CEO, W. J. Gaffney, Inc., San Francisco 1976- ; mem. Nat. CofC; clubs: Frontier Boys, Garcia Gun Club, dir. of Childrens' Garden 1979-80; mil: s/sgt. USAF; Republican; Catholic; rec: hunt, fish, sailing, horseback riding. Res: 20 Fairhills Dr. San Rafael 94901 Ofc: W.J.Gaffney Inc., 696 Pennsylvania Ave. San Francisco 94107.

GAGAR, ELEUTERIO CASTRO, certified public accountant; b. May 26, 1935, Philippines, nat. 1975; s. Arsenio D. and Julieta G. (Castro) G.; m. Virginia J. Calderon, Oct. 8, 1960; children: Marievel, b. 1961; Juliet, b. 1966; Jonathan, b. 1968; Emmanuel, b. 1970; edn: AA, Phil. Coll. of Commerce 1954; BS, Far Eastern Univ., Manila 1957; spl. courses in acctg., taxation, UCLA, LACC, Becker CPA Rev. School, 1973-; real estate courses, Anthony Schs.; CPA, Phil. 1963, Calif. 1982; lic. Real Estate Broker, Calif. 1983. Career: acct. Unitours, Inc., Club Universe 1969-71; internal auditor So. Calif. United Food & Comml. Wkrs. Unions and Food Employers Joint Trust Funds, Inglewood 1972--; CPA, pvt. practice, Los Angeles 1982--; owner/ real estate broker/ finl.

cons. Fund Invest Research and Fin. Svcs., Los Angeles 1983--; pres./ secty. bd. Astrex Internat., Inc., L.A. 1979-81; real estate salesprsn. ERA Comml. and Resdtl. Realty, L.A. 1978-82; mem: Am. Inst. of CPAs; Calif. Soc. of CPAs; Filipino Accts. of So. Calif.; UCLA Alumni Assn.; Rosary Group of Atwater; YMCA, Glendale; Democrat; Catholic; rec: raising quails, gardening, fishing. Res: 3937 Revere Ave Los Angeles 90039 Ofc: So. Calif. United Food and Commercial Wkrs. Unions and Food Employers Joint Trust Funds, 3405 W Imperial Hwy, Ste 305, Inglewood 90303

GAINES, ROBERT FRANKLIN, insurance broker; b. Oct. 21, 1925, Oakland; s. Frank Stewart and Louise (Moore) G.; m. Winifred Breuner, Feb. 24, 1951; chil: Bob, b. 1952, Clare, b. 1954, Ted, b. 1958, Peter, b. 1960, Margaret, b. 1962; edn: BS, UCB 1949. Career: spl. agent Phoenix Assurance Co., 1949-52; ind. agent Robert F. Gaines, 1952-58; partner Gaines & Corlett, 1958-74; pres. Insurance Associates of Sacramento, 1974--; chmn. bd. Mercantile Bank, 1982-; dir. John Breuner Co. 1972-82. Honors: hon. D.Div., Church Divinity Sch. of the Pacific; mem: Independent Ins. Agents & Brokers of Sacto. (pres.); Pioneers-Sacramento (bd. mem.); Sact. Sym. Assn. (pres. 1982-4); Sutter Club; Republican; Episcopal; rec: birding. Res: 630 Wilhaggin Dr. Sacramento 95825 Ofc: Insurance Assocs. of Sacramento, 2100 Northrop Ave. Bldg. 500, Sacto 95825.

GALE, ADELITO MOLINA, thoracic surgeon; b. Oct. 30, 1933, Philippines, nat. 1970; s. Anastacio V. and Ricarda B. (Molina) G.; m. Ann Belden, Nov. 17, 1962; children: Mary Ann, b. 1963, Amy, b. 1964, Marsha, b. 1967, Arick, b. 1969, Jonathan, b. 1972, Nicholas, b. 1978; edn: AA, Sto. Tomas Univ., Manila 1951, MD, 1956. Career: intern St. Johns Hosp., Lowell, Mass. 1957-58; surgery esident St. Peters Hosp., Albany, NY 1958-61, Wyckoff Heights Hosp., Brklyn 1961-62, cardiovascular surgery res. St. Francis Hosp., Roslyn, L.I., NY 1962-64, Hahnemann Med. Sch. & Hosp., Phila., Pa. 1964-66; surgical staff VA Hosp., Phoenix, Az. 1967-71; pvt. practice Thoracic Cardiovascular Surgery, Escondido, Ca. 1971--; Diplomate: Am. Bd. of Surgery 1965, Am. Bd. Thoracic Surg. 1966; Fellow: Am. Coll. of Surgeons 1971, Am. Coll. Chest Physicians 1969; mem: AMA, CMA, San Diego Co. MEd. Soc., Soc. of Thoracic Surgeons, Pilipino Med. Assn. SD (pres.); Health Services Adv. Bd. S.D.Co.; gov. body Health System Agcy. S.D.-Imperial Co.; bd. dirs. Bank of Rancho Bernardo; bd. edn. Poway Unified Sch. Dist.; Republican; Catholic. Res: 17361 Grandee Pl San Diego 92128 Ofc: 151 East Third, Escondido 92025

GALIONI, ELMER F., psychiatrist; b. Jan. 17, 1924, San Francisco; s. Peter A. and Julia (Biron) Galioni; edn: AB, UC Berkeley, 1943, MD, UC San Francisco Med. Sch., 1946, internship, US Naval Hosp., San Diego, 1946-47; residency in psychiatry, Langley Porter Clinic, S.F., 1949-52; m. Avis, Dec. 8, 1962; chil: Paul, Craig, Joan (Hoschler), Claudia (Joslin); career: Dir. of Clin. Demonstration Pgm., Stockton State Hosp., 1950-51; staff psychiatrist, Langley Porter Clinic, 1951-52; dir. of clin. services, Stockton State Hosp., 1952-58, assoc. medical dir., 1958-61; DeputyDirector, Dept. of Mental Hygiene, 1961-72; director, Mental Health Services, ESKATON American River Healthcare Center, Sacramento 1972--; cons. N.I.M.H., 1963-; asst. clin. prof., Dept. Psychiatry, UC Davis Med. Sch., 1969-; Diplomat, Am. Bd. of Psychiatry and Neurology, 1953; cert. by Am. Psychiatric Assn., Mental Hosp. Adminstrn., 1958p; mem: AMA, CMA, Sacto. Co. Med. Soc.; Fellow, AAAS; Fellow, Am. Psychiatric Assn., past pres. Central Calif. District branch; Sacto. Area Mental Health Assn., bd. dirs. 1972-5; Am. Assn. for Geriatric Psychiatry; Am. Assn. of Psychiatry and the Law; publs: arts. in med. jours. & books; spl. interests: Mental Health Pgm. Adminstrn., Forensic Psychiatry; mil: lt.jg (M.C.) USNR 1947-49; res: 708 Elmhurst Cir. Sacramento 95825 ofc: 4747 Engle Road Carmichael 95608.

GALLAGHER, NEIL DENNISON, physician, surgeon; b. Oct. 17, 1923, Scranton, PA; s. Leo Aloysius and Daisy Uzella (Belles) G.; m. Tally Rago, June 21, 1951; 1 dau: Michele, b. 1956; edn: DC, Penn. Coll. of Chiropractic, 1944; MD, Hahnemann Med. Coll. 1949. Career: research res. Gen. Practice 1950-60; genetics research Sonoma State Hosp. 1960-2; med. dir. classified research proj. NASA, Calif. Med. Facility 1963-4; fellowship, postgrad. med. and cons. Presbyterian Hosp., S.F. 1967-9; med. dir. Home Health Care Dept., Sacto. Med. Ctr. 1970-2; staff mem. Solano Co. Hosp. 1972-3; gen. practice 1974-8; med. dir. Physicians Weight Clinic 1978--; lectr. Am. Cancer Soc. 1964-9; cons. Presbyterian Hosp., S.F. 1968-9; awards: plaque of commdn., NASA 1964; Cert. of Excellence in Med. Edn., Am. Med. Assn. 1969; mem: Am. Med. Assn. of Family Practitioners; pres., Vacaville Chpt., Nat. Exchange Club; Am. Soc. of Bariatric Physicians (ASBF); author: med. column in local newspaper; med. dir. classified pgm. for NASA 1963-4; mil: USNR; Methodist; rec: music, magic, numismatics. Res: 119 Anita Ct Vacaville 95688 Ofc: Physicians Weight Clinic, 619 Buck Ave, Ste B, Vacaville 95688

GALLAWAY, ELIZABETH LOUISE, aerospace engineer; b. Apr. 16, 1944, Detroit, Mich.; d. Jack Frank and Elizabeth Helen (Kepko) Paster; div.; edn: BS in aero. engrg., Embry Riddle Univ. 1965; Nat., State Bd. cert. in embalming, L.A. Coll. of Mortuary Sci. 1973; postgrad. engrg. courses, CSU Northridge; FAA pvt. pilot cert. 1975. Career: actress/model Shirley Hamilton Inc., Chgo. 1966-71; reservationist/bkpr. Hertz Corp., Miami and Chgo. 1966-67; flight dispatcher Northwest Orient Airlines, Chgo. O'Hare Fld. 1968-71; lab. tech. LAC/USC Med. Ctr., Los Angeles 1971-73, autopsy asst. 1975; electroencephalograph tech. Electographic Labs., Encino 1976; embalmer/ autopsy asst./ asst. funeral di. Bastian and Perrot Mortuary, Northridge 1978-81; devel. engr., qualification plan coord., MX State IV, Rockwell Int'l Rocketdyne Div., Canoga Park 1982--; honors: recognition for contbns. to successful first flt. test of the Peacekeeper Stage IV on June 17, 1983, Rockwell Int'l.; mem: AIAA, Nat. Assn. Female Execs., Rockwell Int'l Club; rec: flying, fencing, horseback riding. Res: 20711 Vanowen St, 219, Canoga Park 91306 Ofc: Rocketdyne, 6633 Canoga Ave, CB09, Canoga Park 91304

GALVERY, DAVID B., interior designer; b. Dec. 19, 1928, Los Angeles; s. Francis B. and Sarah S. (Saniger) G.; edn: Los Angeles Coll. 1946-48; Chouinard Art Sch. 1948-50; ASID, Am. Soc. of Interior Designers. Career: interior designer, W.J. Sloanes in San Francisco 1952-55 in Beverly Hills 1955-65, with J.H. Biggar, Pasadena 1965-78; owner/ designer David Galvery Interior Design, So. Pasadena 1978--; awards: ASID commdn. 1980-1; Nat. Council for Interior Design Qualifications; mem: ASID (bd. mem. 1980); Pasadena Jr. Philharmonic (Showcase House com. 1981, 82, 84); publs: Designer West Mag.; Republican; Ch. of Relig. Sci. Res: 461 Prospect Circle So. Pasadena 91030 Ofc: POB 8364 San Marino 91108

GAMBLE, THOM LEE, architectural firm principal; b. Jan. 25, 1947, Spokane, Wash.; s. Hubert Arthur and Irene Bernice (Ficker) G.; m. Sandra June Killen (dec. 1979), May 9, 1970; m 2d. Elaine Marie Lucia, Mar. 20, 1982; children: Ryan, b. 1977; Nick, b. 1979; edn: Bach.Arch, Wash. State Univ. 1971; grad. stu. in forestry, 1971-2. Career: owner Niles Hardware & Supply, Fremont 1972; admin. asst. to proj. arch. Terra Calif., Rossmoor, Walnut Creek 1973; proj. admin. The Villages Proj. Terra Calif., San Jose 1976; founder/ prin., design & consulting firm Gamble, Connolly, Amonson, now archtl. firm of Gamble, White, Amonson, vice pres. 1983--; pres. So. Div., Building Indus. Assn. of No. Calif. 1982; mem. bd. dirs. Building Indus. Assn. (Div. bd. 1979-84, Regnl. bd. 1981-84); mem. Calif. Building Ind. Assn. bd. dirs. 1982-3; mem. Calif. Building Indus. Assn., Californians for Housing, Audubon Soc.; Republican; Lutheran; rec: travel, ski, fish, nature photog. Res: 3011 Oakham Dr San Ramon 94583 Ofc: Gamble, White, Amonson, 43551 Mission Blvd, Ste 7, Fremont 94539

GAMBOA, GEORGE CHARLES, educator, oral surgeon; b. Dec. 17, 1923, King City; s. George Angel and Martha Ann (Baker) G.; m. Winona Mae Collins, July 16, 1946; children: Cheryl, b. 1948; Jon, b. 1951; Judith, b. 1953; edn: DDS, Univ. of the Pacific Coll. of Phys. & Surgeons 1946; MS, oral surgery, Univ. Minn. 1953; AB, zoology, USC 1958; EdD, USC 1976. Career: assoc. clinical prof., grad. pgm. Oral Surgery, USC 1954--; assoc. prof., grad. pgm. oral surgery, Loma Linda Univ. 1958--; part-time practice Oral Surgery, San Gabriel; chmn. Dept. of Oral Surgery, Sch. of Dentistry, Loma Linda Univ. 1960-3; mem. exec. com. Profl. Staff Assn., LAC-USC Med. Ctr. 1977-; mem. (v.chmn. Profl. Edn. sub-com.) Calif. Div., Am. Cancer Soc. 1978-; chmn. Safety Svcs. Com., W. San Gabriel chpt. ARC 1981-; honors: Omicron Kappa Upsilon; mem: So. Calif. Soc. of Oral and Maxillofacial Surgeons; So. Calif. Acad of Oral Pathology; Marsh Robinson Acad. of Oral Surgeons; Internat. Assns. of Oral and Maxillofacial Surgeons; Diplomate, Am. Bd. of Oral and Maxillofacial Surgeons; Am. Acad. of Dental Radiology; pres., Alhambra Lions Club, 1968; mil: lt. jg USNR, dental ofcr. 1946-8; Republican; Seventh-day Adventists; rec: golf, water skiing. Res: 1102 Loganrita Ave Arcadia 91006 Ofc: 132 So. Mission Dr San Gabriel 91776

GAMBORG, OLUF LIND, senior research scientist; b. Nov. 9, 1924, Stenderup, Denmark, Canadian res./perm. res. USA; s. Peter Andersen and Anna Marie (Antonsen) G.; m. Gertrude Christensen, July 11, 1953; children: Brian Lind, b. 1955; Cheryl Marie, b. 1958; Linda Joanne, b. 1960; edn: BSc in Agri, w/distinction, Univ. of Alberta 1956 MSc biochem., 1958; PhD biochem., Univ. of Saskatchewan 1962. Career: assoc./sr. research scientist, Nat. Research Council of Canada Lab., Saskatoon 1958-79; sci. research dir. in plant cell biology, in the Founding of the Internat. Plant Research Inst., San Carlos 1979-81; sr. resrch. fellow 1981--; Internat. orgnzr. and instr. High Tech. courses and symposia sponsored by UNESCO for developing countries (Brazil 1978, Peking, China 1981); awards: Gold Medal of the Canadian Soc. of Plant Physiologists 1977; spkr. internat. scientific symposia, confs., and wrkshps.; mem: Am. Soc. Plant Tissue Culture; Internat. Cell Res. Orgn.; UNESCO; Scand. Soc. Plant Physiologists; mng. ed. Plant Cell Reports, Internat. Sci. Journal; author over 130 publs. and booklets; mil: served in Danish Air Force; Lutheran; rec: swim, jog, golf, family hist. Res: 1404 Solana Dr Belmont 94002

GAMELIN, STEVEN MARK, financial analyst; b. Feb. 13, 1945, St. Peter, Minn.; s. Francis Clifford and Ruth Mathilda (Vickner) G.; m. Beth Freeman, Feb. 6, 1976; 1 son: Chad, b. 1969; edn: Univ. of Minn. 1967; Midland Lutheran Coll. 1967-8; Black Hawk Coll. 1968-9; BA, bus. adm./fin., CSU Fullerton 1973; Calif. Gen. Contractors lic. 1982; Calif. Real Estate Brokers Lic. 1978. Career: commercial loan ofcr./ asst. mgr. Crocker Nat. Bank, 1973-8; gen. mgr. Bridgecreek Realty Invest. Corp., Westminster 1978-83; loan mgr. Farmer's Ins. Gp. Federal Credit Union, Los Angeles 1983-1984; mgr. ops. Water and Power Employees Credit Union, Los Angeles 1984--; mem: Nat. Assn. of Realtors; Nat. Assn. of Contractors; Hidden Lakes Investment Club; Kay Pro Users Gp.; mil: USN 1963-7; rec: guitar music, sports, art, woodworking. Res: 1652 Clear Springs Fullerton 92631 Ofc: Water and Power Employees Credit Union, 1053 Sunset Blvd Los Angeles 90012

GANDSEY, LOUIS JOHN, petroleum & chemical engineering consultant; b. May 19, 1921, Greybull, Wyo.; s. John Wellington and Leonora Francis (McLaughlin) G.; m. Mary Louise Aluiso, Nov. 10, 1945; children: Mary, b. 1946; Catherine, b. 1948; John, b. 1953; Michael, b. 1958; Laurie, b. 1960; edn: AA, Compton Jr. Coll. 1941; BS, UC Berkeley 1943; M.Eng., UCLA 1958; Profl. Engr., State of Calif. 1958. Career: var. positions with Richfield then ARCO 1943-69; with ARCO 1969 77: mgr. Supply & transport, Chgo 1969-70; mgr., planning, NY 1970-1; mgr. coord. & supply, Los Angeles 1971-5; mgr. domestic crude, ARCO, 1975-77; v.p. Lunday-Thagard Oil Co., So. Gate 1977-82; cons. Templeton & Los Angeles 1982--; coll. tchr., chemistry, petroleum, petroleum refining; mem: Am. Chemical Soc.; Pacific Energy Assn.; publ: arts. in Petroleum Refiner, World Oil Chemical Processing; mil: pvt. Corps of Engrs., US Army 1946; Republican; Catholic; rec: farming, horses, cattle. Res: Route 1 Box 16A Templeton 93465 Ofc: POB 1519 South Gate 90280

GANTZ, SANFORD PAUL EDWARD, investment real estate and management co. president; b. Sept. 30, 1939, Brklyn.; s. Meyer and Anna (Ochs) G.; m. Marilynn Miller, Aug. 17, 1974; children: Jacqueline, b. 1965, Debra, b. 1967; stepsons: Jack, b. 1962, Jim, b. 1965, Richard, b. 1967; edn: BSEE, highest honors, Pratt Inst. 1962, MS, UCLA 1965; lic. real estate broker, Calif. 1981. Career: engr. Hughes Aircraft, Culver City and TRW, Redondo Bch., 1963-71; real estate sales Forest E. Olson, Inc. 1971-74; apt. house sales firms of Wagner/ Jacobson and H. Bruce Hanes, 1974-75; prin. Ivar/Gantz Co., Inc. (apt. house sales & mgmt.), 1975--; owner/pres. Gantz Investment Properties, Inc., Tarzana 1981--; dir: Ivar/Gantz 1975-, Gantz Inv. Prop. Inc. 1981-; instr. math, physics, engr. LA Jr. Colls. 1971-; honors: Tau Beta Pi, Eta Kappa Nu, Masters & Doctoral fellowships to UCLA; Jewish; rec: basketball, lake power boating, photog. Ofc: Gantz Inv. Prop., 18344 Oxnard St., 2d Fl.. Tarzana

GANZ, JULIAN, JR., retail furniture chain executive; b. Oct. 9, 1929, Los Angeles; s. Julian A. and Betty (Huff) G.; m. Jo Ann Schaaf, June 18, 1951; children: J. Taylor, b. 1953; Whitney H., b. 1956; edn: BA, honors, Stanford Univ. 1951. Career: co- owner/ chief exec. 18 McMahan Furniture Stores, Calif. and Ore.; bd. dirs. The Gap Stores, Inc. (NYSE); awards: co- recipient (with wife, Jo Ann) Pres.'s Medal, Grad. School, City Univ. of NY 1979; mem: Los Angeles Co. Museum of Art (pres. bd. trustees); Museum of Modern Art, NYC (Intl. Council); Friends of Am. Arts at Yale (exec. com.); Nat. Gallery of Art, Wash. DC (Collector's Com.); The Beach Club, Santa Monica; Confrerie des Chevaliers du Tastevin; works: Jo Ann and Julian Ganz, Jr. Collection of 19th Century Am. Art (paintings and sculpture) exhibn. orgnzd. in 1982 by Nat. Gallery of Art, Wash. DC, later touring Amon Carter Mus. (Ft. Worth) and LA County Mus. of Art; Republican; Episcopal; rec: art collection, skiing, fishing. Res: 137 So Rockingham Ave Los Angeles 90049 Ofc: McMahan Furniture Stores, POB 1251 Santa Monica 90406

GARBER, CHESTER STANTON, businessman, lawyer; b. Nov. 28, 1943, Fresno; s. Chester and Virginia Lee (Trimmer) G.; m. Emilia Ting, MD, June 20, 1981; edn: BA, Univ. of San Francisco 1963; MA, 1968; JD, S.F. Law Sch. 1971; mem. Calif. State Bar; lic. Calif. Real Estate Broker; Registered Rep., SEC; Calif. Securities Agt. lic.; Insurance lic.: life, disability; lic. comml. pilot (multi engine and instrument ratings). Career: (past) pres./ CEO: John's Italian Restaurants Inc., Garmoh Investments Co. Inc., Maurtee Investment Co. Inc., Stage Lounges Inc., 418 Geary Corp; currently: pres./ chmn. bd./ CEO: C.S. Garber, Inc.; Garber Petroleum, Inc.; Xanadu Mines, Inc.; Eldorado Mines, Ltd.; Golden Valley Aero, Inc.; asst. treas. of Emilia C. Ting, M.D., Inc. (lic. med. corp.); mem: Calif. State Bar; Aircraft Owners & Pilots Assn.; Nat. Assn. of Real Estate Brokers; Nat. Assn. of Security Dealers; Am. Mgmt. Assn.; Downtown Club, Fresno; nationally published profl. wildlife photg.; mil: capt. Spl. Forces, US Army, silver, bronze stars, DSC, Purple Heart (4); rec: gardening, martial arts, firearms. Ofc: C.S. Garber & Assoc., 83 E Shaw, Ste 250, Fresno 93710

GARBUTT, ALFRED W., III., chiropractor; b. Jan. 24, 1952, Uniontown,PA; s. Alfred W., Jr. and Menichina (Firmani) G.; edn: CSU, 1970-1, 1974-5; D.C., Palmer Coll. of Chiropractic 1978. Career: hd. of Chiropractic Dept. Shaw Health Ctr., Hollywood 1979; co-dir. Chiropractic Health Care Ctr., Beverly Hills 1980-3; adminstrv. advis. and treating Dr. Beverly Hills Chiro. Ctr., Beverly Hills 1981-2; cons. to Olympic Team Doctors for Israel and Kenya; dir. Chiro. and Athletic Enhancement Ctr., Hollywood; cons./dr. top level Am. atheletes & USA Olympic Team; part time faculty, Pepperdine Univ. and New York Coll. of Chiro.; chmn. bd. Sports Related Research, Inc.; awards: John Connolly Meml. Awd., Palmer Coll. of Chiro. 1978; Who's Who in Am. Coll. and Univs. 1978; Outstanding Young Men of Am. 1979; mem: Calif. Info. Bureau (pres. 1977-8); Parker Chiro. Research Found.; Found. for Chiro. Research; Calif. Chiro. Assn.; Acupuncture Soc. of Am.; Nat. Acad. of Research Biochemists; Elks; publs: art. on nutrition, Today's Professional, 1979; resrch: athletic enhancement, TMJ (jaw) funcion, redesign sleep supports; Republican; Scientology; rec: photog., writing, sports, marksmanship, martial arts. Res: Glendale Ofc: Chiropractic and Athletic Enhancement Center, 1980 Hillhurst Ave Los Angeles 90027

GARCIA, RONALD ANTHONY, engineer; b. Feb. 15, 1954, Key West, Fla.; s. Gabriel E. and Helen Margaret (Stickland); edn: Cuesta Comm. Coll. 1970; diploma, San Luis Sr. High 1972; BSc, indsl. engring., CalPoly, SLO 1977; MBA, 1982; Calif. Reg. Engr. in Tng.; Calif. lic. Real Estate Broker; FAA lic. pilot. Career: real estate sales, Pacesetter Realty, San Jose 1978-80; assoc. real estate broker ERA-PTC Realty, San Luis Obispo 1980--; produce and prodn. scheduler Libby, McNeil & Libby, in Sunnyvale 1976; mfg. project engr./supr. Watkins-Johnson Co., San Jose 1977-80; nuclear engr. (civil & mech.) Pullman Power Prods., Avila Beach 1983--; awards: top referral assoc., Electronic Realty Assocs. 1982; Calif. State Scholarship 1972-3; Alpha Phi Mu, (chpt. pres. 1976, 77); mem: Am. Inst. of Indsl. Engrs.; Nat., Calif. Assn. of Realtors; March of Dimes; Muscular Dystrophy Assn.; Grass Roots; rec: flying, investments, child psychology, outdoor sports. Res: 543 Felton Way San Luis Obispo 93401 Ofc: Pullman Power Products, Diablo Canyon Rd Avila Beach 93424

GARDINER, SAMUEL WHITTIER, judge, lawyer; b. Sept. 28, 1902, Larkspur; s. James Allen and Adda Estella (Holtz) G.; m. Susan Fenton, June 26, 1927; m. 2d. Barbara Geddes Rengort, Sept. 11, 1971; children: Diane (Wilkinson), b. 1928; Samuel, Jr., b. 1931; Constance (Birkie), b. 1935; edn: AB, UC Berkeley 1923; JD, 1925; admitted to Calif. State Bar. Career: atty./ partner: Martinelli & Gardiner 1933-49, Gardiner, Riede & Elliot 1949-64; atty. Marin Muni. Water Dist. 1942-64; Superior Court judge 1964-73; ch. Democratic Central Com., Marin Co. 1944-52; del. Dem. Nat. Convs. (1944, 48, 52); cpgn. chmn. for Marin for Pat Brown, Alan Cranston, and J.F. Kennedy campaigns; currently ret., part time law practice; mem: Marvelous Marin (County CofC) pres. 1939; Rotary Club of San Rafael, pres. 1940; Marin Shrine Club, pres. 1938; Democrat 1933-80, Repub. 1980-3; Presbyterian; rec: bridge, fly fishing. Res: 170 La Cuesta San Rafael 94904

GARDNER, JAMES HARKINS, executive; b. July 15, 1943, Evanston, IL; s. James Floyd and Charlotte (Hogan) Gardner; edn: BS, Purdue Univ., 1965; MBA, Harvard Univ., 1968; chil: Lee, b. 1970. Career: vice pres., Geomet, Inc., 1968-78; pres. Risk Management Resources, Inc., San Francisco, 1978--; prof., bus. statistics, No. Virginia Coll., 1968-70. Mem: Commonwealth Club of Calif.; Masonic Lodge; Sigma Nu frat., comdr. 1963-64. Mil: Lt.Cmdr., USPHS, 1968-70. Res: 111 San Pablo Ave., San Francisco 94127; Office: Risk Mgmt. Resources, 500 Sansome, #205, San Francisco 94111.

GARDNER, NORD ARLING, management consultant; b. Aug. 10, 1923, Afton, Wyo.; s. Arling A. and Ruth (Lee) G.; m. Thora Marie Stephen, Mar. 24, 1945; children: Randall Nord; Scott Stephen, Craig Robert, Laurie Lee; edn: BA, Univ. Wyo. 1945; MS, CSU Hayward 1972; MPA, 1975; postgrad. Univ. Chgo., Univ. Mich., UC Berkeley. Career: Commnd. 2d.lt., advanced through grades to lt. col. US Army, 1942-64, ret. 1966, (Army Commendn. medal); personnel analyst Univ. Hosp. UC San Diego 1946-8; coord. manpower devel. UC Berkeley 1968-75; univ. tng. ofcr. San Francisco State Univ. 1975-80, personnel mgr 1976-80; exec. dir. CRDC Maintenance Tng. Corp. (nonprofit), S.F.; pres./dir. Sandor Assocs. Mgmt. Cons., Pleasant Hill; instr. Japanese, psychol., supervisory courses, 1977-8, Advis. Council S.F. Comm. Coll. Dist.; mem: Retired Ofcrs. Assn.; Am. Soc. Tng. and Devel.; No. Calif. Human Rels. Council; Am. Assn. Univ. Adminstrs.; Internat. Personnel Mgrs. Assn.; Coll. and Univ. Personnel Assn. (W. Coast rep.); Internat. Platform Assn.; Am. Legion; clubs: Commonwealth of Calif., UCB Faculty, University (SF); listed nat., internat. biographical ref. books; author: To Gather Stones, 1978; Republican. Res: 2995 Bonnie Ln Pleasant Hill 94523 Ofc: 615 Grant Ave, 4th Floor, San Francisco 94108

GARNER, CHESTER ALEXANDER, botanist, biomedical foundation executive; b. Sept. 25, 1897, Lebanon,Ind.; s. Abner Anderson and Effie Almyra (Alexander) Garner; m. Frances J. Schotthoefer, Sept. 21, 1923; chil: Edmund Gale, b. 1925, Joan (Taylor), b. 1927; edn: BSA, Purdue Univ. 1921, MS,(tchg.fellow)Iowa St. Coll. 1924, postgrad. Univ. of Ill. 1925-6, USC 1928; tchg. cred. Am.Inst.Agri.1928; career: dir. War Gardens, 1918, Anderson, Ind., Purdue Agr.Ext., Ft. Wayne, 1919; tchg. fellow Horticulture, Iowa St. Coll., 1921-22; assoc. horticulturist, US Dept.Agri., Wash., 1922-25; assoc. prof. olericulture, Univ. of Ill. 1925-26; in chg. Agri. Tchg. & Projects, So. Imperial Co., 1927-28; tchr. biol.,agr., Hi Sch., Jr. Coll., Fullerton 1928-32; cons./contractor in agri., 1933--; dir./entomologist Rotenone Chem. Co., 1933-36; exec.cons. Agronomy, Horticulture, Beaco-Canengco Ltd., Montreal; explorer, Am. Colombian Corp., Magdalena River Lands of Loba, 1940; cons./contractor US Corps Engr., Los Angeles, Puerto Rico 1940-43; civilian chief (food-health), w/Adm. Ingram for Coord. InterAm. Affairs, Mil. Region 6, Bahia Brazil 1943-4. awards: Purdue Univ. scholarship to Iowa St. Univ., 1921; Harvard Chair, Inst. Tropical Resrch, Barro, Colorado Is., Panama 1939-40; L.A. CofC awd., devel. fgn. commerce, 1942. Mem: Alpha Gamma Rho frat. (1916-21), Masons 1921-, The Planetary Soc., Alzheimer Soc. publs: Manual of Med. Botany, Botanical Manual of Emollients for Burns & Scalds; mil: Stu. Army Tng. Corps, 1916-21; Republican; Methodist; rec: jungle botanizing, music (vol. musical therapy in hosps.); res: 1007 Camino Magenta, Thousand Oaks 91360; ofc: Harmony Found., POB 1746, Thousand Oaks 91360.

GAROUTTE, SALLY JETER, textile-quilt historian; b. Nov. 9, 1925, Kokomo, Indiana; d. Harry Dee and Myrtle Gladys (Cook) Jeter; m. Bill Garoutte, July 18, 1948; children: Brian, b. 1949; Susanna, b. 1951; David, b. 1954; Katherine, b. 1956; edn: San Diego State Coll. 1943-5; RN, S.D. County Hosp. Sch. of Nursing 1948; UC Berkeley 1948-9; BA, Goddard Coll., Vermont 1974-6. Career: nursing 1948-56; real estate sales 1958-60; served on Marin Co. (Calif.) Human Rights Commn. 1964-68, Mill Valley (Calif.) Planning Commn. 1967-70; founder/ coord. Am. Quilt Study Gp., Mill Valley 1979--; mem: Am. Quilt Study Gp.; Am. Assn. of Textile Chemists and Colorists; Am. Assn. for State and Local History; NOW; East Bay Heritage Quilters; Calif. Hist. Soc.; publs: num. arts on quilts and textile hist. emphasizing No. America 1650-1950; editor/pub. three vols.: Uncoverings, 1980; Uncoverings, 1981; Uncoverings, 1982; Prot. Address: American Quilt Group, 105 Molino Ave Mill Valley 94941

GARRETT, ELDRIDGE DEE, speech pathologist; b. Dec. 8, 1944, Oakland; s. Eldridge Dee, Sr. and Madalyn (Loyde) G.; m. Patty , June 16, 1967; children:

Eddie, b. 1971; Ernie, b. 1973; edn: BA, Pasadena Nazarene Coll. 1967; MA, Univ. of Redlands 1971; Elem. and Sec. Tchg. Cred., Speech Therapy Cred., UofR 1971; Adminstrv. Cred., CSC San Bernardino 1975; cert., Calif. Bd. of Med. Examiners 1976. Career: speech pathologist Redlands Unified Sch. Dist. 1969-76; pres. Garrett Extraction 1971-6; pres. Garrett Extraction Chemical Co. of Redlands, 1971-6; pres. Garrett & Assocs., Speech Pathologists Inc. 1976--; pres. Riverside Hearing and Speech Center 1--; cons. Redlands Unified Sch. Dist., Univ. of Redlands Speech Therapy Dept., Point Loma Nazarene Coll. Speech Dept.; mem: Point Loma Coll. Alumni Bd.; Calif. Speech and Hearing Assn.; Calif. Assn. of Speech Pathologists in Pvt. Practice; Riverside CofC; Corona Norco CofC; Calif. Assn. of Health Facilities; Republican; Nazarene; rec: back packing, fishing, tennis. Res: 424 Wilbar Circle Redlands 92373 Ofc: Riverside Hearing and Speech Center, 3739 Arlington Riverside 92506

GARSIDE, BEN CHARLES III, securities investment advisor; b. May 25, 1925, Denver, Colo.; s. Ben Charles Jr. and Eloise Nadene (Eisele) G.; m. Charlyn Louise Pyles, Sept. 4, 1949; children: Pamela, b. 1953; Deborah, b. 1956; Victoria, b. 1957; Cynthia, b. 1958; edn: BA, Stanford Univ. 1949; AA, Control Data Inst. 1970; investment advisor, Sec. & Exch. Com. 1970. Career: 2nd Lt., Aerial Navigator, Army Air Corps., Europe 1943-5; dist. staff asst. Pacific Telephone, San Rafael 1949-51; 1st Lt., Aerial Navigator, USAF, Korea 1951-3; acct. exec. Den Whitter & Co., Santa Ana 1954-70; ed./pub. The Garside Forecast, Tustin 1970--; sr. partner Garside & Co., (invest. mgmt.), Tustin 1975--; sr. v.p./ dir. Market Timing and Research, (var. annuity timing), Huntington Beach 1978--; guest lectr. Cal. State Fullerton, West Coast Univ., Golden West Coll., and Santa Barbara City Coll.; num. seminars and TV appearances related to securities; awards: Stock Market Timer of Yr., Timer Digest, Ft. Lauderdale, Fla. 1982; Top 2 percent in Po, NY, NY 1981-4; mem: Tech. Securities Analysts Assn.; Internat. Assn. of Fin. Planners; mil: 2nd Lt., Navigator, Army Air Corps. 1943-45; 1st Lt., Navigator, USAF 1951-3; distng. flying cross, Air Medal w/ 3 Oak Leaf Clusters; Republican; Protestant; rec: golf, swimming, trout fishing. Res: 5200 Irvine Blvd, No. 370, Irvine 92714 Ofc: Garside & Co., 17772 Irvine Blvd, Ste 102, Tustin 92680

GARTHE, DAVID JACK, lawyer; b. July 27, 1946, Minneapolis, Minn.; s. John Joseph and Edith Lee (Dickerson) G.; m. Mary Quigley, Mar. 4, 1972; 1 son: Gregory, b. 1977; edn: UC, Davis 1968; JD, 1971. Career: atty. Brunson, Brunson & McKinnon, San Francisco 1972-4; atty. Boornazian, Jensen & Garthe, Oakland 1974--; dir. Equitec Mutual Fund 1980-2; arbitrator, Am. Arbitration Assn. 1978-82; honors: law review, The Order of The Coif, Nat. Legal Honor Soc. 1973-; mem: Order of the Coif; Am. Bar Assn.; Alameda Co. Bar Assn.; Am. Arbitration Assn.; Sigma Alpha Epsilon, frat.; author: The Investigation of Robbery as part of The Prevention and Control of Robbery, Vol. IV, pub. The Center on Admin. of Criminal Justice, UC Davis 1973; mil: S/ Sgt. USAR 1968-74; Democrat; Catholic; rec: athletics. Res: 3054 Holyrood Dr Oakland 94611 Ofc; Boornazian, Jensen & Garthe, 1504 Franklin St Oakland 94612

GARVIN, BURDETTE MERL, JR., business appraiser; b. July 7, 1943, Curtisville, Penn.; s. Burdette M. Sr. and Florence E. (Lewetag) G.; children: Todd R., b. 1966; Richard E., b. 1968; edn: AS, Chaffey Coll. 1971; cert. bus. appraiser, Inst. of Bus. Appraisers; Calif. real estate broker 1968. Career: business opportunity broker 1964--; owner Garvin Appraisals, San Barnardino; expert witness on bus. goodwill- court witness; spkr. to profls.; bus. cons.; honors: Lambda Chi Frat. 1970; Internat. Bus. Brokerage Assn. 1979; mem: Inst. of Bus. Appraisers, Inc.; Kiwanis; Elks, Aircraft Owners Assn.; Pilots Assn.; ed./ pub. Expert Corner, newletter to attys.; Republican; Protestant; rec: pilot. Res: 27525 Crestforest Dr, Cedar Pine Park); mail: POB 6325, San Bernardino 92412; Ofc: Garvin Appraisals, 975 No. D Street San Bernardino 92410

GARY, JAMES RESER, realtor; b. Sept. 18, 1941, Dallas, TX; s.u James Welch and Mary Else (Reser) G.; m. Linda BS, in BA, Univ. of Denver 1963; realtor, Nat. Assn. Real Estate 1977. Career: salesman Proctor and Gamble Co., Los Angeles 1963; stock broker Paine Webber Jackson & Curtis, Beverly Hills 1964-70; real estate salesman Gribin Von Dyl, Woodland Hills 1971-3; v.p. Day Realty, Woodland Hills 1973-8; pres. James R. Gary & Co., Ltd., Woodland Hills 1978--; chmn. bd. David Gibson Escrow Co., Woodland Hills 1983; chmn. bd. Glanfinnan Music, Ltd. 1984; mgr. Gleann Mor Pipes & Drums; Century City Lions Club (pres. 1973); Santa Monica JAYCEES: Woodland Hills CofC; State Senator ED Davis Com. (fin. chmn. 1980, 84-); exec. producer: Scottish folk music record; mil: 1st Lt., US Army, Armor 1966-9; Republican; Presbyterian; rec: pipe music, fishing. Res: Woodland Hills Ofc: James R. Gary & Co., Ltd., 21747 Erwin St Woodland Hills 91367

GASKINS, FRANCIS EARLE, III, company executive; b. Oct. 2, 1943, Miami, Fla.; s. Francis Earle, Jr. and Harriet Elizabeth (Thomsen) G.; m. Anne Field, Mar. 18, 1972; 1 son: Courtney, b. 1975; edn: AB, Princeton Univ. 1965; MBA, Harvard Bus. Sch. 1967. Career: founder/ chmn. Videotape Prods. Co., Santa Monica 1972-79; founder/ pres. Disc/3 Co., Santa Monica 1976-79; founder/ pres. Gaskins & Co., Santa Monica 1969-81; founder/ chmn./ CEO American Training Internat., Los Angeles 1981--; bd. dirs. Kurs Marlar & Sauage; mem: ADAPSO (bd. Micro Computer Sect.); Princeton Club; Harvard Bus. Sch. Assn.; Republican; Protestant; rec: wind surfinng, running. Res: 203 24th St Santa Monica 90402 Ofc: American Training International, 12638 Beatrice St Los Angeles 90066

GASIVODA, GUIDO, real estate investments, property management executive; b. June 4, 1913, NYC, NY; s. Paul and Teresa (Cellini) G.; m. Marie Leslie Meskimen, Dec. 19, 1935; 1 dau: Karen Lee Finney, b. 1945; lic., Calif. Real Estate Bd. 1952. Career: automotive sales 1929-37; self employed, automotive garage 1937-41; supvr. electrical maintenance, Moore Drydock Co. 1941-3; electical inspector US Maritime Com. 1943-5; self employed retail bus. 1945-53, real estate investment and mgmt., 1953--, pres. G. Gasivoda & Assoc., Inc.; v.p. Redwood Mobile Estates, Inc.; mng. partner Haven Assoc., Charter Assoc., Bel Moon Co., County Assoc.; owner/ mgr. svl. real estate holdings in Calif.; awards: Distng. Businessman Awd., 1983; San Mateo Grand Jury 1971; Belmont CofC; mem: St. Francis Kiwanis Club, S.F. (pres. 1953); Mounted Patrol of San Mateo Co.; Harbor Devel. Assn. (pres. 1979); San Mateo Co. Horsemen Assn.; Republican (Presdtl. Task Force); rec: Western horsemanship, boating, fishing. Res: 2316 Warner Range Menlo Park 94025 Ofc: G. Gasivoda & Assoc., Inc., 100 Harbor Blvd Belmont 94002

GATES, FRANCIS, legal information services consultant, lawyer; b. Apr. 28, 1927, Sacramento; s. Earl E. and Adele (Lavallee) G. (both parents 2d gen. Californians b. Placer Co.); div.; 1 son, David W., b. 1953; edn: AB, UC Berkeley 1952; BLS (MLS certified now), 1954; JD, San Francisco Law Sch. 1963; career: reference librarian Grad. Social Sci. Lib. UCB, 1954-60; law librarian Calif. Continuing Edn. of the Bar (CEB), 1960-63; law librn. and Research Atty, CEB, 1963-70; assoc law librn./ asst. prof. USC Law Center, 1970-72, law librn./asst. prof. 1972-73, law librn./prof. 1973-75; law librn./ prof. of law Columbia Univ. Law Sch., NYC 1975-81; legal information svcs. cons., librn., lawyer, San Francisco 1981--. Exec. bd. Am. Assn. of Law Libraries (AALL), 1975-77, 79-82; pres. AALL 1980-81; AALL liason to Assn. of Legal Adminstrs. 1983-, v. ch. Libraries Com., facil. & tech. div., Sect. on Law Office Mgt., Am. Bar Assn. 1983-; Referee State Bar Court, State Bar of Calif. 1983-; honors: Phi Beta Kappa 1952; Coif (fac., USC 1973); mem: State Bar of Calif.; AALL, Spl. Libraries Assn., Am. Bar Assn., San Francisco Bar Assn., W. Pac., No. Calif., So. Calif. chpts, AALL; publs: contbg. author: The Private Law Library In The High-Tech Era (Practising Law Inst., 1983); Calif. Law Office Handbook, Calif. Cont. Edn. of the Bar; other profl. publs.; mil: sgt. USAF 1945-8; christian; rec: gardening, wine tasting, cooking. Ofc: legal information services consultant, atty. at law, POB 12303, San Francisco 94112

GAVER, KENNETH DARREL, psychiatrist- hospital medical director; b. Jan. 12, 1925, Santa Barbara; s. Morris Fred and Nina Annis (McEwen) G.; m. 2d. Dona Averill, Aug. 6, 1969; children: Linda, b. 1952; Paul, b. 1953; Jananne, b. 1956; edn: BA, UC, Berkeley 1946; MD, Univ. of Tenn. Coll. of Med. 1948. Career: rotating internship, US Naval Hosp., Oakland 1949-50; psychiatric res. tng, US Naval Hosp., Nat. Naval Med. Ctr., Bethseda, Md. 1952, US Naval Hosp., San Diego 1952-3; Ore. State Hosp., Salem, Ore. 1953-4; Ind. Univ. Med. Ctr. 1955-6; dir. of edn. and research and electroencephalographer, Ore. State Hosp. 1955-8; asst. prof. of psychiatry Univ. Ore. Med. Sch., Portland 1958-9; pvt. med. practice- psychiatry, neurology and electroenceph., Salem, Ore. 1959-65; Mental Health Div., State of Ore., Salem Ore. 1965-71; asst. adminstr. 1965-6; adminstr. 1966-71; Ohio Dept. Mental Health and Mental Retardation, Columbus, Ohio 1971-4; dir. designee 1971-2; dir. 1972-4; commnr. Texas Dept. of Mental Health and Mental Retardation, Austin, Tx. 1974-8; Health and Human Svcs. Sys. Cons., Austin, Tx. 1978; med. dir. Del Amo Hosp., Torrance 1978--; Diplomate in Psychiat., Am. Boars Psychiat. & Neurology 1957; cons., advisor num. state bds. and nat. orgns.; pres. Nat. Assn. of State Mental Health Pgm. Dirs. 1973-5; councillor Accreditation Council for Psychiat. Facilities, Jt. Commn. on Accred. of Hosps. 1974; liaison mem. nat. Adv. Mental Health Council, HEW 1973-6; mem. Commn. on Mental Illness and Human Svcs., So. Regl. Edn. Bd. 1975-8; mem. Task Force on Orgn., President's Commn. on Mental Health 1977-8; chmn. Standards Com., Nat. Assn. of Pvt. Psychiat. Hosps. (trustee 1983-) 1980; v.p. Whisper, Inc., cons. firm, Austin, Tx.; extensive legislative testimony: Ore., Ohio, Tex., US House of Reps. and US Senate; num. profl. publs.; mem: Ore. Med. Assn.; AMA, Marion- Polk Co. Med. Soc.; Am. Psychiat. Assn.; Ohio Pschiat. Assn.; Texas Dist. Br., Am. Psychiat. Assn.; No. Pacific Soc. of Neurol. and Psychiat.; AAAS, Travis Co. Med. Soc.; Tex. Med. Assn.; Am. Assn. on Mental Deficiency; So. Calif. Psychiat. Soc.; South Bay Psychiat. Soc.; mil: Lt., MC USNR. Res: 1520 Paseo del Mar Palos Verdes Estates 90274 Ofc: Del Amo Hosp., 23700 Camino del Sol Torrance 90505

GAVIRA, HORACIO EDWARD, electrical engineer; b. Aug. 1, 1926, Mexico City, nat. 1963; s. Miguel and Luz Maria (Mendez) G.; m. Brunhilde Klement, May 28, 1955; children: David, b. 1957; Helga, b. 1961; edn: diploma, (ESIME), Coll. of Mech. and Electrical Engring., Mexico City 1960; MSEE, CSU, L.A. 1978; Reg. Profl. Engr. State Calif. 1983. Career: design analyst Magnetic Research Corp., Hawthorne 1956-9; elec. engr. Inet-Sprague div. Teledyne Inc., Gardena 1959-64; mem. tech. staff TRW Sys., Inc., Redondo Bch. 1964-70; sr. elec. engr./supvr. Static Power, Inc., Newport Bch. 1970-6; proj. engr. Teledyne Inet, Torrance 1976-9; work package mgr. TRW Space and Tech. Gp., Redondo Bch. 1979--; honors: scholarship award, 1953, Indus. Electrica de Mexico (subs. Westinghouse); W.C. Miller Literary Award for best art. (coauthor w/wife) 1974, Plus Ultra mag., The Azteca Numismatic Soc., L.A.; mem: senior mem. IEEE; So. Calif. Meter Assn.; COY (Career Opps. for Youth, TRW spons. outreach pgm. for minority youth; past dir. radio pgm. in Spanish to reach families in the barrio); interpreter mem. Flying Samaritans, South Bay chpt.; mem. Toastmasters TRW Club 2189 (1st, Humorous Speech Contest 1968); pres. TRW Spanish Club (tchr. Sp. lang./culture)Patentee: Voltage Level Detector, pat. pend.: Failsafe Multiple Transformer Circuit Configuration; Republican; Catholic. Res: 11350 Walcroft St Lakewood 90715 Ofc: TRW STG, M2/2362, One Space Park Redondo Beach 90278

GAVLICK, STEPHEN GEORGE, certified public accountant; b. May 24, 1946, Passaic, NJ; s. Stephen and Martha (Zenda) G.; m. Linda Gavlick, May 1, 1971; children: Scott, b. 1974; Matthew, b. 1976; Meredith, b. 1978; edn: BS, Wilkes Coll. 1968; additional major, Rutgers Univ. 1973; CPA, State Bd. of Accountancy 1976. Career: fin. analyst Blue Cross 1969-73; staff acctnt. Sunnabend & Fink, CPAs 1973-5; staff acctnt. Asinow Ramin & Co. 1975-7; partner Asinow Ramin & Co. 1977-9; partner Ramin Gavlick & Co. 1979--; mem: Am. Inst. of CPAs; Calif. Soc. of CPAs; Knights of Columbus; Cub Scout of Am.; YMCA Indian Guides; Catholic; rec: Puaie collecting. Res: 6093 Ronald Cr Cypress 90630 Ofc: 800 So Brookhurst St, Ste 2B, Anaheim 92804

GAYLORD, ROBERTA IRENE, speech pathologist; b. Jan 18, 1922, Detroit, Mi; d. Lloyd Rutherford and H. Irene (Slagel) Worden; mother, Irene Worden, author, received Internatl. Mark Twain award for book 'Our Falling Image'; MA edn., Calif. State Univ., San Jose, 1973; BA CSUSJ, 1969; m. Richard Cody Marsh, July 5, 1941; m. 2d., Harold Bernard Gaylord, Apr. 5, 1959; children: Sandra, b. 1944. Career: producer, writer commentator, 'Star's Stairway Radio Show,' KWKW, Pasadena, 1949-54; co-owner, Gaylord Constrn. Co., West Covina, 1963-67; language, speech and hearing spec., Moreland Sch. Dist., Campbell, 1969-82; consultant 1982--; also v.p. Gaylord Constrn. Co., 1963-67; reviewed stage productions and interviewed celebrities on Star's Stairway Show 1949-54. Recipient: Voice of Democracy Award, Veterans of Foreign Wars, 1973-74. Mem: Calif. Speech-Language-Hearing Assn., 1969, nominating comm., 1976; Santa Clara Co. Speech-Hearing Assn., chmn. Hosp. comm. 1974, secty. 1975, legislator chmn 1976; Life mem. CTA; Sigma Alpha Eta, 1967; Amer. Fedn. TV Radio Artists, 1949; Pi Lambda Theta 1982; Internatl. Platform Assn., 1982, People to People Internatl., 1979. Author: TORP Program, Research in Speech Pathology, 1978-79. Republican. Rec.: travel, dancing, bridge. Res.: 3312 Sudbury Rd., PO Box 1067 Cameron Park, 95682.

GAYMAN, PATRICIA GYNETH H., chiropractor; b. Aug. 16, 1938, San Pedro; d. Norman Alan and Olive Delone (Jensen) Smith; m. Merrill Gayman, Mar. 29, 1969; children: Cheryl, b. 1954; Robert, b. 1956; Karla, b. 1956; Kym, b. 1957; Leland, b. 1958; Deirdre, b. 1960; Stacy, b. 1962; edn: Monterey Peninsula Coll. 1958-9; DC, Palmer Coll. of Chiropractic 1964; Shasta Coll. 1971-3; DC, Calif. State Bd. of Chiropractic Examiners 1964. Career: chiropractic practice, Monterey Peninsula 1964-8; assoc. Dr. G.E. Anderson, D.C., Hayward 1968-9; assoc. Dr. Neal Swanson, D.C., Redding 1974-9; Gayman Chiropractic Ofc., Redding 1979--; Holistic Living Edn. classes 1979-83; Stress Reduction and Imagery classes 1980-3; guest lectr. Civic orgns. & TV and radio appearances; m: Sigma Phi Chi Sor. (pres. 1962); Women of Chiropractic Profl. Soc.; Regents Pacific States Chiropractic Coll.; Family Planning, Inc.; Quota Club of Redding; Acad. Parapsychology and Medicine; Metaphysical Exploration Ctr.; Democrat; Ch. of Relig. Sci.; rec: cont. chiro. edn., metaphysical studies. Res: 72 Churn Creek Rd Redding 96002 Ofc: Gayman Chiropractic Ofc., 1065 W Cypress Ave Redding 96001

GAZZERA, STEPHEN, JR., lawyer; b. July16, 1928, San Francisco, CA; s. Steve and Mary (Fresia) Gazzera; BA, Univ. Santa Clara; JD, Univ. Santa Clara, 1952; m. Peggy Fowler, July 26, 1959; children: Stephen, III, b. 1960; Michael Jeffrey, b. 1961; Nicole Joie, b. 1963. Career: partner, Law Office of Gazzera & Antonioli, 1954--; also mem., multi Bar Assn. Comms. Commencing on date of inception of practice through approximately 1975. Recipient: Outstanding graduate of Univ. of Santa Clara class of 1952; honoree of the William Paca Lodge of the Sons of Italy. Mem.: Rotary Club; Kiwanis Club; Elks Club; Los Altos Golf & Country Club; Sunnyview Family Club; William Paca Lodge; Italian Mens Club. Mil.: lst Lt., Army Artillery, 1952-53; Commendation Medal, Asiatic Theater Ribbons (Korean war service). Republican, Repub. Party rep. Catholic. Rec.: golf, hunting, fishing. Res.: 1225 Magdalena Ct., Los Altos 94022; Office: Gazzera & Antonioli, 1134 W. El Camino Real, Mountain View 94040.

GBADEBO, MICHAEL ADETOKUNBOH, electrical engineer; b. Oct. 3, 1953, Lagos, Nigeria, nat. 1982; s. Samuel Adewusi and Dorothy Adekunbi (Pacheco) F.; m. Julia Gbadebo, Aug. 2, 1980; children: Yinka, b. 1981; edn: BSEE, San Jose State Univ. 1980; profl. engr. (P.E.), State of Calif. 1983. Career: asst. engr. Underwriters labs. 1980-1; assoc. proj. engr. 1981-2; safety engr. Mohawk Data Scis. 1982-3; sr. standards engr. Molecular Computer 1983--; cons., pres. Rockford Engring. Svcs. 1983--; mem: U.S. Tech. Adv. Gp. (USTC-74) WG6 1983--; Nat. Soc. of Profl. Engrs.; IEEE, Computer and Power Soc.; Episcopalian; rec: ping- pong, travel, reading. Res: 1370 Crailford Court San Jose 95121

GEE, HENRY W., real estate broker, investment consultant; b. Nov. 26, 1922; m. Eudora Ma, Mar. 16, 1952; chidren: Nancy Ann, b. 1953; Faline J., b. 1958; Cindy D., b. 1959; edn: Western Bus. Coll., Albuquerque, NM; LaSalle Ext. Univ., Chgo., Ill. 1958; LLB, Am. Sch. of Law, Chgo. 1957; Univ. of New Mexico, Albuquerque 1960-3; MAI I., Univ. of Okla. 1967; MAI II., USC 1968; UC Berkeley 1972; grad. Realtor's Inst. 1975. Career: owner/ mgr. real estate ofc. Albuquerque, NM 1960-9; owner/ mgr. Gee Realty & Inv. Co., Mtn. View 1970--; dir.: Mtn. View Community Svc. 1974-6; Mtn. View CofC 1976-81; Downtown Bus. Assn., Mtn. View; Calif. Assn. of Realtors 1979, 80; Mtn. View Chpt. United Way; Mtn. Bd. of Realtors; mem: Mtn. View Bd. of Realtors (pres. 1980); San Jose Bd. of Realtors; Nat. Assn. of Realtors; Mtn. View CofC; Mtn. View Central Bus. Assn.; Chinese Am. Citizens Alliance (pres. Albuquerque Lodge 1961-2; pres. Peninsula Lodge 1971-2); Stanford Area Chinese Club; Mtn. View Kiwanis Club; rec: photog., bowling. Res: 891 Cascade Dr Sunnyvale 94087 Ofc: Gee Realty & Investment Co., 786 W Dana St Mountain View 94041

GEE, NANCY ANN, lawyer; b. June 30, 1953, Albuquerque, NM; d. Henry W. and Eudora L. (Ma) G.; edn: BS, UC Davis 1975; JD, Univ. of Santa Clara 1978. Career: lab. asst. NASA Ames Research Ctr.; atty. assoc. William K. Wilburn, a profl. corp.; currently, atty. at law, sely employed, Mountain View; honors: Calif. State Scholar; mem: Chinese American Citizens Alliance (pres. Peninsula Lodge 1980, 81); Chinese Am. Citizens Alliance, Grand Lodge (spl. asst. to the Grand Pres. on Women Affairs, 1981; 1st woman elected as a Grand exec. 1983); Santa Clara Co. Bar Assn.; Soroptimist Internat.; rec: photog., music, stained glass. Res: 891 Cascade Dr Sunnyvale 94087 Ofc: Nancy Ann Gee, atty. at law, 682 W Dana St Mountain View 94041

GEE, VIRGINIA CATHERINE, recruitment administrator; b. May 19, 1941, San Francisco; d. Chew Wing and Sue (Jeong) Hom; m. Herbert H. Gee, May 12, 1962; 1 son: Christopher Lawrence, b. 1963; edn: AS, San Francisco City Coll. 1959; BS, Univ. of San Francisco 1981. Career: supr. Bus. Ofc. Pacific Tel. Co., S.F. 1959-63, Public Office mgr. 1963-66, mgmt. instr. 1966-68, Urban Affairs rep. 1968-70, personnel staff mgr. 1970-74; recruitment adminstr. Stanford University, Stanford 1974--; Gov. Brown apptd. Appeal Hearing Ofcr./ commnr. Calif. Apprenticeship Council, 1974-, Gov. Deukmejian apptd. 1983-, chair 1984-; commnr. Federal Com. on Apprenticeship 1975-84; Cert. Mediator, Nat. Ctr. for Collaborative Planning Public Service Apptments; Mayor Feinstein apptd. v.p. San Francisco Pvt. Indus. 1980-82 and dir. S.F. Conservation Corp. 1984-; cons. Asian Art Mus. of S.F.; honors: Hon. Citizen of Louisville, Ky.; recogn., Stanford Fed. Credit Union, Chinese Am. Inst. of Engrs. (SF), TIDE Proj.-Calif. Dept. Edn., YWCA Central Hqtrs (SF); mem. Commonwealth Club of SF, Nat. Soc. for Fundraising Execs., Am. Soc. for Pers. Admin., No. Calif. Human Resources Council, Am. Soc. for Tng. & Devel., Northeast Medical Services (bd. vp), SF Squash Club, UC Alumni Assn. (life), Stanford Univ. Alumni Assn. (life), Museum Soc., Soc. for Asian Art, Calif. Comm. Coll. Placement Assn. (v.p.), Bay Area Profl. Womens Network (bd.), Chinese Am. Citizens Alliance (SF, bd.), YWCA (bd., treas.), Asian Pacific Personnel Assn. (pres.); Republican; Catholic; rec: model ship building. Res: 1422 Clay St San Francisco 94109 Ofc: Stanford Univ. Old Pavilion, Stanford 94305

GEIGER, DAVID CLAYTON, university executive; b. May 26, 1935, Mayo, Fla.; s. David Clayton Jr. and Shelley (Pridgeon) G.; m. Helen Womack, Jan. 4, 1959; children: Mark, b. 1960; Mike, b. 1961; edn: diploma, Portland Electronic Coll. 1962; energy auditor, Calif. State Energy Com. 1981. Career: supvr. Litton Computer Corp., Colorado Springs, Colo. 1964-9; tech. II press opr. Hewelett/ Packard, Colo. Spgs., Colo. 1969-72; upholsterer, Freightliner Corp., Portland, Ore. 1972-4; owner/ mgr. Artic Circle, Portland 1974-8; owner/ mgr. Dave's Restaurant, Portland 1978-80; mgr. ops. Pepperdine Univ., Malibu 1980--; mex; The Assn. of Physical Plant Adminstrs. of Univ. and Colls. 1981-; Republican; Christian; rec: gem stones, scuba. Res: 1331 Morrow Circle Thousand Oaks 91360 Ofc: Pepperdine Univ., 24255 Pacific Coast Hwy. Malibu 90265

GEISE, HARRY FREMONT, meteorologist, philanthropist; b. Jan. 8, 1920, Oak Park, Ill.; s. Harry and Rosalind (Muser) G.; children: Marian Apgar, b. 1955; Gloria Peterson, b. 1943; triplets: Barry, Gary, Harry, b. 1976; edn: Univ. of Chgo. 1938-9; Meteorologist Svc. Sch., Lakehurst, NJ 1943-4. Career: pvt. weather svc., Chgo. 1937--; chief meteorologist Kingsbury Ord., 1943; meteorol. radio sta. WLS and Prarie Farmer newspaper 1941, 42, 46; assoc. Dr. Irving P. Krick, meteorol. cons. 1947-9; media dir., dir. Pac. div. 1955-59; Army Air Corps. research, developed new temperature forecasting technique, Calif. Inst. of Tech. and Am. Inst. Aerological Research 1948-9; cond. weather and travel shows: WBKB- TV, Chgo,; radio sta. WOPA, Oak Park, Ill., 1950-1; pvt. weather svc. 1954; staff meteorol., San Jose Mercury and News: radio KSJO, KNTV, San Jose; KHUB, Watsonville; KGO-TV, S.F.; cond. The Weather and You' series, Columbia Pac. radio network 1956-8; Panorama Pac. Weather Show, KNXT- TV, CBS, L.A. 1957-8; prod. over 70 daily radio pgms. in U.S. 1959; est. WEATHER Center for CBS, NY (demonstrated forecasts 2 yrs. in advance), WCBS-TV 1966-7; pvt. weather svc., incl. commercial accts. and radio sta. 1962-81; Nat. Defense Exec. Reservist 1968-75; instr. meteorol.: Santa Rosa Jr. Coll. 1964-6; Sonoma State Coll. 1967-8; issued first week in advance forecasts to pub.; recognized relationship between specmfied solar emissions and maj. changes in earth weather pattern 1956; initiated thunderstorm warning sys. using radio static known as Sferics (1st discovered in 1936), which became model for US Ord. plants 1942; Calif. 1st tchg. cred. based on outstanding eminence in meteorol. 1964;a discovered a relationship between a particular weather type and rash type tornado outbreaks in Midwest, US 1965; origin. transatlantic weather radio pgm. from Geneva to London to Calif. to Paris to S.F., Dec. 1965-77. Author: USA: Voice of America 1968; svl. TV films, arts. publ. in newspapers, mags., trade and progl. journals, num. radio and TV stations.; spkr. environmental problms.: Rotaray; CofC; AAUW; Commonwealth Club of Calif.; CBS Stations; mem: Am. Meteorol. Soc.; Foreign Royal Meteorological Soc.;mil: Aerologist, USMC, 1943-5, WWII; rec: world travel, writing, reading. Res: 4100 Folsom, 3D, Sacramento 95819 and 566 Rainbow Dr Napa 94558

GEISELMAN, PAULA J., physiological psychologist; b. June 30, 1944, Ironton, Ohio; d. Paul and Rosemary (Dawson) Parsley; m. Dr. R. Edward Geiselman, Mar. 20, 1976; edn: AB, high honor, Ohio Univ. 1971; MS, 1976; C.Phil., UCLA 1982; PhD, 1983. Career: instr. Ohio Univ., Athens, Ohio 1974-6; resrch. asst., tchg. asst., UCLA 1977-82, tchg. fellow 1982-3, staff resrch assoc. 1983, vis. asst. prof. UCLA, 1983--; honors: the UCLA Medal; hon. life mem. and Outstanding Grad. Student, UCLA Alumni Assn.; Grad. Woman of the Year, Assn. of Academic Women; Sigma Xi; Chancellor's Banner Marshall for UCLA Commencement (1983); NIMH fellowships 1977-81; mem: Soc. for Neurosci., AAAS, Women in Neurosci., Assn. of Academic Women, Western Psychol. Assn., (hon.) British Brain Resrch Assn., (hon.) European Brain and Behavior Soc.; publs: num. sci. jour. arts., papers; rec: opera, ballet, museums. Res: 2450 E. Del Mar Blvd, 7, Pasadena 91107 Ofc: Dept. of Psychology, Franz Hall, UCLA, 405 Hilgard Ave Los Angeles 90024

GEISEN, WALTER MARTIN, engineer; b. Apr. 28, 1928, Elmwood Place, Ohio; s. George William Sr. and Charlotte Ann (Rogers) G.; m. June Koss, June 19, 1948; children: Nancy, b. 1949; Eric, b. 1951; Jeffrey, b. 1955; Timothy, b. 1957; edn: LLB, Williams Coll. 1965; reg. profl. engr. Calif. and Canada 1977. Career: with General Electric Co. 1953--; engring. supvr., Evandale, Ohio, 1953-8; field engring. supvr., L.A. 1958-63; mgr. svc. shops sales, Evandale, OH 1963-5; proj. engr., Edward AFB 1965-7; design, drafting mgr., Edwards AFB 1967-70; pgm. mgr., Mojave 1970-80; mgr.- mfg. engring. 1980-2; Honorable Order of Kentucky Colonels 1964; mem: Soc. of Mfg. Engrs.; Soc. of Flight Test Engrs.; Antelope Valley Aero Museum (founder/ dir. 1968-72; pres. 1972-5); No. L.A. Co. Planning Council; Death Valley 49ers, Inc.; mil: Chief Warrant Ofcr., USAR 1949-60; Republican, Central Comm., Ohio 1954-8; Chirstian; rec: flying, hunting, community related activities. Res: 44526 Lowtree Ave Lancaster 93534 Ofc: General Electric Co., POB 700 Mojave 93501

GELMAN, STEVE, editor; b. Mar. 15, 1934, NY, NY; as. Abraham and Sydelle (Korman) G.; m. Rita Golden, Dec. 11, 1960; chidren: Mitchell, b. 1962; Jan, b. 1963; edn: BA, Brooklyn Coll. 1955; MS, Columbia Univ. Grad. Sch. of Journalism 1957. Career: mng. ed. Sport Magazine; art. ed. Life Mag.; cons. ed. New West Mag., Look Mag., TV Guide Mag., Sport Mag., Time Inc.; west coast ed. Viking- Penguin Publ. Co.; pres. Mag. Sports Writers Assn. of Am. 1962; author: 14 pub. books; mil: US Army. Ofc: TV Guide, 9000 Sunset Blvd. Los Angeles 90069

GENCO, JOHN FRANCIS, sales consultant; b. Apr. 2, 1919, Brooklyn, NY; s. Stefano Luke and Mary (Onorato) G.; m. Mildred Ruby Fries (dec.), June 1, 1942; children: Joanna Phillips, b. 1944; Susan Perry, b. 1945; Mary Jane, b. 1949; Calif. Sch. of Ins. 1960; sales tng. conf. 1962; career recogn. conf. 1962; IDS- R&R, Estate Protection Course in Adv. Fin. Planning 1978. Career: with Investors Diversified Svcs., Inc./ IDS Life Ins. Co., Fresno 1974--; salesman 1959-63; dist. mgr. 1963-73; reg. rep. 1974-84; cons. for new reps., IDS 1975-84; awards: Man of the Year 1963; Pres.'s Club bd. dirs. (Top 20 in Nat.) 1963, 66; IDS Millionaire 1963-84; IDS Quality Award & Outstanding Leadership in Sales 1977; mem: Life Underwriters Tng. Council (LUTC) 1972; IDS Diamond Club 1963; Eagles Lodge, Fresno; Dante Club, Fresno; constructed and flew first gas engine powered model airplane in Fresno 1935; first radio controlled model airplane in Fresno 1937; mil: Cpl., US Army/ Air Force 1943-6, Asia-Pacific War Zone; Republican; Catholic; rec: golf, wood working, classic automobiles. Res: 516 W Swift Ave Clovis 93612 Ofc: IDS, America Express, 5528 No Palm, Ste 111, Fresno 93704

GENERAL, JOHN ARTHUR, defense electronics executive; b. July 26, 1943, Dunfermline, Scotland; s. Leonard Arthur and Margaret Cullen (Malpas) G.; m. Susan Dewald, Dec. 24, 1964; children: Sean, b. 1965; Matthew, b. 1970; edn: Columbia Univ. 1960; BS, w/ distn., US Naval Acad. 1965; MS, OPS analysis, Navy Postgrad. Sch. 1972; naval aviator, USN 1967; subsplst., OPS analysis, USN 1975; subsylst., Command and Control, USN 1976. Career: aviator, USN, USNA Annapolis; VT1, VT3, VT5 Pensacola; VT28 Corpus Christi; VP31 San Diego; VP31, VP50 NAS Moffett; NPGS Monterey; First Fleet staff, San Diego; Third Fleet staff, Pearl Harbor, 1965-76; pgm. mgr., Stanford Research Inst., Menlo Park 1976-78, 1979-80; field ofc. mgr. Ketron Inc., Melo Park 1978-9; deputy dir. Special Electronic Systems, ESL Inc., Sunnyvale 1980-4; pres./ founder/ CEO Delfin Systems, Inc., Sunnyvale 1984--; dir. Delfin Sys. Inc. 1984-; dir. BROMS- Slavish, Inc. 1974-5; awards: Columbia Univ. Trust Fund Scholarship, US Naval Acad.; Fulbright Scholarship Cand., US Naval Acad.; grad. letter of commdn. for personal Leadership and High Ideas of Duty, Honor, and Loyalty'; Navy League Jr. Ofcr. of the Yr.;, Honolulu; USN White House Fellows Cond.; mem: Assn. of Old Crows; Navy League; Naval Inst.; Defense Preparedness Assn.; US Naval Acad. Info. Ofcr.; Elks; Stanford Area Youth Basketball; Palo Alto AYSO; Little League; PTA; PCL Baseball; community writer, Honolulu Sun Press 1974-6; mil: lcdr, USN 1965-76; cdr, USNR.R 1976-, Airmedal (2), Navy Unit Commdn., Vietnam Campaign (5 stars); Expert Pistol; Episcopal; rec: coaching, fishing. Res: 532 Channing Ave Palo Alto 94301 Ofc: Delfin Systems, 328 Gibraltar Dr Sunnyvale 94086

GENO, RICHARD EARL, life insurance agency president; b. Mar. 20, 1942, Oakland; s. Claude Earl (dec.) and Florence Jacqueline Geno; m. Joan Horgan, June 14, 1964; children: Jennifer, b. 1965; Deborah, b. 1967; Kristin, b. 1968; Richard II, b. 1969; Lauren, b. 1976; Jodi, b. 1978; Stephanie, b. 1980; edn: BS, UC Berkeley 1964; MS, The American Coll. 1979; CLU 1970; Chartered Fin. Cons. 1982; Cert. Fin. Planner 1983. Career: agent College Life Ins. Co. 1964-74; general agent 1974-82; pres. Richard F. Geno & Assoc. Ins. Svcs., Inc., San Jose 1979--; agency mgr. The Bankers Life 1982--; bd. dir. San Jose Gen. Agent's and Mgr. Assn. 1975-(pres. 1980-1); bd. dirs. San Jose Chpt. Chartered Life Underwriters 1981-; bd. dirs. Leading Life Ins. Producers f No. Calif. 1978-80 (pres. 1979); bd. dirs. Peninsula Life Underwriters 1971-2; awards: Jack Richter Meml. Awd.,"Underwriter of the Year, San Jose Life Underwriters Assn. 1980; Million Dollar Round Table 1965-; Co. Sales Leader

(1972, 76, 78) and No. One Agency (1978, 80, 81, 82), College Life Ins. Co.; mem: Nat. Assn. of Life Underwriters; Am. Soc. of CLUs; Leading Life Ins. Producers of No. Calif.; Assn. for Adv. Life Underwriting; publs: arts. in ins. and estate planning mags.; Republican; Catholic; rec: Little League baseball, coaching basketball, racquetball. Res: 347 Costello Ct Los Altos 94022 Ofc: Richard E. Geno & Assocs., Ins. Svcs., Inc., The Geno Bldg, 1042 West Hedding San Jose 95826

GEORGE, ANGELA DAWN', marriage, family, child therapist; b. Apr. 18, 1937, St. Kitts, West Indies, US citizen; d. James Edmond and Aileen Kathleen (Phillips) Mestier; m. Donald J. George, June 29, 1974; children: Kathleen, b. 1956; Steven, b. 1959; edn: BA, Coll. of New Rochelle 1960; MS, Notre Dame Univ. 1 65; MA, Fielding Inst. 1980; marriage, family, child counselor, State of Calif. 1981. Career: mathematics tchr. secondary & collegiate levels 1960-77; mem. Ursuline Nuns 1954-74; tchr. coll.-prep. acad.: Dallas, Tex. 1960-3; New Rochelle, NY 1963-7; Alton, Ill. 1967-9; Coll. of New Rochelle, NY 1969-71; UC Santa Barbara 1zw2-3; Marymount Jr. High 1975-7; intern Santa Barbara Co. Mental Health 1978-80; pvt. practice, spl. relationship and bereavement counseling, and foscusing, 1980--; instr. wkshps., Casa de Maria Retreat Center and Cont. (pres. 1975); faculty, Edn. of Santa Barbara (focusing 1982, pres. Myers- Briggs); spkr. local gps.; focusing coord., Santa Barbara 1982 (Gendlin, Focusing, The Focusing Illustrated, Chgo., Ill.); mem: Assn. Humanistic Psychologoy; Internat. Transactional Analysis Assn.; Community Environment Council, Santa Barbara; Peace Resource Ctr., Santa Barbara; author: Focusing on the Hospice Patient, Focusing Folio, Vol. 2, 1982; Democrat; Catholic; rec: hiking, wind surfing, travel. Address: 888 San Ysidro Lane Santa Barbara 93108

GEORGE, GARRY LEONARD, anesthiologist; b. Dec. 26, 1947, Nashville Tenn.; s. L. C. and Martha Louelle (Higgs) G.; edn: BS, Middle Tenn. State Univ. 1970; MD, Univ. of Tenn. Sch. of Med. 1973; anesthesiologist, Univ. of Texas Dept. of Anes., John Sealy Hosp., Galveston, Tx. 1978. Career: intern St. Joseph Hosp., Memphis, Tenn. 1973-4; Capt. USAF Med. Corps., 2yrs. active duty, 4 mos. sch. aerospace med., flight surgeon 2yrs., Korea and Calif. AFBs; res. anesthesiology John Sealy Hosp., Galveston, Tex. 1976-8; staff anesthes. Baptist Meml. Hosp. 1978-81; freelance anes., So. Calif. 1981-3; staff anes., El Cajon Valley Hosp. 1983--; mem: Am. Med. Assn.; Am. Soc. of Anesthesiol.; Calif. Soc. of Anes.; founder pvt. real estate rentals, 6 units; mil: flight surgeon, Capt., USAF Med. Corps. 1974-6; rec: real estate, sailing, travel. Res: 7968 Mission Center Court San Diego 92108; Garry L. George, MD, Inc., POBH 33182 San Diego 92103

GEORGIO, JUDY ANGELA, construction contractor; b. Mar. 17, 1930, Cranston, Rhode Is.; d. Armand Francis and Louise Luna (Procaccini) Fiori; m. Louis Georgio (dec. 1979), May 15, 1948; children: Gregg, b. 1949; Michael, b. 1958; Ron, b. 1951; Jon, b. 1960; edn: So. Calif. Sch. of Bus., No. Hollywood 1959; contractors lic., Calif. & Nevada. Career: contractor; first female mail carrier in San Fernando Valley; Litton Computers and General Instrument Ofc. Mgmt. 1975; currently: pres. Gothic Landscaping, Calif. and Nevada; owner J. Georgio & Sons, Inc.; honors: featured on cover of Outdoor Mag. w/ husband; awarded Home Beautification Awd. of 1980; mem: contractor lic. Landscapers Assn.; CofC; Athletic Assn. of San Fernando Valley; Catholic; rec: sports. Address: J. Georgio & Sons, Inc., 16787 Knollwood Dr Granada Hils 91344

GER, JAMES YUAN-LONG, obstetrician-gynecologist; b. Sept. 22, 1944, Nantou, Taiwan, nat. 1979; s. Tong-So and Yu-Nu (Shih) G.; m. Janice, Nov. 27, 1971; children: Michael, b. 1973; Christine, b. 1976; edn: MD, Taipei Med. Coll. Sch. of Med. 1970. Career: intern St. Mary Hosp., Waterbury, Conn. 1973-74; ob-gyn. resident Brooklyn-Cumberland Med. Ctr., Brooklyn, NY 1974-75; junior and senior res. Boston City Hosp., 1975-77; currently, ob-gyn., pvt. practice, Hawaiian Gardens; Diplomate American Bd. of Obstetrics & Gynecology; Fellow Am. Coll. of Obstetrics & Gynecology; mem: Am. & Calif. Med. Assns.; mil: 2nd lt. med. ofcr. Chinese Navy. res: 6260 Majorca Cir Long Beach 90803; Ofc: 21520 S Pioneer Blvd, Ste 103, Hawaiian Gardens 90716

GERICKE, DOUGLAS NEIL, lawyer; b. Sept. 23, 1938, Ukiah; s. Otto Luke and Catherine Rose (Levi) G.; m. Frances Souza, Aug. 27, 1960; children: John, b. 1960; Kristin, b. 1963; Marlene, b. 1964; Neil, b. 1975; edn: AB, St. Mary's Coll. 1960; JD, Citrus Belt Law Sch. 1976; atty. at law, State Bar of Calif. 1976. Career: deputy probation ofcr. Alameda Co. 1961-5; parole agent Calif. Youth Authority, Oakland & Sacramento 1965-73; community svc. cons. Calif. Youth Authority, Los Angeles 1973-7; honors: Calif. Delegate 1980; White House Conf. on Families; listed: Who's Who in the West; mem: Calif. State Bar Assn.; San Bernardino Co. Bar Assn.; Nat. Welfare Fraud Assn.; Aquinas H.S. Bd. (pres. 1982-3); Elks; Calif. Historical So.; Republican; Catholic; rec: youth and adult soccer coach. Res: 2561 E Del Norte Dr Highland 92346 Ofc: District Atty.'s Ofc., 316 No Mt. View San Bernardino 92415

GERKEN, WALTER B., life insurance company executive; b. Aug. 14, 1922, New York, NY; s. Walter A. and Virginia (Bland) G.; m. Darlene Stolt, Sept. 6, 1952; children: Walter C., b. 1953; Ellen, b. 1955; Beth, b. 1956; Daniel, b. 1958; Andrew, b. 1961; David, b. 1964; edn: BA, Wesleyan Univ. 1948; MPA, Maxwell Sch. of Citizenship- Pub. Affairs, Syracuse Univ. 1958. Career: supvr. budget and adminstrn. analysis State of Wisc. 1950-6; investment spl. Northwestern Mutual Life Ins. Co. 1954; investment research ofcr. 1956-9; investments mgr. 1959-67; financial v.p. Pac. Mutual Life Ins. Co. 1967-9; exec. v.p. 1969-72, pres. bd. dirs. 1972--; dir: Carter Hawley Hale Stores, So. Calif. Edison Co., Times- Mirror Co., Whittaker Corp.; chmn. Calif. Roundtable; chmn. Los Angeles United Way; bd. of trustees Occidental Coll.; Trustee Emeritus, Wesleyan Univ.; bd. dirs. Milwaukee Schs. 1965-7; clubs: Stock Exch., Balboa Bay, Pac. Union, S.F. California, Metropolitan (Wash DC); mil: capt., navigator, USAF 1942-6, WWII, decorated DFC,, Air Medal, British Coastal Command Citation. Res: Corona del Mar Ofc: 700 Newport Center Dr Newport Beach 92660

GERMAN, DANA J., certified public accountant; b. July 14, 1950, Foweler; d. Hans A. and Phyllis Elizabeth (Oxford) Jensen; m. Stephen German, June 24, 1972; children: Matthew, b. 1980; Sarah, b. 1983; edn: BS, CSU, summa cum laude, Fresno 1972; CPA; Am. Inst. CPAs; Calif. State Soc. of CPAs. Career: staff acctnt. Price Water House, Los Angels 1972-5; mgr. Design Furniture, Reedley 1975-7; secty./treas. Stephen L. German Accountancy Corp., Reedley 1977--; instr. Reedley Coll.; guest lectr. Reedley Coll. 1978-; awards: Bank of Am. Achievement Awd. 1968; Good Citizenship Awd., DAR, 1968; Phi Kappa Phi; Beta Gamma Sigma; Beta Alpha Psi; mem: Am. Inst. of CPAs; Calif. State Soc. of CPAs; Am. Women's Soc. of CPAs; Bus. & Profl. Women; Calif. Women for Agriculture; Sierra Kings Hosp. Aux.; chmn. Reedley Parks & Rec. Commn.; Reedley Hist. Soc.; Kings River Arts Council; Democrat; Mennonite Brethren; rec: gardening, cooking. Res: 19283 E American Reedley 93654 Ofc: Stephen L. German Accountancy Corp., 1423 11th Street Reedley 93654

GERNHARDT, LOUIS ALLAN IV, company executive; b. Dec. 8, 1949, San Francisco; s. Louis Allan III and Jeanette Diane Hunt (Cooper) G.; m. Catherine Meyerhoff, July 3, 1971; children: Louis V, b. 1978; Nicholas, b. 1980; Clayton, b. 1981; Chance, b. 1983. Career: nat. svc. mgr. Apeco Corp., Evanston, Ill. 1970-2; with Taylor Made Ofc. Sys., Inc., Concord 1972--; sales rep. 1972-3; sales mgr. 1973-7; v.p. sales 1977-82; v.p./gen. mgr. 1982-3; pres. Information Sys. Div., 1983--; bd. dirs. Taylor Made Ofc. Sys., Inc. 1977-; gen. partner Sequoia Leasing Ltd. 1978-; awards: sales mgr. of the yr. 1975, 76, 77; regl. sales mgr. of yr. 1977, Taylor Made Ofc. Sys., inc.; mem: Nat. Ofc. Machines Dealers Assn.; No. Calif. Ofc. Machine Dealers Assn.; Am. Bowling Congress; spkr: Dealer Diversification in the 80's, on copiers and duplication at Dataquest Internat. Conf.; mil: Sgt., US Army 1966-9, GCM, Awd. of Merit; Republican; Catholic; rec: athletics, bottle collecting, sports memorabilia. Res: 1228 Krona Lane Concord 94521 Ofc: Taylor Made Office Systems, Inc., 1035 Detroit Ave Concord 94521

GERSCH, CHERYL LYNNE, marketing executive; b. Dec. 16, 1953, Oakland; d. Herman T. and Frances Louise (Schatte) Gersch; edn: BA, jour., Univ. Houston 1978. Career: advt. sales exec., Daily Cougar, 1974-76; advt. director Roots Natural Footwear, Houston, Tex. 1976-78; sales rep. MCA Distbg. Corp., 1981; district mgr. Magnetic Video (now 20th Century-Fox Video), 1981-82; dir. mktg., W. Div. Neighborhood Video Club, 1982--; cons. Hollywood Video Library, 1983, Jomarc Prodns., 1984-; mem: Texas Record Peddlars Assn. 1978-81, Country Music Assn. 1978-81, Houston Solar Energy Soc. 1980; publs: writer/photog. Daily Cougar 1976-8; Republican: Christian; rec: golf, cooking. Res: 6600 Beachview Dr, Apt. 310, Rancho Palos Verdes 90274 Ofc: Neighborhood Video Club, 904 Silver Spur Rd, Ste 412, Rolling Hills Estates

GERSHFELD, SEMYON, construction co. executive; b. Nov. 17, 1931, Odessa, USSR, nat. 1984; s. Michael and Hanna (Kuschnirskai) G.; m. Rosa, Oct. 14, 1954; children: Michael, b. 1956, Jack, b. 1957; edn: grad. Kaevskoe Mil. Schs. 1952; BS in C.E., Moscow Constrn. Inst. 1965; Calif. Reg. Civil Engr. 1983, Gen. Engring. Contr. A, 1978, Gen. Bldg. Contr. B, 1977. Career: foreman, constrn. supt., project mgr., chief engr., USSR, 1961-75; project supt. RN & GSA Construction, Inc., USA 1976-79; sr. struc. designer Jacobs Engring. Group, Inc., 1980-82; pres. SMG Constrn. & Engring., Inc., Buena Park 1979--; recipient good work and conduct awards (4), USSR; mem. Orange Co. Athletic Club; mil: capt. arty., 1949-61; Republican; rec: sport. Res: 8110 Woodland Dr Buena Park 90620 Ofc: SMG Construction & Eng. Inc., 8117 Woodland Dr. Buena Park 90620

GERSTEN, HARRY ROBERT, real estate executive; b. Apr. 10, 1946, Reno, Nev.; s. Milton and Mary (Uzekevich) G.; m. Cynthia Kathryn Greek, May 2, 1969; 2 sons, Andrew, b. 1970, Matthew, b. 1975; edn: AA, Rio Hondo Coll. 1969; BS, CSU San Diego 1973; Calif. lic. R.E. Broker; (CRA) Cert. Review Appraiser 1983; (RMU), Reg. Mortgage Underwriter 1983; (CPM), Cert. Property Mgr. cand. 1984. Career: project mgr. and systems coord., The Gersten Cos., Beverly Hills 1971-80; real estate ofcr. California First Bank, San Diego 1980--; R.E. cons. prin., Gersten Ent.; listed Who's Who in Real Estate 1983, Who's Who in Fin. and Indus. 1984; mem. Inst. of R.E. Mgmt., Nat. Assn. of Realtors; sr. mem. Nat. Assn. of Review Appraisers and Mortgage Underwriters; mem. Mensa, Chula Vista Assn. for Gifted Children, RX-7 Club of Am.; mil: sp4 US Army 1969-71; rec: swim, tennis, sports cars, stamps. Res: 230 Camino Entrada Chula Vista 92010 Ofc: California First Bank, 530 B St, Ste. 700, San Diego 92101

GESSON, BRUCE HARVEY, physician, anesthesiologist; b. Nov. 16, 1942, Brooklyn, NY; s. Irwin and Sarah (Krames) G.; m. Joan, June 7, 1970; 2 daus.: Elizabeth, b. 1971, Lisa, b. 1975; edn: BS, City Coll. NY 1964; MD, Univ. of NY at Buffalo 1968; Anesthesiologist, UCLA Med. Ctr. 1975. Career: intern, Charity Hosp. of La., Tulane Univ. 1968-9; res. Cedars of Lebanon Hosp., L.A. 1969-70; served to maj. US Army Med. Corps, W.Ger. 1970-73; res. in anesthesia, UCLA Med. Sch. and Hosp., 1973-5; pvt. practice, Modesto, Calif. 1975--, clin. practice of anesthesiol. with subsplty. in pain control work; chmn. Dept. Anesthesia, Meml. Hosp. of Stanislaus Co. 1981-3; awards: Avon, State Univ. of NY, SUNY at Buffalo scholarships, Fellow in Tropical Med. 1967; mem: Fellow

Am. Coll. of Anesthesiol., AMA, CMA, Stanislaus Co. Med. Assn., Am., Calif. Soc. of Anesthesiol., Internat. Assn. for Study of Pain; clubs: Civic, Nat. Assn. of Watch and Clock Collectors, Sportsman of Stanislaus; Republican; Jewish; rec: clocks, jogging, golf, racquetball. Address: Bruce H. Gesson MD, Inc., 1004 Shaftesbury Ct. Modesto 95350

GETTINS, JAMES MORGAN, investment broker; b. May 2, 1937, San Francisco; s. Harry D. and Lucile (Magon) G.; m. Nancy, Sept. 5, 1959; children: Cindi, b. 1961, Jim Jr., b. 1962, Shawn, b. 1968, Shannon, b. 1973; edn: BS in ind. mgt., CSU San Jose 1960. Career: pres. Gettins, Daley, Inc., Los Altos 1979-82; v.p./dir./founder Morgan Petroleum, Inc., Monterey 1981--; pres. Gettins Finl. Group, Los Altos 1982--; Republican; Prot. Res: 24624 Summerhill Ave Los Altos Hills 94022 Ofc: 4984 El Camino Real, Ste.212, Los Altos 94022

GHEZZO, ANTHONY PAUL, purchasing agent, b. July 27, 1927, Ravenna, Italy, nat. 1961; s. Simeone S. and Caterina M. (Fenoglio) G.; m. Joanne F. Padovani, Aug. 4, 1962; children: Mark, b. 1964, Alan, b. 1964, Paul, b. 1971; edn: school tchr., Inst. Magistrale Gov., Florence, Italy 1945; Profl. Desig. Purch. Mgmt., UCLA 1969. Career: dept. mgr. Italian Ministry of Fin., Tax Div., Dept. Insp Corps, Florence, Italy 1946 56; buyer for the Sisters of the Third Order of S.F. (Peoria, Ill.) eleven hospitals, 1957-62; asst. purch. agt./dept. mgr. for May Co. dept. stores, 1963-67; v.p./sr. purch. agt, Corporate Purch. for all Home Savings of Am. branches (over 260) and subsids. 1967--; mem. Purch. Mgmt. Assn.; mil: Ital. Underground (Resistance) 1944; Ital. Army Inf. 1950-51; Democrat; Catholic; rec: photog., travel. Res: 1335 No Michillinda Ave Pasadena 91107 Ofc: Home Svgs of America, 4900 Rivergrade Rd Irwindale 91706

GHONIEM, NASR MOSTAFA, professor of engineering; b. Mar. 5, 1948, Alexandria, Egypt, nat. 1980; s. Mostafa H. and Etmad (Elzarka) G.; m. Virginia Lea, June 19, 1976; children: Amira Anne, b. 1980, Adam Tarek, b. 1982; edn: BS, Univ. of Alexandria 1971; M.Eng., McMaster Univ. (Can.) 1974; MS, Univ. Wisc. 1975, PhD 1977. Career: tenured prof. of engring. (nuclear) Univ. of Calif., Los Angeles 1977--, spec. in devel. of fusion energy as alternative energy source; pres./cons., Materials and Fusion Consulting; honors: Young Man of Am. Award 1978; mem. Am. Nuclear Soc., bd. dirs. Egyptian-Am. Scholars Assn.; publs: over 45 arts. in field in sci. jours., conf. proceedings; rec: gardening. Res: 10415 Danube Ave, Granada Hills, CA 91344 Ofc: 6288 Boelter Hall, UCLA, Los Angeles CA 90024

GHORMLEY, JOHN HARNED, building contractor; b. Aug. 11, 1936, Greenfield, Iowa; s. Clarence Emmett and Dorothy (LaNeece) H.; m. Anne Doran, May 25, 1960; 2 daus.: Lynne, b. 1961, Rebecca, b. 1966; edn: undergrad. Purdue Univ. 1954-5, BS in C.E., Univ. Wisc. 1959; Reg. Profl. Engr. Calif. (1962), Fla. (1971), Ind. (1974). Career: assoc. engr. Douglas Aircraft Co., El Segundo 1959; civil engring. assoc. City of Torrance 1959-62; City Engr./Dir. of Pub. Works, City of Gardena 1962-65, City Adminstrv. Ofcr., 1965-70; partner Benner and Ghormley Civil Engrs., Santa Paula 1970-75; vice pres. Ervin, Ghormley, Johnson & Assocs., Los Angeles 1975-77; pres. Bonita Homes Inc., Oceano 1977--; honors: award for outstanding service, Gardena Valley CofC 1968; mem. South Co. Economic Devel. Assn. (pres. 1983-4); clubs: Gardena Valley Kiwanis 1968-70, Ojai Optimist (pres. 1976), Gr. Pismo Bch. Kiwanis 1981-, Masons; Republican; Presbyterian; rec: flying. Res: POB 356, 980 Branch Mill Rd Arroyo Grande 93420 Ofc: Bonita Homes Inc., PO Drawer B, Oceano 93445

GIANNOTTI, DAVID ALLEN, lawyer; b. May 27, 1947, Rome, NY; s. Dominick and Florence M. (Wilkinson) G.; m. Kathy Hanna, June 5, 1982; edn: BA in pol. sci., Ithaca Coll. 1969; JD, Emory Univ. Sch of Law 1971; admitted to practice in Ga. (1972), Tenn. (1972), NY (1976), Calif. (1981). Career: assoc. law firm Stophel, Caldwell & Heggie, Chattanooga, Tenn. 1972-75; assoc. counsel Hooker Chemicals & Plastics Corp., Niagara Falls, NY 1975-76, assoc. general counsel Regulatory Affairs 1976-78, counsel Environ. Affairs (Houston, Tex.) 1978-81; counsel Environ., Health & Safety, Occidental Petroleum Corp., Los Angeles 1981--; spkr. various profl. devel. seminars for Executive Ent. (1977-8), Chem. Mfrs. Assn. (1977), Texas Bar Assn. (1982,3), ABA (1983), Practicing Law Inst. (1983); awards: Internat. Moot Ct. Team (3d in regl. competition); Am. Jurisprudence awards; scholarships to Ithaca and Emory Univs.; mem: Bar Assns. of Ga., Tenn., Calif., L.A. County; Am. Bar Assn. (sects. on Bus., Natural Resources, Litigation, Tort and Ins. Practice); Chem. Mfr's. Assn. Ad Hoc Superfund Litigation Gp. 1982-, and Chem. Regulations Adv. Com. 1975-8; mem. Empire State (NY) CofC Environ. Conserv. Com. 1975-80; Warner Woods Homeowners Assn. bd. dirs.; Republican; Episcopal (youth sponsor/advisor 1974-5); rec: piano, phys. fitness. Res: 21931 Burbank Blvd., 48, Woodland Hills 91367 Ofc: Occidental Petroleum Corp. 10889 Wilshire Blvd, Ste. 1500, Los Angeles 90024

GIBBS, GEORGE KARROLL, b. June 9, 1911, Grace, Ida.; s. John Chester and Clara (McClellan) G.; m. Myrtle Trimmer, Jan. 29, 1939; children: Rose Marie, b. 1939, Gregory, b. 1949; edn: BS in agri., Univ. of Ida. 1934. Career: area dir. Rural Resettlement, Boise, Ida. 1934-37; soil scientist Calif. Soil Conserv. Svc., Berkeley 1937-52; soil conserv. expert UN Food and Agr. Orgn., 1952-53; soil conservationist Soil Cons. Service, Watsonville, Ca. 1953-56, Soil Cons. Service Area Fresno, 1956-72; soil scientist FMC Internat. Op., San Jose 1973-74; currently semi-ret., real estate broker, Fresno; cons. on soil conserv. for UN in Iraq 1952-3; cons. in irrigation devel., FMC Corp. in Nigeria 1973-4; awards: Union Pacific coll. scholarship 1930; appreciation, UN, 1953; award of merit, Calif. Assn. of Soil Cons. Districts; mem: Soil

Terresa Lynn, Raymond Ivis. Career: with Motor Freight Co. 1948, Auto Parts House 1950, fractional H.P. engine repair 1952, sales mgr. auto parts distbr., Calif. 1956, owner/pres./bd. chmn. Western Wholesale Co. (div. Glemar Inc.), anaheim 1959--; dir. trade adv. com. Small Engine Repair; instr. Fractional Engine Repair, 10 yrs., instr. Calif. Dept. of Corrections, 5 yrs.; mem. CTFMA (pres. 1981), Shriners (v.p. Orange Co. club 1984), Masons, Scottish Rite, Elks, DeAnza Caballeros, Nat. Greyhound Assn.; Christian; rec: collectibles. Res: RR1, Box 311, Corona 91720 Ofc: Western Wholesale Co. 1200 No Bluegum St Anaheim 92806

GIBBS, JACQUELINE, educator, business owner; b. Mar. 12, 1942, Newnan, Ga.; d. George W. and Isma (Howard) Gibbs; edn: BS, Tenn. A&I State Univ. 1962; MA in adm., CSU Hayward 1973; acctg., LaSalle Ext. Univ. 1977; num. tax seminars annually, 1975-; study tour Brit. schools, spons. UCSB 1972; cert. IRS Enrolled Agent 1978. Career: math. teacher pub. schools, Kansas City, Mo. 1962-67, Berkeley (Ca.) Unified Sch. Dist. 1967-81; IRS tax examiner, 1967; tax preparer, 1970-78, with Tax Corp. of Am. 1970-75; math. instr. Peralta Coll. Dist., 1974-82; prop. Gibbs' Bookkeeping & Tax Service, Oakland 1978-82, 1984--; co-pres. Digital Acctg., Inc. 1983-4; awards: grantee Pearl S. Buck Found. 1976; cert. of leadership devel., Cornell Univ. 1977; Outstanding Sec. Tchr., Berkeley; mem: Nat. Assn. of Accts., Nat., Calif. Assn. of Enrolled Agts., Bay Area Women Entrepreneurs, Consumer Affairs Tax Preparer Pgm., Coalition of 100 Black Women, Nat. Assn. of Tax Consultants, Nat. Notary Assn., Nat. Council of Negro Women (life; state orgnzr.; leadership tng. seminars), Nat. Assn. Female Execs.; past chpsn. Berkeley Tchrs Negotiating Com. 1974; Prot. Res: 811 York, 109, Oakland 94610 Ofc: 262 Grand Ave, Ste 210, Oakland 94610

GIBBS, RAYMOND ROGER, community services director; b. Feb. 25, 1946, Palmer, Mass.; s. Burnham Raymond and Mary Marjorie (Schmidt) G.; m. Susan Gilman, Sept. 3, 1966; children: Eric, b 1969, Justin, b. 1972; edn: AA, Shasta Coll. 1966; BA, CSU Chico 1969; Reg. Recreator No. 1306, Calif. 1969. Career: engring. aide City of Red Bluff, 1964-67, recreation supvr., 1967-71; dir. Parks and Comm. Services, City of Colusa, 1971--; instr. Yuba Coll. 1973 ; chmn. Comm. Rels. Com., Colusa Comm. Hosp. 1983-; honors: Pride Award, Colusa Co 4-H, 1975; Lion of the Year 1976, Colusa Lions Club; mem: Calif. Parks & Rec. Soc. (pres. 1981); Rotary; Colusa Unified Sch. Dist., Friends of Music (pres.), Redskins Athletic Found. (bd.); Am. Field Svc. Exchge Pgm.; Stagehands Civic Theatre Orgn. (past pres.); publs: art., Western Cities Mag. 3/78; mil: sgt. E5, Calif. Army NG 1970-76 (hon. grad. Ft. Belvoir, Va. Engring Sch.); Republican; Methodist; rec: softball, skiing, boating. Res: 309 Hartley Dr Colusa 95932 Ofc: City of Colusa 425 Webster St, POB 1063, Colusa 95932

GIBEL, ILA MARIE, real estate broker; b. Sept. 13, 1941, Chico; d. Charles Eldon and Nina Mae (Bolton) Ingraham; m. Robert Gibel, Jan. 27, 1968; children: Loren, b. 1963; Karen, b. 1969; edn: AA, Yuba Jr. Coll. 1962; BA, CSU Los Angeles 1967; lic. R.E. Broker, Calif. 1983. Career: secty. Prudential Life Ins. Co., Chico 1959; internat. banking secty. Crocker Nat. Bank Credit Dept., San Francisco 1960; secty. Chico YMCA, Chico 1960-6; secty. Steel & Arostegui, Attys. at Law, Yuba City 1962; dept. secty. Underwriting Dept. Royal Globes Ins. Co., S.F. 1962-63; legal secty. Shirley, Saroyan, Cartwright & Peterson, Attys. at Law, S.F. 1964; asst. dept. secty. CSU Los Angeles Engring. Dept. 1967-68; mng. supvr. Avco Investment Corp., Newport Beach 1973-83; broker assoc., Century 21 Osborne, Marks & Assoc., San Juan Capistrano 1983--; awards: Merryman Awd., Avco Fin. Svcs. 1979; Million Dollar Club, Avco Fin. Svcs. 1982; mem: Nat. & Calif. Assns. Realtors; Tau Sigma Nu; Republican; Ocean Hills Comm. Ch.; rec: research and preparation family genealogy. Res: 31165 Via Cristal San Juan Capistrano 92675 Ofc: Century 21 Osborne, Marks & Assoc., 31931 Camino Capistrano San Juan Capistrano 92675

GIBSON, ALAN POWNALL, real estate brokerage president; b. Aug. 22, 1935, Oakland; s. Ralph Brown and Ruth Alice (Pownall) G.; m. Jayne Magstadt, Feb. 18, 1984; children: Craig Pownall b. 1969, Bradley Kent, b. 1971; edn: BA, CSU San Jose 1959; MA, CSU San Diego 1965. Career: teacher Edwin Markham Jr. High, 1959-62, Saratoga High Sch. 1962-78; real estate sales agt. Ram Realtors, 1972-74, Contempo Realty, 1974-80; pres. Contempo Realty-Avy, 1980-83; pres. Gibson Props. -Better Homes & Gardens, San Jose 1983--; honors: Teacher of Year, Saratoga H.S. 1964; pres. Almaden Valley Breakfast Group 1982; mem: Nat., Calif. (dir.) Assn. of Realtors; San Jose Real Estate Bd. (Multiple Listing Com.); mil: E3, USNR; Republican; Rel. Sci.; rec: golf, swim, tennis. Res: 6653 Copperwood Cir. San Jose 95120 Ofc: Gibson Properties/Better Homes & Gardens, 5029 Almaden Expy. San Jose 95118

GIBSON, DAVID JAMES, physician/rheumatologist, b. May 1, 1945, Cincinnati, Ohio; edn: AB, Asbury Coll. 1967; MD, Univ. of Ky. 1971; medical intern/res. Ind. Univ. Med. Ctr. 1971-3; resrch. fellow Harvard Med. Sch., Arthritis Univ, 1973-5; postgrad., rheumatol., Santa Barbara (Ca.) Med. Found. Clinic, 1977-9; cert. Am. Bd. Internal Med. 1978; State Lic. Ky., Ind., Mass., Calif. Career: major USAF, M.C., chief div. rheumatology, USAF Med. Ctr., Keelser AFB, Miss. 1975-77, regl. cons. in rheumatol., DOD, 1975; att. phys. Wadsworth VA Hosp., Los Angeles and Santa Barbara Cottage Hosp., 1977; med. dir. Beverly Manor Convalescent Hosp., 1983-; bd. trustees Health Force Mgmt. Group, In. 1981; lectr. with Western Inst. for Med. Studies 1982; faculty, La. State Univ., New Orleans 1975, UC Los Angeles, 1977, USC, 1980; bd. trustees Meml. Rehab. Hosp., S.B. 1978-; mem: Am. Rheumatism Assn., Rheumatism Socs. of La., New England, So. Calif.; Am., Santa Barbara (pres.)

Soc. of Internal Med.; Underseas Medicine Soc.; Soc. of AF Physicians, AMA, CMA, Santa Barbara Co. Med. Soc.; Am. Coll. of Physicians; AAAS; Arthritis Found. (chpt. bd. 1977-); United Scleroderma Found. (chmn. Med. Adv. Bd. 1980); bd. dirs. S.B. Med. Found. Clinic 1981; num. med. jour. publs., presentations. Address: POB 1200, Santa Barbara 93102

GIBSON, GAYNOR ALLISON, educator; b. Aug. 25, 1919, San Francisco; s. Ray Atherton and Alice Eleanor (Kroehncke) G.; m. Manuela Gabellini, Oct. 19, 1947, Florence, Italy; children: Cynthia Rae, b. 1948, Micaela, b. 1953, Gregory, b. 1954, Regina, b. 1957, Randy, b. 1963; edn: Cert. Engr., Stanford Univ., 1942-3; Univ. of Md., 1959-60; hon. MA, UCLA Ext. Div. 1981; Calif. Life Teachers Cred., Jr. Coll. Career: grocery chain mgr. Keystone Grocers, San Francisco 1935-38; decorator florist Podesta & Baldocchi, S.F. 1938-42; enlisted man to lt. col. US Army Signal Corps, 1942-63 (instr. communications and Italian interpreter, 1942-45, contracting ofcr., world-wide 1945-63); asst. chief contracts, plans, procedures, tng. CalTech Jet Propulsion Lab., Pasadena (contract negotiator/adminstr. for "Ranger" Moon Pgm.) 1963-67; sr. contracts adminstr., Navy Phoenix F-14/AWG-9 Radar Pgm., Hughes Aircraft Co., 1967-81; dean of instrn., Procurement & Contracts Tng. Schs. & Consultants, Altadena 1981--; instr. Pasadena City Coll. 1962-, head Purch. & Contracting Dept.; master instr. UCLA, curriculum adv. com. UCLA Ext. Div.; instr. CUS Northridge 1980-, Northrop Univ. 1982-3; instr Hughes Aircraft Co., all sites, 1967-81; honors: Calif. Scholarship Soc. 1935; Fellow, Nat. Contracts Mgmt. Assn. 1981; National Educator of Year 1982-3; mem: Retired Officers Assn., Reserve Officers Assn.; Mil. Order World Wars; Navy League; Pasadena CofC; Purch. Mgmt. Assn. of Los Angeles. Program coordinator to estab. Profl. MS degree in Acquisition and Contracts Mgmt., Northrop U. 1982-3; author textbooks in field; mil. decorations (11) incl. Army; Commend., Berlin Airlift, Presdtl. Cit., Korean Medal; Repub.; Catholic; rec: language studies, golf. Address: Procurement & Contract Tng Schools & Cons., 411 W. Altadena Dr Altadena 91001-1236

GIBSON, PAULA LAUREN, lawyer; b. July 2, 1956, Denver, Colo.; d. Richard C., Jr., and Thelma C. Gibson; edn: BA, UC Los Angeles 1978; JD, Southwestern Univ. Sch of Law 1981; admitted State Bar of Calif. 1981. Career: research asst., Hon. Norman Pittlack, L.A. Superior Ct. 1981; law clerk intern, Hon. Consuelo B. Marshall, U.S. Dist. Ct., Central Dist. of Calif., 1981; law clerk, Potter, Bradish & Ellinghouse, Encino 1981-2; legal counsel, Calif. State Dept. of Corporations, 1982--; student mem. Am. Bar Assn. Journal Advis. Bd. 1980-1; honors: chancellor's marshall, UCLA 1978; Silver Key Award (2), ABA, 1981; Who's Who in Am. Colls. & Univs. 1981; mem: Am. Bar Assn. (Corps., Banking, Bus. Law sect.; Patent, Trademark & Copyright Law sect.), LA County bar Assn. (Legal Svcs. for Poor com.), State Bar of Calif. (Bus. Law); publs: book rev., ABA Jour. 1981; art., The Commentator 2/80; rec: fashion photog. Res: 8457 Farralone Ave Canoga Pk 91304 Ofc: Dept. of Corps., 600 So Commonwealth Ave, 16th Flr., Los Angeles 90005

GIDDINGS, DAVID WIGHT, company executive; b. Feb. 5, 1954, Lynwood; s. Edwin and Manya (Koshko) G.; edn: CSU Fullerton, 1972-78. Career: pres. D.W. Giddings Co., Inc., Brea 1972--; secty./chief fin. ofcr. Elsinore Aerospace Services, Inc., Downey 1982--; owner Jet Set Enterprises, Irvine 1983--; mem: BBB of L.A. and Orange Co.; Republican; Catholic; rec: computers, electronics. Res: 5151-38 Walnut Ave Irvine 92714 Ofc: Elsinore Aerospace Services, Inc. 9701 Lakewood Blvd, Ste 103, Downey 90241

GIEDT, GLORIA H., social worker; b. Feb. 3, 1938, Oakland; d. Bernham Arthur and Myrtle Lucille (Jackson) Handling; m. George Morton Rose, Aug. 31, 1956, div.; chil: Lori Ann, b. 1958, Daniel, b. 1961; m. 2d Robert Richard Giedt, July 30, 1971; edn: AA, Harbor Jr. Coll., 1975; BSG, magna cum laude, USC, 1977; MSW, UCLA, 1979; Lic. Clin. Soc. Worker (L.C.S.W.), Calif., 1982. Career: vol. Exceptional Childrens Found., 1963-69; gerontology intern Southland Lutheran Home, Norwalk 1976; casework counselor intern Martin Luther King Jr. Hosp., 1977-78; adminstrv. intern Harbor Regional Ctr., L.A. 1978-79; clin. social worker M.L.K.Jr. Hosp., 1979-81, San Pedro Penin. Hosp., 1981-83, F.H.P., Long Beach 1983--; cons. Clearview Convalescent, 1979--; spkr. community presentations, San Pedro 1981-83; merit awards: Alpha Gamma Sigma 1974, Town & Gown Jrs. 1976, 77, Alumni Merit Scholar 1976-78. Mem: W. Gerontol. Soc. 1975-; Nat. Assn. of Soc. Workers; NERTA-AARP; Golden Era Assn. Publs: Needs Assessment of Elderly Developmentally Disabled Clients of Harbor Regl. Ctr. (1979); Democrat; Methodist; rec: oil painting. res: 1836 Peninsula Verde Dr. Rancho Palos Verdes 90717. ofc: F.H.P., 2925 N. Palo Verde Ave. Long Beach.

GIEM, ROSS NYE (JR.), physician, surgeon; b. May 23, 1923, Corvallis, Ore.; s. Ross Nye and Goldie Mary (Falk) G.; m. 1944, m. 2d. 1970; div.; children: John Charles, b. 1945, David Ross, b. 1946, Paul Andrew Lincoln, b. 1951, James Lawrence, b. 1954, Ross N. III, b. 1957, Matthew John, b. 1968, Julie Ann, b. 1973; edn: BA, La Sierra Coll. 1948; MD, Loma Linda Univ. 1953; MD lic. to practice med., Calif., Mo., Ill.; Bd. Cert. in General Surg., Am. Bd. Surg. 1961. Career: currently emergency dept. physician, St. Luke Hosp., Pasadena; (past) paramedic instr., instr. resident (MD) physicians in emergency med., MDs in surgery, RNs (nurses) in trauma classes (So. Ill. Univ. School Med.); med. practice in Sacramento, Los Angeles, Pasadena, Calif., Rolla and St. Louis, Mo., Belleville, Ill.; gen. surg./chief examiner, St. Louis VA Hosp. 1969-71; past mem./ chmn. various med. profl. groups and hosp. staffs; mem: (FACS) Fellow Am. Coll. Surg. 1963; (FACEP) Fellow Am. Coll. Emerg. Phys. 1973; Pan Am. Surg. Assn., Brit. Med. Soc., AMA, CMA, Am. Heart Assn., Med. Assns. Mo., St. Louis, Ill.; publs: 2 arts., Calif. Med. Journal; mil: sgt.

US Army 1943-46, ATO medal; Ind.; Prot.; rec: graphic arts, music, tennis. Ofc: St. Luke Hosp. E. Washington St, Pasadena 91107

GIFFORD, BROOKS, lawyer; b. Apr. 22, 1910, Chgo.; s. Robert Ladd (noted inventor, educator, financier, philanthropist; listed Who's Who in Am. 1926-62) pres. Glen Campbell-LA Open Golf Found.; mil: E5 USCGR; Republican; Catholic; rec: sail, ski, travel. Res: 4314 Glencoe Ave Marina del Rey 90291 Ofc: Mfrs. Finl. Services, 3333 Wilshire Blvd Los Angeles 90010

GIFFORD, ERNEST MILTON, JR., educator; b. Jan. 17, 1920, Riverside; s. Ernest Milton and Mildred Wade (Campbell) G.; m. Jean Duncan, July 15, 1942; 1 dau., Jeanette, b. 1948; edn: BA, UC Berkeley 1942, PhD, 1950. Career: asst./ assoc./ prof. of botany and botanist in the Experiment Station, Univ. of Calif., Davis 1950--, chmn. Dept. of Botany, UCD, 1963-66, 1973-77; chief editor Am. Jour. of Botany, 1975-80; awards: Merek Senior Postdoctl. Fellowship 1956-57; John Simon Guggenheim Fellowship 1966-67; Fulbright Research Scholar to France 1966-67; Nato Sr. Fellowship to France 1974; recipient Cert. of Merit, Botanical Soc. of Am. 1981; mem: Sigma Xi, Botanical Soc. of Am. (pres. 1982), Internat. Soc. of Plant Morphologists (v.p. 1980-4), Am. Inst. of Biological Scis., Calif. Botanical Soc.; co-author: (textbook) Comparative Morphology of Vascular Plants (3rd ed., 1974); 85 research publs.; mil: col. (ret.) US Army 1942-73, Bronze Star medal; rec: gardening, photog. Res: 1023 Ovejas Ave Davis 95616 Ofc: Dept. of Botany, Univ. of California, Davis 95616

GILBERT, ALORA JEAN GILES, marketing executive; b. Oct. 23, 1947, Calexico; d. Clifford L. and Vera L. (Randles) Giles; m. Maurice Gilbert Jr., Mar. 28, 1983; edn: AA, Pierce Jr. Coll. 1967; BA in psych., UC Santa Barbara 1980. Career: statistical clerk So Calif. Gas Co. 1970-73; field merchandiser Warner Elektra, Atlantic Corp., 1977-79; promotion/mktg. mgr. Warner Bros. Records, San Francisco 1979--; coordinator Eleanor Curry Fund, San Mateo; mem. Nat. Assn. for Female Execs. Inc.; awards: Bay Area Promo. Dir. of Year 1983, Profl. Dance Music Assn.; Outstanding Young Women of Am. 1982; various Gold Records for promo., mktg. 1979-. Rel: A.M.E.; rec: writing (plays, poetry, short stories), theatre. Res: 855 35th St. Oakland 94608 Ofc: Warner Brothers Records 680 Beach St San Francisco 94109

GILBERT, KIRK SPARKMAN, physician; b. Oct. 4, 1954, La Jolla; s. Alton Keith and Mary Katherine (Sparkman) G.; m. Marsha, Sept. 5, 1982; edn: BS, honors, Univ. of Wash. 1976, MD, honors, 1980; Dip. Am. Bd. of Family Physicians 1983. Career: intern, resident, Family Practice Pgm., UCLA, Santa Monica Med. Ctr.; physician pvt. practice, Santa Barbara 1983--; past advis. bd. L.A. Basin Area Health Edn. Center; honors: Phi Beta Kappa, Faculty Medalist (1975), Pres.'s Medalist, Sigma Nu Frat. National Scholar of Year (1976), Alpha Omega Alpha (1979), King Co. Chpt. of The AAFP: Theodore J. Phillips Award (1980); mem: Am. Acad. Family Physicians, Med. Soc. of Santa Barbara Co., S.B. CofC, S.B. Nat. Hist. Mus., Textile Mus. (Wash DC), past sr. mem. Nat. Ski Patrol System; Ind.; Unitarian; hobbies incl. entomology, numismatics, textiles: weaver spec. in pile carpets. Res: 1711 Hillcrest Rd Santa Barbara 93103 Ofc: Kirk S. Gilbert, MD, 200 N. LaCumbre Rd, Ste A-B, Santa Barbara 93110

GILBERT, NANCI ELAINE, real estate broker/developer; b. Jan. 10, 1943, Honolulu; d. James Carl and Josephine Adell (Sullivan) Gilbert; gr.granddau. of founder of first real estate co. in Calif., McCarthy Real Estate, L.A. Edn: grad. Punahou Sch, Honolulu 1961; AS in Radio & TV, Endicott Coll. 1963; real estate courses, USC, 1981, Coll. of Marin, 1978; Calif. real estate sales lic. 1978, R.E. broker lic. 1981. Career: residential real estate sales, 1978-; currently devel. cost-efficient residential bldg. projects in Sacramento area; developer/ owner/broker RRR Properties; pres./owner Crystal Bay Holding Co.; owner/ broker Russian River Resort Properties; cons.: The Alexander Co. 1983-, Ward Ent. 1981-, Las Baulines Nurseries 1982-; bd. dirs. Shane Distbrs. 1983-. Recipient num. sales awards, President's Club, 1974, Multi-Million Dollar Club, 1983, Million Dollar Club, 1981-2. Mem: Sacramento, Sonoma Co., Marin Co. Board of Realtors; Nat. Assn. for Female Execs. Inc., Sacto. Women's Network, Women in Bus. in Sonoma Co., Bay Area Career Women, The Smithsonian Assocs (nat. mem.), Alpine Explorers and Adventurers Club (pres. 1984), Nat. Geographic Soc.; Republican; Episcopal; rec: x-c skier, class. guitar, scuba, wildlife photog. Res: 6670 Oakhill Dr Roseville 95678 Ofc: RRR Properties 8125 Sunset Ave, 188, Fair Oaks 95628

GILBERT, ROBERT EDWARD, manufacturing co. president; b. Nov. 7, 1923, Oakdale; s. Amos Lawrence and Emma Teresa (Banks) G.; m. Beverly Stone, Dec. 9, 1945; children: Charles, b. 1948, Robert, b. 1951, Terry, b. 1953, David, b. 1956, Michael, b. 1962; edn: BS, UC Berkeley 1947. Career: warehouseman, salesman/partner, sales mgr., v.p./ currently pres. & chief exec. (1981-), A.L. Gilbert Co., Oakdale 1940-; pres. Oakdale Comml. Feed Yard, 1970-83; dir. Berry Seed & Feed Co. 1954-76, dir. Oakdale Feed & Seed Co. 1962-; honors: Hon. Young Farmer, Modesto J.C. 1963, State Grange Dairy Merit 1969; mem: Calif. Grain & Feed, Calif. Cattle Feeders, Nat. Cattlemen, Am. Feed Mfrs.; clubs: Modesto Elks, SES, UPEC, West Expo., CofC, BSA Exec. Com., Stanislaus Taxpayers Assn.; works: study of relationship of parity pricing of milk and beef (1978); mil: lt.jg USNR PTO, 3d, 5th, 7th, 9th Fleet; Republican; Episcopal; rec: Calif. hist., travel, ranching. Res: 566 No Second Ave Oakdale 95361 Ofc: A.L.Gilbert Co. 304 No Yosemite Oakdale 95361

GILES, JEAN HALL, business executive; b. Mar. 30, 1908, Dallas, TX; d. Clarence D. (chem.-mining engr., U.S.-Mex.; dec.) and Elizabeth (McIntyre) Overton (dec.); gr.-granddaughter of Lottie Hargrove, author 'Texas History in

Rhyme'; m. Alonzo Russell Hall, II, Jan. 23, 1923 (dec.); m. 2d., Harry Edward Giles, Apr. 24, 1928; div. 1937; children: Mrs. Kenneth Crawford (Marjorie Jean Hall) Hodges, Jr.; Alonzo Russell Hall, III; Janice R. Giles; Marjean Ruth Giles (hon. student). Career: realtor-notary, L.A. Co., 1948-61; bldg. contractor-propr., L.A. Real Estate Exchange; partner, Tech. Contractors. Dir. Vol. Corps, L.A. Area War Chest; Capt., commanding ofcr., orgn. S.W. L.A. unit, 1942; Maj., Natl. Exec. Ofcr., 1943-44; Children's Hosp. Benefit, 1945-46; coord., Motor Corps., L.A. Area War Chest, 1944-45; Capt., Communications Corps, U.S. Hdqtrs. Mem.: past: L.A. and Natl. Realty Bds.; Amer. Inst. of Mgmt.; Women's Div., L.A. CofC.; Los Fiesteros de L.A.; Hollywood Chpt., Natl. Fedn. of Bus. and P Profl. Women; L.A. World Affairs Council; Hist. Soc. of So. Calif.; L.A. Art Assn.; Assistance League of So. Calif. Democrat, Inspector, Precinct 747. Protestant. Rec.: golf (scorer, 18 yrs., Los Angeles Open and others). Office: P.O. Box 36474, Los Angeles 90036.

GILES, WALTER EDMUND, health care executive; b. Aug. 9, 1934, Omaha, Nebr.; s. Walter E. and Julia Margaret (Shively) G.; m. Dana Foster, Sept. 29, 1970; children: Sue, b. 1956, Theresa, b. 1958, Kimberly, b. 1960, Nadine, b. 1962; edn: BA, Univ. of Nebr. 1977; certified: Alcoholism Counselor (nat. assn. 1974, Calif. assn. 1978); Sr. Profl. Counselor, State Nebr. 1974; Biofeedback Counselor, Behavioral Therapy & Resrch Inst. 1980. Career: med. technologist Univ. of Nebr. Coll. of Medicine, Omaha 1960-65; sci. sales, Donley Medical, Lincoln, Nebr. 1965-70, alcoholism counselor Vets. Adminstrn. 1970, coordinator Municipal Cts. 1970-77; dir. Orange Co. Employee Assistance Network, Santa Ana 1977-78; adminstr. Advanced Health Ctr., Newport Bch. 1978-81; pres. Greatwest Health Services Inc., Orange 1981--; adv. bd. Human Svcs. Dept. Saddleback Coll. 1979-81; bd. Alcoholics for Christ 1983-; alcoholism expert witness Dist. Court; mem: (charter) Nebr./Calif. Assn. of Alcoholism Counselors; Nat. Assn. of Alcoholism Counselors; Assn. of Labor Mgmt. and Cons. on Alcoholism; Nat. Council on Alcoholism; Rotary, Elks, CofC, Masons; past v.p. Junior CofC, Nebr. 1958; profl. papers in field; Republican; Christian; rec: photog. Res: 2113 Ave. Espada, San Clemente 92672 Ofc: Greatwest Health Services Inc. 1653 E. Lincoln Orange 92665

GILKEY, DAVID PAIGE, chiropractor; b. Mar. 24, 1954, San Jose; s. Elwin P. and Phyllis E. (Graun) G.; m. Janet, Jan. 6, 1974; edn: AA, San Jose City Coll. 1976; DC, Los Angeles Coll. of Chiropractic 1979, postgrad. pgm. sports medicine 1983-4; BA in humanities, New Coll. of Calif. (S.F.) 1981; postgrad. pgm. Am. Coll. of Chiropractic Orthopedics 1979-81; grad. work in pub. adm., CSUSJ 1983-; Calif. Chiropractic Assn. cert. in disability eval. (1980), ind. medical exam. (1982). Career: chiropractor 1979-, owner pvt. practice, spec. in orthopedics, San Jose 1980--; mem: Dip. Nat. Bd. of Chiropractic Examiners; L.A. Coll. of of Chiropractic Alumni Assn.; Am. (Council on Roentgenol. and Orthopedics), Calif. Chiropractic Assn.; Santa Clara Soc. (past pres., Dr. of Year 1983); Am. Coll. of Chiro. Orthopedics, Toastmaster Internat.; Sheriff's Adv. Bd. Santa Clara Co.; BBB; Biocentrics Inst. (instr./cons.) 1983, Republican; rec: coins, stamps, motorcycles. Res: 1037 Fairview Ave San Jose 95125 Ofc: 2937 Union Ave San Jose 95124

GILLIGAN, DOREEN ELAINE, real estate broker; b. Canada, nat. 1958; d. Neil and Ada (Rothwell) McArthur; m. Timothy Gilligan, Oct. 18, 1952; career: Westwood real estate broker and owner interior improvement co., currently; previously with Bank of Toronto, Vancouver, BC; Lansdown Race Track, Vancouver; bank officer, Bank of America; American City Bank. Mem: Toastmistress, Canon Explorers, Sierra Club, Twilite Hikers; rec: camping, hiking, travel; res/ofc: 10959 Rochester Ave. Los Angeles 90024.

GILLILAND, DONALD REGINALD, recreation and hotel industry executive; b. Aug. 18, 1943, Birmingham, Ala.; s. Roy and Fannie Elizabeth (McCarley) G.; 1 son, Scott, b. 1968; edn: BS indsl. mgmt., Auburn Univ. 1966; MS in mgt., honors, Fla. Internat. Univ. 1974; lic. real estate broker, Fla. 1970. Career: power sales/cons. Fla. Power & Light Co., Miami 1966-73; real estate broker Jerry D. Starr Realty, Miami 1970-73; pres. Jockey Club Realty Co., Miami 1973-75; sec./treas. SMC&G, Los Angeles 1976-78; dir. membership/ sales Marina City Club, Marina del Rey 1975-80, v.p. mktg. 1980--; exec. com./ bd. dirs. Aero Club of So. Calif. (owner of the Spruce Goose) 1982-; mem: Nat. Aeronautic Assn., Am. Soc. of Travel Agents, Hotel Sales & Mgmt. Assn.; mem. Miami Jaycees, So. Miami Rotary, Internat. Chili Soc. (founding), US Tennis Assn.; clubs: Jockey (Miami), Marina City, Mountaingate Country, Racquet (Palm Springs); winner of 1981 Catalina Is. Chili Cookoff, competed in 1981 World Championship Chili Cookoff; mil: E5 USAR, 1966-72; Republican; Prot.; rec: tennis, cooking, travel. Res: 4344 Promenade Way, 200P, Marina del Rey 90292 Ofc: Marina City Club, 4333 Admiralty Way Marina del Rey 90292

GILLILAND, WARREN LEE, automotive brake design engineer; b. July 5, 1946, Omaha, Nebr.; s. Max Frederick and Lorraine Marguerite (Cooper) G.; m. Katherine Lemich, Nov. 13, 1965; 1 son, Max, b. 1975; edn: L.A. Valley Coll. 1964-70, L.A. Pierce Coll. 1976-80; protege of Franklin B. Airheart, foremost expert on disc brakes in world. Career: nat. sales mgr., chief designer Hurst Airheart Products, Chatsworth 1968-74; service mgr. various auto dealers So. Calif., 1975-79; consulting engr., owner Warmax Design Co., Westlake Village 1979--; designer: brake systems on the Disneyland Autotopia cars, Bart Train, assisted in design of Indianapolis Racing Brakes; author: Winning the Auto Repair Game (in progress); Republican; Christian; rec: bowling (190av.). Address: 891 Hartglen, Westlake Village 91361

GILLOOLY, JESSICA ANNETTE, family counselor; b. Nov. 5, 1947, Okla. City, Okla.; d. Royce Wayne and Audrey Louise (Feaster) Barron; m. Gregory Gillooly, June 24, 1979; edn: BS, Univ. of Mo. 1968-70; MA, CSU Los Angeles 1977; Contg. edn. courses 1977-; MFCC, Marriage, Family & Child Counselor, Calif. 1979; Std. Calif. Tchr. Credential, Comm. Coll. Instr. Cred. Career: current pvt practice MFCC, Los Angeles; psychology instr. (part-time) Glendale Community Coll. 1980-, lectr. to New Horizons Adult Re-Entry Pgm., Glendale Com. Coll. 1981-; awards: Acad. Scholarship 1967-68, Sigma Phi Alpha 1970, Phi Kappa Phi 1977; mem. Calif. Assn. for Counseling & Devel., Calif. Assn. of Marriage & Family Therapists; works: devel. original pgms. incl.: L.A.County Dept. Hlth. Svcs. Dental Hlth. Pgm. for L.A. Co. Elem. Schools (coauthor); Basic Nutrition Sch. Pgm. for children with Learning Disabilities; pre-natal edn. for teenage couples; intro. to dental clinic for patient (aged 2 to 15); parenting pgm. (for minority first time mothers); psychology of women coll. course; others. Democrat; Methodist; rec: hiking, gardening, wine devotee. Res: 3734 Sheridge Dr Sherman Oaks 91403 Ofc: 850 Colorado Blvd Ste. 204, Los Angeles 90041

GILMORE, ROBERT BARRY, computer co. president; b. Jan. 18, 1936, Hattiesburg, Miss.; s. Arthur Lavonne and Georgia (Jordan) G.; m. Darla Rife, June 22, 1973; children: Katherine, b. 1957; Gilbert, b. 1960; Robert, b. 1962; edn: music edn., Univ. of So. Miss. 1954-57; Desig: Parachutist, US Parachute Assn. 1965; CDP, and ICCP, 1984. Career: mgr. data processing MFC Services, Jackson, Miss. 1966-67, with NCR Corp. 1970-79; support splst., Dayton, Ohio 1970-72; proj. mgr. software support, San Diego 1972-77; mgr. sys. software mktg., Dayton, Ohio 1977-79; mgr. software support Microdata Corp., Irvine 1979-81; pres. Capricorn Computing, Inc. (NCR affiliate software house), Mission Viejo 1981--; instr. computer scis. Saddleback Comm. College 1983-84; mem. Elks; mil: m/sgt. Miss. Army Nat. Guard 1950-63; Republican; rec: golf, sailing, music. Res: 27622 Pasatiempo Mission Viejo 92692

GILSTRAP, GLENN EUGENE, distributing co. executive; b. Jan. 20, 1928, Orange County, Ind.; s. Ivis Truman and Mary Alice (Larimore) G.; m. Marjorie June Heacock, Dec. 6, 1946; children: Glennda June, LaDonna Jean, and Elizabeth (Robertson) G.; m. Roberta Conner, July 2, 1960; children: Frederick Vern, b. 1961, Harold Dorin, b. 1962, Kari Elizabeth, b. 1964; edn: BA, CSU Long Beach, 1971, MSc, CSU Dominguez Hills 1976, MPA, Univ. of S.F., 1982. Career: draftsman, City of Los Angeles, 1956-58; engineering aide Co. of L.A. 1958-63; civil engring. asst. City of Torrance 1963-72, environmental quality adminstr. 1972-79; dir. of community devel. City of Porterville, 1979-82; deputy dir. Devel. Svcs. City of Huntington Beach, 1982--; mem: Am. Planners Assn., Am. Public Works Assn., Am. Water Works Assn., Exchange Club Porterville, Los Angeles Air Quality Mgmt. Com. 1978-9; Aikido (martial art) instr. 1965-; publs: Airport Noise Control Pgm., Torrance 1978, Animal Control Study 1977; mil: E4, USAF 1954-56; Republican; Sci. of Mind; rec: orange grower, Aikido, jog, fishing, writing. Res: 911-7 Georgia St Huntington Beach 92648 Ofc: City of Huntington Beach, 2000 Main St Huntington Beach 92648

GIN, WILLIAM TIP, structural engineer; b. Nov. 15, 1948, Dick Hoi, Kwangtung, China; s. Tip Tung and Fung Ming (Yee) G.; m. Linda M., Aug. 12, 1971; children: Jeffrey, b. 1972, Jennifer, b. 1974; edn: AA, Merritt Coll. 1968; BS Arch. Engr., Cal Poly Univ. 1971; MS in C.E., CSU San Jose 1977; Calif. lic. Profl. Engr. 1975; Comm. College Instr. cred. Career: struc. designer Robinson & Assocs., San Francisco 1971-73, asst. engr. Tudor Engrng. Co., 1973-75; bridge engr. Deleuw Cather, 1975-76; engr. Parsons Brinckerhoff, Quade & Douglas Inc., 1976-77; struc. engr. Kaiser Aluminum, Oakland 1977-78; struc. engr. Naval Facilities Engrg Com, San Bruno 1979--; instr. Laney Coll., Oakland 1976-; mem. Soc. of Am. Mil. Engr.; Prot.; rec: tennis, ski. Res: 436762 Excelso Dr Fremont 94539 Ofc: WestNavFacEngCom, POB 727, San Bruno 94066

GINSBERG, ALBERT BASIL, account executive; b. Nov. 13, 1927, Winnipeg, Can.; nat. 1972; s. Maurice Harold and Thelma (Rackow) G.; m. Mona Axelrod, Mar. 29, 1954; children: Andrea, b. 1956, Dana, b. 1960; edn: BS, Univ. of Alberta 1948. Career: mfrs. rep., Western Canada 1948-60; parking cons., owner/opr. of Canada wide parking facilities, 1961-68; securities acct. exec. Shearson Hammill, 1968-74; acct. exec. Prudential-Bache Securities, 1974--, v.p. investments; product lectr., Prudential-Bache; awards: Millionaires Club 1980; Chairmen's Council 1978-84; mem: San Diego Stock & Bond Club (vp 1984), Bnai Brith, United Jewish Fedn. of San Diego (legal & tax adv. com. Comm. Found.); clubs: Stardust CC, San Diego Athletic; mil: lt. Royal Can. Ord. Corp 1945-58; Republican; rec: golf, swim, photog. Res: 6450 Brynwood Way San Diego 92120 Ofc: Prudential-Bache Securities 701 B Street San Diego 92101

GISVOLD, JEANINE FOSTER, lawyer; b. Dec. 29, 1944, Denver, Colo.; d. Eugene S., Sr., and Olga Mary (Daniels) Foster; div.; 1 son, Mark T. Gisvold, b. 1970; edn: BS, nursing, Univ. of Colo. 1967; MS in nursing, UC San Francisco Med. Ctr. 1968; JD, Hastings Coll. of the Law 1977; R.N., Calif. 1967; admitted to Calif. State Bar 1977. Career: staff nurse, Denver and San Francisco, 1964-68; cons. to mental instns. throughout Central Am., Resrch. project, 1968; psychiatric clin. nurse splst. chief adminstrv. nurse, dir. Crisis Intervention Ctr., Marin Co. Comm. Mental Health Center, 1968-72; supr./asst. dir. Nursing, Marin Gen. Hosp., San Rafael 1969-74; law clerk Werchick & Werchick, S.F. 1975-77; atty. law firm Shaw, Kuhn & Thomas, San Rafael 1977-81; trial atty. spec. in personal injury litigation, Shaw & Gisvold, Inc. 1981--; elected bd. dirs. Marin Gen. Hosp. Dist. 1979-87; bd. dir. Center Point, 1980-1, Womens Way, 1983; mem: Calif., San Francisco Trial Lawyers Assn., Queens Bench, ABA, Marin Bar Assn., NOW, Nat. Womens Polit. Caucus; owner of state and nat. historical landmark: the Dollar Mansion in San Rafael, upon completion of restoration will be open to public periodically; Ind.; Catholic; rec: restoration Victorian houses, antiques. Res: 115 J Street San Rafael 94901 Ofc: Shaw & Gisvold, Inc. 515 Northgate Dr 94903

GLASS, JOHN DOUGLAS, senior reliability engineer; b. Sept. 26, 1943, Launceston, Tasmania; s. Everard Wm. and Patricia Anne (Ryan) G.; m. Susan Barry, Dec. 15, 1973; children: Joanna, b. 1976, John, b. 1978, William, b. 1981; edn: ATC, C.B. Teachers Coll. (Melbourne) 1963; B.App.Sci., west Aus. Inst. of Tech. (Perth) 1967; BS, Univ. of Melbourne, 1970; Dip.Ed., Univ. of Tasmania (Hobart) 1973; M.Ed., Chapman Coll. 1976; MA, UC Dominguez Hills 1977; MS, Rochester Inst. Tech. 1983; ASQC Cert. Rel. Engr. 1983; cred. tchr. (primary, sec., tertiary) Calif., Australia. Career: tchr. Christian Brothers, Aus. 1961-71; head of math dept. Hutchins Sch., Hobart, Tas. 1972-3; dir. learning ctr. Monterey Peninsula Coll., Ca. 1974-5; tchr. San Carlos Sch., Monterey 1974-5; head of math/sci. depts., Broadland House, Launceston 1976-7; head math dept. Marian Coll., Launceston 1977-8; Quality Ass. dir. Leatherback Industries, Hollister, Ca. 1979-80; mgr. Reliability Dept., Teledyne McCormick Selph, Hollister 1980--, frequently on location throughout USA as troubleshooter/ failure analyst on aerospace systems which use ordnance. Cons., ABC-TV Sec. Math. Series, Melb. 1969-70; mem. Victorian HSC Math Curric. Bd. 1970-1; State Examiner, Tech. Reporting, Tasmanian Edn. Dept. 1977-8; awards: Hist. of Sci. Exhbn. (1st Pl.) Univ. of Melb. 1970; mem: ASQC, Mensa, Australian Science Tchrs Assn., AOQC, St. Vincent De Paul Soc., Jaycees; publs: many arts. on ordnance; art. Jour. of HOS 1971, AOQC Symp. 1984; Liberal; Catholic; rec: all sports, lapidary. Res: 1681 Sunset Dr Hollister 95023 Ofc: Teledyne McCormick Selph 3601 Union Rd Hollister 95023

GLASS, TIMOTHY JOSEPH, financial executive; b. July 29, 1951, Hackensack, NJ; s. James Richard and Frieda Betty (Hess) G.; 2 sons, Robert, b. 1969, Jason, b. 1973; edn: BS in acctg., Univ. of Akron 1974; C.P.A. 1981. Career: sr. acct. Price Waterhouse & Co., Newport Beach 1974-79; v.p. fin. E.T.C. Carpet Mills, Ltd., Santa Ana 1979-82; currently, controller Herbalife International, Culver City; mem. Calif. Soc. of CPAs, NE Santa Ana Residents Assn. (bd. dirs. 1981); Republican; Catholic; rec: reading. Res: 1018 E. Buffalo Ave Santa Ana 92706 Ofc: Herbalife Intl. 5721 Slauson Ave Culver City 90230

GLASGOW, EMMETT FREDRICK, auto customizing co. owner; b. Jan. 23, 1929, Southgate; s. Emmett April and Mabel Teresa (Eels) G.; m. Shirley Goodfellow, June 14, 1957; children: Cynthia, b 1955, Terry, b. 1958. Career: self-empl. 1968-, owner three companies: Cardinal Spray Painting, Street Customs Ltd., and Cardinal Limousine, in Garden Grove; many customized cars have been featured in nat. auto mags., Hot Rod, Super Chevy, 1001 Truck & Van Ideas, Custom Rods and Street Machine; num. articles (How-To) incl. The ABC's of Street Rod Painting (pub. by Argus); created six customized Camaros for motion picture, Eat My Dust; author two books: Do It Yourself Customizing (1975), Van Customizing (1976); mem. El Bekal Shrine (pres. Oriental Band 1983); mil: cpl. US Army 511 Airborne, 1955-57; Democrat; Prot.; rec: gardening. Res: 10701 Parliament Ave Garden Grove 92640 Ofc: Street Customs Ltd. 11737 Cardinal Cir Garden Grove 92643

GLASSY, MARK CHARLES, research scientist; b. July 2, 1952, Tacoma, Wn.; s. Frank Joseph and Lorraine (Gay) G.; m. Donna, June 8, 1974; 2 sons, Jason, b. 1979, Matthew, b. 1980; edn: BS, Univ. of San Francisco 1974; Ind. Univ. Sch. of Med. 1974-5; PhD in biochem., UC Riverside 1978. Career: postdoctoral research fellow Dept. Molecular Immunol., Scripps Clinic & Resrch Found. 1978-81; asst. resrch immunologist, UC San Diego Cancer Center 1980--; teaching asst. UCSF 1973-4, Ind. Univ. 1974-5, UCR 1975-8; awards: sci. paper, Am. Chem. Soc. Student Affils., 1974; Earle C. Anthony Fellowship 1976-7, Chancellor's Patent Fund 1978, NIH research awards 1978-9, 1983-6, fellowship 1979-81; Am. Cancer Soc. grantee 1981-2; mem: Am. Chemical Soc., AAAS, NY Acad. of Sci., Fedn. of Am. Scientists; mem. Acad. of Sci. Fiction, Fantasy, and Horror; Count Dracula Soc.; Patent Pend.: All Human Monoclonals to Diagnose, Treat Cancer; num. sci. arts., abstracts, book chapters; Democrat; Catholic; rec: sci-fi (extensive pvt. collection). Res: 10246 Parkdale Ave San Diego 92126 Ofc: UCSD Cancer Center, Ste T-011, San Diego 92103

GLEBERMAN, FRANK MARTIN, financial services co. principal; b. Jan. 26, 1938, Cincinnati, Ohio; s. Myron Fernando and Betty (McKim) G.; edn: USC Sch. of Business, 1955-60; CLU, Am. Coll./Bryn Mawr, 1969; Gen. Securities Rep., NASD. Career: asst. advt. mgr. Carnation co., 1961-2; life ins. agt. New York Life Ins. Co., 1962-66, asst. mgr. 1966-70, supt. So. Pacific Region, 1971-74, gen. mgr. 1970-71, 1974-78; asst. general agt. Mass. Mutual Life, 1978-80; prin./mgr. Manufacturers Financial Services, Los Angeles 1981--; bd. dirs: Westways Inc., Western-Mayflower Moving and Sotorage, Modern-Mayflower Moving and Storage, Great Amer. Moving & Storage, Lorentine Corp.; owner Frank M. Gleberman Gen. Mgmt. Consulting; writer, lectr., holds seminars, confs. in finl. plnng. & ins.; chmn. LA Unified Sch. Dist. Underutilized Sch. Sites Com.; honors: resolutions, L.A. City Council and Co. Bd. Supvrs. 1973; KNX Radio Citizen of Week 1977; mem: Nat., Calif., L.A. Assn. of Life Underwriters; Inst. of Certified Finl. Plnnrs.; Am., L.A. Co. Soc. of CLU; NASD (chmn. The Finl. Plnng. Study Group); orgns: Nat. Assn. for People with Disabilities (pres.), LA County Easter Seal Soc. (past pres./ bd. chmn.); LA Jr. Chamber of Commerce (past pres./ bd. chmn.; past pres. Charity Found.), LA Area CofC (past dir.), Commerce Assocs. of USC (past pres./ bd. chmn.), USC Assocs. (life), Calif. Yacht Club; fmr. dir. LA Civic Light Opera Assn.; fmr. v.chmn. LA Open Golf Tournament Advis. Com., past

icology, Alcohol Rehab.; mil: USPH 1970-4; Jewish; rec: tennis, woodwkg., computer pgmmg. Res: 339 Magellan San Francisco 94116 Ofc: 350 Parnassus, Ste 609, San Francisco 94117

GLEN, JAMES WILLIAM, dentist; b. Oct. 2, 1950, Simcoe, Ont., Canada, nat. 1962; s. Carl Eugene and Nola Bowen (Moss) G.; m. Kathy, Aug. 27, 1977; 2 daus., Rebecca, b. 1980, Elizabeth, b. 1982; edn: BA, Univ. of La Verne 1973; DDS, UC Los Angeles 1981; alumnus, L.D. Pankey Inst. of Post Grad. Dental Edn. Career: assoc. dentist with Dr. Leon Roisman of American Dental Council, 1981; owner pvt. practice, La Jolla 1983--; dental ins. cons. San Diego County and Municipal Employee's Assn. 1981; honors: UCLA Award in Team Dentistry Utilization 1981; mem: Pre-Fellow Acad. of Gen. Dentistry, Am., Calif. Dental Assn., S.D. Co. Dental Soc.; rec: aviation. Address: 6633 La Jolla Blvd La Jolla 92037

GLENN, LARRY RAY, company president; b. Feb. 1, 1937, Santa Monica; s. Chester A. and Lucile (Brown) G.; m. Joyce, Mar. 21, 1959; children: Cheryl Lee, b. 1960, Brenda Lee, b. 1961, Leslie Robert, b. 1961; edn: BA, Woodbury Coll. 1955. Career: sales, Taverner & Fricke Paper Co. 1954-63, Atlas Spec. Bag Co. 1963-69; sales mgr. Acteson Paper Co. 1969-78; sales/gen. mgr. Pak West Paper Co. 1978-81; owner/pres. The Paper Company, Inc., Glendora 1981--; served on City of Glendora General Plan Com. 1972; mem. Glendora Coordinating Council (v.p.), Glendora Holiday Basket Pgm., chmn. Band Shell Project (funding); mem: Sales & Mktg. Execs. of Orange County, Execs. Assn. of Orange Co., Glendora CofC (chief amb.), Execs. Assn. of San Gabriel Valley (pres.), Kiwanis; mil: airman USNR 1954-63; Republican; Rel. Sci.; rec: hunt, hike, camping. Address: The Paper Co. Inc 317 No Westridge Ave Glendora 91740

GLINCHER, ERWIN MARK, life and disability insurance executive; b. Mar. 22, 1929, Everett, Mass.; s. Abraham and Rae (Avratin) G.; m. Sharen Grey, Aug. 1, 1950; children: Wendy, b. 1952, Betsy, b. 1956, Debby, b. 1958; edn: JD, Suffolk Law Sch. 1952; Life Underwriters Tng. Council 1971. Career: sales mgr. Helene Curtis Industries, 1959-63; pres. Paris-Ace Beauty Supply Co., 1963-65; life ins. indus. 1965-79, gen. agent American General Life Ins. Co., 1979--; recipient num. awards, Myasthenia Gravis Found., N.Y. and L.A.; Temple Beth Am Honor Roll 1983; mem: Nat., Western, L.A. Life Underwriters; Million Dollar Round Table (Qual., Life); Myasthenia Gravis Found. (Nat. vice pres.; past pres., bd. dir. L.A. chpt.); Shriners; Democrat; Jewish; rec: tennis, Swimming. Res: 6637 Maryland Dr Los Angeles 90048 Ofc: American Gen. Life Ins. Co. 6363 Wilshire Blvd, Ste 419, Los Angeles 90048

GLOR, PETER JOHN, engineering specialist; b. Jan. 25, 1944, Batavia, NY; s. Eldon Merritt and Ora Elizabeth (Putney) G.; children: Steven Kent, b. 1970, Jason Marc, b. 1972, Jennifer Lynn, b. 1978; edn: BA, Purdue Univ. 1967, MA, Iowa State Univ. 1974. Career: Air Intercept Controller, USS Canberra, 1967-69; Combat Info. Ctr. Ofcr., USS Connole, 1969-70; Logistic advisor to Vietnamese Navy Logistic Support Cmd.,j Saigon 1970-71; asst. prof. of naval sci. Iowa State Univ. 1971-74; combat cargo ofcr/chief engr. USS Barbour Cty. 1974-76; plans ofcr/public affairs ofcr. Naval Beach Gp. One, Coronado 1976-77; Logistic rep. to sr. logistic splst., General Dynamics-Convair Div., San Diego 1977-82, engineering splst. 1982--, coordinator for all logistic resrch & devel.; mem. DOD/Industry Working Gp., and Aerospace Indus. of Am. Panel on Logistic Support Analysis; honors: Phi Eta Sigma 1962; mem: Convair chpt. Nat. Mgmt. Assn., US Naval Inst., Soc. of Logistic Engrs., San Diego Zool. Soc., Sigma Nu frat. 1964-7; pub. tech. papers; mil: cmdr. USNR, Navy Commend., Combat Action, Vietnam Cmpgn. ribbons, Chief of Naval Tng. Commendation 1974; Methodist (choir, bldg. com.); rec: choral music, photog., painting. Res: 5310 Repecho Dr, V103, San Diego 92124 Ofc: General Dynamics Convair Div, P3-2620 Kearney Villa Rd San Diego 92138

GLORIG, ARAM, physician; b. June 8, 1906, Manchester, Eng.; US citizen; s. Aram and Beatrice (Allen) G.; div.; 2 daus. Patricia, b. 1947, Deborah, b. 1951; edn: BS, Atlantic Union Coll. 1931; MD, Loma Linda Univ. 1938. Career: intern Lawrence Meml. Hosp., New London, Conn. 1937-8, res. Willard Parker Hosp., NYC 1939-40, Henrietta Egleston Hosp., Atlanta, Ga. 1940-1; major US Army M.C., chief, ENT, various hosps. Iceland, Eng., Ger., 1942-46; dir. Audiology and Speech Correction Ctr., Walter Reed Army Med. Ctr./ and dir. Tech. Resrch in Hearing Dept. of Army/ and chief, Audiol. and Speech Correction, VA, Wash DC 1947-53; dir. of resrch. The Los Angeles Found. of Otology, and Noise Resrch. Ctr., 1953-64; dir. Callier Ctr. for Communication Disorders, 1964-77, Dir. Emeritus 1977-; cons. indsl. and forensic otology Otologic Med. Group, Inc., L.A. 1977--; assoc. dir. resrch House Ear Inst., L.A. 1977--; teaching, num. med. instns., univs. 1949--; Dean Emeritus, Univ. of Texas, Dallas, 1977-; Calif. lic. Provider Cont. Edn. for RNs, 1981-3; mem: Acoustical Soc. of Am. (Fellow), Am. Acad. Opthalmol. and Otolaryngol. (Fellow), AAAS, Am. Auditory Soc. (founding pres. 1972), Am. Indsl. Hygiene Assn. (past pres. No Tex. Sect.), Am. Laryngol., Rhinol., Otol. Soc. Inc. (Fellow), AMA, Am. Otol. Soc. (Fellow), Am. Speech and Hearing Assn. (Fellow, life), Royal Soc. of Med., etc.; awards: Ignacio Berraquer (1968), Citizenship, WFAA (1969), Am. Acad. of Ophthal. and Otol. (1971), Amplifon Center for Resrch. Study, Milan, Italy (1979), Carhart Meml., Am. Auditory Soc. (1979), Mem. of Honor, XV Intl. Cong. of Audiol., Krakow, Poland (1980); author four books, num. med. arts.; Republican; Prot.; rec: golf, sailing. Res: 6225 Riviera Cir Long Beach 90815 Ofc: Otologic Med Gp. 2122 West 3rd St Los Angeles 90057

GLUNTS, DONALD E., real estate co. president; b. Feb. 5, 1952, Chelsea, Mass.; s. James D. and Georgia (Gabor) G.; m. Jan, Sept. 16, 1979; edn: Santa

Monica City Coll. 1969-71, Anthony R.E. Schools 1972, 74; Calif. lic. R.E. Broker 1974, Alcohol Beverage Control lic. 1981. Career: mgr. Crown Realty, Venice 1972-76; pres. D.G. Realty, Inc., Venice 1976--; prop. Ports of L.A. Liquors, Pac. Palisades; founding dir. Executive Savings and Loan, Marina Del Rey, 1984-; dir. Venice/Marina del Rey Area Bd. of Realtors, 1978-84; awards: Venice of America, 1983; profl. recognition awards; Master Real Estate Appraiser 1982; mem: CAR, Venice/Marina del Rey Bd. of Realtors, Nat. Council of R.E. Exchangors, R.E. Appraisers Assn.; Jewish; rec: travel. Res: 2228 Prospect Ave Venice 90291 Ofc: D.G. Realty, Inc. 1009 W. Washington Blvd Venice 90291

GO, BLANDINO CHAN, engineer; b. June 2, 1957, Concepcion, Phil.; s. Juanito and Tomasa (Chan) G.; edn: BS, metal. eng., Mapua Inst. of Tech. 1979; MS in mech. eng., CSU Long Bch 1983; BS (cand.),app. econ., Univ. of S.F. 1984; Cert. Mfg. Engr. 1983. Career: metallurg. engr. Thermo-Electron Corp., Los Angeles 1979-81; resrch engr Northrop Corp., Hawthorne 1981--; mem: Am. Soc. for Metals, The Metallurg. Soc. of AIME, Computer Club of So. Calif., Toastmaster Intl.; Democrat; Catholic; rec: chess, tennis. Res: 241 So Ave 57, No 206, Los Angeles 90042 Ofc: Northrop Aircraft, One Northrop Ave, 5072/51, Hawthorne 90250

GODDARD, HERBERT HARRY, real estate broker; b. June 25, 1903, Edgemont, S.D.; s. Herbert and Carrie (Lehr) G.; m. Bernice Boss, Mar. 31, 1928; children: Beverley, b. 1929, Joanne, b. 1930, James Herbert, b. 1941. Career: building trades (carpenter), L.A. 1923-28; trainee to mgr. S.H. Kress Co., No. & So. Calif., 1928-40; variety store owner, Long Beach area 1940-45; Shipyards fabrication splst., Wilmington 1942-45; real estate broker, Arcadia 1946--; dir. (pres. 1968) Arcadia Bd. of Realtors 10 yrs., Realtor of Year 1971, vice pres. Area 16, Calif. Assn. of Realtors; Civitan Citizen of Year 1959; Legion of Honor DeMolay 1975; mem: Masons, Scottish Rite, Shriners (S.G.V. pres. 1963), High Twelve Club Arcadia (charter pres. 1960, State pres. 1967), pres. Ensign Mayo High Twelve Loan Fund 1974-84, Rotary, Arcadia CofC (pres. 1954), Arcadia Hist. Soc. (pres. 1980); chmn. Arcadia Historical Commn., 1984; Republican; Prot.; rec: fishing, photog., club work. Res: 11 West Longden Ave Arcadia 91006 Ofc: 1010 Baldwin Ave, Ste A, Arcadia 91006

GODFREY, DAVID B., business broker; b. June 16, 1935, Lowell, Mass.; s. David and Julia (Guenard) G.; m. Donna Blair, Feb. 14, 1978, children: Stephanie, b. 1969, Erin (Webb), b. 1971; edn: BS, E.E., Duke Univ. 1957; MS, E.E., Ohio State Univ., 1968; MBA, real estate, Golden Gate Univ. 1984; lic. Calif. Real Estate Broker 1983. Career: chief deputy adminstr, Bur. of Workers Compensation, St. of Ohio, 1975-77; pres./gen. partner Pride Properties (350 units comml. & R.E. holdings and gen. contracting firm), Cols., Ohio 1969-76; chief of avionics engring. General Dynamics, San Diego, Ca. 1978-79; mgr. bus. mktg. Geddling & Burk, San Francisco 1981-83; broker/owner Calif. Business Associates, S.F. 1983--; Dir. Small Business Inst., SBA, 1984; adj. prof. Golden Gate Univ. Grad. Sch. Small Bus., 1983-; publs: arts. in various mags., National Mall Monitor, Jour. of Parapsychol.; rec: tennis, reading. Ofc: Calif. Business Assocs. 1885A Lombard St San Francisco 94123

GODFREY, GLEN KEOKI, city official; b. Aug. 8, 1934, Eugene, Ore.; s. Glen and Elizabeth (Robertson) G.; m. Roberta Conner, July 2, 1960; children: Frederick Vern, b. 1961, Harold Dorin, b. 1962, Kari Elizabeth, b. 1964; edn: BA, CSU Long Beach, 1971, MSc, CSU Dominguez Hills 1976, MPA, Univ. of S.F., 1982. Career: draftsman, City of Los Angeles, 1956-58; engineering aide Co. of L.A. 1958-63; civil engring. asst. City of Torrance 1963-72, environmental quality adminstr. 1972-79; dir. of community devel. City of Porterville, 1979-82; deputy dir. Devel. Svcs. City of Huntington Beach, 1982--; mem: Am. Planners Assn., Am. Public Works Assn., Am. Water Works Assn., Exchange Club Porterville, Los Angeles Air Quality Mgmt. Com. 1978-9; Aikido (martial art) instr. 1965-; publs: Airport Noise Control Pgm., Torrance 1978; Animal Control Study 1977; mil: E4, USAF 1954-56; Republican; Sci. of Mind; rec: orange grower, Aikido, jog, fishing, writing. Res: 911-7 Georgia St Huntington Beach 92648 Ofc: City of Huntington Beach, 2000 Main St Huntington Beach 92648

GODRICH, DAVID WILLIAM KENNETH, real estate co. executive; b. Oct. 24, 1927, Versailles, France; nat. 1958; s. John Frederick and Helena Irene Grace (Fraser) G.; m. Margaret (Brown), Mar. 16, 1963; children: Anthony, b. 1956, Carol, b. 1957; edn: R.I.C.S. (surveyor, Eng.) Coll. of Estate Mgmt. 1951; Calif. lic. Gen. Contr., Real Estate Lic. Career: Kemp & Hawley, London, articled pupil; sr. property mgr. Coldwell Banker & Co., 1951-64; mktg. mgr. Great Lakes Realty 1965-66; v.p. real estate & constrn. Dean Witter & Co. 1967-77; nat. mgr. of real estate Transcon Lines 1977-80; v.p. leasing & prop. mgmt. August Financial Corp., Long Beach 1981--; Calif. Dept. R.E. approved lectr. on Leasing, Constrn., Prop. Mgmt.; founder of Dean Witter & Co. R.E. Dept.; mem. Past Pres. Club So. Cal. Cricket Assn.; mem: Royal Inst. of Chartered Surveyors, Eng. 1951, Smithsonian Inst., So. Calif. Cricket Assn. 1951-, B.O.M.A. Orange Co.; author: A Gaggle of Geese; Old Haberdashers Book on Nouns of Assemblage (collective nouns); mil: Radar A.B. RC-3, Royal Navy, Eng. 1945-48, 1939-45 Service Star, Atlantic Star, Def. Medal, Victory Medal, Sharpshooter; Republican; Episcopal; rec: etymology, music, horticulture. Res: 22242 Buenaventura St Woodland Hills 91364 Ofc: August Fin. Corp. 4401 Atlantic Ave, Ste. 400, Long Beach 90807

GOERGEN, JAN ROGER, financier; b. Dec. 11, 1935, Caledonia, MN; s. Cass Leon and Flavia Joyce (Evans) G.; m. Karen Rolli, June 25, 1977; edn: BA, Univ. of Minn. 1957; Harvard Bus. (Ext.) 1958-9, London Sch. of Econ. 1968-9, Univ. of Caracas 1977-82, PhD cand., Internat. Econ. Career: Merrill Lynch & Assocs. Investment Corp. 1959-62; vp-finance, sr. v.p., exec. vice pres., pres., pres./chief op. ofcr., currently chmn./chief exec. with Intercap, Ltd. and its affils.; (current) Congl. Advis. Council, US Senatorial Bus. Advis. Bd., Am. Economic Council Found., Nat. Found. for Philanthropy; honors: Eagle Scout, BSA 1950; John Sargeant - Pillsbury Fellow (Univ. Minn. Found. 1964); One of Minn.'s Outstanding (JC's 1967); Order of Bolivar (Venezuela 1980); mem: Internat. Assn. of Finl. Planners, Am. Soc. of Profl. Cons.; clubs: Rancho Santa Fe Garden Club, Univ. of Minn. Found., Eagle Scout Alumni Assn., Big Brother, Little League Football. Works: mng. an investment portfolio for an OPEC member nation (value 3 billion dollars 1975, to over 14 billion value in 1984); devel. first program to achieve infinite leverage in the purchase of US equity securities (1962); estab. first co. to survey and accurately project mutual fund perf. (1964); asstd. in design of first series of US oil and gas lmtd. partnerships (1966); asstd. in design of first offshore real estate investment trust (1968), trust grew to be largest single owner/mgr. of US properties in just four years; designed first combination travel resort prop. ownership concept (1972); mil: 2d lt. US Army (Battlefield Comm.) 1951-52, Purple Heart, Silver Star; Episcopal; rec: travel, tennis, fishing, swim. Res: POB 1485, Rancho Santa Fe 92067 Ofc: Intercap, Ltd. POB 607, Rancho Santa Fe 92067

GOETTIG, DONELLA C., management analyst, b. Sept. 28, 1932, Pana, Ill.; d. Dwight and Elva (Pope) Culberson; m. Alan Goettig, Aug. 7, 1954; children: Jeff, b. 1957, Susan, b. 1959, Jon, b. 1960; edn: BS in office mgt., Univ. of Ill. 1957. Career: instr. Bus. Edn. Dept., Cerro Coso Comm. College, Ridgecrest, 1963-76; management analyst, Mgmt. Div. Ofc. of Fin. and Mgmt., Naval Weapons Center, China Lake 1976-79, Mgr. Office Systems (Mgmt. Information Sys. Div.), Ofc. of Fin. and Mgmt. NWC, 1979--, Mgr. Xerox Office Information System, 1982-4; mem. Office Careers Advis. Group (Burroughs H.Sch., Cerro Coso Coll.); recipient Sustained Superior Performance Award, NWC China Lake 1981; mem: Internat. Information/Word Processing Assn., Women's Aux. Ofcrs. Club (pres. 1967), Pink Ladies Hosp. Aux., Girl Scouts Area Chpsn. 1971-2; Republican; Prot.; rec: ski, hike, fishing, sewing. Res: POB 2141 Ridgecrest 93555 Ofc: Naval Weapons Ctr (Code 0844) China Lake 93555

GOETZ, BRUCE EUGENE, farmer/processor; b. May 17, 1927, San Francisco; s. George C. and Georgia R. (Farnsworth) G.; m. Carol Baur, Feb. 2, 1951; children: Linda, b. 1951, Bruce Jr., b. 1953, Daniel, b. 1956, Tim, b. 1958, Tracey, b. 1963; edn: Laney Jr. Coll. 1947-9. Career: audio-visual repairman, Oakland Board of Education, 1949-50; real estate salesman Anza Realty, 1950-51; insurance agt. (asst. mgr., instr. new agts., claims adjustor) Unity Mutual, United Ins., Prudential Ins., General Agent, John Hancock, 1951-66, farmer/processor Green Valley Blueberry Farm, 1966--; founding pres. Sonoma County Farm Trails (bd. dirs. 8 yrs); advis. com. General Plan for Sonoma Co.; chmn. advis. com. Forestville Sch. District; Strawberry advis. com., Calif. State Farm Bureau; mem. Sonoma Co. Farm Trails, Sonoma Co. Farm Bureau, Lions Club, Druids 121; mil: sgt. USAAF 1945-47; Democrat; Methodist; rec: golf, bowling, square dancing. Address: Green Valley Blueberry Farm, 9345 Ross Sta. Rd. Sebastopol 95472

GOFFMAN, JERRY M., psychologist; b. Feb. 6, 1940, Brooklyn, NY; s. Ben and Esther (Bregman) G.; 1 son, David, b. 1969; edn: BA, CSU San Diego 1964, MS, 1969; PhD, U.S. Internat. Univ. 1972; Psychologist, Calif. Bd. MQA 1981. Career: research director Center for Prisoner of War Studies, San Diego 1969-77; program mgr. Domestic Violence Intervention Pgm., San Bernardino County Dept. of Mental Health, 1977-81; psychologist, founder/coord. Batterers Anonymous (self-help counseling pgm. for men who batter women; currently with 30 chapters in 14 states) 1981--; mem. Inland Psychol. Assn.; chmn. San Bernardino Co. Sch. Attendance Rev. Bd. 1979; speaker num. confs., profl. assns.; arts. in mil., med., psych. journals; mil: USAR; rec: computer hacker. Res: 1729 No Colwyn Ave Highland 92346 Ofc: Batterers Anonymous, POB 29, Redlands 92373

GOLDBERG, ANDREA RACHELLE, marriage, family and child therapist; b. Sept. 6, 1950, Los Angeles; d. Anchel and Joy Lee (Levy) G.; edn: BA, USC 1975, MA, Pepperdine Univ. 1977; Lic. Marriage, Family and Child Therapist, Calif. 1980; Hypnosis BBSE Cert. 1982 Career: pvt. practice MFCT/clin. cons. Creative Counseling & Guidance Center, Sherman Oaks, 1980-82, also pvt. practice MFCT in West Los Angeles, and Pomona (In-patient & Out-patient Facilities) 1980-82; pvt. practice in Marriage, Family, and Child Therapy, West Covina 1982--; instr. Learning Tree Open Univ., Thousand Oaks 1982-; mem: Am., Calif. Assn. of Marriage and Family Therapists, Calif. State Psychol. Assn., Am. Assn. of Biofeedback Clinicians, Am. Assn. for Counseling and Devel.; bd. trustees, Bridge: Away Across, Inc. 1979-83; mem. The Menniger Found. 1984-; lectr. in field of general psychol. 1981-, wkshops in family comm., self-esteem and assertiveness; Republican; Jewish; rec: horseback riding, oil painting. Res: 3011 Adornos Way, Burbank 91504 Ofc: Private Practice, Home Savings Bldg., 100 So Vincent Ave, Ste 404, West Covina 91790

GOLDBERG, ARNOLD NORMAN, real estate broker; b. Dec. 22, 1944, Norwich, Conn.; s. Julius and Marion (Rutchik) G.; 1 dau. Susan, b. 1965; edn: AA, Sacto. City Coll. 1964; Calif. lic. real estate broker. Career: actor, electrician, sound, props., asst. to prods. Lewis & Young Prodns., Sacramento Music Circus, 1957-66; toured Mexico and S. Am. with "Carousel" and "Showboat", US State Dept. spons. tour, 1966; secty. R.G. Cooley Constrn Inc., 1981-83; pres./real estate broker California Lake Lands Inc. (R.E. appraiser, investor, developer; packaged home sales), 1983--; mem: Nat., Calif., Assn. of Realtors;

Nevada Co. Bd. of Realtors; Moose; Democrat; Jewish; rec: philately, theatrical lighting, elec. wiring. Res: 14907 Lake Lane, Nevada City 95959 Ofc: California Lake Lands Inc. POB 1272, Nevada City 95959

GOLDBERG, DAVID ARTHUR, physician; b. Apr. 23, 1944, Milwaukee, Wisc.; s. Max S. and Beatrice (Ansfield) G.; m. Cheryl, Aug. 20, 1967; children: Jason, b. 1973, Dana, b. 1976; edn: BS, Univ. of Wisc. 1966, MD, U. of Wisc. Med. Sch. 1970. Career: internship, res. (Int. Med.), fellowship (Nephrology), USPHS Hospital, San Francisco 1970-74; fellowship in Neph., VA Hosp., S.F. 1974-75; pvt. practice, San Francisco 1975--; asst. clin. prof. of med. UC San Francisco; co-dir. Intensive Care Unit, St. Joseph's, SF 1976-8; staff: Marshal Hale Hosp. (med. dir. Alcohol Care Unit 1980-2), Mt. Zion Hosp., French Hosp., St. Mary's Hosp., Univ. Calif. Hosp., (S.F.); Dip. Am. Bd. of Internal Med. 1973; Dip. Am. Bd. of Nephrology 1978; mem: AMA, CMA, SF Med. Soc., Am. Heart Assn.; spl. interests: Occupational Toxicology, Alcohol Rehab.; mil: USPH 1970-4; Jewish; rec: tennis, woodwkg., computer pgmmg. Res: 339 Magellan San Francisco 94116 Ofc: 350 Parnassus, Ste 609, San Francisco 94117

GOLDBERG, M. RICHARD, hand surgeon; b. May 23, 1946, NYC; s. Samuel and Florence (Nussbaum) G.; m. Celeste, Oct. 4, 1975; children: Dara, b. 1978, Sharon, b. 1980; edn: BS, Univ. of NY 1968; MD, NY Med. Coll. 1972; Gen. Surgery & Orthopedic Tng., Albert Einstein Coll. of Med.; Hand Surgery Tng., Univ. of Colo. Med. Ctr.; Hand Surgeon. Career: hand surgeon Hand Surgery Assoc., Sacto.; asst. clin. prof. UC Davis Med. ctr.; honors: grad., cum laude, Hon. Univ. in Biological Socs.; mem: Am. Coll. of Surgeons; Am. Acad. Orthopedic Surgeons; Am. Soc. for Surgery of the Hand; Western Orthopedic Assn.; diplomat Am. Bd. of Orthopedic Surgery; No. Eastern Calif. chpt. Arthritis Found. bd. dirs.; Republican; Jewish; rec: golf, skiing. Res: 4805 Brompton Ct Carmichael 95608 Ofc: 2 Scripps Dr, Ste 210, Sacramento 95825

GOLDBERGER, MARVIN LEONARD, educator, physicist; b. Oct 22, 1922, Chicago, IL; s. Joseph and Mildred (Sedwitz) Goldberger; cousin, Dr. Joseph Goldberger, discoverer of Pellagra cure; BS, Carnegie Inst. of Tech., 1943; Ph.D., Univ. Chicago, 1;948; m. Mildred Ginsburg, Nov. 25, 1945; children: Joel S., b. 1952; Samuel M., b. 1949. Career: asst. to assoc. prof., Univ. Chicago,m 1950-55; prof. 1955-57; Higgins Prof. of Mathematical Physics, Princeton Univ., 1957-77; Joseph Henry Prof. of Physics, Princeton Univ., 1977-78; chmn., Dept. of Physics, Princeton Univ., 1970-76; pres., Calif. Inst. of Tech., 1978--; also mem., Gen. Motors bd., 1980; mem., President's Sci. Adv. Comm., 1965-69; adv. comm., Office of Sci. and Tech., 1969--. Recipient: Sc.D., Carnegie-Mellon Univ., 1979; Sc.D., Univ. of Notre Dame, 1979; D.H.L., Hebrew Union Coll., 1980; LL.D., Occidental Coll., 1980; Heineman Prize for Mathematical Physics. Mem.: Natl. Acad. of Scis.; Amer. Physical Soc.; Amer. Acad. of rts & Scis.; Fedn. of Amer. Scientists; chmn. 1972-73; Amer. Philosophical Soc.; Council for Foreign Rels.; Comm. on Internatl. Security and Arms Control; Nuclear Safety Oversight Comm. Mil.: SSgt., USA Corps of Engrs., 1943-46. Democrat. Jewish. Rec.: gourmet cooking, jogging, scuba diving. Res.: 415 S. Hill Ave., Pasadena 91106; Office of the President Calif. Inst. of Technology, Pasadena 91125.

GOLDMAN, JERRY B., insurance agent; b. Mar. 17, 1953, Detroit, Mich.; s. Hyman and Lucille (Schwartz) G.; m. Harriet Zaff, Oct. 5, 1975; children: Phillip, b. 1977, Erik, b. 1978, Brooke, b. 1983; edn: acctg., CSU Northrodge 1972. Career: general ins. agent, spec. in life, disability income, medical, estate planning, prin. J.B.Goldman Ins. Services, Woodland Hills; awards: Million Dollar Round Table, Nat. Sales Achievement, Nat. Quality Award; mem. San Fernando Life Underwriters; Boys Little League, Temple Mens Club; Democrat; Jewish; rec: motorcycling. Res: 117 Springdale Ct. Thousand Oakds 91360 Ofc: J.B.Goldman Ins. Services, 5955 De Soto Ave, Ste 232, Woodland Hills 91367

GOLDMAN, WARREN DALE, warehouse leasing co. president; b. Apr. 27, 1937, Hollister; s. Homer Ward and Lela Florence (Babbitt) G.; m. Mary Lou Molinari, Apr. 26, 1957; children: Jeffrey, b. 1958, Stephen, b. 1961; edn: Hartnell Jr. Coll. eve. sch., 1969-77. Career: started as carpenter 1960, then foreman 1964, supt. 1967, estimator/salesman 1969, partner 1976, Salinas Steel Builders Inc., pres./sole owner 1981--; founder/gen. partner Goldman Land and Devel. Co., 1963--; founder/gen. partner Goldman and Molinari Warehouse Leasing, 1973--; dir. Bank of Salinas; mem: Rotary, Elks, Sons of Italy, Native Sons of the Golden West, Presidents Club of Calif., Internat. Airshow; mil: USNR; Republican; Episcopal; rec: golf, football, duck hunting. Res: 44 Los Laureles Ave Salinas 93901 Ofc: Salinas Steel Builders Inc. 1161 Terven St Salinas 93901

GOLDNER, RUTH, psychotherapist-marriage & family counselor; b. June 16, 1915, Sacramento; d. Bernard and Gertrude (Blumberg) Freidberg; m. Sanford Goldner, July 24, 1938; 1 son, Steven, b. 1943; edn: BA, UC Berkeley 1937; cert. counseling splst. UCLA 1973; MA, Goddard Coll. 1976; lic. Marriage, Family, Child Counselor, Calif. 1976. Career: actress/dir. in theatre and radio, NYC, San Francisco, Berkeley, Sacto., 1936-55; group wkr. in improvisational tecniques with teen-agers, Christadora Settlement House, NYC, 1937-8; pub. rels. and bus. exec. Pasternak Advt. Agcy., Los Angeles 1955-68; research wkr. Resthaven Psychiat. Hosp., L.A. 1968-9; counselor So. Calif. Counseling Ctr., L.A. 1973-7; pvt. practice marriage, family and individual counseling/ supr. of Intern-trainees, Hollywood-Sunset Comm. Clinic, L.A. 1977--; field faculty for MA degree student in psychol.; condr. weekly sem. in Focusing (Gendlin)

technique; mem: Am. Assn. for Counseling and Devel., Calif. Assn. for Marriage, Family and Child Counselors; clubs: California, NOW; Democrat; rec: writing, theatre. Address: 3209 Silverado Dr Los Angeles 90039

GOLDSMAN, GENE, lawyer; b. July 22, 1951, Neward, N.J.; s. Leon and Betty (Goldwater) Goldsman; edn: BA, Seton Hall Univ., 1973, JD, Pepperdine Univ. Sch. of Law, 1976; m. Cher DiLiberti, Dec. 18, 1980; son, Aron Matthew, b. 1981; career: law clerk, John K. Trotter, Inc., 1975-77; Law Offices of DiLiberti & Goldsman, Santa Ana 1977--; instr. Orange Co. Bar Assn. Educational Pgm., Grades 4-6; guest speaker, Fullerton Jr. College; mem: Calif. Bar Assn., American, Calif., Orange County Trial Lawyers Assns., ACLU, Cardozo Soc.; res: 156 Monarch Bay, South Laguna; ofc: Law Offices of DiLiberti & Goldsman, A Profl. Law Corp., 611 Civic Center Dr. W., Suite 200, Santa Ana 92701.

GOLDSTEIN, ADELL ROBERTA, health care administrator, b. May 2, 1944, Chgo.; d. Benjamin and Bertha Baim; m. Alan Goldstein, June 9, 1963; children: Gail Rose, b. 1964, Devora Shoshana, b. 1966, Israel Joseph, b. 1969; edn: AA, LA City Coll. 1964; dip. int. design, Internat. Corres. Schs. 1967; cert. int. design, Interior Designers Guild 1972; dietetic asst. Pasadena Jr. Coll. 1974; BA in home econ., CSU Los Angeles 1976, MS in health care adminstrn. CSULA Sch of Bus. & Econ. 1980; lic. Nursing Home Adminstr. 1973; cert. Dietary Supr., Am. Dietetic Assn., & P.C.C. Career: co-adminstr. /dietary supr. Sunshine Terrace Conv. Hosp., Los Angeles 1973--; asst. adminstr. / dietary cons. Hayworth Terrace 1, L.A. 1963--; dietary cons. Hayworth Terrace 11, 1965-, and Shalom Retirement Hotel, 1972-; interior designer/cons. Adell Interiors, 1972--; prin. Adell's Cons. for Health Care Planning, 1980--; instr. LACC Student Pgm. tng. RNs and Dietary Supervs., 1977-80, Cont. Edn. courses; bd. dirs. Shalom Hotel 1971-; bd. dirs. Hayworth Terrace 1968-; mem: Hosp., Instn., Ednl., Food Service Soc. (L.A. chapter founding pres.; Calif. State Sec. 1977); Fellow Am. Coll. of Nursing Home Adminstrs.; H.S.A. Agency; Residential Care Fac. Owners Assn.; C.A.H.F; L.A.H.A.; orgns: vol. investigator LA Co. Bur. of Consumer Affairs 1975-8; active PTA, 1972-9; bd. mem. LA Mikvah Soc.; mem. Am. Mizrachi Women, Emunah Women of Am., Bikur Cholem Soc., Neshei Agudath Yisroel Bd. 1971-4; rec: piano, needlepoint, fencing. Res: 138 No June St Los Angeles 90004 Ofc: Supreme Bus. Services, c/o Shalom Hotel, 330 No Hayworth Ave Los Angeles 90004

GOLDSTEIN, MICHAEL STUART, computer systems co. executive; b. Apr. 22, 1945, NYC, s. David and Ann (Klotz) G.; m. Penny J. Donaldson, May 4, 1968; children: David John, b. 1971, Darren Stuart, b. 1979; edn: BA, UC Los Angeles 1966. Career: promotions mgr. Transamerica Fin., Los Angeles 1966-70; Western regional mgr. Trans Union Systems Corp., Los Angeles, Chgo., 1970-78; pres. Mutogo Data Corp., Irvine 1978--; condr. num. seminars in field; cons. in computer systems; mem: Data Entry Mgmt. Assn., Data Processing Mgmt. Assn., Am. Mgmt. Assn.; Democrat; Jewish. Ofc: Mutogo Data Corp. 15560-E Rockfield Blvd Irvine 92714

GOLDSTEIN, ROBERT STANLEY, contractor; b. Jan. 11, 1923, Kansas City, Mo.; s. Leo Roy and Doris (Binks) G.; edn: Northwestern 1946-47. Career: soldier of fortune Africa (8 yrs.), last personal envoy to US for Col. Ojuku, Biafran War; pres./ chmn. bd. Federated Advtg., 1970-78; gen. contr./ pres./ chmn. bd. Pittsburgh Metals 1974-84; honors: TV and Radio Pub. Svc., Mayor Sam Yorty, City of L.A. 1973, and Calif. State Assemblyman Hank Arklin, 1970; mem. State Congl. Advisory Bd.; mil: lt. col. US Army Air Corps; Republican; rec: flying, horse racing. Res: 7224 Hillside Los Angeles 90046 Ofc: Pittsburgh Metals, 808 S Vermont Los Angeles 90005

GOLDSTRICH, JOSEPH DANIEL, physician; b. May 13, 1938, Dallas, Tx.; edn: BS, SMU, 1959; MD, UT Southwestern Med. Sch., 1964; cardiology fellow, Dallas VA Hosp. 1969-70; USPHS postdoc. fellow in metabolism, UT Southwestern Med. Sch. 1970-71. Career: mil. capt., Chief of Preventive Med., US Forces, Dominican Repub. (1965-6), Ft. Benning, Ga. (1966-7); pvt. practice of cardiology, Dallas 1973-75; nat. dir. of edn. and comm. pgms. American Heart Assn., Dallas, Tx. 1975-77; cardiologist Longevity Ctr., Santa Barbara, Ca. 1977-78; dir. Heart Center, Dallas 1979-81; med. dir. Pritikin Longevity Ctr., Santa Monica 1981-2; currently, pvt. practice of nutritnl. med. and cardiol., Pacific Palisades; fmr. faculty, Southwestern Med. Sch., UT Health Sci. Ctr., No. Tx. State Univ.; awards: Undergrad. Scholarships, SMU 1958-9; Kappa Mu Epsilon 1959; Army Commend. Medals 1966, 67; Who's Who in Tx. 1973-4; (FACC) Fellow Am. Coll. of Cardiology 1977; fmr. bd. dirs.: Dallas Free Clinic, Council on Alcoholism, Cardiac Inst., City Council's Drug Abuse Council, Diabetes Assn. Inc., Am. Heart Assn., (Dallas). Address: Joe D. Goldstrich, MD, FACC, POB 5445, Santa Monica 90405

GOLDWATER, MYRA, real estate broker; b. Nov. 14, 1913, St. Louis, Mo.; d. Joseph Abraham and Fannie (Rindsberg) Schoenfeld; m. Gerald Benjamin Goldwater (dec. 1966), Aug. 4, 1940; 1 dau., Teree Goldwater Peck, b. 1942; grad. Los Angeles H.S. 1930; cert. GRI (Graduate R.E.Inst.), Calif. Assn. of Realtors 1978. Career: owner/opr. of Studio Art of California (social printing plant estab. by Goldwater family in 1906, Los Angeles), operative head 1943-61, sold in 1964; real estate agt., Palm Springs 1963-, broker/owner Myra Goldwater, Realtor in Palm Springs 1967--; commnr. Pres. Reagan's Commn. on Housing 1981-2; apptd. advis. com. Federal Home Loan Mortgage Corp (Freddie Mac) 1984-; ex-ofcio. mem. HUD Task Force on Deregulation 1982; mem. Coordinating Council of Riverside Co. (CRA), 8 yrs.; dir. Nat. Assn. of Realtors 1978-85 (Realtor Found. 1982-3, Res. MLS com., PAC Cong. Liaison Subcom.); dir. Calif. Assn. of Realtors 1973-84 (exec. com. 1977; num. coms., chmnships; CREPAC trustee 1982-5; Legal Action Fund trustee 1983-88; Regl. v.p. 1975,6; liaison to Calif. Escrow Assn. 1979-81); Palm Springs Bd. of

Realtors (pres. 1973,4; Realtor of Year 1981); past bd. dirs. P.S. CofC, United Way of Desert; Republican (vp Calif. Repub. Assem. 1980-4; dir./past pres. P.S. Repub. Assem.); Jewish. Address: Myra Goldwater, Realtor, 246 So. Palm Canyon Dr Palm Springs 92262

GOLDWASSER, ESTHER MARIE, lawyer; b. Sept. 3, 1949, Milwaukee, Wisc.; d. Donald B. and Arlis V. (Rifkin) G.; edn: Bs, Univ. Calif. 1972; JD, (salutatorian) Armstrong Coll. 1978. Career: solo practice law in Los Angeles 1979-82; litigation atty. partnership law practice in Bay Area, 1982--; scholarship awards: Farmers Ins. Gp. 1975-6, Soroptomists of San Leandro 1976, Am. Business Womens Assn. 1975, 76, 77, West Pub. Co. 1977; mem: Alameda Co. Bar Assn.; (fmr) San Fernando Valley Women Lawyer's Assn. (charter), San Fernando Vly Bar Assn., Los Angeles Co. Bar Assn.; mem. Am. Businesswomen's Assn.; Democrat; Jewish; rec: lace crocheting, horseback riding. Ofc: 2608 Central Ave, Ste. 3, Union City 94587

GOLTERMANN, ANNETTE, real estate broker; b. Sept. 14, 1939, San Rafael (4th gen. Californian); d. Anthony Peter and Bess Vivian (McNeill) Garatti; m. Kenneth Conrad Goltermann, Dec. 21, 1963; children: John Kenneth Conrad Casey, b. 1970; April Elizabeth, b. 1972; edn: AA, Coll. of Marin 1959, DA, CSU San Jose 1961; Calif. State Tchg. Cred. 1961. Career: teacher Healdsburg Sch. District, 1961-64, Petaluma City Schs. 1964-69, substitute tchr. Sonoma Co. Schs. Two Rock Sch. Dist. 1976-79; real estate broker Goltermann Real Estate, Petaluma 1982--; v.p. Goltermann Constrn. Inc. 1964--. Commnr. of Housing & Urban Devel. Sonoma Co. 2d Sup. Dist. 1981-. Awards: life mbr. Million Dollar Sales 1979, Sonoma Co. MLS. Mem: Calif. Tchg. Assn. 1961-70; Calif. Bd. of Realtors, Petaluma Council of Realtors, Sonoma Co. MLS, Petaluma CofC; Cinnabar Sch. PTA pres. 1976-7; Calif. Cong. of PTA 1961-70, 1975-; AAUW (1st vp 1975); Dominican (Convent Sch.)Alumnae Assn.; Cinnabar Sch. Site Council 1978-82, Cinnabar Edn. Found.(sec 1982-); Republican; Prot. Rec: entertaining at home, gardening, family genealogy, youth work. Address: Goltermann Real Estate 1060 Skillman Ln. Petaluma 94952

GOMER, CHARLES JOSEPH, radiation biologist; b. Mar. 13, 1950, Jersey City, NJ; s. Frank Edward and Eleanor Josephine (Geiger) G.; m. Patricia Nash, June 28, 1975; 1 dau: Alison, b. 1983; edn: BS, St. Lawrence Univ. 1973; PhD, State Univ. of NY, Buffalo 1978. Career: post doctoral fellow, Los Alamos Nat. Lab., Los Alamos, NM 1978-80; asst. prof. pediatrics USC Sch. of Med., Los Angeles 1980--; bd. of sci. dirs. Photofrin Med. Gp.; awards: New Investigation Research Awd., Nat. Cancer Inst., Nat. Inst. of Health; mem: Am. Assn. of Cancer Research; Radiation Research Soc.; publs: 30. Res: 1241 Amberwood Dr Duarte 91010 Ofc: Childrens Hospital, 4650 Sunset Blvd Los Angeles 90027

GOMEZ, ROBERT HUERTA, company president; b. June 2, 1952, Woodland, Ca.; s. Librado Martinez and Consuelo Maria (Huerta) G.; m. Donna Birrueta, Dec. 24, 1982; edn: dip. Edison H.S. 1970; dip. automotive repair, Pacific Tech. Inst. 1971. Career: driver delivery, counter sales Lou's Auto Supply, Inc., Stockton 1971-77, owner/pres. 1977--; Republican; Mormon; rec: sports. Res: 945 No Sutter St Stockton 95202 Ofc: Lou's Auto Supply, Inc. 1322 So El Dorado Stockton 95206

GONZALES, ROBERT ALPHONSE, real estate broker; b. Apr. 13, 1918, Los Angeles; s. Juan and Concepcion G.; m. Jennie Jan. 6, 1946; children: Charles, b. 1961; Roberta Renee, b. 1968; edn: grad. Garfield High Sch. 1937; Calif. lic. real estate broker. Career: real estate sales in family bus. (estab. by father in 1925), Juan Gonzales Realty, Los Angeles 1944-50; owner/broker R.A. Gonzales Realty, L.A. 1950--, (now joined in the bus. by his son, Charles, recently returned from Mormon Mission work in Argentina) awards: Golden Gloves boxing featherweight champion of the Pacific Coast 1936; orgnzr. First and Alma Sts. Boys Club, spons. by the Sheriff Dept.; mem. Community Affairs Soc.; mil: enlisted man USAF 1940-44, svc. in Iceland, Eng.; Mormon; rec: phys. fitness. Res: 700 De Palma Way, Montebello 90640 Ofc: R.A.Gonzales Realty, 6319 Whittier Blvd Los Angeles 90022

GONZALEZ, JUDITH SCHOLASTICA, nursing home administrator; b. Dec. 24, 1945, Chgo., Ill.; d. Russell Homes and Helen Marie (Field) Smith; m. Joseph Felix Gonzalez, Feb. 14, 1973; children: Christopher, b. 1974; Anthony, b. 1976; edn: LVN, Compton Coll. 1975; AS, 1977; BA, Dominguez State 1980; MBA, 1982; Calif. lic. voc. nurse 1976, teaching credential nursing 1981, lic. nursing home adminstr. 1981. Career: critical care nurse Long Beach V.A. Hosp. 1969-75; emerg. room & I.C.U., Long Beach Comm. Hosp. 1976-8;: dir. of staff/ adminstrv. asst. in tng. Western Medical Ent., Glendale 1979-81; lic. adminstr. Am. Health Ctrs., Newport Bch. 1981-2, Delma Corp., Huntington Bch. 1983--; co. recognition, Adminstr. of the Yr. 1983; mem: Calif. Assn. of Health Facilities (chmn. Peer Assist. Com., statewide and O.C. chpt.; bd. mem. at large O.C. chpt., Comm. Care com., Mem. com.; editor O.C. Chpt. News); Calif. League of Long Term Care Nurses (coms.); ARC instr. C.P.R.; Nat. League Nursing; Catholic; rec: running, painting, dancing. Res: 11954 Agnes Cerritos 90701 Ofc: Delma Corp., 18851 Florida St Huntington Beach 92648

GOOCH, WILLIAM THOMSON, manufacturing company executive; b. Feb. 9, 1942, Reno, Nevada; s. William Ozwald and Anna Cecilia (Thompson) G.; m. Linda Jean Betts, Jan. 6, 1968; children: Teresa, b. 1968; Aaron, b. 1971; edn: AA, Santa Rosa Jr. Coll. 1965. Career: with Optical Coating Laboratory Inc., Santa Rosa 1962--; tchn. 1962-70; inspection svcs. mgr. 1971-3; tchnl. prods. div. quality assurance mgr. 1974-82; gov. prods. div. quality assurance mgr.

1983--; ind. cons. Prod. Quality and Quality Control 1981-; employee counselor 1983-; technl. review com. 1982-; awards: ABCD Awd., Lifespring 1983; mem: Russian River Fly Fishers; Foothills Homeowners Assn.; Lifespring; Santa Rosa Jr. CofC; mng. ed./prin. author: Optical Coating Lab. Ops. manual (Santa Rosa ops.) and the Govt. Prods. Div. Qual. Ass. manuals; mil: nat. def. deferral; Republican; Prot.; rec: human potential tng., fly fishing, camping. Res: 5405 Idlewood Road Santa Rosa 95404 Ofc: Optical Coating Laboratory, Inc., 2789 Northpoint Pkwy Santa Rosa 95401-7397

GOOD, ROBERT EUGENE, chiropractor; b. Aug. 28, 1935, Stillwater, Okla.; s. Robert Eugene and Geraldine Lee (Graham) G.; edn: BS, Univ. of Okla. 1958; DC, Los Angeles Coll. of Chiropractic 1976; DC, Calif. 1976. Career: USN commission 1958; Lt.jg. Engring. ofcr. USS Laffey DD-724 1960-1; research engr. rank Lt(jg) US Bureau of Reclamation 1961-72; chiropractic practice, Santa Barbara 1977--; mil: Lt.jg., USN 1958-61; Democrat; Christian. Res: 434 E Valerio Santa Barbara 93101 Ofc: 1811 State Street Santa Barbara 93101

GOODALE, CHARLES CHESTER, JR., irrigation company president; b. Dec. 11, 1935, Visalia; s. Charles Chester Sr. and Marie Elinore (Da Shiell) G.; m. Barbara Ann Rector (div.), Jan 30, 1960; children: Charles Edward, b. 1960; Chester Michael, b. 1960; Timothy Joel, b. 1962; Kelly Luan, b. 1969; edn: AA, Coll. of Sequoias 1956; BS, CSU Fresno 1961. Career: hd. sales engr. Muller Irrigation, Terra Bella & Madera 1961-79; hd. sales engr. Applied Irrigation, Fresno 1979-80; gen. mgr./ pres./ chmn. bd. A & G Irrigation, Madera 1980--; awards: Sequoia Medal, Sequoia Council of Boy Scouts of Am. 1979; honors: Chi Beta Alpha hon. agricultural frat. 1959; mem: Terra Bella Lions Club; mil: Sgt., Calif. Nat. Guard (Army Nat. Guard) 1957-8; Republican; Methodist; rec: photog., hiking, canoeing. Res: 708 Claremont Madera 93637 Ofc: A & G Irrigation, 214 So Gateway Dr Madera 93637

GOODE, VERN EVERT, manufacturing co. executive; b. May 31, 1939, Pontiac, Mich.; s. Dolph Evert and Beatrice Edith (Hartung) G.; m. Joan C. Isaacs, June 29, 1958; children: Kevin, b. 1959; Karen, b. 1961; edn: AMA courses in mgmt., budgeting & fin. planning, 1970, 1983. Career: engr. apprentice General Motors, Pontiac, Mich. 1957-60; engr. cons., San Jose 1960-8; mgr. prod. engring. Caelus Memories 1968-73; dir. engring. Memorex, Santa Clara 1973-4; v.p. mgmt. IPS, Sunnyvale 1974-5; pres. Dical Inc., San Jose 1975-8; pres. Caelus Memories 1978--; Am. Nat. Standards Inst. 1968-75; mem: past, Civil Defense Desert/ Alpine Rescue Svc.; PTA (local pres.); Co. Bowling League (pres.); Co. Recreation Club (pres.); Golden Gate Water Ski Club (pres.); author: techl. art., Computer Media, pub. Small Systems World, Dec. 1980; Republican; Protestant; rec: water sports, snow skiing, raquetball. Res: 6645 Mt. Forest Drive San Jose 95120 Ofc: Caelus Memories, 1015 Timothy Dr San Jose 95133

GOODING, FREDERICK WAYNE, SR., physician - physiatry; b. July 11, 1951, Phila.; s. Gurney Franklin and Ethel Maime (Bell) G.; m. Sheila Wall, Aug. 9, 1975; children: Frederick Jr., b. 1974; Johan Demetrius, b. 1976; Shane Kyla, b. 1980; edn: BS, Princeton Univ. 1973; MD, Howard Univ. Coll. of Med. 1977; splst. in Physiatry (phys. med. & rehab.). Career: intern, UC Irvine 1977-8; spl. res. tng. UCLA, Wadsworth, VA 1978-80; chief of physical med. dept., Watts Health Found., Nat. Health Svcs. Corps. 1980-1; pvt. practice, Lynwood, 1981--; sports med. H.S. students; Nat. Conf. lectr.; prospective assoc. prof. PSRO, academia w/ Martin Luther King, Jr. Hosp. tng. pgm.; awards: No. 1 Sports Doctor, Jordan H.S. 1981-2; mem: CMA; AMA; IPA; NHSC; Lynwood, Inglewood CofC; Acad. Physical Med. and Rehab.; Princeton Univ. Alumni Assn.; inventor (pat. pend.): improved therapeutic transcutaneous electrical nerve stimulator, sci exhib. Franklin Inst., Analog Computer 1969; Christian; rec: sports. Res: 6250 Mosley Ave Los Angeles 90056 Ofc: 3584 Century Blvd, Ste C, Lynwood 90262

GOODLEY, PAUL C., research & development engineer; b. Feb. 23, 1941, Henderson, KY; s. Charles S. and Barbara E. (Griggs) G.; edn: BS, Murray State Univ. 1972. Career: cheml. techn. Monsanto Co. 1964-8; Murray State 1968-72; Abbott Labs 1972-8; sci. II, Research Lab. MSU 1978-80; R&D engr. 1980--; lab. dir. Murray State Univ. 1977-80; honors: Sigma Zi hon. sci. research soc.; mem: Am. Chem. Soc. for Mass Spectrometry; Am. Assn. for Adv. of Sci.; Kentucky Acad. of Sci.; Bay Area Mass Spectrometry Soc.; ACS Analytical Chem.; North Chgo. H.S. Sci. Seminar Series; publs: 28 publs. in field journals 1971--; mil: PFC, USAR 1963-9; rec: flying, coins, computers. Res: 10110 Parkwood Dr, No. 18-2, Cupertino 95014 Ofc: Hewlett- Packard Co., 1601 California Ave, Palo Alto 94304

GOODMAN ALEX W., chamber of commerce executive; b. Apr. 12, 1924, Los Angeles; s. Julius and Golda (Skulnick) Goodman; edn: BA in pub. adm., UCLA, 1950; US Chamber of Commerce Inst., Univ. Santa Clara, summers 1965-71; m. Shirley Anderson, July4, 1968; four children; career: Fire capt., Los Angeles County Fire Dept., 1948-65; chamber of commerce exec., Rosemead, Temple City, Buena Park, West Covina, 1965-76, mgr. San Clemente Chamber of Commerce, 1976--; mem: Federated Chambers of Commerce of Orange County (pres. 1982-83), Calif. Assn. of C. of C. Execs.; mil: m/sgt. US Army, 1944-47; rec: golf; res: 301 Calle Villario San Clemente 92672 ofc: San Clemente Chamber of Commerce 1100 No. El Camino Real, San Clemente 92672.

GOODMAN, FRANCES CARLA, psychotherapist; b. July 29, 1918, NY, NY; d. Louis M. and Jennie (Gaffen) Gold; div.; children: Joel, b. 1948; Sheldon, b. 1951; Gary, b. 1958; edn: BA, CSU, Los Angeles 1975; MS, USC 1977; psychotherapist, marriage, family and child therapist, State Calif. Bd. of Behavioral

Sci. Examiners 1978. Career: pvt. practice 1978--; currently in Beverly Hills; bd. dirs. So. Calif. Psychotherapy Affiliation; bd. mem. Gp. Psychotherapy Assn. of So. Calif.; honors: Psi Chi nat. hon. soc.; mem: Calif. Assn. of Marriage, Family, Child Therapists; Am. Orthopsychiatric Assn.; KCET; So. Poverty Law Ctr.; Simon Wiesenthal Ctr.; author: 3 short stories, pub. Compassionate Viewpoint, 1970; rec: writing novels. Res: 4193 Holly Knoll Dr Los Angeles 90027 Ofc: 9363 Wilshire Blvd, Ste 216, Beverly Hills 90210

GOODMAN, GLEN STUART, security systems co. executive; b. Jan. 22, 1950, Cleveland, Ohio; s. Louis and Belle (Kravitz) G.; edn: BBA, Ohio Univ. 1972; Western States Law Sch. 1973; pvt. investigator, State of Calif. 1979. Career: supvr. Broughton Foods, Athens, Ohio 1969-72; asst. res. dir. Lakeview Inc./ Ohio Univ. Res. Life, Athens, OH 1969-72; corp. security dir., asst. v.p. San Diego Fed. Savings & Loan Assn., San Diego 1972-9; v.p./ regl. dir. NAVCO Security Systems, San Diego 1979--; cons. to mgmt./ pvt. investigator, Glen S. Goodman Investigations, 1979--; mem: Calif. Assn. of Lic. Investigators; San Diego Co. Check Investigators; Rotarian; Soc. for Adv. of Mgmt.; Republican (Repub. Assocs.); Jewish; rec: tennis, jogging. Res: 6089 Cumulus Lane San Diego 92110 Ofc: NAVCO Security Systems, 16600 Aston St Irvine 92714

GOODMAN, SUSAN JANE, real estate broker; b. June 71, 1946, Suffern, NY; d. Irving Howard and Sylvia Helen (Maistroff) G.; edn: AA, Rider Coll. 1966; Calif. lic. real estate broker 1983. Career: real estate agt. Grubb & Ellis Comml. Brokerage Co., Los Angeles and Beverly Hills (top ten producer every year; spec. in sales/leasing ofc. bldgs., investments), 1976-84; broker Bailes & Associates, Westwood 1984--, spec. in ofc. leasing and investments; mem. Nat. Assn. of Women in Comml. Real Estate (1st v.p. L.A. chpt.); United Jewish Fund (R.E. Div.); rec: running, athletics. Res: 1078 Superba Ave, Venice 90291 Ofc: Bailes & Associates Inc. 10920 Wilshire Blvd, Ste 750, Los Angeles 90024

GOODRICH, WILLIAM CHARLES, association executive; b. Nov. 16, 1943, Denver, CO; s. Herbert Lynn and Francis L. Goodrich; edn: BBA, Columbia Univ., 1980; CLU, Amer. Coll., 1975; m. Mary Nelms, Jan. 30, 1963; chil: Lesha, b. 1963; Lori, b. 1963; Billie Louise, b. 1969. Career: vice pres., Custom Color, Inc., 1967-69; asst. dist. mgr., Ind. Order of Foresters, 1969-72; pres., American Financial Union, 1972-78; sr. vice pres., Western Growers Assn., 1978--. Honors: natl. sales achievement aed., 1975, 76, 77; natl. quality award, 1974, 76, 77, Natl. Assn. Life Underwriters. Mem: Masons; Calif. Fraternal Congress, FIC Section, past pres.; Amer. Soc. of Chartered Life Underwriters; Natl. & Long Beach-Orange Co. Assn. of Life Underwriters. Republican. Protestant. Rec: micro computers, chess, swim. Res: 13721 Solitaire, Irvine 92714; Office: Western Growers Assn., 17620 Fitch, Irvine 92714.

GOODRICH, WILLIAM SAYER, insurance broker; b. Dec. 30, 1918, San Francisco; s. William Henry and Sally Veronica (Sayers) G.; m. Evelyn Tate, June 25, 1981; edn: BA, UCLA 1943. Career: self-empl. ins. broker, Beverly Hills 1946-61, spec. in motion picture/t.v. fields 1961; partner Charles, Ryan & Rivers, Los Angeles 1961-71; avocado rancher 1972-7; ret. 1977-; v.p./ dir. Charles, Ryan & Rivers 1962-71; mem: Fallbrook CofC; Fallbrook Music Soc.; Calif. Yacht Club; Vista Valley Country Club; publs: RV Travel Log, 1978; mil: Lt.(jg), USNR 1942-57; Republican; Episcopal; rec: boating, RVs. Res: 2591 Daisy Lane Fallbrook 92028

GOODROW, LARRY EDWIN, SR., company executive; b. Jan. 27, 1949, San Jose; s. Florence Mae Deal Goodrow; m. Beverly Battaglia, Jan. 9, 1971; children: Angelique Lynette, b. 1971; Larry, Jr., b. 1973; edn: bus. degree, San Jose City Coll. 1973; lic. real estate salesman 1975, broker, 1979; life & disability ins. lic. 1977. Career: cost analyst, gen. constrn. Pacific Gas & Elec. Co. 1969-76; ofc. mgr. Golden Plan of California 1976-8; salesman Morrow Realty 1977-8; pres. Best Financial Svcs., Inc. 1978-83; pres. Lighthouse Mortgage Co. 1983--; tchr. seminars in field; honors: winner two 300 rings, achievement awds., twenty 700 patches (for 700 or better series in bowling), Am. Bowling Assn.; mem: Nat. Assn. of Realtors; San Jose Real Estate Bd.; Nat. Bowling Congress; Am. Bowling Congress; PAL Soccer; Pacific Baseball; fund raising, San Jose Christian Sch.; Prot.; rec: bowling, baseball, soccer. Res: 7139 Cahen Dr San Jose 95120 Ofc: Lighthouse Mortgage Co., 2077 So. Bascome Ave Campbell 95008

GOODWIN, ADELIA A., company president; b. Nov. 1, 1936, Hutchinson, Kans.; d. Harold P. and Mildred A. Guizlo; m. Dr. V. Charles Bachman, Feb. 14, 1979; children: Sandra A. Goodwin, b. 1960; Douglas K. Goodwin, b. 1963; edn: BA, Berean Christian Coll. 1983; MA (cand.), 1984. Career: graphic arts supvr. MRC Dept. Wichita State Univ., Wichita, Kansas 1975-80; founder/ pres. Studio Dee, Long Beach 1980--; co-founder/ assoc. minister Berean Ch. of the Scriptures, Long Beach; honors: Woman of the Yr. 1983, 1983; Hon. D.Min. 1982, Coll. of Life; mem: Long Beach CofC; Christian; rec: 6801 Millmark Ave Long Beach 90805 Ofc: Studio Dee, 2234 E Broadway Long Beach 90803

GOOLSBY, JE, advertising executive; b. Jan. 25, 1936, Livingston, Tenn.; s. John Y. and Nina; children: Ellen Frances, b. 1964, Desiree Monique, b. 1968, Cjaer Zorba, b. 1970; edn: Art Center Sch. 1953-4, El Camino Coll. 1958-9; BA, UC Santa Barbara 1963; Santa Barbara Bus. Coll. 1964. Career: building designer/ contr./ prin., 1964-65; publications mgr. Human Factors Research, Inc., Santa Barbara 1966-70; art dir. KVZK-TV, Pago Pago, Samoa 1970-72; art dir./publs. mgr. UCSB, 1972-76, graphic design instr., 1975; graphic designer/ prin., Santa Barbara 1976-80; advt. mgr. Sloan Technology Corp., S.B. 1981--;

owner Horizon Tours, a lmtd. partnershp. 1979-80; awards: Best Trade Mag., Best Archtl. Graphics, Greater S.B. Advt. Club, 1975; mem: S.B. Art Mus., S.B. Hist. Soc., Gr. S.B. Advt. Club; mil: sgt. US Army 1955-57, GCM, German Occ.; Democrat; Unitarian; rec: design. Res: 2322 White Ave, Santa BArbara 92109 Ofc: Sloan Technol. Corp., 605 E. Montecito St Sta Barbara 93103

GORDON, FORREST LYLE, life insurance executive; b. Feb. 4, 1926, Rich Hill, MO; s. Fay Ward and Martha Blanche (Caton) G.; m. Onie Elizabeth Orr, Sept. 11, 1946; children: Carol Diane (Kobe), 1949; David Ward, b. 1967; edn: Evang. Tchr. Tng. Cert., Bible Inst. of L.A. 1953; CLU, Am. Coll., 1977; dip., Inst. of Ins. Mktg., LSU (Baton Rouge, La.) 1973. Career: Coxswain/ deep sea diver, US Coast Guard 1943-6; fireman, sr. fire insp./capt. Los Angeles City Fire Dept. 1946-62; life ins. agent, unit mgr., gen. agent, currently dist. mgr.(San Fernando Valley), Fidelity Union Life Ins. Co., Dallas, Tex. (Home Office) 1965--; instr. Home Ofc. Ins. Sch. 1979; instr. Life Underwriters Tng. Council 1981; num. profl. awards incl. Awd. of Excellence 1978, Centurian Awd. 1982, Agcy. Man of Yr. 1965, 79, 80; MDRT 1981, Nat. Sales Acheivement Awd. 1969, Hall of Fame 1980. Mem. San Fernando Valley Life Underwriters (past bd. dirs.); lic. Baptist minister 1976-, Bible tchr., chmn. Missions, 1st Baptist Ch. of Reseda; publs: num. ins. arts.; church constn.; mil: USCG, WWII, Pac., Eur. theaters; Republican; Res: 6440 Baird Ave Reseda 91335 Ofc: Fidelity Union Life Ins. Co., POB 500 Dallas, Texas 75221

GORDON, JAMES BENNETT, JR., marriage, family & child counselor; b. Aug. 20, 1946, Newark, NJ; s. James B. and Marian Monica (Miller) G.; edn: BA, Cal Lutheran Coll. 1968; MA, Azusa Pacific Coll. 1975; PhD in prog., Univ. without Walls, 1984; Lic. MFCC, Calif. Bd. of Behav. Sci. Examiners 1978. Career: opr., family care home, Dept. Mental Health 1970-8; resource splst. (spl. edn. tchr.) Conejo Unified Sch. Dist. 1969-83; limited pvt. practice in counseling 1978--; owner/ opr. Gordon Charter & Limosine Svc., 1980--; recipient hon. svc. awd., PTA of Conejo 1979; mem: Conejo Adv. Bd. (past); Conejo Future Found. Com. on Youth; Com. of Tchr. Licensing & Preparation CLC & Cal Paly (team mem.); Westlake (Interfaith) Ecumenical Council; Boy Scouts of Am.; works: screen role in ABC-TV movie 1983; mem. coll. orch. (bassoon); coauthor (MFC) profl. conf. papers 1976; Republican; Lutheran; rec: travel, ski, 4 wheeling. Res: 2516 Young Ave Thousand Oaks 91360 Ofc: Counseling Center of the Oaks, 80 Long Ct Thousand Oaks 91360

GORDON, LARRY DUANE, financial executive; b. Nov. 26, 1937, Park Rapids, Minn.; s. Kurvin Harry and Anna Murr (Shipley-Barton); m. Katherine Marie Stoll, Oct. 17, 1978; children: Larry D., Jr., b. 1956; Burvin A., b. 1958; Pamela S., b. 1961; Twyla R., b. 1963; Ben A., b. 1966; Jermayne L., b. 1971; Justin E., b. 1982; Brandon A., b. 1982; edn: M, Univ. of Tokyo, 1957; Univ. of Maryland 1955-6; Univ. of Minn. 1954-; Allan Hacock Jr. Coll. 1965-8. Career: asst. br. mgr. Granite Consruction 1962-5; acctnt. Sambo's Restaurant 1968-9; fin. advr. Hastings Harcourt III; sr. v.p./ controller, Helena-Chemform Chemical Co.; bd. dirs. Prof. Express; bd. dirs. ASI Draperies; awards: Dist. Svc. Awd., State of Tenn. 1978; PA, State Calif. 1966; mem: Calif. Veterans Assn; Elks; Lions; Kiwanis; author: sci-fi. novel, Hallowed Ground; num. arts., Journal of Accountancy; mil: S/Sgt., US Army Paratrooper 1952-62; S/Sgt. USAF Air Guard 1982-; Jewish; rec: music, writing, art. Res: 931 W Duarte Rd Arcadia 91006 Ofc: ASI Draperies, 5221 W Jefferson Los Angeles 90016

GORDON, LEONARD WALTER, aluminum products company executive; b. May 1, 1926, Detroit, MI; s. Walter Stanley and Mabel (Furrow) Gordon; attended Cass Tech., 1944; Wayne State, 1946-47; m. Gertrude Organek, Sept. 27, 1952; children: Denise, b. 1954; Donna, b. 1955; Leonard, b. 1962; Sandra, b. 1966. Career: clerk, Atlantic Pacific Tea Co., Detroit, MI, 1942-53; plant mgr., Rogers Industries, Detroit, 1953-62; v.,p., Elixir Industries, Gardena, CA, 1969-81; General Manager, International Aluminum Products Corporation, 1981--. Republican. Catholic. Rec.: fishing, hiking. Res.: 4987 Silver Arrow, Rancho Palos Verdes 90274; Office: International Aluminum Products Corporation, 777 Monterey Pass Road Monterey Park 91754.

GORDON, ROBERT LESTER, university professor; b. Oct. 19, 1928, Akron, Ohio; s. Norman Lester and Loa Irene (Rickert) G.; m. Ruth Gordon, Dec. 18, 1948; children: Constance, b. 1949; Richard, b. 1953; Jeffrey, b. 1954; Jonathan, b. 1957; Jenifer, b. 1961; edn: Kent State Univ. 1946-9; Am. Floral Art Sch. 1949; BS, Cal Poly State Univ. 1977. Career: librarian, Kent State Univ., Kent, Ohio 1946-9, 51; hd. designer, Airport Florist, Akron, OH 1949-51; self empl. Gordon's Floral Art Shoppe, Akron 1951-6; hd. designer mgr. Collins' West Towne Florist, Akron 1956-65; asst. dir. Am. Floral Art Sch., Chgo., Ill. 1965-7; prof. Ornamental Horticulture Dept., Cal Poly. State Univ., San Luis Obispo 1967--; prin. Floral Design Studio, S.L.O.; lectr. and demonstr. on floral design in all 50 states, Europe, Japan, and So. Africa; featured designer for nat. convs. of Garden Clubs, Am. Inst. of Floral Designers and Profl. Floral Commentators Internat.; mem: Am. Floral Designers; Am. Acad. of Florists; Profl. Floral Commentators Internat.; Soc. of Am. Florists; Calif. Garden Clubs, Inc.; Miss City of S.L.O. Pageant Bd. (pres., exec. dir.); S.L.O. Wedding Guild (pres.); author: Profl. Floral Design for the Beginner; host: (16 1/2 hour) TV series; publs: arts. floral trade mags.; Republican; Presbyterian; rec: profl. singer. Res: 532 Monterey St san Luis Obispo 93401 Ofc: California Polytechnic Univ., O.H. Dept., San Luis Obispo 93407

GOREHAM, WILLIAM BARNS, insurance executive; b. June 17, 1938, Des Moines, Iowa; s. Bert Sheldon and Ada Mae (Barns) G.; m. Roxana F. Pajerski, Dec. 19, 1959; children: Nicole D'Ann, b. 1970; Desiree Anne, b. 1972; edn:

BA, Drake Univ. 1960. Career: life ins. agent Central Life of Iowa, Des Moines 1960-4; gen. agent Provident Life & Accident, Des Moines 1964-9; v.p./ gen. mgr. Financial Ins. Svcs., Inc., subs. U.S. Fin. Corp., San Diego 1969-72; v.p./ secty. Hayne- Goreham & Assocs., Inc., San Diego 1972-4; pres. William B. Goreham & Assocs., Inc., S.D. 1974-6; chmn. bd./ CEO William B. Goreham & Assocs., Inc., S.D. 1976--; awards: Pres.'s Cabinet, Provident Life & Acc. Ins. Co.; mem: MDRT (life & qual.); Atlas Health Club; mil: Iowa Air NG, 6 yrs.; Republican; Prot.; rec: golf, handball. Res: 1702 Soledad Ave La Jolla 92037 Ofc: Goreham & Assocs., 7857 Convoy Ct, Ste 206, San Diego 92111

GORGIE, FRANK JONATHAN, manufacturing company executive; b. Dec. 3, 1923, Canfield, Ohio; s. Paul and Susan Gorgie; edn: BS, Western Reserve, 1937-41; m. Rosalia Magda, March 21, 1964; chil: Frank Jonathan, b. 1965, Pearl Lynn, b. 1967; career: pres., Gorgie Manufacturing, Canfield, Ohio, 1946-66; pres., Gorgie International Mfg., Santa Ana, Calif., 1966-77; Chmn. of the Bd., National Energy Research Corp., Newport Beach, 1977--; Dir., Covalence International, Costa Mesa; Manufacturer's Safety Award; Mem.: American Management Assn, Better Business Bureau, Newport Harbor Area C. of C., Orange Co., C. of C., Gideon's Bible Assn., Assn. of Federal Investigators, Natl. Pres. and Life Member of Natl. Counter Intelligence Corp. Assn., Life Member, BPO-Elks, Chairman, Am. Red Cross, Listed in National Social Register; Inventor of electric travel iron and automatic breaklight indicator; Mil: Spec. Agent in Charge, Intelligence Unit, 5 Bronze Stars, EFO Ribbon, Ribbons for five mil. campaigns; Republican; Protestant; rec: golf, res.: 9812 La Cresta Circle, Huntington Beach, 92646 ofc: National Energy Research Corp., 881 Dover Dr., Ste 25, Newport Beach 92663.

GORSKI, THOMAS MARTIN, psychotherapist, consultant; b. Nov. 1, 1944, Toledo, Ohio; s. Ted E. and Sophia B. (Lucas) G.; m. Karen Louise, Sept. 16, 1978; edn: BA, Univ. Notre Dame 1967, M.Theol. 1971; Univ. Catolica de Puerto Rico 1967-8; Univ. Catolica de Chile 1968-9; MSW, St. Louis Univ. 1977; instr. cred., Calif. Com. Coll. 1981-; LCSW, Calif. 1981; NASW Reg. of Clin. Soc. Wkrs. 1982, NASW Acad. of Cert. Soc. Wkrs. 1979; Am. Assn. Marriage & Family Therapists 1979. Career: instr. Coll. de San George, Satiago de Chile 1967-9; researcher Inst. de Boliviano de Estudio y Accion Social, La Paz, Bolivia 1968; tchr./ counselor Mercy H.S., Farmington, Mich. 1971-3; dir. of counseling svc. Council for Retarded, Bishop Noll Inst., Hoosier's Boys Town, Schererville, Ind. 1973-6; dir. counseling svcs. St. Joseph's Hosp., South Bend, Ind. 1977-80; part time pvt. practice 1977-81; clinical dir. Kern View Com. Counseling Clinic, Bakersfield 1980-2; pvt. practice psychotherapy, Bksfld. 1982--; cons. to local schools, hosps., and bus., 1982 ; instr.: Bakersfield Coll.; Mercy Coll.; Notre Dame Univ.; Bellermino Inst., Santiago de Chile; mem: Nat. Assn. of Soc. Wkrs. Register of Clinical Soc. Wkrs.; Am. Assn. of Marriage Family Therapists; Acad. of Cert. Soc. Wkrs., Key Club; Big Brothers/ Big Sisters, Notre Dame Alumni; Ministerial Assn. of Wasco/ Schaffer; publs: articles in profl. jours., newspapers, mags.; Catholic; rec: carpentry, fishing. Address: 2704 Idaho Street Bakersfield 93305 Ofc: 671 Palm Ave Wasco 93302

GORT, LINDA LEE, social worker; b. May 16, 1948, East St. Louis, Ill.; d. Robert F. and Jacqueline G. (Dennis) Mantle; m. Thomas Gort, Jan. 2, 1978; 1 son, Adam, b. 1980; edn: BS in sociol., E. Ill. Univ. 1970; MSW, George Williams Coll. 1975; C.S.W., Ill. 1975; Acad. of Cert. Social Workers (ACSW), 1977; Lic. Clinical Social Worker (LCSW) 1981. Career: AFDC worker Ill. Dept. Public Aid, 1969; parent coordinator Joliet (Ill.)-Will County Day Care Ctr., 1970-71; foster home placement supr. Ill. Dept. Children Family Services, Chgo. 1971-72; pgm. coordinator/dir. Ray Graham Assn. for the Handicapped, Addison, Ill. 1975-78; state hospital liaison San Gabriel Valley Regl. Ctr., Covina 1978-80; therapist Family Svc. Assn. of Am., Orange, Riverside & San Diego Counties, 1980-84; therapist in pvt. practice, Fallbrook 1982--: medical social worker for 2 home hlth agencies, 1982-; cons. Fallbrook Conv. Hosp.; pub. speaker, advocacy for handicapped, aged; founder/devel. Drug Hotline, Joliet, Ill. 1970-72. Honors: apptd. Gov's Com. on Handicapped 1976; DePaul Univ., Rehab Svcs Tng Pgm. 1976. Mem: Nat. Assn. of Social Workers, Social Workers in Home Health Services, Jobs Daughters. Author: Different Patterns of Alcoholism As They Relate to the Middle Aged Female Alcoholic; Parent Handbook, 1977, Ray Graham Assn. for Handicapped. Methodist. Rec: travel, Agatha Christie. Res: 2885 Alta Vista Fallbrook 92028

GOTTLIEB, ALAN RUSS, physician; b. Sept. 28, 1953, Brooklyn, NY; s. Martin and Evelyn (Gertner) G.; m. Cynthia Gottlied (div.), Jan. 1, 1976; children: Christen Lael, b. 1976; edn: BA, magna cum laude, St. Univ. of NY, Buffalo 1974; MD, Univ. of Mich. 1978; MPH in progress, UC Berkeley 1984; lic. physician and surgeon, Bd. of Med. Quality Assurance 1979. Career: research asst. Mt. Sinai Sch. of Medicine, NY, NY 1973-4; internship, flexible med. Highland Gen. Hosp., Oakland 1978-9; family practice res. San Joaquin Gen. Hosp., Stockton 1979-81; staff phys. St. Joseph's Hosp., Stockton 1981, emergency dept. Vesper Meml. Hosp., San Leandro 1981--; guest instr. Delta Coll. Sch. of Nursing 1981-; honors: scholastic achievement awd., State of New York 1970, Phi Beta Kappa 1974; mem: Dip. Am. Acad. of Family Practitioners; Curriculum Com., UCB Sch. of Public Health; YMCA Indian Scouts; Sierra Club; works: tumor virus research, publs. 1973-4, Mt. Sinai Sch. of Med.; research in med. care utilization, UCB and Vesper Meml. Hosp. 1983-4; Democrat; Jewish; rec: travel, skiing, scuba. Res: 2 Anchor Drive, No. 397, Emeryville 94608 Ofc: Vesper Memorial Hosp., Emergency Dept., 2800 Benedict Dr San Leandro 94577

GOTTSCHALK, IRVING JOSEPH, business owner, ret.; b. Nov. 7, 1951, Los Angeles; s. William M. and Matie (Rosenfield) G.; m. Lorraine Marqusee, May 15, 1955; children: Suzanne, b. 1958; Joni, b. 1960; edn: BA, UCLA 1937. Career: engring. plnnr. Rockwell Internat. (fmrly No. Am. Aviation) 1956-58; master pgmmr. Hughes Aircraft 1968-71; owner Gottschalk Sales (restaurant equip.) 1972-79; comptroller Wm. Gottschalk Jr. (brother), misc. bus. ents. 1972-79; chmn. Fathers Action Com., L.A. City Schs. Volunteer & Tutorial Bureau 1974-76; bd. dirs. Jeffrey Found. for Handicapped 1981-82; task force chmn./ exec. bd. Sr. Citizen Affairs & Volunteer Svcs., L.A. City Fedn. of Comm. Coord. Councils; awards: Volunteer Svc. Awds., L.A. City Schs. & Fedn. Comm. Coord. Councils; mem: Masons, Lions Club (Jeffrey Found.); Active volunteer Community Svc. Desk, L.A.; Steering Com. KCET-TV pgm. Your Children-Our Children; publs: pub. monthly Lions news; contbr. monthly neighborhood newspaper; contbr. Poetic Anthology, 1984; mil: sgt. US Army Infantry 1941-45, Overseas Medal, GCM; Democrat; rec: journalism, philanthropy, volunteer. Res: 2145 Balsam Ave Los Angeles 90025

GOULD, CARL MAURICE, lawyer; b. Oct. 14, 1913, Toronto, Canada, nat. 1943; s. Samuel and Bess (Green) G.; m. Joyce Cappelle, Dec. 16, 1949; children: Beth, b. 1951; Tony, b. 1958; edn: Univ. of Toronto Sch. of Med. 1930-3; LLB, Loyola Univ. Sch. of Law 1942; JD, 1942; admitted to Calif. State Bar 1943, US Supreme Ct. 1950. Career: atty. (splst. in labor rels. law rep. mgmt.) law firm Hill, Farrer & Burrill, Los Angeles 1943-, partner 1945--; frequent spkr., seminar leader on labor rels. and benefit plans; witness; apptd. Arbitrator, Am. Arbitration Assn. 1963; mem: State Bar of Calif.; Am. Bar Assn. (labor law sect.); Inst. of Indsl. Rels, UCLA; Fed. Bar Assn.; Internat. Bar Assn.; Los Angeles Bar Assn.; Am. Judicature Soc.; Internat. Soc. for Labor Law; The Canadian Soc. of Los Angeles; Toluca Lake Property Owners Assn.; Loyola Alumni Assn.; author textbooks: ; textbooks: When and How to Go to the Labor Boad (Univ. Calif.); Dissecting the Trust Agreement and Mergers and Dissolution of Benefit Funds (Internat. Found. of Health, Welfare and Pension Plans Inc.); contbr. two chpts., Advising California Employers (Calif. CEB); profl. journal articles; mil: Tech 5, US Army Med. Admin. Corps.; rec: family, theatre arts, sports. Res: 4240 Navajo Street, Toluca Lake Station, No Hollywood 91602 Ofc: Hill, Farrer & Burrill, 445 So Figueroa St, 34th Flr, Los Angeles 90071

GOULD, RICHARD CLARKE, electrical contractor; b. Aug. 5, 1940, Los Angeles; s. Clarke Richard and Mabel Isabel (Iancola) G.; m. Linda Jean Christensen, Aug. 16, 1963; children: Timothy Scott, b. 1967; Tamara Stacey, b. 1969; edn: cert. competency, S.D. Co. Enr. Dept. 1969; cert. journeyman electrician, Elec. Wkrs. Local 569; journeyman wireman, Mesa Coll. and San Diego City Coll. 1969-74; various Calif. contractors lic. 1976, 78, 81, 83; Career: material handler Bell Electric, San Diego 1960-2; purch. agent Ling Oliver Electric, San Diego 1963-5; sound techn. Constrn. Electronics, 1965-7, apprentice electrician Oliver Elec. Inc., 1967-70; electrician, foreman, supt. Oliver Elec. Inc., 1970-6; owner Gould Electric, San Diego 1976-8, pres. Gould Electric, Inc., San Diego 1978--, cons. Pacific Beach Town Council awards: coach, minor league champs, Mission Bay Little League 1978; recognition, Mission Bay and Colt Little Leagues 1980, Pacific Beach Town Council 1982, 83; mem: Zoo Execs.; Zoological Soc. of San Diego; Pacific Beach Town Council; S.D. Apartment Assn.; IBEW Local 569; SDNECA; German Shorthair Pointer Club of S.D.; S.D. Comm. Child Abuse Council; Mother Goose Parade Assn.; Zoo Affils.; Zoo Boosters; Nat. Fdn. of Ind. Bus.; Nat. Electrical Contractors Assn.; Pacific Beach Hist. Soc.; sponsor, Isuzu Andy Williams San Diego Open; Mission Bay Little League; Restor. State of Liberty; PTA; Reuben H. Fleet Space Mus.; S.D. Police Depts. Comm. Alert Pgm.; Republican Nat. Com.; Lutheran; rec: gun and coin collecting, hunting, swimming. Res: 1312 Chalcedony St San Diego 92109 Ofc: Gould Elecric, Inc., 1959 Grand Ave San Diego 92109

GOWER, WILFORD DENNIS, real estate broker, instructor; b. May 17, 1918, Livermore, Ky; s. Woodie Wilford and Louella L. (Dempsey) G.; m. Jean E. Block, Dec. 27, 1952; children: Linda, b. 1941; Phillip, . 1947; Wilford, Jr., b. 1955; Marianne, b. 1957; Elise, b. 1964; edn: BS, Western Kentucky Univ. 1940; MBA, Syracuse Univ. 1956; PhD, The American Univ. 1963; Comm. Coll. Instr. Cred. (life), bus., mgmt. real estate, Calif. 1980; lic. real estate broker, Calif. 1973-. Career: High Sch. teacher, Webster Co., Ky. 1940-42; served 2d lt. to maj. US Army, 1942-63 (decorated 3 Bronze Stars w/valor device, Combat Inf. badge, various battle medals and commendns.), inf. ofcr. WWII, sr. advisor/ cmdr. Japanese Forces (of 6000) 1950-52, R&D dir. 1952-55, comptroller Ft. Lewis, Wn. 1956-59, chief of plnng. Eighth Army, Korea 1959-60, chief of policies & plans (5 Divnl. Areas), R&D Ofc. Pentagon (mem. approx. 10 Army and DOD mgmt. coms.; mem. Army Chief of Staff Advis. Com.) 1960-63; mgr. budgets & property, Rocketdyne Div., asst. gen. mgr. Jet Engines Div., Rockwell Intl. 1963-64; treas. Greer Hydraulics Inc. 1965-66; real estate broker (offices in 4 counties) 1973--; author/lectr. on real estate concerns; honors: Kentucky Col., Gov. of Ky. 1981; mem: Nat., Calif., local real estate bds., orgns.; Nat. Roster of Scientist and Engrs. of US 1941; Masons, Scottish Rite, CofCs, L.A.Town Hall; Republican; Prot. Res: 26881 Canyon Crest San Juan Capistrano 92675

GRADY, EUGENE JOSEPH, JR., city executive; b. Jan. 21, 1924, Biloxi, Miss.; s. Eugene Joseph and Lily Marjorie (Rushing) G.; m. Irene Harnandez, Jan. 17, 1969; children: James, b. 1946; Victor, b. 1949; Irene, b. 1951; Maurice, b. 1956; Ernest, b. 1959; edn: UC Berkeley Sch. of Public Health 1947; San Diego State Coll. 1952; Southwestern Coll. 1972; Reg. Sanitarian, Calif. 1948; Calif. Comm. Coll. Life Tchg. Cred. for Bldg. & Housing Insp. Career: environmental health sanitarian, San Diego Co. Health Dept. 1947-53; insp. bldg. & housing, City of Chula Vista 1953-66, dir. bldg. & Housing 1966--; mem: Intl. Conf. of Bldg. Officials (pres. S.D. chpt. 1961), Calif. Bldg. Ofcls. (pres. 1972-3), Nat. Environ. Health Ass. (pres. Calif. chpt. 1954), Intl. Assn.

of Plumbing & Mech. Ofcls., Am. Water Works Assn., ACI (pres. S.D. Intl. chpt. 1979), Nat. Assn. Housing and Redevel.; mem. Calif. Comm. Coll. statewide advis. com. on Bldg. Insp. Curriculum; mem. Southwestern Comm. Coll. Advis. Com.; recognition awards: Chula Vista Lions Club, Calif. Bldg. Ofcls. Assn., Am. Bus. Womens Assn. (Boss of Yr 1977); mil: boatswain mate2, USN 1942-5, Pac. War Zone medal; Republican; Catholic; rec: hunting, fishing, farming. Res: 6275 Otay Mesa Rd San Diego 92173 Ofc: City of Chula Vista, 276 4th Ave Chula Vista 92173

GRAEBER, CHARLES CALVERT, geologist/mineralogist; b. Jan. 8, 1949, Los Angeles; s. Charles Calvert and Martha Viault Graeber; m. Kerith Stiles, May 6, 1978; edn: BS, geological engr., Colorado Sch. of Mines 1972. Career: mineral sales Pala Internat. 1972-80; owner/ opr. Cal Graeber Fine Minerals & Gems, Fallbrook 1980--; cons.: local firms, San Diego, Utah ,World, and San Bernardino Co. Museums of Natural Hist.; mem: Fallbrook Gem & Mineral Soc.; Friends of Mineralogy; Catholic; rec: golf, tennis, diving. Address: 333 Sky Vista Fallbrook 92028

GRAFF, MARC DAVID, psychiatrist; b. Nov. 5, 1948, Chgo.; s. Norman and Phyllis Lenore (Firestone) G.; m. Laura, Sept. 24, 1972; children: Rebecca, b. 1977, Benjamin, b. 1979; edn: BA, UC Berkeley 1970; MD, Univ. of Chgo. 1974; intern, resident Univ. of Rochester, 1974-78; lic. MD in Calif. 1975, Penna. 1978, New York 1975. Career: asst. and fellow in psychiat. U. of Rochester, 1974-77, instr. in psychiatry 1977-78; asst. prof. psychiat. Western Psychiat. Inst. and Univ. of Pittsburgh, 1978-80; graduate fellow Rand Grad. Inst., Santa Monica 1980-81; ptnr. Southern Calif. Permanente Medical Group, 1981--; asst. clin. prof. psychiat., UC Los Angeles 1981-; cons. The Rand Corp. 1981; honors: in zoology, UCB 1970, in psychiatry, Univ. of Chgo. 1974; mem: Am. Psychiatric Assn., AAAS, Assn. for Public Policy Analysis and Mgmt., Calif. Turtle and Tortoise Club (pres. San Fernando Vly chpt. 1983); Democrat; Jewish (Reform); rec: turtles, tortoises. Res: 19949 Arminta St Canoga Park 91306 Ofc: So. Calif. Permanente Med. Gp., 16800 Devonshire, Ste. 200, Granada Hills 91344

GRAFF, RONALD ALBERT, clergyman, educational computer software developer; b. Mar. 15, 1940, Denver, Colo.; s. Albert Henry and Queen Mab (Foster) G.; m. Barbara Jean Vanderkilt, Dec. 9, 1960; children: Judith, b. 1964, Laurie, b. 1966, Timothy, b. 1969; edn: BA, Biola Coll., magna cum laude, 1962; B.D. (M.Div. equiv.), Talbot Theol. Sem. 1962, D.Min. candidate; ordained minister, Nat. Fel. Brethren Chs. 1966. Career: pastor Community Brethren Ch., Los Angeles 19656-72, Grace Brethren Ch., Mission Viejo 1972-76, assoc. pastor/supt. of schs. Mission Hills Christian Ctr., Laguna Hills 1978-80; instr. Prison Fellowship In-Prison Seminars, 1979--; bd. dirs. Alpha Family Counselling, 1980-; dir. Living Hope Ministries, 1981-, spkr. daily radio ministry, 1981-2; conf. spkr. various chs.; adminstrv. asst. Indsl. Hydrocarbons, San Dimas 1976-78; v.p. Ops., Wabash Computer Systems, El Toro 1980-83; v.p. The Wabash Apple (computer retailing chain, distbr., sch., software dev.), 1981-3; pres. Ednl. Systems Software, El Toro 1982--; pres. Learning Technologies (pub. The Discovery Ency., for use with microcomputers), Laguna Hills 1983--; frequent guest, radio/t.v. media, computer rel. subjects; spkr. num. confs., seminars; chmn. Truth for Youth Crusade, Montebello 1968; mem: Nat. Fellowship of Brethren Chs. (So.Cal. & Az. Dist. moderator 1971-2, v.chmn. Dist. Youth Bd. 1968); E. L.A./Montebello Ministerial Assn. (chmn. 1969-70); Talbot Alumni Assn. (pres. 1970). Works: author: Learning is Fun With The Computer (Innovative Comp. Prods. 1978); Reveille, Arise and Build (Comm. Brethren Ch. 1968); patentee: Illuminated Wax Form; computer pgms.: Shell Games (1979), and Elementary, My Dear Apple, (1980, Apple Comp. Corp.), Class Records, and Supermath (1982, Ednl. Systems Software), The Discovery Ency. (1983, Learning Tech.); Republican; non-denom. Christian; rec: travel. Address: Learning Technologies, 25041 MacKenzie Laguna Hills 92653

GRAHAM, ALICE MAY, lawyer; b. Mar. 18, 1950, NY, NY; d. Howard and Sylvia (Berkin) G.; 1 dau., Vered Naomi Yakovee, b. 1974; edn: BA, UCLA 1972; JD, Loyola Law Sch. 1978; atty. at law, Calif State Bar 1978; real estate broker, Calif. Dept. of Real Estate 1980. Career: partner Ray Consultants, Beverly Hills 1978-81; v.p. 1979-81; atty. at law, pvt. practice, Beverly Hills 1981--; Of Counsel, Law Ofcs. of Gary Smolker, Beverly Hills 1982--; mem: Am. Bar Assn.; Calif. State Bar Assn.; Real Property Sect., Los Angeles Co. Bar Assn.; Assn. of real Estate Attys.; Women Lawyers Assn.; Beverly Hills Bus. & Profl. Women; Jewish Fdn. Council Facilities Mgmt. Com.; Sch. Adv. Com., Beverly Vista Sch.; Democrat; Jewish. Res: 333 So Doheny Dr, No. 4, Beverly Hills 90211 Ofc: Alice M. Graham, 361 No Canon Dr Beverly Hills 90210

GRAHAM, DEBORAH JANE, psychologist, college administrator, marriage family child therapist; b. Oct. 29, 1953, Uvale, Tex.; d. Archie Jackson and Della Jane (Reitzer) G.; edn: BS, Baylor Univ. 1976; MA, Azusa Pacific Coll. 1980; PhD, U.S. Internat. Univ. Career: corp. youth pgm. dir. T Bar M Racket Clubs, Inc., Dallas, Tex. 1976-7; marriage, family, child therapist, (adminstr. 1980-), Lister Psychological Svcs., Costa Mesa 1978--; tchr. Newport- Mesa Sch. Dist., Newport Beach 1978-9; placement spl. for the handicapped, No. Orange Co. Comm. Coll. Dist. 1979-81; coord. Spl. Student Found. Scholarship, Baylor Univ. 1974; Calif. Grad. Fellowship, Calif. Student Aid Commn. 1979-82; State Scholarship awd., Calif. Sch. Employees Assn. 1980; mem: Delta Psy Kayya, profl. women in phys. edn. hon. frat., (pres. 1975-6); Am. Assn. of Health, Phys. Edn., & Recreation; Am., Calif. Assn. of Marriage, Family, Child Therapists; Calif. Assn. of Post- Secondary Educators of the Disabled; Orange Co. Com. for Employment of the Handicapped; Am. psychological Assn.; Am. Coll. of Sports Med.; Am. Orthopsych. Assn.; Baptist; rec:

tennis, golf, water sports. Ofcs: Cypress Coll., 9200 Valley View Cypress 90630; Lister Psychological Services, 2970 Harbor Blvd., Ste 210, Costa Mesa 92626

GRAHAM, EDMUND LOWELL, lawyer; b. July 17, 1937, Sanford, NC; s. George Malcolm and Virginia (Cameron) G.; m. Victoria Milland, Jan. 22, 1969; children: Travis, b. 1972; Alex, b. 1977; edn: AB, Univ. of No. Carolina, Chapel Hill 1960; JD, UCLA 1968; civil trial lawyer. Career: dir./ treas. Vacation Inds., Inc. 1971-8; dir./ advr. Torrance Nat. Bank 1978--; civil trial lawyer Lowell Graham Law Corp. 1968--; mem: Calif. and Los Angeles Trial Lawyers; So. Bay and L.A. Co. Bar Assns.; So. Bay 500 Club; Soc. of Old Crows; Republican: Lincoln Repub. Club (pres. 1977); Calif. Del. to Rep. Nat. Conv. 1977, 78; Los Angeles Co. and Calif. State Rep. Central Coms.; mil: B-52 combat crew mem., USAF 1960-5; maj. Calif. Air NG 1966-72, USAF Commdn. Medal; Presbyterian; rec: golf, travel. Res: 1209 Via Gabriel Palos Verdes Estates 90274 Ofc: Lowell Graham Law Corp., 21515 Hawthorne Blvd, Ste 1130, Torrance 90503

GRAHAM, KENT, financial systems executive; b. Mar. 7, 1948, St. Paul, Minn.; s. Fred and Charlotte (Bluhm) G.; edn: BS, San Jose State 1971; MBA, Pepperdine 1979. Career: data control supvr. Blake, Moffet & Towne 1971-3; hosp. adminstr., fin. & mgmt. sys. dir. Mt. Zion Hosp., San Francisco 1973--; mem: Medi-Serv Credit Union; San Francisco Jewish Comm. Ctr.; rec: music, athletics. Res: 435 Franconia St San Francisco 94110 Ofc: Mt. Zion Hosp., 1600 Divisadera St San Francico 94116

GRAHAM, WILLIAM MEADE, psychotherapist, clinical social worker; b. Apr. 15, 1948, Cleveland, Ohio; s. Joseph John and Elizabeth Paige (Taylor) G.; m. Penelope Jean Aron, Aug. 30, 1968; children: Elton, b. 1971, Geoffrey, b. 1981; edn: BA, CSC Stanislaus 1973, MSW, honors, CSU Fresno 1978; LCSW (lic. clin. soc. wkr.) Calif. 1980; Calif. Comm. Colls. Instr. cred. 1982. Career: intern, under Exec. Dir. Fresno Co./City Commn. on Aging, 1976-77, designed and implemented the successful Sr. Citizens discount pgm. for seniors of Fresno; intern- adminstrv. asst. Fresno Empl. & Tng. Commn., 1977-8; psychiat. soc. wkr. Kings Co. Mental Hlth. Svcs., Kings View 1979-82, planned & devel. a Day Treatment pgm. for severely disturbed children, adolescents of Kings Co. 1979-80, comm. svc. splst. 1980-82; psychotherapist self-empl. pvt.practice, Lemoore 1982--; instr. Coll. of th Sequoias 1982-3; Republican; Episcopal; rec: farming, gardening, fishing, skiing. Res: 3535 W. Dorthea, Visalia 93277 Ofc: William M. Graham, LCSW, 339 W. D Street, Ste. M, Lemoore 93245

GRAIL, DONALD JOHN, manufacturing co. executive; b. Oct. 30, 1930, Cleveland, Ohio; s. John and Gertrude (Warren) G.; ; children: Kevin, b. 1956, Randall, b. 1962, Donald Jr., b. 1967; edn: BA, Denison Univ. 1952. Career: stockbroker, Cleveland 1955-67; gen. mgr. Mameco Internat., US and Euro. Mktgs., 1967-72; pres. Durasurf, Inc. (dev. one coat poly acrylate stucco and decking sys.), L.A. 1972-75, (name chg.) The Grail Co., 1975-83; chmn. bd. Grailcoat, Inc., Newport Beach 1983--; cons. with num. firms in US, Eur., Japan re the use of acrylic polymer modified cement; trustee Common Market W. Europe Seminar Spkrs. Assn., Amsterdam, Holland 1971; patents: co-inventor Modifying cement utilizing acrylic polymers; inventor (pat.pend.) Lightweight modified cement roofing tiles; mil: 2d lt. US Army 1952-4, Korean Combat ribbons, Commendn. medal. Res: 267 Baywood Dr Newport Beach 92660 Ofc: Grailcoat, Inc. 881 Dover Dr, Ste. 14, Newport Beach 92663

GRALL, CARL JOSEPH, coin dealer, ret.; b. May 22, 1916, Detroit, Mich.; s. Peter Joseph and Cleona Lilly (Daugherty) G.; nephew of Carl V.P. Daugherty, dist. atty. Detroit; m. Mary Goodrich, 1942 (div. 1948); 1 dau. Kristi, b. 1964. Career: owner, Farmer Joe's Mkt., Hawthorne, Calif. 1946-50; owner Farmer's Daughter Stamps &: Coins, Redondo Beach, 1951-60; owner The Money Bag, Torrance, 1960-67; pres. San Pedro Farms Inc., 1967-72; chmn. bd. Colorsound Inc., West Covina 1965-69; founding pres. Teletype Coin Dealers Assn. of Calif., 1963--; owner Lawndale Jewelry & Loan, 1973-78; also investment counseling, Teletype Coin Dealers; mem. Masonic Lodge West Adams 565, L.A. Golden West Comdry 43, L.A. Royal Arch Masons 33, Cryptic Masons of Calif. 35, Knight Templar of Cal. 43, Peace Ofcrs Shrine Club, So. Bay Shrine Club, L.A. Consistory, 32nd deg. Masons (life), Al Malaikah Temple (life); mil: chief warrant ofcr. USCG, 1943-45; Republican (supporting); Christian; rec: fishing, numismatics. Res: 1609 Plaza Del Amo, Torrance 90501

GRANATH, RONALD ALEX, manufacturing co. executive; b. Feb. 16, 1942, Los Angeles; s. John Alex and Mathilda (Hendrickson) G.; m. Kenna Lee Emberton, Oct. 4, 1963; children: Kenneth John, b. 1966; Carrie Ruth, b. 1968; edn: Foothill Coll. 1961-3. Career: engineering aide Reflection Ednl. Prods., Mt. View 1963-66; tech. video maint. Memorex Corp., Santa Clara 1966-69, instr. Video Magnetic Recording Theory, 1967; instr. Video Theory, Foothill Coll., Los Altos 1968; asst. engr., engring. adminstr. Internat. Video Corp., Sunnyvale 1969-77; maint. engr. Versatile Video Inc., 1977; engring. svcs. mgr. Harris Video Systems, 1978-81, prodn. control/mat. mgr. 1981--; mem. Am. Prodn. & Inventory Control Soc.; BSA (pub. rels.), South Valley Welcome Wagon Gourmet Club; Republican; Baptist; rec: photog. Res: 6274 Camino Verde Dr San Jose 95119 Ofc: Harris Video Systems, 1255 E. Arques Ave Sunnyvale 94086

GRAND, GLORIA JEAN, computer co. executive; b. Jan. 16, 1945, Joplin, Mo.; d. Frank Vincent and Anita Marian (Allegretti); edn: BA, CSU Los Angeles 1968, MA, 1975; Calif. Real Estate Lic. 1978. Career: art teacher Santa Monica High Sch., 1970-78, and Santa Monica Coll. 1975-78; exec. adminstr.

Inst. of Health, Beverly Hills, 1978-81; dir. mktg. Computer Devel. Inc., Newport Beach 1982--; tchr. inservice tng., right/left brain transference in the classroom; awards: CSU Internat. Studies Pgm. Scholar, Univ. of Florence, Italy 1968; mem: (past) Calif./Santa Monica Art Tchrs Assn. (pres.); Nat. Trade Show Exhibs. Assn.; works: 1st place, art, Bur. de Tourissme, Florence, Italy 1969; "2 for the show" 2 woman exhib. Robert's Art Gallery, S.M. 1978; Christian; rec: skiing, tennis, painting, drawing, photog. Res: 3336 Via Lido-C, Newport Beach 92663 Ofc: Computer Development Inc. 151 Shipyard Way, Berth C Cabin 2, Newport Beach 92663

GRANNIS, (BERTHA) IONE WILKINS, public assistance executive; b. Oct. 12, 1902, Malden, Mo.; d. Claude Moore and Georgia Pearl (Ray) Wilkins; m. Eugene Oregon Farrow, July 18, 1926; m. 2d. Charles Webster Grannis, July 20, 1949, div. 1967; children: Berti Farrow, b. 1927; David Farrow, b. 1929; edn: AB in sociol., Chapman Coll. 1939; Cert. Soc. Wrk., USC 1945; Cert. Gerontology, USC Leonard Davis Sch. of Gerontology 1977; grad. stu. humanities, Pacific Oaks Coll. 1981-. Career: currently Andrus Vol. on campus USC Leonard Davis Sch. of Gerontol.; sch. tchr., Cape Girardeau, Mo. 1919-21; minister's wife, South Africa, 1926-28; USO director for YWCA-USO in Santa Ana, Ca., Tonopah, Nev., Tacoma, Wash., and Catalina Is., Ca., 1941-44; soc. wkr./supr. Los Angeles Bur. of Public Assistance, and Bur. of Adoptions, 1945-57, 1958-60, soc. wkr. Salvation Army Home for Unwed Mothers, 1960-67; mem. Nat. Assn. of Social Workers, Western Gerontol. Soc., YWCA Pasadena, Calif. Sierra Club 1947-, Nature Conservancy, KCET, UN Assn. of the US, NOW, AARP, Older Womans League; publs: contbr. Volunteer News (Andrus Ctr., USC), Pacific Oaks Coll. publs.; Democrat; Unitarian-Universalist; rec: writing, singing. Res: 3932 Roderick Rd Los Angeles 90065

GRANT, BRADLEY CAMERON, physician; b. Aut. 10, 1954, Olean, NY; s. Dr. Murray and Trudy (Shein) G.; edn: BA, Western Maryland Coll. 1976, D.O. Coll. Osteopathic Med. and Surg. 1979; Dip. Nat. Bds. 1980, Cert. Basic, Advanced Cardiac Life Support; lic. Colo., Mo., Calif., Ill. Career: physician, Peak Nine Medical Center, Breckenridge, Colo. 1980-81, Comm. Health Ctr., Garden Grove, Ca. 1981; pvt. practice, pres./med. dir. Lake Elsinore (Ca.) Family Medical Clinic, Inc., 1981--; team phys. Elsinore H. Sch.; asst. prof. Calif. Osteopathic Med. Sch.; bd. trustees Casa Colina Rehab. Facility; honors: Phi Beta Epsilon, Beta Beta Beta, Sigma Sigma Phi, USPHJ Scholarship; mem: Am. Osteopathic Assn., United Am. Acad. of Osteo., Osteo. Alumni Assn., Am. Coll. Sports Medicine, Am. Osteo.. Acad. Sports Med., Am. Coll. of Emerg. Phys., Am. Coll. of G.P.s, Denver Med. Soc. (Profl. Peer Rev. bd.), Colo. Osteo. Soc., Orange Co. Osteo. Soc., Riverside Co. Med. Soc., Calif. Osteo. Phys. Soc. (conv. plnng. com.), San Bernardino Osteo. Med. Soc. (grievance com.); num. presentations, publs. in field; mil: USPHS 1979-80; Jewish; rec: athletics, travel, music, theatre. Res: 33351 Adelfa Lake Elsinore 92330 Ofc: Lake Elsinore Family Medical Clinic, Inc. 17037 Lakeshore Dr Lake Elsinore 92330

GRANT, DAVID BROWNE, metal finishing co. executive; b. Apr. 21, 1915, Sharonville, Ohio; s. David John and Catherine Emma (Browne) G.; m. Elizabeth Connolly, May 17, 1942; children: Ann G. (Villa), b. 1943; Elizabeth (Williams) b. 1944, David C. b. 1947, Susan B. b. 1949, Mary Margaret b. 1951, James B. b. 1953, Patricia J. b. 1958; edn: AB, cum laude, Colgate Univ. 1936; LLB, Yale Univ. Sch. of Law 1939. Career: atty., pvt. practice, Detroit, Mich. 1939-41; asst. sales mgr./ asst. to pres. Empire Toll Co., Detroit 1941-46; sales rep. Stone Tool Co., Los Angeles 1946-47; owner Tool Electrolizing Co., Los Angeles 1947-51; owner/ pres. Stone Tool Corp., Los Angeles 1949-52; owner Electrolizing Sales, Inc. 1951-72; owner/ pres. Electrolizing Co./ Electrolizing, Inc., Los Angeles, Santa Clara, and Houston, Tex. 1951--; dir. Electrolizing, Inc. 1951-; bd. consultors Marymount H.S., Los Angeles; mem: M&M Assn.; L.A. CofC; Inst. Aero. & Astro.; Am. Soc. Metals; Metal Finishing Assn., So. Calif.; Phi Gamma Delta; Phi Beta Kappa; Jonathan Club; Braemar, Spring Valley & Irvine Coast Country Clubs; mil: commun. ofcr., lt. USNR 1942-45; Republican; Catholic; rec: golf, boating, swimming. Res: 3 Northampton Ct Newport Beach 92660 Ofc: Electrolizing, Inc., 1947 Hooper Ave Los Angeles 90011

GRANT, DOROTHY LUCIA, real estate sales executive; b. June 5, 1923, Biola, Calif.; d. John and Martha (Jaschiniak) Jerkovich; m. Charles Lindy Grant, May 27, 1959; 1 son, Bruce Charles, b. 1948; edn: grad., Sawyer Sch. of Business 1942; various real estate courses, Lumbleau R.E. Sch.; Calif. lic. R.E. Broker Assoc. 1965. Career: bookeeper/secty. Harbor Belt Line R.R., San Pedro 1942-48; ofc. mgr. Victor Adding Machine Co., Long Beach 1950-59; broker assoc. Marcus W. Meairs Realtors, Riverside 1961-82, James W. Miller Real Estate Co., 1981--; sales awards: Top Ten (1976, 77, 78, 79), Million Dollar Club (79); mem. Riverside Bd. of Realtors 1961-; advis. bd. YWCA 1978-82; Republican; Lutheran (organist 1938-45, recording sec.); rec: photog., int. decor., gourmet cook. Res: 4530 Toyon Rd. Riverside 92504 Ofc: James W. Miller Co., Realtors 5924 Magnolia Ave Riverside 92506

GRANT, JON BARTON, dentist; b. July 17, 1943, Elmhurst, Ill.; s. Russell Sutherland and Louise Winona (Brown) G.; m. Patricia Rodley, June 26, 1983; edn: undergrad., Colo. State Univ. 1961-3; DDS, Univ. of Nebr. 1968. Career: group practice of dentistry, Colorado Springs, Colo. 1968-74, pvt. practice, Foster City 1974--; mem: FAGD, Fellow Acad. of Gen. Dentistry (pres. Colo., regional v.p., nat. dir.); Acad. of Dental Group Practice (founding, charter treas.); FAIDS, Fellow Acad. of Internat. Dental Studies; FADI, Fellow Acad. of Dentistry Internat.; Am. Assn. of Endodontists; Am. Soc. of Preventative Dentistry; Am. Acad. of Dental Gp. Practice; Nat. Analgesial Soc. (nat. v.p.); Am., Calif., San Mateo Co. Dental Socs.; Rotarian (pres. Foster City), Foster City CofC (pres.); awards: World Record in Parachuting 1977; San Francisco Mags. 100 Most Eligible Bachelors 1981; rec: water/snow skiing. Res: 2990 Summit Dr Hillsborough 94010 Ofc: 1289 E. Hillsdale Blvd Foster City 94404

GRANT, SHIRLEY MAE, tourism/conventions executive; b. Feb. 4, 1936, Barberton, Ohio; d. Chester C. and Virginia (Crispin) Culp; m. Stewart Kennedy Grant (dec.), June 19, 1960; children: Michelle, b. 1961; Sabrina, b. 1963; Michael, b. 1968; edn: AA in bus., Graceland Coll. 1956; BS in edn., CSU Long Beach 1965, MS in counseling, 1974; elementary tchg. cred.; community coll. tchg. cred. (bus., real estate adm., counseling); Calif. lic. real estate broker; Role Tng. Director, Middle Mgmt. Seminar, CSULB 1973. Career: mgr. Virginia's Restaurant, 1950-56; asst. registrar Graceland Coll., 1956-58; adminstrn. asst. CSC Long Beach, 1958-61; owner/mgr. resdtl. income units, 1958-78; elem. sch. teacher (Vista USF, Rossmoor Elem. Sch.) 1965-70; asst. to Dean of Admissions & Records, 1970-74, dir. Sch. & Coll. Rels., CSU Fullerton and CSU Dom. Hills, 1974-79; owner/broker Bennett & Co., 1980-82; tourism/convention coordinator Knott's Berry Farm, 1982--; mem. state steering com. Calif. Women in Higher Edn. 1974-5; honors: Danforth Scholar 1954; MECHA 1978; mem: Phi Delta Kappa (pres. 1974), Calif. Assn. Realtors, CofC, Buena Park Visitor & Conv.; Unitarian/ Reorg. LDS; rec: travel, camping, breeding Silky Terriers. Res: 5409 Arrowhead Ave Buena Park 90621 Ofc: Knott's Berry Farm, 8309 Beach Blvd Buena Park 90620

GRANTON, SAMUEL RICHARD, real estate broker-consultant; b. Sept. 3, 1922, Buffalo, NY; s. Frank Charles and Marie (Costanzo) G.; m. Esther Fracasso, May 10, 1950; children: Gregory S., b. 1951, Gina A., b. 1953; edn: BS in soc. sci., City Univ. of NY, 1950; dip., real estate acctg. & law, Weaver Sch. of Real Estate, 1954; grad. studies, Claremont Grad. Sch., 1955-6; grad. US Armed Forces Inst. 1947-52, Anthony Sch. of Real Estate 1967; spl. courses, San Bernardino Valley Coll. 1955-67; lic. real estate broker, Calif., Okla.; life teaching cred., real estate, Calif. Comm. Colls. Career: land title searcher/ title examiner & sr. escrow ofcr. Security Title Ins. Co., San Bernardino 1952-69; real estate counselor- exchangor, Nat. Assn. of Securities Dealers rep., 1969-71; asst. v.p./escrow mgr. First California Title Co. of San Diego, 1971-72; v.p./nat. escrow ofcr., Commercial Standard Title Ins. Co., S.D. 1972-75; owner, Gran Terra Realty & Mgmt. Services Co., Cardiff by the Sea 1975- ; pres. United Seminars of America, 1978--; exec. v.p. Gran Terra Landscape Inc., 1979--; bus. cons. (high tech.), Granton & Son & Assocs., 1982-; internat. bus. cons./assoc. Creative Systems Engrs. (mech./elec. engring. cons.); real estate instr. Mira Costa, Palomar, Grossmont Colls., 1971-; honors: Direct Commn. by Pres. Truman, 2d lt. USAF, 1942-52; mem: Calif. Assn. of R.E. Teachers, Calif. Escrow Assn. (Cert. Sr. Escrow Ofcr.), Am. Escrow Assn., Interex Exchangers Assn., mem. World Trade Ctr. of San Diego Inc.; Seat (INEX) Internat. Investment & Bus. Exchg., London, Eng. & Sydney, Aust.; publs: arts. in real estate, escrow indus. mags.; rec: stamps, coins, First Edition books. Res: 1652 Traveld Way, Encinitas 92024 Ofc: Gran Terra Realty & Mgmt Svcs Co. 2157 Newcastle Ave, Cardiff by the Sea 92007

GRASSL, THEODORE PETER, newspaper executive; b. Nov. 12, 1931, Stratford, WI; s. Ferdinand V. and Rebecca M. (Fandre) Grassl; BBA, Univ. Wisc., Madison, 1959; m. Marlene Palmer, Aug. 25, 1962; children: Melody, b. 1959 (adopted). Career: sys. supv., Control Data Corp., Minneapolis, MN. 1967-69; bus. sys. mgr., Minneapolis Star & Tribune Co., Minneapolis, MN, 1969-71; data processing mgr., Minneapolis Star & Tribune Co., 1971-74; dir. acctg., Minneapolis Star & Tribune Co., 1974-75; bus. mgr., Trenton Times Corp., Trenton, MJ, 1975-76; v.p., gen. mgr., Trenton Times Corp., 1976-78; gen. mgr., L.A. Herald Examiner 1978--; v.p. Hearst Community Newspapers, 1981--; instr., Pillsbury Acctg. Devel. Pgm.; instr., Control Data's After Hours Pgm. Beta Alpha Psi, 1957. Mem.: New Trenton Corp., bd. dirs., 1977; CofC, Mercer Co., bd. dirs. 1977; Natl. Campers and Hikers Assn., state assn. pres., MN, 1973-75; Boy Scouts of Amer., bd. dirs. 1976-77; Geo. Wash. Council. Numerous publ. items on data processing esp. project mgmt. and on camping; major seminar, Control Data (1960s); Mil.: DK2, USN, 1951-55. Republican. Roman Catholic. Rec.: tennis, oil painting, camping. Res.: 12401 Littler Pl., Granada Hills 91344; Office: Los Angeles Herald Examiner, 1111 S. Broadway, Los Angeles 90015.

GRATNEY, THOMAS JEROME, managerial economist; b. Apr. 1, 1944, Altadena; s. R. Emery and Margy C. (McBain) G.; m. Sandra Brooks, Jan. 13, 1974; children: Thomas J., II b. 1969, Kimberly Dawn b. 1979; edn: UC Santa Barbara 1963; Univ. of Ariz., Tucson 1966. Career: mgr. Prolight Industries, Fullerton 1971-77; mgr. ITT, Costa Mesa Div. 1977-79; senior ptnr. Shoreline Services (mgmt. consulting), 1979--; dir. Half Moon Bay Aquaculture Project (study comml. feasibility of lobster farming) 1983-; honors: Internat. Assn. of Chiefs of Police Hall of Fame for devel. safety equip. for law enforcement personnel; mem: Internat. Assn. of Chiefs of Police 1974-, Calif. Aquaculture Assn.; author outdoor survival book: One Way Out (1983); mil: cmd. sgt. major Academy US Army 1963-; US Army Key Member Consultant 1982; Democrat; Methodist; rec: fishing, camping. Res: 340 Shelter Cove Dr Half Moon Bay 94019 Ofc: Shoreline Services 700 Mill St Half Moon Bay 94019

GRATT, BARTON MICHAEL, professor, dentist; b. Aug. 23, 1945, Chgo.; s. Jack and Bette Vivian (Goldbloom) G.; m. Karren, June 3, 1979; edn: DDS, UC Los Angeles 1971; dip. Am. Bd. of Oral Maxillo Facial Radiology 1981. Career: pvt. practice of dentistry, 1971-75; asst. prof., Oral Radiology, UCSF Sch of Dentistry, 1975-79, assoc. prof., Sect. of Oral Radiology, UCLA Sch. of Dentistry, 1979--; prin. investigator NIH resrch. grant; cons. to the Xerox Corp., Gen. Elec. Corp., and IWG Corp.; Fellow Am. Bd. of Dental Radiology; mem.: Internat. Assn. for Dental Research (sec-treas So. Calif. Sect.),

Am. Dental Assn., Am. Fund for Dental Health (vol.); works: originator of Dental Xerogradiography; developed the UCQC Dental Radiology Quality Assurance System; over 30 sci. publs.; Democrat; rec: pottery making. Res: 2619 Federal Ave Los Angeles 90064 Ofc: UCLA Sch of Dentistry Los Angeles 90024

GRAY, DENIS LEON, orthodontist; b. Dec. 22, 1937, La Grande, OR; s. Raymond Lorenzo and Freeda Genevieve (Kennedy) Gray; BS, Oregon State Univ., 1960; DMD, Univ. of OR Dental Sch., 1963; Ortho., Northwestern Univ. Dental Sch., 1970; m. Milda Maria Bacevicius, May 11, 1974. Career: gen. dentist, Denis Leon Gray, DMD, San Jose, 1963-68; orthodontist, Denis Leon Gray, DMD, Inc., Tustin, 1970--. Honors: Phi Eta Sigma, OR State Univ., 1958; Delta Phi Omega, Univ. of OR Dental Sch., 1962; Marshal Award, Univ. of OR Dental Sch., 1962. Mem.: Amer. Assn. Orthodontists; Pacific Coast Soc. of Orthodontists; Calif. State Soc. of Orthodontists; Amer. Dental Assn.; Calif. Dental Assn.; Orange Co. Dental Assn.; Psi Omega, dental frat., treas. 1962; Phi Delta Theta, scholarship chmn., 1959. Republican. Protestant. Rec.: cars, real estate, reading. Res.: 38 Mission Bay Dr., Corona del Mar 92625; Office: Denis Leon Gray, DMD, Inc., 18102 Irvine Blvd., Tustin 92680.

GRAY, GARY DAVID, communications engineer; b. Nov. 7, 1942, Orange; s. Albert Eldred and Wilda Minerva (Fender) G.; m. Mary Reilly, 1981; children: Holly Anne, b. 1965; David Christian, b. 1967; edn: AA, engrg., Fullerton Jr. Coll. 1962; BS eng. (electrical), cum laude, CSU Long Beach 1969, MSEE 1974; Reg. Profl. Electrical Engr., Calif., Wash DC; Chartered Electronic & Radio Engr., England; FCC Lic. Comml. & Amateur Radio Opr.; Calif. Comm. Coll. Life Instr. Cred. Career: comm. engring. asst., 1969-71; comm. project engr., 1971-76; comm. engr., 1976-82; chief communications engr., GSA/Comm. Div., County of Orange, Calif. 1982--; cons. comm. engr. (part-time); honors: Nat. Award for Innovative Leadership, IEEE O.C. Sect. 1976-7, Tau Beta Pi, Eta Kappa Nu; mem: Fellow Radio Club of Am.; Fellow Inst. for Adv. of Engring.; IEE Sr. mem./chmn. O.C. Sect. 1974-5; Instn. of Electronic & Radio Engrs., England; pres., Calif. Public-Safety Radio Assn., 1980 & 1984 (So. CA Chpt. of APCO); mem. Calif., Nat. Socs. of Profl. Engrs.; So. Calif. Fire Frequency Coordinator, CPRA/APCO; assoc. mem. Calif. Fire Chiefs Assn.; assoc. mem. O.C. Peace Ofcrs. Assn.; publs: profl. jour. arts.; Republican; Christian; rec: amateur radio WB6HUG. Ofc: Orange County Communications, 481 The City Dr South, Orange 92668

GRAY, JAN CHARLES, retail food chain executive; b. June 15, 1947, Des Moines, Iowa; s. Charles Donald and Mary C. Gray; BA econ., UC Berkeley 1969; JD, Harvard Law Sch. 1972. Career: assoc. atty. Halstead, Baker & Sterling, Los Angeles 1971-75; vice pres. & gen. counsel/Pub. Affairs, Ralphs Grocer Co., Los Angeles 1975--; judge pro tem, Los Angeles Municipal Court, 1977-; arbitrator, Amer. Arbitration Assn., 1977-; real estate broker, 1973-; instr. UCLA Ext. div.; Retail Food Mktg. Law, 1976-: Retail Food Mktg. Indus., 1977-; instr. Cerritos Coll., 1980-81; speaker, rent control, State Bar Conv., 1979; trustee So. Bay Univ. Coll. of Law, 1978-79; mem. Bd. of Visitors, Southwestern Univ. Sch. of Law, 1983-; mem: Am. Bar Assn., various sections: State Bar Calif., del. Conv. 1976-81; L.A. Co. Bar Assn., Corp. Law Dept. Exec. com. 1975-76, 1979-, Barristers exec. com. 1974-75, 1979-81; L.A. Bar Journal exec. com. 1973-75; San Fernando Valley Bar Assn., chmn. Real Prop. section 1975-77; Calif. Retailers Assn., Supermarket Com. 1977-; Food Marketing Inst., Govt. Rels. Com., 1977-, Govt. Affairs Council, 1977-. Gov't Apptmt: L.A. County Private Industry Council, 1982-; publs: articles in legal periodicals, contbg. author, book: Life or Death: Who Controls? (Springer Pub. 1976); mil: USAR; Democrat (State and L.A. Co. Central Coms., 1980; del. 1980 Dem. Nat. Conv.); Catholic; rec: tennis, travel. Res: POB 407, Beverly Hills 90213 Ofc: Ralphs Grocery Co., POB 54143 Los Angeles 90054

GREEN, GEORGE, radio station executive; b. May 23, 1931, Calif.; m. Mimi, Aug. 23, 1958; children: Jeff, b. 1961; Randy, b. 1963; Jamie, b. 1965; edn: BA, UC Los Angeles 1955. Career: page NBC-TV, Hollywood 1954-56; local salesman KPAL, Palm Springs 1956-57, KRHN FM, Los Angeles 1957-59; local acct. exec. KABC TV, L.A. 1959-60; local acct. exec. KABC Radio, 1960-65, general sales mgr. 1965-79, v.p./gen. mgr. 1979--; chmn. So. Calif. Broadcasters 1984; honors: Life Saver of the Year 1983, Advt. Indus. Emergency Fund; mem. bd. dirs. L.A. Ad Club, Multiple Sclerosis; mil: cpl. USAF 1951-52; rec: racquetball, golf, skiing, scuba diving. Res: 4765 Park Encino Lane Encino 91436 Ofc: KABC Radio 3321 So La Cienega Blvd Los Angeles 91436

GREEN, HOWARD CHESTER, jurist; b. Sept. 6, 1916, Fresno; s. Thomas Butler and Ida B. (Bomar) Green; edn: JD, Baylor Univ., 1953; m. Jeanne McCarty, Apr. 26, 1944; 1 dau., Kelly, b. 1953; career: Deputy Fresno County Recorder, 1938-50 (except for Army Service WWII); teacher, Comml. subjects, Fresno City Coll. Night Sch., 1947-48; attorney, sole practitioner, 1954-82; Six years, Judge Pro Tem, Madera County Superior Court; Judge, Chowchilla Judicial District, 1958-82; judge who handled the original appearances of the defendants in the Chowchilla School Bus Kidnapping case, 1976; as Judge Pro Tem, Madera Co. Sup. Court heard leading case on "in lieu" lands, Jay vs. Madera Lumber Co. (decision upheld on appeal); as vis. judge, Fresno Muni. Ct., declared the "No-Knock" provisions of CAL-OSHA unconstnl. in People vs. Salwasser (upheld by appellate cts.), decision quoted in US Congl. Record, 4/4/77; honors: Internat. Order of DeMolay, Chevalier Degree 1941, Legion of Honor Degree, 1976; mem: Calif. State Bar, 1954-; Judges and Constables Assn. (prior); Delta Theta Phi Law frat. 1951-; Rotary (prior); Chowchilla Dist. C. of C. secty. 1958-9; mem., Parade Announcer, Chowchilla Spring Festival, 25 yrs.; Chowchilla Planning Commn. 1957-58; chmn.

March of Dimes 1956-60; Dean of Boys, Madera Co. 4-H Camp, 1965; exec. com. Sequoia Council BSA 1956; Madera Golf and CC; Madera County Bar Assn. 1954-; Masons 1941- (Master Chowchilla Lodge #485, 1966); Scottish Rite, Fresno Bodies; asst. ed. Baylor Law Rev., 1952-53; mil: s/sgt. US Army 1941-45; (insp./ct. reporter for Insp. Gen's Section, Hq. Third Army); Republican; Methodist; rec: antique car restoration, square dance, fish, hunt, golf; res: 604 Ventura Ave. Chowchilla 93601.

GREEN, JENNIFER ANN, artist, photographer; d. Hubert and Helen Margaret (Herbst) Hunsucker; div.; children: Kimberly, Wendy, Barbara; edn: BA, Univ. of Colo.; stu. Acad. of Art S.F., two yrs.; spl. courses, Coll. of Arts & Crafts, Oakland, Coll. of Marin. Career: artist in oils, watercolors, pastels, pencil, oilpastel, mixed media; subjects: portraiture and figures of people at their work, animals, and currently doing a long study (10 to 30 paintings in series) in watercolor of the restored old wooden tugs of S.F. bay and rivers; paintings on permanent exhbn. in S.F. National Maritime Museum; Hamilton AFB Reception Center, the Dogs for Blind Sch. (San Rafael), Napa State Hosp.; num. photographs of the tugs on different jobs and locales (collected by the tug cos. for office display); rep. by S.F. Ship Model Gallery, the Solarium (Nat. Maritime Mus.), others; rec: hiking, windsurfing, people, nature. Address: POB 2624, San Rafael 94912

GREEN, JOHN JEFFREY, agricultural executive; b. Feb. 1, 1939, Berkeley; s. Robert Clarke and Deborah (Bixby) G.; m. Leslie Vido, Apr. 14, 1973; children: Elizabeth, b. 1962; John, b. 1964; Joey, b. 1966; edn: BS, Mich. State Univ. 1960; MBA, 1963; lic. Real Estate Broker, Calif. 1969. Career: mkt. & ops. analyst/ feedlot mgr./ grain buyer J.G. Boswell Co., Los Angeles 1963-67; real estate broker Coldwell Banker & Co., San Francisco 1967-71; sales analyst/ v.p. Great Plains Western Corp., Whittier 1971-73; regl. v.p. Fields Investment Gp., Portola Valley 1973-78; gen. mgr. Richard A. Glass Co., Indio 1978-81; pres. The Samuel Edwards Assocs., Santa Paula 1981--; mem./ bd. dirs: Fillmore-Piru Citrus Assn., Santa Barbara Lemon Assn., Ventura Co. Farm Bureau, Ventura Co. Citrus Growers Assn., Pleasant Valley Vegetable Coop.; Bixby Ranch Co. (past); honors: Scabbard & Blade Hon. 1960; Blue Key Hon. 1960; mem: Ventura Co. Bd. Realtors; Lobero Theatre Found.; Rotary Club; Bohemian Club; Santa Barbara Polo & Racquet Club; mil: 1st lt. US Army QMC 1961-62; Republican; Episcopal; rec: tennis, camping, equestrian. Res: 8782 Ladera Ln Montecito 93108 Ofc: The Samuel Edwards Assocs., 124 N 10th St, POB 711, Santa Paula 93060

GREEN, WILLIAM WARREN, lawyer; b. Nov. 9, 1950, Fresno; s. Charles Clark and Annabel (Fitzke) G.; edn: BA in econ., Univ. of Calif. 1972; JD, La Verne Law Sch. 1976; admitted Calif. State Bar 1977. Career: atty. in pvt. practice, Green & Green, Attys. at Law, Dana Point, 1977--, spec. in worker's comp. law, personal injury; guest lectr. on wkmn's comp. law to medical convs.; honors: Calif. State Scholar 1968; mem. Long Beach Police Ofcrs Assn., Calif. Applicants Attorneys Assn.; author: Calif. Workmen's Compensation Law Forms & Guides (in prog. 1984); mil: capt. US Marine Air Corps; Republican; Catholic; rec: aviation. Res: 3301 Tempe Huntington Harbour 92649 Ofc: Green & Green, Attys. 24265 De Leon Dr Dana Point 92649

GREENE, IDA, educator, counselor; b. May 28, 1938, Minters, AL; d. Willie O'Neal and Rosetta (Ulmer) Greene; edn: Provident Hosp. Sch. of Nursing, 1962; BA, CSU San Diego 1970, MS 1975; 1 son, Eddie, b. 1974. Career: dir. Nursing Service, Vista Hill Hosp.; career counselor San Diego State Univ.; instr. San Diego Community Colls.; psychiatric nurse, El Cajon Valley Hosp.; teacher/counselor S.D. City Schs.; licensed Marriage and Family Therapist; mgmt. cons. I.G. Enterprises, 1978--; honors: Psi Chi awd psychology, 1969; mem: Toastmasters, Women in Sales, Nat. Council of Negro Women, Women in Mgmt., Women in Comm. Svcs; Coauthor book: The Black Triumph; Methodist; rec: swim, tennis, ski. Address: I.G. Ent., 2910 Baily Ave, San Diego 92105

GREENE, JOHN NATHANIAL EUGENE, govt. counter-intelligence agent; b. Oct. 11, 1924, Tulsa, Okla.; s. Jack Herman and Della Maude G.; children: Kevin, b. 1954, Tracy Ann, b. 1956; edn: AA, E. Ore. Coll. 1947; BA, Northwestern State Coll. 1950; MA, Univ. Miss. 1951; AA in R.E., UCLA 1959; grad. work, USC 1960-61; lic. Real Estate Broker 1960, Calif. Bldg. Contr. 1963; Cert. Pilot single engine land. 1947. Career: editor Santa Barbara Star, 1956-7; publs. dir. Univ. of Santa Barbara, 1957-60; owner/mgr. Campus Realty, Isla Vista Realty, and John E. Greene Associates Builders, 1960-69; intelligence operative for CIA detached duty with US State Dept. in Central Am., 1969--; college lectr. on intell. activities, 1969-; honors: 1965 Lions Intl. Man of the Year; 1975 BBB Cert. of Merit; 1981 Presidential Commendn. for M.I.A. op. in Laos; 1983 Presdtl. Commendn. for ops. in El Salvador, Honduras and Nicaragua; mem: CofC (pres. 1961); Isla Vista Bus. Orgn. (pres. 65, 6, 7); supvr. apptd. mem. Goleta Valley Cityhood Commn. 1966; Isla Vista Com. for Cityhood (pres. 1967); Contractors Assn. of S.B.; Goleta Valley Comm. Hosp. Bd.; Nat. Bd. of Consumer Arbitrators; editor BBB South Coast Report; mil: gunnery sgt. USMC 1942-45, 3 unit Presdtl. Cits., 2 Purple Hearts, 3 Silver Stars, Navy Cross; Libertarian; Prot.; rec: fishing, swimming, sailing, flying. Address: San Francisco

GREENE, ROBERT FINLAY, physician; b. Apr. 2, 1942, Portland, Ore.; s. Wm. Raymond and Ferne Finlay (Moyer) G.; m. Elizabeth Macdonald, June 27, 1964; children: Nathan, b. 1968, Rebecca, b. 1971, Bethany, b. 1979, Philip, b. 1981; edn: Stanford Univ. 1960-63; B. of Med. Sc., MD, Univ. of Calif. S.F. 1967; dip. Am. Bd. of Orthopedic Surg. 1983. Career: Smith, Kline and French

Fgn. Fellowship, Tanzania, 1966; rotating internship Santa Clara Valley Med. Ctr. 1967-8, gen. surg. res. 1968-9; active duty US Navy in Oakland and S.Vietnam, 1969-71; missionary doctor (leprosy work, language stu.) S. Vietnam, 1971-75; orthopedic res. Stanford Univ. 1975-78; missionary orthopedic surgeon, Zaire (French language stu. & tropical medicine Belgium), 1978-82; solo pvt. practice of orthopedics, Madera, 1982--; honors: Alpha Omega Alpha 1967; Diplomate Am. Bd. of Orthopedic Surgeons 1983; mem: Calif. Med. Assn., Fresno-Madera Med. Soc., Christian Med. Soc., Rotarian; mil: lt. USN 1969-71; Republican; Christian & Missionary Alliance. Res: 2321 National ave Madera 93637 Ofc: 115 South A Street Madera 93638

GREENE, VICTORIA JOANNE, advertising agency president; b. Sept. 4, 1949, Clarkston, WN; d. James Patrick and Betty Jean (Morgan) Martin; m. James Greene (div.), Sept. 3, 1970; edn: BA, Univ. of Ida. 1971; Art Center Coll. of Design 1975-6. Career: sole prop. Gamma Co., Los Angeles 1976-, pres./ CEO Gamma Advt. & Mass Mktg. Agcy. Inc. 1982--; mem. Olympic Task Force for 1984 Olympic Games; awards: award of excellence for Transam. Assurance Co. (client), Life Ins. Advts. Assn. 1981, 2; mem: Advt. Club of L.A., U.S. Olympic Soc., L.A. Area CofC, L.A. Athletic Club, LA County Art Mus. sponsor; owner/opr. 80 acre ranch for breeding and raising thoroughbred horses; rec: equitation, skiing, tennis, art collector. Res: 5047 El Adobe La Crescenta 91214 Ofc: Gamma Advertising & Mass Marketing Agency Inc. 1150 So Olive, Ste. 2817, Los Angeles 90015

GREENE, YVONNE MARGARET, real estate broker; b. Aug. 6, 1932, New Orleans, La.; d. Isadore and Eugenia (Khaten) La Fargue; m. Sen. Bill Greene, Mar. 30, 1962; children: Alisa, b. 1966; Jan, b. 1968; edn: AA, Am. River Coll. 1982; BS, Univ. of San Francisco 1984; GRI, Grad. Realtors Inst. 1978; RECI, Real Estate Cert. Inst. 1981. Career: social service investigation, City of Los Angeles, 1960-66; real estate sales, Moss and Moss, Cooper Realtors, Sacto. 1974-80; asst. mgr. Kiernan Realtors, Land Park Office, 1980--; honors: Sacramento's 100 Most Influential Women, Sacto. Observer Newspaper, 1975; hon. fellow Harry S. Truman Library, 1975-84; Civic Activities Awd., Sacto. Bd. of Realtors, 1979; Kiernan Realtors - Top Producer 1981, Sales Leader 1980; mem: Nat., Calif. Assn. of Realtors 1974-; Sacto. Bd. of Realtors (mbrshp. com. 1980), Women's Council of realtors, Nat. Assn. Profl. Saleswomen, Nat. Assn. Notaries; orgns: Urban League, Women's Civic Imp. Club, Jack and Jill of Am. Inc., Calif. Legislative Families Club, Calif. Museum Found.; Democrat; Catholic; rec: flower arranging, cake decorating. Res: 1750 59th Ave Sacramento 95822 Ofc: Kiernan Realtors 1906 Fruitridge Rd Sacrameno 95822

GREENFIELD, LARRY DAVID, physician, diagnostic radiologist, nuclear medicine, thyroid oncologist; b. Mar. 23, 1944, NYC; s. Samuel and Gertrude (Schwartz) G., edn: BA, USC 1965; MD, Chgo. Med. Sch. 1969; intern, resident LAC/USC Med. Center 1969-71; MS (NIH Traineeship) UCLA Ctr. of Hlth. Scis. 1971-73; res./chief res., Radiation Therapy, Harbor Gen. Hosp. 1973-76; Diplomate Nat. Bd. of Med. Examiners 1970; Cert., Am. Bd. of Nuclear Med. 1973, Am. Bd. of Therapeutic Radiology 19776. Career: phys. in nuclear medicine, Olive View Med. Center, Van Nuys 1972-73, estab. Thyroid Clinc 1973; sr. phys. Nuclear Med., City of Hope Nat. Med. Ctr., Duarte 1973-76, dir. Nuclear Med., Radiation Oncologist, Thyroid Oncology Service 1977-80, cons. Nuclear Med. and Thyroid Oncology 1980--; dir. staff Dpt. Radiol. UCLA-Harbor Med. Ctr., Torrance, assoc. mem. UCLA Comprehensive Cancer Ctr., L.A. 1977--; clin. asst. prof. Radiation Oncol. & Nuclear Medicine, UCLA Ctr. for Hlth. Scis. 1979-; vis. prof. Chgo. Med. Sch. 1975-; frequent lectr. Awards: Roche Labs clerkship 1969; stu. on SS Hope in Ceylon 1968; Award of Merit (as Post founder, 1st advisor LAC/USC Med. Ctr.) Med. Explorer Post 362, 1970; fellowship, Am. Med. Writers Assn. 1981; Disting. Alumnus 1980, Chgo. Med. Sch.; Alpha Epsilon Delta, Phi Delta Epsilon. Mem: Am. Endocurietherapy Soc., Soc. of Nuclear Med., Am. Coll. of Radiol., Calif. Radiological Soc., Calif./ So. Calif. Radiation Therapy Soc., Am. Soc. Therapeutic Radiologists, World/ Calif.,/ L.A. co. Med. Assns., Am. Radium Soc., Am. Thyroid Assn., So. Calif. Acad. of Clin. Oncology, No. Am. Hyperthermia Group, Am. Coll. of Nuclear Physicians. Editor, Noninvasive Medical Imaging, An Internat. Jour., num. med. publs. Republican. Jewish. Rec: antique telephones, rollerskating. Res:10536 Rochester Los Angeles 90024 Ofc: Brotman Medical Ctr. Dept. Diagnostic Radiology, Radiation Oncol. Culver City 90230

GREENLAW, RUSSELL COOLEY, engineer; b. Apr. 14, 1945, Oakland; s. Morrison Bronk and M. Suzanne (Cooley) G.; m. Christine Paden, Aug. 31, 1969; children: Kimberly, b. 1974, Craig, b. 1977; edn: BS in civil eng., Univ. of Pacific 1967; MS, engrg., Univ. Calif. 1969; Reg. Mech. Engr., Calif. 1971, Reg. Civil Engr. 1973. Career: structural naval architect Mare Island Naval Shipyard, 1966-68; asst. prof. of civil engring. Univ. of Pacific, 1969-72; self empl. 1972-76; mech. engr. Lawrence Lilvermore Lab., 1976-79; self empl., prin. Russ Greenlaw & Assocs. (P.E., civil, mech., marine), 1979--; prin./pres. Civil Computing Corp. 1981--, spec. in computer software; honors: Outstanding Graduate 1967, Engineers Council of Sacramento Valley; mem: ASCE (Task Force on state -of-art computer practices; pres. Central Valley Br. 1973;); assoc. mem. Structural Engrs. Assn. of Cenral Calif.; assoc. mem. Soc. of Naval Architects & Marine Engrs.; publs: num. profl. journal articles, tech. papers; author/pub. PropStar Users' Guide (1984), various users' manuals, 1980-; Republican; Prot.; rec: sailing, flying. Res: 2073 Mars Rd Livermore 94550 Ofc: Russ Greenlaw & Assocs. 2111 Research Dr, Ste. 1, Livermore 94550

GREENWELL, ROGER ALLEN, scientist; b. Dec. 4, 1941, Santa Maria; s. George C. and Bessie Florence (Sutton) G.; m. Jeannine Pendleton, July 25, 1969; 1 son: George Eli; edn: AA, Hancock Jr. Coll. 1961; BS, Calif. Poly. Coll. 1968; BS, US Internat. Univ. 1974; DBA, 1981. Career: mathematician Naval Weapons Ctr., China Lake 1968; ops. research analyst, Corona 1969-70; ops. research analyst, Comdr. Naval Forces, Vietnam 1968-69; mathematician Naval Electronics Lab. Ctr., San Diego 1970-77; scientist Naval Ocean Sys. Ctr., San Diego 1977-84; sr. scientist Science & Engring. Assoc., Inc., San Diego 1984--; cons. fiber optics and econ. analysis; mem: Ops. Research Soc. Am.; Inst. Mgmt. Sci; AIAA; Soc. Allied Weight Engrs.; Soc. Photo Optical and Instrumentation Engrs.; mil: US Army 1964-67; works: contbr. book chpts., govt. publs. and movie in field. Res: 3778 Eagle St San Diego 92103 Ofc: Science and Engineering Assoc., Inc., 3111 Camino Del Rio N, Ste 1004, San Diego 92108

GREER, FRANK LACY, building contractor; b. Oct. 31, 1927, St. Johns, Ariz.; s. Lloyd and Thelma (Lackey) G.; m. Beth Harkey, Sept. 7, 1946; children: Cath Marie, b. 1947, Rodger Lloyd, b. 1952, Sally Ann, b. 1954; Calif. Lic. Contr. 1953. Career: vice pres. B & G Constructors, 1955-62; pres. Greer Bros. Enterprises, 1962--; investment counselor/trustee Greer Bros. Ent. Defined Benefit Plan 1978-; co-owner Greer-Wood, 1968-73, Town and Country Devel., 1982-; mem. Elks; active in LDS Ch. as Sunday Sch. teacher, missionary, Boy Scout Troop leader, fund raising, 1957-73; mil: USMC 1943-45, Purple Heart Battle of Iwo Jima; Republican; Ch. of Jesus Christ of Latter Day Saints; rec: collector rare Am. coins Early Dates. Res: 708 E. Park Lane Santa Ana 92701 Ofc: 133 No. Pixley, Orange 92668

GREER, LARRY, lumber broker/company president; b. Dec. 8, 1941, Yuma, Ariz.; s. Grant and Esther Greer; m. Florinze, May 25, 1969; children; Marquis F., b. 1970, Electa S., b. 1976, Yolanda M., b. 1979; edn: bus. adminstrn., Contra Costa Coll. 1975-7, UC Berkeley 1977-8. Career: asst. opr. Texaco Sales Terminal, 1960-65, sr. opr. 1967-71; ins. agent Golden State Mutual Ins., 1971-72; spl. agent/bus. ins. Prudential Ins., 1972-77; pres./chief of staff, A.T.A.P Internat., 1979--; current devel. projects incl. a marina devel., 15 mil. dollar comml. resdtl. devel., single family housing devel., 1980-. Honors: Outstanding Nat. Student, Scholarship, UCB; while in Jr. Coll. authored Student Body Bill which passed Calif. Assem. and Senate, vetoed by Gov. Brown 1978; mem: orgnzr. Gr. Richmond Housing Corp. 1973; founding pres./CEO, Gr. Richmond Comm. Devel. Corp. 1971-78; founding pres. Gr. Richmond Social Svcs. 1974; mem. Richmond Economic Devel. Com. 1977; past pres. Contra Costa Comm. Coll. 1975-6; Evangelist; rec: horsebreaking and riding, fishing. Res: 4720 Overend Ave Richmond 94804 Ofc: ATAP Intl. POB 663 Richmond 94804

GREGG, BARRY DAVID, financial executive, consultant; b. San Diego; s. Wm. F. and Anga C. (Serum) G.; edn: BS, USC 1976; MBA, UC Los Angeles 1977; MBT, USC 1982; cert. in mgmt. accting., Inst. of Mgmt. Acctng. 1980; enrolled agent, IRS 1982; CFP (cert. fin. plnnr.) Coll. for Fin. Plnng. 1984. Career: sr. fin. analyst Memorex Corp., Santa Clara 1978-79; product line finance mgr. Beckman Instruments Inc., Brea 1979-81; prin. B.D. Gregg & Co., Newport Beach 1981--; adjunct lectr. in accting. CSU Fullerton 1980-81; mem: Fin. Mgmt. Assn., Am. Mgmt. Assn., Nat. Assn. of Accts., Am. Acctg. Assn., Data Processing Mgmt. assn., Internat. Assn. for Fin. Plnng., Inst. of Certified Fin. Planners; mem. Mensa; mil: USAF 1970-74. Ofc: B.D.Gregg & Co., 8033 Sunset Blvd, Ste 4027, Los Angeles 90046

GREGG, RICHARD, lawyer; b. May 24, 1946, Cananea Sonora, Mexico, nat. 1966; s. Enrique Francisco and Carolina (Rivas) G.; m. Jean Pharris, June 2, 1973; 1 dau: Jessica Raquel, b. 1983; edn: BA, CSC Dominguez Hills 1972; JD, UC Davis 1977; admitted to Calif. State Bar 1977. Career: adminstrv. analyst City of Redondo Beach Police Dept. 1972-4; student intern Yolo Co. Public Defenders Ofc. 1976; student legal asst. Dept. Motor Vehicles, Sacramento 1976-77; atty. The Baccardo Law Firm 1983--; court interpreter, Sup. Ct. of Yolo Co. 1975--; awards: Dist. Toastmaster of the Year 1981, 82; mem: Yolo Co. Bar (pres. 1983); Calif. Trial Lawyers Assn.; Santa Clara Co. Bar Assn.; Toastmasters; Safe Harbor Crisis House, Inc.; La Raza Lawyers Assn.; mil: 1st lt. US Army 1966-9, Army Commdn., Air Medal; Democrat. Res: 17200 Los Robles Way Los Gatos 95030 Ofc: 111 W St. John Street, Ste 1100, San Jose 95115

GREGORIAN, RAPHAEL PAUL, international trade co. president; b. July 11, 1929, Kislavodsk, USSR, nat. 1957; s. Paul and Olga Ilinichna (Sharikova) G.; m. Joyce Gorham, July 4, 1976; children: Tatiana, b. 1959; Gina, b. 1962; edn: AA, Am. Univ. of Beirut 1948; BS, Univ. of Mich. 1950; BA, USC 1952; MS in engring. scis., UC Berkeley 1957, doctoral work in Soviet Studies; Stanford Univ. Exec. Pgm. 1969. Career: research engr. Sylvania Electric 1956-61; electronics mktg. mgr. Europe, Sylvania Internat. (GTE), Geneva, Switzerland 1961-4; internat. mktg. mgr. MEC div. of Teledyne and Melabs, a div. of SCM 1964-6; founded subsidiary for Melabs, Brussles, Belgium 1966-9; pres./ CEO Melabs, S.A. 1969-70; currently: owner/ pres./ chmn. Calif. Internat. Trade Corp.; pres. Calintra Services; mem. small bus. com. US-USSR Trade & Econ. Council 1982-; lectr. on US-USSR trade; cons. IBM, Technicon (div. of Revlon), E.I. duPont de Nemours & Co.; awarded over 30 diplomas from USSR CofC and Indus. and Ministry of Fgn. Trade of the USSR for new companies in the market; Presdtl. E (excellence in export for a small electronics co.) awd. 1967; Republican; Russian Orthodox; rec: atique collecting, travel, languages. Res: 550 Kingsley St Palo Alto 94301 Ofc: 285 Hamilton Ave, Ste 520 Palo Alto 94301

GREGORY, CALVIN LUTHER, insurance agent, educator, counselor; b. Jan. 11, 1942, Bronx, NY; s. Jacob and Ruth (Cherchian) G.; m. Carla Deaver, June 30, 1979; edn: AA, L.A. City Coll.; BA, CSU Los Angeles 1964; M.Div.,

Fuller Theol. Sem. 1968; M.Re.Edn., Southwestern Sem. 1969; D.D., Otay Mesa Coll, San Diego 1982; PhD in religion, Universal Life Ch., Inc. 1982; Ordained minister Am. Baptist Conv. L.A. 1970; real estate lic., Calif. 1969; Notary Public, Calif. 1969. Career: USAF Chaplain, Edwards AFB 1970; pastor First Baptist Ch., Boron, CA 1971; ins. agent Prudential Life Ins. Co., Ventura 1972; mgr. Prudential Ins. Co., Thousand Oaks 1973; casualty ins. agent Allstate Ins. Co., Thousand Oaks 1974; pres. Ins. Agcy. Placement Svc., Thousand Oaks 1975--; counselar Wilshire Presbyterian Ch., Los Angeles, fmrly. Hd. Youth Minister, 1974; tchr., polit. sci. Maranatha H.S., Rosemead; investor - owner apt. bldgs., real property 1974--; awards: president's citation, Prudential 1972; WLRT, Prudential 1972; Top- 20 Salesman awd., Southwestern Co. 1967; mem: Forensic Club, CSU, L.A. 1963; Apartment Assn. L.A. 1975-; Republican; rec: travel, video tapes, jogging. Res: 3307 Big Cloud Circle Thousand Oaks 91360 Ofc: Insurance Agency Placeme, Jr., Aug. 14, 1946; children: Donald, b. 1952; Robert, b. 1954; John, b. 1956; Mark, m. 1965; edn: AA, Santa Rosa Jr. Coll. 1950; BA, Sonoma State 1963; MA, 1970; GRI, Grad. Realtors Inst. 1976, CRS, cert. resl. spl. 1978, Nat. Assn. of Realtors; sr. cert. mem., IREA; Internat. Cert. Appraiser (pending). Career: college instr. 1970-4; real estate salesprsn. 1973; owner/broker Real Estate Information Center, Inc., Sonoma 1975--; precentor (relig. soloist) First Ch. of Christ Scientist, Sonoma 1965-; honors: GRI; CRS; Million Dollar Club (life); mem. Women's Soc. of Christian Svc. for outstanding svc. 1965-; VFW Distng. Svc. 1983; mem: Nat. Assn. of Realtors; Sonoma Co. Multiple Listing Svc., Bd. of Realtors 1973- (dir. 1976-8, mem. Edn. Com., chmn. Million Dollar Club, Sonoma Council); soloist Sonoma Valley Chorale; recordings: relig. solo music, Infinite Power of Love; Republican; Christian Sci.; rec: music, writing, sewing. Res: 327 Napa Street E., Sonoma 95476 Ofc: Real Estate Information Center, Inc., 481 First Street W., Sonoma 95476

GREGORY, EVELYN ILENE, real estate broker; b. May 26, 1930, Canton, Ill.; d. Joseph Alfred and Gladys Irene (Benson) Kidd; m. Frank D. Gregory, Jr., Aug. 14, 1946; children: Donald, b. 1952; Robert, b. 1954; John, b. 1956; Mark, m. 1965; edn: AA, Santa Rosa Jr. Coll. 1950; BA, Sonoma State 1963; MA, 1970; GRI, Grad. Realtors Inst. 1976, CRS, Cert. Resl. Splst. 1978, Nat. Assn. of Realtors; Sr. Cert. Mem., IREA; Internat. Cert. Appraiser (pending). Career: college instr. 1970-4; real estate salesprsn. 1973; owner/broker Real Estate Information Center, Inc., Sonoma 1975--; precentor (relig. soloist) First Ch. of Christ Scientist, Sonoma 1965-; honors: GRI; CRS; Million Dollar Club (life); mem. Women's Soc. of Christian Svc. for outstanding svc. 1965-; VFW Distng. Svc. 1983; mem: Nat. Assn. of Realtors; Sonoma Co. Multiple Listing Svc., Bd. of Realtors 1973- (dir. 1976-8, mem. Edn. Com., chmn. Million Dollar Club, Sonoma Council); soloist Sonoma Valley Chorale; music recording: Infinite Power of Love (religious solo); Republican; Christian Sci.; rec: music, writing, sewing. Res: 327 Napa Street E., Sonoma 95476 Ofc: Real Estate Information Center, Inc., 481 First Street W., Sonoma 95476

GREGORY, SIDNEY YOUNG, stockbroker, financial consultant; b. July 12, 1920, Iowa Park, Texas; s. Sidney Young and Frances Belle (Hanks); first cousin, Nancy Hanks (dec. 1983), ch. Nat. Endowment for the Arts under three Presidents; m. Rosemary Friel, Dec. 17, 1945; chil: Dennis, b. 1948; Nancy, b. 1951; Janice, b. 1956; Drew, b. 1959; edn: BA, Univ. Tex. 1947; teaching cred. Chapman Coll. 1953; assoc. N.Y. Stock Exchange, Nat. Assn. Security Dealers 1955-; assoc. Am. Coll. of Sports Medicine, 1980-; mem. US Cycling Fedn. 1978-. Career: mem. Texas State Legislature (House of Reps.), Austin 1946-50 comml. mktg. Victor Adding Machine Co., Long Beach, Ca. 1950-52; teacher Tustin Public Schools 1955-56; stockbroker Dean Witter & Co., 1955-62; stock broker, finl. cons. Shearson/American Express, 1962--, Newport Beach ofc. mgr. 1962-8; instr., securities and investments, Golden West Coll. 1975-80. Awards: gold medal (bicycle 25 mile time trial) 1983 Senior Olympics. Mem. Battleship Texas Commn. 1948; pres. Red Hill Breakfast Club 1965; mem. Lions Club. Author: The Stampede Theory (stockmarket book, 1968); authored legislation that revised tng. schs. for juvenile delinquents, state of Texas 1949. Mil: maj. (transport pilot) USMC 1943-45, 1952-55; pol: conservative; rec: bicycle racing, nat. class. Res: 1000 W. MacArthur #29, Santa Ana 92707 Ofc: Shearson/Am Exp, 19000 MacArthur, Penthouse, Newport Beach 92660

GREGORY, WAYNE BRIAN, nylon equipment designer; b. Feb. 7, 1948, Hartford, Conn.; s. Harvey Gerald and Monica Myrtle (Nash) G.; m. Susan Arlene Smithson, Nov. 1, 1970; 1 dau: Heather Nicole, b. 1980; edn: San Diego City Coll. 1967-70. Career: tech. cons. Alpenlite Prods., Claremont 1973; prod. engr. Snow Lion Corp., Berkeley 1973-5; R & D dir. Gerry Outdoor Sports, Denver, Co. 1975-6; retail stores mgr. Frostline Kits, Inc., Northglenn, Co. 1976; owner/ pres. Gregory Mountain Prods., Inc., San Diego 1977-83; v.p. research & devel. Bianchi Internat., Temecula 1983--; guest lectr. for Boy Scouts of Am., Sierra Club, other orgns.; honors: Eagle Scout; Eagle Scout and BSA Scout leader 1973-; works: leader in innovative fabric concept, outdoor equip. and industry trends; mil: E-4, USAR 1970-6; Republican; LDS; rec: woodworking, backpacking. Res: 1647 Tecalote Dr Fallbrook 92028

GRELLA, NOREEN M., social worker; b. Sept. 16, 1946, Mineola, NY; d. Marchiano M. and Stephanie (Andrazek) G.; edn: BA, Rider Coll. 1968; MSW, Univ. of Penna. 1970; LCSW, Calif. Bd. of Behavioral Sci. Examiners. Career: social wkr. Contra Costa Co. Social Svc. 1970-4; soc. wkr. Childrens Home Sc. 1974; soc. svc. Child Welfare 1975-81; sr. soc. wkr. 1981--; pvt. practice Psychotherapist 1978--; lectr. Cal State Fullerton and USC 1976--; Gubernatorial appointment State Adv. Gp. on Juvenile Justice & Delinquency Prevention 1983; Senator John Seymour's Womens Issues Task Force 1983; awards: Orange Co. Child Abuse Council Awd. 1976-78; honors: Childrens Bureau Fellowship 1968; mem: So. Calif. Network of Exec. Women; Orange Co. Rape Crisis Network Unit; past ch. O.C. VOTERR orgn.; O.C. Employees Assn.; So. Calif. Juvenile Ofcrs. Assn.; Nat. Womens Pol. Caucus; publs: profl. papers, keynote spkr. 1982; Republican; Catholic; rec: photog., skiing. Res: 4233 E Fairhaven Orange 92669 Ofc: Noreen M. Grella & Assocs., 3822 Campus Dr Newport Beach

GRIBOW, DALE SEWARD, lawyer; b. June 18, 1943, Chgo.; edn: BA, USC 1965; JD, Loyola Univ. 1968; adv. legal studies, UCLA and USC. Career: deputy public defender Los Angeles Co. 1970-4; sr. partner Gribow, Benjamin & Sandler 1974-6; Law ofcs. of Dale S. Gribow, APC, Beverly Hills 1976--; owner: Exec. Credit Control Inc., Nutritional Biological Corp.; judge prom tem: West Los Angeles Municipal Ct. 1977, Los Angeles and Beverly Hills Municipal Cts. 1983; founder Concerned Adults for Dubnoff Sch. for Handicapped Chidren, L.A. 1971, pres. 1973-6; bd. dirs.: Dubnoff Ctr. 1974-82, Thalians, Guardians, Westside Chpt. Kidney Found., Variety Club, L.A. Boys & Girls Club, Ctr. for the Inprovement of Child Caring, Pips, Marbles, J. Daniels, Aspen Mktg., Anti-Defamation League legal steering com.; univ. guest. lectr.; Dist. Atty's Adv. Bd.; City Atty's Adv. Com. Awards: Dale Seward Gribow Day, 1/8/82, by proclamation Mayor and City Council of Bev. Hls.; Commendations., City of L.A. (1977, 80, 82), Calif. Assembly (1982), Gov. Jerry Brown, US Sen. Cranston, Cong. Henry Waxman (1982); David Schloss Meml. Awd. 1974; mem: Am., L.A. Co., Bev. Hills., W. Hollywood, San Fernando Valley. bar assns.; Calif., L.A. trial lawyers assns.; Calif. Attys. for Criminal Justice; L.A., San Fernando Vlly. criminal cts. bar assns.; L.A. Jr. CofC; USC Alumni, Pres.'s Club, Commerce Assocs., Blue Key Alumni; Legion Lex; Thalians, City of Hope, Vista Del Mar, Friars Club, Variety Club; Bnai Brith; Simon Weisenthal Ctr. for Holocaust Studies; LA World Fair Council. Ofc: 9777 Wilshire Blvd, Ste 918, Beverly Hills 90212

GRIFFIN, ROY JESSE, distributing company executive; b. Dec. 1, 1924, Morrisville, Miss.; s. Charles Jesse and Laura Elizabeth (Westphall) G.; m. Laura M. Ramsey, Nov. 19, 1944; children: Robert Eugene, b. 1947; Dennis Charles, b. 1949; Kathleen Ann, b. 1960. Career: hardware sales Thompson Diggs Co., Calif. 1946-9; hardware sales Sears Roebuck, Sacto. 1949-50; quality control U.S. Govt., McClelland Field, Sacto. 1950-3; mgr. hardware dept. Dolans Bldg. Materials, Sacto. 1953-8; salespsn. to gen. mgr. Wilco Supply, Oakland 1959--; mem: Masons; Rotary of Oakland; Jobs Daus., Walnut Creek; Music Boosters, Northgate H.S.; mil: AMM 3/c, USN 1942-5; Republican; Prot.; rec: travel, golf. Res: 637 Manhasset Ct Walnut Creek 94598 Ofc: Wilco Supply, 5960 Telegraph Ave Oakland 94609- 1597

GRILLOS, JOHN MURDICK, company president; b. Feb. 19, 1942, Cheyenne, Wyo.; s. Murdick John and Betty Mae (Anderson) G.; m. Patricia Paschall, July 9, 1966; children: Christina, b. 1970; Stephen, b. 1972; edn: BS, Ill. Inst. of Tech. 1969; MBA, Univ. of Chgo. 1971. Career: engr. Western Electric, Chgo., Ill. 1966-9; proj. mgr. Inst. for Computer Research, Univ. of Chgo. 1969-72; bus. unit mgr. Am. Mgmt. Sys., Arlington, VA 1972-9; v.p./ regl. mgr. Am. Mgmt. Sys., San Mateo 1979-83; pres. Tesseract Corp., San Francisco 1983--; instr. Ill. Inst. of Tech. 1970; instr. USMC 1964; dir. Univ. of Chgo. Alumni Fund 1972-4; chmn. bd. Evertec, Inc. 1981-3; mem: Univ. of Chgo. Nat. Alumni Fund; publs: Distribution Logistics in Forest Products Companies, Industry Mgmt. Assn. 1981; A Guide to Systems Development, Hewlett Packard Gen. Sys. Users Gp. 1978; Distribution Processing: Why Consider It ?, Auerbach Mgmt. Perspectives vol. 1-05-11, Auerbach Pubs., Inc. 1976; Pricing EDP Services, Computer Decisions, 1974; A Guide to Managing Centralized Data Processing in the Public Sector, State Govt. 1974; mil: Sgt., USMC reserve 1963-9, GCM; rec: sailing, photog., racquetball. Res: 1919 Hilman Ave Belmont 94002 Ofc: Tesseract Corp., 101 Howard San Francisco 94120

GRIM, DOUGLAS PAUL, lawyer; b. May 12, 1940, Bellingham, WA; s. Paul R. and Vivian I. (McMillen) G.; children: Caryn, b. 1970; Devin, b. 1972; edn: BA, Lawrece Coll. 1962; LLB, Stanr: assoc. Hanna and Morton, L.A. 1966-72; of counsel Harris, Noble, Huler & Gallop, L.A. 1972-5; partner law ofcs. of Douglas P. Grim, L.A. 1975--; instr. Golden Gate Univ. Sch. of Law 1975;awards: Michael F. Tobey Awd., L.A. Jr. CofC 1972; listed: Who's Who in Am. Law, 1st, 2nd, 3rd eds.; honors: student body pres., Lawrence Coll. 1962; mem: Calif., L.A. Co., and Am. Bar Assns.; L.A. Area Council Boy Scouts; L.A. Jr. CofC; Wilshire Kiwanis; Uptown Investment Club (pres. 1978); Jonathan Club; Riviera Tennis Club; publs: arts. legal journals; Methodist; rec: tennis, polo, skiing. Res: 247 So Lorraine Blvd Los Angeles 90004 Ofc: Law Offices of Douglas P. Grim, 523 W Sixth Street Los Angeles 90014

GRIMES, DONALD L., life insurance agency executive; b. Mar. 6, 1929, Little Falls, Minn.; s. Austin L. and Kathryn M. (Kenna) G.; m. Ellen Kaufman, Dec. 29, 1962; children: Daniel, b. 1965; Peter, b. 1967; Jessica, b. 1969; edn: St. Thomas Coll., St. Paul 1946-48; BA, Univ. of Minn. 1954; CLU, Am. Soc. of Chartered Life Underwriters 1970; Chartered Fin. Cons. (CHFE), The Am. Coll., Bryn Mawr 1983. Career: gp. sales Travelers Ins. Co., Hartford, Conn. and San Francisco 1955-7; acct. exec. Marsh & McLennan, San Francisco 1957-61; supvr. Aetna Life, S.F. 1961-3; mgr. life & benefits dept. Western State Ins. Brokers, S.F. 1963-7; brokerage agcy. mgr. The Bankers Life, S.F. 1967--; bd. dirs. S.F. Life Underwriters Assn. 1972-6; dir. S.F. Chpt. CLUs 1973-5; mem: S.F. Estate Planning Council; S.F. Life Underwriters Assn.; S.F. Chpt. CLUs; Variety Club of No. Calif.; Merchants Exch. Club; Marines Meml. Club; mil: Sgt., USMC 1950-3; rec: real estate investments. Res: 117 Alpine Terrace San Francisco 94117 Ofc: The Bankers Life, 505 Sansome, Ste 1000, San Francisco 94111

GRIMM, LUCIEEN CHARLOTTE, fashion designer; b. Apr. 28, 1921, Berlin, Germany; naturalized, 1952; d. Fritz George and Marie Charlotte (Mietz) Henschel; attended Victoria Oberlyzeum, Berlin, 5 yrs., 1931-36; studied fashion, Coll. Fashion Design, Germany, 1936-39. Career: fashion designer, Germany, 1940-52; fashion designer of Antiguelaces, bridal gowns, dresses, L.A., 1952--; bus. owner, Lucieen, L.A., --. Listed as Fashion Designer of Berlin, Germany, 1952. Mem.: Art Guild, Berlin. Protestant. Res.: 752 S. Wilton Place, Apt. 1, Los Angeles 90005; Office: Lucieen, 225 N. Larchmont Blvd., Los Angeles 90004.

GRIMSHAW, DONALD HARVEY, logistics engineer; b. June 22, 1923, Turtlecreek Twp., Ohio; s. Percy and Louella (Harvey) Grimshaw; edn: AA, El Camino College, 1956; AB, Calif. State Univ., at LA, 1959; Univ. of So. California, 1959-61; m. Jean Mrazek, November 18, 1950; chil: Randall, b. 1951, Kimberley, b. 1954, Stuart, b. 1957, Paul, b. 1960, Heather, b. 1963, Matthew, b. 1966; career: tech. staff specialist, TRW Defense Systems Group, Redondo Beach, 1965--; research writer, State of Calif., Dept. of Water Resources, Los Angeles, 1962-65; research engr., Northrop Corp., Hawthorne, 1957-62; research asst., Douglas Aircraft Co., Santa Monica, 1954-57; research asst., Hughes Aircraft Co., Culver City, 1951-54; honors: won Republican nomination for US Representative in Congress, 31st Congressional District of California, in 1978 and 1980 elections; Mem.: Executive Committee of Calif. State Republican Committee, Los Angeles Co. Central Committee, and 53rd Assembly District Central Committee; mem. Society of Logistics Engineers, American Institute of Aeronautics and Astronautics, Soc. fo Tech. Communications; Lawndale C. of C., PTA, Boy Scouts of America; works: three articles published in SPECTRUM, the journal of the Soc. of Logisics Engineers; Managing editor of SPECTRUM, 1966-68; mil: Chief Electrician's Mate, US Naval Reserve, 1942-45, 1947-51. Decorations for WWII and Korea; Republican; Presbyterian; rec: photography, golf, tennis; res: 3616 West 157th Street, Lawndale 90260 ofc: TRW Defense Systems Group, 1 Space Park, Redondo Beach 90278.

GRODIN, JOSEPH RAYMOND, jurist; b. Aug. 30, 1930, Oakland; s. Michael and Celia (Falk) Grodin; edn: BA, UC Berkeley, 1951, JD, Yale Law Sch., 1954, PhD, London Sch. Economics, 1960; m. Janet Sasser, July 20, 1952; daus.: Sharon, b. 1956, Lisa, b. 1961; career: practiced law, specializing in labor law, firm of Neuhart & Grodin, San Francisco 1955-71; Law Prof., Hastings Coll. of the Law, 1972-79; Associate Justice, Calif. Ct. Appeal, Dist. 1, Div. 1, 1979-80, Presiding Justice, Calif. Ct. Appeal, Dist. 1, Div. 2, San Francisco, 1981--; vis. prof. Stanford Law Sch. 1976-77; mem. Calif. Agric. Labor Rel. Bd., 1975-76; mem: Phi Beta Kappa, Order of the Coif, Am. Jewish Congress; publs: Union Govt. & the Law, 1960, num. law review articles; Dem.; Jewish; rec: backpacking; res: 2926 Avalon Ave., Berkeley 94705 ofc: State Bldg., San Francisco.

GROLEAU, JAMES EDWARD, insurance consultant; b. May 20, 1934, Hawkesbury, Ontario, Canada, nat. 1965; s. Antonio Joseph and Mae (Simpson) G.; m. Huguette G. Martin, Aug. 16, 1956; 1 dau: Lynda, b. 1957; edn: St. Marie's 1948-50; La Salle Ext. Univ. 1950-2; assoc. in risk mgmt., Ins. Inst. of Am. 1976. Career: acctnt. Pascal Hardware, Montreal, Canada 1950-2; spl. agent Western Assurance Co., Montreal 1952-9; underwriter Ins. Co. of No. Am., Los Angeles 1 br. underwriting mgr. Commercial Union Ins., L.A. 1964-8; casualty mgr. Jas. Econn G Co., L.A. 1968-9; v.p. Bayly, Martin & Fay, L.A. 1969--; v.p. Risk Treatment Services, L.A. 1969--; chr. var. ins. classes at ins. cos.; ednl. dir. BMF; cons.; Knight of the Year, Knight of Columbus 1975-6; mem: Ins. Cos. Edl. Dirs. Soc.; Moose Lodge; Knights of Columbus (PGK); Masons; Scottish Rite; Shriners; Republican; rec: golf, fishing, travel. Res: 127 So Elm St Alhambra 91801 Ofc: Bayly, Martin & Fay, Inc., 3200 Wilshire Blvd, Ste 1200, Los Angeles 90010

GROOM, KEVIN LEE, mechanical engineer; b. Jan. 13, 1956, Honolulu, Hawaii; s. Wayman Keith and Leatrice (Conerly) G.; m. Kimberly Groom, Aug. 14, 1982; edn: BS, in ME, UC Irvine 1978; MS, in ME, CSU Fullerton 1983; profl. engr. in mechl. engring., State of Calif. 1982. Career: sr. engr. Bethel Power Corp., San Clemente 1978--; tech. support to the crafts re installation of piping sys. San Onofre Nuclear Generating Station; participant devel. of Mgmt. Ability Pgm., Bechtel 1982-; mem: ASME (assoc.); Nat. Soc of Profl. Engrs. (assoc.); mem. Energy and Natural Resources Adv. Bd., Calif. Assem. Richard Robinson; UC Irvine Alumni Assn.; publs: sci. papers; Democrat; Christian; rec: backpacking, photog., sailing. Res: 213 Candice Pl Vista 92083 Ofc: Bechtel Power Corp., POB 450 San Clemente 92672

GROSS, BARRY, data systems company executive; b. Jan. 25, 1950, NY, NY; s. J. George and Roslyn (Lippman) G.; m. Pat Huber, May 14, 1977; edn: BA, Union Coll. 1972; MBA, Rutgers Grad. Sch. of Bus. 1974. Career: CPA Kenneth Leventhal & Co., Newport Beach 1974-6; corp. controller/ CFO The Housing Gp., Irvine 1977-81; partner/ v.p. Interface Data Systems, Anaheim 1981--; mem: Am. Inst. CPAs; Calif. Soc. of CPAs; rec: marathon running, triathlons, cabinet making. res: 3672 Hamilton Irvine 92714 Ofc: Interface Data Systems, 2990 E La Jolla Anaheim 92806

GROSS, SYDNEY, real estate developer; b. May 18, 1921, Czech., nat. 1943; m. Sarah Velick, Feb. 8, 1942; children: Harold, b. 1948; Barry, b. 1951; Lori, b. 1955; edn: BA, business 1939. Career: owner Belknap Distbrs., Detroit, Mich. 1944; sales Carlgate Corp., L.A. 1958; owner Blue Chip Realthy Investments, L.A. 1959; pres. Gross Enterprises, Inc. Encino 1960--; awards: Fernando Awd., US CofC; mem: Encino CofC; B.P.O. Elks; Al Malaikah Shrine; mil: US Army 1942-4; rec: community planning, high rise office devel. and constrn., creative real estate devel. Res: 4169 Clear Valley Encino 91436 Ofc: 16000 Ventura Blvd, Ste 1200, Encino 91436

GROSSBERG, RICHARD MALCOLM, lawyer; b. July 30, 1922, St. Louis, Mo.; s. David and Goldie Lucille (Bass) G.; m. Constance J. Brink, May 22, 1976; children: Michael, b. 1950; Gail, b. 1951; Stephen, b. 1965; edn: AA, UCLA 1942; JD, USC 1950; State Bar of Calif. 1951. Career: deputy legisltv. counsel 1951-2; base legal ofc., McClen AFB 1952-3; atty., pvt. practice 1953--; mem: Calif., San Diego Co., and No. Co. Bar Assns.; San Diego Trial Lawyers Assn.; Calif. Attys. for Criminal Justice; Mensa; No. Co. Serenity House, Inc.; mil: AUS 1942-6; Lt., USCGR; Democrat; Jewish; rec: sports. Res: 260 Riverview Way Oceanside 92054 Ofc: Richard M. Grossberg, Lawyer, 355 W Vista Way Vista 92083

GROSSHANS, KARL H., metal fabrication co. executive; b. Sept. 25, 1947, Ludwigsburg, W. Germany, nat. 1962; s. Jacob and Marie (Wieland) m. Christine VandeBerg, Apr. 29, 1972; children: Michael, b. 1975; Kevin, b. 1982. Career: with Lodi Door Inc., Lodi 1969-81: shipping & receiving 1969-79, plant mgr. 1979-81; gen. foreman Cal-Rak Corp., Stockton 1982--; mem: ASM, Loyal Order of Moose; mil: Sgt. E5, USMC 1965-9, scout-sniper, Vietnam; Lutheran; rec: wood working, water skiing, motorcycles. Res: 1148 Tamarack Dr Lodi 95240 Ofc: Cal-Rak Corp., 1821 E Charter Way Stockton 95205

GROSSMAN, AVRAM SAMUEL, computer scientist/consultant; b. Apr. 15, 1951, Los Angeles; s. Louis and Sylvia (Teitelbaum) G.; edn: AA in math., Santa Monica Coll. 1971, BS in Biol., CSU San Diego 1974. Career: analyst Naval Electronics Lab. (now NOSC), San Diego 1973-75; owner Technical Research Labs (biomedical resrch), San Diego 1975-; designer (AS/5 console) National Advanced Systems, S.D. 1976-78; technical support Itel Internat., Germany and London, Eng. 1978-80; cons. in Europe, Grossman & Assocs. 1980-82; dir. Tech. Support, Eagle Computer Co. 1983-84; prin./dir. G & A, Computer Consultants, 1984--. Mem. Sierra Club (leader); publs: contbr. EDN Mag. 1976-7; 2 patent apps. 1976; alternate (wholistic) health and biomed. research. Democrat; Jewish; rec: flying, sailing. Address: Grossman Assocs. 749 Grayling Bay Costa Mesa 92626

GROSSMAN, REGINA VALDEZ, psychotherapist; b. Apr. 29, 1946, Oakland; d. Robert K. and Louisa (Valdez) Mitchell; m. Dr. Stephen Grossman, July 26, 1972; edn: MSW, UC Berkeley 1971; Postmasters cert. in Comm. Mental Health, 1973; MPH, 1973; JD, UCLA Sch. of Law 1980; LCSW, lic. clin. soc. wkr., Calif. 1974. Career: soc. wrk. staff Children's Hosp. of Oakland 1973-4; Stanford Univ. Med. Ctr. 1974-6; dir. soc. wrk. Kaiser Hosp., So. SAN Francisco 1981-3; cons. to legal profession re psycho-social aspects of family law; pvt. practice 1983--; past administrv. research for Judge C. Reynoso (now Cal. Supreme Ct. Justice); UCLA Judicical extern in Marin Co. Superior Ct.; honors: California State Fellowship 1964; mem: Trial Lawyers Assn. of San Mateo Co., Profl. Connections for Women, Palo Alto Chpt., rec. computers, photog., sports. Res: POB 291 San Carlos 94070 Ofc: 560 Oxford Ave, Ste 5, Palo Alto 94306

GROSSMAN, RICHARD A., lawyer; b. Oct. 26, 1939, Detroit, Mich.; s. Moses M. and Alice May (Aronson) G.; div.; children: Justine, b. 1970; Adam, b. 1974; edn: BA, Wayne State Univ. 1963; JD, Univ. of Mich. 1969. Career: speech writer, staff, U.S. Senator Robert F. Kennedy 1967; staff, chief counsel, NASA 1967; U.S. Tax Ct. 1971; U.S. Supreme Ct. 1974; sr. partner Grossman & Levintahl 1974-7; sr. partner Law Ofcs. of Richard A. Grossman 1977--; judge pro tem: Municipal Ct. of Calif., Beverly Hills 1973-7; Sup. Ct. of Calif., Co. of L.A. 1980-2; chmn. Justice William O. Douglass Annual Awd. 1976-82; pvt. law practice, Bev. Hls. 1981-; cons. to Govt. andInd. on internat. bus. and security matters 1979--; pres./ dir. Public Counsel, The Public Interest Law Ofcs. of the L.A. Co. and Bev. Hls. Bar Assns. 1975-82; chmn. Fed. Judicial Survey 1978; vis. prof. Claremont Grad. Sch. 1973-4; awards: Humanitarian Awd. for Relief Efforts for Ctr. for Pediatric Plastic and Recons. Surgery, Rep. of Vietnam 1972; honors: Pi Sigma Alpha 1962; mem: Am. Bar Assn. (subcom. Internat. Copyright Law concerning Berne Conv.); Los Angeles Co. Bar Assn.; Beverly Hills Bar Assn. (chmn. Small Claims Ct. Com., Judge Pro Tem); Internat. Maccabee League (soccer); publs: poetry, I Am A Young Man, Vol. I & II, 1973-5; mil: capt. USMC, Silver and Bronze Stars, Navy Cross, Purple Heart, Gallantry Cross, Honor Medal, Navy Marine Corps. Medal; Democrat; Jewish; rec: mountain climbing, painting, travel. Ofc: Law Offices of Richard A. Grossman, 9601 Wilshire Blvd, Ste 200, Beverly Hills

GROTLE, GERALD KNUTE, travel agency president; b. Sept. 6, 1932, Seattle, Wash.; s. Knute C. and Marguerite M. (Hansen) G.; edn: BS, CSU Long Beach 1954; MA, UCLA 1955; CTC, cert. travel counselor, Inst. of Cert. Travel Agents 1976. Career: Pan American World Airways, Los Angeles 1956-7; World Travel Bureau of Anaheim, Inc. 1957--; pres. 1967--; v.p. 1983--; pres. Orange Co. Travel Agents Assn. 1972-3; area v.p. So. Calif. Chpt. The Am. Soc. of Travel Agents; awards: Inst. of Cert. Travel Agents, life mem. 1967-; Orange Co. Travel Agents Assn. life mem. 1982-; num. awds. from airlines and cruise oprs., Kiwanis Club, City of Anaheim, Boy Scouts of Am.; mem: Orange Co. Travel Agents Assn. (pres. 1972, 73); Am. Soc. of Travel Agents; Inst. Cert. Travel Agents; Kiwanis Club; Magic Island, Newport Beach; Orange Co. Apartment Owners Assn.; publs: (thesis) Evaluation of a Travel Agency for Purchase, Sales Mgmt. for Travel Agents 1977, num. reprints; num. travel arts. on ship orientated travel; Republican; Prot., dir. Christ Chapel, Santa Ana; rec: travel, sailing. Res: 113 Orange Hill Lane Anaheim Hills 92807 Ofc: World Travel Bureau of Anaheim, Inc., 839 So Harbor Blvd Anaheim 92805

GROVE, SYLVAN (Bud) EDWARD, computer consultant, administrator; b. Dec. 23, 1939, Detroit, Mich.; s. Sylvan Duward and Laura May (Beal) G.; div.; 1 dau: Cherie Kim, b. 1970; edn: Macomb Coll., Mich.; No. Montana Coll.; Maryland Univ. Career: served to E4, USAF 1958-65; electrician Chevrolet; electronic splst. Hughes Aircraft, 1958, Gen. Motors, 1965-72; electronic spec. Hughes Aircraft, El Segundo 1972-, equipment eng. 1979-80, adminstr. 1982--; pres. Toppless Computer, Carson 1983--; computer cons. hardware and software; mem: Software Writers Internat. Guild; SME; IEEE; Nat. Computer Graphics Assn.; Hughes Aircraft computer Assn. (HESEA); mil: E-4, USAF 1958-65; rec: chess, computers, creating software. Res./ Toppless Computer, 21111 Dolores, No. 146, Carson 90745 Ofc: Hughes Aircraft, 2060 Imperial El Segundo 90245

GRUBER, FRED JOE, software development executive; b. Aug. 9, 1956, Los Angeles; s. Isaac and Ruth (Selski) G.; m. Susan Jo Waldman, Oct. 2, 1983; edn: USC 1977-9. Career: with Nova Stylings, Inc., Los Angeles 1973--; acttg. clerk 1973; inventory mgr. 1974-6; v.p. 1976--; secty. 1980--; dir. 1981--; pres. Solutions Plus, Inc., Los Angeles 1983--; software cons. FMF Ind. 1982-3; Deutsch Fasteners 1983; mem: City of Hope; United Jewish Appeal; Republican Nat. Com.; Pres.'s Adv. Bd.; Heritage Found.; Gopac; Republican; Jewish; rec: skiing, racquetball, sailing. Res: 17132 Escalon Dr Encino 91316 Ofc: Nova Stylings, Inc., 812 W 8th Street Los Angeles 90017

GRUBER, MILDRED ANN, fruit products co. executive; b. Nov. 18, 1905, Chetopa, Kansas; d. Thomas Marvin and Mary (Morgan) Brookshire; m. Emanuel V. Gruber (dec.), Nov. 18, 1931; children: Mary Kathryn (Cooper), b. 1934; Emanuel Vincent II, b. 1936; Marvin Ellsworth (dec.), b. 1938; edn: tchr. cert., Kansas State Tchrs. Coll. 1924. Career: elementary school teacher, Chetopa, Kans. 1924-30; v.p./chmn. bd., Sunshine Fruit Products Co., Los Angeles --; recipient recognition awards Am. National Red Cross 1948, Grand Cross of Color, Order of Rainbow 1954, Victory Chest 1945-6, BSA Den Mother 1948; active in PTAs, Masonic Orders; Republican; Presbyterian; rec: ceramics, crocheting. Res: 4047 W. 103rd. Inglewood 90304 Ofc: Sunshine Fruit Products Co. 6080 So. Hoover Los Angeles 90044

GRUENWALD, JON RAY, engineering co. executive; b. Feb. 26, 1947, Berlin, Wisc.; s. Raymond John and Ruth D. (Gomol) G.; m. Janice Valee Squires, Jan. 25, 1969; 1 son, Jordan Jon, b. 1981; edn: BCA, Univ. of Wisc. 1972; mgmt., Internat. Correspondence Sch. 1977; VFR pilots lic., Morey Pilot Tng. 1975; Reg. Profl. Engr. and Designer, Wisc.; reg. profl. engr., Calif. Career: electrician Gruenwald Elec., Princeton, Wisc. 1960-5; Mayr Elec., Sheboygan, Wisc. 1966-67; elec. mgr. Academy Elec., Madison, Wisc. 1968-75; environ. cons., Environmental Consultants, Madison 1974-6; elec. supt. Thompson Elec., Hibbing, Minn. 1976; res. engr. Metcalf and Eddy, Boston, Mass. 1976-7; proj. mgr. Pieper Elec., Milwaukee 1978-9; elec. engr. Bople Engring., Newport Beach 1979-80 (sub-contr. to Donald F. Dickerson Assocs., Frankfort, Ger.); v.p. elec. div. and asst. prodn. mgr. Donald F. Dickerson Assocs., Van Nuys 1980-2; Electrend, Fullerton 1883--; lectr. on elec. sys., Univ. of Wisc. 1968-72; mem: Internat. Brotherhood of Elec. Wkrs.; IEEE; Inst. of Illuminating Engrs.; Nat. Soc. of Profl. Engrs.; Nat. Pilots Assn.; Univ. of Wisc. Alumni Assn.; Protestant; rec: photog., stained glass, antiques. Res: 28101 Juneda Dr Saugus 91350 Ofc: Electrend, 3519 W Commonwealth Ave Fullerton 92633

GRUETER, SHIRLEY EDNA, antique dealer; b. July 5, 1918, Kansas City, Kansas; d. Earl Willard and Olive Josephine (Teehan) Kaufman; m. Joseph Grueter, Nov. 22, 1937; children: Shirley, b. 1938; Catherine, b. 1939; Robert Andrew, b. 1941; Virginia, b. 1943; Joseph Edward, b. 1956; edn: writers course, Famous Schools, 1969; Pasadena City Coll. 1973-5. Career: mgr./ owner Grueter's Shooting Supplies, San Gabriel 1945-65; owner Shirley Grueter Antiques, Temple City 1975--; former tchr. ammunitions reloading; exhibitor at monthly antiques shows; mem: Sierra Madre Woman's Club; Sierra Madre Hist. Essicks House benefit chmn.; rec: art (oils), photog., pianist. Res: 9073 E Hermosa Dr Temple City 91780 Ofc: Shirley Grueter Antiques 9157A, Las Tunas Dr Temple City 91780

GRUND, EDWARD LEOPOLD, department store executive; b. March 30, 1945, Baltimore, Md.; s. Leopold and Rosalie L. (Molder) G.; m. Constance Haynsworth, May 31, 1969; edn: BA, Univ. of Md. 1963-7. Career: exec. trainee Hecht Co. (div. May Dept. Stores) Wash DC 1966-67, dept. mgr., divisional mdse. mgr. 1968, transferred to G. Fox & Co. (div. May Dept. Stores), Hartford Conn./spl. asst. to V.P & Gen. Ops. Mgr., asst. store mgr., buyer sporting goods, 1968-73; joined J. Homestock (div. R.H.Macy Co.) Dedham, Mass. store mgr., regional mgr. NY & NJ, v.p. stores, 1973-78; joined Broadway Dept. Stores (div. Carter, Hawley, Hale), Los Angeles as gen. mgr. 1978, regional mgr. L.A. store regions 1980, executive v.p. stores, 1982--; Frederick Atkins com. chmn. 1983; clubs: Rotary; United Way of San Diego; WASI Salk Inst. of La Jolla; S.D. Hist. Soc.; North Co. (S.D.) Concert Assn.; Pasadena Hist. Soc.; Ronald Mac Donald House of S.D.; San Diegans Against Childhood Cancer; Republican; Episcopal (Vestry; S.D. Archdio. Conv. del.); rec: sailing, antiques. Res: 1217 Lorain Rd San Marino 91108 Ofc: The Broadway Dept. Stores, 3880 No Mission Rd Los Angeles 90031

GRUNDLER, DENNIS EUGENE, systems programmer/ software engineer; b. Sept. 10, 1959, Topeka, Kansas; s. Edward James and Marjorie Joan (Potter) G.; edn: AS, Yuba City Coll. 1980; BS, EECS, UC Berkeley 1982. Career: assoc. mem. pgmg. staff Xerox Corp. 1982-3; mem. pgmg. staff I, Xerox Corp. 1983; mem. pgmg. staff II, Xerox Corp. 1983--; awards: Eagle Scout, Boy Scouts of Am. 1973; mem: Inst. of Electrical and Electronic Engrs. 1981-; Assn.

of Computing Machines 1984; rec: backpacking, camping, electronic kit bldg. Res: 660 Mariposa Ave, No 206, Mountain View 94040 Ofc: Xerox Corp., 3450 Hillview Ave Palo Alto 94304

GU, ALSTON LEE-VAN, engineer; b. Apr. 7, 1941, Szechwan, China, nat. 1975; s. Wan-Yin and Man-Yin (Hsu) G.; m. Judy Wu, Apr. 12, 1969; children: Arthur, b. 1970; Alice, b. 1977; edn: BS, Nat. Tailsan Univ. 1963; SM, Mass. Inst. of Tech. 1966; ME, 1967; ScD 1969. Career: research asst. Mass. Inst. of Tech., Cambridge, Mass. 1964-9; mem. tech. staff Bell Telephone Laboratory, Wippany, NY 1967; sr. research sci. Mechnl. Tech. Inc., Latham, NY 1969-76; sr. engring. spl. Ai Research Mfg. Co., Torrance 1976-9; proj. engr. Ai Research Mfg. Co., Torrance 1979--; adjunct prof. Mechnl. Engring. Dept. Union Coll. 1972-5; guest lectr. Mechnl. Engring. Dept. CSU 1978-9; awards: recognition, Design Engring. Conf. 1975, 77 and Western Design Engring. Conf. 1978, 82; mem: ASME; Sigma Xi; 21 tech. papers publs. in profl. journs. 1968-; 5 patents pend.; Prot.; rec: sports, music. Res: 5832 Sunmist Dr Rancho Palos Verdes 90274 Ofc: AiResearch Mfg. Co., 2525 W 190th Street Torrance 90509

GU, ZU HAN, research scientist, educator; b. July 29, 1941, Shanghai, China; s. Hong-Shon and Jian-Ming (Zhang) G.; m. Ying Lin, Dec. 16, 1969; 1 dau. Jian-Lin, b. 1973; edn: BS, Jiao-Tong Univ., Shanghai 1964; MS, UC San Diego 1983; PhD degree pgm. UCSD 1982-. Career: research scientist Opto-electronics/laser application; lectr. Jiao-tong Univ., Shanghai 1964-76, asst. prof. 1976-80; vis. scholar/research scientist, Univ. Calif. San Diego 1980-82, postgrad. stu. Elec. Engring. Dept. UCSD 1982--; cons. in China to num. hosps., factories; awards: Fellowship for sci. resrch. abroad, Chinese Govt.; mem. Optical Soc. of Am., Internat. Soc. for Optical Engineering (SPIE), Laser Soc. of China (Shanghai Com.); research spec.: computer generated holograms, image coding and restoration, pattern classification and recogn., optical scanning device, detect and display tech. in laser application; publs: (4) sci. jours.; rec: travel, music, tennis. Res: 3911 Miramar Rd, Apt H, San Diego 92037 Ofc: UCSD, Dept EECS/C-104, La Jolla 92037

GUALIANO, MICHAEL JOSEPH, JR., computer service co. president; b. Feb. 17, 1955, San Diego; s. Michael Joseph and Constance Joan Gualiano; m. Janna M. Glenn, Oct. 18, 1981; edn: computer techn., 1979 computer engring., Am. Internat. 1980. Career: restaurant mgmt. 1973-6; pet store owner, Anaheim 1976-9; founder/pres. Systems Up, Inc., 1981--; chief exec. new co. in Bay Area to be formed in 1984; works: designer spl. computer equip.; mil: S/Sgt., ROTC; Democrat; Catholic; rec: computer pgmmg., musician, wood work. Res: 21422 Broken Arrow Dr Diamond Bar 19765 Ofc: Systems Up, Inc., 450 E Chapman Ave Orange 92666

GUARDINO, EDWARD FRANCIS, chiropractor; b. Mar. 11, 1952, Barcelona, Spain, nat. 1969; s. Agustin and Maria Guardino; edn: Santa Monica City Coll. 1972; AA, Am. Jr. Coll. of Barcelona 1973; BA, New Coll. of Calif. 1974; D.C., Cleveland Chiropractic Coll. 1973-77; Career: clin. dir. Diaz Chiropractic Gp., Redondo Beach 1981; gen. dir. Laforte Chiropractic Gp. 1980; owner/ opr. Mid Bay Clinic, Los Angeles 1982, White Stone Chiropractic Clinic, Santa Ana 1982-3; owner/opr. Westchester Chiropractic Clinic, L.A. 1983--, pres. Edward F. Guardino D.C. Inc. 1983-; sports industry cons./So. Calif. bus. dir. Indsl. Chiropractic Svcs. 1983--; Outstanding Young Men of Am., Jaycees 1982; mem: The Am. Assn. of Nutrition & Dietary Cons.; Calif. Chiro. Assn.; Christian Chiro. Assn.; Lions Internat.; dir./D.Div., White Stone Ministries 1979; language interpreter during (Assem. of God) missionary Central Am. Tour 1978; Hope Chapel Del Rey; rec: bike racing, competitive jet-ski. Res: 5157 W 58th Ladera Hghts 90056 Ofc: Westchester Chiropractic Health Ctr., 8908 So Sepulveda Blvd Los Angeles 90045

GUBSER, ANN KATHLEEN, company executive; b. July 9, 1941, Montreal, Quebec, Canada; nat. 1960; d. Francis Patrick and Mary Evelyn (O'Brien) Sweeney; m. Ray E Gubser, June 26, 1961; children: Paul, b. 1962; Gail, b. 1963; Greg, b. 1965; Adam, b. 1969; edn: BA, Immaculate Heart Coll., L.A. 1963; cont. edn., UCLA Ext., SCU Dom. Hills. Career: elected mem. bd. trustees Hermosa Beach City Sch. Dist. 1977-81; salespsn. TCI (bus. telephone systems), Manhattan Beach 1978-81, asst. to pres. 1981; asst. to sr. v.p., Direct Sales Div., Inter-Tel, Inc., Buena Park 1981-3; mgr., Mktg. Svcs.,j ComSystems, Inc., Van Nuys 1983; mgr. Adminstrn., Inter-Tel, Inc., Buena Park 1983--; spkr., Career options for women, UCLA and UC Irvine ext. pgms.; awards: Calif. State Legislature Commdn. 1981; recognition, So. Bay Children's Health Ctr. 1976, Hermosa Beach Sch. Dist. 1976, 80; mem: Women in Mgmt.; So. Bay Coalition for Alternatives to Domestic Violence; Hermosa Beach Sch. Bd. (pres. 1978, 80); Am. Martyrs Parish Bd. (Manhattan Beach) pres. 1972-3, dir. Innercity Summer Day Camp 1973-4; CSBA Legislative Network; advis. bd., Hermosa Bch. 1736 Runaway Project 1978; comm. advis. bd., Richstone Ctr. for the Prevention of Child Abuse; Republican; rec: backpacking, camping, Calif. history. Res: 34 17th Street Hermosa Bech 90254 Ofc: Inter-Tel, Inc., 67669 8th Street Beuna Park 90620

GUCHEREAU, RAOUL EMILE, accountant/real estate broker; b. Nov. 1, 1922, New Orleans, La.; s. Raoul Morris and Marie Inez (Alline) G.; m. Thelma Irene Guchereau, Sept. 23, 1943; children: Donald; Kenneth; Jerome; edn: BA, Loyola Univ. 1960; realtor, Nat. Assn. of Realtors 1963. Career: tax collection audit div. Internal Revenue Svc., New Orleans 1946-52; cost acct. Bethlehem Steel, Los Angeles 1952-8; real estate sales agt., Whittier 1960-63; self-empl. accountant, L & R Bookkeeping Tax Service, Whittier 1960--, real estate broker 1963--, forms investment real estate syndications; gen. partner

Errol Mahal Prods. 1983--; honors: Order of the Arrow, Scouter of Year 1963, Los Angeles BSA Council; Hon. mem. PTA 1963; Little League mgr. (6 years) with Maverick League Champions; mem: Calif. Assn. Realtors 1960-; Nat. Assn. of Tax Consultants, Whittier CofC; orgns: YMCA Indian Guides 1954-60; BSA (16 yrs., Whittier Dist. bd.), planning all activities for scouting pgm. in Cubs, Scouts, and Explorers; mil: 1C USN 1942-45, PT decor.; Democrat; Catholic; rec: photog. Res: 10909 Theis Ave Whittier 90604 Ofc: L&R Bookkeeping, 15051 Leffingwell Rd, Ste. 201, Whittier 90604

GUENTHER, CHARLES R., business executive, consultant; b. Apr. 21, 1948, Santa Ana; s. Stanley George and Wilma Eliza (Zentner) G.; m. Ann Marie Eyerly, Aug. 31, 1966; children: Andrea, b. 1967; Christian, b. 1978; edn: AA, Santa Ana Coll. 1968; BA, CSU Fullerton 1970; MA, 1974; Airline Transport Pilot Cert. Career: busboy, cook, cement mason, elec. techn., charter pilot, flight instr., tchg. asst., research asst., admin. analyst prior to 1971; sr. personnel analsyt City of Santa Ana 1971-4; pres./sr. cons. Wollack, Waibel and Guenther, Inc. (mgmt. conssultants), Fair Oaks 1974-7; dir. human resources, Mercy Health Care Orgn., Sacramento 1978-84; labor rels. cons. 1978-; exec. dir. Foundation Health Plan, Sacto. 1984--; lectr. Grad. Sch. Bus. Adm. Golden Gate Univ.; awards: NSF Research Fellowship 1970; mem. Am. Soc. for Personnel Adminstrn.; frequent guest spkr. law enforcement, personnel & labor rels.; arts. in profl. journals; Republican; Ch. of Jesus Christ L.D.S.; rec: aviation, sport fishing, alpine skiing. Res: 2039 Shelfield Dr Carmichael 95608 Ofc: Foundation Health Plan, 5030 El Camino Ave Carmichael 95608

GUERIN, ANNETTE CATHERINE, construction co. executive; b. Nov. 12, 1958, San Diego; d. Alfred Henry and Clara Catherine (Board) G.; edn: AA, Mesa Jr. Coll. 1978; BBA, CSU San Diego 1984. Career: admin. staff spl. Pacific Tel. Co., San Diego 1978-81; mgr. of admin. & fin. Southland Electric, Inc., San Diego 1981--, also Affirm. Action dir. Equal Employment Opp. 1984--; awards: 1st runner up Miss Toys for Tots (USMC) 1977; mem: Nat. Assn. of Women in Constrn; Am. Mgrs. Assn.; advisor Jr. Achievement, Pac. Tel. 1981; San Diego Police Dept. cheerleader 1978-9; Mesa Coll. cheerleader 1976-8; Republican; Christian; rec: travel, interiar decorating, water skiing. Res: 2735 Ariane Dr, No 176 A, San Diego 92117 Ofc: Southland Electric, Inc. of San Diego, 11211 Sorrento Valley Rd, Ste P, San Diego 92121

GUGAS, CHRIS, polygraphist, author; b. Aug. 12, 1921, Omaha, Nebr.; s. Nicholas and Vera (Henas) G.; m. Anne Claudia Setaro, June 27, 1942; children: Chris, Jr., b. 1943; Steven E., b. 1946; Carol (Hawker), b. 1951; edn: DD, Ch. of Living Sci. 1968; BA, pub. adminstrn. 1970; MA, USC 1977; postgrad. CSU Los Angeles; PhD, Univ. of Beverly Hills 1983. Career: asst. dir. L.A. School Security, Los Angeles Bd. of Edn. 1949-50; CIA agent, U.S. Govt. 1950-4; L.A. Bd. of Edn. 1955-7; dir. Central Bureau of Investigation, L.A. 1962; public safety dir. Omaha, Nebr. 1963-5; dir. Profl. Security Consultants, Hollywood 1966--; security cons.; business, t.v., motion picture industries; instr. L.A. Polygraph Inst.; Las Vegas Polygraph Inst.; exec. dir. The Truthseekers; mem: founder Nat. Bd. of Polygraph Examiners; Am. Polygraph Assn. (pres. 1971-2); Special Agents Assn. (pres. 1960); Marine Corps League (pres. 1945); Combat Correspondents Assn. (pres. 1970); Red Cross Council (pres. 1939); Calif. Peace Ofcr. Assn.; Silver Dollar Club; author: The Silent Witness: A Polygrahist's Casebook, Prentice-Hall 1979; columnist: Los Angeles Daily Journal, Security World Mag.; contrib. over 150 arts. on crimonology; newspapers, mags., trade journs.; mil: USMC 1940-9, decorated Presdtl. Unit Cit., 4 Battle Stars, 3 Navy Unit Cits.; Greek Orthodox; rec: electronics, writing, sports. Res: 4018 DIxie Canyon Ave Sherman Oaks 91423 OFc: 1680 No Vine St, Ste 400, Hollywood 90028

GUGGENHEIM, WOLF Z., physician, internist; b. Mar. 28, 1932, Western Europe; s. Willy and Betty (Schlesinger) G.; m. Vivian ; children: Arye, b. 1967; Achiezer, b. 1972; edn: MD, Univ. of Zurich 1959; lic. MD, Switzerland (1959), NY (1964), Cal. (1966). Career: intern State Univ. New York, Glensfalls Gen. Hosp. 1960-1; res. physician, internal med. N.Y. Polyclinic Hosp. Med. Ctr. 1961-3; sr. res./NIH Fellow Joslin Diabetes Ctr., Harvard Med. Sch. 1963-4; physician/internist, solo pvt. practice 1964--; fulltime instr. Internal Med., N.Y. Med. Coll. 1964-7; prof. of medicine (Distinguished Professorship) Touro Coll. 1975-8; recipient Klaus Found. Postgrad. Merit Scholarship 1959-60; mem: Am. Diabetes Assoc., So. Calif. affil.; Graduate Council, Univ. of Zurich; mil: capt., inf./ field intell., I.D.F.; rec: classical music, swimming. Res: 2 Ketch St, Marina Peninsula, Marina Del Rey 90291 Ofc: 804 Venice Blvd Venice Beach 90291

GUNDERMAN, GARY EDMUND, lawyer; b. Sept. 15, 1934, Compton; s. Gus Herbert and Corinne Catherine (Dixon) Gunderman; edn: AA, UCLA, 1957, JD, Hastings Coll. of Law, 1961; m. Rosemary Baker, June 20, 1980; chil.: Pamela, b. 1955, Linda, b. 1957, Connie, b. 1959, Cynthia, b. 1959, Gus, b. 1963, Tiffany, b. 1965; career: assoc. atty., Voegelin, Barton, Harris & Callister, Los Angeles 1962-64; partner, Cossaboom & Gunderman, Santa Ana 1964-67, Gunderman & Riddet, Santa Ana, 1968-69; sole practitioner, Santa Ana 1969--; instr. of law, Pacific Coast Univ. 1972-74. Mem: Orange Co. Bar Assn., Calif. Trial Lawyers, Am. Trial Lawyers, State Bar of Calif. standing com. on legislation, Family Law Section. Mil: sgt. US Army Inf. 1953-56; Democrat; Prot.; rec: hunting, fishing; res: 9982 Thistle, Fountain Valley 92708 Law ofc. Gary E. Gunderman, 900 No. Broadway, Ste. 712, Santa Ana 92701.

GULIAN, ANOOSH JANE, oriental rug appraiser/retailer; b. Jan. 20, 1923, Los Angeles; d. Haroutune Garabed and Eugenie (Kassabian) Haroutunian; widow; two daus., Gloria Jayne Ainslie, b. 1949; Laura Jean Gulian, b. 1953;

edn: dip. Metropolitan Business Sch. 1943; Cert. Oriental Rug Appraiser, Oriental Rug Retailers Assn. 1980. Career: typist, clerk, US Army Induction Sta., L.A. 1943, US Army Finance Dept., 1944, US Army Traffic Dept., 1945-6; prop. Gulian Oriental Rugs, Sherman Oaks, 1975-84; cert. oriental rug appraiser, 1980--; mem. Oriental Rug Retailers Assn.; Daughters of Vartan; Ladies Guild of Ararat Old Age Home and Conv. Hosp.; Republican; Prot.; rec: backgammon, phys. fitness, dancing. Res: 14636 Hesby St Sherman Oaks 91423

GUNDERSON, JAMES DONALD, JR., lawyer; b. May 14, 1947, Oakland; s. James Donald, Sr., and Bettygene (Otto) G.; m. Marilyn Melton, June 15, 1968; children: Jeremy, b. 1973, David, b. 1981, Christine, b. 1983; edn: grad. AUS Aviation Sch., Hunter Army Airfield, Savannah, Ga. 1969 AA, Santa Rosa Coll., highest honors, 1973; BA, (Dean's Scholar), CSU San Jose 1974; JD magna cum laude, Univ. of Santa Clara 1977; lic. comml. pilot, FAA 1970; admitted to Calif. Bar 1977, US Dist. Ct. (No. Calif.)1977, US Ct. of Appeals (Ninth Dist.) 1978, US Supreme Ct. 1982; Calif. Real Estate Broker lic. 1980. Career: Small unit cmdr. and combat helicopter pilot with 20th Engr. Brigade, Vietnam 1969-70; Small unit cmdr., 3d Armored Cavalry, Ft. Lewis, Wn. 1970-72; atty. assoc. Kouns & Marshall, San Jose 1977-80; partner law offices of Fields & Gunderson, 1980--; pres./bd. chmn. Westland Brokerage Corp., 1983--; honors: Pi Sigma Alpha; recipient appreciation certs. as mediator and arbitrator 1981, 82, 83, Judges of the Santa Clara Co. Judicial Dist.; mem: Am., Canta Clara Co. Bar Assns.; Legal Panel, Calif. Assn. of Realtors 1980; arbitrator, Neighborhood Small Claims Ct., Santa Clara Co. Judicial Dist. 1980; South Valley YMCA; mil: capt. USAR, Bronze Star, Vietnam, Army Air Medal, 15 Awards, Vietnam 1969-70, Nat. Def. Medal, Vietnam Service Awd. (2), Mil. Aviator; Republican; Prot. Res: 780 Upton Ct. San Jose 95136 Ofc: Fields & Gunderson, 1625WIG), investment banker; b. July 6, 1937, Dusseldorf, Germany; s. Heinrich and Ilse (Schuster) G.; div.; children: Andrew, b. 1971, Annabelle Kathryn, b. 1973; edn: LLD, Heidelberg Law Sch. 1963; JD, Wurzburg Law Sch. 1964. Career: Foreign Guest Tng. Pgm., The Chase Manhattan Bank, NA, NY, 1964; mgmt. trainee Dresdner Bank A.G., Frankfurt, 1964-65; financial v.p., Pipeline Constrn. Div., Thyssen A.G., 1965-66; v.p. and partner, Loeb, Rhoades & Co., Investment Bankers, 1967-75; dir. and mem. exec. com. Sunbelt Properties, Inc., 1975, v.chmn. of bd., 1976-, pres. 1978-81, mil. served in W. Ger. Army, sgt. ROTC, dischg. 1959; clubs: The Recess (NYC), Annabelle's (London); Prot.; rec: skiing. Ofc: 600 B Street San Diego 92110, 375 Park Avenue, NY, NY 10152

GUNDLACH, HEINZ L(UDWIG), investment banker; b. July 6, 1937, Dusseldorf, Germany, s. Heinrich and Ilse (Schuster) G., div., children. Andrew, b 1971, Annabelle Kathryn, b. 1973; edn: LLD, Heidelberg Law Sch. 1963; JD, Wurzburg Law Sch. 1964. Career: Foreign Guest Tng. Pgm., The Chase Manhattan Bank, NA, NY, 1964; mgmt. trainee Dresdner Bank A.G., Frankfurt, 1964-65; financial v.p., Pipeline Constrn. Div., Thyssen A.G., 1965-66; v.p. and partner, Loeb, Rhoades & Co., Investment Bankers, 1967-75; dir. and mem. exec. com. Sunbelt Properties, Inc., 1975, v.chmn. of bd., 1976-, pres. 1978-81; mil: served in W. Ger. Army, sgt. ROTC, dischg. 1959; clubs: The Recess (NYC), Annabelle's (London); Prot.; rec: skiing. Ofc: 600 B Street San Diego 92110, 375 Park Avenue, NY, NY 10152

GUNN, ANDREW JAY, lawyer; b. Dec. 11, 1956, San Antonio, Tex.; s. Leonard Darrell and Louella Mae (Higgins) G.; m. Beverly Ann, Jan. 7, 1978; 1 dau: Kelly Mae, b. 1981; edn: UC Riverside 1975-77; BS, Western State Univ. 1979; JD, 1980; LLD, Western State Univ. Coll. of Law 1980. Career: US Forest Svc., Del Rosa, summers 1975, 78; Inter-Regl. Hot Shot Fire Suppression Crew, US Forest Svc., Mormon Rocks Engine Co., summer 1976; law clerk MacLachlan, Burford & Arias, San Bernardino 1979-80; currently, assoc. atty. Law Ofcs. C.L. Vineyard, San Bernardino; Judge Pro Tem, San Bernardino Municipal Ct.; awards: Lawyers Wives Scholarship 1979; mem: Am., Calif. & San Bernardino Co. Bar Assns.; A.T.X. (bd. dirs.); Democrat; rec: hunting, fishing. Res: 3394 Lynwood Dr Highland 92346 Ofc: Law Offices of C.L. Vineyard, 330 North D St, Ste 430, San Bernardino 92401

GUNN, JAMES MICHAEL, lawyer; b. Mar. 3, 1945, Houston, Tex.; s. Rodney Wilbur and Ola Geneva (Anders) G.; m. Kimberly Stiglich, Aug. 16, 1975; 1 dau. Jennifer Michelle, b. 1976; edn: BS, CalPoly Univ., Pomona 1967; MBA, USC, 1969; JD, La Verne Coll. 1976; admitted to Calif. State Bar 1977. Career: Continuation School teacher, Azusa Unified Sch. Dist. 969-72; acct. mgr. NCR Computer Div., Los Angeles 1972-73; teacher Azusa Unified Sch. Dist. 1973-77; Deputy District Atty., Co. of San Bernardino 1977-80; atty. law firm of McVittie, Gutierrez & Bidart, Chino 1980; atty. solo pvt. practice, Ontario 1980--; past chmn. Azusa Educators Assn. Human Rels. Com.; past mem. CTA Standing Com. on Human Rels.; honors: Teacher of the Year 1975, Foothill Jr. High Sch.; recognition, District Atty. of San Bernardino Co., Calif. State Assembly; mem: Calif., West End Trial Lawyers Assns.; Calif., E. Los Angeles Co. (secty.), San Bernardino Bar Assns.; mil: USNR 1968-9; Democrat; Prot.; rec: water/snow skiing. Ofc: James Michael Gunn, APC, 1047 W. Sixth St, Ste. 107, Ontario 91762

GUPTILL, WILLIAM KEITH, certified public accountant; b. jAug. 20, 1930, Fertilla; s. Sidney Earl and Dorothy Marie (DeRose) G.; m. Olga Bulat, Mar.

25, 1961; 1 dau., Tayna Ann, b. 1967; edn: AA, Citrus Jr. Coll. 1956; BS, L.A. State Coll. 1959; CPA, Calif. 1968. Career: staff acct., Gerald Case, CPA, Pomona 1959; controller, Win Ward Co., Montclair 1960; internal auditor, R.O. Schultz, West Covina 1960-63; self-empl. accountant, Covina 1964-66; staff acct. Stegall 7 Easley, Covina 1966-68; partner Parke, Guptill & Co., 1968, mng. partner 1982--; spec. in dealership accting. in So. Calif., have 10.7 percent of total auto dealerships; cons. for num. auto dealerships, bldr. devel., Sec. Pac. Nat. Bank -leasing; chief finl. ofcr. Firebird Internat. Raceway Park, Az. 1983-; dir. Pacific Auto Supply 1962-, North Bend Industries 1975-, Allen Homes, Inc. 1979-, Orange Co. Internat. Raceway 1980-; frequent lectr. on income tax matters to auto dealer groups; mem. Univ. of LaVerne, Spl. Coms.; mem: Am. Inst. CPAs, Calif. Soc. CPAs, West Covina CofC; club: South Hills CC; mil: sgt. USAF 1951-55, GCM, Sharpshooter medal; Republican; Methodist; rec: hunt, fish, golf, ski. Res: 2573 San Andres Way Claremont 91711 Ofc: Parke, Guptill & Co., 2626 E. Garvey, Ste. 101, West Covina 91791

GURLING, GARY ALLEN, engineer-hybrid/microelectronics; b. Apr. 10, 1946, National City; s. Edward Francis and Anita May (Laird) G.; m. Beverly Ruskow, Jan. 27, 1979; edn: BSEE, CSU San Diego 1973. Career: tech. asst., draftsman, designer, assoc. engr. General Dynamics/Electronics Div., San Diego 1966-, currently senior engr. in hybrid/microelectronics, 1979--; mem: Internat. Soc. for Hybrid Microelectronics, Internat. Electronics Pkging. Soc.; Democrat; Christian; rec: photog., skiing, gardening. Res: 6821 Rolando Knolls Dr La Mesa 92041 Ofc: General Dynamics/ Electronics Div., POB 85310, M/Z 7234-R, San Diego 92041

GURNEY, CAROL A., office expansion service executive; b. June 1, 1949, East Orange, N.J.; d. Wm. J. and Lily M. (Curran) G.; edn: Franklin Jr. Coll. 1967. Career: with Dancer Fitzgerald Sample, Inc. (advt. agcy.), Torrance 1973--; secty. exec. vice pres., 1973, office mgr. 1975, personnel director 1978, vice pres. personnel & office mgmt. 1981-83; prin./owner Carol Gurney Associates, Office Expansion Services, Los Angeles 1983--; mem. Los Angeles Advt. Women (bd.; com. ch.); rec: tennis, ski, travel, art. Address: Carol Gurney Assocs., 10745 Ashton Ave Los Angeles 90024

GUSTAFSON, VANCE A., investments executive; b. Aug. 14, 1931, San Diego; s. Carl Earl and Florence (Vance) G.; m. Marilyn Joyce Franke, June 28, 1958; children: Stefen E., b. 1961, Richard V., b. 1964; edn: BA, Claremont McKenna Coll. 1957; Reg. Prin. NASD. Career: sales, Hill, Richard & Co., San Diego 1957-60; branch resident mgr. Lester Ryons & Co., S.D. 1960-69, asst. mgr. (merger) Hornblower & Weeks, 1969-71; branch res. mgr. Dupont Glore Forgan, Los Angeles 1972; sales, Kidder Peabody & Co., S.D. 1973-74; branch mgr. Hornblower & Weeks, S.D. 1975-78; sales Western Fin. Corp., San Diego 1978--; awards: Top Ten Percent Sales nationally, Hornblower & Weeks 1971; past pres. Univ. Club of San Diego (1968); mem: Stock & Bond Club 1958- (bd. mem. 1965-6), Internat. Assn. of Fin. Planners; club: San Diego Yacht (pres. Angler's Gp. 83); mil: s/sgt. USAF 1950-53; Republican; Prot.; rec: sailing, fishing, hunting (birds), skiing. Res: 2570 Willow St San Diego 92106 Ofc: WEstern Fin. Corp. 530 B Street, Ste. 2409, San Diego 92101

GUTIERREZ, ARTURO FERNANDO, jurist; b. Apr. 13, 1948, Los Angeles; s. Jose Arturo and Maria Elena (Ascencio) Gutierrez; edn: Pasadena City Coll., 1966-69, CSU Los Angeles, 1969-70, JD, Loyola Law Sch., 1974; m. Yvonne Shaw, Aug. 16, 1975; chil: Art, b. 1976, Audra, b. 1978; career: Los Angeles Municipal Court Clerk 1971-75; Ventura Co. Public Defender 1975-81; judge, Municipal Court Ventura County 1981--; prof. of law (evidence), Southern Calif. Inst. of Law, Ventura; honors: 1981 Municipal Trial Judge of the Year, Trial Lawyers Assn. Mem: Mexican-Am. Bar Assn., pres., 1981; Channel Counties Legal Services, dir. 1980; Calif. Judges Assn.; rec: skiing, scuba, chess; ofc: Ventura Co. Municipal Ct., 800 S. Victoria Ave. Ventura 93009.

GUTIERREZ, OLGA, psychiatrist/educator; b. Dec. 29, 1929, Buenos Aires, Argentina; d. Gabriel and Soledad (Garcia Bueno) G.; grandau. of Jose San Roman, Dean, Sch. of Medicine, Spain; div.; 1 son, Luis Eduardo, b. 1961; edn: immunologist, Inst. Pasteur, Paris 1959; PhD in biochem., Univ. Buenos Aires 1954, MD, 1967; 3d. postgrad. phys. in psychiatry, USC 1980. Career: ednl. asst. Univ. Buenos Aires, 1953-58; research fellow, Inst. Pasteur, Paris, 1958-60; ednl. chief and research assoc. Univ. Buenos Aires, 1960-70; resrch. fellow Superior Council of Biol. Resrch, Madrid, Spain 1970-71; resrch. fellow, Reproductive Biol., OB-Gyn, USC, 1971-74; pvt. practice of med., Buenos Aires, 1975-77; postgrad. phys. tng. in psychiatry, USC 1978-80; adult psychiatrist LAC/USC Med. Ctr. 1981, child and adolesc. psychiatrist, 1982, forensic psychiatrist USC Inst. of Psychiat., Law and Behavioral Scis., Dept. of Psychiatry 1984--; awards: Golden Medal, Univ. of Buenos Aires 1952, Faculty of Med. awd. 1954, Acad. of Med. awd. 1966; Jr. Chamber awd. 1968; mem: Soc. of Chem. of Uruguay (corres. mem.); Acad. of Pharm. and Biochem., Arg.; Microbiol. and Immunol. Assn.; AMA; Biochem. Assn.; publs: over 15 sci. arts. rel. to medicine; guest appearances on t.v. and radio on psychiatric issues; Catholic; rec: sports, swimming, sailing, tennis. Res: 101 California Ave, Apt 507, Santa Monica 90403 Ofc: 271 LAC/USC Medical Center, 1937 Hospital Pl Los Angeles 90033

GUYAN, LINDA LEE, information systems executive; b. Feb. 28, 1947, San Bernardino; d. Oous Leonard and Iva Lee (Reaves) Himes; div.; children: Anthony, b. 1965, Timothy, b. 1967; lic. Calif. Dept. Real Estate 1980. Career: library asst. City of San Bernardino, Rowe Branch Lib. 1969-70; medical asst. Kaiser Hosp., Fontana 1970-80; word processing opr. Air Force Regl. Civil Engr., Norton AFB 1980-81; project mgr. Office Automation Systems, Science Applications, San Bernardino 1981--; mem. Assn. of Info. Systems Profls.;

Prot.; rec: reading. Res: 2060 South Date, Bloomington 92316 Ofc: Science Applications 412 Hospitality Ln, Ste. 204, San Bernardino 92408

GUYER, PAUL MEYER, lawyer; b. Sept. 8, 1923, Lynchburg, Va.; s. Charles Max and Jeannette (Hecht) Guggenheimer; m. Ann Guyer, July 26, 1943; children: Michael, b. 1944, Tom, b. 1946, Richard, b. 1957, James, b. 1959, Lisa, b. 1962; edn: BS engring., West Coast Univ. 1942; JD, Southwestern Univ. Sch of Law 1965; admitted Calif. State Bar 1966. Career: vice pres. National Bus. & Prop. Exchange, 1948-52; pres. Union Interchange Inc., 1952-65; pres. law corp., Paul M. Guyer Inc., Los Angeles 1968--; dir. Union Interchange Inc., Coronet Mortgage & Finl. Corp.; awards: outstanding leader, BSA, 1949; recognition by the state govs. o Feliz Kiwanis (pres.); publs: num. mag. arts. rel. to real estate and landlord- tenant law; mil: USAF 1942-45; Republican; Christian Sci.; rec: flying, skiing. REs: 3311 Beaudry Terr Glendale 91208 Ofc: Paul M. Guyer Inc. 4477 Hollywood Blvd Los Angeles 90027

GUYETTE, PHILIP ANTHONY, industrial educator; b. Aug. 15, 1948, Fresno; s. Harold Joseph and Anne Elizabeth (Smith) G.; d. Janet Niederfrank, Nov. 12, 1983; edn: AA, Fresno City Coll. 1971; BA, CSU Fresno 1973, MA, 1974; Standard Sec. Teaching Credential, Vocational 8.1 Auto Tchg. Cred., Community Coll. Tchg. Cred. (Calif.). Career: comml. farm work, Ernest Hogsett, Fresno 1961-72, also mechanic part-time; brakeman-switchman A.T. & Santa Fe R.R., summers 1967, 69-71, 74-75; self empl. Auto General Repair Shop, Fresno 1975-78; automotive instr. Corcoran (Calif.) Unified Sch. Dist. 1975-79; prin. Quinn Co., caterpillar dealership 1979--; service tng. instr./ mechanic 1979--; honors: Outstand Young Men of Am. 1979; mem: Calif. Indsl. Edn. Assn. (life), Vocational Indsl. Clubs of Am. (advisor 1975-9); mil: sgt E5, US Army 1967-69, supr. maint. on track & wheeled veh., Korea; rec: pvt. pilot, farming. Res: 3043 So Cherry Ave Fresno 93706 Ofc: Quinn Co. POB 12625, Fresno 93778

H

HA, PHAM PHUOC, real estate broker, import co. executive; b. Mar. 11, 1937, Saigon, Vietnam, nat. 1982; d. Hoa Van and Thua Thi (Tran) Pham; m. Bodja Trong Dzung Ha, Oct. 5, 1956; children: Charles T., b. 1957, Tivonne D., b. 1959, David D., b. 1961, Mindy M.D., b. 1962, Stephanie P., b. 1963, Lien D., b. 19656, Nicholas D., b. 1967, Anthony D., b. 1969, Kim D., b. 1971, Christine T.Y., b. 1975; edn: law cert. (4th yr.), Saigon Univ. Sch. of Law 1971; AA, DeAnza Coll. 1978; BA, CSU San Jose 1980; Calif. lic. real estate salespsn. 1981, real estate broker 1983. Career: Govt. Nat. Bank ofcr., Vietnam 1958-70; owner/dir. Thien-Nga Import & Export Co., 1971-75 (came to USA as refugee); counselor Community Companions (wk. with MDs and psychiatrists for mentally ill clients), San Jose 1979-82; counselor State Dept. of Rehab. (social adjustment couns. for Asian Refugees), part time 1979-82; real estate sales Internat. Real Estate Network, Santa Clara 1982, broker/mktg. mgr. (co. name changed) Nat. Financial Network, 1983--; also mktg. mgr. Swanee Co. Import & Export; mem: Nat., Calif. Assn. of Realtors, Nat. Assn. for Female Execs., Vietnamese Martial Arts Assn., Vietnamese Lawyers Assn., IBM/Credit Union Clubs; Republican; Budhism; rec: music, swim, tennis, photog. Res: 5540 Bollinger Rd San Jose 95128 Ofc: 2470 El Camino Real Santa Clara 95051

HAAK, HAROLD H., university president; b. June 1, 1935, S. Harold John Andrew and Laura (Kittleson) H.; m. Betty Steiner, June 25, 1955; children: Alison, b. 1963, Janet, b. 1965; edn: BA, Univ. of Wisc. 1957, MA, 1958; PhD, Princeton Univ. 1963. Career: asst./assoc. prof. of political sci., San Diego St. Coll. 1962-69, prof. of public adminstrn. and urban studies and dean Coll. of Profl. Studies, 1969-71; academic v.p. CSU Fresno, 1971-73; chancellor Univ. of Colo. at Denver, 1973-80; president CSU Fresno, 1980--; chmn. Denver Metropolitan Study Panel, 1976-77; bd. dirs. Fresno Economic Devel. Corp., 1981-, Fresno Philharmonic, 1981-, Fresno Chamber of Commerce, 1981-; awards: Distinguished Service Award, Denver Regl. Council of Govts. 1978; mem: Phi Beta Kappa, Phi Kappa Phi, Blue Key; club: Sunnyside Country. Res: 4411 N. Van Ness Blvd Fresno 93704 Ofc: California State University, Fresno 93740

HAAS, ELSON MARK, physician, author, lecturer; b. Aug. 14, 1947, Detroit; s. Martin M. and Shirley (Ellis) Haas; edn: pre-med., Univ. of Mich. 1965-8, MD, 1972. Career: internship, Highland Hosp., Oakland 1972-3; phys. Alameda Co. Health Care Clinics and City of Berkeley Clinics, 1973-76, also apprenticeship/practice Bolinas Health Service in natural and preventive med. (biofeedback, acupuncture, nutrition, herbal med.); physician pvt. practice, 1975--, currently 3 offices; co-creator/partner (w/ B.S. Argisle) Health Harvest, Unltd. (health ednl. products); lectr./teaching seminars in preventive medicine; host TV show: To Health (series), San Jose Cable; author: Staying Healthy With The Seasons (1981; English, Spanish, German eds.); designer products: Sole Sox, Acupuncture T-shirt, Chakra T-shirt, num. others. Rec: tennis, bicycle, running, music (flute, drums). Ofc: Wellness Med. Group, 25 Mitchell Blvd. #8, San Rafael 94903; Center for Health Awareness, 1762 Hamilton Ave, San Jose 95125

HAAS, PETER E., industrialist; b. Dec. 20, 1918, San Francisco; s. Walter A. and Elise (Stern) H.; m. Miriam Ruchwarger, Aug. 26, 1981; children: Peter E., Jr., Michael Stern, Margaret Elizabeth; edn: AB, Univ. Calif. 1940; MBA cum laude, (Baker Scholar) Harvard Grad. Sch. of Business 1943. Career: Levi Strauss & Co., 1945--: asst. prodn. mgr. 1948-51, vice pres./dir. 1952-58, exec. v.p. 1958-70, pres. 1970-81, chief exec. ofcr. 1976-81, chmn. bd. 1981--; Dir: Am. Tel. & Tel. Co., Crocker Nat. Bank; mem. Golden Gate Nat. Rec. Area Citizens Adv. Com.; trustee United Way of the Bay Area; bd. govs. United Way of Am.; v.chmn./dir. S.F. Bay Area Council; co-chmn. No. Calif. U.S. Olympic Com.; awards: Bus. Statesman of the Year 1982, Harvard Bus. Sch. Assn. of No. Calif.; CEO of the Year 1981, Fin. World Mag.; Big Brothers of SF Bay Area Award for contbn. to Youth 1963; Time Mag. leader of tomorrow 1953; clubs: Pacific-Union, Concordia-Argonaut, The Family; Republican; Jewish. Res: 2800 Broadway, San Francisco 94115 Ofc: Levi Strauss & Co., 1155 Battery St San Francisco 94120

HAAS, WALTER A., JR., industrialist; b. Jan. 24, 1916, San Francisco; s. Walter A. and Elise (Stern) H.; m. Evelyn Danzig, Mar. 6, 1940; children: Robert Douglas, b. 1942, Elizabeth Jane, b. 1944, Walter Jerome, b. 1949; edn: AB, Univ. Calif. 1937; MBA, Harvard Grad. Sch. of Business 1939. Career: Levi Strauss & Co., 1939--: personnel mgr. 1946, v.p./dir. 1952, pres./dir. 1958, bd. chmn./CEO 1970, dir./chmn. Exec. Com. 1981--; Dir: Bank of Am., BankAm Corp., United Air Lines Inc./UAL Inc., Mauna Kea Properties; owner Oakland Athletics Baseball Co.; mem. Trilateral Commn.; v.p. Levi Strauss Found.; adv. council Reading is Fundamental, Inc.; mem. SRI Internat. Adv. Council; awards: 1984 Alumnus of the Year, UC Berkeley; 1983 American Image Apparel Industry Hall of Fame Award, Men's Fashion Assn.; hon. LLD, Wheaton Coll. 1983; 1982 Chancellor's Award, UCB Found.; 1976 CEO of Year, Fin. World Mag.; hon. Phi Beta Kappa Soc. 1976; num. others; clubs: Bohemian, The Family, Lake Merced Golf, Pacific Union, Calif. Tennis; mil: maj. QMC, WWII, 52 mos. active duty; Republican; Jewish. Res: 2666 Broadway, San Francisco 94115 Ofc: Levi Strauss & Co. 1155 Battery St. San Francisco 94111

HABIB, MOUNIR R., communication and computer scientist; b. Apr. 21, 1944, Suez, Egypt, nat. 1975; s. Riad and Alice Habib; m. Fumiko Matsumoto, Aug. 4, 1973; children: Mark, b 1974, Marsha, b. 1982; edn: BS in Electronic Eng., honors, Alexandria (Egypt) Univ. 1965; MS in Electronic Eng., Univ. of Bridgeport, Conn. 1972. Career: asst. dir. Railways Telecomm., Alexandria, Egypt 1965-68; design eng. positions with Wells Fargo, NYC 1968-70, Homes, NYC 1970-71, Wagner Elect., Livingston NJ 1972-73; test design engr. and senior software designer Stromberg-Carlson Longwood, Fla. 1973-79; senior system engr. GTE Spring, Burlingame, Ca. 1979-81; sci. staff Bell Northern Research, Mt. View 1981--; instr. electronic eng. RETS Inst., Nutley, NJ 1973; mem: IEEE, Smithsonian Instn. (Nat. Assoc.), YMCA, little league baseball; Democrat; Christian Orthodox; rec: painting, gardening. Res: 218 Prairie Dog Lane Fremont 94539 Ofc: BNR, 685A E. Middlefield Rd Mountain View 94043

HADDIX, CHARLES E., legislative and regulatory consultant; b Nov. 23, 1915, Astoria, Ore.; s. Charles and Mattie (Wilson) H.; m. Betty Lee Wylie, Aug. 22, 1948; children: Bruce W., b. 1951, Anne C., b. 1953, C. Brian, b. 1955; edn: Grad. US Maritime Officers Sch., 1943; spl. courses, Golden Gate Univ. 1951, UC San Francisco 1952. Career: national sales mgr. Radio Station KLX, Oakland, 1953-55; West Coast mgr. Forjoe & Co., AM-TV sales rep., 1955-60; v.p. Calif. Spot Sales, Radio California 1958-60; v.p. Radio Station KLIP, Fowler, Ca. 1961-63; medical sales rep. Ives Labs. Inc., Sanger 1964-73; State Gov. Relations Cons., Marion Laboratories Inc., 1973-; Central California Forum on Refugee Affairs, 1983-; Calif. Legislative Advocate 1968-, Ariz., Nev., N.Mex., Ore., Wash. 1975; mil: served with Marina Mercante Nat., Repub. of Panama, 1945; mem: US Naval Inst., Internat. Oceanographic Found., Am. Mus. of Naval History, Ore. & Clatsop County Historical Socs., Manuscript Soc., Toastmaster Internat. (ACT), Commonwealth Club of Calif. Address: 3218 North McCall, Sanger 93657

HADDON, (CLARA) JOAN, sales executive; b. Nov. 30, 1935, Rockwood, Tenn.; d. Arch and Clara (Guettner) Howard; m. Richard Haddon, Sept. 10, 1960; children: Mimi, b. 1970, Tim, b. 1966; edn: BA, Berea (Ky.) Coll., 1957; grad. stu. Boston Univ. 1959-60. Career: tchr. 10 years Mich., Palm Springs Unified Schs., Santa Monica Schs., San Francisco Unified Schs.; Shaklee coordinator, organized nationwide sales force, 1970--; condr. leadership tng. seminars; recipient Shaklee leadership awards at convs. in Mex., Austria, Eng.; mem. AAUW 1960-66; bd. mem. Desert Mus. (Palm Springs) Sunday afternoon concerts; Democrat; Meth.; rec: travel. Address: 1037 Tamarisk, Palm Springs 92262

HAGE, STEPHEN JOHN, radiology administrator; b. July 22, 1943, Chgo.; s. Steve and Irene (Lewandowski) H.; m. Constance Simonis, June 10, 1967; edn: AAAS, YMCA Comm. Coll. 1969; R.T., Am. Regis. of Radiologic Technologists. Career: x-ray tech. Highland Pk. (Ill.), Ill. 1966-68; tech. supr. Therapeutic Radiol. Dept., Hines (Ill.) VA Hosp. 1968-70; chief technologist Gottlieb Mem. Hosp., Melrose Pk., Ill. 1970-71; adminstrv. asst. Radiol. Dept., and radiologic physics instr. So. Chgo. Comm. Hosp., 1971-79; radiology adminstr. Cedars-Sinai Med. Ctr., Los Angeles 1979--; free lance radiologic cons. 1972-; honors: 1st place, Ill. State Soc. Radiologic Techs. Essay Contest (1966), Phi Theta Kappa; mem: AAAS, Health Physics Soc. (Midwest), Am. Soc. Radiol. Techs. Am. Hosp. Radiol. Adminstrs. (charter, chmn. Long Range Plnng. Com. W. Region 1981-82); frequent guest lectr., faculty lectr., univs., colls., hosps.; mem. editl. bd. Administrative Radiology (monthly publ.), 1982 ; contbg. ed./columnist Medical Imaging Adminstrator (mo.), and Radiology Mgmt. (qrtrly. jour. AHRA); num. tech. jour. articles; mil: lance

cpl. USMC 1961-64; Catholic; rec: motorcycling, writing sci-fi. Res: 7540-7 Corbin Ave Reseda 91335 Ofc: Cedars Sinai Med. Ctr. 8700 Beverly Blvd, Ste. 5416, Los Angeles 90048

HAGLUND, E(DWARD) ARTHUR, corporate production manager ret.; b. Mar. 9, 1928, Havre, Mont.; s. Gustave Ragnar and Florence Jeannette (Webber) H.; m. Barbara Jean Bangeman, June 11, 1950; children: Katherine Marie, b. 1952, James Edward, b. 1956; edn: BS in bus., Univ. Mont. 1952; Univ. of Wash. Grad. Sch. 1953. Career: prodn. plnng. supr. Kaiser Aluminum, Spokane, Wash. 1953-57, Mill plnng. supr., prodn. plnng. supt. (Ravenswood, W.Va.) 1957-63, Computer Systems supr., Corp. Sys. mgr. (Oakland, Ca.) 1963-69, Mill Services mgr. (Toledo, Oh.) 1970, Finl. Plnng. supr. (Oakland) 1971-72, Corp. mgr. Prod. Planning (Oakland) 1973-83, ret.; mem: Am. Prodn. & Inventory Control Soc. (Primary Metals Coord.); honors: Active Legion of Honor, Internat. Order DeMolay (1982); trustee Masonic Homes of Calif. 1979-83, Calif. Masonic Found. 1983-82; mem: Phi Delta Theta Frat., Jaycees (charter pres. Ravenswood, W.Va. 1959-63), Toastmasters (past club pres.), BSA Scoutmaster 1964-69, Masons (Grand Lodge, F&AM of Calif. Grand Master 1983-84), Shriners; publs: arts. in profl. jours., California Freemason, New Age Mag.; mil: yeoman 3/c USN 1946-48; Republican; United Methodist; rec: golf, woodworking, x-c skiing. Res: 543 Silverado Dr Lafayette 94549 Ofc: Masonic Grand Lodge, F&AM of Calif., 1111 California St San Francisco 94108

HAHN, JAMES KENNETH, city controller of Los Angeles; b.July 3, 1950, Los Angeles; s. Kenneth F. and Ramona Bell (Fox) H.; BA in Eng., magna cum laude, Pepperdine Univ. 1972; JD, Pepperdine Sch. of Law 1975; admitted to Calif. State Bar 1975. Career: law clerk District Attorney of Los Angeles, 1974; deputy city atty., City of Los Angeles, 1975-79; founding ptnr. law firm Horner and Hahn, Marina del Rey 1979-81; elected City Controller of Los Angeles 1981--; honors: Young Alumnus of Year 1983, Pepperdine; Who's Who in Am. Colls. and Univs. 1972; v.chmn. Corp. Allocations Com. United Way of L.A.; bd. dirs. Pepperdine Univ. Alumni Assn.; Ch. of Christ; rec: photog. Res: 8738 Delford Ave Los Angeles 90045 Ofc: City Hall, 200 N. Spring St, Rm. 220, Los Angeles 90012

HAIG, DOUGLAS YACOUBIAN, mechanical engineer; b. Dec. 27, 1910, Kayseri, Turkey, nat. Sept. 28, 1932; s. Haigazoon K. and Eunice (Emuryan) Y.; m. Marie Ashjian, Aug. 26, 1945; children: Lucille, b. 1946, Gladys, b. 1948, Stephen, b. 1954, Debora, b. 1955; edn: stu. Ill. Inst. of Tech. (nights) 1934-40; AA, L.A. City Coll. 1964; DC, L.A. Coll. of Chiropractic 1950. Career: draftsman/asst. in development of Automatic Gear Transmissions for autos, Oscar H. Banker (brother-in-law), Chicago 1933-; currently engineering design analyst CDI Corp., Culver City, Ca. and Calif. lic. Dr. of Chiropractic, Encino, mem. Calif. Chiropractic Assn., spl. interest. natural methods of health care; Republican; Catholic. Res: 16732 Magnolia Blvd Encino 91436 Ofc: CDI Corp. 5901 Green Valley Circle, Ste. 160, Culver City 90230

HAIM, DAVID, computer marketing co. president; b. Nov. 2, 1920, Istanbul, Turkey, nat. 1968; s. Samuel and Maria (Bigerano) H.; m. Suda J. Bobbitt, Dec. 1, 1962; children: Sam J., b. 1963, Suda M., b. 1965; edn: BS, Univ. of Istanbul, Turkey 1942; Dr., Medical Sch., Rome, Italy 1946; Grad. Sch. of Bus. Admin., UCLA 1968. Career: sales mgr. Olivetti (Italy), Rome 1956-58; district mgr. Olivetti Mexicana, Mexico City 1958-60; area mgr. Olivetti-Underwood Corp., NYC 1960-63; area mgr. Olivetti Corp. of America, Los Angeles 1964-69, national sales mgr., Systems Sales, NYC 1970-71, west coast mgr. Agency Div., 1971-72; founder/pres. Minicom Systems, Los Angeles 1973--; clubs: Los Angeles Tennis, Wilshire Country; Republican; Catholic; rec: tennis, classical music. Res: 214 N. Rossmore Ave Los Angeles 90004 Ofc: Minicom Systems, 1636 Wilshire Blvd Los Angeles 90017

HAINES, RICHARD FOSTER, research scientist; b. May 19, 1937, Seattle; s. Donald Hutchinson and Claudia May (Bennett) Haines; m. Carol Taylor, June 17, 1961; 2 daus: Cynthia Lynn, b. 1965, Laura Anne, b. 1970; edn: Univ. of Wash. (Seattle) Coll. of Engring. 1955-7; BA, psych., Pac. Lutheran Coll. 1960; MA, psych., Mich. State Univ. 1962, PhD in Exptl. Psych. 1964; lic. FAA Pilot Ground Sch. Career: engring aide Boeing Airplane Co., Seattle 1957; grad. teaching fellow Mich. State Univ. Dept. of Psychol. 1962-3, NIH pre-doct. fellow, 1963-4; Nat. Resrch Council resident postdoct. resrch assoc. NASA-Ames Resrch Ctr. 1964-67, sr. resrch scientist, Man-Vehicle Resrch Div., 1967--; sci. cons.: Stanford Univ., TRW Systems, City of Los Angeles, Pac. Tel., local attys., others; dir./chmn. N. Am. UFO Fedn. Inc.; bd. mem. The Center-Counselling for Drug Abuse. Honors: Alumnus of the Year, Pac. Lutheran Univ. 1972; NASA-Tech. Brief Award, 1976; Palo Alto Mayor's Distinguished Svc. Award 1968. Mem: Aerospace Med. Assn. (assoc. fellow); Optical Soc. of Am.; The Internat. Soc. of Air Safety Investigators (chpt. bd.dirs.); Sigma Xi. Patentee (2). Publs: Observing UFOs (Nelson-Hall Pub., 1980); UFO Phenomena and the Behavioral Scientist (Scarecrow Press, NJ, 2979); approx. 45 sci. journal arts., 15 NASA Tech. Reports, 20 UFO arts. Republican; Christian; rec: photog., writing, UFO studies. res: 325 Langton Ave. Los Altos 94022 ofc: AMES Research Ctr. NASA, Moffett Field 94035.

HALDANE, DONALD ROBERT, real estate broker, business executive; b. Dec. 13, 1944, Detroit, Mich.; s. George Ward and Lourie (Rowlen) Haldane; m. Jane Elizabeth Uhl, July 25, 1965; 2 sons: Michael, b. 1967, Eric, b. 1972; edn: CSU Long Beach 1962-5; AA, Cypress Coll. 1968; Golden West Coll. 1982; lic. real estate broker, Calif. 1981. Career: vice pres. Republic Van's Storage, Inc., Los Angeles 1970-73; v.p. Lido Van & Storage, Inc., Fountain

Valley 1973-74; v.p. Pan Am. Van Lines, Huntington Bch. 1975-78; pres. Newport Van & Storage, Inc., Cypress 1975-80; investor, real estate broker, 1978--; Republican; rec: racquetball, ski; address: 16775 Old Stagecoach Rd. Applegate 95703.

HALE, CAROLE DIANE JEZIORSKI GORDON, real estate appraiser/consultant; b. Feb. 19, 1943, Los Angeles; d. Anthony John and Vivian (Smith) Jeziorski; m. 2d. Roger Hale, Feb. 14, 1982; 1 son (by previous m.), William Gordon, b. 1966; edn: AA, Orange Coast Coll. 1976; num. spl. profl. courses; Calif. lic. Real Estate Broker 1980-; MAI, Am. Inst. of R.E. Appraisers 1983. Career: secty./asst. Brabant Real Estate & Appraisals, Huntington Park 1971-73; sales agt. Tarbell Realtors, Costa Mesa 1974-75; assoc. appraiser Roger A. McInnes, MAI, Tustin 1974-76; asst. mgr./appraisal ofcr. Calif. First Bank, El Segundo 1976-78; asst. v.p. Appraisal Dept., So. Calif. Region, The Bank of California, L.A. 1978-84; prin., The Hale Co., Real Estate Appraisals & Consultation, 1984--; mem. Am. Inst. of Real Estate Appraisers (MAI), co-ch. Profl. Advance. Mem. Com. 1984; publs: arts. in trade publs.; Republican; Protestant. Address: The Hale Co., 2251 Woodhollow Ln Chino Hills 91710

HALES, NORMA M., credit union executive; b. Feb. 7, 1933, Brooklyn, NY; d. Robert J. and Rita R. (Surrette) Jordan; m. Robert L. Hales, June 18, 1967; 1 son, Robert L., Jr., b. 1968; edn: stu. Am. River Coll. 1980-83, Dale Carnegie courses 1983. Career: working in credit unions since 1954; var. mgmt. positions, 1959--; mgr. Western Electric personnel credit union, NYC 1959, serviced NY-NJ Credit Unions on The Service Bureau Data Proc. System, 1968-70; mgmt., School Employees C.U., Sacramento 1970-, currently v.p. mgr. central ops., Golden 1 Credit Union, Sacto.; mem.: Sacto. Valley Chpt., Calif. Credit Union League (past bd. dirs. 5 yrs.; chmn. Edn./dir. Regl. Learning Ctr. 1984); Credit Women Internat.; Comstock Club; recipient spl. appreciation award for svc., Calif. C.U. League. Res: 5344 Maui Way Fair Oaks 95628 Ofc: The Golden 1 C.U., 1108 O Street Sacramento 95814

HALEY, PATRICIA MARIE, personnel executive; b. May 17, 1944, St. Louis, Mo.; d. James Chauncey and Virginia Marie (Foley) Magill; m. Richard Bland Haley, Aug. 25, 1962; children: Michael, b. 1963, Timothy, b. 1968; edn: stu. Santa Ana Coll. 1978-; Calif. lic. Notary Public 1979; cert. General Insurance, Ins. Inst. of Amer. 1979; accred. personnel mgr. Am. Soc. Personnel Adminstrn. 1982. Career: secty. Citizens Nat. Bank, St. Louis, Mo. 1962-65; sales secty. Statis. Tabulating Co., St. Louis 1965-69, Home Ins. Kansas City, Mo. 1970-72; sales secty., div. v.p., personnel coord., currently personnel/admininstrv. service mgr. American States Ins., Santa Ana 1974--, Quality Commitment facilitator Santa Ana Div. 1982; recipient United Way cmpgn. awards 1981, 82, 83; mem. Am. Soc. Personnel Adminstrs., P.E.R.M.A.; club: Dana West Yacht; Republican; Catholic; rec: sportfising (2d place winner w/ husband, Catalina Gold Cup Tourn. 10/83), writing short stories. Res: 23336 Caminito Lazaro Laguna Hills 92653 Ofc: American States Ins. Co. 400 N. Tustin Santa Ana 92705

HALFON, SUSANA, lawyer, b. July 9, 1950, Mexico City, Mex.; nat. 1973; d. Salomon and Rebeca (Magrisso) Halfon; 1 son, Rodolfo Vidaurri, b. 1980; edn: BA, UC San Diego 1972; JD, UCB Boalt Hall 1975; study abroad pgm. Univ. De Bordeaux 1970-71; admitted to Calif. State Bar 1978. Career: legal asst. Calif. Agri. Labor Relatios Bd., Sacto., San Diego, 1975-77; project dir. State of Calif. Commn. on the Status of Women, Sacto. 1977-78; head lobbyist, Calif. Rural Legal Assistance, Migrant Pgm., Sacto. 1978-81; legal advisor to board, Public Employment Relations Board, Sacto. 1981--; honors: recognition for drafting and helping pass legis. on migrant education, Statewide Migrant Parent Adv. Com., and Sacto. Bee (newspaper); mem: Centro Legal, Sacto. (bd. dirs. 1983), La Raza Lawyers Assn. (exec. bd.), MAPA; Democrat; rec: aerobics. Res: 3995 H Street Sacramento 95819 Ofc: PERB, 1031 18th St, Ste. 203, Sacramento 95814

HALL, BETTY, real estate broker; b. Oct. 5, 1937, Los Angeles; d. August and Dorothy (Jones) Koedel; m. Randall Collins, Apr. 17, 1982; children: Robert, b. 1961, James, b. 1965; edn: stu. Ohlone Jr. Coll. 1979; Anthony R.E. Schs.; Calif. lic. real estate broker 1976. Career: real estate sales & inv., 1972-, real estate broker Red Carpet Realtors, Fremont 1976--; awards: Red Carpet Realtors top ten prod. (1976, 77, 79, 80, 81); Million Dollar Club, So. Alameda Co. Bd. Realtors (SACBOR) 1976-; mem. San Jose Real Estate Bd., SACBOR, Womens Council of Realtors, Fremont Jr. CofC; publs. in field of time mgmt., motivational sems.; Republican; rec: inter. decor., cooking, community wk. Res: 4633 Mowry Ave Fremont 94538 Ofc: Red Carpet Realtors 43505 Mission Blvd Fremont 94538

HALL, EARL DAVID, electrical engineer; b. Apr. 22, 1951, Columbus, Ohio; s. Earl B. and Martha J. (Lawhead) Hall; m. Petra Middecke, Jan. 12, 1981; children: Sebastian, b. 1974; Joshua, b. 1982, Russell, b. 1983; edn: AA, DeVry (Ohio Inst. of Electronics) 1971. Career: electronic tech. Paul H. Henson Resrch Ctr., Delaware, Oh. 1972-74; engring. cons. NCR Corp., Cambridge, Oh. 1974; engrg. tech. splst. NCR Corp., W. Columbia, S.C. 1974-79; systems integration engring. cons. Siemens Corp., Boca Raton, Fla. 1980-82; test engr. Telcom Technologies Inc. Ontario, Ca. 1982-83; elec. engr. product devel., Ferix Corp., Fremont 1983--; mem. DeVry Alumni Assn.; BSA Cubmaster; works: designed 1st family of NCR microcomputer systems 1976; designed, installed 1st EP6X sys. in W. Ger. 5/81; Democrat; United Brethren; rec: scuba, computers. Res: 35256 Aquado Ct. Fremont Ofc: Ferix Corp. 48571 Milmont, Fremont 94538

HALL, HAROLD CECIL, chartered life underwriter; b. June 9, 1922, Upland; s. Herbert Clinton and Mildred (Smith) H.; m. Sylvia Joy Hurley, June 23, 1946; children: Gay Linele, b. 1949, Gary Randall, b. 1953, Janette Gail, b. 1957, Nanette Dale, b. 1957; edn: spl. courses, Chaffey Jr. Coll., Texas Christian Univ.; CLU, American Coll. 1971. Career: freight agt., Pacific Elec. Ry., Los Angeles 1947-53; sales rep. Louisville & Nashville, Ry., L.A. 1953-59; sales rep. Paxton Trucking, 1959-63; agt. Pacific Fidelity Life Ins. Co., Covina 1963-66, asst. mgr. 1966-69, general agent 1969---, owner Hall Ins. Agcy.; instr. ins. courses, LUTC, 1971-77; mem: Life Underwriters Assn. (pres. 1976-7), Estate Planning Council (pres. 1979), Chartered Life Underwriters (pres. 1985-86), Toastmasters (past pres.), Los Angeles CofC Spkrs. Bur.; publs: arts. in trade mags.; mil: sgt. (Codes & Cyphers), 8th AF, Eng. 1942-45; Republican (campaigner); Latter-Day Saints; rec: gardening. Res: 254 E. Hurst St Covina 91723 Ofc: Hall Ins. Agcy POB 214, Covina 91723

HALL, HOWARD HARRY, lawyer; b. Jan. 9, 1933, Syracuse, NY; s. Harold Gibner and Mildred Ethel (Way) H.; children: Carol, b. 1959, Kristen, b. 1962; edn: BA, Syracuse Univ. 1953, JD, 1959; admitted NY Bar 1960, US Supreme Ct. 1964, Calif. Bar 1978. Career: trial attorney NY law firm 1960-, later estab. own law firm spec. in trial of both civil and criminal cases; prin. Law Ofc. of Howard H. Hall, Paramount, Ca. 1978--; Commnr. of Edn., Syracuse, NY 1963-67; Phi Delta Phi Legal Frat. (pres. 1959); mem: Calif. Trial Lawyers Assn., Calif. Bar Assn., Phi Gamma Delta Frat., NY Trial Lawyers Assn., Upstate Trial Lawyers Assn. (bd. dirs.), Masons (32 deg.); publs: contbr. Syracuse Law Rev.; lectr. var. Bar groups; mil: capt. USMC 1953-56; Republican; (Reagan for Pres. Campgn. Com. 1980); Prot.; rec: classial music. Law Office of Howard H. Hall, 15730 Paramount Blvd Paramount 90723

HALL, JANICE WALLER, real estate broker; b. Nov. 15, 1939, Shreveport, La.; d. Robert Wm. and Annie Maxine (McGinty) Waller; m. Raymond G. Hall, Jr. Sept. 8, 1959; children: Jon Bradley, b. 1962, Julie Ann, b. 1964, Jacklyn Christine, b. 1971; edn: stu. Stephen F. Austin State Coll.; Calif. lic. real estate broker; GRI, Grad. Realtor Inst., Calif. Assn. Realtors. Career: supr. Word Processing Ctr., Sch. of Health, Loma Linda Univ.; mgr./owner/broker Century 21 Loma Linda Realty, Loma Linda currently; mem. Calif. Assn. of Realtors (dir. 1983), San Bernardino Valley Bd. of Realtors (dir. 1983, honored as Realtor Associate for 1982); Loma Linda CofC; Repulican; 7th-Day Adventist; rec: Pathfinder Youth Gp., skiing, water sports. Res: 1340 Mohave Dr Colton 92324 Ofc: Century 21 Loma Linda Realty 24557 University Ave Loma Linda 92354

HALL, J. WENDELL, lawyer; b. Sept. 30, 1938, Springville, Utah; s. Arthur LeRoy and Della Marie (Jensen) H.; m. Kay Christensen, July 10, 1964; children: Douglas, b. 1968, Tecia, b. 1971, Scott, b. 1977; edn: BA, Brigham Young Univ. 1964; JD, Univ. of Santa Clara 1974. Career: claims adjuster Liberty Mutual Ins. Co., 1964-66, claims supr. 1966-72; claims mgr. Am. Re-Insurance Co., 1972-74; atty. Leonard & Thomas, 1974-76, Leonard, Thomas & Hall, 1976-80, asst. mng. ptnr. Thomas, Hall & Kirby 1980--; honors: Pi Sigma Alpha; mil: splst. E6 USAR 1962-68; Republican; LDS Ch. representative in Taiwan & HongKong 1958-61; rec: photog. Res: 1274 Greenbrook Dr Danville 94526 Ofc: Thomas, Hall & Kirby, 1415 Oakland Blvd, Ste 100, Walnut Creek 94596

HALL, MANLY PALMER, lecturer, author, philosophical society founder; b. March 18, 1901, Peterborough, Ont., Can., nat. 1904; m. Marie Bauer, Dec. 6, 1950. Career: founder/pres. Philosophical Research Soc. Inc., Los Angeles 1934--; author 40 books incl. Encyclopedic Outline of Masonic, Hermetic, Qabbalistic and Rosicrucian Symbolical Philosophy (1928); Lectures on Ancient Philosophy (1947); First Principle of Philosophy (1949); Healing, The Divine Art (1950); Search for Reality (1967): Buddhism and Psychotherapy (1967); num. articles, taped lectrs., booklets; honored for distinguished service as lectr., author, tchr., City of Los Angeles 1e Soc. (life), N.M. Hist. Soc. (life), Soc. Rosicruciana in Civitatibus Foederatis (hon. 8 deg.), Mark Twain Soc. (hon.), Indian Assn. of Am., Am. Fedn. Astrologers, Internat. Soc. Gen. Semantics, Am. Soc. Psychical Research (past pres.), Fedn. Philat. Clubs of So. Calif., Masons (33 deg.). Address: Philosophical Research Society Inc., 3910 Los Feliz Blvd Los Angeles 90027

HALL, PETER VINCENT, mortgage insurance co. executive; b. Apr. 14, 1934, Ft. Wayne, Ind.; s. Wm. B.F. and Sarah (Niezer) H.; m. Sherrill Tucker, Apr. 4, 1959; children: Sarah, b. 1960, Mary, b. 1963, Timothy, b. 1966, William, b. 1969; edn: AB econ., Georgetown Univ. 1957; MBA fin., Stanford Univ. 1962. Career: home builder, Traverse City, Mich. 1958; asst. mgr. Advance Mortgage Corp., 1959; mgr. General Equity Investment Corp., 1962-64; pres. Colonial Inv. Corp., 1964-70; pres. Argus Finl., 1970-73, chmn. bd. 1980-82; exec. v.p. PMI Mortgage Corp., 1973-78, pres. 1978-80; pres. PMI Mortgage Ins. Co., 1982--; chmn. Sears Mortgage Securities Corp., 1983--; mem. Western Adv. FNMA (Federal Nat. Mtg. Assn.); mem. Mortgage Bankers Assn.; club: University (SF); mil: ensign USN 1958-59. Res: 600 Eucalyptus Ave Hillsborough 94010 Ofc: PMI Mortgage Insurance Co., 601 Montgomery St San Francisco 94111

HALL, RUTH MARIE, health agency executive; b. July 13, 1914, St. Louis, Mo.; d. John Sylvester and Minna Emma (Giese) Henger; children: John Herron, b. 1937, Nancy Herron, b. 1939, Thomas Herron, b. 1941, Susan Hall, b. 1943; edn: Western Reserve Univ. 1957-61. Career: dir. Family Lounge, Cleveland (Ohio) Clinic Hosp., 1958-65; asst. adminstr. Residence Halls, University Hosps., Cleveland 1965-67; exec. dir. Easter Seal Soc. of Solano

County, Ca. 1968--; honors: Golden Apple Award, Vallejo Elem. Sch. Adminstrs. Assn. 1970, Esther Elder Smith Award (for conthn. to disabled) 1971; mem: Nat./Calif. Easter Seal Exec. Assn., Nat. Assn. for Female Execs., Soroptimists, Women of the CofC, Vallejo Music Theatre, Vallejo Sym. League, Mira Theatre, Republican Women of Solano Co.; works: enameling on metal, exhib. Cleveland Mus. of Art, May Show 1956, 57, 58, 60; Presbyterian; rec: needlepoint, knitting. Res: 488 Corcoran St Vallejo 94589 Ofc: Easter Seal Society, 119 Larwin Plaza Vallejo 94590

HALLADAY, KAREN SUE, real estate broker, financial planner; b. July 26, 1943, Stockton; d. Dr. Louis and Eleanor Sue Keene (Sandberg) Jacques, Jr.; m. Wayne Halladay, Feb. 4, 1967; edn: BA, 1965 and MA, 1967, with highest honors, CSU San Jose; postgrad. wk., philos., UC Berkeley 1970-76; Calif. Std. Elem. Tchr. credential, Jr. Coll. Instr., Comm. Coll. Counselor cred.; Reg. Representative, Reg. Investment Advisor Agt.; Finl. Planner; Calif. lic. R.E. Broker. Career: elem. sch. tchr. Lompoc Unified Sch. District, 1967-70; instr. Alan Han Jr. Coll., Santa Maria 1968-70; coll. instr./supr. student teachers, St. Marys Coll., Moraga 1974-76; real estate agt. Marcus Co. and Stephen R. Payne, Walnut Creek, 1977-81; realtor/owner Halladay & Assocsurity Pacific Real Estate, Walnut Creek; acct. exec. WZW Financial Services; mem: Nat./ Calif. Assn. of Realtors, Contra Costa Bd. of Realtors (profl. stds. panel 1981-), San Joaquin Bd. of Realtors, Internat. Assn. for Finl. Plnng., Toastmasters Intl.; Democrat; Episcopal; rec: hiking, river rafting, wine appreciation. REs: 2365 Hagen Oaks Dr Alamo 94507 Ofc: Sec. Pacific Real Estate, 587 Ygnacio Valley Rd. Walnut Creek 94596

HALLER, RONALD JAMES, real estate financial executive; b. Nov. 24, 944, Cleveland, Ohio; s. Ely and Eileen C. (Dobson) H.; m. Heidi Lasnik, Apr. 4, 1965; children: Eric, b. 1966, Monica, b. 1970, Tristan, b. 1983; edn: AA, data proc., Cuyahoga Comm. Coll. 1969; BBA in acctg., cum laude, Cleveland St. Univ. 1966; MBA pgm. Case-Western Reserve Univ. 1966-68; CPA, State of Ohio 1968, Fla. 1973. Career: accountant Ernst & Ernst & Co., Cleveland, Oh. 1965-68; asst. controller Preferred Properties Inc., Cleveland 1968-70; asst. treas./asst. controller Northern Union Holdings Corp., Cleveland 1970-71; controller Associated Estates Corp., Cleveland 1971-72; controller/dir. of adminstrn. James Burt Inc., Tampa, Fla. 1975-76; first v.p. fin./sec. treas (CFO) Coldwell Banker Residential Real Estate Services Inc., Fountain Valley 1976-83; pres. Pan Pacific Equity Corp., Laguna Hills 1983--; instr. acctg. and data proc. courses, Cuyahoga Comm. Coll. 1968-70, Tampa Univ. 1972-73; mem: Am. Inst. of CPAs 1968-76, Ohio Inst. of CPAs 1968-73, Fla. Inst. of CPAs 1973-76, Nat. Assn. of Accts. 1966-76j, Beta Alpha Psi (acctg. hon.), fin. Little League coach, mgr.; author: JBI Property Mgmt. Computer System, for use on IBM System 32 (mktd. nat. by IBM 1975-78); Republican; Methodist; rec: weight lifting, wood working, tennis. Res: 27084 Pinario Mission Viejo 92692 Ofc: Pan Pacific Equity Corp., 23297 South Pointe Dr, Ste 230, Laguna Hills 92653

HALLETT, NORMAN, commodity options executive; b. Mar. 23, 1949, Bronx, NY; s. Leo George and Esther (Sivowitz) H.; m. Tisha Ramsdell, July 18, 1981; edn: BA, math., Univ. Cinn. 1973; cert., Commodities Series 3. Career: gen. mgr. Gold Boot Shoe for the Potter Shoe Co., Cincinnati 1975-76; gen. mgr. for New York Times Clothing Stores, Cincinnati 1976-77; restaurant mgr. Frisch's Restaurants, Cinti., 1977-78; night club mgr. American Events Corp., Cinti. 1978-79; regional v.p. International Trading Group, Ltd. (largest retail options firm in US), San Mateo 1979--; recipient many ITG sales awards; mem. Save the Children; Television interviewer (1-1/2 years), Bob Gray producer, TV-60 KCSM, San Mateo; num. appearances on TV-48 San Jose, Ask the Expert; avocation: voice. Res: 30 Tripp Ct. Woodside 94062 Ofc: International Trading Group, Ltd., 60 East 3rd Ave San Mateo 94401

HALLIBURTON, GENE DENNIS, national automobile club president; b. Sept. 17, 1919, Kennett, MO; s. William Elija and Minnie Ola (Fowler) Halliburton; attended Univ. of Ind., 1939-41; Univ. of Calif., 1949-51; m. May Gardner, Apr. 3, 1955; chil: Randall Bryan, b. 1959; Susan Marguerite, b. 1969; Kathryn Elizabeth, b. 1961; Gardner William, b. 1963; career: passenger agent, Transworld Airlines, Kansas City, MO, 1939-44; instr., USAF, Air Training Command, USA, 1944-47; mgr., Whitcomb Travel Agency, S.F., CA, 1947-49; pres., Dist. Sales Mgr., Natl. Automobile Club, S.F., 1949--; pres. chief exec. ofcr., Natl. Automobile Club, S.F., 1974--; pres. Amer. Automobile Touring Alliance; dir., Alliance Internationale de Tourisme, Geneva, Switzerland. Recipient: Man of the Year, Eastbay Ins. Man's Assn., 1960, 61. Mem.: pres., Oakland Ins. Forum, 1960; pres., Ins. Fieldman's Assn., 1961; chmn. bd. govs., S.F. Pub. Rels. Round Table, 1967; v. chmn., Calif. Commn. for Driver Edn., 1968-71; adv. panel, Governor's Traffic Safety Commn., 1969; ofcr., dir., Calif. Traffic Safety Found., 1971; pres., Ins. Co. Mgrs. Assn. of No. Calif., 1976. Produced and moderated four half-hour panel discussions on How To Buy Insurance, which was aired weekly on three Bay Area radio stations, 1961. Mil.: SSgt., USAF, 1944-46. Republican; Protestant; rec: photography, travel, camping. res.: 300 Vernon St., Oakland 94610 ofc: Natl. Automobile Club, One Market Plaza, Suite 300, San Francisco 94105.

HALLINAN, LAUREN POPLACK, lawyer; b. June 22, 1947, d. William T. and Eleanor Edith (Wolf) Poplack; m. Patrick Hallinan, Feb. 14, 1982; edn: BA, Newcomb Coll. 1970, JD, Tulane Univ. Law Sch.; admitted to Calif. State Bar 1974. Career: assoc. Faulla, Braun & Martel, 1974-77; atty. National Economic Devel. Law Center, 1977-81; ptnr. Hallinan, Osterhoudt & Poplack, San Francisco 1981--, spec. criminal law, urban issues; instr. Hastings Coll. of the Law 1982--; lectr. Legal Services Corp. 1978-81; bd, dirs. Nat. Center for Appropriate Technology 1979-81; nat. chpsn. Nat. Comm. Devel. Block Grant Task Force empl. com. 1979-; honors: Order of the Coif 1974, Tulane Law Rev. editor

1972-74; mem: Calif. State Bar Assn. (del. Bar Conf. 1977, ed. Legal Svcs. Sect. newsletter 1977), Calif. Women Lawyers, ACLU; publs: arts. in law jours.; contbg. author/ed. Community Devel. Block Grants (Nat. Econ. Devel. & Law Ctr., Berkeley 1978). Res: 19 Ridgecrest Rd Kentfield 94907 Ofc: Hallinan, Osterhoudt & Poplack 345 Franklin St San Francisco 94102

HALLINAN, PATRICK SARSFIELD, lawyer; b. Dec. 12, 1934, San Francisco; s. Vincent and Vivian (Moore) H.; m. Lauren Poplack, Feb. 14, 1982; children: Casey, b. 1971, Neil, b. 1978; edn: AB, Univ. Calif. 1959; LLB, Hastings Coll. of the Law 1962; MA in Anthropology, UC 1970, PhD Cand.; admitted to Calif. State Bar 1963. Career: ptnr. law firm Hallinan, Osterhoudt & Poplack (and predecessor firm), San Francisco 1963--, currently senior partner; apptd. City Commnr., pres. Bd. of Permit Appeals, S.F. 1974-77; bd. dirs. Calif. Attorneys for Criminal Justice; lectr. Hastings Coll. of Trial Advocacy 1983; num. publs. in sci. journals on archaeological subjects; listed, Martindale Hubbell, Best Lawyers in Am. Res: 19 Ridgecrest, Kent Woodlands 94907 Ofc: Hallinan, Osterhoudt & Poplack, 345 Franklin St San Francisco 94102

HALLINAN, VINCENT, lawyer; b. Dec. 16, 1896, San Francisco; s. Patrick and Elizabeth (Sheehan) H.; m. Vivian Moore, Aug 16, 1932; children: Patrick, b. 1934, Terence, b. 1936, Michael, b 1939, matthew, b. 1940, Conn, b. 1942, Daniel, b. 1948; edn: AB, Univ. of San Francisco 1919, LLB, 1923. Admitted to Calif. Bar 1920, US Supreme Ct. Bar 1946. Career: defense atty. pvt. practice spec. in jury trials nationally publicized criminal cases: Hanford Windmill Murder (1928), Frank Egan, S.F. Public Defender (1932), Irene Mansfeldt (1945), Harry Bridges (1949); Presidential candidate of Progressive Party in 1952; hon. mem. I.L.W.U.; author: Lion In Court (Putnam Sons NY 1963); A Clash of Cultures; mil. ofcr. USN 1918-19; Ind.; rec: boxing, football. Res: 1080 Chestnut San Francisco 94109 Ofc: 819 Eddy, San Francisco 94109

HALLOCK, BRAVEN SCOTT, manufacturing co. executive; b. Feb. 24, 1956, Covina; s. Robert, Duane and Cherry Leoma (Llewellyn) H.; edn: BA in pol. sci. and BS in eco n., USC, 1983. Career: store mgr. The Instep (Adidas Athletic Equip.) Menlo Park 1976-79; asst. corporate credit mgr. Thermacote-Welco Co., Pasadena 1980-81; asst. mgr. M.I.S. Dept., Hughest Aircraft Co., E.D.S.G. Div., El Segundo 1982; regl. adminstrv. mgr., West Coast, Liquid Carbonid Corp., Irwindale 1983--; So. Calif. Office asst. for fmr. US Sen. S.I. Hayakawa (Calif.); awards: Fellowship grant, USC 1983-84; mem. Credit Mgrs. Assn. of So. Calif. 1981-; Past Master Counselor, charter mem. Los Altos Chpt., Order of DeMolay; Republican; Lutheran; rec: sports, outdoors. Res: 615 S. Santa Paula Ct San Dimas 91773 Ofc: Liquid Carbonic Corp. 16125 Ornelas St Irwindale 91706

HALLORAN, KAREN GAY, security co. owner; b. July 1, 1956, Burbank; d. Richard Lawrence and Arline Jean (Brockmiller) Mahan; m. Leslie Halloran, May 5, 1977; chil: Kimberly, b. 1978; Erinn, b. 1980; Keven, b. 1983. Career: exec. asst. Scandicrafts, Inc., Camarillo 1976-79; owner Lock-Tronic Security Services, Simi Valley 1979--; honors: Who's Who of Am. High Sch. Students 1973. Charter mem. Kiwanians, Simi Vly.; Girl Scout Leader; Republican; Christian; rec: stained glass, cooking. Address: Lock-Tronic Security Services, 2285 N. Tracy Ave. Simi Valley 93063

HALPER, DONALD KENNETH, lawyer; b. Aug. 26, 1933, NY, NY; s. David Leonard and Frances Naomi (Orkin) H.; m. Renee, Nov. 17, 1978; children: Mark Robert, b. 1965, Beth Denise, b. 1968; edn: BBA, Western Reserve Univ. 1956; JD, Cleveland St. Univ. 1960; admitted to Ohio Bar 1961, Calif. Bar 1971, US Tax Ct., US Supreme Ct., Federal Dist. Cts. in Ohio, Calif. Career: pvt practice of law, Cleveland, O. 1961-64; law clk. Superior Ct., Los Angeles 1964-65; atty., Vets Adm., L.A. 1965-69, IRS, L.A. 1969-73, pvt. practice law, L.A. 1973-74; directing atty. Legal Aid, L.A. 1974-75; deputy dist. atty., L.A. 1975-78; pvt. practice law, L.A. 1978--; law prof. Glendale Coll. of Law 1962, L.A. City Coll. 1973-75; judge pro tem L.A. Municipal Ct. 1980-; family law mediator L.A. Superior Ct. 1978-; arbitrator, Am. Arbitrn. Assn.; chmn. adv. council Coldwater Cyn Elem. Sch.; hon. life PTA; mem: San Fernando Valley Bar Assn., Calif. Dist. Attys. Assn., Kiwanis, Bnai Brith; lectr., author on wills, probate, estate plnng., consumer law, child support, family law and paternity, 1961-; mil: sp4 US Army 1957-63; Democrat; Jewish; rec: writing, golf, tennis. Res: 16661 Lahey St Granada Hills 91344 Ofc: Donald K. Halper, 14401 Sylvan St, Ste. 107, Van Nuys 91401

HALVERSON, DAVID REX, retail co. exective; b. Jan. 4, 1957, Long Beach; s. David R., Sr. and Susan (Terry) H.; m. Pamela Jo Carroll, May 28, 1983; edn: Claremont McKenna Coll. 1974-76; cert. audio cons., Soc. Audio Consultants 1977. Career: major appliance sales/asst. mgr. with Los Angeles corp. in Alhambra and Burbank 1977; audio/video cons. Federated Group, Hollywood 1977-79, floor supr., mdse. mgr., sales mgr., gen. mgr. various locations (Montclair, Temple City, W.L.A., Westminster), 1979-82; district mgr. (six stores), Federated Group, 1984--; mem. Soc. Audio Cons. 1976-; Democrat; Prot.; rec: photog., basketball. Res: 1312A Diamond Bar Blvd, Diamond Bar 91765 Ofc: Federated Group, 5665 E. Union Pacific Ave Commerce 90022

HALY, JANE MARIGER, marriage, family and child counselor; b. Apr. 19, 1931, Monterey Park; d. Mark Farnsworth and Louise (Merrill) Mariger; m. George Haly, Jr. July 22, 1949; children: Carolyn, b. 1952, Susan, b. 1952, Julie,

b. 1953; edn: BS, Lindenwood Colls. 1980; MA, Azusa Pacific Univ. 1982; Calif. lic. MFCC, 1981. Career: optician, Murray Weber, MD, Canoga Pk. 1975-79; licensed optician, B. Davidorf, MD, Woodland Hills 1979-80; therapist California Family Study Ctr., Westlake Vil. 1980-81, MFCC therapist/ptnr. Assocs. in Counseling 1983--; bd. dirs. Addiction Control Treatment Services; cons. Camp Care Life Style Center; recipient profl. volunteer award, CLARE Found. 1981-82; mem. Calif. Assn. Marriage & Family Therapists; rec: travel, scuba diving, biking. Res: 29500 Heathercliff Rd, 115, Malibu 90265 Ofc: Associates in Counseling, 2660 Townsgate Rd, Ste. 110, Westlake Village 91361

HAMILTON, BRANDON LESLIE, system engineer; b. Nov. 26, 1947, Chgo.; s. Eugene Alexander and Gloria Lee (Gladney) H.; edn: AA, Kennedy-King Coll. 1975; BS, Univ. Ill. 1979. Career: nuclear engineer cons. Stone and Webster Engrng., Boston, Mass. 1972-74; self empl. engineering tutor, Chgo. 1974-77; sci. research pgmmr., Univ. of Ill., Chgo. 1977; physics lab asst., Ill. Inst. of Tech., Chgo. 1977; tutor/instr. Inroads Inc., Chgo. 1975-78; strategic analyst Analytic Services, Arlington, Va. 1979-80; nuclear/computer engr. So. California Edison, San Clemente, Ca. 1980-84; satellite test dir. Aerojet Electrosystems, Azusa 1984--; mem. Operations Research Soc. of Am. 1978-80; mem. Mathematical Assn. of Am.; D.C. Student Math. Soc. (newsletter ed. 1979-80); Omega Psi Phi Frat.; publs: tech. papers, sci. reports; mil: E5 USN 1968-72, Nat. Defense Medal, Honorman; rec: jogging, scuba, swimming. Res: 211 Grand Ave, 412, Long Beach 90803 Ofc: Aerojet Electrosystems, 1100 West Hollyvale St, Azusa 91702

HAMILTON, JACKSON DOUGLAS, lawyer; b. Feb. 5, 1949, Cleveland, Ohio; m. Laurie Williams, Dec. 19, 1971; children: Jackson D. Jr., b. 1976, William Schuyler, b. 1980; edn: BA, Colgate Univ. 1971; JD, Univ. Penna. Law Sch. 1974. Career: assoc. lawyer firm of Mihaly, Schuyler & Burton, Los Angeles 1974-76; firm of Brawerman & Kopple, Beverly Hills 1976-77; firm of Cooper, Wyatt, Tepper & Plant, L.A. 1977-78; firm of Freedman & Sobel, Beverly Hills 1979; firm of Flame, Sanger, Grayson & Ginsburg, Encino 1980-83; firm of Wood, Lucksinger & Epstein, Los Angeles 1983--; adj. prof. Univ. of San Diego Law Sch. Grad. Tax Pgm. 1981; asst. editor Entertainment Law Reporter, 1979-; cons. Sports Law, Calif. Senate 1983 ; mem: Am. Bar Assn. (Tax Sect., Internat. Law Sect.), Internat. Fiscal Assn.; contbg. writer to The Tax Lawyer, The Los Angeles Daily Journal Report, Calif. State Bar Jour., The Internat. Tax Jour., Taxes-The Tax Mag.; Republican; Presbyterian; rec: tennis, sailing. Res: 1760 Sunset Ave Santa Monica 90405 Ofc: Wood, Lucksinger & Epstein, 1900 Ave of the Stars, Ste. 1700, Los Angeles 90067

HAMILTON, JOHN RICHARDSON, III, database administrator; b. May 13, 1952, Hagerstown, Md.; s. John Richardson, Jr. and Anne Sophia (Earley) Hamilton; m. Eileen Budnaitis, Feb. 11, 1984: children: Marna, b. 1966, Darren, b. 1970, Daniel, b. 1973; edn: BSGS (comp.sci.), US Mil. Acad., West Point, 1974. Career: senior database analyst CTB/McGraw-Hill, Monterey, Ca. 1977-81; database adminstr. National Semiconductor, Santa Clara 1982; mgr. Database Adminstration, ESL, Sunnyvale 1983; senior cons. NDBS Inc., Redwood City 1983--; tchg. Public Utils. Commn. 2/84; cons. GECC 3/84; cons. Charles Schwab Inc. 1983-84; cons. US Fleet Leasing 1984-; mem. Cullinet Regl. Users Gp., Order of DeMolay, BSA, Am. Sportsmans Club, Assn. of (West Point) Graduates; mil: 2d lt. US Army 1974-76; Republican; rec: Gundogs (train, breed), hunting, microcomputer software. Res: 1130 Polk Ln San Jose 95117 Ofc: NDBS, Inc. 350 Bridge Pkwy, Ste. 206, Redwood City 94065

HAMILTON, RONALD RAY, jeweler, b. Apr. 17, 1939, Alton, Ill.; s. Clarence E. and Lovie C. (Hamby) H.; m. Diane Cho, July 3, 1981; edn: BA, UC Los Angeles 1970, cert. real estate, UCLA 1974, cert. govt. supvn., E.LA Coll. 1978; Gemological Inst. of Am. 1981-82; Calif. lic. real estate broker 1976. Career: instr. Data Proc. Sch. for USN, San Diego 1962; computer opr. UC Los Angeles 1975; senior real estate agt. City of Los Angeles, in chg. of property mgmt., 1980; owner Hamilton's Jewelry, San Pedro currently; frequent guest spkr. var. groups on all aspects of jewelry, 1981-; mil: P.O. 2/c USN 1962; Democrat; Prot.; rec: ocean sailing, guitar, chess. Res: 21144 S. Budlong Torrance 90502 Ofc: Hamilton's Jewelry, 28032 S. Western, San Pedro 90732

HAMLIN, CARL TED, gemologist-jeweler; b. Jan. 2, 1939, Ducan, Okla.; s. Carl Cecil and Clara Savanna (Anderson) H.; m. Marilyn Miller, Mar. 11, 1980; 1 son, Garrett Carl, b. 1968; edn: computer op. San Diego Coll. 1964; tchr. cred., CSU San Diego 1974; cert. GIA, Gemological Inst. of Am. 1971. Career: owner/opr. manufacturing jewelry firm, Hamlins Mfg. Jewelers, El Cajon 1969-; lectr., tchr., gemcutter and master craftsman; awards: for jewelry designs num. shows 1973-78; mem: Retail Jewelers of Am., Calif. Retail Jewelers Assn., San Diego Gemological Soc., Tourmaline Gem and Mineral Soc., Exchange Club of Am. (treas.); publs: newspaper columns 1973-75, research in field; mil: A/2 USAF 1956-60; Republican; Prot.; rec: travel. Res: 7231 Big Oak St San Diego 92114 (POB 565, La Mesa 92041) Ofc: Hamlins Mfg. Jewelers 2234 Fletcher Pky, Ste.F, El Cajon 92020

HAMMER, ARMAND, industrialist; b. May 21, 1898, New York, N.Y.; s. Julius and Rose (Robinson) Hammer; edn: BS, Columbia Univ., 1919, MD, 1921; m. Frances Barrett, 1956; 1 son; career: president Allied Am. Corp., NY, NY 1923-25, A. Hammer Pencil Co., NY, London, Moscow 1925-30, Hammer Galleries, Inc., NY, NY 1930--, J.W. Dant Distilling Co., NYC, Dant, Ky. 1943-54; pres., bd. chmn. Mutual Broadcasting System, NY, NY 1957-58; bd. chmn., CEO, Occidental Petroleum Corp., Los Angeles 1957--; chmn., M. Knoedler and Co., Inc., NY, NY 1972--; bd. dirs. Canadian Occidental Petroleum Ltd. 1964-; founder, hon. chmn. Armand Hammer College, 1981-; mem. Grad. Sch. of Mgmt. Bd. of Visitors UCLA 1957-; mem. Los Angeles Petroleum Club 1960-; bd. govs. Eleanor Roosevelt Cancer Found., 1960-; apptd. mem. National Petroleum Council 1968-; bd. trustees, L.A. Co. Mus. of Art 1968-; bd. trustees, chmn. exec. com., Salk Inst. for Biological Studies 1969-; bd. dirs. L.A. World Affairs Council 1969-; adv. com. Com. for a Greater Calif. 1969-; founder mem. L.A. Music Ctr.; bd. dirs., bd. govs. UN Assn. of USA 1970-; bd. govs. Ford's Theatre Soc. 1970-; bd. dirs. Planned Parenthood World Pop./L.A. 1970-; hon. mem. Royal Acad. of Arts, London, Eng. 1975-; bd. dirs. Assocs. of the Harvard Bus. Sch. 1975-; bd dirs. Am. Petroleum Inst., Wash. DC 1975-; LAC-USC Cancer Assocs. 1975-; bd. dirs. Calif. Roundtable 1976-; founder mem. Pepperdine Assocs. 1976-; nat. trustee, National Sym.; mem. James Smithson Soc., Smithsonian Nat. Assocs.; pres., Found. of the Internat. Inst. of Human Rights, Geneva 1977-; bd. dirs. Century City Cultural Commn.; asv. com. Fogg Art Mus.; adv. council The Friendship Forces; bd. trustees United for Calif.; exec. mem. Energy Research and Edn. Found.; charter mem. Nat. Vis. Council of Health Scis Faculties, Columbia Univ.; trustee The Capitol Children's Mus.; bd. dirs. Corcoran Gallery of Art; hon. mem. The Jockey Club; bd. dmrs. Keep America Beautiful, Inc.; mem. L.A. Council Navy League of the US; bd. dirs. Bus. Com. for the Arts, NYC; Fifty-Year Club of Am. Medicine; Fellows for Life of New Orleans Mus. of Art; Com. on Artic Oil and Gas Resources; UNICEF Nat. Support Council; adv. council Am. Longevity Assn., Inc.; Univ. Okla. Assocs.; hon. mem. Royal Scottish Acad., Edinburgh, Scotland; adv. bd. Ctr. for Strategic and Internat. Studies, Georgetown Univ.; L.A. Olympic Citizens Adv. Commn.; Fine Arts Com. of US State Dept.; chmn. President's Cancer Panel 1981-; Mayor Bradley's Task Force for Africa/L.A. Rels. 1981-; Internat. Bd. Govs., Bob Hope Internat. Heart Research Inst. 1982-. Life mem., AMA, N.Y. Co. Med. Assn., Alpha Omega Alpha, Mu Sigma, Phi Sigma Delta; presented Pres. F.D.R.'s Campobello residence as U.S.-Canadian Peace Park in presence of Pres. Kennedy and Prime Minister Lester Pearson, 1964; mem. Lotos Club 1973-; mem. Internat. Inst. of Human Rights 1978- (sponsored Peace Confs., Oslo, Norway 1978, Campobello Peace Park 1979, Warsaw, Poland 1980, Aix-en-Provence, France 1981; founded the Armand Hammer Center for Cancer Biology and Research, Salk Inst., 1969; estab. the Julius and Armand Hammer Health Scis. Center, Columbia Univ., 1977; awards: (hon.) LL.D., Pepperdine Univ. (1978), Southeastern Univ. (Columbia Univ.), (hon.) D.H.L., Univ. Colo. (1979), (hon.) D.Pub. Svc. Salem Coll, (1979), (hon.) LL.D., Aix-en-Provence Univ., France (1981); decorated comdr. Order of the Crown (Belgium), comdr. Order of Andres Bellow (Venezuela), Mexican Order of the Aztec Eagle, ofcr. Nat. Order of Legion of Honor (France), Order of Friendship Among Peoples (Soviet Union), Royal Order of the Polar Star (Sweden), Grand Officer to the Merit of the Republic (Italy), Knight Comdr's Cross (Austria); recipient Internat. Achievement Award (1982), World Trade Club of S.F., Maimonides Award (1980), L.A. Jewish Community, Entrepreneur of the Year (1980), USC, num. others; author, The Quest of the Romanoff Treasure, 1936; subject of books (by Robt. Considine); 'The Remarkable Life of Dr. Armand Hammer' and 'Larger Than Life'; mil: US Army Med. Corps 1918-1919; ofc: Occidental Petroleum Corp., 10889 Wilshire Blvd. Ste. 1500, Los Angeles 90024.

HAMMOND, GEORGE DENMAN, physician, researcher, administrator; b. Feb. 5, 1923, Atlanta, GA; s. Percy Waters and Elizabeth Taylor (Denman) H.; m. Florence Williams, Mar. 30, 1946; children: Lane Elizabeth Clark, b. 1949, Christopher Scott, b. 1951, Bruce Benedict, b. 1953, Kirk Denman, b. 1955; edn: BA, chem., Univ. N.C., Chapel Hill 1944; MD, Univ. Penna. Sch. of Med. 1948; rotating intern Penna. Hosp., Phila. 1948-50; res. pediatrics, Childrens Hosp. of Phila. 1952-53; sr. res., Ped., UC San Francisco 1953-54. Diplomate Am. Bd. of Pediatrics 1956; Fellow Am. Acad. of Ped. 1958. Career: research fellow/assoc., asst. prof. pediatrics, UC Sch. of Med., S.F. 1954-57; USC Sch. of Medicine, L.A. asst. prof./assoc. prof./prof. ped. 1957--, deputy chmn. Dept. Ped., 1970-71, assoc. dean USC Sch. of Medicine, 1981--; dir. LA County-USC Comprehensive Cancer Ctr. 1971-81; dir. Kenneth Norris Jr. Cancer Resrch Hosp. & Inst., 1979-81; chmn. Childrens Cancer Study Gp., USC 1968-; bd. dirs. Calif. Div. Am. Cancer Soc. 1974-; apptd. by gov. to State Calif. Cancer Adv. Council 1980-; mem. editorial bds: Medical and Pediatric Oncology (1974-), Oncology (1976-), Am. J. Clin. Oncol. (1977-), J. Hematologic Oncol. (1981-); awards: Fellow Giannini Found. 1954-56, Am. Cancer Soc. Scholar in Cancer Resrch 1964-65, distinguished alumnus awd. Univ. N.C. at Chapel Hill 1974, The Adm. Chambliss Award of the Navy League 1979, Lucy Wortham James Clin. Resrch. Awd. 1984; mem: Internat. Soc. Hematology, Am. Soc. Hematology, Am. Assn. for Cancer Research, Am. Soc. of Clin. Oncology, Soc. Internat. Pediatrie; num. sci. publs; mil: cmdr. M.C. USNR (ret.) active duty 1942-45, 1950-52, naval flight surgeon 1950; Republican; Prot.; rec: classic car restoration, photog. Res: 851 S. El Molino Pasadena 91106 Ofc: USC School of Medicine, 2025 Zonal Ave, KAM 506, Los Angeles 90033

HAMPTON, COLETTE PIAT, high fashion designer; b. Sept. 21, 1933, Amiens, France; d. Andre Charles Julian and Hama (Micheline) Piat; div. Dr. Antoine Scheckenberger; children: Alexander Christian, b. 1958, Antoine Eric, b. 1959, Sophie Colette, b. 1961; edn: Baccalaureate, Notre Dame, 1945-49; deg., art hist., cum laude, Sch. of Ecoile Beaux-Arts 1950-52. Career: began art/design career travelling with architect father, with first couture design at age 13; awarded spl. authorization by Cambre des Metiers to conduct profl. bus. before age of 21 years; high fashion designer, Modiliste Haute Couture, with pvt. clientele in E. France, Paris, Carmel, San Francisco; pvt. fashion shows in Pebble Beach, currently; Catholic; rec: art hist., piano, literature. Address: Colette Piat High Fashion, POB 415, Carmel 93921

HAN, MAN HI, doctor of oriental medicine, educator, clergyman; b. Apr. 18, 1934, Seoul, Korea; nat. 1980; s. Han Boo Gol and Han Bong sam; edn: Master,

Dahlmah Bum Eursah Temple, 1966; Phd, Columbia Pacific Univ., 1979; OMD (Dr. Oriental Med.), and PhD (oriental med.), Samra Univ. Health Sci., 1983. Career: Buddhist monk, Suh Deuk Sah Temple, Korea, 1950--, estab. Tahl Mah Sah Temple, Los Angeles, 1973; abbot Buddhist Temple of America, L.A., 1976; clinical staff/prof. The California Acupuncture College, L.A. 1981; Rev./dir. Suh Doh Sah Buddhist Temple of Am., L.A. 1982--; Dir.: Oriental Medical Ctr. 1979, Oriental Health Foods (herbs co.) 1974, Oriental Acupuncture Ctr. 1977; mem: Acupuncture Assn. of Am., Korean Am. Acupuncture Assn., Internat. Angah Council, Beverly Hills CofC, Korean Community Assn.; mil: Rep. of Korea Army 1957; rec: mountain climbing. Address: Suh Doh Sah Buddhist Temple of America, 674 Crenshaw Blvd Los Angeles 90005

HAN, SANG YOUL, manufacturing co. chief executive; b. Dec. 2, 1938, Seoul, Korea, nat. 1976; s. Chong Soo and Do Chee (Kim) H.; m. Dora Mesa, Dec. 13, 1969; children: Sang II, b. 1971, Steven, b. 1973, Monica, b. 1975, Michael, b. 1981; edn: AA, Pasadena City Coll. 1960; BS, USC, 1962, grad. wk. 1963-64; Calif. lic. Profl. Engr. (Civil), Land Devel., General Building Contractor. Career: vp-operation, Dallons Instruments Div., International Rectifier Corp., El Segundo 1972; chief engr., Chromalloy American Corp., City of Industry 1978; project mgr. Filtrol Corp., Los Angeles 1981; pres./CEO, Han Industrial Corp., Pomona 1984--; Dir. Han Enterprises, Pasadena 1975-; mem. Nat. Assn. of General Contractors; Rotary Club of Pomona; Republican (medal of merit, Repub. Pres. Task Force 1983); Christian; rec: reading, swimming. Res: 452 N. Greer Covina 91724 Ofc: Han Industrial Corp. 401 S. Main St, Ste. 210, Pomona 91766

HANDA, MANOHAR LAL, engineer; b. Apr. 10, 1929, Jhelum, Punjab, Pakistan, nat. 1977; s. Gian Chand and Maya Devi (Kochhar) H.; m. Ruchira Nanda, Oct. 3, 1954; 2 sons: Sanjiv, b. 1956, Vikas, b. 1958; edn: BA (hons. math.), Punjab Univ. 1948, BS, 1952; M. Eng., UC Berkeley 1965; Reg. Profl. Engr. states of Calif., Mich., Iowa, Okla. and Penna. Career: asst. engr., Punjab State Govt., India 1952-61, senior design engr. 1961-64; asst. engr. Raymond Kaiser Engr., Oakland, Ca. 1965-67, senior design engr. 1967-72, struct. design supr. 1972-80, principal engr./project design engr. 1980--; mem: ASCE, Am. Concrete Inst., Am. Inst. of Steel Constrn., Prestressed Concrete Inst., Internat. Conf. of Building Officials; publs: article, revs. ACI Jour. 1981; rec: study religions/ philosophy. Res: 1484 Christina Ct. Hayward 94545 Ofc: Raymond Kaiser Engr. 300 Lakeside Dr (POB 23210) Oakland 94623

HANDWERGER, RICHARD MICHAEL, physician/eye surgeon; b. Dec. 28, 1945, NY, NY; s. Irv and Anne (Gersh) Handwerger; edn: BA, Hunter Coll., 1967; PhD, Columbia Univ., 1969; MD, Columbia Med. Sch., 1973. career: developed corneal (eye) transplant service for Kaiser Permanente, So. Calif., 1977-82; private solo practice of ophthalmic medicine, Beverly Hills 1982--, attend corneal confs., Jules Stein Eye Inst., UCLA; active in public edn. & awareness (mass media) regarding corneal and organ transplant information. Diplomate, Am. Bd. of Ophthalmology 1979; Fellow, Am. Acad. of Ophthalmol. 1980. mem: Los Angeles Ophthalmol. Soc., Los Angeles Co. Med. Assn. Republican; rec: piano, photog., astronomy, enology. ofc: 435 N. Roxbury Dr. #409, Beverly Hills 90210

HANGARTER, JOAN B., chiropractor; b. Mar. 16, 1949, NYC; d. Sid and Helen (Goldman) Abramowitz; m. Peter Hangarter, June 7, 1981; edn: BS, Boston Univ. 1970, MS, Long Is. Univ. 1975, DC, L.A. Coll. of Chiropractic 1979. Career: therapist/coord. drug abuse pgms. in New York and in West Covina, Ca. 1970-76; assoc. doctor Awender Chiropractic Corp., S. San Francisco 1980-81; self empl. Family Chiropractic Office, S.S.F. 1981; chiropractor, Berkeley Holistic Health Ctr., 1981-82; owner/dir. Solano Chiropractic Ofc., Berkeley 1982-; instr. classes, lectr. and public spkr. in Bay Area on nutrition, stress and health radio, TV appearances; mem: American, Calif. Chiropractic Assns., Council of Women Chiropractors, Parker Chiro. Research Found.; bd. dirs. Berkeley Boosters Assoc., bd. dirs. Solan Ave. Merchants Assn.; rec: river rafting, skiing, scuba. Res: 7126 Marlborough Terrace Berkeley 94705 Ofc: Solano Chiropractic 1738 Solano Ave Berkeley 94707

HANIFF, ABEL M., real estate broker; b. Apr. 6, 1947, Lautoka, Fiji Islands; s. Doctor M. and Habiban (Bibi) H.; m. Samshun, Dec. 18, 1973; children: Arifa, b. 1975, Waheeda, b. 1977, Riyaaz, b. 1979; edn: grad. Seattle Comm. Coll. 1970; Anthonys Real Estate Schs. 1972, 76; Calif. lic. real estate broker 1976-. Career: came to USA 1967, fulltime wk. as hotel busboy, bldg. maint., Seattle area during college yrs., 1967-70; real estate broker, 1976-; realtor/owner Red Carpet-Abel Haniff & Assoc., Oakland 1979--; dir. Red Carpet Council Systems; mem. Oakland Board of Realtors, MLS; Nat. Assn. Real Estate Brokers; Nat. Fedn. of Independent Bus.; Republican; Middle Eastern; rec: music (band player), sports. Res: 6624 Simson St Oakland 94605 Ofc: Red Carpet-Abel Haniff & Assoc., 3001 High St, Ste. B, Oakland 94619

HANKER, GREGORY JAMES, orthopaedic surgeon; b. Mar. 11, 1947, NYC; s. Theodore James and Gloria (O'Lear) H.; m. Mary Pat, Sept. 6, 1969; children: Corey, b. 1975, Kelly, b. 1981; edn: AB, cum laude, St. Louis Univ. 1969; MA, Univ. of Ariz., Dept. Math. 1971; MD, Case Western Reserve Univ. Sch. of Med. 1981. Career: grad. teaching assoc. Dept. Math., Univ. of Ariz. 1969-73; served to capt. USAF-R, 1969-, senior pilot/aircraft comdr., aeromedical evacuation of patients throughout Europe, Africa, Gr. Brit., and the Middle East, 1969-77; USAF Reserve tactical airlift pilot, 1977-81; resident in orthopaedic surgery, UC Los Angeles Medical Center, 1981--, instr. UCLA med. students in musculoskeletal disease; honors: Distinguished Graduate, and Air Tng. Cmd. Commanders Trophy, USAF, 1973; NSF grantee 1970; Pi Mu Epsilon (math.) 1968; USAF coll. scholarship 1966-69, med. sch. scholarship 1980-81; mem. AMA, USAF Reserve Assn., Alpha Delta Gamma; works: devel. USAF C9-A Life Support audio-visual tng. package; devel. flt. ops. computorized flight plan system; responsible for the yearly publication of USAF effectiveness reports for Squadron level; Republican; Catholic; rec: swim, running, racketball. Res: 9742 Swinton Ave Sepulveda 91343 Ofc: UCLA Medical Ctr, Div. Orthopaedics, 10833 LeConte Ave Los Angeles 90024

HANKS, MAJA, lawyer; b. Nov. 7, 1950, San Francisco; d. Bill and Sigrid (Seppala) Hanks; edn: BA, CalPolytech., Pomona 1972; JD, LaVerne Law Sch. 1977; stu. Univ. of Uppsala, Sweden; admitted to Calif. State Bar 1977. Career: law clk. Law Offices of Ronald B. Schwartz, Newport Bch. 1973-77; atty. Law Firm of Lewis, Rouda & Lewis, San Francisco 1977-78; atty. sole practitioner/pres. Maja Hanks, P.C., S.F. and Newport Bch., 1978--; lectr. Nat. Women in Law Conv. 1980, SFSU 1981, Calif. Trial Lawyers Assn. 1980, 81, 82, 83, Am. Trial Lawyers 1983; instr. trial advocacy, Hastings Coll. of Law 1981; Am. Trial Lawyers Assn. Nat. Coll. of Advocacy, Univ. of Nev. 1983; honors: one of ten most successful young women trial lawyers in USA, Time Mag. 1983; mem: S.F. Trial Lawyers Assn. (ofcr.), Calif. Trial Lawyers Assn. (bd. govs.), Am. Trial Lawyers Assn., Calif. Women Lawyers, Queens Bench S.F., Bay Area Lawyers for Individual Freedom; publs: arts. in law jours.; rec: scuba. Res: 137 Crescent Ave Sausalito 94965 Law Offices of Maja Hanks, Ivy Court, 368 Hayes St San Francisco 94102

HANLEY, JAMES ROBERT, real estate broker; b. May 23, 1935, Milwaukee, Wisc.; s. Lucian J. and Margaret E. (Romano); m. Robin Boone, Sept. 6, 1972; children: Christine, b. 1959, Scott, b. 1961, Valerie, b. 1963, Michael, b. 1964, Troy, b. 1969, Jamie, b. 1979; edn: BS, Utah State Univ. 1966; MS, Southern Ill. Univ. 1967; lifetime tchr credentials in Ill. (1974), Mich. (1968), Calif. (1970); Calif. lic. real estate broker (1980). Career: head coach/athletic dir. Milwaukee Track Club, 1960-63; grad. asst./track coach So. Ill. Univ. 1966-68; asst. prof. edn. Lake Superior STate Coll. 1968-70; English instr. Duarte (Ca.) H.S., 1970-73; editor Shape Up Mag., Woodland Hills 1973-74; dir. athletics/ Phys. Edn. Dept. chmn. Tinley Park (Ill.) H.S. 1-3-76; mgr. Century 21 West Covina, Ca. 1976-83; head track/x-c coach Covina H.S., 1977-81; broker/owner Century 21, Covina 1984--; freelance writer, publicist Senior Olympics 1971-74; resrch. analyst Weider Internat. 1972-74; lectr. PTA and sch. functions; weekly health & fitness columns in 6 newspapers in Ill., Calif.; awards: Achievement of Year 1966, Utah State Univ.; fellowship, So. Ill. Univ. 1967; Canadian Indoor Shot Put recordholder 1962; Cen. 21 Centurion Award 1983, Million Dollar Club, 1976-83; Wisconsin Athlete of the Year 1962; All-American Track, Milwaukee Track Club 1962. Mem: Nat. Edn. Assn., Nat. Assn. of Realtors, Covina Valley Bd. of Realtors, Nat. Coaches Assn., Nat. Assn. Athletic Dirs., Nat. Notary Assn., CofC, YMCA, PTA, Elks; publs: over 50 arts. in Parade Mag., All American Athlete, Mr. America, Esquire, Athletic Jour., Scholastic Coach, Shape Up, Retirement Living, Muscle Mag., others; Democrat; Christian; rec: writing, jogging, golf. Res: 1101 Wingate St Covina 91724 Ofc. Century 21, 961 N. Azusa Ave Covina 91723

HANLEY, ROBERT LEE, company president; b. Sept. 4, 1927, Des Moines, Iowa; s. John James and Mary Irene (Butler) H.; m. Barbara Jean Downs, Dec. 20, 1947; children: Michael R., b. 1951; Vicki J., b. 1955; edn: undergrad. Iowa St. Coll. 1946-49, BS, Drake Univ. 1951. Career: sales application engr Sterling Elec. Motors, Los Angeles 1951-59, sales trainer 1958-59, District Sales mgr., San Francisco 1959-63; founder/prin. R.L. Hanley & Asso. (sales rep. & consulting co.), Burlingame 1963-64; founder/pres./CEO Hanley-Brewton & Assocs. (sales rep., cons. in mech. and elec. power transmission), San Mateo 1964--; chmn. adv. bd. Sumitomo Machinery of Am. 1980-84; pres. adv. bd. Sterling Elec. Motors, Div. A.O. Smith, 1982; honors: top producing sales engr. in US 1957/8, top producing sales rep. 1982/3, Sterling Elec. Motors; rep. of year 1982, Sumitomo Mach. of Am.; mem: MANA, EMEA, AB & PTD; past pres. Little League, Belmont; Parks and Rec. Commn., Belmont 1968; Masons, Elks, Bayside Tennis Club, Lake Almanor Country Club; publs: tech. papers in trade jours. 1976, 79; mil: USNR; Republican; Episcopal; rec: computer, golf, fishing. Res: 2714 Belmont Cyn Rd Belmont 94002 Ofc: Hanley-Brewton & Associates, 257 N. Amphlett Blvd San Mateo 94401

HANN, GARY MARSHALL, lawyer; b. June 24, 1952, Los Angeles; s. Saul A. and Helen (Moray) H.; m. Joanne H., July 11, 1982; edn: JD, San Fernando Valley Coll. of Law 1980. Career: law clk. for Hillsinger and Costanzo, products liability unit, 1978, for Robert Moray, 1979; assoc. Law Offices Sydney Gordon, civil litigation unit, 1981; gen. ptnr. Kotler & Hann, Newhall currently; judge protem Newhall Municipal Ct.; dir. Whittier Human Rights Com. 1981; awards: Am. Jurisprudence (1980), Human Rights Com. (1974); mem: LA Trial Lawyers Assn., LA County bar Assn., Calif. Trial Lawyers Assn., Santa Clarita Valley Atty. Assn.; founding chmn. Santa Clarita Valley Battered Womens Shelter 1983; Common Cause, Sierra Club, Alliance for Survival, Comm. Hotline; coauthor: A Marital Dissolution Manual for Poor and Battered Women; Democrat; rec: swimming, scuba. Ofc: Kotler & Hann, 23942 Lyons Ave, Ste. 202, Newhall 91321

HANNA, MARY ELLEN MARTIN, real estate broker; b. Jan. 21, 1932, Winner, S.Dak.; d. Raymond Vincent and Clara Hazel (Talcott) Hughes; m. Donald Martin, 1949-77; children: Vicki, b. 1950, Debra, b. 1952, Michael, b. 1954, Gregg, b. 1957, Tamara, b. 1960; m. 2d. Richard G. Hanna, Jan. 14, 1979; edn: stu. De Anza Coll. 1976-79, Foothill Coll. 1982, Univ. of Phoenix 1984; Calif. lic. Cosmetology 1965, Real Estate Broker 1979, Subject Tchr. Credential 1982. Career: hairdresser Reflections of Beauty, Mt. View; owner Mary Martins Coiffures, Sunnyvale, Hair-O-Scope Beauty Salon, Mt. View; sales assoc.

Van Vleck Realtors, Sunnyvale, Condominium Splsts., Sunnyvale; broker assoc. J.M. Daley & Assocs., Palo Alto; currently v.p./branch mgr. Cornish & Carey Realtors, Cupertino; mng. gen. ptnr. MMH Investments, a lmtd. ptnrshp.; tchr. adult edn. courses, Mt. View, Los Altos; mem: Nat., and Calif. Assn. of Realtors; San Jose, and Sunnyvale Boards of Realtors; Internat. Order of Rainbow for Girls, Mothers Club (pres. Fremont, Ca. 1966, 68), Girl Scouts ldr. 1959-63; Republican; Rel. Sci.; rec: travel, cooking. Res: 110 Woodleaf Way, Mountain View 94040 Ofc: Cornish & Carey, 19960 Stevens Creek Blvd Cupertino 95014

HANNUM, STEPHEN BURGE, mortician; b. June 17, 1955, New London, Conn.; s. Arthur and Patricia (Burge) H.; m. RoseMarie Krumnow, June 27, 1981; edn: Mortuary Sci., Cypress Coll. 1981; San Diego City Coll. 1975-77; CSU San Diego 1977-77. Career: embalmer, Lewis Colonial/Benbough Mortuary, San Diego 1981, arranger, dir. 1982--; arranger, dir., embalmer Erickson-Anderson Mortuary, La Mesa 1981, grief counselor Ericson-Anderson Mortuary, Nov. 1981--; mgr. El Cajon Mortuary 1983--; mem: San Diego County Funeral Dirs. Assn., Masons, Shriners (Al Bahr Shrine Pipe Band drum major/ pres. 1982), Scottish Rite Bodies; Democrat; So. Baptist; rc: hiking, camping, photog. Res: 5103 E. Falls View Dr San Diego 92115 Ofc: Erickson-Anderson Mortuary, 8390 Allison Ave La Mesa 92041 El Cajon Mortuary, 624 El Cajon Blvd. El Cajon 92020

HANOVER, NORMAN L., lawyer; b. Dec. 23, 1936, Chgo.; s. Harold and Esther (Silverberg) H.; m. Mary Lou, Mar. 28, 1982; children: Frederick, b. 1962; Matthew, b. 1964; Marci, b. 1966; Cammie Weber, b. 1955; Sherry Berz, b. 1958; Gary Berz, b. 1960; Lenny Berz, b. 1962; edn: JD, Loyola Univ. 1960. Career: law practice, San Bernardino; bd. dirs. YMCA; advisor S.B. Co. Medical Assistants Assn.; Operating Receiver/Trustee, Federal Bankruptcy Ct.; Superior Ct. Receiver, S.B. & Riv. Co.; judge protem Domestic Rels. Dept.; commnr. protem Municipal Ct. and Small Claims; chmn. budget com. S.B. Co. Unified Sch. Dist.; mem. State Bar of Calif. (chmn. Local Adminstrn. Com. Dist. 4 1973-74; mem. Bankruptcy Law Adv. Com., Calif. Bd. of Legal Splzn.), Am. Bar Assn., Calif. Trial Lawyers Assn.; Jewish; rec: sports. Res: 3152 Parkside San Bernardino 92404 Ofc: 141 No. Arrowhead, Ste. 5, San Bernardino 92408

HANSEN, KATHRYN G., products distributor; b. Nov. 5, 1908, Chgo.; d. Edmund M. and Margaret Jo (O'Donnell) Gibbon; tching. cert. Chgo. Tchrs. Coll. 1934; B.Sc., edn., DePaul Univ. 1942; M.Ed., Loyola Univ. 1946; doctoral stu. Univ. Chgo. 1965-66; grad. stu. George Wms. Coll., Art Inst. Chgo., Bowling Green Univ.; m. Ralph Ingram Hansen, Aug. 15, 1951. Career: tchr. English for Adults, Chgo. Bd. Edn. 1947-58, tchr. and art coord. Chgo. Bd. Edn., 1965-69, dir. Project Family Life, Chgo. 1956-69; founder Chgo. Edn. News, 1962; originator, lectr. TV pgm. Brush-Up-On-Art (closed circuit TV, Laguna Hills 1972-73); ind. distbr. Shaklee Food Products 1973-77; supr. Everliving Products Aloe Vera, 1980--; writer/reporter City News Service, Cinc., Oh.; freelance writer, 1st 5 yrs churches Laguna Hills, Leisure World; currently writing book of poetry; poems pub.: New Voices in Amer. Poetry (1979), Acad. of Poets, Poet Mag., Internat. Poet Society (World); mem. National Council Sr. Citizens (secty. local chpt. 1983); awards: cert. Newspaper Inst. Amer., NY 1982; So. Calif. Bdcstg. KGER Radio (Childrens Safety Campaign 1981-82);recipient NEA hon. dinners, engraved gold locket, Ch. Women United (1975), num. ribbons for art exhibs.; mem. Pres. Task Force to dedicate Am. flag in Capitol Rotunda for K.G. Hansen 1982; elected v.p. Court 2000 St. Nicholas Catholic Daughters; ecumenical rep. Archdiocese of L.A. Roman Cath. Ch. 1973-75; cons. Women Aglow Calif.; mem: AAUW, Internat. Platform Assn., Ch. Women United, Laguna Hills Religious Council, Laguna Hills Research Com., NEA (life), founder Delta Kappa Gamma Cook Co. Coord. Council, (life) Chgo. Art Inst.; Republican; Catholic; rec: art, writing. Res: 2240-0 Via Puerta Laguna Hills 92653

HANSEN, NANCY MARIAN, real estate broker; b. Aug. 3, 1955, Watsonville; d. Everett Earl and Marian Elizabeth (Bradley) H.; edn: Cabrillo Coll. 1973-77; Calif. lic. Real Estate Broker 1980. Career: real estate sales agt. 1977-79; broker/ptnr. Watsonville Properties, 1980--; spkr., The R.E. Field, Monte Vista and Watsonville High Schs. 1982; mem. Watsonville Bd. of Realtors 1977- (dir. 1983, sec. treas. 1984; MLS chpsn. 1983); jDemocrat; Catholic; rec: swimming, cooking, bowling. Res: 267 Hames Rd Watsonville 95076 Ofc: Watsonville Properties, 30-B East 5th St. Watsonville 95076

HANSON, DIANA LEE, clinical social worker; b. July 17, 1942, Glendale; d. Paul and Orva (Cooper) Peck; children: Brett, b. 1968, Darrick, b. 1969; edn: AA, Los Angeles Valley Coll. 1972; BA, CSU Northridge 1975; MSW, USC 1978; PhD Cand., Cambridge Grad. Sch. Psychology 1982-83; LCSW, Calif. 1981. Career: student counselor LA County Probation Dept. 1971-72; psychiatric soc. wkr. intern Camarillo St. Hosp. 19347-76; med. soc. wk. intern LA/USC Med. Ctr., 1976-77; clin. soc. wkr. Metropolitan St. Hosp. 1978; Casewk. supr. National Found. for Treatment of Emotionally Handicapped 1978-79; psychiat. soc. wkr. Gateways Hosp. and Mental Health Ctr. 1979-81; Lic. Clin. Soc. Wkr., Private Practice, Los Angeles 1981--; dir. counseling pgm. Ocean Park Comm. Ctr., Santa Monica 1982-83; asst. clin. prof. USC, 1983-; guest lectr. CSU Northridge, Pub. Hlth. Dept. 1981-82; conducted tng. in State Dept. of Pub. Soc. Svcs. Cultural Awareness Pgm. on Empathy and Working with Minority Clients, 1982; guest lectr. UCLA Sch. of Soc. Wk., 1982; cons. Alcoholism Ctr. for Women 1981-; mem. Calif. Womens Commn. on Alcoholism 1982-83; adv. com. Gay and Lesbian Comm. Svcs. Ctr. LA, 1982-83; mem: Nat. Assn. of Soc. Wkrs., Gay and Lesbian Academic Union (co-ch. LA 1979, exec. com. Nat. Bd. Dirs. 1980-83), Soc. for Clin. Soc. Wkrs.; publs:

presentor, NASW Symp. 1981, Calif. Womens Commn. on Alcoholism 1982; Democrat; rec: backpacking. Address: 3215 Isabel Dr Los Angeles 90065

HANTOS, PETER, computer engineer; b. Apr. 14, 1949, Budapest, Hungary; s. Andor and Terry (Graf) H.; edn: MS, Tech. Univ. of Budapest 1973, PhD, 1980. Career: asst. prof. and mgr. Minicomputer Center, Dept. of Automation, Tech. Univ. of Budapest 1974-79; vis. asst. prof. Dept. of Electrical and Computer Engring./Sci., UC Santa Barbara 1979-80, 1981-2; senior systems pgmmr. Inst. for Coord. of Computer Techniques, Budapest 1980; software engr. Spacelabs Inc., Los Angeles 1982-84; cons. mem. Pgmmg. Staff, Xerox Corp., El Segundo 1984--; senior mem. IEEE; publs: 30 papers, tech. reports and presentations in field; rec: literature. Res: 8570 Hollywood Blvd Los Angeles 90069 Ofc: Xerox Corp., OSD, (N1-07) 701 S. Aviation, El Segundo 90245

HARBERT, WILLIAM JAMES, general contractor; b. May 25, 1911, Greeley, Nebr.; s. James William and Myrtle (Butcher) H.; m. Dorothy J. Moore, Mar. 4, 1933; 1 dau. Diane, b. 1936. Career: refinery-research dept. Union Oil Co., Los Angeles 1934-69; gen. contractor (custom homes, golf course, club house, med. bldgs., restaurants, etc.) 1946-63; semi-ret.; gen. contracting cons. So. Heating & A/C Co., Long Beach; mem: Long Beach Petroleum Club; Kiwanis Club, Uptown Long Beach; Long Beach 20-30 Club; YMCA (Camp Oaks Bd. Mgmt. Exec. Com.); works: aided in devel., constrn. & maint. Long Beach Girl Scouts Camp, Skyland Ranch, Idlywild; devel., constrn., maint. Long Beach Boy Scout Camp Tahquitz; Republican; Christian; rec: painting oil portraits, growing orchids & cymbidiums. Res: 16222 Monterey Ln, Apt. 345, Huntington Beach 92649

HARBISON, STEPHEN FRANKLIN, lawyer; b. Dec. 28, 1943, Santa Monica; s. Edward Franklin and Gertrude Stockton Deacon (Blakney) H.; m. Mary Lou Kohrman, Sept. 3, 1966; children: Mark, b. 1967; William, b. 1970; edn: AB, Stanford Univ. 1965; LLB, 1968; admitted to Calif. State Bar 1969. Career: assoc. atty. Flint & MacKay, Los Angeles 1969-72; partner Argue, Freston, Pearson, Harbison & Myers, Los Angeles 1972--; mem: Los Angeles, Calif. & Am. Bar Assns.; Assn. of Bus. Trial Lawyers; Jonathan Club; L.A. Jr. CofC (Art Found.); L.A. City Com. on Automotive Repair Facilities; Carmel Bach Festival; Nat. Methodist Found. for Christian Higher Edn.; L.A. Master Chorale Assn.; Stanford Law Soc. of So. Calif.; Stanford Club of L.A. Co.; Republican; Methodist; rec: racketball, tennis, antique cars. Res: 1130 Georgina Ave Santa Monica 90402 Ofc: Argue, Freston, Pearson, Harbison & Myers, 626 Wilshire Blvd, Ste 1000, Los Angeles 90017

HARDIE, MARION, family therapist; b. Dec. 17, 1929, Modesto; d. R. Keith and Dorothy Mildred (Williams) Hardie; m. H. Wayne Clay, July 22, 1950; children: Vicki Lorraine, b. 1954, Caryl Jean, b. 1961, H. Wayne, Jr. b. 1963, Patricia Anne, b. 1968; m. 2d. Mendel H. Lieberman, June 3, 1973; edn: BA, elem. ed., San Francisco St. Univ. 1957; MA, Acad. of Arts & Humanities, 1980; Calif. Tchr. Credentials (life): Gen. Elem., Std., Adult (psych., family living), Basic Pupil Personnel and Supervn., Splst. Learning Handicapped, Calif. Comm. Colls. (psych., counseling); Calif. lic. MFCC Marriage Family Child Counselor 1980. Career: tchr. Turlock (Ca.) Unified Sch. Dist. 1949-50, 51-2, S. San Francisco USD 1957-60, Oak Grove Sch. Dist., San Jose 1970--: currently tchr. primary educationally handicapped 1977--; counselor pvt. practice, 1973--; instr. American Acad. of Family Studies, Scotts Valley 1980-; ldr. seminars in Transpersonal Psych. CSU San Jose 1975-76; spkr./workshops: Sunnyvale Adminstrs., S.J. Public Health Nurses, S.J. Childrens Ctr., Santa Clara Tchrs. Assn., Oak Ridge Elem. Tchrs., Brandaise Parents Gp., Palo Alto Parents without Ptnrs., AAUW, others; coauthor with Mendel H. Lieberman, Resolving Conflicts: Everybody Wins (Unity/Orenda Pubs. 1981); mem: Nat., Calif., South Bay Teachrs. Assns., Nat. Sex Forum, Internat. Transactnl. Anal. Assn., Assn. for Humanistic Psychol., Calif. Assn. Marriage and Family Therapists, Am. Assn. Marriage and Family Counselors, No. Calif. Hypnosis Assn.; Democrat; Humanist; rec: painting, graphics, knitting. Address: 13393 Sousa Ln Saratoga 95070

HARDIN, DENNIS RALPH, dentist; b. Oct. 25, 1941, Long Beach; s. Ralph Hartshorn and Dorothy Alice (Boby) H.; m. Mary-Ellen Foliart, May 29, 1977; children: Robb Dennis, b. 1980; Brooke-Ellen, b. 1982; edn: BS, CSU Northridge 1964; DDS, Univ. of the Pacific, S.F. 1969. Career: pvt. practice 1972-77; owner gp. practice 1977-80; v.p./ dental dir. Comm. Dental Svcs. 1980--; awards: Nat. Dental Hon. Soc. TKO 1969-; mem: Am. Dental Assn.; Calif. Dental Assn.; Am. Endodontic Soc.; Adv. Com. on Health Ins. to Calif. Senate 1983-; TKO Nat. Dental Hon. Sco.; OKU Dental Hon. Soc.; mil: lt. USN 1969-72, Calif. and Vietnam. Res: 1808 Paseo Del Mar Palos Verdes Estates 90274 Ofc: Community Dental Services, 2235 Sepulveda Blvd Torrance 90501

HARDIN, EUGENE, physician; b. Dec. 6, 1941, Jacksonville, Fla.; s. Moses Henry and Edith (Lee) H.; m. Jocelyn, Jan. 8, 1967; children: Jeffrey, b. 1970; Gregory, b. 1974; edn; BS, Fla. A & M Univ. 1964; MD, Univ. of So. Fla. 1977; internal med., King Med. Ctr. 1980; physician/ surgeon, Calif. 1978; internist King-Drew Ctr. 1980. Career: staff pharmacist VA Hosp., Palo Alto 1967-74; medic/ pharmacist, Ft. Hood, Tex., Long Bihn, Vietnam 1974-77; med. resident King-Drew Med. Cr. 1977-80; assoc. prof. CSU Dominguez Hills, part-time 1978-81; asst. prof. emergency med. King-Drew Med. Ctr., Los Angeles 1980--; dir. Carson Med. Gp., Carson 1981--; awards: Most Outstanding Res., King-Drew Med. Ctr. 1980; Superior Perf. Awd., VA Hosp., Stanford 1974; AMA Phys. Recgn. Award 1982; mem: AMA; Am. Coll. of Physicians; Alpha Kappa Mu nat. hon. soc. 1964; Carson CofC; lectr., Headaches, Diferental Diagnosis, Harbor Gen. Hosp 1983; mil: Spec. E-5 US Army 1968-69; Foreign

Svc. Medal; Vietnam Svc. Medal; GCM; Democrat; Protestant; rec: tennis, fihing, jogging. Res: 1144 Oakfair Ln Harbor City 90710 Ofc: Carson Medical Group, 542 E Carson St Carson 90745

HARDING, JENNY LOUISE, construction industry financial executive; b. Apr. 10, 1946, Portland, Ore.; d. Charles C. and Lu Emma (Brown) Olberding; 1 dau., Julie Anne, b. 1980; edn: BS, acctg., CSU San Diego 1977; MBA, National Univ. 1980; Calif. lic. Real Estate Broker 1981. Career: corporate controller Snyder-Langston Inc. (comml. builder), Irvine 1982--; div. controller Genstar Devel. Inc. Broadmoor Homes Div., San Diego 1978-81; corp. controller Internat. Housing Systems Inc., San Diego 1977-78; gen. acctg. supr., then asst. controller Avco Comm. Developers Inc. San Diego 1967-74; mem. Nat. Assn. of Accountants, Nat. Assn. for Female Execs., Sierra Club; Democrat; Catholic. Res: 22992 Caminito Olivia Laguna Hills 92653 Ofc: Snyder-Langston, Inc. 17962 Cowan Irvine 92714

HARDING, JOHN BRIARD, JR., computer co. executive; b. Sept. 4, 1934, Boston, Mass.; s. John Briard and Mary (Chamberlin) H.; m. Patrizia Turco-Sillitti, Feb. 28, 1972; children: Stefano, b. 1973; William, b. 1976; Dumitilla, b. 1960; edn: BA, math., UCLA 1956. Career: sys. rep. IBM Corp. 1960; automation analyst, Allied Corp. 1961-62; pres. FACTS, Inc., 1962-63; pres. International Data Processing Corp. 1964-73; dir. of data proc. Westinghouse Electric Corp., Milan, Italy 1973-74; prof. Univ. of Petroleum & Minerals, Saudi, Arabia 1974-76; data sys. advr. Aramco 1976-80; pres. Steven P. Williams Assocs. 1980--; assoc. prof. Pratt Inst. of Tech. Grad. Sch. of Eng. 1968-69; expert cons. United Nations 1965-66; publs: La Programmazione Strutturata (Structured Programming), pub. CRM, Italy 1977; rec: tennis. Res: 304 S Elm Dr Beverly Hills 90212 Ofc: Steven P.Williams Assoc., 8530 Wilshire Blvd, Ste 309, Beverly Hills 90211

HARDY, ANNA GLORIA, psychotherapist; b. Nov. 25, 1929, Teaneck, NJ; d. Sardo Joseph and Lillian (Cuccinotta) Gentiluomo; m. Robert A. Hardy, Jr. May 3, 1953; children: Lisa, b. 1955, Robert, b. 1957, Steven, b. 1961; edn: MA psych., Univ. of Laverne, 1970; MA psych., Pepperdine Univ. 1982; lic: RN, State of NY (1951-), Calif. (1958-); Sch. Audiometrist, Calif. 1976, Sch. Nurse Service cred. (life) 1980, MFCC (Marriage, Family, Child Counselor) 1983. Career: operating rm. nurse Rockville (NY) Minor Surg., 1951-52; pediatric ofc. nrs. Dr. D. Berliner, Hewlett, NY 1953-54; gen. staff nrs. Pomona (Ca.) Valley Comm. Hosp., 1959-60; sch. nrs. Ontario-Montclair Sch. Dist., 1970-72; Newport-Mesa Unified Sch. Dist., Newport Bch. 1974-81; pvt. practice MFCC, Newport Beach 1983--; mem: Orange Co. Sch. Nrs. Orgn. 1976-81; Nat. Assn. of Sch. Nurses 1976-81; Psi Chi; Calif. Assn. Marriage and Family Therapists, vol. first-aid instr., CPR instr. Red Cross 1977-81, vol. counselor/ therapist Laguna Bch. Free Clinic 1982-; Republican; Catholic; rec: tennis, gardening. Address: Ann Hardy, RN, MFCC, 901 Aleppo St Newport Beach 92660

HARGIS MILLIGAN, CARINA MARCIA, social worker; b. May 31, 1955, Chgo.; d. Ira Clair and Geraldine Marie (Kelley) Hargis; m. Dennis Milligan, Aug. 22, 1981; edn: BS, honors, Univ. of Central Ark. 1977; MS, CSU Fullerton 1980; MFCC, Marriage, Family & Child Counselor, Calif. 1982; Sch. Psychologist, CSUF 1981; Pupil Personnel Svcs., CSUF 1980. Career: counselor Fullerton Union H.S. Dist., Fullerton 1977-78; counselor, Centralia Sch. Dist., Buena Park 1978-80; counselor Cornelia Connelly H.S., Anaheim 1980-82; tchr. Long Beach Unified Sch. Dist. Long Beach 1982-83; marriage, family & child counselor, pvt. practice, Buena Park 1983--; tchg. cons. & assessing svcs.; mem: Am. & Calif. Presonnel & Guidance Assns.; Am. Psychological Assn.; Calif. Assn. of Marriage Family Therapists; Catholic; rec: swimming, bicycling, yoga. Res: 8209 Santa Inez Way Buena Park 90620 Ofc: Social Services Agency, 501 N Brookhurst, Ste 200, Anaheim 92801

HARKLESS, CATHERINE GALE, lawyer; b. Wooster, Ohio; d. Robert Oliver and Iota Patricia (Stauffer) Ebert; m. James Harkless, May 22, 1971; children: Michael James, b. 1974; Kelley Christine, b. 1976; edn: BA, Denison Univ. 1973; grad., cum laude, Aurora Coll. 1972; JD, magna cum laude, Calif. Western Sch. of Law 1980; amitted to practice, Calif. 1980. Career: law clerk Jove (Defense lawyer); atty. Treitler & Assoc., San Diego 1980--; spkr. law rel. seminars; honors: Am. Jurisprudence Awards, Trusts & Wills 1979, Remedies 1980; mem: Calif. & San Diego Co. Bar Assns.; Trial Lawyers Assn.; Childrens Hosp. Aux.; Republican; Protestant; rec: flying, sports. Res: 175 Alameda Blvd Coronado 92118 Ofc: Treitler & Assoc., 8334 Clairemont Mesa Blvd, Ste 207, San Diego 92111

HARLEY, ROBISON DOOLING, JR., lawyer; b. July 6, 1946, Ancon (C.Z.) Panama; s. Robison Dooling and Loyde Hazel (Gouchenauer) Harley; m. Suzanne P. Bendel, Aug. 8, 1975; children: Arianne Erin, b. 1980, Lauren Loyde, b. 1982; edn: BA, Brown Univ. 1968; JD, Temple Univ. 1971; LLM (criminal law), Univ. of San Diego 1982; cert. criminal law splst. Calif. State Bar (1981); admitted to US Supreme Ct., US Ct. of Mil. Appeals, various Federal Dist. and Circuit Cts. throughout the US; Certified Criminal Trial Advocate, Nat. Bd. Trial Advocates 1982, Career: judge advocate (trial counsel, def. counsel, mil. judge, asst. staff judge adv.) USMC, 1971-75; asst. agency dir. Safeco Title Insurance Co., Panorama City 1975-77; criminal defense atty. law firm of Cohen, Stokke & Davis, Santa Ana 1977--; instr. Orange Co. Coll. of Trial Advocacy; judge pro tem Orange Co. Municipal Cts.; mem: Am., Calif., Penna, NJ and Dist. Columbia Bar Assns.; Calif. Attys. for Criminal Justice, Calif. Pub. Defenders Assn., Nat. Assn. of Criminal Defense Lawyers, Orange Co. Bar Assn. (Judiciary Com., Adminstrn. of Justice Com., Criminal Law Sect.), O.C. Trial Lawyers Assn., Assn. of Trial Lawyers of Am., Calif. Trial

Lawyers; bd. dirs. Legal Aid Soc. of O.C.; mil: maj. USMC(R), cert. of congratulations, Commandant USMC, cert. of commendn., Comdg. General, USMC; Republican; Prot.; rec: sports, phys. fitness. Res: 18225 Bayberry Way Irvine 92715 Ofc: Cohen, Stokke & Davis, 540 N. Golden Cir, Ste. 300 , Santa Ana 92705

HARMATA, DONALD DAMIAN, lawyer; b. Mar. 3, 1950, Hopewell, Va.; s. John James and Rosalie Evangeline (Tomko) Harmata, Jr.; m. Georgiana Lougee, Aug. 19, 1972; edn: BA, Va. Polytechnic Inst. and State Univ. 1972; JD, Coll. of Wm. and Mary, 1975. Career: lawyer, pvt. civil practice, Sacramento 1978--; editor/pub. California Procurement Publs., Sacto. 1979-82; instr. CSU Sacramento, 1981-2; mem: State Bar of Calif. (exec. com. Public Law Sect. 1981-4), Gov's Small Business Advisory Com. (ch. State Pgms. and Procurement Com. 1981-2); Calif. State Legislature's Public Procurement Adv. Com. 1984; mil: capt. USAF, Judge Adv. Gen's Corps, Sacramento Air Logistics Ctr. 1975-79, AF Commend. Medal. Res: 4616 Jan Dr. Carmichael 95608 Ofc: 2110 21st St., Ste. 125, Sacramento 95818

HARMON, KATE PEARL (L), psychotherapist/school psychologist; b. Nov. 1, 1898, NYC; d. Jacob and Anna (Ruben) Lapin; m. Walter Harmon (dec.) Apr. 20, 1933; edn: dip. Savages Sch. for Health & Phys. edn., NYC 1923; BS, New York Univ. 1932, grad. wk. 1933; MA, Loyola Univ. (Los Angeles) 1964, stu. USC Law Sch. 1956, UCLA 1947-52, Univ. of Hawaii 1952; Calif. credentials: Psychologist, Physical Edn., General Sec. Edn., MFCC (Marriage, Family Child Counselor). Career: dir. phys. ed. (Junior, Senior, Adult) Oakland Pub. Schs. 1924-30; retail sales/mgmt. Marshall Field, Sears, Sally Frocks, Chgo.; personnel mgr. Federal Civil Service, L.A., 10 years; counselor LA Pub. Schs., sch. psychol. Hawthorne Sch. Dist.; lic. MFCC private practice; chief psychiat. soc. wkr. Child Guidance Clinic, Hawthorne 6 yrs.; mem: AAUW, L.W. Academians, Calif. Assn. MFCT, Nat. Assn. Retired Tchrs., Nat. Assn. Ret. Federal Employees (pres. LW 970); pres. Mutual No. 75 Leisure World 1978; pres. Wilshire Blvd. Temple Seniors; mil: cpl. Air Force WWII, GC; Democrat; Temple Judea, L.W. (first trustee, dir.); rec: drama, music. Res: 5517 Paseo Del Lago E. Apt 2, Laguna Hills 92653

HARNER, MARGARETE SCHLIEP, corporate broker; b. July 5, 1940, W. Berlin, W. Germany, nat. 1970; d. Max and Maria (Mueller) Schliep; m. Ray Harner, June 4, 1962, div. 1982; chidren: Koreen, b. 1963; Gabrielle, b. 1967; Colette, b. 1968; Muriel, b. 1969; edn: AA, Santa Monica City Coll. 1976; Fulbright Scholarship 1961-62; Calif. lic. R.E. Broker 1981. Career: real estate agt. Century 21 O'Donnell Assoc. 1975-82; asst. v.p. Blumenave Internat. Realty 1982-83, corp. broker 1983--; honors: Million Dollar Salespsn 1977; mem: Santa Monica Sister City Assn., German Am. Club of Santa Monica. Res: 639 Seventh St Santa Monica 90402 Ofc: Blumenave International Realty, Inc., 4337 Marina City Dr, Ste 549 E, Marina del Rey 90292

HARPER, LYNNE LESLIE, b. Nov. 26, 1930, Greenville, Miss.; d. Wm. Melvin and Mary Belle (Harris) H.; edn: BS, UC Los Angeles 1961; JD, Peoples Coll. of Law 1980. Admitted to Calif. State Bar 1980. Career: social wkr., supvr., deputy director, district dir. Los Angeles County Dept. Social Services, 1960-80, ret.; pvt. law practice, 1980--: extensive pro bono legal wk.; of counsel to non-profit corp. Commonground Wome Comm. Center LA; honors: recognition award, Black Employees Assn. of LA County 1979; mem. Calif. Bar Assn., Calif. Trial Lawyers Assn., LA Trial Lawyers Assn., Assn. of Trial Lawyers of Am., Calif. Women Lawyers Assn.; mem. NOW (Calif. State treas. 1974-76), ACLU, NAACP, Nat. Lawyers Guild; mil: sgt. WACs 1951-55; Democrat; rec: camping. Address: 1229 High Point St Los Angeles 90035

HARRELL, TOMMY FRANCIS, systems engineer; b. Mar. 25, 1943, Chgo.; s. Tommy F. and Margaret Cecelia (McDonald) H.; m. Barbara Thomas, Nov. 13, 1971; 1 dau. Vicki, b. 1972; edn: BS in EE, Tri-State Coll. 1965; MA in bus. ad., Highlands Univ. 1971. Career: engr. in satellite navigation and data acquisition for ocean resrch., Westinghouse Elec. Ocean Resrch and Engrg Labs, Annapolis, Md. 1965-67; engr. in digital interface design, Apollo Manned Space Flt. Bendix Field Engr., Beltsville, Md. 1968; sales engr. Honeywell Sales & Mktg. Careers Inst., Framingham, Mass. 1969-70; cons. engr. clients Western Elec., Gould Ocean Research, Ohio Nuclear 1971-76; systems analyst in mfg. systems, Sprague Elec., Lansing, N.C. 1977-80, Transamerica Delaval, Oakland 1981--; mem: Am. Prodn. and Inventory Control Soc. (founding pres. Mission Peak chpt., Fremont 1983); Robotics Soc. of Am.; Aircraft Owners and Pilots Assn.; forming users group Expert Systems on micro-computers. Works: devel. seagoing Data Acquisition System on exhib. Expo 67 in Montreal, Can.; devel. for Transam. Delaval an automated and integrated Purchasing, Chg Notice and Request for Quote System 1981-3; devel. (copyrighted) barcoding sys. for small businesses (using IBM PC) for meeting govt. Logmar requirements; Republican; rec: Japanese Joinery, stockmkt. Res: 2485 Shoreline Dr #204, Alameda 94501 Ofc: Transamerica Delaval, 550 85th Ave Oakland 94621

HARRINGTON, DONALD TIMMONDS, computer programmer/analyst; b. Feb. 11, 1957, Detroit, Mich.; s. Daniel Bolton and Betty Jane (Childs) H.; m. Lauren Peterson, June 21, 1981; stu. De Anza Coll. Career: pgmmr. Shugart Assoc. 1979-80; contractor Qume Corp., San Jose 1980-81; pgmmr./analyst Smith Kline Instr., Sunnyvale 1981-83; analyst Zilog Inc., Campbell 1983--. Musician: Santa Clara Co. Honor Band 1972, America's Youth in Concert Europe Tour 1972, 1st bass clarinet, CBDA Honor Band 1975; Democrat; Lutheran; rc: golf, philately, woodwkg. Res: 1473 Saturn Ct. Milpitas Ofc: Zilog Inc. 1315 Dell Ave Campbell 95008

HARRINGTON, EVERETT LAWRENCE, sales executive; b. Jan. 15, 1950, Durham, N.C.; s. Eugene Arthur and Margie Henrietta (Gunn) H.; m. Denise Little, Aug. 1971; children: Everett, Jr. b. 1974, Krestin, b. 1977; edn: Assoc. (EE), United Electronics Inst. 1970; BS, Univ. of S.F. 1978. Career: apprentice Gen. Elec. Model Shop, Louisville, Ky. 1968-71; electronic warfare tech. USN, aboard ship, outside contracts coordinator, Naval Air Sta., Alameda, Ca. 1971-79; sales engr. GE Co., Oakland 1979-80; facilities mgr. U.S. Instrument Rentals (subs. of U.S. Leasing), San Mateo 1980-81, regl. sales mgr. USIR 1981--; mem. Am. Mgmt. Assn., Precision Measurement Soc.; awards: Million Dollar Club, U.S. Leasing, 1981, 82, Petty Ofcr. of the Month 1972 USS Coral Sea, P.O. of the Yr. 1977 NAS Alameda; mil: E6 USN 1971-79, GCM, Nat. Defense; Republican; Baptist; rec: coaching little league sports, jogging. Res: 5257 Bayview Dr Richmond 94804 Ofc: US Instrument Rentals 700 S. Claremont St, Ste 220, San Mateo 94402

HARRINGTON, GEORGE GARY, educator; b. Mar. 3, 1943, Los Angeles; s. George Owen and Madeline Agnes (Eyraud); m. Nancy R. Johnson, May 31, 1969; edn: BA, econ., CSU Northridge 1965; MA, econ., UC Riverside 1967; MS, sch. adm., CSU Hayward 1977; Calif. Credentials: Supervision, Elem., Secondary Tchr., and Comm. College Instr. Career: tchr. Livermore Valley Unified Sch. Dist., 1975-81, math dept. ch. Junction Middle Sch. 1975-76; elemtary principal Mt. Pleasant Sch. District, San Jose 1981--; orgnzr. state exemplary math. pgm.; coach sch. chess club/team 1970-76, girls basketball and softball 1974; recipient Outstanding Principal award, Mt. Pleasant Sch. staff 1983; mem. Phi Delta Kappa (chpt. pres. 1983), Livermore Educators Assn. (negotiation team ch.1975), Northridge JC, Pleasanton Population Growth Com.; publs: Modified Lodestar Individualized Upgraded Math Pgm. (1976); Christian; rec: travel, computers, chess, shogi. Res: 3446 Bordeaux Pl Pleasanton 94566 Ofc: Valle Vista School 2400 Flint Ave San Jose 95148

HARRINGTON, HARLAND JAMES, quality professional/quality engineering executive; b. Jan. 16, 1929, Johnson City, NY; s. Frank O. and Carri May (Sanders) H.; m. Marguerite Holtzmaster 1965; 1 son, James Steven, b. 1968; edn: AA, electronics, Broom Tech. Coll. 1953; BS gen. engring., Univ. of Beverly Hills 1978, MBA, 1980; MS Quality Systems, Columbia Pacific Univ. 1981, PhD Quality Engring., 1982. Career: apprentice tool maker, IBM, 1947-, then worked in Devel. Engring.; Mfg. Engring., Prod. Engring. depts.; cons. on reliability to IBM, San Jose (temporary assignment) 1963; var. mgmt. promotions to current position, Quality Profl./project mgr., IBM; honors: Benjamin Lubelsky Award as outstanding QC Profl. in Calif., 1978; ASQC Adminstrv. Applications Silver Ann. Award as outstanding contrib. to QC in Mgmt. Sci. field over past 25 years, 1980; IBM Awards Banquet, recognition for service in field of quality, 1981; John Delbert Award for outstanding contbns. to field of mgmt., Internat. Mgmt. Council, 1982. Mem: ASQC (chmn. Internat. Chpt., dir.), Internat. Mgmt. Council (v.p., dir.); chmn. adv. com. on Quality Reliability, CSU San Jose; chmn. adv. com. Mgmt. Studies, San Jose City Coll., West Valley Coll.; num. articles and tech. publs., USA and internat.; frequent speaker worldwide; mil: seaman 1/c USNR 1947-55; rec: fishing. Res: 16080 Camino Del Cerro Los Gatos 95030 Ofc: IBM, 5600 Cottle Rd San Jose 95193

HARRINGTON, ROGER ELI, engineer, manufacturer, distributor; b. Apr. 10, 1917, New Haven, Conn.; s. Fred Eli and Hannah (Steele) H.; m. Phyllis S. (dec.), Feb. 14, 1941; children: Bruce, b. 1944, Ronald, b. 1947, Douglas, b. 1950, Keith (dec), b. 1955; edn: BA, Wesleyan Univ. 1939. Career: mechanical contracting until 1966; indsl. security field, 1966--; devel. an extreme angle Surveillance Camera now used extensively by savings and loan offices, banks in Calif., Ariz., Hawaii; owner CAM-Wide Camera (distbn. co.); maj. stockholder/dir. Optics of Kansas (mfg.); active in youth-oriented community groups; Republican; Prot. Address: 4200 Virginia Vista Long Beach 90807

HARRIS, EARL ELEZAR, writer, entrepreneur; b. Nov. 23, 1889, Pueblo, Colo.; s. Frederick William and Lizzie Alice (Bottorff) H.; m. Maybelle Urch, 1910, dec. 1969; children: Maybelle Frances, Elmer Earl, Muriel Alice, Doris Alta, Ivan Arnold, Kenneth Lloyd, Zelma Louis; m. 2d. Alta Austin, 1975; edn: Oakland Polytech. 1910; Nat. Salesmens Inst., Chgo. 1921; Newspaper Inst. of Am. 1975. Career: conductor Key System, Okla. 1912-16; family ranch, Silt, Colo. 1917-19; partner Harris Hdw. & Implement Co. 1932-41; sales rep. var. small cos. 1925-31; traveling sales rep., Colo. Springs Music Co. 1932-41; field dir./ asst. to Pacific area supvr. Am. Red Cross, Overseas 1942-46; traveling sales rep. H.T. Bennet Music Co., Santa Brabara 1946-48; owner Harris Music Co., Arroyo Grande 1949-52; pres. Mid-State Enterprise Energizers, Inc. 1983--; author 3 books: Pioneer Memories, Sketches of One Mans Life, How Red Cross Helped; free lance writer, newspaper, mags., periodicals; awards: 5th pl. nat. writing contest, Rocky Mountain Writers Guild, Inc. 1982; mem: 100F Lodge (past Grand master); Better Bus. orgns.; Santa Barbara Co. Sr. Citizens gps.; works: invented first dirt mover, pat. 1907; crossed the prairie twice by Prairie Schooner as a youngster; Republican (Pres. Task Force); Christian Sci. Res: 4844 Hernandez Dr Guadalupe 93434

HARRIS, ELIHU MASON, lawyer, state official; b. Aug. 15, 1947, Los Angeles; s. Elihu M. and Frances M. (Cunningham) H.; m. Kathy Neal, Aug. 14, 1982; edn; BA, CSU Hayward 1968; MA, UC Berkeley 1969; JD, UC Davis 1972; Calif. lic. real estate broker. Career: admin. asst. to Assemblyman John Mills 1972-74; asst. to Congresswoman Yvonne Burke 1974-75; exec. dir. National Bar Assn. 1975-77; currently, atty. Harris, Alexander, Burris & Culver; Democrat; Methodist. Ofc: 364 14th St Oakland 94612

HARRIS, LAWRENCE L., YMCA executive; b. Sept. 11, 1943, Santa Monica; s. Herman David and Sadie (Helbling) H.; m. Deborah Gould, Feb. 3, 1980;

edn: BA, CSU Long Beach 1972; Coll. of the Desert 1962-64. Career: pgm. dir. YMCA, downtown Long Beach 1972-74; recreation ldr. L.A. City Parks & Recreation Dept. 1975-78; pgm. dir. YMCA, Palisades- Malibu 1978-79; site supvr. Nat. Park Svc., Santa Monica Mountains N.R.A. 1980; The Foothill Family YMCA, Pasadena, pgm. dir. 1980, YMCA Senior Dir. (cert. Nat. Council of YMCAs, 1982), assoc. exec. dir. 1982; exec. dir. 1983--; mem. Internat. World Svc. Com.; Profl. Resource in Day Care & Sports Pgmmg. for the YMCA Assn.; honors: one of twelve senior dirs. in So. Calif. selected for the exec. devel. pgm. 1983; mem: Assn. of Profl. Dirs. of YMCAs; Kiwanis Club, Pasadena (Key Club); Com. mem. for Boys & Girls); Bus. Alliance with Youth Proj. of Pasadena; works: redesigned & organized after sch. day care pgm., sports pgms. & front ofc. sys. for YMCA 1981-82; mil: hosp. corpsman 3/ c USN 1966-70, Vietnam Svc., Bronze Star; Pres. Unit Citation; Vietnam Campaign; Democrat; Jewish; rec: Pasadena historical research, house restoration. Res: 1078 N Michigan Ave Pasadena 91104 Ofc: Foothill YMCA, 2750 New York Dr Pasadena 91107

HARRIS, LEONARD GEORGE, construction co. executive; b. Aug. 25, 1936, Sydney, N.S.W., Australia; s. Bertrand Pierce and Dorothy (Fowler) H.; m. Mavis Bridge, Aug. 30, 1958; children: Robert, b. 159; Max, b. 1963; edn: ME, honors, Sydney Univ. of Tech. 1957; bus. admin. I.C.S., Scranton, Pa. 1973. Career: ships surveyor Naval Dockyards, Sydney, Australia 1954-57; estimator/ project engr. Internat. Combustion, Sydney, Aus. 1957-62; field constrn. engr. C.F. Braun & Co., Sydney 1963-65; constrn. supt. CF Braun & Co., Alhambra, Calif. 1966-72, constrn. mgr. 1972-79, pres./ gen mgr. C.F.Braun Constructors Inc., Alhambra 1980--, pres./ gen. mgr. World Wide Constrn. Ops.; bd. dirs. Nat. Contractors Assn.; v.chmn. Nat. Contractors Assn. Exec. Com.; Protestant; rec: racquetball, fishing, hunting. Res: 20752 Alicante Ln Huntington Beach 92646 Ofc: C F Braun Constructors Inc., 10005 Freemont Ave Alhambra 91802

HARRIS, MARION KIRK, civil engineer, Ret.; b. June 12, 1914, Sacramento, s. Marion Alva and Nettie (Ireland) Harris; AA, Sacramento Jr. Coll., 1934; BS, UC Berkeley, 1951. Career: Clair A. Hill & Assoc., Redding, CA, 1947-49, 51-55; Ruth & Going, Inc., San Jose, 1955-58; Mark Thomas & Co., San Jose, 1958-62; Calif.-Pacific Engrs., San Jose, 1962-66; Ruth & Going, Norton S. Curtis, San Jose, 1966-75; retired, 1975. Honors: BS, cum laude, UC Berkeley, 1951; Daniel W. Meade prize, UC Berkeley, 1950. Mem.: BPOE No. 1973; AWS; ACSM; AAAS; Tau Beta Pi; Chi Epsilon; Sigma Xi. Author: Civil Engring. (ASCE Journ.), June 1965, 'Planning & Anchoring 12 Miles of Big Pipe,'; holder of five patents in automotive steam power, 1970-80. Mil.: RT 1/C, USNR, 1944-46. Republican. Protestant. Rec.: old car renovation. Res.: 4755 Dolores Ave., P.O. Box 2017, Atascadero 93423.

HARRIS, MICHAEL EARL, health care administrator; b. Aug. 16, 1955, Chgo.; s. Earl Jr. and Mattie (Prince) H.; m. Lynnell Victoria Bennett, Feb. 12, 1976; edn: BS, USC 1977; MS, CSU Los Angeles 1980. Career: asst. dir. So. Calif. Perinatal Dispatch Ctr., Huntington Meml. Hosp., Pasadena 1976-79; asst. dir. personnel Maxicare Health Plans, Inc., Hawthorne 1980-81; dir. of personnel Hawthorne Comm. Med. Gp., Inc., Hawthorne 1980-81; patient care adminstr. Northridge Med. Gp., Northridge 1982--; instr. in health care admin., degree pgm. Univ. of LaVerne; awards: Calif. Scholarship Fedn. life mem.; UCLA Alumni Scholar; mem: Personnel & Indsl. Rels. Assn.; Am. Mgmt. Assn.; Med. Gp. Mgmt. Assn.; Democrat; Baptist; rec: coin collecting. Res: 1603 Helmick Street Carson 90746 Ofc: Northridge Medical Group, 8530 Reseda Blvd, Administrv. Ofc., Northridge 19324

HARRIS, NORMA MARANI, welding co. president; b. July 1, 1925, Weed; d. Pietro and Matilde (Sbarbaro) Marani; grad. McClatchy H.S. 1943; m. Kent Harris, Oct. 6, 1946; children: Joanne, b. 1947, Kathleen, b. 1950, Marilee, b. 1954, Kent, b. 1962. Career: personnel bd. 1943-46, supr. mail room 1946-70, teacher aide Colfax Grammar Sch., Placer Hills Sch., Placer H.S., 1970-73; bookkeeper, counter clerk, 1973, pres. Harris Wldg. Inc., Citrus Hts. 1974--; mem. Placer H.S. Welding Adv. Bd. 1976-; Metals Adv. Bd., Sierra Coll. 1981-83; adv. dir. Alex Brown Bank 1979-82; exec. bd. Com. to Preserve the Courthouse for the Courts; mem: Placer County Contractors Assn. (1st Woman Dir.; Scholarship chpsn.); Auburn Area CofC (pres. 1982); Golden Chain Council (pres. 1982-83); Sierra Coll. Found. Bd. (pres. 1976-83); Order Sons of Italy in Am. (Venerable 1st Woman, Roseville Lodge 1981-83); Bus. & Profl. Womens (Woman of Achievment 1982); Soroptimist Intl. of Auburn (2d v.p. 1983); American Legion Aux.; Calif. Native Daughter; Auburn Merchants Council; Gold Country Fair Booster; Applegate Civic Ctr., past. dir. 20th District Agri. Fair Auburn; Citrus Hts. CofC; Roseville CofC; orgnzr. Applegate Well Baby Clinic 1958-68; Colfax Parents Club, Placer Hills PTA; Republican; Catholic (choir); rec: jogging, swim, poetry. Res: POB 238 Applegate 95703 Ofc: Harris Welding Inc. 8475 Auburn Blvd Citrus Hts 95610

HARRISON, BRIAN YORKE, stevedoring co. executive; b. Sept. 20, 1927, Port Talbot, South Wales, Britian, nat. 1959; s. Roland Yorke and Beatrice Irene (Richards) H.; m. Margaret Noreen Pickering, Oct. 12, 1954; 1 dau. Joyce Barbara, b. 1958; edn: 2nd Mate, Tech. Coll., Cardiff, Wales 1947, 1st Mate, 1951, Master, 1954; Master Mariner Unltd. lic., British Ministry of Transport 1954. Career: asst. port capt. Furness, Withy & Co., Los Angeles 1955-58; port capt. William J. Rountree & Co., L.A. 1958-64; Associated Banning Co. (acquired by Metropolitan Stevedore Co. 1967), stevedore supt. 1964-67; adminstrv. asst. 1973; v.p. 1980; exec. v.p. 1981; pres./chief exec. Metropolitan Stevedore Co. 1982--, mem. bd. dirs.; awards: Rotary & Boys Club of Am. Awds.; mem: Master Contracting Stevedore Assn.; Los Angeles Steamship Assn.; Propeller Club of US; Wilmington Rotary (past pres.); Boys Club of

Wilmington (past pres.); Episcopal Seamens Ctr. (past pres.); Los Angeles Harbor Masonic Lodge; Marine Square Club; Palos Verdes Golf Club; Virginia Country Club; Long Beach & Internat. City Club, Long Beach; mil: British Merchant Marines, Ministry of War Transport, WWII Svc.; Republican; Episcopal; rec: golf, nautical memorabilia, travel. Res: 7359 Via Lorado Rancho Palos Verdes 90274 Ofc: Metropolitan Stevedore Co., 211 Marine Ave Wilmington 90744

HARRISON, LEROY EUGENE, real estate broker; b. July 15, 1936, Portland, Ore.; s. Willard LeRoy and Dorthy Goldia (Kliensmith) H.; m. Virginia Ruth Mersberg, Dec. 20, 1981; children: Rodney, b. 1959; Cindy, b. 1961; edn: auto. svc. & maint. cert., Pacific Union Coll. 1956; AA, San Bernardino Valley Coll. 1958; R.E. cert., 1967; Calif. lic. R.E. Saleman 1964, R.E. Broker 1969. Career: real estate salesman 1964-69; owner/ broker San Bernardino Realty, San Bernardino 1970-71; broker Hangtown Realty, Placerville 1971-73; owner/ broker Harrison Realty, Camino 1973-82; owner/ broker Ranchland Realty, Stockton, Atascadero 1982-83; broker Arroyo Grade Realty, Arroyo Grande 1983; owner/ broker Beach & Country Properties, Arroyo Grande 1983--; honors: Million Dollar Salesman Awd., El Dorado Co. Bd. Realtors 1977; mem: Pismo Coast & Atascadero Bds. Realtors; Calif. & Nat. Assns. Realtors; Farm Land Inst.; Pollock Pines, Atascadero & Arroyo Grande CofC; works: builder of race engines 1968; Republican; Seventh Day Adventist; rec: modified & antique autos. Res: 571 Gularte Rd Arroyo Grande 93420 Ofc: Beach & Country Properties, 123 W Branch Arroyo Grande 93420

HARRISON, RAYMOND W., insurance co. executive; b. Sept. 13, 1950, Los Angeles; s. Raymond Willis and Mary Jean (Adcox) H.; m. Judith Love, Oct. 18, 1969; children: Jori Anne, b. 1977, Holli, b. 1979, Shellie, b. 1981; edn: Midwestern Baptist Coll. 1971-72; grad. (highest honors) Life Ins. Mktg. Inst. Purdue Univ. 1975-76; LUTCF (Life Underwriter Tng. Council Fellow), ChFc (Chartered Fin. Cons.), CLU (Chartered Life Underwriter), American Coll. Career: asst. mgmt. supermkt. 1966; life ins. underwriter Mutual Security Life, Sacramento 1972-, cons. to Home Office, regl. mgr. for No. Calif. 1980--; honors: Qual. Million Dollar Round Table (10), Career Builder Award; mem. Nat. Assn. of Life Underwriters, MDRT, General Agents & Mgrs. Conf., Sacto. Assn. of Life Underwriters (past bd.); youth wk. vol., Easter Seals, var. charities cpgns.; Republican; Calvary Baptist (Deacon, trustee); rec: pvt. pilot, photog., pub. spkg. Res: 911 Fawn Ct Roseville 95678 Ofc: Mutual Security Life, 1540 River Park Dr, Ste 110, Sacramento 95815

HARRY, HERBERT SYDNEY, II, oil co. executive; b. Mar. 9, 1925, Torrance; s. Herbert Sydney and Mary V. (Halpin) H.; m. Barbara Weigand, Jan. 17, 1944; children: Robin, b. 1945; Kimith, b. 1948; Herbert III, b. 1950; Michael, b. 1963; edn: BA, USC, 1950; Calif. lic real estate broker. Career: Union Oil Co. of Calif. 1950--; landman, Sactramento 1953, senior landman, Bakersfield 1955, Div. landman, 1957; asst. mgr. of Lands, Los Angeles 1963; mgr. of Lands 1967--; Dir: Dentalloy Inc., Calif. Offshore Operators Inc.; dir. L.A. Petroleum Club; dir. R.M. Pyles Boys Camp; honors: founding chmn. Wildcat Invitational. (1970-); Tenn. Squire 1977; Wildcat of the Yr. 1980; mem: Am. Assn. of Petroleum Landmen (dir. 1968-70; chmn. Wildcat Com. 1975); Pub. Lands Com. of Western Oil & Gas Assn.; Golfs Golden Circle; works: Acquisition of Lands With a City Address, Southwerter Legal Found., Mathew Bender & Co., 1965; mil: torpedoman 1/c USNR 1943-45, So. Pacific Camp.; Asiatic Camp.; Merit. Awd.; Republican; Catholic; rec; golf, swimming, spectator sports. Res: 225 S Lake Ave Pasadena 91101 Ofc: Union Oil Co. of Calif., Union Oil Center, Los Angeles 90017

HART, BETTY JANE, manufacturing and service co. executive; b. June 25, 1926, Dallas, Tex.; d. Earl Richard and Mary Jane (McClure) Hart; edn: El Camino Jr. Coll. 1948-9, Mgmt. Action Pgm. 1976. Career: printing apprentice to asst. mgr. Vogue Printing Co., Los Angeles 9146-52; founder/pres./CEO Hart Bindery Service, L.A. 1952--; adv. com. LA Trade Tech. Coll. 1963-65, 75-76; awards: Printing InTech. Found. (Pittsburg, PA) Naomi Berber Mem. Award 1979; Internat. Assn. of Printing House Craftsman awards 1977. Mem: Womans Graphic Art Soc. of LA, Printing House Craftsman of So. Calif., Printing Indus. Assn. of So. Calif. (dir., past pres. Trade Graphic Finisher Sect., past pres. Master Printers Sect.), Master Printers of Am. Arlington, Va. (past dir.); Republican; Prot.; rec: golf. Res: 4042 Midway Culver City 90230 Ofc: Hart Bindery Service, 3290 E. 26th St Los Angeles 90023

HART, EDWARD A., JR., college president; b. Dec. 10, 1928, Oakland; s. Edward A. and Marion (Glaser) H.; m. Josephine C. McCarthy, July 15, 1951; children: William, b. 1953; Brenda, b. 1955; Theresa, b. 1956; Alice, b. 1961; Howard, b. 1962; edn: AB, UC Berkeley 1951; MA, 1957; EdD, 1966; Calif. lic. Life Creds. Tchg. & Admin., State Dept. Edn. Career: tchr. Lodi Union H.S. 1955-56; tchr./ dept. chmn./ football coach Castro Valley H.S. 1956-61; tchr./ football coach/ dir. of athletics Chabot Coll., Hayward 1961-68; asst. dean of instrn./ assoc. dean of students 1968-75; asst. supt. for gen. devel. Saddleback Comm. Coll. Dist., 1975-79; pres. Saddleback Coll. No., Irvine 1979--; lctr. on mgmt. style, Saddleback Bus. & Ind. Spkrs. Bureau; honors: mem. State Chancellors Com. on Capital Outlay; mem: Assn. of Calif. Comm. Coll. Adminstrs.; Calif. Comm. Coll. CEOs; Rotary Club of Laguna Hills; mil: 1st lt. US Army Airborne Infantry, Bronze Star; rec: computer programming, antique clock restoring, racquetball. Res: 33741 Windjammer Dr Laguna Niguel 92677 Ofc: Saddleback Coll. North, 5500 Irvine Center Dr Irvine 92714

HART, LARRY C., lawyer; b. Dec. 24, 1942, Lawton, Okla.; s. Clifford c. and Evelyn M. (Dupler) H.; m. Nina M., Sept. 3, 1982; edn: ABA, Otero Jr. Coll. 1963; BS, Colo. State Univ. 1967; JD, Loyola Univ. Sch. of Law 1974; admitted to practice, Calif. State Bar 1974. Career: assoc. atty. Law Ofcs. Ned Good, Los Angeles 1974-76; assoc. atty. Hagenbaugh & Murphy, L.A. 1976-77; pres./ founder firm. of Hart & Michaelis 1977, Los Angeles 1977--, Chgo. 1981-83; instr. aviation law USC; Los Angeles Co. Superior Ct. Arbitration Hearing Ofcr.; mem: Assn. of So. Calif. Defense Counsel; Aviation Ins. Assn.; Defense Research Inst.; Lawyer-Pilot's Bar Assn.; Am. Bar Assn. (Tort & Ins. Sect.); Calif. Bar Assn.; admitted to Federal Bar for Central, Northern & Eastern Dists. of Calif. & US Ct. of Appeals, Ninth Circuit; works: The Legal Profession's Contribution to Flight Safety, presented to 8th Orient Airlines Assn. Flight Safety Sem., Manila, Philippines, 10/83; rec: cert. pilot, skiing, scuba diving. Res: 4000 Via Opata Palos Verdes Estates 90274 Ofc: Hart & Michaelis, 9841 Airport Blvd, Ste 822, Los Angeles 90045

HART, LUCY SHUTTLEWORTH, speech pathologist; b. Mar. 29, 1945, Indpls., Ind.; d. Wendell Riley and Mary Malinda (Bell) Shuttleworth; m. Richard K. Mason, Aug. 30, 1969; m. 2d. Phillip H. Hart, Oct. 15, 1982; 1 son, Justin C. Mason, b. 1973; edn: BS, Purdue Univ. 1966; MEd, Univ. of Virginia 1967; post grad., Butler Univ. 1975; Cert. of Clinical Competence, Am. Speech & Hearing Assn. Career: speech pathologist The Medical Center, Columbis, Ga. 1970; resource spec. Pub. Schs., Salt Lake City, Utah 1972; lang., speech & hearing clinician, Pub. Schs., Indpls., Ind. 1974; dist. mgr. Jafra Cosmetics, Concord 1978; realtor assoc. E.R.A. Kenworthy Realty, Concord 1980; speech pathologist Ric Outman & Assoc., Walnut Creek 1982--; student tchg. supvr. Florida State Univ., Tallahassee, Fla. 1967; student tchg. supvr. Auburn Univ., Auburn, Ala. 1970; awards: Branch Sponsoring Awd., Jafra Cosmetics 1978; Listing Salesprsn. of the Month, E.R.A. Kenworthy Realty 1980; mem: Am. Speech & Hearing Assn.; Nat. Assn. Re.altors; Calif. Assn. Realtors; Contra Costa Bd. Realtors; Delta Gamma Soc. Sorority Alumni Assn.; Purdue Univ. Alumni Assn.; Univ. of Virginia Alumni Assn.; World Wings (Assn. of Former Pan American Stewardesses); Am. Assn. of Univ. Women; Sierra Club; Presbyterian; rec: English equitation, organaic gardening, tennis. Res: 4375 Dorset Ct Concord 94521 Ofc: Ric Outman & Assoc., 1844 San Miguel, Ste 308A, Walnut Creek 94596

HART, RICHARD VARL, bank executive; b. Feb. 16, 1927, Gettysburg, S.Dak.; s. Clifford Kenneth and Ethel Ida (Manfull) H.; m. Gudrun Werner, May 27, 1979; cihldren: Clifford, b. 1953; John Driscoll, b. 1969; edn: grad. Univ. of Wash Pacific Coast Banking Sch. 1978. Career: loan trainee to br. mgr. Security Pacific Nat. Bank, Los Angeles 1964-73; secty./ treas. JED Devel. Corp., Santa Ana 1973-74; br. mgr. Community Bank, Los Angeles 1974-78; exec. v.p./ COO/ bd. dirs. Union Bank, Tucson, Ariz. 1979-81; sr. v.p./ br. adminstr. Community Bank, Los Angeles 1981; exec. v.p./ br. adminstr. 1982-83; exec. v.p./ chief credit ofcr./ bd. dirs. 1983--; bd. dirs. Union Bank, Tucson, Ariz. 1979--; mem: Bank Admin. Inst.; Robert Morris Assocs.; Arizona Opera Co., La Canada- Flintridge Country Club; Marina City Club; mil: CPO, USN 1945-64; Republican; Methodist; rec: golf, boating. Res: 707 Starlight Heights Dr La Canada 91011 Ofc: Community Bank, 2955 Fletcher Dr Los Angeles 90065

HART, ROBERT LYN, building/engineering contractor; b. Sept. 1, 1943, Miami, Okla.; s. Robert E. and Lenah Ruth (Negim) Hart; m. Rosemary Ziehn, Apr. 28, 1962; chil: Robert David, b. 1963; Karen Lynn, b. 1967; edn: AA, Am River Coll. 1957; BA, CSU Sacto. 1961. Career: constrn. supt., dir. Robert E. Hart, Inc., 1959-65; gen. supt. Lund Constrn., Sacto 1966; partner Hart Constrn., Sacto 1967-8; owner/pres. Kingdom Konstrn., Sacto 1969--; cons. devel. projects, partner Armstrong-Hart Devel. Co. 1979-, partner RDR Devel. Co. 1983-. Mem. Pres. Council, Letourneau Coll., Long View, Tex.; mem: Building Indus. Assn., Gen. Contractors Assn., Sacto Builder's Exchange; life mem. NRA; Lions (dist. secty. 1975); Scoutmaster Troop 6, Sacto 1961. Mil: US Army 1961-7. Presbyterian (elder & adm. Fair Oaks Presbyn. Mariner Fleet 1983-4); rec: hunt, camp. res: 8579 Willings Way, Fair Oaks 95628 Ofc: Kingdom Konstruction, 2945 Ramona Ave, Sacramento 95826

HART, WILLIAM ROBERT, clinical social worker; b. July 31, 1936, Denison, Tex.; s. Wm. R., Sr. and Avo Pauline (Henley) H.; m. Andrea Jean Spafford, Sept. 30, 1961; children: Dennis, b. 1962, Eric, b. 1969, Jodi, b. 1971; edn: AA, L.A. Harbor Coll. 1965, BA, CSU Dominguez Hills 1967, MSW, Smith Coll. Sch. for Social Wk. 1972; LCSW (Lic. Clin. Soc. Wk.), Calif. 1977, Mich., NY. Career: soc. wkr. L.A. County Dept. Pub. Soc. Svcs. 1968-70, National Jewish Hosp., Denver 1970-72, Berkshire Mental Health Clinic 1971-72; sr. psychiat. soc. wkr. Broome County Mental Health Clin. 1962-75, also faculty part-time Broome Comm. Coll., pvt. practice psychotherapy Twin Tiers Human Svcs. 1973-76; mem. Mental Health Task Force of New York-Penn. (5-county plnng. commn.) 1973-76; Day Care Project coord. Univ. of Mich., Ann Arbor 1976-77; clin. soc. wkr. Dept. of Mental Health, San Bernardino Co. (Ca.) 1977-81; pvt. practice/ptnr. Redlands Psychol. and Family Services 1981-82; clin. dir. Victor Valley Counseling Svcs. 1982-83; chief inpatient treatment The CareUnit, San Bernardino Comm. Hosp., 1983--. Address: 3607 North D St San Bernardino 92405

HARTLINE, ROBERT HIND, regulatory bank official; b. June 13, 1925, Wash. DC; s. William Raymond and Anne Isabel (Hind) H.; m. Mary Dunham, Oct. 3, 1953; children: Mary Anne, b. 1955; Robert Jr., b. 1957; Franklin, b. 1958; Thomas, b. 1959; Kathryn, b. 1961; John, b. 1963; Ralph, b. 1964; Charles, b. 1968; edn: BA, The George Washington Univ. 1950. Career: The Hecht Co., Wash. DC 1945-54; sales rep. Addressograph- Multigraph Corp., Wash. DC 1954-55; mgmt. trainee Nat. Metropolitan Bank (Am. Security), Wash. DC 1955-60; sr. fin. analyst Fed. Home Loan Bank Bd., Wash. DC 1960-74; currently, sr. v.p., San Francisco; honors: Phi Beta Kappa 1950; Outstanding

Svc. Awd., Fed. Home Loan Bank Bd. 1973; m: Alpha Kappa Psi, profl. bus. frat; St. Isidore's Roman Catholic Ch. (Minister of Music); Cub- Boy Scouts of Am. (former); mil: aviation cadet, US Army Air Force 1943-45; capt. USMCR 1948-56; Catholic; rec: music, gardening, golf. Res: 2468 Lavender Dr Walnut Creek 94596 Ofc: Federal Home Loan Bank of S.F., 600 California St San Francisco 94120

HARTMAN, ALFRED A., financial consultant; b. May 31, 1932, NY, NY; s. Joseph and Anna Hartman; m. Darlene Artell, Apr. 16, 1955; children: Mark, Christopher, Theresa, Elizabeth, Marguerite, Thomas, Hansel, Anthony, Katherine, Anna, Mary-Claire, Paul-John, Peter, Maria, Jeremy, Samuel, Jennifer, Amalia, William, Benedict; desig: Certified Pension Consultant, Am. Soc. of Pension Actuaries. Career: regl. sales mgr. Kimball Systems (div. Litton Indus), Atlanta, Ga. 1964-68; pension cons. Employee Benefit Consultants Inc., Santa Ana 1968-70; founder/pres. The Hartman Group Inc. (Pension Adminstrs.), Orange 1970-80 (sold to American Retirement Systems); founder/pres. Calif. Pension Investment Research Inc., Newport Beach 1981-83; co-founder/pres. Image Printing Systems Inc., Orange 1981--, Computrans Tariff Systems Inc., Orange 1982--, Loanserv Inc., Orange 1983--; founder/bd. chmn. American Electronic Mail Inc., Orange 1981--; founder/pres. Glenmary Consultants Inc., Orange 1981--; gen. ptnr. 3 lmtd. ptnrships; lectr., pension admin., CSULA 1977-80; dir. Team Effort Inc., Riverside 1984-; honors: Family of the Year, Right to Life League, LA 1980; mem. Am. Soc. of Pension Actuaries 1973-81, Western Pension Conv. 1970-80, Knights of Columbus; performer: Irvine Master Chorale 1975-76, University Glee Club, Yale Univ. 1983-, San Clemente Civic Light Opera prodns. 1963, 74; mil: A/1c USAF 1952-54, GCM; Republican; Catholic; rec: golf, woodworking, photog. Res: 42 Wildcat Springs Dr Madison CT 06443 Ofc: Image Printing Systems Inc. 303 W. Katella Ave, 2nd Flr, Orange 92667

HARTMAN, CAROL ALAYNE, artist; b. Dec. 29, 1948, Sidney, Montana; d. Alvin O. and Verna C. (Houglum) Fisher; m. Boyd J. Hartman, Mar. 17, 1969; children: Allan, b. 1969; Brad, b. 1971; edn: BA, Montana State Univ. 1971; grad. work, Univ. of Neveda 1979-81; MA, cand., CSU Fresno 1982--; artist, CSUF 1984. Career: dir. advtg. graphics Learavia, Reno, Nev. 1973; graphic artist Univ. of Nevada Reno, Reno, Nev. 1973-76; art. instr. Reno Recreation, Reno, Nev. 1976-80; owner/ artist/ prodn. design Hartman Graphics, Reno, Nev. 1973-81, Fresno, Calif. 1981--; lectr. Fresno Chpt. on Women in Art 1982; awards: 1st pl. news feature, 2nd layout design, Nevada Press Women 1980; mem: Art Dirs. & Artists Club of Sacto.; Nat. Fedn. Press Women; NPW; CPW; Internat. Assn.; of Bus. Communicators; CSUF Bulldog Found.; Delta Gamma Alumni; MSU Alumni; AAUW; UNR Faculty Club; works: first NYC solo exhibit of artwork: Locked Doors (45 pieces), at SOHO 20 Invitational Space 9/83; prod./editor first City of Reno Employee News Mag. 1978; Lutheran; rec: campnig, gold panning, x-country skiing. Address: 1366 West Tenaya Fresno 93711

HARVEY, BARBARA LEE, certified public accountant; b. Jan. 22, 1940, Valparaiso, Ind.; d. Delbert and Evelyn Pauline (Hill) Collinsworth; div.; children: Cheryl, b. 1962, Caren, b. 1963; edn: AA, Citrus Coll. 1973, BA, CSU Fullerton 1976, MBA, 1982; CPA, Calif. 1980. Career: Vacco Industries, South El Monte 1976-77, Prager & Fenton, Hollywood 1977-78, McGladrey, Hendrickson & Co., Arcadia 1978-81, Mills & Elliott, Tustin 1981-82, City of Hope, Duarte 1982--. Awards: Bank of Am. awd. 1974; mem. Friends of the Claremont Library (pres. 1980-84), City of Claremont rep. on library affairs to County of L.A. 1981-84; Democrat; rec: sci-fi, bicycling. Res: 1366 LaFayette Rd.-J, Claremont 91711 Ofc: City of Hope, 1500 E. Duarte Rd Duarte 91010

HARVEY, JOSEPH BIVENS, superior court judge; b. Nov. 5, 1927, Hankow, China; s. Earle Rolston and Mary Lee (Mullis) Harvey; BA, Occidental Coll., 1949; JD, Hastings Coll. of Law, 1952; m. Jo Ann Robinson, June 17, 1952; children: Jean, b. 1953; Warren, b. 1954; Thomas, b. 1956; Mary, b. 1962; Katherine, b. 1963. Career: research atty., Ct. of Appeal, First Appellate Dist., S.F., 1953-54; dep. dist. atty., San Diego Co., 1954-56; assoc. counsel, Dept. of Alcoholic Beverage Control, Sacramento, 1957-59; dep. atty. gen., State of Calif., Sacramento, 1959; asst. exec. secty., Calif. Law Revision Commn., Stanford, 1959-67; partner Herrick, Gross, Mansfield, Harvey & Miller, and successor firms, Palo Alto, 1967-70; sole practice, Susanville, CA, 1970-77; partner, Harvey & Bradbury, Susanville, 1977-78; judge, Superior Ct. of Lassen Co., Susanville, 1979--; also lectr., Calif. Continuing Edn. of the Bar. Honors: Order of the Coif; Thurston Soc. Mem.: Calif. State Bar Assn., 1953-78; Palo Alto Bar Assn., 1967-70; Lassen Co. Bar Assn., 1970-78, pres. 1975; Susanville Rotary Club, 1971--; Lassen Co. Taxpayers Assn., 1976-78, pres. 1977-78. Author of numerous articles incl. 'Rights and Duties Upon Termination of a Lease,' 54 California Law Review 1141 (1966); 'Judicial Notice,' Calif. Evidence Code Manual 375 (CEB 1966); 'Evidentiary Burdens and Presumptions,' Calif. Evidence Code Manual 399 (CEB 1966); 'Evidence Code Section 1224 -- Are An Employee's Admissions Admissible Against his Employer?' 8 Santa Clara Lawyer 59 (1967). Draftsman, co-draftsman of legislation incl. Calif. Evidence Code (1965 Stat. Ch. 299), Calif. Arbitration Act (1961 Stat. Ch. 461), Rescission of Proceedings (1961 Stat. Ch. 1621), Taking Possession and Passage of Title in Eminent Domain Proceedings (1961 Stat. Ch. 1613), Separation of the Nondelinquent from the Delinquent Minor in Juvenile Ct. Proceedings (1961 Stat. Ch. 1616). Mil.: Seaman 1/C, USN, 1945-46; 1st Lt., USAF, 1952-53. Democrat. Presbyterian, elder. Rec.: backpacking, choral directing, quartet singing. Res.: 8 Fairway Dr., Susanville 96130; Office: Superior Court, Courthouse, Susanville 96130.

HARVEY, LEE G., electrical contractor; b. Apr. 15, 1927, Candler, N.C.; d. Ralph and Bessie Lee (Penland) Welch; m. Lyle Greene (dec.); m. 2d. Richard Harvey, June 15, 1972; children: Sherri, b. 1953, Lyle, Jr. b. 1954, Jeffrey, b. 1961, (stepchil.) David, Cathy, Judy; edn: Long Beach City Coll., Southwestern Comm. Coll., Mesa Comm. Coll.; Calif. lic: Electrical Contractor 1976, Landscape Contr. 1980, Cert. Nurseryman 1977. Career: gen. mgr. South Bay Electric Corp., National City and South Bay Plumbing Co., 1970-80; gen. mgr. South Bay Apartments Constrn. Co., National City 1973--; owner antique retail bus.; honors: among the first women to qualify for electrical contractor license; publs: short stories, poetry; creator limited editions of porcelains; Republican; So. Baptist, pres. San Diego So. Baptist Womens Orgn. 1954-61, taught mission studies throughout state, estab. camps for youth in So. Calif.; rec: collector Madame Alexander dolls. Res: 5235 Glen View Pl Bonita 92002 Ofc: South Bay Apts. Const. Co. 1615 Hoover National City 92050

HARVEY, VIC, real estate broker; b. Apr. 18, 1931, NY, NY; s. Henry and Beatrice (Yarmoff) Feldman; m. Judy Raskin, July 7, 1978; children: Jay, b. 1956, USA Jo, b. 1957, Dayna Jean, b. 1959; edn: JD, Mid Valley Coll. of Law 1978. Career: came to Calif. in 1954, var. sales jobs 1954-60; real estate sales agt. 1960, partner 1961, became sole owner 1966-, broker/owner Century 21 Vic Harvey, Realtors, Woodland Hills 1974--, top selling Cen.21 Ofc. in the S.F. Valley 1976-83; instr. sales tng. seminars S.F. Board of Realtors; awards: Cert. of Merit for public svc., City of L.A. 1973; mem: S.F. Vly. Bd. of Realtors (v.p. 1970, chmn. Multiple Listing Com. 1968), Woodland Hills CofC; publs: The Vic Harvey Story (sales manual), cartoonist for AUS 4th Inf. newspaper, Germany; mil: pfc US Army 1952-54; Democrat; Christian; rec: tennis, dancing. Res: 23128 Park Sorrento Calabasas 91302 Ofc: Century 21 Vic Harvey Realtors, 21744 Ventura Blvd Woodland Hills 91364

HARWICK, BURTON THOMAS, manufacturing co. president; b. July 4, 1923, Deer Lodge, Montana; s. Thomas and Christine (Larsen) H.; m. Betty Corinne Burns, June 20, 1947; children: W. Thomas, b. 1948; B. Terence, b. 1949; Bonnie Christine, b. 1951; Beverly Anne (Carrol), b. 1953; edn: AB, UC Berkeley 1951; UCLA 1956-61. Career: research analyst No. Am. Aviation (The Old Radiation Lab.), Berkeley 1951-54, research splst. No. Am. Aviation, Downey 954-56; proj. engr./ supvr. Atomics Internat., Canoga Park 1956-60; pgm. mgr./ supvr. 1960-70; pres. Hochheiser Electronics Corp., Burbank 1970-72; pres. Dynatrol Nat. Corp., Sun Valey 1972--; tchr. elec. USN 1943-46; guest spkr. IEEE; mem: Nat. Trust of Historic Preservation; L.A. Co. Mus. of Art.; UC Berkeley Alumni Assn.; Fair Housing Council, San Fernando Valley; Literacy Refugee Com., Thousand Oaks; patentee: US & 17 foreign countries on nuclear particle monitoring; mil: chief elec. tech. USN 1943-46; Reserves 1946-50; Presbyterian (elder); rec: woodworking, travel. Ofc: Dynatrol National Corp., 8088 San Fernando Rd Sun Valley 91352

HASELTINE, JO ANN ELLEN, non-profit organization executive; b. Dec. 31, 1947, Seattle, Wash.; d. Herbert Mortimer and Loraine May (Moses) H.; edn: AA, Coll. of Marin 1969; BS, Columbia Pacific Univ. 1982. Career: dir. dining room and extra staff mem. spl. activities, Campfire Girls Summer Camp Program 1968-71; nursery school tchr. var. schs. Marin County, part-time 1968-70; office clk. US Govt., incl. US Army Corps of Engrs., San Francisco 1971-81; founder/exec. dir. Marin Puzzle People, Inc. (a non-profit orgn. for learning disabled adults), San Rafael 1977--; cons. on Learning Disabilities: Richmond Sch. Dist., Union City Sch. Dists., De Anza Coll., Merritt Coll., and Mission Valley Coll., 1979-; honors: Federal Executive Bd. 1981 nominee Federal Employee of the Year, outstanding consumer award Calif. Council on Developmental Disabilities 1981, S.F. Bay Area Volunteer Activist awd. 1981, Calif. Assn. of Post-Secondary Educators Frank Lanterman Award 1983; mem: Assn. for Children with Learning Disabilities, Calif. Assn. for Neurologically Handicapped Children, Calif. Protection and Advocacy Inc. (Review Com. 1978-82), Spl. Edn. Adv. Bd. Marin County Schs. 1980-83; author: Socialization of Learning Disabled Adults: Why and How to Organize a Group; mil: AF Basic Tng. Pgm., Lackland AF Base, Tx. 1975, mem. USAR 1975-; Democrat; Episcopal; rec: swim, dog tng., equestrian. Res: 164 N. San Pedro Rd, Apt 1-303, San Rafael 94903 Ofc: Marin Puzzle People Inc. 1368 Lincoln Ave, Ste 105, San Rafael 94901

HASKELL, GREGG OWEN, civil engineer; b. Dec. 1, 1952, Oakland; s. Owen Wesley and Zelia Juanity (Ulrich) H.; edn: BSCE, No. Ariz. Univ. 1974; ME, UC Berkeley 1978. Career: engrs. asst. H.J. Degenkolb & Assoc., Cons. Engrs., San Francisco 1972-73; engr. in tng. 1974-75; proj. engr. Owen W. Haskell, Inc., Oakland 1977-78; civil engr. Ruthoff & Englekirk Inc. 1979-80; civil engr. Forell/ Elsesser Engrs., Inc., S.F. 1980--; tchg. asst. UC Berkeley 1974-75; awards: Outstanding Civil Engr., NAU Sch. of Civil Eng. & Tech. 1974; Outstanding Engr., NAU Coll. of Eng. 1974; mem: NAU Soc. of Eng. Exec. Council (pres. 1974); Am. Soc. of Civil Eng.; Structural Engrs. Assn. of No. Calif.; ASCE SEAONC (Cont. Edn. Com.); author: Free Vibrations and Near- Field Acoustic Radiation of a Simply Suporrt Cylindrical Shell; coauthor: w/ Gary W. Rogers, Acoustic Radiation of a Vibrating Rectangular Membrane, 24th Annual Am. Inst. of Aero. & Astro., Reg. IV Student Conf. 1974; Republican, Melones Dam Advoc. 1975; Methodist; rec: pvt. pilot, archery, skiing. Res: 71 Lafayette Cir Lafayette 94513 Ofc: Forell/ Elsesser Engrs., Inc., 631 Clay St San Francisco 94111

HASLETT, JOHN ADAMS, JR., company president; b. July 17, 1934, Pasadena; s. John Adams and Ruth Carolyn (Montgomery) H.; m. Diann Noroby, July 30, 1977; edn: BA, Pomona Coll., Claremont 1956. Career: with John A. Haslett Co. 1960--; salesman 1960; gen. mgr. 1971; pres. 1978; mem: Los Angeles Retarded Childrens Found. (pres. 1971-72) Ironwood Country Club, Palm Desert; Balboa Bay Club, Newport Beach; mil: lt. j.g. USN 1959; Republican; Baptist. Res: 16641 So Pacific Sunset Beach 90742 OFc: John A. Haslett Co., Inc., 4740 E 26th St Los Angeles 90040

HASSELBECK, GRACE IRENE, rehabilitation counselor-educator; b. May 7, 1923, Medford, Mass.; s. Walter A. and Doris E. (Maxfield) Basse; edn: BA, Univ. of Redlands, 1949, MA, 1949; widow; l dau. Dorene, b. 1945; career: Rehabilitation Counselor/ teacher for the blind, State of Calif. Dept. of Rehabilitation, Long Beach, 1951--; mem. exec. bd. So. Calif. chapter, American Assn. for Workers for tha Blind, 1982; mem. community adv. bd., KLON pub. radio, 1980-81; mem. Sweet Adelines, Inc. pres. 1974-76; Republican; Prot.; rec: gardening, boating, fishing, travel; res: 3480 Harding St., Long Beach 90805 ofc: State of Calif. Dept. of Rehabilitation, 3530 Atlantic Ave. Ste. 201, Long Beach 90807.

HASSMAN, GEORGE IRA, physician; b. May 14, 1953, Jersey City, NJ; s. Rubin William and Selma (Weissfeld) H.; edn: BA, w/ distn., Boston Univ. 1974; MD, Univ. of Miami Sch. of Med. 1979. Career: intern Pacific Med. Ctr., San Francisco 1979-80; physician, gen. practice 1980-81; ophthalmology res., Univ. of Ill. 1981-82; MD, gen. practice, San Francisco 1982--; honors: Psi Chi hon. soc. 1974; diplomate, Nat. Bd. of Med. Examiners; mem: Am. Med. Assn.; works: Pseudomonas Corneal Ulcer With Extended- Wear Soft Contact Lenses, Archives of Opthalm. 10/83; rec: classical pianist. Address: 4101 23rd St San Francisco 94114

HASTINGS, AGGIE (AGNES) MARY, civic worker; b. Oct. 11, 1922, Buffalo, NY; d. Joseph Anthony and Sophie (Meyers) Smith; m. Donald Hastings, June 17, 1948; children: Donna Marie, b. 1949, Donald L., b. 1955; edn: BA, intl. studies, Golden Gate Univ. 1973; grad. stu. journalism, radio and TV writing, San Franciso St. Univ. and San Jose St. Univ., 1974-77; travel indus. course, Canada Coll. 1983; Cert. Paralegal. Career: secty., Lib. clk. State of Calif., Civil Service, worked in various state agencies, PUC, WCAB, Langley Porter Psychiatric Clinic, and Caltrans, 1963-80; during WWII worked for Army and Navy as insp. on bombsights and radio eqpt. (in Buffalo and Syracuse, NY) 1943-45; then with Assoc. Press as dictaphone typist/copy girl, and reporter for Syracuse Post Standard; Paralegal volunteer: S F Public Defender's Office, Lawyers' Com. for Urban Affairs (Immigration Clinic at La Raza Legal Clinic, S.F.), 1983-; US Govt. Census Enumerator 1980; volunteer: jail aide Service League, San Mateo Co. 1978; USO and Travelers Aid, SF Airport 1978, judge insp. election polls San Mateo Co. 1977-; freelance writer, reporter; mem: Golden Gate Univ. Alumni, Sigma Delta Chi, Intpnat. Platform Assn., Alcoholism Adv. Bd. of San Marin Co. 1977, Amer. Red. Cross, Palo Alto, Adult Benevolent Assn.; Republican, Catholic; rec: writing, photog., comm. work. Res: 11722 Calle Vivienda Rancho Bernardo 92128

HASTY, ROBERT GENE, clergyman; b. Dec. 5, 1941, Rock Island, Ill.; s. Russell K. and Helen Jane (Gaunt) H.; m. Barbara Jo Phillips, Nov. 25, 1963; children: Robert Jr., b. 1964; Richard K., b. 1967; edn: BM, USC 1963; MM, 1968; DMA, 1971; Rel.M., Sch. of Theology, Claremont 1976; ordained minister, Disciples of Christ Ch. 1977. Career: instr. USC 1964-75; visiting prof. Sacto. State Univ. 1972; dir. Festival Choir & Chamber Singers, USC Idylwild 1977-80; dir./ founder Summerfest Music Camp 1981--; assoc. minister First Christian Ch., Bakersfield 1977-79; chair, music dept. Pacific Christian Coll. 1979-80; assoc. minister First Christian Ch., Pomona 1973-77; owner, The Hasty Note 1981--; currently, sr. minister First Chirstian Ch., Norwalk; guest conductor: So. Calif. region honor choirs, 1981 Gen. Assembly of the Christian Ch. Anaheim Conv. Ctr., First Annual High Sch. Choir Night Dodger Stadium 1980; ednl. cons. Glendale Coll., East L.A. Coll., Irvine; honors: USC Chamber Singers Award 1963, Music Edn. Awd. 1963, USC Alumni Awd. 1963, USC Skull & Dagger frat. 1969; mem: Kern Co. Music Educators Assn. (pres. 1967-68); Phi Mu Alpha Sinfonia frat. (pres.); So. Calif. Vocal Assn.; Kiwanis; rec: coin collecting, real estate. Res: 2174 Pami Circle Orange 92667 Ofc: First Christian Church, POB 253, Norwalk 90650

HATCH, WILLIAM BARRETT, research and development co. president; b. Sept. 13, 1924, Centralia, Wash.; s. William Barrett and Peggy Jo (Cosgrove) H.; m. Karina B. Conrads, Oct. 11, 1980; edn: BS, Univ. of Wash. 1951. Career: missile engr. Sperry, Pt. Mugu 1951-54; dir. of R&D Aerophysics Dev. Corp., Santa Monica 1954-57; proj. engr. DART missile guidance receiver, Electronics Sys. Devel. Corp., Ventura 1957-60; elec. dept. mgr. TE Co., Santa Barbara 1960-62; principal engr. Raytheon Co., Goleta 1962-79; currently, pres. Hatch Research & Devel. Co.; elec. warfare cons. Naval Research Lab. & Applied Physics Lab.; awards: 5 pontents; mem: Assn. of Old Crows; Ch. of Jesus Christ, LDS (priest); publs: Computer Use In Electronic Warefare, 1978; developed first transistorized guidance sys. 1957; mil: electrician 2/c USN 1943-46; Republican; rec: fishing, camping, hiking. Res: 4331 Modoc Rd Santa Barbara 93110 Ofc: Hatch R&D, 115 S La Cumbre Ln Santa Barbara 93105

HATCHER, KELSEY WALLACE, real estate broker; b. Dec. 8, 1913, Woodland; s. Earle Kelsey and Venus Virginia 9Bullivant) H.; m. Elizabeth Ann Duffy, Mar. 21, 1970; children: Nancy, b. 1940, John, b. 1942, William, b. 1948; Calif. lic. Real Estate Broker 1970. Career: self employed farmer, Woodland, Calif. 1932-68; sales/repairs Amos Metz Rentals, Woodland 1968-70; mgr. Victor Welding Supplies 1970-73; broker/owner Hatcher Real Estate, 1973--; also farming; pres. Yolo Zamora Water District; dir. Marys Cemetery Dist.; mem: Yolo County Farm Bur., Assoc. Farmers, Beet Growers Assn., Tomato Growers Assn., Farm Labor Assn., Nat. Assn. of Realtors, Masons, Elks, Lions; Republican; Episcopal; rec: travel, hunting, fishing, sports. Res: 103 Casa Linda Dr Woodland 95695 Ofc: Hatcher Real Estate, 612 Main, Woodland 95695

HATCHETT, DONNA JANE, public affairs executive; b. Aug. 4, 1945, Wichita, Ks.; d. Vester P. and Jane J. (Sexton) VanZant; m. James C. Hatchett, July 10, 1965; children: Jamie JoAnn, b. 1966; Marissa Jane, b. 1970; edn: AA, Fullerton Coll. 1976; BA, CSU Fullerton 1979; MA, Univ. of Redlands 1984. Career: pub. info. asst. Co. of Orange 1976-78; pub. info. asst. City of Irvine 1978-79; pub. info. ofcr. Rancho Santiago Comm. Coll. Dist. 1979--; Leaders of the 80's, Inst. for Leadership Devel. 1984; awards: Fullerton Coll. Journalism Alumni Awd. 1981; Outstanding Young Woman of Am. 1980; Outstanding Woman Communications Student, Women in Commun., Inc. 1979; Fullerton Coll. Woman of the Yr. 1976; Fullerton Coll. Journalist of the Yr. 1976; Democrat; rec: volleyball, sports. Res: 2811 Bayberry Way Fullerton 92633 Ofc: Rancho Santiago Comm. Coll. Dist., Santa Ana Coll., 17th and Bristol Sts Santa Ana 92706

HATFIELD, DALE CHARLES, banker; b. May 26, 1931, Springfield, Ill.; s. C. Ray and Gladys (Shumate) H.; m. Lura Ann Northrop, 1957; children: Dana, b. 1960, Dean, b. 1962, Dianne, b. 1969; edn: BS, Bradley Univ. 1953; MBA, Univ. Denver 1963. Career: research mgr. Boise Cascade Corp., Boise, Ida. 1963-67; asst. secty., Bank of California, Marketing, Southern Div., Los Angeles, 1967-68, asst. v.p. 1969, vice pres. Home Office, San Francisco 1975--; (respons. for bank's ins. pgm. mgmt. and capital budget); mem. American Bankers Assn. (spr. 1976-80, Faculty cmn. seminars nationwide 1977-80, dir. Ins. and Protection Div. 1976-78, chmn. Ins. Com. ABA 1976); mem. Calif. Bankers Assn. (spkr. statewide 1975-, chmn. Emergency Planning Task Force 1981-, chmn. Ins. Com. CBA 1978-80); mem. Gov's Task Force on Earthquake Preparedness 1980-, Calif. State Fin. and Monetary Svcs Com 1981-, Calif. CofC (Ins. & Employee Benefits Com. 1978-), No. Calif. Risk & Ins. Mgmt. Soc. (dir. 1976-78), Am. Mgmt. Assn. (Ins. Seminars 1975-76); Faculty, The School for Bank Admin. B.A.I., 1983; pres. Orinda Assn. 1975; bd. dirs. Contra Costa Co. Easter Seal Soc. 1974-76; dir. Orinda Youth Assn. 1976-7; mem. Masons, Commonwealth Club of Calif., Moraga Country Club; publs: Guidlines for Disaster Planning (C.B.A. pub. 1982); quoted frequently in banking publs.; mil: 1slt. USAF, Republican, Presbyterian (Elder). Res: 25 Cedar Ln Orinda 94563

HATFIELD, DONALD H., real estate developer, rancher; b. June 22, 1929, Bozeman, Mont.; s. Ralph H. and Edith Vivian (Morgan) Crabb; m. Dolores Viola Rodiak, Sept. 25, 1965; children: Christy Gale, b. 1952, Jack, b. 1957, Jay, b. 1960; edn: stu. San Mateo Jr. Coll., Univ. of Colo.; BA in econ., Univ. Calif. 1951; JD, Univ. of San Francisco Law Sch. 1968; admitted to practice State Bar of Calif.; Calif. lic. Real Estate Broker; lic. Contractor, Calif., Nev. Career: economist Calif. & Hawaii Corp., S.F. 1953-55; building contr. self-empl., Burlingame 1956-72; atty./ptnr. Bruen, Kaufman & Hatfield, S.F. 1972--; real estate devel., owner Four Rent Inc., Las Vegas, Nev. 1976--; rancher/owner Dyer (Nev.) Ranch Co. 1977--; dir./prin. Fallon (Nev.) National Bank, Am. National Bank (Aurora, Colo.); dir./pres. exec. com. Commercial Bank of San Francisco; owner/pub. Review Miner (Lovelock, Nev.); maj. shareholder Lahontan Valley News (Fallon, Nev.). Mem: Am. Bar Assn., Calif. Trial Lawyers Assn., Bar Assn. of S.F., Nev. County Hist. Soc., Death Valley 49ers Inc., Nat. Cattlemen's Assn.; clubs: The Plaza (Honolulu), E. Clampus Vitus (Nevada City); works: residential design Homes by Hatfield (1960-66); Republican; Episcopal; rec: fly fishing, gardening. Res: 230 Main St Nevada City CA 95959 Ofc: Four Rent Inc. 1801 E. Tropicana Ave, Ste. 29, Las Vegas, NV 89109

HATH, DAVID COLLINS, college dean; b. Mar. 13, 1944, San Diego; s. Collins Maxwell and Dorothy (Laird) H.; m. Deborah Shively, Apr. 9, 1976; 2 sons: Derek Collins; Douglas Alan; edn: AA, Porterville Coll. 1964; BS, CSU Fresno 1966; MA, Chapman Coll. 1972; post grad. Pepperdine Univ., UC Irvine. Career: indsl. rels. rep. Ford Motor Co., Automotive Assem. Div. 1966-68; instr. Tustin Union H.S. Dist. 1968-69; instr./ counselor/ counseling psychologist Orange Unified Sch. Dist. 1969-75; dean cont. edn. div. Rancho Santiago Comm. Coll. Dist., Orange 1975-83; dean Orange Canyon Campus, Rancho Santiago Comm. Coll. Dist., Orange 1983--; mem. Orange Intercultural Edn. Commn. 1973-75; Rehab. Inst. of Orange Co. (Easter Seals Found.) 1979-; Vocational Edn. Adv. Com.; Calif. Dept. of Food & Agri. Regl. Edn. Accreditation Com. 1980-84; awards: Eagle Scout, Boy Scouts of Am. 1956; William T. Hornaday awd. 1958; Bus. Awd., Outstanding Achiev., Bank of Am. 1963; W.P. Bartlett Found. Awd. 1964; Mgmt. Commdn., Ford Motor Co. 1968; Comm. svc. awds; Outstanding Young Men of Am., Jaycees; mem: Rehab. Inst. of Orange Co. (Comm. Adv. Bd.); Assn. of Calif. Sch. Adminstrs.; Assn. of Calif. Comm. Coll. Adminstrs.; Calif. Assn. Marriage & Family Therapists; Calif. Comm. Coll. Cont. Edn. ASsn.; Calif. Personnel & Guidance Assn.; Phi Delta Kappa; Jr. Achiev. Adv. Rep.; Chapman Coll. Comm. Clinic Adv. Bd.; YMCA Indian Guides, Orange CofC; Republican; Presbyterian; rec: camping, gardening, jogging. Res: 10744 Rancho Santiago Blvd Orange 92669 Ofc: Rancho Santiago Comm. Coll. Dist., Orange Canyon Campus, 8045 E Chapman Ave Orange 92669

HATHAWAY, DOROTHY ELEANOR, antique dealer; b. Nov. 13, 1928, Los Angeles; d. Charles Willis and Eleanor Margaret (Breuning) Robbins; m.

James Alderman Hathaway, Dec. 30 , 1950; children: Christine, b. 1951; Linda, b. 1953; Laurene, b. 1954; James Jr., b. 1958; Cecile, b. 1961; edn: art major, Glendale City Coll. 1946-47; shorthand, Metropolitan Trade Sch. 1953. Career: secty. to TV comic Jim Hawthorne 1949-50; model Lola Whitehead Agcy. 1947-50; prodn./ stage mgr. Euterpe Opera Club (Dorothy Chandler Pavillion) 1965-69; owner Tioga Lodge Historical Site Resort 1969-80; owner Tioga Lodge Antiques 1970-, (name chg.) Hathaway House Antiques 1978--; tchr. antiques class, Malaga Cove Adult Sch. 1982; conducted auctions, Tioga Lodge 1970-77; mem: Catholic Daughters of Am. (25 year pin 1977); Am. Legion Aux. (Chaplain); columnist Bridgeport Chronicle, Mono Herald 1972-76; Republican; Catholic; rec: arts, crafts. Res: 130 The Village, Condo 302, Redondo Beach 90277

HATHAWAY, ODELL S., II, (Jay), motion picture producer/director; b. Mar. 3, 1941, Los Angeles; s. James Lawrence and Lucille Marie (Harding) H.; m. Marjorie Berry, Dec. 10, 1962; chldren: Odell, b. 1961; Susan, b. 1963; Constance, b. 1964; James John, b. 1965; Robert, b. 1969; Ann E., b. 1977; edn: Columbia Coll., Chgo. 1959-60; grad., Van Nuys H.S. 1958. Career: prod./dir. Jay Hathaway Prodns., Sherman Oaks 1965--; exec. dir. Am. Acad. of Husband-Coached Childbirth, Sherman Oaks 1970--; bd. advs., Nat. Assn. Parents & Profl. for Safe Alternative Childbirth (NAPSAC); mem: Acad. TV Arts & Scis.; Soc. of Motion Picture & TV Engrs.; author: w/ wife, Children at Birth, and, The Bradley Method; prod./dir. more than 20 films on childbirth edn.; Republican; Episcopal; rec: pvt. pilot. Res: 4846 Katherine Ave Sherman Oaks 91423 Ofc: American Academy of Husband-Coached Childbirth, POB 5224 Sherman Oaks 91413

HATTIER, THOMAS HOWARD, management information systems executive; b. Sept. 23, 1949, Erie, Pa.; s. Emile Clark and Judith Gehrig (West) H.; m. Dawn Irene Wilson, Mar. 22, 1967; children: Thomas Jr., b. 1967; Richard, b. 1970; Robert, b. 1974; Lisa, b. 1977; edn: cert. Computer Ednl. Inst. 1968; BSBA, Drexel Univ. 1978. Career: computer pgmr. Gen. Accident Ins. Co., Phila., Pa, 1968-69; logistics spec. Gen. Electric Co.,, Re-Entry & Environmental Systems Div., Phila. 1969-76; proj. support/ admin. splst. Gen. Elec. Co., Space Div., Valley Forge, Pa. 1976-78, mgr. pgm. cost/schedule control, 1978-81; mgr. pgm. plng. & control, GE Co., Space Div., Sunnyvale 1981-84; currently, mgr. computer application ctr. support, Gen. Elec. Co. Corporate Information Systems, Bridgeport, Ct. 1984--; cons. individual and small business finl. plng. & income tax; honors: Alpha Sigma Lambda 1978; Profl. Recgn. Pgm. Awd., Gen. Elec. Co. 1979; 5 Gallon Blood Donor Awd., Red Cross 1983; mem: Gen. Electric Elfun Soc.; YMCA; Santa Teresa Hosp. Volunteer Pgm.; works: devel. Software Devel. Cost & Resource Estimation Model, used for large scale scientific computer tng.; Democrat; Catholic; rec: game, book and coin collecting. Res: 3 Pilgrim Ln Monroe, CT 06468 Ofc: General Electric Co., 1285 Boston Ave, Ste 31EW, Bridgeport, CT 06602

HAU, BETTY RUGEN, nutritionist, real estate broker; b. Jan. 15, 1947, Ling, Shantung, nat. 1979; d. Chang-Sheng and Shih-Lin (Yueh) Hao; edn: BS, Fu-Jen Catholic Univ. 1969; MS, No. Ill. Univ. 1971; reg. dietitian, Am. Dietetic Assn. 1974. Career: real estate broker H & W Realty, Monterey Park 1980--; mgr./ cons. Hao's Auto Svc., Alhambra 1981--; mgr. R.T. Lee Auto Sales, Los Angeles 1983--; mem: Am. Dietetic Assn.; Calif. Assn. Realtors; So. Calif. Shantung Province Assn.; rec: dancing, travel. Res: 332 S Pomelo Ave, A, Monterey Park 91754 Ofc: H & W Realty, 716 E Garvey Ave, Ste IIC, Monterey Park 91754

HAUN, RALPH EDWIN, commercial real estate investment co. president; b. Dec. 10, 1940, Whittier; s. Ralph Edwin and Dorothy Maude (Utter) H.; m. Diane Butler, Jan. 25, 1964; edn: BS, CSU San Jose 1963; MS, 1964; postgrad. wk., Univ. Calif. 1972; Calif. Jr. Coll. Tchg. Credential 1972; Real Estate Broker Lic. 1978. Career: mgmt. analyst Hood Corp., Whittier 1969; gen. mgr. Auto Electric Eng. Co., Anaheim 1970-71; v.p./ gen. mgr. Trabaca Prods. of Calif., Costa Mesa 1971-78; comml. R.E. sales Stout & Assoc., Newport Beach 1978-80; pres. Haun Raab Webster & Co., Inc., Newport Beach 1980--; mem: Apart. Assn. of Orange Co.; R.E. & Ins. Club; Soc. for Adv. of Mgmt.; spkr., var. local govtl. meeting & functions; mil: 1st lt. US Army Infantry 1966-69, Bronze Star, Army Commdn. w/ V, Air medal, Purple Heart; Republican; Protestant; rec: drawing, painting, photog. Res: 21162 Castlerock Rd Laguna Beach 92651 Ofc: Haun Raab Webster & Co., Inc., 5 Upper Newport Plaza Newport Beach 92660

HAVAS, MAURICE, logistician; b. Jan. 8, 1948, Amsterdam, Holland, nat. 1959; s. Gustav and Jeannette (Van Weezel) Havas; m. Patsy Edwards Dec. 30, 1981; chil.(by previous marriage): Jacki, b. 1968, Carrie, b. 1970, Daniel, b. 1975; (stepdau.) Robyn Stettler, b. 1968; edn: BS, Weber State Coll., Ogden, Ut. 1976; cert., Utah St. Univ. 1967, cert., Hill AFB, 1969; Certified Profl. Logistician, 1978. Career: card punch machine opr. Defense Depot, Ogden, Ut. 1966-7; aircraft flt. line mech., Ogden (Utah) Air Logistics Ctr., 1967-72, supply clk. to suprv. supply clk., 1972-74, inventory mgmt. splst., 1974-76, supply systems analyst, 1976-79, suprv. inventory mgmt. splst., 1979-81; AF Logistics Insp., AF Inspection and Safety Ctr., Norton AFB, 1981--. Recipient suggestion awards, Def. Supply Agcy. 1968, USAF 1972, (2) 74, 1980; 3 performance awds., USAF, 1982, 83; Boss of Year 1980, Am. Bus. Women's Assn., Ogden chpt. 1980; appreciation, Fed. Employed Women and Spanish Spkg. Pgms., 1977; selection into AF Logistics Exec. Cadre, 1980; appreciation, Utah chpt. Soc. of Logistics Engrs. 1977. sr. mem. Soc. of Logistics Engrs. (Profl. Qualifications Rev. Bd.1980-; inventory control com. mgr. Tech. Activities Div. 1982-; Utah SOLE Bd. Advisors 1977-81; chmn. Ut. SOLE Chpt. 1, 1976-7); Jewish; profl. publs.; rec: computer pgmg., auto mechs., fgn. coins. Res: 1331 Parker Ct., Redlands 92373 Ofc: Hdqtrs, AF Insp./Safety Ctr./ IGBLS, Norton AFB 92409

HAWES, JOHN ALLAN, marriage and family therapist; b. Dec. 11, 1957, Wash. DC; s. Melvin Albert and Donna Isabel (Stout) H.; m. Joanne Pollard, June 21, 1980; edn: BS, magna cum laude, USC 1980; MA, Azusa Pacific Univ. 1983; Calif. Reg. MFCC Intern, 1983. Career: individual and group therapist Azusa Pacific Univ. Counseling Ctr. 1981-82; drug abuse intervention therapist Arcadia Presbyterian Ch. 1982; pgm. splst. drug abuse prevention & edn. HOY (Help Our Youth) Comm. Clinic 1982-83; marriage & family therapy intern, HOY 1982--, and pgm. supvr Drug Abuse Prevention & Edn. 1983; marriage & family therapy cons. Neurological Learning Ctr. 1983; mem: Los Angeles Co. Drug Abuse Prevention Network; Calif. Assn. Marrige & Family Therapists; works: research, conditioned taste aversion & conditioned illness paradigms, AUSC 1978-79; Republican; Protestant; rec: philately, athletics, camping. Res: 140-B N Canyon Blvd Monrovia 91016 Ofc: HOY Community Clinic, 128 Wheeler Ave Arcadia 91006

HAWKINS, AVERILL ERIC, insurance agent; b. Dec. 7, 1936, Dinuba, Calif.; s. Averill Evans and Irene Ellen 9schonher) H.; m. Barbara Steele, Apr. 3, 1955; children: Christopher, b. 1957; Darren, b. 1959; edn: AA, eng., Reedley Coll. 1956; CLU, Am. Coll. of Chartered Life Underwriters 1972. Career: life & health insurance agt. Bankers Life Nebr., Dinuba, Ca. 1962--; instr. Life Underwriters Assn., 1965-66; dir. Sierra Masonic Family Club Ins., 1983-; profl. awards: Hall of Fame 1966-82, Sower Club 1967-79, Nat. Sales Achievement 1973-81, Nat. Quality Awd. 1967-84, Centurion Club 1976, Sower Round Table 1975, 76, 78, Actuaries Honor Roll 1974-84; Masonic Light Award 1982; mem: Fresno Life Underwriters Assn. (dir. 1972/3), Calif. Assn. Life Underwriters, Nat. Life Underwriters Assn., Fresno Chp. CLUs, Nat. Assn. CLUs, Nat. Guard Assn. of Calif., Nat. Guard Assn. of the US; orgns: Kiwanis (pres. 1964, lt. gov. 1970/1); Masons; Dinuba Plnng. Commn., Dinuba Indsl. Plnng. Commn. (v.chmn. 1972/3); CofC; publs: arts. in company mag.; mil: currently Brig. Gen. Army Nat. Guard; decorated Merit Svc. medals (2), Calif. Medal of Merit, Gov's Unit Cit., Merit Unit Cit., GCM; Republican; Presbyterian (elder); rec: motorcycle touring, tennis. Res: 781 Harvard Ave, Dinuba 93618 Ofc: Averill E. Hawkins, CLU, 531 N. Alta, Suite D, Dinuba 93618

HAWKINS, LELAND BARNES, III, real estate executive; b. Apr. 4, 1926, Moneta; s. Leland Barnes, Jr. and Jessie Geneva (Luckensmeyer) H.; m. Jane Louise Albrecht, Sept 26, 1959; children: Joanna Louise, b. 19061; Katherine, b. 1963; Frederick Barnes, b. 1967; edn; BA, Univ. of Redlands 1949; UC Davis 1983; cert. in real estate, Wharton Sch., Univ. of Penn. Career: power cons. indsl. sales Metropolitan Div. So. Calif. Edison 1952-56; coll. rep. Prentice Hall 1956-58; So. Calif. sales mgr. Occidental Chem. Co. 1958-76; gen. mgr. Brookside Properties 1977--; dir. Foothill Investments 1983--; chmn. Calif. Delegation to European Congress celebrating the Bicentennial of the Treaties of Paris & Versailles 1983; awards: Meritorious Svc. Awd., Riverside Chpt. Calif. Soc. Sons of the Am. Revolution; mem: SAR (National Soc. trustee 1984-, pres. Calif. Soc. 1983-84); Affiliated Cities Rental Owners Assn. (past v.p., dir.); Affiliated Cities Apartment Assn.; Am. Legion; Redlands Hist. Soc.; Orange Belt Mineralogical Soc.; Redlands Gem & Mineral Soc.; Classic Car Club of So. Calif. Univ. of Redlands Fellow; City of Redlands Traffic Commnr.; Winter Concert Assn.; works: ed. Patriot Volunteer 1983-84; mil: US Army 1943-45; USMCR 1947-52; Republican; Congregational; rec: desert exploration, opera, Am. & European history. Res: 1521 W Cypress Ave Redlands 92373 Ofc: Brookside Properties, POB 646 Redlands 92373

HAWKINS, RICHARD MICHAEL, lawyer; b. July 23, 1949, Nevada City; s. Robert Augustus and Virginia June (Hawke) H.; m. Linda Lee, Sept. 27, 1975; 1 dau: Alexandra Michelle, b. 1978; edn: BS, UC Davis 1971; JD, UC Hasting Coll. of Law 1974; M.Law-Taxation, Univ. of Pacific McGeorge Sch. of Law 1983; admitted to Calif. State Bar 1974. Career: assoc. atty. Larue & Francis, Nevada City 1974-75; partner 1976; partner Larue, Roach & Hawkins, Nevada City 1977-78; of counsel Berliner & Ellers, Nevada City 1978-80; partner Berliner, Spiller & Hawkins, 1981; sole practitioner Richard M. Hawkins, A Profl. Corp. 1981--; honors: Order of the Coif, Thurston Soc., Phi Kappa Phi, Bancroft Whitney Award 1973; mem: Am., Calif. & Nevada City Bar Assns.; 49er Fire Dept. Protection Dist. (Bd. Commrs., Fire Chief); Democrat; Catholic; rec: running, swimming, tennis. Res: 13343 Red Dog Rd Nevada City 95959 Ofc: 305 Railroad Ave, Ste 10, Nevada City 95959

HAYES, JAMES CLYDE, artist; b. May 28, 1946, Clovis, N.M.; s. Christopher C. and Willow Grace (Hoyle) H.; edn: Univ. of NM 1966-9; stu. architectl. rendering w/ Yum Kee Fu, AIA Hong Kong, China (now in Albuquerque NM), portraiture w/ R.C. Gorman, Garo Antresian, w/ British sculptors Pearson and Young. Career: artist, painter spec. in combining history with art; reproduction prints of his paintings available in S.F. shops in St. Francis Hotel, Fairmont, The Opera Shop, Grace Cathedral, many others; one of his Windmill prints presented to Queen Beatrix of Holland by the dir. of S.F. Parks and Rec. Dept., 1982; his paintings of historically significant buildings in San Francisco printed as cards and prints for sale on site include: the Conservatory purchased by S.F. Garden Club to commemorate restoration and raise funds for maint.; oil painting of the Second Flood Mansion printed into cards for graduation ceremonies by the Hamlin Girls Sch., 1983; Stuart Hall Boys Sch. at Sacred Heart, the 3d. Flood Mansion, purch. watercolour of their sch. 1981; the San Francisco Opera House and Louis M. Davies Sym. Hall paintings used on Christmas cards by the trustees two yrs.; watercolour paintings of Grace

Cathedral (sold to Dean Gillespie) and Trinity Episcopal Ch. (blt. 1890, pre-earthquake structure), 1981. Address: 100 Harbor Blvd. Sp.4, Belmont 94002

HAYES, WILLIAM RICHARD, business executive; b. Apr. 5, 1921, Yonkers, NY; s. Albert Aloysius and Laura Julia (Crimmins) H.; m. Anne E. Hannan, May 22, 1943; children: Thomas, b. 1945; Timothy, b. 1947; Robert, b. 1950; Susan, b. 1952; Daniel, b. 1955; edn: UC Riverside 1954-57; Univ. of Omaha 1958-61. Career: exec. v.p. BKC, Inc., Bethesda, Md. 1978-81; v.p. ops. HBV, Inc., Sacramento, Ca. 1981-82; v.p. western region Mantech Internat. Corp. (Alexandra, Va.), Los Angeles, San Diego 1982--; dir. HBV Inc.; cons. Rakan Aviation, Rome, NY; mem: Order of Daedalians; Air Force Assn.; Sacto.; Nat. War Coll. Alumni; Rancho Bernardo Swim & Tennis Club; Eastview Swim & Tennis Club; mil: maj. gen. USAF, DSM Legion of Merit, DFC, Bronze Star; Republican; Catholic; rec: tennis, squash, racquetball. Res: 17665 Drayton Hall Way Rancho Bernardo 92128 Ofc: Mantech Internat. Co., 8352 Clairemont Mesa Blvd San Diego 92111

HAYTON, BRADLEY PAUL, psychologist; b. July 24, 1952, Inglewood; s. Roy Kenneth and Constance Alice (Brown) H.; edn: BA (psychol., Bible), Biola Univ. 1974; M.Div., Bethel Theol. Seminary 1976; MS (clin./comm. psych), CSU Fullerton 1979; MA (marriage, family, child counseling), Biola Univ. 1980; MA (mod. Euro. hist.), UC Irvine 1983; PhD (psych.), US Internat. Univ. 1983. Career: tchr. assistant, 1978-81; behavior splst. II, College Hosp., Cerritos 1978-83; psychologist/ alcoholism counselor Moorings, Long Beach 1982--; asst. prof. Calif. Christian Inst., Anaheim 1983--; adj. asst. prof. Azusa Pacific Univ., Azusa 1983--; mem: Nat. Emotive Therapy Inst.; Christian Assn. for Psychological Studies; Assn. of Labor Mgmt. Admin.; Cons. on Alcoholism; publs: contbr. to Journ. of Christian Reconstruction, Christianity & Civilization, Journ. of Psychology & Christianity, Journ. of Theol. & Psychol., Christianity Today, Reformed Journ., Fundamentalist Journ., Geneva Review; Republican; Christian; rec: singing, backpacking, skiing. Res: 6210 W Ocean Front Newport Beach 92663 Ofc: Azusa Pacific University, Psy. Dept., Azusa 91702

HAZBOUN, VIVECA, psychiatrist; b. Nov. 2, 1949, Ramallah, Jordan, nat. 1971; d. Albert Anthony and Helen (Kalaris) H.; edn: BA, Immaculate Heart Coll. 1970; MS, USC 1972, MD, 1976. Board Certified in Adult Psychiatry. Career: tchg. asst. USC Grad. Sch.; clin. instr. in clin. psychiatry/fellow in child and adolescent psychiatry/chief child resident LA County-USC Medical Center 1980-81; ward chief Children's Inpatient Psychiatric Service, and asst. prof. clin. psychiat. LAC-USC Med. Ctr. and USC Med. Sch., 1981--; pvt. practice in child, adult and adolescent psychiatry, Los Angeles 1981--; awards: recognition, L.A. Child Guidance Clinic 1980, Papal Awd. for article re Papal Pilgrimage to the Holy Land; mem: So. Calif. Psychiat. Soc., L.A. Psychoanalytic Inst., Am. Acad. of Child Psychiatry, So. Calif. Soc. for Child Psychiat., Am. Arab Univ. Graduate Club, L.A. Athletic Club; publs: med. journal arts., poetry (French) in Gesture; Catholic; rec: dance, swim, painting. Res: 2045 Kenilworth Ave Los Angeles 90039 Ofc: 4815 Hollylwood Blvd Ste. 25, Los Angeles 90027

HAZELTINE, HERBERT SAMUEL, lawyer; b. Dec. 12, 1908, Huntington Beach; s. Herbert S. and Emma (Phelps) H.; m. Frances Sue Coffin, Aug. 5, 1936; children: Susan Connell, b. 1940, Ann Hyde, b. 1948, Lynn H., b. 1952; edn: AB, Stanford Univ. 1931; JD, Harvard Law Sch. 1934; hon. JD, USC, 1979. Career: lawyer assoc. Evans & Boye, 1935-41; partner Adams, Duque & Hazeltine, 1945--; pres. La Bolsa Title Co.; life trustee USC; mem: Am. Bar Assn., Corp. Sectys. of Am.; mil: cmdr. USNR, 1942-45; Republican; Protestant; rec: golf. Res: 495 Orange Grove Cir. Pasadena 91105 Ofc: Adams, Duque & Hazeltine, 523 W. 6th St Los Angeles 90014

HEADLEE, ROLLAND DOCKERAY, executive director, Town Hall of Calif.; b. Aug. 27, 1916, Los Angeles; s. Jesse William and Cleora (Dockeray) H.; desc. Thomas Wight, English emigrant to Mass. 1634; stu. UCLA; m. Alzora Burgett, May 13, 1939; 1 dau: Linda Ann (Pohl), b. 1946. Career: asst. mgr. Finance Assocs. 1946-59; fin. & bus. cons. R.D. Headlee & Assocs 1959--; acct. exec. and cons. Walter E. Heller & Co. 1962-65; exec. v.p. Genrus Engring. Corp. 1965-67; exec. dir. Town Hall of California, 1967--; Dir.: Am. Internat. Bank Mfrs. Assocs., Starfire Engring. Co., (past) Genuss Engring., Jolie Cosmetics; Moderator, Town Hall on the Air, nat. radio pgm.; guest lectr. USC Sch. Eng. 1977, 78; tchr. Comparative Religions 1954-69; honored by formal resolution: US Senate, 92d & 95th Sessions; US Cong., 91st Session; Calif. State Assembly, 1971, 76; City of L.A. 1971; mem: Town Hall (life) Detroit Econ. Club; Mensa Internat.; L.A. World Affairs Council; L.A. Stock Exch. Club; US Power Squadron; US Coast Guard Aux., flotilla commdr.; Westport Beach Club; Commonwealth Club; Newcomen Soc.; Com. on Foreign Rels.; BSA, Sea Scout Counselor; Oceanic Soc.; publs: ed. ll anthologies concerning over 20 subjects; guest writer, var. trade publs.; mil: 1st lt., gen. staff ofcr., lt.jg USCGR, post WWII; Republican; Methodist (adult supt.,

v.chmn. bd.); rec: skiing, gem/mineral collector, sailing, equestrian. Res: 8064 El Manor Ave Los Angeles 90045 Ofc: Town Hall, R.D. Headlee Assocs., 523 W 6th St, Ste 232, Los Angeles 90014

HEARN, JOHN ROBERT, construction co. president; b. May 17, 1927, NY; s. John Joseph and Marguerite M (Conyers) H.; m. Frances C. Walsh, June 18, 1949; children: Barbara Jean, b. 1957; John F., b. 1962; edn: cert., Coll. of Armed Forces; courses, San Antonio Jr. Coll., San Mateo Jr. Coll.; BBA, St. John's Univ. 1960; Calif. Lic. Class A Engring. Contractor. Career: equip. mgr. Merritt Chapman & Scott Corp., NYC 1965; asst. equip. mgr. Bechtel Corp., San Francisco 1966; constrn. mgr. E.O. Wickberg Constrn. Co., Perth Amboy, NY 1970; v.p./ gen. mgr. Lapadula & Villani of Calif., Long Beach 1971; v.p./ gen. mgr. Constrn. Machine Movers, El Monte 1975; pres. Fran & Jack Eng. & Constrn. Co., Glendora 1980--; eng. cons. San Bon Constructors, San Dimas; Q' clearing for Top Secret work for Dept. of Energy; honors: Delta Mu Delta, St. Johns Univ. 1958; past pres. PTA Pomona Catholic H.S. 1974; mem: Knights of Columbus; Elks; Toastmasters; mil: pfc US Army 1945-47; Republican; Catholic; rec: fishing, golf, swimming. Res: 122 Carlet St San Dimas 91773 Ofc: Fran & Jack Engring & Construction Co., 225 S Glendora Ave, Ste 396, Glendora 91740

HEARST, RANDOLPH APPERSON, publishing co. executive; b. Dec. 2, 1915, NYC; s. William Randolph and Millicent (Willson) H.; m. Catherine Campbell, Jan. 12, 1938, div. 1982; children: Catherine; Virginia; Patricia; Anne; Victoria; m. 2d. Maria C. Scruggs, May 2, 1982; edn: student, Harvard 1933-34. Career: asst. to ed. Atlanta Georgian 1939-40; asst. to. pub. San Francisco Call-Bull. 1940-44, exec. ed. 1947-49, pub. 1950-53; pres./ dir./ CEO Hearst Consol. Publs., Inc. and Hearst Publ. Co. Inc. 1961-64; chmn. exec. com. The Hearst Corp. 1965-73, chmn. bd. 1973-, dir. 1975-; pres. San Francisco Examiner 1972-; trustee Hearst Found.; mem: Piedmont Union; Piedmont Driving (Atlanta); Burlingame Country Club; Pacific Union; Press (San Francisco); mil: capt. USAAF Air Transport Command 1943-45; Catholic. Ofc: 110 5th St San Francisco 94103

HEATH, TED HARRIS, research engineer; b. May 24, 1951, Durango, Colo.;s. Parrish Richard, Sr. and Dixie (Harris) Heath; m. Jane, Aug. 31, 1974; children: Geoffrey Edwin, b. 1980; Sally Jane, b. 1981; edn: BS, CSU Long Beach 1979; Reg. Profl. Mech. Engr., Calif. Career: mech. engr. US Dept. of Navy, Mare Island Naval Shipyard 1980; research engr. So. Calif. Edison Co., Rosemead 1981-83; resource contracts engr. 1983-84; research engr. 1984--, renewable energy cons to pvt. individuals 1983-; mem: Tau Beta Pi; Soc. of Naval Architects & Marine Engrs.; Am. Soc. of Mech. Engrs.; Am. Wind Energy Assn.; mil: P.O. 2/c (machinist mate), USN 1970-74, Nat. Defense; Republican; Episcopal; rec: sports, camping. Res: 1230 Cottowood St Ontario 91761 Ofc: Southern California Edison Co., 2244 Walnut Grove Ave Rosemead 91770

HEATHERINGTON, DONALD WILLIAM, insurance co. executive; b. Dec. 10, 1929, Cereal; s. George Wesley and Sadie (Heins) H.; m. Audrey Kinsel, May 30, 1952; children: Dean Arthur, b. 1957; Kimberly Victoria, b. 1959; edn: Camrose Lutheran Coll. 1944-47; CLU (chartered life underwriter), CFP (chartered fin. plnnr.), American Coll. 1971; Fellow Life Mgmt. Inst. Career:' with Manufacturers Financial Group 1948--: agent. 1948-52; adminstrv. mgr. 1952-62; asst. v.p. 1962-72; gen. mgr. 1972--; pres. Hartford Life Underwriters Assn. 1960; national dir. Gen. Agents & Mgrs. Conf. (GAMC); awards: Nat. Mgmt. Awd., GAMC 1974-84; Master Agency Bldr. (Top 100 Agencies) 1983; mem: San Francisco GAMA (pres. 1980); S.F. Life Underwriters Assn.; Olympic Club; Jr. CofC; Republican; Presbyterian; rec: golf. Res: 18 Pepper way San Rafael 94901 Ofc: Manufacturers Financial, Steuart St Tower, One Market Plaza, Ste 1010, San Francisco 94105

HEATON, DEAN REED, technology co. executive; b. June 21, 1936, Larned, Ks.; s. Clyde Jacob and Mildred Ruth (Reed) H.; m. Virginia Mac Donald, Aug. 25, 1973; children: James, b. 1958; John, b. 1960; Michael, b. 1961; Leslie, b. 1963; edn: BSEE, Indiana Inst. of Tech. 1960. Career: elec. engr. Philco Corp., Fairfax, Va. 1960-62; mgr. Custome Engring. Honeywell Corp., Annapolis, Md. 1962-70; dir. mktg. Aiken Industries, College Park, Md. 1970-78; v.p./ gen. mgr. Microwave Prods. Div., TRW Microwave 1978--; mem: IEEE; AIAA; AOC; Sons of the Am. Revolution; num. arts. in electronic journs.; mil: radioman USN 1954-57; rec: genealogy, ancient history, golf. Res: 682 Rustic Ln Mountain View 94040 Ofc: TRW Microwave, 825 Stewart Dr Sunnyvale 94086

HEBERT, RAYMOND EARL, JR., consulting firm president; b. June 23, 1937, Los Angeles; s. Raymond E., Sr. and Marcella (Bente) H.; m. Karen Liner, Feb. 18, 1977; children: Shelly, b. 1962; Stac Allan, b. 1965; edn: BS, UCLA 1959; MBA, Univ. Calif. 1963. Career: sales & mktg. Armour & Co. 1961-64; mktg. dir. Hunt/ Wesson Div. Norton Simon, Inc. 1964-67; exec. v.p. AMR Internat. Inc. 1967-70; pres. MCI, Inc. 1970-77; pres. Wilshire Mktg. Corp., Div. Knopp Comm. Corp. (pub. Architectural Digest, GEO & Bon Appetit Mags.) 1977-82; pres. Hebert & Assoc., Inc., Beverly Hills 1982--; mem: Nat. Republican Commerce, Junior Chamber (pres.), Young Pres. Assn.; Nat. Com. Boy Scouts of Am.; clubs: Union League (NY), Jonathan (LA); mil: lt.jg USN, fighter pilot; rec: skiing, tennis, sailing. Res: 1296 San Ysidro Dr Beverly Hills 90210 Ofc: Hebert & Assoc., Inc., 9701 Wilshire Blvd Beverly Hills 90212

HECHT, H. MICHAEL, retail department store chain president; b. Oct. 17, 1939, Buffalo, NY; s. Harold M. and Elizabeth (Liveright) H.; m. Brenda Clucas, June 16, 1962; children: Elizabeth, b. 1965; Thomas, b. 1967; John, b. 1969; Christopher, b. 1976; edn: BA, honors, Dartmouth Coll. 1961; MBA, honors, Amos Tuck Sch. of Bus. Admin. 1962. Career: v.p./ dir. of stores Hecht Co., Wash. DC 1969; v.p./ gen. merch. mgr. Meier & Frank, Portland, Ore 1970; exec. v.p. G. Fox & Co., Hartford, Ct. 1972; exec. v.p. merch. The Broadway, Los Angeles 1975; pres. The Broadway, L.A. 1984--; mem: United Way, L.A. (sect. hd.); bd. dirs. KIDSPACE (a participatory museum); Jonathan Club, L.A.; rec: snow skiing, body surfing. Res: 1560 Charlton Rd San Marino 91108 Ofc: The Broadway 3880 N Mission Rd Los ANgeles 90031

HECKMAN, DONALD REX, II, lawyer; b. May 30, 1946, St. Joseph, Mich.; s. Donald Rex and Betty Ann (Blakeman) H.; m. Lisa, May 30, 1981; edn: BS, honors, UC Berkeley 1968; JD, UC Berkeley Boalt Hall 1973; admitted to practice, Calif. State Bar 1973; Cert. Tax Splst. 1979. Career: process engr. Shell Chem. Co., Martinez 1968-70; atty./partner Wilke, Fleury, Hoffelt, Gould & Birney, Sacto. 1973--; instr. grad. tax pgm. Golden Gate Univ. 1979-; lectr. cont. edn. pgms. Calif. CPA Found. for Edn. & Research 1981-; honors: Outstanding Undergrad. Citation, Chem. Eng. Dept. Golden Gate Univ.; Phi Beta Kappa; Tau Beta Pi; mem: Am. Bar Assn. (Tax Sect.) Calif. Bar Assn. (Tax Sect.); Sacto. Co. Bar Assn. (Bar Liaison Com.); Active 20-30 Club of Sacto. No. 1 (pres. 1984); Sacto.- San Joaquin Chpt. Muscular Dystrophy Assn.; Sacto. Estate Plng. Council (bd. dirs.); publs: paper on Use of Corporations to Hold Real Property, presented 1981 Corp. Tax Plng. Conf.; Republican; Congregationalist; rec: stamps, x-country skiing, golf. Res: 844 Santa Ynez Way Sacramento 95816 Ofc: Wilke, Fleury, Hoffelt, Gould & Birney, 555 Capitol Mall, Ste 1100, Sacramento 95814

HEDGECOCK, JAMES LEE, chiropractor; b. Oct. 26, 1943, Torrance; s. James Lee, Sr. and Florence Ellen (Bowling) H.; m. Rosalind Russell, May 13, 1972; children: Mary, b. 1964; Jeffery, b. 1965; edn: DC, Cleveland Coll. 1968; PhD neurology acupuncture, Univ. of Pasadena 1976; DC, Calif.; Acupuncture proficiency, Hong Kong Acupuncurist Fedn. 1973; cert. in nutrition & sports med., USC 1983; cert. in vascular diagnosis, Internat. Acad. of Neuro-Vascular 1980. Career: pvt. practice, Torrance 1969-72; dean of faculty Univ. of Pasadena Chiro. Coll. 1972-73; dir. of clinics/ dean postgrad. studies 1973-75; pres. Hedgecock Health Group; pvt. practices Newport Beach and Pasadena; cons. indsl. work injuries; mem: Orange Co. Chiro. Soc.; Calif. Chiro. Assn.; Parker Chiro. Research Found.; Med. Spec. Com., Calif. Health Review Journ.; rec: artist, sculptor. Res: 2690 Park Ave Laguna Beach Ofc: Hedgecock Chiropractic, 4321 Birch St, Ste E, Newport Beach 92660

HEDGES, PATRICIA ANN, psychologist; b. Aug. 23, 1955, Bellflower; d. Paul Willis and Helen (Atwood) Hedges; edn: BA, Pepperdine Univ. 1978; MA, Antioch Univ. 1981; MFCC reg. intern., Bd. of Behav. Sci. Examiners 1983. Career: psychiatric aide Charter Med. Hosp., Long Beach 1978s81; MFCC trainee, Helpline Youth Counseling, Bellflower 1981-82; MFCC reg. intern, So. Calif. Pain Control Inst., Long Beach 1981-82; coord./resrchr. Pain Control Pgm., Joseph Moskowitz, MD, Inc., Long Beach 1982-83; MFGG/ pain mgmt. counselor Patricia Hedges, MA, MFCC, Long Beach 1983--; mem. Calif. Assn. of Marriage and Family Therapists; publs: The Effects of The Arts on Children: From Birth Through Preschool Age, Annual Conf. for Calif. Assn. of Marriage & Family Therapists, San Diego 1982; Democrat; Protestant; rec: sewing, swimming, tennis. Res: 6533 Fairman St Lakewood 90713 Ofc: Patricia Hedges, MA, 3605 Long Beach Blvd, Ste 210, Long Beach 90807

HEDISH, MARC STUART, computer programmer/systems designer; b. June 14, 1965, South Bend, Indiana; s. Norman David and Sandi Lee (Levin) H. Career: computer programmer 1977--; owner Mammoth Computer Svcs., Van Nuys 1980--; sys. design & installation, High Sierra Reservations 1980; sys. cons. Community Svcs. Agency 1980-81; mem: Los Angeles Valley College Hillel Council (honor award 1983); City of Hope (Maxine Glabman Vision of Hope chpt.); copyrights: Data Management System III (8/80), Data Management System IV (1981), Poster 1.0 (1982); Democrat; Jewish; rec: electronics, computers, jazz music. Address: Mammoth Computer Services, 6830 Mammoth Ave Van Nuys 91405

HEDRICK, DANIEL LEE, automobile dealer; b. Jan. 9, 1929, Portland, Ore.; s. Earle Wesley and Mary (Talmadge) H.; m. Mary Lou Cleland, Aug. 5, 1950; two sons: Stephen, b. 1951 (PhD, asst. prof. UCSD); Donald, b. 1957 (asst. gen. mgr. family dealership); edn: LA City Coll. 1947-8; UCLA 1948-9. Career: service op. dept. Milliken Chevrolet, Culver City 1951-56, mgmt., Chevrolet Div., General Motors Corp. 1956-77, pres./dealer-opr. Dan Hedrick Chevrolet, Inc., San Fernando 1977--; bd. dirs. Quintec Mfg., Costa Mesa; recipient Comm. Svc. Award, San Fernando CofC 1980, 82, 83; mem: S.F CofC (exec. bd.), S.F. Kiwanis Club (past pres.), Woodland Hills Country Club; Republican; Episcopal; rec: water ski, boating, old car restoration. Res: 4516 San Blas Ave Woodland Hills 91364 Ofc: Dan Hedrick Chevrolet Inc. 753 San Fernando Rd San Fernando 91340

HEFFLEFINGER, CLARICE MAE, real estate broker; b. Oct. 5, 1937, Oregon, Ill.; d. Ralph Wayne and Wyota A. (Nashold) Thorpe; m. Jack K. Hefflefinger; children: Kevin, Deborah, Jack, Kenneth; edn: AA, Coll. of the Sequoias 1967, certs. in Ins., R.E., Bus. courses; Fresno State Coll. 1956. Career: var. positions, banking & insurance, 1956-76; real estate 1977--; substitute tchr. Tulare City Schs. 1979--; rep. State Assemblyman Don Rogers, 33rd Dist., Tulare Co. 1982--; chmn. Tulare Co. Draft Bd.; awards: Realtor of the Yr. 1983 Tulare Bd. Realtors, appreciation cits. from Am. Legion, Amvets;

mem: Nat. Assn. Realtors; Calif. Assn. Realtors (dir.); Tulare Bd. Realtors (pres. 1982, dir. 1984); Republican Nat. Com.; Republican Womens Fedn., Tulare; League of Women Voters; Tulare CofC (Booster Club); Tulare Amvets Aux. (pres. 1983-84); Republican; Protestant; rec: dancing, playing piano. Res: 1351 William Tulare 93274 Ofc: Lewis Real Estate, POB 1213 Tulare 93275

HEFLER, DAVID A., data processing executive; b. May 31, 1943, NY, NY; s. Bernard L. and Vera Francis (Schindel) H.; m. Jean Riggs, Oct. 25, 1969; children: Andrew, b. 1971; Adam, b. 1974; Rachel, b. 1977; edn: BS in bus. adm., Fairleigh Dickinson Univ. 1966; AS in data proc., Mt. San Antonio Coll. 1978; MA, mgmt., Univ. of Redlands 1983. Career: sales & mktg. mgr. Genuine Parts Co., Napa, Anaheim 1973-76; data processing pgmr./analyst, data processing mgr. Sparling Div. Envirotech Corp., El Monte 1976-78; sys. analyst Beckman Instruments, Fullerton 1978-79; ADP plng. analyst So. Calif. Edison, Rosemead 1979-82; mgr. data processing hardware svcs. Securty Pacific nat. Bank, Glendale 1982--; mem: Boy Scouts of Am.; Reserve Ofcrs. Assn.; conbr: Communications for Management and Business, by Norman Sugband, pub. Scott Froesman, 1982; mil: maj. US Army 1966-73, nuclear weapons ofcr., currently, USAR; rec: travel, photog. Res: 1086 Nashport St LaVerne 91750 Ofc: Security Pacific Nat. Bank, 701 N Brand Blvd Glendale 91203

HEIFERMAN, ANNABELLE, city official; b. Oct. 5, 1922, Luthersville, Ga.; d. Walter S. and May Bell (Sprayberry) Cruse; m. Joseph Heiferman, Sept. 2, 1947; children: James, b. 1941, Dana, b. 1944, Carolyn, b. 1948, David, b. 1959, Tobi, b. 1961; edn: BA in bus. adm., Univ. of Ga. 1944. Career: mdse. exec. R.H. Macy & Co., Atlanta, Ga. 1948-57; vice pres. Joe Heiferman Inc. (jewelry co.), Beverly Hills 1959-; elected to City Council 1982--, currently vice-mayor, City of Beverly Hills; community recognition awards incl. Calif. Cong. PTA, and Maple Center bd. dirs.; led drive for zoning ordinance to provide senior housing in B.H.; past pres. B.H. Senior Adult Assn. 1978-81; served on B.H. Housing and Comm. Devel. Com.; active in League of Women Voters, Am. Cancer Soc., City of Hope, Junior Blind, Childrens Hosp., founding bd. B.H. Meals on Wheels pgm.; Democrat; Jewish. Res: 607 N. Foothill Rd Beverly Hills 90210 Ofc: City of Beverly Hills, 450 N. Crescent Dr Beverly Hills 90210

HEIKEL, HARVEY ALLEN, marketing executive; b. Mar. 31, 1941, Cleveland, Ohio; s. Samuel Emil and Helmi Sharon (Samo) H.; edn: BA intl. studies, and BSBA intl. trade, Ohio State Univ. 1965; MBA, Golden Gate Univ. 1973. Career: research/admin. asst. Amer. Mktg. Assn., 1964-65; customer rels./ pgmr. Electronic Data Sys., Dallas, Tex. & San Francisco, Calif. 1969-71; field sales rep., regl. sales mgr., dist. sales mgr., S.F. 1971-82; dir. mktg. R.J. Bambeck Co., Santa Ana 1982--; partner Market Probe Internat., internat. mkt. research 1975--; awards: honors: Scabbard & Blade 1965; Anchor & Chain, Ohio St. Lacrosse Team 1962-64, co-capt. 1964; mem: Alpha Tau Omega; Navy ROTC; Ohio State Univ. Athletic Council; Council of Fraternity Pres. (Ohio St. U.); Columbus, Grange City, & San Francisco Lacrosse Clubs; mil: capt. USMC 1965-69, Vietnam Campaign, Navy Unit Cit.; Christian; rec: skiing, native plants, travel. Res: 100 J Bridgeway, 150, Sausalito 94965 Ofc: R.J. Bambeck Co., Irvine Indsl. Complex, 1921 E Carnegie Ave Santa Ana 92705

HEINDL, CLIFFORD JOSEPH, physicist, executive researcher; b. Feb. 4, 1926, Chgo.; s. Anton T. and Louise (Fiala) H.; edn: BS, Northwestern Univ. 1947; MA, 1948; MA, Columbia Univ. 1950; PhD, 1959; Oak Ridge Sch. of Reactor Tech. 1954-55. Career: sr. physicist Bendix Aviation Corp. Research Labs., Detroit, Mich. 1953-54; asst. sect. chief atomic energy div. Babcock & Wilson Co., Lynchburg, Va. 1956-58; supvr. nuclear & reactor physics gp. Jet Propulsion Lab., Pasadena 1959-65; tech. mgr. research & adv. devel. Jet Propulsion Lab., Calif. Inst. of Tech. 1965--; mem: Am. Inst. of Aero. & Astro., Health Physics Soc.; Am. Physical Soc.; Am. Nuclear Soc.; author: var. sci. & tech. papers; mil: sgt. US Army Med. Corps 1944-46, WWII. Res: 179 Mockingbird Ln, So. Pasadena Ofc: 4800 Oak Grove Dr Pasadena 91103

HEINEMANN, HEINZ, scientist; b. Aug. 21, 1913, Berlin, Germany, nat. 1944; s. Felix and Edith (Boehm) H.; m. Elaine Silverman, Feb. 12, 1948; children: Susan Carol, b. 1948, Peter Michael, b. 1951; : PhD, Univ. of Basle, 1938. Career: lab. supvr. Attapulgus Clay Co., Phila. 1941-48; section chief Resrch., Houdry Process Corp., Phila. 1948-57; dir. Chem. Engring. Resrch., The G.W. Kellogg Co., NY 1957-69; mgr. Catalysis Resrch., Mobil Res. & Dev. Corp., Princeton, NJ 1969-78; staff senior scientist Lawrence Berkeley Lab., Univ. of Calif. 1978--; lectr. chem. eng. dept. UCB; honors: elected Nat. Academy of Engring. 1976; Gerphree Award, Am. Chem. Soc. 1971; Houdry Award, Catalysis Soc. 1975; Cat. Club of Phila. Award 1976; mem: Am. Chem. Soc., Catalysis Soc., Fellow Am. Inst. Chem. Engring., Royal Soc., Internat. Congress Catalysis (pres. 1956-60); publs: 135 profl. papers and patents. Res: 1588 Campus Drive Berkeley 94708 Ofc: LBL Bldg. 62, University of California Berkeley 94720

HEINO, PAMELA SUE, speech pathologist; b. Mar. 29, 1949, Salina, Kansas; d. Alfred V. and Donna J. Heino; edn: BA, UC Santa Barbara 1971; MA, Univ. of the Pacific 1972. Teaching Credentials: Adminstrv. Services 1982, Std. Tchg. 1980, Comm. Colls. 1973; State lic. Speech Pathologist 1974. Career: Middle Severe Language Delayed/ Aphasia Tchr. Splst., Los Angeles Co. Supt. of Schs. 1972-3, primary SLD, 1973-4, presch. SLD, 1974-5, diagnostic SLD, 1975-7, pgm. splst. for SLD/A, 1977-79, 1980, high sch. SLD/A tchr. splst., 1980-81; pgm. splst. in spl. edn. for five school districts: Ha. Dists., 1981--; speech pathol. in pvt. practice, Redondo Beach 1979--; instr. UCLA Ext., 1980-; profl. spkr. var. confs. 1981-, radio talk show guest; cons./instr. Citrus Comm. Coll.; v.p. Koenig Ent. Inc. 1981-; v.p. RLN Ent. Inc. 1981-; ptnr. NHB Associates 1981-; dir. of mktg. Pacific Devel. Assocs. 1982-; awards: Cert.

Clin. Competence, Am. Speech and Hearing Assn. 1975; Fed. Grad. Fellowship, UOP 1972; mem: Am., Calif. Speech and Hearing Assns., Calif. Assn. for Neurologically Impaired Children, Assn. of Calif. Sch. Administrs., Calif. Assn. of Program Splst. (chm. local orgn. 1982-), Irena Twnhse Assn. (pres. 1982-), Marina City Club: Republican; Christian; rec: travel, int. design, singing. Res: 717 C North Irena Ave Redondo Beach 90277 Ofc: Lawndale School District 4161 W. 147th St Lawndale 90260

HEINRICHS, CHARLES LEONARD, engineering executive; b. Aug. 6, 1933, Reedley; s. Abraham Benjamin and Sarah Doris (Koop) H.; m. Nancy Germann, Feb. 24, 1957; children: Debra, b. 1958; Patrice, b. 1960; Gregory, b. 1961; David, b. 1965; edn: BA, Northwest Mo. State Univ. 1958; MBA, Pepperdine Univ. 1980. Career: analyst No. American Aviation, Neosho, Mo. 1959-61; jr. statistician Bendix Corp., Kansas City, Mo. 1961-62; reliability engr. Gen. Dynamics Corp., San Diego 1962-65; sr. scientist Booz- Allen Applied Research, Inc., Ft. Leavenworth, Ks. 1965-66; sect. hd. Gen. Dynamics Corp., Montreal, Canada & Rochester, NY 1966-70; engring. mgr. Hughes Aircraft Co., Los Angeles 1970--; adult edn. instr. 1959-65; indsl. commun. cons. 1969-; awards: Outstanding Toastmaster of the Yr., Area 7, Dist. 33, Toastmasters Internat. 1978; mem: Soc. of Logistics Engrs.; Toastmasters; Reliability, Maintainability Logistics Symposium; Nat. Spkrs. Assn.; publs: sci./tech. papers, Gen. Dynamics Reliability Panel 1964, ASQC 1967; mil: airman 1/c USAF 1951-55, GCM; Libertarian; Protestant; rec: jogging, fishing. Res: 755 N Verna Ave Newbury Park 91320 Ofc: Hughes Aircraft Co., 8433 Fallbrook Ave Canoga Park 91304

HEINZER, ERNEST ROBERT, factory representative, exporter and importer; b. Apr. 6, 1943, San Francisco; s. Ernest Alfred and Janet (Watson) H.; edn: BA, San Francisco State 1965. Career: Jr. H.S. tchr. 1967-70; Ernest A. Heinzer Co., San Francisco (oldest wholesaler of juvenile furniture in Western US) 1970; currently, owner Ernest A. Heinzer & Sons Co., S.F.; Fine Arts Mus. of S.F. (bd. dirs. Graphic Arts Council); The Olympic Club; The Walpole Soc. of London; works: paints, designs juvenile bedding, toys & clothing. Republican; rec: art collecting, gardening. Ofc: Ernest A. Heinzer & Sons Co., 933 Treat Ave San Francisco 94110

HEISLER, TREY HARRY, lawyer; b. Dec. 2, 1949, Opelika, Ala.; s. Irving Dan Jules and Bett Mae (Karnoff) H.; m. Pamela-Beth Stearns, Feb. 3, 1980; children: Jeremiah, b. 1982; Adam, b. 1983; edn: UC Santa Barbara 1967-69; BA, UCLA 1971; JD, Univ. of San Fernando Valley Coll. of Law 1975; admitted to practice, Calif. State Bar 1976. Career: sales assoc. Bullocks 1970-76; atty. assoc. Singer & Rudolph 1976-78, Singer, Rudolph & Braun 1978-79; assoc. Korte, Crain & Parente 1979-81, partner Korte, Crain & Heisler 1981--, splst. Workers Compensation; honors: Am. Field Svc., Academic 1966; mem: founder, So. Bay Workers Compensation Council; Calif. Defense Attys. Assn.; Democrat; Jewish; rec: golf, hiking, backpacking. Res: 18871 Kilfinan St Northridge 91326 Ofc: Korte, Crain & Heisler, 5455 Wilshire Blvd, Ste 1706, Los Angeles 90036 & 235 Montgomery St, Ste 1823 San Francisco 94104

HEISMAN, MICHAEL ALAN, podiatrist; b. Dec. 30, 1950, Albany, NY; s. Bertram Charles and Lenore (Wolinsky) H.; m. Marleen, June 5, 1978; children: Nicole, b. 1979; Brian, b. 1982; edn: BS, State Univ. Coll. at New Paltz, NY 1973; MS, Rensselaer Poltechnic Inst. 1975; DPM, Calif. Coll. of Podiatric Med. 1978; podiatrist, Calif. 1978. Career: pvt. practice, San Jose 1978-83; staff podiatrist San Jose State Univ. 1980-83; staff podiatrist Crestwood Manor Physciatric Facility 1978--; sports podiatrist San Jose State Univ. Basketball Team 1980--; chief Valley Med. Ctr., Podiatry Clinic 1979--; med. staff San Jose Gen. Hosp., Valley West General Hosp., Santa Clara Valley Med. Ctr., O'Conner Gen. Hosp.; mem: Central Coast Podiatric Med. Assn.; Am. Podiatry Assn.; Calif. Podiatric Med. Assn.; Am. Coll. of Sports Med.; Podiatric Sports Med. Assn.; Pacific Coast Health Assn.: Works: Antibiotic Extraction from Selected Soil Samples, Eastern Coll. Sem. Journ. 1973; Synergistic Effects of Selected Bacteria in Use of the Ecologen, New Brunswick Med. Bulletin 1975; rec: running, sports medicine. Res: 806 Midvale Ln San Jose 95136 Ofc: 1706 Willew Street, Ste E, San Jose 95125

HEKMAT-PANAH, SOHEIL, physician; b. Nov. 26, 1947, Tehran, Iran; naturalized 1981; s. Morad and Houran (Shenassa) Hekmat; edn: BS, microbiol., Mich. State Univ., 1970, MD, Univ. of Mexico, 1975; m. Afsaneh Kohen, 1982; career: residency in internal medicine, White Memorial Medical Center, Los Angeles; currently, Medical Director of Angelus Convalescent Hosp., Inglewood, Marlinda Convalescent Hosp., Lynwood, Hillcrest Medical Clinic, Inglewood; Jewish; rec: collector, antiquest, stamps & coins; res: 1300 Midvale #607, Los Angeles 90024 ofc: Hillcrest Med. Clinic 511 E. Manchester Blvd., Inglewood 90301; Brentwood Med. Center, 11633 San Vincente Blvd. #320, Los Angeles 90049.

HELD, BRUCE JAY, industrial hygienist; b. Apr. 10, 1933, Allentown, Pa.; s. Warren H. and Evelyn (Muschlitz) H.; m. Peggy Anderson (dec.); m. 2d. Beryl Siemer, Feb. 16, 1973; children: Karen, b. 1956, Bruce, b. 1958, Karl, b. 1961, Kurt, b. 1961, Glen, b. 1964, (step): Kenneth, b. 1961, Beryl Katherine, b. 1962, Kerrie, b. 1969; edn: BS, Cornell Univ. 1955; MPH (IH), Univ. of Mich. 1964; Calif. Reg. Profl. Safety Engr., Cert. Safety Profl. Career: indsl. hygienist Nat. Lead of Ohio, Cincinnati, 1956-59; indsl. hygienist US Atomic Energy Commn., Idaho Falls, Ida. 1959-63, Atomics International, Canoga Park, Ca. 1964-67, Sandia Labs., Livermore 1967-71, Allied Gulf Nuclear Corp., Barnwell, S.C. 1971-72; asst. group ldr. for R&D, Los Alamos (NM) Sci. Lab., 1972-75; leader Indsl. Hygiene Group, Lawrence Livermore Nat. Lab., Livermore, Ca. 1975--; bd. dirs. Board of Cert. Safety Profls. of the America 1974-79 (pres. 1978); mem. (Gov. Reagan apptee) State Environmental Quality Study Council 1969-71; expert witness for OSHA sev. health std. hearings; faculty Environ. Sci. Dept., CSU Hayward 1976-; mem. Health and Safety Adv. Com., (past chmn. Breathing Apparatus Panel 1979) Internat. Assn. Fire Fighters; cons. on respiratory protection pvt. indus.; US rep. of the Internat. Atomic Energy Agcy. meeting to revise Respirator and Protective Clothing Std., Vienna, Austria 1982; mem. Am. Indsl. Hygiene Assn. (1959-), Am. Conf. of Govtl. Indsl. Hygienists (1959-), Veterans of Safety, Internat. Soc. for Respiratory Protection (1st pres. 1982); NFPA Fire Fighter Breathing Apparatus Com. 1978-; publs: author/ coauthor 5 books in field, num. journal arts., conf. papers; rec: model railroading. Res: 534 Yosemite Dr Livermore 94550 Ofc: LLNL, POB 5505, L-384, Livermore 94550

HELD, CARL PETER, physician, pain center medical director; b. Mar9. 22, 1934, NY; s. Otto Peter and Alice Gloria Heald; children: John, b. 1970; Douglas, b. 1973; edn; Ba, Allegheny Coll. 1959; MD, 1963; resident internal med., Univ. of Colo. 1964-66; psychiatric res., Wash. Univ., St. Louis 1966-69. Career: med. doctor, Headache & Backache Inst., a Pain Ctr. in Tustin; mem: Orange Co. Med. Assn.; Calif. Med. Assn.; CofC; Sierra Club; Toastmasters; developed pain pgm. which eliminates common types of severe, long term pain problems; mil: enlisted US Army Med. Corps. 1955-57; rec: cooking, dancing. Res: 29 Woodwind Irvine 92714 OFc: Headache & Backache Inst., A Pain Center, 17400 Irvine Blvd Tustin 92680

HELDT, JOHN JOURDAN, educator, quality engineer; b. Dec. 19, 1919, Evansville, Ind.; s. Carl Anton and Marcella Clara (Bosse) H.; m. Marguerite Walton, May 11, 1946; children: John, b. 1950, Nicholas, b. 1951, Rebecca, b. 1953, Marguerite, b. 1954, Angela, b. 1955, Janet, b. 1958, Marcella b. 1963; edn: The Inf. Sch., Ft. Benning, Ga. 1944; BSEE, Univ. of Evansville, 1949; MSEE, So. Methodist Univ. 1961; PhD, Sussex Coll. of Tech., England 1975. Reg. Profl. Engr. (elec., mech., quality) in Ind., Tex., Calif.; Calif. State Expert Examiner for Quality Registration. Career: water well and pump wk. for Heldt-Monroe Co., Evansville, Ind. 1949-51; AUS combat engr., Korea 1951-52; welding engr. RCA Whirlpool, plant engr. Hoosier Cardinal Corp., Evansville 1952-57, metallurgical process analyst General Dynamics, Ft. Wor th (authored a process patent for 17-7 ph stainless steel heat treatment) 1957-63; senior resrch. engr. Lockheed Co., Sunnvale 1962-70, Senior Procurement Product Assurance Engr. 1970, senior PA Engr. GTE Lenkurt, San Carlos, 5 years; sr. staff engr. Ampex, Sunnyvale, 2 years., and Memorex, Santa Clara, 2 yrs.; head Product Assur. Design Support, Watkins-Johnson Co., San Jose 3 yrs.; currently prin. engr. Quality Systems, Fortune Systems Inc., Belmont; educator: devel. Master's Degree in Quality Mgmt. pgm. for Univ. of Phoenix, taught all courses for first two pilot pgms., authored all text modules and tchg. aids for pgm., and with W.E. Land organized Bachelor's Quality Pgm.; organized seminars for Am. Inst. for Quality and Reliability and Penton Learning Systems through USA; instr. quality engring. courses De Anza Coll. 1970-; mem. Quality Assur. Adv. Coms., De Anza Coll., Univ. f Phoenix; Mentor for Quality Degree Pgm., Columbia Pacific Univ.; honors: Fellow ASQC 1981, recipient E.L. Grant Award, ASQC 1983, and 17 awards for ASQC seminar presentations (internat., regional, local); patentee; contbg. writer/editorial bd. Quality Mag. (Hitchcock Pub.); mil: 2d lt. Inf. 71st Div., Eur. WWII; 1st lt., Korea 1951-52, Bronze Star, Commendn., Battle Stars; Democrat; rec: volleyball, swim. Res. 2205 Riordan Dr San Jose 95130 Ofc: Fortune Systems Inc. 300 Harbor Blvd Belmont 94002

HELFAND, STEPHEN LEWIS, physician-neurology; b. Apr. 24, 1953, Brooklyn, NY; s. Alan Jay and Rita Rachel Zelda (Wolffe) H.; m. Sharon K. Inouye, MD, Aug. 28, 1983; edn: undergrad. S.U.N.Y., Binghamton 1971-73; BS, honors, Stanford Univ. 1975; MD, Albert Einstein Coll. of Med. 1979; Diplomate Nat. Bd. Med. Examiners 1980. Career: med. intern Montefiore Hosp., NY 1979-80; clin. resident in neurol. Mass. Gen. Hosp., Boston 1980-83; vis. scholar in neuroimmunology Queen's Univ., Kingston, Ont., Can. 1981; postdoctl. fellow in developmental neurobiology/ cons. in neurol., Stanford Univ. 1983--; awards: NSF fellowship 1975, Am. Medical Students Assn. nat. research awd. 1zw7, Roche Award in Neuroscis. y77, MRC Fellowship in Neuroimmunol. 1979, Queen's Univ. Devel. Fund Awd. 1981, Sandoz Awd., Boston Soc. Psychiatry/Neurol. 1983; mem: Am. Acad. of Neurology, Boston Soc. of Psychiatry and Neurology, Mass. Med. Soc., NY Acad. of Scis.; author chapter in NK Cells and Other Natural Effector Cells (Academic Press 1982), over 15 sci. publs.; Democrat; Jewish; rec: creative writing. Res: 396 Imperial Way, 315, Daly Cit 94015 Ofc: Dept. Biol. Scis. Stanford University Stanford 94305

HELLER, JOHN A., computerized information systems consultant; b. Oct. 5, 1953, Monroe, Mich.; s. Thomas George and Marilyn (Knowles) H.; m. Margert S. Walsh, Oct. 17, 1982; edn: BS, Rensselaer Polytech. Inst. 1976. Career: material supvr. Leviton Mfg., NY 1975-77; proj. mgr. 1977-78; mng. mfg. control sys. Bendix, Tenn. 1978-79; mgr. mfg. material sys. Bendix, NY 1979-81; mgr. mfg. control sys. McGraw Edison, NJ 1981; dir. applications devel. MRP Sys., Calif. 1981-82; independent cons. mgmt. efficiency sys. 1982--; dir. applications support Reliable Data Sys., Calif. 1983--; awarded NY Regent Scholarship; mem: Soc. Mfg. Engrs.; Am. Prodn. Inventory Control Soc.; USR Gp.; UNIOPS; PICONET; designed MRP Sys. to run on Micros; engr. software for a speech synthesis bd. using pulse code modulation technology; Catholic. Res: 3943 El Camino Real, Apt 19, Palo Alto 94306 Ofc: Management Efficiency Systems, 3790 El Camino Real, Ste 213, Palo Alto 94306

HELLINGSON, KENNETH ROY, general contractor; b. Feb. 10, 1945, San Diego; s. Charles and Antoinetta (Petrich) H.; m. Jackie Haddad, Dec. 3, 1965;

children: Tanya, b. 1966, Tyler, b. 1973; Calif. lic. B Gen. Building Contractor. Career: with Rohr Corp. 1965-68; owner Ken Hellingson / General Contracting, 1968--, projects incl. new homes, remodeling, and restoration of hist. homes; honors: recognition for youth work, La Jolla (1975-) coach baseball, soccer, baseball, founder pres. Pinto League (lst div. of Pony Baseball) 1981-; Democrat; Presbyterian; rec: ski, bicycling, coaching sports. Res: 6219 La Jolla Mesa Dr La Jolla 92037 Ofc: Ken Hellingson, POB 2139, La Jolla 92038

HELLMAN, BARNET RICHARD, software consultant; b. Feb. 10, 1956, New Martinsville, W.Va.; s. J. Walter and Charlotte R. (Raimist) H.; edn: USAF Acad. 1974-78; BS, Worcester State Coll. 1980; MS, Univ. of New Haven 1984; cert. data proc., Worcester State Coll. 1980. Career: pgmr./ analyst R.R. Donnelley & Sons Co., Old Saybrook, Ct. 1981-82; data processing mgr. Allied Refrigeration Inc., Long Beach 1983; cons. J.D. Edwards & Co., Newport Beach 1984--; adj. lectr. Univ. of New Haven, Grotene Ext. 1982; mem: DATA; mil: cadet USAF 1974-78; Jewish; rec: philatelist, sci-fi. Res: 156 Ximeno Ave, 2, Belmont Shores 90803 (POB 90844 Long Beach 90809) Ofc: J.D. Edwards & Co., 3822 Campus Dr, Ste 205, Newport Beach 92660

HELM, RICHARD EUGENE, alarm co. president; b. Jan. 27, 1936, Winterset, Io.; s. Harry David and Mabel Florence (McCasslin) H.; m. Leah, Aug. 2, 1958; children: Arlan, b. 1959; Bryan, b. 1960. Career: worked in electronics, mechanical, electrical fields for var. cos. incl. Packard Bell Elec., Denver, Colo. 1961; Ling Elec., Anaheim 1962-63; Richfield Auto Mech., Anaheim 1964-67; U.S. Polymeric Corp. Maint. Mech., Santa Ana 1969-73; elect. wk. for Airco, Gen. Tire, Uniroyal Tire, Executive Motor Hms., 1973-778; elect. installation GW Alarm Co. Alarm & Elect., Tustin 1978-81; founder/owner/pres. Fireball Alarm Co., Anaheim 1981--; recipient recogn. award for outstanding wk. at Navy L.B. Shipyard, Gt. Western Alarm Co. 1977; gp. leader Boy Scouts; mil: airman 2/c USAF 1957-60, TAC Missile Badge, GCM; Christian; rec: electronics, travel, photog. Address: Fireball Alarm Co., 1840 E Redwood Ave Anaheim 92805

HELMAN, JOHN CLINTON, periodontist; b. Jan. 28, 1944, Maywood; s. Oliver Brigg and Jennie Angelina (Tasso) H.; m. Mary Ann Pudoff, June 10, 1967; children: Elizabeth Victoria Ann, b. 1978; Andrew George Clinton, b. 1981; edn: BA, Long Beach State Coll. 1966; DDS, Univ. of the Pacific 1970; cert. in periodontics, Wadsworth V.A. Hosp. 1976-78. Career: asoc. gen. dentist Charles A. Eliason, DDS, Alameda 1970-71; with Naismith Dental Gp., San Francisco 1971-76; resident periodontics Wadsworth VA Hosp., L.A. 1976-78, chief res. 1978; assoc. periodontist Oslas, Oliver & Arndt Periodontal Corp., El Cerrito & assoc. prof. periodontics, UOP Sch. of Destistry 1978-79; assoc. prof. periodontics UOP Sch. of Dent., S.F. 1980-82; self- empl. periodontist, So. Lake Tahoe 1979--; honors: Ki Psi Phi scholarship key UOP 1970; mem: ADA, CDA; Alameda Co., Berkeley, Sacto. Dist. & San Francisco Dental Socs.; Am. Acad. Periodont.; Calif. & Western Socs. Periodont.; So. Calif. Soc. Oral Path.; Larkspur Volunteer Firemen Assn.; Lake Valley Fire Dept.; publs: art., J. Dent. Res. 1979--; Republican; Episcopal; rec: landscaping, fishing, hiking. Res: POB 16604, So. Lake Tahoe 95706 Ofc: Jon C. Helman, DDS, 2155 South Ave, Ste 34, POB 9051, So. Lake Tahoe 95731

HELSPER, JAMES THOMAS, physician; b. Mar. 29, 1924, Mnpls., Minn.; s. Salvius John and Gretchen Louise (Gleissner) H.; m. 2d. Carolyn Harrison, Dec. 26, 1975; children: James Thomas, Jr., b. 1955; Richard Scott, b. 1957; Paige Carla, b. 1961; Brian Harrison, b. 1981; edn: BS, St. Vicent Coll., Latrobe, Pa. 1945; MD, Jefferson Med. Coll. 1947; grad. stu. Univ. of Penn. 1949-50. Career: intern Med. Ctr., Jersey Ctiy 1947-48, res. internal med. 19487-49; res., surgery: US Naval Hosp., Portsmouth, Va. 1951-52; Queens Hosp., NYC 1952s53; Meml. Ctr. for Cancer, NYC 1953-57; currently, pres. Tumor Clinic Med. Gp., Pasadena; assoc. clinical prof. of surgery (tumor), USC Sch. of Med., Los Angeles; asst. clin. prof. surgery, Loma Linda Univ. Sch.of Med. (past); surgical staff: Huntington Meml. Hosp., Calif. Hosp. Med. Ctr., St. Luke Hosp., Methodist Hosp. of So. Calif., Hosp. of Good Samaritan, L.A. Kenneth Norris, Jr. Cancer Hosp., L.A.; attending surgeon L.A. Co. USC Med. Ctr.; chief surgical tng. svc. Huntington Meml. Hosp. 1962-; cons. clin. pgm. Pasadena Found. for Med. Research 1960-81; Pasadena Found. for Med. Research 1960-; bd. dirs. Huntington Med. Research Insts. 1982-; mem: Am. Cancer Soc. (bd. dirs. Calif. div. 1967-, pres. L.A. Co. Unit 1970-71); Am., Calif. & L.A. County Medical Assns. (coms. on cancer); Pasadena Med. Soc.; L.A. Surgical Soc.; Am. Fedn. Clin. Oncologic Studies; Am. Soc. Clin. Oncology; Soc. Surgical Oncology; Soc. Head & Neck Surgeons; Am. Radium Soc.; Am. Coll. Surgeons; Pan-Pacific Surgical Assn.; World Med. Assn.; WHO; AAAS; Flying Physicians Assn.; research: devel. Stoma Button (named for author) for laryngectomy patients; num. arts. in med. journs., art. in Aero mag., 9/77; mil: capt. USNR-R, active 1943-45, 1950-52; Republican; Catholic; rec: flying, sailing, photog. Res: 580 Arbor St Pasadena 91105 Ofc: Tumor Clinic Med. Group, 635 E Union Pasadena 91101

HELZER, PAUL LAURENCE, chiropractor; b. Mar. 21, 1952, Glendale; s. Wesly Paul and Kathaleen Winona (Stubbs) H.; m. Beverly Arlene, Aug. 13, 1983; children: Jenifer Ruth, b. 1974, Ginger Kathaleen, b. 1976; edn: AA, San Antonio Jr. Coll. 1971; DC, Palmer Coll. 1974; PhD, psych., Newport Univ. 1982. Career: dr. of chiropractic/ dir. Helzer Chiropractic Clinic, Bellflower; mem. Los Angeles Coll. of Chiropractic Ext. faculty; frequent lectr.; columnist for local newspaper; contbg. writer sev. mags., research jours.; author: Interpyschic Defense Mechanisms (1982), Wholistic Living for the New Age (1983); invited (among 30 selected chiropractors) by govt. China (PRC) to lectr. and tch. in Chinese univs., hosps. 1983; recipient jourenalism awd. Parker Chiro.

Research Soc. 1981, 82, 83; mem. Am., Calif., Internat. chiropractic assns.; Lion Club (pres. 1983); Christian; rec: scuba, writing, travel. Res: 12461 Fallcreek Cerritos 90701 Ofc: Helzer Chiropractic Clinic, 9461 Flower St Bellflower 90706

HEMMING, MICHAEL JOHN, lawyer; b. June 14, 1948, Los Angeles; s. Gerald Patrick and Katherine Ellen (Simpson) H.; m. Leoti Lynn, June 21, 1966; children: Michael G., b. 1966; Ryan, b. 1972; edn: AA, East L.A. Jr. Coll. 1969; BA, CSU L.A. 1971; JD, Western State Univ. Coll. of Law 1976; admitted to practice, Calif. State Bar 1977. Career: salesman ABC Stadium Concessions 1962-72; machinist apprentice Union Pacific Railroad 1966-69; meter reader So. Calif. Edison Co. 1969; constrn. acct. 1969; jr. acct. 1969; accountant 1970-71; jr. auditor 1971-73; assoc. auditor 1973-75; sr. auditor/ contract adminstr. 1975-79; gen. counsel DWD Mgmt. Co. 1981--; atty. at law 1977--; dir. DWD Mgmt. Co.; mem: Calif., Los Angeles Co. & Eastern Bar Assns.; Diamond Bar CofC; Republican; rec: chess, coin & stamp collecting. Res: 23560 Gold Nugget Diamond Bar 91765 Law Ofcs. of Michael J. Hemming, 22632 Golden Springs Dr, Ste 230, Diamond Bar 91765

HEMPHILL, ALAN POLK, television broadcasting co. executive; b. Aug. 22, 1933, Montgomery, Ala.; s. Alan P. and Elizabeth Orr (Evans) H.; m. Jean Tilden Baker, June 8, 1957; children: Elizabeth, b. 1958, Alan, b. 1960, Laurie, b. 1964; edn: BSEE, US Naval Acad. Annapolis 1957. Career: served to Lcdr. USN 1957-77; comdg. ofcr. US Naval Reserve Tng. Center, Vallejo, Ca. and ofcr. in chg. USS Pampanito, 1963-64; project ofcr. Information Flagship Data Sys. Devel., Naval Electronics Lab., San Diego 1967-69; nat. dir. Remember the Pueblo cmpgn. 1968; ofcr. in chg. Chollas Hts. Transmitter Sta., San Diego 1976-77; mgr./broker Prestige Properties Real Estate, San Diego 1977-80; founder/ gen. ptnr./ dir. of mktg. Orion Business Systems, S.D. 1981-82; pres./ CEO, Oak Broadcasting Systems, Glendale (Channel 52), 1981-82, chmn. bd. dirs. 1982-83, bd. dirs./trustee of 50ˆ stock of Oak Industries, Oak Bdcstg. Systems (approved by FCC), 1982--; honors: qualifed for Submarines (ofcr. 1961), qual. for command of Submarines (1966); mem: Kiwanis Internat. (pres. Rancho Bernardo 1980-81), Green Valley Civic Assn. (pres. 1974, chmn. 1976), Junior Achievement of North County (bd. chmn. 1978); contbg. columnist Escondido Times Advocate (1980), regular columnist (Rancho) Bernardo News 1981-; Libertarian; rec: creative writing. Res: 16241 Del Norte, Poway 92064 Ofc: Oak Broadcasting Systems Inc. 1139 Grand Central Ave Glendale 91201

HEMPHILL, DEAN DELON, real estate broker; b. Aug. 31, 1934, Martinez; s. Wertz (Doc) and Vera (Dowrellio) H.; m. Patricia Ann Mefferd, Mar. 5, 1960; children: Julie, b. 1961; Steven, b. 1970; edn: AA & AS, R.E. bus., Napa Coll. 1976; AA & AS, bus. mgmt., 1978; Anthony Sch. 1973; R.E. broker, R.E. Cert. Inst. Career: real estate salesprsn. Town & Country Estates 1971-73; broker/ owner 1973--; mem: San Francisco Corral Westerners Historical Soc. (pres. 1982); E Clampus Vitus Napa County Historical Soc. (pres. 1980); St. Andrews Soc., S.F.; works: Key to City San Francisco 1949 for pastel art work; mil: airman 1/c USAF 1954-58, GCM; rec: California history. Address: Town & Country Estates, 865 El Centro Ave Napa 94558

HEMPHILL, ROBERT GARY, clothing store chain owner; b. May 2, 1957, Oakland; s. Benjamin Robert and Norman Jo (Manties) H.; edn: BS, San Diego State Univ. 1980. Career: owner/ partner Greenhill Arabians (Arabian horse breeding) 1983--; chief fin. advr. More The Woman, Inc. (two retail stores) 1983--; owner The Clothes Vault (three stores), Oakland 1983--; awards: Rookie of the Yr., Rugby Football, SDSU 1977, Most Valuable Back, 1979; mem: Oakland CofC; The Fund for Animals; Calif. Marine Mammal Rehab. Ctr.; Old Aztecs Rugby Football Club; analyst (vol.), San Diego Police Dept. 1979-80; Presbyterian; rec: rugby, animal rehabilitation. Res: 1200 Lakeshore Ave, 22E, Oakland 94606 Ofc: The Clothes Vault, 1764 Broadway Oakland 94612

HENDERSON, CARL GREGORY, chiropractor; b. Feb. 21, 1947; s. Robert Milton and Vella Rose Henderson; children: Michael, b. 1967; Jeanna, b. 1970; Jennifer, b. 1975; edn: DC, Los Angeles Coll. of Chiro. 1979; ND, DO, Anglo-Am. Inst. Career: fmrly. with Kaiser Gpysum Co.; self- defense instr.; currently, pvt. practice, doctor of chiropractic, Fallbrook Chiro. Ctr.; owner On-Guard Tng. Inst. (lagest teargas/ self defense sch. in Calif.); creator self defense sys. for women; lectr. worldwide on chiropractic, self defense and Boy Scouts; author/ pub. Deseret Alphabet Primer 1972; writer/ prod. movie, Women Be Aware, 1982; awards: Grand Champion, USFE Karate Championships, Europe 1968; num. presidential sports awds.; Black Belt in Nippon Kenpo; mem: Am. Chiro. Council on Mental Health (pres.); Calif. Chiro. Assn.; Phon- A- Thon organizer; Boy Scouts of AM. (organizer awd., Scouters Key, Scouters tng. awd., Den Ldrs. Tng. Awd., Commnr. Arrowhead Awd., Awd. of Merit); mil: USAR, 3 yrs. Ofc: Fallbrook Chiropractic Center, 125 W Fig St Fallbrook 92028

HENDERSON, DANIEL ROBERT, business excutive; b. May 3, 1944, Indpls., Ind.; s. Robert Harry and Barbara Jacquiline (Maloney) H.; m. Ellen Veronica, June 24, 1967; children Nicole, b. 1972; Katherine, b. 1975; Rory, b. 1977; Emily, b. 1978; edn: BS, Univ. of Cinncinnati 1968; MBA, Univ. of Ariz. 1969; profl. engr., Ohio. Career: cost analyst Well Fargo Bank, San Francisco 1971-72; proj. mgr. Scott-Buttner Corp., Oakland 1972-73; contracts coord. Arabian Am. Oil Co., Saudi Arabia 1973-74, project & pgms. engr. 1974-75; asst. mgr. cost. control Davy McKee Inc., Cleveland, Ohio 1978-79; mgr. proj. control Sohio Constrn. Co., San Francisco 1979-82, mgr. plng. & budgets 1982-84; bd. chmn. Hystrix Corp., Lafayette, Ca. 1984--, bd. chmn. Athletic

Analysis Corp. 1984--; inventor: Swing Analyzer, a device for analyzing golf and other athletic swings, pat. pend.; Republican; rec: sports, home repair. Address: Hystrix Corp., 826 Las Trampas Lafayette 94549

HENDERSON, DAVID JOHN, computer co. executive; b. Sept. 22, 1945, San Francisco; s. John Murray and Hazel Martha (Dunbar) H.; edn: AA, Coll. of San Mateo 1965; AB, San Francisco State Univ. 1966. Career: ins. agent Metropolitan Life ins. Co., Hayward 1970-73; subrogation adjuster Ins. Co. of No. Am. dba Recovery Svcs. Internat., San Francisco 1973-75; gen. mgr. Pacific Pub. Carriers, S.F. 1975-77; acct. exec. Western Ins. Assoc., S.F. 1977-80; ins. investigator, Ins. Co. of No. Am., S.F. 1980-83; founder/ pres./ CEO Estate Design Sys., Inc., Fremont 1983--; computer cons. Estate Design Sys., Inc. 1983-; mem: Nat. Notary Assn.; New Bus. Admin.; Marines Meml. Club, S.F.; segt. USAF 1966-70, Reserve 1972, Air Force Svc., Air Force Commdn.; Republican (Pres. Task Force 1984); Episcopal; rec: music, yachting, travel. Res: 1205 Old Canyon Rd Fremont 94536 Ofc: Estate Design Systems, Inc., POB 7223 Fremont 94537

HENDERSON, JOAN ELAINE (Elaine O. Eure), artist, poet; b. Nov. 12, 1943, San Antonio, Tex.; d. Clarence George and Joan Elaine (Ferguson) Ornduff; m. Roy Calvin Eure, Sr.; m. 2d. Don Henderson (dir., film prodn. mgr. for EPCOT, Walt Disney), July 25, 1982; chldren: Anna Celeste, b. 1967; Roy Calvin, Jr., b. 1970; Andrew Quinten, b. 1972; edn: AA, Sacred Heart Coll. for Women, Cullman, Ala. 1963; Univ. of So. Miss. 1963-77. Career: currently, pres. E.Y.E., Inc., Especially Yours by Elaine, Inc. (estab. to advance careers of artist & creative acceptance of fine arts & crafts); past mem. So. Miss. Art Assn.; Internat. Soc. of Artists; painting in permanent collection Jackson, Miss.; active in womens movements; rec: scuba, needlework, sailing. Address: 1079 E Olive Ave Burbank 91501

HENDERSON, TERRANCE R., savings and loan executive; b. Sept. 21, 1942, Erie, Penn.; s. Russell A. and Jean E. (Thompson) H.; m. Linda A. Baker, June 15, 1968; 1 dau: Cari Ann, b. 1974; edn: BS, Penn. State 1965; MBA, 1967. Career: ops. mgr./ applications devel. mgr., pgm./ analyst E.D. du Pont 1968-80; mgr. bus. info. sys. Levi Strauss, US Gps. II & III, Karet & Dallas field ops., San Francisco 1980--; Urban League Data Processing Adv. Com.; Data Processing Adv. Com., San Diego Comm. Coll. Dist.; mem: AFCOM, Assoc. for Computer Ops. Mgrs.; Methodist; rec: woodworking. Res: 15335 Skyridge Rd Poway 92064 Ofc: Home Federal Savings & Loan, 5545 Morehouse Dr San Diego 92121

HENDERSON, VICTOR WARREN, physician, behavioral neurologist; b. Aug 20, 1951, Little Rock, Ark.; s. Philip S. and N. Jean (Edsel) H.; m. Barbara Curtiss, May 24, 1975; children: Gregory, b. 1978; Geoffreey, b. 1980; Stephanie, b. 1982; edn; BS, summa cum laude, Univ. of Georgia 1972, MD, Johns Hopkins Univ. 1976; diplomate, nuerology, Am. Bd. of Psychiatry & Neurology 1981. Career: intern, internal med. Duke niv. Med. Ctr., Durham NC 1976-77; res. neurology Wash. Univ. Sch. of Med., Barnes Hosp., St. Louis, Mo. 1977-80; fellow, behav. neurology Boston Univ. Sch. of Med. (Aphasia/ Neurobehavior Research Ctr., Boston Veterans Admin. Hosp.), Boston, Mass. 1980-81; instr. neurology Boston Univ. Sch. of Med., Boston, Mass. 1980-81; asst. prof. USC Sch. of Med.; co-dir. USC Neurobehavior Clinic at Good Samaritan Hosp.; cons. Adult Head Injury Svc., Rancho Los Amigos Hosp., Downey; awards: Nat. Merit Scholarship; 1968-72; Stanley Grey prize in psychology, Univ. of Ga. 1972; Phi Beta Kappa 1972; mem: Am. Acad. of Neurology; Internat. Neuropsychology Soc.; Nat. Head Injury Found.; Behaviorl Neurology Soc.; Los Angeles Soc. of Neurology And Psychiatry; publs: frequent contbr., med. arts., sci. publs. 1980-; coauthor: book, Neurologic Logic, 1984; Protestant. Ofc: USC School of Medicine, Dept. of Neurology, 2025 Zonal Ave Los Angeles 90033

HENDRICKS, WALTER, corporate finance executive; b. May 23, 1925, NY, NY; s. Morris and Dora (Kirschbaum) H.; m. Elaine Held, June 27, 1948; children: Eric Robert (b. 1951, dec. 1979), Audrey Pam, b. 1954, Cherly Susan, b. 1956; edn: BA, Brooklyn Coll. 1952; MBA, NY Univ. Grad. Sch. of Bus. Adm. 1961; CFA, Chartered Finl. Analyst, Inst. of CFA 1968. Career: junior analyst Du Vals Consensus Inc., 1949-50, First Nat. City Bank of NY, 1950-55, Foster & Adams 1955-57; resrch. dir. Chas W. Scranton & Co. 1957-69; v.p./ resrch. dir. Morgan Olmstead Kennedy & Gardner 1969; v.p. resrch and corp. fin. Sierrega & Co., Redmond Luxenburg & Co., J. Shapiro & Co., United Securities Co. of Am., Gregerson & Co., Parker Jackson & Co., consecutively 1970-73, v.p. corp. fin./mgr. Investors Finl. Corp. 1973-79; v.p. corp. fin. M.S. Wien & Co., Am. Western Sec., Marsan Securities, Brentwood Securities, Private Ledger Fin. Svcs., 1979-83, D.H.Blair & Co., 1983--; asst. prof. econ. Quinnipiac Coll. 1958-67, instr. New Haven Coll. 1958-67, UCLA 1968-69; mem: Inst. of CFAs, Finl. Analysts Fedn., NY Soc. of Security Analysts; works: responsible for taking over 30 companies public, 1959-81; mil: sgt. US Army 1943-46; Democrat; Jewish; rec: stamps. Res: 10753 Weyburn Ave Los Angeles 90024 Ofc: D.H. Blair & Co. Inc. 9033 Wilshire Blvd, Ste 304, Beverly Hills 90211

HENDRICKSON, BENJAMIN SHERMAN, psychotherapist, ret.; b. Jan. 23, 1931, Springlake, NJ; m. Rishelle Tobin, Oct. 19, 1982; children: Steven D., b. 1953, Sharon J. Welch, b. 1955, Wendy C. Curtier, b. 1956, Casey J., b. 1979; edn: ThB, S.T.D., L.I.F.E. Bible Coll. 1970; BA, MA, Azusa Pacific Coll. 1971, 72; ThD, Fla. State Theol. Sem. 1972; PhD, Am. Internat. Univ. 1979; Calif. lic. MFCT, Marriage Family, Child Therapist 1973; Tchrs. Cert. 1971; Reg. Hypnotist; Reg. Sex Therapist; Reg. Sex Educator. Career: internship Calif. Family Study Ctr., N. Hywd. 1971-72; intern Family Counseling Ctr. of A.V., Lancaster 1972-73, dir. 1973-75; exec. dir. Valencia Counseling Svc. 1976-78, Lancaster Counseling Svc. 1975-78; pvt. practice, 1978-82, ret.; prof. Univ. of La Verne 1978-9; regent Fla. State Christian Coll.; regent Alpha Psi Omega; Diplomate. Am. Psychotherapy Assn.; Diplomate Am. Bd. Pastoral Counseling; Fellow Am. Coll. of Clinic Adminstrs.; Fellow Internat. Council of Sex Educators; mem: Am. Security Council, Am. Legion (life), Disabled Am. Vets. (life), Retired Ofcrs. Assn. (life); CA rep. Congl. Advis. Bd.; charter mem. Presdtl. Task Force; mil: Lt. Col. USAF ret., Missile Badge, Air Medal, Pres. Unit Cit., UN, Nat. Def., Korean Svc. medals, GCM, Air Crew Wings; Chaplain, LTC, Civil Air Patrol ret.; Republican; Prot.; rec: photog. Res: 45800 N. 10th St. East, 158, Lancaster 93535

HENDRIKSEN, ELDON SENDE, author/ professor; b. Oct. 20, 1917, Alhambra; s. Henry Andrew and Margot Antonie (Sende) H.; m. E. Kathleen Podmore, Oct. 18, 1942; children: Margot, b. 1946; Dan, b. 1949; edn; BS, UC Berkeley 941; MBA, 1947; PhD, 1957; CPA, Calif. 1953. Career: prof. bus. admin. Wash. State Univ. 1955-75; visiting prof. of acctg. Univ. of Ill. 1970-71; sr. Fulbright-Hayes Scholar, Univ. of Queensland, Brisbane, Australia 1976; prof. Univ. of Santa Clara 1978, 180-83; currently, author; ed. The Accounting Review 1970-72; Recipient award, Am. Inst. of CPAs, Notable Contrbn. to Acctg. Literature 1980; Wash. State Univ. Faculty Invited Address 1969; mem: Am. Acctg. Assn.; Am. Inst. CPAs; author: Accounting Theory, Richard D. Irwin, Inc., 1965, rev. 1970, 77, 82 (Japanese, Spanish, Chinese- Taiwan, French & Swedish translations); num. books & arts.; mil: lt. USNR 1941-45; Lutheran; rec: gardening. Res: 10510 Deodara Dr Cupertino 95024

HENKE, EDGAR EDWIN, sales & marketing executive; b. Dec. 13, 1927, Ontario, Calif.; s. Edgar Wilbur and Thelma Eugenie (Britain) H.; m. Rocille Mickey, Jan. 17, 1950; children: Melissa Anne, b. 1956, Jennifer Lee, b. 1958, MaryBeth, b. 1963, Joanna, b. 1966; edn: AA, Ventura Coll. 1947; BS, edn., USC 1952; MA, edn., Stanford Univ. 1956; Spl. Secondary Tchg. Cred. 1952. Career: started 14 year profl. football career as rookie with Los Angeles Dons, 1949, with Winnepeg Blue Bombers, Canadian Football League (All-Canadian recogn.) 1950, with the San Francisco 49ers (All-Pro Nat. Football League honors, played in Pro-Bowl) 1951 52, player/ asst. coach Calgary Stampeder profl. football club 1955, S.F. 49ers (All-Pro/All-Star recogn.) 1956 60, player/ coach St. Louis Cardinals (first recipient of Old Pro Award) 1961-62; coll. coaching Univ. of the Pacific and CSU San Jose, two years; then gen. sales mgr. System 99 (gen. commodity common carrier transp. co.), Oakland v.p./dir. of sales 1974--; toured with the Harlem Globe Trotters (played 7 games) 1958; honors: athletic honors high sch. and coll.; spl. alumni recognition, Faculty, Ventura Coll. 1964; spl. team commendn. as mem. Warrior Football Team, Nat. Service Champs 1953, by Cmdg. Gen. of Fort Ord, Maj. Gen. Robt. N. McClure; Man K. Andorc Wild Trout Conservation Award, 1974; Order of the Jassid, Sierra Pacific Fly Casters of Van Nuys 1977; Sportsman of Year 1978, Calif. Outdoor Sportswriters; hon. mention (6th), Fedn. of Fly Fisher's 1982 photo contest; mem: Calif. Fisheries Restoration Found., Oakland (advisor); Rowdy Creek Hatchery Proj., Smith River (sponsor); Fedn. of Fly Fishers, El Segundo; Trout Unlmtd. (Denver); Izaak Walton League of Am.; Fly Fishers of Ore. (Portland); Friends of the Ventura River (life); Nat. Rifle Assn.; Calif. Waterfowl Assn., S.F.; Ducks Unlmtd.; Nat. Football Alumni Assn.; Trojan Football Alumni Club; mediated 8 year project to present redwood sculpture, The Indomitable Salmon, (carver, Floyd L. Davis) to Humboldt Co. Prairie Creek Fish Hatchery, 1974; publs: num. arts., editorials in var. publs. re preservation of our cold water fishery resources; testimony Congl. Hearing Records, Klamath River Indian Fishing Rights; mil: cpl. US Army Inf. 1953-55, 3 individual commendns.; Democrat; Prot.; rec: sports, hunting, flytying. Res: 3433 Woodstock Ln Mtn View 94040 Ofc: System 99, 8201 Edgewater Dr Oakland 94621

HENKE, RAY LANGE, lawyer; b. May 31, 1953, Pomona; s. Burton Leyhmon and Wilma (Lange) H.; edn: BA, high honors, Univ. of Hawaii 1976; JD, Univ. of San Francisco 1979; admitted to Calif. State Bar 1979. Career: practicing atty. Butler, Jefferson, Dan & Allis, medical malpractice, aviation products liability; honors: law review, moot court honors, USF; mem: Am., Calif., Los Angeles County Bar Assns, Am., Calif., Los Angeles Trial Lawyers Assns.; publs: arts., Advocate law jour. 1980; rec: martial artist. Ofc: Butler, Jefferson, Dan & Allis, 626 Wilshire Blvd, Ste. 914, Los Angeles 90017

HENLEY, RICHARD MERLE, business executive, entrepreneur; b. Mar. 15, 1952, Portland, Ore.; s. Roy F. and Grayce L. (Roatch) H.; m. Jan Talbert, Feb. 14, 1984; edn: AA, Barstow Jr. Coll. 1972; BA cum laude,, CSU Long Beach 1974, grad. wk. 1974; mgmt. Hubbard Tng. Acad.; cert. Drug Rehab. Splst., Narconon Tng. Ctr. 1974-75; Calif. State lic: Gen. Constrn. Contr., Plumbing Contr., Solar Contr. Career: clk. J.C. Penneys, 1966-68; mgr. gp. of Texaco Stations, 1968-72; Narconon, counselor, L.A. Rehabilitation Center (vol. wkr. up to 80 hrs. wkly. to rehab. drug addicts), 1974-76, nat. adminstr. Narconon U.S. (25 offices), 1976-77, estab. Delaware br. 1977; formed Henley Ents. 1975, became largest volume br. ofc. in Water Refining Co. Network 1979-80; founder/ bd. chmn. Northland Environmental Inc., Burbank 1980--, water purification and renewable energy field, So. Calif. Factory rep. for Sunland Solar; chmn. bd. dirs. Sunland National Dealer Assn. 1982-84; num. tv, radio, press interviews re solar industry; recipient volume trophies & awards for 10 offices set up across USA, Sunland and Northland cos.; mem: Calif. Lic. Contrs. Assn., Solar Energy Industries Assn., calif. SEIA, State CofC, Nat. Fedn. of Ind. Bus., US Dept. of Commerce Exporters Directory; spkr. Renewable Energy Technologies Symp. and Internat. Expo. (RETSIE 84); gen. secty.

Nat. Assn. of People Who Care (NAPWC) 1979; publs: Employer's Bill of Rights, Employee's Bill of Rights (1983), Calif. CofC, and Nat. Fedn. Ind. Bus.; contbg. writer: Solar mag., Sun Up, Sunspots, Energy Collector, Apartment Reporter, Bnai Brith, Properity, WISE News; expert marksman (NRA) Rifle team placed 3d in state; Republican; Scientologist; rec: flying (helicopter, ultralight), skiing. Res: 6058 Delphi St Los Angeles 90042 Ofc: Northland Environmental Inc. 1115 Chestnut St Burbank 91506

HENNESSY, JAMES LAWRENCE, JR., mortgage finance executive; b. Apr. 24, 1949, San Francisco; s. James L. (Capt. USN ret.) and Jane Catherine (Edgerly) H.; m. Claudette Coffee, July 31, 1976; 1 dau. Kerry Boone, b. 1983; edn: BA hist, Univ. of San Diego 1971. Career: sales coord. Redman Indus., Riverside 1972, zone mgr., Phoenix, Az. 1973; bus. devel. ofcr., comml. loan ofcr. Florida Fed. S&L, St. Petersburg, Fl. 1974-5; with PMI Mortgage Ins. Co. 1976--, regional rep. to reg. mgr., San Diego 1976-82, area sales mgr. Calif., Az., Nev. 1983, currently vice pres./gen. mgr. W. USA; frequent pub. spkr. various So. Calif. trade assns., mtg. lenders 1976-; honors: 1967 Calif. Scholarship Fedn., 1971 Phi Alpha Theta (hist. hon. soc.), 1982 Reg. Mgr. of the Year, PMI Mortgage Ins. Co. Mem: San Diego Mortgage Bankers Assn. (dir. 1981), Calif. Mtg. Bankers Assn. (conv. comm. chmn. 1979, 81); past chmn. S.D. Young Mtg. Bankers; mil: Calif., Az., Fla. Nat. Guards; Republican; rec: watersports, photog., hist., writing. Ofc: PMI, 14181 Yorba St., Ste. 206, Tustin 92680

HENNING, JOHN F., JR., publisher; b. Nov. 28, 1923, San Francisco; s. John F., Sr. and Mary Ellen (Bashore) H.; m. Frances R. Sorensen, Jan. 4, 1947; children: John (Jeff) F. III, b. 1952; Robert T., b. 1961; edn: BA, w/ distn., Stanford Univ. 1947. Career: promotional & gen. assignment San Francisco Examiner 1947; asst. mgr. Sunset Book Div. Lane Pub. Co. 1951, sales rep. Sunset Mag. 1954, advtg. mgr. 1959, v.p. 1963, asst. publisher 1967, assoc. pub. 1972, v.p./gen. mgr. 1974, pres./assoc. pub./bd. dirs. 1982--; mem: Western Assn. of Food Chains; Wine & Food Soc. of S.F; The Illuminators; Advtg. Club of S.F; World Trade Club; Am. Soc. of Travel Agents; The Family; Stanford Golf Club; mil: lt. j.g. USNR, WWII aviator; Presbyterian; rec: ranching, hunting, photog. Res: 48 Alameda de las Pulgas Atherton 94025 Ofc: Lane Publishing Co., Willow & Middlefield Rds. Menlo Park 94025

HENRICKSON, RICHARD L., clergyman/public relations executive; b. Dec. 23, 1947, Minot, N.D.; s. Leonard B. and Ione M. (Buen) Henrickson; edn: BA, St. Olaf Coll. 1969; M.Div., Princeton Theo. Seminary 1973; MA, NY Univ. 1983; ordained, Lutheran Ch. in Am. 1975. Career: asst. dir. A Christian Ministry in National Parks, Nat. Council of Churches, NYC 1973-75; pastor Christ Lutheran Ch., Manhattan 1975-81; dir. of devel. Seamen & International House, Luth. Ch. in Am., 1981-83; dir. of devel. Redwood Terrace Lutheran Home, Escondido 1983--; lectr., Am. & Eng. lit., Baruch Coll., City Univ. of NY 1983; Community Adv. Council, Beth Isral Med. Ctr., NY 1976-83; Ethics & Resrch Bd, Cabrini Med. Ctr, NY 1977-83. Mem: Nat. Soc. of Fund Raising Execs., Assn. of Lutheran Devel. Execs., Am. Assn. of Pastoral Counselors, Escondido CofC; (Manhattan): Community Bd. No. 5, Comm. Learning Ctr., Neighbors (Senior Advocacy Org.). Rec: literature, horticulture, travel, ski. Res: 3895 Colina Dorada Dr. San Diego 92124 Ofc: Redwood Terrace Lutheran Home, 710 W. 13th Ave Escondido 92025

HENRIKSON, PHILIP HILL, nuclear engineer; b. Mar. 25, 1944, Vallejo; s. Otto and Emma Miralda (Hill) H.; m. Melody Henderson, Dec. 24, 1969; children: Kerry, b. 1970; Heidi, b. 1971; Mica, b. 1972; Aaron, b.3 1973; Ammon, b. 1977; Leah, b. 1979; edn: BS, Univ. of Nev. 1966; MS, Univ. of Idaho 1972; JD, Lincoln Univ. 1978; lic. atty., Calif. & Fed. Cts. 1979; lic. profl. nuclear engr., Calif. 1976. Career: lab. asst., Desert Research Inst., Atmosperic Phyiscs Div., Univ. of Nevada 1964-66; nuclear submarine eng. ofcr. USN 1966-70; nuclear gp. supvr. Bechtel Architect Engr., Norwald 1971-73; pgm. mgr. General Electric, San Jose 1973-80; mgr. nuclear licensing, Penn. Power & Light, Allentown, Pa. 1980-82; nuclear safety pg. ldr. So. Calif. Edison, Rosemead 1983--; awards: Fleischman Forestry Scholarship 1962; Nat. Sci. Found. Fellowship 1970-71; Nat. Collegiate Athletic Assn. Track Champion 1966; mem: State Bar of Calif.; Am. Bar ASsn.; Am. Nuclear Soc.; Toastmasters; Freeman Inst.; works: Am. Nuclear Soc. paper on Accelerated Licensing, 1980; mil: lt., USNR 1970-80, Vietnam Vet.; Republican; LDS; rec: triathlons. Res: 9138 Cedargrove Ave Whittier 90605 Ofc: Southern California Edison, 2244 Walnut Grove Ave, G01, 316, Rosemead 91770

HENRY, ANDRE FRITZ, physician; b. June 24, 1942, Port-au-Prince, Haiti (WI); s. Anthony and Carmina (Nicoleau) H.; m. Marlene, Mar. 15, 1969; children: Yanick, b. 1971; Carl Andre, b. 1972; Patrick, b. 1975; Marlene S., b. 1977; Steeve, b. 1979; edn: physician & surgeon, Univ. Nacional de Cordoba Sch. of Med. 1968; PhD, Univ. Nacional de Buenos Aires, Argentina 1975. Career: prof. fisiologia, Univ. Nac. de Corboba 1969-71; chief nuclear med. dept., San Lucas, Argentina 1975-77; attache de press/attache culturel, Haitian Embassy, Argentina 1972-78; physician for Los Angeles County, 1980-81; v.p. Lincoln Hosp. Med. Cr. 1982-83, chief med. staff 1983-84; pvt. practice med., Los Angeles 1980--; clin. instr. family & preventive med. USC 1982-; mem: Am., Calif., L.A. Co. Med. Assns.; Am. Coll. of Gen. Practice; Haitian Inst. of calif.; num. publs.; Democrat; SDA; rec: business administration, golf. Res: 685 Ridge Dr Glendale 91206 Ofc: Henry Medical Corporation, 443 S Soto Street Los Angeles 90033

HENRY, ANNIE LOUISE, corporate executive; b. Nov. 4, 1910, San Francisco; d. Thomas McLean and Belle Victoria (Miller) Allan; m. John Howard

Henry, Jan. 1, 1937; 1 dau. Annabel A., b. 1943; edn: BS, Univ. Calif. 1931. Career: general office and secty. underwriting dept. Calif. State Auto Assoc. 1931-33; mgr. Dickinson Warren Secretarial Sch., 1933-37; tchr. comml. subject, Commerce High Sch., S.F. (nights) over ten years; secty. Head Office, Dept. of Employment; ptnr. Allan Automatic Sprinkler, 1951-, incorporated 1955, secty./treas. Allan Automatic Sprinkler Corp. of So. Calif. 1956--; founder, secty. treas. A & H Fabco, 1964--; founder, secty. treas. A & T Pipe Fabricators, So. Calif. 1973--; Republican; Presbyterian. Res: 114 Stratford Drive San Francisco 94132 Ofc: Allan Automatic Sprinkler Corp. 439 Eccles Ave South San Francisco

HENRY, JAMES NATHAN, psychotherapist, clergyman; b. Apr. 8, 1929, Midwest, Wyo.; s. Charles Phillip and Ora Ann (Shelton) H.; m. Mary Kay brown, Apr. 8, 1967; children: Linda, b. 1946, Michael, b. 1949, Patricia (step), b. 1946, Barbara (step), b. 1950; edn: AA, Orange Coast Coll. 1969; BA, MA, Chapman Coll. 1970, 74; D.Min., Calif. Graduate Sch. of Theology 1974; PhD, Newport Internat. Univ. 1978; lic. MFCC, Marriage Family Child Counselor, Calif. Career: ordained Baptist minister 32 years, lost eyesight 1966, returned to coll. (earned 5 degrees); Blind rehabilitation counselor, psychiatrist asst., Dr. J. Needler 1971-75; asst. minister First Baptist Ch., dir. Costa Mesa Counseling Service 1971-76; MFCC pvt. practice, non-denom. minister, pres. Abundant Christian Dynamics Inc., 1974--; religious counseling pgms. on radio and TV, 1970-82; honors: Spl. recogn. as first Blind Psn. to receive Doctorate, Calif. Grad. Sch. of Theol.; mem: Calif. Assn. MFCC (mem. com. 1974-6), Trinity So. baptist Assn. (Morals and Stds. Com. 1981-2); Riverside County Mental Hlth Adv. Bd. 1978-; spl. com. Patton State Hosp. 1982; chmn. bd. ADAR 1978-9; chmn. bd. Boys and Girls Club of the Desert 1978-9; Lions Club; mil: sgt. USMC 1943-5, USNR 1946-50, USMCR 1950-57, Purple Heart, GCM, Asia.Pac. 2 Battle Stars, ATO Victory medal, Pres. Comm., Navy Unit Comm.; Republican; rec: phys. fitness, collector swords. Res: 17989 Corkill Rd, 141, Desert Hot Springs 92240 Ofc: James N. Henry MFCC, 1548 N. Palm Canyon Dr Palm Springs 92262

HENRY, WARD JAMES, III, chiropractor; b. May 17, 1948, Seattle, Mash.; s. Ward James, Jr. and La Rene Dale (Stephens) H.; edn: AA, Orange Coast Coll. 1972; BS, UC Irvine 1974; DC, Los Angeles Sch. of Chiro. 1980; DC, Calif. Career: clinic intern orthopaedic & radiology Thie Chiro. Gp., Pasadena 1978-80; clinic intern orthopaedic Dr. Rome Hanning, Naples 1979-80; chiropractor/ sports physician, Seal Beach 1980-83, Sunset Beach 1983--; team chiropractor Belmont Shore Rugby Tean 1981-; cons. physician Los Angeles City Jr. Football League 1982-83; chiropractor: world class amateur tennis, Avra Jain, John Grale, Fanny Bollen; profl. atheletes, Bob Welch, pitcher, Brian Bowers, football; mem: Nat. Sports Injury Council; publs.: arts., J. Biochem. 1979, Uncle Jam Mag. 10/82, Singles Mag. 11/83; mil: Ftgsn, USN 1967-69, Vietnam Svc., Nat. Defense; Episcopal; music, surfing, skiing. Res: 615 Ocean Ave Seal Beach 90740 Ofc: Sunset Beach Health Center, 16222 Pacific Coast Hwy, Huntington Beach 92649

HEPNER, EDWARD MARSHALL, international business consultant; b. Feb. 16, 1938, Vancouver, B.C., Canada; s. Eli and Nerene (Welch) H.; m. Pauline Pena, Sept. 1, 1979; children: Richard, b. 1968; Lisa, b. 1970; edn: BA, honors, Univ. of British Columbia 1962; MA, 1964; MBA, USC 1984. Career: officer Canadian Foreign Svc. (19 yrs.), served in Kenya, Germany & US 1965-83; Consul of Canada, Los Angeles 1978-83; pres. Canadian Comml. Advisers, Inc. (designed to assist US, Canadian, Asian & European bus. persons operating in No. America or Overseas), Los Angeles 1983--; diplomat; lectr.; writer; tchr.; bus. cons.; awards: Canadian Univ. Scholarships 1961, 62, various public spkg. awds.; mem: Profl. Assn. of Foreign Svc. Ofcrs.; Am. Mktg. Assn.; Am. Mgmt. Assn.; Town Hall; L.A. CofC; Canada- Calif. CofC; USC MBA Alumni Assn.; Nat. Assn. of Immigration Consultants; num. civic orgns.; num. arts. var. publs. incl. Calif.'s "Energy Detente" and USC Symposium on Canada- US Relations, 1982; Presbyterian; rec: tennis, golf, chess. Res: 13934 Bora Bora Way, 314E, Marina del Rey 90292 Ofc: Canadian Commercial Advisers, Inc., Los Angeles

HERINGER, JOHN NELSON, physician; b. Oct. 22, 1948, Rugby, N.Dak.; s. Roland Arthur and Margery Ruth Heringer; m. Eileen, Sept .20, 1980; children: Todd, b. 1972, Bryce, b. 1974; John Paul, b. 1982; edn: BA, Occidental Coll. 1969; MD, Univ. of Ariz. 1973. Career: emergency physician Bay Gen. Hosp., Chula Vista 1974-78; emergency physician Santa Teresa Hosp., San Jose 1978-79; dir. of emergency dept. O'Conner Hosp., San Jose 1979-81; physician family practice, pres./med. dir. Emergi-Stop Medical Clinic, San Jose 1981--; national faculty mem. Am. Heart Assn. 1980-; mem: Am. Coll. Emergency Physicians; Santa Clara Co. Med. Soc.; Calif. Med. Soc.; mil: lcdr, USPHS 1974-76; Republican; Protestant; rec: woodworking, hiking. Res: 18803 Hilltop Way Saratoga 95070 Ofc: Emergi-Stop, 3002 Leigh Ave San Jose 95124

HERLT, EMMIALINA HARU, health care administrator; b. Feb. 1, 1937, Kula, Haui, Hawaii; d. Taneshige and Ine (Yamasaki) Endo; m. John L. Herlt, Nov. 19, 1960; 1 dau: Laura Ann, b. 1963; edn: BSN, Univ. of Ha. 1959; MPH, UCLA 1973; reg. nurse, Calif.; pub. health nurse, Bureau of Consumer Affairs. Career: PHN & actng dir. of nurses Boulder Co. Health Dept. 1965-67; nursing care coord. San Fernando Valley Home Health Agency 1968-70; exec. dir. Visiting Nurse Assn., Pasadena & San Gabriel Valley 1973-79; dir. Profl. Nurses Bureau Home Health Agcy. 1983--; organizing/ dir. ops./ sales, a new Home Health Agency; awards: Scholarship, Univ. of Hawaii 1955-59; Speech Dept. Awd., Univ. of Hawaii 1959; mem: Commn. of Aging; Hospice of Pasadena; Hospice Orgn. of So. Calif.; Zonta Internat. (Pasadena Club pres.

1980-82); Delta Sigma Rho; mil: lst lt. US Army 1958-60; rec: Bonsai, cooking, golf. Res: 555 S Grand Ave Pasadena 91105 Ofc: Professional Nurses Bureau, 3660 Wilshire Blvd, Ste 1040, Los Angeles 90010

HERNANDEZ, MANLIO A., real estate broker; b. June 21, 1933, Tlacolula, Oaxaca, Mex., nat. 1957; s. Hesiquio J. and Martina V. (Aguilar) H.; m. Felicitas Calvo, Nov. 15, 1960; children: Jamie, b. 1961; Jorge, b. 1962; Xochitl, b. 1972; edn: Cal Poly, SLO 1975-; R.E. broker, Calif. 1979. Career: retail clerk Economy Army & Navy Store, Oxnard 1958-60; store mgr. 1961-75; owner 1976--; R.E. sales 1979-82; R.E. broker 1982--; currently, owner Realty Investments, Grover City; awards: Union Civica y Cultural Mexicana, UCCM 1969-73; Svc. Awd. (social studies), Calif. Central Region 1974; Top Producer, Internat. R.E. Network 1983; mem: Pismo Coast Bd. Realtors; Pismo Coast MLS; Santa Maria MLS; Economic Opportunity Commn. (commnr. 1965-68); adult/ youth Soccer League; Parent Advrs. & Student Alliance (PASA); invention: cuff for trousers to enlarge pants or sleeves of sports coat, pat. pend.; Libertarian; Catholic; rec: civics, refinishing antique furniture. Res: 1168 Brighton, POB 888, Grover City 93433 Ofc: 1168 Grover City 93433

HERNANDEZ, VIDAL, real estate broker; b. Feb. 9, 1935, Bogota Columbia, nat. 1967; s. Antonio Jesus and Margarita (Ospina) H.; m. Leonor, July 20, 1963; edn: AA, Pasadena City Coll. 1964; tchg. credentials (life) data processing, UCLA 1967; computer sys. & pmg. IBM, Control Data, Xerox 1977; Calif. lic. R.E. broker 1982. Career: data processing opr. IBM, Los Angeles; jr. pgmmr. Coldwell Banker, Los Angeles 1964-67; electronic data processing coord. Xerox Corp., Pasadena 1967-77; realtor assoc. Bona Real Estate Co., Pasadena 1977-83; broker/ pres. Vileo Investments, Pasadena 1983--; awards: Real Estate Sales Master Leader, Bona Real Estate Co. 1978-82; mem: YMCA; Boy Scouts of Am.; Democrat; Lutheran; rec: skiing, flying, golf. Res: 540 Gloria Rd Arcadia 91006 Ofc; Vileo Investments, 501 N Hill Ave Pasadena 91106

HERNANDEZ-BRAVO, LUIS RAUL, insurance co. executive; b. June 2, 1943, Pilares Sonora, Mex.; immigrated to US 1966 with wife (nat. US cit.); s. Carlos Hernandez Rodriguez and Arminda Bravo de Hernandez, m. Annette Margareta Bjorklund, Aug. 13, 1966; children: Adriana, b. 1967, Karlana, b. 1971, Tamara, b. 1974, Tania, b. 1977; edn: BA, Burnely Sch. of Profl. Art 1967; spl. courses Univ. Wash., Seattle; cand. CLU (Cert. Life Underwriter). Career: display mgr. Rohdes of Seattle, Wash. 1967-68; advt. sales Ketchikan Daily News, Alaska 1968-71; advt. dir. El Mexicano St. Newspaper, Mex. 1971-72; agent (Hon. Roll producer) Auto Club of So. Calif. 1973-77; agt. (Hon. Ring) Allstate Insurance 1977-79, dist. sales mgr. 1980-84, market sales mgr., S.E. San Diego County, 1984--; awards: Key Manager, 1zr1-83; mem. Lions Club, Toastmasters Intl., World Wide Marriage Encounter; works: orig., designed "Southeastern Log" state wide news publ., Ketchikan (Lew Williams, pub. 1970); created murals in Tougass Trading Post (1971, Ala.), Seattle Center (1968); art instr. Ketchikan Pub. Library 1968; rec: golf, painting. Res: 1406 Kim Pl Chula Vista 92011 Ofc: Allstate Ins. Co. 744 Jamacha Rd El Cajon 92020

HERNDON, KENNETH BRYAN, publishing co. executive; b. Mar. 4, 1943, Detroit, Mich.; s. Bryan and Mildred (McGaugh) H.; m. Mary Ellen, Nov. 9, 1968; children: Bryan, b. 1970; Kevin, b. 1975; Denis, b. 1975; edn: AA, Detroit Inst. of Arts 1963, BS, Woodbury Univ. 1968. Career: prodn. mgr. East/ West Network, Los Angeles 1968-80; v.p. prodn. Calif. Business, L.A. 1980--; cons./ prodn. dir. Douglas Publishing and Health & Care mags.; awards: 1st pl. awd., Health & Svcs. Graphics awd., USC 1967; mem: Western Publishers Assn.; Democrat; Catholic; rec: back packing, fishing, drawing. Res: 812 Irving Dr Burbank 91504 Ofc: California Business News, Inc., 6420 Wilshire Blvd, Ste 711, Los Angeles 90048

HERR, LARRY B., sales co. executive; b. Dec. 23, 1924, Lancaster, Pa.; s. Larry B. and Ruth F. (Foltz) H.; m. Margaret Ansley, Aug. 18, 1948; children: James, b. 1956; Steven, b. 1957; edn: BS, Drexel Univ. 1948. Career: salesman L.B. Herr & Son, Lancaster, Pa. 1948-54; pres. Mara-Long-Marsh, Inc., San Diego 1954-64; pres. Parron Hall Office Interiors, San Diego 1964--; bd. dirs. State Compensation Ins. Fund 1972--; mem: Nat. Ofc. Products Assn.; Kiwanis Club, San Diego; San Diego CofC; Univ. Club of San Diego; Republican; Episcopal; rec: skiing. Res: 854 Bangor St San Diego 92106 Ofc: Parron Hall Office Interiors, 820 W Ash St San Diego 92101

HERRAN, JUAN JOSE, physician; b. Aug. 1, 1950, Sancti-Spiritus, Cuba, nat. 1970; s. Jose and Evangelina (Garcia) H.; edn: BS, 1972, MD, Univ. of Puerto Rico. Career: resident internal med. VA Hosp., Rio Piedras, P.Rico 1976-79; clin. instr. NY Medical Coll., Lincoln Hosp. affiliation, Bronx, NY 1979-80; Stanford Univ. Med. Center, 1980-83, mem. Heart and Lung Transplant Com. 1982-83; pulmonary medicine splst., Whittier, Ca. 1983--; clin. dir. Dept. of Respiratory Med., Whittier Hosp. Med. Ctr.; mem: Los Angeles Co. Med. Assn., Am. Coll. of Physicians, Am. Coll. of Chest Physicians; orgns: Metropolitan Opera and S.F. Opera Guilds; publs: research abstracts on Pulmonary Physiology; rec: classical music, opera. Res: 6308 Comstock, Apt F, Whittier 90601 Ofc: Colima Internal Medical Group, 10155 Colima Whittier 90603

HERST, PERRY STERN, JR., real estate executive; b. Sept. 18, 1929, Chgo.; s. Perry Stern and Gertrude (Browarsky) H.; div.; children: Perry III, b. 1965; Craig, b. 1966; edn: BA, Brown Univ. 1951; MBA, Harvard Grad. Sch. 1953. Career: loan ofcr. Equitable Finance Corp., Chgo. 1957; R.E. leasing & devel. broker Arthur Rubloff & Co., Chgo. 1958-64; v.p. Tishman- Gateway Inc., Chgo. 1964-68; sr. v.p. Tishman Realty & Constrn. Co., Inc., Los Angeles 1968-77; pres. 1977--; awards: Humanitarian Awd., Nat. Conf. of Christians & Jews 1976; Civic Achiev. Awd., The Am. Jewish Com. 1979; mem: Lamda Alpha; Urban Land Inst.; L.A. area CofC (Long Range Plng. Com.); Los Angeles Mayor's Economic Council; Nat. Conf. of Christians & Jews; The Am. Jewish Com.; Jr. Achiev. of So. Calif.; UCLA Chancellor Assocs.; mil: lt. sr. grade USN 1954-56; Republican; Jewish; rec: fishing, hunting, tennis. Res: Malibu Ofc: Tishman West Management Corp., 10960 Wilshire Blvd, Ste 700, Los Angeles 90024

HERTWECK, E. ROMAYNE, educator; b. July 24, 1928, Springfield, Mo.; s. Garnett P. and Gladys (Chowning) H.; m. Alma Louise Street, Dec. 16, 1955, 1 son: William Scott, b. 1970; edn: BA, Augustana Coll. 1962; MA, Pepperdine Coll. 1963; EdD, Ariz. State Univ. 1966; PhD, US Internat. Univ. 1978. Career: night ed. Rock Island Argus Newspaper, Ill. 1961-62; grad. tchg. asst. Pepperdine Coll., Los Angeles 1963; counselor, VA, Ariz. State Univ., Tempe, Ariz. 1964; assoc. dir. conciliation ct. Miracopa Co. Superior Ct., Phoenix, Ariz. 1965; instr. Phoenix Coll. 1966; prof. psychol. Mira Costa Coll., Oceanside, Calif. 1967--; chmn. psychol. counseling dept. World Campus Afloat, S.S. Ryndam, spring 1970; instr. edn. dept., Univ. of San Diego, part- time 1968-69; lectr. bus. mgmt. dept., San Diego State Univ., part-time 1980--; instr. Chapman Coll. Residence Ctr., Camp Pendleton 1969--; bd. dirs. Christian Counseling Ctr., Oceanside 1970--; mem: Kiwanis; Carlsbad Club; Am., Western & No. San Diego Co. Psychol. Assns.; Am. Personnel & Guidance Assn.; Phi Delta Kappa; Kappa Delta Pi; Psi Chi; Republican; Protestant; rec: travel, golf, photog. Res: 2024 Oceanview Rd Oceanside Ofc: Mira Costa College, Oceanside

HESS, EDWARD JORGEN, university librarian; b. Feb. 18, 1925, Hamburg, IA; s. Edward A. and Luella (Nelson) Hess; BA, soc. sci. and secondary edn., Peru State Coll., NE, 1949; MA, polit sci., USC, 1954; MS, lib. sci., 1957; Ph.D., lib. sci., 1970. Career: tchr., Jr. High and High Schs., MO and CA, 1950-56; lib. cataloger, San Diego State Univ., 1957-58; serials lib., 1958-59; lib. supr. tech. services, 1961-63; lib. dir., Lompoc Pub. Lib., 1965-66; asst. lib. and chief of tech. services, Calif. State Univ., Northridge, 1966-67; asst. lib. and chief of pub. services, 1967-69; full time 1969-70; asst. prof. 1970-76; asst. univ. lib. for pub. services, USC, 1976--. Calif. Community Coll. Lib. Credential, valid for life, Contbg. author, California Librarian, other publs. Editor, California Librarian, 1969. Mil.: AUS, 1943-46. Mem.: Calif. Lib. Assn., chmn., bylaws comm., 1968-69, parliamentarian 1968, councilor 1975-77; Amer. Lib. Assn., Calif. correspondent for ALA Yearbook, 1976; Amer. Soc. for Information Sci.; Calif. Soc. of Librarians, CLA; So. Calif. Tech. Processes Group; Beta Phi Mu; Kappa Delta Pi. Mem.: Sierra Club, 1967--; Ratl. Trust for Historic Preservation, 1972--; Western Photog. Collectors Assn., 1974--; Friends of the Chinatown Lib., 1977--. Rec.: photography, travel. Res.: 517 N. Vista Bonita Ave., Glendora 91740; Office: Univ. Lib., USC, Los Angeles 90007.

HESS, JUDITH FERNE, school administrator; b. Aug. 15, 1941, Pontiac, Mich.; d. Wm. Roy and Reba Fern (Dailey) Lane; edn: BS, So. Ill. Univ. 1962; MS Ed., Univ. Ill. 1964; PhD, Calif. Grad. Inst. 1975; Calif. lic. MFCC (Marriage Family Child Counseling), lic. Ednl. Psychology; Tchr. credentials: Gen. Pupil Personnel, Gen. Adminstrn., Secondary Tchg. Career: secty. Nat. Teachers of Eng., Champaign, Ill. 1963-64; tchr. Peoria (Ill.) Hts. Comm. H.Sch. 1962-63; counselor/psychologist Charter Oak Unif. Sch. Dist., Covina, Ca. 1964 69; psychologist, dir. Title III, Glendora Unif. Sch. Dist. 1969-81; program mgr. San Bernardino Co. schs. 1981-82; coordinator Spl. Svcs., Hesperia Sch. Dist. 1983--; career mgr. Career Plnng. Center Branch, Monrovia 1978; commnr. State Bd. of Behav. Scis., Sacto. (5 times); honors: PTA (2), and Ill. Normal scholarships; Nat. Hon. Soc., Pi Lamba Theta, Delta Kappa Pi; mem: Delta Kappa Gamma Soc. Intl.; Assn. Calif. Sch. Adminstrs.; Council Exceptional Children; Nat. Assn. MFCC; mem. Altrusa; bd. mem. Job, Inc. 1983-; publs: art., The Catalyst (Fall 83), num. ednl. tng. manuals and kits, 11 cassette tapes, 3 slide and tape presentations; devel. Exemplary status SpEd pgm., 1984; Republican; Prot.; rec: travel. Res: 16330 Cabrillo Dr Victorville 92392 Ofc: Hesperia School District 9144 Third, Hesperia 92345

HESSLINK, ROBERT LOUIS, company executive; b. Mar. 25, 1931, Swink, Colo.; s. Joseph Abner (dec.) and Estelle Blanche (Cooper) H.; m. Frances O'Neill; children: Charles W., b. 1951; Robert L. Jr., b. 1956; edn: AA, LaJunta Jr. Coll. 1952; num. A.F. spec. schs. Career: with Am. Gen. Capital Plng., parttime 1958-73; Tucson, Ariz. 1958-61; rep. Moses Lake, Wash. 1961-63; res. mgr., Amarillo, Tex. 1963s66; dist. mgr., Riverside, Calif. 1973--; honors: Millionaire Club Awd. 1978--; 500,00 Club Awd. 1974-77; mem: Order of Daedalian; Frat. Order of Mil. Pilots; Flight 30; 200 Mem.; The Retired Ofcrs. Assn. (local & nat.); Nat. ASsn. of Uniform Svcs.; Internat. Assn. of Fin. Plnrs., Orange Co. chpt.; Riverside City Coll. Tiger Backers Club; mil: lt. col. USAF 1953-73, ret., Bronze Star; Air Medal w/ 4 Oak Leaf Cluster; Air Force Commdn. w/ 1 Oak Leaf; spec: pilot, instr. pilot, wing standardization evaluator, instrument instr., aircraft KC-135 tanker; Democrat; Protestant. Address: American Capital Financial Services, 2997 Woodhaven St Riverside 92503

HESTEHAVE, BORGE TAGE, maufacturing co. executive; b. Aug. 29, 1923, Elsinore, Denmark, nat. 1967; s. Frederik Marentius and Kamma Marie (Jorgensen) H.; m. Marianne Rejkjaer, Aug. 29, 1948; children: Kjeld, b. 1951; Judy, b. 1956; edn: The Latin Sch. of Elsinore 1941; The Tech. Coll. of Elsinore 1941-45; mech. eng., The Tech. Inst. of Copenhagen 1946-48. Career: plant engr. AMBA Co., Copenhagen 1949-51; works mgr. Pomos Ltd., Santiago de Chile 1951-55; tool designer Artcraft Engineering, Los Angeles 1956-58; plant engr. Flintkote Co., L.A. 1958-60; plant mgr. Latchford Glass, L.A. 1960-61; plant mgr. Kerr Plastics, Santa Ana 1961-63; gen. mgcr. Magi-Cup, Berkeley

1963-38; plant mgr. Trans Containr, Upland 1968-69; pres./ chmn. bd. Bomatic, Inc., Ontario 1969--; mem: Soc. of Plastics Engrs.; Soc. of Mfg. Engrs.; Ontario CofC; patentee: injection blow molding machines, others; mil: Royal Danish Navy 1948-49; Republican; Protestant; rec: sailing, flying, tennis. Res: 8031 Beechwood Dr Alta Loma 91701 Ofc: Bomatic, Inc., 1841 E Acacia St Ontario 91761

HESTON, RICHARD EARL, insurance broker; b. Dec. 31, 1940, Youngstown, Ohio; s. Clifford James and Goldie Ellen (De Witt) H.; m. Kathleen Marie Moon, Jan. 2, 1973; children: Brian David, b. 1968, Caleb Joshua, b. 1973, Seth Jeremiah, b. 1977; edn: stu. Mt. San Antonio Jr. Coll., CalPoly Pomona, CSC San Bernardino. Career: musician/ music tchr. self empl., 1959-70; owner Glen-East Music Store, 1970-73; purch. agent in Los Angeles 1976-83; ins. agt. Farmers Insurance 1976-83, broker/owner Heston Insurance Agency, Fontana 1983--; mem. United Farmers Agents Assn., PIA, Big I; awards: recognition for civic svc., United Way, American Red Cross, City of Fontana, Rialto, San Bdno.; LUTC Underwriting award, Life Masters ins. award, Commercial Masters of Ins. award. Mem: chmn. Bur. of Franchise City of Fontana; treas. Merrill Comm. Services of Fontana; chmn. Fontana Youth Devel.; bd. mem. Am. Red Cross (Fontana, San Bdno.), United Way Regl. Bd.; Little League Baseball mgr., sponsor 9 yrs.; Exchange Club; Fontana Mummers; works: semi-profl. vocalist in San Bdno., L.A. Counties 1950s-; Conserv. Baptist; rec: treasure hunting, art, historical museums. Res: 17490 Grevillea Fontana 92335 Ofc: Heston Insurance Agency 16752 Foothill Blvd Fontana 92335

HETRICK, ROBERT CHARLES, JR., securities firm executive; b. Apr. 29, 1939, Pottstown, Penna.; s. Robert and Grace Hetrick, Sr.; m. Bonnie Kay McDougall, Mar. 16, 1963; children: Stephen, b. 1972, Matthew, b. 1977, Melissa, b. 1977; edn: BSBA, Univ. Rochester 1962; MBA, UC Berkeley 1967. Career: mgr. trainee Gen. Elec. Co., Schenectady, NY 1963; stockbroker, vice pres. Smith Barney & Co., Los Angeles 1967--; life mem. Presidents Club; orgns: Santa Monica Protective Assn. (dir.), Pacific Palisades Baseball Assn. (treas.), Jonathan Club; mil: lt. USN 1963-66, Vietnam Svc.; Republican; Presbyterian; rec: coaching soccer/baseball. Res: 1127 Georgina Ave Santa Monica 90402 Ofc: Smith Barney & Co., 800 W. Sixth St, Los Angeles 90017

HEVENLY, JUDY ANN, author/astrologist, b. Feb. 1, 1938, Port Elizabeth, South Africa; d. Trevor and Mavis (Butt-Thompson) Doorly-Jones; m. Robert P. Heverly, 1968, div. 1970; ed. Holy Rosary Convent, Collegiate H.Sch. (Port Elizabeth); Asso. in Rel. Sci., United Ch. of Rel. Sci. 1976; D.Div., Ch. of Gospel Ministry Inc. 1978; Career: actress, London, Eng. appearing in such movies as Charles Chaplin's "Countess from Hong Kong," Dick Lester "The Knack," "Goldfinger" (James Bond), Francois Truffaut's " Fahrenheit 451," "Alfie" w/ Michael Caine, 1970-73; writer/catalogue designer Southeby Parke Bernet, Los Angeles 1973-74; asst. to rep. Hong Kong Trade Council, L.A. 1976-79; astrologist/ psychic/ metaphysician, Los Angeles Holistic Group, 1979--, pub./v.p. P.S.I. Publishing Co., 1979--; author: Pages of Your Mind (novel) 1984; writer, Globe Newspapers, W.Palm Beach, Fla. 1979-; columnist/ astrologist, Courier Diplomatique, Wash DC, 1983-; vpm mem: L.A. Press club, Internat. Directory of Astrologers/Psychics, Spiritualists Soc. of Gr.Brit., British Actors Equity Assn., Psychic Guide 1982-83, Book Publicists of So. Calif.; works: accurately predicted more than 100 major nat. and internat. events, featured in publs. incl. The Nat. Enquirer, Star, Globe, Examiner, The London TV Times, Fate, Psychic Guide; interviews in The LA Times, Herald Examiner, Valley Daily News, Civic Center News, Israeli Times, Esoteric News; num. radio, TV appearances; Republican; Ch. Rel. Sci.; rec: politics, travel, writing. Res: 14411 Kittridge Van Nuys 91405 Ofc: Hevenly World Publishing, POB 3895, Van Nuys 91407 Los Angeles Wholistic Group, Ste 421, Box 6010, Sherman Oaks 91413

HEWITT, SCOTT, security investigator; b. Dec. 19, 1953, Los Angeles; s. George Lynn and Roselyn (Hyun) H.; m. Lori Spencer, Sept. 10, 1977; 1 son: Jeffrey, b. 1983; edn: BS in criminal justice, CSU Los Angeles 1976; pvt. investigator, Calif. 1983. Career: security mgr. May Co., Calif. 1977-79; adminstr. security pgms. Hughes Helicopters, Culver City 1979-83; sr. investigator 1983--; loss prevention agent J.W. Robinsons, Santa Monica 1981-84; awards: for svc., May Co. 1980; for svc., Hughes Helicopters Fed. Credit Union 1982; mem: Los Angeles- Orange Co. Peace Ofcrs. Shrine Club; Am. Soc. for Indsl. Security; Masons, Los Angeles; Venice United Methodist Ch.; Long Beach Scottish Rite; El Bekel Shrine, Long Beach; Republican; Methodist; rec: sports. Res: 2428 Beverly Ave, Apt C, Santa Monica 90405 Ofc: Hughes Helicopters, Bldg. 17, M/S T55, Culver City 90230

HEWLETT, WILLIAM REDINGTON, industrialist; b. May 20, 1913, Ann Arbor, Mich.; s. Albion Walter and Louise (Redington) H.; m. Flora Lamson, Aug. 10, 1938, dec. 1977; children: Eleanor Louise, b. 1942, Walter Berry, b. 1944, James Sterry, b. 1947, William Albion, b. 1949, Mary Joan, b. 1951; m. 2d. Rosemary Kopmeier Bradford, May 24, 1978; edn: BA 1934, E.E. 1939, Stanford Univ.; MS, Mass. Inst. of Tech. 1936; Hon. Degrees: LLD, UCB 1966, LLD, Yale Univ. 1976, DSc, Kenyon Coll. 1978, DSc, Polytech. Inst. of NY 1978, Eng.D, Univ. of Notre Dame 1980, Eng.D, Utah State Univ. 1980, Eng.D., Dartmouth Coll. 1983, LLd, Mills Coll. 1983. Career: co-founder/ptnr. Hewlett-Packard Co., Palo Alto 1939-46, dir. 1947-, exec. VP 1947-64, pres. 1964-68, pres./CEO 1969-77, chmn. Exec. Com./ CEO 1977-78, dir./chmn. of Exec. Com. 1978--; dir. Utah International Inc. 1974-; trustee Calif. Acad. of Scis. (Hon.) 1969-; trustee (chmn. bd. trustees 1980-) Carnegie Inst. of Wash. 1971-; awards: Calif. Mfr. of Year 1969, Calif. Mfrs. Assn.; Business Statesman of Year 1970, Harvard Bus. Sch. of No. Calif.; Medal of Achievement, 1971, Western Electronic Mfrs. Assn.; IEEE Founders Medal 1973; Industrialist of Year 1973 (w/ David Packard), Calif. Mus. of Sci. & Indus. 1973; Herbert Hoover Medal, 1977, Stanford Univ. Alumni Assn.; mem: Nat. Acad. of Engring. 1965-, Nat. Acad. of Scis. 1977-, Fellow Am. Acad. of Arts & Scis. 1970-, Fellow IEEE (pres. 1954), Instrument Soc. of Am. (hon. life), The Franklin Inst. (life fellow); clubs: Bohemian, Pacific-Union, Menlo Country (Woodside), Century Assn. (NYC); coauthor sev. tech. arts.; holds patents on R.C. Oscillators and other electronic devices; mil: lt. col. US Army Signal Corps WWII 1942-45, Army Commendn.; Republican; Presbyterian; rec: ski, golf, photog. Ofc: Hewlett-Packard Co. 1501 Page Mill Rd Palo Alto 94304

HEYWOOD, KENNETH TRUE, real estate broker; b. Mar. 17, 1928, Panguitch, Utah; s. Edgar True and Clara Fulton (Syrett) H.; m. Lorraine Padelford, July 21, 1950; children: David, b. 1954; Robert, b. 1955; Rebecca, b. 1962; Carlton, b. 1964; Valerie, b. 1969; Chrystal, b. 1971; edn: BA, Ariz. State Univ. 1952, MA, 1962; Calif. tchr. credentials: gen. adminstrn., standard svcs. supvn., std. designated svcs., pupil personnel, gen. secondary, gen. elem. Career: tchr. Wasco High S/D, Wasco 1967-69; vocational counselor Dept. Human Resources Devel., Bakersfield 1969-70; counselor, counselor supvr., pgm. dir. Regl. Occupational Ctr. of Kern 1970-79; coord. vocational & career edn. Ofc. of the Kern County Supt. of Schs. 1979-80; salesman/ broker Wingate Real Estate, Wasco 1980--; awards: Tchr. of the Year, Kern Co. Supt. of Schs. Ofc. 1980; mem: Nat. Edn. Assn.; Calif. Teachers Assn.; Nat. & Calif. Vocational Edn. Assns.; Bakersfield Calif. East Stake High Council; Republican; LDS; rec: family activities, gardening. Res: 1224 Second St Wasco 93280 Ofc: Wingate Real Estate, 1701 Hwy 46, Wasco 93280

HICK, KEN W., manufacturing company president; b. Oct. 17, 1946, New Westminister, B.C., Canada; s. Les W. and Mary I. (Warner) H.; 1 son, David W., b. 1969; edn: BA, E. Washington St. Coll. 1971; MBA, Univ. of Wash. 1973, PhD, 1978. Career: regional mgr. Hilti Inc., Stamford, Conn. 1975-79; gen. mgr. Moore Internat., Portland, Ore. 1979-80; v.p. sales/mktg. Phillips Inc., Anaheim, Ca. 1980; owner/pres./CEO KC Metal Products Inc., San Jose 1981--; mem. Bd. of Fellows Univ. of Santa Clara; mem. Am. Inst. of Timber Constructors, Nat. Assn. of Business Economists, Am. Mgmt. Assn.; mil: s/sgt. USAF 1963-66, Commendn. Medal; num. arts. in business journals; Republican; Catholic; rec: aviation/ pilot. Res: 566 Cambrian Way Danville 94569 San Jose Ofc: KC Metal Products Inc. 1960 Hartog Dr San Jose 95131

HICKEY, ROGER LEE, metrologist; b. Sept. 26, 1949, San Diego; s. Chester Oliver and Atlantis Rose (Munro) H.; m. Debra Tunnell, Aug. 4, 1972; children: Rebecca, b. 1976; Randy, b. 1978; Rachael, b. 1981; edn: BA, Calif. Baptist Coll. 1983; BS, 1983. Career: electronics tech./ metrologist Bear Medical Sys., Inc. 1982--; instr. physical sci. Calif. Baptist Coll.; awards: Outstanding Achiev. in Sci., Calif. Baptist Coll. 1982; mem: Nat. Conf. of Standards Labs. (delegate); IEEE; ASQE; PMA; Am. Nat. Red Cross (instr.); mil: ET-2 USN 1969-79, GCM (2), Combat Action, Vietnam Svc., Navy Expoditionary; Baptist; rec: pvt. pilot, amateur radio, fly fishing. Res: 8190 Garfield Ave Riverside 92504 Ofc: Bear Medical Systems, Inc., 2085 Rustin Ave Riverside 92507

HICKS, LEWELLYN WESTCOTT, insurance executive; b. June 20, 1920, Fresno; s. Henry Kincheloe and Daisy (Monney) H.; m. Margaret Carson, Jan. 9, 1944; children: L. Westcott Jr., b. 1945; Susan Wente, b. 1949; edn: BA, UC Berkeley 1947; Inst. Ins. Mktg., So. Methodist Univ. 1953; UCLA Grad. Sch. of Bus. 1970-71; CLU, Am. Coll. 1956. Career: personnel interviewer State of Calif. 1950-51; agent State Farm Ins. Co., Oakland 1951-52; asst. dist. mgr. 1953-54; asst. regl. dir. Maryland, Va., Del., DC 1955-57; regl. agcy. v.p. State Farm Ins., Home Ofc., Bloomington, Ill. 1958-69; agcy. dir. regl. ofc., Westlake Village 1970-74; agcy. mgr., Oxnard, Ventura 1974--; honors: mem. State Farm Millionaires Club 1977-83, pres. awd. Ventura Co. Assn. of Life Underwriters 1982-83; mem: Ventura Co. Life Underwriters (past pres., Nat. Com.); Agents & Mgrs. (past pres.); Nat. ssn. of Life Underwriters (Nat. Council); Am. Coll. of Life Underwriters; Masons, Shriners; mil: lt., aviator USN 1941-46, mem. Black Cat Squadron; Republican; Presbyterian; rec: skiing, swimming, Brittany Spaniels. Res: 1840 Stonesgate St Westlake Village 91361 Ofc: State Farm Ins. Co., 500 Esplanade Dr Oxnard 93030

HIDALGO, RICHARD, real estate broker; b. Feb. 16, 1919, Floresville, Tx.; came to Santa Barbara, Ca. in 1919; s. Thomas Garcia and Severa Navarro (Ramirez) H.; m. Maria Hernandez, June 24, 1950; edn: AA in R.E., Santa Barbara City Coll. 1983; GRI Grad. Realtors Inst., CAR; Calif. R.E. sales/ broker lic. 1960-; Comm. Coll. Tchr. Credential (1971). Career: sales in appliance div. family retail bus. until 1957, owner retail store 1958-60; real estate salesman, investor, 1960-, broker/owner Hidalgo Realty, Santa Barbara; mem. Grand Jury 1963-4; Police and Fire Commnr. 1965; Realtor of Year 1970; mem. S.B. City Council 1971-72; dir. (pres. 1979) Old Spanish Days; dir. (chmn. 1982) Metro. Transit Dist.; dir., past pres. (1978) S.B. Uptown Lions; S.B. Northside Bus. Assn. (pres. 1983); mem. CofC; devel. the S.B. Sister City Program (1972); hon. life mem. Native Sons of Golden West; Republican; Baptist; rec: music. Res: 835 Arguello Rd Santa Barbara 93101 Ofc: Hidalgo Realty 835 Arguello Rd Santa Barbara 93103

HIGBE, CLIFTON MELTON HARVIN, lawyer; b. Sept. 13, 1932, Columbia, S.Carolina; s. William Wellington and Agnes Irene (Shaw) H.; m. Anne Jensen, Feb. 14, 1980; children: Clifton Jr., b. 1956; Elizibeth, b. 1958; Randall, b. 1959; edn: Fla. State Univ. 1956-57; AA, Am. River Coll. 1962; JD, U.O.P./ McGeorge Sch. of Law 1970. Career: gen. mgr. Comstock Steel Co. 1958-64; owner/ broker The Higbe Co., Sacto. 1964--; sales mgr. Sacto. bus. dist. Pacific

Telephone Co. 1966-71; atty. at law, Clifton M.H. Higbe, Sacto. 1971--; instr. bus law; lectr. tax deferred exchanges, ethics; awards: Am. Jurisprudence Cert. 66; mem: Am., Calif. & Sacto. Co. Bar Assns.; Nat. Assn. of Home Bldrs.; Bldg. Indus. Assn.; Sacto. Real Estate Exch. Gp.; Nat. Fedn. of Ind. Bus.; Kiwi Growers of Calif.; Calif. Republican Assn.; mil: 1st lt. USAF 1950-58; Republican; Baptist; rec: swim, running, gemstone collector. Res: 700-4 Woodside East, Sacramento 95825 Ofc: The Higbe Co., 1555 River Park Dr, Ste 202, Sacramento 95815

HIGGINS, WINIFRED C., newspaper production executive; b. Jan. 26, 1934, Raleigh, NC; d. Meredith L. and Rachel D. (Allen) Shumaker; 1 dau. Charlotte, b. 1953; edn: Univ. of Okla., San Bernardino Valley Coll. Career: typesetter opr. News Mirror, Yucaipa and Calimesa, 1963; mark-up psn. The Desert Sun, Palm Springs 1973, asst. composing foreman, 1975, asst. prodn. mgr. 1977, prodn. mgr. 1979--; honors: Resolution, State of Calif. Assembly (spons. by Cong. Jerry Lewis), 1978; Woman of Achievement, Yucaipa Valley Bus. and Profl. Womens Club (1973), League of Women Voters, San Brdno. Co. (1976) for aiding residents of Calif. State Womens Prison, Frontera to obtain college edns.; mem: Calif. Fedn. of Bus. and Profl. Womens Clubs (Individual Devel. Instr. 1975-, certifies new Instrs. 1980-; state P.R. ch. 1980, state conv. hostess 1983); San Orco Dist. (San Brdno. and Orange Cos.) Calif. Fedn. of Bus. and Profl. Women (pres. 1977; estab. Leadership Tng. Sem. 1983); publs: Pub. Rels. Manual for Calif. Fedn. BPW, 1978; Republican; Presbyterian; rec: gardening, piano, public spkg. Res: 590 Ave K, (POB 83) Calimesa 92320 Ofc: The Desert Sun, 611 S. Palm Canyon Dr Palm Springs 92262

HIGUE, GEORGE JOHN, dentist; b. Mar. 21, 1915, Los Angeles; edn: DDS, USC, 1940; m. Mary Kellam, Dec. 31, 1960; 1 child, Michell, b. 1945; private practice dentistry, self-employed, Bell, Ca. 1945--; Fellow, Royal Soc. of Health, Fellow, Internat. Coll. of Dentists, Fellow, American Coll. of Dentists, Fellow, Am. Acad. of Applied Nutrition; recipient distinguished service awards, Am. Soc. of Dentistry of Children (1966, Dallas, Tex.), Bell CofC (1972), Calif. Assembly Resolution of Commendation (1980); mem: So. Calif. Soc. of Clinical Hypnosis, pres, 1978-79; Orange Co. Soc. of Clin. Hypnosis, treas. 1980, 81, 82; American Soc. of Clin. Hypnosis, treas. 1979; Bell-Maywood Rotary Club, pres. 1941, 32 years of perfect attendance; So. Calif. Soc. of Dentistry for Children, pres. 1951, Pierre Fauchard Acad. (internat. hon. dental orgn.), pres. 1974; Bell C. of C., pres. 1951, 1966; chmn. L.A. County Children's Dental Health Day, 1951; publs: adminstrv. & sci. dental articles; mil: maj. Dental Corps. AUS, 1940-46, 1 Battle Star; Republican; Prot; rec: boating, fishing, golf; res: 3351 Bounty Cir., Huntington Harbor 92649 ofc: 4327 Gage Ave. Bell 90201.

HILL, ALBERT ANDREW, lumber co. owner; b. Apr. 22, 1915, Iron River, Wisc.; s. Hjalmer Andrew and Ida Mary (Sorvisto) H.; m. Margaret Silver, July 14, 1937; children: Albert Alan, b. 1938; Ronald Steven, b. 1944; stu. gen. mdsg., Palo Alto Adult Edn. 1954. Career: fireman City of Palo Alto 1939-47; lumber merchant, Palo Alto Lumber 1948-60; sales Builder's Hardware 1960-67; warehouseman Fremont High Dist. 1967-78; ret.; co-owner Palo Alto Lumber Co.; mem: Palo Alto Masons; Boy Scouts of Am.; Palo Alto Lawn Bowls (pres. 1981); De Molay (Adv. Com., Dad Advr.); Barron Park Fire Dist. (fire chief); Republican; Lutheran; rec: lawn bowls, golf. Res: 2131 Barbara Dr Palo Alto 94303

HILL, BESSIE JUNE SEATON, accountant, artist; b. Nov. 15, 1922, Perkins, Okla.; d. Alexander J. and Tabitha (Thomas) Seaton; m. Harold H. Hill, July 4, 1945; edn: Loma Linda Univ. 1940-1, Madison Coll. campus So. Missionary Coll. 1941, Longmeyers Bus. Coll. 1945-6; AA (2), Coll. of the Desert, 1963-80; spl. courses, CSU Long Beach, Anthony Schs.; Calif. lic. Real Estate Broker, Notary Public, Voc. Tchg. Credential (acctg., real estate) 1980-6. Career: chief acct. Coachella Valley County Water Dist. 1948-57; acct. Massey Sand & Rock/ Wade G. Ellis, CPA, 1957-60; fin. ofcr./chief acct. City of Indio, 1960-66; self-empl. acct. 1967-71; controller Riviera Hotel & Country Club, 1971-72; controller/treas. Desert Hot Springs Co. Water Dist. 1973-79; auditor/ofc. mgr. West San Bernardino Co. Water Dist. 1981-82; artist, painter (American Indians, Westerns, Lndscps., Seascps.), awards for still-life in juried shows; mem: Desert Art Center Inc., Yucca Valley Art Assn. Inc., Fontana Art Assn. Inc., CSCSB Acctg. Assn., Soroptimist Intl.; 7th-Day Adventist; rec: outdoor life, art. Res: 45-146 Monroe St Indio 92201 Ofc: Computer Mgmt. Svc., POB 4546 Palm Springs 92201

HILL, BRIAN EARL, lawyer; b. Aug. 26, 1954, Hardwick, Vt.; s. Bruce Philo and Dorothy Delia (Godfrey) H.; edn: AA, Hancock Jr. Coll. 1974; BA, UC Santa Barbara 1977; JD, Univ. of S.F. 1981. Career: admitted to practice State Bar of Calif. 1981; judicial atty. for Judge Hugh Evans, Third Dist. Court of Appeal, Sacto. 1981--; honors: rep. UC Student Lobby, 1976; extern to fmr. Calif. Supreme Ct. Justice Frank Newman; Rotary Scholarship to Univ. of Edinburgh 1984-85; mem: Young Lawyers of Calif., Am. Bar Assn., Calif. Bar Assn., Volunteers in Parole; Democrat; Catholic; rec: sports, reading. Res: 2315 T Street Apt. B, Sacramento 95812 Ofc: Court of Appeal, 119 Library & Courts Bldg. Sacramento 95814

HILL, DORCAS M. EAVES, surgeon; b. Dec. 2, 1946, Pittsburgh, Pa.; d. Jehu R. and Marie Bernice (Morris) Eaves; div.; 1 child, Ceceli b. 1970; edn: cert. med. lab. tech., BCH Hosp. 1967, BA, Univ. Mass. 1973, MD, Boston Univ.

Sch. of Medicine 1977. Career: intern, resident Gen. Surg., UC Irvine Medical Center, 1977-82, asst. prof. of surgery UCIMC, 1982--: first woman to receive faculty apptmt. Dept. of Gen. Surgery UCI; chief administrv. resident Gen. Surg., instr. Residents and Med. Students; instr. Advance trauma life support 1982, instr. Advance cardiac life support 1979-; mem: AMA, Nat. Assn. of Residents and Interns, UCI House Staff Assn., A.W.A.; candidate Am. Coll. of Surgeons; Democrat; Jewish; rec: tennis, jogging, swim. Res: 15 Song Sparron Irvine 92714 Ofc: UCI Medical Center, 101 City Drive So. Orange 92668

HILL, DOUGLAS EMERY, certified public accountant; b. Oct. 21, 1946, Burbank; s. Lawrence Grant and Lucille Ellen (Arney) H.; m. Eugenia Yvonne Ubillus, Oct. 21, 1972; children: Christian, b. 1975; Alan, b. 1979; edn: BS, CSU Northridge 1970; cert. of completion, Peace Corps. Tng. Pgm. 1970; MS, bus. admin., CSU Northridge 1976; AICPA, Golden Gate Univ. 1980-; CPA, Calif. 1980. Career: spl. tax acct. Greyhound Lines, Inc., Western Div., San Francisco 1975-79; staff acct. Philip J. Andrews, CPA, San Carlos 1979-81; sr. staff acct. Bierman, Solomon, Ross & Petrick, CPAs, Woodland Hills 1981-82; owner Douglas E. Hill, CPA, Newbury Park & Thousand Oaks 1982--; mem. Peace Corps, tchr. other P.C. volunteers 1972-73; cons./ employee ABMI 1973; awards: Jr. Rose Bowl, CSUN 1967; Peruvian People School to School Pgms, fluent Spanish, State Dept. 1973; mem: AICPA; Calif. Soc. CPAs (Peninsula chpt., L.A. chpt.); San Fernando Valley Discussion Gp.; CSUN Alumni; Conejo Valley CofC; AYSO; works: num. Peace Corps publs. 1972-73; Democrat; Catholic; rec: creative writing, outdoor sports. Res: 91 Bluefield Newbury Park 91320 Ofc: 550 St Charles Dr, Ste 204C, Thousand Oaks 91360

HILL, (EDITH) MARLENE, speech pathologist; b. June 19, 1947, Oberlin, Ks.; d. John Albert and Margaret Ann (Germeroth) H.; edn: BA, Univ. of No. Colo. 1969; MS, speech pathology & audiology, 1973; CCC, Cert. Clinical Competency 1976. Career: speech pathologist Kern Co. Supt. of Schs., Bakersfield 1973-75; speech pathologist Meml. Rehab. Found. Ctr., Santa Barbara 1975-80; assoc. prof. UC Santa Barbara 1977; speech pathologist, pvt. practice, Santa Barbara 1980--; mem: Am. Speech & Hearing Assn.; rec: fiddler. Address: 958 Isleta Ave Santa Barbara 93109

HILL, EDWIN LEROY, real estate broker, mortgage co. president; b. Sept. 21, 1944, Taft; s. Howard LeRoy and Madeline Ethyl (Burlock) H.; edn: BS, San Jose State 1968, Secondary Edn. (life) Tchr. Cert. 1969, MS, 1973; Calif. lic. Real Estate Broker 1980. Career: realtor assoc. 1971-80; realtor Cabrillo Co. 1980-82; All Brokers, Porsche Properities, Inc. (formerly Allstate Realtors) 1982--; pres. DeAnza Mortgage, Cupertino 1983--; dir. Calif. Assn. Realtors 1981-83; bd. dirs. Central Valley Realtor Gp.; rep. to state assn. C.A.R. (1983) for San Jose Bd. Realtors Equal Opportunities Com. (won award for Bd.), devel. I.D. Badges for S.J. Bd. of Realtors 1978-81; mem: San Jose Real Estate Bd., Nat. & Calif. Assns. Realtors; Phi Delta Kappa (past pres.); Sigma Pi (Alumni Assn.); mil: E-6, USAR, Expert Rifle; Democrat; Methodist; rec: tennis, bowling, yachting. Res: 1137 Via Jose San Jose 95120 Ofc: De Anza Mortgage, 20009 B Stevens Creek Blvd Cupertino 95014

HILL, JERRY L., real estate brokerage president; b. Apr. 1, 1948, Berwyn, Ill.; s. Leonard W. and Jeannette V. (Karstens) H.; m. Janice Lindsay, Dec. 24, 1966; 1 son: T. Robert, b. 1980, edn, BS, w/ distn., San Jose State 1976. Career: self-empl. fin. plnr., San Jose 1972-80; R.E. sales ERA Marquis & Hill., San Jose 1978--, company pres. 1979--; former dir. Mountain Computer; instr. income tax' applications to real estate and client counseling; awards: No. 1 Calif. Ofc., ERA Marquis & Hill 1982-83, and top sales awd. ERA Marquis & Hill. 1983; mem: San Jose Real Estate Bd.; Almaden Golf & Country Club; developed: combination funding concept for use with fin. plng.; mil: capt. US Army 1966-72, Airborne & Jumpmaster qualified, Combat Inf. Badge, Bronze Star; Episcopal; rec: tennis, financial analysis. Res: 7071 Wooded Lake Dr San Jose 95120 Ofc: ERA Marquis & Hill, 1510 Parkmoor Ave San Jose 95128

HILL, KENNETH ALEXANDER, savings & loan executive; b. Mar. 25, 1946, Albany; s. Alexander and Freda Virginia (Walker) H.; m. Mary Louise Bradbury, June 10, 1945; children: Scott C., b. 1970; Todd A., b. 1977; edn: AA, DeAnza Coll. 1975; BS, San Jose State Univ. 1975; realtor, Nat. Assn. Realtors 1978. Career: salesman Referral Realty, San Jose 1975-78; realtor/ owner AKT-1 Real Estate Svc., Stockton 1978-82; field coord. State Savings & Loan, Stockton 1982; corp. broker/ v.p. 1982-83; real estate mgr./ v.p. Am. Savings & Loan, Stockton 1983--; corp. broker FCA Real Estate Equities, Inc., subs. Am. Savings & Loan 1983--; mem: Stockton, Calif. & Nat. Assns. Realtors; Rho Epsilon Nat. R.E. frat.; San Jose State Univ. (chpt. pres. 1975); Alumni; mil: photog. mate E-4 USN 1967-69, Armed Froces Expedit. Medal, Nat. Defense, Vietnam Svc.; Democrat; Protestant; rec; sailing, real estate cons., photog. Res: 4609 Dunman Ave Woodland Hills 91364 Ofc: American Savings, 7120 Hayvenhurst, Ste 305, Van Nuys 91406

HILL, LORIE ELIZABETH, psychotherapist; b. Oct. 21, 1946, Buffalo, NY; d. Graham and Elizabeth Helen (Salm) H.; edn: Univ. of Manchester, Eng. 1966-67; BA, Grinnell Coll. 1968; MA, Univ. Wisc. 1970; MA, CSU Sonoma 1974; PhD, Wright Inst. 1980. Career: English instr. Univ. of Mo. 1970-71; therapist trainee Valley Children & Youth, Pleasanton 1975-76; adminstr./ supvr. Antioch-West & Ctr. for Ind. Living, San Francisco & Berkeley 1975-77; dir. of tng. Ctr. for Edn. & Mental Health, S.F. 1977-80; exec. dir. 1980-81; instr. MA pgm. in psychol. John F. Kennedy Univ., Orinda 1981; psychotherapist, pvt. practice, Berkeley 1981-83, Oakland 1983--; organizer against nuclear war; found. mem. Psychotherapists for Soc. Responsibility; spkr. non- sexist psychology; mem: Nat. Abortion Rights Action League; Sane (Anti-nuclear orgn.); Nat. Orgn. Women; Demo. Socialist; rec: sports, travel. Res: 3028 Brookdale Ave Oakland 94602 Ofc: 312 Hudson St Oakland

HILL, LOWELL STANLEY, designer, business owner; b. Feb. 5, 1934, Fort Sheridan, Ill.; s. Jack and Velma Opal (Borton) H.; m. Barbara Matilde Suarez, Nov. 9, 1957; children: Lowell, b. 1958, Velma, b. 1959, Barbara, b. 1961, Sandra, b. 1962, Stanley, b. 1964; edn: Univ. of Mo. 1953-56; Chaffey Coll. 1959; AA, Mt. San Antonio Coll. 1962, tchrs. credential 1967. Career: illustrator US Army, Ft. Leonard Wood, No. 1953-56; mgr. Stout Sign Co., Long Beach 1957-58; lead man Circuit Bd. Div. Gen. Dynamics, Pomona 1959-63; tech. advr./ store mgr. E.W. Dorn Co., Gardena 1963-70; tchr. los Angeles Trade Tech. Coll., L.A. 1966-68; owner/ designer/ cons. Lowell S. Hill Enterprises, Ontario 1970--; guest spkr.: Cal Poly Univ., Pomona; Mt. San Antonio Coll., Walnut; Foundation Sch., Montebello; guest technical trainee Zurich Bolting Mfg. Co., Switz. 1975; honors: Hon. Chief, Nez Perce Nation 1970; mem: Screen Printing Internat.; Nat. Small Bus. Assn.; Calif. Assn. Independent Bus.; Trade Adv. Com., L.A. Trade Tech. Coll.; Am. Indian Week (v.p 1968-); Boy Scouts of Am. (ldr. 1972-75); research: European methods as applied to design, mfg. of screen printing rel. prods.; original designs of metal frames; imported the first Harlacher screen stretcher from Switz. into USA, 1980; mil: sgt. E-5 AUS 1953-56, mem. Champion Pistol Team 1955; Republican; Catholic; rec: target shooting, hunting, archery. Res: 775 W 24th St Upland 91786 Ofc: Lowell S. Hill Enterprises, 5416 Mission Blvd Ontario 91761

HILL, MARION, refrigeration engineer, community activist; b. May 20, 1914, Longview, Tex.; s. George and Georgia (Richardson) H.; m. Kathylen, Aug. 1965; children: Crystal, Karen, Roger, Wendell, Marion Delores; edn: YMCA Trade Sch. NYC 1938; mech. eng. refrig., NY Tech. Inst. 1948; Reg. Refrigeration Engr. Career: serv. engr. Carrier Air Contitioner, Bronx, NY 1954; engr. Hotel Gov. Clinton, 1955; serv. engr. Hughes Aircraft Co. Culver City 1965-77; owner Marion Hill Air Conditioner Contracting, 1978-80; community activist, Public Opinion Polls, Calif. So. Area Youth Advisor, 1979-; Membership Head Start Health Advisory, Inglewood; honors: recognition for service, Project Head Start, US Dept. of Commerce, NAACP (nat., regl., L.A. awards), 25 Year Cert. RSES Engineer Soc., Bur. of Census City of LA, Councilman Robert Farrell. Mem: Youth Work Organizer, NAACP, Nat. Conf. Ore. & St. Louis, Mo.; author: To Help You Become Successful; coauthor: White Man What Do You Know About The Negro (1943); extremely active in early civil rights movement (worked through Pres. Roosevelt in 1942 to open employment to skilled blacks in Kaiser Shipyard, Portland, Ore.); mil: US Army Corps of Engrs.; Democrat (fmr. Demo Central Com.); Prot.; rec: hunting, fishing. Res: 2129 W. 74th St Los Angeles 90047

HILL, R. TOM, ecosystem management consultant; b. Aug. 25, 1940, Bloomington, Ind.; s. Lark and Annabelle Lee (Sexton) H.; edn: BA, Taylor Univ. 1962; M.Div. Louisville Presbyterian Theol. Sem. 1965; MA, Rosemead Grad. Sch. of Psychology 1973; PhD, cum laude, Calif. Grad. Sch. of Theol. 1978; Calif. lic. Marriage, Family, Child Therapist 1974. Career: assoc. minister Kenwood Park United Presbyterian Ch., Cedar Rapids, Iowa 1965-66; Navy chaplain (active duty), 1966-69; minister, First United Presbyn. Ch., Delphos, Oh. 1969-71; adj. faculty Calif. Grad. Sch. of Theol., 1976-78; pvt. practice therapist (spec. in stress reduction of relationship problems) 1974--; Naval Reserve chaplain with Navy, Marines, and Coast Guard 1963--; temp. assignments incl. Naval Tng. Ctr., San Diego 1983, Navy Family Support Pgm. & Family Advocacy Pgm., Wash. DC 1983, staff instr. Navy Chaplains Sch., Newport, RI 1982, Naval Air Sta. Miramar 1981; mem. US Naval Reserve, Calif. Assn. of Marriage and Family Therapists, Reserve Officers Assn., Covina CofC; publs: poems: Chaplain (1977), Soar With The Eagle (1983), contbr. ch., mil. publs.; mil: chaplain, lt.cmdr. USNR 1963-, (active 1966-69) Navy Commendn. medal 1983; rec: amateur prospecting, jogging. Res: 16775 Brookport St Covina 91722 Ofc: R.Tom Hill, PhD, 626 S. Second Ave, Ste C, Covina 91723

HILLERTS, ROXIE LEE BERRY, educator; b. June 7, 1938, Warren, Ohio; d. Harvey Leroy and Winifred Esther (Biery) Berry; m. Rodney Hillerts, Dec. 29, 1971; edn: BA, Northwestern Univ. 1960; MA, CSU Los Angeles 1965; MA, Marriage Family Child Counseling, Azusa-Pacific 1980. Career: tchr. counselor Los Angeles City Schs. 1960-77; edn. splst. Youth Job Tng. Pgm., Glendale Schs. 1977-81; devel. exemplary federally funded pgms. for youths 16-21; edn. splst. Regl. Occupational Pgm. (computer aided drafting & design pgm. in conjunction w/ Jet Propulsion Lab, Pasadena), County ROP and Glendale Schs. 1981--; tch. Bi-lingual Parent Edn. Wrkshps., Effective Parenting Sems., Glendale Unified Sch. Dist. 1982-83; mem: Phi Delta Kappa, USC; Phi Lambda Theta, CSU Los Angeles; Calif. Assn. Regl. Occupational Pgms./ Ctrs.; Assn. Calif. Sch. Adminstrs.; Calif. Assn. Marriage Family Therapists; Democrat; rec: cooking, physical activities. Res: 4845 Commonwealth Ave La Canada 91011 Ofc: 223 N Jackson St Glendale 91206

HILMO, WALTER JACK, manufacturing-construction co. executive; b. Mar. 9, 1941, Pocatello, Id.; s. Walter Jay and Katie June (Christiansen) Tranmer; m. Nancy Ann Woolf, June 11, 1966; children: David, b. 1968; Heather, b. 1971; Michael, b. 1972; Robert, b. 1974; Bryce,b . 1977; Justin, b. 1980; Chad, b. 1984; edn: BA, Brigham Young Univ. 1966; MBA, Pepperdine Univ. 1982; Comm. Coll. Instr. Credential, Calif. 1983. Career: (past) cost acct. Profo Tools, Vernon; cost acct. Weiser Locks, So. gate; asst. controller Orchid Paper, La Palma; corp. cost analyst Amtek, Carlsbad; controller Fuller Co., Compton; controller Rood Systems, Inc., Fontana; currently, asst. gen. mgr. Western Engineering Sys., Chino; instr. acctg. Orange Coast Coll.; cons. mgmt. &

acctg. San Clemente Gen. Hosp.; mem: Nat. Assn. Accts.; Am. Inst. Corp. Controllers; Orange Co. Council of Boy Scouts of Am. (El Capitan Dist. commnr.); Republican; LDS; rec: camping. Res: 10632 Melric Ave Garden Grove 92643 Ofc: Western Engineering Systems, 13950 Yorba Ave Chino 91710

HILTON, LOIS ESTELLE, business consultant; b. Jan. 23, 1933, Woodville, Miss.; d. John Willard and Johnnie May (Mut) Carter; m. Owen Hilton, June 13, 1959, div.; children: Brenda, b. 1960, Ray, b. 1961, Karen, b. 1967; edn: BA, phil., CSU Los Angeles 1955; grad. work CSULA 1955-57, CSULB 1964-65; int. design, LaSalle Univ. 1958; lic. real estate, Tex., Calif. Career: buyer, D.H. Holmes, 1955-59; regional mgr. (Houston)/nat. sales trainer Coles Cross-Ref. Inc. 1959-63; prin. Wholesale Automobile Brokerage firm 1963-70; prin. Rhama Distbrs. Internat. (skin care prods.), and comml. real estate mgr. Seaback Investment Corp., Houston 1970-74; dir. Schaeffer's Pvt. Sch., Arlington, Tx. 1975-79; counselor Dynamic Personnel, Arlington ;1980-81; nat. sales tnr. V.R. Bus. Brokers, Dallas 1981-2; bus. cons. 1983--, cons. James E. Day & Assocs. S.A. (Mex.), Magna Marine Svcs. Inc. (St. Thomas); gen. mgr. Margaritas, Int. Imports, Houston 1983--. Mem. Nat. Assn. Female Execs. Inc., Internat. Platform Soc., Royal Geo. Soc., Eng., Eastern Star; Republican; rec: piano, swim. Res: 1253 N. Reeder Ave Covina 91724 Ofc: 1101 Post Oak Rd, 9632, Houston, Tx 77056

HILTON, RICHARD A., private investigator; b. Feb. 10, 1948, San Bernardino; s. David Roy and Ruth (Bartels) H.; m. Kathleen Susan Lemaster, Aug. 22, 1970; children: Gregory David, b. 1973; Jason Richard, b. 1978; edn: BA, UC Santa Barbara 1970. Career: claims rep. Calif. State Automobile Assn. 1970-73; claims rep. Hartford Ins. Co. 1973-78; field adjuster Chambers & Barber Adjusters 1977-78; mgr. Western Claims Adjusters 1978-79; owner, Hilton Claims Svc. & Rick Hilton, Pvt. Investigator 1979--; mem: Central Coast Claims Assn. (pres. 1982), CAIIA, NFIB; Toastmasters; YMCA Indian Guides chief 1979-82; AYSO soccer coach 4 years; rec: golf, skiing, boating. Ofc: 405 Alberto Way, Ste E, Los Gatos 95030

HILTON, WILLIAM BARRON, world-wide hotel chain president; b. Oct. 23, 1927, Dallas, TX; s., Conrad Nicholson and Mary Barron (Saxon) Hilton; m. Marilyn June Hawley, Chicago, June 20, 1947; children: William Barron, Jr., b. 1948; Hawley Anne, b. 1949; Stephen Michael, b. 1950; David Alan, b. 1952; Sharon Constance, b. 1953; Richard Howard, b. 1955; Daniel Kevin, b. 1962; Ronald Jeffrey, b.1963. Career: founder-gen. partner, Vita-Pakt Citrus Prods. Co., 1948--; dir., Hilton Hotels Corp., 1954--, v.p. 1954-66, pres.-chief exec. ofcr. 1966--; Pres., San Diego Chargers Ltd., 1961-66; pres. Amer. Football League, 1965; dir. Mfgrs. Hanover Trust Co., 1970; dir., Conrad N. Hilton Found.; trustee, City of Hope; trustee, advis. bd., Dir. Sports, Inc.; dir. Realty Com. on Taxation; sponsor. Mil.: Photographers Mate, USN, hon. disch. 1946. Awards: Hotel Man of Year, Penn State, 1969. Mem.: L.A. World Affairs Council; Chevalier of Confrerie de la Chaine des Rotisseurs; Bel-Air Country Club, 1951--; L.A. Country Club, 1979; Desert Horizons Country Club, 1980; Bel-Air Bay Club, 1968--; Magistral Knights Sovereign Mil. Order of Malta. Rec.: hunting, fishing, photography. Res.: 1060 Brooklawn Dr., Holmby Hills 90024; Office: 9990 Santa Monica Blvd., Beverly Hills 90212.

HIMELSEIN, LEONARD, manufacturing/import-export co. executive; b. Oct. 21, 1945, Johannesburg, S.Africa; s. Abe and Sarah (Chaitowitz) H.; m. Sheila Joseph, Jan. 10, 1971; children: Felicia, b. 1973, Wayne, b. 1974; edn: Damelin Coll. 1964. Career: trainee mgr. O.K. Bazaars, Johannesburg 1965, dept. mgr./buyer Ackermans, 1968, dir. Taj Mahal Mfg. Co. (diamond dealers and jewellery mfrs.), Johannesburg 1969-74; mng. dir. 1975-80, bd. chmn. 1981--; mng. dir. Himelsein Prop. Co., Johannesburg 1977--; bd. chmn. Czar Jewellers, Boputhatswana, S.A. 1981--; pres. National Pacific Corp. dba Himelsein Inc., Los Angeles 1981--; dir. Internat. Wines & Spirits, Ariz. 1984--; honors: feature subject, Personalities In The Diamond Trade, The Diamond News and S.A. Jeweller (1971); mem. Diamond Club of S.A. 1973- (chmn. Dept. Manpower & Util. 1980), Jewelry Mfrs. Assn. (exec. com. 1973-81); v.p. Pacific Jewish Center; bd. Emmanuel Streisand Sch. Res: 12841 Woodbridge St, No. 6, Studio City 91604 Ofc: Himelsein Inc 606 S. Hill St, Ste 603, Los Angeles 90014

HINDIN, MAURICE J., judge; b. Oct. 10, 1910, Los Angeles, CA; s. Theodore J. and Ida Hindin; BS, USC, 1933; LLB, 1935; LLD; m. Dorothy Sweet, Salt Lake City, Aug. 11, 1938; children: Arthur T., b. 1943; Carol, b. 1950. Career: admitted to practice law, Calif., 1935; admitted to practice before U.S. Supreme Ct., 1942; formerly sr. partner, Hindin & Hindin law firm, Beverly Hills. Mem.: Amer. and L.A. Co. Bar Assns.; assoc., ARRL, Amer. Trial Lawyers Assn.; Friars Club. Rec.: owner-operator amateur radio sta., W6EUV. Office: Court and Chambers, Los Angeles County Courthouse, Los Angeles.

HINCKLEY, STEWART CRAIG, real estate and mortgage broker; b. Feb. 15, 1934, Redlands; s. L. Stewart and Bertha Green (Craig) H.; m. Jane Kathleen Hanson, Feb. 13, 1981; children: Anne Marie, b. 1959; Laura, b. 1961; Thomas Craig, b. 1965; edn: BA, Claremont Mens Coll. 1958; Calif. lic. R.E. broker. Career: sales The Glidden Co., San Francisco 1958-59; lending ofcr. Bank of Am., Costa Mesa 1959-62; admin. asst. Howard B. Lawson Co., Orange 1962-63; partner/ gen. mgr. Hinckley Orange Grove Co., Redlands 1963--; R.E. broker S.C. Hinckley R.E. Investments, 1967--; pres. Investment Property Specialists, Inc., 1978-82; currently, pres. H & A Financial, Atascadero; cons. Flotran, Inc. 1978-79; dir. I.P.S. Investments 1978-80; mem: Farm Bureau; Calif. Farmer; Atascadero Bd. Realtors; Free to be Sober Ministries; Proj. New Hope (drug & alcohol rehab. & supports pgms.); mil: QMSN, USNR 1954-56; Republican; Protestant; rec: distance running, skiing. Res: 8400 San

Gregorio Rd Atascadero 93422 Ofc: H & A Financial, 7350 El Camino Real, Ste 201, Atascadero 93422

HINDIYEH, OMAR M., engineering construction co. president; b. Apr. 29, 1938, Jerusalem, nat. 1954; s. Mohammad Musa and Zenab Wafa (Dajani) H.; grandfather, Shiek Musa Hindiyeh; m. Darlene Hall (educator), Jan. 31, 1953; children: Omar, b. 1955; Sami R., b. 1957; Diane D., b. 1960; edn: BS, Civil Eng. 1951; postgrad. UC Berkley 1955, CSU San Jose 1975; Calif. lic: Gen. Engring. Contractor, Gen. Bldg. Contr., Solar Contr.; Profl. Engr., Real Estate Salesman; US Soccer Fedn. Referee 1970-. Career: County engr. Napa County 1955-56; US Federal engr. Mare Is. Shipyard, Pub. Works, Vallejo 1956-57; Wheelus Air Base, Tripoli, Libya 1957-60; field engr. Port of Oakland 1960-63; civil engr. transp. City of San Jose 1968/80; chmn. bd./ pres. OSO Developers, Inc. (eng. constrn. contractor), San Jose 1979--; chmn. bd. For You Inc. (health spa), San Jose 1979-81; pres. CMI Gp. (cons., mgmt.), San Jose 1980-81; Adult Edn. tchr., Napa Valley Even. Sch. 1955-57; awards: recognition membership campaign, Inst. of Transp. 1977, Mercury News Safety Poster contest 1978; mem: South Bay Transp. Assn. (pres. 1980); Inst. of Transp. Engrs.; Am. Inst. of Concrete; Lions Club; Tennis Club; PAL Football; San Martin Homeowners Assn.; US Scoutmaster, overseas 1963-68; publs: Traffic Accident Prevention (gp. ldr.); San Jose- Palo Alto Bs. Demo. Proj. Plan; Tarffic Engring. User Selected Info. Retrieval Sys.; mil: engr. US Army, Ft. Ord. 1952-54; rec: soccer, tennis, travel. Res: 265 Hindiyeh Ln San Martin 95046 Ofc: OSO Developers, Inc., 320 San Jose Ave San Jose 95151

HINES, RODNEY LEE, artist; b. Feb. 15, 1954, Ashland, Ohio; s. Earl Lealand and Donna Jean (Houston) H.; edn: The Columbus Coll. of Art & Design 1972-73; field study, Nature & Reality, in Mohican Country, Loudonville, Ohio 1974-78; Master Designer craftspsn. in glass. Career: prop. Rodney's Gift Shoppe (sales & commns.), Ashland, Ohio 1968-72; prop. Hines Stained Glass, Ashland, Loudonville & Mansfield, Ohio 1973-81; prop. Hines, San Francisco (creating line of tranquility sculpture & mystical symbols in glass) 1981--; instr. The Mansfield Art Ctr., Mansfield, Ohio 1975-81; lectr. Philosophical Aspects of Stained Glass; exhibitor & wholesaler to art instns. & fine galleries; mem: Ohio Designer Craftsmen; The Medocino Art Ctr.; The San Francisco Art Inst.; works: devised Glass Beads Between Glass technique; Reg. copyrights on line of Tranquility Sculpture; sculptor of 3-dimensional glass castles. Address: HINES, 150 Gardenside San Francisco 94131

HINKLE, JOHN HARRY, JR., lawyer; b. Dec. 5, 1946, Ft. Sheridan, Ill.; s. John Harry and Sarah Mebus (Wright) Hinkle; edn: BA, CSU San Jose 1970, JD, Lincoln Univ. 1976. Career: police ofcr. city of San Jose 1969-74; legal aide, staff atty. law firm Lanviere & Dickerson, San Jose 1974-77; pres. Miller & Hinkle, APC (gen. practice law firm empl. 8 attys.), San Jose 1977--; partner Homeland Props. (R E brokerage, prop met.) 1978--; partner Miller & Hinkle investment, tax gp., 1980--; bd.dirs. Dermatech, Inc.; assoc. prof. Lincoln Univ., San Francisco 1978-; mediator, arbitrator Superior Ct., Sta.Clara Co.; mem. bd. Vietnamese Law Clinic, San Jose. Recipient Abe Ziner Meml. Award, 1970-77. mem: Am. Bar Assn., Sta.Clara Co. Bar Assn. (arbitrator fin., client rels. coms.), Sta.Clara Co. Barristers' Club, Calif. Trial Lawyers Assn., Volunteers in Parole 1977-, Sigma Nu frat.; clubs: San Jose Racquet, Dwntwn Athletic. Republican. Protestant. rec: tennis, guitar, banjo, juggling. Res: 87 Rankin Ave San Jose 95110 Ofc: Miller & Hinkle, APC 635 N. First St San Jose 95112

HINKLE, THOMAS LYNN, lawyer; b. May 30, 1939, Fresno; s. Robert Kenneth and Agnes Gertrude (Wilder) H.; m. Genevieve Dutke, June 27, 1970; children: Mark, b. 1971; Karen, b. 1973; edn: BA, Univ. of San Francisco 1961; JD, UC Hastings Coll. of Law 1971; admitted to practice, State Bar of Calif. 1972. Career: deputy dist. atty. County of Ventura, San Buenaventura 1971-74; assoc. atty. Heily, Blase & Ellison, Oxnard 1974-77, partner (Ventura) 1977--; lectr. legal subjects to law students, legal sectys., civic orgns., & lawyers gps. 1981, 82; Judge Pro Tempore, Ventura Co. Municipal Ct. 1979; awards: Hastings Alumni Assn. Awd., Moot Ct. Performance 1970; Moot Ct. Bd., Hastings Coll. of Law. 1970-71; Outstanding Chpt. pres., Calif. Trial Lawyers Assn. 1982; mem: Calif. & Ventura Co. Trial Lawyers Assns.; Ventura Co. Bar Assn.; mil: capt. US Army 1962-68, Bronze Star, Vietnamese Medal of Hon., Army Commdn., Vietnamese Campaign, Vietnam Svc., Nat. Defense; Republican; Catholic; rec: youth sports. Res: 1125 Horizon Dr Ventura 93003 Ofc: Heily, Blase & Ellison, 5550 Telegraph Rd Ventura 93003

HINMAN, HAZEL GIBB, educational psychologist; b. July 5, 1910, Jennings, Ks.; d. Clarence Eugene and Mary Josephine (Lippincott) Gibb; m. L.M. Hinman, Sept. 2, 1931; children: Michael b. 1937, John b. 1940, Rebecca b. 1941, Robert b. 1943; edn: Univ. of Ks. 1930-31; BA in Eng.lit., Univ. of Redlands, 1956, MA, with distinction, 1958; Claremont Grad. Sch. 1959-65; Calif. credentials: (life) School Psychologist, Elem., Jr. High Sch., H.S., Jr. Coll. Tchr.; MFCC, Marriage Family Child Counselor. Career: elem. tchr., Mt. Baldy, Ca. 1954-58, Riverside Unified Schs. 1958-9; tchr. Claremont Unified Schs. 1959-62, school psychometrist 1962-65, sch. psychologist 1965-76; Pederson Psychol. Corp., Inc. 1980-81; self empl. Ednl. Psychologist, MFCC, 1981--; honors: Pi Lambda Theta, Alpha Iota; mem: Calif. Tchrs. Assn. (life), Nat. Tchrs. Assn., Calif. Assn. of School Psychologists, Calif. Assn. of Psychologists & Psychometrists, Claremont Tchrs. Assn., PTA; mem: Claremont Sym. (1st violinist), Univ. of Ks. Sym.; area rep. Provo (Utah) Canyon Sch.; publs: Gifted Children's Pgm., Bibliotherapy bklet., Claremont Sch. Sys.; Republican; Methodist; rec: crafts, hiking, swim. Res: 56778 Free Gold Dr Yucca Valley 92284

HINO, JAMES HIROSHI, engineering consulting co. president; b. May 27, 1954, Honolulu, HI; s. Shigeru and Betsy Masuye (Hirota) H.; m. Paula Sasaki, Aug. 29, 1976; 1 dau: Jennifer, b. 1981; edn: BS, magna cum laude, USC 1976; MS, 1977. Career: engr. Jet Propulsion Lab., Pasadena 1974-77; research engr. Honeywell (tng. & control sys. ctr.), W. Covina 1977-79; eng. cons. Telos Computing, Santa Monica 1979-81; pres. Magnus Systems, Inc., Newport Beach 1981--; honors: Phi Kappa Phi 1976; Tau Beta Pi 1975; Eta Kappa Nu 1975; mem: Assn. for Computing Machinery; MENSA; rec: computer architecture, software design. Address: Magnus Systems, Inc., 1521 Dorothy Ln Newport Beach 92660

HINSON, JAMES RANDOLPH, safety and health consultant; b. July 21, 1944, Charlotte, NC; s. Fred Homer and Margie (Smith) H.; m. Janet Marie Bardwell, May 29, 1964; children: James Everett, b. 1970; Jason Raymond, b. 1974; Jennifer Lynn, b. 1980; edn: AS, Canada Comm. Coll. 1976; BS pgm., human rels., USF (1985); Instr. Indsl. Safety, US Dept. Labor, OSHA 1972, 1973; Police Ofcr. Stds. & Tng., Calif. 1966; Comm. Coll. Instr. cert., US Santa Cruz 1975; cert. investigation techniques, FBI 1964; Reg. Profl. Engr., Calif. 1977; Cert. Hazard Control Mgr. (Master), 1976. Career: field supt. Rudolph & Sletten, Mt. View 1968-70; asst. to v.p. constrn. MacKay Homes Div. of Kaiser Aetna, Menlo Park 1970-72; CEO Safety & Health Consultants, Foster City 1972--; pvt. instr. hazard control 1972-; instr. Canada Comm. Coll. 1973-76; bd. dirs. No. Calif. Constrn. Inst.; consulting: Employer Agt. OSHA Hearings, Expert Witness civil & criminal state and fed. courts; recipient Awd. of Merit in Safety Edn., Nat. Safety Council, Redwood City 1975; mem: Am. Soc. of Safety Engrs. (Constrn. Div., S.F. Bay Area treas. 1984); Rotary (bd. Foster City 1984); Nat. Soc. Profl. Engrs.; Nat. Safety Mgmt. Soc.; Internat. Assn. Hazard Control Mgrs.; mil: seaman USN; Republican; Methodist; rec: health & safety issues, pub. speaking. Res: 745 Coronado Ln Foster City 94404 Ofc: Safety & Health Consultants, POB 4866, Foster City 94404

HINSVARK, KENNETH DUANE, lawyer; b. May 16, 1926, Clear Lake, S.Dak.; s. Jacob Adolph and Clara Idiana (Moen) H.; m. Madelyn Maloney, Mar. 26, 1966; children: Barrett, b. 1955; Cheryl, b. 1956; BA, UC Berkeley 1949, LLB, UC Boalt Hall 1951, JD, 1974. Career: deputy dist. atty., San Bernardino Co. 1951 52; atty. Safeway Stores, Oakland & Los Angeles 1953 60; real estate mgr. Safeway Stores, Omaha, Nebr. 1960-62; atty., sole practitioner, Orange Co. 1962-74; Palm Springs 1975--; atty./ gen. partner American West Investment Co.; honors: Phi Beta Kappa, UC Berkeley 1949; mem: Lions Club, Oakland Cosmopolitan (pres. 1956); works: one of first to spec. in shopping center law, developed 35 shopping ctr. in Calif., Nevada, Ariz., N.M., Utah & Wash.; mil: 2nd lt. US Army 1944-46, Nat. Guard 1948-49, Philippine Lib.; Democrat; Protestant; rec: tennis, ski, swim. Res: 770 W Sunny Dunes St Palm Springs 92262 Ofc: American West Investment Co., 559 S Palm Canyon, Ste B212, Palm Springs 92262

HINTZ, JOHN LESLIE STEVEN, demolition contractor; b. June 8, 1928, Chgo.; s. John Alfred and Anna Hintz; m. Betty Herrmann, Nov. 26, 1960; children: Brian John, b. 1961; Michael Kevin, b. 1963; Kathleen Diane, b. 1964; edn: AA, Los Angeles City Coll. 1953. Career: advtg. Proctor & Gamble, Los Angeles 1952; Wholesales Roofing & Material, L.A. 1953-59; Valley Credit & Collectin, Alhambra 1959-61; pres. Hintz Wrecking Co., Inc., L.A. & Burbank 1961--; recipient Cert. of Awd. for svc. to children, Oak Hill Sch. 1979; mem: Nat. Demolition Assn.; L.A. Better Bus. Bureau; Elks Club; Burbank CofC; Soc. to Preserve & Encourage Radio Drama, Variety & Comedy; YMCA Indian Guides song ldr. 1969-72; mil: cpl. USMC 1946-48, sharp shooter; Republican; Catholic; rec: collecting radio pgms for museum (2nd largest collection in world). Res: 615 E. Walnut Ave Burbank 91501

HINZ, WILLIAM ALFRED, lawyer; b. May 4, 1949, St. Charles, Ill.; s. Alfred William and Carol Ida (Johnson) H.; m. Debra, Dec. 29, 1977; 1 son: Matthew, b. 1982; edn: BA, Adams State 1972; JD, Western State 1980. Career: solo law practice, Orange, Ca. 1982--; instr. Nat. Univ. 1981-; mem: Am., Calif. & Harbor Bar Assns.; publs: You and Small Claims Court, 4/83; Republican; Lutheran; rec: tennis, fishing. Res: 1010 Bonnie Ann Ct La Habra 90631 Ofc: Law Ofc. of William A. Hinz, 1110 E Chapman, Ste 200, Orange 92666

HIRSCH, FRANK CHRISTOPHER, financial planner; b. Dec. 19, 1948, San Bernardino; s. Bernard V. and June Ruth Hirsch; m. Lesley Ann Johnson, Dec. 19, 1970; children: Corey Ann, b. 1974; Timothy Mitchell, b. 1976; edn: AA, Antelope Valley Coll. 1972; BA, CSU Northridge 1975; MST, Northrop Univ. Sch. of Law 1983; accredited pension adminstr. 1983, Nat. Inst. of Pension Adminstrs. 1983. Career: asst. patrolman/ plnr. US Forest Svc. 1970-71; exec. dir. proj. Neal (Narcotics Edn. & Redab.) 1971-74; sr. plnr. Mayors Ofc. of Criminal Justice Plng., City of Los Angeles 1974-75; Frank C. Hirsch & Assoc., Environmental Plnrs. 1974-75; Frank. C. Hirsch, Fin. Plnrs. 1976--; pres. American Investment Advisors; v.p. Great Am. Securities; instr. grad. tax pgm. Northrop Univ. Sch. of Law; mem: Inst. CFPs; Nat. Assn. Life Underwriters; Western Pension; Am. Soc. of CLUs; Nat. Assn. of Pension Adminstrs.; mil: Vietnam 1968-69; Republican; Catholic; rec: flying. Ofc: HIS Corporation, POB 4020, Lancaster 93534

HIRSCHFELD, TOMAS B., chemist; b. Dec. 20, 1939, Montevideo, Uruguay, nat. 1975; s. Rudolf H. and Ruth (Nordon) H.; m. Judith Berggrunn, Nov. 3, 1963; children: Noemi, b. 1964; Dina, b. 1968; Susan, b. 1975; edn: BS in chem., Vasquez Acevedo Inst., Uruguay 1957; MS, chem., Nat. Univ., Uruguay 1961, PhD chem. eng. 1965, PhD chem. 1975. Career: asst. prof. Nat. Univ., Montevideo 1965-68; vis. scientist No. American Rockwell, Thousands

Oaks, Ca. 1966-67; staff scientist Block Engring., Cambridge, Mass. 1968-71, chief scientist 1971-79; sr. scientist Lawrence Livermore Nat. Lab., 1979--; indsl prof. Indiana Univ., Bloomington 1978-83; adj. prof. Univ. of Wash., Seattle 1983-, cons. 1979-. Honors: IR-100 awd. 1975, 79, 81, 83; Meggers awd. 1978; elected chmn. 1985 Internat. FT-IR Conf., 1985 Gordon Conf. Analytical Chem.; mem: Fellow Optical Soc. Am. (mem. editorial bd.); IEEE (senior); Am. Chem. Soc. (editorial bd.); Coblentz Soc. (gov. bd.); Soc. Applied Spectroscopy (editorial bd.); Soc. Photoptical instrum. Eng. (guest ed.); Am. Microbeam Soc.; Soc. Analytical Cytology; publs: 150 journal, book arts.; 110 patents; 200 profl. papers; Jewish. Res: 1262 Vancouver Way Livermore 94550 Ofc: Lawrence Livermore National Lab. 7000 East Ave Livermore 94550

HISE, MARK ALLEN, dentist; b. Jan. 17, 1950, Chgo.; s. Clyde and Rose T. (Partipilo) H.; edn: AA, Mt. San Antonio Coll. 1972; BA, highest honors, UC Riverside 1974; MS, Univ. of Utah 1978; DDS, UC Los Angeles 1983. Career: hd. guitar instr. Associated Music Co., West Covina 1967-70; sheet metal wkr. Western Htg. & Plumbing, San Francisco 1974-75; high sch. tchr. Northwest Acad., Houston, Tx. 1978-79; course chmn./instr. Medical Coll. Preparation Program, UCLA 1980--; assoc. dentist , Dr. Robt. Aubell, P.C., Crescent City 1983; dentist pvt. practice, Arcata 1983--; instr. Allied Health Scis., Coll. of the Redwoods, Eureka 1984-; lectr., seminar ldr. on Preparing for Med. Sch., major univs.; awards: Henry Carter Scholar, Calif. State Scholar, and Regents Scholar, Univ. Calif., 1973, 1974; Calif. State Fellow 1975; NIH Fellow 1975-79; Am. Soc. for Pharmacol. & Exp. Therapeutics grantee 1979; early grad. from UCLA Dental Sch. 1983; mem: Am., Calif. Dental Assns., Nat. Soc. for Med. Resrch., AAAS, Acad. of Gen. Dentistry; publs: arts. in sci. journals, mag. & newspaper arts., textbook in prog. (The Med. Coll. Admission Test); spkr. on orig. research nat. sci. meetings; Ind.; Catholic; rec: guitar, writing. Res: 4606 McKinnon Arcata 95521 Ofc: Mark A. Hise, MS, DDS, 1225 B Street Arcata 95521

HISER, EDWARD THOMAS, manufacturing co. executive/ educator; b. Nov. 16, 1945, E. St. Louis, Ill.; s. Eugene Earl and Hazel Ida (Hesse) H.; edn: BS, So. Ill. Univ. 1971; MS, 1974; Resource Splst. cred., Calif. 1980. Career: spl. edn. tchr. retarded and learning disabled, Fairview Hghts., Ill. 1972-77; spl. edn. resource splst. Los Angeles City Schs. 1977-83; exec. v.p. Everlite Fuel Corp., Century City 1983--; dir. Everlite Fuel Corp. 1983-; dir. Lawson Chem. Prod. 1981-84; awards: 4 year State Scholarship, Chmn. of Spl. Edn. Dept., Los Angeles 1968; mem: Am. Fedn. of Tchrs.; Calif. Tchrs. Assn.; Calif. Assn. of Resource Specs.; VFW; Alpha Delta Chi svc. frat. (pres.); Delta Psi Omega; PTA; Sierra Club; works: fed. proj., Creating Lesson Plans for Minimal Brain Dysfunction Students, 1976; mil: sgt. US Army 1966-68, Soldier of Unit Awd., 97th Artillery Gp., Vietnam; Democrat; Metropolitan Comm. Ch.; rec: vol. work in prisons with illiterates, hiking, travel. Res: POB 97 Inverness 94937 Ofc: Everlite Fuel Corp., 2049 Century Park E, Ste 5243, Century City 90067

HITCHCOCK, VERNON THOMAS, lawyer; b. Feb. 21, 1919, Selma, Ind.; s. Lucian Elmer and Lola Alice (King) H.; m. Betty K. Orr, May 24, 1949; children: Brenda, b. 1950; Linda, b. 1953; Nancy, b. 1955; Debra, b. 1957; Randolph, b. 1960; edn: BS, agric., Purdue Univ. 1940; JD, Stanford Univ. 1953; admitted to practice, Calif. State Bar. Career: naval aviator, USNR, US & Pacific 1941-45; airline pilot Southwest Airways, S.F. 1946; airline pilot TWA, Kansas City, Mo. & San Francisco, Calif. 1947-51; atty. at law., pvt. practice, Healdsburg 1954-55; deputy atty. gen., State of Calif., Sacto. 1956; deputy county counsel, Sonoma Co., Santa Rosa 1957-65; exec. dir. Libyan Aviation Co., Tripoli, Libya 1966-67; legal counsel Sonoma Co. Schs., Santa Rosa 1967-82; pvt. practice, law 1982--; partner/ farm mgr. GHJ Farms 1982--; originator of Freedom Under Law pgm. for tchg. jr. and sr. high sch. students about Am. law; mem: Sonoma Co. Bar Assn.; Reserve Ofcrs. Assn., US; Commonwealth Club, Calif.; Naval Order of US; US Naval Inst.; Quiet Birdmen; Ind. Order of Odd Fellows; Am. Security Council; Alpha Zeta, Purdue chpt.; Indiana 4-H Club; mil: commndr. USNR 1941-69; Republican; Episcopal; rec: trumpet (mem. Las Gauinas Valley Sanitary Non- Marching Band, Terra Linda). Address: 3411 Sidney Square Santa Rosa 95405

HITTLEMAN, MILES LESLIE, wholesale hardware co. owner; b. Apr. 24, 1929; s. Cyrus Harold and Matilda (Blum) H.; m. Geraldine, Oct. 18, 1968; children: Nina, b. 1952; Robin, b. 1955; Scott, b. 1970. Career: owner Las Vegas Conv. & Trade Show Co., Las Angeles 1962-65; dist. saes mgr. Ideal Brushes, Inc., No. Hollywood 1965-71; nat. sales mgr. Nat. Aerosols, Inc., L.A. 1971-78; nat. sales mgr. Ideal Brushes, No. Hollywood 1978-79; owner Wholesales Hardward Co.; pres./ Associated Surplus Dealers Assn. 1961; recipient sev. Kiwanis awds., Pacoima 1975-77; mem: Assoc. Surplus Dealters Assn.; City of Hope; Boy Scouts of Am., Sea Scouts; works: trade shows in Las Vegas, Nevada 1962; mil: hospitalman l/c USN 1946-51, GCM, WWII, So. Pac. Asiatic; Republican; Hebrew; rec: fishing, sports. Address: Miles Hittleman & Assoc., 8545 Kester Ave Panorama City 91402

HIX, THOMAS CHARLES, real estate brokerage president; b. Aug. 10, 1953, Los Angeles; s. Donald Kieth and Helen Julia (Blagdon) H.; edn: BA, CSU Northridge 1976; Calif. lic. R.E. broker 1976; lic. broker dealer, mem. NASD. Career: salesman Pantano Realty, Belmont 1975-77; founder/pres. Transbay Corp. (real estate syndication & brokerage co.) 1977--; founder pres. Trans-Corp. Securities 1983--; rec: sailing, skiing. Res: 2706 Coronet Blvd Belmont 94002 Ofc: Transbay Corp., 707 Bradford St Redwood City 94063

HIXON, EVA MARA, real estate broker; b. Sept. 21, 1932, Barger, Tex.; d. Martin B. and Mabel Catherine (Smith) Mara; m. Virgil Carl Hixon, Aug. 7,

1948; children: Gary b. 1949, Vickie Kay b. 1955; Calif. Real Estate Lic. 1974, Broker 1977. Career: fmr. dept. store sales clk. (5 yrs), dir. sales mgmt. Stanley Home Products (3 yrs), bus. ptnr. with husband 1963-74; real estate sales 1974-, broker/owner C & H Realty, Clovis 1977--; honors: Cow Palace color guard; mem: Farm Bur., Realty Board, Exchange Clubs, Calif. State Horsemens Assn. (v.p. Region 15), La Caballestra de Fresno Ladies Parade Gp. (v.p./capt.), PTA (pres.), CofC, Booster Club; Republican; Ch. of Jesus Christ of L.D.S.; rec: equestrian, swimming, bartering. Res: 1385 Sunnyside Clovis 93612 Ofc: C & H Realty 1924 Minnewawa Clovia 93612

HJERSMAN, ROY FREDERICK, business owner; b. July 29, 1918, Oakland; s. Carl Johan and Elvi Terese (Bomark) H.; m. Margaret DellaVedowa, Feb. 5, 1943; children: Peter, b. 1946; Margaret, b. 1948; Roy, b. 1953; Cynthia, b. 1958; edn: Oakland City Coll. 1936. Career: apprentice Office Equipment Co. 1937; apprentice United Ofc. Machine Co. 1938; apprentice Underwood Typewriter Co. 1938-42; instr. US Army 1943-44; owner Inland Typewriter Co. (teleprinters & carrier/ repeater), 1944--; cons. San Quentin Prison Vocational Pgm. 1951--; honors: chmn. emeritus San Quentin Trade Adv. Council 1975; Paul Harris Fellow, Rotary Internat. 1977; life mem. PTA 1947; mem: East Bay Ofc. Machine Dealers Assn.; Walnut Creek Rotary; Heather Farms Garden Club; Am. Soc. Dowsers; Civic Arts Assn.; Boy Scouts of Am. (asst. dist. commnr. 1967-71); publs: num. arts, Your Man Friday, trade publs. 1949-83; mil: cpl. US Army Signal Corps 1942-44, GCM; Republican; Presbyterian; rec: antique office machines, travel, photog. Res: 1468 Rancho View Dr Lafayette 94549 Ofc: Inland Typewriter Co., POB 2184, Walnut Creek 94595

HOAG, RICHARD WINSTON, manufacturing/distribution co. president; b. Feb. 7, 1936, Buffalo, NY; s. Leo Daniel and Grace Winston (Shephard) H.; m. Anita Whithouse, May 10, 1980; children: R. Scott, b. 1959; S. Michael, b. 1964; edn: BS, Canisius, 1958. Career: sales/ mktg., mfg. & foreign ops. exec.: from sales to v.p. sales Max Factor; v.p. sales/ mktg. Mattel Toy Co.; currently, pres./ COO Computers Internat.; bd. dirs: Vector Graphics, (Thousand Oaks), Interac, Inc. (Woodland Hills), Chantal Cosmetics (Westwood). Res: 6824 Las Olas Way Malibu 90265 Ofc: Computers International Inc., 3540 Wilshire Blvd Los Angeles 90010

HOAGLAND, GRANT TAYLOR, lawyer; b. June 21, 1949, Los Angeles; s. Dallas Abram and Marydene (Oldham) H.; edn: BA, cum laude, CSU Long Beach 1974; JD, Western State Univ. Coll. of Law 1978. Career: atty. law ofcs. Erwin Sobel 1979-80; Legal Clinic of Jacoby & Meyers, Cerritos 1980--; awards: Am. Jurisprudence Awd. for Remedies II, Western State Univ.; BSA Order of the Arrow, Eagle Scout; mem: Am. & L.A. Co. Bar Assns.; Am. & L.A. Trial Lawyers Assns.; Elks Club; commnr./chmn. South Gate Parks & Recreation Commn.; Latter Day Saints; rec: skiing, racquetball, musicianship. Res: 9231 Dearborn Ave South Gate 90280 Ofc: Legal Clinic of Jacoby & Meyers, 11444 South St Cerritos 90701

HOBBS, JANICE KAY, financial planner; b. May 17, 1956, Orange, Ca.; d. Robert Dean and Irene Rose (Gardner) Hobbs; edn: BS in B.A., summa cum laude, San Diego St. Univ. 1978; MBA, USC 1983; MSBA cand. USC 1985; Calif. lic: R.E. Broker 1981, Life and Disability Agt. 1984, Variable Annuities lic. 1984; CFP, Coll. Fin. Plnng. 1985; Gen. Securities Reg. Rep., NASD 1984. Career: mgr. Brickyard Restaurant, Orange 1978-79; real estate broker Hobbs-Alan Realtors, Orange 1979-84; owner Jan Hobbs Property Mgmt. Co., Orange 1982--; fin. planner Innovative Fin. Planning Services, Tustin 1984--; exec. adv. bd. California City Bank 1983--; R.E. cons. Century Am. Corp.; mem: Nat. and Calif. Assn. of Realtors, East Orange Co. Bd. Realtors (Budget & Fin. Com. 1982), Internat. Assn. of Fin. Planners, Inst. of CFPs, USC Profl. Business Womens Assn.; vol. So. Calif. Spl. Olympics; wks: feasibility study for Wiltern Theater Hist. Site, L.A. 1982; Republican; Presbyterian; rec: softball coach, racquetball. Res: 2615 E. Denise Ave Orange 92667 Ofc: Innovative Financial Plnng Services, 17542 E. 17th St, Ste 400, Tustin 92680

HOBBS, RICHARD LEIGHTON, physicist; b. Nov. 3, 1942, Boston, Mass.; s. Irving Leighton and Gergrude Otelia (Peterson) H.; edn: BA, physics, Northeastern Univ. 1966; grad. courses, astronomy, comp. sci., Boston Univ. 1966-70. Career: senior systems engr. Dynalectron Corp., Norco Div.; reentry physicist and weapon systems analyst: Titan and Minuteman Intercontinental Ballistic Missiles (ICBMs), SR-71 and U2 spy planes, Space Shuttle, B-1 Bomber, Air Launched Cruise Missiles (ALCMs), and MK92 Fire Control Sys and 76mm Gun Mounts for FFG-7 Class frigates, Vandenberg AFB, Edwards AFB, FLTAC, Corona and the Uwajalein Missile Range; honors: Engr. of the Quarter, Fall 1983, Dynalectron Norco Div.; mem. Am. Inst. of Physics 1961-66 (treas.); Planetary Soc.; Urantia Found.; num. sci. publs.; Ind.; Christian; rec: travel, archeol. Res: 4002 River Ave Newport Beach 92663 Ofc: Dynalectron Corp. 2727 Hamner Av Norco 91760

HODGES, A. CLIFTON, lawyer; b. Sept. 5, 1941, Glendale; s. Alvin Cooper and Betty Jane (Burnett) H.; l son, Clayton Thomas b. 1976; edn: Glendale Coll. 1959-61; BS in E.E., CSU Los Angeles 1963; JD, USC Law Sch. 1969; admitted Calif. State Bar 1970. Career: pvt. practice law, Law Offices A. Clifton Hodges, 1970--, splst. in plaintiff/personal injury law since 1976; judge pro tem San Bernardino Co.; Lawyer Referral Service spl. panel; arbitrator, S.B. Co.; mem: Am. Trial Lawyers Assn., San Bernardino Co. Bar Assn., State Bar Assn., Am.

Bar Assn., CTLA, LA County Bar Assn.; mem. Mockingbird Cyn Home-owners Assn., Am. Quarter Horse Assn., Pacific Quarter Horse Racing Assn.; speaker var. profl. meetings, law day seminars for sch. students; Nat. Unity Party (Organizing Com.; Empire campaign chmn. John Anderson for Pres. 1980) rec: Quarter Horse racing, power boating. Res: 15810 Lindina Dr Riverside 92504 Law Offices A. Clifton Hodges, 290 North D St, Ste. 724, San Bernardino 92401 and 4200 Campus Dr Newport Beach 92660

HODGES, PATRICIA MARIE, psychologist;b. Feb. 18, 1931, Gary, Ind.; d. Claude and Helen (Jelke) Kim; m. John Hodges, Sept. 6, 1969; children: Kay b. 1958, Karen b. 1960, Bill b. 1964; edn: PhD, Claremont Grad. Sch. 1970; lic. psychologist, Calif. Career: pvt. practice, pres. Claremont Psy Services Inc.; prof./ chair Dept. of Psy. CSU Los Angeles; faculty The Fielding Inst.; awarded sev. govt. resrch. grants in psychology; mem: APA, WPA, CSPA, SPSSI, SRCD; author: Language w/o Speed, numerous articles; Unitarian; rec: ski. Res: 1712 Finecroft, Claremont 91711 Ofc: Claremont Psy Services, 201 W 4th St Ste 204, Claremont 91711

HODGES, WALTER ALONZA, JR., personnel executive; b. Dec. 18, 1945, Upland; s. Walter Alonza Sr. and Mary Margaret (Truitt) H.; m. Paula Jones, Jan. 27, 1979; children: Denise, b. 1971; Joseph, b. 1968; edn: AS, Pierce Jr. Coll. 1966; BS, Phila. Coll. of Textiles & Sci. 1968. Career: safety & tng. mgr. Anchor Hocking Corp., Los Angeles, Jacksonville, Fla., Connellsville, Pa. 1969-74; personnel supvr. Hyland D. Mobex Corp., Fullerton 1976-79; v.p. personnel, Western Div. Automatic Data Processing, Inc., La Palma 1979--; mem: Am. Soc. for Personnel Adminstrs.; United Way, Orange Co.; Democrat; Christian; rec: antique automobiles; Res: 23451 Schooner Dr, POB 5093, Canyon Lake 92380 Ofc: Automatic Data Processing, 5355 Orangethorpe Ave La Palma 92380

HOFERT, JACK, lawyer; b. Apr. 6, 1930, Phila., Pa.; s. David and Beatrice (Schatz) H.; m. Marilyn, Sept. 4, 1960; chilren: Dina, b. 1963; Bruce, b. 1966; edn: BS, UCLA 1952; MBA, 1954; JD, 1957; admitted to practice, Calif. State Bar 1958; CPA, 1959; lic. R.E. broker 1965. Career: fin. v.p. Pacific Theatres Corp., Los Angeles 1962-69; self- empl. bus. cons. & acquisitions finder, L.A. 1969-74; mgr. tax dept. Peat, Marwick, Mitchell & Co., L.A. 1974-77; dir. of taxation Lewis Homes, Upland 1977-80; atty. & bus. cons. 1980--; owner/pres. Di-Bru, Inc., L.A. (bus. consulting co.) 1981--; dir. Cinerama, Inc. 1965-69; tchr. income tax courses, UCLA Ext. pgm. 1962-69; honors: Order of the Coif, staff UCLA Law Review; mem: State Bar of Calif.; Am. Inst. CPAs (past); Calif. Soc. CPAs (past); publs: approx. 12 arts. in tax & bus. mags.; mil: seaman apprentice USN 1948-49. Address: 2479 Roscomare Rd Los Angeles 90077

HOFFER, EDWARD ANDREW, business owner, community leader; b. Oct. 18, 1925, Muncie, Ind.; s. Vern Howard and Charline Leslie (Ingersoll) H., brother, Robert M. Hoffer, pres. Wisc. Gas Co.; m. Charlotte Schneppe, Aug. 17, 1946; 1 son: Edward E., b. 1949; edn: grad., Indiana Bus. Coll. 1948. Career: asst. purchasing agent. Durham Mfg. Co., Muncie, Ind. 1948-56; asst. buyer/ hd. of shop at home svc. Broadway Dept. Stores, Los Angeles 1956-62; buyer R.H. Thomas Co., Pasadena 1962-63; owner Hoffer's Carpet & Drapery Store, Camarillo 1963--; honors: Voted 1980 Man of the Yr.; num. orgns. awds.; mem: Camarillo Rotary Club; Camarillo CofC (v.p. 1964, dir. 1982-, pres. 1983-84); Am. Cancer Soc., Ventura chpt. (pres. 1970-71); Camarillo Comm. Bank (founder/ dir. 1979-); Ventura Co. BSA; Camarillo Trade Club; Camarillo Boys Club; Somis Water Protection Dist.; Magic Castle, L.A.; mil: yeoman 2/c USN 1942-46; Republican (campaign chmn. var. people 1963-82); Protestant- Lutheran; rec: stamp & coin collecting, swimming, magic. Res: 277 Geneive Cir Camarillo 93018 Ofc: Hoffer's Carpet & Drapery Store, 462 Dawson Dr Camarillo 93010

HOFFER, M. MARK, orthopedic surgeon; b. July 15, 1935, New York; s. Philip and Rose Hoffer; m. Margo, June 12, 1960; children: Michael b. 1962, David b. 1963, Rebecca b. 1971; edn: Union Coll. 1953-56; MD, Univ. of Chgo. 1960. Career: internship US Navy, 1960; submarine medicine USN 1961-64; orthopedic residency Oscharn Clinic, New Orleans 1964-68; orthopedic fellowship Rancho Los Amigos Hospital, Downey 1969, currently chief Childrens Orthopedics Service and Childrens Reconstrv. Service; prof./chief of orthopedics Univ. Calif. Med. Sch. Ofc: Rancho Los Amigos Hospital, Downey 90242

HOFFMAN, ARON HERSHEL, certified public accountant; b. Nov. 17, 1944, Berkeley; s. Ben F. and Sylvia Hoffman; m. Linda Trimbo, Dec. 28, 1970; children: Dawniele Beth, b. 1974; Stephanie Kay, b. 1978; edn: BS, Golden Gate Univ. 1969. Career: staff acct. Haskins & Sells, CPAs 1969-71; mgr. Hemming Morse & Co., CPAs 1972-74; pres. Hoffman & Madsen, Accty. Corp., San Mateo 1974--; deputy mayor & councilman, City of San Mateo 1984-85; prof. in acctg. Golden Gate Univ. 1974-75; lectr. Calif. CPA Found. 1974--; mem: Am. Inst. CPAs; Calif. Soc. CPAs; Calif. Peace Ofcrs. Assn.; works: staff tng., Calif. CPA Found.; Republican; rec: reading. Res: 503 Princeton Rd San Mateo 94402 Ofc: Hoffman & Madsen, 675 Mariners Island Blvd, Ste 106, San Mateo 94401

HOFFMAN, CHARLES DANIEL, corporate president; b. June 27, 1934, Fredericksburg, Pa.; s. Floyd Davis and Dorothy May (Hoy) H.; m. F. Michele Sciortino, July 10, 1982; 1 son: Lance Hoffman, b. 1962; edn: Penn. State Univ. 1954-55; Yale Univ. 1955-58. Career: mgr. Wrights Town House Restaurant, Richmond, Va. 1958-60; owner/ pres. Art Producers, Inc., Wash. DC 1960-64; editor Boat/ US Newsletter, Wash. DC 1964-65; Mid- Atlantic regl. dir. VISTA pgm., Wash. DC 1965-67; regl. tng. dir. OJT Pgm., Inst. of Scrap Iron & Steel,

Wash. DC 1967-69; nat. tng. dir. 1969-71; cons., Wash. DC 1971-73; founder/ pres./ CEO Self Directed Placement Corp. 1973--; rec: horse breeding, fox hunting. Res: 2930 Cowley Way San Diego 92117 Ofc: Self Directed Placement Corp., 3010 Cowley Way San Diego 92117

HOFFMAN, CHARLES L(ARRY), business consultant; b. Aug. 6, 1938, Flint, Mich.; s. Charles L., Sr. and Loretta E. (Russell) h.; m. Carol Ann Mentor, July 11, 1981; children: Michele, b. 1967; Jacquie (adptd.); Danny (adptd.); Graydon Whelan (step), b. 1973; edn: AA, Saddleback Coll., Irvine 1978. Career: nat. sales mgr./ v.p. mktg. Washington West Trade Corp., Los Angeles 1969-75; owner C. Larry Hoffman & Assoc. 1975-80; chmn. bd./ CEO Hoffman Business Consultants 1980--; partner Irvine Meadows Amphitheatre; former chmn. Irvine City Plng. Commn.; mem: Irvine CofC (past pres.); Cystic Fibrosis, Orange Co.; mil: E-4 US Army 1961-63; Republican; So. Coast Comm. Ch.; rec: gourmet cooking. Res: 21 Rainstar Irvine 92714 Ofc: Hoffman Business Consultants, Inc., 2300 Michelson Dr, Ste 300, Irvine 92715

HOFFMAN, HOWARD TORRENS, company president; b. Dec. 30, 1923, East St. Louis, Ill.; s. Edmund Howard and Beulah Esther (Hood) H.; brother, G.D. Hoffman; m. Ruth Ann Koch, June 19, 1947; children: Howard Torrens, b. 1951, Jean Gisele, b. 1955, Glenn Kevin, b. 1956; edn: BSEE, Iowa State Univ. 1950; MSEE, Thomas Univ. 1972, PhD, mgmt. sci., 1977; Reg. Profl. Engr. 1955. Career: section head Joy Mfg. Co., St. Louis 1950-55; electronics sys. engr. McDonnell Aircraft Corp., St. Louis 1955-57; exec. engr. ITT Labs (Farnsworth Electronics), Ft. Wayne, Ind. 1957-58; mgr. Missile Sys., Litton Industries, College Park, Md. 1958-60; div. mgr. Teledyne-Ryan, San Diego, Ca. 1960-66; pres./chief exec. ofcr. Hoffman Assocs., San Diego 1966--; bd. chmn./exec. dir. H & R Assocs., S.D. 1968--; v.p., engr. Digital Devel. Corp., 1976-77; independent mgmt. consultant; honors: Merit Cert. for contbns. to electronics and aerospace industries, 1970; United Crusade Comm. Svc. Award 1972; Comm. Leader Awd. 1975; listed Who's Who in Am., Who's Who in Aviation, others; mem: IEEE, Am. Inst. Aero. & Astro., Nat. Soc. of Profl. Engrs., Nat. Mgmt. Assn., Am. Mgmt. Assn., Internat. Platform Assn., Armed Forces Comm. & Electronics Assn., Assn. of the US Army, DAV; publs: Intrinsic Safety, DC Amplifiers, Space Radars, Lunar Landing Radars Mgmt. Controls; patents in field; mil: Office of Mil. Govt. for Germany, Berlin, US Army 1943-46, Bronze Star, Combat medals, Medical Badge; Independent; Presbyterian; rec: stamps, electronics, woodworking, gardening. Res: 5545 Stresemann St San Diego 92122 Ofc: Hoffman Associates, POB 22010, San Diego 92122

HOFFMAN, IRWIN DONALD, periodontist; b. Dec. 27, 1935, Brooklyn, NY; s. Henry and Etta (Rubin) H.; m. Rochelle Schwartzman, Sept. 2, 1966; children: Renee, b. 1969; Risa, b. 1972; edn: BA, Brooklyn Coll. 1952-56; DDS, NY Univ. Coll. of Dentistry 1960; MSD, 1968; cert. of Splty. Periodontics, 1968; dental lic. N Y 1960, Calif. 1962. Career: gen. practice, dentistry 1960-66; periodontic practice 1966--; currently, pres. Irwin D. Hoffman, DDS, MSD, Inc.; awards: dental research awd., NYUCD 1960; NY State postgrad. partial tuition awd. 1967; mem: Am. Acad. Periodontology; Calif. Soc. Periodont.; Internat. Assn. Dental Research; Am. & Calif. Dental Assns.; Orange Co. Dental Soc.; Sci. Research Soc. of Am.; So. Coast Priodontal Gp.; Wilderness Soc.; Environmental Defense Fund; Natural Resources Defense Council; Friends of Irvine Coast; So. Coast Repertory Theatre; Orange Co. Philharmonic Soc.; Shorecliff Residents Assn., Inc. (past pres.); num. publs. in industry journs.; mil: capt. Dental Corps. USAF, active duty 1960-62. Res: 130 Shorecliff Rd Corona del Mar 92625 Ofc: Irwin D. Hoffman, DDS, MSD, Inc., 18821 Delaware St, Ste 201, Huntington Beach 92648

HOFFMANN, MARK REINHARD, theoretical chemist; b. Oct. 3, 1958, St. Paul, Minn.; s. Gerhard Reinhold and Heidi Barbara (Tritthaler) H.; edn: BA, Northwestern Univ. 1980; PhD, UC Berkeley 1984. Career: lab. tech. H.B. Fuller Co., St. Paul, Minn. 1978; lab. tech. Sinclair & Valentine, Inc., W. St. Paul, Minn. 1979; tchg. asst. UC Berkeley 1980-82; research asst. Univ. of Calif., Lawrence Berkeley Lab., 1980--; honors: Alpha Lambda Delta 1977; mem. Am. Physical Soc. 1978; num. sci. journal publs.; Catholic; rec: hiking, chess, photog. Res: 2299 Piedmont Ave, 401, Berkeley 94720 Ofc: Univ. of California, Dept. of Chemistry, Berkeley 94720

HOFFMAN, MARVIN, computer software consulting co. president; b. July 27, 1933, Wauwatosa, Wisc.; s. Sam and Anna (Cohen) H.; m. F. Evelyn Lazar, Sept. 28, 1955; children: Loren b. 1959, Darryl b. 1960; edn: BA in math., CSU Northridge 1962; postgrad. wk., CSU and UCLA; Life Tchg. Credential Bus. Data Processing. Career: systems supr. North Am. Rockwell 1961-66; dir. 6000 Software Devel., Control Date Corp. 1966-69; dir. software devel. Ampex Corp. 1969-72; mgr. software devel. F&M Systems Co. 1972-73; dir. R&D Div. Computer Machinery Corp. 1973-76; fwunder/pres./bd. chmn. XXCAL, Inc. (multi-branch data processing consulting and human resource co.), Los Angeles 1976--; chmn. bd. Executive Systems Inc.; bd. dirs. Software Mfg. Inc.; instr./mem. adv. com. L.A. City Coll.; honors: Alpha Gamma Sigma 1958; mem: W.L.A. CofC 1981-; nat. past pres. Vaide & Sel Users Group 1962-72; past mem. DAMA, ACM; mil: AG2 USN 1952-56, Korean, Far East Cpgn., GC; Democrat; Jewish; rec: ski, golf, jogging. Res: 2423 S. Beverly Dr Los Angeles 90034 Ofc: XXCAL Inc. 11500 Olympic Blvd Los Angeles 90025

HOFFMAN, ROBERT STOCKING, aerospace industry executive; b. Aug. 7, 1944, Cincinnati, Ohio; s. Herman Miller and Lois Wahler (Stocking) H.; m. Susan Lee, Jan. 18, 1969; children: Jonathan, b. 1971; Kyle, b. 1976; edn: BS, Univ. of Ariz. 1967; MS, 1975; JD, Loyola of Los Angeles 1980; admitted to Calif. State Bar 1980. Career: payload devel. engr. USAF- SAFSP, Los Angeles

Air Force Station, L.A. 1973-77; br. mgr. USAF- SAMSO, L.A. AFS 1977-79; staff engr. TRW, Redondo Beach 1979-81; asst. proj. mgr. TRW, Redondo Beach 1981-82; proj. mgr. satellite communs. 1982--; honors: Blue Key Hon. 1965-66, Who's Who in Am. Colls. & Univs. 1967, Air Force Sys. Command's Outstanding Spkr. 1971-72; mem: Sigma Pi Sigma (pres. 1965-66); Fed., Calif. & L.A. Co. Bar Assns.; Toastmasters; Jaycees; Boy Scouts of Am. (Eagle Scout 1961, asst. scoutmaster 1969-73, cubmaster 1981-83, asst. dist. commnr. 1983, dist. commr. 1983-84); Rotary; publs: contbr. Optical Scis. Ctr. Tech. Report, Univ. of Ariz., 5/75; mil: maj. USAF 1967-79, Merit. Svc., AF Commdn., Organizational Excellence Awd., AF Unit Cit.; Republican; Methodist; rce: scuba diving, skiing, photog. Res: 7091 Sunlight Dr Huntington Beach 92647 Ofc: TRW, One Space Park, 03/2234, Redondo Beach 90278

HOFMAN, ERNEST PERSHING, real estate broker/developer; b. Sept. 12, 1918, Chgo.; s. ERnest H. and Irene Elizabeth (Schumacher) H.; m Drennan Smith, Jan. 19, 1947; edn: AA, Bakersfield Coll. 1938. Career: flying instr./ commercial pilot Scott Flying Service 1942; flight ofcr., US Army Air Corps 1944, flt. instr./supr. with Flying Cadets 1944-46, Long Beach & Palm Springs Ferry Command, Air Transport Cmd. in Africa, Arabia & India; owner/opr. Service Station in Shafter, Ca. 1946; insurance agt./ins. agency owner 1949--; realtor, 1958--; gen. contractor/pres. Hofman Builders Inc. (141 new homes, 3 office bldgs.) 1969--; honors: Award of Merit, Kern County bd. of Trade 1962, Paul Harris Fellow, Shafter Rotary Club; mem: Bakersfield Bd. of Realtors, Calif., Nat. Assn. of Realtors, Bakersfield CofC, Rotary, Masons, Scottish Rite, Shriners, Assistance League of Bakersfield adv. bd., The Retired Officers Assn., Shafter Hist. Soc.; mil: maj. USAF ret. 1978, Asia-Pac. Serv., Euro. African Middle Eastern Serv., WWI Victory medals; Republican; Congregational; rec: travel, photog. Res: 3338 El Encanto Ct Bakersfield 93301 Ofc: Hofman Builders Inc. 2901 H Street, Ste 2, Bakersfield 93301

HOGAN, FORESCEE MARIQUEE, sportswear manufacturer, designer; b. May 30,1957, Los Angeles; d. Forace and Dorothy Iona (Hardiman) Hogan; edn: AA, profl. modeling cert., Brooks Coll. 1977; BA, bus. ad., Loyola Marymount Univ. 1980; Profl. Fashion Design cert., Univ. of Paris, La Sorbonne, 1979. Career: asst. designer Barbara Barbara, Junior Dress Mfr., 1977; freelanced during sch. yrs. for var. entertainment groups, small movie houses (CBS, Am. Film Inst.); exec. tng. prgm. Bullocks, 1980; fashion designer/pres./ owner Flips (sportswear & dress mfg. co.), founder/ptnr. Flips of Forescee-M&Co. 1981--; instr. Woodbury Univ. 1983-, Brooks Coll. 1984; recipient Golden Dome Award 1976, 77, Black Achievement Award, Loyola Marymount Univ. 1980; recognition for creative designs in trade publs. Calif. Apparel News (3/82, 5/83), Womens Wear Daily (9/82); mem. Ephebian Soc.(life), Winter Fox Ski Assn.; Democrat (New Frontier Dem. Club, Spkrs. Bur. 1984); christian; rec: tennis, costume design, skiing. Res: 972 W. 244 St Harbor City 90710 Ofc: Forescee-M&Co, dba Flips, 824 S. Los Angeles St, Ste 507, Los Angeles 90014

HOHN, BRUCE ANDREW, lawyer; b. Sept. 19, 1946, Lynwood (4th gen. Californian); s. Andrew Vincent and Mary Grace Hohn; m. Catherine Burke, Dec. 31, 1967, div. 1977; children: Margaret Grace, b. 1969; Garth Andrew, b. 1983; edn: BSL, Glendale Univ. 1975; admitted to practice Calif. State Bar, all State and Fed. Cts. Calif. 1977. Career: fmr. self empl. municipal contr., mng. salvage bus.; currently lawyer pvt. practice in Downey; mem. Am., Southeast Bar Assns.; Republican; Catholic; rec: hunt, fish, golf. Res: 10001 Frontage Rd South Gate 90280 Ofc: Bruce A. Hohn, 11510 S. Downey Ave Downey 90241

HOLDEN, JACKIE LOU, real estate broker; b. Aug. 15, 1946, Allegan, Mich.; d. James Allen (dec.) and Betty Ruth (Cassidy) Melvin; m. Joseph Holden, Sept. 2, 1982; children: Roni Sue Wittkoski, b. 1967; Thomas James Wittkoski II, b. 1969; edn: spl. courses, San Diego Evening Coll. 1979, Western Mich. Univ. 1966, Anthonys R.E. Schs. 1981, 82. Career: asst. property mgr. Trust Dept. San Diego Trust & Savings Bank 1973; escrow ofcr. Safeco Title Ins. Co. 1975-77; escrow loan ofcr. Home Savings 1977-78; escrow ofcr. Heartland Escrow 1978-79; br. mgr./ escrow ofcr./ sales rep. title ins. Winfield Title 1979-81; escrow mgr. Commonwealth Title 1981; broker/corp. secty. Silver Cowgirl Realty Co. 1981--, also mortgage banker cons.; broker Silver Cowgirl Financial; recipient Salesmanship award, Safeco Title 1976-78; mem: Nat. Notary Assn.; Womens Council of Realtors; San Diego City Escrow Assn.; San Diego CofC; S.D. East Co. Bd. Realtors; Calif. & Nat. Assns. Realtors; Toastmasters Intl.; Democrat; Methodist; rec: vol. work, missions. Res: 6928 Coleshill Dr San Diego 92119 Ofc: Silver Cowgirl Realty, 9355 Lavell St La Mesa 92041

HOLDEN, JOHN MORGAN, stage director/ educator; b. June 21, 1922, Cincinnati, Oh.; s. Reuben Andrus and Grace (Morgan) H.; edn: AB, Yale Univ. 1944; MFA, UCLA 1951; Life Comm. Coll. Tchg. Cred., Calif. Career: mgr. dir. Stumptown Players, Guerneville 1952-54; instr. drama & English Athens Coll., Athens, Greece 1963-64; asst. prof. theater & humanities Porterville Coll., Portervill 1966-83; dir. Porterville Bar Theater 1971-84; currently, dir. Three Rivers Players, Three Rivers & columnist Mineral King Pub., Exeter; dir. Visalia Comm. Players, Visalia; columnist/ art ed. valley Voice Monthly, Visalia; awards: acting & dir. awds., Porterville Bar Theater, Visalia Ice House Theater; mem: Am. Theater Assn.; So. Calif. Ednl. Theater Assn.; mil: 1st lt. Army Inf. 1943-46, Bronze Star; Democrat; Presbyterian; rec: piano, swimming. Address: 42640 Sierra Dr Three Rivers 93271

HOLDEN, JOHN OLIVER WENDELL, educator; b. May 29, 1940, Morristown, Pa.; s. Edgar Wendell and Eleanor Lois (Fields) H.; m. Jean Ann Wagner, Oct. 7, 1961; children: Steven Vernon, b. 1962; Tracy Jean, b. 1963;

Nancy Sue, b. 1965; edn: AA, Valley Jr. Coll. 1964; cert. Contg. Edn., Nat. Assn. Trade & Tech. Schs. 1979-. Career: mgr. reservations ticket ofc. Nat. Airlines, Inc., Los Angeles 1958-67; pres./ CEO Holbury Internat., Inc., San Diego 1967-72; dir. dispaly- merchandising Contempo Casuals, Inc., L.A. 1972-75; pres./ CEO Chateau Properties, Inc., Hollywood 1975-84; dir. edn. Acad. Pacific Travel Coll., Hollywood 1978-83; exec. dir. Acad. Pacific Bus. & Travel Coll., Hollywood 183--; secty./ bd. dirs. Airline Schs. Coll., Inc.; secty./ bd. dirs. S.W.S. Corp.; bd. dirs. Acad. Pacific Travel Agcy.; mem: Am. Soc. of Travel Agents (allied mem.); Republican; Protestant; rec: travel. Res: 6221 Hollymont Dr Hollywood 90068 Ofc: Academy Pacific Business & Travel Coll., 6253 Hollywood Blvd Hollywood 90028

HOLDER, JEANETTE FRANCES, real estate broker; b. July 22, 1932, Detroit, Mich.; d. Evert Willis and Rosa Marguerite (Englehart) Gamble; m. Donald K. Holder, Mar. 11, 1950; children: Susann M., b. 1954; Donald K. Jr., b. 1957; edn: Santa Barbara City Coll. 1972; Hancock Coll., Santa Maria 1983; R.E. broker, Calif. 1972. Career: profl. model Patricia Stevens Studios, Detroit, Mich. 1949-62; mgr. (3 clubs) Silhouette/ Am. Health Studios, Detroit, Mich. 1958-62; secty./ mgr. Carpinteria Valley CofC, 1967-69; owner/ broker Casa La Cumbre Real Estate, Santa Barbara 1969--; mem: Santa Barbara Bd. Realtors, S.B. Fashion Guild. Address: Casa la Cumbre Real Estate, 1665 La Cumbre Ln Nipomo 93444

HOLGATE, GEORGE JACKSON, university president; b. Feb. 19, 1933, Lakewood, Ohio; s. George Curtis and Melba (Klein) H.; l dau. Leigh M.; edn: BM, Baldwin-Wallace Coll. 1953; MS, Univ. So. Calif. 1955, EdD, 1962; PhD, Riverside Univ. 1970, LLD. Career: exec. v.p. Sierra Found., 1953-56; tchr. Oxnard High Sch. and Ventura Coll., 1956-62; campus coord. Congo Polytech. Inst., 1962-64; pres. Riverside Univ., 1965--; bd. dirs. Lincoln General Corp. 1972-77. Music condr.: Ojai Festival, 1945, Ventura Co. Concert Chorale and Chamber Singers, 1956-60, Ventura Bach Festival, 1958, Columbia Orch. 1960; awards: US Jr. CofC Distinguished Service Award 1962; bd. dirs: Riverside Sym. Orch., Riverside Opera Assn., Calif. Assn. for Pvt. Edn., Calif. Council of Business Schs.; mem. Phi Mu Alpha Sinfonia, Phi Delta Dappa; mil: flotilla comdr. USCG Aux. 1983-; Democratic State Central Com. of Calif. 1962, Dem. nominee for Cong. 1962; rec: music, fishing, sailing, flying. Ofc: 890 Indian Hill Blvd Pomona 91767

HOLGUIN, RUDOLPH JOSEPH, physician-family medicine; b. July 22, 1953, Los Angeles; s. Edward Robert and Frances (Dominquez) H.; m. Diane M., June 21, 1975; children: Ramon b. 1978, Fernando b. 1979, Armando b. 1979, Alejandro b. 1982; edn: BS, UC Irvine 1975, MD, UCI Med. Sch. 1979; lic. Family Medicine Doctor, Calif. 1980. Career: Family Practice residency, 1979-82; phys. Kaiser (Date Street Clinic) Fontana 1982; faculty mem. San Bernardino Co. Family Medicine Residency 1982--; dir. McKee Health Ctr. 1982-83; practicing Emergency Room (ER) Phys., 1983--; dir. Fontana Family Health Ctr. 1983--; clin. med. instr. UC Irvine Med. Sch.; Fellow Am. Acad. of Family Practice, Advance Trauma Life Support Instr. Cert., Diplomate Am. Bd. of Family Practice; mem: Am./Calif./ San Bernardino-Riv. Acads. of Family Practice, Soc. of Tchrs. of Family Med., Clin. Instrs. of Adv. Cardiac Life Support; rec: tennis, racquetball, camping. Res: 2172 Magnolia Ave Rialto 92376 Ofc S.B. County Med. Center Dept. Family Practice, 780 E. Gilbert, San Bernardino

HOLLAND, KENNETH MURRAY, petroleum engineer; b. Dec. 28, 1925, Long Beach; s. Jens Olai and Clara Huey (Geiger) H.; m. Marily, Aug. 13, 1955; children: Eric C., b. 1959; Thomas D., b. 1961; edn: BS, UC Berkeley 1950; MS, USC 1957; Reg. Profl. Engr. (petroleum), Calif. Career: engr. Standard Oil of Calif. 1950-73: engr. prod. & reservoir, La Habra 1950-58, engr. drilling & prod., La Habra, San Francisco 1959-66, engr. reservoir, Huntington Beach, Carpinteria 1967-73; sr. engr. evaluation Chevron USA, San Francisco 1974-77; sr. engr. assoc. Chevron Oil Field Research Co., La Habra 1978; sr. reservoir engr. Chevron Geosciences, Houston, Tex. 1979-80; sr. eng. assoc. Chevron Oil Field Research Co., La Habra 1981--; lectr. on secondary recovery, USC 1958; honors: Tau Beta Pi 1949; mem: Soc. Petroleum Engrs. (Jr. Gp. chmn. 1954); Balboa Bay Club; Dover Shores Assn.; coauthor: Single- Well Evaluation for Miceller Polymer Recovery, Soc. Petroleum Engrs. 10/83; mil: lt. j.g. USNR 1943-46; Republican; Presbyterian; rec: sailing, skiing, gardening. Res: 1716 Santiago Dr Newport Beach 92660 Ofc: Chevron Oil Field Research Co., POB 446, La Habra 90631

HOLLAND, ZACHARY STEPHAN, III, apparel industry executive; b. Oct. 17, 1938, Brooklyn, NY; s. Norman Ned and Sylvia Shirley (Schindler) H.; thrice married and div.; 2 daus. Randi Alyssa, Kimberly Dawn; edn: Pace Coll. 1957-62. Career: pres. ZSH Inc., a mktg. orgn. in the womens fashion industry specializing in designer & junior apparel; in 1974 pioneered the concept of designer jeans, dba Antonio Guiseppe, showed as only American mfr. in Spring 1976 in Paris and London; profl. public speaker re alcohol and drug abuse, prison reform; mem: Beverly Hills CofC & Civic Assn., Toastmasters Internat. (area gov.); Jewish; rec: skydiving, stained glass, carpentry, guitar. Res: 428-A S. Spalding Dr Beverly Hills 90201 Ofc: ZSH Inc., 110 E. 9th St, Ste B1153, Los Angeles 90079

HOLLANDER, JOHN DIRK, podiatrist; b. Mar. 27, 1954, NY, NY; s. Gerrard and Argate L. (Palmer) Hollander; m. Robin L. Anderson, June 6, 1982; edn: BA, Alfred Univ. 1974; B. Basic Med. Sci., Calif. Coll. Podiatric Med., 1980, DPM, 1981. Career: lab. tech. Cardio-Vascular Research Inst., Moffitt Hosp., San Francisco 1976-79; functional orthotic mfg., Foot Comfort Ctr., Anaheim 1980-81; res. surg. and podiatric med. Doctors Hosp., Anaheim 1980-81; currently pvt. practice, Santa Rosa Foot Health Center; tch. inservice tng. to nurses in num. hosps.; team doctor Star Skate World Speed Skaters; mem: Am. Podiat. Med. Students Assn. 1977-80, Podopediatric Soc. (charter), Acad. of Ambulatory Foot Surgery 1981, Am. Podiatric Circulatory Soc., Am. Acad. Podiatric Sports Med. (assoc. 1983), Am. Podiatry Assn., Calif. Podiatric Med. Assn., Redwood Empire Podiatry Assn., Am. Running and Fitness Assn.; researcher nat. study of neonates and foot related problems; rec: run, swim, ski, scuba. Res: 493 Patten Sonoma 95476 Ofc: Santa Rosa Foot Health Center, 1421 Montgomery Dr Santa Rosa 95405

HOLLEMAN, JOHN JOSEPH, college president; b. Oct. 25, 1932, Oakland; s. Joseph W. and P. Grace (Kingham) H.; m. Nancy Bracken, Mar. 1956; children: Jennifer, b. 1960; Linda, b. 1962; John, b. 1964; edn: BA, UC Berkeley 1956; MA, 1958; EdD, Nova Univ. 1983. Career: instr. Merritt Coll. (designed new biology curriculum; intro. oceanography & marine biol. pgms.) 1957-74; chmn. Dept. Biological Sci. 1966-70; coord. instrn. 1967-70; chmn. Sci. & Math. Div. Merritt Coll. 1975-77; pres. Vista Coll. (264 locations, 600 courses, 13,500 students), Berkeley 1977--; cons./ environ. biologist Dames & Moore, Soil Engrs. & Geologists 1971-78; mem: Nat. Task Force of 2-yr. Coll. Biologists, Am. Inst. Biological Sci. 1970-71; dir. HEW Urban Chem. Tech. Itern Proj. 1973-75; dir. NSY Human Beings & Their Environ. 1977-80; Task Force, locally funded constrn. projs., Chacellors Ofc., Calif. Comm. Colls. 1980; cons. Am. Inst. Biol. Scis. 1974-75; mem: Am. & Calif. Assns. of Comm. & Jr. Colls.; Am. Assn. of Higher Edn.; Ecological Soc. of Am.; Nat. Assn. Biology Tchrs.; Am. Inst. Biol. Scis. (adv. council Proj. Biotech 1971-76); Biol. Soc. of Wash.; Calif. Malacazoological Soc.; W. Soc. of Natuarlists; W. Soc. of Malacologists; Calif. Acad. of Scis.; So. Calif. Soc. of Scis.; Peralta Found.; Rotary; Berkeley Breakfast Club; Berkeley & Oakland CofC; Herrick Health Care Found.; num. arts.in scholarly journs. mil: cpl. US Army 1950-52; rec: youth soccer coach, referee. Res: 164 Greenbrook Dr Danville 94526 Ofc: Vista College, 2020 Milvia St, Ste 480, Berkeley 94704

HOLLENBECK, CECIL DOW, company president; b. Jan. 27, 1931, Glendale, Ariz.; s. Frank Ralph and Cora B. (Watson) H.; m. Wanda Linn, Oct. 14, 1950; children: Trudy, b. 1954; Randy, b. 1956; Stacy, b. 1960; Carol, b. 1965; Darel, b. 1965. Career: plasterer Anderson & Anderson, National City 1949-52; with Delp Plastering, La Mesa 1947-48, 1954-59; plasterer apprentice 1947-48; plastering foreman 1954-59; lathing supt. 1959-64; plastering supt. of gun crew 1964-68; plastering supt. 1968-76; gen. supt. 1976-81; owner/ gen. mgr./ pres. Delp Plastering 1981--; mem: San Diego Plasterers Assn.; mil: sgt. US Army Airborne 1952-54; Republican; Baptist; rec: motorcycles. Res: 5239 Alzeda Dr La Mesa 92041 Ofc: Delp Plastering, 8160 Center St La Mesa 92041

HOLLINGSWORTH, RAYMOND CLARK, industrial film producer; b. June 19, 1927, San Francisco; s. William Fay and Erica (Eschler) H.; m. Isabelle Crikos, Sept. 6, 1952; chilren: Donna b. 1948, Diana b. 1955, Marc b. 1956, Linda b. 1956; edn: 2d Class FCC Radio Telegraph lic., Pacific Radio Sch., 1945; 1st Class Radiotelephone lic. S.E. Signal Sch., US Army, 1954; spl. courses, City Coll. of S.F., Heald's Coll., UC Berkeley. Career: writer, dir., audio-visual prod. Edn. & Tng. Dept., United Airlines (photog. all UAL stock footage for aircraft in-flite, etc. Library, L.A. 1960-73) ret. 1983; photog. opening scenes of film, Guess Who's Coming to Dinner?, for Stanley Kramer; prod. film, In Your Hands, used by local Pub. Health Depts. in Bay Area; prod. film for UAL Flt. Dept., Incapacitated Flight Crew Member, now a std. for flt. tng. among internat. air carriers (over 75 copies of film sold; film won IATA and Air Safety Found. awards 1973-74); prod. film: Let's Talk Back for United Air Lines, 1983; tchr. A-V seminars, Univ. of Nev., Reno (Coll. of Judiciary); mem. curriculum bd. City Coll. of SF; honors: US judge rep. C.I.N.E. to 2nd Int. Film Festival, Thessloniki, Greece 1973; jury chmn. Am. Film Festival for Tng. Film/TV category, 1973-; pre-screener for S.F. Film Fest.; mem: A-V Mgmt. Assn. (Western dir. 1971), Info. Film Prods. Assn. (nat. v.p. mem. 1970), Soc. of Motion Picture and TV Engrs. 1967-, Masons (3d degree), Soc. of Antique Modelers (Frisco Vultures club 1940s), lic. Acad. of Model Aeronautics; works: narrated over 400 tng. films; recipient Cindy film award, IFPA, 1959, and sev. Indsl. Photog. awards 1960-62; mil: Merchant Marine Radio Ofcr. 1945-47, sgt. US Army 1954-56, sgt. Nat. Guard 1948-54; Republican; Lutheran; Rec: radio controlled aircraft models, computer tech. Res: 482 Sylvan Ave San Bruno 94066

HOLLIS, JOHN LESTER, accountant; b. Oct. 11,1944, Knoxville, Tenn.; s. Lester Garland and Rosa Marietta (Sliger) Hollis; m. Linda Anderson, July 16, 1977; 2 daus.: Melanie, b. 1978, Chandra, b. 1980; edn: AA, Modesto Jr. Coll. 1969; BA, CSC Stanislaus 1970; MBA, Golden Gate Univ. 1981. career: comml. note teller Wells Fargo Bank, Modesto 1964-67; chief acct. Varco Pruden, Turlock 1970-73; corp. treas./dir. Valley Constrn. Co., Modesto 1973-76; acctg. supr. Gen. Foods Mfg. Corp., Modesto 1976--, chmn. Public Affairs Com. 1981-; instr. Modesto Jr. Coll. 1979-81; spkr. for various orgns.; mem. citizens adv. com. Stanislaus Co. Area Assn. of Govts.; mem: Nat. Assn. of Accts. 1970-(pres. 1978); Sportsmen of Stanislaus; E Clampus Vitus Hist. Soc. 1973-6; Lions 1973-6. mil: sgt. Calif. Army Nat. Guard 1965-71. Republican (Young Repubs. 1969-73), Death Penalty Iniative, chmn. for Stanislaus Co. 1971. 1st Baptist Ch. Modesto (bd.deacons 1983-6). rec: racquetball, water ski, woodworking. Res: 3600 Ganado Wy, Modesto 95356 Ofc: General Foods, POB 3659, Modesto 95352.

HOLLOWAY, GEORGE, lawyer; b. Dec. 27, 1946, Los Angeles; s. George Washington and Annie Lee Holloway; edn: BA, CSU Los Angeles 1972; JD, Univ. of W. L.A. Sch. of Law 1981; cert. of film prodn., UCLA 1975; admitted to Calif. State Bar 1982. Career: actor, mem. screen actors guild; currently, sole practitioner Law Ofcs. of George Holloway, Los Angeles; mem: Am. & Calif. Bar Assns.; Calif. Trial Lawyers Assn.; Compton Lawyers Assn.; mil: sgt. US Army; Baptist; rec: tennis, golf, racquetball. Address: Law Ofcs. of George Holloway, 3125 W Vernon Ave Los Angeles 90008

HOLLOWAY, GILBERT NEWTON, III, sales co. president; b. July 24, 1941, San Jose; s. Gilbert Newton Jr. and Madeleine (Lewis) H.; m. Georgianne Albaugh, Mar. 29, 1969; children: Daryn, b. 1973; Dyann, b. 1976; Gib IV, b. 1979; edn: BS, San Jose State Univ. 1963; MBA, USC 1967; Std. Tchg. Credential, Calif. 1968, Splty. Jr. Coll. (life); instrument rated pvt. pilot. Career: mktg. rep. Xerox, Los Angeles 1966-68; mktg. cons. Canadian Govt., cons. ofcs. in Los Angeles 1968-69; tchr. mktg. course East L.A. & El Camino Coll. evening sessions 1968-70; estab./ owner/ pres. Holloway Sales, Inc. (mfrs. agent selling sports equip. & apparel in Western states), Mariposa 1969--; dir. TRED 2, Inc. (mfr. of athletic shoes); awards: Falstaff Achiev. Awd.; Sales Agcy. of yr., Brooks Athletic Shoes, Saravac Gloves & Majestic Athletic Wear 1983; mem: Mfrs. Agents Nat. Assn.; Sporting Goods Agents Assn.; Aircraft Owners & Pilots Assn.; Youth City of Am. (dir./ treas.); Merced Country Club; bd. deacons chmn. The Little Church in the Hills, Mariposa; mil: helicopter rescue crewman E-5 USN 1959-62; Republican; rec: flying (own Cessna Turbo 210), golf, tennis. Res: 5880 Mt Bullion Ridge Rd, Mariposa 95338 Ofc: Holloway Sales, Inc., POB 1945, Mariposa 95388

HOLLOWAY, ROBERT ANTHONY, clinical psychologist; b. Aug. 30, 1946, Okla. City, Okla.; s. Maurice Earl and Gertrude (Van Hooser) H.; Chandra Mc Nary, June 23, 1984; 1 son: Justin Anthony, b. 1982; edn: BA, honors, Chapman Coll. 1979; MA, 1981; PhD, Calif. Grad. Inst. 1982; tchg. credentials, Calif. St. Dept. Edn. 1980, Calif. Real Estate Lic. 1982. Career: outside sales rep. to v.p. Bay area American Millionaires, inc. 1982--; dir. Drug & Alcohol Pgm., Germany 1977-78; staff therapist Capistrano by the Sea Psychiatric Hosp. 1981-82; pvt. practice, Tustin 1981-82; mem: Am. Psychological Assn.; Am. Testing & Evaluation; Am. Mgmt. Assn.; Boy Scouts of Am.; Pop Warner Football; Kids Against Alcohol & Drugs; publs: arts., Single in Orange Co. Mag. 1981; conduct sems. on self devel. & wealth consciousness; mil: hospitalman 3/c USN 1964-67; E3 US Army 1970-78: Purple Heart, Vietnam, Joint Svc. Commdn., Navy Achiev. & Commdn., Vietnamese Cross of Gal., MC Combat Action, Combat Medic; Republican; Protestant; rec: stamps, ice skating, travel. Address: Robert A. Holloway, PhD, 336 Dolphin Isle Foster City 94404

HOLMES, CHANDLER, steel co. owner; b. Sept. 25, 1929, Evanston, Ill.; s. George and Florence Holmes; m. Eva Kibler, May 8, 1980; children: Margaret Etta, b. 1958, Karen Chandler, b. 1961; edn: AB, Wabash Coll. 1951; MBA, Harvard Univ. 1956. Career: salesman, var. mktg. pos. Kaiser Aluminum Co. 1956-62; v.p. sales Interant. Anodizing Co., Chgo. 1962-69; trade assn. exec. Steel Svc. Ctr. Inst., Cleveland, Ohio 1969-79; currently, pres./ owner Chandler Holmes Steel Co., Huntington Beach; tchr.- lectr. on mgmt. Steel Svc. Ctr. execs. 1969-79; mem: Steel Svc. Ctr. Inst.; mil: lt. s.g. USNR; Republican; Presbyterian; rec: skiing, golf, tennis. Res: 16941 Bedford Ln Huntington Harbor 92649 Ofc: Chandler Holmes Steel Co., 5901 Warner AVe Huntington Beach 92647

HOLMES, STEPHEN LEE, commercial pilot/ mortgage broker; b. Nov. 1, 1941, Pomona; s. Alba Lee and Frances Del (Pedley) H.; m. Codean Marie, Feb. 2, 1964; children: Tawny, b. 1965; Jeffrey, b. 1970; edn: AA, Chaffey Jr. Coll. 1965; AS, Mt. San Antonio Jr. Coll. 1980; R.E. cert.; airline transport pilot, FAA 1970; flight examiner, FAA 1975; vocational tchrs. cred. in aviation, Calif. 1970. Career: flight instr. 1965-68; qualified crew (Boeing 707, 727, Convair 880, Lockheed L1011), TWA 1968--; airline transport pilot rating 1970; mem: ALPA; Foothill Baptist Ch.; FAA Aviation Safety Counselor; W. San Bernardino Bd. Realtors; works: author/originator first state ROP curriculum for aviation edn. 1970; tchr. ground & flight tng. (all levels); Republican; Baptist; rec; flying, skiing, travel. Res: 1716 Orangewood Ave Upland 91786 Ofc: Associated Mortgage, 5206 Benito St, Ste 202, Montclair 91703

HOLT, ROSANNA COLUCCI, real estate executive; b. Aug. 5, 1953, Pitts., Pa.; d. Pasquale and Santina Colucci; m. John Edward Holt, Aug. 5, 1978, div.; 1 son: Stanley Pasquale, b. 1979; edn: BA, CSU Los Angeles 1976; grad., Lumbleau/ Chamberlin Real Estate Sch. 1981; MA, Univ. of San Francisco 1983; Calif. R.E. sales lic. 1980, R.E. broker lic. 1982; Notary Public, Calif. 1982; Tchg. Cred., Calif. 1983. Career: tchr. Los Angeles Co. Unified Sch. Dist., L.A. 1976, 1979; v.p. Western Pacific Investments, Huntington Beach 1977; career cons./ ofc. mgr. Avant Garde Personnel, Century City, Beverly Hills 1980; broker/owner Holt Realty, San Marino 1982--; pub. spkr. on edn., property mgmt., property renovation, real estate loans & real estate investment; honors: Kappa Delta Pi 1977, scholarship CSULA 1971; mem: CSULA Alumni Assn., USF Alumni Assn., Calif. Tchrs. Assn., Nat./ Calif. Assn. Realtors, West San Gabriel Bd. Realtors; orgns: Alpha Phi Omega, Red Cross, March of Dimes, Heart Fund, United Way; Christian; rec: antiques, research, music. Ofc: Holt Realty, 1613 Chelsea Rd, Ste 111, San Marino 91108

HOLTSMARK, ERIC B., architect; b. July 25, 1937, Malmköping, Sweden; s. Bent Erling and Birgit (Egerstrom) H.; m. Aase Kristoffersen, Sept. 5, 1975; children: Devon b. 1963, Eric, II b. 1964, Mindi b. 1977, Jenni b. 1979, Nicole b. 1984; edn: Midland Sch., 1950-55; B.Arch., UC Berkeley 1963; cert., Inst. d'Urbanisme (1960-61), L'Ecole des Beaux Arts (1960-61), Paris. Reg. Architect, ca. 1978; Reg. EIT, Ca. 1965; NCARB, 1982. Career: journeyman carpenter (7 yrs), var. constrn. trades, 1951-63; resident engr. Masonic Home, Union City (hosp. project) 1963-64; proj. coordinator Bechtel Internat. San

Francisco for Tarapur Nuclear project, India 1964-66; field engr. Bechtel Pacific Corp. Ltd., Tasmania (iron mine & townsite) 1966-67; sr. engr. var. hotel projects, Bechtel Corp., NY 1968-69; proj. mgr. and architect Bechtel Internat. Ltd., Helsinki, Finland (Hotel Inter-Continental) 1969-72; proj. mgr. Bechtel Intl. Ltd., London, England (Hotel Inter-Continental) 1972-76; proj. mgr. Bechtel Inc., S.F. (Saudi Arabia projs.) 1976-78; architect/owner Commercial & Hotel Development, S.F. (hotels and other projects in USA, Europe, West Indies, Mid East) 1978--; owner Mark-Bentland Properties (Calif. inv. co.) 1975--; mem: Phi Kappa Tau (1955-7), Project Mgmt. Inst., S.F. 1977-79, AIA No. Calif. 1978-81, Soc. of Am. Reg. Architects 1980-82, Nat. Trust for Hist. Preservation 1980--; Republican (Presdtl. Task Force 1982-); author: In Thee I Trust (accts. of travel alone through Russia 1960), pub. in Paris 1960; Ind.; rec: tennis, skiing, swim. Res: 321 Scenic Ave Piedmont 94611 Ofc: Commercial & Hotel Development, 1 Nob Hill San Francisco 94108

HOLYCROSS, ROBERT LEE, business owner; b. Jan. 17, 1933, Columbus, Ohio; s. Gerald and Evelyn (Carson) H.; m. Thelma Ruth Diets, Dec. 4, 1976; children: Adam, b. 1975, Tracy b. 1970; edn. Ohio State Univ., 1978; cert: Profl. Bowling Instr., AMF 1960-1. Career: bowling lanes mgmt., Denver, Colo. 1949-1975, Columbus, Ohio 1975-79, Vallejo 1980-; owner Vintage Bowl & Pizza Parlor, Vallejo 1980--; also real estate salesman and Distbr. rep. Federal Machines (vending); past bd. chmn. Cherryvale Recreation Ctr. Boulder, Colo.; mem: District Semi-Pro Bowlers of Ohio, (dir. 1977); Dist. Tournament Bowler's Assn., (pres 1978-9); Am. Legion, Moose Lodge, CofC, Kiwanis, Elks, W. Vallejo Mare Island Little League. publs: Bowling Handbook 1961. mil: USN 1951-54 Korea; Mormon; rec. hunting, fishing. Res: 101 Marla Dr American Cyn 94589 Ofc: Vintage Bowl & Pizza, 4215 Broadway Vallejo 94589

HOLZMAN, ROBERT MARVIN, marketing co. president; b. Apr. 7, 1942, Chgo.; s. Leonard Charles and Reva (Circle) H.; children: Daniel, b. 1966; Sean, b. 1969; Tamar, b. 1969; edn: BS, CSU Northridge 1964. Career: sales rep. Westinghouse Electric Appliance Div. 1964-68; dist. mgr. Westinghouse Elec. Supply Co. 1968-70; pres. Marketing West Inc., No. Hollywood 1970--; lectr. mktg. & sales, USC & Pepperdine Univ.; recipient sales awards: Norelco Lighting Co., Sanyo Electric Inc.; rec: antique cars, sailing, scuba diving. Res: 24 Yawl St Marina Del Rey 90292 Ofc: Marketing West, Inc., 13333 Saticoy St, No. Hollywood 91605

HOM, ART B., psychiatric social worker; b. June 28, 1947, Oakland; s. Teong F. and Yen H. (Yee) H.; m. Edna, Aug. 29, 1970; children: Christina b. 1977, Benjamin b. 1978, Deborah b. 1981; edn: BA, UC Berkeley 1969, MSW, 1972; LCSW, Calif. BBSE 1975. Career: psychiatric soc. wkr. Crisis Clinic, Mount Zion Hosp. and Med. Center, San Francisco 1972-78; mental health counselor City Coll. of S.F., 1976-78; pvt. practice, Treatment of Families and Adults, Organizational cons., 1981; asst. dir. Crisis Clinic Mount Zion Hosp. and Med. Ctr., S.F. 1978-82; director 1982--; lectr., asst. clin. prof. UCSF Dept. Psychiat. Sch. of Medicine, 1978--; honors: 10 Year Service award, Mt. Zion Hosp. & Med Center, SF, 1982; Social Work Staff of the Year (group award), Nat. Assn. of Social Wkrs., SF 1980; mem: Nat. Assn. of Social Wkrs., Orthopsychiatry, Bay Area Asian Social Wkrs (founder/ch. 1979), Asian Community Mental Health Svcs (bd. dirs. 1979-, ch. 1981-), Westside Comm. Mental Hlth. Ctr. (bd. dirs.); publs: contbr. chapters three textbooks; mil: splst.6, USAR 1970-76, Commendn.; Democrat; mem. Elect Harry Gin for School Board Com., 1983; Chinese Ind. Baptist Ch.; rec: opera, fishing, jogging. Res: 98 Crestmont Dr Oakland 94619 Ofc: Mount Zion Hospital & Med Ctr, POB 7921, San Francisco 94120

HOM, STANLEY CHIN, clinical social worker; b. Sept. 21, 1952, San Francisco; s. Thomas and Lang Kim (Leong) Chan; edn: BA, soc. welfare, UC Berkeley 1974, BA, econ. 1974, MSW, 1977; LCSW, Calif. Career: psychiatric group counselor Manzanita Halfway House, Union City 1975; psychiat. soc. wkr. Napa State Hosp., Imola 1977-79, Child & Family Mental Health, Oakland 1979-80; sr. psychiat. soc. wkr. Family, Youth & Children Svcs., Berkeley 1980-82; pgm. coord. Mental Health Court Pgm., Berkeley 1982; lic. clinical soc. wkr., pvt. practice, Passageways Counseling Ctr., Fremont 1980--; cons. San Lorenzo Unified Sch. Dist. 1983-; mem: Nat. Assn. of Soc. Workers, NASW Reg. of Clin. Soc. Wkrs., Internat. Council on Soc. Welfare, The Psychotherapy Inst.; adv. bd. Casey Family Pgm. 1982-; adv. bd. Shelter Against Violent Environment, Inc. 1982-; bd. mem. Berkeley Children's Svcs., Inc. 1981-3; founder, Safety Assurance for Families Through Education (SAFE), prevention pgm. for child sexual abuse; Democrat. Res: 1410 Addison St, Apt B, Berkeley 94702 Ofc: Passageways Counseling Center, 3535 Capitol Ave, Fremont

HOME, (GEORGE) DE FORREST, lawyer; b. Jan. 31, 1901, Los Angeles; s. George Kimball and Alice Minerva (Hanly) H.; m. Lucie Hartzell, Sept. 5, 1924; 1 son, DeForrest b. 1939; edn: BA, Pomona Coll. 1922; JD, Columbia Univ. Law Sch. 1925. Career: lawyer; lectr. Forensic Medicine, UCLA Medical Sch. 1950-57; mem. American College of Trial Lawyers; past pres. San Fernando Valley Boy Scouts; past pres. Pomona Coll. Alumni Assn.; 32nd degree Mason; P.A.D. Law Frat.; Rotarian; Lakeside Golf Club, Rancho Bernardo Golf Club; Republican; Prot.; rec: golf,fly fishing. Res: 17287 Campillo Dr San Diego 92128

HONACK, MICHAEL HENRY, artist/inventor; b. Jan. 3, 1948, Kansas City, Mo.; s. Henry Albert and Margaret Eileen (Wright) H.. Career: creative jeweler 1967--, designs wearable art containing electronic displays (micro-

electronic systems typically the size of a quarter), which reflect light and motion; pres. Freeman Michael Assocs. Inc. (devel./mfr. micro-electronic systems, kinetic displays for use in body adornment), Saratoga 1980--; inventor: Hybrid micro-circuit with LED displays (1981-83), circuits with artist-designed Liquid Crystal Displays (1984); extensive travels in Europe, Far East, 1970s. Address: Freeman Michael Associates Inc. 14201 Worden Way Saratoga 95070

HONDA, RONALD TAMOTSU, electro optics engineer; b. Feb. 11, 1949, Reedley; s. Edwin N. and Rose S. (Ogata) H.; edn: AS, Reedley Coll. 1969; BS, UCLA 1971. Career: electro optics engr. Ford Aerospace 1972-76, research & devel. engr. 1977-82, senior R&D engr. 1983, engring. splst. R&D, senior electro optics engr. 1984--; mem. Nat. Mgmt. Assn.; patents (2): Optical Scanning Apparatus, and Optical Scanning Apparatus driven by common source; Republican; rec: skiing, radio contolled airplanes, fishing. Res: 36 Windjammer Irvine 92714 Ofc: Ford Aerospace & Communications Corp., Ford Rd Newport Beach 92660

HONG, HYUN SHICK, mortgage banker/ real estate consultant; b. Feb. 21, 1954, Seoul, Korea, nat. 1974; s. Soong Bok and Eun Young (Lee) H.; m. Chanhee Suh, Sept. 8, 1979; children: Andrea, b. 1981; Teresa, b. 1983; edn: BS, CSU Los Angeles 1978; (GRI) Grad. Realtors Inst., Calif. Assn. Realtors. Career: real estate broker Ace Realty, Artesia 1980-81; owner/ broker Golden Bell Realty, Cerritos 1981--; owner/ mortgage banker East-West Financial Co., Cerritos 1982--; mem: CSU Korean Student Assn. (pres. 1976); Korean Student Assn. of So. Calif. (pres. 1977); Nat. & Calif. Assns. of Realtors; Realtors Nat. Mktg. Inst.; rec: swimming. Res: 1144 N San Gabriel Blvd Rosemead 91770 Ofc: East-West Financial Co., 17100 Norwalk Blvd, Ste 108, Cerritos 90701

HONEYSETT, WILLIAM L., newspaper publisher; b. Aug. 13, 1937, Wenatchee, Wash.; s. Harlan H. and Thelma O. (Vaughn) Honeysett; ed. Univ. of Puget Sound 1956-58, Wash. State Coll. 1958-62; m. Norma Wilson, June 23, 1962; children: Michelle, b. 1964; Richard, b. 1967. Career: with Bellingham Herald, Bellingham, Wash.: display advt. sales 1958-62, retain advt. mgr. 1962-66, asst. to pub. 1966-67, bus. mgr. 1967-70, gen. mgr. 1970-71, pub. 1971-77; pres. & pub. The Sun, San Bernardino, Ca. 1977--, apptd. v.p. Gannett Southwest and Pacific Newspaper Group, 1981. Instr. newspaper advt., mgmt. W. Washington Univ. Awards: Citizen of Achievement, League of Women Voters 1979; Urban Leader of the Year 1980, Inland Area Urban League. Mem.: (Bellingham, Wash.) Rotary, YMCA Bd., United Way, Yacht Club, Golf and CC; (San Bernardino) chmn. Bd. of Councillors, mem. Advisory Bd., Calif. State San Bernardino; YMCA, bd. dirs.; Arrowhead United Way, bd. dirs.; Inland Action bd.; Natl. Orange Show bd.; St. Bernardine Hosp. Found. bd.; San Bernardino Co. United Way long-range planning task force chmn.; Tournament of Roses Parade, bd. dirs.; San Bernardino C. of C. bd. dirs.; Inland Empire Cultural Found., pres.; Am. Calif. Newspaper Publishers Assn.; Allied Daily Newspapers, bd. trustees; Allied Foundation, bd. trustees. Mil.: Air Natl. Guard 1960-66. Mem. Redlands United Ch. of Christ, chmn. bd. trustees. Rec.: gardening. Res: 1525 Crown, Redlands 92373. Office: The Sun, 399 N. 'D' St., San Bernardino 92401.

HOOD, JACQUI C., lawyer; b. June 29, 1946, Vallejo; d. Wm. Edward, IV and Jacqueline Brent (French) Jones; m. Arthur P. Sacchetti, Feb. 14, 1978; children: Stephen Patrick b. 1964, Erin Dolores b. 1965, Shelley Anne b. 1966, Timothy Michael b. 1968; edn: BS, summa cum laude, and MPA, summa cum laude, Univ. of So. Calif., 1977; JD, Yale Law Sch., 1980; admitted to Calif. State Bar 1980. Career: payroll supr. Container Corp. of Am., 1970-73; US Postal Svc., New Haven, Conn. 1978-80; law clk. Taft, Stettinius & Hollister, Cin., Ohio 1979; litigation atty. McKenna, Conner & Cuneo, Los Angeles 1980-82; legal counsel Wm. T. Thompson Co., Torrance 1982--; exec. dir. A Natural Concern, Venice 1983--; rep. Council for Responsible Nutrition Legislative Affairs Com., 1982-; awards: Service Award, Los Angeles Sch. Bd. 1982, Fletcher Bowron Award for Outstanding Promise in Pub. Adminstrn. 1977; John M. Pfiffner Award 1977; mem: Calif. State Bar (Legal Svcs. for Prisoners com. 1980-), Wilshire Bar Assn. (gov. 1982-; Bull. editor 1983-4), LA County Bar Assn./LA County Medical Assn. Legal/Med. Relations Com. (1981-), Young Executives Forum (NFDA); publs: art., Labor Law Jour. 4/81, paper, USC microfilm library 6/77; Democrat (So. Calif. Area coord. Californians with Hart cpgn.; Nat. Demo Credentials Com., 1984 Nat. Conv. del.); Jewish; rec: pianist; cancer therapist (vol.). Res: 17698 Walnut St Fountain Valley 92708 Ofc: Wm. T. Thompson Co. 1317 W. Washington Blvd Venice 90291

HOOK, LYNNE O'NEILL, psychotherapist; b. Dec. 13, 1929, Liverpool, England, nat. 1965; d. Phillip Peter and Mary Jane O'Neill; m. Albert Louis Hook, June 3, 1972; children: Lynne, b. 1963; Jay, b. 1971; edn: BA, w/ distn., San Jose State Univ. 1981; MA, Univ. of Santa Clara 1983; PhD in psychology, Laurence Univ. (Santa Barbara), 1984. Reg. Intern, Calif. Bd. Behav. Sci. Career: ofc. svcs. supvr. Mars Candies, Burlingame 1965-67; adminstrn. MSD, Lockheed Missiles & Space Corp. 1973-80; gp. facilitator/ intern Juvenile Hall, San Jose 1981; family counselor/ intern. Foothill Coll., Los Altos 1983; reg. intern. with Dr. Erle Kirk, Psychologist, Mt. View 1983--; honors: Phi Kappa Phi; Psi Chi; mem: Am. Psychological Assn.; Calif. Assn. Marriage & Family Therapists; Nat. Council on Alcoholism; Toastmistress; Democrat; rec: camping, travel. Res: 783 Steuben Dr Sunnyvale 94087 Ofc: 1057 El Monte Ave, Ste D, Mountain View 94040

HOOPER, ROBERT ALEXANDER, filmmaker/ lawyer; b. Apr. 13, 1947, Annapolis, Md.; s. Posey Alexander and Louise (Hickey) H.; ed; BA, UC San Diego 1969; JD, UC Davis 1974; MFA, UCLA 1982; admitted to Calif. State Bar 1975. Career: staff research assoc. UCSD Med. Sch. 1970-72; law clerk, Legal

Aid Soc., Santa Cruz Co. 1973-75; adminstv. analyst to chmn., County Bd. Supvrs., San Luis Obispo 1975-76; producer Documentary Film Project, Scripps Instn. of Oceanography 1977-78; film series dir., US Environmental Protection Agency, Wash. DC 1979-81; currently, producer and cons. Planned Parenthood, ABC News 20/20; cons. Canadian Bdctg. Corp., Toronto on pgms.: Not in My Backyard, and Radon Factor; instr. UCSD Ext.; his films have appeared on PBS, ABC World News Tonight, ABC Close-Up, ABC 20/20, CNN and CBC (fifth estate pgm.); mem: Calif. Bar; Environmental Defense Fund; San Diego Co. Conciliation Ct.; Assn. Family Conciliation Cts.; films: Radon Factor, CBC 1983; The Deep, ABC 1983; Not In My Backyard, CBC 1982, num. film documentaries; Democrat; rec; scuba diving, back packing. Res: 1552 Camino Del Mar, Del Mar 92014 Ofc: Planned Parenthood, 2100 Fifth Ave San Diego 92101

HOOPER, STEVEN JOE, corporate president; b. Dec. 26, 1949, Cleveland, Ohio; s. Phillip F. and Phyllis A. (Teaford) Hooper; edn: BS, Kent State Univ., 1972; career: owner Ethison & Hooper Enterprises, Aspen, Colo. 1974-76; owner, pres., CEO, Beautiful Daydreams, Inc. (yogurt/ice cream mfg. & distbn. co.), Dana Point, 1976-- (co. was the first to develop and market frozen yogurt in the USA; co. currently mfg. 18 dirrerent products in Los Angeles for nat. distbn.); pres., Neo-socks, Inc. (neoprene ski & windsurfing apparel), Dana Point (1980--; dir. Market West Brokers, Denver, Colo.; publs: Beginning Biology (lab. manual), 1971, The Making of A Beautiful Day (in dairy & ice cream field), 1980; Republican; Protestant; rec: skiing, tennis; res: 24181 Vista D'oro So. Laguna 92677 ofc: Beautiful Daydreams, Inc. PO Box 327 Dana Point 92629.

HOOPES ROBERT STEVEN, chiropractor; b. Nov. 12, 1953, Merced, s. Robert Charles and Evelyne Rosetta (Duncan/ Asther) H.; m. Shirley, Feb. 26, 1977; children: Jaeson, b. 1977; Katrina, b. 1979; edn: AA, Fresno City Coll. 1974; DC, Palmer Coll. of Chiro. 1977. Career: lectr. var. health groups; host radio broadcasts on chiropractic & nutrition as alternatives for health; one year intern, with awards, Palmer Coll. 1976-77; clinical practice, pres. Hoopes Chiropractic Office Inc., Fresno 1982--; mem: Exec. Assn. of Fresno (dir. 1979); Yennis Acupuncture Research Found. (dir. 1980-81); Calif. Chiro. Assn.; Internat. Coll. of Applied Kinesiology; Internat. Acad. of Nutrition; Republican; Christian; rec: golf. Res: 4865 E Cornell Fresno 93703 Hoopes Chiropractic Office Inc., 2053 N Fresno St Fresno 93803

HOOSE, WINSTON PETTUS, financial planning executive; b. Oct. 3, 1946, Los Angeles; s. Harned Pettus and Elisabeth S. (Smith) H.; edn: BA, Whittier Coll. 1968; JD, USC Law Ctr. 1971; CLU, cand. Career: Vista volunteer lawyer, Ctr. for Law & Poverty, Los Angeles 1971-72; trust ofcr. United Calif. Bank L.A. 1973-75, trust ofcr., S.F. Hdqtrs. & secty., Trust Investment Com. 1975-77, mgr. pension trust accts., S.F. 1977-78; credit ofcr./ analyst, L.A. Hdqtrs. & S.F. Main Ofc. 1978-79; fin. plng. exec., Levine Financial Group, San Francisco 1979--; Whittier Coll. Endowment Com. 1984; bd. dirs. San Francisco Jaycees 1979-80; awards: New Agent in the Country for Mutual Benefit Life Ins. Co. in Number of Cases, 1980; New Assoc. of Year 1980, Levine Fin. Gp.; Delta Sigma Rho- Tau Kappa Alpha, nat. spkg. frat. 1968; Phi Sigma Alpha, polit. sci. frat. 1968; mem: S.F. & Nat. Life Underwriters Assns.; Million Dollar Round Table; Phi Alpha Delta, Ross chpt.; Nat. Spkrs. Assn.; S.F. Rotary; Big Brothers of the Bay Area; Jr. Achiev., Bay Area; Whittier Coll. No. Calif. Alumni chpt.; William Penn Soc.; Whittier Coll. Frat.; publs: United Calif. Bank Trust Mgmt. Tng. Pgm. 1973; Democrat; Ch. of Relig. Sci.; rec: biking, phys. fitness, youth orgns. Res: 441 Via Hidalgo, 20, Greenbrae 94904 Ofc: Levine Financial Group, 1 California St, Ste 2400, San Francisco 94111

HOOVER, DANIEL WAYNE, advertising and public relations executive; b. Apr. 10, 1947, Van Nuys; s. Perry Franklin and Vera Wanda (Johnson) H.; m. Joan Carol Motta, May 29, 1971; 1 son, Timothy Daniel, b. 1975; edn: BA, CSU Northridge 1969. Career: Los Angeles Times, L.A. 1965-70; profl. entertainer, self- empl., Pacific states 1968-70; regl. sales mgr. No. American Svcs., Inc., Orange Co. 1970-71; dir./ pres. Innovative Med. Sys., Inc., Fullerton 1971-72; exec. v.p. Hoover & Assocs./ Hoover Communications Group Inc., Fullerton & Phoenix, Ariz. 1972-74; chmn./ pres. Estey-Hoover Inc., Newport Beach 1975--; mem. Am. Assn. Advtg. Agencies, Nat. Com. on Client Svc., NY, NY 1979-83; guest lectr. colls. & civic orgns.; awards: Young Man of the Yr., Am. Legion 1965; 330 Yard Intermediate Hurdles, Calif. State Coll. Champion (1980); Golden Orange Creative Avtg. Awds., O.C. Advtg. Fedn. 1975-81; Overall Outstanding Achiev. Awd., Internat. Assn. Bus. Communicators 1980; mem: Am. Assn. Avtg. Agencies; Western State Advtg.; Orange Co. Profl. Assn.; Bus. Forum; Exec. Council of O.C.; Indsl. League of O.C. (Govt. Affairs Comm.); Family Svc. Assn. O.C.; O.C. Arts Alliance; United Way Communications Com., O.C..; Sun Valley Jr. Coord. Council; 552 Club Hoag Hosp.; Greentree Homeowners Assn. (dir., pres.); clubs: Irvine YMCA (founder Great Irvine Campout 1984); Rotary, Pi Kappa Alpha; feature columnist in var. bus. publs.; Republican; Christian; rec: sailing, skiing, singing. Res: 4241 Brookside Irvine 92714 Ofc: Estey-Hoover, Inc., 3300 Irvine Ave, Ste 225, Newport Beach 92660

HOPCUS, SHARRON ALMEDIA, manufacturing co. executive; b. Oct. 19, 1942; d. Norval W. and Dorothy M. (McGraw) Wilson; m. Eugene Hopcus, June 16, 1962; children: Melody, b. 1963e; Shanna, b. 1964; edn; trade & indsl. tchg. cert. 1971-78; Oscar Rose Jr. Coll.; Okla. Univ.; Okla. State Univ.; Okla. State Tech.; cosmetologist, Paul Beauty Coll. 1968. Career: tchr. secondary edn. Choctaw (Okla.) High Sch. 1971-79 (dept. hd.; Pep Club sponsor; VICA Club Sponser, local, co. & state levels); production control & personnel mgr. Eck-Adams Corp. Flewelling Div., South Gate, Ca. 1979--; curriculum writer, State Dept. of Voc. Edn. 1976; honors: recognition, Vocational Indsl. Clubs of Am. 1975, Princess Tri Alpha (Beta Sigma Phi) 1983; mem: Okla. Vocational. Tchrs. Assn.; Nat. Vocational Tchr. Assn.; publs: Profl. Cosmetology Practices (1976-77); Democrat; Catholic; rec: reading/ writing. Res: 11931 Gonsalves St Cerritos 90701 Ofc: Eck-Adams Corp., 12411 Industrial Ave South Gate 90802

HOPKINS, BARBARA P., public relations executive; b. Sept. 26, 1948, Santa Monica; d. Philip Rising and Caroline Jean (Dickason) Peters; m. Philip J Hopkins, May 23, 1981; Edn: AA, Santa Monica Coll., 1971; BS, CSU San Diego 1976; grad. stu., UCLA, 1981-2. Career: gen. partner, Signet Properties, Los Angeles 1971--; tech. editor, C. Brewer & Co., Hilo, Hawaii 1975; ed. Aztec Engineer, San Diego, 1976; regional publicist, YWCA, San Diego 1977; Campaign Cons. Repub. Congl. and Assem. Candidates, San Diego 1978-79; Public Opinion Pollster, Los Angeles Times, 1982; pres., Humbird Hopkins Inc., Los Angeles 1979--; ASCE 1975-76, Am. Soc. of Mag. Photo. 1980. Listed in: Who's Who Among Students in Am. Univ. & Coll. 1976; Personalities of Am.; Personalities of the West & Midwest; mem:IEEE 1974-76; Internat. Assn. of Bus. Communicators; Sales & Mktg. Exec. Assn. Orgns: Mayor's Council on Libraries, Los Angeles; Wilshire Blvd. Property Owners Assn.; Comml. & Indus. Props. Assn. (founding mem.); docent Mus. of Sci & Indus. Publs: The Layman's Guide to Raising Cane-A Guide to the Hawaiian Sugar Industry, 1976; The Students' Survival Guide, 1977, 2d ed. 1978. Rec: writing, travel, opera. Ofc: Humbird Hopkins Inc., POB 49813, Barrington Station, Los Angeles 90049

HOPKINS, CECILIA ANN, college administrator; b. Feb. 17, 1922, Havre, Mont.; d. Kost L. and Mary (Manaras) Sofos; m. Henry E. Hopkins, Sept. 7, 1944; edn: BS, Mont. State Coll. 1944; MS, San Francisco St. Coll. 1958, 2d. MA, 1967; PhD, Calif. Western Univ. 1977. Career: business tchr. Harve H.S., 1942-44; secty. George P. Gorham Real Estate, 1944-45; escrow secty. Fox & Carskadon Realtors, 1945-50; escrow ofcr. Calif. Pacific Title Ins. Co. 1950-57; bus. tchr. Westmoor H.S., 1957-58; instr. Coll. of San Mateo, 1958--, chpsn. Real Estate Dept. 1963-76, dir. Div. of Business 1976-; cons. Calif. State Dept. Real Estate, Sacto.; chpsn. Comm. Coll. Adv. Commn., 1971-72; adv. com. Comm. Coll. Chancellor 1976-; adv. com. Comm. Coll. R.E. Edn. Endowment Fund 1977; project dir. Career Awareness Consortium Com. 1976-; appt. to State Dept. of R.E. Commnrs. Adv. Com. for Edn. and Resrch. 1983-; awards: RECI (Real Estate Certificate Inst.) Award, Calif. Assn. of Realtors 1982; CBEA (Calif. Bus. Education) Commendn. for devel. real estate curriculum and devotion to bus. edn. 1978; Soroptimist Intl. (San Mateo - Burlingame) Woman of Achievement 1979; mem: Delta Pi Epsilon (nat. secty. 1968-9), Calif. Assn. of Real Estate Tchrs. (state pres. 1964-5, hon. dir. 1965-), S.F. State Coll. Counseling and Guidance Alumni Assn., Calif. Bus. Tchrs. Assn., Alpha Gamma Delta, Theta Alpha Delta, Phi Lambda Theta, AAUW; coauthor: Calif. Real Estate Principles (John Wiley & Sons 1980); rec: travel, antiques, hiking. Res: 504 Colgate Wy San Mateo Ofc: College of San Mateo 1700 W. Hilldale Blvd San Mateo 94402

HOPKINS, FRANKLIN LEE, SR., advertising executive; b. Sept. 13, 1940, Cincinnati, Ohio; s. Oscar Vern and Mary Winifred (Hirons) H.; m. Grace A. Jay, Jan. 17, 1960, div. 1971; children: Franklin Lee; Gray Jay; Jody Lyn; Kelly Todd; m. 2d. Margaret Edith Schlarman, July 17, 1977; children: Darin, Jeff, Lisa Horgan; edn: Cincinnati Univ. 1965-67; Cincinnati Art. Acad. 1962-64. Career: US Pub. Health assignment 1961-64; art. dir. Gable Advt., Cin., Columbus, Ind. 1964-66; art dir./ percentage owner Avery Studio Art, Columbus 1966; art. dir./ acct. exec. Bauer Kemble, Spicer Advt., Cin.. 1966-69; designer/ creative dir. Cambell, Turner & Assocs., Inc., Cin. 1969-73; v.p./ creative dir. William E. Wilson Advt., Palos Verdes, Los Angeles 1973-75; designer/ owner Franklin L. Hopkins Assocs., Inc., Fountain Valley 1978--; awards: Awd. of Merit, Chgo. Art Dirs. 1965; 1st pl. awds., Cin. Art Dirs. 1968 & Los Angeles Indsl. Advt. Club 1973; mem: Orange Co. Advt. Fedn.; Fountain Valley CofC (1st v.p.); Omni; Kiwanis; Masons; mil: USN 1958-61; Res: 18938 San Blas St Fountain Valley 92708 Ofc: 10101 Slater Ave, Ste 220, Fountain Valley 92708

HOPKINS, SYLVIA RUTH, accountant; b. June 16, 1934, Annapolis, Md.; d. Willard and Doretha (Arnold) Triska, Jan. 21, 1983; edn: BS, San Diego State Univ. 1965; MBA, Pepperdine Univ. 1976; postgrad. courses, seminars. Career: chief acct. Alessio Corp. & subsidiaries, San Diego 1966-70; chief acct. Typagraph Corp., San Diego 1970-72; asst. controller, Plessey Envirenmental Sys., San Diego 1972-75; asst. corp. controller, Morris Shenker Ent., San Diego 1975-77; chief acct., Hydro- Products, San Diego 1977-79; assoc. exec dir. internal ops. United Way of San Diego Co. 1982--; mem: Nat. Assn. Accts.; Hosp. Financial Mgmt. Assn.; Am. Guild of Patient Acct. Mgr.; Loma Riviera Condominium Assn. Bd. Govs.; works: create art objects, rep. Kesler Art Gallery; rec: creating art objects, bldg. miniature doll furniture. Res: 4356 Loma Riviera Ct San Diego 92110 Ofc: United Way San Diego County, 7510 Clairemont Mesa Blvd San Diego 92117

HOPPE, BERT RAYMOND, commercial photographer; b. Jan. 14, 1946, Burlington, Iowa; s. Kenneth Henry and Ethelbert (Mix) H.; edn. Imperial Valley Coll. Career: photographer/owner Hoppe Photography, El Centro 1964--: comml. photog., instant passports, team photos, conventions, reunions, weddings, aerials, spl. events, conventional photog., spl. investigative photos with Law Enforcement ofcls.; photo analysis expert court witness; instr. photog., 4H youth groups, others; awards: Top Winner, Western Fairs Assn., 1965 through 1983; Nat. Newspapers Award for Photog. Achievement, 1964; mem. Optimist Club, Bowling Assn.; Republican; Presbyterian; rec: bowling, fishing, gardening. Address: Hoppe Photography, 1708 Ross Ave El Centro 92244

HOPPING, RICHARD LEE, college president; b. July 26, 1928, Dayton, Ohio; s. Lavon Lee and Dorothy Marie (Anderson) Hopping; edn: BSc & D. Optometry, So. Coll. of Optomatry, 1952, (hon.) D. Ocular Sci., 1972; m. Patricia Vance, June 30, 1951; chil: Ronald, b. 1952, Debra, b. 1954, Jerrold, b. 1956; career: practice optometry, Dayton, Ohio 1953-73; president, Southern Calif. Coll. of Optometry, Fullerton 1973--; pres. elect, Assn. of Schools and Colls. of Optometry, 1981-; trustee, Assn. of Ind. Calif. Colls. and Univs., 1973-; chmn., Adv. Research Council, American Optometric Found., 1976-; chmn., Awards Com., Am. Acad. of Optometry, 1981-. honors: Optometrist of Yr. 1962, Ohio State Optometric Assn.; Optimist of the Yr. 1956, Dayton View Optimist Club; one of Ohio's ten outstanding Young Men of the Yr., 1960, Jr. C. of C.; Sigma Alpha Sigma; Beta Sigma Kappa; Fellow, Am. Acad. of Optometry; Fellow, Am. Public Health Assn. Mem: American Optometric Assn. (pres. 1971-2, bd. trustees 1966-73, chmn. num. coms., Referee in Practice Mgmt., Journal, 1977-); Opio Optometric Assn. (pres. 1964-65, chmn. various coms.); Miami Valley Optometric Soc. (pres. 1958-59); Calif. Optometric Assn. (Long Range Planning Com. 1974-77, 1981-); publs: num. articles on vision and health care; Republican; Presbyterian; res: 2741 Anacapa Pl. Fullerton 92635 ofc: So. Calif. Coll of Optometry, 2001 Associated Road, Fullerton 92631.

HORAN, CAROLE PUGH, school administrator/ boutique owner; b. July 1, 1944, Chgo.; d. Hillard B. and Goldie L. (Lawson) Williams; children: Scott, b. 1965; Deborah, b. 1968; Danielle, b. 1978; Anthony, b. 1980; edn: BA, Central State Coll. 1966. Career: dir. Winner Business Sch. 1971-73; dir. Holoman Career Inst. 1973-75; adminstr. Dorothy Brown Sch., spl. edn. sch. 1975--; owner Little Like Me Fashion Petite Boutique 1982--; awards: Comm. Svc. awd., C.I.T.I.E.S. 1981; mem: Urban League; NAACP; Calif. Assn. Pvt. Spl. Edn. Schs. (CAPSES); Black Edn. Assn.; Carson CofC; publs: Reach Out and Touch $$$, 1982; Ch. of Relig. Sci.; rec: golf, swimming, balloon decorations. Res: 1783 Gladwick St Carson 90746 Ofcs: Little Like Me, 111 E Carson St, Ste 6, Carson 90745; Dorothy Brown School, 3502 S Normadie Ave Los Angeles 90007

HORNADAY, WILLIAM HARRY DELYN, lawyer/ business consultant; b. Oct. 20, 1945, Los Angeles; s. William H.D. and Patricia Lee (Leach) H.; edn: BA, UCLA 1974; JD, UCLA Law Sch. 1977; admitted to State Bar of Calif. 1977. Career: asst. dean students UCLA 1975-77; atty. Columbia Pictures 1977-78; exec. dir. Creative Affairs, Avco Embassy Pictures Corp. 1979-80; currently atty./bus. cons. in pvt. practice, partner Alcanter & Hornaday, A Profl. Law Corp., Beverly Hills; coord. UCLA Entertainment Symposium (Exec. Com.) 1976; honors: UCLA Law Review 1976-77; mem: Beverly Hills & Los Angeles Bar Assns.; Los Angeles Copyright Soc.; Am. Film Inst.; works: ed. The Legal and Related Business Aspects of Independent Film Production, 1976; Republican; Relig. Sci.; rec: creative writing, racquetball. Res: 7566 Rosewood Ave, 8, Los Angeles 90036 Ofc: Alcanter & Hornaday, 9701 Wilshire Blvd, Ste 550, Beverly Hills 90210

HORNBECK, MARGUERITE ELMA, educator; b. Oct. 4, 1901, Great Bend, Kans.; d. Richard Elmer and Jonette Still (Cowgill) Hornbeck; Gr.Grandfather Andrew Still, MD, the founder of Osteopathy; Gr.Grandniece of Robert Louis Stevenson; m. Don Carlos Barrett (dec.), Atty., June 3, 1937; edn: BA, UC Berkeley 1926, MA, 1931; postgrad. wk., edn., Stanford Univ. 1954, Univ. of the Pacific 1956, 57; Gen. Life Sec. Tchr. Credential. Career: general science tchr. (gr. 8, 9), and Visual Aid coordinator, San Francisco Unified Sch. District, 1927-67, ret.; orgnzr. school Science Fairs, had youngest Grand Award winner in S.F. Sci. Fairs; vol. Sabin Polio Public Immunization Cpgn.; vol. Fed./State tax counselor for the Elderly; honors: First tchr. recipient Conservation Tng. Scholarship in Calif.; Pi Lambda Theta; photographed the burning of the Carrier of Sputnik I in skies over Los Angeles (the only photo of the event, US Govt. has copy); life mem: Univ. Calif. Alumni Assn., Stanford Univ. Alumni Assn., Calif. Tchrs. Assn., Nat. Tchrs. Assn., Nat. Retired Tchrs. Assn., Calif. Retired Tchrs. Assn.; mem: US Intl. Secretariat; Service Info. Dir. for UN Conf. on Internat. Orgn., S.F. 1945; vol. civilian service in 2d Army Secret Command, WWII; dir. school First Aid Ctr., WWII; Republican; Episcopal; club: Past Matron OES; rec: photog., breeding Fancy Siamese cats, creating (prize winning) crochet patterns. Res: 101 Laidley St San Francisco 94131

HOROWITZ, DAVID CHARLES, consumer correspondent; b. June 30, 1937, NY, NY; s. Max Leo and Dorothy (Lippman) H.; m. Suzannc E. McCambridge, 1973; 2 daughters; edn: BA, hons. journ., Bradley Univ. 1959; MSJ, Northwestern Univ. 1960; CBS Fellow, Columbia Univ. 1962-63. Career: editor-in-chief Tazewell Co. (Ill.) Newspaper, 1956; reporter Peoria (Ill.) Journ. Star, 1957-60; reporter, columnist Lerner Newspapers and Chgo. City News Bureau, 1959-60; newscaster KRNT Radio-TV, Des Moines 1960-62; news writer/prod. ABC Radio Network, NYC 1963; Far East corr. NBC News, 1963-64; pub. affairs dir. WMCA, NYC 1964-66; corr.-edn. editor, Consumer Ombudsman, KNBC News Action Reporter, L.A. 1966--, spec. features: Consumer Guideline, Of Consumer Interest, Consumer Close/Up; nat. syndicated pgm. David Horowitz Consumer Buyline, Fight Back! with David Horowitz; worldwide Apollo 15 splashdown, 1971; Calif. earthquake 2/9/71; Dem. Conv. 1972; advisor UCLA publs.; writer num. articles. Awards: Natl. Radio-TV Daily Award for Krebiozen - Hope or Hoax for Cancer, 1963; won Emmy for consumer ombudsman, KNBC Newsservice; Emmy awards for comsumer reporting 1973, 75, 77, 82 (two), 83; citations for Pub. Serv., City and County of L.A., State of Calif., 1979; City of Hope Spirit of Life Awd. 1979; US Postal Insps. Awd. 1981; Calif. St. Distinguished Citizen, 1982; US Consumer Product Safety Commn. 1982; Calif. Consumer Affairs Assn. 1982; distinguished achiev., Vista Del Mar 1981; Jewish Fedn. Council honoree 1981; Media Award Nat. Soc. of Consumer Affairs Profls. 1982; recogn. Humane Soc. of the US, LA Co. Bd. Suprs., LA Press Club, LA Co. Commn. on Alcoholism, Work Tng. Pgm. for Developmentally Disabled Young Adults; TV talk show guest: Tonight, Dinah, Phil Donahue, Hour Mag., others; feature subject in Time Mag. (1/4/82), TV Tuide (5/15/82); mil: USNR 1954-62; mem. bd. dirs: Nat. Bdcst. Edn. Conf., Am. Cancer Soc. Calif. Div., LA Jewish Home for Aged, The Silent Network, The Young Musicians Found. Inc.; adv. bd. S.H.A.R.E., Inc.; patron LA Co. Art Mus.; mem. Acad. TV Arts and Scis., Internat. Radio-TV Soc., Radio-TV News Dirs. Assn., Nat. Edn. Writers Assn., The Guardians, Sigma Delta Chi, Phi Delta Kappa, Overseas Press Club of Am., Friars Club; author: Fight Back and Don't Get Ripped Off (1979); synd. columnist Des Moines Register and Tribune synd., 1981-. Ofc: 3000 W. Alameda Ave Burbank 91523

HORTON, BARBARA BOYD, psychotherapist; b. Apr. 30, 1939, Brooklyn, NY; d. Robert Van Scoy and Helen Mary (Cameron) H.; m. John Moss, Aug. 29, 1983; children: David, Carly (dec.), and Kym DiIorio; edn: BA, Cornell Univ. 1960; Simmons Sch. of Soc. Wk. 1964-65; MA, US Internat. Univ., San Diego 1980; marriage family child counselor intern, Bd. Behav. Examiners 1983. Career: sales agt. Donna Mundor Realtors, Laguna Beach 1974-76; pgm. dir. Women Shelter, Long Beach 1977-78; bus. ctr. instr. Saddleback Coll., Irvine 1980-82; info. sys. lab instr. Cypress Coll., 1980-81; co-dir. Human Options, Battered Womens Shelter, So. Orange Co. 1982--; bd. mem. Orange Co. Mental Health Assn. 1971-73; chair Orange Co. Comm. Friends Pgm., Calif. State Comm. Friends Com. 1971-73; mem: Assn. Marriage, Family & Child Therapists; Am. Assn. Info. Sys. Profls. (Hon. Soc. 1983); Am. Assn. Univ. Women; Mothers Against Drunk Driving (MADD); rec: swimming, bicycling. Res: 24721 Rollingwood El Toro 92630 Ofc: Human Options, 428 Park Ave Laguna Beach 92651

HORTON, BERNARD RAY, investment advisor, company president; b. Sept. 17, 1948, Yakima, Wash.; s. Kenneth Leo and Florence Frances (Odowichuck) H.; m. Lennette Radman, May 6, 1978; children: Bernard, b. 1967; Dannette, b. 1968; edn: AA, Phoenix Coll. 1970; BS, Univ. of Ariz. 1972; CFP, Coll. Fin. Plng. 1980. Career: cost acct. Anderson Clayton Inc., Poenix, Ariz. 1968-69; bus. sys. corns. Valley Nat. Bank, Az. 1970-73; dir. mktg. Montana Bank, Great Fall, Montana 1973-74; AVP dir. R&D, Bank of Idaho, Boise, Idaho 1974-76; v.p. prof. svcs. div. Am. Nat. Bank, Bakersfield 1976-77; founder/ dir. 49er Savings & Loan, Oakhurst 1979-83; dir. Summa Health Plan, Fresno 1984-; pres. Inst. for Retirement Plng., Fresno 1977--; mem: Inst. CFPs; Internat. Assn. for Fin. Plng.; Fresno CofC; works: created computer software pgm., FINTRAK, for financial svcs. firms used nationally; sev. arts. on personal financial plng., profl. & trade journs.; mil: E-5 USN 1966-67, Vietnam; Repubilcan; Christian; rec: golf, camping, bicycling. Res: POB 119 Oneal's 93645 Ofc: Institute for Retirement Planning, 723 E Locust, Ste 122, Fresno 93710

HORTON, JEFFREY THOMAS, dentist; b. Feb. 7, 1942, Louisville, Ky.; s. Hammond Spalding Horton and Catherine (Olrich) Horton Lyle; edn: BS, USC 1965, DDS, 1971. Career: engr. Pacific Lighting (natural gas wholesaler) Engring. Dept.; estab. dental practice, Murrieta 1971--; primary organizer Murrieta Health Fair 1973-74; pres. Murrieta CofC 1974-75; founder/chmn. bd. Butterfield Savings & Loan Assn. 1978-1983; bd. dirs. Butterfield Equities Corp. 1983--; awards: Butterfield S&L named Nat. Top Performer in class w/ Return on Assets by Fed. Reserve 1982; mem: Am., Calif. & Tri-County Dental Assns.; Southwest Territory Gen. Plan; Murrieta & Temecula CofC; Republican; Congregational; rec: water sports, hot air balloon pilot. Res: 28500 Via Princessa, 6, Murrieta 92362 Ofc: 41516 Kalmia Murrieta 92362

HORTON-HIGHFILL, LINDA FAYE, private investigator; b. Sept. 2, 1947, Sulpher Springs, Tex.; d. Edgar Allen and Vera Faye (Davis-Montgomery) H.; children: Michael Anthony, Jennifer Lyn; edn: Fresno City Coll.; BA in soc. welfare, magna cum laude, CSU Fresno 1976; Calif. lic. Private Investigator 1980. Career: hearing rep. Fresno County Legal Svcs., 1975; stu. probation ofcr. Fresno Co. Probation Dept., 1975; deputy probation ofcr. Fresno and Madera Co. Probation Depts., 1977-78; claims investgator The Zenith Insurance Co., Fresno 1978-79, 1982--; owner L.F. Highfill and Assocs., pvt. investg. agcy. spec. in Wkrs. Comp., Civil and Camera Surveillance, 1980-82; mem: Fresno Indsl. Claims Assn.; (past) Ventura Co. Profl. Womens Netwk., V.Co. CofC, V.Co. Ins. Womens Assn., San Fernando Valley Adjusters Assn., Kern Co. Adjusters Assn.; Ind.; Prot.; res: 6040 N. Rafael Fresno 93711 Ofc: The Zenith, 2547 W. Shaw Fresno 93711

HORWIN, LEONARD, lawyer; b. Jan. 2, 1913, Chicago, IL; s. Joseph and Jeanette Horwin; ed. BD, hons., UCLA, 1933; LLB, cum laude, Yale Law Sch., 1936; m. Ursula Helene Donig, Beverly Hills, Oct. 15, 1939; children: Noel S., b. 1940; Leonora Marie, b. 1947. Career: assoc. with pioneer law firm, Lawler, Felix and Hall, 1936-39; partner, (Jack W.) Hardy and Horwin, attys. for L.A. Examiner, Sterling Elec. Motors, others, 1939-42; partner, Witkin-Horwin Review Course on Calif. Law, 1939-42; lectr., labor law, USC Law Sch., 1941; counsel, Bd. of Econ. Warfare and mem. requirements com., War Prodn. Bd., 1942-43; attache, U.S. Embassy, Madrid, Spain, 1943-47; Amer. repr. in Spain, Allied Control Council for Ger., 1945-47; lectr., Spanish lang., on Amer. Constitutional Law, Amer. Cultural Inst., Madrid, 1945; lectr., foreign affairs, Town Hall, others, 1949; pvt. law practice, 1950--. Elected to Beverly Hills City Council, 1962, Mayor Pro Tempore, 1963, Mayor of Beverly Hills, 1964; chmn., com. on municipal ct. reorgan., League of Calif. Cities, 1963-65; dir., So. Calif. Rapid Transit Dist., 1964-66; del. L.A. Regional Transportation Study, 1964-66; del. L.A. Regional Transportation Study, 1964-66; pres. Friends of Santa Monica Mtns. State Park, 1964-66; com. chmn., Transportation Comm., L.A. Goals Council, 1966-70; chmn., Beverly Hills Rent

Control Adjustment Comm., 1980. Author: numerous articles on legal subjs.; editor, Yale Law Journ., 1934-35; Awards: winner, Yale Univ. Israel H. Peres Prize for legal writing, 1934-35; winner, Yale Univ. Edward D. Robbins Meml. Prize, 1935-36. Judaism. Rec.: community projs. and activities, hunting, riding, skiing. Res.: 434 El Camino Dr., Beverly Hills; Office: 121 S. Beverly Dr., Beverly Hills 90212.

HORWITZ, ROBERT PERRY, mechanical engineer/ real estate broker; b. Dec. 2, 1932, Los Angeles; s. Gus and Doris A. (Roe) H.; div.; children: Lori, b. 1953; Robert, b. 1955; Jamie, b. 1961; James, b. 963; edn: BSME, honors, CSU Los Angeles 1958; Reg. Profl. Engr., Calif. 1965; lic. R.E. broker, Calif. 1970. Career: senior proj. engr. Peerlees Pump Div., FMC Corp., Los Angeles 1955-66; prod. supvr. Hydroaire Div., Crane Co., Burbank 1966-68; proj. mgr. Task Corp., Joy Mfg. Co., Anaheim 1968-73; sr. proj. engr. ITT J.C. Carter Co., Costa Mesa 1973-74; eng. mgr. Airco Cryogenics, Irvine 1974-78; eng. mgr. Aurora Pump, Gen. Signal Corp., City of Industry 1978-80; R.E. broker Newport Harbor-Costa Mesa Bd. Realtors 1980--; sr. proj. engr. ITT Jabsco Prods., Costa Mesa 1981--; mem: Nat. & Calif. Assns. Realtors; Am. Soc. of Mech. Engrs.; Instrument Soc. of Am.; works: patents in field of turbomachinery 1963-83, num. arts. in tech. journs.; Republican; Protestant; rec: skiing, boating, bridge. Res: 2047 Sea Cove Ln Costa Mesa 92627 Ofc: XCaliber Realty & Investment, 1525 Mesa Verde Dr E, Ste 121, Costa Mesa 92626

HOSFELDT, ROBERT MARSHALL, cable television executive; B. Apr. 23, 1933, Los Angeles; s. Paul Carpenter and Alma Dora (Snyder) H.; m. Blanche Fritzar, June 18, 1957; children: Brett, b. 1958 (dec); Bobbie, b. 1961; edn: BA, San Jose State 1959; MA, 1961; MBA, Pepperdine Univ. 1978. Career: announcer/ dir., pgm. dir., v.p./ gen. mgr. KNTV, San Jose 1959-65; exec. v.p./ gen. mgr. Gill Cable, San Jose; prof. broadcast mgmt., San Jose State Univ.; dir. Calif. Cable Television Assn.; awards: PAL Citizen of the Yr., Nat. Participant of Yr., Tower Awd., San Jose; mem: Rotary Club (bd.); Calif. Cable TV Assn.; Sparton Found. (past pres.); San Jose PAL (past pres.); San Jose Nat. Alumni Assn. (past res.); works: recipient Innovator Awd., Arbitron for Outstanding use of Broadcast Research; mil: PO 1/c USN 1951-55; Republican; Lutheran; rec: jogging, roadracing. Res: 15 Kite Hill Rd Santa Cruz 95060 Ofc: Gill Industries, 1302 N 4th St San Jose 95112

HOSKINS, GARY ALLAN, computer co. president; b. Mar. 8, 1952, Seattle, Wash.; s. Allan Walter and Margaret (Wilson) H.; m. Penelope Weston, Aug. 16, 1981; children: Amanda b. 1969, Jamie b. 1974, Daniel b. 1977; edn: computer sci./data proc., Coll. of Marin. Career: data proc. mgr. Holiday Magic, San Rafael; software engr. Singer Business Machines, San Leandro; tech ofcr Internat Computers Ltd., Bracknell, England; systems analyst CyberData Corp., Monterey; currently: pres./dir. Intec Micro Technology Limited, Pacific Grove; dir. Intec (Reading) Limited, Reading, Eng.; Republican; rec: camping, hiking, skiing, swim. Ofc: Intec Micro Technology Limited, 990 Benito Court Pacific Grove 93950

HOSKINS, JOHN HERBERT, real estate broker; b. June 5, 1927, Somerville, Mass.; s. Halford Lancaster and Edna Alice (Charles) H.; m. Martha Ann Peterson, Apr. 24, 1954; children: Alison, b. 1957; Carolyn, b. 1958; Clifford, b. 1967; edn: BA, Swarthmore Coll. 1959; R.E. broker, Calif. 1977. Career: analyst Dept. of Defense 1949; analyst field research unit Far East Command, Yokosuka, Japan 1950-52; Dept. of Defense, Wash. DC 1952-54; v.consul Consular Affairs, Calcutta (India) Consulate Gen. 1956-61; Middle East Affairs, Dept. State, Wash. DC 1961-63; 2nd secty. Political Sect., US Embassy, Tehran, Iran 1963-68; US Embassy, Saigon, Svn. 1968-69; US Embassy, Phnom Penh, Cambodia 1970; 1st secty. Cento coord., US Embassy, Ankara, Turkey 1971-74; Iran desk, Dept. State, Wash. DC 1975; currently, bd. dirs. Better Homes of Lafayette; awards: Top Producer, Mason-McDuffie Co., Orinda 1977-81; mem: World Affairs Council of No. Calif.; Campolindo Homeowners Assn.; mil: 2nd lt. USAR 1954-61; rec: tennis, skiing. Res:199 Calle La Mesa Moraga 94556 Ofc: Better Homes Realty, 3701 Mt Diablo Blvd Lafayette 94549

HOSKINS, NANCY MARGARET, county executive; b. Feb. 21, 1948, Milwaukee, Wisc.; d. Donald Henry and Terry (Mahynski) Dettlaff; edn: BS, Wisc. State Univ. 1970; spl. courses, Univ. Calif.; Calif. Real Estate Lic.; indsl. engring. cert., Booz-Allen and Hamilton Internat. Cons. Career: sales, mgmt., Hearst Corp. 1966-72; instr. Wisc. State School Sys., 1970-74; systems analyst to mgr. Adminstrv. Services, County of San Diego, 1974--; chpsn. Supvsy. Com. S.D. Co. Credit Union; recipient recogn. for vol. work in estab. Crime Victims Fund; mem: Women in Mgmt., La Jolla Contemp. Art Mus. Art Council, Toastmasters, North Coast Repertory Theatre; sponsor first 8k race to benefit Child Abuse Preventn. Found. of S.D. Co. 1984; Republican; rec: running, tennis, writing. Res: 13942 Mango Dr Del Mar 92014 Ofc: County of San Diego 7949 Mission Center Rd San Diego 92108

HOSKINSON, JOHN DONALD, JR., marketing executive; b. Dec. 5, 1946, Buffalo, NY; s. John Donald, Sr. and Virginia Mary (Fallon) H.; m. Janice Blackford, July 31, 1971; children: Jeffrey, b. 1973; John III, b. 1977; edn: BBA, cum laude, Ohio Univ. 1973; MBA, Central Mich. 1975-77; MBA, Newport Univ. 1978; PhD, 1980; comml. pilot, FAA 1971. Career: product mgr. Masonite Corp., Dover, Ohio 1975-77; ops. mgr. Western Region, Masonite Corp., La Mirada 1977-79; sales mgr. Flintoke, Los Angeles 1979-80; br. mgr. Flintoke/ Genstar, Riverside 1980-81; nat. sales mgr. Gruber Sys., Valencia 1981-83; v.p. mktg. 1983--; assoc. prof. bus. mgmt. Stark Tech. Coll., Canton, Ohio 1975-77; cons. Video Concepts, Redlands 1982-83; mem: Data Processing Mgmt. Assn.; Am. Mgmt. Assn.; Am. Mktg. Assn.; Nat. Acctg. Frat. (Beta Alpha Psi); Acctg. Hon. Soc., Ohio Univ.; AYSO (asst. coach);u Canyon Aquatics (Com-

petition Com.); YMCA (Indian Guides); developed: Standard Job Cost Sys., Masonite 1972; implemented five year mktg. plan, Gruber 1982; mil: capt. US Army 1965-71; aviator, paratrooper, Vietnam Svc., Vietnam Camp., Commdn. Medal, Air Medal w/ 4 Oak Leaf Culster, Combat Inf. Badge, Nat. Def.; Republican; rec: personal computing, family video prodns., youth sports. Res: 23702 Rotunda Rd Valencia 91355 Ofc: Gruber Systems, 25636 Avenue Stanford Valencia 91355

HOSP, F. PHILLIP, lawyer; b. Aug. 24, 1944, Wichita Falls, Tex.; s. Franz Phillip and Helen Theda (McNatt) H.; m. Maureen Petry, Nov. 17, 1978; children: Phillip, b. 1980, Megan, b. 1981; edn: BA, USC 1966; JD, Loyola Law Sch. 1969; admitted to Calif. State Bar 1970. Career: assoc. atty. Spray Gould & Bowers, Los Angeles 1970-76; partner Hartman Hosp Richard & Schlegel, Pasadena 1976--, currently, ofcr./ principal; dir. Golden State Sanwa Bank; judge pro tem, Los Angeles Superior Ct. 1980-83; mem: Am., Calif., Los Angeles Co. & Pasadena Bar Assns.; Calif. Mus. of Sci. & Industry (adv. bd.); So Calif. Profl. Golfers Assn. (adv. bd.) Crescenta Canada YMCA (dir.) Oakmont CopC; Jonathan Club, Los Angeles; Soc. of Bacchus; Republican; Catholic; rec: golf. Res: 5351 Vista Lejana, La Canada-Flintridge 91011 Ofc: Hartman, Hosp, Richard & Schlegel, A Profl Corp, 94 S Los Robles Pasadena 91101

HOTCHKIS, PRESTON, lawyer; b. 1893; edn: Univ. of Calif.; hon. LLD, Whittier Coll. (1957), Pepperdine Coll. (1955); m. Katharine Bixby S. 1923; two daus.; m. 2d Georgina Mage, Feb. 1981. Career: seaman to ensign US Navy, WWI, 1918-19; co-founder, dir., vice pres. Pacific Finance Corp. 1920; dir., exec. v.p. Pacific Indemnity Co. 1926; dir. exec. com. Consolidated Western Steel Corp. 1929; dir. pres. Central Business Properties Inc. 1929; dir. pres. vice-chmn. Founders Insurance Co. 1946; chmn. bd. Bixby Ranch Co. Los Angeles. Mem: pres. Calif. Alumni Assn. 1934-36; regent Univ. of Calif. 1934-36; War Manpower Board for S. Cal. 1942-45 US Rep. Econ & Social Council 1954-55; past mem. Hoover Commn. Task Force Fed. Lending agencies; Official Host, City of Los Angeles; chmn. Greater LA Area War Chest Campaign; current: trustee Mills Coll., Harvey Mudd Coll., Southwest Museum, Good Hope Med. Found. (v.p.); co-founder Hon. Dir. Past Pres. LA World Affairs Council; Japanese Philharmonic Soc., LA; mem. Mayors Adv. Com.; Girl Scouts of US Nat. Ad. Council; chmn. Local Agcy. Formation Comm. LA County; Southland Water Com.; pres. bd. Pepperdine Coll.; adv. council Univ. of Redlands; adv. council Calif. State Parks Found.; dir. Property Owners Tax Assn. of Calif. Inc.; dir. Metropolitan Water Dist. of So. Calif. 1978; trustee Calif. Alumni Found., Univ. Calif.; publs: History of Lost Angels Camp; clubs: California (LA), University (LA), Valley Hunt (Pasa.), Pacific Union (SF), Bohemian (SF), Twilight (SF);. Res: 1415 Circle Dr San Marino 91108 Ofc: 523 West Sixth St Los Angeles 90014

HOUGARDY, ROBERT GRAY, financial planner-consultant; b. Feb. 24, 1931, Henryetta, Okla.; s. Oscar Daniel and Evelyn Mildred (Gray) H.; m. Jeanne Grove, Dec. 28, 1957; children: Peter, b. 1959; Nevin, b. 1960; Elizabeth, b. 1961; Matthew, b. 1963; edn: USAF Univ. Ext. 1952-53; BBA, Woodbury Univ. 1955; UCLA Ext. 1957-58; CFP, Coll. for Fin. Plng. 1980. Career: mktg. assoc. Frito Co. 1955-58; mktg. analyst Frito Lay 1958-67; stockbroker Reynolds Securities- Mitchen Jones & Templeton 1967-79; fin. cons. Shearson American Express 1979-82; v.p./ asst. mgr. 1982--; tchr. mktg. San Jose State 1959, Cabrillo Coll. 1970-83; tchr. fin. & retirement plng., Dominican Hosp. Found. 1983; mem: Coll. for Fin. Plng.; Assn. of Fin. Plnrs.; Rotary; Soquel Dist. Unified Sch. Bd (pres. 1971-75); mil: t/sgt US Army Air Force 1947-53, Distng. Unit Citation w/ 3 Bronze Stars, Korean Svc., United Nations Svc.; Republican (Central Com.); Catholic; rec: tennis. Res: 133 Kenny Ct Santa Cruz 95065 Ofc: Shearson American Express, 555 Soquel Ave Santa Cruz 95062

HOUSMAN, LELAND B., cardiothoracic surgeon; b. Oct. 30, 1942, El Paso, Tx.; s. Henry Louis and Esther Ruth (Bleeker) H.; m. Carolyn Senkowsky, Feb. 7, 1974; children: Scott b. 1976, Keith b. 1978; edn: BS, Univ. of Texas 1963; MD, Baylor Coll. of Med. 1967. Career: internship Methodist Hosp., Houston 1978; residency (chief res. gen. surg. 1972-3) UC San Diego 1968-1973, (chief res. cardiopulmonary surg. 1974-5) Univ. Ore. 1973-1975; pvt. practice Cardiothoracic surgery, San Diego 1975--; instr. instr. Dept. Surg., Univ. Ore. Med. Sch. 1971; Dept. Surg. UCSD 1971-73, Div. Cardiac Surg. UCSD 1975-; honors: Instrument flying instr.; Baylor Coll. of Medicine Outstanding Intern Award 1967-8; mem: Fellow Am. Coll. of Cardiology, Fellow Am. Coll. of Chest Physicians, Fellow Am. Coll. of Surgeons, Soc. of Thoracic Surgeons, Fellow Internat. Coll. of Surgeons, Fellow Internat. Cardiovascula Soc., AMA, Albert Starr Cardiac Surg. Soc.; contbr. 43 publs. (1970-82) in Archives of Surgery, Surgery, Annals of Thoracic Surgery, J. of the Am. Med. Assn., etc.; mil: lt. cmdr. USNR 1963-77; Republican; Jewish; rec: tennis, flying. Res: 4878 Avion Way San Diego 92115 Ofc: 3400 Fourth Ave San Diego 92103

HOVINGH, JACK, nuclear engineer; b. May 5, 1935, Grand Rapids, Mich.; s. Peter and Hermina (Kraker) H.; children: Mary b. 1959, Mark b. 1960, dec. 1982; edn: BSE, mech. eng., Univ. of Mich. 1958, BSE, math, 1958; MS, engrg. sci., UC Berkeley 1973. Reg. Profl. Engr. Calif. Career: nuclear engr. Lawrence Livermore National Lab., Livermore 1958--; honors: Pi Tau Sigma 1957, Univ. Mich. Regents Alumni Award 1953, listed: Who's Who in Tech. Today - Energy, Who's Who in Frontier Sci. and Tech., Internat. Who's Who in Engineering; mem: American Nuclear Soc.; works: pioneer in design and analysis of both magnetically and inertially confined fusion reactors. Res: 4250 Muirwood Dr Pleasanton 94566 Ofc: Lawrence Livermore National Lab., POB 808, Livermore 94550

HOVLAND, CARL MICHAEL, lawyer; b. Dec. 26, 1941, Los Angeles, CA; s. Carl Oscar and Marie Kathryn (Toomey) Hovland; JD, Univ. Calif., Berkeley. 1967; BA, UC Berkeley, 1964; children: Ami Victoire, b. 1968; Carter J., b. 1973. Career: atty., assoc., Law Firm Betts & Loomis, 1967-69; atty., assoc., law firm Shield & Smith, 1969-71; atty., partner, Law Firm, Shield & Smith, 1972-73; atty., assoc., Law Firm, Peacock & Sullivan, 1975-80; atty., partner, Law Offices Harold Syllivan, 1975-80; also judge pro tem., L.A. Municipal Ct.; arbitrator, Amer. Arbitration Assn., 1975--; arbitrator, L.A. Superior Ct., 1973--; Recipient: Cert. of Recog. as Trial Lawyer, Negligence and Product Liability Specialist, Calif. Trial Lawyers Assn., 1978. Mem.: Amer. Bd. Trial Advocates, rank of Adv., 1972--; Amer. Bar Assn., 1967--; Calif. Bar Assn., 1967--; Calif. Trial Lawyers Assn.; L.A. Trial Lawyers Assn.; Amer. Trial Lawyers Assn. Republican. Catholic. Rec.: tennis, horseback riding, fishing, skiing, boating. Res.: 24 Cinchring Rd., Rolling Hills 90274; Office: Carl Hovland, No. 1 Manchester Blvd., Suite 500, Inglewood 90301.

HOWARD, DUNCAN LENT, real estate co. president; b Sept. 4, 1940, San Francisco; s. Lot Duncan, Jr. and Elizabeth (Lent) H.; m. Madeline Ann Domning (dec. 1983), June 18, 1967; children: Lent b. 1968, Lyman b. 1969; edn: AA, Pre-law, San Francisco City Coll. 1968; BA, govt., Univ. of S.F. 1970; Calif. lic. R.E. Broker, Realtor. Career: gen. supt. George Howard Trucking & Excavating Co., Marin Co. 1962-65; asst. to sales mgr. Engs Motor Truck Co., Hegenberger Rd, Oakland 1965-67; real estate sales, resdtl., Coldwell Banker & Co., S.F. 1971-72; R.E. sales/mgr. S.F. office, W. Bruce Shafer & Co., Realtors 1972-73; asst. to the pres. Cushman & Wakefield of Calif., S.F. 1973-76; exec. v.p., chief adminstrv. fin. and ops. ofcr. Owen Ent. Inc. (R.E. Dev. and Fin.), S.F. 1978-80; owner/pres. Duncan Howard Co., Real Estate 1976--; mem. Nat. Adv. Council Small Bus. Adminstrn. (subcoms. on Women in Bus., Taxation) 1981-83; fund raiser for Big Brothers, Boy Scouts of Am., United Way (chmn. 1979), Burks Sch. of S.F.; candidate for US Congress 1983 (5th Congl. Dist. of S.F.); mem: S.F. Chamber of Commerce (Crime Prev. Com.); Nat., Calif. Assns. of Realtors, S.F. Bd. of Realtors; Cow Hollow Homeowners Assn. (bd. dirs.); Assocs. of Childrens Hosp. of S.F. (past pres.); adv. bd. chmn. Inst. of Neurobehav. Scis. of Frank Gerbode Resrch. Found.; bd. dirs. S.F. Zoo Soc.; pres. St. Luke's Sch.; bd. chmn. Cathedral Sch. for Boys; Republican (S.F. Central Com.; S.F. Fin. Com.; campaign wkr.); Episcopal; rec: jog, tropical fish, fishing, duck hunting. Res: 65 Normandie Terrace San Francisco 94115 Ofc: Duncan Howard Co. 505 Sansome St, Ste 1502, San Francisco 94111

HOWARD, JAMES EDWARD, software co. president; b. July 18, 1942, Los Angeles; s. John Andrew and Mary Alice (Vare) H.; children: John, b. 1966, Cynthia, b. 1968, Cheryl, b. 1971, Christine, b. 1975; edn: PhD, UCLA, 1969. Career: engr./ tech. & program mgmt. in antenna and radar R&D, Hughes Aircraft Co., Culver City 1964-77; sr. mem. corp. staff (mng. R&D contracts) Mark Resources, Marina Del Rel 1977-81; pres./founder Howard Software Svcs. (devel., mktg. fin. software for personal computers), La Jolla 1981--; publs: num. tech. papers on radar and adaptive antennas (e.g. IEEE Trans.) 1968-, devel. computer software & manuals (pub. HowardSoft) 1968-; rec: classic cars, jazz. Ofc: HowardSoft, 8008 Girard Ave, Ste. 310, La Jolla 92037

HOWARD, MURRAY, realty co. president; b. July 25, 1914, Los Angeles; s. George A.J. and Mabel (Murray) H.; edn: BS, UCLA 1939; lic. pub. acct. Career: mgr. Foundries, Inc. 1945-59; pres./ chmn. bd. Howard Mach. Prods., Inc. 1949-63; chmn. bd. Murray Howard Realty, Inc. 1961-62; pres./ chmn. bd. 1962--; pres./ chmn. bd. Ranch Sales, Inc. 1968--; pres./ chmn. bd. Murray Howard Devel., Inc. 1969--; bd. dirs. Shur-Lok Corp. 1969--; dir. Airshippers Pub. Corp., La Brea Realty & Devel. Co.; mem: Gov. Warren's Calif. Minority Commn.; Nat. Assn. Cost Accts. (past v.p./ dir.); Nat. Assn. Mfrs.; Delta Tau Delta. Res: 3771 Lockland Dr Los Angeles 90008 Ofc: 1605 W Olympic Blvd, Ste 404, Los Angeles 90015

HOWE, ROBERT BRUCE, mechanical engineer; b. Feb. 15, 1955, Tacoma, Wash.; s. Douglas Orville and Marion Dorothy (Osgood) H.; m. Susan E. Snyder, Dec. 18, 1977; edn: BS, Wash. State Univ. 1978; Reg. Profl. Engr., Calif. 1982. Career: prodn. eng. Hewlett- Packard Co., Palo Alto 1978-80; mech./ optical design engr. Optimetrix, Mt. View 1980-82; mgr./ devel. engr. Shugart Assoc., Santa Clara 1982-83; mech. design engr./ supvr. InSystems, San Jose 1983--; cons. engr. Optimetrix 1982; tutor, Mt. View H.S. 1978-79; mem: ASME; Republican; rec: carpentry, shooting. Res: 691 High Glen Dr San Jose 95133e Ofc: InSystems, 1972 Concours Dr San Jose 95131

HOWELL, RICHARD JAMES, aerospace engineer; b. Jan. 9, 1935, San Bernardino; s. Weldon Olin and Barbara May (Mulligan) H.; div.; 1 son, Wesley, b. 1958; edn: AA, Mt. San Antonio Coll. 1965; BS, mech. eng., West Coast Univ. 1974, BS, elec. eng., 1974. Career: elec. engr. General Dynamics, Pomona 1959-73; elec. engr. USN, Corona 1974-75; elec. engr. Metron Corp., Upland 1975-78; sys. analyst Chemsult A.G., Dhahran, Saudia Arabia 1978-79; sys. engr. TRW, Inc., Norton AFB, San Bernardino 1980--; pres. Howell Eng. Co., Bryn Mawr 1963--; awards: Svc. Awd., asst. football coach, City of Chino Pop Warner Football Assn. 1969; mem: Soc. of Automotive Engrs.; Am. Soc. Mech. Engrs.; The Fibonacci Assn.; donor of ancient Arabian antiquities to San Bernardino Co. Mus., UCLA Dept. Geology, Big Bear Valley Hist. Soc.; publs: num. original works in math. & eng. mathematics; mil: sgt. USAF 1955-59, GCM, Nat. Defense Svc., Air Force Longivity Svc.; Democrat; Presbyterian; rec: high performance Pontiac automotive engineering. Res: 1125 Pine Ave, Apt 6B, Redlands 92373 Ofc: TRW, Inc., 953/2433 Norton AFB, San Bernardino 92409

HOWES, BENJAMIN DURWARD, IV, dentist; b. Jan. 28, 1957, Pasadena; s. Benjamin D., III and Mary Cynthia (Marble) H.; edn: AB, USC 1979; BS, 1981; DDS, 1983. Career: dentist, Newport Beach 1983--; instr. cardiopulmonary resuscitation, USC Dept. of Anesthesia & Medicine; mem: Am. & Calif. Dental Assns.; Acad. of Gen. Dentistry; Valley Hunt Club; Jonathan Club; Kappa Alpha Order; research: area of temporal mandibular joint & muscle dysfunction syndrome; Republican; Episcopal; rec: golf, sailing, skiing. Res: 1018 E Balboa Blvd Balboa 92661

HOWORTH, BEA BORGES, marketing and public relations executive; b. Feb. 18, 1936, Teaneck, NJ; d. Charles and Ruth Robinson (Carter) Borges; m. David Howorth (ednl. film prod. Golden Coast Films, Santa Barbara), May 6, 1967; edn: BS, home ec./fashion design, Skidmore Coll. 1953; grad. wk. UC Santa Barbara 1960-61; MS, Edn. Adminstrn., Pepperdine Univ. 1980; Calif. Comm. Coll. tchr. cred. (life); CMD (Cert. Mktg. Dir.), Internat. Council of Shopping Ctrs. 1973. Career: costume dept. for Rockettes and Corps de Ballet, Radio City Music Hall, NYC 1954; designer Dilks Designs, Bermuda 1955-57; Fashion Ofc. Bonwit Teller, Fifth Ave., NY 1958; fashion coord. H. Liebes, San Francisco 1959, with Sunset Mag. advt. ofc. 1960-61; exec. dir. Downtown Santa Barbara Retail Merchants Assn. 1964-66; pub. rels. staff Sears, Roebuck & Co. Pac. Coast Area, L.A. 1966-67; opened La Cumbre Plaza regl. shopping ctr. in Santa Barbara for Ernest W. Hahn Inc., mktg. dir./gen. mgr. until 1976, transf. to Corp. Information, Hahn Corp. Hdqtrs., L.A. 1976, worked on new shopping center openings throughout US, then mktg. dir. University Towne Centre, La Jolla; currently dir. mktg./pub. rels. (Hahn's newest ctr.) Palm Desert Town Center, Palm Desert; instr. S.B. Comm. Coll. 1973-81; honors: S.B. Advt. Woman of Year 1969, recogn. Am. Advt. Fedn., award for best use of color in newspaper advt. 1967; mem: Am. Mktg. assn., Internat. Council of Shopping Centers, So. Calif. Mktg. Dirs. Assn., Desert Advt. Club, (past mem. San Diego Ad Club, past bd. mem. S.B. Ad Club); Phi Delta Kappa (edn. hon.); Palm Desert CofC (bd. dirs. 1984); author: Fashion Show Handbook (ICSC 1971), writer ednl. scripts for Golden Coast Films, S.B. 1973-; Republican; Episcopal; rec: sailing, collect ship models. Res: 74-952 Chateau Cir Palm Desert 92260 Ofc: Palm Desert Town Center, Mgmt. Ofc. 72-840 Hwy 111 Palm Desert 92260

HOY, MARJORIE ANN, professor of entomology; b. May 19, 1941, Kansas City, Ks.; d. Dayton Junior and Marjorie Jean (Acker) Wolf; m. James Hoy, Dec. 22, 1961; 1 son: Benjamin, b. 1970; edn: AB, Univ. of Ks. 1963; MS, UC Berkeley 1966; PhD, 1972. Career: instr. Fresno State Univ. Dept. Biology 1972; research entomologist Conn. Agric. Exptl. Sta., New Haven, Ct. 1973-75; research entomologist US Forest Svc., Hamden, Ct. 1975-76; asst. prof. Dept. Entomology, UC Berkeley 1976-80; assoc. prof. 1980-82; prof. 1982--; chair Sci. Adv. Panel, Gypsy Moth Eradication, Calif. Dept. Food & Agric.; honors: Phi Beta Kappa; NSF Grad. Fellowship; NIH trainee; visiting prof., Hewbrew Univ.; vis. scientist, DSIR, New Zealand; mem: Entomological Soc. of AM.; Acarology Soc. of Am.; Internat. Orgn. for Biological Control; AAAS; Sigma Xi; publs: editor 3 books, approx. 85 sci. papers and arts. in tech. journs. and semipopular publs.; rec: gardening, hiking, piano. Res: 1004 Grizzly Peak Blvd Berkeley 94708 Ofc: Univ. of California, 201 Wellman Hall, Dept. Entomology, Berkeley 94720

HOYT, JACK W., university professor; b. Oct. 19, 1922, Chgo.; s. Claire A. and Fleta (Wheeler) Hoyt; edn: BS, Ill. Inst. of Tech., 1944, MS, UCLA, 1952, PhD, 1962; m. Helen Erickson, Dec. 27, 1945; chil: John, b. 1948, Katheryn, b. 1952, Annette, b. 1959, Denise, b. 1964; career: engineer, National Advisory Com. on Aeronautics, Cleveland, Oh. 1944-48; engr., Naval Ocean Systems Center, San Diego 1948-79; prof. of mechanical engring., US Naval Acad., Annapolis 1976-77, Rutgers Univ. 1979-81, San Diego State Univ. 1981--; awards: Freeman Scholar, ASME, 1971; Gilbert Curl Award, USN, 1975; mem: ASME, NY Acad of Scis., Soc. of Naval Architects and Marine Engrs.; publs: num. technical pubs. in hydrodynamics; rec: jogging, woodworking, stamps; res: 4694 Lisann St., San Diego 92117 ofc: San Diego State Univ., San Diego 92182-0191.

HSIU, HWEI-CHIH, architectural/environmental planning co. executive; b. Sept. 7, 1927, Nanking, China, nat. 1973; s. Yana and Qualan (Chu) H.; m. Julia, Dec. 17, 1960; children: Patricia, b. 1961; Helen, b. 1964; Thomas, b. 1970; edn: BS, Taiwan Coll. of Eng. 1953; M.Arch., Univ. of Ill. Grad. Sch. 1960; lic. contractor, A & B, Calif. Career: chief physical plnng. W.L. Pereira & Assoc., Los Angeles 1960-65; prin. eng. chief of community plnng. Bechtel Corp., L.A. 1965-70; dir. plnng. AVCO Comm. Devel., Inc. 1970-73; founder/ pres. HCH & Assoc. 1973-; chmn. bd., San Diego 1983--; urban devel. advsr. to V.P. of the Repub. of China 1969; mem: Nat. Assn. of Env. Profls.; The Urban Land Inst.; Am. Plnng. Assn.; UCSD Chancellors Assocs.; Zoological Soc. of S.D.; Zoo Boosters; Republican; rec: photog. Res: 17218 Cloudcroft Dr Poway 92064 Ofc: HCH & Assoc., 4877 Viewridge Ave San Diego 92123

HU, STEVE SENG-CHIU, research executive/ college president; b. Mar. 16, 1924, Yangchou, Kiangsu Province, China; s. Yubin and Shuchang (Lee) H.; m. Lily Li-wan Liu; children: April, b. 1962; Yendo, b. 1963; Victor, b. 1964; edn: BS, Chiao-Tung Univ., Shanghai 1941; MS, Rensselaer Polytech. Inst. 1942, DSc, Mass. Inst. of Tech. 1942. Career: tech. dir. Douglas Aircraft's China Aircraft/ China Motor Pgms., Calif. & NJ 1943-48; tech. dir. Kelley Eng. Co., NY & Ariz. 1949-54; sys. engr./ meteorological spec. RCA Corp., Ariz. 1955-58; cons. gas dynamics Aerojet Gen. Corp. 1958-69; research scientist Jet Propulsion Lab., Calif. Inst. Tech. 1960-61; tech. dir. Northrop Corp. & Northrop Space Labs., Ala. 1961-72; pres. Univ. of Am. United Research Inst., and Am. Technical College, Calif. & Taiwan 1973--; dir. Century Research,

Inc., Gardena 1973--; nat. dir./ exec. v.p. Am. Astronautical Soc., Wash. DC 1963-71; ed. AAS Proceedings of Missiles & Aerospace Vehicle Scis.; prof., part- time, Univ. Ariz. 1957-58, USC 1959-63, 1968-71; Univ. of Ala. 1963-68; Auburn Univ. 1964-66; CSU 1968-71; awards: Salisbury Prize & Sloan Prize, M.I.T. 1942; Merit. Cert. & cash awd., Commn. of Aeronautical Affairs, Repub. of China 1945; Merit Cert. & cash awd. for sci. achiev. & dynamic ldrshp., Northrop/ NASA Space Labs. 1966; mem: Am. Astronautical Soc.; Inst. of Aero. & Astro.; Nat. Assn. of Tech. Schs.; works: tech. dir. Northrop/ NASA Electronic Guidance Sys. for Lunar Landing Vehicle Pgms. 1963-68; author: Theory of Guidance/ Control and Optimization for Tectical/ Strategic Missiles and Aerospace Vehicles, pub. Univ. of Ala./ Century Research, Inc. 1969, 73; rec: opera music, dancing, travel. Res: 19635 S Vermont Ave Gardena 90247

HUANG, CARL KUO-CHANG, hotel owner; b. Sept. 22, 1937, Taiwan, Republic of China; s. Tien Hsi and Yon Pong Huang; m. Show China, Jan. 24, 1964; children: James, b. 1966; Jane, b. 1968; edn: BA, Nat. Taiwan Normal Univ. 1962; MA, 1970; MA, UCAL 1971. Career: primary sch. tchr., Taiwan 1955-57; H.S. tchr., Taiwan 1965-67; coll. instr., Taiwan 1965-67; owner Manhattan Motel, Glendale 1975-81; opr. Glendale Motel 1978-81; owner Town House Motel, Van Nuys 1978 79; mng. partner New Orlean Hotel 1979, Joined franchise of Travelodge, sole owner Inglewood Airport Travelodge 1981--; mem. bd. First Bank of Inglewood (Orgn.); mem: Inglewood CofC; Westchester/ LAX CofC; Calif. Hotel & Motel Assn.; LA Chinatown Lion Club; publs: Dr. Sun Yat Sen' Theory of Political Power, 1970; From Man to Class; Karl Marx's Key Idea 1972; rec: writing. Res: 1508 E Orange Grove Glendale 91025 Ofc: Inglewood Airport Travelodge, 3900 W Century Blvd Inglewood 90303

HUANG, DAVID MAO-CHING, lawyer; b. Dec. 23, 1940, Tainan, Taiwan, R.O.C.; s. Shin-Bou and Shih-Chih (Lai) H.; m. Ben-Fang, Mar. 28, 1970; children: Joanne, b. 1976; Karin, b. 1979; edn: LLB, Soochow Univ. 1963; LLM, Nat. Taiwan Univ. 1969; MCL, Univ. of Wash. 1971; PhD, 1975; admitted to Calif. State Bar 1979. Career: legal asst. Graham & James, San Francisco 1975-76; assoc. prof. of law Soochow Univ., Taipei, Taiwan, R.O.C. 1976-78; atty. at law, Cerritos, Ca. 1979--; awards: Ford Found. Fellowship 1970-71; mem: Am., Calif. & Los Angeles Co. Bar Assns.; So. Calif. Chinese Lawyers Assn.; Chinese Bus. Assn., Inc. (dir. 1983); publs: Maritime Liens in the Republic of China, Journ. of Maritime Law & Commerce Vol. 8, 1977; mil: lt. Chinese ROTC 1963-64; Christian; rec: music, tennis, travel. Res: 17417 Mapes Ave Cerritos 90701 Ofc: Law Ofcs. of David Huang, 12140 Artesia Blvd, Ste 104, Cerritos 90701

HUBBARD, CHARLES RONALD, corporate programs executive; b. Feb. 4, 1933, Weaver, Ala.; s. John Duncan and Athy Pauling (Lusk) H.; m. Betty McKieroy, Dec. 29, 1951; 1 son: Charles Ronald II, b. 1957; edn: BSEE, Univ. of Ala. 1960. Career: engr./ mktg. & pgm. mgr. Sperry Corp., Huntsville, Ala., 1960-71; sect. head 1971-74; sr. staff engr. Honeywell, Inc., Clearwater, Fla. 1974-76, mng. 1976-79; chief engr., Honeywell, Inc., W. Covina, Calif. 1979-82, assoc. dir. eng. 1982-84, assoc. dir. Advanced Products, 1984--; dir. S&H Office Supplies, Huntsville, Ala. 1972-74, West Covina, Calif. 1984-; mem: IEEE (Govt. Rels. Com.; Controls Gp.); publs: Saturn V/ Apollo and Beyond, Am. Astronautical Soc., 1967; mil: s/sgt. USAF 1953-57; Methodist; rec: jogging, golf. Res: 5460 Willowick Cir Anaheim 92807 Ofc: Honeywell, Inc., 1200 E San Bernardino Rd, West Covina 91790

HUBBARD, DAVID ALLAN, clergyman, educator; b. Apr. 8, 1928, Stockton; s. John King and Helena (White) H.; m. Ruth Doyal, Aug. 12, 1949; 1 dau. Mary Ruth b. 1955; edn: BA, Westmont Coll. 1949; BD, Fuller Theol. Sem. 1952, Th.M, 1954; PhD, St. Andrews Univ., Scotland 1957; DD (hon.), John Brown Univ. 1975; LHD (hon.), Rockford Coll. 1975; Ordained to ministry, Conservative Baptist Assn. 1952. Career: Interim pastor Montecito Comm. Ch. 1960-62; asst. prof., chmn. Dept. Biblical Studies and Philosophy, Westmont Coll. 1957-63; spkr., The Joyful Sound, an internat. radio bdcst. 1969-80; exec. v.p. Fuller Evangelistic Assn. 1969--; pres./prof. Old Testament, Fuller Theol. Sem. 1963--; lectr. Loma Linda Univ. 1982; Staley lectr. Messiah Coll. (Grantham, Pa.) 1982; Tipple lectr. Drew Univ. (Madison, NJ) 1979, E.T. Earl lectr. Pacific Sch. of Religion (Berkeley) 1978; vis. lectr. num. univs., sems. 1955-; mem: Am. Acad. of Religion & Soc. of Biblical Literature, Inst. for Biblical Research, Nat. Assn. of Profs. of Hebrew, Soc. for Old Testament Study, Evangelical Book Club (adv. bd.), Assn. of Governing Bds. (bd. govs.), Pioneer Ministries Inc. (bd. of ref.), Cong. on Biblical Exposition (coms. of ref.), The Ministers' Permanent Library, Word Inc. (edtl. bd.), Assn. of Theol. Schs. in US and Can. (exec. com.; pres. 1976-8), Gen. Council Latin America Mission Inc., Evangelicals for Soc. Action (nat. adv. bd.), Religious Book Club; mem. Town Hall of Calif., Twilight Club of Pasadena, Pasa. Urban Coalition (chmn. 1968-71), Univ. Club of Pasa., Rotary Club of Pasa. (hon.); author: Beyond Futility (Eerdmans 1976); Chinese Ed. 1981, Living Spring Publs., translated by Silas Chan; Book of James: Wisdom that Works (Word, 1980); Colossians Speaks to the Sickness of Our Time (Word, 1976); num. other publs.; Am. Baptist. Res: 1777 La Cresta Dr Pasadena 91103 Ofc: Fuller Theological Seminary, 135 N. Oakland Ave Pasadena 91101

HUBER, ELBERT WILLIAM (Bud), aerospace co. executive; b. Aug. 8, 1944, Austin, Tex.; s. Elbert Wm., Sr. and Maxine Audrey (Hill) H.; edn: BA, Univ. of Tex., Austin 1968; MA (Nat. Security Affairs), US Naval Postgrad. Sch. 1975. Career: pgmr. analyst Am. Gen. Life Ins. 1962-64; submarine svc., restricted line (intelligence), USN 1968-79; mgr. data network eng. corp. staff

Hughes Aircraft Co., Long Beach; splst. in CCITT X.25 packet switched data comm. field; owner pvt. computer- related consulting svc.; mem: Assn. for Computing Machinery; IEEE; Whitman Brooks Found.; publs: Hughes Aircraft Experiences in X.25 Packet Switching, IEEE 4/83; mil: Lcdr USN 1968-79; rec: swimming. Res: 149 Quincy Ave Long Beach 90803 Ofc: Hughes Aircraft Co., POB 9399 Long Beach 90810

HUBER, JAMES EDWIN, administrative services executive/ automotive importer; b. Nov. 24, 1940, Rochester, NY; s. George Leadley and Fern Helen (Loucks) H.; m. Valerie Anderson, July 13, 1968; edn: BS, CSU Los Angeles 1972. Career: with Toyota Motor Sales, USA, Inc. 1972--: acct. 1972-74; fin. analyst Vehicle Pgms. 1974-76; adminstr. Vehicle Pgms. 1976-77; import svcs. mgr. 1977-79; nat. admin. svcs. mgr. 1979-82; nat. purchasing & admin. svcs. mgr. 1982--; Corp. Donations Com. mem. 1982-; Corp. Hdqtrs. Plng. Task Force, telecommun. chmn. 1980-82; mem: Telecomm. Assn.; local political action gps.; mil: E-5 US Coast Guard Reserve 1963-69; Republican; Catholic; rec: boating, fishing, hunting. Res: 4380 Cerritos Ave Long Beach 90807 Ofc: Toyota Motor Sales, U.S.A., Inc., 19001 S. Western Ave Torrance 90509

HUBERMAN, BERNARD ABEL, physicist; b. Nov. 7, 1943, Buenos Aires, Argentina; s. Leon and Sara (Jasovich) H.; m. Caryn Yasowitz, Sept. 20, 1970; children: Lara, Andrew; edn: M.Phys., Univ. of Buenos Aires 1966; PhD, Univ. of Penn. 1971, D.Phil., 1971. Career: research staff Xerox Palo Alto Research Ctr. 1971-82; visiting scientist Inst. Laue, Lanpwin, Frances 1976; lectr. Dept. Applied Physics Stanford Univ. 1975-80; cons. prof. 1980--; vis. prof. Univ. of Paris, Francee 1981; principal scientist Xerox Palo Alto Research Ctr. 1982--; fellow, Am. Physical Soc. 1981; trustee Aspen Ctr. for Physics 1981-; fellow Japan Soc. for the Promotion of Sci. 1982; works: 70 orig. publs. in theoretical physics; invented self-repairing adaptive parallel computer, 1983, pat. pend. Res: 4152 Georgia Ave Palo Alto 94306 Ofc: Xerox Palo Alto Research Center, Palo Alto 94304

HUBERT, EARL GUS, business owner; b. Sept. 7, 1928, Mitchell, S.Dak.; s. Carl Frederick and Clara Amelia (Tremaine) H.; m. Diane Uidla Federkiewicz, July 4, 1974; 1 son, Steven, b. 1954; edn: BS, Dakota Wesleyan Univ. 1950; MA, Univ. So. Dakota 1957; postgrad. wk. USC 1960-63. Career: asst. bacteriologist Wichita Gen. Hosp., Wichita Falls, Tex. 1957-58; research microbiologist Veterans Admin. Ctr., Los Angeles 1958-72; prodn. mgr. Cal Labs, No. Hollywood 1972-78; owner Flower World Retail Shop, Canoga Park 1978-81; owner Earl G. Hubert Ins. Agency, Canoga Park 1981--; ed. The Southern California Microbiology, Newspaper of Am. Soc. Microbiology, So. Calif. Br. 1968-72; mem: Am. Soc. Microbiology (So. Calif. br.); Canoga Park CofC; Kiwanis, Canoga Park; Elks; coauthor. 30 scientific papers on research in pyelonephritis; contbr. to book, Microbial Protoplasts, Spheroplasts & L-Forms; mil: lt. j.g. USN 1950 55; Protestant, rec. welding, art, flying. Res: 9855 Burnet Ave Sepulveda 91343 Ofc: Earl G. Hubert Insurance, 21201 Victory Blvd, Ste 125, Canoga Park 91303

HUBKA, DALE LEWIS, company president; b. Jan. 3, 1949, Riverside; s. Melvin Dale and Shirley Hazel Hubka; m. Sandra Jean, Apr. 13, 1972; 1 son, Derek, b. 1971; edn: electronics tech., USN Sch. 1968; Ohlone Coll. 1972-73. Career: founder Fuseco as ptnrship with wife, 1975, incorporated in 1979, estab. 2nd location, Seattle, Wash. 1980, pres. Fusecom, Inc. (wholesale distbr. fuses and related hardware) 1979--; cons. to mfrs. (Bussmann, Littelfuse, etc.) on mktg. trends & products --; awards: Bachelor of Fuseology, Littelfuse; Overcurrent Protection, Reliance Electronic Marketing & Sales, Bussmann; mem: EAC, S.F. Bay area; CofC (Mem. Com.); mil: E-4, USN, Vietnam; Republican; rec: boating, camping, building radio controlled equipment. Res: 4802 South Point Byron 94514 Ofc: Fusecom, Inc., 3601 Edison Way Fremont 94538

HUDSON, DAVID LEE, accountant; b. Apr. 29, 1956, Greenville, SC; s. David Earl and Shirley Marguerite (Hayward) H.; m. Mari, July 26, 1980; edn: BSBA, cum laude, Biola Univ. 1980; MBA Program, CSU Long Beach 1983-; CPA, Calif. 1982. Career: staff acct. Fox & Co., CPAs, Los Angeles, Newport 1980-82; internal auditor, UCLA, Los Angeles 1982-83; internal auditor, Burlington Northern Air Freight, Inc., (subsidiary of the Pittston Co.), Irvine 1983--; tchg. asst. auditing couse Biola Univ., La Mirada 1982-83; Fin. Com. Granada Hght. Friends Ch. 1982-; mem: Am. Inst. CPAs; Calif. Soc. CPAs; INst. of Internal Auditors, Inc.; Accts. Adv. Com., Assemblyman Frank Hill, 52nd Assembly Dist. Calif. Legislature; Republican; Evangelical; rec: skiing, running, tennis. Res: 15325 Santa Gertrudes Ave, J202, La Mirada 90638 Ofc: Burlington Northern Air Freight, Inc., 18200 Von Karman Ave Irvine 92715

HUDSON, KEITH GRAHAM, manufacturing management specialist; b. Aug. 10, 1944, Birmingham, England, nat. 1981; s. George Ernest and Winifred G. (Stokes) H.; div.; children: Kevin, b. 1967; Dean, b. 1970; edn: BSC, mech. & prodn. eng., Bromsgrove Tech. Coll., England 1965; BSC, indsl. mgmt., Univ. of Ottowa, Canada 1974. Career: mgr. indsl. eng. Huyck Canada, Arnprior, Ontario 1969-74; mgr. mfg. Atco, Alberta 1974-77; pres. M.C.I., Calgary, Alberta 1977-80; pres. Produtec Corp. (productivity & efficiency consulting svc. for mfg. cos.) 1980--; mem: Am. Inst. Indsl. Engrs. (pres. 1983); rec: boating. Res: 1715 Strand Way, B6, Coronado 92118 Ofc: Produtec Corp., 8333 Clairemont Mesa Blvd, Ste 200, San Diego 92111

HUDSON, MICHAEL CRAIG, civil engineer; b. Mar. 20, 1951, Lynwood; s. John William and Grace Carlene (Wilde) H.; m. Marina Harris, Feb. 14, 1973; children: Christina, b. 1975; Michael, b. 1976; John, b. 1978; edn: BSCE, Calif.

Polytech. Univ. 1974; Reg. Civil Engr., Calif. 1977. Career: civil engr. asst. Los Angeles Co. Flood Control Dist., Los Angeles 1974-78; reg. engr. A S L Consulting Engrs., Pasadena 1978-82; proj. engr. 1982--; mem: Am. Soc. Civil Engrs.; Nat. Soc. Profl. Engrs.; Nat. Rifle Assn. of Am.; Republican; Latter-day Saints; rec: hunting, trap shooting, bicycling. Res: 3148 S Eighth Ave Arcadia 91006 Ofc: A S L Consulting Engineers, 3280 E Foothill Blvd, Ste 160, Pasadena 91107

HUDSPETH, JOHN BERNAL, architect; b. Nov. 28, 1912, Oakland; s. Charles Ernest and Orraetta (Higgins) H.; m. Francis Birbeck, Oct. 23, 1934; 1 son: David Kent, b. 1943; edn: AB, UC Berkeley 1936. Career: asst. architect Edwin Lewis Snyder, Arch., Berkeley 1932-33; asst. to arch. Frederick L.R. Confer, Arch., Berkeley 1933-36; architl. draftsman Warren C. Perry, Archit., San Francisco 1937; chief arch./ asst. plant mgr. Alameda Shipyard of the United Engring. Co., Ltd. 1942-45; civil engr. (structural) County of San Mateo, Redwood City 1971-75; arch.. 1976-82; chief architect John B. Hudspeth, Arch., Berkeley 1937-42, Oakland 1945-71, Berkeley 1981--; mem. Chi Psi frat.; archtl. works: Shipyard facilities, United Eng. Co., Ltd., Alameda & S.F. 1942-45; Burbank Sch. and John Swett Sch., Oakland 1950; Inst. of Transp. & Traffic Eng., UC Richmond Field Sta. 1952; Olinda Sch., Olinda, Contra Costa Co. 1957; Grass Valley Sch., Oakland 1957; Brekeley Albany Municipal Ct. Bldg., Berkeley 1958; White Sch. Union City 1960; Intensive Care Unit, Oak Knoll Naval Hosp. 1960; Fire House 13, Oakland 1961; El Ranch Verde Sch., Union City 1963; Galbraith Golf Club House, Oakland 1966; Chi Psi Lodge, UC Berkeley 1968; admin. bldg., library and the soils and pavements testing labs., UC Richmond; Republican; Christian; rec: golf, painting. Address: 548 Wildcat Canyon Rd Berkeley 94708

HUFF, MADELEINE ANDREE, insurance broker; b. Apr. 3, 1932, Nouatre, France, nat. 1964; d. Andre Edouard and Yvonne (Debout) Lassagne; m. Isaac Wilford Huff, Jr. July 20, 1959; 1 dau. Danielle Yvonne b. 1953; edn: C.A.P. (clerical), Ecole Pigier, 1950; desig. translator from Spanish lang., from English lang., Soc. Pour La Propagation des Langues Vivantes 1950; Calif. lic. Gen. Insurance Broker 1964. Career: D.AC for Am. Govt. in France, 1954-59; secty. R.W.Parker, Salinas, Ca. 1959-64; ptnr. Parker & Huff Ins. Agcy., Salinas 1964-66, sole owner 1966-72; owner investment props., Salinas 1972-; sec.treas. Independent Ins. Agents Assn. Salinas 1964-68; v.p. Alisal CofC 1968; awards: AUS War Office awards (2) 1958; mem. 10-10 Travel Club, Am. Legion, VFW Aux.; Republican; Catholic; rec: music, gourmet cooking, travel. Res: 19045 Buena Lane Salinas 93908

HUGHES, ELAINE M., clinical social worker; b. Dec. 29, 1925, Seattle, Wash.; d. Arthur Thorval and Magda (Michaelsen) Kjellmann; m. Hugh Hughes, May 5, 1972; edn: AA, Imperial Valley Coll. 1964; BA, CSU San Diego 1966; MSW, USC 1977; LCSW, Calif. Career: adoption wkr. Imperial Co. Adptn. Agcy., El Centro 1966-68, Orange Co. Adptn. Agcy., Santa Ana 1968-; clin. soc. wkr. Child Health, Orange Co. Public Health, 1977-79; childrens svc. wkr. Dept. Pub. Soc. Svcs., Los Angeles Co. 1980-81; family counselor US Navy, Long Bch. 1981-82; chief of svcs. Family Service, USMC, El Toro 1983--; hosp. cons., lic. clin. soc. wkr. in pvt. practice; mem. Nat. Assn. Soc. Wkrs, Acad. of Cert. Soc. Wkrs.; Lutheran. Ofc: USMC Air Station, Bldg 58, El Toro 92709

HUGHES, RALPH ELSTO, manufactured homes dealer; b. Mar. 5, 1919, Donavon, Ill.; s. John Ralph and Agnes Maria (Emmert) H.; m. Margery Brown, Mar. 5, 1981; children: Ralph E., Jr., Sidney Dianne, Fredrick E., and Kenneth E.; edn: forestry, Univ. of Idaho 1939; sci., Purdue Univ. 1942. Career: supply chief USMC (20 yrs.); celrk US Post Ofc. (3 yrs.); sales, sales mgr., area mgr., dealer/ owner Mesa Mobile Homes, Barstow & Victorville; mem: Calif. Manufactured Homes Assn.; Masons (Master); mil: m/ sgt. USMC 1940-63; Republican; Protestant; rec: ranching in Hunkley. Res: 15567 Kasota Rd Apple Valley 92307 Ofc: Mesa Mobile Home, 31047 E Main St Barstow 92311

HUI, HELEN YUEN HING, lawyer; b. Jan. 3, 1944, Hong Kong; edn: BA, Smith Coll. 1967; MSW Gerontology Fellowship, UC Berkeley 1970; JD, UC Hastings Coll. of Law 1974. Career: Student Service asst. S.F. Chinatown - North Beach English Language Ctr., 1967-68; instr. Sociol. Dept. S.F. City Coll. 1970-71; summer intern S.F. ACLU Legal Dept. 1973; law clk. Hardesty & Lau, S.F. 1973-74, atty. assoc. 1975-77; ptnr. Lau & Lee, Attys. at Law, S.F. 1977-9; ptnr. Lee & Hui, Attys. at Law, S.F. 1979--; civic vol.: editl. staff/dir. East/West Chinese Am. Journal; dir. Chinese Newcomers Service Ctr. 1977-; dir. North East Medical Service 1977-; fmr. dir. Hastings Childcare Ctr. (1980-1), SF Chinatown YWCA (1970-2); mem. Am. Bar Assn., Am. Immigration Lawyers Assn., Asian Am. Bar Assn. of Greater Bay Area, Bar Assn. of S.F. Ofc: Lee and Hui, 300 Montgomery St, Ste 1000, San Francisco 94104

HUI, JOHN SHUI-LUN, real estate developer/broker; b. May 7, 1955, Hong Kong; s. Hui Sui-Chow and Nancy; edn: Imperial Coll. 1974; BS, Cal Poly, Pomona 1980; Calif. lic. real estate broker, gen. contractor, 1983. Career: sales Cathay Realty 1978; sales Founders Realty & Westramona Devel. Inc. 1982; pres. J. & J. Real Estate & Devel. Inc. 1983--; pres. Monte Devel. Inc., Asia Am. Investment, 1980-83; rec: fishing. Res: 210 N McPherrin, Unit B, Monterey Park 91754 Ofc: 801 S Garfield, Ste 105, Alhambra 91801

HULL, LARRY ARTHUR, real estate broker; b. June 28, 1940, Los Angeles; s. Eugene H. and Almira V. (Deering) H.; m. D. Irene Dempsey, July 31, 1966; children: Douglas, b. 1967; Caren, b. 1970; edn: BS, San Jose State Univ. 1970. Career: asst. mgr. Security Finance, San Jose 1964-66; loan ofcr. Crocker Nat. Bank, San Jose 1966-68; cost acct. Sylvania, Mt. View 1968; property supvr.

Fidelity Property Mgmt., San Jose 1969-70; secty./ treas. Advanced Properties, Inc., San Jose 1970-72, pres./ chmn. bd. dirs. 1972--; mem: San Jose Real Estate Bd.; Santa Cruz Bd. Realtors; Tri-Co. Apart. Assn.; Santa Cruz CofC; Calif. Motel Assn. (pres. 1975-76); Kiwanis, Blossom Valley Club; Optimists, Miracle Mile Club; mil: pfc US Army 1961-64; Republican; Presbyterian; rec: golf, tennis, racquetball. Res: 1545 Puerto Vallarta Dr San Jose 95120 Ofc: Advanced Properties, 4100 Moorpark Ave, Ste 125, San Jose 95117

HULME, ALLAN DENNISON, educator; b. Aug. 18, 1947, San Francisco (4th gen. Californian); s. Capt. Kenneth Allan and Edna Mavis (Ohman) H.; edn: AA, Coll. of Marin 1967; BA in econ., honors, San Diego St. Univ. 1969; MA in sch. admin., San Francisco St. Univ. 1972; Calif. Std. Elem. Tchr. Credential (life), Std. Secondary Cred. (life), Std. Adminstrn. Cred. (life); Real Estate Broker lic. 1982; minister, Ch. of Gospel Ministry. Career: elementary sch. tchr., Novato 1971--, devel. tchg. pgm. of Gifted and Talented children 1979; real estate broker; recipient Hon. Service Award, Loma Verde Sch. PTA 1976, School Master of Year, Marin Co. 1980; mem: Profl. Educators Group of Calif. (state dir.; pres. Marin chpt. 1979, 80), Bahia Homeowners Assn.; publs: newspaper articles; mil: Nat. Guard (Armor) 1969-70; Republican; Lutheran; rec: sailing, swim, camping. Res: 2573 Topaz Dr Novato 94947 Ofc: Loma Verde Sch, 399 Alameda de la Loma, Novato 94947

HULTQUIST, ALLEN WARD, computer co. executive; b. Dec. 3, 1950, North Platte, Nebr.; s. Allen E. and Dolores Marlene (Ward) H.; m. Cheryl O'Neal, Mar. 29, 1980; 1 son, Michael Allen b. 1982; edn: AA, chem., Shasta Comm. Coll. 1971, BS, chem. CSU Chico, 1973, computer sci. 1973-74. Career: grad. tchg. asst. CSU Chico, 1973-74; field customer support analyst Information Systems Design, Santa Clara 1974-79; sr. scientific programmer Applied Technology, Sunnyvale 1979; sr. staff analyst Information Systems Design, Santa Clara 1979-80, product mgr. Manufacturing Systems, 1980-81; product mgr. Electronics Mfg., Control Data Corp., Santa Clara 1981-, mgr. Product Devel. 1983-84; v.p. mktg. Fab Trak Inc. (mfg. software applications), Palo Alto 1984--; cons. sci/engrg. computer applications; mem: IEEE, Soc. of Mfg. Engrs., Semiconductor Equip. and Materials Inst.; publs: A Yield Enhancement System, Micro-Electronics Measurement and Test Seminar (5/81); Democrat; Prot.; rec: golf, tennis, softball. Res: 1891 Camacho Wy San Jose 95142 Ofc: Fab Trak Inc., Palo Alto

HUMISTON, DAVID MICHAEL, lawyer; b. Sept. 16, 1954, Denver, Colo.; . John David and Fumiko (Hirata) H.; edn: BA, UC Los Angeles 1976; JD, UC Hastings Coll. of the Law 1979. Career: assoc. law firm Cotkin, Collins, Kolts and Franseell, L.A. 1979-83, law firm Sedgwick, Detert, Moran & Arnold, 1983--; pres. Los Angeles Chpt. and mem. bd. dirs. Hastings Coll. of the Law Alumni Assn. Recipient Gov.'s Award, Calif., 1972; mem: Pi Gamma Mu, Omicron Delta Epsilon, Am. Bar Assn., Calif. State Bar Assn., Los Angeles County bar Assn., Advocates for the Arts; Republican; Prot.; rec: photog., classical music, golf. Res: 230 S. Madison Ave, No. 305, Pasadena 91107 Ofc: Sedgwick, Detert, Moran & Arnold, 3600 Wilshire Blvd, Ste 1934, Los Angeles 90010

HUMPHREYS, GEORGE A., real estate broker; b. Jan. 9, 1939, Boston, Mass.; s. Joseph and Eleanor (Hammond) H.; 1 dau. Adrianne, b. 1969; edn: BSEE, Northeastern Univ. 1962; MBA, Boston Coll. 1969. Career: mgr. Harvy Won Computer Systems, San Diego 1972-75; sales engr. Acco Datamaster, City of Commerce 1975-77; real estate broker Trendsetter Realty, Escondido 1977-82; founding dir. Hidden Valley National Bank, 1982--; mil: capt. US Army 1963-67; Republican; rec: travel, sailing, wind surfing. Address: George A Humphreys Inc. 12925 Caminito Del Canto Del Mar 92014

HUNDSHAMER, FRANCIS X., credit service co. president; b. Dec. 2, 1926, Syracuse, NY; s. Alois L., Sr. and Rosalie (Sabeske) H.; m. Julianne Hopstein, May 15, 1948; children: Thomas, b. 1949; Patricia, b. 1950; Lenny, b. 1953; James, b. 1957; edn: mil. ofcr., Cherry Point Marines 1944; qual. cert., Bureau of Collection & Investigative Svcs. 1966. Career: ins. broker, Syracuse, NY 1947-59; owner/ opr. Premiere Prodns. (comml. record co., recording & distbr. pop. records) 1957-59; Calif. Collector, Valley Credit Exchange, San Gabriel 1959-66; corp. pres./ chmn. bd. Orange Credit Svc., Orange 1966--; mem. Elks; works: song writer/ poet, 6 pub. items; mil: lt. USMC 1943-49 WWII, 1950 Korea, Ribbons (13), Battle Stars (5), US Pres. Unit Cit., Korean Pres. Unit Cit.; Republican; Catholic; rec: rose bushes. Res: 642 Sharon Rd Arcadia 91006 Ofc: Orange Credit Service, 550 E Chapman 92666

HUNT, A. THOMAS, lawyer; b. Mar. 15, 1940, Auburn, NY; s. Alvin C. and Alice Marian (Thomas) H.; m. Eleanor Shellard, June 2, 1962; children: Kenneth b. 1966, A. William b. 1966, A. Thomas b. 1968; edn: BA, magna cum laude, St. Lawrence Univ. 1962; JD, with honors, Harvard Law Sch. 1965; admitted to New York bar 1968, California bar 1973. Career: vis. lectr. in law, Univ. of Khartoum, Khartoum, Sudan 1965-67; assoc. Polletti, Freidin, Prashker, Feldman & Gartner, NY, NY 1967-71; staff atty. Employment Sect. Civil Rights Div. US Dept. Justice, Wash DC, 1971-72; chief Employment Discrimination Dept., Center for Law in the Public Interest, Los Angeles, Ca. 1972-81; ptnr. Taylor, Roth & Hunt, A Law Corp., Los Angeles 1981--, lead atty. in approx. 30 major employment discrimination class actions (incl. Davis v. Co. of LA Fire Dept. 1979, Blake v. City of LA Police Dept. 1979, Craig v. Co. of LA Sheriffs Dept. 1980); vis. prof. Southwestern Univ. Sch. of Law; honors: Phi Beta Kappa, Omicron Delta Kappa; recipient US Dept. Justice Spl. Achievement Award 1972; spl. achieve. award for pvt. practitioners, Equal Empl. Opp. Commn. 1974, 77; feature profile, Los Angeles Daily Journal (daily legal newspaper) 11/82; listed, The Best Lawyers in Am. (1983); mem: Am. Bar Assn. (Labor Com., Equal Empl. Opp. Sect. 1981-), Los Angeles County Bar Assn.; publs: contbr. Sudan Law J. 1966; Democrat; rec: cooking, baseball. Res: 3510 Stoner Ave Los Angeles 90066 Ofc: Taylor, Roth & Hunt 617 S. Olive St, Ste 1100, Los Angeles 90014

HUNT, DANIEL STOCKTON, magazine publishing executive; b. Nov. 12, 1936, Los Angeles; s. George Smith and Mireille (de Martelly) H.; m. Carolyn Schutt, June 4, 1973; 1 dau. Bentley Anne, b. 1976; edn: BA, Yale Univ. 1961. Career: senior editor Cycle World Mag. 1969-72; mktg. dir. Bond/ Parkhurst/ Bond 1972-73; pub. Cycle World, Pickup, Van & 4WD, Sea Magazines, 1974-79; v.p. mktg. Trailer Life Pubs. 1980--; pres. Princeton Data, 1983--; mem. Western Publs. Assn.; works: (computer software) Princeton Data Legal Billing; num. arts. in computer mags. (ie. Byte, Interface Age, Dr. Dobb's Journ.). Res: 359 Princeton Dr Costa Mesa 92626 Ofc: T L Enterprises, Inc., 29901 Agoura Rd Agoura 91301

HUNT, HUBBARD, animation equipment manufacturer; b. Feb. 13, 1900, Evanston, Ill.; s. Myron and Harriet Holland Boardman H.; m. Helen Jack Henderson, Apr. 27, 1935; edn: Valpariso Univ.; UC Berkeley. Career: prod. tng. films, Walt Disney Prodns., during WWII; travel films, South America, Belem Manaus, Laticia & Rio; Emerald Mines & Life in Bogota; owner/ pres. Fax Company (mfr. animation equipment & supplies), Pasadena; mem: Avdtg. Club of Los Angeles; Tournament of Roses Assn.; mil: 143 field artillery, WWI; Republican; Presbyterian; rec: designing animation special equipment. Res: 1077 Laguna Rd Pasadena 91105 Ofc: Fax Co. 374 S Fair Oaks Ave Pasadena 91105

HUNT, ROBERT G., oral maxillofacial surgeon; b. July 10, 1945, San Diego; s. Harvey G. and Pauline A. (Nazarovic) H.; m. Diane, Apr. 26, 1975; 1 dau: Christine, b. 1981; edn: AA, Mesa Coll. 1971; DDS, USC 1976; BS, Univ. Nebr. 1979; MD, 1979. Career: physician, surgeon & dentist; currently, pvt. practice oral maxillofacial & reconstructive surgery of the jaws, San Diego; chmn. Blood Reserve Com. San Diego Co. Dental Soc.; v.p. Nat. Cred-A-Chek, Inc.; diplomate. Nat. Bd. Med. Examiners, Nat. Bd. Dental Examiners, Am. Bd. Oral Maxillofacial Surgery; fellow, Am. Assn. Oral Maxillofacial Surgeons; mem: Am. Med. Assn.; Am. Dental Assn.; So. Calif. Acad. of Oral Pathology; Paul Revere Study Club (pres.); Phi Kappa Phi; Omikron Kappa Upsilon; Mensa; contbr: San Diego Co. Cancer Soc. publs.; mil: s/sgt. USAF 1965-70, ret. Res: 4205 Trias St San Diego 92103

HUNT, ROBERT CHARLES, data processing executive; b. Jan. 14, 1934, Detroit, Mich.; s. Russell Frances and Blanche Maye (Pratt) Hunt; m. Joann Inda, June 3, 1961; chil: Steven, b. 1965, Kevin, b. 1969, Allen, b. 1972; career: data processing supr. Standard Accident Ins. Co., Detroit, Mich. 1957-58; asst. dir. Data Processing, Grossmont Union High Sch. District, La Mesa, 1962-80; dir. Data Processing, Sweetwater Union High Sch. District, Chula Vista 1980--; mem: DECUS-Digital Equip. Corp. Users Soc., installation del.; Bajalug-local DEC Users Group, Starlight Terrace Homeowners Assn., bd. mem., El Chobibo Dance Club, pres. 1979-80; mil: spc-5 US Army; Democrat; Catholic; rec: dancing, woodworking; res: 3931 Nereis Dr. La Mesa 92041 ofc: Sweetwater Union High Sch Dist. 1130 5th Ave. Chula Vista 92011.

HUNT, JERRY ALLEN, systems analyst/engineer; b. May 27, 1937, Hastings, Nebraska; s. Frank Albert and Helen Marie (Kluver) H.; M. Evelyn Watson, Jan. 23, 1955; children: Steve, b. 1959; Dani, b. 1960; Kenneth, b. 1961; Kurt, b. 1963. Edn: BS, Bus. Adm. (mgmt), Franklin Univ., Columbus, Ohio, 1965. Career: systms. analyst Continental Oil Co., Midland, Tx. 1973-77; owner/ mgr. Hunt's Service Bereau, Hastings, NE 1977-78; Systms. analyst Mobil Oil Corp., Denver 1978-79; sr. systms. analyst Johnson Controls, Inc., Santa Ana 1979-82, & comp. consultant 1982-83; sr. analyst Pertec Computer Corp., Irvine 1983--.; area commisioner, BSA, Columbus, OH 1968; junior achievement advisor Continental Oil Co., Midland, TX 1975-76; loan officer West Texas Fed. Credit Union, Midland 1976-77. Awards: Manager's Cert., Am. Mgmt. Assn., 1981. Mem: Data Processing Mgmt. Assn., 1980--; Internat. Database Mgmt. Assn. 1984--. Works: bus. article, Savvy Mag., 1983; comp. article, Datamation Mag., 1983. Mil: E4 USAF 1954-60, Nat. Def. Medal (Europe), GCM. Republican; Catholic. Rec: freelance writing, travel, music. Res: 1017 E. 19th St Santa Ana 92706 Ofc: Pertec Computer Corp., 17112 Armstrong Ave Irvine 92714

HUNTER, ART, stock broker; b. Apr. 24, 1933, Fairport Harbor, Ohio; s. Albert and Mary (Kapostasy) Dexter; m. Chip Aquino; children: Terry, b. 1958; Caroline, b. 1963; edn: BS, Univ. of Notre Dame 1954. Career: profl. football, L.A. Rams, Green Bay Packers, Pittsburgh Steelers, Cleveland Browns, 11 yrs.; currently, acct. exec. Merrill Lynch, Santa Ana; awards: All American; All-Pro; mem: NFL Players Assn.; NFL Alumni Assn.; mil: PFC US Army 1955-56; DNS; rec: sunning, gardening. Res: 1376 S.E. Skyline Dr Santa Ana 92705 Ofc: Merrill Lynch, 1000 N Main St Santa Ana 92702

HUNTER, BETTY KATHERINE, speaker/ executive search consultant/ public relations executive; b. May 28, 1945, Los Angeles; d. Robert Cecil and B. Fay (McLean) H.; Edn: BS psychol., Univ. of So. Cal., 1967, postgrad., 1968. Career: educational consultant Los Angeles Unified Sch. Dist., 1968-80; exec. search consultant Korn/Ferry Internat., LA 1980-81; speaker/ exec. search / pub. rels. exec. Betty K. Hunter, LA 1982; bd. dir. USC Commerce Assn. 1974-; lecturer USC 1982-, lectr. UCLA 1982-; radio/tv personality. Awards: PTA Hon. Life Award (edn.), 1976; fundraising award, USC Grad. Sch. Bus., 1983. Mem: USC Educare; Nat. Speakers Assn.; Internat. Platform Assn.; Junior League LA; Las Floristas; Hollywood Bowl Juniors; LA World Affair Council; Town Hall of CA.; Calif. Repub. Assn.; Republican. Res: 4201 Via Marina #265 Marina Del Rey 90292. Ofc: Betty K. Hunter, 2029 Century Park E., Ste 580 Los Angeles 90067

HUNTER, DAVID CROXTON, surveyor; b. Mar. 17, 1924, Detroit, Mich.; s. George Croxton and Carolyn Louise (Jones) H.; m. Sara Gagliardi, Jan. 1, 1957; children: Janet b. 1957, Carol b. 1959, George b. 1960, Evelyn b. 1962, Jennifer b. 1970; edn: BS in geol., Univ. of Mass. 1950; Reg. Profl. Land Surveyor, Calif. Career: pres. Hunter Land Surveying, Inc. 1979--; past pos. with Aerial Mapping Cos., Kaiser Engrs., Cerro Corp., Bechtel Corp., Arthur G. McKee, Morrison-Knudsen; mgmt. and engring. (32 years) in surveying and constrn. fields incl. aerial mapping, layout and control of hydroelectric projects, alumina plant, copper mine devel. in Chile, copper plant expansion in Mexico, iron ore marine terminals in Brazil, land devel. in Calif.; cons. Anaconda Copper Co., 1980, Los Pelambres Copper Mine mapping in Chile; mem. Am. Soc. of Photogrammetry, Calif. Land Surveyors Assn.; mil: pvt. US Army 1943-46; Republican; Prot.; rec: skiing. Res: 8327 Hidden Valley Circle Fair Oaks 95628 Ofc: Hunter Land Surveying Inc. POB 190, Lower Lake 95457

HUNTER, DAVID LEROY, physician, lawyer; b. Mar. 3, 1949, Maddock, N.Dak.; s. Robert Irving and Marie (Liudahl) H.; edn: BA, N.D. St. Univ. 1971; MD, Univ. of Minn. (Mnpls.) 1974; med. internship Stanford Univ./Santa Clara Valley Med. Ctr. 1974-75; JD, Harvard Univ. Law Sch. 1978. Diplomate Nat. Bd. of Med. Examiners 1975; Fellow Am. Coll. of Emergency Physicians 1983; Dip. Am. Bd. of Emerg. Med. 1982; admitted Calif. bar. 1978. Career: practiced emerg. medicine, Melrose-Wakefield Hosp., Melrose, Mass. 1975-78; emerg. phys. Alexian Brothers Hosp., San Jose 1978--, dir. Emergency Dept., chmn. Emerg. Com. 1980-; Medico-legal Cons. 1979--; ptnr. Calif. Emergency Physicians Medical Group; honors: Alpha Omega, Phi Eta Sigma, Phi Kappa Phi; mem: Calif. Bar, Harvard Law Sch. Assn., Am. Soc. of Law and Medicine, Am. Coll. of Emerg. Physicians, Santa Clara Co. Med. Soc., Calif. Med. Assn.; active in Guide Dogs for the Blind, Scotts Valley Com. for Orderly Growth, San Lorenzo Valley Prop. Owners Assn., var. community issues; Republican (Calif. Repub. Party, Calif. Assem.); Prot.; rec: breeding and raising Am. Kennel Club cert. German Shepherds. Res: 784 Lockhart Gulch Rd Scotts Valley 95066 Ofc: Alexian Brothers Hospital 225 N. Jackson Ave San Jose 95116

HUNTER, GLENN C., vascular surgeon; b. Dec. 24, 1944, Cape Town, So. Africa; s. Leslie C. and Margaret H. (Turner) H.; m. Susan Lawrence, Feb. 21, 1981; edn: MB, CHB, w.honors, Univ. of Cape Town Med. Sch. 1968. Career: surg. intern, resident Somerset Hosp., Cape Town 1969-73; trauma (accident) surg. res., Luton and Dunstable, England 1973; gen. surg. res. Kimberley, S.A. 1974, County Hosp., Hereford, Eng. 1974-76; Liverpool Royal Infirmary 1976; research fellow in microcirculation, UC San Francisco 1977-78; clin. instr., vascular surg., Univ. of Ariz. Coll. of Med., Tucson 1979-80; asst. prof. of surg., UC Davis 1981--; staff surgeon, VA Med. Center, Martinez 1981-, chief Vascular Surgery 1983--; liver transplants, resrch.; honors: Class Prize in Pathology, Univ. of Cape Town; Fellow Coll. of Surgeons, S.A. 1973-; Fellow Royal Coll. of Surgeons, Edinburgh 1973-; mem. Assn. for Academic Surgery, Assn. for VA Surgeons, East Bay Surg. Soc.; Prot.; rec: fishing. Res: 585 Capitol Dr Benicia 94510 Ofc: Veterans Adminstrn. Medical Center, 150 Muir Rd Martinez 94553

HUNTER, JEFFREY CHARLES, consumer and office products co. executive; b. Oct. 19, 1938, San Diego; s. Theodore Lee and Dorothea (Wilson) H.; edn: BS, CSU San Diego 1962, MS, 1964; postgrad. wk. Univ. Wash., Seattle 1964-65, MAM, Univ. Redlands 1979. Calif. Comm. Coll. Tchr. credentials in bus. and chem. Career: all with Avery International: Avery Label div. senior chemist, paper and materials, research dept. 1966-71; material lab. supr., research dept. 1971-76; product devel. splst. Avery Label Resale div. 1976-79; project mgr. Consumer Div., 1979--, Consumer and Office Products Group, Avery Internat.; grad. business instr. Univ. of Redlands 1980-, faculty mem. Coll. of Profl. Studies, Univ. of San Francisco 1981-; state chmn. curriculum design com. Coll. of Profl. Studies 1982, 83, 84. Mem: Council of Reprographics Execs., Assn. of MBA Execs., Am. Chem. Soc., Tech. Assn. of the Pulp & Paper Indus., Kiwanis Intl.; publs. in field; Republican; Episcopal; rec: numismatics, scuba diving. Res: 923 N. San Antonio Pomona 91767 Ofc: Avery Label Div. Avery Internat. 777 E. Foothill Blvd Azusa 91702

HUNTER, JENNIFER JOAN, clinical social worker; b. Apr. 5, 1950; d. Charles William and Phyllis Joan (Altamira) H.; edn: BA, Univ. of No. Colo. 1973; MA, 1974; MSW, Univ. of Ks.; CSW, Univ. of Ks. 1979. Career: speech pathologist, fed. pgms. title I, Pine Ridge Indian Reservation Pine Ridge, S.Dak. 1974-75; speech pathologist Sewall Rehab. Ctr., Denver, Colo. 1975-77; CSW, head trauma unit, physical med. & rehab. Northridge Hosp. Med. Ctr. 1979--; organizer/ profl. liason Proj. Headway 1983; cons. traumatic head injury, hosps., ins. cos., & interest gps.; mem: NASW (Ks. chpt.); Am. Head Trauma Alliance (Profl. Adv. Bd.); works: concept development, Calif. Head Injury Rehab. Ctr., Inc. 1982; Democrat; Catholic; rec: gourmet cooking, piano, aerobics. Res: 1927 Glendon Ave, 1, Westwood 90025 Ofc: Northridge Hosp. Medical Center, 18300 Roscoe Blvd Northridge 91328

HUNTER, LEON, housing authority executive; b. May 13, 1929, Edna, Okla.; s. Roosevelt and Emma Lee (Fisher) H.; m. Lula M. Simien, Nov. 18, 1967; children: Maxine, b. 1946; Sharon, b. 1948; Leon Jr., b. 1949; Joey, b. 1954; Kenneth, b. 1955; Gregory, b. 1957; Debra, b. 1966; edn: AA, Contra Costa Jr. Coll. 1972; BA, San Francisco State Univ. 1978; desig. Pub. Housing Mgr., NAHRO 1978. Career: tenant rels. advsr. Richmond Housing Authority, Richmond 1968-72, leased housing negotiator 1972-76, asst. pub. housing dir. 1976-79, pub. housing dir. 1979--; pres. No. Calif. & Nevada Exec. Dirs. Assn. 1984; mem: Nat. Exec. Dirs. Assn.; NAHRO (life); Pub. Housing Authorities Dirs. Assn.; Masons; USF Alumni Assn.; Democrat; Methodist; rec: golf, bowling. Res: 5201 Victor Ave Richmond 94804 Ofc: Richmond Housing Authority, POB 515, Station A, Richmond, 94808

HUNTER, WILLIAM CARLTON, lawyer; b. Dec. 24, 1939, Wilmington, Delaware; s. Carlton E. and Virginia Odell (Talbott) H.; m. Kathleen Donovan, Sept. 10, 1971; children: J. Craig, b. 1963; W. Douglas, b. 1965; Anne, b. 1975; Will, b. 1978; edn: BS, Univ. of Virginia 1961, JD, 1969; MBA, Golden Gate Univ. 1972; admitted to practice, Calif. State Bar & US 9th Circuit Ct. of Appeals 1970. Career: assoc. atty. Lillick, McHose, Wheat, Adams & Charles, San Francisco 1970-71; Garret McEnerney II, San Francisco 1971-74; partner Hunter, Boyd & Murray, Santa Rosa 1977-82; sole practice, Healdsburg 1982--; assoc. prof. Golden Gate Univ. Grad. Bus. Sch. 1973-76; prof. Empire Law Sch. 1976-81; counsel Calif. Coastal Alliance 1974; mem: Am., Calif. & Sonoma Co. Bar Assns.; Calif. Trial Lawyers Assn.; Redwood Empire Trial Lawyers Assn. (pres.); Healdsburg CofC (bd. dirs.); Healdsburg Boys Club (bd. dirs.); Westside Sch. Dist.; Kiwanis; mil: capt. USMC 1961-65; rec: tennis, woodworking. Res: 7559 Mill Creek Rd Healdsburg 95448 Ofc: William C. Hunter, 141 North Street, POB 328, Healdsburg 95448

HUNTINGTON, RICHARD B., engineering and constructors co. executive; b. May 4, 1924, Kans.; s. Ben and Julia E. (Wilson) H.; m. Betty Ann Huffman, Aug. 7, 1949; two children; edn: elec. engrg., Univ. of Me. 1943; BS in M.E., Univ. Calif. 1946; Calif. Reg. Profl. Engr. (Mech.), lic. engring., bldg., plumbing, elec. and air condtg. contractor. Career: co-owner Ben Huntington & Sons, 1946-52; co-owner University Heating, 1952-67; co-owner/CEO/bd. chmn. University Industries, 1967--, (employs over 1200 in USA), prin. subs. are Univ. Mechanical & Engring. Contractors, University Financial (R.E. devel. projs. in Calif., Ariz., Alaska), Univ. Mech. Contrs. of Ariz., Univ. Contractors Internat., S.A. (engrs., contr. mech. systems overseas) and Univ. Energy; dir. La Jolla Bank & Trust Co.; honors: Tau Beta Pi; mem. Am. Soc. Htg. Refrig. Air Contg. Engrs.; trustee The Bishops Sch. (past pres., bd.), trustee La Jolla Cancer & Research Found.; mem. Kiwanis, Navy Club, San Diego Yacht Club, Univ. Mgmt. Assn., CofC, President's Roundtable; mil: maj. USAR; Republican; Presbyterian; rec: radio amateur. Res: 5761 Rutgers Rd La Jolla 92037 Ofc: University Industries 3430 Caminito Del Rio N. San Diego 92108

HUNTLEY, MALLARD RICHARDS, insurance broker; b. Jan. 23, 1935, Hartford, Conn.; s. Mallard Joseph and Ada Josephine (Holloway) H.; children: Jennifer, b. 1963; Sean, b. 1964; Erin, b. 1970; edn: BA, Univ. of Tulsa 1956; MBA, Stanford 1961. Career: pub. rels. dir. Calif. Optometric Assn. 1961-64; pres. Huntley-Sheehy, Inc., Marysville 1964--; v.p./ dir. Wallis Trane Svc. Agcy. of Sacramento; pres./ chmn. bd. Mallard, Inc.; mem: Peach Tree Country Club (pres. 1976-77); Rotary Club (Marysville pres. 1975-76); bd. chmn. Rideout Meml. Hosp. 1979, 80, 84; Rideout Inst. for Devel. (pres. 1970, 72); Independent Agents Assn. (Yuba Co. pres. 1965); mil: capt. USAF 1956-59, navigator, bombador B-47; Republican; Methodist; rec: golf, tennis, racquetball. Res: 4838 Fruitland Rd Marysville 95901 Ofc: Huntley-Sheehy, 520 Olive St Marysville 95901

HUNTLEY, SHIRLEY ANNE CONKLIN, personal and business communication consultant; b. Sept. 7, 1927, Kansas City, Mo.; d. Clare Cleophas and Helen Marie (Kerr) Conklin; m. Robert G. Huntley, Feb. 2, 1956; children: Steven G., b. 1959; R. Scott, b. 1961; edn: BA, William Jewell Coll. 1949; MA, Azusa Pacific Univ. 1983, grad. study, USC 1983; marriage, family & child counselor intern, BBSE 1982. Career: pub. rels. Mass. State Republican Com. 1952; secty. advtg. mgr. Kansas City Star 1953; secty. Calif. State Assemblyman/ secty. Interim Commn. on Pub. Utilities & Corps. 1955-56; campaign coord. US Congl. Campaigns (2) 1956-58; co- owner AVCOM (Audio- Visual Commun.), No. Hollywood 1966--; marriage, family & child counselor Santa Anita Counseling Ctr., Arcadia 1982--; currently, personal & bus. communications cons.; dir. AVCOM, No. Hollywood 1977--; dir. ABBECTRON, Orange 1983; counseling staff Santa Anita Counseling Ctr., Arcadia 1982-; mem: Hotel Mgrs. Assn.; Am. Soc. Tng. Dirs.; So. Calif. Soc. Assn. Execs.; Am. & Calif. Assns. Marriage & Family Therapists; Pasadena CofC; Inglewood PTA; Inglewood Womens Club; Alpha Gamma Delta Alumnae (pres.); Phi Sigma Kappa Mothers Club (pres.); Inter- Frat. Mothers Council, USC; Pasadena Panhellenic Assn. (delegate); San Marion Newcomers Club; Republican Womens Culb; works: home improvement & restorations; Republican; Presbyterian; rec: writing, public speaking, sailing. Res: 363 N Myrtle Ave Monrovia 91016 Ofcs: Santa Anita Counseling Center, 226 W Colorado Blvd Arcadia 91006; AVCOM, 5422 Fair Ave, No Hollywood 91601

HURFORD, DAVID DEAN, JR., realty services co. executive; b. July 4, 1951, Los Angeles; s. David Dean and Patricia Jean (Woodard) H.; edn: AB, Stanford Univ. 1973; MA, Occidental Coll. 1974; lic. real estate broker, Calif. 1976. Career: Coro Foundation Fellow, San Francisco 1974; municipal fin. cons. Bartle Wells Assocs., S.F. 1975-76; with Coldwell Banker & Co., Los Angeles 1976--: staff salesman 1976-80, sales cons. 1980-82, senior sales cons. 1982-83,

v.p. institutional realty svcs. 1983--; awards: Top Salesman Awd. 1982, 83; Distng. Achiev. Awd., Coldwell Banker; fellow, Rotary Internat. Found. 1980; mem: Los Angeles Bd. Realtors; Town Hall; Coro Assocs.; United Way; Jonathan Club; Explorers Club; rec: backpacking, travel, photog. Res: Pasadena Ofc: Coldwell Banker & Co., 533 Fremont Ave Los Angeles 90071

HURLEY, JOSEPH DERMOT, healthcare services executive; b. July 8, 1921, NY, NY; s. Wm. J. and Rose Lena (Rush) H.; m. Helen Dick, Sept. 21, 1950; children: Kathleen b. 1951, Michael b. 1953, Joseph b. 1958, Jeanette b. 1961; edn: BS, Ore. State Univ. 1948. Career: sales rep./supr. Proctor & Gamble, San Francisco 1948-55; gen. mgr. Dy-Dee Wash, S.F. 1955-59; sales mgr. Pacific Chemical, Seattle 1960-61; gen. mgr. Angelica Healthcare, Los Angeles 1961-71, vice pres. mktg. (largest hospital linen service nationwide), Angelica Healthcare Services Group Inc., Anaheim 1972--; lectr. UCLA, CSU Northridge 1963-; mem. United Hosp. Assn. Edn. Com. (Recognition Award, only non-hosp. associated recipient) 1965-; Found. mem. Healthwest 1978-; Found. mem. Northridge Med. Ctr. 1978-; avocation: opr. free job placement svc. for hosp. administrators; mil: pfc US Army Inf., Silver Star, Croix de Guerre; Republican. Res: 10910 Des Moines Northridge 91326 Ofc: Angelica Healthcare, 600 N. Euclid Ave, Ste 301, Anaheim 92801

HURLEY, ROBERT DONALD, chiropractor/ educator; b. Apr. 28, 1941, Everett, Wash.; s. Donald Robert and Mary Elizabeth (Dacre) H.; children: Scott, Charles; edn: AA, Santa Barbara City Coll. 1962; BS, Pacific Christian Coll.; grad. stu. psychol., Grad. Div. Calif. Family Study Ctr., Azusa Pacific Coll. 1979-81; DC, Los Angeles Coll. Chiro. 1972; lic. DC, Calif. 1972, Wash. 1979; Calif. Comm. Coll. Health Instr. Credential. Career: practice of chiropractic (12 yrs.); health instr. (8 yrs.); faculty, Los Angeles Coll. of Chiropractic 1979-, Calif. Comm. Coll. Sys. 1975-; chiropractic clinic dir.; dir. Santa Barbara Chiro. Soc.; historian/ researcher/ legis. & media person Calif. Chiro. Assn.; honors: past Master Councilor, Santa Barbara Demolay; mem: Calif. & Am. Chiro. Assns.; Santa Barbara Chiro. Soc. (past pres. 1983); Nat. Physical Therapy Assn.; Mensa, Masons, Scottish Rite, Toastmasters; works: Alternative Grade Sch., Santa Barbara 1974; mil: US Army, active 1962, reserves 1962-68; Universalist; rec: sailing, tennis. Address: 1919 State St, Ste 207, Santa Barbara 93101

HURLEY, WILLIAM LAWRENCE, hotel management executive; b. Aug. 21, 1950, Chgo.; s. Jerry and Mausolene Esther (Hoppers) H.; m. Karla Dickinson, Sept. 11, 1971; children: Patrick, b. 1979; Ryan, b. 1981; edn: BS, Univ. of Denver 1972. Career: mgmt. trainee The Sheraton Corp. 1972-74; Front Office mgr. Sheraton Boston 1974-76; res. mgr. Sheraton Houston 1979; mgr. Sheraton Boston 1980-81; gen. mgr., Miramar Sheraton 1982-83; gen. mgr. Monterey Sheraton 1984--; bd. dirs. Santa Monica Conv. & Visitors Bureau 1982-83; mem. Calif. Hotel & Motel Assn.; Republican; Methodist; rec: woodworking. Res: 27422 Vista Del Toro Salinas 93908 Ofc: Monterey Sheraton Hotel, 350 Calle Principal Monterey 93940

HURST, JAMES HENRY, real estate broker-developer; b. Feb. 10, 1932, Portland, Ore.; s. Roy Ronsley and Nelle Minnie (Heckes) H.; m. Sharon K., May 14, 1981; children: James, b. 1953; Terrie, b. 1955; William, b. 1959; Kelley R., b. 1971; edn: Univ. of Ariz.; lic. real estate broker, contractor, Calif. 1956, 75. Career: active realtor & ofcr. sev. development cos., 1954-: incl. Hurst-Reed Inc., Champion Land Investment Co.; currently, pres. Hurst Realty & Devel. Co., Inc. & Nelroy Corp. Constrn., 1975--; awards: Gold Nugget Awd. for Park in Sierra Oaks subdiv. (winner class A-2), Bldg. Indus. Assn. 1983; mem: Sacto. Home Bldrs. Assn.; Placer Co. Contractors Assn.; Sacto. & Placer Co. Bds. Realtors; Am. River Brokers Exch. (past pres.); Carmichael & Auburn Rotary Culb; Sacto. Metro. CofC; works: custom homes; mil: PO 3/c USN 1952-54; Republican; Episcopal; rec: fishing, camping, dog showing. Address: Hurst Realty & Development Co., 9225 Country Club Ln Auburn 95603

HURST, PATSY SUE, sales and marketing executive; b. Jan. 30, 1957, Jamestown, Tenn.; d. Oliver Judge and Charlene Ruth Hurst; edn: BS, Tenn. Tech. Univ. 1979. Career: asst. sales mgr. Village Boutique, Cookeville, Tenn. 1979-80; computer opr. Toyota Central, Los Angeles 1980; payroll/const. secty. Mitchell Cement Contracting Co., Panorama City 1980, office mgr. 1980, project mgr. 1981-82; exec. secty., Bldg. & Leasing mgr., Frank T. Howard Contracting Co., Orange 1982-, asst. mktg. dir. 1983, vice pres. mktg. & sales, Howard Bldg. Corp., Orange (branch ofc) 1983--; cons. Hurst Credit Systems, 1983; high sch. honors incl: Top 10 of Class, pres. Future Homemakers of Am., Future Farmers of Am. Sweetheart, Varsity Cheerleader Capt., Sch. Newspaper staff; mem. Soc. for Marketing Profl. Services (Awards Com. 1983-4), Building Owners & Mgrs. Assn. (mktg. rep.), Soroptomist, Bus. & Profl. Women; rec: aerobics, golf, tennis. Res: 1730 Rogers Pl, 47, Burbank 91203 Ofc: Howard Building Corp. 1717 W. Orangewood, Ste I, Orange 92668

HURT, ROBERT GLENN, investment securities co. executive; b. Jan. 31, 1919, Pasadena; s. Dr. Leslie M. (past pres. AVMA) and Effie Mae (McKim) H.; edn: AB, USC, 1940; postgrad. Harvard Bus. Sch. 1941. Career: trainee Calvin Bullock, Ltd., NYC 1946; asst. to west coast head, L.A. 1946-49; northern div. head, 1949-53; resident and senior v.p. Calvin Bullock, Ltd., San Francisco 1954--; honors: Order of Kentucky Colonels; mem. Alpha Delta Sigma, Phi Kappa Psi, Andreas Canyon Club, Stock Exchange Club of San Francisco, Stock Exchange Club of Los Angeles, Harvard Club, Pres. Circle USC, Am. Legion, Reserve Officers Assn.; mil: pvt. to lt. col. AUS Inf. 1941-46; comdr. Mil. Order of World Wars; Cathlic. Res: 937 Ashbury St San Francisco 94117

Ofc: Calvin Bullock, Ltd., 931 The Mills Bldg., 220 Montgomery St San Francisco 94104

HUSS, WILLIAM W., lawyer; b. Sept. 9, 1932, Gastonia, NC; s. William W., Sr. and Helen Cannon (Tillotson) H.; m. Marlene Marie Coleman, Jan. 31, 1976; children: Matthew Louis, b. 1961; Charlyn Tillotson, b. 1964; Damon Alexander, b. 1968; edn: AA, L.A. City Coll. 1958; BS, USC 1962; JD, USC Sch. of Law 1965; admitted to practice: Calif. State Bar, US Dist. Ct. 1965, US Ct. of Appeals, US Ct. of Mil. Appeals, US Ct. of Claims, US Ct. of Customs & Patent Appeals, Supreme Ct. of US 1969. Career: estab. law firm Huss & Crawford (practice ltd. to civil litigation- products liability, personal injury, profl. malpractice, prop. damage & ins. law), Los Angeles 1980--; fmr. assoc./ partner in sev. L.A. law firms spec. civil trial law; judge pro-tem, L.A. Municipal Ct.; arbitrator Personal Injury & Bus. Litigation Panels, L.A. Superior Ct.; arbitrator, Am. Arbitration Assn.; moderator/ instr. Cont. Edn. of the Bar, Calif. State Bar; instr. tort law Ins. Ednl. Assn.; honors: Hale Ct. chmn. 1964, Practice Ct. chmn. 1963, USC Sch. of Law; Sigma Pi Alpha, hon. lang. frat.; Martindale & Hubble A-V rating; mem: Am. Legion; Jonathan Club; Assn. of So. Calif. Defense Counsel; Calif. State Bar; Naval Reserve Ofcrs. Assn.; US Naval Cryptologic Veterans Assn.; Am. Bar Assn.; Mensa; St. James Sch., L.A. (chmn. 1967-82); publs. ed., Findings & Conclusions, Assn. of So. Calif. Def. Counsel 1970-72; columnist, Insurance Journ. 1981; mil: capt. USNR Judge Advoc. Gen. Corps, cmdg. ofcr. Los Angeles Law Co. 11-2, 1973-75; Republican (Co. Central Com. 1965-72); Episcopal; rec: percussive music, archeol., hiking. Res: 800 West 1st St, No 708, Los Angeles 90012 Ofc: Huss & Crawford, 205 S Broadway, Ste 204, Los Angeles 90012

HUSTON, JEFFREY B., chartered life underwriter; b. Apr. 27, 1945, NYC; s. A. Arthur and Jacquelin B. (Hawkins) H.; m. Lynn M. Kinder, Dec. 20, 1969; 1 son: Dru J., b. 1972; edn: BA, Chapman Coll. 1968; CLU, Am. Coll. 1976. Career: agent/ unit mgr. Reserve Life 1968-70; gen. agent United Fidelity Life 1970-76; gen. agent Central Life 1976--; cons./ tng. dir. Trans American Occidental Life 1973-75; cons./ asst. dir. mktg. Best Life 1983; awards: Nat. Quality Assurance Awd. (10 yrs.); mem: NALU; CLU; GAMA; Cosmopolitan Club (chart. pres.); Jaycees (pres.); Republican; Lutheran; rec: exercise, racquetball. Res: 1133 Naples Ave Placentia 92670 Ofc: Central Life, 17742 Irvine Blvd, Ste 200 Tustin 92680

HUTCHESON, JERRY DEE, consulting electrical engineer; b. Oct. 31, 1932, Hammon, Okla.; s. Radford Andrew and Ethel Mai (Boulware) H.; brother, Radford Roland Hutcheson, NM Dir. of Missions, So. Baptist Conv.; m. Lynda Weber, Mar. 6, 1957; edn: BS, Eastern NM Univ. 1959, postgrad., Temple Univ. 1961-62; postgrad., Univ. NM 1964-65; reg. elec. engr., Calif. Career: research engr. RCA 1959-62; sect. head Motorola 1962-63; research physicist Dikewood Corp. 1963-66; sr. tech. staff Signetics Corp. 1966-69; eng. mgr. Littons Sys 1969-70; eng. mgr. Fairchild Semiconductor 1971; eqpt. eng. gp. mgr. Teledyne Semiconductor 1971-74; dir. eng. D.C.A. Reliability Labs. 1974-75; founder, pres./ CEO VLSI Research, Inc., San Jose 1975--; mem: Masonic Lodge (Master Mason); Nat. & Calif. Socs. of Profl. Engrs.; Profl. Engrs. in Pvt. Practice; Profl. & Tech. Cons. Assn.; Semiconductor Eqpt. & Materials Inst.; coauthor/ pub: The VLSI Capital Equipment Outlook, 1980; contbr: var. arts. in profl. journs. 1960-; research, integrated circuits and process equipment 1960-; mil: USAF 1951-55; Democrat (Precinct Com. 1964-66); Presbyterian; rec: philately, oil painting, tennis. Res: 5950 Vistaloop San Jose 95124 Ofc: VLSI Research Inc., 1754 Technology Dr, Ste 226, San Jose 95110

HUTCHFUL, GEORGE ALEX, orthopaedic surgeon; b. May 18, 1945, Cape Coast, Chana, W. Africa; s. Joseph Samuel and Maria Brew (Simons) H.; m. Constance King, June 27, 1976; edn: BS, Howard Univ. 1967, MS, 1969, MD, Howard Univ. Coll. of Med. 1974. Career: instr. biology Lincoln Univ., Jefferson City, Mo. 1969-70; med. rotating intern LA County-USC Med. Center, L.A. 1975-76; surgical resident UC Davis, Sacramento Med. Center, 1975-76; asst. resident Orthopaedics, Univ. Rochester, Strong Mem. Hosp., Rochester, NY 1976-78; res. Orthopaedics, Howard Univ. Hosp., Wash DC 1978-81; asst. chief of orthopaedics Valley Medical Center, Fresno 1981-82; staff orthopedist Family Health Program, Long Beach 1982--; faculty UCSF San Joaquin Valley Tchg. Pgm.; instr. medical postgrad. housestaff, Valley Med. Ctr. of Fresno; honors: AMA Phys. Recogn. Award 1980-83, Beta Kappa Chi (sci. hon.) 1969; mem. AMA, CMA, San Joaquin Valley Orthopaedic Assn.; articles in med. journals; Ind.; Methodist; rec: tennis, bicycling, skiing, jazz. Res: 4682 Warner Ave Huntington Beach 92649 Ofc: Family Health Program, 2925 N. Palo Verde Ave Long Beach 90815

HUTCHINS, LEWIS DEE, real estate broker/developer; b. Mar. 23, 1944, Fresno; BS, acctg. & bus., CSU San Jose 1971; MBA, info. systems, USC 1972; Calif. Tchg. Credential; Calif. lic: CPA, Real Estate Broker, Gen. Bldg. Contr. Career: residential and comml. builder and developer, pres. Citcon Corp., San Jose; (past): v.p., reg. mgr. Genstar Pacific Investments; v.p. fin. Broadmoor Homes; mgr. Prudential Ins.; auditor Arthur Young & Co.; honors: Deans Scholar, Phi Kappa Phi; mem: Am. Inst. CPA, CCalif. soc. of CPAs, BIA, Home Builders Council, Sales & Mktg. Council; mem. Beta Alpha Psi, Beta Gamma Sigma; mil: sgt. E5, US Army, Bronze Star, Army Commendn. Medal. Res: 4763 La Pinta Way San Jose 95129 Ofc: POB 10278, San Jose 95157

HUTCHINSON, LORRAINE KAY, marriage, family and child therapist; b. Aug. 27, 1951, Pittsburg, Calif.; d. Louis V., Sr. and Alice G. (Jackson) Green; m. Chester Hutchinson, Feb. 27, 1976; children: Treasure, b. 1976; Reginald, b. 1976; edn: BS, Univ. Santa Clara 1973; MA, Azusa Pacific Univ. 1983; marriage family child counselor intern, Calif. BBSE 1983. Career: instr./ counselor Opportunities Industrialization Ctr. 1973-74; dir. presch. pgm. Emmanuel Baptist Ch. 1978-81; marriage, family & child counselor intern Center For Family Learninga, San Jose 1983; volunteer cons./ marriage, family & child intern, Arbutus Youth Assn. 1982-; honors: life mem. Calif. Scholarship Fedn. 1969; mem: Calif. Assn. Marital & Family Therapy; Christian Assn. for Psychological Studies; Democrat; Baptist. Res: 3579 Rowley Dr San Jose 95132 Ofc: Center for Family Learning, 5150 Graves Ave, Bldg 6D, San Jose 95129

HUTCHINSON, OTIS HALE, civil engineer; b. Nov. 28, 1928, Los Angeles; s. Ralph W. and Edith (Kitt) H.; m. Margaret A., Aug. 6, 1960; edn: BS, Univ. of Ariz. 1952; reg. civil engr., Calif. 1961. Career: with State of Calif. Dept. of Transp.: subprofl. 1946-50; jr. civil engr. 1950-56; asst. bridge engr. 1956-60; assoc. bridge engr. 1960--; mem: Naval Reserve Assn. (pres. Sutter chpt. 1975-77; pres. 12th dist. 1981-83); Boy Scouts of Am. (Explorer Advr. 1956-63); mil: commdr. USNR 1952-78; Republican; Protestant; rec: philately, hunting. Res: 4931 Bowman Oaks Way Carmichael 95608 Ofc: State of California, Dept. of Transportation, POB 1499, Sacramento

HUTCHISON, WILLIAM LEE, computer co. executive; b. Dec. 25, 1952, New Kensington, Pa.; s. William John and Carolyn Louise (Becker) H.; edn: BS, Grove City Coll. 1974. Career: mktg. rep. IBM, Los Angeles 1974-77; nat. sales instr. Basic Four, Irvine 1977-78, sales mgr., L.A. 1978-81; branch mgr., Irvine 1981-82; v.p. sales Micro Five, Irvine 1982--; awards: Rookie of the Yr., Western Reg. IBM 1976; Republican; Lutheran; rec: music, sports. Res: 901 Hyde Ct Costa Mesa 92626 Ofc: Micro Five, 3560 Hyland Costa Mesa 82626

HWANG, KWANG HAN, diplomat; b. July 20, 1937, Kangwon Province, Republic ofKorea; s. C. G. and S. S. (Hahm) Hwang; m. Jean Ock Suh, May 28, 1966; children: Young Mi b. 1967, Young Sil b. 1968, Chang Suk b. 1973; edn: BA, Korean Mil. Academy 1961. Career: commnd. 2d lt. Korean Army 1961, Comdr. Korean Army Mechanized Unit, 1974-76; Defense Attache to the Korean Embassy, Saudi Arabia 1977-80; Retired Brigadier General, entered Ministry of Foreign Affairs, 1980-; Ambassador to Repub. of Ghana 1981-83; Korean Consul General, Los Angeles 1983--; honors: Korean Presidential Award, other nat. honors; rec: golf, travel. Res: 627 S. Rossmore Ave Los Angeles 90036 Ofc: Korean Consulate General, 5455 Wilshire Blvd, Ste 1101, Los Angeles 90036

HYDE, PAUL RODNEY, banker; b. Dec. 27, 1953, El Paso, Tex.; s. Gerald Rodney and Lola Josephine (Nessen) H.; m. Polly J., Jan. 24, 1976; children: Shawn, b. 1977; Rebecca, b. 1979; Brian, b. 1981; edn: AA, Santa Barbara City Coll. 1976; CFP, Coll. of Fin. Plng., Denver, Colo. 1982. Career: comml. loan ofcr. Wells Fargo Bank; v.p./ mgr. First Pacific Bank, Beverly Hills Ofc.; currently, v.p./ mgr. Valley State Bank, Universal City Ofc.; pres. Hyde Fin. Svcs., Inc.; Republican; Ch. of Jesus Christ of LDS (tchr. early morning seminary class, Old Testament); rec: sports, photog. Res: 636 Corwin Ave Glendale 91206 Ofc: Valley State Bank, 3575 Cahuenga Blvd W, Universal City 90068

HYMAN, HERBERT MIKE, aerospace engineer; b. Apr. 14, 1940, NY, NY; s. Joseph and Lilian (Grey) H.; m. Reva Rothenberg, Nov. 4, 1978; 1 son: Brian Leigh, b. 1980. Edn: BA, Cal. State Long Bch., 1962; MBA, Golden State Univ., 1979; BSCS, West Coast Univ., 1983; DBA (in prog.) US Internat. Univ., 1983-; cert. mgr. Ints. of Cert. Profl. Mgrs., 1982. Career: Mgmt., avionics, automatic test equip., data base, info. & comm. systems, Rockwell Internat., 1963--.; design engr., sr. field engr., avionics proj. office, integraton engr., logistics engr. supr., proj. engr.; instr. CM pgm., Rockwell candidates, 1980-; field engr./tech. adv. to DOD, Vietnam & Europe, 1966-75. Awards: Engr. of the Month, Rockwell 1/83; Group Achievement Award, NASA, 1982. Mem: Nat. Mgmt. Assn. (cert. prgm. mgr.); Inst. of Cert. Profl. Mgrs.; Masons, Scottish Rite, Shriners, US Handball Assn.. Rec: electronics/comp., handball, golf. Res: 5003 Oxford Dr. Cypress 90630. Ofc: Rockwell Internat., 12214 Lakewood Blvd. Downey 90241

I

IAMELE, RICHARD THOMAS, law librarian; b. Jan. 29, 1942, Newark, N.J.; s. Armando Anthony and Evelyn (Coladonato) Iamele; edn: BA, Loyola Univ. of Los Angeles, 1963, M.S.L.S., USC, 1967, MD, Southwestern Univ. Sch of Law, 1976; m. Marilyn Berutto, Aug. 21, 1965; chil: Thomas, b. 1966, Ann Marie, b. 1968; career: Cataloger, Univ. of Southern Calif., Los Angeles 1967-71; cataloger, Los Angeles County Law Library, 1971-77, reference librarian 1977-78, asst. librarian 1978-80, librarian 1980--; mem: State Bar of Calif., American Bar Assn., Am. Assn. of Law Libraries, So. Calif. Assn. of Law Libraries; Republican; Roman Catholic; ofc: L.A. Co. Law Library, 301 West 1st St. Los Angeles 90012.

IANNACCONE, FRANK JAMES, lawyer; b. June 27, 1950, NY, NY; s. Frank and Anna Lucille (Ferrara) I.; m. Cathy Durkes, Sept. 15, 1969; edn: AA, Mooropark Coll. 1972; BA, CSU Northridge 1973; JD, Southwestern Univ. 1976. Career: pvt. practice law, Los Angeles 1977; sr. partner firm of Licker, Rothstein, Delchop & Iannaccone 1978-80; owner/sr. ptnr. Law Ofcs. of Frank James Iannaccone, Inc., Thousand Oaks 1980--; awards: Commdn. Awd., EPIC

(Ednl. Participation in Communities) 1973; Am. Jurisprudence Awards (Evidence and Community Property) 1975; mem: Am. Bar Assn.; Internat. Netsuke Collectors Soc.; Internat. Oceanographic Found.; L.A. Co. Mus. of Art.; Thousand Oaks CofC; Republican; rec: sailing, surfing, travel. Res: 16601 Marquez Ave Pacific Palisades 90272 Ofc: Law Ofcs. of Frank J. Iannaccone, Inc., 100 E Thousand Oaks Blvd, Ste 137, Thousand Oaks 91360

IANTORNO, PAT PETER, pharmacist; b. Dec. 21, 1948, Long Beach; s. Sam James and Sayoe Margaret Iantorno; m. Julie, Aug. 10, 1973; children: Eric, b. 1975; Jordan, b. 1982; edn: AB, UCLA 1971; BS, Univ. of Ariz. 1974; D.Pharm., Univ. Pacific 1975; Clinical Doctorate, 1975; lic. Pharm. in Calif., Ariz., 1974. Career: pharmacist El Cajon Med. Pharmacy 1976; pres. Iantorno Pharmacies, Inc. 1978; founder/pres. Iantorno Clinic Pharmacies, Inc. (estab. 19 prescription oriented medical ctr. pharmacies 1978-82) 1978--; dir. Encinitas Med. Pharmacy 1976; dir. Medco Drugs 1978; mem: Calif. Pharmacists Assn. (pres. 1978); Am. Pharmacists Assn.; Chem. People Nat. Proj. (panel); Drug Task Force, Escondido; Council for Retail Pharmacy Roles, Univ. of So. Calif. Coll. of Pharm.; invention: automatic pill counter for retail pharmacy usen, 1977; composer, piano music 1978, 82; Repubilcan; rec; music, writing. Res: 1756 Tatterham Rd Leucadia 92024 Ofc: Iantorno Clinic Pharmacies, 317 N El Camino Real, Ste 404, Encinitas 92021

IBBETSON, EDWIN THORNTON, development co. president; b. Apr. 17, 1923, Los Angeles; s. Robert Edwin and Ann E. (Thornton) Ibbetson; m. Harriet Alice Hudson, Dec. 28, 1947; children: Elizabeth Ann (Mrs. Phillip Hitchcock), Douglas Hudson, Gregory Bruce, Timothy Edwin, Julia Katherine (Mrs. Martin Zilinskas), Erika Alice (Mrs. Tor Hertzog). Career: with Union Devel. Co., Cerritos 1944-, pres. 1961--; partner Paramount Constrn., Cerritos 1948-; v.p. Valley Properties Inc., Imperial Valley 1962-; pres. Union Farms Inc., Cerritos 1962-81; chmn. bd. dirs. Dutch Village Bowling Ctr. Inc., Lakewood 1965-; partner Ibbetson-Marsh Realtors 1975-; vice chmn. bd. Equitable Svg.& Loan Assn. 1977-; bd. dirs.(chmn. 1977-9) Garden State Bank 1974-79; bd. dirs.(sec. 1979-82, chmn. 1983-) Met. Water Dist. So. Calif., 1959-; chmn. Bellflower Water Devel. Com. 1965-; chmn. Los Angeles Co. Real Estate Adv. Com. 1974-; bd.dirs. Armed Services YMCA, Long Beach 1962-72; trustee St. Mary's Hosp., Long Beach. honors: Young Man of Year 1959, Bellflower Jaycees; Hon. Pres. for Life, Calif. Assn of Realtors, 1980; Realtor of Year, Bellflower Dist. Bd. Realtors, 1962, 67, 71; Bellflower Kiwanis Man of Year 1983. Mem: Am. Soc. Real Estate Counselors (fov., pres. 1977), Calif. Assn. Realtors (treas. 1972-7, dir.), Internat. Real Estate Fedn., Nat. Assn. Realtors (dir.), Nat. Inst. Real Estate Brokers (cert. comml. investment mem.), Inst. Real state Mgmt. (cert. property mgr.), Urban Land Inst., Rancho Los Cerritos Bd. Realtors (1961), Central Basin Water Assn. (dir.), Calif. Real Esanis (pres. 1958), Internat. Traders, So. Calif. Tuna (Long Bch). mil: USNR 1943-46. Roman Catholic. Ofc: 16550 Bloomfield Ave, Cerritos 90701

IBRAHIM, LAILA SOBI, financial planner; b. Aug. 8, 1957, Cairo, Egypt, nat. 1976; s. Sobi Alexander and Angele Rezk (Metguli) I.; edn: bus./econ. major, UCLA 1975-78; CPF, Coll. of Fin. Planning. 1981. Career: sales rep. John Naylor Corp., Fountain Valley 1978-80; Registered Rep. Innovative Financial Planning Svcs., Inc., Tustin 1980--, Reg. Prin./vice pres. currently; mem: Internat. Assn. Fin. Plnrs.; Inst. CFPs; Republican; Christian; rec: sports. Res: 1 Escapade Ct Newport Beach 92663 Ofc: Innovative Financial Planning Services Inc., 17542 E 17th St, Ste 400, Tustin 92680

ICHINAGA, GARY RONALD, electronic mfg. co. executive; b. Jan. 5, 1953, San Jose; s. Howard Kazuo and Yoshiye (Kawaguchi) Ichinaga; edn: AA, cert. in electronics tech., Cerritos Coll. 1979. Career: supr. Electro Services, Inc. 1977-78; prodn. mgr. JKL Mfg., 1978-79; prin. IBT Printed Circuits, 1979-81; prodn. mgr. Pioneer Circuits, Inc. 1981-82; vice pres./gen. mgr. Superior Plastics, Inc., Paramount 1982--; mem. Japanese Am. Citizen League; Democrat; Buddhist; rec: electronics, sports, music. Res: 11124 Excelsior Dr. %16, Norwalk 90650 Ofc: Superior Plastics, Inc. 7303 Madison St. Paramount 90723

IGI, GEORGE KAZUO, clinical services director; b. Feb. 23, 1941, Los Angeles; s. Sadao and Etsuko (Ikitake) I.; m. Cynthia Heard, Mar. 22, 1977; children: Kelly, b. 1965; Amanda, b. 1978; Melissa, b. 1981; edn: AA, Los Angeles City Coll. 1966; BA, CSU Northridge 1967; MSW, USC 1969; Calif. LCSW Lic. Clin. Soc. Wkr. 1972; Acad. Cert. Soc. Wkrs. 1972. Career: psychiatric soc. wkr. Junipero Serra Boys Club, Los Angeles 1969-71; deputy probation ofcr. III, Los Angeles Co. Probation Dept. 1971-72; dir. clinical svcs. Calif. Youth Homes, Inglewood 1972-76; exec. dir. The Sycamores, Altadena & instr. CSU Los Angeles Soc. Welfare Dept. 1976-77; dir. clin. svcs. Calif. Youth Homes 1977--; conf. chmn. first Nat. Asian- Am. Mental Health Conf. 1972; chmn. Nat. Asian- Am. Mental Health Fedn. 1972-74; bd. mem. Asian- Am. Comm. Mental Health Tng. Ctr. 1972-76; bd. dirs. Oriental Svc. Ctr. 1969-71; awards: 2nd degree Black Belt, 1970; mem: NASW; Asian Am. Soc. Wkrs. (cofounder 1969, pres. 1970-71); USC Sch. of Soc. Wrk. Alumni Assn.; Bd. Behav. Sci. Examiners, Calif.; Judo Black Belt Assn. of Am.; YMCA (Indian Princess); USC Sch. of Soc. Wrk. Admissions Com.; Venice Boys Club (Judo instr.); works: principle or coauthohr num. grants for Nat. Asian- Am. Mental Health Assn.; first ant. Asian- Am. Mental Health Conf. under NIMH sponsorship; mil: airman 1/c, USAF; Democrat; Catholic; rec: Judo, gardening. Res: 2224 Via Alamitos Palos Verdes Estates 90274 Ofc: 442 Warren Ln Inglewood 90302

IGLEHART, DONALD LEE, educator; b. May 11, 1933, Baltimore, MD; s. Marion McDonnal (dec.) and Ruth Roberta (Gillen) I.; m. Sheralee Florence Hill, Jul. 15, 1961; children: Kent, b. 1964; Mark, b. 1966, 1961. Career: postdoctl. research fellow Oxford Univ., 1961-2; asst./assoc. prof. of operations research Cornell Univ., 1962-67; prof. ops. research Stanford Univ., 1967--; prin./dir. Control Analyst Corp., 1971-77; dir. Renhart Corp., 1983--. Awards: fellow, Inst. Mathematical Stats.; fellow, Churchill Coll., Cambridge Univ.. Mem: Operations Research Soc. of Am.; Inst. Mathematical Stats.; Bernoulli Soc.; publs:; over 70 papers (1962-) topics: probability theory, statistics, queueing theory, simulaton, and inventory theory; mil: lt. USN 1956-58; rec: tennis, piano. Res: 833 Tolman Dr. Stanford 94305. Ofc: Stanford University, Dept. Operations Research Stanford 94305

IGO, LOUIS DANIEL, lawyer, educator; b. Sept. 21, 1939, Boston, Mass.; s. Luther Louis and Martha (Baker) I.; 1 son, John Daniel b. 1958; edn: BS in Econ./Acctg., Mo. Valley Coll. 1963; postgrad. tax law Univ. Mo., K.C. 1964-66; JD, Univ. Tulsa 1967; postgrad. Okla. Sch. Accountancy 1967-68, USC 1979; admitted to Okla. bar 1968, US Dist. Ct. (No. Dist.) Okla. 1968, US Tax Ct. 1973, Calif. bar 1973, US Dist. Ct. (Cen. Dist.) Calif. 1973, US Ct. Mil. Appeals 1982, US Ct. Appeals (9th Cir.) 1982, US Supreme Ct. 1973. Career: acct. Lipoff, Sharlipp, Pasmen & Co. K.C., Mo. 1963-64; asst. to sales mgr. Lynn Ins. Group, K.C., 1965-66; cost acct. Gulf Oil Corp., K.C., 1966; contract/ real estate Texaco Inc., Tulsa, Okla. 1968-70; acct. Arthur Young & Co. Long Beach, Ca. 1970-71; self empl. practicing atty., Los Angeles 1973--; prof. law and acctg. Los Angeles Community Coll. Dist., 1972-83; mem: LA County Bar Assn., Japanese Am. Bar Assn.; Arbitrator Am. Arbitration Assn.; Cert. Trial and Defense Counsel; Cert. Legal Assistance Ofcr.; orgns: Elks, Masons, Scottish Rite, Shriners, Naval Reserve Assn., Sigma Alpha Epsilon, Alpha Phi Omega, Phi Alpha Delta, Reserve Ofcrs. Assn.; mil: US Army 1964-68; comdr. JAG Corps, USNR 1968-, Mil. Magistrate 1980-; author scripts and syllabus for Law for the '70's (Instrnl. TV award, 1976); revised the Time Life Family Legal Guide, 1976; Ind.; Episcopal; rec; sailing, walking, hunting. Res: 16552 Sell Circle Huntington Beach 92649 Ofc: LACC, 855 N. Vermont Los Angeles 90029 Law Ofc: 16216 Hawthorne Blvd Lawndale 90260

IKHARO, ISMAILA IBRAHIM, insurance agent; b. Aug. 19, 1952, Auchi, Nigeria; s. Chief Ibrahim and Achaja Meremu Offako (Afegbua) I.; m. Hauwa Eve Ahmed, Sept. 12, 1978; child: Teslim, b. 1982; edn: BSc, Wilberforce Univ. 1979; MSc, Wright State Univ. 1981; MBA, Golden Gate Univ. 1983; Life & Disability Ins. Lic. Career: classroom tchr., local sch. bd., Auchi 1972-73; tutor, State Sch. Bd., Benin-City 1974-76; data processing Ohio Dept. Nat. Resources, Columbus, Ohio 1977; founder Ishmael Enterprendre, Fairborn, Ohio 1980-82; ins. agent John Hancock Ins., Daly City 1983--; awards: Fiestco Academic Scholarship, Wright State Univ. 1981; mem: Am. Mgmt. Assn.; MBA Execs.; Alpha-Cee Klub; Orgn. Concerned Citizens; research: boating and boat usage in Ohio; Muslim; rec: tennis. Res: 1130 3rd Ave, 403, Oakland 94606 Ofc: John Hancock Co., 207 Southgate Ave Daly City 94015

IMKER, FRANZ W., school faciities executive; b. Jan. 18, 1929, San Jose; s. Frederick W. and Hazel W. (Naas) I.; m. Marilyn Mottitt, Aug. 11, 1950; children: Frederick W., b. 1952; Eric F., b. 1951; edn: AB, (Engring. Dept. honors) San Jose State 1951; MBA, Stanford 1953; comm. coll. tchg. cred., Calif. 1965. Career: ret. Lt. Col. USAF, 1953-75, budget ofcr., acctg. & fin. ofcr., comptroller; facilities mgr. Santa Cruz City Schs. 1976--; fin. ofcr. Post 64 Am. Legion; awards: Coolice Scholar, Stanford Univ. 1952; Republican; Protestant; rec: philately. Res: 2395 Delaware Ave Santa Cruz 95060 Ofc: Santa Cruz City Schools, 133 Mission St Santa Cruz 95060

INGRAM, ROBERT BRUCE, lawyer; b. July 19, 1940, Des Moines, Io.; s. Earl J. and Frances F. (Forquer) I.; m. Judith J., Sept. 10, 1966; children: Stephanie, b. 1973; Ashley, b. 1976; Robert, b. 1977; edn: Univ. of Iowa 1958-61; BA, Drake Univ. 1962; Drake Law Sch. 1962-63; JD, William & Mary Sch. of Law 1970; trial lawyer. Career: trial lawyer, law ofcs. Melvin Belli 1971-78; trial lawyer, law ofcs. Robert B. Ingram, San Rafael 1978--; honors: Key note spkr., Georgia State Bar 1979; mem: Am., Calif. & San Francisco Trial Lawyers Assns.; Am. Bar Assn.; Elks Club; Rafael Racquet Club; Am. Heart Assn., Marin chpt.; arts. in law reviews; Presbyterian. Ofc: Robert B. Ingram, A Profl. Conp., 4340 Redwood Hwy, Ste 352, San Rafael 94903

INMAN, PAUL BARRON, business owner; b. July 18, 1956, Van Nuys; s. Carl B. and Wanda Mary (Yaco) I.; m. Elisabeth Huebner, June 20, 1981; children: Melissa b. 1982, Amber b. 1984; edn: AA, Antelope Valley Coll. Career: owner Inman's Courier Service, 1976-77; bus. devel. rep. Transamerica Title, 1-7; audit clk. Bank of Am. 1979-82; owner Desert Couriers Lancaster 1981--; Republican; Christian. Res: 44141 Gingham Ave Lancaster 93534 Ofc: 115 W Ave J, Ste D, Lancaster 93534

INMAN, WANDA MARY, real estate broker; b. Dec. 6, 1925, Italy (parents Am. cit.); d. Victor and Elizabeth (Mohr) Yaco; m. Carl Barron Inman, May 4, 1952; children: Paul, b. 1956; Gail, b. 1957; edn: AA, Antelope Valley Coll. 1981; Univ. of Ill. 1944-46; Cert. Senior Escrow Ofcr., Calif. Escrow Assn. Career: escrow ofcr. Bank of Am., Lancaster 1969-75; hd. escrow dept. 1975-83; realtor Roberson Realty, Pearblossom 1983--; escrow instr. Antelope Valley Coll. (sev. sems. for real estate cont. edn.) 1977-; Ecrow Assn. of Antelope Valley (pres. 1977); Foothill & Palmdale Bds. Realtors; Republican; Christian; rec: travel. Res: 7518 W Avenue A, Lancaster 93534 Ofc: Roberson Realty, 12822 Pearblossom Hwy, Pearblossom 93553

INNERBICHLER, LEO JOSEPH, engineer; b. Mar. 19, 1927, Gallup, NM; s. Fred Harry and Juanita (Jaramillo) I.; m. Mabel Baca, Dec. 24, 1951; children: Jennifer, b. 1955; Stephen, b. 1959; edn: Univ. of Okla. 1944-45; Grad. Meteorology, UCLA 1951-52; BS, US Naval Acad., 1950; M.Bus.Econ., Claremont 1966. Career: systems engring. splst., design gp. supvr./ section head & pgm. mgmt. assignments General Dynamics, Pomona 1956-76; proj. engr. adv. sys. research & definition/ eng. cons. Flight Systems, Inc., Newport Beach 1976--; pres. L.J.I. Assocs. (real estate brokerage ofc.) 1975-; mem: Omicron Delta Epsilon, econ. hon. soc.; Sister City Assn., Upland, Ca., Caborca, Mex. & Meldura, Australia (pres.); coauthor: Applied Systems Enigneering Techniques, 1965; author: Resource Allocation Under Conditions of Uncertainty, 1966; mil: pvt. US Army 1944-46; midshipman, USN 1946-50; lt. col. USAF, 1950-56, Reserves 1956-70; rec: oil/ Chinese brush painting, antique furniture restoration. Res: 2298 Waterman Costa Mesa 92627 Ofc: Flight Systems, 1901 Dove Newport Beach 92660

INNES, JOHN HERBERT, electronic manufacturing executive; b. July 8, 1937, Merced (4th gen. Californian); s. George Alexander and Phyllis Tutin (Hopps) I.; m. Catherine Franklin (4th gen. Californian), May 7, 1966; children: Matthew, b. 1967; Marcus, b. 1969; edn: ME Bus., Univ. of Colo. Career: prodn. mgmt. Del Monte Corp. 1962-67; mgr. semiconductor ops. Fairchild Semiconductor 1967-70; founder/ mgr. bi-polar ops. Intersil, Inc., Santa Clara 1970-75; founder/ v.p. ops. Cronus Precision Prods., Santa Clara 1975-80; pres. Livermore Communications, Livermore 1981-83; v.p. ops. Tanon Mfg., Inc., Milpitas 1983--; founder/ dir. Livermore Communs. & Tanon Mfg. Inc.; honors: Community Awd., Chmn. of Pleasanton Indsl. Gen. Plan 1983-84; commnr. Plng. Commn., Pleasanton 1984; mem: YMCA (Century); Elks; Castlewood CofC; patentee: 1st digital stopwatch, watch, stopwatch electronic circuit; Republican; Catholic; rec: pvt. pilot, water sports, golf. Res: 1586 Foothill Rd Pleasanton 94566 Ofc: Tanon Mfg., Inc., 1841 Tarob, Ste G, Milpitas

INSKEEP, EDWARD C., school administrator; b. Nov. 13, 1941, Oceanside; s. Charles Carey and May (Blount) Inskeep; m. Connie Wright, jan. 25, 1963; chil: Timothy, b. 1968, Dale, b. 1966; edn: AA, Mira Costa Jr. Coll. 1961; AB, San Diego State Univ. 1964; MA, CSU Long Bch 1969; PhD, U.S. Internat. Univ. 1979; teaching credentials (for life): elem., sec., adult, jr. coll. (computer sci.), Calif State (health & accident, life ins.); elem. adminstrn. and gen. adminstrn. credentials. Career: fmr. sch.teacher, gr. 3-12, instr. teacher tng. 6 yrs.; vice prin. De Mille Jr. High Sch., Long Beach 1982--; instr. computer sci. various colls.; cons. to bus. re computers; author: Apple Execution (art. and computer pgm. sold to Personal Computing); mem: Phi Delta Kappa, Assn. Long Beach Educ. Mgrs., Orange Co. Assn. Computing Machinery, Assn. Calif. Sch. Adminstrs.; Republican; prot.; rec: arc & gas welding, glassblowing, tennis. Res: 2130 Kallen Ave., Long Beach 90815 Ofc: De Mille Jr. High 725 E. Parkcrest, Long Beach 90808

INSTITORIS, EMIL ZOLTON, consulting co. executive, b. July 27, 1927, Detroit, Mich.; S. Michael and Margaret (Dont) I; m. Shirley Melton, Oct. 24, 1978; 1 dau: Paulette Mueller b. 1945; edn: BA, Jackson State Univ. 1972; MBA, 1974; PhD, Thomas A. Edison 1976; ciln. psychologist, Plam Beach Tng. Ctr. 1976. Career: process engr. quality sandards Gen. Motors Fisher Body Div., Detroit, Mich. 1950-58; asst. supt. quality control 1958-63; supt. quality control 1963-68; dir. ops. Skyways Airport Hotel 1969-70; bd. chmn./ pres. Skpways Ent., Inc. 1971 ; cons. maj. hotel chains, UCLA & USC Cont. Edn. pgms.; mem: fellow, Am. Acad. Behav. Sci.; fellow, Assn. for Soc. Psychology; fellow, Am. Coll. of Clinic Amdinstrs.; Am. Bd. Examiners in Psychotherapy; Nat. Psychological Assn.; Am. Psychotherapy Assn.; Am. Assn. Profl. Hypologists; Nat. Psychiat. Assn.; United Assn. of Christian Counselors; Am. Assn. Rel. Counselors; Am. Mgmt. Assn.; Am. Entrepreneurs Assn.; Alphi Psi Sigma; Delta Epsilon Omega; mil: tech. 4th gr. US Army 1945-48, Euro., Am. Theatre, Occ. Forces Ribbon, GCM; Republican (Pres. Task Force); Catholic; rec: writing, collect fire arms, restore mil. vehicles. Res: 447 W Via Escuela Palm Springs 92262 Ofc: Skyways Ent., Inc., POB 45907 Los Angeles 90045

IPPOLITO, MACEL CONNIE, sales and marketing co. president; b. Dec. 31, 1935, Torrington, Wyo.; d. Roy Edward and Georgia Elaine (Morrow) Nearing; m. Carl Ippolito, Oct. 7, 1978; att. var. jr. colls. Career: fmr. receptionist to adminstr. on Apollo Pgm. for MIT (Instrumentation Lab.), Cape Kennedy, Fla.; chief ops. Carson Gp. (physician search gp.), Manhattan, NY; corp. asst. secty., Shapell Inds.; currently, pres. Four Seasons Greenhouses of Calif. (mktg. solariums) Glendale; honors: active in 4-H and won Wyoming State Garden Judging Contest; Republican; Protestant; rec: equestrian, golf, cooking. Res: 4715 Caheunga Blvd Toluca Lake 91602 Ofc: Four Seasons Greenhouses of Calif., 1849 Dana St Glendale 91201

IRANI, BIJAN, metallurgist; b. Sept. 5, 1951, Hamadan, Iran; s. Alinaghi nd Molook (Matin) I.; m. Carmella, July 23, 1981; edn: AA, Santa Barbara City Coll. 1973; BS, Calif. Polytech. Univ. 1976; grad. stu, USC. Career: shop metallurgist Thero Electron Corp. 1976-77, plant metallurgist 1977-78, chief metallurgist 1978-82; gen. mgr. So. Calif. Aluminum Treating Co. 1983--, quality control mgr./ chief metallurgist; tchr. Cerritos Comm. Colls.; tchr. metallurgical engr. Am. Soc. for Metals; honors: ASME Awd., Am. Soc. for Metals (ASM); mem: ASM (edn. chmn.); publs: sev. papers on stress corrosion 1976, and heat treating of high strength metals 1978; Moslem; rec: equestrian, philately. Res: 458 E. Tujunga Ave, F, Burbank 91501 Ofc: Cal-Doran Metallurgical, 2830 E. Washington Blvd Los Angeles 90023

IRETON, JOHN MELVILLE, manufacturing co. owner; b. Nov. 25, 1926, Santa Barbara (4th gen. Californian); s. Arthur Charles Wm. and Marie Genevieve (Estes) I.; ances., Henry Ireton, Gen. and son-in-law of Oliver Cromwell; m. Marion Wait, Nov. 30, 1957; children: Peter b. 1949, Patrick b. 1951, JohnJr. b. 1958, Kathryn b. 1959, Curt b. 1961, Elizabeth b. 1963, Mary b. 1964; edn: Black Fox Mil. Inst. (Hollywood, Ca.); Univ. of Hawaii, Honolulu. Career: div. mgr. White Truck and Constrn. Eqpt. Div., Schumann Carriage Co., Honolulu 1948-58; White Motor Co., Cleveland, Milwaukee, Los Angeles to 1965; self-empl., joined briefly in coop. effort with Dutton Mfg. Co. later to become His Business, Inc., a Christian ministry in design, mfg. and mktg. co. of construction dqpt. products for the electrical industry; mil: USAAFR 1944-47; Republican; Christian; rec: sailing. Res: 9250 Brier Crest Dr. La Mesa 92041 Ofc: His Business, Inc. 5803 Kearny Villa Rd San Diego 92123

IRICK, PATRICIA CAMILLE, fast foods co. executive; b. Nov. 11, 1936, Los Angeles; d. John Richard and Dorothea D. (Pearce) Collins; edn: BS in Edn., Univ. of Houston 1958; M.Ed., Stephen F. Austin, 1964; Texas Tchr. Cert. (life): Supvsn/Adm., Elem., H.S.; pgmmg. tech. Control Data Inst. 1973. Career: math. instr. Dallas (Tx.) Independent School Dist. 1961-70; supr. Lower Sch. Math Dept. The Hockaday Sch., Dallas 1970-72; data center coord., mgr. I/O Control Dept., Gambles Datamation Ctr, Burbank, Ca. 1973-79; mgr. computer ops./tech. support Collins Foods Internat. Inc. 1979--; honors: outstanding young educator, Dallas Jr. CofC 1969; rec: writer short stories, oil painting, bridge. Res: 6500 Green Valley Circle, 135, Culver City 90230 Ofc: Collins Foods Inter. Inc. 5400 Alla Rd Los Angeles 90066

IRICK, ROBERT LEE, materials center president; b. Aug. 14, 1930, Competition, Mo.; s. Melvin Hollege and Delphia Ruth (Handley) I.; edn: BA, Southwest Mo. State Univ. 1955; cert. Yale Ins. of F.E. Languages, 1951-52; MA, Harvard Univ. 1958, PhD, 1971. Career: rep. The Hannaford Co., Inc.; pres. Chinese Materials Center, Hong Kong, 1978--; pres./ chmn. bd. dirs. Chinese Materials Center, Inc., S.F. 1974-81; mng. dir. Taiwan Ent. Co., Ltd., Taipei, 1970--; res. dir. Calif. State Internat. Programs, Taipei, 1966--; mng. dir. Chinese Materials and Research Aids Service Center, Inc. Taipei 1964-74; also adj. assoc. prof./ prof. Nat. Chengchi Univ. 1976-79, Nat. Chungkung Univ. 1974-75, adj. prof. Nat. Taiwan Univ. 1981-; instr. Yale Univ. 1957; secty. Adv. Bd., Sino Am. Commn. workshop on coop. in scis. and humanities, Taipei 1965-71; hon. director World-Wide Ethical Soc. 1981-; honors: Boys Nation, Lebanon H. Sch. No. 1 grad., Debate Letter 1951, Who's Who Among Students in Am. Colls. and Univs. 1955, Intl. Who's Who in Edn., Men of Achievement, Who's Who in the World, Intl. Director of Scholars & Splsts. in the Third World, Who's Who in Library and Information Services, Directory of Am. Scholars, The Intl. Book of Honor; mem: past pres. Harvard Club of Taipei, Am. Univ. Club (Taipei), Assn. for Asian Studies Inc., Ann Arbor (Com. on East Asian Libraries), Chinese Lang. Tchrs. Assn., Kappa Alpha Order 1950-51, Presidents Club Southwest Mo. State Univ., Smithsonian Assocs., num. publs. incl. 50th Ann. edition SMSU Ozarko; mil: TSgt. USAF 1951-55, Commendn.; Methodist, rec. collect cookbooks. Ofc. 2F, 17 Alley 7 Lane 217 Chunghsiao E. Rd., Sec. 3 Taipei, Taiwan 100, ROC.

IRWIN, JANET KATHRYN, marketing co. executive; b. May 21, 1937, Waterford, MI; d. Thomas R. and Alma M. (Tuttle) Corbin; m. Thomas Irwin, Feb. 8, 1982; 1 son, Cameron Corbin Smith, b. 1966; edn: BA, Mich. State Univ. 1959. Career: dir. broadcast media, MacManus, John & Adams Advtg., Mich. 1959-60; acct. exec. David Parry Public Relations, Los Angeles 1960-66; owner/pres. Janet Smith Pub. Rels, L.A. 1966-73; Dir. Bodrell Smith & Assocs. 1966-74; western regl. mgr. Marer and Brass, L.A. 1974-76 pres. J. Corbin Smith Investments, Santa Monica 1976-81; regl. mgr. Calif., Bernard Haldane Assocs., L.A. 1979--; honors: runner up Miss Mich. Contest 1955; pres. Buckley Parents Assn. 1972-73; mem. Bus. and Profl. Women, Chamber of Commerce; Republican; Prot.; rec: tennis, music. Res: 11740 Wilshire Blvd Los Angeles 90025 Ofc: Bernard Haldane Assoc. 8484 Wilshire Blvd, Ste. 800 Beverly Hills 90211

ISAACSON, BORIS, inventor, researcher; b. Dec. 28, 1926, Brooklyn, NY; s. Frank and Gussic (Cohen) I.; div.; children: Cory Michael, b. 1955; Dean Robert, b. 1961; edn: BA, Brooklyn Coll. 1950. Career: lighting dir. NBC TV, 1950-60; pres. Solartile, Inc., Milolite Ind., Sun Energy Prod., Van Guard Mfg. 1961; pres. New Age Kitchens, No. Hollywood; founder/ pres. Living Food Soc., No. Hollywood 1983; currently, owner/ inventor Tomorrow Now; pres. Taxpayers for Unitax, No. Hollywood; instr. TV Lighting, Columbia Coll.; mem: Soc. of TV Lighting Dirs.; No. Hollywood CofC; Parents Without Partners; patentee: Air Depollution Dome, 1973; Inflatable Blower, 1976; Inflatable Windmill, 1978; Solar Shingle, 1977; mil: elec. mate 3/c USNR, WWII; Ind.; Agnostic; rec: tax reform. Res: 11019 Cumpston St, No. Hollywood 91601 Ofc: Tomorrow Now, 11015 Cumpston, No. Hollywood 91601

ISELEY, ROBERT CRAIG, lawyer; b. Sept. 18, 1948, Pasadena; s. Ralph Craven and Jane Elizabeth (DeMonte) I.; m. Lieselotte C., Nov. 30, 1973; children: Michael, b. 1967; Clifford, b. 1969; edn: AA, Pasadena City Coll. 1968; BA, UC Berkeley 1970; JD, Loyola Law Sch. 1977; admitted to practice, Calif. State Bar, Calif. Supreme Ct. 1980; lic. Real Estate Broker, Calif. Career: br. mgr. Gen. Electric Credit Corp. 1972-78; investment advr. Spartan Brokerage Gp. 1979-82; law partner Plefka & Iseley, Attys. at Law 1981-82; atty., Robert Craif Iseley, Atty. at Law 1982-83; currently, atty. Robert Craig Iseley, A Profl. Corp., Sacto.; dir. Red Shield Servicing, Inc. 1982; cons. Sacramento Financial Orgn.; honors: Phi Beta Kappa, UCB 1970; mem: Am., Calif., Sacto. bar assns.; Sacto. County Bar Assn.; Sacramento Fin. Orgn.; publs: (legal decisions): Triangle Mgmt. v. Allstate S & L (21 B.R. 699, 1982), Golden Plan of California (25 B.R. 183, 1982); Democrat; Protestant; rec: sports, home remodel. Res: 116 Glenville Cir Sacramento 95826 Ofc: Robert Craig Iseley, A Profl. Corp., 451 Parkfair Dr, Ste 7, Sacramento 95825

ITAGAKI, BRIAN HIRO, spine orthopaedic surgeon; b. Oct. 12, 1946, Honolulu, Hawaii; s. Shigeru and Yuriko Mavis (Takahashi) Itagaki; m. Gale Hamaoka, Sept. 27, 1970; children: Lynn, b. 1974, Lisa, b. 1977; edn: BA, Univ. Hawaii, 1968; MS, Univ. Ill. 1969; MD, Univ. Hawaii 1977. Career: capt. USAF 1969-73; systems analyst IBM 360 Computer, Command Post Japanese Briefer to visiting Dignataries, SAC Hdqtrs., Offutt AFB 1970-73; orthopaedic surgery resident (chief res. 1981-2) UC Irvine Med. Ctr. 1977-82; awards: Spinal Surgery Fellowship, Rancho Los Amigos Hosp. 1982-3, Outstanding Cadet AF ROTC Summer Camp 1968, 1st place Biomed Research Forum, and rep. to Nat. Sci. Research Forum (Galveston, Tex.), Univ. Hawaii Sch. of Med. 1974, UCI Med. Ctr. Outstanding Resident & Tchr. 1978, Quarterly Med. Record Award 1979; mem: AMA, Am. Coll. of Surgeons (cand.), Antibiotic Review subcom. UCI Med. Ctr. 1982; team phys. Garden Grove H.S. football team 1978-81; publs: art. Aviation Space Environmental Medicine, 6/76, research in lumbar spine fractures 1981-2; Prot.; rec: running, gardening. Res: 6556 Sattes Dr Rancho Palos Verdes 90274 Ofc: Rancho Los Amigos Hospital, Spinal Deformities, HB130, 7601 East Imperial Hwy Downey 90242

IVEY, WILLIAM GILBERT, calibration services executive; b. Apr. 12, 1929, Jacksonville, Fla.; s. Joseph Josha and Francina (Taylor) I.; m. Imalda Davis, Feb. 12, 1951; children: Gilbert, b. 1952; Jacqueline, b. 1954; Cynthia, b. 1957; edn: AA, El Camino 1959; lic FCC Radio Telephone w/ Radar endorsement, 1980-5. Career: aircraft elec. North American, Checkout F100 Line, El Segundo 1953-56; sr. techn. Northrop Ref. & Transfer Std., Hawthorne 1956-64; metrology splst. DC & LF Standards TRW DSSG, Redondo Beach 1964-70; metrology engr. 1970-72; metrology supvr. gen. calibration 1972-81; sect. head calibration svcs., TRW O&SG, Redondo Beach 1972--; mem. Los Angeles Personnel Dept. Examining Bd. 1979; cons. Willow Brook Jr. High 1980, Compton Comm. Coll. 1980; awards: John Quincy Adams Mgmt. Excellence Awd., Precision Measurement Assn. 1983; Quality Circle Leadership Awd., TRW 1980-81; Man of the Month, Precision Measurment Assn. 1984; mem: Precision Measurement Assn. (pres.); Bootstray; Youth Motivation Task Force; Mead Valley CofC; Amateur Radio Club of TRW (pres. 1979); mil: s/sgt. E-5 USAF 1948-53, radar tech. & air police supvr., WWI Victory, GCM, Japanese Occupation; Democrat; SDA; rec: amateur radio, hunting, fishing. Res: 930 W 132nd Street Compton 90222 Ofc: TRW/ OSG, One Space Park, S/365, Redondo Beach 90278

IZZO, JOSEPH GEORGE, JR., writer; b. Oct. 21, 1950, Hollywood; s. Joseph G. and Florence (Graganella) I.; m. Kristine, July 3, 1976; edn: BA, English, CSU San Jose 1973; MA, edn., Santa Clara Univ. 1975. Career: founder Izkinelli Publs., 1974; coauthor/pub. 1st Ed., A Forkful of San Jose (1975) 2d. and 3d. eds. (1975-78); coauthor/pub.: A Forkful of the Peninsula (1979), A Forkful of Contra Costa. Diablo Valley (1979); founder/exec. editor J.K. West Publications, 1981--, author/pub. The First Business Companion to Silicon Valley, and (bestselling) South Bay Hot Plates; other works: Guilty Parties (novel), Guilty Parties (screenplay), Forkful (screenplay), Deathbell (screenplay); restaurant critic, San Jose Mercury News 1980-; tch. writing and reading Moorpark Juvenile Court Sch.; mem. American Lung Assn., GreenPeace USA, Childcare Partner, San Jose Sym., San Jose Art Museum; Republican; Catholic; rec: phys. fitness. Res: 6325 Benzo Dr San Jose 95123 Ofc: JK West Publications, POB 18758, San Jose 95158

J

JABIN, MARVIN (MARK), lawyer; b. Mar. 28, 1929, Brooklyn, NY; s. Sol and Belle (Paikoff) J.; m. Lelia Honig, May 13, 1952; children: Valerie, b. 1957; Gregory, b. 1958; Anthony, b. 1965; Desiree, b. 1970; edn: AB, NYU 1952; BS, UCLA 1954; JD, UCLA 1957. Career: partner law firm Jabin & Jabin, Monterey park 1958--; v.p. CVJ Constrn., Inc., Monterey Park 1977--; partner sev. real estate devel. cos. in Los Angeles Co. 1979--; asst. prof. bus. law SCU Los Angeles 1972-75; arbitrator, Am. Arbitration Assn. 1963-; Judge Pro Tem, Alhambra Municiple Ct. 1981-; mem: Am., Los Angeles Co. Bar Assns.; San Gabriel Valley Bar Assn. (pres. 1975); Monterey Park Rotary; CSU Los Angeles Adv. Council; mil: tech. 5th gr. M.C., US Army 1946-49; rec: music, chess, photog., art. Ofc: Jabin & Jabin, 701 S Atlantic Blvd Monterey Park 91754

JACKSON, JAMES JOHN, certified public atherine (Devereaux) J.; m. Danuta (Stocerz) Jackson, PhD, MD (noted Polist immunologist), Jan. 23, 1980; edn: BS, honors, Univ. of Ill. 1968; MBA, pgm., UC Berkeley 1968. Career: acct. Walter K. Sears, CPA, Albany 1969-72; CPA Shigeji Takeda, CPA, Los Angeles 1973-75; CPA 1975-77; v.p. Greenberg & Jackson, an Accty. Corp., Hollywood 1978--; Edmund J. James Scholar, Univ. of Ill. 1965-68; mem: Beta Alpha Psi, nat. acctg. frat.; Calif. Soc. CPAs; Publs: art., An Analogy Between Communism & Freudian Psychology, Univ. of Ill. Green Caldron Mag., 1965; Ch. of Scientology; rec: stu. religion, travel. Res: 2526 N Greenbrier Santa Ana 92706 Ofc: Greenberg & Jackson, 1770 N Vermont, Ste 108, Los Angeles 90027

JACKSON, JAMES PHILIP, lawyer; b. June 11, 1931, Portland, Ore.; s. Rein Everett and Elsie (Gilbert) J.; m. Gloria Coffey, July 25, 1959; children: Lynn, b. 1960; Scott, b. 1960; edn: BA, Williamette Univ. 1953; LLD, Univ. of Colo. 1957; admitted to practice, Oregon bar 1958, Calif. bar, 1960. Career: atty.

League of Ore. Cities, Eugene, Ore. 1958-59; atty., State of Calif., Sacramento 1960-62; asst. city atty. City of Santa Rosa 962-65; asst. city atty. City of Sacramento 1965-68, city attorney 1968--; pres./ v.p. City Attys. Assn. of Calif. 1977-79; bd. dirs. League of Calif. Cities 1983-; mem: Ore. & Calif. State Bars; Sacto. Co. Bar Assn.; Rotary Club, Sacto.; Presbyterian Ch. (Elder); mil: Spec. 4 US Army 9154-56; Presbyterian; rec: skiing, running. Res: 45 Moonlit Cir Sacramento 95831 Ofc: City of Sacramento, 812 10th Street, Ste 201, Sacramento 95814

JACKSON, JOSEPH, physiotherapist; b. Feb. 25, 1935, Greenville, Miss.; s. Mose and Lola B. (Duncan) J.; children: Dwight, b. 1960; Toni & Terri, b. 1961; edn: AA, Los Angeles City Coll. 1963; BS, SCU Long Beach 1978; lic., Bd. Med. Examiners 1971. Career: currently, dir. physical therapy dept. Community Hosp., Gardena; pres./ owner Community Physical Therapy Ctr., Inc. 1975--; dir. physical therapy dept. Edgemont Hosp., Hollywood 1981-; awards: Spl. Citation, Post Ofc. 1969; Suggestion Awd., L.A. Postal Svc. 1969; mem: Am. Physical Therapy Assn.; UCLA Alumni Assn.; Calif. Guest Home Owners Assn.; CSU Long Beach Alumni Assn.; Am. Red Cross; A I A frat.; founder: Jackson's Found. for the Disabled 1969; Republican; SDA; rec: basketball, carpentry. Res: 1934 W 22nd Street Los Angeles 90018 Ofc: Community Physical Therapy Center., Inc., 725 S Long Beach Blvd Compton 90221

JACKSON, KENNETH DWIGHT, real estate broker; b. Oct. 14, 1931, Los Angeles; s. Francis Edward and Mildred Evelyn (Regan) Jackson; m. Roselle M. George, Dec. 26, 1956, div. 1979; chil: Roselle Diane, b. 1958, Kenneth Dwight Edward, b. 1959, Keith David, b. 1960, Kevin Douglas, b. 1962, Kieley Donald, b. 1966; edn: BS, Univ. Calif. 1961; lic. real estate broker, Calif., Nev. Career: real estate broker/mgr. offices in Palm Springs and Incline Village, Nev.; mil: sgt. USAF 1951-5; Republican; Catholic; res: 345 Mariscal Rd. Palm Springs 92262.

JACKSON, LOY S., accounting executive; b. May 11, 1943, Deport, Tex.; s. Oda S. and Bertha May (Grizzle) Jackson; 1 dau., Kristina Marie, b. 1971; edn: AS, Worcester Jr. Coll. 1970, BS in bus. mgmt., Clark Univ. 1976. Career: asst. credit mgr. Honeywell Computer, Control Div., Farmingham, Mass. 1966-69; credit mgr. Harrington & Richardson, Worcester, Mass. 1969-71; Dist. credit mgr. Simplex Time Recorder Co., Gardner, Mass. 1971-78; corp. credit mgr. Gulf & Western, New Bedford, Mass. 1978-80, Whittaker Corp., Santa Ana, Ca. 1980-82; mgr. customer acctg. Del Mar Window Coverings, div. Beatrice Foods Co., Westminster 1982--; cons., estab. br. ops., Whittaker Medical, 1982; guest lectr. various Chambers of Commerce nationwide 1975-77; mem: Nat. Assn. of Credit Mgmt. 1968- (dir. Worcester, Mass. chpt. 1975-78), Soc. of Profl. Credit Mgrs., Nat. Assn. of Accountants 1966-76; mil: Airman 1c USAF 1961-66; Democrat; Methodist; rec: jog, swim, ski, art. Res: 16783 Beach Blvd. Huntington Beach 92647 Ofc: Del Mar Window Coverings, 7150 Fenwick Ln Westminster 92683

JACKSON, MICHELE CHICKERELLA, lawyer; b. Jan. 17, 1954, Redwood City; d. Joseph A. and Enessa (Mandy) Chickerella; m. Warren Jackson, Aug. 14, 1976; edn: BA, Stanford Univ. 1976; JD, Univ. of S.F. Law Sch. 1979; admitted to practice, State Bar of Calif. 1979, US Dist. Ct. (No. Dist.), Ninth Circuit Ct. of Appeals. Career: extern. Hon. Wiley Manuel, Calif. Supreme Ct., San Francisco 1978; atty., Furth, Fahrner, Bluemle & Mason, S.F; mem: Am. Bar Assn. (antitrust & litigation sects.); State Bar of Calif.; S.F. Bar Assn.; Barristers Club; NOW; Democrat; rec: hiking, ballet & symphony. Res: 60 Dorado Terrace San Francisco 94112 Ofc: Furth, Fahrner, Bluemle, & Mason, 201 Sansome St, Ste 1000, San Francisco 94104

JACOBS, GARRY LAWRENCE, management consultant; b. July 29, 1946, NYC; s. Walter C. and Lucille (Hirsch) Jacobs; m. Leslie Phelps, June 14, 1970; edn: BA, UCLA 1968, Univ. of Hawaii Med. Sch. 1970-71. Career: asst. secty. The Mother's Service Society (social sci. resrch inst.) Pondicherry, India, conducting postgrad. research in economic devel., literary criticism, and corp. mgmt., 1973--; mem. Commn. on Devel., Internat. Union of Anthropological and Ethnological Scis. 1983-4; mgmt. cons. to Rhone Poulenc Nederlands, 1983; recipient 1982 Investigative Journalism award for best art. pub. in Indian Journal; mem. Am. Economics Assn. 1981-2. works: designed new model for economic indicators to measure devel. in India (1980-3); two books in progress; address: 1100 Soscol Road %3, Napa 94558; Mere Cie, POB 5343, Napa Valley 94581-0343

JACOBSEN, MICHAELENE MARIE, company president; b. May 22, 1952, Mishawaka, Ind.; d. Michael S. and Barbara A. (Uhl) Hess; m. J. Sidney Jacobsen, July 10, 1976; edn: BA, Indiana Univ. 1973; lic. pvt. investigator, Calif. 1982. Career: campus police ofcr. Univ. of Notre Dame, Notre Dame, Ind. 1973-76; security mgr. Bullocks Northern Calif., Walnut Creek 1976-79; regl. security mgr. Joseph Magnin, San Francisco 1979-81; chmn./pres. Store Analysis, Inc., Oakland 1981--; pvt. investigations & consulting.; mem: Nat. Assn. of Chiefs of Police; Internat. Assn. Women Police; Women Police of Indiana; Am. Soc. for Indsl. Security; Spinsters & Dames, Piedmont. Address: Store Analysis, Inc., 6760 Moore Dr Oakland 94611

JACOBSON, ALEXANDER D., computer software co. executive; b. Dec. 1, 1933, NY, NY; s. Seymour Irving and Annabelle (Maibach) J.; m. Rebecca Davies, Oct. 24, 1971; children: Julie, b. 1959; David, b. 1962; edn: BS, UC Los Angeles 1955, MS, 1958; PhD in elec. engr., Calif. Inst. of Tech. 1964. Career: with Hughes Aircraft Co. 1955-77: mem. tech. staff, doctoral fellow Microwave Lab., Culver City 1955-61; Hughes Research Lab.: tech. staff 1961-68, head Displays Resrch Section 1968-72, assoc. mgr. Exploratory Studies Dept.,

Malibu 1972-76; mgr. Liquid Crystal Display Pgms Indsl. Products Div., Carlsbad 1976-77; independent cons. 1977-79; pres./CEO, Inference Corp., Los Angeles 1979--; honors: Tau Beta Pi, Pi Mu Epsilon, Sigma Xi hon. socs.; best paper IEEE profl group in Antennas & Propagation 1967; best paper awd., Soc. for Info. Display, 1972 Internat. Meeting; works: 36 technical papers; holder or co-holder 12 patents. Res: 12256 Canna Rd Los Angeles 90049 Ofc: Inference Corp. 5300 W. Century Blvd Los Angeles 90045

JACOBSON, LYNN ANNE, national sales executive; b. Nov. 5, 1953, San Diego; d. Deneen R. and Jeanette (Verhafren) Brinks; m. Jay Kihm Jacobson, June 16, 1974. Career: cashier, office mgr., dept. mgr. Builders Emporium, San Diego 1971-74; sales rep. for various giftware cos., Los Angeles 1974-78; salespsn. United Silver & Cutlery Co., 1978, supr. 1981, Western Regnl. sales mgr. 1982; nat. sales mgr. Bradley Import Co., L.A. 1983--; City of Hope patron 1974--; Republican (Pres. Task Force); Catholic; rec: ballet, bicycling, motorcycling. Res: 422 S. Lucia, Redondo Beach 90277 Ofc: Bradley Import Co. 1424 N. Spring St Los Angeles 90012

JACOBSON, RONALD JOEL, artist/ lawyer; b. May 17, 1948, Chgo.; s. Abraham and Julia Eva (Lazarus) J.; edn: City of London Coll. 1969; Otis Art Inst. 1970-71, 1976-78; BA, USC 1970; JD, UC Los Angeles 1973; admitted to practice, State Bar of Calif. 1973. Career: one- man shows: COR Gallery, Los Angeles 1978; Knights, Ltd., Beverly Hills 1979; Ross Lawrence Silver Gallery, L.A. 1981; gp. shows: Fisher Gallery, L.A. 1970; Gallery Plus, L.A. 1976; L.A. County Mus. of Sci. and Industry 1979; Form & Function Gallery, Atlanta, Ga. 1983; assoc. counsel, Bank of Am. Legal Dept., L.A. 1974-78; assoc. counsel Paramount Pictures Corp., L.A. 19-81; counsel Filmways, Inc., L.A. 1981; sr. assoc. Stein & Kahan, Santa Monica 1982; of counsel Katsky, Ker & Hunt, L.A. 1982-83; senior atty. Paramount Pictures Corp., Network TV Prodn. Div. Profl. Artist 1983--; mem: State Bar of Calif.; Los Angeles Copyright Soc.; Municipal Elections Com. of Los Angeles (Bd. Govs.); Soc. & Pub. Art Resource Ctr. (bd. dirs.); produced: over 50 original oil painting, 450 serigraphs; Democrat; Jewish; rec: health, body building. Res: 3860 Hollypark Pl Los Angeles 90039 Ofc: 5555 Melrose Ave Los Angeles 90038

JAFFE, LAWRENCE JAY, psychiatrist; b. Aug. 23, 1950, NYC, s. Leonard Eilperin und Hortense (Bock) J.; edn: BS, Univ. of Maryland 1972; MD, Autonomous Univ., Guadalaja 1975; MD, Downstate Med. Ctr. 1976; psychiatric res., UCSD Med. Ctr. Dept. of Psychiatry 1981; bd. cert., Am. Coll. of Psychiatry & Neurology 1983. Career: chief res., attg. staff, clinical instr., Dept. of Psychiatry, UCSD Sch. of Med. Univ. Hosp. 1981; cons / liason psychiatrist Renal Transplant Com., UCSD Med. Ctr. 1981; staff psych. SDSU Student Health Svcs. Ctr. 1981; pvt. practice gen. psychiatry 1981; supvi./ tchg. psychiatric residents & med. students; awards: Outstanding Grad. Resident, UCSD Dept. of Psychiatry 1981; mem: San Diego Psychiatric Soc., Am. Psychiatric Assn.; publs: The Importance of Drug Use Histories in a Series of Alcoholics, Journ. of Clinical Psychiatry, Vol. 42, No. 6, 6/81; Democrat; Jewish; rec: sports & athletic activities, music. Res: 2235 Montgomery Cardiff 92007 Ofc: Mission Valley Psychiatry, 2525 Camino Del Rio So., Ste 215, San Diego 92108

JAFFE, N. MARK, computer graphics consultant; b. Mar. 6, 1944, Havre de Grace, Md.; s. Joseph and Leah (Leibowitz) J.; m. Marli Schatz (dec. 1978), Aug. 11, 1965; children: Jennifer, b. 1967, Timothy, b. 1969; edn: BS, math., Drexel Univ. 1975. Career: math analyst Gen. Elec. Co., King of Prussia, Pa. 1967-77; applications engr. Vector General Inc., Woodland Hills, Ca. 1977-79; independent software contracting, 1979-80; film prodn. software support Information Int'l, Culver City 1980-82; systems & appls. support Bechtel Power Corp., Norwalk 1982-83; independent graphics cons., 1983--; computer graphics pgmmg. instr. Pierce Coll. 1979-80; mem. ACM/SIGgraph (past ch. LA chpt.), NCGA; film credits: Real Life (computer graphics animation), Looker (computer graphics animation), Tron (tech. support); Democrat; Christian; rec: acting, photog., roller skating. Address: Jaff's Perfetc Produx Co. 24118 Friar St Woodland Hills 91367

JAFFE, SAM, agent-film producer; b. May 21, 1901, NYC; s. Max and Naomi Jaffe; m. Oct. 9, 1926; children: Naomi, Barbara (Kohn), Judith (Tolmach). Career: associated B.P. Schulberg, independently producing: The Virginian (silent film); Capital Punishment; Rich Mans Wives, Poor Mans Wives; others; produced for RKO Dimplomanics w/ Wheeler & Woolsey: Emergency Call (Wm. Boyd & Pat O'Brien); The Fighting Sullivans (Fox Damon & Pythias for MGM); co-prod. Born Free (Columbia), award winner for Best Family Picture; agent for Humphrey Bogart, Lauren Bacall, Fredric March, Donald O'Connor, David Niven, Errol Flyn; chmn. Infantile Paralysis Drive; Res: 272 Lasky Dr Beverly Hills

JAIN, ASHOK KUMAR, neurosurgeon; b. Oct. 28, 1946, Narowal, Kashmir, India; s. Amar Nath and Bagwanti Jain; m. Reena (also M.D.), May 30, 1970; children: Neelam, b. 1978; Sacha, b. 1981; edn BS, MD, All India Inst. of Med. Scis. 1970. Career: surgical intern Rochester Gen. Hosp., Rochester, NY 1970-71; res. gen. surgery Univ. of Rochester Surgery Pgm., Rochester, NY 1971-73; res. neurosurgery Victoria Gen. Hosp., Dalhousie Univ., Halifax, Nova Scotia, Canada 1973-77; solo pvt. practice neurosurgery, Redding 1977--; mem: Shasta Trinity Med. Soc.; CMA; Calif. Assn. Neurological Surgeons; Congress of Neurological Surgeons; Am. Coll. of Surgeons; Republican (Nat. Com.); rec: philately, philosophical studies, travel. Res: 1590 Ganim Ln Redding 96001 Ofc: Ashok K. Jain, A Med. Corp., 2105 Court St, POK 4212, Redding 96099

JAIN, DESH B., engineer; b. Dec. 3, 1941, Kot Radha Kishan, India; s. Tirath Dass and Ram Pyari Jain; m. Nirmal, Feb. 6, 1967; children: Anju, b. 1968, Anita, b. 1971, Nisha, b. 1979; edn: BS, physical scis. Panjab Univ., India 1963, BS, chem. engrg., 1966; mech. engring. stu. CSU Long Beach 1980-81; grad. Nat. Inst. for Tng. in Indsl. Engring.; Dale Carnegie Courses; Calif. lic. Profl. Engr. (chem., 1982; mech., 1983). Career: assoc. lectr. chem. eng., Nat. Dairy Research Inst., Karnal, India 1967-68; chem. engr. Hindustan Zinc Ltd., Udaipur, India 1968-74; chem. engring. mgr. Luxfer USA Ltd. Riverside, Ca. 1976-77; R&D chem. engr. Garrett Energy Resrch & Engring., Ojai 1977-78; engring. gp. So. Calif. Edison Co., Redondo Bch. 1978-81; senior engr. Instrumentation Gp., The Ralph M. Parsons Co., Pasadena 1981-83; air quality engr. South Coast Air Quality Mgmt. Dist., El Monte 1983--; mem: (fmr.) Instrument Soc. of Am., var. academic & sports (cricket) clubs: publs: sev. stories and arts. in univ. journals 1963-67; Hindu; rec: table-tennis, swimming, tennis. Res: 13734 E. Felson St Cerritos 90701 Ofc: South Coast Air Quality Mgmt. Dist., 9150 Flair Dr El Monte 91731

JAMES, ANN MARIE, personnel executive; b. July 29, 1922, Pueblo, Colo.; d. John Jack and Caroline Lena (Fabrizio) Cardinale; m. Leon G. James, Sept. 18, 1948; children: Deborah Ann (Ottow), b. 1950, Leon G., Jr. b. 1931; ed. pub. schs. Career: civil svc. clk. US Govt. Ordnance Depot, Pueblo Air Base, AF Hdqts. Colorado Springs, Colo., Rent Control Board, Pueblo, Colo., 1943-48; secty. National Trade Schools, Calif.; personnel dir., buyer Hinshaw's Dept. Stores Inc. Whittier 1969--; Democrat; Catholic; rec: crafts. Res: 9403 Carron Dr. Pico Rivera 90660 Ofc: Hinshaw's, 8480 Quadway Whittier 90607

JAMES, ART, radio & television announcer/ master-of-ceremonies; b. Oct. 15, 1929, Dearborn, Mich.; s. Samuel and Olga (Fedchenia) Efimchik; children: Jeffrey Hamilton, b. 1957; Jennifer, b. 1960; edn: BA, Wayne State Univ. 1952. Career: announcer in Saginaw & Detroit; host dozen network TV game shows over 25 years, including: Concentration, Say When, The Who What or Where Game; devel. and produced num. audience participation pgms. for maj. networks, also two off-Broadway Plays in NY; guest lectr. univ. ext. courses in broadcast announcing & non-fiction writing; contbg. writer, TV Guide; mem. Meeting Planners Internat.; mil: US Army 1952-54; rec: pvt. pilot (comml), golf, Russian linguist. Res: 9950 Durant Dr Beverly Hills 90212 Ofc: Art James Productions, 8833 Sunset Blvd, Ste 306, Los Angeles 90069

JAMES, BILLY EUGENE, real estate broker; b. Jan. 1, 1943, Mena, Ark.; s. Oval C. and Verna Christel (Keeton) Cordell; m. Cheryl E. Joki, June 1, 1980; children: Barbara, b. 1967, Sharlene, b. 1964; Stephanie, b. 1968; Susan, b. 1970; Shawna, b. 1970; edn: AA, Grossmont Coll. 1981; AS, Southwestern Coll. 1965; LSIT cert., Calif. 1981; R.E. broker lic., Calif. 1983. Career: draftsman, City of Chula Vista 1967-69; designer/ draftsman, Inter City Engrs., San Diego 1969-72; R.E. salesman, Century 21, San Diego 1972-82; principal proj. engr. Rick Engr. Co., San Diego 1972--; owner/ broker James Realty, San Diego 1983--; mem: San Diego Bd. Realtors; Calif. & Nat. Assns. Realtors; Multiple Listing Svc.; San Diego Zoological Soc.; Nat. Geographical Soc.; The Smithsonian Assocs.; Republican; Methodist; rec: gardening. Res: 7347 Rondel Ct San Diego 92119 Ofcs: Rick Engineering Co., 5620 Friars Rd San Diego 92110 Ofc: James Realty, 1516 W Redwood St, Ste 107, San Diego 92101

JAMES, CHARLES LEE, JR., computer design engneer; b. Jan. 23, 1949, Anderson, S.C.; s. Charles Lee and Juanita (Campbell) J.; m. Virginia Nelson, Sept. 2, 1972; children: Amy, b. 1968; Christopher, b. 1977; edn: AS in electronics, San Diego Evening Coll. 1977 (1974-83). Career: indsl. x-ray tech. Conam Inspection Inc., Rahway, NJ 1968; elec. tech. Non- Linear Sys., Inc., Del Mar 1973; elec. tech. US Elevator Corp., San Diego 1974; assoc. devel. engr. Univ. of Calif. San Diego, Ctr. for Astrophysics and Space Sci. Dept., X-ray and Gamma-ray astronomy & solar physics gp. 1974--; owner James Computer Repair 1982-; awards: Gp. Achiev. Awd., Head-1, NASA 1978; mem. bd. dirs. San Diego Co. Churches of God, bd. trustees Clairemont Ch. of God, S.D., Eldorado Homes, Inc. and Ch. of God Homes Inc., Oceanside; coauthor: Scripps Canyon Sea Structure, pub. Marine Journ. Vol. 17 No. 4, 1983-84; computer sys. design, HEAD-1 Experiment, NASA Computer Sys. Design & Maint. 1977; mil: AE-2 USN 1969-73, Nat. Defense, Merit. Unit Cit., Armed Froces Expedit. Medal (Korea), Vietnam Campaign, Vietnam Svc. w/ Bronze Star; Republican; Ch. of God; rec: sports, auto repair. Res: 8263 Hydra Ln San Diego 92126 Ofc: University of California, San Diego, CASS C-011, La Jolla 92093

JAMES, DOT, foundation executive; b. Sept. 14, 1938, San Antonio, Tex.; d. Royal Percy and Eloise (Ohlen) J.; edn: BA, So. Methodist Univ. 1960; MA, Stanford Univ. 1962; MPA, Univ. of San Francisco 1985; gen. secondary tchg. cred., Calif. 1962. Career: mgmt. analyst, Dept. of Navy 1963-65; H.S. English tchr. Gilroy H.S. & Caldwell (ID) H.S. 1965-71; travel mag. ed., Boise Cascade 1971-73; chief editor Venus mag. 1973-75; partner/ CEO F.S. Button Mfg. Co. 1975-83; freelance writer/ ed. 1965--; currently, exec. dir. AIDS Found., Santa Clara Co.; commnr. City of San Jose Parks & Recreation Commn. 1972-73; awards: NDEA Inst. in Eng. Fellowship 1967; Coe Found. Inst. in Am. Studies Fellowship 1969; mem: NEA/ CTA/ GTA; AFT/ CFT; Nat. Assn. Female Execs.; Bay Area Career women; Stanford Bay Area Porf. Womens Club; San Jose & Los Gatos CofC; BBB of Santa Clara Co.; NOW, Calif.; Womens Athletic Assn., San Jose; Alpha Delta Pi (pres. 1956); works: Biography of John Knott, Tex. Hist. Soc. Archives; creator/mfr. Feminist-slogan buttons 1975-83, housed in Womens Collection, Smithsonian Instn. 1975-83; Democrat; Humanist; rec: cartooning, golf, philately. Res: 4260 Camden Ave San Jose 95124 Ofc: AIDS Foundation, Santa Clara Co., 715 N First St, Ste 10, San Jose 95112

JAMES, PAMONA RITHA, clinical social worker; b. Sept. 3, 1915, Lincoln, Nebr.; d. Thomas and Ritha Venora (Woods) Banks; m. Clinton James, Aug. 10, 1952; edn: BA, Univ. of Nebr. 1945; MSW, 1949; LCSW, Calif. 1969. Career: social ins. claims examiner Soc. Security Admin., San Francisco 1974-79; med. soc. svc. cons. State Calif. Dept. Soc. Welfare, S.F. 1965-70, 1972-73; psychiatric soc. wkr. State Calif. Dept. Mental Hygiene, Oakland & Hayward 1954-58, 1961-65; ret. 1979; med. soc. svc. cons. State Calif. Dept. Soc. Welfare 1965-70, 1972-73; cons. States in Ninth Reg. Soc. Security 1974-79; honors: Psi Chi, psychology hon. soc. 1944; mem: NASW; Acad. Cert. Soc. Wkrs.; Univ. Nebr.- Lincoln Alumni Assn.; Presidio Ofcrs. Club, S.F; Calif. Nat. Assn. Ret. Fed. Employees; Smithsonian Assocs.; Alta Sierra Property Owners Assn.; Alta Sierra Womens Nine Hole Golf Club; Episcopal; rec: golf. Res: 123 Hanley Dr Grass Valley 95945

JAMES, THOMAS JEFFERSON, IV, livestock breeding consultant; b. Mar. 25, 1947, Miami, Fla.; s. Thomas Jefferson and Dorothy (Davis) James III; m. Jeanne Louise Ramey, Oct. 13, 1969; children: Heidi, b. 1970; Thomas, b. 1976; John, b. 1978; edn: AA, West Hills Jr. Coll. 1967; BA, Calif. State Polytech. Univ. 1971; Lic: real estate sales, Calif. 1974; Calif. life tching. cred. (vocational agri.) 1974. Career: employee trainer Diablo Mfg., Visalia, Castro Valley 1971-73; agri. supr./instr., Sacto. Co., Elk Grove 1973-74; ranch real estate sales Bob Cook Realty, Clements 1974-83; owner/mgr. Cow Horse Country Mfg. Co., Clements 1976--; prin. James Trucking Co., Clements 1979; genetics coordinator Timeshare Breeding Service, Elk Grove; mem. World Shorthorn Cattle Com.; agri. teacher; bd. dirs. Nat. Reined Cowhorse Assn. (non-pro rep.). Honors: Nat. Quilland Scroll 1965. Rec: stock horses. Res: 12190 East Jahant Rd., Acampo 95220 (POB 118 Clements 95227) Ofc: Timeshare Breeding Svc 8788 Elk Grove Blvd, Ste. E, Elk Grove 95624

JAMISON, KARIN EHRENCLOU, physician; b. Oct. 22, 1930, Los Angeles; d. Eric Rudolph and Beda Alexia Seraphia (Gronquist) Ehrenclou; m. W. Blake Jamison, June 22, 1957; children: Eric, b. 1958; Elin, b. 1960; Tim, b. 1961; Mark, b. 1963; edn: AB, Occidental Coll. 1953; MD, USC Sch. of Med. 1957; physician & surgeon, Calif. 1958. Career: outpatient clinic physician/ attg. physician Tuberculosis Sanitarium, San Diego Co. Gen. Hosp., San Diego 1959-60; pvt. family practice, Lompoc 1961-73; primary care physician, Vandenbreg AFB Hosp. 1974-80; emergency physician, Lompoc Dist. Hosp., Lompoc 1980--; honors: Alpha Omega Alpha, hon. med. soc. 1957; mem: Calif. Acad. Family Physicians; Am. Acad. of Family Physicians; Fellow Am. Bd. Family Physicians; Campfire Girls (Lompoc Council); Lompoc Comm. Concerts (bd. dirs.); Sierra Club; Great Books Club; works: quiltmaker (8 during past 6 yrs.); Republican; Unitarian; rec: gardening, bicycling, running. Res: 29 Cambridge Dr Lompoc 93436 Ofc: Lompoc District Hospital, 508 E Hickory Lompoc 93436

JANG, SUDEOK, lawyer; b. May 1, 1947, Young-Joo, Korea; s. Unhak and Hwasoon (Lee) J.; m. Insuh, Apr. 7, 1973; children: Seongjoon, b. 1974; Sungwoo, b. 1979; edn: BA, Hankuk Univ. of Foreign Studies 1971; M.Pub.Admin., Seoul Nat. Univ. 1975; MBA, UCLA 1980; JD, 1980; admitted to practice, State Bar of Calif. 1981; arbitrator, Am. Arbitration Assn. 1982. Career: asst. dir. Adminstrv. Mgmt. Bureau, Ministry of Govt. Admin., Repub. of Korea 1972-75; letters of credit negotiator, Union Bank Internat. Dept., Los Angeles 1975-76; atty. at law, Law Firm Graham & James, Los Angeles 1980-83; partner, law firm Finley, Kumble, Wagner, Heine, Underburg, Manley & Casey, Beverly Hills 1983--; diplomatic trainee, German Found. 1974; tchg. asst. UCLA Grad. Sch. Mgmt. 1977; plng. ofcr. Security Pacific Nat. Bank 1977; mngl. trainee, Repub. of Korea 1972-73; awards: Highest Citation of Pres., Hankuk Univ. of Foreign Studies 1971; Virginia-Florence Scholarship, UCLA Sch. of Law 1977; mem: Am. Arbitration Assn.; Am. Mgmt. Assn.; Am., Calif., Korean-Am. & Los Angeles Bar Assns.; Fin. Lawyers Conf.; publs: Analytic Criteria for Reorgn. 1975; Technique for Communications Satellite Mktg. 1980; rec: golf, literature, sprint. Res: 23285 Hamlin St Canoga Park 91307 Ofc: c/o Finley, Kumble, 9100 Wilshire Blvd, Ste 10-E, Beverly Hills 90212

JANISSE, THOMAS LEO, emergency medicine physician; b. Aug. 25, 1946, Detroit, Mich.; s. Emile C. and Rita M. (Willis) J.; m. Cherryl D. Luallin, Oct. 20, 1980; children: Laura D., b. 1981; Jill M., b. 1983; edn: John Carroll Univ. 1964-66; Loyola Univ. Ext., Rome, Italy 1968; BA & BS, Marquette Univ. 1966-69; MD, Wayne State Univ. Sch. of Med. 1975; physician & surgeon, Calif. 1976. Career: pediatrics Kaiser Permenente Hosp., Oakland 1975-76; emergency med. physician, Kaiser Permenente Hosp., Walnut Creek 1976-77; emergency med. physician Amador Hosp., Jackson 1977--; secty./ treas Med. Exec. Com. Amador Hosp. 1983; chmn. Quality Assurance Com. Amador Hosp. 1983; dir./principal instr. Premedic & Mobile Intensive Care Nursing Tng., Amador Co. 1983; awards: Fed. Grantee, Emergency Med. Svcs. 1983; grantee, Literature, Nat. Endowment for the Arts 1981; grantee, Coord. Council of Literary Mags., NY 1981; mem: Am. Coll. Emergency Physicians, Emerg. Med. Svcs. Adv. Bd. Amador Co., Emerg. Med. Care Com. Amador Co.; works: prod. Hometown Radio Review; mem./founding bd. Amador County Arts Council; publisher, Peninhand Press; editor/pub. 6 vols. of The Volcano Review (lit. & arts periodical) 1979-; ed./pub. book, The Argonaut Mine Disaster, 1982; Catholic; rec: literature, the arts. Res: 19723 Sutter Creek-Volcano Rd Volcano 95689 Ofc: Amador Hospital, 108 Court St Jackson 95642

JAPENGA, JACK WALLACE, radiologist; b. June 22, 1928, Chgo.; s. Jacob Martin and Theresa Alberta (Jaax) J.; m. Laurena Booker, Nov. 1, 1952; children: Wm. Martin, Ann Theresa, Charles Albert, Diana; edn: PhB, Univ. Chgo. 1949, MD, 1953. Career: intern USPHS Hosp., San Francisco 1953-54;

resident in radiology Univ. Chgo. 1956-59; practice medicine specializing in radiology, Glendora, Ca. 1959--; mem. staffs Magan Med. Clinic (Covina), San Dimas Comm. Hosp., Foothill Presbyn. Hosp. (Glendora), Glendora Comm. Hosp.; chmn. pub. health commn. County of Los Angeles 1975-82; fmr. chief of staff Glendora Comm. Hosp., San Dimas Comm. Hosp.; dir. InBank, InBancorp.; honors: Commendation for civic service, L.A. County Board of Supervisors; mem: Am., Calif. (bd. of dels.), L.A. County (past pres. Foothill Dist.) med assns., Am. Coll. Radiology, L.A. Radiol. Soc., Calif. Radiol. Soc., Am. FEdn. Physicians and Dentists (pres. Calif. Council), Glendora Radiol. Assn. Inc. (pres., dir.), Am. Thermographic Soc.; mil: USPHS 1953-56; Republican. Res: 2452 N. Cameron St Covina 91724 Ofc: 210 S. Grand St Glendora 91740

JAPENGA, LAURENA BOOKER, pediatrician; b. Nov. 6, 1927, Greensboro, N.C.; d. William Gray and Nina Emmaline (Park) Booker; m. Jack Wallace Japenga, Nov. 1, 1952; children: William, b. 1953; Ann. b. 1955; Charles, b. 1957; Diana, b. 1961; edn: Univ. of N. Carolina 1944-47; MD, Duke Univ. 1951; pediatric intern & res., Duke Univ., 1951-53, 1955-59; physician & surgeon, Calif. 1953. Career: pvt. practice pediatrics, Covina, Glendora, San Dimas, 1961--; currently, chief of staff San Dimas Hosp., San Dimas; instr. Univ. of Chgo. 1951-52, 53; instr. Mt. Zion Hosp., San Francisco 1953; mem: L.A. Co. Med. Assn.; Am. Acad. Pediatrics. Res: 2452 N Cameron Ave Covina 991724 Ofc: 1330 W Covina Blvd San Dimas 91773

JARAMILLO, ANDREW CECIL, physician; b. Feb. 23, 1948, Albuquerque, N.M.; s. Estunislado Andrew and Albita (Bacu) J.; m. Pebbie, June 12, 1977; 1 son: Andrew Cecil Jr., b. 1980; edn: BS, Univ. of NM 1972; MD, 1976. Career: family practice, Tulare 1977-81; v.p. Tulare Dist. Hosp. med. staff, Tulare 1981; med. dir. emergency svcs. 1981--; emergency svcs. physician; surgical asst.; mem: Tulare CofC; CMA; Tulare Co. Med. Assn.; Am. Coll. Emergency Physicians; Tulare Dist. Hosp. Med. Staff; mil: N.M. Air Nat. Guard 1966-72; USAF, active duty 1969-70; Republican; Catholic; rec: computer science, desert horticulture. Res: 651 Helene St Tulare 93274 Ofc: Tulare District Hospital, 869 Cherry Ave Tulare 93274

JARZOMBEK, STANLEY JOSEPH, JR., computer and information systems integrator; b. May 27, 1955, McAllen, Tex.; s. Stanley J. and Virginia Anna (Pfeifer) J.; m. Paula Jeannine Zaedow, July 27, 1974; edn: BA in computer sci., Univ. of Tex., Austin 1980, and BBA in data proc. & anal., 1980; MS, info. sys., AF Inst. of Tech. 1982; grad. wk. in systems mgmt. USC 1982-. Career: served to capt. USAF 1980--: systems devel. ofcr. AF Inst. of Tech. (AFIT), Wright Patterson AFB, 1980-82; systems integration ofcr., currently network systems integrator, Sunnyvale AFS, Calif. 1982--, chmn. AF Satellite Control Network Configuration Mgmt. Gp. 1983-, chmn. AF Satellite Control Facility Change Control Wkg. Gp. 1983-, v.p. AF Inst. of Tech. Engineering Council 1980-81; mem. AF Language Control Bd. 1982-; Software Quality Assurance Seminar lectr. 1983-; pres. Sunnyvale AFS Co. Grade Officers Council 1983-84; awards: AF Assn. Co. Grade Officer of the Year (CGOY) 1984; AF Satellite Control Facility CGOY 1983; Who's Who in Aviation and Aerospace (Janes) 1983; Outstanding Young Men of Am., US Jaycees 1982; 1980 CACTUS Outstanding Student, Univ. of Texas at Austin; 1980 Disting. Grad. at UT, Mortar Board, Omicron Delta Kappa. Mem: ACM, IEEE, AIAA, DOMA, AFA, Ada/ Jovial Users Group, UT Data Proc. Alumni Assn., US Jaycees, Toastmasters Int. (CTM, Toastmaster of Yr. 1983, Area F4 Gov.), UT Ex Students Assn., asst. Scoutmaster BSA; publs: software quality ass. applications, contbr. 8th West Coast Compukr Faire 1983; mil: AF Commendn. Medal, GCM; Republican; Catholic; rec: backpacking, camping, public spkg. Res: 112 Falkirk Ct Sunnyvale 94087 Ofc: USAF Satellite Control Facility, POB 3430, Sunnyvale AFS 94088

JASPER, WILLIAM JOSEPH, electronics engineer; b. Mar. 3, 1949, Washington, Mo.; s. Joseph Franz and Orpha Amelia (Roehrs) J.; div.; 1 son: Jeffrey, b. 1975; edn: BS, Univ. of Mo., Rolla 1972. Career: Failure Analysis engr. Hughes Aircraft Corp., Culver City 1973-75; equip. engring. mgr. Burroughs Corp., San Diego 1975--; instr. Palomar Coll., San Marcos, 1982-83; honors: Sigma Pi Sigma, physics hon. 1969; Awd. for Tech. Excellence, Burroughs MCG 1984; mem: Intercollegiate Knights 1968; publs: (4), Burroughs MCO Technology Review 1979; patentee: Audio Differential Voltmeter 1982. Res: 341 James St Escondido 92027 ofc: Burroughs Corp., 16701 W Bernardo Dr San Diego 92128

JAVAHERIAN, HADI, engineer; b. Sept. 3, 1956, Mashhad, Iran, nat. 1982; s. Ahmad and Moulood (Milanizadeh) J.; m. Linda Preuninger, Jan. 30, 1982; edn: BSME, Univ. of Wash., Seattle 1980; postgrad. degree in energy, Swiss Fed. Sch. of Tech., Lausanne, Switz. 1981. Career: research engr. asst. Applied Thermal Lab., Lausanne, Switz. 1980-81; vice pres./rep. So. Calif., Robertson & Assocs. Inc., Canoga Park, 1982-83; gen. mgr. Willy Loi Enterprises Inc., Van Nuys 1983--; mem. ASME (assoc.); rec: jewelry, soccer, travel. Res: 7439 Woodman Ave, No. 29, Van Nuys 91405 Ofc: Willy Loi Enterprises Inc. 5510 Sunnyslope Van Nuys 91401

JAZAYERI, M. ROBERT, physician; b. Aug. 6, 1921, Iran; s. Mohamad Javad and Batool (Mortazavi) J.; m. Zari, June 6, 1950; children: Azar, b. 1950; Behzad, b. 1953; Azita, b. 1959; Amin, b. 1964; edn: MD, Teheran Med. Coll. 1951; dip. in diseases of skin, St. John Hosp., London 1968; resident in dermatology, Jorjani Hosp., Iran 1965-67. Career: gen. practitioner Jorjani Gen. Hosp. 1965-67; res. dermatology, Iran 1967-69; St. Johns Hosp., London, Eng. 1969; gen. practice & dermatology, pvt. clinic, Iran 1979; intern Pacific Hosp. (1 yr.); estab. med. practice M. Robert Jazaferi, MD, Santa Ana 1983--; chmn.

Khusisten Province Council 1975-79; rec: soccer, swimming, chess. Res: 46 Oakdale Irvine 92714 Ofc: M. Robert Jazaferi, MD, 1913 E 17th, Ste 107, Santa Ana 92701

JEFFRIES, RICK NEIL, clinical social worker; b. Aug. 4, 1952, Savannah, Ga.; s. Kenneth Dewitt and Dorothy Ann (Brown) J.; edn: Univ. of Ark. 1970-72; BA, CSU 1976; MSW, 1979; LCSW, Calif. BBSE 1981. Career: stu. intern Wintu Intensive Treatment Pgm., Sacramento 1978-79; youth counselor Oak Spl. Counseling Pgm., Ione 1979-80; casework splst. Northern Reception Ctr.- Clinic, Sacto. 1979-80; youth counselor Wintu, Sacto. 1980; casework splst. Wintu Intensive Treatment Pgm., Sacto. 1980--; cons. adolescent psychotherapy, James Inst. 1981, Sacto. City Sch. Dist. 1982, Diogenes Youth Svcs. 1983; tchg. stress reduction Calif. Youth Authority 1981-; awards: Academic Achiev. Awd., Criminal Justice Tng. Ctr. 1979; mem: Diogenes Youth Svcs. (bd. dirs.); Dittmar Neighborhood Assn. (pres. 1980-); works: pioneered use of Ericksonian Hypnosis & Neuro-linguistic pgmmg. at Wintu Intensive Treatment Pgm. 1980; Implemented Adolescent Sexual Offender Treatment, Wintu 1981; Democrat; Methodist; rec: alpine skiing, bicycling, racquetball. Res: 645 Dittmar Way Sacramento 95819 Ofc: N.R.C.C./ Wintu, 3001 Ramon Ave Sacramento 95826

JELLA, SUSAN ANN, corporate executive; b. June 21, 1947, San Rafael; d. Clayton Kimball and Evelyn (Menary) Rice; children: David, b. 1968; Brian, b. 1973; Steven, b. 1977; edn: UC Berkeley 1971-72; BA, honors, CSC Sonoma 1972; AA, Santa Rosa Jr. Coll. 1972; pvt. pilot lic., FAA 1980; lic. real estate broker, Calif. 1972. Career: gen. mgr. Vintage Properties & Fireside Realty 1979-82; v.p. sales & mktg. Barratt Homes (internat. co.), 1982; pres./ chmn. bd. Diversified Bus. Securities, Inc. and subs. cos. Vintage Realty, Vintage Travel, and Vintage Promotions (a general real estate firm, a travel agcy. spec. in sports travel and celebrity events and a promotional agcy. for celebrities), 1972--; tchr. real estate 1980; dir. travel agency; honors: life mem. Million Dollar Club 1978; mem: Sonoma Co. Bd. Realtors; 20-30 Womens Club; Soroptomists; Junior League; Capitol Flyers; Crocker Art Docents; publs: essay, Presbyterian Today (1960); Democrat; Episcopal; rec: antiques, flying, travel. Res: 724 Woodside Ln E, Apt. 14, Sacramento 95825

JELLEY, JOSEPH G., real estate co. president; b. Apr. 19, 1937, Blairsville, Pa.; s. Joseph G. and E. (Freidline) J.; m. Patricia A. Tremellen, July 29, 1982; children: Joseph, b. 1957; James, b. 1959; Joanna, b. 1961; John, b. 1962; edn: BS, cum laude, Tri-State Univ. 1957; GRI, Calif. 1978; Cert. Residential Splst., Nat. Assn. Realtors 1979; cert. R.E. broker, mgr. 1980. Career: sale mgr. Robert Hall Co., NY 1962 64; merchandising supt. Sears Roebuck & Co., NY 1964-70; Midwest dist. sales mgr. Melville Shoe Co., Foxmoor Div., NY 1971-74; sr. regl. v.p. V.E. Howard & Co., Del Mar 1975-76; founder/ pres. Westeren State Pacific Pines Corp., Del Mar 1976--; pres. The Jelley Co., Inc. (R.E. brokerage, comm2./ res. leasing); pres. Pacific Pines Devel. Corp.; pres. Del Mar Morgage Co., Inc.; fin. dir. Patjel Ltd., Inc. 1981; profl. lectr./ cons., fin., mktg., mgmt.; recipient num. corp. awds.; mem: Torrey Pines Plng. Com. (chmn.); Del Marr 200 (Fin. Com.); Nat. & Calif. Assns. Realtors; San Diego Bldg. Contractors assn.; No. Co. Youth Svcs. Bureau; publs: num. arts. on fin. and real estate, San Diego Co. newspapers, periodicals; rec: creative design, writing. Res: 13635 Pine Needles Dr Del Mar 92014 Ofc: Western State Pacific Pines Corp., 1110 Camino Del Mar Del Mar 92014

JENNINGS, EDWARD CLINTON, III, mortgage broker; b. Jan. 8, 1945, Antioch; s. Edward C., Jr. and Velma Grace (Luhrman) J.; m. Judith Kay Nelson, July 27, 1970; edn: BS, Calif. Polytech. St. Univ. 1969, MBA, 1975; contg. real estate edn.; Calif. lic. R.E. Agt. 1973, Broker 1975. Career: stockbroker Merrill Lynch, Pierce, fenner & Smith, 1971-73; mgr. (75 sales agts. residential sales) Allstate Realtors, 1975-77; co-owner United Realtors, 1977-80; pres. Jennings Financial Corp. (loan brokerage) 1980-82; owner/ broker Midstate Mortgage, San Jose 1982--; mil: 1st lt. US Army 1969-71, Viet Nam. Address: 133 Skowhegan Ct San Jose 95139

JENNINGS, PETER RALPH, software author/executive; b. July 15, 1950, Bedford, Beds., England; s. Geoffrey and Liesl Astrid (Behm) J.; m. Jane Elizabeth Barkley, Aug. 18, 1973; edn: BSc, McMaster Univ. 1971; MA, State Univ. NY at Stony Brook 1972; MBA, McMaster Univ. 1974. Career: founder/ pres. Micro-Ware, Ltd., Toronto, Ont., Can. 1976-83; cofounder/ dir. PEAC Media Research, Inc., Toronto 1978--; cofounder/ chmn. VisiCorp, San Jose 1979-81, vice chmn. 1981--; partner Assoc. Venture Investors, Ltd., Menlo Park 1982--; dir: VisiCorp, San Jose; Gavilan Computer Corp., Campbell; Vivid Sys., Inc., Palo Alto; Vasona Corp., Campbell; Tallgrass Technologics Canada, Inc., Toronto; PEAC Media Research, Inc., Toronto; Digitrol Computers, Inc., Waterloo, Canada; awards: ICP Million Dollar AWd., VisiDex sales 1982; mem: Fellow Internat. Soc. for Philosophical Enquiry; software author: Micro-Chess, 1977; Micro-ADE, 1978; VisiDex 1981; inventor: Program Evaluation Analysis Computer, 1978; Chess Mate, 1977. Res: 125 Hill Top Dr Los Gatos 95030 Ofc: VisiCorp, 2895 Zanker Rd San Jose 95134

JENSEN, GERALD RANDOLPH, graphic artist;s b. Aug. 12, 1924, Kalispell, Montana; s. Hans Clemen and Mabel E. (Everson) J.; m. Helen Levine, Dec. 11, 1943; 1 dau: Marjorie, b. 1955; edn: G.Th., Life Coll. 1945; Litt.D., Internat. Acad. 1970; MA, Union Univ. 1976; PhD, 1978. Career: regl. & nat. dir. youth & Christian edn. Internat. Ch. Foursquare Gospel, Los Angeles 1946-54; dir. San Francisco area Youth for Christ 1955-60; v.p. Sacred Records, Whittier 1960-63; dir./ ed. internat. publs. Full Gospel Businessmens Fellowship 1963-69; pres. Triangle Productions, BUrbank 1970-79; pres. Claiborne/ Jensen Adv. 1980-82; pres. Jerry Jensen & Assocs., Santa Fe Springs 1982--;

bd. dirs.: Friends in the West, Seattle, Wash.; Internat. Bible Inst., Santa Fe Springs; Outreach Korea, Torrance; World Missioary Assistance Plan; Wings of Healing; Total Health Mag.; Am. Bible Soc.; Revival Fires; The Methodist Hour; Jimmy Snow Evangelistic Assoc., Nashville, Tenn.; awards: design, Dynamic Graphics, 1961; Christian Edn. Awd., Internat. Bible Inst. 1980; Spl. Svc. Awd., Golden Gate Univ. 1983; works: acts, Asian ed., Scandanavian, European & Spanish eds. Voice Mag., Full Gospel Businessmens Fellowship 1977-; youth mags., Vision, Young America, Today's Youth, Campus, View, Charisma Digest; Republican; Protestant; rec: art collection, golf, travel. Res: 12402 St. Mark Garden Grove 92745 Ofc: Jerry Jensen & Assoc., 9926 Pioneer Blvd, Ste 107, Santa Fe Springs 90670

JENSEN, HELEN MARIE, real estate broker; b. Apr. 10, 1923, Waxahachie, Tex.; d. Ben S. and Johnnie L. (Thedford) Likins; widow; two daus: Charlotte b. 1942, Jeanne b. 1946; stu. Long Beach Jr. Coll., Delta Coll.; Calif. lic. real estate broker. Career: sales mgr. Don Schneider Realty, Downey 1956-60; broker/owner Candlewood Realty, Whittier 1960-63, Foothill Realty, Fullerton 1963-76, specialized in exchanges with Landmark Homes, repossessions, residences, land, income devel.; fmr. realtor assoc. Riverboat Realty, currently with Beck & Ratto Realtors, Stockton 1984--; mem: Stockton Bd. of Realtors, (past) Downey Bellflower, Whittier, North & East Orange County bd. of realtors; names Salesman of Year (2 times), Downey Bd. Realtors, Hometown Speech Contest finalist, State of Calif.; mem: Bus. & Profl. Women, 1956-59; num. exchange groups; publs: stories, poems in Delta Showboat mag.; Baptist; rec: squaredancing (Lodi Promenade, Boots & Bonnets clubs). Res: 8535 Burns Pl Stockton 95209 Ofc: Beck and Ratto Realtors, 8102 Kelley Dr, Ste E, Stockton 95209

JENSEN, PETER LADD, mining co. president; b. Feb. 16, 1951, San Diego; s. George David and Margaret Ann (Ladd) J.; m. Vbolratana, Aug. 19, 1972; children: Ploypailin, b. 1981; Poomi, b. 1983; edn: BS, Mass. Inst. of Tech. 1974; MS, 1974; Reg. Profl. Chem. Engr., Calif. Career: mfg. engr. Standard Oil of Calif., El Segundo 1974-76; chief process engr. C.E. Miller Corp., Irvine 1976-80; pvt. investor, San Diego 1980-; pres. Yuba Natural Resources, San Diego 83--; honors: Sigma Xi; mem. Cuyamaca Club; Episcopal; rec: water sports. Res: 2158 Balboa Ave Del Mar 92014 Ofc: Yuba Natural Resources, 701 B, Ste 1460, San Diego 92101

JENSEN, RITA PAULA, real estate broker; b. May 22, 1932, Los Angeles; d. Lawrence Charles and Marguerite Willeta (Thomas) Fox; m. Leroy Jensen (dec.); 1 dau: Tamara, b. 1968; edn: Long Beach City Coll. 1951-54; Long Beach State Univ. 1955-56. Career: reliability engr. Vickers Eng., Torrance 1960-64; math. analyst McDonnell Douglas, Huntington Beach 1966-69; real estate sales, Real Estate Store, Long Beach 1971-75, Coltrane & Co., Long Beach 1975-77 Top Sail Properties, Long Beach 1977-80, broker/pres. JTM Brokerage, Long Beach 1980--; bd. dirs. Long Beach Bd. Realtors; mem: Nat. & Calif. Assn. Realtors; Civic Light Opera; Republican; Catholic; rec: travel. Res: 37 61st Pl Long Beach 90803 Ofc: JTM Brokerage, 312 Redondo Ave Long Beach 90814

JENSEN, STANLEY PHILIP, mechanical engineer designer; b. Mar. 27, 1951, San Mateo; s. Philip Albert and Florance Hellen (Henderson) J.; edn: AS, W. Valley Coll. 1972; BS, UC Davis 1974; Reg. Profl. Engr. M20933, Calif. 1979. Career: mech. engr. US Army Corps of Engs., Sacramento Dist., Monterey Resident Ofc. 1975-80; mech. design engr. Gen. Svcs. Admin., Region 9, San Francisco 1980--; awards: suggestion awd., 2- value engring. awds, Sacto. Dist. Corps. of Engrs. 1975-81; mem: Am. Soc. Heating, Refrigerating & Air Conditioning Engrs. (assoc.); Soc. of Am. Mil. Engrs.; works: first 3D x-ray; Republican; Lutheran; rec: programming, holography, golf, volley ball. Res: 28504 Mission Blvd, 922, Hayward 94544 Ofc: General Services Administration, 525 Market St San Francisco 94105

JENSEN, THOMAS PETER, engineering consultant/company owner; b. Dec. 10, 1944, Superior, Wisc.; s. Clifford George and Betty Louise (Peterson) J.; edn: AAS, Milwaukee Inst. Tech. 1966; BSEE, Edison State 1984. Career: metrology engr. Globe Union, Milwaukee, Wisc. 1966-71; elec./ optic. engr. ITEK Corp., Milwaukee, Wisc. 1971-75; mfg. engr. Cushman Electronics, Sunnyvale ; proj. engring. cons. TJ Ent. 1975-83; sustaining (electronics/ computer) engr. Tandem Computers 1983--; consulting (proj. mgmt.) Perkin-Elmer, Kaiser Electronics, Telemon; mem: Fellow Feathers, hang gliding club, S.F.; mil: E-5 USAR; Democrat; Lutheran; rec: hang gliding. Address: TJ Enterprises, 883 Bruce Dr Palo Alto 94303

JENSSEN, FINN CHRISTOPHER, scale co. president; b. Mar. 21, 1943, Albany; s. Finn Leopold and Helen F. (Geurts) J.; m. Elisabeth Thomassoff, Dec. 12, 1975; children: Julie, b. 1969; Olivia, b. 1978; Amanda, b. 1982; edn: BS, San Jose State Univ. 1966. Career: pres. Jenssen Scales, Inc., San Jose 1972--; mem: Nat. Scale Mens Assn. (chmn. No. Calif. Div. 1983-84); Better Bus. Bureau; San Jose State Alumni Assn.; Cancer Soc.; Pres. Council San Jose State Univ.; San Jose Mus. of Art; Republican; Protestant; rec: fishing, swimming, travel. Res: 922 Sundance Dr Fremont 94539 Ofc: Jenssen Scales, Inc., 635 Hulet St San Jose 95125

JESSE, ROSALIE CRUISE, clinical psychologist; b. July 25, 1938, Northview, Mo.; d. Harold Washington and Ida Marie (Kegley) Cruise; 1 son: Rick, b. 1959; edn: AA, Grossmont Coll. 1971; BA, cum laude, w/ distn., San Diego State Univ. 1973; MA, w/ spl. commdn., Calif. Sch. of Profl. Psychology 1975; PhD, 1977; Lic. Clin. Psychologist, Calif. 1980. Career: dir. Inst. for Adv. Psychological Studies, Calif. Sch. of Profl. Psychology, San Diego 1978; dir. counseling & pgm. devel. East Co. ACCORD, El Cajon 1977-80; dir. Family Counseling Ctr., El Cajon 1980; clin. psychologist Forensic Svcs., San Diego Co. Mental Health 1981-83; pvt. practice clin. psychol./prin. Alvarado Center for Psychology, S.D. 1977--; instr. UCSD Ext. 1981; honors: Psi Chi 1973; mem: Acad. of San Diego Psychologist, Am. Psychological Assn.; publs: The Role of the Psychologistc in the Acute General Hospital, The Profl. Psychologist, 1977; The Interpersonal Effects of Alcoholism, in The Impact of ALcoholism (ed. Steven Bucky) 1979; Democrat; Protestant; rec: swimming, travel, photog. Address: 6330 Alvarado Ct, Ste 203, San Diego 92120

JESSER, JAMES T., landscape architect; b. Dec. 13, 1938; edn: BA, CalPoly Pomona, 1966; Calif. Lic. Landscape Architect No. 1601. Career: fmr. lndscp. designer San Dan Nursery (Brea), Acorn Landscape Co., Union Standard Landscape Corp. (Capistrano Bch.); current landscape architect/prin., James T. Jesser & Assocs., Laguna Beach; public wks. incl: Doheny Gazebo ocean overlook (appeared in Sunset Mag. 5/81), Del Obispo Ball Park, Pines Ocean View Park (Capistrano Bch. Park Dist.); landscape design for Plaza De Propseridad (comml. shopping center project), winner City of San Juan Capo. Landscape Award; Lemonwood Mobile Estates (residential comm., Ventura), winner Calif. Mobile Home Assn. award; other projects for Howard Johnson, Inc., El Torito theme restaurants, Dana Point Harbor areas, var. indsl. parks and custom residences. Address: James T. Jesser Landscape Architect, 1065 Miramar St Laguna Bch 92651

JESSUP, WARREN T., patent lawyer; b. Aug. 1, 1916, Eureka; s. Thurman Warren and Millie (Johnson) J.; m. Evelyn Via, Sept. 13, 1941; children: Thurman, b. 1943; Paul, b. 1947; Stephen, b. 1950; Marilyn, b. 1952; BSEE, USC 1937; JD, George Washington Univ. 1942. Career: engr. General Electric Co., Schenectody, NY 1937-38; patent assoc. Gen. Elec. Co., Wash. DC 1938-42; patent counsel Eleventh Naval Dist., Pasadena 1946-50; patent atty. Huebner, Beehler, Warel, Herzig, Los Angeles 1950-56; patent atty., Los Angeles 1956-68; patent atty. Jessup & Beecher 1968--; instr. UCLA Engring. Ext. 1951-65; instr. UCLA Grad. Engring. Sch. 1965-75; honors: Eta Kappa Nu; Phi Delta Phi; Order of Coif; Tau Beta Pi; mem: Am. & Los Angeles Patent Law Assns.; Hidden Valley Municipal Water Dist. (pres. 1978-); Kiwanis; Conejo Valley Hist. Soc.; publs: arts, Jour. Patent Office Soc., contbr., Ency. of Patent Practice (Reinhold); mil: commdr. USNR 1942-46; Baptist; rec: equestrian, cartography. Res. Thousand Oaks Ofc: Jessup & Beecher, 875 Westlake Blvd, Ste 205, Westlake Village 91361

JEWELL, JOHN HUTTSELL, librarian; b. May 13, 1940, Kansas City, Mo.; s. Jack Huttsell and Corrinne Elizabeth (Fye) J.; m. Carol Thompson, June 16, 1961; 1 dau: Teresa Elizabeth, b. 1972; edn: BA, Univ. of Ks. 1961; MA, Univ. of Denver 1969. Career: dir. WTTV, Bloomington, Ind. 1962-64; intern, Fresno Co. Free Labrary 1967-69; science librarian 1970-76; coord. reference svcs. 1976-82; principal librarian reference svcs. 1982--; honors: Phi Betta Kappa; Beta Phi Mu; mem: Calif. Alliance of Info. & Referral Svcs. (bd. dirs.); Epilepsy Soc. of Fresno (bd. dirs.); Spl. Libraries Assn.; Am. & Calif. Library Assns. Res: 2901 N Teilman Ave Fresno 93705 Ofc: Fresno County Free Library, 2420 Mariposa Fresno 93721

JIN, GORDON, data processing center director; b. Aug. 10, 1949, San Francisco; s. Hung B. and Ngar F (Lee) J.; edn: BSEE, Heald Eng. Coll. 1971; DeVry Sch. of Electronics 1968. Career: messenger Fed. Reserve Bank of Chgo. 1967; data assembly clerk Wells Fargo Bank, San Francisco 1968, A.V.P. mgr. 1978; dir. Fed. Home Loan Bank of S.F. 1980, A..V.P. dir. 1982--; mem. IEEE 1970; bd. dirs. San Francisco Volunteers Bureau; Junior Achievement S.F.; Democrat; rec: skiing, boating, outdoor activities. Res: 1535 S Diamond Bar Diamond Bar 91765 Ofc: Federal Home Loan Bank, 19935 E Walnut Dr Walnut 91789

JOHNS, W. LLOYD, university president; b. May 25, 1930, St. Louis, Mo.; s. William C. and Beatrice G. (Schoenen) Johns; edn: BS, Northeast Mo. State Coll., 1952, MA, 1956, EdD, USC, 1966, post doctoral, Inst. for Ednl. Mgmt., Harvard Univ., 1974; m. Dorene Ann Hill, Oct. 11, 1975; chil: Victoria (Parsons), Michelle Lynn, Terri Lee; career: teacher (music, vocal and instrumental), public schools K-12, Mo. 1950-54; prin., Shelbina (Mo.) Elem Sch./dir., Shelbina H.S. Band, 1954-56; prin./adminstr., Ophelia Parish Jr. H.S. (demo-lab. sch. on Northeast Mo. State Coll. campus) 1956-57; teacher (math., sci.) Sequoia Jr. H.S., Fontant 1957-58, prin. 1959-60; prin., Alder Jr. H.S., Fontana 1960-63, Fontana Sr. H.S., 1963-65; asst. prof./prof. of Ednl. Adminstrn., CSU Northridge 1965-75, also asst. to the Dean Sch. of Edn. 1968-70, dir. Audio Visual Services 1970-72, assoc. v.p. Bus & Adminstrv. Affairs 1972-75; vice pres. Adminstrv. Affairs & Ednl. Services, CSU Sonoma 1975-76, v.p.-in-chg. and acting president 1976-77; exec. v.p. CSU Sacramento 1977-78, pres. 1978--; faculty, (dir., 1975) Nat. Leadership Tng Pgm in Area of the Deaf, sponsored by Rehabilitation Services Adminstrn., Wash. DC, 1966-75; vis. prof., Pepperdine Univ. 1969-74; mem. Com. on the Humanities, Am. Assn. of State Colls and Univs. 1979-82; ch., Found. of CSU Sacramento 1979-82. Frequent speaker, exec. seminars, profl. & bus. groups, service orgns. Honors: music scholarship, Northeast Mo. State Univ. 1948-52; Alpha Phi Sigma (scholastic), Kappa Delta Pi (profl.), Blue Key, Phi Delta Kappa, (profl. edn); Resolution, L.A. City Council 1975; Associated Students award, CSU Sacto 1977-79; hon. life mem. Sacto Musicians' Union 1978; appreciation, Sacto Athletic Hall of Fame 1979; Baldwin Lectr., Annual Outstanding Educator Series, Northeast Mo. State Univ. 1980; Service award, USAF Assn. Sacto chpt. 1981; Sr. advisor Gov.'s Exec. Fellows Program, Sacto. 1982; bd. dirs.: Salvation Army, Sacto Co. Community Action against Drug Abuse, Golden Empire Çouncil BSA, Comstock Club, Sacto. United Way, Sacto. Metropolitan C of C, Theatre Ballet of Sacto.; cons., Sacto Jr. League; sponsor, Gov.'s Prayer Breakfast 1981, 82; pres., bd. dirs. Helping Hand Fund; exec. council, AF Assn. Author num. scholarly publs., arts. Mem. Sacto. Newcomers (past pres.), Sacto Sym. League, Univ. Affils., Am. Heart Assn., Psi Delta Sigma, Inc., Camellia Festival Assn. (Gold-Coater, bd. dirs.); rec: profl. trumpet player, woodworking, gourmet cooking; res: 333 Wyndgate Rd. Sacramento 95825 ofc: Calif. State Univ. 6000 J St. Sacramento 95819.

JOHNSON, ALBERT, JR., physician; b. June 19, 1934, Moneta, Va.; s. Albert D. and Ora P. Johnson; edn: BA, Lincoln (Pa.) Univ., 1956, MS, Howard Univ., 1958, Ph.D., Univ. of Ill., 1961, M.D., Howard Univ., 1966, MPH, Johns Hopkins Univ., 1968, aerospace medicine, Sch. of Aerospace Med. (San Antonio, Tex.) 1972; m. Antonia Bennett, May 29, 1975; career: Senior Flight Surgeon USAF 1965-77, USAF Reserve 1977--: Medical examiner, Sch of Aerospace Medicine (working w/pilots & astronauts); Aerospace Med. examiner, Andrews AFB, for @ 40 returning Vietnam P.O.W.s; assigned to support the President of USA (1972-74) in flights at Andrews AFB; Director of worldwide Aerospace Medicine for Medical Evaluation (incl. med. evaluation for Gen. Omar Bradley, Mrs. Mamie Eisenhower, Supreme Ct. Justice Thurgood Marshall), 1975-76; Director of Aerospace Medicine, Phong Rang, Vietnam; Family Practice physician, So. Calif. Permanente Medical Group, West Covina 1977--; recipient Associate Fellowship, Aerospace Med. Assn. Mem AMA, ASMA. Publs: medical research papers, presentations internat. confs.; mil: lt. col. USAF 1965-; decorated Vietnam, Air, Markmanship, National Def. Medals; Democrat; Baptist; res: 16537 Circle Hill Lane, Hacienda Hgts 91745 ofc: So. Calif. Permanente Medical Group 1249 Sunset Ave. W. Covina 91790.

JOHNSON, BARBARA SEGRESS, psychotherapist; b. Apr. 27, 1943, Fresno; d. Robert Monroe and Christine Fay (Clark) Segress; edn: BA, psychology, Pacific Coll., 1977, MA in counseling, Summa Cum Laude, CSU Fresno, 1980; m. Richard Johnson, 1964; chil: Darlene Joelle, b. 1966, David Paul, b. 1969; career: California li censed Marriage, Family, Child Counselor; Placement tng. Valley Guidance Ctr. Fresno, 1977; family counselor Fresno Co. Jail, Women's Sect., Valley Missions 1978; marriage & family counselor Northwest Counseling Svc., Fresno 1978-79; founder/dir./ counselor New Hope Counseling Service, 1979-80; marriage & family counselor Fresno Counseling Service, 1980-81; marriage & family therapist/co-owner Fresno Counseling & Therapy Group, 1981--; faculty, Advanced Studies Dept., CSU Fresno 1981-; awards: Krommer Scholarship 1976-77, Harris Memorial Scholarship 1979; life time Calif. Comm. College Cred.; mem: Calif. Assn. of Marriage & Family Therapists (clin. mem.) 1980-, Christian Assn. of Psychological Studies 1980-, Phi Kappa Phi; publs: contbr. to New Hope and Valley Mission newsletters; Republican; Presbyterian rec: tennis, travel, swimming; res: 6555 N. Bethel Clovis 93612 ofc: Fresno Counseling & Therapy Group 3772 N. First St. Fresno 93726.

JOHNSON, DAVID DEAN BRIAN, structural engineer; b. Feb. 7, 1956, No. Hollywood; s. Charles Walton and Marcia Miriam (Baile) J.; edn: BS, CSU Northridge 1980; Reg. Profl. Civil Engr. 34859, Calif. 1982. Career: design draftsman Aircraft Component Repair Co., Sun Valley 1977-79; struct. designer/ darftsman John Chan & Assoc., Struct. Engrs., Van Nuys 1979-80; proj. struct. engr. KPFF Consulting Engrs., Encino 1980--; mem: Am. Soc. Civil Engrs.; Structural Eng. Assn. of So. Calif.; Am. Concrete Inst.; Republican; Methodit; rec: handball, racquetball, wine tasting. Res: 19241 Nordhoff St, 27, Northridge 91324 Ofc: KPFF Consulting Engineers, 16000 Ventura Blvd, Ste 802, Encino 91436

JOHNSON, DEANNA DEWENE, airline sales executive; b. Mar. 14, 1941, Benkelman, Nebr.; d. Dewey Daniel and Annie Marie (Gunther) Gerdes; 1 dau: Cara, b. 1973; edn: spec. courses, Weaver Airline Sch. 1960-61, Braniff Tng. Sch. 1961, Northwest Airlines 1961. Career: opr. and accts. receivable Benkelman Telco, Nebr. 1957-61; ticket agent Braniff Airways, Minpls.- St. Paul, Minn. 1961-77, Los Angeles 1977-78, reservation mgr. (temp.) 1978-79, reservation supvr. 1979--; instr. Travel & Tourism, Mnpls. Vocational Sch. 1972; apptd. mem. Adv. Bd. Bloomington (Minn.) Outreach Homes 1975; honors: sev. Mrs. Jaycee of the Month (1972-77); mem: BRAC Union; Bloomington (Mn.) Mrs. Jaycees (state del. 1974); Stadium Queens Bowling League (pres. 1975-77); Jefferson PTA; Burbank Dialogue Gp. NCCJ 1981-; Burbank Vikings Youth Cheerleader pgm. (team mother 1982); Democrat; Methodist; rec: needlework, people, travel. Res: 824 E Groton Dr Burbank 91504 Ofc: Northwest Airlines. 5757 W Century Blvd, Ste 380, Los Angeles 90045

JOHNSON, DOUGLAS WAYNE, technical services executive; b. Feb. 26, 1946, Pittsburgh, Pa.; s. Clarence Harold and Shirley Lou (March) J.; m. Jolene Anderson, June 25, 1971; 1 dau: Andrea, b. 1974; edn: AA, Bakersfield Coll. 1967; BS, CSU Fresno 1973; adv. cert., The Commn. on Peace Ofcr. Stds. & Tng. 1981. Career: computer sys. cons./ sem. lectr.; police ofcr./ dir. tech. svcs. Madera Police Dept., Madera 1974--; exec. dir. Public Safety micro-Software, Madera Apr. 1983--; corp. ofcr. Criminal Justice Seminar Assocs. Inc., El Toro 1984--; awards: Distinguished Profl. Police Service, Hanford Police Dept. 1983; Tho Noble Order of Field Mice, USAF, Strategic Air Command, Grand Forks AFB 1970; Meritorious Conduct, Madera Police Dept. 1975; mem: Calif. Law Enforcement Assn. (pres. Records Supvrs., Central chpt. 1980-81); Madera City Peace Ofcrs. Assn.; Peace Ofcrs. Research Assn. of Calif.; Civil Air Patrol (Mission pilot 1972-74); publs: writer/ publisher: Public Safety micro-Software "ANALYST", S.T.A.R.S. (Subpoena Tracking & Reporting Sys.), March 1984 (software for law enforcement); contbg. writer (title cover art.) Law & Order Mag. 5/79; Texas Instruments Profl. Pgm. Exch.: Offender Census, Investigative Manpower, Patrol Workload Analysis, others; mil: sgt. E-4 USAF 1967-71, Nat. Def., Unit Cit. (2), GCM; Republican; rec: painting, computer pgmmg., photog. Res: 25575 Sybil Way Madera 93638 Ofc: Madera Police Dept., 203 W Fourth St Madera 93637

JOHNSON, EDDIE LEROY, computer data processing systems consultant; b. Apr. 10, 1946, Yuma, Ariz.; s. Joe Nathan and Elizabeth Lavern (Frazier) J.; m. Wilma Jean Scott, Dec. 12, 1970; children: Ersula, b. 1977, Edwinna, b. 1979, Erica, b. 1983; edn: computer sci. courses, Contra Costa Jr. Coll. 1979-80, Laney Jr. Coll. 1975-76; elec. tech., Ariz. Western Jr. Coll. 1965-67. Career: apprentice elec. meterman Pacific Gas & Electric, Fresno 1971-73; profl. computer opr. Electronic Data Sys., San Francisco 1973-78; methods analyst Levi Strauss & Co., S.F. 1978-79; sys. cons. Bank of Am. NTSA, S.F. 1979--; mem. Bay Area Urban Bankers Assn., NAACP; mil: aviation elec. tech. 2/c E-5 USN 1967-70; Democrat; Baptist (Deacon); rec: travel. Res: 2943 Gomer Dr Richmond 94806 Ofc: Bank of America, 1455 Market St, Ste 3486, San Francisco 94103

JOHNSON, GENIEL D., real estate broker; b. Sept. 18, 1935, Grover, Wyo.; d. LaMonte Welker and Verda Ann (Astle) Draney; m. Dawan Johnson, May 29, 1953; children: Eric, 1954; Howell, b. 1955; Neil, b. 1957; Bard, b. 1959; Keri, b. 1965; edn: AA, soc. sci., honors, Lake Tahoe Comm. Coll. 1976; AA, real estate, honors, 1978; stu. Lake Tahoe Comm. Coll. 1983-. Career: sales agent Sierra Nevada Realty, So. Lake Tahoe 1977, South Tahoe Properties, So. Lake Tahoe 1977, Ed Phelps Realty, Inc., So. Lake Tahoe 1978-83, broker assoc. Coldwell Banker, So. Lake Tahoe 1983--; mem: Nat. & Calif. Assns. Realtors; So. Lake Tahoe Bd. Realtors (Ethics Com., PAC); past Cub Scouts den mother and So. Tahoe Steppers (girls track) chaperone; Republican; Mormon; rec: hiking, swimming, needlework. Res: 128 Cattleman's Tr, So. Lake Tahoe 95731 Ofc: Coldwell Banker, 1123 Hwy 50 Tahoe Paradise 95708

JOHNSON, HERMAN DOWELL, university financial executive; b. Sept. 11, 1925, Rillito, Ariz.; s. Robert Ralph and Ora Mae (Curtis) J.; m. Janet Joslin, May 7, 1946; children: Christine b. 1948, Laura b. 1952; edn: stu. Colo. Coll. 1943-44, Univ. of Okla. 1944-46; BS, UCB 1948; Armstrong Coll. 1948-49; Indsl. Coll. of the Armed Forces 1966-68. Career: senior acct. UC Berkeley 1952-55; acctg. ofcr. UCSD 1955-69, budget acctg. ofcr. UCSD 1959-65, asst. to vice chancellor Bus. and Finance, 1966-67, asst./acting vice chancellor Administrn. 1967-69, vice chancellor Bus. and Finance, UCSD 1969 ; mem: Torrey Pines Rotary (pres. 1976/7), Western Assn. of Coll. and Univ. Bus. Ofcrs. (pres. 1975/6), Nat. Assn. of Coll. and Univ. Bus. (pres. 1982/3), Univ. of Calif. Retirement System Governing Bd. 1970-73; mil: served to maj. (ret.); rec: furniture refinishing, golf, fishing. Res: 1625 Malden St San Diego 92109 Ofc: UCSD, Q-007 La Jolla 92093

JOHNSON, JAMES BRUCE, dentist; b. Oct. 4, 1948, Covina; s. James Oliver and Frances Marie (Platz) J.; m. Elizabeth Bellissimo, Jan. 24, 1970; children: Joel Bryant, b. 1973; Erich Robert, b. 1976; Lauren Elizabeth, b. 1978; edn. BS, Univ. of Calif. 1976; BA, Fresno State 1971; DDS, UC San Francisco 1976. Career: gen. dentistry practice, self-empl. 1976 ; bd. diro. Northcast YMCA 1983, chmn. fundraising 1981-83; honors: Century Club, Northcast YMCA, recognition, Glendale Comm. Coll. Senior Citizen Pgms.; mem: Am. & Calif. Dental Assns.; Democrat; Protestant; rec: early Am. furniture restoration, scuba diving, backpacking. Res: 5148 Argus Dr Eagle Rock 90041 Ofc: 4867 Eagle Rock Blvd Eagle Rock 90041

JOHNSON, JAMES RUSSELL, special education programs administrator; b. Oct. 2, 1938, San Diego; b. Carroll Edmund and Aleta Ethel (Sheller) J.; m. Nancy Jeanne Marble (Scott), Aug. 27, 1960; children: James Russell, II b. 1961; Jeffrey Randell, b. 1966; Jennifer Nan, b. 1970; edn: BA, San Diego State Univ. 1960, MA, 1964; D.Ed. Univ. of La Verne 1979; Calif. Tchr. Credentials (life): Gen. Elem., Exceptional Child-M.R., Elem. Admin., Gen. Admin., Gen. Sec., Learning Handicapped, Severely Handicapped. Career: summer sch. principal, La Mesa- Spring Valley Sch. Dist., La Mesa 1964, 66; asst. principal, La Mesa 1965-68; instr. CSU Ext., Fullerton & San Bernardino 1968-74; adj. prof. Univ. of La Verne, 1980--; dir. spl. edn. Corona-Norco Unified Sch. Dist., 1968--; actg. principal Victress Bower Sch. for Exceptional Students, Corona 1974, 75; awards: Outstanding Adminstr., Temescal Masonic Lodge 1984; Hon. Life Mem. Maryland Ave PTA 1968; Cont. Svc. awd., Garretson Elem. PTA 1972; Leadership Cert., Ctr. for Developmental Disabilities 1971; Spl. Commdn., Proj. I.D.E.A.L. 1969; bd. dirs. Peppermint Ridge Home for Developmentally Disabled; arts. in ednl. journals; Republican; Methodist; rec: stained glass windows, antique refinishing, camping. Res: 296 Coronado Dr Corona 91720 Ofc: 300 Buena Vista Corona 91720

JOHNSON, JAY ARTHUR, electronics co. president; b. Mar. 26, 1942, Spokane, Wash.; s. Robert William and Virginia Ruth (Cheatham) J.; m. Charlotte Ann Traveres, July 14, 1961; children: Chris, b. 1962, Jeff, b. 1967; edn: AS, US Navy Sch. 1961; stu. Long Beach City Coll. 1962-63, Fresno City City 1963-65, CSC Fresno 1966; B lic., US Soccer Fedn. 1979. Career: pgm. analyst No. American Aviation 1962-63; svc. mgr. AV Electronics Inc. 1964-68; prodn. mgr. 1068-70; gen. partner Central Calif. Electronics 1968-74; chief exec. ofcr. Central Calif. Electronics, Inc. 1974--; varsity coach Fresno H.S. 1980-83; awards: Harold S. Young Awd. 1980; Cert. of Commdn. Fresno Unified Sch. Dist. 1983; mem: Nat. Sound Contractors Assn.; Nat. Fire Protection Assn.; Calif. Automatic Fire Alarm Assn.; Fresno Jr. Soccer League; Fresno Metro Soccer League; Calif. Youth Soccer Assn. (staff coach); Nat. Soccer Coaches of Am. Assn.; mil: E-5 USN, GCM, Vietnam; Republican; rec: soccer, skiing. Res: 615 W Robinwood Fresno 93704 Ofc: Central California Electronics, 93 E Belmont Fresno 93701

JOHNSON, JOAN ELISE, anesthesiology supervisor; b. July 6, 1932, Baltimore, Md.; d. Harry Scott and Ida Myrtle Monks; m. Dr. Walter Lauren Johnson, June 30, 1955, div. 1968; children: Charles b. 1957, Lauren b. 1958,

Dana b. 1960, Arthur b. 1965; edn: pre-nsg. Univ. of Md. 1965; RN, Union Mem. Sch. of Nsg., Balto., Md. 1953; undergrad. stu. Johns Hopkins Univ. 1954; CRNA (Cert. Reg. Nse. Anesthetist), Barnes Hosp. Sch. of Anesthesia Wash. Univ., 1956; BA, Redlands Univ. 1976, MA in human resource mgmt., 1980. Career: instr. Anesthesia Project Hope, Peru 1961-63, and English instr. Peruvian Am. Cultural Ctr.; free-lance anesthetist, San Diego, Ca. 1963-68; staff anesthetist Kaiser Found. Hosp., S.D. 1968--: supvr. Nurse Anesthesia/ mgr. Dept. of Anesthesiologia; lectr. var. mgmt. topics, chem. dependency; program coord. Kaiser Regl. Anesthesia Symposium 1983; mem: Am. Assn. Nurse Anesthetists (nat. del. 1975, govt. rels. com. chair 1979-82), Calif. Assn. jof Nurse Anesthetists (pres. 1978-9, chair nominating com. 1982-84), Calif. Soc. of Anesthesiol., Am. Heart Assn. CPR, Anesthesia Hist. Assn., Am. Mgmt. Assn., Nat. Assn. of Female Execs., Center for Womens Studies S.D., Humane Soc., Green Peace; Cubscouts Den Mother 1969-72; Brownie, GSA ldr. 1962-75; mgr. Bobby Soxs 1965-75; publs: sev. arts. on labor unions and nsg., photog. slide lectures; Republican; Methodist. Ofc: Kaiser Permanente 4647 Zion Ave San Diego 92120

JOHNSON, JUDITH S., health care management executive; b. Oct. 25, 1943, Coatesville, Penna.; d. Wm Rice and Virginia Grace (Elder) Shellenberger; m. Martin Blake, Oct. 2, 1982; children: Karen, b. 1963, Carole, b. 1966; edn: BA in math., summa cum laude, Gwynedd Mercy Coll. 1974; MBA in prog., UCLA. Career: mktg. mgr. Lemmon Pharm. Co., Sellersville, Pa. 1974-76; mgr. TRW Electronics, L.A. 1977-78; dir. mktg. American Medical Int., Beverly HIlls 1978-80; ops. mgr. Nat. Medical Ents., LA 1980-82; owner/pres. Phase 5 HealthCare Systems Inc., Torrance 1982--; vice pres. New Market Mgmt. Services, Long Beach 1984-; dir. Physicians of Gr. Long Beach Med. Group, 1984-; cons. to hospitals in Outpatient Practice devel.; cons. to healthcare electronics indus.; honors: Who's Who in Am. Colls. & Univs. 1974, Sigma Phi Sigma, Kappa Gamma Pi; mem: Medical Group Mgmt. Assn., Am. Coll. of Medical Group Adminstrs., Women in Business, LA; Republican; Catholic; rec: pianist. Res: 2086 Middlebrook Rd Torrance 90501 Ofc: Phase 5 HealthCare Systems Inc. 3465 Torrance Bl, Ste G, Torrance 90503

JOHNSON, LAMAR LEE, electrical contractor; b. May 22, 1937, Warthen, Ga., s. Luther Hunter and Susie Kate (Harrell) J.; m. Donna Daphne Kruse, Mar. 3, 1961; chidren: Virgil Lamar, b. 1961; Tammie Trelaine, b. 1963; Wyatt Lee, b. 1964; Todd Sumner, b. 1983. Journeyman Electrician. Career: elec. lineman Washington County EMC, Sandersville, Ga. 1961-63, San Diego Gas & Elec. Co., San Diego 1963-79; elec. contr./owner/pres. Johnson Elec. Co., Chula Vista 1979--; awards: Safe Driving Awd., S.D. Gas & Elec. Co.; mem: Assoc. Bldrs. & Contractors, Inc.; Assem. of God Ch.; mil: BMSN USN 1957-61; Democrat, Protestant. Address: Johnson Electric Co., 1480 Max Ave Chula Vista 92011

JOHNSON, LEE ANN, author; b. May 21, 1945, Corpus Christi, Tex.; d. Lemuel Robert, Jr. and Evelyn Jane (Gilliam) Loving; m. Donald E. Johnson, June 17, 1963; edn: BA, Univ. of Tex. 1967; MA, UCLA 1968; PhD, 1972; JD, UCB Boalt Hall 1981; admitted to practice, State Bar of Calif. 1981. Career: asst. prof. Dept. of English Michigan State Univ. 1972-76; Fulbright- Hays lectr. Univ. of Seville, Spain 1975-76; vis. lectr. Holy Names Coll., UC Davis 1976-77; vis. lectr. Sch. of Internat. Studies, Tokyo, Japan 1978-79; assoc. McCutchen, Doyle, Brown & Emersen, San Francisco 1981-82; presented papers at var. scholarly confs. 1972-76; law clerk Shozawa & Nakamura, Tokyo 1978-79; awards: Grad. Woman of the Yr., UCLA 1972; Fulbright Hayes Lectr., Spain 1975-76; UC Berkeley Law Review 1979-81; mem: Authors Guild; Calif. Writers Club; Am. & Calif. Bar Assns.; Modern Lang. Assn.; author: Mary Hallock Foote (book length biography) (Boston, G.K. Hall 1980), num. mag. arts. (in Ninteenth- Century Fiction, Twentieth Century Literature, Ariz. Qtly.); Democrat; Protestant; rec: tennis, jogging. Address: 45 Golf Rd Pleasanton 94566

JOHNSON, MERLIN ELMER, lighting consultant; b. Nov. 22, 1931, Sebastopol; s. Wm. Elmer and Mary Louise (Pierini) J.; m. Peggy Jean, Oct. 4, 1952; children: Duane b. 1953, Glenn b. 1956, Eric b. 1959; edn: undergrad., Phoenix (Ariz.) Coll. 1950; M.E. (mech. eng.) USAF Chanute Field, Ill. (Univ. of Ill. affil.) 1952; spl. courses, Santa Rosa Jr. Coll. 1954, I.C.S. 1955, Samuel Gompers, 1960; Calif. lic. gen. electrical contractor 1968. Career: plant supt. (classified govt. wk.) Rudolf Wendel Inc., Santa Rosa 1953-59; custom lighting design, installations Casella Lighting Co., San Francisco 1959-69; pres. Artistic Lighting Corp., San Rafael 1969--; pres. Merlin Johnson & Assocs., Palm Desert 1980--; creating custom lighting designs/installations nationwide, Canada, and Japan; patents pending for optical framing projection equip.; mem: Assoc. Builders & Contrs., Am. Bldrs. & Contrs. Assn., Illuminating Engring. Soc.; Masons; Scottish Rite, Shriners; mil: A2C USAF; rec: music; res: 44-85 San Clemente Cir Palm Desert 92260 Ofc: Merlin Johnson & Associates, POB 1338, Palm Desert 92261

JOHNSON, PETER EDWARD, JR., manufacturing co. executive; b. Nov. 7, 1947, Palo Alto; s. Peter E and Josephine M. (Ross) J.; div.; children: Jeanene, b. 1974; Jason, b. 1977; edn: BA, Univ. of Phoenix 1982. Career: insp. Watkins-Johnson Co. 1970-77, quality engr. 1977-82, senior quality engr. 1982-83, head prod. assurance inspection 1984--; mem: Am. Soc. Quality Control, (chmn. San Francisco sect.); Univ. of Phoenix Alumni Assn. (pres.); publs: contbg. writer, The Gate 1983; mil: sgt. USAF 1966-69; Democrat; Christian; rec: construction, gardening. Res: 870 El Camino, Apt 35, Mountain View 94086 Ofc: Watkins-Johnson, 3333 Hillview Ave Palo Alto 94304

JOHNSON, QUENTIN DENNIS, accountant, realtor; b. Aug. 12, 1919,

Hooper, Nebr.; s. Christian William and Lillian Myrtle (Peterson) J.; m. Mary Siders, Sept. 22, 1945; children: Patricia, b. 1946; Mark, b. 1948; edn: Midland Coll., Fremont, NE 1939-40; BS in acctg, USC 1949; lic: Calif. Pub. Acct. 1948; Enrolled Agent, IRS 1961; Calif. Real Estate Broker 1982. Career: acct. Gen. Motors Chevrolet Div., Van Nuys 1949-51; pub. acct. Loomis & Johnson, San Fernando 1951-52; pub. acct. sole practitioner, San Fernando 1953-77; controller M.F. Daily Investment Co., Camarillo 1978; sales assoc. Mac Elhenny, Levy & Co., comml./ investment div., Oxnard 1979-81; real estate broker Quentin D. Johnson, Realtor, Ventura 1982--; pres. San Fernando Valley chpt. Soc. of Calif. Acct. 1959-60, bd. dirs. 1956-59; dir. Los Posas Plaza Trade Club 1978; awards: recognition for civic service, City of San Fernando 1976, Robert G. Morton Post, VFW 1974; Resolution, Hon. Jim Keysor, 41st Assembly Dist. 1971; mem: Nat. Soc. of Pub. Accts.; Soc. of Calif. Accts. (S.F. Valley chpt. pres. 1959-60); Ventura Bd. Realtors; Nat. Assn. Realtors; City of San Fernando mayor 1971-72, city councilman 1969-76; chmn. City Personnel Bd.; mem. City Economic Devel. Com.; treas. San Fernando Fiesta; dir. CofC; Rotary (past pres. San Fernando, past mem. Camarillo, current mem.), dir. Ventura Rotary); Am. Legion; VFW; mil: tech. sgt. US Army Engrs. 1940-45, GCM; Republican; Catholic; rec: music, fishing, travel. Address: 3832 W Pacific Coast Hwy Ventura 93001

JOHNSON, RACHEL QUEENESTA, disability programs administrator; b. Sept. 21, 1947, Vallejo; d. Alfonso and Vernita (McKinney) Brown; m. Ronald Johnson, Dec. 26, 1965; children: Angela b. 1966, Ronald Jr. b. 1967, Ciceli b. 1974, Rhachelle b. 1949; edn: Solano Comm. Coll., Santa Rosa Comm. Coll., Sonoma State Univ., var. profl. workshops, tng. insts.; lic. Psychiatric Technician. Career: therapist Sonoma State Hosp., 1966-69; mgmt., resident tng. and care, Napa State Hosp., 1970-78, Sonoma St. Hosp., 1978-80; program adminstr. (residential pgm. for mental and devel. disabled), Alpha-Omega Inc., Vallejo 1980--; rec: youth wk., exercise. Res: 126 Mira Loma Vallejo 94590 Ofc: Alpha-Omega Inc. 1410 Georgoa St Vallejo 94590

JOHNSON, RICHARD ALAN, wholesale food co. president; b. Oct. 12, 1952, Berkeley; s. Clayton Errold and Elisabeth Johnson; m. Melissa Robin Cardenas, Aug. 23, 1953; apprentice mach., automotive mech.; then driver, worked var. positions up to mgr., A.C.O. Inc. (wholesale foods) 1972-76; opened auto repair bus. 1976-81, built show cars listed in Car Craft Mag. and Custom Rodder Mag., 1979-80; owner/pres. Santa Cruz Poultry Inc. (wholesale food co.), 1982--; mem. Food Executives Assn. of Las Vegas, Nev. 1973-75; recipient sev. awards in hobby related orgns.; breed, ride and show German Hanovarian Horses in Hunter & Jumper events; Republican; rec: restoring exotic cars, water ski, scuba dive. Res: 120 Travis Ln Watsonville 95076 Ofc: Santa Cruz Poultry Inc. 111 Dubois Rd. Santa Cruz 95060

JOHNSON, RICHARD LLOYD, physician; b. Feb. 16, 1918, Weaverville; s. Lloyd Godfrey and Elizabeth Avis (Henderson) J.; m. Merrie Louise Buchanan, Dec. 30, 1967; children: Elizabeth b. 1947, Ellen b. 1951, Victoria b. 1952, Caroline b. 1954; edn: AB, UC Berkeley 1939; MD, UC Med School, San Francisco 1942. Career: intern, Sacramento Co. Hosp. 1942-43; residency Internal Med., Milwaukee Co. Hosp., Wis. 1946-48; solo practice Internal Medicine, Sacramento 1949--; med. dir. Sacto. Convalescent Hosp. 1976-; senior staff mem. Sutter Comm. Hosps., chief Dept. of Med. 1965-76, chmn. of staff 1966; sr. staff mem. Mercy Gen. Hosp., chief Dept. of Med. 1960; participant White House Conf. on Aging 1961, 81, Calif. Conf. on Aging 1960; mem. Calif. State Bd. Medical Examiners 1965-69, secty.treas. 1967-69. Mem: AMA, CMA (del. 1977 Long Term Care com. 1980), Sacto. County Med. Soc. (pres. 1978; ed. Sacramento Medicine 1955, 79, 80), Sacto. Soc. Internal Med. (pres. 1974-75), Calif. Soc. Internal Med. (pres. 1980), Am. Soc. Internal Med. (del. 1976-77, 80), Calif., Sacto. Co. Heart Assns.; mem. Gov's Adv. Com. on Aging, 1958-65; chmn. Health Sect., Comm. Welfare Council 1961; trustee United Crusade Sacto. 1963; Sacto. Co. Mental Health Adv. Com. 1973-75; mem. Masons, Scottish Rite, Shrine, SAR, New England Hist. Genealogy Soc.; mil: capt. US ARmy M.C. 1943-46; Episcopal; rec: genealogy, Calif. hist. Res: 200 Tivoli Way Sacto 95819 Ofc: 2600 Capitol Ave Suite 301, Sacramento 95816

JOHNSON, RONALD JOHN, commodity broker, market analyst; b. Oct. 3, 1946, Long Branch, NJ; s. Wilbur W. and Adeling G. Johnson; m. Nancy Eileen Murphy, Sept. 22, 1982; edn: AA, Pasadena City Coll. 1966; BS, CSU Los Angeles 1968; grad. bus. pgm., CSULA 1970; desig.: Assoc., Commodity Futures Trading Commn. & Nat. Futures Assn. Career: research anal. Market Research Assoc. Inc., Pasadena 1965-68; commodity broker M.S. Commodities/ Rosenthal & Co., Pasadena 1970-72; commodity broker Enterex Commodities/ Kipnis Commodities, Newport Beach 1972-74; commodity mgr. Hornblower & Weeks, Hemphill Noyes, Orange 1974-79; pres. Mages & Johnson Inc. dba Archer/Heinold Commodities, Santa Ana 1979--; host daily TV show, The Futures & Options Review, KSCI (Ch. 18) 1982-; nat. spkg. tour, Am. Entrepreneurs Assn. Fin. Opportunity Expo. 1980-81; honors: Traders Club, Hornblower & Weeks (3 yrs.); mem: Santa Ana CofC; publs: spl. reports & newpaper arts. on economic matters; guest spkr. Financial Inquiry, nat. TV show, E.F. Hutton; mil: E-5 USNR, reserve 1963-68, active 1968-70; Republican; Catholic. Res: 2325 Heliotrope Dr Santa Ana 92706 Ofc: Archer/ Heinold, 970 W 17th St, Ste F, Santa Ana 92706

JOHNSON, ROY ROBERT, physician; b. Sept. 16, 1945, Long Beach; s. Lawrence Edwin and Ruth Kathryn (Donnelly) J.; m. Karen D. Ryn, June 14, 1969; children: Robert, b. 1975; Kimberly, b. 1976; edn: AA, Santa Ana Jr. Coll. 1970; BA, Fullerton State Coll. 1972; MD, UCLA 1976. Career: residency, UC

Irvine Med. Ctr., Orange 1976-79; family physician, pvt. practice, Valley Center 1979--, splst. treatment rattlesnake ond venomous bites; awards: Mead Johnson Award 1979; Outstanding Resident and Tchr., UCI Med. Ctr. 1977, 78; mem. Am. Assn. Family Practice; Rotarian; mil: served in USN, Sailor of the Month (Balboa Naval Hosp. 9/68); Republican; Episcopal; rec: herpetology, fishing. Res: 13777 Little Pond Rd Valley Center 92082 Ofc: 28743 Valley Center Rd, Ste 3, Valley Center 92052

JOHNSON, THOMAS REED, education administrator; b. Apr. 26, 1951, Youngstown, Ohio; s. Quentin LeRoy and Mary Jane (Scarmuzzi) J.; m. Catherine Virginia, May 18, 1982; 1 son, Aaron, b. 1983; edn: BA, San Jose State Univ. 1974; MA, lang. pathol., Humboldt State Univ. 1975; MA, edn., Calif. Lutheran Coll. 1978. Career: speech pathologist Bakersfield City Schs. 1975-79; lang. splst. Dept. of Youth Authority, No. Calif. 1979-83; dir. edn. Lincoln Christian Acad., Stockton 1983--; estab. spl. edn. in 10 schs., Dept. Youth Authority; lectr. on juvenile delinqcy. and spl. edn.; mem: Am. Speech, Lang. & Hearing Assn. (Cert. of Clin. Competence, 1978); Council of Exceptional Children; Assn. of Christian Schs., Internat.; State Legis. Com. on Edn.; Republican; Protestant; rec: ship design & model bldg., Mid. East hist. Res: 8260 Bennett Stockton 95212 Ofc: Lincoln Christian Academy, 1700 Porter Way, Stockton 95207

JOHNSON, WYATT THOMAS, JR., newspaper publisher; b. Macon, Ga., Sept. 30, 1941; s. Wyatt Thomas and Josephine Victoria (Brown) J.; A.B. in Journalism, U. Ga., 1963; M.B.A., Harvard, 1965; m. Edwina Mac Chastain, Dec. 19, 1963; children Wyatt Thomas III, Christa Farie. Reporter, mgmt. trainee Macon Telegraph and News, 1957-65; White House fellow, 1965-66; asst. press sec. to Pres. U.S., 1966, dep. press sec., 1967, spl. asst. to Pres., 1968, exec. asst., 1969-70; exec. v.p., dir. Tex. Broadcasting Corp., Sta. KTBC-AM-FM-TV, Austin, 1970-73; exec. editor, v.p., dir. Dallas Times Herald, 1973-75, publisher, 1975-77; pres. Los Angeles Times, 1977-1980s; Publisher and Chief Executive Officer 1980--. Mem. Pres.'s Commn. on White House Fellows, 1979, Neiman Fellows Selection Com., Harvard U., 1977. Pres. adv. bd. Henry W. Grady Sch. Journalism, 1974-75. Bd. dirs. U. Ga. Sch. Journalism, Peabody Awards, ARC; Chrm. of Bd., Lyndon B. Johnson Found. Named Nat. Man of Year, Sigma Nu, 1962, Outstanding Young Man of Ga., Jr. C. of C., 1967. One of Five Outstanding Young Texans, Tex. Jaycees, 1969, One of 10 Outstanding Men of U.S., 1975. Mem. Am. Newspaper Pubs. Assn., Newspaper Advt. Bur. (dir.), Ga. Alumni Soc. (pres. 1979), Council on Fgn. Relations N.Y., Sphinx Soc., Young Pres.'s Orgn., Gridiron Soc. (Ga.), Sigma Delta Chi, Sigma Nu. Harvard Business School Alumni. Methodist. Coauthor: Automating Newspaper Composition, 1965. Home: 2235 Chaucer Rd, San Marino, CA 91108. Office: Los Angeles Times, Times Mirror Sq., Los Angeles, CA 90053.

JOHNSTON, DANA CHRIS, mortgage co. executive; b. Apr. 15, 1954, San Mateo; s. Delman and Mildred (Lobb) J.; edn: BS, CSU San Jose 1976; Calif. lic. Real Estate Sales (1980), Life and Disability, Notary. Career: branch mgr. Fireside Thrift Co., 1977-79; loan dept. head Western Thrift and Loan Assn., 1979-80; investment and loan cons. Cutler Mortgage Inc., 1980; loan agt. Peninsula Mortgage Corp., 1980-82; vice pres. of adminstrn. American Coast Mortgage Corp., Redwood City 1982--; Republican; rec: skiing, football, softball. Res: 939 Aberdeen Dr Sunnyvale 94087 Ofc: American Coast Mortgage Corp. 961 Woodside Rd, Suite D, Redwood City 94087

JOHNSTON, MICHAEL BLAINE, manufacturing co. executive; b. Dec. 21, 1946, Memphis, Tenn.; s. James Blaine, Jr. and Martha Louise (Allday) J.; m. Mary Dowd (exec. dir. Am. Cancer Soc. Kings Co.), Feb. 14, 1982; edn: BSIE, Miss. State Univ. 1971; Co-operative Edn. Grad. 1971. Career: with Armstrong Rubber 1971--: indsl. engr., Little Rock, Ark. 1971-72, New Haven, Conn. 1972-74, indsl. engr./ mgr. scheduling, Nashville, Tenn. 1974-78, currently indsl. engring. mgr./ quality circles facilitator/ mgr. Material Preparation Div., Hanford, Calif. 1978--; honors: Alpha Pi Mu, IE hon.; Tau Beta Pi, eng. hon.; mem: Am. Inst. Indsl. Engrs.; Kings Co. Grand Jury; Kings- Hanford Kiwanis Club; Kings Co. Spl. Olympics; Am. Cancer Soc.; mil: 1st lt. Army Nat. Guard, Miss., Conn. and Tenn. 1968-76; Republican; Methodist; rec: golf, fishing, civics. Res: 1379 W Malone Hanford 93230 Ofc: The Armstrong Rubber Co., POB 129, Hanford 93232

JOLLEY, JEAN EVANS, writer and publisher; b. June 15, 1926, Conway, S.C.; d. Thomas Maxcy and Ludie (Shuler) Evans; m. Jack Wm. Jolley, June 30, 1944, div.; 1 dau. Janet b. 1945; ed. pub. schools; ordained minister, Pentecostal Holiness Ch. (1956); cert. svc. Calif. Pvt. Postsec. Ednl. Instn. (1983). Career: reporter Columbia (S.C.) Record daily newspaper 1940-44; editor var. Calif. community newspapers, 1945-69 incl. 20 years with Herald Am. Newspaper Gp., L.A. and Orange Counties; edit. dir./writer Morris Cerullo World Evangelism, 1971-82; currently self empl. mgmt. and media cons. to religious orgns., free lance writer, rel. publisher; faculty Cathedral Bible Coll., Escondido 1983-; Management by Objectives Seminars 1982-; staff minister West Adams Foursquare Ch., L.A.; bd. dirs. Black Comm. Center of CSU San Diego 1978-80; recipient Distinguished Service Award, US Jaycees 1967; num. honors as editor 1945-69; first woman mem. Buena Park Kiwanis Club 1967; mem. Evangelical Press Assn., jHarvestime Intl. Network (corp. secty.); author: Toni, the Story of a Black Saint (1976), ghostwriter approx. 30 rel. books; publ. 6 books; Republiccan; Ch. of Foursquare Gospel; rec: golf, fishing. Address: 204 E. 11th Ave Escondido 92025

JONES, ALLEN KENNETH, educator; b. Apr. 16, 1928, Flagstaff, Ariz.; s. Allen Stokes and Pauline Louise (Lockwood) J.; m. Patricia Ann Moeller, Mar.

2, 1958; children: Elizabeth, b. 1949; Allen Lynn, b. 1950; Douglas, b. 1952; Patricia, b. 1953; Debra, b. 1955; Kenneth, b. 1962; edn: BS, Ariz. State Univ. 1950; MA, Chapman Coll. 1975; Calif. lic: Gen. Elem. Life Tchg. Cred. 1968; Nat. Assn. Securities Dealers lic. 1981; Real Estate lic. 1977; Life/ Disability Ins. lic. 1981. Career: mgr./ pressonel instr. Standard Oil Co. of Calif., Phoenix, Ariz. & Modesto, Calif. 1955-56; self- empl., Modesto 1966-68; asst. principal/ tchr. Sylvan Union Sch. Dist., Modesto 1968--; pres. Sylvan Dist. Educators Assn. 1982-83; chmn. Calif. Tchrs. Assn. Stanislaus Co. Svc. Ctr. 1983-, rep. Stanislaus County to C.T.A. State Council 1983-86; mem: Sylvan Dist. Educators Assn.; Calif. Tchrs. Assn.; Nat. Assn. Securities Dealers; Stanislaus Math. Council; Nat. Assn. Realtors; Modesto Bds. Realtors; Democrat; Presbyterian; rec: lapidary, golf, fishing. Res: 1424 Glen Aulen Dr Modesto 95350

JONES, BETTY DE WITT, computer programming executive; b. June 24, 1933, Logan, Kans.; d. Loren Leroy and Virga Hazel (Coombs) DeWitt; m. Wilmer L. Jones, Nov. 24, 1982; children: Stephen J. and Karyn Sue Washburn. Career: sr. pgmmr. Varian Assocs. Palo Alto 1968-75; project leader R. L. Polk, Detroit, Mich. 1977-78; owner Custom Computer Consultants, Carson City, Nev. 1978-80; dir. MIS/asst. v.p. Gits Ents., Chgo. 1980; sr. pgmmr./ analyst Harrah's Reno 1980 81; sr. analyst Dillingham Constrn., Pleasanton, Calif. 1981-83; mgr. pgmmg. Atherton Indus., Menlo Park 1983--; bd. dirs. Upland Hills Ecolog. Awareness Ctr., Lake Orion, Mich.; asst. tchr. pilot pgm. Head Start, summer 64. Res: 2707 Newlands, Belmont 94002 Ofc: Atherton Ind. 260 Constitution Dr Menlo Park 94025

JONES, CLINTFORD ROSS, engineering co. executive; b. Nov. 5, 1934, Schenectady, NY; s. Maynard Carlton and Evalina (Witbeck) J.; m. Alba Riveros, May 11, 1963; edn: BS, metallurg. eng., Mo. Sch. of Mines 1958; MS, materials sci., Northwestern Univ. 1976; MBA, Loyola Marymount Univ. 1982. Reg. Profl. Engr., Ill.; Reg. Profl. Engr. (metallurgical, chemical), Calif. Career: with P.R. Mallory, Lab. for Physical Sci., Burlington, Mass. 163-67; senior metallurgist Handy & Harman, Fairfield, Conn. 1969-71; project engr. Holmes & Narver, Orange 1974-76; sr. project engr. Jacobs Engring. Gp., Pasadena 1976-81; prin. engr. C.F. Braun, Alhambra 1981--; bd. dirs. Escalon Sch. for Atypical Children, Pasadena; awards: NY State Regents Scholarship, Leopold Schepp Found. Scholarship, Am. Foundrymans Scholarship, ARPA Fellowship; mem: Am. Inst. of Mining & Metallurgical Engrs. (v. chmn. So. Calif. Sect. 1976-78), Am. Soc. of Metals, Nat. Calif. Soc. of Profl. Engrs., Am. Chem. Soc., Mensa, Town Hall of Calif., Toastmasters Intl. (past area gov.); publs. in field; holder of 13 U.S. patents; rec: woodworking, lapidary. Res: 20262 Ravenwood Ln Huntington Beach 92646 Ofc: C.F.Braun & Co. 1000 S. Fremont Ave Alhambra 91802

JONES, DOUGLAS N., family counselor, educator; b. Jan. 6, 1933, Los Angeles; s. Ralph L. and Maxine J. (Buzzard) J.; m. Sharon Kreps, Aug. 9, 1957; children: Lori, b. 1960, Gail, b. 1964, Karen, b. 1967; edn: BA, Univ. of La Verne 1955; MRE, Calif. Baptist Theol. Sem. 1960; MA, CSU Los Angeles 1962; post masters wk. in counseling psychol., UCLA, CSUF, CSULA, Loyola-Marymount Univ.; Calif. Sec. Tchg. Credental (1956), Gen. Pupil Personell Svcs., Counseling (1966), Gen. Adminstrv. and Supvsn. (1977), Sch. Psychologist (1980); lic. MFCC (Marriage Family Child Counselor). Career: athletic dir., coach Upland Coll. 1958-64, assoc. prof. 1963; counselor Chino Sch. Dist. 1964-71; psy. & sociology prof. Saddleback Coll. 1973-82; psy. prof. (parttime) Univ. of La Verne Grad. Sch. 1982-; tchr., counselor Irvine Unified Sch. Dist. 1971-83; MFCC pvt. practice, counselor Mission Comm. Psychological Services, Capistrano Bch. 1982--; awards: 4 Sport Letterman, Univ. of La Verne and Cal Baptist, 1954-55; Coach of the Year, Upland Coll. 1958-59; ed. coll. newspapers Mt. SAC and Univ. La Verne; mem. Nat. Educators Fellowship, Fellowship of Christian Athletes, Calif. Assn. of Sch. Psychologists; author: Counselee's Resource Guide; Republican; Baptist; rec: basketball, tennis, volleyball. Res: 32862 Barque Way Dana Point 92629 Ofc: Mission Community Psychological Services, 26875 Calle Hermosa, Suite 12, Capistrano Beach 92624

JONES, EDWARD THOMAS, physician; b. Dec. 19, 1938, Weymouth, Mass.; s. Philip Thomas and Mary Geraldine (Connolly) J.; children: Edward, Jr. b. 1966; Thomas b. 1967; edn: BS, Holy Cross, 1960; MD, Tufts Med. Sch. 1964. Career: intern Rhode Island Hosp. 1965, res. 1966-68; pvt. practice ophthalmology 1968--; bd. dirs. Richmond Hosp. 1975-80; mem: Fellow, Am. Acad. of Ophthalmology; US Chess Fedn.; East Bay Ophthalmology Soc; mil: capt. US Nat. Guard 1965-71; Republican; rec: computer programming, chess. Res: 90 Elizabeth Way San Rafael 94901 Ofc: 2101 Vale Rd San Pablo 94806

JONES, GARY LA ROY, plant engineering manager; b. Feb. 18, 1935, Vernon, Tex.; s. Earl Roy and Pauline Vera (Pearce) J.; m. Paulette DeFrancisco, Aug. 23, 1969; 1 son: Brian, b. 1974; edn: BS, John F. Kennedy Univ. 1973; AA, Coll. of San Mateo 1967. Career: elec. tech. Varian Assoc., Palo Alto 1958; methods analyst Eimac Gp., San Carlos 1965; indsl. engr. Varian Assoc., Palo Alto 1968; plant eng. mgr. Varian Instruments, Walnut Creek 1974--; chmn. Shadelands Indsl. Park Assn. 1981-83; awards: Certs. in Bus. Admin. & Acctg., J.F. Kennedy Univ. 1972; Cert. in Indsl. Mgmt., Coll. of San Mateo 1867; Cert. Mfg. Engr9., S.M.E. 1977; mem: Soc. of Mfg. Engrs.; Am. Inst. Indsl. Engrs.; Walnut Creek CofC; F&AM Lodge, Los Altos; Scottish Rite, Oakland; Shrine, Aahmes Temple, Oakland; mil: P.O. USNR 1952-64, Korean Svc., Nat. Defense, Aircrew Wings; Democrat; Methodist; rec: boating, skiing, fishing. Res: 1610 Eve Dr Concord 94521 Ofc: Varian Instruments, 2700 Mitchell Dr Walnut Creek 94598

JONES, HAROLD THOMAS, JR., manufacturing co. controller; b. Sept. 14, 1938, Los Angeles; s. Harold Thomas Sr. and Opal (McNatt) J.; m. Anita Eriksson, May 17, 1964; children: Erik, b. 1967; Ellis, b. 1970; edn: BS, USC 1961; lic: CPA, Calif. Career: staff auditor Haskins & Sells, CPAs, Los Angeles 1961-65; asst. controller Leisure World Found., Laguna Hills 1965-69; controller Diversified Health Svcs., Van Nuys 1969-70; asst. v.p. fin. Nat. Medical Ent., Brentwood 1970-78; controller Livingston Med. Prods., Modesto 1978-81; controller Stanislaus Food Prods., Modesto 1981--; mem: Am. Inst. CPAs; Calif. Soc. CPAs (Sa Joaquin chpt.); Alpha Kappa Psi Alumni (past pres.); USC Commerce Assocs.; Central Calif. Apart. Assn. (bd. dirs.); YMCA (Father & Son Trailblazers; Indian Guides); mil: payroll Spec. 5 USAR 1961-65; Republican; Ch. of Relig. Sci.; rec: investments, genealogy, travel. Res: 1100 Potomac Way Modesto 95355 Ofc: Stanislaus Food Products, 1202 D St, POB 3951, Modesto 95352

JONES, JAMES HAROLD, corporate executive; b. Aug. 26, 1930, Harrison, Ark.; s. Charlie and Pearl (Wood) J.; m. Peggy Lou Bort, Apr. 2, 1960; children: James Bort, b. 1963, Cliff Ownbey, b. 1965, Lee Christopher, b. 1967, Kenneth Carson, b. 1974; edn: BSBA, Univ. of Ark. 1953; So. Grad. Sch. of Banking, So. Meth. Univ. 1960; Adv. Mgmt. Pgm. Harvard Bus. Sch. 1966. Career: asst. cashier, v.p., exec. v.p. Republic National Bank of Dallas, 1958-69; bd. chmn., CEO, pres., dir. First Commerce Corp. (one-bank holding co.), and subs. First Nat. Bank of Commerce, also bd. chmn./CEO First Commerce Realty Investors (REIT), New Orleans, 1969-75; deputy chmn., pres., CEO, dir. Bancal Tri State Corp. (one-bank holding co.), and subs. The Bank of California, San Francisco 1975; owner, dir., pres., CEO, First Resources Corp., San Mateo 1976--; owner, CEO, bd. chmn. Jameson Pharm. Corp., 1983--; owner, chmn. exec. com. Kahan & Lessin Co., 1983--; owner, dir. K & L Nutritional, Inc. 1984--; dir. Wal-Mart Stores Inc. 1970-; fmr. faculty Sch. of Banking of the South (LSU), Southwestern Grad. Sch. of Banking (SMU); mem. Devel. Council Univ. of Ark. 1973-; past pres. New Orleans Bank Clearning House; chmn. Gulf South Minority Purch. Council (US Dept. Commerce) 1972-74; Louisiana chmn. U.S.Svgs. Bonds (US Treas. Dept.) 1973-75; Metro chmn. Nat. Alliance of Businessmen (JOBS) in coop. with US Dept Labor, 1974-75; awards: 1974 Hornblower Awd., New Orleans Pub. Rels. Soc. of Am.; Nat. Cystic Fibrosis Resrch. Found. Service Awd.; New Orleans CofC Service Awd. 1972, Carnation Awd. for Outstanding Volunteer Svc.; mem. Phi Lambda Chi; Baptist. Res: 862 Chiltern Rd Hillsborough 94010 Ofc: 100 S. Ellsworth, Ste. 811, San Mateo 94401

JONES, LEON LAMONT, psychotherapist; b. Mar. 14, 1930, Glendale; s. Orval Herbert and Dana Ruth (Fields) J.; m. Kathryn Dutt, Apr. 3, 1964; 1 son, Nicholas b. 1965; edn: BA, CSU Los Angeles, 1955, state psychometrist credential; USC, 1961-64; MSW, CSU San Diego 1967, Calif. LCSW (clin. soc. wkr.) MFCC (marriage family child counselor) 1968 Career: supveg child welfare wkr. Dept. of Public Soc. Service 1962-68, supvsg. psychiatric soc. wkr. Dept. of Mental Health, 1969-73; clin. dir. Pasadena Guidance Clinic Adult Service, 1973-77; currently psychotherapist pvt. practice, Pasadena; clin. faculty USC 1974-77, CSU Sch. of Nsg. 1975-77, Antioch Coll. 1976-77; apptd. Pasa. Human Relations Com. 1976-77; mem. Acad. of Cert. Soc. Wkrs, Soc. for Clin. Soc. Wkrs.; cons. to Pasa. Comm. Hosp. 1975-76, Huntington Meml. Hosp. PT Service 1973-77, Foothill Family Service 1977-79; mil: cpl. US Army 1952-54, Korean Pres. Unit Cit., UN, Korean Svc., Nat. Def., American (2 bronze stars) medals; rec: collect toy metal soldiers. Res: 1471 Arroyo View Dr Pasadena 91103 Ofc: Leon Jones, MSW, Marriage & Family Counselor APC, 547 E. Union St Pasadena 91101

JONES, LOLA MARIE, insurance agency owner; b. Dec. 20, 1930, Pierce, Col.; d. Edwin Thomas and Bertha Violet (Nicks) Smith; children: Jerry, b. 1949; Stephen, b. 1952; Penelope, b. 1954. Career: US Fidelity & Guaranty 1961-68; Paris R. Masek Ins. Svc. 1968-75; Miner Harkness Ins. 1975-80; Christian Ins. Agcy. 1980-83; owner, Lola M. Jones Ins. Svc., Sierra Madre 1983--; elected (first woman) bd. govs. Am. Agents Alliance; named Underwriter/ Agent of the Yr. 1981 for Calif., Nat. Auto & Cas. Co.; mem: Am. Agents Alliance; Republican; Baptist; rec: quilting. Res: 136 W Montecito Sierra Madre 91024 Ofc: Lola M. Jones Insurance Service, 55 1/2 N Auburn Sierra Madre 91024

JONES, PROCTOR PATTERSON, diplomat, Honorary Vice Dean, San Francisco Consular Corps; b. May 25, 1916, Cleveland, Oh.; s. John Beverly and Ferne (Patterson) J.; desc. William Whipple, signer Declaration of Independence; desc. of the family de Savignac who settled Detroit in 1701 with Cadillac; desc. John Jones, first English-born child in Montreal (1760); m. Martha Martin, Nov. 29, 1947; children: John, Martha, Proctor Jr., Jessica, Melinda, Greta; edn: AB, Western Reserve Univ. 1937, LLB, JD, 1948; grad. wk. Harvard and Stanford Univs., 1949. Reg. with US Treasury Dept., admitted to practice US Tax Ct., 1951, US Supreme Ct., 1965. Career: owner, mgr. Summer Theatre, Cedarhurst, Long Is.; tchr. Western Reserve Univ., Cleveland Coll. 1947; exec. dir. Experiment in Internat. Living, 1949; tax counsel, Redwood City, Ca. 1951-52; adv. dept. S.F. Newspaper Agcy., 1953; legal ed. Bancroft Whitney Publ. Co., S.F. 1954-59; owner Proctor Jones Photog. Studio, S.F. 1959-77; hon. consul general of Tunisia, 1977--; bd. chmn. Proctor Patterson Jones-Ferne Beverly Ford Found.; awards: num. profl. photography awards, DFA (hon.), Baldwin-Wallace Coll. 1976; One of 50 Outstanding Californians, 1951, Fortnight Mag.; mem. bd. dirs. French-Am. Bilingual Sch.; bd. Seadrift Prop. Owners Assn.; past pres. Presidio Hts. Assn. of Neighbors 1976; mem. Republican State Central Com. 1949-52; past mem. Young Republicans of Calif. (treas.; pres. San Mateo Co. chpt.); bd. dirs. Stinson Beach Co. Water

Bd.; bd. dirs. Calif. Water, Transit & Defense Proj. 1952; mem: SF Opera, SF Symphony; clubs: Bohemian, Union (Cleveland), St. Francis Yacht; mil: capt. USAF 1941-46, Spl. Svcs. Div. War Dept. Staff WWII; Democrat (Nat. Fin. Com.); Episcopal; rec: collection of travel materials. Res: 330 Seadrift Rd Stinson Beach 94970 Ofc: Consulate General of Tunisia, 3401 Sacramento St, San Francisco 94118

JONES, ROBERT RICHARD, consultant; b. Sept. 13, 1925, Canton, Oh.; s. Robert Hall and Clara (Channell) J.; div.; children: Melinda Lou b. 1953, Christopher b. 1955; edn: BA, UCLA 1951; MA, NY Univ. 1962; postgrad. wk. Univ. of Pa. Wharton Sch. of Bus. 1974; PhD Cand., Golden Gate Univ. 1979-; Ga. State Univ. Sch. of Ins. 1966; CLU, Chartered Life Underwriter, Am. Coll. 1978. Career: info. ofcr. US Dept. of State, news corres. Voice of Am., NYC, 1950-53; nat. mgr. mktg. NY Life Ins. Co., NYC 1953-66; asst. v.p. Gulf Life Ins. Co. 1966-68; dir./chief exec. Gulf Holding Corp., Jacksonville, Fla. 1966-69, and pres. Fla. Growth Co., 1968-69; asst. v.p. Aetna Variable Annuity Life in Wash. DC, Hartford, Conn., 1969-72; dir. specialized mktg. Hartford Variable Annuity Life, Hartford Ins. Gp. (subs. ITT), Hartford, Conn. 1972-78, planned, devel. internat. ops. 1975; cons. Robert R. Jones and Assocs., San Francisco 1978--, spec. in devel. of life and health sales through property-casualty firms; cons. to SRI Intl., Financial Industries Center, Intl. Mgmt. & Economics Gp.; acad. honors: J.N. Flint, and NBC Radio Scholarships, UCLA, 1949, 1950; Ednl. Theater Awd., UCLA, 1950; TKA (forensics hon.), Phi Mu Alpha Sinfonia (profl. hon.), Music Frat., Debate and Oratory Champion, 1946-7, Ohio State Oratory, 3d Pl. 1946; mem: Marines Mem. Club, NY Univ. Alumni Assn. (pres. 1964), Parents Without Partners (intl. pres. 1961), UCLA Alumni Assn, NY (pres. 1965), Old First Concerts, SF (dir.), Internat. Assn. for Fin. Plnng., SF (dir., v.p.), Peninsula Chpt. Am. Soc. of CLUs (dir.); mil: radio tng. ofcr. AFRS 1943-46, Am. Cpgn., Victory, Euro, Middle Eastern and African Cpgn. medals; rec: pvt. pilot, Jaguar XKE. Res: 904 Peninsula Ave, 408, San Mateo 94401

JONES, RUSSELL EUGENE, electrical engineer; b. May 24, 1928, Baltimore, Maryland; s. Charles William and Charlotte Maud (Richards) J.; m. Lucille A. Crandall, Nov. 23, 1950; children: Richard, b. 1954; Robert, b. 1956; Laurie, b. 1963; edn: BSEE, Johns Hopkins Univ. 1957; MSEE, Drexel Univ. 1967; Calif. Comm. Coll. Instr. Credential 1981. Career: design engr. aircraft antennas Martin-Marietta Corp. 1967-65; prin. radar design engr. Bendix Corp. 1965-77; gp. head antenna design Hughes Aircraft Co. 1977--; instr. celestial navigation, Long Beach City Coll.; awards: Distng. Ednl. Achiev., US Power Squadrons 1982; mem: IEEE; Long Beach Power Squadron (commdr. 1983); Maryland Cruising Club (commodore 1970); 1984 Olympics Yachting Competition (chief support craft communicator); publs: art., The Ensign Mag. 5/82; contbg. ed. The BURGEE yachting mag.; fmr. profl. photographer (num. photos pub.); mil: lt. US Army 1950-53, Korean Svc.; Republican; Protestant; rec: yachting, amateur radio (KE6YI), photog. Res: 3032 Kittrick Dr Los Alamitos 90720 Ofc: Hughes Aircraft Co., POB 92436, Mail R2/ A102, Los Angeles 90009

JONES, TOBBIE T., JR., accountant; b. May 17, 1949, Dallas, Tex.; s. Tobbie T., Sr. and Marietta (Bell) J.; m. Jacquline B. Snowden, Sept. 22, 1972; children: Tunisia, b. 1973; Tobi, b. 1975; edn: BA, Bishop Coll. 1973; stu. No. Tex. State Univ. 1973-74; certs. in pers. mgmt. & supvn. and minority dynamics, City of Dallas 1973. Career: admin. asst. City of Dallas Parks & Rec. Admin., 1972-74; asst. exec. dir. Charles Drew Home Health Agcy., Dallas 1974-79; sr. acct. Tng. & Research Found., Inglewood, Calif. 1980--; owner Executive Acctg. & Tax Svcs., Inglewood 1984--; awards; Music Scholarship, Bishop Coll. 1969-71; mem. Dallas County Comm. Action Executive Bd. 1969-70; Phi Beta Lambda (pres. 1970-71); Urban Mgmt. Assts. of No. Tex. 1970-74; Republican; Baptist; rec: fishing, golf. Res: 531 E Hazel, Apt 5, Inglewood 90302 Ofc: Training & Research Foundation, 340 E Kelso Inglewood 90302

JONES, WYMAN, city librarian; b. Dec. 17, 1929, St. Louis, Mo.; s. Jay Hugh and Nina Marie (Dallas) J.; sons: Gregory Foster, Mark Jay, Manson Matthew, Ross Christopher; edn: BA, Adams State Coll. 1956; MLS, Univ. Tex. 1958. Career: chief sci. reorg. dept. Dallas Public Library 1958-59; chief of Branches 1956-64; dir. Ft. Worth City/ County Public Lib. Sys. 1964-70; dir. Los Angeles Public Library System, 1970--; library building & system planning cons. 1963-; mem: Am., Calif. Library Assns.; author: (with E. Castagna) The Library Reaches Out (1964); publs: monthly column in Library Journal (1964), arts. in profl. pubs.; mil: USAF 1951-55. Res: Promenade West, 880 W First St Los Angeles 90012 Ofc: Los Angeles Public Library, 630 W Fifth St Los Angeles 90071

JORDAN, DANIEL ARTHUR, real estate co. executive; b. Mar. 18, 1936, Fresno; s. Rev. Philip Anselm and Marion Leona (Durman) J.; edn: BS, summa cum laude, Calif. Lutheran Coll. 1978; MBA, USC 1981. Career: senior sales assoc. Brown Realtors, Thousand Oaks 1978-81; v.p. TB & A Development Co., Los Angeles 1982--; bd. dirs. Poipu Kai Resorts, Kauai, Hawaii; bd. dirs. Stonebridge, Deer Valley, Utah; honors: Alpha Mu Gamma; Calif. Scholarship Fedn. (life); Who's Who Am. Univ. & Coll. Students 1978; Million Dollar Circle, Nat. Assn. Home Bldrs. 1980; mem: Nat., Calif. Assns. Realtors; Los Angeles Bd. Realtors; USC Career Svcs. Ofc. (bd. dirs.); USC Real Estate Assn.; Republican (Pres. Task Force); Lutheran; rec: skiing, hiking, swimming. Res: 2408 Moreno Dr Los Angeles 90039 Ofc: TB & A Development Co., 1520 Wilshire Blvd Los Angeles 90017

JORDAN, HOWARD VIVIAN, JR., political scientist/ farmer; b. Nov. 3, 1921, National City; s. Howard Vivian and Madeleine (Miller) J.; m. Dolores E. Schmidt, Jan. 16, 1945; children: Robert A., 1945; Howard V. III, b. 1948; Michael D., b. 1951; edn: AA, Santa Ana Coll. 1967; BA, San Bernardino State Coll. 1974; lic. real estate broker, Calif. 1964. Career: capt. USMC 1941-62; real estate broker, insurance broker, self- empl. 1962-82; county supvr. deputy, San Bernardino Co. 1982-83, ret.; pres. Royal Ent. Inc. 1971-72; pres. Pine Cove Water Dist. 1976-80; v.p. Construction West 1980; honors: gov. Pacific Southwest. Dist. Optimist Internat. 1978-79; mem: Ret. Ofcrs. Assn.; Pan Am. Optimist Club, Los Angeles; mil: capt. USMC 1941-62, Bronze Star; Republican; Catholic; rec: coins, stamps, gardening. Res: 21972 Viento Rd Apple Valley 92307

JORDAN, R(AYMOND) BRUCE, management consultant/educator; b. Mar. 10, 1912, Holland, Mich.; s. Albert Raymond and Aimee (Best) J.; m. Dorothy Caig, June 6, 1942; edn: BA, CSC Sacto 1952; MBA, Stanford Univ. Grad. Sch. Bus. 1959; Calif. Standard Teaching Cred.; Lic. Public Acct. Career: acct.-auditor State Bd. Equalization, State Dept. Employment 1947-48, mgmt. analyst 1948-52, chief analyst 1952-59; chief mgmt. analyst Hdqtrs Ofc., State Dept. Mental Hygiene, 1959-63; bus. adminstr. Atascadero State Hosp. 1963-68, Patton State Hosp. (San Bernardino) 1968-70; mgmt. cons. hosps. Victoria, B.C. Can. 1970-72; health services mgmt. consultant, No. Calif. 1973--; cons. to Nat. Govt. of Iran in mgmt. tng. and instr. Ministry Staffs, Univ. Tehran (1956); adj. prof. Golden Gate Univ. 1983-, instr. Monterey campus (Gen. Mgmt., Personnel & Labor Rels. Mgmt, Hlth Svcs. Mgmt.) 1972-; instr. Sacto City Coll. 1951-62, UC Davis 1963, Cuesta Coll. 1967-8, Monterey Penin. Coll. Served as treas. Experience, Inc. (distbr. free vegetables, aid in craft sales) 1973-78; pres. Monterey Co. Ombudsman Pgm. 1976-; founder/mem. adv. bd. Monterey Co. Sr. Hearing Ctr. 1977-; bd. dir. Monterey Co. Senior Aide Pgm.; adv. bd. Alliance on Aging; founding pres. Concerned Senior Citizens, Monterey Penin. Club 1974-7; adv. Monterey Sr. Day Care Ctr. 1977-8. Author: two books (mgmt. field), various profl., ednl. publs., Task Force Report on Hlth & Welfare Agcy., Gov.'s Reorgn. Plan 1959; originator whole dollar acctg. in Calif. State Govt.; Recipient Bronze Achievement Awd, Mental Hosp. Svc. 1963. Mem: Toastmasters Internat. (Able Toastmaster), fmr. Rotarian. Mil: US Army, So. Pac. 1943-6. Prot. Rec: mosaics. Address: R. Bruce Jordan, MBA, 110 41st St, 705, Oakland 94611

JORDAN, RICHARD BUCKNER, stockbroker; b. Nov. 30, 1930, Redlands; s. Leslie Lafayette and Mildred (McCay) J.; m. Constance Burch Eddy, Mar. 28, 1959; edn: BA, Yale 1957. Career: stockbroker Dean Witter & Co. 1958-76; stockbroker Bateman Eichler, Hill Richards 1976--; mem: Muscular Dystrophe Soc., Fresno (pres. 1970); Fresno Arts Ctr. (pres. 1981-83); University Club CSUF; mil: QM2 USN 1951-54, GCM; Republican; Episcopal; rec: philately. Res: 5081 N Van Ness Ave Fresno 93711 Ofc: 1551 E Shaw Ave Fresno 93710

JORDAN, WILBERT CORNELIOUS, physician; b. Sept. 11, 1944, Wheatley, Ark.; s. William and Annie Mae (Tolson) J.; edn; AB, Harvard 1966; MD, Case Western Reserve 1971; MPH, UCLA 1978. Career: physician, Govt. of India, World Health Orgn. Smallpox Eradication Pgm. 1973-74; assoc. epidemiologist, Dist. of Columbia 1973-76; pub. health chief, South area, Los Angeles County, 1977-80; actg. chmn. Dept. of Community Med., Charles R. Drew Postgrad. Med. Sch. 1978-80; practitioner, infectious disease, Los Angeles; assoc. prof. Chas Drew Med. Sch.; asst. prof. UCLA; UCLA Med. Sch. Admissions Com.; dir. ofc. of quality assurance, Martin Luther King Gen. Hosp. 1977--; mem: Nat. Med. Assn.; Assn. of Am. Med. Colls.; Am. Pub. Health Assn.; Am. Coll. of Physicians; NAACP; publs: sev. arts. on infectious diseases; mil: USPHS 1973-76; Democrat; Baptist; rec: jogging, gospel music, jazz. Res: 2380 Venus Dr Los Angeles 90046 Ofc: 3200 S Susana Rd, Ste 304, Compton 90221

JORNACION, OSCAR LICTADA, certified public accountant, publisher, co. president; b. Oct. 13, 1951, San Juan, Philippines; s. Eleuterio Pimentel and Consuelo (Lictada) J.; m. Gilda Arroyo, June 15, 1980; 1 son, Grant, b. 1981; edn: BS in bus. adm., magna cum laude, Univ. of the East, 1973; profl. devel. courses, Calif. St. Univ. 1975-76; MBA, Pepperdine Univ. 1982. Career: auditor Price Waterhouse, Phil. 1973-74; accounting supr. Price Waterhouse, Los Angeles, Ca. 1974-77; mgr. acctg., Ticor Mortgage Ins., L.A. 1976-77, dir. of acctg. 1977-81; pres. Western Mectrix Co., L.A. 1979-81; practicing CPA, 1981--, pres. Perma-Ware Marketing co., L.A. 1982--; newspaper, magazine & directory publisher, California Examiner, 1983--; mem: Am. Entrepreneurs Assn., Los Angeles CofC; Republican; Catholic; rec: tennis, jogging. Res: 7511 Laurel Grove Ct North Hollywood 91605 Ofc: California Examiner, 2901 W. Beverly Blvd Los Angeles 90057

JOSEPH, PHYLLIS F., accountant; b. July 9, 1938, Omaha, Nebr.; d. Hershel H. (dec) and Zelda (Charney) Freedman; m. Allan J. Joseph, Sept. 1, 1958; children: Elizabeth, b. 1962; Susan, b 1964; Debbie (dec., 1969); Katherine, b. 1973; edn: BS, Univ. of Wisc. 1960; MBA, UC Berkeley 1980; CPA, Calif. 1982. Career: tchr. Madison Pub. Schs., Madison, Wisc. 1960-63; cons./ pgmr. Western Ops., Inc., San Francisco 1967-70; senior asst. acct. Deloitte Haskins & Sells, S.F. 1980-82; senior acct. Smith & Lange, CPAs, S.F. 1982-83; currently, acctg. policy coord. Wells Fargo Bank, S.F.; Kaiser Aluminum/ Berkeley Bus. Sch. Learning Partnership 1980; honors: Beta Alpha Psi (pres. 1979-80); Beta Gamma Sigma, Univ. of Calif. Honor Soc. 1979-80; mem: Calif. Soc. of CPAs; City of Mill Valley Parks & Recreation Commn. (v.chmn. 1976). Res: 2461 Washington St San Francisco 94115 Ofc: Wells Fargo Bank, NA, 475 Sansome St, Ste 1056, San Francisco 94111

JOSHI, CHANDRASHEKHAR JANARDAN, physicist; b. July 22, 1953, Wai, India; s. Janardan Digambar and Ramabai (Kirpekar) J.; m. Asha Bhatt, Jan. 18, 1982; edn: BSc, London Univ., U.K. 1974; PhD, Hull Univ., U.K. 1978. Career: research assoc. Nat. Research Council of Canada, Ottawa 1978-81; research engr. Univ. of Calif. Los Angeles 1981-83, adj. assoc. prof. UCLA 1983--, co-dir. Laser-Plasma Interactions Lab, UCLA; tchr. Electromagnetics & Quantum Electronics, UCLA; cons. Lawrence Livermore Lab.; honors: Citation, Inst. of Nuclear Engrs., U.K. 1974; mem: APS, IEEE; publs: over 30 in areas of laser- plasma interaction, lasers, plasma physics and collective accelerators; rec: travel. Res: 825 Ocean Park Blvd, Apt B, Santa Monica 90405 Ofc: UCLA, 405 Hilgard Ave Los Angeles 90024

JOYCE, STEPHEN MICHAEL, lawyer; b. Mar. 19, 1945, Los Angeles; s. John Rowland and Elizabeth Rose (Rahe) J.; m. Bernadette, Aug. 18, 1973; 1 dau: Natalie, b. 1982; edn: BS, CSU Los Angeles 1970; JD, Univ. San Fernando Valley 1976; admitted to Calif. State Bar 1976, US Ct. of Claims 1981. Career: partner law firm Gold & Joyce, Beverly Hills 1976--; bd. dirs. Safety Edn. Treatment Ctr., San Fernando Valley; mem: Los Angeles Trial Lawyers Assn.; Calabasas Racquetball Club; Calabasas Athletic Club; Appeal pub. Joyce v. U.S. (2 Ct. Cl. 226, 1983); mil: pvt. US Army; Democrat; Catholic; rec: racquetball, golf, fishing. Res: 1724 Barcelona Ct Calabasas Park 90302 Ofc: Gold & Joyce, 241 S Beverly Dr Beverly Hills 90212

JOYFUL, MARYANN CONNERLY, education consultant; b. Monmouth, Ill.; d. Stanley S. and Mary J. (Blevins) Connerly; children: Marypat Green, b. 1953; Mike Cole Kessenick, b. 1955; edn: BA, CSU San Francisco 1952; MA, CSU Los Angeles 1961; EdD, Calif. Western Univ. 1976. Career: educator Torrance Unified Schs., 1956-66; instr. UC Los Angeles, 1965-66; educator L.A. City Schs., 1966-67, 1968-76; adminstr. Shiprock Bur. of Indian Affairs Elem. Sch. 1967-68; pres. Joyful House Inc., Rancho Palos Verdes 1972--; consultant Small Bus. Adminstrn., L.A., 1972, cons. Head State Pgms., 1965-67; publisher: weekly newsletter on Bus. in Nursery Schs., monthly newsletter on small business; honors: Nat. Outstanding Leader in Elementary Edn., 1976; Palos Verdes Penin. Pacesetter of the Year 1973; mem. NOW; rec: writing, dancing, hiking. Ofc: Joyful House Inc. POB 2232, Palos Verdes 90274

JUAREZ-URIBE, JOEL, cardiologist; b. Dec. 10, 1948, Acapulco, Mex.; s. Joel Juarez-Guzman and Gloria (Uribe-Garcia) J.; m. Lourdes Sanchez-Diaz, Sept. 5, 1971; children: Joel b. 1973, Jacob b. 1975, Jessica b. 1978; edn: BS, Univ. of Guerrero, 1965; MD, Univ. of Mexico Med. Sch. 1973; internist Univ. of Texas Med. Sch. 1973-1976; cardiology fellowship Emory Univ. Sch. Med. 1976-1979; diplomate Am. Bd. of Cardiovascular Disease 1979; diplomate Am. Bd. of Internal Med. 1976. Career: assoc. prof. of medicine, Univ. of Mex. Med. Sch. and chief, Dept. of Medicine, Gen. Hosp. of Acapulco, 1979-82; cardiologist pvt. practice, Chula Vista, Ca. 1983--; staff cardiol. Bay General Hosp., Chula Vista Community Hosp., Alvarado Comm. Hosp. (S.D.); mem: San Diego county Med. Soc., AMA, Calif. Med. Assn., Soc. Mexicana De Cardiologia; Catholic; rec: classical music, sailing. Res: 383 Surrey Dr Bonita 92002 Ofc: 401 H Street, Suite 8, Chula Vista 92002

JUE, JEFFREY, social worker/administrator; b. July 23, 1943, San Francisco; s. Stanley and Aimee (Owyang) J.; m. Linda Valerio, Nov. 17, 1962; children: Christine, b. 1963; Leslie, b. 1969; edn: BA, San Francisco State Univ. 1968; MSW, UC Berkeley 1970; LCSW, Calif. 1972. Career: dir. Child Adolescent pgm., dir. Mobile Emergency Svcs., tng. dir. Outpatient dept., Stanislaus Co. Dept. of Mental Health, Modesto, 1972-79, clin. svcs. mgr. 1979-81; dir. client svcs., Western Regl. Ctr. for Developmentally Disabled, Inglewood 1981-82; mental health dir. Merced Co., Merced 1982--; instr. Chapman Coll., Modesto Jr. Coll.; awards: Soc. Wkr. of the Year - Adminstn., NASW 1982; mem: Nat. Assn. Soc. Workers, Calif. Primary Prevention Network (bd. dirs. 1983); rec: skiing, tennis, racquetball. Res: 124 Oakhurst Ct Merced 95340

JUE, THOMPSON KIT, distribution co. executive; b. Nov. 10, 1950, Vallejo; s. Yoot Jeung and Yit Kay (Der) J.; m. Regina Vons, Apr. 20, 1974; children: Ronald, b. 1978; Alena, b. 1976; edn: Merritt Coll. 1968-70; BS, CSU Hayward 1970-72; CPA cert. 1975. Career: auditor Main Lafrentz & Co., CPAs, San Francisco 1972; auditor Amfac, Inc., Burlingame 1975; asst. controller Amfac Elec. Supply Co., Burlingame 1975; regl. controller Amfac Drug Supply Co., San Mateo 1976; controller Keyston Bros., Inc., S.F. 1977, chief fin. officer 1981--, v.p., bd. dirs. 1983--; mem. Asian Pacific Personnel Assn.; Republican; rec: jogging, carpentry, gardening. Res: 1085 Rudgear Rd Walnut Creek 94596 Ofc: Keyston Bros., 1000 Brannan St San Francisco 94103

JUKKOLA, GEORGE DUANE, physician; b. Feb. 28, 1945, Aliquippa, Pa.; s. Waino Helmer and Bedelia (Pyle) J.; m. Gretchen Strom, Feb. 14, 1970, div. 1984; children: David, b.1973; Jeffrey, b.1978; edn: BA, UC Berkeley 1970; MD, Univ. of Pittsburgh 1975; splst. Obstetrics & Gynecology. Career: intern, res. obstetrics/ gynecology Arron Gen. Med. Ctr., Arron, Ohio 1975-78; pvt. practice, Ob/Gyn., Parkview Comm. Hosp. & Riverside Comm. Hosp. 1978--; dir. Parkview Profl. Ctr. 1981--; co- founder Family Birthing Center, Riverside 1981-; bd. cert. Am. Board Ob/Gyn. 1981; mem: Am., Calif. & Riverside Co. Med. Assns.; Fellow Am. Coll. Ob/Gyn; Am. Assn. Gynecologic Laparoscopists; Mensa; research: computer analysis of cesarean section morbidity 1976-78; mil: USAF 1965-69, Air Medal w/ 4 Oak Leaf Clusters; Republican. Res: 2580 Carlton Pl Riverside 92507 Ofc: George D. Jukkola, MD, Inc., 3865 Jackson St, Ste 38, Riverside 92503

JULEEN, GARY LE ROY, marriage, family and child therapist; b. Dec. 24, 1946, San Diego; s. Runard Albert and Ruth Mabel Juleen; edn: BA, San Diego State Univ. 1973; MA, Nat. Univ. 1980; PhD, Profl. Sch. of Psychological Studies 1984; lic. marriage, family & child therapist, Calif. BBSE 1982. Career: trust ops. supvr. Crocker Nat. Bank, San Diego 1971-74; exec. dir. Logos Found. Inc., San Diego 1974-79; asst. ops. supvr. San Diego Trust & Savings Bank 1979-81; dir. treatment svcs. Green Valley Ranch, Ramona 1981-83; dir. Pelican Family Inst., San Diego 1982--; adj. faculty Univ. of La Verne 1983; awards: Eagle Scout, Boy Scouts of Am. 1961; Staff of the Year 1983, Youth Devel. Inc.; mem: Calif. Assn. Marriage & Family Therapists; Christian Assn. of Psychological Svcs.; San Diego Evangelical Assn.; Alpha Gamma Omega frat., San Diego State Univ.; Assembly of God. Res: 7805 Tommy Dr, Apt 69, San Diego 92119 Ofc: Pelican Family Inst., 810 Emerald St, Ste 115, San Diego 92109

JUNCHEN, DAVID LAWRENCE, pipe organ builder; b. Feb. 23, 1946, Rock Island, Ill.; s. Lawrence Ernest and Lucy Mae (Ditto) J.; edn: BSEE, highest honors, Univ. of Ill. 1968. Career: founder/ owner Junchen Pipe Organ Corp., Woodstock, Ill. 1975-80; mng. dir. Baranger Studios, South Pasadena 1980-81; contbr. Ency. of Automatic Musical Instruments; awards: key to City of Rock Island, Ill. 1957; Outstanding Freshman in Engring., Univ. of Ill. 1963; mem: Am. Inst. of Organbldrs.; Am. Theatre Organ Soc.; Musical Box Soc.; Automatic Musical Instrument Collectors Assn.; Tau Beta Pi; Eta Kappa Nu; composer/ arranger over 100 music roll for automatic musical instruments; author: Encyclopedia of Am. Theatre Organs, 1983. Address: 280 E. Del Mar, Ste 311, Pasadena 91101

JURI FERNANDEZ, HUGO OSCAR, physician-surgeon/educator; b.Oct. 2, 1948, Cordoba, Argentina; s. Alfredo Elias and Florentina (Fernandez) Juri; m. Carmen Boroccioni, Dec. 23, 1972; children: Gustavo, b. 1975, Robert, b. 1979; edn: BS, Gral Paz Mil. Inst. 1965; MD, Cordoba National Univ. 1971. Career: neurosurg. dept. Cordoba Nat. Univ. Med. Sch., 1972; intern Union Hosp. Fall River, Mass. 1973; surgical resident (chief res. 1977) Sisters Hosp., Buffalo, NY 1974-77; Fellow Head and Neck Surg., asst. clin. instr. ENT Dept., State Univ. of NY at Buffalo, 1978; chief of surgery Bellavista Comm. Hosp., Los Angeles 1978, chief of staff 1979; chief of surg. Beverly Hills Hosp., West L.A. 1979, and dir. laser surgery, conducting a pioneer clin. trial of use of CO2 Laser Beam in Decubitus Ulcers (Medicare Adm. Pgm); surgical practice, Alpha Medical Group, Los Angeles and instr. (6 months a yr.) Cordoba Nat. Univ. (370 year old instn.) Argentina; mem. local med. soc., Argentinian Assn. of Head and Neck Pathol. (treas. Cordoba Assn.); num. sci. presentations internat. profl. meetings; mil: lt.; Catholic. Res: 18038 Gallinette St Rowland Ht 91748 Ofc: Alpha Medical Group 3467 Whittier Blvd Los Angeles 90023

JUST, GERALD E., lawyer; b. Jan. 31, 1942, Millis, Mass.; s. Wilmington and Grace (Wobble) J.; m. Jane Manant, Oct. 8, 1961, children: Tina, b. 1962, Debbie, b. 1963, Jayne, b. 1964; edn: LLM, USC, 1964-72, admitted to practice Calif. State Bar. Career: lawyer pvt. practice, pres. Just Law Corp., Bel Air; honors: City Law Award 1980, State Law Award, 1981; mil: E5 US Army; rec: race car racing. Res: 2040 West Rosecrans Ave Gardena 90249 Ofc: Just Law Corp. Bel Air

JUSTUS, ADALU, designer, writer, lecturer; b. Aug. 5, 1928, Lawrenceville, Ill.; d. Edward G. and Zerma E. (Johnston); m. Gary H. Justus, Jan. 8, 1974; children: Rick b. 1948, Marlene b. 1950, Jeff b. 1952, Jamie b. 1954, Melinda b. 1955, Brett b. 1968. Dip. in custom-fitting, Symbra-Ette. Career: designer of custom undergarments, brassieres, etc.; original pattern maker, prototypes in custom-bra and prosthesis field; opr. lic. Child-Care Center, 1968-73; owner The Elegante Lady, Hesperia 1973--; direct sales Symbra-Ette (Calif.), 1974--, held tng. seminars 1977; designer undergarments (2 patent appls.) incl. strapless bra for large sizes and exclusive side-hook design bra, and direct sales, Command Performance (mfg. co. Waco, Tex.) 1977--; free-lance writer, author book for women on Self-Image; other publs: In the Shadow of Death (1960), Body & Soul (TV screenplay 1963), Mommy, Please Don't Kill Me (1983), You Are Elegant in God's Sight (1984); instr. Breast Clinic, Victor Valley Hosp., instr. classes for nurses in breast self-exam., V.V. Hosp., St. Mary's of the Desert (Apple Valley); Am. BSE instr., Mastectomy Adv. V.V. Br. American Cancer Soc.; respons. for obtaining grant from the Irvine Found. to estab. blood donor center for Hemophilia Found. in Orange Co.; counselor to approx. 15,000 women and husbands re Mastectomies; honors incl. Miss America Pageant Award (1978, 79), recognition from num. civic orgns. as speaker for Hemophilia Found.; mem: ASTM, Hesperia CofC, Hemophilia Found. (bd. mem. L.A. 1967-71; pres. O.C. chpt. 1969-71), Am. Cancer Soc., founder Victor Valley Women Against Abortion; Republican; Presbyterian; rec: doll clothes patterns, 7 grandchildren. Address: The Elegante Lady, 18019 Danbury Ave Hesperia 92345

K

KABOT, PAUL GARY, consulting design engineer; b. June 15, 1935, Compton; s. Paul and Agnes (Cowan) Kotab; m. Mary Jane Yeths, June 28, 1953; children: James, b. 1954; William, b. 1956; Donna, b. 1959; edn: Compton Coll. 1956-57, 1960-62, Santa Monica City Coll. 1959. Career: machine designer Protonics Design, Gardena 1965; prod. devel. mgr. Falcon Plastics, Oxnard 1965-71; chief engr. Promold Inc., Van Nuys 1971-72; cons. engr. free lance var. cos. 1972-73; dir. research & devel. Plasta Medic Inc., El Segundo 1973-75; owner Kabot Design Engring., Newbury Park 1975--; cons. engr. Matel Inc. 1959-62; cons. engr. Smith Aviation 1957; mem: Soc. of Plastic Engrs., Am. Soc. of Metals; rec: electronics. Res: 108 Dena Dr Newbury Park 91320 Ofc: Kabot Design Engineering, 996 Lawrence Dr, Ste 203, Newbury Park 91320

KACHANI, DJAFAR, jewelry importer; b. Jan. 1, 1935, Ardabel, Azarbajjan; s. Mir Rahem and Alaweye Kachani; m. Elle Schmidt, Mar. 17, 1967; children: Daniela b. 1968, Thomas b. 1972, Stephan b. 1976, Andrew b. 1983; edn: med. stu. Univ. Innsbruck, 1966; bus. courses, W.Germany 1978. Career: import-export bus., Innsbruck, Austria 1968; owner Kachani Jewelry Import, 1978--; Islam; rec: sports, music, equestrian. Address: D. Kachani Jewelry Import, 33541 Calle Miramar San Juan Capistrano 92675

KAFOURE, STEVEN GEORGE, tax practitioner; b. Oct. 21, 1948, Indpls., Ind.; s. William George and Frances Hanna (Risk) K.; m. Dory Lynn Rigopoulos, July 14, 1984; edn: BS, Indiana Univ. 1966-70; stu. environmental engrg. Univ. of Cincinnati 1971; Std. Tchg. Cred., Calif. 1974; Lic. Ins. Agent, Calif. 1981; Reg. Tax Practitioner, Calif. Career: instr. Poway Unified Sch. Dist., Poway 1974-80; tax preparer Tax Corp. of Am., San Diego 1977-80; tax preparer/ ins. agent prin., San Diego 1984--; Pro-Trac Fin. Advisory Panel 1983-84, Sci. Dept. Hd. and dist.- wide curriculum devel., Poway Unified Schs. 1979-80; awards: Student Conserv. Aide, Grand Canyon Nat. Park 1972; Ruggels Awd. for Ind. Univ. Outstanding Freshman Gymnast 1967; Nat. Merit Scholar 1966; mem: Internat. Assn. Fin. Plng.; L-5 Soc.; San Diego Zoological Soc.; Phi Kappa Tau frat.; Birds of Indiana (sponsor); Indianan Univ. Arts & Sci. (sponsor); Christian; rec: philately, backpacking. Res: 17941 Aguamiel Rd San Diego 92127 Ofc: Steven Kafoure, 16776 Bernardo Center Dr, Ste 203, San Diego 92128

KAGAN, ROBERT MICHAEL, real estate executive; b. Apr. 15, 1943, Oakland; s. Harry and Irene (Manuck) K.; edn: AB, UC Berkeley 1965, MBA, 1969. Career: cons. Urban Research & Devel., San Francisco 1969-70; cons. Larry Smith & Co., Los Angeles 1970-71; senior acquisitions analyst Kaiser-Aetna, Oakland 1971-72; pres. Kagan-Bennett, Inc., Oakland 1972-82; v.p. Cal Fed Ent., S.F. 1982--; adj. prof. Golden Gate Univ., S.F.; cons. P.M. & E.; cons. Wells Fargo Bank; honors: Am. Field Exch. Student to Finland 1960, comm. svc. awd. City of Piedmont 1961, Calif. Real Estate Assn. scholarship 1968; mem. Commonwealth Club, S.F; Republican; Jewish. Res: 2150 Lakeshore Ave Oakland 94606 Ofc: Cal Fed Enterprises, 505 Sansome St, Ste 1905, San Francisco 94111

KAGAN, THEODORE JAY, seminar instructor; b. Sept. 9, 1944, Brklyn; s. Murray and Elizabeth (Silverman) K.; edn: AAS, NYC Comm. Coll. 1966; BS, Woodbury Univ. 1971; career:advt. sales United Western Newspapers, 1971-5, Larchmont Chronicle 975-6, Meredith Newspapers, Los Angeles 1976-8, San Bernardino Sun, 1978-81; seminar instr., cons. on time mgmt., goal setting, keynote spkr. Positive Dimensions, San Bernardino 1981--; mem. Nat. Spkrs. Assn., Toastmasters Internat. (area gov.); contbg. author, Great Persuaders (Royal Pub. Co., Glendora) cartoon series: Corkey (outdoor enjoyment through edn. theme), In Touch, 1982; mil: E4 US Army 1966-8; Democrat; Jewish; rec: backpacking, camping. Address: 5312 Dogwood St San Bernardino 92404

KAHLE, OMAR ALFONSO, real estate broker; b. June 26, 1915, Angus, Ont., Canada, derivative citizenship; s. Herman V. and Bula A. (Leggette) K.; m. Katherine Foote, July 14, 1940; children: Omar Jr., b. 1941; Vance, b. 1945; Monica, b. 1951; Regina, b. 1955; edn: civil eng. stu. Northeastern Univ. 1935; Mass. Inst. Tech. 1936; Lumbleau Sch. of Real Estate 1970; Golden West and Orange Coast Colls. 1974. Career: stock mgr. Jiffy Mfg. Co., Charlestown, Mass. 1937-38; owner Kahle Rental Svc., Roxbury, Mass. 1939-41; rivet passer Bethlehem Steel Shipyard, E. Boston 1942; apprentice diesel mechanic Clark-Wilcox Co., Boston 1943; stock mgr. Fogg Nozzle Co., Los Angeles 1943-44; elec. plant mech. Am. Airlines, Monterey, Mex. 1945-46; carpenter A.F.L. Union Hall, Hamilton, Ont., Can. 1947-50, in Los Angeles & Orange Co., 1951-70; real estate agt. Seymore Realty, Century 21- Ladera Rlty., Huntington Beach 1970-75; broker/owner Kahle Realty, Costa Mesa 1975--; recipient Lister/ Salesman of the Yr., Century 21 Ladera Rlty. 1974; Blue Ribbons for clay modeling and free hand drawing, Athol Co. Fair 1923; mem: Newport Harbor Elks Lodge; N.H. Costa Mesa Bd. Realtors; Huntington Beach Real Estate Bd. 1971-75; Republican; Catholic; rec: ballroom & square dancing. Res: 924 Dogwood St Costa Mesa 92627 Oc: Kahle Realaty, 870 W 19th St Costa Mesa 92627

KAHN, JUDITH FAYE, administrator; b. June 9, 1944, Wash. DC; d. J. Leon and Helen (Margolis) Kahn; edn: BA, Univ. of So. Fla. 1967; MA, San Francisco State Univ. 1973. Career: owner/ opr. Kahn's Candles 1974-77; developer/ conductor Cafe Walks (combination hist. tour of S.F. neighborhood & intro. to best S.F. cafes) 1983--; tchr. (soc. studies, English) at jr. and sr. high sch. levels, 1976--; mem: Calif. Tchrs. Assn.; Am. Assn. for State & Local Hist.; Jewish Democratic Club; author/pub. Indulge Yourself: A Guide to San Francisco Neighborhood Cafes and Coffeehousese (1982); Democrat; Jewish; rec: painting, tennis, rafting. Res: 355 24th Ave San Francisco 94121 Ofc: Kahn Publishing, 355 24th Ave San Francisco 94121

KAISER, DARYL WILLIAM, certified public accountant; b. Apr. 30, 1942, Chico; s. Otto Henry and Gertrude Marie (Quadros) K.; m. Margaret Olivarez,

June 30, 1962; children: Carisa, b. 1963, Heather, b. 1965, Lisa, b. 1967, Timothy, b. 1968; edn: BA, CSU Chico 1964; CPA, Calif. 1968, FAA instrument rated pilot 1979, lic. real estate broker 1983. Career: var. acctg. positions, Redding, Red Bluff, Chico, 1962-68; CPA/vice pres. Matson & Isom Accountancy Corp., Chico 1968--; past instr. municipal acctg. CSU Chico; elected mem. Butte Co. LAFCO (Local Agcy Formation Commn.) 1983-; elected mem. (chmn. 1984) Chico Area Recreation & Park Dist. 1980-; mem: Am. Inst. of CPAs, Calif. Soc. CPAs, Chico CofC (treas.), Butte Creek Country Club, Elks, Rotary, Y's Mem Club (pres.), Jaycees (treas.), Chico Tennis Club (treas.); Republican; Catholic; rec: tennis, flying. Res: 1259 E. 1st Ave Chico 95926 Ofc: Matson & Isom Acctcy Corp. POB 1638, Chico 95927

KALLAY, THOMAS, professor of law; b. July 14, 1937, Budapest, Hungary, nat. 1956; m. Chitra Rao, Mar. 20, 1963; children: Maya b. 1966, Thomas b. 1970; edn: AB, UCLA 1958, JD, UCLA Sch. of Law 1962; Fulbright fellow, Univ. of Heidelberg, W.Ger. 1959-60; admitted to State Bar of Calif. 1963. Career: deputy atty. gen. State of Calif. 1967-70; senior research atty. Calif. State Ct. of Appeals 1970-72, 1976-77; assoc. and partner Kaplan, Livingston, Berkowitz & Selvin, Beverly Hills 1972-76; prof. of law Southwestern Univ. Sch. of Law 1977--; vis. prof. of law, UCLA Sch. of Law 1981; mem. New Motor Vehicle Bd., State of Calif. 1973-74, 1975-76; honors: Phi Beta Kappa 58, Fulbright Fellow 1959-60; mem; Nat. Hwy. Safety Adv. Com. (apptd. by Pres. Reagan); articles in law journals and revs.; mil: lt. commdr. USNR 1963-67; Republican (State Central Com. 1974-78); Methodist; rec: tennis. Res: 451 18th Santa Monica 90402 Ofc: Southwestern University School of Law, 675 South Westmoreland Los Angeles 90005

KALTENBACH, HUBERT LEONARD, newspaper executive; b. Jan. 3, 1922, Sandoval, Ill.; s. Adolph Leo and Elizabeth Margaret (Nagel) K.; m. Theodora S. Hunt, June 15, 1946; children: Shirley Jean, b. 1948; Jeffrey Leo, b. 1951; edn: USN Aviation Cadet Sch., 1942; BA, UCLA 1947. Career: Copley Newspapers: News-Pilot, San Pedro 1946-78: asst. circulation mgr. 1946-56, circulation mgr./ indsl. rels. dir. 1956-64, asst. to publisher and indsl. rels. dir. 1963-65, publisher 1965-78; The Daily Breeze, Torrance 1969-78: asst. to pub. 1969-70, publisher 1970-78, pres. The Copley Press Inc., 1978--, dir. 1968-, Exec. Com. 1979-; pres. So. Calif. Assn. Newspapers 1972-74; mem: Calif. Newspaper Pubs. Assn. (pres. 1979); Western Newspaper Industrial Relations Bureau (pres. 1973, 74); Calif. Pres. Assn. (pres. 1983, 84); US Navy League; Assn. of Naval Aviation (life); US Naval Inst.; Am. Newspaper Pubs. Assn.; La Jolla Country Club; Point Ferman Masonic Lodge; San Pedro & Torrance CofC; San Diego Press Culb; United Way, L.A., S.D. Counties; mil: lt. USNR 1942-46, naval aviator; Republican; Protestant. Res: 1630 Valdez Dr La Jolla 92037 Ofc: The Copley Press, Inc., 7776 Ivanhoe Ave, POB 1530, La Jolla 92037

KAM, ALEX MANCHOI, electronic importer; b. Nov. 14, 1953, Canton, China, nat. 1972; s. Cheuk Kee and Chiu Yung (Yip) Kam; m. Choi Yee, Sept. 18, 1977; children: Michelle, b. 1978, Michael, b. 1980; edn: BS, chem. engr., UC Los Angeles 1975; grad. wk. bus., CSULA. Career: aerospace indus. engr., splst. in adhesive bonding, Hughes Aircraft Co., 1975-81; founder/pres./ chief exec. Ace Wholesale, Los Angeles 1981--, importer watches, radios, telephones, calculators, etc.; dir: United National Bank (Monterey Park), Allied Securities, Top Champion Co.; honors: Phi Eta Sigma (1971); mem. SAMPE, Monterey Park CofC, Assn. Inst. of Chem. Engineer (1972-75), Chinese Profl. Assn. (M.P.). Res: 1118 Wandering Dr Monterey Park 91754 Ofc: Ace Wholesale, 451 S. Los Angeles St Los Angeles 90013

KAM, PAUL HING-KWOK, university administrator; b. Nov. 6, 1947, Canton, China; s. Rev. Scheng and Roly (Lo) Kam; m. May Poon, Feb. 1, 1975; 1 dau. Vannessa, b. 1979; edn: BS in mktg., 1975), BS in hotel & rest. mgmt., 1977, Calif. Poly Univ. Career: asst. dir. to dir. food service, Azusa Pacific Univ., 1973-76, dir. auxiliary service, 1976-79, dir. general and aux. services, 1979--; listed Who's Who in the West; mem: Nat. Mgmt. Assn., Nat. Assn. of Coll. Aux. Services, Phys. Plant Adminstrs. of Univs. and Colls., Nat. Assn. Coll. Univ. Services, Pi Sigma Epsilon; Christian; rec: basketball, tennis; res: 1307 S. Glendora Ave. Glendora 91740 ofc: Azusa Pacific Univ. Hwy 66 at Citrus, Azusa 91702.

KAMBOJ, PREM K., physician; b. Feb. 2, 1950, Patiala, India; s. Hans Raj and Kunti Devi (Gandhi) K.; m. Meena, Sept. 4, 1976; children: Amit, b. 1979; Amol, b. 1980; edn: Mahendra Coll., Patiala, India 1967; MB, BS, Med. Coll., Patiala 1967-72. Career: residency in pediatrics Blank Children's Hosp., Des Moines, Iowa 1977; staff phys. Woodward State Hosp., Woodward, Iowa 1977-78; pvt. practice pediatrics, Tulare, Calif. 1978--; chief of med. staff. Tulare Dist. Hosp., Tulare 1982-83; Fellow Am. Acad. of Pediatrics; Diplomate, Am. Bd. Pediatrics 1979; mem: CMA Am. Acad. Pediat.; Tulare Co. Med. Soc.; Rotary; rec: tennis, table tennis, travel. Res: 1626 Coelho Tulare 93274 Ofc: Prem K. Kamboj, MD, Inc., 963 Gem St Tulare 93274

KAMERER, PHILIP FINLEY, building and development co. executive; b. Dec. 6, 1938, Lima, Ohio; s. Henry Alden and Madge (Mitchell) K.; m. Gail Young, Aug. 19, 1966; children: Nancy, b. 1970; Shelley, b. 1972; edn: BA, Ohio State Univ. 1960; MBA, UC Berkeley 1968; Calif. lic. Real Estate Broker. 1976. Career: right of way agent Calif. Div. of Hwys., San Francisco 1964-66; land agent Boise Cascade Bldg. Co., Hayward 1968-71; land acquisitions Hofmann Co., Concord 1971-75; real estate mgr. Shortstop, Benicia 1975-77; devel. mgr. Citation Bldrs., San Leandro 1977--; honors: Glenn Willaman Found. Award Calif. R.E. Assn. 1968; mem: Bldg. Industry Assn., Commonwealth Club, Crow Canyon Athletic Club (San Ramon); mil: lt. USNR 1960-66; Democrat; Episcopal; rec: white water rafting. Res: 615 Logan Ln Danville 94526 Ofc: Citation Builders, 2777 Alvarado St San Leandro 94577

KAMHOLTZ, STANLEY, financial planning co. president; b. May 10, 1928, Brooklyn, NY; s. John Sigmund and Anna (Schwartz) Kamholtz; m. Marilyn Heckler, May 30, 1953; chil: Valerie Jean, David Stuart, Mark Lawrence, Terry Lynn, George Harrison; edn: stu. Ohio State Univ. 1948, Bklyn. Coll. 1950, UCLA, 1965-8; Coll. Financial Planning, 1980-1; Regis. investment adviser. Career: mgr. Universal Advt. Agcy., L.I., NY 1952-53; chief insp. engring. liaison Republic Aviation, Farmingdale,NY 1952-5, proj. adminstr., writer, 1957-59, tech. writer top secret projects, 1959-60; contract adminstr. Support Svcs Airesearch, Torrance 1960-68; agt. John Hancock Ins. Co., Torrance 1968-70, supr. 1971-74, supr., fin. planner, 1974-79; owner/pres./CEO Financial Planning Assocs. Inc., Torrance 1979--; regional dir. Fin. Advisory Clinic; writer, author, lectr. Honors: BSA Award of Merit, Regis. Campmaster, BSA; dist. commnr. BSA 1962-4, commnr. 1964-. Mem. Calif. Assn. Underwriters (ethics chmn.), Am. Rocket Soc., Instrument Soc. Am., South Bay Estate Planning Assn., Internat. Assn. Fin. Planners, Inst. Cert. Fin. Planners, Writers Guild, Nat. Assn. Life Underwriters, AF Assn., Aircraft Owners and Pilots Assn., Power Squadron, B'nai B'rith (pres.); mil: USAF 1946-49, Purple Heart, Victory Medal, Knighted: Royal Order of Garter 1947; Republican; Jewish; res: 823 Eastman Pl. San Pedro 90731 ofc: Fin. Planning Assocs. Inc. 2733 Pacific Coast Hwy Ste 305 Torrance 90505

KAMINE, BERNARD SAMUEL, lawyer; b. Dec. 5, 1943, Okla. City, Okla.; s. Martin and Mildred Esther K.; m. Marcia P. Haber, Sept. 9, 1982; children: Jorge H., b. 1973, Benjamin H., b. 1983; edn: BA, Univ. of Denver 1965; JD, Harvard Univ. 1968. Career: deputy atty. general Calif. dept. of Justice, 1968-72; asst. atty. gen. Colo. Dept. of Law, 1972-74; assoc. Shapiro & Maguire Law Corp., 1974-76; Law Offices of Bernard S. Kamine, 1976--; instr. Glendale Univ. Coll. of Law, 1970-72; lectr. Calif. Continuing Edn. of the Bar 1979, 82; judge pro tem Municipal Cts. 1974-; panel of arbitrators, Am. Arbitration Assn. 1976-; mem. Calif. Judicial Council Adv. Com. on Legal Forms, 1978-82; mem. Los Angeles Superior Ct. Arbitration Adminstrv. Commn. 1979-, arbitrator L.A. Sup. Ct. Constrn. Law Panel, 1979-. Mem: Am., Calif. Bar Assns., Los Angeles Bar Assn. (chpsn. Superior Cts. Com. 1977-9; chpsn. Constrn. Law Subsect., Real Prop. Sect. 1981-3; exec. com. of delegation to State Bar Conf. of Dels. 1980-2), Reserve Officers Assn. (chpt. pres. 1977-8), Assoc. Gen. Contractors of Calif., Engrg. Contractors Assn. (chpsn. APWA com. 1983-), So. Calif. Contractors Assn., Anti-Defamation League (regional bd. Pac. S.W. Regiion). Contbr. profl. jours., law revs. Mil: maj. USAR. Democrat (L.A. Co. Dem. Central Com. 1982-4). Jewish. Rec: jogging. Law Offices of Bernard S. Kamine, 350 S. Figueroa, Suite 250, Los Angeles 90071

KAMMERER, HELMUT JEAN, chemist; b.Oct. 18, 1926, Zurich, Switz.; s. Jean George and Emma (Winkler) K.; m. Gerda W. Zobl, Dec. 18, 1949; children: Roger b. 1950, Felix b. 1951, Regula b. 1953, Agnes b. 1953, Katharine b. 1962; edn: BS in chem., Basel Univ., Switz. 1947; MA, Byzantine Hist., Magdalen Coll., Oxford, Eng. 1950. Career: ink div. Labitzke, Zurich (paint and printing ink mfrs.), 1950-54; R&D, Tyro, Luzern (adhesives and splty. products), 1954-59; with Kady (mfr. silk screen printing inks), Perpignan, France 1959-62; ind. cons. for Adhesives, Paints and Inks in Barcelona, Spain 1962-65; tech. dir. Indus. Levantina de Pinturas, Valencia, Spain 1965-69; owner Tyrocol (water and solvent based adhesives), Valencia, Sp. 1970-76, co. merger with Insoco (adhesives for shoe & leather indus.) 1976, tech. dir. Tyrocol Div. Insoco, Alicante, Spain 1976-81; chemist Gans Ink & Supply, Los Angeles, Ca. 1981; v.p. resrch & devel., TW Graphics Group, City of Commerce 1981--; mem. L.A. Ink Production Club, L.A. soc. for Coatings Technol., Swiss Soc. Helvetia, Swiss Park Inc., ACLU; mil: lt. ABC Svc. Swiss Army; Orthodox. Res: 345 S. Alexandria Ave Los Angeles 90020 Ofc: TW Graphics Group, 7220 E. Slauson Ave, City of Commerce 90040

KAN, LILY LIANG, real estate broker; b. Sept. 3, 1951, Taipei, Taiwan, R.O.C., nat. 1978; d. Tung (legislator, R.O.C.) and Given-Chin (Chang) Liang; m. Yisen Kan, Jan. 25, 1972; 1 dau: Jennifer, b. 1977; edn: BA, Taipei, Taiwan. Career: real estate sales agt. Cal Robison & Assoc., Reno, Nev. 1977-79; pres./ broker Kan Realty, Reno, Nev. 1979--; broker assoc. Coldwell Banker, Palos Verdes, Calif. 1981--; honors: Million Dollar Club 1977-; Gold Circle Coldwell Banker Real Estate Svc. Co.; mem: Nat. Assn. of Realtors (Calif. & Nev.); Chinese School South Bay (PTA, treas.); Christian; rec: piano, oil painting. Res: 1521 Via Fernandez Palos Verdes Estates 90274 Ofcs: Coldwell Banker, 27421 Hawthorne Blvd Rancho Palos Verdes 90274; Kan Realty, 2075 Market St Reno, Nev. 89502

KANDA, KULDIP SINGH, pharmaceutical co. executive; b. Oct. 4, 1951, Jullundur, India; s. Mast R. and Pushpa R. (Karval) K.; m. Neena Dhunna, Jan. 22, 1976; children: Sonia, b. 1977; Robert, b. 1981; edn: pre-med., D.A.V. Coll. (1 yr.); B.Pharm., Kasturba Med. Coll. Career: chief pharmacist/ owner Kanda Medicos, Jullundur, India 1974-76; mfg. supvr. Vita Fresh Vitamin Co., Garden Grove 1976-79; prodn. mgr. Health Crafters, Los Angeles 1979-80; pharmacist/ mfg. mgr. P. Leiner Nutritional Products, Torrance 1980--; cons. in mfg. planning; mem: Am. Pharmaceutical Assn.; Lions Club; La Mirada Tennis Club; past mem./chmn. Leo Club, Jullunder; rec; tennis, cricket, gold replicas. Res: 13014 Clearwood Ave La Mirada 90638 Ofc: P. Leiner Nutritional Products, 1845 W 205th St Torrance 90501

KANG, TAE WHA, research institute president; b. Feb. 18, 1945, Chejoodo, Korea; s. Chan Bok and Kap Soon (Song) K.; m. Young Ae, Aug. 20, 1973; children: Joon, b 1976; Susie, b. 1979; edn: BS, Yonsei Univ., Korea 1970; grad. wk., So. Ill. Univ. 1970-71; PhD in biol., Ill. Inst. Tech. 1976; Lic. Med. Tech., Calif. Career: postdoctl. fellow, Univ. of Edinburgh, Scotland 1975-76; chmn. Chem. Dept. Bio-Technics Labs. Inc., Los Angeles 1976-77; med. tech. Baldwin Park (Calif.) Comm. Hosp. 1978-79; adj. prof. Pacific Western Univ., Encino 1983--; lab. director and pres. Bio- Science Research Inst. Inc., Chino 1979--; consulting microbiologist, UHI Corp., L.A. 1983-; honors: British Med. Fellowship 1976-77; Predoctl. Research Grant, US Army Research Ofc. 1975; Nat. Sci. Found. Trainee 1971-75; mem: Sigma Xi; Am. Soc. for Microbiology; Am. Assn. for Clin. Chem.; num. arts. & conf. presentations; rec: mountain climbing. Res: 3307 Adrienne Dr West Covina 91792 Ofc: Bio-Science Research Inst., 4813 Cheyenne Way Chino 91710

KAPELCZAK, JOHN PAUL, computer systems analyst; b. July 15, 1948, Chelsea, Mass.; s. Edmund John and Helen C. (Kantorowski) K.; m. Lynda See, July 3, 1976; edn: BS in physics, CSU San Diego 1971. Career: mem. tech. staff, computer pgmmr. Logicon Inc., San Diego 1971-77; computer pgmmr. NCR, San Diego, 1977-8, telecommunications system analyst, 1978-9, proj. supr. of telecomms., 1979-81, telecommunications sr. systems analyst, 1981--; pres. Country Apple Devel. Inc. (real estate devel. corp.), 1978-80; sr. cons. Telecomms. Resrch & Devel. Ideas Group, NCR, S.D. 1983-4; rep. S.D. Indsl. Recreation Council 1976; mem: Logicon Employees League (pres. S.D. chpt. 1975-6), Patrons of Palomar Coll., S.D. Zoological Soc.; Democrat; Catholic; rec. bus. analysis, computers, softball, gardening. Res. 15485 Villa Sierra Rd Valley Center 92082 Ofc: NCR Corp., 16550 W. Bernardo Dr San Diego 92127

KAPLAN, OSCAR JOEL, university professor; b. Oct. 21, 1915, NY, NY; s. Philip and Becka (Uttef) Kaplan; edn: BA, UCLA, 1937, MA 1938, PhD, UC Berkeley, 1940; m. Rose Zankan, Dec. 28, 1942; chil: Stephen Paul, b. 1944, Robert Malcolm, b. 1947, David T. A., b. 1951; career: assoc. prof. of psychology, Univ. of Idaho, So. Br., 1941-45; prof. of psychology and dir. Center for Survey Research, CSU San Diego 1946--; vis. prof. of public health, UCLA, 1965-66; awards: Western Gerontological Soc. award for outstanding contbns. to gerontology, 1977; outstanding university professor, CSU San Diego Alumni Assn., 1982; mem: Am. Psychological Assn., Am. Assn. for Public Opinion Research, Gerontological Soc. of Am. Author (books): Mental Disorders in Later Life, 1945, rev. 1956; Psychopathology of Aging, 1979; res: 5409 Hewlett Dr. San Diego 92115 ofc: CSU San Diego, San Diego 92182-0350.

KAPLAN, ROSE Z., opinion research analyst; b. May 13, 1916, St. Catherines, Ont., Can.; naturalized 1945; d. Max and Sophia (Kramer) Zankan; edn: BA, Univ. of W. Ontario, 1937, teaching cred., London (Ont.) Normal Sch., 1938; m. Oscar J. Kaplan, Dec. 28, 1942; chil: Stephen Paul, b. 1944, Robert Malcolm, b. 1947, David Theodore Abel, b. 1951; career: teacher, Hillcrest Progressive (pvt. parochial) School, Toronto, Onc., Can. 1938-39, Edith Cavell (public) School, Riverside, Ont. 1939-40; director of field work, Southwest Surveys, San Diego, Ca. 1956-66; pres., Economic Behavior Analysts, Inc., San Diego 1966--; mem: Faculty Womens Club, CSU San Diego 1946-, Market Research Assn. (nat.) 1970-, So. Calif. Market Research Assn. 1980-; publs: num. articles in profl. journals; res: 5409 Hewlett Dr. San Diego 92115 ofc: Economic Behavior Analysts Inc. PO Box 15338 San Diego 92115.

KARANT, YASHA JACK, research physicist; b. Apr. 20, 1950, Los Angeles; parents: Harold and Viola Cornelia (Louis) K.; edn: stu. Brown Univ. 1968-69; BA, honors, Immaculate Heart Coll. (joint pgm. w/ Cal Tech) 1975; PhD, UC Berkeley 1980. Career: research asst. USC 1975; grad. stu. research assoc. UC Berkeley 1975-80; staff scientist Lawrence Berkeley Lab. 1980--; currently, mng. physicist Interactive Computer Assisted Measurement Sys., Relativistic Heavy Ions Gp., Nuclear Sci. Div., Lawrence Berkeley Lab.; honors: 1st Place Latin, Alpha Mu Gamma 1966, Phi Eta Sigma, Sigma Xi; mem: Am. Physical Soc.; Forth Interest Gp.; Alpha Chi Sigma; invited spkr. Gordon Research Conf. 1982, num. articles in sci. journals; rec: clarinet, hiking, photog. Res: 810 Arlington El Cerrito 94530 Ofc: Lawrence Berkeley Laboratory, Bldg. 50 Rm 245, Berkeley 94720

KARATZ, BRUCE E., real estate executive; b. Oct. 10, 1945, Chgo.; s. Harry Robert and Naomi Rae (Goldstein) K.; m. Janet Louise Dreisen, July 21, 1968; children: Elizabeth, b. 1970; Matthew, b. 1971; Theodore, b. 1978; edn: The Blake Sch. 1963; BA, Boston Univ. 1967; JD, USC Law Sch. 1970; admitted State Bar of Calif. 1971. Career: lawyer Keatinge & Sterling, Los Angeles 1970-72; assoc. corp. counsel Kaufman & Broad, Inc., Los Angeles 1972-73, dir. forward planning (Irvine), 1973-74; pres. Kaufman & Broad Provence, Aixen Provence, France 1974-76; pres. Kaufman & Broad France, Paris, Fr. 1976-80; pres. Kaufman & Broad Devel. Group, Los Angeles 1980--, dir. Kaufman & Broad, Inc., Los Angeles; mem. Young Presidents Orgn.; honors: Humanitarian, Man of the Year, NCCJ, Los Angeles 1982; trustee Pitzer Coll. (Claremont) 1983-; bd. govs. Cedars-Sinai Med. Ctr., L.A., 1983-; bd. dirs. CORO Found., L.A. 1984-; founder Mus. of Contemporary Art, L.A., 1981; Democrat; Jewish; rec: modern art, skiing, travel. Res: 160 So Thurston Ave Los Angeles 90049 Ofc: Kaufman & Broad Development Group, 11601 Wilshire Blvd, 11th Flr., Los Angeles 90025

KARDEL, KARL CHRISTIAN, designer- contractor; b. Nov. 21, 1940, Charlotte, Mich.; s. Hans Emil and Karen Magrethe (Werge) K.; div.; children: Sissel, b. 1970; Kaj-Emil, b. 1972, Camilla, b. 1975; edn: BA, UC Berkeley 1963; Heller Scholar, UC 1964. Career: contractor/ colorist/ designer 1963--; founder/ pres. Karl Kardel Co. Inc.; owner Karl Kardel Sales Co. (interior design co.); pres. Mica-Shield Waterproofing Co. 1976; lectr. UC Sch. of Architecture 1979; lec 1979-80; lectures on Art, Color & Architecture, Pacific Design Ctr. 1981; awards: Civic Arts Awd., Berkeley 1978; Berkeley City Council; Maharishi Civic Awd. 1982; mem: Delta Phi Epsilon, UCB; Berkeley CofC; Bi- Centennial Commn. for City of Oakland 1976; Berkeley Repertory

Theater (bd. dirs.); Berkeley Architl. Heritage Assn.; works: restored Berkeley Main Library incl. Sgraffito murals 1976; num. public & pvt. works; responsible for reintroduction of the American archtl. color revival: colors for the oldest Jewish temple in Calif., and Calif. State Capitol Mall colors 1981; Republican; rec: architectural heritage, classic car collecting, skiing. Res: 140 Olive St. 94611 Ofc: Karl Kardel Co. Inc., 4926 E 12th St Oakland 94601

KARLSTROM, LESLIE RUTH, lawyer; b. Jan. 23, 1955, Wash. DC; d. Otto LeRoy and Esther Ruth (Kessler) Karlstrom; edn: Mex. law studies, Univ. de Libro Derecho 1979; BA, honors, George Mason Univ. 1977; JD, Univ. of Puget Sound 1980; admitted to practice District of Columbia, Calif. bars, 1981, 1982. Career: legal intern Schmidt & Linde, Friday Harbor, Wash. 1978; legal intern, Ortega & Assoc. (pvt. Mexican firm), Mexico City 1979; legal trainee, pvt. Mexican firm and internat. law firm, Mex. City 1980-81; pvt. law practice, spec. immigration/ internat. law, Leslie R. Karlstrom, Livermore 1982--; Immigration Clinic, S.F., Domestic Abuse Clinic, Livermore; honors: undergrad. honors in Spanish, German & French; mem: Am., Calif., Wash. DC, Alameda Co., San Francisco, & Livermore- Pleasanton bar assns.; Womens Bus. Network; Mex.-Am. Legal Com. ABA; works: Latin Am. legal studies, Mex. City & Guatemala 1979; multi- lingual sessions/ drafts & research for foreign investors incl. tech. transfers; rec: travel, swimming. Res: 1147 Batavia Livermore 94550 Law Offices of Leslie R. Karlstrom, 2258 Third St Livermore 94550

KARMELICH, BEN L., savings & loan co. president; b. Sept. 19, 1925, San Pedro; s. Frank and Franka (Cvitanich) K.; m. Marie Uglesich, July 12, 1958; children: John b. 1959, Ben Jr. b. 1962, Mark b. 1963, Brian b. 1967; edn: AB, UC Berkeley 1949; grad. wk. Univ. So. Calif. Career: pres./chief exec. ofcr. Highland Federal S&L, Los Angeles, 1968--; sr. v.p. Fishermen & Merchants Svgs., San Pedro, 1965-68; asst. v.p. Coast Fed. Svgs., L.A. 1951-65; also pres. HFS Corp., L.A. 1978--; bd. dirs. Highland Fed. S&L; instr. L.A. Harbor Jr. COll. 1965-67; chief exec. of a top 200 most profitable svgs. & loan in USA, 1978-1983, by U.S. Svgs. & Loan League, Chgo. hqtrs. Mem: Fed. S&L Conf., Calif. (bd. dirs.); (past) mem. San Pedro Kiwanis, 20 yrs. (pres. 1965), Toastmasters S.P. (pres. 1968); 25 yr. mem. San Pedro CofC, and Yugoslav Amer. Club, S.P.; num. tech. publs.; rec: swim, bicycling. Res: Rancho Palos Verdes Ofc: Highland Federal, 6301 N. Figueroa Los Angeles 90042

KARR, JAMES, real estate appraiser; b. Mar. 9, 1940, Sofia, Bulgaria, nat. 1973; s. Georgy and Maria (Barakova) K.; edn: geology, Sofia State Univ., Bulgaria 1962; var. real estate courses, 1974-83. Career: geologist GeoLabs, Inc., Santa Ana 1968-74; R.E. appraisers Mariners Savings & Loan Assn., Newport Beach 1974-76; estab./ pres. (3 corps.) J.K. Property Appraisals, Inc., Southland Appraisals Svcs., Inc. & Right Time Investments, Inc. 1976--; awards: Pres. Achiev. Awd., Republican Nat. Com. 1982; mem. assoc. Soc. of Real Estate Appraisers, Orange Co. chpt.; Republican; Christian; rec: horses (breed, show). Res: 5001 Paseo Segovia Irvine 92715 Ofc: Southland Appraisal Servicse, Inc., 14771 Plaza Dr, Ste E, Tustin 92680

KARR, PENNY JANE, psychotherapist; b. Oct. 28, 1941, Alameda; d. Ferd Otis and Arlene Hale (Rose) Drayer; children: Laura, b. 1963, Christopher, b. 1965; edn: BA, CSU Sacto. 1969, MSW, 1974. Calif. lic. Marriage, Family & Child Counselor 1975-, Clin. Soc. Wk. 1978-. Career: substitute tchr. Waterville H.Sch., 1968; assoc. dir. Mental Health Assn., Sactamento 1969-72; intern. for MFCC lic., Sacto. 1975-77; psychotherapist and family counselor, pvt. practice, Sacto. 1975--, expert witness in child custody, sexual abuse; supr. interns in MFCC, 1982-; cons. Mercy Extended Care Facility, Sacto.; lectr. to schools, colleges, churches, community groups, radio & TV; mem: Christian Assn. for Psychol. Studies (area coordinator), Nat. Assn. for Christians in Soc. Wk., Soc. for Clin. Soc. Wk., Diabetes Assn. of Sacto., Mental Health Assn., Acad. of Religion & (Mental) Health, Nat. Assn. of Soc. Wkrs.; recogn. awards: Comm. Interaction Pgm. 1980, Nat. Found. March of Dimes 1968, Nat. Soc. Autistic Children 1972, Sen. Lyons Club 1969, Mental Health Assn. 1978, Am. Diabetes Assn. 1977, 78; Republican; Christian (local ch. ldr.); rec: Biblical research, water sports. Ofc: 1555 River Park Drive, Ste. 206, Sacramento 95814

KASHYAP, BHAGWATI PRASAD, researcher; b. Oct. 5, 1948, Durg, Madhya Prdesh, India; s. Keshaw Ram and Dewa Bai (Verma) K.; m. Laxmi, Aug. 12, 1983; edn: B.Eng., Govt. Coll. of Eng. & Tech., Raipur, India 1971; M.Eng., Indian Inst. of Tech. 1975; PhD eng., Indian Inst. of Tech. 1980. Career: junior research asst. Indian Inst. of Tech., Kanpur, India 1974-75; senior research asst. 1976-80; jr. research engr. Research & Devel. Center for Iron & Steel, India 1980; post-doctoral research engr. Dept. of Mech. Eng., UC Davis 1981--; awards: Nat. Scholarship, Govt. of India 1966-71; mem. Am. Soc. for Metals; publs.: num. sci. papers; Hindu; rec: poetry, writing. Res: 330 J St, Apt 30, Davis 95616 Ofc: Dept. of Mechanical Engineering, Univ. of California Davis 95616

KASSIS, DONALD JAMES, county real estate executive; b. May 4, 1930, Williston, N. Dak.; s. Eli Joseph and Elizabeth Veronica (Zinnie) K.; m. Mary Lou Augustine, June 27, 1959; children: David, b. 1960; Joan, b. 1961; Elizabeth, b. 1960; Jacqueline, b. 1966; edn: AA, Sacto. City Coll. 1950; BA, CSU Sacto. 1959; cert. in real estate UC Davis 1965. Career: mgr. Stop-N-Shop Markets 1957-60; real estate property mgr. County of Sacramento 1960-79, real estate supvr., property mgr. 1979--; property mgr. D & P Investments 1980; mem: Toastmasters Intl. (ATM 1980; past pres., Natoma); Internat. Platform Assn.; St. Mary's Social Club, Catholic Diocese of Sacto. (pres. 1981-83); publs: Policy and Procedures for Acquisition of Real Estate Property Manage-

ment; Lease- Purchase Methods and Procedures for Acquisition of Real Estate; mil: US Army 1951-53; Republican; Catholic; rec: public speaking, R.E. inv., dancing. Res: 2630 Notre Dame Dr Sacramento 95826 Ofc: County of Sacramento, 927 7th St, Rm 220, Sacramento 95826

KATZ, SAM, artist; b. Aug. 17, 1909, Odessa, Russia, nat. 1912; s. Benjamin and Golda (Zack) K.; m. Helen R., June 28, 1936, dec. 1979; 2 sons, Barry b. 1943, Jerry, b. 1948; m. 2d. Doryce L., Mar. 8, 1981; edn: Metropolitan Art Sch. NY, Nat. Acad. of Design, NY (1934), The Art Students League, NY, Ecole Des Beaux Arts, Paris. Career: art director/artist Montclair Printing, N.J. 1929, then with David Weils & Sons, NY; free lance artist, N.J. 1947; art director, coml. illus. and design, var. printing houses, advt. agencies and art studios, incl. Wadsworth Advt. Agency, Shmidt Art Service, NY, 1948-56; moved to Calif. 1956--, designed jewelry (in wax ready for casting), wood sculpture, posters, packaging design, restorer paintings, portrait painting in all mediums; currently spec. in fine art painting and portrait commissions; nat. recognition for his "Margarita Girls" done for Jose Quervo Tequila; num. gold medal and blue ribbon awards; his paintings in pvt. collections in USA, Can., Europe; mem: Calif. Art Club, Am. Inst. of Fine Arts, Am. Artists Profl. League, Desert Mus. Civic Art Club (P.S.), L.A. Sym., Viennese Culture Club (L.A.), Civic Art (P.S.); mil: pfc 9th Inf. Div. AUS 1944-46; Hebrew; rec: wood sculpture. Studio: 1802 Barona Rd Palm Springs 92264

KATZAKIAN, BOZANT, banker; b. Jan. 1, 1915, Kingsburg, Calif.; s. Garabed S. and Dovie (Emersian) K.; m. Lorraine Dickson, Aug. 13, 1942; children: Ronald b. 1944, Terry b. 1947, Reginald b. 1951, Jennifer b. 1954. Career: entered real estate field 1949, founder/ptnr. Katzakian & Schaffer, Realtors, 1955-82; founder/bd. chmn. Bank of Lodi 1983-; mem., pres. Lodi Bd. of Realtors 1964-66; reg. v.p. Calif. Assn. Realtors 1955-74 (exec. com. 1976); Lodi City Council 1956-64 (mayor 1958-64); bd. dirs. (pres. Central Valley Dist.) League of Calif. Cities 1960-64; orgns: Frat. Order of Eagles (pres. 1942), Lodi Grape Festival and Wine Assn. (pres. 1956), Lions Club (pres. 1956), Masons, Scottish Rite, Shrine, Native Sons, Lodi Dist. CofC (Outstanding Citizen of Yr 1968); Democrat; Protestant; rec: fishing. Res: 503 W Pine St Lodi 95240 Ofc: Bank of Lodi 701 S. Ham Lodi 95240

KAUFMAN, CARY STEVEN, surgeon; b. Jan. 5, 1948, Los Angeles; s. Carl Lazar and Betty (Halperin) K.; m. Linda, Mar. 25, 1972; children: Casey b. 1975, Lauren b. 1979, Amanda b. 1973; edn: BS in chem., cum laude, UCLA 1969; MD, UCLA Sch. of Med. 1973; Diplomate Am. Board of Surgery 1981. Med. lic. Wash. 1975, Calif. 1975. Career: resident in surg., Univ. of Wash. 1973-75, Harbor/UCLA Med. Ctr. 1975-79; general and vascular surgeon pvt. practice, Long Beach; att. surgeon Long Beach Meml. Hosp. 1979--; clin. asst. prof. surg. UCLA, 1979--; mem: Fellow Am. Coll. of Surgeons, Long Beach Surgical Soc., Calif. Med. Assn., LA County Med. Assn.; med. adv. Reach for Recovery Pgm. Am. Cancer Soc.; Long Beach CofC; contbr. med. journals; Democrat; Jewish. Res: 4202 Rousseau Ln Palos Verdes 90274 Ofc: Cary S. Kaufman MD, 701 E. 28th St, Ste. 301, Long Beach 90806

KAUFMAN, JULIAN MORTIMER, television executive; b. Apr. 3, 1918, Detroit, Mich.; s. Anton and Fannie (Newman) K.; m. Katherine Likins, May 6, 1943; children: Nikki, b. 1944; Keith, b. 1946. Career: publisher Tucson Shopper, Tucson, Az. 1948-50; TV account exec. KGO-TV, Am. Broadcasting Co. 1951-52; TV station mgr. KPHO-TV, Phoenix, Ariz., Meredith Bdctg. Co., 1952-53; v.p./ gen. mgr. XETV (Ch. 6), Bay City TV Inc., San Diego 1953--; v.p./ bd. dirs. Spanish Internat. Network; awards: Peabody Awd. 1970; S.D. Press Club Headliner Awd. 1978; Govs. Awd. NATAS (S.D.) 1984; mem: Sigma Delta Chi; Nat. Acad. TV Arts & Scis.; San Diego CofC; Better Bus. Bureau; San Diego Tourist & Conv. Bureau; publs: arts. in Broadcasting mag., TV Aye Mag.; mil: warrant ofcr. j.g. USAAF 1942-46; Republican. Res: 3125 Montesano Rd Escondido 92025 Ofc: Bay City Television Inc., 8253 Ronson Rd San Diego 92111

KAUFMAN, MURRAY JAMES, oil co. executive; b. June 23, 1950, Pittsburgh, Pa.; s. Jerome J. and Rita Belle (Lando) K.; edn: AA, Los Angeles Valley Coll. 1970, BA, CSU Northridge 1972. Career: asst. news editor KFWB Radio, Los Angeles 1972-74; reporter BBC Radio One, London, Eng. 1972-75; dir. public rels. Clark Ortone Inc., Northridge 1972-75; revenue ofcr. US Dept. of Treasury, Hollywood, 1975-80; hypnotherapist in pvt. practice, 1980-82; oil leasing rep. Federal Lease Filing Service, Malibu 1982--; pres./bd. chmn. Terra Firma Resources, Inc. (Wilmington, Dela.) 1982-; honors: Tau Alpha Epsilon (1970), Adv. Hypnotic Techs. cert., UCLA 1981; spl. achieve. awd. US Dept. Treas. 1980; mem. Quantum Illuminati, Acad. of TV Arts & Scis. 1970-72; Republican; Christian; rec: hypnosis. Res: 18014 Sherman Way Reseda 91335 Ofc: Federal Lease Filing Corp. 28990 Pacific Coast Hwy Malibu 90265

KAUFMAN, STEVEN LEE, electronics engineer; b. Feb. 22, 1949, Yankton, S. Dak.; s. Orlando Joe and Marjorie Gwendolyn (Christensen) K.; m. Susan Lynn Rafter, June 5, 1976; edn: BSEE, S.Dak. Sch. of Mines & Tech. 1971. Career: elec. engr. GS-12 Pacific Missile Test Ctr., Point Mugu 1971-78; senior engr. Raytheon ESD, Goleta 1978--; mem: Sigma Tau; Eta Kappa Nu; Pi Mu Epsilon; Assn. of Old Crows; Raytheon Mgmt. Club; Republican; Mennonite; rec: alpine skiing, stained glass. Res: 4915 Coral Way Oxnard 93030 Ofc: Raytheon ESD, 9380 Hollister Ave Goleta 93117

KAUFMAN, TONY M., insurance agent; b. May 16, 1953, Shreveport, La.; s. Jewel F. and Gertrude Kaufman; m. Janese Brody, Mar. 4, 1972; 1 dau. Analise J. b. 1973; edn: CLU (chartered life underwriter), American Coll. 1982. Career: ins. agt. Mutual of New York, 1977-79; pres. Tony M. Kaufman

Insurance Assocs. Inc., Lguna Hills, Ca. 1979--; v.p. Family Group Homes for underprivileged children in Orange Co., 1980-; awards: Million Dollar Round Table 1977- (Life & Qualifying mem. 1983), Top of the Table; US Life President Club (1982, 83); Mutual of NY Top 50 mem. (1979), Pres. Club (1977, 78); mem. Saddleback Breakfast Club (pres. 1982); rec: golf, chess. Res: 27681 Paseo Barone, San Juan Capistrano 92675 Ofc: Tony M. Kaufman Ins. Assocs. Inc. 23181 Verdugo Dr Laguna Hills 92653

KAVANAUGH, NORMAN WALTERS, lawyer; b. May 1, 1927, Santa Barbara; s. Isak Andreas and Josephine (Swanson) K.; m. Lee Simpson, Sept. 25, 1983; children: Matthew Whitney, b. 1957; David Bond, b. 1960; edn: BA, Yale Univ. 1950; LLD, Stanford Univ. 1953; admitted to practice, Calif., Dist. of Columbia bars 1953, NY bar 1958. Career: fmr. partner law firm Wilson, Jones, Morton & Lynch (San Mateo), Basye, Prior, Kavanaugh & Clark (Burlingame), Bronson, Bronson & McKinnon (San Francico); currently practice law, Burlingame; pres. San Mateo Co. Bar 1969; lectr. Cont. Edn. of the Bar; counsel Peninsula Comm. Found.; mem: Legal Aid Soc. of San Mateo Co. (pres.1965); San Mateo Union H.S. Bd. of Trustees (past pres.); Volunteer Bureau of San Mateo C. (past pres.); Am. Red Cross, S.M. (past pres.); United Bay Area Crusade (Allocations Com.); editor text on Calif. Probate Law for Matthew Bender, Legal Publishers, S.F; mil: 1st lt. USAF 1953-55; Episcopal. Res: 1056 Shoreline Dr San Mateo 94404 Ofc: Norman W. Kavanaugh, 405 Primrose Rd Burlingame 94010

KEATHLEY, JACKSON PHILLIP, agricultural consultant; b. Mar. 22, 1942, Dustin, Okla.; s. Luster and Stella (Liles) K.; m. Florence Paulsen, Sept. 2, 1967; children: Laura Beth, b. 1970; Craig Phillip, b. 1973; cdn: BS, Okla. State Univ. 1965; MS, 1966; PhD, Univ. of Ga. 1972. Career: sr. research biologist Dow Chem. Co., Walnut Creek 1872-74; field research & devel. rep. Gulf Oil Chem. Co., Concord 1974-80; devel. rep. E.I. du Pont de Nemours & Co., Menlo Park 1980-82; agricultural cons./pres. Keathley Agricultural Services, Concord 1982--; mgr. Jr. Optimists Baseball League 1982-; honors: Am. Legion Award 1960, Sigma Xi 1970, Gamma Sigma Delta 1972; mem: Entomological Soc. of Am.; Weed Sci. Soc. of Am.; Au. Phystopathological Soc.; Am. Mosquito Control Assn.; Am. Regis. of Profl. Entomologists; AAAS; Calif. Council of Agri. Prod. Consultants Assn.; Council of Agri. Sci. & Tech, Calif. Weed Conf.; Calif. Pest Control Advrs.; pub. papers in sci. and trade journals; mil: lt. commdr. USN 1966-78; Democrat; Baptist; rec: softball, basketball, woodworking. Address: Keathley Agricultural Services, 3602 Dumbarton St Concord 94519

KEARNEY, MICHAEL JOSEPH, recreation specialist; b. Apr. 3, 1948, Fort Dodge, Iowa; s. Wm. Joseph and Mary Bernice (Collins) K.; div.; 1 dau. Deborah Michelle, b. 1972; edn: cert. rec., Palomar Comm. Coll. 1975, BS in rec & leisure studies, CSU San Jose 1978. Career: intern with Vaxjo, Sweden Rec. Dept., Fall 1978; mgr. Whirlin Wheels Skateboard Park, Escondido 1979-80; counselor Boys and Girls Aid, El Cajon 1980-82, supr. 1984--; pgm. dir. Armed Services YMCA, San Diego, 1982-83; awards: merit cert., Palomar Coll. Associated Student Govt. Exec. Council, 1975; cit. for leadership, Nat. Rec. & Park Assn. Student Branch, 1976; mem: Calif. Parks and Recreation Soc. (state bd. dirs. 1976-7), Nat. Rec. & Park Assn. (S.W. region student rep. 1977); mil: E5 US Army 1969-71; rec: outdoors, basket weaving. Res: 4338 Felton St San Diego 92104

KECK, DARRYL LOWELL, social worker; b. Sept. 30, 1948, Oakland; s. Lowell Hugh and Inez Irene (Rivers) K.; m. Susan, Jan. 7, 1978; son Peter, b. 1980; edn: AA, Laney Jr. Coll. 1969; BA, CSU Sacto. 1972, MSW, 1978; Calif. Lic. Clin. Soc. Wkr. 1982. Career: leader/ asst. dir. camp Oakland Recreation 1967, 70, 72; patient rep. Marshall Hosp., Placerville 1976; counselor New Morning Youth Svcs., Placerville 1976-79; social wkr. El Dorado County, Placerville 1979--, contract psychotherapist, El Dorado Co. Wo/ Mens Ctr. 1980-82; cons. St. Patricks Counseling Ministries & pvt. practice 1982--; mem. New Morning Youth Svcs. (v.p., bd. dirs. 1979-81); Democrat; Catholic; rec: parenting, sports. Res: 1320 Dimity Ln Placerville 95667 Ofc: El Dorado County- Adoptions, POB 1637, Placerville 95667

KEELEY, CONRAD WARNER, JR., chartered life underwriter; b. Feb. 10, 1919, Monterey; s. Conrad Warner and Blanche Corey (Littlefield) K.; m. Barbara Moser, May 11, 1946 (dec. 1975); 1 son, Conrad Warner III, b. 1948; m. 2d. Bernadine Savage Steel, Feb. 15, 1977; edn: AB, San Jose State Univ. 1941; CLU, Am. Coll. of Life Underwriters 1965. Career: Monterey Peninsula rep. Connecticut Gen. Life Ins. (CIGNA) 1946--; pres. Monterey Bay Life Underwriters Assn. 1964-65; mem. Monterey Bay Chtp. of CLUs (pres. 1971-72); instr. Life Underwriting Tng. Council; Monterey City Councilman 1947-51; chpt. chmn. Monterey Red Cross 1962; recipient John Keppleman Award for Public Svc. 1966; mem. Monterey Peninsula Country Club, Monterey Hist. & Art Assn. (bd. dirs. 1978-83) Monterey- Peninsula CofC (past bd. dirs.); mil: lt. USNR 1941-46 (grad. Midshipmen's Sch., Northwestern U. Chgo. 1942) C.O. (S.C. 641) Solomon Islands, (APD 70) Okinawa & Japan, 4 battle stars Asia-Pac. Theatre; Protestant; rec: golf. Address: 1035 San Carlos Rd Pebble Beach 93953

KEENEY, EDMUND LUDLOW, Scripps Clinic president emeritus; b. Aug. 1908, Shelbyville, Ind.; s. Bayard G. and Ethel (Adams) K.; m. Esther Cox Loney Wight, Mar. 14, 1950; children: Edmund L. Jr., Eleanor (Smith); edn: AB, Ind. Univ. 1930; MD, Johns Hopkins Univ. 1934. Career: intern Johns Hopkins Hosp., 1934-35, res. 1935-36, instr. in med. 1940-48; est. medical practice, spec. in allergy, San Diego 1948-55; pres., dir. Scripps Clinic and Research Found., La Jolla, 1955-77, pres. Emer. 1977--. Bd. trustees, Univ. of

San Diego, 1974-; dir. Allergy Found. of Amer.; author: Practical Medical Mycology (publ. Charles C. Thomas, 1955), contbr. articles, papers in allergy, immunology, mycology to profl. jours.; ed. bd. Journ. of Allergy; dir. research on fungus infections Ofc. of Sci. Research and Devel., USN, WWII, 1942-46; mem: AMA 1938- (sec. Sect. on Allergy 1964-65); fellow Am. Acad. of Allergy 1940- (pres. 1963-64); Soc. for Clin. Investigation 1945-; Fellow Am. Coll. of Phys. 1946-; Diplomate Am. Bd. of Internal Med., subspecialty allergy; Western Soc. for Clin. Research 1948-; Western Assn. of Phys. 1955-; Calif. Med. Assn. (sci. bd. dirs.); Rotarian; Eldorado CC; Phi Beta Kappa, Alpha Omega Alpha, Beta Theta Pi; Republican; Presbyterian; rec: golf, fishing, swim. Res: 338 Via del Norte La Jolla Ofc: 10666 N. Torrey Pines Rd La Jolla 92037

KEHAR, ADNAN AHMED, certified public accountant; b. June 15, 1957, Karachi Sind, Pakistan; s. Dr. Bashir Ahmed and Mumtaz (Soomro) K.; edn: AA, El Camino Coll. 1975; BSc, CSU Northridge 1977; MBA, CSU Dominguez Hills 1979; CPA, Calif. 1982. Career: fmr senior acct./auditor Del Ferguson Accts. Inc., Beverly Hills; chief acct./ ofcr. mgr. Mihal Corp., Gardena; currently, owner Kehar & Co., CPAs, Canoga Park; cons. electronic high tech. (start up & public cos.); mgmt. advisory svcs. to small bus. & public cos.; recipient El Camino Alumni Honor Soc. Award; mem: Calif. Soc. CPAs, Am. Inst. CPAs, Muslim, rec. sports. Address: Kehar & Co. CPAs, 20234 Cantara St, Ste 303, Canoga Park 91306

KEHIAIAN, GAITAG, private investigator; b. July 7, 1949, Constantza, Romania; s. Aram and Cristina (Harutunian) K.; m. Giuseppina, Jan. 28, 1982; desig: Officer 3 Engineer, Navy Univ. of Giurgiu 1967-71; PI, Am. Police Acad., Wash. DC; Romanian Police Acad., Bucharest; Calif. lic. Class A. Career: security consultant for pvt. firms and corporations; private investigator/owner Lightning Detective Agency, Los Angeles; honors: Cert. of Appreciation, J. Edgar Hoover Memorial by Am. Police Hall of Fame; mem: Am. Fedn. of Police; Internat. Police Congress; Internat. Assn. Investigators and Special Police; US Gongressional Adv. Bd.; mil: sgt. Spl. Forces 1972; Catholic; rec: electronics, fishing, travel. Res: 902 N Normandie Ave, Apt 4, Los Angeles 90029 Ofc: Lightning Detective Agency, POB 75667, Los Angeles 90075

KEIPER, FRANCIS PITMAN, JR., electrical engineer; b. Apr. 13, 1929, Wash. DC; s. Francis Pittman and Helen Margaret (Fien) K.; m. Jo Ann Vagg, June 8, 1952, div. 1978; children: Susan, b. 1953; Sharon, b. 1956; Francis II, b. 1958; edn: Bach. E.E., Cornell Univ. 1951. Career: student engr., research scientist Philco Corp., Phila., Pa. 1948-62; engring. splst., principal engr. Philco Ford Co., Willow Grove, Pa, 1962-73; principal engr. Philco Ford Co., Sierra Electronic Opn., Menlo Park 1974-75; principal engr., chief engr. Lear Siegler Inc., Sierra Elec. Div., Menlo Park 1975 ; IEEE, Solid State Circuits Com. (1953-56) & Telecommun. Standards Com. (1979-); honors: Eta Kappa Nu 1951; mem. IEEE; approx. 20 patents incl. Transistor Applications, Color TV, Reading Machines, Pattern Recognition, Telecom Mesuring Equip.; sci. conf. papers; Unitarian. Res: 1398 Thunderbird Ave Sunnyvale 94087 Ofc: LSI Sierra, 3885 Bohannon Dr Menlo Park 94025

KEISER, KATHLEEN MAY, quality engineer; b. July 23, 1942, Santa Monica; d. Milton Leroy and Margaret Elizabeth (Shopbell) Keiser; edn: Cert. Drafting, Santa Monica City Coll. 1963; BS Electronics, CSU Long Beach 1968; profl. certs. in Occupational Health & Safety, Supvsn., QA, Golden West Coll. Career: calibration tech. and test engr. Rockwell, Anaheim 1968-73, process quality engr. (QE) 1973-74; procurement QE 1974-79, senior procurement quality rep., Rockwell, Downey 1979-82; pgm. & rec. insp. QE, Parker Hannifin Corp., Irvine 1982--; mem: ASQC, SWE; Republican; rec: walking, travel. Res: 1361 Laguna Rd, 11-3, Tustin 92680 Ofc: Parker, 18321 Jamboree Irvine 92715

KELL, JAMES C., computer co. executive; b. Aug. 23, 1941, Stockton; s. Lauren E. and Barbara P. (Joy) K.; m. Judy A., Mar. 3, 1962; children: Julie, b. 1963; Jennifer, b. 1973; edn: BS, UC Berkeley, 1970; CPA, 1972, Calif. Career: mgmt. cons. Coopers & Lybrand, San Francisco 1969-73; var. finl./ project/ mktg. exec. positions, Bechtel Corp., S.F 1973-81; v.p. fin. Nutech, Inc./ pres. Nutech Computer Sciences, Inc., San Jose 1981-83; currently, pres. Opticom Corp., San Jose 1983--; founder Consumer Marine Supply 1979; founder Soundman Prodns. Inc., 1982; Founder Opticom Corp. 1983; honors: Phi Beta Kappa 1969, Ernst & Ernst Acctg. Found. Award 1969, John Dolbeer Scholarship 1970; mem: AICPA; Beta Alpha Psi (pres. 1969); rec: sailing. Res: 1701 Copper Hill Dr Morgan Hill 95037 Ofc: Opticom Corp., 6895 Via Del Oro San Jose 95119

KELLER, BRUCE ELLIOTT, financial/personal manager; b. Nov. 22, 1946, Newark, NJ; s. Gerald J. and Sylvia (Kendler) Keller; edn: BS, Seton Hall Univ. 1968; JD, San Fernando Valley Coll. of Law 1979. Career: undergraduate public accounting, 1964-68; devel. financial mgmt. practice, 1968-76; owner financial bus. mgmt. firm, Keller Hill Michaels & Rushmore, Los Angeles 1979--; rec: tennis. Address: Keller Hill Michaels & Rushmore, 2049 Century Park East Los Angeles 90067

KELLER, JAMES DONALD, certified public accountant; b. Aug. 1, 1934, Laramie, Wyo.; s. Chester Lee and Devota Emma (Collins) K.; m. Georgiann E., July 14, 1956; children: Yoland, b. 1957; Cynthia, b. 1959; Steve, b. 1960; Teri, b. 1961; Ken, b. 1962; John, b. 1964; Jackie, b. 1966; edn: BS, Univ. of Wichita 1962; CPA, Calif. 1980; enrolled to practice, IRS 1975. Career: traffic mgr. The Boeing Co., Wichita, Ks. 1957-60; James D. Keller Co., Accts. & Auditors, Wichita, Ks. 1960-66; planner Lockheed MSD-Ops., Sunnyvale

1966-73; public acct. prin. James D. Keller, Sunnyvale 1973-76; partner Keller & Panetta, CPAs, Sunnyvale 1976--; dir. KPH Transportation Co., Inc. 1981-; dir. World Wide Investors, Inc. 1980-82; mem: Calif. Soc. CPAs; Soc. of No. Calif. Accts.; Knights of Columbus; spkr. num. civic clubs & orgns.; mil: AO3 USN 1951-55, num. svc. awds.; Democrat; Catholic; rec: ceramics, fishing. Res: 2996 Camargo Ct San Jose 95132 Ofc: Keller & Panetta CPAs, 510 S Mathilda Ave, Ste 7, Sunnyvale 94086

KELLER, MICHAEL A., music library director; b. Apr. 5, 1945, Sterling, Colo.; s. Ephraim Richard and Mary Patricia (Warren) K.; m. Carol Lawrence, Oct. 6, 1979; children: Kristen,b. 1958, Paul, b. 1971, Laura, b. 1981; edn: BA, cum laude (biology, music), Hamilton Coll., Clinton, NY 1967; MA (music hist.) St. Univ. of NY at Buffalo 1970; MLS (academic librnshp.) SUNY at Geneseo 1972; postgrad. SUNY at Buffalo ABD, 1970-. Career: acting undergrad. librarian, Cornell University, 1976, music librn./senior lectr. in musicology, 1973-81; head Music Library, Univ. Calif. Berkeley, 1981--; cons., library and music dept.: Univ. of Alberta, Edmonton (1983), Brown Univ. (1983), Rutgers Univ. Libraries (1982), Bates Coll. (1976), Colgate Univ. (1976); awards: UCB Medal (Bronze) 1983; Nat. Music Clubs Spl. Commendn. 1978; var. resrch. grants, CU Coll. of Arts and Scis. (1973-81), travel grant for study in Italy 1980; Nelson Clark Dale Prize, Hamilton Coll., 1967; mem: Am. Library Assn., AAUP, Music Library Assn., Internat. Assn. of Music Libraries, Am. Musicological Soc.; mem. Cayuga Hts. Vol. Fire Co.; articles in scholarly and music library jours., reviews, var. newsletters; three new indexes to musical lit. (1980); contbr. New Groves Dictionary of Music and Musicians (London: Macmillan, 1980); mil: s/sgt. NY Army Nat. Guard 1968-74, instr. Land Mine Warfare, NY OCS, 1973-74; rec: sailing, skiing, wine. Res: 1756 Marin Ave Berkeley 94707 Ofc: The Music Library, University of Californai, 240 Morrison Hall, Berkeley 94720

KELLOGG, BRUCE MICHAEL, real estate investor; b. Jan. 3, 1947, Buffalo, NY; s. Harlan Wood and Hilma Moore (Yarrington) K.; m. Diane Mancuso, Dec. 25, 1979; children: Jeremy, b. 1972; Catherine, b. 1974; Michael, b 1980; Elizabeth, b. 1982; edn: BS, Rutgers Univ. 1969; MBA, Golden Gate Univ. 1976. Career: real estate investor 1973--; proprietorship in 5 Bay area counties, spec. owning & rehabilitating low income properties; 1982 inventory approx. 200 properties; trader stocks & commodities using advanced statistics & computers, -1973; mem: Nat., Calif. & Tri-Co. Apartment Assns.; Nat. Multi Housing Council; Nat., Calif. Assn. Realtors; San Jose Bd. Realtors; Internat. Platform Assn.; publs: arts. in Commodity Journal Mag. (7/72, 1/73, 3/73) on computer comparison of systems for commodity trading; Republican; Catholic; rec: family outings; Address: POB 18174 San Jose 95158

KELLY, ALISON OLIVER, artist; b. Oct. 6, 1952, Galveston, Tex.; d. Louis Lloyd and Audrey (Houlgrave) Oliver; m. Scott Matthew Kelly, May 6, 1983; 1 dau: Mary Margaret, b. 1983; edn: AB, Tobe Coburn 1972; BA, Margrethe Skolen 1974. Career: fmrly. with Salomon Bros., NY, Margit Brandt Design, Copenhagen; currently self-empl., childrens gifts; lectr. on micro computer, Salomon Bros.; works: Hand illustrated books for Charles Revson, Joseph W. McCarthy, Mrs. Richard A. Giza, others; Republican; Episcopal; rec: all art. Addres: 3643 Mosswood Lafayette 94549

KELLY, CARL HALL, III, pharmacist; b. July 27, 1945, Henderson, Nev.; s. Carl Hall and Dorothy Dean (Mason) Kelly; edn: Linfield Coll. 1963-4, BS, Ore. State Univ., 1969; m. Barbara Brown, Mar. 3, 1973; chil: Erin, b. 1977, Brent, b. 1979, Brandon, b. 1982; career: pharmacy intern, Salem (Ore.) Meml. Hosp., 1966-69; pharmacist, Sav-On Drugs, Chula Vista, Ca. 1969-71; pharmacy mgr., White Front Pharmacy, La Mesa 1971-75; co-developer, Santa Ana/Tustin Clinic Pharmacy, Santa Ana 1973; co-founder, Pink's Plantation Tree Farm, Mill City, Ore. 1977--; owner/pharmacist, White Front Pharmacy/K&L Nutrition, La Mesa 1975--; pres., Telbat, Inc., Santa Ana 1979-; profl. advisor, Advisory Bd. for Alternative Pursuits Inst., Inc., 1977; Kappa Psi frat. v.p.; 1969; works: You and Your Nutrition, a TV interview, Ch.8, San Diego, 1978; Republican; Roman Catholic; rec: aquatic sports, numismatics, skiing; res: 351 Ave. De Las Rosas Encinitas 92024 ofc: White Front Pharmacy/ K&L Nutrition 5280 Baltimore Dr. La Mesa 92041.

KELLY, FRANK LIND, scientist, corporate executive; b. Oct. 7, 1932, San Diego; s. Frank R. and Ethel E. Kelley; m. Marlene Alban, July 5, 1953; children: Kevin, b. 1958, Erin Marie, b. 1961, Karlin, b. 1963, Kyle, b. 1965; edn: BA, CSU San Diego 1959, grad. studies CSUSD 1959-62, CSU Northridge 1963-65, UCLA 1966. Career: aviation electronic tech. USN, 1951-55 (Combat Aircrew Award, Korean Service Medal, GCM); physicist General Dynamics, San Diego 1956-62; senior scientist Lockheed Calif. Co., Burbank 1962-67; mgr. Plasma Sciences Labs., Van nuys 1967-71; mgr. ops. Carson Astronomical Instruments, Valencia 1971-75; senior v.p. ops. Pacesetter Systems Inc., Sylmar 1975--; co. director Plasma Sciences Labs., 1967-71; cons. to indus. and USAF in field of Plasma Physics 1966-71; recipient num. awards for service, Boys Scouts of Am. Mem: Am. Physical Soc., AAAS, IEEE, AIAA; Patentee (1966, 1977, others pend.); sci. journal arts.; rec: hiking, camping. Res: 10544 Densmore Granada Hills 91344 Ofc: 12884 Bradley Ave Sylmar 91342

KELLY, MARTIN BERNARD, agri-business real estate developer/broker; b. Feb. 22, 1938, NY, NY; s. John J. and Margaret T. (Ward) K.; m. Debbie Lyn Kleven, July 29, 1981; 1 son, Sean, b. 1975; edn: AA, US Armed Forces Inst., Wash DC 1958; AA, real estate/law/agri., Antelope Valley Coll.; dip. police sci., Delahanty Inst. NY; dip. Lumbleau R.E. Sch.; dip. H&R Block Adv. Income Tax Sch. Career: investigator Equifax Corp., Santa Monica, 1960-63; sales mgr. Internat. Order of Foresters (frat. life ins.), Sherman Oaks, 1963-69; v.p./dir. mktg. Physicians and Surgeons Assn. (3d largest ppd. hlth plan in US),

Los Angeles 1969-72; founder/exec. dir. Comm. Action for Medical Plans (consulting), 1972-75; pres. Country Properties (gen. real estate), Green Valley 1975--; franchise owner H & R Block ofc. (tax, acctg.), Green Valley 1975--; pres. Green Valley Homes (devel. co.), 1979--; owner Deer Creek Ranch (trains, breeds Arabian Horses), 1974-; past owner/opr. Mr. Kelly's (night club), Playa del Rey 1962-64, Sportsman's Lodge (youth hostel), Mammoth Lakes 1964-74, Mammoth Accom. Ctr. (reservation svc.), 1967-72; Four Seasons Sports Club, 1972-75; honors: Hon. Mayor of Green Valley 1981/2; recipient sev. sales achievement awards; mem: Knights of Columbus, Intl. Order of Foresters (Prince), Four Seasons Sport Club (past pres.); publs: contbg. columnist, Vanguard (1979-80), Antelope Valley Press (1982-); History of Green Valley (1981), num. poems; mil: sgt. USMC 1955-58, Korea, Japan with 1st Air Wing; Republican; Catholic; rec: skiing, tennis, equestrian, mountaineering. Res: 38800 San Francisquito Cyn Rd Green Valley 91350 Ofc: Country Properties, 39804 San Francisquito Cyn Rd Green Valley 91350

KELLY, TERRY JON, energy co. executive/ airline pilot; b. Apr. 7, 1944, Detroit, Mich.; s. Jesse Oliver and Dorothy Evelyn (Niemela) K.; m. Karen Stucky, July 8, 1978; children: Steven, b. 1979; Krystal, b. 1982; edn: AA, Los Angeles Harbor Coll. 1964; BS, CSU Los Angeles 1967; CFP -Cert. Finl. Planner, Coll. of Finl. Plnng. 1983; Calif. lic. Real Estate Broker 1980; Reg. Principal, Nat. Assn. Security Dealers 1982. Career: agcy. mgr. San Francisco Life, Los Angeles 1961-68; flight instr. Brackett Air Svc., Pomona 1968-69; bus. devel. ofcr. Union Bank, San Jose 1974-75; airline pilot, United Airlines, Inc. Los Angeles 1969--; v.p. Tamco Energy, Inc., Languna Hills. 1981--; v.p./ dir./ prin. Tamco Energy Inc., Tamco Industries Inc. 1981-; pres./ dir./prin. Crown Group Inc. 1983-; mem: Orange Co. Petroleum Assn.; Internat. Assn. of Fin. Plnrs.; Inst. CFPs; Airline Pilots Assn.; Toastmasters; mil: sgt. USAFR 1966-70; Republican; Christian; rec: flying, swimming, sailing. Res; 28421 Dapple Grey Dr Laguna Hills 92653 Ofc: Tamco Energy Inc., 23461 South Pointe Dr, Ste 115, Laguna Hills 92653

KELLY, WILSON CALVERT, veterinarian; b. Feb. 12, 1921, Stockton; s. James Albert and Lottie F. (Hughes) K.; m. Patricia H. McNamara, Sept. 23, 1944; children: Tim, Patrick, Kirk, Maureen, Neil; edn: BS zool., Colo. State Univ. 1950, DVM, 1952; stu. Stockton Jr. Coll. 1939-40, UC Davis 1938-9, 1940-41. desig. Naval Aviator, NAS, Corpus Christi, 1942. Career: USN, WWII, 1941-46; sq. cmdr. Navy Fighter Squadron, NAS, Denver, Colo. 1949-51; veterinarian pvt. practice, small animal practitioner 1952-83; apptd. to Bd. of Examiners in Veterinary Med. by Gov. Reagan, 1969-76 (pres. 1973); honors: appreciation award "to the father of the AHT Program", Bd. of Exam. in Vet. Med. and the Animal Health Technician Exam. Com., 1983; mem: Baja Bush Pilots (charter 1970); Stockton Aeronautical Assn. (pres. 1980); Calif. Acad. of Vet. Med. (charter 1976, pres. 1984); No. Calif. Vet. Med. Assn. (past pres. two terms); Am. Vet. Med. Assn.; Am. Animal Hosp. Assn.; No. San Joaquin Vet. Med. Assn.; AOPA; authored Animal Health Technician Act, adopted as part of the Calif. Veterinary Practice Act; mil: lt. cmdr. USNR 1941-46, D.F.C. (2), Purple Heart, Air Medals (13), Batt. Stars (11), Pres. Unit Cit.; Republican; Episcopal; rec: pvt. pilot, trout fishing, travel. Res: 12250 N. Lower Sacramento Rd Lodi 95240 Ofc: Animal Clinic 7575 Pacific Ave Stockton 95207

KELSEY, KATHERINE LOUISE, artist; b. Cleveland, Ohio; d. Adam and Katie (Breckel) McKee; m. Francis Overstreet Kelsey, July 6, 1950; edn: BS, and AM, Columbia Univ., NY; Escuela de Pintura & Escultura, Mex. City; spl. studies Cleveland Sch. of Art, John Huntington Polytechnic. Career: instr./ head Art Dept., Andrews School, Willoughby, Ohio (16 yrs.); artist/owner Contemporary Arts (bus. rentals of paintings), Berkeley 1960s--; num. exhibs. in mus. & galleries: paintings, sculptures, textile designs, ceramics, lithographs, etchings, sold through museums and galleries; recipient 1 Special Award, 2 first prizes, num. hon. mentions; life mem. Cleveland Mus. of Art; mem: S.F. Museum Soc., Humane Soc., YMCA, Kelsey Kindred; Ind.; Presbyterian; rec: swimming. Res: 1753 Lexington Ave El Cerrito 94530 Ofc: Contemporary Arts, 2318 Shattuck Ave Berkeley 94704

KELSEY, LEO HAROLD, manufacturer's agent; b. Mar. 27, 1952, Casper, Wyo.; s. Harold Franklyn and Audrey (Cohee) K.; m. Pamela Baird, Jan. 14, 1978; 1 child, Eryn, b. 1976; CKD (cert. kitchen designer), Soc. Certified Kitchen Designers 1982. Career: sales/designer Everitt Kitchen Center, Ft. Collins, Colo. 1972-73; owner Cabinet Creations Unlmtd., Greeley, Colo. 1973-78; sales/designer Elm Distbrs. Denver, Colo. 1978-7-9; pres. KB Associates, Foster City, Ca. 1980--; nat. bd. dirs. National Kitchen and Bath Assn. 1983-85, recipient NKBA merit award for svc. to indus. (1982, 83, 84), past pres. NKBA Mtn. States Chpt. 1978, pgm. chmn. No. Calif. Chpt. 1981. Res: 135 East O'Keefe, 3, Menlo Park 94025 Ofc: KB Assocs. 1169 Chess Dr, Ste. I, Foster City 94404

KEMP, DAVID GEORGE, real estate broker; b. Feb. 23, 1943, Los Angeles; s. George Paul and Arlene Rose (Wysuph) K.; m. Olga Leticia Rocha, Dec. 17, 1977; children: Diane Olga, b. 1981; Paul David, b. 1983; edn: AA, Los Angeles Pierce 1964; BA, UC Santa Barbara 1966; AS, Southwestern 1981; MBA, Nat. Univ. 1985; lic. R.E. broker, Calif. 1982. Career: recreation dir. Los Angeles City 1960-69; dir. of aquatics Santa Monica City 1975-76; exec. dir. Pinedale Improvement Orgn., Fresno 1977-79; asst. housing mgr. San Diego Housing Commn. 1979--; mem: San Diego Apt. Assn.; So. San Diego Bay Cities Bd. Realtors; Soc. of Real Estate Appraisers; Inst. of Real Estate Mgmt.; works: annexed the unincorporated territory of Pinedale to the City of Fresno through petition process 1979; Democrat; Christian; rec: tennis, swimming, chess. Res: 1404 Ridgeback Rd, Apt G, Chula Vista 92010 Ofc: San Diego Housing Commission, 121 Broadway, Ste 400, San Diego 92101

KEMP, JAMES PATRICK, physician; b. July 18, 1936, Charleston, W.Va.; s. James P. and Virginia Lee (Gilardi) K.; m. Judith, Apr. 26, 1969; children: Tiffany, b. 1963, Cynthia, b. 1967; edn: BA in biol. Univ. of Va. 1958, MD, 1962. Career: pediatric intern Univ. of Fla. 1962-63, ped. resident, Emory Univ. 1963-65; mil. svc. US Naval Hosp., San Diego 1965-67; ped. allergy/ immunology res. Univ. of Calif., San Francisco 1967-69; pvt. practice Pediatric Allergy, 1969--, pres. Pediatric Allergy Medical Group, APC, San Diego; assoc. clin. prof. of pediatrics, UCSD; mem: Fellow: Am. Acad. of Allergy and Immunol., Am. Coll. of Allergy, Am. Assn. of Certified Allergists, and Am. Acad. of Pediatrics; mem. AMA, CMA, S.D. County Med. Soc., Calif. Soc. of Allergy and Clin. Immunol. (pres. 1979), S.D. Allergy Soc. (pres. 1971), S.D. Pediat. Soc., Asthma & Allergy Found. of Am. (past pres. S.D. chpt.); Rotary (S.D. ofcr.); publs. in med. journals; num. research projects (45); mil: lcdr. USNR 1965-67; Republican; Protestant; rec: skiing, camping, ranching. Res: 3264 Curlew St San Diego 92103 Ofc: Pediatric Allergy Medical Group 7920 Frost St, Ste. 100, San Diego 92123

KENDRICK, STEPHEN HAYES, manufacturing co. executive; b. Oct. 3, 1949, Palo Alto; s. Marron and Mary Elizabeth (Roth) K.; m. Katharine Lewis, June 26, 1971, 1 dau. Claire, b. 1981, edn. BA, Williams Coll. 1972, MBA, Harvard Bus. Sch. 1976. Career: with Schlage Lock Co., San Francisco 1976--: spl. projects coordinator 1976-77; materials sys. mgr. 1978-79; proj. mgr. 1980-81; div. mfg. eng. mgr. 1982--; dir. E.D. Bullard Co. 1983-; trustee Thacher Sch.; dir. Russian Hill Neighbors; assoc. Children's Hosp. SF; mem: Soc. of Mfg. Engrs., Am. Production & Inventory Control Soc., Sierra Club, ACLU, NPG, POS; Republican; rec: mountaineering, squash. Res: 1020 Broadway San Francisco 94133 Ofc: Schlage Lock Co., 2401 Bayshore Blvd San Francisco 94134

KENLY, ROD BRENT, electronics engineer; b. June 4, 1954, Phoenix, Ariz.; s. John and Betty Blair (Votaw) K.; m. Sharon Rhonemus, Oct. 1, 1979; 1 son: Jeremy, b. 1981; edn: BSEE, Northern Ariz. Univ. 1979; EIT, State of Ariz. Bd. of Tech. Regis. 1979. Career: electronics engr. Motorola, Phoenix, Ariz. 1975, State of Ariz., Phoenix 1976; elecrical engr. Bechtel Power Corp., Joseph City, Az. 1977; electronic engr. Naval Weapon Ctr., China Lake, Calif. 1979-83, supv. elec. engr. 1983--; tchr. basic pgmmg. Cerro Coso Comm. Coll. 1983-; mem: IEEE; Indian Well Valley Trap & Skeet Club; Silver Trowel & Flagstaff F&AM; Phoenix Scottish Rite Bodies; publs: tech. memorandums, AIM-9M Free Flight Analysis 3/84; Republican; Presbyterian; rec: trapshooting, leatherwork. Res: 748 W Dolphin Ridgecrest 93555 Ofc: Naval Weapons Ceneter, CODE 3622, China Lake 93555

KENNA, TIMOTHY WILLIAM, lawyer; b. March 10, 1949, Orange, Ca., s. Wilfred Patrick and Maxine (Neilsen) K.; m. Kathleen Ikola, June 17, 1972; children: Daniel Patrick b. 1977, Todd Joseph b. 1980; edn: BA, honors, UC Santa Barbara 1971; JD, Univ. of San Francisco 1975. Career: judicial extern Hon. Allison M. Rouse, Calif. Ct. of Appeals 1974; assoc. atty. law firm Nelson, Liker & Merrifield, Los Angeles 1975-76; assoc. atty. law firm Jones & Wilson, L.A. 1976-81, ptnr. 1982, mng. ptnr. 1983--; honors: Letters & Science Scholar, California State Scholar, assoc. ed. USF Law Rev. 1974; mem: American Bar Assn. (Fidelity & Surety Com.), Los Angeles Co. Bar Assn., Surety Producers Assn. (support mem.) 1981-83, Surety Claims Assn. 1981 83, Defense Research Inst. (DRI) 1982-83. Major trials: Penncorp Fin. Inc. v. Penn Gen. Agencies (1980), Stonewall Ins. Co. v. Food Fair Stores Inc. (1982) pub. Business Insurance Mag. 1/82; mem. La Canada Flintridge Tournament of Roses Assn. 83-84, Descanso Gardens Guild 83-84, Colonial Williamsburg Found. 79-84, UCSB Alumni Assn., USF Alumni Assn.; Democrat; Catholic; rec: camping, fishing, racquetball,contemporary choir. Res: 1519 Riendo Ln La Canada 91011 Ofc: Jones & Wilson, 11620 Wilshire Blvd Ste 300, Los Angeles 90025

KENNEDY, BARBARA DIANE, company president; b. June 21, 1952, Pasadena; d. Charles B. and Josephine (Ewing) K.; edn: BA, CSU Los Angeles 1976; cert., Sound masters/ Recording Eng. 1982. Career: owner Wallcoverings by Barbara, Los Angeles 1975-83; owner Kennedy Enterprises, Pasadena 1982--; pres. Tappercize Inc., Pasadena 1983--; vice pres. E & B's Cookies, L.A. 1984--; spkr. entrepreneurship Pasadena Schs., health/ nutrition/ vitamins through T/Z Assocs.; awards: Sportsmanship Trophy 1969; Most Outstanding, Drill Team 1970; musical works: composed finale, Pasadena's Dah Doo Review, scholarship fundraising; prod. all Tappercize music/ videos; composed/ arranged, Who Oh Why (radio) 1982; Republican; rec: songwriting, skiing. Res: 2002 1/2 E Orange Grove, B, Pasadena 91104 Ofc: Tappercize Inc., 121 W Green St Pasadena 91105

KENNEDY, BILL WILLIAM, dentist; b. Feb. 10, 1956, Barataria, Trinidad, nat. 1979; s. John A., Sr. and Evelyn E. (Pierre) K.; m. Yvette Jackson, July 5, 1980; children: Shani, b. 1974; Mischa, b. 1979; Trecha, b. 1982; edn: BS in psychobiology, UCLA 1978; DDS, 1979; lic. dentist, Calif. 1983. Career: gen. dentist Dr. Howard M. Stein Dental Corp.; presently, clinic director, Dr. Charles H. Moore Dental Corp. 1983--; mem. Nat. Dental Assn. Action Com.; dir. Metropolitan State Hosp. Volunteer Pgm.; honors: Most Valuable Athlete, UCLA 1975; mem: Nat. & Am. Dental Assns.; Internat. Assn. for Study of Pain; Phi Beta Sigma; Canadian Nat. Track & Field Team (sprinter); Christian; rec: 3302 Sawtelle Blvd, 14, Los Angeles 90066 Ofc: 5517 Holmes Ave Los Angeles 90058

KENNEDY, JACK DEWEY, chiropractor; b. Oct. 24, 1957, Garden Grove; s. Thomas Stevens and Joan Dee Kennedy; edn: CSU Chico 1975-78; BS, Los Angeles Coll. of Chiropractic, 1980, DC, 1981. Career: physical therapist Glendale Physical Therapy, 1980-82; assoc. dir. Burbank- Glendale Chiropractic, Glendale 1982-83; director Anaheim Chiropractic, 1983--; tchr. spinal care classes to public; scoliosis screenings; Diplomate Nat. bd. Chiro. Examiners; mem: Am., Calif. & Orange Co. Chiro. Assns.; Big Brothers of Am.; Spl. Olympics; Orange Co. Toastmasters; research: to explain theraputic effects of laughter & emotions in the healing process 1978-, to be pub. circa 1986; Republican; rec: weight lifting, sports medicine, comedy. Res: 1308 E Harvard St, 5, Glendale 91205 Ofc: Anaheim Chiropractic, 925 E Lincoln Ave Anaheim 92805

KENNEDY, JAMES JOSEPH JOHN, landscape architect; b. Oct. 27, 1932, Holyoke, Mass.; s. James Joseph and Maybelle Eva (Beaudoin) K.; m. Mary Ann Daly, Sept. 1, 1956; children: John, b. 1957; James Michael, b. 1959; Jeanne, b. 1960; James Joseph, b. 1962; edn: Holyoke Jr. Coll. 1952-53; Univ. of Mass. 1953-54; Univ. of San Francisco 1956; BS, Univ. Mass. 1959, B.Landscape Arch., 1960; Reg. Land. Arch. Calif. 1963, Tenn. 1972, Fla. 1975. Career: chief layout engr. M.A. Gammino Constrn., Providence, R.I. (Conn. Expressway) 1957-58; junior, asst., assoc., senior landscp. arch. State of Calif. Div. Architecture, 1960-63; landscp. arch., irrigation cons. Seaworld, 1963-69, 1983-; landscape architect J.J.J. Kennedy & Assocs. 1964--; irrigation cons. SD G&E Substation (1982); cons. La Jolla Devel. Co., 30 Shopping Centers, No./ So. Calif., water mgmt. 1982-; awards: Nat. AIA Award 1976; Pacific Plaza Shopping Center; SGPA Architects; Calif. Council of Land. Arch., Seaworld Skytower and Atlantis Restaurant (1968); Calif. Garden Club, Szalay Residence (1967); mem: Am. Soc. of Landscape Arch., Am. Inst. of Landscape Arch., Calif. Roadside Council, Coronado Floral, San Diego Floral, Knights of Columbus; works: water conservation, slope erosion control by use of most updated electronics; mil: cadet, nav. USAF 1954-56; Catholic; rec: model radio control aircraft, bird observer rel. to plant materials. Res: 2426 Alto Cerro Circle San Diego 92109 Ofc: J.J.J.Kennedy and Assocs. 3755 Ocean Front Walk Suite 6, San Diego 92109

KENNEDY, JOHN MARIUS, aerospace staff engineer; b. Sept. 13, 1921, NY, NY; s. Edward and Annette (Chevalier) K.; m. Adele Pattin, Nov. 26, 1952; children: Jo Emily b. 1956, Edward b. 1959; edn: BS in elec. eng., Lehigh Univ. 1944; cert. comm. photog., Sch. of Modern Photog., NY 1947; course wk. New Sch. of Soc. Research, NYU, UCLA, and USC; courses in Adv. Tech. Edn. Pgm., Hughes Aircraft, var. mgmt. sems.; Reg. Profl. Engr., NY. Career: cmdg. ofcr. Marrak and Sondrestrom Fjord Army Air Bases, Greenland, 1946; asst. supt. ops. Caltex Oil Plant, Hankow, China, 1948; design engr. Edo Aircraft, Long Island, NY 1952; engr. the Austin Co., Special Devices Div., Manhattan, NY 1955; engr. Nemos Corp. (Appliances) Bronx, NY 1956; engr. Mergenthaler Linotype Co., Brklyn., NY 1962; staff engr. Hughes Aircraft Co., El Segundo, Calif. 1962--, conceptualize and design equip. for space, aircraft, shipboard, and ground vehicles; honors: mem. Republican Senatorial Inner Circle 1984; commendn. for personal contbn., Guidance and Controls Div. and cert. of achieve., W.B. Dudley, USAF Cmdr. AFPRO Cost Reduction Pgm. 1966; recogn. for contbn. to success of Pioneer Venus Space Probe Program; mem: The Nat. Writers Club (profl.), Acad. of Sci. Fiction, Horror and Fantasy Films, Pacific Asia Mus. (Pasadena), L.A. County Mus. of Art; author: Making Electricity Work (Thomas Y. Crowell 1959), contbr. Am. Poetry Anthol., Vol. II (1983); mil: parachutist, US Inf., WWII; rec: write, collect Chinese paintings. Res: 11676 Chenault Brentwood Los Angeles 90049 Ofc: Hughes Aircraft Co. 2175 Prk Place, E50/A227, El Segundo 90245

KENT, ALLEN JOSEPH, lawyer; b. June 23, 1939, Jamaica, NY; s. Allen I and Katherine Elizabeth (Sullivan) K.; m. Doreen McIninch, July 14, 1963; children: Darin, b. 1964; Ryan, b. 1967; Allison, b. 1969; edn: AB, UC Berkeley 1962; JD, Golden Gate Univ. Sch. of Law 1966; admitted to Calif. State Bar 1967. Career: assoc. Morgan, Wenzel, Morris & Polich, Los Angeles 1966-68; assoc. Carroll & Anderson, Indio 1968-70; partner Barbagelata, Carmazzi, Arnold & Kent, San Francisco 1970-76; assoc. gen. counsel Kaiser Aetna & Kacor Realty, Oakland 1976-80; sole practitioner Law Ofcs. Allen J. Kent, S.F. 1980--; lectr. constrn. law, CSU Sacto. 1972; dir. Spinol Corp., O'Keeffe's Inc. 1980-; honors: J.C. of the Month, Palm Springs Jaycees 1969; mem: No. Calif. Constrn. Inst.; Am. Arbitration Assn.; Calif. Trial Lawyers Assn.; Am. Legion; Elks; Palm Springs Jaycees; Rotary Club; mil: cpl. USMC 1960-66; Democrat; Catholic; rec: sailing, hiking, jogging. Res: 119 Starlite Dr San Mateo 94402 Ofc: Ghirardelli Square, 900 North Point, Chocolate Bldg, 4th Flr, San Francisco 94109

KENT, LAWRENCE, educator, banker; b. Feb. 21, 1935, Dayton, Ohio; s. Charles Ernest and Roma Flae Thomas Hollopeter; edn: AA cum laude, Los Angeles City Coll. 1977; BA cum laude, CSU Northridge 1-9; MA in edn., San Francisco State Univ. 1981; PhD in gen. edn. admin., Miami Univ. (Ohio), 1984; att. City Coll. of S.F., Skyline Coll., L.A. Valley Coll., Pima Coll., 1973-82. Career: banker, Ohio, Ariz., Calif., 1953-76; deputy county auditor, Montgomery Co., Ohio 1968-70; with CSUN Libraries, 1978-79; SFSU Sch. of Edn., 1979-81; Fellow, Miami Univ., Oxford, Ohio 1982-85; honors: Phi Delta Kappa Diamond Jubilee Graduate Honors Award, SFSU, 1981; Nat. Honor Soc. 1953; listee: The Hereditary Register of the USA, 1973-78, Los Angeles Blue Book, 1979-84; mem: AAUP, Phi Alpha Theta, Phi Delta Kappa, Pi Lambda Theta, Sons & Dau. of the Pilgrims, Sons of the Am. Colonists, Huguenot Soc. of Am., Huguenot Soc. Founders of Manakin, SAR (Calif.), SAR, Soc. War of 1812, St. George's Soc. of NY, St. David's Soc. of NY, First Families of Ohio, Soc. of Indiana Pioneers, Mil. Order of the Loyal Legion, Mil. Order of the Stars & Bars, Sons of Union Veterans, Sons of Confederate Veterans, Sons of Sherman's March to the Sea, Am. Edn. Fin. Assn., Am. Ednl. Resrch. Assn.; publs: co-ed. SFSU The Ed. Admin. Research & Ldrshp. Handbook: Programs and

Services (1980); staff CSUN Sunburst 1979; mil: Fin. Corps, US Army 1956-8 (Korea), USAR 1958-62; Republican (cand. for San Mateo County Comm. Coll. Dist. bd. trustees 1981); Episcopal. Res: P.O.Box 2834 Dayton, Ohio 45401

KENTNER, WILMA BERNICE, professional color consultant, corporate executive; b. May 23, 1929, Cheyenne, Wyo.; d. Wm. Bristol and Roberta (Allbee) Tufford; m. Dean George Kentner, May 9, 1948; children: Cynthia Ann (Krause), b. 1949, Jim Lew, b. 1952, Denice Marie (Baldree), b. 1956, Nora Eileen (Jackman),b. 1959, Claudean Kay,b. 1964; edn: cosmetol., Cheyenne Beauty Coll. 1947. Career: owner Powder Box Beauty Salon, North Platte, Nebr.; ptnr./v.p. Ednl. and Cosmetic Divs., Color Me A Season Inc. (a Color Coded Cosmetic) and an educational trade school (tchg. art of color consultation); author textbook for Color Consultants: Tie Me Up With Rainbows (1981), A Rainbow In Your Eyes (1983); newspaper column, Contra Costa Times Adv., Color Me A Season (1979); pioneer in the field of Color Consultant, involved in founding nat. orgn. for profl. color consultants; mem: Color Marketing (Wash. DC); honors: Mrs. North Platte in Mrs. America Contest 1956; Democrat; Ch. of Jesus Christ of Latter Day Saints (past Relief Soc. Pres. (5 Wards), Primary Pres. (3 times), Young Womens Mutual Pres.); rec: lecturing, color. Res: 1657 Thornwood Dr Concord 94521 Ofc: Color Me A Season Inc.1070A Shary Circle Concord 94518

KERBY, DONALD L., landscape co. owner; b. May 25, 1936, Oakland; s. Robert and Mrs. (Peterson) K.; m. Marie Smith, Aug. 28, 1953; children: Frederick, b. 1954; Vickie, b. 1956; Jeff, b. 1958; Julie, b. 1961; Don, Jr. b. 1962. Career: owner Don Kerby Landscaping (landscaping, sprinkler repair & landscape maintenance cos.), Stockton 1970--; mem: Ducks Unlimited; Stockton Better Bus. Bureau; CofC; mil: E5 USAF 1954-58. Res: 6810 Angelica Circle Stockton; Den Kerby Landscaping, POB 7448, Stockton 95207

KERNER, FRANCIS XAVIER, lawyer; b. Apr. 6, 1907, San Francisco; s. Louis Philip and Mary Gertrude (Uren) K.; m. Virginia Cain, OCt. 1, 1934; children: Peter, b. 1938; Joan, b. 1938; edn: AB, Univ. of S.F. 1929; LLD, Stanford Univ. 1932. Career: law clerk Linforth Cannon 1932-33; atty. Farm Credit Admin. of Berkeley (now Sacto.) 1933-45; partner Kerner, Colangelo & Imlay, San Francisco 1945--; mem: Nat. Council of Farmer Cooperatives (Legal & Tax Com.); Agricultural Council of Calif. (assoc.); Nat. Soc. of Accts. for Cooperatives; publs: Income Tax and Cooperatives, Calif. Farm & Ranch Law 1967; Securities & Capital Structures of Farmer Cooperatives in Calif., Hastings Law Jour. 309, 1968; Democrat; Catholic. Res: 6650 Crosswood Circle Citrus Hghts 95610 Ofc: Kerner, Colangelo & Imlay, 114 Sansome St, Ste 500, San Francisco 94104

KERR, MAUDE ESTHER, executive; b. Oct. 29, 1912, Culver, Kans.; d. Solomon Richard and Etta May (Aldaffer) Redding; m. Jack Kerr, July 3, 1931; children: Barbara, b. 1932, William, b. 1935, Herbert, b. 1937, Joanne, b. 1946; edn: Normal Tng. Tchrs. Cert., Culver, Ks. 1931. Career: owner w/ husband var. businesses, 1937-57 incl. wrecking yard in Ft. Worth, Tex., restaurant, cocktail lounge in Ariz. 1957; trucking industry, 1965-, co-founder truck driving school, Orange, Ca. in 1977, owner/adminstr. Federal Truck Driving Sch. Inc., San Diego 1977--; mem: Orange CofC (Woman of the Year, Womens Div. 1975); Santee CofC (dir. 1979); Grossmont Condominium Assn. (pres. 1981-83); Am. Business Womens Assn. (treas. 1983-84); Progressive Speakers Toastmaster Club (pres. 1981); Am. Business Womens Assn.; El Cajon CofC. Res: 5750 Amaya, No. 48, La Mesa 92041 Ofc: Fed. Truck Driving School of San Diego Inc. 2966-B Fletcher Pkwy El Cajon 92020

KERRY, ALAN ERNEST, executive/real estate developer; b. Dec. 24, 1949, Canonsburg, Penna.; s. Theodore Harvey and Dorothy Edna (St. Denis) K.; m. Susan L. Thomas, May 2, 1975; children: Michael, b. 1968, Lannin, b. 1980; edn: BA in pol. sci., honors, Penna. State Univ. 1971, MPA, honors, 1973; Calif. lic. real estate broker 1980. Career: adminstrv. asst. Alcoa Properties Inc. (R.E. subs. Aluminum Co. of am.), Century City 1973-74; mgr. Century City Shopping Ctr. Alcoa Properties Inc., Century City 1975-76; mktg. mgr. Alcoa Prop. Inc., Century City 1977-79; buyer Aluminum Co. of Am., New Orleans, La. 1979-80; leasing dir. and devel. mgr. High Rise Div. Watt Industries Inc., Santa Monica and Century City, Ca. 1980-83, v.p. and leasing dir. 1983--; guest lectr. UCLA Ext. courses in real estate, 1981, 82; tchr. Office Leasing Sems. 1982-83, tchr. Junior Achievement pgm. 1982-83; honors: Pi Sigma Alpha, Phi Kappa Phi, Phi Beta Kappa; mem: Rotary Intl. Century City Club (bd. dirs. 1982-85), Century City CofC (bd. dirs., exec. com. 1981-; R.E. Forum chmn. 1982, 83); Cubmaster and asst. Scoutmaster BSA 1977-79; adv. bd. (chmn. 1981-83) L.A. Unified Sch. Dist. Magnet Pgm. Portola Jr. H.S.; Republican; Prot.; rec: golf, ski, backpacking. Res: 16618 Lorillard St Granada Hills 91344Ofc: Watt Industries Inc. 1875 Century Park East, Ste 1110, Los Angeles 90067

KERSHAW, RONALD GRANT, internal auditor; b. July 6, 1950, Moscow, Idaho; s. Hyrum Watkins and Mildred (Hanks) K.; edn: BS, Brigham Young Univ. 1975, MBA, Golden Gate Univ 1984; cert. internal auditor, Inst. Internal Auditors 1978. Career: internal auditor Del Monte Corp. 1975-76, senior internal auditor 1976-79; internal auditor Consolidated Capital 1979, mgr./ internal audit 1980-82, v.p. /internal audit 1982--; mem. Profl. Acctg. Pgm. Adv. Com., UC Berkeley 1982-84; mem: Inst. of Internal Auditors (pres. 1984-85); publs: Auditing Like An Owner Should, Concepts 1982; Republican; LDS. Res: 3533 Twenty- first St San Francisco 94114 Ofc: Consolidated Capital, 1900 Powell St, Ste 1000, Emeryville 94608

KERSTEIN, STEVEN, stockbroker; b. Sept. 11, 1957, Los Angeles S. Ralph

and Geraldine V. (Mullen) K.; edn: BS, USC 1979. Career: stockbroker Merrill Lynch Pierce Fenner & Smith, Pasadena 1979--; guest lectr., fin. & mktg., USC, Pasadena City Coll. 1979-; honors: Pres. Club, Merrill Lynch 1980-83; Alpha Lambda Delta 1975; mem: Pasadena Bond Club; Soc. for Adv. of Mgmt.; Youth Sym. West (conductor 1976-83); principal clarinetist, Brentwood-Westwood Sym., Highland Park Sym., Southeast Sym., American Youth Sym. and West Valley Chamber Orch.; Republican; rec: music, racquetball, skiing. Res: 440 San Juan Pl Pasadena 91107 Ofc: Merrill Lynch, 225 S Lake Ave Pasadena 91101

KESSEL, ROBERT WILLIAM, clinical social worker;b. Aug. 13, 1934, Everett, Mass.; s. Charles W. and Celia (Kaplan) K.; children: Kim, b. 1963, Lynne, b. 1967; edn: AB, Boston Univ. 1957; MSW, Univ. Mich. Sch. of Social Wk. 1961; DSW, USC Sch. of Soc. Wk. 1971; contg. postgrad. stu. spl. courses; Calif. LCSW, MFCC. Career: senior medical soc. wkr. St. John's Hosp. & Health Center, Santa Monica 1981--; dir. profl. svcs. Boys Republic, Farmington Hills, Mich. 180-81; vis. lectr. Santa Fe (N.M.) Sch. of Natural Med. 1980-; prof. Univ. of Humanistic Studies, S.D. 1978-82; co-founder, clin. adminstr. Inst. for Creative Living, La Jolla 1977-80; clin. cons. two drug rehabilitation pgms. in S.D. County 1978-80; faculty UCSD Ext. pgm., holistic med., 1977-78; co-founder, clin. adminstr. Center for Holistic Arts, San Diego 1974-76; assoc. prof. S.D. St. Coll. Sch. of Soc. Wk. 1969-74; tng. supr. Calif. Dept. Soc. Svcs. 1968-69; mem: AAUP, Council on Soc. Wk. Edn., Am. Assn. of Mental Deficiency, NASW, Acad. of Cert. Soc. Wkrs., Orthomolecular Med. Soc., Iridologists Internat. (charter); Democrat; rec: ski, swim, chess. Res: 420 Raymond, 15, Santa Monica 90405 Ofc: St. Johns Hosp. & Health Ctr. 1328 22nd St Santa Monica 90404

KESSELMAN, SHERIDAN, ABEL, rehabilitation counselor; b. May 25, 1946, Phila., Pa.; d. Saul Walter and Mollie Sylvia (Tabach) Abel; m. Stanley W.W. Kesselman, May 3, 1969; children: Brittany, b. 1977; Jared, b. 1980; edn: BA, CSU Northridge 1968; Secondary Tchr. Cred., CSULA 1971; MA, Chapman Coll. 1973; state lic. Marriage, Family & Child Counselor, MFCC, 1973; nat. Cert. Rehabilitation Counselor, 1976. Career: tchr. Marshall High Sch., Los Angeles 1971-72; pvt. practice psychotherapy, marriage, family & child counselor, Beverly Hills. 1973-76; rehab. counselor State Dept. of Rehabilitation, L.A. 1973-79; rehab. counselor/dir. Sheridan Kesselman Rehab. Services Inc. (wkg. with handicapped, industrially injured wkrs.), Encino 1979--; TV, radio talk show guest expert on teenage emotional problems; mem: Calif. Assn. Marriage, Family & Child Counselors; Calif. Assn. Rehab. Profls.; rec: gardening, salinig, tennis. Res: 4150 Rolomar Dr Encino 91436 Ofc: Sheridan Kesselman Rehabilitation Services, Inc., 15910 Ventura Blvd, Ste 1833, Encino 91436

KESSLER, JOHN EDWARD, JR., real estate investor; b. Nov. 19, 1932, Detroit, Mich.; s. John Edward and Frances Mae (Park) K.; m. Rosalie Engel, 1963; children: Rosalie Lynne b. 1964, John, III b. 1968, Kortney Rae b. 1972; edn: BA in acctg. Mich. St. Univ. 1956; LLB, Wayne Univ. 1956; LLD, LaSalle Univ. 1961. Career: jet pilot USMC, 1956-61; CPA, Price Waterhouse & Co., 1961-63; real estate broker, developer, past owner/pres. San Francisco Real Estate co. (3 offices and 86 sales agts.), project director Sierra Springs; owner recreational newspaper, Recreation Gazette (200,000 circ.) 1974-75; mgr./ owner personal R.E. portfolio, currently; mil: 1st lt. USMC, 1956-61. Res: 23 Stanton Way Mill Valley 94941

KESSLER-MARKS, JUNE H., therapy center president; b. Dec. 8, 1935, Cambridge, Mass.; d. Albert H. and Winnie (Block) K.; m. Nov. 8, 1947, div.; children: Andrew H., b. 1948; Michael A., b. 1951; edn: BA, Immaculate Heart Coll. 1977; MA, 1979; PhD, Calif. Graduate Inst. 1983; lic. marriage, family & child therapist. Career: bd. dirs. United Nations Ctr.; intern (psychology), Hospice Parkwood Hosp., Los Angeles Free Clinic; currently, pres. Beginnings Therapy Center Inc.; mem: Calif. M.F.T.; L.A. Mus.; KPFK; Foreign Affairs Council (past); rec: potter. Res: 4820 Swinton Ave Encino 91316 Ofc: Beginnings Therapy Center, Inc., 1011 N Fairfax Ave Hollywood 90046

KESTER, VIRGIL MAYNARD, JR., trucking co. owner; b. Dec. 7, 1935, Santa Cruz; s. Virgil, Sr. and Myrtle Irene (Bailey) K.; m. Marlene Packer, Nov. 14, 1954; children: Linda, b. 1955; Donald, b. 1957; David, b. 1960; Lisa, b. 1961; edn: Hartnell Jr. Coll. 1953. Career: owner/pres. of an automobile club 1953; teamster Granite Constrn. Co. 1954; owner Kester & Son Paving & Grading 1955; owner K & T Trucking 1959--; co-owner Cabrillo Sand & Gravel Co., 1966, expanded quarry ops. to incl. material from Calif., other states & Mexico, 1969; devel. water trucks for emergencies and fire suppression 1982-83; currently, owner K & T Trucking, and Larry's Dumpster Svc.; mem. Teamsters 1954-; Operating Engrs. 1963-; pres. Engrs. Grading Contractors Assn., Monterey Bay 1970; mem: Calif. Trucking Assn.; Aptos CofC (past pres.); Santa Cruz Elks; Knights of Columbus; Am. Red Cross, Watsonville; Family Motor Coach Assn.; works: designer constrn. equip. and constrn. (on site) job projects.; Democrat; Catholic; rec: travel. Res: 1000 Day Valley Rd, Aptos 95001 Ofcs: Larry's Dumpster Service; K & T Trucking, POB 939, Aptos 95001

KETELL, HERBERT R., construction co. president; b. Oct. 17, 1903, Jefferson, Iowa; s. Dr. H.C. and Mabel (Huston) K.; m. Marlene Rose, 1960; children: Thomas C., b. 1964; Herbert, Jr. b. 1937; Wm. Kent, b. 1929; edn: BA, Pomona Coll. 1926. Career: builder/ pres. Ketell Construction Co. (40 yrs.)--, built 3059 homes on contract, Kaiser Shipyard wkrs.; author: (book) Keys To a Good Life; pres. Spring Valley Comm. Center Booster Club; pres. Spring Valley Parks & Recreation Council; pres. Portland Zoo Commn., Portland,

Ore.; honors: Community Center main hall named Ketell Hall; poet laureate, Man of the Yr., Kiwanis Club of Spring Valley; elected Mr. Spring Valley, CofC; mem: Masons; Kiwanis; Hist. Soc. of S.V.; CofC; Valle de Oro Plnng. Gp.; Portland Homes Bldrs. Assn.; Helix South Tennis Club; Republican (del. at large Calif. Repub. Assem.); rec: tennis, bridge, swimming. Address: Ketell Construction Co., 10014 Cristobal Dr Spring Valley 92077

KETTENHOFEN, ERNEST NILE, ship captain, public official, investor; b. July 17, 1917, Portage, Wisc.; s. Ernest Wm. and Alta M William Nile, b. 1946, Linda Dean, b. 1947, Becky Michele, b. 1949, James Ernest, b. 1954; edn: BS, Calif. Maritime Acad. 1941; lic. First Class Pilot, Unlmtd. Masters, USCG. Career: capt. US Maritime Svc. and USNR, WWII, in action Atlantic, Pacific, Mediterranean; past mem./chmn. Marin Co. Bd. of Supervisors, commnr. Calif. Dept. of Navigation and Ocean Devel., commnr. Calif. Dept. of Boating and Waterways; currently real estate investor, prin., opr. (R.E. & investment cos.): Kett-Jenn Co., The Locators R.E. Co., Marin Lands, Inc., E.N.K. Props., E.N.K. Assocs., Chamberlands, Inc., Tahoe Ski Bowl Inc., Quail Lake Water Co., Kettco Investments, Piner Assocs.; founder (non-profit): Chamberlands Bch. & Mtn. Club, Tahoe Ski and Tennis Club, Anchorage Home Owners Assn., Gate Five Rd. Assessmt. Dist.; past bd. dirs. Marin Gen. Hosp., and Found. mem., past bd. govs. Calif. Maritime Acad.; past chmn. Marin Co. Employees Retirement Bd.; bd. dirs. Redwood Bank. Founding mem., dir.: Mental Health Adv. Bd., Comprehensive Health Planning, Coll. of Marin Found., Help Elevate Low Income People, Welfare Adv. Bd., Lost Springs Ranch for Single Parents; mem. Sailors Union of Pacific (Master, Mates & Pilots); mem: Richmond-El Cerrito Bd. of Realtors (v.p.); mem: Rotary, Kiwanis, Oceanic Soc. (founder, S.F. Bay chpt.), Sr. Coordinating Council of Marin (chmn.), Marinship Prop. Owners Assn., BSA (Jr. Asst. Scout Master, Eagle w/Gold Palm 1932-6), DeMolay (jr. counselor 1936-7). Recipient num. awards, citations in all fields. Donor 500 acres as a State Park in Lake Co. Republican; Prot.; rec: outdoors, philanthropy. Res: 125 Anchorage Rd Sausalito 94965 Ofc: Indsl. Ctr. Bldg., Gate Five Rd Sausalito 94965

KEVER, J. WARREN, agronomist; b. Jan. 24, 1923, Valdasta, Tex.; s. Autie Travis and Bonnie Katherine (Combest) Kever; edn: BS in agronomy, Texas A & M, 1947, M. Horticulture, Univ. Mo., 1950; m. Yvonne McIntosh, Sept. 16, 1950; chil: Tom, b. 1953, Kathy, b. 1954, Leslie, b. 1954, Connie, b. 1962; career: teacher, Veterans Agriculture School, McKinney, Tex. 1948-49; agri. research, Univ. Calif., Davis 1950-52; sales rep., John Pryor Fertilizer Co., Salinas 1952-54, Hayes-Simmons Co., Mission, Tex. 1954-55, The Triangle Co. (fertilizer), Salinas, Ca. 1955-69; sales, research, prin., bd. dirs. The John Pryor Co., Salinas 1969--; mem: Elks, Combest Family Assn. (pres. 1975-77), Calif. Fertilizer Assn.; publs: writer: story of John Pryor Co., Solutions Mag., 1980; agronomic research relating to local fertilizer usage; mil: pfc, Army Artillery 1943-45 (Germany); rec: geneology; res: 531 Ambrose, Salinas 93901 ofc: John Pryor Co. 1505 Abbot St. Salinas 93902.

KEYSTON, RONALD SCOTT, engineering co. president; b. Mar. 17, 1951, San Mateo; s. George Noel, Jr. and Jane M. (Simonds) K.; m. Yvonne L. Hansen, June 1974; children: Ronald, Jr., b. 1979; Daniel, b. 1980; Cheries, b. 1983; edn: BS in ag. bus., Cal Poly 1974. Career: v.p. Anza Engring. Co. 1975-76; pres. Keyco Landscaping Corp. 1976-82; pres. Keyco Engring. Corp. 1982--; mil: 1st lt US Army Corps Engrs.; Republican; Christian. Res: 2445 Park Rd Redwood City 94062 Ofc: Keyco Engineering Corp., 1290 Old Bayshore, Burlingame 94010

KHALSA, KRIS, advertising agency executive; b. Sept. 30, 1944, Poughkeepsie, NY; s. Anthony, Sr. and Nunzia (Aiello) Stellavato; m. Kathleen Malec, May 29, 1983; children: Anthony III, b. 1963; Joseph, b. 1964; Nadine, b. 1972; edn: Marist Coll. 1962-63; Calif. Comm. Coll. Tchg. Cred. (life), Kundalini Yoga & Comparative Meditation, 1976. Career: adminstr. Kundalini Research Inst., Pomona 1973-78; owner Nanak's Landscape Co., Pomona 1977-78; acct. exec. G.R.D. Ent., Los Angeles 1979-81; catering and wholesale prods. mgr. Golden Temple Conscious Cookery, L.A. 1978-80; founder/ pres. Pacific Advtg. & Print Connection (div. Mondra Corp.); nat. dir. 3HO Prison- Ashram Proj. 1975-78; pgm. dir. Kundalini Juvenile Diverson 1976; recipient Cert. of Achiev., Cal Poly Pomona, Counselors Conf. on Drug Abus 1975; mem: Concerned Businessmens Assn. of Am. (bd. dirs.); Am. Nat. Red Cross; Reseda CofC; CSU Northridge Alumni Assn.; Smithsonian Assocs.; Nat. Audubon Soc.; Yoga meditation lectr., panelist, num. workshops and classes: Claremont Colls., UCLA, Mt. SAC, other instns. 1973-82; Democrat; Catholic; rec: music. Res: 1535 Westgate Ave, 7, Los Angeles 90025 Ofc: Print Connection Pacific Advertising, 6117 Reseda Blvd, Ste 206, Reseda 91335

KHALVATI, MEHDI JOHN, design automation systems corp. president; b. May 4, 1953, Tehran, Iran; s. Abolhassam and Mahin (Farhadian) K.; edn: BS, Tehran Univ. 1975; MS, Univ. Calif. Berkeley 1977, PhD, 1981. Career: designer National Iranian Oil Co., 1975; senior engring. aid, UC Berkeley 1977-81; supr. engring. Impell Corp., San Francisco 1981-84; principal/pres. Design Automation Systems Corp., Alameda 1984--; instr. UC ext. 1981; awards: Pahlavi Found. Fellowship 1976-81; mem: ASCE, ASME, ACM, Univ. Calif. Alumni Assns.; pres. micro-computer club Impell Corp. 1982-84; rec: skiing, swimming. Res: 1191 Vacation Dr Lafayette 94549 Ofc: Design Automation Systems Corp. 420 Central Ave, Ste. 210, Alameda 94501

KHAN, ISKANDAR, consulting engineering co. executive; b.Oct. 8, 1947, Peshawar, Pakistan, nat. 1978; s. Abdul Qadir and Esaf (Zai) K.; m. Ghazala Khanzada, May 27, 1981; edn: B.E., Univ. of Peshawar, 1968; M.A.Sc., Univ. of Toronto 1970. Career: staff engr. Woodward-Clude, Clifton, NJ 1970-73; project engr. Dames & Moore, Westwood, Los Angeles 1973-75; senior engr. Ertec Western, Long Beach 1975--; real estate investor, Calif., Ariz.; recipient Gold Medal and Pres. commendn., Govt. of Pakistan, 1968; mem: ASCE, Structural Engrs. Assn. of So. Calif., Soil & Foundation Engrs. Assn., Soc. for Marketing Profl. Services, Soc. of Am. Mil. Engrs.; author: Urta Lifafa (1960); rec: golf, tennis, ski. Res: 13751 Beach St Cerritos 90701 Ofc: Ertec Western, 3777 Long Beach Blvd Long Beach 90807

KHANNA, DAN M., manufacturing co. executive; b. June 11, 1946, New Delhi, India, nat. 1979; s. Late Din Dayal and Krishna Kumari (Puri) K.; m. Savita Bajaj, Dec. 1, 1976; 1 child: Pooja, b. 1978; edn: BS, Calif. Polytech. State Univ. 1972; MBA, Univ. Santa Clara 9179; Calif. (life) Comm. Coll. Instr. Cred. in bus. & indsl. mgmt., 1979. Career: indsl. engr., senior indsl. engr., supvr I.E., mgr. indsl. engring. Peterbilt Motors Co., Newark 1973-75; mfg. mgr. Cochran Western Corp., Div. of Western Gear, Salinas 1975-76; materials mgr, Computer Div. Rolm Corp., Santa Clara 1977-80; materials & MIS mgr. Altos Computers 1980-81; v.p. ops. Nestar Systems Inc., Palo Alto 1981-83; currently, bd. chmn./ pres. Cosmosys Internat. Inc., San Jose 1983--; dir. Murphy Computer Svcs., Gentech; tchr. acctg. Gavilan Coll.; mem: assoc. AIIE; Soc. of Mfg. Engrs.; Hindu. Res: 2895 Richgrove Ct San Jose 95148 Ofc: Cosmosys Internat., Inc., 1735 N 1st St, Ste 312, San Jose 95112

KHOSLA, VED MITTER, oral and maxillo-facial surgeon-educator; b. Jan 13, 1926, Nairobi, Kenya; s. Jagdish Rai and Tara V. Khosla; bro.-in-law, Dr. Aran Amar, Assoc. Prof. & Chief of Urology, Kaiser Hosp. & U.C. Med Center; L.D.S., Royal Coll. of Surgeons, Edinburgh 1950, F.D.S., 1958; L.D.S., Coll. of Dental Surgeons, Sask., Can., 1962; m. Santosh Chabra, Oct. 11, 1952; children: Ashok, b. 1956; Siddarth, b. 1962. Career: Pvt. Practice, Sask., Can., 1962-67, San Mateo, Ca., 1967--; Acting Asst. Prof. to Prof. of Oral Surgery & Chief, Oral & Maxillo-Facial Surgery, Univ. Calif. and San Francisco Gen. Hosp. Med. Center, 1967--, Oral Surgery Cons., San Quentin State Prison, 1968-, Dir., Postdoctoral Studies in Oral Surgery, Univ. Calif., 1968- Lectr. in Oral Surgery, VA Hosp., S.C., 1970-; mem. Post-doctoral Com. (Hosp. and Interns) 1968-; mem. S.F. Gen Hosp. Planning Com. 1968-; Lectr., Univ. of Pacific, 1971 . Bd. Examiners: Sr. Oral Surgery Students, Sr. Dental Hygiene Students, Postdoctoral students-Master's Candidates in Dental Surgery. Granted personal coat of arms by H.M. Queen Elizabeth II, 1959. Recipient Govt. of Kenya scholarship, 1945; Tchr. Award, UC Dental Sch. 1969; 1st Hon. Mention, photog., SAMAEATON Med Arts 1970, elected Fellow, American College of Dentists, 1982. Fellow: Royal Coll. of Surgeons (Edinburgh) Internat. Coll. Dentists, Internat. Coll. Applied Nutrition, Internat. Assn. Oral Surgeons, Royal Soc. Health, AAAS; Diplomate, Pan Am. Med. Assn.; mem. Brit., Am. Soc. Oral Surgeons: Can., Am., Calif. Dental Assns.; Am. Dental Soc. Anesthesiology, Am. Acad. Dental Radiology, N.Y. Acad. of Scis., Internat. Assn. Maxilliofacial Radiology, Omicron Kappa Upsilon, U.C. Sch. Dentistry Alumni Assn. Contbr. articles to profl. jours. Rec. gardening, photog. Res: 1525 Lakeview Dr., Hillsborough, CA 94010.

KHURI, WALID AFIF, surgeon; b. Aug. 1, 1942, Jerusalem, nat. 1978; s. Afif Salim and Marie J. (Da'Doush) K.; m. Paula Twigg, Oct. 28, 1953; children: Marie, b. 1974, Nadia, b. 1976, Afif, b. 1981; edn: BS, Am. Univ. of Beirut, 1962, MD, 1966. Career: physician Arabian American Oil Co., Dhabran, Saudi Arabia, 1966-68; surg. resident Berkshire Med. Ctr., Pittsfield, Mass. 1968-69, surg. res., chief res. W. Va. Univ. Med. Ctr., Morgantown, W.Va. 1969-73; chief of surg. Mattie Williams Hosp., Richlands, Va. 1973-79; surgeon/ adminstr. Palestine Hosp., Amman, Jordan (temp.); Fellow Am. Coll. of Surgeons (FACS) 1976; Fellow Internat. Coll. of Surgeons (FICS) 1977; mem. Virginia Surg. Soc., S.W. Va. Country Club; Episcopal; rec: golf, fishing. Address: 57 Stevenson Lane, Atherton 94025 (temp.) POB 460, Amman, Jordan

KIEFER, ROBERT HARRY, manufacturing/distributing co. executive; b. Apr. 25, 1945, Tonopah, Nev.; s. Martin Leon and Anne Alice (Abrahamson) K.; m. Nancy Resnick, June 19, 1966; children: Courtney, b. 1968, Reed, b. 1970, Tyler, b. 1974; edn: BA, Univ. of Minn. 1967. Career: advt. mgmt. trainee G.E. Co., Schenectady, NY 1968; v.p. mktg. comm., Alexander & Alexander, Mnpls. 1968-72; dir. mktg. comm., Minnetonka Inc., Minnetonka, Minn. 1972-75; pres. Direct Mktg. Svcs. Inc., Mnpls. 1975-80; pres. Vet Derm Products Inc., Mission Viejo, Ca. 1980--; Dir. Pilots Internat. Assn. 1970-72, Am. Businessmens Group Ins. Trust 1976-78; guest lectr. Univ. of Minn. 1970-75, mem. Journalism Curriculum Rev. Com. 1970-72. Awards: Outstanding Young Men of Am. 1975-83; Champion Paper Corp. 1983 graphics award; Mead Paper Corp. graphics awd. 1982;; best display, Veterinary Exhibitors Assn., 1980; awards, Midwest Mail Mktg. Assn. 1978, Direct Mktg. Assn. of Am. 1971, others. Mem: chpt. pres. Nat. Profl. Advt. Frat. 1967; v.p. Midwest Mail Mktg. Assn. 1970-2; Minn. Alumni Assn.; San Diego Direct Mktg. Club.; So. Cal. Direct Mktg. Club. Orgns: San Clemente CofC, S.C. Aquatic Team (pres. 1980), S.C. Ocean Festival (v.p. 1979), San Juan Cap. CofC (bd. dirs.), San Onofre Surfing Club, Hobie-spons. Ski Team (capt. 1982); publs:ep.; Jewish; rec: surf, ski, camping. Res: 31822 Paseo La Branza, San Juan Capistrano 92675 Ofc: Vet Derm Products Inc. 28321 Marguerite Pkwy, Ste. 201, Mission Viejo 92692

KIEHNE, ANNA M., accountant; b. Dec. 15, 1947, Dreston, Minn.; d. Alvin H. and Anna M. (Goldsmith) K.; edn: BA in bus. adm., Winona State Univ. 1969; CSU Los Angeles 1974-78; certs. Basic Petroleum Tech., ECA/Intercomp. 1981, Flexible Budgeting, NAA 1982. Career: acct. Murray Howard Realty, L.A. 1974-78; staff acct. Bowest Corp., La Jolla 1978-79; acctg. supr. Majestic Investment, Denver, Colo. 1979-81; adminstrv. acct./ofc. mgr. ECA/ Intercomp., Denver 1981-83; systems analyst Home Savings of Am., L.A.

1983--; listee: Who's Who in West 1984-85, Am. Biographical Inst. 1984; mem: Nat. Assn. of Accts., Nat. Assn. of Female Execs., Nat. Womens Polit. Caucus (newsletter ed. L.A. Metro chpt.); vol. Am. Heart Assn., Special Olympics, Am. Volksport Assn.; Election judge; Democrat; Lutheran; rec: hiking, x-c skiing. Res: 2445 E. Del Mar Pasadena 91107 Ofc: Home Savings of America, 3731 Wilshire Blvd Los Angeles 90010

KIERNEY, ROBERTA CATHERINE, lawyer; b. Jan. 22, 1941, Bayonne, NJ; d. Stephen V. and Alice C. (Angeli) Lignow; m. Carl E. Kierney, Mar. 3, 1962; children: Lynn, b. 1962, Philip,b. 1964, Christa, b. 1965, Jennifer, b. 1970; edn: Immaculata Coll. 1958-9; BA, math., Caldwell Coll. 962; grad. wk. (MPA), CSU Chico 1973-75; JD, Univ. of Pac. McGeorge Sch. of Law 1979; admitted to Calif. bar 1979. Career: law clk. Nev. Co. County Counsel's Ofc., Nev. City, Ca. 1978-79, Kenneth H. Leach, Penn Valley, Ca. 1979; atty./pres., Law Ofc. of Roberta C. Kierney, A Prof. Corp., Grass Valley 1979--; bd. dirs. Nev. Co. Domestic Violence Coalition, and Nev. Co. Legal Assistance Inc., 1980-81; mem: Am. Bar Assn. (Family Law, Gen. Practice, Real Prop. and Probate Sects.), Am. Trial Lawyers Assn., Calif. State Bar (Estate Plnng. & Probate, Family Law, Real Prop., Tax Law Sects.), Calif. Women Lawyers, Nev. Co. Bar Assn. (pres. 1982), Placer Co. Women Lawyers; del. State Bar of Calif. Conf. of Dels.; charter mem. Calif. Grand Jurors Assn.; Nev. Co. Grand Jury (foreman); Catholic. Res: 11693 Brunswick Pines Rd Grass Valley 95945 Law Office of Roberta C. Kierney, APC, 128 Glasson Way, Grass Valley 95945

KIESER, JAMES ARTHUR, contractor; b. Feb. 11, 1915, Wessington Springs, S.Dak.; s. William and Gretta L. (Brewer) K.; m. Hazel Wheeler Hall, Feb. 14, 1948; 1 dau: Sondra, b. 1941; edn: Dakota Wesleyan Univ. 1933-35. Career: self-empl., S.Dak. 1933-36; mgr. Singer sewing Machine Stores, Santa Barbara, Santa Monica, Pasadena 1939-50; owner/ pres. Atom Heating Co., a Calif. Corp. 1948--; bd. dirs. Los Angeles Inst. of Heating & Air Cond. (1968, 69, 70, Man of the Year 1969); mem. Calif. Lic. Contractors Assn.; Glendale CofC (Com. on Energy Conservation); Gateway Kiwanis, Glendale (pres. 1983-84); Self-Aid Wrkshp. for the Retarded; Hist. Soc. of Glendale; YWCA Adv. Council; Glendale Coord. Council (pres. 1981-82); Verdugo Club, Glendale; Elks (48 yrs); Mayor's Com. for Employment of the Handicapped; Democrat; Protestant; rec: travel, photog. Res: 1601 Arboles Dr Glendale 91207 Ofc: 4587 Brazil St Los Angeles 90039

KIESLING, ELIZABETH HEATH, speech and language pathologist; b. Apr. 22, 1951, Sacramento; d. Louis Alexander and Patricia Elizabeth (Heath) Kiesling; edn: BA, and MA, comm. disorders, Univ. of the Pacific, 1973, 74; Calif. Tchr. Cred. Speech and Language Splst.; lic. Bd. Med. Qual. Exams. in Sp. Pathol.; Cert. Clin. Competence, Am. Speech Lang. Hearing Assn. (ASHA) 1979. Career: speech and language splst., San Mateo County Schools, 1974--: classes for the deaf and severely hard of hearing, 1974-78; integrated severe disorders of language pgm., 1978--; mem: Calif. Speech, Lang. & Hearing Assn. (CSHA), ASHA, Vista Townhouses Assn. (bd. dirs.), Delta Delta Delta Sor. Alumnae (treas. 1982-4), S.F./Penin. Pacific Club (UOP alumni) founding bd. dirs. 1981-; Junior League of Palo Alto; Republican; Protestant; rec: sports, crafts, gardening. REs: 556 Vista Ave Palo Alto 94306 Ofc: Integrated Dysphasia Program, 65 Tower Rd, Rm 28, San Mateo 94402

KIESSIG, RUSSELL OWEN, executive; b. Dec. 14, 1932, San Francisco; s. Otto Charles and Netha D. (McCord) K.; m. Carol Hansen, Oct. 12, 1968; children: Richard, b. 1959; Stephanie, b. 1961; Priscilla, b. 1970; Randall, b. 1973; edn: BA, San Fracisco State 1957. Career: industrial sales and personnel wk. 1957-65; employment mgr. William Coleman PhD, Westwood 1966; mgr. indsl. rels. Litton Ind. Mellonics Div., Sunnyvale 1967-69; founder/ pres. Professional Resources Assocs. Inc. (profl. & tech. recruitment co.), Mt. View 1969-77; founder/ pres. Sycamore Mineral Springs Resort, Inc., San Luis Obispo 1975--; founder/ pres. San Juan Capistrano Hot Springs Resort Inc., San Juan Cap. 1979--; cons. profl. & exec. staffing; founding bd. mem. Internat. Soc. of Comml. Spa Operators; Republican; Protestant; rec: deep sea fishing. Res: 33701 Pequito Dana Point 92629 Ofc: San Juan Hot Springs, 35501 Ortega Hwy, POB 58, San Juan Capistrano 92693

KIEU, DAO QUANG, physician; b. Nov. 20, 1930, Vietnam, nat. 1982; s. Thuc Chi (dec.) and Ket Thi (Nguyen) K.; m. (Camxuan) Swan Nguyen, Dec. 31, 1957; 1 child: Anhthu, b. 1967; edn: P.C.B. (Physics, Chem., Biol.) Hanoi Faculty of Sci. 1952; MD, Saigon Med. Sch. 1959; Univ. of Ark. Med. Scis. 1975-78; Cert., Ark. State Med. Bd. 1978; Cert., Calif. Bd. Med. Qual. Assur. 1980. Career: med. practice, Vietnam 1959-75; physician Nat. Health Svc. Corps 1978-80; physician Los Angeles Unified Sch. Dist. 1980-81; physician South Health Ctr. of L.A. Co. 1981--; mem: Los Angeles Pediatric Soc.; Physicians Assn. of L.A. Co.; Am. Veneral Disease Assn.; Am. Acad. Family Physicians; Am. Occupational Med. Assn.; Buddhist. Res: 14533 Larch Ave Lawndale 90260 Ofc: South Health Center, 1522 E 102nd St Los Angeles 90002

KILBURN, KAYE HATCH, professor of medicine/educator; b. Sept. 20, 1931, Logan, Utah; d. H. Parley and Winona Hatch K.; m. Gerrie Griffin, Jun. 7, 1954; children: Ann Louise, b. 1958; Scott Kaye, b. 1961; Jean Marie, b. 1963; edn: BS, Univ. Utah, 1951; MD, Univ. Utah Coll. Med., 1954. Career: asst. prof. med. Washington Univ. Med. Sch., St Louis, Mo., 1960-62; assoc. prof. med./ chief med. serv. VA Hosp., Duke Durham, NC, 1962-69; prof. med. & dir. envir. med. Duke Univ. Med. Sch., Durham, NC, 1969-73; prof. med./assoc. prof. anat. Univ. Mo. Columbia, 1973-77; prof. med./prof. community med. Mt. Sinai Sch. Med., NY, NY, 1977-80.; mem. bd. Scienific Counsellors Div. of Cancer Prevention & Control Nat. Cancer Inst.; awards: Research Career Dev. Award, Nat. Inst. Environmental Health Sci., 1968; mem: Am. Pys. Soc.; Am. Soc. Path.; Am. Soc. Cell Biol.; Am. Thoracic Soc.; AAAS; Am. Heart Assn.; So. Soc. Clin. Invest.; Mid Western Soc. Clin. Invest.. Publs: 135 scientific papers, 1957--; mil: capt. US Army MC 1958-60; Democrat; Unitarian; rec: hunt., swim., travel. Res: 3250 Mesaloa Ln. Pasadena 91107. Ofc: USC Med. Sch., 2025 Zonal Ave. Los Angeles 90033

KILEY, DANIEL PATRICK, dentist; b. Aug. 11, 1951, San Fernando; s. John Francis and Patricia Elaine (Shrader) K.; m. Deborah Baranek, Nov. 30, 1974; 1 son: Matthew, b. 1979; edn: BS, cum laude, Univ. of San Francisco 1973; DDS, UCLA 1977; lic. to practice, Calif. 1977. Career: pvt. practice family dentistry 1977--; currently, pres. Daniel P. Kiley, DDS, Inc., La Verne; instr. basic cardiac life support, Gr. L.A. Affil. American Heart Assn.; honors: Regent Scholar, Univ. of Calif. 1973-77; Outstanding Young Men of Am. 1976; mem: Am. & Calif. Dental Assns.; Claremont Kiwanis (pres. 1983-84); La Verne CofC (Comm. Liaison chmn.); Univ. of S.F. (Pres.'s Ambassador 1980-); Republican; Catholic; rec: gourmet cooking, gardening. Res: 2670 Sweetbriar Dr Claremont 91711 Ofc: Daniel P. Kile, DDS, Inc., 2187 Foothill Blvd La Verne 91750

KILEY, MARY-LOUISE, psychiatric social worker; b. Apr. 10, 1952, Newton, Mass.; d. Edward Joseph and Louise Agnes (Daly) Kiley; m. Norman Eric Swanberg, Dec. 30, 1978; edn: BA, cum laude, Smith Coll. 1974; MSW, Boston Coll. Grad. Sch of Social Wrk 1977; L.C.S.W., Lic. Clin. Social Worker, 1980. Career: social wrkr Newton & Wellesley Nursing Home, Wellesley, Mass. 1975-6; adoption & foster care soc. wrkr Catholic Charities, Brockton, Mass. 1977-8; soc. wrkr. Catholic Soc. Svc., Los Angeles 1978-9; psychiatric soc. wrkr Family Health Program, Long Bch. 1979-81, Kaiser Permanente Dept. Psychosocial Svcs., La Mesa 1982--, self-employed businesswoman. Appearances on L.A. and Orange Co. radio talk shows, print media interviews, 1981. Mem: Acad. of Cert. Social Workrs, Nat. Assn. Social Workers; World Trade Assocs. Publs: art., Social Casework (2/77); bldr./owner w/husband geodesic dome home, 1982. Democrat. Catholic. Rec: racquetball, camping, sewing, aerobics. Res: 14815 High Valley Rd. Poway 92064 Ofc: Kaiser Permanente 8010 Parkwy Dr La Mesa 92041

KILLEBREW, MIRIAN CLAIRE (SHARPE), sales company president; b. Oct. 25, 1920, Indianapolis, IN; d. Randle Percy and Lucille Edith (Horton) Sharpe; mother's Casey family history, Samuel Clemens (Mark Twain); John Sharpe, paternal grandfather, one of three men to first discover Gold in Australia (mining engr.); AA, Placer Coll., (now Sierra Coll.), 1940; m. James Artell Killebrew, Sept. 14, 1940; children: Dorothy Jean, b. 1942; Deborah Jean, b. 1957. Career: v.p., K & H Sales, Inc., pres. 1946-76, 1976--. Mem.: Castro Valley chpt. No. 572, O.E.S., 1961; San Leandro CofC, 1950; Alta Mira Club, San Leandro, 1979; Oakland Museum Assn., 1978; All Saints Episcopal Ch., San Leandro, 1948; Natl. Right to Work Comm., 1974; BBB/Eastbay, exec. service, 1965; Natl. Fedn. of Independent Business, 15-yr. mem. Anglican-Episcopalian, treas., Alter Guild. Rec.: golf, needlepoint, reading. Res.: 18397 Magee Way, Castro Valley 94546; Office: K & H Sales Inc., 1800 Williams St., San Leandro 94577.

KILPATRICK, ALAN T., chartered life underwriter; b. Oct. 4, 1941, Los Angeles; s. Paul Wm. and Lillian Pauline (Jackson) K.; m. Jo Ann Kubasek, Apr. 6, 1968; children: Laura, b. 1972, Jason, b. 1979; edn: UC Berkeley 1959-62; BS, CSU Hayward 1970; CLU, Coll. of Life Underwriters 1969. Career: ins. agt. Mutual of Omaha, 1965-70; ins. agt. Allstate Ins. Co., 1970-73; ins. broker, Kilpatrick Insurance Agency, 1973-76; ins. broker/pres. C/K Ins. Agency, 1976--; acct. exec. Poulton Assocs., 1980--; finl. plnnr. Independent Financial Planners, 1976--; real estate inv. mgr. own co. 1971-; pres. Action Internat. (wholesale/retail distbn. co.) 1979--; gen. ptnr. Rental Properties Assocs. 1983--; mem: Internat. Assn. of Fin. Planners Inc., Ind. Insurance Agts. Assn., Oakland CofC (afil.); Small Yacht Racing Assn., commodore Venture 24/25 Fleet of No. Calif. (1984); mil: sp4 US Army 1966-67, Parachutist Badge, Vietnam Cmpgn., Viet. Svc., Nat. Def. medals; Republican (past pres. Oakland Young Repubs.); Congregational; rec: soccer coach, sailing, travel. Res: 806 Matadera Cir. Danville 94526 Ofc: Poulton Associates 140 Franklin St Oakland 94607

KIM, CHANG MIN, maintenance co. executive; b. Aug. 11, 1956, Seoul, Korea; s. Daw Jum and Young (Wha) Kim.; edn: Han Kook Univ. of Foreign Studies 1976; BA, UCLA 1983. Career: intern trade splst. Dept. of Comm. 1982; partner Rams Maintenance Co. 1980--; partner The Golden Fashion Emc., 1983--; field sanitarian, US Arm 1977-80; mem: Los Angeles CofC; Victory Presbyterian Ch., Dialogue, Korean Tutoral Proj.; publs: ed., Victor, Victory Presbyterian 1983; ed. Dialogue, UCLA Dialogue 1981, 82; mil: Spec. 4 US Amry 1977-80; Democrat; Presbyterian; rec: soccer, baseball, basketball. Res: 1341 S Hoover St, 5, Los Angeles 90006 Ofc: Golden Fashion/ Rams Maint., 939 S Broadway, Ste 306, Los Angeles 90015

KIM, HONG GI, obstetrician-gynecologist; b. Apr. 7, 1944, Nagoya, Japan; Korean, nat. 1945; s. Bong-Soo and Soon-Duk (Jang) K.; m. Hee Suk, Jan. 17, 1982; edn: MD, Med. Coll. of Yonsei Univ., Seoul, Korea 1971; bd. cert. Am. Board of Obstets. and Gynecol. 1982. Career: internship in gen. surgery, Huron Road Hosp., Cleveland, Ohio 1975-76; intern, resident in ob-gyn, Cook County Hosp., Chgo. 1976-80; med. staff Vallejo Gen. Hosp., Vallejo, Calif. 1981--, chmn. Dept. of Obstets. and Gynecol. 1982-; awards: Intern of the Year 1977, Cook County Hosp.; Phys. Recognition Award in CME, AMA 1982; mem: Am. Med. Assn., Calif. Med. Assn., Fellow Am. Coll. Ob.-Gyn.; mil: capt. Korean Army 1972-75; rec: tennis, golf, equestrian. Res: 320 Avian Dr. Vallejo 94590 Ofc: Hong Gi Kim, MD, Ob-Gyn, 1360 N. Camino Alto, Ste 206, Vallejo 94590

KIM, JUNG CHUL, business owner; b. Apr. 6, 1926, Seoul, Korea; nat. 1974; s. Ri Hyon and Do Hyon (Hong) K.; m. Jang Ho, Apr. 10, 1957; children: Yong Sung, b. 1958; Yong Rim, b. 1959; Yong Joo, b. 1961; Masters Degree, Gunkook Univ. 1959. Career: Katusa personnel ofcr. Korea Mil. Adv. Gp. (KMAG) 1963-68; camp mgr. Chulai Base, Philco Ford Corp. 1968-70; owner Meadowmaid Farms, Los Angeles 1974-79; owner, Long Beach Suzui, Long Beach 1979--; personnel mgmt., Adjutant Gen. Sch. 1959; honors: Master Achiev., US Suzuki Corp. 1982, 83; Achiev., Personnel Mgmt., KMAG 1963; mil: maj. Adjutant Gen. Corps; Presbyterian. Res: 7501 Los Trancos Cir La Palma 90623 Ofc: Long Beach Suzuki, 2441 Long Beach Blvd Long Beach 90806

KIM, KWANG EUN, acupuncturist/chiropractor/herbalist; b. Sept. 15, 1938, Seoul, Korea, nat. 1974; s. Ick Chae and Tan (Ock) K.; m. Kyung Sook Yoo, Jnue 17, 1966; children: Sion, b. 1967; Yale, b. 1969; Royle, b. 1975; edn: BA, Union Christian Coll., Seoul 1960; MA, Yonsei Univ., Seoul 1962; DC, Cleveland Chiropractic Coll. 1973; M.Herb., Emerson Coll. of Herbology 1981; PhD, cand., Donsbach Univ. 1982. Career: pvt. practice acupuncturist, chiropractor, herbalist, nutritionist; pres. Dr. Kwang Eun Kim, DC, Inc., Los Angeles; v.p. Korean Chiro. Assn. of US; pres. Korean Ch. Music Assn.; clin. asst. tchg. Cleveland Chiro. Coll., L.A. 1972-73; mem: Am. Chiro. Assn.; Found. for Chiro. Edn. & Research, USA; fellow, Research Council on Botanic Medicine, Can.; Am. Acupuncture Assn.; Am. Nutrition & Herbal Med. Assn.; Republican; Presbyterian; rec: pictures, coins, stamps. Res: 645 Hillcrest Ave, Flintridge 91011 Ofc: Dr. Kwang Eun Kim, DC, Inc. 252 S Oxford Ave Los Angeles 90004

KIM, STEVE SUNKI, financial analyst; b. Jan. 4, 1941, Seoul, Korea, nat. 1975; s. Eung N. and Ok (Kyong) K.; m. Seung Hee, Apr. 4, 1970; children: Michael, b. 1972, Christine, b. 1974, Austin, b. 1979; edn: LLB, Seoul Nat. Univ. 1964; BS, acctg., UC Los Angeles 1969; MBA, USC, 1974. Career: cost acctg. supr. Roberts Consol. Industry Div. Champion Internat. Corp., 1969-74; cost acctg. mgr. Lightolier, Inc., 1974-78; asst. controller, div. controller Internat. Foodservice, Div. Acton Foodservice Corp., 1978-82; fin. director/corp. controller Sparling Instrument Inc., El Monte 1982--; mem. Assn. of Corporate Controller; So. Baptist; rec: tennis, skiing. Res: 19731 Blythe St Canoga Park 91306 Ofc: Sparling Instrument Co. Inc. 4097 N. Temple City Blvd El Monte 91731

KIM, WON, acupuncturist; b. May 1, 1954, Seoul, Korea; s. Sun Kuk and Hyun Kyun (Shin) K.; edn: BA, Han Yang, Seoul 1976; BA, S.A.M.R.A. 1982; OMD, So. Baylor Univ. 1983. Career: acupuncture doctors asst., Gardena Acupuncture 1980; acupuncturist, Kyung Hee Acupuncture & Chiro. Gp., Los Angeles 1982--; volunteer acupuncture treatment for elderly in Korean Comm.; mem: Korean Artists Club (Calif.); Classical Guitarists Assn. (L.A.); mil: surgical doctors asst. Korean Army, Seoul, Korea 1978; Jae Il Korean-Am. Ch.; rec: oil painting, golf, classical guitar. Res: 16424 S Western Ave, 3, Gardena 902117 Ofc: Kyung Hee Acupuncture & Chiropractic Gp., 3115 W Olympic Blvd Los Angeles 90006

KIM, YOUNG HOON, lawyer; b. May 3, 1936, Seoul, Korea, nat. 1968; s. Hyung Ik and Soon Kil (Han) K.; m. Kang, June 13, 1982; 1 son: Eric, b. 1973; edn: BSCE, Univ. of Mich. 1960; MBA, Golden Gate Univ. 1974; JD, San Francisco Law Sch. 1978; Reg. Profl. Engr., Calif.; admitted to State Bar of Calif. Career: civil engr.: A. Benesch & Assoc., Chgo., Ill. 1960-67, US Army Corp. of Engrs. 1968, US Dept. of Navy, Ocean Eng., Vallejo 1969, San Francisco Port Commn., S.F. 1970, US Forest Svc., S.F. 1971, S.F. Pub. Utilities Commn. 1972, S.F. Municipal Railway 1974; currently, atty. at law, pvt. practice for Korean communities, S.F.; past dir. Multi Services Center for Koreans; cons./ advr. Korean churches, civic orgns. & svc. orgns. needing Korean spkg. atty.; mem: San Francisco & Calif. Bar Assns.; Am. Immigration Lawyers Assn.; ASCE (inactive); Mt. Diablo Pilots Assn.; Aircraft Owner & Pilots Assn.; Methodist; rec: flying, travel, photog. Res: 291 31st Ave San Francisco 94121 Ofc: Law Ofcs. of Y.H. Kim, 605 Market St, Ste 900, San Francisco 94105

KIM, YOUNG JOON, insurance agent; b. Nov. 22, 1945, Inchon, Korea, nat. 1981; s. Sok Young and Kyung Hee (Han) K.; m. Kath S., Oct. 5, 1974; children: Rachel, b. 1975; Sarah, b. 1977; Patrick, b. 1981; edn: BA, Han Kook Univ. of Foreign Studies 1970. Career: senior master agent Equitable Life Assurance Soc. of the US; honors: Agent of the Yr., Gen. Agents & Mgrs. Assn. of Orange Co.; Nat. DSF Leader, Equitable Life Assurance Soc. of US; mem: Nat. Assn. of Life Underwriters; Million Dollar Round Table; rec: golf. Res: 3288 Heatherfield Dr Hacienda Hght 91745 Ofc: The Equitable Life Assurance, 1055 N Main St, Ste 700, Santa Ana 92702

KIM, YUNG-TAE, physician; b. July 19, 1951, Seoul, Korea, nat. 1979; s. Chong-Suhl and Sun-Shon (Choe) K.; m. Jin-Soo, June 19, 1980; edn: AB, USC, 1974; MD, Georgetown Univ., 1978. Career: physician, obstet-gynecolog. practice, Northridge, Calif.; mem. Am. Med. Assn., Calif. Med. Assn., Jr. Fellow of Am. Coll. of Obstet. & Gynecolog.; rec: philately, photog. Res: 18556 Brasilia Dr Northridge 91326 Ofc: Yung-Tae Kim, MD, 8833 Reseda Blvd, Ste D, Northridge 91324

KIMME, ERNEST GODFREY, mathematician/engineer/co. president; b. June 7, 1929, Long Beach; s. Ernest G. and Lura E. (Dake) K.; m. Jeanne Bolen, Dec. 5, 1978; children (by previous marriage): Ernest G., b. 1954, Elizabeth E., b. 1956, Karl, b. 1967; edn: BA, magna cum laude, Pomona Coll. 1952; MA, Univ. of Minn. 1954, PhD, 1955. Career: grad. instr. Oregon St. Univ., 1955-57; tech. staff Bell Tel. Labs/Research, Murray Hills, N.J. 1957-65 (supr. Mobile

Radio Research, 1962-65); head applied scis., Collins Radio Co., Newport Beach, Ca. 1965-72; research engr. Northrop Electronics, Hawthorne 1972-74; mgr. GPS Devel. Pems, E.W. Dept., Interstate Electronics Corp., Anaheim 1974-79; tech. director, spl. communications pgms., Gould NSD, El Monte 1979-82; pres./chief scientist Cobit Inc., Anaheim 1982--; adj. prof. Pepperdine Univ. Ext., El Toro 1974-76; mem: Am. Math. Soc., Soc. for Ind. and Applied Math., IEEE (chmn. Saddleback subsect. 1977-8); num. research publs. (40) 1955-; Republican; Protestant; rec: music. Res./mail: 301 Starfire, Anaheim 92807 Ofc: Cobit Inc., 227 N. Sunset City of Industry 91744

KIMURA, HIROSHI, chemist; b. Dec. 20, 1927, Dallas, Tex.; s. Seizo and Chiyo (Nose) K.; m. Yoshiko, Mar. 12, 1957; children: Karen, b. 1958; Sharon, b. 1961; edn: BS, UCLA 1958. Career: senior engring. aid UCLA, 1957-59; mem. tech. staff Hughes Aircraft Co. 1959-61; sr. scientist Korad Corp. 1961-68; sect. head Hughes Aircraft Co. 1968--; honors: Sigma Xi Soc.; mem: Am. Crystal Growers Assn.; Japanese Applied Physics Soc.; Porter Valley Country Club; works: patents in crystal growth; num. publs. in sci. journs.; mil: cpl. US Army 9153-55; Democrat; rec: golf, tennis, music. Res: 19130 Pala Mesa Rd Northridge 91326 Ofc: Hughes Research Labs., 3011 Malibu Canyon Rd Malibu 90265

KINDLER, JUDITH MARIE, textile designer, manufacturer; b. Feb. 14, 1949, Buffalo, NY; d. Donald S. and Janet F. (Harbeck) Cornell; m. Christian Kindler, July 31, 1979; 1 dau. (step), Radha Kindler; edn: Fine Arts stu., Villa Maria Coll. 1968-69, Kent State Univ. 1969-70, CEU, UC Berkeley Ext. 1980, spl. courses, Canada Coll. 1981. Career: interior designer, 6 years; textile designer/mfr., 1982--, devel. line (over 90 designs) of hand painted fabrics for the home furnishings indus.; custom designer of fabrics for corporate design applications (Bell Tel. Co., Sitmar ocean cruise ships); rep. by Chalfonte St. Giles (San Francisco), The Kipp Collection (Los Angeles), Andre Matenciot Co. (NYC), and designer showrooms nat.; mem. Nat. Home Fashions League; rec: skiing. Ofc: Judith Kindler Textiles 118 King St San Francisco 94107

KING, BENJAMIN EARL (Tom), lawyer; b. July 10, 1929, Camden, Ark.; s. Ben E. and Henrietta (Weitzman) K.; edn: BS, Univ. of Ore. 1951; LLB, UCLA Sch. of Law 1956; admitted State Bar of Calif. (1957), US Supreme Ct., US Ct. of Appeals (9th Cir.), US Dist. Cts. (So., Central, No., Eastern dists. Calif.). Cert. Civil Trial Splst., Nat. Bd. of Trial Advocacy. Career: Deputy Attorney General, State of Calif. 1957-60; prin. law firm of Buchalter, Nemer, Fields, Chrystie & Younger, APC, Los Angeles 1963--; mem. L.A. County Commn. on Judicial Procedures 1975-78; Vol. Hearing Referee, State Bar Courts, 1978 ; lectr. Calif. Contg. Edn. of the Bar; Fellow Am. Coll. of Trial Lawyers 1982--; mem: Am. Bar Assn., Assn. of Bus. Trial Lawyers (bd. govs. 1983-, editor ABTL Report 1980-82), L.A. County Bar Assn. (edtl. bd. Bar Bull. 1966-71), Lawyers Advisory Council, Constnl. Rights Found. 1981-; articles in Am. Bar Assn. Jour., Calif. Lawyer, Los Angeles Lawyer, other profl. publs.; contbr. chapters in Calif. Condemnation Practice and Calif. Civil Procedure During Trial, (Calif. CEB); author: In the Shadow of the Giants-Mountain Ascents Past & Present (A.S.Barnes & Co. Inc. 1981); articles in Sport, Summit, Carte Blanche, Travel, Sir, Scholastic Coach, L.A. Times, Mainichi (Tokyo), Nippon Times (Tokyo), The Statesman (Calcutta), other publs.; clubs: American Alpine, L.A. Athletic; Democrat; Jewish; rec: skiing, mountaineering. Ofc: Buchalter, Nemer, Fields, Chrystie & Younger, APC, 700 S. Flower St, Ste 700, Los Angeles 90017

KING, CURTIS HOWARD, realty co. president; b. July 4,. 1949, Great Falls, Mont.; s. Robert Carl and Ione Marie (Randolph) K.; m. Sharon Ann Jones, July 30, 1977; children: Steven, b. 1983; Kristin, b. 1984; edn: BS, Cal Poly 1971, Secondary Tchg. Credential, 1972, MS, 1974; Calif. Real Estate Sales lic., 1978, R.E. Broker lic., 1981. Career: secondary tchr. Fairfield- Suisun Unif School Dist. 1972-79; sales agent Allstate Realtors, Vacaville 1978-80; pres. K & K, Inc., dba American West Realty 1981-- and Ashland Properties 1979--; counselor/ tchr. Am. Inst. for Foreign Study 1976-77; investment counseling/cons. Allstate Realtors 1978-80, Am. West Realty 1981-; honors: v.p. Fairfield-Suisun Unif. Tchrs. Assn. 1978; Salesman of the Yr., Allstate Reltors 1979, 80; mem: No. Solano Co. Bd. Realtors; Nat. & Calif. Assns. Realtors; Inst. Real Estate Mgmt.; Vacaville Cofc; Calif. Real Estate PAC; Issues Mobilization PAC; Democrat; Methodist; rec: pvt. pilot, skiing, travel. Res: 179 Cheyenne Dr Verties (Ste. C) 501 E Monte Vista Vacaville 95688

KING, (LILLIE) DALE, mining and water dowser; b. Aug. 13, 1904, Comanchie County, Tx.; d. Robert and Sabina (McRae) Johnson; m. Oscar Lloyd King, Sr. Aug. 13, 1921; children: Oscar L., Jr. b. 1922, Mae-Dale, b. 1924, Sabina, b. 1929; ed. public schs.; elec. engring. courses, UC Berkeley; art stu., Famous San Francisco Artists; soc. wk. trainee, Galveston. Career: jr. elec. engr. Kaiser Plant, Richmond, Ca. 1942-44; recreation dir., City of Richmond, 1945, Lafayette Grammar Sch., 1947-48; owner/opr. The Craft Shop (won two awards for Good Design, S.F. Mus. of Art), Lafayette 1949-53; instr. Acalanes Union Hi. Sch. Adult Edn., 1954-55; prin. Dale King's Studio (weaving, dress designing), Apple Valley 1957; opr. Apple Valley Inn Gift Shop, 1958; owner Tumbleweed Interiors (int. decor.), Apple Valley 1959-61; owner Designing Woman Shop, Hesperia (Ca.) Inn, 1962-64; soc. dir. Deep Creek Guest Ranch, Apple Valley 1965; owner/opr. Terri Lee Ranch (guest ranch, art ctr.), 1962-67; owner Dale Kings Mines (11 mines), prospecting the precious metals, 1958--, water dowsing (sev. water wells per mo. for desert homes) 1971--; mem. United Mining Councils of Am. Inc., Victor Valley Council; Cactus Wren Garden Club; Fed. Womens Club; Republican; Prot.; rec: prospecting, UFO contacts. Res: 21138 Kingsdale Rd, POB 1024, Apple Valley 92307

KING, DAVID WALSH, oil co. owner; b. Feb. 14, 1950, Staten Is., NY; s. Norman MacLeod, III and Mary Katherine (Walsh) K.; m. Beverly Ann, July 3, 1978; children: Lindsay Meagan, b. 1980; Travis Morgan, b. 1981; edn: AA, bus., San Francisco City Coll. 1977-79. Career: gp. claims supvr. Metropolitan Life Ins., San Franicsco 1970-79; acct. exec. Abe Oil, Inc., Newark 1979-81; owner King Oil Co. Hercules 1982--; mem: Am. Petroleum Re-Refiners; mil: sgt. E-5 US Army 1967-70, Vietnam; Protestant; rec: basketball, softball. Address: King Oil, 133 Bobolink Way Hercules 94547

KING, FRANKLIN W., lawyer; b. Aug. 8, 1942, Alexandria, La.; s. William F. and Helen Kathleen (Weaver) K.; edn: BA, Univ. of Ala. 1965; JD, Duke Univ. Law Sch. 1972. Career: law practice, San Francisco; listed Who's Who in American Law, 1980; mem: Am., Calif. Bar Assns.; Am., Calif. Trial Lawyers Assns.; Phi Delta Theta legal frat.; Phi Kappa Phi; mil: maj., Judge Advoc. Gen. USAF 1965-69, USAFR 1970-; rec: sports, music, theatre. Ofc: 12555 Post St, Ste 744, San Franciscoa 94109

KING, FREDERICK EARL, security-loss prevention executive; b. Sept. 21, 1925, Topeka, Ks.; s. Fredric Earl and Iva Dell (Smith) K.; m. JoAnn Perrilard, June 10, 1972; children: Michael, b. 1958; Robin, b. 1950; edn: police scis., East L.A. Coll. 1956, Apple Valley Jr. Coll. 1955-56, Mt. San Antonio Coll. 1956-63. Career: deputy sheriff, Los Angeles Co. 1955-59; dist. atty. Los Angeles Bureau of Investigations 1959-64; police cons. US Dept. of State Ofc. of Public Safety 1964-68; asst. sec. dir. Market Basket 1971-82; prin. King Security Consultant Svcs. 1982--: loss prevention mgr. Trak Auto, West Coast (1983), dir. of security ABC Mkt. Corp., Los Angeles 1983--; in service tng. advr., Vietnam Nat. Police 1956-57; awards: Medal of Merit, Vietnam 1957; mem: So. Calif. Robbery Assn.; Am. Soc. for Indsl. Security; L.A. Co. Peace Ofcrs. Assn.; Internat. Narcotic Enforcement Assn.; Internat. Assn. of Chiefs of Police; L.A. Co. Dist. Atty. Invest. Assn.; Palm Springs Police Ofcrs. Assn.; Calif. Assn. Lic. Investigators; Elks; Anaheim CofC; publs: state law enforcement publs. 1955-59; mil: GM 2/c USN, WWII, Korea; Democrat; Protestant;; rec: tennis, equestrian, photog. Res: 5022 Budlong St Anaheim 92807 Ofc: ABC Markets, 5318 S Main Los Angeles 90037

KING, GEORGE (H.S.H. Prince de Santorini, Count de Florina), Archbishop; b. Jan. 23, 1919, Wellington Shropshire, Eng.; s. George and Mary King; ed. Guisborough Public Sch., Eng.; m. H.S.H. Princess Monique Noppe, Jan. 30, 1971. Career: author 30 pub. books; lectr./tchr./broadcaster on religious subjects; prod./dir. num. 16mm docu. films and video-tape prodns.; prod. num. ednl. cassettes; founder/pres. The Aetherius Soc., (reg. by Fed. Govt. as a Relig., Sci., and Edn. Orgn.) and Metropolitan Archbishop The Aetherius Churches; founder/pres. Grand Magistry, Mystical Order of St. Peter (reg. UCCI); founder/pres. Coll. of Spiritual Scis., London, Eng.; mem. Supreme Council, The Sovereign Mil. Orthodox Dynastic Imperial Constaninian Order of St. Georges (reg. UCCI); prof. human rels., mem. North-West London Univ. Reg. of Adv. Consultants for schools and colls.; internat. adv. bd./ordained minister Internat. Evangelism Crusades Inc., Calif.; nat. adv. bd. Nat. Chaplains Assn. USA; mem. Confedn. of Chivalry, Eng.; recipient Peace Prize (1982), Intl. Evangelism Crusades Inc., Peace and Justice Awd. (1981), UCCI; num. chivalric titles and awards incl. Gold Medal for outstanding svc. to humanity, Imperial House of Byzantium; mil: Cabinet Minister Republic of Free Poland, Army Gen. Polish Armed Forces (in Exile); WWII Def. Medal (Brit), Cross of Merit w/ Swords (Poland), Internat. Acad. of Criminology (patron), Am. Fedn. of Police, Royal Nat. Lifeboat Instn. (Brit. Govt.), Nat. Rifle Assn., Calif. Rifle and Pistol Club; mem. Nat. Adv. Bd. Am. Security Council Found. Address: 6216 Afton Place Hollywood 90028

KING, MARTHA LOUISE, real estate broker; b. Aug. 5, 1915, Delaware, Ohio; d. Roy Henry and Charlotte May (Abrams) Braumiller; widow; children: Carl Anderson, b. 1934; Roger Anderson, b. 1938; Bonnie King, b. 1953; edn: Dr. C.J. McClaskey, Real Estate Law, Fla. 1967; Anthony R.E. Sch. 1969, 72; lic. R.E. Broker, Calif. 1972. Career: chief inspector Delo Screw Co., Delaware, Ohio 1943-46; charity work St. Justin CH., Santa Clara 1955-64; real estate sales, Land Brokers, Inc., Fern Park, Fla. 1968-69; real estate broker, own ofc., Martha King Realty, Calif. Hot Springs 1972--; mem: Orange Belt Bd. Realtors; Winter Park-Orlando Bd. Realtors; Poterville CofC; Calif. Hot Springs Elementary Sch. Bd.; Tulare Co. Hist. Soc.; publs: newsletter, Wood Chips and Pine Cones; Republican; Catholic; rec: music, nature. Res: Rt 4 Box 720, Oakwood Rd, California Hot Springs 93207 Ofc: Martha King Realty, Rt 4 Box 720, Mtn. 56 Rd, California Hot Springs 93207

KING, MAUREEN CAROLE VICTORIA, psychotherapist; b. Oct. 28, 1953, Los Angeles; d. Jerimiah and Elsie (Berman) King; edn: BA, UC Santa Barbara 1977; MA, honors, CSU Los Angeles 1979; doctl. pgm. Calif. Grad. Inst. 1980-; Calif. lic. MFCC, Marriage Family Child Counselor. Career: recreational therapist Children's Hosp. of L.A. 1979; senior staff clinician Wilshire West Sch., Santa Monica 1979--; psychotherapist pvt. practice; cons. Palmer Drug Abuse Program, and Cry Help; honors: Psi Chi; mem. Calif. Assn. of Marriage Family Therapist (West Side afil.), Am. Psychoanalytic Soc., Am. Psych. Assn., City of Hope; rec: equestrian, sailing, skiing. Res: 1640 Durango Ave Los Angeles 90035 Ofc: 3300 Castle Heights, Ste 3, Los Angeles 90034

KING, RICHARD B., executive; b. Aug. 25, 1917, Pierre, S.Dak.; s. Harry A. and Rhea (Gifford) K.; m. Elizabeth Ann, Dec. 19, 1982; children: Robert, b. 1942; Rebecca, b. 1941; edn: Long Beach Polytech. 1935. Career: owner King Printing Co., Long Beach; owner/ pres. graphics div. Crown Consultants; mem: Kiwanis, Long Beach; Nat. Assn. Accts. (pres. 1959, 60); Long Beach Aquarium Soc. (pres. 1950-51); Pacific Hosp. of Long Beach Found. (pres. 1983-84); Republican; Protestant; rec: sailing, fishing. Res: 666 E Ocean Blvd, 2504, Long Beach 90802 Ofc: King Printing Co., 2684 Dawson Ave Long Beach 90806

KING, ROBERT JACKSON, educator; b. Feb. 6, 1940, Madison, Wisc.; s. Joel Jackson and Dorothy (Wegoner) K.; m. Claire Colt, July 4, 1970; 1 dau. Angela b. 1974; edn: att. Central Mich. Univ. 1958/9, No. Mich. Univ. 1959/60; AB, CSU Chico 1965, MA in phys. edn., 1971. Career: tchr/coach Cordova High Sch., Rancho Cordova 1966-67, Mira Loma H.S., Sacramento 1967-82, Del Campo H.S., Fair Oaks 1982--; Sac-Joaquin Section chmn. Cross-country 1970-75, 1979-83; Capital Valley League chmn. Track & X-C, 1970-82; Capital Athletic League chmn. Track 1982, 83, 84; awards: Calif. State H.S. Cross-Country Coach of Year 1977; District 8 (6 western states) H.S. Coach of Year 1977; runner-up Nat. Coach of Year 1977; Sacto. Union X-C Coach of Year 1976, 77, 78; mem. Nat. X-C Coach of Year selection com. 1978. Mem: Calif. Tchrs. Assn., San Juan tchrs. Assn., Nat. Edn. Assn., Calif. Coaches Assn., Nat. Coaches Assn.; orgnzr./spons. Mira Loma Track Boosters and Del Campo Track Boosters orgns.; frequent spkr. sports clinics; mil: sp4 Army Nat. Guard 1963-69; rec: running, constrn. contr., auto repair. Res: 34 Meadowbrook Davis 95616 Ofc: Del Campo H.S. 4925 Dewey Dr Fair Oaks 95628

KING, ROSEMARY LOUISE, forecaster/dance instructor; b. Sept. 15, 1945, Pittsburgh, Pa.; d. Henry Forrest and Helen Louise (Polanosky) Kimble; m. Norman King, Aug. 17, 1968. Edn: BA, summa cum laude S.F. State Coll., 1973; MA, UC Berkeley, 1974; C Ph, 1977; Calif. Comm. Coll. teaching credential, 1977. Career: SF Ballet/Pacific Ballet, SF 1963-69; dance teacher Powell-Reilly Studios, SF 1971-73; dance/statistics instr. UC Berkeley, 1973-77; bio-statistician US Govt., Palo Alto, 1977-78; systems analyst Pacific Tele., SF 1978-82 (toll messag econometric); forecaster Pac. Bell, SF 1982--; dancer and dance tchr. Baptiste Ctr. of Yoga/Dance, 1983--. Awards: Florence Hale Stephenson Award, SFSU, 1973. Mem: Am. Assn. of Health, Phys. & Rec.; Nat. Assn. of Female Execs.; AAUW; United Way vol., Am. Cancer Soc. (team leader), SF Opera Guild; orig. research pub. Univ. of Mich. 1976.; Republican; Catholic; rec: needlework, gourmet cook., travel. Res: 123 Dellbrook Ave San Francisco 94131. Ofc: Pacific Bell, 116 New Montgomery St, Rm 220, San Francisco 94105

KINGSLEY, ROBERT, Court of Apeal Justice; b. Oct. 8, 1903, Cedar Falls, Iowa; s. Frank Åmos and Angeline (Van Niman) K.; m. Doris Field Forbes-Manson, June 12, 1937; m. 2d. Ninon M. Hogan, July 3, 1976; edn: AB, AM, Univ. of Minn., 1923; LLB, 1926; S.J.D., Harvard Univ. 1928. Career: instr. in law, Univ. of Minn., 1926-27; Thayer Fellow Harvard Law Sch. 1927-28; asst. prof. law, USC, 1928-30, prof. 1930-, vice dean Sch. of Law 1947-51, assoc. dean 1951-52, dean 1962-63; justic, Ct. of Appeal, 1963--; mem: past pes. Jr. CofC, Music Found., past pres. L.A. Music Guild, secty. L.A. Civic Light Opera Assn. 1948-; trustee L.A. Co. Bar Assn. 1963; Delta Theta Phi frat., University Club (L.A.), Nat. Lawyers Club (Wash DC); Congregational. Res: 231 S. Citrus Ave Los Angeles Ofc: 3580 Wilshire Blvd Los Angeles 90010

KINKADE, H. KEITH, antique dealer; b. Feb 21, 1929, Cromwell, Iowa; s. George and Mabel Grace (Blosser) K.; m. Evelyn Varsell, July 23, 1960; edn: BS, Drake Univ. 1950. Career: tchr. in San Jose, Calif. 1958-72; owner, Classic Antiques, San Jose 1972--; mem: Nat. Assn. Dealers in Antiques, Inc.; Antique Dealers Orgn. of No. Calif., Inc.; Am. Soc. of Appraisers (assoc.); Am. Cut Glass Assn.; Republican; Presbyterian; rec: cut glass, bridge. Res: 2655 Cottle Ave San Jose 95125 Ofc: Classic Antiques, 2210 Lincoln Ave San Jose 95125

KINNEY, JACK ALANSON, scientist; b. Sept. 11, 1921, Port Allegany, Pa.; s. Alanson M. and Hazel B. (Greer) K.; m. Shirley Davis, Nov. 10, 1953; children: J. Alleyn, b. 1946, Jothen S., b 1948; edn: MA, Univ. of Chgo. 1951. Career: Delinquency Prev. coordinator, Ill. Youth Commn., Rock Is. 1951-52; Employee utilization tech. Rock Is. Arsenal, 1952-53; head Personnel Res. Ofc. Ordnance Civilian Personnel Agcy., Rock Is. 1953-57; staff asst. to Chief Scientist, Army Resrch. Ofc., Durham, N.C. 1957-61; dir. Spec. Sys. Div. US Naval Personnel Resrch. Lab. Wash DC 1961-65; senior staff Inst. of Naval Studies,Center for Naval anal., Cambridge, Mass. 1965-66; supvsy. staff assoc. Arthur D. Little Inc., Cambridge, Mass. 1966-74; senior scientist Anacapa Scis. Inc., Santa Barbara 1974--; awards: Pres's. award, Arthur D. Little Inc. (1973), recogn. for outstanding performance, Australian Dept. of Bus. & Consumer Affairs (1979); mem: Internat. Assn. of Law Enforcement Intell. Analysts (v.p.), Internat. Assn. of Chiefs of Police, Acad. of Criminal Justice Scs., Assn. for Criminal Justice Research, Western & Pacific Assn. of Criminal Justice Educators, Am. Judicature Soc., Soc. of Police & Criminal Psychology, Am. Soc. of Criminology, Nat. Council on Crime & Delinquency, Federal Criminal Investigators Assn., Am. Soc. for Indsl. Security, Pilots Internat. Assn., Col. Confederate Air Force Ghost Squadron; publs: num. sci. papers, arts. profl. presentations worldwide (spec. fields of urban terrorism, internat. narcotics control, bank sec., personnel mgt.); mil: 1st lt. USAAF 1942-46, decorated Air Medal w/2 Oak Leaf clusters, Purple Heart, ETO 3 stars, ATO, Victory; Ind.; Prot.; rec: music, hist., golf, flying. Res: 5182 Vista Bahia Santa Barbara 93111 Ofc: Anacapa Sciences Inc., PO Drawer Q SBA 93102

KIRBY, JOHN CLAYTON, general management consultant; b. Jan. 13, 1945, Pittsburgh, Pa.; s. John C. and Virginia (Gillispie) K.; m. Carol Dubins, Mar. 17, 1983; edn: BS, and MS, Univ. of Pittsburgh, 1967, 68; MBA, Harvard Univ. 1970. Career: senior economist Standard Oil (Indiana), 1970-74; senior v.p. Management Analysis Center (Ca.) 1974-83; v.p. Towers, Perrin, Forster & Crosby/ Cresap, McCormick and Paget, Inc., 1983--; chief exec. ofcr. Plant & Field Service Corp., 1984; honors: MS Thesis presented SPE World Conf. 1970; Tenneco Fellowship, Harvard 1968; R.C. Baker Fellowship, Univ. of Pittsburgh

1967; 1981 US Internat. Skeet Shooting Champion; 1983 Invitation to Tryouts for 1984 Olympic Shooting Team, Intl. Skeet; mem: Soc. of Petroleum Engrs.; Harvard Club (Boston, NYC), Harvard Bus. Sch. Assn. (LA), Jonathan Club (LA), Town Hall of Calif. (LA); publs: 20 arts. and books on Internat. Fin., Corp. Strategy; Republican; Episcopal; rec: sailing, x-c skiing, biathlon athlete. Res: 105 N. Beachwood Dr Los Angeles 90004 Ofc: CMP, Inc. 1925 Century Park East, Ste. 1500, Los Angeles 90067

KIRIAZES, MARK LEONIDAS, data processing executive; b. Nov. 30, 1944, Chgo.; s. Marcos L. and Florence Therese (Weber) K.; m. Sandra Mullins, Dec. 28, 1963; 1 dau. Tammy, b. 1964; edn: BGS, Univ. of Nebr., Omaha 1975; Webster Coll. 1981-82. Career: capt. USAF, 1962--: Wing Missile Facilities instr., Little Rock AFB, Ark. 1965-69, Wing Evaluator, Missile Facilities 1970-71; computer ops. supr. HQ SAC, Offutt AFB, Nebr. 1971-75; non-commnd. ofcr. in chg. Base Data Automation, Lases Field, Azores, Portugal 1975-77; non-commnd. ofcr. in ch. SWCS Computer Tng., Offutt AFB, NE 1977-78; pgmmr./analyst Mission Essential Back-up NORAD, Colo. 1978-82; chief Data Automation Div. Castle AFB, Calif. 1982--; senor computer sci. and psych. instr. Big Bend Comm. Coll. Euro. Div., Portugal; listed Top Computer Exccs. in US, Applied Computer Research; mem. Pen and Sword Soc.; mil. decorations: Jt. Service Commendn. Medal, AF Commendn. Medal w. 2 Oak Leafs, others; Democrat; Catholic; rec: bird watching, hunting, camping. Res: 2270 Santa Cruz Dr Atwater 95301 Ofc: 93 BMS/AD, Castle AFB 95342

KIRK, CASSIUS LAMB, JR., lawyer, investor; b. June 8, 1929, Bozeman, Mont.; s. Cassius L. and Gertrude V. (McCarthy) K.; edn: AB, pol. sci., Stanford Univ. 1951; JD, UC Berkeley 1954. Career: assoc. law firm of Cooley, Godward, Castro, Huddleson & Tatum, San Francisco 1956-60; staff counsel business affairs, Stanford Univ. 1960-78; chief bus. ofcr., staff counsel, Menlo Sch. and Coll., Menlo Park 1978-81; pres. Elberli-Kirk Properties, Inc., Menlo Park 1981--; faculty, UC Santa Barbara Wkshop for Coll. Adminstrs. 1965-73; pres. Menlo Towers Assn., 1978-79, 82-83; mem. Palo Alto CofC (bd. dirs. 1968-70); mem. Calif. Bar, Order of the Coif, Phi Sigma Alpha, Phi Alpha Delta, Stanford Faculty Club; law rev. arts.; mil: sp3 US Army, Occ. Ger., GCM; Republican; rec: jogging, travel, opera. Address: Eberli-Kirk Properties Inc. 1330 University Dr, No. 52, Menlo Park 94025

KIRK, ROBERT ELMER, chiropractor; b. Aug. 18, 1945, Missoula, Mont.; s. Robert Hursy and June Loretta (Luse) K.; two sons: Thomas Allen, b. 1969, Wayne Donald, b. 1974; edn: eng. courses, Portland State Univ. 1963-4, 1968-9, premed. stu. 1971 2; DC, Los Angeles Coll. of Chiropractic 1976, Career, dr. of chiropractic, Dr. Keith Havet, Los Angeles 1976; dr./ofc. mgr. Burpee Chiro. Office, Santa Ana 1977; clin. faculty Los Angeles Coll. of Chiro., Glendale 1978-9; dr./owner Villa Marina Chiropractic Office, Marina Del Rey 1978--; honors: Sigma Chi Psi; appreciation, Boys and Girls Club of Venice, Venice CofC; mem: Los Angeles Coll. of Chiropractic Alumni Assn. (pres. 1978), Venice-Marina Rotary (dir. 1981, 84), Venice Boosters Assn./LAPD (vp 1982), Venice CofC (pres. 1982); mil: sgt. USAF 1964-68; Republican; Presbyterian; rec: theater, art. Res: 900 Cedar St, 305, El Segundo 19245 Villa Marina Chiropractic Ofc. 13450 Maxella Ave Marina Del Rey 90292

KIRKHAM, ROGER CRAIG, general contractor; b. Nov. 12, 1945, Los Angeles; s. Kenneth L. and Mary E. (Wilson) K.; children: Tracy, b. 1973; Toddi, b. 1974; Todd, b. 1977; edn: AS, in acctg., Oregon Tech. Inst. 1968, BS in bus. admin. Calif. St. Polytech. Coll. 1970; FAA lic. pvt. pilot; Calif. Contractors lic. 1975. Career: jr. acct. Weyerhauser Corp., Ore.; pres./ owner Insurance Repair, Insurance Interiors, Irvine 1970-81; currently, owner/ gen. contractor Kirkham-Anderson, Inc., Irvine; founder Liberty National Bank; awards: Contractor of the Yr., Nat. Assn. Remodelers Industry 1982; mem: Nat. Assn. of Remodelers Ind.; Toastmasters; YMCA; mil: 2nd lt. US Army; Protestant; rec: snow skiing, pvt. pilot, scuba diving. Res: 18162 Joshua Ln Santa Ana 92705 Ofc: Kirkham-Anderson, Inc., 17751 Mitchell Irvine 92714

KIRKLAND, BERTHA THERESA, asst. project engineer; b. May 16, 1916, San Francisco; d. Lawrence and Therese (Kanzler) Schmelzer; m. Thornton Crowns Kirkland, Jr. (dec. 1971), Dec. 27, 1937; children: Kathryn Elizabeth b. 1943, Francis Charles b. 1945. Career: supr. hospital operations, American Potash & Chemical Corp., Trona, 1953-54; office mgr. T.C. Kirkland, Electrical Contractor 1954-58; sec.treas., dir. T.C. Kirkland Inc., San Bernardino 1958-74; electrical estimator/engr. ADD-M Electric, Inc. San Bernardino 1972-83; vice pres. 1974-82; elec. estimator/engr. Corona Industrial Electric, Inc. Corona 1982-83; asst. project engineer Fischbach & Moore, Inc. Los Angeles 1984--; mem. Arrowhead Country Club; Episcopal. Res: 526 East Sonora St San Bernardino 92404 Ofc: Fischbach & Moore, Inc. 4690 Worth St Los Angeles 90063

KIRKORIAN, IRA, builder-developer; b. Oct. 11, 1910, Madera; s. Kosrof and Stella Kirkorian; m. Marguerite Haggard, Feb. 18, 1938; 1 son: Kent, b. 1938. Career: farmer, Fresno 1928-45; home builder, Fresno 1945-51; founder Kirkwood Village apt. complex, Kirkwood Plaza Auto & Shopping Ctr. and the Winchester Auto Ctr. in Campbell while building homes in Campbell, Los Gatos, Saratoga and San Jose 1951--; developed property (640 acres) into vineyard, Fresno 1973; purchased Barengo Vineyards, Lodi 1976; sold/ traded vincyards 1980-81 for shopping centers in Napa, Milpitas and Sunnyvale; purch. shopping center, Salinas 1982; currently, owner/ mgr. indsl., comml. and resdtl. properties; recipient num. awards for creativity, design and values, Parade of Homes (of Campbell, Co. of Santa Clara Supvrs. & Sanitation Dist.; Kiwanis; Rotary; Campbell CofC; City of Campbell Comml. & Indsl. Com.; Protestant; rec: golf, sport activities, travel. Res: 305 Norlene Way Grass

Valley 95945 Ofc: Ira Kirkorian, Builder Developer, 1820 W Campbell Ave Campbell 95008

KIRWAN, MARIANNE HIGENBOTTAM, stockbroker; b. Dec. 4, 1938, Edmonton, Alberta, Can.; d. Arthur and Kathleen Gwendolyn (Gough) Higenbottam; m. Kevin Kirwan, June 16, 1962; 1 son: Kevin, Jr. b. 1963; edn: Santa Monica Col. 1975-76. Career: stockbroker Dean Witter Reynolds, Beverly Hills; assoc. v.p. 1977--; dir. First Business Savings & Loan, Westchester; mem: Junior League of Los Angeles, The Beach Club; Republican; Episcopal. Res: 700 Kingman Ave Santa Monica 90402 Ofc: Dean Witter Reynolds, 9470 Wilshire Blvd Beverly Hills 90212

KISSLER, HAROLD B., JR., real estate management executive; b. Aug. 23, 1942, Seattle, Wash.; s. Harold Benjamin and Maxine A. (Clark) K.; m. Francine Tosi, Apr. 6, 1968; edn: BS, CSU Fresno 1968; Cert. Property Mgr., Inst. of R.E. Mgmt. Career: acct. exec. E.F. Hutton & Co., Fresno 1968-72; founder/prin. Manco West, Inc., Fresno 1972--, currently pres./bd. chmn./sole stockholder; mem. Fresno City Coll. Housing Mgmt. Adv. Com. 1983-84; mem: Nat. Assn. of Realtors (Inst. of R.E. Mgmt. bd. govs. 1984-87, San Joaquin Chpt. pres. 1978-80); Fresno Bd. of Realtors; Calif. Apartment Assn. Rental Housing Assn. of Central Calif.; Community Assns. Inst. 1975-; Internat. Council of Shopping Ctrs.; mem. Downtown Rotary, CSUF Alumni Assn., CSUF Bulldog Found., Fresno Zool. Soc., Fresno Co. and City CofC, Fresno Conv. Bur.; mil: E4 USAR 1966-72; Republican; rec: skiing, bus. devel. Res: 554 E Saginaw Fresno 93707 Ofc: Manco West Inc. 5424 N. Palm Ste 108, Fresno 93704

KITADA, SHINICHI, biochemist; b. Dec. 9, 1948, Osaka, Japan; s. Koichi and Asako (Seki) Kitada; edn: MD, Kyoto Univ., 1973, MS in biol. chem., UCLA, 1977, PhD in biol. chem, 1979; career: intern, Kyoto University Hosp. 1973-74; resident physician in Chest Disease Research Inst. 1974-75; research scholar, Lab. of Biomedical and Environmental Scis., UCLA, 1979--. Awards: Japan Soc. for the Promotion of Sci. Fellow 1975-76; Edna Lievre Fellow of Am. Cancer Soc. 1981-82. Mem. American Oil Chemists Soc., Sigma Xi, N.Y. Acad. of Scis. Publs: articles in profl. jours. Presbyterian; rec: swimming, tennis; res: 478 Landfair Ave. #5, Los Angeles 90024 ofc: Lab. of Biomedical and Environmental Scis, 900 Veteran Ave. Los Angeles 90024.

KITAY, JOYCE MARILYN, clinical social worker; b. Sept. 22, 1934, Los Angeles; d. Norman and Rose Ella Budne (Schlank) Roybark; m. Jerry Kitay, Dec. 24, 1965; children: Jill, b. 1969; Chad, b. 1971; edn: BS, UCLA 1957; MSW, USC 1961; MA, Pepperdine Univ. 1976; PhD, cand., US Internat. Univ.; Calif. LCSW (Lic. Clin. Soc. Wkr.), MFCC (Marriage, Family & Child Counselor). Career: soc. wkr./ soc. wrks. supvn. Calif. State Dept. of Mental Health 1961-66; social wkr. Jewish Family Svc., Long Beach 1966, Family Svc. of Whittier, Family Svc. of Los Angeles, Salvation Army Family Svc., 1966-78; currently, pvt. practice, Manhattan Beach; honors: pres. Psi Chi psychology stu. hon. soc., Pepperdine Univ. 1975; mem: Nat. Assn. of Soc. Wkrs., Fellow Soc. for Clinical Work; rec: water sports, guitar, travel. Ofc: 2100 Sepulveda, Ste 11, Manhattan Beach 90266

KITTLESON, HAROLD ALVER, electronic mfrs. representative; b. Jan. 9, 1912, Malta, Ill.; s. Elon Edwin and Anna Olena (Hobbet) K.; Great Uncle Ole Kittleson invented and patented barbed wire (1875); m. Ella Hartshorn, Apr. 5, 1941; 1 dau. Betty Ann (York) b. 1942; edn: tchr. cred. Iowa State Tchrs. Coll., Cedar Falls 1932; elec. engrg. Iowa State Coll., Ames 1934-38; cert. Microwave Engring., Cal. Tech., 1941; cert. USN Radar Sch., Phila. 1943; tech. & bus. courses, Lockheed Co., Sperry Electronic Corp. (NY), MIT, UCLA; bus. mgmt. certs., Stanford Univ., 1961-62. Career: wk. on family farm, Woden, Iowa, -1932; country school tchr., Iowa, 1932-34; resrch. asst., E.E., Iowa State Coll, 1936-39; chief elec. engr. American Pubs. supply, Lynn, Mass. 1939-40; hd. electronic test equip. engring. an design, Lockheed Aircraft, No. Hollywood, Ca. 1940-43; coordinating engr. AEW Proj., MIT Radiation Lab., Cambridge, Mass. 1944-45; founder/owner/pres. Kittleson Co. (electronic mfrs. rep), Los Angeles 1946--, Continental Components 1955-60; lectr. Lockheed Aircraft 1943; cons. No. Am. Phillips Co. 1957, Gen. Equip. Corp. 1958, Fairchild Recording Equip. Corp. 1960, Airtron 1965; recipient appreciation profl. orgns., Presbyn. Ch.; guest of honor sev. banquets; No. 1 Booth Choice (1000 exhibitors), WESCON Show and Conv. 1969. Mem: Internat. Platform Assn., Electronic Reps Assn. (pres. 1950), Mfrs. Agents Nat. Assn. (pres. 1955), Precision Measurement Assn. (charter, internat. pres. 1970-72), Meals for Millions Found (bd. trustees 1975-80); active in charity fundraising; publs: tech. reports, mkt. studies, book on family recollections (2 vols. completed); US patent applicant (1983); Republican (Election Bd.); Presbyterian (commnr. Gen. Assem.); rec: painting, cosmology, exptl. gardening. Address: 20315 Runnymede Canoga Park 91306

KIZER, KENNETH WAYNE, physician; b. May 28, 1951, Decatur, Ind.; s. Homer Martin and Ellen (Howland) K.; m. Suzanne A., Aug. 26, 1972; children: Kelly Christina, b. 1978, Kimberly Casey, b. 1980; edn: BS w.distinction, Stanford Univ. 1972; MD, w. honors, UCLA 1976, MPA, 1976; postgrad. tng. with USN and UC San Francisco; splty. tng. and certification in emergency med., toxicology, occupatnl. and preventive medicine, and diving and hyperbaric medicine. Career: var. jobs incl. fireman, lab. asst. during coll. years; diving med. ofcr., submarine squadron med. ofcr. and Group med. ofcr. Explosive Ordnance Disposal Gp. One, USN, 1977-80; pvt. practice emergency med. in Hawaii, 1978-80, Calif. 1980--, pres. Environmental and Emerg. Health Services Inc.; cons. Diving and Hyperbaric Med., 1980--; dir. Emergency Medical Services Authority, State of Calif. currently; frequent lectr. med.

meetings, symps.; honors: Navy League of US Nat. Sea Service Award (1980); finalist (nom. by Secty. of the Navy) 1980 Rockefellar Found. Public Service Awds.; DOD Humanitarian Service Medal; Outstanding Jr. Officer of Hawaii 1979, and Spl. Achieve. Awd., Navy League of US, Honolulu Council; AMA Phys. Recogn. awds.; Mosby Book Scholarship, UCLA 1976; Alpha Omega Alpha; SAR Citizenship Awd. 1968. Mem: Calif. Med. Assn.; Am. Coll. of Emerg. Phys.; Undersea Med. Soc. (pres. N.Pac. chpt. 1981-82); founding pres. Hawaii Undersea Med. Assn. (1978-80); Wilderness Med. Soc., San Mateo (founder, pres. 1984); Diving Control Bd., UCB (1980-); tech. adv. Fed. Fire Fighters of Calif., Sacto. (1983-); mil: USN 1976-77, lt. USNR; Republican; rec: scuba diving, swimming, hiking, racquet sports. Res: 10 San Benito Way Novato 94947 Ofc: Emergency Medical Services Authority 1600 9th St, Rm 400, Sacramento 95814

KJOSS-HANSEN, BENTE, executive health center director; b. Mar. 9, 1948, Tonsberg, Norway, nat. 1966; parents: Consul Arnold Mayer and Aase Francisca (Christensen) Kjos-Hansen; edn: BS, Univ. of Maine 1966; MS, Univ. of No. Colo. 1976; EdD, 1983. Career: asst. prof. Wash. State Univ., Pullman, Wash. 1976-78; asst. prof. Univ. of No. Colo., Greeley, Colo. 1978-80; instr. San Diego State Univ., 1980; stress seminars, Health & Fitness Pgm., Scripps Hosp. 1981-82; currently, dir. Ctr. for Executive Health, Scripps Meml. Hosp.; cons. cardiac equip., Havik Med. Gp. 1983; cons. preventive med. pgm. Megatex Corp. 1983; listed Who's Who in San Diego Women; mem: Heart in Industry (Am. Heart Assn.); No. Am. Soc. for Psychology of Sport & Physical Activity; Women in Bus.; ABIRA; Special Olympics vol.; works: the Executive Stress Monitor, a portable EKG device implemented for high stress individuals to monitor on the job response to stress; Lutheran; rec; skiing, tennis, dog training. Res: 10150 Campo Rd Spring Valley 92077 Ofc: Center for Executive Health, Scripps Hosp., 9834 Genesee, Ste 111, La Jolla 92037

KLAWE, WITOLD LUDWIG, biologist; b. Jun. 9, 1923, Piotrkow Trybunalski, 1961; s. Alfons and Anna Maria (Gampf) K.; m. Barbara Mary (Hillsdon), Jun. 13, 1955; 1 son: David Michael, b. 1960; edn: BA, Univ. Toronto, 1953, MA, 1955. Career: instr. dept. zoology Univ. Toronto, Canada, 1953-55; jr. scientist/ scientist/ senior scientist Inter-American Tropical Tuna Comm., 1955--; concurrently mem. of working groups, expert panel for facilitation of tuna research, FAO of the UN. Recipient var. scholastic awards, Univ. Toronto. Mem: Am. Inst. of Fishery Research Biologists, AAS. Publs: num. sci. publs. and books pertaining to fisheries for tuna, billfish and related species. Res: 6151 La Pintura Dr. La Jolla 92037. Ofc: Inter-American Tropical Tuna Commn., c/o Scripps Inst. Oceanogrphy La Jolla 92037

KLEIN, JACQUELINE SMOLINSKY, lawyer; b. Nov. 13, 1932, Detroit, Mich.; d. Henry J. and Tillie (Gottlieb) Smolinsky; m. 2d. Paul Drucker, June 27, 1978; children: David Alan, Deborah Carol, and Steven Jay Klein; edn: BA, Wayne St. Univ. 1954; JD, honors, Western State Univ. Coll. of Law 1975; admitted to Calif. State Bar 1975. Career: tchr. Detroit public schs. 1954-61; office adminstrn. in Calif. 1961-72; currently supervisory atty. Office of Hearings and Appeals (Soc. Security Adminstrn.), W. Los Angeles; spkr. civic groups, var. legal assns. on Soc. Sec. Disability evaluations; mem. Editl. Adv. Council, West Pub. Co. re soc. sec. publs.; honors: law rev. editor 1975; recogn. for outstanding contbns. in pro bono and low fee legal svcs., Calif. State Bar (1982), Bet Tzedek legal svcs. (1981, 82); mem. L.A. County Bar Assn. (Soc. Sec. Sect.), Calif. State Bar, Federal Bar Assn., Nat. Orgn. of S.S. Claimant's Reps., Pioneer Women, Hadassah; Jewish. Res: 8567 Clifton Way Beverly Hills 90211 Ofc: US Govt., Rm 8200, 11000 Wilshire Blvd Los Angeles 90024

KLEIN, LAWRENCE ROBERT, securities broker; b. May 27, 1938, NY, NY; s. George Samuel and Miriam Gertrude (Billig) K.; m. Joan Kramer, Sept. 17, 1960; children: Lisa, b. 1962; Amy, b. 1965; Randi, b. 1970; edn: MBA, Adelphi Univ. 1965; BA, NYU 1960; CFP, UCLA 1981; R.I.A., SEC. Career: Merrill Lynch Pierce Fenner & Smith 1960-80; Shearson American Express 1980-84; resident v.p. mgr. Bateman Eichler Hill Richards, Century City Ofc., 1984--; instr. UCLA Grad. Sch. of Business; honors: Instr. of the Yr. UCLA 1982; mem: Beverly Hills Mgrs. Assn.; Scottish Rite; Masons; Jewish; rec: working with handicapped. Res: 715 Arroyo Oaks Dr Westlake Village 91362 Ofc: Bateman Eichler Hill Richards, 1900 Ave of Stars Los Angeles 90067

KLEIN, PATRICK CARL, pharmacist; b. Feb. 17, 1947, Long Beach; s. Laverdes Peter and Marianne Martha (Kramer) K.; m. Kathleen, June 14, 1980; children: Emily Lavine, b. 1981; Andrew Patrick, b. 1983; edn: D.Pharm., Univ. of the Pacific 1973; reg. pharmacist, Calif. 1973. Career: with Payless Drug Store 1973--; staff pharmacist, Stockton 1973-78; chief pharmacist, Salinas 1978-82; chief pharamicst, Arroyo Grande 1982--; instr. short course Cuesta Coll. 1983; mem: San Luis Obispo Hospice (bd. dirs.); Central Coast Pharmaceutical Assn. (bd. dirs.); Salinas Valley Hospice (lectr.); Visiting Nurse Assn., Monterey Co. (pharm. cons., lectr., Profl. Affairs Com. mem.); Calif. Pharmaceutical Assn.; mil: s/sgt. USAF; Republican; Catholic; rec: fly fishing, cycling, jogging. Res: 151 Carmelde Ln Grover City 93433 Ofc: Payless Drug Store, 1400 Grand Ave Arroyo Grande 93420

KLEINBERG, JUDITH G., law professor, legal journalist; b. Jan. 28, 1946, Hartford, Conn.; d. Burleigh B. and Ruth (Leven) Greenberg; m. James P. Kleinberg, Aug. 30, 1970; children: Alexander, b. 1975, Lauren, b. 1977; edn: BA w. honors, Univ. of Mich. 1968, cert. (Fr. lit.) Alliance Francaise, Paris 1964; JD, UCB Boalt Hall Sch. of Law 1971, Boston Univ. Sch. of Law 1968-69; admitted to Calif. and Federal bars 1972. Career: press aide and speech writer State Sen. Milton Marks (S.F.), 1974; legal and consumer affairs TV reporter and docu. prod., 1974-76; pvt. practice, 1972-77; asst. prof. of law, adminstrn. and legal processes, Mills Coll., Oakland 1977--; freelance legal journalist and video documentary prod. (recent mini-docs appeared on syndicated public TV in Calif. for The Calif. Journal prod. in Sacto.); bd. dirs. (N.Calif.) Calif. Abortion Rights Action League; bd. trustees The Head-Royce Sch., Oakland; honors: Theta Sigma Phi (profl. women journalists hon.) 1968-; Am. Jurisprudence Awd., Contracts; assoc. ed. Calif. Law Rev. 1970-71; mem: State Bar of Calif. (Com. on Free Press and Fair Trial); S.F. Bar Assn.; AFTRA, 1974-; ACLU. Res: 30 Bay Tree Ln Berkeley 94708 Ofc: Mills College, Oakland 94613

KLEINE, MICHAEL PHILLIP, aerospace procurement supervisor; b. Apr. 4, 1950, Glendale; s. Irving Harry and Shirley Lee (Adler) K.; m. Barbara, May 20, 1978; edn: BA, philos., CSU Northridge 1972; JD, Loyola Law Sch., L.A. 1980; admitted to Calif. State Bar 1981, US Ct. of Appeals (9th Cir.), US Dist. Ct. (Central dist.), US Claims Ct., 1982. Career: supervisor, Materiel Procurement, Jet Propulsion Lab., Pasadena 1983--, senior contracts analyst, 1980-83; fmr. veteran's counselor, ofc. mgr., US Dept. of Justice, Wash DC 1975-80, (intern pgm.) contract splst/negotiator HQ Space Div., USAF, El Segundo 1978-80; instr. JPL course, Contract Mgmt., 1982-; honors: Ephebian Soc., Kiwanis Scholarship, Calif. State Scholarship, 1968; Newman Soc. Awd. 1972; mem: Nat. Contract Mgmt. Assn. (pres. San Gabriel Valley hpt. 1983-84), Federal Bar Assn., Pasadena Bar Assn.; mil: E4 US Army 1973-75, Nat. Defense Medal; rec: gardening, aerobics, running. Res: 521 La Mesa Place Pasadena 91103 Ofc: Calif. Inst. of Tech./Jet Propulsion Lab. 4800 Oak Grove Drive Mail Stop 511/406, Pasadena 91109

KLETZKY, OSCAR ALBERTO, physician; b. Dec. 6, 1936, Santa Fe, Argentina (nat. pending); s. Mauricio and Rose (Selzer) K.; m. Leonor R., Mar. 30, 1963; children: Claudia, b. 1964, Sigal, b. 1966, Ariel, b. 1971; edn: MD, Cordoba (Argentina) Univ., 1961; postgrad. OB-Gyn., Tel Aviv Univ. Med. Sch.; lic. MD in Argentina (1961), Israel (1964), Calif., USA (1976). Career: resident in OB-Gyn. Clinicas Hosp., Cordoba, Arg. 1961-62, Hasharon Hosp., Tel Aviv, Israel 1966-71; instr. Tel Aviv Univ. Med. Sch., 1971-72; Ford Found. Fellow in Reprod. Biol., USC Sch. of Medicine, LA County-USC Med. Ctr., Los Angeles 1972-75; asst. prof./ assoc./ prof. Dept. of Ob. and Gyn., USC Sch. of Medicine, Los Angeles 1974--, dir. Reproductive Endocrine Lab., USC 1976--; awards: Squibb Prize (2), Pacific Coast Fertility Soc. 1973, 1979; mem: Pac. Coast Fertility Soc., Soc. for Gynecol. Investigation, Am. Fertility Soc., Endocrine Soc., Am. Fedn. for Clin. Resrch.; publs: num. sci. and med. journal articles, reviews; reviewer for Am. J. of Obstets. and Gynecol., Contraception, Clin. Endocrinology and Metabolism, J. of Endocrinol. (Italy); mem. Am. Youth Soccer Assn.; mil: capt., phys., Israeli Army 1965; Jewish; rec: skiing, tennis, soccer. Res: 251 N. Rexford Dr Beverly Hills 90210 Ofc: Women's Hospital, 1240 N. Mission Rd, Rm L-1013, Los Angeles 90033

KLIMOSKI, DAVID BRUCE, personnel consultant, consulting chemical engineer; b. June 20, 1946, Denver, Colo.; s. Stephen and Helen W. (Schon) K.; m. Marilyn Simpson, Aug. 29, 1970; edn: BS chem. engrg. Univ. of Colo., Boulder 1968; grad. stu. Chem. Eng., UC Berkeley 1970-71; Reg. Chem. Engr., Calif. 1977; Employment Agcy. Lic., Calif. 1978. Career: design engr. Standard Oil Co. of Calif., S.F. 1968-73; sr. project engr. Procon, Inc. Div. Universal Oil Products, Walnut Creek 1977; sr. project engr. Enserv, Inc., Concord 1978; owner Professional Design Services, Consulting Engineer 1978--, and Concord Personnel Service, Placement Agency, 1978--; dir. Chief Equipment Corp., Denver, Colo.; recipient Community Service Award (Profl. Design Services), Peralta Comm. Coll. Dist., East Bay Skills Ctr., Oakland; mem: Instrument Soc. of Am., Am. Inst. of Chem. Engrs. (Sr. Mem.; No. Calif. Sect. mem. com.), Calf. Assn. of Personnel Consultants; mem. Concord CofC; Indus. Edn. Council Office support task force, Contra Costa County; adv. com. Engring. Aide Pgm., Regl. Occ. Pgm.; Central Contra Costa County Employer Adv. Group; Employ. Adv. Com. East Bay Skills Ctr., Oakland; rec: golf, swim. Ofc: Professional Design Services, 1820 Galindo St Ste 230, Concord 94520

KLOTZ, GEORGE CHRISTIAN, insurance agency president; b. Jan. 17, 1932, Yuma, Ariz.; s. George Dewey and Helen (Schmidt) K.; m. Elizabeth Mendosa, Jan. 19, 1955; children: Katy, b. 1955, Linda, b. 1958, Julie, b. 1961; edn: Riverside City Coll. 1950-51; Am. Coll. of Life Underwriters 1970-81. Career: ptnr. George Alexander Clothing, Banning 1955-59; owner George Klotz Used Cars, 1960-64; agent Lutheran Mutual Life Ins. Co., Waverly, Iowa 1964-, supr. 1968-, agency mgr. 1969-, pres. George Klotz Ins. Agency, Inc., Montclair, Ca. 1982--; recipient Top Mgr. Honors, Lutheran Mutual Life Ins. Co.; Citizen of the Year, City of Montclair, Calif.; mem. Nat. Assn. of Life Underwriters 1968-, Calif. Assn. of Life Underwriters (trustee 2 terms), Pomona Valley Life Underwriters (past pres.); past pres. Optimist Club; co-author book How to replace Social Security in the US; mil: E5 Sgt. US Army 1951-54; Republican; Lutheran; rec: travel. Res: 9784 Surrey Ave Montclair 91763 Ofc: George Klotz Insurance Agency Inc. 9625 Monte Vista Ave, Ste 108, Montclair 91763

KNELL, CHARLES ANDREW, lawyer; b. Oct. 11, 1941, Wash DC; s. Charles A. and Evelyn Joy (Riley) K.; m. Marcia Dion, Oct. 22, 1966; children: Nisa, b. 1967, Sarah, b. 1969, Nora, b. 1972; edn: BA, Carroll Coll. 1963; JD, Univ. of Mont. 1966; admitted to Mont. State Bar 1966, Calif. State Bar 1968. Career: estate tax atty. Internal Revenue Service, S.F. 1967-70; Ware & Fredenrich, 1970-71; Danaher, Gunn & Klynn, 1971-73; atty. Charles A. Knell Profl. Law Corp., Palo Alto 1973--; bd. dirs. El Camino Hosp.; bd. govs. El Camino Found.; bd. govs. El Camino Ins. Exchange; instr. real estate law, Foothill Coll., lectr. pvt. orgns.; mem. Calif., Santa Clara County and Palo Alto Bar Assns., Palo Alto Fin. Planning Forum, Internat. Common Law Soc. (bd. dirs.), Los Altos Kiwans (past pres.); bd. dirs. San Jos Diocese Cursillo

Secretariat; seminar spkr. 1970-, Nat. Signage Assn. conv. (1980); Democrat; Catholic; rec: racquetball. Res: 498 Azalea Way Los Altos 94022 Ofc: Charles A Knell PLC, 2 Palo Alto Sq, Ste 530, Palo Alto 94304

KNOPF, SUSAN MARIE, psychiatric social worker; b. Oct. 28, 1945, San Rafael; d. Gedge William and Catherine Marie (Jordan) K.; edn: Ab, UC Berkeley 1967; MS, Columbia Univ. Sch. of Soc. Work 1971; Calif. Comm. Coll. Instr. Credential 1978; LCSW, Calif. 1980; Acad. Cert. Soc. Wkrs., NASW 1981. Career: soc. wkr. Contra Costa Co. Soc. Svc. Dept. 1967-69; soc. svc. practitioner Marin Co. Dept. Pub. Soc. Svcs. 1971-72; soc. wkr./ pgm. dir. Trinity Sch. for Children, Ukiah 1973-80; psychiatric soc. wkr. Mendocino Co. Mental Health Svcs. 1980--; instr. Mendocino Comm. Coll. 1979, 81; ed. for content, book by Douglas W. Orr, MD and Nancy A. Adams, R.N. 1982; agcy. supvr. Student Field Experience, CSU Chico 75-80; honors: fellowships, Columbia Univ. 969-71; mem: Social Svcs. Union, AFL-CIO, Contra Costa Co. chpt.; Nat. Conf. on Soc. Welfare; Mendocino Co. Mental Health Assn.; NASW; Calif. Native Plant Soc. (charter mem. Sanhedrin chpt.); The Rural Inst., Ukiah; Democrat; Catholic; rec: swimming, cooking, travel. Res: 460 Todd Rd Ukiah 95482 Ofc: Mendocino County Mental Health Services, 564 S Dora Ukiah 95482

KNOX, ALAN ANTHONY, lawyer; b. Dec. 27, 1940, Orange; s. Joseph Allen and Marjorie (Campbell) K.; 1 dau. Melanie, b. 1973; edn: AB, Univ. of Redlands 1962; JD, Pepperdine Univ. 1970; admitted to Calif. State Bar 1972, US Dist. Ct. 1973. Career: title cons. to First American Title Ins. Co., Santa Ana 1964-70; mem. Debenture div., Perpetual Trustee Co., Ltd. Sydney, Australia 1971; assoc. Mitchell, Hart & Brisco, attys. at law, Santa Ana, Ca. 1972-74; pvt. practice 1974-77; mem./dir. Knox & Coombs, A Profl. Corp., Santa Ana 1977--; arbitrator Am. Arbitration Assn., lectr. Calif. Contg. Edn. of the Bar; mem: State Bar of Calif. (Real Prop. SEct.), Calif. Trial Lawyers Assn., Orange County Bar Assn. (chmn. Real Prop. Sect.1977); dir. Orange Comm. Service Cena4r, Inc. (non-profit child svcs. orgn. spons. Head Start, Day-Care and pre-sch. pgms. in El Modena); Elks; publs: contbr. Orange County Bar Jour. (1974), Real Prop. News (1980), Escrow Update (1982); Republican; Episcopal; rec: sailing. Ofc: Knox & Coombs APC, 888 N.Main St, Ste 905, Santa Ana 92701

KNOX, ELMER DALE, respiratory therapist; b. Jan. 15, 1948, Turlock; s. Jess D. and Velma (Denton) K.; m. Loretta Balentine, Nov. 29, 1969; children: Brandon, b. 1970; Jonathan, b. 1972; Certified Respiratory Therapy Tech., NBRC 1974. Career: respiratory therapy tech. Doctors Med. Ctr., Modesto 1972-75; supvr. respiratory therapy dept. Manteca Hosp., Manteca 1975--; area mgr. Cure Care, Inc., Modesto 1980--; awards: Volunteer of the Yr., Stanislaus-Toulumni Heart Assn. 1980; Bronze Svc. Awd., Calif. Heart Assn. 1983; mem; Calif. Soc. for Respiratory Care; Nat. Bd. for Respiratory Care; Am. Assn. for Respiratory Therapists; Am. Heart Assn.; mil: spec. 5/c US Army, medic; Democrat; rec: golf. Res: 1505 Sylvan Meadows Modesto 95355 Ofc: Cura Care, 1400 Lone Palm Ave Modesto 95355

KOBOSA-MUNRO, LYN ANN, mental health center administrator; b. Sept. 29, 1938, Pittsburgh, Pa.; d. John Joseph and Madeleine (Hillgrove) Munro; m. David Kobosa, May 30, 1975; children: Allison, and Erica Sedey; edn: BS, Univ. of Pittsburgh 1960; Univ. Mich. 1963-64; MSW, USC 1973; Calif. lic. MFCC (marriage family child counselor), LCSW (lic. clin. social wkr.). Career: family therapist Family Service Yspsilanti, Mich. 1963-64; counselor Planned Parenthood, Los Angeles 1972-73; adoptions wkr., County of Los Angeles 1973; adminstr. Hathaway Childrens Svcs, Lake View Terrace 1973--; cons. Valley Village Group Homes for the Developmentally Disabled, L.A. 1978-81; honors: Phi Beta Kappa, Mortar Bd., Coll. Hall of Fame (1960), Univ. Mich. Fellowship 1962; mem: bd. dirs. Rappline (adolescent hot line) 1970-74; Soc. of Archtl. Historians 1981-; Los Angeles Conservency 1980-; Nat. Assn. of Soc. Wkrs.; L.A. Dance Alliance, So. Cal. Clogging Assn.; publs: Sexuality in the Aging Woman, Health and Soc. Work (11/77); Unitarian; rec: Appalacian Mtn. dance: clogging. Res: 16750 Parthenia St Sepulveda 91343 Ofc: Hathaway 11600 Eldridge Ave, Ste. 200A Lake View Terrace 91342

KOCH, JACK ANTHONY, podiatrist; b. June 30, 1950, Chgo.; s. Henry Carl and Genevieve Josephine (Klimek) K.; edn: AS, Harper Coll. 1970; BA, Univ. of Wisc., Eau Claire 1973; DPM, Ill. Coll. of Podiatric med. 1978; grad. pgm. (MBA), Pepperdine Univ. 1983-; Lic. Podiatrist, Calif 1978. Career: podiatrist, pvt. practice, Los Angeles 1983--; mem: Am., Calif. & L.A. Co. Podiatry Assns.; Sierra Club; rec: skiing, travel, photog. Res: 216 S Hamilton Dr B, Beverly Hills 90211 Ofc: 321 N Larchmont Blvd, Ste 524, Los Angeles 90004

KOCH, LEON HENRY, building contractor; b. April 7, 1906, Oowgiac, Mich.; s. Henry F. W. and Minnie (Stahl) K.; m. Margaret Alfield Fredricksen, Dec. 31, 1934; children: Ivan, Clinton, June, Earl, David, Neil, Robert; edn: business courses, Santa Rosa Jr. Coll.; Calif. Gen. Building Contr. B-1 Lic. 39332. Career: with Ellis Ahlstrom building contractor, Santa Rosa, 1927-29; self empl. building trades, 1929--; bldr. residences, comml. bldgs., subdivs., country estate of Wilshire Heights, Santa Rosa; Army and Navy Base wk. for Radich & Brown, var. other contractors, WWII, 1941-44; recipient Santa Rosa Chamber of Commerce Award past pres. General Contractors, S.R., 1948-49; mem. Elks; mil: cadet 1920-22; Ch. of Christ. Address: L. Henry Koch, 527 Grant St Vallejo 94590

KOECKRITZ, ANN ELIZABETH, nursing home administrator; b. Mar. 26, 1945, Swan River, Manitoba, Can., nat. 1974; d. David and Lydia (Krause) Lausman; m. Karl Koeckritz, Dec. 11, 1965; children: Mark, b. 1966; Scott, b. 1971; edn: cosmetol., Lapin Bros. Schs. of Beauty, Inc. 1966; No. Orange Co. Comm. Coll. 1980; nsg. home adminstr., Adminstrs. in Training Pgm. 1981; Preceptor, Nsg. Home Adminstr. field. Career: cosmetologist Mirada Hills Beauty Salon, La Mirada 1972; purchasing agent Miraga Hills Convalescent Hosp., La Mirada 1975; ofc. supvr. computer sys. tech. Sunhaven Conv. Hosp., Fullerton 1979, activity leader 1980, asst. adminstr. 1981, admintstr. 1982; adminstr. Huntington Drive Conv. Hosp., Arcadia 1983--; honors: cosmetology, Adv. Student and Student of Yr. Trophy; mem: Haskell Jr. High and Gahr H.S. PTAs. Res: 11009 Gonsalves Pl Cerritos 90701 Ofc: Huntington Drive Conv. Hospital, 400 W Huntington Dr Arcadia 91006

KOEHLER, LLOYD K., regional personnel executive; b. Dec. 30, 1942, Spring Valley, Ill.; s. Lloyd F. and Martha Pauline (Campbell) K.; div.; children: Chuck, b. 1960, Scott, b. 1963, Kristy, b. 1972; edn: BA, psych., Univ. of So. Fla. 1968. Career: counselor Youth Opportunity Center, St. Petersburg, Fla. 1964-69; personel rep., then Equal Empl. Opp. coordinator GTE Data Services, Tampa, Fla. 1969-73; div. personnel supr. Eckerd Drugs Inc., Clearwater, Fla. 1973-75; pers. mgr. Gulfstar Yachts Inc., St. Pete., 1975-79; pers. mgr. United Div. of Howmedica (Pfizer Inc), Largo, Fla. 1979-81; regional pers. mgr. Pfizer Inc., Lucerne Valley, Ca. 1981--; honors: Equal Emply. Opportunity Award, Tampa Urban League (1972, 73), mem. Com. of 100, Pinellas County, Fla. (1980, 81); dir. Lakewood Jr. Spartans Youth Football 1972-77 (pres.'s awd. 1972, 73); vol. youth sports: baseball, football, track and field; Republican; Presbyterian; rec: sports, phys. fitness. Res: 20012 Talihina Rd Apple Valley 92307 Ofc: Pfizer Inc., POB 558, Lucerne Valley 92356

KOEHN, SAMUEL PETER, real estate broker-developer; b. Nov. 13, 1953, Merced, Ca.; s. Samuel C. and Ida V. (McCollum) K.; m. Dr. Mary L. Coelho, June 11, 1983; edn: Bach. Urban Geog., CSU San Jose 1975, Masters, 1980; grad. bus. adm. pgm., CSU Fresno, currently; Calif. lic. Real Estate Broker 1981, Gen. Building Contractor 1982. Career: engineering assoc., asst. city plnnr., City of Atwater, 1977-79; assoc. plnnr., acting plnng. dir., City of Madera, 1980-84; bldg. constrn. and real estate bus. owner, Northwest Development Co., Madera; co-owner Can Am Devel. Co.; guest spkr. var. service clubs, profl. assns.; honors: Sigma Iota Epsilon (bus. hon.); mem: Nat. Assn. of Realtors, Calif. Assn. of Realtors, Monterey Co. Bd. of Realtors, Soc. of Calif.Accts., Am. Planning Assn., Calif. Inst. of Technology Transfer; Ex-officio mem. City of Atwood Plnng. Commn., 1978-79, City of MaderaPlnng. Commn. 1982-83; publs: Calif. Environmental Quality Act: A tool for geographic planning (1979); Republican; Catholic; rec: sailing, skiing. Res: 310 Spencer Monterey 93940 Ofc: 1252 West 21 Street Merced 95340

KOELZER, KATHLEEN WINTER, group travel consultant; b. Apr. 16, 1946, San Jose, Ca.; d. Lloyd C. "Bud" (US Olympic coach) and Helen (Delatour) Winter; m. William Koelzer, Dec. 17, 1982; edn: BA, UC Los Angeles 1968; spl. courses, Univ. of S.F. Guadalajara, Univ. of Mexico City, 1966; cert., Cruise Lines Internat. Assn. 1978. Career: flight attendant World Airways, Oakland, Ca. 1968-71; sales rep. (first woman to hold pos.) World Airways, 1971-74; co-founder Char-Tours, San Francisco, 1974; founder/owner Travel Education, Inc., Seattle, Wash. 1975; founder/pres./bd. chmn. Travel Reps., Inc., Santa Ana 1977--; awards: Princess Cruise lines Top 100 (1977-83), US Del. to China Internat. Tourism Conf. (3/83); mem: Pacific Area Travel Assn., Cruise Lines Internat. Assn.; bd. dirs. Loving Kindness (direct food relief gp.) 1983-84; Western states briefing mgr. The Hunger Project, 1982; bd. mem. Orange Co. Holiday Project 1981; author: The China Fact Book (1978); Democrat; rec: travel, jogging. Res: 620 9th St Huntington Beach 92648 Ofc: Travel Reps. Inc. 435 S. Broadway, Santa Ana 92701

KOELZER, WILLIAM, marketing consultant; b. May 25, 1942, Lansing, Mich.; s. Charles Robert and Lois Audrey (Young) K.; m. Kathleen Winter, Dec. 17, 1982; children (by prev. marriage): Jacqueline, b. 1967, Shelley, b. 1972; edn: AA, Orange Coast Coll. 1965; BA in journ., CSU San Jose 1968; desig: APR, Accredited Counselor, Public Rels. Soc. of Am. 1974. Career: editor,Mich. Out-of-Doors, Lansing, 1968, Otsego County Herald Times, Gaylord, Mich., 1968-69, Mich. North, 1968-69; v.p. Cochrane Chase, Livingston & Co., Inc. 1969-75; pres. Gold Rush Ice Cream Co., Arcata, Ca. 1977-78; v.p. Basso & Assocs., Newport Beach 1979-80; pres. Koelzer & Assoc., Irvine 1980-83; exec. v.p./owner Travel Reps., Inc., Santa Ana 1983--; US Del. to First China Internat. Tourism Conf., 1983; bd. dirs. Pilot Rock, Inc., Arcata 1978; past bd. dirs. Arcata CofC; awards: Top mktg. award 1975, L.A. chpt. Pub. Rels. Soc. of Am., Orange Co. Chpt. PRSA Top Awards (2), 1982; campaign mgr. Hank Appleton for Humboldt County Supr. (1976); regl. promo. dir. The Hunger Proj.-W. 1982; mem. Lew Epsteins Newport Beach Men's Club; author: Scuba Diving: How To Get Started (1976); senior editor, Marketing Problem Solver (1973); mil: E5 USNR 1961-63; Democrat; rec: scuba diving, writing novels, travel. Res: 620 9th St Huntington Beach 92648 Ofc: Travel Reps Inc. 435 S. Broadway Santa Ana 92701

KOENIG, FREDERICK P., engineering co. executive; b. Dec. 12, 1909, Cincinnati, Ohio; s. Gustave and Julia (Christian) K.; m. Teresita Jimenez, Oct. 15, 1977; 1 dau: Teresa E., b. 1949; edn: BS, UC Berkeley 1940; Reg. Mech. Engr., Calif. Career: welding engr. Consolidated Corp. Ship Bldg. Div., Wilmington Div. 1942-45; chief engr. Pacific Valve & Pump Co. 1945-48; welding engr. Paramount Steel Corp., Paramount 1949-52; cons. engr., Long Beach 1952-54; pres. Koenig Controls & Equip. Co., Long Beach 1954-68; pres. & CEO Koenig Eng. & Equip. Co., Long Beach 1968--; mem: Pacific Enrgy Assn.; So. Calif. Meter Assn.; Long Beach Art Assn. (pres. 1968-69); inventor/mfr. Koenig Liquid Discharge Vessel, used in USA and fgn. countries in natural gas process & refineries 1958--; Republican; Lutheran; rec: design equipment. Res: 23661

Algiers Mission Viejo 92691 Ofc: Koenig Engineering & Equipment Co., POB 2637, Mission Viejo 92690

KOFFORD, CREE-L, lawyer; b. July 11, 1933, Santaquin, Utah; s. Cree C. and Melba N. (Nelson) K.; m. Ila Jean Macdonald, Sept. 11, 1953; children: Kim, b. 1954; Janes, b. 1957; Bradley, b. 1962; Quinn, b. 1965; Tracy, b. 1966; edn: BS, Univ. of Utah 1955; JD, USC 1961. Career: partner Munns and Kofford, San Marino 1962-68; mng. partner Munns, Kofford, Hoffman, Hunt & Throckmorton, Pasadena 1969--; frequent spkr. liability related topics, var. engrg. socs. & constrn. indus. convs.; recipient appreciation certs: Constrn. Consultants Bd. of Ch. of Jesus Christ of Latter-day Saints, 1981; Am. Soc. of Plumbing Engrs.; Refrigeration Svc. Engrs. Soc.; mem: Boy Scouts of Am., San Gabriel Valley Council; Am. (constrn. ind. sect.), Calif. & L.A. Co. Bar Assns.; University Club; publs: num. arts. in profl. journs.; reg. contbr. under title "Legal Briefing," Plumbing Engineer pub. by Am. Soc. of Plumbing Engrs. 1973-; "Real Estate and the New Tax Law," pub. in the Real Estate Mkt. Advr. 1982; Republican; Ch. of Jesus Christ of Latter-day Saints; rec: equestrian. Res: 1330 Rodeo Rd Arcadia 91006 Ofc: Munns, Kofford, Hoffman, Hunt & Throckmorton, 199 N Lake, Ste 300, Pasadena 91101

KOHAN-MATLICK, JOHN PAUL, video co. owner; b. Dec.11, 1945, Seattle, Wash.; s. Benjamin Maurice and Lillian (Warrener) Matlick; m. Felisa Kohan, Nov. 6, 1980; children: Zebedee, b. 1972, Zoelinda, b. 1971, Michelle, b. 1969, David, b. 1969; edn: Univ. of Wash. 1964-67. Career: photojournalist Toronto Star Weekly, MacLaine's Mag. Toronto, Can. 1967-69; prod. "Kent State--Student View" and "Nerve Gas Unnerves", for Nat. Edn. TV, SEattle, Wash. 1968-69; cinematographer "Doors in Concert", Toronto 1969; owner/mgr. Universal Color Labs, Palo Alto 1970-73; spl. projects mgr. Spiritual Sky Scented Products, Culver City 1974-76; creator of spl. effects Amicus Prodns., Hollywood 1976-77; owner/pres./dir. of photog., Video-It, Inc., Hollywood 1978--; dir. of photog. on the West Coast for "Lifestyles of the Rich and Famous" (syn. weekly TV pgm.); awards: ITVA First Place Award for Point of Sales VideoProgram, 1982; rewarded for conducting ind. investigation of corruption at Royal Canadian Mint, worked with Gen. Intell. SEct./Internal Affairs of the Royal Can. Mounted Police, 1969-70; mem: ITVA; Assn. Multi-Images Internat.; Hollywood CofC; works: co-inventor process of printing both slides & prints from a universal color negative film (1970); invented single tube film processor for proc. up to 36 rolls of 35mm film at once (1973); silver-tubing cutting machine (1974); alcohol-free process of mfg. incense (1975); redesigned an $80,000 Flat Pack Machine (1976); invented "Star Wars" wand (1976); pioneered devel. of 3/4" video prodn. as a bdcst. medium (1978-84); designed rear screen projection sys. for transf. slides to videotape with movement and spl. effects (1979); Intl. Soc. Krishna Consciousness, Judaism; rec: coins/stamps, orchid care, travel. Res: 10750 Franklin Ave Culver City 90230 Ofc: 1016 N. Sycamore Ave Hollywood 90038

KOHLENBERGER, STEPHEN MICHAEL, design co. president; b. Mar. 30, 1956, Orange; s. David Wesley and Charmian (Cavaghan) K.; edn: stu. Fullerton Coll., CSU Fullerton, Saddleback Coll., Orange Coast Coll. Career: electronic tech., Century Data, Anaheim 1972-74; var. pos. with CSU Fullerton 1974-78, incl. asst. sys. mgr. Computer Center, hd. cons. Quantitative Methods Dept., proj. coord. Mktg. Dept.; systems coord./pgmmr. Byte Shop, Placentia 1977-78; chief tech. UMI, Anaheim 1979-80; dir. engring. Xymec Inc., Irvine 1980-81; pres. Kohlenberger Designs, Tustin 1979--; software publisher; Automobile market simulation pgm., author of microcomputer op. sys. and coauthor of 2d. microcomputer op. sys.; designed electronic multiplexor now mfd. in Japan; designed 2 electronic printers; created pgm. to link largest Hard Disk drive currently avail. to IBM Pers. Computer; mem: Assn. for Computing Machinery, IEEE; Irvine CofC, Orange County CofC; rec: philosophy, computers, electronics. Res: 13841 Tustin East Dr, 223, Tustin Ofc: Kohlenberger Designs, POB 2237 Orange 92669

KOHRS, CHRISTOPHER MARTIN, psychotherapist; b. Aug. 3, 1944, Berkeley; s. Lewis Paul and Charlotte (Irwin) K.; m. Nancy Lombardi, July 14, 1980; edn: AB, psych., CSU San Diego 1967, MS, clin. psych., 1969; Calif. Marriage, Family & Child Therapist, 1972. Career: probation ofcr. L.A. County, 1969-81, splst. in child custody, guardianship, juvenile supvn.; family crisis intervention (sole) counselor, L.A. County Probation pilot proj., 1972-77; (proj. slated for 90 days, cont. 5 years, success rate 14 higher than Dept. av.); psychotherapist pvt. practice, Redondo Bch. 1977-81, Carlsbad 1981--, and also in Del Mar; lectr.; mem: North Co. (S.D.) Psychol. Assn. (chmn. Liason Com.), Calif. Assn. of Marriage and Family Therapists, Carlsbad Rotary, Toastmasters (best spkr. awds.), Del Mar CofC; publs: paper on delinquency preven. for Calif. Legislature 1976; book on psychol. growth (in prog.); Ind.; Christian; rec: white water rafting, gliding, jazz combo ldr. Res: 6783 Heath Ct Carlsbad 92008 Ofc: So. Calif. Psychotherapy Affiliates, 2885 Hope St, Carlsbad; Center for Personal Growth, 13355 Stratford Ct, Del Mar

KOJOORI, SHAKROKH SHARIATMADARI, wig designer/mfr. of hair goods; b. Aug. 18, 1947, Teheran, Iran; s. Ali S. and Zahra Kojoori; m. Marlene, May 21, 1978; children: Jonah, b. 1978, Lilah, b. 1980; edn: BS in econ., National Univ. 1970, MS, 1972. Career: real estate sales agt. Star Realty, Century City; real estate broker/owner S. Kojoori and Assoc., Beverly Hills; wig designer and mfr. of hair goods, Michaeldino Wig Designs, Redondo Beach 1980--; mfr. custom hairpieces for clients nat., active in theatrical hair work for Universal Studios (Incredible Hulk), Disneyland, M.G.M. Grand Hotel, Las Vegas, Ice Capades, Madame Oink of Pizza Time Theatre, and motion pictures (White Buffalo, Grizzly Adams); West Coast distbr. Top Head (adv. hair replacement prod.); mem. Nat. Assn. of Real Estate Brokers; rec: philately,

photog., travel. Ofc: Michaeldino Wigs, 1926 S. Pacific Coast Hwy, Ste 110, Redondo Beach 90277

KOLDHEKAR, SATISH M., b. Nov. 8, 1952, Baroda, Gujarat, India, nat. Am. 1981; s. Mukundrao and Malati (Paradkar) K.; m. Dr. Vaijayanti W. Deshmukh, MD, Jan. 18, 1982; 1 dau. Ami, b. 1983; edn: BS in ME, Sardar Patel Univ. 1974; MS in mech. eng., Ariz. State Univ. 1980. Career: test engr., resrch & devel., ITT General Controls, Glendale 1980-82; devel. engr., biomed. R&D, Xerox Medical Systems, Pasadena, 1982; project engr., aerospace med., Scott Aviation (div. Figgie Intl. Co.), Monrovia 1983--; awards: 1st prize, grad. students W.C. Sect. AIAA, 1980; stu. mem. AIAA, 1978-9, ASME 1978-9, Internat. Solar Energy Soc. 1979-80; patentee: Bullet resistant optical lens system (1983); publs: Aerospace Scis. meeting, St. Louis, Mo. 1981; rec: bldg. prototypes of new bio-med. product ideas. Res: 6830 No Rosemead Blvd, %23, San Gabriel 91775 Ofc: Scott Aviation, 1900 Walker Ave, Monrovia 91016

KOLL, DONALD M., construction co. executive; b. Mar. 29, 1933, Santa Monica; s. Milton Lee (dec.) and Edna (Grube) K.; m. Dorothy Brittingham, July 16, 1955; sic children; edn: BA, Stanford Univ. 1955; Lic. Gen. Contractor, Calif. Career: v.p. K.W. Koll Constrn. Co. 1958-62; pres. The Koll Co. 1962-83; currently, chmn./ CEO The Koll Co., Newport Beach; bd. dirs: Grubb & Ellis Comml. Brokerage Co., Atlas Hotels, Wells Fargo & Co., Wells Fargo Bank, The Irvine Co., Economic Devel. Corp. of Orange Co.; awards: Man of the Yr., Nat. Assn. Indsl. Ofc. Parks 1983; Presidential appointee: World Bd., United Service Orgn. and Bd. Advrs. of National Air & Space Museum; mem: Boy Scouts of Am. (exec. bd.); UC Irvine bd. overseers; Commn. of the Californias; World Bus. Council, Inc.; Urban Land Inst.; Gr. Irvine Indsl. League; CofC; Young Pres. Orgn.; Smithsonian Instn.; mil: capt. USAF; Episcopal; rec: boating, snow skiing, hunting. Ofc: The Koll Company, 4490 Von Karman Ave Newport Beach 92663

KOLTAI, LESLIE, community college system chancellor; b. Apr. 6, 1931, Karcag, Hungary; s. Nicholas and Marie Koltai; edn: BA, Univ. of Budapes, 1954; MA, UCLA, 1960, Ed.D., 1967; hon. LL.D., Pepperdine Univ., 1975; hon. D.H.L., Univ. of Judaism, L.A., 1978; m. Katherine Erdos, 1953, Hungary; children: Steve, b. 1954, Marian, b. 1962, Robert, b. 1964. Career: Asso. prof. and dept. chmn., Pasadena City Coll., 1960-67, dean of instnl. research, 1967-68; pres. and chancellor, Metro. Community Coll. Dist., Kansas City, Mo., 1968-72; chancellor, L.A. Community Colls., (system of 10 colls., 145,000 students) 1972--. adj. prof., USC, 1979-, UCLA, 1975-; faculty, Claremont Grad. Sch., Higher Edn. Mgmt. Inst., 1979-; Trustee, Carnegie Found. for Advance. of Mem. Nat. Panel for Study of Am. Hi Sch.; trustee, Ednl. Resources Information Ctr., UCLA; honors: Citizen of the Yr. 1962, Nat. Citizenship Day Com.; Outstanding Service Awards, Fed. Exec. Board, L.A., 1976; Rehabilitation Services Adminstrn., Wash. DC, 1977; Kappa Tau Alpha, journalistic hon.; Alpha Mu Gamma, fgn. lang. hon.; humanistic services award, Black Faculty & Staff Assn., 1981; hon. mem. Chicano Faculty Assn., 1981; misc. civic awards; mem. Am. Council on Edn., Ednl. Record com., com. on Fgn. Students in U.S.; Monterey Inst. of Internat. Studies, Nat. Advisory Council; Brookings Instn. nat. adv. panel, Financing Postsecondary Edn.; Am. Council on Edn., adv. bd. Visiting Execs. Program, nat. panel for Advanc. of Women in Higher Edn. Adminstrn.; bd. dirs. Am. Assn. for Advanc. of Humanities; nat. adv. bd. Council on Learning; No. Am. Council, Internat. Assn. Univ. and Coll. Presidents; bd. dirs. League for Innovation in Community Colls.; Am. Assn. Community and Jr. Colls., nat. com. Internat. Rels. and Cooperation; Assn. of Governing Bds. of Univs. and Colls., Adv. Council of Presidents. Res: 3820 Ballina Cyn. Rd. Encino 91436. Ofc: 617 West 7th St., L.A. 90017.

KOMETANI, GEORGE, mechanical engineer; b. Oct. 7, 1937, Auburn, Wash.; s. Kizo and Sakaye (Terada) K.; m. Betty Kishaba, Mar. 21, 1964; children: Cheryl, b. 1966; Ellen, b. 1969; edn: BS, UCLA 1962. Career: design engr. Douglas Aircraft Co., Culver City 1962-63; design engr. Whittaker Corp., Canoga Park 1963-69; engr. MTS, Hughes Aircraft Co., El Segundo 1969-70; engr./ pgm. mgr. Space Vector Corp., Northridge 1970--; works: devel. & launch of Conestoga, the first comml. rocket, 9/82; Republican; Methodist; rec: woodworking, physical fitness, skiing. Res: 12429 Stanwood Pl, Los Angeles 90066 Ofc: Space Vector Corp., 19631 Prairie St Northridge 91324

KOMYATHY, GABOR, hotelier; b. Mar. 10, 1944, Budapest, Hungary; s. Dr. Aladar and Maria (Fuzessery) K.; edn: Masters, F.Liszt Acad. of Music, Bpest, 1963-68; Masters, Coll. for Hotel & Food Indus., Bpest 1975-78; desig: CTC, Cert. Travel Counselor, ICTA, Wellesley, Mass. 1983. Career: regl. mng. dir. Ibus Travel Co., Lake Balaton Region, Hungary 1972-75; dir. sales and mktg. Danubius Hotel & Spa Co., Budapest, 1975-78; dir. internat. mktg. The Beverly Hilton Hotel, Beverly Hills, Ca. 1979-83; National Olympic Com. service mgr., LAAOC, Los Angeles, 1984; senior ptnr. California Consultants, mktg. and mgmt. cons. firm, L.A. 1983--; honors: commendn., County of Los Angeles, 1983; mem: British-Am. CofC, German-Am. CofC, French-Am. CofC, Danish-Am. CofC, Beverly Hills CofC, ATME, AHMA; bd. dirs. Hungaria Sport Club; Guest Lecture Series spkr., USC, 1982; rec: classical music, sports, literature. Res: 3700 Sepulveda Blvd Los Angeles 90034 Ofc: LAOOC, Los Angeles 90084

KONOPISOS, JAMES WILLIAM, sales executive; b. July 30, 1922, Sunrise, Wyo.; s. Wm. Dimitrios and Anastacia (Pantazopoulos) K.; m. Zoe J. Jamison, Dec. 2, 1945; children: Theodore, b. 1946, Stacy Elaine, b. 1952. Career: dist. mgr. General Electric Co., 1972-75, area sales mgr. 1975--; fmr. bus. owner in Phoenix, Ariz. 1955-66; mem: Escondido CofC (life, 1969), Ambassadors Esc. Chamber (life, 1969), Kiwanis Club of Esc. (pres. 1972; lt. gov. Div. 37 1974/5), Kiwanis Internat. (life, 1975); mil: sgt. USAF 1942-45; Republican; Greek

Orthodox; rec: stamp/coin & plate collection. Res: 1542 Jeffrey Ave Escondido 92027 Ofc: General Electric, 3554 Kettner Blvd San Diego 92101

KONRAD, RITA CHRISTA, real estate broker executive; b. Aug. 18, 1951, Gelsenkirchen, W. Germany; d. Hans Johann and Elisabeth (Nagel) Konrad; edn: Business Night Sch., Ger. 1964-66; Bus. Coll. (Jr. Coll.), Ger. 1966-68; Executive Broker Series, USC 1982. Career: exptl. assembly, ITT Jennings, San Jose 1969-71; bookkeeper/office mgr. Martino's Furniture, San Jose 1971-72; surgical asst./ofc. mgr./bkkpr. John Bowler, DDS, San Jose 1972-77; prop. American Auction Assoc., Santa Clara 1977-80; prop. Silver & Gold Jewelry Co. (wholesale & retail), Santa Clara 1977-80; real estate agt. Nat. Financial Network, Santa Clara 1980--, real estate broker/mgr. currently; public spkr. var. R.E. related workshops and meetings; mem: Nat. Assn. of Realtors, Calif. Assn. of Realtors, San Jose Real Estate Board; fmr. mem. Nat. Auctioneers Assn., Santa Clara CofC; rec: writing poetry, gourmet cooking. Res: 1472 Calabazas Blvd Santa Clara 95051 Ofc: National Financial Network, 2470 El Camino Santa Clara 95051

KOPENY, LOUIS CLARENCE, lawyer, indsl. engineer, mgmt. consultant; b. Mar. 31, 1926,Chgo.; s. Louis Joseph and Caroline (Zapfel) K.; m. Elizabeth Macaluso, Nov. 23, 1946; children: Betty Lou (Wojciechowski), b. 1948; William J., b. 1950; Carol Anne (Jones), b. 1954; June Ellen (Havlena), . 1956; Robert L., b. 1957; edn: Ph.B., Northwestern Univ., 1951; MBA, CSU Fullerton, 1970; JD, Western State Univ. 1980. Calif. Reg. Profl. Engr.; Calif. Jr. Coll. Tchr. Credential; admitted to Calif. State Bar. Career: indsl. engr. Motorola Inc. and Motorola Canada, Ltd., Toronto 1951-55; chief indsl. engr., Radio-TV Div., Westinghouse Elec. Corp., Metuchen, NJ, 1955-57; mng. assoc. Mgmt. Services Dept., Arthur Young & Co., Los Angeles and NYC, 1957-61; mgmt. cons., self-empl., Sepulveda, Ca. 1961-62; asst. to Oper. V.P., Autonetics Div. Rockwell Internatl., Anaheim 1962-70; prin. (mgmt. cons.) Arthur Young & Co., Santa Ana 1970-75; ops. mgr./indsl. engr. Knott's Berry Farm, Buena Park 1975-82; atty. pvt. practice, Yorba Linda, 1982--; instr. UCI Ext. 1969-73; adj. prof. National Univ. 1982-83; honors: Beta Gamma Signa 1970; mem: Am. Inst. of Instl. Engrs. (sr.), State Bar of Calif., Masons; mil: yeoman USNR 1943-46, ATO, Asia-Pac. Theater (1 star), Philippine Liberation (1 star), Victory Medal; Republican; Lutheran; rec: gun collector, fishing, barbershop singing. Address: 5721 Casa Loma Ave Yorba Linda 92686

KOO, WILFRED, real estate investment co. executive; b. May 29, 1953, Hong Kong; s. Daniel and Rose (Wong) K.; m. Linda, July 17, 1976; children: Maureen, b. 1981; Lorraine, b. 1983; edn. BA, Univ. of Redlands 1975, MBA, USC 1977; CPA cert., Calif. 1982. Career: supvg. senior acct., audit, Peat Marwick, Mitchell & Co., Los Angeles 1977-80; supvsg. senio. tax splst. Peat, Marwick, Mitchell & Co., Century City 1980-81; tax mgr. Kal Kan Foods, Inc., Vernon 1981--; v.p./secty. Rheingold, Inc., San Diego 1980--; mng. dir. Baxendale N.V., Diamond Bar 1981--; dir. Rheingold, Inc. 1981-83; mem: CPA, Calif.; Calif. Assn. CPAs; San Diego CofC; Republican; Catholic. Address: Baxendale N.V. c/o, 3359 S Falcon Ridge Rd Diamond Bar 91765

KOPARI, LESLIE ARPAD, JR., software development engineer; b. Aug. 29, 1952, Pecs, Hungary, nat. 1963; s. Leslie A. and Maria Antalne (Schwabach) K.; m. Ann Matalamaki, Sept. 22, 1972; 1 son: Armand, b. 1973; edn: stu. Univ. of Minn., Duluth 1970-72; AS, Tidewater Comm. Coll. 1979; BS, Old Dominion Univ. 1981. Career: sales rep. Ency. Britannica, Norfolk, Va. 1976-77; tchg. asst. Old Dominion Univ., Norfolk, Va. 1979-81; pgmr. analyst Hewlett-Packard, Cupertino 1981-83; software devel. engr. 1983--; mem: Assn. for Computing Machinery; IEEE; Las Cumbres Amateur Radio Club, Santa Clara Co.; Advent Lutheran Ch., Morgan Hill (Ch. Council, Property Com.); mil: musician 2/c USN 1972-77, GCM, Nat. Defense; rec: music, amateur radio, youth athletics. Res: 2515 Gitana Ct Morgan Hill 95037 Ofc: Hewlett-Packard Co., 19310 Pruneridge Ave Cupertino 95014

KORAN, DENNIS HOWARD, editor; b. May 21, 1947, Los Angeles; s. Aaron Baer and Shirley Mildred (Kassan) Koran; BA, UC Berkeley, 1970; stu. Univ. of Leeds, Eng. 1966-67; m. Roslynn Cohen, April 6, 1979; 1 son, Michael, b. 1981. Career: co-founder and co-editor Cloud Marauder Books, Berkeley 1967-71; founder, editor Panjandrum Books, Los Angeles, 1971--, also ed. Panjandrum Poetry Journal; VISTA Volunteer 1970-71, served as a govt. consultant working with Seminole Indians in Okla. Awards: Ephebian Society 1964; grants for publishing from: Coordinating Council of Literary Mags. (NYC) 1971, 73, 75, 78; Natl. Endowment for the Arts, Literature Program 1974, 76, 78, 80-81. Mem.: Coordinating Council of Literary Mags., 1971-; Poets and Writers, Inc. (NYC), 1975-; Lovers of the Stinking Rose (Berkeley) 1973-. Publs.: VACANCIES. Poems 1969-75, pub. Mothers' Hen Press, San Francisco 1975; num. poems in lit. mags. including Beatitudes, Amphora, Poetry Now, SF Phoenix, Fuse, & Skywriting: non-fiction book in progress: Before the Dawn: A Chronicle of the Sixties. Democrat. Jewish, pres. Temple Youth Group 1964. Rec.: rare books, philately, bike riding. Res.: 5428 Hermitage Ave., No Hollywood 91607. Office: Panjandrum Books, 11321 Iowa Ave., Ste. 1, Los Angeles 90025.

KORF, HAROLD EDWARD, university library director; b. Oct. 28, 1925, Osakis, MN; s. Herman and Elizabeth (Reller) Korf; gr.-grandfather, Graf von Korf of Russia; BA, Univ. Calif., Berkeley, 1949; BLS, Univ. Calif., Berkeley, 1953; m. Evelyn Parsons. Career: assoc. dir., Humanities & Social Sci., Stanford, 1957; librarian, Bus. Sch., Golden Gate Univ., 1960-70; assoc. prof., Humanities, Golden Gate Univ., 1965--; dir., Golden Gate Univ. Lib., 1970--; bd. dirs., Strybing Arboretum Soc., S.F.; res. World Trade Library, 1977--. Mem.: AAUP; Special Libraries ssn. Independent. Unitarian. Rec.: gardening. Res.: 1549 Beach St., San Francisco 94123; Office: Golden Gate Univ., 536 Mission San Francisco 94105.

KORNFIELD, HARRISON JAMES, physician; b. Jul. 19, 1931, Oakland; s. Sanford and B. Geraldine (Jacobs) K.; m. Christine L. Baker, Aug. 3, 1975; children: Alisa, b. 1976; Aaron, b. 1979. Edn: AB, UC, 1952; MD UC Sch. Med., 1956; Am. Bd. Surgery, 1962. Career: intern Highland Alameda County Hosp., Oakland, 1956-57; resident/chief res. surg. Kansas Univ. Med. Ctr., 1957-61; chief surgery Perrin AFB, Tex., 1961-63; chief surgery Sunnyvale Med. Clinic, 1963--; chmn. bd. dirs./CEO, 1974-79; chief of staff Valley Med. Ctr. 1974-77; chief surgery El Camino Hosp., 1974-75. Mem: San Jose Surgical Soc. (past Pres.); Am. Coll. of Surgeons (past council mem.). Res: 26209 Dori Ln. Los Altos Hills 94022. Ofc: Sunnyvale Medical Center, 596 Carroll St. Sunnyvale 94086

KORODY, ANTHONY V., photographer/ corporate executive; b. Mar. 4, 1951, Los Angeles; s. Paul Alexander and Erica (Goetter) K.; edn: Webb School of Calif. 1970, journalism maj. USC, 1970-72; m. Jaimie C. Levy, Mar. 13, 1982. Career: freelance photog. for: Black Star, Life, Newsweek, 1970; picture editor of Daily Trojan, 1971; one of orig. 13 photographers/founders of SYGMA Agence de Press, Paris (today the largest photo syndicate in world) 1973--; freelance photog. for: People, Time, Fortune and Newsweek, 1978--; co-founder/v.p./dir. Image Stream Inc. (a multi image prodn. co.), 1978--; founder/ CEO Fourth Estate Press (photog. corp.), 1978--; contbg. photog. People Weekly Mag., 1979-; lectr. Art Center; mem: NPPA, Sigma Delta Chi, Assn. for Multi Image; works: cover photographs on: Time, Newsweek, People (18), McCall's, U.S. News, Paris Match, and Stern Mags.; Republican (Presdtl. Task Force); Catholic; rec: radio control cars. Ofc: Image Stream Inc. 5450 W. Washington Blvd Los Angeles 90016

KOSAKURA, TAKESHI, industrial designer/ business executive; b. Feb. 3, 1932, Berkeley; s. Takeo and Somie (Ilda) K.; m. Phyllis T. Kusumi, Apr. 19, 1958; children: Steven T., b. 1959; Lori H., b. 1961; Mark, b. 1965; edn: BPA, Art Ctr. Sch. 1957; MBA, Pepperdine Univ. 1980. Career: automotive stylist Ford Motor Co., Dearborn, Mich. 1957-60; art dir. Menasha Corp. 1960-62; v.p. design Roberts & Kosakura, Inc., Orange 1962-65; pres. Roberts & Kosakura, Inc. (became Kosakura & Assoc., Inc. 1972), Anaheim 1965--; honors: Citation, City of Detroit Resolution for participation in creation of mural presented by Ford Motor Co. to city; mem: Anaheim CofC; US CofC; Suburban Optimists; Orange Co. Advtg. Club; works: mural, Wayne County Airport (Detroit); publs: Self Perceived Creative & Non Creative Workers Attitudes Towards Routine Job Tasks; mil: cpl. US Army 1952-54; Republican; Buddhist; rec: painting, skiing, golf. Res: 10871 Pembroke Dr Santa Ana 92705 Ofc: Kosakura & Assoc., Inc., 1321 N Blue Gum St Anaheim 92805

KOSKI, JEANNE MARIE, programmer/analyst manager; b. Nov. 24, 1946, Long Beach; d. Eugene Michael and Beva Marie (Hyman) Empe; div.; children; Kenneth, b. 1964; Stephanie, b. 1966; Christopher, b. 1967; Rochelle, b. 1971; edn: AA, honors, Am. River Coll. 1982; stu. CSU Sacto. 1982-, McGeorge Sch. of Law 1983-. Career: owner/ mgr. Western Auto Assoc. Store, Ft. Bragg 1972-80; pgmmr./analyst mgr. Minicomputer Assoc. Inc., Sacto. 1982--; mem: Assn. for Computing Machinery; Am. Bar Assn. (student div.); IEEE (stu. div.); Soroptimist, Ft. Bragg; Aircraft Owners & Pilots Assn.; Golden Key Nat. Hon. Soc.; Mendocino Co. 4-H Club Council; Democrat; Lutheran; rec: private pilot. Res: 2619 Rio Oso Rd Rio Oso 95674 Ofc: Minicomputer Assoc., Inc., 2160 Royale Rd, Ste 24, Sacramento 95815

KOSTENBAUDER, DANIEL, international tax attorney; b. Oct. 4, 1950, Danville, Penn.; s. Daniel F. and Nancy J. (Friday) K.; m. Robin Welles, Apr. 4, 1980; edn: BA, Yale Univ. 1972; JD, NY Univ. 1975, LLM in taxation, 1979; admitted to practice, NY bar 1976, Calif. bar 1981. Career: assoc. Everett, Johnson & Breckinridge, NY 1975-80; tax atty. Hewlett- Packard Co., Palo Alto 1980-81; senior tax atty. 1981--; spkr. World Trade Inst. sem., San Juan, P.R. 11/82; honors: Robert E. Lewis, Jr. Trophy, Yale Univ. 1972; Note & Comment Editor, NYU Law Sch. Journ. of Internat. Law & Politics 1974-75; mem: Am. Bar Assn. (Sect. Sci. & Tech., Div. of Computer Law Com. on Taxation); NY State Bar Assn.; Yale Club of Peninsula (dir.); Republican; Protestant; rec: tennis. Ofc: Hewlett-Packard Co., 3000 Hanover St Palo Alto 94304

KOTT, PAUL TERRENCE, real estate co. president; b. Mar. 27, 1954, Lynwood; s. Wm. Irving and Eleanor Ruth (Faris) K.; m. Lisa Robinson, Mar. 14, 1981; 1 dau. Krystin Lynn, b. 1982; edn: BA, USC, 1977; Calif. lic. real estate broker 1981. Career: real estate sales agt. 1978-, top sales producer, Carl Rau R.E., Anaheim 1979-81; broker/pres. Paul Kott Realtors, Anaheim 1982--; mem: Anaheim Bd. of Realtors (bd. dirs.), West Orange Co. Bd. of Realtors, Calif. Assn. of Realtors, Nat. Assn. of Realtors, Anaheim CofC, Phi Gamma Delta frat., Acad. of Magical Arts; coauthor collegiate book: Banco De Saber (Book of Knowledge); active in magical arts, co-instr. course in magic, CSU Fullerton; Republican; Christian; rec: magic, pianist. Res: 945 N. West St Anaheim 92801 Ofc: Paul Kott Realtors 504 N. State College Blvd Anaheim 92806

KOULETSIS, JOHN, quality assurance engineer; b. Sept. 16, 1925, NYC; s. George and Bertha (Pantzis) K.; m. Mary Kontopoulos, June 18, 1950; children: Patricia, b. 1951, Victoria b. 1953, George, b. 1955; edn: San Diego Jr. Coll. 1957; desig. Statistical Qual. Control, 1957. Career: aircraft insp. Rorh Industries Inc., Chula Vista 1957-, Quality Assurance engr. 1980--; nominee for the Pride Program (1976) Rohr Ind. and recipient employee commendn. from Douglas Aircraft rep.; musician (bass viol player) Big bands and combos for pvt. clubs and mil. bases, 1940-80; mem. Jack LaLane Hlth Club; mil: USN 1943-46, Asia.Pac. Campgn., Victory, Philippine Liberation, ATO Cpgn.

medals; Ind.; Greek Orthodox; rec: music instruments collection. Res: 9149 Madison St LaMesa 92041 Ofc: Rohr Ind., Foot "H" St, Chula Vista 92011

KOZAK, STEPHEN VINCENT, JR., county executive; b. July 7, 1951, Agna, Guam; s. Maj. Stephen V. (USAF Ret.) and Estelle Agnes (Potomski) K.; edn: BA, Cal State Polytech. Univ. Pomona, 1973; MBA, UC Riverside 1975; MBA, econ., CSU Fullerton 1981; airport plnng. & design, Sch. of Civil Engring. Ext., Ga. Inst. of Tech., 1983. Calif. Comm. Coll. Instr. Credential (life) Pub. Svc. & Adminstrn., 1979. Career: data analyst Aeronutronic Ford Co., JPL/ NASA Support Pgms., Pasadena 1971-75; staff/aide II, Orange County Adminstrv. Office, Santa Ana, 1975-77; exec. asst. to Supr. Thomas F. Riley, 5th Dist., Orange Co. Bd. Supervisors, Santa Ana 1977-81; Plans & Programs mgr. John Wayne Airport, Orange Co., Santa Ana 1981--; treas. Sch. of Arts Alumni Adv. Council, Cal State Polytech Univ., Pomona 1982-, charter mem. Alumni Career Adv. Network, 1979-; charter mem. Career Plnng. and Placement Alumni Netwk., UC Riv. 1983-, mem. UCR Alumni Assn. Scholarship Pgm. Com. 1983-84; Public mem. Comm. Video Adv. Bd. City of Orange 1982; honors: Outstanding Young Man of Am. 1981-2, US Jaycees; mem: The Acad. of Political Sci., The Western Govtl. Research Assn., The Planetary Soc., AAAS, Town Hall of Calif., Pi Sigma Alpha; United Way Campaign office coord. 1979-; rep. O.C. Gen. Aviation Citizens Adv. Gp. 1980-82; panel spkr. 35th Ann. Conf. Airport Oprs. Council Internat. 1982; author: Operating Budgets: A Practical Approach for Improving Budgetary Control for the County of Orange (Nat. Assn. of Accts. Manuscript Author Award 1980-81); Republican; Catholic; rec: softball,skiing, photog. Res: 2005-33 W. Culver Ave Orange 92668 Ofc: John Wayne Airport, Orange County 18741 Airport Way N. Santa Ana 92707

KRACHT, JAMES E., software engineer; b. Dec. 10, 1954, Two Rivers, Wisc.; s. William H. and Frieda B. (Buschmann) K.; m. Linda S Luistro, Jun. 9,1984. Edn: AA, Bethany Lutheran Coll., Mankato, MN, 1975; BA (math & comp. sci.), Univ. Wisc., Madison, 1977; MS, 1978. Career: mem. tech. staff Bell Labs, Naperville, Il., 1978-80; research/develop. engr. GTE Sylvania, Mt. View, 1980-81; software engr. Intel Corp., Santa Clara, 1981-82; computer Scientist Cdex Corp., Los Altos, 1984-84; software engr. Teknowledge, Palo Alto, 1984--. Awards: Nat. Merit Scholarship, 1973; Univ. Wisconsin Fellowship, 1977. Mem: Assn. for Computing Machinery; IEEE Computer Soc. Independent; Lutheran. Rec: creative writing, running. Res: 255 S Rengstorff Ave, %107 Mountain View 94040 Ofc: Teknowledge, 525 University Ave Palo Alto 94301

KRAFT, GARRY G., chiropractor; b. Oct. 6, 1945, San Francisco; s. Basil and Frances Gannon; edn: Orange Coast Coll. 1971-72, Univ. of Colo. 1975-77; DC, Los Angeles Coll. of Chiropractic 1982. Career: parts dept. mgr. Hueberger Volkswagen, Colorado Springs, Colo. 1972-75; veterans counselor, Vets. Outreach Pgm. of Univ. of Colo., 1976-77; salesman Santa Monica (Ca.) Volkswagen 1978; lab. and tchg. asst. L.A. Coll. of Chiropractic, 1980-81; staff chiropractor Hobson Chiropractic/Medical Clinic, Glendale 1982-83; co-owner/ staff chiropractor Citrus Health Center (chiro./med. clinic) Azusa, 1973--; awards: grantee, Springwell Research and Trust for emergency med. care pkg.; Outstanding Senior Awd., LA Coll. of Chiro. 1981; Who's Who in Am. Colls. & Univs. 1981; Diplomate Nat. Bd. of Chiro. Examiners 1981; mem: Am. Chiropractic Assn. (past pres. Student Chpt. LACC); Calif. Chiro. Assn.; Alumni Assn. of Sigma Chi Psi (past pres. LACC chpt.); Glendora CofC, Azusa CofC, Red Cross vol.; mil: sgt. US ARmy 1977-79, Army Commendn., Nat. Def., Vietnam Svc., Vietnam Cpgn. medals; Democrat; rec: off road racing, sailing. Res: 18632 Gallarno Dr Covina 91722 Ofc: Citrus Health Center 472 S. Citrus Ave Covina 91702

KRAFT, HENRY ROBERT, lawyer; b. Apr. 27, 1946, Los Angeles; s. Sylvester and Freda S. Kraft; m. Terry, July 21, 1968; children: Diana, b. 1972, Kevin, b. 1975; edn: BA, hist., San Fernando Valley St. Coll. 1958; JD, USC Law Sch. 1971; admitted to Calif. State Bar 1972. Career: law clk. US Atty's Office, Los Angeles 1970; assoc. Trope & Trope, Century City 1970-72; San Bernardino County Deputy Public Defender 1972-78; ptnr. Piazza, King &: Kraft 1978; sole practice, 1978-82; Victorville Deputy City Atty. 1978; Needles Acting City Atty. 1978-79; ptnr. Kraft, Hegner & Hodge, Victorville 1982--; Barstow City Atty., Redevel. Agency Atty., Barstow Comm. Hosp. atty., 1980--; honors: Pi Sigma Alpha (pol. sci. hon.), Phi Alpha Theta (hist. hon.); mem: San Bernardino County Bar Assn., Calif. State Bar, Am. Bar Assn., High Desert Bar Assn. (pres. 1982), Calif. Trial Lawyers Assn., Calif. Attys. for Criminal Justice, Calif. Soc. for Healthcare Attys., League of Calif. Cities, Calif. Public Defenders Assn., YMCA, Optimists, Cub Scouts, Victorville, Barstow, & Apple Valley Chambers of Commerce; Democrat; Jewish; rec: camping. Res: 14705 Keota Rd Apple Valley 92307 Ofc: Kraft, Hegner & Hodge, 16239 Victor St Victorville 92392

KRAKOWER, DAVID, financial manager/certified public accountant; b. Mar. 4,1953, Houston, Tex.; s. Joseph David and Rae (Graham) K.. Edn: BA economics, Stanford Univ., 1975; MBA finance, Wharton Grad., 1977.; CPA, Calif., 1980. Career: senior accountant Price Waterhouse, San Francisco, 1977-80; asst. controller Wells Fargo Leasing, SF, 1980-82; mgr. fin. analysis Federal Reserve Bank of SF, 1982--. Mem: AICPA, Calif. Soc. of CPAs; rec: Chinese calligraphy, tennis, Calif. wines. Res: 714 A Cole St. San Francisco 94117 Ofc: Federal Reserve Bank of S.F., 101 Market St. San Francisco 94105

KRAL, VIVIAN LAURIE, lawyer; b. June 12, 1954, San Francisco; d. Bohumil J. and Margery (Bullert) K.; edn: AB, Stanford Univ. 1975; JD, UCB Boalt Hall

1978; admitted to State Bar of Calif. 1978. Career: assoc. firm of Thoits, Lehman & Love (spec. civil litigation & appellate practice), Palo Alto 1980--; honors: Phi Beta Kappa, Stanford Univ. 1975; mem: Am., Calif., San Mateo & Santa Clara Co. Bar Assns. Res: 10 Murray Ct San Mateo 94403 Ofc: Thoits, Lehman & Love, 525 University Ave, Ste 1219, Palo Alto 94301

KRAMP, ALBERT LEE, contractor; b. Dec. 17, 1944, Placerville; s. Albert Leland and Luella E. (Hutchings) K.; m. Diana M., Nov. 6, 1964; children: Tracy, b. 1970; Tammy, b. 1973. Career: insulator Sacramento Insulation, Stockton Branch (9yrs.); estimator (2 yrs.); mgr. Stockton Custon Plastering, Stockton (3 yrs.); currently, owner Al Kramp Specialties, Stockton; conduct free energy conservation wrkshps.; awards: Cert. of Appreciation, Stockton Police Youth Activities, Sr. Projs. 1983; mem: Better Bus. Bureau (dir.); PG&E Contractors Adv. Bd.; Bd. of Comm. Involvement Panel; Stockton Energy Com.; Insulation Contractors Assn. of Calif.; active var. civic orgns.; Democrat; Baptist; rec: hunting, fishing. Res: 2736 Telegraph Ave Stockton 95204 Ofc: Al Kramp Specialties, 1702 E Alpine Ave, POB 8867, Stockton 95208

KRASNER, OSCAR JAY, co. president/educator; b. Dec. 3, 1922, St. Louis, Mo.; s. Benjamin and Rose (Persov) K.; m. Bonnie Kidder, June 4, 1944; children: Bruce, b. 1951, Glenn, b. 1954, Scott, b. 1956, Steve, b. 1958, Michael, b. 1960, Bettina, b. 1962; edn: BS, Washington Univ., St. Louis, 1943; MA, Univ. Chgo. 1950; MS, USC, 1965, and DBA, 1969. Career: staff Exec. Office of the Secty. US Navy Dept., 1944-51; hd. Indsl. Engring. Branch, Naval Ordnance Plant, Indpls. 1951-55; supv. consultant Business Research Corp., Chgo. 1955-56; mgr. VTOL Project Plnng. 1956-61; exec. advisor Long Range Plnng. No. Am. Aviation, 1962-64; dir. Tech. Resources Analysis, Corporate Ofc., No. Am. Aviation (then No. Am. Rockwell), 1965-70; pres. Solid State Technology Corp., 1968-71; prof. of mgmt. Pepperdine Univ. 1970--; pres. Rensark Assocs., Long Beach 1976--; dir: Utah Computer Industries 1981-, Seethaler Internat. Corp. 1981-; bd. govs. Assn. of Venture Founders 1982-; nat. adv. bd. Nat. Congress of Inventor Orgns. 1983-; mem. Acad. of Mgmt., World Future Soc., Internat. Council for Small Business; num. articles in field of strategic plnng. and entrepreneurship research; mil: US ARmy 1942-44; Jewish. Res: 4709 Autry Ave Long Beach 90808 Ofc: 2151 Michelson Dr Irvine

KRAUS, ARTHUR DELLAR, financial planner; b. Nov. 14, 1939, Los Angeles; s. Arthur E. and Alice D. (Dellar) K.; m. Irene Simon, Apr. 3, 1966; children: Mark, b. 1959; Mitchell, b. 1971; Michael, b. 1972; Matthew, b. 1974; edn: BS, USC 1962; CLU, American Coll. 1967, ChFC (Chartered Fin. Cons.) 1983. Career: agency mgr. Pacific Mutual Life 1960--; v.p. Financial Mgmt. Svcs., Los Angeles 1983--; pres. FMS Securities, Inc.; dir. Fin. Mgmt. Svcs.; instr. Agcy Mgmt. Tng. Course 1983-84; awards: Nat. Mgmt. Awd. 1983; Regl. Citation Awd., Pacific Mutual 1983; mem: Nat. Assn. Life Underwriters; Gen. Agents & Mgrs. Assn.; Internat. Assn. of Fin. Plnrs.; Americans for Democratic Action (nat. bd. dirs.); Cardinal Gold; Univ. Synagogue (bd. trustees); mil: HM-3 USCGR 1957-65; Democrat; Jewish. Res: 2565 Cordelia Rd Los Angeles 90049 Ofc: Financial Management Services, 10880 Wilshire Blvd, Ste 1206, Los Angeles 90024

KRAUSE, LAWRENCE ALLEN, personal financial advisor; b. Oct. 28, 1939, Chgo.; s. Leo and Sylvia Harriet (Bergman) K.; m. Donna Ferkel, Aug. 14, 1971; children: Danielle, b. 1976; Alexis, b. 1981; edn: BA, State Univ. of Iowa 1961; CFP, Coll. of Fin. Plnng. 1978; Real Estate Broker, State of Ill. 1967; Reg. Securities Principal, SEC, 1980. Career: exec. v.p. JOBS Inc., Waukegan, Ill. 1961-62; pres. Inventory & Bus. Controls, Inc., Waukegan 1963-66; real estate broker Schoen Realtors, Rockford, Ill. 1967-69; reg. rep./ investment banker Reynold & Co., San Francisco 1970-75; dir./ coord. fin. plnng. dept. Sutro & Co., Inc., S.F. 1975-79; pres. Lawrence A. Krause & Assocs. Inc., S.F. 1979--; pres. KW Securities Corp., pres. KW Financial Svcs. Inc.; adj. prof. fin. plnng. San Francisco State Univ. 1982-; adv. com. Golden Gate Univ.; faculty USC 1984; adv. bd. Technology Funding, Inc. 1984; honors: elected Fin. Plnnr. of the YR., San Francisco 1982; Fin. Writers Awd., Financial Plnnr. Mag. 1981; mem: Nat. Center for Fin. Edn. Inc.; Internat. Assn. for Fin. Plnng. Inc. (pres. S.F. chpt. 1980-82); Inst. CFPs; Am. Canecr Soc. (S.F. Unit); Concordia- Argonaut Club; publs: monthly column, Hedging Your Dollars, Calif. Bus. mag. 1979-; author chpt., Financial Planning for the Professional, in Your Book of Financial Planning, 1983; author sect., Forms and Planning Aids Volume, Financial and Estate Planning, Commerce Clearing House; mil: sp5 US Army 1961-67; Republican; Jewish; rec: equestrian, skiing, golf. Res: 672 Matsonia Dr Foster City 94404 Ofc: Lawrence A. Krause & Assocs., Inc., 500 Washington St, Ste 750, San Francisco 94111

KRAYE, HOWARD, executive; b. Apr. 3, 1941, Chgo.; s. Phil M. and Frances (Binder) K.; m. Saundra J. Schneier, June 30, 1963; children: Tamra Linn, b. 1965; Kevin Michael, b. 1969; edn: BS, USAF Acad. 1963; MS, Purdue Univ. 1965; Reg. Profl. Engr. Calif. 1981. Career: pres. Plast-Alum Mfg., Inc., Glendale; pres. Conserdyne Corp., Los Angeles; chmn. Calif. State Energy Bank 1981-; chmn. Calif. Solar Council 1980-; honors: L.A. Energy Conservation Awd. 1982; L.A. City Council Awd. for civic involvement 1983; mem: Internat. Solar Energy Soc.; Calif. Solar Energy Inds. Assn.; Newhall Sch. Newspaper advr.; publs: sev. arts. for nat. & internat. alternate energy jours.; mil: capt. USAF, Commdn. Medal; Republican; Jewish; rec: white water rafting, skiing. Res: 25345 Avenida Ronada Valencia 91355 Ofc: Conserdyne Corp., 11611 San Vincent Blvd, Ste 1050, Los Angeles 90049

KRCMAR, JANET, librarian; b. June 9, 1936, Moorehead, Minn.; d. Minet Lafayne and Anabel (Lee) Dixon; m. 2d. Ludwig Leopold Krcmar, IV, Dec. 27,

1964; children: Kirk, b. 1955, Corey, b. 1957, Kim, b. 1962, Nancie, b. 1963; edn: BA, L.A. State Coll. 1957; D.Litt. (hon) Hamilton St. Univ., 1973. Career: dir. Tanglewood Sch. for Girls, 1956-58; librn. Riker Labs. 1958-62, Thompson-Ramo-Woodridge 1962-64; supr. of documentation, The Bunker-Ramo Corp., 1964-82; contbr. num. arts. to Spec. Lib. Journ.; ed. Oasis; ed. Library Mgmt. Bulletin 1982-3; mem. Jeff Corey Players (1955), Circle Theatre Group (1956); honors: Award of Great Green Angel, Girl Scouts, 1975; leadership awds., YWCA-L.A., 1976; Human Resource of US, Am. Bicentennial Resrch. Inst., 1976; Calif. State Figure Skating Champion 1955; Most Outstanding Drama Student, Valley Coll. 1956; scholarship awd., Univ. Women, 1955-56; recogn., L.A. chpt. Am. Soc. for Information Sci., 1970; mem: Am. Lib. Assn., Calif. Lib. Assn., Assn. of Computing Mach., Nat. Councilor-at-lg. Am. Soc. for Inf. Sci. 1978-; L.A. City Sch. career guidance bd. 1964-, (trade tech.) L.A. Colls. Adv. Bd., ofcr. Spl. Libs. Assn. 1965- (pres. 1977-8), Calif. Ind.-Edn. Council (pres. 1968, bd. 1976-), Am. Fedn. of Mineralogists, pres. Simi Valley Art Assn., Union; mem. Pi Delta Pi, Alpha Psi Omega, Alpha Mu Gamma, Sierra Club; Episcopal; rec: art, mineralogy, skating. Res: 1529 Kane Ave Simi Valley Ofc: Arete Associates, 5445 Balboa Blvd Encino

KREH, KENNETH ERWIN, financial- business consultant; b. May 31, 1934, Flint, Mich.; s. Oscar and Doris (Brugger) K.; m. Beverly, Apr. 7, 1962; children: Kristy, b. 1963; Kent, b. 1965; Kurtis, b. 1967; edn: Indsl. Tech., Gen. Motors Inst. 1957; BS, Univ. of Mich. 1960; MBA, Univ. of Detroit 1969; CFP 1982; EA 1984. Career: indsl. tech. 1960-71; TRW, Ill. Inst. Tech.; Research Inst., Gen. Electric, Chgo. & Detroit; mktg. exec. Resdel Eng. & Altec Corp., 1971-76; prin., financial and bus. planning, Kreh & Assocs. 1976--; dir. Indsl. Plnnrs. Mgmt.; instr. USC, and Calif. St. Univ.; honors: Beta Gamma Sigma; pres. North Central chpt. Numerical Control Soc.; pres. Bloomfields Hill Imp. Assn.: mem: City Club of San Marino; Internat. Assn. Fin. Plnnrs.; Inst. CFPs; Univ. of Mich. Alumni Club, L.A.; Bond Club; publs: num. arts. on auto. mfg., bus. & personal plnng.; mil: US Army 1956-57; Protestant; rec; computer pgmmg., photog. Res: 1450 Lorain Rd San Marino 91108 Ofc: Kreh & Assocs., 532 El Dorado St, Ste 200, Pasadena 91101

KREISLER, MARTIN H., financial manager; b. Aug. 11, 1944, Los Angeles; s. Sol S. and Win (Levine) K.; children: Ari, b. 1974; Marc, b. 1975; edn: BS, CSU Long Beach 1966; MBA, USC 1971. Career: volunteer Peace Corps, Ghana, Africa 1966-69; asst. controller Daylin Med. & Surgical, Los Angeles 1971-72; asst. controller Technicolor, Inc., L.A. 1973-76; asst. v.p. Security First Gp., L.A. 1977 78; chief finl. ofcr. Calif Assn. Realtors, L.A. 1979--; treas. No. American Raceco, Inc.; secty./ treas. Calif. Assn. Realtors Mortgage Asst. Corp., Carrie Mac; mem: Balboa Village Homeowners Assn.; YMCA (Indian Guides); Nat. Assn. Accts., USC MBA Club; publs: Basis Guide to Financial Management and Board Structure (1982); Republican; Jewish; rec: off road race cars. Res; 9030 Dempsey Ave Sepulveda 91343 Ofc: California Assn. of Realtors, 525 S Virgil Los Angeles 90020

KRINDLE, DANIEL JASON, lawyer; b. Jan. 6, 1940, Winnipeg, Manitoba, Can.; s. Sam E. and Sophie (Rosen) K.; edn: BA, honors, Univ. of Manitoba 1961, LLB, 1965; Barrister and Solicitor, 1965, Man., Can. Career: assoc. D'Arcy, Irving Haig & Smethurst, Barristers & Solicitors, Winnipeg 1965-70; assoc. law firm of Gibson, Dunn & Crutcher, Los Angeles, Ca. 1971-73, law firm of Haight, Dickson, Brown & Bonesteel, L.A. 1973-78; atty., Daniel Jason Krindle A Profl. Law Corp., Los Angeles 1978--; arbitrator: Los Angeles Superior Ct., Fee Dispute Com. (L.A.), and Am. Arbitration Assn.; recipient commendns. for legal articles, Atty. Gen. of Manitoba (1963), Govt. of Canada (1976); mem: Law Soc. of Manitoba, Manitoba Bar Assn., Am. Bar Assn. (sustaining), LA Trial Lawyers Assn. (sustaining), Calif. Trial Lawyers (sustaining); mem. Beverly Hills, Century City Bar Assns. (bus. litigation sect.); Cert. of Experience Products Liability, P.I., Med. Malpractice, Dosmetic Relations (Calif.); author: Medical Illustrations for the Purpose of Settlement & Trial (1984); mem. Thalians Pres. Club, Bev. Hills Mens Charities Orgn., Soc. of the Founders of Hebrew Univ. of Jerusalem; rec: football, aerobics, wt.lifting. Res: 1284 Monte Cielo Dr Beverly Hills 90210 Ofc: Daniel Jason Krindle APLC, 10880 Wilshire Blvd, Ste 1900, Los Angeles 90024

KRIZ, JOSEPH ALOIS, educator, writer, business consultant; b. Mar. 16, 1920, Oshkosh, Wisc.; s. Rudy Aloyious and Catherine Ann (Klemmer) K.; m. Doloris Hesser, Aug. 5, 1944; children: Susan Terese (McKechnie),b. 1955, Mary Kay (Cox), b. 1957; edn: BS, US Naval Acad. 1942; MBA, Columbia Univ. 1952; postgrad. stu. GBS Harvard, UC Berkeley. Career: served to Comdr. Supply Corps, USN, 1942-63; tours as Comptroller/Supply Dir. of two major Navy air stations; Supply Ofcr. of Aviation Supply Ship during Korean War, prof., four years, US Navy Postgrad. Sch. (estab. 1st grad. bus. sch. in US Mil.); lectr. Univ. of Texas, Arlington, 1 yr.; lectr. UC Berkeley, 2 yrs.; prof./ Small Bus. Coord. Diablo Valley Coll., Pleasant Hill 1965-84, ret.; guest lectr. 1984-; vol. SCORE/ACE pgm. of the Small Bus. Adminstrn. 1970-; creator/ instr. course in Logistics fr Peruvian Naval Acad., Lima, Peru 1949; vol. cons. to Contra Costa County Bd. of Suprs. (new civil svc. personnel code) 1969-71; mem. PROBE study group of the Commn. for Study of Higher Edn. 1972-75; past cons. Allis Chalmers Corp., and Santa Fe Indus.; honors: num. ltrs of commendn., (6) area ribbons from mil. duty WWII, Korean War; Beta Gamma Sigma (bus. hon.), Beta Alpha Psi (acct. hon.), Bus. Tchr. of Year 1973-4 (Diablo Vly Coll), Fellow Found. of Econ. Ed. (1969, 1974); mem: Am. Mgmt. Assn., Soc. for Advanced Mgmt., Western Mktg. Assn. (bd. govs. 1979-81); author: Your Dynamic World of Business (McGraw Hill 1974), other texts and short arts.; author suspense novel: Conch Chowder (1984); Republican; Catholic; rec: bridge, sports. Res: Palma Vista 25, Diablo 94528

KROELLIAN, FRANZ MANUK, accountant, systems analyst; b. Sept. 15, 1948, Brockton, Mass.; s. Franklin L. and Mary Elaine (Kayian) Kroell; edn: BS in B.A., Walla Walla Coll. 1970; MA in edn., CSU San Diego 1977, MBA (cand.), tax plnng., 1984; Calif. Lic. Tax Preparer; Calif. Std. Sec. Tchr. credential, Comm. Coll. Instr. cred. Career: youth pastor Christian Ch., La Mesa 1970-71; adminstrv. trainee Fin. Mgmt. Dept., City of San Diego 1971-72, junior acct. Human Resources Dept., 1972-73, jr. asst./assoc. acct. Dept. of Public Wks. 1973-74; auditor & controller Health Svcs., County of San Diego, 1977-82; business edn. instr. Escondido Union High Sch. Dist., 1982-83, study sabbatical, 1983-4; honors: nationwide Latin Exam. honoree; svc. awd. County of S.D.; mem: Soc. of Calif. Accts., Calif. Business Edn. Assn., Sierra Club, Am. Film Club, Armenian Youth Cultural Soc., Delta Upsilon Frat., Commodore 64K Coastal Users Gp. (pres.), Old Globe Theatre Ushers Gp. (v.p.); sev. scholarly publs., pub. poetry; Republican (cpgn. Gov. Deukmejian); rec: backpacking, windsurfing, pets. Address: Manuk Korellian POB 99911 San Diego 92109

KRONER, MARVIN, distributing & manufacturing co. executive; b. Apr. 9, 1918, Phila., Pa.; s. Paul and Ethel (Sunshine) K.; m. Esther Parra, Apr. 22, 1950; children: Lynn, b. 1956; Patricia, b. 1958; Paul, b. 1961; edn: Los Angeles Jr. Coll. 1937. Career: sales Ida Lubin Co., Los Angeles 1940-43; sales Ben Kluger Co., L.A. 1946-48; pres. Acme Thread & Supply, Inc., L.A. 1948--; curently, v.p Mark Textile Corp; dir./ pres. Coalition of Apparel Indus. in Calif. 1984-; fmr. pres./dir. Textile Assn. of L.A. 1975-77; mem.Mitsui Mfrs. Bank/ L.A. adv. bd.; honors: Man of the Yr., Textile Assn. of L.A. 1971; citations, City of Los Angeles 1973, 1975; mem: Merchant Club; Fashion Indus. Club (charter); Wine & Food Soc., San Fernando Valley; Los Angeles Athletic Club; Del Rey Yacht Club; Magic Castle; The Springs Club (Rancho Mirage); CAIC; TALA; The Guardians; ACLU; ADA; mil: boatswains mate 2/c USNR, maritime svc.; rec: running, internat. travel. Res: 15430 Valley Vista Blvd Sherman Oaks 91403 Ofc: Acme Thread & Supply, Inc., 826 S Los Angeles St Los Angeles 90014

KREUGER, EDNA ELIZABETH, optical & sporting goods co. executive; b. July 24, 1922, Detroit, Mich.; d. John Morgan and Lillian Winifred (Doherty) Thomas; m. Dr. Richard H. Krueger; children: Richard Heinrich; Thomas Eduard; Paul Eric; edn: BS, Wayne State Univ. 1942; grad. wk. UCLA 1975-77; Calif. Inst. Tech. 1977-84; USC 1973-83; Loyola Marymount 1980-81. Career: owner/ gen. mgr. Krueger Constrn. Co., Airjet Ventilator Co., S.C. Steel Fabricators, and S.C. Heating & Ventilating Co., 1943 66; ofc. mgr. Pacesetter Homes 1964-66; dir. personnel Salfed Corp. Kentucky Fried Chicken 1966-70, asst. gen. mgr. 1968-70; personnel mgr. Bushnell 1970-, dir. personnel, 1979, dir. human resources Bushnell, Div. of Bausch & Lomb 1980--, v.p. So. Coast Comm. Hosp.; Capistrano Beach Club bd. dirs.; personnel mgmt. instr. Pasadena City Coll. 1980; mem. Personnel & Indsl. Rels. Assn. (exec. bd. dirs. & chprsn. Dist. III; moderator 1983 Annual Conf.); Exec. Women Internat. (exec. com.); Am. Mfrs. Assn.; Am. Soc. for Personel Admin.; San Gabriel County Adv. League; Pasadena CofC; Womens Civic League; West Point Army/ Navy '83 Found; Nat. Assn. for Female Execs.; Soroptomist; Bus. & Profl. Women; Internat. Assn. of Personnel Women; L.A. Basin Equal Opportunity League; Calif. Inst. Tech. Svc. League Bd.; Pasadena Urban League; publs: newsletter, Bushnell Banner 1972-80; newsletter, Three's A Crowd, Personnel & Indsl. Rels. Assn. 1983; mil: observer USAF 1962-63, So. Calif.; Republican (Central Com.); rec: public speaking, sailing, photog. res: 1150 Fairview Ave Arcadia 91006 Ofc: Bushnell, Div. of Bausch & Lomb, 2828 E Foothill Blvd Pasadena 91107

KUEI, CHIH-CHUNG, computer programmer; b. June 30, 1950, Taipei, Taiwan; s. Shu-Yew and Jing-Hong (Chi) K.; m. Kady Tan, Feb. 6, 1977; 1 child: Fan-Chin, b. 1979; edn: BS, Chung-Yuan Univ. 1972; M.Computer Sci., Stevens Inst. of Tech. 1980. Career: math. instr. Chung-Yu Jr. Coll., Taiwan 1974-78; research asst. Stevens Computer Graphics Lab., Hoboken, NJ 1979-80; computer pgmr./ analyst Computer Sharing Svcs., Inc., Oakland, Calif. 1980-82; computer pgmr. Tricad, Inc., Milpitas 1982--; mem: Assn. for Computing Machines; IEEE (Computer Soc.); Catholic; rec: bridge, chess. Res: 267 Edwin Way Hayward 94544 Ofc: Tricad, Inc., 1655 McCarthy Blvd Milpitas 95035

KUHL, PAUL BEACH, lawyer; b. Jul. 15, 1935, Elizabeth, N.J.; s. Paul Edmund and Charlotte Imogene (Hetche) K.; m. Janey Stadheim, Jun. 24, 1967; children: Alison, b. 1969; Todd, b. 1970. Edn: BA, Cornell Univ., 1957; LLB, Stanford Univ., 1960; admitted State Bar of Calif. 1961. Career: attorney Law Offices of Walter C. Kohn, San Francisco, 1961-63; atty. Sedgwick, Detert, Moran & Arnold, San Francisco, 1963--.; lecturer, Calif. Continuing Edn. of the Bar, faculty Hastings Coll. of Trial Advocacy; advocate, Am. Bd. Trial Advocates, 1983. Mem: Defense Research Inst.; No. Calif. Assn. of Defense Counsel; San Francisco Trial Lawyers Assn.; Am. Bar Assn. Mem. Canon Tennis Club, Tahoe Tavern Property Owners Assn. (sec./pres.). Mil: Lt., US Coast Guard Reserve, 1961-68; Republican. Rec: tennis, music. Res: Box 574 Ross 94957 Ofc: Sedgwick, Detert, Moran, & Arnold, 111 Pine St. Suite 1100, San Francisco 94111

KUHN, CHARLES E., corporate executive; b. Nov. 29, 1919, Cincinnati, Oh.; s. Leo and Vivian K.; m. Elma Jane Smith, Nov. 17, 1944 (div.); m. Patrica L. McVicar, Nov. 27, 1974 (div. 1980); m. Rena Horten, Jun. 1, 1980 (div. 1983); children: Karen Jo Ann, James Roland. Edn: Purdue Univ., 1938-39. Career: v.p. Fansteel Metal Corp., 1950-55; Hills McCanna Co. 1955-58; v.p. Dresser Mfg. Div. of Dresser Ind., Inc., 1958-60, pres. 1960-64; group v.p./dir. Parent

Co., 1964-65, exec. v.p. 1965-68, pres./chief op. ofcr. 1968-70; pres./dir. Wylain Inc., Dallas. chmn. bd. and CEO 1970-82; bd. dirs.: General Portland, Inc., Dallas Bay; Beer Distr., Rendondo Bch; Am. First Corp.: Am. Gas Assn., Florida Council of 100, Pennsylvania Soc., Canadian Gas Assn.. Mil: USNR 1940-42. Res: 1654 Mandeville Canyon Rd. Los Angeles 90049. Ofc: POB 800443 Dallas Texas 75380

KUIVENHOVEN, ROY JOHN, SR., company president; b. June 30, 1939, Los Angeles; s. John and Ramona Mary (Coronel) K.; m. Anita, Apr. 15, 1960; children: Roy Jr., b. 1961; David, b. 1962; Paula, b. 1965; John C., b. 1982; edn: BA, Los Angeles State 1964. Career: sales engr. Otis Elev.; br. mgr. ITT Wire & Cable; distbr. Mil. Spec. Supply; gen. mgr., Adv. Elec. Sales; v.p. sales Y-R Assoc.; currently, pres. Kal Wire Co., Inc. & chmn. bd./ corp. dir. Computer Cable Indus. Inc.; mem: Islam Shrine (pres.); Crippled Childrens Soc., Santa Clara (mem. bd.); mil: sgt. E-5 US Army; Republican; Catholic; rec: classic vehicles (40 in collection). Res: 14615 Gallant Fox Morgan Hills 95037 Ofc: Computer Cable Industries, Inc., 2971 Mead Ave Santa Clara 95051

KUKLIN, JEFFREY PETER, talent agency executive; b. Dec. 13, 1935, NY, NY; s. Norman Bennett and Deane Kuklin; m. Jensina Olson, 1960, div. 1969; son, Andrew b. 1967; m. 2d. Ronia Levene, June 22, 1969; children: Adam b. 1971, Jensena b. 1974, Jeremy b. 1975; edn: AB, Columbia Coll. 1957; JD, Columbia Law Sch. 1960. Career: program atty., Am. Broadcasting Co., NYC 1969-72, L.A. 1972-73, also assoc. dir. contracts 1970-73; bus. affairs atty. Internatl. Famous Agency, Los Angeles 1973-74, v.p. bus. affairs & law, West Coast 1974-75; v.p. legal & bus. affairs, Billy Jack Ent., Culver City 1975-76; bus. affairs exec. William Morris Agency Inc., Beverly Hills 1976-79, hd. TV bus. affairs 1979-81, vice pres./hd. TV Bus. Affairs Dept. 1981--; listed, Who's Who in Am. Law; mem. Acad. of TV Arts & Scis. 1973-, L.A. Copyright Soc. 1973-, Am. Bar Assn. 1962-. Res: 30312 Eaglebrook Dr Agoura Hills 91301 Ofc: William Morris Agency Inc. 151 El Camino Dr Beverly Hills 90212

KULCZYCKI, STEVEN EDWARD, television program executive; b. May 1, 1950, Chgo.; s. Edward and Jean Norman (McNielly) K.; m. Jody Singer, Nov. 25, 1983; children: Briana S. Landau, b. 1968; Jenna S. Singer, b. 1973; edn: Drake Univ. 1968-9, BA, Univ. Minn. 1972; Adv. Mgmt. Pgm. The Wharton Sch. of Bus., Univ. Penna. 1983. Career: general mgr. University Community Video, Mnpls. 1973-75; deputy dir. Pgmmg., KTCA-TV, Mnpls./St. Paul 1978-80, v.p. Broadcasting, 1980-83; vice pres. Pgmmg. KCET-TV, Los Angeles, 1983--; honors: Film Festival Awards competition winner for a list of TV prodns. incl. the Chicago Internat., Atlanta, others; mem. Nat. Acad. of TV Arts and Scis. Res: 12741 Bloomfield St Studio City 91604 Ofc: KCET-TV, 4401 Sunset Blvd Los Angeles 90027

KULKA, PHYLIS CHRISTINE, psychotherapist; b. Dec. 6, 1921, Auckland, N.Z., nat. 1948; d. Trevor Francis and Olive R. (Bray) McCarthy; m. Frank L. Kulka (dec. 1981), Aug. 11, 1944; children: Kathleen, b. 1947, Ronald, b. 1950; edn: BA, National Univ. 1980; MA, Profl. Sch. of Psychol. Studies, 1982; PhD, Golden State Univ. 1983; desig: Marriage, Family, Child Counselor Intern, BBSE Calif. 1983. Career: primary grade school tchr. in sev. states and Hawaii, 22 years; pvt. practice psychotherapy, Vista, Calif. 1983--; cons. EternalHills Mortuary; instr. Profl. Sch. for Psychol. Studies 1982; honors: recogn. for outstanding public svc. as mem. Crime Prevention Commn., City Council of Vista; mem: Assn. for Humanistic Psychology, No. County Psychol. Assn., Am. Psychol. Assn. (assoc.), Senior Citizens, Disabled Am. Vets., Lifeline Comm. Svcs.; author: Psychic Surgery: A study to determine correlation of specific personality traits and successful psychic surgery (6/83); Democrat; Catholic; rec: gardening and preserving the harvest. Address: 1044 Prospect Pl Vista 92083

KUM, JIMMY LEE, business owner; b. Aug. 24, 1923, San Francisco; s. Dat. T. and Shew S. Kum; m. May O., Mar. 31, 1964; children: Robert J.,b. 1965; Lawrence J., b. 1967; David J., b. 1970; edn: AA, City Coll. of San Francisco 1948; BS, Univ. of Calif. 1951; MBA, Columbia Pacific Univ. 1980; JD, Southland Univ. 1983; Calif. Comm. Coll. Instr. Credential; lic. Public Acct., Real Estate Broker, Ins. Broker, Notary Public. Career: gen. mgr. Kum's Svcs. Co.; author: Basic Understanding Pertaining to Real Estate; mem: Nat. Soc. Pub. Accts.; Nat., Calif., and San Francisco Assns. Realtors; Chinese Am. Citizens Alliance; mil: US Army Signal Corps; Democrat; Baptist; rec; baseball, football, tennis. Address: 3814 Moraga St San Fracisco 94122

KUMAGI, TOM TAKETO, lawyer; b. Feb. 21, 1927, Dines, Wyo.; s. Frank Kikuji and Tommie Tamai (Tsuru) K.; m. Pierrette, Oct. 18, 1974; edn; BS, Univ. of Utah 1950; MA, 1952; JD, Western State Univ. 1972; admitted to practice, State Bar of Calif. Career: senior staff engr. Hughes Aircraft Co., Culver City, Los Angeles, Fullerton 1952-63; staff scientist Rockwell Internat., Anaheim 1963-74; atty. at law, pvt. practice, Garden Grove 1974--; honors: Phi Beta Kapp 1950; Phi Kappa Phi 1950; Sigma Pi Sigma 1949; mem: Calif. State Bar; Orange Co. Bar Assn.; Los Angeles Trial Lawyers Assn. (former); Japanese Am. Citizen League (past pres. Orange Co. chpt.); patentee: early basic computer design incl. error detection & correction, machine tool control, and magnetic sensors, also Laser Radar sys.; sev. tech. publs. on missile trajectory analyses, perturbation theory and oblateness effects; mil: US Army 1945-46; Republican; rec: computer handicapping. Ofc: 12570 Brookhurst St, Ste 1, Garden Grove 92640

KUMANO, AKIHIKO, mechanical engineer; b. Dec. 2, 1951, Tokyo, Japan, nat. 1976; s. Taminori and Mariko (Kanasaka) K.; m. Kazuko, Sept. 19, 1975; children: Kaoru, b. 1977; Yoko, b. 1980; edn: BS, Seikei Univ., Tokyo 1975; M.Eng., Penn. State Univ. 1976; PhD, UC Berkeley 1980; Reg. Profl. Engr., Calif. 1982. Career: research engr. Seikei Univ., Tokyo, Japan 1975; research asst. Penn. State Univ. 1975-76, UCB 1977-80; senior adv. engr. Shugart Assoc., Sunnyvale 1980-81; tech. leader/ project mgr. Nutech Engrs. Inc., San Jose 1981-83; senior engr. Seagate Technology, Scotts Valley 1983--; Research Fellow, supvsr. R&D activities, UC Berkeley 1980--; cons., senior consultation for utility industry, Nutech Engrs. Inc. 1983-; honors: Rep. of Grad. Class, Seikei Univ. 1975; Research Asst., UCB 1977-80; Earle C. Anthony Tuition Scholarship, UCB 1977; mem: Am. Soc. of Mech. Engrs. (assoc.); patents: (1) Japan, and (2) US (pend.); publs: sev. tech. papers incl. 2 NSF reports, conf. presentations, 1976-; Res: 10461 Davison Ave Cupertino 95014 Ofc: Seagate Technology, 900 Disc Dr Scotts Valley 95066

KUMASAKA, ANDREW KAORU, psychiatrist; b Mar. 27, 1950, Chgo.; s. George and Yuriko (Kawaguchi) K.; m. Carmen Arriaga, Aug. 15, 1981; edn: BA, Stanford Univ. 1972; MD, UCLA 1976; Calif. Lic. Physician & Surgeon, 1976. Career: staff psychiatrist So. Calif. Permanente Med. Gp., Los Angeles 1980-81; staff psychiatrist Santa Cruz Co. Mental Health Svcs., Santa Cruz 1981-83; staff psychiatrist, Dominican Mental Health Unit, Santa Cruz 1983; currently, pvt. practice psychiatry; cons.: Benjamin Rush Clinic, Venice 1979-80, Harbor Hills Locked Skilled Nursing Facility, Santa Cruz 1983, Lifespan, Santa Cruz 1983, Nuevo Paseo Gp. Homes, Santa Cruz 1982-83; honors: Superior top rating, Nat. Piano Playing Auditions 1957-68; Nat. Merit Semi-Finalist 1968; Japanese Am. Citizens League, Jr. Citizen Award, Seattle, Wash. 1968; Diplomate Am. Bd. of Pyschiatry & Neurology 1983; mem: Dominican Santa Cruz Hosp., Comm. Hosp. of Santa Cruz, Santa Cruz Gen. Hosp. (med. staff); Family Svcs. Assn.; works: design & constrn. Seattle Mus. of Sci. & Ind. 1970; Multi- media presentation on relocation of Japanese-Americans during WWII, Stanford Univ. 1972; Discussion of Sexual Disfunction Treatment in US, Network TV, from Tokyo, Japan 1980; presented course on Morita Psychotherapy, UCLA- NPI 1980; contbg. writer book chpt., Flowing Bridges: Silent Waters (1984); rec: writing poetry, piano, basketball. Res: 181 La Cima Soquel 95073 Ofc: 1595 Soquel Dr, Ste 410, Santa Cruz 95065

KUMMER, ROBERT W., JR., banker; b. May 31, 1936, Pittsburgh, Pa.; s. Robert, Sr. and Mary Louise (Preskar) K.; m. Barbara Tanzola, Sept. 20, 1980; children: Christopher, b. 1963, Mark, b. 1964, David, b. 1966, David Hillman, b. 1966, Tricia Hillman, b. 1969, Peter Hillman, b. 1970; edn: BA, Oberlin Coll. 1958, UC Berkeley 1960. Career: director of devel. Oberlin College, 1960-62; sr. vice pres./gen. mgr. Union Bank, Los Angeles 1962-81; chmn. bd./CEO, 1st Business Bank, L.A. 1981--; mem: Independent Bankers Assn., Calif. Bankers Assn., Am. Bankers Assn., CEO Club of Los Angeles; orgns: Big Brothers of Gr. LA, United Way, Am. Cancer Soc., Jonathan Club, Oakmont CC; Republican; Catholic; rec: golf, hiking, travel. Res: 1925 West Mountain, Glendale 91201 Ofc: 1st Business Bank, 601 West Fifth St Los Angeles 90071

KUNC, JOSEPH A., physicist; b. Nov. 1, 1943, Baranowicze, Poland; s. Stefan and Helena (Kozakiewicz) K.; edn: MS, Warsaw Tech. Univ. 1969, PhD in plasma physics, 1974. Career: assoc. prof. Warsaw Technical Univ. 1974-79; vis. prof. Nat. Bureau of Standards, Atomic and Plasma Radiation Div. Wash DC, 1978; research affiliate Calif. Inst. of Tech., 1982-83; assoc. prof. Dept. of Physics, Univ. So. Calif., 1979--; awards: Fellowship, Nat. Bur. of Stds. USA, 1978, merit cert., 1979; var. resrch., tchg., and merit awards, Warsaw Tech. Univ., 1971-78; mem: The Am. Physical Soc., IEEE; Catholic; rec: skiing, sailing. Res: 3565 Linden Ave Long Beach 90807 Ofc: Phys. Dept. SHS-274, University of Southern California, Los Angeles 90007

KUNZMAN, E. EUGENE, psychiatrist; b. Feb. 16, 1937, Elmira, NY; s. Edward Eric and Jenny Farnham (Bradigan) K.; m. Lucy Ann, June 19, 1965; children: Robert, b. 1968, Susan, b. 1971; edn: AA, Pasadena City Coll. 1957; MD, USC Sch. of Med. 1963; bd. cert. Am. Bd. of Psychiatry and Neurology 1976. Career: child psychiatric cons. Five Acres Home for Boys and Girls, Altadena 1972-77; staff psychiatrist/coord. Children's and Adolescent's Services, San Gabriel Valley Mental Hlth. Ctr., Arcadia 1972-76, Arcadia Mental Hlth. Ctr., Arcadia 1978--; medical dir. Center Against Abusive Behavior, Pasadena; asst. prof. of psychiat. L.A. Co.-USC Med. Ctr., 1976-79, assoc. clin. prof. of psychiat. Dept. Psychiat. USC Sch. of Medicine, 1979--; mem: Am. Psychiat. Assn., So. Calif. Psychiat. Soc., Calif. Forensic Mental Hlth. Assn., San Marino City Club; mil: lt. comdr. USPHS, 1966-68; Republican; Presbyterian; rec: coins/stamps, coll. football statistics. Res: 1862 Warwick Rd San Marino 91108 Ofc: Arcadia Mental Heath Center, 330 East Live Oak Ave Arcadia 91006

KUNKEL, ELDRED JOHN, real estate developer; b. Oct. 24, 1931, Marion, S.Dak.; s. Gustav Lawrence and Marie Bertha (Hiebert) K.; m. Evelyn Schellenberg, May 19, 1951; children: Cheryl, b. 1954; Bruce, b. 1958; Brad, b. 1958; edn: BA, San Jose State Univ. 1953. Career: constrn. supt. Plett Constrn. 1955-58; owner Eldred Kunkel Bldrs. 1958-69; pres. Kunkel-Thomas Co. 1968-74; pres. Eldred Kunkel Assocs., Campbell 1975--; mem. Plaza Bank Adv. Panel 1980-; real estate broker 1973-; mem: Realtors Nat. Mktg. Inst., comml. investment div.; vocal soloist; Republican; Mennonite Brethren (ch. moderator); rec: reg.. breeder Tex. Longhorn cattle and Paint horses. Ofc: Eldred Kunkel Assoc., 1350 Dell Ave., Ste 202, Campbell 95008

KUNKEL, GINA RAE, product design engineer; b. June 15, 1959, Detroit, Mich.; d. Ray George and Shirley E. (Farsakian) K.; edn: BS, mech. engr., Mich. State Univ. 1982, BS, packaging engr. 1982; grad. stu. bus. ad., Pepperdine Univ. currently. Career: senior acct. M.S.U. Sch. of Pkg., East Lansing, MI 1978-80; mech.- pkg. engr. Digital Equip. Corp., Maynard, MA 1980; sys.

L

engr./ cons. J.D. Seagram & Sons, NYC 1981; senior research asst./ cons. M.S.U. Sch. of Pkg., MI 1980-82; product design engr. Hughes Aircraft Co., Los Angeles 1982--, leader of Quality Circle 1984, respons. engr. Authority Leasat , 1982-83, electronic packaging 1984; honors: Achiev. Awds. (2), Hughes Aircraft 1983; Cost Improvement 1983; v.p., M.S.U. Sch. of Pkg. 1982; Jr. of the Yr., MSU 1981; mem: Soc. of Plastics Engrs. (MSU rep. 1980); Am. Soc. Mech. Engrs. (affiliate); Soc. of Pkg. & Handling Engrs.; Hughes Running Club; Electronic Pkg. & Prodn.; publs: Influence & Response of Can Shipping Containers to the Rail Mode of Transportation, MSU Sch. of Pkg. 1982; Republican; Presbyterian; rec: computer simulation and consulting, electronic packaging and logistics. Res: 615 S Prospect, Apt 201, Redondo Beach 90277 Ofc: Hughes Aircraft Co., POB 92919, 530/ P323, Los Angeles 90009

KUNIN, RICHARD A., physician; b. Oct. 22, 1932, Mnpls.; s. Maxim and Jeannette (Simons) K.; m. Matilda Lucretia Manning, Feb. 16, 1961; 1 son, Gregory Maxim, b. 1962; edn: BS in chem., Univ. of Minn. 1953, MD, Univ. Minn. Med. Sch. 1955; diplomate Am. Board Psychiatry and Neurology (in psychiatry) 1962. Career: asst. res. in psychiatry NY Hosp., Cornell Med. Ctr. (Payne Whitney Clinic) 1956-59; post doctoral special fellow in neurophysiology Stanford Univ. Med. Ctr., dept. of neurology 1962-63; pvt. practice psychiatry and general medical practice 1963--; pres. SF Acad. of Hypnosis, 1970; pres. Orthomolecular Med. Soc., 1979-81; author: Meganutrition (McGraw Hill 1980), Meganutrition for Women (McGraw Hill 1983); mil: capt. US Army M.C. 1959-61. Address: 2698 Pacific, San Francisco 94115

KUO, RICHARD WU-CHIAO, Asian/internat. trading co. owner, educator; b. Jan. 22, 1913, Anhwei, China; nat. 1979; s. Kuo Yuen-Hsuen and Tsun Shu (Liang) K.; brother, Gen. Kuo Chi-Chiao, ret. Minister of Nat. Defense, Taiwan, China; m. Sylvia Shou-Cheng Sung, Feb. 22, 1974; children: Pai-Hua, b. 1948, Tiao-Hua, b. 1936, O-Hua, b. 1939, Mai-Hua,b. 1950, Wei-Hua, b. 1955; edn: BA, Wash. State Univ., Pullman, 1930, MA, 1932; DCS (comml. sci.), NY Univ., 1935. Career: prof. Dept. of Finance & Industry, CSU Fresno 1971; vis. prof. Morgan State Coll. (Baltimore, Md.) 1971-72, Amer. Grad. Sch. of Mgmt. (Glendale, Ariz.) 1972; prof./dept. chmn., Dept. Indsl. & Bus. Mgmt., 1973-74 and acting dean Coll. of Commerce, Nanyang Univ., Singapore, 1966; prof. Provincial Chung Hsin Univ., Taiwan 1961-62; gen. mgr. China Devel. Corp. 1950-62; adv. China Agri. Devel. Corp. (subs. Farmers Bank of China, Taiwan) 1950-62; bd. dirs. Chinese Petroleum Corp., Taiwan 1950-56; mem. British Inst. of Mgmt , Am Mktg Assn ; author num articles and books on monetary systems. Res: 544 Colusa Ave El Cerrito 94530

KURAHASHI, TEISEI, company executive; b. Jan. 3, 1934, Tokyo, Japan; s. Sadamu and Tazuko (Fukano) K ; m. Kazuko, Oct. 19, 1958; 1 child Michiko, b. 1959; edn: BA, cum laude Keio Univ. 1957. Career: with Nippon Steel Corp. 1969-81, Nippon Steel USA, Inc. 1981--; mgr. export sales 1969; mgr. corp. plng. 1974; deputy gen. mgr. corp. plng. 1978; exec. v.p. 1981--; v.p. Japan Bus. Assn. of So. Calif.; mem: Japan Bus. Assn. of So. Calif.; Calif. CofC; University Club; Breamar Country Club; Los Coyotes Country Club; Methodist; rec: classical music. Ofc: Nippon Steel U.S.A., Inc., 611 W 6th St, Ste 2900, Los Angeles 90017

KURAN, PETER GAVIN, motion picture visual effects co. owner; Sept. 6, 1956, E. Orange, NJ; s. Jack Peter and Patricia (MacDonald) K.; edn: BA, Cal-Arts 1978. Career: animator Lucasfilm, Star Wars 1977; animator Universal, Battlestar Galactica 1978; animation supvr. Lucasfilm, Empire Strikes Back 1979; owner/ pres./ chmn. bd. VCE (Visual Concept Engring.), Inc. 1980--; handling visual effects for motion pictures: Dragonslayer, Conan- the Barbarian, Star Trek II, Return of the Jedi, others; awards: Special Effects Award for The Howling, Acad. of Sci. Fiction Fantasy and Horror 1978; Unitarian. Res: 1220 Cole Pl, No 9, Hollywood 90028 Ofc: VCE, Inc., 1157 N Highland Ave Hollywood 90038

KUTASI, LESLIE THOMAS, textile manufacturing co. president; b. Nov. 2, 1950, Budapest, Hungary, nat. 1962; s. Sigmond and Veronika Kutasi; m. Michelle Gaither, Aug. 26 1972; children: Jason, b. 1977; Lauren, b. 1979; edn: BA, USC 1972; MBA, 1973. Career: pres. Stanton-Kutasi Co., Los Angeles 1970--; dir. Textile Assn. of Los Angeles; honors: USC Entrepreneur of the Yr., 1981; mem: Young Pres. Orgn.; Riviera Tennis Club; rec: tennis, skiing, building radio control models. Res: 501 Loring Ave Los Angeles 90024 Ofc: Stanton-Kutasi Co., 1024 S Maple Ave Los Angeles 90015

KVITASH, VADIM I., physician; b. Mar. 19, 1936, Odessa, USSR; married, two daus.; edn: MD, Odessa Med. Sch. 1961; splty. cert., Virology, 1965; PhD, Mechnikov's Sci. and Resrch. Inst. of Virology and Epidemiology, 1969. Career: pediatrician in chg. Novo Ivanovsk (USSR) Hsop. 1961-64; cons. phys./ virologist, resrchr. 1965-70; asst. prof. pediat. Odessa Med. Sch., 1970-74; resrch. asst., assoc. Immunopathways Lab., San Francisco 1976--; founder/dir. Balascopy Inst., S.F. 1980--; resident Dept. Pathol., Mt. Zion Hosp. and Med. Ctr., S.F. 1981-82; phys. pvt. practice Allergy-Immunology, S.F. 1982--; awards incl. Laureate, All-Soviet Union Competition, Best Research Wk. of Young Scientists 1968; mem. S.F. Med. Soc., Calif. Med. Assn., Am. Assn. for Clin. Immunol./Allergy, Internat. Corresp. Soc. of Allergists, Drug Info. Assn.; Am. Assn. for Med. Systems and Informatics, Soc. for Gen. Systems Resrch., Am. Assn. for Artificial Intell., AAAS; publs: (51) books and journal arts. Address: Balascopy Institute, 2352 Post St San Francisco 94115

LACAS, MARK ALAN, manufacturing co. executive; b. Oct. 17, 1956, Chgo.; s. Leo L. and Mary Ann (Chapman); edn: elec. engring., mgmt. major, Purdue Univ. 1977-78; Career: owner custom mfg. firm (indsl. controls for the mfg. industry), spec. in design of audio electronics, 1972-78; chief designer, transp. vehicle monitoring systems, Tora-Flite Inc., Syracuse, Ind. 1973-78; project engr., hybrid microcircuits, CTS Microelectronics, Lafayette, Ind. 1978-80; senior R&D engr. (computerized flt. and maint. trainers to support jet aircraft), Northrop Aircraft, Hawthorne, Ca. 1980-83, cons. Northrop Aircraft/engring. dir. VLSI Networks, 1983--; pres. Fast Feedback Technologies 1983--; awards: 1st School Sci. Fair (Conn.) 1970, 1st Regional Sci. Fair (Ind.) 1975; major winner 1975 Internat. Sci. and Engring. Fair; NASA award expense paid trip to view Apollo-Soyuz blastoff; awards from US Dept. of Transp., Gen. Motors, Am. Astronautical Soc., Am. Patent Lawyers Assn., US Patent Office, FASST, and US Army; mem. IEEE Computer Soc., FASST, Int. Soc. of Hybrid Mfgrs.; inventions: Microtest-100 Personal Computer based Digital Multi meter (1983), Transp. monitoring System (1975); rec: music, sailing, flying. Res: 1717 Harriman Ln Redondo Bch 90278 Ofc: Fast Feedback Technologies 2631 Manhattan Bch Blvd Redondo Beach 90278

LADD, STEVEN GERALD, public administrator; b. Jan. 13, 1946, Delano; s. Scott Gerald and Marjorie Zola (Kelley) L.; m. Susan Hall, June 29, 1973; 1 son: Douglas, b. 1964; edn: Univ. of the Pacific 1963-67; BA, Calif. State Coll. 1974; MA., Vandebilt Univ. 1976. Career: deputy dir. Kern Co. Plng. Dept. 1976--; Bakersfield City Charter Commn. 1979; awards: CSB Alumni of the Yr. 1984; Vanderbilt Univ. Scholar 1974-76; Tenneco Inc. Scholarship 1963-67; mem: Am. Soc. for Pub. Admin. (pres. 1983); CSB Alumni Assn. (pres. 1982); Mensa; mil: s/sgt. USAF 1967-71; Democrat; Disciples of Christ; rec: racquetball. Res: 7208 Mignonette Bakersfield 93308; Ofc: Kern Co. Planning Dept., 1103 Golden State Ave Bakersfield 93301

LAGESON, ERNEST BENJAMIN, lawyer; b. Dec. 19, 1932, Sharon, N.Dak.; s. Ernest and Eunice (McLean) L.; m. Jeanne Marie Lettiere, Apr. 12, 1955; children: Kristine Jeanne, b. 1962; Ernest B., III, b. 1967; edn: AA, UC Berkeley 1952, BS in bus. adm., 1954, LLB, UCB Boalt Hall 1959; admitted to Calif. State Bar 1960. Career: deputy district atty., Ofc. of the Contra Costa County Dist. Atty., Richmond 1959-60; assoc. (gen. litigation dept.) Bronson, Bronson & McKinnon, San Francisco 1961-, partner 1967--, currently senior ptnr., senior trial atty.; mem: Am. Bar Assn., Calif. Bar Assn., S.F. Bar Assn., Ass. of Defense Counsel (bd. dirs. 1974-76), Internat. Assn. of Defense Counsel (v.chmn. Aviation Com. 1980-83), Defense Research Inst. (Calif. State Chmn. 1977-8, Pacific. Regl. V.P. 1978-80, bd. dirs., v.p./Info. 1983-4) (honored as Outstanding State Chmn. 1977); American bd. of Trial Advocates; clubs: Commonwealth Club of Calif., Richmond CC; instr. Calif. Contg. Edn. of the Bar; contbr. law journals; mil: lt.jg USNR, Active Duty 1954-56; Republican; Catholic. Res: 55 Arlington Ct Kensington 94707 Ofc: Bronson, Bronson & McKinnon, 555 California St, Ste 3400, San Francisco 94104

LA GREEN, ALAN LENNART, association manager; b. May 20, 1951, Burbank; s. Lennart F. and Mary (Cassara) LaGreen; m. Wendy Diane Gilmaker, Jun 28, 1975; 1 dau. Cara, b. 1980; edn: BA, jour., USC 1972, grad. stu., CSU Northridge 1973-4. Career: pub. rels. asst. Dames & Moore, Los Angeles 1972-75; asst. publisher Orange County Illustrated, Newport Beach 1975; mbrshp mgr. Toastmasters Internat., Santa Ana 1975-79, pub. affairs mgr., district adminstn. & programming, 1979--; freelance writer; mem: Am. Soc. of Assn. Execs. (Section bd. mem. 1976-7), Pub. Rels. Soc. of Am., Meeting Planners Internat., Toastmasters; publs: art., Passenger Train Jour. 10/79; Republican (Calif. Repub. Assem., asst. campaign mgr. Royce for State Senate 1982); Presbyterian; rec: railroads, photog. res: 120 W. 20th St. Santa Ana 92706 ofc: Toastmasters Int'l 2200 N. Grand Ave Santa Ana 92711

LAI, CAN DINH, accountant; b. Jan. 1, 1936, Hanam, Vietnam, nat. 1981; s. Bang Dinh and Man Thi (Tran) L.; m. Oanh Ngoc Hoang, Nov. 18, 1966; children: Trang Lai, b. 1967; De Lai, b. 1972; edn: LLB, Univ. of Saigon Law Sch., Vietnam 1964. Career: atty. at law, Saigon, Vietnam 1966-75; acct. General Steamship Internat., San Francisco 1979--; real estate broker, S.F. 1981--; pres. Saigon Bar Assn. 1972; mem: San Francisco Bd. Realtors; Vietnamese Friendship and Mutual Assistance Orgn., Bay Area; mil: NCO, Vietnamese Air Force 1956-66, Medal of Merit; rec: tennis, social activities. Res: 2535 44th Ave San Francisco 94116 Ofc: General Steamship International, 400 California St, San Francisco 94116

LAM, MARKS HUNG-SING, corporate executive; b. Jan. 16, 1947, Hong Kong, nat. 1975; s. Wah and Lai Ming (Fung) Lam; m. Yuk Ling Lee, Feb. 15, 1977; chil: Quanen Y., b. 1977, Kenneth Y., b. 1978; edn: BA, San Francisco State Univ. 1974, grad. stu. 1975; lic: real estate broker, Calif. (1978), notary public (1979), real estate appraiser, Soc. of Govtl. Appraisers (1979), travel agt. diploma, Internat. Travel Sch. (1975). Career: founder/sales mgr. Lam's Travel Service Ctr., San Francisco 1974-77; founder/gen. mgr. United Calif. Communication, Inc. (Cable TV ch. 23, S.F.), 1975-77; owner/broker U.S.Property Investments Co. (real estate brokerage and constrn. firm), S.F. 1978--; v.p./ exec. mgr. Fitdy Corp. (trading co.), S.F. 1984--. Mem: SF Real Estate Board; Nat. Notary Assn; Soc. of Govtl. Appraisers; S.F. CofC; Internat. Air Traffic Assn. rec: music, philosophy, community work. res: 1927 32nd Ave San Francisco 94116 ofc: US Property Investments 1321-A Powell St. San Francisco 94133; Fitdy Corp. 950 Stockton St., #401, San Francisco 94108

LAMAR, JUDITH MERRILL, service co. executive; b. July 5, 1945, Oshkosh, Wisc.; d. Erwin Clarence and H. Maxine (Allen) Merrill; m. Robert V. Lamar Jr., Dec. 28, 1965, div. 1979; children: Robert, III b. 1969, James A. b. 1972; edn: Univ. of Ariz. 1963-67; cert. in escrow, Palomar Coll. 1979; Cert. Escrow Ofcr., Calif. Escrow Assn. 1979. Career: travel agent Miramar Travel Agcy., San Diego 1975-77; escrow secty. Rancho Escrow Co., San Diego 1977-79, escrow officer, 1979-80, sole owner, 1980-83; instr. Palomar Coll. Contg. Edn. Pgm. 1983; panelist for Women in Agric. in Third World Countries Forum (4/83); served in Dominican Republic as a vol. administering oral polio vaccine to children; dir. to volunteers in Internat. Service and Awareness 1983-84; chmn. telephone team for S.D. Action Support Center for the End Hunger Televent; mem: No. S.D. County Escrow Assn. (pres. 1983), Calif. Escrow Assn. (dir. 1983), Am. Escrow Assn. (del. Ann. Conv. 1983), Toastmasters (ATM 1983), Soroptomists, founding mem. Profl. and Exec. Women of the Ranch 1982; Republican; United Methodist; rec: cultural anthropol., travel. Res: 17541 Matinal Rd San Diego 92127

LAMBERT, CHARLES GORDON, lawyer; b. Jan. 20, 1949, Wash. DC; s. Henry Dee and Mary Elizabeth (Hooper) L.; m. Laurel Babeaux, div.; 1 dau. Lisa, b. 1977; edn: diploma Inst. Le Rosey 1967; La Sorbonne 1970; BA, Pomona Coll. 1971; JD, Univ. of Denver 1973; admitted to practice Colorado bar 1974, Calif. bar 1980. Career: landman Ladd Petroleum Corp., Denver 1973; Land rep., Chevron Oil Co., Denver 1974-75; Natural Gas rep., Chevron USA, Inc., Denver 1975-79; exec. ofc. staff Standard Oil Co. of Calif., San Francisco 1979, staff asst. to the V.P.- Legal, 1979-80; atty. Chevron USA Inc., S.F. 1980-81; staff atty. Chevron Shipping Co., S.F. 1981--; of counsel Saunders & Saunders 1981-; awards: Am. Jurisprudence Awards, Evidence and Civil Procedure 1973; mem: Denver Assn. Petroleum Landmen; Rock Mountain Natural Gas Assn.; Am. Bar Assn. (Sci. & Tech. Sect.); French Quarter Condominium Assn.; S.F. Bay Club; Anchorage Condo. Assn.; Episcopal; rec: tennis, sailing, bridge. Res: 201 Jamaica Tiburon 94920 Ofc: Chevron Shipping Co., 555 Market St, Rm 1734, San Francisco 94105

LAMBERT, DUANE RICHARD, educator; b. Apr. 11, 1950, Murray, Utah; s. Paul Woodbury and Barbara La Rue (Zwahlen) L.; m. Wendy Hunter, Apr. 22, 1974; children: Jennifer, b. 1975; Richard, b. 1978; Jason, b. 1982; edn: BS, Brigham Young Univ. 1974; MBA, Univ. of Utah 1977; JD, Univ. of Utah Coll. of Law 1977; CPA, Calif. 1979. Career: staff acct. Touche Ross & Co., San Francisco 1977-79; acct. in charge, Harris, Kerr, Forster & Co., S.F. 1979-80; vis. assoc. prof./lectr. UC Berkeley 1982-83; assoc. prof. CSU Hayward 1980--; lectr. for Professional Education Ltd., Danville 1982-; honors: Phi Kappa Phi 1974; Beta Gamma Sigma 1974; mem: Am. Bar Assn. (Sect. Corp. Banking & Bus.; Sect. Pub. Contract Law); Utah Bar Assn.; Am. Bus. Law Assn.; Western Regl. Bus. Law Assn.; coauthor: Study Guide to Accompany Business Law Text and Cases, jointly pub. Harcourt Brace Jovanovich Inc. & Bancroft-Whitney Co.; Republican; L.D.S. Ch.; rec: reading, camping. Res: 223 Newton St Hayward 94544 Ofc: California State Univ., MB 2121, Hayward 94542

LAMBERT, LARRY M(AX), insurance services co. president; b. Oct. 5, 1942, Charter Oaks, Iowa; s. Winfred Eugene and Helen E. Lambert; edn: Wichita State Univ. 1960-64; children: Robin b. 1963, Stan b. 1966, Steven b. 1968, Stuart b. 1973. Career: flight line instr. Beech Aircraft, Wichita, Ks. 1963-65; insurance agt. Penn Mutual Life Ins. Co., Wichita 1965-68, dist. mgr. 1968-69, assoc. gen. agt. 1969-72, gen. agent in training, Penn Mutual Life Ins. Co., Phila. 1972; gen. agent, Penn Mutual Life Ins. Co., Long Beach, Calif. 1972-79; pres. L.B.L. Ins. Services, Inc., Long Beach 1979--; pres. Lary Lambert & Assocs.; pres. Finl. Counseling Resources Inc.; instr. Long Beach City Coll. 1978-79; mgmt. cons., 1972--. Awards: Sales & Mktg. awards 1966, 68; Nat. Mgmt. Award, 1975-76; Community Service award, Long Beach Assn. of Life Underwriters, 1982; pres. Goodwill Industries 1978, 79; chmn. bd. trustees, Earl & Loraine Miller Children's Hosp. Med. Center; bd. dirs. Memorial Hosp. Med. Center and Found.; mem: Long Beach Assn. of Life Underwriters (pres. 1975-6, secty. Past President Council), Calif. Assn. Life Underwriters (pres. 1983-4, chmn. State Newsletter 1979-82); Republican; Lutheran; rec: running, golf. Res: 383 Bayshore Dr Long Beach 90803 Ofc: Larry Lambert & Assocs. 3633 E. Broadway Long Beach 90803

LAMBERTI, IRENE, chiropractor/ author; b. Oct. 14, 1950, Rockville Centre, NY; d. Joseph and Virginia Lamberti; edn: BA, Nazareth Coll. 1972; DC, Western States Chiro. Coll. 1978; DC, Calif. 1980. Career: chiropractor, pvt. practice spec. sports injuries, Marin Co. 1980--; media rep. Bay Area Chiro. Assn. 1982--; host radio talk show, Health Matters, 1983--; designer Lamberti Sports Design (high tech. sports wear clothing), 1983--; awards: Botterman Awd., Calif. Chiro. Assn. 1982, 83; mem: San Anselmo CofC (bd. dirs.); Calif. & Bay Area Chiro. Assns.; author, Pumping Iron Without Pain, a preventive & self care guide for weight tng. injuries; rec: running, bicycling, weight lifting. Ofc: Chiropractic Health Center, 25 San Anselmo Ave San Anselmo 94960

LAMBRIDIS, NIKOS, computer science instructor; b. Jan. 25, 1954, Thessaloniki, Greece; s. Themistoklis and Irene Lambridis; m. Cathleen, Sept. 17, 1983; edn: BS, electronic physics, Univ. of San Francisco, 1979, BS in biophysics 1980, MS in bioengring. 1981, MS in C.S., 1983; Calif. Tchr. Credential. Career: instr. computer sci. Computer Learning Center; asst. prof. Univ. of San Francisco, Golden Gate Univ.; founder/ instr./ organizer First Soccer/ Computer Day Camp for Kids; founder/ owner Lambridis Seminars for Adults in Computer Literacy; cons./ tchr. computer sys., ofc. automation; cons./ inmplement computers in all soccer camps throughout US; mem: Data Processing Mgmt. Assn.; Am. Computing Machinery; Am. Mgmt. Assn.; Democritos, Greek- Am. Profl. Soc.; Greek-Am. Athletic Club; publs: art., Effects of COBOL in Medical Data, Computer Analysis on C.T. Scanners; book, CONDOR, the Data Base System; Democrat; Greek-Orthodox; rec: soccer (mem. Greek Olympic Team 1976). Address: Lambridis Seminars, 2602 Pacific Ave San Francisco 94115

LAMBROSE, DOUGLAS, financial services company president; b. Aug. 10, 1946, Schenectady, NY; s. C. Gustave and Anne (Aliferis) Lambrose; BS, N.Y. Univ., 1970; m. Susan Rosmarin, May 14, 1977; chil: Joshua, b. 1976; Jessica, b. 1979. Career: financial planner and cons. for over 12 yrs.; enrolled agent before IRS, a Calif R.E. Licensee; presently pres. financial services co. in Newport Beach, Calif. specializing in acctg., tax preparation and planning, investments; numerous consulting positions. Honors: grad. with honors; Phi Alpha Kappa academic frat.; v.p., Finance Soc., co-ed. and contrib. to Enterprise, NYU Publication, 1969-70 Who's Who in Finance, 1982. Mem: Amer. Economic Council; Internatl. Assn. of Finl. Planners; Univ. Athletic CLub. Contrib. to Enterprise, 1969-70; presently planning book to help doctors and other profls. understand business principles. Rec: sailing, skiing, reading. Res: 28 Glenn, Irvine 92714; Office: One Newport Place, 1301 Dove St., Newport Beach 92660.

LANAHAN, DANIEL JOSEPH, lawyer; b. Jan. 13, 1940, Brooklyn, NY; s. Daniel J. and Mary (Maguire) L.; m. Suzanne Sheehan, Aug. 18, 1962; children: Mary Patricia, b. 1963; Karen Marie, b. 1964; Maureen Claire, b. 1966; edn: JD, San Francisco Law Sch. 1969; admitted to Calif. State Bar 1970; Life Comm. Coll. Tchg. Cred. (Law), Calif. 1971. Career: claims adjuster/ claims mgr. Consolidated Insurances Co., NYC, Phila., San Francisco 1961-68; staff asst. Insurance Del Monte Corp. 1968; claims mgr. El Dorado Ins. Co. 1968-70; lawyer/ dir. Ropers, Majeski, Kohn, Bentley, Wagner & Kane, S.F. 1970--; corp. secty./ dir. Bay Area Bank 1979-; tchr. law San Mateo Comm. Coll. Dist. 1971-74; mem: San Mateo, San Francisco, Calif. & Am. Bar Assns.; Assn. of Defense Counsel; Defense Research Inst.; Redwood City CofC; S.F. CofC; publs: handbook, Laws of Arrest, Search and Seizure, Firearms, 1975; mil: sp4, US Army 1957-61, GCM; Republican; Catholic; rec: equestrian, golf. Res: 1540 Cordilleras Rd Redwood City 94062 Ofc: Ropers, Majeski, et al., 235 Montgomery St, Ste 620, San Francisco 94104

LAND, JUDY, real estate broker; b. Oct. 6, 1945, Phoenix, Ariz.; d. Stanford Karl and D. Latanne (Hilburn) L.; children: Neal McNeil, III b. 1973; Tahnee McNeil, b. 1975; edn: AA, Merritt Coll. 1968; R.E. Broker Lic., Anthony's Real Estate Sch. 1976; MBA, Burklyn Bus. Sch. 1981. Career: gen. mgr. Ace Rent-A-Car, San Francisco 1968-72; R.E. agent, J.W. Welch Co., San Diego 1972-76; v.p. mktg. & land acquisitions Brehm Communities, San Diego 1977; pres. land sales The Land Co., Del Mar 1978-83; dir. land sales Harry L. Summers, Inc., La Jolla 1983--; honors: The Spike Club, Building Indus. Assn.; mem: Home Builders Council (bd. dirs.; Building Indus. Assn. (Mem. Com.); San Diego Econ. Devel. Corp.; Nat. Assn. Women in Comml. Real Estate; San Diego Republican Businesswomen; San Diego Bd. Realtors; San Dieguito Bd. Realtors; Olympics Exec. Com.; City Club San Diego; S.D. Econ. Devel. Corp.; Republican; rec: decorating, shopping, flying. Res: 916 Begonia Ct Carlsbad 92008 Ofc: Harry L. Summers, Inc., 9404 Genesee Ave, Ste 140, La Jolla 92037

LANDAKER, STEPHEN DAVID, physician; b. Dec.2, 1951, Charleston, S.C.; s. Chester Lavaughn and Mary Catherine (Hogan) L., Sr.; edn: Ore. State Univ. 1969-70; BS, Univ. of Nev., Reno 1973; MD, Tufts Univ. Sch. of Medicine 1978. Career: internship, Navy Regl. Medical Ctr., San Diego 1978-79; Naval flight surgeon, Naval Aerospace Med. Inst., Pensacola, Fla. 1979-80; USN Branch Clinic, El Toro MCAS, Santa Ana, Ca. 1980-83; residency orthopedic surg. Naval Hosp., San Diego 1983--; awards: AMA Physicians Recognition awd. 1982; mem: AMA, Soc. of Naval Flight Surgeons, Aerospace Med. Assn.; mil: lt. comdr. USN Medical Corps 1978-; Democrat; Episcopal; rec: swimming, skiing, sailing. Res: 4660 Huggins St San Diego 92122 Ofc: Naval Hospital, San Diego

LANDERO, REYNALDO RIVERA, physician; b. Oct. 3, 1941, Manila, Philippines; s. Frisco C. and Maria R. Landero; edn: BS, pre-med., Univ. of the East, 1962; MD, Manila Central Univ. 1967; m. Lydia Buenavetura, May 5, 1960; children: Rey Raleigh III, b. 1961; Loreei, b. 1963; Rosanna, b. 1965; Rey Rainier IV, b. 1969; Rey Randall V, b. 1974. Career: rotating intern North Gen. Hosp., Manila 1966-67, St. Thomas Hosp., Akron, Ohio 1968-69; resident internal medicine, Long Beach VA Hosp./ UC Irvine, 1969-71; chest disease fellowship Wadsworth VA Hosp./ UCLA /Harbor Gen. Hosp., Los Angeles 1971-73; pvt. practice internal medicine-Diseases of the chest, 1973--; prin. Landero Med. Clinic, Carson and Norwalk Profl. Ctr., Norwalk, 1973--; clin. instr. in medicine, USC, 1974--; prin. Filipinos Auto Body Shop; chmn. CONPUSO (Confedn. of Phil., US orgns.), 1979; leader Phil. Community Affairs, L.A.; honors: Resolutions, commendn. for comm. leadership, L.A. County Bd. Suprs. and L.A. Mayor Tom Bradley (1971); Comm. Leadership Award, COMPUSO Pres.'s Ball (1971); Fellow Phil. Coll. of Physician (USA); mem: Calif. Med. Assn., Calif. Soc. of Internal Med., L.A. Co. Med. Assn. (Chest Sect.), Trudeau Soc., Long Beach Filipino Doctors Assn., Phil. Med. Soc. of So. Calif., Phil. Profl. and Tech. Soc. (past pres.), AMA, Am. Soc. of Internal Med., Am. Thoracic Soc., Am. Heart Assn., Assn. of Phil. Practicing Physicians; mem. United Couples of Carson (past pres.), Casa Dominguez Filipino Assn., Phil-Am. Assn. of Carson, Phil. PAC, Lions (bd. dirs.), Share and Care Apostolate Found. Inc. (bd. dirs.); Catholic; rec: swim, walk. Res: 1416 Via Andres Palos Verdes Estates 90274 Ofc: 23411 S. Main St Carson 90745

LANDERS, NEWLIN J., contractor/ business executive; b. July 10, 1906, N. Salem, Ind.; s. De Loy and Pearl (Paige) L.; m. Margaret Rechat (dec.); children: Larry; Marlin; m. 2d. Vernette Trosper, May 2, 1959; edn: Bus. Contractors Sch.; courses in personnel mgmt. Career: fmr. owner/mgr. Landers Mach. Co., Bell Gardens and E.L.A.; owner Havasu Landing, Ca.; ptnr. Selwyn-Landers Valve Co., E.L.A.; owner/mgr. Navajo Tract, Apple Valley; prop. Landers Air Strip, Gas Sta. and Water Delivery Co.; founder, Landers, Calif. (donated land for fire sta. and Homestead Valley Womens Club). Awards: Bus.Man of Week, KJST Radio Sta., Joshua Tree, Ca. 1969; mem. Sheriff Rangers, Yucca Valley (recogn. Landers Vol. Fire dept.; bd. dirs. Landers Moose Lodge; life mem. Intercontinental Biographical Assn.;Am. Biog. Inst. Research Assn. Life Fellow Awd. (1981); Comm. Leaders of Am. 1972; Landers Community Dinner in honor of founder on his 75th birthday (1981); mem. Nat. Wildlife Fedn.; rec: pvt. pilot, Citizens radio band. Res: 904 Landers Ln Landers Ofc: 1105 Landers Ln Landers 92284

LANDERS, VERNETTE, author/school district counselor (ret.); b. May 3, 1912, Lawton, Okla.; d. Fred and La Verne Trosper; m. Maj. Paul A. Lum (dec.), 1955; chil: William Tappan; m. 2d. Newlin Landers, May 2, 1959; chil: Larry, Marlin; edn: AB, honors, UCLA 1933, MA, 1935; EdD, 1953; tchg. life diploma 1940; gen. pupil personnel svcs. life diploma 1970. Career: tchr. Montebello (Ca.) schs., 1935-45, 1948-50, 1951-59; prof. Long Beach City Coll. 1946-47, Los Angeles State Coll. 1950; dean of girls 29 Palms H.S., 1960-65; dist. counselor Morongo Unified Sch. Dist., 1965-72; coord. Adult Edn., 1965-67; dir. Guidance Proj., 1967; chg. clk., vol. Landers Post Office, 1962-83; secty. Landers Volunteer Fire Dept. 1972; v.p. Landers Assn. Inc., 1969-71; dir. Desert Ears, emerg. radio serv. 1970-73; contbg. writer var. mags., jours. 1944--; recogn. awards: Intl. Biog. Centre (1973), Intl. Acad. of Poets, London, Eng. (1973), hon. dip. Univ. of Arts, Parma, Italy (1982), hon. dip. Leonardo DaVinci Intl. Acad., Rome, Italy (1982), Intl. Personnel Research Assn. (1972), Intl. Who's Who in Poetry (1980); author: Impy (74), Talkie (75), Impy's Children (75), Nineteen O Four (76), Little Brown Bat (76), Slo Go (77), Who and Who Who (78), Sandy The Coydog (79), The Kit Fox and the Walking Stick (80), Poems in New Voices in Amer. Poetry (74, 75), An Anthol. on World Brotherhood and People (81); mem: Am., Calif., Personnel and Guidance Assns., NEA, Calif. Tchrs. Assn., Nat. Wildlife Fedn., Nat. Hist. Soc., Internat. Platform Assn., Nat. League of Am., Penwomen, Bus. and Profl. Womens Club (pres. Montebello 1940), Toastmistress (pres., Whittier 1957), Soroptimist (Soroptimist of Year, 29 Palms, 1967), Desert Mem. Hosp. Guild (life), Hi Desert Playhouse Guild (life), Homestead Valley Womens Club (life), Phi Beta Kappa, Pi Lambda Theta, Sigma Delta Pi, Pi Delta Phi, Mortar Bd. Prytanean Spurs, Landers Garden Club; Community Ch.; rec: wild animals, flying. Res: 905 Landers Ln Landers 92284

LANDES, ROBERT ALTON, clinical pharmacist, b. Aug. 31, 1942, Inglewood; s. Glenn Alton and Edith Irene (Demmon) L.; edn: AA, Compton Coll. 1962; D.Pharm., USC 1966; UCLA 1981-83; MBA pgm., CSU Los Angeles 1983-; reg. pharmacist, Calif. 1966, Nevada, 1966. Career: staff pharmacist Titus Pharmacy, Santa Ana 1966-68; owner/ pres. Robert's Reports, Torrance 1983--; clin. pharmacist St. Francis Med. Ctr., Lynwood 1968--; exec. bd. Inst. for Adv. in Human Svcs.; preceptor Calif. State Bd. Pharmacy 1975-; clin. instr. USC Sch. of Pharm. 1976-80; honors: Rho Chi 1965; Horton and Converse Awd. for Excellence in the practice of pharmacy 1966; mem: Am. & So. Calif. Socs. Hosp. Pharmacists; Am. Mktg. Assn.; Orange Co. Soc. Hosp. Pharmacists (Clin. Svcs. Com.); Phi Delta Chi; S.F. Med. Ctr. Critical Care Com.; Am. Assns. for Adv. of Sci.; USC Alumni; Southwood Homeowners Assn.; Am. Running and Fitness Assn.; presentations: Devel. of Clinical Pharmacy Svcs., ASHP, San Antonio, Tex. 1978; Hand- Held Calculators and Clinical Pharmacokinetics, ASHP, San Francisco 1980; Digoxin Predictability, ASHP, New Orleans 1981; arts. in profl. journals; Republican; Baptist; rec: cycling, weight training, philately. Res: Robert's Reports, 21321 Marjorie Ave Torrance 90503 Ofc: St. Francis Medical Center, 3630 Imperial Highway Lynwood 90262

LANDRUM, LEE WELLLINGTON, lawyer; b. Aug. 11, 1923, Pecos, Texas; s. Robert Rosser and Esther (Hershenson) L.; m. Sandra, Nov. 17, 163; children: Susan b. 1951, Ross Anthony b. 1948; edn: BS, USC 1943; LLB/JD, USC, 1949. Admitted to Calif. State Bar 1950, all state cts., US Supreme Ct., Circuit Ct. of Appeals, and US Dist. Ct. Career: practising trial atty. (spec. trial of civil cases) 1950--; bd. dirs. Tender Loving Zoo, Inc. (orgn. which provides small petable animals to brain damaged children); mem. State Bar of Calif., LA County Bar Assn. (1972-3); mil: lt (jg) USNR 1942-46, So. Pac. WWII 1944-5; rec: writing, painting, pianist, culinary arts. Ofc: 180 Newport Center Dr Newport Beach 92660

LANE, WILLIAM KENNETH, physician; b. Nov. 5, 1922, Butte, Mt.; s. John Patrick and Elizabeth Marie (Murphy) L.; m. Gilda Parision, Aug. 21, 1954; children: William S., b. 1955; Francine Deirdre, b. 1958; edn: Univ. of Montana 1940-41; Carroll Coll. 1941-43; MD, Marquette Univ. Sch. of Med. 1946; intern Queen of Angels Hosp., L.A. 1946-47; res., 1954-56; urology res. VA Hosp., Long Beach 1956-58. Career: pvt. practice internal med., San Franisco 1947-51; USN M.C., Korean War, Far Eastern Theatre 1951-54; physician, VA Hosps., Long Beach, Oakland, Palo Alto 1956--; lectr. psychology of the elderly, Foothill Coll. 1972-74; Honorary Cheyenne Indian, conferred by Rev. Hoffman, No. Cheyenne Indian Sch., Ashland, Mt. 1966; mem: Am. Geriatric Soc.; Nat. Assn. VA Physicians; San Francisco Co. Med. Soc.; AMA; Audubon Soc.; St. Vincent de Paul Soc.; Cupertino Landscape Artists; publs: Acute Bacterial Infections in the Elderly Male, Am. Geriatrics Soc. Vol. 16 No. 3, 1968; mil: pfc US Army 1943-46; lt. USN 1951-54, med. ofcr. USS Skagit.

GCM, WII Victory, Korean Svc., Far East Theatre; Republican; Catholic; rec: oil and watercolor painting, hiking. Res: 1023 Yorkshire Dr Los Altos 94022 Ofc: Stanford VA Medical Center, 3801 Miranda (171), Palo Alto 94304

LANG, JAMES ALAN, manufacturing co. executive; b. Feb. 21, 1922, Chgo.; s. Walter E. and Thelma Marie (Colbrun) L.; m. Joanne H. Norris, June 28, 1975; children: Mary, b. 1949; Lindsey, b. 1951; edn: BSEE, Colo. Univ. 1948; stu. Dartmouth Coll. 1940-42; postgrad. wk., indsl. eng., Ill. Inst. of Tech. 1949-50. Reg. Profl. Engr. Calif. Career: apparatus engr. Automatic Electric Co., Chgo., Ill. 1948-50; product design engr. & system engr. Motorola Inc., Chgo. 1950-58; district sales mgr. Motorola Communications & Electronics, Los Angeles 1958-62; sales mgr. Microwave RCA, Camden, N.J. 1962-71; product mgr. Microwave, Wescom Inc., Santa Clara 1972-79; system engring. mgr. GTE Lenkurt, San Carlos 1979-80; product line mgr. Radio Products Telecomm. Div. Calif. Microwave, Sunnyvale 1980-83; pres. J.A.L. & Assocs., Los Altos 1984--; cons. to tech. coms. Assn. of American Railroads 1965-; mem: IEEE (exec. com. Santa Clara Valley Sect. 1980-82, chmn. IEEE Comm. Soc. 1981-82), Radio Club of Amer., Sigma Nu Frat. (treas. 1947 Colo. Univ.); Colorado Ski Team 1947; works: coholder patent on Single Tone signalling for mobile radio selective calling (1952), coholder patent for REA Telephone radio Telephone party line signalling (1953); mil: s/sgt. USAF 1942-46, Philippines svc., Battle Star; Republican; United Methodist; rec: skiing, sailing, bridge, woodworking. Res: 24591 Summerhill Ct Los Altos 94022 Ofc: California Microwave Inc. 990 Almanor Ave Sunnyvale 94086

LANGE, KELLY, television anchorperson; b. Flushing, Long Island, NY; d. Edmund V. and Alice (Reason) Scafard; 1 child, Kelly Snyder; edn: BA, English, Merrimack Coll., N. Andover, Mass. Career: Ladybird reporter from helicopter, KABC Radio, Los Angeles 1967-72; news reporter and co-host Sunday Show, KNBC-TV, 1w1-81; weather caster, KNBC News, 1971-76; anchorperson, 1976--, anchor 4 and 6 p.m. hour news Mon. thru Fri.; host: Strange As It Seems 1981, Take My Advice 1975-76, NBC's Rose Parade 1975-82, Kelly's LA 1975-; interviews: film stars, politicians, govt. leaders; Vacation anchor, NBC's Nightly News, 1976 ; Vacation host, Today Show, 1976--, Tomorrow Show 1976-81; speaker num. clubs and orgns.; rec: fgn. travel, restoring antiques, cars, skiing. Ofc: 3000 W. Alameda Ave Burbank 91523

LANGEWIS, CORNELIS, engineer; b. Apr. 10, 1918, Wormerveer, The Netherlands, nat. 1959; s. Cornelis and Elizabeth (Mol) L.; m. Hillegonda Root, July 27, 1939; children: Elisabeth, b. 1941; Cornelis, b. 1945, Christiaan, b. 1946; Johan, b. 1949; Hillegonda Arlene, b. 1956; edn: electr. engr., Tech. Coll., M.T.S., Amsterdam 1938; cert. analytical chemist, Sch. of Chem., Zaandam, The Netherlands 1941; Reg. Profl. Engr. (control sys., 1975) (mfg. engr. 1976), Calif. Career: design engr. Marley Co , Ks City Mo. 1954-56; mgr. devel. eng. pkg. div. Kaiser Aluminum & Chem. Corp., Oakland 1956-78; founder/ pres. Langewis Consulting & Engring., Inc., Walnut Creek 1978--; organizer and chmn. tech. seminars spons. by Soc. of Mfg. Engrs. (Oakland, 1978; Tampa, Fla. 1979; Chgo. 1979; Oakland 1980; Clearwater Beach, Fla. 1981); mem: Soc. for Metals, Soc. of Mfg. Engrs.; 19 US patents on tools, machinery, controls, etc. for Can Mfg. indus.; publs: tech. papers, MF79-970 Ironing of Cans, 1979, MF79 971 Draw & Ironed Can Mfg. , 1979; MF80-908 Can Mafg. 1980, MF81-965 Two Piece Can Mfg., 1981; MF79-972 Reducing Metal Weight of Can, 1979, pub. by Soc. of Mfg. Engrs.; art., Reducing the Cost of Cans, Food Eng., 4/79; var. chpts. in tech. books, Pressworking & Metal Forming, Soc. of Mfg. Engrs.; Republican; rec: woodworking, photog. Address: 41 Kevin Ct Walnut Creek 94596

LANGFORD, HUGH ANDREW, management consultant; b. Mar. 25, 1936, St. Louis, Mo.; s. Edmond A. and Isabel Barnes (Noee) L.; m. Janet Guillory, Feb. 18, 1967; children: Alicia, b. 1970, Ransom, b. 1971; edn: BS in C.E., Univ. of Mo. at Rolla 1963; MS, mgmt. sys., USC 1969; Armed Forces Staff Coll. 1975; Indsl. Coll. of the Armed Forces 1976. Career: design engr./test engr., McConnell Aircraft Corp., St. Louis 1957-59; served to lt. col. USAF, 1959-79: fighter pilot/instr. pilot, 1959-68; USAF Mgmt. System Review Director, 1969-71; USAF Pgm. Mgr., 1972-75; USAF Staff Ofcr., 1975-79; assoc. cons. 1977-79; CEO, Langford and Assocs. (consulting firm), Pasadena 1977--; cons./lectr. to Nat. Aeronautical Space Adminstrn. (NASA), US Navy, US Army; mem. Chi Epsilon (C.Eng. frat.), Tech. Mktg. Soc. of Amer.; bd. dirs. Pasa. Chamber Orch.; Grade chmn. Polytech. Sch. Annual Fund Cpgn.; publs: Performance Measurement and Program Mgmt. - A Look Ahead (1981); mil. decorations inc. DFC, Merit. Service, Air Medal w/ 10 Oak Leaf clusters, AF Commendn. w/ Oak Leaf cluster, Presdtl. Unit Cit. for Extraordinary Gallantry, Combat Readiness, AF Outstanding Unit Awd., GCM, Nat. Def., Repub. of Vietnam Commendn. w/ 3 Bronze Stars, others; Episcopal; rec: flying, hunting, travel. Ofc: Langford and Assocs. 830 S.Oakland Ave Pasadena 91106

LANGLAND, GAYLE F., systems engineering executive; b. Nov. 18, 1934, Cleveland, Ohio; d. James Arthur and Leona Margaret (Kirchner) Foukal; m. Arthur H. Langland, Feb. 18, 1977; edn: BA, Ohio Wesleyan Univ. 1957. Career: school tchr. (3 yrs.); with IBM (23 yrs. to current) from instr. to systems engr. to systems engring. mgr.; IBM Executive Loan to Los Angeles Olympic Organizing Com., deputy dir. Equestrian 3-Day Event (Rancho Santa Fe) 23rd Olympiad, 1984; Republican; Presbyterian; rec: equestrian, skiing, fly fishing. Res: 31010 Stardust Ln Valley Center 92082 Ofc: IMB/ NMD, 1550 Hotel Circle San Diego 92108

LANNI, MARY LOU, educator; b. Los Angeles; d. Anthony Warren and Lucille (Leahy) Lanni; dir. desc. of Israel Putnam (one of four maj. gens. of

Am. Revolution) and Rufus Putnam (built armaments at West Point, led settlers to Ohio); edn: Immaculate Heart Prep.; BSc, MS, USC. Career: tchr., pvt. schs., Los Angeles Co. chs. 1960; L.A. Unif. Sch. Dist. 1961--; supvg. tchr. UCLA Tchr. Tng. 1961-64; master tchr., USC Tchr. Tng. Pgm. 1965-79; partner Greenhill Stables (Thoroughbred horse racing), 1967-70; dir. pub. rels. Delta Design 1981--; cons. for ednl. film. 1972; filmed interview for Japaneses TV, American Education: Science Applications, 1974; tchr. math., sci. and soc. sci. insvc. classes for tchrs. 1965--; author part of teachers exam. for Sch. dist. 1970; awards: UCLA Math. Conf., Computer Programming Am. Legion Essay Awd.; USC awds. for svc. to tchg. profession 1972-76; NSF Marine Edn. Pgm. Grant & Cert. 1978-79; Eng. as a Second Lang. Tng. Pgm. Cert. 1980-81; mem: Phi Beta Kappa; L.A. Opera Assocs.; Commerce Assocs.; USC Intergreek Soc.; Trojan Culb; editor for publs: Americans, Then and Now, and Geometry, Use It; rec: skiing, painting, antiques. Res: POB 5496 Beverly Hills 90210

LANNON, DENNIS EDWARD, chiropractor; b. Nov. 15, 1947, Covina; s. Edward James and Betty Sue (Calison) L.; m. Carol, July 30, 1978; 1 dau: Jolie, b. 1969; edn: BA, Univ. of LaVerne 1970; naval flight ofcr., Navy Flight Sch. 1972; DC, Cleveland Chiro. Coll., L.A. 1979. Career: chiropractor, sports injury splst., owner Lannon Chiropractic Office; awards: Volunteer Svc. Awd., YMCA 1983; mem: Calif. Chiro. Assn.; Saddleback Valley CofC; Saddleback YMCA Bd. Mgrs.; Rotary; mil: capt. USMC 1974; Republican; Catholic; rec: sports. Res: 22712 Woodlake Ln El Toro 92630 Ofc: 23361 El Toro Rd, Ste 202, El Toro 92630

LAN, CARL GUSTAV, architect; b. Oct. 19, 1907, Gothenburg, Sweden; s. Carl and Ida (Sjon) G.; m. Iris Meyer, Dec. 21, 1935; children: Douglas, b. 1937; Randolph, b. 1938; edn: City Coll. of NY 1925-26; Columbia Univ. 1926-30. Career: chief engr. inspector U.S. Dept. of Argriculture, Wash. DC 1935-38; supvg. architect Fed. Housing Admin., Wash. DC 1938-48; partner John H. Graham & Assoc., Architects, Wash. DC 1947-55; tech. dir. Nat. Assn. of Home Bldrs., Wash. DC 1948-52; v.p. archit. Earl W. Smith Orgn., Berkeley 1952-55; internat. practice, archit., ofcs. in Seoul, Korea 1955--; research, lectg., real estate economics, Hotel consultation; recipient Citation & Medal of Achiev., Pres. of Korea; mem: Am. Inst. of Architects; Bldg. Research Adv. Bd., Nat. Acad. of Scis.; Southwest Research Inst.; Seismological Soc. of Am.; Prestressed Concreted Inst.; Urban Land Inst.; works: thesis, Earthquake Constrn. 1954; advr., urban redevel. to Pres. of Korea after Korean War/ dir. ednl. pgm. 1955-56; guest lectr. var. univs. 1949-62. Address: Carl G. Lans, A.I.A., Architect, 21821 Fairlane Cir Huntington Beach 92646

LANSING, FAIZA S., engineer/ scientist; b. Dec. 29, 1946, Port Said, Egypt, nat. 1978; d. Shaker S. and Nozha A. (Seifane) Benjamin; m. Fikry Lansing, Aug. 2, 1970; children: Hany, b. 1971; Christian, b. 1976; edn: Bs, Cairo Univ. 1970; MS, Syracuse Univ. 1976; PhD, USC 1981; Reg. Profl. Engr., Calif. 1978. Career: instr. Port Said Inst. of Tech., Cairo, Egypt 1970-73; devel. engr. Carlyleu Compressor CO., Syracuse, NY 1973-75; mem. tech. staff Rockwell Internat., Los Angeles 1975-77; engr. Jet. Propulsion Lab, Pasadena 1977-79; sr. engr. Envirogenics Sys. Co., El Monte 1978-79; research assoc./ asstc. USC, Los Angeles 1979-82; mem. tech. staff TRW, Redondo Beach 1982-83; asst. proj. scientist, Jet Propulsion Lab., Pasadena 1983--; faculty, CSU, Los Angeles, part- time 1980-; cons. Environgenics Sys. Co. 1979-80; awards: Cost Saving Awde, Carlyle Compressor Co. 1974; mem: Soc. of Women Engrs.; Am. Physcial Soc.; Huntington Sch. and Valentine Sch. PTAs; author/ coauthor: 15 tech. papers in mech. engring. fields and geophysical fluid dynamics; Democrat; Coptic Orthodox; rec: reading. Res: 1809 E California Blvd San Marino 91108 Ofc: Jet Propulsion Lab., Calif. Inst. of Tech., 4800 Oak Grove Dr, mail stop 138-308, Pasadena 91109

LANSING, FIKRY L., engineering executive; b. Oct. 20, 1946, Sohag, Egypt; s. Louis and Rafika L. (Guirguis) L.; m. Faiza Benjamin, Aug. 3, 1970; children: Hany F., b. 1971; Christian F., b. 1976; edn: PhD.M.D., Syracuse Univ. 1972-75; MSME, Cairo Univ. 1971; BS.M.D., Cairo Univ. 1966. Career: lectr. Cairo Univ., Cairo, Egypt 1966-72; sr. engr. Jet Propulsion Lab, Caltech, Pasadena 1975-76; tech. staff 1976-77; tech. gp. supvr. 1977--; career lectr. USC Los Angeles 1980-; sev. tech. presentations in profl. socs., sems. and annual confs.; awards: NASA Tech. awds. 1977, 80, 80; tchg. research asst. Syracuse Univ. 1972-75; hon. bachelors degree, Cairo Univ. 1966; mem: ASME; Am. Inst. Aero. & Astro.; AAUP; Sigma Xi tech. soc.; Nat. Profl. Engrs.; author/ coauthor: 29 tech. arts., 5 NASA new. tech. items, pats. pend. in areas of direct energy conversion, solar energy, kinetics of chem. reactions, A/C, flames and power cycles; Republican; Christian (Coptic); rec: swimming, writing, photog. Res: 8734 Huntington Dr San Gabriel 91775 Ofc: Jet Propulsion Laboratory, 4800 Oak Grove Dr Pasadena 91103

LARGE, DAVID JAMES, electrical engineer; b. Dec. 31, 1940, Puyallup, Wash.; s. Wm. Henry, Jr. and Alice Arminta (Cox) L.; m. Sally Jo Shepherd, June 28, 1963; children: Sean, b. 1970, Cynthia, b 1972; edn: BSEE, Calif. Inst. of Tech. 1963; CSU San Jose 1964-5, DeAnza Coll. 1975, West Valley Coll. 1976. Career: project engr. Eimac Div. Varian Assocs., San Carlos 1963-67; sr. devel. engr. Varian Assocs., Palo Alto 1967; section hd. Instrument Devel., Kruse Electronics div. Systron Donner Corp., Sunnyvale 1968-73; senior mem. tech. staff Avantek Inc., Santa clara 1973-78; chief engr. Gill Cable TV, San Jose 1978-82; v.p. engring. Gill Industries, San Jose 1982--; bd. dirs. Mtn. Charlie Water Co. 1981-; mem: IEEE (senior), Soc. of Cable TV Engrs. (sr.), Nat. Cable TV Assn. (engring. subcom. on networking and archit.), Alumni Assn. Caltech, Computer Using Educators of Santa Clara Co., Lyceum BSA (Monterey Bay Area Council); inventions: Cavity Input Tuner (1965), Active Diode Oscillator (1971); publs: 10 tech. arts. in nat. mags., 1966-83; 6 tech. papers, regl. & nat. confs. 1976-83; Ind.; rec: house constrn., electronic musical instr. design. REs: 26175 Pierce Rd Los Gatos 95030 Ofc: GIll Industries 234 Gish, San Jose 95112

LARK, DONALD HUGH, cogeneration consultant; b. Jan. 3, 1920, Bostwick, Nebr.; s. George William and Elizabeth Bessie (Parsons) L.; m. Kathryn Peak, Oct. 31, 1965; children: Donna Rae, b. 1943; Dennis, b. 1946; Richard, b. 1947; edn: BS, Columbia Coll. 1940. Career: engr. Standard Oil Co. of Calif., El Segundo 1945-59; pres. Louvers & Lark, Inc. & Globe Chem Internat., Inc., Los Angeles 1959-64; Gen. Contractors Engineering Consultant, San Diego 1964-66; proj. mgr. Kelco Div. Merck & Co., Inc., San Diego 1966-83; cogeneration cons. Energetics Sys., San Diego 1983--; tchr. struct. eng. & basic chem. classes Kelco Div. Merck employees 1972-75; Distng. Grad. ROTC Class 1940; Engr. of the Yr., Am. Inst. Plant Engrs. 1973-74; mem: Corrosion engrs.; Plant Engrcs (pres. 1975); Assn. of Energy Engrs. (pres. 1983-84); San Deigo Ofc. of Emergency Mgmt. (San Carlos Area Leader); Masonic Lodge; Elks; air and water pollution cons. to State Assemblyman Larry Stirling; publs: arts. in Congeneration Mag. 1981; Energy Engr. 1983-84; Plant Engring. Mag. 1984; mil: Bos'n 1st USCG 1942-45; ESSL USN 1948-50; sgt. AUS 1950; Republican; Methodist; rec: lecture on entomology, photog. for insects. Address: Energetics Systems, 7871 Compass Lake Dr San Diego 92119

LARRIVA, RICHARD PHILIP, lawyer; b. Sept. 25, 1948, Los Angeles; s. Rudolph and Martha Gloria (Palma) L.; m. Marsha Friedel, May 20, 1972; 1 dau: Marissa, b. 1982; edn: BA, CSU Northridge 1971; JD, Southwestern Univ. Sch. of Law. 1974; admitted to practice, Calif. State Bar 1974. Career: assoc. atty. Black & Warden, Encino 1974-76; assoc. atty. Zonni Ginoccio & Taylor, Santa Ana 1977-79; sr. assoc. atty. Callaham Mc Mune & Willis, Tustin 1980--; mem: Am., Calif. & Orange Co. Bar Assns.; Calif. Trial Lawyers Assn.; So. Calif. Assn. of Defense Counsel; Orange Co. Jr. All Am. Football (coach 1977-; bd. dirs. 1980); Democrat; Catholic; rec: coaching youth football, water skiing, photog. Res: 38 Fort Sumter Irvine 92714 Ofc: Callahan, Mc Cune & Willis, 17321 Irivne Blvd Tustin 92680

LARSEN, KAJ MOGENS, linear metrologist; b. Nov. 17, 1928, Bronshoj, Kopenhagen, Denmark; s. Hans Ernest and Agnes Augusta Marie Jenssine (Jensen) Larsen; m. Birgit Ingrid Kristensen, Nov. 26, 1955; edn: Tech. Coll., Kopenhagen, Denmark 1943-47. Career: aprentice finemechanic, Denmark; insp. controller G.N.T. Automatic Telefonvej Gladsaxe, Kopenhagen 1949-71; instrument svc. man Dial Indicator Lab, No. Hollywood, Ca. 1971-72; miniature machining Stowe Ingineering, Gardena 1972-73; senior linear metrologist Loral E.O.S. (former Xerok), Pasadena 1973--; mem: Nat. Mgmt. Assn.; Soc. of Mgmt. Eng.; Danish Viking Club, Orange Co.; mil: telegraf pioneer, Telefon & Telegraf Kompagny, Danish Army; Protestant; rec; outdoor activities, gardening. Res: 3018 Blandford Dr Rowland Hghts 91748 Ofc: Loral E.O.S., 300 N Halstead St Pasadena 91109

LARSON, GLEN SHELDON, physical therapist/executive; b. Sept. 3, 1949, Ephraim, Utah; s. Sheldon R. and Gladys (Petersen) L.; div.; edn: BS, honors, Univ. of Utah 1975. Lic: Nursing Home Adminstr., Calif.; Reg. Physical Therapist, Calif., Utah. Career: with Therapy Services, Inc., Salt Lake City, also L.D.S. Hosp., Dept. of Pulmonary Phys. Therapy, 1974-75; Beverly Manor Convalescent Hosp., Escondido, Ca. 1975-76; cons. Longer Life Found. Inc. 1978--; pres./bd. chmn. Larson Physical Therapy, Inc. El Cajon 1976--; co-owner/bd. dirs. Western Leisure Care, Inc. 1982--; owner/dir. Country Hills Residentl. and Retirement Ctr. 1982-; honors: rep. State of Utah at two Presidential Leadership Confs., Wash DC, 1967, 68; listed Who's Who in Am. Jr. Colls. 1969; mem: Am. Physical Therapy Assn., Calif. Chpt. APTA; mil: E5 US Army 1972-75; Republican; L.D.S.; rec: skiing, hunt, racquetball. Res: 11720 Joyas Ct San Diego 92124 Ofc: Larson Physical Therapy Inc. 590 Front St El Cajon 92020

LARSON, H. PHILLIP, marketing co. executive; b. Jan. 18, 1938, Onawa, Ia.; s. Dale Newton and Mary Ethel Bell (Kimble) L.; children: Teri Lynne, b. 1959; Steven Dale, b. 1962; edn: Coll. Equiv., 1 yr., Mil. GED. Career: v.p. Liqui-Brush Corp. 1966-68; pres./ owner Pacific Prods. 1969-72; v.p. Friendly, Inc. 1972-73; sales mgr. Bookkeepers Svc. 1973-76; group coord. Ideal Inc. 1976-78; nat. tng. dir. Golden Youth Mktg. 1978-80; gen. mgr. Herbalife Internat. Inc. 1980--; mil: E.G. USN 1955-66, Nat. Defense, GCM, Vietnam Svc.; rec: sports, ednl. reading. Res: 9416 Zelzah Ave Northridge 91325 Ofc: 5721 Slauson Ave Culver City

LARSON-CZISNY, MAXINE LUCILLE, real estate broker; b. Feb. 7, 1950, Seattle, Wash.; d. Jerome Benjamin and Lucille Maxine (Johnson) L.; m. Edward Raymond Czisny, Apr. 9, 1983; edn: BA, Univ. of Wash. 1970; MBA, Univ. of Ore. Grad. Sch. 1972-3; MBA, UC Irvine Grad. Sch. 1978-9; Calif. lic: Real Estate Sales 1978, Real Estate Broker 1982, Notary Public 1981; Comm. Coll. Lifetime Instr. Credential 1978. Career: internat. flt. attendant Trans World Airlines, 8 years; sales broker Goldenwest Realtors, Lake Forest 1980--; recipient Top Producer Award 1983, top honors in 1980, 81; mem: Nat., Calif. Assn. of Realtors; Irvine, and Newport Beach-Costa Mesa Bd. of Realtors; AISCEC Internat. Bus. Orgn. 1970; Alpha Chi Omega, AAUW; fundraising gps. for Orange Co. Albert Sitton Home, and O.C. Music and Performing Arts Ctr.; spkr. on sales techniques; Republican; Christian; mem. Newport Bch. Tennis Club, Newport Bch. Sporting House; rec: boating, skiing. Res: 12 Canyon Island Dr Newport Bch 92660 Ofc: Goldenwest Realtros 23642 Rockfield Rd Lake Forest 92630

LARTIGUE, GEORGE ROY, social worker; b. June 25, 1940, Reddell, La.; s. Louis R. and Thelma (Frank) L.; m. Barbara, May 30, 1976; children: Jackie,

b. 1963, Marcus, b. 1966; edn: BA, magna cum laude, Grambling Coll. 1962; MSW, West Va. Univ. 1964; Psychiat. Soc. Wkr., 1964; LCSW, Calif. 1978. Career: clin. soc. wkr. Vets. Adminstrn. Ctr., Dayton, Ohio 1964-67; chief Soc. Svcs. Dept., Miami Valley Child Devel. Ctrs. (8), Dayton 1967-68; dir. Action Inc. 1968; tchr. Charles Drew High Sch., Eunice, La. 1968-9; soc. wkr. Kern _Co. Welfare Dept., Bakersfield, Ca. 1969-70, psychiat. soc. wkr. Child Guidance Clinic, Bksfld. 1970-81, dir. Cons. and Edn Dept., 1981--; cons. Lowell Youth Ctr., 1978; adj. lectr. CSC Bksfld. 1974-76; cons. Friendship House 1983-; cons. Candidates Forum for Ward 1 City Council, A. Phillip Randolph Inst., 1983; honors: Alpha Kappa Mu, Sigma Rho Sigma, spkr. National Honor Soc. Conv. Wash DC (1960); Man of the Year 1976, S. Bksfld. Kiwanis Club; Black Achieve. Awd., People's Missionary Baptist Ch. 1980; Merit Svc. Awd. Private Industry Council 1983; mem: Nat. Assn. Soc. Wkrs., Acad. of Cert. Soc. Wkrs. (1966-9); Kiwanis (past pres. S. Bksfld.); Kern Child Abuse Prev. Council (pres. elect); Citizens Adv. Council to Bksfld. City Sch. Dist.; bd. mem. Comm. Health Advis. Council of Target Area Pgms.; bd. Mental Hlth Assn. Kern Co.; bd. Martin Luther King Cultural Ctr.; Assoc. Ministers Alliance, People Loving People Outreach Prison Ministry, bd. mem. St. John Housing Manor; Alpha Phi Alpha frat.; bd. mem., pres. Black Amer. Political Assn. of Calif.; profl. conf presentations; Democrat; Prot.; rec: singing, writing sermons and speeches. Res: 3901 Lillian Way Bakersfield 93309 Ofc: Child Guidance Clinic 3628 Stockdale Hwy Bakersfield 93309

LASKA, MARK SROL, dentist; b. Apr. 26, 1945, Pittsburgh, Pa.; s. Sol and Lena Irene (Berman) L.; m. Joan Dunlap, 1973; children: Shawn b. 1963, Sheila b. 1964, Shaye b. 1976; edn: UC Los Angeles 1963-66; DDS, USC Sch. of Dentistry 1970. Career: dentist Group Dental Service, 1970-81, head dentist Group Dental Service, A., 1973-81, dental dir. Group Dental Serv., 1980-81; pvt. practice, Los Angeles 1981--; assoc. with S. Jay Welborn, Pasadena 1981-82; mem: Zeta Beta Tau frat., Alpha Omega dental frat., L.A. Dental Soc. (Comm. on Dental Care, 1981-84), Calif. Dental Assn., Amer. Dental Assn., Acad. of General Dentistry; mem. Los Angeles Olympic Citizens Advis. Commn., and L.A. Olympic Medical/Dental Advis. Commn. (1984); bd. dirs. Hollywood Los Feliz Jewish Comm. Ctr. 1979-84 (chmn. phys. ed. com. 1981-2); YMCA; bd. dirs. Laughlin Park Homeowners Assn. (pres. 1981, treas. 1983); Democrat; Jewish; rec: politics, racquetball, running. Res: Los Angeles 90027 Ofc: 3460 Wilshire Blvd, Ste 104, Los Angeles 90010

LASKOSKI, DANIEL LEWIS, medical diagnostics co. sales executive; b. Dec. 10, 1948, Muskegon, Mich.; s. Lewis Stanley and Lois Lillian (Sherman) L.; m. Peggy Maass, Dec. 16, 1972; 1 child, Robin, b. 1980; edn: BA, Kalamazoo Coll. 1971; MBA, Pepperdine Univ. 1982. Career: sales rep. Chgo., Upjohn Lab Procedures 1972-73, hosp. sales rep., Kansas City 1973-74, dist. sales mgr., San Francisco 1974-77, mgr. sales & svc. Western reg., Woodland Hills 1977-81; nat. sales mgr. Bio Rad Labs., Richmond, Ca. 1982 ; mem. Upjohn Lab Procedures Nat. Mktg. Bd. 1977-81; honors: Nat. Hon. Soc. 1967; Salesman of the Yr. Upjohn 1972; mem: Bio Medical Mktg. Assn.; Sales Execs. of No. Calif.; Sleepy Hollow Homeowners Assn.; Kalamazoo Coll. Alumni Assn.; Pepperdine Alumni Assn.; Republican; Methodist; rec: tennis, basketball. Res: 145 Van Tassel Ct San Anselmo 94960 Ofc: Bio Rad Laboratories, 2200 Wright Ave Richmond 948047

LASORDA, TOM CHARLES, L.A. Dodgers manager; b. Sept. 22, 1927, Norristown, PA; s. Sabatino and Carmella (Covotta) Lasorda; Edn: Norristown H.S., 1945; m. Joan Miller, 1950; chil: Laura, b. 1952; Tom Jr., b. 1958. Career: former left handed pitcher; pitched in major leagues with Brooklyn Dodgers of Natl. League. Played with Kansas City Athletics of Amer. League, one of 19 mgrs. to win pennant in 1st year of managing in Natl. League. Second mgr. in Natl. League history to win pennants in 1st two years as manager, 1977-78. Managed Natl. League All-Stars, 1978-79; managed Dodgers in world series of 1977-78; managed the Dodgers to the 1981 World Series Championship; brought the World Championship back to Los Angeles after an absence of 16 yrs.; second time selected as Mgr. of the Year in the Natl. League, 1982; third All Star game as manager. Recipient: Minor League Mgr. of Year, 1970; Natl. League Mgr. of Year, 1977. Mem: St. Mary's, Fullerton, CA, v.p. Variety Club. Mil: Cpl., USA, 1945-48. Catholic: res: 1473 W. Maxzim, Fullerton 92633; Office: L.A. Dodgers, 1000 Elysian Park Ave., Los Angeles 90012.

LATHAM, R. GEORGE, JR., urban planner/ development co. president; b. Aug. 25, 1953, Roseville; b. Ralph G. and Helen V. (Harrison) L.; edn: BA, UC Berkeley 1975; MA, USC 1977; desig: APA, Assoc., Am. Plnng. Assn.; ULI, Urban Land Inst. Career: independent contractor, plnng., devel. & constrn. of comml. & residential projs. in South Placer Co. 1977-79; pres. Latham Devel. Corp., Roseville 1979--; mem. var. plnng. related coms., City of Roseville; honors: Residential Application, Tile Inst. (1981); mem: APA, ULA, USC Alumni Assn., Comstock Club, Sutter Club, local CofC, Theta Delta Chi; works: innovative approaches in community devel. plnng. and public space environment; Republican (Nat. Task Force, conv. rep. 1976); Catholic; rec: skiing, tennis. Res: 5322 Terrace Oak Fair Oaks 95628 Ofc: Latham Development Corp., 729 Sunrise, Ste 403, Rosville 95678

LAU, BING SIN, county administrator; b. Sept. 10, 1946, Hong Kong; d. Chun-Kau and Lai (Chui) Sin; m. Henry Lau, June 6, 1970; 1 son, Ryan, b. 1980; edn: BA, Internat. Christian Univ. (Tokyo) 1968; MSW, Univ. of N.C., Chapel Hill 1970; MPA, CSU-The Consortium 1978; LCSW, Calif. BBSE 1981. Career: social wkr. supr. Murdoch Center, N.C. 1971-74; soc. wk. cons. Resthaven Community Mental Health Center, 1974-75; psychiat. soc. wkr. L.A. County Dept. of Health, 1975-78, adminstrv. asst. 1978-79; contracts and grants

adminstr. L.A. Co. Dept. of Mental Health, 1980--; field instr. Sch. of Soc. Wk. Univ. of N.C. 1971-74, East Carolina Univ., Greenville; devcl. the first successful normalization (de-instnl.) and community placement pgm. for the developmentally disabled in State of N.C.; mem: Nat. Assn. of Soc. Wkrs., Am. Soc. for Public Adminstrn., Inst. of Cert. Finl. Planners (provisional); L.A. County Asian Amer. Employees Assn. (pres. 1979-80); Asian Amer. Womens Network; Amer. Assn. of Individual Investors; rec: travel. Res: 1948 Crest Dr Los Angeles 90034 Ofc: L.A. Co. Dept. of Mental Health 2415 W. 6th St Los Angeles 90059

LAU, ELIZABETH K.W., clinical social worker; b. Jan. 7, 1940, Hong Kong, nat. 1971; d. Boon-Lop and Chik–Yee (Tsang) Lai; m. Edmond Lau, June 5, 1965; children: Melissa, b. 1968, Ernest, b. 1971; edn: BA, Brigham Young Univ. 1963; MSW, Univ. of Kans. 1965; Calif. lic: LCSW 1969; Academy Cert. Soc. Wkr., NASW 1967. Career: psy soc. wkr. Cameron House, San Francisco 1965-68; supr. Outpatient Clinic, Northeast Comm. Mental Health Ctr., S.F. 1969-73; clin. director Chinatown Child Devel. Ctr., S.F. 1973-75; child mental health coms. & pgm. splst. Kai Ming Headstart Pgm., S.F. 1975-77; clin. soc. wkr. VA Medical Ctr., Palo Alto 1977--; cons. Medical & Family Mailbox, Chinese Times, SF, 1980-83; co-dir. Victory Garment Mfg. Inc. 1980-83; mental hlth cons. HeadStart Pgm., SF 1975-77; recipient performance awards, VA Med. Ctr. 1969, 1983; mem. Nat. Assn. of Social Wkrs. 1965-; v.p./exec. bd. Zion Lutheran Ch. & Sch., S.F. 1981-83; author 3 books: Innovative Parenting (3rd printing 1982), How to Love Your Children (1983), Help Your Children to Develop Good Habits (1983) (Pub. in Chinese language, Hong Kong); Republican; Lutheran; rec: reading. Res: 470 Ortega St San Francisco 94122 Ofc: VA Medical Center, 3801 Miranda Ave Palo Alto 94304

LAU, FUNG YEE, import-export co. owner; b. Oct. 18, 1928, Canton, China, nat. 1967; d. Yu and Yuet Chow (Ma) Chung; m. Sum Lau (dec.), Apr. 16, 1950; children: Jeannie, b. 1951; May, b. 1952; Karen, b. 1965. Career: prop. The Ying Co. 1949--; mem: Lung Kong Tin Yee Assn.; Republican; rec: travel. Res: 2167 14th Ave San Francisco 94116 Ofc: The Ying Co., 1120 Stockton St, San Francisco 94133

LAU, SOPHIE, real estate broker, b. Oct. 8, 1942, China; d. Han-Tung and Y.S. Liu; m. Jeffrey Lau, May 12, 1962; children: Gina, b. 1963; Kennan, b. 1964; edn: BA, San Francisco City Coll. 1962; R.E. courses, Anthony/ Lumbleau Real Estate Schs. 1974; Calif. lic. real estate broker. Career: owner/ mgr. Oriental Restaurant, San Bruno 1966-69; owner/ mgr. Sophie's Internat Trading, San Francisco 1969-73; v p / gen. mgr. Good Earth Realty, Inc., S.F. 1973--, pres./ gen. mgr. Good Earth Ent., Inc., S.F. 1982--; hon. counselor H.T. Engr. & Contractors 1978-; advr. Calif. Nat. Bank 1982, 83; dir. S.F. Chinese CofC 1980, 81; pres. Chinese Real Estate Assn. 1981, chprsn. bd. 1982, advr. 19833; mem: San Francisco Bd. Realtors; Chinese- Am Bilingual Edn. Com; S F-Taipei Sister City Com.; World Buddhist Temple Coll. (hon. counselor); Jen Sen Buddhism & Taoism Assn.; No. Beach Improvement Assn.; Republican; Buddhist/ Taoism; rec: equestrian, skiing, cooking. Res: 1434 Larkin St San Francisco 94109 Ofc: Good Earth Realty, Inc., 785 Columbus Ave San Francisco 94133

LAUB, DONALD D., farmer; b. July 22, 1933, Fresno; s. Henry and Anna (Rietz) L.; m. Clara B. Fogal, Aug. 28, 1954; children: Debra Ann, b. 1956, David, b. 1958, Diane, b. 1960, Donna, b. 1963; edn: Kellogg Fellow, Agricultural Edn. Found. 1973-75. Career: farmer, grape grower; pres. Laub Ranches Inc.; ptnr. J & L Vineyards; dir. Guild Wineries & Dist. (1984); 2d. v.p. Fresno County Farm Bureau (1984); trustee Washington Union High Sch. (1984); dir. Twilight Haven Convalescent Home; dir. Calif. Assn. Winegrape Growers (1984); mem. Calif. Winegrape Insp. Com. (1984); mem. Farm Bureau; mil: served US Army and Reserv., 8 yrs.; rec: collector Amer. cut crystal. Res: 6051 So. Fruit, Fresno 93706

LAUDENSLAGER, WANDA LEE, speech pathologist/ real estate broker/ building contractor; b. July 22, 1929, San Jose; d. Victor Vierra and Florence Lorene (Houck) Silveria; m. Leonard Laudenslager, Apr. 26, 1952; children: Leonard II, b. 1953, Dawn Marie, b. 1954; edn: AA, Coll. of San Mateo 1960; BA, CSU San Jose 1962; BA, 1965. Calif. tchr. credential 1962, std. supvn. 1971, std. designated svcs. 1971; lic. audiometrist, 1966, speech pathologist 1974; lic. real estate broker 1978, gen. bldg. contractor 1979. Career: speech pathologist, Newark Unif. Sch. Dist. 1962-65, dist. coord. Speech, Lang. and Hearing Dept. 1965--; self- empl. R.E. broker, gen. bldg. contractor; honors: Alpha Gamma Sigma 1960; Phi Kappa Phi; Pi Lambda Theta; Kappa Delta Pi 1962; mem; Am. Speech Lang. & Hearing Assn.; Assn. of Calif. Sch. Adminstrs.; Newark Sch. Adminstrs. Assn.; Nat./ Calif. Assns. Realtors; So. Alameda Co. Bd. Realtors; Republican; Presbyterian. Res: 3773 Logan Dr Fremont 94536 Ofc: Newark Unified Sch. Dist., 5715 Musick Ave Newark 94536

LAUER, GEORGE, chemist; b. Feb. 18, 1936, Vienna, Austria; nat. 1951; s. Otto and Alice (Denton) L.; m. Sandra Comp, Oct. 1, 1983; children: Julie, b. 1964, Robert, b. 1970; edn: BS, UCLA 1961; PhD, Calif. Inst. of Tech. 1967. Career: jr. chemist North Am. Aviation, 1961-63; research assoc. Rockwell Science Ctr., Thousand Oaks 1967-68, mem. tech. staff 1968-70, group leader 1970-75, div. mgr. Environmental Resrch & Tech., Westlake Village 1975-78, director Rockwell Internat., Newbury Park 1978--; mem: Air Pollution Control Assn., Am. Chemical Soc., Assn. for Computing Machinery, Calif. Desert Air Working Group; LA County Museum; works: 53 publs., 20 presented papers, 3 patents; mil: Sp4 US Army 1957-59; Jewish; rec: music. Res: 6009 Maury Ave Woodland Hills 91367 Ofc: Rockwell Intl. 2421 W. Hillcrest Newbury Park 91320

LAUFENBERG, PATRICK CHRISTOPHER, chiropractor; b. Dec. 27, 1941, London, Eng., nat. 1965; s. George Ernest and Clara Emily (O'Neill) L.; m. Nancy Jean Boehm, Sept. 24, 1965; 1 son: Sean, b 1970; edn: DC, Palmer Coll. of Chiropractic 1973; DC, Calif. St. Board. Career: indsl. med. supvr. Bethlehem Steel Corp., Pinole 1965-69; pvt. practice, Dublin 1974--; mem. Nat. Bd. Chiro. Examiners 1974-79; awards: John Connolly Meml. Awd. 1973; mem: Internat. Chiropractors Assn.; Calif. Chiro. Assn.; Dublin CofC; author: Thompson Technic Manual, 1974; Kinesiology as Applied to Chiropractic, 1973; Biomechanics of the Pelvis- Monographs, for Am. Chiro. Assn., ed. 1981; New Dimensions in Neurological Diagnosis, Digest Chiro. Econ., 1976; Business Letter Reference Manual, 1979; Listen to the Music (chronicle of Am. music) 1982; mil: hospitalman 3/c USN 1960-64, GCM; rec: music collection, computer applications, lecturer. Res: 4778 Ganner Ct. Pleasanton 94566 Ofc: 6978 Village Pkwy Dublin 94568

LAUFMAN, GERALD EDWARD, aerospace co. executive; b. Oct. 25, 1929, Los Angeles; s. Louis Leslie and Margaret Catherine (Fitzgerald) L.; m. Patricia Muller, Jan. 11, 1964; children: James, b. 1965; Christopher, b. 1974; edn: AA, Compton Coll. 1949; UCLA 1950; MBA, honors, Pepperdine Univ. 1979; pvt. pilot; SEL, Dept. Trans. 1977. Career: dir. of engring. Arnoux Corp., Culver City 1959-61; chief engr. SKG Corp., Santa Ana 1961-63; senior mem. adv. tech. staff Marquardt Corp. 1963-65; mgr. equip. pgms. activity Satellite control facilities opn. Ford Aerospace & Commun. Corp., Sunnyvale 1965--; major pgms. mgr. (RIS, RIPS, EWTR, etc.) Proposal mgr. for the automation of remote satellite tracking stations; principal designer first solid-state telementry decommutation sys. (SKG Mark IV); mem: Armed Forces Commun. & Electronics Assn.; Little League, PTA, Home & Sch. Clubs; works: Disclosures rel. to error correction sys. and telemetry synchronization schemes; mil: AL-3 USNR 47-52; Republican; Protestant; rec: general aviation, golf. Res: 3073 Westfield Ave San Jose 95128 Ofc: Ford Aerospace & Communications Corp., 1260 Crossman Ave Sunnyvale 94089

LAUGHTON, BARRIE ALLAN, insurance co. executive; b. July 13, 1934, Calgary, Alberta, Can., nat. 1953; s. Allan Aubrey and Rita (McAndrews) Laughton; m. Carol Marston, June 24, 1956; children: David, b. 1957; Suzanne, b. 1959; James, b. 1962; Paul, b. 1964; edn: AA, Modesto Jr. Coll. 1956; BA, CSU Sacto 1958; CLU (Chartered Life Underwriter) 1965, ChFC (Chartered Finl. Cons.) 1984, The American Coll., Bryn Mawr, Pa. Career: cost acct. McClellan AFB, Sacramento 1958-9; with N.Y. Life Ins. Co., 1959-: agt., asst. mgr., Sacramento, 1959-64, regional mgr. of sales devel., San Francisco, 1964-66, gen. mgr., Santa Clara, 1966-74, gen. mgr., Fresno, 1974--; recipient co. awards for devel. leading new agents in Central and Mid-Pacific regions. Mem: Fresno General Agts. & Mgrs. Assn. (past pres.); Fresno Estate Planning Council, Fresno Life Underwriters Assn. (awds chmn); Fresno Chartered Life Underwriters; charter mem. Fresno Big Brothers 250 Club; Republican; Catholic; rec: ski, fish, golf. Res: 7869 E. Saginaw Fresno 93727 Ofc: New York Life 1180 E. Shaw Ave, 201, Fresno 93710

LAUNER, LELAND CONVIS, company president; b. June 14, 1918, Los Angeles; s. Albert and Lulu C. Launer; m. Betty Bissitt, June 21, 1941; children: Lawrence b. 1943, Luanne (Kreutzer) b. 1946, Leland Jr. b. 1955, Alan b. 1959; edn: BA in bus. adm., Univ. of Redlands, 1940; JD, USC Sch. of Law 1948; US Naval Supply Corps Sch., Harvard Grad. Sch. of Bus. Admin., 1944-45; contg. edn. 1952-; admitted to Calif. State Bar 1948, US Dist. Cts. (No., So.), US Dist. Ct. of Appeals, US Tax Ct. 1950, USAF Bd. of Contract Appeals. Career: summer empl. City of Fullerton engring. dept., So. Calif. Edison Co. maint. div., Douglas Aircraft Co., 1941-44; asst. mgr. Indsl. Relations, Douglas Aircraft Co. Inc., 1946-51; exec. v.p., chief exec., dir., prin. Fletcher Aviation Corp. (now A.J. Industries), 1951-59; atty. at law Launer, Chaffee & Launer, Fullerton, 1951-59; v.p./secty. Interstate Engring. Corp., Anaheim 1959-65; atty. at law Launer, Chaffee, Ward & Orman, Fullerton 1965-78; pres./chief exec./dir. Shafco Industries Inc., Anaheim 1979--; dir. Towner Mfg. Co., Santa Ana; Municipal Judge pro tem, and Arbitrator, Am. Arbitration Assn.; mem: Orange County Bar Assn., Calif. Bar Assn., No. Orange Co. YMCA, Kappa Sigma Sigma, Phi Alpha Delta legal frat.; past mem. Fullerton Community Chest (dir.), Kiwanis Club (dir.); No. Orange County YMCA (mem. 49 years, past pres.); Univ. of Redlands (fmr. pres. Alumni Assn., fmr. v. chmn. Bd. Trustees and Exec. Com.); fmr. Bd. Overseers Johnston Coll.; fmr. chmn. Advis. Bd. CSU Fullerton; fmr. mem./chmn. O.C. Aviation Commn. (11 yrs), So. Calif. Aviation Council Inc. (12 yrs); mil: lt (jg) USNR, Active Duty 1944-46, Reserv. 1946-51; United Methodist; rec: fishing, camping. Res: 304 Ave Carlos Newport Bch 92660 Ofc: 2850 E. Coronado St Anaheim 92806

LAURENCE, PETER A., financial planner; b. May 27, 1945, San Franisco; s. A. A. and Beth C. (Caldwell) L.; m. Sheryll M. Horton, July 26, 1969; children: Todd, b. 1966; Alana, b. 1977; Alisa, b. 1978; edn: AA, Diablo Valley Coll. 1969; Calif. lic. real estate sales, 1969, R.E. Broker, 1971; GRI, Grad. Realtors Inst., CAR 1975, Cert. Res. Splst. 1980; Securities 7 Lic., SEC 1983; Career: mgr. American Realty 1969; part owner/ broker Better Homes Realty 1974--; v.p. Ygnacio Investments Inc. 1982--; pres. Laurence Financial Planning 1984--; dir. Calif. Assn. Realtors 1980, 81; dir. Contra Costa Bd. Realtors 1978-81; awards: Better Home Realtor of the Year; mem: Contra Costa Bd. Realtors; Nat. & Calif. Assns. Realtors; nat. Assn. Securities Dealers; Concord Century Club; Diablo Scholarships; CofC; Republican; LDS; rec: golf, skiing, travel. Res: 60 Mt Rushmore Rd Clayton 94517 Ofc: Better Homes Realty, 1511 Treat Blvd, Ste 100, Walnut Creek 94598

LAUSEN, P. SANDER, optician; b. Oct. 29, 1934, Aarhus, Denmark, nat. 1971; s. Daniel Severin and Ragnhilde (Faurholt) L.; m. Jytte Rasmussen, Jan. 25, 1958; children: Pia, b. 1960; Rene, b. 1963; edn: BS, Inst. of Tech., Copenhagen, Denmark 1956; M.Ophthalmic Optics 1972; bd. cert. Am. Bd. Opticianry 1967; Fellow Nat. Acad. Opticianry 1967. Career: dispensing optician C.F. Mc William Ltd., Auckland, NZ 1957-65; dispensing optician/ mgr. Superior Optical Co., Newport Beach 1965-74; mgr. Victor Optical, Laguna Hills 1974-76; ownr Continental Eyewear, Newport Beach 1976--; awards: Man of the Month (2), and Awd. of Merit Hi-Lite, Superior Optical Co. 1971; mem; Calif. Soc. Ophthalmic Dispensers; Newport Beach Tennis Club; Newport Ctr. Toastmasters; Conservation Caucus; research: Aniseikonia and Iseikonic Lenses; Republican; Lutheran; rec; soccer, tennis. Res: 56 Promenade Irvine 92715 Ofc: Continental Eyewear, 2523-A Eastbluff Dr Newport Beach 92660

LAUTARET, MAVIS H., social worker; b. Oct. 14, 1920, Vallejo; d. Stanford Kingsley and Mildred Gladys (Kadow) Claunch; m. John Daniel Lautaret, Oct. 6, 1979; children: Kaaran Poncetta, b. 1946; Mark Poncetta, b. 1951; edn: BA, honors, Univ. of Calif. 1975. Career: owner/ broker/ mgr. Poncetta Realty 1958-76; social worker 1977--; adult svcs: Monterey Co. Nutrition coord.; staff to Senior Citizens Adv. Com.; case mgmt. of impaired adults; organization senior citizen convs., liaison Bd. of Suprs., liaison Alliance on Aging, liaison Natividada Med. Ctr.; pres. Monterey Co. Nutrition Bd.; v.p. Suicide Prevention Ctr.; recipient National award, Membership Drive Salinas Area Republican Women, Fed. 1966; mem: Salinas Area Republican Central Com. (pres. 1966); Calif. Republican Central Com. (Agric. Com. 1964-68); Corral de Tierra Golf & Country Club; publs: arts. in San Jose Mercury & San Francisco Examiner (1942); Republican; rec: golf, fishing, tennis. Res: 1238 Via Paraiso Salinas 93901 Ofc: Monterey County Dept. of Social Svcs., POB 299 Salinas 93902

LAVENTHOL, CAROLE COODY BECKER, artist designer; b. Sept. 8, 1939, San Diego; d. Allen K. and Myrtice (Hall) Coody; m. Richard Laventhol, Oct. 26, 1969; 1 dau. Alison b. 1971; edn: BA, San Diego St. Univ. 1961, MA, fine arts, 1965; Calif. Secondary Tchr. Cred. 1961. Career: tchr. San Diego Unified Sch. Dist. 1961-66; owner Etcetra Art Gallery & Boutique, 1966-68; owner Carole Laventhol Interior Design, 1972--: stringer Better Homes & Gardens mag. 1974-75, designer Furniture Forum 1968-69, Design Center Inc. 1968-71; profl. exhibiting artist (museums & galleries) 1961--; owner Carol Laventhol Fine Art (art cons.); instr. Mesa Coll. 1968, Cal-Wester Univ. 1965; founder pres./bd. dirs. SDSU Art Council 1978-; TV Auctioneer in the Arts, PBS-TV, 1978, 79, 80; awards: Bank of Am. Award- Art 1957, Reader's Digest Awd. 1957, Calif. Scholarship Fedn. (life), Painting of the Year Awd., J.C.C. 1981, purch. awd. S.D. Mus. of Art 1963, Angel Flight Nat. Officer 1961, Sweetheart of Sigma Chi (1960, SDSU); mem: Artists' Equity, S.D. Artists Guild (v.p.), Kappa Pi (hon. art frat.), La Jolla Mus. of Art, SD Mus. of Art, American Craft Council; mem. Globe Theater Guilders, Charter 100; Dimensions; KPBS Auction Vols.; La Jolla Country Day Sch. (fashion show com.); exhibs: sev. one woman shows 1961-, group shows incl. SD Mus., La Jolla Mus., Long Beach Mus., Tucson Mus. of Art; rec: gardening, music, theater. Res: 4021 Miller St San Diego 92103 Ofc: Carole Laventhol Fine Art, 518A Island Ave San Diego 92120

LAWICKI, LEONARD JOSEPH, real estate broker; b. Jan. 22, 1933, Buffalo, NY; s. Leon and Mary (Szymanski) L.; m. Geraldine Warmus, Apr. 19, 1954; children: Robert b. 1955, Mark b. 1958, Donna b. 1963, Debora b. 1967, Deanna b. 1967; edn: AA, Eri County Tech. 1953; cert. Bryant Bus. Sch. 1955; Calif. lic. real estate broker. Career: asst. motor eng. Westinghouse Electric, Buffalo, NY 1953; prodn. control Bell Aircraft 1955-57; quality control engr. Sylvania Elec., Buffalo, NY 1957-65; eng. material release McDonnell Douglas 1965-66; sales mgr. Seymour Realty, 1966-73; vice pres. Coastal Cities Realty, 1973-75; broker/owner ERA Realty Lawicki and Assoc., Anaheim 1976--; pres. CPL Investments; ptnr. D & L Prop. Mgmt.; ptnr. L & D Finl. Arrangers; sales awards: Top Sales and Top Listings 1972, 3 Million Dollar Club 1977-80, most listings solo 1980, Anaheim Bd. of Realtors; top sales awds. Seymour Realty 1966-73, Katella Realty 1974; mem: Anaheim Bd. of Realtors (dir. 1979-84, pres. 1982, PAC), Calif. Assn. of Realtors (dir. 1979-82, R.A.P., Mem. at Large 1983); mem. Anaheim Police Honorarys, CofC, Sister City (Mito, Japan), Heritage Com.; mem. Anaheim Meml. Hosp. Double 11 Club; mil: sgt. US Army, GCM, Euro. Occ. Medal; Republican; Catholic; rec: swim, golf, public spkg. Res: 1676 Ord Way Anaheim 92802 Ofc: ERA Realty Lawicki & Assoc. 1691 S. Euclid St Anaheim 92802

LAWRENCE, E. ABBOTT, III, company president; b. Sept. 21, 1940, Somerville, NJ; s. Edgar A. and Mary Elizabeth (Weill) Lawrence, Jr.; Edn: BA, Princeton Univ., 1962: Career: media analyst & acct. exec., Leo Burnett Co., Chicago, 1962-66; natl. sales mgr., KTLA-TV, Los Angeles, 1966-68, gen. sales mgr. 1968-71; owner, Sports Sales Specialists, Los Angeles, 1971-74; owner, pres., Abbjohn, Inc., L.A., 1972---; dba Brennan's Pub, Marina del Rey, 1972---; dba, Brennan's Pub, Manhattan Beach, 1974---; dba Pancho's Restaurant, Manhattan Beach, 1977---. Recipient commercial remodeling award, Manhattan Bch. C of C, 1977; City Scroll, Manhattan Beach City Council, 1977; Great Menus Award, Natl. Restaurant Assn., 1978. Mem: Manhattan Beach C. of C. Republican. Episcopal. Rec: fishing, boating, golf. Res: 4013 Strand, Manhattan Beach 90266; Office: Abbjohn, Inc., 4089 Lincoln Blvd., Marina del Rey 90291.

LAWRENCE, PATRICIA ANN, library director; b. Nov. 3, 1946, Bowling Green, Ohio; d. Frederick Nelson and Myrtle Jesse Mawer (Barton) Gossman; m. Hugh G. Lawrence, Sept. 1977; edn: BA, Bowling Green State Univ. 1968;

MLS, UC Berkeley 1977; Calif. County Librarians Cert., 1978. Career: director Sausalito Public Library 1977; asst. lib. dir. Marin County Library 1977-79, Napa City County Library 1979-83; library director Pacific Gas & Electric, San Francisco 1983--; mem. Special Library Assn., Am. Library Assn., Sausalito Hist. Soc., Sausalito Womens Club; publs: bibliographies on Commercial Sail. Res: POB 1156 Sausalito 94965 Ofc: PG&E, Room 1220, 77 Beale St San Francisco 94103

LAWRENCE, RICHARD ALEX, lawyer; b. Aug. 15, 1952, Los Angeles; m. Denise May, Dec. 16, 1973; 1 son, Gregory Scott, b. 1980; edn: BA, UC Los Angeles 1974, JD, 1977. Career: community services rep. L.A. City Council, 1972-74; assoc. atty./law clk. Ebben, Brown, Winfield & Canzoneri, 1976-78; senior deputy & legal counsel to Supvr. Edmund D. Edelman, L.A. County Bd. of Supervisors, 1978-81; atty. Law Offices of Sheldon H. Sloan, P.C., Los Angeles 1981--; honors: Phi Beta Kappa, Distinguished Advocate Awd. UCLA Law Sch. (1977), commendns., L.A. County Bd. of Supvrs. (1981, 82); mem. bd. commnrs. (chmn. 1982), L.A. County Housing Authority, 1978-82; mem. L.A. County Housing Commn. 1983-; bd. dirs. xnorah Housing Found. 1983-; bd. dirs. Metro Region, Jewish Fedn. Council 1982-; bd. dirs. Alternative Living for the Aging 1983-; mem. Am. Bar Assn. (v.chmn. Housing and Urban Devel. Law Subcom., Adminstrv. Law Sect. 1979-82); mem. govt. rels. com. L.A. Music Center 1982-; Democrat; Jewish. Law Offices of Sheldon H. Sloan, PC, 8481 Melrose Pl Los Angeles 90069

LAWSON, HENRY SPENCE, IV, data processing director; b. Jan. 20, 1955, Los Angeles; s. Henry S., III, and Arden Merle (Gray) Lawson; m. Marcia Wells, Apr. 17, 1983; edn: CSU San Diego 1975-78. Career: pgmmr., supvr. Hewlett-Packard, 1978-82; dir. data proc. Runner's World Magazine, Mountain View 1982--; prin. Timing of Races co.; mem. Runner's World Racing Team; runner (marathons 2.25 best); active in community theater (dir., actor, dancer, chorus) 1974-; Republican; Lutheran. Res: 10556 Merriman Rd Cupertino 95014 Ofc: Runner's World 1400 Stierlin Rd Mountain View 94043

LAY, JAMES SAMPSON, agricultural chemical co. executive; b. Apr. 7, 1922, Owensboro, Ky.; s. George and Hester Lucille (Stone) L.; m. Merri Rubley, Aug. 13, 1950; edn: BS, Mich. State Univ. 1950; M.Agric., 1951; D.Pharm., Ferris State Coll. 1953, Reg. Pharmacist, Mich. 1954, Calif. 1960. Career: tchr. vocational agric. Marshall, Mich. 1950-51; pharmacist Rubley Drug Store, Battle Creek, Mich. 1954-55; med. rep. Eli Lilly & Co., St. Joseph, Mich. 1955; agric rep. Eli Lilly & Co. (Elanco Prods. Div.), Denver, Colo. 1956-59 and Fresno, Calif. 1959-61; tech. svc. rep. Elanco Prods. Co., Indpls., Ind. 1961-62, field svc. mgr. 1962-65, Western regl. sales mgr., Fresno 1965-70; Western distribn. mgr. Eli Lilly & Co., Fresno 1970-72; industry affairs advisor Elanco Prods. Co., Fresno 1972-83; dir. Calif. Grain & Feed Assn. 1968-70; dir. Western Agric. Chems. Assns. 1975-78, 1980-83; chmn. bd. WACA 1983, 84; awards: Outstanding Mem. Awd., Western Agric. Chem. Assn. 1980; Appreciation Awd., Calif. Women for Agric. 1979; mem: Westernh Sect. Am. Soc. Animal Sci. dir. 1972-73; Fresno Agric. Roundtable; Rotary: Sequoia Council BSA; Fresno City & Co. CofC; Valley Employers Assn.; Masons; Shrine; Jesters; mil: lt. paratroops US Army 1942-46, Pres. Citation (2); Bronze Star, Purple Hearts (2), Dutch Awd., French Awd., Arrow Head & (3) Stars; Democrat; Protestant; rec: golf, travel. Res: 4895 E Butler Ave, 103, Fresno 93727 Ofc: Elanco Products Co., 3131 S Willow, POB 10097, Fresno 93745

LAYTON, EDWARD NORMAN, construction co. president; b. June 29, 1928, Kellogg, Idaho; s. Ernest Alfred and Ruth Eloise (Thwing) L.; . Mary Katherine Ketchum, June 29, 1948; children: Norman, b. 1950; Cheryl, b. 1954; Terri, b. 1957; Dennis, b. 1958; edn: cert. bus. mgmt., UCLA 1957; lic. General Contractor Bl, Calif. 1958. Career: cowboy for Davis Ranch, Ariz. 1944; shop foreman Fiat Metal Products 1948; carpenter 1949-52; carpenter supt. Casnor Constrn. 1952-63; v.p./ part owner 1964-77; founder/ pres. Ed Layton Constrn. Co. 1978--; bd. chmn. Tri-County Investment Gp. Inc. 1976-; Building Industry Assn. So. Calif. (dir. 1976-84, v.p. labor 1981-83, chmn. Labor Negotiation Com. 1982-83); awards: Citizen of Yr., Walnut Valley 1975; Cabrillo awd. for excellency of constrn. (La Mirada City Hall), Architects Inst. of Am. 1970; Gold Nuggent awd. of merit, Pacific Coast Bldrs. Conf. 14 Western States, for excellence of comml. remodel 1981; mem: Bldg. Indus. Assn., Pasadena San Gabriel Valley chpt. (Comml. Indsl. Council); Nat. Assn. Home Bldrs.; Mens Club Queen of Valley Hosp.; N.A.H.B. Spike Club (So. Calif. labor policy dir.); So.Calif. Aracheol. Survey Assn.; Kiwanis Internat. (Cal-Nev-Ha Found.); Calif. Country Club; works: first fiberglass domed bldg. for projection and display of stellar films of spac flights 1965; rewrote master labor agreement for B.I.A. 1980; constrn. over 200 million projs.; Republican (Pres. Task Force); Protestant; rec: amateur archeologist, lapidarest, minerologist. Res: 404 S Lemon Ave Walnut 91789 Ofc: Ed Layton Construction Co., Inc., POB 60, Walnut 91789

LAZAN, clothing designer; b. Oct. 9, 1957, Sn Francsco; d. Richard Burdon and Janet Kay (Smith) Deal; m. Kent Smith, Dec. 4, 1975; edn: cert. tailoring, Chesapeake (Va.) Tech. & Voc. Center 1973-4; AA, Tidewater Comm. Coll. 1976; BFA, Virginia Commonwealth Univ. 1980; cert. diver, NASLI 1975. Career: seamstress/tailor Leggetts (dept. store) Norfolk, Va. 1974-76; supvr. alterations Thalhimers (dept. store) 1976-77; freelance designing, tailoring, fashion cons. for pvt. clients in Virginia and Wash DC area, 1972-80, in greater Los Angeles area, 1980--; designer/owner Lazan boutique in Malibu, 1981-82; designer/patternmaker Charles Ray Limited Creations Inc., Topanga 1983-84; pvt. clients include sev. champion figure skaters (internat.), the 1974 Buffalo Bills' Linebackers, num. show business celebrities; costume designer credits: Matchmaker (graduate film, CSU Long Beach 1983), Future World Expo '83 (L.A. Conv. Ctr.), The Seduction (feature movie 1981), Jim Bray Roller Boogie (roller skating show 1981), Longshot (feature movie 1981); num. profl. awards incl. First Pl. Best use of Fabric, Burlington Industries (1978); mem. Toastmasters Intl., Malibu CofC; publs: Dad's Car Cure Schedule Book (1983); Sci. of Mind; rec: dream analysis, jogging, photog. Res: 22660 PCH No. 13, Malibu 90265 Ofc: POB 612, Malibu 90265

LAZARUS, DAVID, real estate broker; b. Sept. 16, 1938, Fresno; s. David H. and Mary (Kolajian); div.; children: Brian, b. 1962; Julie, b. 1969; edn: AA, Fresno City Coll. 1959; desig: GRI, Grad. Realtors Ins., CAR; charter mem. Nat. Mktg. Inst. Career: owner/ pres. Herald Realty, Inc. 1967--; dir. Calif. Assn. Realtors 1973-77; chprsn. Fresno Bd. Realtors Multiple Listing Svc. 1974; awards: Boss of the Yr., Nat. Assn. Profl. Saleswomen 1983; mem: Nat. & Calif. Assns. Realtors; Fresno Bd. Realtors; United Way; Fresno Co. Landmarks Commn.; Fresno Co. & Clovis- Big Creek Hist. Socs.; Nat. Assn. Watch & Clock Collectors; British Cab Soc.; mil: USCG 1959-72, Reserves, USCG Band mem.; Republican; Protestant; rec: antiques, British Cabs, photog. Res: 3406 N Locan Fresno 93727 Ofc: Herald Realty, Inc., 1520 E Olive Fresno 93728

LAZZARO, ANTHONY DEREK, university executive; b. Jan. 31, 1921, Utica, NY; s. Angelo Michael and Philomena (Vanilla) L.; m. Shirley M. Jones, Dec. 20, 1941; 1 dau: Nancy Lee (Ferri), b. 1948; BS, USC 1948; LLD, honors, Pepperdine Univ. 1974; Reg. Profl. Engr., Calif. 1968. Career: with USC 1948--: asst. 1948-65, assoc. bus. mgr. 1965-71, dir. campus devel. 1960-71, assoc. v.p. 1971-72, v.p. bus. affairs 1972--; dir. Republic Fed. S&L Assn. 1961-; RFS Devel. Corp. 1974-; RFS Mortgage Corp. 1976-; cons. US Dept. of HEW; chmn. United Students Aid Funds Adv. Bd. 1976; ednl. adv. bd., Coll. & University Bus.; mem: Citizen Com. Palos Verdes Bd. Edn. 1955-57; Hoover Urban Renewal Adv. Com., City of L.A.; Western Assn. Schs. & Colls. Accrediting Comms.; Western Assn. Coll. & Univ. Bus. Ofcrs. (pres. 1972); Nat. Assn. Coll. & Univ. Bus. Ofcs. (pres. 1978); Phi Kappa Phi; Tau Beta Pi; mil: lt. s.g. USN 1941-46. Res: 4012 Via Largavista Palos Verdes Estates 90274 Ofc: USC University Park, OWH 100, Los Angeles 90089

LEAF, MARILYN GROSSMAN, clinical social worker; b. Jan. 7, 1942, Detroit, Mich.; d. Dr. Sol C. and Pauline (Fried) Grossman; div.; 2 sons: Matthew b. 1968, Jeffrey b. 1975; edn: BA in edn., Univ. of Mich. 963; MSW, Univ. of Chgo. Sch. of Soc. Svc. Admin. 1965; lic: LCSW, Calif.; Cert. Soc. Wkr. , Ill. 1968-73. Career: clin. soc. wkr. Psychiatric and Psychomatic Inst., Michael Reese Hosp., Chgo. 1967-68; psychotherapist, med. student supvr., La Cabida Childrens' Hosp., Chgo. 1969-71; pvt. practitioner, Chgo. 1971-73; cons. Ancona Montessori Sch., Chgo. 1971-72; asst. tchr./profl. vol. Thalians Comm. Mental Health Center, PIPS Warm Line & Cheerful Helpers Nursery Sch., Los Angeles 1977-78, clin. soc. wkr. Northridge Hosp. Med. Center, Northridge 1978-80, currently oncology soc. wkr. and coordinator Eating Disorders Pgm., 1980--; Hospice Volunteer supvr. Northridge Hosp., supvr. Valley Beth Shalom Counseling Ctr., 1980-; pvt. practice, 1979--; Task Force Jewish Hospice Bur. 1982; awards: Branstrom Freshman Prize, Univ. of Mich. 1960; Alpha Lambda Delta 1960, Wyvern Woman's Hon. 1962; listed Who's Who of Am. Women 1983; mem: Nat. Hospice Orgn., So. Calif. Hospice Assn., Nat. Assn. of Social Wkrs., Acad. Certified Soc. Wkrs., Fellow Soc. Clin. Soc. Skrs.; Jewish Fedn. Council of Greater L.A.; Democrat; Jewish; rec: drawing, water color painting, racquetball. Res./pvt. practice: 4732 Del Moreno Dr Woodland Hills 91364 Ofc: Northridge Hospital Med. Ctr. 18300 Roscoe Blvd Northridge 91328

LEAKE, ALBERT ERNEST, JR., sales and marketing executive; b. Aug. 13, 1938, Glendale; s. Albert Ernest, Sr. and Ida Tuni (Pietala) L.; div.; children: Lisa, b. 1963; Lorene, b. 1969; edn: BS, Univ. of Nev. 1960; UCLA Bus. Sch. 1976-79. Career: with Pacific Telephone 1962-80: sales mgr. 1962, prodn. mgr. 1963, bus. ofc. mgr. 1964-65, div. mgr. 1966-70, dist. mgr. 1971-75, dist. sales mgr. 1976-80; v.p. sales & mktg. Westec Plastics 1980-81; owner Precision Mktg. Assocs. 1982--; partner Precision Molding Assocs. 1982--; owner/ mng. partner Performance Motoring Assoc. 1983--; awards: Salesman of The Year 1960; Boss of the Yr., Reno 1970; Outstanding Pres., Nev. Jaycees 1970; JCI Senator 1971; Alfa Romeo Competition Race Driver of Year 1976; Outstanding Young Men of Am. 1972, 73; mem: Calif. (pres. 1960), Reno (pres. 1970) and US Jaycees; Nevada State Fair Board (pres. 1972); Better Bus. Bureau of No. Nev. (pres. 1972); Campfire Girls Bd. Dirs. (pres. 1974); PTA (pres. 1973); Kiwanis; Sports Car Club of Am.; Sales & Mktg. Execs. Assn.; works: No. Calif. Regional Roadracing Champion (1974, 75, 76) SCCA Divisional Champion (1976); mil: PO 2/c USNR 1958-64; Republican; Presbyterian/ Methodist; rec: auto restoration & racing, motorcycles. Res: 14304 Hwy 9 Boulder Creek 95006 Ofc: Performance Motoring Assoc., 695 Creek Dr Boulder Creek 95006

LEAKE, MICHAEL JOSEPH, real estate syndicator; b. Aug. 20, 1943, San Francisco; s. Kenneth and Eleanor L.; m. Ligia Bustamonte, Aug. 20, 1981; children: Bobby, Mark Frances, Erica, Jed; edn: BS, Santa Clara Univ. 1965, MBA, 1967. Career: exec. trainee and top aide to top L.A. exec., So. Pacific RR, 1967-70; nat. sales trainer Sylvania, Home Entertainment Div. 1970; life ins. agt. Conn. Mutual Life 1970-72; pres. Gary Dodson Photography, Rancho Cordova 1971-74; real estate syndicator, chmn. bd. Leake & Co. Investments, 1974--; pres. PMI Records; bd. dir. Superior Beverage; majority stockhldr. Homeq Corp., Sports Life Style International; mem. Torrance C. of C.; seven inventions; Republican; Catholic; rec: golf, tennis, bridge, poker. Res: 519 Paseo De Los Reyes, Redondo Beach 90277 Ofc: 21515 Hawthorne Blvd. Ste. 440, Torrance 90503

LE BLANC, RUSSELL LOUIS, real property broker; b. Mar. 18, 1954, San Jose; s. James Nathaniel and Lela Margariete (Breed) LeBlanc; edn: De Anza Coll., West Valley Jr. Coll., San Jose St. Coll.; Calif. lic. Real Estate Broker 1979. Career: brick mason, carpenter, plumber, DePersia's Construction, South Tahoe 1-3-74; ski instr., 1973-74; test technician Beckman Spinco Instruments, Palo Alto 1974-75; machinist United Centrifugal Pumps, San Jose 1975-77; real estate sales agt./broker, Van Vleck Realtors, San Jose 1977-79; cons. Residential Home Exchangers, San Jose 1980-82; pres. LeBlanc & Associates, San Jose 1979--; bd. dirs. Dist. 93 Machinist Credit Union 1975-81; Exec. Bd. Local 504, Dist. 93 Mach. Union 1976-77; mem: San Jose Bd. of Realtors (Grievance Com. 1979-82), Calif. Assn. of Realtors, Nat; Assn. of Realtors; Monterey Penin. Yacht Club; rec: sailing, skiing, tennis. res: 1687 Sandyrock Ct San Jose 95125 Ofc: LeBlanc & Associates POB 6002 San Jose 95150

LE BOUEF, JOHN FREDERICK, lawyer; b. Dec. 19, 1939, Oswego, NY; s Theodore Francis and Dorothea Jeannette (Hopkins) L.; edn: BA, State Univ. of NY, Oswego 1964; JD, Pepperdine Univ. Sch. of Law 1973. Career: atty. John F. Le Bouef, Los Angeles 1973--; judge pro tem, Los Angeles Municipal Ct.; mem: Calif., Los Angeles County & Beverly Hills Bar Assns.; Calif. Trial Lawyers Assn.; Criminal Cts. Assn. of the Bar; Calif. Attys. for Criminal Justice; Phi Alpha Delta; Republican; Catholic; rec: sailing, volleyball, handball. Ofc: John F. Le Bouef, Atty., 521 N. La Cienega Blvd, Ste 6, Los Angeles 90048

LECKIE, BERNARD ARTHUR, lawyer; b. Dec. 10, 1932, Los Angeles; s. Arthur Bernard and Lorene Dorothy (Kiesan) L.; m. Maryanne Hammatt, Dec. 21, 1959; children: Scott, b. 1962, Karin, b. 1964; edn: BS, USC Sch. of Commerce, 1959, LLB, JD, USC Law Sch. 1959. Career: deputy dist. atty. Los Angeles, 1960-61; atty. firms of Betts, Ely, & Loomis, 1961-63, Ely, Kadison & Quinn, 1963-65, Bernard A. Leckie, Atty. at Law, 1964-80, partner law firm Meserve, Mumper & Hughes, 1980--; instr. P.E. law, LA City Adult Edn., 1960-62; instr. R.E. Practice, LA City Coll. 1962-66; honors: Law Week Award, USC Law Class, 1959. Mem: Am., Los Angeles Co., and Orange Co. Bar Assns., LA Co., Orange Co. Trial Lawyers Assns., C.T.L.A., A.T.L.A., Am. Judicature Soc., Martindale-Hubbell A.V. rating, State Bar of Calif., Investigation Com. in Disciplinary matters, Phi Delta Theta (social), Phi Delta Phi (legal); mil: cpl. US Army 1951-53; Republican; Protestant; rec: sports, tennis, running, golf. Ofc: 5190 Campus Dr Newport Beach 92660

LECKRONE, DANIEL EDWIN, lawyer; b. Feb. 1, 1938, Hammond, Ind.; s. Ivan and Alice Dorothy (Secor) Leckrone; m. Helena Jane McNary; children: Daniel, b. 1963, Susan E., b. 1969, John C., b. 1967; edn: BS, Indiana Univ. Sch. of Bus. 1960, JD, Ind. Univ. Sch. of Law 1963; admitted to practice law: Indiana 1963, US Ct. of Mil. Appeals 1966, US Dist. Ct. (So. Dist. Ind.) 1966, Ill. 1970, US Supreme Ct. 1971, Calif. 1975. Career: capt. US Army, Judge Advocate Gen's Corp., 1963-66; assoc. atty. Cox, Zwernor, Gambill & Sullivan, 1966-70; staff atty. Container Corp. of America, 1970-71; v.p./counsel Marsh Supermarkets, Inc. 1971-74; general counsel, Domestic, Memorex Corp., 1974-78; v.p. Law, Memorex Internat. Ltd., 1978-82; secty. and corp. counsel, Memorex Corp., 1981-82; pres. Daniel E. Leckrone Profl. Law Corp., San Jose, Ca. 1982--, chief legal ofcr., secty. var. public and pvt. cos.; mem: Santa Clara Co., Am., Ind. State Bar Assn., State Bar of Calif., Internat. Bar Assn., Fellow Ind. Bar Found.; clubs: Rotary, Elks. Res: 19251 Douglass Ln Saratoga 95070 Ofc: Daniel E. Leckrone PLC, Lloyd's Bank Bldg, Ste. 300, San Jose 95113

LEDFORD, GARY ALAN, designer, builder, developer; b. Dec. 30, 1946, San Diego; s. Loren Oscar and Madge Francis (Condon) L.; m. Linda Halbert Barker, Jan. 7, 1979; children: Kelly, b. 1969; Jeanne, b. 1970; Robert, b. 1972; Kevin, b. 1973; edn: CE, US Army Engrg. Sch. 1967; grad. courses in structures, Univ. of Colo. 1969. Career: platoon dr., co. comdr., Battalion Civil Engr., US Army Corps of Engrs. (Airborne), Vietnam, 1969; pres. Mastercraft Contractors, Inc., Colorado Springs 1969-73; v.p./ gen. mgr. K.L. Redfern, Inc., Orange, Calif. 973-75; 1975--: pres. Mojave Feed & Fuel Corp., mng. partner Apple Valley Mall; instr. (Command & Staff), Us Army Eng. Sch., Ft. Belvoir, VA 1966 (Nike Missile Support Sys.); awards: 2nd pl. design, Colo. Springs Parade of Homes 1972; mem: Urban Land Inst.; Nat. Assn. home Bldrs.; Nat. Rifle Assn.; Nat. Chinchilla Breeders Assn.; VFW; Gray Panthers; Internat. Council of Shopping Ctrs.; works: design, engineering, constrn. projects incl. 26 shopping ctrs., 44 restaurants, 3 Edwards Theatres, 3 schools (L.A. Bd. Edn), Malibu Grand Prix (Pomona), over 100 svc. stations, num. indsl. bldgs., medical facilities, and var. mil. projects; design & devel. contractor computer software (copyrighted 1979), Tuffcore Bldg. Sys. (pat pend. 1981), Alcohol Separation Process (pat. pend. 1982); mil. decorations: Bronze Star (2), Army Commdn. (2), Purple Heart; Republican; Protestant; rec: hunting, equestrian, chess. Res: 14415 Erie, Apple Valley 92307 Ofc: Ledford Industries, 11401 Apple Valley Rd Apple Valley 92307

LE DOUX, THIERRY JAMES LOUIS, design engineer; b. Mar. 27, 1950, Yakima, Wash.; s. Robert-Eustace Gerard and Barbara Lucinda (Crawford) L.; m. Marilyn Ruth Bruno, Jul. 31, 1971. Edn: AS computer sci., Grossmont Coll., 1980. Career: supervisory technician Frontier, Inc. 1974-75; sr. tech. TRE/ Security and Service Comm., Santa Ana 1975-76; field svc. engr. EDS, Inc., Irvine 1976-77; assoc. engr. Spectral Dynamics, San Diego 1977-79; customer svc. engr. Perkin-Elmer Corp., 1979-82; design engr., microcomputer design for nat. defense projects.; sr. partner Electronics Computer Consultants, Santee; instr. Brunswick Inst. of Tech., San Diego. Awards: Engr. of the Year in microcomputer design, San Diego Electronics Assn., 1980; Outstanding Young Men of Am., US Jr. CofC, 1981. Inventions in field of weather monitoring. Mil: Sgt. E-5 USN, USAR 1968-77, Combat Action Ribbon, Vietnam Cpgn. and svc medals, Vietnamese Gallantry Cross w/ Oak Leaf, Navy Unit Commend.; Republican; Protestant. Rec: meteorology, football, baseball, tennis. Res: 10737 Second St. Santee 92071 Ofc: Logicon, Inc, 3911 Sorrento Valley Blvd Dept. 1700, San Diego 92101

LEE, ALFRED JEROME, certified public accountant; b. Oct. 30, 1958, Ft. Lauderdale, Fla.; s. Filander and Alberta (Bell) L.; m. Regenia Moore, May 10, 1980; edn: BA, Dillard Univ. 1980. Career: acctg. asst. Atlantic Richfield Co., Dallas, Tex. 1978-79; acctg. asst. Mobil Oil Co., New Orleans, La. 1979-80; acctg. intern IBM, Dallas, Tex. 1979; Peat, Marwick, Mitchell & Co., Los Angeles 1980-83; internal audit MCA Inc. (Universal Pictures) 1983; dir. fin. reporting MCA Records, Inc., Universal City 1983--; honors: Nat. V.P. Alpha Kappa Ma hon. soc. 1979-80; mem: Nat. Assn. Black Accts.; Alphi Phi Alpha Frat. Inc.; Democrat; Baptist; rec: music. Res: 7422 Hazeltine Ave, 12, Van Nuys 91405 Ofc: MCA Records, Inc., 407 Lankershim Blvd Universal City 91608

LEE, CHOK KAU BINKY, physicist/ engineer; b. Aug. 6, 1948, Canton, Kwongtung, China, nat. 1979; s. Ching-Lam and Choi Ha (Lam) L.; m. Viola Chan, Aug. 30, 1974; edn: B.Eng., CSU San Francisco 1972; M.Nuclear.Eng., UC Berkeley 1973; PhD, UCLA 1979; Reg. Profl. (Mech). Engr. Calif. 1982. Career: with Thermxchanger Inc. 1970--: draftsman 1970-72, engr. 1972-73, cons. 1973--; engr. Nuclear Svcs. Corp. (aka Quadrex Corp.) 1973-76, cons. 1976--; postgrad. research engr. UCLA 1976-79; senior research splst. R & D Assocs. 1979--; tech. papers reviewer for J. of Solar Energy Engring., J. of Physico Chem. Hydrodynamics; mem: ASME (assoc.); ANS (stu.); Westwood Gardens Civic Assn.; publs: 4 journ. publs. and over 10 tech. conf. papers in fields of Nuclear reactor safety, Bubble collapse dynamics, Turbulent interface heat & mass transfer, Ocean thermal energy conversion, Nuclear weapons effects- radiative coupling & cratering, High pressure poperties of geologic materials; rec: chess, music. Res: 10746 Ayres Ave Los Angeles 90064 Ofc: R&D Associates, 4640 Admiralty Way, Ste 974, Marina del Rey 90291

LEE, CLIFFORD LEROY, newspaper circulation manager; b. Jan. 1, 1948, Lodi; s. George Sherman and Frances (Cross) Lee; m. Adoracion Soriano Silva, Sept. 6, 1969; 2 daus: Gabrielle, b. 1970, Danielle, b. 1972; edn: BA, CSC Stanislaus 1970. Career: circulation mgr. Advance-Register, Tulare 1975-77; circ./mktg. dir. The Press-Tribune, Roseville 1977-80; circ. mgr. Ontario (Calif.) Daily Report 1981, Lake County Record-Bee, Lakeport 1982--. Mem: Cal-Western Circ. Mgrs. Assn. (recipient awards: Best Carrier Publicity 1978, 79; Best Carrier Newspaper 1979); Internat. Circulation Mgrs. Assn.; Republican; Catholic; rec: golf, chess, tennis. Res: 5267 Tenino Way, Kelseyville 95451 Ofc: Lake County Record-Bee 495 N. Main St Lakeport 95453

LEE, EUN WOO, real estate broker; b. Dec. 3, 1926, Taegu, Korea, nat. 1982; s. Chong Ok and Im Yi (Lim) L.; m. Kyong, Sept. 15, 1955; children: Grace, b. 1956; Lily, b. 1957; John, b. 1961; Susan, b. 1962; edn: AA, Harbor Coll. 1979; BA, CSU Dominguez Hills 1981; Real Estate Broker lic. Calif. 1978. Career: v.p./chief ed. Donghwa News Agcy., Korea 1956-73, Wash. correspondent 1958-64, Tokyo correspondent 1972-73; exec. dir. Miryung Co., Seoul, Korea 1973-75; R.E. broker, Torrance 1976-84; Sun Realty, 1st American Realt, currently, owner/ broker Hope Realty, Torrance; honors: Elec. Pres., Kwanhoon Journalist Club, Korea 1966; mem: Korean Eds. Assn., Seoul; Internat. Press Inst.; Calif. Assn. Realtors; Journalist Club, Korea (pres. 1966); Torrance Korean United Methodist Ch. (elder, layleader); mil: capt. ROK Army, Korea 1950-55; Methodist. Res: 22546 Berendo Ave Torrance 90502 Ofc: Hope Realty, 23643 Arlington Ave Torrance 90501

LEE, GEORGE MING-CHI, engineer; b. Feb. 22, 1932, Hahn-Kow Hurbeei, China; came to USA 1979; s. Tsu-Fen and Annie Chie-Yun (Chao) Lee; m. Ming-Fen, Sept. 8, 1958; edn: BS, Tsin-Hwa Univ., Peking 1953, MS, 1956; Calif. Reg. Mechanical Engr. 1982. Career: asst. prof. Harbin Civil Engineering Inst., China 1956-79; design engr. (computer software) Fluor Engineers Inc., Mining and Metals Div., Redwood City 1980--; mem. Amer. Soc. of Mech. Engrs.; publs: over 20 tech papers on devel. of Belt Conveyor Engring. Computer Pgms., 1982-83; rec: microcomputers, classical music, bridge. Res: 75 Arch St, 202, Redwood City 94062 Ofc: Fluor Engineers Inc. Mining and Metals Div. 10 Twin Dolphin Dr Redwood City 94065

LEE, JAE KU, company president; b. Mar. 20, 1938, Seoul, Korea; s. Chung Hee and Chin Hee (Cho) L.; m. In Pin Kim, May 27, 1964, 1 dau: Elisa, b. 1968; edn: BA, Kun Kuk Univ. 1964; MA, 1968. Career: exec. dir. Hwashin Retail & Mfg. Co., 1967; pres. Moolim Bldg. Material Prods. Co., Inc. 1969; pres./ CEO Dai Ocho USA, Inc. 1975; mem: Korean Am. Assn. (pres.); Korean Comm. Orgn. (S.F. & Bay Area rep. 1979); Northwestern US Dist. of the Adv. Council on Peaceful Unification Policy, R.O.K. (pres.); orean Am. Edn. Ctr.; Korean Am. Political Assn.; Multi Svc. Ctr. for Koreans; S.F., Seoul Sister City Commn.; No. Calif. Korean Soccer Assn.; mil: R.O.K. Army 1959-61; Republican; Baptist; rec: music, table tennis. Address: 655 Ellis St, Penthouse, San Francisco 94109

LEE, JAMES H., business owner/ language instructor; b. Nov. 26, 1921, Pyong Yong, Korea; s. Byimg P and Ching I. (Chae) L.; m. Susan K., June 19, 1954; children: Ellie I., b. 1955; Edward I., b. 1957; edn: AA, Yin- Sei Univ., Korea 1947; AA, Monterey Peninsula Coll. 1962; BA, Monterey Inst. Foreign Study 1974. Career: instr. foreign lang. Degense Language Inst., Monterey 1956--; currently, owner motel bus., Lighthouse Lodge, Pacific Grove; mem: Acad. Adv. Council, Defense Lang. Inst.: Christian; rec: music. res: 241 Via Gayuba Monterey 93940 Ofc: Lighthouse Lodge, 1249 Lighthouse Ave Pacific Grove 93950

LEE, JOHN FRANCIS, corporate president/ CEO; b. Sept. 19, 1918, Boston, Mass.; s. Michael Francis and Catherine Mary (Arrigal) L.; div.; children: Anne- Marie, b. 1946; Robert Paul, b. 1947; Virginia Louise, b. 1948; Jacqueline, b. 1966; edn: BS, The Citadel 1947; MS, Harvard 1948; DSc, Univ. of London 1968; DLitt., honors, Univ. of Malaga 1972. Career: asst.- assoc prof. Univ. of Maine 1948-52; Broughton dist. prof. of eng., NC State Uni. 1952-61; pres. State Univ. of NY, Stony Brook 1961-62; spl. advr./ cons. Nat. Sci. Found., Wash. 1962-71; pres./ CEO Internat. Devel. Svcs., Inc., Wash. 1962-71; pres./ CEO Promotorco, S.A. (Europe), Luxemborg 1971-79; pres./ CEO Intercontinental Mgmt. Cons., Inc., Torrance 1979--; dir: Volos, Ltd., Banco Hispano- Americano; Equity Corp., Chase Overseas Investments, INc.; Promotorco, S.A.; Creative Search Corp.; vis. prof. CSU System White HOuse Conf. on Interant. Cooperation 1965; personal rank of Ambassador, ICEM-Argentina Negotiations 1966; participant Dept. of State Foreign Policy Conf. 1970, 71; honors: Chevalier Legion D'Honeur, France 1973; Southern Cross, Brazil 1965; Order of Bernardo O'Higgins, Chile 1966; Ambassador of Goodwill, No. Carolina 1961; mem: IEEE; AIAA; Sigma Xi; Tau Beta PI: OSA; Pi Tau Sigma; Am. Foreign Svc. assn.; SPIE; ISHM; author: Theory and Design of Steam and Gas Turbines, McGraw- Hill 1954, 2nd ed. (7th prntg.) 1961; coauthor. Thermodynamics, w/ F.W. Sears, Addison Weseley Pub. 1955, 2nd ed. (10th prntg.) 1962; publs: over 70 profl. arts.; mil: maj. US Army 1941-45, Bronze Star, Purple Heart; rec: tennis. Res: 6702 Los Verdes Dr Rancho Palos Verdes 90274 Ofc: Intercontinental Management Consulatants, Inc., 3838 Carson St, M/S 110, Torrance 90503

LEE, KATHRYN EILEEN, psychiatric social worker; b. Sept. 2, 1942, Grand Forks, N.Dak.; d. Robert E. and Bette Mae (Hewitt) L.; m. Thomas E. Zinkle, July 16, 1983; edn: BA, Univ. of Minn. 1964; MSW, Ariz. State Univ. 1972; LCSW, Calif. 1979; NASW 1984; ACSW. Career: soc. svc. practitioner, Child Protective Svcs., San Bernardino 1972-74; psychiat. soc. wkr. Riverside Co. Mental Health, Riverside 1974; clin. soc. wkr. Comm. Mental Health Ctr. of Escambia Co., Pensacola, Fla. 1974-77; mental health clinician II, San Bernardino Co. Mental Health Unit, San Bernardino 1978-82; mental health clinician III, San Bernardino Co. Geriatric Assessment Ctr., SanBernardino 1982-83; chief soc. wkr. Riverside Comm. Hosp. Knollwood Ctr., Riverside 1983--; participant wrkshps., Women & Alcohol and Helping Your Alcoholic Before He/She Hits Bottom 1974-77; cons. soc. wkr.: Northwest Fla. Home Health Agcy., Inc., Pensacola, Fla. 1976-77; Med. Ctr. Clinic, Dialysis Ctr., Pensacola 1977; Desert Alcoholism Coilition, Hayman Ctr., Palm Springs 1978-79; awards: Tuition Scholarship, Ariz. State Univ. 1971; mem: NASW; Soc. of Clin. Soc. Wkrs. Res: 12125 Country Club Ln Grand Terrace 92324 Ofc: Riverside Community Hospital- Knollwood Center, 5900 Brockton Riverside 92506

LEE, MARGARET ANNE, psychotherapist; b. Nov. 23, 1930, Scribner, Nebr.; d. Wm. Christian and Caroline Bertha (Benner) Joens; m. Robert Lee, May 21, 1950, div. 1971; children: Lawrence b. 151, James b. 1953, Daniel b. 1954; edn: AA, Napa Coll. 1949; journalism major UCB, 1949-50; BA, CSC Sonoma 1975; MSW, CSU Sacto. 1977; Calif. lic: Comm. Coll. Tchr. Credential, MFCC (Marriage Family Child Counselor), LCSW (Lic. Clin. Soc. Wkr.), 1978. Career: eligibility wkr./supr. Napa Co. Dept. Social Svcs. 1968-75; part-time instr. Napa Valley Coll. 1978-83; psychotherapist, self-empl., Napa Valley Center, 1977--; bd. mem. Napa Child Devel. Center 1980-, chair 1982-; elected, Napa Valley Coll. Bd. of Trustees 1984-88; honors: (contracted polio- quad., 1954, confined to wheelchair) Self Mag. Fresh Start Award 1984; guest of honor, luncheon, Congl. Caucus on Womens Issues, Wash DC (2/84); mem. Nat. Assn. of Soc. Wkrs.; Napa County Council Economic Opportunity (bd. dirs.); Mental Health Assn. of Napa Co. (bd. dirs.); Napa chpt. Nat. Women's Polit. Caucus; March of Dimes vol.; columnist local news for Napa Register 1946-50, contbg. writer S.F. Chronicle, Redbook, The Lutheran mag.; Democrat (Napa Dem. Caucus); Lutheran. Res: 15 Camilla Dr. Napa 94558 Ofc: Margaret A. Lee, 1100 Trancas, Ste 300, POB 2099, Napa 94558

LEE, MARTIN VINCENT, lawyer/ certified public accountant; b. June 20, 1955, Los Angeles; s. Jack C. and Betty (Quon) L.; m. Joanne Lam, Aug. 28, 1982; edn: BS, USC 1977; JD, UCLA Law Sch. 1982; CPA, State Bd. of Accty. 1980. Career: staff acct. Ernst & Whinney, Los Angeles 1977-78; semi sr. Kenneth Leventhal, L.A. 1978-769; dir./ mgr. Yee Sign Chong Co., Inc., L.A. 1977--; gen. partner FAMCO Investment, L.A. 1981--; assoc. Luce, Forward, Hill, Seffer & Mongels 1982--; dir. First Public Svgs. & Loan Assn.; mem: Calif. Soc. CPAs; Republican; Christian. Res: 1748 Webster Ave Los Angeles 90026 Ofc: Luce, Forward Hill Seffer & Mangels, 1900 Ave of the Stars, 4th Flr, Los Angeles 90067

LEE, NANCY MAUDE, publishing co. executive; b. Aug. 29, 1950, NYC; d. Henry Lawrence and Thea Gerda (Gerhardt) L.; edn: BA, UCLA 1973; Univ. of Goettingen, Germany 1971-72; cosmetic retailing, Giggey Hilt's Coll. of Retail Tng. Career: dir. tng. Consumer Div. Lee Pharmaceuticals, So. El Monte 1975-77; corp. pub. rels. dir. 1977-81; owner Mother Goose Distributing 1979--; pub. rels. cons. First Interstate Bank 1982; mktg. cons. Resources for Infant Educators; mem: UCLA Alumni Assn.; Daughters of Am. Revolution; Los Angeles Athletic Club; UCLA Pub. Rels. Club; couathor/ pub. a new concept in children's safety, pub. in sev. languages; Republican; rec: reading, writing, gourmet cooking. Address: Mother Goose, 512 Winston Ave Pasadena 91107

LEE, RUSSEL HEWLETT, general surgeon; b. May 19, 1926, Palo Alto; s. Russel V. and Dorothy (Womack) L.; m. Elizabeth Plumb, June 20, 1947;

children: Virginia, b. 1950; Phyllis, b. 1953; Eric, b. 1955; Stanley, b. 1956; edn: AB, BS, Stanford Univ. 1947; MD, Stanford Univ. Sch. of Med. 1949. Career: research assoc. St. Bartholomew's Hosp., London 1955; joined Palo Alto Med. Clinic 1956, partner 1958-, elected exec. vice director 1965-81, exec. dir. 1981--; instr. surgery, clin. prof. surgery Stanford Univ. Sch. of Med. 1956--; bd. dirs. Blue Shield of Calif. (chmn. Med. Policy Com.); chmn. bd. Preferred Providers of Am., Inc. 1982--; founder Bd. of Lifeguard HMO 1970-83; honors: Phi Beta Kappa, Stanford Univ. 1946; Alpha Omega Alpha hon. med. frat. 109; mem: Santa Clara Co. Med. Soc. (pres.); Am. & Calif. Med. Assns.; fellow, Am. Coll. of Surgeons (chmn. Com. on Apllicants); Pacific Coast & Western Surgical Assns.; bd. dirs. Peninsula Meml. Blood Bank; Palo Alto CofC; Palo Alto Med. Research Found.; Santa Clara Co. Safety Council Bd. Dirs.; Comm. Council of Palo Alto; publs: 23 publs. in med. journs.; mil: lt. USNR 1943-45, USN 1949-51; rec: woodwork, wild life photog. Res: 640 Los Trancas Portola Valley 94025 Ofc: Palo Alto Medical Foundation, 300 Homer Ave Palo Alto 94301

LEE, SHEILA SHUN-FONG, engineer; b. Aug. 2, 1954, Hong Kong; d. Kin and Mui Yuk (Ling) Lee; m. Daniel Lo, Aug. 13, 1983; edn: BS, CSU Fresno 1977; MS, Carnegie-Mellon Univ. 1978; Profl. Engr., Calif. 1982. Career: bridge engr. Howard, Needles, Tammen & Bergendoff, Kansas City 1978-82; structural engr. Nutech, San Jose, Ca. 1982-83; assoc. Chris Tse & Assoc., Consulting Engrs., Santa Clara 1983--; awards: B. Wilson Scholarship 1976; mem: Nat. Soc. Profl. Engrs.; Am. Soc. Civil Engrs.; Kansas Eng. Soc.; Friendship Club; rec: racquetball, tennis. Res: 311 Falcato Dr Milpitas 95035 Ofc: Chris Tse & Assoc., 5711 Thomas Rd, Ste 7, Santa Clara 95054

LEE, STEVEN SOK-YOL, real estate broker/journalist; b. Dec. 3, 1934, Seoul, Korea, nat. 1984; s. Yoo Ky and Jung Ja Lee; m. Julia Kim-Ju, Jan. 21, 1963; children: Charles, b. 1965; Suzanne, b. 1967; edn: BA, Univ. of Foreign Studies 1958; diploma, journalism, Indian Univ. 1962; diploma, journ., Editorial Study Ctr., Cardiff, U.K. 1969; R.E. Broker lic., Calif. 1981. Career: with Dong-A Ilbo, Seoul, Korea 1965-75: Saigon correspondent 1965-67, Tokpo correspondent 1970-72, features ed. 1973 74, advtg. mgr. 1974-75; West Coast correspondent Voice of America, USA 1981--; currently, owner/ broker Steven Lee Realty; v.p. Korea Journalist Assn., honors. In-hon Medal of Honor, Korea Govt.; Awd. for Best Newes Story of Yr., Korean Newspaper Publishers Assn.; mem: Sigma Delta Chi; Nat Assn. Realtors; Southbay Korean- Am. Realty Assn.; The Korean Press Club of Am. (pres.); edited 2 vols. research books on No. Korea's foreign policy; Christian; rec: fishing, camping. Res: 24238 Park St Torrance 90505 Ofc: Steven Lee Realty, 23643 Arlington Ave Torrance 90501

LEE, TOMMY RYAN, lawyer; b. Aug. 6, 1948, Novato; s. Wendell Ray and Anita June (Calkins) L.; m. Linda, Dec 5, 1975; children: Ryan, b. 1978; Joseph, b. 1981; Jacqueline, b. 1983; edn: AA, Coll. of Marin 1968; BS, Sonoma State Univ. 1973; JD, Lincoln Univ. 1978. Career: gen. counsel/vice pres. L. Ferdig & Co., Inc. 1977-78; atty. at law, pvt. practice, Novato 1978--; mem: Am., Calif., Marin County Bar Assns.; Am. Trial Lawyers Assn.; Rotary Club, Novato; fmr. dir. Nova-Ro Senior Citizens Complex; bd. dirs. Novato Human Needs Ctr.; Novato CofC (Ambassadors Club; Legis. Action Com.); mil: sp5, JAG Corps, USAR 1970-77; Republican; Protestant; rec: snow/water skiing, hunting. Res: 1881 Marion Ave Novato 94947 Ofc: 1450 Grant Ave, Ste 210, Novato 94947

LEE, VIVIAN INEZ, administrative contracting officer; b. May 27, 1941, Teague, Tex.; d. Sanford and Annie Beatrice (Moseley) Burks; m. Wilford C. Lee, Dec. 24, 1961; children: Avery Bernard b. 1964, Adedra LaSette b. 1969, Nina LaDawn b. 1976; edn: L.A. City Coll. 1959-61, Merrit Coll. 1966-69, St. Mary's Coll. (Moraga) 1977-78, Vista Coll. 1979-80. Career: govt. civil service, 1965--, currently administrative contracting officer, DCASMA-SF, in San Bruno, Calif.; EEO Rep. 1976-77, EEO Counselor 1977-79; recipient recognition awds. Naval Postgraduate Sch., Monterey (1980), Dept. of Navy Ofc. of General Counsel (1983), DCASMA-SF (1976, 81, 82), Outstanding Performance Award (1972); mem: NCMA, Gold Rush Chpt., Sacramento; Nat. Bapt. Convention of Am. (past pres. Calif. Junior Womens Aux.; v.p. Matrons Aux. Mt. Zion Dist. Assn.); PTA (past pres.); publs: Career Counseling and You (1978-9), Black History Observance, Profiles in Black (1982), Profiles of Federal Women (1977); Democrat; Baptist; rec: bowling, sewing. Res: 1607 Alcatraz Ave Berkeley 94703 Ofc: DCASMA-SF, 1250 Bayhill Dr San Bruno 94066

LEE, WENDELL, manufacturing co. pharmacologist; b. Sept. 16, 1946, Manking, China, nat. 1956; s. Henry and Alice Lee; m. Gayle Meyer, Nov. 12, 1966; children: Jenny, b. 1967; Justin, b. 1980; Chrstine, b. 1983; edn: BS, UCLA 1972; PhD, USC 1976. Career: chemist, part- time (4 yrs.); free agent/ cons. (4 yrs.); quality assurance mgr. (4 yrs.); currently, v.p. regulatory affairs/ quality assurance ORMCO, Glendora (4 yrs.); mem: ASQC; RAPS; WHO; AMA; works: group theory relationship to toxicity; rec: classical guitar, chess, tennis. Res: 4326 Hillside Dr Banning 92220 Ofc: ARMCO, 1332 S Lone Hill Ave Glendora 91740

LEE, YOUNG WOO, insurance co. financial officer; b. July 13, 1941, Seoul, Korea, nat. Sept. 9, 1980; s. Jong J. and Boo S. (Kim) Lee; m. Julie Cho, Sept. 23, 1973; children: Samuel b. 1975, Grace b. 1980; edn: BS, CSU Hayward 1974; Calif. lic. Real Estate Broker 1978; Enrolled Agent, IRS, US Dept. Treas. 1978; CPA cert. (pending 1984). Career: chief accountant Valley of California (Valley Realty), Dublin 1975-77; internal auditor and asst. treas. American

Home Shield Corp., 1978-82, controller /asst. treas. 1982--, also treas. American Mortgage Service Inc. and Compu Fund Inc., 1982--; honors: academic award, Korean and Am. Womens Club 1974, Pres.'s award for distinguished service, Am. Home Shield Corp. 1981; mem. Nat. Assn. of Enrolled Agents, Calif. Assn. of Enrolled Agents; Republican; Seventh-day Adventist; rec: landscaping. Res: 702 Arboles Place San Ramon 94583 Ofc: American Home Shield, 7950 Dublin Blvd, Ste 300, Dublin 94568

LEESON, ALAN MARSHALL, corporation president; b. Dec. 4, 1937, St. Paul, Minn.; s. Louis and Ada (Dubov) L.; m. Sally Benson, Sept. 7, 1974; children: Kristin, b. 1967; Jeffrey, b. 1969; edn: BS, summ cum laude, Univ. of Ariz. 1963; PhD, cand., UCS Berkeley 1973; CPA, Ariz. 1964, Calif. 1965. Career: senior auditor Arthur Young & Co., San Francisco 1963-65; fin. plnng. mgr. Raychem Corp., Menlo Park 1965-68; founder/ pres. Spectrum Label Corp., San Carlos 1968--; dir. Flexographic Tech. Assn. 1983; pres. San Carlos Sch. Bd.; honors: Eagle Scout, BSA 1952; Univ. Scholarship Awds. 1962, 63; Phi Kappa Phi 1963; Beta Gamma Sigma 1963; Haskins & Sells Award. 1963; Key for Top Bus. Grad., Delta Sigma Pi 1963; mem: Alpha Kappa Psi; San Carlos CofC; Am. Inst. CPAs (pres. 1965); San Mateo Arts Council; Better Bus. Bureau; Univ. of Ariz. Life Alumni; Univ. of Ariz. Old Main Club; works: company received Top Award in nat. competition spons. by Flexographic Tech. Assn. 1983; mil: airman USAF 1956-60, Distng. Unit Citation w/ Cluster; Republican; rec: music, travel, photog. Res: 1087 Hewitt Dr San Carlos 94070 Ofc: Spectrum Label Corp., 1000 Washington St San Carlos 94070

LEFEBVRE, PEGGY ANDERSON, advertising agency executive; b. Dec. 2, 1951, Springfield, Mo.; d. Paul William and Norma Jean (Turk) Anderson; m. Donald E. Lefebvre, July 25, 1980; edn: BA, cum laude, Univ. of Ill., Chgo. 1974. Career: artist Associated Foods, Salt Lake City 1974-77; art dir. Bell & Howell, Salt Lake City 1977-80; owner Lefebvre Advtg., Anaheim 1980--; dir. Vortex Export Mgmt. Co. 1982-; mem: Women in Mgmt.; works: one woman show: Ward Galley, Chgo. 1974, Atrium Galley, Salt Lake City 1975; Republican; Presbyterian. Res: 502 E. Buffalo Ave Santa Ana 92706 Ofc: Lefebvre Adertising, 1717 S State College Blvd, Anaheim 92804

LEGASPI, CONSUELITO UBAY, accountant; b. Sept. 30, 1942, Manila, Philippines, nat. 1971; s. Jose L. and Patrocinio U. (Ubay) L.; m. Grace Macagba, Oct. 22, 1966; 1 son: Nicholas II, b. 1967; edn: BBA, Univ. of the East 1965; notary pub., Calif. 1974; real estate broker, Calif. 1974. Career: asst. payroll mgr. Bullock's, Pasadena 1968; accts. payable supvr., Bethlehem Steel Corp., Los Angeles 1971-82; dept. acct. Los Angeles Times 1982--; realtor/ broker C.U. Legaspi & Assoc., So. Pasadena 1974--; mem: Nat. & Calif. Assns. Realtors; Real Estate Cert. Inst.; Nat. Notary Assn.; Civil Air Patrol, USAF; mil: 1st lt. Philippine Army 1963-66, infantryman; Catholic. Res: 330 Camino Del Sol, So. Pasadena 91030 Ofc: Los Angeles Times, Times Mirror Square, Los Angeles 90053

LEGG, DONNA ELAYNE, municipal government official; b. Mar. 13, 1935, Framingham, Mass.; d. Walter Irving and Mabelle Ruth (Hocking) Maker; div.; children: Marilyn Estelle (Kemper), b. 1956; Thomas Nealon, b. 1958; Steven Jay, b. 1959; Malaine Diane (Sanchez), b. 1962; Philip Clark, b. 1964; edn: Framingham Tchrs. Coll. 1953-54; x-ray tech., Boston City Hosp. 1954-55; Northeastern Univ. 1954-55; AA, Merced Comm. Coll. 1976; Notary Public, Calif. Career: with City of Atwater 1968--; secty. to Public Works Supt. 1968-75; secty. to City Engr./ Dir. of Pub. Works 1975-81; secty. to City Engr./ Dir. Parks & Recreation 1980-81; secty. to Chief of Police/ Records Supvr. 1981--; elected Atwater City Clerk 1980--; awards: Base-Community Council Awd. for Outstanding Contribution to Military- Civilian Harmony 1976; mem: Nat. Notary Assn.; City Clerks Assn. of Calif. (Central Valley Div.); Merced Co. United Way; Merced Co. Commn. on the Status of Women; Salvation Army Svc. Ext. Unit.; Soroptimist Internat. (pres. 1979-80); Toastmasters Internat. (Atwater Chatelaines, pres. 1979-80); San Joaquin Valley Youth Svcs.; United Methodist Ch. (secty. to bd. trustees); Atwater CofC; Republican; Methodist; rec: history. Res: 2020 Fruitland Ave Atwater 95301 Ofc: City of Atwater, 750 Bellevue Rd Atwater 95301

LEHMANN, A. SPENCER, chemical engineer, oil co. executive (ret.); b. Sept. 23, 1916, Los Angeles; s. Aldo M. and Elsie (Thompson) Lehmann; m. Rosalie Belle Lowther, Dec. 28, 1943; twin sons: Lawrence S., b. 1945, Bruce A., b. 1945; edn: AB, chem., Stanford Univ. 1938, PhD, chem., Brown Univ. 1941; Regis. chem. engr., Calif. #0477. Career: research chemist Naval Research Lab, Anacostia, Wash.DC 1941-42; resrch. chemist Brown Univ., Manhattan Dist. Project, 1942-44; sr. engr. (Y-12 Tenn.) Eastman, Oak Ridge, Tenn. 1945; resrch chemist Shell Develop. Co., 1946-52; various tech. mgmt. positions incl. refinery mgr., gen. mgr. technical depts., gen. mgr. research orgn. & facilities, Shell Oil Co., 1952-76; past chmn. Am. Petroleum Inst. com. on technical data; dir. Fallbrook Public Utility Dist. 1983-; dir. Farm Bureau 1980-83. Honors: Phi Beta Kappa, Sigma Xi, appreciation cert. Am. Petroleum Inst. Mem: Am. Chem. Soc., Am. Inst. Chem. Engrs., Rotary Club of Fallbrook (pres.elect), Fallbrook CofC (v.p./dir.), Vista Valley CC; mil: 2d lt. Ordnance Dept. USAR 1941-42; rec: avocado grower. res: 1917 Santa Margarita Dr. Fallbrook 92028

LEHMKUHL, RICHARD URBAN, life underwriter; b. June 14, 1938, Milwaukee, Wisc.; s. Harry D. and Marcella (Felsecker) L.; m. Sally Rae Steffens, Aug. 19, 1967; children: Jeffrey Vandervort (step), b. 1960; Courtney C. Lehmkuhl, b. 1968; edn: Marquette 1956-58; Loyola Univ. 1964-65; San Fernando Coll. 1965-66; Grad. LUTC, Life Underwriter Assn. of Los Angeles.

Career: agent Washington Nat. Ins. Co., Los Angeles 1968-81; agent Farmers Ins. Gp. 1981--; tchr. adv. life ins. courses, Los Angeles Life Underwriters Assn.; awards: Wash. Nat. Agent of the Yr., Los Angeles Gen. Agents & Mgrs. Assn. 1977; Man of the Yr., Pacific Palisades Rotary 1982-83; mem: Los Angeles Life Underwriters Assn.; Pacific Palisades Rotary Club; mil: airman l/ c USAF 1959-63; Republican; Catholic; rec: surfing, skiing, backpacking. Res: 567 Erskine Dr Pacific Palisades 90272 Ofc: Richard U. Lehmkuhl Insurance Services, 12327 Santa Monica Blvd, Ste 201, Los Angeles 90025

LEIDY, PHILIP BRUCE, clinical pathologist; b. Dec. 30, 1949, Los Angeles; s. Charles William and Norma Ruth (Rosendale) L.; m. Colleen, June 1, 1972; children: Kimberly, b. 1976; Melinda, b. 1979; Lindsey, b. 1983; edn: Rio Hondo Coll. 1968-72; BA, Westmont Coll. 1972; MA, Fuller Theological Sem. 1976; PhD, Fuller Grad. Sch. of Psychology 1979; lic. Psychologist, Calif. BMQA 1981. Career: psychological asst. Creative Counseling Ctr., Hollywood 1979-80; psychol. asst. Live Oak Counseling Ctr., Glendora 1978-81; psychol. asst. Hacienda Psychological Svcs., Hacienda Hghts. 1979-81, clin. psychologist 1981--, jr. partner 1983--; clin. asst. prof. Fuller Grad. Sch. of Psychology 1981-82; honors: Outstanding Young Men of Am., Jaycees 1983; mem: Am. Psychological Assn.; Christian Assn. for Psychol. Studies; Whittier Area Baptist Fellowship (Bd. Overseers, var. coms., tchr. on death, divorce & step families); Republican; Baptist; rec: jogging, racquetball, photog. Res: 9949 Winfield Ave Whittier 90603 Ofc: Hacienda Psychological Services, 2440 S Hacienda Blvds, Ste 104, Hacienda Heights 91745

LEINBERGER, CHRISTOPHER BROWN, consulting firm executive; b. Jan. 2, 1951, Charleston, W.Va.; s. Fredrick Arthur and Helen B. Leinberger; m. Madeleine McDougal, Aug. 25, 1973; children: Christopher Jr., b. 1978; Rebecca, b. 1981; edn: BA, Swarthmore Coll. 1972; Coro Found. (L.A.) 1973; MBA, Harvard Bus. Sch. 1976. Career: asst. to pres. ARA Food Svcs. in Los Angeles, Phila. & NYC, 1973-77; dir. concept devel. Saga Corp., Menlo Park 1977-79; exec. v.p. Robert Charles Lesser & Co., Beverly Hills 1979-82, pres./ partner 1982--; honors: Fellowship, Nat. Sci. found. 1970; NCAA Scholar-Athlete 1972; Coro Found. Fellow 1972-73; mem: Urban Land Inst.; Nat. Assn. Corp. Real Estate Execs.; Jonathan Club; Beyond War Proj.; Zamarano Club (rare books); publs: arts. in Mortgage Banker, N.Y. Times, Wall Street Journ.; L.A. Times; Bus. Week, others; Democrat; Creative Initiative Found.; rec: bird prints, map collecting, backpacking. Res: 411 California Terrace Pasadena 91105 Ofc: Robert Charles Lesser & Co., 8484 Wilshire Blvd, Ste 340, Beverly Hills 90211

LEISNER, JAMES WINGE, investor; b. Feb. 23, 1924, Evanston, Ill.; s. Paul Winge and Florence Mary (Heath) L.; grandfather, Adolph Winge Leisner, dir. of Bank of Denmark, dec. 1923; m. Linda Daniel, Mar. 30, 1973; 1 dau. Kimberley b. 1956; edn: BS in polit. sci., honors, Northwestern Univ. 1950; MA, USC, 1977; CPA, Univ. Ill., 1956. Career: salesman Procter & Gamble, Chgo. 1945-46; salesman A.B.Dick Co., Milwaukee, 1946-48; mktg. analyst A.C. Nielsen & Co., Chgo. 1950-52; mgr. corporate mergers, Alexander Grant & Co., 1952-53; ptnr. Peat, Marwick, Mitchell & Co., Los Angeles 1953-75, mng. ptnr. L.A. office, 1959-72, v. chmn. bd. dirs. 1960-72, retired partner 1973-; bd. dirs. Merle Norman Cosmetics Inc. 1973-75; bd. dirs. Air California 1973-81; bd. dirs. Westgate-Calif. Corp. 1973-81. Honors: Phi Beta Kappa (1950), Phi Kappa Phi (1977), Bishop's Awardof Merit, Episcopal Dioscese of L.A. (1964), comm. svc. award, United Way of L.A. (1975); mem: YMCA of Metro. L.A. (v.p., dir. 1962-68); L.A. Area CofC (dir. 1963-69); Calif. Soc. of CPAs (dir. 1966-69); Am. Inst. of CPAs; v.p., dir. United Way of L.A. 1967-75; dir. Urban Coalition of L.A. 1968-70; councilor, USC 1970-; chmn. bd. dirs. Children's Hosp. Council of So. Calif., dir. Hosp. Council of So. Calif., and dir. Nat. Assn. of Children's Hosps., 1978-80; trustee Univ. of Redlands 1972-74; mem. San Gabriel Country Club (dir. 1969-72), Newport Harbor Yacht Club (dir., treas. 1984); mil: capt. US Inf. 1943-46, 2 Bronze stars for valor; Republican (L.A. Repub. Fin. Com. 1968-72); Episcopal (trustee L.A. Diocese); rec: skipper of a sloop, Newport Bch. Res: 4872 Basswood Ln Irvine 92715

LE MASTER, EVERT EUGENE, real estate loan co. owner; b. Aug. 8, 1929, Akron, Ohio; s. Russell B. and Bertha V. LeMaster; m. Judy K. Larson, July 14, 1979; edn: Akron Univ., Univ. of Kentucky, LaSalle Univ. 1953-59. Career: v.p./ dir. loan ops. Aid Investment & Discount, Akron, Ohio; supvn./ co. acquisitions leader GAC Finance & Finance America; broker/ owner Lee Financial & Suncrest Home Loans; currently, pres. Help U Borrow, Inc., Garden Grove; Court apptd. overseer trust violation; honors: Past Pres. Hot Stove League; mem: local, state Real Estate Bds., Elks, Moose, Masons; author book on real estate lending; mil: cpl. US Army (101 Airborne & 314th Army Band); Lutheran; rec: wood working. Res: 12841 Dungan Ln Garden Grove 92640 Ofc: Help U Borrow, Inc., 12062 Valley View, Ste 116, Garden Grove 92645

LE MASURIER, ROBERT ARTHUR, engineering co. president; b. Dec. 31, 1946, Honolulu, Hawaii; s. Dr. Robt. S. and Joyce Reese (Munn) LeMasurier; children: Lisa Jean b. 1976, Robert Jr. b. 1981. Career: draftsman for various cos., 1967-73, engrg. mgmt. (Bl Bomber & classified comm. sys. projs.) Hughes Aircraft, and Rockwell Internat., 1973-74, 1974-78; mgmt. pos. Odetics Co., Anaheim, 1978-80; founder/pres./bd. chmn. Total Concept Eng. Inc., 1980--; comp. assoc. Phillip Ultrasound, Cameo Electronics, var. cos.; coll. instr.; mil: USAF 1964-66, GCM, Weapons Expert; rec: martial arts, scuba diving, surfing. Res: 10142 Constitution Dr Huntington Bch 92646 Ofc: Total Concept Eng. Inc. 2122 S. Grand Ave, Ste J, Santa Ana 92705

LEMMI, CARLOS A. E., educator; b. Oct. 29, 1936, Buenos Aires, Argentina, nat. 1969; s. Emilio Atilio Guido and Mria Nidia (Linera) L.; div.; 2 sons: Dennis Alberto b. 1965, Kervin Lee b. 1970; edn: pharmacist, Univ. of Buenos Aires, 1958, biochemist, 1960; PhD, UC Los Angeles 1974; lic: Medical Lab. Tech., Calif. 1964-; researcher - controlled substances reg., Dept. Justice DEA 1979-. Career: chief of applied investigation Brand Labs. (Argentina) and tech. dir. Parke-Davis of Argentina; came to USA in 1963; worked in Gastric Physiology w/ Dr. James Thompson., 1964-67; tchg. (microscopic anatomy) UCLA, 1972-, asst./assoc. prof. anatomy, UCLA Sch. of Med. 1976--, NIH Research grants ($290,000), as Principal Investigator invited presentations in USA and Europe (Vienna, Paris, Aberdeen); mem. Surgery Exec. Com. Harbor-UCLA Medical Ctr. 1975--; frequent guest spkr. med. groups; author 83 sci. publs. (2 books, 5 book chapters, 46 resrch. papers, 30 abstracts); mem: Am. Soc. of Zoologists, Am. Inst. of Biolog. Scis., NY Acad. of Sci., Am. Soc. of Anatomists, Internat. Soc. for Devel. and Comparative Immunology, Resrch. & Edn. Inst. Inc. (REI) of Harbor-UCLA Med. Ctr.; (inactive): L.A. Transplant Soc., Soc. for Cryobiology, Am. Soc. for Extra Corporeal Technol., Electron Microscopy Soc. of Am., So. Calif.; FCC Radio Amateur Lic. (WB6MCW) 1969-, mem. Radio Amateur Civil Emergcy. Svc., LA Co. Civil Defense, 1976-; active PTA (1976-9), Cub Scout ldr. (1975); FAA lic. pvt. pilot 1982-; scubadiver cert. 1976-. Res: 4024 Emerald St, 205, Torrance 90503 Ofc: Harbor-UCLA Medical Center, Dept. of Surgery, 1000 W. Carson St, F6, Torrance 90502

LENGFELD, HELEN FOORMAN, voluntary service organization founder/ president; b. June 26, 1898, San Francisco; d. Isaac and Sadie (Samuels) Foorman; m. Louis Lengfeld, July 27, 1918; children: Lewis F. b. 1919, Frances H. (Meyer) b. 1920; ed. private schs., pvt. tutors. Career: secty., then pres. No. Calif. Women's Golf Assn., 1925-35; West Coast mem. U.S. Golf Assn. Women's Com. 1936-44; founder Pacific Women Golfers (now 9000 members with an annual "Helen Lengfeld Day"; Calif. vice pres., pres., and nat. 1st v.p. American Womens' Voluntary Services (400,000 members during WWII) 141-53; editor/ publisher The National Golfer (20 years) 1950s-60s; founder/ pres. United Voluntary Services (50,000 mems.) 1953--; mem. Vets. Admin. Voluntary Services Nat. Com. 1946-; founder/chmn. Calif. Junior Girls' Golf Tourn. 1946-; founder/chmn. Calif. Womens' Golf Croup 1946-60; founder/ chmn. Calif. Womens' Amateur Golf Championship 1966 ; founder/chmn. Calif. Womens' Senior Golf Tourn. 1972-; organizer volunteer-staffed "Havens" (social clubs) in 42 veterans' hosps.; organized extensive voluntary svcs. on mil. bases; orgnzr. USAF Golf Tournaments (18 yrs); recipient nat. V.A. honors, num. awards; mem. Peninsula Golf & Country Club (1912-), others; Republican. Res. 250 Woodridge Rd Hillsborough 94010 Ofc: United Voluntary Services, 30 Second Ave San Mateo 94401

LENIHAN, JAMES JOHN, insurance broker; b. July 31, 1928, San Francisco; s. James John and Ellen Veronica (Begley) L.; m. Anne Morrissey, May 6, 1950; children: James, b. 1951; Linda, b. 1953; Susan, b. 1955; Timothy, b. 1957; Colleen, b. 1961; edn: BS, Univ. of San Francisco 1980; Chartered Property Casualty Underwriter, Am. Inst. Prop. & Liability Underwriters 1971. Career: spl. agent Pacific Nat. Fire Ins. Co., San Francisco 1950-52; mgr. ins. dept. J.V. Manfredi Co. 1952-61; v.p. in chg. insurance ops. Henderson-Lenihan, Inc. 1961-72; pres./ owner Lenihan Ins., Inc. 1972-76; v.p./prin. Flamer & Co. (largest independently owned property & casualty ins. agcy. S.F. Penin.), Los Altos 1976--; past pres. Foothills Ins. Agents Assn. 1960-62; awards: Young Man of the Year 1961, Mtn. View Jaycees, Outstanding Young Men of Am.; Citizen of the Year 1966, City of Mtn. View; mem: Foothills Assn. of Ins. Agents; Soc. of CPC4; Mtn. View CofC; Santa Clara Valley Water Dist.; Mtn. View Police Activities League; Democrat; Catholic. Res: 49 Showers Dr, 435, Mountain View 94040 Ofc: Flamer & Co., 330 Distel Circle Los Altos 94022

LEOF, DAVID BENJAMIN, physician; b. Aug. 7, 1938, Phila., Pa.; s. Emanuel and Irene (Kauffman) L.; children: Pamela Natasha, b. 1965; Anton David, b. 1968; edn: BA, Trinity Coll. 1960; MD, Yale 1965; psychiatrist, UC Med. Ctr., Langley Porter Neuropsychiatric Inst. 1970. Career: postgrad. tng., fellowship, Langley Porter, Maudsley Hosp., London, Inst. of Psychiatry, London & C.G. Jung Inst., San Francisco; psychoanalyst/ psychiatrist, pvt. practice 1970--; asst. clin. prof. of psychiatry UC Medical Center, San Francisco; awards: James Hudson Brown Fellow, Yale Univ. to St. Thomas Hosp., London 1962-63; Steinman Fellow, Maudsley Hosp., London; Jr. Phi Beta Kappa Trinity Coll. 1959; mem: Am. & No. Calif. Psychiatric Socs.; C.G. Jung Inst., S.F.; French American Bilingual Sch., San Francisco (past pres. parents); publs: Innervation of the Human Lung, Journ. of Anatomy, London 1964; mil: lt. commdr. US Pub. Health Svc. 1965-67; rec: scuba diving, sailing, sculpting. Address: 2907 Fillmore St San Francisco 94123

LEONARD, GENEVA K., real estate broker; b. June 8, 1920; d. William A. and Myra Frances (Davis) Kilpatrick; m. Daniel A. Leonard, Aug. 31, 1940, div. 1968; children: Judith L. (Fanucchi), b. 1941; Danelle L. (Gordon), b. 1947; Janelle L. (Dennison), b. 1947; Martha J., b. 1952; edn: Visalia Comm. Coll. 1939; real estate courses, Adult Edn. 1958, Anthonys Schs. 1968. Calif. lic. R.E. Broker 1968. Career: sales mgr. Strachan Realty 1967, realtor own office, 1968--; awards: Production Awd. in Real Estate Sales, Fresno Realty Bd. 1959; mem: Fresno Realty Bd., Fresno Multiple Listing Svc.; Fresno Womens Div. CofC; Democrat; Protestant; rec: ancient history, Bible study & history. Address: G.K. Pat Leonard, Realtor, 1323 W Browning Fresno 93711

LEONARD, GWEN T., loan processing specialist; b. June 26, 1926, Denver, Colo.; d. S.R. and Jeanette (Bulkley) Trythall; m. L. W. Leonard, Jan. 1, 1953; 1 son, Lester T. b. 1956; edn: Barnes Sch. of Bus. 1943-44, Pasadena City Coll., UCLA Ext., Mt. San Antonio Coll.; Savings & Loan League courses Woodbury Coll. 1958-62; Cert. Senior Escrow Ofcr., Cert. Sr. Loan Escrow Ofcr., 1960, Calif. Escrow Assn.; Calif. lic. Real Estate Broker 1959-; Calif. (life) Tchr. (R.E.) Cert. 1966. Career: escrow coordinator ofcr., PBX opr., Davis-Baker Realty, Pasadena 1943-56; cost acct., escrow ofcr. Eastridge Dev., La Mesa 1957-58; escrow ofcr. (Sale & Loan) Home Savings & Loan Assn., Arcadia 1958-60, Escrow Mgr./asst. secty. 1960-81, Loan Processing Depot mgr., 1981-83; loan proc. splst. Conventional Loan Admin., Home Savings of America, Savings of Am., & Ahmanson Mtg. Co., 1983--, respons. for loan proc. training pgm. nationwide for Home Svgs. and Subsidiaries; chmn. Edn. Com. Escrow Associates of San Gabriel Valley, 1966-75; advisor Mt. San Antonio Coll. real estate and escrow certificate pgms. 1968-; prof. of real estate Mt. SAC, 1966-81; prof. R.E. Lic. Renewal Seminars, Mt. SAC 1979-; lectr. pvt. mortgage ins. cos.; honors: two spl. awards for ednl. tng., Escrow Assoc. of San Gab. Valley and CEA, 1970, 1982; Outstanding Business woman, L.A. Bus. & Profl. Women Assn. 1978; mem: Escrow Assoc. of San Gab. Valley 1958-, CEA, 1958-; (fmr.) Soroptimist Club of Arcadia-Monrovia (pres. 1969-70), Friends of Library Arcadia, Pasa. power Squadronettes; publs: cons. on textbooks (escrow procedures), Title Ins. & Trust Co.; Republican; Prot.; rec: gardening, boating, teaching. Res: 3530 Damien Ave, 273, La Verne 91750 Ofc: Home Svgs of America, 3731 Wilshire Bl, Ste 780, Los Angeles 90010

LEONG, MARGARET ELIZABETH WOO, psychiatric social worker; b. June 23, 1943, Peoria, Ill.; d. Herbert Ying Yick and Kate H. (Jue) Woo; m. Dr. Tony Chan Leong Jr., Feb. 9, 1974; edn: AA, Merritt Coll. 1965; BA, San Francisco State Univ. 1968; MSW, UC Berkeley 1974; PhD, Wright Inst. 1983; LCSW, Calif. 1980. Career: Teacher's Corp intern, Urban Tchr.'s Corp., Chgo., Ill. 1968-69; tchr. Martin Luther King In-Community Sch., Berkeley 1969-70; field work asst. East Bay Chinese Youth Council, Oakland 1970-72; comm. aide Oakland Pub. Schs., Oakland 1970-71; comm. liaison Alameda Co. Mental Health Svc., Oakland 1975-76; patients rights advoc. 1976-80; psychiatric soc. wkr. 1976--; Alameda Co. Mental Health Asian Caucus & Ethnic Minority Employees Caucus; Alameda Co. Health Care Svcs. Affirmative Action Com. & Tng. Com.; recipient NIMH Grant 1972-74, Carnegie Grant 1972-74, Univ. Grant In-Aid 1973-74; mem: Social Services Union 535; UC Berkeley Alumni Assn; NIMH Sub-com. (E. Oakland Mental Health Citizens Com.); UCB Sch. of Soc. Welfare Counseling Proj. (comm. cons. Calif. Ctr. Proj.); Cub Scouts (den mother); History, Culture & Current Problems of Racial & Ethnic Minorities Com.; Democrat; rec; teddy bear collection, gardening. Res: 334 Newton Ave Oakland 94606 Ofc: Alameda Co. Mental Health, Asian Unit, 285 17th St, 3rd Fl., Oakland 94612

LEONG, RUSSELL KENT, graphic designer; b. Nov. 21, 1946, San Francisco; s. Yun Kim and Ethel (Jear) L.; edn: BA, CSU San Jose 1970. Career: senior designer Wadsworth Publishing Co., Belmont 1970-73; art dir./ designer Russell Leong Design, Palo Alto 1974--; design faculty, Design Dept. CSU San Jose 1980-; awards: Bronze Medal, Western Art Dirs. Club Annual show 1975; Murphy Awd. (Gold), San Jose Advtg. Club 1980; Gold Awd., San Francisco Soc. of Communicating Arts 1980; Merit Awd., Communication Arts Mag. 1978; mem: Western Art Dirs. Club; Inst. Graphic Designers, S.F.; Am. Inst. Graphic Arts.; S.F. Soc. of Comml. Art; rec: surfing. Res: 975 Inverness Way Sunnyvale 94087 Ofc: Russell Leong Design, 535 Ramona St, Ste 33, Palo Alto 94301

LEPORIERE, RALPH DENNIS, quality engineer; b. Nov. 8, 1932, Elizabeth, NJ; s. Maximo and Christian Leporiere; m. Judith Louise Crowhurst, Nov. 19, 1960; children: Bonnie Ann, b. 1961; David Anthony, b. 1964; edn: BS, Rutgers Univ. 1954; postgrad. wk. Coll. of the Holy Names, Oakland 1965-66. Career: chemist NY Quinine & Chem. Works, Inc., Newark NJ 1954-55; asst. to chief chemist/ quality control C.D. Smith Pharmaceutical Co., New Brunswick, NJ 1955-56; asst. supvr. qual. control White Labs, Inc., Kenilworth, NJ 1958-60; staff cons. qual. eng. Calif. & Hawaiian Sugar Co., Crockett, Calif. 1960--; chmn./ instr. Qual. Control Dept. Laney Coll., Oakland 1967--; chmn./ asst. prof. JFK Univ., Martinez 1967-72; instr./mem. Adv. Com. Annual Stat. Short Course, UC Davis 1969-; mem: Fellow Am. Soc. for Quality Control (S.F. & East Bay Sects.); Toastmasters (Vallejo chpt. pres. 1965); Am. Statistical Assn.; Am. Chem. Soc.; Am. Canyon Co. Water Dist. (pres. 1973-83, v.p. 1971-73); Listed: Who's Who in the West 1970-; mil: Med. Svc. Corps, US Army Environmental Health Labs, Edgewood, MD 1956-58. Res: 618 Kilpatrick St Vallejo 94589 Ofc: Calif. & Hawaiian Sugar Co., 830 Loring Ave Crockett 94525

LESH, ANGELA DAWN, marketing research executive; b. Dec. 23, 1947, Altadena; d. Olin Eugene and Betty Jean (Carroll) L.; edn: BA, UC Davis 1970; MA, Sacto. State Univ. 1971. Career: jr. research analyst Doremus, San Francisco 1971-73; mktg. research analyst Medical Care Found., Sacto. 1973; dir. mktg. research Wells Fargo Bank, S.F. 1973-78; senior project mgr. Shaklee Corp., S.F. 1978-79; pres. A. Dawn Lesh & Assoc., Kensington 1979-81; dir. mktg. research Bank of Am. 1981--; mem: Commonwealth Club, S.F.; Calif. Aggie Alumni Assn., Davis; Am. Mktg. Assn.; Women in Communication; Advtg. Research Found. (Finl. Research Council); Bank Mktg. Assn., Chgo.; publs: journal article, Leadership Through Positioning, A.R.F.; Democrat; Methodist; rec: running, pottery, travel. Res: 1612 Ocean View Kensington 94707 Ofc: Bank of America, 120 Montgomery St, Ste 1174, San Francisco 94104

LESLIE, ROBERT ROHRER, marina boating industry executive; b. June 27, 1927, Los Angeles; s. Harold D. and Martha (Rohrer) L.; m. Uta Ferguson; children: Kenneth b. 1952, John b. 1954, Kerry b. 1957, James b. 1962; edn: BS,

USC, 1950. Career: general agt. Leslie & Hess Agency, Northwestern Nat. Life Ins. Co., L.A. 1952-69; exec. v.p. Marina del Rey Lessees Assn., Marina del Rey, 1969--; exec. v.p. Marina del Rey CofC, 1972-76; owner Robert R. Leslie & Assocs., Consultants and Yacht Brokers, Mrina del Rey, 1978--; Calif. Marine Parks & Harbors Assn. state pres. 1975-76; Nat. Boating Fedn. pres. 1983-84; honors: Marina del Rey Yachtsman of the Year 1975; Pacific Coast Yachting Assn. Yachtsman of Yr. 1976; Calif. Assembly Resolution 1976; Marina del Rey Citizen of Yr. 1983; mem: So. Calif. Yachting Assn. (staff commodore 1972), Pac. Coast Yachting Assn. (staff commodore 1975), Calif. and Transpacific Yacht Clubs, Native Sons of Golden West (pres. Ramona, 1983), SAR, Sigma Alpha Epsilon social frat., Masons, Shriners, Marina City Club; speaker on Marina and Boating Economics to various groups statewide; mil: lt. USCG, WWII and Korea; Republican; Presbyterian; rec: sailing, powerboating, racing and cruising. Res: 13900 Marquesas Way, Apt C-82, Marina del Rey 90292 Ofc: 14120 Tahiti Way Marina del Rey 90292

LESNIAK, RONALD S., consulting firm executive; b. Mar. 13, 1948, Oak Park, Ill.; s. Joseph J. and Pearl V. (Wroczynski) L.; m. Theresa A. Sperry, Jan. 23, 1971; children: Jeffrey, b. 1973; Andrew, b. 1975; Philip, b. 1977; David, b. 1980. Career: staff engr. GTE Automatic Electric Co., Northlake, Ill. 1970-76; mgr. customer support ITT Telecommun., Des Plaines, Ill. 1976-78; mktg. mgr. Rolm Corp., Santa Clara, Ca. 1978-83; exec. v.p. Alverson Lesniak & Assoc., Inc., Belmont 1983--; awards: Pres. Club Awd. for outstanding achiev., Rolm Corp. 1982; mem: Entrepreneurs Alliance, Santa Clara; Scotts Valley Little League; Catholic (choir dir.); rec: golf, tennis, racquetball. Res: 1520 Vine Hill Rd Santa Cruz 95065 Ofc: Alverson Lesniak & Assoc., Inc., POB 79, Belmont 94002

LESSNER, RONALD DENNIS, lawyer; b. Feb. 8, 1947, Los Angeles; s. Eugene and Vivian Lessner; edn: BA, CSU Northridge 1969; JD, Southwestern 1972; admitted to Calif. State Bar 1973. Career: atty., pvt. practice spec. personal injury 1973--; mem: Los Angeles, Santa Monica, Beverly Hills Bar Assns., Calif.,and L.A. Trial Lawyers Assns.; rec: skiing, travel. Res: 12258 Sunset Pkwy Los Angeles Ofc: Ronald D. Lessner, A Law Corp., 2120 Wilshire Blvd, 3rd Flr, Santa Monica 90403

LEUNG, LAI-SUNG ERIC, eye surgeon; b. Apr. 30, 1944, Shanghai, China, nat. 1980; s. Chi-Hsuei and Kwai-Han (Lee) L.; m. Kay-Lee Huang, July 5, 1969; children: Loh-Sze b. 1975, Loh-Shan b. 1977; edn: AB, Columbia Univ. 1966; MD, Johns Hopkins Univ. 1970; surg. intern., UC San Diego 1970-71; resident ophthalmologist Univ. of Penna. 1971-74; Diplomate Am. Bd. of Ophthalmology 1976; FACS, Fellow Am. Coll. of Surgeons 1978. Career: estab. pvt. practice ophthalmol., San Francisco 1975--; tchg. staff St. Mary's Hosp. Med. Center, S.F.; active staff French Hosp., and Chinese Hosp., S.F.; Fellow Am. Acad. of Ophthalmology 1977; mem. Chinese Comm. Health Care Assn. (dir. 1983); Assn. of Chinese Comm. Physicians (dir. 1983); Am. Assn. of Ophthal.; S.F. Med. Soc.; Calif. Med. Assn.; dir. North Peninsular Mandarin Sch. 1979-83; dir. Chinese Newcomer Services 1982-83; advisor American Nat. Bank, S.F. 1983; med. journal arts., profl. presentations; rec: sailing, skiing, basketball, travel. Res: 126 Valdeflores Dr Burlingame 94010 Ofc: L. Eric Leung, MD, Inc. 929 Clay St San Francisco 94108

LEUNG, TOM, banker; b. Nov. 10, 1926, Hong Kong; s. Cheuk and Foon Leung; m. Glory, Aug. 10, 1947; children: Kitty, b. 1949; Frank, b. 1950; edn: MBA, Golden Gate Univ. 1972; Real Estate Broker lic., Calif. 1979. Career: bus. mgr. Hongkong & Shanghai Banking Corp., San Francisco 1964-76; v.p. Olympic Savings, S.F. 1977-78 chmn. bd./ pres./ CEO Sincere Savings Bank, San Francisco 1979--; mem: Economic Opportunity Council, S.F.; columnist: Tom Leung's Column, Chinese Times, S.F. 1967-79; rec: writing, football. Res: 583 15th Ave San Francisco 94118 Ofc: 526 Columbus Ave San Francisco 94133

LEUTY, GERALD JOHNSTON, osteopathic physician-surgeon; b. July 23, 1919, Knoxville, Iowa; s. Johnston William and Mable Geraldine (Johnston) L.; m. Norma Jean Hindman, Dec. 30, 1964; children: Barbara, b. 1970; Patrick, b. 1975; edn: AA, Kemper Mil. Sch. 1939; Coll. of Mortuary Sci. 1941; Drake Univ. 1946; DO, Coll. of Osteopathic Med. & Surgery 1949; lic. Osteopathic Physician & Surgeon, Calif. 1975. Career: motician/ embalmer, Des Moines, Ia. 1940; aeronautical engr. Boeing Aircraft Co., Wichita, Ks. 1942; bacteriologist US Army Med. Corp. 1942, 46; osteopathic physician- surgeon, Knoxville, Ia. 1949, 56; clin. dir. Leuty Osteopathic Clinic, Earlham, Ia. 1956-77; osteopathic physician- surgeon, gen. practice, Santa Rosa, Ca. 1977--; lectr. Coll. of Osteopathic Med. & Surgery, Des Moines, Ia. 1975; preceptor instr. Coll. of Osteopathic Medicine of the Pacific, Pomona 1981-83; honors: Life mem. Am. Med. Soc. of Vienna 1970; Fellow, Internat. Coll. of Angiologiae 1980; OPSC Awd. 1981; mem: Iowa Osteopathic Soc. (pres. 6th dist. 1974); Soc. of Osteopathic Physicians; No. Calif. Osteopathic Med. Soc. (pres. 1981); Osteopathic Physicians & Surgeons of Calif. (pres. 1982); Am. Osteopathic Assn. (House of Delegates); Am. Acad. of Osteopathy Calif. Div.); Lions Club, Knoxville, Ia. (pres. 1946); Am. Legion, Ia. (6th dist. commdr. 1974-75); works: Eitiology of Primary Atypical Pneumonia 1944; mil: sgt. US Army M.C. 1942-46, Respiratory Disease Commn.; Republican; Presbyterian; rec: travel, photog. Res: 5835 La Cuesta Dr Santa Rosa 95405 Ofc: 4275 Montgomery Dr Santa Rosa 95405

LE VECQUE, CHARLOTTE ROSE, psychiatric social worker; b. Nov. 11, 1944, Darby, Penn; d. George Alfred and Charlotte Vivian (Bunsart) L.. Edn: BS, Western Michigan Univ., 1966; MSW, Adelphi Univ., 1968.; LCSW, lic. clin. soc. wkr. NY 1968, Calif. 1974; ACSW, NASW, 1970. Career: psychiat. social worker Patton State Hosp., Patton, CA, 1968; Sr. psychiat. soc. wkr.

dept. mental health So. Bejo Co. Hosp., 1971-74; dept. psychiat. So. Cal. Permanente Med. Grp., Fontana and Canyon Crest, 1974--; LCSW, dept. psychiat. So. Cal. Prmanente Med. Grp.; Nat. Assn. of Soc. Wrks. (mem. at large); guest lectr. Clin. Psycho Internship; speaker health topics seminars. Awards: Orange Empire Dog Club service award, 1983. Mem: NASW; fellow, SCSW; Nat. Registry Health Care Providers (charter); ASCW. Orgns: Palm Springs Kennel Club; Am. Fox Terrier Club; Western Fox Terr. Breeders Assn. (bd. govs., ed. Kliptails); Santa Ana Valley Kennel Club; San Bejo Humane Soc; San Bejo Horseman's Assn; Democrat. Rec: Fox Terrier breeding, exhibs., tng., horseback riding. Res: 3465 E. Holly Circle Dr Highland 92346 Ofc: SCPMG, 5225 Canyon Crest Dr Riverside 92507

LEVIE, ALBERT company president; b. Jan. 11, 1917, Mnpls., Minn.; s. Siegfried and Betty (Klein) L.; m. LaVonne Joan Battle, Sept. 27, 1953; children: James, b. 1941, Tim, b. 1943; Barbara, b 1946; Brad, b. 1955; Glenn, b. 1959; edn: BA, UCLA 1940. Career: owner Antelope Valley Refrig. Co., Palmdale 1940-47; pres. Elgee Meats, Los Angeles 1946-75; pres. Gullivers, Inc. 1972--; instr. UCLA 1951-; adj. prof. Cal Poly, Pomona 1982-; mem: CRA, NRA; Assoc. Meat Jobbers (pres. 1953); author: Meat Handbook, AVI Publishing, (4th ed.) 1963; var. wrkshps. and papers on meat and food svc.; D.T.S.; Jewish; rec: golf, skiing, photog. Res: 1816 San Ysidro Beverly Hills 90210 Ofc: Gulliver's, Inc., 12540 Beatrice St, Ste 200, Los Angeles 90066

LEVIN, BARRY LEE, lawyer; b. Mar. 6, 1947, Chgo., Ill.; s. Julius and Pearl (Green) L.; m. Renee Gail, Mar. 8, 1969; children: Jennifer Jo b. 1972, Brandy Erin b. 1976, Elly Lynn b. 1981; edn: AA, Los Angeles Valley Coll. 1975; BA, CSU 1976; JD cum laude, San Fernando Valley Coll. of Law 1980; mem. Calif. State Bar. Career: patrol, narcotics, detectives and vice, Los Angeles Police Dept. 1969-80; deputy dist. atty. Los Angeles County Dist. Attorneys Office, 1981; criminal trial lawyer sole practitioner 1982--; pro bono representation of indigent Vietnam combat veterans; represent police officers in pension hearings; mem. State Bar of Calif., Federal Bar, Amer. Bar Assn., Calif. Attys. for Criminal Justice; mil: ssg E6 US Army Airborne 1965-68, 2 tours Republic Vietnam, 3 Purple Hearts, Bronze Star w/V, Air Medal; Republican; Jewish; rec: scuba diving, boxing, baseball. Res: 20444 Pacific Coast Hwy Malibu 90265 Law Office of Barry L. Levin 1100 Glendon Ave Penthouse Westwood Village 90024

LEVIN, EDWARD HART, business owner; b. Aug. 31, 1942, Beverly Hills; s. Charles Y. and Hortence (Margolies) L.; m. Laurie Ann Maxson, Apr. 3, 1982; children: Tracy b. 1965, Scott b. 1966, Terry b. 1967, Cary b. 1969; edn: BS, Univ. of Heildberg, W. Ger. 1967; certs: Physician's Asst. SP-2 (1974), Respiratory Therapist (1972), Cardiographic Tech. (1980). Career: tech. dir. Cardio-Pulmonary Services 1967-71, Golden State Meml. Hosp. & Med. Center 1971-73, Univ. of Penna. Med. Ctr. 1973-74; tech. dir. ICU, CCU, MCU, US Govt. Hosp., Landsthual, W.Germany 1974-78; respiratory therapist Barlow Hosp. (for respir. disease) 1978-79; tech. dir. Santa Fe Mem. Hosp. and Med. Ctr. 1978-80, Oxnard Comm. Hosp. 1980; owner two janitorial cos.: B & E Comml. Sanitation & Building Maint. 1980--, and Quality Building Maint. 1983--; tchg. coord. for respiratory therapy, jr. coll., 1969; mem. American Legion, Ventura Trade Club; mil: E5 US Army 1963-66, GCM, Purple Heart; Ofc: B&E Commercial Sanitation & Bldg. Maint., QBM, 433 E. Main, Ste. 10, Ventura 93001

LEVIN, MILTON B., insurance underwriter; b. Jan. 4, 1910, Rhode Island; s. Samuel and Rebecca (Fradin) L.; m. Ruth R. Robinson, June 16, 1940; 1 dau: Linda b. 1945; 2 grandchildren: Robin b. 1971, Richard b. 1968; edn: BA, Brown Univ. 1931; Boston Univ. 1950-55; CPCU, Am. Inst. Property & Casualty Underwriters 1955. Career: credit mgr. United Utilities Retail Chain, R.I.; owner Milton B. Levin Ins. Agency, R.I. 1934-53; partner Goldsmith & Levin Co., Ins. Brokers, R.I. 1953-55; pres. Milton Goodman & Assocs. Ins. Agcy., Los Angeles 1956-71; merged Milton Goodman & Assocs. with Stein, Antignas, Kent, Inc. 1975; cons. Wellington Agencies, Inc., L.A. 1975-79; ofc. broker/ cons. Triangle Ins. Inc., Sherman Oaks 1980--; mem: Soc. of CPCUs, Boston, Mass. & Los Angeles chpts.; Rhode Island Assn. Ins. Agents, Inc. (panel expert); Speakers Bureau (Property Ins. Com.); Boy Scouts of Am. (Scout Master); Menorah Lodge (Master Mason); publs: Critique & Comments in the Daily News, San Fernando, Ca. (1984) and in the Standard, New England's Ins. Weekly (1942-43); mil: US Army, WWII; Republican Cand. for Councilman, Prov. R.I. 1938; Democrat. Res: 5400 Yarmouth Ave Encino 91316 Ofc: Triangle Insurance, Inc., 4340 Fulton Ave Sherman Oaks 91423

LEVINE, MILTON MARTIN, manufacturing co. executive; b. Nov. 3, 1913, McKeesport, Penn.; s. Harry and Mary (Weisan) L.; m. Mauricette Paulette Schneider, Dec. 1, 1945; children: Harriet, b. 1949; Steven, b. 1952; Ellen, b. 1957. Career: sales mgr. Wolk Furniture Co., Homestead, Pa. 1940; salesman May- Stearns, Pittsburgh, Pa. 1942; salesman Ohringer Furniture, Braddock, Pa. 1946; currently, chmn. Uncle Milton Inds., Inc., Culver City; honors: Man of the Yr., Westside Jewish Comm. Ctr. 1962; chmn. UJWF 1962; Comm. Chest 1962; mem: Am. Pet Products; Nat. School Supply; Toy Whslers. Assn.; Am. Toy Mfrs. Assn.; Masonic Blue Lodge; Scottish Rite; Al Malaiki Temple; Westgate Masonic Club; inventor: Ant Farm; Dwarf Tree Kit; Fossil Hunt; author: Ant Facts & Fantasies; You Can't Get There From Here; mil: 1st sgt. US Army Engrs., GCM, Meritorious Unit; ETO 4 Battle Stars; Democrat; Jewish; rec: golf, baseball. Res: 5106 Huck Finn Ln Culver City 90230 Ofc: Uncle Milton Industries, Inc., 10325 W Jefferson Blvd Culver City 90230

LEVINE, SIDNEY, school administrator; b. May 12, 1929, Belvedere; s.

Morris and Rose (Nitovitch) L.; m. Edith Jurman, Aug. 23, 1958; children: Marcy, b. 1959; Sharon, b. 1962; edn: BA, UCLA 1950; MA, 1954; CSU Northridge 1958-63; Calif. Tchr. Credential (1954), Pupil Personnel (1956), and Adminstrv. (1970). Career: hd. counselor Mann Jr. High Sch. 1968-72, Nobel Jr. High Sch., San Fernando 1972-73; tchr./ counselor Maclay Jr. High Sch. 1973-74; hd. counselor Sepulveda Jr. High Sch. 1974--; acct. exec. Tchrs. Mgmt. & Investment Corp.; honors: Faculty Chmn. 1959-60; Treas., Secondary Head Counselors Org. of Los Angeles 1977-79; mem: Secondary Head Counselors Orgn. of L.A.; Assoc. Adminstrs. of L.A.; Calif. Personnel & Guidance Assn.; Phi Delta Kappa; Educare; Sch.- Comm. Adv. Council; works: developed group counseling pgm., assisted in devel. gifted magnet school, Sepulveda Jr. High 1974-83; mil: sgt. US Army 1950-52; Hebrew; rec: sports, philately, photog. Res: 5009 Woodman Ave, 112, Sherman Oaks 91423 Ofc: Los Angeles Unified Schools, 450 N Grand Los Angeles 90051; Teachers Management & Investment, POB 2500, Newport Beach 92660

LEVINE, STANLEY BRYANT, pathologist; b. June 27, 1942, St. Louis, MO; s. Morris Harold and Frances Ida Levine; father, Dr. Morris H. Levine, former pres., Rocky Mountain Radiology Soc.; Edn: BS, Tufts Univ., 1963; MD, Harvrd Univ., 1967. Career: anatomic pathology res., Yale New Haven Med. Ctr., New Haven, CT, 1967-69; clinical pathology res., Walter Army Med. Center, Wash. D.C., 1969-71; chief pathologist, US Army Hosp., Saigon, So. Vietnam, 1971-72; chief of clinical pathology, Letterman Army Med. Center, San Francisco, 1973-74; chief of hematology, Metropolitan Hosps., Portland, OR, 1974-77; chief clinical pathology, O'Connor Hosp., San Jose, 1977---; also asst. clinical prof., Clinical Pathology, nuclear med., Univ. Oreg. Med. Sch., 1977; also lectr., Hematopathology course, Armed Forces Inst. of Pathology, 1977-80. Mem: Amer. Soc. of Clinical Pathologists; Coll. of Amer. Pathologists; Soc. of Nuclear Med.; Amer. Coll. of Nuclear Physics; Amer. Med. Assn.; Calif. Med. Assn.; Santa Clara Co. Med. Soc.; Phi Delta Epsilon frat. Papers publ: Clinical Nuclear Medicine, 1977; Achieves of Pathology, 1977, 73, 74; Amer. Journ. Surg., 1970. Mil: Maj., AUS, 1969-74; Bronze Star, Vietnam Service. Rec: softball, tennis, racquetball. Res: 3180 Loma Verde Dr., Apt. 11, San Jose 95117; Office: O'Connor Hosp., 2105 Forest Ave., San Jose 95117.

LEVIT, WILLIAM HAROLD, lawyer, retired judge; b. Jan. 11, 1908, San Francisco; s. Morris and Fannie (Jacobs) Levit; Edn: AB, Stanford Univ., 1928; JD, Stanford Law Sch., 1930; m. Barbara Kaiser, June 9, 1933; chil: Jacqueline Levit Weiss (Superior Ct. Judge), b. 1936; William H., Jr. (Attorney), b. 1938. Career: partner, Long & Levit, Attys., San Francisco and Los Angeles, 1930-42, 1946-62, Of Counsel, 1976-78; Judge of the Superior Court of Calif., Los Angeles County, 1962-76, retired 1976; Of Counsel, Stroock & Stroock & Lavan, Los Angeles and New York, 1978---. Mem: Judicial Council of Calif., 1969-71; Dean, Calif. Judicial Coll., 1971; instr., Judicial Adminstrn. USC Law Center, 1968-77; governing bd., Calif. Center for Judicial Edn. and Research, 1973-76; mem. Faculty, Natl. Judicial Coll., 1965-68, 1973; mem., Inst. of Judicial Administration. Fellow, Amer. Coll. of Trial Lawyers; hon. mem., Italian Bar, 1944---. Publs: co-author: New Legal Precedent Regarding Psychiatric Examinations, The Amer. Journ. of Psychiatry, May 1965; contrib. Calif. Law Rev., Judicial Council of Calif., legal texts. Mil: Lt. Col., US Army, Judge Advocate Gen.'s Dept., 1942-46; awarded Bronze Star Medal. Rec: golf, swimming. Res: Beverly Hills; Office: Stroock, Stroock & Lavan, 1801 Century Park East, Suite 900, Los Angeles 90067.

LEVY, DAVID STEVEN, university administrator; b. Mar. 9, 1955, Los Angeles; s. Henry and Gloria Grace (Barouh) L.; edn: BA, Occidental Coll. 1977, Masters, 1979. Career: student loan officer Bank of America 1975-78; asst. dir. finl. aid, Calif. State Coll. San Bernardino 1978-79; finl. aid counselor CSU Northridge 1979-80; assoc. dir. finl. aid CSU Dominguez Hills 1980-82; dir. financial aid Occidental Coll. 1982--; honors: Phi Beta Kappa, Mortar Board, Delta Phi Epsilon, Psi Chi, Phi Alpha Theta, Sigma Alpha Epsilon, recipient Richter Fellowship (1976), CSU Adminstrv. Fellowship (1981-82); listed Who's Who in the West, Internat. Youth in Achieve., Comm. Leaders of Amer., Personalities of Amer.; mem: Calif. Postsec. Edn. Commn.; Calif. Student Aid Commn. (Computer Search Scholarship Adv. Com. 1981-82); Occidental Coll. Mortar Bd., Alumni Pres., 1979-82; Nat. Assn. of Student Finl. Aid Adminstrs. 1977-; Western Assn. of Student Finl. Aid Adminstrs. 1977-; Calif. Student Finl. Aid Adminstrs. 1977-; publs: contbr. Calif. Student Aid Commn. Workbook (1977-); rec: music, literature, the arts. Res: 3522 Henrietta Ave La Crescenta 91214 Ofc: Financial Aid Office Occidental College 1600 Campus Rd Los Angeles 90041

LEWIS, CALVIN THOMAS, JR., restaurateur; b. May 11, 1949, Memphis, Tenn.; s. Calvin Thomas, Sr. and Willodean (Gambill) L.; m. Pamela Peters, July 16, 1977. Career: asst. mgr. The Crab Cooker, Newport Beach 1969-73; owner/ mgr. The Seafood Broiler, Glendale 1973-76; owner/ mgr. The Fish Market, Palo Alto 1976-83; currently, cons. Cameron's Seafood, Pasadena; mem: Nat. & Calif. Restaurant Assns.; NCDXC; ARRL; NCCC; Lutheran; rec: radion communications, computer sciences. Res: 1220 Brookmere Rd Pasadena 91105 Ofc: Cameron's, 1978 Colorado Pasadena 91107

LEWIS, GENE RAYMOND, chartered life underwriter; b. Dec. 1, 1937, Des Moines, Ia.; s. Raymond E. and Mollie Irene (Thompson) L.; m. Beverly Block, June 21, 1958; children: Mark b. 1960, Kathy b. 1962, Steve b. 1966, Sheri b. 1972; edn: grad. (ministerial degree) Depeu Bible Coll. 1959; CLU, American Coll. 1970, ChFP, 1981. Career: Youth for Christ director, Des Moines, Iowa 1956-59; self-empl. Denver, Colo. 1959-65; insurance agent, dist. mgr. Metropolitan Life, Fresno, Ca. 1965-76; general agent Mutual Security, Fresno 1976--; mem. Mutual Security Advisory Bd.; Leading Gen. Agt. of Co. 1980-81; instr. CLU courses 1979, LUTC courses 1978; past pres. Stockton Life Underwriters 1972; bd. mem. Words of the Gospel Radio Pgm.; mem: Charter Finl. Plnnrs. of Fresno, Fresno Life Underwriters, Fresno Charter Life Und., Mutual Security Charter Life Und.; Republican; Mennonite Brethren Ch.; rec: hunting, active in youth wk. Res: 5494 N. Angus, Fresno 93710 Ofc: Mutual Security, 1300 W. Shaw, Ste A1, Fresno 93711

LEWIS, M. DAVID, physician; b. Oct. 13, 1946, Imperial, Nebr.; s. Betty Blair; 1 son, Matthew David; edn: AB, Univ. of Mo. 1969; MD, Univ. of Colo. 1973; residency Wilford Hall USAF Medical Center 1973-76, chief res. psychiatry 1976. Career: chief Dept. of Mental Health, USAF Academy, Colo. 1976-79, med. supr. Drug and Alcohol Abuse Com. 1978-89; med. dir. Arapahoe Mental Hlth Center, Englewood, Colo. 1979-80; psychiatric/medical supr. Vernon C. Grounds Family Counseling Ctr., Englewood, Colo. 1977-81; med. dir., PAASA Pgm., Queen of Angels Hosp., Los Angeles 1979-81; currently: chief of staff Coldwater Cyn. Hosp., No. Hollywood; med. dir. substance abuse pgms. Coldwater Cyn. Hosp., Pasadena Comm. Hosp.; clin. prof. Dept. Psy., UC Los Angeles. Consultant Republican Nat. Com. 1978-; bd. dirs. Am. Inst. of Applied Politics, Westminster Coll. (S.L.C., Ut. 1979-); phys. for SS Universe Campus, World Campus Afloat, Chapman Coll. 1973; cons. Inst. for Shipboard Edn. 1978-79; honors: Univ. of Mo. Football Team 1964-68, Sugar Bowl Team 1966, Disting. Military Cadet, ROTC, 1968; mem: AMA, Am. Psychiatric Assn., Soc. of AF Psychiatrists (charter, past v.p.), So. Calif. Psychiat. Soc. Address: 6421 Coldwater Cyn Ave No. Hollywood 91606

LEWIS, RONALD GEORGE, automotive corporation executive; b. Sept. 14, 1942, Orange; s. George Oliver and Phyllis Eleanor (Alfrey) L.; m. Nora Kathleen Lee, Aug. 26, 1967; children: Kristine, b. 1969; David, b. 1972; edn: AA, Santa Ana Coll. 1962; BA, San Jose State Univ. 1965; post grad., 1965-66; post grad., Pepperdine 1968, 1969-70; Spl. Secondary (1965), Gen. Secondary (1966), and Standard Life (1972) tchg. credentials, Calif., Automotive Smog Equip. Installers Lic., Bureau of Auto Repair 1972-77. Career: dir. aquatics City of Santa Ana 1963-69; automotive instr. Sunny Hills H.S., Fullerton 1966-72; with Nissan Motor Corp. 1972--; tech. tng. instr., Los Angeles Reg. 1972-74; dist. svc. mgr. 1974-75; consumer rels. mgr. 1975-76; regl. svc. mgr. I, Nissan Motor Corp., San Francisco region 1976-81; regl. svc. mgr. II, Los Angeles region 1981-82; nat. mgr. Consumer Relations, Carson 1982--; automotive adv. bd. Rio Hondo Coll. 1975; advis. com. Career Expo, Humbolt County Schs. 1978, awards: Eagle Scout, BSA 1959; Man of the Year 1962, Santa Ana Coll.; Tech. Awd., Hon. Mention, Nissan Motor Corp. 1976; mem: Epsilon Pi Tau (pres. 1965-66); Calif. Indsl. Edn. Assn.; Soc. of Automotive Engrs.; Soc. Consumer Affairs Profls.; Am. Mgmt. Assn.; Sigma Chi; Homeowners Assn.; Parent Tchr. Orgn.; works: devel. & implemented current Nissan Customer Care Pgm., incl. Mediation/ Arbitration Dispute Resolution Mechanism 1982-83; Republican; rec: bicycling, swimming, restoration of vehicles. Res: 7562 Indigo Ln La Palma 90623 Ofc: Nissan Motor Corporation, 18501 S Figueroa St Carson 90248

LEZAK, DANIEL SHERWIN, corporate executive; b. Dec. 1, 1933, Chgo., Ill.; s. Nathan and Jeanette Lezak; m. Cheryl Corol, Nov. 19, 1983; children: Jeffrey, Gary, Scott; edn: BS in acctcy., Roosevelt Univ.; Certified Public Acct., Calif. 1963. Career: tax dept. Armour & Co., Chgo. 1957; internal auditor Revel Inc., Venice, Calif. 1958; controller and treas. Remanco Inc., Santa Monica 1962; empl. with Hughes Aircraft; sec.treas., then asst. to the pres. Winsco Instruments and Controls (merged into Genisco Tech. Corp.); empl. with John Reitz & Co., Los Angeles; pres. Internat. Recreation & Sports Inc., -1971; splst. in revitalizing troubled cos. 1970--; current: pres. Lezak Group, Inc. (OTC); dir.: Enterprise Technologies Inc., Lucky Chance Mining Corp., Apexx Investing Co., Lezak Group Inc., General Residential Corp., Bio Recovery Technology Inc.; mem. Calif. Soc. of CPAs; mil: splst 1/c US Army 1953-55; Republican; Jewish. Res: 987 Tahoe Blvd Incline Village NV 89450 Ofc: Lezak Group Inc. 23501 Park Sorrento Calabasas 91302

LI, LYMAN G., architect; b. Aug. 17, 1925, Toy Sing, Kwangtung, China, nat. 1963; s. Wah Sign and Fong (Shee) L.; m. Betty L. Ng., M.D., Aug. 4, 1956; children: Berdine, b. 1959; Gary, b. 1962; Carl, b. 1964; edn: BS, Heald Coll. 1948; UC Ext., San Francisco 1948-52; Univ. VA Ext. 1953-54; George Washington Univ. 1956; Reg. Archit., D.C., Calif.; cert. Nat. Council of Archit. Registration Bd. Career: Ryan & Lee Archits., San Francisco 1948-52; Faulkner, Kingsbury & Stenhouse, Archits., Wash. DC 1952-56; Vincent G. Kling, Archits. 1956-57; Meyers & Evers, Arcits., S.F. 1957; Wurster, Bernardi & Emmons, S.F. 1958; assoc. archit. Paul A. Ryan, S.F. 1958-68; proj. archit. Robert B. Liles, Inc., Marin Co. 1968-83; archit. V.A. Med. Ctr., S.F. 1983--; Chinatown Tech. Adv. Com., San Francisco Planning Commn. 1964-65; mem: Am. Inst. Archits.; Internat. Platform Assn.; works: Carmelite Monastery, San Jose; St. Mary's Cathedral, S.F.; Convent of Sacred Heart Schs., S.F., Menlo Park; mil: AUS 1943-45, Bronze Star, Purple Heart, European, African and Middle Eastern Campaigns, WWII Victory, Am. Campaign, Battle Stars (3); Protestant; rec: arts, skiing. Res: 501 Park Way Mill Valley 94941 Ofc: Engineering Service, V.A. Medical Center, San Francisco 94121

LI, YUAN-YU PETER, architect; b. Feb. 27, 1945, Chung-King, China; s. I-Kuang and Chiao-Lan (Sun) Li; m. Cheng-Yun Lee, Mar. 19, 1948; 1 child, Robin, b. 1976; edn: Bach. Arch., Chung-Yun Coll. of Sci. & Engring., Taiwan 1969; M.Landscape Arch., Iowa St. Univ., Ames 1973; Reg. Architect, Calif., mem. AIA, 1983. Career: past arch. with var. architectural and engring. firms incl. Gin Wong Associates, L.A. and Ralph M. Parsons Co., Pasadena; currently architect/pres. Delta 79, Inc., Alhambra; honors: Phi Kappa Phi, Sigma Tau Delta, recognition award Alhambra Beautiful, Alhambra CofC, 1983; mem. Los Angeles CofC; Catholic; rec: tennis, swimming, softball. Res: 8625 E. Roccus Ln San Gabriel 91775 Ofc: Delta 79, Inc. 114 S. Monterey St Alhambra 91801

LIBANOFF, ARTHUR, podiatrist; b. May 17, 1931, Chicago; s. Leo and Sylvia (Goodman) Libanoff; Edn: BS, Univ. of Ill., 1953; DPM, Ill. Coll. of Podiatry, 1959; m. Erliss Ruff, 1955. Career: pvt. practice, 1960—, at 740 W. La Habra Blvd., La Habra; residency pgm., Beach Community Hospital; credential comm., Podiatric Surg., Beach Community Hospital. Honors: Dean's list, Univ. of Ill., 1949; pres., Durlacher Honor Soc., Ill. Coll. of Podiatry, 1955; pres., German Club, Univ. Ill., 1950. Mil: Cpl., US Army, 1955-57. Jewish. Office: 740 W. La Habra Blvd., La Habra 90631.

LIBOVE, JOEL MICHAEL, electrical engineer; b. Apr. 11, 1954, Cleveland, Ohio; s. Charles and Rosa (Greenspan) L.; m. Barbara Sacks, Dec. 26, 1982. Edn: BS, Cornell Univ., 1976; MSc, UC Berkeley, 1978; PhD, 1981. Career: research asst. UC Berkeley. 1977-79; chief engr. Dual Systems Corp., Berkeley 1979-82; v.p. research Dual Systems, 1982--, bd. dirs. 1981-. Honors: NY State Regents Scholarship 1972-76, Tau Beta Pi, Eta Kappa Nu, Sigma Xi, Earle C. Anthony fellow. Mem: NY Acad. of Sciences; IEEE; AAAS. Sci. inventions. Rec: hiking. Res: 1771 Highland Pl. Berkeley 94709 Ofc: Dual Systems Corp., 2530 San Pablo Ave. Berkeley 94702

LICCARDO, SALVADOR A., lawyer; b. Mar. 15, 1935; edn: BA, Univ. of Santa Clara 1956, JD, 1961; admitted to Calif. State Bar, 1962, Federal Ct. (9th Cir.), 1961, US Supreme Ct. 1966. Career: atty./ptnr. law firm Caputo, Liccardo, Rossi, Sturges & McNeil, San Jose; lectr. Contg. Edn. of the Bar, Calif. Trial Lawyers Assn.; lectr. Kans. Trial Lawyers Conv. 1983; lectr. Nat. Assn. of Legal Investigators Conv., Ore. 1983; mem: Am. Bar Assn. 1962-; Calif. Bar Assn. (Med. Malpractice Com. 1975); Santa Clara County Bar Assn. (Exec. Com., Bd. Trustees, Secty., 1972; Medical-Legal Liaison Com. 1978); Assn. of Trial Lawyers of Am.; Calif. Trial Lawyers Assn. (chief editor Journal 1981; bd. govs. 1977-81); Inner Circle of Advocates; Am. Bd. of Profl. Liability Attys.; Trial Lawyers for Public Justice, Wash DC (bd. dirs. 1983); articles in legal jours.; mil: 1st lt. US Army 1956-58. Office: Caputo, Liccardo, Rossi, Sturges & McNeil, 960 West Hedding St, 2d Flr, San Jose 95126

LICHTMAN, DAVID ISADORE, computer consulting co. president; b. Jan. 4, 1946, Two Egg, Fla.; s. Nathan and Anna (Kron) L.; m. Anita Fishman, Sept. 3, 1967; edn: BA, Fla. Atlantic Univ. 1967; MA, Univ. of South Fla. 1970; EdD, Univ. of So. Calif. 1973. Career: tchr. Exceptional Children Pgm., Palm Beach County Schs., Fla. 1967-69; instr./writer Auburn Univ., 1970-71; US Office of Edn. Fellow, USC, 1971-73; asst. prof. Edn., Univ. of S.C., 1973-78; senior staff mem. National Information Center for Spl. Edn. Materials, 1978-80; info. splst. Lockheed-California Co., 121-82; pres. Educational Computer Applications Inc., 1980--; spkr. num. nat., internat. confs. incl. 1981 Technology Assisted Learning Industry Conf., The Am. Soc. of Profl. Consultants, and Data Proc. Mgmt. Assn.; mem: Consultants Roundtable (1983 chpsn.), Trainers Assn. of So. Calif. (pres. 1982); publs: assoc. editor Jour. of the Council for Exceptional Chil., fmr. dept. ed. Edn. Unlmtd.; arts. and comments in num. mags. incl. Creative Computing, Chart Your Course, The Profl. Cons., The L.A. Bus. Jour., Fortune Mag. Address: ECA Inc., PO Box 1000, Arleta 91331

LICHTY, CARLETON, hotelier; b. May 1, 1915, Sunnyside, Wash.; s. Guy C. and Fern (Kramer) L.; m. Jean Pearce, Nov. 21, 1945; children: Lizbeth (Gladwill), b. 1950; Dr. Guy C., II, b. 1952; Lorraine (Adams), b. 1958; edn: BS, USC 1937. Career: gen. mgr. U.S. Grant Hotel, San Diego 1945-61; mng. dir. Hotel del Coronado, Coronado 1961-63, exec. v.p. 1964-68, pres./gen. mgr. 1968-82, v.chmn. bd. 1982--; awards: Resort Exec. of the Yr., Am. Hotel & Motel Assn. 1981; Hotel Man of the Yr., San Diego Hotel Sales Mgrs. 1984; Man of the Yr., San Diego Conv. & Visitors Bureau 1983; mem: San Diego Hotel & Motel ASsn. (pres. 1965); Calif. Hotel & Motel Assn. (pres. 1973); San Diego CofC (pres. 1979); San Diego Conv. & Visitors Bureau (pres. 1980); San Diego Econ. Devel. Corp.; mil: lt. commdr. USN 1941-45; Republican; Protestant. Res: 156 H Ave Coronado 92118 Ofc: Hotel del Coronado, 1500 Orange Ave Coronado 92118

LIDDELL, RICHARD WARREN, bank executive; b. Mar. 7, 1945, Tooele, Utah; s. Byron LaVarre and Echo Mae (Kirk) L.; m. Judi Kohler, Aug. 19, 1966; children: Richard, b. 1967; David, b. 1969; Marty, b. 1976; Joseph, b. 1979; Thomas, b. 1981; edn: BS, Univ. of San Francisco 1977; Real Estate Broker lic., Calif. 1983; Notary Public, Hawaii 1978. Career: asst. mgr. Kapiolani Br. First Hawaiian Bank, Honolulu 1977; loan review ofcr. 1978; mgr. 1979; AVP, premises liaison ofcr. Bank of Am., San Francisco 1980, v.p./ regl. real estate mgr. 1981, v.p./ senior real estate plnnr. (internat.) 1982; currently v.p./ principal constrn. leader The Crocker Bank, S.F.; instr. Am. Inst. of Banking, Honolulu 1978-79; honors: Cand. for CPM, Inst. of R.E. Mgmt., Nat. Bd. Realtors; mem: Bldrs. Exch., Santa Rosa; Kaneohe Flotilla, US Coast Guard Aux.; Lions Club, Honolulu; works: Future of Real Estate In California, Univ. of S.F. 1977; International R.E. Management Information System, Bank of Am. 1983; created, Mgrs. Seminar on Comml. Lending for First Hawaiian Bank 1978; Republican; Ch. of Jesus Christ of LDS; rec: aviation, astronomy, scuba diving. Res: 1709 Woodcrest Dr Concord 94521 Ofc: The Crocker Bank, One Montgomery St, 21st Flr, San Francisco 94104

LIEBERMAN, MYRON ARRON, real estate development co. president; b. Jan. 19, 1940, Chgo.; s. Herman and Rose (Raitzer) L.; m. Arlene, Aug. 21, 1968; 1 son: Scott, b. 1973; edn: BS, CSUN 1963; MS, 1968; postgrad. wk. UCLA 1970-72; desig: ASCP/MT 1963; Am. Soc. Clin. Pathologists 1968; Am. Soc. Sch. Adminstrs. 1971. Career: chief of labs. Kaiser Hosp. 1966; tchr. L.A. City Schs. 1967-69; chief of labs., Bio-Chem Procedures 1968; sch. principal Woodcrest Schs. 1969-80, adminstr. 1971-83; pres. Woodcrest Schools Inc.; pres. Riverside Devel. Co. 1980--; pres. MDM Real Estate Investment Co. 1983--; pres. advsry. bd. Commerce Nat. Bank 1983-85; awards: Kiwanis service award, San Fernando Valley Coll. civic award, San Fernando Valley Beautiful Building award; mem: Am. Soc. Sch. Adminstrs.; L.A. Bd. Realtors; S.F. Valley Culture Soc.; Tarzana (pres.) & Woodland Hills CofC; So. Calf. Edn. of Young Children; Encino Shrine Club; B'nai B'rith; Toastmasters; Optimists; works: clin. research, Vet. Hosp., Los Angeles 1964-65; bulletin ed. var. civic orgns. 1980-84; mil: sp4 US Army 1961-68; Democrat; Jewish; rec: golf, boating. Res: 3931 Stone Canyon Sherman Oaks 91403 Ofc: Riverside Development Co., 6043 Tampa, Ste 5, Tarzana 91356

LIERSCH, ANDREWS F., community services organization president; b. Jan. 9, 1936, Milwaukee, Wis.; s. Andrew John and Carolyn Marie (Fox) L.; m. Karen Kitsteiner, July 19, 1980; children: Stephanie b. 1961, Andrea b. 1963, Andrew b. 1974, Michael b. 1976; edn: BS in bus. adm., Ariz. State Univ. 1961. Career: mgr. market research Motorola, Phoenix, ARiz. 1961-67; dir. mktg. services Electronic Industries Assn., Wash DC 1967-69; dir. business plnng. Fairchild Camera and Instrument, Mt. View, Ca. 1969-72; dir. major pgms. Signetics Corp., Sunnyvale 1972-74; pres. Olympus Inc., Cupertino 1974-76; pres./CEO Goodwill Industries, San Jose 1976--; bd. chmn. Uvira Inc. 1978-79; chmn. bd. trustees, Goodwill of Santa Clara County Trust, 1981-; ex-officio dir. Goodwill Bd. Dirs. 1979-; RSA Region IX Planning Advis. com. 1981-82; cons. US Dept. Edn. 1981; mem: Federal Tech. Assistance Panel 1980-; Nat. Rehabilitation Assn. 1977-; Rotary Club of San Jose (dir.), Comm. Campership Fund Bd., San Jose CofC; Republican; Prot. Res: 2882 Forbes Ave Santa Clara 95051 Ofc: Goodwill Ind. 1080 N. 7th St San Jose 95112

LIEUTARD, EMILE AUGUSTE, real estate broker, accountant; b. Oct. 14, 1909, San Francisco; s. Auguste E. and Leonie Sarah (Broussal) L.; m. Alice Marie Soulie, Sept. 19, 1931; 1 dau. Claudette Alice, b. 1932; edn: San Francisco public schs., Healds Bus. Coll., S.F. Coll. of Bus., S.F. Law Sch., and US Treas. Dept. courses; Calif. lic. Public Acct., Real Estate Broker; realtor, Nat. Assn. Realtors. Career: asst. auditor Calif. and Hawaiian Sugar Refining Corp., and treas./gen. mgr. C & H Federal Credit Union, until 1942; with US Govt. Treasury Dept., 1942-47; self-empl. cons./ acct./ ptnr. Lieutard and Lenoir, San Francisco 1947-52; broker/realtor dba Realty Associates, San Mateo 1952--; owner Antiques de France (antique shop), San Mateo; mem. Sigma Delta Kappa (legal frat.), Nat. Assn. of Pub. Accts., San Mateo-Burlingame Bd. of Realtors, Nat., Calif. real estate assns.; Commonwealth Club, Native Sons of the Golden West, Elks; mem. French Hosp. Assn., S.F. (fmr. dir.); Republican; Catholic; rec: fishing. Res: 538 Alhambra Rd San Mateo 94402

LIEUX, PIERRE A., veterinarian; b. July 5, 1925, Maisons Laffitte, France, nat. 1956; s. Frederic S. and Leone (Cheron) L.; m. Pamela Wallin; children: Marilyn Jean b. 1951, Michele b. 1954, Eric b. 1956, Deanna b. 1962, Jean Pierre b. 1965; edn: DVM, Univ. of Paris, Alfort (France) 1949. Career: postgrad. tng. Equine Research Station, Newmarket, UK, Fulbright research fellowship, Univ. of Ky., Lexington; residency, Haggyard, Davidson, McGee, veterinary firm, Lexington, Ky. 3 years; resident veterinarian Sneed Stock Farm (equine breeding), Hemet, Ca. two years; pres. Pierre A Lieux DVM Inc., pvt. equine practice, Riverside, 1955--, supvr. sev. large thoroughbred breeding farms, approx. 1300 broodmares; awards: research grantee, Calif. Thoroughbred Breeders Assn. (2), Animal Health Found.; mem: Am. Veterinary Med. Assn., Calif. Vet. Med. Assn., So. Calif. Vet. Med. Assn. (chmn. Equine Sterility Com.), Am. Assn. of Equine Practitioners, Soc. of Theriogenoly, charter mem. Calif. Academy of Vet. Medicine; articles in vet. med. literature; frequent lectr. profl. assns. 1954-; Republican; rec: photog., equitation, fencing. Address: Pierre Lieux D.V.M., Inc. 4728 Riverside Dr Riverside 925409

LILEY, BOBBY, engineer/physicist, lawyer; b. Jan. 13, 1933, Pactolus, N.C.; s. James Henry and Louise (Carney) L.; m. Helen Frances, Feb. 6, 1957; children: Fasha b. 1960, Abric b. 1963, Zalen b. 1965; edn: BS in physics/math, N.C. A&T State Univ. 1955; MS in applied physics, UCLA 1960; MS in engrg., UCLA 1972; JD, Glendale Coll. of Law 1977; admitted to Calif. State Bar 1978. Career: research engr. North American Aviation Inc., Los Angeles 1956; sr. resrch. engr. Space and Info. Systems Div. of NAA Inc., Downey 1960-61; sr. engr. Space General Corp., El Monte 1961-63; resrch. splst., lead engr., project engr., prin. investigator at Rockwell Internat., Seal Beach 1963-79, supvr. of engring., project mgr. 1979--; lawyer, sole practitioner, Los Angeles 1978--; instr. math and chem., Academic Advancement Pgm., UCLA (1972); pres. General Bd. United Christian Church 1982-; honors: Rockwell Internat. Engr. of the Month (1981), L.A. Council of Black Profl. Engrs. Applied Science Award (11/83), commendn., Dept. of Air Force for wk. on Global Positioning Satellite Pgm. (4/77); Sigma Pi Sigma (physics hon.), Nu Beta Epsilon (law hon.); mem. Am. Nuclear Soc., Am. Geophysical Union, AIAA, L.A. Council of Black Profl., Phi Beta Sigma frat. engrs.; pres. Miss. Aid Project; works: Slope Control Wheel - Wheel Brake Control System patent (5/64); NASA Tech. Briefs (1969, 71); num. tech. publs.; tech. paper in high energy nuclear modelling for proton-induced proton and neutron spectra (1967, Nuclear Sci. and Engrg.); mil: AF ROTC; Democrat; Disciples of Christ; rec: oil painting. Res: 1878 Copa Way Monterey Park 91754 Ofc: Rockwell Intl., 12214 Lakewood Blvd Downey CA Law Ofc: 3701 Wilshire Blvd Ste 700, Los Angeles 90010

LILLIE, MILDRED L., judge; b. Jan. 25, 1915, Ida Grove, Ia.; d. Ottmar A. and Florence E. (Martin) Kluckhohn; m. Cameron L. Lllie, Mar. 18, 1947 (dec. 1959); m. 2d A. V. Falcone, Aug. 27, 1966; edn: AB, UC Berkeley 1935; JD, UC Boalt Hall of Law 1938; hon. degrees: LLD, Western States Univ. Coll. of Law 1966; LLD, Pepperdine Univ. 1979; admitted to practice, State Bar of Calif. 1938, Fed. Ct. 1942, US Supreme Ct. 1961. Career: with the City Atty.'s Ofc., Alameda 1938-39; pvt. practice, Los Angeles 1946-47; judge, Municipal Ct., City of L.A. 1947-49; judge, Superior Ct., Co. of L.A. 1949-58; Justice, Ct.of Appeal, State of Calif. 1958--; assoc. Justice Pro Tem, Calif. Supreme Ct. 1960, 77, 78, 81, 82; mem: L.A. area CofC (bd. dirs. 1975-82); L.A. Athletic Club; Western State Univ. Coll. of Law. (exec. & admissions bd.); Ebell Club of L.A.; L.A. Ballet Guild; Am. Heart Assn.; Civic Light Opera Assn.; Les Dames de Champagne; Fed., Am. and L.A. County Bar Assns.; Calif. Judges Assn.; Pepperdine Univ. Assocs.; NCCJ (bd. dirs.); Catholic; rec: painting, cooking, writing. Res: 510 S Burnside Ave Los Angeles 90036 Ofc: 3580 Wilshire Blvd Los Angeles 90010

LILLIG, THOMAS STOTT, company president; b. Sept. 25, 1943, Annapolis, Md.; s. Everett Houston and Jean Kathleen (Stott) L.; m. Janice Sproul, June 12, 1965; children: Robert, b. 1967; Mark, b. 1970; Kim, b. 1974; edn: BS, Ore. State Univ. 1965; MBA, Univ. of Wash. 1972; USN: Nuclear Power Sch. 1965-66; Submarine Ofcrs. Sch. 1966; Polaris Missile Weapons Ofcr. Sch. 1968. Career: fin. analyst Standard Oil of Calif. 1972-74; mgr. fin. analysis, CBS Retail Stores 1974-76; mgr. budgets Golden West Financial 1976-78; coord. Shortstop Inc. 1978-79; dir. Exxec Inc., dba Systems/ Financial Gp. 1979--; awards: NROTC Scholarship, Ore. State 1961-65; Standard Oil Fellowship, Univ. of Wash. Grad. Sch. of Bus. 1970-72; mil: lt., USN 1965-70, nuclear sub. ofcr., Nat. Defense Svc., Vietnam Svc., Qual. in Submarines, Merit. Unit Commdn.; rec: camping, fishing, history. Res: 4489 River Ash Ct Concord 94521 Ofc: Systems/ Financial Group, 155 Montgomery St, Ste 901, San Francisco 94104

LIM, EUSEBIO GAN, otolaryngologist; b. Aug. 14, Manila, Philippines; s. Bien Liong and Bella (Gan) Lim; Edn: MD, Santo Tomas, 1952; AA, Santo Tomas, 1947. Career: otolaryngologist, Union Med. Clinic, Huntington Park, CA. Fellow of Internatl. Acad. of Cosmetic Surgery. Mem: Los Angeles County Med. Assn. Catholic. Rec: photography, car racing. Res: 11730 Sunset Blvd., Los Angeles 90049; Office: Union Medical Clinic, 5421 Pacific Blvd., Huntington Park 90255.

LIMJOCO, JAIME YAP, certified public accountant; b. July 29, 1934, Iloilo City, Philippines, nat. 1976; s. Gaudencio Dizon and Magdalena Solitario (Yap) L.; m. Milagros Aquino, Apr. 17, 1971; children: Jude b. 1961, James b. 1973; edn: BE in commerce, magna cum laude, Iloilo City Coll. 1955; MS in acctg. Roosevelt Univ. 1967; MBA, taxation, Golden Gate Univ. 1979; Dale Carnegie courses 1979; cert: CPA, Phil. (1959), Calif. (1973). Career: accountant G.A. Machineries, Inc. Philippines 1956-59; internal auditor Ysmael Steel Mfg. Co., Phil. 1959-65; S.F Firestone and Co., CPA firm, 1967-69; acct. Grand of Calif., Oakland 1969-70; staff accountant Peter Brethauer, CPA, 1970-71, Business Mgmt. Consultants, 1971-73, Lefort & Co., CPAs, 1973-74; acct. Fono Enterprises, San Francisco 1974-83; ptnr. Cunocar Accounting Service, Berkeley 1983--; mem: The Calif. Soc. of CPAs, 1973-; Soc. of Calif. Accts. 1973. Res: 922 Gellert Blvd Daly City 94015 Ofc: Cunocar Accounting Service, 2020 Stuart St Berkeley 94703

LIN, ALICE KO-CHIEN, real estate investment co. executive; b. Jan. 2, 1943, China, nat. 1975; d. Wei-Ming and Lan-Ying (Kuo) Ho; m. Heh-Sen Lin, June 8, 1968; children: Andrew b. 1969, David b. 1977; edn: BS in biol., Nat. Chung-Hsing Univ., Tai-Chung, Taiwan 1966; MS biol., Univ. of New Hampshire 1968; ASCP Pgm., Medical Sch., Case Western Reserve Univ. 1970; clin. chem. pgm. Northeastern Univ. 1972. Career: chief histologist Clin. Dept., Forest City Hosp., Cleveland, Oh. 1968-69; resrch. assoc. Bio-chemistry Lab., Dept. Biology, Case Western Reserve Univ. 1969-70; senior med. technologist Clin. Chemistry Dept. Children's Hosp. Med. Ctr., Boston, Mass. 1971-75; group leader clinical tests and tng. super. junior med. technologists; real estate investment assoc. Century 21, La Palma, Calif. 1978-79, Real Estate Center Corp., Cerritos 1979-80; exec. v.p. Lin & Co. (real estate investments, devel. co.), Cerritos 1981--; dir. California Four Devel. Co. 1981-; cons. Hanson Ho Architectural Design and Devel. Co. 1982-; awards for real estate sales 1979, 1980, Million Dollar Club; mem: Nat. Assn. of Realtors; publs: resrch. in field of juvenile hormone of insects; resrch. & devel. of universal DDD heart pacemakers (patents pend.); rec: vol. tchg. ABC Sch. Dist., travel. Ofc: Lin and Company, 17311 S. Moonglow Circle Cerritos 90701

LIN, CHORNG-LIEH, chemist-chemical engineer; b. Aug. 30, 1938, Taichung, Taiwan, nat. 1973; s. Lien-San and Pei-Suan (Chien) L.; m. Jen Jen Chen, Nov. 28, 1970; children: Angela, b. 1973; Steven, b. 1976; edn: BS, Cheng-Kung Univ. 1961; MS, Miami Univ. 1966; PhD, Univ. of Pitts. 1971. Career: R&D chemist Wei-Chuan Food Co., Taipei, Taiwan 1963-64; tchg. asst. Miami Univ., Oxford, Ohio 1965-66; tchg. & research asst. Univ. of Pittsburgh, 1966-71; senior scientist Jet Propulsion Lab., Pasadena 1971-77, tech. staff 1977-82; pres. Hansia Inc., Pasadena 1982--; cons. Ta-Fong Chem. Co. 1972-82, cons. Amtech, Inc. 1981-; mem: Phi Lambda Upsilon; Sigma Xi; Am. Chem. Soc.; So. Calif. Taiwanese Assn.; W. San Gabriel Valley Bd. Realtors; publs: over 20 tech. publs. on food, pharmaceutical & atmospheric chemistry 1963-83; mil: 2nd lt. Taiwanese Army 1961-62; Democrat; Presbyterian; rec: music, swimming, skiing. Res: 2990 Oneida St Pasadena 91107 Ofc: Papa Lions, Inc., 658 W Garvey Ave Monterey Park 91754

LIN, TE HUA, physicist; b. Apr. 25, 1951, Yunlin, Taiwan, ROC; s. Tung-Hou and Tsai-Jie (Tsai) L.; m. Yueh-ying, Dec. 28, 1975; children: Erwin, b. 1979, Eric, b. 1981; edn: BS, Tunghai Univ. 1973; stu. Rensselaer Poly. Inst.; PhD, UC Berkeley 1983. Career: senior process eng. Intel Corp., Santa Clara 1983--; rec: tennis. Res: 908 Minnesota Ave San Jose 95125 Ofc: Intel Corp. 3601 Juliette Ln Santa Clara 95051

LINDAUER, JAMES THOMAS, computer software executive; b. Dec. 3, 1949, Evansville, Ind.; s. Alfred Thomas and Dorothy Loretta (Scheessele) L.; m. Christina Reid, Feb. 16, 1974; 1 dau: Allison, b. 1982; edn: BS, Purdue Univ. 1969; 1st Cl. Radio Tel. Lic., FCC 1980. Career: sales engr. Varian Assoc., Palo Alto 1969-74; mktg. engr. Avantek, Santa Clara 1974-76; mkt. mgr. 1976-80; dir. mktg. Compact Engring., Palo Alto 1980-83; v.p./ gen. mgr. Compact Software, Inc., Palo Alto 1983--; mem: IEEE; Decathlon Club; Republican; Catholic; rec: skiing, travel, photog. Res: 874 Lockhaven Dr Los Altos 94022 Ofc: Compact Software, Inc., 1131 San Antonio Rd Palo Alto 94303

LINDBERG, DEXTER CLAYTON, real estate executive; b. May 12, 1938, Edmonton, Alberta, Can.; s. Eddy Bertram and Verna Adelina (Lofgren) L.; m. Catherine Elliot, June 8, 1962; edn: RIA, Soc. of Mgmt. Accts., Univ. of Alberta 1966; Appraisal Inst. of Can., Univ. of Guelph and Univ. of Western Ontario 1975-76. Career: var. pos. with predecssor and subs. co. of Genstar Corp. 1967--; exec. asst. to pres., Edmonton 1967s68; controller, Edmonton 1969; treas, Vancouver, B.C. 1970-71; corp. property mgr., Edmonton & Toronto 1972-75; asst. secty. Toronto 1977; v.p. Land & Housing Div., Edmonton & San Francisco 1977--; gen. mgr. Genstar Comml. Devel. 1981; v.p. Sutter Hill Ltd. 982--; v.p. Sutter Hill Mgmt. (Southwest) Inc. 1982-83; v.p. Sutter Hill Devel. Ltd. 1983--; dir. Genstar Devel. Inc., Sutter Hill Ltd.; mem: Soc. Mgmt. Accts. (profl.); Appraisal Inst. of Canada (profl.); Internat. Inst. Valuers; Mississaugua Golf & Country Club; Commonwealth Club of Calif.; publs: Canadian Developers Operating in the U.S., AIM, 2/80; Republican; Protestant; rec: golf. Res: 2368 Lariat Ln Walnut Creek 94596 Ofc: Genstar Corp., Four Embarcadero Ctr., San Francisco 94111

LINDSAY, GEORGE FRANKLIN, electronics engineer, b. May 4, 1937, Whittier; s. George White and Thelma Estella (Samples) L.; m. Carol Ann Baatenburg Dejong, Feb. 18, 1978; children: Catherine, b. 1962; Michael, b. 1964; Natalie, b. 1965; Mark, b. 1965; Christine, b. 1970; Candice, b. 1980. Edn: Cal. Inst. of Tech., 1955-59; BS (math) CSU LA, 1965. Career: electronics tchn. Naval Ordanance Test Station, Pasadena, 1959; digital design engr. Naval Undersea Ctrs., Pasadena & San Diego, 1960-82; supr. electr. engr. Naval Ocean Systems Ctr., 1982--. Awards: Bank of Am. Award in Math., 1955; Quality Step Increase, Naval Undersea Warfare Ctr. 1967, 75, Achievement, 1974, US Patents: Inverse Wiedemann Effect Torsional Delay Line Method Filter Device ,1968, and patented variations 1968, 1969 (2), 1972 (2); Republican; Scientology. Rec: scientol., woodwork.. Res: 1612 Pepper Dr. El Cajon 92021. Ofc: Naval Ocean Systems Ctr., San Diego 92152

LINDSEY, JOHN HALL, JR., data base specialist; b. July 29, 1938, Malvern, Ark.; s. John Hall and Francis Jeanette (Stuart) L.; m. Renetta Louise Harms, July 14, 1962; children: Sabra Ann, b. 1968; Lemecia Sue, b. 1970; Lance Lee, b. 1975; edn: AA, Ark. Polytech. Coll. 1956-58; BS, Okla. State Univ. 1961; BS, Univ. of Utah 1964; MBA, USC 1968. Career: data base adminstr. Nat. Cash Reifster Corp., Rancho Bernardino 1966-73; data base cons., self-empl., Los Angeles 1973-75; data base adminstr. Kal Kan Foods, Inc., Vernon 1975-77; data base supvr. Kaiser Steel Corp., Fontana 1977-79; data base adminstr. Wester Gear Corp., Lynwood 1979--; founder Poly Sys., Inc., 1968; guest lectr. USC 1975-76; cons. Comarc Design Sys. 1973-82; guide 1979-82; cons. SDI Ind. Sys.a 1978-80; mem: L.A. Integrated Data Base Mgmt. Sys. Users Gp. (pres. 1983); Data Dictionary Proj. Guide Internat. (proj. ldr. 1980-81); Mt. Baldy Aquatics (pres. 1978-79); Assn. for Sys. Mgmt., Long Beach (past pres.); Soc. for Mgmt. Info. Sys.; Nat. Mgmt. Assn.; Ontario Comm. Credit Union; Affiliated Cities Apart. Owners ASsn.; publs: arts. computer journals; mil: sp3, Ark. Nat. Guard 1956-64; Republican; Presbyterian; rec: swimming, restoring houses, travel. Res: 1556 N Cypress Ave Ontario 91762 Ofc: Western Gear Corporation, Corp. Computer Ctr., 2600 E Imperial HwyfLynwood 90262

LINEBERGER, JEANNIE ELIZABETH, lawyer; b. Jan. 31, 1946, Wash. DC; d. Donald Victor and Jeanne Marie (Houghten) Wengrovius; edn: BS, CSU Long Beach 1968; JD, Western State Univ. 1981; Comm. Coll. Law Instr. Credential, Calif. Career: airline stewardess Am. Airlines 1968; med. technologist Meml. Hosp., Long Beach 1969-76; pharmaceutical rep., Ortho Pharmaceuticals 1976; med. tech. Meml. Hosp. 1977-83; atty. Carroll, Faile & Hahn, Long Beach 1983--; honors: Cert. of Awd. for the Long Beach Zoo; mem. Am. Soc. of Clin. Pathologists; Long Beach Zoo; Am., Calif., Los Angeles Co. & Long Beach Bar Assns.; Los Angeles Trial Lawyers Assn.; research: future space missions, No. Am. Space & Aviation 1986; microbial contamination of jet fuel, McDonnell- Douglas Corp. 1966-67; Ch. Relig. Sci.; rec: skiing, birds, tropical fish. Res: 4823 Hayfer Lakewood 90712 Ofc: Carroll, Faile & Hahn, 3629 Atlantic Ave Long Beach 90807

LINGERFELT, ERMA REBECCA, company officer; b. Sept. 14, 1915, Planada; d. Milton Merle and Elma Ruth (Weaver) Reiman; m. Garland Lingerfelt, Dec. 29, 1940; children: Garland Jr., b. 1942; Kathryn, b. 1946; David, b. 1951; edn: pvt. sec., Armstrong Bus. Coll. 1935; UC Berkeley 1934. Career: secty. Agricultural Conservation Ofc., Merced 1937; ofc. personnel mgr. 1938-39; payroll 1940; ofc. mgr./ secty. Lingerfelt Turkey Farms 1940-74;

secty./ treas. Lingerfelt Orchards, Inc. 1974-84; currently secty./ treas, Lingerfelt Orchards, Inc.; mem: Ballico PTA (pres. 1957, 58); Am. Legion Aux.; Republican; Ch. of Jesus Christ of LDS; rec: gardening. Address: Lingerfelt Orchards, Inc., 10086 N Ballico Ave Ballico 95303

LINGERFELT, GARLAND DARREL, agriculturist; b. May 27, 1916, Maud, Okla.; s. Clifton Jasper and Myrtle Elizabeth (Lane) L.; m. Erma Reiman, Dec. 30, 1940; children: Garland Darrel, b. 1942; Kathryn Ruth, b. 1946; David Merle, b. 1951; edn: Modesto Jr. Coll. 1936-37; UC Berkeley 1937-38. Career: player St. Louis Browns Profl. Ball Club and San Antonio Ball Club, Tex. League 1939; mem. Calif. Poultry Improvement Adv. Com. 1949; currently, pres. Lingerfelt Orchards, Inc.; pres., Ballico Almond Hulling Co.; mem: Am. Legion; 4AI Lions Internat. (pres. Delhi Ballico Lions, 1965, district gov. 1969); works: Trapnested turkeys for breeding 1946-56; mil: tech. sgt./ undercover agent 1942-45; Republican; Ch. of Jesus Christ of LDS; rec: fishing. Address: Lingerfelt Orchards, Inc., 10086 N Ballico Ave Ballico 95303

LINGLE, ROBERT LEO, savings and loan executive; b. Nov. 27, 1941, Dubuque, Ia.; s. Leo Albert and Ruth Evelyn (Bruesch) L.; m. Bonita Bilbery, June 30, 1979; children: Darrin, b. 1968; Todd, b. 1970; edn: AA, Pasadena City Coll. 1962; BS, CSU Los Angels 1964; CFA, Inst. of Chartered Fin. Analysts 1974; Real Estate Broker, Calif. 1975. Career: mgmt. trainee Security Pacific Nat. Bank, Los Angeles 1964; portfolio mgr. 1965-68; trust investment ofcr. Union Bank, L.A. 1968-77, v.p. real estate lending 1977-80; v.p./ real estate mgr. Bank of Calif., San Bernardino 1980-82; v.p./ mgr. Beverly Hills S&L 1982-83; senior v.p. Cal American Svgs. & Loan 1983--, mem. sr. loan com.; awards: SPOKE Awd., Jaycees 1972; mem: Inst. CFAs; Soc. Real Estate Appraisers (L.A. chpt.); RIM Real Estate Internat.; Bldg. Ind. Assn. (Orange Co.); Hacienda Hghts. Drug Abuse Council (past) YMCA Fund Raising, San Bernardino; San Bernardino CofC; Republican; Lutheran; rec: skiing, travel. Res: 1234 Nashport La Verne 91750 Ofc: Cal American Savings and Loan Assn., 888 S West St, Ste 201, Anaheim 92802

LINLEY, JAMES RICHARD, insurance co. executive; b. Apr. 19, 1935, Harbor Beach, Mich.; s. William Richard and Margaret Alice (Kenney) L.; m. Suzanne Penn, Feb. 14, 1970; children: Brad, b. 1965; Lisa, b. 1963; edn: bus. admin., Mich. State 1956. Career: Allstate ins. Co. 1964-77; mgr. marine div. Nat. American Ins. Co. 1977-80; asst. v.p. 1980-81; v.p. 1981-83; v.p. Commerce Svc. Corp. 1983; v.p. Hospital Ins. Svcs., Inc. 1983--; mem: Marine Underwriting Assn. of So. Calif.; Republican; Presbyterian; rec: skiing, travel. Res: 4904 Marshall Creek Dr LaVerne 91750 Ofc: Hospital Insurance, 525 S Virgil Ave Los Angeles 90020

LINN, JOY, investment banking firm president; b. Nov. 8, 1936, Monterey Park; d. Herbert A. and Kathleen L. (Reynolds) Shuttleworth; edn: AA, Fullerton Coll. 1974; desig: Cert. Senior Escrow Ofcr., Calif. Escrow Assn. 1980; Life Comm. Coll. Tchr. (real estate) Credential. Career: personnel dir. Camac Corp., Bristol, Va. 1970-72; escrow ofcr. Walker & Lee, Whittier 1972-74; adminstrv. dir. Christ Church, Anaheim 1974-76; escrow br. mgr. Tarbell, Buena Park 1976-77; mgr. escrow dept. Chartered Bank of London, Vista 1977-79; mgr. loan & escrow depts. Hawthorne Savings & Loan, Vista 1979-81; pres./chief exec. Pathways Assocs. Inc., Anaheim 1981--; mem: CEA (regl. pres. & dir. State Bd. of Calif. Escrow Assn.), ASCAP, Jobs Daughters, Young Republicans, Abingden Soc. for Preservation of Native Art; works: composed/ preformed, The Story Lady (record for children), & The Star (a Chirstmas Story); contbg. mem. Calif. Christian Inst. of Human Rels. (4 yrs.); dir. Pathways to Happiness (non profit svc. orgn.); mil: s/sgt. USAF 1954-55; rec: writing, directing. Res: 1100 N Acacia, Unit 10, Anaheim 92805 Ofc: Pathways Associates Inc., 2111 W Crescent Ave, Ste A, Anaheim 92801

LINTON, THOMAS DENSMORE, JR., patent attorney; b. May 2, 1925, Auburn, Ky.; s. Thomas D. and Sally Ruth (Price) L.; m. Sally Diane Kleinhen, Dec. 19, 1953; children: Thomas, III b. 1956, Elizabeth Diane b. 1959, Jennifer Leigh b. 1962, Garwood Price b. 1964; edn: BS, US Naval Acad. 1949; JD, Univ. of Ariz. 1958; cert. patent law, US Patent Office 1960; cert. exec. mgmt., USC 1966; Reg. Patent Atty.; admitted to practice Ariz. State Bar. Career: served to lt. cmdr. US Navy 1943-55, Reserve 1955-, Korean Pres. Unit Cit.; patent counsel Industrial Div. Garrett Corp. 1960-62; patent counsel/general counsel Harvey Aluminum Corp. 1962-66; pvt. patent practice, Los Angeles and Phoenix, Ariz. 1966--; law practice, Phoenix; participant in var. emerging hi-tech. cos.; mem: L.A. Patent Law Assn., State Bar of Ariz. (Corp. and Banking Sect.); clubs: Calif. Yacht, L.A. Athletic, Braemar Country, Riviera Country; Presbyterian; rec: sailing, music, farming. Res: 3404 Colville Place Encino 91436 Ofc: 16530 Ventura Blvd, Ste 600, Encino CA 91436; 100 W. Washington St, 13th Flr. Phoenix AZ 85003

LIPPITT, ELIZABETH CHARLOTTE, writer; b. San Francisco, d. Sidney Grant and Stella Lippitt; edn: Univ. Calif., Mills Coll. Career: writer, performer satirical monologues, popular singer; contbg. writer to 80 newspapers, 1960s--: Shreveport Journ., Miami Herald, St. Louis Globe-Democrat, Jackson News, Union Leader, Orlando Sentinel, Phoenix Republic, Tampa Tribune, Birmingham Post Herald, Speak Up (Toronto, Can.); num. other publs.; honors: Congress of Freedom Awards (6) for arts. on national affairs; listed num. biographical dictionaries; vocalist performer Internat. Biog. Congress, Los Angeles (1981), NYC (1983); mem: Metropolitan Club, Olympic Club, Nat. Adv. Bd. Amer. Security Council, IPA, Commonwealth Club, Nat. Assn. R.R. Passengers, Nat. Trust for Historic Preserv., Amer. Conservative Union, Guide Dogs for the Blind, humane and anti-vivisection orgns. (9), Friends of Animals, Com. for Humane Legislation, Amvets, Childrens Village Home

Soc., Congressional Club, Young Americans for Freedom, Freedoms Found., World Anti-Communist League; Catholic; rec: swim (50 mi. swim for ARC). Res: 2414 Pacific Ave San Francisco 94116

LIPPITT, LESLIE W., company executive; b. July 12, 1952, Joplin, Mo.; s. Merreil D. and Betty Lane (Strater) L.; m. Cynthia K. Porter, Jan. 30, 1982; children: Sean, b. 1983; edn: AA, Calif. Coll. Mort. Scis. 1976; BS, USC 1975; Embalmers Lic. 1976; Funeral Dir. Lic. 1980. Career: embalmer Price/ Daniel Mort., Los Angeles 1975-77; personal supvr. Mottel's Mort., Long Beach 1977-78; asst. mgr. Evans- Brown Mort., Sun City 1978-81; gen. mgr. Mead Mort./ O'Donnell Funeral Home, Barstow 1981--; honors: Mu Sigma Alpha 1976; mem: Calif. Funeral Dirs. Assn.; Barstow CofC; Barstow Optimist Club; Mojave Valley Hospice; Advis. Bd. for City Council; Republican; Protestant; rec; sports, creative crafts. Res: 616 E Main St Barstow 92311 Ofc: Barstow Mortuaries, Inc., 36930 Irwin Rd Barstow 92311

LIPPSTREU, DAN, golf professional; b. Dec. 11, 1941, Fairfield; s. Edward M. and Martha (Adamczyk) L.; m. Linda Lafferty, Sept. 3, 1966; children: Donna, b. 1971; Pamela, b. 1973; edn: BA, Chico State Univ. 1964; desig: PGA Class A Profl. 1972. Career: asst. golf pro Green Valley Country Club 1965; touring PGA golf profl. 1969; asst. golf profl. Willow Park Golf Course 1971; golf porfl. Las Positas Golf Course, Livermore 19762--; bd. dirs. No. Calif. PGA; pres. Jr. Golf Assn. of No. Calif. awards: Nat. Jr. Golf Promoter of the Yr. 1983; NCPGA Jr. Golf Promoter of the Yr. 1982, 1983 (2); NCPGA Merchandiser of the Yr. 1982; mem: PGA of Am. (No. Calif. Bd. Dirs.); JGANC (pres. 1983, 84); NCPGA (pres. 1981); Livermore CofC; works: set up 7 jr. golf camps in No. Calif.; hosted JGANC Annual Match Play Tourn. (3 yrs.); hosted Golf Digest Long Drive 1981, 82; hosted NCPGA Apprentice Pro Cup matches 1981; formed Las Positas Jr. Golf Assn.; mil: USAR 1965-71; rec: all sports. Res: 4572 Winter Ct Pleasanton 94566 ofc: Las Positas Golf Course, POB 1048, Livermore 94566

LIPSETT, JOYCE K., artist; b. Jan. 5, 1934, Pasadena; d. Jack R. and Genevieve (Gonzalez) Teutschman; m. James R. Lipsett, Aug. 3, 1961; children: Steven Michael Gibson b. 1952, (stepchil.) Ronald Wayne Lipsett b. 1957, Gail Elaine Lipsett (Johnson) b. 1958. ed. public schs.; stu. stone & portrait, Surdez Sch. of Sculpture (Woodbridge). Career: treas. Lodi Art Center 1973; artist, sculpture -clay and stone, 1972--; tchr. sculpture Lodi Art Ctr. 1983--; recipient num. awards for sculpture, juried in over 20 shows in No. Calif.; mem. Lodi Art Center, Lodi Womens Club, fmr. 4-H Leader; Christian; rec: horses, art. Res: 23045 N. Sowles Rd Acampo 95220

LIPTON, KENNETH MICHAEL, lawyer; b. June 11, 1954, Hollywood; s. Gary and Millicent Audrey (Stein) L.; edn: AA, UC Santa Barbara 1974; BSL, Univ. West L.A. 1978, JD, 1978; admitted to practice, State Bar of Calif. 1978. Career: solo law practice 1978--; awards: Sears Art Scholarship, Idyllwild Sch. of Music and the Arts (USC), Barnsdall Park Exhibits; works: zinc plate etchings; rec: art, music. Address: 5900 Sepulveda, Ste 400, Van Nuys 91411

LISKA, JAMES GEORGE, quality assurance specialist; b. Apr. 17, 1943, Newport, R.I.; s. James Victor and Gertrude E. (Munch) L.; m. Gail M. Harper, July 1, 1973; edn: BA, No. Ill. Univ., Dekalb 1964; spl. courses, Nat. Foremans Inst. Waterford, Conn.; cert. in supvsry. devel., Midwest Indsl. Mgmt. Assn. 1975. Career: insp., tool and gage insp. Hills-McCanna Corp., Carpentersville, Ill. 1964-66; inspection leadman, Diversey Engring. Co., Chgo. 1966-70; supt., insp. foreman R.J. Frisby Mfg. Co., Elk Grove Village, Ill. 1970-76; quality control mgr. CR Industries (prin. product: Oil Seals), Elgin, Ill. 1976-78; mgr. Process Quality Engring. (MX Ballistic Missile), Aerojet Strategic Propulsion Co., Sacramento, Calif. 1978--; mem. Am. Soc. of Quality Control, Soc. of Mfg. Engrs.; designed/blt. own passive solar home. Res: 4544 Stoneyridge Rd Placerville 95667 Ofc: Aerojet Strategic Propulsion Co., POB 15699C, Sacramento 95813

LITFIN, RICHARD ALBERT, news service executive; b. Sept. 9, 1918, The Dalles, Ore.; s. Bernard R. and Alberta (Knappenberger) L.; m. Marie Foley, June 28, 1944; children: Mari, b. 1945; Tom, b. 1946; Mercedes, b. 1949; Regina, b. 1952; Anthony, b. 1952; Angela, b. 1956; edn: BJ, Univ. of Mo. Career: with United Press Internat. 1946--; bureau mgr., Olympia, Wa. 1946-47; bus. rep. Pacific NW 1946-52; bus., gr. Pacific Div. 1953-56; div. mgr. 1956-75; v.p. Western zone 1977-80; sr. v.p. 1980-83; mem: bd. fellows, Univ. of Santa Clara; Sigma Alpha Epsilon; Sigma Delta Chi; Alpha Delta Sigma; Sons of Am. Revolution; mil: ensign USNR 1941-42, Battleship Ohio, assigned Fighting 12, USS Saratoga 1943, D.F.C., Air Medal w/ Stars; Republican; Catholic. Res: 1790 Oak Ave Menlo Park

LITTLE, LAWRENCE ALAN, hospital pharmacy services director; b. Jan. 23, 1947, Downey; s. Eugene R. and Naomia L. (Murphy) L.; edn: Long Beach City Coll. 1964-66; Pharm.D., UC San Francisco 1970; Reg. Pharmacist, Calif., Nev. Career: staff pharmacist French Hospital, S.F. 1970-76, asst. dir. of pharmacy, 1976-79, dir. of pharmacy, 1979-80; assoc. dir./dir. of pharmacy svcs., Herrick Hospital, Berkeley 1980--; asst. clin. prof. of pharmacy UCSF 1982--; cons. Pharmacy Group Purchasing Pgm., Hospital Council of So./No. Calif. 1979-; mem: Am. Soc. of Hosp. Pharmacists, Calif. Soc. of Hosp. Pharmacists, No. Calif. Soc. of Hosp. Pharmacists; publs: art. A.J.H.P. (3/82); rec: photog. Res: 750 Stonegate Dr So. San Francisco 94080 Ofc: Herrick Hospital & Health Center, 2001 Dwight Way Berkeley 94704

LITTLE, RICHARD CARUTHERS, entertainer; b. Nov. 26, 1938, Ottawa, Ontario, Canada; s. Lawrence Peniston and Elizabeth Maud (Willson)

Little; brothers Fred Little and Chris Little, residing in Canada; Edn: diploma, Lisgar Collegiate, Jr. Matrick, 1958; m. Jeanne Worden, oct. 16, 1971; chil: Bria, b. 1977. Career: TV: Rich Little Christmas Carol, Rich Little Washington Follies, Great Pretenders I and II, Jimmy Stewart Tribute, Jack Lemmon Tribute, Fantasy Island, Hawaii 5-0, Judy Garland Show, You Asked For It, Policewoman, Love Boat, Chico and the Man, KopyKats, Tonight Show, Hollywood Squares, Midnight Special, Julie Andrews Show, various talk shows. Feature films: Another Nice Mess and Dirty Tricks. Nightclubs: all major clubs in U.S. incl. MGM Grand in Las Vegas, Sahara Tahoe, Riviera Hotel, Boardwalk Regency, Mill Run Theater. Benefits incl. Amy Karen Cancer Benefit, Share and Boy Scouts Spokesman. Recipient: Entertainer of the Year, Las Vegas; AGVA Comedy Star of the Year; Cleveland Amory Best Guest on a TV Talk Show, Ottawa's Favorite Son, Montreux Festival Golden Rose for Rich Little's Christmas Carol. Mem: AFTRA, SAG, ACTRA, AEA; AGVA; ATAS. Anglican. Rec: tennis, skiing, video. Office: Rich Little Prodns., Inc., 9200 Sunset Blvd., Suite 607, Los Angeles 90069.

LITZENBERG, ROBERT LEROY, chief executive, consulting civil engineer; b. June 8, 1928, Toledo, Ohio; s. LeRoy and Hulda Bertha (Schreier) L.; m. Nancy Ann Baldwin, June 5, 1958; children: John, b. 1965; Roy, b. 1966; Daniel, b. 1970; Mary Beth, b. 1972; edn: B.Civil. Eng., The Ohio State Univ. 1958, MS in C.E., 1958; MBA, Wayne State Univ. 1964; Reg. Civil Engr., Calif. Ariz., Ohio & Mich. Career: sanitary engr. Hagen & Sawyer, Detroit, Mich. 1958; sr. sanitary engr., Detroit Dept. of Health, Detroit, Mich. 1959; proj. engr. Parke, Davis & Co., Detroit, Mich. 1959-63; v.p./ gen. mgr. Brown Hutchinson, Inc., Detroit 1963-72; treas. Kenton City Schs., Kenton, Ohio 1977-79; pres. Litzenburg & Assoc., Kenton, Ohio 1972-79; pres. BCL Assoc., Inc., Long Beach 1979--; sr. corp. mgmt. & conslg. engr. spec. on sanitary engring. & harzardous waste mgmt. (over 20 yrs.); honors: Tau Beta Pi; Chi Epsilon; Sigma Xi; Outstanding Svc. Awds., Engring. Soc. of Detroit, Mich. 1970-71; mem: Redondo Beach Youth Basketball; AYSO Soccer; Tordono Little League; PTA, West H.S., Torrance; Band Assn., W. Torrance H.S.; works: The High Temperature fluid wall reactor, Detroit, Mich. 1964; The shift from land, an Engineering perspective, Las Vegas 1983; mil: cpl. MPCID 1950-52; rec: coaching youth sports, mechanical work. Res: 21313 Kent Ave Torrance 90503 Ofc: BCL Associates, Inc., 444 W Ocean Blvd, Ste 1400, Long Beach 90802

LIU, JIIN-TARN, architect-city planner; b. Oct. 30, 1946, Canton, China; s. Shen-Chuan and Chui-Yi (Lau) Liu; m. Jennifer Fu, Sept. 1, 1976; children: Sharon b. 1979, Charles b. 1982, James b. 1982; edn: BS in engrg. Nat. Cheng Kung Univ. Taiwan 1969; Master of Profl. Studies in Internat. Devel., Cornell Univ. 1976; MS in engrg., CSU Fullerton 1982; Reg. Profl. Civil Engr., Calif. 1982; Reg. Architect (1969), Profl. Arch. Engr. (1969), Profl. City Planner (1971), Taiwan. Career: engr. Taiwan Provincial Public Works Bureau, Taiwan 1970-75, section chief 1976-78; structural engr. Fluor Engineers Inc., Irvine, Calif. 1979--; part time prof. Chinese Cultural Univ., Taipei 1976-78; cons. Wan Tai Engineer Inc., Taipei 1976-78; works: planner for Lin Ko New Town, the first planned newtown in Taiwan (1975), planned population 200,000 (short term), 450,000 (long term); completed 19 city, newtown, new community plans and 2 regional plans, 1970-78; resrch. publ. (Studies of Planning Procedure for Taiwan's City Planning, 1978); architect/engr. num. indsl. structures, comml. buildings, houses, hotels, motels, schools; mem. Chinese Inst. ofCivil Engr., Chinese Inst. of Architect, Chinese Inst. of City Planning; mem. United Way; mil: 2d. lt. Army Engring. Corp. Taiwan 1969-70; rec: tennis, fishing, chess, painting. Res: 3747 E. Roberta Dr Orange 92669 Ofc: Fluor Engineer Inc. 3333 Michelson Dr Irvine 92730

LLORENTE, RAFAEL, retail business owner; b. Feb. 6, 1921, Santa Clara, Cuba; s. Rafael Angel and Catalina (Castro) L.; m. Olga Perez, Sep. 3, 1949; children: Rafael, b. 1952; Graciela, b. 1955. Edn: M. in phys. ed., Inst. Nac. de Edn. Fisica, 1948. Career: personnel adm./gen. adm. RHC Cadena Azul ;founder/owner Rafael's Interiors, Habana, Cuba, 1953. Orgns: mem. bd. dir. Circulo Guinero, LA, 1965-66, 1977-78; mem. St. Vicent Paul Soc., 1967-69. Republican; Catholic. Rec: photo., aviation. Address: 13457 Bryson St. Panorama City, Calif. 91402

LLOYD, JACK B., entertainment consultant; b. Mar. 31, 1927, Chgo.; s. Jack and Hortense (Breslau) Levine; m. Phyllis Wexler, July 8, 1951; children: Robert, b. 1955; Alison, b. 1957; edn: BS, USC 1951. Career: asst. to gen. mgr./ mdse. mgr. Harris & Frank 1951-53; ins. investigator, varios cos. to 1965; assoc. Irving Granz Prodns., concert producer 1965-68; American Productions (dir./ prod. Beach Boys Concerts) 1968-679; v.p. The Visual Thing 1969-70; ed./ publisher assoc. Tolin Publishing 1970-72; personal mgr: Jose Ferrer, Jim Backus, Mamie Van Doren, et al 1970-75, entertainment consultant/ publicist (dba Advent Internat.), Van Nuys 1975--; publicist Zugsmith & Assoc., Inc.; mem: VIPs for United Cerebral Palsy/ Spastic Childrens Found.; Exec. Com. for Fund Raising, Howard Keel Celebrity Golf Tourn.; works: ed./ writer, What's Happening Mag., 1970; cons./ ed. Official Talent & Booking Directory, 1970-78; producer, talent, Bob Hope/ Air Force Assn. Golf Tourn. 1982, 83, 84; Democrat; Jewish; rec: creative writing, photog. Res: 5908 Aldea Ave 91316 Ofc: Advent International, POB 7325 Van Nuys 91409

LLOYD, LANCE JOHN, chemical engineer; b. Aug. 5, 1936, Sydney, N.S.W., Australia; s. Walter William Scott and Ella Beatrice (Hobden) L.; m. Judith Ann Garnock, Dec. 5, 1964; children: Kylie, b. 1966; Jaimie, b. 1968; Andrew, b. 1970; edn: B Eng., honors, Univ. of Sydney 1958; M.Eng. Univ. of New. So. Wales 1966; Cert. of Eng., Inst. of Chem. Engrs.; fellow, Inst. of Dirs., Australia. Career: var. chem. engr. pos., U.K.; in charge A.C.I. Dimet & Brick Facilities, Univ. of New So. Wales; currently, reg. pres. A.C.I. America Inc., Newport Beach; dir. ACI Am., Inc., Kintruss Corp., Inc., McCullough Sys., Inc., ACI Galls Prods., Inc., DTH Ent., Inc., Overmyer Corp., Inc., ACI Am. Holdings Inc., ACI Internat. Bv, Am. Consolidated Industries Inc.; mem: Inst. Chem. Engrs., U.K.; Balboa Bay Club; Liberal (Australia); Methodist; rec: rugby football, field hockey. Res: 1845 Port Stanhope Pl Newport Beach 92660 Ofc: ACI America Inc., 1811 Quail St, 2nd Flr, Newport Beach 92660

LLOYD, MICHAEL BANCROFT, lawyer; b. July 4, 1950, Orange; s. Kenneth Bancroft and Evelyn Ann Lloyd; m. Judy, Jan. 6, 1973; chldren: Christian, b. 1978; Alison, b. 1980; edn: BA, CSU Fullerton 1972; JD, Pepperdine Univ. 1975; admitted to practice 1976; Comm. Coll. Law Tchg. Cred., Calif. Career: cert. legal intern Aitken, Bradshaw & Andres, Santa Ana 1973-75; atty. Law Ofcs. Harold Gamer, Beverly Hills 1976; deputy pub. defender Riverside Co. 1976-79; atty. Law Ofcs. Michael B. Lloyd, Riverside 1980; partner Imburg & Lloyd, APC, Riverside 1981--; honors: Outstanding Young Men of Am., Jaycees 1983; Democratic Gold Key Awd. 1981; mem: Am., Calif. & Riverside Trial Lawyers Assns.; Am. & Riverside Co. (Law Steering Com.) Bar Assns.; Calif. Attys. for Criminal Justice Assn.; Amicus Pepperdine; Republican; rec: golf, tennis. Res: 1423 Rimroad Riverside 92506 Ofc: Imburg & Lloyd, APC, 4075 Main St, Ste 500, Riverside 92501

L'LYLE, IRIS, iridologist/nutritionist; b. Jan. 11, 1929, Washington, La.; d. Lucius and Marie (LeDoux) Motte; m. 2d. Art Beasley L'lyle, Dec. 18, 1976; children: Glenn Honore b. 1949, Sybil b. 1950, Diane b. 1952, Anita b. 1953, Monica b. 1954, Laura b. 1955; edn: N.D., Bernadean Univ. 1976; BS dietetics, CSU Long Beach 1980; PhD, Donsbach Univ. Sch. of Nutrition, 1984. Career: nurse, 25 years, involved in holistic health movement; iridologist/nutritionist cons. Los Angeles area, 4 years, El Cajon, 1981-83, founder/owner Nutritional Counseling Service, Long Beach 1984--; mem. Christian Business Women of S.D., Am. Assn. of Nutrition & Dietary Consultants, Iridologist Internat., Nat. Health Fedn.; Democrat; Baptist; rec: gardening, needlewk. Address: Iris L'lyle, PhD Iridologist/Nutritionist, 7051 Natal Dr, Ste 83, Westminster 92683

LO, WILLIAM WEI-HSING, engineer; b. Apr. 15, 1950, Hong Kong, China; s. Tac-Haim and Fu-Shien (Twang) L.; m Emily Feng, Jan. 16, 1978; 1 dau: Jeniffer, b. 1982; edn: BS, Taipei Inst. of Tech. 1971; MS, Kansas State Univ. 1979. Career: elec. engr. Taiwan Power Co., Taipei, Taiwan 1976; research asst. Kansas State Univ., Manhattan, Bs. 1978; sr. engr. Control Data Corp., Omaha, Nebr. 1982; sr. engr. Ibis Sys. Inc., Westlake Village 1983; currently, principal engr. Pertec Peripherals Corp., Chatsworth, awards. tech. excellence, Control Data Corp. 1981; mem: IEEE; Christian; rec: research in computer based robotic systems field. Res: 2779 N Velarde Dr Thousand Oaks 91360 Ofc: Pertec Peripherals Corp., 9610 De Soto Ave Chatsworth 91311

LOBBAN, PETER EDWARD, scientist; b. Nov. 9, 1944, Atlanta, GA; s. Fred Peter and Frances Elizabeth (Conrad) L.; m. Nina Baller, Dec. 28, 1969; 1 son: Andrew, b. 1975. Edn: BS (life science), Mass. Inst. of Tech., 1962-66; PhD (biochem.), Stanford Univ., 1966-72, MS in E.E., 1974-76. Career: postdoctoral fellow Univ. Toronto, 1972-74; sr. engr. Varian Assoc., Palo Alto, 1976-82; sr. scientist Sequoia-Turner Corp., Mt. View, 1982--. Mem: Phi Lambda Upsilon, 1965; hon. Woodrow Wilson Fellowship, 1966; mem. IEEE 1975--. Publs: Sci. Jour. arts. Rec: camp., kayak., woodwork.. Res: 273 Lowell Ave. Palo Alto 94301. Ofc: Sequoia-Turner Corp., 755 Ravendale Dr. Mt. View 94043

LOBDELL, ROBERT C., newspaper executive; b. Jan. 1, 1926, Mankato, Mn.; s. Darwin Norman and Hilda Cecelia (Peterson) L.; m. Nancy Lower, July 12, 1952; children: Teresa (Johnson), b. 1953; Robert John, b. 1955; William Scott, b. 1960; James Marston, b. 1962; edn: AB, Stanford Univ. 1948; LLD, 1950; admitted to practice, State Bar of Calif. 1951, US Supreme Ct. Bar 1964. Career: atty., legal dept. Bank of America, Los Angeles 1951-52; atty./ corp. ofcr. Youngstown Sheet & Tube Co., Youngstown, Ohio 1952-65; asst. gen. counsel/ asst. secty. The Times Mirror Co., Los Angeles 1965-70, v.p./ asst. secty. The Times Mirror Co. and v.p./ gen. counsel Los Angeles Times 1970--; secty./ trustee Pfaffinger Found., Los Angeles Time Fund; mem Inst. for Corp. Counsel (chair, gov.); Constitutional Rights Found. (Lawyers Adv. Council); Am., Calif., Los Angeles County Bar Assn.; dir.L.A. Co. Bar Found.; Am. Soc. of Corp. Sectys.; Beta Theta Pi; Univ. Club; publs: co- ed., Southern California Conference on The Media and the Law, 1977; mil: pfc Army Air Corps 1944-45, 1st lt. USAR 1951-52; Episcopal; rec: tennis, jogging, music. Res: 925 Hillside Dr Long Beach 90815 Ofc: Los Angeles Times, Times Mirror Square Los Angeles 90053

LOBODOVSKY, KONSTANTIN K., electrical/mechanical engineer; b. Sept.ariovich) L.; m. Barbara Morgan, Feb. 7, 1975; edn: BS, elec. eng., Heald Coll. 1973; BS, mech. eng., 1978; Calif. Comm. Coll. Tchg. Credential; Cert. Energy Auditor. Career: with Pacific Gas & Electric Co. 1955--; draftsman 1955; land dept. surveyor, computer draftsman, land mgmt. real property admin. 1957; San Fracisco liaison, city & co. depts., illuminating engr., indsl. power engr. 1973; energy conservation svcs. techl. svcs. unit, sr. energy svcs. engr./ proj. mgr., staff instr./ lectr. 1979--; instr. math. & elec. engr. Heald Engring. Coll. Evening Div. 1968-77; dean of engring. & tech. schs. Heald Coll. Even. Div. 1977-79; awards: Energy Engr. of the Yr. (Bay Area chpt.) 1980, (13 Western States) 1981, Assn. of Energy Engrs., Atlanta, Ga.; Spkr. Awd., Pacific Gas & Electric 1979; mem: Assn. Energy Engrs. (pres. 1979-81; Exec. Com.); World Energy Engring. Congress Adv. Bd.; Russian Orthodox Ch. West Coast Diocese (tech. advr., bd. mem.); Engrs. Club of San Francisco; S.F. Proj. S.A.F.E.; US patent; tech. publs. in field, 1979-84; mil: sp4 US Army Honor Guard/Drill Team 1961-63, GCM, Expert Rifle, Letters of Commdn.,

Spl. Assignment to Pentagon; Republican; Russian Orthodox; rec: photog. Res: 591 32nd Ave San Francisco 94121 Ofc: Pacific Gas and Electric Co., 77 Beale, Ste A1251, San Francisco 94106

LOCATELLI, PAUL LEO, university administrator; b. Sept. 16, 1938, Santa Cruz; s. Vincent D. and Marie J. (Piccone) L.; edn: BSc, Univ. Santa Clara 1961; M.Div., Jesuit Sch. of Theol., Berkeley 1974; BDA, USC 1971; Cert. CPA, Calif. 1965. Career: profl. acct. Lautze & Lautze (Wolf & Co.) 1960-64, 74; lectr. Jesuit Sch. of Theol., Berkeley 1973-74; with Univ. of Santa Clara 1974--: prof. of acctg. 1974--; assoc. dean Sch. of Bus. 1976-78; academic v.p. 1978--; bd. trustees: Seattle Univ., Seattle, Wash. 1983; Univ. of San Francisco 1979-; Bellarmine Coll. Prep. 1975-; chmn. jury for the Calif. Mus. Sci. and Industry 1978-79, and chmn. for selection of Industrialist of the Yr. 1979; honors: Teacher of the Yr. 1977-78, Beta Gamma Sigma 1978; mem: Am. Inst. & Calif. Soc. of CPAs, Am. Acctg. Assn.; Democrat; Roman Catholic Jesuit Priest; rec: photog. Address: University of Santa Clara, Santa Clara 95053

LO CELSO, MICHAEL ALBERT, insurance broker; b. Dec. 3, 1934, Chgo., Ill.; s. Albert Ernest and Therese Rose (Intrieri) L.; m. Donna, Oct. 3, 1958; children: Michele Anne, b. 1963; Monique Marie, b. 1966; edn: LLD, La Salle Ext. 1974; desig: C.P.I.M., 1983. Career: salesmgr. E.B. Randall & Sons Ins. 1959-60; unit supvn. Safeco 1960-62; unit hd., umbrella supvr., dist. mgr. Tri-Co. Area (2 yrs.), underwriting mgr. San Diego area (1 yr.), house ofc. San Francisco area (1 yr.) Crum & Forster 1962-71; mktg. v.p. Wilshire Insurance 1971-74; mktg. mgr. Ed Lee Kozberg & Son 1974-81; currently, owner America Ins. Agcy. (div. Locelso & Estey Ins. Agcy. Inc.); faculty mem./ adv. bd. I.E.A. 1971-; rep. W.A.I.B. Produce Liaison Council to I.S.O.; awards: Student of the Yr., St. Mels 1954; 26 var. trophies 1949-70; All Star Short Stop, Class B Softball 1966, 67; Spoke, Spark & Speak Up Awds., Key Man Awd., Duarte Jaycess; mem: Western Assn. Ins. Brokers (pres.); Duarte Jaycees (pres.); Scripps Miramar Home Owners Assn. (pres.); Casualty Underwriters Club, Los Angeles; Ins. Council for City of Hope; West Side Ins. Women; Nat. Assn. Ins. Women; coauthor: umbrella manual, Industrial Indemnity; mil: Naval Intelligence 1955-59; Catholic; rec: bridge, sports, art collection. Res: 3655 Hightide Dr Rancho Palos Verdes 90274 Ofc: America Insurance Agency, 17000 Ventura Blvd, Ste 208, Encino 91316

LOCKE, JOHN CLAYTON, telecommunications engineering executive; b. March 15, 1956, Glendale; s. Marvin Clayton and Irene (May) L.; m. Cynthia M. Roos, Feb. 18, 1978; 1 son, Jeffery, b. 1982; edn: BS in elec. & electronics eng., cum laude, CalPoly Univ. 1981; computer tech., Control Data Inst. 1975; part-time teaching cred., Calif. 1983. Career: engrg. aide Alston Div. Conrac Corp., 1975-79; v.p. engrg./prin. Dimas Corp., 1979-82; v.p. engrg. Telcom Technologies, Ontario 1982--, bd. dirs. 1983-; instr. computer tech. Mt. San Antonio Coll. 1983-4. Honors: full scholastic scholarship, Control Data Inst. 1974; guest spkr. CalPoly Univ.; Eta Kappa Nu (mem. 1980, spkr. 1980, 81). Resrch: fiber optics in telecommunications, 1980. Republican; Baptist; rec: x-c runner, racquetball. Res: 1101 Eaton Rd San Dimas 91773 Ofc: Telcom Technologies 3072 East G St Ontario 91764

LOCKE, RALPH VERNON, manufacturing co. marketing executive; b. Jan. 23, 1936, Berkeley; s. Ralph Sherman and Lylia Jane (Miller) L.; m. Lynne Ransler, June 5, 1981; children: Steven, b. 1960; Kevin, b. 1961; Craig, b. 1963; Stacey, b. 1966; Amy, b. 1968; edn: San Francisco State Coll. 1956-59. Career: v.p. sales Diamond Springs Lime Co., Diamond Springs 1957-62; mgr. mktg. & sales A. Teichert & Sons, Sacto. 1963-78; gen. sales mgr. Granite Rock Co., Watsonville 1978-82; v.p. mktg. Basalt Rock, Napa 1982--; pres. Sacto. Bldrs. Exch. 1968; pres. Aggregate & Concrete Assn. 1974, 75; mem: Lyons Club, Rotary Club, Kiwanis; mil: spec. 3 US Army 1954-56; Republican; Presbyterian; rec: sports car racing, skiing, tennis. Res: 1990 Yount St, POB 3238, Yountville 94599 Ofc: Basalt Rock, 2301 Napa- Vallejo Hwy, POB 2540, Napa 94558

LOCKHART, JAMES BICKNELL, JR., manufacturing co. president; b. Mar. 27, 1918, Taunton, Mass.; s. James Bicknell and Charlotte Bradford (Babbitt) L.; m. Mary Ann Riegel, Oct. 2, 1943; children: Joan Riegel b. 1944, James B., III b. 1946, Ann Murchie b. 1948, Brenda Margaret b. 1950; edn: BS, Yale Univ. 1940, MBA, Northwestern Univ. 1941, MS, US Naval Acad. 1945. Career: cost acct. Gen. Electric Co., Mass. 1941-43; mgmt. cons. MacDonald Bros., Mass. 1945-48; chief indsl. engr. Riegel Paper Corp., N.J. 1948, purchasing agt. 1948-50, asst. to v.p. Prodn. 1950-51, mill mgr. 1951-54, N.Y. mgr. indsl. & merchant sale 1954-57, dir. 1952-67, corp. secty. 1955-63, corp. controller 1958-63, v.p. 1957-63; pres./CEO, Isolite Corp., Hawthorne, Calif. 1978--; past dir: Ridge Water Co. Inc., N.J.; Bartelt Engring., Ill.; Conwed Internat., Minn.; Fiber Conversion Co., Ga.; Sonic Engring. Corp., Conn.; Internat. Acoustical Testing Labs Inc., Minn.; Wood Conversion Industries, Minn.; Magnus Products Corp., Mich.; Mica-Wood Corp., Wisc.; First Trust Co., Minn.; exec. com. Specialty Paper & Board Assn., NY 1957-58. Honors: permanent exhib. named in honor, Minn. Science Mus. 1974; award of honor, The Wisdom Soc. 1975; service awards, Big Brothers of St. Paul, Minn. (1975), Big Brothers/Big Sisters of Am. (1977); key to City of San Bernardino, Calif. (1977); listed, Who's Who in Amer.; founder/dir. Old Town Restorations, Minn. 1970; mem: Mayflower Soc., Nat. UN Day Com., 1978; mil: lt. USNR 1942-46, cmdr. minesweeper, Victory, Pacific Theatre, Amer. Theatre, Phil. Liberation medals; Republican; Episcopal; rec: travel. Res: 635 E. Palmdale Ave Orange 92665 Ofc: Isolite Corp. 3232 W. El Segundo Blvd Hawthorne 90250

LOCKNESS, DORIS ESTELLE, aviatrix; b. Feb. 2, 1910, Bryant, Pa.; d. Lewis Watson and Harriette Estelle (Myers) Erwin; m. 2d. Robert Lockness, Apr. 10, 1948; children: Donna, b. 1928; Paul, b. 1930; David, b. 1932; Ronald, b. 1933. Career: student pilot, Wilmington, CA 1938; pvt. pilot, Long Beach 1939-40; WWII service military pilot, Women's Airforce Service Pilots (WASP), 1943; comml. pilot, Long Beach 1962; flight instr., Long Beach, Santa Monica, Van Nuys 1964-68; qual. in single and multi-engined airplanes, seaplanes and helicopters, commd. ofcr. Confederate Air Force, 1982, grade Col.; Received Fedn. Aeronautique Internat. sporting lic. (FAI) Balloon Fedn. of Am. 1982; comml. pilot instr. hot air balloons 1983; continues flying activities in personal aircraft; mem: Ninety-Nines Internat. (treas. Cameron Park chpt. 1983); chair Direct Relief Found., San Fernando Valley chpt. Ninety-Nines, 1980-82; OX5 Aviation Pioneers (life); Whirly-Girls, Internat. Womens Helicopter Pilots Inc.; Seaplane Pilots Assn.; Air Force Assn.; Balloon Fedn. of Am.; Sacto. Valley Pilots Assn.; Sacto. Jaguar Car Club; Republican; Lutheran; rec: cross country flying; exhibits Jaguar sports cars in concour'd' elegance events (num. 1st pl. trophies). Res: 2572 Sterling Dr Rescue 95672 mail: POB 1455 Cameron Park 95682

LOERA, JESSE PHILLIP, electrical enngineer; b. Oct. 29, 1948, Los Angeles; s. Apolonio and Delfina (Yanez) L.; edn: AA, E. Los Angeles Coll. 1968; BS, CSU Los Angeles 1974. Career: analyst/ research Electronics Research Div. Rockwell Internat., Anaheim 1970-73; biomed. engr. intern Cardiology Div. Harbor Gen. Hosp., Torrance 1973-74; elec. engr. Hoffman Electroncis Corp., El Monte 1974-75; tech. staff Jet Propulsion Lab, Pasadena 1975--; pres. J.P. Loera & Assoc., Eng. & Mgmt. Consultants 1982--; honors: Outstanding Young Men of Am., US Jaycees 1984; Outstanding Alumni of E. Los Angeles Coll. 1983; mem: Soc. of Hispanic Profl. Engrs. (Data Processing Com.; advr. to Nat. Pres. 1981-83; Publicity Com.); Progress for Youth Orgn., Inc. E. L.A.; Exptl. Sys. for Edn. Inc.; Mexican-Am. Communications Found.; guest spkr. Symposium on the Frontiers of Meso America (Tegucigalpa, Honduras 1975), Symp. on the Processes of Change of Meso America (Guanajvajo, Mex. 1977); Republican; Catholic; avocation: mgmt. consulting splst. in sys. analysis, strategic plng. & info. sys. Res: POB 50363 Pasadena 91105 Ofc: Jet Propulsion Laboratory, 4800 Oak Grove Dr, MS:238-601, Pasadena 91109

LOESCHKE, DONALD RAYMOND, steel co. president; b. Dec. 9, 1929, Milbank, S.Dak.; s. Raymond Karl and Kohar Elizabeth (Lepian) L.; m. Diane Scott, Nov. 15, 1952; children: Nadia b. 1954, Tanja b. 158; edn: BA, Hillsdale Coll. 1957; Univ. of Mich. 1959; Mich. State Univ. 1958-59; Tchr. Cert., State of Mich. 1957. Career: tchr. Warren Consolidated Schs., Warren, Mich. 1957-64; pres., exec. secty. Warren Edn. Assn. 1964-65; vice pres. Gemini Equip. Sales Inc., Detroit 1965-66; mktg. mgr. S. Vincen Bowles Inc., Sun Valley, Ca. 1966-70; pres. Hercules Container Industries, Montebello 1971-75; pres. Arpico Steel Corp., Montebello 1976--; honors: Man of the Year, Greater Los Angeles Solid Waste Mgmt. Assn. 1972; mem: Calif. Refuse Removal Council, Gr. L.A. Solid Waste Mgmt. Assn., Calif. Disposal Assn., San Bernardino-Riverside Disposal Assn., San Diego Disposal Assn., Orange County Disposal Assn., Montebello CofC; mil: pfc US Army Inf. 1948-51, Purple Heart, UN Medal; Democrat; Prot.; rec: sports. Res: 4421 North Ohio, Yorba Linda 92686 Ofc: Arpico Steel Corp. 1718 S. Greenwood Ave Montebello 90640

LOEWY, PETER H., lawyer; b. Oct. 2, 1955, NY; s. Herbert and Ruth (Berger) L.; edn: BA, summa cum laude, City Coll. of NY 1976; JD, Rutgers Univ. 1979; admitted to practice state & fed. bars of NY, NJ, Fla., and Calif. Career: law clerk Wellisch Metzgertleone, Coral Gables, Fla. 1978; atty. Fragomen Del Rey & Bernsen P.C., NY 1979-82, mng. atty., Los Angeles 1982-83; partner real estate devel., Loewy Del Sol Properties 1984; v.chmn. Comm. Plnng. Bd., NY 1980-81; honors: Phi Beta Kappa; mem: Rutgers Internat. Law Soc.; Assn. of Trial Lawyers; Assn. of Immigration & Nationality Lawyers; So. Calif. Squash Racquets Assn.; Fifth Ave Squash Club; publs: ed., Immigration Law Report, Clark Boardman; rec: squash. Res: 25 Spinnaker 12, Marina del Rey 90292 Ofc: Fragomen Del Rey & Bernsen P.C., 1901 Ave of the Stars, Ste 460, Los Angeles 90067

LOFLAND, JERI IRENA, interior design co. president; b. Oct. 16, 1928, Detroit, Mich.; d. Edward J. and Maryanna (Stolarczyk) Jromin; m. James E. Lofland, Sept. 4, 1955; children: Martin James, b. 1957; Leslie, b. 1957; edn: Cass Tech., Detroit 1949; interior design, Phoenix Coll. 1960; desig: AID, Am. Inst. of Design 1948. Career: model/ sales Saks 5th Ave, Detroit, Mich. 1948; owner/ co. exec. Irena's Shopping Svc. 1949-51; actress/ TV commercials, Hollywood 1951-65; Irena's Interiors, Los Angeles 1965-66, Newport Beach 1966--; real estate & investments 1950--; currently, pres. Irena's Interior Design & Real Estate Investments & chmn. bd. Ice Cream Industries, Newport Beach; dir. tng. int. design students, Irena's, Newport Beach 1969-74; awards: Dorris-Hyman Awd., Designer of the Year 1961, Phoenix; mem: Screen Actors Guild; Am. Fedn. Radio & TV; judge, Miss Calif. (Riverside), and Miss Universe (Palm Springs); affilated with Dorothy Shriver Modeling Sch. (Newport Bch) 1978-83; Downtown Beauty Com. Lake Elsinore, 1983; soc. dir. Barney Oldfield County Club (Sherman Oaks) 1953-54; soc. com. Balboa Bay Club (Newport Beach) 1968-70; chmn./soc. dir. Club Iona (Newport Beach) 1976-77; works: booklet on Religious Faith, 1978; Hotel Art Rendering for int. design competition 1962; Republican; Catholic/ Jewish; rec: art collection, antiques. Res: 711 Lido Park Dr 92663 Ofc: Ice Cream Industries, 3355 Via Lido, Ste 300, Newport Beach 92663

LOFTON, JAMES LESTER, private investigator; b. Nov. 21, 1942, Orlando, Fla.; s. Richard B. and Rosie B. (Lewis) L.; m. Rosemary Marie Davis, Mar. 17, 1962; children: Debra b. 1963, Diana b. 164, Michael b. 1965; edn: BA, San Diego St. Coll. 972; JD, Western St. Univ. 1983; Calif. lic: Nursing Home Adminstr. 1971-76, Investigator. Career: fmr. comml. abalone diver, roofer, dry-wall contractor, shipyard foreman; pres. American Medex Assn. 1970-72; adminstr./co-owner 39-bed Nursing Home Facility, San Diego 1972; cons. corp. mergers & acquisitions, 1972-74; administr. Carrol Ents., El Cajon 1975; para-legal asst. Louis M. Karp, Federal Bankruptcy Judge (ret.) 1976; pvt. investigator, sole prop. Falcon & Ferret, public document resrch. and investg. firm (assisting num. law firms and corps.), 1977--; asst. organized crime law enforcement splsts, 1981-; mem: Nat. Assn. of Former Intell. Officers; mil: E4 USN Hosp. Corps. GC, Commendn.; Republican; Prot. Res: 2819 Polk St San Diego 92104 Ofc: Falcon & Ferret Intelligence Ops. POB 33623 San Diego 92103

LOGAN, ROLAND D., chiropractor; b. Aug. 6, 1936; S. Roland P. and Margaret Nadine (Reynolds); m. Jeanne Crenshaw, Aug. 11, 1982; children: Michael, b. 1958; Bruce, b. 1960; Bob, b. 1962; Lynette, b. 1965; Angie, b. 1970; edn: DC, Palmer Coll. of Chiro. 1972; DC, Bd. Chiro. Examiners 1973. Career: mgr. beauty coll., Chico 1960-63; life underwriter Equitable of NY 1963-66; owner/ opr. hair salon; chiropractor/ pres. Logan Chiro. Ofcs., A Profl. Corp., Modesto 1972--; mem: Calif. & Stanislaus- San Joaquin Chiro. Assns.; Rotary; Republican; Unity Ch.; rec: water skiing, travel. Ofc: Logan Chiropractic Offices, 321 E Granger Ave Modesto 95350

LOGUE, MURL FRANCIS, mfg. engineer, company president; b. Feb. 9, 1921, Pittsburgh, PA; s. Fred D. and Mary Ellen (Crawley) Logue; Cert. Mgmt. Engring., Pittsburgh Tech. Inst., 1953; stu. data processing & computer programming, San Joaquin Delta Coll., 1964-65; stu. and instr., USN Mahinists Sch., Norfolk, VA, 1943; m. Charlene Brown, Mar. 11, 1978; chil: Kathleen, b. 1946 (dec.); Michael Francis, b. 1949; step-chil: Karen (Mrs. Gary Gervase); David Bobitt, b. 1959. Career: supr., West Penn Machine Shops, Pittsburgh, 1946-53; supr. of methods engring., Lewis Machinery Div. of Blaw Knox Corp., 1953-56; chief tool engr., Bucyrus Erie Corp., Erie, PA, 1956-57 chief mfg. engr., Tel Autograph Corp., Los Angeles, 1957-60; chief engr., Anderson Die Casting Co., L.A., 1960-62; senior tool engr., Norris Industry, L.A., 1962-64; mgr mfg. engring., Super Mold Corp., Lodi, 1964-66; chief machine tool engr., Norris Industry, Riverbank Army Ammo. Plant (responsible engr. for plant layout & equipment of largest US facility, 60 and 81mm mortar shells; engr. responsible in planning & constrn. of most advanced facility in world, prodn. of hot pressed tech. ceramics, cermets and sialons), 1966-67; mfgrs. rep., 1967-71; pres., Logue Associates Inc. (successor to M.F. Logue Assoc.), mfg. engrs. & consultants, Newman, 1971---. Dir., Fan-Fi Corp., 1972; natl. lectr. for Soc. of Mfg. Engrs., 1970-76. Profl Engr., Calif., 1978---. Mem: Woodbridge Lodge F&AM, 1965---; Soc. of Mfg. Engrs., sr. mem. 1965---; US Congressional Adv. Bd., 1981-82. Patent (applicant) for new energy saving shower head; designed prodn. machinery for mil. hardware (Sparrow, Shrike, and other missiles). Mil: MM1/c (acting CMM), USN, 1942-45. Republican. Baptist. Rec: boating, fishing, hunting. Address: Logue Assocs. Inc., 29435 Sanches Rd., Newman 95360.

LOMBARDO, SALVATORE THOMAS, real estate broker-investor; b. Nov. 23, 1931, Providence, R.I.; s. Salvatore and Emma (DeRobbio) L.; m. Patricia Ruth Lippnik, Apr. 23, 1960; children: Thomas b. 1963, Gerald b. 1965; edn: AA, Pasadena City Coll. 1953, BS, Woodbury Univ. 1951, BA, UC Los Angeles 1957, MS, USC, 1963. Career: founder/pres. Lombardo Enterprises, pvt. income property investment co. 1960--, and pres. Patrician Real Estate, in Northridge 1977-81, moved to Westlake Village 1981--; devel. Imperial House (1st large co-operative complex in the S.F. Vly.), Sherman Oaks 1980; quoted re alternate sources of financing real estate in California Business mag. 10/83; mem. San Fernando Valley Bd. of Realtors; treas. Chaminade Coll. Prep. Booster Assn. 1981-82; mil: cpl. US Army; Republican; Catholic; rec: music. Address: Patrician Real Estate, Lombardo Ent. 1655 Upper Ranch Road Westlake Village 91362

LONG, DEBORAH ANN, special education assistant, realtor associate; b. Dec. 11, 1949, Buffalo, NY; d. Willie, Jr. and Georgia Effie (Hardy) Fisher; m. James Ellis Long, Dec. 19, 1970; children: Kimberley Ann b. 1971, Anthony Fitzgerald b. 1973; edn: AA, Grossmont Coll. 1977; stu. Chapman Coll., 1983-. Cert. Medical Lab. Asst., ROP 1975; grad. Military Ombudsman (counselor). Career: research tech. Searle Labs., Skokie, Ill. 1969-73; spl. edn. asst. Mission Beach Sch., San Diego 1975--, integration monitor, S.D. Unif. Sch. Dist.; realtor assoc. Century 21/Hawkins Realty, S.D., 1980--; recipient appreciation, USS Denver LPD-9 (1980) and Fleet Tng. Center (1982), Mil. Ombudsman; mem: Nat. Assn. of Female Execs., Negro Bus. & Profl. Womens Club (sec. 1982), The City Club (1981-3), Dimensions of San Diego; Girl Scout co-ldr., bd. mem./pres. Parent Tchr. Gp. (PTG) Holy Spirit Sch.; Ombudsman for Military Personnel & Dependents; works: devel. solvent systems to check purification of Prostaglandins; Democrat; Baptist; rec: racquetball, coaching Girl's Soccer, computers. Res: 8673 Potrero St San Diego 92114 Ofc: Mission Beach School, 818 Santa Barbara Pl. San Diego 92109; Century 21/Hawkins Realty, 1005 N. Euclid Ave San Diego 92114

LONG, FAY ELEANOR, social worker; b. Apr. 7, 1934, Rimbey, Alberta, Can., nat. 1959; d. Lewis Samuel and Nellie May (Henderson) Cole; div.; 1 son: Lewis C. Long, b. 1952; edn: BA, cum laude, Sacto. State Coll. 1965; MSW, Sacto. State Univ. 1970; desig: Lic. Soc. Wkr., MFCC (Marriage, Family & Child Counselor), Calif. Career: welfare worker III Sacramento Co. 1965-68; soc. wkr./ parole agent Calif. Youth Authority 1969-76; supvg. correctional counselor II Calif. Dept. Corrections, Folsom State Prison 1976--; first woman lodge casework supvr. Preston Sch. Calif. Youth Authority 1969; first woman supvr. Folsom State Prison 1976; first woman supvr. Security Housing Unit., Folsom Frisno 1979; mem: Calif. Probation Parole Assn.; Calif. Assn. Mgrs.: Psi Chi; Republican. Res: 9312 Appalachian Dr Sacramento 95827 Ofc: Folsom State Prison, POB W, Represa 95671

LONG, JAMES LENERE, judge; b. Dec. 7, 1937, Wintergarden, FL; s. James Joshua and Susie Lenere (Ward) Long; sister, June LaVerne Long, instr. Sch. of Social Work, CSU Sacto.; bro., Elton Ward Long, assoc. prof. in Criminal Justice Dept., CSU Sacto.; Edn: BA, San Jose State Coll., 1960; JD, Howard Univ. Law Sch., 1967. Career: law clerk for Neighborhood Legal Services Found., Wash., D.C. (while law student); grad. legal asst., Legal Air Soc., Sacto. Co., Legislative Counsel Bur., 1967-69; pvt. practice, criminal and civil law, Sacramento, 1970---; apptd. Sup. Ct. Judge, 1982---; spec. legal counsel, NAAC, Western Region, 2 yrs.; non-legal exp: Juvenile Hall Counselor, Dep. Probation Officer, Sacramento Co.; asst. clerk, Calif. State Assem.; asst. prof., Criminal Justice Dept., CSU Sacramento. Awards: NAACP Riverside Branch, McGeorge Sch. of Law; recipient Resolution Calif. State Legislature, 1970. Mem: NAACP, bd. dirs. Sacto. chpt.; bd. dirs., Oak Park Project Area Com. (P.Z.C.); bd. dirs., Stanford Home Found., Observer Found.; Sacto. Legal Aid Soc.; Federal Bar, Eastern Dist. of Calif.; Bar of Supreme Ct. of U.S.; Amer., Calif. State, Sacramento Co. Bar Assns.; Calif. Trial Lawyers Assn.s; Calif. Sacto. Assn. Black Lawyers; Charles Houston Bar Assn. Mil: 2nd Lt., USAR. Co-author: (w/brother) of book American Minorities: The Justice Issue, Prentice-Hall Inc., 1975. Res: 3439 4th Ave., Sacramento 95817; Office: Courthouse, Dept. 22, Sacramento 95814.

LONG, ROSALEE MADELINE, law librarian; b. Aug. 27, 1931, Concordia, KS; d. James Allen and Mary Clara (McConnell) Vincent; Edn: AB in L.S., Kans. State Univ. at Emporia, 1953; JD, Univ. of Santa Clara, 1973; admitted to practice law in Calif., 1976; m. Robert Long, 1954. Career: cataloger, San Jose State Univ., 1954-56; head Cataloging Dept., 1956-58; cataloger, Stanford Law Library, Stanford Univ., Stanford, 1958-60; head Cataloging Dept., 1960-74; Spl. Projects Librarian, 1974-75; Assoc. Law Librarian, 1975---. Faculty mem., Amer. Assn. of Law Libraries Inst., Univ. of Minn., 1974. Awarded Law Sch. Scholarship, Amer. Assn. of Law Libraries. Mem: State Bar of California, American Assn. of Law Libraries. Publs: author notation (w/Merryman), 1966; Stanford Law Library Classification (w/ Merryman), 1968. Rec: music, golf. Res: 1175 Plum Ave., Sunnyvale 94087; Office: Stanford Law Lib., Rm. 220, Stanford 94305.

LOPES, FOSTER STEVEN, educator; b. Dec. 17, 1929, New Bedford, Mass.; s. Joseph M. and Cremilda (Pedro) L.; m. Iva (Lee) N. Matlock, June 26, 1954; children: Deborah, b. 1954; Cheryl, b. 1956; Stephanie, b. 1961; edn: AA, San Jose City Coll. 1957-59, BA, CSU San Jose 1962, MA, 1964; Calif. Tchr. Std. Supv. Cred. 1965. Career: tchr. lang. arts/ soc. studies, Santa Clara Unif. Sch. Dist. 1962-68; tchr. driver edn. 1968-71; tchr. soc. studies (civics/ Am. problems) 1971-; trustee W. Valley Joint Comm. Coll. Dist. 1969-85; mem: Calif. Tchrs. Assn.; Phi Delta Kappa; Santa Clara Coimbra (Portugal) Sister City orgn.; Portugese-Am. Club; mil: airman 2/c USAF 1951-55; Democrat; Catholic; rec: swimming, gardening. Res: 2647 Birch Tree Ln Santa Clara 95051 Ofc: West Valley Joint Community College District, 14000 Fruitvale Ave Saratoga 95070

LOPEZ, AGUSTIN CARIG, life insurance agency executive; b. Aug. 28, 1908, Manaoag, Pangasinan, Philippines; s. Anastacio Y. and Benedicta Delin (Carig) L.; m. Mary Lois Dickson, June 24, 1945; children: David Carig b. 1946, Peter Dickson b. 1950; edn: AB, internat. rels., UC Berkeley 1937, MA in philos. 1940. Career: agent West Coast Life Insurance Co., 1937-39, district agt. 1939-42, general agent for state of Calif., Western Life Ins. Co. 1942--; gen. insurance underwriter and broker, 1940--; semi-ret. 1973; past mem. local life underwriter and gen. ins. assns.; recipient National Quality Awards (5) for excellence, Nat. Assn. of Life Underwriters; mem. Univ. of Calf. Alumni Assn.; active in religious and fraternal and charitable orgns.; listed Who's Who in Methodism (1952), Who's Who in Am. (1954-56); author: The Taming of a Dream; United Methodist; rec: bicycling. Res: 6634 Chabot Rd Oakland 94618 Ofc: Western Life, 1540 San Pablo Ave Oakland 94612

LOPEZ, ANTHONY BONILLA, public administrator; b. Dec. 12, 1945, El Paso, Tex.; s. A. Tafoya and Ophelia (Bonilla) L.; edn: AA, Long Beach City Coll. 1973; BS, CSU Long Beach 1974; postgrad., para-legal cert. Univ. San Diego 1975; Personnel Mgmt. & Employee Rels. cert., Univ. Calif. 1980. Career: adminstrv. services dir. City of Coachella, 1982--; fmr. dir. Human Services/Grant's Ofcr., City of Desert Hot Springs; cons. non-profit orgns., dir. Anthony B. Lopez and Assocs.; program dir. Stanton Reachout Pgm.; campus minister, orgnzr. Newman Club, Golden West Coll.; adminstrv. intern Long Beach City Police Dept. and City of Paramount, intern L.A. County Harbor Patrol, Marina del Rey; asst. mgr. TransAm. Corp. Honors: Phi Kappa Phi, Gold Nugget Award, CSULB; mem: Municipal Finance Officers Assn., Internat. Personnel Mgmt. Assocs., Internat. City Mgmt. Assn. (afil.), Public Risk & Ins. Mgmt. Assn., Calif. Soc. of Municipal Finance Ofcrs., Am. Soc. for Pub. Adminstrn., Am. Mgmt. Assn., Municipal Mgmt. Assts. of So. Calif., Toastmasters Intl., Coachella Valley Rotary Club; Catholic; rec: tennis. Res: POB 735 Coachella 92236 Ofc: City of Coachella, 1515 Sixth St Coachella 92236

LOPEZ, JERRY, video systems co. owner; b. Sept. 3, 1951, Tucson, Ariz.; s. Juan Bojorquez and Mary (Lopez) L.; m. Sylvia, May 25, 1974; children: Inez, b. 1980; Vicente Francisco, b. 1982; edn: BA, CSU Northridge 1976; Instr. Cable Television, Calif. 1981. Career: tech. Theta Cable TV, Santa Monica 1973-76; head tech. Premier Channel, Burlingcame 1976-78; head tech. Mediapoint Inc., Orange 1978-81; instr. cable tv, No. Valley Occupational Ctr.

1981-83; owner/ pres. ops. Dial One Action Commun., Van Nuys 1979--; rec: furniture making, home movies, parenting. Res: 466 Giano Ave La Puente 91744 Ofc: Dial One Action Communications, 14811 1/2 Oxnard St Van Nuys 91411

LOPEZ, MARY, real estate broker; b. Feb. 22, 1926, Durant, Okla.; d. Juan E. and Ramona (Perez) Santos; m. Tony Menchaca, Jan. 7, 1946; children: Shirley Ann b. 1946, Judy Gayle (Aldredge) b. 1948; edn: AA, Contra Costa Coll. 1968; BA in criminology, UC Berkeley 1970; att. Univ. San Jose 1945; Calif. Real Estate lic. 1952, Broker lic. 1954. Career: legal secty. for Harry Houser, San Jose, 1945-52; real estate agt. Chet Rogers Realty 1952, Joe Powell, Richmond 1953, realtor self-empl. 1954--; mgr. retail business; interpretor (Spanish translation) courts of law; charter mem. City of Richmond Human Relations Commn. 1964; mem: West Contra Costa Bd. of Realtors (pres. Womens' Council 1982), Calif. Assn. of Realtors, Nat. Assn. of Realtors; charter mem. West Contra Costa Hispanic Forum 1983-; mem. Bus. & Profl. Women (BPW Woman of Achievement Awd. 1983); CofC; Univ. of Calif. Alumni Assn. (life), Alpha Gamma Sigma Hon. Soc., CofC; bd. dirs. Am. Red Cross (10 yrs); United Bay Area Crusade chpsn. for Richmond (twice); artist: one woman exhib. Contra Costa Coll. (1974); amateur musician (guitar, clarinet), played with concert band sev. years; Republican; cand. for Richmond City Council; Prot.; rec: lapidary, music. Res: 2631 Bissell Ave Richmond 94804

LO PICCOLO, PIERINA EMILLIA, opera singer, restaurateur; b. Dec. 11, 1901, Italy, nat. 1923; d. Angelo and Josephine (Campagnoni) Piubeni; m. Salvatore Lo Piccolo, 1948; 1 dau: Josephine, b. 1926; edn: RN, Evangeline Booth Hosp; voice maj., Scuola Musicale di Milano 1937; BA, Shaw Univ. 1975. Career: prima donna, 25 operas; performer, motion pictures; profl. voice tchr.; partner, w/ husband, Lo Piccolo's Unique Mus. Restaurant, Burbank (dishes from historically famous dinners, atmosphere of history, music & song); founder The Home & Family Life Mus., Burbank (depicting family life from inception of USA); recorded the history of the Nat. Anthem, Lib. of Congress; honoros: named city historian, Burbank; Awd. of Commdn. for Vision Expanded Into Action & Awd. of Merit for Cultural Advancement, exec. bd. Womens Council of Burbank 1965; Outstanding Woman of Community, Tri-Valley Dist. of Calif.; Woman of Achiev., Magnolia Park Bus. & Profl. Womens Club; Nat. Singers Awd., Ministry of Cultural Arts, Italy 1937; Christian (pastoral counseling). Res: 4011 W Magnolia Blvd Burbank 91505

LOPPNOW, DAVID HUNT, radar engineering executive; b. Jan. 2, 1934, Milwaukee, Wisc.; s. Lester Alfred and Irma Iva Loppnow; m. Sharon Lee Gray, June 21, 1958; cihldren: Jeffrey, b. 1959; Randall, b. 1961; Heather, b. 1966; edn: AB, Ripon Coll. 1955; post grad., Univ. of Hawaii, UCLA, Georgia Tech. & George Wash. Univ. Career: sr. pgmr. analyst System Development Corp., Santa Monica 1959-62; eng. gp. leader Litton Data Sys., Van Nuys 1962-66; senior mem. tech. staff ITT Gilfillan, Van Nuys 1966--; mem: IEEE; Assn. Old Crows; Gilfillam Mgmt. Assn.; works: Low Level Surveillance Radar Design, 1983; Adaptive Clutter and Interference Suppression for the Surveillance Radar Environment 1984; mil: lt. j.g. USNR 1955-59, naval aviation observer; Republican; Protestant; rec· theater, music, travel. Res: 22577 Waterbury St Woodland Hills 91364 Ofc: ITT Gilfillan, 7821 Orion Ave, POB 7713 Van Nuys 91409

LORENTZEN, KAY WILBUR, veterinarian; b. Mar. 31, 1920, San Francisco; s. Dr. Kay Gustav and Carolyn Frieda (Stettin) L.; m. Barbara Nunes, June 24, 1945; edn: AA, San Benito Jr. Coll. 1939-41; VMD, Univ. of Penn. 1943-47; grad. Command and Gen. Staff Coll., US Army 1972; Stanford Univ. 1941-43. Career: pvt. practice, Santa Rosa 1947-50; Col. US Army Veterinary Corp, (USA, Alaska, Germany, Vietnam) 1950-77; retired as Western Regl. Army Veterinary Consultant Letterman Army Med. Ctr. 1977; mem: Nat. Eagle Scout Assn.; Am. & Calif. State Vet. Med. Assns.; Ret. Ofcr. Assn.; mil. decorations: Legion of Merit, Bronze Star, Meritorious Svc. w/ Oak Leaf Cluster, Vietnam Campaign w/ yr. bar, Armed Forces Hon. Medal l/c, Vietnam Unit Cit., Cross of Gallantry; Republican; Protestant; rec: golf, swimming, model trains. Res: 211 Donald Dr Hollister 95023

LORESCO, ALEJANDRO, real estate broker; b. Feb. 25, 1924, Calasiao, Pangasinan, Philippines, nat. 1949; s. Pedro and Ramona Zulueta (Abulencia) L.; m. Remigia Domagas, May 4, 1954; children: Juanita, b. 1954; Salvador, b. 1955; Alejandro Jr., b. 1959. Career: ins. agent 1960--; real estate salesman 1973-75; real estate broker 1975--; owner/ realtor/ ins. agent Loresco Realty & Ins., San Diego 1978--; mem: Filipino Investment Corp.; United Filipino Merchants; San Diego Bd. Realtors; Pangasinan Assn. of San Diego; Pampnga Assn.; Dagupan City Assn.; So. Bay Comm. Assn.; Filipino Assn. of Nat. City; United Assn. of So. Calif., Imperial Beach; mil: USN 1946-65, WWII, Korean, Cuban Crises, Vietnam & China Svc. Medals; Catholic; rec: equestrian, swimming, dancing. Res: 3225 Kennelworth Ln Bonita 92002 Ofc: Loresco Realty & Insurance, 2332 Reo Dr San Diego 92139

LORRAINE, EVA, ballet company artistic director; b. Jan. 5, Chicago; d. Yoseph Fortuna (composer, conductor) and Sara (White) Cassatta (changed to Cassidy); grad. St. Xavier's Acad.; AB, Eng. lit., Univ. Chicago (assoc. tchrs. hn. deg.); stu. with Adolph Bolm, Bronislava Nijinska, Mordkin, Ambrozini and Preobrajenska, Paris, Fr.; accredited teacher-choreographer. Career: actress, Essanay Studios, 20 motion pictures incl. Mary McAllister pic. "Pants," before age of 12 yrs.; Broadway debut as Eva Lynn in Earl Carroll Vanities, Naughty Riquette, Passing Show; star of film, It Happened in Paris; ballet soloist, Chicago Opera (at 16 yrs.); apptd. George White's Scandals; dir., choreographer, 7 Broadway shows, Schuberts Theaters; prima ballerina, Manhattan Mary; staged ballet, Down, Simple Simon (Ziegfeld), 1931-33; Orphans of the Storm, Ft. Lee Studios, 1933; ballet soloist, Michael Mordkin Ballet in Les Sylphides, Giselle; Euro. tour w/David Appolon for Paramount, Our American Pavlova, 1936-39; Ziegfeld Follies, 1937-40; contract with MGM, Republic Studios, protege-asst. to Maria Ouspenskaya, 1940-49; Carnegie Hall debut, 1948; founder, dir., choreographer, Calif. ballet Co. of L.A., debut Hollywood Bowl 1954; artistic dir., L.A. Festival Ballet, Pasa. Civic Ballet; guest choreographer, ballerina, Vienna and London Festivals, 1971, Chicago Ballet Ctr., 1972; currently artistic dir., Amer. Ballet Center Performing Arts, Oak Park Civic Ballet (repertory opera): "The Magic Flute," "Tannhauser," "Merry Widow," "Nutcracker Ballet"; created orig. choreography for ballets: Boccaccio, Command Performance, Rhapsody in Blue, Western Symphony, Concerto, Mischief Maker, Mukunda. Recipient Governors Award for outstanding merit, 1979; L.A. Critics Art Award for 1st Calif. Children's Ballet, 1954. Mem: Dance Masters of Amer., SAG, AEA, AFTRA, CofC. Rec: writing, costume design, painting. Res: 136 N. Marion, Oak Park, IL 60302.

LOSCHIAVO, JOHN JOSEPH, university president; b. Feb. 25, 1925, San Francisco; s. Joseph and Anna (Re) LoSchiavo; edn: AB, Gonzaga Univ., Spokane 1948, MA, 1949; STL, Alma Coll., Los Gatos 162. Career: instr. philosophy, theol., Univ. San Francisco, 1950-52, 61-62, dean of students, 1962-66, v.p. for student affairs 1966-68; pres. Bellarmine Coll. Prep., San Jose 1968-75; pres. USF, 1977--, trustee USF, 1964-68, 1969-, chmn. 1970-73; dir. assn. of Jesuit Colls. and Univs., 1977-; exec. com. Assn. of Independent Calif. Colls. and Univs.; mem: NCCJ Inc. (bd. mem. No. Calif. 1982-), Alpha Sigma Nu (life), The Olympic Club 1977-, The Bohemian Club 1978-, Il Cenacolo 1977-; Democrat; Roman Catholic, ordained RC priest. Rec: golf, swimming. Res: Xavier Hall, Univ. of San Francisco, San Francisco 94117 Ofc: University Center, 424, Univ. of S.F., San Francisco 94117

LOUGHEED, ARTHUR LAWRENCE, insurance agency president; b. Aug. 11, 1944, Fresno; s. Evan A. and Irene E. (Westby) L.; div.; children: Christopher, b. 1967; Jennifer, b. 1969; Evan, b. 1975; edn: Albion Coll. 1963-64; AA, Orange Coast Coll. 1964; USC Grad. Sch. of Law 1964-65; MS, finl. svcs., American Coll., Bryn Mawr 1980; desig: CLU, Am. Soc. Chartered Life Underwriters 1973; Chartered Property and Casualty Underwriter, Soc. of Ch. Prop. & Cas. Und. 1980. Career: Farmers Ins. Gp., Los Angeles, served Santa Ana, Calif. & Pocatello, Idaho; agent./ Div. Agcy. mgr./ Regional life mgr. Aetna Life & Casualty Ins. Co., Hartford Conn., served Los Angeles 1974-77; mgr. of estate, bus. & pension sales CNA Ins. Cos., Chgo., Ill., served Los Angeles & Chgo. lzw7-81; reg. dir. life sales ofcs./ nat. dir. mktg. & sales lng. Lougheed, Talbot & Assoc. Ins. Svcs., Inc. 1981--; currently, pres./ gen. agnet The Bershire Life Ins. Co., San Diego; lectr. on ins. Glendale Coll., Univ. of Ill., Chgo., De Paul Univ., Chgo., UC San Diego, UC Irvine; reg. instr./ sem. leader Ins. Ednl. Assn. of San Francisco; honors: Alpha Gamma Sigma 1964; Toppers Club, Farmers Ins. Gp. 1965-69; Regionaire, Aetna Life & Casualty 1975-; Nat., Calif., San Diego & Glendale/ Burbank Assns. of Life Underwriters; Am. Soc. CLUs; Soc. Chart. Property & Casualty Underwriters; Saddleback Kiwanis, Mission Viejo; San Diego CofC; editor assoc. CALUnderwriter mag. 1976, contbr. articles in finl. field various nat., regl. publs.; photog. work pub. var. newspapers and mags.; Republican; Luthern; rec: fishing, history, literature. Res: 6982 Wisconsin Ave La Mesa 92041 Ofc: Lougheed, Talbot & Assocs., 2515 Camino del Rio S., Ste 226, San Diego 92108

LOURDEAUX, WALLACE JOSEPH, historical restoration co. owner; b. May 20, 1945, San Francisco; s. Albert Francis and Mildred Nevada Rose (Park) L.; m. Roseanna D. Fiedor, Mar. 28, 1978; 1 son: Joseph, b. 1979; edn: B.Arch., Univ. Ore. 1968; Gen. Bldg. Contractors Lic. Career: designer Welton Becket Architecture, San Francisco 1969-71; owner Redwood Design, Corte Madera 1971-75; owner Historical Restoration & Devel. Co., Petaluma 1975--; awards: Merit Awd. for Hist. Preservation, Co. of Sonoma; Best Preservation City of Petaluma, Sonoma Co., City of Fairfax, Marin Co.; mem: Petaluma Redevel. Agency, Sonoma Co.; Fairfax Redevel. Agcy., Marin Co.; Phi Delta Theta; Optimists Club of Am.; works: innovative means of restructuring bldgs. for readaptive uses 1971-83; Republican; Catholic; rec: archaelogy, history of architecture. Res: 9 Summit Dr Corte Madera 94925 Ofc: Historical Restoration, 7 Fourth St Petaluma 94952

LOUTTIT, GORDON JAMES, lawyer; b. June 29, 1947, Detroit, Mich.; s. James Gordon and Winifred Margaret (Mullen) L.; edn: BA, UCLA 1969; JD, 1972. Career: counsel State of Calif. Dept. of Corporations 1972-74; atty. Hahn Cazier Hoegh & Leff, Los Angeles 1974-78; asst. gen. counsel Whittaker Corp. (NYSE) 1978--; gen. counsel/bd. dir. Yardney Corp. (Amex), 1980--; awards: Calif. State Scholar 1965-69; mem: Am. & Los Angeles Co. Bar Assns.; L.A. Co. Mus. of Art.; Mus. of Contemporary Art; Republican; Presbyterian; rec: art, architecture, classic sports cars. Res: 217 Bayview Dr Manhattan Beach 90266 Ofc: Whittaker Corporation, 10880 Wilshire Blvd Los Angeles 90024

LOVELACE, RALPH EDGAR, electrical engineer; b. Jan. 25, 1936, Pough Keepsie, NY; s. Harry James and Gladys (Birdsall) L.; m. Carol Ann Noren,

Oct. 18, 1958; children: Deborah, b. 1959; Patricia, b. 1964; David, b. 1966. Edn: BEE, Clarkson Coll of Tech., 1958; MSEE, Univ. of Conn., 1964. Career: engr. Link Div. General Precision, Binghamton, NY, 1958-60; des. engr. Norden Div. UAC, Norwalk, Conn., 1960-66; int. cir. des. engr. Sylvania, Woburn, Mass., 1966-69; mgr. Linear IC Design General Electric, Syracuse, NY, 1969-73, sect. head Analog IC Design, 1973-84; sr. staff splst. Signetics, 1984--.; tchr. Elec. Engring. Bridgeport Engring. Inst., Conn., and Cogswell Coll., San Francisco. Mem: sr. mem. IEEE; BSA Scout Troup leader. Profl. papers IEEE, five US patents; Republican; Catholic. Rec: camp., sail. Res: 288 Belblossom Way Los Gatos 95030 Ofc: Signetics, 811 E. Argues Ave, MS 1661, Sunnyvale 94088-3409

LOVELL, FREDERICK WARREN, physician; b. June 13, 1922, Astoria, Ore.; s. Sherman M. and Ruby J. (Dunn) L.; m. June Hendrickson, June 13, 1981; children: Peggy, b. 1952; Sherman, b. 1954; Robert, b. 1956; Mary Jo, b. 1959; Tina, b. 1961; edn: BS, honors, Univ. of Oregon 1949; MS, Northwestern Univ. 1952; MD, 1953; diplomate, Am. Bd. Pathology 1959. Career: pilot, Army Air Forces 1943-46, chief aerospace pathology Armed Forces Inst. of Pathology 1957-60; cons. FAA, USA 1961-75; cons. Civil Aeronautics Authority, Repub. of China, Taiwan 1967-73; clin. prof. of pathology Univ. of Wash. 1961-81; chief pathologist Northwest Hosp., Seattle, Wash. 1960-79; chief medical examiner-coroner County of Ventura 1981--; v.p. Lovell Auto Co., Astoria Ore, 1946-; honors: Profl. Svc. Citation, FAA 1975; Phi Beta Kappa 1949; Sigma Xi 1949; mem: Am. Acad. of Forensic Scis. 1983; Nat. Assn. Med. Examiners 1976; Rotary; Delta Upsilon; Phi Beta Pi; publs: num. publs. re aviation safety & the medical profession; mil: col., USAFR 1939-73 (ret.), Air Medal w/ 2 Clusters; Republican; Lutheran; rec: aviation, history, outdoors. Res: 5401 Topa Topa Dr Ventura 93003 Ofc: Ventura County Medical Examiner, 3291 Loma Vista Rd Ventura 93003

LOVELY, CLEMENT FRANCIS, real estate broker; b. July 24, 1909, St. Louis, Mo.; s. Clement Charles and Anna (Cleary) L.; m. Carmen Cruz, Aug. 20, 1962; children: June b. 1940, William b. 1944, Janet b. 1947; edn: BS, St. Louis Univ. 1933. Calif. lic. real estate broker 1974. Career: dir. of mktg. Amerace Corp., NYC 1962-63, International Dioxcide Inc. NYC 1963-70; ret. 1970-73; self-empl. realtor, 1974--, senior assoc. broker with Century 21 Jack Carter Realty Inc.; awards: 10 Million Dollar Club; mem: Chem. Mktg. Assn. (life); fmr. mem. Am. Chem. Soc., Tech. Assn. of Pulp & Paper Assn.; dir./v.p. Bernardo Home Owners Corp.; dir. Del Norte Corral of the Westerners (hist. assn.); dir. Rancho Bernardo Hist. Soc.; Rancho Bernardo Anglers Club, Rockhounds Club, Racquet Club; Mil. Order of World War Officers; patent: Pulverdent Chlorine Dioxide Compositions; num. articles in trade journals, 1962-69, relating to water treatment, sewage plant deoderizing; mil: lt. cmdr. USNR 1942-55, Am. Theatre, Pacific Theatre 2 Battle stars, Philippine Liberation medal; Republican; Christian; rec: tennis, equestrian, fishing. Res: 17076 Montura Dr San Diego 92128 Ofc: Century 21 Jack Carter Realty Inc. 12405 Rancho Bernardo Rd San Diego 92128

LOVETT, TERRY EDWIN, lawyer, real estate broker; b. Sept. 1, 1942, St. Claire, Mich.; s. Edwin Pharoe and Eva (Cookenmaster) L.; m. Janna Howe, May 5, 1977; children: Cory b. 1967, Dina b. 1968, Lon b. 1971, stepdaus: Lisa b. 1964, Laurie b. 1966; edn: grad. Hwy. Patrol Acad. 1966; JD, Southwestern Univ. Sch. of Law 1972; admitted to Calif. State Bar 1973; Calif. lic. Real Estate Broker 1978. Career: electronic engrg. Hughes Aircraft Co., Culver City 1963-66; Calif. Highway Patrolman 1966-73; pvt. law practice 1973--; real estate broker-developer, 1978--; co-owner Group Syndicated Investments (GSI) and American Pacific, both real estate and mgmt. cos., Westminster; v.p. adminstrn. The Management Team, Inc.; Gen. Ptnr. in num. Calif. Lmtd. Partnerships; lectr. seminars on R.E. investments, Immigration and Naturalization law in Hong Kong, Taiwan, Singapore (1983); mem. Calif. State Bar (hearing ofcr. Malpractice Com.), and local bar assns.; mem. Nat. Assn. of Realtors, Orange Co. Bd. of Realtors; Masons; mil: E3 USN 1960-63, Airborne Radio and Radar; rec: pvt. pilot, skiing, jogging. Res: 8821 Baywood Dr Huntington Bch 92646 Ofc: GSI & American Pacific, 9061 Bolsa Ave, Ste 204, Westminster 92683

LOWE, LAWRENCE CELO, insurance broker; b. Dec. 26, 1935, Palestine, Tex.; s. Byrd and Azell (Murchison) L.; children: Lawrence, b. 1960; Mark, b. 1961; Kevin, b. 1964; Peter, b. 1968; edn: AA, City Coll. of San Francisco 1956; San Francisco State 1956-57oe; Golden Gate Coll. of Law 1958. Career: mgr. Roos Atkins, Oakland 1958-61; mgr. Admarc Assoc., Berkeley 1961-63; mgr. Service Assoc., Inc., Oakland 1963-64; v.p. East Bay Ins. Mart Inc., Oakland 1964--; cons. Collier Encyclopedias 1960-61; honors: Informational Svc. Award of the Year, State of Calif., 1955; Grand Marshall, Miss America Contest, City of San Francisco 1955; mem: Alpha Phi (pres. 1955)); Franklin Canyon Golf and Country Club (pres. 1968-70); Oakland Chinese Golf Club; Democrat; Baptist; rec: golf. Res: Ballena Village, 1370 Third St 102, Alameda 94501 Ofc: East Bay Insurance Mart Inc., 3603 Piedmont Ave Oakland 94611

LUBACH, RINSE CORNELUS ANTONIUS, restaurateur; b. Jan. 20, 1911, Amsterdam, The Netherlands; s. Rinse Jan Augustinus and Maria Wilhelmina (Houtman) L.; m. Johanna Wilhelmina Vandeberge, Jan. 11, 1933; 1 son: Rinse Bob, b. 1936. Career: restaurant apprenticeship, The Netherlands, Europe (4 yrs.); supvr. feeding of French Olympic Athletes, Amsterdam 1928; asst. mgr. Bel-Air Country Club, Los Angeles 1937; later worked concurrently as food & beverage dir. Bel- Air Hotel, Ocean House, US Grant Hotel, San Diego; founder/owner Lubach's Restaurant, San Diego 1956--; dir. Emeritus of Calif. Restaraunt Assn.; v.consul The Netherlands in San Diego 1958-; awards: titled Knight in the Order of Orange-Nassau (one of The Netherlands highest honors), by Queen Juliana 1977; Americanism Medal, Daughters of the Revolution 1980; mem: San Diego Conv. & Visitors Bureau (past pres.), chmn. CONVIS Cruise Ship Com., and vice chmn. Cruise Ind. Consortium; Rotary; Central City Assn.; Combined Health Agencies Drive. Res: 10309 Grand View Dr La Mesa 92041 Ofc: Lubach's, 2101 N Harbor Dr San Diego 92101

LUCERO, BARBARA LUCILLE, interior decorator; b. Oct. 9, 1920, Tilorn, Nebr.; d. Russel D. and Emma L. (Hayes) Roseborough; m. Edward Lucero, Oct. 1, 1948; 1 dau: Donna Rae, b. 1942; edn: costume design, Trade Tech. Coll. 1950-53; AA, Pasadena City Coll. 1979. Career: owner Jo-Baba Interiors, Los Angeles 1954--, Amway Distbr. 1980--; honors: Amway Distributorship Silver Inner Circle 1980, Gold Inner Circle 1981, Retail Awd. 1983, Producer Awd. 1983; Democrat; Catholic; rec: gardening, sewing, crosswords. Address: Jo-Baba Interiors, 1441 Paso Real, Ste 99, Rowland Heights 91748

LUDEMAN, BARTON LEE, human resources executive; b. Mar. 27, 1930, Pueblo, Colo.; s. Rudolph C and Lois E. (Irwin) L.; edn: BSBA, advt. journ., Univ. of Coll. 1952, MPS in personnel svcs., 1957. Career: employment interviewer US Dept. of Employment 1956-59; asst. dir. of personnel Univ. of Denver 1959-63, coll. relations coord. First Western Bank, dir. trng., human resources devel. dir., asst. dir. personnel Lloyds Bank Calif. 1963-80; pres. Bart Ludeman Assoc., Inc. 1980--; trainer seminars for Univ. of Denver, UCLA, Rio Hondo Comm. Coll.; guest instr./ lectr. CSU Long Beach and Northridge; awards: Gordon Bliss Awd., ASTD 1975; mem: Am. Soc. for Tng. & Devel. (pres. 1978); Am. Soc. for Personnel Admin.; Assessment Ctr. Congress; Calif. Cooperative Edn. Assn. (pres.-elec. 1977); Nat. Assn. for Indus.- Edn. Cooperation (bd. dirs. 1981-); publs: articles in ednl. journals, most recently: In the Private Sector, There is a Choice (New Directions for Cont. Edn., 10/81), Assessment... Measuring Management Skills to Increase Productivity (League for Innovation in Comm. Colls. 1982), A Strategy for Business- Synergy at Work (Bus. to Bus. 7/83); mil: USAF 1952-56; Republican; Episcopal; rec: writing, politics, marketing. Res: 6737 Stearns St Long Beach 90815 Ofc: 1379 E 28th St Signal Hill 90806

LUDLUM, DOUGLAS KENT, distribution executive; b. May 16, 1949, Alva, Okla.; s. Robert A. and Bonnie J. (Roberts) L.; m. Sandra G. Baker, May 24, 1970; children: Christopher, b. 1975; Michelle, b. 1977; edn: Univ. of the Americas, Mex. City; AA, Golden West Coll. 1971; BS, CSU Long Beach 1975. Career: area mgr. K-Mart, Montclair 1974-76; asst. controller Glastron- Carlson, Anaheim 1976-77; indsl. engr. Customfininshing, Westminster 1977-79; controller/ gen. mgr. LaSalle-Deitch Co., Tustin 1979--, cons./ owner Sandi & Assoc. 1979-, awards: Comm. Leadership awds., Irvine Co. 1981-83; mem: Lions Club; Walnut Maint. Assn. (past pres.); Heritage Park Homeowners Assn. (pres.); works: Tech. Bulliten trade, gen. mgmt. 9/83; Republican; Methodist; rec: computer science, camping, foster child program. Res: 1 Heritage Irvine 92714 Ofc: LaSalle-Deitch Co., 215 W First St, Ste 105-1, Tustin 92680

LUFRANO, ANTHONY ALBERT, social work agency executive director; b. Mar. 18, 1940, McKees Rocks, Penna.; s. Albert Charles and Phyllis (Magnelli) L.; m. Mary Kay Stanton, Nov. 14, 1970; children: Chris, b. 1973; Matthew, b. 1975; Patrick, b. 1978; edn: BA, Univ. of Pittsburgh 1962; MSW, 1964; ACSW, Acad. Cert. Soc. Wkrs. 1966. Career: director guidance & counseling/ coord. Domestic Peace Corps for the Boys Club of McKees Rocks, Inc., McKees Rocks, Penna. 1964-66; coord. Volunteer Svcs. of Alegheny Co., Pitts., Penna. 1966-69; assoc. dir./ dir. of plng. & allocations United Way of Mercer City, Sharon, Penna. 1969-72; assoc. dir./ dir. plng. United Way of Allen Co., Ft. Wayne, Ind. 1972-76; agcy. rels./ plng./ budget dir. Region V, United Way of Los Angeles, L.A. 1976-78; assoc. exec. v.p. Crippled Childrens Soc. of L.A., 1978-82; currently, pres./ chief exec. ofcr. Family Service of Los Angeles; former P/T instr. soc. scis. & humanities, Penna. State Univ., St. Francis Coll., Ft. Wayne, Ind.; cons. MBO & Fundraising to sev. agencies; devel. Crippled Childrens Soc.'s World's Greatest Working Truck Show 1981; awards: Boy of the Yr., Boys Club of Am. 1958; Nat. Hon. Awd., for Pgm. Excellence 1966; Spl. Awd. Outstanding Leadership, Crippled Childrens Soc. 1982; United Way Leadership Awd. 1969-78; Architectural Awd., Soc. of Am. Reg. Archs. & SFV sect. Am. Inst. Archs. 1983; mem: ACSW; NASW; Am. Camping Assn.; Scouting for Handicapped Com.; L.A. Co. Council of Voluntary Agencies; Evaluation & Strategic Plng., Family Svc. Am.; Pub. Rels. Com., Western Reg., Family Svc. Am.; Consortium of So. Calif. Family Svc. Agencies; Univ. Club of L.A.; works: Serving the Handicapped- A Coordinated Approach for Mercer County, Pa. & Brookfield Township, O., Sharon, Pa. -1970; Community Perceptions of Human Needs & Services in Allen Co., Fort Wayne, Ind. 1976; rec: theatre, painting, song writing. Res: 18820 Dukas St Northridge 91326 Ofc: Family Service of L.A., 1521 Wilshire Blvd Los Angeles 90017

LUGASH, JEFFREY BRENT, lawyer; b. Nov. 15, 1940, Cleveland, Ohio; s. Sam and Lillian (Schuster) L.; m. Susan Levitt, Aug. 30, 1970; children: Spencer Brent, b. 1972; Blake Lawrence, b. 1977; edn: AA, Los Angeles City Coll. 1961; BA, UCLA 1963; JD, Hastings Coll. of Law 1966. Career: atty., sole practitioner (spec. civil litigation) 1969--; (received possibly first punitive damage awd. against parents & grandparents for child stealing); bd. dirs. Dr. Pepper Bottling Co., So. Calif. 1974; judge pro-tem, W. L.A. Municipal Ct., Small Claims Div. 1980-83; arbitrator, Los Angeles Co. Bar Assn. Com. on Atty.- Client Rels. 1979-83; City of Commerce Indsl. Council/ CofC Basic Bd. Dirs. 1982-83; directing atty. City of Commerce Indsl. Council's Gp. Legal Plan 1980-83; honors: Justice (pres.), Jackson Temple chpt. Phi Alpha Delta law frat. 1965-66; Pres. Gr. Los Angeles chpt. Hastings Coll. of Law Alumni Assn. 1982; mem: L.A. Co. Bar Assn.; L.A. Trial Lawyers Assn.; Assn. Bus. Trial

Lawyers; Beverly Hills Mens Profl. Assn.; Hastings Coll. of Law Alumni Assn.; City of Hope (Founders Gp.); founder mem./dir. Calif. Citizens Action Gp.; Republican; Jewish; rec: tennis, golf, skiing. Res: 4369 Hayvenhurst Ave Encino 91436 Ofc: Jeffrey B. Lugash, 6055 E Washington Blvd, Ste 721, Commerce 90040

LUHN, ROBERT KENT, writer, editor; b. Nov. 25, 1953, Oakland; s. Joel Adrian and Norma Jeanne (Arnold) L.; m. Alison Shiroma, Oct. 12, 1983; edn: AB, UC Davis 1976. Career: free lance writer, credits: PC World, PC, PC Welt, Media and Methods, American Film, Dramatics, Paper Cinema, The Hudson Review, Book Forum, The San Francisco Chronicle, The Nantucket Review, Executive Update, Owlflight, Grapevine Weekly, Different Drummer; assoc. editor PC World Magazine; market research analyst Decision Devel. Corp. 1981-83; honors: New West Writers' Award (1977); listed, Who's Who in the West (1984), Who's Where Among Writers (1983); mem: No. Calif. Science Writers Assn.; ACLU; AFI; Common Cause Now; Found. for Nat. Progress; Southern Poverty Law Ctr.; author: More Words At Play (St. Martins), book anthologies: Horizon Press Editions (1983); Democrat; rec: writing, tennis. Res: 2674 A Baldwin Ln Walnut Creek 94596 Ofc: PC World, 555 De Haro St San Francisco 94177

LUKE, SHERRILL DAVID, judge; b. Sept. 19, 1928, Los Angeles; s. Mordecai David (dec.) and Venye Alfasetta (Richards) L.; m. Anne Bradford, Aug. 22, 1959; children: David, b. 1960; Melana, b. 1962; edn: BA, UCLA 1950; MA, UC Berkeley 1954; JD, Golden gate univ. 1960. Career: asst. city mgr., Richmond 1953-61; urban affairs secty., Gov.'s Ofc., Sacto. 1961-65; atty. at law, L.A. 1965-67; dir. pgm. devel. Mayor's Ofc., Wash. DC 1967-69; urban affairs dir. Aetna Life & Casulty, Hartford, Ct. 1969-73; atty. at law, L.A. 1973-78; chief. dep. assessor, L.A. Co. 1978-81; judge of the municipal ct., L.A. Judicial Dist. 1981--; con. Ford Found. 1966; dir. Urban Design & Devel. Corp. 1969-70; adj. prof. Loyola Law Sch. 19979-; student body pres., UCLA 1949-50; pres. L.A. City Plng. Commn. 1973-76; lectr. Cont. Edn. of the Bar 1980-81; mem: Kappa Alpha Psi, Upsilon chpt. (pres. 1948-50); UCLA Alumni Assn. (gen. counsel 1966-67; v.p. Scholarships & Admissions 1975); The UCLA Found.; Lambda Alpha land econs. hon.; mil: 1st lt. USAF 1954-56; Democrat (Calif. Demo. Council); Unitarian; rec: tennis, running. Res: 286 Trino Way Pacific Palisades 90272 Ofc: Los Angeles Judicial Ditrict, 110 N Grand Ave Los Angeles 90012

LUM, MARGARET CHAN, lawyer; b. Sept. 20, 1929, Sacramento; d. Si Chon and Liang Shee (Liange) Chan; m. Tom Lum, Nov. 23, 1958; children: Paul L., b. 1959; Thomas G., b. 1961; edn: AA, Sacto. City Coll. 1949; BS, Stanford Univ. 1952; BA, UC San Francisco 1970 and CSU Sacto. 1971; JD, McGeorge Sch. of Law, Univ. of the Pacific 1979; admitted to practice, Calif. State Bar 1980. Career: staff nurse S.F. Visiting Nse. Assn. 1952-55; school nurse San Juan Unified Sch. Dist. 1955-61, Fairfield Unif. Sch. Dist. 1967-70, Travis Unif. Sch. Dist. 1970-76; part-time staff nse. Summer Migrant Camp, Solano County Hlth Dept 1967-70; atty. at law pvt. practice, solo 1981-81, assoc. Moe & Lum, 1981--; mem. Yolo-Solano Air Pollutin Control Dist. Hearing Bd. 1983-; legal cons. Ong Ko Met Assn. 1982-; dir. Lum & Young Farms, Inc. 1972-; awards: scholarship, Am. Assn. of Univ. Women 1949; mem: Calif. State Bar (Estate Plng. & Bus. Law sects.); Solano Co. Bar Assn.; Asian Bar Assn., Sacto.; Am. Immigration Lawyers Assn.; Calif. Women Lawyers; McGeorge & Stanford Alumni Assns.; Calif., Calif. Sch. & Stanford Nurses Assns.; Calif. Tchrs. Assn.; Dixon CofC; Soroptimists; Dixon Womens Network; Enchanted Hills Aux.; Sacto. Symphony Assn.; Chinese Culture Found.; Calif. Women for Agric.; publs: pub., Journal of School Health, Vol. XLIII, No. 6, 1973; asst. nurse ofcr., US Pub. Health Svc. Reserves 1952-60; Comm. Ch.; rec: Chinese antique coins, art objects & cooking; travel. Res: 805 Hillview Dr Dixon 95620 Ofc: Moe & Lum, 805 N Lincoln St Dixon 95620

LUM, MORRIS HARVEY, real estate broker; b. Mar. 5, 1954, Sacramento; s. Thornton and Betty BQ (Yee) L.; edn: Sacto. City Coll.; Am. River Coll.; GRI (Grad. Realtors Inst.), Calif. Assn. Realtors 1978; CREA (Cert. R.E. Appraiser), Calif. Assn. R.E. Appraisers 1983. Career: real estate salesman Rylander & Co., Sacto. 1973-74, ERA/ Rylander, Sacto. 1974-75; tng. & sales mgr. Home Finders Realtors, Sacto. 1975-79; real estate salesman Better Homes Realty, Rancho Cordova 1979-81; owner/ broker The Lum Co., Realtors 1981--; awards: Top Producer, ERA/ Rylander & Co., Realtors 1974; mem: Nat. Assn. Realtors; Calif. Assn. Realtors (Real Estate Syndication Div.); Sacto. Bd. Realtors; Calif. Assn. Real Estate Appraisers (senior mem.); Ben Ali Keystone Cop Patrol (1st lt. 1984), Emir Shrine Club, Ben Ali Temple; Scottish Rite Freemasonry, Valley of Sacto.; Zorah Grotto, M.O.V.P.E.R. of Sunnyvale; Concord Lodge, Sacto.; Am. River Lodge, Rancho Cordova; Chinese Acacia Club of Oakland, S.F.; Romeo Owners Club. Address: The Lum Company, Realtors, 331 22nd St Sacramento 95816

LUM, PAUL, real estate broker; b. Aug. 8, 1949, San Francisco; s. Quan and May Lum; m. Arlene, Aug. 15, 1971; children: Cheryl b. 1972, David b. 1977, Michel b. 1981; edn: AA in real estate, Merritt Coll.; BA, San Francisco St. Univ. 1973; Calif. lic. R.E. Broker, Contractor, Notary Public; RECI, Real Estate Cert. Inst. Career: real estate sales Land West Realty, 1972-78; owner/ pres. Parkgate Realty & Investment Co. Inc., 1978--; mgr. 250rental units and commercial bldgs. in Oakland, 1973--; owner Parkgate Property Mgmt. 1979-; awards: recognition, Kiwanis Intl. (coached Spl. Olympics), Oakland Better Bus. Bur., Oakland CofC; mem. Calif. Assn. of Realtors (State dir. 3 yrs; life mem. PAC); Oakland Bd. of Realtors (dir. 1980-, chmn. Traders Marketing Club); Alameda Apartment House Assn. (bd. dirs.); sponsor, Oakland Chinese Comm. Council Inc., Red Cross -Housing, Housing Authority, Citizen for Better Oakland 1983-; mem. Toastmasters (adm. v.p.), Oakland Athletic Club. Address: Parkgate Realty & Investment Co. Inc. 262 Grand Ave Ste. 100, Oakland 94610

LUND, SVEN GEORGE, importer/manufacturer saunas; b. Dec. 23, 1930, Sweden; nat. 1961; s. Josef and Maria Edla (Lindgren) Lund; m. Gerda Hevroy, Dec. 18, 1967; Calif. lic. Gen. Bldg. Contractor, 1970. Career: gen. builder, finished carpentry, Chgo. 1956-63, San Francisco 1963-, spec. in sauna baths 1964-, prop. Sven's Sauna, Mill Valley 1967-84, San Rafael 1984--; mfr. pre-fab sauna kits, importer TYLO Heaters; architl. cons. sauna design. Mem. Swedish Am. CofC; Mt. Tam Racquet Club; works: miniature model sauna rooms; mil: Swedish Air Force 1950; Republican; Lutheran; rec: reading, tennis, soccer. Res: 115 William Ave Larkspur 94939 Ofc: Sven's Sauna Tylo Heaters, 3070 Kerner Blvd., L, San Rafael 94901

LUNDBERG, DONALD LEE VERN, educator; b. Aug. 11, 1915, Red Oak, Iowa; s. Charles A. and Ada B. (Swanson) L.; m. Mildred Peaslee (dec. 1976); m. 2d. Verna Stover Aug. 4, 1983; children: Suzanne b. 1948, Carl b. 1950, Eric b. 1958; edn: BA, State Univ. of Iowa 1938; BS in BA, USC 1941; MA, CSC Stanislaus 1966; Nat. Univ. of Mexico (summer) 1937; Tchg. credentials: Iowa (1938), Calif. (1955), Pupil Personnel Counseling (1957). Career: high sch. tchr. Arthur, Iowa 1938-39, H.S. & Jr. Coll. tchr. Creston, Iowa 1948-54; Fulbright tchg. grantee, Aleppo, Syria 1954-55; tchr. Thomas Downey H.S., Modesto, Calif. 1955-57, counselor, 1957-65, estab. the Am. Field Svc. Program and Tchr. Asst. Pgm.; counselor Modesto Jr. Coll. 1965-76, estab. the Peer Tutoring Pgm., dir. Internat. Student Pgm.; ret.; owner/mgr. 3 ranches; honors: 9th fastest marathon runner in 65-69 age group nationally and fastest 10K runner age 68 in 1982, Nat. Data Running Center, Tucson; life mountain climber, all peaks in Mexico, all 14,000 ft. peaks on West Coast, many climbs in Europe, S.A., and Himalayas. Mem: Nat. Assn. of Foreign Student Affairs, local, state, nat. edn. assns.; pres. Modesto Toastbreakers Toastmasters 1960; pres. Waterford Lions Club 1982-3; ch. YMCA World Service Com. 1981-82; Audubon Soc. (donor $100,000 to buy land for wildlife refuge Stanislaus County 1978); active lifelong in conservation projects; mil: s/sgt. USAF 1942-46, S.W. Pacific. Res: 2113 Patterson Rd Modesto 95355

LUNDBERG, JAN CHRISTIAN, energy information co. executive; b. Aug. 2, 1952, Mex.; s. Daniel and Mesa Vernell (Dobson) Lundberg; edn: Ecole Des Roches, Overseas Sch. of Rome; Am. Comml. Sch. of Athens, Greece; UCLA; UC Riverside. Career: mgr. Share of Market, Lundberg Survey, Inc., 1972-5; editor Lundberg Letter, 1973-6, pub. 1976-8, contbg. ed. 1979-; pres. Independent MarketSurvey, 1976-7; v.p. Lundberg Survey, Inc., No. Hollywood 1979--. Publs: contbg. author (chpt. 1), Energy and Sea Power, Pergamon Press, recorded 2 albums, Prologue; rec: sailing, racquetball. Address: Lundberg Survey, Inc. PO Box 3996, No. Hollywood 91609

LUNDELL, DONALD RUSSELL, engineering executive; b. Sep. 7, 1940, Benjamin, Utah; s. Russell T. and Leola (Tanner) L.; m. Gail Peters, Jun. 1, 1963; children: Russell, b. 1964; John, b. 1966; Suzanne, b. 1969; Victoria, b. 1972; David, b. 1975; Robert, b. 1977. Edn: AA, E. Ariz. Jr. Coll. 1959; BS in EE. Univ. Ariz. 1964; MSEE, Santa Clara Univ. 1968. Career: various engring. and mgmt. positions, IBM Corp., 1964-82; sr. v.p. of engring. Atasi Corp., 1982--; lectr. physics San Jose St. Univ. 1970-71. Awards: Silver Beaver, BSA, 1980. Republican; Mormon. Res: 3290 Godfrey Ave Gilroy 95020 Ofc: Atasi Corp., 2075 Zanker Rd San Jose 95139

LUNDGREN, CARL GUNARD, dentist; b. July 30, 1924, Provo, Utah; s. John G. and Hazel Marie (Olsen); m. Marjorie, June 15, 1973; children: Christine (Cummings) b. 1951, Cynthia b. 1952, Ronald b. 1953, Barbara (Tippins) b. 1956; edn: AA, Compton Coll. 1943; DDS, USC, 1946. Career: naval dental ofcr. USNR 1946-48; dental intern Los Angeles County Hosp. 1949; gen. dentist pvt. practice, Hawthorne 1949-74, Lawndale 1974--; asst. clin. prof. USC Sch. of Dentistry 1971-76; awards: Calif. Assembly Resolution 1975, Hawthorne CofC Service Awd. 1980; life mem. USC Dental Assocs. 1982; mem: Fellow Acad. of Gen. Dentistry (1975; So. Calif. Editor), Fellow Internat. Coll. of Dentists (1977, Editor Dist. 13), Fellow Acad. of Dentistry Internat. (1982), Western Dental Soc. (pres. 1977, Editor 1979-81), Am. Dental Assn., Calif. Dental Assn. (del. 1977); mem. Hawthorne Kiwanis (pres. 1957, Legion of Honor Award), CofC (pres. 1967), YMCA (pres. 1969), Hawthorne Parade chmn. 28 yrs.; publs: 24 editorials in dental journals; TV appearances re dentistry (Jerry Lewis Telethon 1977, NBC Health Fair 1978; dental spokesman num. seminars, orgns.; mil: lt. (jg) USNR 1946-48; Republican; Prot.; rec: scuba diving, underwater photog., tennis. Res: 59 Silver Saddle Ln Rolling Hills Est. 90274 Ofc: Carl Lundgren, DDS Inc. 14722 Hawthorne Blvd Lawndale 90260

LUNENSCHLOSS, EDWARD VINCENT, manufacturing co. consultant; b. Feb. 18, 1930, Los Angeles; s. Edward Joseph and Mary Mae (Daugherty) L.; m. Joyce Shoneberg, Sept. 28, 1952, div. 1981; children: Eric, b. 1962; Kristen, b. 1964; edn: AA, Univ. of Hawaii; BS, Northrop Univ., Los Angeles; Gen. Contractor Lic., Calif. Career: chief engr./ partner Mason Electric Corp. 1963-67; pres./ gen. mgr. ERA Mfg. Corp. 1967-69; gen. mgr. Air Pax Pacific Div. Ferrodyne Corp., 1969-75, pres./ gen. mgr. 1975-79; small bus. consultant 1979--, cons. engring. & mktg./ dir. Knuth Hinge Co., Inglewood; cons. GLM Ent.; advr. (past dir.) San Gabriel Valley Bank; assoc. dir. Impact Drug Rehab. Houses; recipient Hon. Awd., Impact Drug Rehabilitation Houses 1978; mem: Am. Mgmt. Assn., Hamilton, NY; Consultant Capacities Gp., NY; Rotarian; Impact Drug Rehab. Houses (past pres.); commnr. L.A. Co. Obscenity & Pornography Commn. (past chmn. 2 terms); patents (14) relating to switches &

relays; mil: ensign USN, dischg. 1951; Republican; Catholic; rec: scuba diving. Res: 1417 Greenfield Arcadia 91006 Ofc: Knuth Hinge Co., 509 S Hindry Ave Inglewood 90301

LUONG, SANH CAM, telecommunications engineer; b. Dec. 3, 1957, Saigon, Vietnam; s. Kim and Lien Phung (Trinh) L.; edn: BS, honors, CSU Los Angeles 1982; MS, 1984; engr.-in-tng. Calif. State Bd. Reg. Profl. Engrs. 1983. Career: supt. Animal Food Experimental Farm, Saigon, Vietnam 1975-78; spl. asst. United Nations High Commnr. for Refugees (UNHCR), Bangkok, Thailand 1978-79; tchr. asst. Castelar Elem. Sch., Los Angeles, part- time 1979-82; commun. engr., microwave sys. & telephone network design, Los Angeles Dept. of Water & Power, Los Angeles 1982--; honors: Tau Beta Pi; Phi Kappa Phi; Eta Kappa Nu; Pi Delta Pi; mem: IEEE; Communication Soc.; Power Engrs. Club; Christian; rec: tennis. Res: 1302 Shamwood, West Covina 91790 Ofc: Los Angeles Department of Water & Power, 1216 W 1st St Los angeles 90026

LUPER, ARCHIE WILLIAM, restaurateur/entrepreneur; b. Jan. 12, 1912, Elk City, Okla.; s. Wm. Andrew and Elizabeth Sarah (Sharp) L.; m. Francile Jeanette Sands, Jan. 20, 1941; children: Denese b. 1954, Archie, Jr. b. 1956; grad. public schs. Drumright, Okla.; stu. culinary arts, Cordon Bleu Sch. (Paris), Montana Hotel and Restaurant Sch. (Lucerne, Switz.). Career: estab. food service bus. in Okla. 1941-; opened 1st Loop's restaurant in Ventura, Calif. 1947-, founder/owner/opr. 13 restaurants, 3 cafeterias, wholesale and retail bakery, 96 unit motor-hotel, produce co., and other ents., 1947--; named to American Restaurant Mag. Hall of Fame (1960); bd. dirs. Calif. Restaurant Assn.; bd. dirs. (co-chmn.) Four Seas Coll. Singapore; bd. trustees City of Hope, Los Angeles; Church of Christ preacher and missionary advisor internat.; spkr. num. seminaries & Bible Colls., civic meetings; author Loop's Cook Book (1965), Loop's Franchise Manual (1965), God's Angel in China (1984); biography pub. in God Is My Partner (Roberts and Sons 1984); invention: Rubber Sleeve for Amphibious Jeeps to keep water out of differential gears and transmission (1941); Republican; Ch. of Christ; rec: travel. Res: 215 Lang St Ventura 93003 Ofc: Luper Enterprises Inc. 3159 E. Main St Ventura 93003

LUPINI, FRANK, engineer; b. June 27, 1945, Perugia, Italy, nat. 1963; s. Amedeo and Irma (Mattiacci) L.; m. Ilia Prosepe, June 24, 1978; children: Stephen b. 1979, Daniel b. 1982; edn: BS in engring., CSU Los Angeles 1967, MS, in E.E. 1970. Calif. Real Estate lic. Career: senior systems engr. Avionic self defensive systems (B-52, F-15, F-111, B-1), rockwell Internat., Anaheim 1967-71; sr. engr. (design & devel. DD-963 Combat Sys.), Litton Indus. Culver City 1971-72; dir. sys. integration (aircraft carrier anti-ship missile defense) Hughes Aircraft Co., Fullerton 1972-76, hd. Foreign Systems Gp. (electronic def. sys.), 1976--; condr. seminars on Electronic Warfare; honors: Tau Beta Pi, Eta Kappa Nu; mem. IEEE, Assn. of Old Crows; founding pres. Italian Young Adult Catholic Club of Los Angeles, 1971-76; Alpha Phi Omega nat. svc. frat.; publs: sci. paper, Military Electronics Expo., Anaheim (1979); Catholic; rec: ski, hunt, fish, travel. Res: 2215 Seaview Dr Fullerton 92633 Ofc: Hughes Aircraft Co 1901 Malvern Ave M.S. 618/P-415, Fullerton 92634

LUPTON, RALPH LEANDER, workers compensation appeals board judge, ret.; b. May 31, 1906, Toledo, Ia.; s. John Lawrence and Susan Louise (Clark) L.; grandfather, Leander Clark, co. judge, Tama Co., Ia. (legislator, Ia. House Reps., lt. col. Union Army, Civil War); m. Winifred Lowe, Dec. 30, 1933, dec. 1970; children: Leslie Ann, b. 1938; William, b. 1942; edn: Cornell Coll., Ia. 1024-26; BS, Northwestern Univ. 1928; JD, 1931. Career: gen. law practice, Iowa 1931-38; asst. auditor Occidental Coll., L.A., Calif. 1938-39; auditor Sales tax div. State Bd. of Equalization, L.A. 1940-41; head legal dept. 1942; sr. trial atty./ head of subrogation dept. State Compensation Ins. Fund, in Law of Subrogation 1944-57; judge Workers Compensation Appeals Bd. 1957-69, ret.; instr. Claims Dept. State Compensation Ins. Fund, Law of Subrogation 1944-47; awards: Gold Medal, winner Big Ten & Nat. Wrestling Championship 1926-29 (125- pound class); Hall of Fame, Cornell College 1974, All American Honor Roll, Northwestern Univ. 1928; mem: Phi Delta Theta; Beta Gamma Sigma; Phi Alpha Delta; Elks; Lions (Lion Tamer); Sierra Club; Wilderness Soc.; Audubon Soc.; Nat. Parks & Conservation Assn.; Nat., Calif. & Iowa Bar Assns.; publs: contbr. law journals and revs.; Workmens Compensation Law, Due Process: Conduct of Trial, Examination and Cross Examination, for judges of state compensation appeals bd., 1969; Democrat; Methodist (deacon); rec: mtn. climbing (Mt. Whitney 10 times), dancing, bridge, historical novels. Res: 1516 Rock Glenn Ave 208, Glendale 91205

LUPU, ANDREI NICOLAE, urologist; b. June 11, 1924, Bucharest, Romania, nat. 1969; s. Nicolae Gheorghe and Elena Maria (Limburg) L.; m. Helga, Aug. 12, 1972; children: Elena Maria, b. 1973; Nicolae Andrei, b. 1975; edn: BS, Lyceum Titu Maioerescu, Bucharest 1942; MD, & D.Sc., Univ. of Bucharest 1949; intern, Med. Faculty, Hosp. Floreasca, Univ Bucharest 1948 51; resident UCLA Sch. of Med. 1972-75; MD, Bd. Cert. Urologist, Calif. 1974. Career: instr. surgery Univ. Bucharest, Hosp. Floreasca, 1948-51, Hosp. Coltea 1951-57; fellow urology Hosp. Ed Herriot, Univ. of Lyon, France 1958-59; fellow surgery/ urology UCLA Sch. of Med. 1960-61; research surgeon UCLA Dept. of Physiology 1963-72; clin. instr. surgery/ urology UCLA Sch. of Med. 1975-77; co-chief urology sect., Sepulveda VA Hosp. 1975--; chief div. of urology Olive View Med. Ctr., Van Nuys 1976--; asst. prof. surgery/ urology UCLA Sch. of Med. 1977-81; assocp prof. surgery/ urology 1981--; awards: for scientific exhibits, Western Sect. Am. Urological Assn.; mem: Royal Soc. of Med.; Am., Calif. & L.A. Co. Med. Assns.; L.A. Urological Soc.; Soc. of Govt. Svc. Urologists; fellow, Societe Internationale D'Urologie; Am. Urological Assn. (Western sect.); Assn. of Clin. Urologists; Am. Coll. Surgeons (Urological sect. rep., So. Calif. chpt.); Am. Heart Assn.; Assn. of Mil. Surgeons of US; Willard E. Goodwin Soc.; Am. Assn. for Adv. of Sci.; Pacific Palisades Tennis Club; num. publs. in sci. journs. 1945-; mil: lt. Romanian Army 1942-44; rec: pianist, tennis. Ofc: Division of Urology, UCLA Medical Center, 10833 Le Conte Ave Los Angeles 90024

LURIE, ABRAHAM M., real property management firm president; b. Nov. 21, 1923, Des Moines, Ia.; s. Nathan and Tillie (Livingston) L.; children: Leslie (Ralston), b. 1951; Scott, b. 1956; edn: BS, Ohio State Univ. 1948; grad. studies, Loyola Univ. Law Sch. 1952-53; UCLA Law Sch. 1953-54. Career: CPA, Leonard & Jacobson; CPA, Touche, Niven & Co. 1948-53; solo acctg. practice 1953-57; lawyer/CPA dual practice, 1957-64; senior partner Lurie & Skaug (CPA firm), Beverly Hills 1968-73; CPA, Braverman, Lurie & Co., Beverly Hills. 1968-73; chmn. bd./ pres. Real Property Mgmt., Inc., Marina del Rey 1973--; honors: Man of the Yr., Boys & Girls Club of Venice 1981; Citizen of the Yr., Marina del Rey CofC 1981; mem: Calif. Bar Assn.; Am. Assn. of Atty./ CPAs; County of L.A. Economy & Effiency Commn. (Comm. Rels. Task Force); L.A. World Affairs Council; Co. of L.A. Land Devel. Coordinating Ctr. Advis. Com.; mil: pvt., Infan., US Army 1943-46. Res: Los Angeles; Ofc: Real Property Management, Inc., 444 Washington St Marina del Rey 90291

LURIE, KAREN ANN, corporate controller; b. Oct. 24, 1957, Jersey City, NJ; d. Hilbert and Patricia Louise (McKnight) L.; edn: BS, USC 1980. Career: staff acct. Owens- Illinois Forest Prods. Div., Los Angeles 1977-78; corp. controller Armstrong Pacific Corp., Santa Fe Springs 1980--; honors: Miss California Teenager, Miss America Teenager, Inc. 1975; mem: American Mensa, Ltd. 1980-; Phi Beta Phi; USC Orange Co. Young Alumni Club; Republican; Presbyterian, Protestant; rec: needlwork, sports, travel. Res: 14420 E Eastridge Dr Whittier 90602 Ofc: Armstrong Pacific Corporation, 11845 E Telegraph Rd Santa Fe Springs 90670

LUSKEY, ROBERT L., JR., publishing company executive; b. Jan. 31, 1941, Roanoke, VA; s. R. Lee and Elsie Vera (Reid) Luskey; Edn: BA, USC, 1963; m. Margaret Langhans, Feb. 20, 1965; div.; chil: Robert Lee III, b. 1966; Matthew Christian, b. 1968. Career: sales rep., Luskey Brothers & Co., Inc., Anaheim, 1963; pub. rels. dir., 1964; v.p., 1966; exec. v.p., 1971; pres., 1981; exec. comm. mem.: Natl. Yellow Pages Service Assn. 1980-83, Assn. No. American Directory Publishers 197483, Western Independent Directory Publisher Assn. 1977-79. Mem: pres., Western Independent Directory Publishers, 2 terms; pres., Assn. North American Directory Publishers, 2 terms; v.p., Natl. Yellow Pages Service Assn.; Theta Chi frat., Beta Tau chpt., pres. Mil: SSgt. (E-6), Calif. State Natl. Guard, 1970. Democrat. Roman Catholic. Rec: theatre, opera, writing. Res: 14 Blue Lagoon, So. Laguna 92651; Office: Luskey Brothers & Co., Inc., 608 E. Broadway, Anaheim 92805.

LUSKIN, BERNARD JAY, community college president; b. June 3, 1937, Pittsburgh, Pa.; s. Morris and Esther (Helfand) L.; 1 son: Ryan, b. 1966; edn: AA, Long Beach City Coll. 1959; BA, CSU Los Angeles 1961; MA, CSU Long Beach 1964; EdD, UCLA 1970. Career: bus. instr. Roosevelt H.S., Los Angeles 1959-60; bus. instr. Costa Mesa H.S., Costa Mesa 1960-63; prof. bus. & computer sci. Orange Coast Coll., Costa Mesa 1963-65; dean fed. proj./ assn. dir. vocational edn./ assoc. dean admissions & records Orange Coast Coll., Costa Mesa 1965-69; v.chancellor ednl. plng. & devel. Coast Comm. Coll. Dist., Costa Mesa 1969-76; pres. Coastline Comm. Coll., Fountain Valley 1976-82; pres. Orange Coast Coll., Costa Mesa 1982--; adj. prof. Claremont Grad. Sch., and Pepperdine Univ.; coord. doctoral practicum in adminstrn., Kellogg Fellow, University Fellow, UCLA, 1967-70; Govt. Rels. Splst. Pgm. 1972; honors: Outstanding Graduating Senior in Bus. Edn., CSU Los Angeles 1961; Hall of Fame, Long Beach City Coll. 1980; UCLA Distng. Leadership. Awd. 1982; mem: Am. Assn. Comm. & Jr. Colls. (chmn. bd. dirs.; chmn. Commn. of Cont. Edn.); Nat. Council for Resource Devel.; Task Force of Calif. State Univs. & Colls. Gen. Edn. Breadth Policy; Nat. Sci. Found. Adv. Commn.; author: 6 books, 4 monographs, 45 arts., 1 film, 1 TV series (20 half-hrs., nom. Emmy, won John Swett Awd.); mil: USN 1956-58; rec: swimming, fishing. Res: 16621 Melville Circle Huntington Beach 92649 Ofc: Orange Coast Coll., 2701 Fairview Rd, POB 5005, Costa Mesa 92628

LUTCHANSKY, HERMAN, real estate executive; b. Jan. 23, 1925, Detroit, Mich.; edn: Western State Univ. Coll. of Law, 2 yrs.; Calif. Comm. Coll. Lifetime Tchr. cred.; GRI, Grad. Realtors Inst. Career: wholesale food bus., Detroit and San Diego, 27 yrs.; current: real estate broker, cons., owner/ investor, instr., property mgr., syndicator; pres. King Midas Real Estate Corp., San Diego; author/publisher: The Real World of RE Investing (8th ed.); instr. Calif. Contg. Edn. Pgm.; mem. San Diego Bd. of Realtors, NAR, CAR, Real Estate Securities and Syndication Inst., Nat. Council of Exchangors (Gold Card), sev. exchange groups; Masons, Shriners; mil: USN, GCM. Res: 2428 Amity St San Diego 92109 Ofc: 950 Hotel Circle, North, Ste G, San Diego 92108

LYNGE, NANCY BORDEN, real estate broker; b. Aug. 4, 1939, Los Angeles; d. Robert F. and Kathryn A. Miller; m. Dennis Lynge, July 16, 1977; children: Mark Borden b. 1963, Robin Borden b. 1965; edn: BA indsl. psych., USC 1960, NSF scholar/ grad. stu. research psych. 3 years; spl. courses, Cypress Comm. Coll., Anthony Sch., H&R Block; Community Coll. Tchr. credential life (R.E.); Calif. lic. Real Estate Broker (1982), Tax Preparer (1984). Career: research psychologist Pacific State Hosp., Pomona 1 yer; currently: real estate broker, tax cons., investment counselor; co-owner Lake Perris Real Estate; v.p.

Tryland Corp.; honors: Alpha Gamma Delta (1957), Am. Contract Bridge League Life Master (1972); past pres. Inland Empire Bridge Assn.; author: Beginning Bridge (pub. 1964), instr. bridge on World Cruise 1974; Republican; Presbyterian; rec: genealogy. Res: 1380 Halifax Dr Riverside 92506 Ofc: Lake Perris Real Estate, POB 1178, Perris 92370

LYNN, MORRIS RICHARDSON, (JR.), lawyer; b. Nov. 1, 1946, Cincinnati, Ohio; s. Morris Richardson, Sr. and Opal Louise (Gilbert) L.; m. Carole Lynn, Dec. 26, 1969; children: Brian, b. 1972; Steven, b. 1973; edn: BA, UCLA 1968; JD, UC Hastings Coll. of Law 1971. Career: assoc. atty. Hill, Farrer & Burrill, Los Angeles 1971-73; assoc. atty. White, Price, Peterson & Robinson, San Diego 1974-77; partner Peterson, Gamer, Muns & Price, San Diego 1977-80; partner Muns, Mehalick & Lynn, San Diego 1980--; pres. Hastings Coll. of Law Alumni Assn., San Diego chpt. 1983-84; awards: Blue Key Nat. Hon. frat; Letterman, UCLA Varsity Basketball Team, NCAA Champs. 1966-67; mem: Am., Calif. & San Diego Co. Bar Assns.; Calif. & San Diego Trial Lawyers Assns.; mil: 1st lt. US Army 1972, Reserves; Democrat; Protestant; rec: sports. res: 8289 Sugarman Dr La Jolla 92037 Ofc: Muns, Mehalick & Lynn, 1200 Third Ave Ste 1024, San Diego 92101

LYON, CHRISTOPHER, opthalmologist; b. Jan. 9, 1947, Liverpool, Eng., nat. 1979; s. Wm. George and Lilian Martha (Knight) L.; m. Cheryl Candos, Apr. 7, 1974; 1 dau. Ashley Elizabeth b. 1zrl; edn: BS (hon.) Univ. Hull, England 1967; MS in biol., Univ. Malawi, Africa 1970; PhD, biol. sci., Univ. Rhode Island, USA 1973; MD, Univ. Aut. de Cd. Juarez 1979; Calif. lic. MD, PhD, 1981. Career: asst. lectr. in biology Bunda Coll., Malawi, Africa 1967-69, Soche Hill Coll. Univ. Malawi 1969; head biology master St. Bonaventure's High Sch., Liverpool, UK 1970; grad. asst. in virology Univ. R.I. 1970-72, instr. in biophysics 1973; cancer resrch. scientist Roswell Park, Buffalo 1973-76; asst. resrch. prof. in cell biol. St. Univ. of NY at Buffalo 1976; chief resident in ophthalmol. NY Med. Coll. 1981; ophthalmologist Ross Loos INA, Anaheim, Calif. 1982; ophthalmologist pvt. practice Orange and Long Beach 1983--; clin. instr. in ophthal. UC Irvine 1983--; advisor Braille Inst. 1983-; honrs: Fellowships, UN & Brit. Govt., Univ. Malawi 1967, Univ. R.I. 1970-73; mem: Am. Acad. of Ophthal., AMA, Calif. Assn. of Ophthal., NY Acad. of Scis., NY State Ophthal. Soc., Am. Soc. of Cell Biologists, Contact Lens Assn. of Ophthal., AAAS, Am. Microscopy Soc., Electron Microscopy Soc. of Am., Orange County Soc. of Ophthal., Irvine Med.-Dental Soc., Irvine Civic League; publs: 24 sci. research papers; Republican; rec: photog., micro-photog., jogging. Res: 20 Belmonte Irvine 92714 Ofc: Orange County Eye Associates 2623 E. Chapman Ave Orange 92669

LYTLE, JAMES RAYMOND, gemologist; b. June 17, 1947, Chattanooga, Tenn.; s. Raymond and Diane (Roberts) L.; m. Heidi Dwane, May 26, 1972; edn: BA, Sonoma State 1974; Grad. Gemologist, Resident Diamond Grad., Gemological Inst. of Am. 1984. Career: researcher Ctr. for Internal Research, Cordoba, Argentina 1974-76; tech. writer Scientific Mktg. Assocs., Lanham, Md. & cab driver Yellow Cab of Arlington, Va. 1976-77; independent buyer/ seller/ appraiser gemstones, J & H, Ltd., San Francisco 1978--; pub. talks on geology of gem formation and rel. subjects; mem: Gemological Inst. of Am. Alumni Assn.; mil: E-3 USN,, Vietnam Svc. w/ Bronze Star. Address: J & H Ltd., 2180 Union St San Francisco 94123

LYTLE, JOHN JAMES, oral and maxillofacial surgeon; b. Mar. 19, 1934, Pittsburgh, Pa.; s. John Willis and Lillian Myrtle (Coulson) L.; m. Marcia Lou Deakins, Aug. 25, 1953; children: John L. (M.D.), b. 1956; Mark A. (J.D.) b. 1959; Robert J. b. 1964; Susan L., b. 1969; edn: DDS, Univ. of So. Calif. 1958, MD, 1965; Lic. in Dentistry and Medicine, Calif. Career: residency in oral surgery L.A. County General Hosp. 1959-61, Rotating intern, 1965-66; dir. of Hospital Dentistry USC 1966-68, asst. prof. oral surgery USC Dentistry & Medicine 1967-74, assoc. prof. 1974-77, clin. prof. & chmn. 1977--; chief of Oral & Maxillofacial Surgery L.A. County USC Med. Center 1977--; chief of med. staff Memorial Hosp. of Glendale 1979, bd. trustees 1979-, pres. 1984-85; bd. dirs. Central Bank of Glendale 1979-. Fellow Am. Coll. of Dentists 1968; dir. Am. Bd. of Oral & Maxillo. Surgery 1981; mem: So. Calif. Soc. of Oral & Maxillofacial Surgeons (pres. 1981), Am. Assn. of Oral & Maxillo. Surgeons, ADA, AMA; bd. dirs. Ednl. Found. of Am. Assn. Oral & Maxillo. Surgeons 1981-; bd. dirs. Glendale Coll. Found. 1983-, Glendale Sym. Assn. 1983-; sci. publs. (25) in field; Republican; Presbyterian; pres. Antigua Yachts West Inc. sailing yacht distbn. Res: 2757 Hampstead Rd Glendale 91206 Ofc: McMillan & Lytle Inc. 655 No. Central Ave Ste 151, Glendale 91203

LYTTON, SHELDON HARRY, lawyer; b. Sept. 20, 1942, Chgo.; s. William H. and Sylvia (Ichilson) L.; m. Susan D., May 2, 1982; chidren: Deborah, b. 1966; Jennifer, b. 1969; Chris, b. 1974; edn: BS, Northwestern Univ. 1963; grad. studies, UCLA 1964; JD, UCLA Sch. of Law 1973; admitted to practice, State Bar of Calif. Career: atty. O'Melveny & Myers, Los Angeles 1973-78; spl. asst. Atty. Gen., Calif. 1978; chief of staff Lt. Gov. ofCalif. 1979; partner Finley, Kumble, Wagner, Heine, Underberg & Manley 1980--; chmn. bd. Center National Bank, Woodland Hills; dir. Curb Communications; honors: chief editor UCLA Law Review 1972-73; winner, Roscoe Pound Moot Ct. Competition 1972; Outstanding Advoc., Los Angeles Moot Ct. Comp. 1972; mem: Cedars Sinai Med. Ctr. bd. govs. 1980-; Commn. of the Californias (del. 1980-82); Calif. Commn. of Citizen Participation exec. dir. 1980-82; author: Non-Stop to London (Avon 1969), Mustang (Avon 1969); legal art: Taxability of the Widow's Allowance (19 UCLA Law Review 1972); Republican. Ofc: Finley, Kumble, Wagner, et al, 9100 Wilshire Beverly Hills 90212

M

MA, FENGCHOW CLARENCE, agricultural engineer; b. Sept. 4, 1919, Kai-feng, Honan, China, immigrated to USA 1972; s. Chao-Hsiang and Wen-Chieh (Yang) Ma; m. Fanny Corvera-Acha, Jan. 20, 1963; 1 son: Fernando, b. 1964; edn: BS, Nat. Chekiang Univ. 1942; post grad., Iowa State Univ. 1945-46; Regis. Profl. Engr., Calif. 1977. Career: agric. engr./ chief dept. of ops. Agricultural Machinery Ops. & Mgmt. Ofc. MOAF/ CNRRA/ UNRRA, Shanghai, Chinaa 1946-49; sr. farm machinery splst. Sino-Amer. Jt. Commn. on Rural Reconstrn., Taipei, Taiwan, ROC 1950-62; agric. eng. advr. Food & Agric. Orgn. of the UN (assigned to Bolivia, Peru, Chile, Ecuador, Liberia, Honduras, Grenada & Bangladesh), Rome Italy 1962-80; cons. agric.engr. IRI Research Inst., NY, assigned to USAID financed projects in Guyana, 1981-82, in Peru 1983--; mem: Am. Soc. of Agric. Engrs.; publs: A Preliminary Study of Farm Implements Used In Taiwan Province, JCRR Plant Ind. Series No. 4, Taipei, Taiwan, ROC 4/ 55; On The Agricultural Mechanization in Taiwan, JCRR Plant Ind. Series No. 14, Taipei, 7/ 57; Brief Report on the Agricultural Mechanization in Taiwan, 5th Internat. Congress of Agric. Eng., Brussels, Belgium 1958; Implications on Rice Field Mechanization in Taiwan, 10th Pacific Sci. Congress, Honolulu, Hi., 7/ 61; Preliminary Study of Farm Implements Used in Vietnam, CIM Pub. Series No. 24, Saigon, Vietnam 1962; Mechanization of Small Farms in Taiwan, UN Conf. on the Application of Sci. & Tech. for the Benefit of Less Developed Areas, Geneva, Switzerland 1963; rec: stamp and coin collection. Res: 1004 Azalea Dr Sunnyvale 94086 Bus. Mail: POB 70096 Sunnyvale CA 94086

MACALUSO, DAMIAN JOHN, manufacturing plant executive; b. May 8, 1947, Hartford, Conn.; s. Joseph Francis and Amelia Teresa (Tonon) M.; m. Marylou Kosak, Nov. 24, 1973; children: Marykate, b. 1974; Jennie Anne, b. 1977; Laura Beth, b. 1979. Edn: BA, Univ. Conn. 1978; MBA, Pepperdine Univ. 1983. Career: div. prodn. General Motors Corp., Bristol, Conn. 1974-78; gen. supr. Torin Information Systems Div., Torrington, Conn., 1978-81, plant supt., Van Nuys, Calif. 1981-83; plant mgr., Torin Egineered Blowers Div., Clevepak Corp., Van Nuys, 1983--. Mem: Am. Mgmt. Assn. Mil: sgt. USMC 1968-70, Vietnam svc., 3 Purple Hearts; Republican; Catholic. Rec: gardening, stamps, baseball. Res: 455 Highview St. Newbury Park 91320 Ofc: Torin Corp., 16300 Roscoe Blvd. Van Nuys 91320

MACCHIARINI, PETER, artist-sculptor; b. Aug. 27, 1909, Santa Rosa, Calif.; s. Daniele and Brigida (Mancini) M.; m. Virginia deHaas, May 28, 1949; children: Laura (Langdon) b. 1935, Nella (Ueligitone) b. 1951; Daniel Max b. 1953; edn: basic tng. in marble carving, clay modeling, archtl. drawing and gen. scis.; Art Acad., Pietrasanta, Italy 1924-28; stu. Calif. Sch. of Fine Arts, S.F. Career: marble carver, P. Grassi & Co., San Francisco 1928-31; WPA Theatre and Art Projects, S.F. 1935-40; self-empl. artist designing and mfg. jewelry and sculpture, 1945--; instr. in jewelry & metalwork, Mills Coll. 1952, 55; frequent lectr. for var. museums, pvt. orgns., radio and TV throughout the Bay Area; sculpture and jewelry rep. in permanent collections of State of Calif., the Oakland Mus., Home Svgs & Loan Assn., and City and County of San Francisco, and num. pvt. collections; mem. organizing com. of first S.F. outdoor Art Festivals (in Hoteling Pl. and the Ferry Bldg.) 1939, 40, 41, secured city sponsorship for the Art Festival in 1946-, participating artist in every S.F. Art Festival (1939-) and winner more awards than any other individual artist; num. 1st, 2d, purchase prizes, hon. mentions for jewelry and sculpture: L.A. County Fair 1949-, Calif. State Fair 1950-, Oakland Art Mus., S.F Art Commn., others; mem. Artists Equity 1950-55; charter mem. S.F. Metal Arts Guild 1951-54; Affiliated Art Groups Bay Area 1951-56 (pres. 1954); clubs: S.F. Italian Athletic Club 1944-, Assoc. Lucchesi nel Mondo 1980-; rec: photog. Address: 130 Russia Ave San Francisco 94112

MAC DONALD, BRUCE ALLEN, electronics executive; b. Nov. 24, 1949, Hanford; s. Delbert and Doris Lena (Short) MacDonald; m. Delora, Nov. 7, 978; 2 sons: Brian, b. 1970, Robert, b. 1978; edn: BA, CSUN, 1970. Career: stock clerk Sensor Technology, 1969, buyer 1971, materials mgr. 1974, v.p. material 1980, v.p. mfg. Sensor Tech/Dyneer, currently; founder/pres. Corlund Electronics, Newbury Park 1982--; mil: E4 USNR 1972; Republican; Presbyterian; rec: water/snow ski; res: 29322 Trailway Ln Agoura 91301 ofc: Corlund Elect. 3543 Old Conejo Rd. #101 Newbury Park 91320

MAC DONALD, RICHARD ROSS, information systems consulting co. executive; b. Aug. 20, 1945, Annapolis, Md.; s. Frank Wadsworth and Henrietta Maria (Scott) M.; m. Cheryl A. Peffer, Aug. 31, 1968; children: Brian R., b. 1972; Garrett C., b. 1975; edn: BS, US Naval Acad. 1967; MBA, Golden Gate Univ. 1979. Career: proj. engr., nuclear engr., eng. supvr., proj. eng. mgr., Bechtel Power Corp. 1971-79; sr. proj. mgr. TERA Corp. 1980-82; v.p. ops. TERA Info. Eng. Corp. 1982--; cons. TERA Corp. 1980-; mem: Sigma Pi Sigma; YMCA (Indian Guides); works: Evaluating Decommissioning Costs for Nuclear Power Plants, Decontamination and Decommissioning of Nuclear Facilities, Plenum Press 1980; mil: LCDR N 1967-71; Republican; Catholic. Res: 14 Mt Eden Pl Clayton 94517 Ofc: TERA Information Engineering Corp., 2150 Shattuck Ave Berkeley 94704

MAC DONALD, TERRY LYNN, planning and control executive; b. Sept. 16, 1944, Loma Linda; s. William Edward and Adela Gloria Foster (Valdez) M.;

m. Maxine Hendrickson, May 11, 1979; 1 dau: Toni Elizabeth Dust, b. 1970; edn: AA, Barstow Comm. Coll. 1972; BA, Univ. of Redlands 1983; Qualified Mgr./ Pvt. Patrol Opr., Bur. of Consumer Affairs 1983; Qual. Mgr./ Pvt. Investigator, 1982. Career: lt. San Bernardino Co. Sherriff 1967-82; work control mgr. Boeing Svcs. Internat., Ft. Irwin 1983-84; pvt. patrol opr. 1982--; owner/ opr./ pvt. investigator, Victorville 1982--; instr. Sheriff's Acad. 1975-80; instr. Barstow Comm. Coll. 1978-80; instr. Barstow High Sch. 1978-79; traffic pgm. dir. Loma Linda- Grand Terrace 1980-82; honors: Ofcr. of the Month, Sheriff's Ofc. 1972; Class Rep., Univ. of Redlands 1982-83; mem: BPOE, Barstow; BSI Employees Golf Club (pres. 1983-84); BSI Employees Basketball Club (pres./ coach 1983-84); Barstow- San Bernardino- Apple Valley Youth Football Pgm.; Republican; Protestant; rec: golf, youth activities. Res: 1517 Church St Barstow 92311 Ofc: Boeing Services, 281 Barstow Rd Fort Irwin 92310

MAC DONALD, SANFORD ROBERT, investment co. pres.; b. Jan.12, 1941, Los Angeles; s. Sanford Christian and Carrie (Nolton) M.; m. Linda Cardillo, Feb. 10, 1962; 1 dau. Lisa Lorraine b. 1963; edn: El Camino Coll. 1959-61. Career: insurance broker Pacific Fidelity Life Ins. Co. Los Angeles 1963-69; op. mgr. Airport Parking Co., LA Intl. Airport 1961-69; regl. mgr. Ampco Auto Parks, Phoenix, Az. 1969-74; gen. mgr. United Auto Parks, Denver, Colo. 1974-76; ops. dir. Parking Concepts Inc., Los Angeles 1976--; pres. Diversified Investments Co., L.A. 1982--; sales cons. Southwestern Petroleum Corp., Ft. Worth, Tx. 1984--; recipient top sales award Pacific Fidelity Life Ins. 1964, top regl. mgr. ABMI Parking, Phoenix 1972 ; mem./ pres. Phoenix Parking Assn. 1972-74, Bus. & Govt. Council 1973-74, Phoenix Metro. CofC; mem: Am. Mgmt. Assn. (NY), The Am. Film Inst. (Wash DC), Nat. Geographic Soc. and Smithsonian Instn.; apptd. to Govtl. Affairs Council Denver Co. 1975; mem. Youth for Christ USA Found. 1984; Republican; Christian; rec: music, theater, water sports. Res: 5772 Garden Grove Bl, 197, Westminster 92683 Ofc: Diversified Investments Co. 11925-F Grevillea, Hawthorne 90250

MAC DONELL, RICHARD ANTHONY, mobile park developer; b. Feb. 12, 1927, Hibbing, Minn.; s. Randolph Alexander and Loretta (St. Germain) M.; m. Helen Watt, July 24, 1954; children: Glenn Richard, b. 1955; Suzanne Jane, b. 1956; Gregory Scott, b. 1958; Debora Kay, b. 1959; Alexander Randolph, b. 1960; Roger James, b. 1962; Stuart John, b. 1963; Janette Clarice, b. 1964, Linda Kathleen, b. 1966; Richard Allen, b. 1968; edn: BA, Univ. of Minn. 1949. Career: state secty./ treas Western Mobile Home Assn. 1955-57; pres. Trinity Lake Corp. 1963-67; owner Ranchero/ Thunderbird Mobile Home 1958--; secty R.A. Mac Donell Oil Co. 1960--; cons. Community Sys. Housing Corp. 1970--; pres./ chmn. bd. RAM Corp. 1979--, pres. Stuart's Mobile Home Sales 1980--; mem: Rotary 1954-64; Serra Club 1960-70; CofC 1961-; clubs: Menlo Country, St. Francis Yacht, Marin Yacht; mil: med. corpsman USN 1945-46; Republican; Catholic; rec: fishing, hunting, golf. Res: 230 Atherton Ave Atherton 94025 Ofc: Ranchero/Thunderbird, 954 Henderson Ave Sunnyvale 94086

MAC GREGOR, JAMES PATTISON, general contractor executive; b. Apr. 21, 1932, Boston, Mass.; s. James Pattison Fleming and Susan (Harrison) M.; m. Beverly, Jan. 8, 1951; children: Raymond, b. 1952; Donna, b. 1958; Robert, b. 1963; edn: BSME, Northeastern Univ. 1957; Profl. Engr., Mass. 1969, Cali. 1978. Career: with General Elec. Co., 1957-80: test engr., Lynn, Mass. and Schenectady, NY 1957-58; gear engr., Lynn, Mass. 1958-59; field engr., Boston, Mass. 1959-60; marine supt., Boston, Mass. 1960-65; mgr. turbine quality control, Fitchburg, Mass. 1966-72; dist. mgr., San Francisco 1972-76; reg. mgr., El Monte 1976-80; gen. mgr. Schnitzer-Levin Marine Co., S.F. 1980-82; pres. Bay Western Indsl. Maintenance Co., Richmond 1982-83; pres. Stockmar Inds., Inc., Richmond 1983--; dir. Bay Western Indsl. Maint., Inc. 1982; dir. Stockmar Inds. Inc., Northwestern Indsl. Maint. Inc., Power Maint. Inc., and Stockmar Inds. Intermountain Inc. 1983; awards: Denny Awd., 1962, and Cordiner Awd., Gen. Elec. Co. 1963; mem: Soc. of Naval Architects & Marine Engrs.; Am. Soc. of Naval Engrs.; Soc. of Port Engrs. of S.F.; Propeller Club of US; Pacific Coast Elec. Assn.; Northwest Elec. Light & Power Assn.; Lafayette-Moraga Soccer Club; Wollaston Lodge AF&AM; mil: aviation machinist mate 3/c, USN 1950-52; Republican; Protestant; rec: running, bowling, racquetball. Res: 1092 Country Club Dr Moraga 94556 Ofc: Stockmar Industries, Inc., 500 B Street Richmond 94801

MACHADO, MARIO J., television broadcaster, producer; b. Apr. 22, 1935, Shanghai, China; s. Carlos Jacinto M.; edn: British pub. sch., Shanghai (multilingual: Portuguese, 2 Chinese dialects); St. Johns Mil. Acad., L.A.; St. Francis Xavier Coll; bus. mgmt. degree Univ. of Hong Kong; Univ. of Wash. Career: with IBM five yrs.; controller nat. company; creator/co-pub. Soccer Corner (1st Amer. soccer mag.); founder/pres. Specials' Ink, Sports Inc., Primo and Trident Publs., MJM Communications; profl. bdcstr. 1967--. Host, nat. syndicated series MEDIX, KRLA Connection, Good Day LA, and California People (KTTV-Metromedia); co-host Noontime (KNXT); analyst for sporting events, KHJ-TV, L.A., 1967--; bdcst. World Cup Soccer Championships (ABC-TV) Spain 1982, Mex. 1970, Ger. 1974, Argentina 1978; voice of soccer for CBS-TV Network, 1968, 76; host, Star Soccer (English PBS netwk.); bdcst. Football League Cup Final, Wembley, 1977; host, The Best of the World Cup (Spanish Intl. Netwk.); host weekly series It Takes All Kinds (KNXT); host for Asian comm., Sunset (series); in-flt. narrator: TWA's Executive Report, Singapore Airlines; narrator indsl. film/video tapes for major corps.; movie credits incl: Blue Thunder, Scarface, King Kong, Brian's Song, Oh God; celebrity guest appearances; voice of Virginia Slims Championships, L.A.; co-prod. w/ Doron Kauper, documentary on Irving Stone; prod. Internat. Stars in Concert and Una Serata Italiana (for Internat. Student Center, UCLA); prod. World Song Festival in America, and Golden Gate to Spruce Goose Chase; awards: Interceptor Award for best documentary, S.F., 1975; Asian of the Year, L.A. City Asian-Amer. Assn., 1978; Seven Emmy and Emmy nominations, 1971-77. Founder youth soccer league, San Fern. Valley; hon. dir. Amer. Youth Soccer Orgn. (AYSO); host benefit tennis tourn.; dir. John Rossi Youth Found.; Catholic; rec: record collection, tennis, soccer. Res: 5750 Briarcliff Rd Los Angeles

MACHINIST, BENJAMIN, ANTHONY, automobile distributor co. executive; b. Oct. 13, 1931, Lowell, Mass.; s. Benjamin and Vincentia Evelyn (Grady) M.; m. Barbara Cambria, June 13, 1953; children: Kathryn, b. 1963; Jocelyn, b. 1967; edn: BS in Bus. Adm., cum laude, Holy Cross Coll., Worchester, Mass. 1953; MBA, Boston Coll. Grad. Sch. of Mgmt. 1961. Career: dir. dealer rels., Nissan Motor Corp., in U.S.A., var. locations, 1970--: nat. dealer orgn. mgr.; nat. sales plnng. mgr.; L.A. regl. sales mgr.; N.Y. regl. sales mgr.; nat. sales adminstrn. mgr.; sales adminstrn. asst.; chmn. NMC/USA TV Communication Task Force 1977; chmn. NMC/ USA Regl. Performance Recogn. Awd. 1977-81; exec. secty. NMC/USA Dealer Policy Review Bd. 1979-; honors: recognition awards: NY Region Datsun Dealer adv. bd. (1973), Nat. Datsun Dealer Adv. Bd. (1978, 79-80, 80-81, 81-82), fund raising recog., Pres. Carter (1979), and Pres. Reagan (1982), Highly Appreciated Friend Awd., Signal Hill (Calif.) Rotary Club 1983; mem: Costa Mesa CofC (Mem. Com.); Automotive Hall of Fame, Inc. 1982-83; mil: s/sgt. US Army 1954-56, GCM; Republican; Catholic; rec: music. Res: 13 Banyan Tree Ln Irvine 92715 Ofc: Nissan Motor Corp. USA, 18501 S Figueroa St Carson 90248

MAC INNES, JOHN NEALON, electronics executive, ret.; b. Oct. 21, 1908, Boston, Mass.; s. Angus Archie, Sr. and Carrie Ellis (Babbitt) M.; m. Elizabeth Walters, Nov. 27, 1946; children: Ian b. 1935, Jean b. 1938, Gael; edn: BS, Trinity Coll. 1930; grad. stu. Columbia Univ., Univ. of Dela., Dartmouth Coll. Career: head math. dept. St. Andrew's Sch., Middletown, Dela. 1930, asst. headmaster 1948; exchange prof. Marlborough Coll. Wiltshire, Eng. and Rugby Sch., Rugby, Eng.; ops. research Ryan Aeronautical Co., San Diego, Ca. 1956; ops. research General Dynamics Corp., San Diego 1958, ret. 1969, mktg. cons. 1970-75; taught Naval Strategy and Tactics San Diego NTC 1966-70; awards: Rotarian of the Year (Coronado) 1978, DOD (ARPA) Appreciation Award 1968, Am. Red Cross Awds. 1980, 81; mem: Navy League, Naval Inst., Rotary Club Coronado (pres. 1980-81), Residential Assoc., Coronado Floral Assoc. (pres. 61); directorships: Coronado Hosp./Found., Red Cross, 4th July Comm. Palomar Mt., Mutual Water Co., Coronado Playhouse; works: Gold/Blue Ribbons: Flower Arranging, Weaving (wool tweed); mil: capt. USN Ret.: Air Defense USN, Solomon Is.; USMC 1st Marine Amphib., CIC Ofcr. USS San Jacinto CVL-30; decorations: Silver Star, Legion of Merit, Bronze Star (2), Purple Heart, Naval Reserve medals, 12 Area and campaign medals; Pres. Unit Cit. (2), Navy Unit Cit.; Republican; Episcopal; rec: antique restor., woodworking, mountains. Res: 649 Margarita Ave Coronado 92118

MACINTYRE, DONALD J., college president; b. Oct. 17, 1939, Detroit, Mich.; s. Donald Maclellan and Ellen (McGrath) Macintyre; m. Antoinette Shen, June 2, 1979; chil: Honey, b. 1962, James, b. 1964, Michele, b. 1964, John, b. 1965; edn: AB, Univ. of Detroit 1961, MA, Univ. of Iowa 1963, PhD, 1966. Career: history prof. Univ. of the Pacific, Stockton 1966-73; dean/acting pres. St. Francis Coll., Biddeford, Me. 1973-75; v.p. academic affairs Univ. of San Francisco, 1975-79; pres. Metropolitan State Coll., Denver, Colos. 1979-81; pres. Canada Coll., Redwood City 1981-83; pres. Skyline Coll., San Bruno 1983--; labor/mgmt. rels. cons.: Indsl. Rels. Workshop Seminars, Inc. 1978-, assoc. John A. Scalone and Assocs., Orinda 1977-, cons. Colo. State Bd. of Agriculture 1979, chief negotiator Univ. of San Francisco 1975-79; frequent keynote speaker, panelist, workshop leader ednl. confs.; num. talks, comm. groups. Awards: resrch grants, UOP, 1969, 70, 70-1; distinguished tching. award, students of UOP 1971; Henry Clay Award, Univ. of S.F. 1976; hon. mem. Internat. Cultural Soc. of Korea 1979; Don Quixote Awd., Nat. Hispanic Univ. Convocation 1983. Mem. Nat. Adv. Council on Telecommunications Edn., Wash.DC 1984-; bd.dirs. Chinese Culture Found., S.F. 1983-; adv. bd. European Univ. of Am. 1982-; trustee Nat. Hispanic Univ. 1982-. Publs: edtl. bd. The State of Hispanic Am. (1981-), journal arts. Rec: tennis. Res: 27 Midway, Mill Valley 94941 Ofc: Skyline Coll. 3300 College Dr. San Bruno 94066

MACK, FRANK GRAHAM, real estate broker; b. Nov. 12, 1920, Oakland, 3d. gen. Californian; s. Warren E. and Lesley Eleanor (MerGuire) M.; m. Louise Mildred Lawson (3d. gen. Californian), Apr. 23, 1950; children: Susan, b. 1944; Karen, b. 1945; edn: BS, Menlo Jr. Coll. 1939-40; BS, San Jose State 1947. Career: self-empl. real estate broker and insurance agent, owner Frank Mack Realtor, 1947--; honors: Chmn. Tax Appeals Bd., Co. of Santa Clara (4 yrs.); mem: L.A. Bd. of Realtors; Los Altos Bd. Realtors; March of Dimes, Los Altos (1st chmn.); Am. Legion; Elks; mil: US Army Signal Corps 1942-46; Republican; Methodist; rec: golf. Address: Frank Mack, Realtor, 1075 Echo Dr Los Altos 94022

MACK, GREGORY VICTOR, control systems engineer; b. Dec. 24, 1953, Pineville, La.; s. Henry Eli and Mary Elizabeth (Lee) M.; m. Cynthia Eleby, Dec. 18, 1977. Edn: stu. Mastbaum Tech. 1971; AS, Lincoln Coll. 1975; BS chem. engr., Drexel Univ. 1982. Career: refinery tech./oper. Gulf Oil, Phila. 1972-76; automation engr. Greeley & Hansen Engrs., Phila. 1976-82; sr. control systems engr. Kentron Internat.- THUMS Long Beach Oil Co. Proj., Prudhoe Bay, Alaska Proj., San Ramon, Ca. and Prudhoe Bay 1982--. Mem: Am. Inst. of Chem. Engrs., Astronomical Soc. of the Pacific, US Chess Fedn. Participant in design and implementation of the largest distbd. control system worldwide, Sohio Alaska oilfield. Rec: astronomy, chess, tennis. Res: 2938 Calais Dr. San Ramon 94583 Ofc: Kentron Intl. Inc., One Annabel Ln., Ste. 103, San Ramon 94583

MAC KAY, MELVILLE FRANK, dentist; b. Sept. 24, 1929, Winnipeg, Man., Can., nat. 1959; s. Victor Lancelot and Christina (Wilson) M.; m. Linda Denham, June 30, 1968; children: Douglas Scott, b. 1959; Melinda, b. 1969; Shaun, b. 1977; edn: AA, East L.A. Jr. Coll. 1954; DDS, Loma Linda Univ. 1958. Career: lic. mech. engr., Calif. 1951-54; dental practice, 1958--; tchr. oral surgery Loma Linda Univ. 1966-68; mem. C.D.I.P. com., San Joaquin County; mem: San Joaquin Dental Soc. (pub. rels. com.), Sertoma Internat. (Sertoman of year), Arabian Horse Assn.; works: blt. Salute (42 ft. sail boat); mil: lt. commndr. Royal Canadian Navy; Republican; Protestant; rec: equestrian, sailing, photog. Res: 5391 Covey Creek Cir Stockton 95207; Ofc: Melville Frank MacKay, DDS, 4255 Pacific Ave Stockton 95207

MAC KENZIE, JEANNE L., geriatric nurisng consultant; b. Apr. 28, 1939, Calif.; d. Stanley Fuller and Jeannette Barbara (Quast) Davis; children: John Douglas, b. 1960; Gary Gordon, b. 1962; edn: BS, San Francisco State Coll. 1960; Med. Surg. Nsg., Stanford Univ. 1958; tchr., edn. series, UC Ext., Santa Cruz 1974; grad. studies, Geriatric Nursing, San Jose State Univ. 1978-; lic: R.N., Pub. Health Nse., Nursing Home Adminstr., (life) Std. Designated and Comm. Coll. (nsg. edn.) Tchg. credentials. Career: aide Sequoia Hosp., Red-wood City 1957-60; RN, 1960-64; nurse Devenshire Oaks Conv. Hosp. 1964-66; Grays Harbor Comm. Hosp., Aberdeen, Wash. 1967; Redwood City Sch. Dept., Redwood City, Calif. 1968; Drs. Richards, Porter & Levenson 1969; dir. nirs. svc. Capitola Extended Care Hosp., Capitola 1970; Lark Manor Conv. hosp., Los Gatos 1971- 78; relief adminstr., Inservice Edn., dir. nursing svc. Marcus Manor Conv. Hosp., San Jose 1978-79; instr. nsg. assts. San Jose Regl. Vocational Ctr. 1979-; staff nurse San Jose Hosp. 1979-; nsg. cons. num. extended care facilities, Los Gatos areo 1979-; honors: Lucina K. Lordon Nursing Awd. 1978; Resolution of Commdn., League of Friends of Santa Clara Co. Commn. on the Status of Women 1982; Lic. Provider for Cont. Edn., BRN and BENHA 1982; mem: Calif. Nurses Assn.; Am. Coll. of Nursing Home Adminstrs.; Peninsula Long Term Nurses Assn.; Republican; Protestant; rec: beekeeper. Res: 18105 La Verne Los Gatos 95030; POB 415, Redwood Estates 95044

MACMEEKEN, JOHN PEEBLES, lawyer; b. Aug. 15, 1924, Newark, NJ; s. John West and Esther Helen (Strong) M.; m. Mary L. Swanberg, Nov. 26, 1949; children: Carol M. Luther, b. 1950; John West M., b. 1952; Susan G. M., b. 1956; edn: JD, Harvard Univ. 1948. Career: atty. assoc. Chickering & Gregory, San Francisco 1948-60, partner 1960-82; partner Pettit & Martin, S.F. 1982--; dir: Glenbrook-Sterling Corp., Lanark West Co., Portland Hills Co.; mem: Am. & Calif. Bar Assn.; Outlook Club of Calif., World Trade Club, Common-wealth Club of Calif., Berkeley Tennis Club, Golden Gateway Tennis Club, Oakland-Dalian Friendship Assn. (dir.); Alpha Delta Phi; Delta Phi Epsilon; mil: US Army 1942-45; Republican; Congregational; rec: fly fishing, tennis, painting. Res: 5708 Glenbrook Dr Oakland 94618 Ofc: Pettit & Martin, 101 California St, Ste 3500, San Francisco 94111

MACRI, PAULINE FRANCES, pharmacist; b. Oct. 25, 1957, San Francisco; d. Frank Rocco and Anna Macri; edn: BS, Univ. of the Pacific 1980; RPH (Reg. Pharmacist) lic. in Calif. 1980, Nev. 1981. Career: intern pharmacist Los Altos Pharmacy, Los Altos 1980; chief pharmacist Clifford's Pharmacies, Menlo Park 1980-82; chief pharmacist Walgreens, Santa Clara 1982--; pharmacy cons. Adult Day Health Ctr., Visiting Nurse Assn. of San Mateo Co., Inc. 1981-; bd. dirs. San Mateo Pharmacists Assn., Inc. 1981-82; v.p. 1982-; TV comml. actress 1976-80; fashion model 1982-; honors: UOP Cheerleader 1979-80; Leadership Awd., Cheerleading Camp 1979; mem: Lambda Kappa Sigma (profl. frat.); Am. & San Mateo Co. Pharmaceutical Assns.; Calif. Pharacists Assn.; Calif. Pharmacists PAC; works: Choosing the proper sunscreen, art. printed & distbd. in community 1980, 82; Republican; Cathoic; rec: body conditioning, dancing. Res: 755 Arlington Rd Redwood City 94062 Ofc: Walgreens, 2012 El Camino Real Santa Clara 95050

MADDOX, GARY RAYMOND, chiropractor; b. May 6, 1950, Indpls.; s. George H. and Opal Virginia (Godwin) M.; m. Lourdes De La Concepcion, June 15, 1977; children: Casey b. 1973, Jamie b. 1977, Micheal b. 1983; edn: AA, Santa Rosa Comm. Coll. 1973; DC, Palmer Coll. of Chiropractic 1977; spl. tng. w/ Dr. Leroy Perry in Olympic Sports 1983; Lic. DC in Hawaii, Calif.; Cert. in Disability (Industrial) Evaluation 1980. Career: staff dr. Boston Chiropractic Office 1977, Latch Chiro. Office 1978; dir./doctor Maddox Chiropractic Office, Santa Rosa, Ca. 1980--; family practice, sports injuries, indsl. accidents; honors: Who's Who in am. Colls. & Univs. 1977; Pi Tau Delta 1977; mem: Nat. Safety Council, Calif. br.; Calif. Chiro. Assn. (Key Doctor Legis. Pgm.); Parker Chiro. Research Found.; Am. Chiro. Assn.; Santa Rosa CofC; Indep.; Christian; rec: sports. Res: 642 Wright St Santa Rosa 95401 Ofc: Maddox Chiropractic Office 1400 Guerneville Rd, Ste 3, Santa Rosa 95401

MADDOX, GRACE BERYL, government economist, ret.; b. Hayward, WI; d. McPherson C. and Grace Mary (Bailey) Maddox; BA, Amer. Univ., Wash. D.C., 1954; MA, econ., Amer. Univ., Wash. D.C., 1958. Career: US Interstate Commerce Commn., 1937-39; Dept. of Justice, 1939-45; Dept. of State, 1945-47; Central Intelligence Agency, 1947-56; Fed. Trade Commn., 1956-67; served on staff of Francis Biddle, US Mem. Internatl. Military Tribunal, Nuremberg, Germany, 1945-47. Co-author of several industry reports publ. by Fed. Trade Commn., 1956-67. Superior Service Awards, Fed.

Trade Commn., 1962-67. Mem: Daughters of Amer. Revolution; Phi Delta Gamma; Amer. Economic Assn. Co-author: "Antibiotics Manufacture," 1958; "Food Marketing," parts I, II (1962), III (1965). Presbyterian. Rec: oil painting. Res: 5796 Encino Rd., Apt. 5, Goleta 93117.

MADEWELL, CHARLES JAMES, construction manager; b. Aug. 3, 1944, Phila., Pa.; s. Charles and Dorothy Mildred (Hosking) M.; m. Sandra Norton, b. Aug. 17, 1968; cihldren: Timothy Charles, b. 1971; Jennifer Ann, b. 1980; Andrew Charles, b. 1983; edn: BS, Rutgers Univ. 1966; US Steel Mgmt. Pgm.; Bethany Coll. 1976; Lic. Profl. Engr., Calif. (1974), NJ (1975) and Wash. (1978). Career: field engr. Am. Bridge Div. US Steel Corp., NY & Los Angeles 1966-70; proj. engr., Los Angeles 1971-783; proj. mgr. 1974-78; mgr. field ops. Adams & Smith, Inc., Pleasant Hill 1979-80; proj. mgr. Dillingham Constrn., Inc., Pleasanton 1981--; proj. mgr. Dillngham/ Tokola, A Joint Venture for the Golden Gate Bridge Deck & Sidewalk Replacement, 1983--; mem: Am. Soc. of Civil Engrs.; Nat. Soc. Profl. Engrs.; Am. Mgmt. Assns.; BSA (Pack chmn., Webelos ldr., 1980-2); mil: Army ROTC 1962-64; Republican; Presbyterian; rec: backpacking, skiing. Res: 614 Timpanoqos Ln Danville 94526 Ofc: Dillingham Construction, Inc., 7100 Johnson Dr Pleasanton 94566

MADISON, DAVID GARY, chiropractic orthopedist; b. June 14, 1952, Yuma, Ariz.; s. Dempsey H. and Norma M. Madison; m. Jeannie M., Aug. 26, 1963; 1 dau. Melissa, b. 1979; edn: stu. UC Riverside 1969-72; DC, Los Angeles Coll. of Chiropractic 1976; postgrad. Cert. in Orthopedics 1979; Diplomate Am. Bd. of Chiropractic Orthopedists 1982; Cert. Disability Evaluator. Career: gen. chiropractic practice 1976-79; chiropractic orthopedist 1979--, spec. in neuro-musculo-skeletal problems; Fellow Acad. of Chiropractic Orthopedists 1983; mem. Am. Coll. of Chiro. Orthopedists (secty. 1981-2), Am. Chiro. Assn. (ACA Councils on: Orthopedics, Nutrition, Sports Injuries, Roentgenology), Calif. Chiro. Assn. (Peer Rev. state chmn. 1983), Riverside County Chiro. Soc. (v.p. 1977-9), Found. for Medical Care of Riv. (Peer Rev. 19780-); frequent lectr. in field; mem. Elks Lodge; Indep.; Lutheran; rec: family. Res: 5931 Normandie Pl Riverside 92506 Ofc: 5386 Arlington Ave Riverside 92504

MADNI, ASAD MOHAMED, engineering executive; b. Sept. 8, 1947, nat. US Citizen 1983; s. Mohamed Taher and Sara Alimohamed (Wadiwalla) M.; m. Gowhartaj, Nov. 11, 1976; edn: dip. in advanced electronics RCA Insts. Inc., NY, NY 1968; BS, UC Los Angeles 1969, MS 1973. Career: engring. reader (undergrad. and grad. courses) UCLA, Los Angeles 1969-73; senior electronics instr. Pacific State Univ., Los Angeles 1969-71; senior electronics auditor Pertec Corp., Chatsworth 1973-75; proj. engr. Systron Donner Corp. Microwave Div., Van Nuys 1975-80, senior engr. 1980-81, engring. mgr. 1981-82, dir. of Engring. and dir. of Advanced Programs Technology, 1982--, respons. for devel. of num. industry firsts in the field of intelligent instrumentation conceptualization and design; tech. adv. to Test and Measurement World mag. (Interfield Pub. Co., Boston); profl. presentations worldwide (incl. the Pentagon), workshop ldr., track ldr.; senior mem. IEEE 1976-, mem. Assn. of Old Crows, Nat. Rifle Assn. of Am. (life); works: 3 U.S. Patents (2 pats. pend. in area of electronic warfare), num. tech. articles in sci. publs.; rec: art collector, music. Res: 3582 Greenfield Ave Los Angeles 90034 Ofc: Systron Donner Corp. Microwave Div. 14844 Oxnard St Van Nuys 91411

MAFFINI, MARTHA WAHL LEEMAN, educator; b. Jan. 20, 1939, Hartford, Conn.; d. William F. and Virginia (Yenney) Wahl; m. William L. Maffini, July 8, 1982; children: Harry Leeman, b. 1972; Amy Leeman, b. 1974; Cara Maffini, b. 1983; edn: BS, Univ. of Vermont 1961; M.Ed., Boston Univ. 1965; postgrad., Clark Sch. for Deaf, Smith Coll. 1967; credentials: tchr. deaf and hard of hearing. Career: tchr. speech dept. Central Inst. for Deaf, St. Louis, Mo. 1965-66; supvr. lang. problem classes Horace Mann Sch. for the Deaf, Boston, Mass. 1966-69; tchr. hard of hearing Haman Elem. Sch., Santa Clara, Calif. 1970-75, Wilson Jr. High, 1975-80, tchr. communicatively handicapped Buchser Jr. High, 1980--; Master Tchr. audiology, CSU San Jose 1978-83; ednl. cons. Mass. Eye & Ear, Boston 1967; awards: HEW Fellow 1964-65, Alpha Delta Pi Scholarship Awd. 1961, Outstanding Young Women in Am. 1972; mem: Am. Speech & Hearing Assn.; Alexander Graham Bell Assn. for Deaf; Alpha Delta Pi; Girl and Boy Scouts; YMCA; St. Andrews Sch. Parent- Volunteers; Support 4-H; profl. publs. in field; Espiscopal; rec: sewing, collecting Early American Primitives. Res: 65 S Milton Ave Campbell 95008 Ofc: Santa Clara Unified Schools, Lawrence Station Rd Santa Clara 95051

MAFFUCCIO, DANIEL JOHN, refinery executive; b. July 25, 1926, Pittsfield, Mass.; s. Joseph and Carmella (Mondelli) M.; m. Shirley Jungles, Aug. 26, 1950; children: Joseph, b. 1952; Daniel, b. 1955; James, b. 1956; edn: BS, Brown Univ. 1947; Reg. Profl. Engr., Ill. 1956, La. 1968. Career: Texaco Inc. 1947--: engr. at Lockport Refinery 1947; proj. engr. Texaco Corp. Engring. Dept., Houston 1960; staff engr. Refining Managerial, Houston 1964; chief engr. Louisiana Plant, Convent, La. 1968; asst. plant mgr. Eagle Point Plant, West-ville, NJ 1971; plant mgr. Los Angeles Plant, Wilmington 1978--; mem: Nat. Petroleum Refiners Assn.; Am. Mgmt. Assn.; Western Oil & Gas Assn.; Wilmington CofC; mil: lt. j.g. USNR 1944-52, Active Svcs. 1944-46; Republican; Catholic; rec: oil painting, drawing, golf. Res: 28178 S Ridgecove Ct Rancho Palos Verdes 90274 Ofc: Texaco Inc., 2101 E Pacific Coast Hwy Wilmington 90744

MAGGARD, SARAH ELIZABETH, educator; b. Nov. 17, 1948, Whittier; d. William Alexander and Laura Belle (Redford) M.; edn: BA, Whittier Coll. 1970; MA, 1971; JD, cum laude, Western State Univ. Coll. of Law 1981; Elem. and Sec. Tchg. Creds. 1971; admitted to State Bar of Calif. 1982. Career:

currently: tchr. (English) Rowland Unified Sch. Dist.; pvt. part-time law practice spec. in wills and trusts; honors: Am. Jurisprudence Awards. 1979, 80; Law Review assoc. ed. 1979-80; mem: Am., Calif., and Los Angeles Co. Bar Assns.; Lawyers Club of L.A.; Athenian Soc.; Delta Phi Upsilon; Republican; Baptist; rec: spectator sports. Res: 10319 Tigrina Ave Whittier 90603 Ofc: Alvarado Intermediate School, 1901 Desire Rowland Hghts 91748

MAGNESS, TIMOTHY, health and saftey executive; b. Feb. 3, 1949, Lawton, Okla.; s. John Wilbur and Margurite J. (Lefevere) M.; m. Marian Gail Howell, Jan. 19, 1968; children: Andrea, b. 1971; Amber, b. 1974; edn: AA, Santa Ana Coll. 1975; AA, Golden West Coll. 1978; BA, CSU Fullerton 1980; grad. stu. MBA pgm., Nat. Univ. 1983-. Career: protection ofcr., sgt., lt. Hughes Aircraft Co. 1973-1976, hd. security dept. 1977, hd. enviromental health & safety (indsl. security) 1980--; mem. Corp. Health Comm.; tchr. Golden West Coll. 1978; Nat. Safety Council; Forklift Safety; Chemical Safety; CPR Instr., Am. Heart Assn.; Mgmt. Club, Hughes Aircraft, Newport Beach (pres. 1984); Semiconductor Safety Gp., So. Calif.; Am. Soc. Indsl. Security; mil: sgt. E-5 USMC 1967-73, Vietnam, Vietnamese Cross of Gal., Combat Action Ribbon, Air Medals (7); Democrat; Catholic; rec: racquetball, softball. Res: 2114 Candis Santa Ana 92706 Ofc: Hughes Aircraft Company, 500 Superior Ave Newport Beach 92663

MAGNIN, CYRIL ISAAC, retail trade executive, philanthropist; b. July 6, 1899, San Francisco; s. Joseph and Charlotte (Davis) M.; m. Anen (Newman), Jerry; edn: stu. Univ. Calif. 1919-22; LLD, Univ. of the Pacific 1967; PhD in Fine Arts (hon.), Univ. of San Francisco 1978; MFA (hon.) Acad. of Art Coll. 1979. Career: fmr. pres., chmn. of bd. Joseph Magnin Co., Inc., San Francisco; gen. partner Cyril Magnin Investments, Ltd.; chmn. of bd. Lilli Ann Corp.; dir. Spectrum Foods, Inc.; chief of protocol, City and County of San Francisco 1964--; v.p. Calif. Mus. Found.; exec. mem. Asian Arts Mus. SF; mem. Blyth Zellerbach Com.; bd. dirs. March of Dimes Nat. Found.; pres. Calif. Assn. A.C.T.; bd. dirs., exec. com. Fine Arts Mus. SF; trustee Am. Cancer Soc., SF Opera Assn., Boys Town Italy; pres. bd. advs. Calif. Culinary Acad.; honors: Decorated Star of Solidarity (Italy), Legion of Honor (France), Comdr. Brit. Empire, Cross of Order of Merit (Fed. Repub. Germany), Order of Phoenix (Greece), Comdr. Royal Order North Star (Sweden), Order de Isabel La Catolica (Spain); Calif. Maritime Award 1959; Man of Year 1962, NCCJ; Retailer of Year 1962; Booker T. Washington awd. 1962; recogn., City and County Los Angeles (1965), SF Jr. CofC (1969), Nat. Asthma Center (1978), Fashion Inst. Design and Mdse. (1978), Cath. Youth Orgn. (1978), Coro Found. (1980); mem: Gr. SF CofC (past pres., chmn.), Mason (Shriner) 33rd degree; clubs: St. Francis Yacht, Villa Taverna, World Trade (dir.); author: Call Me Cyril (McGraw-Hill 1981) Res: Mark Hopkins Hotel, San Francisco 94106 Ofc: 444 Market, Ste 2430, San Francisco 94111

MAGOWAN, PETER ALDEN, grocery chain store executive; b. Apr. 5, 1942, NYC; s. Robert Anderson and Doris Merrill Magowan; edn: BA, Stanford 1964; MA, Oxford Univ. 1966; Johns Hopkins Sch. of Adv. Internat. Studies 1968. Career: with Safeway Stores 1968--: store mgr., Wash. DC 1968-70; dist. mgr. Houston, Tex. 1970; retail ops. mgr. Phoenix, Ariz. 1971-72; div. mgr. Tulsa, Okla. 1973-76; mgr. internat. div., Toronto, Can. 1976-78; western reg. mgr., San Francisco 1978-79; dir. 1979, chmn. bd./ CEO 1980--; dir. Pacific Gas & Electric Co.; dir. Food Mktg. Inst.; mem: Johns Hopkins Sch. of Advanced Internat. Studies (adv. council); Bus. Roundtable; US CofC (dir.); THe Hudson Inst. (dir.). Ofc: Safeway Stores, Inc., 4th & Jackson Sts., Oakland

MAGSINO, FRANCISCO DE LAS ALAS, artist; b. Dec. 3, 1937, San Jose, Mindoro, Philippines; s. Roman Panganiban and Juanita Ramirez (De Las Alas) M.; m. Florinda Domingo, Aug. 21, 1976; children: Daniel, b. 1974; Frank, b. 1980; edn: B.Fine Arts, Acad. of Art 1971. Career: artist Woman's World Mag., Philippines 1962; illustrator artist Hontiveros Assocs., Phil. 1964-66, Adver. Inc. 1966-67; art. dir. Hontiveros Assocs. 1967-68; art director (part-time) Hubbert Advtg., San Francisco 1969-72, Philippine News, S.F. 1972-75; artist, self- empl., Vallejo 1973--; awards: 3rd Place painting category, World Sci. Fiction Conv. 1974; Best of Show, Western Artist of Am., Reno 1982; Best of Show, Western Artist of Am., Cody, Wyo. 1983; Gold Awd., Silver Awd., Bronze Awd., Western Artist of Am. 1983; mem. Western Artist of Am.; rec: bowling, fishing. Address: 150 Westminster Way Vallejo 94591

MAIN, RICHARD B., strategic marketing consultant; b. July 27, 1949, San Diego; s. Richard G. and Irene E. (Johnson) M.; m. Rita D. Graef, Dec. 27, 1975; children: Rickey, b. 1971; Mickey,b . 1978; edn: BSEE, Cooks Inst. of Elec. Eng. 1972; dipl. Capitol Radio Eng. Inst. 1974; BSBA, Univ. of NY 1983-84; Reg. Profl. E.I.T., Calif. Career: chief engr. Univ. Engd. Sys. 1972-76; sys. engr. Ford Aerospace 1976-77; eng. mgr. Neptune UES 1977-79; founder/ pres. Zendex Corp. 1979-82; eng. mgr. Signetics Microsys. 1983-84; pres. Zebu Corp. 1981--; strategic plnr. Communication Machinery Corp., Santa Barbara; mem: IEEE; Rotary; publs: tech. arts. Electronic Design 2/82 and Electronics Mag. 3/84; Republican; Unitarian; rec: motorcycle hill climbing. Ofc: Zebu Corp., 663 Bernardo Sunnyvale 94087

MAIN, STEVEN THOMAS, information systems co. president; b. Dec. 24, 1942, Los Angeles; s. George A. and Willine D. (Fasel) M.; m. Joan Kaplan, July 12, 1964, div. 1984; children: Lauren, b. 1966; Kristen, b. 1968; Adam, b. 1971; edn: BS, CSU Long Beach 1971. Career: mgr. The Broadway, Los Angeles 1971-76; mgr. Carter Hawley Hale, L.A. 1976-79; dir. The Emporium, San Francisco 1979-82; v.p. The Robert A. McNeil Corp., San Mateo 1982-83; pres.

Systems Technology Mgmt., Inc., San Mateo 1983--; dir. Ikon Finl. Systems; tchr. mgmt. and data processing South Bay Adult Sch. 1974-79; Democrat; Episcopal; rec: numismatics, antique autos, tennis. Res; 207 Shady Glen Rd Walnut Creek 94596 OFc: Systems Technology Management, Inc., 2700 Campus Dr, Ste 302, San Mateo 94403

MAJIDI-AHY, GHOLAMREZA, engineer; b. Apr. 27, 1958, Tehran, Iran; s. Mehdigholi and Pourandokht (Motameni) M.; edn: BSEE, honors, UC San Diego 1980; MSEE, 1981. Career: asst. pmmgr./ research asst. UC San Diego 1979-80; tchg. asst. 1981; G.A. FET amp design engr. Harris Microwave Semiconductor 1981-83; sr. engr. 1983--; tchr. elec. eng. grad. courses, Univ. of Santa Clara; awards: Univ. of Calif. Scholarship 1979; mem: IEEE (Elec. Devices Soc.); Microwave Theory & Techniques Soc.; works; NSF research proj. on Ionospheric Scintillation, sci. publs. (2) in Journal of Atmos. Terres. Physics, IEE, London; rec: volley ball, swimming, skiing. Res: POB 5071 Stanford 94305 Ofc: Harris Microwave Semiconductor, 1530 McCarthy Blvd Milpitas 95035

MAJUMDAR, SAMPRAKASH, computer engineer; b. Oct. 30, 1946, Barisal, Bangladesh, nat. 1979; s. Subodh Chandra and Sankari (Chakravorty) M.; m. Maitrayi, Feb. 24, 1978; l son: Devdoot, b. 1982; edn: BSEE, Bangladesh Univ. of Eng. & Tech. 1969; MSEE, Tex. Tech. Univ. 1975. Career: grad. research asst. Texas Tech. Univ., Lubbock, Tex. 1974; sr. engr. Litton Data Sys., Van Nuys 1975-76; tech. staff TRW, Redondo Beach 1979--; tchr., UCLA; pres. Microsys (microprocessor & computer tng.); mem: IEEE; dir. Jhanker (nonprofit orgn. to promote music & culture of S.E. Asia); publs: paper, Distbd. Operating Sys., 1st Internat. Conf. on Distbd. Data Proc. Sys., IEEE, Huntsville, Ala. 1979; Hindu; rec: fine arts, teaching, music. Address: Microsys, 3651 Greve Dr Rancho Palos Verdes 90274

MAKI, WAYNE ALLEN, service co. executive; b. Dec. 11, 1944, Stambaugh, Mich.; s. John Theodore and Ailie Elsie (Laukaniemi) M.; m. Diane Joyce Gonzales, Sept. 20, 1964; children: Christine, b. 1965, Austin, b. 1969. edn: AA, Orange Coast Coll. 1978; BS, Univ. Redlands 1981; MBA, Pepperdine Univ. 1982; desig: Account Exec./Indus. Cons., AT&T Comms. 1984. Career: communication tech., AT&T, Oakland 1963-67, engring. assoc./supr. (San Francisco) 1967-71, sales supr. 1971; acct. supr. AT&T, Tacoma, Wa. 1971-74; regl. acct. mgr. AT&T, Orange, Ca. 1974-82, national acct. mgr., (Laguna Hills) 1982--; civic speaker AT&T Spkrs. Bur. 1984; bd. dirs., sponsor Am. Youth Soccer Orgn. 1984; mem. Am. Mgmt. Assn., Am. Mktg. Assn.; Republican; Catholic; rec: golf, running, youth coach. Res: 1763 New Hampshire Dr Costa Mesa 92626 Ofc: AT&T Communications, 23421 S. Pointe Dr, Ste. 100, Laguna Hills 92653

MAKOWSKI, TEEN FREDELL, financial planner; b. Jan. 30, 1928, Jerome, Ariz.; d. Ernest Wilbur and Hazel Dell (Boyer) Fredell; m. Edward C. Makowski, Nov. 18, 1964, div.; children: Kristine Elizabeth, b. 1968, Michael Edward, b. 1966; edn: BS in phys. ed., Univ. of Ariz. 1950; MA in edn., Ariz. State Univ. 1954; MA in spl. edn., San Francisco State Univ. 1978; Nat. Assn. Securities Dealers lic.; Calif. Life Ins. lic.; Life Sec. Teaching Credential, Gen. Pupil Personnel Cred., Learning Handicapped Tchg. Cred., Adminstrv. Edn. Cred. Career: teacher (phys. ed., tennis coach, dir. dancing drill team), Glendale, Az. 1950-60; tchr., PE Dept. ch., counselor Fremont Union H.S. Dist., Sunnyvale, Ca. 1962-69; owner Teen Pom Pon School (subcontractor with Nat. Cheerleaders Assn., instr. summer camps and clinics in W. US) 1960-72; substitute tchr San Mateo Elem. Sch. Dist. and Fremont UHSD, 1972-75; project dir. in fed. funded pgms. for spl. edn. (devel. Slice of Life Pgm. for Calif. Dept. of Edn.) 1976-83; finl. planner Waddell & Reed, San Jose 1984--; instr. CSU San Jose; cons. in career-voc. edn. for special edn. Honors: recognition by Council for Exceptnl Children for the Slice of Life pgm.; pgm. validated for national use by US Dept. of Edn.; pgm. included in CEC book of exemplary pgms., 1982. Mem: Santa Clara Council for Exceptnl Chil. (pres.); CANHC; Calif. Assn. for Work Exp. Educs.; Am. Soc. for Tng. & Devel.; Computer Using Educators; fmr. Cub Scout Den mother, Jobs Daus. mother. Publs: Job Awareness Inventory test, Mafex Pubs. 1981; ednl. jour. arts.; Lutheran; rec: skiing, travel, painting. Res: 950 Elsinore Dr Palo Alto 94303 Ofc: Waddell & Reed 1530 The Alameda, 200, San Jose 95126

MALAMUD, CARLOS DAVID, real estate investor/developer; b. Feb. 11, 1953, Mexico City; s. Isaac Carlos and Agustina (Russek) M.; edn: JD (equiv.), honors, Univ. Iberoamericana 1976; Anthony Sch. of R.E. 1983; Calif. lic. Real Estate Broker 1983. Career: legal counsel Promotora e Inmobiliaria Juarez, S.A. de C.V., Mexico City 1976--; gen. ptnr. Galleria-Paseo Assoc., San Diego 1979; gen. ptnr. TCRM Equities 2 Ltd., San Diego 1980-; secty. I.G.C. Corp., San Diego 1977-; secty. Sunbelt Real Estate, San Diego 1983; mem: Rotary Club of La Jolla (World Comm. Svc. chmn.; Paul Harris sustaining mem.); Toastmasters of La Jolla (secty.); World Affairs Council of S.D.; San Diego/Taichung, Taiwan Sister Cities Com.; author: Derecho Funerario (Editorial Porrua, Mexico City 1979), first book written on Mexican Funeral Law; rec: water sports, travel. Res: 5940 Camino de la Costa La Jolla 92037 Ofc: Sunbelt Real Estate, 4990 Mission Blvd San Diego 92109

MALATESTA, ROSALIE ELINOR, accountant; b. Feb. 10, 1938, San Francisco; d. Albert Angelo and Alba (Botto) M.; edn: AA acctg., Am. River Coll. 1974; Sacto. State Univ., 1974-76. Career: bookkeeper D. E. Pomerantz & Co., CPA, San Francisco 1956-63, 66-67; cost acct. Roberts Constrn. Co., San Mateo 1963-65; staff acct. Goldsmith, Exline & Seidman, CPA, San Mateo,

1969-71, Phil A. Baender, Acct. Corp., Danville, 1976-80; ofc. acct. United Calif. Brokers, Danville, 1980-81; prop. Professional Bookkeeping Systems, Alamo 1981--. Mem: Nat. Assn. of Accounting; Commonwealth Club; Sierra Club; Oakla. Museum Assn., various singles orgns.; Republican; Christian. Rec: plants, jazz, golf, hiking, cuisine. Res: 517 Garden Creek Pl. Danville 94526. Ofc: Professional Bookkeeping Systems, 3237 Danville Blvd. Alamo 94507

MALAVENDA, PETER S., computer retail corporate president; b. May 9, 1936, Meriden, Ct.; s. Peter Joseph and Josephine Rose (Bordonaro) M.; m. Patricia Simeone, Nov. 1, 1958; chldren: Lori, b. 1960; Peter, b. 1961; Daniel, b. 1962; edn: BS, Univ. of Conn. 1975. Career: owner /mgr. Modern Pest Control Co., Southington, Ct. 1961-64; pres. Scottsdale Tram, Scottsdale, Ariz. 1965-67; owner/ mgr. Mal's Trenching & Backhoe, Inc., Phoenix, Ariz. 1967-71; nat. accts. mgr. Stanley Works Drapery Hardware Div., Wallingford, Ct. 1971-81; owner/ gen. mgr. Computer Plus, Westminster, Calif. 1981--; pres. Profl. Sales Develop Inc.; mktg. mgr./ cons. Starlite Ent.; awards: Toastmaster Spokesman Awd. 1981; Salesman of the Yr., Stanley Works 1972, 74; mem: PTA (pres. 1970); Indep. Order of the Forestors (Teen Sponser 1972); Toastmasters; Profl. Computer Dealers Assn. (v.p.); Stanley Forum; mil: airman 1/c USAF 1954-58, GCM, SAC, Korean War, Humanitarian Awd.; Democrat; Presbyterian; rec: sports cars, photog. Res: 1700 W Cerritos Ave 213, Anaheim 92804 Ofc: Computer Plus, 14300 Beach Blvd Westminster 92683

MALBOEUF, ANN LYNN, real estate broker/ marketing consultant; b. Nov. 13, 1946, Berkeley; d. Stanley and Katherine Ellen (Pitcher) Colberson; chldren: Michael, b. 1969; Gregory, b. 1971; Susan, b. 1973; edn: BA, Holy Names Coll. 1968. Career: tchr. Sacred Heart Sch., Oakland 1968-70; Leta Burns Real Estate, Orinda 1976-77; Century 21 Tri City Realtors, Lafayette 1978-82; assoc. broker Wallace, Underwood & Scofield, Orinda 1982--; pub. rels./ mktg. cons. Citicorp Savings, Oaklands 1982--; honors: Million Dollar Club 1976-78; Two Million Dollar hClub 1979, 83; Top 50 Nationwide, Century 21, 1979; mem: Contra Costa Bd. Realtors; Jr. League, Oakland East Bay (Family Svc. Guild pres. 1979; chmn. Pub. Rels. Com.); Spinsters and Dames (pres. 1980); Orinda Country Club; Lakeview Club, Oakland; Art Docent Orinda Schs.; Orinda Intermed. Sch. Parent Club; Del Rey Parents Club; Am. Assn. of Univ. Women, Berkeley; Republican; rec: creative writing. Res: 14 Hilldale Ct Orinda 94563. Ofc: Wallace Underwood, 89 Moraga Way Orinda 94563

MALDONADO, JUAN, insurance agency president; b. Dec. 17, 1942, Falfurrias, Tex.; s. Gilberto and Anita (Garza) M.; m. Maria M. Kennedy, Aug. 12, 1967; chldren: J. Eric, b. 1969; Andrea Marie, b. 1971; Aaron Gilbert, b. 1975; edn: stu. Santa Ana Coll. 1966-71, Orange Coast Coll. 1969-70, profl. courses USC. Career: with Union Central Life Insurance Co. 1970--: agent, Santa Ana 1970, Orange Co. unit mgr. 1973, asst. mgr. Los Angeles agency 1975, mgr. of Orange Co. for UCL 1979, mgr. Spl. Mktg. Agency 1982--; pres. Juan Maldonado Insurance Assoc., Inc. 1984--; mem. Knights of the Round Table; mem. Golden Key Soc.; honors: Presidents Club (1973-), Leaders Circle (1982-), Inner Circle (1983-), Union Central Life Ins. Co.; mem: Orange Co. Life Underwriters Assn.; Million Dollar Round Table; Pres.'s Field Adv. Cabinet, Union Central Life; Orange Co. Latin Am. Businessmen Assn.; Baja Oso Homeowners Assn.; Viejo Little League Bowling League (pres.); mil: USMC 1961-65; Republican; Catholic; rec: racquetball, bowling, travel. Res: 26952 Marbella Mission Viejo 92691 Ofc: Juan Maldonado Insurance Associates, 1600 N Broadway, Ste 960, Santa Ana 92706

MALDONADO, KIRK FRANCIS, lawyer; b. Mar. 7, 1950, Omaha, Nebr.; s. Manuel and Orpha Mae (Kovar) M.; edn: BA, Univ. of Nebr. at Omaha 1975; JD, Creighton Univ. 1978; LLM, taxation, Georgetown Univ. 1981. Career: atty. Employee Plans and Exempt Orgns. Div., Office of Chief Counsel, Internal Revenue Service, Wash DC 1978-81; atty. Gibson, Dunn & Crutcher, Newport Beach 1981--; listed, Who's Who in Am. Law; mem. American, Calif., Nebr. bar assns.; publs: articles in J. of Taxation, Tax Mag., Taxation for Lawyers; rec: weight lifting. Res: 637 Baywood Dr Newport Beach 92660 Ofc: Gibson, Dunn & Crutcher, 800 Newport Center Dr Newport Beach 92660

MALDONADO, ROBERTO, sales and marketing executive; b. Jan. 26, 1935, Madrid, Spain, nat. 1963; s. Andres and Meri (Bermejo) M.; m. Dolly Torres Figueroa, Aug. 18, 1956; children: Robert, b. 1959; Eric, b. 1963; edn: AA, Univ. of Madrid 1953; BS, physics, NY Univ. 1959; BS, math., 1959; MS, 1961. Career: dist. mgr. IBM, The Svc. Bureau Corp. 1959-70; v.p. mktg. System Develop. Corp. 1970-80; v.p. internat. mktg. Pertec Computer Corp. 1980-82; v.p. mktg. 1982--; dir. Bantam Computer Corp.; awards: 100 Percent Club of IBM 1967, 68, 69; mem: NY Univ. Foreign Student Dept. (Cultural chmn.); orgns: Cub Scout Master, P.V. (1966-69), Beconsfield, Quebec, Can. (1972-73); soccer coach, P.V. 1965-70, 1974-76; Republican; Catholic (Mens Club); rec: exercise, golf. Res: 4321 Via Azalea Palos Verdes Estates 90274 Ofc: Pertec, 11712 Armstrong Ave Irvine 92714

MALEC, EDWARD, blueprint executive; b. Aug. 1, 1936, Chgo.; s. Edward Joseph and Marie Stella (Mastalski) M.; m. Joan Nielsen, Oct. 28, 1973; children (by previous marriage): Mary, b. 1960; Marcia, b. 1962; edn: Outstanding Achiev. Awd., Lane Tech. H.S. 1950-45; computer sci., Southwestern Coll. 1964-66. Career: counselor YMCA Boys Camp, Upper Scott Lake Mich. 1952, 53, 54; asst. shipping clerk, Ill. Baking Corp. 1952-54; blue print mgr., supvr. blue print dept., head blue print dept., prodn. controller San Diego Blue Print 1958-74; mgr. Chico Blueprint 1974-77; owner/ opr. Action Blueprint, National City 1977--; music instr.; soloist La Jolla Symphony 1957; recipient

Appreciation Awd. for Contbn. in Support of Youth Activities, Sweetwater Union H.S. Dist. 1981; named Mr. Music, most versatile musician in NTC Band, San Diego Union (1956); mem: Elks, Chula Vista; Elks Nat. Found.; National City CofC; Nat. City Kiwanis; mil: musician 2 USN 1954-58, Nat. Defense, GCM; Republican; rec: gardening, fishing, music. Res: 3614 Linbergh St San Diego 92154 Ofc: Action Blueprint, 116 National City Blvd National City 92050

MALLEK, JAMES RUDOLPH, social services consultant; b. Apr. 3, 1926, Neenha, Wisc.; s.. Rudolph and Ann Mallek; m. Rosa, Feb. 11, 1947; 1 son: James Randolph, b. 1953; edn: BA, San Diego State Univ. 1959; MA, UCLA 1966; MSW, 1969; JD, Western State Univ. 1976; Cert. Soc. Wkr., NASW, ACSW. Career: supvg. probation ofcr. Los Angeles Co. Probation Dept., Los Angeles 1965-82; pres. Jayarem, Inc., Bellflower 1982--; dir. Correctional Inst. for Contg. Edn. 1976-79; v.p. Calif. Probation, Parole & Correctional Assn. 1976-79; mem: Fellow, Nat. Assn. for Family Life; Am. Assn. for Marriage, Family & Child Counselors; Tri- City React, Inc.; Masons; Scottish Rite; Shriners; Radio League of Am.; So. Calif. CIC Assn.; works: Personality Affect on Probation Officers, Social Works, Nov. 1969; mil: CWO US Army 1943-64, Army Commdn., GCM, Nat. Svc. Defense Medal; Ch. of Relig. Sci.; rec: amateur radio, photog. Res: POB 1214 Bellflower 90706

MALLEN, RAYMOND EDWARD, import/distribution co. president; b. May 14, 1947, Jersey City, NJ; s. Edward Gerard and Catherine Sarah (Simmons) M.; m. Marilyn Hasley, Feb. 14, 1982; 1 dau. Mallory Ryan, b. 1983; edn: BS, Fairleigh Dickinson Univ. 1969. Career: order desk clerk Boman Industries 1970, district salesman 1971, regional sales mgr. 1972, zone sales mgr. 1975, Eastern sales mgr. 1977, branch mgr. 1978; transf. to Calif. home office as nat. dir. sales & mktg./bd. dir. Car Stereo Distbr. 1980--; owner/pres. Auto Alarm Distbr. dba D.B.R. Security Systems, Los Alamitos 1982--; advisor to USC (MBA) Bus. Sch. 1980-81; Republican; Catholic; rec: travel, photog., music, video equip. Res: 26592 Naccome, Mission Viejo 92691 Ofc: D.B.R. Security Systems, 10359 Los Alamitos Blvd Los Alamitos 90720

MALONE, PATRICIA ANN, podiatrist; b. Nov. 8, 1952, San Jose; d. Woodene Pillsbery and Dorothy (Doughty) Jones; m. Jim F. Malone, Feb. 2, 1979; edn: BS entomology, CSU San Jose 1975; BS med. sci., Calif. Coll. Podiatric Medicine 1976, DPM, 1978; lic. Podiatrist, Phys. and Surgeon of the Foot, Calif. BMQA 1978. Career: podiatric physician Coddington Podiatry Group, Santa Rosa 1978-80; quality control entomologist State of Calif. Medfly Proj., Los Gatos 1980-81; podiatric phys. Malone and Malone Podiatry Corp., Bakersfield 1981--, spec. in foot care of elderly; v.p. Beverly Hills Foot Consultants 1982-; mem. Hypnotists Union, Local No. 472; bd. dirs. Redwood Empire Ballet Com.; mem: Pacific Coast Entomol. Soc.; Affiliated Podiatrists of Calif.; Assn. for Women in Sci.; Sigma Delta Epsilon- Grad. Women in Sci. Inc.; AAUW; publs: gen. info. booklets re foot problems for general public; Democrat; rec: amateur cartoonist, author unpub. novel, jazz dancer. Ofc: Malone & Malone Podiatry Corp., 5752 Stine Rd Bakersfield 93309

MALONEY, DOUGLAS JAMES, county counsel; b. May 26, 1933, San Francisco; s. James Douglas and Loretta Patricia (O'Connel) M.; m. Ruth Elenore Hill, Dec. 31, 1976; children: Lynne, b. 1956; Karen, b. 1958; Douglas Jr., b. 1961; Susan, b. 1962; Pamela, b. 1963; edn: BS, Calif. Maritime Acad. 1954; JD, Univ. of San Francisco 1958. Career: deputy county counsel Sonoma Co. 1959-60; asst. county counsel Marin Co. 1960-62, county counsel 1962--; dir. Living History Centre; dir. Irish Am. Bar Assn.; dir. Irish Forum; corp. counsel Marin Sym. Assn.; mem: Nat. Assn. of Co. Civil Legal Ofcrs. (pres. 1977-78); Calif. County Counsels and Dist. Attys. Assn. (pres. 1973-74); Am. Bar Assn.; works: num. plays (1970-); book reviews, Pacific Sun; law review arts.; Democrat; Catholic; rec: theatre production, writing. Res: 12 Germaine Pl Novato 94947 Ofc: County of Marin, Ste 342, Civic Center, San Rafael 94903

MALONEY, JOHN GERALD, mechanical engineer; b. June 18, 1940, Orange; b. John Francis and Dorothy Fern (Toney) M.; m. Barbara Anderson, July 18, 1964; edn: BSME, Loyola Univ., L.A. 1963; MSME, USC 1966; MBA, CSU Fullerton 1976. Career: eng. splst. General Dynamics, Pomona 1963-83; pres. Maloney's Transmission Svc. & Automatic Transmission Parts of Orange Co., Orange 1979--; staff scientist Brunswick Corp., Defense Div., Costa Mesa 1983--; honors: Tau Beta Pi 1975; mem: assoc. fellow, Am. Inst. of Aero. & Astro.; Soc. of Automotive Engrs.; Diamond Bar Lions Club; publs: papers in the Shock and Vibration Bulletin 1975, 76. Res: 1825 Leaning Pine Dr Diamond Bar 91765 Ofc: Brunswick Defense, 3333 Harbor Blvd Costa Mesa 92626

MALONEY, KENNETH FRANCIS, oil development consultant/company president; b. April 7, 1918, Wilkes-Barre, Pa.; s. Joseph James and Agnes (Kennedy) Maloney; m. Lois Long, Feb. 14, 1941; children: Kenneth Long, b. 1945, Susan Kathy, b. 1950; edn: BS ChE, Bucknell Univ., 1949, and MS ChE, 1955; Reg. Profl. Engr. West VA, PA, CA. Career: engineer, refinery process foreman, refinery supt., general supt. of oil ops., mgr. plants & pipelines, mgr. mfg. & oil supply (NYC), chief engr. Arabian-American Oil Co., 1947-68; asst. to the president, Wilkes Coll., 1968-69; mgr. Elk Refinery, Energy Engr. Pennzoil, 1969-79; senior scientist/project mgr. KVB (devel. combustion technology), Irvine, Calif. 1979--; pres. Calpenn Assocs. (oil devel. consulting co.), 1971--; bd.dirs. Eureka Pipeline Co. 1972-5; Derr lectr. Bucknell 1979; guest lectr. local civic groups, Wilkes-Barre and Oil City, Pa.; mem. AiChE; Patent pend.: tech. devel. for coal fired stokers; devel. successful pgm. for EPA, 1982.

mil: lt. AC, 1942-5. Republican. Presbyterian. rec: ski, tennis, scuba. res: 433 Locust Laguna Bch 92651. ofc: KVB, 18006 Skypark Blvd., Box 19518, Irvine 92714.

MALOOLY, BARBARA ELLEN, real estate company executive; b. Jan. 26, 1940, Ackley, IA; d. Wilke J. and Dorothy Geraldine (Wagner) Eilders; Edn: stu., Mt. San Antonio Coll., 1971-76; real estate, Mt. San Antonio Coll., 1974; exchange, Natl. Inst. of Exchange, 1978; condo devel., Calif. Assn. of Realtors, 1982; m. Richard Malooly, 1957; div; chil: Cynthia, b. 1959; Carol, b. 1960; William, b. 1962; Richard, b. 1966. Career: waitress and mgr., Diamond Bar Country Club, Diamond Bar, CA, 1963-71; real estate sales, Diamond Bar Realty, 1971-72; real estate sales, Red Carpet Realty, Diamond Bar, 1972-74; broker, owner of Gallery of Homes, Diamond Bar, 1974; pres., Malooly Realty Inc., Diamond Bar, 1977; trng. and tchg. real estate for So. Calif. Regional Gallery of Homes, 1977-78. Honors: 1971, top listing and sales award; 1974, top sales and listing award and top overall award from So. Calif. Regional of Red Carpet. Mem: Hacienda Bd. of Realtors, 1973---; Walnut Valley CofC, 1975---; Diamond Bar Womens Club, 1977; No. Orange Co. Bd. of Realtors and West San Bernardino Co. Bd. of Realtors, 1978---; Amer. Bus. Womens Assn., 1980-81; Political Affairs, Legislative Affairs, and Local Govt. Affairs chmn., Hacienda Bd. of Realtors, 1980-81. Currently writing book. Presbyterian. Rec: sailing, golfing, fishing, ceramics. Res: 870 Golden Prados, Diamond Bar 91765; Office: Gallery of Homes, 574 N. Diamond Bar Blvd., Diamond Bar 91765.

MALPASS, DANA DENISE, publisher; b. Dec. 16, 1949, Baltimore, Md.; d. Herbert Holmes, Jr. and Lois Elaine (Leonhardt) Malpass; edn: manicurist lic., Castro valley Beauty Coll. 1979. Career: publisher, manicurist, beauty trade show producer; founder/editor/pub. Mainly Manicuring (now a 20-page monthly trade newspaper with distbn. to 24,000profls. internat.), 1982--; mem. Calif. Nail Fashion Com.; founder/ofcr. Mainly Manicuring Ednl. Advis. Com.; mem: Calif. Cosmetology Assn., Barbers and Beauty Assn. for the Unification of Nail Artists; vol. (English tchr., maint. instr.) Mission Voc. Center, S.F; Democrat; Unity; rec: arts and crafts, travel, career devel. Res: 1120 Hollywood Ave, Apt 2, Oakland 94602 Ofc: Mainly Manicuring, 4403-A Piedmont Ave Oakland 94611

MALTBY, JEAN E., JR., corporate safety coordinator; b. May 30, 1943, Tacoma, Wash.; s. Jean E., Sr. and Frances Frieda (Ladzinski) M.; children: Tammy b. 1967, Tracey b. 1967, Paul b. 1970; edn: num profl courses, spl courses Coll. of San Mateo, Calif. State Univ.; var. certifications: Nt. Safety Council, Internat. Safety Council, Am. Mgmt. Assn. Career: draftsman City Hall, Newport, R.I., 1970; instrument repairman San Francisco Instrument Co., 1971 73; repair shop mgr. Johnson & Joseph Co., S.F. 1973-74, mfg. mgr. Davis Instruments Corp., San Leandro 1974-76; mfg. mgr. Gould Inc., Controls Div. Rundell Products, REdwood City 1976-78; mfg. engring. cons. J.T. Marsh & Assocs. Inc., mgmt. cons., Newport Beach 1979; supvr. Indsl. Engring., supvr. Maint., Corporate Safety coordinator and supvr. Facility Planning, MDS Qantel Corp., Hayward 1978--; mil: E5, USN 1960-70, decorated GCM (2), Vietnam Svc. (3), Hostile Fire (2); Democrat; Catholic; rec: philately, golf, table tennis. Res: 1010 Lynn St Livermore 94550 Ofc: MDS Qantel 4142 Pt Eden Way Hayward 94545

MAN, GUY KEE, engineer; b. May 27, 1951, Hong Kong; s. Hon-Kwong and Sau-Ching (Luk) M.; m. Debra Ching, Dec. 15, 1979; edn: BS, honors, Univ. of Redlands 1974; BS, Stanford Univ. 1975; Engr., 1978; PhD, 1979; Reg. Profl. Engr. (mech.), Calif. Career: tchg. asst. Dept. of Mech. Eng. Stanford Univ. 1975-78; senior engr. Jet Propulsion Lab Guidance & Control Sect., Caltech Pasadena 1979-81, tech. gp. leader Control Analysis Group, 1981--; cons. in Dynamics, Controls and Seismic Analysis 1982-; mem: Am. Soc. of Mech. Engrs.; Calif. Soc. of Profl. Engrs.; Nat. Soc. of Profl. Engrs.; Sigma Xi; publs: arts. in var. tech. journs.; rec: painting, hiking, photog. Res: 20113 Cassia Ct Cerritos 90701 Ofc: Jet Propulsion Lab, Caltech, 4800 Oak Grove Dr Pasadena 91109

MANCINO, DOUGLAS MICHAEL, lawyer; b. May 8, 1949, Cleveland, Ohio; s. Paul and Adele (Brazaitis) M.; m. Carol Ann, June 16, 1973; edn: BA, cum laude, Kent State Univ. 1971; JD, summa cum laude, Ohio State Univ. 1974; admitted to practice Supreme Cts. of Calif., Ohio, D.C. Ct. of Appeals, US Dist. Ct. (No. Dist. Ohio), US Tax Ct. Career: atty. law firm Baker & Hostetler, Cleveland, Ohio ofc. 1974-80; ptnr. Memel, Jacobs, Pierno & Gersh, Century City, L.A. ofc. 1980--; lectr. profl. orgns. on legal, tax, health care subjects; mem: Am. Bar Assn. (Tax Sect., Bus. Sect., Real Prop., Probate, and Trust Sect.), State Bar of Calif. (Tax and Bus. Law sects.), Ohio State Bar Assn., Gr. Cleveland, Dist. of Columbia, Beverly Hills (ch. Health Law com.) bar assns., Nat. Health Lawyers Assn., Am. Soc. of Hosp. Attys., Calif. Soc. for Healthcare Attys.; publs: arts. in legal and trade journals in legal, healthcare areas; Democrat; rec: skiing, golf, tennis. Res: 2727 Patricia Ave Los Angeles 90064 Ofc: Memel, Jacobs, Pierno & Gersh, 1801 Century Park East, Los Angeles 90067

MANDEL, BENJAMIN JORGE, dentist; b. May 13, 1944, Mexico City; nat. 1975; s. Mauricio and Victoria (Eskenazi) M.; m. Olga Sherr, Dec. 27, 1970; children: Joshua b. 1980, Jonathan b. 1983; edn: BS, chem., UC Berkeley 1966; MS, chem., Polytech. Inst., Mexico 1969; postgrad. biochemistry advanced studies, Univ. of Wisc. 1970-71; DDS, NY Univ. 1975. Career: research assoc. Univ. of Wisc. 1970-72; gen. practice resident VA Hosp., Martinez, Ca. 1975-76; pvt. practice dentistry, Santa Clara 1976--; cons. Mission Convales-

cent Home, 1976-77; fmr. cons. Child Health & Disability Prevention Pgm.; KRON Health Fair volunteer 1980, 81; founder, chmn. Santa Clara Co. Periodontology Study Club; lectr. on T.M.J. disorders and relationship to headache, back and neck pain, (Hawaii, and internat.) 1982; elected mem. Calif. Dental Bd. of Examiners; mem: Santa Clara Dental Soc. 1975- (hosp. com. 1977, dental health com. 1982); Western Soc. of Peridontol. (bd. dirs. Santa Clara Co. Orthopedic Study Club); Am. Soc. of Clin. Hypnosis; Am. Dental Assn.; Calif. Dental Assn. (table clinic presentation 1983 Anaheim meeting); Hispanic Amer. Dental Assn.; Amer. Acad. of Periodontology (assoc.); Alpha Omega frat. publs: art., Australian J. of Chem. 1970; resrch. in pain control 1971-2; rec: cello player, opera, ballet, painting. Res: 46553 Chaparrel Dr Fremont 94539 Ofc: Ben Mandel, DDS, Inc. 1150 Scott Blvd Santa Clara 95050

MANER, ETHRIDGE LESTER, realtor/ business owner; b. Sept. 24, 1932, Knoxville, Tenn.; s. Ethridge Lee and Katherine Elizabeth (Webb) M.; m. Emily Caraway, July 3, 1954; children: Lisa Ann, b. 1962; Mark Lester, b. 1964; edn: BS, Univ. of Tenn. 1959; Adv. Mgmt., Ohio State 1970. Career: v.p. Curlee Clothing Co., St. Louis, Mo. 1960-72; Mono Co. Bd. Supvrs., Mono Co. 1980-82; chmn. 1981-82; owner Mono County Realty, Mammoth Lakes 1972--; co- owner High Sierra Travel Svc., Bishop and Mammoth Lakes 1982--; Tch. Adv. Com., Apparel Industry; apparel indus. cons. Adv. Com. to Devel. Sports Interest in The Nat. Forests of Calif.; awards: Awd. of Spl. Merit in recgn. of faithful svc. and contbns., Am. Apparel Mfrs. Assn. 1974; Pres.'s Awd., Mammoth Lakes CofC; recipient commendations, Calif. Senate Rules Com. and Calif. Ofc. of Emergency Svcs., 1983; Resolution, Calif. State Assembly 1983; mem: Rural Counties Supvrs. Assn. of Calif. Co. Supvrs. Assn. of Calif.; Mammoth Lakes Lions Club (pres. 1979-80); Mammoth Lakes CofC (pres. 1978-79); Elks; Jaycees; works: Nat. Adv. Com. to Develop Metric Standards for USA and Canada; mil: USAF 1951-55 (incl. 25 combat missions in B-29 over Korea), Air Medal w/ Oak Leaf Cluster, Korean Svc., Nat. Defense, UN Svc.; Republican; Episcopal; golf, aviation, skiing. Res: 280025 Grindelwald S Mammoth Lakes 93546 Ofc: High Sierra Travel, 621 West Line St Bishop 93514

MANGALIMAN, CESAR PACIS, real estate specialist/broker; b. Oct. 29, 1925, Philippines, nat. 1955; s. Anacleto and Trinidad Somera (Pacis) M.; m. Victoria Usi Bonifacio, Sept. 16, 1950; children: Magdalena M. (Hall) b. 1951, Amelia b. 1952, Cesar B. Jr., b. 1?5, Fides M. (Rojo) b. 1957; edn: Olympic Coll. (Bremerton, Wn.) 1955-56; UC Ext. SF 1961-62; City Coll. of S.F. 1975-81; Lumbleau Real Estate Sch. 1975; Calif. lic. Real Estate Broker 1977-. Career: chief yeoman, personnel and administrative splst. (E7) US Navy 1946-66: Captain's Writer on board the USS Ranger (CVA-61) and personnel and adminstrv. spls. on sev aircraft carriers, Vietnam, Korea, the Phil.; asst. to Plans and Programs Ofcr., mem. staff of Comdr. Western Sea Frontier, and Comdr. Pacific Reserve Fleet (respons. for short and long range contingency war plans, Top Secret clearance); currently Dept. of Army civilian employee/ mgr. facilities (real estate) program in coord. with GSA and Corps of Engrs. for new offices, relocations, expansions and upgrades for nine subordinate commands, HQs 6th Recruiting Brigade (W.), Presidio of S.F. 1978--; also real estate broker Phi-Am Realty, S.F. 1975--; mem. Calif. Real Estate Assn. 1975-77; Officers Club Presidio of S.F.; Mr. and Mrs. Club of Calif.; Masantol Club; mil. decorations: GCM (5), WWII, Vietnam-Korean Svc., Armed Forces Expdtn., Adm. Byrd's South Pole Exped.; Democrat; Catholic; rec: wrestling, fishing, volleyball. REs: 8 Knott Ct San Francisco 94112 Ofc: HQS, DA, 6th Recruiting Brigade (W), Presidio of San Francisco 94129

MANGER, CHARLES CHRISTIAN, III, physician-ophthalmologist; b. Jan. 16, 1944, Mare Is.; s. Charles C. and Helen Frances (Alexander) Manger; Edn: BS in math & nuclear sci., USN Acad., Annapolis, 1965; pre-med., Harvard Univ., 1971; MD, USC, 1976; internal medicine internship, 1976-77; ophthalmology residency, 1977-80, L.A. Co./USC Med. Center; m. Carol Granone, June 4, 1977. Career: fully qualified in submarines/electrical and reactor officer, Nuclear Submarine Force, 1965-70; served on Ballistic Missile Submarine USS Nathan Hale, 3 yrs.; researcher in Hypertension Lab., NYU Med. Center, 1971-72; MD degree and postgrad. studies, 1972-80; pvt. practice in Ophthalmology, Laguna Hills, 1980---; clin. instr. of ophthalmology, USC (eye surgery); mem. adv. council Natl. Hypertension Assn. Honors: Student body pres., USC Sch. of Med., 1973-74; Diplomate, Amer. Bd. of Ophthalmology, 1981. Mem: Orange Co. Med. Assn.; Orange Co. Soc. of Ophthalmology; Calif. Med. Assn.; AMA; Amer. Acad. of Ophthalmology. Medical staff: South Coast Hosp., So. Laguna; Western Medical Center, Tustin; Saddleback Comm. Hosp., Laguna Hills; Mission Community Hosp., Mission Viejo. Publs: hypertension research (3), clin. ophthalmol. research (1). Mil: Lt., USN, 1965-70, Polaris Patrol Medal. Republican. Roman Catholic. Rec: golf, swimming, tropical and saltwater aquariums Res: 28631 Placida Ave., Laguna Niguel 92677; Office: C.C. Manger III, M.D., Inc., 23561 Paseo de Valencia, Suite 46, Laguna Hills 92653.

MANGUM, DANNY LEE, quality assurance engineer; b. July 26, 1933, Salt Lake City, Utah; s. Cleddy Merrill and Lillian Beatrice (Schell) M.; m. Jacqueline Louise Cordle, Mar. 4, 1955; children: David, b. 1956; Sandra, b. 1957; Angela, b. 1959; Leslie, b. 1962; Teresa, b. 1964; edn: AA, Allan Hancock Coll. 1976. Career: field insp.: Convair Astronautics Div. Gen. Dynamics Corp., Palmdale 1957-60, Fairchild AFB, Wash. 1960-61, RCA Svc. Co., Beale AFB, Calif. 1961-62, Martin Marietta Corp., Vandenberg AFB 1962-64, Rocketdyne, Div. NAA Rocket Site, Edwards AFB 1964-66; with Martin Marietta Corp., Vandenberg AFB 1966--; insp. field site 1966-69, engr./ sr. engr. quality field 1977-81, lead Quality Assurance & Engring., 1981--, (aerospace pgms.

involved with: Titan 34D, Peacekeeper, Titan III, Apollo, Gemini, Titan II, Titan I, Atlas E, F-106, & F-102); honors: Annual Awds., Operational Performance, Martin Marietta Corp., Denver, Colo. 1983; Gold Medallion Awd., Martin Marietta 1976, 83; Engr. of the Yr., Air Force Assn., Robert H. Goddard chpt. 1982; life mem., Alpha Gamma Sigma, Aquarius chpt., Allan Hancock Coll. 1976; mem: Martin Marietta Mgmt. Club; Nat. Mgmt. Assn.; Youth Football League, Lompoc (Ways & Means chmn. 1970); Youth Softball League (mgr./ coach 1967-77); mil: sgt. US Army 1951-54, Combat Inf. Badge, UN Svc., Korean Svc. w/ Bronze Star, Nat. Def. Svc.; Republican; Protestant; rec: home computer, camping, fishing. Res: 209 North W St Lompoc 93436 Ofc: Martin Marietta Corp., POB 1681, Vandenberg AFB 93437

MANKIN, WILLIAM DEAN, business owner/executive; b. Feb. 13, 1934, Carterville, Mo.; s. Charles Pearl and Helen Mamie (Land) M.; m. Patricia Jean Erby, Aug. 10, 1964; 1 dau. Cheri, b. 1966; edn: BA, Wichita Univ. 1961; MA, Wash. Univ. 1967; MBA, Pepperdine Univ. 1982. Career: sales rep. IBM, Kansas City, Mo. 1961-66; gen. mgr. Texas Instruments, Inc., Houston, Tex. 1966-71; v.p./ gen. mgr. Newark Electronics, Los Angeles 1971-73; dist. sales mgr. Fairchild Camera & Instrument, Santa Ana 1973-82; exec. v.p./ gen. partner Centaur Corp., Irvine 1982--; sales awards: Salesman of Year, IBM (1962), Texas Instruments (1969), Western Area Salesman of Yr., Fairchild (1979); mem: Exchange Club of Newport Beach; Albert Pike Masonic Lodge; mil: PO 1/c USN 1952-56, Nat. Defense, GCM, Purple Heart; Republican; Protestant; rec: racquetball, bicycling, golf. Res: 21 Snowberry Irvine 92714 Ofc: Centaur Corporation, 18006 Skypark Circle, Ste 106, Irvine 92714

MANN, ROBERT LE ROY, pharmacist; b. May 11, 1914, Westby, Montana; s. Ernest Otto and Minnie Henrietta (Voitel) M.; m. F. Lucille Foster, Dec. 17, 1945, (dec.); m. 2d. Virginia Nourse, Oct. 12, 1974; children: Ruth, b. 1953; Charles, b. 1957; edn: BS, and D.Pharm., USC 1951; Calif. Contractors Lic. 1936. Career: pharmacist Horton & Converse, Beverly Hills 1951, Sav-On Drug (#11), Inglewood 1951-79, ret.; honors: Rho Chi Soc., USC; mem. Kiwanis Club; works: mem. 70 voice choir, Packard Motor Co., on KFI; piano accompanist for tenor soloist, KFOX (now KERN), Long Beach; baritone sect. vocal choir (6 country tour of Europe); mil: s/sgt., instrument splst., USAF 1943-45, England; Republican; Presbyterian. Res: 2605 Harriman Ln 4, Redondo Beach 90278

MANN, SANTA SINGH, business management executive; b. June 28, 1933, Ganganager, India; s. Dalip Singh (dec.) and Kartar K. (Sahota) Mann; naturalized, 1968; BSEE, Univ. Ariz., 1968; MS, math, UCSD; MS, physics; m. Balbir Kaur Sandhu, July 8, 1951; chil: Sohn; Babu; Sahib; Prem. Career: mgr., Transdata Inc., San Diego; sr. staff engr., Hoffman Elec. Corp., L.A.; exec. v.p., Electro Technology, Inc., S.D.; cons., Arvin Industries & Rohr Corp.; bus. mgmt. exec., Hayward, 1966—; 1st Indian to own 25,000 acres in Calif. Bd. dir., MPS Corp., S.D.; chmn. several non-profit corps. Mem: Natl., Calif., So. Alameda Co., Yuba Co. and Sutter Co. Bds. Realtors. Sikhism, pres. Internatl. Sikh Forum. Res: 2103 S. King Rd., P.O. Box 21393, San Jose 95151.

MANNHEIMER, RALPH I., financial planning executive; b. Aug. 14, 1930, Frankfort, Ger., nat. 1953; s. Joseph and Paula (Loewenstein) M.; m. Maxene Schnadmill, Dec. 20, 1953; children: Jody, b. 1957; Marcie, b. 1965; edn: AA, L.A. City Coll. 1955; BS, San Fernando Valley State Coll., 1960; CLU, Chartered Life Underwriter, The Am. Coll. 1969. Career: adminstrn., suprvn., proj. control mgr. Rocketdyne Div. No. Am. Aviation, Canoga Park 1959-65; ins. agt. Mass. Mutual Life Ins. Co., Woodland Hls. 1965-73; pres. Perquisites Inc., Sherman Oaks 1973--; instr. group ins., Independent Agents Assn. Honors: recognition, City of Los Angeles 1980, Temple Solael president, 1973; Ansel Adams Photo Award winner. Mem: L.A. County Art Museum; Friends of Photography; CLU (pres. San Fernando Vlly chpt. 1979-80); Nat., Calif. Assn. Life Underwriters; Bnai Brith (pres. Woodland Hls. Lodge 1964-65); Sierra Club. Mil: CNG 1949-50, Sgt. US Army 1950-52; UN Svc., Combat Svc. w/ bronze star, Army of Occ. Japan medals; Democrat; Jewish; rec: travel, photog., camping, racquetball. Res: 24525 Eilat St. Woodland Hills 91364 Ofc: Perquisites Inc., 21243 Ventura Blvd., Ste. 119, Woodland Hills 91346

MANNING, KENNETH RUSSELL, developer; b. Oct. 24, 1951, Alhambra; s. Travis L. and Norma Jean (Bartlett) M.; m. Susan M. Speicher, Sept. 9, 1972; children: Keith, b. 1974; Kari, b. 1977; edn: BS, Calif. Potytech. Univ., S.L.O. 1974. Career: v.p. Manning Constrn., Inc. 1973-80; pres. Tri- Pacific Devel., Inc. 1980--; advr. La Puente Valley Regl. Occupation Pgm.; honors: Man. of the Yr., Hacienda Hghts. Republican Womens Club 1979; Outstanding Young Men of Am., Jaycees 1972; mem: Hacienda La. Puente Unif. Sch. Dist. Bd. of Edn. (pres. 1982-83); L.A. Co. Youth chmn. 1983-84; CofC; Hacienda Hghts. Kiwanis (pres. 1978-79); Republican (L.A. Co. Central Com.); rec: snow skiing, golf. Res: 2317 Sarandi Grande Hacienda Heights 91745 Ofc: Tri-Pacific Development, Inc., 1930 Bon View, Ste 12, Ontario 91761

MANNING, MICHAEL M., certified public accountant; b. Nov. 23, 1939, Los Angeles; s. Earl Francis and Isabel Mary (Hanley) M.; father, Capt. Earl F. Manning, US Merch. Marine, WWII (veteran of 2 sinkings, 19 days in lifeboat sailed 1200 mi. in lifeboat to safety); m. Phyllis M.H. Underwood, 1963; children: Phyllis E., b. 1964; Helen, b. 1965; twins, Patrick and Michael G., b. 1969; edn: BS, Golden Gate Univ. 1961-64; CPA, 1971; FAA Cert. comml. pilot Instrument Rating (Land & Sea). Career: pub. acct., staff acct. 1960-64; res. auditor in charge States Steamship Co., Maritime Admin., Dept. of Commerce 1965-70; principal, pub. acctg. firm Michael M. Mannig, CPA 1971-80; partner, pub. acctg. firm. Manning & Carroll, CPAs 1980--; client rel. directorship of Nat. Real Estate Fund ($ 20,000,000 R.E. Investment Trust); mem: Fed. Govt. Acct. Assn.; Am. INst. of CPAS; Soc. of Calif. Accts. (No. Bay pres. 1976-77, pres. elec. 1975-76); Calif. Soc. of CPAs, S.F.; Marin Estate Plng. Council; Rotary, Mill Valley; Elks, San Rafael; Native Sons of the Golden West; mil: SK3 USNR 1957-65; Republican; Catholic; rec: music (active in var. Dixieland & big bands), flying, jogging. Address: Manning & Carroll, CPAs, 169 Miller Ave Mill Valley 94941

MANNING, TRAVIS LIONEL, general contractor; b. Nov. 9, 1920, Forgan, Okla.; s. Roy and Velencia Velna (Mitchell) M.; m. Norma, Feb. 8, 1947; children: Bradley Travis, b. 1950; Kenneth Russell, b. 1951; Lois Ann, b. 1957; edn: AA, Pasadena Jr. Coll. 1940; BE in CE, USC 1946; Reg. Civil Engr., Calif. 1949; Lic. Surveyor, Calif. 1947; Gen. Contractor, Calif. 1968. Career: asst. dist. engr. L.A. Co. Road Dept. 1948-52; pvt. practice, consulting engr. 1952-59; dir. pub. works, City of El Monte 1959-64; dir. Upper San Gabriel Valley Municipal Water Dist. 1964-82; mem. bd./ pres. Hacienda La Puente Unif. Sch. Dist. 1969-74; dir. Metropolitan Water Dist. 1973-78; mem. bd./ pres. Mt. San Antonio Comm. Coll. 1975-81; gen. contractor 1964--; currently, owner Tri- Pacific Development, Inc., Ontario; chmn. bd. Tri-Pacific Devel., Inc.; chmn. bd. Tri- Pacific Fin. Inc.; mng. gen. partner Dunes Properties Ltd.; mng. gen. partner High Desert Park Ltd.; mng. gen. partner Bon View Indsl. Plaza; honors: Cert. of Appreciation, Selective Svc. Sys., Pres. Nixon and Gov. Ronald Reagan; mem: So. Calif. Water Utilities Assn.; 20/ 30 Clubs (internat. pres. 1955-56); Rotary Club (pres. 1962-63); Kiwanis Club (pres. 1980-81); Republican; (L.A. Co. Exec. Com.; del. for Pres. Reagan, Nat. Conv. 1968, 76, 80); rec: golf. Res: 12725 Golf Course Dr, SVL 311, Victorville 92392 Ofc: Tri-Pacific Development, Inc. 1930 Bon View 12, Ontario 91761

MANRIQUE, MARTIN, home furnishings designer/business owner; b. Jan. 4, 1923, Leon Gto., Mex., nat. 1952; s. Aurelio Flores and Luz Marie Manrique; m. Emma Jimenez, Mar. 24, 1949; children: Richard, b. 1950; Victor, b. 1955; Martha, b. 1957; Norma, b. 1962; edn: Inst. Politecnico Nacionale 1941-43; W.L.A. Coll. 1977-78. Career: foreman Alwyn Studios; foreman Home Furniture Co.; designer Schenasi Decoration, Beverly Hills; foreman Chambers & Sons, Los Angeles; owner Manrique Custom Upholsters, L.A. 1961--; apptd. to Calif. Dept. of Consumer Affairs Bureau of Home Furnishings Adv. Bd., Gov. Brown Jr. 1981, reapptd. 82-; composer/ lyricist, num. works include oratory: The Creation, comprising 17 songs; Democrat; Presbyterian; rec: songwriing. Res: 8806 Glider Ave Los Angeles 90045 Ofc: Manrique Custom Upholsterers, 4333 1/2 Degnan Blvd Los Angeles 90008

MANUEL, LEE M., real estate investment co. president; b. Aug. 13, 1936, Los Angeles; s. Paul V. and Vivian J. (Jackson) M.; m. Sally Marsden, 1959; children: Stephen b. 1965, Stacey Ann b. 1971; edn: BS, USC 1958; profl. desig. in Investment Real Estate, and certs. in R.E. Fin., R.E. Mktg., UCLA; GRI-grad. Realtors Inst. of Calif.; Calif. lic. real estate broker; NASD lic. principal. Career: active in real estate fin. and inv. field 1960s-; bd. chmn./CEO of Oak Capital Corp., Sherman Oaks; dir. Warner Financial; fmr. v.p. Nationwide Constrn. Lending for Weyerhaeuser Mortgage Co.; fmr. v.p. Lifetime Fed. Svgs. and Loan; mem: Nat. Assn. Realtors; Calif. Assn. Realtors (dir.); San Fernando Valley Bd. of Realtors (past pres.; dir. SFVBR Federal Credit Union); Real Estate Securities and Syndication Inst. (Fed. Taxation Com.); Phi Gamma Delta (past pres.); rec: skiing, tennis. Res: 412 N. Kenwood St Glendale 91206 Ofc: Oak Capital Corp. 4645 Van Nuys Blvd, Ste 100, Sherman Oaks 91403

MARCHAND, DANIEL WELLS, realtor-appraiser; b. Nov. 13, 1951, Oakland; s. Claude Charles and Marilyn (Wells) M.; edn: real estate courses, Chabot Jr. Coll. 1973-74; (GRI) Graduate Realtors Inst., CAR 1975; (CRS) Cert. Residential Splst., NAR 1979. Career: gen. real estate brokerage firm, incl. sales (res., comml., & indsl.), develop., appraisals, property mgmt., investment counseling, estate plng. & mortgage lending 1971--; currently, pres. MW Assoc., Inc., A. Calif. Real Estate Corp.; advr./ cons. Alameda Co., City of Hayward, attys., developers, realtors, banks, pvt. individuals & bus., & mortgage cos.; appraiser I.R.S., gen. real estate values, probate of estate; witness, Superior Ct, Alameda & Contra Costa Co.; honors: Named Who's Who in Resdtl. Real Estate, Nat. Assn. Realtor 1981-84; life mem. Million Dollar Club; life mem. Achievement Club, So. Alameda Co. Bd. Realtors; mem: Alameda Co. Assessment Appeals Bd.; Calif. Assn. Realtors (Interbd. Arbitration Com.); Internat. Orgn. of R.E. Appraisers; So. Alameda Co. Bd. Realtors; Nat. Assn. Realtors; Contra Costa Bd of. Realtors; Alameda Co. Apart. Owners Assn.; Alameda Co. Property Owners Assn.; Hayward Rotary; St. Rose Hosp. Adv. Bd.; Alameda Co. 100 Club; mil: airman USAF 1970; Republican; Protestant; rec: equestrian, skiing. Res: 2625 Warwick Pl Hayward 94542 Ofc: MW Associates, Inc., 25805 Mission Blvd Hayward 94544

MARCHETTI, JOSEPH JOHN, general contractor; b. Oct. 8, 1945; s. Vincent and Fanny Marchetti; m. Franca, Oct. 19, 1969; children: Bridget, b. 1974; Diana, b. 1979; edn: San Francisco State Univ. 1963-64; Healds Architl. Coll. 1964-67; lic. Gen. Contractor, Calif. Career: proj. mgr. Emanual Mfg. Corp. 1968-70; proj. mgr. Feiler Bros. Corp. 1971-75; div. mgr./ estimator Plant Bros. Corp. 1976-78; co- owner/ v.p. Feiler Bros. Corp. 1978--; owner/ v.p./ gen. mgr. Traditional Woodworks Corp. 1982--; honors: Awd. for Excellence, Woodwork Inst. of Calif. 1978; Crazy Shirts, Sec. Pacific Nat. Bank, Fishermans Wharf 1979; Hibernia Bank Exec. Ofc., Compass Rose Rm., The Westin St. Francis hotel 1981; mem: Assoc. Gen. Contractors of Calif.; Carpenters Apprentice Com.; Elks Club; Sons of Italy; Press Club, S.F.; Marine's Meml. Club, S.F.;

Italian Catholic Fedn.; Woodwork Inst. of Calif.; works: oil paintings, constrn. designs & space plans on var. proj. incl. Claremont Hotel, Oakland; mil: sgt. USMC; Democrat; Catholic; rec: oil painting, bicycling, football. Res: 1440 Vancouver Burlingame 94010 Ofc: Feiler Bros. Corporation, 184 Harbor Way, So. San Francisco 94080

MARCUS, JOHN RICHARD, lawyer; b. Apr. 28, 1930, St. Helena, Calif.; s. Elias George and Dorothy Olive (Jones) M.; div.; children: David b. 1952, Debbie b. 1955, Cathy b. 1956, Nancy b. 1958, Jonathan b. 1970; edn: BA, Walla Walla Coll. 1951; JD, UCLA Law Sch. 19; postgrad. courses, Loma Linda Univ. Med. Sch.; admitted to Calif. State Bar 1956, US Dist. Ct. 1956, US Supreme Ct. 1963. Career: atty. at law, San Bernardino; businessman, San Bernardino, El Monte; arbitrator, Am. Arbitration Assn.; judge pro tem in Municipal and Superior Cts.; fmr. mem. Hearing Bd. South Coast Air Quality Mgmt. Dist.; past pres. Legal Aid Soc. S.B. Co.; mem: Am. Bar Assn., San Bernardino Co. Bar Assn., Am. Bd. of Trial Advocates (chpt. sec.treas. 1983-4), Calif. Trial Lawyers Assn., Law Sci. Inst. of Am., Lawyer-Pilot's Bar Assn.; Masons, Shriners, Elks, Native Sons of Golden West, Rotary (past pres. Lake Arrowhead), S.B. Council Navy League of US (past pres.), Nat. Fedn. of Indep. Business. Address: 357 W. 2nd St, Ste 11, San Bernardino 92401

MARGARITIS, JOHN PAUL, public relations executive; b. June 8, 1949, NY, NY; s. George H. and Mary (Liakos) M.; m. Charlene Corenman, Feb. 21, 1982; edn: BA, Washington Jefferson Coll. 971; M.Media, New Sch. for Soc. Research, NY 1977. Career: acct. exec. Hank Boernor & Assoc., Uniondale, NY 1974-75; acct. exec. Manning, Selvage & Lee, NY 1976-77; acct. supvr. General Electric Co., NY 1977-79; v.p./ dir. of client svcs. Burson- Marsteller, Chgo., Ill. 1979-80, Los Angeles, Calif. 1980-82; v.p./ gen. mgr./ partner Fleishman-Hillard, Los Angeles 1982--; mem: Pub. Rels. Soc. of Am.; Publicity Club of NY; L.A. CofC; Town Hall; Boy Scouts of Am. (L.A. Council); Washington- Jefferson Coll. Calif. Alumni Assn. (bd. dirs.); Jonathan Club; mil: 1st lt. US Army Signal Corps 1972-74, Army Commdn., Nat. Defense Svc.; Republican; Greek Orthodox; rec: swimming, tennis Res: 4342 Redwood Ave 202, Marina del Rey 90292 Ofc: Fleishmann-Hillard, Inc., 444 S Flower, Ste 2600, Los Angeles 90071

MARGERUM, BARRY LEIGH, marketing executive; b. Oct. 11, 1951, Trenton, NJ; s. Raymond Edmond, Jr. and Alvira (Konopka) M.; edn: BS, Princeton Univ. 1969-73; MBA, Stanford Univ. 1976-78. Career: mktg. rep. IBM, Newark, NJ 1973-76; asst. to pres. Epsilon Data Mgmt., Burlingame, Mass. 1978-79; prod. mgr. Apple Computer, Cupertino, Calif. 1978-80; dir. of mktg. GriD Systems Corp., Mtn. View 1980-82; dist. mgr. 1983--; honors: capt. Princeton Wrestling Team 1973; 3rd EIWA Wrestling Championships 1971; mem: Am. Mgmt. Assn.; Princeton Alumni Wrestling Assn.; Foster Parent; Republican; Episcopal; rec: fine arts, squash, skiing. Res: 928 Wright Ave 502, Mountain View 94043 Ofc: Grid Systems Corporation, 2535 Garcia Ave Mountain View 94043

MARGULIS, LYNN LOUISE, clinical social worker; b. July 25, 1951, London, Ont., Canada; d. John Charles and Peggy E. (Norman) Sinclair; m. Harvey Glen Margulis, Feb. 23, 1978; edn: AA, Fresno City Jr. Coll. 1973; BA, summa cum laude, CSU Fresno 1975, MSW, 1979; (LCSW) Lic. Clin. Soc. Wkr., Calif.; (ACSW) Acad. of Cert. Soc. Wkrs. Career: fmr. soc. wkr. Fresno County Mental Health, Community Care, Acute Psychiatric Unit, Residential Care and Rehabilitation programs; psychotherapist, Rape Counseling of Fresno, currently and also afil. with Bullard Counseling Center of Fresno; estab. Info./Referral Support Group on PMS; cons. to Assn. for Retarded Citizens; volunteer wkr. Mental Health Assn., Big Brothers/Big Sisters of Fresno; honors: Phi Kappa Phi; mem. ACSW, Mental Health Assn. of Fresno, League of Women Voters; publs: writer on women, aging, and pre menstrual syndrome in local newspaper; Democrat; Ch. Relig. Sci.; rec: photog., antique art collecting. Res: 1220 E. Bremer Fresno 93728 Ofc: Rape Counseling 3006 N. Fresno St Fresno 93703

MARHOEFER, GORDON JOSEPH, chartered life underwriter, lawyer; b. Aug. 25, 1932, Detroit, Mich.; s. Edwin Louis and Lucy Cecilia (Cavanaugh) Marhoefer; m. Patricia Black Nutter, 1978; children: George, b. 1956; Clifford, b. 1956; Thomas, b. 1958; Robert, b. 1960; (step) Darci, b. 1969; edn: BA, Loyola Univ., L.A. 1954; CLU, Am. College 1966; JD, Loyola Law Sch. 1972; ChFC, Am. College 1983. Career: Pacific Mutual Life Ins. Co., L.A.: adminstrv. trainee 1955-7, agent (Sherman Oaks) 1957-9, adminstrv. asst. 1959-61, mgr. of conservation 1961-4, mgr. advanced underwriting, 1964-7, dir. estate & bus. planning, 1967-72; life underwriter/atty., Newport Beach 1972--; CLU instr.; Life Mgmt. Assn. instr. Mem: Million Dollar Round Table, Life and Qualifying mem. 1977-84; Newport Bch-Irvine Estate Planning Council (founding dir., finl. ofcr. 1982-3, secty 1983-4); Calif., Orange Co. Bar Assns.; Am. Soc. of CLUs; Nat. Assn. Life Underwriters; Mensa; Alano Club of Costa Mesa (v.chmn. 1975-6); Burbank Parochial Baseball League 1968-71. Publs: arts. in profl. jours. Republican (first pres., Burbank Young Repubs.). Catholic. Rec: photog., camping. Res: 342 Sydney Ln Costa Mesa 92627 Ofc: Massachusetts Mutual Life Ins. Co., 610 Newport Ctr Dr, Ste 1300 Newport Bch 92663

MARIANO, ELPIDIO CRUZ, surgeon; b. Nov. 16, 1946, Philippine; s. Domingo G. and Amparo S. (Cruz) M.; m. Edna S. Rivera, Jan. 14, 1973; children: Edward, b. 1973; C. Michael, b. 1977; Catherine, b. 1981; edn: BS, Univ. of Santo Thomas 1966; MD, cum laude, 1971. Career: res. surgery Univ. of Santo Tomas, Philippines 1971-73; res. surgery CMDNJ, New Jersey Med. Sch.,

Newark, NJ 1973-74; res. surgery CMDNJ, Rutgers Med. Sch., Piscataway, NJ 1974-78; chief res. surgery 1978-79; instr. surgery 1979-80; asst. prof. surgery 1980-83; attndg. staff Petaluma Valley Hosp., Petaluma 1983--; mem: Fellow Am. Coll. of Surgeons; Fellow Southeastern Surgical Congress; Assn. for Acad. Surgery; publs: num. arts. in med. journs.; Catholic. Address: 106 Lynch Creek Way, Ste 9B, Petaluma 94952

MARIETTA, MARY BLACKFORD, social worker; b. Mar. 17, 1929, Gallup, N.Mex.; d. Clyde Walter and Edna (Elder) Blackford; m. George ALbert Marietta, June 18, 1967; children: Eric Keven Sweat (dec.) 1955-1957; Cynthia Eileen Moriarty, b. 1956; edn: BS,. Ariz. State Univ. 1951; MSW, UCLA 1957. Career: soc. wkr. L.A. County Dept. of Public Assisstance, Los Angeles 1953-57; deputy probation ofcr., L.A. Co. Probation Dept. 1957-68; clin. soc. wkr. L.A. Co. Probation Dept., Las Palmas Sch. for Girls 1968-70; dir. soc. svcs. Epworth Village, York, NE, 1970; clin. soc. wkr. Lancaster Mental Health Ctr., Lincoln, NE 1971-77; sr. soc. wkr./ MSW San Diego Co. Dept. of Soc. Svcs. 1977--; clin. soc. wkr. Family Svcs. Assn., part- time 1978-80; pvt. practice, LCSW, Oceanside, part- time; chmn./ v.chmn. No. County Child Abuse Task Force 1981, 82; secty. San Diego Child Abuse Council 1982; chmn. Grief Ctr., Lincoln, NE 1975-77; cons. Adolescent Gp. Home, Lincoln, NE 1974-77; awards: Freshman Scholarship, ASU 1947; Brotherhood Awd., ASU 1950; mem: NASW; Acad. Cert. Soc. Wkrs.; No. County Psychological Assn., Vista; Baha'i Faith, Oceanside; Local Spiritual Assembly, Oceanside; Palomar Chorale gp., Palomar Coll., San Marcus; Baha'i Faith; rec: gardening, dancing, sewing. Res: 3426 Apricot Tree Way Oceanside 92054 Ofc: San Diego County Dept. of Social Services, 311 S Tremont Oceanside 92054

MARINE, ERWIN, investment advisor; b. Aug. 21, 1924, NY; s. Charles Rudulf and Claire (Fox) Marino; m. Luanne Roberts, Jan. 26, 1976; 1 son: Scott Charles, b. 1954; edn: BS mech. eng., Univ. of Okla. 1945; BS indsl. eng. , USC 1956; Reg. Investment Advisor.; Reg. Profl. Engr., Calif. Career: controller Kam Corp., Honolulu, Hi. 1970; chief engr. Cathy Corp., Westlake Village 1977; pres. Marine & Marine Inc. , Thousand Oaks 1979; real estate broker Fred Sands Investment Div., Westlake Village 1981; rep. Investors Diversified Svcs., Ventura 1983; owner/ fin. advisor and tax planner, Erwin Marine Financial, Westlake Village 1984--; lectr. Univ. of Hawaii 1972; lectr., Learning Tree; guest lectr. UCLA 1982-e; awards: Hillel Awd., Univ. of Okla 1944; mem: Conejo CofC (Profl. Com.); Internat. Assn. for Fin. Plnnrs.; works: 1st pl., Piano Competition, NYC 1938; 1st pl., La Canada Art Sch. 1954; estab. mfg. ops. in Hong-Kong, Philippincs, Taiwan, Mex. & Spain 1970-, estab. initial industrialization of border industry, Texas & Calif. 1968; mil: lt. USN 1945, Pacific Theatre; Republican; Jewish; rec: music, art; Res: 2155 Wimbledon Circle Westlake Village 91361 Ofc: Erwin Marine Financial, 2659 Townsgate Rd, Ste 101, Westlake Village 91361

MARINER, WILLIAM MARTIN, chiropractor; b. Jan. 2, 1949, Baltimore, Md.; s. Wm. Joseph and Ellen (Dexter) M.; edn: AA, Phoenix (Az.) Coll. 1976; BS, L.A. Coll. of Chiropractic 1979, DC, summa cum laude, 1980; lic. D.C. in Calif., Ariz., 1980. Career: health food store mgr. Guru's Grainery, Phoenix, Az. 1975; physical therapist A.R.E. Clinic, Phx. 1975-76; research dir. G.R.D. Healing Arts Center, Phx. 1975-76; adminstrv. asst. to acadcmic dcan, Los Angeles Coll. of Chiro., L.A. 1977-80; adminstrv. cons. Calif. Acupuncture Coll., L.A. 1978, faculty mem. 1978-80; founder/pres. and clinical dir. Pacific Healing Arts Center, Del Mar 1980--; honors: Outstanding Senior 1980, Am. Chiro. Assn., Delta Sigma 1980, National Dean's List 1979-80, Phi Theta Kappa 1976; mem: Am. Chiropractic Assn. (Council on Nutrition, Council on Mental Health), Calif. Chiro. Assn., Internat. Coll. of Applied Kinesiology, Holistic Dental Assn., Holistic Chiro. Assn., British Homeopathic Assn., Assn. for Humanistic Psychology, San Diego Chiro. Soc., Del Mar CofC; author/pub. various patient edn. materials; Democrat; Sci. of Mind Intl.; avo: prayer minister, personal growth, natural healing. Res: 428-B "A" St Encinitas 92024 Ofc: Pacific Healing Arts Center, 318 Ninth St, Stc A, Del Mar 92014

MARJAN, MANOUCHEHR, architect; b. Feb. 2, 1932, Tehran, Iran; s. Ali-Asghar and Marzieh (Allahyari) M.; m. Darakhsahn Ghahremani, Nov. 19, 1960; children: Marjaneh, b. 1962; Negin, b. 1963; edn: Teheran Univ. 1950-55; PhD, Rome Univ. 1958. Career: founder/ sr. partner/ mng. dir. Marjan Consulting Engrs., Teheran, Iran 1958-78; currently, architect, Bahar Arch., Newport Beach; tchr. arch., Nat. Univ. of Iran 1960-63, Teheran Univ. 1963-67; honors: Student Profiency Awd. in Edn., Rome Univ. 1958; Proficiency Awd., Ministry of Edn., Iran 1958; Proficiency Awd., Ministry of Housting & Devel. 1971; mem: Am. Inst. of Arch.; Syndicate of Architectural Cons. of Iran (bd. dirs.); Iranian Soc. of Consultants (bd. dirs.); Iranian Imperial Club; fluent in Persian, Italian, French and English; Moslem; rec: antiques, painting. Res: 22 Candlebush Irvine 92715 Ofc: Bahar Arch., 5015 Birch, Ste 2, Newport Beach 92660

MARKER, CLIFFORD H., company president; b. Apr. 3, 1899, Ligonier, Pa.; s. Denny C. and Nancy Maude (Clifford) M.; (the Clifford and Marker families came to W. Penna. prior to 1800, see Hist. of Westmoreland Co., Pa.); m. Beryl Schuler, 1924 (dec.); m. 2d. Voris Linthacum, 1936, (dec.); children: Clifford, b. 1925; Charles, b. 1926 (dec.); Marc L., b. 1941; edn: BA, Amherst Coll. 1921 (Delta Upsilon frat.); USC Law Sch., Calif. Inst. Tech. Career: pres. Selected Investments, Inc. 1930s; pres. Internat. Engring. Co. 1937-42; spec. personal rep. Lockheed Aircraft Corp. 1942-43; personnel dir. The Owl Drug. Co. 1943-48; indsl. rel. dir./ v.p./ corp. dir. Sav-On Drugs, Inc. 1948-82; pres./ chmn. bd. Refiners Petroleum Corp. 1965-81; pres./ dir. Voris, Inc., Reno, Nev. 1947--; commnr. Dept. of Water & Power, L.A. 1960-64, pres./ mem. bd. 1962;

1st v.p./dir. L.A. Water & Power Assocs. 1977-83; former chmn. adv. bd. Booth Meml. Hosp., L.A.; mem: Metro L.A. Salvation Army (adv. bd. 1966-84); mem. Pepperdine Univ. Assocs. Founding 400, 1977-; Circle of L.A. County Mus. of Art (pres.); The Univ. Club of L.A.; L.A. Country Club; pvt. turf clubs of Santa Anita & Del Mar; mil: SATC Ofcrs. Tng., Plattsburgh, NY 1918, hon. disch. US Army 1918; Republican; Presbyterian. Res: 2401 Bowmont Dr Beverly Hills 90210

MARKER, MARC LINTHACUM, bank executive, lawyer; b. July 19, 1941, Los Angeles; s. Clifford Harry and Voris (Linthacum) Marker; Edn: Harvard School; AB, UC Riverside, 1965; JD, USC, 1967; m. Sandra Yocom, Aug. 28, 1965; chil: Victor, b. 1970; Gwendolyn, b. 1974. Career: asst. v.p., asst. secty., Security Pacific Natl. Bank, Los Angeles, 1970-73; chief counsel, Security Pacific Leasing Corp., San Francisco, 1973— and secty. 1980—; pres., secty., counsel, Security Pacific Leasing Services Corp., 1977—. Mem: Amer. Assn. of Equipment Lessors Lawyers Com., 1977-81; Comml. Law Instr., Amer. Inst. of Banking, 1971-72; dir., Refiners Petroleum Corp., pvt. oil & gas drilling co.), 1977-81; dir. & secty., Voris Inc., pvt. co., 1973—. Mem: Univ. Club of L.A. Presentations; Practicing Law Ins., Amer. Assn. of Equip. Lessors, 1976—. Mil: Cmdr., USCGR 1966—. Republican. Lutheran. Rec: scuba diving, mountaineering. Res: 41 Lakeside Dr., Corte Madera 94925; Office: Security Pacific Leasing Corp., 4 Embarcadero Ctr., #1200, San Francisco 94111.

MARKHAM, KEITH GEORGE, flight test center executive; b. Nov. 22, 1926, Ontario, Ore.; s. George Reynolds and Anna Isabelle (Anderson) M.; m. Lela Hartley, Aug. 29, 1952; children: Diane, b. 1954; Marilyn, b. 1956; Nancy, b. 1957; Stephen, b. 1959; Glen, b. 1960; Alan, b. 1966; Carol, b. 1967; edn: BS, Brigham Young Univ. 1953; MS, UCLA 1977. Career: at Air Force Flight Test Ctr., Edwards AFB 1953--; physicist flight research br.; range sys. engr.; supvr. range engineering & scheduling ofc.; chief range ops. br.; currently, chief range sys. eng. sect.; awards: Outstanding Performance Awd. 1983; Letter of Aprreciation, Maj. Gen. Robert T. March, HQ USAF; Boy Scouts of Am. Dist. Awd. of Merit 1976; mem: Range Comndrs. Council (Optical Systems Gp.); Soc. of Photographic Instrumentation Engrs. (past); Air Force Assn.; Timers Aero Club; Ch. of Jesus Christ of LDS (Bishop 1956-63, High Council 1967-79, Stake Pres. 1979-82); Boy Scouts of Am.; works: designed sev. speed courses where world speed records were estab. by aircraft, Edwards AFB; Republican; Ch. of Jesus Christ of LDS; rec: model aircraft, gardening. Res: 44914 N 15th St W, Lancaster 93534 Ofc: 6521 Range Squadron/ ENRER Stop 200, Edwards AFB 93523

MARKOTA, IVAN STEPHEN, JR., producer, acting academy owner; b. Apr. 26, 1927, Los Angeles; s. Ivan and Clothilde (Szymanski) M.; m. Frieda Lippitt, July 4, 1976; two children: Cindy b. 1959, Mitchell b. 1961; edn: BA, Columbia Coll. 1962, MA 1964; dip. D. Rouzer Sch. of Motion Picture Production, 1970. Career: construction industry, 1958-73; professional actor, 1963-73; producer, stage (theatre), 1974--, and producer for Cable-TV; exec. dir./owner Van Mar Acad. of Motion Picture & TV Acting (250 students), schs. in Hollywood and Dallas, 1967--; mem: Acting Coaches & Teachers Assn. (pres.), American Theatres Assn., American Film Inst., Screen Actors Guild, AFTRA, Actor's Equity Assn., Hollywood CofC, L.A. CofC, Better Bus. Bur.; mil: US Merchant Marines; sgy, helping people. Res: 950 N. Kings Rd, 218, Los Angeles 90069 Ofc: Van Mar Academy of Motion Picture & TV Acting, 7710 Santa Monica Blvd Hollywood 90046

MARKS, HATTIE GENEVE, real estate broker; b. Aug. 25, 1922, Indianola, Utah; d. Richard Leo and Grace Adilade (Nelson) Spencer; m. Paul Dan Marks, June 25, 1950; 1 dau. Sharon Geneve (Scarpino) b. 1944; edn: AA, Allan Hancock Jr. Coll. 1975; cert. of R.E., Allan Hancock Coll. 1972; Chuck Chatam Sch. 1970; grad. Richard R. Reno Sch. of Taxation and Exch. 1980; GRI, grad. Realtors Inst. 1980. Career: real estate salespsn. Culberson Co., Lompoc 1967-75, Village Realty 1975-83, realtor/broker Geneve Marks, Lompoc 1984--; awards: Lompoc Woman of the Year 1984; Key Person Award, Lompoc Valley Bd. of Realtors 1982; service awards Lompoc Valley Flower Festival Assn. (Flower Festival Queen Coronation Ball decorations chmn. 1980, 81, 82, 83); mem: Calif. Assn. Realtors, Lompoc Valley Bd. of Realtors (Comm. chmn. 1982); CofC (Ambassador); Quota Club of Lompoc (pres. 1982, Quotarian of Year 198, 83); Santa Barbara Co. Heart Fund Assn.; Art Assn. of Lompoc; Neighborhood Watch Pgm. (chmn. 1982-84); works: local artist, calligrapher, designer parade floats (Sweepstake Winner 1981) for Flower Festival Parade; mil. wife 19 years; Democrat; L.D.S. Ch.; rec: sewing, painting, needle art. Address: 208 Princeton Lompoc 93436

MARLOW, CHRISTOPHER WILLIAM, business owner; b. July 18, 1955, Detroit, Mich.; s. Walter William and Blanche Ann (Sehlerth) M.; edn: att. Orange Coast Coll. 1975, Santa Ana Coll. 1978. Career: piano/ saxophone player 1971--; sales mgr. Organ Exchange, Anaheim Plaza 1976; salespsn. Colton Piano Organ Co., Santa Anan 1980; owner Marlow Music, Garden Grove 1981--; dir. Youth Orchestra; pvt. music tchr.; mem. Curriculum Com. for Vocational Music, Orange Coast Coll.; bd. dirs. Music Associates; mem: Nat. Assn. of Music Merchants; Am. Red Cross (Disaster Volunteer); Speakers Bureau; Republican; Christian; rec: study of British History. Res: 12322 Sungrove Garden Grove 92640 Ofc: Marlow Music, 8915 Westminster Ave Garden Grove 92644

MARMOLEJO, RONALD PETER, podiatrist; b. Dec. 4, 1949, Madera; s. Eno G. and Frances M. Baldrica (Martinez) M.; m. Joyce Brown, July 16, 1975; 1 dau: Courtney, b. 1983; edn: AS, Fresno City Coll. 1972; BA, CSU Fresno 1976; BS, Calif. Coll. of Podiatric Med. 1980; DPM, 1982; DPM, Nat. Bd. of Podiatry Examiners 1982. Career: extern, CCPM, Ft. Ord, Kaiser Vallejo and VA Fort Miley, San Francisco 1978-82; solo practice, podiatrist (spec. biomechanics, sportsmedicine and conservative treatments of the lower extremities), Ofcs. in Porterville, Lindsay and Springville 1982--; staff Sierra View Dist. Hosp.; staff Lindsay Dist. Hosp.; staff Visalia Comm. Hosp.; free foot screenings, Porterville H.S. and Annual Health Fair; Annual Carrer Day, Poterville Rotary; mem: Am. Podiatry Assn.; Calif. Med. Podiatry Assn.; Mid- Valley Podiatry Assn.; Rotary; CofC; Porterville H.S. Booster Club; research: effects of progressive systemic sclerosis (scleroderma) on the lower extremities; mil: 1st lt. Calif. Army Nat. Guard, Nat. Def., Expt. M16, M14, M60; Republican; Baptist; rec: radio controlled airplanes, tennis. Res: 580 W Union Ave Porterville 93257 Ofc: Porterville Podiatry, 620 W Grand Ave Porterville 93257

MARQUIS, WILLIAM G., retirement facility administrator; b. May 6, 1934, Spokane, Wash.; s. GErald W. and Betty (ShulenbergerO M.; m. Mary Anne Blount, Feb. 5, 1964; 1 dau. Melora Anne, b. 1970; Calif. lic. Real Estate Broker 1979, R.E. Agt. 1958; Calif. lic. Community Care Adminstr. 1978. Career: independent owner five Fast Food restaurants 1959-69, founder/pres. Char-Burger Internat., 20-unit Fast Food chain in San Diego (sold to Arbys); v.p. John B. Chadwell & Co. (bus. brokerage) 1975-76; pres. Western Bankers Consulting and Business Brokerage, 1976-80; current: pres./co-owner Gardens Inc., also adminstr. 245 unit full service retirement facility; founder Sun Savings and Loan, S.D. and Landmark Thrift & Loan, S.D.; mem. Lions Club (Host) of S.D.; mil: sp2/c US Army. Res: 1522 So Orange Ave El Cajon 92020 Ofc: 5480 Marengo Ave La Mesa 92041

MARRONE, STEPHEN, ANTHONY, chiropractor; b. Aug. 2, 1929, NY, NY; s. Anthony and Felicia; m. Gemma M., Oct. 5, 1957; children: Lisa, b. 1958; Stephen, b. 1960; Jeffrey, b. 1961; Gemma, b. 1962; edn: BS, NYU 1951; DC, Chiropractic Inst. of NY 1957; postgrad., Los Angeles Coll. of Chiropractic 1958; DC lic., Calif. 1958. Career: aeronautical engr. Republic Aviation, NY (4 yrs.); corp. mgr. tech. employment Combustion Engring., NY (3 yrs.); senior proj. staff engr. Nuclear Central Station & Space Power Atomics Internat., Los Angeles (9 yrs.); cert. x-ray supvr./ opr. Calif. 1972--; currently, DC, S.A. Marrone, DC, A Chiropractic Corp., Westlake Village; pres./ chmn. bd. Internat. Health Care Svcs. 1972-83; awards: Doctor of the Year, Calif. Chiro. Assn. 1968; Gov. apptd. mem. Los Angeles Co. Med. Quality Review Com., Bd. of Med. Quality Assur. 1981-85; mem: Calif. Chiropractic Assn. (pres. San Fernando Valley Soc. 1981); Los Angeles County Chiro. Soc.; Kiwanis (Tarzana pres. 1969, 72); research: proj. dir. Chirokinetics (a chiropractic technique), Los Angeles Coll. of Chiro.; Republican; Knights of Columbus. Res: 2410 Oakshore Dr Westlake Village 91361 Ofc: S.A. Marrone, DC, A Chiropractic Corp., 4625 Lakeview Canyon Rd Westlake Village 91361

MARSEGLIA, MICHAEL MARK, radiologic technologist; b. Feb. 19, 1955, Phoenix, AZ; s. Vincent James and Margaret Mary Marseglia; edn: BS, Radiologic Tech., Loma Linda Univ., 1982. Career: staff radiologic technologist, Arroyo Grande Community Hosp., Calif., 1979-80; Twin Cities Community Hosp., Templeton, 1980-81; staff radiologic technologist, Loma Linda Univ. Medical Center, 1981-82; clin. instr. radiologic tech., 1982---; part-time instr., Chaffey Coll., 1982---. Awards: Mallinckrodt Awd., 1979; Squibb Awd., 1982, Loma Linda Univ. Mem: Amer., Calif. Soc. of Radiologic Technologists. Republican. Rec: weightlifting. Res: 1544 Fairway Dr., Paso Robles 93446.

MARSHALL, JOHN FREDERICK, real estate broker; b. June 9, 1951, Los Angeles; s. Jack W. and Louella D. (Rulliam) M.; edn: BS, Ariz. State Univ. 1974; Calif. lic. Real Estate Broker. Career: mgr. Calif. Land & Cattle Co., King City 1975-76; salesman USA Real Estate Inc., Modesto 1976-82; salesman, retail comml., Coldwell Banker, Fresno 1982--; mem: Internat. Council of Shopping Ctrs.; Kiwanis, E. Fresno; Mosdesto Relays Inc. (bd. dirs.); Republican; Episcopal; rec: pvt. pilot, snow skiing, history. Res; 593 W San Jose A, Fresno 93704 Ofc: Coldwell Banker, 1510 E Shaw Ave, Ste 103, Fresno 93710

MARSHALL, JOSEPH I, investment company executive; b. Feb. 23, 1927, Hoboken, NJ; s. Joseph I., Sr. and Genevieve (Dunlap) M.; m. Maureen Mc Ilroy, Oct. 28, 1949; children: Maureen, b. 1951; Michael, b. 1961; Eileen, b. 1962; edn: Rutgers Univ. 1946-49; desig: Internat. Fin. Plnnr. Career: v.p. Bankers United Life Assurance, Oakbrook, Ill. 1962-70; Independent Financial Consultants, Encino, Calif. 1970-77; v.p./ dir. of agencies Kemper Financial Svcs. 1977--; cons: sales & mktg., Kemper Fin. Svcs. 1975-77; sales & mktg., University Life Ins. Co. 1970-73; Comml. Bankers Life Ins. Co. 1972; Investor's Guarantee Life Ins. Co. 1971-72; Hawaii Corp. 1972; awards: Ins. V.P. of the Yr., Kemper Fin. Svcs. 1982; Leader Presidents Club, Prudential Ins. Co. 1955; mem: Internat. Assn. of Fin. Plnnrs.; Knights of Columbus; Life Underwriters, San Fernando Valley; Porter Valley Country CLub; publs: ads, newspaper & trade mags.; sales brochures for prods.; mil: PHM 3/c USN 1944-46; Democrat; Catholic. Res: 19144-1 Index St Northridge 91326 Ofc: Kemper Financial Services, 120 S LaSalle St Chicago, Ill. 60603

MARSHALL, TREVOR GORDON, electronics consultant; b. Nov. 16, 1948, Adelaide, So. Australia; US Res.; s. Jeffery Gordon and Cynthia Olive (Overall) M.; m. Frances Elizabeth Schuman, June 1, 1970; edn: B.Eng., Univ. of Adelaide 1974; M.Eng., 1978; D.Phil., Univ. of W. Australia 1984; MIEE,

Instn. Elec. and Electronics Engrs. 1974. Career: tutor Elec. Eng. Dept. Univ. of Technology, Lae, Papua, New Guinea 1974; lectr./ assoc. prof. Elec. Eng. Dept. W. Australian Inst. of Tech. 1975-78, cons. Wait-Aid Ltd., 1978-81; senior engr. Nucleus Ltd., Sydney, Australia 1981-82; proj. engr. Cambrian Systems, Inc., Westlake Village, Calif. 1982-83, senior cons. Cambrian Cons., Inc., Calabasas 1983--; SYSOP tech. RCP/ Ms., Thousand Oaks 1982-; awards: Reg. 10 Student Paper Prize, IEEE 1973; SONY Electronics Prize, Australian Broadcasting Commn. 1979; mem. IEEE; num. publications; two patents (Australia); mil: 1st lt. Australian Army Reserve 1964-73. Res: 3423 Hill Canyon Ave Thousand Oaks 91360 Ofc: Cambrian Consultants, Inc., 23930 Craftsman Rd Calabasas 91302

MARSTON, RICHARD WELDEN, lawyer; b. May 8, 1933, Ithaca, NY; s. Winthrop Simon and Sylva Orabelle (Jones) M.; m. Margaret Scholz, Feb. 29, 1960; children: John, b. 1962; Ann, b. 1964; Robert, b. 1965; edn: BS, UC Berkeley 1955; JD, UC Hastings Coll. of Law 1963; Cert. Arbitrator, Calif. Career: pvt. practice law, San Jose 1964-68; municipal atty. San Jose, Glendale, Beverly Hills & Burbank 1968--; currently, senior asst. city atty., Burbank; judge pro tem Los Angeles Municipal Ct.; mem: Calif. Bar Assn. (Pub. Law Sect.); Los Angeles Co. Bar Assn.; Kiwanis, Glendale; So. Calif. Genealogical Soc. (dir.); mil: capt. USAFR 1971; Republican; Catholic; rec: dist. running, backpacking, geneology. Res: 1224 Imperial Dr Glendale 91207 Ofc: City of Burbank, 275 E Olive Ave Burbank 91502

MART, STEPHEN, ARTHUR, visual consultant; b. June 17, 1952, Fresno; s. Dale and Madeline Ann (McClurg) M.; m. Jerry Ogle, Sept. 19, 1980; edn: Famous Artists Sch., Westport, Conn. 1968; BA, San Jose State Univ. 1970-74. Career: internat. ops. mgr. Loomis Courier Svc., Inc., San Francisco 1974-78; owner Luminsions, San Francisco, now The Visual Planning Co., Guerneville 1978--; consultant; designer/prod. visual hardware & software, sculptures and spl. effects; designer/ opr. stage lighting for over 300 performances of approx. 200 performers; works: Hexaweb (hexagonal sculpture) Guerneville 1983, Visual Effects Screen and Lighting Sys. (3- story interior w/ 500 piece lighting sys. for pvtly. owned dancehall/ cabaret theater) 1983; mem. The Planetary Soc., The Smithsonian Assn., DeYoung Museum; Democrat; Protestant; rec: graphic arts, photog. Address: 16881 Armstrong Woods Guerneville 95446

MARTELL, MAURINE, business owner; b. Sept. 6, 1932, El Campo, Tex.; d. Nathan and Carrie (Davis) Burleson; div.; children: Angelle Juanita Clarke, b. 1971; Denise Rene Harris, b. 1953; Victoria Marlene Harris, b. 1954; edn: AA, Los Angeles City Coll. 1951. Career: profl. musician (pianist, arranger, organist) 1948-60, (extensive travel) 1964-80, owner Martell's Fashions & Records Shop 1961-63; pres. Tell-Mar Record Co., pres. Reen-Mar Publishing Co.; mem: NAAFAD (fashion designers); composer: musical, The God Within- A Prayer Away; Just Around the Corner (May Be the Sunshine of Your Life); You Must Go Back To God- Nothing is Impossible, 1979; Democrat; Baptist; rec: chess, music coach. Res: 1647 W 52nd St Los Angeles 90062 Ofc: Martell's Fashions & Records, 5342 1/2 S Crenshaw Blvd Los Angeles 90043

MARTIN, DAVID RALPH, association executive; b. Mar. 8, 1913, Alton, Ill.; s. David Ralph and Bertha (Rhea) M.; m. Settimia Petti, Apr. 26, 1941; edn: AB in econ. (cum laude) Harvard Univ. 1935; Nat. Tng. Schs., Confs. for (BSA) Scout Execs. (1936-68). Career: editor and asst. dir. of publications, Nat. Hqtrs. Boy Scouts of Am., NY 1935-43; chief Retail Advt., US Ofc. of War Information, Wash DC 1943-45; dir. pub. rels. US Fgn. Economic Adminstrn., Pac. Area, Honolulu 1945; dir. press rels./acct. exec. Wm. B. Remington Advt. Agcy., Springfield, Mass. 1946; chief ed. Book Dept., Science Research Assocs. (publishers) Chgo. 1947; pub. relations counselor, Bakersfield, Calif. 1948; Dist. Scout Exec., BSA, Bksfld. 1949-51, Los Angeles 1951-53; asst. Scout Exec. and Field Dir. BSA, L.A. 1953-57; deputy regl. exec. National Council BSA, L.A. 1957-72, ret. 1972; realtor assoc. Ed Laird Realty, San Luis Obispo 1972-78; realtor Red Carpet Real Estate, arroyo Grande 1978-81; mem: SLO Bd. of Realtors 1972-81; Masons; Elks; Republican (State Central Com. 1975-6, SLO Co. Central Com. 1975-79, pres. Estero Repub. Men's Club, Morro Bay 1975-77); hon. trustee Martin and Osa Johnson Safari Mus. (Chanute, Ks.); author: A Boy Scout Sails with the Sea Devil (Putnam: NY), co-author: Three Boy Scouts in Africa (Putnam: NY); columnist: The State of Things, pub. in The Central Coast Times, SLO (1974-79); Prot. Res: 1234 Bolton Dr Morro Bay 93442

MARTIN, JOSEPH, JR., lawyer; b. May 21, 1915; edn: BA, Yale Univ., 1936, LLB, Yale Law Sch. 1939; mem. State Bars of Calif., NY, and D.C. Career: assoc. Cadwalader, Wickersham & Taft, NY, 1939-41; USN (to Lt. Cmdr.) 1941-46; ptnr. Wallace, Garrison, Norton & Ray, San Francisco 1946-55; ptnr. Allan, Miller, Groezinger, Keesling & Martin, 1955-70; Pettit, Evers & Martin 1973-, (Pettit & Martin); Gen. Counsel, Fed. Trade Commn., Wash DC 1970-71; US Rep., Geneva Disamarment Conf. (rank, Ambassador) 1971-76. Fellow, Am. Bar Found.; mem. Pres's Advis. Com. for Arms Control & Disarmament, 1974-78; pres. S.F. Public Utilities Commn. 1956-60; Repub. Natl. Committeeman for Calif. 1960-64; dir. Nat. Fair Campaign Practices Com. 1965-; dir. Arms Control Assn. 1977-; dir. Legal Assistance to the Elderly; Arcata Corp., 7/28/82; Sunworld Internat. Airways Inc., 11/13/81; Shaughnessy Holdings Inc., 1983; vis. fellow Stanford Univ. Northeast Asia-U.S. Forum on Internat. Policy, 1980-; treas. Repub. Party of Calif. 1956-58; dir. Patrons of Art & Music, Calif. Palace of Legion of Honor, 1958-70, pres. 1963-68; clubs: Pacific-Union (S.F), Burlingame CC, Yale (of N.Y.); honors: Official Commendation, Outstanding Service as Gen. Counsel, FTC, 1973;

Disting. Hon. Award, US Arms Control & Disarm. Agcy. 1973; Lifetime Achievement Awd., Legal Assistance to the Elderly, 1981. Address: c/o Pettit & Martin, 101 California St, 35th Fl., San Francisco 94111

MARTIN, PAULA H., educational consultant; b. Nov. 22, 1949, Chgo.; d. Hugo M. and Ann E. (Clark) Zschau; edn: BA, So. Ill. Univ.-Carbondale 1971; M.Ed., Loyola Univ., Chgo. 1975; Ed.D., Univ. of San Francisco 1981; stu. Mangold Idiomas, Madrid, Spain, 1971, Univ. Autonoma, Mexico City, 1974. Career: tchr. bilingual pgms., Chgo. Public Schs./part-time instr. of English as a Second Language for adults, Chgo. Comm. Colls., 1972-75; evaluator (large scale bilingual pgms. in six cultural communities), San Francisco Public Schs., 1975-78; evaluator, Title IV Desegregation Assistance Center proposals and projects, Berkeley, 1978-79; independent consultant dba California Evaluation Services, San Francisco, 1976--; projects incl. US Dept. of Edn. and state-funded ednl. pgms. pertaining to bilingual edn., bilingual vocational edn., and profl. credential pgms. for adults. Mem: Am. Ednl. Research Assn., Nat. Assn. for Bilingual Edn., Teachers of English to Speakers of Other Languages, Evaluation Network, Evaluation Research Soc., Calif. Assn. of Program Evaluators, Commonwealth Club, S.F; publs: contrib. Evaluation News and ERIC (a nat. data base), Evaluation Section, Educational Redesign (1978), San Francisco Unified Sch. Dist.; Democrat; Christian; rec: study Zen, Vedanta, metaphysicial works. Address: California Evaluation Services, 2090 Green St, No. 27, San Francisco 94123

MARTIN, ROBERT NELSON, chiropractor; b. Sept. 21, 1919, Youngstown, Ohio; s. Robert Nelson and Helen (Robinson) M.; m. Clara Bailes, Dec. 8, 1939; edn: L.A. Coll. Physiotherapy 1945; DC, L.A. Coll. Chiropractic 1948. Career: fireman US Coast Guard 1936-39; baker CCC 1939-40; bartender, Gorman, Ca. 1940-42; welder Aircraft Components, Inc. 1942-45; self- empl., Pasadena 1950--; mem: FOE-2310, Van Nuys (pres. 1951-52); Am. Coll. of Chiropractic Orthopedists; Am. Council Chiro. Orthopedists; Pan-Aero Flyers; Christian; rec: flying, fishing, golf. Res: 8739 Tilden Ave Van Nuys 91402 Ofc: Robert N Martin, RPT, DC, 15 N Euclid Ave, Ste 214, Pasadena 91101

MARTIN, STEPHEN J., lawyer; b. Mar. 20, 1930, Montclair, NJ; s. Willis Elwin and Katherine Elizabeth (Lyons) M.; m. Kathleen Lyons, May 10, 1958; children: Christopher John, b. 1964; Therese Marie, b. 1966; edn: PhB, Univ. of Notre Dame 1951; JD, Univ. of Mich. Law Sch. 1954; LLM, NYU Law Sch. 1959; CPA cert 1957; admitted to State Bar of Mich. 1954, State Bar of Calif. 1960. Career: pub. acctg. staff Touche, Ross, Bailey & Smart, Detroit, Mich. 1954-58; assoc. Pillsbury, Madison & Sutro, San Francisco 1959-66, partner, 1965--; mem: Am. Bar Assn. (Council ABA Sect. of Taxation, Wash. DC 1981-83, chmn, Sales, Exch. & Basis Com 1977-79); Calif Bar Assn; Am. Bar Found.; Am. Coll. of Tax Counsel; Am. Inst. of CPAs; Calif. Soc. CPAs; World Trade Club, S.F; Bankers Club, S.F; S.F. Tax CLub; publs: Corporate Takeovers and Property Distbns: The Stark Contrast, 35th Annual Inst. on Fed. Taxation, 1983; Salvaging the Distressed Real Estate Venture, Univ. of San Diego 2nd Annual R.E. Tax Inst. 1982. Res: 60 Denise Dr Hillsborough 94010 Ofc: Pillsbury, Madison & Sutro, POB 7880 San Francisco 94120

MARTIN, THOMAS ALLAN, prosthetics manufacturing co. owner; b. Aug. 26, 1936, Havre, Mont.; s. James S. and Ruby W. Martin; m. Susan M. Alfaro, July 30, 1969; children: Marian b. 1962, Pamela b. 1964, Mark b. 1973, Thomas b. 1979; edn: postgrad. courses in prosthetics, UC Los Angeles, NY Univ., Annastift (Hanover, W.Ger.); Cert. Orthotist and Prosthetist, Am. Bd., Wash DC. 1973. Career: SFC E7, US Army 1954-75: selected to research the thalidamide pgm. in W. Germany; att. Naval Prosthetic Research Lab. Oak Knoll Naval Hosp., Oakland, Ca. 1965-66; worked with Dr. Juan Monroes (World Hlth Orgn.) to estab. a Rehabilitation Ctr. for Viet Namese Army, 1966-69; senior NCO Orthopedic Svc., Dept. Army, 1969-75: restruc. the orthotic/prosthetic facility Frankfurt, Ger. 1969-71; redesigned the orthotic-prosthetic facility (fmrly. at Letterman Gen. Hosp.); estab. the tng. pgm. for military orthotists (still current); restruc. the orthotic-prosthetic lab. at Kosair Crippled Chil. Hosp. Louisville, Ky.; faculty mem. Delgado Coll. New Orleans; created guest lecture series for orthopedic residents Tulane Univ. 1978-79; wrote 24 (self-paced learning pgm.) tech. manuals for orthotist/ prosthetist students; current owner Baja Orthotic and Prosthetic Co.; mem: Ky. Orthotic-Prosthetic Assn. (founding pres. 1976); Louisiana Orth.-Prosth. Assn. (sec.treas. 1978); Am. Orth. and Prosth. Assn. (Edn. Accred. Commn. 1978-); Am. Bd. of Certification (Contg. Edn. Com. 1980-); mem. CofC (bd. dirs., Pres. Award, Chula Vista); Bi Nat. Health Council, Bay Gen. Hosp. 1982; mem. Hansons Disease Commn. 1983; v.p. Le Tip, Chula Vista Chpt. 1983; publs. in med. journals; mil. decorations: Combat Medic Badge, Bronze Star, Vietnam.; Republican; Prot.; rec: coach Little League, Pop Warner Football. Res: 1438 Platano Ct Chula Vista 92011 Ofc: Baja Orthotic & Prosthetic Svc. 205 Church Ave Chula Vista 92010

MARTINEZ, FRANK R., college president; b. Dec. 28, 1921, Los Angeles, CA; s. Frank and Caroline (Bassett) Martinez; BA, polit. sci., Univ. Redlands, 1947; MA, hist., USC, 1953; EdD, 1963; m. Lois M. Martinez, Mar. 16, 1951; children: Larry F., b. 1953; Jay, b. 1955; Mark b. 1956; Barbara, b. 1960. Career: instr. and counselor, Citus Coll., 1947-52; adminstrv. dean, 1962-64; asst. supt., Ednl. Services, Cuesta Coll., 1964-77; pres., supt., 1977--. Mem: San Luis Obispo Co. Civil Service Commn., 1974-78. Mil: USMC, 1942-46, So. Pacific. Mem: Rotary Club, pres. 1959-60. Presbyterian, elder. Rec: bullfighting. Res: 2383 Sunset Dr., San Luis Obispo 93401; office; P.O. Box J, San Luis Obispo 93406.

MARTINEZ GANDARA, JULIO ANTONIO, librarian; b. Oct. 4, 1931, Santiago, Cuba; naturalized 1968; s. Julio and Maria (Gandara) Martinez; PhD, UC Riverside, 1980; MA, Univ. Minn.; MALS, Univ. Mich., 1967; BA, So. Ill. Univ., 1963. Career: assoc. librn., San Diego State Univ., 1980—, sr. asst. lib., 1976-78, asst. librn., 1973-76; also coord. Chicano collection, S.D.S.U. Library; ed., Cognition and Brain Theory, Journl. Recipient: So. Ill. Tuition & Activity Awards, 1958-61. Mem: Natl. Librns. Assn.; Amer. Lib. Assn.; Soc. for the Interdisciplinary Study of the Mind; Calif. Lib. Assn., Coll. & Univ. chpt.; Mensa. Author: Book, Chicano Scholars and Writers, Metuchen, N.J., Scarecrow Press, 1979; book, Chicano Literature: A Reader's Encyclopedia, Westport, Conn.: Greenwood Press, forthcoming; 5 scholarly papers, 18 book reviews, Cyclopedia of Chicano Literature, ed. in press. Citizens Party. Rec: chess, Beethoven. Res: 5642 Hamill Ave., San Diego 92120; Office: Univ. Lib., General Ref. Dept., San Diego State Univ., San Diego 92182.

MARTINEZ, JOSE ANTONIO, physician; b. June 10, 1938, Santa Ana, El Salvador, Central Am.; s. Manuel A. and Mercedes (Sandoval) M.; m. Gloria Bendeck, 1966; children: Jose Antonio, b. 1967; Evelyn, b. 1969; Leslie, b. 1973; Carlos Manuel, b. 1980; edn: Bach. in Letters & Sci., Nat. Inst., El Salvador 1957; MD, Sch. of Med., El Salvador 1967. Career: ob-gyn. splst. Alma Med. Gp., Panorama City 1971-76; ob-gyn. tng., Baltimore (4 yrs.); pvt. practice 1976--; ob-gyn. residency, El Salvador 1966-69; asst. prof. El Salvador Sch. of Med. 1969-71; mem: Am. Coll. of Ob-Gyn.; Am. Fertility Soc.; Am. & Calif. Med. Assns.; Assn. of Gyn-Laparoscopists; L.A. Obstetrical Soc.; Med. Coll. of El Salvador; L.A. County Med. Soc.; Catholic. Res: 16441 Sunburst St Sepulveda 91343 Ofc: Serra Medical Clinic, 14673 Parthenia St Panorama City 91402

MARTINO, PHILIP RAY, chiropractor; b. Sept. 1, 1953, St. Albans, NY; s. John and Rosalie (Gummer) M.; edn: AA, Miami- Dade Jr. Coll. 1973; BS, DC, Palmer Coll. of Chiro. 1977; Toftness Postgraduate Sch. of Chiropractic 1977. Career: chiropractor, pvt. practice, Santa Barbara; lectr. improving health habits and life before birth class (covering human embryo's development); mem: Calif. Chiro. Assn. (past treas.); Palmer Orating Club; Winchester Canyon Gun Club; Am. Tae-Kwon-Do Fedn.; works: painting; stained glass; Christian; rec: surfing, trap & skeet shooting. Ofc: 122-A W. Figueroa Santa Barbara 93105

MARVIN, ARTHUR ELTON, real estate investment broker; b. Feb. 22, 1936, Troy, NY; s. Frank Charles and Mary Katherine (Aiken) M.; edn: AA, Erie Tech. 1959; BS, Univ. of Ariz. 1966; Calif. lic. Real Estate Broker 1982; Nat. Exchanger, NCE. Career: metallurgical engr. Atomic Energy Commn., Los Alamos, NM 1966; engr. McDonnell Douglas 1970; pres. Steelmans, Inc., Huntington Park 1976; broker/ owner Century 21 Carrington Realty 1982--; instr. real estate seminars; honors: Top Salesman, Whitaker Metals 1968; President, Pony/ Colt/ Thoroughbred League, Garden Grove; mem: Nat. Council Exchangers; Huntington Beach- Fountain Valley Bd. Dirs.; Elks; Boys Club com.; works: founder, Real Estate Club of Calif.; author: Foreclosing-Profits and Pitfalls; mil: sgt. US Army 1956-57; Catholic; rec: golf. Res: POB 5425 Garden Grove 92645 Ofc: Century 21 Carrington Realty, 16509 Brookhurst St Fountain Valley 92708

MASON, CHERYL WHITE, lawyer; b. Champaign, Ill.; d. John Russel and Mary Lucille (Birden) White; m. Robert Mason, Oct. 10, 1972; children: Robert, b. 1973; Daniel, b. 1976; edn: BA, Purdue Univ. 1972; JD, Univ. of Chgo. 1976. Career: assoc. O'Melveny & Myers 1976-81; exec. dir. Public Counsel, Los Angeles 1981--; adj. prof. Loyola Law Sch.; honors: Distng. Svc. Awd., Purdue Univ. Black Cultural Ctr. 1980; mem: Am., Los Angeles County, Langston bar assns.; Black Women Lawyers; Women Lawyers of Los Angeles; Westminster Neigborhood Assn. (bd. dirs.); Democrat; Christian. Res: 3844 W 27th Los Angeles 90018 Ofc: Public Counsel, 3535 W Sixth, Ste 100, Los Angeles 90020

MASON, KATHRYN ANN, radiation biologist; b. Sept. 21, 1946, Taylor, Tex.; d. Charles Richard and Rubye Afa (Roepke) M.; edn: BSc, Tex. A&M Univ. 1969; MSc, Sam Houston State Univ. 1976. Career: research tech. Dept. of Exptl. Radiotherapy, M.D. Anderson Hosp., Houston, Tex. 1969-76, senior research asst. 1976-80; splst. Dept. Radiation Oncology, UCLA 1980--; reviewer, radiation research; reviewer med. physics; cons. design & mgmt. of animal research facilities; honors: Sigma XI Research Awd. 1976; mem: Radiation Research Soc.; Jonsson Comprehensive Cancer Ctr. (assoc.); Beverly Glen Assn.; num. arts. in med. journs.; Democrat. Res: 2154 N. Beverly Glen Los Angeles 90077 Ofc: UCLA, Dept. of Radiation Oncology, CHS B3-171, Los Angeles 90024

MASRI, MERLE SID, biochemist; b. Sept. 12, 1927, Jerusalem, Palestine, nat. 1954; s. Sid R. and Fatima (Muneimne) M.; m. Maryjean Anderson, June 28, 1952; children: Kristin, Allan, Wendy, Heather; edn: BA, UC Berkeley 1950, PhD, 1953. Career: research asst. UC Berkeley 1950-53; research assoc. hematology Michael Reese Hosp., Med. Research Inst., Chgo., Ill. 1954-56; currently, research biochemist Western Regl. Research Ctr., Agricultural Research Svc., USDA, Berkeley; honors: USDA Spl. Service Award 1966, Superior Svc. Gp. Award 1976, and Merit Awd. 1977; listed num. biographical publs.; mem: Am. Chem. Soc.; AAAS; Am. Oil Chemists Soc.; No. Am. Thermal Analysis Soc.; NY Acad. of Scis.; publs (100: contbr. research articles to sci. journs., num. presentations, nat. & internat. profl. sci. meetings & confs.; rec: pvt. pilot. Res: 9 Commodore Dr Emeryville 94608 Ofc: Western Regional Research Center, USDA, 800 Buchanan St Berkeley 94710

MASS, EDWARD GEORGE, cruise co. executive; b. Jan. 26, 1944, Wyandotte, Mich.; s. Edward George and Catherine Jane (Corrigan) M.; edn: BS, Eastern Mich. Univ. 1967. Career: sales mgr. Northwest Airlines, Ft. Lauderdale, Fla. 1975-80; regl. sales dir. Sitmar Cruises, Miami, Fla. 1980-83; v.p. sales Sitmar Cruises, Los Angeles 1983--; mem: Am. Soc. of Travel Agents; mil: lt. US 1967-71, Vietnam Svc.; rec: athletics. Res: 4346 Redwood Ave Marina Del Rey 90291 Ofc: Sitmar Cruises, 10100 Santa Monica Blvd, 11th Flr, Los Angeles 90067

MASSA, EDWARD CLEMENT, real estate/insurance broker; b. May 7, 1907, Hayward; s. Manuel Maria and Camilla (Cotta) M.; widower; two children: Michael b. 1938, Valerie (Lozowicki) b. 1948; edn: AB, St. Mary's Coll., Moraga 1929; JD, Univ. of Notre Dame 1933; grad. stu. Stanford Univ. Career: realtor, insuror, developer, cattle ranch owner; handled real estate transactions for num. corporations, developers, public utils., insurance cos., corp. and individual investors; connected family ins. agcy. estab. 1990s; mem. Bd. of Regents St. Mary's Coll. 1970-80; mem. Community Council Sch. of Bus. and Economics, CSU Hayward, mem. CSUH Affiliates, Pres. Circle; secty. Past Presidents Assn. U.P.E.C. (a Portuguese Frat. Life Ins. Co., Calif. -Nev.); mem. Com. of Four rep. Portuguese of origin or birth in Calif. on mission to Fayal, Azore Is. (volcanic eruption mercy mission, 1958); mem. Nat. Ital. Am. Found.; (past): chmn. US Small Bus. Adminstrn. San Francisco Dist. Advis. Council (48 counties); mem. SBA Nat. Advis. Council; awarded citation for svc., SBA (1977); past orgns: pres. St. Mary's Coll. Nat. Alumni Assn. 1957-8, dir. Notre Dame Univ. Alumni Club of No. Calif., chmn. Infantile Paralysis Com. (Hayward), CofC (ofcr., coms.), United Crusade (bd. dirs.), So. Alameda Co. Bd. of Realtors, Hayward Merchants Assn. (pres.), others; book in prog.; Republican; Catholic; rc: music, lecturing, travel. Res: 22566 Norwood Dr Hayward 94541 Ofc: POB 89, Hayward 94543

MASSA, EMIDDIO, educator; b. Aug. 5, 1928, Havertown, Penna.; s. Joseph and Nicolina (Matricardi) M.; m. Mae Lanza, Sept. 16, 1951; children: Joy, b. 1952, Emiddio Jr., b. 1954, Patricia Ann, b. 1956, Eric, b. 1958, Michael, b. 1967; edn: BS, Geo. Washington Univ. 1956, MBA, fin. mgmt. 1963; MBA, real estate, National Univ. 1982; FAA lic. Comml. Pilot 1979; Calif. lic. Fin. Mgr. 1981. Career: served all ranks through cap. USN 1946-79, served overseas French Morocco 1950, Germany 1959, Argentina 1972-75, comdr. Naval Air Reserve, San Diego 1978-79, ret. Jan. 1980; decorated Legion of Merit, others incl. Vietnam, Korea, WWII; currently prof. Aerospace Scis./ chmn. Aerospace Studies Dept., National Univ., San Diego 1983--; airport mgmt. cons. for City of San Diego; dir. Aerospace Mus. of S.D.; mem: Nat. Mgmt. Assn. (pres. Nat. Univ. chpt. 1984), Calif. Colls. and Mil. Educators (treas.), S.D. Navy League (v.p. 1983-4), Naval Inst.; dir. Uptown Plnng. Com.; capt. Crime Stop Neighborhood Watch; publs: Naval Reserve Forces-One Navy? (1970 Naval Inst.); Republican; Catholic; rec: aviation, politics, antique cars. Res: 1401 Sassafras St. San Diego 92103 Ofc: National Univ. 4141 Camino Del Rio So. San Diego 92108

MASTERS, SANDRA ORLINE, real estate broker; b. Jan. 6, 1936, Willamantic, Conn.; d. Dan and Vera Ellen (Korner) Haigh; m. Charles Masters, Aug. 18, 1973; children: Kimberly b. 1960, Kristen b. 1972, David b. 1965; edn: Assoc. Bus., Burdett Coll. 1957. Career: secty. Sylvania, 1958-67; adminstrv. asst. Stanford Univ., 1969-72, Data Disc., 1972-74; real estate broker ERA Allstate Realtors, 1975--; recipient sales awards 1980, 81, Million Dollar Club; mem. Eastfield League, Tahoe Racquet Club; Republican; Episcopal; rec: swimming, skiing, piano. Res: Creston Oaks Arabians, Creston Rd, Paso Robles 93446

MATARE, HERBERT FRANZ, physicist; b. Sept. 22, 1912, Aachen, W.Germany, nat. 1967; s. Joseph Peter and Paula (Broicher) M.; m. Ursula Krenzien, Dec. 2, 1939; children: Felicitas b. 1944, Vitus b. 1955; edn: BS (Abitur) Realgymnasium Aachen/Univ. Geneva 1933; MS (Dipl.Ing.) in physics, Univ. Aachen 1939; PhD (Dr.Ing.) electronics, Univ. of Berlin 1942; PhD in solid state physics, Univ. Paris 1950. Career: head Microwave Lab., Telefunken, Berlin, W.Ger. 1939-45; dir. Semiconductor Lab., Westinghouse, Paris, Fr. 1946-52; founder/pres. Intermetall Inc., Dusseldorf, W.Ger. 1952-56; head Semiconductor R&D, Gen. Tel. & Electronics Co., NY 1956-59; dir. of resrch. TEKADE, Semiconductor Dept. Nuernberg, W.Ger. 1959-61; hd. Quantum Electronics Dept. The Bendix Corp.Research Labs., Southfield, Mich. 1961-63; tech. dir./ mgr. Lear-Siegler Research Labs. Santa Monica, Ca. 1963-64; asst. chief engr. Douglas Aircraft Co., Santa Monica 1964-66; sci. advisor Rockwell Internat. Anaheim 1966-69; pres. ISSEC (Internat. Solid State Electronics Consultants) 1970--; asst. prof. Univ. Aachen, W.Ger. 1936-45; vis. prof. UCLA 1968-69; vis. prof. CSUF 1969-70; Fellow IEEE, NY 1976-; mem. emeritus NY Acad. of Sci.; hon. mem. Inst. for the Advancement of Man; mem: Am. Physical Soc. (Solid State Div.), Electrochem. Soc., Thin Film Div. Am. Vacuum Soc. AAAS; publs: over 100 papers in sci. journals; two books: Microwave Receiver Technology (1951), Defect Electronics in Semiconductors (1971); approx. 60 patents, incl. First transistor patents from 1948 (Westinghouse, Paris), Semicondr. diode mixer theory and tech., 1st vacuum growth of silicon monocrystals and patent on levitation (1952), growth and study of bicrystals (1955-60), first low temp. transistor (1958, GTE), devel. optical heterodyning with bicrystals (1963), 1st crystal-to-crystal optical comm. link (1961) LPE for LED's (1975); rec: astronomy, biology. Address: 141 Medio Dr Los Angeles 90049

MATEUS, BARBARA JEANNE, real estate appraiser; b. Sterling, Colo.; d. Clarence E. and Catherine B. (Gertge) Monroe; m. Ermelindo N. Mateus, June 24, 1972; edn: AA, Northeastern Jr. Coll. 1968; BS, Colo. State Univ. 1970; lic. Real Estate Broker, Calif.; desig: Senior Real Property Appraiser Soc. of R.E.

Appraisers 1983; Career: dept. secty Cost Estimating Dept. Singer-Kearfott, San Marcos 1970-72; exec. secty. to finl. controller Home Federal 1972-74; staff appraiser Home Federal Savings & Loan, San Diego 1974-78, resdtl. income supvr. and tng. coord. 1975-78, senior appraiser 1979-80, appraisal ofcr. 1980--; proj. analyst 1981-82; major loan appraiser 1982--; asst. v.p. Home Federal Savings 1980; mem: Soc. of R.E. Appraisers (pres. S.D. 1983); Cabrillo Civic Clubs of Calif.; Portugueses Hist. Soc.; Golden Hill Comm. Action Orgn.; Democrat; Catholic; rec: Portuguese language, piano, travel. Res: 1644 Granada Ave San Diego 92102 Ofc: Home Federal Savings, 701 Broadway San Diego 92101

MATEWOSIAN, RALPH, real estate broker/developer; b. Dec. 29, 1939, Novorossissk, Russia; s. Zakar and Astghik (Gregorian) M.; edn: AA, Fresno City Coll. 1962; BA, Fresno State Univ. 1971; Calif. Std. Tchg. Credential 1972. Career: Arrow Electric Motor Repair 1964-69; tchr. Fresno Unified Sch. Dist. 1972-79; realtor-developer, owner Ralph Matewosian Realty, Fresno 1977--; mem: FTA; Calif. Tchrs. Assn.; NEA; Fresno Bd. Realtors; Nat. and Calif. Assns. Realtors; mil: sp4 US Army 1962-64. Address: 755 W Sierra, Ste 107, Fresno 93704

MATHENY, HENRY GRIFFY, lawyer; b. Apr. 21, 1933, Los Angeles; s. Lemuel John and Esther Anne (Halford) M.; m. Luise E. Ehrich, July 1, 1970; children: David, b. 1957; Kelly, b. 1962; John, b. 1963; Dagmar, b. 1973; edn: San Jose State 1951-53; BS, Fresno State 1958; Loyola Univ., L.A. 1960; LLD, (JD), UCLA 1964. Career: adjuster Orange Coast Adjusters, Los Angeles 1960, 64; atty. Vaughan, Brandlin, Robinson & Roehmer, L.A. 1965-67; atty. Rus, Hoffman & Mills, Sacto. 1967-71; partner Rust, Armenis & Matheny, Sacto. 1971-73; partner Barrett, Newlan & Matheny 1973-79; pres. Matheny, Poidmore & Sears, Profl. Corp. 1979--; prof. of Law, Lincoln Law Sch., Sacto. 1972-; arbitrator Superior Cts. of Sacto., El Dorado & Yolo Cos.; arbitrator Am. Arbitration Assn.; honors: 2V Rating, Martindale Hubbell; mem: Amer., Sacto. County Bar Assns.; Calif. Trial Lawyers Assn.; No. Calif. Assn. of Defense Counsel; Elks; CofC (Auburn); mil: Sp3 US Army 1953-55; Republican; Episcopal. Res: 3011 Morse Ave Sacramento 95821 Ofc: Matheny, Poidmore & Sears, 2100 Northrop, Bldg 1200, Sacramento 95821

MATHERS, GARY AMES, insurance broker; b. Sept. 18, 1944, Glendale; s. Marvin E. and Jeanne C. (Tritchler) Mathers; m. Suzanne P. Hall, Nov. 16, 1969; 1 dau., Andrea Kathryn, b. 1979; edn: BSc, CSU San Jose, 1972. Career: insurance mktg., 1972--; owner Community Insurance, San Jose; devel. first discounted gp. auto and homeowner ins. pgms. for employees in Silicon Vly. Awards: Commercial Masters, Topper Club, num. sales awds. Mem. Santa Clara Co. Bar Assn. Arbitration Com.; mem. Spartan Blazer; Republican; Prot.; rec: golf, hunting. Res: 1614 Sparkling Wy San Jose 95125 Ofc: Community Ins. POB 1213 San Jose 95108

MATHIS, REED ALEXANDER, clinical pharmacist/nuclear pharmacist; b. Mar. 17, 1952, Takoma Park, Md.; s. Herbert Barlow, Jr. III and Marjorie Ruth (Reed) Duncan; edn: UCLA 1970-72; BS, microbiology, USC 1975; BS, pharm., Univ. of Wisc. 1978; D.Pharm., USC 1982; grad. pgm. (MS in nuclear pharm.), USC 1982-. Career: hosp. clin./nuclear pharmacist in charge Professional Pharmaceutical Assoc., Marina del Rey 1982--; clin. pharmacist VA Hosp., Wadsworth, Los Angeles 1983--; hosp. pharm., Rx Relief Pharmacist Splsts., San Diego 1983--; honors: Nat. Sci. Found. Stipend 1968, Wash. DC Jr. Acad. of Scis. 1968-70; mem: Calif. Pharm. Assn.; USC Gen. Alumni Assn. (life); Am. Security Council; Com. of Ten Thousand; Freemason, Elysburg, Pa.; Williamsport, Pa. Consistory; publs: The De Sanctis- Cacchione Syndrome: A UV Repair Defect (Reed, Cleaver, Sugarman, Mathis) Annal. Derm. 1975; Republican (Nat. Congl. Com.; Pres. Task Force); Presbyterian; rec: X-C skiing, swimming, microbiology. Res: 500 Jackson Pl 311, Glendale 91206 Ofc: Professional Pharmaceutical Associates, 4037 Via Marina, H312, Marina del Rey 90291

MATHYS, MARC G., oil co. corporate counsel; b. May 29, 1955, Bern, Switzerland, nat. 1960; s. Guy Paul and Heidi Simone (Bruegger) M.; edn: Schweizerische Alpine Mittelschule Davos, Switz. 1972-73; USAF Acad. 1973-75; BS, UCLA 1977; JD, Pepperdine Law Sch. 1980; Hague Acad. of Internat. Law.; Engr. in Tng. 1982; admitted to practice Calif., Indian, and Okla. Bar Assns. Career: asst. engr. Southern Calif. Edison 1976; safety engr. Liberty Mutual 1977; advtg. bus., self- empl. 1978-80; hearing ofcr./ indsl. engr./ Lake Co. Deputy Coroner, Indiana 1980-81; currently corp. counsel/ secty ECC Oil Co., Fresno; secty. ECC Resources Corp., Equity Drilling Co.; mem: Soc. of Prof. Engrs.; Am., Calif. & Fresno Co. Bar Assns.; Big Brothers; publisher: Tax Briefs, circular (on going) covering changes in oil and gas taxation, arts.; mil: USAF 1973-75; Army Guard 1980-81; Republican; rec: scuba diving, pilot. Res: 13040 E Belmont Sanger 93657 Ofc: ECC Oil, 1535 E Olive Fresno 93728

MATISOFF, BERNARD S., consulting engineer/ designer; b. Apr. 4, 1930, Los Angeles; s. Samuel and Reva (Sorrich) M.; m. Louise Breskin, June 20, 1953; children: Martin, b. 1957; Glen, b. 1963; edn: mech. design, drafting, L.A. Trade-Tech. Coll.; BSE, West Coast Univ. 1957; Reg. Profl. Engr., Calif.; Cert. Mfg. Engr., Soc. of Mfg. Engrs. (splst. electronics pkg. design and engring.; ops. research; mfg. engring.). Career: supvr. lab svcs., Computer Control Co., Los Angeles 1960-68; mgr. mfg. engring. Data Recall Corp., El Segundo 1968-70; mgr. mfg. Califone Internat., L.A. 1974-75; engr. Litton Industries, Woodlands Hills 1975-77; mgr. tech. svcs. Vector General Inc., Woodland Hills 1977-79; engr. EMM-SESCO, Chatsworth 1979-80; cons. engr./ designer B.

Matisoff & Assoc., Woodland Hills. 1980--; currently chief editor PME Data Svc., Quarterly (pub. by Van Nostrand Reinhold Co., NY, NY); author: Handbook of Electronics Manufacturing Engineering (1978), Handbook of Electronics Packaging Design and Engineering (1981), Van Nostrand Reinhold Co.; contbr. profl. & tech. mags.; mil: SK/ 3 USN 1948-52, UN Svc.; Hebrew; rec: nature photog. Address: 20745 Clarendon St Woodland Hills 91367

MATORY, WILLIAM EARLE, JR., plastic and reconstructive surgeon; b. Nov. 20, 1950, Richmond, Va.; s. Dr. Wm. Earle and Dr. Deborah (Lore) M.; edn: BS chem./math., Yale Univ. 1972; MD, Howard Univ. Coll. of Med. 1976; MD postgrad. fellow Harvard Med. Sch. 1981, UC San Francisco 1983. Career: jr. resident gen. surg., Beth Israel Hosp., Boston, Mass. 1976-79; chief res. 1980; fellow gen. surg. Lahey Clinic, Boston 1979; sr. res. gen. surg. Mass. Gen. Hosp. 1980; chief res. plastic & reconstrv. surg. St. Francis Hosp./UC San Francisco, 1981-83, fellow 1983; Hand Fellowship, 1983, plastic & reconstrv. surgeon, St. Francis Meml. Hosp., 1983-; awards: grand Prize 1978, Nat. Student REsearch Forum, Galveston, Tx.; presentation competitions: 1st Prize Norfolk Flap Symposium (1983), 2d. Prize Calif. Soc. of Plastic Surgeons (1983), 1st Prize, Nat. Med. Assn. (1983); mem: Am. Soc. Plastic & Reconstrv. Surgeons, Calif. Med. Soc., Big Brothers of Am.; arts. in med. journals; rec: raquetball, tennis, chess. Res: 2310 19th St San Francisco 94107 Ofc: St. Francis Memorial Hosp. 900 Hyde St San Francisco 94109

MATSCHULLAT, ROBERT WAYNE, investment banker; b. Nov. 21, 1947, St. Cloud, Minn.; s. Wayne Emil and Harriet Jane (Bowman) M.; m. Ariane Hardin, June 16, 1970; children Clare Corrine, b. 1982; Robert Carter, b. 1983; edn: BA, Stanford Univ. 1969; MBA, w/ honors, 1972. Career: asoc. Morgan Stanley & Co., NY 1972-77; v.p. Salomon Brothers Inc., San Francisco ofc. 1977-83; mng. dir. 1984--; mem: San Francisco Golf Club; The Olympic Club; The Bankers Club of S.F; rec: golf. Res: 947 Green St San Francisco 94133 Ofc: Salomon Brothers Inc., 555 California St, Ste 3900, San Francisco 94104

MATSON, JAMES GEORGE, architect; b. Sept. 29, 1948, NY; s. George Donald and Margaret Jane (Hawkes) M.; edn: B.Arch., Univ. of Va. 1972; M.Arch., Harvard Univ. 1974; Reg. Architect, Pa. 1977, Calif. 1982. Career: senior arch. Dept. of Plng. & Devel., City of Trenton, NJ 1974-77; proj. arch. Bittorf, Holland & Christianson, Archs. Ltd., Edmonton, Alberta, Can. 1977-79; job capt. Charles Kober Assoc., Los Angeles 1979-80; proj. arch. Kamnitzer & Cotton, Archs., L.A. 1980--; honors: Design Awd. for Comm. Coll. Bldg., City of Edmonton 1981; mem: NCARB; Am. Inst. Archs.; Sycamore Rosewood Apart. Corp.; Sierra Club; Nat. Trust for Historic Preservation; Smithsonian Inst.; Univ. of Va. Alumni Soc.; So. Calif. Soc. of Arch. Historians; publs: arts. on manufactured housing, shopping mall storefronts, book rev., L.A. Architect 1982-83; Democrat; Protestant; rec: renovation of old houses, travel.Res: 450 N Sycamore Ave 11, Los Angeles 90036 Ofc: Kamnitzer & Cotton, Archs., 6330 W San Vicente Blvd, Los Angeles 90048

MATSON, JOHN WILLIAM, II, publisher; b. Sept. 15, 1944, Nashville, TN; s. John William and Janet Louise (Reese) Matson; AB, William Penn Coll., 1968; AM, Creighton Univ., 1971. Career: security ofcr., Pinkerton, Inc., Los Angeles Office, 1972-76; title clerk, TransAmerica Title Ins. Co., L.A., 1976-80; owner, John William Matson II, A.M., Publr., Beverly Hills, 1980--. Honors: Cert.of Appre., L.A. Co. Heart Assn., 1964; History Award, William Penn Coll., 1968, Mem. Cert., Phi Alpha Theta, Creighton Univ., 1970; Cert.of Appre., Natl. Police Ofcrs. Assn., 1972. Mem: preceptor, Glendale Chpt., Order of DeMolay, 1959; mem., Glendale Coll. Circle K, 1963; mem., Theta Eta chpt., Phi Alpha Theta, Creighton Univ., 1970; mem., #22-S, Fla. Assn. of Pvt. Investigators, 1977---. Currently conducting research for book on improved gasoline economy for vehicles. Libertarian. Episcopalian. Rec: historical research, European folk music. Res: 535 Woodbury Rd., Glendale 91206; Office; John William Matson II, A.M. Publshr., 256 S. Robertson Blvd., Suite 5350, Bevelry Hills 90211.

MATTESON, WILLIAM ROBERT, real estate co. president; b. July 14, 1922, Kellhier, Minn.; s. Charles James and Maude Jesse (Jones) M.; children: Robert, b. 1952; Lorraine, b. 1962; edn: BS, Bryant A & Stratton Coll. 1948; PhD, bus. mgt., Internat. Coll. 1982; Calif. lic: Road Builder, Gen. Contractor, Real Estate Broker. Career: past pres. Title Realty Co.; past chmn. bd. Portafone Corp.; past chmn. bd. S.U.S. Enterprises, Diversified Corp.; current: pres. P.S. I Love You Realty; pres. Matteson Constrn. Co.; bd. dirs. num. Mutual Funds, and other corps.; bd. dirs. Angelview Crippled Childrens Hosp.; author/ lcctr. var. colls. statewide; awards: Mexico- US Cultural Exch. Awd.; mem: Internat. Congress of Shopping Ctr. Developers; Palm Springs Bd. of Realtors; Palm Springs CofC; The Magic Castle; Aircraft Owners & Pilots Assn.; author, 1st Am. book on Timeshare: The Prepaid Vacation; inventor and developer of the cordless telephone; mil: ETO US Army 1942-45, Bronze Star, Purple Heart, Pres. Citation (2); Republican (pres. The Republican Club; So. Calif. Co-Chmn. of the President's Club; v.p./Coordinating Counsel; 3d. Dist. Repub. Central Com.; pres. P.S. Repub. Assembly); Presbyterian; rec: pilot, golf. Res: 190 Hermosa Pl Palm Springs 92262 Ofc: 2825 E Tahquitz- McCallum Way Palm Springs 92262

MATTHEY, BERNARD PAUL, JR., real estate broker/developer; b. Oct. 19, 1927, Armenia, N.D.; s. Bernard Paul and Frances Harriet (McLeod) Matthey; m. Marjeanne Macdonald, 1953; children: Bernard b. 1953, Thomas b. 1955, Laura b. 1957, Mary b. 1967; edn: BS, US Mil. Acad., 1950; BSEE, Univ. Ariz., 1963; MS, Shippensburg State Coll., Pa., 1972. Career: served to Col. US Army (Ret.) 1950-76, commanded at each level from platoon to group (of battalions); comdr. 127th Signal Battalion, Vietnam 1969-70; comdr. Signal Group, US Army, Alaska and dir. of engring., US Army Communications Command; decorated Legion of Merit (3); real estate broker/developer 1980--, pres. Capistrano Assocs. Real Estate, Inc.; gen. ptnr. Vista la Serena land devel.; honors: recogn. awards, Kiwanis Internat. 1979, So. Orange County Bd. Realtors 1980; mem: San Juan Capistrano Citizens for Responsive Govt. (chmn. 1976-77); San Juan Cap. Kiwanis Club (pres. 1979-80); Calif. Assn. of Realtors (dir. 1979-); So. Orange Co. Bd. of Realtors (dir., treas. 1979-, chmn. Civic Affairs Com. 1978-); mem. exec. com. Saddleback Coll. Angel Bd., Saddleback Coll. Found., 1980-; Republican; Presbyterian (ruling elder); rec: flying, skiing, fishing. Res: 33861 Calle Acordarse, San Juan Capistrano 92675 Ofc: Mission Realtors 31501 Camino Capistrano, San Juan Capistrano 92675 and Vista la Serena 530 CAmino de Estrella, San Clemente 92672

MATTINSON, GERTRUDE MAUDE, public accountant; b. Aug. 24, 1899, Pierpont, SD; d. Percey M. and Blanche E. (Sherwood) Bezanson; paternal forefathers from Besancon, Fr. settled in Nova Scotia in 1750; maternal gr. grandparents came from Wurtenberg, Ger., in a home-made boat, settled in Iowa 1852; uncle, Maynard Bezanson, authored The Peace River Trail (instrumental in opening up country north of Edmonton, Alb, Can.); widowed 1927; children: Shirley L. (Morano), b. 1921; Wilton H., b. 1922; edn: Benzanson Pub. Sch., Alberta, Can.; grad., Pasadena Bus. Coll. 1928. Career: chief auditor/ pvt. secty. to the mgr. Hotel Green, Pasadena 1928-36; chief acct., Treesweet Prods. Co., Santa Ana 1936-45; asst. comptroller/ ofc. mgr. Thompson Glass Co., L.A. 1945-46; comptroller/ ofc. mgr. CBS Steel Force & Motionair Inc., Vernon 1946-51 (1st woman comptroller in US, 1948); secty./ treas./ comptroller Nat. Electroncis Corp., L.A. 1952-53; ofc. mgr./ asst. to pres. Superline Prods. Co., Compton 1953-55; Nat. Rug Co. & Furniture Co. of Am., L.A. 1955-56; secty./ treas./ comptroller Lee Steel Co., Bell Casting Co., Cottage Mfg. Co. & Willard Mfg. Co., Huntington Park 1956-66; secty./ treas. comptroller/ bd. dirs. Nat. Technology Inc., Western Technology, Inc., Santa Ana 1966-69; pvt. acctg. practice 1969--; recipient sev. USO. service awds, WWII (incl. 2500 hr. svc.); honors, Bus. & Profl. Womens Club of L.A.; mem: Womens Div., L.A. CofC; L.A. Creditmen's Assn.; L.A. Credit Womans Assn. (past pres.); Bus. & Profl. Womens Club; Soroptimist, Saddleback Valley (charter); Leisure World Hist. Soc. (charter); 1st Nighter of Saddleback Cll.; Democrat; Christian Scientist; rec: equestrian; dancing. Res: 4900 E Telegraph RD, G-40, Ventura 93003

MATYAS, EMIL H., employee benefits and advertising co. executive; b. Aug. 21, 1926, Footedale, Penn.; s. John W. and Mary (Stredney) M.; m. Jane C. Smith (assoc. food ed. Bon Apetit Mag.), 1948; children: Anne L., b. 1952; Susan M., b. 1954; James C., b. 1956; edn: AB, USC 1948; UCLA Inst. Indsl. Rels. 1952. Career: ofc. boy Marsh & McLennan, Los Angeles 1948, employee benefits dept. 1956; employee benefits mgr. Bayly, Martin & Fay, L.A. 1962, v.p. employee benefits 1965; pres. Robison-Matyas Co., L.A. 1965--; chmn. Oxford Ins. Mgmt., L.A. 1969--; chmn. Indoor Advtg. Co., L.A. 1975--; honors: Nat. Found. of Employee Benefit Plans, spkr./panel moderator Group Mgrs. of L.A. (spkr., PIRA panelist); mem: Internat.Found. of Benefit Plans: Independent Agents Assn.; Sigma Alpha Epsilon (Alumni pres.); works: avtg. prods., pats. pend. (3); author, art., Pension Plan Nat. Reciprocity; SUB Pay Plan art.; mil: USN 1946. Res: 2044 Edgewood Dr, So. Pasadena 91030 Ofc: Oxford Insurance Management, 3600 Wilshire Blvd, Ste 1820, Los Angeles 90010

MATYCHOWIAK, FRANCIS ANTHONY, psychiatrist; b. May 20, 1926, Pinckneyville, Ill.; s. Thaddeus Joseph and Ida M. (Kellerman) M.; m. Sally Kayser, Oct. 28, 1950; edn: BA, Miami Univ., Oxford, Ohio 1947; BS, Univ. of Ill. 1947; MD, Univ. of Ill. Coll. of Med. 1950. Career: intern Indianapolis Gen. Hosp., Ind. 1950-51; psychiatry resident VA Hosp., Palo Alto, Calif. 1954-56; pvt. practice, Knightstown, Ind. 1951-52, Bakersfield Calif., 1956--; cons. Calif. Correctional Inst., Tehachapi 1958-; dir. psychiatry, A. Med. Group, Inc., dba Sans Doloroso Inst.; recipient Resolution of Commdn. for contbns. on Mental Health Adv. Bd., Kern Co. 1957-73; mem: Am. Med. Assn.; Calif. Med. Assn. (Ad Hoc Task Force to evaluate Dr. of Mental Health Proj., UC-Mt. Zion chmn. Com. on Negotiations; Med. Staff Steering Com.; Staff Surveyor Devel. Sub-Com.; Liaison Com. to State Hosp. Med. Staffs; Task Force on Child Abuse; Commn. on Mental Health & Developmental Disabilities; Conrad bd. dirs.; Task Force to monitor CLEX (Membshp. com.); Kern Co. Med. Soc. (pres. 1974); Am. Psychiatric Assn.; Am. Acad. of Clin. Psychiatry; Am. Coll. of Forensic Psychiatry; mil: lt. MC USNR, active 1952-54; Republican; Catholic; rec: gardening, oenophile, photog. Res: 601 Walnut Ave Bakersfield 93305 Ofc: Psychiatry, A Medical Group Inc., 1901 Truxtun Ave Bakersfield 93301

MATZDORFF, JEFFRY ALAN, manufacturing co. executive; b. Apr. 12, 1954, Springfield, Ohio; s. Gary G. and Marianne I. (Terner) M.; edn: BA in econ., UC Irvine 1976. Career: co-founder w/ father and brother, Gary's Leather Creations, 1976--; sailed across Pacific to Hawaii (43 ft. sailboat), 1975; sailed across Atlantic, Florida to Portugal (50 ft. sailboat), 1981; honors: Jr. Commodore, Windjammer Yacht Club 1969; Junior National USA Sailing Champ., Coronado 15, 1971; mem: Los Angeles Athletic Club; Sigma Chi Alumni (Orange Co. chpt.; founder Eta Sigma chpt.); Calif. Yacht Club; inventor leather working machines (pat. pend. 1982); Republican; Jewish; rec: sailing, sailboat racing. Res: 11645 Montana, Ste 302, Brentwood 90049 Gary's Leather Creations, 2430 S. Hill St Los Angeles 90007

MATZINGER, KENNETH MARSHALL, certified public accountant; b. Nov. 6, 1956, Eglin Air Force Base, Fla.; s. Kenneth Oscar and Shirley Mae (Whaley) M.; m. Linda, Jan. 6, 1979; 1 son, Daniel b. 1981; edn: bs, CSU Sacto. 1979; CPA, Calif. 1982. Career: acctg. with Coleman 7 Caine, CPAs in South Lake Tahoe, Ca. and Minden, Nev.: staff acct. 1979-82, senior acct. 1981, ptnr. and shareholder 1982--; mem: Am. Inst. of CPAs, Calif. Soc. of CPAs, South Lake Tahoe CofC; rec: skiing, swimming, var. outdoor sports. Address: PO Box 738, South Lake Tahoe, CA 95705 Ofc: Coleman & Caine, CPAs 3459 Lake Tahoe Blvd, Ste C, South Lake Tahoe 95705

MAULDIN, NORMA JEAN HUMPHRIES, company executive; b. Aug. 16, 1923, Gordonville, Tx.; d. James Wiley and Lynna Leota (Noel-Crain) Humphries; m. William Mauldin, Feb. 28, 1942; children: Col. Bruce Patrick b. 1943, Dr. William Timothy II b. 1946; edn: Christ Church Coll. Oxford, 1983; Warnborough Coll., Oxford Univ. 1977; Westfield Coll., Univ. of London, 1978; MS, Hardin-Simmons Univ., 1961; BS, USC, 1943. Career: co-prod. Internat. Air Shows, TV and live; pres. Mauldin and Staff, P.R., Los Angeles 1957-80; pres. Stardust Aviation, Santa Ana, 1980--; honors: Hon. Kentucky Col., Best Dressed, and Woman of the Year; del. Nat. Demo. Issues Conv. Louisville, Ky. 1975; mem: Internat. Platform Assn., Am. Mgmt. Assn., Army-Navy Country Club, Art Club (Ga.), Newport Bay Yacht Club (Ga.), Virginia Garden Club, Savannah Country Club, Mu Phi Epsilon, Townhall of Calif., World Affairs Council, L.A. Mus. of Sci. and Indus., L.A. Mus. of Modern Art, Bowers Art Mus., Newport Beach Art Mus., Newport Beach Demo. Club, Demo. Women Orange Club (past v.p.), Nat. Women Politic (chmn. women); author: Cliff Winters the Pilot, The Man (1961), The Consummate Barnstormer (1962), The Daredevil Clown (1963); Democrat; Episcopal; rec: flying, skydiving, parakiting. Res: 1013 W. Elliott Pl. Santa Ana 92704; Sec. Homes: 112 Eighth St. Seal Beach 92740; Hawaiian Ocean View Estates, Capt. Cook, Hawaii 96704; Flying M Ranch, Vale OR; 105 E. 45th St Savannah GA 31405 Ofc: Stardust Aviation, POB 3388, Santa Ana 92703

MAUND, GAY ELIZABETH, audiologist; b. Dec. 3, 1945, Philadelphia, Pa.; d. Walter Thomas and Eleanor Logan Maund; edn: BA, Marymount Coll. 1967; MA, USC, 1969; Spanish lang. stu. National Univ., Mexico City. Career: audiologist, USC-LA County Med. Center, Los Angeles 1969-70, Veterans Adminstrn. Outpatient Clinic, L.A. 1970--, coordinator Hearing Aid Issuance Pgm., largest hearing aid pgm. in USA with four satellite clinics, also public relations ofcr. VA Outpatient Clinic, L.A. 1979--, acting adminstrv. asst. to Chief Medical Adminstrv. Ofcr. 1982; assoc. coordinator of Quality Assurance 1984; part-time faculty CSU Los Angeles and CSU Northridge, 1971-75; awards: for superior profl. performance, Vet. Adminstrn. (1980, 81, 82), Disting. Fed. Employee 1977, narrator Disting. Fed. Employee Awards Ceremony 1978, Spl. Contribn. Award 1982; mem: Council for the Handicapped, L.A. City; Am. Speech and Hearing Assn.; rec: skiing, tennis, cooking, sewing. Office: VA Outpatient Clinic, 425 S. Hill St Ste G70, Los Angeles 90013

MAUPIN, OWEN LILBURN, small business counselor; b. Dec. 22, 1918, Red Bluff; s. Fred and Virginia Pearl (Hendricks) M.; m. Georgene Hormel, Aug. 1, 1942; children: David Owen, b. 1944; Fredric George, b. 1946; Deidre Jayne, b. 1948; edn: Calif. Polytech., S.L.O. 1938-39; AA, Taft Jr. Coll. 1941; BS, Univ. of Md. 1965. Career: franchisee with General Business Svcs., a nat. orgn. hdqtrs. Rockville, Md. 1977--: S.E. Calif. regl. dir., (L.A., Riverside, & San Bernardino Cos. & portions of Kern, Inyo & Mono Cos.) Gen. Bus. Svcs.; Designate Trainer for Bus. Counselors; pres. Gen. Bus. Svcs. Adv. Council; honors: Counselor of the Yr., Western Div. Gen. Bus. Svcs.; Frannie Awd., Internat. Franchise Assn.; Golden Circle Awd., Gen. Bus. Svcs. for bus. growth 1978, 80, 81; mem: E. San Bernardino Kiwanis Club (pres. 1983-84); Inland Empire Trade Club; San. Bernardino CofC; Toastmasters (past pres.); mil: aviator, carrier pilot, capt. USN 1941-68, WWII, Korea, Pacific Fleet, Atlantic Fleet, S.E. NATO hdqrts., Europe, Navy hdqtrs., Pentagon; Democrat; Congregational; rec: snow skiing, golf. Res: 6369 Center St Highland 92346 Ofc: General Business Services, 412 W 17th St San Bernardino 92405

MAURO, CHARLES SALVATORE, JR., computer research and development executive; b. June 29, 1958, Englewood, NJ; s. Charles Salvatore Sr. and Georgia Merriman (Whitney) M.; m. Claudette Carol Cuny, Sept. 8, 1979; edn: Univ. of Santa CLara 1976-78. Career: researcher Low Pressure Wind Tunnel (Marswit), Nasa Ames Research Ctr., Sunnyvale 1977-78; software engr. Apple Computer, Inc., Cupertino 1978-80; pres. Advanced Logic Sys., Inc., Sunnyvale 1980-83; dir. research & devel. Mouse Systems, Santa Clara 1983--; mem: Nat. Assn. of Rocketry; Nat. Geographic Soc.; publs: sev. mag. arts. & books incl., Apple Founder Steve Wozniak & Myself, Omni Mag. 7/83; Logic Design, Advanced Logic Systems, Integrated Circuits Mag.; Republican; Catholic; rec: philately, sci-fi, model rocketry, flying. Res: 2383 Lincoln Village Dr San Jose 95125 Ofc: Mouse Systems, 2336H Walsh Ave Santa Clara 95051

MAWLA, NATHERA, artist/real estate broker; b. June 6, 1942, Mosel, Iraq, nat. 1972; d. Georges and Sabeeha (Jabory) Hadid; m. Khalid Mawla, Sept. 29, 1961; children: Gary b. 1963, Ted b. 1966, Tina b. 1968; edn: Colo. Univ. in Boulder 1962-64; AA in bus., San Jose City Coll. 1970; BA in art, CSU San Jose 1974, MFA 1976; Calif. Adult Tchg. cred.; spec. courses Acad. of R.E., USC, Anthony Sch. Career: real estate broker C&C Realtors, Cupertino; art instr: Los Gatos Adult Edn. 1977-8, Metropolitan Adult Edn. 1977-8, lectr. SJCC 1976, tchg. asst. CSUSJ 1974; author/pub. Middle Eastern Cook Book (1969); exhib: SF Mus. of Modern Art (1978), La Mamelle Gal., SF (1977), Word Work Gal., San Jose (1977), Camera Work Gal. (1976), Quay Gal. (1974), CSUSJ (1974), Helen Euphrat Gal., De Anza Coll. (1975), SF Art Inst. (1975), S.J. Inst. of Contemp. Art. (1982); mem: life alumni CSUSJ; League of Arab Am.

Women (pres.); vol. tchr. Idylwild Children's Ctr. 1966-69; Democrat; Christian; rec: travel. Res: 16167 Greenwood Rd Monte Sereno 95030 Ofc: S&C Realtors 19960 Stevens Creek Blvd Cupertino

MAXIMOFF, ROBERT HENRY, corporate/financial planning executive; b. Nov. 29, 1924, Bartlesville, Okla.; s. Vladimir and Florence Nadine (Plunkett) M.; m. Helen Patten Hanson, Sept. 16, 1950; children: Christopher Carl, b. 1953; James Timothy, b. 1961; edn: AS, Kansas City Jr. Coll. 1943; BS, Univ. of Ill. 1947; diploma, Adv. Mgmt. Inst. Northwestern Univ. 1981. Career: design & research engr. Panhandle Eastern Pipeline Co., Ks. City, Mo. 1947-50; mech. splty. designer M.W. Kellogg Co., NYC 1950-51; piping designer/ stress analst Foster Wheeler Corp., NYC 1951-52; with Standard Oil of NJ (Exxon) & affiliates 1952-75: Southeast Asia advsr., Econ. & Supply, Esso Eastern Inc., Kuala Lumpur, Malaysia 1962-64; refinery mgr. Esso Standard Malaysia, Port Dickson, Malaysia 1964-65; mgr. Plng. Coordination, Esson Eastern Inc., NY 1966-67, and asst. treas. 1967-68; dir. Esso Standard Malaysia, Kuala Lumpur, Malaysia, also dir. Esso Standard Ltd., Singapore 1968-71; mgr. Corp. Plnng. and Fin., Esso Australia, Sydney, Aus. 1971-75; with Bechtel Corp., San Francisco 1975--: exec. engr., procurement 1975-76; plnng. mgr., refinery & chem. 1976-78; actg. plnng. mgr., corp. mktg. 1978-79; mgr. plng. & admin. nuclear fuel ops. 1979--; honors: Beta Gamma Sigma; mem: Corp. Plnnrs. Assn.; Am. Nuclear Soc.; Mid- Penin. Sym. Assn.; Mensa; Harvard Club of S.F.; publs: Conversion to Integrated Planning, Darling Downs Inst., Queensland, Aus. 1972; mil: cpl. US Army 1943-45; Presbyterian; rec: Asian affairs, history, anthropology. Res: 1847 Juarez Ave Los Altos 94022 Ofc: Bechtel National, Inc., POB 3965 San Francisco 94119

MAXUM, BERNARD J., energy systems co. owner; b. Nov. 4, 1931, Bremerton, Wash.; s. Marion L. and LuElla M. Maxum; m. Marilyn Jo Bruce, June 20, 1959; children: Laurie b. 1960, Linda b. 1961, Michael b. 1963, Karen b. 1964, Kristine b. 1967; edn: BS, honors, Univ. Wash. 1955; MS, USC, 1957; PhD, UC Berkeley 1963. Reg. Profl. Engineer, Calif. Career: architl. designer and bldg. contractor, 1952-54; coll. instr. USC, UCB, 1955-63; mgr., chief engr., Aerospace Opns., MTS, 1963-70; owner Semcor Assocs. (engrng. design, consulting), Mission Viejo 1970--, owner Semcor Energy Systems (wholesale distbr. energy products and systems: solar, wind, photovoltaics, energy conservation), 1978--; lectr., seminars; honors: Hughes Fellow 1956-57, Ford Found. Fellow 1960-62; mem: ASHRAE, IEEE, Calif. Solar Indus.Assn., Am. Inst. Physics, CofC; 40 publs. in engring. and research; Catholic; rec: skiing, bicycling, bridge. Res: 26552 Montebello Pl. Mission Viejo 92691 Ofc: Semcor Energy Systems 25651-G Taladro Circle Mission Viejo 92691

MAY, CHARLES HARRISON, optometrist; b. Aug. 5, 1922, Allergan, Mich.; s. Charles Sylvester and Mabelle (Rowan) M.; m. Athena Marinos, Nov. 1, 1964; edn: UC Berkeley 1943, Univ. Notre Dame 1944, Cornell Univ. 1944; OD, No. Ill. Coll. Optometry 1946. Career: dr. of optometry, San Bernardino 1947-, San Diego 1967-, Los Angeles 1973 ; staff optometrist Patton State Mental Hosp., 1948-; bd. dirs. US Home Svgs. & Loan; bd. dirs. National Eye Research; chmn. Internat. Soc. of Orthokeratology; recipient Grand Honours, Nat. Eye Research Found. 1981; listed, Who's Who in the West 1972-73, Men of Achievement 1974; mem: S.D. Opera, S.D. Symphony, Old Globe Theatre, S.D. Yacht Club, La Jolla Beach & Tennis, Circum Navigators, NCCJ, Salvation Army, Navy League, Salk Inst., S.D. Optometric Soc., S.D. Mental Health, S.D. Childrens Hosp.; works: developed science Orthokeratology (correction of vision for myopic to 20/20 thru refitting of contact lenses), author of official manual of instrns.; mil: lt. USN 1942-45; Republican; Greek Orthodox; rec: sailing. Res: 857 Armada Terrace San Diego 92106 Ofc: Alvarado Medical Center, 6495 Alvarado Rd, 101, San Diego 92120

MAY, GARY L., architecture and design co. president; b. Aug. 26, 1941, Bozeman, Mont.; s. Doran C. and Alice M. (Torgrimson) M.; 1 dau. Stacey, b. 1970; edn: US Army Signal Corp., Ft. Monmouth, NJ 1961; Gen. Contractor, Calif. 1983. Career: mgr. Dial Finance Co., Ks. City, Mo. 1964; gen. mgr. Control Data Corp., Santa Fe Springs, calif. 1964-72; sr. v.p. Bank Plnng. Assoc., Los Angeles 1972-80; pres. Coordinated Financial Interiors, Fountain Valley 1980--; pres. C.U. Plnng. & Bldg., Fountain Valley 1980--; bd.dirs. Orange Co. Realtors Credit Union; honors: Jaycee of the Yr., Month, Quarter; Pres. Council, Secty., Pres. & Proj. Chmn., San Rafael Jaycees; mem: Orange Co. Builders Assn.; mil: s/sgt E-6 US Army 1960-62, GCM, Sharp Shooter Rifle; Lutheran; rec: bicycling, bowling, golf. Res: 7892 Northlake Dr, 106, Huntington Beach 92647 Ofc: Coordinated Financial Interiors, 17330 Newhope St Fountain Valley 92708

MAYBERRY, MILDRED DOTSON, social worker, ret.; b. July 12, 1919, Cleveland, Ohio; d. James H. and Rebecca J. (Trevillion) D.; edn: att. Spelman Coll.; BA, Lincoln Univ. 1943; MSW, Atlanta Univ. 1953, Loyola Univ., Univ. of Chgo.; cert. NASW. Career: med. soc. wkr. Cook Co. Hosp., Chgo., Ill. 1953-58; psychiatric soc. wkr./ supvr./ dir. mental health clinic, Dept. of Health, Chgo. 1958-60; med. soc. wkr. Gr. Chgo. Chpt. Muscular Dystrophy of Am., Inc., Chgo. 1960-64; dir. pub. health soc. svc. (responsible for devel. & admin. of soc. wrk. component for fed. funded projs.) Dept. of Health 1964-72; psychiat. soc.wkr. Dept. Mental Health of Calif., Sacto. 1972-76; pub. health soc. wrk. cons.; ret. 1983; tnr. Allied Health Profls., non- profl., Ill.; Community Fund. Reviewing Com., Ill.; White House Conf. on Children; Commn. on Handicapped Children, Ill.; Sacto. State Sch. of Soc. Wrk. Adv. Bd.; Suicide Prevention Exec. Bd., Sacto.; Planned Parenthood Exec. Bd., Chgo. 1969-72; honors: Alpha Kappa Delta, Atlanta Univ. 1952; mem: NASW; Nat. Conf. on Soc. Welfare; Am. Pub. Health Assn.; Ill. Pub. Health Assn.; Ill. Welfare Assn.; Nat. Council on Soc. Wrk. Edn.; Black Assn. of Soc. Wkrs.; Alpha Kappa Alpha; Nat. Urban League; NAACP; Suicide Prevention; Nat. Assn. of Sch. Age Parents; works: Early Indentification & treatment of handicapping conditions in children 1971; Protestant; rec: knitting, crochet, volunteer. Res: 2614 Sobrante Way Rancho Cordova 95670

MAYER, SUSAN J. PARKER-, property management executive; b. Mar. 3, 1947, Milwaukee, Wisc.; d. Glenn H. and Jeanne Elizabeth (Nordness) Parker; m. Kenneth D. Mayer, Jan. 22, 1983; edn: BA, San Diego State Univ. 1970; Lumbleau Real Estate Sch.; real estate courses, UCLA; desig: Real Property Adminstr., Bldg. Owners & Mgrs. Assn. 1983; Calif. lic. Real Estate Broker. Career: adminstrv. asst. to v.p. leasing/ mktg./ mgmt. Ketchum Peck & Tooley, Los Angeles 1971-75; property mgr. Tooley & Co. 1975-79; asst. v.p. Wells Fargo Realty Advrs. 1979-81; property mgr. Murdock Mgmt. Co. 1981-83; gen. mgr. Triton Property Mgmt. Co. 1983--; bd. dirs. Bldg. Owners & Mgrs. Assn. (wrkshp. com. Annual Los Angeles Conv.; real property adminstrs. classes for BOMI designation, L.A.); mem: Women in Mgmt.; Bldg. Owners & Mgrs. Assn.; Republican; Ch. of Relig. Sci. Res: 13050 Maxella Ave 3, Marina del Rey 90292 Ofc: Triton Property Management Co., 10850 Wilshire Blvd, Ste 550, Los Angeles 90024

MAYNARD, ISABELLE, social worker; b. Mar. 3, 1929, Tientsin, China; nat. 1954; d. Abraham and Sophie (Joffe) Zimmerman; div.; 1 dau. Judith Anne Maynard Malings b. 1948; edn: BA, UC Berkeley 1954, MSW, 1956; Calif. (LCSW) Lic. Clin. Soc. Wkr. Career: casewkr. and groupwkr. Internat. Inst. of San Francisco, 1956-66; psychiat. soc. wkr. S.F. Gen. Hosp. Outpatient psychiatric, 1966 67; cons. Internat. Inst. of Oakland, 1966-67; soc. wk. supvr. Contra Costa County Soc. Svcs. Child Protective Svcs., 1968--; pvt. practice, Berkeley 1975-79; supr. of MSW students for Univ. Calif., SF State Coll., and Hayward State Coll., 1960-82; tchg. workshops in child abuse and neglect, 1972-78; honors: Warrington Stokes Award for contbns. in field of Child Abuse and Neglect Prevention (1982); recogn. awards (1982, 1981); mem. Bay Area Theatre Workers Assn.; actress One-Act Theatre Co. of S.F. 1976-; publs: short stories and poetry in S.F. Fiction Monthly, Present Tense, Agada, Shmate, J.A.C.O.B.; Democrat; rec: acting, writing, weaving. Res: 6 Admiral Dr, 476, Emeryville 94608 Ofc: 3431 McDonald Ave, Richmond

MAYNARD, MICHAEL ERNEST, manufacturing co. president; b. Mar. 17, 1934, Franklin, N.H.; s. Charles Leonel and Ruth Evelyn (Doyle) M.; m. Sally Provost, Nov. 8, 1963; children: Michael Jr., b. 1964; Stephen, b. 1966; Shelena, b. 1966; edn: US Armed Forces Inst. 1960 63. Career: mgr./ food supvr. Howard Johnson Restaurant 1963-65; svc. mgr., prod. mgr., v.p. research & devel., pres. Automation D.S.S., Inc. 1966-82; pres./ engr. Misa Mfg., Inc., Design 1982 ; pres./ dir. mktg. Automatic Dishwashing Sys., Inc. 1983--; mem: Retail Bakers Assn. of Am.; Calif. Restaurant Assn.; Royal Order of Moose; inventions: Egg Master, Helper I, Helper II; mil: E-4 USN 1960-63; Republican; Catholic; rec: spl. project research, organist. Res: 11401 Jacalene Ln Garden Grove 92640 Ofc: Misa Manufacturing, Inc., 7766 Westminster Ave Westminster 92683

MAYO, JOHN BLOUNT, public relations agency owner/ educator; b. Jan. 9, 1938, Richmond, Va.; s. John B. and Lillian (Hargrave) M: M. Nita Louise Kellam, May 30, 1965; children: Carolyn Lee Matthews, b. 1962; Sara Louise, b. 1967; John Kellam, b. 1969; Kathleen Elizabeth, b. 1974; edn: BA, Univ. of N.C. 1960; MA, Univ. of Tex., Austin 1966; MA, Am. Univ., Wash. DC 1976. Career: Cdr, USN (ret.), active duty USN as Spl. Duty (Public Affairs) Ofcr. 1960-80: deputy pub. affairs ofcr. Submarine Force Atlantic 1966-68; asst. pub. affairs ofcr. First Naval Dist. 1968-69; pub. affairs ofcr. Naval Material Command 1969-70, Naval Air Sys. Command 1980-81, Naval Forces Vietnam 1971-72; dir. research & evaluation Naval Internat Rels. Activity 1972-73, dir. print media 1973-75; dir. audiovisual ops. Ofc. of Info., Navy Dept. 1975-76; asst. chief of staff Eleventh Naval Dist. 1977-80; dir. pub. rels./ prof. mktg. National Univ., San Diego 1980-82; corp. commn. dir. Robert Keith & Co., Inc. 1983; pres. Mayo & Assoc., Inc. 1983--; awards: Donald M. Mackey Awd., Navy League of US 1981; No. San Diego Co. Press Club Publicity Awd. 1982; PR Caseworks, Special PR Event of the Year Awd. (King Kong), 1983; mem: Navy League of US (San Diego Council bd. dirs.); Pub. Rel. Soc. of Am. (bd. dirs., profl. devel. chmn.); San Diego Press Club; Am. Assn. of Individual Investors Computer Gp./ San Diego Computer Soc. Investors Gp.; Nat. Univ. Alumni Assn. (life); author: Bulletin From Dallas: The President is Dead (Banner Books 1967); Methodist; rec: personal computing, photog. Res: 17023 Cloudcroft Dr Poway 92064 Ofc: Mayo & Assoc. Inc., 16776 Bernardo Center Dr, Ste 110B, Rancho Bernardo 92128

MAYSE, HENRY CARL, consultant; b. Apr. 20, 1922, Temple, Tex.; s. Henry Carl and Clara Carrie (Riemann) M.; m. Kathleen Cameron, Oct. 9, 1948; children: Helen (Carnes), b. 1949; Rio (Reng), b. 1952; Phyllis (Biggs), b. 1954; edn: Art Center Coll. of Design 1946-49. Career: art dir. Kenyon & Eckhardt, NY 1949-52; designer No. American Aviation, El Segundo 1952-58; designer Litton Inds., Van Nuys 1958-62; tech. dir. Warner Bros., Burbank 1962-75; designer/ R&D v.p. Loquitur Co., Woodland Hills 975-77; designer/ pres. The Mayse Co., Canoga Park 1977-83; pres. 1983--; tech. cons. Taiwan Chinese Govt.; cons. US CIA/ OSS; bd dirs. Loquitur Co.; mem: L.A. Profl. Club; British Athletic Assn.; Soc. of Ant. of Scotland; Noemics Soc.; works: Books: Frostfire; Wheel of Ixion; Inventions: Loquitur Weapons System, Colt Submachine Gun; Other: The Noemics (ethical sys.), The Eleusides Concept. Mil: capt. US Army Air Corps 1940-45, DFC, AM, BS; Republican; Christian Sci.; rec: oil painting, British Antiquities, Archaeo- physics. Ofc: The Mayse Company, 20354 Gilmore St Canoga Park 91306

MAZAREI, HOSSEIN, industrialist; b. Mar. 17, 1935, Shiraz, Persia; s. Bagher M. and Naier (Shariah) M.; m. Fereshteh Banu, Apr. 6, 1958; two sons: Victor B. b. 1962, Richard B. b. 1963; edn: grad. Nemazi, 1957; AA, Pierce Coll. 1961; BS engring. Calif. Polytech. Univ. SLO 1963; MA in cinematography, Columbia Univ. 1965; JD/LLB, La Salle Univ. 1973. Career: pres. Hossco Petroleum Inc. offices in Kuwait, Abu Dabi, Geneva, Riyahd, and London; import/export bus. liason between heads of state of various Middle Eastern countries; past cons. to OPEC (pre-Khoemeni); owner two corps. (textile indus.): Westher Financial Inc. dba Texprint Internat. and CIM (Corp. Indsl. Mgmt.); owner/landlord of chain of service stations; real estate investor; recipient Gold Medal award for contbns. to Persia's 2,500 Year Centennial; mem. Optomist Club Intl.; works: drawings of ancient Persopolis; Republican; Agnostic; rec: flying, tennis, golf. Res: 4419 Valley Spring Dr North Ranch Westlake Village 91362 Ofc: Hossco Petroleum Inc. 16311 Ventura Blvd, Ste 1080, Encino 91436

MAZILU, TIBERIU, electrical enineer; b. June 5, 1946, Resita, Rumania; s. Sebastian and Hildegard (Kabat) M.; m. Doina Izvernariu, Nov. 15, 1974; 1 dau: Jaime Kara, b. 1983; edn: BSEE, Polytech. Inst. Timisoara/ Romania 1969; MSEE, UCLA 1977, EE, 1979, PhD, 1981. Career: elec. engr. Rhig Inst., Romania 1969-71; microwave researcher Spinner GmbH, Munich, Ger. 1971-75; research asst. UCLA 1977-80; staff engr. Bunker Ramo, Westlake Village 1979-82; staff engr., tech. staff Hughes Aircraft Co., Canoga Park 1982--; cons. elec. engr. Malco A Microdot Company 1980; recipient technology contrbn. awards (2), Bunker Ramo 1981; mem: IEEE (Microwave Theory & Techniques Soc.); publs. in tech. journals, presentation, Nat. Radio Sci. Meeting 5/82; mil: soldier Army, Romania 1970; Catholic; rec: classical music, painting, camping. Res: 4800 Adele Ct Woodland Hills 91364 Ofc: Hughes Aircraft, 8433 Fallbrook Ave Canoga Park 91304

MAZZA, LEE ANN, business owner; b. Jan. 7, 1932, Calif.; d. Antonio and Agostina (Miguel) Gonsalves; children: Jamie R., b. 1959; Sandra Lynn, b. 1962; edn: Am. River Coll. 1960; NY Sch. of Int. Design 1963; No. Am. Travel Sch. 1970; Anthony's Real Estate 1975. Career: owner Matilda's Antiques & The Fashion Shed; pres. Samba Beverage Inc.; owner T.M.'s Interiors; currently, exec. gov./ regl. v.p. Who's Who International; Who's Who Internat. Social Orgn. for Single; honors: Exch. Student, Am. Field Svc.; mem: Soroptimist; Alpha Nu; works: interior decor; Democrat; Catholic; rec: entertaining, dancing, travel. Address: 3815 Robertson Ave Sacramento 95821

MC ANALLY, DON, editor, publisher; b. Oct. 27, 1913, Sewell, NJ; s. James C. and Ina (MacLeod) M.; m. Edith P. McKinney, Dec. 11, 1934; 1 dau: Shirley Ann English; edn: John Wanamaker Cadet Inst., Phila.; Sales Analysis Inst., Chgo. Career: reporter/ed. Woodbury Daily Times, NJ 1932-45; ed. Owens-Illinois Co. Publs., NJ and Ohio 1945-47; asst. advtg. mgr. Libbey- Owens-Ford Glass Co., Toledo, Oh. 1947-53; sales promotion mgr./ prod. sales mgr. LOF Glass Fibers Co., Toledo 1953-59; ed. Pacific Oil Marketer, Los Angeles 1960-66; owner Hovercraft of So. Calif. 1975-76; pub. Calif. Businesswoman 1978; ed./pub. O & A Mktg. News 1966--, Calif. Senior Citizen News 1977--, The Automotive Booster of Calif. 1974--; awards: Man of the Year, Pacific Oil Conf. 1977; Spl. Award, Automotive Affiliated Representative 1979; appreciation, Western Oil Ind. TBA Gp. 1971, Douglas Oil Ex-Employees 1980; v.p. So. Calif. Chapt. Automotive Hall of Fame 1984; award winning editor, Toledo Club of Printing House Craftsmen 1950; Good Neighbor award, Toledo, Oh. 1948; Dinner guest of honor, So. Calif. Petroleum Indus. Golf & Tennis Tournament 1984. Mem: Lions Club, Calif. Indep. Oil Marketers Assn., Masquers (Hywd.), Silver Dollar Club (S.F.Vly), Roorag (L.A.), Automotive Booster Club of Greater L.A., OX 5 Aviation Pioneers, Nat. and So. Calif. Wing, Greater L.A. Press Club. Address: 4409 Indiana Ave La Canada 91011

MC ATEE, GARY LEE, medical electronics service co. owner; b. Oct. 13, 1949, Marion, Ind.; s. Dallas Wilbur and Hazel Mae (Flook) M.; m. Debra Saegar, Aug. 2, 1980; children: Katherine, b. 1972; Michael, b. 1974; Jonathan, b. 1982; Kimberly, b. 1983; edn: ASEET, Purdue Univ. 1971; desig: BMET, 1980. Career: regl. svc. mgr. Alpex Computer Co. 1971-74; tnr. regl. svc. coord. Intrnat. Medical Corp. 1974-80; owner Medical Repair Svcs. Co. 1980-81; owner Western Electronic Sales & Tech. 1981--; mem: Med. Equip. Repair Assn.; Christian; rec: raising Dobermans, salt water fishing. Res: 662 Kingman Dr Vacaville 95688 Ofc: W.E.S.T., POB 1313 Vacaville 95696

MC BRIDE, NORMAN L., JR., veterinarian; b. in Noble, Ill.; s. Norman I. and Anna McBride; m. 2d. Betty Jane Settliffe Rasmussen, May 24, 1966; children: (by previous marriage) Katheryn Anne (Coutts), Deanna Elizabeth (Cutler), and Stephen Lewis, (step) Linda Marie and Kathleen Anne Rasmussen; edn: att. schs. in Evanston, Ill.; DVM, Univ. of Toronto, 1938; postgrad. tng. in Milwaukee, Chgo. Career: veterinarian practice, Pasadena 1943--, spec. in orthopedic surgery; researcher on diseases and bacteriology of the canine ear; pioneer resrch. in animal kidney transplants; cancer resrch; mem. faculty USC Sch. of Medicine, 1953--; coauthor two textbooks on veterinarymedicine; lectr. nat., internt. in orthopedics and diseases and surgery of the canine ear; mem: Calif. State Vet. Medicine Assn. (Humane Com., contg. edn. com.), Am. Animal Hosp. Assn. (exec. bd., past nat. program cmn.), Am. Vet. Med. Assn. (Small Animal Sect.); mem. Sci. Assn. Univ. of Toronto; Univ. of Toronto Alumni Assn. of So. Calif. (past pres.); Omega Tau Sigma; clubs: Lions, Masons, Elks, Irvine Coast Country, DeAnza Country, Borrego Springs Country; publs: subject of Time mag. article. Address: 2103 Yacht Daphne Newport Beach 92660

MC BRIDE, TERRY LYNN, controller; b. Feb. 29, 1952; s. Neil Benjamin and Marian Ellen (Hayes) McB.; m. Marianna Davis, June 5, 1982; edn: BS, Bob Jones Univ. 1975. Career: chief acct. Whittier Coll., Whittier 1975-79; asst. mgr. ACST Credit Unive, Whittier 1979; staff acct. Daring, Wold & Agee, CPAs, Whittier 1979-80; controller Calif. Radio Sales, Inc., Montebello 1980-81; comptroller Whittier Coll. 1981--; Republican; Free Evangelical; rec: photog. Res: 23051 Paseo Dr Terrado, 4, Diamond Bar 91765 Ofc: Whittier College, 13406 E Philadelphia St, POB 634, Whittier 90608

MC CABE, DONALD LEE, physician; b. Nov. 5, 1925, Phila., Pa.; s. Joseph Grant and Agnes Muriel (Lee) McC.; m. Jean Smallwood, June, 1977; children: Geoffrey, b. 1951; Timothy, b. 1953; Eleanor, b. 1957, Traill, b. 1963, (step) Karyn, and Derek; edn: Ursinus Coll.; Haverford Coll.; DO, Phila. Coll. of Osteopathic Med. 1950. Career: country physician, Towanda, Pa. 1951-68; psychiatric physician, Harrisburg State Hosp., 1969-73; Delaware Valley Mental Health Found. 1974; psychiatric practice 1969-74; general and psychiatric med. practice, Sacto., Calif. 1974--; past. pres. Am. Coll. of Gen. Practice (Pa. & Calif.); Osteo. Physicians & Surgeons of Calif.; ed. Journ. of O.P.S.C.; clin. research in kryptopyrroles; mem: Fellow Am. Coll. Gen. Practice; Am. Pub. Health Assn.; Acad. Psychosomatic Med.; Internat. Biographical Assn.; Internat. Acad. for Med. Preventics; Constitutional Patriots Assn.; works: paintings, logo designs, author: A Diary From Orient; num. med. publs.; mil: USNR V-12s, Ursinus Coll. 1944-46; Republican; Christian; rec: sailing, painting, photog. Res: 3221 Greenwood Ave Sacramento 95821 Ofc: 3530 Auburn Blvd, Ste 3, Sacramento 95821

MC CAFFERY, ROBERT LEO, contract engineering firm president; b. Apr. 0, 1939, Breckinridge, Minn.; s. Leo Andrew and Dorothy Rose (Marick) McC.; m. Jane Newland, June 15, 1979; children: Lori, b. 1963; Robin, b. 1964; Michael, b. 1967; Kelli, b. 1969; Marie, b. 1970; Michele, b. 1970; Melissa, b. 1980; edn: AA, Eastern Ariz. Jr. Coll. 1961; bus. admin., CSU Los Angeles 1962-68. Career: engr. Rockwell 1961-67; cons. engr. 1967-70; proj. engr. TRW 1970-74; pres. Eagle Engring. Svcs., L.A. 1974--; honors: listed, Jane's Who's Who, Com. to Save Hughes Flying Boat, Calif. State Assembly Resolution 1980, L.A. County Bd. of Supvrs. Resolution 1980; Rotarian of Year 1980, Venice Marina Rotary Club; Public Rels. Soc. of Am./LA Chpt. Prisms Award 1980; mem: Nat. Fedn. of Independent Bus.; Action Counsel; Aero Club of S.C. (dir.); AIAA; Aerospace Mus. Exec. Com.; Internat. Fellowship of Flying Rotarians; AOPA; NAA; Venice Marina Rotary (pres. 1981-82); BSA-Comm. Chmn. (US & Westchester), bd. Boys & Girls Club (Venice); Red Barons; Elks; Marina City Club; Venice Boosters Assn. Adv. Bd. Marina Mercy Hosp.; mil: s/sgt. USAF 1956-60; Republican; rec: flying, water skiing, photog. Res: 701 29th St Manhattan Beach 90266 Ofc: Eagle Engineering Services, Inc., 5710 W Manchester, Ste 104, Los Angeles 90045

MC CALLON, LARRY KEITH, manufacturing co. executive; b. Oct. 21, 1939, Mayfield, Kentucky; s. Clyde Dawson and Annie Dee (Burnett) McC.; m. Su-Chun Lee, Apr. 10, 1981; children: James, b. 1954; Bryan, b. 1956; David, b 1960; edn: BS, engr. math., Univ. of Mich. 1962; BS, aero. engr., 1962; MS, Air Force Inst. of Tech. 1963. Career: major USAF 1962-83; analyst Air Force Foriegn Tech. Div. 1963-66; research assoc. Lawrence Livermore Lab. 1966-69; br. chief Air Force Weapons Lab 1969-71; R&D div. chief US Mil. Assistance Gp., Korea 1975-81; pgm. ofc. br. chief Air Force Space div. 1981-83; ret. USAF 19883; proj. mgr. Strategic Missile Test Mgmt. Northrop Electroncis Div. 1983--; honors: Tau Beta Pi, eng. hon. soc. 1961; mem: Am. Ist. Aero. Astro.; Air Force Assn.; Am. Defense Preparedness Ass.; mil. decorations: Bronze Star, Defense Meritorious Svc.; Air Force Meritorious Svc. w/ Oak Leaf cluster; Joint Svc. Commdn.; Republican; Protestant; rec: bridge, gardening. Res: 9752 La Cresta Cir Huntington Bach 92646 Ofc: Northrop Electronics Division, 2301 W. 120th St Hawthorne 90250

MC CANDLESS, BIRK STEVEN, real estate development co. president; b. Dec. 2, 1947, Palo Alto; s. Charles Sprague and Jean Anna (Birkland) McC.; m. Mary Schloss, May 12, 1970; children: Mary Ann, b. 1977; Kathryn Malone, b. 1979; Laura Birkland, b. 1984; edn: BS, USC 1969; MBA, Univ. of Santa Clara 1974. Career: asst. to pres. C.S. McCandless, Engrs. & Developers, Palo Alto 1974-76; founder/ pres./CEO McCandless Mgmt. Corp., Palo Alto 1976--; founder/ pres. McCandless Devel. Corp., Palo Alto 1978--; mem: Urban Land Inst.; San Jose, Sunnyvale & Santa Clara CofC; Elks Club, Palo Alto; mil: lt. USNR 1969-72; Republican; Episcopal; rec: pvt. aviation, physical fitness, dist. running. Res: 129 Smith Creek Dr Los Gatos 95030 Ofc: McCandless Companies, 710 Lakeway, Ste 200, Sunnyvale 94086

MC CANDLESS, CHARLES SPURGEON, ceramic tile contractor, b. July 2, 1907, Encampment, Wyo.; s. Charles Sumner and Jenny (Nelson) McC.; m. Bessie A. Brand (dec. 1979), Sept. 3, 1929; children: Lorna b. 1932, Charles b. 1934, Janet b. 1937, Fred b. 1943; ed. home study, State Voc. Cert. 1935. Career: founder/owner Charles McCandless Tile, Orange County 1924--, incorporated 1960, still active as field supt. and corp. pres. Charles McCandless Tile Inc. (oldest tile contracting firm op. under continuous ownership and name in So. Calif.) opened San Diego br. in Carlsbad, 1979; (his sons Charles and Fred, active in the firm, became major stockholders in 1960) fmr. instr. Trade Sch., Santa Ana Schs., 4 years; honors: Tile Contractor of the Year 1966, 13 Western States; Charles Mowers Award, Orange County Builders Assn.; mem. Contractors Assn. So. Calif. (Jt. Arbitration Bd., 10 yrs.); Past Master Orange Grove Masonic Lodge 1951; Salvation Army advis. bd. 20 yrs.; works: installed the tile in first house blt. in San Clemente, also in the Ole Hanson residence, and Hambottom res., later to become Casa Pacifica The Western White House;

recent projs. of firm incl. Disney World (Fla.), San Onofre Nuclear Plant (for Bechtel), all of South Coast Plaza and Satellite Bldgs. (Costa Mesa); mil: pvt. CNG 1932-35; Republican; Presbyterian (Elder); rec: Vintage Fords (1914, 1920, 1928, 1933, 1955). Res: 213 River St Orange 92666Ofc: Charles McCandless Tile Inc 636 Poinsettia St Santa Ana 92701

MC CANN, KENNETH EDWARD, manufacturing co. executive; b. May 28, 1935, Chgo., Ill.; s. John Henery and Florence Elizabeth (Kidd) McC.; m. Donna K. Hamilton, Nov. 27, 1954; children: Renee, b. 1957; Gregory, b. 1961; edn: BBA, Chapman 1978; Contractors Lic., Calif. 1978. Career: sr. elec. lab tech. ITT Kellogg 1958-62; sr. design evaluation engr. NCR Corp. 1962-64; prod. evaluation supvr. 1964-78; quality assurance mgr. NCR Corp. 1978-81, Atari Inc. 1981-83, System Industries Inc. 1983--; mem: Am. Soc. for Quality Control; Loyal Order of Moose; Am. Legion; mil: photog. mate-2 US Naval Air Reserve 1953-65; Republican; Catholic; rec: flying. Res: 1545 Willowhave Ct San Jose 95126 Ofc: System Industries, 1855 Barber Ln Milpitas

MC CANN, RUTH VIRGINIA, electronic mfg. co. executive; b. Mar. 2, 1934, Portlavaca, Tex.; d. Thomas Kemp and Victoria (Haws) McCann Sr.; edn: cert. in materials mgmt., San Diego State Univ. 1981; cert. in purchasing mgmt., UCSD, 1983. Career: buyer Topaz Inc., San Diego 1967-74; purchasing agt. OAR Corp. (electronic mfg. co.), San Diego 1974-75, mgr. of materials, 1975--; mem.: APICS; Purchasing Mgmt. Assn. San Diego chpt. 1972- (dir. 1979-81, sec. 1982-3, 1st VP 1983-4, S.D. chpt. 1st woman pres. 1984-5); rec: jog, bike; res: 3833 Ingraham St. A306, San Diego 92109 ofc: OAR Corp. 10447 Roselle St. San Diego 92121

MC CANN, WILBUR E., economist; b. Mar. 30, 1911, Street, Md.; s. Wilbur and Laura (Robinson) McC.; m. Elsie Groff, Dec. 12, 1936; children: Joyce, b. 1940; Clark, b. 1942; edn: BS, Univ. of Maryland 1933; MS, 1934. Career: economist Dair Industry, Wash. DC 1934-43; head research dept. Los Angeles CofC, L.A. 1946-56; pvt. econ. research activities 1956-83; Wilbur McCann, Economic Consultant 1957-68; pres. Western Economic Research Co., Inc. 1969--; mem: Am. Statistical Assn.; Nat. Assn. Bus. Economists; Lamba Alpha frat.; Los Angeles Area CofC; Riviera Country Club, Pacific Palisades; works: developed the first multi- color map depicting results of Census, noted for creation of small area data for practical applications in bus. & govt.; mil: lt. USN Aviation Br. 1943-46; Democrat; Methodist; rec: golf. Res: 13831 Chandler Blvd Van Nuys 91401 Ofc: Western Economic Research Co. Inc., 13437 Ventura Blvd Sherman Oaks 91423

MC CARROLL, NEIL FRENFELL, II, lawyer; b. Mar. 24, 1944, Los Angeles; s. Neil G. and Mary (Hannin) McC.; m. Ase, Aug. 5, 1967; 1 child, Morgan, b. 1971; edn: BS in law, USC, 1967, JD, 1969; admitted to Calif. State Bar 1969. Career: assoc. Keatinge & Sterling (corp. securities practice) 1969 71; or. assoc. Stephens, Jones, Lafever & Smith (gen. corp., corp. sec. practice) 1971-75; sr. counsel City National Bank 1975-82; ptnr. McCarroll & McCarroll, 1982--; of counsel Rosen, Wachtell & Gilbert APC, and Myron Blumberg A Law Corp.; dir: Letek Corp., Schats Dutch Bakeries Inc.; mem. Am. Bar Assn., State Bar of Calif., Internat. Bar Assn., L.A. County Bar Assn., Los Feliz Improvement Assn. (dir.); clubs: Century West, Snowcreek Athletic; legal counsel Com. to incorporate Mammoth Lakes. Address: 250034 Valley Vista Dr (POB 9200) Mammoth Lakes 93546

MC CARTHY, ADAIR BERNARD, real estate executive; b. Oct. 5, 1931, San Francisco; s. Adair Bernard and Josephine Clement (Halverson) McCarthy; m. June Barber, Sept. 23, 1961; 1 dau. Kathleen, b. 1967; edn: BA in acctg., cum laude, San Jose State Univ. 1956; Graduate Realtors Inst. 1973. Career: owner McCarthy Real Estate Co., San Francisco 1963-75; pres., dir. McCarthy Group Inc. (real estate devel. & sales), Sausalito 1979--; sr. v.p. The Innisfree Cos., Sausalito 1975--; pres. Innisfree Marketing Assocs., Sausalito 1975--. Honors: Sigma Alpha Epsilon frat. (pres. 1955); mem: Nat. Assn. of Realtors, Calif. Real Estate Assn., No. Calif. Sales & Mktg. Council, Marin Co. Real Estate Board, S.F. Real Estate Bd., No. Calif. Bldg. Industry Assn.; mem. The Marin Co. Mediation Svcs Advis. Com.; mil: USN 1948-52; rec: hiking, philately, vineyard grower; res: 79 Greenwood Way Mill Valley 94941 ofc: The Innisfree Cos. 2656 Bridgeway Sausalito 94965

MC CARTHY, EDWARD JOSEPH, III, computer co. president; b. Jan. 22, 1955, Chgo., Ill.; s. Edward Joseph, Jr. and Diane Marie (Paschen) McC.; m. Carolyn Jean Brown, Sept. 7, 1980; edn: BS, CSU Long Beach 1977; MBA, 1979. Career: sales mgr. Quikdata (computer timesharing firm), Long Beach 1976-78; dir. Delphi Systems Inc. (computer sys. house), No. Hollywood 1978-81; Western US mgr. Computer Sharing Svcs. (computer timesharing firm), Denver Colo.; pres./CEO Promethean Sys., Inc. (computer sys. house), Santa Monica 1981--; dir. Western Reserves (oil exploration & drilling co.); mem: Los Angeles CofC; Santa Monica Jaycees; Santa Monica Kiwanis; Republican; Catholic; rec: skiing, ice hockey. Res: 8968 W 25th St Los Angeles 90034 Ofc: Promethean Systems, Inc., 1434 6th St, Ste 6, Santa Monica 90401

MC CARTHY, JOHN CHARLES, lawyer; b. Nov. 14, 1923, Chgo., Ill.; s. Thomas James and Margaret Mary (Schollmeyer) McC.; m. Lorraine Donovan, Feb. 5, 1960; children: Michael, b. 1961; Mary, b 1962; Sheila, b. 1964; edn: Maimi Univ. 1942-44; BSBA, USC 1947; JD, UCLA 1952; admitted to State Bar of Calif. 1953. Career: pvt. practice law, Claremont 1954-63; director of the Peace Corps in Thailand (US Govt.), Bangkok 1963-66; partner law firm Young, Henrie & McCarthy, Pomona 1966-75; pres. law firm John C. McCarthy, Inc., Claremont 1975--; lectr./writer for var. legal groups (incl. Calif. State Bar, Assn. of Am. Trial Lawyers, law schs., Calif. Trial Lawyers Assn.,

others); honors: Alumnus of the Year 1973 UCLA Law Sch., nat. chmn. Environmental Law Sect. Assn. of American Trial Lawyers 1972-74; mem: Calif. Trial Lawyers Assn. (pres. 1969); University Club (pres. 1969); publs: (book and cassettes) Sucessful Techniques in Handling Bad Faith Cases (1973), (book) Punitive Damages in Bad Faith Cases (3d ed. 1983), (book) Punitive Damages in Wrongful Discharge Cases (1984) (pub: Lawpress Corp. Tiburon, CA); Democrat; Catholic; rec: lecturing, skiing, golf. Res: 1920 Indian Hill Blvd Claremont 91711 Ofc: Law Offices of John C. McCarthy, Inc., 401 Harvard Ave Claremont 91711

MC CARTHY, MARY PHYLLIS MASCITTI, social worker; b. Oct. 12, 1928, Leominster, Mass.; d. Pelino and Anna Pelina (DiNino) Mascitti; m. Walter Joseph McCarthy (dec.), May 21, 1955; edn: BS, UC Los Angeles 1954; MSW, Catholic Univ. of Am. 1963; PhD, Bryn Mawr Coll. 1976. Catholic Sister (Sisters of Soc. Svc.), Calif. LCSW. Career: court soc. wkr. and county adoption supr. Muskegon County (Mich.) Juvenile and Circuit Cts., 1951-54; soc. wkr. UCLA Student Counseling Ctr., Catholic Soc. Svc. Vallejo, Georgetown Univ. Hosp. Wash. DC, pre 1963; clin. soc. wkr. pvt. practice 1965--; workshops and lectures on psychological, sociological and social welfare, 1965-; cons. to Regis House Settlement Pgm, also gen. councilor/treas. Sisters of Social Service, 1974-76; instr. Immaculate Heart Coll. and Mount Saint Mary's Coll., 1963-68; dir. Holy Family Adoption Service, L.A. 1963-70; currently: dir. Quo Vadis Family Center, and cons. Nat. Family Plng. Tchrs. Assn., Torrance 1980--; Social Systems analyst, 1976--; bd. mem. Natural Family Plng. Pgm., St. Joseph Hosp., Orange 1981-; cons. World Hlth Orgn. Nat. Family Plng. Resrch. Study in Colombia, S.A. 1977; awards: NIH grant 1962 & 1971; Distinguished Ldrshp. in Research 1976, Cedars-Sinai Med. Center, L.A. Mem: Nat. Assn. of Soc. Wkrs. (bd. dirs. L.A. 1966-71), Acad. of Cert. Soc. Wkrs. (certification bd. 1970-74), Calif. Clin. Soc. Wkrs., Nat. Conf. of Soc. Wkrs., Internat. Conf. of Soc. Welfare, Am. Assn. of Soc. Welfare History, Nat. Conf. of Catholic Charities; mem. Sigma Kappa Sor., L.A., Torrance CofC, Palos Verdes Penin. Coordinating Council, Torrance Coord. Council; publs: arts. in med journals, family plng. confs.; Catholic Sister (SSS); rec: art, gardening. Res: 1120 Westchester Pl Los Angeles 90010 Ofc: Quo Vadis Family Center, 3715 W. Lomita Blvd, Ste. 129, Torrance 90505

MC CARTHY, RICHARD JOHN, family counselor; b. July 17, 1955, Tulsa, Okla.; s. John Eugene and Alice Mary (Fritton) McC.; m. Susan, June 26, 1982; edn: BS, Univ. of Utah 1977; MA, Loyola Marymount Univ. 1979; MFCC-Marriage, Family & Child Counselor, Calif. 1983. Career: research asst. Veterans Hosp., Salt Lake, Utah 1976-77; asst. prof. psychology Marymount Coll. 1979-82; counselor So. Bay Therapeutic Clinic, Torrance 1978-81; pres. Internat. Developmental Sys., Lomita 1980-83; dir. aquatic sports Marymount Coll. 1978--; counselor Quo Vadis Family Ctr., Torrance 1981--; psychiatric soc. wkr., pvt. practice 1983--, dir. Marriage & Family Clinic, Hermosa Beach 1984-; v.p. Faculty Senate Marymount Coll. 1980-81; honors: capt. Univ. of Utah Diving Team 1976; Psi Chi nat. psychology hon. soc. 1979; mem: Calif. Assn. Marriage & Family Therapists; Masters AAU Diving; works: memory research, 1976; Republican; Catholic; rec: swimming, diving, skiing. Res: 26410 Rolling Vista Dr Lomita 90717 Ofc: Quo Vadis Family Center, 3715 W Lomita Blvd, Ste 129, Torrance 90505

MC CARTHY, ROBERT WILLIAM, financial planner/ corporate executive; b. Feb. 15, 1936, Chgo.; s. John James and Katherine (Horan) McC.; m. Frances Grooms, July 11, 1975; children: Robert, b. 1957; Donald, b. 1959; Kelly, b. 1977; edn: Loras Coll. 1954-55; Northwestern Univ. 1955-58. Career: pres. R.W. McCarthy & Assocs., Inc. (fin. plng., investments, investment counseling, tax plng., real estate devel., limited partnerships, venture capital projs.), Irvine; chmn. exec. com./bd. dirs. Continental Gen. Insuranceman, Inc. 1982-; State Adv. Com. to Pres. of US 1982-; mem: Internat. Assn. of Fin. Plnrs.; Nat. Assn. Securities Dealers; Nat. Assn. Tax Cons.; Nat. Assn. Reg. Reps.; Aircraft Owners & Pilots Assn.; Am. Assn. Arbian Horse Owners; Republican; Catholic; rec: raising/ breeding Arabian horses, flying, travel. Res: 5735 Crest de Ville, Villa Park 92667 Ofc: R.W. McCarthy & Assoc. Inc. 611 Anton Blvd, Ste 780 Costa Mesa 92626

MC CARTNEY, RICHARD LEE, entrepreneur; b. July 7, 1938, Hood River, Ore.; s. Howard Eugene and Dorothy Mary (Hiday) McC.; m. Faye Auvon Woodruff, Feb. 24, 1968; children: Celeste b. 1959, Debbie b. 1961, Adrian b. 1962; edn: AA, Chabot Coll.; LLB, LaSalle Univ. 1968; desig: Calif. lic. Real Estate Broker 1762, Calif. Comm. Colls. Instr. cred. 1975; Notary Public; Reg. Practitioner, ICC (1975), Fed. Maritime Commn. (1976); CPM (Cert. Purchasing Mgr.), Nat. Assn. Purch. Mgmt. 1976. Career: asst. purchasing agt. Enterprise Div. De Laval Turbine, Oakland 1959-66; purch. agt. Gen. Electric Co., San Leandro 1966-69; commodity splst. Fairchild Semiconductor, Mtn. View 1969-70; self-empl. real estate indus. 1970-72; mgr. of purchasing Ecolaire Environmental, Pleasant Hill 1972-80, Instru. Div. Varian Assoc., Palo Alto 1980-81; 1981--: owner/mgr. Camaraderie (art gallery & custom frame shop), and Runner Up (a courier svc.); cons. in physical distbn.; instr. (phys. distbn. mgmt. courses) Chabot Coll. and UC Ext., Berkeley 1974-; mem: Berkeley CofC, Nat. Fedn. of Indep. Bus., Assn. of Transp. Practitioners, Am. Purch. Soc. (life), So. Alameda Co. Bd. of Realtors; mem. Calif. Acad. of Scis. (life), SF Mus. Soc., SF Zool. Soc.; mil: cpl. USMC 1956-59; Republican; Pastor, The Interim Ch. of Jesus Christ; rec: tchg., computer pgmg. Res: POB 1605, San Leandro 94577 Ofc: Camaraderie 2820 Telegraph Ave Berkeley 94705

MC CARTY, CYNTHIA BROWN, real estate broker; b. July 25, 1938, New Orleans, La.; d. Robert William and Mabel Louise (Ockman) Brown; edn.

grad. St. Joseph Acad. 1956; Calif. lic. Real Estate Broker. Career: employed McDonnell Douglas Sacramento Test Center and Kwajalein, Marshall Islands, 12 years; in real estate 15 years: curent owner/broker Heritage Land and Homes (two offices) Placerville, and Coloma; mem. Placerville City Planning Commn. 4 years; recipient Award for Outstanding Scouting Contribution; mem: Nat. Assn. Realtors, Calif. Assn. Realtors (Syndication Div.), El Dorado Co. Bd. Realtors; 99s (internat. orgn. for woman pilots); El Dorado CofC; Toast-mistress (past pres.); Asst. Dist. Comm. Boy Scouts of Am.; Democrat; Catholic; rec: flying, golf, outdoor sports. Res: 3148 Verde Robles Dr Camino 95709 Ofc: Heritage Land and Homes, 82 Main St, Placerville 95667

MC CARTY, MICHAEL LAWRENCE, restaurateur; b. Feb. 10, 1953, Mt. Kiscoe, NY; s. John Thomas and Carol May (Holly) McC.; m. Kim Lieberman, Jan. 29, 1984; edn: Andover Exeter Sch. Year Abroad/France 1969-70; BA, Univ. of Colo. 1975; CAP, L'Ecole D'Hotellerie de Paris 1974; Grande Diplome, Cordon Bleu, Paris 1974; Cert., Cornell Univ. Sch. of Hotel & Restaurant Mgmt. 1974. Career: founder/ opr. three restaurants, Paris & Colo.; currently, Michael's (restaurant), Santa Monica; bd. dirs./ treas. corp. founder Am. Inst. Wine & Food; Chaine de Rotisseurs (Maitre Grillardin); Society of Bacchus; mem: Fraternity of Friends (Music Ctr.); Music Ctr.; Mus. of Contemporary Art; Pres. Circle Los Angeles Co. Mus. of ARt.; Mus. Modern Art, NY; Whitney Mus., NY; Republican; Episcopal; rec: contemporary art collection, food & wine, tennis. Res: 3222 Rambla Pacifico Malibu 90265 Ofc: Michael's 1147 Third St Santa Monica 90403

MC CARTY, NIELSEN WARE, real estate broker/ educator; b. July 26, 1926, Chattanooga, Tenn.; d. James Loomis and Blanche Roberta (Arnold) Ware; m. Warren Kendall McCarty, Apr. 18, 1953; children: Kendall Loomis, b. 1956; Daniel Lewis, b. 1958; edn: BS, Univ. of Chattanooga 1948; Calif. Tchrs. Cred., USC 1963; Real Estate Broker Lic., LA Pierce Com. Coll. 1982. Career: chemist Emerson P. Poste 1948-51; cons. chem. engr., research analyst, Atomic Energy Research Dept. No. American Aviation 1951-53; research engr. Atomics Internat. Div. Rockwell Internat. 1953-56; tchr. math., sci. L.A. Unified Sch. Dist. 1963-77; real estate sales Century 21 Victory Realty 1977-82; real estate broker Nielsen's Realty 1982--; tchr. math. Reseda H.S., L.A. Unif. Sch. Dist. 1984--; mem: Gamma Sigma Epsilon; Am. Chem Soc. (Section editor, Chattanooga 1949-51); San Fernando Valley Bd. Realtors; SF Valley Alumnae of Kappa Delta (pres.); P.E.O.; Valley Univ. Women (pres.); Canoga Park Womens Club (pres.); SF Valley Panhellenic Assn.; Republican; Episcopal; rec: tennis, bridge, gardening. Address: Nielsen's Realty, 6131 Fenwood Ave Woodland Hills 91367

McCLATCHY, JAMES, newspaper publisher; b. Sacramento; s. Carlos and Phebe (Briggs) McClatchy; Edn: AB, Stanford Univ., MS, Columbia Univ. Career: newspaper reporter, editor and publisher, chmn. bd., McClatchy Newspapers. Publisher: Tiburon Ark, Tahoe World. Mil: pilot, USAF. Office: 21st & Q Streets, Sacramento 95813.

MC CLEES, N. SUSAN, stockbroker; b. Oct. 4, 1946, San Francisco; d. James Wycoff and Genevieve Marie (Mathews) McClees; edn: AA, Coll. of Marin 1967; AB, UC Berkeley 1969; M.Music, Dominican Coll. 1971; Calif. Life Tchg. Cred.; lic: Broker, Insurance, Assoc. Commodity, Options. Career: music tchr. 1971-72; dir. of music Katharine Branson Sch. 1972-74; profl. photographer Oakland Raiders, Oakland Stompers, Seattle Seahawks, Calif. Miss World, 1976-79; stockbroker 1981--: currently, assoc. v.p. Dean Witter Reynolds, Santa Rosa; profl. violinist, 1st violin, Santa Rosa Symphony; awards: 1st place Region 7, Porsche Club of Am. 1981, and 1st place in Sonoma & Marin Co. 1982; mem: Mensa; Bay Area Career Women; Women's Found. (Seminar Com.); Democrat; rec: race cars. Res: 3 Palm Ave Corte Madera 94925 Ofc: Dean Witter Reynolds, 703 2nd St Santa Rosa 95402

MC CLINTOCK, ESTHER RAY, real estate broker, financial planner; b. June 3, 1922, Silver Springs, Fla.; d. Clyde Fowler and Harriet (Smith) Ray; m. J. Lee McClintock, May 19, 1945, dissolved; 2 daus: Kathleen, b. 1947, Theresa, b. 1949; edn: spl. courses, Orange Coast Coll., Santa Ana Coll. 1949-53; real estate courses, Valley Coll. 1968-69, UCLA 1975-76, John Carey Inst., Lumbleau and Anthony Schs. of R.E.; Calif. lic. Real Estate Broker 1970, Mortgage Loan Broker, Underwriting Mem. Local 776, Film Editor & Video Tape Editors 1965-84. Career: fmr. exec. secty. var. motion picture executives; past asst. editor for Warner Bros, 20th Century-Fox, Universal Studios and Paramount Studios; owner/broker McClintock Realty and Financial Services, Beverly Hills 1970--, fmrly with offices in Escondido and Lancaster; pres. Calvane, Inc. 1975-76; honors: Thespians; mem: Epsilon Sigma Alpha (sec.treas. 1946-8), Beta Sigma Phi (1952-70), Los Angeles, Escondido bds. of realtors (on leave of absence), Westside Brokers Assn., L.A. MLS, L.A. CofC, Bus. & Profl. Womens Club; Republican (Nat. Senatl., Nat. Repub., Pres. Task Force); Sci. of Mind; rec: genealogy, cooking. Res: 329 Teloma Dr Ventura 93003

MC CLUNG, JOHN ROBINSON, JR., advertising executive/editor; b. Sept. 14, 1914, Sewanee, Tenn.; s. John Robinson and Mary Merle (McCall) McC.; m. Edith Eve Logue, Feb. 3, 1944; children: John, b. 1946; Bonnie, b. 1948; Marilyn, b. 1952; edn: BA, Kansas State Univ. 1937. Career: reporter Manhattan Mercury, Kansas 1934-36; editor Kansas State Royal Purple (awarded All American Pacemaker) 1936-37; advtg. staff & editor, home office house mag., Aetna Life & Casualty, Hartford, Ct. 1938-41; acct. exec./ assoc. mgr. Kirschner & Co. (advtg. agcy./ publ. firm), San Francisco & Palo Alto, 1946-61, Palo Alto 1962-65; ed. Nat. Insurance Adjuster Mag. 1963-65; v.p. Art Blum

Agcy. (Pub. Rels.), San Francisco 1966; founder/ chmn./ pres. McClung Avtg. Agcy., Inc., Palo Alto 1967--; current ed. The Beta Theta Pi (founded 1872, oldest continuously pub. fraternity mag.) 1977-; past pres. Beta Theta Pi, S.F. Bay Area Alumni Assn. (elected pres. of Nat. Convention 1965; Dist. Chief Calif. 1954-62); mem: Sigma Delta Chi; S.F. Advtg. Club; S.F. Adcrafters (pres. 1955); Peninsula Advtg. Club; P.A.L.O. Club; Fraternity Editors Assn.; mil: capt. Signal Corp. 1941-45, ofcr. in chg of Gen. MacArthurs GHQ Intercept Ctr. (1944), GHQ Signal Ctr. (1945), Hollandia, New Guinea, Pacific Theater Commun. Ctrs.; Republican; Methodist; rec: sports, travel. Res: 746 Josina Ave Palo Alto 94306 Ofc: McClung Advertising Agency, Inc., POB 60699 Palo Alto 94306

MC CLURE, ROBERT STUART, milling co. president; b. July 3, 1928, Los Angeles; s. James Gordon and Dorothy Grace (Horne) McC.; m. Virginia Grace Haddad, Dec. 5, 1959; children: Joel G., b. 1961; Margaret, b. 1962; Andrew S., b. 1963; edn: BS, UC Davis 1950. Career: foreman Safeway Stores Meat Processing Plant, Los ANgeles 1954-59; plant supt. Safeway Meat Processing, Wilmington, Dela. 1959-61; mgr. Consolidated Milling Co. L.A. Branch 1961-72; regl. mgr. 1972-77; owner/ mgr./ pres. 1977--; mem: Fountain Valley Lodge F&AM; Santa Ana Valley AASR Masons; El Bekal Shrine, Anaheim; mil: sgt. 1/c US Army 1950-53; Republican; Protestant; rec: sailing, travel. Res: 24942 Tocaloma Ct Laguna Hills 92653 Ofc: Consolidated Milling, Inc., 8610 Central Ave Stanton 90680

MC COLLOCH, MELVIN LEE, company executive; b. Sept. 12, 1936, Grand Junction, Colo.; s. Joe Wilson and Bernice Lucille (Shelly) McC.; m. Irene Morales, Sept. 3, 1965; children: Mykel, b. 1958; Randi, b. 1959; Joe, b. 1961; edn: BS, Fresno State Coll. 1957. Career: with Nickel Enterprises, 1957--: gen. foreman, Merced Co. ops. 1957-59; gen. supt. Kern Co. ops. 1959-63; gen. supt. Calif. ops. 1963-69; v.p. 1969-77; operations mgr. 1977--; pres. Olcese Water Dist. 1977-; v.p. ops. Rio Bravo Resort Golf and Tennis Club 1978-; v.p. bd. Rio Bravo Tennis Club 1978-; chmn. bd./ v.p. Kern River Whitewater Club 1979-; chmn. bd./v.p. La Hacienda, Inc. 1979-; dir. Rio Bravo Homeowners Assn. 1979-81, Cattle King Homeowners Assn. 1980-81; dir. West Kern Conservation Dist. 1982, 83, 84; awards: State Farmer Degree 1954; Young Business Man of the Yr., Merced Co. 1960; Advertisement Pizazz Awd. 1981, 82, 83; mem: Lions Club; 20-30 Club; 3rd Degree Masonic Temple; Exchange Club (pres. 1964-65); mil: US Army 1952-53, Korea; Democrat; Protestant; rec: tennis, golf, hunting. Res: Star Rt Box 1C, Bakersfield 93301 Oc: Nickel Enterprises, Star Rt 4 Box 801, Rio Bravo Annex, Bakersfield 93306

MC COLM, PATRICIA ALICE, production co. executive; b. June 5, 1946, Emporia, Kansas; d. George Lester and Emma Victoria (Davis) McC.; edn: BA, Univ. of Ariz. 1968; MA, Univ. of Minn. 1971; tchr. tng. course, Royal Ballet Sch., London 1974-75; profl. stage, Ecole Jacque L'Coq, Paris 1975; JD, Golden Gate Univ. Sch. of Law 1984; EdD, in progress, Univ. of San Francisco 1985. Career: promotion/ prodn. asst. WCCO- TV, Mnpls., Minn. 1969; instr. Augsbury Coll. Mnpls., Minn. 1969-71; sole prop. Presidio Interiors, San Francisco 1971-73; instr. Am. Conservatory Theatre, S.F. 1975; lectr. in broadcasting S.F. State Univ. 1976-79; dist. mgr. Sony Video Prods. Co./ Sony Corp. of Am. 1979-80; instr. City Coll. of S.F. 1982-83; legal extern FCC, Wash. DC 1983; sole prop. Media Arts Wrkshp. & Prodn. Co., S.F. 1977--; awards: First Female Dist. Mgr. in the Video Ind., USA 1979; Alpha Epsilon Rho nat. radio-tv frat. 1969, Phi Beta music & speech frat. 1970; Miss Minneapolis 1970-71, Miss America Pageant; mem: Am. Bar Assn.; Am. Women in Radio & TV; Am. Fedn. of TV & Radio Artists; Am. Guild of Musical Arts; Screen Actors Guild; Speech Commun. Assn.; Delta Zeta, Beta Iota; Sigma Delta; rec: ballet, acting, Maltese show dog breeding. Ofc: Media Arts Workshop, 579 Miramar Ave San Francisco 94112

MC CONAHY, CLARENCE ALBERT, JR., business owner; b. Aug. 18, 1924, Altoona, Penn.; s. Clarence Albert, Sr. and Fleda Bertha (Morgan) McC.; m. Loretta Mae Miller, Sept. 5, 1950; children: Ralph, b. 1952; Lee A., b. 1955; Lora L., b 1960; edn: acctg. Skadron Bus. Coll. 1950; AA, San Bernardino Valley Coll. 1959. Career: deputy city treas. City of San Bernardino 1950-53, chief deputy city treas. 1953-62; owner/ mgr. South Coast Press (aka South Coast Rubber Stamps) 1962--; honors: hon. mem. Santa Claus Inc. of Greater San Bernardino 1970; Rotarian of Year 1977, S.B. Rotary; mem: San Bernardino Jaycees (pres. 1959); Santa Claus Inc. (pres. 1969); So. Calif. Marking Club (pres. 1974-75); S.B. Rotary Club (pres. 1980-81); Marking Device Assn. (bd. dirs., rep. Southwest US); Interact Clubs (Pacific & S.B. H.Schs.); YMCA; Arrowhead Country Club; mil: pfc US Army 1943-46; Democrat; Protestant; rec: golf. Res: 3120 Sierra Way San Bernardino 92405 Ofc: South Coast Rubber Stamps, 261 S Arrowhead Ave San Bernardino 92408

MC CORD, ALBERT BYRON, economic development corp. president; b. June 19, 1944, Hereford, Tex.; s. C.V. and Edna Murrell (Thornboro) McC.; 1 son, James Byron b. 1977; edn: BBA, Eastern N.Mex. Univ. 1967. Career: chief indsl. devel. New Mex. Commerce & Ind. Dept., Santa Fe, N.Mex. 1973-82; pres. Fresno Co. Econ. Devel. Corp., Fresno 1982-84; pres. SEDCORP (Solano Econ. Devel. Corp.), Fairfield 1984--; Calif. Assn. for Local Econ. Devel. (bd. dirs., Seminar Staff, Gov. Econ. Devel. Task Force) 1983-84; N. Mex. Indsl. Devel. Execs. Assn. (bd. dirs.) 1980-82; awards: Gov.'s Appreciation Awd., State of N. Mex. 1982; Albuquerque Indsl. Devel. Svc. Commdn. 1982; mem: Am. Econ. Devel. Council; Calif. Assn. for Local Econ. Devel.; Rotary; publs.: Fresno Business Prospectus (1982, 84); N.M. Industrial Fact Book (1974, 76, 78, 80); rec: sailing. Res: 1222 Hartford Circle Fairfield 94533 Ofc: SEDCORP, 2750 N. Texas St, Ste 380, Fairfield 94533

MC CORD, CHARLES LEE, physician; b. Apr. 8, 1951, Moorhead, Minn.; s. Bernard Grosvenor and Margarett (Wood) McC.; edn: BS, Syracuse Univ. 1973; MD, SUNY Upstate Med. Ctr. 1977; Intern, Resident, Cedars Sinai Med. Ctr., L.A. 1981; Bd. Cert. Am. Coll. of Obstetrics & Gynecology (FACOG) 1983. Career: physician, Mullikin Med. Ctr., Artesia 1981-83; currently, Redondo Beach Medical Gp., Redondo Beach; awards: Bd. Cert., Am. Coll. of Obs. & Gyn. 1983; mem: L.A. Co. Med. Assn.; L.A. Ob/ Gyn. Soc.; Am. Assn. of Gyn. Laparascopists; Christian; rec: flying, tennis, travel. Res: 2808 1/2 Manhattan Ave Manhattan Beach 90266 Ofc: Redondo Beach Medical Group, 502 Torrance Blvd Redondo Beach 90277

MC CORMACK, CAROLE JEAN, mortgage broker; b. May 17, 1942, Portland, Ore.; d. Henry Claire and Grace Lorraine (Brigner) Rolphe; div.; 1 dau. Kelley Christine b. 1972; Calif. Tchr. cred., Creative Fin., 1980. Career: escrow secty. Mortgage Refinance Co., L.A. 1963-65; secty. Anderson Lithograph, L.A. 1965-67; asst. branch mgr. Home Savings & Loan, Lakewood 1967-73; self- empl. Loan Document Service, Anaheim 1973-76; spot loan mgr. Suburban Coastal Corp., Tustin 1976-80; v.p. Am. Real Estate Inst., Costa Mesa 1980-81; public rels./ broker rels. San Marino Savings & Loan, Irvine 1981; br. mgr. Great Southwest Mortgage, Tustin 1981-83; owner/ pres. Lighthouse Finl. Center, Inc., Tustin 1983--; tchr. Calif. Sch. of Mortgage Banking 1984-; awards: Top Producer, Suburban Coastal 1976-80, Top Funder 1976-80; sev. guest spkg. appreciation awards, Bd. of Realtors, Calif. 1980; mem: East Orange Co. & Huntington Beach- Fountain Valley Bds. Realtors; Realty Investment Assn. of Orange Co.; Assn. of Profl. Mortgage Women; mil: A/2c USAF 1960-62; Episcopal; mem. National Walking Horse Assn., Calif. Fox Trotter Assn. (dau. won Junior Champion, 11 and under, 1982 CFTA; won High Point, 1982 NWHA) raise & train Thorobred/ Foxtrotter/ Tennesee Walking Horses. Res: 3531 Pedley St Norco 91670 Ofc: Lighthouse Financial Center, Inc., 14771 Plaza Dr, Ste M, Tustin 92680

MC CORMACK, VIRGINIA CARRILLO, lawyer; b. Oct. 3, 1948, Milwaukee, Wisc.; d. Charles S. and Marie R. (Carrillo) McC.; m. Peter T. Healy, Aug. 9, 1980; 1 son, Brendan b. 1981; edn: BA, UC Berkeley 1971; JD, UC Davis 1979. Career: atty. assoc. Tolpegin, Imai & Tadlock. San Francisco 1979--; awards: Study Grant Internat. Law, Strassbourg, France 1978; mem: Am., Calif. Bar Assns.; Internat. Forum Discussions; poetry pub. in Coll. mags. 1966-70; Democrat; Catholic; rec: running, swimming, literature. Res: 1801 Grant St Berkeley 94703; Tolpegin, Imai & Tadlock, 235 Montgomery, Ste 950, San Francisco 94104

MC COWN, HARVEY JIM, certified public accountant; b. Sept. 14, 1941, Bakersfield; s. Jim and Grace (Taylor) McC.; m. Joanne Hanson, June 13, 1964; children: Steven b. 1966, Alan b. 1970, Debborah b. 1972, Rachel b. 1975; edn: BS in acctg., UC Berkeley 1964, MBA in acctg. 1965; CPA cert., Calif. 1967-, Ida. 1974-. Career: summer intern Main La Frantz & Co., Oakland 1964; staff acct. Price Waterhouse & Co., San Francisco 1965-66; acct. McCown, Cole & Krause, Bakersfield 1966-68; tax dept. Arthur Anderson & Co., 1968-76 (in S.F. 1968-74; hd. Tax Dept., Boise, Ida. 1974-76); partner Jim & Harvey McCown, CPAs (fmrly McCown & Krause), Bakersfield 1976--. Instr. in taxation and acctg.: CSU Bakersfield, Real Estate Edn. Council (Ida.), Am. Bankers Assn., and Univ. Calif.; instr. in-house tng. classes Arthur Andersen & Co.; public spkr. on Economic Recovery Tax Act of 1981; panelist on tax and estate plnng.; honors: Beta Gamma Sigma, Beta Alpha Psi; mem: Calif. Soc. of CPAs (state bd. dirs. 1982-84, pres. Bakersfield chpt. 1983-84, state taxation com. 1978-82); Estate Planning Council (dir. Bakersfield chpt. 1979-85, mem. Boise chpt.); Idaho CPAs Soc. (state taxation com. 1975-76); Amer. Inst. of CPAs; Kiwanis, Jaycees; author: Real Estate-Federal Taxation (1976); Republican; LDS (elder); rec: gardening, skiing. Res: 3204 Sunview Dr Bakersfield 93306 Ofc: Jim & Harvey McCown, CPAs 1415 18th St, Ste 506, Bakersfield 93301

MC COY, CHARLES W., JR., lawyer; b. Nov. 3, 1946, Wash. DC; s. Charles W. and Mary Kay (Hammond) McC.; m. Jan Hodge, June 12, 1971; children: Justin, b. 1968; Seth, b. 1971; Jamie, b. 1980; edn: BS, Purdue Univ. 1968; JD, honors, Univ. of Tex. 1975. Career: partner law firm Sheppard, Mullin, Richter & Hampton, Los Angeles 1975--; Judge Pro Tem, Los Angeles Municipal Ct.; Am. Bar Assn. (Monograph Com., Antitrust Scct.); Calif. and Los Angeles Bar Assns.; Assn. of Bus. Trial Lawyers; contbg. author: Fundamentals of Legal Research (Found. Press. 1976); author: Kelly's Love (romantic novel); mil: capt. USMC, Navy Commdn. Medal w/ Combat V; Republican; Presbyterian (Elder); rec: tennis, skiing, golf. Res: 2513 E Thackery West Covina 91791 Ofc: Sheppard, Mullin, Richter & Hampton, 333 S Hope St, 48th Flr, Los Angeles 90071

MC COY, ROY EDGAR, banking executive; b. May 26, 1928, Glendale; s. Walter Clinton and Martha (Langton) McCoy; m. Louisce McKee, Dec. 27, 1954; children: Loren b. 1956, Nancy b. 1956, Gretchen b. 1958, Robert b. 1964; edn: BA, Univ. of Nebr. 1952. Career: owner/pres. Interpose Internat. Inc. (mfr. skate boards), 1975-76; branch mgr. Great American Federal Bank, currently regional mgr./sr. v.p., San Diego; dir. Coronado Tax Commn.; mem: Coronado Chamber of Commerce (pres.), Coronado Council Navy League of the US (pres.), Coronado Hist. Assn. (past pres.), Rotary, San Diego University Club, Eagle Scout BSA; mil: capt. US Navy 1952-75, decorated Legion of Merit, Bronze Star, Commendn., Vietnamese Cross of Gal., Medal of Honor 1/ c; Republican; rec: woodworking, politics. Res: 624 J Ave Coronado 92118 Ofc: Great American Federal, 600 B St San Diego 92183

MC COY, WILLIAM EDWARD, III, engineer, computer scientist; b. Jan. 9, 1939, Oakland; s. Wm. Edward and Mary Venable (Tuckerman) McCoy; edn:

BS gen. sci., and BS math., honors, Ore. State Univ. 1977, BS computer sci., 1980; MS computer sci., CSU Chico 1982. Career: electronic tech. Pan Am. World Airways, Yuma (Ariz.) Test Sta. 1960-61; logic designeer/asst. analyst Hughes Aircraft Co., Culver City 1962-65; pgmmr. Balter Publications, Hawthorne 1966-67; pgmmr. analyst Atlantic Richfield Co., Los Angeles 1968-69; pgmmr. analyst Autographics, Monterey Park 1969-70; cons., L.A., 1971, electronics engr. Naval Weapons Ctr., China Lake 1980-81; j engr. EDP Appls., SP Communications, Burlingame 1981--; instr. computer & info. sci., Coll. of San Mateo 1982; honors: Phi Beta Chi, UCC Honor Soc., Phi Kappa Phi (life); mem: AAAS, IEEE & IEEE Computer Soc., ACM, Soc. for Computer Simulation (mem. at lg. 1981-2), AIAA, Toastmasters (CTM), Jaycees (Buena Park treas. 1964, Hawthorne state dir. 1967, v.p. 1968); DAV (life); Calif. Assn. Physically Handicapped (life); Knights of Columbus Ridgecrest (Dep. Grand Knight 1981); works: Multi input & output pgm. controlled switch (pat.pend.); mil: A/2c electronic tech. USAF 1956-60; Republican; Catholic; rc: microcomputers, horse racing, cryptography. Res: 1124 Paloma, 1, Burlingame 94010 Ofc: SP Communications, One Advian Ct Burlingame 94010

MC CRARY, BARBARA JO, mobile home sales co. owner; b. Jan. 6, 1934, Quinton, Okla.; d. Nan V. (Murrell) Brackett; m. m. Bill Johnston, div.; children: Julie, b. 1952, Terry Ellen (Hauff) b. 1954, Vickie Lynn b. 1956; m. 2d. Jerry Lee McCrary, Oct. 19, 1973; desig: Calif. Ins. Lic. (life) Fire & Casualty, Calif. lic. Contractor, P.U.C. lic. for freight of mobile homes, etc.; lic. Mobile Home Dealer, Calif. Career: retail sales clk., Merced 1968-69; automobile sales Town & Country Chrysler, Merced 1969; sales Travelon Trailer Co., Modesto 1973; ptnr. Bill's Trailer Sales, Merced 1974-77; owner McCrary's Mobile Homes, Merced 1977--; mem. Merced, Mariposa Horsemans Assn.; Republican; Prot.; rec: dance, fish, gardening. Res: 3670 N. Santa Fe Dr Merced 95340 Ofc: McCrarys Mobile Homes, 1950 N. Ashby Rd Merced 95340

MC CULLOUGH, PATRICIA ANN, hospital administrator; b. Oct. 11, 1937, Hoquiam, Wash.; d. Irvin Earl and Margaret (McNamara) Albertson; m. Donavon McCullough (dec.), June 13, 1968, 1 son. John Olson, b. 1963, edn. BA, summa cum laude, Seattle Univ. 1971; MA, Pacific Lutheran Univ. 1974; Cert. Mental Health Adminstr., Assn. Mental Health Adminstrs. Career: chief alcohol & drug rehab. US Army, Ft. Lewis, Wash. 1972-78; CareUnit Hosp. (formerly Alcenas), Kirkland, Wash. 1978-80; CareUnit Hosp. (formerly Care Manor), Orange, Calif. 1980-81; Crossroads Hosp., Van Nuys 1981-82; hosp. adminstr. Comperhensive Care Corp. 1978--; honors: Outstanding Student, Coll. of Arts & Scis., Seattle Univ. 1971; Fed. Employee of the Yr , Pierce Co , Wash. 1974; Outstanding Performance (2), US Army 1974, 78; Outstanding Employee Awd., Comprehensive Care Corp. 1980; mem: United Hosp. Assn. (advr. 1984); Assn. Mental Health Adminstrs.; Nat. Council on Alcoholism; L.A. Cofc, Crenshaw Cofc, ALMACA; mil: A/2c USAF 1957-60; Presbyterian. Res: 1015 N Kings Rd 118, Los Angeles 90069 Ofc: Comprehensive Care Corp. dba CareUnit Hospital of Los Angeles, 5035 Coliseum Los Angeles 90016

MC CULLOUGH, RICHARD JOSEPH, contractor; b. Feb. 11, 1947, San Francisco; s. Robert James and Evelyn Marie (Lawler) M.; m. Gayle Louise Zanella, Mar. 21, 1972; 1 dau. Lecia Marie, b. 1977, edn. Healds Coll. 1967-71, AA, City 1968; SF Comm. Coll. 1972-8; cert. High Rise Fire Safety Director; cert. Cardio Pulmonary Resuscitation. Career: contractor/ project mgr /chief engr. Holiday Inns, S.F. & Hawaii, 1971-83, Four Seasons Clift Hotel, S.F.,. 1981-84; owner Kaatz Contractors Inc., marble maint. and metal refinishing, San Francisco 1984-- served on S.F. Civil Service Commn. Oral Exam Bd. for selection of Chief Engrs. Recipient two PG&E Energy Conservation; mem: Nat. Fire Protection Assn., Nat. Assn. of Power Engrs., fmr. mem. Local 39 Exec. Bd.; Democrat. Res: 414 Sixth St Petaluma 94952 Ofc: Kaatz Contractors Inc. 292 Ocean Ave San Francisco 94112

MC CUTCHEN, CHARLOTTE BARNWELL, physician; b. Oct. 31, 1944, Camp Lejeune, N.C.; d. James Malcolm and Emily Strother (Dunovant) McC.; edn: BS, Univ. of S.C. 1966; MD, Med. Coll. of Va. 1970. Career: residency tng. Vanderbilt Univ. 1972-74; instr. neurology & lab. medicine, Univ. of Wash. Sch. of Med., Seattle, 1974-77; asst. clin. prof. neurosciences UC San Diego 1977--; cons. UCSD Internal Med. Gp. 1980-; bd. dirs. Western Electroencephelographic Soc. 1983-86; secty. Am. Epilepsy Soc. 1982-85; mem: San Diego Neurological Assn.; S.D. County Epilepsy Soc.; Western EEG Soc.; Am. EEG Soc.; Am. Acad. of Neurology; A.U.R.A.; publs: num. arts. in med. journs.; Episcopal; rec: sailing, backpacking, gardening. Res: 5559 Dalen Ave San Diego 92122 Ofc: S.D.V.A.M.C., 3350 La Jolla Village Dr San Diego

MC DANIELS, JOHN LEA, lawyer; b. May 30, 1940, San Francisco; s. John Hale and Vivian Marie (Lea) McD.; edn: BA, Stanford Univ. 1962; JD, San Francisco Law Sch. 1969. Mem: Internat. Bar Assn.; Am. Bar Assn.; Commonwealth Club; Cercle de l'Union; The Wine & Food Soc. of S.F.; Internat. Food & Wine Soc.; Inns of Court Society in Calif.; The Assocs. of the Stanford Univ. Libraries; The Friends of the Bancroft Library); St. Thomas More Soc. of S.F.; bd. dirs. Bay Area USO; mil: Spec. 4/c AUS 1962-64; Catholic. Res: 1250 Jones St San Francisco 94109 Ofc: John Lea McDaniels, 40 First St, 3rd Floor, San Francisco 94105

McDERMOTT, RICHARD SCHICK, government official; b. July 13, 1923; Las Animas, CO; s. Raymond B. and Freda C. (Schick) McDermott; AB, Western State Coll., Gunnison, CO, 1947; JD, Univ. of Colo.,Boulder, 1950; m. Dorothy E. Thompson, Jan. 6, 1952; chil: Denise, b. 1954; Reuel, b. 1956; Brian, b. 1958; Gerald Abbott, b. 1946; Keith Abbott, b. 1949. Career: admitted to Colo. Bar, 1951; pvt. practice in Las Animas, CO, 1951-57; acting field solicitor, Dept. of Interior, Gallup, NM, 1957-59; admitted to NM Bar, 1959; partner, firm of Perry & McDermott, Gallup, 1959-65; realty officer, Bureau of Indian Affairs, Crow Agency, MT. 1965-68; realty officer, Bur. of Indian Affairs, Palm Springs, CA 1968-70; dir., 1970—; com. mem. for improvement of land title records, American Bar Assn., 1965-68; mem., Indian Law Comm., Federal Bar Assn., 1966—; pres. 16th Jud. Dist., Colo. Bar Assn., 1956; mem. comm. to correlate problems with Med. Soc., New Mex. Bar Assn., 1962-65; pres., McKinley Co. Bar Assn., 1962. Honors: pres., Las Animas, Colo., Bd. of Edn., 1955-57. Mem: bd. dirs., Univ. Colo. Law Alumni Fund, 1960-62; Family Consultation Service, ARC, Big Brothers, Palm Springs Sr. Center 1980-81, United Way of the Desert 1977—; v.p., McKinley Co. PTA Council, 1961-62; Palm Springs CofC, chmn. Economic Devel. Com., 1977-78; dir. 1973-76, 1978-81; Theta Chi, Phi Alpha Delta, Knife & Fork pres. 1964; Rotarian, club pres., 1962-63, 1975-76. Mil: AUS, ETO, 1942-46. Methodist, trustee, delegate to annual conf., 1980—. Res: 701 Ocotillo Ave., Palm Springs 92262; Office: Bureau of Indian Affairs, 441 S. Calle Encilia, Suite 8, Palm Springs 92262.

MC DONALD, LOUIS MARTIN, computer scientist; b. Dec. 8, 1956, Chgo.; s. Louis John and Eve Ruth (Lauth) McD.; m. Elizabeth Abeyta, Aug. 7, 1982; edn: BS, Cal Poly, Pomona 1981; MS, USC 1984. Career: computer tech. Bureau of Land Mgmt., Riverside 1979-80; computer pgmr. Walter Dorwin Teague Assoc., Inc., Pomona 1980-81; gp. head Hughes Aircraft, El Segundo 1981--; awards: Nat. IEEE Computer Soc. Scholarship 1981; Nat. Register of Outstanding Coll. Seniors 1981; Outstanding Young Men of Am., Jaycees 1982; mem: IEEE (Computer Soc., Cal Poly Pomona Student br. pres. 1979-81); ACM; Bits & Chips Computer Sci. Club (pres. 1979-81); Upsilon Pi Epsilon computer sci. hon. soc. (pres. 1980-81); Democrat; Catholic. Res: 8804 Reading Ave Westchester 90045 Ofc: Hughes Aircraft, POB 92426, R2/ A158 Los Angeles 90009

MC DONALD, MARGARET FOLEY, lawyer; b. Long Beach; d. James LaSalle and Nora Margaret (Foley) McDonald; 2 children (both adopted 1969), Elyse Caron Vosburg, b. 1954; Lawrence Andrew Hoytt, b. 1952; edn: AB, USC 1967; JD, Southwestern Univ. Sch. of Law 1980; USC Sch. of Bus. Admin. 1976-78; admitted to practice Calif. State Bar (1980), US Dist. Ct., Central Dist. (1981), US Ct. of Appeals, 9th Circuit (1981). Career: atty. Silver & Freedman, Los Angeles 1981--; investment advr. McDonald & Co., L.A. 1970-81; mem: Coro Assocs; Tax Law Soc. (Curriculum Com.), Southwestern Univ.; Los Angeles World Affairs Council. Ofc: Silver & Freedman, A Profl. Law Corp., 1888 Century Park E, Ste 1620, Los Angeles 90067

MC DONALD, SAMMANTHA HAYWARD, utility co. customer service executive; b. Nov. 18, 1949, Pasadena; d. Louis George and Ethelyn Georgia (Hale) Nichols; m. 2d. Jerry McDonald, July 30. 1983; children: Nicole Charise Hayward, b. 1972; John Thomas Mc Donald, b. 1973; Christopher McDonald, b. 1975; edn: AS, San Diego Mesa Coll. 1976; BBA, Nat. Univ. 1980; MBA, 1983. Career: customer info. rep., San Diego Gas & Elec. Co. 1970-72, 1974-80; customer info. analyst 1980-81; customer svc. supvr., Beach Cities Dist. 1981--; sem. leader/ tnr./ mem. Energy Spkrs. Corps; awards: Sch. Citizens Adv. Com. Svc. Awd., San Diego City Schs. 1975; Awd. of Excellence, Best Internal Commun., Internat. Assn. of Bus. Communicators 1983; mem: Career Womens Assn.; Dimensions; Am. Mgmt. Assn.; Mira Mesa Scripps Ranch CofC; Democrat; rec: creative writing, arts & crafts. Res: 13530 Longfellow Ln San Diego 92129 Ofc; SDG&E, 4901 Morena Blvd, Ste 210, San Diego 92117

MC DONOUGH, THOMAS REDMOND, scientist/ writer/ lecturer; b. Oct. 4, 1945, Boston, Mass.; s. Redmond Augustus and Sophie Theresa (Stankewich) McD.; edn: SB, MIT 1966; PhD, Cornell Univ. 1973. Career: tech. MIT Instrumentation Lab, Cambridge, Mass. 1964; staff mem. MIT Sci. Tchg. Center 1966; NASA trainee, Cornell Univ., Ithaca, NY 1969-71; postdoctoral researcher 1973-75; NASA/ Nat. Acad. of Scis: res. research assoc. Jet Propulsion Lab, Pasadena 1976-77; lectr. in engring. Calif. Inst. Tech. 1979--; coord. of search for extraterrestrial intelligence, The Planetary Soc., Pasadena 1981--; cons. Jet Propulsion Lab, Pasadena 1978-81; cons. Avco Embassy Pictures, Hollywood 1981; cons. New Pictures Gp., Hollywood 1982--; honors: scholarship, NY State Regents 1962; citation, NASA 1979; fellow, British Interplanetary Soc. 1977; Outstanding Toastmaster, JPL/ Caltech Toastmasters 1978; Outstanding Pro- Space Achiev., Nebraskans for the Adv. of Space Devel. 1982; mem: Am. Astron. Soc.; Am. Physical Soc.; Am. Geophysical Union; Authors Guild; Internat. Astron. Union (Commn. on Search of E.T. Intelligence); Sci. Fiction Writers of Am.; Toastmasters Internat. (past pres.); Platform Assn.; Am. Inst. of Aero. & Astro.; First Mars Landing Soc.; L-5 Soc.; Mensa; Nat. Space Inst.; works: arts. & stories pub. in Analog, Starlog, Sky & Telescope, Creative Computing, Personal Computing, others; sci. papers in Nature, Icarus, Science, J. Geophys. Research, Atmosphere of Titan (NASA); rec: stereoscopic photog., hiking. Ofc: Califorina Institute of Technology, 138-78, Pasadena 91125

MC DOWELL, ALLENE SIEBE, manufacturing co. executive; b. June 9, 1934, Boise, Idaho; d. Edward Louis and Lucile (Philpott) Siebe; m. Daniel McDowell, Sept. 8, 1956; edn: AA, Boise State Univ. 1954. Career: secty. Idaho Power Co., Boise, Idaho 1954-565; with. Firestone Tire & Rubber Co. 1956-82; secty. 1956-64; asst. ed./ comm. rels. asst. 1964-68; ed./ personnel asst. 1968-79; ed./ photographer/ actg. salary personnel mgr. 1979-82; personnel adminstr. Kirkhill Rubber Co., Brea 1983--; mem: Personnel & Indsl. Rels. Assn.; Los Angeles Rubber Gp.; Republican; Protestant; rec: sailing, fashion

design, photog. Res: 13441 Springdale St Westminster 92683 Ofc: Kirkhill Rubber Co., 300 E Cypress St Brea 92621

MC DOWELL, JENNIFER, publisher/composer; b. May 19, 1936, Albuquerque, NM; d. Willard A. and Margaret (Garrison) McDowell; grandfather, Lemuel Addison Garrison, fmr. pres. Central College (Pella, Iowa); mother, Margaret F Garrison, author; uncle Lon Garrison, supt. Yellowstone Nat. Park 1955-63. Edn: BS, UC Berkeley 1957; MA, CSU San Diego 1958; MLS, UCB 1963; PhD, Univ. Ore. Eugene 1973; m. Milton Loventhal, July 2, 1973. Career: high sch. tchr. Abraham Lincoln H.S., San Jose 1960-61; freelance ed., Soviet field, 1961-63; research asst., sociol., Univ. Ore. 1964-66; ed./ pub. Merlin Papers, San Jose 1969--; ed./pub. Merlin Press, 1973--; res. cons. sociol., San Jose 1973--; music publisher Lipstick and Toy Balloons Pub. Co., San Jose 1978--; resrchr., writer Merlin Research and Writing Center, 1980--; co-creator musical comedy: Russia's Secret Plot to Take Back Alaska (1983); tchr. writing workshops 1969-73; manuscript reader for Journ. of the Sci. Study of Religion, 1974-; on the list of composers for Paramount Pictures, 1981-; co-prod. radio shows, Sta. KALX, Berkeley 1971-72; songs (3) featured in Survey of Am. Music for Bicentennial Year; Awards: doctoral fellowship 1971-73, AAUW; Calif. Arts Council grant 1976-77; profl. awards: Am. Song Festival (1976-79), Poetry Orgn. for Women (1979), Bill Casey Meml. Award (1980), listed in Directory of Am. Poets and Fiction Writers 1980; composer for Harold C. Crain Award (1980) winning play, Simple Gifts by Nancy Gilsenan; honors: Kappa Kappa Gamma, Sigma Alpha Iota, Phi Beta Kappa, Beta Phi Mu; mem: Soc. for the Sci. Study of Relig., Soc. for the Study of Relig. nd Communism, Am. Sociological Assn., Poetry Orgn. for Women, Feminist Writers Guild, Internat. Womens Writing Guild; author: Black Politics (1971), Contemporary Women Poets an Anthology (1977); contrib. many arts. in Bulletin of Bibliography, Jour. for the Sci. Study of Religion, San Jose Studies; contbr. poems, essays to num. mags. incl. Women's World, Women Talking, Women Listening, X a Journal of the Arts, others; composer over 60 songs. Democrat; Prot.; rec: tennis, Calif. native plants, hiking. Ofc: Merlin Press, POB 5602, San Jose 95150

MC DOWELL, LOREN L., real estate broker; b. Nov. 14, 1931, Soldier, Ks.; s. Lester P. and Edith Ivo (Wiles) McD.; m. Patricia Patton, Oct. 10, 1950; children: James, b. 1952; Steven, b. 1954; Daniel, b. 1956; Cathy, b. 1957. Career: real estate salesman, San Diego 1956-59; real estate broker (spec. land acquisitions & sales), San Diego 1959-67; owner Surfside Mortgage Co., San Diego 1967-70; v.p./ head acquisitions/ chief appraiser Sea Coast Investment Co., S.D. 1970-72; independent R.E. appraiser, 1972--; V.A. appraiser; v.p. Sea Coast Trust Deed Co. 1970-72; honors: Master Exchangor Awd., Title Ins. & Trust 1972; mem: Nat. Assn. R.E. Appraisers; Soc. of R.E. Appraisers; publs: author/pub. Curbside Appraisal Report, 1982; mil: fire control tech., PO 2/c, GCM, Korean Conflict Medal; Republican; rec: fishing. Res: 11508 Creek Rd (POB 554) Poway 92064

MC DUFFIE, MALCOLM, oil co. executive, ret.; b. Nov. 14, 1915, San Francisco; s. William Chester and Mary (Skaife) McD.; m. Mary de Surville, Dec. 8, 1951; children: Cynthia, b. 1952; Duncan, b. 1955; edn: BA, econ., Stanford Univ. 1940. Career: O.C. Field Gasoline Corp. 1940-41; Wilmington Gasoline Corp. 1941-42; with Mohawk Petroleum Co. 1945-80; pres./ dir. 1969-80; dir. Reserve Oil & Gas Co. 1973-80; sr. v.p. 1977-80; spl. asst. to pres. Getty Oil Co., Los Angeles 1980-82; ret.; bd. of overseers Huntington Library, Art Gallery & Bot. gardens; bd. dirs. Calif. Inst. of Tech. Assoc.; mem: Nat. Petroleum Refiners Assn.; Indep. Refiners Assn. of Calif. (pres. 1967-69, 1977-78); Am. Petroleum Inst.; Rancheros Visitadores; Chevalier du Tastevin; Clubs: California, (LA), Bohemian (SF), Valley Hunt, Annandale Golf (Pasadena), Birnam Wood (Sta Barbara); Republican; Episcopal; rec: hunting, fishing. Res: 2060 Lombardy Rd San Marino 91108

MC EUEN, JAMES ANDREW, manufacturing engineering executive; b. Aug. 2, 1936, Thatcher, Ariz.; s. Vernon Perry and Beatrice (Woods) McE.; 1 dau. Cynthia Ann; Calif. Reg. Profl. (Mfg.) Engr. 1981. Career: planning engr. wire harness designer Hughes Aircraft, El Segundo & Fullerton 1959-62; wire harness designer Nortronics, Hawthorne 1962-63; plng. engr., senior devel. mfg. engr. Hughes, El Segundo & Canoga Park 1963-71; supvr. mfg. eng., head of plng., head of microelectronics, head of material control 1973--; mem: Soc. of Mfg. Eng.; Loyal Order of Moose; mil: airman 2/c USAF 1955-58; Republican; Mormon; rec: model ships, radio controlled airplanes. Res: 1115D Catlin St Simi Valley 93065 Ofc: Hughes Aircraft, 8433 Fallbrook, Canoga Park 91304

MC FADDIN, MARY MONTGOMERY, fashion commentator, company president; b. Jan. 20, 1953, d. Jacob and Pearlene Harris; edn: diploma, Lear Siegler Inst., Md. 1971-72; West Los Angeles Coll. 1977-79. Career: owner M & M McFaddin Productions (acting, dancing, modeling, jazzercise wkshops), Los Angeles; fashion commentator, coordinator in Los Angeles, throughout US, and Europe, Africa; awards: Outstanding Young Woman Am. 1982, appreciation for community svc. Cong. Augusta S. Hawkins; mem. NAACP, Nat. Assn. of Profl. Bus. Women, Los Angeles Investor Group (treas.). Res: 4129 W. 59th Pl Los Angeles 90008 Ofc: M&M McFaddin Productions, 3343 W. 43d St Los Angeles 90008

MC FARLAND, BOBBY LYNN, engineering computer specialist; b. Jan. 20, 1928, Wichita, Ks.; s. Edwin Ted and Ethel Mae (Allen) McF.; m. Mary, Aug. 3, 1950; children: Beverly, b. 1952; Robin, b. 1957; Michel, b. 1963; edn: BSChE,

Tex. Tech. Univ. 1949; MS, UCLA 1960; Reg. Profl. Engr. (CH2413) Calif. Career: principal engr. Aerojet Gen., Azusa 1950-64; propulsion splst., Rocketdyne Div. Rockwell, Canoga Park 1964-73; tech. staff LMEC Div. Rockwell, Canoga Park 1973-76; sr. staff engr. Energy Sys. Gp. Div. Rockwell, Canoga Park 1973--; guest lectr. USC 1977--; bd. dirs. H.T.R.I., 1978-; awards: Rockwell Pride Awd. 1972; Div. Engr. of the Yr. 1978, 80; Boy Scouts Awd. of Merit 1979; JPL Commdn. 1977; mem: AIAA; AICHE; Toastmasters; Methodist Men; Boy Scouts; Optimists; wks: engring. papers, patentee, author: DEAP, TAP-6, TAP-7, 2 DABLATE & STESEP computer codes; mil: T5 US Army 1946-47; Democrat; Methodist; rec: electronic repair, camping, micro computers. Res: 17175 Gunther St Granada Hills 91344 OFc: Rockwell, 8900 De Soto Ave Canoga Park 91344

MC FARLAND, DON, business excutive; b. Dec. 18, 1933, Los Angeles; s. Gordon and Robina (McNiven) McF.; m. Judith Lindberg, Dec. 18, 1955; children: Gary Donald, b. 1957; Daniel Ryan, b. 1958; Laura Gladys, b. 1964; Douglas Walter, b. 1966; edn: BS, USC Sch. of Commerce 1956. Career: svc. mgr. Bullocks, Los Angeles 155; mgr. Childrens Castle, L.A. 1955-58; mgr. pckg. & mail order depts. Lindberg Nutrition 1958--; bd. dirs. Nutrition Supply, treas. 1965-, pres. 1979--; bd. dirs. Natures Best, v.p. 1975-79, pres. 1979-83, honors: Skull & Dagger (hon.) USC; mem: Trojan Football Alumni Club, USC (past pres.), USC Sch. of Commerce Club, Trojan Club; Nat. Nutritional Foods Assn.; Am. Nutrition Soc., So. Bay chpt.; Republican; Protestant; rec: jogging, world travel. Res: 5 Coveview Dr Rancho Palos Verdes 90274 Ofc: 3945 Crenshaw Blvd Los Angeles 90008

MC GADDEN, JOSEPH RAYMOND, logistician, cryptologist; b. Apr. 2, 1935, Lowell, Mass.; s. Joseph Walter and Elizabeth Grace (Foster) M.; engaged to m. Ruth Marie Albee Dunn (dau. Sir Clarence J. Albee, mem. Royal French Order of Soldats de Verdun 1918; rel., poet/playwright Edward Albee; desc. of Adm. Byrd), 10/6/84; children: William, Charles, Robert, Scott; and Alan, Sheila, Gary Dunn; edn: Lowell Tech., 1967-71; Fla. Inst. of Tech. 1976; Orange Coast Coll. 1964; Chapman Coll. 1965; Adult Voc. Teaching Cert., Mass. 1970; Cryptologist, NSA/CSS 1978; (cand. 1984) Cert. Profl. Logistician (CPL). Career: avionics supr. USMC 1953-66; with GTE Systems, 1966--; proj. supr. communication satellites, GTE, Waltham, Mass. 1966 70, supr. LEAA Projects 1970-72; mgr. EW & Recon Projects, Ops. Group, GTE Mountain View, Ca. 1973-79, mem. tech. staff SIGIN Improvement Pgms, 1980-82, tech. support/ logistics/ configuration mgr. 1982-3, logistics mgr. Space Resrch. Projects 1983--; cryptologic ofcr. USNR Security Gp., cons. to Naval Weapons Sta., Newport, RI 1969; awards: Cryptol. Svc. to Country, USNCVA 1979. Mem. Mensa, Soc. Logistics Engrs., ASTD, US Naval Inst., Am. Soc. for Tng. & Devel., USN Cryptol. Assn.; GTE Employees Assn. (vp 1979); sponsor San Jose Civic Light Opera, S.J. Performance Group; publs: sev. tech., sci. publs. mil: USMC 1953-66, USAF 1968-1972; chief warrant ofcr. USNR 1982-; Air Crewman Wings, combat action, Vietnam svc., Valorous unit (28 combat and svc. decorations); rec: theatre, jogging. Res: 302 Curie Dr San Jose 95119 Ofc: GTE Systems, 100 Ferguson Dr Mountain View 94039

MC GILL, STEPHEN KENNETH, company executive; b. Feb. 13, 1949, Atlanta, Ga.; s. Stephen Kenneth Sr. and Edris Carol (Sadenwater) McG.; edn: MBA, UC Berkeley 1978; BAE, Ga. Inst. of Tech. 1971. Career: sales engr. Allen Bradley Co., San Francisco 1972-78; dist. mgr., Ft. Lauderdale, Fla. 1978-80; mgr. of ops. Wyle- Emg, El Segundo 1980-81; mgr. ops., San Diego 1981-82; dir. ops. San Diego/ Connector Divs. 1982-83; part owner: fin. advr. Curcuit Svcs., Inc., Santa Clara 1979-83; bd. dirs. Circuit Svcs., Inc. 1979-83; mem: SME; IEEE; Optimist Internat. (chmn. Solona Beach Adopt A Sch. Pgm.); Republican; Baptist; rec: skiing, flying, Russian language. Res: 930 Via Mil Cumbres, 120B, Solana Beach 92075 Ofc: Wyle, Emg., 9525 Chesapeake Dr San Diego 92123

MC GINN, JANE LEOCHA, real estate broker; b. Oct. 14, 1948, Annapolis, Md.; d. Victor Stanley and Nancy Irr (Clarke) Leocha; children: John, b. 1968; David, b. 1970; Daniel, b. 19785; edn: AA, West Hills Coll. 1982; Meridian Jr. Coll. 1968; Reedley Jr. Coll. 1978; Univ. of Md. 1966-67; Calif. Reg. Dental Asst. (1978), lic. R.E. Broker, 1984. Career: sales assoc. ERA Town & Country Realtors, Lemoore 1980-82; sales assoc. Centurion Realtors, Lemoore 1982; broker/ owner Century 21 Creative Realty, Lemoore 1982--; dir./ chmn. grievance com. Kings Co. Bd. Realtors 1982-; secty. Pioneer Square Merchants Assn. 1983-; honors: Outstanding Young Women of Am. 1983; mem: Kings Co. Womens Trade Club; Kings Co. Navy League; Assn. Naval Aviation; Lemoore CofC; campaigner: Pashayan for Congress (Steering Com. 1983-); Maroot Supvr. Com. 1982; Republican (Central Com., Steering Com.); Catholic; rec: equestrian, golf, riflery. Res: 1560 Antelope Dr Lemoore 93245 Ofc: Century 21 Creative Realty, 1152 N Lemoore Ave, Ste 101, Lemoore 93245

MC GINTY, BRIAN DONALD, lawyer/ writer; b. June 22, 1937, Santa Barbara; s. Donald Bruce and Natalia Vallejo (Haraszthy) McG.; edn: AB,. UC Berkeley 1959; JD, 1962. Career: practicing atty., Monterey County, Ca. 1963-73; journalist/ wirter 1973--; author over 100 arts. in popular journs. & mags.; lectr. polit. sci. Hartnell Coll., Salinas 1963-64; awards: Awd. for Best Writing, Nat. Hist. Soc. 1976; author: Haraszthy at the Mint; The Palace Inns. Res: POB 1698 San Francisco 94101

McGLORY, JANE ALICE, community youth center founder; b. Apr. 22, 1932, Los Angeles, CA; s. John Edward and Eva Pansy (Knox) Bragg; attended Metro. Bus. Sch., 1950-53; UCLA ext., 1959-63; m. Albert McGlory, Oct. 31, 1962; children: William, b. 1952; Johnny, b. 1960; Dino, b. 1964; Joseph,

b. 1971. Career: clerk, L.A. Co., 1951-54; dep. sheriff, L.A. Co. Hall of Justice, L.A., 1954-58; asst. supv., UCLA Ext., L.A., 1959-67; volunteer community worker, 1967--. Received award from Pacoima Community Youth, 1978; Thomas Jefferson Humanitarian Award, Amer. Inst. for Pub. Serv., 1979; Humanitarian Award, Angeles of the Valley Eastern Star chpt., 1980, Mem: Pacoima Comm. Youth Culture Center, founder, pres., 1977--; Pledgerville Sr. Citizens Villa, Inc., board mem., finance comm. 1980—. Democrat. Seventh-Day Adventist, treas. Rec: reading, writing. Res: 11755 Dronfield Ave., Pacoima 91331; Office: Pacoima Comm. Youth Culture Center, 11243 Glenoaks Blvd., Pacoima 91331.

MC GOVERAN, DAVID ORNAN, consulting firm executive; b. Mar. 17, 1952, Pittsburgh, Ca.; s. Lowell Benage and Tressie Jane (Sanders) McG.; m. Mary Rhodes, July 7, 1978; 1 child, Lauren b. 1984; edn: Diablo Valley Coll. 1970-73; BS, physics, Univ. Chgo. 1976; grad. wk. Stanford Univ. 1978-79. Career: physics assoc. Stanford Research Ins. 1976-79; electronics engring. instr. Professional Engring. Inst., Belmont, Ca. 1978-79; prof./dept. chmn. Computer Sci. and Bus. Mgmt., Condie Coll., San Jose 1979-80; sales support mgr. GCA Corp., Santa Clara 1980-82; CAM Sys. mgr. Synertek, Santa Cruz, 1982-83; pres. Alternative Technologics, Santa Cruz 1976--; author two books: Electronic Engineering Technicians Handbook (1980), Night Moods (1982); inventor: Cable Connecting Tool (Pat. 1978), Slide Tube (copyright 1972), Fasttrack Semicondr. Automation Sys. (1983), others; contbg. writer sci. books, journals; recipient num. science awards and scholastic merit awds. 1967-75 incl. Univ. Chgo. scholarships, Calif. Scholarship Found.; mem: IEEE, ACM, IDM Users Group, founder/pres. Inst. for the Advance. of Noetics, Chgo. 1975-78; Alternative Natural Philosophy (dir. 1978-), NY Acad. of Scis., Meninger Found. (charter fellow 1978), Data Proc. Mgmt. Assn., Assn. for Humanistic Psychol. (life), Assn. for Transpersonal Psychol., AAAS, Md. Neurological Soc. 1976; founding pres. Delta Rocket Soc. 1966; rec: guitar, mathematical logic, philos. Res: 15905 Bear Creek Rd Boulder Creek 95006 Ofc: Alternative Technologies 150 Felker St, Ste E, Santa Cruz 95060

MC GOWAN, CHARLES DAVID, housing developer; b. Dec. 20, 1949, San Francisco; s. Wm. Charles and Pauline (Krisfalusy) McG.; edn: BA, sociol., Univ. Notre Dame 1971; M.Urban Plng., CSU San Jose 1982. Career: cons. City of Gilroy, 1976-77, housing and comm. devel. grant coordinator 1977-80; devel. ofcr. Housing Authority, County of Santa Clara, San Jose 1980--; mem. Plng. Com., Advis. Council of Council on Aging of Santa Clara County, Inc., 1982-; awards: Calif. State Scholarship, Univ. Santa Clara Scholarship, 1967; mem: Am. Planning Assn., Am. Inst. of Cert. Planners (charter), Nat. Assn. of Housing and Redevel. Officials (housing com. Pac. Southwest Regl. Conf. 1983-), Calif. Winetasters Guild (pres. 1982-3), Assn. of Local Housing Finance Agencies (Profl. Devel. and Publs. com. 1983-); author: A Housing Plan for the Housing Auth. of the County of Santa Clara 1982-87 (1982); editor Plng. Study of Franklin McKinley Sch. Dist., San Jose (1975); mil: USN 1971-74, USNR 1974-77, Nat. Def. Ribbon, Commendn.; Democrat; rec: backpacking, hiking, winetasting. Res: 980 Alice Ln Apt 3, Menlo Park 94025 Ofc: Housing Authority of the County of Santa Clara, 999 W. Taylor St San Jose 95126

MC GOWAN, JOYCE MAE, oil treatment operator; b. Jan. 10, 1933, Colorado Springs, Colo.; d. James Berton and Ina Mae (Wickle) McG.; m. Louis Banducci, July 1, 1978; children: Cynthia, b. 1951; Terri, b. 1959; Karen, b. 1960; Renee, b. 1970; edn: Compton Coll. 1950. Career: with Gulf Oil, Yorba Linda Oil field 1975--; field hand roustabout 1975; gauger 1976; sr. opr. 1983--: oil treatment, gas treatment, care of crude oil tank battery & wells in field; Christian; rec: camping. Res: 2065 W Ontario Corona 91720 Ofc: Gulf Oil, 4573 Casaloma Yorba Linda

MC GRAIN, JOHN PATRICK, investor; b. Aug. 23, 1945, Los Angeles; s. Jack Freeman and Muriel Teresa (Arnold) Runyon; m. Nancy H. Abel, Dec. 28, 1968; edn: BA, UCLA 1967; Reg. Options Principal, NASD Principal, Br. Ofc. Mgr., 1979. Career: v.p./ dir. R.M. Evans & Co., Los Angeles 1969-71; securities broker Bateman, Eichler, Hills, Richard & EF Hutton, L.A. 1972-77; nat.'s fixed income mgr. Loeb Rhoads Hornblower/ Shearson, L.A. 1977-79; v.p./ mgr. Wagenseller & Durst, L.A. 1979-80; sales mgr. Bache, Halsey, Stuart, Shields, L.A. 1980-81; v.p./mgr. Thomson McKinnon Securities, Inc., L.A. 1981--; dir: PlantMinder 1981-, Pacific Waste Mgmt., Pasa. 1983-, Conversion Industries USA, Inc., Pasa. 1983-; Western Congeneration, Inc., Pasa. 1983-; awards: Leadership Awd., Nat. Elks Club 1963; Calif. recipient Hearst Senate Youth Pgm. 1963; State Pres. Calif. Assn. of Student Counsils 1963; Leadership Awd. Am. Legion 1962; mem: Pasadena Bond Club; rec: equestrian, golf. Res: 707 Sierra Meadow, Sierra Madre 91024 Ofc: Thomson McKinnon Securities, 213 S. Euclid Pasadena 91101

MC GREGOR, IAN PETER ROBERT, optician; b. Apr. 3, 1929, London, England; s. John Donaldson and Louis Winifred McGregor; m. Jill May, Nov. 26, 1949; adopted son, Gerald, b. 1946; desig: Masters in Ophthalmic Optics, Am. Board of Opt. 1975; Nat. Registry of Contact Lens, Examiners Tchg. Credential; Calif. instr. cred. for Nat. Contact Lens examiners. Career: controller and tech. rep. Combined Optical Industries, Slough, Bucks, Eng.; dispenser for Superior Optical L.A., Calif. 1957-60; sales rep. W. Coast reg. Revlon Corp., 1960-63; owner optical dispensing ofc., Pasadena 1963-66; supr. optical dept. Magan Med. Clinic, Covina 1966-77; dispensing optician, contact lens cons., owner Lake Optical, Duarte 1980--; instr. optics and contact lenses, Crafton Hills Coll. 1973-, full-time 2 yrs.; mem: Contact Lens Soc. of am.,

Pacific Coast Contact Lens Soc. (Charter), Calif. Soc. of Ophthalmic Dispensers (Charter), Fellow Nat. Acad. of Opticianary; fmr. mem./ofcr. Toastmasters, Civitan; publs: contracts for 6 books on ophthalmic optics (Warren Green Pub., St. Louis, Mo.); Republican; Ch. of England; rec: writing, optical resrch., soccer coach. Res: 313 Clarkview Dr Duarte 91010 Ofc: Lake Optical 1740 E. Huntington Dr, Ste 203, Duarte 91010

MC GUIRE, JOHN FRANCIS, lawyer; b. Aug. 29, 1945, NY, NY; s. John F. Sr. and Gertrude (Quast) McG.; m. Lynne, June 9, 1968; children: Kerry b. 1970, John b. 1971, Patrice b. 1975, Brian b. 1976; edn: BS, US Naval Acad. 1968; MS, So. Ill. Univ. 1971; JD, Marquette Univ. 1975. Career: Press Officer to the Sec. of Defense, 1971-73; assoc. law firm McInnis, Fitzgerald, Rees & Sharkey, San Diego 1975-78; ptnr., mng. ptnr. Thorsnes, Bartolotta, McGuire & Padilla 1978--; honors: Order of the Barristers (1975), Thomas Moore Scholar (1975), Outstanding Trial Lawyer (1982), Trial Lawyer of the Year 1983; mem. Am., Wisconsin, and Calif. bar assns.; Disabled American Veterans, Order of the Purple Heart, Sons of St. Patrick; mil: lt. USN, Navy Achieve. Medal in Combat V, Navy Commendn. Medal in Combat V, Purple Heart, Jt. Service Commendn. medal, num. campgn. medals; Democrat; Catholic; rec: surfing, lacrosse. Res: POB 2492 Rancho Santa Fe 92067 Ofc: Thorsnes, Bartolotta, McGuire & Padilla 225 Broadway, Ste 1125, San Diego 92101

MC GUIRE, MICHAEL JOHN, water quality manager, b. June 29, 1947, San Antonio, Tx.; s. James Brendan and Opal Mary (Brady) McG.; m. Deborah Marrow, June 19, 1971; 1 son, David b. 1980; edn: BSCE, Univ. of Penna. 1969; MS, environmtl. engring. Drexel Univ. 1971, PhD, 1977; Reg. Profl. Engr. Calif., New Jersey, Penna. Career: proj. engr. Philadelphia (Pa.) Water Dept. 1969-73; research assoc. Drexel Univ. 1976-77; prin. engr. Brown and Caldwell Consulting engrs., Pasadena, CA 1977-79; water quality engr. The Metropolitan Water Dist. of So. Calif., L.A. 1979-84, Water Quality Mgr. 1984--; consulting environmtl. engr. 1979-; cons. to Nat. Acad. of Sci., Safe Drinking Water Com. 19787-79; bd. trustees Am. Water Works Assn. Research Found. 1983-; honors: academic achieve. awd. Am. Water Works Assn. 1978, Sigma Xi, Sigma Tau (eng. hon.) 1969, Diplomate Acad. of Environmtl. Engring.; listed Who's Who in the West 1981-85; mem: Am. Water Works Assn. (chmn. Edn. Div. 1982, v. chmn. Jt. Tng. Coordinating Com. 1982, Calif-Nev. Sect. Edn. Adminstr. 1978-81 and chmn. Water Qual. and Resources Div.); Am. Chemical Soc.; ASCE; Internat. Assn. on Water Pollution and Control 1972-; Water Pollution Control fedn.; Sigma Nu 1966-; publs: co-editor w/ I.H. Suffet: Activated Carbon Absorption of Organics from the Aqueous Phase (2 vols.), 1980), and Treatment of Water by Granular Activated Carbon (1983); author over 50 tech. publs. on trace contaminant control in the water treatment process; rec: swim, scuba dive, personal computers. res: 209 Rennie Ave Venice 90291 Ofc: The Metropolitan Water Dist. of So. Calif. POB 54153, Los Angeles 90054

MC INTIRE, DAVID RUSSELL, contract management executive; b. July 20, 1953, San Pedro; s. Thomas Floyd and Ruby (Pierce) McIntire; m. Velma Fox, June 15, 1974; 2 sons: Brian, b. 1980, Kevin, b. 1982; edn: BS cum laude, CSU Long Beach 1975, MBA, 1976, num. spl. courses. Career: financial analyst Aeronutronic Ford, Newport Beach 1976; sr. financial analyst W. Devel. Labs. Ford Aerospace, Palo Alto 1977-78; sr. contract adminstr. Watkins-Johnson Co., San Jose 1979-80, head, Contracts Palo Alto Plant, 1983--; bd. dirs. Inst. for Medical Research, Valley Med. Ctr. 1979-80; Republican; Christian Ch.; rec: woodworking, racquetball, tennis, scuba. Res: 5773 Barnswell Way San Jose 95138 Ofc: Watkins-Johnson Co. 3333 Hillview Ave Stanford Industrial Park, Palo Alto 94304

MC INTOSH, GREGORY CECIL (PRINCE), engineering co. president; b. Dec. 19, 1949, Ft. Hood, Tx.; Prince (hereditary title), Principality of Outer Baldonia, 1966; (nat. citizen, Principality of Outer Baldonia); s. Horace Samuel and Phyllis Mary (Mountford) McI.; m. Carol Ann Hackett, Oct. 14, 1978; edn: BA, philos., honors, CSU Dominguez Hills 1975-81; att. El Camino Coll. 1971, L.A. Harbor Coll. 1968-70; Cert. APT Pgmmr., UCC 1981; Cert. Compact II Pgmmr., MDSI 1980. Career: mgr. Lundquist-McDonalds, San Pedro 1968-70; salesman United-Overton, Inc. El Segundo 1970-73; supr. International Rectifier, El Segundo 1973-75; salesman Volume Shoe Corp., Gardena 1975-76; mgr. Levitan Mgmt. Corp., Gardena 1976-79; substitute tchr. Lawndale Elem. Sch. Dist., 1979; pres./CEO H.M.S. Engineering Inc., Gardena 1979-80; machine shop foreman/ maint. supr./ numerical control pgmmr. Essick-Hadco Mfg. Co. Div. Figgie Internat. Inc., 1980--; mem: Numerical Control Soc. (pres. L.A. Chpt. 1982-3, 1983-4), North Am. Nietzsche Soc.; past pres. CSU-DH Philosophy and Chess Clubs; orgns: Holiday Project; publs: Joniper, The Littlest Elf (radio play bdcst. 12/83); Keynote spkr. Grad. Class, Wilshire Computer Coll. (6/83); Libertarian; Zen Buddhist; rec: painting, chess, poetry. Res: 2929 W. 190th St, 101, Redondo Bch 90278 Ofc: Essick/Hadco Mfg. Co. 1950 S. Santa Fe Ave Los Angeles 90021

MC INTOSH, WILLIAM VERNON, energy management consultant; b. Sept. 6, 1945, Long Beach; s. Clarence Vernon and Esther Christine (Hedman) McI.; m. Audrey Louise Brown, Apr. 24, 1976; 1 son: Joseph, b. 1979; edn: BA, San Francisco State Univ. 1975. Career: with Pacific Gas and Electric Co. 1967--; elec. engring. estimator, San Francisco 1967-76; comml. rep. 1976-77; illumination engr. 1977-80; power engr. 1980-82; currently sr. energy mgmt. engr.; co- founder/ bd. dirs. Assn. of Profl. Energy Mgrs. 1983-; honors: Resolution of Commdn., County of Marin 1983; "Bill McIntosh Day," City of Novato, Aug. 6, 1983; mem: Assn. Profl. Energy Mgrs.; Illuminating Eng. Soc. of No. Am.; Pacific Coastc Elec. Assn.; Pacific Coast Gas Assn.; City of Novato (Plng. Commnr.); Novato Youth Ctr.; Commonwealth Club of Calif.; S.F. Highe Twelve Club (past pres.); S.F. Educator Lodge F&AM of Calif.; Elks, Novato; Republican; Presbyterian; rec: home construction, gardening. Res: 28 Mendocino Ln Novato 94947 Ofc: Pacific Gas and Electric Company, 245 Market St, Rm 743, San Francisco 94106

McINTYRE, ROBERT MALCOLM, utility company president; b. Dec. 18, 1923, Portland, OR; s. Daniel A. and Bessie W. (Earsley) McIntyre; BA, UCLA, 1950; graduate work, UCLA, USC, Columbia Univ.; m. Marilyn Westcott, Aug. 27, 1949; chil: Julie, b. 1951. Career: various management positions, Southern California Gas Co., 1952—: v.p., 1970; sr. v.p., 1974; dir., 1975—, pres. 1980—, also pres. Pacific Lighting Service Co., 1980—, dir. 1975—. Past dir. and mem. Pacific Coast Gas Assn., mem. American Gas Assn., Trustee of Inst. of Gas Technology. Awards: Forty-Niner Club Award, Pacific Coast Gas Assn., 1979; Natl. Hispanic Scholarship Award, for originating and chairing Hispanic of the Year Award Dinner in 1980; Mex. Amer. Legal Defense and Ednl. Fund (MALDEF) Award for outstanding service, corporate responsibility, 1981. Dir., Los Angeles Area CofC; dir., Natl. Conf. of Christians and Jews; trustee, exec. com. mem., L.A. Orthopaedic Hosp.; mem., Lowman Club, L.A. Orthopaedic Hosp., Dir., Hoag Meml. Hosp. Presby.; dir., United States-Mex. CofC; dir., L.A. Co. Academic Decathlon; mem., Hon. Bd. of Govs. of Japanese Amer. Cultural and Comm. Center; mem., Korean Amer. Centennial Comm.; dir., Calif. Council for Environmental and Economic Balance; dir., Calif. Found. on the Environment and the Economy; mem., bd. govs., lifetime mem., Town Hall of Calif.; dir., Mexican American Legal Defense and Ednl. Fund (MALDEF); chmn., 36th Navy Ball Comm.; Corp. bd. mem., L.A. United Way; mem., exec. cabinet, Orange Co. United Way; mem., Commn. of the Californias; mem., L.A. Mayor Bradley's Ad Hoc Comm. on City Finances; 1982 chmn., Plaza de la Raza Business Industry Adv. Bd.; mem., Huntington Library Soc. of Fellows; mem., L.A. Music Center Founders; mem., Newport Harbor Art Museum Business Council; mem., Orange Co. Bus. Comm. for the Arts Steering Comm.; mem., L.A. Olympic Citizen Adv. Comn.; mem., UCLA GSM Dean's Council; mem., Pepperdine Univ. Assocs.; mem., USC Assocs.; mem., Calif. Club; L.A. Club; Phi Kappa Psi. Mil: served to Lt.(s.g.), USN, 1942-46, Combat Stars for Pacific and China Theaters. Republican. Presbyterian. Rec: golf, tennis, boating. Res: 511 Via Lido Nord, Newport Beach 92663; Office: So. Calif. Gas Co., 810 S. Flower St., Los Angeles 90017.

MC KAY, LARRY WAYNE, real estate broker; b. Sept. 1, 1945, Compton; s. Earl Lloyd and Jeanne Louise (Rattelman) McK.; m. Patricia R. Buckley, Aug. 14, 1970; children: Sara Ann, b. 1982; Neil Allen, b. 1983; edn: BS, honors, Woodbury Coll. 1969-72; San Francisco State Univ. 1972; lic. R.E. Broker, Calif. 1975. Career: assoc. broker Value Realty, San Jose 1975-76; branch mgr. Transamerica Title Ins., Castro Valley 1976-79; asst. co. mgr. Commonwealth Land Title Ins., Hayward 1979-80; exec. v.p. Abre, Inc.- Allied Brokers, Dublin 1980; lectr./ cons. Larry McKay Real Estate Seminars 1980--; assoc. broker The Ryness Co., Danville 1980--; mem: Am. Mktg. Assn.; San Jose & So. Alameda Co. Real Estate Bds.; works: lectr. on creative financing & escrow procedures throughout No. Calif. for R.E. Ind.; mil: 1st lt. US Army 1966-69; Republican; Protestant; rec: skiing, camping, fishing. Res: 62 Summer Rim Cir Sacramento 95823 Ofc: The Ryness Company, 801 San Ramon Valley Blvd Danville

MC KEE, BRUCE DEAN, clinical social worker; b. Apr. 22, 1944, Chgo.; s. Robert Lester and Gertrude Hazel McKee; m. Nancy Kerr, Nov. 22, 1967, div. 1977; 1 son: Colin, b. 1969; edn: Univ. of Colo. 1962-64; UC Davis 1964; BA, CSU Sonoma 1967; BSW, CSU Fresno 1975; CSW, Calif. 1978. Career: probation ofcr. County of Santa Cruz 1970-73; soc. wkr. Acute Psychiatric Unit, Fresno Co. Dept. Mental Health 1975-76; chief of svc. North Outreach Mental Health Svc., Pinedale 1976-82; dir. Outpatient Mental Health Svcs., Total Life Ctr., St. Agnes Med. Ctr., Fresno 1982--; grad. level tchg. CSUF 1981-, undergrad. tchg. 1978-81; consulting to human services agencies, schs.; awards: NIMH Grantee Tulane Univ. 1975-76, Phi Kappa Phi 1975, apptd. to Boys Clubs of Am. Help-A-Kid pgm. 1977; mem: NASW; Mental Health Assn.; Fresno Youth Soccer Assn.; works: ldr. wrkshps. Children and the Law, 1979-82; Paul Masson- Avenue of the Giants Marathons 1979-81; co-founder gestalt inst. Fresno 1982-83; mil: E-4 US Army 1968-70, Vietnam, GCM, Air Medal- CIB, Spl. Honors; Democrat; Protestant; rec: backpacking, skiing, photog. Res: 6051 Augusta Fresno 93710 Ofc: Saint Agnes Medical Center, 1245 E Herndon Fresno 93710

MC KEEHAN, DAVID WILLIAMS, computer scientist/engineer; b. May 8, 1955, Arlington, Va.; s. John Badger and Juanita (Schroeder) McK.; edn: BA physics/ comp. sci., Ithaca Coll. 1978. Career: jr. engr., now tech. dir. Kaiser Electronics, San Jose: tech. dir. Image Processing and Kaster Graphics; mem: IEEE; ACM; AFCEA; S.F. Bay Area AdaTEC (founder); works: devel. aircraft landing sys. using machine vision to restore pilots vision in bad weather 1981; Republican; rec: aircraft modeling. Res: 4251 Norwalk Dr San Jose 95129 Ofc: Kaiser Electronics, 2701 Orchard Pkwy San Jose 95134

McKELVEY, GEORGE IRWIN, III, college administrator; b. May 5, 1925, Glen Ridge, NJ; s. George and Florence McKelvey; AB, Univ. Rochester, 1950; MA, Univ. of Rochester, 1957; m. Velma Vergara, 1959; chil: George Stuart, b. 1965. Career: exec. secty., Alumni Assn., Univ. Rochester, 1950-54; dir., Alumni rels., 1954-56; assoc. dir., Alumni Council, 1956-57; dir., devl., Harvey Mudd Coll., 1957-58; v.p., devel. and planning, 1968; dir., Bates Found. for Aeron. Edn. Raymond M. Alf Museum. Mil: Aviation Cadet,

USNR, 1943-44; Ensign, USMS, 1945-46. Mem: Council for the Adv. and Support of Edn.; Univ. Club, L.A.; Men's Garden Club, L.A.; Psi Upsilon. Presbyterian. Office: Harvey Mudd Coll., Claremont 91711.

MC KENNA, THOMAS J., aerobatic pilot; b. May 12, 1908, Meadowbrook, Pa.; s. John and Bridget (Cassidy) McK.; grad. Catholic Schs., Berwyn, Pa. 1927; grad. flying sch., Wilmington, Del. 1938; soloed a Jenney Airplane, Camden, NJ 1928; pvt., comml. & instr. rating 1938. Career: pilot instr. combat flying to Royal Air Force pilots 1940-42, to US Army Cadets 1942-44, War Eagle Field, Lancaster, Ca.; currently, only aerobatic flight instr., Santa Barbara Airport (1976 150 h.p. Citabria), Mercury Air Ctr. 1981--; (most famous pupil, Frank Tallman whose movies incl. The Great Waldo Pepper, and TV series Baa-Baa Black Sheep); subject of arts. in num. publs. incl. Pvt. Pilot, Gen. Aviation News and sev. books.; mem: Quiet Birdmen; Santa Barbara Pilots Assn.; OX5 Pioneers of Am.; Santa Barbara Flying Club; S.B. Aero Club Inc.; Antelope Valley Aero Mus. Inc.; Republican; Catholic. Res: 1312 Shoreline Dr Santa Barbara 93109 Ofc: Mercury Air Center, Santa Barbara Airport

MC KENNON, JOHN EARLE, hotel management executive, b. Mar. 30, 1917, Clarksville, Ark.; s. Dr. Parma Dixon and Inez (Winingham) McK.; m. Mary Frances Heeney, Jan. 28, 1946; children: John Earle Jr. b. 1949, James Heeney b. 1954; edn: Fort Smith Jr. Coll. 1935-37; Cert. Hotel Adminstr., Am. Hotel & Motel Ednl. Inst. 1982. Career: var. pos. to asst. mgr. Southwest Hotels, Little Rock, Ark. 1937-49; asst. catering mgr. Heidelberg Hotel (Albert Pick Chain) Baton Rouge, La. 1949-52; dir. food & bev./ exec. asst. mgr. Aladdin Hotel, K.C., Mo. 1952-56; gen. mgr. MacDonald Prop. Inc. (Conrad Hilton - Spearl Ellison) 1956-67 (Murray Hotel, NM, Lafayette Hotels in San Diego, Long Bch.); v.p. Hotel Div. Denny's, Inc. 1967-73 (mng. dir. The Grand Hotel, Anaheim; v.p. Imperial Hawaii Hotel, Honolulu); v.p/gen. mgr./ prin. of group that purchased Grand Hotel, 1973-74; cons. 1974--, dir. rehabilitation/reorgn. of Biltmore Hotel, L.A. 1974-76; pres./chief adminstrv. ofcr. Westwater Hotels (18 hotels and motels) 1977-79; pres./CEO McKennon-Holden Hotels, Inc. 1980-83; exec. dir. Hotel Div. H. B. Development Co., 1983--. Profl. awards: recogn., Anaheim Area Visitor and Conv. Bur. (1968); Joe Minster Award as outstanding hotel man of year 1969 for Calif.; Medal of Amities Gastronomiques Internat., Wine Indus. of France (1969). Mem: Calif. Hotel & Motel Assn. (chmn. bd. 1983, pres. 1982, exec. com. 1979-); Am. Hotel & Motel Assn. (bd. dirs. 1974-); Am. Hotel Assn. Directory Corp. (1971-); LA Convention Bur. (exec. bd. 1975 6); Anaheim Area Vis. & Conv. Bur. (pres. 1972); Anaheim CofC (bd. 1969-74); dir. N.M. Hotel Assn. 1956-59; past pres. Long Beach Orange County Restaurant Assn.; served on advis. bds. Salvation Army; bd. dirs. N.Mex. Tuberculosis Assn., St. Mary's Hosp. (Long Bch.), and Easter Seals Assn. (O. Co.); publs: series of five arts., Lodging Mag.; Catholic; rec: farming, hunting. REs: 2210 N. Mantle Lane Santa Ana 92701 Ofc: H. B. Development Co. 17821 East 17th St Ste 295, Tustin 92680

MC KERNAN, THOMAS VINCENT, JR., automobile club executive; b. June 20, 1944, Alexandria, La.; s. Thomas Vincent and Mae Marie (Gassiott) McK.; m. Judith Havenner, Mar. 27, 1971; children: Megan, b. 1979; Shannon, b. 1981; edn: BS, CSU Los Angeles 1981; MBA, 1984; Cert. Data Processor, Inst. for Certification of Computer Profls. 1981. Career: svc. rep. Auto Club So. Calif., Pasadena 1966-69, pgmr., Los Angeles 1969-72, supvr. computer pgmg. 1972-74, asst. mgr. ins. sys. 1974-75, mgr. ins. sys. 1975-77, mgr. computer sys. 1977-79, group mgr. data processing 1979-80, dir. data proc. 1980-83, asst. v.p. Fin. & Admin. Auto Club of So. Cal., L.A. 1983--; mem: Ofc. Automation Council, L.A.; Soc. for Mgmt. of Info. Sys. (Adv. Council); CSULA Sch. of Bus.; Jonathan Club; Republican; Catholic; rec: skeet shooting, micro computers, classic automobiles. Res: 333 W Camino Real Arcadia 91006 Ofc: Automobile Club So. Calif., 2601 S Figueroa Los Angeles 90007

MC KINNEY, GEORGE DALLAS, clergyman; b. Aug. 9, 1932, Jonesboro, Ark.; s. George Sr. and Rosie Anna (Thompson) McK.; m. Jean C., June 15, 1957; children: George b. 1958, Grant b. 1961, Gregory b. 1962, Gordon b. 1966, Glenn b. 1969; edn: BA, magna cum laude, Ark. State Univ. (Pine Bluff) 1954; MA, Oberlin Sch. of Theol. 156; PhD, Calif. Grad. Sch. of Theology 1974; Qual. tchr./coll. (life); Calif. Lic. MFCC (Marriage Family Child Counselor) 1969, Ordained Elder, Ch. of God in Christ 1954. Career: dir. Chagrin Falls Park (Ohio) Comm. Center 1955-56; Protestant Chaplain, Toledo State Mental Hosp. 1956-57; counselor Family Court, Toledo, O. 1957-59; senior probation ofcr. San Diego County Prob. Dept. 1959-65; asst. dir. Economic Com., San Diego 1965-71; minister St. Stephen's Ch. of God in Christ, San Diego 1962--; author: The Theology of the Jehovah's Witness (Zondervon Pub. House 1962), Pastoral Counselor Handbook (1981), var. relig. pamphlets. Honors: one of 20 authors who made significant contbn. to Evangelical Christian Literature, Christianity Today (1962); community svc. awd. Bus. & Profl. Women; Outstanding Man of Year 1969, Internat. Assn. Aerospace Wkrs. Dist. 50; J.F. Kennedy Awd. for service to Youth; Outstanding Pstor, SDSU Blakc Students; 1975 NAACP Award for contbns. in relig. field, San Diego; Democrat; Pentecostal; rec: swimming. Res: 5848 Arboles San Diego 92120 Ofc: St. Stephen's Ch. of God in Christ, 5825 Imperial Ave San Diego 92114

MC KINNEY, RONALD CLAGGETT, horticulturist; educator; b. Sept. 30, 1928, Gresham, Ore.; s. Charles C. and Lucile E. (Saling) McK.; m. Evelyn Hadachek, July 1, 1953; children: Regina b. 1956, Denise b. 1958; edn: BA, E. Washington Univ. 1953; stu. CSU San Diego 1957-61; MA, US Internat. Univ. 1973; Calif. Tchg. Credentials: General Elem. (1961), Gen. Junior High 91961), Pupil Personnel Svcs. (1973). Career: asst. dir. Tng. and Recreation, Ryan Aeronautical, San Diego 1957; pres. Valor, Inc., S.D. 1958; mgr. Drug Mart, Inc. 1959; tchr. Cardiff-By-The-Sea 1961, tchr., counselor Chula Vista City Schs. 1962--; owner Evon Orchids (wholesale, retail), S.D. 1973--; spkr. var. garden clubs and orchid socs. statewide 1977-; workshop instr. for novice orchid growers; cons. to interior designers; recipient num. awards for growning and exhibiting orchids; mem: Nat. Edn. Assn., Calif. Tchrs. Assn., Chula Vista Elem. Educators Assn. (Building and Grievance rep. for NEA, CTA, CVEEA); mem. Am. Orchid Soc., Cymbidium Soc. of Am., Honolulu Orchid Soc., S.D. County Orchid Soc., Palomar Orchid Soc., Orange Co. Cymbidium Soc.; past bd. dirs: Nat. Radio Assn. (Reno, Nev.) 1969-71, Calif. State Radio Assn. Sacto. 1971, pres. 1972-74; publs: two research pamphlets: History and Flora and Fauna of San Clemente Island (1954), Fingertip Facts for the Enthusiast (1982); mil: lt. cdr. USNR 1947-70; Republican; Prot.; rec: philately. Address: Evon Orchids, 4355 Huerfano Ave San Diego 92117

MC KINSTRY, GARY WHITMORE, retailing executive; b. Apr. 11, 1944, Hartford, Conn.; s. Roger Edwards and Doris Juliet (Smith) McK.; edn: BA, Colby Coll. 1966; MFA, Univ. of Miss. 1968. Career: design cons. Ostrer House, Boston, Mass. 1972-73; interior designer Bloomingdale's, Boston, Mass. 1973-75; asst. display mgr. Bloomingdale's, Garden City, NY 1975-76, visual merchandise mgr. Macy's, White Plains, NY 1976-77; home furnishings fashion coord. Jordan Marsh, Miami, Fla. 1977-80; sales promotion fashion dir. Breuners, San Ramon 1980--; career cons. The Fashion Group of Boston 1974; awards: architecture, Dodge Prize 1966; mem: Spokane City Club, Spokane Civic Theatre; works: filmstrip/tape (display) Houghton-Mifflin Pub., Boston 1974; mil: capt. USAF 1968-72; AF Commdn., Uniformed Svcs. Commdn.; Episcopal; rec: drawing, piano, organ. Res: 501 Monarch Ridge Dr Walnut Creek 94596 Ofc: Breuners, 3201 Fostoria Way San Ramon 94583

MC LAREN, JUANITA H., real estate broker; b. Aug. 30, 1911, Queen City, Tx.; d. Wm. Richard and Lucille (Blaydes) Henderson; m. Lloyd Thomas Dorsey, July 5, 1935; m. 2d. David G. McLaren, Dec. 1947; children: Joe b. 1932, Thomas b. 1941, Juanita b. 1948; edn: H.S. grad. Atlanta, Tx. 1930; real estate courses Cal. St. Polytech. Coll. 1964, De Anza Coll. 1983, Calif. lic. Real Estate Broker 1960-. Career: realtor spec. in subdivisions, and sale of land, owner/broker, Cupertino 1960--; exclusive leasing agt. for shopping ctrs. (Goulds Shopping Ctr. San Jose) and apartment complex; purch. broker for var. individual and corp. developers for num. subdivisions in Cupertino, Saratoga, San Jose; sold old mining town, Helena (Hwy 299); honors: Resolution, for water conservation dist. bonds, Bd. of Supvrs. 1963; Resolution, Calif. Senate 1971; Woman of Achievement, San Jose Mercury News 1975; aptd. (first woman to serve) by Cupertino City Council to Archtl. and Site Approval Com. 1968-74; elected (first woman) pres. Cupertino CofC 1979-80, chmn. of bd. 1980-81; mem. Cupertino Historical Soc. (v.chmn. Landmarks com. 1967); mem. Nat. Assn. Real Estate Bds., (pres. San Jose Chpt. Women's Council NAREB 1965), Calif. Real Estate Assn., San Jose Real Estate Bd. (CREA Dir. and Ofcl. Del. 1966); Nat.Inst. of Farm and Land Brokers (fmr.); Internat. Traders Club; mem. (past) Commonwealth Club of Calif., Nurses Edn. Fund of Santa Clara Co., Tri-Co. Apt. Homeowners, Century Club YMCA; Republican (Fedn. Women); Methodist; rec: aerobic exercise. Res/Ofc: 22101 Lindy Lane Cupertino 95014

MC LAUGHLIN, JOSEPH CHARLES, physician; b. Oct. 5, 1922, Calgary, Alberta, Can., nat. 1946; s. John Angus and Gertrude (Gagnon) McL.; m. Dorothy, Jan. 30, 1959; children: Cheri, b. 1956; Lisa, b. 1960; Kelly, b. 1961; Joe Jr., b. 1962; Wendy, b. 1964; edn: St. Cloud Tchrs. Coll. 1946-48; Univ. of Minn. 1949-51; Sacto. State Coll. 1952-53; MD, Temple Univ. 1957; Physician & Surgeon, Calif. 1958. Career: intern UC San Francisco Hosp. 1957-58; physician Co. of San Diego Health Dept. 1958-59; pvt. practice, family med., La Jolla 1959-81; chief of clinics & commun. med. Armed Forces Hosp., Ministry of Def. & Aviation, Kingdom of Saudi Arabia 1981--; honors: fellow, Am. Acad. of Family Practice; fellow, Royal Soc. of Health, London; mem: Scripps Meml. Hosp. (Med. Exec. Com.); Am. Med. Assn.; Am. Acad. of Family Practice; Kiwanis Club, La Jolla; publs: Q-fever Associated Hepatitus, Western Medicine, 1/ 59; mil: radio opr./ navigator, flying ofcr., Royal Canadian Air Force 1941-45, King's Commdn. for valuable service in the air; Republican; Christian; rec: skiing,. scuba diving, wind-surfing. Res: 4032 Mt Acadia San Diego 92111 Ofc; Box 570 Dhahran Airport, Dhahran, Saudi Arabia

MC LEOD, SALLY ANN, certified public accountant; b. Dec. 5, 1947, Albany, Calif.; d. John J. and Florence A. (Valencia) Hitzenhammer; m. Kenneth McLeod, June 3, 1967; children: Jeffry b. 1974, Christopher b. 1982; edn: AA, honors Chabot Coll. 1974; BS in acctg., honors, CSU San Jose 1977. Career: staff accountant Peat, Marwick, Mitchell & Co., San Jose 1978-779; senior acct. Scruggs & Bryant, San Jose 1979-82; prop. Sally A. McLeod, CPA, San Jose 1982--; mem: Amer. Inst. of CPAs, Calif. Soc. of CPAs, Nat. Assn. of Accountants, Network of Women Entrepreneurs (treas. 1982, 83); Catholic. Address: Sally A. McLeod, CPA, 2733 Mabury Square San Jose 95133

MC MAHAN, CELESTE TINA, architectural project manager; b. Jan. 4, 1948, Denver, Colo.; d. Frank and Jean Dolores (Graves) McMahan; m. George Richards, Dec. 2, 1977; edn: BA, Univ. of Colo. 1976; M. Urban & Regl. Plng., Univ. of Colo. 1977; postgrad. wk. in arch., 1977. Career: housing sales coord. Great Western United, Colorado City, 1970-74; dir. of parks and recreation City of Edgewater, Colo. 1975-76; planner, City of Aurora, Colo. 1976-77; project mgr./architect Stanford Univ., 1977-79; designer/ facilities plnr. Sacramento Savings and Loan, 179-80; project mgr. Crocker Bank, (Calif.) 1980-81; project mgr. (corp. real estate) Bank of America, (Calif.)

1981--; owner McMahan Consulting (interior design firm) 1979--; awards: Univ. of Colo. grantee 1974-77; WICHE Intern 1976; Who's Who in Am. Women (1984); mem: Am. Inst. of Architects (assoc.), Orgn. of Women Architects, Nat. Assn. of Female Execs., Nat. Assn. of Corporate Real Estate Execs., Stanford Univ. Alumni Assn., Commonwealth Club of Calif.; commn. mem. Archtl. Review Bd. Environmtl. Beautification Commn. Menlo Park, 1978; apptd. to Gov's Housing Policy Com., Denver 1976; bd. dirs. San Francisco Traditional Jazz Found.; bd. dirs. S.F. Friends of the ARts; publs: A Market Analysis of Downtown Aurora (1976); Housing Market and Pop. Projections (1976); photog.: Tales From the Old Country (1984); Episcopal; rec: photog., traditional jazz, art. Res: POB 1568, Vallejo 94590 Ofc: Bank of America 560 Davis, San Francisco 94111

MC MAHON, JOSEPH ANTHONY, physician-surgeon; b. May 19, 1935, Pawcatuck, Conn.; s. Francis J. and Theresa (Lo Priore) McM.; edn: classical grad. (highest hons.) La Salle Acad. 1953; BS, Univ. of Notre Dame 1957; MD, NY Medical Coll. 1962; MD, Calif. BMQA 1983. Career: internship and surgical residency, Bellevue Hosp., NYC 1962-66; private practice, Pawcatuck, Conn. 1967-82; Indian Health Service 1977-82: clin. dir. Ft. Yates P.H.S. Hospital Schurz, Nev., Red Lake, Minn., N.Dak.; medical dir. Alpha Medical, Los Angeles 1983--; cons. physician Mullinax Holistic Clinics (Valencia & Upland, Ca.); med. dir. Fairway Med. (Walnut, Ca.); awards: Fellowships (stu. hypertension) Columbia Univ. 1961, (stu. med. ethics) Univ. of Tex. 1977; mem: AMA, Alpha Kappa Kappa, Aesculapian Club (v.p. 1957); mil: pending apptmt. col. Army Nat. Guard 1446th Mobile Hosp. Unit. Calif.; Republican; Catholic; rec: equestrian, tennis, music.REs: 1231 Francisquito Ave West Covina 91790 Ofc: Alpha Medical 3210 W. Vernon Ave Los Angeles 90008

MC MAHON, LYNN KEITH, chiropractor; b. Coco Solo Naval Hosp., Panama C.Z.; d. Herbert Anthony and Mary Lea (Pike) Keith; m. Brian G. McMahon, Oct. 2, 1982; edn: AA, Chabot Coll. 1972; DC, cum laude, Life Chiro. Coll. 1981; Cert. X-Ray Supvr. & Opr. Career: dental hygienist, 1972-78; chiropractor Finneran Chiro. Clinic, Newhall 1982--; CPR instr., Red Cross 1983; chiro. info. instr. Finneran Chiro. Clinic 1983; diplomate, Calif. Bd. Chiro. Examiners; Am. & Calif. Chiro. Assns.; Career Womens Network; Am. Red Cross; works: estab. volunteer dental clinic, plaque control pgm., instr. plaque control, Synanon; estab. lay lecture pgm., Finneran Chiro. Clinic; Catholic; rec: wind surfing, snow skiing. Res: 23660 Via Delfina Valencia 91355 Ofc: Finneran Chiropractic Clinic, 24460 Lyons Ave Newhall 91321

MC MAHON, PATRICK JAMES, manufacturing co. executive; b. Dec. 10, 1947, NY, NY; s. Patrick Joseph and Mill (Gillet) McM.; m. Patricia Joan O'Rourke, May 1, 1971; children: Michael, b. 1972; Bradley, b. 1977; edn: BA, Univ. of Notre Dame 1968. Career: with Mack Trucks, Inc. 1971--; salesman, Newburgh, NY, Staten Island, NY and Elizabeth NJ; asst. br. mgr. Queens, NY; br. mgr. Newburgh Poughkeepsie, Newark and Los Angeles; currently, branch mgr. Mack Trucks, Inc., Los Angeles; Ofc: Mack Trucks, Inc., 2340 E Olympic Blvd Los Angeles 90021

MC MAHON, TIMOTHY MASSEY, lawyer; b. Oct. 7, 1950, Santa Barbara; s. Timothy Ferris and Natalie (Browning) McM.; m. Ann, June 26, 1971; children: Kimberly, b. 1978; Timothy Ryan, b. 1981; edn: BA, UC Davis 1972; JD, UC Hastings Coll. of Law 1975; admitted to Calif. State Bar, lic. Calif. Real Estate Broker. Career: deputy dist. atty. Alameda County, 1976-80; atty. McNamara, Lewis, Houston, McClure & Ney (Walnut Creek) 1980; lawyer assoc. with Lewis, Archer & McComas, Inc., now Archer & McComas, Inc., Walnut Creek; bd. govs. Hastings Coll. of Law Alumni Assn.; mem: Alameda Co., Contra Costa Co., and Calif. Bar Assns.; Contra Costa Barristers Assn.; Alameda-Contra Costa Trial Lawyer Assn.; Republican; Protestant; rec: fishing, hunting, racquetball. Res: 112 Mandala Ct Walnut Creek 945696 Ofc: Archer & McComas, 1299 Newell Hill Pl, Ste 300, Walnut Creek 94596

MC MASTERS, JAMES HOWARD, real estate executive; b. Aug. 8, 1944, San Mateo; s. Howard James and Florence Marie (Neilsen) McM.; m. Ann Johnsen, Aug. 14, 1977; children: Rayna b. 1979, Kendra b. 1981; edn: AA, Foothill Jr. Coll. 1967; BS, CSU San Jose 1970; lic. Calif. Real Estate Broker 1973. Career: sales agt. Grubb & Ellis Co., Oakland 1972-76; principal owner McMasters Realty Inc., Walnut Creek 1977; ptnr./pres. McMasters & Westland Commercial Real Estate Inc., Walnut Creek 1977--; ptnr. Consol. Regional Equities 1980--; ptnr. Asian Assocs. 1981--; awards: American Spirit of Honor Award 1971, Wall Street Journal Awd. 1970; listed, Who's Who Am. Colls. & Univs. 1970, Who's Who in Real Estate in Am. 1981-2; mem: Contra Costa Bd. of Realtors, Calif. Assn. of Realtors, East Bay Brokers Assn. (pres. 1983), Inernat. Council of Shopping Centers (pgm. chmn. 1981-2); mem. Walnut Creek Civic Arts Regional Center Com. 1981, BSA Regl. Advis. Com. 1981-3; works: chief statistician US Army Proj. Volar (All Volunteer Army) 1971; mil: sp4 Human Resources Research Orgn. 1971; Republican; Episcopal; rec: Black Belt Karate. Res: 1633 Rocksprings Place Walnut Creek 94596 Ofc: McMasters & Westland, 590 Ygnacio Valley Rd, Ste 200, Walnut Creek 94596

MC MILLAN, TOMMIE JOE, radio broadcasting executive; b. Apr. 3, 1945, Denver, Colo.; s. James and Helen Eugenia (Perry) McM.; div.; 1 son, Leland Joseph b. 1981; edn: stu. E.Los Angeles Coll., Santa Monica City Coll., W.L.A. Coll., 1966-69; cert. PMD (Motion & Time Study), Booze, Allen Hamilton 1967. Career: regional dir. Nationwide Advt. Co., L.A., Phoenix, 1969-71; exec. v.p. Peterson, Masters & McMillan Advt., Beverly Hills 1972-73; nat. sales mgr. Pacific FM Broadcasters, KLOL AM&FM, San Francisco 1973-74; local sales mgr. RKO General, KRTH-FM, Los Anges 1974-78; nat. sales mgr.

Cox Bdcstg. KFI-AM, KOST-FM, Los Angeles 1978-82; v.p. general sales mgr./station mgr. Gannett Bdcstg. KDSO and KEZL, San Diego, 1982-83; nat. sales mgr. KNX-AM, CBS Bdcstg. Inc., Los Angeles 1983--; exec. v.p., bd. mem. McMillan Bus Lines, Phoenix, Ariz.; pres./founder Greater San Diego Advt. Golf Assn.; honors: City of Boston award as mem. of Prime Recovery Team aboard USS Wasp for Gemini (2, 3, 4, & 6) Space Capsule recoveries (1965); recogn. for fundraising (Loman & Barkley Invitational, Westlake Village) for Calif. Inst. for Cancer Resrch., UCLA (1981); mem. So. Calif. Broadcasters Assn.; past pres. (1982), bd. dirs. North Ranch Country Club; founder, Dr. Frank Scott, Aztec Invitational Golf Tourn. & Fund Raiser for San Diego St. Univ.; So. Calif. Advt. Golf Assn. (past pres.); Gr. San Diego Advt. Golf Assn.; San Francisco Advt. Golf Assn.; mil: E5 USN 1962-66, Vietnam Service, Cit.; Republican; Methodist; rec: golf, motorcycle x-c racing, skiing. Res: 5318 Don Pio Dr Woodland Hills 91364 Ofc: KNX-AM CBS Inc., 6121 Sunset Blvd Los Angeles 91364

MC MILLEN, MARY LOU, real estate broker; b. June 22, 1935, Washington, Pa.; d. Clyde Johnson and Mary Cecile (Cochran) Henry; children: Lynda, b. 1956; Kenneth, b. 1957; Robert, b. 1960; Gregory, b. 1964; edn: BA, CSU Long Beach 1965; undergrad. (hons.) CSU Fullerton 1962-64, Stanford Univ. 1953-55; Calif. Gen. Elem. Tchr. Credential 1965; R.E. Broker lic. 1978. Career: tchr. in Mission Viejo 1966-69; real estate sales Alpine Realty, Big Bear Lake 1975-76, Lomas Santa Fe, Realty Execs., and McMillen Investments, in San Diego North County, 1976-84; currently, broker/ inv. counseling/ fin. plng. Mc Millen Investments, Encinitas; awards: Million Dollars Club, Realty Executives 1978, 79; mem: Calif. Assn. Realtors; Docent of Marine Biology, Scripps Inst. of Oceanography; AAUW; Toastmistress; Childrens Hosp.; Republican; Presbyterian; rec: horticulture, skiing, art. Address: McMillen Investments, 840 Val Sereno Dr Encinitas 92024

MC MURRAY, WAYNE TAYLOR, building contractor; b. Sept. 13, 1924, Pasadena; s. Donald D. and Madge (Poggi) McM.; m. Jean Crowell, May 19, 1951; children: Robert, b. 1953; Kenneth, b. 1955; Katherine, b. 1959; edn: BS, Calif. Inst. of Tech. 1945; MBA, USC 1956. Career: proj. engr. C.F. Braun & Co., Alhambra 1946-58; plant mgr. Dynacolor Corp., Los Angeles 1958-59; pres. Weymouth Crowell Constrn. Co., L.A. 1960--; pres./ dir. Coastal Municipal Water Dist. 1979-; dir. Tri-Cities Municipal Water Dist. 1977-78; chmn. Water Adv. Com. of Orange Co. 1984; mem: Calif. Inst. of Tech. Alumni Assn.; Constrn. Laborers Health & Welfare; mil: lt. USNR 1943-46; Republican (Orange Co. Central Com. 1983). Res: 2012 Calle de Los Alamos San Clemente 92672 Oc: Weymouth Crowell Construction Co., 1918 Riverside Dr Los Angeles 90039

McNAMEE, GILBERT WILSON, librarian; b. Aug. 6, 1918, Harrisonburg, VA; s. John Hobson and Armenda VeDora (Southwick) McName; Edn: BA, George Wash. Univ., Wash., D.C., 1954; MLS, UC Berkeley, 1964. Career: librarian, US Depository Collection, Internatl. Civil Aviation Orgn., Wash., D.C., 1949-56; mem., Airport Use Panel, Wash., D.C., 1957-58; librarian, Documents and business depts., San Francisco, CA, 1959-67; asst. dir., Bay Area Reference Center, San Francisco, 1967-72; dir., Bay Are Reference Center, San Francisco, 1972-78; principal librarian, Business Library, San Francisco, 1978---; cons., Library subjs.; conducted library workshops, US, Canada, Australia. Honors: Phi Beta Kappa, 1953. Mem: Calif. Libr. Assn., pres. 1976; Calif. Soc. of Librarians, pres. 1972; Amer. Library Assn., Council mem. 1974-78, 1980-83. Contrib. to Library Journal, American Libraries, Synergy. Mil: USAF, 1941-45. Democrat. United Brethren. Rec: gardening, photography, travel. Res: 1767 Green St., San Francisco 94123; Office: SFPL Business Library, 530 Kearny St., San Francisco 94108.

MC PIKE, WILLIAM ROGER, lawyer; b. Feb. 18, 1951, Fresno; s. James B. and Cassina JoAnn (Herd) McPike; (father, arbitrator Am. Arbitration Assn.; mother, real estate broker); pat. gr.grandparents (Beaty) came to Calif. in 1881 from Carrollton, Mo.; m. Patricia Ann, June 24, 1979; children: Patrick b. 1975, Roger b. 1980; edn: AA, Fresno City Coll. 1972, BA, CSU Fresno 1974, JD, Humphreys Coll. of Law 1980; admitted to Calif. State Bar 1980; Calif. Real Estate lic. 1976-. Career: insurance claims rep. Calif. State Automobile Assn. and New Hampshire Ins., 1976-78; real estate devel., market cons., acquisition agt. for developers Leo Wilson & Co. of Fresno, and San Joaquin Devel. Co. Inc., 1978-81; pvt. law practice, William R. McPike, Atty. at Law, Fresno 1980--; corp. counsel San Joaquin Dev./Brokerage Co. Inc., 1980-82; honors: Alpha Gamma Sigma (1970), Student Senator Fresno City Coll. 1969; mem: Am. Bar Assn., Calif. State Bar Assn., Fresno County Bar Assn.; legal counsel to Save the Abused Youngsters; auditor of 1983 Miss Fresno County Pageant; works: photog. entry 1983 Fresno County Fair; 1965 Art Award, Robert Louis Stevenson Sch. Pebble Beach; Republican; Methodist; rec: numismatics, fishing, travel. Res: 133 Fountain Way Fresno 93704 Ofc: William R. McPike, Atty at Law, 2350 W Shaw Ave, Ste 117, Fresno 93711

MC QUAY, CLARK DOWNING, orthodontist; b. Apr. 7, 1924, Alhambra; s. Charles D. and Ginevra (Clark) McQ.; m. Audrey Hill, July 22, 1950; children: Timothy Clark, b. 1951; Carolyn (Tucker), b. 1952; Diane Patricia, b. 1954; Robin Elizabeth, b. 1956; Alison Hill, b. 1960; edn: DDS, USC 1950; Grad. Orthodontics, USC 1951; Destint- Orthodontist, Calif. 1950. Career: pvt. practice orthodontics, Westwood Village and Brentwood 1951--; dental staff St. Johns Hosp. Med. Ctr.; bd. dirs. Summit Health Ltd. 1969-; mem: Pacific Coast Soc. of Orthodontics; Am. Assn. of Orthodontists; Am. Med. Assn.; Western Dental Soc.; USC Dental Assocs.; Beverly Hills Acad. of Dentistry (pres. 1978); Delta Sigma Delta, L.A. Grad. chpt. (past pres.); Century Club, USC (past pres.); Rotary (past pres. L.A.- Brentwood Club 1980); Westlake Sch.; YMCA; Los Angeles Country Club; Bel Air Bay Club; L.A. Mens Garden Club; mil: Inf. Med. Det. US Army 1943-45, Purple Heart; Republican; Episcopal; rec: gardening, golf, skiing. Res: 15010 Altata Dr Pacific Palisades 90272 Ofc: 11980 San Vicente Blvd, Ste 602, Los Angeles 90049

MC SHANE, JOHN PAUL, systems analysis executive; b. Aug. 27, 1932, Hammond, Ind.; s. James Henry and Mary Anne (English) McS.; m. Mornette Williams, Oct. 29, 1955; children: Kathleen b. 1956, Bridget b. 1957, Terese b. 1959, Patrice b. 1960, Maureen b. 1962, John b. 1964; edn: BS, elec. eng., Univ. Notre Dame 1954; MS, systems mgmt., USC 1983. Career: assoc. design engr. Lockheed Aircraft Corp., Burbank 1955-56; engr. spls. product perf. analysis Sperry-Univac, St. Paul, Minn. 1956-58; sr. hdqtrs. engr. G.E. Computer Dept., Phoenix, Ariz. 1958-67; senior splst. Systems Analysis, McDonnell Douglas Astronautics, 1967--; mem. Notre Dame Alumni (ofcr., Man of the Year Awd.); civic svc. (15 yrs.), City of Westminster incl. Merit Commn. Traffic Commn., Project Ldr. spl. Traffic Systems sgudy, Police Advis. Com., Beautification Commn., chmn. City Goals Com. (author Environmental Element), Mayor's apptee. to Spl. Dists. Com.; youth vol. work in Little League bd., team mgr., parish youth basketball pgm.; Catholic (past pres. Parish Council, ed. Parish News, Youth Religion tchr.). Res: 5071 Cambridge Ave Westminster 92683 Ofc: McDonnell Douglas 5301 Bolsa Ave Huntington Beach 92637

MC WALTERS, JAMES G., commercial brokerage co. executive; b. Oct. 7, 1940, NYC; s. John and Mary McWalters; m. Patricia Rohweller, Apr. 19, 1975; edn: Midshipman/BS in Aeronautical Engr. and Nuclear Sci. (top 2^ in grad. class), US Naval Acad., Annapolis 1964. Career: precision machinist, Arizona Gear, Tucson 1958-60; prodn. supr. No. Am. Aviation, Downey, Calif. 1960; founder/pres. Advanced Protective Systems, Inc., San Diego 1969-71, merged with Sterling Security Svc., 1971; with Grubb and Ellis Comml. Brokerage Co. 1972-78: investment mktg. 1972-3, mgr. new tract sales, San Diego 1973-4, Los Angeles sales mgr. 1974-5, mgr. Investment Bus. Devel. 1975-6, Investment Div. coordinator 1974-8, mgr. L.A. Comml. Brokerage Co. 1975-8, vice pres. 1974-8, bd. dirs. 1976-8; pres. Vistar Comml. Brokerage Co., 1980; exec. vice pres./regional dir. Merrill Lynch Commercial Real Estate (developed commercial real estate brokerage network in western states), 1981--; mil: served in USN 1960-69; conducted first boarding and search opns. on minesweeper Excel, Vietnam 1964-5, 3 yrs. abd. nuclear submarine Snook, Vietnam Service Star; rec: flying, golf, tennis, ski. Res: Glendale Ofc: Merrill Lynch Comml. Real Estate, 640 S. Olive St. Los Angeles 90014

MEDLEY, DONALD BRUCE, educator; b. Sept. 20, 1932, Monroe, Mich.; s. Hugh Lloyd and Nurnie (Clawson) M.; m. Louise Spencer, Sept. 1, 1956; children: Brian b. 1958, Sherrie b. 1961, Anthony b. 1964; edn: BVE, CSC Los Angeles 1971; MA, CSU Los Angeles 1972; Ed.D, Brigham Young Univ. 1976; desig: CDP, Data Proc. Mgmt. Assn. 1963; Executive Acct., I.C.S., 1967; Calif. tchr. creds. Comm. College Instr. (1971), Supr. (1974), Sec. Voc. (1976); CDE (DP) and DBE (Bus.), Data Edn. Cert. Council (1976). Career: machine opr./sect. supr. USAF 1952-56; senior mach. opr. Willy Motors Inc. 1956-7; supr. Data Proc., Kobacker Stores Inc. 1957-9; pgmmr. Hughes Aircraft, 1959-60; mgr. data proc. ops. Telecomputing Corp. 1960-62; sr. computing analyst Rocketdyne Div. No. Am. 1962-67; sr. mgmt. systems designer Xerox Data Systems 1968-70 (half time); data proc. instr. /wk. exp. coord. Moorpark Coll. 1963-82; pres. Evaluation Techniques Consortium Inc. 1977-81; staff computer splst. US Dept. Agri. SEA-CDSD, 1980-81; prof./chmn. Computer Info. Sys. Dept., Calif. State Polytech. Univ., Pomona 1981--; gen. chmn. 1983 Nat. Computer Conf. Anaheim; mem: D.P. Mgmt. Assn., IEEE Computer Soc., ACM, Soc. of Data Educators, Assn. of Women in Computing, (past) Optimists; wks: sev. papers on computing pgms. and systems; Programming Principles With Cobol I, II (2 vols., South-Western Pub. Co. 1984, 9/84); mil: Airman 1/c USAF 1952-56; Republican; Prot.; rec: fishing. Res: 11425 Marquette Ln Pomona 91766 Ofc: Calif. State Poly Univ., 3801 W. Temple Ave Pomona 91768

MEEKS, DASHIELL SHAWN, utilities co. engineer; b. Apr. 2, 1948, Newark, NJ; s. Charles Augustus and Ada Lucille (Roberts) M.; m. Carol Miller, Oct. 11, 1974; edn: BS, Lehigh Univ. 1969; MBA, Murray State Univ. 1979; Engr. In Tng., Calif. 1980; Reg. Profl. Engr. (mech.), Calif. 1982. Career: research engr. Kaiser Aluminum & Chem. Corp., Oakland 1969-73; proj. engr. W.R. Grace & Co., Lexington, Mass. 1973-79; sr. engr. San Diego Gas & Elec. Co., San Diego 1979--; spkr. Career Day, S.D. Jt. Council of Eng. Socs. (1980-81), Lions Internat. (1982), S.D. Council of Black Engr. (1980, 81, 82), Serra Jr. H.S. (1983); judge, San Diego Nat. Student Sci. Competition, S.D. Elem. Inst. of Sci. 1982; awards: Scholastic Scholarship, Frat. Order of Masons 1969; Outstanding Young Men of Am., Jaycees 1983; mem: Am. Soc. for Metals; No. Calif. & S.D. Councils of Black Engrs.; Ohio Valley Mgmt. Club; Am. Inst. of Indsl. Engrs.; Sigma Alpha Mu, Sigma Kappa chpt.; United Way of Owensboro; Cliff Hagan Boys Club; Dynamic Toastmasters; works: presentation, Pacific Coast Elec. Assn. Conf., L.A. 3/83; Presbyterian; rec: basketball, bridge, chess. Res: 6432 El Perico Ln Carlsbad 92008 Ofc: San Diego Gas & Electric Co., 990 Bay Blvd Chula Vista 92011

MEENA, EDWARD J., real estate - author; b. Apr. 2, 1922, Vicksburg, Miss.; s. Elias and Mamie (Abraham) M.; m. Warene Shurden 1951, div. 1956; edn: AA, Miss. State Univ. 1946-48. Career: Meena Landscaping and Floral Co., Clarksdale, Miss. 1948-55; MGM Studio, Culver City 1955-74; Tempa Geiger-Century 21 Realtors, Brentwood & Encino 1974--; dir. of S&S Pub.; honors: founder, Pet Defenders; mem: Theta Xi; L.A. Co. Mus. of Art; Royal Oaks Found.; L.A. World Affairs Council; Nat. Exchange; coauthor: Star Maker, Star Breaker; author: Bride of Annadale; Methodist. Res: 5721 Babbitt Ave Encino 91316 Ofc: Tempa Geiger & Assoc., 16430 Ventura Blvd Encino 91436

MEER, RONALD LEE, finance executive; b. Aug. 30, 1955, Denver, Colo.; s. Morey M. and Sylivia E. (Rubinstone) M.; edn: BSM (bus. mgmt.), Pepperdine Univ., grad. stu. fin., Golden Gate Univ. Reg. Representative NASD. Career: gen. mgr. retail sales div. Goodyear Tire & Rubber Co., Torrane 1974-76; product coord. and R/D cons. W.R. Grace Corp., 1976-78; dir. corporate services (designed Exec. Devel. Pgm.) Merrill Lynch, Pierce, Fenner & Smith, Inc. Laguna Hills/ Newport Bch. 1978-83; dir. corp. svcs. Prudential-Bache Securities Inc. Newport Beach 1983--; instr. Saddleback Coll., Orange Coast Coll., 1982-; co-founder/dir. The Cathy Rigby Regl. Sport Center, Irvine 1980--; co-founder/cons. D & M Communications, Oceanside 1982-83; mem: Orange County Finance Soc., So. Calif. Assn. of Strategic Planners, Orange County Bus. Com. for the Arts; publ: contbr. Executive Mag. (1981); rec: pvt. pilot (multi-eng., instrument). Res: 26531 Fresno Dr Mission Viejo 92691 Ofc: Prudential-Bache Securities 1301 Dove St Newport Bch 92660

MEGUIAR, MALCOLM FLOYD, manufacturer; b. June 16, 1915, Pasadena; s. Frank Jr. and Sadie Jane (Habenicht) M.; m. Mabel Ruth Hudson, Nov. 27, 1934; children: Larry Gordon b. 1935, Barry James b. 1942; edn: Pasadena City Coll. Career: bd. chmn. Meguiar's Mirror Bright Polish Co. Inc., Irvine (sales throughout US and 7 foreign re-packaging plants); co. was founded by (father) Frank Meguiar, Jr. in 1901, son, Barry is corp. president currently. Charter pres. Pasadena Lancer Club, charter v.p. Pasa. (now Pt. Loma) Coll. Crusader Club, charter mem., dir. Pasa. Quarterbacks; bus. advis. bd. Pasa. City Coll. and chmn. bd. govs. of Alumni Assn. (awarded lifetime Gold Pass to all coll. events); charter rep. Troop 21, Boy Scouts of Am.; past pres. Pasa. Boys Club (hon. lifetime mem.); awarded Orv Mohler Trophy, for contbn. to sports in So. Calif., Sports Ambassadors, 1961; mem: Tournament of Roses Com. (hon. life mem.); Jr. CofC (life); Pasa. Kiwanis Club (senior mem.); Salvation Army (Man of Year 1968); Pasa. University Club; Pasa. CofC, Balboa Bay Club; patron: YMCA (N.E. Br.), athletic teams (45years) Softball, Baseball, Little League, AAU Basketball, Bowling, Track and Field, Volleyball, Indianapolis 500 and Riverside Grand Prix. Ofc: Mirror Bright Polish Co. Inc. 17275 Daimler Ave Irvine 92714

MEIER, STEPHEN C., media communications co. executive; b. Apr. 22, 1950, Los Angeles; s. Erwin William and Betsy (Ross) Meier; m. Carol Williams, Apr. 20, 1974; children: Charles, b. 1978; Marilyn, 1980; edn: AB, Occidental Coll. 1972; MBA, Harvard Bus. Sch. 1977. Career: budget analyst Joint Legis. Budget Com., Calif. Legislature 1973-75; mgr. Corp. Communications & Community Services, The Times Mirror Co. 1977-79, dir. Pub. Affairs 1979-83, asst. to the Pres. 1983--; mem: Oneonta Club, So. Pasadena; United Presbyterian Ch. (elder). Ofc: The Times Mirror Company, Times Mirror Square, Los Angeles 90053

MEKIS, NICK ANTHONY, general contractor-developer; b. Feb. 11, 1925, Watsonville; s. Michael and Catherine Mekis; m. Betty Drape, Mar. 20, 1960; children: Jayne Lynn, b. 1950; Kurt Eric, b. 953; edn: Petroleum Engr., Harbor Jr. Coll. 1955-56; lic. Gen. Contractor, Calif. Career: owner Nick Mekis Concrete Constrn., Long Beach 1952-62; owner Nick Mekis General Contractor/ Developer, Long Beach 1962--; pres. Mekis-Ross Devel. Corp. 1978-81, v.p. 1980--; v.p. Fairways Homeowners Assn., Palm Springs; honors: Mayor/ Councilman City Signal Hill 1974-78; dir. Metropolitan Waster Dist. 1974-78; dir. L.A. Co. Mosquito Abatement Dist. 1974-78; mem: Repub. Nat. Com.; Calif. Repub. Com.; Calif. Contract Cities (Polit. Action Com.); Travelers Aid Soc., Long Beach; Long Beach Elks; Am. Legion; mil: m/sgt. US Army 1943-46, 1950-52, num. medals; Republican; Catholic; rec: horseless carriage auto club. Address: 2400 E 23rd St Signal Hill 90806

MELIA, ANTHONY FRANCIS, JR., insurance broker; b. Sept. 3, 1933, Gretna, Nebr.; s. Anthony Francis Sr. and Hazel (Bishop) M.; edn: BA, Univ. of Nebr. 1957; cont. edn. UCLA & Los Angeles City Coll.; desig: CIC, Soc. of Cert. Ins. Counselors 1980; Notary Pub., Calif. 1967. Career: founder/ owner Melia Ins. Inc. 1967; changed to Nat. Bus. Ins. Agency upon acquisiton of Titan Agencies 1980; pres./ owner National Business Insurance Agency, Los Angeles 1967--; lectr./ author; mem: Profl. Ins. Agents of Calif. & Nev.; Metropolitan Elections Com. of L.A.; L.A. Bus. & Profl. Assn. (pres. 1981-); contbg. writer: NEXUS Mag. 1984, frequent interviews & arts in Bay Area Reporter (1982), Frontiers Mag. (1983), & L.A. Times (1/84); mil: corp. US Army 1953-55, Nat. Defense Svc., GCM, Army of Occupation Medal; Democrat; rec: photog., collector historic autographs/ signatures; Res: 1020 Carol Dr Los Angeles 90069 Ofc: NBIA, 1017 N La Cienega, Ste 306, Los Angeles 90069

MELLINGER, ROBERT LOUIS, lawyer; b. June 25, 1956, McKeesport, Pa.; s. Robert L. and Ines Dina (Agostini) M.; m. Doris Ana Padron, Nov. 17, 1984; edn: BA in psych., BA in poli-sci., Washington & Jefferson Coll. 1978; JD, Southwestern Univ. Sch. of Law 1981; admitted Calif. State Bar 1983. Career: law clk. Lloyd H. Fuge, Esq., Clairton, Pa. 1979, William F. Brown, Esq., Beverly Hills, Ca. 1980, Mental Health Advocacy Services, Inc., 1980; legal journalist Metropolitan News, 1980; law clk. Navarro & Maas, 1980-81; assoc. atty./law clk. E.L. Sanabria & Assocs. 1981-83; East L.A. Community Center/ Immigration Clinic, 1980; asst. in pub. rels. Southwestern Univ. 1980-81; assoc. atty. Peter L. Lago, A Law Corp., Downey 1983--; dir./treas./ pub. rels. Santa Monica Amateur Boxing Club, A Non-Profit Corp., 1982-; honors: Outstanding Young Men of Am. 1980, US Jaycees; Who's Who Among Students in Am.

Univs. & Colls.; Internat. Youth in Achieve., Young Comm. Ldrs. of Am. 1981; editor-in-chief The Commentator (law sch. newspaper) 1979-81, 3 distinguished svc. awards, Southwestern Univ.; mem: Am. Bar Assn., Assn. of Trial Lawyers of Am., Calif. Bar Assn., Italian Am. Lawyers Assn., Greater L.A. Press Club, Phi Alpha Delta Law Frat. Intl. (treas. 1981), Amateur Athletic Union of the USA (life), USA Amateur Boxing Fedn., Real Estate Law Forum, Olympic Alumni Orgn.; Catholic; rec: sports, music. Res: 373 S. Hoover St, Apt. 201, Los Angeles 90020 Ofc: Peter L. Lago, ALC, 12651 Lakewood Blvd, 2d Fl., Downey 90242

MELLOTT, SHARON LEE, chiropractor; b. Nov. 9, 1939, Thief River Falls, Minn.; d. Melvin Ingolf and Evelyn Irene (Olson) Sabo; m. Keith D. Mellot, Aug. 11, 1962; 1 son, Kevin Gerard, b. 1965; edn: Pacific Lutheran Univ. 1957-58; Reg. Radiologic Technologist, Univ. of Ore. Med. Sch. 1960; DC, Palmer Coll. of Chiro. West 1982; postgrad. roentgenology, Western State Coll. of Chiro. 1982; Diplomate, Am. Bd. Chiro. Examiners 1982; DC lic. State Bds. Maine, Calif. (1982), Nev., Idaho, Colo. & Wyo. (1983). Career: radiologic tech., Seattle, Sacto., So. S.F. bay areas 1960-79; owner/ opr. The Transcriber, med. sectl. svc., Sunnyvale 1975--; chiropractor/ clin. dir./ owner Sierra Chiro. Clinic, Saratoga 1982--; instr. anatomy & physiology, East- West Ctr. for the Healing Arts 1983; honors: Hon. DC Degree, No. Calif. Coll. of Chiro. 1980; mem: Internat. Chiropractors Assn.; Am. Chiro. Assn. (Council on Roentgenology); Good Shepherd Lutheran Home Aux.; Saratoga Womens Breakfast CLub; Civitan Club of Sunnyvale; Am. Scandinavian Stu. Exch.; Multi Handicapped Research Found.; Aux. for Hearing Research; Rubella Parents of Calif.; needlework exhibitor: var. local comm. shows; author/ presentor: monologue, Kate Luther- A Woman for All Ages; Republican; Lutheran; rec: needlework, music. Res: POB 492 Saratoga 95071 Ofc: Sierra Chiropractic Clinic, 1221 Saratoga-Sunnyvale Rd Saratoga 95070

MELNIKOW, DAVID GREGORY, manufacturing co. executive/ real estate broker; b. Apr. 19, 1927, San Francisco; s. Henry Peter and Caroline (French) M.; m. Theresa Molinaro, Sept. 13, 1958; children: David Jr., b. 1953; Christopher, b. 1955; Matthew, b. 1956; edn: BA, UC Berkeley 1951; R.E. Broker, Calif. 1980. Career: police sgt. Berkeley Police Dept. 1956-70; gen. mgr. Wholesale Produce Co., Santa Rosa 1970-79; broker/ owner real estate firm, Cameron Park 1980-83; pres./ gen. mgr. Gatrean Homes, Cameron Park 1980--; pres. Green Valley Equity Fund 1982-83; v.p. Wicket Inc. 1982-83; mem: Contra Costa & El Dorado Co. Bds. Realtors; Navy League; Elks Club; mil: firecontrolman 3/c USN 1945-46; Republican; Catholic; rec: boating, fishing. Res: 3082 Emerald Ct Cameron Park 95682 Ofc: Gatrean Homes, 3260 Cameron Park Dr Cameron Park 95682

MENDELOW, SAMUEL MARVIN, educational computer software co. president; b. June 27, 1931, Buffalo, NY; s. Albert and Frida M.; m. Marilyn Nortman, Mar. 8, 1962; children: Donna, b. 1963, Debra, b. 1964, Robert, b. 1965; edn: bus. adm./ music, Univ. Miami 1950-52. Career: vice pres. General Aerospace Materials Corp., Plainview, NY 1952-62; pres. Aerodynamics Indus. Inc., Farmingdale, NY 1962-67; founder/v.p. EDP Indus. Inc., Los Angeles 1967-76; pres. QC Resources Group, L.A. 1977-82; pres. NET Systems, Inc., L.A. 1977-82; pres. Compass Software Corp., Encino 1984--; pres. CourseWare Research Corp., Encino 1984--; dir. Publishers Support Group, Inc., Encino 1984-; chosen by Govt. of Israel to exclusively rep. all indsl. products mfd. in Israel for export to US (1966); rep. (various tech. products mfd. for export to Israel) Grumman Internat. Corp.; honors: bus. chmn. United Cerebral Palsey (NY 1954), student guest condr. Tampa (Fla.) Sym. Orch. (1948); mem: Am. Soc. of Composers, Authors and Pubs.; Am. Soc. for Nondestructive Testing, Inc.; Masons, Pi Lambda Phi. Guest panelist 8th Ann. W.Coast Computer Faire, S.F. 1983; rec: music, golf, tennis, swim. Res:4949 Genesta Ave Encino 91316 Ofc: Compass Software Corp. 17000 Ventura Blvd Ste 220, Encino 91316

MENDELSON, JERRY LEONARD, franchise marketing executive; b. Dec. 11, 1933, Chgo.; s. Joseph Ralph and Florence (Offer) M. Career: senior acct. exec. incentives/mktg. E.F MacDonald Co. 1970-75; pres. J.L.M. Co. (incentive co., mktg. to maj. So. Calif. corps.) 1975-80; pres. Damiana Co. (franchise consulting) 1980-83; owner Mendelson's Frame & Gallery, Balboa Penin 1983-; pres. Grandma Lee's Bakery & Eating Place (fast food sandwich & bakery franchise) 1984--; founding pres. Roosters (mens charitable orgn.); community svc. involvement for alcohol and drug dependent; mil: USN 1951-54, Aircraft Carrier duty, Korean Conflict; Republican; rec: boating. Res: 322 Montero Ave Balboa 92661 Ofc: Grandma Lee's, 1301 Dove St, Ste 1050, Newport Beach 92660

MENDELSON, SAMUEL, certified public accountant; b. Sept. 13, 1921, San Francisco; s. Ira and Tillie (Cohen) M.; m. Irene June, 1961; children: Alan, Lawrence, Debra, Gladys, Robert Bruce, Jeffrey, Timothy; edn: BS, UC Berkeley·1943; MS, Golden Gate Uni. 1948; D.Laws., 1955; lic. CPA, Calif. 1948. Career: staff acct. Hood & Strong, CPAs 1946-49; prin. CPA practice 1949--, currently, senior partner Samuel Mendelson & Co., San Francisco; mil: capt. USMC 1942-46; Ofc: Samuel Mendelson & Co., 47 Kearny St, San Francisco 94108

MENDERSON, WILLIAM THOMAS, insurance co. executive, ret.; b. July 21, 1924, McKeesport, Pa.; s. Thomas Kerr and Agnus Helen (Wood) M.; m. June Izard, Aug. 3, 1946; children: Sue Ann, b. 1948; Sally Jane, b. 1950; Sandra Elizabeth, b. 1954; edn: BS, Ariz. State Univ. 1948; profl. courses, Life Ins. Agcy. Mgmt. Assn. Sch., Hartford, Conn. 1952, 56; 57. Career: with New York

Life Ins. Co., 1948-84: ins. sales, Phoenix, Az. 1948, asst. mgr. 1949, tng. supr., N.Y., 1951, general mgr., Reno, Nev. 1952, Sacramento, 1960-84. Mem. Insurance Ednl. & Devel. Com. 1976. Profl. awards: Presidents Trophy, New York Life 1956; Grand Slam awd. 20 consec. years; recruiting awds for 35 yrs. Mem: Estate Planning Council 1952-60; Life Undertraining Tng. Council; Life Underwriters Assn. 1952-84 (state legis. chmn. Nev., 1954-60); Gen. Agents & Mgrs. Assn. 1952-84; Elks 1954-60, Masons, Shriners. Publs: ins. sales & tng guides, 1948-84. Mil: served in US Army ETO 1943-46, Croix de Guerre, Bronzestar, 5 battle stars; Republican; Presbyterian; rec: golf, travel. Res: 300 Dunbarton Cir Sacramento 95825

MENDOZA, CHRISTIAN DANIEL, financier/broker; b. July 2, 1951, San Jose; s. Emilio Aguiniga and Juanita Franco (Reyes) M.; edn: grad. Bellarmine Coll. Prep. San Jose 1969; stu. UC Santa Cruz 1973, Univ. of Hawaii 1974-75; BS, Santa Clara Univ. 1977; R.E. Broker lic. Calif. 1981. Career: broker/ exec. Merrill Lynch, Inc., San Jose 1979-80; broker/ agent Ortiz Investments/ Realty, Inc., San Jose 1980-83; broker/ partner Treico Financial, Ltd., Sunnyvale 1983; pres./ broker Christian & Associates Finance, San Jose 1983--; earned highest bank commn. paid to date on West Coast ($26,000, Standard Fed. Bank of Md. 1983); mem: Teen Challenge (chmn. fund raising); Full Gospel Businessmens Fellowship Internat.; Democrat; Catholic; rec: weight lifting. Res: 1800 Stokes St 185, San Jose 95126 Ofc: Christian & Associates Finance, 3003 Moorpark, Ste 203, San Jose 95128

MENDOZA, SONIA, electronic components co. president; b. Feb. 2, 1945, Cairo, Egypt; d. George and Helen (De Natale) Rayes; m. Richard Mendoza, Feb. 17, 1968; children: Katherine, b. 1969; Anthony, b. 1970; Tania, b. 1974; Michael, b. 1976; edn: sectl., Westchester Bus. Sch. 1963. Career: sales promotion mgr. Air France Cargo, Los Angeles 1965-70; cargo sales mgr. asst. UTA French Airlines, L.A. 1970-72; internat. sales rep. Ivory Air Forwarding, Santa Clara 1979-80; ofc. mgr. American Components Inc., Santa Clara 1980-82; pres. Alamo Electronic Components, Inc., San Jose 1981--, involved with computer clubs, and servicing of computer peripheral and strong customer rels.; mem: Silicon Valley Computer Soc. Res: 16360 Jackson Oaks Dr Morgan Hill 95037 OFc: Alamo Electronic Components, Inc., 6940 Santa Teresa Blvd, Ste 3, San Jose 95119

MENNEN, JULIE MARIE, psychotherapist; b. Jan. 8, 1956, Glendale; d. Dr. Paul (MD) and Trudie (Booklin) M.; m. Clyde Wickham, Aug. 15, 1982; edn: BA, cum laude, CSU Long Beach 1977; MA, Calif. Sch. of Profl. Psychology, San Diego 1979; PhD, 1982; Lic. Marriage, Family & Child Counselor, Calif. 1983. Career: psychological asst. Steve Savlov, PhD, Laguna Hills 1981-82; marriage, family & child counselor (MFCC), pvt. practice, Tustin Psychology Ctr., Tustin 1982-83; MFCC, Psych. asst., pvt. practice, Neil Ribner, PhD, La Jolla 1982--; drug prevention splst. Pathways, San Diego, part-time 1981--; group facilitator Ctr. for Neurologic Studies, San Diego, 1983-; vol. counselor, Parents United 1981-; honors: recogn., Saddleback Valley Bus. & Profl. Womens Club 1982; mem: Solana Beach Leads Club; Career Connections; AAUW (Del Mar-Leucadia br.); San Diego Child Abuse Coordinating Council; S.E. Child Sexual Abuse Review Com.; Orange Co. Child Sexual Abuse Network; CSPP Alumni Assn.; CSULB Alumni Assn.; publs: Before It Happens: A Handbook for Parents on the Prevention of Child Sexual Abuse, Manuscript 1983; Incest, Why Me?, Thursday's Child, June 1983; Incest: Speaking the Unspoken, Thursday's Child, May 1983; rec: sailing. Res: 1029 Hermes Ave Leucadia 92024 Ofc: Julie Mennen, PhD, 8950 Villa La Jolla Dr, Ste 1132A, La Jolla 92037

MENO, GLENN ANTHONY, printed circuit board designer; b. Jan. 11, 1957, San Diego; s. Jesus Cruz (dec.) and Brigida (Javier) M.; m. Patricia Ann. Borja Pereira, Apr. 2, 1977; edn: San Diego City Coll. 1975-79; San Diego Mesa Coll. 1979; desig: Reg. Rep., NASD 1981; Life Only Agent, Calif. 1981. Career: supship eng. draftsman 32nd St. Naval Sta., San Diego 1974-78; elec. drafter NCR, Rancho Bernardo 1978-80; PCB designer Manpower co., San Diego 1980-81, Spin Physics 1981-82, Dynair Electronics 1982-83, TSA 1983; RB designer, Senior Design 1983-84; consulting/finl. plnng. prin. GNP Docuservice, eng. & fin. svcs., Spring Valley 1984--; mem: Nat. Assn. Securities Dealers; Sons & Daughters of Guam Club, San Diego; Republican; Christian; rec: investments, computers, chess. Address: GNP Docuservice, 9243 Warmwood Ave Spring Valley 92077

MENON, NIRMALA KRISHNA, biochemist; b. May 18, 1944, Trivandrum, Berala, India, came to USA 1973; parents: Balakrishna Krishnapillai and Ponnamma Bhagavathiamma (Pillai) Menon; m. Madhaven Menon, Aug. 27, 1966; children: Murali, b. 1967; Anupama, b. 1977; edn: BS, Univ. of Kerala, India 1964; MS, 1966; D.Phil., Univ. of Saugor, Sagar, India 1972. Career: research fellow Univ. of Saugor, India 1968-69; resrch. fellowship Lab. of Biomed. & Environ. Sci., UCLA 1969-72; postdtl. trainee neurobiology research Hosp. for Sick Children, Toronto, Canada 1972-73; rsearch assoc. II Brain Behavior Research Ctr., Sonoma State Hosp., UCSF 1974; postgrad. research neurologist UCLA -Reed Neurological Research Centre & Neuropsychiatric Inst. 1974-76, asst. research neurologist 1976-78; asst. research biochem. UCLA-Lab. Biomed. & Environ. Scis. 1983--; tchr. occuptnl. course on nutrition & brain devel., Sch. of Pub Health, UCLA 1979-82; honors: Nat. Research Svc. Awd., NIH 1981-83, Outstanding Paper, Am. Oil Chemists Soc. 1983; mem: Soc. for Neuroscience; Am. Oil Chemists Soc.; British Brain Soc. & European Brain & Behavior Sci. (hon. mem.); Sigma Xi; AAAS; Assn. of Academic Women, UCLA; contbr. 24 publs. in sci. journs. 1970-; Hindu; rec: Indian classical music. Res: 9009 Whitaker Ave Sepulveda 91343 Ofc: Laboratory of Biomedical & Environmental Sciences, 900 Veteran Ave, Univ. of Calif., Los Angeles 90024

MERCURIO, GLORIA CARMEN, real estate broker; b. Mar. 19, 1931, Medford, Mass.; d. Daniel and Rose Ann (Toscano) Tarallo; m. Frank Mercurio, Dec. 15, 1951; children: Stephen, b. 1953; Frank, b. 1955; Daniel, b. 1958; Horace,b. 1959; R.E. Broker Lic., Calif. 1975. Career: real estate salesman Arndt Assoc. 1969-, Century-21 Arndt Assoc., Monterey 1972; broker/ owner Mercurio Real Estate, Monterey 1979--; mem. Monterey Bd. Realtors (secty., edn. chmn., 1981, grievance com. 1983-84, balloting chmn. 1977); Hon. Life Mem. PTA (past pres: Thomas O. Larkin 1965-66; Walter Colton Jr. H.S. 1968-69; Monterey H.S. 1970); mem: Zonta Internat.; Monterey Civic Club; Monterey Penin. Hosp. Aux. (pres. 1983); Childrens Home Soc.; Democrat; Protestant; rec: singer-soloist (mem. Choraleers). Res: 698 Madison St Monterey 93940 Ofc: Mercurio Real Estate, 452 Pacific St Monterey 93940

MERDLER, JOSEPH, lawyer; b. Feb. 12, 1935, Bronx, NY; s. Morris and Esther (Steller) M.; m. Margot H. Halperin, Mar. 28, 1957; 1 dau. Marci, b. 1965; edn: BS, UCLA 1957; JD, Southwestern Univ. Sch. of Law 1963; Reg. Sanitarian, Calif. 1957; Arbitrator, Am. Arbitration Assn. 1981; admitted to Calif. State Bar 1964. Career: pub. health sanitarian 1957-64; atty. sole practitioner, Sherman Oaks 1964-65; partner Merdler & Gabourie, Attys., Sherman Oaks 1965-73; partner Astor & Merdler, Attys., Northridge 1973--; lectr. Pub. Health Law., CSU Northridge 1976-77; lectr. East L.A. Coll. 1979; Reserve Police Ofcr., San Fernando Police Dept. 1981-; Judge Pro Tem, Los Angeles Municipal Ct. 1971-; judge pro tem Burbank Municipal Ct. 1983; honors: Outstanding Svc., Metal Trades Council AFL- CIO 1974; Order of DeMolay Legion of Honor 1972; Specific Achiev. Awd., Dayton Amateur Radio Assn. 1980; mem: Am. & Calif. Bar Assns.; Am. Judicature Soc.; Phi Alpha Delta; Calif. Peace Ofcrs. Assn.; Northridge CofC; Encino Shrine Club (pres. 1971); Almalaikah Temple; Los Angeles Scottish Rites; F&AM; Personal Communications Found. (pres. 1979-); So. Calif. DX Assn.; Am. Radio Relay League; Jewish; rec: amateur radio. Ofc: Astor & Merdler, Attys., 9036 Reseda Blvd, Ste 203, Northridge 91324

MEROLLA, VICTOR ANTHONY, insurance co. executive; b. May 26, 1949, San Francisco; s Victor Umberto and Millie (Israel) M.; m. Bonnie Jean Smith, June 30, 1974; div. 1984; 1 dau. Gina Marie, b. 1981; edn: BS, Univ. Santa Clara 1971; grad. stu. MBA Pgm. Calif. Coastal Univ. 1984; certified AAI (Accred. Advisor of Insurance) 1984; ARM (Assoc. Risk Mgr) and CPCU (Cert. Prop. Cas. Underwriter) in progress. Career: bus. sales rep. Liberty Mutual Ins. Co., San Jose 1975-77; mktg. rep. Safeco Ins. Co., Burlingame 1977-78; account rep Philadelphia Mfg. Ins. Co., Walnut Creek 1979 80; regl. sales dir. Fireman's Fund Ins. Co., San Rafael 1979-81; exec. sales rep. Employee Benefits Ins. Co., San Francisco 1981-82; bus. agent/mgr. Nationwide Insurance Co., Walnut Creek 1982--; awards: ROTC Acad. Scholar awards: ROTC Acad. Scholar 1969; mem: Alameda-Contra Costa Ins. Forum (pgm. dir. 1983/4; sec-treas. 1985); Ins. Mktg. Assn. of the East Bay; Shriners; Jobs Daus. (past assoc. guardian); Univ. of Santa Clara Alumni Assoc. (pres. elect East Bay Alumni Assoc.); Bronco Bench & Theatre Arts; Toastmasters Internat.; Masons; Scottish Rites; high school football coach, San Ramon 1979-82; mem. San Ramon Soccer Club (adult); Republican; Catholic; rec: sports, music, theatre. Address: 629 Hartley Dr. Danville 94526

MERRIFIELD, DONALD PAUL, S.J. university president, clergyman; b. Nov. 14, 1928, Los Angeles; s. Arthur S. and Elizabeth Marian (Baker) M.; edn: BS (physics) Calif. Inst. of Tech. 1950; MS (physics) Univ. of Notre Dame 1951; Ph.L. (philosophy), St. Louis Univ. 1957; PhD (physics) Mass. Inst. of Tech. 1962; STM (theol.), Univ. of Santa Clara 1966. Career: instr. physics Loyola Univ. of L.A. 1961-62; lectr. Univ. of Santa Clara Eng.Sch. 1965; cons. theoretical chem. Jet Propulsion Lab, CalTech, 1962-69; pres. Loyola Univ. of L.A. (now. Loyola Marymount Univ.) 1969--; awards: S.T.D., USC (1969), service award CalTech (1971); Soc. of Sigma Xi (sci. hon.); mem: Assn. of Independent Calif. Colls. & Univs. (exec bd., past pres.), Independent Colls. of So. Calif. Inc. (bd.), Santa Marta Hosp. Found. (bd.), Inner City Law Center (bd.); Assn. of Jesuit Colls. & Univ. (bd.); Catholic priest/Soc. of Jesus; rec: sailing, swimming. Address: Loyola Marymount Univ., Loyola Blvd at W. 80th St Los Angeles 90045

MERRIFIELD, WILLIAM POWERS, lawyer; b. Mar. 11, 1941, Carmel; s. Charles Wellington (DDS) and Clara Louis (MD) (Powers) M.; children: Catherine Lynn, b. 1963; Gregory Todd, b. 1966; edn: Stanford Univ. 1958-59; BA, w/ honors, CSU Long Beach 1966; JD, Pepperdine Univ. 1975; admitted to State Bar of Calif. 1978; lic. Real Estate Broker, Calif. 1982. Career: with Rockwell Internat. 1960-80: research engr. (devel. inspection sys. for Apollo/ Saturn spacecraft) 1960-66; contract pricing splst. 1966-75; mgr. pricing (respons. for negotiation of maj. cost proposals B-1 pgm., supvr. 50 employees) 1975-80; applications engr. CTS Keene, Paso Robles (design custom elec. components) 1981; real estate atty. Polin-Truchan & Cooper, San Luis Obispo 1982--; in-house instr. num. classes Rockwell Intl. 1960-80; honors: Alpha Kappa Psi 1966; listed Who's Who in Am. Law (2d ed.); mem. Am., Calif. and San Luis Obispo bar assns.; Nat., Calif., San Luis Obispo and Scenic Coast realty bds.; Lions; Elks; San Luis Obispo CofC; coauthor: paper, Radiography of one to five inch thick beryllium sections (using med. techniques in an indsl. application- Bucky/ Potter Grids, etc.); mil: cpl. E-4 USMCR 1959-65; Republican; Congregational; rec: local politics, painting, skiing. Res: 1975 8th St Los Osos 93402 Ofc: Polin-Truchan & Cooper, 486 Marsh St San Luis Obispo 93401

MERRILL, GEORGE WILLIAM, mechanical engineer; b. Feb. 16, 1954, Dugway, Utah; s. George Wynn and Lou Ella (Boyd) M.; edn: BSME, San Diego State Univ. 1977; Reg. Profl. Engr., Calif. 1981. Career: research asst. Naval Oceanographic Systems Ctr. (NOSC), San Diego 1976-77; mech. engr. Mare Island Naval Shipyard, Vallejo 1978--; senior mech. engr. M T M Consulting Engrs., Sonoma 1982--; awards: Spl. Achiev. Awd. (1982), Sustained Superior Performance (1983), Dept. of the Navy; mem: Am. Soc. of Mech. Engr.; Soc. of Automotive Engrs.; Calif. Acad. of Sci.; Nat. Geographic Soc.; Republican; rec: electronics, photog. Res: 105 Foothill Blvd Napa 94558 Ofc: Mare Island Naval Shipyard, Code 442, Stop 032, Vallejo 94592

MERRILL, THOMAS ST. JOHN, ophthalmic photographer; b. Feb. 21, 1946, Jersey City, NJ; s. Willard St. John and Frances Minnie (Havlieck) Merrill; edn: Fairleigh Dickenson Univ., 1963-64; Germain School of Photog., 1967-68; m. Marie Knoetig, Mar. 19, 1967; chil: Monica M., b. 1971; Michelle S., b. 1974. Career: photographer, Veteran's Adminstrn. Hosp., NY, 1967; dir., Manhattan Eye. Ear and Throat Hosp., NYC, 1967-70; medical photographer, Don Allen Studio, NYC, 1970-71; chief ophthalmic photographer, Mt. Sinai Sch. of Medicine, NYC, 1971-76; Univ. of Calif., Irvine, Calif., 1976---; instr., Biological Photo. Assn. Internatl. meeting, 1982. Mem: Biological Photographic Assn., bd. dirs.; Ophthalmic Photographers Soc., bd. dirs.; VFW, life mem. Works: photographs used worldwide in medical lectures, various journal articles. Mil: Sp/4, US Army, 1964-67; Vietnam Service. Lutheran. Rec: camping, fishing, motorcycling. Res: 4395 Goldenrod Ct., Chino 91710; Office: UCI Dept. of Ophthalmology, Irvine 92717.

MERRYMAN, CRYSTAL C., graphic arts executive; b. Feb.11, 1945, San Diego: d. Victor J. and Shirley C. (Hatter) Czerkas; m. M.B. "Det" Merryman, June 20, 1964; 1 d. Ashley Krista b. 1968; edn: stu. CSU Los Angeles 1962-64; AA, Grossmont Comm. Coll. 1977; BA in journ., w/distinction CSU San Diego 1979. Career: media buyer Hubbert & Assoc. Advt. Inc. 1964-66; self empl. as asst. pub. of polit. hist. text. 1967-68; advt. mgr. Central Fed. Savings 1971-74; advt. cons. 1974-78; pres./gen. mgr. Eucalyptus Productions Inc. (typesetting and graphic arts firm) , San Diego 1978--; guest spkr., Journ. Dept., CSU San Diego; honors: company won 2 awards for typesetting excellence, Nat. Type X Expo., 1983, NYC (only S.D. firm and one of only four Calif. cos. honored); mem. Citizens Adv. Council, East Co. Perf. Arts Ctr. 1981-84, Long Range Adv. Plnng. Com. 1984; mem: Internat. Printing Week Orgnl. Com. 1984, Printing Indus. of Am. Inc., San Diego Employers Assn.; orgns: East County Perf. Arts Center (past pres ; bd. dirs. Curtain Raisers 1978); v.p. S.D. Sym. Pops Assn.; S.D. Jr. Theatre Adminstry. Com., bd. dirs. L.A. Chamber Orch. 1982-83; mem. S.D. Sym. Assn., S.D. Opera Assn., English Speaking Union, Friends of Journalism SDSU; Democrat; Catholic; rec: antiques, travel. Res: 9105 Molly Woods Ave La Mesa 92041 Ofc: Eucalyptus Productions Inc. 3678 Fifth Ave San Diego 92103

MERRYMAN, MICHAEL B. "Det", publisher; b. Jan. 7, 1942, Los Angeles; s. Clarence B. and Jayne (Stidger) M.; m. Crystal C. Czerkas, June 20, 1964; 1 dau. Ashley Krista, b. 1968; edn: CSU Los Angeles 1958-63. Career: var. pos. in political admin. & mktg. incl. exec. dir. Calif. Democratic State Central Com. (2 yrs.), 1968-78; pres. publishing & mktg. co. (nine statewide publs.) 1978-82; pres. Applause Mag., San Diego 1972-82; v.p./ dir./ publisher Performing Arts Network 1981--; v.p./ dir./ CFO Eucalyptus Prodns., Inical presenter, through M.B.M. Ent.; mem: Ctr. for World Music; Curtain Raisers; Festival for the Californias; SDSU. Arts. Council (bd.); S.D. Civic Light Opera; S.D. Opera Assn. and Galaxy Steering Com.; S.D. Pops Assn. (pres.); S.D. Repertory Theatre; S.D. Sym. Assn.; past mem: Alliance of Calif. Arts Council (pres.), Calif. Confedn. of the Arts (pres.), Coll. Park Hosp. adv. bd., COMBO (bd.), L.A. Chamber Orchestra (bd.), Old Globe Theatre (ROP adv. bd.); Democrat; Catholic; rec: theatre, sports, golf. Res: 9105 Molly Woods Ave La Mesa 92041 Oc: 3680 Fifth Ave San Diego 92103

MESKE, ERICH V(INCENT), real estate broker; b. June 9, 1913, Bakersfield; s. Joseph and Mary (Kefer) M.; edn: BS, UC Berkeley 1941; MS, San Jose State Univ. 1964; Real Estate Cert., UC Berkeley Ext. 1963; lic. R.E. Broker, Calif. 1964. Career: sales clk., dept. mgr., asst. buyer Mens Clothing Depts. Hale Bros. (now Broadway stores), San Francisco; asst. mgr. Smiths, Oakland; accts. payable Hales, Smiths, Roos Brothers (now Atkins) dept. stores in Berkeley, Oakland, 1941-42; engr. US Engineering Dept., Honolulu HI; indsl. engr. Columbia Steel Co., Pittsburg, Ca. 1943; engr. US Dept. Engring., S.F. & Oakland, 1944-46; real estate appraiser Contra Costa County, 1959-63, Federal Housing Adminstrn., S.F. 1964-70; rehabilitation & codes spls. Dept. Housing & Urban Devel., L.A. 1970-76; cons. 1970-76; awards: sev. cash awards FHA and HUD; Commendn., L.A. County Bd. of Supvrs. 1976; mem. Sierra Club (life) 1948-; Democrat; rec: oil painting. Address: POB 2551 Redding 960999

MESNICK, RICHARD, training director; b. Oct. 16, 1943, Los Angeles; s. Charles and Dora Mesnick; m. Harlene Goldberg, July 4, 1973; 1 dau. Wendy, b. 1967; edn: BA, UCLA 1966, MBA, 1969. Career: tchr. secondary sch., Oakwood Pvt. Sch. 1969-71; mgmt devel splst. Mattel Toys 1971-73; dir. of tng. Ernest & Julio Gallo Winery, Los Angeles; cons., curriculum Mktg. Dept., Univ. of Va.; mem: Nat. Soc. of Sales Tng. & Devel.; ASTD; Big Brothers; Nat. Racquet Ball Assn.; publs: Consultative Selling Paper (1982), motivational seminar; Jewish; rec: racquet sports, travel. Res: 25 Northstar 3, Marina del Rey 90291 Ofc: Ernest & Julio Gallo Winery, 2650 Commerce Way Los Angeles 90040

MESSINEO, S. BERNARD, metallurgical engineer; b. Feb. 19, 1923, Turtle Creek, Penn.; s. Samuel and Margaret Marie (Franciullo) M.; m. Dolores M. Soltis, June 5, 1948; children: Diana Marie, b. 1949; James Arthur, b. 1956; Bernard Alan, b. 1953; Carol Ann, b. 1961; edn: BS, honors, Univ. of Pittsburgh 1949; MBA, Pepperdine Univ. 1971-72. Career: var. metallurgical pos. Wheeling Steel Corp., Wheeling, W. Va. 1949-66; with Kaiser Steel Corp. 1966-83, as metallurgical engr./supvr., supt. Metallurgy, supt. Tech. Svc., mgr. Quality Control, Claims mgr., supt. of Foundry, mgr. Tin Mill Tech.; metallurgical cons. Con Zinc Riotinto (CRA) 1984; chief metallurgist Pacific Steel Co., Fontana 1984--; var. seminars New Holland Inc. (1976), Reliance Steel (1975), Rohr Aircraft 1973, 74; guest lectr. Southwest Coll.; presented paper, High Strength, Low Alloy Steel for the Construction Industry, ASM Golden Gate Sem. 1968; honors: Sigma Tau 1948, Sigma Gamma Epsilon 1948; mem: Am. Soc. for Metals; Am. Iron & Steel Inst.; Am. Soc. for Testing Materials; American Legion; Knights of Columbus; VFW; Univ. of Pitts. Alumni Assn. of L.A.; patent: A Method of Producing Tin Plate for Lithography w/ direct printed UV cured inks, 1984; mil: aviation machinist mate 1/c USN Air Corps 1942-46, Air Medal, GCM, European Campaign, Am. Campaign, Victory Medal; Republican; Catholic; rec: desert fauna, swimming, hiking. Res: 1694 Shamrock Ave Upland 91786 Ofc: Pacific Steel Co., POB 217 Fontana 92335

MESTAD, ORVILLE LAVERNE, dentist; b. Mar. 22, 1923, Decorah, Iowa; s. Clarence Benjamin and Edna Belinda (Larsen) M.; m. Shirley, July 20, 1948; children: Cynthia Ann, b. 1955; Ronald Matthew, b. 1956;edn: BS, USC 1949; DDS, USC Sch. of Dentistry 1953. Career: pvt. practice dentistry, self-empl., pres. ORVCO Corp.; clin. instr. USC Sch. of Destistry 1953-57; organizer/ chmn./ dir. Foothill Independent Bank; dir. Citrus Coll. Found.; dir./ v.chmn. Foothill Presbyterian Hosp. 1972-83; honors: Alpha Tau Epsilon, La Touche Award operative excellence, USC (1953), exceptional svc. awd. Foothill Presbyterian Hosp. 1972-82; mem: Am. Dental Assn.; San Gabriel Dental Soc.; Acad. of Dentistry, Odontic Seminar, USC; Arcadia Lions; mil: US Army 1943 45, Bronze Star; Republican; Presbyterian (Elder); rec; snow skiing, rock climbing, flying. Res: 1144 Indian Springs Dr Glendora 91740

METCALF, ROBERT J(ack), securities firm chief executive; b. May 25, 1938, Vernal, Utah; s. Robert Andrew and LaRue Pack (Morgan) M.; m. Heather Compson, Mar. 25, 1970; children: Eric, b. 1962, Sean, b. 1965; edn: stu. N. Mex. Mil. Inst. 1956, El Camino Jr. Coll. 1957; BS in fin., UCLA 1961. Career: co-founder, CEO, chmn. bd. Value Equities, San Diego 1983--; mem. La Jolla Contemporary Art Mus.; L.D.S.; rec: running, skiing, handball. Res: 347 Dunemere Dr. La Jolla 92037 Ofc: Value Equities 9191 Towne Centre Dr San Diego 92122

METCHO, MARY TRUE, psychotherapist; b. Apr. 15, 1933, Fairplay, Mo.; d. Bert G. and Flora (Davis) True; m. John Lindblad, 1952, div. 1976; m. 2d. John Metcho, Feb. 26, 1984; children: Michael, b. 1954; Lawrence, b. 1960; Jennifer,b. 1966; edn: UC Berkeley 1950-52; BA, Sonoma State Univ. 1972; MSW, CSU Sacto. 1975; LCSW; MFCC; ACSW; Cert. Hypnotherapist; Cert. Reichian Therapy. Career: State of Calif. Veterans Home 1975-79; Chrysalis Assoc. 1979-81; currently, pvt. practice psychotherapist & cons., True Assoc., Berkeley; spkr. & sem. pgms. on stress mgmt.; mem: Nat. Spkrs. Assn.; No. Calif. Hypnosis Soc.; Republican; Unity; rec: art- abstract expressionism, metaphysics. Res: 2 Skander Ct Pleasant Hill 94523 Ofc: True Associates, 1623A Martin Luther King Jr Way, Berkeley 94709

METTLER, RUBEN FREDERICK, manufacturing and electronics co. executive; b. Feb. 23, 1924, Shafter; s. Henry Frederick and Lydia Mettler; m. Donna Jean Smith, May 1, 1955; two sons: Matthew, Daniel; edn: BS in E.E., Calif. Inst. of Tech. 1944, MS, 1947, PhD, elec. & aero. eng., 1949. Career: asso. div. dir. systems research and devel. Hughes Aircraft Co. 1949-54; spl. cons. to asst. sec. def. 1954-55; asst. gen. mgr. guided missile research div. Ramo-Wooldridge Corp. 1955-58 pres. TRW Space Technology Labs. (Ramo-Woodlridge merged with Thompson Prods. in 1958 forming TRW) 1958-65; pres. TRW Systems Group 1965-68; asst. pres. TRW Inc. 1968-69; pres. TRW Inc. 1969-77, chmn. of bd. and CEO, 1977--; dir: BankAm. Corp., Merck & Co. Inc.; v.chmn. bd. trustees Calif. Inst. of Tech.; trustee Cleveland Clinic Found.; trustee Com. for Economic Devel.; chmn. The Business Roundtable; trustee The Conference Board; dir. Nat. Action Council for Minorities in Engineering Inc.; mem. Pres. Reagan's Nat. Productivity Adv. Com.; honors: Sigma Xi, Eta Kappa Nu, Tau Beta Pi, Theta Xi; mem: Nat. Acad. of Engring., Fellow IEEE, Sci. Research Soc. of Am., Fellow Am. Inst. of Aero. and Astro.; honors: Keta Kappa Nu award for Nation's Most Outstanding Young Electrical Engr. 1954; one of Ten Outstanding Young Men in Am. US Jaycees; Engring. Socs. of So. Calif. Engineer of the Year 1964; CalTech Alumni Disting. Svc. Awd. 1966; Nat. Human Rels. Awd., NCCJ 1979; hon. DHL, Baldwin-Wallace Coll. 1980; Merit. Civilian Service Awd., Dept. of Def. 1969; Excellence in Mgmt. Awd. Industry Week mag. 1979; patents: Rocket Launch Control Sys. (1954), Aircraft Control Sys. (1959), oil well logging sys.; Ofc: TRW Inc. One Space Park, Redondo Beach 90278

METZGER, TIMOTHY PAUL, computer operations executive; b. June 19, 1954, St. Paul, Minn.; s. Paul F. and Marie M. (Behele) M.; m. Alice M. Cariaga; 1 child, Tashiana b. 1983; edn: BS in Indsl. Eng., Univ. of Iowa 1976; MS, I.E., Iowa State Univ. 1978; MBA in fin., Golden Gate Univ. 1984; Cert. Mfg. Eng. Calif. Career: graphic artist Key Mfg. Inc. Janesville, IA 1974-76; design engr. Universal Indus. Inc., Waterloo, IA 1973-76; mfg. engr. Winnebago Indus. Inc., Forest City, IA 1976-77; indsl. engr. Westinghouse Elec. Corp., Sunnyvale 1978-80; field svc. engr. Westinghouse Elec. Corp., Portland,

Ore. 1980-81; sr. mfg. engr. Westinghouse Elec. Corp., Sunnyvale 1981-83, ops. supr. Marine Div. computer op., 1983--; cons. in comp. appls. (data base) Integrated Computer Applications Corps. 1983-; mem. Soc. of Mfg. Engrs., Soc. of Automotive Engrs., Computer Automated Systems Assn.; coauthor El-Con (patented 1973), Universal Indus.; Republican; Lutheran; rec: pvt. pilot, skiing, golf. Res: 3359 Rocky Mtn Drive San Jose 95127 ofc: Westinghouse Electric Corp. 401 E. Hendy Ave Sunnyvale 94088

METZLER, YVONNE LEETE, travel agency owner; b. Jan. 25, 1930, Bishop; d. Ben Ford and Gladys Edna (Johnson) Leete; m. Richard Metzler, June 2, 1950; children: David, b. 1951; Regan, b. 1953; Erin, b. 1957; edn: UC Berkeley. Career: vocational instr. Ukiah Jr. Acad., Ukiah 1963-64; acct. W.W. Woodward, P.A./ Clarence White CPA, Ukiah 1971-73; partner/ owner Redwood Travel Agency, Ukiah 1973-76; owner/ mgr. A-1 Travel Planners, Ukiah 1976--; owner A-1 Travel Planners, Willits 1979--; mem: Ukiah Plnng. Commn. ; Ukiah CofC (pres. 1981, 1982); Ukiah Bus. & Profl. Womens Club 1964-79 (treas. 1977-8); Am. Soc. of Bus. & Profl. Womens Clubs 1968-9; Soroptimists (Ukiah pres. 1977-78); Am. Soc. of Travel Agents 1973-; Mendocino Co. CofC (dir. 1981); Republican (Central Com. 1979-80); Protestant; rec: travel. Res: 1112 W Standley St Ukiah 95482 Ofc: A-1 Travel Planners, 505 E Perkins St Ukiah 95482

MEYER, IVAH GENE, clincial social work consultant; b. Nov. 18, 1935, Decatur, Ill.; d. Anthony Joseph and Nona Alice (Gamble) Viccone; m. Richard Anthony Meyer; children: Steven Anthony, Stuart Allen, Scott Arthur; edn: grad., w/ distcn., Phoenix Coll. 1964; BS, honors, Ariz. State Univ. 1969; postgrad. wk., USC, PhD cand. US Internat. Univ. Career: soc. wkr. Florence Crittenton Maternity Home 1969; soc. wkr. Family Svc. of Phoenix 1970-73; faculty assoc. Ariz. St. Univ. Grad. Sch., Sch. of Soc. Wrk., Family Svc. of Pomona Valley 1973-80; supvr./ faculty assoc. USC Grad. Sch. of Soc. Wkr. & Pitzer Coll. Undergrad. Sch. of Psychology; founder Chino Counseling Ctr., pvt. practice; also, exec. dir. Soc. Svc. Dept. Christ Anglican Ch., Pomona and co-counselor with Dr. William Carson Thompson, Rector; honors: listed num. biographical refs.; mem: Nat. Assn. Cert. Soc. Wkrs.; NASW; Clin. Soc. of Soc. Wkrs.; Republican; Catholic; rec: needlepoint, gardening, entertaining. Res: 778 Via Montevideo Claremont 91711 Ofc: Chino Counseling Center, 12632 Central Ave Chino

MEYER, JEFFERY WILSON, agricultural chemicals sales executive; b. June 22, 1923, San Francisco; s. Wilson and Mabel (Wilson) M.; m. Janet Busse, Jan. 28, 1945; children: Pamela, b. 1949; Elizabeth, b. 1952; edn: BS, UC Coll. of Agric. 1948. Career: with Wilson & George Meyer & Co. 1948--: sales, Los Angeles 1948; mil. service 1950-52; mgr. of Coke Dept. WGM, San Francisco 1952; v.p. Agric. Dept. 1956; pres./ dir. 1959-; chmn. bd./ CEO/ pres. 1973-; bd. dirs. Barclays Bank of Calif. Mem: Calif. Acad. of Scis. (v.chmn.); Norwegian American CofC (past pres.); Point Reyes Bird Observatory (dir.); Internat. Fertilizer Assn.; Bohemian Club; Pacific-Union Club; Cercle de l'Union; St. Francis Yacht Club; Menlo Country Club; California Club; publs: underwater photos; mil: 1st lt. US Army 1942-52, active duty WWII and Korean War (5 yrs.), Combat Inf. Badge, Bronze Star, GC, Asia-Pac., Battle Star Luzon, US Theater, Jap. Occ., WWII Victory, Nat. Def., Phil. Presdtl. Unit Cit., Phil. Victory medal; Episcopal; sports fishing, operate 50' TS diesel. Res: 3880 Ralston Ave Hillsborough 94010 Ofc: Wilson & George Meyer & Co., 270 Lawrence Ave, So. San Francisco 94080

MEYER, MICHAEL LAURENCE HAROLD, entertainment executive, lawyer; b. May 3, 1957, Los Angeles; s. Marvin Burton and Nan Ryan (Ullman) Meyer; edn: dip., Phillips Acad., Andover 1974; cert., Pushkin Inst., Moscow 1977; BA, Amherst Coll. 1978; JD, USC Law Sch. 1981; admitted Calif. Bar 1981. Career: pres. Michael Meyer & Assocs., personal mgmt. & prodn., personal mgr /dir. bus. affairs/dir. dramatic devel. Larry A. Thompson Org. 1981--; editor-in-chief Entertainment, Publishing & Arts Handbook (1983-), Entertainment Law Journal (1981-3); prof. USC/CCE (Entertainment Tax Symposium, and The Bus. Side of Entertainment). Honors: Shattuck Award, USC Law Sch. Mem: Calif., Beverly Hills, Century City Bar Assns., Phi Alpha Delta Law frat.; clubs: Magic Castle, Pips. Publs: mag. arts.; Democrat; Jewish; rec: magic, tennis. Res: 704 N. Beverly Dr. Beverly Hills 90210 Ofc: Michael Meyer & Associates, 9665 Wilshire Blvd, Ste. 400, Beverly Hills 90212

MEYERS, JOHN OWEN, III, lawyer; b. Sept. 21, 1947, Detroit, Mich.; s. John O. and Elizabeth J. (Marcotte) M.; m. Reta B., May 18, 1969; edn: BA, San Diego State Univ. 1970; JD, Univ. of San Diego 1973; admitted to practice, State Bar of Calif. 1973. Career: deputy public defender Imperial County. 1971-74, deputy dist. atty. Imperial County 1974; atty., Imperial County 1976-77; assoc. atty. Reich, Adell, Crost & Perry, Pomona 1977-79; atty. John Owen Meyers A Profl. Law Corp., Pomona 1979--; dean & proaf. Am. Coll. of Law, Anaheim; secty. Am. Coll. of Law Corp.; mem: Calif. Trial Lawyer Assn.; E. L.A. Co. Bar Assn.; Jaycees, El Centro (pres. 1976); chmn. Imperial Co. Com. on Substance Abuse 1976; rec: writing, skiing. Res: 504 Via Florida San Clemente 92671 Ofc: John Owen Meyers, APLC, 300 S Park, Ste 499, Pomona 91766

MEYSENBURG, JOHN HAROLD, electronic engineer; b. Dec. 2, 1934, Primrose, Nebr.; s. Harold Peter and Agnes Gertrude (Puetz) M.; m. Mary Ann Augustine, June 17, 1967; children: Peter b. 1971, Amy b. 1976; edn: Radio Engring. Inst. 1954-55, Ricker Coll. 1958, Pasadena City Coll. 1967-71. Career: tech. rep. field engr. Philco Corp. 1959-61; senior tech. TRW Semiconductors 1961-64; sr. electronic tech. in R & D, Quality Control (Project Apollo Spacecraft), Allen Jones Electronics, 1964-65; sr. electronic tech. TRW System, 1965-67; electronic engr. (test asst.) Jet Propulsion Lab., 1967--: helped develop: High Power Solid State Microwave Switch (1968), Micromin and NASA Std. Transponder (1969-75), RF Test System (1975), Transmitter for Total Hip Joint Biotelemetry System (1980), Solid State X Band Transmitter (1981), ISPM Down Converter (1980-81); honors: mem. of the JPL Flight Team to deliver an X-band Down Converter to the Galileo Spacecraft; 1953 Bausch & Lomb Hon. Science Award; co-inventor on a patent for Beam Lead Integrated Circuit Test Fixture (1974); 3d. place (color slides - subject lighting), L.A. Photog. Center (1956); Boy Scouts of Am. counsellor; mil: Airman 2/c 1954-59, GCM; Democrat; Catholic; rec: photog., radio expt. Res: 6725 Brentmead Ave Arcadia 91006 Ofc: Jet Propulsion Laboratory 4800 Oak Grove Dr Pasadena 91009

MICHAELS, ANDREA ELIZABETH, entertainment production agency executive; b. Dec. 14, 1943, Rab, Yugoslavia, nat. 1954; d. Peter and Lelja Louise (Kauders) Gerson; 1 son: Jonathan Brian, b. 1970; edn: BA, UCLA 1974. Career: v.p. Ron Rubin Prodns., Santa Monica 1973--; bd. dirs. Meeting Planners Internat. 1983-84; mem. chmn. Nat. Assn. of Catering Execs. 1982 84; bd. dirs. Hotel Sales Mgmt. Assn. 1983; write poetry/ short stories (pvt. pub.); breed, race and show horses; Jewish. Res: 3040 Madler Action 93510 Ofc: Ron Rubin Productions, 2901 Wilshire Blvd, Ste 441, Santa Monica 90403

MICHAELS, MICHAEL DANIEL, lawyer; b. Sept. 1, 1954, Los Angeles; s. Michael Daniel and Olga Milicent (Petkovich) M.; edn: BA, magna cum laude, USC 1976; JD, Loyola Univ., L.A. 1979; admitted to State Bar of Calif. 1981. Career: law clerk Hon. Clarke E. Stephens, Assoc. Justice of Calif. Court of Appeal (2d Dist.) Los Angeles 1981-82; assoc. atty. Good & Novack, Pasadena 1982--; honors: Phi Beta Kappa; Phi Kappa Phi; mem: Am., Calif. Bar Assns.; Calif. Trial Lawyers Assn.; Plaintiff Trial Lawyers Assn. of L.A.; YMCA; Democrat (Californians for Brown 1978; resrch. for debates w/ Evelle Younger, Brown Campaign, 1978); Serbian Orthodox; rec: dist. running, volleyball, softball. Res: 1621 S Pomona Ave, D 23, Fullerton 92632 Ofc: Good & Novack, 35 S Raymond Ave, Ste 200, Pasadena 91105

MICHAELI, JOHN EDWARD, communications executive; b. Nov. 20, Los Angeles; s. John Francis and Anna Gertrude (LaVelle) M.; m. Mary Ann Lee, Sept. 1, 1984; edn: BA, Calif. State Univ. 165, MA, 1980. Career: publicist, MGM, 1965-67; publicist, then dir. of publicity & advtg.; currently VP-Communications, Hanna-Barbera Productions, 1967--; recipient num. honors for public service; mem. Acad. of Motion Picture Arts & Scis., Acad. of TV Arts & Scis., Publicists Guild, SDT; mil: USCG. Ofc: Hanna-Barbera, 3400 Cahunga Blvd Los Angeles 90068

MICHAUD, GERALD FREDRICK, advertising agency creative director; b. June 16, 1949, Rochester, NY; s. Eric Joseph and Dorothy Celeste (Daigle) M.; m. Jennifer Solomon, May 1, 1982; edn: BA philos., magna cum laude, Univ. of Detroit 1971, MA, relig. studies, 1976; cert. Internat. Inst. of Relig. Communications, New Orleans 1975; St. John's Provincial Seminary, Plymouth, Mich. 19727-75. Career: editor, Pastoral Life mag., Canfield, Oh. 1972; promotion dir. Alba House Communications, Canfield 1972; editor, Media Focus, Dearborn, Mich. 1973-76; public relations staff, Youth for Understanding, Ann Arbor, Mich. 1977-79; editor, EDM Digest, Farmington, Mich. 1978-80; creative director, Cal-Ad Company, Burbank, Calif. 1980-82, (name chg.) Dimon & Associates, 1982--; cons. to End Hunger Network, L.A.; cons. to The Resource (bus. netwkg. directory), Toluca Lake; honors: Eagle Scout 1966, John C. Vismara Philosophy Award 1972, Alpha Sigma Nu Nat. Jesuit Hon. Soc. 1972; mem: Art Directors of Los Angeles, Nat. Assn. of Printers & Lithographers, Detroit Archdiocesan Pastoral Council 1974-75; orgns: End Hunger Network, The Hunger Project, The Rainbow Circle, Inst. for Synergy in Action, Design for a Positive Future; works: filmstrip pgms: Friendship with God, Continuing the Ministry of Jesus, Christians & Politics, (1972); Democrat; Catholic (mem. Society of St. Paul religious order 1967-75); rec: tennis, rel. studies. Res: 443 S. Niagara Burbank 91505 Ofc: Dimon & Assocs. 3001 N. San Fernando Blvd 91505

MICHELETTI, MICHAEL JAMES, tele-communication contractor, real estate broker; b. Oct. 29, 1947, San Francisco; s. George Peter and Ida Irene (Ribero) M.; m. Ophelia Butler; children: Darcy, b. 1971, O'Landa, b. 1980, Mardono, b. 1982, Veronica, b. 1984; edn: BA, high honors, UC Riverside 1970; MBA, San Jose State Univ. 1980. Career: with Pacific Tel. Co. 1970-77; instr. CSUSJ; broker/owner Monmeth Properties, 1977-80; owner Sacramento Prewire Co., Sacto. 1980--; broker/owner Comwell Real Estate, Sacto. 1981--; instr. Yuba Coll. 1984; mem. Calif. Contractors License Bd., Nat. Bd. of Realtors; publs: art. in Financial Stable Mgmt. Res: 1504 Columbia Dr Woodland 95695 Ofc: Sacramento Prewire Co. 8170 Belvedere Dr Sacramento 95826

MICHIE, BARBARA E., insurance agent; b. Sept. 23, 1944, Colman, S.Dak.; d. C.R. and Vivian (Rosen) Stratton; m. A. Douglas Michie; children: Stewart; Jeffery; Andrew; Matthew; edn: BA, Univ. of So. Dakota 1966. Career: soc. wkr. Los Angeles & San Diego Cos. 1966-73; salesman/ makeup artist Ambiaga Inc. 1977-79; territory salesman Ried & Sibell 1979-81; founder/prin. Michie Ins. Agency 1982--; mem: Nat. Assn. of Ins. Women; Nat. Assn. of Profl. Saleswomen; Experience Unltd.; orgns: Widow Workshop, Widow Persons Bureau, Alumni Resources; Lutheran; rec: boating, travel. Address: Michie Insurance Agency, 19 Ray Ct Danville 94526

MICKEY, NORMAN LEE, social work executive and video dating service owner; b. Oct. 2, 1939, Antioch, Calif.; s. James Raymond and Jennie Virginia (Moglie) M.; m. Deanna Rolerson, 1961, div. 1968; 1 dau: Cathy, b. 1965; edn: BA, psy., San Jose State Coll. 1964; AA, Diablo Valley Coll. 1959. Career: founder/ owner/ dir. Video Introductions, Concord 1977--; soc. wrk. supvr. Contra Costa Soc. Svc. Dept. 1969--; soc. wkr. Contra Costa Co. Soc. Svc. Dept., Pittsburg & Pleasant Hill 1964-69; mem: Contra Costa Co. Central Labor Council (exec. bd. 1972-75, del. 1970-72); Soc. Svc. Union S.E.I.U., AFL-CIO (Contra Costa Co. chpt., founding pres. 1967-68); Contra Costa Housing Authority tenant appeal referee 71-81; author/pub. Romantic Reminders (Copyright 1980). Res: 420 Brookside Dr Antioch 94509 Ofc: Video Introductions, 1810 C Willow Pass Rd Concord 94520

MIDDLETON, CHARLES BAKER, clergyman/counselor; b. Jan. 20, 1908, Gibtown, Tx.; s. Robert and Olive Clarinda (Gregg) M.; m. Alma Margaret McFarlen, Oct. 10, 1926; 1 dau. Margaret Charlene; edn: dip. in Auctioneering, Ft. Smith, Ark. Auction Sch. 1965; AA in real estate, San Diego City Coll. 1972; BA in Bible, National Christian Univ. 1974; PhD in human behav., La Jolla Univ. 1979; 9 hon. awards, var. instns., 1972-80. Career: minister, Church of Christ, 1932-- in Texas, Okla., Ark., New Mex. 1932-41, Wyo., Ida., Mont., Tex., Ariz. 1941-51; has preached every Sunday for 46 years (1938-); has helped estab. num. churches in Texas, Calif., and Mont.; minister, counselor, auctioneer, real estate broker, 1965--; mem. So. Assn. of Marriage Counslors, National Auctioneers Assn., Calif. Assn. of Realtors; publs: printed and radio sermons on the Church, Marriage, Home; Middleton-George debate on 7th-Day Adventism; Republican; Rec: 4465 36th St San Diego 92116 Ofc: Church of Christ, 7277 Fulton St San Diego 92116

MIDLAM, KEVIN WAYNE, lawyer; b. Nov. 8, 1939, Bluffton, Ohio; s. Donald Sheldon and Mildred Pauleyne (Pitzen) M.; div.; children: Victoria, b.1970; Christopher, b. 1972; edn: BS, Willamette Univ. 1961; JD, Willamette Univ. Coll. of Law 1963; admitted to State Bar of Calif. 1964. Career: deputy city atty., San Diego 1964-65; assoc./ partner, pvt. practice Johnson & Midlam 1965-78, assoc. & adj. prof. Western State Coll. of Law and sd Coll. of Law 1973-77; partner Ault, Midlam & Deuprey 1978--; mem: San Diego Co. Bar Assn. (bd. dirs. 1976-78, treas./ pres. 1978); State Bar of Calif. (bd. gov. 1979-82, v.p. 1982); mem: Am., Calif. & San Diego Co. Bar Assns.; Fellows of Am. Bar; San Diego Co. Regl. Criminal Justice Adv. Bd. (chmn. 1975-76); Boy Scouts of Am. (San Diego Co. Council); 1st United Methodist Ch. (admin. bd. 1977-79, 1981-); Republican; Methodist; rec: swimming, golf, travel. Res: 325 S Sierra St, 43, Solana Beach Ofc: Ault, Midlam & Deuprey, 5030 Camino de la Siesta San Diego 92108

MIECKE, GARY G, engineer/manager; b. March 22, 1946, Buffalo, NY; s. Erwin A. and Ella (Duell) Miecke, Edn. A.A. L.A.C.C. 1972 B.A. Cal Poly Pomona 1976. Career: engineer/manager, Selective Services Corp. 1972--; president Omni Corporation 1975---; consulting. Awards: Professional Engineer. Mem: Inst. of Ind. Engineering. Research/Consulting for Easter Seal Foundation, Orange CA. Mil: Sgt. Army 1967-69 Vietnam. Rec: sailing, swimming. Res: P.O. Box 17697, Los Angeles 90017; Office: Selective Services, P.O. Box 17697, Los Angeles 90017.

MIELKE, CLARENCE HAROLD, JR., physician; b. June 18, 1936, Spokane, Wash.; s. Clarence Harold and Marie Katherine (Gillespie) M.; m. Marcia Rose, July 5, 1964; children: Elisa, b. 1966; John, b. 1968; Kristina b, 1970; edn: BS, Wash. State Univ. 1958; MD, Univ. of Louisville 1963; postgrad. internal med., UC San Francisco 1967, hematology, USC 1968, Tufts Univ. 1969-70. Career: asst. prof. med.: USC 1967-68; Tufts New Eng. Med. Ctr. 1968-71; UC San Francisco 1971-80; assoc. prof. med. UC San Francisco 1980--; chief hematology research Pacific Med. Ctr. 1981--; co-dir. Inst. Cancer Research 1983--; ed. Journal Clinical Apheresis; dir. Hematology Immunology Lab. and Blood Bank Medical Research Inst.; mem: Fellow Am. Coll. of Physicians; Fellow Internat. Soc. of Hematology; Fellow Am. Coll. of Angiology; Am. Soc. of Hematology; Am. Heart Assn.; AHA Council on Thrombosis; Am., Calif. Socs. Internal Med.; Calif., San Francisco Med. Socs.; author: approx. 100 medical related articles two books, and contbr. sev. books, ed.; mil: maj. USAR 1967-76; Democrat; Episcopal; rec: wine making, hunting, fishing. Res: 129 Kinross Dr San Rafael 94901 Ofc: Pacific Medical Center, POB 7999 San Francisco 94920

MIILU, JOHN RAYMOND, lawyer; b. July 2, 1938, Berkeley; s. Edwin Francis and Jessie Marion (Milliken) M.; edn: AB, UC Santa Barbara 1960; JD, UC Berkeley Boalt Hall 1963; admitted to practice, var. Fed. Cts., State Bar of Calif. 1964. Career: pvt. practice law, Oakland and Sunnyvale 1964-68; chief staff atty. The St. Paul Companies, San Francisco 2968-73; counsel Bechtel Corp., S.F. & Wash. DC 1977-79; div. counsel/ asst. secty. Bechtel Power Corp., Norwalk 1979--; exec. v.chmn. Am. Bar Assn. Forum Com. on the Constrn. Industry 1978; lectr. Georgetown Univ. Internat. Investment Negotiation Ctr.; mem. Internat., Am., Calif. and Los Angeles Co. bar assns.; Republican; rec: sailing, travel. Res: 16715 Castaway Ln Huntington Beach 92649 Ofc: Bechtel Power Corp., 12400 E Imperial Hwoy Norwalk 90650

MIKALSON, ROY G., college president; b. July 21, 1921, Eureka, MT; s. Lawrence and Barbara Mikalson; Edn: BA, Univ. Wash., 1947; MA, 1948; PhD, Univ. Calif. Berkeley, 1964; m. Eva M. Johnson, July 31, 1949, Missoula, MT; chil: Steven A., b. 1950; Barbara G. (Brownstne), b. 1953; Jeffrey R., b. 1949; Thomas L., b. 1960. Career: instructor, Montana Univ., Missoula, 1948-49; instr., Lower Columbia Coll., Longview, WA, 1950-62; Dean of evening coll., Coll. of Marin, Kentfield, CA, 1964-66; pres., Clackemas Community Coll., Oregon City, OR, 1966-68; pres., Modesto Jr. Coll., 1968-71; supt., pres., Santa Rosa Jr. Coll., 1971---; YMCA bd. dirs.; Family Information Center bd. dir.; bd. dirs., Cal. Community Colleges Chief Exec. Officers. Mil: served AUS, Infantry, 1940-45, So. Pacific; 7 campaigns, 4 decorations. Mem: Elks, Rotary International; Commonwealth Club. Rec: writing, hiking, golf, swimming. Res: 4050 Alta Vista, Santa Rosa; Office: 1501 Mendocino Ave., Santa Rosa 95401.

MIKESELL, MARY JANE, communication specialist; b. Oct. 29, 1943, Rockledge, Fla.; d. John and Mary Christine (Leighty) Wagner; edn: BA, CSU Northridge 1967; MA, Pacific Oaks Coll. 1980; PhD Cand., California Graduate Inst., 1983-; Calif. lic. (MFCC) Marriage, Family, Child Counselor. Career: tchr. Los Angeles Unifiec, LA 1966-69; photo lab. dir. Oceanograficos de Honduras, Roatan, Honduras, C.A., 1969-70; supr. LA Life Insurance Co., 1970-72; customer serv. rep. Beverly Hills Fed. S&L, B.H. 1972-73; staff CSU Northridge 1974-78; hd. of ofc. svcs. Pacific Oaks Coll., Pasadena 1978-79; prodn. supr. Frito-Lay Inc., LA 1979-81; circulation supr. Daily News, Van Nuys 1981-82; ednl. therapist/Intern MFCC, Barr Counseling Ctr. and Victory-Tampa Psychol. Ctr., 1982--; projects coord. Rockey & Assoc., Brentwood 1983--; consult, lecture, tch., 1973--; Olympic Project coord. Gold Medal Bobsled Team, 1983-84; press staff ATAS Emmy Awards ceremonies, 1983; staff Southland Olympic News Bur. 1983-; staff, 7-11/Bicycling Mag. Internat. Grand Prix Cycling race, 1983; Sub-Center Steward at the 1984 Water Polo Venue at Pepperdine-Press ops.; mem: Nat. Assn. for Female Execs., AAUW, Planetary Soc., Calif. Scholarship Fedn.; CSUN Anthropol. Club 1975-77; works: photog. exhib. Canoga Park Mission Gal. (1966), all photos for the Soo Yin Trade Co. catalog (1977), brochure photos for Miss China Town (1977), Archealogy Today (multi-media presentation); Democrat (San Fernando Valley vol.); Judeo-Christian; rec: photog., writing, amateur laser research. res: 14318 Tiara, 4, Van Nuys 91401 Ofc: Carlson, rockey & Assoc. 11777 San Vicente, Ste 907, Los Angees 90049; Barr Counseling Ctr. 5955 De Soto Woodland Hills 91367

MIKKELSEN, JUANITA LESLIE HILL, ranch owner; b. July 4, 1926, Fresno; d. Leopold Pete and Eveline Ily (Osterode) Hill; div.; two children: Sheila Karen, b. 1950; John Paul, b. 1952; edn: Holmby Coll., L.A. 1943-44; lic. real estate sales, Calif. 1965. Career: asst. bookeepear, Family Creamery 1942-46; co- owner/ mgr. Mikkelsen Butane Ce. 1949-62; real estate ssales 1965-82; antique shop owner 1970-75; owner/ mgr. reantals 1972--; owner/ mgr. ranch 1975--; mem: Ladies Oriental Shrine of No. Calif.; Calif. Women for Agric.; Farm Bureau; Nat. Fedn. of Independent Bus.; Am. & Pacific Coast Quarter Horse Assns.; U.S. Equestrian Team; Senatorial Club; Pres. Task Force; Republican; Episcopal; rec: remodeling/ designing homes, animal training, civic affairs. Res: 34600 Road 140 Visalia 93291

MIKULICICH, NIKOLA MARIO, lawyer; b. Dec. 6, 1940, Berlin, Germany; s. George Frederick and Irmgard (Pravitz) M.; m. Joan, June 21, 1968; children: Nikola Jr. b. 1972, Catherine b. 1972; edn: BA, CSC Los Angeles 1963; LLB, JD, UCLA Sch. of Law 1966; admitted to State Bar of Calif. 1968. Career: atty. assoc. Anderson, Adams & Bacon, Rosemead, Ca. 1967-69; deputy dist. atty., Dist. Attorney's Ofc. County of Los Angeles, 1969--, current hd. Medicolegal Section; lectr. for Los Angeles DA's Speakers Bur. 1970-; advisor for DA's Office on medicolegal matters; mem. of the Joint LA Co. Bar and LA Co. Medical Assn. ad hoc Bio Ethics Com.; spkr. and cons. to BMQA, frequent lectr. var. med. groups; mem: San Gabriel Valley Bar Assn. 1968-69; Assn. of Deputy Dist. Attys. LA County 1972- (Bio Medical Ethics Com. 1982-); Calif. D.A. Assn. (chmn. Medicolegal Com.); LA County Select Citizens Com. on Life Support Policies; fmr. mem. S.G.V. Rotary, UCLA Law Sch. Alumni, PAD Law Frat.; Republican (past pres. CSULA chpt. Young Repubs.); Catholic; rec: pvt. pilot, skiing, skin diving. Res: 348 Paseo De Gracia Redondo Beach 90277 Ofc: LA County District Atty's Office 210 West Temple St Los Angeles 90012

MILAM, LARRY JOE, cosmetic and health care products co. president; b. July 10, 1945, Paris, Tenn.;s. Clarence G. and Abbess (Lax) M.; m. Judy Melton, Aug. 20, 1965; 1 son, Jason b. 1973; edn: BS, agri. edn., Univ. of Tenn. 1967; grad. wk. Univ. of Fla., Gainsville and Rollin Coll., Winter Park, 1980-81; desig. Agriculture Mgmt. Splst., USDA 1981. Career: tchr. Williamson Co. High Sch. 1967-69; national instr. Tradition Inc., Orlando, Fla. 1969, state dir.- Louisiana and Ark., 1970, divnl. sales adminstrn. Western (18 states) Div., Reno, Nev. 1970-71, divnl. sales adminstr. Central (15 states) Div., Indnpls. 1971-72; pres. Camelon Cosmetics Inc., Macon, Ga. 1973; pres. Koscot Cosmetics Inc., Orlando, Fla. 1973; pres. Group III Inc., Financial Consultants, Orlando 1972-74; pres. Pleasure Tours Internat. Inc., Orlando; pres. New Spirit Internat. Inc., St. Paul, Minn. 1980-81; founder/pres./ bd. chmn. New Spirit of America Inc. 1982--; bd. dirs. WeCare Products Inc., Kissimmee, Fla. 1979-80; recipient Outstanding Young Educator Award 1968, Williamson Co., Tenn. Jaycees; hon. mem. Phi Kappa Phi (1967), Businessman of the Week (1976), WHOO Radio; mem: San Dimas CofC, Am. Red Cross (Disaster Shelter mgr. 1979), past pres. Orlando Leadership Council; past dir. Junior Achievement Pgm. 1968-9; works: devel. unique cosmetic formulas; Democrat; Baptist; rec: numismatics, landscape design. Res: 130 E. Via Vaquero San Dimas 91773 Ofc: New Spirit of America Inc. 458 W Arrow Hwy San Dimas 91773

MILANES, DIONISIO RAMOS, real estate broker; b. Jan. 16, 1925, La Union, Philippines, nat. 1975; s. Esteban Rivera and Encarnacion (Ramos) M.; m. Nora Maja Gustilo, Dec. 3, 1960; children: Ferdinand b. 1961, Steven b. 1963, Madee b. 1968; edn: LLB, Far Eastern Univ., 1954; desig: atty. & counselor at law, Supreme Ct. of the P.I.; Calif. lic. Real Estate Broker; realtor, CAR, NAR, S.F. Bd. of Realtors; lic. Notary Public; reg. Income Tax Preparer. Career: practising atty., Manila, Phil. 1955-56; govt. atty., Civil Service Dept., Phil. 1956-68; coll. instr. Trinity College, Phil. (owned and mng. by Americans) 1963-68; tourist in US 1969; insurance underwriter, 1970; spl. investigator San Francisco Dept. of Social Services 1972-81, collections ofcr. 1982-83, eligibility appeals splst. 1983--; pres. Milanes Realty & Inv. Corp., 1979--; mem: SF Board of Realtors, Calif. Assn. of Realtors, Nat. Assn. of Realtors, Better Business Bur., US Chamber of Commerce, Filipino American Social Svcs. Employees Assn.; Episcopal; rec: fishing. Res: 21 Girard St San Francisco 94134 Ofc: Milanes Realty & Inv. Corp. 2527 San Bruno Ave San Francisco 94134

MILANI, JAMES EDWARD, dentist; b. Dec. 6, 1956, Greenbrae; s. Edward Wayne and Shirley May (De Maretti) M.; edn: BA, Univ. of the Pacific 1979; DDS, Univ. of Pacific Sch. of Dentistry 1982. Career: instr. fixed prosthodontics & dental anatomy Univ. of Pacific Sch. of Dentistry (1 yr.); pvt. practices, Belvedere and Lucerne; currently, solo group practice, Lucerne; pre-clin. instr. Univ. of Pacific Sch. of Dentistry 1982-83; honors: Am. Coll. of Stomatologic Surgeons 1982, Am. Acad. of Oral Pathology 1982; mem: Am. & Calif. Dental Assn.; Redwood Empire Dental Soc.; Lake County Health Council; Republican; Lutheran; rec: snow skiing, backpacking, golf. Res: 9631 Timberline Ct Kelseyville 95451 Ofc: 6075 Hwy 20, Lucerne 95458

MILAZZO, DAVID Y., architect; b. Feb. 27, 1945, Bakersfield; s. Anthony Alfred and Reeba Allen (Young)M.; m. Linda Gold, Aug. 21, 1968; 1 son, David Anthony, b. 1974; edn: AA, Bakersfield Jr. Coll. 1970; BA, Cal Poly State Univ.,S.L.O., 1974; cert. Nat. Council of Architectural Registration Bds. Career: draftsman/designer, Fisher & Wilde Architects, Ventura 1974-75f; Ken Sorensen Architect, Bakersfield, 1975-76; principal ptnr. in charge of design Clement/Milazzo & Assocs., 1976-83; Milazzo & Associates, Architects, 1983--; cons. to City of Bakersfield: Zoning Ordinance Review Adv. Com., Planning Commnr., Redevelopment Agcy. Design Rev. Bd.; mem. bd. dirs. Kern River Found.; awards: Golden Empire Chpt./AIA Design of Excellence award, 1981; Bakersfield CofC awards: Most Attractive Comml. Building (1982, 83), Most Attractive Comm. Landscaping (1982, 83); mem: Am. Inst. of Architects (corp.mem.), Golden Empire Chpt.; Downtown Business Assn. (bd. dirs.); Italian Heritage Dante Assn. (bd. dirs.); Pres.'s Assn. of CSU Bakersfield; works: primarily the design and constrn. of contemporary architecture; mil: s/sgt USAF 1965-69, decorated Vietnam, France; Republican; Prot.; rec: photog. Res: 2432 Spruce St Bakersfield 93301 Ofc: Milazzo & Assocs., Architects 1200 Truxtun Ave, Ste. 120, Bakersfield 93301

MILES, CARTER EARL, construction co. president; b. Sept. 24, 1918, Amos, Montana; s. Charles and Ethlyn Blanche (Potts) M.; m. May Taylor, Feb. 9, 1946; children: Vicki, b. 1947; Gary, b. 1951; edn: BS, agric. eng. Ore. State Univ. 1942; BS, civil eng., 1948. Career: jr. civil engr. East Bay Municipal Utility Dist. 1948-51; partner Richards & Miles, Oakland 1951s53; estimator Robert Miller Co., Richmond 1953s54; estimator McGuire & Heter, Oakland 1954-61; co-owner/pres. Albay Constr. Co., Martinez 1961--; East. Bay Dist. dir. Assn. Gen. Contractor of Calif. (Collective Bargaining Com.); No. Calif. Piping Contractors (Millwright Trust Fund dir. 1978-83, bd. dirs. 1980-84); awards: appreciation, Am. Gen. Contractors of Calif. 1977, 81; mem: US and Calif. Chambers of Commerce; Nat. Fedn. Independent Bus.; Contra Costa Builder Exchange; Tripartite Com. of Labor, Bus. & Users; Little League and Adult Softball, Bowling Team; Republican; Protestant; rec: golf, travel. Res: 950 Vista Del Diablo Martinez 94553 Ofc: Albay Construction Co., 865 Howe Rd (POB 2568) Martinez 94553

MILES, DONALD FREDERICK, lawyer; b. Apr. 11, 1949, Marysville, Calif.; s. Frederick J. and Janet Marie (Johnstone) M.; m. Rebecca, Feb. 20, 1982; 1 dau. Stacey b. 1983; edn: AA, honors, Yuba Coll. 1969; AB econ., honors, Stanford Univ. 1971; JD, UC Hastings Coll. of the Law 1974; admitted to State Bar of Calif. 1974. Career: law clk., Hon. William P. Clark, Jr. (now Secty. of the Interior), Calif. Supreme Court, 1973-75; instr. legal rhetoric, Hastings Coll. of the Law, Univ. of Calif. 1974-75; assoc. atty. Pettit & Martin, San Francisco 1975-80, elected to ptnrship, 1980; shareholder/ptnr. Rogers, Joseph, O'Donnell & Quinn, S.F. 1981--; adj. faculty UC Hastings Coll. of the Law, 1980--, faculty and demonstrating atty. Hastings Nat. Coll. of Trial and Appellate Advocacy, 1983-; Defense Steering Com. Sutter Hosps./Miofsky Multi-Party Litigation, 1979-83; lectr. State Bar of Calif./UC Contg. Edn. of the Bar, 183-; lectr. CPCU/Am. Inst. for Property & Liability Underwriters/Ins. Inst. of Am.; lectr. East Bay Chief Executives Counsel, 1983; honors: Order of the Coif (1974), Thurston Hon. Soc. (1973-4), Bank of Am. Man of the Year (1969), Chi Psi Nat. Fellowship (1971), Valedictorian/ Student Body Pres. Yuba Coll. (1969), pres. Chi Psi Frat., Stanford (1971), Demolay Chevalier Award, Superior Calif. Demolay Assn. Medal of Honor, Past Master Councilor, Demolay, Marysville; mem: Am. Bar Assn., Defense Research Inst., No. Calif. Assn. of Def. Counsel, San Francisco Bar Assn., S.F. Barristers, Hastings Alumni Assn.; bd. dirs. Stanford Bay Area Juniors 1976-9; mem. Olympic Club, Stanford Alumni Assn. (Class rep. 1971-), E Clampus Vitus; contbr. legal publs.; Republican; Presbyterian; rec: scuba diving, backpacking, photog. Res: 495 Willow Court, Novato 94947 Ofc: Rogers, Joseph, O'Donnell & Quinn, APC, 505 Sansome St, 14th Flr, San Francisco 94111

MILES, PATRICIA ANN, teacher, businesswoman; b. Oct. 29, 1942, Vicksburg, MS; d. William McKinley and Hazel Lucille Thomas; children:

RaJendra b. 1964, Shawndra b. 1972; edn: Bach. Music Edn., Jackson St. Univ. 1963; Pepperdine Univ. 1966-68, CSULA 1966. Career: substitute tchr. Fontana Schools, 1965-72j, Special Edn. tchr./ dept. chair 1970-72; Summer Girl Friday, Kelly Girls, 1966, 1974--; acctg., White Front Stores (part-time), 1967; Los Angeles City Schs. Home Tchr. 1974-79; ER Tchr., Jefferson High Sch., Poly Tech, Mulholland Jr. H.S., 1980; Amway Distributor 1982--; lectr., A Positive Thinker; beauty cons.; mem: CTA, NEA, UTLA, Delta Sigma Theta Sor., Council of Exceptional Children 1966-72, Music Educators Nat. Conf. 1964-74, National Council Negro Women; mil: P.O. USNR/ CINCPAC/ WWMCCS ADP 119, Encino; rec: swimm, travel, helping people. Res: 3727 W. 107th St Inglewood 90303 Ofc: Pat's International, POB 4838, Inglewood 90302

MILES, PATRICIA VIVIAN, real estate broker; b. Oct. 8, 1940, Sacramento; d. Charles Patrick and Gwendelyn Vivian (Griffiths) Clarke; m. Donald John Kessel, June 6, 1957; children: Peggy b. 1958, Donna b. 1959, John b. 1963, Patricia b. 1970; m. 2d William Douglas Miles, July 17, 1975; edn: Elk Grove Coll., 1978 Anthony Schs., 1972; Calif. lic. Real Estate Broker. Career: var. pos. retail sales, 1955-67, sorter Hunt Wesson, 1968-72; real estate sales, Milano Realtors 1972-75, Miles Real Estate 1976-77; owner/broker/mgr. Realty World Miles and Assocs., Sacramento 1977--; recipient sev. sales awards, Sacto. Bd. of Realtors Listing Awd.; mem. Sacramento Bd. of Realtors, Calif. Assn. of Realtors, Soroptomist Club, Valley Hi Country Club, Mather AF Ofcrs. Club/Wife; Nat. Republican Com.; rec: sew, piano, concerts. Res: 4843 St. Augustine Dr Elk Grove 95624 Ofc: Realty World Miles and Associates 7127 Southland Park Dr Sacramento 95831

MILGRIM, DARROW A., educator/administrator; b. Apr. 30, 1945, Chgo.; s. David and Mickey (Man) M.; m. Laurie Stevens, Apr. 15, 1983; 1 son, Derick, b. 1976; edn: BA, CSU San Bernardino 1968; Calif. Elem. & Sec. Tchg. Cred. 1969 (CSUSB), and Adminstrv. Supvn. Cred., 1973 (USC); Cert. Camp Director, Am. Camping Assn. 1975. Career: tchr. Rialto Unif. Sch. Dist. 1969-70; tchr. Las Virgenes Unif. Sch. Dist. 1970-76; dir. Calamigos Star C Ranch 1970-84; owner DM Ins. Svcs. 1981--; exec. dir. Calamigos Star C Ranch Summer Camp 1984--; dir. Soc. Calif. Camping Assn. 1973-84; chmn. Pvt. Independent Camps Western US 1978-; dir. Calif. Camping Legis. Adv. Council 1975-; dir. PIC Nat. Adv. Council 1978-; awards. disting. svc. award Am. Camping Assn. 1983; mem: Calif. Tchrs. Assn.; Am. Camping Assn.; Western Assn. of Independent Camps (pres. Soc. Calif. sect. 1981); editor: State Camping Legislative Notes 1976-79; mil: E-7 USAR 1965-71; Democrat. Res: 3293 N Sawtooth Ct Westlake Village 91362 Ofc: DM Insurance Services, POB 6173 Thousand Oaks 91360

MILLANG, STEVEN JAMES, accountant; b. May 12, 1949, Inglewood; s. Irven Hiram and Lois Nadine (Matson) M.; edn: BSBA, CSU Pomona 1972; MBA, CSU Long Beach 1979; lic. Real Estate Broker, Calif. 1982. Career: revenue agt. Internal Revenue Svc., Los Angeles 1973--; tchr. contg. edn. Tax Seminar, CSU Long Beach 1984; mem: Calif. Polytech. Univ. Pomona Alumni Assn.; Long Beach State Univ. Alumni Assn.; mil: E-3 Calif. Army Nat. Guard 1971-77; rec: collecting antiques, wine making. Res: 12484 Benson Ave Chino 91710 Ofc: Internal Revenue Service, 300 N Los Angeles St Los Angeles 90053

MILLER, ANN LEE, real estate broker; b. Sept. 8, 1917, Phila., Pa.; d. Harry A. and Mollie (Adelman) Cooper; m. David Miller, Mar. 20, 1939; children: Bonnie, b. 1941; Howard, b. 1951; edn: BA, Temple Univ., Phila. 1939. Career: credit mgr. Albert Einstein Medical, Phila. 1952-65; exec. dir. Ponce- De- Leon Nursing Home, Phila. 1965-68; asst. adminstr. Albert Einstein Med. 1968-72; mgr. patient accts. Hahneman Medical, Phila 1972-76; currently, real estate broker, self- empl., Carlsbad; honors: Chaplain of Four Chaplains Awd. 1965; Top R.E. Producer, C-21 local ofc. 1979, 80; mem: Eastern Star Assoc. Matron. Address: Ann/ Dave Realty, 2814 Luciernaga St Carlsbad 92008

MILLER, ELY ROBERT, real estate syndication executive; b. Nov. 15, 1930, Milwaukee, WI; s. Herbert H. and Molly (Belfer) Miller; edn: B.S., Univ. of Wisconsin, 1953; m. Yvonne Fishbein, June 28, 1970; chil: Richard, b. 1965, Jeff, b. 1972, Brian, b. 1977. Career: president, Bob Miller Co., Milwaukee, Wisc., 1954-62, v.p. A.L. Grootemaat & Son, Inc., Milwaukee, Wisc., 1962-69, president, Remanco, Div. of Inland Steel, Chicago, Ill., 1970-78, senior v.p., Robert A. McNeil Corp., San Mateo, Calif., 1978---; bd. mem. Inland steel, Dir., A.L. Grootemaat & Son, Inc. Dir., Robert A. McNeil Corp., 1978---; Dir. Milwaukee Bd. of Realtors, 1973; Certified mem. of the IREM faculty for IREM's course, 701: Art of Mangaging the Management Office offered throughout the U.S. & Canada, 1976-82. Instructor in real estate management at the Univ. of Wisconsin Sch. of Commerce, 1962. Awards: property mgmt. of the year, Milwaukee, Wisc., 1967, Milwaukee Man of the Year City of Hope, 1972, Journal of Property Mgmt. Award, 1977, Elected to Admissions IREM's prestigious Academy of Authors, 1982. Mem: Inst. of Real Estate Mgmt., 1982, chperson of the property mgmt. committee of the Amer. Chpt. of the Intern. Real Estate Fed., 1982, chmn of the rental housing subcommittee of the State & Municipal Legislation Committee for the Natl. Assn. of Realtors, 1982; natl. pres., Inst. of Real Estate Mgmt., 1980; Gov. councillor, IREM 1982, Sec./Treas., IREM 1979, Regional v.p. IREM, 1972-73-74, pres. Milwaukee chpt. of IREM, 1970. Journal of Property Mgmt. Articles, 1977, 1977, 1981. Mortgage banking, 1982, tax shelter digest, 1982. Mil: 1st Lt., U.S.A., (Korea). Rec: jogging, basketball. Res: 339 Alberta Way, Hillsborough 94010; Office: The Robert A. McNeil Corp., 2855 Campus Dr., San Mateo 94403.

MILLER, EMERSON WALDO, government accountant/ financial manager; b. Jan. 27, 1920, Green Island, Jamaica, W.I., nat. 1957; s. Adolphus Eustace and Catherine Sarah (Dixon) M.; m. Olive Claire Ford, Apr. 10, 1945; children: Cheryll, b. 1945; Hellena, b. 1947; Emerson, b. 1949; Oliver (Rhodes Scholar 1978), b. 1953; Donald, b. 1957; Selwyn, b. 1960; edn: att. Univ. of Toronto 1938-43, UC Berkeley 1950-61; BS, State Univ. of NY, Albany 1976; BA, honors, Charter Oak Coll. 1979; ACI dip., Inst. of Commerce (London, Eng.) 1941; FAE dip., (cf. MBA/ CPA), Intern. Acct. & Exec. Corp. of Can. 1945; FFCS dip., Faculty of Sec. & Admin. (Guilford, Surrey, Eng.) 1945; ACEA dip., Assn. of Cost. & Exec. Accts. (London) 1982. Career: cost acct. Poirier & Mclane Corp., NYC 1941-42; principal Emerson Miller & Co., Intern. Acct., Chartered, Kingston, Jamaica W.I. 1942-49; lectr., acctg. & bus. law, Jamaica Sch. of Commerce, Kingston, Jamaica W.I. 1945-48; Tax Examiner/ Conferee Internal Revenue Svc., S.F. 1963-64, sect. chief 1965-70, branch chief 1970--; maj. segment fin. mgmt. activities Gen. Svc. Admin., US Govt., S.F., Credit Com. chmn. 1969-81, treas. 1981--; dir. VARO-SF Fed Credit Union, S.F. 1982-; Calif. Edn. VP, GSA-SF chpt., Internat. Toastmasters Club 1965-68; instr., govt. acctg., GSA-SF 1966-69; mem. Mgmt. Improvement Com., Fed. Exec. Bd. 1973-74; pres. S.F. chpt. Assn. of Govt. Accts. 1973-74; honors: GSA Special Achiev. Awd. 1969, mem: Am. Acct. Assn.; Nat. Assn. Accts.; Assn. of Govt. Accts. (SF chpt. pres. 1973-74); Am. Mgmt. Assn.; Fin. Mgmt. Assn.; British Inst. of Mgmt.; Am. Judicature Assn.; British Social and Athletic Club 1970; Inst. of Commerce assoc. 1941; Fellow, Internat. Accts. & Execs. Corp. of Canada 1945; Fellow, Faculty of Sec. & Admin. 1945; Assn. of Cost & Exec. Accts. (assoc.) 1982; Fellow, Royal Econonomic Soc. 1962; publisher: Classified Buyers Dir. (Jamaica) 1948; rec: gardening, cricket. Res: 505 Coventry Rd Kensington 94707 Ofc: 525 Market St San Francisco 94105

MILLER, GARY ALLEN, commercial appliance service representative; b. Jan. 17, 1951, Missoula, Montana; s. Carl Franklin and Marion Aileen (Rand) M.; m. Carol Jeanne Hanna, June 11, 1976; edn: cert. Computer Design & Analysis, Brunswick Inst. 1983; AS, Grossmont Coll. 84. Career: appliance rebuilder Calif. Meter Svc., San Diego 1975; head mechanic Insta-Tune, Phoenix, Ariz. 1975-76; security guard Purolator Security, Phoenix 1976; field serivceman California Meter Svc. 1977-79; line mechanic Castle Plymouth, Chula Vista 1979; currently, field svc. rep. Art's Inc., San Diego 1980--; mem: Masterworks Choral, Bakersfield 1974; research: interfacing small home computers, using machine language, with other data gathering machines; mil: sgt. E-5 US Army 1970-73; US Army Nat. Guard, San Diego 1979-81; Assembly of God; rec: music, photog. Res: 10133 Peaceful Ct Santee 92071 Ofc: Art's Incorporated, 2888 Adams Ave San Diego 92116

MILLER, GARY N., chiropractor; b. Dec. 6, 1944, Denver, Colo.; s. Dr. Leo F. and Caroline M. (Smith) M.; edn: BS, Univ. of Iowa 1967; Bach. of Human Biol., Nat. Coll. of Chiropractic 1972, DC, 1972. Career: cancer resrch. asst. Univ. of Iowa med. coll., Iowa City, IA 1968; non-commnd. ofcr. in chg. of Physical Therapy Sect. 801st Gen. Hosp., Chgo., and Letterman Hosp., San Francisco, 1972-74; resident staff, mem. bd. dirs. Berkeley Free Clinic and Wholistic Center 1974-75; dir. San Francisco Headache Clinic 1976-79; corp. pres. San Francisco Chiropractic Clinic, 1976--; lectr. and instr. on medical/ legal sports and personal injury, wkrs. compensation, and nutritional subjects at med. colls., univs., hosps., and profl. state assns., presentations on radio and t.v.; apptd. Indep. Medical Examiner, Calif. State Indsl. Accident Commn. 1979; postgrad. instr. L.A. Coll. of Chiropractic; guest lectr. Internat. Sports Fedn., Monte Carlo, France 1982; honors: Who's Who Among Students 1973; Doctor of the Year 1983, Calif. Chiro. Assn.; Doctor of the Year 1977 and 1980, S.F. Chiro. Soc.; Who's Who in Chiropractic Internat. 1981; mem: Am., Calif., Bay Area chiropractic assns., San Francisco Chiro. Soc., Bay Area Chiro. Research Soc.; Knights of Columbus (3d deg.), Sacramento St Merchant Guild, Film Festival of Fine Arts, Industrial Claims Assn.; works: Orthopedic Dental Pillow (1979), Chiropractic Back Book (1983), Calif. Chiro. Assn. New Doctors' Manuals, journal contbr.; mil: SP4 US Army 1972-74; Republican; Catholic; avo: to contrib. to harmonious human existence. Res: 8 Place Moulin Tiburon Ofc: 3637 Sacramento St San Francisco 94118

MILLER, HARRY DANIEL, lawyer; b. Apr. 17, 1931, Oakland; s. Ralph Daniel and Luciele Grace (Snavely) M.; m. Jean, Dec. 23, 1950; children: Kjerstin, b. 1958, Daniel b. 1959, Carl, b. 1964; edn: BA, UC Berkeley 1952, JD Boalt Hall of Law, 1957; grad. legal stu., Ford Found. Scholar to Sweden 1957-58; admitted to Calif. State Bar 1958. Career: practice of law, founding partner of Miller, Starr & Regalia, Oakland 1958--; adj. prof. of law Univ. of San Francisco Law Sch. 1977-; mem: Alameda County Bar Assn., Am. Bar Assn., State Bar of Calif., Supreme Ct. Bar, trustee Alta Bates Found.; bd. dirs. Assoc. Homebuilders of the Greater East Bay 1973-74; mem. Legal Action Com. Calif. Assn. of Realtors 1973-77; coauthor: Current Law of California Real Estate, 4 vols. (Bancroft Whitney 1963); contbg. author Calif. Real Estate Sales Transactions (Calif. CEB 1967); editor Scandinavian Studies in Law (1958 Stockholm Inst. for Scand. Law); arts. in law jours.; mil: lt. USNR (SC) 1952-54; Republican; Prot.; rec: ski, tennis, golf. res: 2 Nelson Court Orinda 94563 Ofc: Miller, Starr & Regalia, One Kaiser Plaza Oakland 94612

MILLER, JAMES THOMAS, real estate broker; b. Nov. 6, 1947, Louisville, Ky.; s. Joseph J. and Joan (Thomas) M.; m. Melanie Sandy, Feb. 28, 1980; childern; Brooke, b. 1972; Bart, b. 1975; Kurt, b. 1979; edn: BBA, Morehead State Univ. 1969; MBA, Pepperdine Univ. 1975; M.Mktg., CSU San Bernardino 1976-79; lic. R.E. Broker, Calif. 1981. Career: pharmaceutical salesman Pfizer Labs, Tustin 1973-75, Lederle Labs., Los Angeles 1975-80; broker/ property mgr. Sunset Gp., San Bernardino 1980--; mem. Econ. Council, San Bernardino

CofC; mem. Pvt. Industry Council, San Bernardino;; honors: Nat. Hon. Soc. 1965; Marine Corp Tennis Champion 1972; pres. Jr. Achievement 1963; mem: Riverside Tennis Assn. (pres.); Riverside Little League (sponsorship chmn.); research: non-verbal communications in mktg., 1978; mil: capt., USMC 1969-72; Republican; Disciples of Christ (chmn. trustees); rec: land investments, racquetball, golf. Res: 4343 Brentwood Riverside 92506 Ofc: Sunset Brokers, 348 W Hospitality, Ste 102, San Bernardino 92408

MILLER, JEFFREY CRAIG, manufacturing co. president; b. Jan. 7, 1948, Phila., Pa.; s. Bernard and Sylvia (Weizer) M.; edn BA, cum laude, Glassboro State Coll. 1974. Career: dist. sales mgr., div. sales mgr., national sales trainer I.C. System 1976-80; dist. sales mgr. throughout Calif. 1980--; currently, founder/ pres./ chmn. bd. Vital-Link Inc., No. Highlands; mem: Phi Epsilon (pres. 1971); coach Fresno State Womens Gymnastic Team 1979; coach Glassboro State Coll. Gymnastic Team 1971; designed Vital-Link Lifesaving System 1980; mil: E-6 USN; Jewish; rec: windsurfing, flying, diving. Res: 500 N Street Sacramento 95814 Ofc: Vital-Link Inc., 5610 Lura Way, North Highlands 95660

MILLER, JOHN JOSE, jurist; b. uly 28, 1932, Savannah, GA; s. Fred and Minnie (Edmond) Miller, Sr.; Edn: AB, Talladega Coll., 1954; LLB, Howard Univ., 1957; Walter Perry Johnson Fellow, UC Boalt Hall of Law; chil: Duncan, b. 1962; Heather, b. 1964; Robin, b. 1973. Career: mem., Calif. Assembly, 1966-78; chmn. Assembly Judiciary Comm., 1974-78; mem., Judicial Council, CA, 1974-78; minority leader, 1970-71; pres., Berkeley Bd. of Edn., 1966; mem., Berkeley Housing Adv. Appeals Bd.; library trustees; Bishop's Comm. Episcopal Ch. of the Good Shepherd; v. chmn. Comm. on the Structure of the Judiciary; mem., Comm. on Finance, Insurance and Commerce, Assembly; pvt. practice, Berkeley-San Francisco; justice, Ct. of Appeal, 1978—. Honors: class and student body pres., Talladega Coll; Avery Speech Award; Recipient, Man of the Year Award, Chr. by Side of the Road, Berkeley, 1965; Public Official of the Year Award, Los Angeles Trial Lawyers Assn., 1975; Outstanding Service Award, Contra Costa Trial Lawyers Assn., 1976; Legislator of the Year Award, Calif. Trial Lawyers Assn., 1976. Mem: Amer. Judicature Soc.; Alpha Phi Alpha frat.; Men's Club, UC Berkeley. Assoc. Editor Howard Law Journal, 1956-57; author several articles on taxation, Howard Law Journ. Democrat. Episcopalian. Rec: chess, orchid growing, gardening. Office: Justice, Court of Appeal, San Francisco 94102.

MILLER, KENNETH RUSSELL, JR., financial planning co. president; b. Mar. 7, 1946, Bellevue, Pa.; s. Kenneth Russell, Sr. and Velma Jean (Barto) M.; m. Sharon Sanders, Nov. 27, 1981; children: Thomas b. 1971, Kimberley b. 1973, Michael b. 1977; edn: LUTC, Life Underwriters Tng. Council 1979; NASD Registered Rep.; Calif. Life & Disability Lic.; Calif. Dept. Real Estate Lic. Career: radio & TV Announcer 1967-70; trucking indus. mgmt. with AllTrans Express, Watsonville and then whse. mgr. Bekins Moving & Storage, Burlingame -1973; ins. agt. Mass Mutual, San Jose 1973-79; individual financial planning firm, 1979-81; joined Money Concepts, Internat. Inc., 1982-, founder/ pres. and finl. planner Money Concepts of Santa Clara County, 1982--; awards: Rookie of Year nom. San Jose Life Underwriters, Presidents Club 1978, Salesman/Year 1982 for USA, Money Concepts Internat., MCI Millionaires Club, MCI Eagles Club, 1983 Opportunity Seminar of the Year Presenter; mem: San Jose Life Underwriters Assn., San Jose Real Estate Board, Reg. Rep. IFS Capital (Mem. firm NASD); mil: cpl. USMC 1964-67, Vietnam Vet.; Prot.; rec: organic gardening, youth soccer. Res: 1949 Wright Ave Sunnyvale 94087 Ofc: Money Concepts/Santa Clara County, 690 W. Fremont Ave, Ste 7, Sunnyvale 94087

MILLER, LENORE SUMNER, realtor, actress; b. Aug. 29, 1909, Sumner, IL; d. Libern and Corinne Celestine (Heath) Sumner; Edn: BA, Univ. of Chgo., 1928, bus.. adm., Northwestern Univ., 1930, theology, Biola Coll., 1950; studied ballet under Mlle. Theo Hughes and Prof. Sheehan at Circle Ballet School, Indpls.; m. Edward Miller (dance partner), 1924, div. 1927; Chil: Betty, b. 1924. Career: owner/prod./choreographer various dance cos. performing in Kansas, Tex., Okla, Miami and Havana, during 1930s; played the Orpheum Circuit, then Loew's; dancer/actress, Hollywood, movies including My Fair Lady, Hello Dolly, 42nd Street, State Fair; played in the pit for silent movies in Sumner, Ill. 1921-24, recipient num. awards from Amer. Legion, Eastern Star, Masonic fund raisers; citation for A.W.V.S. and C.D.V.O. (selling most bonds in NYC); Mem: Eastern Star (Silver Star chpt.); Order of the Amaranth (Alhambra Ct., Royal matron); Degree of Honor Protective Assn. (Santa Monica chpt. and Van Holly chpt.); Santa Monica Lyric Chorus (past pres); Nat. Soc. of Arts and Letters (sponsored by Nancy Davis Reagan); Women of the Moose (musician, 5 yrs.); The Troupers (life mem., Gold Card); S.A.G., S.E.G.; Hollywood Ladies Comedy Club (pres. 5 yrs., life mem. Gold Card); mem. Episcopal Guild (little ch. Around the Corner, NYC); Show-Womens past press Club World-Wide; works: prod. num. shows (following vaudeville pattern) for various orgns. 1960—; Author: Skid Row; sev. short stories; autobiography in progress; Republican. Methodist. Rec: music, dancing. Res/ Office: Green Earth Realty, 737 N. Mansfield Ave., Hollywood 90038.

MILLER, MONA DUETSCH, lawyer; b. Feb. 9, 1953, Coral Gables, Fla.; d. Dr. Irvin and Freda (Smukler) Deutsch; m. Steven Jeffrey Miller, Aug. 21, 1977; edn: AB, w/ distn. Cornell Univ. Coll. of Arts & Scis. 1973; JD, Stanford Law Sch. 1977; admitted to State Bar of Calif. 1977. Career: assoc. litigation dept. McKenna & Fitting, now McKenna, Conner & Cuneo, Los Angeles 1977--, partner 1983--; bd. dirs./ secty. Calif. Atty. Fed. Credit Union 1983; honors: Phi Beta Kappa 1973; Alpha Lamda Delta 1972; Raven & Serpent 1972; moderator, Panel on Constrn. Loan Breakdowns, Real Property Sect. L.A. Co. Bar Assn. 1981; mem: Am. Bar Assn.; L.A. Co. Bar Assn. (Real Property sect., Comml. Law & Bankruptcy sect.); Stanford Law Review 1976-77; Stanford Journs. of Internat. Studies 1975-76; Jewish; rec: classical piano. Res: 1916 Roscomare Rd Los Angeles 90077 Ofc: McKenna, Conner & Cuneo, 3435 Wilshire Blvd, Ste 2800, Los Angeles 90010

MILLER, PHILIP DANIEL, physician; b. Dec. 12, 1946, Estacada, Ore.; s. Abraham and Olive Margaret (Bucher) M.; m. Laurie Terrat, Sept. 22, 1980; edn: BS, Ore. State Univ. 1969; MD, Univ. of Ore. 1972; Board Cert. in Ob-Gyn. 1980. Career: intern L.A. Co. USC Med. Ctr., Los Angeles 1972-73; res. Kaiser Hosp., L.A. 1974-77; staff physician, Kaiser Hosp., Santa Clara 1977--; honors: Alpha Omega Alpha 1971; mem: Shufeldt Soc.; Med. Soc. of Santa Clara Co.; Peninsula Ob-Gyn. Soc.; Libertarian; Protestant; rec: automobile restoration, woodworking, photog. Res: 19953 Wright Dr Los Gatos 95030 Ofc: Kaiser Hospital, 900 Kiely Blvd Santa Clara 95051

MILLER, PHOEBE AMELIA, computer software marketing consultant; b. Jan. 13, 1948, Evanston, Ill.; d. William Prescott and Elizabeth Helen (Lucker) Miller; edn: BA, honors, Univ. of Wisc. 1970; grad. work, Stanford Univ. 1973; MBA, Golden Gate Univ. 1978; ICP Sales Tng. 1979. Career: optics analyst Coherent Radiation, Palo Alto 1970-72; engr. Bechtel Inc. 1972-77; asst. div. mgr. Rand Info. Systems, San Francisco 1977-79; sr. mktg. rep. Computer Scis. Corp., S.F. 1979-81; sr. mktg. cons. Quasar Sys. Inc., Walnut Creek 1981--; awards: Quasar Pres.'s Awd., 1982, 83; V.P. Achiev. Club, Computer Scis. Corp. 1981; Awd. of Merit, for tech. contrbn., Bechtel Corp.; publs: contbr. Nat. Structural Engring. Conf. 1976. Res: 439 Greenwich San Francisco 94133 Ofc: Quasar Systems Inc. (Cognos Corp.), 1801 Oakland Blvd, Ste 100, Walncutive; b. Feb. 17, 1942, Dallas, Tex. S. William P. and Cornelia (Thompson) M.; m. Mary Lee Conatser, Jan. 31, 1964; children: Tom, b. 1965; Cheryl Lee, b. 1968; edn: BA, Baylor Univ. 1965; postgrad. wk. Univ. of Tex. 1971, So. Methodist Univ. 1970. Career: personnel adminstr. General Motors 1966-689; salaried personnel analyst LTV Aerospace 1968-71; personnel adminstr. Texas Industries Inc. 1971-75; personnel mgr. Dobbs Houses Inc. 1975-76; dir. gen. svc. Six Flags Over Texas 1976-79; dir. gen. svcs. Six Flags Magic Mountain 1979-82; v.p./ gen. mgr. 1982--; mem: Santa Clarita Valley CofC (bd. dirs.); Santa Clarita Valley Boys & Girls Club (bd. dirs.); St. Stephens Spl. Sch. (bd. dirs.); Baptist; rec: golf. Res: 25562 Avenida Frasca Valencia 91355 Ofc: Six Flags Magic Mountain, POB 5500 Valencia 91355

MILLER, RICHARD THOMPSON, amusement park executive; b. Feb. 17, 1942, Dallas, Tex. S. William P. and Cornelia (Thompson) M.; m. Mary Lee Conatser, Jan. 31, 1964; children: Tom, b. 1965; Cheryl Lee, b. 1968; edn: BA, Baylor Univ. 1965; postgrad. wk. Univ. of Tex. 1971, So. Methodist Univ. 1970. Career: personnel adminstr. General Motors 1966-689; salaried personnel analyst LTV Aerospace 1968-71; personnel adminstr. Texas Industries Inc. 1971-75; personnel mgr. Dobbs Houses Inc. 1975-76; dir. gen. svc. Six Flags Over Texas 1976-79; dir. gen. svcs. Six Flags Magic Mountain 1979-82; v.p./ gen. mgr. 1982--; mem: Santa Clarita Valley CofC (bd. dirs.); Santa Clarita Valley Boys & Girls Club (bd. dirs.); St. Stephens Spl. Sch. (bd. dirs.); Baptist; rec: golf. Res: 25562 Avenida Frasca Valencia 91355 Ofc: Six Flags Magic Mountain, POB 5500 Valencia 91355

MILLER, STANLEY RAY, sound system consultant; b. Oct. 25, 1940, Lincoln, Nebr.; s. Maurice Winston and Blanche Fern (Mosier) M.; div.; two children: Cordie Lynne b. 1967, Neil Andrew b. 1971; edn: BA, Kearney State Coll. 1965. Career: founder/pres./chief exec. ofcr. Stanal Sound Ltd., 1962--, cons. engr./ audio mixer for sound systems and concerts; chief live concert mixing engr. for Neil Diamond, 1969-, designed, mfd. and toured large sound systems, worldwide 1964-, has toured sound systems for Simon & Garfunkel, Johnny Cash, Christy Minstrels, Young Americans, Bill Cosby, Mac Davis, Dolly Parton, Pink Floyd, Bob Dylan, John Denver, The Osmond Brothers, Donnie & Marie Osmond, Tom Jones and Englebert Humperdink, 1964-; dir. sound svcs. at the Universal Amphitheatre, Greek Theatre, Pantages Theatre, and the Wilshire Theatre (L.A.), Pacific Amphitheatre (Costa Mesa), Golden Gate Theatre (S.F.), Poplar Creek Music Theatre (Chgo.); respons. for functional design of more than ten different models of Yamaha Sound Mixing Consoles, as well as other Yamaha products for Concert Sound Indus.; lectr. num. colls., Audio Engring. Soc. nat. convs., Altec Sound Contractor Dealer Nat. Tng. Meetings; mem. Audio Engring. Soc. 1958-, Profl. Entertainment Prodn. Soc. (treas.), BPOE Lodge 984; Democrat; Lutheran. Res: 3336 Primera Ave Hollywood 90068 Ofc: Stanal Sound, Ltd. 16123 Valerio St Van Nuys 91406

MILLER, WALTER IRWIN, JR., financial planner; b. Dec. 10, 1935, Sioux City, Iowa; s. Walter I. and Marian (Krommenhoek) M.; m. Marie L. Thiesen, July 30, 1955; children: Deborah Ann Miller Tice, Susan Marie, Mark Frederick, Douglas Walter; edn: BA, CSU San Diego 1961; CLU, Am. Coll. of Life Underwriters 1969; CFP, Coll. for Finl. Plnng. 1973; ChFC, Coll. of Life Underwriter, NASD Finl. Principal 1979 Reg. Investment Advisor 1980. Career: exec. Pacific Tel., San Diego 1961-64; salesman, sr. vice pres. College Life and University Life Ins. Co., Indpls. and Okla. City, 1964-68; pres./CEO Capital Growth Planning and Capital Growth Resources, and affil. cos., San Diego 1968--; pres. El Cajon Valley Gen. Contractors, Inc.; bd. dirs. Pacific States Chiropractic Coll. 1978-9. Mem: Nat. Assn. of Securities Dealers, Internat. Assn. of Fin. Planners, S.D. Assn. of Fin. Planners, Certified Inst. for Fin. Planning, Calif. Broker-Dealer Assn. (dir. 1982), Am. Coll. for Life Underwriters, S.D. Assn. Realtors, El Cajon CofC; mil: seaman USN 1953-57; Republican; Unitarian; rec: constrn., car restoration. Res: 1185 Hub Court, El Cajon 92020 Ofc: Capital Growth Plnng. 422 S. Pierce St El Cajon 92020

MILLER, WILLIS LEE, rancher; b. Feb. 3, 1921, Akron, Ohio; s. William Lee and Nina Mae (Bell) M.; m. Dorothy Rhea Murdy, June 22, 1945; children: William Lee, Norma Jeanne, Walter James, Dorothy Willene, Marilyn Louise, Katherine Anne, Wesley Stephen; edn: stu. Univ. Calif., Davis. Career: farming and ranching in Westminster, Calif. 1946--; owner/ pres: Willis L. Miller Ranch Co. 1967--, Los Alisos Ranch Co. 1967--, Springdale Equipment Co. 1960--; dir: Riverside Asso. Fed. Land Bank, County Nat. Bank; Deacon, elder Presbyterian Ch. 1948-; mem. Farm Bureau; mil: pilot US Army Air Force, WWII, ETO, decorated DFC with oak leaf cluster, Air medal with 5 oak leaf clusters; Republican; Address: 13070 Old Bolsa Chica Rd Westminster 92683

MILLIGAN, NITA RAMONA, real estate/ mineral, oil and gas broker; b. Oct. 25, 1929, Union City, Okla.; d. George S. and Reta Jane (Cook) Howard; m. Caleb Ross Milligan, Mar. 28, 1963; edn: spl. courses, Anthony Schools, USC, Bakersfield Coll.; Calif. lic. Mineral, Oil & Gas Broker 1982, Real Estate Broker 1979. Career: real estate sales assoc. Paul Jacobs Myers, Bakersfield 1979, Community Marketing, Inc., Bksfld. 1980, Mr. Ken Colley, Tehachapi 1981; currently real estate broker Great American Marketing, and mineral oil & gas broker Paris Energy, Bakersfield; honors: recogn., Nat. Found. March of Dimes 1976, Kern County Shrine Club 1974, Advertising Club of Kern Co. 1976, Junior Achievement 1974, 75; mem: Am. Assn. of Petroleum Landmen, Bakersfield Assn. Petroleum Landmen; Nat., Calif. Assn. of Realtors, Bakersfield Bd. of Realtors; Republican; Presbyterian; rec: golf, swim, bowling. Res: 937 Panorama Dr Bakersfield 93305 Ofc: Paris Energy, POB 1569, Bakersfield 93301

MILLIKAN, JACK WATSON, lumber milling executive; b. June 30, 1919, Murphysboro, Ill.; s. Elzie C. and Edith (Rolens) M.; m. Geraldine F. Moise, Apr. 11, 1942; children: Nancy Lee, John C. (DDS), Kenneth Charles; edn: AA, Compton Coll. 1939; mktg., UCLA 1939-41. Career: salesman Penberthy Lumber Co., Los Angeles 1950-55; exec. v.p. Lane Lumber Co., Los Angeles (now. Lane Stanton Vance Lumber Co., Hardwood) & pres. Custom Mills Inc., City of Industry 1955--; pres. So. Calif. Hardwood Lumber Assn. 1961-82; pres. Pacific Coast Hardwood Lumber Assn. 1975 (secty. 1974); pres. Internat. Hardwood Prods. Assn., Wash. DC; honors: mem: Industry Hills Exec. Security Com.; Friendly Hills Country Club; Whittier Bruin Club; Boy Scouts of Am. (Com.) works: hardwood lumber arts., Calif. Lumber Merchant Mag. 1962-82; active in revision of Nat. Hardwood Lumber Footage Grading Rules; mil: capt. USNR Intell. 1942-74, Amphibious Forces, Submarine Svc., Meritorious Unit. Commdn., Pacific Theatre, Am. Theatre; Republican (Pres. Task Force); Methodist; rec: boating, skiing, furniture building. Res: 8419 Scranata Dr Whittier 90603 Ofc: Custom Mills, Inc., Lane Stanton Lumber Co., 14710 Nelson Ave City of Industry 91744

MILLS, AMY BETH, boutique owner; b. May 30, 1952, Santa Monica; d. Paul and Anne Scott Mills; edn: UC Northridge 1970-72. Career: jr. mgmt. Field's retail chain (Calif.); mgmt., Andrades, Maui Hawaii; in-flt. hostess Continental Airlines, Chgo. and Denver; bus. mgr. Campbell Hall Sch., Los Angeles; owner/designer Golden Girl Jewelry Co., Los Angeles; current owner of splty. boutique, The Country Life (spec. in Americana country art and interiors), Los Angeles, 2d shop in Sedona, Ariz. in planning; instr. classes in decor and design through shop; wedding cons./designer; publish mail-order catalog; mem. Studio City CofC; rec: exercise, running, racquetball; collect Americana artifacts. Res: 12712 Moorpark, 205, Studio City 91604 Ofc: The Country Life, 12206 Ventura Blvd Studio City 91604

MILLS, EUGENE SUMNER, college president; b. Sept. 13, 1924, West Newton, Ind.; s. Sumner Amos and Lela (Weatherly) M.; m. Dorothy Wildman, Oct. 22, 1945; children: David b. 1956, Sara b. 1960; edn: AB, Earlham Coll. 1947; MA, Claremont Grad. Sch. 1949, PhD, 1952. Career: instr. of psychology Whittier Coll. 1950, asst./assoc./prof. of psychol. and chmn. Dept. of Psychol. 1952-62; prof. of psychol. Univ. of New Hampshire, Durham, NH 1962-79, chmn. Dept. of Psychol. 1962-65, dean Grad. Sch., coordinator of Research, 1963-67, dean Coll. of Liberal Arts, 1967-70, acad. vp, 1970-71, provost, 1971-74, president 1974-79; pres. Whittier Coll. and Whittier Coll. Sch. of Law, 1979--; prof. of psychol., Whittier Coll. 1979--; vis. prof. Univ. of Victoria, BC summers 1958, 60; honors: LLD, New Hampshire Coll. 1979; grantee Danford Found., NSF; merit cit. for extraordinary leadership in higher edn., Claremont Grad. Sch. 1980; mem: Fellow American Psych. Assn., Western Psych. Assn. 1962-79, Eastern, New Hampshire (pres. 1969-70, dir. 1967-70) Psych. Assns., Sigma Xi, Phi Kappa Phi, Omicron Delta Kappa, Indep. Coll. of So. Calif. (bd. dirs. 1979-); exec. bd. LA Area Council Boy Scouts of Am.; bd. trustees Southwest Mus., Town Hall of Calif., Friends Assn. for Higher Edn., California Club; author: George Trumbull Ladd: Pioneer American Psychologist (1969); arts. in profl. psych. jours.; Republican; Soc. of Friends; rec: travel, reading, sailing. Res: 13952 Summit Dr Whittier 90602 Ofc: Whittier College, P.O.Box 634 Whittier 90608

MILLS, PATRICIA HUNTER, portfolio manager; b. Dec. 22, 1949, Salisbury, Rhodesia (now Harare, Zimbabwe); d. Donald Garfield and Elsie (Hunter) Edmondson; m. Todd Mills, May 17, 1975; 1 dau: Tyra, b. 1982; edn: BA, Univ. of Natal S. Africa 1970; CFA designation, Univ. of Va. 1981-. Career: secty. Town Plnng. Appeals Bd., Natal, So. Africa 1971-72; travels in Australia 1972-73; secty. So. Highlands Area Authority, Papua, New Guinea 1973-74; travels in New Zealand, Columbia, Ecuador, Peru, Bolivia, Central Am. & Mex. 1974-75; travels in Am. 1975-77; v.p. portfolio/ mgr. marketable securities, Loomis, Sayles & Co., Los Angeles 1977--; mem: Los Angeles Assn. of Investment Women (exec. bd., com. ch.); Los Angeles World Affairs Council; rec: restoration of present home (castle built in 1911 by former Lt. Gov. of Calif., A.J. Wallace), travel. Res: 5455 Castle Knoll La Canada 91011 Ofc: Loomis, Sayles & Co., 700 S Flower St, Ste 2110, Los Angeles 90017

MILNER, HOWARD M., real estate broker/developer; b. Sept. 21, 1937, Los Angeles; s. David and Rose (Devron) M.; children: Mara Lynn b. 1967, Debra Faye b. 1971; edn: AA, L.A. City Coll. 1957; cert. in real estate, UCLA 1962; Calif. lic. Real Estate Broker. Career: senior store planner Broadway Dept. Stores 1959; exec. dir./property mgmt. Palm Properties, 1960; nat. real estate director Fotomat Corp. 1968; dir. of real estate Copper Penny Coffee Shops, 1970; vice pres./dir. R.E. & Constrn., Jerry Lewis Cinema Theatres, 1972; independent real estate broker/developer, Milner Properties, Los Angeles 1980--; v.p./investment advisor/bd. dir: Swiss American Finl. Corp., HESA Global Investments Ltd., HESA Global Mortgage Corp., 1980-85; property mgr. Hersch and Co., Los Angeles, 1985, mng. dir. for multi-unit apt. bldgs. and K-Mart Shopping Ctrs. throughout So. Calif., Colo., Utah, Kans., Ind., Nebr., Ore.; guest lectr. var. orgns. on real estate acquisition, devel. & national franchise expansion; mem. Mayor's Comml. Devel. Com., City of Los Angeles; honors: Eagle Scout, BSA 1952; Ford Motor Scholarship, Achitecture; mem: Am. Inst. of Indsl. Engrs., Am. Soc. of Mil. Engrs., Internat. Real Estate Fedn., Calif. R.E. Assn., Inst. of R.E. Mgmt., Internat. Council of Shopping Centers, A.I.A., Toastmasters, Shriners, City of Hope; mil: US Army Corps of Engrs. 1957-59; rec: jogging, racquetball, golf. Ofc: Milner Properties 8000 Blackburn Ave Los Angeles 90048

MINDEL, EARL LAWRENCE, nutritionist, author; b. Jan. 20, 1940, St. Boniface, Manitoba, Can.; s. William and Minerva Sybil (Galsky) M.; m. Gail Jaffe, 1971; children: Alanna, b. 1972; Evan Louis Ashley, b. 1976; edn: BS, pharmacy, ND State Univ.; PhD, nutrition, Univ. of Beverly Hills 1980. Career: pres. Kis Min Inc. 1965-71; secty./ treas. Natural Organics Inc. 1971--; pres. Adanac Mgmt. Inc. 1979--; bd. dirs. Nat. Bancorp. 1981-; prof. and mem. bd. dirs. Donsbach Univ. School of Nutrition, 1980-; Dale Carnegie instr.; bd. dirs. Western L.A. Regl. CofC; awards: L.A. City Proclamation Awd. of Achiev. 1981; mem: Masons, Scottish Rite, Shrine, Kappa Psi pharm. frat., Am. Nutrition Soc., Nat. Health Fedn., Am. Pharmaceutical Assn., Calif. Pharmacists Assn. (charter), Am. Acad. of Gen. Practice of Pharmacy, Internat. Coll. of Applied Nutrition, Nutrition Found.; author: Earl Mindell's Vitamin Bible, (nat. best seller) (Warner Books 1980, paperback reprint 1981); Earl Mindell's Vitamin Bible For Your Kids (Rawson-Wade, paperback reprint, Bantam Books 1982); Earl Mindell's Quick and Easy Guide to Better Health (1982); Earl Mindell's Pill Bible (Bantam Books 1984); rec: antique collecting, golf. Address: Adanac Management Inc., 709 N Hillcrest Rd Beverly Hills 90210

MINII, TRINH NGOC, computer systems design engineer; b. Feb. 11, 1952, Hanoi, Vietnam, nat. 1978; s. Trinh Dinh Duyen and Ta Thi Vy M.; m. Dieuhang Tran, July 19, 1981; 1 dau. Cynthia, b. 1983; edn: BS, summa cum laude, Westcoast Univ. 1980; career: design engineer Control Data Corp., Anaheim 1979-80, sr. design engr. Basic Four Corp., Tustin 1980-1, Technology Marketing Inc., Irvine 1981-3, Computerbase, Irvine 1983--, prin. designer advanced next gen. computer systems; mem: IEEE, Computer Club; Buddist; rec: classical guitarist, poet. Res: 20756 Ivy Cir. Yorba Linda 92686 Ofc: Computerbase, 7 Studebaker, Irvine 92714

MIRA, THOMAS KELLY, communication consultant; b. Apr. 7, 1941, NY, NY; s. Anthony Agathon and Irene (Kelly) M.; m. Patricia Frances Edwards, Feb. 7, 1970; children: Nicole P., b. 1976; Michael T., b. 1972; edn: BA, Loyola Univ., L.A. 1969; MS, Kensington Univ. 1983; D.Phil., 1984. Career: community relations asst. So. Calif. Edison Co. 1970-71; community rels. rep. 1971-72; environmental communications cons. 1972-74; mgr. environmental commun. 1974-77; pres./ CEO Thomas K. Mira Inc., Newport Beach 1977--; faculty Calif. Inst. of Tech. 1984; faculty Internat. Univ. for President, Young Presidents Orgn. 1984; honors: Outstanding Young Man of Am., Jaycees 1983; Police Athletic League Svc. Awd. 1982; mem: Pub. Rels. Soc. of Am.; Am. Assn. of Profl. Cons.; Costa Mesa CofC; publs: Survival on the Platform, Exec. Mag. 1980; Republican; Catholic. Res: 939 Glodenrod Dr Costa Mesa 92626 Ofc: Thomas K. Mira Inc., 100 Newport Center Dr, Ste 200, Newport Beach 92660

MIRABELLA, JOSEPH, building contractor; b. June 19, 1922, Nicosia, Sicily, nat. 1953; s. Joseph and Palma (Campagna) M.; m. Alicia, Dec. 29, 1979; children: Joseph III, b. 1981, Renata Luisa b. 1958, Palma Rita b. 1955, Roland Robert b. 1951. Calif. lic. Gen. Building Contractor 1969. Career: carpenter, foreman, supt. var. construction cos. in Calif. 1950-, owner/contr. Joseph Mirabella Construction, 1969--; mem. I.C.F., Elks, Knights of Columbus; mil: s/sgt Italian Navy, Three Crosses Al Valor Militare; Democrat; Catholic; rec: collector stamps, antiques. Address: Joseph Mirabella Construction, 918 Newton St San Fernando 01340

MIRJAHANGIR, FRANK FAROKH, consulting engineer; b.June 15, 1942, Tehran, Iran; s. Habib and Malek (Afrashtem) Mirjahangir; edn: Masters in bus. admin., Long Beach St. Univ., 1971, Bachelor of Sci. in civil engr., Calif. St. Poly C Pomona, 1966; m. Maureen Hicky, Dec. 1971; chil: Michael, b. 1972, Christopher, b. 1974, Patrick, b. 1979. Career: currently consulting engr. in field of civil struc. engrg., chief structural plancheck engr. city oh H.B., 1982-73. structural plancheck egr. county of Ventura, 1972-73. Assist. Civil engr. city of L.B., 1970-71. Civil structural engr, Bechtel Corp. Norwalk, 1966,69. owner of Amiran. Const. Co., dir. of prof. design group. Awards: past pres. of Hunt. Beach, Municipal Employee Assoc., mem. Who's Who in Orange Co., Mem: Kiwanis International. Republican. Rec: fishing, snow skiing. Res/Office: 5942 Brassie Circle, Hunting Beach 92649.

MIRKIN, JEFFREY MIRKIN, car rental co. executive; b. Nov. 5, 1952, Los Angeles; s. Morris J. and Judith Carol (Lindenberg) M.; m. Allison Radford, May 23, 1981; 1 son, Matthew b. 1983; edn: BA psychol., magna cum laude, UC Berkeley 1974; MBA, USC, 1981. Career: asst. to the president, MJM Hydrotech., Los Angeles 1974-78; systems director Budget Rent-a-Car LAX, 1978-79; owner Bruno's Chartreuse restaurant, L.A. 1980--; asst. gen. mgr. Budget Rent-a-Car LAX, 1981-83; exec. vice pres. Budget Rent-a-Car SoCal, 1983--; bd. dirs. California Standard Indemnity, 1982-; bd. dirs. Advanced Touch Systems, 1983-; honors: Phi Beta Kappa (1974), Honor Student Soc. 1972, 73, 74; mem. Los Angeles Chamber of Commerce; Democrat; rec: astronomy, photog., computer pgmmg., tennis. Ofc: Budget Rent-a-Car, 150 S. Doheny Dr Beverly Hills 90211

MISKUS, MICHAEL ANTHONY, electrical engineer; b. Dec. 10, 1950, East Chicago, Ind.; s. Paul J. and Josephine (Forstra) M.; m. Jeannie Ellen Doumanni, June 24, 1949; edn: BS, elect. engring. tech., Purdue Univ. 1972; cert. mgmt. Ind. Central Coll. 1974, cert. mgmt. Ind. Univ., Purdue Univ., 1975. Career: maint. mgr./supr. Diamond Chain Co., Indpls. 1972-76; plant and primary elec. engr. Johnson Baby Products Co., Park Forest South, Ill. 1976-81; plant engr. Sherwin-Williams, Emulsion Plant, Chgo., Ill. 1981-82; prin. Miskus Consultants, Industrial and Commercial Electrical Consultants, Olympia Fields, Ill.; staff facilities engr., acting director plant engring. Bourns Inc., Riverside 1982--; instr., elect. tech. pgms., Moraine Valley Comm. Coll., Prairie State Coll., 1978; recipient P & Q Cost Reduction Award 1983, Bourns Inc., "Utility Rate Analysis"; mem: IEEE, Industrial Applications Soc., Indsl. Electronics & Control Soc. (sr.), Assn. of Energy Engrs., Illumination Engrs. Soc. of North Am., Internat. Platform Soc.; research: electrostatic precipitator, Purdue Univ. 1971-72; Republican; Lutheran; rec: skiing, sailing. Res: 5475 Canyon Crest Dr, 12, Riverside CA 92507 Ofc: Miscon Ltd., POB 292, Olympia Fields, Ill. 60461; Bourns Inc., 1200 Columbia Ave Riverside CA 92507

MISSETT, JUDI SHEPPARD, founder/president Jazzercise, Inc.; b. Mar. 10, 1944, San Diego; d. Del Winifield and June Virgie (Nelson) Sheppard; m. John Vincent Missett, Dec. 23, 1966; childern: Shanna Suzanne, b. 1968; Brendan John, b. 1982; edn: BS, Northwestern Univ. 1966; cert: Presidential Physical Fitness, Ronald Reagan, 1983. Career: profl. dancer since age of 3; danced under Gus Giordano and Matt Mattox; corp. pres./owner/originator and choreographer of Jazzercise Inc., Chgo. 1969-70, Carlsbad 1970--; tchr. 2,500 instructors in physiology and jazz dance technique via videocassette; 300,000 students receive nat. in-house newsletter; honors: Leukemia Soc. Award (1983); City Keys to Boise, New Orleans, Albuquerque, Red Oak (IA), Cleveland, O., and Minnpls.; Spl. Olympics Award.; Dance for Heart; Girl Watching Award-top 10 (1983); mem: Am. Coll. of Sports Med.; Adopt-A-School; Com. of 200; Am. Assn. of Fitness Dirs. in Bus. Industry; CAHPERD; Boys & Girls Clubs; CofC; Friends of the Library; Womens Resource Ctr.; works: choreographed football half-times; columnist, 45 newspapers (Register Tribune Syndicate); jazzercise newsletter (300,000 circ.); rec: dancing, choreography. Ofc: Jazzercise Inc., 2808 Roosevelt St Carlsbad 92008

MISTRY, CHANDRAVADAN M., physician; b. Oct. 13, 1943, Vesma, Gujarat, India; s. Madhavbhai G. and Bhaniben M. Mistry; m. Kamuben, June 23, 1970; edn: premed. stu. Bhavans Coll., Univ. of Bombay 1962-64; MBBS, S.C.B. Med. Coll. (Cuttack Orissa, India) Utkal Univ. 1971. Career: Dept. of Med., Univ. Tng. Hosp., Lusaka, Zambia, Africa; resident internal med. Shadyside Hosp., Pitts., Pa. 1977-80; physician/ splst. Los Angeles Co. Mira Loma Hosp. 1981--; pvt. practice, Valley Internal Med., Med. Gp., Lancaster, part- time; staff: Antelope Valley Med. Ctr., Lancaster; Lancaster Comm. Hosp., Lancaster; publs: contbr. med. journs. of Zambia & East Africa, 1972-73; Hindu; rec: music, photog. Res: 44011 Halcom Ave Lancaster 93534 Ofc: Valley Internal Medicine Medical Group, 910 Lancaster Blvd, Ste 1, Lancaster 93534

MITCHELL, DOCIA MILLICENT, real estate broker; b. Oct. 28, 1912, Mayland, Tenn.; s. Jeff and Miranda (Vickers) Davidson; m. Eugene D. Maddox Nov. 8, 1935, div. Oct. 10, 1945; 1 son, Patrick Eugene b. 1937; m. 2d. Robert Mitchell, Apr. 17, 1949; Calif. lic. Real Estate Broker 1976. Career: housekeeper, Cookville Shirt Factory, 1928-36; wkr. Columbia Mills, Los Angeles 1936-37, leadwoman, Lockheed Aircraft, Burbank, 1942-63, ret.; real estate broker, San Diego currently; mem. San Diego Bd. of Realtors 1965-80; Republican; Baptist; rec: bowling. Res: 8634 Chantilly Ave San Diego 92123

MITCHELL, EARL LAMONT, corporate president; b. Feb. 12, 1912, Sacramento; s. John Wesley and Hilda Maude (Schvalle) M.; m. Doris Aagaard Becher, Sept. 14, 1934; children: Earl, b. 1937; Mary, b. 1940; Jean, b. 1944; att. Jr. Coll. 2 years. Career: Pacific Coast sales rep. Covill Mfg. Co., San Francisco 1932-45; pres./ treas. Mitchell Ent. Inc., owner State Plbg. & Htg. Supplies, San Carlos 1942--; mem: Assn. of US Army ill Golf & Country Club; No. Calif. Seniors Golf Club; Senior Assn. NCGA; Seniors Assn. of Am.; Republican; Christian Science; rec: golf, work. Res: 3950 Sand Hill Rd Woodside 94062 Ofc: State Plbg. & Htg. Supplies, 1000 American San Carlos 94070

MITCHELL, MICHAEL CHARLES, lawyer; b. Feb. 13, 1947, Los Angeles; s. Dominic Chester and Dorothy Marie (Dolmage) M.; m. Ingrid Burkard, June 21, 1969; children: Daniel, b. 1974; Alicia, b. 1974; edn: BA, Loyola Univ., L.A. 1969; JD, Loyola Univ. Sch. of Law 1972; admitted to Calif. State Bar 1972. Career: law clerk Hanna & Morton, Los Angeles 1970-72; assoc. atty. 1972-79; partner Anglea & Buford, Pasadena 1979-82; counsel for Appellee, Darusmont v. United States, US Supreme Ct. 1980; sr. partner MacFarlane, Lambert & Mitchell, Pasadena 1982--; legal advr. Lions Eye Found. of So. Calif. 1978-; legal advr. L.E.F. Meml. Trust 1980-; area chmn. Scout- O- Rama, San Gabriel Valley Council, Boy Scouts of Am. 1982, 83; dir. Pasadena Jaycees Found. 1983-; tlegal advr. Tournament of Toys & Star News Charities; trustee Pasadena Lions Meml. Trust; awards: Distng. Svc. Awd., Pasadena Jaycees 1982; mem: Am., Calif., Los Angeles Co. & Pasadena Bar Assns.; Phi Alpha Delta; Pasadena Lions Club (pres 1980-81); Pasadena Tournament of Roses Assn.; Arcadia Elks Club; Pasadena CofC; Pasadena Univ. Club; Quarterbacks Club of Pasadena; publs: arts. in L.A. Co. Bar Journ. (11/77), L.A. Lawyer (12/78); Republican; Catholic; rec: philately, racquetball, photog. Res: 1007 Entrada Way Glendora 91740 Ofc: MacFarlane, Lambert & Mitchell, 35 N Lake Ave Pasadena 91101

MITCHELL, RICHARD PAUL, sales executive, teacher, writer; b. Feb. 2, 1939, Brooklyn, NY; s. Richard Francis and Helen (Olive) M.; m. Cynthia Skolnik, Mar. 1, 1980; edn: BS, St. Francis Coll. 1961; Graduate Fellow San Diego St. Coll. 1964-5, USC 1962, Yeshiva Univ. 1962-3, Adelphi Univ. 1963-4. Career: tchr. mathematics, NY, 1961-66; salesman Wang Labs., NYC 1966-69; salesman Computer Mach. Corp., L.A. 1969-70; independent contr., self-empl. 1970-77; sales engr. Hewlett-Packard, L.A. 1977-79; dist. sales mgr. Terak Corp., L.A. 1979-82; Western Dist. sales mgr. Lundy Electronics, L.A. 1982-83; dist. sales mgr. Zitel Corp., 1983--; instr. Los Angeles Comm. Coll. 1981-; mem: IEEE, The Acad. of Magical Arts, The Magic Castle, UCSD Pascal Users Soc., Apple Users Soc., The Unofficial LACC Computer Club (pres. 1981); coauthor: Positive Expectation Handicapping (Foothill Press 1983); arts. in Gambling Times (7/80), The MicroComputer Investor (1982); rec: writing, pgmg., magic, softball. Res: 4455 Los Feliz Blvd Los Angeles 90027

MITCHELL, ROBERT RALPH, city manager; b. July 19, 1928, Emporia, Ks.; s. Ralph B. and Susan Hazel (Ace) M.; m. Lois Amerine, Apr. 11, 1954; children: Janice, b. 1955; Julia, b. 1957; R. Brian, b. 1959; Edith Susan, b. 1964; edn: certs., Univ. of Chgo. and Penna. State Univ.; BS, Emporia State Univ. 1950; MPA, Univ. of Ks. 1958. Career: admin. asst. to city mgr., Ferguson, Mo. 1954-56; borough mgr./ secty. Holidaysburg, Pa. 1956-59, Sharpsville, Pa. 1959-63; city mgr. Webster City, Io. 1963; municipal financial analyst J.B. Hanaur & Co., Beverly Hills 1964-65; Marche & Co., Los Angeles 1965; city mgr. Coachella, Calif. 1965-68; city mgr, Duarte 1968-75; city mgr. Baldwin Park 1975-76; city mgr., Loma Linda 1977--; adj. faculty Ctr. for Pub. Policy & Admin., CSU Long Beach 1976-; pgm. adv. bd. Calif. State Coll. San Bernardino 1983; honors: 25 Yr. Svc. Cert., Internat. City Mgmt. Assn.; Commdns. from City Council of Loma Linda, Mayor of Baldwin Park, City Council of Duarte, City Council of Coachella, The Burgess & Council of Sharpsville, Pa.; mem: Internat. City Mgmt. Assn.; Inland Empire City Mgrs. Assn. (pres. 1982-83); Am. Soc. for Pub. Admin.; Rotary, So. San Bernardino (pres. 1984-85); Masons, Yorkrite, Scottish Rite; mil: spl. agent US Army Counter-Intell. Corp 1951-54; Presbyterian; rec: old cars, wedgwood. Res: 11721 Martin St Loma Linda 92354 Ofc: City of Loma Linda, 11128 Anderson St Loma Linda 92354

MITCHELL, WILLIAM J., city councilman; b. Feb. 24, 1933, San Diego; s. Arnold Robert ad Marguerite Marie (Dunn) M.; children: William, b. 1964; Robin, b. 1970; edn: BS, Univ. of Calif. 1958; cont. edn., San Diego Bd. Realtors 1979-84. Career: owner/ broker Bill Mitchell Real Estate 1958-77, Santa Barbara, Newport Beach, La Jolla; owner English Antiques 1973-75; deputy mayor City of San Diego 1981; city councilman City of San Diego 1977--; exec. com. Santa Barbara Bd. Realtor 1964-65; v.p. Real Estate Brokers Assn. of La Jolla 1975-76; dir. Newport Harbor Bd. Realtors 1960-61; honors: Judge Ralph Knox Awd., Real Estate Brokers Assn. 1972; Maharishi Awd., 1st in Govt. 1982; San Diego Police Dept. Awd. 1978; mem: Masons, Scottish Rite, Save Our Heritage Orgn., Hist. Soc., Scottish Games (medalist), La Jolla Town Council, San Diego- Yokohama Sister City Soc.; founder/ dir. Neighborhood Awareness Program Against Crime (1976-78), I Report Crime pgm. (1981), San Diego Police Horse Patrol (1982), San Diego Crime Commn., Alcohol & Drug Abuse Prevention Task Force; mil: s/sgt. USAF 1951-55, GCM, Korean Svc., UN Svc. w/ Battle Star, Nat. Defense Svc., ROK Pres. Unit Citation; Republican; Presbyterian/ Metaphysical; rec: ship model constn., poetry. Res: 17555 Drayton Hall Way San Diego 92128 Ofc: 202 C Street San Diego 92101

MITOCK, MARK STEVEN, educator/adolescent therapist; b. May 9, 1945, Los Angeles; s. Barnett and Sara (Rosberg) M.; m. Marijane Ronson, Nov. 7, 1971; children: Danielle Cara, b. 1975; Brandi Joy, b. 1983; edn: BA, UCLA 1967; MS, USC 1970; Calif. Std. Secondary Tchg. Credential (1968) Adminstrv. Tchg. Cred. (1979) Splst. Learning Handicapped (1975); MFCC- Marriage, Family & Child Counselor, BBSE 1979. Career: tchr./ therapist Camps Miller/ Kirkpatrick, Malibu, L.A. Co. Dept. of Probation 1970; tchr./ therapist Wm. Workman High Sch., La Puente Unif. Sch. Dist. (dept. chmn. spl. edn. dept.) 1971-74; founder/ dir.: Pathways Sch., Sherman Oaks 1974-80; Wilshire West Sch., Santa Monica 1972--; Parkside Acad., Van Nuys 1980--; pvt. practice (splst. adolescent and family treatment) 1979--; cons. Spl. Edn. Overseas Tng. Pgm., Lakenheath, Eng. 1979; honors: grad. fellow, USC 1970; mem: Calif. Assn. Marriage & Family Therapists (W. L.A. Chpt.); Gp. Psychotherapy Assn. of So. Calif. (chmn. Ethics Com.); Zeta Beta Tau frat., UCLA; Santa Monica CofC (Edn. Com.); Sch. Community Attendance Com. (in conjunction w/ Santa Monica Police Dept.); Community Outreach Pgm. (adolescents w/ lng. & emotional disorders), Santa Monica & Van Nuys; rec: river rafting, paddle tennis, films. Res: 4857 Winnetka Woodland Hills 91364 Ofc: Wilshire West School, 1516 19th St Santa Monica 90404

MITSUOKA, J. CHRIS, clinical pharmacist; b. Sept. 19, 1948, Visalia; s. Noboru and Miyoko Ann (Katano) M.; m. Kyoko Toyota, June 26, 1971; children: Jevon Chris b. 1976, Trenton James b. 1981; edn: BA, Univ. of Redlands 1970; Dr. Pharm., UC San Francisco 1974; res. UCSF, 1975. Career: clin. pharm. Dept. of Pharm. and dir. pharmacokinetics Dept. of Pathol., UC Davis Med. Ctr., Sacto., 1977--; asst. prof. of clin. pharm., Coll. of Pharm., Creighton Univ., Omaha, Nebr. and clin. coord. of pharm., VA Hosp., Omaha, 1975-77; honors: John Walter Millar Award, UCSF, Carey Scholarship, UCSF, Rho Chi Soc.; forensic awards: Univ. of Redlands Debate Team 1968-70, San Fernando Valley Univ. Invitnl. Tourn. 1st Pl., Ariz. State Univ. Roadrunner Tourn. 4th Pl., Univ. of Calif. Prev. Tourn. cert. award; mem: Am. Soc. of Hosp. Pharmacists, sacto. Valley Soc. of Hosp. Pharmacists; publs: num. arts., sci. papers in profl. journals; num. sci. presentations nat. profl. meetings 1975-; Democrat; Buddhist; rec: fishing, judo, computers. Res: 6830 Wavecrest Way, Sacramento 95831 Ofc: Univ. of Calif. Davis Medical Center, Dept. Pharmacy, 2315 Stockton Blvd Sacramento 95817

MIYAMOTO, SAM SHIGERU, international co. executive; b. Mar. 22, 1927, Brawley, Calif.; s. Shininchi and Masu (Shiosaki) M.; m. Jean Kageyama, 1960; children: Sharon, b. 1962; Julie, b. 1967; Steven, b. 1969; edn: BS, USC. Career: with Mitsubishi Internat. Corp., 28 yrs.; mgr. of machinery 1969; asst. to gen. mgr. 1976--; spl. interest in developing trade between Japan and Calif. and creating opportunities for Calif. business (big and small) in internat. world trade; Democrat; Protestant; rec: camping, bowling, golf. Res: 849 Ridgecrest St Monterey Park 91754 Ofc: Mitsubishi International Corp., 555 S Flower St Los Angeles 91754

MIYOSHI, DAVID MASAO, lawyer; b. Jan. 2, 1944, Overton, Nev.; s. Joseph Masaru and Jean Michiye (Horikiri) M.; m. Teruko, July 14, 1977; children: Mark, b. 1980; Brandon, b. 1981; edn: BS, USC 1966; JD, Hastings Coll. of Law 1973; MBA, Harvard Univ. 1978; Cert. of Completion, Waseda Univ. Tokyo 1976; admitted to State Bar of Calif. 1973. Career: liaison atty. Matsuo & Korsugi law ofc., Tokyo, Japan 1974-76; atty./ mgr. real estate dept. Mori & Ota law ofc., Los Angeles 1978-80; atty./ asst. head Far East ops. dept. Morgan, Lewis & Bockius, Los Angeles 1980-82; pres./chmn. bd. Trans-Continental Investment Inc. & Dai-Ichi Mortgage Corp., Los Angeles & Tokyo 1982--; dir. Miyoka Assn. 1983; dir. Avalon Auto Parts 1980; dir. PC-9 Ent. Inc. 1983; honor: Beta Gamma Sigma 1966; mem: Am. Bar. Assn. (Internat. Bus. & Real Property Divs.); Calif. Bar Assn.; Japanese Am. Republican Soc. Trust; Japanese Am. Citizens League; publs: Condominiums, Securities or Real Estate? (Horei legal publ. Tokyo, Japan 1976); mil: capt. USMC, Naval Commdn.; Republican; Baptist; rec: pvt. pilot, tennis, golf. Res: 4307 Newton St Torrance 90505 Ofc: Dai-Ichi Mortgage Corp., 700 S Flower St, Ste 2200, Los Angeles 90017

MIYOSHI, RICHARD YUTAKA, dental laboratory owner; b June 2, 1956, San Francisco; s. Joseph Kaname and Sachiko (Komiya) M.; edn: AS, dental lab. tech., City Coll. of S.F. 1977; BS in health sci., cum laude, CSU San Francisco 1980, cert. higher edn. 1981; Cert. in Dental Lab. Tech., Nat. Bd. 1980; Calif. Comm. Coll. Instr. Cred., 1982. Career: dental lab. tech. Eaton Dental Laboratory, San Francisco 1975-77, NK Dental Lab., 1977-79; certified dental lab. tech. Dent-Arts Dental Lab., S.F. 1979-80, L & L Dental Lab., 1980-81, Cardinal Dental Lab., Oakland 1981-82; faculty mem. City Coll. of S.F., 1981--; dental lab. owner, 1983--; listed in Who's Who in the Dental Laboratory Indus. directory 1981, 82; mem: Certified Dental Lab. Technologists, Nat. Assn. of Dental Labs.; rec: photog., painting, jewelry. Res: 582 19th Ave San Francisco 94121 Ofc: 200 Valley Drive Brisbane; City College of San Francisco, 50 Phelan Ave, Ste S104, San Francisco 94112

MODJTAHEDI, PARVIZ MODJI, marketing/administration executive; b. June 11, 1939, Tehran, Iran; USA Perm. Res.; s. Mahammed Ali and Suzanne Jeanne (Van De Nostande) M.; children: Bijan, b. 1961; Susan, b. 1969; edn: BA, London Univ. 1966, MSc, 1968. Career: asst. London Univ. 1968; mgr. productivity svcs. Iran Nat. Airline, Tehran 1969-72; dir. of tng. IDRO, Tehran 1972-76; v.chancellor Farabi Univ., Tehran 1976-79; assoc. prof. mktg. Tehran Univ. 1970-79; mktg. exec. Bowmont Corp. Corp., London & Calif. 1979-82; chief exec./ pres. Firstworld Travel of Orange Co. Inc., Newport Beach 1982--; honors: 1st Class Honors, London Univ. 1968; Paul Harris Fellow, Rotary Internat. 1978; mem: Am. Mgmt. Assn.; British Inst. of Mgmt. (assoc.); Indsl. Mgmt. Inst.; fellow, British Soc. of Commerce; Rotary Club, Newport Harbor (past pres.); CofC; Balboa Bay Club; publs: var. mktg. & mkt. research papers 1970-80; rec: music. Res: 3110 Park Newport Newport Beach 92660 Ofc: Firstworld Travel of Orange County Inc., 567 San Nicolas Dr, St 210, Newport Beach 92660

MOELLER, MARLO ALFRED, restaurant owner; b. Aug. 7, 1929, Wheaton, Minn.; s. Arthur Henry and Loretta (Baumgartner) M.; m. Joyce Ingram, Jan. 14, 1955; children: Vicky b. 1955, Kevin b. 1957, Scott b. 1963; edn: Navigator, AF Basic Nav. Sch., James Connally AFB, Waco, Tx. 1955, Squadron Officer Sch., Maxwell AFB, Ala. 1960; desig. Flight Navigator, FAA 1966. Career: served to major, USAF 1951-71, became a Master Navigator, flew with V.I.P.s, 1961-71, flew in SouthEast Asia, 1967-68, served on num. boards, served as U.S. Customs, Immigration and Plant Quarantine Ofcr., ret. in 1971 with over 10,000 accident free flying hours; decorated Air Medal w/4 oak leaf clusters, Navy - Marine Pres. Unit Cit. w/star, Nat. Def. Svc. Medal bronze star, AF Longevity Svc. Awd. w/ 3 oak leaf clusters, Southeast Asia medal, AF Reserve medal, GCM, Merit Svc., Korean Svc., UN Svc., Repub. of Vietnam., Nat. Def. Svc. medals; real estate sales agt. in Colorado Springs, Colo. 1971-74; ptnr. Belgian Waffle Inn, Santa Ana, Calif. 1974-, pres./sole owner 1977--; mem: Retired Officers Assn. (TROA); Indep.; Christian. Res: 26432 Estanciero Mission Viejo 92691 Ofc: Belgian Waffle Inn, 3820 S. Plaza Dr Santa Ana 92704

MOFFAT, CLARK GORDON, financial planner; b. May 25, 1956, Glendale; s. Gordon Howard and Barbara Lee (Brooks) M.; m. Elizabeth Nobles, June 27, 1978; children: Jonathan, b. 1979; Michelle, b. 1980; Cameron, b. 1983; edn: BS in fin. plng., Brigham Young Univ. 1980; (CFP) Cert. Fin. Plnnr. 1984. Career: Diversified Financial Program 1980-81; Personal Financial Planner 1981-83; assoc. plnnr. Surety Investment Svcs., Los Angeles 1983--; bd.dirs. Denton Osteopathic Hosp., Denton, Tex. 1980-83; mem: Internat. Assn. Fin. Plnnrs. (L.A. chpt.); Freeman Inst.; Boy Scouts of Am. (Eagle Scout); Ch. of Jesus Christ of LDS (missionary Sydney, Aus. 2 yrs.); rec: sailing, golf. Res: 3214 Montrose Ave La Crescenta 91214 Ofc: Surety Investment Services, 4050 Wilshire Blvd, Ste 507, Los Angeles

MOFFITT, JOHN PAUL, lawyer; b. Oct. 12, 1942, Compton; s. Robert Allen and Enid Ruth Moffitt; m. Linda R. Holte, July 11, 1964; children: Monique R., b. 1968; Robert M., b. 1983; edn: BA, Occidental Coll. 1964; JD, Calif. Western Univ. Sch. of Law 1967; admitted to State Bar of Calif. 1967. Career: summer mgmt. tng. pgm. Security Pacific Nat. Bank 1960-66; assoc., law ofcs. Goodstein & Moffitt 1967-71; partner, law firm Jackson & Goodstein, then (name chg.) Goodstein, Copes & Field, 1972-79; partner, law firm Dewar & Moffitt 1979--; prof. bus. law, L.A. Comm. Colls. 1972-74; judge pro tem, W. L.A. Municipal Ct. 1977-78; awards: Home Fed. Savings & Loan Scholarship, 3d. year law sch. outstanding student award; mem: Am. (Banking & Bus. Law sect.), Los Angeles County, Century City (bd. dirs.) bar assns.; Am. Ajudicature Soc.; mem. Sch. Bd. St. Matthews Parish Sch., Pac. Palisades; Occidental Coll. Alumni Assn. (William Stuart Young Soc.); Sunset Mesa Property Owners Assn.; publs: arts. in law revs.; Republican; Episcopal; rec: gardening, tennis. Res: 18301 Clifftop Way Malibu 90265 Ofc: Dewar and Moffitt, 1900 Ave of the Stars, Ste 950, Los Angeles 90067

MOHAMED, JOSEPH, SR., business owner; b. Mar. 19, 1928, Omar, WV; s. Mose (Moski Mohamed Al Habal) and Minnie Elizabeth (Martin) M.; gr.grandfathers Jesse Testerman and Cable Martin fought in the Civil War; m. Shirley Medieros, June 22, 1979; children (by previous marriage): Joseph Jr. b. 1948, James R. b. 1951, John W. b. 1951, Leslie Louise b. 1957; edn: AA, Sacramento Jr. Coll. 1951; BA, CSU Sacto. 1954. Lic. Calif. State Contractor, engring., gen., landscape, excavating-grading-paving, solar; Agri. Pest Control Opr.-Contractor, Agri. Pest Control Adviser, R.E. Broker, lic. Common Carrier hwy. transp.; lic. comml. pilot, rotor, instrument, flight instr. Career: worked on family ranches, farms in Lodi and Stockton areas, -1945; estab. a comml. trucking opn., hauled produce and lumber, Calif. and Nev., 1949-52; estab. the Mexican Co. of Agri. and Livestock, Ltd., Ensenada, Baja, Calif., Mex., devel. 2500 acres raising grain & row crops, 1953-57; opr. air charter service, Baja Calif., Mex. 1953-57; owner Quintair Inc. of Calif., an air charter service, 1957--; small scale farming in Sacto. Valley area, hay, orchard crops, raise and show horses, 1958--; R.E. investor, 1949--; R.E. subdivider, developer, 1970--. Mem. Masons, Shriners, Scottish Rite, Elks, Sacto Univ. Alumni Assn., Sacto City and Co. Mus., Elk Grove Hist. Soc., Sacto. and Calif. State Horsemans Assns., Amer. Heart Assn., Sacto Metro CofC, 1972-, Landscape Contractors Assn. 1952-58 (past pres.), Navy League of US (past pres.), Reserve Ofcrs. Assn. (v.p.), Assn. of US Army, Nat. Rifle Assn. (life), Calif. State Hwy. Patrol Aux., Sacto Co. Sheriff's Dept. Reserve Deputy, Sacto. Co. Sheriff's Mounted Posse (dir. active riding mem.), Elk Grove CofC, Sacto Safety Council, Ore. Shakespeare Festival Assn., Sacto. Regl. Arts Council, Civil Affairs Assn., Calif. Rental Assn., Sacto./Calif./Nat. Apartment Assn., Sacto. Country Music Assn. (life), Friends of Sacto. Hist. Soc. (contrib.), McClellan Aviation Mus. Found. (dir.), Easter Seal Soc. for Crippled Children (contrib.), Comstock Club of Sacto, Commonwealth Club SF, Sacto Bd. of Realtors, Calif./Nat. Assn. of Realtors, Am. River Coll. Found., Salvation Army, YMCA; apptd. mem. Gov's Emergency Drought Task Force 1977; mil: enlisted US Army 1946, commnd. 2d lt. 1947, ret. col. USAR 1978; Legion of Merit, Merit Svc., 2 Army Commendn. medals; Republican (Pres. Task Force); Moslem; rec: photog., hunting, riding. Address: 4405 College Oak Dr Sacramento 95841

MOHAMMADI, RASHED, computer systems specialist/engineer; b. Jan. 3, 1955, Karachi, Pakistan; s. Khurshid Mahamadi and Noor Jehan (Soofi) M.; edn: BS, math., Karachi Univ., 1974; stu. elec. eng. dept., Univ. of Nebr., Lincoln 1974-75; BS, elec. eng., Tex. Tech. Univ. 1977. Career: electronics tech. troubleshooter Calculator Div., Tex. Instruments 1976-77, field customer engr. in data systems group, 1977-, currently tech. splst. main frame computer systems and peripherals, Texas Instruments Inc., Irvine, Ca.; instr. sys. engineers, computer dealers: communications and networking seminars; honors: award cert. as valuable mem. tech. support, Texas Instruments, L.A. 1984; mem: Pakistani Am. Assn. (Alhambra chpt. dir. 1984); vol. envoy aid for Pakistan, L.A. Olympics; chmn. youth gp. Islamic Center of San Gabriel Valley 1983-4; Islam; rec: tennis. Res: 13579 Lily Pl Chino 91710 Ofc: Texas Instruments Inc. 17891 Cartwright Rd, Irvine 92714

MOHAN, SHAMANNA, dentist; b. May 10, 1951; Bangalore, Karnataka, India; d. Byrathi Muniswamappa and Savithri (Apajappa) Shamanna; m. Kajeswari Mohan, Mar. 25, 1976; children: Vilekha, b. 1977; Vikash, b. 1981; edn: Bach. of Dental Surgery,, Govt. Dental Sch., India 1974; Calif. lic. Dentist. Career: assoc. Sunshine Dental Gp. 1980-81; owner/ pvt. practitioner

Golden State Dental Gp., Long Beach 1981--; mem: Karnataka State Dental Council; rec: racquetball, bowling, tennis. Res: 7912 Comstock Cir La Palma 90623 Ofc: Golden State Dental Group, 5399 Orange Ave Long Beach 90805

MOHR, CAROLYN STEVENS, psychiatrist; b. July 28, 1935, New Orleans, La.; d. George and Myrtle Caroline (Watts) Stevens; twp children: Steven, b. 1962; Gina, b. 1963; edn: BS, Xavier Univ. 1950-54; MS, Tuskeegee Inst. 1960-61; MD, Tulane Sch. of Med. 1976. Career: chief coord. med. edn. reinforcement & enrichment pgm. Tulane Med. Sch. 1973-74; psychiatric res. M.L. King Hosp. 1976-79; chief res. 1978-79; pvt. practice 1980--; staff psychiatrist sev. hosps., L.A. 1979--; med. dir. KAZI Residential Drug Pgm. 1981-; med. dir. JAMAA Drug Treatment pgm. 1978-81; asst. prof. Charles Drew Post Grad. Med. Sch. 1979-81; acting dir. Psychiatric Emergency- Walk in Clinic Svc. and chief Crisis Evalutian Unit, Martin Luther King Hosp. 1979-81; mem: Inglewood Physicians Assn.; Black Women Physician Assn.; LAX CofC; Inglewood CofC; Alpha Kappa Alpha; Spl. People in Comm. Affairs (SPICE); Democrat; Catholic/ Ch. of Relig. Sci.; rec: sky diving, gardening, sailing. Res: 5643 Chariton Ave Los Angeles 90056 OFc: Carolyn S. Mohr, MD, 336 E Hillcrest Blvd, Ste 507, Inglewood 90301

MOIR, RALPH WAYNE, physicist; b. Jan. 21, 1940, Bellingham, Wash.; s. Francis Leroy and Florence Augusta (Hershey) M.; m. Elizabeth ranstead, June 8, 1963; children: Sara, b. 1965, Steven, b. 1967, Christina, b. 1969; edn: BS, UC Berkeley 1962; ScD, MIT, 1967. Career: research physicist, group leader, project leader, Lawrence Livermore National Lab.; dir. resrch. pgms. in magnetic fusion energy field, spec. in direct energy conversion and fusion breeder research; coinventor of Yin-Yang Magnet configuration; 5 patents; num. technical articles; mem: American Nuclear Soc. (tech. pgm. chmn.), Fellow American Physical Soc., Am. Future Soc., Americans for Energy Independence, Scientists and Engrs. for Secure Energy, Negative Population Growth; mem. Boys Scouts; Republican; Unitarian; rec: hunting, fishing, farming. Res: 1730 Murdell Ln Livermore 94550 Ofc: Lawrence Livermore National Lab., POB 554, Livermore 94550

MOISE, LAURIE LEE, equitation instructor and lecturer; b. Jan. 24, 1954, San Diego; d. Donald F. and Joyce Lorraine (Beech) Campbell; m. A. Steven Moise, Sept. 2, 1978; 1 son: Adam Christopher, b. 1983; edn: BS in animal sci., Calif. State Polytech. Univ., Pomona 1976; Brit. Horse Soc. asst. instr. cert., Curland Equestrian Ent. (Somerset, Eng.) 1977; M.Agric., Cal Poly Pomona 1979. Career: asst. to dir. of nutrition Moorman's Mfg. Co., San Rafael 1978; columnist, The Feed Bin, for the Pony Express weekly, Norco 1979-83; head equitation instr. J.K. Kellogg Arabian Horse Ctr./ lectr. animal sci. dept. Calif. Polytech. Univ., Pomona 1979--; honors: Outstanding Young Women of Am. 1981; mem: Gamma Sigma Delta; Am. Soc. of Animal Scientists; Sigma Xi; De Anza D.O.G. Club; Orange Empire Dog Club; Inland Empire Golden Retriever Club; Golden Retriever Club of Am.; publs: The Effect of Cottonseed Meal on Growth of Young Horses, Journ. of Animal Sci., 8/81; Democrat; Methodist; rec: raising & showing Golden Retrievers. Res: 243 Seventh St Norco 91760 Ofc: Cal Poly University, 3810 W Temple Pomona 91768

MOLAND, GERHARD MICHAEL, child welfare adminstrator; b. Dec. 1, 1937, Eau Claire, Wisc.; s. Oscar Gerhard and Pearl Eloise (Buntz) M.; m. Cheryl Trimmer, July 18, 1970; children; Mary, b. 1971; Michael, b. 1972; Christopher, b. 1976; edn: BA, Carlton, b. 1959; MSW, USC 1968; (LCSW) Lic. Clin. Soc. Wkr., Calif. 1968; ACSW NASW (1968-82). Career: probation counselor Los Angeles Co. Probation Dept., Downey 1963-64; with L.A. Co. Dept. of Pub. Soc. Svcs. 1964--; soc. wkr., Long Beach 1964-68; child welfare wkr., Long Beach 1968-69; child welfare supvr. 1969-72; pgm. analyst, El Monte 1972-75; deputy regl. svcs. adminstr., Norwalk 1975-80; head emergency responce proj., El Monte 1980-81; dir. child sexual abuse proj., El Monte 1981; dir. emergency protective svcs., El Monte 1981--; therapist Long Beach Family Svc. 1968-; instr. Long Beach City Coll. 1972-83; adv. com. Project High Risk 1983; mem: Nat. Assn. Soc. Wkrs.; Long Beach Petroleum Club; Long Beach Youth Soccer Orgn. (coach); Webelos leader, Long Beach; mil: lt. USNR 1959-66; rec: coaching youth soccer. Res: 3811 Pine Ave Long Beach 90807 Ofc: Los Angeles County, Dept. of Public Social Services, 4024 N Durgee, El Monte 91732

MONEY, RUSTY, artist; b. Nov. 16, Oak Lawn, IL; d. Clarence Louis and Hazel Mae (LeVroix) Krieger; pat. grandmother Fredricka Prang Krueger posed for Charles Dana Gibson's famous Gibson Girls series; edn: Emilita Terry Art Course, Washington Sch. of Art, Texas A&M Univ., Ariz. State Univ., 1959-61; pvt. study under Xivair Gonzales (Life Mag. staff artist Series on Egypt), Ariz. artist Wm. Schimmel; m. 1948; div. 1971; chil: Breton Rice, Melisa Rice Foltz. Career: began drawing at age 5, with ink drawings of Gibson as ideal; began painting about 1950---; devel. special technique (in oils that appear to be watercolors); freelance profl. artist, currently in Escondido; her series (4) of lmtd. edition Plates, Figurines (7), Lithos (2) are sold throughout USA and Canada; her paintings in num. pvt. collections. Recipient 1963, 64 Gold Cup 1st Prize Ariz. Annual Shows, Mesa Art League Awards, 1st Pl., Calif. 1980, Hazeltine Collection; num. other awards. Mem: Internatl. Fine Art League; Amer. Art Assn.; World Wide Artists Assn.; Orange Co. Art Assn. Republican. Lutheran. Rec: aiding young people, vol. counseling. Studio: 1651-147 So. Juniper, Escondido 92025.

MONJI, MICHAEL ALLAN, landscape contractor/ distributor; b. Feb. 11, 1951, St. Paul, Minn.; s. Fred and Gladys Dorothy (Bierdorf) M.; edn: AA, Bakersfield Coll. 1973; BS, CSC Bakersfield 1975. Career: owner Michael

Monji Landscaping/ Valley Sprinkler & Nursery, Bakersfield 1969--; pest control opr./advsr.; tchr. weed & fertilization control, CSC Bakersfield; honors: winner three Statewide Landscaping Awards, 19 local Landscape Awds.; mem: Calif. Landscape Contractors Assn. (pres. Bakersfield chpt. 1982-83); Democrat; Catholic; rec: sports, skiing. Address: Valley Sprinkler, 2600 Brundage Ln Bakersfield 93304

MONK, SYDNEY C., publishing co. executive; b. Feb. 2, 1954, San Francisco; s. James A. and Diana Charla (Williams) M.; edn: Sonoma State Univ. (2 yrs.). Career: pres. Calif. Readers Service, Lafayette 1981--; sales rep. Western Readers Service 1981; bd. dirs. Proj. One, San Francisco 1975-81; mem: Sierra Club; Hegira Found. (bd. dirs., apptd. pres. 1980-); Republican; Episcopal; rec: rock climbing, camping, skiing. Res: 1947 Reliez Valley Rd Lafayette 94549 Ofc: California Readers Service, POB 1355 Lafayette 94549

MONROE, STANLEY EDWIN, surgeon; b. June 26, 1902, Bangor, MI; s. Samuel E. and Ella M. Monroe; Edn: AB, Univ. of Mich., 1925; MD, Rush Med. Coll., 1936; m. Ruth Williams, June 14, 1933, dec. Dec. 10, 1981; m. 2d., Flora Quinn, Aug. 6, 1982. Career: intern, Evanston (IL) Hosp., 1935-36; resident surg. 1936-37, asst. surgeon 1940-41; clin. asst. surg., Northwestern Univ., 1938-39, instr. surg. 1940-41, asst. to Dr. Frederick Christopher, 1937-41; chief surg., VA Hosp., Tucson, 1947-49; surg. Aramco, Saudi Arabia, 1950-51; pvt. practice, Chula Vista, CA, 1952-82; founder of Monroe Clinic; served from WAC TR Center. chief surg., 4th Gen. Hosp., Surgical Cons., AFWest Pac, Australian Base Surg. Honors: AOA, Phi Beta Pi; founder, Soc. of Academic Achievement. Mem: Masons, Chula Vista Lodge; Univ. Club, San Diego. Numerous medical publs., author of med. phrase book with vocabulary, also Spanish ed. Democrat. Protestant. Rec: fly fishing, book collector, travel. Res: 2 Palomar Dr., Chula Vista 92011.

MONTAGNESE, JAMES JOSEPH, stockbroker; b. June 13, 1922, Gypsum, Ohio; s. Rocco and Carmela (Petulla) M.; m. Rose Borning, June 22, 1946; children: Rocco b. 1963, Carmela b. 1965; edn: Simmons Inst., Valley Coll., Chaffey Coll. Career: General Industries Co., Elyria, Ohio 1945; Bendix Westinghouse, 1946; co-owner Naros Gift Shop, Fontana, Ca. 1948-63; stockbroker 1963--, asst. mgr. and accout v.p. Paine Webber, Redlands, currently; recipient num. profl. awards; mem: pres. 20-30 Club, Rotary, Elks, Knights of Columbus (3rd degree), Fontana Theater Guild (pres.); works: radio and local tv shows, Little Theater, Civic Light Opera in San Bernardino, app. in minstrel show played at Worlds Fair in NY (1939); mil: tech. sgt. Air Corps 1942-45; Republican; Catholic; rec: theater, music. Res: 23231 Westwood Dr Grand Terrace 92324 Ofc: Paine Webber, 205 East State St Redlands 92373

MONTELONGO, ABEL GONZALES, real estate broker-developer; b. Nov. 24, 1931, Del Rio, Tex. s. Serapio Perez and Juana Montelongo; m. Aileen Hernandez, May 29, 1948; children: Joseph Robert, b. 1949; Juanita Sue, b. 1951; Mary Elaine, b. 1952; Peggy Jo, b. 1953; edn: San Angelo Jr. Coll. 1951-52; Calif. lic: R.E. Broker, Gen. Contractor, R.E. Appraiser. Career: real estate developer, investor; owner Century Realty & Century Investment Co.; v.p. Alianza Internat. Corp.; chmn. bd. First Internat. Bank; mem: Musicians Assn. of San Diego Co.; AFL-CIO; Mexican-Am. Found.; Kingsmen Internat.; S.E.R. Jobs for Progress; Internat. Orgn. of R.E. Appraisers; Musicians Union; Real Estate Bd.; mil. service in Vietnam U.S.O. 1969-70, GS15 desig. (col.); Republican; Assembly of God; rec: music. Res: 233 Chula Vista St Chula Vista 92010 Ofc: Century Realty, 211-B Church Ave Chula Vista 92010

MONTGOMERY, ARTHUR JAMES, landscape architect; b. Nov. 5, 1931, Flint, Mich.; s. Arthur Harold and Verna Eulla (McKinstry) M.; m. Marjorie Small, Sept. 11, 1951; children: Donald, b. 1953; Stephen, b. 1954; Louis, b. 1956; Kenneth, b. 1962; Jennifer, b. 1978; edn: BS, Calif. State Polytech. Univ. 1964; lic. Landscape Arch., Calif. 1980. Career: engr. Pacific Telephone Co. 1952-83, ret.; partner Small & Montgomery 1978-81; landscape architect/prin. A. James Montgomery 1981--; guest lectr. UC Riverside; recipient Awd. of Merit (1969), Silver Beaver (1972), Boy Scouts of Am.; mem: Am. Soc. of Landscape Architects; City of Riverside Design Review Bd.; City of Riverside Park & Recreation Commn.; Republican; Presbyterian; rec: back packing, scouting. Address: A. James Montgomery & Assoc., 2817 Ronald St Riverside 92506

MONTIELLE, E. JAN, educator/therapist; b. Feb. 10, 1940, Cincinnati, Ohio; d. Paul and Catherine (Brauch) Brinkpeter; m. Pascual Martinez, Apr. 26, 1955; div.; 1 dau. Lisa, b. 1967; edn: BS, sec. edn., Univ. of Dayton (Ohio), 1963; MA in counseling, w/distinc., National Univ. 1983; Reg. MFCC Intern (Marriage, Family Child Counselor) Calif. 1983; Trager Psychophysical Integration and Mentastics Practitioner, Trager Inst. 1983. Career: tchr. Fatima High Sch., Dayton, O. 1962-63; tchr./counselor St. Mary's High Sch., Phoenix, Ariz. 1963-66; ednl. cons. Calif. State Dept. of Vocational Rehab., Salinas 1967-69; personnel mgr./buyer Bud Antle Co., Salinas 1970; adminstrv. analyst/asst. registra Univ. Calif., San Diego 1971--; asst. dir. San Diego Trager Center, Del Mar 1983--; pvt. practice, Trager, Encinitas 1983--; awards: Joint award for leadership, and scholarship, National Univ./UCSD (1982); mem: Calif. Assn. of Marriage and Family Therapists, Trager Inst., San Diego Trager Center, S.D. Coalition on Alcohol Problems, Pacific Assn. of Collegiate Registrar and Admissions Officers, UC Staff Assn.; vol. gp. facilitator Scripps Meml. Hosp. Alcohol and Chem. Abuse Treatment Ctr., La Jolla 1983; mem. UCSD Com. on Alcohol and Substance Abuse 1983; mem. Internat. Graphoanalysis Soc. (1978-81), served as resource psn. on identifying learning disabilities through handwriting and referral to sch. pgms.; Democrat; metaphysical; rec:

writing, art, music. Res: 1739 Old Mill Rd Encinitas 92024 Ofc: AC 102/Q-0210R University of Calif., San Diego La Jolla 92093 San Diego Trager Center 1011 Camino Del Mar, Ste 266, Del Mar 92014

MONTOYA, ERNEST ELOY, roofing consultant; b. Mar. 15, 1915, Albuquerque, N.Mex.; s. Elias Robinson and Caroline (Saavedra) M.; m. Alyce Lopez, Dec. 23, 1939; children: Jo Ann, b. 1940; Patricia, b. 1945; Jeanette, b. 1949; Ernest John, b. 1950; Rick Henry, b. 1952; Marybeth, b. 1956; Calif. lic. Roofing Contractor, 1945. Career: roofers helper, apprenticeship 1930s; lic roofer 1945--: roofing consultant, Bakersfield Shingles Wholesale, Bakersfield; supvr. roofing constrn. Camp Roberts, Paso Robles (CA), Florence and Parker (AZ); Camp Beale, Marysville, Vandenberg, Lompoc, and Inyokern (CA) during WWII; mem: Better Bus. Bureau; Bakersfield, Kern Co. Builders Exchange; Bakersfield Knights of Columbus; patentee: TV Monitor (1965); Republican; Catholic; rec: deep sea fishing. Res: 7901 Kroll Way Bakersfield 93309 Ofc: Bakersfield Shingles Wholesale, 4 P Street Bakersfield 93004

MOODY, DANIEL JOSEPH, scientist; b. Dec. 4, 1946, Oak Park, Ill.; s. John H. and Antoinette M. (Gentile) M.; edn: BS, Univ. of W. Mich. 1968; MSEE, Mass. Inst. Tech. 1970; ScD, Calif. Tech. Inst. 1972; PhD, 1972. Career: co developer Josephson Logic Circuit Junction (microcircuit under study by IBM for use in their fifth generation computers); chmn. United Nations Adv. Com. of Emerging Nations Technology; dir. research Health Systems Information Exch.; chmn. bd. Western Star Technology (telecomm. research firm); honors: Research Scientist of the Year, Nat. Sci. Found. 1979; mem: Golden Gate Bus. Assn.; Am. Computer Assn.; NSF; AAAS; Calif. Physicists Club; Computer Users of Am.; Patents: 38 in area of microcomputers and microcircuitry; Research: protocols for paraphysical experiments, proj. involving interactive video in med. & dental databases; mil: telemetrics/ orbit control, NASA 1972-75; rec: photomicography, audiophile. Ofc: TEC/ Helix, 1803 Golden Gate San Francisco 94115

MOOMJEAN, ROSE AGAJANIAN, travel agency executive; b. June 4, 1924, Los Angeles; d. Karl Thomas and Mary (Muradian) Agajanian; m. Ted Moomjean, Aug. 29, 1942. Career: exec. v.p. Camden Travel Agency, Beverly Hills 1976--; Crestview Stationers, Beverly Hills 1966, 73; co-owner/ pub. Big Bear Life Newspaper, Big Bear Lake 1959-62; Limelight News, Big Bear Lake 1949-59; Republican; Protestant; rec: travel. Res: 412 N Palm Dr 504, Beverly Hills 90210 Ofc: Camden Travel Agency Inc., 9250 Wilshire Blvd, Ste LL16, Beverly Hills 90212

MOONEY, DIANE THOMPSON, real estate broker; b Nov. 15, 1941, San Francisco; d. Lowell Eldon and Esther Frances (Cano) Thompson; m. Thomas Patrick Money Jr., July 30, 1966; children: Noelle, b. 1967; Tracy, b. 1970; edn: BS, San Jose State Coll. 1963; grad. studies, 1964-66; lic. R.E. Broker, Calif. 1963. Career: real estate sales agt/ Roger Maason, Sunnyvale 1963, Lowell Thompson, Sunnyvale 1963-64; real estate broker/owner Diane Noel Thompson, Sunnyvale 1964-76; broker R.V. Jones, Los Altos 1976-77, Whitecliff Realty 1977-78; broker/ pres. Diane Thompson Mooney Realty, Los Altos 1978--; mem: Los Altos Bd. of Realtors (Local Govt. chmn. 1982, chmn. Ad. Hoc All Realtor Concept 1983, chmn. Legis. & Local Govt. Rels. 1984); Nat., Calif. Assn. Realtors; Los Altos CofC; Delta Zeta Alumna; works: art awards, Santa Clara County Fair 1964; Democrat (Dollars for Democrats Queen, Sunnyvale 1963; Santa Clara Co. Dollars for Democrats, 1963-64); Catholic; rec: art. Res; 1310 Richardson Ave Sunnyvale 94022 Ofc: Diane Thompson Mooney Realty, POB 122 Los Altos 94022

MOORE, BOBBIE HENDERSON, educator; b. Mar. 29, 1936, Newnan, Ga.; d. Joe Pete (dec.) and Jennie Mae Henderson; div.; 1 dau. Stacey Lynne, b. 1961; edn: BA, Clark Coll., 1957; Atlanta Univ. 1959; M.Ed., USC, 1962; Ed.D., Univ. of San Francisco 1982; grad. wk. Univ. of Calif. 1966, LaVerne Univ. 1972. Career: tchr. Newnan (Ga.) Pub. Schs., 1957-58, Atlanta Pub. Schs., spring 1964; tchr., coord., cons., Berkeley (Ca.) Unified Schs., 1964-69, Los Angeles Unified Schs., 1969--; awards: Clark College Alumni Community Service Award 1978; PTA Hon. Life mem. 1981, Teacher of Year (93rd St. PTA) 1980-81; Red Cross Tchr. of Year (Berkeley) 1969; UNCF Community Award 1978; mem: Calif. Tchrs. Assn., United Tchrs. of L.A. (charter), Nat. Council of Tchrs. of Mathematics, Nat. Council of Negro Women, NAACP, Urban League, Nat. Assn. of Female Execs., Nat. Assn. of Univ. Women, L.A. World Affairs Council, USC Alumnni Assn. (life), EDUCARE (ednl. support group, USC), Clark Coll. Alumni, L.A. (pres. 1972-79), Alpha Kappa Alpha sor.; YWCA; research: children's attitudes toward math and effects of achievement (1981); Methodist (edn. commn. St. Mark United Meth. Ch.); rec: working puzzles, gardening, travel. Res: 1933 Virginia Rd Los Angeles 90016 Ofc: Los Angeles Schools, 450 N. Grand Ave Los Angeles 90012

MOORE, GARY D., commercial interior designer; b. Feb. 13, 1939, Los Angeles; s. Theodore R. and Katherine F. (Chadduck) M.; m. Brooke Bentley, Oct. 13, 1979; children: Kirstin, b. 1964; Christopher, b. 1966; Brent, b. 1968; Heidi, b. 1970; edn: BFA, honors, Art Ctr. Coll. of Desgin 1966. Career: designer General Motors Technical Center, Warren, Mich. 1967; partner Selje, Bond & Stewart, Design Consultants, So. Pasadena 1967-75; pres. G.D. Moore & Co. Inc., Design Cons., Glendale 1975--; designer for maj. Los Angeles law firms & stock brokerage ofcs., splty. restaurants; mil: NCO E-4 US Army 1962; rec: classic autos, travel, photog. Res: 2012 Los Amigos St La Canada-Flintridge 91011 Ofc: G.D. Moore & Co. Inc., 1017 N Pacific Ave Glendale 91202

MOORE, HENRY T., JR., superior court judge; b. Dec. 28, 1932, El Paso, Tex.; s. Henry Trumbull and Bonnie (Platt) M.; m. Lynda Doughty, Nov. 8,

1963; 1 son: Michael, b. 1967; edn: BA, USC 1954; LLD, 1957; LLM, Harvard Univ. 1958; Judge of the Superior Ct., Calif. 1984. Career: assoc./ partner, law firm Moore & Trinkaus 1958-62; partner, law firm, Moore & Moore 1962-76; sole practitioner, Century City & counsel Ward & Heyler 1976-79; sole practitioner (gen. civil & trial practice), Santa Ana 1979-84; judge Superior Court, County of Orange 1984--; So. Coast Regl. Coastal Commn. 1979-; L.A. Superior Ct. Panel of Arbitrators, Orange Co. Superior Ct. Panel of Arbitrators 1979-84; judge pro tem L.A. Municipal Ct. 1979; Orange Co. Tax Reform Com. 1976-77; Citizens Adv. Com. to L.A. City Plnng. Dept. (1971-72), to L.A. City Atty. Burt Pines (1973-74); honors: Phi Beta Kappa, Phi Kappa Phi, Order of the Coif; mem: Mandeville Cyn. Property Owners Assn. (pres. 1971-73); State Bar of Calif. (chmn. local admin. com. 1972) Beverly Hills, L.A. Co. (chmn. pub. rels. com. 1972-74), Orange Co. bar assns.; Am., L.A. & Orange Co. Trial Lawyers Assns.; Assn. of Bus. Trial Lawyers; Internat. Acad. of Law & Sci.; Am. Judicature Soc.; Newport Balboa Rotary Club; Hoag Hosp. 552 Club; Democrat; Presbyterian; rec: racquetball, boating, tennis. Ofc: Courthouse, 700 Civic Center Dr W, Santa Ana 92701

MOORE, JOHN PATRICK, lawyer; b. July 5, 1939, San Francisco; s. Joseph Early and Vera (Forman) M.; m. Carole Calza, Dec. 22, 1977, children: Christina, b. 1978; Elisa, b. 1971; edn: BA, San Jose State Coll. 1963. Career: deputy dist. atty. Los Angeles Co. 1968-70; partner law firm Maher, Moore, Rheinhiemer & Ricks 1971-75; pub. defender Madera County 1975-76; chief prosecutor Calif. Agric. Labor Rels. Bd. 1976-83; currently, pvt. practice law, Fresno; gen. counsel Zamco West, INc. 1983-; chief counsel ALRB Workers Union 1981-83; counsel Fresh Fruit & Vegetable Wkrs., AFL-CIO; mil: sgt. US Army 1962-68; Democrat; Catholic. Res: 1318 E Holland Fresno 93704 Law Ofc: 916 Divisadero Fresno 93721

MOORE, PATRICIA ANNE, real estate broker; b. Nov. 16, 1944, Brooklyn, NY; d. Pat Joseph and Patrina (Travali) Ciardullo; edn: BA, cum laude, Alfred Univ. 1966; MA, cum laude, Univ. of Miami 1968; Tchg. Credentials Fla. 1969, Calif. 1975; Calif. lic. R.E. Broker 1980, Insurance Agent, 1983. Career: tchg. asst. Univ. of Miami, Coral Gables, Fla. 1968; instr. Spanish lang., Univ. of Miami, Fla. 1968-69; tchr. Naples H.S., Naples, Fla. 1969-70; So. American ops. mgr. Emery Airfreight Corp., Miami, Fla. 1970-75; real estate assoc. American Realty, Concord 1975-80; broker/ gen. mgr./ secty. ERA-Kenworthy Realty, Concord 1980--; v.p Gen. Home Loans, Concord 1983--; secty. ERA No. Bay Council; relocation dir. Kenworthy Realty; honors: CWENS 1964, Womens Senior Ct. 1965, Circle (hon. soc.) 1961-62; mem: AAUW; Alpha Kappa Omicron (pres. 1966); Concord CofC; Electronic Realty Assn., No. Bay Council Muscular Dystrophy Assn. Proj. (fund raising); Smithsonian Inst.; Soroptimists of Concord; Republican; rec: modern dance, boating, travel. Res: 1835 Las Ramblas Concord 94521 Ofc: ERA- Kenworthy Realty, 1747 Grant St Concord 94520

MOORE, ROBERT JAY, lawyer; b. Sept. 16, 1950, Sentinel, Okla.; s. Jess Tracy and Arla Elsie (Stubsten) M.; m. Patricia A. Moore, Aug. 18, 1976; edn: AB, honors, Univ. of N.C. at Chapel Hill 1974; JD, UC Los Angeles 1977; admitted to Calif. State Bar 1977, Wash. DC Bar 1978. Career: law clk. to Hon. Ozell Miller Trask, US Ct. of Appeals, 9th Circuit; atty. law firm Gendel, Raskoff, Shapiro & Quittner, Los Angeles 1977-, partner 1983--; awards: John Motley Morehead Foundation Scholar 1968-74; pres. UCLA Soc. of Internat. and Comparative Law 1975-77; lectr. var. panels 1983 Ticor Title Insurers Symp.; author: Taxing the Mobile Home (N.C. Dept. of Natural and Economic Resources); mem: Century City (Sect. on Bus. Orgn.), Los Angeles County (secty. Sect. on Comml. Law and Bankruptcy; Exec. Com.), Calif. (Bus. Law Sect.), American (Sect. on Corp., Banking and Bus. Law; Business BankruptcyCom.) and International (Sect. on Bus. Law) bar assns.; American Soc. of Internat. Law. Address: 1801 Century Park E., 6th Flr., Los Angeles 90067

MOORE, ROBERT KENT, broadcasting executive; b. May 22, 1945, Appleton, Wisc.; s. George Forest and Georgina Maria (Frailey) M.; m. Helen Bookasta, Nov. 3, 1973; edn: BS, Wisc. State Univ. 1967. Career: senior acct. exec. KKDJ Radio 1972-74, KFWB, Westinghouse Radio 1974-76, KABC-TV, AM Broadcasting Co. 1976-78; v.p./ local sales mgr. KLOP-TV, Chris Craft TV Inc. 1978-80; gen. sales mgr. KHTZ Radio, Greater Media Inc. 1980-81, v.p. and gen. mgr. KHTZ Radio, 1981--; guest spkr. UCLA Radio Dept., USC Sch. of Bus., Mktg. Dept.; guest lectr. Univ. of LaVerne Radio & TV Dept.; honors: Radio Sales Mgr. of the Yr. 1980, John Frey, RAG Awd.; mem: So. Calif. Broadcasters Assn. (bd. dirs.); Radio Advis. Bd. Univ. of La Verne; Advtg. Emergency Relief Fund, L.A. (bd. dirs.); Greater L.A. Press Club; Hollywood Radio & TV Soc.; Greater L.A. Cable Club; Presbyterian; rec: tennis player (Sports Ctr. Tennis Ctr. Mens Team). Res: 11292 Laurie Dr Studio City 91604 Ofc: KHTZ Radio, 3580 Wilshire Blvd 90010

MOORE, RONALD MARVIN, physician/ cardiologist; b. May 13, 1929, Loma Linda; s. Marvin Harrison and Ethel Marie (Wagner) M.; m. Anne Marie Tolmosoff, Aug. 23, 1973; children: Janet Lynne, b. 1953; Ronald Marvin Jr., b. 1958; William Wilbur, b. 1963; edn: BA, Union Coll., Lincoln 1952; MD, Loma Linda Univ. Med. Sch. 1958; gen. intern, L.A. Co. Hosp. 1958-59; res. internal med., 1959-61, 1962-63; fellowship cardiology, White Mcml. Hosp., L.A. 1961-62; diplomate Nat. Bd. 1959, diplomate Am. Bd. Internal Med. 1980; Fellow Am. Coll. of Cardiology 1982. Career: tchg. asst. Loma Linda Univ. Med. Sch. 1962-63; att. phys. Valley Med. Ctr., Fresno 1964-73; active staff St. Agnes Hosp., Fresno 1982; active staff Fresno Community Hosp. & Med. Ctr. 1963--, chmn. Dept. of Med., 1974, v.chmn. 1983-84, mem. Exec. Com. and chmn. Dept. of Electrocardiology 1982; honors: Alpha Omega Alpha 1958;

mem: Am., Calif. Med. Assns.; Fresno-Madera Med. Soc. (secty. 1978-79, bd. govs. 1976-79, v.p. 1983-84); Am., Calif., Fresno (pres. 1977-78) Socs. of Internal Med.; fellow, Am. Coll. of Cardiology; mil: cpl. US Army M.C., surg. research unit., Brooke Army Med. Ctr., Ft. Sam Houston, Tex.; Republican; SDA; rec: genealogy, amateur radio, photog. Ofc: Ronald M. Moore, MD, 3636 N First. Ste 141, Fresno 93726

MOORE, WILLIAM JOSEPH, college president; b. Feb. 19, 1932, Siloam Springs, AR; s. Robert Alexander and Nelle Elizabeth (Donly) Moore; BA, 1954; MA, 1955; Univ. Redlands; postgrd. stu. Hong Kong Univ., 1955-56; PhD, Intercollegiate Pgm. of Graduate Studies; Pomona Coll., Claremont Grad. Sch., Scripps Coll., Occidental Coll., Univ. of Redlands, 1963; m. Peggy Perkins, Aug. 24, 1952; chil: Christopher, b. 1957; Kevin, b. 1958; Lisa, b. 1961. Career: instr., San Bernardino Valley Coll., 1956-59; Dean of Instrn., 1969-74; v.p. for Academic Affairs, Univ. of Redlands, 1974-76; pres., Crafton Hills Coll., Yucaipa, 1976—; continuing cons., TRW Systems Group, 1964-71; Labor Arbitrator, 1972—; bd. trustees, Univ. of Redlands, 1976—. Awards: Ford Found. Fellowship, 1954-55; Rotary Found Fellowship, 1955-56; disting. alumnus award, Univ. of Redlands, 1972. Mem: Natl. Labor Panel, Amer. Arbitration Assn., 1976—; Omicron Delta Kappa; World Affairs Council of Inland So. Calif., 1969—, pres. 1973-74; So. Calif. Community Coll. Chief Exec Officers Assn., 1976—, pres. 1981-82; United Way of Redlands Area Bd., 1976—, pres. 1981; bd. trustees, Redlands A.K. Smiley Pub. Library, 1981—. Publ: American Government and Politics: A Reder, NY, Van Nostrand Reinhold Co., 1967, 2d ed., 1971; Monograph for TRW Systems and US Arms Control and Disarmament Agency: Soviet Mil. Strategy and the Problem of US-Soviet Arms Control Agreements, 1967. Democrat. Rec: fly-fishing, fly-tying, gardening. Res: 1537 Crown, Redlands 92373; Office: Crafton Hills Coll., 11711 Sand Canyon Rd., Yucaipa 92399.

MOORMAN, MIRIAM W., psychotherapist; b. Aug. 20, 1925, NY, NY; d. Aaron P. and Bella (Krasnyansky) Wasserman; m. Dr. Herbert K. Moorman, May 18, 1968; children: Uri L. Hertz, b. 1949; Amram A. Hertz, b. 1952; edn: BA in sociol., NY Univ. 1947; MSW, USC 1961; PhD, cand., Internat. Coll.; LCSW, Calif. 1969. Career: social case wkr. L.A. Co. Bureau of Pub. Assistance 1955-57; child welfare wkr. 1958-59; deputy probation ofcr. L.A. County Probation Dept. 1959-62; social case wkr. Council of Jewish Women, L.A. 19862-64; supvg. psychiatric soc. wkr. L.A. Co. Dept. of Mental Health 1964-69; cons./ counselor Poseidon Sch., L.A. 1974-79; pvt. practice psychotherapy, L.A. 1964—; supvr. Homeless Youth Proj., L.A. Free Clinic 1983-; volunteer supvn. of trainees Airport- Marina Counseling Svc. 1983-; honors: Outstanding Svc. Award, Social Work Treatment Svc.; mem: Soc. for Clin. Social Wrk.; Americans for Progressive Israel; Democrat; Jewish; rec: music, folk dance, sculpture. Res: 1870 N Vista St Los Angeles 90046 Ofc: 9201 Sunset Blvd, Ste 209, Los Angeles 90069

MORALES, LARRY HOWARD, engineering co. president; b. Jan. 31, 1942, Los Angeles; s. Lawrence Howard and Freddie Demaris (Spellings) M.; children: Derek b. 1970, Bret b. 1972. Career: partner T&M Land and Cattle Co.; secty., treas. Thomas Mfg. Inc.; mem: Screen Actors Guild (6 yrs.), Nat. & Calif. Cattleman's Assn.; mil: E5 US Army, hon. disch.; rec: cattle ranching, flying, karate. Res: POB 195, Plymouth 95669 (No. Calif.); #14 Santa Bella Rd. Rolling Hills Est. 90274 (So. Calif.) Ofc: Morales Engineering and Mfg. Inc. 149 E. 162nd St Gardena 90248

MORAN, EDGAR M., physician; b. Apr. 28, 1928, Constantza, Romania, nat. 1972; s. Leon and Catty (Rosenblatt) Mayersohn; m. Huguette M. Leger, MD, June 11, 1968; children: Daniel G. b. 1969, Andre A. b. 1971; edn: MD, cum laude, Univ. of Bucharest Sch. of Med. 1952., Career: staff phys. Dept. of Pathology, Hadassah Univ. Hosp., Jerusalem, Israel 1962-65, instr. pathol., Hebrew Univ. 1963-65; asst. in medicine The Mount Sinai Medical Ctr., NY 1968-69; instr. in med., Univ. of Chgo. Pritzker Sch. of Med. 1969-71; asst. prof. Univ. of Chgo. Pritzker Sch. of Med. and The Franklin McLean Meml. Research Inst., 1971-75; assoc. prof. 1975-76; dir. Dept. of Oncology, City of Hope Nat. Med. Ctr., Duarte, Ca. 1976-77; assoc. clin. prof. of med. USC, 1977-78; prof. of med. UC Irvine 1978--; chmn. Cancer Pgm./ chief Section of Hematology-Oncology, VA Med. Ctr., Long Beach 1978--; lectr. Naval Regl. Med. Ctr., Long Beach; honors: Outstanding New Citizen of the Year Award, The citizenship Council of Metropolitan Chgo.; AMA Physician Recogn. Awds. 1969, 73, 76, 79; Searle Award, The 13th Internat. Cong. of Chemotherapy, Vienna, Austria 1983; mem: Am. Fedn. for Clin. Research, Am. Soc. of Hematology, Fellow Internat. Soc. of Hematology, Am. Assn. for Cancer Research, Am. Soc. of Clin. Oncology, Internat. Soc. of Chemotherapy, Fellow Royal Soc. for the Promotion of Health, Fellow NY Acad. of Scis., AAAS, Am. Soc. of Preventive Oncology (founding mem.), Soc. for Hematopathology; research grants: Mayo Found. 1979-82, Nat. Cancer Inst. 1979-83; num. sci. publs. (90; rec: gardening, photog., numismatics. Res: 885 Palo Verde Ave Long Beach 90815 Ofc: Veterans Administration Medical Ctr. 5901 E. 7th St Long Beach 90822

MORELLI, ABDALLAH A., consulting management engineer; b. Feb. 29, 1953, Lebanon, nat. 1984; s. Abdul Monhem A. and Salima S. Morelli; m. Sarah De Carteret, Nov. 11, 1978; children: William, b. 1980; Diana, b. 1982; edn: BS indsl. eng., Calif. Polytech. Univ. 1977; MS indsl./system eng., USC 1981; desig: Cert. Applicator, Work Measurement, Incentive Wages & Job Evaluation, Firestone 1978; Cert. Applicator, Method Time Measurement, MTM Assn. 1979. Career: field supvr. Westside Oil Field Constrn., Taft 1975-77; indsl. mfg. engr. Anderson Desk, Glendal 1977; indsl. engr./ mgr.

prodn. info. ctr., Firestone Tire & Rubber, Southgate 1978-79; sr. indsl. engr./ mgr. indsl. eng. Max Factor & Co., Hawthorne 1980-81; pres. Morelli & Co., Newport Beach 1981--; Supervisory & Credit Evaluation Com. Firestone Credit Union 1978-80; chmn. Productivity Mgmt. Pgm., Inst. of Indsl. Engrs. 1983; mem: Inst. Indsl. Engr. (pres. 1982-83 Pacific Empire; productivity chmn. L.A. chpt.); SBA Consultancy Pgm.; works: Productivity Improvement Pgm. 1980; Employee Involvement Pgm. 1982; rec: stamp and coin collecting. Res: 315 Coronado Balboa 92661 Ofc: Morelli & Co., POB 2422 Newport Beach 92663

MOREN, ULF VILHELM, company executive; b. May 10, 1940, Gothenburg, Sweden; s. Curt Vilhelm and Britt Ingegard (Berndtson) M.; fiancee: Birgitta Halgren; 1 son, Erik Vilhelm; edn: BS, Gotheburg Tech. Coll. 1961; MBA, Berkeley Grad. Sch. of Bus. 1970; lic. Real Estate Broker, Calif. 1983. Career: overseas delivery coord. Volvo AB, Sweden 1961-63; export salesman Daros AB, Sweden 1963-66; mfg. mgr. Ledu Lamp Corp., Stamford, Conn. 1966-69; asst. prod. mgr./ purchasing mgr. Levi Strauss & Co., San Francisco 1978-83; currently, pres. Supercool U.S. Inc., San Rafael; bd. dirs. Bank St. Realtors 1980-; bd. dirs. Mac Enterprises 1981-; metric coordinator, indus. & govt., for Levi Strauss & Co. 1976-77; recipient Canadian Metric Com. Award for Garment Industry Coordination 1977; mem: Marin Co. Bd. Realtors; Nat., Calif. Assns. Realtors; Homes for Living Network; Big Brothers of Marin; Police Activities League; Civil League; Royal Yacht Club of Gothenberg; Onsala Tennis assn.; Young Scandinavians Orgn., S.F; Fall Line Ski Club; works: The Canadian Metric Experience, 1976; Metrics and the Garmet Industry, 1976; How to go Metric, 1977; What Do You Know About Metrics? 1977; mil: sgt. Swedish Army 1961; Republican; Lutheran; rec: sailing, skiing, tennis. Res: 254 Bungalow Ave San Rafael 94901 Ofc: Supercool U.S. Inc., 1004 Irwin St San Rafael 94901

MORETTI, VINCENT CARLO, civil engineer; b. Oct. 1, 1936, Los Angeles; s. Vincent and Marie Lupe (Plank) M.; m. Mary Falkenstien, Nov. 11, 1955, div.; children: Vince, b. 1956; Tony, b. 1957; Gina, b. 1959; Lisa, b. 1961; edn: BSCE, USC 1962; MA, math., Pepperdine Coll. 1965-66; MS in C.E., USC 1972; MBA, Pepperdine Univ. 1981. Regis. Profl. Civil Engr., Calif. 1969; Contractors Lic: B-1 Gen. Bldg. 1974, A Gen. Engring. 1977, C-44 (Solar) 1981. Career: system engr. Space General Corp., El Monte; chief estimator Lubanko & Sons Constrn. Co., El Monte; civil engr., City of Torrance; sole owner The Vincent C. Moretti Co., Redondo Beach; proj. mgr. Jet Propulsion Lab, Pasadena; currently, proj. engr./ mgr./ sect. head TRW Inc., Redondo Beach; eng. cons.; evening instr. in engring., Calif. Comm. Colls. & Calif. Colls. & Univs.; honors: 1st pl. Trophy, Dominquez Hills 10k Race 1980; finished Palos Verdes Marathon 1979; mem: Tau Beta Pi; Skull & Dagger; Chi Epsilon Alumni, USC (pres.); Am. Soc. of Civil Engrs.; active in St. Margaret Mary Parish, founder Third Family (divorce support gp.); publs: (song) Shooting Stars, copyrighted; volume of poems & letters; Republican; Catholic; rec: running, swimming, real estate inv. Res: 25001 Oak St Lomita 90717 Ofc: TRW Inc., One Space Park, 119/ 3830, Redondo Beach 90278

MORGAN, ANNE LILLIAN, nursing home administrator; b. Nov. 17, 1948, Portadown, No. Ireland, nat. 1957; d. John Augustus and Teresa (Haughian) Henderson; m. Jamie Watts, Sept. 24, 1977; children: Morgan E. Watts, b. 1978; Shannon E. Watts, b. 1981; edn: AA, Mt. San Antonio Comm. Coll. 1970; BA, UC Berkely 1973; Tchg. Cred., CSU Hayward 1974; Calif. lic. Nursing Home Adminstr. 1983. Career: tchr., 1975-78; ward clerk Golden Plains Hosp., Hutchinson, Ks. 1979-80; nurses aide Plumtree Hosp., San Jose 1981; phlebotomist Alexian Bros. Hosp., San Jose 1981; asst. to adminstr. Homewood Conv. Hosp., San Jose 1981--; Democrat; Catholic; rec: painting, sewing. Res: 190 N King Rd San Jose 95116 Ofc: Homewood Convelescent Hosp., 75 N 13th St San Jose 95112

MORGAN, HARV THOMAS, newscaster, investigative reporter, foreign correspondent; b. Apr. 1, 1932, West Palm Beach, FL; s. Arthur Vance and Jennie Wofford (Cheatham) Morgan; BA, Hunter Coll., NYC, 1956; grad. work in broadcasting, Columbia Univ., NYC, 1956; grad. work in history, John Carroll Univ., Cleveland, Oh., 1962; div.; chil: Brian, b. 1954; Michael, b. 1964. Career: freelance investigative reporter, self employed, Mill Valley, Calif., 1981---; investigative reporter/fgn. corres., ABC Radio, S.F., 1968-81; newscaster, interviewer, CBS Radio, S.F., 1966-68; newscaster, interviewer, pgm. host, NBC Radio, Cleveland, Oh., 1961-66; pgm. dir., WQTE, Detroit, Mich., 1959-61; pgm. dir., WGKV, Charleston, WV, 1957-59; lectr. in broadcast journalism, S.F. St. Univ., 1970-81. Honors num. radio, TV and print media awards, 1962-80. Mem: Disabled Amer. Veterans, Amer. Federation of TV and Radio Artists; Press Club of S.F. Author of publ. arts. on S.F. Supr. Ct. and Calif. Prisons; currently researching and writing a biography in diary form of Abraham Lincoln, scheduled for publ. 1984. Mil: Sgt., Spl. Svcs. Branch, Army, 1950-52. Baptist. Rec: tennis, stamp collecting, coin collecting. Res/ Office: 507 Barone Lane, Mill Valley 94941.

MORGAN, JACK CLARK, newspaper publisher; b. Oct. 20, 1933, Nephi, Utah; s. Clark Edward and Marjorie (Winn) M.; m. Donna Mae Leishman, July 24, 1958; children: Suzanne, b. 1959; Clark, b. 1961; Cliff, b. 1962; Brad, b. 1968; edn: BA, Brigham Young Univ. 1964. Career: ofc. mgr. trainee Scripps League Newspapers Inc., 1959-60; ofc. mgr./ bus. mgr. Herald and News, Klamath Falls, Ore. 1960-71; pub. The Hanford Sentinel, Hanford 1971--; honors: Citizen of the Yr., Hanford CofC; mem: Calif. Newspaper Pubs. Assn. 1972-; So. San Joaquin Valley Unit CNPA (pres. 1983-84); Rotary; bd. dirs. Kings Co. Secret Witness; Hanford CofC (past pres.); past adv. bd. mem. Salvation Army, Sacred Heart Hosp.; Calif. Shakespearean Festival (bd. mem./

pres. bd. govs.); clk. of bd. Slingerland Inst.; Republican; LDS. Res: 755 Laura Ln Hanford 93230 Ofc: The Hanford Sentinel, 418 W 8th St Hanford 93230

MORGAN, ROGER D., business executive; b. Mar. 14, 1939, Marshall, Mo.; s. Harold W. and Evelyn B. (Griffith) M.; m. Pamela Marie, July 3, 1983; children: Michelle and Scott Morgan, (step) Kelly, Jennifer and Michael Gantous; edn: BA in bus. adm., Colorado Coll., Colo. Springs 1963; BA in fgn. trade, Thunderbird Grad. Sch. of Int. Mgt. Glendale, Ariz. 1964. Career: sales, mktg. and dealer adminstrn., Caterpillar Tractor Co. & Caterpillar Overseas, 1964-73 (Geneva, Madrid and Athens for 7 yrs., then supr. Sales Tng., Peoria); dir. of mktg. Volvo of America, then v.p./gen. mgr. Volvo Penta of Am., 1974-79; v.p. in chg. of heavy equip., land devel. and mfg., Burris Construction Co., San Diego 1979-80, bought export div. of co. in 1980; owner/pres. Intermac. Inc., 1980--, exporter heavy equip. to Mexico prior to economic crisis there, currently selling heavy equip. in US, and land devel. in San Jacinto and Coronado; purchased the the old (53 years) Ferry Boat "San Diego" to return to Coronado for conversion to Restaurant and Dinner Theater; past dir. Nat. Assn. of Engine & Boat Mfrs.; mem. World Trade Assn., San Diego; Coronado Yacht Club; mil: AN, USN 1956-62; Republican; Methodist; rec: flying, hunting, fishing. Res: 530 Pomona Ave Coronado 92118

MORGENSEN, ROBERT ALONZO, manufacturing co. executive; b. Apr. 5, 1946, Dayton, Oh.; s. Otto P. and Eleanor S. (Hill) M.; m. Sheryl Lynn Olson, May 27, 1972; 1 dau. Lauren, b. 1981; edn: BA, Miami Univ., Oxford, Oh. 1969. Career: high sch. tchr. Hamilton Garfield, Hamilton, Oh. 1969-70; sales rep. Procter & Gamble, Cincinati, Oh. 1970-72; sales rep. Inland Chem. Corp. 1972-78; v.p. mktg. Inland Specialty Chem. 1978-81; pres. 1981--; bd. dirs. Inland Specialty 1981-; awards: Salesman of the Year Inland Chem. Corp. 1975, 76, 77; mem: Miami Univ. Alumni Assn.; Calif. Circuit Assn.; Inst. Printed Circuits; Orange Co. CofC; Sons of the Am. Revolution; Republican; Methodist; rec: racquetball, jogging. Res: 31291 Holly Dr, So Laguna 92677 Ofc: Inland Specialty Chemical Corp., 3151 Airway Ave, Bldg J-3, Costa Mesa 92626

MORLEY, JEFFREY JOSHUA, cosmetic dentist; b. Apr. 25, 1953, Los Angeles; s. David Bruce and Renee Sydney (Lubin) M.; edn: Santa Monica Coll. 1970-71; CSU Northridge 1972; CSU San Jose 1972-73; DDS, Univ. of the Pacific 1976. Career: assoc. dentist in pvt. practice, 1976-77; pvt. practice, Novato 1977-82; panel practitioner, Center for Cosmetic Dentistry, San Francisco 1981-82, exec. dir. 1982; currently, pvt. practice, cosmetic dentistry, S.F.; invited lectr. Western Psychological Assn. Annual Meeting 1983; bd. dirs. San Francisco Fashion Quarterly Mag. 1983; mem: Am., Calif., Marin Co. Dental Assns.; Boy Scouts of Am.; research: dental facial esthetics and behavior 1979-83; dental ornamentation in history 1982-83; pioneer in bonding techniques in cosmetic dentistry; Jewish; rec: collect rare Boy Scout memorabilia. Res: 557 Seaver Dr Mill Valley 94941 Ofc: Jeff Morley, 1806 Union St San Francisco 94123

MORRILL, TERRY PATRICK, energy production co. president; b. July 7, 1945, Auburn; s. George Lanham and Joan Emily (Nicol) M.; children: Trent, b. 1970; Chad, b. 1973; edn: BS, Calif. State Polytech. Univ. 1968; desig: Class VIII (tech.), Ch. of Scientology 1975; Calif. lic. B1 Gen. Contractor 1984, C44 Solar Contr. 1984. Career: with Church of Scientology 1968-76: estab. five (Ch. of S.) missions in Calif. profl. counselor/ case supvr. American Saint Hill Orgn. (Ch. of S.) Los Angeles & profl. auditor, Mex. City; profl. case supvr., Pasadena 1968-75; exec. tech. mgr. scientology svcs., L.A. 1975-76; owner/ pres. Terry Morrill Constrn. Co., now Morrill Devel. Co., Los Angeles 1976--, Morrill Bldg. Material, 1978--; pres./ chmn. bd. Pacific Sun Systems, now Pacific Energy Prodn. Sys. Inc., L.A. 1982--; pvt. real estate cons.; mem: Am. Econ. Council (chmn. Glendale chpt. 1979); Calif. Solar Energy Inds. Assn.; World Inst. of Scientology Ent. (WISE, internat. bus. assn.); Glendale CofC; Babe Ruth Baseball Team (sponsor); Apartment Owners Assn.; works: renovation of historic bldgs.; Republican; Ch. of Scientology; rec: pvt. pilot, sports. Res: 631 E Santa Anita, Ste G, Burbank 91501 Ofc: Pacific Energy Production Systems Inc., 540 W Colorado Blvd Glendale 91204

MORRIS, EFFIE LEE, library consultant/lecturer; b. Apr. 20, Richmond, Va.; d. William H. and Erma (Caskie) M; m. Leonard Jones, Aug. 25, 1971; edn: BA, Case Western Res. Univ., 1945; BLS, 1946; MSLS, 1956; EdD, in progress, Univ. of San Francisco 1978-. Career: childs splst. Library for the Blind 1958-63; coord. Childrens Svcs., San Francisco Pub. Lib. 1963-78; senior ed. Harcourt Brace Jovanovich 1978-79; lectr. Childrens Literature, Mills Coll. 1981--; contbg. writer var. profl. publs. honors: The San Francisco Pub. Lib. designated The Effie Lee Morris Hist. & Research Collections of Childrens Literature, Nov. 1981; named mem. Calif. Lib. Svcs. Bd. 1982-84; mem: Childrens Svcs. Lib., Calif. Lib. Assn. (pres. 1969-71) Pub. Lib. Assn. of Am. Lib. Assn. (pres. 1971-72); The Center for The Book of the Library of Congress (Adv. Bd. 1979-); Alpha Kappa Alpha sorority; Altrusa Club. rec: reading. Res: 676 Cleary Ct San Francisco 94109

MORRIS, PAUL J., warden of Calif. state prison at Folsom; b. June 28, 1929, Chicago, IL; s. Paul A. and Catharine (Summers) Morris; edn: various coll. credits totaling approx. 2 yrs.; m. Marva Daly, Dec. 1976; chil: Paul J. II, b. 1952; Catherine Solis, b. 1954; Marie Rubio, b. 1957; Candy, b. 1965. Career: started in 1951 as correctional officer, San Quentin; promoted to Sgt. in 1955 at Tehachapi; Lt. at Camp Minnewawa in San Diego Co. in 1958; three yrs. later, selected to supervise camp training at Calif. Instn. for Men, Chino, remaining there until 1963; promoted to Capt. at Calif. Rehabilitation Center; 1964, ser-

ved as Jail Inspector for Bd. of Corrections before assignment to Sierra Conservation Camp as pgm. adminstr. in charge of central camps; following apptmt. as assoc. supt. at CIM in 1970, moved to Correctional Trng. Facility, Soledad, to assist in reorganization of facility before being named deputy supt.; Feb. 1975, selected by Gov. to be Supt. of Calif. Correctional Center, position held until moving to Folsom, Sept. 1976. Mem: Folsom CofC; Folsom Historical Soc.; Folsom Sports Complex Blue Ribbon Comm.; Economic Devel. Council, City of Folsom; Amer. Correctional Assn. Mil: Pfc., USAF. Rec: reading, fishing, camping. Res: #22, Folsom Prison Grounds, Represa 95671; Office: Folsom State Prison, P.O. Box W, Represa 95671.

MORRIS, ROBERT HUGH, landscape architect, ret.; b. Jan. 11, 1927, Oakland; s. William Henry and Blandine Leah (Franklin) M.; edn: BA, CSU Los Angeles 1961; BS, Calif. Polytech. Univ. Pomona 1970; MS, CSU Sacto. 1973; Lic. Landscape Arch., Calif. 1972. Career: comml. artist Cardinal-Lucky Stores Inc., Sacramento 1953-58; illustrator Lockheed Aircraft Corp. 1958-60; delineator, sr. delineator State of Calif., Monterey & Los Angeles 1960-64; landscape architect, State of Calif., Sacto. 1970-74; recreation planner, State of Calif., Sacto. 1974-82; ret., design cons. Playground for Retarded Children, Grossmont Sch. Dist., El Cajon 1973; mem: Calif. Parks & Recreation Soc. (past mem. 1972-74); senior author: Intertidal Invertebrates of California (Stanford Univ. Press. 1980); mil: sgt. US Army 1945-46; s/sgt. USAF 1950-53; Democrat; Catholic; rec: architecture, art, photog. Res: 3312 26th Ave Sacramento 95820

MORRISSEY, JAD LYNN, heating and air conditioning co. president; b. Jan. 30, 1949, Golden, Colo.; s. Robert William and Marcella Jayne (Veh) M.; m. Peggy Gilstrap, Aug. 21, 1976; children: Callie, b. 1981; Kendra, b. 1983; edn: Utah State Univ. 1967-68; CSU Fresno 1972-76; Contractor Lic. C-20, Calif. 1982. Career: mechanic Baldwin Co., Fresno 1971-81; pres. Baldwin Air Conditioning Co. 1981--; mem: Am. Soc. of Heating & Refrig. Engrs.; NRA; Fresno Better Bus. Bureau; Nat. Fedn. Independent Bus.; US CofC; mil: sgt. US Army 1969-72, Bronze Star; Catholic; rec; woodworking, hunting, fishing. Res: 3852 E Bellaire Fresno 93726 Ofc: Baldwin Air Conditioning Co., 2046 E Home Fresno 93703

MORRISON, BRIAN PATRICK, financial planner; b. Nov. 27, 1954, Norwich, Ct.; s. John Joseph and Irene Elizabeth (Linkus) M.; m. Wendy McAteer, Apr. 24, 1983; edn: AA, Mohegan Comm. Coll. 1975; BS, Univ. of Conn. Storrs 1976; JD, Pepperdine Univ. Sch. of Law 1979, admitted to practice, Supreme Ct. of Calif. 1979; CPA, State Bd. of Accty. 1980; Real Estate Broker 1983; Life & Disability Ins. Agent, Ins. Commn. 1983. Career: staff acct. Russ & Russ, CPAs, Glendale 1978-79; tax acct. Price Waterhouse & Co. Newport Beach 1979-80; gen. partner/ CFO Socal- A Carvel Distributorship, Irvine 1980-83; currently, fin. plnnr. Balanced Financial Management, Orange; mem: Mensa; works: DOD Procurement, Nat. Conttract Mgmt. Quarterly V2/ 78; Republican; Catholic; rec: cooking, skiing, tennis. Res: 1320 Arrow Ln Huntington Beach 92648 Ofc: Balanced Financial Management, 1224 E Katella, Ste 215, Orange 92667

MORRISON, DONALD WILLIAM, reprographic co. executive; b. June 19, 1926, Sacramento; s. Leland Woodson and Norma Marie (Middlehoff) M.; m. Marilyn Louise Lynch, Feb. 28, 1954; children: Kurt Randolph, b. 1957; Wendy Louise, b. 58; edn: BS, Calif. St. Polytech. Coll., SLO 1951. Career: pres. Studio Blueprint & Allied Reprodns. Inc., Walnut Creek & Pleasanton 1954--; dir. Internat. Reprographic Assn. 1978-81; secty./ treas. 1981-82; v.p. 1982-83; pres. 1983-; mem: San Ramon Valley Masonic Lodge (Master 1964); Walnut Creek & Pleasanton CofC; mil: yeoman l/c USN 1944-46; Republican; Protestant; rec: boating, skiing, travel. Res: 372 Cordell Dr Danville 94526 Ofc: Studio Blueprint & Allied Reproductions Inc., 1323 Locust St Walnut Creek 94596

MORRISON, GEORGE THORNTON, JR., pharmacist; b. Mar. 13, 1924, Oakdale; s. George Thornton and Eva Caroline (Holton) M.; m. Shirley A. Murdock, June 25, 1945; children: Kevin; Pamela Ann; edn: Univ. of Tex. 1944-45; BS, Univ. of Calif. 1950; Reg. Pharmacist in Nev. and Calif. 1950. Career: past owner 4 retail pharmacies, 1950-79; current: consulting pharmacist Oak Valley Dist. Hospital; pharmacist for medical center pharmacy and clinic pharmacy; founding pres. Oak Valley Dist. Hosp. Found. 1981-2; mem., chmn., trustee Stanislaus County Bd. of Edn., 14 years; past mem., dir. Oakdale Redevel. Agcy.; past mem. Comprehensive Health Plnng. Commn. (Tri-County); mem. Central Valley, Northern Calif., Calif. pharmaceutical assns.; past bd. mem. Oakdale CofC; past dir. Oakdale Golf & Country Club; mil: pharmacists mate l/c USNR 1942-46, GCM, Am. Theater, Asian Pacific Theater, WWII; Republican; Methodist. Res: 131 West G St Oakdale 95361

MORRISON, GEORGIA LEE, educator; b. Mar. 20, 1930, Bakersfield; d. Gottlieb and Helen Blanch (Kalloch) Koch; m. Harry L. Morrison, Jr. Jan. 18, 1953; children; Christine, b. 1955; Laurey, b. 1957; Harry III, b. 1960; edn: BS, UC Berkeley 1952; MA, John F. Kennedy Univ. 1978. Career: co-founder John F. Kennedy University, Orinda 1964: Registrar and mem. executive, administrv. staffs, 1964-82; dir. of Finl. Aid, 1967-78; Bookstore founder/mgr., 1965-75; founder/ chief adminstr. Career Counseling & Placement Ctr. 1980-82; designer, and Dean of Career Development Pgm. awarding MA degree, 1980-82; JFK Univ. regent 1982--; self- empl. counselor/ consultant 1982-; pres. C.N. Johnston's Inc. 1983-; adv. bd. Career Ctr. Univ. of Calif. WYCA 1981; recipient Kennedy Citation for disting. svc., J.F. Kennedy Univ. 1978; mem: Assn. of Governing Bd. of Univs. & Colls.; Western Gerontology Soc.; Calif.

Personnel & Guidance Assn.; Pacific Assn. of Collegiate Registrars & Admissions Ofcrs.; Diablo Valley Home Economists (pres. 1961); AAUW; bd. mem. Creative Presch. Ctr.; vol. Mt. Diablo Peace Ctr.; Democrat; Unity; rec: collect American Indian baskets & artifacts. Res: 31 Orchard Estates Dr Walnut Creek 94598

MORRISON, JOHN ANTOINE, international strategic planning consultant; b. Sept. 22, 1941, Honolulu, Hi.; s. William Robert Clayton and Evelyn Florence (Funsett) M.; m. Blanca Delia, Dec. 29, 1973; children: Vanessa, b. 1977; Antoine, b. 1979; Erik Michel, b. 1981; edn: Politechnico Nacional, Mex. 1962-64; BA, Univ. of Wash. 1966; MBA, Univ. Nacional, Autonoma, Mex. 1968; postgrad., Univ. of Grenoble, France 1976, Univ. of Bonn, Ger. 1977. Career: dir. internat. mktg. Vinos Europeos, S.A., Bordeaux, France, Mexico City 1973-77; dir. internat. mktg. Internat. Investment Svcs., Ltd., Madrid, Paris, Bonn 1978-82; pres. Loaiza, Morrison, Pena Asociados, San Diego, Mex., Bogota, 1982--; frequent lectr., spkr. on internat. mktg. & foreign mkt. strategies; expert on Latin America; freq. spkr. on bus. in Latin Am.; honors: Mktg. Exec. of the Yr., Internat. Soc. of (W.) European Execs., Paris 1979; Grad., Academie Du Vin, Paris 1979; mem: Chambers of Commerce in France, Ger., Spain, Mex., Chile, Colombia & Brazil; num. world trad assns. in USA, Latin Am. & Europe; Soc. Internac. de Ejecutivos (Madrid); Internat. Soc. of W. European Execs. (Paris); Club Campestre, Club Deportivo (Mex).; publs: num. arts. on foreign investor consulting, strategic mkt. plnng. 1979-83; research: foreign mkt. plnng. and foreign mkt. strategies 1973-; Republican; rec: wine expert and collector, pilot. Res: Box 472 San Ysidro 92073 Ofc: Loaiza Morrison Pena, 557 Blvd. Fundadores Altos, Tijuana, Baja California, Mexico

MORRISON, ROBERT WENDELL, lawyer; b. June 4, 1923, Renovo, Pa.; s. Thomas Cyrill and Edith Louisa (Hall) M.; m. Charlotte Coyne, Dec. 28, 1960; children: Robert Jr., b. 1966; Thomas, b. 1968; edn: BA, Univ. of Penn. 1943; MBA, Wharton Sch. 1947; JD, Columbia Law Sch. 1950; admitted to practice, State Bar of NY 1950, Calif. 1951, US Supreme Ct. 1956, US Ct. Mil. Appeals 1956; Cert. Taxation Splst., Calif. 1973. Career: assoc. in law Columbia Univ., NYC 1950-51; law clerk to Hon. James Alger Fee, US Dist. Ct., Portland, Ore. 1951-52; atty. at law, firm Pillsbury, Madison & Sutro, San Francisco 1952--; taxation splst. 1973-; dir. Laguna Honda Hosp. Volunteers 1976-; bd. govs. Shriners Hosps. for Crippled Children 1977-, v.chmn. 1979, chmn. 1980-82; honors; Phi Beta Kappa 1943; Fellow Am. Coll. of Probate Counsel; mem: Am., Fed., Calif. & San Francisco bar assns.; Reserve Ofcrs. Assn.; Judge Advocates Assn.; Civil Affairs Assn.; Assn. US Army; San Francisco Estate Plnng. Council; Potentate, Islam Shrine Temple 1978; Royal Order of Scotland 1982; mil: col. JAGC, AUS, 1943-46; USAR 1948-80, Legion of Merit; Republican; Methodist; rec: swimming, hiking, tennis. Res: 443 Belvedere Ave Belvedere 94920 Ofc: Pillsbury, Madison & Sutro, POB 7880 San Francisco 94120

MORROW, ODETTE GENEVIEVE, sales and marketing executive; b. Apr. 7, 1935, Teheran, Iran, nat. 1961; d. Antoine Jean and Nabiha Marie (Moughanni) Reboisson; m. Samuel Albin Morrow, Feb. 12, 1956; children: Monique, b. 1957; Denis, b. 1958; Andre, b. 1959; Michelle, b. 1961; Sam Jr., b. 1967; edn: diplome, Ecole Jeanne D'Arc 1950; American Univ., Beirut 1952; cert. Sales & Mktg. Mgmt., The Ednl. Inst. of the Am. Hotel & Motel Assn. 1983. Career: with Holiday Inns Inc. 1967--; current dir. of sales & mktg., San Jose; mem: pres. Hotel Sales Mgmt. Assn. of San Mateo-Santa Clara Co.; Meeting Planners. Internat.; No. Calif. Soc. of Assn. Execs.; Sacramento Soc. of Assn. Execs.; Peninsula Corp. Travel Assn.; San Jose Vis. & Conv. Bur. (chair 1981-82); Women In Bus. San Jose; Tri County Indsl. Recreational Council, Santa Clara; recipient profl. recognition as outstanding mgr., Holiday Inns, 1977, 78; works: started the hotel blitz in conjuction w/ student from San Jose State Univ.; Democrat; Catholic; rec: cooking internat. foods, swimming. Res: 515 Fontanelle Ct San Jose 95111 Ofc: Holiday Inn Park Center Plaza, 282 Almaden Blvd San Jose 95113

MORSHEIMER, FREDERICK THOMAS, retail co. executive; b. Apr. 3, 1948, Gloversville, NY; s. L. Joseph and Emma E. Morsheimer; m. Linda Liljegren, July 7, 1973; children: Megan, b. 1979; Erin, b. 1983; edn: BA, Norwich Univ. 1970; MBA, State Univ. of NY Albany 1982. Career: distbn. ctr. mgr. The Grandoe Corp., Gloversville, NY 1973-75, v.p. Philippine ops. 1976-79, prod. line/ prodn. mgr. 1979, bus. analyst 1980; regl. systems coord. Associated Dry Goods, Western Regl. Data Ctr., Culver City, 1982--; honors: Beta Gamma Sigma, 1982; mem: Data Admin. Mgmt. Assn.; Rotary Club, Gloversville, NY; mil: capt. US Army 1971-73; Republican; rec: cont. education, personal computing. Res: 5900 Canterbury Dr K129, Culver City 90230 Ofc: Associated Dry Goods, 5840 Uplander Way Culver City 90230

MORTAROTTI, JOHN RUSTY, music and effects editor/supervisor; b. Nov. 24, 1946, Los Angeles; s. John Frank and Michaelina Marianna (Plano) M.; engaged: Patricia Donahue; edn: AA, Pasadena City Coll. 1967; CSU Los Angeles 1970-74. Career: audio effects, Los Angeles 1969-73; (music selecting for films) Cinesound, L.A. 1973-76; (music & effects selecting & editing) 1976--, num. shows incl. You Asked For It, Krofft Supershows, Hour Mag., (sound effects editing) The Indianapolis 500 Races; currently, music supvr. The "Breakaway" talk show; collector music from var. film music libraries; mil: spec. 4/c US Amry 1967-69, Marksmanship Badge, Nat. Guard Ribbon; Catholic. Res: 1515 South Ethel Alhambra 91803 Ofc: John R. Mortarotti, 6200 W Third St Los Angeles 90036

MORTIMER, KLAUS HERMAN, importing and wholesale gourmet food co. executive; b. Sept. 25, 1931, Cologne, Ger., nat. 1945; s. Eric Joseph and Ann (Hertz) M.; m. Bridget J., Sept. 4, 1965; children: Eric, b. 1968; Bronwyn, b. 1966; edn: BS, Univ. of Calif. 1954. Career: trainee to dept. mgr. branch store, The Emporium of San Francisco, 1955-60; mgr. Eric J. Mortimer Co., S.F. 1960-61; ptnr. Gourmet Specialties, San Francisco 1961--: secty./ treas. 10 years, pres. 10 years, gen. mgr. 1981--, and pres. Klaus Mortimer Inc.; mil: seaman l/c Navy Air Reserve 1950-58; Republican; rec: skiing, tennis, travel. Res: 60 Surfwood Cir San Rafael 94901 Ofc: Gourmet Specialties, 228 Shaw Rd, So. San Francisco 94080

MORTON, JOHN MARK, hotel manager; b. Jan. 14, 1947, Phila.; s. Thomoas earl, Jr. and Cornelia Virginia (Riordan) M.; edn: AA, Shenandoah Coll., Winchester, Va. 1966; maj. psych. Lebanon Valley Coll., Annville, Pa. 1966-67; BS in hotel adm., Univ. of Nev. 1976. Career: asst. front office mgr. Hyatt Hotel at LAX, Los Angeles 1977-78; front office mgr. L'Ermitage Hotel, Beverly Hills, 1978-80; asst. mgr. The Pointe Resort, Phoenix, Az. 1980-81; res. mgr. Radisson Scottsdale (Az.) Resort and Racquet Club, 1981-82; exec. asst. mgr. L'Ermitage Hotel, B.H. 1982, exec. asst. mgr. El Escorial Hotel (mem. L'Ermitage Hotel Gp.), Santa Barbara 1983-- ("home" White House Press Center when the Pres. is in Calif.); mem. Santa Barbara City Coll. Hotel & Restaurant Mgmt. Conf. Center Advis. Com. 1984; mem: Univ. of Nevada Hoteliers (1976-77), Santa Barbara CofC, S.B. Beach Area Assn.; mil: E5 USAF 1967-73, mem. USAF Thunderbirds, 2 Commendn. Medals for Merit. Svc.; Republican; Methodist; rec: biking, jogging. Address: El Escorial Hotel 625 Por La Mar Circle Santa Barbara 93103

MORTON, WALTER BENSON, JR., consulting electronics engineer; b July 1, 1926, Birmingham, Ala.; s. Walter Benson and Jessie Gertrude (Coe) M.; children: Eric, b. 1952; Rachel, b. 1954; Peter,b. 1956; Bruce, b. 1959; edn: BSEE, Lehigh Univ. 1950; BSBA, 1950; grad. studies, Univ. of Pitts., Univ. of Penna. and Carnegie-Mellon, 1951-53; Reg. Profl. Engr. in Penna. 1982, Calif. 1983. Career: sr. engr. Burroughs- Sperry Univac 1951-55; chief tech. svcs. Beckman Inst. 1956-58; pgm. mgr. Astrodata 1958-60; cons. engr. Xerox, Lockheed, Astrodata, others 1961-73; chief eng. Dressen Barnes 1973-74; cons. Unisen 1974-76; sr. eng. Delta El. & Control 1976; sr. proj. eng. Transrex Corp. 1977-80; proj. mgr./ mgr. design & Devel. Cipher Data Prods. 1980--; dir. Dynamics Inst. 1962-65; lectr./ assoc. prof. CSU Long Beach; honors: Harold Horm Proseminar Prize and Williams Sr. Prize, Lehigh Univ., 1950; mem: IEEE; NY Acad. of Scis.; Am. Assn. for Adv. Sci.; AAAS; publs: papers and letters in var. tech. journs. and proceedings IEEE; mil: lt. (Inf.), US Army; Unitarian. Res: 803 21st St San Diego 92102 Ofc: Cipher Data Products, 10225 Willow Creek San Diego 92102

MOSCA, CARLO ANDREW, education/graphics executive; b. Nov. 10, 1938, Cambridge, MA; s. Antony and Florence (Nardone) Mosca; edn: BS, Boston Univ., 1962; m. Eleanor Eacret, June 5, 1966. Career: staff naturalist and exhibit planner, Trailside Museum, Milton, Mass. 1958-60; teaching intern, Museum of Science, Boston, 1960-61; edn. splst. 1962-66 and supr. School Services 1966-67; instr. in sci. Elliot Pearson Sch., Tufts Univ., 1962-65; nature dir., cons. Morgan Meml. Fresh Air Camps, South Athol, Mass., 1964-67; natural history and physical sci. lectr., 1965-67; dir., Edn., New England Aquarium, Boston, 1967-72; instr., Cambridge (Mass.) Ctr. for Adult Edn., 1969-71; dir., Edn., Sea World, Inc., San Diego 1972-74; and corp. dir., Edn./Graphics, 1974---; advisory coms: Greater San Diego Industry-Edn. Council, treas. 1982; Amer. Assn. of Zoological Parks and Aquariums, v. chmn. Pub. Edn. Com. 1979-82; Amer. Cetacean Soc., edtl. adv. Whale Watcher Journ.; San Diego Comm. Colls., Marine Tech. Adv. Com., 1972---. Awards: Friend of Youth, Goodwill Assocs., Morgan Meml., Goodwill Inn Sch., 1968; The Presidents Awd for dedicated sc., Amer. Assn. of Zoological Parks and Aquariums, 1979. Mem: Amer. Assn. of Museums; Amer. Assn. of Zoological Parks and Aquariums; Amer. Cetacean Soc., S.D. bd. dirs. 1973-78; Assn. of San Diego Educators for the Gifted; Internatl. Oceanographic Found.; Marine Tech. Soc.; Natl. Art Edn. Assn.; Natl. Assn. of Biology Teachers; Natl. Marine Edn. Assn.; Natl. Science Teachers Assn. Numerous publs. Democrat. Catholic. Res: 8211 El Paseo Grande, La Jolla 92037; Office: Sea World, Inc., 1720 S. Shores Rd., San Diego 92109.

MOSES, STEPHEN DAVID, investment company president; b. Nov. 24, 1934, Philadelphia, PA; s. Lester Jacob and Rosalie (Berg) Moses; Edn: JD cum laude, Harvard Law Sch., 1958; BS, in econ., Franklin & Marshall Coll., 1955; m. Annemarie Schleisner, 1962; chil: Kathryn, b. 1963; Stephen Jr., b. 1968; K. Robert (Bobby), b. 1969. Career: atty., Fran Bernstein Gutberlet and Conaway, Baltimore, MD, 1960-65; exec. dir., Balt. Metro. AREA Study Comm., 1961-63; dir., Urban Development Div., Action Inc., Wash., D.C. Honors: Housing Man of the Year, 1970; mem., Bd. of Overseers, Hebrew Union Coll., 1980; bd. of visitors, Franklin & Marshall Coll., 1979---; bd. trustees and oficers, Leo Baeck Temple, 1973---; pres., L.A. Ballet. Author: num. articles publ. in Trade Periodical; lectr. at colleges. Mil: Pfc., Army, 1959. Democrat, Western Regional Chmn., Democratic Natl. Finance Council. Jewish. Rec: tennis, classical music. Res: 149 Denslow Ave., Los Angeles 90049; Office: NIDC, 11812 San Vicente Blvd., 6th Flr., Los Angeles 90049.

MOSLEY, MARIAN JUNE, lawyer; b. Aug. 5, 1929, Great Falls, Montana; d. Theodore and Edith Aileen (Bowman) Kummerfeld; m. Edward Reynold Mosley, Dec. 26, 1965; children: Cary, b. 1950; Laura, b. 1951; Christopher, b.

1966; Caroline, b. 1968; edn: BA, CSU Fresno 1960; grad. work, Univ. of Costa Rica 1964; JD, Humphreys Coll. of Law 1980; admitted to State Bar of Calif. 1980. Career: reservations, stewardess Air American Airlines, Los Angeles 1948-50; sales mgr. Tupperware Inc., Los Angeles 1950-55; tchr. Fresno Unif. Sch. Dist., Fresno 1956-74; atty. at law, pvt. practice, Fresno 1980--; awards: Fullbright Scholarship to study Univ. of Costa Rica and survey tchr. tng. facilities in Central America 1964; mem: Calif. & Fresno Co. (bd. dirs.) Women Lawyers; Fresno Co. Legal Svcs.; Am., Calif. & Fresno Co. Bar Assns.; White Ash Broadcasting Co. (bd.dirs.); Fresno Co. Hist. Soc. (La Paloma Guild); Cancer League; Fresno Med. Soc. Aux.; Fresno Co. Med. Political Action Com.; Am. Assn. of Univ. Women; Nat. Council on Negro Women; works: developed and administered, San Joaquin Valley Home for Youth (behavior modification for juvenile offenders) 1970-78; organized, La Paloma Guild for Fresno Co. Hist. Soc. 1973; Republican; rec: music. Res: 3075 W Kearney Blvd Fresno 93706 Ofc: 808 M Street Fresno 93721

MOSHER, SALLY EKENBERG, company president; b. July 26, 1934, NY, NY; d. Leslie Joseph and Frances Josephine (McArdle) Ekenberg; m. James Kimberly Mosher (dec. 1982), Aug. 13, 1960; edn: B.Mus., Manhattanville Coll. 1956; postgrad. Hofstra Univ. 1958-60, USC 1970-73; JD, USC Sch. of Law 1981; admitted to State Bar of Calif. 1982. Career: musician: pianist, tchr., critic (newspaper), coach, concert mgr., New York and Los Angeles 1957-74; rep. Occidental Life, Pasadena 1975-78; v.p. James K. Mosher Co. Inc., Pasadena 1961-82, pres. 1982--; pres. Oakhill Ent Inc., Pasadena 1984--; assoc. White-Howell Inc., Pasadena; honors: Full Honor Scholarship, Manhattanville Coll. 1952-56; special election Mu Phi Epsilon 1970; mem: Kappa Gamma Pi; Mu Phi Epsilon; Phi Alpha Delta; Associates of CalTech; The Athenaeum; Am., Calif., Los Angeles & Pasadena bar assns.; Pasadena Athletic Club; Upper Rancheros Rd. Assn. (pres. 1981-83); Pasadena Arts Council (ofcr. 1966-8); Junior League, Pasadena (dir. 1966-7); Encounters Concerts (dir. 1966-72); USC Friends of Music (dir. 1973-6), Pasadena Philharmonic Com. (dir.), Fine Arts Club of Pasadena (dir); publs: articles and music revs., 1966-72; Republican; Christian; rec: graphic design. Res: 1260 Rancheros Rd Pasadena 91103

MOSS, CHARLES NORMAN, physician; b. June 13, 1914, Los Angeles; Edn: AB, Stanford Univ., 1940; MD, Harvrd Med. Sch., 1944; MPH, UC Berkeley, 1955; Sr. Flight Surg., USAF, 1956; Dr. PH, UCLA, 1970; Aviation Med. Examiner, FAA, 1970; m. Margaret Louise; chil: Lori Anne, b. 1967. Career: surg. intern, Peter Bent Brigham Hosp., Boston, 1944-45; med. ofcr., US Army; female ward, Birmingham Gen. Hosp., Van Nuys, 1945; Battalion Surg., Shanghai and Peiping, China, 1945-47, med. care for 2500 personnel supr. 18); with USAF, 1949-65; Wing Base Surg., Wing Flight Surg. and Med. Group Comdr., 86th Fighter-Bomber Wing, Germany, 1949-52, med. care 6000, supr. 48 personnel; surg., flight surg., amd med. group comdr., San Antonio Air Material Area, Kelly AFB, TX, 1952-54, med. care for 45,000, supv. of 65 personnel; Preventive Med. Div., Communicable Disease Ofcr., Office of AF Surg. Gen., Wash., D.C., 1955-59, furnished guidance for entire AF; prof. ofcr. for preparation and pub. of num. AF regulations and pamphlets, served on num. bds. and coms. incl. Natl. Acad. of Sci., Natl. Research Council, Army-Air Force Master Menu Bd., US Civil Sevice Examiners; Hosp. Comdr. and flight surg., NATO Hdqtrs., AF & Army, Izmir, Turkey, 1959, med. crae for 10,000, supv. 45; chief, Missile Test and Range Support Div., Staff Surgeon's Office, Atlantic Missile Range and Cape Canaveral, 1959-61, med. care for 18,000, supv. up to 80; safety ofcr. and occupational med., Orlando AFB, FL and Lookout Mtn. AF Station, L.A., 1961-64; ret. Lt. Col., 1965; Med. Dir., No. Amer. Rockwell Corp., L.A. Div., 1969-70; physician, L.A. County, 1970—: Occupational Health Svc., Dept. of Personnel, 1970-73; Chief, Med. Adv. Unit, L.A. Co. Bd. of Retirement, Community Health Servs., 1973-79; med. cons., Health Facilities Div., Dept. of Health Services, 1979-81. Recipient Physician's Recognition Awards, AMA, 1969, 72, 76, 79, 82. Mem: num. profl. assns., Physician for Amer. Weightlifting Team when they won World Championships in Paris, 1950 and Milan, 1951. Presbyterian. Rec: nutrition, weightlifting, photography. Res: 7714 Cowan Ave., Los Angeles 90045.

MOUCK, NORMAN GARRISON, JR., community college superintendent-president; b. Sept. 9, 1928, Omaha, Nebr.; s. Norman G. and Madge Arvilla (Bossoh) M.; m. Dorothy Davis, Jan. 3, 1949; children: Susan, b. 1949; Richard, b. 1952; Teresa, b. 1956; edn: BS, Edinboro State Coll. 1953; M.Ed, UCLA 1956, doctoral studies, 1956-58; MBS, Univ. of Colo. 1959-60; doctoral cand., UCLA 1965-67. Career: dept. chmn./ tchr. math., physics, chem., earch scis. & geography, Fontana H.S. 1954-61; lectr./ supvr. tchr. edn. USC Santa Barbara 1965-66; dir. research & devel./ asst. dean of instrn./ div. chmn./ prof. math. Santa Barbara City Coll. 1961-68; asst. supt. instrn. Santa Clarita Comm. Coll. Dist./ v.p. Coll. of the Canyons 1968-79, interim supt./ pres. Santa Clarita Comm. Coll. District, College of the Canyons 1979, math. instr. 1979-82, supt.-pres. 1982--; cons. Stanford Univ. 1963-64; writer School Mathematics. Group, Stanford Univ. 1964; visting asst. prof. of math., Edinboro State Coll.; honors: Nat. Sci. Found. Fellowship, UCLA 1957, Univ. of Colo. 1959-60; Ebel of Los Angeles Scholarship 1953-54; mem: Kiwanis Club (pres. 1978-79); United Crusade; publs: Elementary Algebra for College Students, H.S. Bear & N.G. Mouck; Mathematics Through Science, Rivesed Parts I-II; mem. writing team Stanford Univ. 1964; mil: surveying and draftsman US Army 1946-59, cartographer 1950-51; Democrat; Presbyterian; rec: swimming, skiing. Res: 28414 Winterdale Dr Canyon Country 91351 Ofc: Santa Clarita Comm. Coll. Dist., Coll. of the Canyons, 26455 Rockwell Canyon Rd Valencia 91355

MOVIUS, WILLIAM ROBERT, otolarngologist; b. Oct. 15, 1913, Billings, Mont.; s. Dr. Arthur James (surgeon, founder of the Billings Clinic) and Joanna Marion (Murray) M.; m. Alice Whitney Burton, Mar. 11, 1944, Mnpls.; children: (twins) Edward Gale (M.D.) and Alice Burton (Mrs. Dennis Painter) b. 1945; John Robert b. 1947; edn: BS, Northwestern Univ. 1936; MB, 1939; MD, 1940. Career: intern Ancker Hosp., St. Paul, 1939-40; instr. anatomy, Univ. of Minn., 1940-41; tchg. fellowship in otolaryngology, 1941-44; mem. Billings Clinic, 1944-47; pvt. practice of otolaryngology,San Diego and La Jolla, 1947-48; ear, nose, throat cons. Scripps Clinic, 1948-74; assoc. prof. of surg. Staff of Children's Hosp., staff Scripps Hosp., 1947-82; mem. exec. com., surg. com. Scripps Hosp.; assoc. clin. prof. of surgery, Div. of Otolaryngology, Vets. Adminstrn., 1971-83; mem: AMA, San Diego Co. Med. Soc., Calif. Med. Assn., Fellow Am. Coll. of Surgeons 1947, Fellow Am. Acad. of Otolaryngology 1948, Fellow Pacific Coast Oto-Ophthalmol. Soc. 1949; Sigma Nu frat.; Phi Chi med. frat.; Mason; Kiwanis 1952-70; Rotary 1970-76; Scoutmaster Troop 565 (La Jolla) 1968-70, Silver Beaver Award 1969; Mission Bay Yacht Club 1947-83 (dir. 1962); Skimmer fleet capt.; Presbyterian elder 1952-61; rec: sailing, yacht racing, mountain climbing, swimming. Res: 2345 Paseo Dorado La Jolla 92037

MOWERY, LEE A., insurance agency president; b. Mar. 26, 1932, St. Louis, Mo.; s. William H., Sr. and Frances M. Mowery; m. Joy Z. Lawrence, June 8, 1952; children: Lesa M., b. 1955; Robin R., . 1958; Christopher L., b. 1963; edn; grad. So. Methodist Univ. Inst. of Ins. Mktg. 1961; BS in bus. adm., Calif. Western Univ. 1970, MS in mktg. 1972; FLMI, Fellow Life Mgmt. Inst. 1974; CLU, Chartered Life Underwriter. Career: agent/ gen. agent Am. Gen. Life Ins. Co., Wichita, Bs. 1955-63; v.p. Investors Reserve Life Ins. Co., Wichita, Bs. 1963-67; v.p. Olympic Life Ins. Co., Dallas, Tex. 1967-69; br. mgr. Los Angeles agency Calif. Western Life Ins. Co. 1969-74; br.mgr. L.A. agcy. Canada Life Assurance Co. 1974-77; br. mgr. L.A. life sales ofc. CNA Ins. Co. 1977-82; pres. Tri- World Ins. Agcy. Inc., Gen. Lines Agcy. 1982--; cons. personal & corp. fin. plnng. & employee benefit plans, Merrill Lynch Pierce Fenner & Smith; mem: Calif. and L.A. Life Underwriters Assns.; L.A. Co. Risk Mgmt. Com.; L.A. Co. Plnng. Commn.; Tax Payers Congress of Calif. Valencia Hills Home Owners Assn. (past pres.) mil: s/sgt. USAF 1951-55; Republican; Methodist; rec: art objects, stain glass design. Res: 25311 Linda Vista Dr Laguna Hills 92653 Ofc: Tri- World Ins. Agency Inc., 3400 Irvine Ave, Ste 115 Newport Beach 92660

MROCZKOWSKI, GEORGE EDMOND, professional treasure hunter; b. May 26, 1925, Milwaukee, Wisc.; s. Theodore and Anna (Glysz) M.; 1 dau: Linda, b. 1949; edn: Army Engrs. Sch., Ft. Belvoir, Va. 1949. Career: ins. sales American Fidelity Life (5 yrs.); currently, retail merchant, Gem & Treasure Hunting Assn.; search & salvage team, Assn. cons. to Govt. Agencies, Military, FBI and local police in recovery ops.; honors: Top Salesman, Million Dollar Producer, Am. Fidelity Life & Constitution Life Ins. Cos.; recogn. for Outstanding Promotion for Mission Reconstrn., Museum and Fiesta, Mission San Luis Rey; mem: Internat Treasure Hunting Soc. of Garrett Electronics; San Diego Hist. Soc.; Old Town CofC; publs: The Professional Treasure Hunter (3rd printing); mil: m/sgt. E-8 USMC 1943-64; Republican; Catholic; rec: photog. Res: 3725 Orion La Mesa 92041 Ofc: Gem and Treasure Hunting Assoc., 2493 San Diego Ave San Diego 92110

MUELLER, JEAN ELAINE, librarian; b. Mar. 5, 1950, Huntington Park; d. Roy Harold and Dorothy Jean (Hansen) M.; edn: BA, CSU Northridge 1972; MSLS, USC 1973. Career: asst. librarian Ethel Percy Andrus Gerontology Ctr., USC Los Angeles 1973-77; chief librarian 1977-83; night asst./ observer Mt. Wilson & Las Campanas Observatories, Carnegie Inst. of Wash., Pasadena 1983--; profl. presentations: ann. meeting Gerontology Soc., S.F. 1977, Toronto 1981; mem: So. Calif. Online Users Gp.; Sci. & Eng. Academic Librarians; Calif. Academic & Research Librarians; Mt. Wilson Observatory Assn.; publs: num. publs. on geronotolgy; co-creator, first online bibliographic database on aging, AGEX, Andrus Gerontological Exch.; Democrat; Methodist; rec: astronomy. Res: Mount Wilson Observatory, Mount Wilson 91023 Ofc: Mount Wilson and Las Campanas Observatories, Carnegie Inst. of Washington, 813 Santa Barbara St Pasadena 91101

MUELLER-VOLLMER, KURT, university professor; b. June 28, 1928,Hamburg, Germany, nat. 1968; s. Kurt and Tilly (Epkens) M.-V.; m. Patricia Bialecki, Aug. 29, 1981; child, Jan David, b. 1967; edn: Matura, Friedrich Wilhelm Gym. 1949; Philosophicum, Univ. of Cologne, 1953; MA, Brown Univ. 1955; PhD, Stanford Univ. 1962. Career: faculty Stanford Univ. 1961--, prof. of German Studies & Humanities/ dir. Grad Pgm. in the Humanities, currently; frequent assignments abroad; also pres. Repac Realty Pacific Inc. internat. property mgmt. firm in Menlo Park, 1973-; honors: senior fellow Nat. Endowment for the Humanities, Wash DC 1979-80; councilmem. Humboldt Soc.; mem. Modern Language Assn. of Am., Schiller Soc., German Am. CofC (S.F.), author sev. books, num. articles in sev. languages: literary criticism, history of ideas, culture hist.; Indep.; Prot.; rec: economics, property mgmt., tchg. Res: 774 Seneca St Palo Alto 94301 Ofc: Stanford University, B 242A, Stanford 94305

MUENCH, JAMAR ANDREA, public administrator; b. Sept. 21, 1940, Los Angeles; d. Charles Frederick and Jamar Rosemary (Young) M.; edn: BA, pol.sci., UCLA 1962; MA in internat. edn., Teachers Coll., Columbia Univ. 1967. Career: Peace Corps vol., Brazil 1963-65; research asst. Business International, NYC 1967-68; various positions in pub. rels., advt., Los Angeles 1969-72; field deputy Assem. Alan Sieroty, 1973-74; adminstrv. asst. Assem.

Speaker Bob Moretti, 1974; legis. analyst City of Los Angeles/LA City Council, 1975-80; exec. dir. LA City Commn. on the Status of Women, 1980--; co-ch. United Way Reg. V, Child Care Needs Study 1984; awards: recognition, Commn. for Sex Equity, LA Unified Sch. Dist. 1983; Pres.'s scholarship, Columbia Univ., 1966. Mem: Nat. Assn. of Female Execs., East Valley Bruins (sec. 1982-4), bd.dirs. San Fernando Vly GSA Council; mem. Citizens Adv. Commn. of LA Olympic Organizing Com.; pres. condominium assn. 1983-4. Democrat; Episcopal; rec: drawing, scuba, skiing. Ofc: Rm. 550-CHE, 200 N. Main St Los Angeles 91606

MUENCH, JERRY FREDRIC, sales/marketing executive; b. Mar. 19, 1935, Abilene, Ks.; s. Fred Theodore and Pearl Elizabeth (Van Dyke) M.; m. Jeanne Sheffield, Apr. 6, 1956; children: Kathy, b. 1960; Michael, b. 1959; edn: AA, Long Beach City Coll. 1956; BSEE, West Coast Univ. 1964. Career: mgr. application engr. Leach Corp. Tech. 1959-69; co-founder/ dir./ secty./ v.p Odetics Inc. 1969--; honors: Group Achiev. Award (Magsat Proj. Team), NASA; mem: Assn. of US Army; Navy League of US; Am. Space Found.; AM. Inst. Aero. & Astro.; Westminster Tenni Club; mil: sp2 Calif. Nat. Guard; Republican (Nat. Com.); rec: running, tennis. Res: 15 69th Place Long Beach 90803 Ofc: Odetics Inc., 1859 S Manchester Anaheim 92802

MULDOON, BETTY PATRICIA, restaurateur; b. Mar. 13, 1953, Chgo., Ill.; d. John Edmund and Alice Therese (McCormick) Muldoon; edn: BA, Knox Coll. 1975; CLM, Univ. 'de Besancon, France 1974; grad. wk. Colo. State Univ. 1975-76; CA, Nat. Cooking Inst. 1979; Performax Tnr., Performax Systems Internat. 1982. Career: restaurant mgr. Shakey's, Denver Colo. 1zw6-79; area supvr. Shakey's Inc., No. Colo. 1979-82; franchise field cons. Shakey's Inc., So. Calif. 1982--; tnr. Performax Sys., restaurant cons. KLC Ent. 1983-- honors: Mgr. of the Yr., Shakey's Inc. 1979; mem: Performax Internat.; author: nat. Delivery Manual, Shakey's Inc. 1984; Republican; Catholic; rec: stockmarket, classical music, culinary arts. Res: 6600 Warner Ave, 102, Huntington Beach 92647 Ofc: Shakey's Inc. 550 N Park Center Dr, Ste 115, Santa Ana 92705

MULLANE, FRANCES HIRSCHMANN, lawyer; b. Apr. 28, 1943, NY; d. Conrad John and Mary Helen (Candela) Hirschmann; m. Allan Mullane, June 19, 1976; edn: JD, magna cum laude, Western State Univ. 1979; admitted to practice, State Bar of Calif. Career: claims clerk Equitable Life Assurance Co., NY 1960-63; gen. ofc. Hirschmann Corp., Vernon 1963-65; quality control inspection & eng., var. companies in So. Calif. 1967-76; atty., self- empl., Norco 1979--; City of Norco Housing Com. 1980; City of Norco Ingalls Park Com. 1983; City of Norco Bus. Lic. Com. 1983-84; awards: Am. Jurisprudence Awds. Evidence I & II Remedies-Corporations, 1979; Prentice Hall Awd., Taxation 1979; mem: Am. & Riverside Co. Bar Assns.; Calif. Trial Lawyers Assn.; Sierra Empire Arabian Horse Assn. (pres. 1980-81); So. Calif. Pinto Breeders & Exhibitors; Norco CofC; Catholic; rec: breeding horses, phnn Mullane, Atty. at Law, 1762 Fourth St Norco 91760

MULLEN, EDWARD BEACH, manufacturing co. executive; b. Oct. 2, 1935, St. Louis, Mo.; s. Edward B. and Marguerite (Stark) M.; m. Nancy Sweet, Aug. 17, 1957; children: Marci, b. 1958; Linda, b. 1960; edn: BSBA, Univ. of Missouri 1957. Career: with US Steel 1959--; comml. trainee, Pittsburgh, Pa. 1959; service rep., Chgo. 1960; sales rep., Kansas City, Mo. 1962; asst. mktg. mgr., Birmingham 1975; asst. sales mgr., Los Angeles, 1976, dist. mgr. sales 1981, current regl. mgr. of sales, US Steel, L.A.; awards: Steel Fellow, Am. Iron & Steel Inst. 1979; USS Manager Devel. Pgm. 1976; mem: Steel Service Ctr. Inst.; Pacific Gas Assoc.; Los Angeles Trade Tech. Mktg. Adv. Com.; Jonathan Club; Rollings Hills Country Club; mil: 1st lt. US Army 1957-59; rec: 1733 Dalton Rd Palos Verdes Estates 90274 Ofc: US Steel, 445 S Figueroa, Ste 3700, Los Angeles 90071

MULLIKEN, DAVID LOMBARD, lawyer; b. Oct. 23, 1943, Chgo., Ill.; s. Alfred Augustus Sr. and Elizabeth (Lombard) M.; gr.-gr.-gr. grandfather, Daniel Webster; m. Noreen Gilman, Dec. 21, 1969; children: David, b. 1978; Douglas, b. 1983; edn: AB, Dartmouth Coll. 1965; MBA, Amos Tuck Sch. of Grad. Bus. Admin. 1966; JD, Univ. of Va. Law Sch. 1975. Career: assoc. atty. Gray, Cary, Ames & Frye, San Diego 1975-80; assoc. Latham & Watkins, San Diego 1980-82; advr. Assemblyman Goggin's CEQA Revision Com. 1982-83; awards: winner William Minor Lile Moot Court Competition, Univ. of Va. Law Sch. 1975.; Stephen Pierre Traynor Awd.; mem: San Diego CofC; State & Nat. Affairs Adv. Council 1980-; San Diego Comm. Resource Panel 1980-, chmn. 1983; Fixed Sources Subcom.; San Diego Associated Gen. Contractor Legal Affairs Com. 1983-; Dartmouth Club of S.D.; S.D. Yacht Club; S.D. Athletic Club; S.D. Tennis & Racquet Club; mil: lt. USN 1967-72, Navy Commdn. w/ Combat V, Merit. Unit Cit., Vietnam Svc. w/ Stars, Vietnam Cpgn., Armed Forces Expeditionary, Nat. Def. Svc.; Republican; Christian Sci.; rec: tennis, sailing, travel. Res: 713 Rosecrans San Diego 92106 Ofc: Latham & Watkins, 701 B St, Ste 2100, San Diego 92101

MULLINS, JACK WAYNE, company president; b. Apr. 15, 1946, Fullerton; s. Jack Gordon and Helen Mollie (Leigh) M.; m. Jean Marie Hodan, July 4, 1969; children: Michelle Marie, b. 1974; Kimberly Denise, b. 1977; edn: Fullerton Coll. 1969-70. Career: mgr. Nat. Drive In Grocery Corp., La Habra 1964-66; route salesman Sparkletts Drinking Water, Santa Ana 1969-74; owner/ opr. Al's Auto Electric, Anaheim 1975-79; owner/ pres. Yorba Linda Auto Parts Inc. 1979--; mem: Calif. Automotive Wholesalers; Indep. Garage Owners of Am.; Automotive Svc. Council; Masons; mil: sgt. US Army Special Forces 1966-69, Bronze Star, US Jump Wings, Vietnamese Jump Wings, Army Commdn.; Republican; Catholic; rec: flying, hunting. Res: 2537 E Hilda Pl Anaheim 92806 Ofc: Yorba Linda Auto Parts Inc. 4981 Valley View Yorba Linda 92686

MUNGER, GEORGE EDWARD, restaurateur; b. Jan. 12, 1940, Milwaukee, Wis.; s. Frank Allen and Cecil Mae M.; m. Piret Korkmann, June 15, 1963; edn: BS, Univ. of Wis. 1963. Career: general mgr. Ace Auto Parks, San Diego, 8 years; designed sev. major stadium parking ops. incl. Dallas Cowboys, Pontiac Silverdome, San Diego Stadium; founder/pres. The Perfect Pan, 1975--, now with 3 cookware stores, 3 cooking schools, 6 restaurants; author cookbook (in prep.); mem: founder Amer. Inst. of Wine & Food, Internat. Assn. of Cooking Schools (past v.p.); Leroy Club; mil: lt. USN 1963-67, Far East; Democrat; Presbyterian; rec: food, wine, skiing. Res: Rt. 1, Box 132A, Sun Valley Rd Del Mar 92014 Ofc: The Perfect Pan, 6610 Convoy Ct, San Diego 92112

MUNICH, JOHN, financial planner; b. Apr. 25, 1926, Akron, Oh.; s. John Sr. and Amelia (Brady) M.; m. Barbara L., June 10, 1951; children: Ken, b. 1955; Sherrie, b. 1957; edn: BS, Kent State Univ. 1952; MS, NY Univ. 1953. Career: contract analyst/ plant eng. asst. No. American Aviation, Downey 1959-61; mgr. of admin. svcs. & prodn. control H.I. Thompson Co., Gardena 1961-63; sr. mgmt. sys. analyst Ford Aeronautics, Irvine 1964-69; self- empl., fin. plnnr./ broker, Garden Grove 1969--; honors: graduate scholarship, NYU 1952-3; Hon. Gp. Kent State Univ.; Mem. Chmn. Soc. for Adv. Mgmt.; mem: Soc. for Adv. Mgmt.; Am. Assn. of Individual Investors; Am. Prodn. & Inventory Control Soc.; Masons; publs: Management By Problem Communication, Systems and Procedures Journ. 1968; mil: PO 3/c USN 1941-44; Republican; Presbyterian; rec: dancing, flying, sports. Res: 12101 Bluebell Ave Garden Grove 92640

MUNSON, DOUGLAS CROW, lawyer; b. Nov. 4, 1938, Modesto; s. Merrill Crow and Sybol Jean (Blankenship) M.; m. Baerbel A.E., Dec. 16, 1978; edn: BA, Stanford Univ. 1960; JD, UC Hastings Law Sch. 1966. Career: assoc. at law with law firm Mullen & Filippi, San Francisco 1967; trial atty., Ofc. of Dist. Atty. S.F. 1968, senior atty. 1969, principal atty. 1970, homicide div. 1972, head atty. Ofc. of the Dist. Atty., S.F. 1982--; faculty Coll. of Criminal Justice Advocacy Hastings Ctr. for Practice Courses; guest lectr. Hastings Law Sch., USF Law Sch., Calif. District Atty. Assn. advanced Prosecutors Sch., S.F. Coroners Ofc. (medical jurisprudence series), S.F. Police Acad.; honors: Outstanding Appellate Advocacy, David E. Snodgrass Moot Ct. Comp., Hastings Law Sch. 1964; Outstanding D.A., S.F. Police Assn. 1981; Outstanding Prosecutor, Calif. Dist. Attys. Assn. 1982; mem: Calif. Bar Assn.; Calif. Dist. Attys. Assn.; S.F. Lawyers Club; Phi Delta Phi (Pomeroy Inn chpt.); mil: sp4 Calif Army Nat. Guard 1963; Republican; Protestant; rec: modeling, sailing, skiing. Res: 870 Pacheco St San Francisco 94116 Ofc: 850 Bryant St, Rm 320, San Francisco 94103

MUNSON, FLORENCE ETHEL, real estate broker; b. Nov. 23, 1898, Palmerston, Ont. Can.; d. Francis Eugene and Annie (Smith) M. Career: real estate broker, 15 years (ret).; fmr. office nurse/mgr. Dr. Franklin I. Harris, San Francisco, 25 yrs.; clerk City of San Francisco, City Hall, later for Parking Authority (auto safety check); driver for Judge Alden Johnson, when in SF, for Stage Door Canteen, and Kaltenborn (radio commentator), during WWII. Mem: SF CofC (1st vp SF Women's CofC 1968-71); Bus. Womens Golf Club of SF; Riviera Republican Womens Club; Santa Barbara Womens Club; Tuesday Swingers (winner 5 golf trophies 1939-45). Republican. Prot. Rec: golf, art, sculpturing. Res: 637 E. Micheltorena St Santa Barbara 93103

MUNTZ, EARL WILLIAM, manufacturing co. executive; b. Jan. 3, 1914, Elgin, Ill.; s. William L. and Margaret (Mooney) M.; children: James, b. 1940; Tina, b. 1952; edn: Elgin, Ill. High Sch. Career: pioneer in car stereo 1928; world's largest automobile dealer 1943; world's largest factory to consumer TV mfr. 1947; mfr. of 1st Am. sports car, Muntz Jet, 1951; mfr. of 1st fibre glass housed air conditioner 1952; inventor car stereo 1958; inventor self contained giant screen TV 1973; pioneer in satellite receivers 1980; world's largest VTR merchandiser 1980; currently, chmn. bd. Muntz Electronics Inc., Van Nuys; honors: Horatio Alger Awd. 1950; 1968 Peterson Pub. Co., Cert. to Modern Motoring, Motor Trend Mag.; Businessmans Awd., L.A. Press Club 1983. Res: 3416 Alana Dr Sherman Oaks 91403 Ofc: Muntz Electronics Inc., 7700 Densmore Ave Van Nuys 91406

MURANAKA, HIDEO, artist; b. Feb. 4, 1946, Mitaka-shi, Tokyo, Japan; s. Nobukichi and Hisae Muranaka; edn: BFA, Tokyo Nat. Univ. of Fine Arts & Music 1970, MFA, 1972; research stu., traditional Japanese painting 1972-73; mural painting, Fresno 1973-74; faculty of Fine Arts. Career: artist, painting, printmaking, traditional calligraphy; art tchr. tradl. Japanese style painting, Togeibijutsu Kenkyu-jo (part-time) in Motosumiyoshi, Kanagawa prefecture, 1969-73; tchr. brush painting and calligraphy, part time, Newman Youth Center, Tokyo, 1970-73; instr. of Sumie painting, Acad. of Art Coll., S.F. 1974-75; instr. brush painting and calligraphy, Acad. Muranaka, S.F. 1976-79; tchr. calligraphy at Soko-Gakuen, S.F. 1981-- and pvt. tchr. brush painting, 1982--; awards: Kasaku Prize, Shell Oil Co. (1971), purch. prizes: Wesleyan Coll. Intl. Exhib. of Prints and Drawings (1980), Owensboro Mus. of Fine Art, Ky. Mid-Am. Bienniel (1982); pencil drawing accepted for The Pacific Coast States Collection, Vice Pres. Mondale's res. in Wash DC, exhib. Nat. Mus. of American Art; art works accepted for Eberhard Faber Art Contest 1974, Rockford Internat. '83 Print and Drawing Biennial, Alabama Works on Paper Exhibn. (touring show) 1983, 18th Nov. Annual- Coos (Ore.) Art Mus.; S.F. Art Festival 1974-77; Two-man Show at Soker-Kaseman Gal., S.F. 1975; mem: Art Exhibn. of Inten, designated Inyu (assn. for artists of traditional Japanese style painting); Lepidopterists Soc.; publs: City Mag. (5/75), S.F. Chronicle (5/75); Christian; rec: music, collecting butterflies. res: 179 Oak St, Apt W, San Francisco 94102

MURPHY, JOHN LEONARD, physicist/audio engineer; b. Mar. 31, 1950, La Plata, Md.; s. Francis Joseph and Sarah Elizabeth (Dameron) M.; m. Sharon L. Alsup, Dec. 24, 1980; edn: BS, physics, Lowell Tech. Inst. 1972; MS, physics, Univ. of Dayton 1974. Career: commnd. ofcr., space systems analyst USAF, 1974-78; chief engr. Ford Audio & Acoustics, Okla. City, Ok. 1978-81; chief engr. Carvin Mfg. Co., Escondido 1981--; mem. Audio Engring. Soc., Acoustical Soc. of Am., IEEE; publs: technical ed./contbg. writer (31 arts. audio topics) Modern Recording Mag. 1978-81; mil: capt. USAF 1974-8, Svcs. Commendn. Medal; rec: music and recording, computing. REs: 1219 Joshua St Escondido 92026 Ofc: Carvin Mfg. Co. 1155 Industrial Ave Escondido 92025

MURPHY, MILES RICHARD, research scientist; b. Dec. 6, 1930, Malaga, Oh.; s. William M. and Martha M. (Kemy) M.; m. Jo Friedlund Feb. 12, 1983; edn: BSIE, Ohio State Univ. 1960; MSc, Stanford Univ. 1971; PhD cand., Calif. Inst. of Integral Studies 1973-. Career: loftsman, No. American Aviation Inc., Columbus, Oh. 1955-61; human factors splst. Philco-Ford Corp., Palo Alto 1961-67; research scientist NASA-Ames Research Ctr., Moffett Field 1967--; honors: Tau Beta Pi, Alpha Pi Mu; mem. Human Factors Soc.; Internat. Ergonomics Soc.; Assn. of Humanistic Guidance Assn.; publs. (37) in human factors and aerospace mcd. fields; mil: airman l/c, Korean Svc, UN Svc., Nat. Defense Svc., GCM; rec: skiing, sailing, flying. Res: 1690 Broadway, 506, San Francisco 94109 Ofc: NASA-Ames Research Center, Moffett Field 94035

MURPHY, RICK L., radio broadcasting executive; b. Jan. 10, 1950, Gene Village; s. Lyle J. and Mary Janet (Wagner) Murphy; m. Janice Reiutz, Apr. 19, 1980; chil: Megan, b. 1981; Ryan Lyle, b. 1983; edn: AA, San Bernardino Vly Coll 1970; BA, CSU San Diego 1973. Career: owner KZUL-AM (Parker, Ariz.), Yavapai Life (Prescott), Yavapai Tribune (Prescott), KBAS/KWAZ Radio (Bullhead City, Ariz.); current: gen. mgr. KCMJ AM/FM Radio, Palm Springs; guest spkr. Telecom Dept., USC. Mem. bd. dirs. Luekemia Soc., Palm Springs chpt.; Democrat; Baptist; rec: business. Res: POB 1626, Palm Springs 92263 Ofc: Westminster Broadcasting, 490 S. Farrell Dr, Ste 202, Palm Springs 92262

MURPHY, RICHARD WILLIAM, JR., banker; b. Apr. 22, 1926, Brooklyn, NY; s. Richard Wm. and Loretta Elizabeth (Rogert) M.; m. Lucy Mae Haynes, June 1, 1952, div. 1984; children: Erin Maureen, Shannon Patricia; edn: San Francisco City Coll. 1955-56; Indsl. Coll. of Armed Forces 1966-68; Am. Inst. of Banking 1964-66; num. spl. courses, var. univs., colls., seminars; Calif. Comm. Coll. tchr. cred. (lifetime), bus., mktg., distbn. Career: served pvt. to capt. USMC (active duty) 1945-58, ret. lt. col. USMCR 1968, press correspondent, jr. editor Stars and Stripes, North China ed. Shanghai 1946, writer / newscaster Armed Forces Radio Service, Tsingtao, China 1946, ed. The Reserve Marine newspaper, Wash DC 1948, sports ed. Camp Lejeune (N C) Globe 1950, pub. info. ofcr., Pearl Harbor, HI 1952-55, pub. rels. ofcr. 12th Marine Corps Reserve (8 Western States), San Francisco 1955-58, pub. rels. cons. 12th MCRRD 1958-65; mktg. mgmt. Wells Fargo Bank, S.F. hdqtrs. 1962-70, L.A. hdqtrs. 1970-72, regl. mktg. mgr. So. Calif. 1972-81, asst. v.p., ret. 1982; vice pres./dir. of mktg. Foothill Independent Bank, Glendora 1982--; instr. Calif. Comm. Colls.; cons. Small Bus. Adminstrn.; pres. Orange Co. chpt. MC Combat Corres. Assn. 1984; mem. Sales & Mktg. Execs. Assn. (bd. dirs. O.C. chpt.); Execs. Assn. of San Gabriel Valley Inc. (pres. 1984); bd. dirs. Am. Heart Assn. (Dist.V); Republican; Catholic. Res: 585 Bonita Apt E, San Dimas 91773 Ofc: Foothill Independent Bank 510 S Grand Ave Glendora 91740

MURPHY, THOMAS F., investment co. president; b. Apr. 29, 1942, Portland, Maine; s. William J. and Marjorie (Moulton) M.; m. Sharon Taylor, Sept. 1, 1963; children: Kelly, b. 1965; William, b. 1967; Kathleen, b. 1970; Patricia, b. 1971; edn: BS, Univ. of Maine, . 1965; MBA, NYU 1966. Career: sys. General Motors Acceptance Corp. 1965-66; mktg. rep. IBM 1966-71; mktg. mgr. ITEL 1971-75; v.p. mktg. Itel Leasing 1975-78; pres. Financial Svcs. Group- Itel Corp. 1978-79; current: pres. TSM Investment Corp.; works: restoration of historical sites, incl. Andrew Young Home, Danville 1983; Catholic; rec: golf. Res: 2441 Roundhill Dr Alamo 94507 Ofc: TSM Inv. Corp., 1600 S Main St, Ste 230, Walnut Creek 94596

MURR, JAMES HENRY, sales engineer/ lawyer; b. Nov. 8, 1918, Lancaster, Penn.; s. Herbert Leon and Fannie Edith (Cramer) M.; children: Priscilla, b. 1942; James H. Jr., b. 1946; edn: BA, Univ. of Chgo. 1941; JD, Glendale Coll. of Law 1976; admitted to State Bar of Calif. 1982. Career: past pos. with General Mills Inc.; currently, Cleveland Twist Drill Co.; mem: State Bar of Calif.; Big Ten Club of So. Calif. (dir.); publs: genealogy, Descendant of Jacob Murr and Catherine Miller; mil: lt. commdnr. USNR, Pacific Theatre, 3 Stars; Presbyterian; rec: skiing, tennis. Res: 928 Wiladonda Dr Lan Canada 91011

MURRAY, MARION A., educator, psychotherapist; b. Oct. 20, 1942, Tulare, Calif.; d. Willis Lewis Sr. and Melvie Margorie (Wilson) Adams; m. Robert L. Murray, Jr., 1959; div. 1979; children: Robert Craig b. 1960, Karyn Michelle b. 1970; edn: AA, El Camino Coll. 1975; BA, psychol., CSU Dominguez Hills, 1977, MA, clin. com. psych., 1979; Calif. LMFCC (Lic. Marriage Family & Child Counselor); Comm. Coll. instr. cred. (life). Career: secty., cons. The Rand Corp., Santa Monica 1966-72; counselor Mid-Cities Comm. Rehab. Ctr., Compton 1978-79; voc. evaluator & coord. Mid-Cities Comm.Rehab.Ctr., 1979; instr. Compton Comm. Coll. 19b7p80; dir. Marion Murray & Assocs., L.A., 1979--; therapist Counseling and Psychol. Assocs., Inglewood 1980-83; v.p. Network Found. Inc. 1979-83; estab. comprehensive instrnl. pgm. for developmentally disabled; designed and implemented a Behavior Modification pgm. for the Exceptional Children's Opportunity Sch. (residentl. facility, L.A.

Unif. non-public sch) 1983; mem: Am. Psychol. Assn. Div. of Comm. Psychol. (27); Western Psychol. Assn.; Calif. Assn. of Marriage & Family Therapists; Nat. Assn. for Retarded Citizens; author: The Complete Travel Training Manual (self-pub. 1981); Democrat; Christian; rec: writing, moddern dance, travel. Res: 13237 S. Avalon Blvd Los Angeles 90061 Ofc: Marion Murray & Assocs POB 61419 Los Angeles 90061

MURRAY, THOMAS TYLER, business owner; b. Jan. 15, 1943, Hanover, Va.; s. Clyde Alvera and Florence Mary (Moran) M.; m. Sarah Keal, Oct. 20, 1965; children: Kim, b. 1966; Stacia, b. 1972; edn: AA, Laney Coll. 1971; Golden Gate Univ. 1971-72. Career: housekeeping supvr. Red Top. Inc., Boston, Mass. 1969-70; sales rep. Pennzoil Co., Alameda 1972-81; owner Home Svcs. Co. 1982--; mem: NAACP; Sales & Mktg. Mgmt. Assn.; Allen Temple Baptist Ch. (Deacon); Com. chmn. Scout Pack; Smithsonian INst. Assn.; Am. Collectors Assn; mil: s/sgt. USMC 1960-69, GCM, Vietnam Svc.; Democrat; Baptist; rec: antiques, gardening, philately. Res: 10818 Ridgeview Ct San Jose 95127 Ofc: Home Services Co., POB 3644 San Jose 95156

MURRAY, WILLIAM EDWARD, electrical engineer; b. Mar 14, 1924, Chickasha, Okla.; s. William Clifford and Blanche Winifred (McIntyre) M.; m. Jeannie Morris, Apr. 27, 1946; children: Robert, b. 1947; Richard, b. 1948; Daniel, b. 1953; John, b. 1955; Alan, b. 1962; edn: BS, UC Berkeley 1947; MSEE, USC 1954; postgrad., UC Irvine 1978-80. Career: br. chief McDonnell Douglas Astronautics Co., Huntington Beach 1974-78; prin. engr./ sci. 1978--; instr. engring., UC Irvine 1978-, UCLA 1960-66, Golden West Coll. 1972-76, CSU Northridge 1974, L.A. Dept. of Edn. 1960-; honors: fellow, Ist. for Adv. of Engring. (1982), IEEE-AES Internat. Tech. Paper Awd. (Wash. DC 1963); mem. Eta Kappa Nu (nat. pres. 1973-74, pres. L.A. Alumni chpt. 1965-66, Western rep. Awards Com. 1983-); mem. IEEE 1940-: treas. L.A. Council 1983-84, chmn. Sections com. 1982-83; chmn. Orange County Sect. 1981-82; gen. chmn. 1982 Reg. 6 Conf., Anaheim; chmn. Power Electronics Splsts Conf. 1977-; secty. Elec. Power/Energy Sys. Panel 1977-; senior mem. IEEE 1970-; mem. Tau Beta Pi, Pi Tau Pi Sigma, Pi Kappa Alpha, Aerospace Electrical Soc., Am. Inst. Aero and Astro. 1962-75; publs: 5 engring. conf. papers; mil: 1st lt. US Army Signal Corps 1943-45, 1950-52; Republican; Methodist; rec: literature, technology, travel. Res: 1531 Wyndham Court Rd Santa Ana 92705 Ofc: Douglas Aircraft Co. 3855 Lakewood Blvd Long Beach 90846

MUSACCHIO, KIRK ANTHONY, lawyer; b. Nov. 11, 1955, Fresno; s. Theodore Alphonsus and Darlene June (Mirigian) M ; edn: BA, Univ. of San Francisco 1977; JD, Univ. of Santa Clara 1980; admitted to State Bar of Calif. 1982. Career: legal editor Matthew Bender & Co., San Francisco 1981-82; senior v.p.-Legal Counsel, Centennial Svgs & Loan Assn., Santa Rosa 1982-; honors: Univ of Santa Clara Law Review comments ed., bd. (1980), Pi Sigma Alpha (ofcr. 1976-77), St. Ives Law Soc. (1976-77), acad. honors for best resrch. paper in Sch. of Bus. (1977) Finl. Execs. Inst., academic scholarship USF 1976-77; mem: American Bar Assn., State Bar of Calif., Assn. of Trial Lawyers of Am., Calif. Trial Lawyers Assn., Commonwealth Club of Calif., Masons, Triple X Frat.; publs: contbr. law revs.; Republican; Catholic; rec: musician. Res: 314 Los Alamos Rd Santa Rosa 95405 Ofc: Centennial Svgs & Loan Assn. 1701 Fourth St Santa Rosa 95404

MUSE, JAMES WILLIAM, US Air Force pilot; b. Apr. 1, 1940, Chickasha, Okla.; s. Raymond Daniel and Elva Ophelia (King) M.; m. Paulina Tayaban, June 1, 1974; children: Jamie, b. 1975; Jennifer, b. 1976; Jessica, b. 1978; edn: N.Mex. Inst. of Mining & Tech. 58-60; Univ. of the Philippines 1972-73; BS, CSU San Diego 1973-74. Career: served to lt. col. USAF 1960--: navigator 1960, electronic warfare ofcr. on B-52 aircraft 1961-66, pilot England, Vietnam, Thailand, Laos, 1966-69; instr. pilot in T-37 aircraft, 1969-71; comdr. Jungle Survival Sch. of Clark AB, Philippines, 1971-73; directed estab. of Inanarro Negrito Village to incl. 1st Nigrito elem. sch., adult edn., medical dispensary, metal foundry and coop. farming, 1972-73; assisted Philippine Armed Forces estab. their 1st Mil. Arms Mus., 1972-73; comdr., 23rd Transp. Squadron, Eng. AFB, LA, 1974-76; chief of aircrew tng., 374 Tactical Air Wing (C-130 aircraft) Clark AB, Phil. 1976-77; chief. of affil. tng. for all Armed Forces, Phil., Okinawa, Japan, Korea, 1977-78; exec. ofcr. and instr. pilot on CT-39 aircraft, Norton AFB, Calif. 1978-82; dir. of misc. aircraft/Internat. Logistics Systems Program Branch, AF Logistics Cmd., McClellan AFB, Calif. 1982--; v.p. Treasurtron Inc., 1982--. Awarded USAF Humanitarian Medal for civilian flood relief, San Bernardino, Calif. 1981; Transportation Staff Ofcr. of Year 1976, Tactical Air Cmd.; 2 Phil. Citations 1972-73; Thailand and Vietnamese Civic Actions medals 1969, 68; Silver Star, DFC w/oak leaf, Merit Svc. w/oak leaf, Air Medal w/12 oak leaf clusters; RVN Gallantry Cross w/ Palm, Laos Order of Million Elephants (for Gallantry), num. others. Mem: Historical Soc. of Phil. 1972-, Assn. of Old Crows1963-73; life mem. Nat. Rifle Assn.; life mem. Calif. Scholarship Fedn.; CofC (Mesa, Az. chmn. mil. affairs com. 1970); Republican; So. Baptist (Sun. Sch. Supt.); rec: archaelogy, lapidary, camping. Res: 12501 Wanderer Rd Auburn 95603 Ofc: USAF, ALC, MMSG, McClellan AFB 95842

MUTSCHLER, LAWRENCE HOWARD, real estate broker/investor; b. Oct. 9, 1934, St. Cloud, Minn.; s. Lawrence V. and Leah Mildred (Luther) M.; edn: Claremont McKenna Coll. 1952-54, BS, USC 1959; Art Center Coll. of Design, 1960; Los Angeles Trade Tech 1978; UCLA 1980-84. Career: developer/ home designer/ builder in Los Angeles area, currently ret. Mem. Bel Air Navy League, Riviera Country Club; Catholic; rec: horses, bridge, collecting antiques & art. Res: 10539 Sunset Blvd Bel Air 90077

MYERS, BOLDEN FRANK FINE, developer, realtor, restaurateur; b. May 29, 1931, Owyhee Country, Idaho; s. George William (Fine) and Elizabeth K. (Kindzer) M.; children: Frank B., b. 1964; Michele E., b. 1965; Kenneth C., b. 1967; edn: San Mateo Jr. Coll. 1954-58; San Francisco Law Sch. 1956-58; Lincoln Law Sch. 1959-61; Real Estate Broker, Calif. Career: owner: Frank Myers Constrn. Co., San Francisco 1964--, Myers Auction Realty 1965--, Colonial House 1975-, Europa Hotel 1980-, Phillips Hotel Bar & Restaurant 1979-, Ste. Claire Hotel (San Jose) 1977-; Veterans Rights activist, dir. Proj. Freedom (to rescue and/ or account for MIAs & POWs); awards: appreciation, Harney Co. Jaycees & US Jaycees; Public. Svc. Awd. for aiding and rescuing Police Ofcr.; mem: Nat. Press Club, S.F.; Aircraft Owners & Pilots Assn.; Tiburn Penin Club; Rotary; S.F. Press Club; works: Biography of Korean War; mil: 2d. lt. (Temp. Field Comm.) US Army 1949-51, Recommended for Congl. Medal of Honor at Hadong, So. Korea, Comb. Inf. Badge; Republican; rec: pvt. pilot, archaeology, Little League. Res: 1221 Jones St, Penthouse, San Francico 94109 Ofc: Frank Myers Construction Co., 3123 17th St San Francisco 94110

MYERS, WADE HAMPTON, JR., computer scientist; b. Nov. 2, 1941, Durham, NC; s. Wade Hampton and Pauline Eugenia (Cross) M.; m. Joyce Yvonne Thornburg, Apr. 17, 1964; edn: BS, Univ. of So. Miss. 1965. Career: sci. pgmmr. General Electric Co., Syracuse, NY 1965, engr. 1966, systems engr. 1967; senior systems engr. Honeywell Info. Sys., Phoenix 1974-76; senior engr. Courier Term. Systems, Phoenix 1977, Intel Corp., Santa Clara 1977; sr. mem. sci. staff BNR Inc., Mtn. View 1979; sr. engr. Signetics Corp., Sunnyvale 1978; microsystems group software mgr. Wade Myers Enterprises, proprietor 1982--; cons. in field; mem: Assn. of Computing Machinery, IEEE, Computer Architecture; Distributed Sys. & Networks. Res: POB 99323 San Francisco 94109 OFc: POB 880068 San Francisco 94188

MYLLENBECK, RICHARD WARREN, public relations executive; b. Apr. 26, 1958, Burbank; s. Warren G. and Olga S. (Smolenzeff) M.; m. Carol Askins, Feb. 14, 1981; edn: AA, DeAnza Coll. 1981; BA, pub. rels., CSU San Jose 1984; career: instr./inflight evaluator US Navy Aviation Anti-Submarine Warfare Oper. P-3C Orion, NAS Moffett Field, CA 1977-81; current tech./supr. Zilog Inc., Campbell 1981-82; prin. sales rep. Frey Racing Ent., Santa Clara 1982-83; owner/prin. Myllenbeck-Helms Public Relations Agcy. 1983--; honors: Phi Kappa Phi 1984, Kappa Tau Alpha 1984; mem: Pub. Rels. Soc. of Am. student orgn. (v.p. 1983); num. mag. arts.; mil. decorations: G-C, Navy Expeditionary, Naval Sea Svc. Deployment medals; Republican; Orthodox Ch. of Am.; rec: auto racing, flying, writing. Address: Myllenbeck-Helms, 860 Williams Way Ste 4, Mountain View 94040

MYSELS, KAROL J(OSEPH), chemist; b. Apr. 14, 1914, Krakow, Poland, nat. 1942; s. Adolf and Janina H. (Rosenberg) Meisels; m. Estella Katzenellenbogen, Mar. 28, 1953; edn: Ingenieur-Chimist, and Lic.-es-Scis., Univ. of Lyon (France) 1937; PhD, inorganic chem., Harvard Univ. 1941. Career: staff mem. Shell Devel. Co., San Francisco 1940-42; research asst./assoc. Stanford Univ., Palo Alto 1941-45; instr. in chemistry, NY Univ. 1945-47; asst. prof. 1947-50, assoc. prof. 1950-54, prof. of chem. USC, Los Angeles 1954-66; assoc. dir. of research R.J.Reynolds Industries, Winston-Salem, NC 1966-70; senior resrch. advisor General Atomic Co., San Diego 1970-79; prin. Research Consulting, La Jolla 1979--; assoc. mem. 1961-69, titular mem. 1969-73, chmn. 1973-79 Commn. on Colloid and Surface Chemistry IUPAC (Internat. Union of Pure & Applied Chemistry), mem. Com. on Physical Chem., IUPAC 1975-79; editorial bds: J. of Chem. Edn. 1958-65, J. Colloid Sci. 1959-67, J. of Physical Chemistry 1961-2, 1976-81, J. Membrane Biology 1969-73, Colloids and Surfaces 1979-, Lanymuir 1984-. Awards: Am. Chem. Soc. Award in Colloid and Surface Chem. 1964, Guggenheim Fellow 1965-6, NSF Faculty Fellow 1957-8 and Senior Postdoctl. 1962-3, Fellow 1962-3, USC Grad. Sch. Research Lectr. 1962, Univ. of Wis. Rennebohn Lectr. 1964, Am. Chemical Soc. Tour lectr. 1971, 74, 77, 78, 80, 81, 82, Phi Lambda Upsilon lectr. U. of Okla. 1975; mem: Am. Chem. Soc. (Councilor 1973-84), Am. Inst. of Chemists (Councilor 1969-76, chmn. Western Chpt. 1961-2), Harvard Club of San Diego, La Jolla Phototravelers (pres. 1981, 82); publs: over 180 publs. incl. 7 books, 11 patents; mil: pvt. VOC, US Army 1942-3; rec: photog. Res: 8327 La Jolla Scenic Dr La Jolla 92037

N

NACK, KATHRYN TIPPIT, architect; b. Oct. 4, 1924, Ft. Worth, Tex.; d. Ralph Leonard and Edeth (Crouch) Tippit; m. Donald H. Nack, Nov. 20, 1955; children: David, b. 1959; Barbara, b. 1961; Susan, b. 1964; stepchildren: Pamela, b. 1946; Emily, b. 1948; Alan, b. 1950; edn: Tyler Jr. Coll. 1941-43; Univ. of Tex. 1943-45; USC 1949; UCLA 1953; Reg. Arch., Calif. 1956. Career: with Kistner, Curtis & Wright, Archs. 1945-53; drafter, San Diego 1945; job captain, Los Angeles 1946-53; designer, Neptune & Thomas, Archs., Pasadena 1953-56; job captain Kathryn T. Nack, Arch., Pasadena 1956-58; dir. of fin./ arch./ computer analyst Nack & Sunderland, Engrs., Los Angeles 1968--; pres. Pasadena Bd. Edn. 1979-, current pres.; Plnng. Commn., Pasadena 1975-79; awards: Second Century Awd., YMCA, Pasadena; Awd. of Merit, Villa Esperanza Sch. for Developmentally Disabled; mem: Zonta Internat.; Civitan Internat.; L.A. Co. Developmental Svcs. Found.; Protestant. Res: 277 S Grand Pasadena 91105 Ofc: Nack & Sunderland, 7462 N Figueroa Los Angeles 90041

NADEMANEE, KOONLAWEE, cardiologist; b. Nov. 14, 1949, Cholburi, Thailand, nat. 1984; s. Boontam and Jaree (Sakhabote) N.; m. Auayporn, June 10, 1975; child: Vim, b. 1981; edn: BSc, Chulalongkorn Univ. 1971; MD, Chulalongkorn Univ. Med. Sch. 1973; Am. Bd. Internal Med., Tulane Univ. 1978; Subsplty. Bd. Cert. in Cardiovascular Disease, UCLA 1981. Career: med. intern Touro Infirmary, New Orleans, La. 1975-76; med. res. 1976-78; cardiology fellow, Dept. of Med., Wadsworth, Va., Los Angeles, Calif. 1978-79; actg. chief Coronary Care Unit./ staff physician cardiology, Wadsworth VA, Los Angeles, Calif. 1981--; asst. prof. med. UCLA Sch. of Med., Los Angeles 1981--; reviewer, Journ. Am. Coll. of Cardiology, Am. Heart Assn., & Annals of Internal Med.; honors: Awd. for Excellence in Cardiology, Touro Infirmary, Tulane Univ.; mem: fellow, Am. Coll. of Cardiology; publs: over 3 dozen articles re Role of newer antiarrhythmic agents in the management of life threatening VT particularly amiodaron, and role of compact holter analog in determining the nature, frequency and duration of trasient myocardial ischemia in patients with coronary artery disease; Buddhist; rec: tennis. Res: 2600 Green Valley Rd Los Angeles 90046 Ofc: Wadsworth VA Hosp., Bldg 500, 691/W111E, Wilshire/ Sawtelle, Los Angeles 90073

NAGEL, SHELLEY BARLAS, psychotherapist; b. June 18, 1943, San Francisco; d. Leon and Ann Egber) Barlas; m. Michael Nagel, Sept. 4, 1966; 1 son: Mark Steven, b. 1969; edn: UC Berkeley 1961-63; nursing, UC Med. Ctr. 1964-66; BA in soc. wk., S.F. State Univ. 1967; MA in counseling psy., Univ. of Santa Clara 1975; PhD in edn., Laurence Univ. 1982. Career: soc. wkr. Mt. Zion Hosp. & Med. Ctr., San Francisco 1967-69; suicide and crisis svc. volunteer, San Clara Co. Mental Health Dept. 1971-73; instr. psychology dept. San Jose City Coll. 1975-76; psychological counselor, cardiac rehab. facility, Los Gatos- Saratoga Comm. Hosp. 1977-81; psychotherapist, pvt. practice 1975--; awards: Svc. Awd., Am. Heart Assn. 1978; Resolution of Commdn. for contributions to the devel. of the community, Santa Clara Co. Commn. on the Status of Women, 1982; mem: Calif. Assn. of Marriage & Family Counselors; West Valley Light Opera (dancer, prodn. of Pal Joey 1977); Am. Heart Assn. (Heart & Stroke Club moderator); Centre for Living with Dying (bd. dirs. 1979-81); Jewish; rec: dance, fashion. Ofc: Shelley Barlas Nagel, 20688 4th St Saratoga 95070

NAGI, MANJIT S., veterinarian; b. Oct. 6, 1936, Kangra, H.P., India, nat. 1976; s. Parmatam Singh and Haribin Kaur (Ahluwalia) N.; m. Harinder, Nov. 24, 1964; children: Rachna, b. 1966; Michael, b 1976; edn: BVSc, Punjab Sch. of Veterinary Sci. 19057; MVSc, Post Grad. Coll. of Animal Sci., Izatnagar 1960; MS, Sch. of Vet. Sci., Wash. State Univ. 1970; lic: Disease Investigation Ofcr.; Avian Pathologist. Career: research asst. pathology Indian Veterinary Res. Inst., Izatnagur, India 1958-62; asst. res. ofcr. disease investigation, Animal Husbandry Dept., Dellhi, India 1962-66; asst. research ofcr. poultry disease, Punjab Agric. Univ., Hissar, India 1966-68; staff research assoc. Virology Dept. Primate Research Ctr., UC Davis 1971-73; state veterinarian Meat Inspection Dept., Calif. 1973-76; fed. veterinarian Meat & Poultry Inspection, USDA 1976-81; veterinary practice 1981--, Livingston Animal Clinic, Livingston; mem: AVMA; CVMA; NSJVMA; Rotary, Livingston; 7 scientific publs; Democrat; rec: fishing. Res: 922 J Livingston 95334 Ofc: Livingston Animal Clinic, i17 3rd Livingston 95334

NAHIN, MELVILLE HOWARD, lawyer; b. July 19, 1929, Chgo., Ill.; s. Ernest B. and Minnette B. (Bernstein) N.; m. Alice S., Jan. 29, 1950; children: Bruce A., b. 1953; Richard L., b. 1956; edn: UCLA 1947-50; JD, Loyola Univ. L.A. 1953. Career: Alvin Hirsch law ofcs. 1953-55; atty. at law, pvt. practice 1973--; currently, pres./chief exec./dir. Nahin & Nahin Law Corp., Los Angeles; dir. Star Finance Co.; honors: 33rd deg. Scottish Rite Mason; Grand Orator, Grand Lodge of Calif.; treas./ bd. govs. Shriners Hosp. Crippled Children 1977-83; Internat. Supreme Council for De Molay 1981; De Molay Legion of Honor, Cross of Honor and Advrs. Honor Key; Isadore Moore Masonic Svc. award, Ionic Masonic Lodge 1972; Vierling Kersey awd., Ionic Lodge 1981; mem: Wilshire Bar Assn. (bd. govs. 1975-81); Am. and Los Angeles Bar Assns.; Los Angeles Trial Lawyers Assn.; L.A. Trial Lawyers Club; City of Hope (med. svc. review com., research review com.); League of Women Voters adv. com.; Hollywood Temple Beth-el; Ionic Masonic Lodge; L.A. Scottish Rite; Al Malaikah Temple Shrine; Vista Del Mar Child Care Ctr.; Child Abuse Listening Line (legal advr.); conbtg. writer, New Age mag., nat. Masonic monthly; contbr. Indiana Free Mason monthly mag.; Democrat; Jewish; rec: sports, politics, spy novels. Res: 1924 San Ysidro Dr Beverly Hills 90210 Ofc: Nahin & Nahin Law Corp., 6399 Wilshire Blvd, Ste 1000, Los Angeles 90048

NAIYER, SHAFIQUE, professional engineer; b. July 15, 1937, Jehanabad, India, nat. 1968; s. Adbul and Zaitoon (Khatoon) Hafeez; m. Fern J. Cook, Jan. 1965; children: Fern, b. 1972; Zakaria, b 1974; edn: ISc, Aligarh Muslim Univ. 1957; BS, Mo. Sch. of Mines & Met. 1963; Profl. Engr., Calif. 1973. Career: Designer Mo. State Hwy. Dept., Kansas City, Mo. 1965-77; civil eng. asst. 1965-66; sr. civil eng. asst. 1966-73; supvg. civil eng. asst. 1973-77; civil engr. Lind & Hillerud, San Marino 1977-79; proj. mgr. Bechtol & Emerson, Los Angeles 1979-82; lead engr. TMSIA, Saudi, Arabia 1982--; currently, owner Videa Works of San Marino; cons. land mgmt., Bechtol & Emerson 1979-82; cons. rapid transit dist., Los Angeles 1977; cons. location of sev. nuclear facilities, Lawrence Livermore Lab. Holmes & Narvar 1978; honors: Scholarship, MSM 1961-63; Juror 1976; mem: Am. Soc. of Civil Engrs.; Islamic Ctr. of So. Calif.; MSM Alumni Assn.; L.A. Co. Road Dept. Tennis Club (pres.); Temple City Tennis Club; Orange Villa Homeowner Assn. (pres.); India Assn. (pres.); Internat. Fellowship (pres.); co-founder/fin. sponsor of Dr. Syed Hasan's Sch. (Insan Sch.; now has 1500 res. students, 130 tchrs.); publs:

photographic book on roadway constrn.; Democrat; Muslim; rec: tennis, golf, photog. Res: 110 N Chapel Ave, 15, Alhambra 91801 Ofc: TMSIA, Box 1779, Dhahran, Saudi Arabia; Video Works of San Marino, 2529 Mission St San Marino 91108

NAKAI, TSUYOSHI ROY, pediatric dentist; b. June 23, 1943, Manzanar; s. Noritatsu and Mistuyo (Nishida) N.; 1 dau: Leslie Akemi, b. 1975; edn: DDS, UC San Francisco Dental Sch. 1968; M.S.D., Univ. of Wash. 1972. Career: gen. dentist, pvt. practice 1968-70; pediatric dentist 1972--; dental kinesiology & nutritional counseling 1978-; guest lectr. UCLA Sch. of Dentistry 1976-77, 82; adv. com. (chmn. 1977), Long Beach City Coll. Dental Asst. Dept. 1975-; dental staff, Childrens Hosp., Long Beach 1974-; Meml. Hosp., Long Beach 1974-; St. Josephs Hosp, Orange, Dental & Oral Surgery Detp. staff Cert. Am. Bd. of Pedodontics 1972; mem: Am. Acad. of Pedondontics; Internat. Acad. of Microendocrinology; Am. Assn. of Dentistry for the Handicap; Calif. Assn. Pediatric Dentistry; rec: racquetball, jogging, skiing. Res: 12501 Camus, No. 5, Garden Grove 92641 Ofc: 4132 Katella Ave, Ste 202, Los Alamitos 90720; 4950 Barranca Pkwy, Ste 306, Irvine 92714

NAKAMURA, HIROMU, psychologist, b. Nov. 6, 1926, Los Angeles, CA, s. Genjiro and Misao (Kamura) Nakamura; Edn: AB, Univ. of Redlands, 1948; MA, UCLA, 1951; Ph.D., USC, 1973; m.Tamaye Yumiba, L.A., Mar. 27, 1955; chil: Glenn Vernon, b. 1957; Colleen Patricia, b. 1962. Career: clin. psychologist intern, Massillon (OH) State Hosp., 1951-52; clin. psychol., Patton (CA) State Hosp., 1952-58; clin. psychol., Pac. State Hosp., Pomona, 1958---; pgm. dir., Lanterman Hosp. and Devel.Center Pomona, 1971---. Contributed articles to profl. journs. Mem: fellow, Royal Soc. of Health; Amer., CA State Psychol. Assns.; Amer. Assn. on Mental Deficiency; Amer. Pub. Health Assn.; Psi Chi. Presbyterian. Res: 3861 Shelter Grove Dr., Claremont 91711; Office: P.O. Box 100, Pomona 91768.

NAKAMURA, JOHN TAKESHI, engineering manager; b. May 31, 1955, Little Rock, Ark.; s. Mickey Mitsuo and Sadako (Nakamura) N.; m. Denise Darlene Minami, Jun. 16, 1979, 1 son. Michael Minoru, b. July 9, 1983; edn: stu., L.A. City Coll. 1972-73; BSEE, USC 1979; MBA, Pepperdine Univ. 1982; career: tech. Aerospace Corp., El Segundo -1977; electronics tech. Sanyo Electric Inc., Carson 1978; tech. engr. Hughes Aircraft Co., Culver City 1978, mem. tech. staff, 1979-82, proj. engr., El Segundo 1983--.; awards: scholarship Electric Club of L.A.; mem: IEEE, 1974-78; USC Engring. Student Council, staff and bus. mgr.: engr. mag. 1973-78; Republican; Presbyterian (deacon); Res: 22307 Avis Court Torrance 90505 Ofc: Hughes Aircraft Co., POB 902 El Segundo 90245

NAKANISHI, ALAN T., optometrist; b. Nov. 2, 1948, San Francisco; s. Joseph M. and Mary T. (Koburi) N.; m. Rea Ginochio, Dec. 2, 1979; 1 child, Chanel b. 1982; edn: BS, Univ. of Calif. 1971, OD, 1973. Career: Doctor of Optometry, Walnut Creek 1973--. Honors: Am. Legion Aux., Calif., awards (1963, 1st pl. 1964, 1965), S.F. Indsl. Arts. Assn. 2d pl. Awd. 1963, DAR Medal Of Honor 1966; Outstanding Young Men of Am. 1979; recogn. awd. Am. Opt. Assn. 1980, 81, 82; Calif. Opt. Assn. Spkrs. awd. 1981, 82; mem: Am. and Calif. Opt. Assns.; Bay Area Opt. Council (bd. dirs. 1979-); Alameda Contra Costa Counties Opt. Soc. (Bulletin ed. 1977-80, dir. 1978-); Nat. Eye Research Found.; Internat. Orthokeratology Sect. 1972-; UC Alumni Assn.; Grad. Students' Hon. Soc.; Am. Opt. Found.; Nat. Assn. of Profls; Better Vision Bur.; Calif. Public Vision League; Internat. Contact Lens Clinic; Council of Sports Vision; Kenneth B. Stoddard Soc.; Fedn. of Am. Scientists; mem. Tradewinds, Diablo Valley Lions Club (v.p. 1983), Japanese Am. Citizens League, Lions Eye Found. (life), O'Hara Handicap Awareness Found.; author: Contact Lens Research Book 1974; Republican; Prot.; rec: scuba diving, music, photog., aquariums. Res: 700 Court Lane Concord 94518 Ofc: 2246 Oak Grove Rd Walnut Creek 94598

NAKANO, FRANK HIROSHI, physician/professor; b. Dec. 21, 1935, Modesto; s. George Gonkichi and Haruko (Harano) N.; m. Josephine van Nieuwpoort, July 25, 1979; children: Genji G., b. 1980; Bastiaan G., b. 1982; edn: BS, honors, UC Sch. of Pharmacy 1958; MD, UCLA Sch. of Med. 1962. Career: asst. clin. instr. medicine, UCLA 1965-67, clin. instr. in med. 1970-74, attndg. general med. 1970-71, cardiac catheterization lab 1977-; attndg. cardiology svcs., L.A. VA Ctr. 1972-74, asst. clin. prof. UCLA 1974--; chief med. svc. Washington Hosp., 1971-73, assoc. chief med. svc. 1973-74, dir. coronary intensive care unit 1972-82, ECG reader 1970--, dir. cardiology svcs. 1972--, chief of staff 1982-84, chmn. cardiology com. Brotman Med. Ctr. 1976-82; currently, cardiologist, pvt. practice; honors: Rho Chi hon soc., Sch. of Pharmacy; Bear Photo Awd. for Scholarship, Sch. of Pharmacy; mem: Fellow Council on Clin. Cardiology, Amer. Heart Assn.; Fellow Am. Coll. of Cardiology; Japanes-American Citizens League; publs: Fatal Lung Scan in a Case of Pulmonary Hypertension due to Obliterative Pulmonary Vascular Disease, in Chest; Computer Enhanced Digital Angiography, in Clin. Cardiology; Computer Enhanced Digital Angiography: Correlation of Clinical Assessment of Left Ventricular Ejection Fraction and Regional Wall Motion, in Am. Heart Journ.; mil: major, chief Cardiology Svc., US Army Japan 1967-69; Republican; Buddhist; rec: raising koi, skiing. Res: 10853 Marietta Ave Culver City 90230 Ofc: 3831 Hughes Ave, Ste 604, Cluver City 90230

NAKASE, GARY SHIGEO, wholesale nursery owner, b. Oct. 20, 1942, Los Angeles; s. Kinchi and Takayo (Maeda) Nakase; Edn: AA, Fullerton Jr. Coll., 1962; BA, Calif. Polytech. State Univ., 1965; m. Debra Toma, June 27, 1975; chil: Nicola, b. 1976; Norie, b. 1977; Natalie, b. 1980. Career: landscaper, gar-

dener, Whittier, 1965-67; owner, Nakase Brothers Wholesale Nursery, Huntington Beach, El Toro, 1967---; secretary, Orange Coast Sports Assn. Buddhist. Rec.: basketball, volleyball. Res: 16521 Graham St., Huntington Beach 92649; Office: Nakase Brothers Nursery, 20571 Canada Rd., El Toro 92630.

NAKATA, TED M., dentist; b. Nov. 8, 1937, Fresno; s. Masao and Haruye (Yamasaki) N.; m. Alice, Dec. 15, 1962; children: Mark, b. 1964; Lisa, b. 1965; Russell, b. 1969; Katy, b. 1970; edn: BS, Univ. of Calif. 1961; DDS, 1961; MS, 1970. Lic. Dentist, 1961; Cert. Periodontology 1970; Diplomate Am. Bd. of Periodontology 1976. Career: pvt. practice 1963-68; tchg. faculty UC San Francisco Sch. of Dentistry 1970-83; currently, pvt. practice periodontics, Fresno; pres. Nat. Found. for the Prevention of Oral Disease 1979-80; pres. Fresno Madera Dental Soc. 1980-81; pres. Calif. Soc. of Periodontists 1983; Council on Edn. & Membership, Calif. Dental Assn.; bd. dirs. Western Soc. of Periodontology; Meeting Site plnng. com. (1985), Am. Acad. of Periodontology, S.F.; honors: Fellowship, Acad. of Dentistry Internat.; mem: Am. and Calif. Dental Assns.; Fresno-Madera Dental Soc.; Calif. Soc. of Periodontists; Am. Acad. & Western Soc. of Periodontology; Nat. Found. for the Prevention of Oral Disease; Nakayama Soc. Club; Valley Dental Care Found.; Fresno-Madera DentalFound.; Parnasis Club, Univ. of Calif.; P & S Club, Univ. of Pacific; publs: Epithelial Regeneration of Wounds, 1971; Chemistry of Human Dental Cementum, 1972; The Effects of Age and Fluoride Exposure on Human Dental Cementum, 1975; mil: capt. USAF 1961-63; Republican; Buddhist; rec: farming, photog. Res: 6235 N Forkner Fresno 93711 Ofc: 4747 N First St, Ste 128, Fresno 93726

NAKAUCHI, EDWARD MITSUO, electronic engineer; b. Sept. 17, 1946, Phila., Pa.; s. Hidemitsu and Hatsue (Tadokoro) N.; m. Linda Mulherin, Oct.; children: Michael, b. 1970; Caryn, b. 1973; Pamela, b. 1975; edn: AA, Orange Coast Coll. 1966; BSEE, cum laude, Northrop Univ. 1969; Cert. Technician, Orange Coast Coll. 1966. Career: elec. engr. Advanced Kinetics, Costa Mesa 1969-70; elec. engr. Electronic Memories, Hawthorne 1970-71; elec. engr. Pertec Bus. Sys., Irvine 1971-74; mgr. HTL-K West, Santa Ana 1974-77; sr. proj. engr. Basic Four Infor. Sys., Tustin 197783; currently, mgr. EMC, Century Data Sys., Anaheim, EMC cons. to num. firms; honors: Outstanding Tech. Paper, Insturment Soc. of Am. 1966; Outstanding Svc. Awd., IEEE 1983; Class Salutatorian, Orange Coast Coll. 1966; Grad. Class Valedictorian, Northrop Univ. 1969; Tau Beta Pi, nat. eng. soc.; mem: IEEE (EMC Soc.); Cub Scouts (Den Ldr., Cubmaster); Boy Scouts of Am. (Commnr.); Explorer Post. (advr.); Girl Scout Olympics (co-chmn.); tech. papers: Static Discharge Problems on Data Processing Equipment, 1975; Predicting Switching Regulator Conducted and Radiated EMI, 1976; Technique for Controlling Radiated Emissions Due to Common- Mode Noise in Electronic Data Processing Systems, 1983; rec: clarinet. Res: 14772 Forrest Ln Westminster 92683 Ofc: Century Data Systems, 1270 N Kraemer Blvd Anaheim 92806

NAMAZIKHAH, MOHAMMAD SADEGH, endodontist educator; b. May 4, 1948, Qum, Iran; s. Mohammad Ali and Pari Namazikhah; m. Saiedeh Saied Shalchi, Aug. 7, 1969; children: Sepideh, b. 1973; Saman, b. 1977; edn: DMD, Nat. Univ. of Iran 1974; Edodontic Cert., USC 1980; MS, USC Sch. of Edn. 1981, AM in edn. 1982. Career: supvr. acctg. Dept. Tehran Distribution, General Tire & Rubber of Iran Co., Tehran, Iran 1967-68; dir. pre- clin. restorative dentistry/ clin. instr. Nat. Univ. of Iran Dental Sch. 1976-77, also pvt. practice, 1974-78; currently asst. prof. endodontics, USC Sch. of Dentistry; pvt. practice in Woodland Hills; honors: Awd., Active Student in Soc. Activities, Univ. Dental Sch.; Orthodontic Prize, Best Student in Orthodontics, Nat. Univ. 1974; Excellence in Tchg., USC; mem: USC Gen. Alumni; USC Sch. of Edn. Alumni; Am., Calif. & San Fernando Valley Dental Assns.; Am. Assn. of Endodontics; research: effect of different irrigation materials on the speed of root canal preparation, USC 1980; comparison of higher education in different countries schools of education, 1981; mil: dentist, lt. capt. Iranian Air Force 1974-76; Moslem; rec: music, travel. Res: 3820 Griffith View Dr Los Angeles 90034 Ofc: Warner Victory Medical Center, 6325 Topanga Canyon, Ste 510, Woodland Hills 91367

NAMVAR, EZRI, mortgage banker; b. Aug. 17, 1951, Tehran, Iran, nat. 1970; s. Hilel and Nosrat (Esmaeilzadeh) Namvar; edn: BS eng., Kans. Univ. 1974, MBA, UCLA 1976. Career: mortgage banker; owner/ pres. Namco Financial, Inc., Los Angeles 1980--; cons. pvt. and instnl. investors; Jewish; rec: ski, photog.; res: 12116 Greenock Ln. Los Angeles 90049 ofc: Namco Finl. 11520 San Vicente #101 Los Angeles 90049

NANEY, DAVID GLEN, lawyer; b. Apr. 21, 1952, Bakersfield; s. Glen Tillman and Olivia Mae (Land) N.; m. Linda, July 19, 1975; children: David, b. 1978; Michael, b. 1980; edn: AA, honors, Bakersfield Coll. 1972; BA, cum laude, UCLA 1974; JD, Loyola Univ 1977; admitted to State Bar of Calif. 1977; Life Comm. Coll. Tchg. Credential, Calif. Career: law clerk Engstrom & Lipscomb, Los Angeles 1976, Robert Farms, Inc., Bakersfield 1977; Greater Bakersfield Legal Assistance, Inc. 1977; atty. Freeman, Freeman & Smiley, Los Angeles 1977-80; partner/ atty. Rosenstein & Naney, L.A. 1980; owner/ atty. Law Ofcs. of David G. Naney, Bakersfield 1980--; instr. Bakersfield Coll. 1981-; temporary judge pro tem, West Kern Municipal Ct. 1982-; mem: Phi Alpha Delta; Am., Calif. & Kern Co. Bar Assns.; Lions Club; Aircraft Owner & Pilots Assn.; UCLA Alumni; Loyal Univ. Alumni; coauthor w/ Douglas K. Freeman, How to Incorporate a Small Business (Practical Law Courses, 1979); Republican; Baptist; rec: model railroading, flying, sailing. Res: 3500 Akers Rd, House 60, Bakersfield 93309 Law Offices of David G. Naney, 1715 Chester Ave, Ste 300, Bakersfield 93301

NANKIVIL, DONALD BRUCE, electronics engineer; b. Aug. 15, 1942, Springfield, Ill.; s. Donald Brewer and Betty Mae (Miller) N.; edn: BSEE with honors, Univ. Fla. 1965, MSEE, 1967. Career: test engr. Boeing Co., Cape Kennedy, Fla. summers 1963-67; technical staff TRW, Redondo Beach 1967-70; mem. air pollution resrch & devel. staff Western Precipitation Div., Joy Mfg., Los Angeles 1970-72; engrg. splst. Ford Aerospace and Communications Corp., Newport Bch 1972--; honors: Florida State H.S. Sci. Fair Winner 1960. Mem: SPIE; Nat. Mgmt. Assn.; Aeronutronic Ski Club. Inventions: method of measuring functions of Photovoltaic diodes; counter-countermeasure passive IR missile sys.; measurement of gyroscopic spin with a beam splitter microscope. Republican; Methodist; rec: dance, tennis, golf. Res: 3001E So. Bradford Ave Santa Ana 92707 Ofc: Ford Aerospace &: Commun. Ford Road Newport Bch 92663

NANOMANTUBE, THOMAS WAYNE, bank computer operations executive; b. Feb. 19, 1953, Falls City, Nebr.; s. Wayne Allen and Lois M. (Federick) N.; edn: BS, CSU Chico 1977; MBA pgm. in fin., Golden Gate Univ. 1978-1980. Career: asst. personnel splst. NASA Ames Research Ctr. 1976-77; mktg. rep. IBM, San Francisco 1977-81; v.p./ mgr. Computing Prods. Mgmt., Crocker Nat. Bank, S.F. 1981--; career advr. Calif. State Univ. Sys.; mem: Press Club of S.F.; Am. Mgmt. Assn.; Am. Banking Assn.; Republican; rec: water skiing, trap shooting, fly fishing. Res: 35965 Carnation Way Fremont 94536 Ofc: Crocker National Bank, 155 5th St, Ste 900/100, San Francisco 94103

NASH, DOROTHY JOANN, certified public accountant; b. Sept. 16, 1937, Phoenix; d. Edward David Hallett and Elizabeth Hallett Breckenridge; m. Robert E. Nash, May 17, 1958; chil: Jeffrey, b. 1960, Steven, b. 1960; edn: BS in acctg., UCB 1958, MS in taxation, CSU Hayward 1980; CPA, Calif. Career: staff acct. tax dept., Coopers & Lybrand CPAs, Oakland 1958-65; currently self empl. CPA spec. in taxation, Orinda; lectr. in taxation CSU Hayward 1979-82, lectr. in acctg. St. Marys Coll. 1982-; apptd. Univ. of Calif. Profl. Acctg. Program Dir. 198– – -8– –; all-day spkr. Colo. State Tax Conf. 1983; frequent guest spkr. on taxation. Honors: passed 4-part CPA exam 1st sitting. Mem: East Bay chpt. CPAs (pres. 1983); CPA Soc. (dir. 1984, taxation com.); Contra Costa CPAs. Orgnzr. annual ski trip to Europe. Republican; rec: ski, woodworking; address: Dorothy J. Nash CPA 40 Evergreen Dr. Orinda 94563

NASH, ED LAWTON, investor/real estate developer; b. June 22, 1942, Hampton, Va.; s. Ed. Lawton Sr. and Esther Sarah (Morris) N.; edn: BA, CSU Los Angeles 1964; MA, Pepperdine Univ. 1968; AA, El Camino Coll. 1977; desig: (CCIM) Cert. Comml. Investment Mem., Realtors Nat. Mktg. Inst. 1980. Career: corp. mgr. compensation & orgn. plnng. Continental Airline 1971-77; pres. Prime Realty, Inc. 1978--; pres. Ed N. Development Co., Inc. 1978-81; chmn. bd./ CEO Enco Internat. Inc. 1983--; former adv. dir. American City Bank; corp. dir./ chmn. investment com. Continental Fed. Credit Union; adv. dir. South Bay Br.; mem: Los Angeles CCIM Chpt.; Realtors Nat. Mktg. Inst.; US Power Squadron; Nat. Council of Exchangors; publs: Effects of Manifest and Induced Anxiety and Experimenter Variabilityf on Simple Reaction Time, Perceptual & Motor Skills Journ. 1966; Republican; rec: boating, skiing, travel. Res: 34 Cypress Way Rolling Hills Estates 90274 Ofc: Prime Realty Inc., 615 Espalanade, Ste 111, Redondo Beac 90272

NAVEJAS, FREDERIK CARLOS, telephone co. executive; b. Mar. 2, 1950, Fresno; s. Felix Lopez and Anita Amelia Navejas; edn: BS, CHE, CSU Long Beach 1976; BA, CSU Dominguez Hills 1978, MPA, 1981. Career: Long Beach asst. plant mgr. Polyplastex United Inc., L.A. 1976-79; prodn. control supvr. McDonnell Douglas Aircraft Corp. 1979-80; engring. mgr. Pacific Telephone & Telegraph Co., Los Angeles 1980-82, San Francisco 1982--; chmn. bd. dirs. Hawaiian Gardens Community Action Council Inc.; Awards: Gold Press Card Award, Sigma Delta Chi 1972; Calif. State Scholarship Awd. 1968; mem: Alpha Kappa Psi, Long Beach DO chpt. (pub. rels. chmn. 1971); Assoc. Students Inc., CSU, Long Beach (pres./ treas. 1972-74); mayor pro tempore, City of Hawaiian Gardens 1979-80; rec: weightlifting, chess, tennis. Res: 12218 East 213 St Hawaiian Gardens 90716 Ofc: Pacific Telephone, 215 Fremont, Ste 423 G, San Francisco

NEAL, CECIL RANDALL, III, business services executive; b. Dec. 26, 1946, Amarillo, Tex.; s. Cecil R. Jr. and Ida Jane (Cox) N.; m. Sharon Ruth Van Sickel, Dec. 9, 1972; children: Janet Rebecca, b. 1975; Cecil Richard IV, b. 1976; edn: BA, Ariz. State Univ. 1970; desig: AIC (Assoc. in Claims), and SIA (Sr. Ins Adjuster), Ins. Inst. of Am. Career: with GAB Business Svcs. Inc. 1970--: senior property adjuster 1970-74; branch mgr. 1974-82; regional mgr. (Calif. & Hawaii) 1982--; honors: T.C. Anderson Awd., Blue Goose 1982; SIA, GAB 1978; Most Valuable Mem., AICA 1981; mem: Internat. Order of the Blue Goose (KGGE 1982); Ariz. Ins. Claims Assn. (pres. 1980); Lions; Masonic Orgns: Scottish Rite, Shrine, Eastern Star; Republican; Christian; rec: fishing. Res: 5752 Sweetwater Yorba Linda 92686 Ofc: GAB, 3450 Wilshire Blvd, Ste 301, Los Angeles 90010

NEAL, JAMES GARY, investment planning executive; b. May 5, 1956, Fresno; s. William Albert and Shirley Jean (Painter) N.; m. Mary Pamela, Jan. 23, 1982; 1 dau. Nicolin Jennifer, b. June 3, 1983; edn: AA, Fresno City Coll. 1976; stu. CSU Fresno 1976-7, San Jose 1977, Hayward 1978; The American Coll. 1978-; grad. Conn. Mutual Grad. Sch. 1983. Life and Disability Lic. 1978-, Nat. Assn. of Securities Dealers 1982-. Career: life and disability ins. salesman, investment plng. exec. Connecticut Mutual Life, Fresno 1978--; spkr., ins. class, CSU Fresno 1981; rep. to The Agents Advis. Com., CML 1983; honors: MVP, St. Mary's Coll. Baseball Sch. 1971; Co. Leaders Club, CML 1980, 81, 82; Agt. of the Year, Fresno Life Underwriters Assn. (FLUA) 1981, Nat. Sales Achieve. Awd. 1981, 82, 83; Million Dollar Round Table (Qual. mem. 1980-), Pres. Blue Chip Assn. CML 1979-; mem: Nat., Calif. Assn. of Life Underwriters, FLUA, Rotary, Fresno Breakfast Tip Club (founder 1980), Lambda Chi Alpha (exec. com.), Aircraft Owners and Pilots Assn., San Joaquin Country Club, Sierra Sport and Racquet Club; works: invented a New Life Ins. Service (Trademark pend. 1984); founder/co-owner of the Fresno Indians, semi-pro baseball team; Republican; Christian; rec: numismatics, pvt. pilot, golf, baseball (coach Babe Ruth). Res: 3610 W. Locust Fresno 93711 Ofc: Conn. Mutual Life 5070 N. Sixth, Ste 189, Fresno 93710

NEFF, NANCY, educational purchasing executive; b. Sept. 9, Mich.; d. John M. and Helen A. (Snyder) Westrick; edn: ASc, Grossmont Coll. 1973; BSc, Western State Univ. 1975; JD, 1977; DD, 1980. Career: airline hostess, model in NY, NY prior to 1971; personnel mgr. Buffums Dept. Store, Fashion Valley 1971-74; aerospace contractor/ contract analyst Rockwell Internat. 1974-77; small & minority bus adminstr. corp. agreement/ corp. agreement coord. (interfaced w/ all Rockwell divs. in Western reg.) 1977-79; deputy dir. Purchasing & Contracting County of San Diego 1979-83; dir. of Purchasing 1983--; spkr: Nat. Assn. Women in Constrn. (1982), Nat. Conf. Public Purchasing Officials, Grossmont Coll. Career Fair; honors: Outstanding Woman of the Yr. 1982; hon. awards: City of San Diego Personnel (1980-81), San Diego Minority Devel. Council (1982); mem: S.D. County Womens Network (pres.); Calif. Women in Govt. (exec. bd. 1981); Nat. Assn. Female Execs. (dir.); Nat. Notary Assn.; Purchasing Mgrs. Assn.; Calif. Pub. Purchasing Officials; San Diego Trial Lawyers Assn.; Delta Theta Phi; S.D. Career Guidance Assn.; No. Co. Connectiens; Presidents Council; Nu Beta Epsilon; No. Co. Repertory Theatre; Young Friends of S.D. Symphony; Young Connoiseurs of S.D. Art.; Calif. Trial Lawyers Assn.; sev. articles in profl. publs; hon. mention, Newsday NY, poetry; rec: theatre arts, flying, aero sports, travel. Res: 10216 Vultee St 212, Downey 90241 Ofc: Nancy Neff, J.D., Compton Unified School Dist. Purch. Dept., 604 S Tamarind Ave Compton 90220

NEFF, SCOTT DAVID, chiropractor; b. Jan. 14, 1953, St. Paul, Minn.; s. Elliott Ira and Mollie (Poboisk) N.; edn: BA, Univ. of Minn. 1978; BS, L.A. Coll. of Chiropractic, 1981, DC, 1981; desig: (DE) Disability Evaluator, Calif. Chiro. Assn. 1983; IME, Indep. Med. Examiner, 1984; Calif. lic. DC, 1982. Career: mng. pres. American Tool Co., St. Paul, Minn. 1974-78; staff doctor Bierly Chiropractice, So. Gate, Calif. 1981; staff dr. Petrikin Chiro. Clinic, Fountain Valley 1982; dir. clinic svcs. White Chiro. Clinics, Hawthorne- Palos Verdes 1982-83; chief of staff The Neff Clinic, Lawndale 1983--; State Disability Evaluator, Independent Med. Examiner; lectr., Fraud in the Chiro.- Med. Health Amalgam, Loma Linda Univ. Dental Sch.; mem. American, Calif. Chiro. Assns.; Los Angeles and L.A. Southwest Chiro. Socs.; Sigma Chi Psi; Sigma Alpha Mu; Fountain Valley Jaycees (dir. 1982); Fountain Valley Boys Club of Am. (bd. dirs. 1982); Lawndale & Westchester Lax CofC; works: inventor, researcher, author: Neuroanatomy of Vertebral Subluxations (viceral-neuromuscular and somato- neuro- muscular pathways) Strain of Arhletisism (physio- somato- system); co- author position paper on chiro., Lymphopathy an Organized Approach, Calif. Council Against Health Frauds; Republican; Jewish; rec: scientific research, writing, music. Res: 28129 Peacock Ridge Rd Rancho Palos Verdes 90274 Ofc: Neff Clinic, 15020 Hawthorne Blvd, Ste G, Lawndale 90260

NEHER, ROBERT LLOYD, JR., health care executive; b. Nov. 24, 1946, Jacksonville, Fla.; s. Robert L. and Betty L. (Wood) N.; m. Carrie Nardella, 1982; stepchildren: Rob; Christine, Buzz; edn: BS, San Diego State Univ. 1970; fellow, CORO FOund. 1970-71; MA, Occidental 1971; postgrad. wk. Univ. Calif. (Riverside, L.A., Berkeley, S.F.) 1972-82; Chief Admin. Ofcr. (1974), Supvr. (1974), Personnel (1974), & Instr. (1972), Comm. Colls. of Calif.; Standard Tchg. Cred., Calif. 1971. Career: fellow, Coro Found., San Francisco 1970-71; admistrv. asst., cand. for Calif. Congressional Dist. 1970-71; instr. Golden Gate Univ. Grad. Sch. of Bus., S.F. 1971; with Imperial Co. 1971-75; drug abuse pgm. & youth devel. dir./ grantsman Econ. Opportunity Commn. 1971-72; comm. pgms. coord./ drug abuse pgm. dir./ mental health adminstr. 1972; adminstr. mental health svcs. & substance abuse pgms. mgr. 1972-75; with Stanislaus Co. 1975-83; co. mental health dir. 1975-77; human svcs. agency dir. 1977-80; exec. dir. western regl. ctr., L.A. 1980-83; exec. dir./ adminstr. San Diego ops. Vista Hall Found., San Diego 1983--; pvt. cons., human resources mgmt. 1979-84; adv. bd. Modesto Jr. Coll. 1976-80; listed in num. biographical publs.; outstanding svc. awds: Vista Hill Found. (1975), Imperial Co. Mental Health Adv. Bd. (1971-75), as instr., Golden Gate Univ., S.F. (1971); mem: Calif. Conf. of Co. Mental Health Dirs. (Long Range Plnng. Commun. Svcs.); Calif. Welfare Dirs. Assn. (Personnel & Staff Devel., exec. bd.); Co. Health Care Adminstrs. Assn.; Assn. of mental Health Adminstrs.; Assn. of So. Cali. Regl. Ctr. (pres. 1980-82); Assn. of Humanistic Psychology; Hosp. Council of San Diego & Imperial Cos.; Nat. Assn. Pvt. Psychiatric Hosps.; Rotary; Mental Health Assn.; Cancer Soc. (pres.); CofC; CORO Found. Assocs.; Modesto Civil Theater; Vista Hill Found.; Commonwealth Club of Calif.; mem. comm. advis. com. San Diego Padres Baseball Team; Republican; Baptist; rec: art. Res: 3776 Via Picante La Mesa 92041 Ofc: Vista Hill Foundation, c/o Mesa Vista Hospital, 7850 Vista Hill Ave San Diego 92123

NEIGHBORS, WILLIAM MILBOURNE, US State Dept. officer, ret.; b. Apr. 22, 1912, Cape Charles, Va.; s. Edmund Luther and Ethel Mae (Milbourne) N.; m. Betty Bier, Feb. 7, 1934; children: Karen Cole, b. 1942; Genie Bassett, b. 1948; edn: Goldey Coll. 1930-32; T.C. Williams, Univ. of Richmond Night Sch. 1935-42; econ., Univ. of Manchester, Eng. 1946-47. Career: asst. secty. Union Life Ins. Co., Richmond, Va. 1935-45; econ. ofcr. US Foreign Svc. 1945-54 (v.consul American Embassy, Manchester & London; econ. ofcr. to all E.

Africa, Kenya); mgr. Chambers of Commerce of Culver City, Reseda, Van Nuys, Woodlands Hills & No. Hollywood 1955--; currently, pub. rels. MPI Label Systems; membership dir. Northridge & Encino CofC; field secty. Mayor Norris Poulsen, L.A. 1958-61; lectr. Knife & Forks Clubs, Exec. Dinner Clubs & L.A. Adult Schs.; bd. mem. Valley Wide Streets & Hwys. 1984; honors: Declaration of Commdn., Soc. of Distng. Citizens 1975; mem: San Fernando Valley Indsl. Assn.; CofC; Masons (lectr. Shrine Hosps. for Crippled Children, asst. secty. Scottish Rite); Rotary (past pres., pub. rels.) ; mil: maj. Civil Air Patrol 1940-45; Aux. USAF; Res: 4360 Coronet Dr Encino

NELSON, BRUCE ARTHUR, lawyer; b. May 24, 1943, Muskegon, Mich.; s. Arthur J. and Ardath F. Nelson; children: Emily, b. 1971; Maggie, b. 1973; edn: BBA, Univ. of Mich.; JD, 1968; admitted to practice, State Bar of Calif. 1969. Career: law clerk Hon. Noel P. Fox, Chief Judge, US Dist. Ct., Grand Rapids, Mi.; assoc. atty. Pillsbury, Madison & Sutro, San Francisco 1969-75; partner 1975-77; partner Morrison & Foerster, S.F. 1977--; gen. counsel, Calif. Employment Law Council 1983-; chmn. bd. Equal Employment Ednl. Pgms. 1982-; mem. bd.: Nat. Conf. of Christians & Jews (1980-), Univ. of Mich. Bd. Devel., Grad. Sch. of Bus. Adminstrn. (1981-), Calif. Bus. Law Inst. (1980-); honors: Phi Kappa Phi, (1964), Beta Gamma Sigma, Valedictorian (1965), Univ. of Mich. BBA Pgm., Order of Coif (1968), Univ. of Mich. Law Sch.; RCA Fellowship in Indsl. Rels; mem: Am. Bar Assn. (Litigation & Labor Coms.); publs: co-ed. Equal Employment Report, ABA 1983-; num. arts. in law journs.; rec: skiing, tennis. Res: 62 Molino Ave Mill Valley 94941 Ofc: Morrison & Foerster, One Market Plaza, Ste 4100, San Francisco 94105

NELSON, C(ARL) ALLEN, specialty merchandise mail order co. owner; b. Feb. 14, 1920, Newton, Kans.; s. Carl Raymond and Marguerite Alice (Allen) N.; m. Betty Jane Johnson (dec. 1978), June 21, 1940; 1 son, Richard Allen, b. 1950; edn: Fort Hays Kansas State Coll. 1938-9, Salt City Bus. Coll. 1939-40; lic. Fire & Casualty/Life & Disability Insurance Agt., Calif. 1948-553, 1965-. Career: central ofc. equipt. instlr. (Long Beach & Whittier 1947-56), supply supr. (Whittier 1956-64), computer opr. (Santa Monica (1964-66), General Telephone Co., 1947-66; agent for Farmers Insurance Gp., Al Nelson Insurance Agency in Long Bch. 1948-53, in Whittier 1966-69, Al Nelson Ins. Agency, Atascadero 1969-75; owner Nelson Enterprises dba Allen's World of Gifts, Knobby Horse, retail & wholesale - splty. mdse., 1983--; design patent (1953) prodn. & mail order of children's "clothes horse" (clothes hanger) Knobby Horse; past pres. Whittier A.M. Y's Mens Club (YMCA Svc. Club) 1964-65, Man of the Year 1965. Best known for his successful battle to repeal the Calif. State Inheritance Tax (1982), testified before Calif. Assem. Revenue and Taxation Com. Hearing on behalf of Assemblyman Don Rogers bill (to repeal tax) AB 264, 1979, appeared in radio, tv interviews on subject and wrote countln behalf of INHERIT (Initiative to Help Ensure the Right to Inherit without Tax); mil: s/sgt. US Army Air Corps 1944-46 (B-29 outfit ground maint., North Field AB, Tinian, Mariannas), GCM, WWII Victory, Asia. Pac. Campaign with 4 battle stars, Disting. Unit Cit.; Republican; Congregational; rec: photog., growing (400) hybrid poplar trees. Res: 15325 Lake Side Lane, Hornbrook 96044 Ofc: Nelson Ent. 15325 Lake Side Lane, POB 10, Ho, Lancaster, Ohio; d. Frank S. and Nancy Ann (Casto) Benson Jr.; m. Patrick Nesbitt 1975, div. 1981; chil: Elizabeth Paige, b. 1977; Patrick Michael Jr., b. 1978; edn: Bradford Jr. Coll. 1967-9; Ohio State Univ. 1972, KKT sorority; stu. Cordon Bleu, London 1973. Career: campaign chmn. for Reagan, Republican primary, Marina Del Rey, 1976; (postprimary) chmn. People for Ford, in chg of vol. groups, orgns., subcoms. in Calif., 1976; mem: Los Angeles Jr. League; C.H.I.P.S. (Colleague Helpers in Philanthropic Svcs); Le Coterie, LA Ballet Guild; Republican; Episcopal. Res: 116 S. Anita Ave. Los Angeles 90049

NELSON, DON ALDEN, certified public accountant; b. Nov. 28, 1927, San Diego; s. Ernest Elmer and Lora Ellen (Swearengin) N.; m. Roslyn Reps, Feb. 12, 1949; children: Linda, b. 1953; Adelaide, b. 1954; edn: BA, UCLA 1948; CPA, Calif. 1951. Career: DeLoitte, Haskins & Sells, Los Angeles Ofc. 1948, partner 1963--; pres. L.A. chpt. Calif. Soc. of CPAs 1972-73; pres. Calif. Soc. CPAs 1983; Council of Am. Inst. of CPAs; trustee Methodist Hosp. of So. Calif.; dir./ v.p. So. Calif. chpt. Nat. Multiple Schlerosis Soc.; dir. Partners Pgm., UCLA Grad. Sch. of Mgmt.; Jacby Assocs. of UCLA Grad. Sch. of Mgmt.; mem. UCLA Chancellor's Assocs. (chmn. 1972-73); mem: Calif. Soc. CPAs (pres. 1983-84); Calif. CPA Found. for Edn. & Research (pres. 1981-83); L.A. Rotary Club; Calif. Club; L.A. Country Club; Jonathan Club (former); Republican; Methodist; rec: paddle tennis, golf. Res: 147 Granville Ave Los Angeles 90049 Ofc: DeLoitte, Haskins & Sells, 333 S Grand Ave, Ste 2800, Los Angeles 90071

NELSON, FRANKLYN LLOYD, psychologist; b. June 21, 1946, Los Angeles; s. Jack W. and Verna Maxine (Lane) N.; edn: BA, CSU Northridge 1969; MA, USC 1973; PhD, 1975; PhD, Calif. Sch. of Profl. Psychology 1983; Lic. Psychologist, Calif. 1979. Career: research assoc. Survey Research Ctr. UCLA 1973-74; research sociologist, Veterans Admin., Los Angeles 1974-76; sr. research assoc. Univ. of Queensland, Brisbane, Australia 1977-78; research psychologist The Inst. for Studies of Destructive Behaviors & the Suicide Prevention Ctr., L.A. 1978--; assoc. dir. SPC Community Treatment Ctr., L.A. 1982--; pvt. practice, clin. psychology, L.A. 1983--; cons. Drug Abuse Pgm. Ofc., L.A. Co. Dept. of Health Svcs., L.A. 1978-80; honors: Alpha Kappa Delta 1970; Psi Chi 1971; NIMH Fellowship 1971-74; Biomed. Scis. Support Grant, NIH 1973-74; mem: Am. Psychological Assn.; Am. Sociological Assn.; Am. Acad. of Political & Soc. Scis.; Sierra Club; Union of Concerned Scientists; publs: contr. arts. to profl. journs.; 19 pub. arts., book chpts. & monographs; Democrat; rec: backpacking. Res: 1041 S Menlo Ave Los Angeles 9006 Ofc: The Robertson Clinic, 1026 S Robertson Blvd Los Angeles 90035

NELSON, GEORGE COOPER, dentist; b. Sept. 13, 1943, Texarkana, Tex.; s. George Cooper Jr. and Martha Mildred (Crockett) N.; m. Rita A., Mar. 21, 1971; children: Khari F., b. 1972; Karma T., b. 1974; Khalid A., b. 1979; edn: DDS, UCLA 1978. Career: practice dentistry, Sacramento. Res: 5 Woodriver Ct Sacramento 95831 Ofc: George C. Nelson DDS, 925 Secret River Dr, Ste F, Sacramento 95831

NELSON, LAWRENCE E., lawyer/ company president; b. Mar. 28, 1949, Los Angeles; s. Edward L. and Jeanne P. (Herbers) edn: Diploma, Webb Sch. for Boys, Claremont 1967; BS, USC 1971; JD, Pepperdine Univ. Sch. of Law 1976; admitted to practice, State Bar of Calif. Career: dist. field rep. Hon. Ronald Cordova, Assemblyman, 74th Dist. 1978-79; atty. at law, pvt. practice; pres. God's Love Co., Newport Beach 1980--; mgr. Willner Mural Co. 1981-; honors: winner, Vincent Dalsimer Moot Court Competition, Pepperdine Law Sch. 1975; Fellowship/ Tchg. Asst., Pepperdine Univ. Law Sch.; Fellow, Pepperdine Liason to Orange Co. Dist. Attys. Ofc.; mem: Calif. State Bar; South Coast Comm. Ch. (chmn. Singles Connection 1983); Orange Co. Performing Arts Ctr., Cabaret chpt. (exec. com./ treas. 1982-83); Toastmasters; The Newport Beach Sporting House; Magic Island; Republican; Christian; rec: theater, sailing, chess. Ofc: Lawrence E. Nelson, Esq., 1300 Quail, Ste 102, Newport Beach 92660

NELSON, PAUL DOUGLAS, lawyer; b. Dec. 22, 1948, Silverton, Ore.; s. Robert Thorsen and Elene Lillie (Douglas) N.; edn: BA, cum laude, Lewis & Clark Coll. 1971; ED, Univ. of Ore. 1974. Career: atty. Hoge, Fenton, Jones & Appel, San Jose 1974-75; atty./ partner Hancock, Rothert & Bunshoft, San Franicsco 1975--; legal counsel Western areas Ski Ins. Pgm.; awards: Nat. Presbyterian Merit Scholar 1967; Student body pres./ student coll. trustee 1970-71; Nat. Moot Ct. Team 1972-74; mem: Am., Calif., Ore. & San Francisco Bar Assns.; S.F. Lawyers Club; Republican; Presbyterin. Res: 744 Longridge Rd Oaklnad 94610 Ofc: Hancock, Rothert & Bunchoft, Four Embarcadero Center, Ste 1000, San Francisco 94111

NELSON, ROBERT F., corporate controller; b. June 14, 1930, Los Angeles; s. Floyd I and Katherine H. (Begley) N ; m. Peggy Woods, Oct. 14, 1950; children: Robert Jr., b. 1951; Raymond, b. 1953; Kathy, b. 1955; Ann,. b. 1960; Richard, b. 1964; Ronald, b. 1965; edn: AA, Mt. San Antonio 1956; BS, CSU 1956; MS, Golden Gate Univ. 1983; CPA, Calif. 1960. Career: sr. acct. Haskins & Sells, Los Angeles 1958-62; internal auditor Conrac Corp., Duarte 1962-64; controller 1965-67; plant controller Nat. cash Register Bus. Forms Div., L.A. 1967 69; corp. controller Walter Carpet Mills Inc., L.A. 1969-74; corp. controller Mand Carpet Mills Inc., L.A. 174-79; corp. controller Hollytex Carpet Mills Inc. (USG Parent Co.), City of Industry 1979--; mem. Calif. Soc. of CPAs; Nat. Assn. CPAs; mil: sgt. USMC 1948-49, 1950-52; Catholic; rec: aerobics, racquetball, tennis. Res: 221 E Miramar Claremont 91711e Ofc: Hollytex Carpet Mills Inc., POB 1255 City of Industry 91745

NELSON, STEVEN ARTHUR, real estate investment banking firm executive; b. May 15, 1945, Hill Air Force Base, Utah; s. Willard Edwin and Verda (Stoker) N.; m. Kathy Jensen, Jan. 21, 1970; children: Patrick, b. 1972; Andrea, b. 1974; Brian, b. 1976; Stephanie, b. 1979; edn: BS, Univ. of Utah 1970; Real Estate Mktg. Cert., CSU Fullerton 1979; Lumbleau R.E. Sch. 1973; Anthony R.E. Sch. 1974-75; Cert., NY Inst. of Finance 1971; R.E. Inv. courses, USC 1982-83. Lic: R.E. Sales 1973, Broker 1975; Insurance Sales 1978; Securities Salesman 1981. Career: acct. exec. Shearson Hammill & Co., Newport Beach 971-73; salesman Larwin Gp., Encino 1973-74; salesman Mission Viejo Co., 1975-76; proj. sales mgr. 1977-78; gen. sales mgr. 1978-79; dir. of sales Bren Co., Newport Beach 1979-81; v.p. sales Balcor/ American Express, Chgo. 1981--; v.p Racquet Inc. 1971-72; v.p. Nelson Equities 1968-78; lectr. CPA cont. edn., Shearson A.E. Pension Investments; awards: Alumni Distng. Svc. Awd., Univ. of Utah 1975; NAHB Million Dollar Circle 1973-77, life mem. 1978; mem: NAHB; BIA; IAFP; NASD; United Way; Delta Sigma Pi; Solitude Ski Patrol; Delta Phi Kappa; pres. Turtlerock Homeowners Assn. 1980-81; Mission Viejo Country Club; Huntington Beach Athletic Club; Boy Scouts SME Com.; works: MVP, City Recreation Softball; High Scorer, City Recreation Basketball; pilot; TAC Ofcr. OCS; sky diver, mem. dance band (bass fiddle); mil: 1st lt. USAR 1963-72, Commdn., Utah Nat. Guard; Republican; Ch. of Jesus Christ of LDS; rec: boating, flying, golf. Address: 3469 Plumeria Pl Costa Mesa 92626

NELSON, STEVEN R., insurance agency president; b. Oct 7, 1946, Hanford; s. Charles P. and Lillian (Kaufman) N.; m. Judy Owen, June 24, 1966; children: Scott, b. 1967; Sean, b. 1968; edn: AA, Coll. of the Sequoias 1966; BA, CSU Fresno 1969. Career: underwriter The Travelers Ins., San Jose 1970-71, senior underwriter, Fresno 1971-74; partner Newton Ins. Agency, Dinuba 1974-76; underwriting mgr. Van Beurden Wigh & Assoc., Kingsburg 1976-78; owner Steven R. Nelson Ins., Dinuba 1978--; cons. Western Carriers Ins. Exch. 1977; recipient merit award, Swana Youth Assn. 1982; mem: Dinuba Mennonite Brethren Ch.; Indep. Ins. Agents of Calif.; Awan Club of the Kingsburg Evangelical Free Ch. (commndr.); Mennonite; rec: competitive road running, olympic discus throwing, hist. Res: 121 Palm Dinuba 93618 Ofc; Steven R. Nelson Insurance, POB 944 Dinuba 93618

NELSON, WALTER W., healthcare financial executive; b. Jan. 9, 1941, San Diego; s. Walter Weems and Betty Carmen (Richards) N.; m. Joanne Sue Sedlacek, Nov. 21, 1981; children: Holli, b. 1960; Barry,b . 1961; Kim, b. 1963; Heidi, b. 1969; edn: CSU Fullerton 1968-72; Bus. Cert., Fullerton Coll. 1966-67; Bus. Cert., Bryan Bus. Coll. 1965; D.Phil., Scientology Aola, PhD 1982; Cert. Qualified Mgr., Calif. 1975. Career: personal staff, Howard Hughes

1963-68; mktg. mgr. Sperry Univac 1968-70; mgr. Delta Tire 1970-73; CBO, United Calif. Bank 1973-75; pres. Proj. Credit Systems 1975-79; v.p. Southland Bus. Bureau 1979-83; v.p. mktg. Financial Healthcare Svcs. 1983--; dir. Kool Kups Corp. 1983-; motivational sems./ spkr. Walter Nelson & Assoc. 1981-; honors: Outstanding Young Men of Am.; Paul Harris Sustaining; mem: HFMA; AGPAM; Howard Hughes Med. Found.; Fullerton So. Rotary; Fullerton CofC; Healthcare Fin. Mgmt. Assn.; Am. Guild Patient Acct. Mgr.; Orange Co. CafC; author: Phase 10, devel. Phase 10 Training; mil: cpl. E-4 USMC 1958-62; Republican; Scientologist; rec: racquetball, sailing. Res: 1260 Venice Ave Placentia 92670 Ofc: Financial Healthcare Services, 1930 Beverly Blvd Los Angeles 90057

NEMETHI, CARL EDWARD, physician-surgeon; b. Feb. 9, 1912, Los Angeles; s. Charles and Caroline (Biedelsphoer) N.; m. Virginia Carberry, June 21, 1939; edn: AB, USC 1933, MD, 1938. Career: surgeon Union Pacific Railroad 1940; regl. med. dir. Am. Can. Co., Flintkote Co., Fibreboard Corp. 1947; health ofcr. City of Vernon 1950; pvt. practice indsl. med. & surgery 1947; founder/ dir. Emergency Unit., Dominguez Valley Hosp. 1963; fouder/ dir. Emerg. Unit. Calif. Lutheran Hosp. 1973; dir. Western Indsl. Med. Assn. 1966; mem: Am., Calif. & L.A. County Med. Assns.; dir. Western Indsl. Med. Assn.; diplomate, Internat. Coll. of Surgeons; Am. Arbitration Assn.; clubs: Los Angeles CC, Birnam Woods (Santa Barbara) CC, Vernon Rotary; num. medical papers on surgeries & injuries of the hand; ext. work on ranch for conservation of wild life in conjunction w/ fish & game, particularly preservation of endangered species of Aleutian goose; mil: maj. USAF 1943-46, Bronze Battle Star, Burma campaign; Republican; Methodist; rec: wildlife. Res: 608 N Elm Dr Beverly Hills 90210 Ofc: Carl E. Nemethi, MD & Staff, 5592 Santa Fe Ave Los Angeles 90058

NEMIR, DONALD PHILIP, lawyer; b. Oct. 31, 1931, Oakland; s. Philip F. and Mary Madelyn (Shavor) N.; edn: AB, UC Berkeley 1957; JD, UC Berkeley Boalt Hall 1960. Career: sr. atty. Law Ofcs. Donald Nemir, San Francisco 1961--; bd. dirs. Summit Found.; mem: Am. Bar Assn.; Phi Delta Phi; Univ. Club, S.F; mil: USNR 1949-54. Res: 370 Marion Ave Mill Valley 94941 Ofc: Law Offices of Donald Nemir, One Maritime Plaza San Francisco 94111

NERI, MICHAEL ANTHONY, physician; b. Feb. 13, 1938, Phila., Pa.; s. Michael D. and Elizabeth R. Neri; m. Linda Joy Bailey, Dec. 31, 66; children: Michael, b. 1970; Stephen, b. 1972; edn: BS, LaSalle Coll. 1960; MD, Hahnemann Med. Coll. 1964; Flight Surgeon, Brook's Sch. Aerospace Med., San Antonio, Tex. 1966. Career: family practice Permanente Med. Gp. of So. Calif. 1968--; physician in charge, Riverside 1972-83; bd. dirs. Mgmt. Assn., Permanente 1970-73; chief of svc. Family Practice 1983; bd. dirs. Kaiser-Permanente; asst. clin. prof. Family Practice, Loma Linda Univ. 1980--; Riverside Gen. Hosp. 1978--; chief of Family Practice Fontana Hosp. 1983--; coordinating chief Family Practice eight Kaiser Hosps. in So. Calif. 1983--; awards: Physicians Recogn. Awds., Am. Med. Assn. 1982, Calif. Med. Assn. 1983; Diplomat, Am. Bd. of Family Practice; mem: Am. Acad. of Family Physicians; Phi Chi; mil: flight surgolic Bishops Synod 1972); rec: travel. Res: 16156 Saddle Crest Pl Riverside 92507 Ofc: Kaiser Permanente, 3951 Van Buren Riverside 92504

NESBITT, BERTRAM IRWIN, exploration co. president; b. June 10, 1915, Regina, Saskatchewan, Can.; s. Lester York and Etta Mae (Wickett) N.; m. Rosina Cozzolino, Aug. 23, 1968; children: Robert William, b. 1942; Doris Dianne, b. 1945; Mary Anne, b. 1948; Betty Kathleen, b. 1954; edn: BASc, Univ. (geological), Assn. of Profl. Engrs. B.C., 1946. Career: geologist Geological Survey of Canada 1935-40; chief geologist Canadian Exploration Co. 1941; chief geologist/ chief engr. Nickel Plate Mine 1941-45; mgr. exploration Western Canada Northwest Territories, Granby Consol. Mining Smelting & Power 1945-48; cons. geological engr./ independent cons. var. mining, oil & indsl. cos. 1948-55; pres. sev. mining & oil exploration companies -1975; pres./ treas./ CEO Oil Securities Inc., Los Angeles 1975--; recipient Tchg. Fellowship, Queens Univ. 1939-41; pres. sev. mining & oil companies; mem: Assn.of Profl. Engrs.; Canadian Inst. of Mining & Metallurgy (life); Am. Inst. of Mining & Metallurgy (life); Soc. of Econ. Geologists; clubs: Capilano Golf & Country (Vancouver), Riviera Golf & Country (L.A.); mil: 1st lt.; Republican; Protestant; rec: golf. Res: 2539 Almaden Ct Los Angeles 90077 Ofc: Oil Securities Inc., 10880 Wilshire Blvd, Ste 1110, Los Angeles 90024

NESBITT, NANCY CASTO BENSON, b. Feb. 19, 1949, Lancaster, Ohio; d. Frank S. and Nancy Ann (Casto) Benson Jr.; m. Patrick Nesbitt 1975, div. 1981; chil: Elizabeth Paige, b. 1977; Patrick Michael Jr., b. 1978; edn: Bradford Jr. Coll. 1967-9; Ohio State Univ. 1972 (KK7 Sorority); stu. Cordon Bleu, London 1973. Career: campaign chmn. for Reagan, Republican primary, Marina Del Rey, 1976; (postprimary) chmn. People for Ford, in chg of vol. groups, orgns., subcoms. in Calif., 1976; mem: Los Angeles Jr. League; C.H.I.P.S. (Colleague Helpers in Philanthropic Svcs); Le Coterie, LA Ballet Guild; Republican; Episcopal. Res: 116 S. Anita Ave. Los Angeles 90049

NESBITT, PATRICK MICHAEL, lawyer; b. Feb. 7, 1944, Detroit, Mich.; s. Frederick Henry and Marie (Labadie) N.; div.; children: Elizabeth Paige, b. 1977; Patrick Michael Jr., b. 1978; edn: ES, US Air Force Acad. 1967; MS, Univ. of Mich. 1968; JD, Whittier Coll. 1981. Career: research engr. USAF 1967-71; pres./ chmn. bd. Patrick M. Nesbitt Assoc. 1971--; mng. partner Nesbitt/ Freshman Devel. Co. 1977--; chmn. bd. Academy Savings & Loan Assn. 1983--; pres. Nesbitt/ Barney Hotel Properties Inc. 1983--; chmn. Bd. P*N Properties Inc. 1983--; honors: Congressional appt. to USAF Academy; grad. scholarship Univ. of Mich.; excellence in design award Am. Inst. of

Archs. 1981; mem: Jonathan Club; Columbus Athletic Club; Marina City Club; mil: capt. USAF 1963-81; Republican; Catholic; rec: skiing, flying, polo. Res: 273 S Glenroy Ave Los Angeles 90049 Ofc: 10880 Wilshire Blvd, Ste 2010 Los Angeles 90024

NESTER, ANDREW CHARLES, company executive; b. Nov. 26, 1935, Clairton, Pa.; s. Andrew C. and Ida May (Inks) N.; m. Lavonne K. Johnson, Nov. 21, 1981; children: Stacey b. 1966, Shannon b. 1969; edn: BSEE, UCLA, 1962. Career: pres. OA Software, Inc. and Sales/Marketing Assistance Corp., San Jose; over 22 years experience in computer, computer peripheral, and software industry; past positions incl. sales mgr. AAI Corp. (mfr. computer controller integrated circuit testers); mktg. dir. Xebec Systems; mgr. Printer Mktg. and mgr. Systems Mktg. at Diablo/Xerox; pres. Professional Resources Technology Inc. (end-user systems co.); v.p. sales/mktg. Disctron Inc. (mfr. disk prods.); mil: Radarman 2/c USN 1954-57. Res: 1433 Brookmill Rd Los LTOS ($)OFC: OA Software Inc./Sales/Marketing Assistance Corp., 2185 The Alameda, San Jose 95126

NEUMAN, HARRY, book co. president; b. Nov. 19, 1913, NY, NY; s. Isak Jacob and Gussie (Pesachinsky) N.; m. Goldie Morantz; children: Jerome I., b. 1941; Richard E., b. 1945; Laurel A., b. 1947. Career: researcher United Lawyers Svc., NY 1932-35; salesman, sales mgr., v.p. Western states, Oxford Book Co., NY 1937-73; pres. Publishers Media, No. Hollywood 1973--; book evaluation cons. Internal Revenue Svc. (former); state pres. Calif. Bookmens Assn. (former); v.p. Oxford Book Co. Inc. (former); honors: Key to the City of San Francisco; mem: Profl. Writers League; Anti-Defamation Bureau Spkrs. Orgn.; Global Interdependence Edn. Assn., CSU L.A.; United Nations Assn.; publs: articles relating to education var. mags; lead art. on edn., State CofC Special issue; Hebrew; rec: music, public spkg. comm. gps., literature. Address: Publishers Media, 5507 Morella Ave, No. Hollywood 91607

NEUMAN, THOMAS, podiatrist; b. May 3, 1947, Czechoslovakia, nat. 1953; s. Sam and Rosalie Neuman; m. Madelyn, June 1, 1969; children: Jason, b. 1977; Adam, b. 1980; edn: Brooklyn Coll. of Pharmacy 1964-67; BS, Long Island Univ. 1967-68; DPM, NY Coll. of Podiatric Med. 1972; Lic. to Practice, NY, Penn. & Calif. Career: res. podiatric surgery Kensington, St. Marys & Lancanau Hosps., Phila., Pa. 1972-73; currently podiatrist, Northridge Foot Gp., Northridge & Antelope Valley Foot Gp., Lancaster; chief of Podiatry, Granada Hills Comm. hosp.; med. cons. Dept. of Soc. Svcs. & Soc. Security Admin.; Diplomate Nat. Bd. of Podiatric Examiners; honors: Man of the Yr., Am. Podiatric Student Assn. 1972; mem: Am., Calif. & Los Angeles Podiatry Assns.; Fellow Acad. of Ambulatory Foot Surgery; Acad. of Podiatric Sports Med.; Am. Diabetes Assn. (bd. dirs. 1979-82); rec: equestrian, American stamps, skiing. Res: 11861 Killimore Ave Northridge 91326 Ofc: Northridge Foot Group, 9535 Reseda Blvd, Ste 100, Northridge 91324 & Antelope Valley Foot Group, 44300 N Division, Ste D, Lancaster 93535

NEWBURY, EDRIS BIGGS, advertising executive; b. July 17, 1902, Long Beach; d. Morton and Jessimin Floy (Gignac) Biggs; m. Charles B. Newbury (dec.); edn: Dipl. Los Angeles Conservatory of Music 1920, Univ. of Calif. Coll. of Music, 1920-24. Career: began tchg. piano at age 12, gave two recitals at age 13; concert pianist and performer for womens' clubs, var. churches (Presbyterian, Methodist, Rel. Sci., New Thot), and Dramatic Soc. affairs, 1926-36; tchr. Night Sch. Adult Edn., Pasadena Conservatory, 1920-30; real estate ofc. mgr., Edwards & Wildey Real Estate, 1929-30; owner advertising bus. 1932-82; named executive broker, Internat. Home Services, 1982-84; created/ bdcst. on KGER Radio, Businessmen's Biographies for Long Beach Red Cross (to get women to make dressings for the wounded); recipient hon. plaque from U.S.Congl. Advis. Bd. from John M. Fisher; mem: So. Pasadena Junior Womens Club (secty) 1920-25, Alhambra Junior Service Club (pres.) 1925-30; works: vol. of poetry; poem pub. (Vantage 1974); art supr. on Long Beach Auditorium mosaic mural; Republican; Sci. of Mind; rec: tennis. Res: 800 E. Ocean Villa Riviera No. 204, Long Beach 90802

NEWCOMBE, JESSE ERNEST, land surveyor; b June 21, 1940, Lakeview, Ore.; s. Ernest and Clare Francis (Down) N.; m. Kares Bassett, Oct. 29, 1977; children: David, b. 1963; Janet, b. 1965; Kimberly, b 1980; edn: Ore. State Univ. 1958-59; Northrop Inst. Of Tech. 1959; Ventura Coll. 1962-64. Career: surveyor Co. of Ventura 1962-69; survey engr. 1969-78; supvg. surveyor Jack K. Bryant 7 ASsoc. 1978-81; v.p. E. & E. Eng. Assoc. Inc. 1981--; pres. Anacapa Surveyors Inc., Camarillo 1982--; mem: Calif. Land Surveyors Assn.; Democrat; Presbyterian; rec: model aviation. Address: Anacapa Surveyors, 5416 Winchester Way Camarillo 93010

NEWGARD, MARK GORDON, oil company executive; b. May 7, 1944, Kalamazoo, Mich.; s. Morris T. and Marion E. (Bangle) N.; m. Jean Baarts, Sept. 3, 1966; m. 2d. Matilda Voss, Feb. 19, 1978; children: Craig, b. 1970; Kimberly, b. 1972; edn: BS, Stanford Uni. 66; MBA, Univ. of Chgo. 1968. Career: with Standard Oil of Calif. (Socal) 1968-80; fin. analyst, San Francisco 1968-70; asst. mktg. mgr., San Jose 1970-72; div. mktg. mgr., Sacto. 1972-74; coord. of computer svcs. dept., S.F 1974-75; regl. mgr. Pacific Basin & Latin Am., S.F. 1975-80; v.p./ gen mgr. Oasis Petroleum Corp., Culver City 1980-83; pres./ CEO Edgington Oil Co. 1983--; dir. Nat. Petroleum Refiners Assn.; mem: Jonathan Club; 20-30 Club of Sacto.; Delta Tau Delta; Republican; rec: skiing, tennis. Res: 10821 Savona Rd Los Angeles 90077 Ofc: Edgington Oil Co., 2400 E Artesia Blvd Long Beach 90805

NEWHOFF, STANLEY NEAL, advertising agency president; b. Jan. 31, 1944, Bronx, NY; s. Norman and Daisy Newhoff; m. Hayde' Mathilde Stekkinger,

June 16, 1969; children: Michelle b. 1970, Angela b. 1972; edn: BA, English, UC Los Angeles 1967. Career: columnist UCLA Daily Bruin, Los Angeles 1963-64; tabulator/asst. supr./asst. dir. of corp. communications, Audience Studies Inc., L.A. 1964-65; advt. copywriter J.R. Bloome Co., L.A. 1969; high sch. English tchr. in Qiryat Gat, Israel, 1969-70; advt. copywriter for L.A. agencies: Dunlap Advt., Foote, Cone & Belding, Dailey & Assocs., Doyle Dane Bernbach, 1970-74; prin./pres. Lerner-Newhoff Advt., L.A. 1974-76; v.p./creative dir. Basso/Boatman Inc., Newport Beach 1976-79; prin./pres. Stanley Newhoff & Assocs. (advt. agcy.) Irvine 1979-81; prin./pres. Newhoff & Prochnow Inc. (advt. agcy.) Costa Mesa 1981--; recipient num. awards for advertising excellence, BPAA and Orange Co. Advt. Fedn., 1975-82; mem: founding dir. Orange County Advt. Guild, Medical Marketing Assn., BPAA; founding pres. Irvine Edn. Found.; mem. Founding Task Force, Nat. Energy Resrch. and Info. Inst.; Mensa; publs. in advt. field; Republican; Jewish. Res: 3931 Claremont St Irvine 92714 Ofc: 3176 Pullman St, Ste 105, Costa Mesa 92626

NEWITT, MONIKA MEYER, realtor; b. Jan. 24, 1945, Menziken, Switzerland, nat. 1966; d. Walter and Lydia Millie (Keller) Meyer; m. Thomas Royal Newitt, M.D., Oct. 28, 1978; 1 dau: Heidi, b. 1980; edn: Long Beach City Coll. 1963-68; El Camino Coll. 1978-80; Calif. lic. R.E. Broker, 1980. Career: secty. Profl. & Pub. Rels. Dept., Calif. Blue Shield 1965-70, editor employee weekly 1969-70; temporary secterial pos. 1972-77; med. secty. Anethesiologists Southwest 1977-80; real estate broker/prin. 1980--; awards: suggestion award, Calif. Blue Shield 1967; sales awards, Century 21, 1979, 80; mem: Calif. Assn. Realtors; Redondo Beach Hist. Soc.; Republican; rec: stained glass, sewing, skiing. Res: 206 Ave D Redondo Beach 90277

NEWKIRK, WILLIAM HENRY, lawyer; b. Aug. 5, 1947, Monterey Park; s. Glen F. and Gladys J. (Rosbrook) N.; edn: BA, UCLA 1970; JD, Southwester Univ. 1974; admitted to practice, State Bar of Calif. 1975. Career: congressional staff employee for Hon. C. Hosmer & Charles Wiggins of Calif. 1972; ins. defense litigation atty. Hillsinger & Costanzo 1975-78; ins. defense litigation atty. Bonne, Jones, Bridges, Mueller & O'Keefe 1978-81; pvt. practice law (spec. med. malpractice & personal injury), Los Angeles 1981--; mem: Los Angeles Trial Lawyers Assn. (bd.govs.), Calif. Trial Lawyers Assn. (PAC), Am. Trial Lawyers Assn.; mil: sgt. E-5 US Army- Calif. Nat. Guard 1970-76; Republican; Methodist; rec: bicycling, tennis, skiing. Res: 11681 Gorham Los Angees 90049 Ofc: Law Offices of William H. Newkirk, 11661 San Vincent Blvd, Ste 1010, Los Angeles 90049

NEWMAN, FRANK C., educator/ former Supreme Court of California Justice; b. July 17, 1917, Eureka; s. Frank J. and Anna (Dunn) N.; m. Frances Burks, 1940; children: Robert; Julie; Carol; edn: AB, Dartmouth 1938; LLD, UC Berkeley 1941; LLM, Columbia Univ. 1947; JSD, 1953; LLD, Univ. of Santa Clara 1978. Career: atty. OPA, NYC and Wash. DC 1942-43; ofc. gen. counsel Navy Dept. 1943-46; prof. of law UC Berkeley 1946-77; dean UC Berkley Law Sch. 1961-66; Jackson H. Ralston prof. internat. law 1974-77; assoc. justice Supreme Court of California 1977-82; visiting prof. to law schs. of Harvard (1953-54), Univ. of Wash. (1952), Salzburg Sem. in Am. Studies, Austria (1954, 64), Strausbourg Inst. of Human Rights. (1970, 71, 75, 77), Ctr. Adv. Study in Behav. Scis. (1957-58); law book editorial bd. Little, Brown & Co. 1956-77; counsel Gov. Calif. Commn. on Unemployed Compensation 1952; cons. Gen. Acctg. fc. 1959; bd. dirs. Fed. Home Loan Bank, S.F. 1962-70; mem: exec. com./ chmn. drafting com. Calif. Constn. Revision Commn. 1964-72; mem. nat. adv. council Amnesty USA; mem. Am. Soc. of Internat. Law; v.p. Internat. Inst. Human Rights; mil: ensign to lt. USNR 1943-46. Ofc: UC Berkeley Sch. of Law (Boalt Hall), Berkeley 94720

NEWMAN, KISTY JONETTE, realty co. personnel executive; b. Oct. 2, 1947, Elko, Nev.; d. Keith M. and Dorothy (Gennette) Williams; m. Thomas L. Newman, July 12, 1979; children: Lisa, b. 1966; Laura, b. 1970; edn: Lumbleau Real Estate Sch. 1976; Santa Ana Coll. 1978, 79, 80; personnel mgmt. cert. stu., UC Irvine 1983-; Calif. lic: Real Estate, Notary. Career: pub. rels. ofcr./ ofc. mgr./ acctg. Mettler Family Mortuary, Garden Grove 1966-77; loan cons. Horizon Co. Inc., Garden Grove 1977-80; dir. personnel & tng./ lic. sch. adminstr. Katella Realty Inc., Anaheim 1980--; annual spkr., Garden Grove Unif. Sch. Dist. Career Days, Employers Adv. Council, Orange Co. 1983-84; honors: Outstanding member, Garden Grove Jr. Womens Club 1973; Silver Spoon award, Garden Grove CofC, Childrens Home Soc., Orange County, 1978; Woman of the Year, City of Garden Grove, CofC 1979; mem: Garden Grove Aux. to Childrens Home Soc. (v.p. 1983-84); Miss Garden Grove Pageant Com. (chmn. 1978); Garden Grove CofC; Childrens Hosp. of Orange Co. (assoc.); Garden Grove Womens Tennis Club (charter); Nat. Notary Assn.; Republican; Protestant; rec: snow skiing, fishing. Res: 10921 Marian Dr Garden Grove 92640. Ofc: Katella Realty Inc., Merrill Lynch Realty Associates Inc., 1741 W Katella Ave Anaheim 92804

NEWMAN, MICHAEL LEE, certified public accountant; b. Dec. 11, 1942, Cleveland, Oh.; s. Edward L. and Irene J. (Onofrio) N.; m. Sharon Pytel, Nov. 16, 1963; children: Christopher, b. 1969; Brock,b . 1975; edn: BS, CSU Los Angeles 1967; CPA, Calif. 1972. Career: jr. acct. James S. File & Assoc., El Monte 1967; staff acct. Harman & Co. CPAs, El Monte 1969, partner, Arcadia 1974; partner, McGladrey Hendrickson CPAs, Arcadia 1977; chief finl. ofcr. Morrow- Meadows Corp., El Monte 1977--; mem: Am. Inst. CPAs; Calif. Soc. CPAs; rec: backpacking, surfing, fishing. Res: 34071 Aurelio Dana Point 92629 Ofc: Morrow-Meadows Corp., 9662 Telstar El Monte 91731

NEWSON, NEIL C., lawyer; b. July 30, 1940, Bronx, NY; s. Leo and Roslyn A. (Myden) N.; m. Linda C., Dec. 16, 1972; children: Debra b. 1965, Michelle b. 1969, Lee b. 1975, Farrell b. 1982; edn: BS, UC Los Angeles 1963; JD, Southwestern Univ. 1967; admitted to Calif. State Bar 1968. Career: national sales mgr. for Biochemical Procedures during undergrad. and postgrad. studies, cons. 1968-; solo law practice, 1968, formed partnership with Theodore Wolfberg, 1969--, currently senior ptnr. law firm of Newson & Wolfberg, P.C., Beverly Hills; v.p. American Reference Laboratories (clin. lab.); co-founder/ dir. of Oral Education Center (charity formed for the teaching of autistic children); mem. Calif. Trial Lawyers Assn., L.A. Trial Lawyers Assn.; publs: sev. arts. in The Mask and Grail; lectr. to clin. lab. groups on aspects of clin. lab. liability; Republican; Jewish; rec: flying, skiing, tennis, golf. Res: Los Angeles 90046 Ofc: Newson & Wolfberg, P.C. 9465 Wilshire Blvd, Ste 610, Beverly hills 90212

NEWSUM, LAWRENCE ELDON, II, chiropractor; b. Feb. 17, 1930, Sioux City, Iowa; s. Lawrence Eldon and Helen (Hilton) N.; m. Michele E., Sept. 15, 1982; children: Allen M., b. 1951; Linda A., b. 1952; Michele M., b. 1955; Lawrence E. III, b. 1957; Mark V., b. 1960; edn: AA, Ft. Dodge Jr. Coll. 1953; DC, Palmer Chiro. Coll. 1958. Career: pvt. practice, Newsum Chiropractic, Lomita; regent. Sherman Chiropractic Coll.; mem: Golden Star Chiropractic Soc., International Chiropractic Soc. (past v.p. Calif. Chpt.), Chiro. Information Bureau (past pres. Bay Harbor chpt.), Calif. Council of Chiropractic (past dir., mem. Chiro. Indsl. Gp.), Parker Alumni Assn. (past pres.); orgns: So. Bay Toastmasters (past pres.), Sertoma Internat. Bay Cities, Lomita Harbor Cities Kiwanis; Peninsula Sym.; Long Beach Civic Light Opera; mil: sgt. US Army 1948-52; rec: gardening, photog. Res: 25 Golden Spur Ln Rancho Palos Verdes 90274 Ofc: Newsum Chiropractic, 24719 Narbonne Ave Lomita 90717

NEWTON, JAMES MITCHELL, civil engineer; b. Sept. 29, 1926, Spokane, Wash.; s. James Edward and MaBelle Violet (Mitchell) N.; m. Mary Fulton, Sept. 18, 1948; children: James Jr., b. 1951; Christine, b. 1953; Terry, b. 1956; Dale, b. 1958; edn: BS, Univ. of Wash. 1951; Reg. Profl. Engr., Wash. 1959, Calif. 1981. Career: with Fed. Hwy. Admin. 1951-81; esign engr. 1951-66; dist engr., Fed. aid Hwy Pgm. in 17 counties, NY 1966-68, NYC & Long Islnd 1968-76; asst. div. adminstr./ dir. eng., Puerto Rico 1976-79; eng. coord., Calif., Nev., Ariz. & Hi. 1979-80; dir. traffic eng. & safety, Calif. Nev., Ariz. & Hi. 1980-81; ret.; mem: Am. Soc. of Civil Engrs.; works: developed design for runaway track arresting facility; mil: sgt. US Army Air Corp 1945-46; Republican; Protestant; rec: genealogy. Res: 844 Spring Dr Walnut Creek 94598

NEWTON, WILLIS HEAD, JR., certified public accountant; b. Apr. 8, 1949, Macon, Ga.; s. Willis Head and Lee Moser Newton; m. Peggy Kontes, Apr. 9, 1982; edn: BA, Dartmouth Coll. 1971; MBA, Stanford Univ. 1976. Career: asst. to pres. Trio Mfg. Co., Forsyth, Ga. 1971-74; audit staff Peat, Marwick, Mitchell & Co., San Francisco 1976-79, audit supvr. 1979-81, audit mgr. 1981--; instr. PMM & Co. Nat. Tng. Pgm. 1981; mem: Am. Inst. CPAs; Calif. CPAs Soc.; Stanford Grad. Sch. of Bus. Alumni Soc.; Dartmouth Alumni Club of No. Calif. (v.p. 1981); S.F. Bay Club; Piedmont Driving Club, Atlanta, Ga.; mil: 2nd lt. US Army Mil. Intelligence 1972-73, Arcom Medal; Baptist; rec: golf, skiing, photog. Res: 2116 Divisadero St San Francisco 94115 Ofc: Peat, Marwick, Mitchell & Co., Three Embarcadero Center, San Francisco 94111

NEY, MICHAEL JAMES, lawyer; b. Nov. 20, 1943, Oakland; s. George William and Mary Monica (Ford) N.; m. Jamie Deren, July 13, 1968; children: Molley McCauley, b. 1976; Deren Michael, b. 1979; edn: BS, Univ. of Santa Calar 1965; JD, John F. Kennedy Law Sch. 1971; admitted to Calif. State Bar 1972. Career: deputy dist. atty. Alameda Co. 1972-73; assoc. atty. law firm Helzel, Leighton, Brunn & Deal, later Brunn, Leighton, Ney & Miller, 1973-75; assoc. atty./ mng. partner firm McNamara, Houston, Dodge, McClure and Ney 1975--; instr. course criminal justice Gavilan Coll. 1972-73; mem: Am., Calif. & Contra Costa Co. Bar Assns.; Santa Clara Alumni Assn., East Bay (past pres.) Delta Sigma Pi (past pres.); arbitrator, Am. Arbitration Assn. & Contra Costa Co.; Our Ladys Home for the Aged, Oakland fund raising com.; mil: yeoman US Coast Guard; Catholic; Res: 1031 Via Nueva Lafayette 94549 Ofc:1211 Newell Ave, Ste 202, Walnut Creek 94596

NG, ERIC SIU-WAH, pharmacist; b. May 26, 1951, Hong Kong; s. Keung and Oi (Lee) Ng; edn: AA, Coll. of the Sequoias 1973; BS, pharm., Idaho State Univ. 1977; BS, biology, 1977; Reg. Pharmacist, Calif. & Nev. 1978. Career: staff pharmacist Physician Med. Pharmacy, Indio 1978; pharmacy mgr., Gemco Pharmacy San Bernardino 1978-80; staff pharmacist, San Gabriel 1980-81; pharmacy mgr./ owner Crossroads Med. Pharmacy 1981--; mem: Am., Calif. & East L.A. Pharmaceutical Assns.; Republican; Christian; rec: jogging, tennis. Res: 400 S Garfield, 4, Monterey Park 91754 Ofc: Crossroads Medical Pharmacy, 750 N Diamond Bar Blvd, Ste 101, Diamond Bar 91765

NG, KIN-FUNG CHARLES, civil/structural engineer; b. Sept. 14, 1953, Kowloon, Hong Kong, nat. 1983; s. Kwok-Leung and Oi-Ching (Leung) Ng; m. Judy Yuen, Aug. 20, 1977; chil: Rebecca C., b. 1981, Teresa C., b. 1983; edn: BS, 1975, MS, 1976, Univ. of Ill., Urbana; Regis. Profl. Engr. (1979), Regis. Structural Engr. (1980), Ill.; Regis. Civil Engr. (1981), Calif. Career: structural engring. (design & analysis of nuclear power generating and radwaste disposal plants): MacDonald Engring. Co., Chgo. 1976-78, Bechtel Power Corp., Ann Arbor, Mich. 1978; struc. engring. splst. Sargent & Lundy Engrs., Chgo. 1978-81; struc. engring. supr., Advanced Technology Div. Bechtel Corp., San Francisco 1981--. Honors: life mem. Chi Epsilon (civil eng.). Mem: Ill. Struc.

Engr. Assn.; Ill. Soc. of Profl. Engrs. 1980-1; assoc. mem. ASCE 1975-7; Christian (trustee Chinese Christian Union Ch., Chgo. 1979-81); rec: sightseeing. Res: 68 Rossmoor Dr. San Francisco 94132 Ofc: Advanced Technology Div. Bechtel National Inc, 45 Fremont St. San Francisco 94119

NG, KIN SENG, pharmacist; b. June 17, 1952, Penang, Malaysia; s. Shou-Yong and Poh Chee (Soo) Ng; m. Trudy Wurangian, May 5, 1977; children: Douglas, b. 1980; Michelle, b. 1982; edn: BS, Univ. of Philippines 1977; MS, USC 1980; Reg. Pharmacist, Calif. 1982. Career: chief pharmacist Hong Kong Adventist Hosp., Hong Kong 1977-79; radiopharmacist Radpharm Inc., Los Angeles 1980-81; pharmacist, Thrifty Durgs, Los Angeles 1981--; adminstrv. council, Hong Kong Adventist Hosp., Hong Kong 1978-79; missionary, Seventh- Day Adventist Ch., Hong Kong 1977-79; awards: Merck Sharp & Dohme Book Awd. 1977; mem: Phi Kappa Phi; Phi Sigma; Seventh- Day Adventist; rec: philately. Res: 19638 Andrada Dr Rowland Heights 91748 Ofc: Thrifty Drugs, 13905 East Amar Rd La Puente 91746

NGUYEN, AN THI, real estate broker; b. May 3, 1940, Saigon, Vietnam; s. Voi Van and Dieu Thi (Tran) N.; m. Tung Vinh, Dec. 27, 1974; edn: AA, Fullerton Coll. 1979; BA, CSU Fullerton 1982; R.E. Broker, Anthony Sch. 1983; R.E. Broker, Calif. Career: writer/ reporter biggest newspaper in Vietnam, escaped from Communists, refugee in America 1976-; staff writer Hornet Newspaper & staff writer Ngawi Viet Newspaper, Orange Co.; curretly, R.E. broker Coldwell Banker, Fullerton; honors: Top Selling Units, Reg. I 1983; Activity Awds.; Quota Buster Awds. 1983; mem: Triing Viiong Assn. (chmn. of press com. 1982-83, 1983-84); works: pub. novel, Vietnam 1966; Buddhist; rec: economics, news, ping pong. Res: 230 W. Knepp, B, Fullerton 92632 Ofc: Coldwell Banker, 529 N. Harbor Blvd Fullerton 92632

NGUYEN, CUC HUU, investment co. president; b. Oct. 20, 1951, Vietnam; s. Lai Hwu and Hanh Thi (Phan) N.; m. Anh-Tuyet Thi Le, Dec. 18, 1976; children: Quoc, b. 1978; Viet, b. 1983; edn: BA, Vietnam 1975; Broker, 1980; Internat. Mgmt. 1981; Investment Soc. 1981. Career: real estate 1978--; owner the Gold Medal Investment & Devel. Co. 1980--; owner Century 21- Gold Medallion Inc. 1982--; honors: Top Winners Circle Awd. 1979-80; mem: Investment Soc.; Vietnamese Volunteer Gp. for Soc. Svc.; Catholic. Res: 2632 Carlo Scimeca Ct San Jose 95132 Ofc: Century 21 Gold Medallion, 298 S Sunnyvale Ave, Ste 105, Sunnyvale 94086

NGUYEN, DAT MANH, physician; b. June 15, 1949, Vietnam; s. Khoai Xuan and De Thi (Pham) N.; m. Phuc, Sept. 6, 1980; 1 son: Christopher, b. 1981; edn: MD, Univ. of Saigon Faculty of Med. 1975. Career: physician, refugee camp, Guam Island 1975; physician asst. to refugees, US Pub. Health Svc., Camp Pendleton 1975; volunteer to Vietnamese refugees, Vietnamese Svc. Ctr., UCI Med. Ctr. 1975-77; counselor aide to non- English spkg. students, Santa Ana Coll., Santa Ana 1977; grad. stu. asst. Metropolitan State Hosp., Norwalk 1977-78; res. tng., gen. med. & internal med., CHgo. 1978-82; currently, internist, v.p./ secty. Nguyen, MD Inc., Westminster 1982--; mem: Calif. & Orage Co. Med. Assns.; Am. Coll. of Physicians; publs: Pancreatic Cancer in Brothers, Annals of Internal Med. 8/82; rec: tennis. Res: 20 Whistling Isle Irving 92683 Ofc: Nguyen MDs Inc., 9118 Bolsa Ave Westminster 92683

NGUYEN, DUC MANH, physician; b. Dec. 26, 1927, Nam Dinh, Vietnam; d. Phuc Manh and Hien Thi (Phan) Manh; m. Han Thi Nguyen, 1968; child: Quynh-Mai Diem, b. 1968; edn: BS, Hanoi Coll., Vietnam 1950; Physics, Chem. & Biology Cert., 1951; MD, Univ. of Saigon, Faculty of Med. 1957. Career: chief of med. sect. Mi. Hosp. of Pleiku & Cap St Jacques, Vietnam Armed Forces 1957-61; chief of zone VI (15 provinces in So. Vietnam), Malaria Eradication Pgm. 1962-64, Health Devel. Admin. 1964-68; pvt. practice, Saigon, Vietnam 1968-75; physician New Hosp., L.S.P., Baton Rouge, La. 1977-78; res. gen. practice Womans Gen. Hosp. & St. John Hosp., Cleveland, Oh. 1978-80; physician Patton State Hosp., Patton, Cali. 1981--; honors: Hon. Mention, Proj. Water Treatment & Distribution in Rural Areas of Vietnam, 1957; Malaria Eradication Campaign, So. Vietnam 1962; mem: Am., Calif. & L.A. Co. Med. Assns.; Am. Gen. Practitioner Assn.; Union of Am. Physicians & Dentists; Am. Lung Assn., L.A. Co.; mil: maj. Med. Corp., Vietnamese Armed Forces; rec: gardening, ping pong, travel. Res: 18805 E Portola Cir, Box 1, Walnut 91789 Ofc: Patton State Hospital, 3102 E Highland Ave Patton

NGUYEN, HAI DANNY, actuary; b. Feb. 3, 1941, Hue, Vietnam; s. Loi Ngoc and My Pho Nguyen; m. Thu Thi, Jan. 28, 1970; children; Betty, b. 1970; Peggy, b. 1972; Danny, b. 1975; Meggy,b . 1983; edn: BS, Univ. of Paris 1961; MS, Univ. of Saigon 1966. Career: h.s. tchr. 1961-65; dir. plnng. & tng. Dept. of Youth, Vietnam 1965-68; prof. electromechanics Mil. Acad. of Vietnam 1968-70; coll. profl., Saigon 1970-75; v.p ops. The Hartman Gp. Inc. 1975-79; pres. Corp. Adminstrs. Inc. 1979--; mgr. Western Union Agcy. of Westminster City & actuary chief The Hartman Gp. Inc. 1975-79; tng. h.s. officials of Vietnam Govt. for rural devel. 1966-68; awards: Tng. Medal, Vietnam Army 1969; mem: Catholic Council in Vietnam in Charge of Explanation of Vatican Council (dir.); works: tng. work & books for Vietnam Officials (32,00 agents); mil: capt. Vietnam Army, Mil. Acad. of Dalat; Catholic; rec: construction, gardening. Res: 16235 Mt Gustin Fountain Valley 92708 Ofc: Corporate Administrators Inc., 9156 Bolsa Ave Westminster 92683

NGUYEN, LOC THE, hospital administrator; b. Sept. 5, 1935, Saigon, Vietnam, nat. 1981; s. Hia Van and Xi Thi (Dao) N.; m. Phi Ma, Aug. 31, 1980; edn: BA, Saigon Univ. Faculty of Letters, 1957; Master in Hosp. Adm., Baylor Univ. 1967; PhD cand. 1983. Lic. Physical Therapist 1976; lic. Nursing Home Adminstr. Career: chief Medical Service Corps (MSC), Office of the Surgeon Gen., Republic of Vietnam Armed Forces, until 4/1975; press. opr. RCA Records Plant, Hollywood 1975-76; phys. therapist Berkley East Convalescent Hosp., Santa Monica 1976--; hosp. adminstr. and nursing home adminstr. cons. for private hosp. projects; mem. Am. Coll. of Nursing Home Adminstrs. 1982; US Cong. Advisory Bd.; mil: col. MSC, RVNAF, decorated Knight of National Order, 30 medals; Republican; rec: tennis, teaching fencing, reading. Res: 501 N. Venice Blvd, 21, Venice 90291 Ofc: Berkley Conv. Hospital 2021 Arizona Ave Santa Monica 90404

NGUYEN, SANG VAN, manufacturing manager; b. Nov. 11, 1950, Saigon, Vietnam; came to USA 1975, nat. 1983; parents: Ho Van and Tan Mai Nguyen; edn: BA in edn. Van Hanh Univ., Vietnam. Career: manufacturing mgr. Power Transistor Co., Torrance 1976--, personnel splst.; mil: 1st lt. 1973-75; Budhist; rec: reading, music, outdoor activities. Res: 15720-1/2 Freeman Ave Lawndale 90260 Ofc: Alan Bradley Co. 800 W. Carson St Torrance 90502

NGUYEN, THU THE, chiropractor; b. July 7, 1935, Vietnam, nat. 1981; s. Chung Tac and Thoa Thi (Tran) N.; m. Phuong Ngo, Jan. 4, 1960; children: Thuyen, b. 1963; Huy, b. 1965; Nang, b. 1971; Richard, b. 1975; Phan The Daniel, b. 1982; edn: 2nd Lt, Dalat Mil. Acad., Vietnam 1954; BA, Saigon Univ. 1962; AA, Black Hawk Coll. 1977; BA, St. Ambrose Coll. 1981; DC, Palmer Coll. of Chiropractic 1981. Career: in Vietnam: platoon leader and co. cmdr. 6th Airborne Battalion 1955-57; 1st Lt., 34th Mortar C Co. Comdr. and Chief, G5 of 22nd Infan. Div. 1957-63; Capt. Intell., Chief Indoctrination Sector 1963-67; Maj., asst. of Deputy Chief of Staff of Op. of Third Corps and Third Mil. Region 1967-70; Col., Chief of Psychol. Warfare Third Corps and Third Mil. Region 1970-72; Di-An Dist. Chief and Sub-Sector Comdr. of Bien Hoa Province, 1972-75; came to USA as refugee, 1975; student, security guard Davenport (Ia.) Art Gallery 1975-81; Doctor of Chiropractic, Garden Grove, Calif. 1981--. Decorated Order National 4th gr. with palm, Army Distinguished 1st gr., 6 Gallantry w/gold, silver stars, 12 other mil. awards; US Army Commendn., Repub. of China Army Merit Decoration. Mem. Internat., Amer., Calif. chiropractic assns.; Buddhist. Res: 2454 Medford Pl Fullerton 92635 Ofc: 10244 Westminster Ave Garden Grove 92643

NICHOLAS, IRVIN DURAND, JR., insurance executive, consultant; b. May 14, 1937, Pryor, Okla.; s. Irvin D. and Helen M. (Milroy) N.; m. Sigrid Knudson, 1960; children: Jim, b. 1969; Amy, b. 1972; Mike, b. 1974; edn: BS, Ore. State Univ. 1961; MBA, Golden Gate Univ. 1974. Career: fin. analyst UC systemwide, Berkeley 1965-69; ins. & risk mgr. 1969-75; v.p. Fred S. James & Co. of Calif., San Francisco 1975-80; sr. v.p. 1980-83; exec. v.p. 1983--; guest lectr. risk mgmt. UC Grad. Sch. of Bus. 1974, 75; pres. Univ. Risk & Ins. Assn. 1975, dir. 1973, 74; mem: Calif. Hosp. Assn. Inst. Mgmt. Com.; Am. water Works Assn.; Risk & Ins. Mgmt. Soc.; Univ. Risk & Ins. Mgmt.; Am. Risk & Ins. Assn.; Alpha Tau Omega; Olympic Club; publs: arts. in profl. publs.; Managing the Library Fire Risk, 1975; Medical Profl. Liability Risk Mgmt. Guidelines, 1974; Accountants Profl. Liability, 1980; mil: capt. USMC 1961-64. Res: 120 Montecito Crescent Walnut Creek 94596 Ofc: Fred S. James & Co., One Embarcadero Ctr San Francisco 94111

NICHOLS, JAMES DAVID, lawyer/rancher; b. Dec. 20, 1944, Los Angeles; s. Robert Booth and Barbara Louise (McLean) N.; m. Dana, Sept. 2, 1966; children: Brandon, b. 1970; Amy, b. 1974; Lori, b. 1980; edn: BS, Abilene Christian Univ. 1968; JD, Southwestern Univ. Sch. of Law 1975. Career: radio announcer (disc jockey) Knot Radio, Prescott, Ariz. 1969-70; location asst. Stanley Kramer Prodns. 1970-71; trial lawyer Bonne, Jones, Bridges, Mueller & O'Keefe Profl. Corp. 1975-80; partner 1980--; pres. Nichols Land & Cattle Co. Inc., Prescott, Ariz. 1983--; instr. bus. law Los Angeles Unif. Sch. Dist. 1980-; honors: Counsel, Internat. Coll. of Surgeons, US Sect.; mem: Christian Legal Soc.; Am. Bd. Trial Advocs.; Los Angeles Riding & Polo Club; Am., Calif. & L.A. Bar Assns.; Assn. of So. Calif. Defense Counsel; Sertoma; Pittsburgh Inst. of Legal Med.; Delta Theta Phi; publs: in Am. Law Inst. 1982; Republican; Christian; rec: ranching. Res: 644 S Reese Pl Burbank 91506 Ofc: Bonne, Jones, Bridges, Mueller & O'Keeye Profl. Corp., 6005 Commonwealth Ave, 17th Flr, Los Angeles 90005

NICKEL, THOMAS ROY, editor, publisher, author; b.Nov. 8, 1900, Everton, Mo.; s. James Benjamin and Clara Ellen (Collins) Nickel); m. Fannabelle Ford, July 29, 1927; m. 2d. Ruth Dowell, Aug. 13, 1961; children: Robert Bruce b. 1928, Sharon June b. 1932, William Wallace Wallace b. 1934, James Douglas b. 1936; edn: AB, Southwest Mo. State Univ. 1927; postgrad. stu., Tibetan Language, UC Berkeley 1944-5. Career: sold first news story to Saturday Blade, Chgo., 1912 (at age 12); owner/ed./pub. Dade County Journal, Everton, Mo. 1917-23; published Midget Mag. (World's Smallest Periodical) 1923-27, invented Nickeliner; staff mem. SMSU, Springfield, Mo. 1924-27 (student dir. publicity; ed. Southwest Standard 1924-27; assoc. ed. Ozarko, sch. annual); asst. gen. mgr. Haynes Corp. Publishers, Los Angeles 1927-30; produced promotional literature for founding of cities of San Clemente and Atascadero, 1928; Notary Public and Publicist, Hollister, Mo. 1932-36; founded Union Mission, Springfield, Mo. 1937; co-founder Full Gospel Business Men's Fellowship Internat. and Voice Mag., 1962; current: founder/pres. Great Commission Internat. and editor Testimony Mag., Hanford; staff mem. Monterey Vistaj Christian Sch., Watsonville, Ca. 1950-55; published: Christianity, All the Recorded Words of Jesus Christ (1925), In Those Days, Upon All Flesh, Miracles Do Happen, Dying Buddhist Korean, God and America (1962-72), Azusa Street Outpouring, The Very Beginning (1981); honors: Medal of Merit presented by Pres. Ronald Reagan 1982, charter mem. Pres. Task Force; Israel State Medal for 25 years service to Israel (1982); mem: Golden Bears, SMSU (life); The Pres.'s Club; founder Hanford chpt. FGBMFI; ofcl. advisor Women's

Aglow Fellowship Internat., Lemoore; mil: Civilian Employee as field ofc. mgr. on Defense Projects at Benicia, Woodland, and Arbuckle, Calif. and prodn. of blood plasma for Armed Forces at Cutter Labs., Berkeley 1943-48; Republican; Assemblies of God; rec: writing, philately. REs: 1300 Whitmore Hanford 93230 Ofc: Great Commission International, 1033 West 7th, Hanford 93230

NICOLAS, JEAN GERARD, physician; b. July 23, 1935, Jacmel, Haiti; s. Henri and Livie (Cambry) N.; m. Deborah Kleinberg, 1976; children: Mischa b. 1977, Sascha b. 1980; edn: BA, Lycee Pinchinat, 1954; MD, Faculte de Med. & Pharm., Port-au-Prince 1960. Career: rotating intern University Hosp., Port-au-Prince, 1959-60; rural medicine, Haiti 1960-61; res. pediatrics Univ. Hosp., Port-au-Prince 1961-62; res. ped., chief resident Lincoln Hosp. and Albert Einstein Coll. of Med., NYC 1962-65; fellow ped-cardiology, Downstate Univ. Med. Sch. and Kings City Hosp., NYC 1965-66, Yale Univ. and Yale New Haven Hosp., Conn. 1966-68; maj. US Army, Fort Ord Hosp. 1968-70; pvt. practice, ped. and ped-cardiology, also clin. instr. in ped., Stanford Univ. 1970-73; res. diagnostic radiology, Stanford Univ. and Stanford Med. Ctr., 1973-76; Cert. Am. Bd. of Pediatrics 1967, Am. Bd. of Radiology 1977; American Coll. of Radiology (appl. pend.); lic. Calif., Conn., New York, Wash., Ore.; mem. AMA, Santa Clara County Med. Soc., 1970-73; publ: Digitalis Tolerance in Young Puppies, J. Pediatrics (1970); rec: music (listener, performer flute & cello). Res: 2984 Tepusquet Canyon Rd Santa Maria 93454

NIELSON, LYNNE CATHERINE, computer co. executive; b. Aug. 8, 1955, Castro Valley; d. Oliver Andrew and Helen Barbara (Cadil) N.; edn: Mass. Commun. Maj., CSU Hayward 1973-78. Career: bus./ advtg. mgr. Daily Pioneer newspaper, CSU Hayward 1974-78; computer ops. mgr. Daughtney's Dept. Store, Castro Valley 1974-78; customer svc. mgr. Mini Systems Inc., Pleasanton 1978--; consulting, devel. curriculum & instrn. IBM personal computers; pub. spkg. engagements; cons. purchasing- implementing a computer; mem: Alpha Phi Gamma; Alpha Phi Omega; Diablo Valley IBM PC Users Gp.; KQED pub. tv.; Republican; Lutheran; rec: computers, backpacking, gourmet cooking. Res: 3467-D Orchard Hill Ct Lafayette 94549 Ofc: Mini Systems Inc., 5726 Sonoma Dr Pleasanton 94566

NIES, BOYD ARTHUR, physician; b. Jan. 12, 1935, Orange; s. Arthur J. and Mary Dora (Sheffer) N.; m. Helen Salter, July 28, 1957; children: Nancy, b. 1958; Linda, b. 1961; Boyd Jr., b. 1971; edn: AB, Stanford Univ. 1956; MD, 1959; Bd. Cert., Internal Med. (1966), Hematology (1972), & Med. Oncology (1975), Am. Bd. of Internal Med. Career: intern in med. UCLA 1959-60; asst. res. med. 1960-61; assoc. res. Wadsworth VA Hosp., Los Angeles 1961-62; clin. assoc. Nat. Cancer Inst., Bethesda, Md. 1961-62; Fellow Hematology, Stanford 1964-65; pvt. practice, internal med. & hematology, Redlands 1965 68; pvt. practice hematology &med. oncology, San Bernardino 1968--, chief of staff St. Bernardine Hosp. 1974; asst. clin. prof. UCLA 1971-82; honors: Phi Beta Kappa; Alpha Omega Alpha; mem: fellow, Am. Coll. of Physicians; Am. Med. Assn.; Am. Soc. of Clin. Oncology; Am. Soc. of Internal Med.; Am. Soc. of Hematology; St. Bernardine Hosp., San Bernardino (bd. dirs. 1975-7); Riverside- San Bernardino Co. Blood Bank (bd. dirs. 1984-); puls: num. arts. in med. journs.; mil: surgeon, US PHS 1962-64; Methodist; rec: philately, tennis, photog. Res: 645 E Mariposa Dr Redlands 92373 Ofc: Inland Hematology Oncology Medical Group Inc., 399 E Highland Ave, Ste 201, San Bernardino 92404

NIGRA, JOHN OSCAR, geological engineer; b. May 26, 1913, El Paso, Tex.; s. John B. and Pauline (Herrera) Nigra; m. Helena Lidonnici, June 29, 1940; 1 son, Roy, b. 1957; edn: BA, Univ. of Tex. Coll. of Mines 1937; MS, Calif. Inst. of Tech. 1946, PhD cand. 1947; ScD, Nat. Univ. of Mex. 1951; grad. stu. Tex. A&M 1937-8, Univ. Mich. 1940, UC Berkeley 1943-4, Claremont/Pomona 1947; Profl. Engr., Regis. Geologist, Cert. Engrg. Geologist, Jr. Coll. Tchr. (life), state of Calif. Career: positions from jr. geologist to prin. geologist spec. in mining geol., petroleum geol, engring. geol. 1937--, domestically with Phelps-Dodge, Sonoma Mining Co., and Barnsdall Oil cos., abroad with Lago Petroleum (Standard of N.J.) in Venezuela, Tex. Petroleum in Colombia, Pemex in Mex., Aramco, NY and Saudi Arabia; jr. coll. tchg. in geological and physical scis., petroleum tech., plane surveying; prof. Engring Coll., Tulane Univ., New Orleans 1951-55, Engring Coll., Baghdad, Iraq 1955-56, Univ. of Rio Grande do Sul, Brazil 1957-58; currently consulting geologist and engr.; cons. to Henningson, Durham & Richardson, Ecoscis Div., Santa Barbara 1977-80 (geotech. baseline investigation for MX Ground Mobile CES, Dept. of AF (SAMSO). Awards: 3 NSF study grants, 1958-61; Fulbright scholar/lectr. in Iraq 1954-5; US State Dept. Smith-Mundt lectr. in Brazil. Mem: Am. Soc. Mining & Petroleum Engrs., Am. Assn. Petroleum Geologists, Geol. Soc. of Am., ASCE, US Power Squadrons. Publs: num. arts., profl. papers on earth sci. subjects; arts. on boating, flying, navigation in nat. mags. Republican. Catholic. rec: ocean cruising, cross-country flying (lic. comml. pilot/flt.instr.), sabre fencing. Res: 3326 Deronda Dr. Hollywood 90068.

NIJSSEN, LEONARD ALEC ROBERT, optometrist-low vision specialist; b. July 13, 1936, Amsterdam, Holland, nat. 1972; s. Bernardus Johannes and Anna Dorothea (deMoor) N.; div.; 1 dau. Carolyn Frances, . 1964; edn: Optometrist, Dutch Sch. of Opt. 1956, Victoria Univ. of N.Z. 1962; Low Vision Splst., Keeler Low Vision Clinic (London) 1980; Calif. lic. Aurologist (1970). Career: optometrist Looman Optometry, Zandvoort, Holland 1954-58; Cocks & Newell Optometrists, Wellington, New Zealand 1959-64; Messier & True Corp., Opthalmologists, 1966-70; self empl. 1970--, splst. in low vision, owner/pres. Nijssen Low Vision and Hearing Center, Modesto (formerly in San Bruno); consulting, guest lectr.; organizer national non-profit philanthropic orgn. to aid the partially sighted; num. media appearances radio, t.v., newspapers nat.; works: Hearing Loss and Hearing Aids (1983); Low Vision (1982); Biorhythmic Cycles (1978); 4 books on eyesight in progress; metaphysical book; mem. Lions Club (hearing & sight dir. 1976-78); mil: 2d lt. Dutch Medical Corps; Republican; rec: metaphysical studies, photog., equestrian. Res: 15277 Cavalieri Rd Sonora 95370 (POB 173, Standard 95373) Ofc: Nijssen Low Vision and Hearing Center, 3025-F McHenry Ave Modesto 95350

NIKOLCHEV, NIKOLA DIMITROV, mechanical engineer; b. Aug. 20, 1923, Pazardjic, Bulgaria, nat. 1977; s. Dimitre Georgiev and Maria Dimitrova (Angelova) N.; m. Grigorina, Sept. 27, 1952; children: Julian,b . 1954; Rina, b. 1956; edn: BS, State Univ., Sofia-Bilg. 1953; Reg. Profl. Engr. (Mech.), Calif. 1983. Career: State Eng. & Constrn. Co., Sofia-Blg. 1953-68 (except 1961-63, 1965-67); Mongolia State Eng. Ofc. 1961-63, 1965-67; Textile Co., Lumumbashy, Congo, Zaire 1969; Stone & Webster Eng., Boston Ofc. 1970-72; Bechtel Corp., San Francisco 1972-80; mech. engr. power & marine divs. Brown & Root Inc., S.F. 1980--; mem: Am. Soc. of Heating, Refrig. & A-C Engrs.; rec: gardening. Res: 6185 Alhambra Ave Pleasant Hill 94523 Ofc: Brown & Root Inc., 200 Porter Dr San Ramon 94583

NILES, WILLIAM LAWSON, business service owner; b. Nov. 19, 1925, Port Jervis, NY; s. Enos McKinley and Florence (Fuller) N.; m. Barbara Slick, Jan. 24, 1970; children: Nancy, b. 1953; Diana, b. 1956; edn: BBA, Univ. of Miami 1950; CSU Northridge 1980-83. Career: fin. analyst TRW, Los Angeles 1954; fin. adminstr. Aerospace Corp., L.A. 1961; fin. adminstr. Xerox Corp., L.A. 1868; adminstr. Ventura Comm. Coll. Dist. 1974-83; owner DGA Bus. Svc., Santa Paula 1983--; mem: Nat. Assn. of Accts., Ventura Co. (pres. 1976-77); mil: cpl. US Army Engrs. 1944-46, ETO Ribbon, 2 campaigns. Republican; Protestant; rec: flying, golf. Res: 6322 Fremont St Ventura Blvd 93003n Ofc: DGA Business Service, 51 Cessna Taxi Santa Paula 93060

NISHIMOTO, RICHARD YOSHIO, advertising/design firm creative director; b. June 27, 1948, Chgo.; s. Tateo Bud and Hisako Frances (Tanaka) N.; edn: Chicago Acad. of Fine Arts 1966-68, Univ. of Ill. 1968-69; BA, Art Inst. of Chgo. 1972-74; BA, Ill. Inst. of Tech./Inst. of Design, 1974-76. Career: dir. of photog., prodn. mgr., acct. exec. Nobart, Inc., Chgo. 1972-76; art director, production dir. Meltzer, Aron & Lemon Inc., San Francisco 1976-78, Foote, Cone & Belding/Honig, S.F. 1978-79, Steve Jacobs Design, Palo Alto 1979-80; director of operations, art dir., prodn. dir. Tycer, Fultz, Bellack, Palo Alto 1980; creative dir. Summit Workshops Inc., Redwood City 1980-82, cons. 1978-80; v.p./prin./creative dir. Quintessential Enterprises, Inc. San Carlos, 1982, San Francisco 1983--; guest lectr. UCB 1976-78; honors: Clifton B. Cates Jr. Award, Chicago, 1974; mem: Art directors Club 1972-, Summit Workshops Inc. 1978-, Marine Corps assn. 1969-, publs. contbr. arts. Metamorphoses Mag. (1982), Holiday Celebration (1978-82); mil: #7 GySgt., USMC, 1969-71, Navy Commendn. medal; Democrat; Buddhist; rec: aikido (a martial art), 1st deg. black belt. Res: 129 Baker St San Francisco 94117 Ofc: Quintessential Ent. Inc. 2400 Pacific Ave, Ste 601, San Francisco 94115

NISSELSON, JANET, educational psychologist; b. Jan. 15, 1918, NYC; d. Max and Clara (Albert) Watnik; m. Cyril Barnert Jr., Mar. 1, 1940, dec. 1947; m. 2d. Michael M. Nisselson, July 1, 1954; children: Cyril Barnert III, b. 1942; Anthony L. Barnert, b. 1943; edn: BA, Hunter Coll. 1938; MS, City Coll. of NY 1956; PhD, Pacific Western 1977; attended, Columbia Univ., NYC & Yeshiva Univ. NYC; Edn. Psych.; Cert. Hypnotherapist; Family Child Counselor. Career: intern child psychology Mt. Sinai Hosp., NYC 1957-58; psychological cons. NYC Childrens Svcs. 1958-59; staff psychol. Psychiat. Clinic for Children, Stamford, Conn. 1961-64; supvg. clin. psychol. Comm. Mental Health, Delaware Co. Mental Health Clinic, Walton, NY 1970-74; senior psychologist, NY Prisons 1975-76; pvt. practice, Granada Hills, Calif. 1976--; tchr. Coll. Alto Canyons, Valencia; volunteer work, Battered Women; mem: Am. & Calif. Psychological Assns. Address: 17163 Courbet St Granada Hills 91344

NOBLE, ROGER SPENCER, company president; b. Feb. 26, 1925, Cleveland, Oh.; s. Phillip Edgar and Mary Martha (Meiche) N.; m. Marilyn Klein, 1977; children: Ronilee, b. 1943; Philip, b. 1943; Mark, b. 1957; Robert, b. 1953; Laura, b. 1954; Nancy, b. 1956; Tim, b. 1958; Gary, b. 1962; edn: BBA, Case Western Reserve Univ. 1949. Career: sales engr./ partner Jackson Machinery, Cleveland, Oh. 11958-62; sales engr. Addy & Whittney Inc., Cleveland 1962-72; branch mgr. Cincinnati Inc., Alhambra 1972-74; eastern regional mgr. Given Internat., Compton 1974-75; sales engr. Am. Machinery & Engring. Inc., El Toro 1975-78; western regl. mgr. Agietron Corp., Irvine 1978-81; founder/ pres. R.S. Nobel Machinery Corp., Irvine 1981--; Soc. Calif. rep., Agietron Corp., Aceira CNC Milling Machines & Machining Ctrs, Scherr- Tumico Comparators, Trinco Bead Blasters, Heidehain Digital Readout, Advanced Machine Design Co. (billet shears & hydraulic presses, etc.); mem:Irvine CofC (v.p.); Lakeshore Maint. Assn.; Nat. Tooling & Michining Assn.; Am. Metal Stamping Assn.; mil: US Army Air Force; Republican (Nat. Com.); Presbyterian; rec: swimming, golf. Res: 8 Lakeview Dr Irvine 92714 Ofc: R.S. Noble Machinery Corp., 197872 Sky Park Circle, Ste D, Irvine 92714

NOLL, HJORDIS ALBERTA, real estate broker; b. July 16, 1909, Billings, Mont.; d. Fredric S. and Anna (Nelson) Westover; m. Ray Noll, June 10, 1939; 1 son: Roger, b. 1940; edn: USC 1929-30. Career: co- owner Noll Realty, San Marcos 1962-68; owner/ broker 1968--; coord./ chmn. orientation pgm. Vista Bd. Realtors 1973-76; 29th dist. chmn. Home Protection Com., Calif. Assn. Realtors; honors: Realtors of the Yr., Vista Bd. Realtors 1974; Woman of th Yr., San Marcos CofC 1982; Proclamation for Pub. Svc., San Diego Co. Bd. Supvrs. 1984; mem: Vista Bd. Realtors (pres. 1975); San Marcos CofC (v.p 183);

Palamarcos Republican Women Fedn. (pres. 1983); Calif. Assn. Realtors (dir. 1974-75); Soroptimists Internat., San Marcos (v.p. 1978); San Marcos Real Estate Assn. (pres. 1978); Republican; rec: antiques, travel. Address: Noll Realty, 650-276 Rancho Santa Fe Rd San Marco 92069

NONG, painter-sculptor; b. Oct. 10, 1930, Seoul, Korea, nat. 1958. Career: pres. Nong Gallery, San Francisco; painter, sculptor; major one-man exhibs. include: Fort Lauderdale (Fla.) Mus. of the Arts, Santa Barbara Mus. of Art, E.B. Crocker Art Gal. (Sacto.), 1965; Georgia Mus. of Art (Athens, Ga.), El Paso (Tex.) Mus. of Art, 1967; Galerie Vallombreuse (Baritz, Fr.) 1970; Nat. Mus. of History (Taipei, Taiwan), Nihonbashi Gal. (Tokyo), Shinsegye Gal. (Seoul) 1971; Nat. Mus. of Modern Art (Seoul), S.F. Zool. Garden, 1975; Tongin Art Gal. (Seoul) 1978; Hartman Rare Art (Dallas) 1981; Korean Cultural Service (L.A.), Choon Chu Gal. (Seoul) 1982; group exhibs. incl. Smithsonian Instn., 1961, Conn. Acad. of Fine Arts, Charles and Emma Frye Art Mus. (Seattle), 1962, Denver Art Mus., 1965, Jersey City Mus., Univ. of Santa Clara (Calif.), 1967, UC Berkeley, 1968, Oakland Art Mus., Gal. des Champs Elysees (Paris), Nt. Sculpture Soc. (NYC), Taipei Provincial Mus., 1971, Gal. Hexagramme (Paris), 1975, Gal. de Arte Misrachi (Mexico City) 1979; rep. in permanent collections: E.B. Crocker Art Gal., Nat. Mus. Hist. (Taipei), Mus. Nat. des Beaux-Arts (Monte Carlo), Inst. de Cultura Puertoriquena (San Juan), Nat. Gal. Modern Art (New Delhi), Asian Art Mus. (S.F.), Nat. Mus. Modern Art and Nat. Mus. (Seoul), Santa Barbara Mus. Art, Consulate Gen. Rep. of Korea (S.F.), Presidential Palace (Seoul), Anchorage Hist. and Fine Arts Mus., Bankers Mtg. Co. of Calif. (S.F.), IBM (San Mateo), Security Pac. Nat. Bank (S.F.), Govt. of the People's Repub. of China (Beijing, and Shanghai), Govt. of Peru, Museo De Arte (Lima), The Korean Emb. (Lima, Peru). Honors: letters of appreciation, Govt. of Repub. of Korea; Cert. of Distinguished Achievement, State of Calif.; Proclamation City and County of San Francisco. Mem: chmn. S.F.-Seoul Sister City Com.; commnr. Asian Art Commn.; hon. mem. Art Soc. Repub. of China; patents: chest of drawers, building; mil: served with AUS and USAF, 1956-60. Res: 999 Green St, 2701, San Francisco 94133. Ofc: Nong Gallery Inc. Hyatt on Union Sq. San Francisco 94108

NORDBY, JUDY LYNNE, real estate co. owner; b. Mar. 6, 1952, Portland, Ore.; d. Herbert Howard and Franceen Evelyn (Mason) P.; m. Frank Nordby, May 3, 1981; children: Jack, b. 1979; Michelle, b. 1983; edn: BA, math., UC Davis 1973; BA, psych., 1973; R.E. Broker, Calif. 1980. Career: records asst. Pacific Telephone, Sacto. 1970; computer pgmmr. Data Mgmt. Assn., Colo. Springs, Colo. 1973-74; founder/ owner The Computery, Vacaville 1977; founder/ owner King Coll. of Real Estate 1975-81; owner Judy Nordby Real Estate, No. Highlands 1981--; honors: CSF Life Mem.; Calif. State Scholarship (4 yrs.); Cal Aggie Alumni Scholarship; Soroptomist scholarship nom.; mem: Nat. Assn. Realtors; Mu Alpha Theta (pres.); Am. Field Svc. (pres.); Chess Club (ofcr.); Fremont Presbyterian Ch. Tennis Team; Grace Baptist Choir Womens Leaders; works: devel. record-keeping sys. for Pacific Telephone 1970; computed new data factor, bearing authors name, graphics/ plotter efficiency, 1974; author, On-Hand Inventory Package, Northstar Computer 1977; author, text books & workbooks for exclusive use, King Coll. of Real Estate 1975-81; Democrat; Protestant; rec: author, photog. Address: Judy Nordby Real Estate, 6508 Larry Way, No. Highlands 95660

NORMINTON, THOMAS M., lawyer; b. Sept. 21, 1948, Los Angeles; s. Vernon Thomas and La Mae (Maggard) N.; edn: UC Irvine 1966-67; AB, UCLA 1970; JD, UC Berkeley Boalt Hall 1973. Career: assoc. Kaplan, Livingston, Goodwin, Berkowitz & Selvin 1973-75; partner Levy & Normington 1975--; co-owner, Les Agnes Restaurant, Santa Monica 1981--; honors: Outstanding graduating senior 1970, UCLA, undergrad. student body pres. UCLA 1969-70, Phi Beta Kappa; mem: Calif, L.A. Co. & Beverly Hills Bar Assns.; UCLA Alumni Assn. (v.p. 1975-78); UCLA Found.; Santa Maria Hist. Soc.; Democrat; Presbyterian. Res: 201 Ocean Ave, No. 505B, Santa Monica 90402 Ofc: Levy & Norminton, 815 Moraga Dr Los Angeles 90049

NORRIS, KATHLEEN ANN, lawyer; b. Feb. 3, 1943; Kansas City, Mo.; d. William Wayne and Bernice Irene (Moline) N.; children: Clayton Albert Taylor, b. 1962; Craig Alan Taylor, b. 1965; Don Norris Udall, b. 1972; Sara Elizabeth Udall, b. 1974; edn: BS, Western State Univ. Coll. of Law 1979; JD, 1980; admitted to practice, State Bar of Calif. 1981. Career: atty., sole practitioner, Corona del Mar; honors: assoc. exec. ed. Law Review, Western State Univ. Coll. of Law 1979-80; Am. Jurisprudence Awd., Contracts 1978; mem: Am., Calif. & Orange Co. Bar Assns.; Calif. & Orange Co. Women Lawyers; Delta Theta Phi; Newport Harbor Republican Women; DAR, William Cabell Chpt.; Zonta Club Int'l., Newport Harbor; Hoag Meml. Presbyn. Hosp. Aux.; Pacific Chorale; Orange Co. Philharmonic Soc., Beacon Bay; Republican; Protestant; rec: softball, tennis, photog. Res: 406 Iris Ave Corona del Mar 92625 Ofc: Atty. at Law, 2721 E Pacific Coast Hwy Corona del Mar 92625

NORTON, BENJAMIN CRANER, JR., business consultant, city mayor; b. Nov. 8, 1920, Los Angeles; s. Benjamin Craner and Grace (Ettlinger) Norton; grandson of Samuel Norton, Polish emigre and early Los Angeles citizen, 1850s; m. Rose Berger, May 8, 1955; chil: Benjamin Craner, III, b.1945, Phillip Adam Savenick, b. 1952; edn: BS in bus.adm., USC 1943. Career: with Norton Bros. & Morris, Inc. (family textile bus. estab. 1904), Los Angeles 1946-58, pres. 1952-58; co-founder Family Trusts (comml., indsl. real estate), L.A. 1953-, sole Trustee dba Norton Bldg. Co., 1955--; bus. cons., 1955--; Public Service: elected councilman, City of Beverly Hills, Apr. 1980-, vice mayor 1982-83, mayor 1983-84; dir., chpsn. Sanitation Dist. #4, Co. of Los Angeles, 1982-83; dir. City of Beverly Hills Parking Authority 1982-83. Honors: 1st pl.(winning over 50,000 entries statewide) high sch. driver safety essay contest spons. by So.Calif.Auto.Club; two Interfrat. Council scholarship awards, 1942, 43; Alpha Delta Sigma nat. profl. advt. frat.; bus. mgr./asst. sports ed. El Rodeo Yearbook, USC; Pi Kappa Alpha social frat.; mem. First Century Families; mil: lt.j.g. USNR 1942-46, decorated Asia-Pac. Area (1 star), Am. Area, WWII Victory; rec: golf. Res: 213 S. Rodeo Dr. Beverly Hills 90212 ofc: Norton Building Co. 757 S. Los Angeles St. Ste.400 Los Angeles 90014

NORTON, MONICA LEE, certified public accountant; b. July 12, 1955, Whittier; d. Gordon Austin and Virginia Lee (Cornett) Christensen; m. Thomas E. Norton, June. 11, 1977; 1 son: Brett,b. 1983; edn: AA, Coll. of the Sequoias 1975; BS, CSU Fresno 1977; CPA, Calif. 1982. Career: asst. to the controller, auto purchasing, Arnold Wiebe Inc., Visalia 1977; controller/ acct. AAA Alarm & Lighting, Visalia 1977-79; jr. staff acct. N.N. Sheklian, CPA, Visalia 1979-80; sr. supvg. staff acct. 1981-82; adminstrv. partner 1982--; awards: Int'l. Order of Job's Daughters Degree of Royal Purple 1981; mem: Am. Inst. of CPAs; Calif. Soc. CPAs; Am. Soc. of Women Accts.; Visalia CofC (Diplomats Com.; Christmas Tree Auction Com.); Republican; Episcopal (Choir); rec: needlework, aerobics, skiing. Res: 1048 Rova Rd Visalia 93277 Ofc: N.N. Sheklian & Co., CPAs,, 201 N Court St Visalia 93291

NORTON, PHILLIP OWEN, lawyer; b. Aug. 5, 1934, Portland, Maine; s. Patrick J. and Edith M. Norton; m. Joyce A., Feb. 19, 1955; children: Jeanne, b. 1956; Patricia, b. 1958; Julia, b. 1960; Peter, b. 1961; Patrick, b. 1963; Paul, b. 1966; edn: AA, Foothill Jr. Coll. 1961; BA, San Jose State Univ. 1971; JD, Univ. of Santa Clara 1976; admitted to practice, State of Calif. 1976; Intermediate Peace Ofcrs. Standards & Tng. Cert., Calif. 1967; Adv. Peace Ofcrs. Standards & Tng. Cert., Calif. 1968. Career: physical edn. instr. Maine State Sch. for the Deaf, Portland, Maine 1954 ; comml. note splst. Am. Trust Co., San Francisco 1955-58; police ofcr. City of Palo Alto 1958-61; pub. safety ofcr. City of Sunnyvale 1961; police ofcr., sgt., lt., City of San Jose 1961-82, ret.; atty. at law, pvt. practitioner, Milpitas 1976--; pres. San Jose Peace Ofcrs. Assn. 1970-71; cons. Pub. employees negotiations Police Emp. Orgns. 1970-73; guest tchr. San Jose State Univ. Pub. Svc. & Admin. 1982-; Peace Ofcrs. Research Assn. of Calif., legal defense fund, Sacto.-Fund atty. 1977-; Calif. Union of Saftey Employees, cons. atty. 1981-; mem: San Jose Peace Ofcrs. Assn. (pres. 1970-71); Peace Ofcrs. Research Assn. of Calif.; Am., Calif. & Santa Clara Co. Bar Assn.; Catholic; rec: genealogy, photog. Address: Phillip O. Norton, Esq., 1466 Saratoga Dr Milpitas 95035

NOTAR, BETTY BRIDGES, educator; b. Dec. 7, 1923, New Orleans, La.; d. Daniel Edward and Helen Ethaline (Bridges) Sanders; m. Charles A. Notar, Sept. 1, 1945; children: Cathie Jo, b. 1946; Bonnie Kae, b. 1951; Toni Ann, b. 1957; Remi Su, b. 1961 (dec.; edn: BS, Seattle Univ. 1949; MEd, Univ. of Wash. 1966; PhD, US Internat. Univ. 1975. Career: secondary tchr. Quilcene (Wash.) High Sch. 1949-50; elem. tchr. Edmonds (Wash.) Grade Sch., 1952-54; sec. tchr. Mojave (Calif.) High Sch. 1955-59, counselor 1959-78, dir. of guidance 1978--; honors: Phi Delta Kappa, Pi Lambda Theta, NDEA Scholarship, Univ. of Wash. 1960; mem: Am. Sch. Counselors Assn.; Am. Personnel & Guidance Assn.; Nat. Vocational Guidance Assn.; Calif. Counseling & Guidance Assn.; Nat. & Calif. Edn. Assns.; Mojave Faculty Assn.; Kern City Juvenile Justice Commn.; Kern Co. Delinquency Prevention Commn.; Order of Eastern Satr, P.M.; Mojave Mineralogical Assn.; World Congress of Profl. Hynotists; works: Relationship of Self Concepts Congruence to Achievement of High School Students, 1975; mil: PFC USMC; Democrat; Methodist; rec: lapidary, travel. Res: 2038 Trinity St Mojave 93501 Ofc: Mojave High School, 15732 O St Mojave 93501

NOTT, ROBERT MARSHALL, real estate broker; b. Sept. 9, 1954, Bethesda, Md.; s. Dwight Dee and Muriel Louise (Marsh) N.; m. Janet Nabiha Buck, Apr. 10, 1976; children: Christian, b. 1978; Justin, b. 1980; edn: CSU Northridge 1977; R.E. Salesman 1978; R.E. Broker, 1982. Career: gen. mgr. Interact Ltd., Van Nuys 1977; salesman Encino Realty & Investment Co., Encino 1978-79; salesman Main St Real Estate Co., Mammoth Lakes 1979; mgr. 1982; co- wner 1984--; cons. to pvt. investor gps.; bd. dirs. Mammoth Lakes Bd. Realtors 1982; arbitration com. mem svc. awd.; mem: Nat. & Calif. Assn. Realtors; Multi-Million Dollar Club; Arbitration Com.; CofC; mil: midshipman US Naval Acad. 1974-75; Republican; Mammoth Lakes Comm. Ch. (elder); rec: golf, skiing, tennis. Res: POB 1340 Mammoth Lakes 93546 Ofc: Main Street Real Estate Company, POB 90 Mammoth Lakes 93546

NOVAK, GLORIA JEAN, librarian; b. Aug. 31, 1934, Detroit, Mich.; d. Julius and Rose (Bortnick) Berkowitz; m. Stefan Novak, Dec. 27, 1957; 1 dau: Genya, b. 1960; edn: Univ. of Mich. 1952-53; UCLA 1953-54; BA, UC Berkeley 1958; MLS, 1968. Career: admin. asst. McCue & Assoc., Archs., San Francisco 1959-66; head current serials East Asiatic Library, UC Berkeley 1969-71, head Engring. Library 1979-81, library space planning 1972--; library building cons: Johns Hopkins Univ. 1980-, Univ. of Md. 1982-, Mills Coll. 1983-, Naval Postgrad. Acad. Monterey 1983-; mem: Am. Library Assn. (Coll.- Univ. Lib. Bldgs., Bldg. & Equip. Sect., Lib. Bldg. Awds., Lib. Bldg. Cons. List); publs: editor (book), Running Out of Space, 1976; contbg. writer: art., Information Bulletin, Western Association May Libraries (11/81), chpt., Austerity Management in Academic Libraries (1984). Res: 6925 Balsam Way Oakland 94611 Ofc: Univ. of California, Main Library, Berkeley 94720

NOVEY, HAROLD S., physician; b. Sept.20, 1926, Baltimore, Md.; s. Allen and Ree (Snyder) N.; m. Lindsay Chance, July 21, 1972; children: Sharon, b. 1966; Ellen, b. 1973; edn: AB, John Hopkins Univ. 1946; Tchg. Fellowship, biology, USC 1946-47; MD, USC 1951; Clin. Prof. of Med., UC Irvine 1980. Career: acting chief allergy- infect. diseases, US VA Hosp., Long Beach 1957-58; pvt. practice med. 1958-83; clin. instr. med. UCLA 1958-65; asst. clin. prof. med. 1965-71; chief allergy-immunology UC Irvine 1971-82; assoc. clin. prof. med. 1972-80; clin. prof. med. 1980--; editorial bds: Annals of Allergy (1972-); Western Journ. of Med. (1979-84), Immunology & Allergy Practice (1979-), Clinical Reviews, in Allergy (1983-); adv. panel on allergy Calif. Med. Assn. 1974-; bd. dirs. Western Soc. of Allergy & Immunology 1983-; honors: diplomate, Am. Bd. of Internal Med. 1958; diplomate, Am. Bd. of Allergy & Clin. Immunology 1973; mem: Am. Med. Assn.; fellow, Am. Coll. Physicians; fellow, Am. Acad. of Allergy & Immunol.; fellow, Am. Coll. of Allergy; Am. Thoracic Soc.; over 50 publs. in peer revs., med. journs. and books; mil: chief of med. Beale AFB, Calif. 1953-55; rec: sailing, boating. Ofc: Univ. of California Irvine Medical Center, 1010 City Dr S, Orange 92668

NOVICK, WALTER E, real estate lawyer/ investor- developer; b. May 25, 1954, Chgo., Ill.; s. William J. and Clara Ruth (Paul) N.; m. Jo-Ann Schwartz, Dec. 21, 1981; edn: BA, honors, So. Methodist Univ. 1976; JD, Univ. of San Diego 1979; Lic. Atty. & Broker, Calif. 1979. Career: assoc. Lowell & Arthur, Attys. at Law, San Diego 1979-80; real estate investment broker, Grubb & Ellis Co., San Diego 1980-83; pres. Walter E. Novick Co., San Diego 1982--; gen. partner, num. real estate partnerships; cons. foreign investment gps. 1982-; ed. Law Review, Univ. of San Diego 1978-79; 2nd pl., I.H. Prinzmetal Writing Comp. 1979; top salesperson, Grubb & Ellis Co., San Diego 1980-83; mem: Am., Calif. & San Diego Bar Assns.; La Jolla Beach & Tennis Club; publs: medical Malpractice: Arbitrating Disputes, 2 Los Angeles Lawyer 34, 3/79; ed. var. legal arts. pub. San Diego Law Review; Republican; rec: tennis, golf. Res: 6131 La Pintura Dr La Jolla 92037 Ofc: Walter E. Norich Co., 2870 4th Ave, Ste 200, San Diego 92103

NOWACKI, WALTER LEO, professional engineer;b. Apr. 25, 1920, Natrona, Pa.; s. Charles S. and Francis V. (Armacki) N.; m. Joyce Ann Pate, July 4, 1946; children: Gregory b. 1948, Steven b. 1950, Michael b. 1952, Mark b. 1954, Kathleen b. 1959, Jeffrey b. 1961; edn: BSME, Iowa State Univ. 1946; BS indsl. mgmt., Purdue Univ. 1952; MBA, Univ. of Chgo. 1961; Exec. Pgm. (XP-17), Univ. of Chgo. 1961; Environmtl. Engrg., USC (Dept. of Defense) 1969; cert., Ops. Research, USC, 1968. Reg. Profl. Engr., Calif. 1965; Ntional Accreditation as Profl. Engr. 1967. Career: Ensign to Lt. Cmdr. (USNR) US Navy 1939-46; Naval Reserve Medal; supt. Mech. Div., American Maize Products 1946 56; plant supt. Chicago Copper & Chemical, Chgo. 1956 57; Div. engr. The Kroger Co., Chgo. 1957-65; dir. of engring. Los Angeles Div., Market Basket, L.A. 1965-82; pres. Food Facility Engring., La Habra 1983; commanding officer Mobilization Div. 9-12; Pres.'s Council (TAFI) Improving Productivity in Food Indus., USC; listed in Community Leaders of Am. (1973-77), Men of Achievement (1975); mem: Nat. Soc. of Profl. Engineers 1950-83, pres. Am. Inst. of Plant Engrs. 1963, pres. County League of Registered Voters 1956, dir. County Disaster Relief Team 1965, dir./guarantor L.A. Civic Light Opera 1973-75, Soc. of Disabled Veterans (cmdr. 1982), City of Hope (founding mem. Food Industry chpt.); works: Nuclear Defenses for Indsl. Plants (1964), Pgmmg. of Facilities Engineering (1975); Republican; Catholic; rec: Civic Light Opera, Inter-Faith Spiritual Ctr.- Covenant House, Exec. Pgm. Club, golf, fish. Address: Food Facility Engineering Inc. 1901 Arbolita Dr La Habra 90631

NUNIS, DOYCE BLACKMAN,JR., historian-author-educator; b. May 30, 1924, Cedartown, GA; s. Doyce B., Sr. and Winnie Ethel (Morris) Nunis; Edn: B.A., U.C.L.A. 1947; M.S. (educ.), U.S.C., 1950; M.Ed., 1952; Ph.D. (hist.), 1958. Career: teacher, Calif. pub. schs. 1948-51; grad. fellowship, U.S.C., 1951-53; lecturer, Dept. of Amer. Civilization & Institutions, U.S.C., 1953-56; instr. in hist., El Camino Coll., Calif., 1956-59; U.C.L.A., 1959-65; assoc. prof., prof. hist., U.S.C., 1965---; trustee, Santa Barbara Mission Archive Library, 1971--, pres., 1972---. Author: (books) "Andrew, Sublette, Rocky Mountain Prince, 1808-53", publ. 1960; "Josiah Belden, 1841 Calif. Overland Pioneer: His Memoir and Early Letters" publ. 1962; "The Golden Frontier: The Recollections of Herman Francis Rinehart, 1851-69", publ. 1964; "The Calif. Diary of Faxon Dean Atherton, 1836-39", publ. 1964; "The Gold Rush Letters of Jasper Smith Hill," publ. 1964; "The Letters of A Young Miner (1849-52)," publ. 1964; "Journey of James H. Bull, Baja Calif. Oct. 1843 to Jan. 1844," publ. 1965; "The Trials of Isaac Graham," publ. 1967; "A Med. Journey in Calif. by Pierre Garnier, M.D.," publ. 1967; "Hudson's Bay Company's First Fur Brigade to the Sacramento Valley, 1829-30", publ. 1967; "Past is Prologue: A Centennial Profile of the Pacific Mutual Life Ins. Co.," publ. 1968; "A Journey on Two Oceans," publ. 1971; "The Vigilance Committee of 1856: Three Views," publ. 1971; "Los Angeles and Its Environs in the 20th Century" (bibliography), publ. 1973; "The Westerners Brand Book Number 14," publ. 1974; "History of Amer. Political Thought" (2 vols.), publ. 1975; "The Mexican War in Baja California," publ. 1977; "A Guide to Historic Places in Los Angeles County" (co-edited), publ. 1978; "A Frontier Doctory by Henry F. Hoyt" (ed.), publ. 1979; "Los Angeles From the Days of the Pueblo by W.W. Robinson" (ed.), publ. 1981; "The Letters of Jacob Baegert," publ. 1982; "The 1769 Transit of Venus [in Baja Calif.]," publ. 1982; "Men, Medicine and Water" (ed.), publ. 1982; contrib. numerous articles to scholarly hist. mags.; ed. So. Calif. Quarterly, 1962---. Awards: Del Amo Found. Grant for research abroad, 1956; Henry E. Huntington Lib. Grant-in-Aid, 1960; John Simon Guggenheim Meml. Fellowship, 1963-64; Award of Merit, Amer. Assn. State and Local Hist., 1965; fellow, Amer. Philosophical Soc., 1969; fellow, L.A. Chancery Archives, 1976; fellow, Calif. Hist. Soc., 1981; mem. many historical societies; L.A. Corral of Wester-

ners; Phi Alpha Theta; Pi Sigma Alpha; Zamorano Club; The Athenaeum (London); research assoc., L.A. Co. Mus. of Natural Hist., 1972. Office: Dept. of Hist., U.S.C., Los Angeles 90089-0034.

NUNN, ERNEST EUGENE, company executive; b. Feb. 16, 1935, Parma, Mo.; s. Ernest F. and Rosa Lee (Pope) N.; m. Jo Ellen Neely, Jan. 25, 1957; children: Julie, b. 1959; Jeffrey, b. 1966; edn: BS, Indiana Univ. 1961. Career: v.p. to chmn. Lazarus Dept. Store (div. of fed. dept. store), Columbus, Oh. 1961-75; pres. Drapery Mfg. Inc., Columbus, Oh. 1975-77; pres. New Ideal Dept. Store, Birmingham, Ala. 1977-80; regl. mgr. Nat. Revenue Corp., Columbus, Oh. 1980-82; pres. Jani-King of Calif. Inc., 1982--; bd. dirs. Better Bus. Bureau, Indpls., Ind. 1973-75; dir. Birmingham CofC 1977-79; mil: sgt. US Army 1956-58; rec: woodworking, golf. Res: 1651 Inez Way Anaheim 92802 Ofc: Jani-King of California Inc., 14700 E Firestone Blvd, Ste 112, La Mirada 90638

NUSSBAUM, LUTHER JAMES, executive; b. Jan. 13, 1947, Decatur, India; s. Leo Lester and Janet Nell (Gladfelter) N.; m. Ginger McCown, Aug. 24, 1968; children: Kari, b. 1975; Kristin, b. 1977; edn: BA, Southwestern, Memphis 1968; MBA, Stanford Univ. 1972. Career: with Cummins Engine Co., Columbus, Ind. 1971-83; asst. to the pres. 1972-73; dir. perf. analysis 1973-74; dir. personnel 1974-75; gen mgr., Mexico 1975-77; gen. mgr. distribution cos. 1977-78; v.p. distbn. 1978-82; v.p. 1982-83; v.p. store ops. Businessland, San Jose 1983--; honors: Phi Beta Kappa 1968; Seidman Awd., Top Econ. Student 1963; mem: Laws Found Bd.; Adv. Team, Delta Found.; Video Alless Ctr. Bd.; rec: painting, sports, music. Res: 43465 Vista Del Mar Fremont 94539 Ofc: Businessland, 3600 Stevens Creek Blvd San Jose 95117

NUYEN, QUINN VAN, accountant; b. Oct. 31, 1936, Langson, Vietnam, nat. 1982; s. Phe Van and Sui Thi N.; m. Lien Nguyen, Nov. 8, 1959; children: Loan, b. 1961; Chi, b. 1963; Thu, b. 1964; Ngoc, b. 1966; Tai, b. 1969; Thao, b. 1971; Mai, b. 1972; Duc, b. 1973; edn: MBA, Univ. Beverly Hills 1983; career: acct. US Gov. and US Embassy, Saigon, Vietnam 1961-75; acct. Collin Groups Australia (Long Beach Br.) 1975-77; gen. mgr./chief fin. officer Culver Co., Huntington Park 1977--; mem: Nat. Acct. Assn. 1976; orgns: PTA Adv., St. Joseph Sch., Vietnam; past leader Catholic Youth, Vietnam; designed computer software system for importers/distrs. 1983; Catholic; rec: music, paint., computers. Res: 6823 Seville Ave Huntington Park 90255 Ofc: Culver Co., 2623 E 54th St Huntington Park 90255

OAKLEY, KURTIS MUNSON, electronics and defense co. executive; b. July 12, 1948, Clarkesville, Ga,; s. Theodore Harold and Rose (Munson) O.; m. Lynn Mori, Mar. 1, 1975; children: Jessica Lynn, b. 1979; Justin Kurtis, b. 1982; edn: B.Ops.Mgmt., CSU Long Beach 1977; MBA, 1978; Cert. Cost Analyst, Inst. of Cost Analysis 1983; Profl. Designation in Govt. Contract Mgmt., UCLA 1980. Career: price- cost analyst TRW, Redondo Beach 1979-81; gen. mgr. Price Prods. Co., Gainesville, Ga. 1981-82; sr. price-cost analyst/mgr. TRW, Redondo Beach 1982-83, mgr. materiel adminstrv. support 1983--; mem: Profl. Mgmt. Assn., L.A. (fin. advr. 1983, 84); Nat. Contract Mgmt. Assn.; Inst. of Cost Analysis; publs: art., Why Should We Stay The Course, Golden West Purchasor, Dec. 1982; mil: PO 3/c USN 1967-71, GCM, Combat Action, Vietnam Svc., Vietnam Campaign; rec: basketball, golf, sports. res: 16761 Viewpoint Ln, 46, Huntington Beach 92647 Ofc: TRW, One Space Park, Bldg. 110/ 1733, Redondo Beach 90278

OBERG, DONALD EUGENE, information systems executive; b. Aug. 1, 1933, McCook, Nebr.; s. Carl E. and Helen Elizabeth (Davis) O.; m. Donna Lofton, June 19, 1954; 2 daus.: Lynn, b. 1959, Kathy b. 1961; m. 2d Carol (Wombaker) Hansford, (dec.), Nov. 18, 1967; m. 3d Juanita (Howard) Melton, June 23, 1978; m. 4th Sharon (McClure) Garrison, Jan. 15, 1983; stepchil: Robin, Mike, Margie, Shawn, Kim, Tami, Kathleen, Sheri; edn: dip. in Russian, Army Lang. Sch. 1954; dip. IBM Corp. Adv. Systems Sch. 1965; BBA in mktg. George Wash. Univ. 1965; Univ. of Md. Grad. Sch. 1967-8. Career: mktg. support & Federal Accts. analyst IBM Corp., Wash DC Regional Ofc. 1957-65; head Tech. Manuals Pub. Gp., IBM/NASA Contract, Goddard Space Flt. Ctr. 1965-69; sr. staff asst. & mem. keyman team to open new IBM Manassas (Va.) Mfg. Plant, 1969-73; estab. retail bus. Massaponax Mini-Mart, Massaponax, Va. 1973-77; with McAuto Computer Systems Health Svcs., Los Angeles 1977-79; dir. info. systems Eisenhower Med. Ctr., Rancho Mirage (Ca.) 1979-82; dir. Info. Svcs. Dept., Hollywood Presbyn. Med. Ctr., Los Angeles 1983--; cert. instr. IBM Corp. Executive Devel. Seminars 1970-73. Mem: Nat. Mgmt. Assn.; Soc. for Tech. Comms. (sr. mem.); founding mem. Indio chpt. D.P. Mgmt. Assn. 1982; dir. Prince Georges Co., Md. Jaycees 1964; past PTA pres. (Virginia Middle Sch.) 1971; mem. Hist. Soc., Spotsylvania Co., Va. 1973-77; devel. brochure for regional distbrn. re Massaponax, Va. Civil War battleground during Bicentennial, 1975-76; mil: security svc USAF 1952-56, Korean Svc, GCM; So. Baptist; rec: golf (Hcp:20), tennis, racquetball. Res: POB 27728 Los Angeles 90027 Ofc: Hollywood Presbyterian Medical Ctr, 1300 No Vermont Ave Los Angeles 90027

O'BRIEN, JOHN STUART, JR., insurance co. marketing executive; b. Nov. 8, 1938, Everett, Wash.; s. John Stuart Sr. and Margaret Beth (Montgomery) O.;

m. Ardyth Kinney, June 30, 1962; children: Barry, b. 1963; Troy, b. 1967; edn: Seattle Pacific Univ. 1957-58; BA, Northwest Coll. 1963; B.Theol., 1964; Regl. Rep., Nat. Assn. Security Dealers; Sch. of Agency Mgmt., Limra 1978. Career: minister, Assemblies of God Ch., Wash. State 1963-67; sales agent New York Life Ins. Co., Everett, Wash. 1967-70; asst. mgr. NY Life Ins. Co., Denver, Colo. & Portland, Ore. 1970-75; agency mgr. Pacific Mutual Life Ins. Co., San Jose 1976-79; field v.p. USLIFE Life Ins. Co., San Jose 1979-81; regl. v.p. UNIMARC Ltd., San Jose 1981-83; regl. dir. of agencies Alexander Hamilton Life Ins. Co., San Jose 1983--; honors: Top New Salesman, New York Life 1967, 68; Top Regl. Recruiter, NY Life 1973; Top Field V.P., USLIFE, quarterly, 1979, 80; mem: Nat., Calif. & San Jose Assns. of Life Underwriters; Gen. Agents & Mgrs., San Jose; Rotary Club; Oakgrove Little League & Sr. League Baseball; Kiwanis Club; YMCA bd. dirs.; Bethel Ch. of San Jose (bd. fin., bldg. bd., ins. com., retirement com., youth choir sponsor, hd usher); Republican; Protestant; rec: racquetball, basketball official, golf. Res: 5058 Barron Park Dr San Jose 96136 Ofc: Alexander Hamilton Life Insurance Co., 1625 The Alameda, Ste 510, San Jose 95126

O'BRIEN, KELLY J., lawyer; b. Dec. 22, 1937, Goliad, Tex.; d. Walter Daniel and Laverne Inez (Lang) Hardin; m. William Joseph O'Brien, Sept. 1960; div.; children: Cindy Lou Browning, b. 1955, Wm. Daniel O'Brien b. 1961; edn: stu. Woodland Univ., MidValley Coll. of Law; JD, San Fernando Valley Coll. of Law; U.S.D. Internat. Law, Oxford Univ., Eng. 1978; Internat. Law, The Hague Holland, 1979; contg. edn. Hastings Coll. of Law 1981, USC, 1982. Admitted to Calif. State Bar 1980, US Ct. of Appeals (9th Circuit) 1982, US Federal Ct. (Central Dist., Ca.) 1980. Career: previous, law clerk Beverly Hills City Attorney; owner Law Firm of Kelly O'Brien, Encino 1980--, staff atty. Women's Legal Clinic, Haven Hills Battered Women's Center; affiliated wk. with Care Unit re alcoholism and drug rehabilitation; honors: achievement awards: Calif. State Gov. Edmund G. Brown Jr., US Pres. Jimmy Carter, US Sen. S.I. Hayakawa, Calif. Sen. (22d Dist.) Alan Sieroty (1978); Resolutions, Calif. State Senate and Assem., 1978; Atty. Gen.'s Staff, State of Texas (1953); Atty. Gen. Girls State, State of Texas (1953); Student Bar pres. Law Sch. (1977-8), Calif. State Student Bar Assn. pres. (1977-8); Law Student of the Year 1978, YWCA; Coro Found. Women's Polit. Affairs 1979, 80. Mem: Amer., Calif. State, Los Angeles County bar assns.; Assn. of Trial Lawyers of Amer.; Calif., Los Angeles, San Fernando Valley Women Lawyers assns.; Calif., L.A. Trial Lawyers assns.; Irisn Amer. Bar Assn. of Calif.; Coro Found. Alumni Assn., Pasadena Playhouse Alumni & Assocs., Nat. Assn. of Female Execs., Order of the Eastern Star, Order of the Rainbow Girls (Grand Cross 1954); founder Calif. State Student Bar Assn. (1976), co-founder Womens Legal Clinic, L.A. (1979); Democrat (State Del. 1979; Dem. Circle 1982); Methodist. Law Offices of Kelly O'Brien, 16027 Ventura Blvd, 4th Flr. Encino 91436

O'BRIEN, RAYMOND FRANCIS, transportation co. executive; b. May 31, 1922, Atchison, Kans.; s. James C. and Anna M. (Wagner) O'Brien; m. Mary Ann Baugher, Sept. 3, 1947; chil: James B., William T., Kathleen A., Christopher R.; edn: BS, Univ. of Mo. 1948; Harvard Adv. Mgmt. Pgm. 1966. Career: acct.-auditor Peat, Marwick, Mitchell & Co., Kansas City, Mo. 1946-52; controller-treas. Riss & Co., K.C., Mo. 1952-58; regional controller Consolidated Freightways Corp. of Delaware (CFCD), Indpls. and Akron, Ohio 1958-61; controller Consol. Freightways, Inc. (CFI), San Francisco, 1961, vice pres. and treas CFI, S.F., 1962-67, named to bd. dirs. 1966, v.p. finance 1967-69, exec. v.p. 1969-75; pres. CFCD, Menlo Park, Calif.1973-75; pres./ chief op. ofcr. CFI, S.F., 1975-77, pres./chief exec. ofcr. 1977-79; bd. chmn./ pres./CEO, Consol. Freightways, Inc., Palo Alto 1979--; dir: Transamerica Corp., Union Bank. Honored as outstanding chief exec. in the motor carrier industry, Finl. World mag. (3 times). Mem: Western Hwy Inst. (pres. 1983-4); The Conf. Bd.; Am. Trucking Assns. (past mem. exec. com.); trustee St. Mary's Coll.; adv. bd. UCB Sch of Bus.; adv. com. Northwestern Univ.; mem. Transp. Ctr., World Trade, Commonwealth, Pacific Union and Palo Alto Clubs, Congl., Burning Tree, Firestone and Menlo Country Clubs. Mil: 1st lt. USAF 1942-5; Republican; rec: swim, fishing, camping, golf. Res: 26347 Esperanza Dr. Los Altos Hills 94022 Ofc: Consolidated Freightways Inc. 3240 Hillview Ave Palo Alto 94303

OCHELTREE, RICHARD LAWRENCE, lawyer;b. Oct. 9, 1931, Springfield, Ill.; s. Chalmer M. and Helen M. (Camm) O.; m. Ann Washburn, Apr. 11, 1958; children: Kirstin, b. 1960; Lorraine, b. 1963; Tracy, b. 1966; edn: AB, Harvard Coll. 1953; LLD, Harvard Law Sch. 1958. Career: v.p. admin./ secty./ gen. counsel American Forest Products Co. Res; 17 Mt Burney Ct San Rafael 94903 Ofc: American Forest Products Co., 2740 Hyde St San Francisco 94109

OCHI, SAM SEIICHIRO, engineer; b. Jul. 19, 1946, Ehime-Ken, Japan, nat. 1959; s. Tad Tadashige and Mae Kikue (Ogawa) O.; m. Muffie Sundell, Aug. 5, 1972; 1 son: Kristopher Kenjiro, b. 1983; edn: BSEE, UC Berkeley 1969, MSEE, 1974. Career: analog design engr. Berkeley Bio-Engring., Berkeley 1970-73; staff engr. Nat. Semiconductor Corp., Santa Clara 1973-77; sr. design engr. Advanced MicroDevices, Sunnyvale, 1977-79; dir. of R&D, Teledyne Semiconductor, Mt. View 1979-83; senior mem., founding mem. tech. staff Maxim Integ. Prods., Sunnyvale 1983--.; Sr. mem. IEEE; 6 patents in integrated circuit and process technol.; design industry's first monolithic A/D using linear differential logic technol. Democrat; Buddhist; rec: classic cars, analog computer techniques; Res: 11208 Mt Crest Dr Cupertino 95014 Ofc: Maxim Integrated Products, 510 Pastoria Ave Sunnyvale 94086

OCHIPINTI, JOHN PHILIP, real estate developer; b. Dec. 21, 1948, Sacramento; s. Charles V. and Susan M. (Baker) Ochipinti; m. Janet Marie Spalding, May 26, 1973; 1 dau. Sara, b. 1978; edn: BA, CSU Sacto 1972, AA, Yuba Coll. 1980; lic.: real estate broker 1978, building contractor 1980. Career: estab. Aztec Real Estate, 1978--, Aztec Development, spec. in bldg. large comml. bldgs. in Yuba Sutter area, 1980--; restaurant franchise owner No. State Wendy's, in Yuba City and Woodland, w/5 planned openings in 1984. Mem. Bd. of Realtors, Rotary, CofC (bd.); clubs: Peachtree Golf & CC, Bodega Harbor CC; Republican; Catholic; rec: golf; res: 605 Queensbury Way, Yuba City 95991 ofc: Aztec Devel. 1290 Lincoln Rd. Yuba City 95991

OCHIPINTI, SIMON CHARLES, mortgage co. executive; b. Jan. 21, 1932, Sacto.; m. Kathleen A. Lynch, Jan. 11, 1958; children: Patricia, b 1958; Daniel, b. 1959; Julie, b. 1966; edn: AA, Grant Tech. Coll. 1953-55. Career: instrumentation engr. Aerojet Gen. Corp., Nimbus 1955-70; real estate sales mgr. Milano Realty, Sacto. 1970-75; br. mgr. Statewide City Mortgage Corp. 1975-79; real estate sales, broker 1979-81; v.p. Statewide City Mortgage Corp. 1981--; Fed. Nat. Mortgage Assn. Underwriter 1979; Real Estate Fin. Instr., Calif. Dept. R.E. for cont. edn. 1978-; honors: Million Dollar Club, Sacto. Bd. Realtors 1974; mem: Calif. Assn. Realtors; Sacto. Bd. Realtors; Calif. Mortgage Bankers Assn.; Sacto. Mortgage Bankers; publs: Real Estate Finance Book, 1983; monthly real estate fin. column, Sacto. Union, 1984; mil: airman 1/c USAF 1950-53; Democrat; Catholic; rec: boating, flying. Res: 7700 Thunderbird Ct Fair Oaks 95628 Ofc: Statewide City Mortgage Corp., 7144 Fair Oaks Blvd, Carmichael 95608

OCKERMAN, PHIL, city volunteer services executive, ret.; b. July 28, 1916, Long Beach; s. Clare C. and Rae (Angelo) O.; m. Doris Mead, May 30, 1941; children: Shirley Rae (Bracken) b. 1943, Jerry b. 1946, Dale b. 1952; edn: AB, Whittier Coll. 1938, Gen. Secondary Tchg. Cred., 1940; MS, CSU Hayward 1975. Lifetime Jr. Coll. Cred. (V.O.Ed.), Recreation 1969, Environ. Ed., Tchr. Ed., 1972; lic. to preach, United Methodist Ch. 1970. Career: tchr. Parlier Union High Sch. Dist., 1940-41; YMCA secty. North Br., Long Beach, Calif. 1941-43, L.B. YMCA Community Secty. 1946-48; exec. secty. Culver Palms YMCA 1948-50; gen. secty. Oroville YMCA 1948-50; exec. secty. East Oakland YMCA, 1955-62; regl. exec. secty. So. Alameda Co. YMCA 1962-65; recreation supr. Volunteer Svcs., Cultural Arts, City of Fremont 1965-75, ret.; (vol.) coord. of Volunteer Svcs./City of Fremont Human Services Dept. 1975--; instr. Camping Edn., San Jose State 1963-6, Ohlone Coll. 1969-74; Fellow Am. Park and Recreation Assn. (1968); Life Mem. Calif. Park and Rec. Assn. (1970); pres./bd. Fremont Assn. City Employees (FACE) 1965- (labor negotiation team 1970); honors incl. Hon. Life Member PTA, Doris and Phil Citizens of the Year 1980; mem. Rotary Club (25 years), Sierra Club, YMCA (bd. dirs.); founder AFTY Inc. (Air for Troubled Youth); exec. secty. Nat. Youth Council on Civic Affairs; bd. S.F. Area Girl Scouts; mil: lt. jg USN 1943-45, lt. cmdr. ret. 1962; Methodist (chmn. bd. trustees). Res: 2698 Sunnycrest Ct Fremont 94539 Ofc: City of Fremont, City Hall Fremont 94538

O'CONNELL, CHRISTINE LOUISE, artist-designer; b. June 30, 1947, Chgo., Ill.; d. Henry Gratton and Louise Wilcox (Coyle) O.; m. John F. Binder, Apr. 16, 1982; stepchildren: Joshua Binder, b. 1966, John Binder, b. 1969; edn: BA, Univ. of Mich. 1968; grad. work, CSU Northridge 1973. Career: asst. to the producer Griffin Prodns., Hollywood 1971-73; adminstr. film pgms. Nat. Broadcasting Co., Burbank 1972-73; dir. motion picture for TV & mini-series, CBS- TV, Studio City 1976-78; dir. movies, mini-series and specials Warner Bros. TV, Burbank 1978-79; v.p. prodn. Sydney Pollack Films, Burbank 1979; fibre artist/ designer/ pres. Spider Woman Designs, Beverly Hills 1980--; honors: Phi Beta Kappa, Zeta Phi Eta, Univ. of Mich. Angell Scholar, Univ. of Mich. Alumni Assn. 4-year Scholarship. Mem: Producers Guild of Am.; works: handwoven interior design art pieces as well as limited edition art couture pieces; wk featured in L.A. Times, the Chgo. Tribune, House Beautiful, Houston Home & Garden, Dallas-Ft. Worth House & Garden. Res: 12229 Falkirk Lane Los Angeles 90049 Ofc: Chris O'Connell, Spider Woman Designs, c/o Proffer, LaPage & Graff, 8665 Wilshire Bl, Ste 303, Beverly Hills 90211

O'CONNOR, CATHERINE, computing services co. executive; b. Jan. 8, 1947, Mahopac, NY; d. Louis A. and Catherine Therese (Sammartino) Freda; 1 son: Matthew, b. 1979; edn: St. Joseph's Univ. 1967-68; Merritt Coll. 1973. Career: mgr. personnel admin. Itel Corp., San Francisco 1973-78; dir. word processing svcs. 1978-79; dir. human resources mgmt. ADP Inc., Hayward 1979--; mem: Nat. Assn. Female Execs.; Bay Area Personnel Assn.; Am. Soc. for Personnel Admin.; No. Calif. Human Resources Council; Internat. Assn. of Personnel Women; rec: snow skiing, bicycling, tennis. Res: 1163 Camino Del Valle Alameda 94501 Ofc: A.D.P. Inc., 2380 W Winton Ave Hayward 94545

O'CONNOR, GEORGE MICHAEL, real estate investor/ insurance broker; b. Apr. 6, 1921, Berkeley; s. James Joseph and Mary Zita (Burns) O.; m. Georgine Dunlop, Oct. 6, 1962; children: Paul, b. 1967; Joyce, b. 1970; edn; BA, UC Berkeley 1942; M.Pub.Admin., USC 1955; real estate & fin., UC Ext. 1966-71; Ins. Broker Lic., Calif. 9153; Jr. Coll. Tchg. Cred., Calif. 1956; Gen. Sec. Tchg. Cred., Calif. 1958. Career: budget analyst, State of Calif. Dept. offin., Sacto. 1949-52; instr. political sci., Wentworth Jr. Coll., Mo. 1956-58; instr. adminstrv. subjects, Naval Air Station, Alameda 1960-63; property mgr./ ins. broker, San Francisco- Oakland area 1963-73; real estate investor/ ins. broker, San Francisco- Oakland area 1973--; mem. Internat. Assn. for Fin. Plnng. 1973-84; mem. Am. Assn. of Independent Investors 1983-84; honors: mem: Phi Delta Kappa 1941; Am. Soc. of Pub. Admin.; am. Soc. of Tng. Dirs.; Citizenship Clearinghouse (Missouri Wrkshp.); United Crusade Spkrs. Bureau, Sacto.; Oakland Symphony Orchestra Assn. (bd. dirs.); Oakland-Piedmont Republican Assembly (pres. 1973-); Berkeley City Commons Club (bd. dirs.); Orinda Country Club; Commonwealth Club; Calif. Hist. Soc.; mil: lt. j.g. USN 1942-45, Asiatic Pac. Campaign Ribbon w/ Bronze Star; Republican; Catholic;

rec; tennis, travel. Res: 27 Muir Ave Piedmont 94610 Ofc: 3450 Lakeshore Ave, Ste 200, Oakland 94610

O'CONNOR, ROBERT HOWARD, mortgage broker-investor; b. Feb. 3, 1944, San Francisco; s. Clarence Dominic and Alberta Louise (Russell) O.; m. Jo Ann Chapman, Nov. 3, 1968; children: Robert Jr., b. 1969; Jacklyn, b. 1971; Brian, b. 1974; Joseph, b. 1979; edn: LLB, Lincoln Univ. Law Sch. 1975. Career: pres. O'Connor Real Estate & Mortgage Co., Burlingame; fin. cons. to individuals & orgns.; pres. Mens Club of Ola Ch., Parish Senator; Jr. Achiev. Advr.; mem: Nat. & Calif. Assns. of Realtors; Nat. Assn. Mortgage Brokers; Nat. Assn. Finl. Cons.; Republican; Catholic.; rec: coaching youth sports, golf. Res: 103 Fey Dr Burlingame 94010 Ofc: O'Connor Mortgage Co., 1815 El Camino Real Burlingame 94010

O'DER, JOHN THOMAS, real estate broker; b. Oct. 31, 1929, Louisville, Ky.; s. John Thomas and Thelma Francis (Jarvis) O.; m. Carol Holton, June 2, 1956; children: Michael, b. 1957; Kathleen, b. 1960; edn: BA, UCLA 1953; cert. of completion, US Naval Postgrad. Sch. 1969-70; realtor, Nat. Assn. Realtors; comml. pilot rating single & multi-engine instr, aircraft 1973, Career: served to comdr. USN 1953-74: aviator, USN (5200 flight hrs., 430 carrier landings); ofcr. in charge heavy attack/ Electronic countermeasures jet acft. detachment 1968-69, (130 combat missions) Vietnam; decorated Bronze Star w/ Combat V, Meritorious Svc. Medal, Air Medals (2), ret. 1974; founder/owner Encinitas Car Wash 1977--; owner/broker real estate ofc. 1978--; mem: Encinitas CofC (mem. H.S. Work Experience Council); San Dieguito Bd. Realtors; Internat. & Calif. Car Wash Assns.; Navy League (S.D. chpt.); Ret. Ofcrs. Assn.; Theta Xi frat.; works: built first total water reclamation plant in car wash, San Diego County 1977; mem. Poway Plng. & Devel. Com. 1975-77; Presbyterian; rec: flying, golf, antique cars, swim. Res: 13064 Camino Del Valle Poway 92064 Ofc: Encinitas Car Wash, 293 N El Camino Real Encinitas 92024

ODER, SUSAN LOUISE, paralegal; b. Mar. 3, 1955, San Diego; d. Robert James and Helon Elizabeth (Moore) O.; edn: AB, magna cum laude, USC 1977; MBA, in progress, UCLA 1983-; Paralegal Cert., Univ. of San Diego 1977. Career: real estate paralegal Loeb & Loeb, Los Angeles 1978, corp. paralegal Parker, Milliken, Clark & O'Hara, L.A. 1979-80; banking paralegal Cohen & Ziskin, L.A. 1981-82; sr. corp. paralegal Buchalter, Nemer, Fields, Chrystie & Younger, L.A. 1983-84; L.A. Paralegal Assn. (LAPA), dir. (1979-83), corp. sect. chair (1980-82), job search cons. (1981-83), v.p. (1982), pres. (1982), newsletter ed. (1983); honors: City Recogn., L.A. Paralegal Assn., Mayor Tom Bradleye, 7/82; mem: Am. Assn. MBA Execs.; L.A. Paralegal Assn.; L.A. Jr. CofC; publs: Paralegal Job Hunting Handbook, LAPA 1982; Organizing California Non- Profit Corporations, LAPA 1980; num. arts. on paralegal profession, 1980-; Republican; Presbyterian; rec: rock hunting, swimming, sailing. Res: 15049 Burbank Blvd, 102, Van Nuys 91411

OEI, KOK-TIN, investor; b. Jan. 10, 1924, Indramayu, Java, Indonesia; s. Han Siong and Ie Boen (Tjan) O.; m. Christina Khoe, June 21, 1952; children: John, b. 1955; Tony, b. 1957; edn: degree, textile engr. Hogere Textile Sch., Netherlands 1952. Career: weigher to asst. mgr. in fathers rice mills, Indonesia; agent, textile dyes, Indonesian import-export firm, Hamburg, Germany (3 yrs.); emigrant to Calif. 1971; investor in apartment bldgs., Northern Calif. 1971--; clerk, Metropolitan Life 1971-80; linguist: Indonesian, Dutch, French, German, English; rec: philately, coins. Res: 2054 Sloat Blvd San Francisco 94116

OFNER, WILLIAM BERNARD, lawyer; b. Aug. 24, 1929, Los Angeles; s. Harry D. and Gertrude (Skoss) Ofner; edn: AA, Los Angeles City Coll. 1950; BA, CSU L.A. 1953; Moyenne Degree, The Sorbonne 1951; JD, Loyola Univ. Law Sch., L.A. 1965; admitted to practice, State Bar of Calif. 1966. Career: draftsman, LADW & P 1953-59; civil eng. asst. DW & P, Los Angeles 1959-67; staff atty. Thomas Moore & Assoc. 1967-69; Law Ofc. William B. Offner, Beverly Hills 1969-73, Los Angeles 1973-80; currently, assoc. Peter Law, Williab B. Ofner, Attys.; pres. Internat. Inc. 1982-83; Torts Lecture, Van Norman Univ. 1971; honors: Scholastic Art Awd. 1947; New Talent Art Exhibit 1953; mem: Lawyers Club, L.A.; Inst. of Sem. Semantics; L.A. Athletic Club; Soc. of Judgment; Van Nuys Toastmasters (pres. 1972); works: water colors, photography 1951-83; oil paintings 1951-66; mil: instr., elec. tech. 2/c USNR 1947-56; Democrat; Jewish; rec: distance running. Res: 105 E Stocker St Glendale 91207 Ofc: Willam B Ofner, 311 S Spring St, Ste 1104, Los Angeles 90013

O'GRADY, STERLING, financial planner; b. July 11, 1944, Muncie, Ind.; s. Eugene and Rossie Josephine (Kuhn) O.; edn: BA, cum laude, UC Santa Cruz 1974; MS, CSU Hayward 1978; LUTC, Life Underwriting Tng. Council 1982; cand., CFP, Coll. for Fin. Plnng., Denver Colo. 1983-84. Career: counselor San Mateo Co., Probation Dept., Belmont & Childrens Svc., San Mateo; asst. br. mgr. Associates Financial Svcs., San Francisco; air freight agent CF Air Freight, Mountain View; reg. rep. John Hancock Companies, San Mateo 1980-83; reg. rep. Judy & Robinson Securities, Menlo Parku 1983--; honors: Qualifier, John Hancock Regl. Hon. Club 1981, 82; John Hancock Millionaires Awd., Mission Dist. 1982; Runner Up, Mutual Fund Sales Awd. 1982; mem: Inst. CFPs; Soroptimits, Redwood City (Svc. Club); Sierra Club, Loma Prieta; UC Alumni Assn.; Buddhist; rec: whitewater rafting, X-C skiing, hiking. Res: 673 1st Lane, So San Francisco 94080 Ofc: Judy & Robinson Securities, 1155 Crane St Menlo Park 94025

O'HALLORAN, LAVERNE M. KATHLEEN, realtor; b. Nov. 15, 1921, Laurium, Mich.; d. Joseph W. and Della K. (Gervais) Shaffer; . John R. O'Halloran Jr., July 15, 1942; children: Sheila Anne (Stoll); Gregory John; Michael John; Maureen Therese (Benelli); Sean Thomas; Margaret Eileen. Career: pres. C&R Investments 1973-74; currently, realtor Kathy O'Halloran Realty, Fresno; mem: Infant of Prague Adoption Agency Aux. 1954-, secty. 1955; pres. Central Calif. CDL 1959-64; pres. Calif. Citizen for Decent Lit. 1961-63; bd. dirs. Nat. Citizens for Decent Lit. 1963-64; Calif. Arts. Soc.; Fresno Art. Ctr.; Republican: chmn., Fresno Co. United Republicans 1962; area coord. Clean Campaign Ballot Initiative 1966; Catholic: pres. Sacred Heart Mothers Club; secty. Sacred Heart Altar Soc.; St. Agnes Svc. Guild 1983; secty. Deanery, Nat. Council Catholic Women; pres. Legion of Mary, Jr. Presidium; rec: gardening, sewing, golf. Address: 3503 N Bond Fresno 93726

OHRN, DAVID RUSSELL, real estate investment counselor, general insurance agent; b. Oct. 25, 1941, Jamestown, NY; s. Russell Herbert and Alice J. Ohrn; div.; edn: Citrus Coll. 1968; Mt. San Antonio Coll. 1970; CSU Fullerton 1973; grad. Life Underwriters Tng. Council, Wash. DC; spl. studies, Saddleback Coll. 1982. Career: credit sales mgr. Sears Roebuck & Co., Covina 1965-74; insurance agt. Mutual of NY, Pasadena 1974-76; Allstate Ins. Co., City of Industry 1976-81; David Russell Ohrn Ins., Dana Point 1982--; realtor assoc. Forest E. Olson Inc., Mission Viejo 1980, Coldwell Banker, Mission Viejo 1981; realtor Pageant Real Estate Laguna Bch. 1981-83, Doheny Realty and Investments, Dana Point 1983--; honors: civic service award, Laguna Niguel CofC (1983), Sales Masters Club (1981), Allstate Honor Ring (1977, 78); dir. Pomona Valley Life Underwriters Assn. 1975-78; dir. Claremont CofC 1976-77; mem: Orange Co. Life Und. Assn., Laguna Beach Bd. of Realtors, Laguna Niguel CofC (charter dir.), Kiwanis Club (pres. Arrow-Azusa Chpt. 1971); mil: sgt. US Army Signal Corps 1959-65; Republican; Relig. Sci.; rec: amateur radio (K6PLV 1957-). Res: 24201 Vista D'Onde, Laguna Niguel 92677 Ofc: Doheny Realty & Investments, 34221 Golden Lantern, Dana Point 92629; Ofc. of David Russell Ohrn, Ins. Agt., 34210 Violet Lantern, Ste B, Dana Point 92629; mail: POB 6161, Laguna Niguel 92677

OKANO, STEVEN YASUAKI, financial planner; b. Feb. 24, 1955, Berkeley; s. William K. and Kimi (Mizuhara) O.; m. Hiroko C. Nishikado, July 28, 1979; children: Jennifer Kiyomi, b. 1980, Lindsey Takimi, b. 1983; edn: BA in environmental/ urban plnng., CSU San Jose 1977, grad. work in cybernetics, 1978-9; Regis Rep, SEC 1984. Career: profl. employment cons. (PEC)/br. mgr. (Craig Agcy.), General Employment Enterprises Inc. (oldest emplymt firm USA), 1978-82; sr. exec. recruiter EDP World Inc. (Bay Area exec. recruiting firm), 1982-83; acct. exec./ finl. plnnr. Thomson McKinnon Securities Inc., San Francisco 1983--; seminar spkr on career plnng., fin. plnng.; awards: num. profl awards, Presidents Club (2); 1st Pl. Architl. Design, City of Berkeley 1973. Mem: Asian Business Network, PEC, San Francisco CofC; past bd. dirs. Japanese Am. Citizens League; Japanese Am. Youth advisor; basketball coach Asian Am. League; mem. Mid-Penin. Citizens for Fair Housing (investigator); orgnzr. volleyball tournament; fundraiser/vol. various sr. citizen projects; Democrat (cand. El Cerrito City Council 1980); Buddhist. Res: 100 Aralia Ct. Hercules 94547 Ofc: Thomson McKinnon Securities Inc. 50 Fremont St. San Francisco 94105

OLDFIELD, BERNARD EDWARD, weapon systems project executive; b. Sept. 10, 1913, Hamilton, Ontario, Can.; s. Glen and May Elizabeth (Bonaney) O.; m. Ethel Marie Cutcliff, Aug. 8, 1981; children: Kenneth G., b. 1936; Janet May, b. 1949; June E. Flowers, b. 1955e; edn: BS, Alfred Univ. 1936; D.Sc., 1972. Career: chief flight test instrumentation, USAF, Edwards AFB 1942-56; pgm. mgr./ dept. mgr. Hughes Aircraft Co., (projs. incl: Falcon, 1st air- to- air missile; Syncom, 1st commun. satellite; Surveyor Moon Lander), Culver City 1956-78; proj. mgr. Veda Inc., Camarillo 1979--; cons. engr., ARO Corp. 1976-78; honors: Pres., Hughes Aircraft Co. Mgmt. Club 1964-65; bd. dirs. 1965-709; sch. bd. Mojave Unif. Sch. Dist. 1953-56; pres. Instrument Soc. of Am., Mojave Sect. 1954; mem: Internat. Test & Evaluation Assn. (charter); assoc. fellow, Am. Inst. Aero. & Astro.; Jet Pioneers of Am.; Rotary Club Internat. (bd. dirs. 1968); Braemar Country Club; Camarillo Springs Golf Mens Club; publs: num. tech. papers; Republican; Methodist; rec: gardening, golf. Res: 6168 Shasta Pl Camarillo 93010 Ofc: Veda Inc., 1317 Del Norte Camarillo 93010

OLDHAM, MAXINE JERNIGAN, realtor; b. Oct. 13, 1923, Whittier; d. John K. and Lela H. (Mears) Jernigan; m. Laurance Oldham, Oct. 28, 1941; children: John Laurence, b. 1942; edn: UC San Diego 1951-80; Western State Univ. 1976-77; LaSalle Ext. 1977-78; AA, San Diego City Coll. 1974. Desig: GRI, Grad. Realtors Inst., CAR 1978. Career: Pacific Telephone, S.D. 1952-57; US Civil Svc. Commn., US Naval Aux., Air Sta., Brown Field, Chula Vista 1957-58; San Diego Bd. of Edn., 1958-59; real estate sales 1966--; realtor Shelter Island Realty, S.D. 1977--; mem: Nat. & Calif. Assns. Realtors; Apt. Owners Assns.; S.D. Bd. Realtors; Calif. Assn. GRI; S.D. Genealogical Soc.; Internat. Fed. Univ. Women; Native Daus. of Am. Revolution; Republican; Catholic; rec: painting, music, theater. Res: 3348 Lowell St San Diego 92106 Ofc: Shelter Island Realty, 2810 Lytton St San Diego 92106

OLESKY, JAMES, microprocessor product executive; b. June 15, 1952, Edison, NJ; s. John Robert Sr. and Roberta (Lecher) O.; m. Kuk Hwa Lee, Nov. 17, 1976; children: Lee Young, b 1978; Jennifer Yong, b. 1980. Career: calibrations tech. Electro Rent Corp. 1979-80; microprocessor prod. mgr. 1980--; mil: tech., s/sgt. USAF 1971-79, Commdn. Medal, NCO Leadership Sch., Leadership Awd.; Republican; Methodist; rec: auto, tv repair. Res: 9740 Sepulveda Blvd, 4, Sepulveda 91343 Ofc: Electro Rent Corp., 4209 Vanowen St Burbank 91505

OLIVIER, PEGGY LOUISE SPROUT, management consultant; b. Feb. 29, 1940, Torrance; d. Ralph Edgar and Melba Pauline (Savage) Sprout; m. Arthur Craig Olivier, July 12, 1964, dissolved 1973; 2 children: Craig Matthew b. 1968, Laura Elisabeth b. 1971; edn: BA, Whittier Coll. 1961; MS, CSU Fresno 1980; spl. courses CSU (Long Beach, San Francisco, San Jose, Hayward) and UC Berkeley. Calif. Tchr. Credentials: Administrv. Service, Sec. Life Dipl., Jr. High Sch. Life Dipl. Career: tchr. Hayward Unif. Sch. Dist. 1961-66; supr. of student tchr. CSU Hayward 1964-66; chair, Alameda County Home Economics Tchrs. 1965-66; regl. supr. UCLA 1966-68; free-lance cons., 1968-73; regl. supr. Bur. of Home Econ., Calif. State Dept. of Edn. 1973-76, cons. Vocational Edn., 1976-78, cons. Commn. on Voc. Edn., 1978-79, mgmt. cons. Office of Grant Adminstrn., Voc. Edn., 1979--; mgr. Calif. Voc. Edn. Data Mgmt. Systems, cons. Voc. Edn. Data Mgmt. Sys. (VEDS of the National Ctr. for Ednl. Statistics), cons. Finl. Status Reports and Mgmt. Systems; honors: Treemy award for Outstanding Tchr., San Lorenzo H.S. Tchrs. Assn. 1962; Valley Homemaker, Herald and News, Hayward (1970); Outstanding Young Woman of Am., 1972; hon. mem. Future Homemakers of Am. Home Econ. Related Occupations (1967, 72, 73); Phi Upsilon Omicron (charter 1975); Gov. appt. Calif. Balance of State Private Indus. Council, 1979-82 (Resolution, Calif. Secty. of State); mem: Am. Home Economics Assn., Am. Vocational Assn., Assn. of Calif. Sch. Adminstrs., Calif. Assn. of Voc. Edn., Calif. Dirs. of Voc. Edn., Calif. Home Economics Assn. (del., conv. com., tchr. edn. chair), Nat. Assn. Supervisors of Home Ec. Edn., Western Assn. of Schs. and Colls., Whittier College Alumni Assn.; vol. Am. Heart Assn., PTA, Cub Scouts ldr., Soroptimist Int'l of Sacto.; arts., reports in ednl. publs.; cons. McGraw Hill 1984-5; Republican; Episcopal; rec: computer, int. decor, tennis. Res: 3413 Whaler Ave Davis 95616 Ofc: Calif. State Dept. Education, Voc. Edn., 721 Capitol Mall, 4th Fl. Sacramento 95814

OLKEN, SHERWIN MICHAEL, physician-radiologist; b. Apr. 16, 1939, Chgo., Ill.; s. Meyer Simon and Rose (Abrams) O.; m. Elaine, Sept. 15, 1963; children: Scott, b. 1965; Douglas, b. 1968; edn: BS, Univ. of Ill. 1961; MD, Chgo. Med. Sch. 1966; Bd. Cert. Radiology, Wadsworth VA Hosp. 1974; Bd. Cert. Radiologist, Am. Bd. of Radiology. Career: radiologist, Beverly Hills 1974-76; radiologist, Kaiser Hosp., W. L.A. 1976-81; diagnostic radiologist/ mem. craniofacial team, So. Calif. Perm. Med. Gp., Kaiser Found. Hosp. 1981--; asst. prof. radiology, UCLA 1977-; area dir. med. edn. & research 1977-81; instr./ lectr./ physicians asst. & nurse practitioner pgm., So. Calif. Perm. Med. Gp.; mem: Am., Calif. & L.A. Co. Med. Asns.; biomed. research: Proteins & Amino Acids 1961; Ultrasonic Diagnosis of Gallbladder Cracinoma 1977; Radiology sign in achiles tendon tear 1978; mil: maj. US army 1967-70, Meritorious Svc. Awd.; Republican; Jewish. Res: 3345 S Colbert Ave Los Angeles 90066 Ofc: Kaiser Hosp., 6041 Cadillac Ave Los Angeles 90034

OLMSTED, JOHN MARTIN, association executive; b. Mar.2, 1937, Wellsboro, Pa.; s. Charles Edwin and Laura Jean (Root) O.; m. Sondra Corken, Aug. 10, 1963; 2 sons, Martin, b. 1967, Jason, b. 1970; edn: BA, Central Mo. State Univ. 1962, MA, 1963. Career: instr. Central Missouri State, 1962-63, No. Illinois Univ. 1964-66, Louisiana State Univ. 1966-68; pres. Martin J. Assocs. 1968-71; assoc. dir. Volunteers of America, Baton Rouge 1971-73; exec. dir. Volunteers of America, Ft.Worth, Dallas 1973-75, Sacramento 1975-82; pres./ CEO/adminstr. Volunteers of America, Calif. Bay Area 1982--, National Exec. Bd., 1981-5. Mem: No. Calif. Soc. of Assn. Execs.; Am. Correctional Assn.; Internat. halfway House Assn.; Rotary (chmn. vocational svc. com.), Lake Merritt Breakfast Club. Mil: sgt. US Army. Protestant; rec: golf. Res: 1117 Holly, Alameda 94501 Ofc: Volunteers of America 1736 Franklin, 1007, Oakland 94612

OLSEN, ALAN RAYMOND, entomologist; b. May 23, 1946, Chgo., Ill.; s. Raymond Fredrick and Grace Lorraine (Sivertsen) O.; m. Angelina Smaserui, Sept. 5, 1970; children: Jeremy, b. 1972; Melissa, b. 1980; edn: BS, Univ. of Ariz. Coll. of Agric. 1971. Career: volunteer US Peace Corps., Palau Islands 1966-69; entomologist US Food & Drug Admin., Seattle field ofc. 1972-78, Los Angeles Dist. 1979-82; supvy. entomologist 1982--; Equal Employment Opportunity Adv. Com., USFDA, Seattle Dist. 1974-77, chprsn. 1977, Los Angeles 1978-79q honors: Awd. of Merit for achievs. in entomology, US FDA 1982; mem: Entomological Soc. of Am.; Pacific Coast entomological Soc.; Assn. of Pacific Systematicists; Assn. of Official Analytical Chemists (assoc. referee 1980-82); Aid Assn. for Lutherans; Altadena Neighborhood Involvement Pgm.; Red Cross Blood Donors; publs: num. arts. in industry journs.; Democrat; Lutheran (Council Deacon); rec: ecology and ethnology of the Palau Islands. Res: 26 E Pine St Altadena 91001 Ofc: U.S. Food & Drug Administration, 1521 West Pico Blvd Los Angeles 90015

OLSEN, DOUGLAS CRAIG, mechanical contractor; b. May 22, 1948, Eureka; s. Galen R. and Lilly M. (Olson) Olsen; m. Dera Novelo, Aug. 22, 1970; children: Matthew, b. 1972; Jason, b. 1974. Career: sheet metal worker Olsen's Heating 1966; v.p. 1971; pres. Olsen's Heating & Sheet Metal Inc., Eureka, 1975--; mem: Humboldt Co. Bldrs. Exch.; Baywood Golf & Country Club; Republican; Episcopal; rec: golf. Res: 691 Hilma Dr Eureka 95501 Ofc: Olsen's Heating, 417 W Wabash Eureka 95501

OLSEN, STEVE ALAN, b. Oct. 25, 1951, Pittsburg, Calif.; s. Stanley Olaf and Gro Sigrid (Thoen) O.; father-in-law: Homer Jerome Blaisdell (inventor, owner/bd. chmn. Blaisdell Mfg. Inc., Brea); m. Victoria Ann Blaisdell, June 23, 1974; children: Wendy Marie b. 1978, Sandra Victoria b. 1982; edn: BA hist., CSU Fullerton 1974; BS mech. eng. (summa cum laude), West Coast Univ. 1979; MS mech. eng., CSU Fullerton 1983. FAA lic. Flight Instr. (Single, Multi-eng.), Flt. Instr.-Instrument, Ground Instr. (Adv.). Career: mechanical/

tooling designer, Tungsten Carbide Mfg., Tustin 1977-78; proj. engr., mfg./ mech. design, Blaisdell Mfg. Inc., Brea 1979-83; mem. tech. staff, Thermal Analysis Gp., Rockwell Internat. Satellite Systems Div., Downey 1983--; honors: Phi Alpha Theta (life, 1973), Alpha Gamma Sigma (life, 1977), Alexander Anderson Engring. Scholarship (1977), University awards: outstanding undergrad. student in engring./outstanding undergraduate student, 1980; mem: The Am. Soc. of Mech. Engrs., Aircraft Owners and Pilots Assn.; part-time flight instr., Fullerton Airport; mil: Ensign USNR 1984; Republican; Lutheran. Res: 811 Casa Blanca Fullerton 92632 Ofc: Rockwell International, Satellite Systems Div. 043, 12214 Lakewood Blvd (AD35) Downey 90241

OLSEN, STEVEN KENT, dentist/ educator; b. Nov. 20, 1944, Spanish Fork, Utah; s. Earl Clarence and Adela Faux Olsen; edn: BS, Brigham Young Univ. 1969; DDS, Univ. of the Pacific Sch. of Dentistry 1974. Career: pvt. practice, gen. & restorative dentistry, dentist- partner Olsen & Pooley, San Francisco 1975--; instr. Univ. of the Pacific Sch. of Dentistry, Dept. of Cont. Edn. 1978--; pvt. practice, endodontics, Salt Lake City, Ut. 1979--; chmn. bd. Am. Dentists Ins. Corp. 1978-80; dir. Wilks & Topper Inc. 1982-; honors: Good Citizen Medal, SAR 1963; life mem. Alpha Epsilon Delta; mem: Am., Calif. & Utah Dental Assns.; Salt Lake Dist. & San Francisco Dental Socs.; P & S Club; L.D.S. Hosp., S.L.C., Ut. (staff 1978-); Coll. of Phys. & Surg. Alumni Assn.; dir. Calif. Inst. for Continuing Edn. 1983-; pres. Nat. Inst. for Cont. Edn. 1983-; publisher, C.I.C.E. Corres. Course 1983-; publs: Accolade, 1963; Lancer Ballade Author, 1963; instrn. & course writer Stanford Palo Alto Inst. of Relig. 1979-81; Republican; Mormon; rec: hiking, travel, world religions. Res: 385 Old La Honda Rd Woodside 94062 Ofc: Olsen & Pooley, One Embarcadero Ctr, Ste 2205, San Francisco 94111

OLSHANSKY, JACK, corporate finance partner; b. Aur. 25, 1929, NYC; s. Max and Ray (Merlin) O.; m. Shirley Dena Krieger, Dec. 31, 1950; children: Donna, b. 1955; Sue, b. 1958; edn: AB, Brooklyn Coll. 1950. Career: var. pos. to pres. McGaw Labs., Div. Am. Hosp. Supply Corp. 1975-78; employment 1959-78; pres. Inspiron Div. C.R. Bard 1979; v.p./ gen. mgr. Cutter Medical 1980-83; currently, ltd. partner Montgomery Securities, San Francisco; cons. Delmed, IMS, Exxon, & Theratech 1979; dir: Windsor Medical 1983-84; Medical Mktg. Assn. 1982-84; Neodontics 1983-84; honors: Recogn., MMA 1980-82 & NITA 1975; mem: ASHP; ASPEN; Binai Brith; publs: arts. in med. mktg.; mil: cpl. US Army 1951-53; Jewish; rec: bridge, golf. Res: 5950 Castle Dr Oakland 94611 Ofc: Montgomery Securities, 600 Montgomery St San Francisco 94111

OLSON, ALBERT MAURITZ, engineer; b. Nov. 1, 1898, Kola, Sweden, naturalized 1931; s. Olof and Christina (Person) Nelson; Edn: BS in engring., Stockholm Inst. of Engring., 1924; various post-grad. courses; m. Gunhild Sundel, Dec. 9, 1925; chil: Lillian, b. 1926. Career: design engr., hydraulic div., W.F. and John Barnes Corp., Rockford, IL, 1936-41; design engr. for indsl. and aircraft hydraulic systems, Sunstrand Machine Tool Co., Rockford, IL, 1941-43; supr. engr., Chain Belt Co., Milwaukee, 1943-51; chief tool engr. for rapid fire howitzer prodn., Ordnance Div., 1951-54; cons. engr., Bolens Products, div. Food Machinery Corp., Port Washington, WI, 1954-55; design engr., and sr. servo mechanisms engr., aircraft hydraulics, mechanisms and controls, Lockheed Aircraft Corp., Los Angeles, 1955-67; Reg. Profl. Engr., CA M-11364; Patents (13) include devel. of seals of all-steel constrn., used in USAF SR71 supersonic aircraft made by Lockheed, to be leakfree under operating condtiions of 550 degrees F. temp. and 3500 psi hydraulic pressure. Mem: (fmr.) Natl. Soc. of Profl. Engrs., CA Soc. of Profl. Engrs. secty. 1961; Amer. Soc. for Metals. Republican. Lutheran. Rec: B/W photography, golf. Res: 1040 Sierra Dr., Turlock 95380.

OLSON, CALVIN ARTHUR, thoracic and vascular surgeon; b. May 17, 1926, Mussoorie United Province, India; s. Arthur Joseph and Helen Anna (Orr) O.; m. Alyse Hansen, Apr. 21, 1948; children: Eric,b . 1952; Karen, b. 1953; Robert, b. 1955; William, b. 1959; Donna, b. 1961; edn: BA, Walla Walla Coll. 1943-46; MD, Loma Linda Univ. 1946-50; diplomate, Nat. Bd. of Med. Examiners 1951; Licentiate British Med. Council, London 1966; Licentiate Med. Council, Canada 1966; fellow, Am. Coll. of Surgeons 1965; diplomat, Am. Bd. of Surgery 1964; Diplomate Am. Bd. of Thoracic Surgery 1966. Career: pvt. med. practice, Crescent City 1955-57; res. thoracic surgery Loma Linda Univ. 1957-62; chief of surgery/ med. dir. Youngberg Adventist Hosp., Singapore 1966-71; chief surgery, Sonora Comm. Hosp. 1971-79; surgeon, Sonora Med. Gp., Sonora 1971--; pres: Tuolomne Co. Med. Soc. (1980-81), Sonora Med. Gp. (1981-83), Sonora Land Devel. Co. (1981-84); bd. dirs. Sonora Comm. Hosp. 1974-84; mem: Singapore Surgical Soc.; Am., Singapore, Calif. & Tuolomne Co. Med. Assns.; Mother Lode Adventist Acad. (sch. bd. chmn. 1972-78); publs: Serum Amylase Levels in Intestinal Obstruction in Dogs, in Surgery, Gynecology & Obstetrics, Jan. 1960; mil: co. commdr., 1st lt. US Army Med. Corps 1953-55, Nat. Defense Svc.; Republican; Seventh-day Adventist (elder). Address: Sonora Medical Group, Four S Forest Rd Sonora 95370

OLSON, HAROLD VERNE, real estate broker; b. Nov. 10, 1916, Lebanon, Ks.; s. William Henry and Myrtle Viola (Payne) O.; m. Marie Pettibone, May 7, 1939; children: William, b. 1941; Harold J., b. 1943; edn: Yuba Jr. Coll.

1959-75; R.E. Broker, Calif. 1964. Career: dir./ broker/ pres. Harold V. Olson Real Estate Inc., Marysville; dir. Calif. Assn. Realtors 1974-75; pres. Sutte Yuba Bd. Realtors 1974; pres. Yuba- Sutter Exch. 1977; honors: Realtors of the Yr. 1972, 74; mem: Sutter- Yuba Bd. Realtors; Yuba- Sutter Real Estate Exch.; Ret. Ofcrs. Assn.; 15th Air Force Assn.; Elks Lodge; Masonic Lodge, White Shrine of Jerusalem; Rotary; Peach Tree Golf & Country Club; mil: CWO-4, USAF 1936-64; DUB w/2 OLC, GCM, ADM, WWII VM, NO3M, UNSM, AFCM, COMM Bib, KSM, AF RM, PTC M w/6 BSS, AF LSA w/1 Slv OLC, ROK PVC; Republican; Preysbyterian; rec: golf. Res: 2204 Buchanan Marysville 95901 Ofc: Harold V. Olson Real Estate, 621 B St, Ste A, Marysville 95901

OLSON, KENNETH E., business executive; b. July 4, 1938, Houston, Tex.; s. Iver Al and Elizabeth L. (Elliot) O.; m. Barbara Braumiller, May 6, 1967; children: Karen, b. 1969; Sherri, b. 1972; edn: BS, Lamar Univ. 1960. Career: founder/ owner Olson Photo Associates Inc. 1962--; cons. to legal profession & police depts. re. photographic reproductions; honors: num. awds. on nat. level for advances in color image forming techniques; mem: Assn. of Profl. Color Labs. (pres. 1984); Profl. Photos of Am.; Photo Mktg. Assn.; Maserati Automobile Club (pres. 1984); Newport Harbor Art Mus. (Bus. Council), Santa Ana Coll. (Adv. Bd.); Long Beach City Coll. (Adv. Bd.); works: tech. arts. & research, The Range Finder Mag. (photog.) & Powerbeat mag. (high performance jet engines); Republican; Lutheran; rec: high performance sports cars & boats. Res: 12991 Springwood Dr Santa Ana 92705 Ofc: Olson Photo Assoc., 527 S Harbor Blvd Anaheim 92805

OLSON, M. JAYNE, retailing executive; b. May 19, 1948, Detroit; d. Rudolph Ralph and Charlotte Josephine (Anzick) Benedict; edn: BS in retailing, Mich. State Univ. 1970. Career: retail mgr./buyer Grande Gourmet Inc., E. Lansing, Mich. 1972-3; dept. mgr./buyer Meijer's Thrifty Acres Inc., Okemos, Mich. 1973-4; deli mgr./supr. 9 stores, National Fast Foods Inc. dba Lavicio's in Wash., Nev., Solana Bch., Ca., 1975-77; owner Jellybean Junction Inc. (children's clothing boutique), Encinitas 1978--. Mem. Encinitas CofC; sponsor local soccer teams for youth 1979-. Print media interviews 1982, 83, rec. phys. fitness, travel. Res: POB 547 Puumene, Maui, HI 96784 Ofc: Jellybean Junction, 439 Encinitas Bl. Encinitas 92024

OMAR, HAL NAJI, real estate broker-consultant; b. Oct. 30, 1930, Basra, Iraq, nat. 1956; b. Oct. 30, 1930; s. Mohammed Naji Al-and Khedija (Ismail) O.; m. Nov. 22, 1952, div. 1961; children: Leila, b. 1953; Diane, b. 1955; Lloyd, b. 1956; Timothy, b. 1958; Darlene, b. 1959; edn: BA, UC Berkeley 1954; MA, San Francisco State Univ. 1960; R.E. Broker, Calif. Career: owner/ opr. Discount T.V. Sales, Anaheim & Garden Grove 1969-72; owner/ opr. The Cottage Coffee Shop, Costa Mesa 1973-74; ins. agent/ broker, Santa Ana 1975-76; R.E. salesman Red Carpet Realtors, Fountain Valley 1977; R.E. Broker, dba Delta West Brokers, Pittsburg, Stockton & So. Lake Tahoe 1979--; res. agent/ proj. mgr. The Maddock Co. (condominium proj., The Ocean Heritage Club), Pompano Beach, Fla. 82; honors: Phi Eta Sigma, UC Berkeley 1950; Fountain Valley & Eastern Costra Costa Bds. Realtors; Nat. Asn. Realtors; Stockton CofC (trade name Tri-Guard Inds. 1982); Homewoners Assn., Ocean Heritage Club (pres. 1982-83); works: book in progress, The Nuts & Bolts of Real Estate Investment; Republican; rec: chess, travel. Res: POB 9972, So. Lake Tahoe 95731 Ofc: 3294 Royal Dr, Ste E, Cameron Park 95682

O'MEA, ROBERT GEORGE, insurance agent; b. June 9, 1950, Los Angeles; s. George Dwyer and Marlyn Kathleen (Kelley) O.; children: Patrick, b. 1981; George, b. 1983; edn: liberal arts, Simon Frazier 1974. Career: Bankers Nat. Ins. Co. 1977; Pres. Adv. Council 1977-84; instr. adv. sales course, Life Underwriting Tng. Council 1983-84; honors: Millon Dollar Round Table 1977-; Top Agency, Bankers Nat. Life 1983-84; Man of the Yr., 1984; mem: San Diego Assn. Life Underwriters; Internat. Game & Fish Assn.; publs: Distemper of Our Time, (winner 2rd annual humanities symposium), Univ. of British Columbia 1973; Republican; Catholic; rec: Marlin fishing (3 time winner Cabo Invitational). Ofc: Robert G. O'Mea & Assoc. Inc., 4950 Waring Rd, Ste 12, San Diego 92120

OMHOLT, BRUCE DONALD, design engineering consultant; b. Mar. 27, 1943, Salem, Ore.; s. Donald Carl and Violet Mae (Buck) O.; m. Darla Faber, Oct. 27, 1972; children: Madison, b. 1964; Natalie, b. 1969; Cassidy, b. 1975; edn: BSME, Heald Coll. of Eng. 1964. Career: real estate salesman R. Lea Ward & Assoc., San Francisco 1962-64; sales engr. Repco Engring., Montebello 1964; var. mfg. eng. & mgmt. pos. Ford Motor Co., Rawsonville, Saline, Owosso & Ypsilanti, Mi. 1964-75; chief engr. E.F. Hauserman Co., Cleveland, Oh. 1975-77; dir. of design & eng. Am. Seating Co., Grand Rapids, Mi. 1977-80; principal Trinity Engring., Grand Rapids, Mi. 1980-81, Rohnert Park, Calif. 1981--; patentee: motorcycle, US pat.; apparatus for removably securing a container to a carrier rack, US pat.; body panel for a motorcycle, US pat.; 2 US & 3 Japanese pats. pend. Res: 1034 Holly Ave Rohnert Park 94928 Ofc: Trinity Engineering, 71 Utility Ct Rohnert Park 94928

ONALFO, DAWN EILEEN, missiles and space co. executive; b. Sept. 21, 1949, Provo, Ut.; d. Don Edward and Ethel Irene (Hussey) Freeman; m. Angelo M. Onalfo, Aug. 4, 1972; children: James, b. 1969; Angelo J., b. 19073; Michael, b. 1977; edn: BS, Univ. of San Francisco 1984. Career: computer pgmmr. Lockheed Missiles & Space Co., Sunnyvale 1974-79; data sys. lead analyst 1978-81; data base adminstr. 1981-82; supvr. 1982--; mem: Am. Soc. for Quality Control (sect. newsletter ed. 1981-83, sect. treas. 1983-84, v.chprsn. ops. 1984-85); Democrat; Mormon; rec: photog. Res: 1967 Junewood Ave San Jose 95132 Ofc: Lockheed, 1111 Lockheed Way, Bldg. 182, Orgn. 8443, Sunnyvale 94086

ONEAL, WILLIAM JAMES, physician; b. June 17, 1914, Chicago; s. James Laughlin and Mildred Dorothy (Jones) Oneal; Edn: AB, Stanford Univ., 1938; MD, 1942; MS, surg., Coll. Med. Evan. 1954; m. Helen Wheeler, Jan. 12, 1942; chil: James, b. 1947; Barbara, b. 1948; Sally, b. 1949; Billy, b. 1952; Susan, b. 1956. Career: intern, L.A. Co. Gen. Hosp., 1941-43; resident surg., Henry Ford Hosp., Detroit, 1943-45; pvt. practice in surg., Pasadena, 1946-53; resident in surg., CA Hosp., L.A., 1954-56; pvt. practice surgery, Pasadena, 1956-58; mem, Los Angeles Tumor Inst., sr. partner & sr. mem. surgical staff, CA Hosp., Los Angeles, 1958-78; ret. 1979---; clin. isntr. in med., USC Sch. of Med, 1950-54. Diplomate American Bd. of Surgery, 1957; fellow, American Coll. of Surgeons, 1959. Mil: Lt., USNR, 1945-46. Republican. Presbyterian. Rec: golf(locally and nationally well known), medalist CA State Amateur, 1954-57. Res: 671 Bradford St., Pasadena 91105.

O'NEIL, SUSAN MARTIN, savings and loan association executive; b. Feb. 16, 1948, Cleveland, Oh.; d. Richard and Estelle Ann (Zucker) Kaplan; m. Harry C. O'Neil Sr., Aug. 8, 1976; edn: BA, summa cum laude, Nat. Univ. 1980; MBA, 1982; Real Estate Broker 1983. Career: br. mgr. San Jacinto Savings, Houston, Tex. 1972-77; maj. loan processor Univ. Savings, Houston, Tex. 1977-78; asst. v.p. maj. loans Farwest Savings & Loan, Newport Beach, Calif. 1978-82; v.p. mj. loans Newport Balboa Savings & Loan Assn., Newport Beach 1982--; mem: Calif. Savings & Loan League (Lending Procedures Com. & Sem. Com.). Res: 2524 Elden Costa Mesa 92627 & 1916 Alessandro Tr Vista 92803 Ofc: Newport Balboa Savings & Loan Assn., 1100 Irvine Ave Newport Beach 92660

O'NEIL, WILLIAM JAMES, lawyer, ret.; b. Dec. 4, 1923, Duluth, Minn.; s. William James and Irene Geraldine (McDonough) O.; m. Gloria Smith, Nov. 28, 1953; children: Timothy, b. 1955; Kathleen, b. 1956; Margaret, b. 1959; edn: BA, Northwestern Univ. 1947; MA, Stanford Univ. 1952; JD, Univ. of S.F. 1952; admitted to practice, State Bar of Calif. 1952. Career: legal dept. Bank of Am. 53-54; atty., S.F./ trial atty. State Compensation Ins. Fund, S.F. 1954, Fresno 1954-61; referee Indsl. Accident Commn., State of Calif., Fresno 1961-62; Mullen & Filippi, Attys., San Francisco 1962-63, partner in charge of Sacto. ofc. 1963-83, ret.; guest lectr. Univ. of Pacific McGeorge Sch. of Law. 1977, 78, 80; Cont. Edn. of the Bar Wkrs. Comp. presentation 1978; mem: Am. & Calif. Bar ssns.; Boy Scouts of Am. (Cub Master, Scout Master, Exec. Bd. Golden Empire Council & Exec. Com., Round table Commnr., Holder Scoutmasters Key); Lions Internat., Carmichael (secty., past pres., past zone chmn., dist. song ldr.); mil: lt. j.g. USNR 1943-46, Am. Theatre, Pacific Theatre. 1 Star, Philippine Liberation; Democrat; Catholic; rec: music, linguistics. Res: 4420 Jasper Ct Carmichael 95608

ONG, GEORGE E., lawyer; b. Jan. 6, 1936, Oakland; s. Chester T.H. and Foon Young (Lee) O.; m. Jennie Y., Aug. 29, 1965; children: Gail, b. 1967; Lori, b. 1970; Ryan,b. 1978; edn: BA, Stanford Univ. 1958; JD, Golden Gate Univ. 1969; admitted to practice, State of Calif. 1971. Career: deputy dist. atty. Alameda County 1971-79 (First Asian apptd. senior trial dep., D.A. Ofc. Alameda Co.); pvt. law practice 1979--; conduct mock (ednl.) trials: Oakland Police Dept., Calif. Hwy Patrol, Oakland Pub. Schs., UCB Boalt Hall. awards: YMCA/ Walter T. Walsh Meml. Scholarship to Stanford; mem: Asian Am., Am., Calif. & Criminal Cts. Bar Assns.; Alameda Co. Bar Assn. (dir. 1981, chmn. Liberty Bell Com. 1978); Trial Lawyers of Am.; Western Trial Lawers; Calif. Dist. Attys. Assn.; Bay Area Prosecutors Assn.; Nat. Assn. Ins. Agents; Calif. Real Estate Assn.; chmn. Law Day, USA 1976-77; Oakland No. Central YMCA (Hi Y Youth counselor); Stanford Alumni Assn.; Stanford Block S Soc.; Orgn. to Met Benevolent Assn.; works: collections on family support, Calif. Family Support Council 1978; Republican; Presbyterian; rec: woodcrafts, scouting, skiing. Res: 659 Kenwyn Rd Oakland 94610 Ofc: George E. Ong, Atty. at Law, 428 13th St, Ste 800, Oakland 94612

ORD, DON GRANT, engineer; b. Nov. 4, 1923, Los Angeles; s. Grant Leland and Nanna Christina (Shettle) O.; m. Lucille Wuster, Apr. 5, 1952; children: David, b. 1954; Scott, b. 1957; Craig, b. 1959; Kimberly, b. 1962; edn: BSE, UCLA 1951; MSEE, CSU Northridge 1970. Career: engr. Northrop Aircraft Co. 1951-55; supvr. Arnoux Corp. 1955-58, 1961-63; Marquardt Aircraft Co. 1958-61; with Rockwell Internat. 1963--; engr. supvr. autonetics div. 1965--; currently mem. tech. staff. VI ASSD Rockwell, Anaheim; tchr. eng., CSU Northridge 1964; honors: Engr. of the yr., Aircraft Systems, 1982; mem: IEEE; Ch. of Jesus Christ of Latter Day Saints (Bishoprie 1962-64, Sunday sch. supvr. 1965-66, high priest gp. ldr. 1966, exec. secty. 1977-); mil: s/sgt. USAF 1942-46; Republican; LDS; rec: computers, skiing. Res: 5412 Willowick Anaheim 92807 Ofc: Rockwell, 3370 Mira Loma Anaheim 92803

ORDOG, GARY JOSEPH, physician, educator; b. June 2, 1954, New Westminster, B.C., Canada; s. Joseph and Jean Ordog; m. Cindy Solodki, June 2, 1979; edn: BS, Univ. of Brit. Columbia 1976, MD, 1979. Career: rotating internship Vancouver General Hosp., 1978-79; Family Practice residency, 1979-80; Emergency Medicine res., Martin Luther King Jr. Gen. Hosp. and Charles R. Drew/ UCLA Postgrad. Med. Sch., Los Angeles, 1980-82; Emerg. Med. Fellowship, King/Drew Medical Ctr., 1982-84, Neurosurgery Research Fellowship, 1982-83; asst. prof. Charles R. Drew/UCLA Postgrad. Med. Sch., 1982--; physician Emergency Medicine, 1982--; honors: Award of Merit, Royal Life Saving Soc. of Canada (1969); Board Certified or Eligible: Am. Bd. of Emergency Med., Royal Coll. of Physicians an Surgeons of Canada (Emerg. Med.), Canadian Coll. of Family Physicians (Emerg. Med. and Family Practice), Am. Bd. of Med. Toxicology; mem. Am. Coll. of Emerg. Physicians, Canadian Coll. of Family Physicians; med. resrch: diving medicine, hyperbaric resrch., traumatology. Ofc: MLK, Jr. Hospital 12021 S. Wilmington Ave Los Angeles 90059

ORMSBY, LIONEL, advertising agency owner; b. Jan. 16, 1909, Oakland; s. Edgar L. and Georgia Council Ormsby; edn: AB, UC Berkeley 1932; m. Lola B. Ensminger; children: John Rush (stepson) b. 1933; Jean Garringer, b. 1946. Career: ed. Pelican Mag., Univ. Calif. 1932; asst. prodn. San Francisco News, 1933-40; asst. acct. exec. McCann-Erickson, Los Angeles 1940-42; acct. exec. Shaw Advt., Los Angeles 1942-46, 56-60; acct. exec. Dozier Eastman & Co., Los Angeles 1946-56; owner Hammer & Ormsby Advt., Los Angeles, Santa Rosa, 1960--; tchr. journ., Alameda H.S. 1932-34, copywriting, LA City Coll. 1950-53; publisher Rexall Reporter 1962-75, BankAmericard Trade Secrets 1969-79, Sales Talk (nationwide newsletter) 1958-83; contbg. writer: Better Homes & Gardens, Am. Home, Readers Digest, Advt. Age, Printers Ink, Sunset, Western Advt., LA Times, LA Herald-Examiner, Seattle Post Intelligencer. Mem: Kappa Sigma (UC, 1930); chmn. Bev. Hills Council BSA 1945; chmn. pub. com. LA TV & Health Assn. 1955-60; bd. dirs. LA Advt. Club (1st vp 1955-65), bd. mem. L.A. Beautiful (pub. dir. 1969-78); bd. Moneytree Mktg. 1981-2. Rec: golf, bridge, fishing, writing. Address: Hammer & Ormsby Advt., 476 Hillsdale Dr Santa Rosa 95405

ORR, JOHN THOMAS, manufacturing co. executive; b. Dec. 17, 1951, Tulsa, Okla.; s. Robert Phillup and Joan Bernadine (Edens) O.; m. Deborah L. Schmidtman, Feb. 18, 1984; children: Aaron, b. 1972; Laurel, . 1970; edn: BS, honors, Tulane Univ. 1974; Univ. of Edinburgh 1972-73; MSEE, Stanford Univ. 1975. Career: design engr. Hewlit- Packard Corp., Cupertino 1975; eng. mgr. Pro- Log Corp., Monterey 1979; co-founder/ gen. mgr. Pilot Instruments, Monterey 1983--; honors: Tau Beta Pi; mem: IEEE; Triton Yacht Club; Republican; Presbyterian; rec: sailing, flying. Res: 222 Lobos Ave Pacific Grove 93950 Ofc: Pilot Instruments, 177 Webster St, Ste A292, Monterey 93940

ORR, GEORGE VERNON, JR., secretary, US Air Force; b. Nov. 12, 1916, Des Moines, Ia.; s. George Vernon and Wilhelmina (Van Niewall) O.; m. Joan Peak, Mar. 31, 1941; children: Carolyn, b. 1947; Robert, b. 1949; edn: BA, Pomona Coll. 1937; MBA, Stanford Univ. 1939. Career: mgmt. trainee Bullocks Dept. Store, Los Angeles 1939-42; partner, Verne Orr Motors 1946-59; partner Verne Orr Co. 1959-62; pres. Investors S&L Assn. 1962-66; Calif. dir. Motor Vehicles 1967-69; Calif. dir. fin. 1970-75; secty. of the Air Force 1981--; past pres: Pasadena Merchants Assn., Family Assistance of Pasadena; L.A. Co. United Way 1963; foreman, L.A. Co. Grand Jury 1962; awards: Man of the Yr., Salvation Army of Pasadena 1970; mem: Kiwanis Club, Pasa. (pres. 1951); Rotary; Carmelita Lodge F&AM; Phi Beta Kappa; Alpha Delta Mu; Univ. Club; Methodist (chmn. bd. stewards, ofc. bd.); mil: ensign, USNR 1942, supply ofcr. Naval Tng. Sch., Chgo. 1943; lt. commdr. USS Mercury AK-42, S. Pacific 1944-45; rec: amateur radio, photog. Res: 1444 Hillcrest Ave Pasadena 91106 Ofc: The Pentagon, Wash. DC 20330

ORR, LEE ERNEST, land development co. executive; b. Apr. 11, 1935, Dillon, Mont.; s. Irving Ernest and Margaret Elizabeth (Reece) O. M. Carolyn Pavacich, Nov. 22, 1970; children: Leanne C., b. 1973; Lee W., b. 1977; edn: BS, Montana State Univ. 1958; Gen. Contractors Lic, Calif. 1973. Career: with Betker Constrn. Corp. 1960-78; constrn. site supt. 1960-70; v.p., Santa Ana 1971-74; pres. 1974-78; with Fredricks Devel. Corp., Santa Ana 1975- 83; v.p. 1975-78; sr. v.p./ bd. mem. 1978-80; exec. v.p./ bd. mem. 1980-83; exec. v.p. Dunn Properties Corp. 1980-83; currently, exec. v.p. Dunn Properties Corp. & v.p. Dunn Propertes of Texas; honors: Arts & Arch. Hon., Delta Phi Delta, Montana State 1956; mem: Nat. Assn. Home Bldrs.; Bldg. Ind. Assn. of So. Calif., Orange Co. chpt.; Orange Co. Model T Club; Sigma Alpha Epsilon (life); Republican; Presbyterian; rec: collect & restore old cars, model railroad, brass collection. Res: 5362 Sierra Roja Rd Irvine 92715 Ofc: Dunn Properties Corp., 28 Brookhollow Dr Santa Ana 92705

OSBERG, JAMES DENNIS, computer systems sales executive; b. Aug. 2, 1951, Monrovia; s. Harvey J. and Myrtle C. (Jenson) O.; m. Elizabeth I. Rennison, b. Apr. 9, 1983; 1 dau: Lacey Elizabeth, b. 1983; edn: AA, Pasadena City Coll. 1971; BS, CSU Los Angeles 1974; Real Estate Broker, Calf. 1974. Career: v.p. Robert Lowe Associates/Prominent Properties, Los Angeles 1973-76; acct. mgr. Agency Records Control Inc., L.A. 1977-70; sales mgr. Delphi Sys. Inc., L.A. 1979-80; owner James Osberg & Assoc., L.A. 1981--; honors: Top Exec. Sales Award, Insurnet 1981; Winners Circle, Insurnet, 1981, 82, 83; mem: Am. Mgmt. Assn.; Alpha Kappa Psi; Republican; Catholic; rec: golf. Res: 3680 Silver Oak Pl Danville 94526 Ofc: Insurnet Inc., 1900 Powell St Emeryville 94608

OSBORN, ROYCE R., hospital radiology administrator; b. Nov. 18, 1925, Gretna, La.; s. Aubrey J. and Leona Marie (Rousseve) O.; m. Paul E. Chachere, Apr. 19, 1952; children: Irene, b. 1953; Linda, b. 1954; Yolande, b. 1956; Royce Jr., b. 1958; Alton, b. 1962; Sabrina, b. 1964; edn: BS, Xavier Univ. 1949; Loyal Univ. Chgo. 1970-71; Reg. Technologist, Am. Regis. of Radiologic Tech. Career: chief technologist Flint- Goodridge Hosp., New Orleans, La. 1955-65; chief tech. Loyola Univ. Med. Ctr., Chgo., Ill. 1969-71; regl. sales rep. Mallinckrodt Inc., Ohio territory 1971-74; tech. adminstr. Duke Univ. Med. Ctr., Durham, NC 1974-77; radiology adminstr. Brotman Med. Ctr., Culver City 1977-79; asst. to diagnostic div. chief UCLA Med. Ctr. Dept. of Radiological Scis., L.A. 1979--; Technologists Rep., Commn. of Technologists Affairs, Am. Coll. of Radiology 1970-71; cons. in radiology, Regl. Med. Conf., New Orleans 1968; nat. sales tng. Mallinckrodt Inc., St. Louis, Mo. 1973-74; honors: R&D of Auxiliary Cassette Holder, 3rd pl. NEMA Awd., Am. Soc. of Radiologic Tech. 1960, Exhibit award 1962; Outstanding Svc., Mallinckrodt Inc. 1974; Gold Awd., Am. Hosp. Radiology Adminstrs. 1984; mem: Am. Soc. of Radiologic Technologist (pres. 1969-70); Am. Hosp. Radiology Adminstrs. (pres. 1981-82); Western Reg. Am. Hosp. Radiology Adminstrs. (pres. 1978-79); author: A Professional Approach to Radiology Admininstration, C. Thomas pub. 1980; contbg. author: Persuading Physicians- A Guide for Hospital Executives, Aspen Press 1984; mil: signalman 3/c USN 1943-46, Victory Medal, So. Pac. Theater; Democrat; Catholic; rec: writing, singing in ch. choir. Res: 938 E Turmont St Carson 90746 Ofc: UCLA Medical Center, Dept. Radiological Sciences, BU-245, Los Angeles 90024

OSGOOD, EDGAR DE PUE, foreign trade co. president; b. Dec. 25, 1918, San Francisco; s. Jack Neville and Correnah DePue Osgood; m. Angela Coppola, Nov. 20, 1983; children: James De Pue b. 1954, Diane Holmes (Matthews), b. 1955; edn: schooled in Switzerland, France, Italy, 1925-31; Heald's Bus. Coll., S.F. 1934; farming major, UC Davis (debating, tennis teams) 1939-40. Career: owner/opr. var. firms: (current) pres./CEO, Osgood Warehouse Co. (warehse. mgmt. personnel ops., mktg., leasing, govt. contr.), San Francisco and Oakland, 1947--, Cargo Services Inc. (export packing), S.F. 1972--, Foreign Trade Services Inc. (Duty free, bonded warehousing), S.F. 1977--, Bay Area Inspection Services (storage warehse), S.F. 1978--; past owner/pres. DePue Warehouse Co. of San Francisco (public warehse and trucking ops.), 1945-70. Hon. Consul General de Cote d'Ivoire (apptd. 1981); chmn. Econ. Sub-com., S.F./Shanghai Friendship Com. (1979-); co-chair March of Dimes Gourmet Gala (1984); Tennis Dir. NFL Alumni S.F. chpt./Youth Tennis Found. Silverado C/C Invitl. Tennis Tourn. (1984); mem./past pres. Alliance Francaise; bd. French Am. Bilingual Sch. 1983-; mem. Calif. State World Trade Commn. Adv. Council 1983-; bd. Friends of Israel 1983-; awards: Youth Service Roscoe Mapes Awd. (1977), Liberty Bell Man of Year 1967, S.F. Bar Assn. and Lawyers Club; honored, S.F. Bd. of Suprs. (1967); Civic Service awd., KABL (1965); Sun Reporter citizen's merit awd. (1958); clubs: Pacific Union, S.F. Tennis, Calif. Tennis, Lagunitas CC (Ross), Cercle de L'Union, Villa Taverna, S.F. CofC, French/Am. CofC; works: chmn. SF Human Rights Commn. 1964-67; pres. Council for Civic Unity 1956-57; co-chmn. SF Com. for Equal Opportunity, credited with passing Fair Employment Practices Commn. Laws, 1955-57; chmn. SF Com. Against Capital Punishment 1960-71; co-founder United World Federalists 1956; mil: aerial navigator USN 1941-45; Republican (pres. Young Repubs. of Calif. 1953; chmn. SF Repub. Central Com. 1960-65, mem. 1954-73); rec: tennis, bridge, dominoes, skiier. Res: 2018 Bush St SF 94115 Ofc: Pier 23, San Francisco 94111

OSHEA, MARTIN LESTER, real estate investment co. executive; b. Dec. 6, 1938, San Francisco; s. Adolph Martin and Maria Karala (Bergmann) O.; m. Barbara Behn, Aug. 2, 1969; children: Laura, b. 1971; Amy, b. 1972; Amanda, b. 1976; edn: BA, Stanford Univ. 1959; Oxford Univ., England 1959-61; MBA, Harvard Bus. Sch. 1963. Career: assoc. corp. fin. dept. Dean Witter & Co., NY 1963-67; assoc. corp. fin. dept. First Calf. Co., San Francisco 1967-69; v.p corp. fin. B. Wilson & Co., S.F. 1969-70; pres. Oshea Co. 1970--; mng. partner Gen. Western Co., S.F. 1967--; trustee First Eastern Realty Trust, Boston 1963-67; dir. Guarantee S&L Assn. of Livermore Valley 1969-71; mem: Commonwealth Club of Calif. (bd. gov. 1975-78, exec. com. 1979); Cow Hollow Improvement Assn. (bd. mem. 1975-); Harvard Club, NYC; Harvard Univ., S.F. (secty. 1972-74); author: Tampering With the Machinery: Roots of Economic and Political Malaise, McGraw Hill, NY 1980; Republican (chmn. S.F. Co. Central Com. 1979-82, v.p. Co. Chmns. Assn. of Calif. 1981-82, Nat. Adv. Council on Adult Edn. 1983-); Catholic; rec: hiking, tennis. Res: 2863 Pacific Ave San Francisco 94115 Ofc: General Western Co., 235 Montgomery, Ste 1656, San Francisco 94104

OSIO, SALVATORE PATRICK, lawyer/ investment banker; b. Feb. 22, 1938, Los Angeles; s. Patrick and Laura Alvarez (Morphy) O.; m. Ursula Pringal, 1966; children: Katrina Marie, b. 1966; Tanya Marie, b. 1968; Salvatore Patrick, b. 1971; edn: LLB, USC 1962; JD, 1962. Career:partner, Carver, Osio & Fuller, Attys., Los Angeles 1963-73; chmn. bd. City Investors Inc., San Diego & L.A. 1973--; instr. real estate investment analysis, UCLA 1967-70; dir. Tchr. Mgmt. & Investment Corp. 1968-70; dir. Reliance Capital Corp. 1970-72; honors: Ephebian Soc., Examiner Hall of Fame 1956-; mem: Jonathan Club; Alpha Tau Omega; Legion Lex; Rancho Santa Fe Golf & Tennis Club; Will Rogers Polo Club; wokrs; Real Estate Investment Analysis- Formulas & Equations, 1969; mil: USAFR 1956-62; Republican; Catholic; rec: equestrian, boating, fishing. Res: 5922 El Montevideo Rancho Santa Fe 92067 OFc; 853 Camino del Mar, Ste 220

OTA, BLAIR GREGORY, oral and maxillofacial surgeon; b. Oct. 4, 1949, Torrance; s. James Tsugio and Kay Helen (Negi) Ota; m. Paula Ann (PhD), July 17, 1971; children: Bowen b. 1972, Jamie b. 1980; edn: undergrad., UCLA 1967-70; DDS, USC, 1974; oral and maxillofacial surgery residency, USC/L.A. County Med. Center, 1974-77; MD, Hahnemann Univ. for the Health Scis. 1981; gen. surg. residency, UC San Diego, 1981-82. Career: oral and maxillofacial surgeon, Gardena 1977-79, 1982--; clin. prof., Oral and Maxillofacial Surgery, USC, 1978--; cons. Canyon Gen. Hosp., Chapman Gen. Hosp., Gardena Community Hosp., Gardena Meml. Hosp., St. Joseph's Med. Ctr., Western Med. Ctr.; honors: Fellow Am. Assn. of Oral and Maxillofacial Surgeons 1982; Fellow Alpha Omega Alpha Nt. Honor Med. Soc. 1981; Resident rep. Marsh Robinson Acad. of Oral and Maxillofacial Surg. 1976; Fellow So. Calif. Acad. of Oral Pathology 1976; Fellow Omicron Kappa Upsilon Nat. Hon. Dental Soc. 1974; Clin. Fellow USC Cancer Fellowship 1973; Alpha Tau Epsilon Hon. Dental Soc. 1971; mem: Am. Dental Assn., Am. Medical Assn., Am. Assn. of Oral & Faxillofacial Surgeons, Calif. Dental Assn., Harbor Dental Soc., Marsh Robinson Acad. of Oral and Maxillo. Surg., Orange County Dental Soc., Orange Co. MEd. Soc., So. Calif. Acad. of Oral Pathol., So. Calif. Japanese Am. Dental Soc., So. Calif. Japanese Am. Med. Soc.; presentation, Maxillary

Segmental Surgery, So. Calif. Soc. of Oral and Maxillofacial Surg. 1976; rec: tennis, surfing, skiing. Res: 4 Bellezza Irvine 92714 Ofc: 1600 W. Redondo Beach Ste 406, Gardena 90247

OTOSHI, TOM YASUO, electrical engineer; b. Sept. 4, 1931, Seattle; s. Jitsuo and Shina (Nakagaki) O.; m. Haruko Shirley Yumiba, Oct. 13, 1963; children: John, b. 1964, Kathryn, b. 1967; edn: BSEE, Univ. of Wash. 1954, MSEE, 1957. Career: electrical engr., mem. tech. staff Hughes Aircraft Co., Culver City 1956-61; tech. staff Jet Propulsion Lab, Pasadena 1961--; honors: Tau Beta Pi, Sigma Xi, num. NASA new technology awards; senior mem. IEEE; num. publs. in profl. journals and progress reports (NASA/JPL), patent; Prot.; rec: choral music, photog., computers. REs: 3551 Henrietta, La Crescenta 91214 Ofc: Jet Propulsion Lab, 4800 Oak Grove Dr Pasadena 91109

OTT, MICHAEL DUANE, lawyer; b. June 9, 1948, San Bernardino; s. Thomas Russell and Beverly Louise (Pentland) O. m. Karen Hiroko Matsumoto, Dec. 23, 1967; children: Jonathan, b. 1969; Steven, b. 1970; edn: BA, UC San Diego 1971; UC Riverside 1971-72; JD, Univ. of Iowa Coll. of Law 1974. Career: law clerk US Dist. Judge A. Andrew Hauk, Central Dist. of Calif., Los Angeles 1974-75; assoc. Friedman, Heffner, Kahaun & Dysart, San Diego 1975-77; atty. Union Pacific Railroad Law Dept., Portland, Ore. 1977; assoc., Kahan, Dysart & Fraser, San Diego 1978-79; sr. deputy co. counsel Co. of Lake, Lakeport 1979-81; sr. deputy co. counsel, Co. of Fresno, Fresno 1981-83; co. counsel, Co. of Madera, Madera 1983--; instr. local govt. law Humphreys Coll. Sch. of Law, Fresno 1982; honors: Notes and Comments ed., Iowa Law Review 1973-74; mem: State Bar of Calif. Am. Bar Assn. (Urban, State & Local Gvt. Law Sect.; Sect. Nat. Resources Law; Litigation Sect.; Govt. Litigation Com.; Fresno Co. Bar Assn.; San Diego Co. Bar Assn. (Legis., Land Use & Legal Ethics & Unlawful Practice Coms.); UC San Diego Alumni & Friends (dir. 1976-76, gen. counsel 1978-79); publs: Pendent Jurisdiction and Minimal Diversity, 59 Iowa Law Review 179, 1973; Close Corporations and the Federal Income Tax Laws-Should the State Label Control?, 59 Iowa Law Review 552, 1974; Democrat (Lake & Fresno Co. Central Coms.); rec: tennis. Res: 8288 N Del Mar Ave Fresno 93711 Ofc: County Counsel, Co. of Madera, 2098 W Yosemite Ave Madera 93937

OTT, RAYMOND EARL, city attorney; b. May 8, 1926, Chgo., Ill.; s. Maurice Earl and Blanche Evelyn (Nelson) O.; m. Foliane Vallee, Feb. 14, 1982; edn: Indiana State Univ. 1944-45; Univ. of Portland 1946-47; JD, USC 1950; admitted to practice, State Bars of Ore. 1950 & Calif. 1953. Career: asst. city atty./ city prosecutor, Beverly Hills 1953-59; city atty., Fremont 1959-69; deputy dir. of contractual rels., Los Angeles Schs. 1969-70; city atty., Palm Springs 1971-79, Beverly Hills 1979-80, Cathedral City 1981--, La Quinta 1982--; mil: A/S V-12 USNR 1944-45; USAR & Calif. Army Nat. Guard 1947-71; lt. col., Judge Advo. Gen. Corps; Republican; Protestant; real private pilot. Res: 72990 Deer Grass Dr Palm Desert 92260 Ofc: City Hall, 68-625 Perez Rd, Ste 16, Cathedral City 92234

OU, WEIMING, engineer; b. Feb. 10, 1952, Tainan, Taiwan; s. Li-Shiu and Wu-Chiu (Hwang) Ou; m. Anchi Chang, Dec. 18, 1976; 1 dau. Tracy, b. 1980; edn: BS in physics, Fu-Jen Univ. 1974; MSEE, Univ. of Houston 1979. Career: research asst. Univ. of Houston, Tx. 1978-79; engr. TRW Microwave, Sunnyvale 1980-81; engr. Varian-SSMD, Santa Clara 1981--; mem. IEEE. Inventions: nondestructive measurement of a dielectric layer using surface electromagnetic waves (1983); research in microwave amplifiers area 1980-. Republican. Rec: fish, ski. Res: 3098 Halgrim Ct. San Jose 95132 Ofc: Varian-SSMD, 3251 Olcott St. Santa Clara 95050

OUSHALEM, ROBERT, lawyer; b. July 21, 1951, Baghdad, Iraq, nat. 1981; s. Baba and Christina (Pera) O.; m. Bella, Nov. 23, 1980; edn: BS, Univ. of NY Brockport 1974; JD, George Mason Univ. 1979; admitted to practice, State of Va. 1979 & Calif. 1980. Career: assoc. law firm Hosterman & Oushalem (spec. immigration & personal liability), San Jose; mem: Am., Calif., Va. & Santa Clara Bar Assns.; Am. Assyrian Commun. Ctr. of San Jose (treas.); Iranian Health Found. (founder); Protestant- Episcopal; rec: skiing, tennis, golf. Res: 4205 Ranwick Ct San Jose 95118 Ofc: Hosterman & Oushalem, 920 Saratoga Ave, Ste 213, San Jose 95129

OVADYA, MUSA MOIZ, electrical engineer; b. Aug. 8, 1957, Istanbul, Turkey; s. Yako and Viyoleta (Maravent) O.; m. Lusi, May 30, 1979; 1 son: Jeffrey, b. 1982; edn: BSEE, Univ. of Rochester 1979; Elec. Engr., Univ. of Rochester 1979. Career: lab supvr. Computer Maintenance Co., Los Angeles 1979-82; sr. engr. Jet Propulsion Lab., Pasadena 1982--; cons. Commuter Computer Corp. 1983-84; publs: A Pipeline Multiprocessor Architecture for High Speed Cell Image Analysis, pub. IEEE Computer Soc. Wrkshp. 1983; rec: basketball, bridge, tennis. Res: 8300 W De Longpre Ave, 301, Los Angeles 90069 Ofc: Jet Propulsion Lab, 4800 Oak Grove Dr Pasadena 91109

OVERTON, LOWELL ROBERT, real estate executive; b. June 20, 1953, Pomona; s. Robert Lightner and Janice Marie (Buffington) O.; edn: AA, Mt. San Antonio Coll. 1974; BA, Calif. State Polytech. Univ., Pomona 1976; BS, 1977; Criminal Justice Cert., 1977; R.E. Borker, Calif. 1981. Career: youth counselor Leroy Boys Home, La Verne; crisis intervention counselor San Bernardino Probation Dept. Ontario; broker assoc. Goldenwest Realtors, Diamond Bar; currently, head res. mktg. div. Goldenwest Investments Internat., Upland; sales tnr.- coord. real estate svcs.; honors: Top Realtors, L.A. & San Bernardino Cos., Goldenwest Realtors & Assocs. 1979; mem: Nat. & Calif.

Realtors Assns.; Am. Assn. of Soc. Wkrs.; Am. Psychological Assn.; Republican; Presbyterian; rec: weight lifting, physical fitness, photog. Res: 1056 Canyon Springs Ln Diamond Bar 91765 Ofc: Goldenwest Investments Internat., 545 N Mountain Ave Upland 91786

OWADES, RUTH M., marketing co. executive; b. Sept. 2, 1944, Los Angeles; d. David and Yonina (Graf) Markowitz; m. Joseph L. Owades, Sept. 7, 1969; edn: BA, Scripps Coll. 1966; Fulbright Scholar Univ. of Strasbourg, France 1967; MBA, Harvard Bus. Sch. 1975. Career: copywriter D'Arcy Advt. Co., St. Louis, Mo. 1970-71; asst. program director KMOX-AM Radio, St. Louis 1971-72; assoc. prod. WCVB-TV, Boston 1972-73; mktg. project mgr. United Brands Co., Boston 1975; mktg. dir. CML Group, Inc. Concord, Mass. 1975-78; founder/pres. Gardener's Eden, Inc. Boston 1978-82; pres. Gardener's Eden Div., Williams-Sonoma, Inc., Emeryville, Ca. 1982; dir. Hellenic Breweries S.A., Athens, Greece. Honors: Goodwill Amb. to Nagoya, Japan 1960; Phi Beta Kappa; mem. Direct Mktg. Assn., Harvard Club of N.Y. Res: 2164 Hyde St. San Francisco 94109 Ofc: Williams-Sonoma Inc. 5750 Hollis St. Emeryville 94608

OWCA, JAMES WILLIAM, manufacturing co. executive; b. Nov 6, 1944, Chgo., Ill.; s William J. and Therese C. (Krause) O.; m. Paula E. Wilberding, June 11, 1966; children: Amy, b. 1967; Andrew, b. 1968; Matthew, b 1976; Katherine, b. 1979; edn: BA, Loras Coll. 1966; MBA, DePaul Univ. 1972. Career: cost acct. U.S. Gypsum, Chgo., Ill. 1966-69; with Teledyne Continental Motors 1969-74; cost acct., Elk Grove, Ill. 1969-70; gen. supvr. 1970-71; mgr. div. acctg., Muskegon, Mich. 1971-72; chief acct. 1972-74; asst. controller Teledyne Wisconsin Motors, Milwaukee, Wisc. 1975-76; controller 1976-81; Teledyne Ryan Aeronautical, San Diego 1981-82; currently, v.p. admin./ controller Teledyne Ryan Electronics, San Diego; mem: Nat. Mgmt. Assn.; Nat. Assn. Accts.; Assn. MBA Execs.; San Diego Zoological Soc.; Knights of Columbus; Republican; Catholic. Res: 17040 Palacio Ct San Diego 92127 Ofc: Teledyne Ryan Electronics, 8650 Balboa Ave San Diego 92123

OWENS, (Jack) JOHN PHILLIP, marketing consultant; b. May 8, 1922, Milwaukee; s. John Richard and Alice Louise (Best) O.; m. Shirley L. Gilmour, Aug. 31, 1947; two daus: Sharron Dee Garvisch, Carole Rochelle Leland; edn: Univ. of Wisc. 1940-1, Milwaukee Sch of Engrg. 1942. Career: with IBM Corp., District Edn. instr., Data Processing mgr., Dist. mgr., Info. Records Div., currently consultant marketing rep.; recipient IBM Mgmt. and Mktg. Awards inel. (22) 100 clubs, (10) Golden Circles, 45 IBM Suggestion Awds., reg. & dist. mgr. awards. Mem. Los Angeles Co. Sheriff's Reserve (Comdr.); mem. L.A. Co. Adv. Commn. for Edn. in Correctional Instns.; mem: Masons, Scottish Rite (32nd Degree); Calif. Peace Ofcrs Assn., L.A. Co. Peace Ofcrs. Assn., Calif. Reserve Peace Ofcrs. Assn., Nat. Sheriff's Assn.; mil: splst (I) 1st cl. USN 1944-46; Republican; Presbyterian; rec: stamp/coin collector. Res: 2030 Maginn Dr Glendale 91202 Ofc: IBM Corp . 355 So. Grand Ave. 22nd Floor, Los Angeles 90060

OWENS, WARNER BARRY, physical therapist; b. Apr. 29, 1939, Detroit, Mi.; s. Wendell Lee and Flora Lucille (Maddox) O.; m. Sandra Olstyn, Nov. 16; children: Jeffrey, b. 1962; Karen, b. 1965; edn: BS, UCLA 1962; Cert. Sch. of Physical Therapy, Childrens Hosp., L.A. 1961. Career: staff physical therapist Valley Physical Therapy Ctr., Van Nuys 1962-63; chief therapist 1963-70; dir. physical therapy St. Joseph Med. Ctr., Burbank 1962-84; exec. v.p. Therapeutic Assocs. Inc., Van Nuys 1970-84; dir: Tetrad & Assocs., McKillip & Owens Inc., Barry- Boyd Leasing Ltd.; honors: past pres. St. Joseph Med. Ctr. Fed. Credit Union; past pres. Internat. Wine & Food Soc., S.F. Br.; mem: Am. Physical Therapy Assn. (chmn. Judicial com. 1981-82); Am. Coll. Sports Med.; Am. Heart Assn.; Republican; Protestant; rec: wine collecting, skiing, golf. Res: 19621 Greenbriar Dr Tarzana 91356 Ofc: Therapeutic Associates Inc., 15243 Van Owen, Ste 102, Van Nuys 91405

OXFORD, HARRY WINNA, JR., chiropractor; b. Jan. 12, 1948, Alameda; s. Harry Winna and Mildred Irene Oxford; edn: AA, Chabot Jr. Coll.; 1971; BS, L.A. Coll. of Chiro. 1975; DC, cum laude 1977; postgrad., Univ. of calif. 1979-82; L.A. Coll. of Chiro. Postgrad. Sch. Orthopedic Cert. Pgm. 1982-84; BS, UC Berkeley; Cert. Chiropractic Disability Evaluator, Calif.; Bd. Eligible Chiro. Orthopedist; Cert. Independent Med. Examiner, Calif. Career: hd. stockboy, salesprsn., pub. rels. dept. Macy's Bayfair, San Leandro 1966-68; clerk, cashier, dist. cashier United Parcel Svc., East Bay, S.F. 1968-71; supvr. Parcel Delivery Svc., San Leandro 1976-77; asst. prof./ research asst. neurophysiology L.A. Coll. of Chiro., Glendale 1976-77; assoc. doctor, pvt. practice, Carl W. La Force Jr., San Leandro 1977-78; DC, pvt. practice, Castro Valley 1978--; team physician San Leandro Catholic Youth Orgn. 1981--; mem. L.A. Coll. of Chiro. Postgrad. Sch. Adv. Com.; honors: Eternal High Alpha, Delta Tau Alpha 1975; Alpha Gamma Sigma 1970; mem: Am. (sports injuries, neurology, roentgenology, technic, nutrition & diagnosis), Calif. & Alameda Co. (past pres.) Chiro. Assns.; Am. Coll. of Sport Med.; Am. Coll. Chiropractic Orthopedists; Castro Valley CofC; US Golf Assn.; publs: poetry pub. Life mag. 1964; num. awds., design/ compositions, for art projects, Chabot Jr. Coll.; research: parapsychology, Man's ability to Taste Color 1969-71; Republican; Lutheran; rec: rosarian, fishinig, art. Res: 3471 Northwood Dr. Castor Valley 94546 OFc: 20406 Redwood Rd, Ste E, Castro Valley 94546

OXX, WILLIAM GARDNER, III, educator, writer, illustrator; b. Jan. 19, 1923, Newport, R.I.; s. Wm. G. and Mary Elizabeth (Bjorkman) Oxx; desc. John Howland of Plymouth Colony; Wm. Arnold, 2d Gov. of R.I.; King David of Scot.; lineage incl. Bliss, Gardner, Greene, Lindsay, Munro families of Bristol and Newport, R.I.; m. May Isobel Anderson, Feb. 11, 1956; children: William IV, (Ensign USN), Sherri Lynn, Jonathan Howland. Edn: AB, hist., Univ. Redlands, 1949, MA, 1951; postgrad. Inst. of Russian Affairs, Columbia Univ.; 6 Calif. State Adminstrv. and Tchg. Credentials, San Fernando Valley State Coll. 1955-61. Career: fellow/instr. hist., Univ. Redlands, 1947-51; L.A. City Schs., instr. US Govt., Russian Hist., Mil. Naval Sci., 1954-84; coached num. So. Calif. Debate League varsity forensic teams (won 75 sweepstakes trophies, 303 gold, silver and bronze medals); apptd. Task Force for Studying Physical Attacks on Calif. Tchrs. 1969-71; dist. asst. chmn. Mayor's Task Force on Narcotics and Drugs, 1; approx. 250 speeches, TV, radio appearances, 1951-. Publs: contbg. ed. (books) Vanguard of Freedom, 1975; The Oxx Family in America, 1973; Bible and Christianity (Lakeside Press) 1952, A Hist. of Flight, 1953; Pictorial Hist. of the World (Simon & Schuster), 1956, America (Ency. Brit. Press), 1954; (coauthor) Brig. Gen. Francis Hudson Oxx, USA (Ret.), The Descendants of Samuel Oxx, Bristol Plymouth Colony; 23 historical, mil. hist. articles; airbrush illustrator Warships of the World, 1946; Army-Navy Jour. of Recognition (vols. 1-24), 1942-45; mem. Naval Intelligence Team under Cmdr. in Chief Adm. Ernest J. King, Pearl Harbor Trial, US Senate, 1945; Rear Commodore, 11th Dist. USCG Aug., 1974-. Awards: 2d place Intercollegiate Western States Championship; James W. Kyle Award for Excellence in Journalism 1949; 1st and 2d Diamond Awards, Nat. Forensic League, 1966, 71. Mem: Univ. Redlands Varsity Debate Team, 1948-50; Pi Kappa Delta (pres.), Alpha Phi Gamma, L.A. Westlake-Wilshire Toastmasters (founder, pres., hon. life pres. 1968), Gen. Soc. Colonial Wars (dep. gov. gen.), Calif. Soc. S.R., SAR (past pres. Gen. Patton chpt.), Soc. Mayflower Descendants, Pilgrim John Howland Soc., Soc. Sons & Daus of the Pilgrims, Soc. War of 1812, St. Andrews Soc. S.F., Hereditary Order, Desc. of Colonial Govs., Mil. Order of the World Wars; hon. life mem. PTA 1959; Republican; Prot.; rec: hist., research, marine art, pvt. library (4000 vols.). Sum. Res. The Whaler, 2481 Kaanapali Pkwy, Lahaina, Maui, HI 96761; No. 162, 439 Ali Wai, Lake Tahoe Keys, So.Lake Tahoe 95705; Res:2429 Leeward Cir Westlake Village 91361

OYGAR, AHMET E., neurosurgeon; b. Apr. 26, 1944, Istanbul, Turkey, naturalized 1976; s. Prof. Ismail Hakki and Zeynep (Torgan) Oygar; Edn: MD, BS, Hacettepe Univ. Med. Sch., 1964-71; chil: Rukiye, b. 1979; Sezen Z., b. 1981. Career: surgical internship, Jacksonville (FL) Univ. Hosp., 1971-72; neurosurgical residency, chief res. 1977-78, Kings Co. Hosp./Downstate Med. Center, Brooklyn, NY, 1972-78; Diplomate American Board of Neurological Surgery, Jan. 1982; lic. phys., FL 1978, CA 1979; pvt. practice, Consulting Neurological Specialties, Palm Springs, currently. Mem: AMA, Calif. Med. Assn., Riverside Co. Med. Assn., Palm Springs Acad. of Medicine, Cong. of Neurol. Surgeons, Calif. Assn. of Neurol. Surgeons, Chevalier de la Confrerie de la Chaine des Rotisseurs Bailliage des U.S.A. Awards: Ofcr. du Palm Academique of French Govt., Merite Civique of Fr. Govt. Publs: arts. in med. journs., profl. presentations med. confs.; First Application of Dorsal Column stimulator in England, 1976. Republican. Moslem. Rec: photography, painting, philately. Res: 2074 Navajo Dr., Palm Springs 92264; Office: Consulting Neurol Specialties, 1330 N. Indian Ave., Palm Springs 92262.

OZOG, RONALD FRANK, tax accountant/ real estate broker; b. Mar. 27, 49, Johnstown, Pa.; s. Stanley Walter and Louise Ann (McLarney) O.; edn: BS, UC San Diego 1974; Enrolled Agent, US Treasury Dept. 1973. Career: tax acct. Ronald F. Ozog, San Diego 1974--; owner/ broker Coastline Realty, San Diego 1974--; chief fin. ofcr. Leisure Retreats of Am. Inc., San Diego 1982--; bd. dirs.: General Recreation Inc., Leisure Retreats of Am. Inc., & Edgewater Financial Inc.; works: devel., financial computer software; mil: cpl. USMC 1968-70; Republican; Catholic. Res: 4651 Pico St, 111, San Diego 92109 Ofc: Leisure Retreats, 1919 Grand Ave, Ste 2F, San Diego 92109

OZORKIEWICZ, RALPH LEO, electronics distributing co. executive; b. June 26, 1946, Wash. DC; s. Leo Edward and Frances Joyce (Sanders) O.; m. Marie Tuholski, Dec. 18, 1977; children: Laura b. 1967, Joy b. 1970, Ryan b. 1980, James b. 1981; edn: BS, engring. mgmt., Univ. of Mo. at Rolla, 1969. Career: district mgr. Texas Instruments, Ft. Wayne, Ind. 1975, Chicago 1975-77, Southwest area mgr., Costa Mesa 1977-80; v.p. Southwestern Gp. Kierulff Electronics, Tustin 1980-81, v.p. mktg., 1981-83, senior v.p. corporate mktg., 1983--; elected founding mem. Acad. of Engineering Mgmt., 1980. Mem: Soc. of Engring. Mgmt., Amer. Electronics Assn., Amer. Mgmt. Assn.; Republican; Catholic; rec: golf. Res: 11912 Skyline Dr Santa Ana 92705 Ofc: Kierulff Electronics, 2585 Commerce Way, Los Angeles 92691

P

PABARCUS, WILLIAM NEIL, lawyer; b. July 2, 1947, Portsmouth, Va.; s. John Peter and Mary Elizabeth (Souza) P.; m. Jo Ann B., June 21, 1972; children: Nicholas, b. 1975; Anthony, b. 1979; edn: AB, San Diego State 1971; JD, cum laude, UC San Diego 1974; admitted to practice 1975. Career: sole practitioner 1975--; assoc. with: Frederick Hetter; Stafford Prante; Henderson & Karp; Mann & Townsend; currently, Joseph R. Irwin; honors: Am. Jurisprudence Award, constitutional law & criminal law; mem: Calif. & San Diego Bar

Assns.; US Dist. Ct. (So. Dist. of Calif.); Catholic; rec: swimming, golf. Res: 2624 Luna Ave San Diego 92117 Ofc: William Pabarcus, 140 Marine View Dr, Ste 201, Solana Beach 92075

PABST, KATHLEEN TOWEY, library director; b. Yorkshire, England; d. Thomas J. Towey; Edn: MLS, MA, BA, UC Berkeley, Grad. Sch. of Librianship; tchg. cert., Durham Univ. Career: library dir., Mechanics Inst. Library, San Francisco; fmrly., librarian, Utah Internatl., Standard Oil of Calif. Corp., US Govt. Agencies. Mem: Amer. Libraries Assn., Calif. Libraries Assn., Spec. Libraries Assn., Commonwealth Club, Tamalpais Conserv. Club. Republican. Office: Mechanics Inst. Library, 57 Post St., San Francisco 94104.

PACE, RUSSELL BROWN, JR., lawyer/insurance co. executive; b. March 6, 1929, Palmyra, Va.; s. Russell B. and Clara Virginia (Jones) P.; m. Margaret Caselli, Aug. 15, 1943; children: Jefferson, b. 1954, Nancy, b. 1957, Russell III, b. 1979, Courtney, b. 1982; edn: BA, Univ. of Va. 1950, LL.B, 1956; admitted to practice US Supreme Ct., US Ct. of Appeals (D.C. Circuit, Tenth Circuit), US Dist. Cts. (D.C., Colo.), Colo. Supreme Ct. Career: pvt. law practice with Davis, Graham & Stubbs, Denver, Colo. 1956-59; with Hogan & Hartson, Wash DC, 1959-68; pvt. law practice in Wash. DC and own investment bus., 1969-73; exec. v.p., gen. counsel, secty. and co-owner of Security First Group, Inc. and Security First Life Insurance Co., Los Angeles 1973-81, vice chmn. bd., co-owner, 1982--; honors: Theta Chi (pres.), Jefferson Soc. (pres.), Lambda Pi, O.O.K., Raven Soc., Baseball (1946-50); Law Rev., Nat. Moot Ct. Competition, John Bassett Moore Soc., Order of the Coif (1953-56). Gov. appointee, Calif. Economic Devel. Commn. 1982-87; co-chmn. The Earthquake Preparedness Com. (L.A. City and Co.) 1984-; pres. Internat. Found. for Learning Disabilities 1983-; founder L.A. Music Center; chmn. bd. Edmund G. "Pat" Brown Inst. of Govt. Affairs 1982-84; chmn. bd. Palmer Drug Abuse Pgm., L.A., Inc. 1981-, mem. nat. bd. trustees 1981-84; fmr. fin. chmn. Princess Grace Gala (1981); mem. The Friends of the Anthony and Elizabeth DuQuette Found. for the Living Arts, Am. Art Council, LA County Mus. of Art, Town Hall, Bel Air Bay Club; mil: s/sgt. to 1st lt. US AF 1950-53, capt. Reserve, Commendn. Medal; Democrat: co-chmn. Nat. Platform Com. (1984), charter mem./dir. Bus. Council, Dem. Nat. Com. 1981-) and chmn. Task Force on Budget and Taxation Matters (1983-); Presbyterian (elder, treas.). Res: 364 N. Bristol Los Angeles 90049 Ofc: Security First Group, (POB 29193, L.A. 90009) 1800 Ave of the Stars, Ste. 1400, Los Angeles 90067

PACKARD, CRAIG WILLIAM, quality assurance executive; b. Nov. 26, 1954, Bethlehem, Pa.; s. Fred Milton and Lucille Florence (Smink) Packard; m. Eileen Ryan, May 24, 1975; 2 daus: Jennifer, b. 1977, Marissa, b. 1982; edn: Penn. State Univ. 1972-3, BS in metallurg. eng., Lehigh Univ. 1976; Cert. Lead Quality Auditor, ANSI, 1982. Career: metallographic investigator Bethlehem Steel Corp., Bethlehem, Pa. 1976-77, product engr. 1977, yield engr. 1977-9, quality assurance engr. 1979-83; quality assurance mgr. Metals Div., Raychem Corp., Menlo Park, Ca. 1983--; mem: Am. Soc. for Metals-LVC (exec. com. 1978-82), ASQC, ASTM; mem. Fremont New In Town Club. Works: devel. portable pneumatic identification tool for semi-finished steel products, 1981. Republican; Episcopal; rec: fishing, table tennis, home repairs; res: 36865 Port Tidewood St. Newark 94560 ofc: Raychem Corp. 300 Constitution Dr. Menlo Park 94025

PACKARD, JOHN TERRELL, investment co. president; b. Dec. 5, 1933, Upland; s. Alden Cass and Florence Eleanor (Eye) Packard; m. Barbara Bentley, March 28, 1956; chil: Dana, b. 1957, Robert, b. 1958, Becky, b. 1961, Leslie, b. 1962; edn: BS, Stanford Univ. 1956, MBA, Stanford Grad. Sch of Bus. 1961; Chartered Fin. Analyst, The Inst. of Chartered Fin. Analysts, 1971. Career: investment counselor Scudder, Stevens & Clark Inc., San Francisco 1961-; vice pres. 1967, exec. v.p. 1973, dir. 1973-, pres. 1983--; gen. partner Scudder, Stevens & Clark, 1971-, dir. 1978-; dir. Scudder Realty Investors, Inc. 1983-. Stanford activities: trustee Stanford Univ. 1978-82, 82-; nat. chmn. Annual Fund 1977-80; trustee (chmn. 1974-6) Bus. Sch. Trust 1971-7; past pres. SF chpt. Stanford Bus. Sch. Alumni Assn.; Stanford Cabinet 1977-81. Trustee, Pacific Sch of Religion 1972-. Honors: Gold Spike Awd. for distinguished svc., Stanford Univ., 1975. Mem: The Security Analysts of S.F. (fmr. dir.), Investment Counsel Assn. of Am.; mem. Commonwealth Club of Calif., Pacific-Union Club, Sunnyvale Planning Commn. 1969-73 (chmn. 1972). Mil: lt. USAF 1956-9. Republican; Presbyterian; res: 12840 La Vida Real, Los Altos Hills 94022 ofc: Scudder, Stevens & Clark Inc. 101 California St., Ste.4100, San Francisco 94111

PACKARD, RUTH MC CREA, clinical social worker; b. May 3, 1920, Cashmere, Wash.; d. Donald Preston and Maud Maggie Adelaide (Richardson) Mc Crea; m. Gail V. Packard, Aug. 8, 1944; children: Margaret, b. 1947; Mary, b. 1948; Martha, b. 1951; Melinda, b. 1957; edn: BA, magna cum laude, Univ. of Puget Sound 1942; MSW, Univ. of Wash. 1964; LCSW, 1969. Career: soc. wkr. Long Beach Gen. Hosp. 1964-68; supvg. med. soc. wkr: Long Beach Gen. Hosp. 1970-81; Rancho Los Amigos Hosp., Downey 1968-69; Univ. of Ore. Med. Sch. 1969-70; dir. clin. soc. wrk., L.A. Co. Calif. Childrens Svcs. 1981--; field instr. UCLA Grad. Sch. of Soc. Wrk. 1972-73; USC 1973-74; CSU Long Beach 1971-81; mem: Children Citizens Adv. Com., Mental Health Assn.; Acad. of Cert. Soc. Wkrs.; NASW; Democrat; Ch. of Relig. Sci.; rec: rug making, Bonsai. Res: 124 West 51st St Long Beach 90805 Ofc: California Childrens Services, 2064 Marengo St Los Angeles 90033

PADAMA, CONSOLACION RESURRECCION, health care administrator; b. Nov. 8, 1941, Manila, Philippines; d. Crispin Tamayo and Enriqueta Resu

(Resurreccion) Mendoza; m. Manuel Padama, Mar. 29, 1964; children: Mary Florence, b. 1964; Glenn, b. 1965; John, b. 1966; edn: BS, Univ. of the East 1962; Nursing Home Adminstr., Ramon Magsaysay Med. Ctr., Cal Haven Nursing Home 1980; Reg. Nurse, Philippines 1962, Calif. 1968. Career: clin. instr. Luzon Colls. Sch. of Nursing, Dagupan City, Philippines 1962-63; UERMMC, Manila, Phil. 1963-64; De Ocampo Meml. Sch. of Nsg., Manila 1964-65; staff nurse Winnipeg Gen. Hosp., Minnipeg, Manitoba, Can. 1965-67; clin. instr. 1967-69; dir. of nurses Fountain View Conv. Hosp., Los Angeles, Calif. 1968-81; dir. of nurses/ co- owner Sycamore Park Conv. Hosp., L.A. 1981--; mem: Long Term Care Nurses; Kapumangi Club; Catholic; rec: camping, fishing. Res: 5406 Los Feliz Blvd Los Angeles 90027 Ofc: Sycamore Park Convalescent Hosp., 4585 N Figueroa Los Angeles 90065

PADILLA, VINCENT PETER, college president; b. May 29, 1925, San Jose; s. Vincent R. and Blanche (Ynostrosa) P.; m. Joyce Mathiesen, Feb. 5, 1947; children: Claudia, b. 1947; Thomas, b. 1954; edn: BA, San Jose State Univ. 1951; MA, CSU Sacto. 1967; Secondary Sch. Admin., Calif. Career: secondary sch. tchr. Sacto. City Unif. Sch. Dist. 1953-68; secondary sch. vice prin., principal 1968-71; with Los Rios Comm. Coll. Dist. 1971--; asst. dean instrn. Cosumnes River Coll. 1971-75, assoc. dean admin. svc. 1975-77; dean of admin. Sacto. City Coll. 1977-79; pres. Cosumnes River Coll. 1979--; mem: Assn. Calif. Comm. Coll. Adminstrs.; Epsilon Pi Tau; Calif. Indsl. Edn. Assn., Sacto. chpt. (pres. 1966); Sacto. Regl. Com. on Cont. Edn.; Calif. Comm./ Jr. Coll. Assoc., Reg. I; Am. Assn. Comm./ Jr. Coll. Adv. Com.; Calif. Comm. Colls. State Commn. of Athletics; Mexican Am. Edn. Assn.; Rotary, Elk Grove; Sacto. Yacht Club; Methodist Hosp., Sacto.; Los Rios Comm. Coll. Dist. Found. Cosumnes River Coll. Found.; mil: hosp. corpsman USNR, active 1943-46, 1951-52, reserve 1947-51; Catholic; rec: boating, cycling, fishing. Res: 8187 Gandy Dancer Way Sacramento 95823; Ofc: Cosumnes River Coll., 8401 Center Pkwy Sacramento 95823

PADUA, BRIGIDO M., real estate broker; b. Oct. 8, 1936, La Union, Philippines; s. Max and Juana Padua; m. Emilia, Nov. 29, 1975; children: Bob; Ricky; Emilie; edn: BS, Nrsit Coll. of Eng. 1962; ECE, Philippine Bd. of Elec. Engrs. Career: pres. Far East Telecomm. Corp., Manila, Philippines; owmner Anita's Furniture; currently, broker/ owner BMP Realty Co., Los Angeles; honors: Product of the Yr., electronics, Philippine Electronics Exec. Com. 1969; mem: Filipino Businessmens Assn. of L.A.; Optimists Club, downtown L.A.; Catholic; rec: fishing, golf. Res: 6400 Bakman Ave, No. Hollywood 91606 Ofc: BMP Realty, 2007 Wilshire Blvd, Ste 904, Los Angeles 90057

PAGAN, JOHN MICHAEL, lawyer; b. July 24, 1953, Santa Monica; s. Leon Howard and Alice Mary (Bambrick) P.; edn: BA, UCLA 1977; JD, Univ. of W. L.A. Sch. of Law 981; admitted to State Bar of Calif. 1981. Career: assoc. law firm Bambrick & Bambrick, Santa Monica 1981--; mem: Am. & Calif. Bar Assns.; Westside Ecumenical Council, UNISEF; Democrat; Catholic; rec: jogging, tennis. Res: 527 9th Santa Monica 90402 Ofc: Bambrick & Bambrick, 2811 Wilshire Blvd, Ste 410, Los Angeles 90403

PAGEN, WILLIAM ROLAND, petroleum co. president; b. Feb. 26, Los Angeles; s. Roland Jocelyn and Minnie (Meyer) P.; children: Patrice b. 1953, Robert b. 1955, John b. 1957; edn: BS, UCLA Sch. of Bus. Adm., 1946. Career: joined Edwin W. Pauley orgn. as accountant in 1946, treas. and dir., 1958, exec. vice pres. 1959, pres./chief exec. ofcr. Pauley Petroleum Inc., 1963--, chmn. bd./pres./CEO, currently; trustee The Edwin W. Paulin Found., Pauley Lifetime Trust, Barbara McHenry Pauley Trust; bd. chmn./CEO Newhall Refining Co. Inc.; pres./dir. Athens Oil Corp., Bayou Oil Co.; pres./dir. Gourmet Concessions, Inland Realty Corp., Via Verde Devel. Co.; bd. chmn./dir. Blacktop Materials Co., Pauley Pacific Inc., Pauley Transp. Inc.; mem. American Petroleum Club (incl. 25-Year Club), Petroleum Accountants Soc., Tax Executives Inst.; mem: dir. KRLA; nat. dir. Mexican CofC; bd. trustees UCLA Found. (pres. 1975-78, chmn. 1978-80, Exec. Com.); LA County Commnr. Small Craft Harbors (chmn. Rent Control Commn., mem. Mediation Com.), Orthopaedic Hosp. bd. of trustees (Adv. Council, Lohman Club, Resources bd. dirs.), L.A. Council for Internat. Visitors (dir.), John D. French Found. for Alzheimer's Disease (dir.); clubs: Petroleum, California, California Yacht (Staff Commodore), Marina City; mil: sgt. USAF 1942; Episcopal; rec: boating, photog., ham radio opr. Res: 875 Comstock Ave Los Angeles 90024 Ofc: 10000 Santa Monica Blvd Los Angeles 90067

PAI, KIHO, pharmacist; b. July 13, 1944, Taegu, Korea; s. Yuwee and Sodeuk (Kim) P.; m Susie Kim, Apr. 30, 1971; children: David; James; edn: BS, Sung Kyun Kwan Univ. Pharmacy Sch. 1965; MS, Seoul Nat. Univ. Pub. Health 1971; PD, Butler Univ. Pharmacy Sch. 1975. Career: pharmacist Indiana Ret. Persons Pharmacy, Indpls., Ind. 1975-77; Calif. Ret. Persons Pharmacy, Long Beach 1977--; awards: Korean Soc. of Indiana 1977; Sung Kyun Univ. Alumni 1978; mem: Indiana Pharmacist Assn. 1975; Calif. Employee Pharmacist Assn. 1977-; Korean Pharmacist Assn. of Calif. (Prof. tchg. instr.) 1983-; Orange Co. Central Y's Mens Club 1983-; Internat. Soc. of Friendship & Goodwill (hon.) 1983-; Universala Esperanto Assn.; Democrat (secty. Asian-Pac. Caucus of O.C.); Christian. Res: 1598 W Tedmar Ave Anaheim 92802 Ofc: Calif. Retired Persons Pharmacy, 201 Long Beach Blvd Long Beach 90802

PALLUCK, ANDREW JOSEPH, health club executive; b. Dec. 5, 1944, Chgo., Ill.; s. Andrew John and Katherine Muriel (Doyle) P.; m. Alexandra Neeb, Aug. 21, 1969; children: Andrew, Jr., b. 1970, Bryan b. 1972, Brent b. 1975; edn: BA, De Paul Univ., Chgo. 1969; Valedictorian, East European Lang. Sch., Syracuse Univ. NY 1964. Career: instr. Holiday Spa Health Culb, Chgo., Ill. 1969-71; asst. mgr. 1971; mgr. 1971-75; area dir. Holiday Spa Health Club, Los Angeles 1975-78; exec. v.p. 1978--; sales & ops. dir. State of Calif., Health & Tennis Corp. of Am.; honors: Mgr. of the Yr. 1973; winner, nat. sales contest, Health & Tennis Corp. of Am. 1973; mem: Santa Ana Jr. Assistance League; mil: sgt. USAF 1963-67, translator for Nat. Security Agency, Berlin, Ger.; Republican; Catholic; rec: weight lifting, water skiing, swimming. Res; 1542 La Loma Dr Santa Ana 92705 Ofc: Holiday Spa Health Club, 6763 Westminster Blvd Westminster 92683

PALMER, DAVID RICHARD, manufacturing co. executive; b. Aug. 4, 1945, South Bend, Ind.; s. Gene Loren and Mary Maxine P.; edn: BA, Claremont Mens Coll. 1967; MBA in fin., Wharton Sch. U. of Penn. 1971, MS in acctg. 1972; MA in mgt., Claremont Grad. Sch. 1979; CPA cert. 1974; Calif. lic. Real Estate Broker, 1975. Career: sr. staff acct. Haskins & Sells, San Francisco 1972-74; sr. fin. analyst Crown Zellerbach Corp., 1974-76, prod. mgr. 1976-7; sr. prod. mgr. Avery Internat., Los Angeles 1977-9, bus. plnng. mgr. 1979-81; vp-mktg. Newcastle Fin. Gp., Orem, Ut. 1981-2; vp-fin. Specialty Shelter Inc., Walnut Creek, Ca. 1982-3; cons. to mgmt. Palmer & Co., Palo Alto 1983--; dir. corp. fin. Micro Power Systems, Santa Clara 1984--; mem: Am. Mktg. Assn., Fin. Plnng. Inst., AICPA, Calif. Soc. CPAs; clubs: Olympic (SF), Merchants Exchange (SF); mil: 1st lt. Airborne Inf. 1967-70, Bronze Star, Vietnam. Res: 3112 Ross Rd Palo Alto 94303 Ofc: Micro Power Systems, 3100 Alfred St Santa Clara 95050

PALMER, FRANK JOSEPH, non-profit organization executive; b. July 22, 1930, Olean, NY; s. George F. and Angelina (Ambroselli) P.; m. Mary Primikiris, Sept. 10, 1951; children: George, b. 1952; Tony, b. 1953; Tom, b. 1958; Frank, b. 1960; Fred, b. 1964; edn: BA, St. Bonaventure Univ. 1957ue; Cert. Fund Raising Exec., Nat. Soc. of Fund Raising Execs. Career: exec. dir. Cattaraugus Co. Health Assn., NY 1957-60; exec. dir. Eyebank Assn. of Am. 1960-66; asst. dir. Rochester Rehab. Ctr. 1966-68; asst. dir. Calif. Heart Assn. 1968-70; deputy dir. Los Angeles Heart Assn. 1970-80; v.p. devel. Am. Heart Assn., Gr. L.A. affiliate 1980--; 2nd v.p. Nat. Soc. of Fund Raising Execs., So. Calif. chpt.; honors: NY State War Veterans Scholarship; Pres.' Club, Franciscans Communications; mem: Nat. Soc. of Fund Raising Execs. (pres. 1982); Granada Hills Booster Club; Franciscan Communications; works: minority pgms., Soc. of Heart Assn. Profl. Staff; faculty mem., Am. Heart Assn.; mil: BMC, USN 1948-52; Democrat; Catholic; rec: gardening, travel. Res: 12007 Eddleston Dr Northridge 91326 Ofc: American Heart Association, 2405 W 8th St Los Angeles 90057

PALMER, GEORGE JOSEPH, structural steel co. executive; b. Mar. 14, 1952, Gardena; s. Maria Elroy and Betty Jo (Alvis) P.; m. Marilyfn Austin, Mar. 27, 1971; children: Julie, b. 1971; Tisha, b. 1979; edn: Cuesta Coll. 1970-72; CSU Bakersfield 1973-75; Bakersfield Jr. Coll. 1973-75; Contractors Lic., Calif. 1980. Career: estab. Mid Coast Welding, 1977, company incorporated 1981; recently selected to construct part of the world's largest Photovoltaic Solar Plant for ARCO Solar, Inc., Carrisa Plains, Calif.; currently, pres./ maj. stockholder Mid-Coast Welding, Atascadero; personal cons. structural steel rel. projs., Co. of San Luis Obispo 1972-; honors: Calif. State Collegiate Wrestling Champion 1972; Calif. Comm. Coll. All Am. 1972; Cuest Coll. Outstanding Athlete of the Yr. 1972; mem: Nat. Fedn. of Independent Bus.; San Luis Obispo Contractors Assn.; Babe Ruth Baseball; AYA Youth Soccer; H.S. Booster; H.S. Wrestling Pgms. (coach); mem. US Wrestling Fedn.; Am. Judo Assn.; Shotocan Karate of Am.; Nat. Assn. Scuba Divers; Solo Pilots Lic.; Catholic. Res: 11800 Old Morro Rd, Atascadero 93422 Mail: POB 1355 Atascadero 193423 Ofc: Mid-Coast Welding, 8260 Via Obra Atascadero 93422

PALMER, THOMAS EARL, software design engineer; b. Jan. 10, 1950, Bakersfield; s. Oran Walker Sr. and Eleanor (Solano) P.; m. Elfie, Feb. 11, 1984; 1 son: Joel, b. 1976; edn: AS, Citrus 1970; BS, Univ. of Alaska 1972. Career: software design engr. Advanced Controls, Irvine; software engr. So. Calif. Edison; currently, software cons. Everett/ Charles Test, Pomona; dir. Datalinc 1981; cons. Everett/ CHarles 1983-84; honors: Rotary Citizen of the Yr.; co-designed test machine tha set a internat. test industry standard for software; mem: Am. Space Found.; Planetary Soc.; works: Kryteron Serios, 1984; Fifty Five Series, 1982-83; Vision (machine), 1982; rec: song writing. Res: 2017 East Yale Ct Ontario 91764 Ofc: Everett/ Charles, 2887 N Towne Pomona 91767

PALOZIE, WALTER JOSEPH, corporation executive; b. Mar. 15, 1919, Hartford, Ct.; s. Peter Andrew and Clara (Trombley) P.; m. Gretchen White, Dec. 7, 1956; Aeronautics Engr., Dept. of Commerce 1948. Career: big band musician, NYC 1941-43; gas station ownwer/ opr., Los Angeles 1946-48; pres. Am. Air Equip. Inc., Paramount 1948--; mem: CofC; Disabled Am. Vets.; mil: t/sgt. US Army 1943-46, European & Pacific Ops.; Catholic; rec: auto racing, big band music. Res: 1821 W Grenadier Dr San Pedro Palos Verdes Estates 90732 Ofc: American Air Equipment Inc., dba Mac Motors, 15142 Paramount Blvd Paramount 90723

PANEK, MILES E., building products and services co. executive; b. Oct. 25, 1923, New Prague, Minn.;e s. Frank and Agnes (Holec) P.; m. Kathryn Buescher, Dec. 27, 1945; children: Christine, b. 1952; Stephen, b. 1956; edn: BSCE, Iowa State Univ. 1947. Career: wth. The Ceco Corp. (bldg. prods. & svcs.), home ofc., Oakbrook, ILl. 1947--; engr., estimator, sales engr, Mnpls., Min. 1947; asst. dist. mgr. Mnpls., Minn. 1954-56; dist. mgr., Cleveland, Oh. 1956-66; dist. mgr., Los Angeles 1966-73; regl. mgr. Western Reg., L.A. 1973-83; v.p. Western Reg., L.A. 1983--; mem. sr. Gp., Ceco Corp.; mem: Structl. Engrs. Soc. of So. Calif.; L.A. CofC (Constrn. Industry); Knights of Columbus, Cleveland, Oh. (Grand Knight 1962-64); Jonathan Club, L.A.; Assn. Gen. Contractors, Calif. (state dir. 1976-77); mil: USN; Republican;

Cathol ic; rec: woodworking, fishing. Res: 1131 Alto Ln La Habra 90631 Ofc: The Ceco Corp., 1450 Mirasol St Los Angeles 90023

PANG, DANIEL, company president; b. Aug. 5, 1943, Luk Fung, China, nat. 1978; m. Patricia Young, May 17, 1967; children: Diana, b. 1967; Selina, b. 1968; edn: diploma, Sydney Tech. Coll. 1964. Career: v.p. Fung Lum Restaurant (USA) Ltd. 1973, pres. 1984--; exec. v.p. Fung Lum Universal Inc. 1978, pres. 1984--; mem: US Congressional Adv. Bd. (spl. advr.); Chineses Comm. Assn. of Santa Clara Co. (pres.) Calif. Nat. Bank Adv. bd.; Campbell-Kee Lung Sister City Com.; Republican (exec. dir. Asian-Am. Repub. Nat. Assn.); Christian. Res: 5100 Riverton Ave, 10, No. Hollywood 91601 Ofc: Fung Lum Universal Inc., 222 Universal Terrace Pkwy Universal City 91608

PANICCIA, PATRICIA LYNN, lawyer/ TV news reporter; b. Sept. 19, 1952, Glendale; d. Valentino and Mary (Napoleon) P.; edn: BA, Univ. of Hawaii 1977; JD, Pepperdine Law SCh. 1981; admitted to practice, State Bars of Hawaii 1981 & Calif. 1982. Career: former profl. surfer (world ranked 1975-79); currently, atty. spec. in media law & t.v. news report/ weekend anchor (under name, Patrician Lynn), KEYT (ABC affiliate), Santa Barbara; appointee, Calif. State Bar Fair Trial & Free Press Com. 1984; mem: Hawaii, Los Angeles Co. & Santa Barbara Bar Assns. Res: 2201 Parkway Dr Santa Barbara 93105 Ofc: KEYT, 730 Miramonte Santa Barbara 93102

PANOFSKY, WOLFGANG KURT HERMANN, physicist/ laboratory director; b. Apr. 24, 1919, Berlin, Ger., nat. 1942; s. Erwin and Dorothea (Mosse) P.; m. Adele Irene Dumond, July 24, 1942; children: Richard Jacob & Margaret Anne, b. 1943; Edward Frank, b. 1947; Carol Eleanor, b. 1951; Steven Thomas, b. 1952; edn: Gelehrtenschule des Johanneums, Hamburg, Ger. 1928-34; BA, Princeton Univ. 1938; PhD, Calif. Inst. Tech. 1942. Career: ofc. scientific R&D proj., Calif. Inst. of Tech. 1942-43; cons. Manhattan Dist. proj., Los Alamos, N.Mex. 1943-45; physicist Radiation Lab., UC Berkeley 1945-446; asst. to assoc. prof. physics, UC Berkeley 1946-51; prof. physics Stanford Univ., 1951-53; prof. & dir. High Energy Physics Lab., Hansen Labs., Stanford 1953-61; prof. &dir. Stanford Linear Accelerator Ctr., Stanford 1961--; Pres.' Scientific ADv. Com. 1960-64; High Energy Physics Adv. Panel to Dept. of Energy 1967-70; Dept. of State Wrkg. Gp., Geneva 1959; cons. Ofc. of Sci. & Tech. of the Pres. 1965-73; cons. Arms Control & Disarmament Agcy. 1959-80; Gen. Adv. Com. to White House 1978-80; Nat. Acad. of Scis. Com. on Internat. Security & Arms Control 1981-; honors: Guggenheim Fellowships 1959, 73; E.O. Lawrence AWd. 1966; Calif. Scientist of Yr. 1967; Nat. Med. of Sci. 1969; Franklin Inst. Awd. 1970; Ofcr., French Legion of Honor 1977; Danz Lectr., Univ. of Wash. 1979; Enrico Fermi Awd. 1979; Cherwell- Simon Lectures, Oxford Univ. 1981; Leo Szilard Awd. 1982; Shoong Found. Hall of Fame in Sci. 1983; mem: Am. Physical Soc. (pres. 1936-); Phi Beta Kappa 1936-; Internat. Union for Pure & Allied Physics 1958; Sigma Ki 1936-; Nat. & Am. Acads. of Scis.; Sierra Club; Stanford-Midpenin. Urban Coalition; publs: textbook, Classical Electricity and Magnetism, w/ M. Phillips, (1955, 62); num. sci. papers in profl. journ.; arts. on arms controls; num. talks on High Energy Physics and Arms Control & Disarmament. Res: 25671 Chapin Ave Los Altos Hills 94022 Ofc: Stanford Linear Accelerator Center, POB 4349 Stanford 94305

PANTUSO, GENE, mens products co. president; b. Jan. 22, 1933, Tooele, Ut.; s. Michael and Emma (Rinaldi) P.; children: Layne, b. 1950; Rebecca, b. 1955; Michael, b. 1957 (dec.); Anthony, b. 1963; ed Pang: Univ. of Utah 1952-55. Career: ofcr./ maj. stockholder Panco Men's Products Inc. 1964--; founder/ pres. Lago Inustries Inc. (mining & recovery of precious metals); gen. partner KenPan Ltd. & Hilltop Industries (br. ofcs. in Auila, Az., opg. millsite & recovery refinery sys.); honors: 3 Regl. Packaging Awds., for Panco Men's Prods. Inc., from Non-Foods Assn., L.A.; mem: Balboa Bay Club, Newport Beach; Irvine Coast Country Club, Newport Beach; Newport Beach Athletic Club; Magic Island, Newport Beach; works: created all pkg. & formulas for prods. manufactured, distributed & mktd. by Panco Men's Prods. INc.; mil: PFC, USAF Spl. Svcs. 1951-52; rec: swimming, tennis, golf. Res: 240 Nice Ave, 109, Newport Beach 92663 Ofc: Panco Men's Products Inc., 2182 E Alton Ave 92714

PAPADAKIS, NICHOLAS ERNEST, real estate co. president; b. July 29, 1947, Long Beach; s. Ernest Nick and Angeline (Gampas) P.; m. Alexandra Pontrelli, May 19, 1983; edn: BS, USC; CSU Long Beach 1970-71; Western State Univ. Sch. of Law 1970-71; Richard LaPore Inst. of Dramatic Arts 1973-75; R.E. Broker, Calif. 1976. Career: exec. v.p. Anchor Corp., San Pedro 1973-84; v.p./ broker Berendo Realty & Mgmt. Corp., San Pedro 1976-84; currently, pres. United Estates, San Pedro; instr. seminars relating to real estate; honors: Am. Legion Award for civic contbns. 1964; recogn., Boy Scouts of Am. 1981; mem: Nat. & Calif. Assns. Realtors; Aman Folk Ensemble (Nat. Bd. Dirs.); works: created/ introduced real estate plan for condominium owners in Calif., Official Govt. Approvals, 1981; Conservative; Greek Orthodox; rec: theater. Res: 3623 S Leland St San Pedro 90731 Ofc: United Estates, 259 W 7th St San Pedro 90731

PAPARIAN, WILLIAM MIHRTAD, lawyer; b. Apr. 3, 1949, Los Angeles; s. William Joseph and Serpouhi (Dickranian) P.; m. Ovsanna Mesrobian, Feb. 14, 1982; edn: BA, CSU Northridge 1981; JD, Southwestern Univ. Sch. of Law 1977. Career: lawyer 1977--; criminal defense; apptd. State Soc. Svcs. Adv. Bd., Gov. Brown 1982; mem: Criminal Cts. Bar Assn.; Calif. Attys. for Criminal Justice; Am. Nat. Comm.; Armenian Profl. Soc.; Armenian Ednl. Found.; mil: cpl. USMC, Vietnam Conflict; Armenian Apostolic. Ofc: 16 N Marengo Ave, Ste 215, Pasadena 91101

PARK, CHUI SUH, pharmacist; b. Aug. 26, 1941, Sinuiju, Korea, nat. 1980; s. Seung Ryong and Jong Nam (Kim) P.; m. Youn Kim, May 4, 1968; children: Clara, b. 1969; Sharon, b. 1977; edn: BS, Seoul Nat. Univ. Coll. of Pharmacy 1964; MS, Seoul Nat. Univ. Grad. Sch. 1967; MS, Purdue Univ. Grad. Sch. 1972; BS, Univ. of Utah Coll. of Pharmacy 1976; Reg. Pharmacist, Calif. & Nev. 1977. Career: research pharmacist Hanil Pharmaceutical Co. Ltd., Seoul, Korea 1966-69; pharmacist De Jay Drugs, Los Angeles 1976-79; pharmacy mgr. Disco Drugs #19, Riverside 1979-80; staff pharmacist Clark Drugs #7, L.A. 1980--; tchg. asst. Purdue Univ. 1971; research asst. Univ. of Utah 1973-74; mem: Am. Pharmaceutical Assn.; Calif. Employee Pharmacist Assn.; Korean Pharmacist Assn. of Calif.; publs: coauthor research art. w/ V.F. Smolen & E.J. Williams, in Journ. of Pharmaceutical Scis., Vol. 64, 520, 1975; Democrat; Catholic. Res: 1831 E Bassett Way Anaheim 92805 Ofc: Clark Drugs, 650 E El Segundo Blvd Los Angeles 90059

PARK, KYONG M., physicist/ chief engineer; b. Jan. 12, 1939, Korea; s. Yoon M. and Bong C. (Yang) P.; b. Bu Cha, Feb. 1, 1972; children: Eugene H., b. 1974; Edwin L., b. 1982 (dec. 1984); edn; BS, Younsei Univ., Korea 1963; MS, Southern Ill. Univ. 1971; Univ. of Okla. 1972-73. Career: instr. Yonsei Univ. 1968; research- tchg. asst. Southern Ill. Univ. & Univ. of Okla. 1969-73; proj. engr. Kavlico Corp. 1977-80; chief enr. 1981--; instr. L.A. Pierce Coll.; honors: Full Scholarship, So. Ill. Univ. 1969-71; Full Scholarship, Univ. of Okla., Nerman 1972-73; mem: Sigma Pi Sigma; Am. Soc. of Physics Tchrs.; Internat. Soc. of Hybrid Microelectronics; IEEE; works: 4 US Patents granted, 1 pend.; mil: 2nd lt., Korean Army 1963-65; Christian; rec: tennis. Res: 21946 Vintage St Chatsworth 91311 Ofc: Kavlico Corp., 20896 Plummer St Chatsworth 91311

PARKER, HENRY WILLIAM, business owner, contractor; b. Oct. 7, 1913, Lindsay, Calif.; s. Edgar Eugene and Alnette C. (Cheek) P.; m. Gladys Elizabeth Grauting, July 27, 1947; children: Henry Wm. Jr., b. 1934, Barbara Jean b. 1935, Richard Paul b. 1938; edn: I.C.S. School 1932-3; Calif. State Contractors Lic. 1948-. Career: with Pillsbury Farms Milling Co., 1931-33; ptnr. Parker Linoleum & Carpet, 1934--, sole owner; co-founder El Monte Tree Planting pgm. with US Forestry Svc., Angeles Nat. Park 1955; honors: El Monte Citizen of the Year, Sid Kading award (1979); mem: El Monte CofC, Auxiliary Police 1940-41, Historical Soc., O.F.P.A. So. Council of Conservation Clubs, Elks, Senior Citizens, Izaak Walton League of Am. (pres. 1955-56), Masons (past Worshipful Master), Scottish Rite, Shriners, Rotarian, past pres. Five Points Rotary Club 1971-72 (Paul Harris Award 1974); sponsor: Boys Club of Am., Boys Club Century Club, Girls Club of Gr. El Monte, 4H Club, Little League; past mem. Five Points Bus. Mens Assn., Native Sons of Golden West; mil: served in US Army 398th Engrs. 3rd Army, regtl. coord. of Spl. Engring., Pres. Unit Cit.; Republican; Presbyterian; rec: camping, fishing, hunting. Res: 2587 S. 10th Ave Arcadia 91006 Ofc: Parker Linoleum & Carpet, 12078 E. Valley Blvd El Monte 91732

PARKER, JIMMY DEAN, distributing co. executive; b. July 6, 1942, Checotah, Okla.; s. Horace Delton and Myrtle Elizabeth (Terry) P.; m. Mary Davidson, Dec. 14, 1961; children: Carl, b. 1962; Craig, b. 1966; Keith, b. 1971; edn: New Mex. Baptist Univ. 1960-61. Career: fast food mgr. Andres, Bakersfield 1962-70; with Glaser Bros., Carpinteria 1962-79, Vernon 1983, Los Angeles 1983--; warehouseman 1962-63; truck driver 1963-65; warehouse mgr. 1965-68; salesprsn. 1968-76; asst. mgr. 1976-77, br. mgr. 1977-83; sr. v.p. ops. 1983--; honors: Los Angeles Confectionery Sales Club 1979; mem: Boy Scouts of Am. (Com. chmn. 1975-76); BOys Baseball, Ojai (v.p. 1977); Republican; Protestant; rec: bowling, golf. Res: 20872 E Fuero Dr Walnut 91789 Ofc: Glaser Bros., 3130 Leonis Blvd Los Angeles 90058

PARKER, MADISON ALDEN, II, accounting co. president; b. Aug. 21, 1942, Nashua, New Hampshire; s. Donald Frederick and Wildie Thayer (Stillings) P.; m. Ruth Marie Gwynn, Sept. 24, 1966; children: Melanie, b. 1968; Madison II,o b. 1969; Stephen, b. 1971; Michael, b. 1972; John, b. 1974; Matthew, b. 1975; Mark, b. 1977; Scott, b. 1978; Tyler, b. 1980; Travis, b. 1981; edn: BS, Brigham Young Univ. 1971. Career: sr. asst. mgr. K Mart, Salt Lake City, Buena Park & Chula Vista 1971-73; founder, tax & acctg. practice 1974; pres./ chmn. bd. Taxamerica Acctg. Inc. 1979--; mem:Nat., Sadleback Valley & Santa Ana CofC; Nat. Assn. for Self- Empl.; AYSO Soccer; Boy Scouts of Am.; publs: author, How to Avoid Income Taxes Legally, 1980; mil: USN 1960; Republican; Ch. of Jesus Christ of LDS; rec: writing poetry, investments, chess. Res: 7064 Filkins Ave Cucamonga 91701 Ofc: Taxamerica Accounting Inc., 2751 E Chapman Ave, Ste 206, Fullerton 92631

PARLEE, NORMAN ALLEN DEVINE, educator; b. Mar. 23, 1915, So. Farmington, N.S., Can.; s. Allen Chipman and Margaret Lavinia (Foster) Parlee; came to U.S., 1953, naturalized, 1959; B.S., Dalhousie Univ., 1935; M.S., 1937; Ph.D., McGill Univ., 1939; postgrad., Cambridge Univ., England, 1959-60; m. Eileen Elliott, Sept. 22, 1938; chil: Cherie (Mrs. Lawrence Clay; Alan. Career: dir., research and devel., Dominion Steel & Coal Corp., Can., 1939-52; prof., metall. engring., Purdue Univ., Lafayette, Ind., 1953-62; prof., extractive metallurgy, Stanford Univ., 1962---; chmn., metallurgy programs, Applied Earth Sci. Dept., 1972---. Recipient Martin Murphy Prize, Engring. Inst. Can., 1948; fellow, Chem. Inst. Can., Amer. Inst. Chemists. Mem: Amer. Inst. Mining, Metall. and Petroleum Engrs.; Amer. Soc. Metals; Canadian Inst. Mining Metallurgy; Nova Scotia Inst. Scis.; Amer. Soc. Engring. Edn.; AAUP; Ductile Iron Soc.; Sigma Xi. Author: (with others) Electric Furnace Steelmaking, 1962; co-editor: Metallurgy at High Temperatures and Pressures, 1963; contrib. articles to profl. journs. Presbyterian. Res: 12145 Edgecliff Pl., Los Angeles 94022; Office: Dept. Applied Earth Scis., Stanford Univ., Stanford 94305.

PARRISH, CATHERINE, real estate broker; b. Nov. 8, 1922, Pulaski, Ga.; d. William and Tollie (Lester) Crum; div.; children: Patricia b. 1944, Glenora b. 1945, Joyce b. 1949, Maurice b. 1962; edn: Teferros Beauty Coll. Syracuse, NY; Merritt Coll. Sch. of Bus., Laney Coll., Alameda Coll., UC Berkeley; Calif. lic. real estate broker. Career: doctor's asst. Kennedy Meml. Hosp. Clinic, Metter, Ga. 1938-39, practical nse. 1939-42, surgical nse. 1942-44; bookbinder McMillan Book Co., Syracuse, NY 1946-47; spl. svcs., Veterans Hosp., Oakland 1947-51; unit mgr. Dreyco Sales, Oakland 1952-55; real estate sales Central Realty and Ray Collins Realty, Oakland 1955-57; real estate owner/ broker/trainer (trained over 200 agts.) Parrish Realty, Oakland 1957-81, resident mgr. 75-unit senior citizens complex Allen Temple Arms, Oakland 1981-83, for HUD, Calif. Housing Fin. Agcy., Am. Baptist Homes of the West. Organized Beautification Pgm. to plant trees on 91st Ave, Oakland (1953); founding bd. dirs. E. Oakland Parent Participation Nursery Sch. Inc.; orgnzr. Career Girls Guild; mem: Beautician Assn. (Syracuse NY), founder/pres. Social and Art Club (Richmond, CA), Merritt Coll. Acctg. Soc. (treas.), Royal Crest Fashion Guild (pres.), Citizens Participation Com. (v.p.), Assoc. Real Property Brokers Inc. (treas.), Bay Area Club of Nat. Assn. of Negro Bus. & Profl. Women Inc. (2d v.p.), Nat., Calif. Assn. of Realtors; Calif. Assn. of Real Estate Brokers (1st v.p.); BBB, Oakland CofC; NAACP; bd. dirs. Voice of Africa Inc.; PTA; apptd. by Mayor John Reading to Bicentennial Com. (1974); apptd. Mayor Lionel Wilson to Oakland Planning Commn. (1978); awards: Bay Area comm. rep. to Pres. Kennedy's Inauguration (1961), Sojourner Truth Award, Nat. Assn. Negro BPW; trophy, Assoc. Real Prop. Brokers Inc., 1962-69, spl. awd. 1976; recogn. award, Allen Temple Baptist Ch. (1980). Res: 9251 East 14th St Oakland 94603

PARRISH, EUDORA MARIE, educator, realtor, tax consultant, manufacturing co. executive; b. Aug. 30, 1927, Woolstock, Iowa; d. Walter Lee and Reva Marie (Tyrell) Parrish; m. Harold Brewer, June 1946; m. 2d. Alfons Vandrics, Sept. 1955; children: Earl, b. 1947; Rita, b. 1950; Althea, b. 1957; edn; BA, UCLA 1970, MA 1974; grad. stu., adm. services cred., CSU Northridge. Career: pub. rels. VTN Engineering, Van Nuys 1951-54; tech. ed. UCLA, Los Angeles 1972-74; tchr. Los Angeles Unified Sch. Dist., 1971--; real estate broker, Van Nuys 1973 ; mgr. Chet's Travel Bed Mfg. and Distbn., Lake Elsinore, Santa Paula and Van Nuys, 1982--; honors: selected for Acad. of PHBAO-ADP (Pgm. for Adminstrv. Tng. Principals of Hispanics, Black, Asians and Others); mem: UCLA Alumni 1974-; San Fernando Bd. of Realtors, Van Nuys; Educare -USC 1983; Phi Delta Kappa (USC); UCLA Masters and Credential Alumni Assn. Grad. Sch. of Edn. 1983; past pres. Mothers Club Bethel 211, N. Hywd.; mem. Valley Sch. Proj. steering com.; Republican; 7th-Day Adventist; rec: constrn. contracting, horses, gardening. Res: 13830 Calvert Van Nuys 91401

PARROTT, JAMES EDWARD, chiropractor, acupuncturist, hypnotherapist; b. Aug. 7, 1924, El Paso, Tex.; s. Insp. John N. and Marie (Doudreaux) P.; m. Mildred Tripp, Aug. 1967; 1 dau. Brynda Monique; edn: DC, L.A. Coll. of Chiro. 1957; CBS Cert., basic sci., Ariz. State 1958; MA, Baptist Comm. Coll.; Oriental Preceptership, acupuncture & herbalogy, Hong Kong Inst. 1960; desig: Profl. Hypnotherapist, Hynotism Tng. Ist. 1979; Cert. X-Ray Supvr.-Opr., Calif. 1979; Cert. Hunter's Safety Instr., Calif. Dept. Fish. & Game. Career: lectr./ tchr. basic scis., Oriental Med.; Acutherapy pioneer in Am. 1960--; chiro./ acupuncturist/ hypnotherapist; bd. chmn. Karmel Kookies Inc.; founder/ pres. San Pedro Prebuilt Homes; honors: Delta Sigma, hon. scholastic soc. of healing arts 1957; mem: Elks; Nat. Rifle Assn. (life); Calif. Rifle & Pistol Club (life); Sigma Chi Omega; works: sculptor; mil: pharmacist 2/c USN, USMC, WWI, Korean War, Korean Pres. Unit Cit., Pres. Unit Cit. USA, Philippine medal, Am. Campaign medal w/ 1 Star, Asia-Pac. w/ 4 Stars, Nat. Def., Victory, UN, Korean Svc. w/ 2 Stars; Democrat (State Central Com.); Catholic (bro. & stu. priesthood, W. Ortho. Cath.); rec: music, art, sculpture. Address: 812 W 5th St Oxnard 93030

PARRY, ROBERT T., economist; b. May 16, 1939, Harrisburg, Pa.; s. Anthony Charles and Margaret Ruth (Troutt) P.; m. Brenda Louise Grumbine, Dec. 27, 1956; children: Robert; Richard; Lisa Louise; edn: BA, magna cum laude, Gettysburg 1957-60; MA, Univ. of Penn. 1960-63; PhD, 1967. Career: asst. prof. econs. Phila., Coll. of Textiles & Sci. 1976-81; exec. v.p./ chief economist 1981--; Sec. Pac. Corp. and Sec. Pac. Nat. Bank; dir. Bunker Hill Income Security; dir. Equity Strategies Fund Inc; lectr. Pac. Coast Banking Sch. 1976-78; honors: Phi Beta Kappa, Gettysburg Coll. 1960; Nat. Defense Edn. Act Fellowship for grad. study 1963; elec. fellow, Nat. Assn. of Bus. Economists 1980; mem: eNat. Assn. Bus Economists (pres. 1979-80); L.A. Chamber (past pres., Council of Econ. Advrs.); Am. Bankers Assn. (chmn. Econ. Adv. Com.); Am. Econ. Assn.; Western Econs. Assn. (exec. cem.); Calif. Bankers Assn. (former dir.); L.A. World Affairs Council; author: num. arts. in bus. & profl. publs. Res: 20529 Vista De Oro Pl Woodland Hills 91364 Ofc: Security Pacific Nat. Bank, 333 S Hope St, Ste H8-12, Los Angeles 90071

PARSINEN, MARK THOMAS, management consultant; b. Apr. 4, 1949, Baraboo, Wisc.; s. Henry John and Irma Helena (Waananen) P.; m. Deidre Moore, Sept. 17, 1972; children: Camrin, b. 1969; Jennifer, b. 1977; Samantha, b. 1980; edn: MBA, honors, Stanford Univ. 1975; BA, cum laude, Univ. of Penn. 1971; Spl. Reading, London Sch. of Econs. 1970. Career: store mgr./ clothing buyer Hart Schaffner & Mark, Hanny's, Phoenix, Ariz. 1972-73; gen.mgr./ treas. Talisman Ent., Menlo Park 1973-75; dir. mktg. Adolph Coors Co., Golden, Colo.; v.p./ ofc. head The Boston Consulting Gp., Los Angeles 1975-83, (one yr. hiatus); v.p./ founder Silicon Solutions Corp., Menlo Park 1983--; dir. Hydroelectric Devel. Inc. (HDI), Denver, Colo. 1981-; honors: Bache Halsey Stuart Scholarship, Stanford 1974; mem: St. Anthony Hall frat. 1968-; Wimbledon Club 1976-78; Camden Hill Club 1976-78; Ladera Oaks Club 1975- (tennis chmn. 1980-81); Republican; rec: skiing, squash, Japanese language. Res: 501 Menlo Oaks Dr Menlo Park 94025 Ofc: Silicon Solutions Corp., 1380 Willow Rd Menlo Park 94025

PARTIDA, H. RICHARD, human resources executive/ private consultant; b. Feb. 16, 1939, Oakland; s. Juan Manuel and Carmen Maria (Partida) Partida; m. Clotilde Martinez, Sept. 1, 1957; children: Denise, b. 1958; Lisa, b. 1961; Richard Jr., b. 1965; edn: BS, Univ. of San Francisco. Career: specifications coord. General Motors, Fremont 1961-63; line supvr. 1963-68; plant labor rels. supvr. Mack Trucks Inc., Hayward 1968-72; personnel mgr. 1972-75; indsl. rels. dir. 1975-79; div. personnel dir. Levi Strauss & Co., San Francisco 1979-81; corp. dir. employment 1981-83; pvt. cons., human resources practices (primarily labor rels. & personnel audits) S.F. 1983--; subs. tchr. Golden Gate Univ., UC Berkeley Ext. Ctr., employment sect. & interviewing 1982-; exec. com. Levi Strauss & Co. 1980-83; honors: Federated Employers, ASTD Panel, JFK Univ., Asian Refugees, East Bay Job Developers, KCBS Talk Radio Pgm.; mem: Am. Soc. Personnel Adminstrs.; No. Calif. Human Resources Council (Plnng. Com.); East Bay Municipal Utiity Dist. (Minority Sourcing); Employment Mgmt. Assn.; Hayword Mayor's Task Force, Jobs for Youth (past); Hispanic Access to Radio & TV (HART); Career Links, stu. job pgm.; works: research paper, Promotional Opportunities for Hispanic Workforce in Sewing Machine Factories; mil: PFC USAR 1958-64; Catholic; rec: early Calif. history, classical music, photog. Address: H. Richard Partida, Consultant, 7936 Stonehurst Ct Pleasanton 94566

PARTON, JAMES (III), lawyer; b.Oct 19, 1951, NY; s. James and Jane Audra (Bourne) P.; m. Diane King, Aug. 22, 1976, (dec.); children: Phillip, b. 1964 (adopted); Christopher, b. 1967; edn: Uppingham Sch., England 1969-70; BA, cum laude, Univ. of Penn. 1973; JD, cum laude, Univ. of San Francisco 1977; admitted to practice, State of Calif. 1977. Career: staff asst. Congressman Michael J. Harrington, Wash. DC 1973-74; judicial clerk Marin Co. Superior Ct., San Rafael 1976; law clerk/ assoc. atty. Ericksen, Lynch, Mackenroth, Arbuthnot & Brennan INc., San Francisco 1976-78; assoc. atty. Lynch & Loofbourrow, S.F. 1978-83; partner 1983--; Alameda Co. Lawyers Com. for Disability Rights 1981-; reader Calif. Com. of Bar Examiners 1978, mem. Am. Bar Assn. (Litigation, Tort & Ins. Practice sects.); San Francisco Bar Assn.; Assn. Trial Lawyers of Am.; Defense Research Inst.; No. Bay Sch. Site Com., Sausalito Sch. Dist. 1978; No. Calif. Alumni rep., The Loomis Chaffee SCh., Windsor, Conn. 1981-; Democrat; rec: photog. Res: 269 Ricardo Rd Mill Valley 94941 Ofc: Lynch & Loofbourrow, 505 Beach St San Francisco 94133

PARTRIDGE-RANKIN, PRISCILLA L., counselor; edn: BA, cum laude, USC 1963; BS, counselors edn. 1965; EdD, counseling psychol. 1974; Sec. Life Cred. 1963; Pupil Personnel Cred. 1966; Supvn. Cred. 1971; single; three children; Career: tchr. Oxnard Unif. Sch. Dist. 1963-65; head counselor Las Virgines Unif. Sch. Dist. 1968-75; faculty mem./ instr. adv. counseling practicum Pacific Christian Coll. 1977--; La Verne Coll. 1977--; Calif. Lutheran Coll. 1975--; counselor Calif. Family Study Ctr. 1975-76; co-founder Assocs. in Growth and Counseling, The Alive Place, Thousand Oaks 1967-81; founder, Assocs. in Marriage & Family Counseling, Partridge-Rankin & Zaboski Inc., ctrs. in Westlake Village & Ventura 1981-; tnr. M.F.C. interns & trainees, psychotherapist, cons. to bus. firms in stress mcgmt., mgmt. tng., spkr./ wrkshp. leader for orgns. nationwide; Oxnard Comm. Coll. Counselor 1975-81; Ventura Co. Comm. Coll. Counselor 1981-; honors: yearbook dedication to ten Senior Women, Helen of Troy 1963; Woman of the Yr. Conejo Valley CofC 1969; AAUW Young Woman ofthe Yr. 1969, 1975; Faculty Senate Pres., Oxnard Coll. 1978; mem: Am. & Calif. Assns. of Marriage, Family & Child Counselors; Am. & Calif. Personnel & Guidance Assns.; Calif. Assn. Women Adminstrs. & Counselors; AAMFC; APGA; public speaker nat., Ind., Wash. DC, Hawaii, N.Mex., etc.; writer var. scholarly journs, newspaper column 1978-80. Address: 91 Calle Escalon Camarillo 93010

PARTRITZ, JOAN ELIZABETH, lawyer; b. July 16, 1931, Chgo., Ill.; d. Norman John and Florence Mae (Russell) P.; edn: BA, Ball State Univ. 1953; MA, honors, CSU Whittier 1963; JD, honors, Loyola Law Sch. 1977; admitted to practice, State Bar of Calif. 1977; US Dist. Ct., Central Dist. of Calif. 1981. Career: copy writer Nelson Advtg. Svc., Los Angeles 1952-53; speech & hearing therapist Port Hueneme sch. Dist., Port Huenme 1953-54; math. tchr. Montebello Sch. Dist., Montebello 1954-77; comedy writer/ performer Foster Prodns., Los Angeles 1980--; law prof. CSU Los Angeles 1978--; atty. Parker & Dally, Pomona 1977--; after dinner & keynote spkr. var. orgns.; cons. Foxtail Publications (ednl. material); honors: Sigma Tau Delta; Kappa Delta Pi; Alpha Pi Gamma; Alpha Psi Omega, Phi Lambda Chi; NSF grants, (3), 1965, 66, 69; Am. Jurisprudence Awd. 1976; Deans Scholarship Awds. (2) 1975, 76; Best of Show, watercolor 1981; mem: Am. Bar Assn. (Tort com., Ins. com.); Calif. Bar Assn.; Women Trial Lawyers; Calif. & Montebello Tchrs. Assns.; Nat. Orgn. for Women; ACLU; Whittier Art Assn.; La Habra Art Asst.; coauthor, California Modern Mathematics Textbook, 1960; Prize winning water colorist, 1981, 81, 83; rep. by Rummel Gallery, Montebello; works in pvt. collections; Democrat; Quaker; rec: painting, comedy writer-performer. Res: 10515 S Portada Dr Whittier 90603 Ofc: Parker & Dally, 100 Pomona Mall West, Ste 300, Pomona 91766

PASCUCCI, VIRGINIA ELLEN, manufacturing co. officer; b. Jan. 5, 1939, Indpls., Ind.; d. Charles Chester and Catherine Margaret (Ackerman) Mc Kee; m. Don Thomas Babbit, Nov. 24, 1960, div.; 1 son: Thomas Charles, b. 1962. Career: fin. plnng. Atlantic Research; ofc. mgr. Gen. Tire Corp.; ofc. mgr. Witney & Sons Masonery; ofc. mgr. Inter-State Tool Co.; para-profl. Apodaca

Finochhaireo & Co., CPA firm; currently, controller Jalisco Mexican Prod. Inc., Artesia; honors: ABC Sch. dist. Appreciation Awd., Career Day; 1st pl. Ladies Net., Frank Cardiel Open 1983, 2nd pl. 1982; mem; Nat. Assn. of Female Execs.; Smithsonian Assocs.; Democrat; Christian; rec: snow skiing, tennis, golf. Res: 1200 Elm, A, San Gabriel 91776 Ofc: Jalisco Mexican Prod. Inc., 17227 Jersey Artesia 90701

PASTEN, LAURA JEAN, veterinarian; b. May 25, 1949, Tacoma, Wash.; d. Frank Larry and Jean Mary (Slavich) Brajkovich; edn: stu. Stanford Univ. 1970; BA in physiology, UC Davis 1970, DVM (regents scholar), 1974; postgrad. Cornell Univ. 1975. Career: Veterinarian, Nevada County Vet. Hosp. Grass Valley, 1975-80; pvt. practice vet. medicine, owner Mother Lode Vet. Hosp. (accred. mem. of American Hospital Assn.), Grass Valley 1980--(Dept. Fish & Game has declared hosp. a Wildlife Sanctuary); afil. staff Sierra Nevada Meml. Hosp.; lectr. in field. Recipient Internatl. Merit Award, Vet. Economics, for most outstanding hospital (1982), cand. for Hospital of the Year award. Mem. AVMA, Calif. Vet. Med. Assn. (ethics com.), Mother Lode Vet. Assn., Am. Animal Hosp. Assn., Nat. Ophthal. Soc., Nat. Pygmy Goat Assn., Nat. Appaloosa Soc., Nat. Assn. Underwater Instrs., Sacramento Valley Vet. Assn. (exec. com.), Denver Area Med. Soc., Internat. Vet. Assn. Am., Endurance Riding Soc., Grass Valley Bus. Women; author (with Dr. Muller) Canine Dermatology (1970), contbr. articles to profl. jours.; Republican; Lutheran. Res: 15978 Shebley Rd Grass Valley 95945 Ofc: 11509 La Barr Meadows Rd Grass Valley 95945

PATEL, PRAFUL J., manufacturing co. executive; b. Dec. 1, 1943, Bakrol, India, nat. 1982; s. Jashbhai M. and Kamalaben J. Patel; m. Bharti, June 3, 1968; children: Hiten, b. 1972; Rina, b. 1978; Nimesh, b. 1978; edn: BS, Sardar Patel Univ. 1968; MEng., Lamar Univ., Tex. 1971. Career: prodn. engr. Busk Action Co., Dallas, Tex. 1971-73; consulting engr. Clow Corp., Bensonville, Ill. 1973-75; v.p. prodn. Jemsons Mfg. Co., India 1975-789; pres. Amesia Internat., Hollywood 1978-80; pres. H.J. Sales Inc. 1981--; cons. engr. & hon. research asst. Symcom Corp., Ahmedabad, India; honors: honor stu., Sandar Patel Univ., India & Univ. of Tex., Arlington; mem: Rotary; Gujarati Cultural Soc., Norwalk; Swaminarayan Sanstha, Whittier; works: research thesis, Production and Middle Management; spl. proj., Productivity Requirement for the Design of Machine Components; Hindu; rec: cricket, swimming, golf. Res: 1424 Tierra Cima Walnut 91789 Ofc: H.J. Sales, 21810 Belshire Hawaiian Gardens 90716

PATRICIAN, MARTY RUTH, child custody mediator-therapist; b. Mar. 12, 1948, Sacto.; d. Albert and Alice (Castro) Barajas; m. Michael Patrician, Nov. 17, 1968; 1 dau: Michele, b. 1983; edn: BA, UC Davis 1972; MSC, Sacto. State Univ. 1975; EdD, Univ. of San Francisco 1983. Career: probation ofcr. Yolo & Sacto. Co. 1973-76; family ct. mediatorm child custody, Sacto. Co. Superior Ct1976--; faculty, Assn. of Conciliation Cts., Calif. chpt., Redding 1980, Monterey 1981; San Diego 1982; com. for Master Degree Students in Counseling, Sacto. State Univ. 1976. 77; guest spkr. var pub. functions, colls., and radio talk shows re. effects of divorce on children, adults & families 1978; honors: C.K. McClatchey H.S. Class Scholarship, UCD Scholarship; UCD Psychology Dept. Citation, Phi Kappa Phi; mem: Assn. of Conciliation Cts.; Mex.-Am. Political Assn.; works: The Night Before Court, Conciliation Ct. Review, 1983; Toward the Best Interest of the Family, Conciliation Ct. Conv., San Diego; Child Custody Terms: Potential Contributors to Custody Conflict and Dissatisfaction, accepted for pub., Journ. of the Acad. of Family Mediators, 1984; Republican; Methodist; rec: film making, snow skiing. Res: 101 Fortado Circle Sacramento 95831 Ofc: Sacramento County Superior Court, Family Court, 720 9th Street Sacramento 95813

PATRICK, CHARLES LEON, real estate broker/ building contractor; b. Feb. 3, 1938; s. Elby Leon and Dorothy Aline (Hicks) P.; m. Carol Sue, Jan. 13, 1961; children; Kelley, b. 1962; LeAnne, b.1966; edn: Bakersfield Coll. 1968-69; Lumbleau Real Estate Sch. 172, 73, 75; UC Santa Barbara 1977; USC 1982; Limited Svc. Cred., Calif. State Dept. of Edn. 1977. Career: draftsman, surveyor, instrument-man, engr. Southern Pacific Transp. Co., Bakersfield 1961-75; general building contr., real estate broker, Bakersfield 1976--; owner Mid-Valley Real Estate, and C.L. Patrick Construction; mem: Bakersfield Board of Realtors, Calif., Nat. Assns. of Realtors, Independent Contractors Assn. 1971-; clubs: Bakersfield Trade, Meudell Lodge Freemasons, Bakersfield Christian Life Schools Booster, Bakersfield College Alumni Assn., UCSB Alumni Assn., Bakersfield Racquet; Republican; Baptist; rec: antique cars. Res: Star Route 4 Box 705, Bakersfield 93306 Ofc: Mid-Valley Real Estate/ C.L. Patrick Construction, 4664 American AvBakersfield 93309

PATRIDGE, JAMES ELTON, JR., real estate broker-investor; b. Nov. 5, 1947, Nashville, Tenn.; s. James Elton Sr. and Evelyn (Powell) P.; m. Mabel Crafton Dec. 22, 1966, div. 1976; m. 2d. Suzanne T. Hamel, July 7, 1983; children: Daniel, b. 1970; Tricia Suzanne, b. 1974 (adopt.); edn: BS, CSU Pomona 1969; BA, Mt. San Antonio Jr. Coll. 1965-67. Career: tchr. La Habra Unif. Sch. Dist., La Habra 1969-70; tchr. San Joaquin Sch. Dist., Irvine 1970-71; Shaklee supvr., self- empl., Irvine 1971-72; real estate agt. Red Carpet Realtors, Santa Ana 1972-75, Orange Realty, Orange 1980--; R.E. investor 1973--; investment cons. 1980--; mem: E. Orange Co. Bd. Realtors 1972-; Nat. & Calif. Assns. Realtors 1972-; Rotary 1973-; Repub. Pres. Task Force 1981-; Nat. Conservative P.A.C. 1980-; Conservative Caucus Inc. 1980-; Nat. Rifle Assn. 1979-; 2nd Amendment Found. 1979-; author: Real Estate, Lmtd. Partnership Prospectuses, 1982; Pentecostal; Omega World Missions (fin. advr.); rec: boating, flying, hunting. Res: 1334 E Barkley Orange 926667 Ofc: J.P. Enterprises, Realtors, POB 5267 Orange 92667

PATTEN, BEBE HARRISON, clergywoman/ educator; b. Sept. 3, 1913, Waverly, Tenn.; d. Newton Felix and Mattie Priscilla (Whitson) Harrison; m. Carl Thomas Patten, Oct. 23, 1955; children: (twins) Priscilla Carla and Bebe Rebecca, Carl Thomas; edn: DD, McKinley-Roosevelt Coll. 1941; D.Litt., Temple Hall Coll. & Sem. 1943. Career: ordained to ministry, Ministerial Assn. of Evangelism 1935; evangelist in var cities of US 1933-50; founder/ pres. Patten Acad. Christian Edn., Oakland 1944--; Patten Bible Coll., Oakland 1945-85; pres.-emeritus/ chancellor, Patten Coll. 1983; founder/ pastor Christian Cathedral of Oakland 1950--; condr. pgm., The Shepherd Hour, San Francisco 1962--; exec. bd. Bar-Ilan U. Assn., Israel; hon. fellow, 1981; Dr. Bebe Patten chair in soc. action estab. 1981; awards: medallion, Ministry of Religious Affairs, Israel 1969; medal, Govt. Press Ofc., Jerusalem 1971; Christian honoree of Year, Jewish Nat. Fund of No. Calif. 1975; Hidden Heroine award, S.F. Bay Council, Girl Scouts USA 1976; Ben-Gurion medallion, Ben-Gurion Research Inst. 1977; mem: Am. Assn. for Higher Edn.; Religious Edn. Assn.; Am. Acad. Religion & Soc. Bibl. Lit.; Zionist Orgn. of Am.; Am. Jewish Hist. Soc.; Am. Israel Pub. Affairs Comm. 1983; works: author, Give Me Back My Soul, 1973; editor, Trumpet Call, 1953--; composer 20 gospel & relig. songs 1948-; listed in num biographical publs.; rec: swimming, tennis. Ofc: 2433 Coolidge Ave Oakland 94601

PATTERSON, CLAYTON ANDREW, certified public accountant, ret.; b. Aug. 9, 1921; No. Bend, Wisc.; s. William Stanley and Annie (Manser) P.; m. Clara Josephine Johnson, May 4, 1968; children: Robert Lewis, b. 1976; William Clayton, b. 1972; Christina Marie, b. 1971; Mark Eldon, b. 1959; Daniel Andrew, b. 1958; edn: BBA, Univ. of Wisc. 1949; CPA, Calif. 1954. Career: CPA/ auditor: Dept. of State Audit, Wisc. 1949-52; Thomas & Moore, CPAs, Los Angeles 1953-54; CPA/ budget, Hughes Aircraft, Los Angeles 1954-55; CPA/ acct. Rockwell Internat. Fin. Div., L.A. 1955-81; ret.; currently, owner Edison Village Apts., Sacto.; mem: Masons; mil: tech. 5 US Army Med. Corp. 1940-45, num. ribbons; Republican; Presbyterian; rec: skiing. Res: Edison Village Apts, 3636 Edison Ave, Apt. 1, Sacramento 95821

PATTERSON, J. MICHAEL, certified public accountant; b. Mar. 6, 1946, Washington, Iowa; s. J. Kenneth and Jo Ann (Ross) P.; m. Marci Flick, Aug. 28, 1979; children: Lori, b. 1964; Lisa, b. 1966; Todd, b. 1970; Staci, b. 1972; edn: BBA, Univ. of Iowa 1968; JD, Univ. of Chgo. 1973; CPA, Iowa 1970, Ill. 1971, Calif. 1973; Realtor, Calif. 1978. Career: with Price Waterhouse; staff, Chgo.; senior, mgr., sr. mgr. Price Waterhouse, San Jose, tax partner, currently; frequent pub. spkr.; mem: Beta Alpha Psi (v.p. 1968); Phi Delta Phi; Am. & Calif. Insts. CPAs; Am., Calif. & Santa Clara (Tax Sect. exec. com.) Bar Assns.; Estate Plnng. Counicl; Am. Electronics Assn. (Tax Subcom.); San Jose Kiwanis (bd. dirs.); Southwest YMCA (bd. dirs.); Santa Clara Co. Trunk & Tusk Club; Childrens Discovery Mus. (bd. advrs.); mil: spec. E-5 US Army 1968-70; Republican (Fin. Com. for Morgan for Senate 1983-); Methodist; rec: sports. Res: 23415 Sunset Dr Los Gatos 95030 Ofc: Price Waterhouse, 121 Park Center Plaza San Jose 95113

PATTERSON, LEE ROY, educator, investor, civic leader; b. Oct. 11, 1904, Chidester, Ark.; s. John Bunyan and Cora Ethel (Kirby) P.; m. Royse Anderson, June 20, 1926; children: Ralph b. 1928, James b. 1932, Stanley b. 1936, Roland b. 1938, Ronald b. 1940; edn: Elem. Life Tchr. cert., Southeastern State Tchrs Coll. 1929, BS, 1932; MA, USC, 1956. Career: tchg. 1923-44 in Oklahoma: elem. sch. tchr./ principal, high sch. tchr./ coach/ prin., supt. of schools 1935-44; owner grocer market, Durant, Okla. 1944-45; moved to Calif. 1945, built 13 rental units, 1945-48; tchr. Los Angeles City Schools, 1949-61, 1965-68, ret.; L.A. Teachers Credit Union bd. dirs. 1951-54; chmn. Tchrs Faculty Gp. 1959-60; currently mng. real estate rentals and mobile home park; elected councilman and mayor of Bell Gardens, two terms, 1961-64; honors: college wrestling championship, 1929; as basketball coach, won county, district, and runner-up in state, 1931; pres. County Athletic Assn. 1934, Scout Master 1930-36; mem: Oklahoma Tchrs Assn. (life mem. 1940), charter mem. Boys Club of Bell Gardens 1961, VIM Senior Citizens Gp. (v.p.), Gideons; pres. Property Owners Assn. of Bell Gardens 1956-61; mem./chmn. Cong. Del Clawson's Academy Interview Com.; works: drew plans and blt. church and high school gymn., 1938, Okla.; blt. mechanism to ring high sch. period bells used 1932-44; Jeffersonian Democrat; Ch. of God (Anderson, Ind.); rec: gardening, grafting, budding (splty: fruit trees). Address: Patterson Materials Co., 5815 Loveland St Bell Gardens 90201

PATTERSON, RICK EDWARD, music composer/ TV producer; b. Aug. 2, 1950, Los Angeles; s. Leland David and Elanor Jane (Kuegeman) P.; m. Nina Cohen, June 5, 1982; edn: AA, L.A. City Coll. 1970; CSU Los Angeles 1972; UCLA 1974. Career: musician 1965-80; T.V. producer, Metro Prodns. 1979; sr. musical dir. Tuesday Prodns. 1978--; pres. R.P.M. Prodns. 1980--; honors: 1st pl., Chgo. Intenat. Film Festival 1983; 1st pl., Best in the West 1983; Golden Real Awd. 1982; 17 Clio Finals ; mem: Musician Local 47; Am. Fedn. of TV & Radio Artists; works: composed/ conducted music for film, A Minor Miracle, starring John Huston & Pele; Libertarian; rec: scuba diving, counseling, skiing. Res: 2406 Caminito Ocean Cove Cardiff by the Sea 92007 Ofc: Tuesday Productions, 4429 Marena Blvd San Diego 92117

PATTON, DOROTHY MARGARET, marketing executive; b. July 20, 1941, Cleveland, Ohio; d. Raymond Charles and Matilda Helen (Rossoll) Taylor; m. Roger Ray Patton, June 15, 1963; 2 daus: Shannon Cathleen, b. 1970; Shareen Lee, b. 1973; edn: BS in sec.edn., Slippery Rock State Coll. 1962; spec. stu., Edinboro State Coll. 1979; Calif. Real Estate lic. 1979; Carnegie sales cert. 1983. Career: teacher : (H.S.) Conneautville, Pa. 1963-5, (Jr.H.) Tucson 1965-7, (elem.) McFarland Schs., 1967-8, (Jr.H.) San Diego Schs. 1968-9;

owner Macrame By Margo, Lakeside, Ca. 1974-9; sales, hardware dept., Sears, El Cajon 1978-9; emplymt. cons. Apple One, Costa Mesa 1980; dir. mktg. MMM Engineering Inc., Anaheim 1981--; spkr., cons. Dale Carnegie Inst., 1983; cons. Newport Beach CofC. Honors: b. with only one arm, yet recipient num. phys. edn. awards in H.Sch.; num. local and state music awds. (Baritone Horn); Nat. Hon. Soc., H.S.; Nat. Music Soc., H.S.; DAR Awd. 1959; Care Awd, Sears, 1979; Outstanding salespsn., Apple One, 1980. Youth vol: mgr. Bobby Sox Softball, Irvine 1980-; vol. AYSO Soccer and Coast Soccer, 1980-. Mem. Jt. Conf. for Increased Use of Minority Bus., 1982-4; site council Irvine Schs.; ICCA (Ind. Computer Cons. Assn.), GATE (Gifted and Talented Edn.), Irvine Forum, The Irvine Found., Culverdale Comm. Assn.; Republican; Methodist (United Meth. Womens Org.); rec: sew, write, camp. Res: 3852 Salem, Irvine 92714 Ofc: MMM Engrg Inc POB 6472 Anaheim 92806

PATTON, JOHN WESLEY, JR., lawyer; b. July 14, 1953, Cleveland, Oh.; s. John Wesley Sr. and Ruby Delores (Hill) P.; edn: BA, Case Westenr Reserve Univ. 1975; JD, magna cum laude, Harvard Univ. Sch. of Law 1979; admitted to State Bar of Calif. 1979. Career: writer assoc. Arnold & Perter, Wash. DC 1976-78; writer assoc. Steptoe & Johnson, Wash. DC 1978-79; summer assoc. O'Melveny & Myers, Los Angeles 1978; assoc. atty. Gibson, Dunn & Crutcher, Los Angeles 1979-81; assoc. atty. Rogers & Wells, L.A. 1981--; honors: Corpus Juris Secundum Awd. 1977-79, Judge W.S. Thompson Internat. Law Awd. 1978, Univ. Pres.'s Scholar 1971; mem: Am., Calif. Bar Assns.; Phi Delta Phi; Democrat; Christian; rec: chess, bicycling. Res: 431 S Burnside Ave, 12G, Los Angeles 90036 OFc: Rogers & Wells, 261 S Figueroa St, Ste 400, Los Angeles 90012

PAULSON, RICHARD, management consultant; b. Feb. 10, 1920, Erie, Penn.; 1 dau: Kathy. Career: test engr. Convair Astronautics, San Diego 1953-63; sr. cons. Bruce Payne Assoc., Los Angeles 1963-65; self-empl., mgmt. cons., Beverly Hills 1965-72; founder/ pres. O.N. Eno Co., Fresno 1972--; author: The ABC's of Time Study, 1978; contbr. arts. on mgmt. to bus. journs., tech. arts. to engring. journs., travel arts., var. mags.; songwriter; designer/ inventor: toys, games, restaurants, artistic & comml. projs.; mil: 1st lt. USAAF 1943-45; ret. USAFR 1963. Ofc: Box 11032 Fresno 93771

PAVESIC, VINCENT DEWAYNE, utility co. personnel supervisor; b. Oct. 14, 1936, Chgo., Ill.; s. Max and Kathryn Amelia (Guzvich) P.; children: Kathy Anne, b. 1958; edn: BA, UCLA 1964; cert. in Pub. Sector Labor Rels., UCLA 1976. Career: coll. textbook publ. Holt, Rinehart & Winston 1966-69; jr. adminstrv. asst. City of Los Angeles Dept. of Water & Power 1969-70; tng. splst. 1970-77; personnel asst./ spl. studies 1977-79; labor rels. rep. 197-82, tng. supvr. 1982-83; personnel supvr./ spl. studies 1983; supvn. instr. E. L.A. Coll. 1973-74; life cred., Calif. Comm. Coll. Dist.; mem: So. Calif. Personnel Mgmt. Assn.; Am. Soc. for Tng. & Devel.; mil: spec. 4 US Army 1958-60; Democrat; rec: pottery. Res: 2008 Andreo Ave Torrance 90501 Ofc: Los Angeles Dept. Water & Power, 111 N Hope, Rm 521, Los Angeles 90051

PAWLEY, CARL JOHN, experimental physicist; b. Feb. 28, 1956, Milwaukee, Wisc.; s. James Arthur and Janet (Vogel) P.; edn: BS, honors, Purdue Univ. 1977; USC 1978; MS, UCLA 1982; PhD, in progress. Career: staff engr. Hughes Aircraft Co., Culver City 1977-78; tchg. asst. USC Los Angeles 1977-78; research asst. UCLA 1978--; presented papers, confs. of: Am. Physical Soc.-Plasma Gp. 1980-84; IEEE- Plasma Gp. 1980-83; 13th Annual Absorption Conf. 1983; guest lectr. UCLA 1980-84; honors: Commencement Spkr., Fairview Park H.S. 1974; mem: Eta Kappa Nu; IEEE; Alpha Phi Omega; Purdue Alumni Assn.; publs. of research: Physcial Review Letters, 1982; Conf. on Plas. Phys., IAENA-CN, 1-2, 1982; Proceedings of 6th Internat. Workshop on Laser Interaction & Rel. Plasma Phenomena, 1984; Democrat; Catholic; rec; backpacking, music. Res; 500 Landfair Ave Los Angeles 90024 Ofc: UCLA, 7702 Boelter Hall, Los Angeles 90024

PAYNE, DONNA LOUISE, stockbroker; b. Apr. 11, 1940, Chelsea, Mich.; d. Frederick George and Geraldine Antoinette (Krusinski) Klink; children: Julia Michael, b. 1980; Lisa Marie, b. 1982; edn: Univ. of Mich., Ann Arbor 1959-60; USC ext.; Commodity Broker, 1982; Life, Disability & Variable Annuity Agent, Calif. 1983; Real Estate Agent, Calif. 1972. Career: ops. staff Shearson Hammill, Santa Barbara 1969-74; ops. mgr. Reynolds Securities, Santa Barbara 1974-78; ops. mgr. E.F. Hutton, S.B. 1978-82; acct. exec. 1982--; ofc. supvr. tng. staff, E.F. Hutton 1978-82; ofc. supvr. tng. staff, Reynolds Securities 1974-78; mem: St. Barbara Parish, Santa Barbara Mission; Catholic; rec: 3704 Ardilla Dr Santa Barbara 93105 Ofc: E.F. Hutton, 12 E Figueroa Santa Barbara 93101

PAYNE, GERRYE EILEEN, psychotherapist/ poet; b. Jan. 20, 1942, Dallas, Tex.; d. Robert M. and Thelma M. (Stone) P.; m. Richard Welin, Jan. 31, 1976; children: Andree Kessel, b. 1965; John C. Kessel, b 1966; edn: BA, UC Berkeley 1965; MA, Eng., CSUS, Rohnert Park 1975; MA, counseling, Univ. of San Francisco 1979. Career: publisher, White Bear Books 1976-79; currently, tchr., Eng. dept. Santa Rosa Jr. Coll., Santa Rosa & psychotherapist Lawrence & Assoc., Santa Rosa; num. poetry readings, Sonoma Co. & San Francisco Bay area; honors: Nat. Endowment for the Arts Awd., Small Press Publs. 1979; mem: Calif. Personnel & Guidance Assn.; Calif. Assn. of Tchrs. of Eng.; poems: Green, 1962; An Amateur Plays Satie, in press; poems & art review in num publs incl. the anthology New Poets- Women; rec: painting. Res: 10582 Barnett Valley Rd Sebastopol 95472 Ofc: Lawrence & Associates, 2525 Cleveland Ave Santa Rsa 95401

PAYNE, L(OUIS) DONALD, engineer/ poet; b. Nov. 29, 1905, Alturas, Calif.; s. Ernest Drury and Blanche Mar (Wallace) P.; m. Jeanette Abbott, Aug. 30, 1931 (dec. 1981); children: Donald Wallace, b. 1935; Grace Abbott, b. 1938; edn: BSEE, UC Berkeley 1981; grad. studies, physics 1931-33. Career: surveyor Calif. Forest Exptl. Sta. 1933-35; entgr. Shell Oil Co., Martinez 1935-37; Shell Devel. Co., Emeryville 1937-39; Pacific Elec. Mfg. Corp. (& takeover Federal-Pacific Elec. Co.), San Francisco & Santa Clara 1941-61; ret.; self guided research, physics, med. & earthquakes; weather forecasting, earthquake forecasting, the physics of light, patterns that phenomena follow, stress, heart attacks; poems in publs: The World of Poetry, In A Nutshell; recipient (3) prizes for poetry; pvt. publs. (3 vols. of book): Earthquake Patterns of the San Francisco Bay Area 1978, 79; pvt. publ. arts: Experiments on Stress Resonance in Man, 1957; On The Origin of Cancer, 1958; On The Fundamental Constants and Conservation Laws of Physics, 1971; mem: Calif. Writers Club; Calif. Fedn. Chaparral Poets; The El Camino Poets of Sacto.; The Ina Coolbrith Circle, S.F.; Nat. Rifle Assn.; rec: sawing wood, mountain climbing. Res: 1543 Beverly Pl Berkeley 94706

PAYNE, ROY C., company executive; b. Oct. 20, 1940, Phila., Pa.; s. S. Roy and Louise A. Payne; m. Susan Marie Calhoun Oct. 19, 1974; edn: BS, Penn. State 1962. Career: mgmt. trainee, ofc. mgr. The Procter & Gamble Distributing Co., (4 cities) 1963-69; mgr. sales admin./ regl. distbn. mgr. Schick Safety Razor Co. Div. Warner Lambert (Internat. distbn. div.) 1969-81; v.p. ops./ v.p./ gen. mgr. Frazik Industries (creative wallcovering), Cerritos 1981--; var. cons. pos. on individual basis; mem: Nat. Council Physical Distribution Mgmt.; Anaheim Police Ofcrs. Hon. Assn.; Artisans; mil: sgt. E-5 USAR 1964-68; rec: racquetball, softball, tennis. Address: Orange County

PAYTON, GEORGE TERRANCE, college professor; b. June 9, 1927, Los Angeles; s. George John and Kathleen Patricia (Allen) P.; m. Waneece F. Arata, Aug. 16, 1953; children: Lynn, b. 1954; Alice, b. 1955; Janet, b. 1957; Casey, b. 1958; Susan, b. 1959; Eileen, b. 1959; edn: BA, San Jose State Univ. 1954; MA, 1956; EdD, USC 1976; Criminologist & Fellow, Am. Assn. of Criminology; Adv. Post Cert., Tng. Supvn. & Admin. Creds. Career: Juvenile officer 1959, sergeant-detective 1960, San Jose Police Dept.; chmn. Law Enforcement pgm., San Jose City Coll. 1961; dir. first Regional Criminal Justice Training Center, Santa Clara County, 1963; instr. Criminal Justice, Evergreen Valley Coll., currently; dir. of Criminal Justice Services, cons. & publs.; honors: distinguished Mil. Graduate, CSU San Jose 1954, Outstanding Educator Award 1971, Outstanding AJ Educator Award, 1975; mem: Internat. Assn. of Chiefs of Police, Internat. Assn. of Identification, Am. Assn. of Criminology, Calif. Peace Ofcrs. Assn. (life), LAE, Nat. Criminal Justice Assn. (Faculty Advisor), Calif. Assn. of Adminstrn. of Justice Educators; lt. San Jose Police Dept. Reserve; publs: Patrol Procedures, Criminal Investigation; 1000 Police Questions; Police Sergeant's Manual (legal book, L.A.) Calif. Criminal Law; Peace Officer's Guide to Criminal Law (Criminal Justice Svcs., San Jose); arts. in Police Chief, Police Mag., Identification News; mil: RD-2 USN 1945-49, Reserv. (Korea) 1950-52, 1st lt. US Army M.P. Reserv. 1954-63; Republican; Catholic. Res: 2207 Golden Dew Circle San Jose 95121 Ofc: Evergreen Valley College 3095 Yerba Buena Rd San Jose 95135

PAZANIN, SANDRA MARIE, financial planner; b. July 31, 1947, Chgo., Ill.; d. Frank J. and Jean E. (Sosnowski) Simmons; m. Robert M. Alverson, Aug. 25, 1979; edn: BA, Univ. of Ill. 1969; MA, Governors State Univ. 1977; CFP, Coll. for Fin. Plnng. 1984. Career: account exec. Randall Gumms Advt., Merrillville, Ill. 1974-76; artist demonstrator Hunt Mfg. Co., Phila. 1976-77; indep. product cons. McGraw-Hill, Paoli, Pa. 1977-78; mgmt. trainee Connecticut General (Cigna Corp.), Chgo. 1978-80, finl. plnnr. Cigna Corp. (Conn. Gen.), Chgo. 1980-82, San Francisco 1982--; awards: Million Dollar Round Table 1979, 80, 81, 82; Cigna Corp. Equity Leaders Club 1981, 82, 83; Outstanding Young Women of Am., 1979; Cigna Corp. Honor Table & Pres.'s Club 1979, 80; mem: Inst. of Certified Finl. Planners, Internat. Assn. for Finl. Planning, Inc., Peninsula Assn. of Life Underwriters, Nat. Assn. of Life Underwriters, Women Life Underwriters Conf.; mem. Bus. Volunteers for the Arts, S.F. chpt.; rec: swimming, weight tng., art. Res: 6 Calypso Ln San Carlos 94070 Ofc: Cigna Corp. 333 Market St, Ste 2400, San Francisco 94105

PAZEMENAS, VYTAS V(ALENTINAS), manager, Infusion Systems, Oximetrix Inc.; b. Feb. 4, 1938, Kaunas, Lithuania; s. Kazys and Mary (Petruska) P.; 1 dau: Lara, b. 1975; edn: BSEE, Penn. State Univ. 1961; MSEE, Univ. of Santa Clara 1966. Career: design engr. GTE Sylvania Inc., Mountain View, 1962-64; advanced devel. engr. Signal Processing Lab., GTE Sylvania, 1965-67; sect. head, Sensors & processors, 1968-71; sr. engring. splst. 1972-73; staff engr., Office of Chief Engr., 1973-76; sr. staff engr. Oximetrix, Inc., Mtn. View, 1976-79; mgr. Infusion Systems, 1979--; also design cons., self-employed, 1975-76. Mem: IEEE, 1961-; US Power Squadron 1970-75 (sr. mem. 1975); Ballena Bay Yacht Club, Alameda (Commodore 1973, 74, 79, dir. 1975, 77, 80), S.F.-Kauai Yacht Race Com. (chmn. 1979-82); patentee: two Electronic Sensors (1969, 74); mil: 1Cpl., USMC, 1955-61; Republican; rec: sailing, skiing. Res: 6298 Lido Ct. Newart 945660 Ofc: Oximetrix Inc. 1212 Terra Bella Ave Mountain View 94043

PEACOCK, EDWARD CHARLES, clergyman/ psychotherapist; b. Feb. 22, 1936, Long Beach; s. Darrel Vern and Beatrice Margaret (Compo) P.; m. Jacquelyn Gaye Miller, Dec. 25, 1959; children: Victoria, b. 1954; Robert, b. 1957; William, b. 1965; edn: BA, CSU Long Beach 1958; M.Div. San Francisco Theol. Sem. 1964; D.Min., 1974; ordained minister, United Presbyterian Ch.; Lic. (MFCC) Marriage & Family Counselor, Psychotherapist. Career: instr./ chmn. Speech & Drama Dept. George Fox College, 1959-61; pastor Aztec Presbyterian Church (1964-6), El Monte Community (66-77), St. Paul's Anaheim (71-78); exec. dir. American Inst. of Family Relations, 1978--; prof. Psych. Dept. num. colls. and univs.; honors: Topper Smith Award (1957, 58), Long Beach State Coll. Gold Nugget Award (1958), Tau Kappa Alpha, Donald Powell Wilson Service Award (1982); mem. Am. Assn. for Marriage & Family Therapy, Am. Acad. of Psychotherapists, Am. Orthospychiatric Assn.; editor: Family Life (1977--); author: The Mind-Brain Phenomenon; Republican; Presbyterian minister; rec: writing, travel. Res: 2347 W. Mall Ave Anaheim 92804 Ofc: American Institute of Family Relations, 4942 Vineland, No Hollywood 91061

PEAKE, BARBARA, psychiatric social worker; b. Feb. 22, 1939, Baltimore, Md.; d. Clarence William and Mary Elizabeth (Bouis) P.; edn: BA, Goucher Coll. 1960; MA, Univ. of San Francisco 1964; MSW, Univ. of Wash. 1972; San Jose State Univ. 1969-70; CSU Fullerton 1979-; LCSW, Calif. 1980. Career: Peace Corps Volunteer: Barquisimeto, Venezuela, S.A., 1966-68; program dir. Children's Social Rehabilitation Services, Santa Ana, Ca. 1975-77; clin. dir. Child Guidance Ctr. of Santa Ana, 1977-80; clin. dir. Child and Family Guidance Ctr., Garden Grove 1980-83, clin. dir. Santa Ana Child Guidance Center, 1983--; cons. Children's Hosp. of Orange County, 1983; cons. Orange, Tustin, Santa Ana, Garden Grove Unified Sch. Dists., 1977-; cons. Orange Co. Social Service Agencies, 1977-; mem. Nat. Assn. of Social Wkrs., American Art Therapy Assn., Internat. Imagery Assn., C.G. Jung Club of Orange County; works: Sculpture Exhibns: Starry Night (Fall 1983), Body Language (Winter 83), CSU Fullerton; Democrat; rec: travel, art, sports. Res: 3733 N. Harbor, 86, Fullerton 92635 Ofc: Santa Ana Child Guidance Center, 1126 W. Edinger Santa Ana 92707

PEARCE, JEANETTE ANN, lawyer; b. Feb. 2, 1943, Columbia, So. Carolina; d. Thomas Marcus and Amanda Elizabeth (Cobb) Bleckley; uncle, Logan E. Bleckley, Justice of Supreme Court of Georgia; cousin, Ty Cobb (baseball fame); m. Nathan Pearce, Dec. 3, 1967; 1 dau: Angelique Nicole, b. 1968; edn: AA, Young Harris Coll. 1963; Am. River Coll. 1966-68; Bach., Lincoln Univ. 1974; admitted to Calif. State Bar 1974. Career: with Proctor & Gamble, Atlanta, Ga. 1963-65; American Cable Electronics, Sacramento, Ca. 1965-75; atty. at law self-empl., Sacramento 1975--; mem: Am. Bar Assn., Calif. Bar Assn., Sacramento County Bar Assn., Women Lawyers of Sacto., Young Lawyers; orgn. vol. liaison for juvenile prisoners; Jewish; rec: music, sports cars, writing. Res: 6748 Hedgewood Dr Sacramento 95842 Ofc: 5405 Palm Ave, Ste 5, Sacramento 95841

PEARLSON, DANIEL DAVID, marketing executive; b. Dec. 22, 1957, Los Angeles; s. Robert M. and Bertha (Abrams) P.; edn: BA, Univ. of Redlands 1979; Linguistic Arts, Acadamie de Commerce, Geneva, Switz. 1973. Career: commercial mktg. rep. Bekins Building Maint. Inc. 1976; sales rep. assigned to Electrics Div., Desco, 1979, dir. Advt. and Promotion, 1981, v.p. market devel., 182, exec. vice pres. Desco Marketing Corp., 1983--; indep. cons. 1982-; lectr. Univ. of Redlands, 1982; awards: KitchenAid Top Ten award, KitchenAid Small Electrics Div., Hobart Corp. (1981); mem: So. Calif. Representatives Assn. 1979-, Housewares Club of So. Calif. 1983-; mem. Municipal Elections Com. of Los Angeles, 1984; chancelor, A.R.C.H.I.V.E.S., 1983; Democrat; agnostic; rec: anthropology, philosophy, strategic games. Res: 725 Almar Ave Pacific Palisades 90272 Ofc: Desco Marketing Corp. 2120 W. 8th St, Ste 304, Los Angeles 90057

PEARCE, RUBERTA MC COY, travel agency executive; b. Aug. 25, 1904, Cicero, Ind.; d. Wm. Morton and Bessie (Bert) McCoy; m. John Wesley Henderson (dec.) June 18, 1928; two sons, John b. 1929, William b. 1932; m. 2d. Solon Pearce (dec.) Mar. 10, 1948; edn: BA in music, UC Berkeley 1925, Graduate Sch. UCB 1925-26; 21 units real estate, UC Ext., S.F.; Calif. lic. Real Estate Broker 1962, Gen. Sec. Lifetime Tchrs. Credential 1945. Career: tchr. various elementary and secondary public schools, Calif. 1926-47; tchr. Diablo Valley Coll., Contra Costa 1955-56; Merritt Coll., Oakland 1960-62; real estate salesman-broker in Danville and Berkeley, 1957-68, Dolphin Real Estate, Pacifica 1970-73; mgr. Henderson Travel, Pacifica 1973-7-; honors: Real Estate Salesman of the Year 1966, Berkeley; mem: Am. Soc. of Travel Agents 1973-, Mensa; State Dir. Calif. Assn. of Realtors 1966, 67; pres. Women's Council Berkeley Bd. of Realtors 1961-62; travel chmn. AARP, Pacifica; accompanist Honolulu Oratorio Soc. (traveled around the world twice), 1951-53; Republican (pres. Pacifica CRA; hd. Goldwater Hqtrs. Berkeley 1964); Ch. of Relig. Sci.; rec: pianist (classical), bridge. Res: 1525 Grand Ave Pacifica 94044 Ofc: Henderson Travel 1277 Linda Mar Ctr Pacifica 94044

PEARSON, BERYL, graphic artist; b. Sept 19, Lancashire, England, nat. 1970; d. John and Lila (Woodward) Shaw; m. Joseph Collier; m. 2d. Lee E. Pearson, 1969; children: Lesley E. (Miller) Collier, b. 1954; Alex Joseph Collier, b. 1959; edn: English schs.; Gamble Inst. of Art Tech. Coll.; Printers Diploma, ITU. Career: artist for a designer, England; graphic artist/printer Andrews Printing Co., Lakewood, Ca. 1971--; fmr. mem. Young Conservative Party, Eng. (2 letters from Sir Winston Churchill), Womens Guild Com., British & Dominion Social Club (pres.; com. mem. 6 yrs.) the only club to fin. sponsor the British and Am. Olympic athletes (one of the oldest British clubs in Calif.); Republican (campaign Nixon for Pres.); Episcopal; rec: oil painting, etching, antique collector. Res: 3722 California Ave Long Beach 90807

PEARSON, RICHARD STEVEN, engineering co. president; b. May 18, 1951, Louisville, Ky.; s. Robert Edward and Pauline (Jacques) P.; m. Mary Ann Martin, Oct. 24, 1981; edn: BS, Western Kentucky Univ. 1974; MCE, cand., Univ. of Ky. 1974-75; MBA, cand. San Diego State Univ. 1976; Reg. Profl. Engr., Calif. Career: design engr. Kentucky Dept. of Transp. 1974, research

engr. 1974-75; special projects engr. M. Rosenblatt & Assoc. (Marine Engring.), San Diego 1975-76; structural engrin. assoc. Deardorff & Deardorff, San Diego 1976-78; founder/pres. Pacific Engineering & Development, San Diego 1978--; dir. Calif.Planning Council; chmn. legis. com. Nat. Soc. of Profl. Engrs.; honors: Man of the Year, Kappa Sigma Frat. 1973; Best Senior Project, W. Ky. Univ. 1974; mem: Jamul-Dulzure Planning Group 1980-83, Land Use Sub-Com.; Calif. Soc. of Profl. Engrs.; Struc. Engrs. Assn.; Kiwanis CLUB: KAPPA Sigma Frat. (Past Grand Master); 94 Club (pres.); works: Pavement Research: Wax Beads, Petrochemical Additives, Heating Devices for Snow Melt (6/74, 12/75); mil: ROTC 1967-74; Republican; Catholic; rec: sailing, tennis, equestrian. REs: 141-4 Proctor Valley Road, Jamul 92035 Ofc: Pacific Engineering and Development, 9471 Ridgehaven Ct, Ste E, San Diego 92123

PEAVEY, CHARLES ALEXANDER, engineering management; b. May 13, 1947, Munich, Ger.; s. Ralph Augustin and Ludmilla Alexandrovna (Maschkoff) P.; edn: Univ. of Maine 1965-70; grad. gemologist wk. in progress, Gemological Inst. of Am.; Nuclear Power Plant Engring., Franklin Inst. 1975. Career: quality control engr. Bechtel Power Corp., Limerick Nuclear Generating Station, Pa.; insp. planner/Div. training, Bechtel Power Corp., San Francisco, Ca.; constrn./startup quality control coord. Bechtel Power Corp., San Onofre Nuclear Generating Station, San Clemente; senior quality assurance engr. Bechtel Power Corp., Los Angeles Power Div., currently; also own/opr. indep. jewelry design and custom mfg. co. spec. in precious stones from worldwide sources; conduct information sessions on energy topics for civic orgns., service clubs, bus. groups throughout So. Calif.; recipient num. speaker's appreciation awards; mem. American Nuclear Soc., British Gemological Soc.; publs: sev. tech. reports and articles on nuclear constrn., inspection, environmental considerations in tech. journals; mil: Airman 3/c USAF, Nat. Defense Service Medal; Republican (Repub. Assocs. of O.C.); Christian Sci.; rec: gemology, classical piano, theatre. Res: 12162 Jentges St Garden Grove 92640 Ofc: Bechtel Power Corp. 12400 E. Imperial Hwy Norwalk 90650

PECK, AARON MARTIN, lawyer; b. Apr. 26, 1939, Osceola, IA; s. Stanley and Leah Peck; Edn: BA, UCLA, 1961; JD, UCLA, 1964; m. Linda Debro, Sept. 4, 1960; chil: Anthony, b. 1965; Dena, b. 1969. Career: law clerk and assoc. atty., Pillsbury, Madison & Sturo, 1964-65; assoc. atty., McKenna & fitting, 1965-69; partner, McKenna, Conner & Cuneo (formerly McKenna & Fitting), 1970—; chmn., Ethics Comm., L.A. Co. Bar Assn., 1981-82; mem., bd. govs., Wilshire Bar Assn., 1981—. Listed, Who's Who in American Law, 2nd ed. Mem: Amer. Bar Assn.; L.A. Co. Bar Assn.; San Francisco Bar Assn.; ilshire Bar Assn.; Calif. Acad. of Appellate Lawyers. Democrat. Res: 706 Thayer Ave., Los Angeles 90024; Office: McKenna, Conner & Cuneo, 3435 Wilshire Blvd.,Los Angeles 90010.

PECK, DONALD EMIL, company executive; b. May 21, 1932, Los Angeles; s. Anton and Anne (Maloune) P.; m. Winifred, July 4, 1965; 1 son: Donald Christopher; edn: BBA, Woodbury Coll. 1959. Career: var. pos. to vice pres. Peck-Lewis Corp. (founded by Mr. Anton Peck in 1947), 1947--, mem. bd. dirs.; mem. Soc. of Mfg. Engrs., Los Angeles Area Mfg. Mgmt. Chpt. (chmn. 1983-4; dedicated service award SME 1973); supporting mem. Zool. Soc. of San Diego; mem. Am. Film Inst., Orange County Trojan Club; mil: YN2, USNR 1952-58; Republican; Prot.; rec: basketball. Res: 13203 Beach St Cerritos 90701 Ofc: Peck-Lewis Corp. 4436 Long Beach Ave Los Angeles 90058

PECK, ROY ROMEYN, engineer, ret.; b. Sept. 18, 1909, Kansas City, Mo.; s. Roy Romeyn Sr. and Mary Emma (Drane) P.; m. Marjorie, May 22, 1983; children: Douglas, b. 1932; Patricia, b. 1936; edn: Kansas State Tchrs. Coll. 1927-29; I.C.S. Civil. Engr., (9) Indsl. Courses Elect. 1930-70; Indsl. Coll. of Armed Forces 1967-68; Instr., var. night sch. courses 1940-49; Reg. Profl. Engr., Calif. 1948. Career: owner/mgr. Roy Peck Associates, 1954-59; cons. various A & E firms, 1959-63; senior design engr. Rockwell Internat. 1963-69 training course rep. Mc Donnell Douglas, 1969-72; project mgr. Daniel, Mann, Johnson & Mendenhall, 1972-76; ret.; current: research in El-Optics & Biophysics; Dept. of Defense cons. Fallout Shelter Analysis (1968), Protective Constrn. (1969); awards: Apollo Achievement Award, NASA, (12) Awards for developments in Space Technology, NASA; mem: IEEE chmn. Calif. Legislative Advisory Commn. 1974-75, IEEE cons. US Legis. Advis. Project 1975-79; dir. El Prado District (County of L.A.) 1966-67; publs: Concepts of Atomic Physics, L.M. Mag. (1952); Ideas for Designers, El. Mech. Mag. (1975); The Energy Problem Report, CILA and IEEE (1974); mil: Radar Cons. Raytheon, Bu. Ships, US & So. Pacific, 1942-45; Prot.; rec: painting, music. REs: 386 S. Burnside, 3D, Los Angeles 90036

PEDERSON, SAM MARSHALL, aerospace software co. executive; b. July 26, 1943, Veblen, S.Dak.; s. E. LeRoy and Ellen (Hestenes) P.; m. Mary Louise Anderson, June 18, 1966; 1 son, Troy, b. 1969; edn: BA, St. Olaf Coll. 1965; MS, Univ. Ill. 1967. Career: resrch asst. Univ. Ill. 1967; mem. tech. staff TRW Systems, Redondo Beach 1967-70; with Space Applications Corp., currently in Santa Ana, 1970-: mem. Tech. Staff 1970-71, Seattle Operation mgr. 1972-76, bd. dir./vice pres. 1974-, Irvine Op. mgr. 1977-82, v.p./dir./general mgr. 1980--; dir. Southland Lutheran Home 1983-; mem: IEEE Computer Soc., Air Force Assn. (patron), AFCEA (corp. mem.); author: The Software Development Project: Planning and Management (Wiley InterScience 1982); Ind.; Lutheran; rec: photog. Res: 2 Hermosa Irvine 92714 Ofc: Space Applications Corp., 200 E. Sandpointe Ave. Ste 300, Santa Ana 92707

PEELER, JOSEPH DAVID, lawyer; b. Sept. 29, 1895, Nashville, TN; s. Joseph David and Virginia Parker (McCue) Peeler; Edn: AB, Univ. Ala., 1915; LLB, Harvard Law Sch., 1920; m. Elizabeth Boggess, Apr. 20, 1927; chil: Stuart Thorne, b. 1929; Joyce, b. 1936. Career: admitted Ky. Bar, 1920, Calif. Bar 1929; practiced law, Louisville, Ky., 1920-29, L.A., 1929---; mem. law firm of Musick, Peeler & Garrett; former mem., bd. dirs., Consolidated Steel Co., Blue Diamond Corp., Tidewater Oil Co., Cyprus Mines Corp. Mem: Calif. Club; Wilshire Country Club; L.A. Club. Mil: Capt., US Air Corps, WWI; Lt.Col., USAC, WWII. Republican. Presbyterian. Rec: golf, fishing, hunting. Res: 131 N. June St.,Los Angeles 90004; Office: One Wilshire Blvd., Suite 2000, Los Angeles 90017.

PENCE, JAMES WILLIAM, insurance agency president; b. Sept. 28, 1928, Richmond, Mo.; s. Walter and Vivian Jane (Reyburn) P.; m. Catherine Marie Shaw, May 28, 1970; edn: BA, Central Mo. State Univ. 1952; cert. of ins., Univ. of Mo. 1954; CSU San Diego 1965; Episcopal Theol. Sch. (Bloy House) 1968-69; cert. of social svcs., UCLA, 1971. Career: field rep. for Missouri and Kansas for Appleton and Cox. Inc., NY, NY 1954; sales rep. Great Central Insurance Co. of Peoria, Ill. 1959; Missouri field rep. Union Ins. Gp. of Bloomington, Ill. 1961; San Diego branch mgr. Nat. Automobile and Casualty Ins. Co. of Los Angeles, 1964; automobile salesman Central Motors Ford in L.A., 1966; eligibility wkr. L.A. County Dept. of Social Services, 1969,j Solano County Welfare Dept., Vallejo 1972; founder/pres. Jim Pence Insurance Agcy. Inc., Vacaville 1977--; mem. American Agents Alliance, Pasadena Calif. Masonic Lodges, 1957-; honors: Ecumenical Commn., Episcopal Diocese of No. Calif. 1980-84; bd. dirs., exec. com., No. Calif. Ecumenical Council, 1981-84, treas. 1983; bd. mem. Vacaville Comm. Action Council, 1979; visitor to World Council of Churches, Vancouver BC 1983; campaigner Kennedy for Pres. (1980), Bradley for Gov. (1982), lobby to Wash DC for Nuclear Freeze (1983); bd. mem., negotiating team Solano County Employees Assn. 1972-75; supvsy. com. CMT Federal Credit Union, Fairfield 1983-4; Vacaville Affordable Housing Campaign Com. 1982; Democrat (v.ch. Solano Co. Dem. Central Com. 1979-84; pres. Vacaville Dem. Club 1979); No. Calif. bd. Americans for Democratic Actions 1979-84; Episcopal; rec: church work. Res: 361 Weatherly Way Vacaville 95688 Ofc: Jim Pence Ins. Agcy. Inc. 643 Merchant St Vacaville 95688

PENDLETON, MARJORIE LUCILE, business owner; b. Apr. 13, 1921, Modesto; d. Paul Marion and Lucile Antoinette (Southworth) Berry; m. George Robert, May 13, 1944; children: Lynne, b. 1946; Janis, b. 1950; Craig, b. 1954; edn: BA cum laude, CSU, Chico, 1942; MA with distinction, CSU, Long Beach 1959; Pupil Personnel Svcs. Credential 1976. Career: tchr. Estancia H.S., Costa Mesa 1965-77, Sch. Psych. Newport-Mesa Unified Sch. Distr. 1977-79; Psych. Tech. Windward Sch. Distr. Kaneohe, Hawaii 1979 80; co founder Balboa Travel Svc., Balboa 1977 .; founder Arbor Frame Shop, Irvine 1981--; instr. economics, Orange Coast Coll. 1966-68. honors: Cardinal Key 1940-2; mem: AAUW 1965; League of Women Voters 1981-83; Red Cross Volunteer 1981-82; Laubach Teacher 1982-83; Univ. Comm. Assn. (treasurer) 1982--; mil: lt. (jg) USNR Supply Corps. 1943-45; Unity Ch.; rec: worldwide travel, needlework, water colors; Res: 24 Foxglove Way Irvine 92715 Ofc: Arbor Frame Shop, 14775 Jeffrey Rd, Ste B, Irvine 92714

PENNELL, LARITA JEANNE, educator; b. Dec. 3, 1927, Portland, Ore.; d. LeRoy Carl and Leona Emma (Flier) Eisele; m. James Kell Pennell, Sept. 2, 1949; edn: BA, Univ. of Ore. 1949; MA, John F. Kennedy Univ. 1979; grad. study: CSU Humboldt, Hayward, Sonoma & San Jose; UC Berkeley 1950-; Univ. de Salamanca, Spain 1967, 68, 80; Univ. de Michoacan, Mex. 1964; Univ. of London, Eng. 1971; Tchr. Credentials: Secondary Edn. (1950), Bilingual Edn. (1979), Designated Svc. (1980), Adminstrv. (1981), Calif. Career: computer science, mathematics educator/faculty Wright School Dist., Santa Rosa 1950-51; Lafayette Sch. Dist., Lafayette 1952-; John F. Kennedy Univ., 1981--; computer cons. Microtime 1983; awards: academic NDEA Grants, US Govt. 1964, 65, 66; WHO (We Honor Ours) Award, CTA-NEA Alcosta Council; mem: Am. Assn. of Tchrs. of Spanish and Portuguese (secty. Bay Area chpt. 1975), Assn. of Mathematics Educators, Lafayette Edn. Assn. (pres. 1983-4); Republican; Catholic; rec: swimming, yoga, computer games. Res: 32 Canyon View Drive Orinda 94563 Ofc: Lafayette School Dist. 3477 School St. Lafayette 94549

PENNELLA, RALPH NICHOLAS, business owner; b. Aug. 30, 1941, Rochester, NY; s. Nicholas S. and Mary E. (Volta-Sousa) P.; m. Ida P. Thibodeau, Nov. 5, 1960; children: Ralph, b. 1965; John, b. 1966; Therese, b. 1972; James, b. 1973; DeAnne, b. 1974; edn: Fullerton Comm. Coll.1961; Adv. Mgmt., Chevron USA 1978; Atlas Tng. Pgms., Brake Svc. (1976), Low Emission (1977), Tune-Up (1978); Dealers Sales & Mgmt., Chevron USA 1975; contg. edn. through seminars, spl. courses. Cert. of Qualification, Nat. Inst. for Automotive Svc., Dept. of Consumer Affairs. Career: station retail sales Standard Oil Co. of Calif., 1962-63, station asst. mgr., 1963-65, station mgr. 1965-67; owner Ralph Pennella Chevron, Pacentia 1967--; awards: Hallmark Award, Chevron USA 1980-; Titan Found. award, CSU Fullerton 1980-81; Nat. Inst. for Automotive Service Excellence 1979; Super 7 Club; mem. Chevron Dealer Assn. 1974-; St. Polycarp Men's Club (pres. 1978-9), Buena Park Knights of Columbus (Grand Knight 1984-5), Orange County Handicap Helpers, Double 11 Club (life saving mem. Anaheim Meml. Hosp.), Cub Scouts 1976, 84; Republican; Catholic; rec: Pinochle, bridge, camping. Res: 7664 Granada Dr Buena Park 90621 Ofc: Ralph Pennella Chevron, 313 W. Orangethorpe Placentia 92670

PENNER, STEPHEN E., lawyer; b. Dec. 9, 1947, Evanston, Ill.; s. Harold E. and Joyce E. (Kennett) P.; m. Lii Tersner, June 29, 1980; 1 dau: Ericka Ann, b. 1982; edn: BS, US Naval Acad. 1971; JD, Calif. Western Sch. of Law 1977. Admitted to State Bar of Calif. Career: lt. US Navy, served in Vietnam as gunnery officer on the USS Turner Joy from 1972 until the last day of the war in Jan. 1973 (fired last shot of Vietnam war as ordered by Pres. Nixon; the ship had been involved in the Tonkin Gulf incident that began the Vietnam war 8 years before); decorated Combat Action Ribbon, Vietnam Campaign, Vietnam Service, Nat. Defense, Expert Rifle, and Expert Pistol medals; senior assoc. law firm Stephen E. Penner & Associates, Santa Barbara currently; mem. Calif. Bar Assn., Equestrian Trails Inc., Santa Barbara Trail Riders; Republican; Prot.; rec: equestrian sports. Offc: Stephen E. Penner & Associates, 1215 De La Vina, Ste K, Santa Barbara 93101

PENOYER, ROBERT HAROLD, electronics engineer; b. Jan. 31, 1947, Detroit, Mich.; s. Harold Elmer and Edith Marie (Thiemer) P.; m. Teresa Garcia, Jan. 24, 1981; children: Shawn, b. 1970; edn: AA, honors, Pasadena City Coll. 1975; BSEE (summa cum laude), West Coast Univ. 1978; MSEE, USC 1981; Reg. Profl. Engr., Calif. 1982. Career: electronics tech. Hoffman Electronics, El Monte 1969-72, senior electronics tech. 1972-75, associate engr. 1975-79, engr. 1979-81; mem./senior mem. technical staff Gould NavCom Systems, El Monte 1981--; electronics instr. (life cred.), Rio Hondo Coll. 1981-; mem. IEEE 1979-; mil: s/sgt. USAF 1966-69, decorated Vietnam Service with cluster, Repub. of Vietnam Campaign, Nat. Def. Svc., AF GCM medals; rec: home computer. Res: 123 N. New Ave Apt. D, Monterey Park 91754 Ofc: Gould NavCom Systems 4323 Arden Drive El Monte 91731

PENT, MICHAEL RICHARD, lawyer; b. Jan. 9, 1946, San Diego; s. Joseph Willoughby Pent and Winifred Ruth (Worrall) Mensforth; m. Patricia Desilet, Dec. 20, 1969; children: Michelle, b. 1973; Mary, b. 1978; edn: BA, Univ. of Fla. 1967; JD, Univ. of Fla. Coll. of Law 1969. Career: deputy dist. atty., County of San Diego, 1974--; judge advocate USAF Ofc. of Judge Adv. Gen., 1970-74; staff atty. Law Inc., Hillsborough Co., Fla. 1970; OEO Pgm : pres. Tierrasanta/Murphy County Chemical People Task Force, 1983-; chmn. Mission Trails Regl. Park Citizens Adv. Com., 1979 ; pres. Tierrasanta Comm. Council, 1976-78; honors: Blue Key (1967), Who's Who Among Students in Am. Colls. and Univs. (1968), Nat. Legal Aid and Defender Recogn. (1969), recogn. for community svc., Mayor and City Council of San Diego (1978), Kiwanis Intl. Distinguished Pres. award (1979), Super-disting. Lt. Gov. awd., CA-NV-HI Dist. (1982), Outstanding Young Man of Am., Nat. Jaycees (1981). Mem: Kiwanis Internat. (Cal-Nev-HA Dist. Foundation v.p. 1983-4, pres. 1984-5), Kiwanis Club of Tierrasanta (pres. 1978-9); Delta Tau Delta Alumni Assn (pres. 1978-80); mil: served to capt. USAF 1970-74, maj. USAFR 1974-; Democrat; Christian; rec: commercial pilot (cert. flight instr) Res: 4014 Tumbor Rd San Diego 92124 Office of District Attorney, 220 West Broadway San Diego 92101

PERCHONOCK, PAUL ROBERT, emergency physician; b. Sept. 3, 1944, Phila., Pa.; s. Meyer and Edith (Balis) P.; m. Judy Ann, Nov. 19, 1982; children: Toni, b. 1967; Deann, b. 1968; Jennifer, b. 1970; Britton, b. 1975; edn: AB, Cornell Univ. 1966; MD, Temple Univ. 1970; cert. American Board of Emergency Medicine 1980. Career: clin. practice of emergency medicine 1972--; co-dir. Alta Bates Hosp. Emergency Dept., Berkeley 1973--; cons. medicolegal emergency med. issues, 1977--; recipient AMA Contg. Edn. Award 1978-83; charter mem. Am. Coll. of Emergency Physicians 1972; Alameda County Emergency Med. Care Com. 1975-83, Alameda Co. Med. Review Panel 1976-83; rec: jogging, Himalayan trekking, skiing. Res: 70 St. James Place Piedmont 94611 Ofc: Alta Bates Hospital, Colby & Webster, Berkeley 94705

PEREYRA-SUAREZ, CHARLES ALBERT, lawyer; b. Sept 7, 1947, Paysandu, Uruguay, nat. 1962; s. Hector and Esther (Enriquez Sajano) P.-S.; edn: BA in hist. (magna cum laude), Pacific Union Coll. 1970; JD, UC Berkeley 1975; admitted to Calif. and Dist. of Columbia Bars. Career: staff attorney Western Center on Law and Poverty Inc., Los Angeles 1976; trial atty. Civil Rights Div. US Dept. of Justice, Wash DC 1976-79; asst. US Atty., Criminal Div., US Atty's Office, L.A. 1979-82; senior litigation assoc. Gibson, Dunn & Crutcher, L.A. 1982--; bd. dirs. Leland House (drug rehab. and juvenile delinquency prevention ctr.); honors: Boalt Hall rep. in nat. clin. pgm. (Georgetown Univ. Law Center, funded by LEAA) Interdisciplinary Criminal Justice Mgmt. Tng. Pgm. (1974); Moot Ct. Bd., staff Ecology Law Quarterly, Boalt Hall Sch. of Law 1973-5; chief editor Campus Chronicle (student newspaper), senior class pres., All-American rating by Assoc. Collegiate Press, Pacific Union Coll.; Democrat; Seventh-day Adventist; rec: tennis, jogging, skiing. Res: 4411 Los Feliz Blvd, 103, Los Angeles 90027 Ofc: Gibson, Dunn & Crutcher, 2029 Century Park East, Ste. 4000, Los Angeles 90027

PEREZ, DENNIS PAUL, real estate broker; b. Sept. 3, 1947, San Jose; s. Joseph C. and Kathryn A. Perez; edn: West Valley Coll. 1965-68; San Jose State Univ. 1969-72. Career: designer Data Technology, San Jose 1969-72; engring. services mgr. Kasper Instr., Sunnyvale 1972-77; real estate broker/owner/pres. Allstate Realtors, Santa Clara 1977-80, National Financial Network Inc., 1980--; pvt. instr. real estate inv. classes; write, sell, manage gen. and lmtd. ptnrships; recipient num. real estate achieve. awards; mem. Sons of Italy (treas. 1972-73) Santa Clara Lodge; Christian; rec: sailing. Res: 2971 Salem Dr Santa Clara 95051 Ofc: National Financial Network Inc., 2470 El Camino Real, Santa Clara 95051

PEREZ, OSCAR, physician; b. Sept. 5, 1945, Monterrey, N.L., Mex., nat. 1963; s. Juan and Carmen (Burford) Perez Molina; m. Yolanda A., May 2, 1975; children: Yanira, b. 1977; Yannelly, b. 1976; Oscar Edward, b. 1981; edn: UCLA 1968; MD, UANL 1975; Physician & Surgeon 1975. Career: postgrad. work Internal Medicine, residency Cook County Hosp. 1975-76, Martin Luther King Hosp., Los Angeles 1976-78; pvt. practice medicine Jose A. Perez, MD, Los Angeles 1978-80, solo pvt. practice, pres. Oscar Perez MD, Inc. Santa Ana 1980--; mem. Orange County Med. Assn.; publs: art., Mexican Pediatrics Jour. 1974; Republican; Catholic; rec: equestrian, swimming, race cars. Res: 15415 Los Molinos St Hacienda Hts 91745 Ofc: Oscar Perez MD Inc. 1125 East 17th St, N-152, Santa Ana 92701

PERILLO, LEONARD RAYMOND, investment co. president/entrepreneur; b. Oct. 29, 1956, Berkeley; s. Leonard Albert and Jinka Anne Jessen (Zoberski) P.; edn: UC Berkeley 1975-6; Oxford Univ., Eng. 1976-7; BBA, CSU Hayward 1979. Career: real estate investment analyst Bellinger, Steinbeck and Roberts, Castro Valley, 1979-80; chief exec. Leonard R. Perillo Investments, 1979--; pres./prin., Jaca-Perillo Constrn., San Lorenzo 1983--; founder/owner Europe-America Imports, 1983--; v.p./bd. chmn. Cloud Enterprises, Orinda 1981--; dir. Cal-Rod Constrn., Castro Valley 1980-81; chmn. advis. bd. Centennial Bank, Hayward 1981-; honors: Sigma Delta Chi (profl. writers) 1977-80, Harlaxton Acad. Soc. 1976-; mem: Calif., Nat. Assn. of Realtors; SACBOR; Commonwealth Club of Calif.; Hayward H.S. Alumni Com. Chmn. 1974-; male model assignments during college, appeared in sev. nat. publs., and on Morning Show TV; Democrat; rec: world travel & study, Am. coins & stamps. Res: 1642 Daniels Dr San Leandro 94577 Ofc: 996 Silverado Ct Hayward 94541

PERKIN, RONALD MURRAY, physician; b. July 31, 1948, Denver, Colo.; s. Robert Murray and Marion Katherine (Thompson) M.; m. Cynthia Louise (Waters), Oct. 4, 1980; 1 son, Matthew Murray b. 1982; edn: BS in engring., honors, Univ. of Colo., Boulder 1970; postgrad. study Johns Hopkins Univ. 1970-71; MD, Univ. of South Fla. Coll. of Med. 1976. Career: pilot/ofcr. US Navy 1973; resident, pediatrics Children's Medical Center, Dallas, Tx. 1976-79, fellowship Ped. Intensive Care, 1979-81, asst. dir. Pediatric Intensive Care, 1981; clin. asst., prof. of ped. Univ. of Texas, Southwestern Med. Sch., Dallas 1981; asst. adj. prof. of ped. UC San Diego Sch. of Med., 1982--, co-dir. Pediatric Intensive care Unit UCSD/University Hosp., 1982--; awards: Lange Annual Award 1975, Mosby Scholarship 1975-6, Outstanding Student in Pediatrics, Surgery and Anatomic Scis. 1976, Alpha Omega Alpha; mem: Soc. of Critical Care Medicine, Am. Heart Assn.; num. articles in med. journals; Republican; Prot.; rec: physical fitness, running. Res: 3664-3D Clairemont Dr San Diego 92117 Ofc: University Hospital, 225 Dickinson St San Diego 92103

PERKINS, DENVER EDWARD, JR., physician; b. Apr. 8, 1941, Temple, TX; s. Denver Edward and Hettie Lois (Randals) Perkins Sr.; Edn: BA in English, VMI, 1963; MD, Univ. Tex., 1973; m. Suzanne Stark, Oct. 5, 1978; chil: Samantha, b. 1969; Rebecca, b. 1969; Brian, b. 1974. Career: physician, director Emergency Dept., St. Paul Hospital, Dallas, 1977-79; pvt. practice, Sonora, Calif., 1979--; director Hospice of the Sierra. Mem: AMA, Calif. Med. Assn. Mil: served to Capt., US Army; armor; Vietnam Svc. medal, Combat Inf. Badge, Bronze Star, Purple Heart, Army Commend. Medal. Republican. Catholic. Rec: skydiving, target shooting, karate. Office: 193 S. Fairview, Ste. B, Sonora 95370.

PERKINS, GEORGE PHILIP, business owner; b. Jan. 7, 1930, Chgo., Ill.; s. James Otis and Irene Ann (Burke) P.; children: Jody, b. 1963; Heidi, b. 1957; Lynn, b. 1962; edn: BS, Univ. of Colo. 1951. Career: owner/mgr. The Lassen Park Ski Area, 1956-66; mgr. The Mineral Lodge and Water System, 1962-76; owner/mgr The Ski Renter, 1969--; pres. George Perkins Ent. Inc. dba the Ski Renter; cons. Mineral Water System; mem. Kappa Sigma Frat. Alumni; author/pub. Hiking Trails of Lassen Volcanic National Park; mil: 2d lt. Finance Corps; rec: photog. Address: The Ski Renter, Box 910, S. Lake Tahoe CA 95705

PERKINS, JO ANN BERESFORD, business owner/ travel consultant; b. Apr. 13, 1931, Red Bluff; d. Harrold Kelsey and Catherine Amanda (Rohwer) Beresford; m. George Perkins, Sept. 10, 1956; children: Heidi, b. 1958; Lynn, b. 1961; Jody, b. 1962; edn: BA, UC Berkeley 1949-53; Lic. Real Estate Broker, Calif. 1978. Career: stewardess United Air Lines 1956-56; owner/opr. Mineral Lodge, 1956-80; owner/opr. Lassen Park Ski Area 1956-66; real estate sales, Western Real Estate Center, 1977-82; owner/opr. Victorian Restaurant, Red Bluff 1979-83 (estab. restaurant in 100-year old Victorian home 1979, in 1980 moved the two-story, 135-ton bldg. restaurant, furnishings intact, to its present location); currently travel cons. Travel Works and comml. real estate sales Kiernan Commercial, Sacramento; past mem. Red Bluff CofC; exec. com. School Bd. Mineral; Republican; Prot.; rec: skiing, photog., travel. Res: 1582 Response Rd, 2064, Sacramento 95815 Ofc: Kiernan Commercial, 1515 30th Street, Sacramento 95816

PERLIS, MICHAEL FREDRICK, lawyer; b. June 3, 1947, NY; s. Leo and Betty F. (Gantz) P.; m. Cynthia Druskin, June 8, 1969; children: Amy Hannah, b. 1974; David Matthew, b. 1978; edn: BSFS, Georgetown Univ. Sch. of Foreign Svc. 1968; JD, Georgetown Univ. Law Ctr. 1971. Admitted Dist. of Columbia Bar 1971-, State Bar of Calif. 1980-. Career: court law clk. Dist. of columbia Court of Appeals, Wash DC; asst. Corporation Counsel, Wash. DC 1972-74;

atty. US Securities and Exchange Commn. Div. of Enforcement, Wash. DC 1974-75, branch chief 1975-77, asst. dir. 1977-80; ptnr. Pettit & Martin, San Francisco 1980--; adj. prof. of law Catholic Univ. of Am. 1979-80; awards: Edmund A. Walsh Gold Medal 1968; Who's Who in American Law (1983); mem. Am., Dist. of Columbia, Calif., San Francisco bar assns.; chmn. ABA subcom. Sec. and Commodities Litigation, Section of Lit. 1982-; works: lectr., var. securities laws and litigation law matters; Democrat; Jewish; rec: art collector. Res: 3 Beechwood Ct. San Rafael 94901 Ofc: Pettit & Martin, 101 California St, 35th Fl, San Francisco 94111

PERNICIARO, GIANVITTORIO, shipping co. executive; b. Dec. 5, 1940, Bari, Italy, nat. 1975; s. Antonino and Anita (Russo) Perniciaro; m. Liliana Peripoli, Nov. 24, 1970; 2 daus.: Patrizia, b. 1964; Elena, b. 1972; edn: spl. courses, English Inst. of Languages, Palermo, Italy 1962, Univ. of Palermo, 1963, Am. Mgmt. Assn., L.A. 1973. Career: interpreter/polyglot, US Govt., Dept. of State, US Consulate General, Palermo, Italy, 1960-68; traffic mgr. AGIP USA, N.Y 1968-69; op. mgr. U.S. Lines, Oakland 1972-74; West Coast ops. mgr. Zim Container Service, 1976--; industry cons. and lectr. Transportation Training Ctr., 1984. Awards: Am. Mgmt. Assn., 1974; Employment Devel. Dept. (E.U.), Oakland, 1976. Mem: The Propeller Club, Port of Los Angeles-Long Beach 1977-, US Senatorial Club 1984. Author: My Baja Book (1981); Container Terminal Operations Textbook (1984). Republican (Presdtl Task Force); Catholic; rec: piano, classical music, motorcycle touring. Res: 1817 Barrywood Ave San Pedro 90731 Ofc: Zim Container Svc 453 So Spring St, Ste 200, Los Angeles 90013

PERO, JEFFREY TOWNE, lawyer; b. Aug. 16, 1946, Utica, NY; s. Chester Daniel and Ella Mae (Towne) P.; m. Bunny, Dec. 19, 1976; edn: AB, Univ. of Notre Dame 1968; JD, NYU Sch. of Law 1971. Career: assoc. lawyer law firm O'Melveny & Myers, Los Angeles 1971; partner 1979; founder Newport Beach Ofc. 1979; currently, in charge in gen. practice, Newport Beach Ofc., O'Melveny & Myers; tchr. law sch., grad. bus. sch. & statewide profl. legal edn. sems., part- time; honors: Root Tilden Scholarship to NYU SCh. of Law, 1968; mem: Am., Calif., Los Angeles & Orange Co. Bar Assns.; Am. Diabetes Assn. (bd. dirs. Orange Co., Calif. chpt.); mil: capt. US Army 1972; Republican; Catholic; rec: num. athletic endeavors. Res: 32641 Caribbean South Laguna 92677 Ofc: O'Melveny & Myers, 610 Newport Center Dr, Ste 1700, Newport Beach 92660

PERRIN, THOMAS, JR., manufacturing co. executive; b. May 10, 1937, Brownstown, Ind.; s. Thomas and Imogene (Beck) P.; m. Elizabeth McDonald, Feb. 23, 1973; children: Tatia, b. 1967; Thomas II, b. 1969; Travis, b. 1974; edn: AA, Ventura Coll. 1975; BA, LaVerne Univ. 1979; MS, 1980. Career: dental tech. Carper Bros. Dental Lab., Denver, Colo. 1958-61; eng. dental tech., Statham Inst. Inc., Los angeles 1962-65; prodn. supt. 1965-74; with Gould Inc., Oxnard 1974--; mktg. engr. 1974-77; mgr. mktg. ad;min. 1977-79; regl. mgr. 1979-81; dir. of sales 1981--; honors: Hon. Roll & Scholarship in Communications, Ventura Coll. 1971; mem: Instrument Soc. of Am.; Techl. Mktg. Soc. of Am.; Nat. Intellectual Soc. (Mensa); works: creator, state- of- the- art process for thin film deposition, 1971; mil: pvt. US Army 1956-58, GCM; Democrat; Portestant; rec: free- lance writing, independent studies. Res: 11897 Lilac Way Fountain Valley 92708 Ofc: Gould Inc. 2230 Statham Blvd Oxnard 93033

PERRY, MICHAEL F., advertising specialties co. owner; b. Sept. 16, 1947, Kenova, W.Va.; s. Elias Lee and Frances Pauline (Davis) P.; m. Arlene Ortiz, Dec. 27, 1967; children: Michelle, b. 1968; Michael, b. 1971; Marissa, b. 1980. Career: bar. mgr. Pacific Finance, Canyon Country 1971-76; sales mgr. R.R. Perry & Co., Los Angeles 1976-82; owner Mike Perry Co., Orange 1982--; mem: Little League (player agent, minor & maj. league); mil: E-5 USAF 1966-69, Accomodation Medal; Democrat; Catholic; rec: sports, motorcycling, engraving. Res: 161 S Poinsettia Orange 92668 Ofc: Mike Perry Co., 840 N Main Orange 92668

PERRY, PHILLIP MICHAEL, company president; b. Nov. 14, 1947, Tucson, Ariz.; s. Eldon Gwain Perry and Doris Edith (Wismer) Perry Noonan; m. Lora T. Stratta, Apr. 14, 1973; edn: bus. acctg., Univ. of Ariz. 1965-70; spl. courses, Grossmont Coll. 1974, San Diego State 1975; var. tech. seminars pumps, controls, hydraulics 1971-. Career: sales engr. Pacific Pumping Co., Los Angeles 1971-76; sales engr. Aurora Pump Co., L.A. 1976-77; pres. Hydro Mechanical Eng. Inc., Fullerton 1977-81, dir. 1977-; pres. Hydrotechnics Inc., Fullerton 1981--; instr. Coll. of the Canyons 1978; guest lectr. Orange Coast Coll. 1978-; awards: Outstanding Sales Achiev., Pacific Pumping Co. 1972; mem: Calif. Water Pollution Control Fedn.; author: Basic Pump Handbook, 1971; Episcopal; rec: micro computers, investments, hunting. Res: 3412 Sunnywood Dr Fullerton 92635 Ofc: Hydrotechincs Inc., POB 5033 Fullerton 92635

PERRY, ROBERT A., lawyer; b. Feb. 16, 1939, Sacrameno; s. Lawrence J. and Emma M. (Del Carlo) P.; m. Barbara, May 22, 1965; children: Jeannine, b. 1966, Scott, b. 1968, Denise, b. 1970; edn: AB, CSC Sacto 1966, JD, McGeorge Sch of Law, UOP 1970; admitted practice law Calif. Bar 1971. Career: pvt. practice law, partner firm Saldine, Perry & Lumley (and predecessor firms) 1972-79; atty. firm Bernhard & Perry, Sacramento 1979-81; sel-empl. solo practice 1981-84; mng. atty. Sacramento Cigna Corp. 1984--; instr. Lincoln Univ. Law Sch. 1972-; mem: Am., Calif. State, Sacramento Co., Italian-Am. Bar Assns.; mem. Unico (Ital. mens orgn.); mil: maj. Calif Army NG; Catholic. Res: 9040 Sierra Valley Ln. Loomis 95650 Ofc: Perry & Yeo, 428 J St., Ste. 360, Sacramento 95814

PERUSSINA, ROBERT DANIEL, certified financial planner; b. May 5, 1955, San Francisco; s. Robert Eugene and Jane Francis (Callaghan) P.; m. Sherry Holcomb, June 19, 1982; 1 son: Daniel, b. 1983; edn: BS, UC Berkeley 1977; CFP, Coll. of Fin. Plnng., Denver, Colo. 1982. Career: fin. plnng. rep. Independent Plnng. Corp. (exec. com., CEO subsidiary Independent Qualified Palns), San Franciso 1977--; plnng. cons. Doctorls Co., Santa Monica 1980-81; dir. S.F. Bay Area chpt. Am. Assn. of Fin. Profls.; sem. spkr. fin. plnng., var. corps. & profl. assns.; honors: past pres., San Francisco Bay Area chpt. Sigma Alpha Epsilon frat.; mem: SAE Alumni Assn.; Cal Beta Alumni Assn.; Internat. Assn. Fin. Plnng.; Inst. CFPs; Am. Assn. Fin. Profls.; publs: author chpt., Wind Energy, in Energy in the Bay Area, UC Berkeley Press, 1977; writer, Bank of Am. Consumer Information Reports, incl. Savings Programs & Ednl. Funding.; Republican; Catholic; rec: sailing, aerobatics, computer programming. Res: 76 Meadow Rd Mill Valley 94941 Ofc: Independent Planning Corp., 1255 Post St, Ste 700, San Francisco 94109

PESSNER, HUBERT OSWALD, lumber sales co. president; b. Nov 28, 1916, Los Angeles; s. Oswin and Carolyn Matilda (Goede) P.; m. Audree Frances Krajack, Apr. 7, 1981; children: Verne Curtis; Kirk Alan; Sandra Gale; edn: AA, Pasadena City Coll. 1937; BS, Ore. State Univ. 1945. Career: asst. mgr. br. yard Patten-Blinn Lumber Co., Los Angeles 1945-47; salesman Ralph E. Barto Lumber Co., Huntington Park 1947-48; salesman Buyer Tarter Webster & Johnson Inc., San Francisco 1948-50; pres./ gen. mgr. West Coast Timber Co., San Rafael 1950--; owner Sugar Pine Sales Co., San Rafael 1959--; mem: Soc. of Am. Foresters; Forest Prods. Research Soc.; Sigma Chi; San Francisco Lumbermans (bd. dir. 1953, pres. 1957-58); Elk Club; United Conservationist & Sportsmen of Marin (bd. govs.); Republican; Protestant. Res: 320 Mountain View Ave San Rafael 94901 Ofc: West Coast Timber Products, 4340 Redwood Hwy, Ste 130, San Rafael 94901

PETERSEN, GARY M., resource conservation co. president; b. Nov. 23, 1947, Santa Monica; s. Kathleen Petersen; m. Alexandra; children: Samantha Kate b. 1976, Jesse Garett b. 1982; att. college in W.L.A. area. Career: founder/pres. Ecolo-Haul, Pacific Palisades 1972--; pioneer of recycling and resource conservation in Calif.; honors: recipient num. honors from City, County and State govts., civic orgns.; recycling award, Calif. Com. for Resource Recovery; 6 time nominee for Tyler Ecology Award, inclusion in The Peter Plan (authored by Laurence Peter); listed Who's Who in Am., Who's Who in the World. Founder/bd. dirs. Calif. Resource Recovery Assn. (CRRA), non-profit statewide orgn. of indus., govt., concerned citizens; mem: State Solid Waste Mgmt. Bd. Steering Com., Cousteau Soc., Calif. Indus. Environmnet Council, Wilderness Soc., Gov's Resource Utilization Task Force, Citizens Solid Waste Environ. Adv. Com. County of L.A., NSF cons. (Com. for Nat. Recycling Policy), advisor US Conf. of Mayors, advisor Nat. Recycling Coalition, mem. World Wildlife Fund, Defenders of Wildlife, Los Angeles Beautiful (bd. dirs.), Santa Monica Beautification and Recycling Pgm. (pres.), So. Calif. Business Mens Assn. Address: Ecolo-Haul, POB 1263, Pacific Palisades 90272

PETERSEN, ROBERT GEORGE, manufacturing co. executive; b. Mar. 31, 1921, Clinton, Iowa; s. Alvin D. and Alvena M. (Gehlsen) P.; m. Norma, Sept. 1, 1949; children: Norman b. 1953, Janice b. 1955; edn: grad. Miles (Iowa) H.S. 1939; tech. courses, L.A. Harbor Coll. 1953-56; Calif. Reg. Profl. Engr./ Control Systems Engring. 1976. Career: technician, then supr. for plant process control instrumentation, Shell Chemical Co. (Div. Shell Oil), 1950-72; ptnr./ v.p. Flowmetrics Inc. (estab. as engring. firm spec. in systems used in Waste Water Mgmt.; mfrs. of flowmeters, Rotometers and Turbine type devices, used in aircraft indus. internat. 1976-), Los Angeles 1972--; training coord. Petro Chem Industry; gen. chmn. SCMA sponsored Instrument Short Course (annual); mem. So. Calif. Meter Assn. (pres. 1967-8), Fellow Inst. for Advancement of Engring. (1981); life mem. Loyal Order of Moose, L.A. Area Counsel BSA; mil: T5 US Army Inf. 1945-47; Republican; Prot.; rec: gardening, hiking. Res: 1953 253rd Place Lomita 90717 Ofc: Flowmetrics Inc. 7447 E. Slauson ave Los Angeles 90040

PETERSEN, THEODORE NEWMAN, lawyer; b. Jan. 20, 1927, Los Angeles; s. Olav Karolus and Mary Cranston (Livingstone) P.; m. Troy Lea Hocker, Nov. 1, 1962; children: Douglas L., b. 1959; Karen L., b. 1963; Erika L., b. 1966; edn: BA, UC Berkeley 1950; LLD, UC Hastings Coll. of Law 1955; admitted to practice, State Bar of Calif. 1955. Career: Law Ofc. of C. Ray Robinson, Los Angeles; Law Ofc. of C. Ray Robinsen, Merced; currently, Law Ofc. of T.N. Petersen, Merced; cons. atty., pgm. w/ Merced Coll. & Merced Bar Assn. for unpaid consultation for coll. students; bd. dirs. Merced Co. Legal Svcs. Orgn.; Calif. Bar. Assn. (com. on Domestic Rels.); Merced Bar Assns. (pres. 1964); mil: aviation machbinists mate 3/c USN Air Corps 1945; Republican; Protestant. Res: 9031 Kraft Planada 95365 Ofc: 1724 M Street Merced 95340

PETERSON, HOWARD COOPER, financial planner, accountant; b. Oct. 12, 1939, Decatur, Ill.; s. Howard and Lorraine (Cooper) P.; edn: BSEE, Univ. of Ill. 1963; MSEE, CSU San Diego 1967; MBA, Columbia Univ. 1969; JD, Calif. Western Sch. of Law 1983; postgrad. law studies, New York Univ. Career: elec. engr. to senior electronics engr. General Dynamics, Convair Div., 1963-68; financial planning and service bus., income tax preparation, real estate brokerage, securities sales, ins. sales, finl. cons., 1970--; pres./dir. Coastal Properties Trust, a real estate inv. trust; pres./dir. E.P.R. Corp., a real estate brokerage; v.p./dir. Equity Programs Corp., NASD securities brokerage; treas./dir. Imperial Screens of San Diego, alarm screens sales; gen. ptnr. Costumes Characters & Classics, costume rentals. Mem: Nat. Soc. of Public Accts., Internat. Assn. of Finl. Plnnrs. Inc., Assn. of Enrolled Agents, Amer. Bar Assn. Ofc: 1335 Hotel Circle South, Ste. 205, San Diego 92108

PETERSON, JOHN ELLIS, hydrogeologist; b. June 15, 1950, Bremerton, Wash.; s. Winfield A. and Phyllis Bernice (Carter) P.; 1 dau: Jennifer, b. 1979; edn: AS, Olympic Coll. 1970; BS, CSU San Diego 1976; BS, w/ distinction, 1978; Reg. Geologist, Calif. 1982. Career: hydrogeologist Hydro-Search Inc., Reno, Nev. 1978-81; co. hydrogeologist, San Diego Co., San Diego 1981--; geology instr. Grossmont Comm.Coll. 1982; pres. Calif. Groundwater Mgmt. Assn.; mem: Nat. Water Well Assn.; San Diego Assn. Geologists; YMCA; Kiwanis Club; works: paper, A County Perspective on Groundwater in Fractured Rock in Proceedings, 14th Biennial Calif. State Groundwater Conf.; paper, Groundwater Mgmt.- San Diego Style in Proceedings Western Regl. Conf. on Groundwater Mgmt. 1983; mil: sonar tech. 3/c USNR, Destroyer svt., Vietnam War; rec: mountaineering, racquetball, running. Res: 4017 Vivian San Diego 92115 Ofc: San Diego County, 5201 Ruffin Rd, Ste 0650, San Diego 92123

PETERSON, NELS STERLING, real estate broker; b. Aug. 21, 1913, Eureka; s. Nels and Katie (Jameson) P.; m. Nellie Whitlatch, June 5, 1971; children: Ronald, b. 1936; Joanne, b. 1957. Career: clerk/ dept. mgr. H.H. Buhne Co. 1929-40; rancher 1940-47; owner/ mgr. Peterson's Sporting Goods 1947-63; partner Hodge & Peterson Realty 1963-72; owner/ mgr. Land Man Realty 1972--; mem: Klamath CofC (past pres.); Calif. State CofC (past); Trinity River Diversion Com., Del Norte Co. (past); Del Norte Co. Boy Scouts (past chmn.); Del Norte Co. Draft Bd. (past). Address: Sterling Peterson Realty (The Land Man), 2123 Harris St Eureka 95501

PETH, MICHAEL ALYN, health care co. executive; b. Aug. 17, 1951, El Paso, Tex.; s. Ivan Harry and Hertha Delores Peth; m. Rita Scherschel, Jan. 26, 1974; children: Christian, b. 1980; Karissa, b. 1982; edn: BA, journalism, CSU San Jose 1983, and Grad. Fin. (magna cum laude), San Jose Univ. 1983. Career: customer svc. mgr. Shofu Dental Corp., Menlo Park 1976-77; lab. bus. asst. Good Samaritan Hosp., San Jose 1977-79; mgr. tech. publs. Technicon Data System, Santa Clara 1979-83; dir. hosp. info. sys. Seton Med. Ctr., Daly City 1983--; dir. hosp. info. sys. St. Catherine Hosp. on Half Moon Bay 1983--; v.p. Hospital Cost Consultants, Daly City 1983--; cons., client firms. for hosp. info. sys. analysis devel.; honor: Mu Alpha Theta 1970; Beta Gamma Sigma 1982, mem: Healthcare Fin. Mgmt. Assn.; Soc. of Med. Computer Observers; Am. Assn. of Med. Sys. & Informatics; Elec. Computing Health Orgn.; publs: A Total Bilirubin Program, pub. Hewlett-Packard Lib., Boblingen, W.Ger. 1973; num. proprietary reference manuals, Technicon Data Sys., Seton Med. Ctr. & Hosp. Cost. Cons.; Lutheran; rec: personal computing, cooking, photog. Res: 4904 Trent Dr San Jose 95124 Ofc: Hospital Cost Consultants, 1784 Sullivan Ave Daly City 94015

PETHEL, DOROTHY LORENE, educator/ nursing and health sciences; b. Aug. 15, 1927, Blythe, Calif.; d. Wm. Jennings and Ruby Coral (Garnett) Hooe; m. James Pethel, Feb. 12, 1958, children: Darlene (Kapelewski), Glenda (Sen wel), Craig; edn: AA, San Bernardino Valley Coll. 1954; AA, nursing, Riverside City Coll. 1960; BS, nsg. CSU Los Angeles 1965; MA, health edn., CSU Sacto. 1970; PhD, hlth. edn., Calif. National Univ. 1979; lic. Marriage, Family and Child Counselor. Career: senior psychiatric nurse, Div. supvr. Patton State Hosp. 1960-66; In-service edn., DeWitt State Hosp., Auburn 1966-69; nsg. instr. Sierra Comm. Coll., dir. Vocational Nsg. Edn. 1979--; conduct workshops for nurses, Calif. Voc. Nurse Educators & Golden West Orthopedic Gp., investigation/advis. com. on CORE project (HEW grant); recipient Hon. Life Mem. for Outstanding Services to young people Oakview Sch., 1973; mem: Calif. Voc. Nse. Educators Assn. (exec. bd.), Golden West Orthopedic Gp. (exec. bd.), Oakview Sch. (exec. bd.), Am. Heart Assn.; CSU Sacto. Academic Affairs Com. (5 yrs.); Sacto. Valley Dirs. of Nsg. Svc. & Edn. Speakers Bur.; Sierra Coll. coms. (Scholarship, Handicapped Students, Emerg. Med. Svc., Comm. Svc.); articles in profl. jours.; editor Medical Surgical Nsg. textbook; copyright: Pethel Attitude Test on Drug Abuse (1971); mem. Orangevale CofC, Holy Family Ch., Confrat. of Christian Mot;s; rec: photog. Res: 8150 Chipwood Way Orangevale 95662 Ofc: Siera Community College 5000 Rocklin Road Rocklin

PETILLO, ANGELA, lawyer; b. Oct. 11, 1949, Long Branch, NJ; d. Angelo F. and Ann P.; edn: BA, Montclair State Coll. 1971; JD, Loyola Univ. Sch. of Law 1980; admitted to practice, State Bar of Calif. 1980, Supreme Ct. of Calif., US Dist. Ct., US Ct. of Appeals. Career: dir./ coord./ instr. Eng. Lang. Pgms.: Title 7, Hoboken, NJ; The Vatican (San Pietro), Vatican City, Rome, Italy; Notre Dame Internat. Sch., Rome, Italy; & The Am. Coll. of Rome, 1971-76; prodn. asst. El Dorado Films, Rome, Italy 1976-77; adminstrv. asst. Dino DeLaurentiis Corp., Beverly Hills 1977-79; atty./ assoc. dir. contracts, Am. Broadcasting Co. Inc., Los Angeles 1981--; cons. Eng. Lang. Pgm., Am. Coll. of Rome 1975; Meetings, L.A. Copyright Soc. 1981-; mem: Am., Calif. & L.A. Co. Bar Assns.; Montclair State Coll. Alumni Assn.; Dante Aligheri Soc.; Town Hall of Calif.; works: profl. photographer, 1976; rec: fluent Italian, travel, skiing. Res: 531 1/2 Glenrock Ave Los Angeles 90024 Ofc: American Broadcasting Companies Inc., 2040 Ave of Stars, Ste 300, Los Angeles 90067

PETRASICH, JOHN M., lawyer; b. Oct. 13, 1945, Long Beach; s. Louis A. and Margaret A. (Moris) P.; m. Kathleen Krenek, July 4, 1969; children: Jason, b. 1971; Jacquelyn, b. 1974; edn; BA, USC 1967; JD, 1970. Career: Fulop & Hardee (formerly Fulop, Rolston, Burns & McKittrick) A Law Corp., Beverly Hills, Newport Beach & NYC: law clerk 1969-70; assoc. lawyer 1971-74; shareholder/ lawyer 1975-82; mem. bd. dirs. 1978-82; lawyer/ founding partner/ bd. dirs./ chmn. Litigation Dept. and chief trial lawyer, McKittrick, Jackson, DeMarco & Peckenpaugh, A Law Corp., Newport Beach 1983--; honors: Order of Coif 1970; asoc. ed. USC Law Review 1969-70; mem: Am.,

Calif., L.A. & Beverly Hills Bar Assns. 1971-; Lawyers Club of L.A. Co. 1971-; Assn. of Trial Lawyers of Am. 1980-; Town Hall of Calif. 1981-. Res: 15 Laurel Tree Ln Irvine 92715 Ofc: McKittrick, Jackson, DeMarco & Peckenpaugh, 4041 MacArthur Blvd, 5th Flr, Newport Beach 92660

PETREE, CLOYCE LAMAR, alcohol rehabilitation center director; b. July 31, 1928, El Reno, Okla.; parents: Cloyce L. and Moreen (Chenoweth) P.; div.; children: James b. 1950, Steven b. 1951, Michael b. 1954, Christopher b. 1955; edn: BA, edn., Central State Coll., Okla. 1952; MS, counseling, Sacto. State Coll. 1970; cert. rehabilitation counselors psy. tng., Univ. of Ore. Medical Sch. 1968; Calif. lic. (MFCC) Marriage, Family and Child Counseling 1971; Comm. Coll. Counselor Cred. (life) 1972; (CAAC) Cert. Alcoholism Counselor 1981. Career: principal, tchr. Seneca (Ks.) Elem. Sch., 1961-62; vocational (alcoholism) aide, Sacramento Alcoholism Center, Dept. Rehab., Sacto. 1966-67, counselor trainee 1967-69, voc. rehabilitation counselor 1969-73; deputy dir. Tng. Dept., Naval Alcohol Rehab. Ctr., Naval Station, San Diego 1973-81, dir. 1981--; bd. dirs. Nat. Assn. Alcoholism and Drug Abuse Counselor (NAADAC); counselor com. Nat. Certification Stds.; mem. Nat. Credentialing Task Force. Honors: Govt. Employee's Insurance Co. (GEICO) Public Svc. Award for contbn. in field of alcoholism, 1982. Mem: Nat. Assn. of Alcoholism Counselors, Am. Assn. for Marriage and Family Therapy, Alcohol and Drug Problem Assn. of No. Am., Calif. Assn. of Alcoholism Counselors (pres.), Federally Employed Women; works: prod. training film (used nat. in grad. schs.) on alcoholism: The Fifteenth American (1967); sev. publs. in field; mil: lt. USN 1946-58; Republican; rec: Small arms, camping, biking. Res: 4465 Kansas, D, San Diego 92116 Ofc: Navy Alcohol Rehabilitation Cent Naval Station, Box 80, San Diego 92116

PETRIC, ROBERTA LEE, speech pathologist; b. Feb. 17, 1951, Elkhart, Ind.; d. James Robert and Eileen Francis (Simons) Wood; m. James William Petric, Sept. 12, 1981; edn: BA, Univ. of Redlands 1973; MS, 1977; Speech Pathologist, Calif. 1979. Career: speech pathologist Alvord Unif. Sch. Dist. (devel. pre-sch. lang. devel. pgm., pgm. in conj. w/ crisis teenage pgm. & probation for skiil in commun. for teenage felons, elem. & h.s. pgms. in spech), Riverside 1973-80; dir. of ops. Regl. Rehab. Cons., Las Vegas, Nev. 1980-83; founder Calif. div. 1983--; pres. Petric & Assoc. Inc. (pvt. speech pathoogy orgn.); honors: Cert. of Clin. Competence, Am. Speech, Lang. & Hearing Assn. 1979; mem: Am. Speech, Lang. & Hearing Assn.; Calif. Speech & Hearing Assn.; Calif. Assn. Health Facilities (assoc.); Panhellenic; Republican; Catholic; rec: skiing, tennis. Res: 2714 Neda Mission Viejo 92692 Ofc: Petric & Associates Inc., POB 3295 Mission Viejo 92690

PETRICK, RICHARD KEITH, employee benefit specialist; b. Oct. 27, 1951, Mineola, NY; s. Edward H. and Lois Anne (Whittaker) P.; edn: BA, Univ. of Ore. 1973; Life & Disability Ins. Lic., Real Estate Lic., Variable Annuity Lic., Calif.; Series 6 Lic., Nat Assn. of Securities Dealers. Career: ins. field underwritier Mutual of New York 1974-81; estab./ owner/ mgr. Richard Petri & Assocs., San Franicso 1981--; bd. dirs. S.F. Life Underwriters Assn. 1979-81; S.F. Life Underwriters Political Action Com. chmn. 1981; honors: Chmns. Awd., S.F. Life Underwriters Assn. 1980, 81; Million Dollar Round Table 1977, 78; Mutual of NY Hon. Club Qualifier 1976-80; mem: S.F. Life Underwriters Assn.; Nat. & Calif. Asss. of Life Underwriters; Commonwealth Club; End Crime Inc. (pres. 1983); Steering Com., San Quentin Comm. Adv. Council; works: mgr. non-profit orgn. dedicated to prisoner rehab.; organized job counseling pgm., San Quentin State Prison 1983; devel. manual for standardized course in skill inventory & job search for inmates; Democrat; Presbyterian; rec: judo (1st degree black belt, Kenpo Karate), tennis. Address: Richard Petrick & Associates, 2424 Fulton St San Francisco 94118

PETTENGILL, MICHAEL KENT, certified fund raising executive/ market research consultant; b. Barre, Vt.; s. Hardy William and Ruth Urbana (Anderson) P.; m. Constance Judith Swift; children: Michelle; Catherine; Kimberly; John; Mansfield Coll.; Wash. Univ.; BSBA, Univ. of Central Calif. 1979; MS, 1981; PhD, 1982; Cert. Real Estate Brokerage, Lee Inst. 1966. Career: with Nat. Found. March of Dimes 1969-75; exec. dir. Penn.- NY chpts. 1969-72; adminstr. Central NY 1971-72; regl. dir. NY-NJ 1972-73; exec. dir. No. Calif. 1973-75; v.p./ independent cons./ CEO Americal Fund Raising Svcs., Sacto. 1975--; v.p. Ask America Mktg. Research, Sacto. 1980--; exec. dir. The Am. Found. of Ednl. Research Inc. 1983--; instr. mkt. research & mkt. profl. svcs., UC Davis Adult Edn. Pgm.; mem. aesthetic adv. commn. Caltrans 1975-81; pres./ admin. chmn./ bd. dirs. El Dorado Hills Comm. Svcs. Dist. 1975-81; chmn. El Dorado Co. Recreation Commn. 1975-77; pres. Mother Lode Rehabilitation Ent. Sheltered Workshop 1975-76; v.chmn. Gp. Health Svcs. Plan 1978-82; trustee Sleepy Hollow Assn. 1974-75; pres./ bd. mem. Chenango Forks Sch. Dist. Civic Assn. 1967-72; bd. mem. Upward Bound Pgm. State Univ. of NY 1967-71; honors: Spl. Recogn. Calif. State Senate 1975; mem: Sacto. Valley Mktg. Assn.; Am. Mktg. Assn.; Am. Assn. of Political Cons.; Nat. Guard Assn. of Calif.; Direct Mail Fund Raising Assn.; Nat. Soc. of Fund Raising Execs.; Sacto. Metro. CofC; dir. Magna Card Inc.; mil: col. Calif. State Mil. Reserve 1979-; Res: 3365 Ridgeview Dr El Dorado Hills 95630 Ofc: 1932 Stockton Blvd Sacramento 95816

PETTIS-HARVILLE, SHIRLEY NEIL, former U.S. congresswoman; b. Mountain View; d. Harold O. and Dorothy McCumber; m. Jery Lyle Pettis, Mar. 2, 1947 (dec.); children: Peter Dwight, b. 1955; Deborah Neil, b. 1958; m. 2d. William Harville, Jan. 16, 1982; edn: Andrews Univ., Mich.; UC Berkeley. Career: mng. dir. Audio-Digest Found. 1953-55; secty./ treas. Pettis Inc. 1953-67; author, newspaper columnist 1967-74; elected to US House of Reps. (to succeed husband, 5-term Congressman, killed in plane crash 1975) Apr. 1975-78; mem. Presidential Commn., Arms Control & Disarmament; dir: Kemper Corp., Lumbermans Mutual, Casualty Ins., Am. Motors & Am. Mfgrs.; rec: equestriam, swimming, flying. Res: 13651 Carlsbad Santa Ana 92705

PEWTHERS, CARROLL DONALD, insurance agency owner; b. Aug. 8, 1936, Eureka, Ca.; s. Carroll and Mary Alice (Wensel) P.; children: Cathleen M., b. 1964, Carol Lee, b. 1961 (dec. 1980); edn: BA, Stanford Univ. 1958; Chartered Life Underwriter, Am. Coll. CLU. Career: agent/supr. New York Life, Palo Alto, 1960-67, gen. mgr., NY Life, San Mateo 1967-75, owner C. Don Pewthers & Assocs. ins. agcy., San Mateo 1975--; mem. Peninsula General Agents & Mgrs. Assn. (pres. 1970), Peninsula Life Underwriters Assn., Am. Soc. of CLUs; past pres. San Mateo Kiwanis Club, past pres., dir. San Mateo Club, Elks, Stanford Alumni Assocs., Stanford Golf Club, Stanford Buck Club, Nat. Rifle Assn.; founder annual C. Don Pewthers Memorial Chili Party 1974-; founder Carolee Pewthers Meml. Scholarship Fund (awarded annually to Alpha Chi Omega, Univ. of Idaho) 1981; Prot. Res: 718 Widgeon Foster City 94404 Ofc: C. Don Pewthers & Ass. 66 Bovet Road, Ste. 353, San Mateo 94402

PEXA, ROBERT JAMES, insurance co. executive; b. Apr. 8, 1932, St. Paul, Minn.; natural s. Raymond Heminger and Louise Mary Olberding; adoptive son of Frank James Pexa; m. Patricia Mingus, Apr. 4, 1959; children: Michael, b. 1960; Kathleen, b. 1961; edn: BA, Univ. of Minn. 1958; CFP, Coll. for Finl. Planning 1983; CLU, Am. Coll. 1980; Assoc. in Mgmt., Ins. Inst. of Am. 1973. Career: with Farmers Ins. Gp. of Companies; agent, primarily in Alameda, Ca. (7 yrs.); regl. sales mgmt., Merced (5 yrs.); currently, dist. sales mgr., Sacto. (9 yrs.); instr. Life Underwriters Tng. Council; awards: coll. stu. abroad, Student Proj. for Amity Among Nations (SPAN); mem: Inst. CFPs; Nat. Ins. Consumer Orgns.; Big Brothers of Am. (past); publs: author, consumer oriented book, The Life Insurance War, used as univ. text, 1980; mil: s/sgt. USAF 1952-56; rec: physical fitness, aerobics. Res: 614 Lyndhurst Ave Roseville 95678 Ofc: Farmers Insurance Group, 3517 Marconi Ave, Ste 202, Sacramento 95821

PFUND, EDWARD T., JR., aerospace co. engineer-executive; b. Dec. 10, 1923, Methuen, Mass.; s. Edward Theodore Sr. and Mary Elizabeth (Banning) P.; m. Marga Andre, Nov. 10, 1954; children: Angela, b. 1954; Gloria, b. 1956; Edward III, b. 1961; edn: BS, magna cum laude, Tufts Coll. 1950; grad. studies, USC 1950, Boston Univ. 1950, Columbia Univ. 1953, UCLA 1956, 58. Career: radio engr. WLAW, Lawrence- Boston 1942-50; foreign svc. staff ofcr. US Dept. of State Voice of Am., Tangiers, Munich, 1950-54; proj. engr. Crusade for Freedom, Radio Free Europe, Munich, Ger. 1955; proj. mgr./ material splst. United Electrodynamics Inc., Pasadena 1956-59; dir. eng./ chief engr. Electronics Specialty Co., Los Angeles & Thomaston, Conn. 1959-61; with Hughes Aircarft, var. locations 1955, 1961--; chmn. Subcom. on Communications, Space Plt. Ops. Gp. 1963, chief Johannesburg Ops. 1961-63; dir. Spacecraft Perf. Analysis and Cmd., 1964-68; pgm. mgr. Lunar Rover Ground Data Sys. Design 1969-70; tech. chmn. Internat. Consortium 1974-78; currently, Middle & Far East Africa and So. American New Business Development mgr.; cons: H.I. Thompson Co., L.A. 1958-60, Andrew Corp., ohgo. 1959, Satelitte Broadcast Assocs., L.A. 1982; faculty, Pasadena City Coll. 1958-60; honors: Phi Beta Kappa; Sigma Pi Sigma; Awd. of Merit, Materials in Design Engring. 1958-59 (design devel. of two unique kinds of coaxial cable having low losses at over 1000 degrees F. for Mach 3 vehicles); Surveyor Test Pilot, Serveyor's Hon. Roll, Aviation Week & Space Technoloy 1966; directed the command control & perf. of all USA unmanned soft lunar landing and the world's first lunar liftoff and translation 1966-68; listed in num. biographical publs.; mem: Am. Inst. of Aero. & Astro. (tech. com. Commun. Sys. 1973-76) 1973-; publs: num. arts. in fields of communications satellites, real- time control and data processing, distributed amplifiers, transmission lines, transistorized telemetering devel. and electrical installation; mil: 2nd lt. US Army Air Corps 1942-46; rec: amateur radio K6OUW (1939-). Res: 25 Silver Saddle Ln Rolling Hills Estates 90274 Ofc: Hughes Aircraft Co., POB 92919, Airport Sta., Los Angeles 90009

PHAM, THAN THI, dentist; b. Aug. 5, 1932, Haiphong, Vietnam; d. Huy Quang and Gian Thi Pham; edn: Baccalaureate I, math., Hanoi, Vietnam 1953; Baccalaureate II, nat. scis., Saigon 1954; Cert., physics, chem., biol., Univ. of Saigon 1955; Diploma of Nat. Dental Surgeon, Univ. of Saigon 1959. Career: with dept. of dentistry for children, Saigon Univ. 1962-75; instr., faculty dental med. 1962-64; lectr. 1964-65; chmn. of clinics/ acting chprsn. 1965-73; asst. prof. 1973-75; deputy chprsn. dept. of childrens dentistry/ faculty of maxillofacial dentistry, Ho Chi Minh City Univ. 1975-78; currently, pres. Monterey Park Dental Gp., Monterey Park; practice gen. dentistry, Saigon 1962-78, Calif. 1982-; honors: Medal of Culture & Edn., Ministry of Edn. 1973; Jessen Internat. Fellowship, Dentistry for Children, The Fedn. Dentaire Internationale 1972; Astra Prize, child dental health, Internat. Assn. of Dentistry for Children. 1975; mem: Am. & Calif. Dental Assns.; San Gabriel Valley Dental Soc.; patron, Internat. Assn. of Dentistry for Children; Girl-Guides of Vietnam (pres. 1966, 67, 75); Pulau Tenga Refugee Ctr., West Malaysia (chprsn. 1979); publs: num. publs. in dental journs.; Buddhism; rec: photog. Ofc: Monterey Park Dental Group, 933 S Atlantic Blvd Monterey Park 91754

PHAM, TRI MINH, physician; b. Aug. 10, 1947, Ha Dong, Vietnam, nat. 1983; s. Giao and Nho Thi (Nguyen) P.; m. Tam Vu, Jan. 20, 1975; children: Alexander Darwin, b. 1975; Caroline Diem Trang, b. 1981; edn; BS, 1965; MD, Saigon Univ. 1972; lic. physician, NJ 1979, Calif. 1980. Career: chief of internal med. Nguyen Hue Hosp., Nha trang, Vietnam 1972-75; assoc. Santa Fe Clinics, Needles, Calif. 1975-78; res. internal med. United Hosp. Med. Ctr., Newark, NJ 1978-81; med. dir. Crestwood Manor Convalescent Hosp. 1981--; staff physician Doctors Medical Ctr., Memorial Hosps., Modesto City Hosp.,

Modesto 1981--; honors: Honor of Vietnamese Army 1974; mem: Am. & Calif. Med. Assns.; Stanislaus Med. Soc.; Modesto No. Rotary Club; mil: capt. med. corps. VietNam Republic Army 1972-75; Buddhist. Res: 4024 Creamery Way Modesto 95356 Ofc: 1130 Coffee Rd, Ste 7-A, Modesto 95355

PHAN, DUNG THANH, engineer; b. July 22, 1947, Saigon, Vietnam, nat. 1981; s. Dat Van and Bay Thi (Le) Phan; m. Lan Q Tran, Sept. 21, 1979; 1 dau. Theresa Q, b. 1981; edn: BA, physics, UC Berkeley 1980; MS in E.E., CSU Los Angeles 1983. Career: entry level engr. to computer program engr. II, Rockwell International, Lakewood 1983--; honors: Phi Kappa Phi, Deans List, honors in math.; mem. IEEE, UCB Alumni Assn.; mil: lt. So. Vietnamese Army, fought with US Armed Forces; Republican; Buddhist; rec: cooking, woodwork. Res: Pasadena Ofc: Rockwell Intl. 2770 E. Carson St Lakewood 90712

PHAN, NGUYEN KIM, physician-surgeon; b. Jan. 23, 19--; Giadinh, Vietnam; s. Dr. Duong N. and Tuong N. Phan; m. Anh-Tu, Sept. 1981; edn: BA, cum laude, UC Berkeley 1971; MD, Univ. of Hawaii Med. Sch. 1976; Res., gen. surgery, Alameda Co. Highland Gen. Hosp. 1976-81. Career: gen. surgeon, Oakland 1982--; consulting surgeon, Oakland Hosp. Med. Staff & Merritt & Providence Hosps. med. staff; honors: Freshman Prize in Biochem., Univ. of Hawaii Med. Sch. 1972; Physician Recogn. Awd., Am. Med. Assn. 1981; Third Prize, Medical Photog., Univ. of Hawaii 1973; mem: Alameda- Contra Costa Co. Med. Assnw.; Calif. Med. Assn.; Am. Soc. of Abdominal Surgeons; East Bay Vietnamese Assn. (bd. dirs.); Asian Community Mental Health Svcs., Oaklanda (bd. dirs.); publs: Duodenal Rupture Following Blunt Abdominal Trauma, Journ. of Abdominal Surgery 1983; Understanding Oriental Medicine: A Treatise, Humanity Litt. Journ. 1981; research: Zen and the Art of Healing; Buddhist; rec: Aikido, chess, photog. Res: 6718 Mokelumne St Oakland 94605 Ofc: 371 9th St, Ste 102 Oakland 94607

PHARIS, RODNEY BARNES, engineering co. executive; b. Dec. 1, 1938, Detroit, Mich.; s. Lloyd Matthew and Mary Nell (Barnes) P.; m. Teri Sanford, Aug. 12, 1978; children: Debbie Joy b. 1960, Mark Scott b. 1963, edn. AA, Foothill Coll. 1975; internat. mktg., CSU San Jose 1974-5, mech. eng., Univ. of Mich. 1965-7. Career: pres. International Motors Co., San Jose currently; pres. Mobility Technology Internat. (during design & devel. of the Cheetah 4-wheel drive vehicle for Lamborghini) 1976-78; asst. mgr. Internat. Engring. and Prodn. Div. FMC Corp., 1972-75; fmr. product engring. design Ford Motor Co.; detail draftsman to senior electromech. design engr. var. cos. in automotive and aerospace indus. 1957-72; recipient recogn. for achievements in automotive engring. in num. US & fgn. mag. articles; apptd. Leader Mem. of the AMA, Fedn. Aeronautique Internationale (1965); Nat. Champion Precision Aerobatics 1954, Glenview Naval Air Station; mem: Soc. of Automotive Engrs., Assn. of the US Army, SCORe Internatl., Nat. Rifle Assn., Am. Defense Preparedness Assn.; patent: Adjustable Pedals (automotive) 1970; publs: Tuned Exhaust Muffler, AMA, 1976; Republican; Lutheran; rec: skiing, flying, photog. Res: 4003 Halkins Dr San Jose 95124 Ofc: International Motors Co. San Jose 95124

PHELAND, ARTHUR DAVID, SR., natural resources consultant; b. Nov. 16, 1919, San Francisco; s. Albert Arthur and Emily Elaine (Hyland) Boullet; m. Rosemarie E. Walsh, Dec. 21, 1958; children: Fern b. 1940, Arthur Jr. b. 1942, Wesley b. 1953, William b. 1953, Belinda b. 1952, Michael b. 1953; edn: stationery engring., Sherman Inst. 1940; self-ed. in fed. and civil law; cert.: Water Pollution Control Assn. 1970. Career: self empl. plumber contractor, 30 years; water pollution control advocate; natural resource consultant; Native American historian, cons. nat. on Hist. of the Pre-Occupiers of this Land; estab. the first Historical Presidence of Archaeological Law, Mendocino County Archaeological Ord. No. 1681 (1976); introduced legislation at State Level to change cemetery and those law to prevent the violation of human burials; recipient Mendocino County Citizens Gold Award for the Advancement of Humanity (2) 1976, 83, County Bd. of Supvrs.; mem: Calif. Archaeology Soc., Calif. Water Pollution Bd. Assn., Am. Mgmt. Assn. Consultants; past pres. Fort Bragg Lions; past comdr. VFW; past charter pres. Native Sons of the Golden West; past pres. Sherman Inst. Alumni; past dir. Indian Health Bd. Calif. and Phoenix, Ariz.; mil: P.O metalsmith 2/c USN WWII 1944-50, Korea, UN medals; Republican; Prot. Native Elder Soc.; rec: archaeology. Res: 323-1/2 S. McPherson St, 11, Fort Bragg 95437 Ofc: Pheland's Ent., POB 1657, Fort Bragg 95437

PHILLIPS, ALMA FAYE, lawyer; b. Aug. 31, 1925, Pitts., Pa.; d. Alexander H. and Jean Z. (Ginsberg) Weinberger; m. Leonard Phillips, Feb. 24, 1946; children: Robin, b. 1952; Susan, b. 1952; Nancy, b. 1954; edn; BA, Univ. of Calif. 1972; JD, San Francisco Law Sch. 1977; admitted to practice, State Bar of calif, Fed. Dist. Ct., Fed. Dist. Ct. of Appeals. Career: sole practitioner, pvt. practice, Oakland 1979--; Judge Pro Tem, Alameda Co. Municipal Ct.; honors: Hon. Life Mem., PTA 1962; Cert. Braille Transcriber, Nat. Library of Congress 1970; mem: Am., S.F. County, Alameda County Bar Assns.; S.F. Lawyers Club; Alameda Co. Arbitration Panel & Client Rels. Com.; Voluntary Legal Svcs. Pgm.; pres. Hiller Highlands bd. dirs.; rec: braille transcribing, weaving, tennis. Res: 24 Schooner Hill Oakland 94618 Ofc: One Kaiser Plaza, Ordway Bldg., Ste 1135, Oakland 94612

PHILLIPS, C. LYLE, data processing administrator; b. Aug. 7, 1942, Topeka, Ks.; s. Clinton and Faye Templeton (Lippencott) P.; m. Marilyn Moon, jan. 30, 1965; children: Laura Lynn, b. 1965; Brian Robert ,b. 1969; edn: grad., Moody Bible Inst. 1964. Career: day supvr. Academics Communications Facility/ UCLA 1964-65; supvr. Sound Dept., Moody Inst. of Sci. 1966-81; data processing adminstr., Moody Inst. of Sci. 1981--; computer cons. Data Equipment Supply 1981-82; mem: Audio Engring. soc.; Digital Equip. Computer Users Soc.; works: built first completely solid state optical film recorder; Republican; Baptist; rec: computer programming. Res: 14534 E Cullen Whittier 90603 Ofc: Moody Institute of Science, 12000 E Washington Blvd, Whittier 90606

PHILLIPS, DEAN PAYNE, business owner; b. Dec. 15, 1914, Cleveland, Ohio; s. Edwin DeRoger and Flora Agnes (Dean) P.; m. Doris Mohn, Dec. 31, 1981; children: Dean R. b. 1940, Jayne M. b. 1957; edn: Journeyman's cert. Cleveland Trade Sch., 1933-37. Career: owner Dean Arts Woodworking, Cleveland, Ohio 1935-42; owner Dean Phillips Picture Framing, Castro Valley, Calif. 1946-80, new concept in custom wholesale picture framing on franchise basis; 1958-76, lectured extensively on picture framing in central Calif.; 1970, co-founder, Profl. Picture Framers Assn. Internat. and first pres. pro-tem; was first Calif. Certificated Adult Edn. Instr. in picture framing; recipient recogn. award for contribs. to indus., Picture Framers Assn. 1977; mem: Castro Valley Mineral and Gem Soc. (charter), Castro Valley Firemans Assn., Kiwanis Internat., Profl. Picture Framers Assn., Sierra Foothills Audubon Soc. (charter); works: introduced modern picture frame mouldings in US, 1936; modern designing utilized surfaces instead of lines, 1946-60; intro. new methods and tools in framing indus., intro. better conservation methods in picture framing, 1958-; mil: WWII Carpenters Mate 2C USN Seabees, 1942-45, Bronze Star, Pac. Theater; rec: fishing, earth scis., wildlife photog. Res: 6312 Janine Ct Magalia 95954 Ofc: Dean Phillips Picture Framing, 5513 Clark Road, Paradise 95969

PHILLIPS, DONALD IVAN, clergyman, educator; b. Apr. 29, 1916, Des Moines, Iowa; s. Douglas Maxwell and Bertha May (Miller) P.; m. Jean Elizabeth Pierce (dec.) June 17, 1939; children: Joanna b. 1940, Donna b. 1943, Barbara b. 1945, David (dec.) b. 1947; m. 2d. Eleanor Isaak Moser, Aug. 9, 1965; edn: BA, Houghton Coll. 1945; No. Baptist Theol. Sem. 1945-6, Los Angeles Baptist Theol. Sem. 1946-7, Western Conservative Baptist Theol. Sem. 1963-4; certs: (2) Hosp. Chaplains' Ministry of Am. Inc. 1975; CSU San Diego 1977; Andrews Univ. 1982; Hosp. Christian Fellowship Seminar 1983. Career: student pastor, churches in New York, Ill., Calif., 1941-47; pastor First Baptist Ch., Tujunga 1947-51; missionary, Brazil, S.A.: Youth for Christ Intl., founder/dir. Brazil Youth for Christ, 1951-55, World Gospel Crusades & Youth for Christ, Intl., 1956-60; mission services dir. King's Garden Inc. Seattle, Wash. 1960-63; campus minister Univ. of Ore. Med. Sch., Portland 1963-65; pastor Baptist Ch., Coeur d'Alene, Ida. 1965-70; pastor Baptist Ch., Riverside, Calif. 1972-74; hosp. chaplain Community Hosp. of San Diego, 1974-76; founder/pres. emeritus New Start, Inc. (drug edn., rehab.) 1976-83, bd. dirs. 1976-; resident chaplain Mission Bay Hosp. & Clairemont Comm. Hosp. 1982--; mem. Rotary Internat., Christian Bus. Men's Com.; author two books: Know Your Enemy, How To Overcome (1960, Brazil); Course (16 lessons) The Why, What, and Who of Addiction; sev. papers in drug abuse field; Republican; Baptist Gen. Conf.; rec: woodworking, writing, poetry. Res: 5483 Gala Ave San Diego 92120

PHILLIPS, DONALD LEWIS, psychotherapist/ clergyman; b. Oct. 6, 1933, Hartshorne, Okla.; s. Guy and Leona Hazel (Barnes) P.; m. Ruthanne Hammons, Dec. 19, 1954; children: Donna, b. 1956; Rodney, b. 1957; Denton, b. 1959; edn; BA, Grand Canyon Coll. 1964; M.Div., Golden Gate Baptist Theol. Sem. 1967; PhD, Univ. of Beverly Hills. 1982; Marriage & Family Therapist 1971. Career: pastor So. Baptist Churches, Calif. & Ariz. 1953-66; dir. of chaplaincy Santa Clara Co. Juvenile Probation Dept. 1968-79; dir. Christian Comm. Counseling Ctr. 1979--; assoc. pastor Christian Comm. Ch. 1970--; prof. No. Calif. Bible Coll. 1972--; mem. Mental Health Assn., Santa Clara Co. 1975-77; tchr. Family Life & Counseling Seminars, USA, Canada, New Zealand, Hong Kong, Taiwan & Japan; pres. Internat. Club, Grand Canyon Coll. 1963; sr. class pres. 1963-64; PTA Treas. Strawberry Point Sch., Mill Valley 1966; mem: Calif. Assn. Marriage & Family Therapists; Nat. Alliance for Family Life; publs: manual, Family & Personal Growth, 1977; Rod & Staff-Christian Counselors manual, 1979; Republican; Baptist; rec: tennis, travel. Res: 1242 Umbarger Rd San Jose 95121 Ofc: 1407 McLaughlin Ave San Jose 95122

PHILLIPS, JAMES LAWRENCE, financial consultant; b. Aug. 26, 1931, Fresno; s. Sidney Frank and Dorothy Maxine (Puccini) P.; m. Maureen Sullivan, May 11, 1962; children: Daniel, b. 1952; Karen, b. 1957; Kathleen, b. 1959; Denise, b. 1960; Cynthia, b 1960; James, . 1969; edn: AS, Memphis Tech. 1951; BS, CSU Fresno 1957; PhD, in progress, Southwestern Univ. 1984; Life, Disability, NASD 1968; CLU, Mass. Mutual 1958. Career: supvr./ brokerage mgr. Mass. Mutual Life Ins. Co. 1957; v.p. G.M. Mazz-Zee Chemical Corp., Fresno ; v.p. Vista Inc. (Mining Op.), Mariposa 1980; currently, cons. Physicians Funding Svcs. Ltd., Fresno; dir. Mazz-Zee Corp., dir. Maz-Zee S.A., Mex.; dir. Anaconda Mining S.A. Mex.; honors: Man of they Yr., Mass Mutual Life Ins. Co. 1958; Nat. Top Ten Awd., VAMCO, Detroit, Mich.; mem: Life Underwriters Assn.; Am. Chemical Soc.; Sub 20-30 (pres. 1960-61); Heart Assn.; Boys Club (bd. dirs.); Fresno Nutritional Hour (bd. dirs.); No. Spartan Baseball League (pres.); Gr. Fresno Spartan League (dir.); works: Zeron, pat. 1978; Universal Rescue Aid Device, 1975; The Pucca Plant (desert magic), co-pub. 1978; rec: Republican; Protentant; rec: sports car racing/ restoration, youth sports coaching. Res: 4081 N Fruit, 109, Fresno 93705 Ofc: Physicians Funding Services Ltd., 2014 Tulare St, Ste 810, Fresno 93721

PHILLIPS, TEDDY STEVE, orchestra director; b. June 15, 1916, Chgo., Ill.; s. Steve S. and Kaliope S. (Phillips) Simms; m. Colleen Lovett, Apr. 18, 1957; children: Joe, b. 1961; Teddy, b. 1963; edn: Univ. of Ill. 1935-39. Career: saxaphone player with big bands across US 1940-45; staff musician Radio Sta.

CBS, Chgo. 1944-45; conductor Teddy Phillips Orch. across country, 1944-55, 1957-62; prin. Teddy Phillips Show, WBKB-TV- ABC, Chgo. 1956-57; conductor Tedd Phillips & Orch.: Ambassador Hotel (L.A.), Flamingo Hotel (Las Vegas), Statler Hotels, Aragon Ballroom, Hilton Hotels (Chgo.) 1962--; pres. P&M Prodns., Woodland Hills 1976--; dir. The Guy Lombardo Orch. 1980--; also TV prod. Great Concert in the Sky; record producer; recording artist; writer, Do the Camel Hump; mem: Musicians Union; Masons; mil: US Army 1940-41; Greek Orthodox. Res: 6252 1/2 Nita Ave Woodland Hills 91367

PHILLIPS, TREVOR, oil co. executive; b. Dec. 27, 1940, United Kingdom; s. Benjamin and Lillian (Balbis) P.; m. Carole Mace, May 1, 1965; children: Jeffrey, b. 1967; Julie, b. 1971; edn: PhD, ULC 1980; CEM, CGS 1983. Career: nat. sales mgr. Scripps- Howard Newspapers 1965-68; research dir. Storer Television 1968-70; self- empl. 1970-76; asst. gen. advtg. mgr. Freedom Newspapers 1976-80; founder/ CEO Western Reserve Oil & Gas Co. 1980--; mem: Elks; Exch. Club; Ambucs; AYSO; Boy Scouts of Am.; mil: E-4 USN 1958-59; Republican; rec: music, arts, golf. Res: 191 Browning Upland 91786 Ofcs: 7845 Emerson Ave Parkersburg, W.Va. 26101 & 1450 E 17th St, Ste 226, Santa Ava 92701

PHILLIPS, WILLIAM CHARLES, insurance co. executive; b. Oct. 27, 1936, Tazoo City, Miss.; s. W.C. and Selma B. Phillips; m. Marylee Alesko, May 15, 1966; children: William Cary, b. 1968; Daniel John, b. 1969; edn: BSME, Auburn Univ. 1960; CLU in progress. Career: engr. NASA 1960-64; sales mgr. Bendix Corp. 1964-69; with New York Life 1969--; sales mgr. 1971; gen. mgr., Downey, Calif. 1976; gen. mgr., Orange 1979--; dir. sales & mkt. recruiting & tng. (approx. 50 agents & staff); honors: Chmns. Trophy, 1982; Presidents Trophy 1983; Forum Leader 1982; Health Leader 1982; Annuity Leader 1982; mem: Gen. Agents & Mgrs. Assn. (pres., Orange; past pres. Long Beach); Toastmasters (pres. 1978); Long Beach Civic Light Orch.; Rolling Hills Country Club; Fram Soccer Club; Sports Gallery, Anaheim; past assoc. Palos Verdes Art Assn.; Republican; Ch. of Christ; rec: racquetball, chess, tennis. Res: 6536 Abbottswood Dr Rancho Palos Verdes 90274 Ofc: New York Life, 1 City Blvd West, Ste 1121, Orange 92668

PHILPOTT, GEORGE MEREL, JR., construction equipment distribution co. executive; b. Oct. 4, 1946, San Mateo; s. George M. and Thelma (Johnson) P.; children: Matthew, b. 1972; Mark, b. 1975; George III, b. 1976; edn: BS, Ariz. State Univ. 1970. Career: field engr.'s aid Pacific Gas & Elec. Co., Big Bend, summers of 1964, 65; asst. ofc. mgr. Gardner- Denver Colo., Phoenix, Ariz. 1967-69; sales mgr. George M. Philpott Co. Inc., So. San Francisco 1970-80; dir. of sales & svc. General Resources Corp., S.F. 1980-82; mng. partner Tri-State Machinery & Supply Co., So. S.F. 1982--; bd. dirs. George M. Philpott Co. Inc.; bd. advrs. General Resources Corp.; mem: Associated Equip. Distributorls (lt. ir. 1983); Constrn. Equip. Distributors Assn. of No. Calif. (bd. dirs. 1982-84, pres. 1983); Rotary Internat.; Phi Kappa Psi; Republican; Episcopal; rec: bicycle touring, tennis. Res: 115 Romero Rd Woodside 94062 Ofc: Tri-State Machinery & Supply Co., 480 Littlefield, So. San Francisco 94080

PHILPOTT-BRYANT, MARCELLE, lawyer; b. Oct. 19, 1933, Chgo.; d. John Alpha and Carmen (Rodriguez) Philpott; div.; children: Jennifer b. 1967, Joel b. 1969; edn: BA, UCLA 1960; JD, Whittier Law Sch. 1974; admitted to Calif. State Bar 1974. Calif. Sec. Tchg. Cred. 1961. Career: counselor L.A. County Probation Dept. 1961-63; sec. sch. tchr. Los Angeles City Schs., 1963-67; lawyer assoc. of Coulter, Vernoff & Brewer, 1975-78; lawyer sole practice, 1978--; arbitrator (US Steel Wkrs. Union and local can cos.); bd. dirs. non-profit mental health orgn.; founder/pres. Attys. for Animal Rights honors: Iota Tau Tau (legal sor.) scholarship award 1975; Hastings Coll. of Advocacy scholarship award 1977; mem./bd. dir. Way Home Counseling Center (1974-), Pasadena Commn. on Status of Women (1977-79), chpsn. San Fernando Valley Drug Abuse Coalition (1974-75), Attys for Animal Rights (nat. pres. 1983-); works: sev. significant lawsuits on behalf of welfare of animals i.e. the San Clemente Is. Goat Case (enjoined USN from shooting 5,000 wild goat inhabitants of island, 1980); Democrat; rec: animal welfare wk. Res: 1051 Chautauqua Blvd Pacific Palisades 90401 Law Office of Marcelle Philpott-Bryant, 1513 Sixth Street, Ste 201, Santa Monica 90401

PICK, MARC GREGORY, chiropractor; b. Nov. 9, 1948; s. David and Beatrice Pick; ed. Santa Monica City Coll. 1969-68, Woodbury Univ. 1968-70; C.D., Cleveland Chiropractic Coll. 1973---, internatl. lectr. on chiropractic Japan, Can., USA 1979---; founder, developer Project Human (dissection & reconstrn. of Human Anatomical Speciman-approx. 6,000 hrs. Human Dissection 1977-82); Faculty mem. Shiokawa Chiropractic Coll., Tokyo, Japan, 1980-, Pasadena Chiropractic Coll. 1977-. Cert. Instr. in Ocipital Tech. (SORSI); Cert. Instr. in Craniopathy (IOS). Awards: Robert Bitterman Award, C.C.A., 1975-76; Pac. Asian Assn. Chiropractic Award, 1979; Outstanding Young Men of Am. Award, 1981. Mem.: Calif. Chirop. Assn., L.A., Metro Soc., pres. 1977-78; Sacro Occipital Research Soc. Internatl., bd. dirs. 1982. Jewish. Rec: bldg. a Human Model, scuba diving, skiing. Res.: 1002 N. Mariposa Ave. #7, Los Angeles 90029; Office: Beverly Hills 90211.

PICKMAN, PHILLIP, executive recruiter; b. May 6, 1938, Minnpls., Minn.; s. Sam and Rose Gertrude (Chiat) P.; m. Leah Rubin, June 17, 1962; children: Kara, b. 1978; Todd, b. 1980; edn: BS, w/ distinction, Univ. of Minn. 1960; MSME, 1962. Career: tech. staff Bell Telephone Labs., Whippany, NJ 1962-65; supvr. opg. sys. research gp. 1065-68; mgr. data processing ops. & equip. Target Stores Inc., Minnpls., Minn. 1968-72; mgr. mgmt. sys. pllng. Dayton Hudson Corp., Minnpls., Minn. 1972-73; dir. info. svcs. Red Owl Stores Inc., Minnpls., Minn. 1973-74; dir. sys. & mgmt. info. Cook United Inc., Cleveland, Oh. 1974-77; regl. v.p. West Coast Data Ctr. May Dept. Stores, Los Angeles, Calif. 1977-80; exec. recruiter Westlake Group Inc., Westlake Village 1980-81; pres. Information Resources Group, Westlake Village 1981--; wrkshp. leader/ guest spkr. EDP mgmt. sems., Am. Mgmt. assn. 1970-72; honors: Pi Tau Sigma (1959) & Tau Beta Pi (1960), Univ. of Minn.; mem: Nat. Retail Merchants Assn. (Terminal Sys. Specifications Task Force 1972-73); G.E. 600 Users Assn. (pres. 1967-68); ESIS Users Gp. (pres. 1974); Planning Bd. Township of Parsippany-Troy Hills, NJ (v.chmn. 1967-68); Morris Co. (NJ) Democratic Co. Com. (1965-68); Jewish Family & Childrens Svc., Minnpls., Minn. (bd. dirs. 1972-73); B'nai B'rith Hillel Found, Univ. of Minn. (adv. bd. 1972-73, 1st v.p. 1973); Congregation Beth Am., Cleveland, Oh. (sch. bd. chmn. 1976-78); Democrat; Jewish; rec: home repair, woodworking, home computing. Res: 1815 Stonesgate St Westlake Village 91361 Ofc: Information Resources Group, 2239 Townsgate Rd, Ste 206, Westlake Village 91361

PICONE, SAMUEL BARTHOLOMEW, JR., physician-surgeon; b. Jan. 24, 1950, Los Angeles; s. Samuel Bartholomew and Gertrude Rose (Elshire) P.; m. Marcia S. Rubenstein, Oct. 22, 1978; edn: BA, UC Berkeley 1972; MD, Chgo. Med. Sch. 1977. Career: res. surgery USC 1978-82; academic appointment, clin. instr. surgery, UC Irvine 1983; currently, pvt. practice surgery, Long Beach; assoc. dir. surgical ICU, Meml. Hosp. Med. Crt.; honors: Alpha Omega Alpha 1977; Merit AWd., L.A. Surgical Soc. 1981; mem: Soc. of Grad. Surgeons LAC/ USC Med. Ctr. 1982; Am. Bd. of Surgery 1982; Am. Soc. of Parenteral & Enteral Nutrition 1982; Am. Coll. of Nutrition 1982; Soc. of Colon & Rectal Surgeon 1982; Episcopal; rec: glass blowing, pottery. Res: 1022 Corning St Los Angeles 90035 Ofc: 3490 Linden Ave Long Beach 90807

PIERCE, J. ELIZABETH STOWE, clinical social worker, ret.; b. Dec. 4, 1921, Susanville; d. Frank Rabineau and Geneva Irene (Turner) Stowe; m. Ernest Pierce, Aug. 21, 1943; children: Randall, b. 1947; Marilyn, b. 1949; Donald, b. 1951 (dec.); edn: AB, CSU San Jose 1943; MSW, USC 1969; UC Los Angeles 1943-46; CSU Long Beach 1959-67; ACSW Nat. Assn. Social Workers 1971; career: para-professional Los Angeles Suicide Prevention Center 1964-67; psychiatric social worker Los Angeles Child Guidance Clinic 1969-75; psychiat. soc. wkr. So. Bay Children's Health Center, Child Guidance Clinic 1969-71, chief soc. wkr. 1971-77, adm. dir., 1976-77; clin. soc. wkr. part-time private practice 1978-82.; honors: Beta Beta Beta Nat. Biology Honor Soc. 1942; honored grad. Biological Sci., CSU San Jose 1943; mem. Nat. Assn. Soc. Wkrs. 1969--.; Orgns: Torrance Health Council 1970-77; Beach Cities Case Conference & Prof. Advisory Bd. -1977; Inter-Agency Council & Mental Health Advisory Bd., So. Bay Health Region, L.A. Co., 1972-77 (corr. secty. 1976); Democrat; Protestant; rec: photo., nature study, needlework; Address: 1582 Griffith Rd Ramona 92065

PIERCE, JAMES DAVID, tax-financial planning consultant; b. Oct. 24, 1928, Los Angeles; s. Craige David and Marcella Alice (Liebscher) P.; m. Joyce Pugmire, Jan. 12, 1951; children: Karla, b. 1947; Carol, b. 1952; Craig, b. 1960; James Jr., b. 1961; edn; BSBA, UCLA 1950; Calif. Life & Health (1972), Fire & Casualty (1973), Ins. Agent; Reg. Rep., NASD 1973; Reg. Tax Preparer, Calif. Career: agent, sales mgr., asst. gen. agent John Hancock Mutual Life Ins. Co., Torrance & Santa Ana 1971-80 ; pres. Profl. Economic Svcs. 1980--; v.p./ CFO Amerian Econ. Resourcese Corp. 1982--; chmn. bd. dirs. P.E.S. Inc. & Financial Plnnrs. Ins. Agency Inc. 1980-; bd. dirs. Am. Econ. Resources Corp. 1982-; co-gen. partner sev. ltd. partnerships; mem: Greater So. Bay chpt. Nat. Assn. Life Underwriters (pres. 1977-78); Internat. Assn. Fin. Plnnrs.; Inst. of CFPs; Jojoba Growers Assn.; Calif. Christmas Tree Growers Assn.; mil: lt. col. US Army 1950-70, ret., Legion of Merit, DFC, Bronze Star, Air Medal, Army Commdn.; Republican; Presbyterian; rec: model railroad and aircraft. Res: 1917 W Carriage Dr Santa Ana 92704 Ofc: Professional Economic Services Inc., 22996 El Toro Rd, Ste 111, El Toro 92630

PIEROSE, PERRY NICHOLAS, physician; b. Aug. 15, 1910, Butte, Mont.; s. Nicholas Peter and Mary (Brant) P.; m. Elizabeth Bissel Van Wormer, 1938; children: Anne, b. 1943; Susan, b. 1945; Gale, b. 1954; edn: AB, Stanford Univ. 1933; Asstship., biochem. research, USC Sch. of Med. 1934, faculty mem. USC Sch. of Med. 1939. Career: pvt. practice internal med., seminar staff St. Vincent L.A. Med. Ctr., Los Angeles & Pasadena; med. dir. Calif. Parthand Cement Co., Los Angeles; med. dir. J.G. Boswell Co., L.A.; mem: Valley Hunt Club; Delta Tau Delta; Nu Sigma Nu Stanford Club; formerly: Bohemian Club, S.F. (courtesy mem. 1945-46 WWII); Flintridge Riding C(UB: L.A. Gaulla Hunting Club, Mex.; Univ. Club, L.A.; mil: capt. M.C. WWII 5th armored div. chief surgery, Ft. McDowell Sta. Hosp., S.F. WWII, four med. commendns.; Republican; Protestant; rec: hunting, gardening, art. Res: 698 La Loma Rd Pasadena 91105 Ofcs: (Main), 2202 W 3rd St Los Angeles 90057; 50 Bellafontaine, Pasadena 91105

PIEVAC, SAM, manufacturing co. executive; b. Sept. 1, 1925, Midland, Pa.; s. Sam and Anna (Symonak) P.; m. Laura B. Wright, Sept. 4, 1953; children: Sam b. 1960, Michael b. 1964; edn: grad. Midland H.S. 1939-43; Loyola Univ., 1947-49. Career: v.p. in charge of sales Underwood & Hale Co., Compton 1952-60; pres. Sam Pievac Co. Inc., Long Beach 1960--; adv. bd. Palm Desert Nat. Bank 1981-; bd. dirs. Pacific Hosp., Long Beach 1983-, mem. Pres.'s Club; mem. Non Foods Merchandisers of the West 1954-(L.A. exec. secty., 8 yrs.); moderator UCLA Sch. of Business, Labor and Mgmt. (helped design course, Non-Food Mdsg., 42 speakers from retail food mktg. indus., 1978); guest lectr. UCLA, gen. mdse. mgmt. & ops., 1979, 80, 81, 82, 83; honors: Citizen of the Year 1983, Exchange Club of Long Beach; recogn. award UCLA 1979; Outstanding Salesman of the Year, Non Food Mdsg. Assn. of the West; mem:

Exchange Club of Long Beach (pres. 1964, dist. gov. 1966); Weingart Family YMCA (bd. 1977-); Long Beach St. Univ. 49er Athletic Found. 1976- (secty. 1983-); Old Ranch Country Club (Seal Beach) 1970-; apptd. by Supr. Deane Dana adv. bd. chmn. Lakewood Golf Course, 1978-; adv. bd. Salvation Army 1970-71; mem. Pres's Circle, Loyola Marymount Univ., CSULB; mil: cpl. US Army Air Force 1943-46; Republican; Catholic; rec: coin & stamp collector. Res: 4539 Clubhouse Dr Lakewood 90712 Ofc: Sam Pievac Co. Inc. 2680 Signal Pkwy Long Beach 90806

PILAR, SALVADOR B., health facilities executive; b. Aug. 16, 1936, Manila, Philippines, nat. 1983; s. Pio P. and Salome B. (Brillantes) P.; m. Generosa Blaza, Apr. 27, 1958; children: Alexander, b. 1959; Salvador, b. 1960; Martin, b 1962; Maria, b. 1964; edn: B.Phil., Univ. of St. Thomas 1958; MA, Ateneo Univ. 1962; MS, Loyola Univ. 1968; UCLA 1980-81; Accredited Personnel Diplomate, ASPA 1978. Career: new prods. mgr. Winthrop Labs., NY/ Far East 1966-68; gp. prodns. mgr. Richardson- Merrell Internat., NY/ Far East 1968-70; dir. personnel Northlake Comm. Hosp., Northlake, Ill. 1970-72; dir. personnel Am. Coll. of Surgeons, Chgo., Ill. 1972-74; dir. admin. Am. Acad. of Pediatrics, Evanston, Ill. 1974-77; personnel dir. Graham Hosp., Canton, Ill. 1977-79; asst. admin. Burbank Comm. Hosp., Burbank, Calif. 1979--; founding dir. Chgo. Compensation Assn.; 3X dir. of the bd. Hosp. Personnel Mgmt. Assn. of So. Calif. 2x dir. Calif. Hosp. Personnel Mgmt. Assn.; dir. Central Ill. Personnel Mgmt. Assn.; dir. Personnel Assn. of Chgo.; mem: Am. Soc. Personnel Adminstrn.; Am. Mgmt. Assn.; Am. Mktg. Assn.; Am. & Chgo. Compensation Assns.; Ill. Soc. for Human Resource Admin.; Conf. of Med. Soc. Execs. of Gr. Chgo.; Soc. of Personnel Adminstr. of Chgo.; Chgo. Hosp. Personnel Mgrs. Assn.; Hosp. Personnel Mgmt. Assn. of So. Calif.; Calif. Hosp. Personnel Mgmt. Assn.; works: The Personnel Function as an Organizational Activity of Chicago Firms, 1978; Automation and Labor, 1967; Catholic; rec: plate collecting, oil painting, photog. Res: 3810 Fairmeade Rd Pasadena 91107 Ofc: Burbank Community Hospital, 466 E Olive Ave Burbank 91501

PILCHER, LAURENCE L., hospital administrator; b. Jan, 16, 1946, South Gate; s. Paul William Sr. and Jettie Lucille (King) P.; edn: BA, Columbia Coll. 1972; BA, Pepperdine Univ. 1974; MPA, 1979; teaching cred. Calif. Comm.; Coll. Career: regional dir. American Kor-Asian Found. 1972-75; adminstrv. dir. Daniel Freeman Hosp. 1975-81; v.p. Presbyterian Intercomm. Hosp. 1981--.; adjunct prof. Sch. of Cont. Edn. Univ. So. Cal. (USC); bd. mem. East Whittier Sch. Dist.; adminstrn. award Daniel Freeman Hosp. 1978; mem: Am. Coll. of Hosp. Adm.; Assn. of Western Hosp.; Hosp. Council of So. Calif.; Republican; Protestant; rec: fitness, running, hiking; Res: 1507 Poppy Peak Dr Pasadena 91105 Ofc: Presbyterian Intercommunity Hospital, 12401 E. Washington Blvd. Whittier 90602

PILLING, GEORGE WILLIAM, lawyer; b. Mar. 25, 1942, Reading, Pa.; s. Hugh Aiken and Lillian Hannah Pilling; 1 dau: Jocelyn Kay, b. 1974; edn: AB, Kalamazoo Coll. 1963; JD, w/ distinction, Univ. of Mich. Law Sch. 1966. Career: law clerk Montgomery, McCracken, Walker & Rhoads, Phila., Penn. 1965; tchr. Boy's Republic (emotionally disturbed boys), Farmington, Mich. 1966-68; law clerk Cooper, White & Cooper, San Francisco 1968; assoc. law firm Pllack & Palmer, Los Angeles 1968-70; staff atty. Western Ctr. on Law & Poverty, L.A. 1970-72; partner law firm Shapiro, Posell & Pilling, L.A. 1972-73; solo practice, George Wm. Pilling, Atty. at Law, L.A. 1974--; pres. LG&N Ent. Inc. (dba Dura- Guide Co., active practice of law concentrating on civil litigation), L.A. 1975--; mem: State Bar of Mich. 1967-; State Bar of Calif. 1968-; ACLU (exec. com., Lawyers Div. 1971-72); Democrat; rec: equestrian, water sports. Res: 3453 Coast View Dr Malibu 90265 Ofc: George Wm. Pilling, 1107-1/2 Glendon Ave Westwood Village Los Angeles 90024

PINCKARD, TERRI ELLEN, writer; b. May 24, 1930, Asbury Park, N.J.; d. Edward Emanuel and Sarah Ann (Frankel) Merat; m. G. Thomas Pinckard, July 14, 1961; children: Cheryl b. 1955, Victoria b. 1956, Vivian b. 1958, Richard b. 1959; edn: AS, Monmouth Junior Coll. 1948; UCLA 1949-51. Career: art layout, copy editor, Lynn-Western Inc., Los Angeles 1952-53; tchr. (Mentally Gifted Minors) Righetti High Sch., 1977-79; lectr. freelance, North Santa Barbara County, 1969-80; free lance writer, 1950--; founder/creator with husband The Pinckard Science Fiction Writers' Salon (annual weekend gathering at the Pinckard Home: Far Horizons, of authors, directors, editors and publishers around the world for stimulating exchange of ideas), 1963-; awards incl: Best Horror Story of the year 1971- in England, France, USA (1973), Solar Pons Soc.; Praed Street Penny Mystery Award 1971; Count Dracula Gothic Lit. Soc.; Mrs. Ann Radcliffs Award 1971. Mem: Solar Pons Mystery Soc., Madame Severance Soc. (founded by Clarence Darrow & Mdme. Severance) 1957-63; Acad. of Sci. Fiction and Fantasy Soc. 1973-; Count Dracula Gothic Lit Soc. 1961- (Gov.); Sci. Fiction Writers of Am. 1970-; The World Sci. Fiction Writers 1975-; lectr., vol. United Cerebral Palsy 1955-63; works: num. non fiction mag. & newspaper articles, 1950s; num. fiction (fantasy, gothic, sci-fi, mainstream) 1950-; collaborator of Weird Tales CBS-TV series (1955); author Centennial musical: The American Spirit (1976); Republican; rec: art. Res: Far Horizons, 2340 Lake Marie Dr Santa Maria 93455

PINDELL, MERL LEE, physician-radiologist; b. Mar. 18, 1893, Madison County, Iowa; s. James Madison and Priscilla Jane (Bishop) Pindell; m. Eva Marie Wallace (dec. 1979) Sept. 28, 1914; 1 son, James Wallace (dec. 1963); edn: New York City Radiology 1917; Cornell Univ. Medical Sch.; MD, Chgo. Coll. of Med. (Loyola Univ.). Cert. Splst. American College of Radiology 1928. Career: med. ofcrs. tng. Camp Fort Riley, Kans. 1916; served in France during WWI; gen. practice of medicine 1918-23; postgrad. sch., Chgo., 1924; resident physician Olive Medical Center, (L.A. County Civil Svc.) 1925-29; chief of radiology, L.A. County Health Dept. 1929-40; radiologist St. John's Hosp., 1940-50; practice in Beverly Hills 1940-58; instr. senior class of med., Loma Linda Univ., and instr. in radiol., St. John's Hosp.; honors: First Award, Radiological Soc. of North Am. (1930); cert. 50 Years Practice of Medicine, AMA (1966); mem. (fmr.): Los Angeles Radiological Soc., Radiological Soc. of No. Am. (pres.), L.A. County Med. Soc. (pres.), Calif. Med. Soc., AMA, Madison County Med. Soc. (pres.); resrch: Early Diagnosis of Tuburculosis, pub. Calif. and Western Medicine, 1928; author: Country Doctor to Beverly Hills Radiologist (1967); mil: lt. Medical Corps France, WWI; capt. Iowa Nat. Guard Brigade Hqtrs. Co.; capt. Evacuation Hosp., Calif. Reserve Corps; Republican; Prot.; rec: astronomy. Res: 302 Evergreen Lane Yreka 96097

PINE, CHARLES JOSEPH, clinical psychologist; b. July 13, 1951, Excelsior Springs, Mo.; s. Charles Edison and La Vern (Upton) P.; m. Mary Day, Dec. 30, 1979; children: Charles Andrew, b. 1981; Joseph Scott, b. 1983; edn: BA, Univ. of Redlands 1973; MA, CSU Los Angeles 1975; PhD, Univ. of Wash. 1979. Career: psychology intern VA Outpatient Clinic, Los Angeles 1978-79; instr./ asst. prof. dept. of psychology Okla. State Univ., Stillwater 1979-80; postdoctoral scholar in Amer. Indian studies & psychol., Inst. of Am. Cultures, UCLA 1980-81; asst. prof. dept. of psychol. & native Am. studies pgm., Wash. State Univ., Pullman 1981-82; cons. 1981, dir. Behavioral Health Svcs., Riverside-San Bernardino Co. Indian Health Inc., Banning 1982--; mem. editl. bd. White Cloud Journ. of Am. Indian & Alaskan Native Mental Health 1982; awards: grantee, Inst. of Am. Cultures, UCLA 1981-82, Inst. of Indian Studies, Univ. of Wash. 1976; mem: Am. Psycholog. Assn. (bd. Ethnic Minority Affairs Task Force on Edn. & Tng. 1982); Western Psycholog. Assn.; Sigma Alpha Epsilon; publs: arts. in profl., scholarly journs.; Republican; Baptist; rec: theatre, music, sports. Res: 365 W Grove Rialto 92376 Ofc: Riverside-San Bernardino Co. Indian Health Inc., 11555 1/2 Potrero Rd Banning

PINE, FLORENCE, accountant; b. Jan. 1, 1918, NY; d. Aaron and Annie (Keller) Kahn; m. Norman Pine, Dec. 15, 1946; children: Kitty, b. 1951; Neil, b. 1955; edn: East Los Angeles Coll. 1963, 64, 81. Career: asst. ofc. mgr. R&K Originals, NYC 1942-46; book keeper/ acct. J.G. Efron, CPA & Assoc., Los Angeles 1947-51, 1964-71; acct. M. Mazur, CPA, L.A. 1972--; honors: City of New York Defense Volunteer Awd. 1945; City of Hope Awds: Angel of Mercy, 1971; Spirit of Life, 1973; Achiev. 1975; Spirit, 1977; Outstanding Svc., 1979; Million Dollar, 1981; Appreciation, 1982; Presidents Awd., 1984; mem: Red Cross (fund raising, Heart & Cancer Funds 1940-46); Montebello Adult Sch. (child study gp., nutrition gp. 1954-57); PTA (budget & fin. dir., recording secty., rep. to Monterey Park Coordg. Council 1958-62); Hadassah Orgn.; City of Hope, Horizon's of Hope chpt. (pres. 1979-). Res: 225 W Riggin St Monterey Park 91754 Ofc: M. Mazur, CPA, 2001 East 14 St, Los Angeles 90021

PINSCHMIDT, ROBERT KRANTZ, quality engineer/ consultant/ educator; b. Oct. 27, 1920, Baltimore, Md.; s. William C. and Edith K. (Krantz) P.; m. Louise Braasch, July 22, 1944; children: Robert K. Jr., b. 1945; John D., b. 1947; Daniel B., b. 1950; Penny E., b. 1958; edn: Cleveland State Univ. 1938-41; BS, Univ. of Colo. 1942; Harvard Grad. ch. of Bus. 1942; MA, CSU San Jose 1970; Cert. Quality Engr., ASQC 1968; Reg. Profl. Engr., Calif. 1978; Cert. Reliability Engr. 1972, Fellow 1979. Career: instr. mgmt. Univ. of Colo., Boulder 1946-48; indsl. engr. Cleveland Graphite Bronze Co., Oh. 1948-49; chief div. of labor statistics State of Ohio, Columbus 1949-50; LCDR USNR Br. Head Q.C. Div. Navy Bureau of Ord., Wash. DC 1950-53; asst. to plant mgr. Landers Frary & Clark, New Britian, Conn. 1953-54; gen. foreman Westinghouse, Baltimore, Md. 1954-59; mgr. staff eng. Lockheed Missiles & Space Co. Inc., Sunnyvale, Calif. 1959--; exec. sec. Product Assurance Adv. Bd.; Quality cons. to industry; coord. DeAnza Coll. Quality Assurance Pgm. (largest in US); prof. quality control, DeAnza Coll. 1967-; Univ. of Phoenix 1981-82, Penton Lng. Sys. 1976-81, Coll. of Notre Dame 1970-78; West Valley Coll. 1970-71, (bus. mgmt.), John Hopkins Univ. 1957-59, Cleveland State Univ. 1949-50; (time & motion study) Univ. of Colo. 1946-48; honors: Testimonial- Edn. Pgms. 1976; Spl. Awd., Idea Fair 1980; Testimonial (Host chmn.), Annual Internat. Quality Congress 1981; B.L. Lubelsky Awd. for Outstanding Contbrn. in field of quality control. 1983; mem: Nat. Mgmt. Assn. 1959-; ASQC 1961- (chmn. Eugene L. Grant Awd. bd. 1978-84; Conf. Mgmt. Bd. 1980-; Reliability & Inspn. Div. 1972-; secty No. Calif. Quality adv. bd. 1975-); Aerospace Idustries of Am. 1978-; Am. Nat. Metric Council (Aerospace Sector) 1981-; Am. Astro. Soc. 1977-82; BSA Scoutmaster 1958-65; Assurances Scis. Found. (sect. treas, dir. of edn.) 1967-; num. scholarly publs., sems.; mil: LCDR USNR active 1942-46, 1950-53, reserve 1946-50; Democrat; Methodist; rec: model trains, restoring old cars, tennis. Res: 16385 Peacock Ln Los Gatos 95030 Ofc: Lockheed Missiles & Space Co. Inc., POB 504, Orgn. 84-02, Bldg. 182, Sunnyvale 94086

PINSLEY, DAVID L., general contractor; b. Dec. 14, 1940, Oakland; s. Max and Mollie (Rubin) Pinsley; m. Kitten Wilson, June 14, 1977; 1 son, Phillip, b. 1968; edn: stu. San Francisco State, 1958-9, UC Berkeley 1959-60, Merritt Coll. 1960-1; lic. gen. bldg. contractor, Calif. 1961-; Nat. Panel of Consumer Arbitrators 1977-; notary public 1977-. Career: expediter and carpenter Federal Bldg. Co., 1955-60; appraiser/loan ofcr. American Svgs & Loan, 1961-2; loan ofcr/appraiser/vice pres. First Lincoln Fin. Corp. (Lifetime S&L), 1963-5; gen. contractor, exec. vice pres. The Pinsley Corp. dba Federal Bldg. Co., 1965--. Mem: Building Indus. Assn. (pres. Remodelers Council 1968-72, bd. mem. 1972-82); Better Bus. Bur. (bd. mem., secty. 1969-); Calif. Bldg. & Safety Inspectors Assn.; clubs: Oakland Athletic, Metropolitan Club of Oakland, Exchange Club of Granada Hills, Mex. Elmhurst Philatelic Soc., Masons, Scottish Rite, Shriners; mil: USCGR 1958-60; Republican; Jewish; rec: philatelist, sports; res: 1555 Lakeside Dr. Oakland 94612 ofc: Fed. Bldg. Co. 10500 MacArthur Blvd. Oakland 94605.

PIPINS, JERRY KEITH, real estate executive; b. June 2, 1943, Ardmore, Okla.; s. Jennings Bryan and Alta Fay (Chitwood) P.; m. Sandra Kemp, Mar. 8, 1969; 1 dau: Michelle Jean, b. 1977; edn: El Camino Coll. 1971. Career: sr. off-site vendor contact Northrop, Hawthorne 1967-73; salesman Fred Fredericks, Torrance 1974-77; v.p. Tri-City Realty, Oceanside 1977-78; owner Wine Cellar Deli., Oceanside 1980-83; pres. Pipins & Assoc., Oceanside 1978--; cons. C.P.S. 1981; honors: Presidential Awd. of Hon., Jaycees 1979; Jaycee of the Month 1978; mem: Oceanside CofC (dir. 1983-); Oceanside Bd. Realtors (dir. 1977); Oceanside/ Carlsbad Jaycees (treas. 1978, v.p. 1979); mil: E-3 USAF 1961-66, Nat. Defense, Outstanding Unit Citation; Republican; rec: golf. Address: Pipins & Associates, POB 329 San Luis Rey 92068

PIROSH, MICHAEL, judge; b. Jan. 26, 1942, Los Angeles; s. Robert and Emily (Fitzpatrick) P.; m. Marjorie Felmus, Dec. 1975; m. 2d. Michele Bernath, Feb. 4, 1979; edn: AB, UC Berkeley 1964; JD, Univ. of San Diego Law Sch. 1968. Career: atty./ dir. of law reform San Fernando Valley Neighborhood Legal Svcs., Van Nuys 1968-69; deputy pub. defender trial atty. Pub. Defenders Ofc., Los Angeles 1969-73; pvt. practice law ofcs. of Michael Pirosh, L.A. 1973-75; deputy denfender trial atty., L.A. 1975-77; supvg. pub. defender Inglewood Juvenile Ct. 1975-76; pvt. practice law, L.A. 1977-80; elected commnr. L.A. Municipal Ct. 1980-81; judge, Municiple Ct., L.A. Judicial Dist. 1981-2; named to L.A. Superior Ct. 1982--; Western coord. Law Students Civil Rights Research Council 1967-68; exec. com., personnel com., exec. ofcr. com. L.A. Municipal Ct. 1981-; awards: Reginald Heber Smith Fellowship sponsored by Harvard & Univ. of Mich. Schs. of Law 1968-69; judge, regl. law sch. Moot Ct. Competition 1981; mem: Calif. Judges Assn. 1981-; L.A. Co. Bar Assn.; Lawyers Club of L.A.; Democrat; Jewish; rec: equestrian, travel, jogging. Res: 1942 San Ysidro Dr Beverly Hills 90210 Ofc: Los Angeles Superior Ct., 111 Hill St Los Angeles 90012

PITLAK, ROBERT THOMAS, manufacturing co. executive; b. May 4, 1938, Jersey City, NJ; s. John Francis and Estelle Dorothy (Marciniak) P.; m. Faith Phillips, June 30, 1962; children: George, b. 1963; Sarah, b. 1977; edn: BS, St. Peter's Coll. 1960; MS, Fairleigh Dickinson Univ. 1968; MBA, Pepperdine Univ. 1979. Career: factory engr. Bausch & Lomb Inc., Rochester, NY 1960-61; prod. mgr. Isomet Corp., Palisades Park, NJ 1961-65; Apollo pgm. engr. Kollsman Instrument Corp., Syosset, NY 1965-69; prod. line mgr. Holobeam Inc., Paramus, NJ 1969-72; field sales engr. Ortec Div. EG&G, Oak Ridge, Tenn. 1972-73; mgr. sales mktg. Appolo Lasers Inc., Los Angeles, Calif. 1973-79; v.p sales & mktg. Interactive Radiation Inc., Northvale, NJ 1979-81; mgr. scientific prods., Appoll Lasers (Allied Corp.), Chatsworth, Calif. 1981--; cons. hi-tech mktg., strategic plnng., new prod. plnng., productivity immprovement, on-line data searching; mem: SPIE; SESA; LIA; works: num. tech. & bus. arts., columnist for Electro- Optical Sys. Design Mag. 1978-83; rec: microcomputers, magic. Res: 1639 Valecroft Ave Westlake Village 91361 Ofc: Apollo Lasers, An Allied Corp., 9201 Independence Ave Chatsworth 91311

PITSKER, PETER BROKAW, management consultant; b. Mar. 14, 1933, San Mateo; s. John Raynold and Dorothy Louise (Brokaw) P.; m. Polly Drake DuBose, Aug. 30. 1958; children: Peter Drake, b. 1959; Amy Frances, b. 1961; Paul Brokaw, b. 1963; John Edwin Allen, b. 1965; edn: BS, Stanford Univ. 1955. Career: refinery engr. Mobil Oil Co., Torrance 1957-60; v.p. mktg. & sales The Foxboro Co., Foxboro, Ma. 1960-62; No. Am. sales mgr. Modular Computer Sys., Ft. Lauderdale, Fla. 1972-75; dir. mktg. & sales General Automation, Anaheim, Calif. 1975-78; v.p./ dir. North & Donahoe (mgmt. consulting engrs.), Santa Ana 1978--; dir./ secty. Triconex, Irvine 1983--; mem: Instrument Soc. of Am.; Am. Inst. of Chem. Engrs.; Robotics Internat./ Soc. Mfg. Engrs.; Assn. for Corp. Growth, Orange Co. chpt.; mil: spec. 3, US Army, active 1955-57, reserve 1957-63; Republican; Protestant; rec: competitive cycling and running (ran 5 marathons incl. Boston Marathon), yacht racinig (2 class champions). Res: 31842 Aguacate Rd San Juan Capistrano 92675 Ofc: North & Donahoe, 1800 E Garry Ave, Ste 114, Santa Ana 92705

PITTMAN, MARIAN SINCLAIR, realtor; b. Feb. 25, 1901, Brklyn.; d. Wm. Moncrief and Della Mae (Heaston) Sinclair; m. Samuel Kemp Pittman, Jr. (dec) May 15, 1934; stepchil: Richard, b. 1930, Marjorie, b. 1932; edn: UC Berkeley 1930-2. Career: secty. E. H. Rollins, Los Angeles 1924-5, Bond, Goodwin & Tucker, San Francisco 1925-9, Bank of Am., Oakland 1932; real estate agt., Fred T. Wood & Assocs., Orinda -1944; realtor/prin. Marian Pittman, Orinda 1944--; currently afil. Realty World, Orinda; founder/partner Orinda Rehab. & Conval. Hosp., Orinda 1967-. Active vol. Hlth. Edn. clinic, Kaiser Hosp. Mem. Contra Costa Bd. of Realtors (pres. Women's Div. 1967; orig. ann. Honor & Roast); Clan Sinclair, Acad. of Scis., S.F; Write your Cong. Club; life mem. UC Alumni Assn. Episcopal. Rec: gardening, scrabble, calico cat. Res: 1049-B Upper Happy Valley Rd Lafayette 94549 Ofc: Realty World 16 Orinda Way Orinda 94563

PIZZICA, STEPHEN V., aircraft company engineer; b. Aug. 6, 1939, Chicago, IL; s. Viro M. and Irene M. (Peterson) Pizzica; BS engring., Northwestern, 1962; MS engring., UCLA, 1969; MBA bus., USC, 1980. Career: mem. tech. staff, sr. staff engr. 1978---; Hughes Aircraft Co., El Segundo, 1962---; lectr., computer usage; profl. electrical engr., CA. Recipient: Hughes Engring. Masters Fellowship, 1967-69; Hughes MBA Fellowship, 1978-80; mem., Beta Gamma Sigma, hon. bus. frat. Mem.: inst. Electrical & Electronic Engrs.: Mem., Soc. for Info. Display; Hughes Mgmt. Club: Natl. Soc. of Profl

Engrs.; CA Soc. of Profl. Engrs. Co-Author technical journ. publ: "CO2 Laser with Simultaneous active and Passive Q-Switching." in Applied Optics, Jan. 1971, based on UCLA Masters paper. Rec.: skiing, running, travel. Res.: P.O. Box 3317, Culver City 90230; Office: Hughes Aircraft Co., P.O. Box 92426, Los Angeles 90009.

PIZZULLI, FRANCIS COSMO, lawyer-bioethicist; b. May 16, 1950, Brooklyn, NY; s. Dominick Lawrence and Rose Nancy (Teracitano) P.; edn: BA, math, UC Santa Barbara 1971; JD, USC 1974; admitted to Calif. State Bar 1975. Career: clerk to Hon. J. Clifford Wallace, 9th Circuit US Court of Appeals (San Diego) 1975-76; Spl. cons. Nat. Commn. for the Protection of Human Subjects of Biomedical and Behavioral Research (Wash DC) 1976-77; assoc. law firm Tuttle & Taylor, Los Angeles 1977-79; assoc. Weissburg & Aronson, L.A. 1979-80; assoc. Engel & Engel, Beverly Hills 1980-81; sole prop. law practice, trial attorney, Santa Monica 1981--; ad hoc commentator on Bioethical issues as guest lectr. to law classes, author and on radio, television (e.g. Cable News Network, KNBC); honors: Order of the Coif, USC Law Ctr., 1974, postdoctoral fellow Hastings Center, NY 1974-75; mem: L.A. County Bar Assn. (founder/chpsn. Biological and Behavioral Technology. Com. 1977; co-chpsn. Bioethics Com. 1981-2), Knights of Columbus, Catholic Big Brothers; publs: Asexual Reproduction & Genetic Engineering, So. Calif. Law Rev. 1974 (reprinted in Biological & Behavioral Technologies and the Law (Praeger 1982); Psychosurgery and Law in The Psychosurgery Debate (W.H. Freeman 1980); Catholic; rec: opera, Renaissance art and hist., track. Res: 24 Mast St, Venice 90291 Ofc: Francis C. Pizzulli, 1299 Ocean Ave, Ste 300, Santa Monica 90401

PLAMONDON, ROBERT JOSEPH, private investigator; b. Jan. 12, 1936, Los Angeles; s. Albert Theophilus and Eleanor Alice (Froehle) P.; m. Sharon Callahan, July 11, 1959; 1 son: Robert J. Jr., b. 1962, dec. 1980; edn: AA, Chaffey Coll. 1972; BS, Citrus Belt Law SCh. 1975; BSBA, UCLA 1958. Career: v.p./ internat.- nat. sales mgr. Evans Prods. Co. (Fortune 500 co.) 1964-70; elected county official, San Bernardino, Constable 1972-78; founded pvt. investigation agency 1978; expanded into 2nd office 1980, 3rd office 1982; founded Am. Sch. of Investigation (profl. acad. to train investigators) 1984; currently, owner ASI Internat. & Am. Sch. of Investigation; dean of sch., instr., cons. for movie & t.v. prodns., exec. protection splst., aircraft accident splst.; honors: Man of the Yr., Kiwanis 1976; mem: Calif. Assn. Licensed Investigators; Nat. Assn. Legal Investigators; Elks; Kiwanis (past pres.); CofC (past pres.); AOPA; works: var. publs. in proflh journs.; arts. on aircraft & pilots; novelist; milm: lt. US Army 1954-56, Army Security Agency; Republican; Catholic; rec; pistol shooting, flying, golf. Res: 8774 Rancho St Alta Loma 91701 Ofc: ASI International, 8968 Archibald Ave, Ste 300, Rancho Cucamonga 91730

PLATT, NORTON R., research and development co. president; b. Apr. 7, 1936, Salt Lake City, Ut.; s. Norton and Inez (Butteane) P.; m. Carol J. Brunt, Aug. 1, 1980; children: Rene, b. 1970; Ronnie, b. 1972; Dalton, b. 1973; edn: BS, Brigham Young Univ. 1961; MBA, USC 1964; PhD, UC Irvine 1979. Career: v.p. Mattell; pres: Miracle Moisture Prods.; Data Systems; Data Prespectives; Human Systems; currently, pres. Swiss American Technologies; grad. research grant in psychobiology; holder of US and Foreign Patents; author: Corporate Aircraft (1964), Land & Taxes (1973); LDS Ch.; rec; psychophysiological research, pvt. pilot. Res: 22 Dewberry Way Irvine 92714 Ofc: 2 Mc Laren, Ste A, Irvine 92714

PLEAS, JOHN EDWARD, JR., electrical engineer; b. Sept. 17, 1946, Memphis, TN; s. John E. and Helen Ann (Simmons) Pleas, Sr.; edn: BSEE, Memphis State Univ., 1976; grad. Defense Systems Mgmt. College, 1981; m. Sandra Dukes, Oct. 26, 1970; chil: Frantz E., b. 1972; Teresa M., b. 1980. Career: broadcast engr., Sonderling Broadcasting Corp., Memphis, 1974-76; design engr., Honeywell Inc., Nashville, 1976-78; project engr., Pacific Missile Test Center (PMTC), Point Mugu, Calif., 1978---; partner/cons., JEM Engineers & Assocs., elec. systems design, safety & energy conservation, Cerritos, 1981—. Regis. Profl. Engr., P.E., Calif. Mem: Natl. Soc. of Profl. Engineers in Pvt. Practice. Mil: Sgt., USAF, 1966-70; Natl. Def. Democrat. Rec: private piot, scuba, guitar. Res: 3910 San Simeon Ave., Oxnard 93034; Office: PMTC-Code #1133, Point Mugu 93042.

PLESSNER, GERALD MAURICE, fund raising co. president; b. Oct. 10, 1934, St. Louis, Mo.; s. Herman and Rose I. (Goldstein) P.; m. Carole Spirtas, May 25, 1959; children: Mitchell Scott, b. 1960; Janice Aurelia, b. 1963; Ellen Beth, b. 1966; edn: BA, Missouri Valley Coll. 1957; Cert. Fund Raising Exec., Nat. Soc. of Fund Raising Execs. 1982. Career: scout exec. Boy Scouts of Am., Pasadena, Calif, Chgo., Ill., Miami, Fla., Pitts., Pa. & St. Louis, Mo. 1957-74; mng. ed. Consumer Newsletter, Los Angeles 1974-76; pres. Fund Raisers Inc., Arcadia 1976--; chmn. Certificate in Fund Raising Pgm., USC; adj. prof., USC; honors: Profl. of the Yr., Nat. Soc. of Fund Raising Execs.; Alumni of the Yr., Missouri Valley Coll.; mem: Nat. Soc. of Fund Raising Execs. (v.p 1983-85); Nat. Exec. Bd. mem. 1983-85; Publicity Club of L.A.; San Fernando Valley Pub. Rels. Round Table; author: three vol., Encyclopedia of Fund Raising; mil: sgt., spl. agt., US Army Counter Intell. Corps; rec: rebuilding player pianos. Address: Fund Raisers Inc., 59 W La Sierra Dr Arcadia 91006

PLOPPER, CHARLES GEORGE, research anatomist/ university professor; b. June 16, 1944, Oakland; s. George Eli and Josephine Vinola (Gates) P.; m. Suzanne May, Nov. 8, 1969; edn: AB, UC Davis 1967; PhD, 1972. Career: chief electron microscopy div., Letterman Army Inst. of Research, Presidio of San

Francisco 1972-75; asst. prof. Univ. of Hawaii Sch. of Med. 1975-77; assoc. prof. Univ. of Kuwait Sch. of Med. 1977-78; sr. staff fellow Nat Inst. Enviromental Scis., No. Carolina 1978-79; faculty UC Davis, Dept. of Anatomy 1979--, asst. prof. 1979-83, assoc. prof. 1983--, dept. chair 1984--; mem. Study Sect. on Respiratory Physiology, Nat. Insts. of Health, Bethesda, Md.; honors: Health Scis. Advancement Awd., NIH 1970-71; Young Investigator Awd., Am. Lung Assn. 1980, 81; mem: Am. Assn. for. Adv. of Sci.; Am. Thoracic Soc.; Am. Assn. of Anatomists; Am. Assn. of Pathologists; Anatomical Soc. of Great Britian; Nature Conservancy; So. Poverty Law Ctr.; Common Cause; num. research publs. and abstracts dealing with cellular biology of the respiratory sys.; mil: capt. US Army 1972-75; Democrat; rec: backpacking, swimming, gardening. Res: 511 Hubble Davis 95616 Ofc: UC Davis Sch. of Veterinary Med., Dept. of Anatomy, Davis 95616

PLUNKETT, ROBERT LAWRENCE, JR., lawyer/ writer; b. Dec. 8, 1951, Denver, Colo.; s. Robert Lawrence and Delores Lorraine (Mathes) P.; edn: BA, UC Santa Cruz 1974; JD, Loyola Univ. Sch. of Law, L.A. 1977; admitted to practice, State Bar of Calif. 1977. Career: atty., Tremaine & Robbins, Los Angeles 1977-78; atty., Bollington, Pennell, Stilz & Bloeser, L.A. 1978-80; atty., John Thomas, L.A. 1980-81; sole practitioner, atty., Sherman Oaks 1981--; honors: Am. Jurisprudence Awd. (2), 1977; Loyola Law Sch. Scholarship 1976; Order of the Pelican 1981; Order of the Dolphin 1980; Grant of Arms 1979; Awd. of Arms 1977; mem: L.A. County San Fernando Valley, Southwest L.A., West Hollywood, Hollywood Bar Assns.; Soc. for Creative Anachronism 1976; works: 1964- Year One- 1974; The Royal Advisor (column running 1980-), Hurgood Through History 1981, 83; rec: medieval study, recreation. Ofc: Robert L. Plunkett, 15303 Ventura Blvd, Ste 800, Sherman Oaks 91403

PODESTO, JOHN B., manufacturing co. executive; b. Mar. 26, 1921, Modesto; s. John B. and Mary Podesto; m. Celesta Tocalino, June 9, 1946; children: Paula, b. 1947; Michele,b. 1950; Gina, b. 1953; Leslie, b. 1957; Jeffrey, b. 1959; edn: BA, St. Marys Coll. 1944; Coll. of the Pacific 1943. Career: pro football, Pittsburgh Steelers, Chicago Bears, 1946-47; farmer, 1947-48; sec.treas. Modesto Tallow Co., 1948--; honors: All America Football 1943; College of Pacific (Coach Amos Alonzo Stagg), Hall of Fame. St. Mary's coll., Univ. of Pacific, Stockton (CA) Hall of Fame, Sportsman of Stanislaus; mem. Sportsmen of Stanislaus, Del Rio Country Club, Elks; mil: USMC 1943-46, capt USMCR; Catholic; rec: golf. Res: 7112 Del Rio Dr Modesto 95356 Ofc: Modesto Tallow Co., POB 1036, Modesto 95353

PODICH, NICHOLAS MARTIN, artist and sculptor; b. Oct. 18, 1914, Watsonville, s. Martin Peter and Ann (Ucovich) P.; m. Marian Guenter, Nov. 10, 1946, children: Nicholas, b. 1948; Cyndel, b. 1950; edn: grad., Watsonville H.S.; grad., O C S 1941 Career: architect, designer Pioneer Builders, Watsonville 1940; profl. baseball pitcher, San Francisco Seals, 1940-41; artist, art director McCarty Co. and successor co., Botsford Ketchum, S.F. 1946-47; artist/art dir. S.F. Publications 1967-80; artist, sculptor, free lance, 1946--; cons. Chevron, Safeway, exhib. gallery shows thruout USA, 1946-79; portrait paintings in permanent collections in Europe and USA; mural in marble dust (10'x10') for House of Soble, S.F.; work on perm. display: St. Joseph Coll., Harrahs Hotel (Lake Tahoe); mem. Soc. of Art Directors-Artists; mil: 1st lt. US Army, PTO, 1941-46; Republican; Catholic; rec: golf, fishing. Address: 965 St. Joseph Ave Los Altos 94022

PODVA, MONTY JAMES, lawyer/energy specialist; b. Nov. 21, 1947, Sacramento; s. James Marion and Alta Veil (Fidler) P.; m. Rebecca Judge, May 2, 1976; children: Anna b. 1978, Sierra b. 1979; edn: BA in hist., UC Davis 1970; MA, Montana State Univ.-Bozeman, 1972-3; JD, Univ. of Pacific McGeorge Sch. of Law 1977; admitted to State Bar of Calif. 1980; Energy Splst., Calif. Energy Commn. 1980. Career: ednl. and leadership cons., S.A.E. Fraternity, Evanston, Ill. 1970-72; Energy Analyst, State of Calif. Div. of Oil & Gas, Sacto. 1973-74; law clerk to retired Justice William O. Douglas, US Supreme Ct., Wash DC, 1977-80; Energy Splst., Calif. Energy Commn., Sacto. 1980--; atty. Law Offices of M. James Podva, Sacto. 1980--; prof. Energy & Natural Resource Law, Wash. DC 1979; prof. Bus. Law, National Univ., Sacto. 1983; awards: Calif. State Scholar 1965, William O. Douglas Distinguished Lectr., 5/80, Yakima Coll., Wash.; Internat. Moot Ct. competition, UOP McGeorge Sch of Law; mem: Capitol City Trial Lawyers Assn., Natural Resources Defense Council, HALT (Help Abolish Legal Tyranny); mem. Calif. Capitol Region Alumni Assn. of Sigma Alpha Epsilon frat.; works: resrch. ed. The Court Years, Autobiography of William O. Douglas, 1977-80; contbr. The Environmental Ethic of Justice William O. Douglas, E.P.A. Jour. Nov/Dec 1979; lead tech. writer, Securing Calif's Energy Future (1983 Biennial Report to Gov. & Legis., Calif. Energy Commn.); Democrat; outdoor rec. Res: POB 161539 Sacto 95816 Ofc: Law Offices of M. James Podva, 800 H St, Ste 302, Sacramento 95816

POLADIAN, ARTIN NISHAN, pharmacist; b. Sept. 30, 1936, Cairo, Egypt, nat. 1974; s. Nishan Yacoub and Khatoun Haroutioun (Keshishian) P.; m. Tchinar-Aida Kupelian, Dec. 9, 1962; children: Tamar, b. 1964; Arto Jr., b. 1971; edn: Cert. Secondary Edn., Coll. De La Salle, Cairo 1957; B.Chem. & Pharmaceutical Chem., Cairo Univ. 1961; D.Pharm., USC 1970. Career: pharm. rep. Pfizer Pharmaceutical Co., Cairo, Egypt 1961-65; owner/mgr. Behnam Pharmacy, Cairo, Egypt 1965-68; staff pharmacist Kaiser Foundation Hosp., Los Angeles 1968-76; pharmacist in chg., Kaiser Permanente Med. Pharmacy, Pasadena 1976--; estab. pharm. preceptorship pgm. 1972, Kaiser Found. Hosp., L.A.; awards: grantee, Alex & Mary Manoukian Edn. Fund, 1969; mem: So. Calif. Hospital Pharamcist, Am. Soc. Hosp. Pharmacists; chmn. Armenian

Rights Council (West Region) of Am.; Parish Council chmn. St. John Armenian Cathedral, Hollywood; treas., bd. dirs. Tekeyan Dickranian Armenian Sch., Hywd.; exec. com. Armenian Democratic League Orgn.; Armenian Apostolic Ch.; rec: drawing, painting. Res: 3323 Ione Pl Los Angeles 90068 Ofc: Kaiser Permanente Med Gp. 450 N. Lake Pasadena 91101

POLANSKY, MICHAEL DAVID, communications corporate executive; b. Apr. 22, 1944, Lynn, Mass.; s. Philip and Lillian (Berman) P.; edn: BS, Tufts Univ. 1972; MA, Univ. of Denver 1974; Cert. Acct. Exec./ Industry Cons., A.T. & T. 1982. Career: meteorological trainee National Weather Svc., Boston, MA & Columbia, S.C., 1962-66; graduate tchg. asst. Univ. of Denver, Colo. 1973-74; Mktg. Sales acct. exec. Pacific Telephone, San Francisco 1978-83; Innovative Systems mgr., Democratic Nat. Conv., Pacific Bell, 1983-84; honors: 1982 Sales Leader Award, 1983 Chairman's Club, Pacific Telephone; mem. Am. Meteorological Soc.; Democrat; rec: meteorology. Res: 70 Beaver St San Francisco 94114 Ofc: Pacific Bell, 633 Folsom Street, Ste 102, San Francisco 94107

POLIMAC-ILLICH, LIGIA KATARINA, chemist; b. Mar. 30, 1930, Miholjac, Yugolslavia; d. Djuro Dimitrie and Maria (First) P.; m. Andjelko Illich, Sept. 7, 1957; child: Vanja, b. 1958; edn: MS, Univ. of Zagreb Sch. of Chem. Tech. 1955. Career: resrch. chemist (drugs and food chemicals) Vetserum, Zagreb, Yugoslavia, 1955-58; mgr. Analytical Lab. DRAVA, Safety Matches Inc., Osijek, Yugoslavia, 1958-59; research group leader, Katran, Organic Ind., Zagreb, Yugoslavia, 1960-62; assoc. prof. Coll. of Organic Chem. Technology, Univ. of Zagreb, 1963-67; analytical chemist Packaging Corp. of America, Los Angeles, Ca. 1968-70; analytical chemist Cyclo Chemical Div. of Alameda Labs. Inc., L.A. 1970-73, mgr. quality control 1973--; mem. Am. Chemical Soc.; Republican; Catholic; rec: dancing, cats. Res: 7444 Yankey St Downey 90242 Office: Cyclo-Products, 1922 East 64th St Los Angeles 90001

POLITE, THERON JEROME, security agency president; b. Feb. 24, 1930, Tampa, Fla.; s. Charlie and Gussie Lee (Shad) Polite; m. Thelma Ford, May 1, 1948; children: Jimmy Lee b. 1944, Celinda Joyce (West) b. 1954, Kenneth Jerome b. 1956; edn: AS in Police Sci., Mtry. Peninsula Coll., Monterey 1970-72; Bach. Adm. of Justice, Golden Gate Univ., 1976, MPA, 1978; desig: Calif. Police Ofcrs' Std. Tng. Basic Cert. 1971; Comm. Coll. instr. credential: Police Sci. (life) 1979; Special Agt., Internat. Police Cong. Wash DC, Internat. Central Bur., Miami; Calif. lic. Pvt. Investigation, lic. Pvt. Security. Career: sgt. 1/c US Armed Forces (AUS, USAF), 1946-69; Auxiliary opr. PG&E Steam Plant, Moss Landing, Castroville 1970; deputy sheriff Montery County Sheriff Dept., 1971-83; pres./mgr. Polite's Private Investigation & Security Agency, Seaside 1983--; councilman, City of Seaside, elected 1982; pres. Comm. Devel. Corp. (CDC) Seaside, 1980-; coll. instr.; dir./exec. bd. mem. Friends Outside in Monterey County; dir./mcm. Mtry Reg. Water Pol. Control Agcy.; dir./ mem. Val. Mosq. Abatement Dist.; honors: Citizen of Year, Omega Psi Phi Frat. 1978, 1982; two Monterey Co. Police Ofcrs Assn. Awards 1972, 73; mem: Nat. Council of Investigation and Security Svc. Inc.; World Assn. of Detectives Inc.; Calif. Assn. Licensed Investgrs.; Masons, Scottish Rite, Kiwanis, NAACP (life, Golden Heritage), Omega Psi Phi Frat., Shriners, ACLU, Am. Legion, Seaside CofC; mil. awards: Bronze Star o.l.c., Army Commendn. o.l.c., Nat. Def. Svc. o.l.c., GCM (6), UN Svc., Korean Svc., Vietnam Svc., Vietnam Campaign, Viet. Cross of Gal. with Palm, Viet. Civil Actions Honor Medal l/c w/Palm, Victor WWII, Combat Inf., Expert Inf.; Democrat (del. for Mondale); Prot.; rec: golf. Address: Polite's Private Investigation and Security Agcy, 1630 Marietta St Seaside 93955

POLK, N. KAREN, engineering technician; b Dec. 20, 1938, Joliet, Ill.; d. Norman Keith and Zalita Jeanette (Holtn) Peterson; m. Carl Albert Polk, June 25, 1960; children: Erick, b. 1961; Allan, b. 1963; Denise, b. 1964; edn: Internat. Rels., Calif. Western (now USIU) 1957-59; AS, Southwestern Coll. 1970-82; AAEE, Southwestern Coll. 1970-82; EE, CSU San Diego 1983-. Career: field interviewer US Census Bureau, San Diego/Imperial Co., 1971-75; clerk typist DOD (Navy) NAS North Island, San Diego 1975-76, electronic engring. tech. (Engr. Designate), 1976--; awards: Superior Performance, US Census Bur. 1973; mem. North Island Profl. Engrs. Assn., Soc. of Women Engrs., IEEE, Toastmistress 1976; Republican; Prot.; rec: golf, tennis, philately. Res: 1548 Max Ave Chula Vista 92011 Ofc: DOD (Navy) NAS North Island, San Diego 92135, Bldg. 317

POLLCHICK, ALLAN LEE, psychologist; m. Linda Brown, Oct. 31, 1970; edn: fellow, Langley Porter Inst., UC Med. Sch., San Francisco 1975-76; PhD, Vanderbilt Univ. 1975; MA, 1973; BA, UCLA 1971. Career: pres. Allan L. Pollchik, PhD, 1976--; instr. San Diego State Univ., 1977--, also cons. Oceanside Sch. System, 1976-; cons. Family Services, Camp Pendleton, 1977-; cons. Project OZ, 1976-80; cons. Chicano Fedn., 1977-79; honors: Nat. Merit Scholar 1967-71; Nat. Sci. Found. Fellow 1972-73; NIMH Fellow 1973-75; mem: No. County Psychol. Assn. (pres. 1980-81); Am. Psychol. Assn.; Interamerican Soc. of Psychol.; Zeta Beta Tau frat.; pres. Seawind Oceanside Homeowners Assn. 1980-81; works: public service radio pgm.: North County Health Spectrum, 1978--; rec: surfing, skiing, weightlifting. Res: 1973 Bluewater Way Oceanside 92054 Ofc: Allan L. Pollchik, Ph.D., 2101 El Camino Real, Ste 203A, Oceanside 92054

POLLOCK, BRUCE C., telecommunications industry executive; b. July 31, 1943, Los Angeles; s. Dr. R. C., Jr. and Dorothy J. (King) P.; m. Carol G., June 17, 1967; children: Elissa M., b. 1974, Leslie I., b. 1974; edn: BS, Univ. of Wash. 1965; JD, UC Berkeley 1968, MBA, 1970; admitted to Calif. State Bar.

Career: financial mgr. Kaiser Cement, 1970-75; legal counsel Kaiser Engineers, 1975-78; vp legal & plnng. Dorntar Gypsum America, 1978-80; mgmt. positions Compath National (telecomm. co.), Oakland, 1980-83, exec. vice pres./chief op. officer, 1983--; bd. dirs. Kaiser Fed. Credit Union 1973-76; mem. Assn. for Corp. Growth (SF chpt.); rec: golf, wines. Address: Compath National, 180 Grand Ave, Ste. 1300, Oakland 94612

POLLOCK, ROY, insurance executive/investor; b. July 13, 1944, Los Angeles; s. Roy W. and Muriel A. (Lewis) P. Career: edn: AA, bus. & scis.; LLM. Career: law enforcement for ten years; insurance indus. 1975--, dist. mgr. Farmers Insurance Group, Capitola; mem. bd. dirs. 4 corps.; head three corps.; honors: Jaycee Man of the Year; mem. var. civic orgns.; mil: lt. USMC, decorated for valor Vietnam; rec: hunting, cars. Ofc: Roy Pollock and Assocs., 1500 41st Ave, Ste 11, Capitola 95010

POMPEI, CARL F., electronics co. chief executive; b. Feb. 13, 1939, Chgo., Ill.; s. Frank and Irene (Eier) P.; m. Donna L. West., Jan. 5, 1963; children: Kimberly (adopt.), b. 1956; Kevin, b. 1963; edn: Univ. of Ill. 1957; Foothill Coll. 1962-66; De Anza Coll. 1967-69. Career: supr. Lockheed Missiles & Space, Palo Alto 1962-63; mgr. Philco-Ford Microelectronics, Santa Clara 1963-68; mgr. American Micro Systems Inc., Santa Clara 1968-69; v.p. Drexler Technology, Palo Alto 1969-73; pres./CEO, NBK Corporation, Santa Clara 1973-82, dir. 1973-; pres./CEO, Probe Technology Corp., Santa Clara 1982--; dir. NCA Corp. 1977-, Sierra Information Systems 1983-, Private Sector Council 1983-; served on Pres.'s Private Sector Survey on Cost Control, Finl. Asset Management (F.A.M.) Task Force, 1983; mem. Nat. Fedn. of Indep. Business, Semiconductor Equip. & Materials Inst., Am. Electronics Assn., Santa Clara Valley World Trade Assn., Am. Soc. for Psychical Research; mil: 2/c Guided Missileman, USN, 1958-62, GCM; Republican; rec: phys. fitness/racquet sports. Res: 1598 Poppy Way Cupertino 95014 Ofc: Probe Technology Corp., 3000 Olcott St Santa Clara 95051

POND, KENNETH JAMES, certified financial planner; b. Aug. 14, 1940, Detroit, Mich.; s. Byron Oliver and Irene Alma (Torikka) P.; m. Norma Ann Woodland, Oct. 28, 1967; children: Bret b. 1970, David b. 1973, Rochele b. 1976; edn: BA, Calif. State Univ. 1966; Registered, NYSE, NY Inst. of Fin. 1969; CFP, Coll. of Financial Planner 1979. Career: real estate cons. LSH Consulting Services, 1966; assoc., senior v.p. investments, Shearson American Express, 1969-79, Presidents Advis. Council 1976, 78, 79; Dean Witter, 1979; finl. plnnr./pres. K. James Pond & Co., Inc. Los Altos 1979--; conducts exec. finl. planning seminars for publicly owned corps.: Spectra Physics 1978, Digital Equip. Corp. 1979, Cordis Corp. 1980, Cermetek Corp. 1982, Valid Logic Corp. 1983; mem: Internat. Assn. of Finl. Plnnrs. Inst. of Certified Finl. Plnnrs.; BSA Scoutmaster; mem. Nat., Calif. Rolls Royce Owners Club; past mem. Toastmasters Intl., Soc. for Adv. of Mgmt., Fly Fishermans Assn.; author/ed. Corporate Spotlight Column No. Calif. Electronic News 1972-; author/commentator TV finl. pgm.: Trendwatch (1974-79); Presbyterian; rec: swimmin, racketball, fishing. Res: 17775 Old Summit Rd Los Gatos 95030 Ofc: K. James Pond & Co Inc. 4966 El Camino Real Los Altos 94022

POPE, JOHN EDWARD, lawyer; b. Dec. 8, 1942, Glendale; s. M. Edward and Minnie (Hartwig) P.; m. Diana Lott, June 30, 1967; children: Deborah, b. 1968; Gregory, b. 1972; Kristen, b. 1975; edn: BS, UC Berkeley 1965; MBA, USC 1967; JD, UCLA 1977; admitted to practice, State Bar of Calif. Career: vice pres./gen. mgr. Eddie Pope & Co. Inc. and Pope Mfg. Inc., Valencia 1967-74; atty. assoc. Cox, Castle & Nicholson, Los Angeles 1977-80; atty. assoc. Irell & Manella, Newport Beach 1980--; dir. Carroll Ave. Restoration Found. 1977-79; lectr. UC Irvine Ext., Light Constrn. and Devel. Mgt. Council, 1982-83; honors: Order of the Coif, 1977, UCLA Law Rev. 1976-7; mem. Am. Bar Assn., State Bar of Calif., Calif. Alumni Assn., Irvine Hist. Soc.; coach AYSO Soccer (1978-83). Res: 6 Sunrise Irvine 92715 Ofc: Irell & Manella, 840 Newport Center Dr, Suite 500, Newport Beach 92660

POPOFF, LARRY MARTIN, wholesale distributor; b. Nov. 8, 1948, Topeka, Ks.; s. Max William and Erma Mae (Smith) P.; m. Jeanie Ann Yarick, Dec. 31, 1978; children: Kevin, b. 1965; Robin, b. 1971; edn: BS, engring., Ore. State Univ. 1969. Career: bldg. insp. City of Rocklin, CA 1970-72; engineering insp., State of Calif., 1972-75; owner wholesale distributorship, Valley Wholesale (material installations sales & service 1974, contractor for service of woodstoves and fireplaces), Sacto. 1974--; cons. energy retail outlets west coast; honors: Eagle Scout 1966, BSA; mem: Calif. Solid Fuel Assn. (pres.); Wood Energy Inst. (bd.); jWood Heat Alliance; orgns: Scoutmaster, Bobby Sox softball; works: design of new type of efficient woodstove; wrote woodstove op. manuals; Democrat; Prot.; rec: golf, tennis, flying. Res: 1609 Truscott Ct Roseville 95678 Ofc: Valley Wholesale, 4555 Auburn Blvd Sacramento 95841

PORCARO, VINCENT JOSEPH, JR., dentist; b. Sept. 26, 1954, Biloxi, Miss.; s. Vincent J. and Mary F. (Starkey) P.; edn: BA, Loma Linda Univ. 1976; DDS, 1982. Career: assoc. dental practice Novato 1982-82, owner dental clinic, Idyllwild, 1983--; dental screening sch. children var. local schs., instns.; mem. Am., Calif. Tri-County Dental Assns., Acad. of General Dentistry, Idyllwild CofC, Anza CofC, Idyllwild Rotary Club (Paul Harris Fellow 1983); works: sculpture; Republican; Seventh Day Adventist; rec: scuba, collecting antique Am. currency. Address: Vincent Joseph Porcaro Jr. DDS, 26770 Hwy 243, POB 1097, Idyllwild 92349

PORCELLI, M. JAY, physician-family practice; b. Oct. 6, 1950, Downey; s. John Joseph and Cressa Beryl (Luhman) P.; m. Marsha Lynn, Jan. 24, 1970; children: Phillip Michael b. 1977, Adrianne Marie b. 1979, Valerie Marie b.

1981; edn: AS, Rio Hondo Coll. 1970; BS, UC Irvine 1972; DO, Chgo. Coll. Osteo. Med. 1974-78; physician and surgeon, Bd. of Osteopathic Examiners 1979. Career: physician and surgeon pvt. practice, dir. med. clinic, Pomona 1979--; cons. phys. Dept. Family Practice, Orange Grove Comm. Hosp. 1979-; hosp. afils. Pomona Valley Comm. Hosp., Doctors Hosp. of Montclair, San Dimas Comm. Hosp., Valley Hosp. (Pomona); bd. dirs. State Med. Assn. (OPSC) 1983-86; asst. prof. Family Practice, Coll. of Osteopathic Med. of the Pacific; honors: Sigma Sigma Phi, UCSB scholarship, Redlands Univ. athletic scholarship, Rio Hondo Coll. (Kiwanis Club award) scholarship; mem: Am. Coll. of Osteopathic GPs (Calif. Soc.); Am. Osteopathic Assn.; Osteopathic Phys. & Surgeons of Calif.; L.A. County Osteopathic Med. Assn. (charter); San Bernardino Co. Osteo. Med. Assn.; Christian Med. Soc.; Am. Heart Assn.; Am. Public Health Assn.; Assoc. Alumni Coll. of Osteo. Med. of the Pacific; mem. YMCA; pub. spkr. womens circles, PTA, elem. schs., high sch. career days; publs: arts. in med. jours.; Republican; Conservative Baptist (bd. trustees Pomona First Bapt. Ch. 1982-4); rec: hunting, skiing, scuba. Address: M. Jay Porcelli, D.O. 1770 N. Orange Grove Ave, Ste 205, Pomona 91767

PORTER, CHARLES ALBERT, manufacturing co. executive/ educator; b. Feb. 16, 1924, Akron, Oh.; s. Dwight Pemperton and Lillie Goaffon Porter; m. Hazel, Aug. 26, 1943; children: Rebecca Lynn, b. 1947; Debra Lee, b. 1953; Cindy Melissa, b. 1966; Dwight Temple, b. 1950; edn: Marine Corp Inst. 1943-46; tchr. edn., UCLA 1961-64; Orange Coast Coll. 1982; L.A. Trade Tech. Coll. 1968, 79, 82. Career: ptnr. first self-service laundry in Orange County, 1947-49; owner Porter Custom (cabinet and fixture co.) 1949-61; instr. building trades, asst./assoc. prof. Cabinetry, Cabinetry Div., Los Angeles Trade and Technical Coll. 1961--; pres. Renaissance Mfg. Co. Inc., 1970-80; owner Legend Enterprises, 1980--; cons. Playmaster corp. 1979-; adv. mem. Fullerton Junior Coll. 1961-, L.A. Trade and Tech. Coll. 1961-, American Bdcstg. Co. Career Opportunities Pgm. 1966; mem. Gov's Indsl. Safety Council 1966-69; adv. Calif. Dept. of Corrections for San Quentin and Chino, 1972-75; mem: Cabinetmakers Assn. of So. Calif. 1970-; The Community of Scholars; Internat. Assn. of Cabinetmakers and Carvers; Soc. De Tallistas Y Ebanitas; Patents: Billiard Tables design (1969), leading designer/mfr. quality billiard tables and accessories in US and Europe; designed/blt. table for the Capitol, Wash DC, which depicts hist. of the US known as The Republic; mil: s/sgt. USMC 1942-46; Republican; Nazarene Ch.; rec: restoration antique autos. Res: 10632 Paloma Garden Grove 92643 Ofc: Legend Enterprises, 2304 West Second St Santa Ana 92703

PORTER, WILLIAM ERNEST, company executive; b. May 11, 1945, Catskill, NY; s. Bernard A. and Mary Jane (Oliver) P.; m. Sharon Brodhead, Jan. 29, 1966; children: De Non, b. 1970; Jerlym, b. 1974; edn: BS, Syracuse Univ. 1967; BS, Purdue Univ. 1969; Ops. Research, Cornell Univ. 1972-73; JD, George Washington Univ. 1979. Career: asst. prof. computer sci., Morehouse Coll. 1969-71; mgr. Systems Engring., Mitre Corp., 1973-76; senior project engr. General Electric 1977-78, pgm. mgr. Info. Systems, 1978-80, mgr. Advanced Info. Systems & Tech., G.E. 1980-81; mgr. Software Engring. R&D, G.E., 1981-83; mgr. G.E. Space Div. Western Operation 1983--; computer sci. instr. Boston Univ. 1973; honors: Phi Beta Kappa (1967), Pi Mu Epsilon (1965), chmn. Software Mission Assurance Conf. (NSIA/AIA/NASA, 1983); mem. Virginia State Bar, Am. Bar Assn.; orgns: United Way, AME choir (Phila.) 1983; publs: The Privacy Act of 1974: A Look At It from a Combined Legal & Technical Perspective, Computers & People (12/76); Democrat; AME; rec: furniture making, singing. Res: 3261 Padilla Way San Jose 95148 Ofc: General Electric 1277 Orleans Dr Sunnyvale 94089

PORTER, WINSTON SEYMOUR, real estate executive, ret.; b. Sept. 17, 1909, Port Maitland, Nova Scotia, Can.; nat. 1935; s. Lyndon E. and Lillian D. (Sanders) P.; m. Ruth Lyon, Sept. 29, 1934; children: Robert G., b. 1938; Lynne Susan, b. 1942; edn: Northwestern Univ. 1936-38. Career: estate of Marshall Field, 1934-42; asst. regional rent director OPA, Chgo. Regl. Office, 1943-46; v.p. Oliver S. Turner & Co., Chgo. 1946-67; v.p. Arthur Rubloff & Co., Chgo. 1967-78; honors: Land Economics Hon. Soc. Lambda Alpha (chpt. pres. 1940); listed, Who's Who in the Midwest 1978, Who's Who in Fin. and Indus. 1981, Who's Who in the West 1982; life mem. Field Mus. Natural Hist. (Chgo.); chmn. Deerfield (Ill.) Planning Commn. 1954-59, Village Trustee 1959-63, pro tem mayor 1960; Building Mgrs. Club of Chgo. (pres. 1963); Chicago Jr. Real Estate Board (pres. 1941); Republican; Presbyterian. Res: 24001 Muirlands Blvd, Greenbriar 281, El Toro 92630

POSNACK, STANFORD, lawyer; b. Oct. 20, 1934, Kansas City, Mo.; s. Harry I. and Celia (Goldstein) P.; m. Judy Fridley, July 15, 1978; children: Laurie, b. 1958; Derek, b. 1961; Mark, b. 1968; edn: Compton Coll. 1952-56; East L.A. Coll. 1956-60; Mt. San Antonio Coll. 1964-67; LLD, La Verne Univ. 1973; admitted to practice, State Bar of Calif. & Calif. Supreme Ct. 1974. Career: atty. at law, self-empl., Azusa, West Covina, 1974--; Los Angeles Juvenile Ct. referee 1981--; previously: air pollution techn. L.A. County Air Pollution Control Dist. 1967-74, var. tech. and prodn. positions, 1951-67; mem. Calif. State Bar Assn., Azusa CofC (v.p. 1975-77), Azusa Rotary Club (bd. 1975-77), Azusa Democratic Club (v.p. 1977-78); rec: bowling, reading. Res: 1133 S. Lark Ellen Ave West Covina 91791 Ofc: Sanford Posnack, 670 S. Sunset Ave, Ste 200, West Covina 91790

POSS, NANCY LUCILE VAN DYKE, private investigator; b. Nov. 20, 1934, Los Angeles; d. Douglas and Bernadette Ann (Le Sage) Van Dyke; children: Charles VanDyke, b. 1956; Wendy K. (Milette), b. 1958; Douglas A., b. 1959; edn: BA, Mt. St. Mary's Coll., L.A. 1956; MA, CSU Long Beach 1971; Lic. Investigator, Calif. 1979. Career: investigator Advise Security Corporation,

Anaheim 1972-74; supr./investgr. Jack Reed Investigations, Fullerton 1974-82; founder/owner Helios Investigations 1982-, chief exec. ofcr. Helios Investigations Inc. 1983--; mem. Council of Internat. Investigators, Calif. Assn. of Licensed Investigators, Inst. of Profl. Investigators (British); club: Canyon Crest Country; Democrat; rec: sailing, tennis, travel. Res: POB 8462, Anaheim 92802 Ofc: Helios Investigations Inc. POB 11783, Santa Ana 92711

POSTGATE, MARY J., medical group administrator; b. May 19, 1939, Grand Junction, Colo.; d. Eli Richard and Doris Mae (Davis) Joe; m. John William Postgate Jr., Sept. 27, 1969; children: Donald L. Beed, b. 1957; (step) John William III, b. 1958; (step) Jennifer Lynn, b. 1960; (step) Mark Steven, b. 1961; (step) Julie Ruth, b. 1962; William Skylor, b. 1969; Beverly Jeannine, b. 1971; edn: acctg.; bus. ad. Bakersfield Coll. 1976-82; Santa Barbara Bus. Coll. 1961. Career: asst. bus. office mgr. Bks Memorial Hosp. 1975-79; accts. receivable mgr. Mercy Hosp. 1979-80; credit mgr. Navy Oil Co. Inc. 1981-83; pres. Fantasy's Gift and Craft, 1980-81; v.p. Gold Leaf Realty, 1979--; administr. Pacific Orthopaedic Medical Gp., 1983--; v.p. Gold Leaf Building Maint. of Kern Co.; mem: Nat. Assn. of Accountant, Credit Mgrs. Assn., Am. Soc. of Women Accountants, Nat. Assn. for Female Execs.; Republican; Prot.; rec: quilting, stichery, travel. Res: 5737 East Brundage Lane, Bakersfield 93307 Ofc: Pacific Orthopaedic Medical Group, 2619 F Street Bakersfield 93301

POULOS, CLARA JEAN, nutrition specialist; b. Jan. 1, 1941, Los Angeles; d. James P. and Clara Georgia (Creighton) Hill; m. Themis Poulos, Jan. 31, 1960; edn: PhD, nutrition, Donsbach Univ. 1979; PhD, biol., Fla. State Univ 1974. Registered Nutrition Specialist. Career: dir. research Leapou Lab., Aptos 1973-76; Monterey Bay Research Ins., Santa Cruz, 1976; nutrition spls. in pvt. practice, Santa Cruz 1975--, dir. of nutrition H.E.L.P.S., 1983--; instr. UC Santa Cruz Ext.; instr. Stoddard Assoc.; Seminars: cons. to Biol-Med. Lab., Chicago Nutra-Med Research Corp., N.Y. Akorn Miller Pharmacal. Chicago-Monterey Bay Aquaculture Farms, Ressurection Distribn. Dartnell Labs.; awards: NaJulander Internat. Research Award 19710, Wainwright Found. Award 1979-. Mem. Internat. Platform Soc., Internat. Toastmistress, Am. Federal Chess Assn., Fellow Intern. Coll. of Applied Nutrition- Am. Nutritionist Assn. Intern; Acad. Nutritional Consultants, mem. Am. Diabetes Assn. Profl., AAAS, Calif. Acad. Sci. Intern, Fishery Assn., Am. Soc. of Clin. Hypnosis Nat. Acad., Research Biological Chemists, Am. Weight Reduction Inst.; publs: articles in profl. journals on alcoholism and hypoglycemia; rec: chess, bowling, photog., swimming. Ofc: Registered Nutrition Specialist, H.E.L.P.S., 1595 Soquel Dr Santa Cruz 95065

POULOS, JOAN GRAHAM, lawyer; b. Almena, Ks.; d. Gilbert Wesley and Opal Z. (Voight) Graham; children: John Stewart, b. 1965; Alexandra Joan, b. 1967; edn: Bach., Univ of Kansas 1968; JD, UC Hastings Coll. of Law 1962; MPA, UC Riverside. Career: attorney in San Diego, Ukiah; mayor pro tem City of Davis, 1972-74; mayor 1974-76; tchr. Intro. to the Common Law Afghanistan (to Afghan judges and prosecutors) USAID, Kabul, Afghanistan; atty. Law offices of Joan G. Poulos, 1978--; contract instr. UC Davis and Humbolt St. Univ., tch. law for Soc. Workers in No. Calif. Counties, 1980-; past instr. family law, legal rights of juveniles and women, UC Ext.; commnr. National Commn. for Uniform State Laws; mem: bd. dirs. Yolo Gen. Hosp., Davis; bd. dirs. New Franklin Soc.; honors: recogn., Soroptomists. Mem: Calif. Elected Women, Calif. Women Lawyers, Women Lawyers of Sacto., ACLU, NOW, Yolo County Bar Assn., State Bar of Calif. (Real Estate Sect.), Am. Bar assn.; mem. Davis Choral; publs: issue editor/contbr. Hastings Law Jour. 1962; Democrat; Prot.; rec: travel. Res: 621 Cordova Place Davis 95616 Law Offices of Joan G. Poulos 1723 Oak, Davis 95616

POWELL, ALEX, lawyer; b. Oct. 10, 1946, Frankfurt a-Mein, Ger., nat. 1952; s. Max and Dorothy Powell; m. Martha Glass, Oct. 1, 1977; edn: BA, Temple Univ. 1968; JD, Univ. of Toledo Sch. of Law 1973. Admitted to Ariz. State Bar 1973, Calif. State Bar 1978. Career: self-empl. atty., Calif. specializing in real estate law, 1978--; self-empl. atty., Ariz., 1973-78; polit. news reporter K-GUN TV, Tucson, Ariz. 1968-70; high sch. tchr. Millville, NJ 1967-68; campaign coord. in Ariz. for gubernatorial cand. and a congl. candidate, 1973; pres./dir. 3-Way Investments, Inc.--; cons. City of Toledo, 1972, on economic devel. of minorities; honors: for innovative exptl. ednl. pgm., 1967-8; Copper Letter, City of Tucson, for media coverage of city & county politics by electronic media. Mem: 20-30 Club, Torrance, 1979; works: exhib. geometric art in oils in juried competition, State of Ohio, 1971, and Toledo Art Mus. purchase shop; Republican; Jewish; rec: swimming, racquetball, fishing. Res: 2007 Mt. Shasta, San Pedro 90732 Ofc: Cornwell & Powell, 21515 Hawthorne Blvd, Ste 1155, Torrance 90503

POWELL, EARL ALEXANDER, III, art museum director; b. Oct. 24, 1973, Spartanburg, So. Carolina; s. Earl Anderson Jr. and Elizabeth (Duckworth) P.; m. Nancy O'Neal Landry, July 17, 1971; children: Cortney, b. 1974; Channing, b. 1978; edn: BA, Williams Coll. 1966; MA, Harvard Univ. 1970; PhD, 1974. Career: curator Michener Collection, Univ. of Texas at Austin, 1974-76; executive curator National Gallery of Arts, Wash. DC 1976-80; dir. Los Angeles County Museum of Art, 1980--; awards: King Olaf Medal, Norway 1978; mem. Walpole Soc., Assn. of Museum Directors, Am. Fedn. of Arts; publs: on American arts; mil: cmdr. USNR; rec: photog. Ofc: Los Angeles County Museum of Art, 5905 Wilshire Blvd Los Angeles 90036

POWERS, NONA LA VAE, custom framer; b. Feb. 24, 1942, St. Anthony, Idaho; d. Russell H. and Della S. (Mathis) Smith; m. Joe M. Powers, Jan. 2, 1963; children: Kira, b. 1964; Joe Jr., b. 1966; edn: AA, San Diego City Coll.; BA, cum laude, CSU San Diego 1976; MA, 1978. Career: custom framer

Potpourri Artist Supply 1977-81; owner Monterey Frames, San Diego 1981--; nat. lectr. for Professional Picture Framers Assn., 1979; color cons. for Letraset USA; lectr. to local PPFA and var. pvt. frame cos., art groups; awards: 3d. Pl., New & Creative Ideas Framing Competition 1979; hon. mention, Print Competition 1979; mem. Profl. Picture Framers Assn.; PTA (pres. 1974); publs: contbg. writer Decor Mag., The Framer mag. Res: 6925 Town View Lane San Diego 92120 Ofc: Monterey Frames 6512-C El Cajon Blvd, San Diego 92115

POZZO, LUIGI PETER, general building contractor; b. Aug. 20, 1912, Los Angeles; s. Emile Anselmo and Carolina Marie (Ferrante) P.; m. Florice Marjorie Moore, June 6, 1943; children: Louis Richard b. 1944, Victor Moore b. 1947, Caroline Florice b. 1959; edn: bus. adm. USC 1931-33; Cert. in Engring. & Architecture I.C.S., 1938-42. Career: constrn. field wk. Pozzo Construction Co., Los Angeles 1933-36, supervisor 1937-42, senior project mgr. 1946-48, supt. of all constrn. and part owner, 1948-65, sole owner/bd. chmn./CEO, Pozzo Construction Co., 1965--; adv. com. Bank of Amer.; bd. govs. USC; pres. Parents League, USC; v.p. bd. dirs. Braille Inst.; bd. trustees St. John's Hosp. and Med. Ctr., Santa Monica; mem. Edwart Frederick Sorrin Soc. Univ. Notre Dame; constrn. counselor for Sisters of Charitiy of the Incarnate Word, Houston; fmr. mem. Pres's Council Loyola H.S.; honors: Knight of Malta-The Sovereign Mil. Hospitaller Order of St. John of Jerusalem of Rhodes and of Malta; Braille Inst. award of merit; Jiggs award, St. John of God, L.A.; Golden Trowel award; Ceramic Inst. award; USC Man of the Year; USC Alumni Assn. service award; Wall Street Journal award; Plastering Inst. award; mem: Skull & Dagger Hon. Soc., Sigma Chi frat., Los Angeles CofC, US CofC, LA World Affairs Council, Town Hall of Calif. (L.A.), USC Assocs., Commerce Assocs. USC Sch. of Bus., Dean's Council UCLA Sch. Arch.; clubs: California, Los Angeles Country; mil: ofcr. 104th USN Constrn. Batt., WWII, two cits.; Republican; Catholic; rec: golf, fishing, travel. Res: 935 Norman Pl Los Angeles 90049 Ofc: Pozzo Const. Co. 2894 Rowena Ave Los Angeles 90039

PRADA, ALFREDO, computer systems consultant; b. July 20, 1933, Bogota, Colombia, nat. 1985; s. Alfredo and Mercedes (Pulido) P.; m. Maria Elena Pulido, June 30, 1973; children: Constanza, b. 1961, Claudia, b. 1961, Alfredo M., b. 1963, Estella, b. 1966; edn: BSEE, Univ. of Tex. 1958; BSIE, Univ. of Mich. 1961; lic. Indsl. Engr. 1964, Elec. Engr. 1964, Colombia. Career: systems analyst and pgmmr. Exxon, Colombia 1959-62; univ. program coordinator, IBM, Colombia 1962-64; systems and pgmmg. mgr. Ecopetrol, Colombia 1962-68; systems gen. mgr. Colgate Palmolive, Central Am. 1968-71; ops. resrch. dept. head Ecopetrol, Colombia 1971-75; ops. resrch. staff splst. A.G. McKee, Cleveland, Oh. 1975-78; systems cons. Computer Scis. Corp., El Segundo 1978-82; prin./pres. Omni Systems Consultants, Lomita 1982--; coll lectr. sev. univs. in Bogota, Col. 1961-74; awards: Good Neighbour Scholar, Univ. of Tex. 1956-8, Orgn. of Am. States (OAS) Scholar, Univ. of Mich. 1960-1; past mem. AIEE, ACM; publs: profl. conf. proceedings 1967, 69, 72; series of arts. in Software News, 5-11/83; rec: x-country, swimming. Address: Omni Systems Consultants, 25837 Oak St, No. 112, Lomita 90717

PRAEGER, DAN ELY, computer peripheral mfg. co. president; b. Aug. 27, 1957, Los Angeles; s. Edward O. and Lea L. (Barbasch) P.; edn: UCLA, West L.A. Sch. of Law. Career: founder/pres. Hustler Messenger Service, Inc., 1977--; Hustler Air Courier, Inc., 1980--; VOAD Systems, 1982--; presenter seminars to indus.; mem. Beverly Hills CofC, The Contemporary Mus.; author: Telephony Mag.; inventor: VOAD Keyboard Phone; Democrat; Jewish; rec: flying, computers, engineering. Res: 435 So Palm, 1, Beverly Hills 90212 Ofc: VOAD Systems, 10960 Wilshire Blvd, 508, Los Angeles 90024

PRATER, STEPHEN DARRELL, general counsel/ law professor; b. Mar. 18, 1954, Seattle, Wash.; s. Darrell Duane and Joanne Lee (Person) P.; edn: BA, w/ distinction, CSU San Jose 1976; MS, 1978; JD, cum laude, Univ. of Santa Clara 1980; admitted to practice, State Bar of Calif. Career: juvenile probation counselor Santa Clara Co. 1974-76; exec. dir. Kids to Camp Inc. 1976-80; prof. admin. of justice dept. San Jose State Univ., part- time 1980-82; currently, v.p./ gen. counsel Allied Mgmt. Svcs. Inc., Santa Clara; served on eight corp. bds.; prof. ins. law Univ. of Santa Clara Law Sch., part- time; honors: Presidents Scholar 1974, 75, 76; mem: Am. Corp. Counsel Assn.; Soc. of Profl. Benefit Adminstrs.; Am. & Santa Clara Co. Bar Assns.; Calif. Trial Lawyers Assn.; Volunteers In Parole; Community Kids to Camp Inc.; serve on adv. bds. to sev. non- profit orgns.; works: honor's thesis, pub. 1978; Democrat; Catholic; rec: public speaking, politics. Res: 472 N Winchester Blvd, 9, Santa Clara 95050 Ofc: Allied Management Services Inc., 2075 Dela Cruz Blvd Santa Clara 95050

PRENOVOST, THOMAS JOSEPH, (JR.), lawyer; b. Nov. 21, 1950, Phoenix, Ariz.; s. Thomas J. and Kathleen Ann (McDonald) P.; m. Amy E., Sept. 2, 1972; children: Thomas J. III, b. 1978, Michael V. b. 1981; edn: BA (cum laude), CSU Long Beach 1972; JD, Loyola Law Sch. (L.A.) 1977. Admitted to practice in Calif. State and Fed. Courts. Career: city planner City of Placentia, 1974; asst. legislative analyst City of Los Angeles 1975-76; law clk. Davis and Killian, Newport Beach, 1976-77; asst. to City Atty. (Santa Ana and Redondo Beach), Law Offices of Charles Post III, Santa Ana 1976-78; atty., Thomas F. Kamph & Assocs., Santa Ana 1979-79; atty., Law Offices of Roger A. Saevig, Irvine 1979--; dir. Centennial Thrift & Loan 1980-; sole lectr. seminar: How to Fin. and Dev. Large Scale Real Estate Projects (Penton Learning Systems, 18-hr. sem.), three presentations nationwide; judge pro tem Orange County Harbor Municipal Ct.; mem. American, Calif. State, and Orange Co. Bar Assns.; Republican; Catholic; rec: tennis, guitar, softball. Res: 249 E. Brookshire Place Brea 92621 Law Office of Roger A. Saevig, POB 16069, Irvine 92713

PRESNICK, BRUCE DAVID, chiropractor; b. Aug. 5, 1947, NY; s. Samuel B. and Eve (Danvetz) P.; m. Laura, Dec. 22, 1976; 1 dau: Zoe Leia, b. 1978; edn: BA, cum laude, Long Island Univ. 1969; DC, Palmer Coll. of Chiro. 1978. Career: v.p. academic affairs Pacific States Chiro. Coll. 1979; actg. pres. 1980-81; dean of chiro. scis. Life Chiro. Coll.-West 1981-82; founder/developer Getting Started sems. 1982; faculty Prep Seminars 1980-83; pvt. practice 1982--; cont. edn. faculty Life Chiro. Coll. 1983; founder Contra Costa Wholistic Network 1983; honors: Outstanding Svc. Awd., Life Chiro. Coll.-West 1983; mem: Internat. Chiropractors Assn. (Congressional Dist. Rep.); Pleasant Hill CofC (bd. dirs.); Democrat. Res: 2027 Norse Dr Pleasant Hill 94523 Ofc: Presnick Chiropractic Office, 670 Gregory Ln, Ste C, Pleasant Hill 94523

PRESTHUS, TONIA LYNN, marketing exeutive; b. Apr. 24, 1949, Chgo., Ill.; s. Robert Vance and Anita (Larsen) P.; edn: Bach., UCLA 1971; Masters, CSU Los Angeles 1974; PhD, Claremont Grad. Sch. 1980; Cert. Spl. Edn. Career: sales mgr. Pro-Max Eng. Corp.; sales mgr. ACS Communications, Santa Monica; nat. projs. mgr. sales div. Wallace- Berrie, Van Nuys; currently, dir. mktg. Metro Bus. Archives, Los Angeles; dir. mktg. Analytichem Internat., Harbor Ctiy; cons. Family Gp. Homes/ Mental Health Doctors-Katella in Orange; mem: Sales & Mktg. Execs.; Am. Mgmt. Assn.; Cornell Univ. (Debating Soc.); patentee: digital electronic locking sys. 1979; Democrat; Lutheran; rec: motorcycles, tennis, skiing. Res: 18 20th Ave, Ste A, Marina Del Rey 90291 Ofc: Metro Business Archives, 1340 E Sixth St Los Angeles 90021

PRESTON, FREDERICK WILLARD, surgeon/ educator, ret.; b. June 27, 1912, Chgo., Ill.; s. Frederick Augustus and Margaret (Atwater) P.; m. Barbara Hess, July 31, 1961; children: Frederick Willard Jr., b. 1943; David Eldred, b. 1948; William Blackmore, b. 1952; edn: BA, Yale Univ. 1935; MD, Northwestern Univ. 1940; MS, physiol., 1942; MS, surgery, Univ. of Minn. 1948; Physician-Surgeon, Calif. Career: surgical intern Presbyterian Hosp., Chgo., Ill. 1939-40; fellow surgery Mayo Clinic, Rochester, Minn. 1941-24, 1945-48; asst. prof. surgery Northwestern Univ. Med. Sch. 1953-58; assoc. prof. 1958-60; prof. 1960-75; chmn. dept. of surgery Santa Barbara Gen. Hosp. 1975-79; dir. surgical edn. Santa Barbara Cottage Hosp. 1975-83; attdng. surgeon V.A. Hosp., Hines, Ill. 1950-53; attndg. surgeon Northwestern Meml. Hosp., Chgo., Ill. 1950-75; staff V.A. Research Hosp., Chgo., Ill. 1953-78, chief surgical svcs. 1953-67; honors: Life Mem. & mem. Bd. Dirs., Schweppe Found. 1962-; Governing Mem., Scheild Aquarium, Chgo., Ill. 1964-75; mem: Am. Assn. for Cancer Research (pres. Chgo. Sect. 1963-64); Am. Coll. of Surgeons (pres. Chgo. Metro. chpt. 1965-66, Councilor 1967-70); Am. Fedn. Clin. Research; Am. Geriatric Soc.; Am. Med. Assn.; Am., Central, Western & Pacific Coast Surgical Assns.; Am. Trauma Soc.; Assn. for Clin. Surgery; Chgo. Acad. of Scis.; Chgo. Surgical Soc.; Mayo Clinic Alumni Assn.; Societe Internationale de Chirurgie; Soc. for Surgery of the Alimentary Tract; Reticuloendothelial Soc.; Univ. Club, Chgo.; La Cumbre Golf & Country Club, Santa Barbara; Santa Barbara Club; Chgo. Literary Club; works: 128 arts. in surgical journs. of chpts. in books, fields of surgery, surgical research, oncology and trauma; mil: lt. to maj. US Army 1942-45, European Theater 1943-45; Republican; Episcopal; rec: gardening, tennis. Res: 755 Via Airosa Santa Barbara 93110 Ofc: Santa Barbara Cottage Hospital, Bath & Pueblo Streets Santa Barbara 93102

PRICE, AUDIE LEE, aerospace engineer/ executive; b. Jan. 31, 1940, Wytheville, Va.; s. Audie Lee and Vivian Alta (Sutherland) P.; m. Barbara Mc Intyre, Aug. 7, 1940; children: Jason, b. 1971; John, b. 1973; edn: BS, Univ. of San Francisco 1978; MBA, Pepperdine 1980; Profl. Engr., Calif. 1977. Career: sr. engr. Whittaker Corp., San Diego 1969-72; proj. mgr. Brunswick Corp., Deland, Fla. 1972-75; mfg. mgr. Whittaker Corp., San Deigo 1975-76; gen. mgr. mfg. div. Acurex Corp., Mtn. View 1976-83; v.p./ gen. mgr. Vantage Assoc. Inc., San Diego 1983--; cons., all- composite airplane, Goldsworthy Beech; plastic tennis racket, Wilson; mem: SAMPE (profl); AYSO (dir. 1982-83); num. publs. re aerospace & electronic warfare; Republican; Methodist; rec: politics, sports, soccer. Res: 2667 Angell Ave San Diego 92122 Ofc: Vantag Assoc., 6355 Nancy Ridge Dr San Diego 92121 PRIGGE, EDWARD KOEHLER, orthopaedic surgeon, ret.; b. July 15, 1905, Los Angeles; s. Henry and Margaret (Kuehler) P.; m. Lenore Worth, Mar. 19, 1932 (dec.); children: Stephen Worth, b. 1936; Norman Kuehler, b. 1938; edn: AB, Univ. of Calif. 1927; MD, UC Med. Sch. 1931; MD, Calif. 1931. Career: pres: med. staff, Meml. Hosp., Modesto 1953; med. staff Stanislaus Co. Gen. Hosp., Modesto 1953-54; Stanislaus Co. Med. Soc. 1958; Del Rio Country Club, Modesto 1964; Sr. Golf Assn. of No. Calif. 1972; ret. 1976; mem. emeritus: Am., Calif. & Stanislaus Co. Med. Assns.; Western Orthopedic Assn.; Am. Acad. of Orthopedic Surgeons; mem: Del Rio Golf & Country Club; Rotary, Modesto; num. arts. in med. journs. & books; mil: coln. AUS Med. Corps 1942-48; Episcopal; rec: painting (water color & oils), golf. Res: 1209 Edgebrook Dr Modesto 95354

PRICE, JOSETTE (CORINELLE) "CORINNE", community education director; b. July 19, 1947, Medan, Indonesia (Dutch citizenship), nat. 1976; d. Willem and Nelly Geertruida (Reynen) van den Ende; m. Robert K. Price, June 21, 1969; edn: early edn. worldwide during extensive travel with parents (in English, Dutch, German, French); AA, Hartnell Coll. 1968; BA, art, sociol., CSU San Francisco 1971; MA in edn., CSU San Jose 1979; Calif. Std. Tchg. Credential, Adult Edn., Arts and Crafts (life) 1974; Adminstrv. Svc. Cred. 1979-. Career: tchr. of arts and crafts and painting, older and handicapped adults 1971-75; coord. Creative Living Pgm., Salinas Adult Sch., Salinas Union H.S. Dist., 1975-80, dir. of Salinas Adult and Comm. Edn., 1981--; mem. Interdistrict Mgmt. Council; comm. involvement: adv. bd. dirs. Natividad Ranches

Inc. (Boys Ranch), Consortium for Job Opp. Bank pgm., Salinas CoC edn. and econ. devel. coms., Hartnell Coll. Local Ednl. Adv. Com. for Vocational Edn.; past Senior Citizen Conf. Com. 1975-80; mem: Assn. of Calif. Sch. Adminstrs. (State Adult Edn. Com., regl. rep. 1981-; chair Statewide Adult Edn. Fall Workshop 1984); Western Assn. of Schs. and Colls.; Calif. Commn. on Teacher Credentialing 1984; Calif. Consortium of Indep. Study; Calif. Council for Adult Edn. (past chpt. pres.); Delta Kappa Gamma Soc. Intl.; Nat. Assn. for Female Execs.; Phi Delta Kappa; cons. var. sch. dists. in field of gerontology, 1975-80; num. workshop presentations; publs: Educational Programs for Older Adults: A Public School's Response (6/82) New Directions for Contg. Education, No. 14; arts. in ednl. jours., Calif. Dept. of Edn. publs.; Democrat; Prot. Res: 15470 Oak Hills Dr Salinas 93907 Ofc: Salinas Union High Sch Dist, 431 W. Alisal St Salinas 93901

PRICE, LAWRENCE LEE, quality assurance engineering specialist; b. June 17, 1935, Detroit, Mich.; s. William G. and Mae D. (Smith) P.;m. Francis Snyder, June 15, 1957; children: Lawrence b. 1959, Kathy b. 1960, David b. 1962, Thersea b. 1964; edn: Lawrence Inst. Tech. (Southfield, Mich.), Wayne State Univ. Career: Support Planner-mgr., Sr. Data splst., Quality Engr. splst., Rockwell International, 1974--; sr. tech. writer, data mgr., comm. support data mgr., Collins Radio Co., 1967-74; engring. writer, General Electric Co., 1961-66; lectr. Coast Line Comm. Coll.; numerous publs.; mil: USMC Reserv. 1953-54, NY Air Nat. Guard, 174th TAC, Fighter Gp. 1965-66; Indep.; Catholic; rec: home computer, writing. Res: 9662 Surfcrest Dr Huntington Beach 92646 Ofc: Rockwell-Int. CCSD, PO Box 11963, Santa Ana 92711

PRIGGE, EDWARD KOEHLER, orthopaedic surgeon, ret.; b. July 15, 1905, Los Angeles; s. Henry and Margaret (Kuehler) P.; m. Lenore Worth, Mar. 19, 1932 (dec.); children: Stephen Worth, b. 1936; Norman Kuehler, b. 1938; edn: AB, Univ. of Calif. 1927; MD, UC Med. Sch. 1931; MD, Calif. 1931. Career: pres: med. staff, Meml. Hosp., Modesto 1953; med. staff Stanislaus County General Hosp., Modesto 1953-54; Stanislaus Co. Med. Soc. 1958; Del Rio Country Club, Modesto 1964; Senior Golf Assn. of No. Calif. 1972; ret. 1976; mem. emeritus: Am., Calif. & Stanislaus Co. Med. Assns.; Western Orthopedic Assn.; Am. Acad. of Orthopedic Surgeons; mem: Del Rio Golf & Country Club; Rotary, Modesto; num. arts. in med. journs. & books; mil: col. AUS Med. Corps 1942-48; Episcopal; rec: painting (water color & oils), golf. Res: 1209 Edgebrook Dr Modesto 95354Ê

PRITIKIN, NATHAN, longevity center founder- director; b. Aug. 29, 1915, Chgo., Ill.; s. Jacob and Esther (Leavitt) P.; m. Ilene Robbins, Nov. 1, 1947; children: Jack, b. 1941; Janet, b. 1949; Robert, b. 1951; Ralph, b. 1954; Kenneth, b. 1956; edn: Univ. of Chgo. 1933-35; D.Sc., (hon.), Kirksville Coll. of Osteopathic Med. 1982. Career: founder/ pres. var. cos. mfg. precision items for electronics and other tech. applications in Chgo. (Ill.), Santa Barbara (Calif.); hon. fellow, Internat. Acad. Preventive Med.; mem: Gov.'s Council on Wellness & Physical Fitness, apptd. by Gov. Brown 1980; inventions: 43 US and Foreign patents in electronics, physics and chem.; coauthor: bestselling book, Live Longer Now, Grosset & Dunlap 1974; author: Pritikin Pgm. for Diet & Exercise (1 yrs. on NY Times Bestseller List), Grosset & Dunlap 1979; The Pritikin Permanent Weight-Loss Manual, Grosset & Dunlap 1981; The Pritikin Promise, Simon & Schuster, 1983. Ofc: POB 5335 Santa Barbara 93108

PRITSKER, KEITH WAYNE, lawyer; b. June 4, 1952, Los Angeles; s. Bentley Donald and Virginia June (Graff) P.; edn: BA, UC Santa Barbara 1974; JD, Southwestern Univ. Sch. of Law 1977; MA, USC 1978; admitted to practice, State of Calif. 1979. Career: asst. mgr. Virginia's Gift and Plaza Stationary, Palm Springs 1969-74; independent contractor Xerox corp., El Segundo 1975; coord. Intermediate Technology Los Angeles, L.A. 1977-78; assoc. law ofcs. Arnold M. Cowan, Redondo Beach 1979; deputy city atty. City of Los Angeles, LA. 1979-83; currently, agency unit criminal div., Los Angeles City Attys. Ofc.; coord. Assoc. Student Academic Affairs Bd., UC Santa Barbara 1973-74; honors: H.M. Frankel Essay Awd., B'nai Brith 1970; Regents Scholarship, Univ. of calif. 1970-74; Outstanding Young Men. of Am., Jaycees 1977; mem: Calif. Dist. Attys. Assn.; Calif. State Bar; L.A. Trial Lawyers; Assn.; United Lodge of Theosophists (assoc.); Sierra Club; Calif. Conservation Proj.; Food First; Thoreau Found.; Shakespeare Soc. of Am.; works: presentation, experimental edn. at First UCSB Conf. on Effective Tchg., UC 1974; Democrat; Jewish; rec: comparative philosoph, backpacking, naturopathy. Res: 8007 W Fourth St Los Angeles 90048 Ofc: City Attorney's Office, 200 N Main ST, Ste 1600, Los Angeles 90012

PROKSCH, RONALD JAMES, certified public accountant; b. Aug. 29, 1939, La Crosse, Wisc.; s. Charles William and Ruby Marie Proksch; m. Emma, Feb. 14, 1969; children: Lynne,b. 1960; Kelleene, k. 1963; edn: Imperial Valley Jr. Coll. 1961-66; Univ. of Ariz. 1967; AA, Coll. of the Desert 1973; BS, magna cum laude, CSC Bakersfield 1978. Career: controller Maggio- Tostado Inc., Thermal 1967-75; v.p. fin. Marshburn Farms Inc., Norwalk 1977; acct. Daniells,

Phillips, Garner & Vaughan, Bakersfield 1978; acct. Mickey, Casanova & Vaske, Bakersfield 1979-80; controller Verdugo Vineyards Inc., Bakersfield 1980-871; controller David Freedman & Co. Inc., Thermal 1981--; honors: Beta Gamma Sigma, CSC 1977; mem: Calif. Soc. CPAs; Beta Gamma Sigma (pres. 1979); mil: airman 2/c Arizona Air Nat. Guard/ Alabama Air Nat. Guard, Reserve 1956-62; Republican; rec: flying. Res: 82 087 Sundown Ct Indio 92201 Ofc: David Freedman & Co. Inc., POB 501, Thermal 92274

PROTHERO, RAYMOND HARROLD, JR., farmer/ businessman; b. Nov. 13, 1923, Santa Ana; s. Raymond Harrold and Doris Sophia (Bargsten) P.; m. Gladys E. Poage, Nov. 9, 1946; children: William A., b. 1947; Robert D., b. 1948; Nancy D., b. 1952; edn: Santa Ana Jr. Coll. 1941-42; Urban Plnng., UC Irvine Ext. 1968. Career: owner Nurseryman 1939-48; owner Citrus Grower 1948-70; owner Land Management 70-84; pres. Prothero Ent. Inc.; pres. El Toro Farmers Mkt. Inc.; Avocado Grower; dir. Orange Co. Farm Bureau; Olive Heights Citrus Assn.; Associated Farmers of Orange Co.; honors: Svc. Awd., El Toro Water Dist. 1983; mem: Orange Co. Farm Bureau; Associated Farmers of Arengo Co.; Saddleback Area Hist. Soc. (pres. 1976); Saddleback Area Coordg. Council; El Toro Sch. Bd.; Saddleback Comm. Hosp. Bd.; UC Irvine Proj. 21 Open Space Study Team; Guidelines for Devel. of Saddleback Valley; Aliso Creek Corridor; El Toro Water Dist. Bd.; mil: quartermaster 3/c USNI 1944-46; Republican; Christian; rec: square dancing, hunting, fishing. Res: 529 Prospect Fallbrook 92028 Ofc: El Toro Farmer's Market, 23512 El Toro Rd El Toro 92630

PROUT, ROSCOE WILLIAM, oral and maxillofacial surgeon; b. Dec. 21, 1925, Denver, Colo.; s. Roscoe William and Elizabeth Barbara (Obinderfer) P.; m. Joan A. Haiden, Aug. 18, 1956; children: Michelle, . 1957; Mary, b. 1958; Lisa, b. 1960; Haiden, b 1967; Roscoe, b. 1970; edn: AB, UCLA 1951; Univ. of Ore. Grad. Sch. 1953; Univ. of Calif. 1956; DDS, Univ. of the Pacific 1960; Oral and Maxillofacial Surgeon. Career: pvt. practice gen. dentistry, Canoga Park 1960-62; res. dept. of oral & maxillofacial surgery L.A. Co. USC Ctr.; instr. dept. of oral surgery USC Sch. of Dentistry 1963 66; pvt. practice oral & maxillofacial surgery, Woodland Hills 1966-76; attdg. staff dept. of oral & maxillofacial surgery L.A. Co. USC Med. Ctr. 1966--; asst. clin. prof. dept. oral & maxillofacial surgery USC Sch. of Dentistry 1968--; currently, pvt. practice oral & maxillofacial surgery, Trazana Med. Square Tarzana; lectr. USC; honors: fellow, Am. Coll. of Dentists 1982; mem: Am. Dental Assn. (House of Delegates 1979-83); Calif. Dental Assn. (chmn. Council on Ins., trustee House of Delegates Council on Ins. 1977-83); San Fernando Valley Dental Soc. (pres., secty., treas., ed. 1979-84); works: Prout Surgical Nerve Stimulator, mktd. by SRS, Napa; mil: USN; Republican, Catholic; rec: photog. Res: 7921 Lake Vista Dr Encino 91316 Ofc: Ross W. Prout, DDS Inc., 19372 Clark, Ste 224, Tarzana 91356

PROUTY, THOMAS PARKER, electronics engineer; b. Jan. 25, 1928, Los Angeles; s. Harold Samuel and Rose Margaret (Becker) P.; m. Carol Ann Norris, Oct. 10, 1982; children: Patrick, b. 1956; Kathleen, b. 1957; Ann, b. 1958; edn: Calif. Tech. 1945-46; AA, El Camino Jr. Coll. 1948; BS, UCLA 1952; Profl. Engr., Calif 1979. Career: engr. Firestone Tire & Rubber Co. 1952-55; sr. engr. Hallamore Electronics div. Lear Siegler 1955-59; chief engr. Newport Scientific Co. Inc. 1959-62; sr. engr. MHD Research Inc. 1962-63; sr. engr. American Astrophysics Inc. 1963-64; chief engr. Lincoln Dynamics Inc. 1964-65; chief edngr. Microdot Magnetics Inc. 1965; sr. engr. splst. AiResearch Mfg. Co. 1965--; amateur radio opr. K6HJH; mem: IEEE (sr.); rec: motorcycles, computer, photog. Res: 18639 Manhattan Pl Torrance 90504 Ofc: 18639 Manhattan Pl Torrance 90504 Ofc: AiResearch Mfg. Co., Dept. 93-7, 2525 W 190th St Torrance 90509

PROVENZANO, JAMES MICHAEL, securities firm executive; b. Aug. 5, 1948, Los Angeles; s. Joseph Russell and Mary Sarah (Mancuso) P.; m. Sharon Evelyn Gutman, Sept. 11, 1976; edn: BS, fin. ins. real estate, Cal Poly Pomona, 1966-70; major fin., Univ. of Ariz. 1966-70; Licensed, NYSC 1973, NASD 1973, Chgo. Bd. of Trade 1973, Calif. & Nev. Ins. Dept. (inactive) 1976-79. Career: 1970, signed with Houston Astros Professional Baseball Team (pitcher), injured shoulder ended baseball career; account exec. Dean Witter Inc., Whittier 1972-74; account exec. Blyth Eastman Dillon Inc., L.A., Las Vegas, Nev. 1974-79; asst. mgr. Dean Witter Ofc., Billings, Mont. 1979-80; broker Merrill Lynch, L.A. 1980-81; assoc. vice pres./asst. mgr. Bateman Eichler Hill Richards, Anaheim 1981--; awards: All League Football Basketball Baseball, Temple City High School (1964 66); full scholarship, baseball, Univ. of Ariz. 1966-70; Academic Honor Roll, and Pres's Hon. List, CalPoly 1971-2; Ranked in Nation: 9th in strikeouts, Collegiate Baseball Statistics 1968; mem. Profl. Baseball Assn. 1970-71; mem. Associated Person Commodities Futures Trading Commn.; Sigma Alpha Epsilon frat. alumni; Western Bass Fishing Assn., Bass Anglers Sportsman Soc.; Democrat; Catholic; rec: hunting, fishing, skiing. Res: 580 Paseo Lucero Anaheim Hills 92807 Ofc: Bateman Eichler Hill Richards, 451 W. Lincoln, Ste 150, Anaheim 92805

PRYOR, ANNIE RUTH, real estate broker; b. Oct. 25, 1936, Ariton, Ala.; d. Homer and Fannie (Kelley) Pryor; edn: Wilson Coll. 1952-4, psychol., Univ of Chgo., 1960s; Nsg. Degree, Grant Hosp., Chgo. 1954-57; Reg. Nurse, Ill., Calif.; Calif. lic. real estate broker. Career: operating room nse., Univ. of Chgo. hosps., 1957-67, as staff nurse, clin. instr., and hd. nse.; op. rm. nse. Sequoia Hosp., Redwood City, Calif. 1968; office nse.; physician asst.; priv. scrub nse., 1969; op. room nse. Los Gatos Comm. Hosp. 1969-79; real estate agt. 1978-82, real estate broker/owner, 1982--; op. room nse. Good Samaritan Hosp., San Jose 1982--; mem. Assn. of Operating Room Nurses, O'Connor

Hosp. Auxilary (vol. Gift Shop), Calif. Assn. of Realtors, Nat. Assn. of Realtors; sponsor Boy Scout Explorer Post No. 850, vol. camp nse.; Republican; Baptist; rec: painting, knitting, table tennis. Address: Pryors Assoc., 671 Division St. Campbell 95008

PRUITT, BUCKLEIGH XAVIER, quality control executive; b. Aug. 4, 1938, Los Angeles; s. Eddie Lee and Elizabeth (Hopkins) Pruitt; A.A., Pruitt Coll of Business 1963; stu. Compton Coll. 1958-59; stu. night classes, L.A. City Coll., Mt. San Antonio Coll., Costa Mesa Coll; m. Donna Bateman, Feb. 14, 1981; Chil: Robyn, b. 1962; Marc, b. 1964; Stacey, b. 1970; Cash, b. 1974. Career: calibration test engr., inspection supr. Rockwell Autonetic Div., Anaheim 1960-68; test quality engineer group leader General Dynamics, Pomona 1968-70; quality program mgr., program quality enineer, group leader Hughes Aircraft Co., Fullerton 1970-79; quality assurance mgr., acting quality director American Telecom Inc., Anaheim 1979-81; quality control mgr. Hydraulic Units (subs. Boeing Co.), Duarte 1981---. Registered Profl. Engr. in Quality Engineering, Ca., 1976. Mem. American Soc. Quality Control, 1981 ; past mem. Hughes Aircraft Mgmt. Club, Natl. Mgmt. Assn. 1968. Co-author: Commercial Workmanship Standards Manual 1980; Military Workmanship Standards Manual 1977. Democrat. Catholic. Rec: chess, coaching youth sports. Res: 1119 Border Ave., Corona 91720; Office: Hydraulic Units Inc., 1700 Business Center Dr., Duarte 91010.

PRZYBYLA, MARY JANE C, supervisor — blood bank serology; b. May 21, 1924, Milwaukee, WI; d. Joseph Herman and Stella Theresa (Lemanski) Przybyla; edn: BS, Mount Mary College, 1946, Grad. work, Stanford Univ., 1947-48; Central Michigan Univ. 1972-78; Certified in Program for continuing Edn. Med. Tech. by Calif. Assoc. of Med. Lab. Tech. June 1972; Career: Med. Tech. St. Mary's Hosp, Tucson, Ariz. 1946-47; spec. Bact. & Blood Bank Palo Alto Hosp, Palo Alto 1947-51; M.T. Spec. Bact. & Blood Bank St. Francis Hosp, San Francisco 1951-52; M.T. Bact. Santa Barbara Cnty. Hosp. Santa Barbara, 1952; Research Inf. Comm. Calif. Public Health Dept., Berkeley 1952; Gen. Med. Tech. Dr. E. W. Tucker, Monterey 1953-55; Supervisor Blood Bank-Serology Silas B. Hays Army Hosp., Fort Ord, 1955---; recipient 8 Dept. of Army outstanding performance of duty awards; Mem: Amer. Assoc. of Blood Banks 1962---; Calif. Assoc. of Med. Tech Sect. local chpt. 1961; mem. since 1961---; Amer. Soc. of Clinical Pathologists, Amer. Soc. of Med. Tech. 1970-79; Bolsa Nueva Homeowners Assoc. treasurer 1980-81. mem. 1975. Co-author: paper "Lewis Antibodies of Long Duration" Calif. Assoc. Med. Tech Meeting 1961; paper presented at Amer. Assoc. of Blood Banks 1962. poster presentation at Amer. Assoc. of Blood Banks 1981. Catholic. Rec: travel, gardening. Res: 15375 Charter Oak Blvd., Salinas 93907, Office: Silas B Hays Army Hosp., Fort Ord 93941.

PUDNEY, GARY LAURENCE, television executive; b. July 20, 1934, Minneapolis, MN; s. Lawrence D. and Agnes (Hansen) Pudney; edn: BA, UCLA, 1956. Career: with Young & Rubicam Advt. Agency, NYC 1960-63, Compton Advt. Agency, NYC 1964-66; v.p. ABC, Inc., 1967---, v.p. spl projects, sr. exec. in charge of talent ABC Entertainment, Los Angeles 1979---; mem: Nat. Cerebral Palsy Found., Hollywood Radio & TV Soc., Acad. TV Arts & Sciences (bd. dirs.). Mil: Capt. USAF 1957-60. Democrat. Lutheran. Office: ABC Entertainment, 2040 Ave. of the Stars, Century City, Los Angeles 90067.

PUGLIA, FRANK VINCENT, lawyer; b. Aug. 1, 1949, Riverdale, MD; s. Frank Vincent and Winnefred Pearle (Crosier) Puglia Sr.; edn: BS law, Western St. Univ. 1974, Juris Doctor, Western St. Univ. 1975; Career: Attorney in private practice 1976-78, 1978-80 Attorney with Lewis, Aex, & Puglia Attorneys at Law 1980---; Attorney in pvt. practice San Diego 92103; Judge pro tem in San Diego Municipal Court; Court Appointed Attorney Class 111; State of Calif. College Instr. Credentials; Awards: Achievement Award-Operation Share 1972, Karate Trophy, Amer. Tae Kwon Do Assn. 1982; Mem: Former Pres. of Balboa Park Athletic Council 1978, Former v.p. of Operation Share 1972; Successful Appeal in the Fourth District Court of Appeals expanding the law of Hearsay Exceptions. See 123 C.A. 3d 677; Mil: Corporal U.S. Marine Corps 1968-70, Force Recon Vietnam. Republican. Catholic. Rec: karate-tae kwon do, scuba diving, sport parachuting, collect gold stamps, breed afghans cooking. Res: 1804 North 39th St., San Diego 92105; Office: Frank V. Puglia, Attorney at Law, 1125 W. Olive, San Diego 92103.

PUGMIRE, AVERILL ARNELL, financial planner; b. April 20, 1920, St. Charles, ID; s. V. Lamont and Myrtle A. (Arnell) Pugmire; edn: Bach. of Mortuary Sci., San Francisco College of Mortuary Sci. 1947; m. Maurine Bodily, June 7, 1944; chil: Gordon, b. 1945; Judy, b. 1947; Thad b. 1951; Amy, b. 1958. Career: route supervisor Gates Towel & Linen Supply 1947-52; Embalmer/Counselor Greenwood Mem. Park & Mortuary 1952-1962; Sales Rep. & Regional mgr. Delger Corp. 1962-71; Sales Rep. & v.p. Financial Planning Counselors 1971-82; Awards: Pres. of San Diego Chpt. of Intern. Assn. of Financial Planners 1976; Secretary of Informed Voters League 1980-82; Dir. of the San Diego Genealogy Assn. 1980-82; Mem: Intern. Assoc. for Financial Planning (one of 6 charter mem.) 1968-82; North Park San Diego Kiwanis Club 1962-82; Bd. of Dir. San Diego Service Center for the Blind 1976-82; San Diego/El Cajon Chpt. Informed Voters League mem. 1976-82. Works: family man 5 married chil., all contributors to Amer. Soc. Services. Mil: WWII Pharmacist Mate 2C Iwo Jima Okinawa Invasions Sept. 1943-Dec. 1945. Church of Jesus Christ of Latter-Day Saints, Mormon, 14 years Bishop. Rec: gardening, jogging. Res: 5017 Hilda Rd., San Diego 92110; Office: Financial Planning Counselors, 7860 Mission Center Ct., #103, San Diego 92108,

PULCRANO, DAN M., newspaper publisher; b. Oct. 1, 1958, New Brunswick, NJ; s. Charles Anthony and Edith (Tanner) Pulcrano; BA, UC Santa Cruz, 1980. Career: ed. in chief, Leviathan, 1977-80; reporter, Santa Barbara News in Review, 1978; cons., L.A. Weekly, 1978-79; adv. dir., Bonita Post, 1978; ed., publ., Santa Cruz Fall Guide, 1980-82; ed., publ., Santa Cruz Weekly, 1981; ed., publ., Los Gatos Weekly, and pres., Los Gatos Communications, Inc., 1982—; journalism instr., UC Santa Cruz, 1978. Mem: Los Gatos Rotary Club, youngest mem. in club's history. Author: articles syndicated nationally for weekly and specialty publications. Res: 16206 Rose Ave., Monte Sereno 95031; Office: Los Gatos Weekly, P.O. Box 65, 114 Royce St., Los Gatos 95030.

PULEC, JACK LEE, neuro-otologic physician; b. July 12, 1932, Crete, NE; s. Anton and Antonette (Divoky) Pulec; edn: B.A., Univ. of Nebr. (Lincoln) 1955, Creighton Med. Sch. (Omaha) 1953-55, M.D., Univ. of Nebr. College of Med. 1957, M.S., Univ. of Minnesota, 1962; m. Marlene Aron, 1951; Chil: Marilyn, b. 1953; Career: Internship-Bishop Clarkson Memorial Hosp. Omaha 1957-58, Res. in Obstet. & Gyn, Univ. of Nebr. College of Med. 1958-59; Res. Otolaryngology, Mayo Grad. Sch. of Med. 1959-62; pvt. practice of Otolaryngology, Omaha, 1962-63, Fellowship in Neuro-otology, L.A. Foundation of Otology 1963-64; Staff cons. in Neuro-otology Mayo Clinic, 1964-69; pvt. practice-Otology-Mayo Clinic 1969-76, pvt. practice, Pulec Ear Clinic, L.A. 1976—; asst. prof. Otolaryngol. Mayo Grad. Sch., 1963-69; assoc. clin. prof., Otolaryngol., USC Sch. of Med. 1974—; Dir. M.S. in Otology, program of USC and Ear Resrch Inst. 1974-76; dir. Temporal Bone Surgical Dissection Lab. 1969-76; dir. Vestibular Test Lab. 1970-75; dir. of resrch. bd. dirs. Ear Resrch Inst. 1974-76; pres. of Ear Internat., 1976—. cons. to minister of health in Abu Dhabi, Egypt, Kuwait, Iran; cons. Nat. Inst. of Neurol. Diagnosis and Blindness 1967-68, US Dept. of Navy 1971—; NASA-Skylab Space Shuttle 1974. Awards: First Annual Prof. Doctor Ignatio Barraquer Meml. award, Chgo. 1965; AMA Billings Bronze Medal, 1969; award for disting. svcs in the ednl programs of Amer. Acad. of Opthalmol. and Otolaryngol., 1971; Dr. S.G. Joshi Meml. Award Gold Medal, India, 1980; mem: AMA, CMA, L.A. Co. Med. Assn., L.A. Soc. of Otol., Resrch Study Club of L.A., Southbay Med. Assn., Amer. Acad. of Opthal. and Otol., Amer. Assn. for Automotive Med., Amer. Audiology Soc., Am. Coll of Surgeons, Amer. Council of otol., Amer. Laryngol., Rhinol. and Otol. Soc. Inc, Amer. Neurotolgy Soc.(v.p. 1976-77), Amer. Otol. Soc., Centurians Deafness Resrch Found. (asst sec. treas 1974), Pac. Coast Oto-Ophthal. Soc., Sigma Xi, NY Acad. of Scis., Barany Soc. (exec. council 1971-74), Fellow Royal Soc. of Med. Works: (12) 16mm color films for medical instrn., (6) medical exhibits in field; resrch in otology and neuro-otology. Republican. Congregational. Rec: travel, camping, automotive engr.. Res: 1054 Vista Grand, Pacific Palisades 90272; Office: Pulec Ear Clinic, 1245 Wilshire Blvd., #503, Los Angeles 90017.

PULLIAM, PAUL EDISON, electrical engineer; b. June 6, 1912, Nickerson, KS; s. George Washington and Hattie Lucy (Vandeventer) Pulliam; edn: ROTC to 2nd Lt., FA-Res, Univ. of Mo., 1937; various spec. courses incl. radar-electornics, completed as a reserve ofcr.; BS in EE, Univ. of Mo., 1951; m. Ila M. Catrett, Feb. 3, 1945; chil: Carol Ann, b. 1946; Paula Ann, b. 1953. Career: elec. engr. Ozark Dam Constructors, bldg. hydroelec. powerhouse ato Bull Shoals Dam in Baxter Co., Ark. 1951-52; mech. plan checker, Clark Co. Bldg. & Safety Dept., Las Vegas, Nev.; construction inspector, Regional Waste Water Treatment Plant, Sacramento Co. Dept. of Pub. Works, Sacto. Lic. Elec. Profl. Engr., Mo., Nev., Calif.; qualified as Guided Missile Officer, Fort Bliss, Tex., 1949; provided two concepts used in devel. of thermonuclear hydrogen bombs, 1949; served as State Advisor on US Congl. Advisory Bd. 1982. Honors: Army Commend. award for suggesting WWII F.A. use of Radar Set SCR-584 and formation of Radar Set SCR-784; named the Polaris Weapon System (1952), named the Pershing Weapon System at Redstone Arsenal, Ala.; provided definition and coined term "afterburner" for jet aircraft thrust reaction in 1949, Ft. Bliss. Mem: Reserve Officers Assn. of the USA (life and 45-yr mem.), IEEE (life mem.), Amer. Soc. of Mil. Engineers, Instrument Soc. of Amer. (sr. mem.). Mil: served Pvt. to Cpl., FA, 1930-34, 2nd Lt. to Maj., FA-Res. US Army, ret. 1972. Democrat. Baptist. Rec: Electric Auto Assn., Sacto. chpt. Res: 7916 Grandstaff Dr., Sacramento 95823.

PUNCHARD, ANTHONY PRICE, immunohematologist, geneticist; b. Aug. 18, 1941, Amitt, LA; s. Thomas J. and Ethel (Fields) Punchard; Edn: Ph.D., UC Berkeley, 1975; USC Sch. of Med., 1970-73; BS, CSU Fullerton, 1963-64; AA, Long Beach City Coll., 1960-61; m. Nancy Espie, Aug. 18, 1980; chil: Anthony Jr.; Donna; Stephanie; Mario. Career: dir. of lab., hematology, So. Calif. Diagnostic Labs, Inc., L.A.; lab. dir., Family Health Center, L.A., —; lab. dir., Crenshaw Park Med. Center, L.A.; research scientist, Bio-Stat Labs., Inc., Hollywood; sr. adv. for med. sci., mem. The U.S. Congl. Advisory Bd. Honors: Appreciation, Center for Disease Control, 1975. Mem: Masons; Knight of Malta, 1981; Worthy Patron of Eastern Star, 1981; Phi Chi med frat. Amer. Assn. of Clinical Pathologists; Coll. of Amer. Pathologists. Works: developed Nordorpharin Vaccine for hemoglobin-S disease, 1975; author: The Last Cavalier, 1983. Mil: 1st Lt., USMC, enlisted in 1958; became fighter pilot; Navy Cross, Purple Heart, Vietnam Cross of Gallantry. Democrat. Catholic. Rec: writing, boating, flying. Res: 1637 Veteran Ave., Apt. 9, Westwood 90024; Office: Charles L. Cooke Family Health Center, 2706 W. Jefferson Blvd., Los Angeles 90018.

PUPLAVA, JAMES JOSEPH, investment advisor; b. Oct. 13, 1950, Whiting, Ind.; s. Joseph James and Helen Ann (Soltis) P.; m. Mary Best, Jan. 8, 1977; children: Ryan James, b. 1978; Christopher Michael, b. 1979; Adam Cole, b. 1981; edn: AA, Phoenix Coll. 1974; BS, cum laude, Ariz. State 1976; MIM, Am. Grad. Sch. of Internat. Mgmt. 1977; CFP, Coll. for Fin. Plnng., Denver, Colo. 1982; RIA, Securities & Exch. Commn. Career: Arthur Andersen & Co., Phoenix, Ariz. 1977-78; principal HTP Inc., Scottsdale, Ariz. 1978-81; principal Puplava-Faulkner, Carlsbad 1981--; fund raising Am. Cancer Soc.; preparing new CME course for Physician at UCSD; honors: Scholarship to Am. Grad. Sch., Ariz. State; mem: IAFP; works: weekly investment art. in San Marcos Courier; mil: C-2 US Army 1971; Republican; Catholic; rec: martial arts, sailing, tennis. Res: 13621 Del Poniente Poway 92064 Ofc: Puplava-Faulkner, 2121 Palomar Airport Rd, Ste 303, Carlsbad 92008

PURCELL, JOSEPH FRED, temporary services co. executive; b. Dec. 14, 1942, Newark, NJ; s. Joseph Joseph and Nevina Susan (Mirabella) Purcell; BA, mktg., Seton Hall Univ., 1965; m. Mary Ellen Nolan, Apr. 21, 1979; chil: Joseph, b. 1965; Michael, b. 1968; Jennifer, b. 1980. Career: sales mgr., Romney Cosmetics, 1967; sales mgr., Westline Products, 1968; pres.: Purcell Employment Systems, Purcell Temporaries, Purcell Tech. Services, Purcell Executive Search, 1969—; various seminars. Honors: L.A. Area Civic Award, Jaycees, 1981. Mem: Acad. of Advanced Traffic, NYC, 1963. Res: 11688 Moraga Lane, Los Angeles 90049; Office: Purcell Group, 4311 Wilshire Blvd., Los Angeles 90010.

PURCELL, TONY LECH, realtor; b. Mar. 30, 1924, Poznan, Poland, nat. 1976; s. Bogdan and Ewa (Wroblewska) Przyluski; m. Feliksa, b. 1948; m. 2d. Alicia, Jan. 28, 1973; children: Gina, b. 1949; Lydia, b. 1952; edn: Bach., Inst. of Econ. 1951; Masters, 1964; Real Estate Salesman (1971), Broker (1975), Calif. Career: rep. (cargo supvr.) Bergman & Jorgenson on Copenhagen, Poland 1952-57; diplomatic assignment, Bucharest, Romania 1957-62; head dept. for Polish Nat. Export- Importer Co. 1962-68; asst. mgr. American Tempering Inc., Union City, Calif. 1968-70; trader Kaiser Trading (subsidiary Kaiser Aluminum), Oakland 1970-71; real estate practice, mid Peninsula, San Mateo Co. 1971--; Rupert Taylor Real Estate, San Mateo 1971-72; Cauchi Realty, S.M. 1972-78; owner/ pres. Purcell Realty, San Mateo 1978--; honors: Life Mem., Million Dollar Club 1973; mem: Nat. & Calif. Assns. Realtors; San Mateo-Burlingame Bd. Realtors; Nat. Notary Assn.; Kiwanis Club; linguist: Eng., Ger., Polish, Rumanian & Russian; mil: Freedom Fighter against Nazi occupation in Poland 1939-40; P.O.M.; Nazi prisons & concentration camps, incl. Berlin- Spandau, liberated by American Army in Mauthausen, Austria (1945), 1940-45; Republican; Catholic; rec: aviation, swimming, tennis. Res: 401 W Hillsdale Blvd San Mateo 94403

PURDY, CHARLES EDWARD, IV, lawyer; b. May 27, 1956, Minnpls., Minn.; s. Charles E. Purdy III and Gene T. (Peirce) Thulin; edn: BA, honors, Univ. of Wisc. 1978; JD, magna cum laude, Univ. of San Diego 1981; admitted to practice, State Bar of Calif. 1981. Career: extern US Ct. of Appeals Judge J. Clifford Wallace 1980; assoc. atty. Ferris, Brennan, et al. 1980-83 currently, sole practitioner (spec. corp. matters), San Diego; regular cons. to var. firms; tchr. on aspects of corp. law, var. instns.; honors: ed., USD Law Review; mem: Am. & San Diego Co. Bar Assns.; publs: on Fourth Amendment and Internat. Terrorism, USD Law Review 1979; regular contbr. edl. pages of Los Angeles and San Diego Newspapers; rec: swimming, writing, skiing. Res: 4528 Boundary St San Diego 92116 Ofc: Charles E. Purdy IV, 2726 Fifth Ave San Diego 92103

PURDY, RUTH MELISSA SANDERS, family therapist/ university professor; b. Nov. 5, 1910, Rock, Okla.; d. Henry Allen and Ada Selena (Payton) Sanders; m. Allen B. Purdy, Sept. 14, 1935; children: Joseph D., b. 1937; John, b. 1941; edn: BA, CSU Long Beach 1951; MA, 1952; PhD, Univ. of Okla. 1966; extensive post doctoral studies. Career: instr. Long Beach City Coll. (estab. & devel. 1st coll. reading lab. & 1st individ.- instrn. adult edn. lab.), Long Beach 1952-58; marriage, family & child therapist Pacific Counseling Ctr., Fullerton 1976-81; dir. Christian Counseling Ctr., Huntington Beach 1981--; adj. prof. Sch. of Psychology, Orange Co. Ctr., Pepperdine Univ., Malibu 1977--; treas Western Coll. Reading Assn. 1974-75; archivist 1979-; secty. Orange Co. chpt. Calif. Assn. Marriage & Family Therapists 1979-80; secty. Calif. Soc. for Hypnosis in Family Therapy 1982--; advr. US Congressional Adv. Bd.; mem: Internat. Reading Assn., Long Beach chpt. (past pres.); PTA; Toastmistress; Am. & Calif. Assns. of Marriage, Family, Child Therapists; Calif. Soc. for Hypnosis in Family Therapy; Western Coll. Reading Assn.; Internat. Coll. for Hypnosis; Council for Exceptional Children; Nat. Alliance for Family Life Inc. (founding clin. mem.); works: PhD dissertation 1966; textbook, English Basics for Clerical Workers, 1981; Republican; Christian; rec: book and stamp collections, travel. Res: 9400 Larkspur Dr Westminster 92683 Ofc: Christian Counseling Center of Huntington Beach, 1207 Main St Huntington Beach 92648

PURI, ARUN K., engineer/investor/restaurateur; b. July 25, 1944, Moga, India, nat. 1980; s. Gopal Krishan and Usha Puri (Kapoor) Puri; Edn: MA, engring., Unif. of Detroit, MI, 1969; m. Urmil Mengi, Mar. 11, 1972; chil: Shalini, b. 1973; Richa, b. 1974. Career: asst. prof., Punjab Engring. Coll., Chandegarh, India; chief engr., Midwest Prestren Concrete, Springfield, IL; sales devel. dir., Rockwin Corp., Santa Fe Springs, CA; mgr., investment, Goldenwest Realtors, Buena Park; mng. gen. partner, Royal Khyber Restaurant, Newport Beach; pres. Frontier Video Games, El Cajon; pres., Arun K. Puri, Inc., La Palma. Awards: Profl. Engr., St. of Calif.; "Most Progressive New Corner" So. Calif. Restaurant Assn., Royal Khyber Restaurant. Rec: tennis, camping. Address: 8 Drakes Bay Dr., Corona del Mar 92625.

PURVES, DAVID WILLIAM, figure skater; b. May 14, 1960, Tubingen, Germany; s. William Kirkwood and Jean Eleanor (McCauley) Purves; edn: BA, Calif. State Polytechnic Univ., Pomona, 1982. Career: mgr., Baskin-Robbins 31 Flavors Ice Cream Store #101, #3077, and #3171, Claremont, 1978---. Awards: Competitive Figure Skating (Ice Dancing): Southwest Pacific Reg. Novice Dance Champ., 1980; Pac. Coast Sectional Novice Dance Silver Medalist, 1980; SW Pacific Reg. Jr. Dance Silver Medalist, 1981; Pac. Coast Sectional Jr. Dance Silver Medalist, 1981; U.S. Natl. Champs. Jr. Dance, Eighth, 1981; SW Pacific Reg. Jr. Dance Champ., 1982; Pac. Coast Sectl. Jr. Dance Champ., 1982; U.S. Natl. Champs. Jr. Dance, Sixth, 1982; U.S. Figure Skating Assn. Gold Dance Medalist, 1982; honors: Dean's List, Honoree for high academic standards, 1982; U.S. Figure Skating Assn. Trial Judge, 1982. Mem: pres., Arctic Blades Figure Skating Club, 1982-83. Rec: photography, music appreciation, art, automobiles, audio equipment. Res: 2817 N. Mountain Ave., Claremont 91711; Office: Baskins-Robbins, 973 W. Foothill Blvd., Claremont 91711.

PURVIANCE, ALBET ROSS, water consultant; b. Apr. 19, 1918, Bellota, CA; s. Bruce Ray and Beth Rozena (Kirk) Purviance; m. Joan Izetta Roehm, July 27, 1941; chil: Albert Ross Jr., b. 1943; Cynthia Ann, b. 1959. Career: Purviance Drillers, 1935-41; So. Pacific Railroad, Sacto., 1941-42; Pan Amer. Engring., Berkeley, 1942-43; Purviance Drillers, Linden, 1943-51; established own bus. 1951; water well driller for Purviance Drillers; foundry moulder helper at S.P. in Sacto.; Cert. High Pressure Electric welder at Pan Amer. in Berkeley; and water well driller; also water cons., locally and area. Mem: Odd Fellows Lodge, Scio 102, Linden, v-grand.; F&AM Mason, Valley Lodge 135, 3rd deg., Linden; Linden O.E.S. 372; Scottish Rite, Stockton, 32nd Deg. Builds and constructs eqpt. as needed for work. Republican, dir. Linden-Peters Fire Dept.; past dir., Linden Co. Water Dist. Methodist. Rec: auto racing, cars, reading. Res: 5060 N. Alfalfa St., Linden 95236; Shop: Ross Purviance Well Drilling, 7930 Waverly Rd.

PURVIS, RENE' CHARLES, educator; b. Apr. 20, 1948, Djakarta, Indonesia, nat. 1966; s. Charles and Johanna (Witveen) Purvis; edn: AA, L.A. Harbor Coll., 1978; BA, CSU Dominguez Hills, 1980; MA, pending fall '82, CSU Dominguez Hills; m. Charlotte Wilms, Aug. 29, 1979; chil: Gina, b. 1976; Wendy, b. 1982. Career: counselor intern, CSU Dominguez Hills, Carson, 1981-82; supv., Castle Park, Redondo Beach, 1982; sub. tchr., Lennox School Dist., Lennox, CA, 1981-82. Mil: E-4, Air Natl. Guard and Army Natl. Guard; USAF E-3, 1975-77. Independent. Non-denominational Christian. Rec: photography, singing/songwriting, bowling, ping-pong. Res: 211 W. Brownwood, #3, Anaheim 92801; Office: Lennox School Dist., 10319 Firmona Ave., Lennox 90304.

PUSSELL, ALBERT, real estate broker; b.Mar. 27, 1915, Los Angeles; s. Barney and Yetta (Bender) P.; m. Ruth Reinglass, June 8, 1936; children: Jo Anne b. 1937, Ronald b. 1943; edn: real estate courses, UCLA Ext. 1960s; Contg. Edn. courses rel. to real estate and investments; Calif. lic. real estate broker 1958. Career: helped parents operate Grocery & Veg. Market, Venice, Calif. 1929; owner A & A Tire Bus., Culver City, 1937; owner/builder apartments, Beverly Hills, 1948; real estate salesman Guy Price Co., Bev. Hills 1952; owner/broker Albert Pussell Realty Co., Bev. Hills 1958-73, builder/mgr. neighborhood shopping centers in L.A. County, 1960s-73; temp. retirement 1973-75; real estate sales George Elkins Co., Newport Beach 1975; owner/broker Albert Pussell Realty, Newport Beach 1978-80, founder/bd. chmn. Pussell Corp. (formed corp. combining R.E. and son's Rare Antique Books), and R.E. broker/mgr. Albert Pussell Real Estate Div. 1980--; fmr. BSA Scoutmaster and active in Juvenile Protection, B.H., 1950s-60s; mem: Federation Internat. Real Estate (FIABCI), Nat. Assn. of Realtors, R.E. Assoc. of Newport Beach-Costa Mesa, Nat. Assn. of Small Bus.; past mem. Optimists, CofC (Culver City); mem. Balboa Bay Club, Six O'clock Club (mens); Republican; rec: boating, fishing. Res: 1221 W. Coast Hwy, 409, Newport Beach 92663 Ofc: Pussell Corp. 1501 Westcliff, Ste. 220, Newport Beach 92663

PUTERBAUGH, KATHRYN ELIZABETH, corporate executive; b. Mar. 5, 1924, Denver, Colo.; d. Fredric John and Cora Kathryn (Zoph) P.; edn: AB, Univ. of Colo. 1945. Career: acct. F.J. Puterbaugh & Co., Denver, Colo. 1946-49; secty./ asst. Hebert Bayer, Aspen, Colo. 1950-51; acct. Himel's, New Orleans, La. 1951-53; asst. controller Berol Pen Co., Va. 1953-54; ofc. mgr./ controller Garratt- Callahan Co., Millbrae, Calif. 1955-65; corp. treas, ibid 1966--; bd. dirs. 1971--; dir. G-C Lubricants Co. 1981-; dir. The Specialty Lubricants Co. 1981-; mem: Nat. Assn. Acts.; Soroptimist Internat. of the Ams., Millbrae- San Bruno; Calif. Republican; San Francisco Mus. Soc.; Mills Meml. Hosp. Assn.; Bear Valley Ski Club; Republican (Nat. Com.); Episcopal; rec: gardening, skiing, golf. Res: 3382 Brittan Ave San Carlos 94070 Ofc: Garratt- Callahan Company, 111 Rollins Rd, Millbrae 94030

PUTHAWALA, AJMEL A., radiation oncologist; b. June 11, 1946, Ahmedabad, India; s. Adbulkadir K. and Sarfunisa A. (Kathawala) P.; m. Nasreen Fjodar, Feb. 15, 1976; children: Raina, b. 1979; Erfan, b. 1981; edn: MB, BS, B.J. Med. Coll., Ahmedabad, India 1969; MD, NY State Univ. 1974; Diploma, Am. Bd. of Radiology 1975. Career: consulting radiation oncology & endocurietherapist: So. Calif. Cancer Ctr., Calif. Hosp. Med. Ctr.; Desert Hosp., Palm Springs; Methodist Hosp. of So. Calif., Arcadia; Martin Luther Hosp. & Med. Ctr., Anaheim; currently, assoc. dir. dept. of radiation oncology, Meml. Med. Ctr. of Long Beach; assoc. clin. prof. radiation sci., UC Irvine; assoc. clin. prof. radiology USC Sch. of Med.; honors: pres. Am. Endocurietherapy Soc. 1982; mem: Am. Coll. of Radiology; Am. Soc. of

Therapeutic Radiology; Radiological Soc. of No. Am.; Calif. Radiological Soc.; publs: num. arts. on interstitial radioactive implants for treatment of var. human cancers; rec: sailing, skiing, hiking. res: 11859 Cresta Verde Dr Whittier 90601 Ofc: Memorial Medical Center, 2801 Atlantic Ave Long Beach 90801

PUTNAM, GREGORY BLANCHARD, architectural management consultant; b. July 23, 1947, Oakland; s. Thomas Milton and Margaret Melanie (Warnecke) P.; m. Caryl Smutz, Aug. 24, 1968; children: Tadd, b. 1074; Eric, b. 1976; edn: BFA, Univ. of N.Mex. 1969. Career: architectural drafter- designer var. firms, Albuquerque, N.Mex.; principal architectural svcs., Albuquerque, N.Mex. 1970-71; v.p. firmwide admin., John Carl Warnecke & Assoc., NY, Wash. DC & San Francisco,Calif. 1971-78; principal/ v.p./ dir. ops. Environmental Plnng. & Research Inc., S.F. 1978-82; pres. Putnam Mgmt. Consultants Inc., Oakland 1982--; exec. com. to BOD, John Carl Warnecke & Assc. 1983; secty., pres. Profl. Svcs. Mgmt. Assn.; dir. Profl. Pgm.; design build automation; honors: AIA, Grad. Sch. Scholarship; Awds. in appreciation of great work &svc. to the design profession, PSMA; mem: AIA (chmn. of cost Svcs. Com. 1974); PSMA (chmn. Edn. & Research Com. 1979, dir. 1983-84); Task Force on Ownership Trasition in the Design Professions 1982; chmn. Land Use & Zoning Com. & delegate, Allied Civic Gp., Indian Springs Civic Assn., Silver Springs, Md. 1973-74; num. arts. in industry journs.; contbg. ed., Progressive Architecture; mil: sgt. New Mex. Air Nat. Guard 1969-71; Republican; rec: art, skiing. Address: Putnam Management Consultants Inc., 902 Longridge Rd Oakland 94610

PUTZKA, GREGORY JAMES, marriage and family therapist; b. May 21, 1952, Minnpls., Minn.; s. Gordon Russell and Elva May (Miller) Pe; m. Margaret A. Fjelstad, Oct. 18, 1980; edn: BS, CSU Sacto. 1976; Calif. Secondary Tchg. Cred. 1976; MS, 1979; Lic. Marriage, Family & Child Counselor, Hynotherapist, Calif. 1982. Career: instr. Cyesis Pgm., Sacto. 1977-79; group leader New Morning, Placerville 1979; counselor: CSU Sacto. Counseling Ctr., White House Counseling Ctr., & Slocan House, Sacto. 1978-80; educator/ tnr. Planned Parenthood, Sacto. 1980--; exec. dir./ chmn. bd. Threshold Ednl. & Counseling Ctr., Sacto. 1980--; cons. El Dorado Co. Sch. Dit. 982; Patient Svcs. Adv. Bd., Planned Parenthood 1975 76; honors: Volunteer Svc. Recogn. Awd., Threshold Ednl. & Counseling Svcs. 1981, 82, 83; mem: Am. Assn. Marriage & Family Counselors; Nat. Council on Family Rels.; Student Coalition, CSU Sacto. (past pres.); Student Rep., Grad. Faculty Com., CSU Sacto; works: contbr. to Nat. Curriculum, MATHTECH INC; mil: s/sgt. E-6 USAR 1971 76, Meritorious Achiev. Awd., Unit Decoration of Valor; rec; scuba diving, bicycling, photog. Res: 346 40th St Sacramento 95819 Ofc: Threshold Educational & Counseling Services, 2618 J St, Ste 4, Sacramento 95816

PYBRUM, STEVEN M., tax accountant, author; b. Mar. 12, 1951, Santa Cruz, CA; edn:BS acctg., real estate, Cal Poly St. Univ. San Luis Obispo 1973; MBA taxation, Golden Gate Univ., 1978. Career: (past) cost acct., Wm. Wrigley Jr. Co.; pub acct., tax dept. with regional firm in Santa Cruz Co.; controller, J.J. Crosetti Co.; currently owner/founder, C.E.O., Steven M. Pyrbum and Assocs. mgmt. consulting firm, Los Osos, San Luis Obispo, Atascadero; owner/founder, Executive Management Services (spec. executive compensation; conducts seminars); instr. of Taxation, Cal Poly State Univ.; ext. edn. pgm.; frequent lectr. Author: "Agri-Business Tax Tips", nationally publ newspaper and mg. column; "Tax Tips" radio program; dir., EMS Educational Found. Honors: Who's Who in the West; Who's Who in Real Estate. Mem: Calif. Soc. of CPAs; Calif. Bar Assn.; Western Growers Assn.; Cattlemen's Assn.; Atascadero CofC, dir., treas.; No. Co. Contractors Assn.; Lions; Elks; Exchange Club. Rec: golf, waterskiing, travel. Address: Steven M. Pybrum & Assocs., 249 Vista Ct., Los Osos 93402.

PYES, ANNETTE, designer/manufacturer; b. Oct. 19, 1926, Winnipeg, Canada; d. David Louis and Isabel (Naiman) Pyes; div. Career: designer/mfgr. Designs By Annette, Los Angeles, 1965-69; Annette Pyes Interiors, L.A., 1969-76; Ann Caron, Inc., Beverly Hills, 1976---. Mem: Thalians, President's Club, 1976. Democrat. Jewish. Rec: sculpture, antiques. Res: 9025 Keith Ave., Los Angeles 90069; Office: Ann Caron, Inc., 9263 West 3rd St., Beverly Hills 90210.

PYLE, DAVID BURTON, management analyst; b. July 26, 1942, San Francisco; s. Bennie B. and Gertrude E. (Tideman) Pyle; edn: AA, Napa Valley Coll. 1964; BS So. Ill. Univ. 1975; grad. work in pub. adminstrn., Golden Gate Univ. 1981---; m. Linda Marie Bright, June 7, 1969; chil: Dion Burton, b. 1976; Daniel William, b. 1977. Career: civilian naval architecture tech., Mare Isl. Naval Shipyard, Vallejo, 1967-73; real property specialist, USAF, Travis AFB, 1973-76; realty specialist, GSA, San Francisco, 1976; property specialist, Dept. of Agriculture, US Forest Service, San Francisco, 1976-80; mgmt. analyst, Mare Island Naval Shipyard, Vallejo, 1980---; life time Calif. Comm. Coll. Instr. Cred.; cons. to Internatl. Fedn. of Profl. and Tech. Engrs. Union Local 11, 1980-81. Honors: Superior Performance Awards Dept. of Navy, 1969, 72. Mem: Amer. Soc. for Pub. Adminstrn.; Amer. Mgmt. Assn.; The Acad. of Political Sci.; council mem., Napa Co. Comprehensive Health Planning Council, 1974-76; mem., O'Brian Park Planning Comm., City of Napa, 1981-82; Golden State Bonsai; Internatl. Bonsai; North Bay Bonsai, pres. 1977-78; Napa Valley Bonsai, pres. 1979, 80. Research: Work Attitudes and Supervisory Styles on Mare Island Naval Shipyard, 1982; Quality Circles Will They Work, 1981. Mil: Sgt., USAF, 1964-70. Democrat. Catholic. Rec: swimming, camping, gardening, bonsai. Res: 748 Jacob Ct., Napa 94558; Office: Mare Island Naval Shipyard, Mgmt. Engring. Office, Vallejo 94592.

Q

QUADRI, FAZLE-RAB G.D., government official; b. Aug. 5, 1948, Dacca, East Pakistan, nat. 1978; s. Gholam Moula and Jehan Ara (Hashim) Q.; children: Ryan Fazlerab b. 1978, Tania Marie Marie b. 1979; edn: AA, W. Wyo. Coll. 1969; BA, CSC San Bernardino 1972; JD, Western State Univ. 1978; admitted to Calif. State Bar 1981. Career: sales rep. American Nat. Insurance Co., 1972-74; budget div. analyst County of Orange, 1974-78: (reviewed over 3,000 state and fed. legislation, trained unit personnel and managed unit budget); County of San Bernardino 1978--: acting legislative advocate 1980, sr. exec. analyst 1981, acting public defender (supr. staff of over 80), and chief executive analyst, 1981--; county rep. on South Coast Air Quality Mgmt. Dist. Bd., County Projects Selection Coms., liaison to County Suprs. Assn. of Calif., Local Govt. rep. on State Hazardous Waste Mgmt. Council, and San Bernardino Co. Municipal Advis. Councils activities; awards: Kiwanis Club Scholarship ((1971-2), Dadabhoy Trust Scholarship (1967-8), American Soc. Scholarships (1963-6)j, Outstanding Young Men of Am. 1981, 82, Presidential Achievement Award 1982; mem: Am., Calif., San Bernardino Co. Bar Assns., Acad. of Polit. Sci., Alumni Assn. CSCSB (bd. dirs.), Statue of Liberty -Ellis Is. Commn.; hon. mem. Rialto Kiwanis Club; publs: sev. poems and arts.; Republican; Islam; rec: reading. Res: 535 E Mariposa Dr Redlands 92373 Ofc: County of San Bernardino, Board Offices, 175 W 5th St San Bernardino 92415

QUADRI, SHERRI MARITA, lawyer; b. Dec. 7, 1948, San Bernardino; d. Wayne D. and Marie S. (Jones) Mathewson; children: Ryan b. 1978, Tania b. 1980; edn: BA, CSC San Bernardino 1971, Std. Secondary Tchg. Credentiao, 1973; JD, Western State Univ. Coll. of Law 1981; admitted to Calif. State Bar 1981. Career: tchr. Aquinas High Sch., San Bernardino 1974-75; adminstrv. asst. City of San Bernardino, 1976-77; adminstrv. services asst., County of Orange, 1977, asst. mgr. Human Resources Pgms., 1977-79; legal intern San Bernardino County Dist. Atty's Office, 1980; attorney, sole practitioner, San Bernardino 1981--; bd. dirs. Inland Counties Legal Services; bd. dirs. Legal Aide Soc.; mem: Am., Calif. State, San Bernardino County (bd. dirs.) Bar Assns.; mem. Sierra Club; treas. Citizens for Jim Ballard (cand. gov. bd. S.B. Comm. Coll. Dist.); Democrat; Presbyterian; rec: hiking, equestrian. Res: 1530 Eureka St San Bernardino 92404 Ofc: Sherri M. Quadri, Atty. 150 West Fifth St, Ste 102, San Bernardino 92401

QUACKENBUSH, RITA JEAN, company president; b. Feb. 13, 1947, Edinburg, Tex.; d. Chalmers Stanford and Deliah May Stromberg; m. Charles W. Quackenbush, Dec. 16, 1978; 1 dau. Carrey Colleen, b. 1981; edn: stu. New College 1964-6, Univ. of Minn. 1966, Univ. of Fin. 1968. Career: insurance cons. Metropolitan Life Ins., Winter Park, Fla. 1969-70; sales rep. Norrell Temp. Svcs., Orlando 1970-71; branch mgr. Staff Bldrs. Internat., Miami & Orlando 1971-74; area mgr. CDI Temp. Svcs., Atlanta, Ga. 1976-79; founder/pres./bd. chmn. Q Services/Q Tech, Santa Clara, Ca. 1979--; co-founder/pres./bd. chmn. Q Bit, Santa Clara 1983--; testified before the: Calif. Commn. on the Status of Women 1981, US Commn. on Civil Rights 1982, Nat. Adv. Council on Vocational Edn. 1983. Awards: 5th pl. Nat. Waterskiing Championship, 1960. Mem. Am. Electron Fin. Com., fin. com. Ed Zschau for Congress 81-82, assoc. Repub. Central Com.). Publs: appeared in Life Mag, 10/82. Rec: flying own plane, waterski. Res: 15990 Oakridge Rd. Morgan Hill 95037 Ofc: Q Tech 4701 Patrick Henry Dr. Bldg. 1, Santa Clara 95050

QUAZI, HEBAB AHMED, engineer/executive; b. Sept. 27, 1939, Bagerhat, Bangladesh, nat. 1978; s. Hemayetuddin Ahmed and Amjura (Khatoon) Q.; m. Selima Begum, Aug. 1, 1962; children: Shahina b. 1966; Tanima b. 1973; edn: BS in chem. eng., Dacca Univ. 1961; Ph.D. Ch.E., Univ. of Newcastle-upon-Tyne, 1965; Bus. Mgmt., UC Los Angeles 1976; Reg. Profl. Engr. (Chemical & Control Sys.), Calif. 1977. Career: asst. prof. of chem. engring. Univ. of Engring. & Tech., Dacca, Bangaladesh 1965-69; sales mgr., ops. mgr., mktg. mgr. Titas Gas Transmission & Distbn. Co., Dacca, Bangl. 1969-71; process engr., systems engr., project coord. Gilbert/Commonwealth Assocs., Jackson, Mich. 1971-73; sr. process engr., sr. chem. engr., project mgr. C.F. Braun & Co., Alhambra, Calif. 1973-77, Murray Hill, NJ 1977-83, Alhambra, Calif. 1983--; vis. lectr. in chem. engring. NJ Inst. of Tech. 1981-83; course dir., gas processing, Center for Profl. Advancement, New Brunswick, NJ 1982-84; mem. Editl. Bd., AIChE Energy Progress Qtrly.; paper reviewer, ACS Indsl. & Engring. Chemistry; ISA Standard Review Bd. mem.; Proposal Review Team mem., NSF; awards: Commonwealth Scholar, U.K.; mem: Am. Inst. of Chem. Engrs. (chmn. Tech. Pgm. Com. Fuels & Petrochem. Div. 1981-4); ASME; Instrument Soc. of Am. (sr.); past mem. Berkeley Hts. Township, NJ Planning Bd. and Environmtl. Commn., 1982-3; publs: 15 tech. papers; Democrat; Islam; rec: tennis. Res: 1219 Calle Vistaso San Dimas 91773 Ofc: C. F. Braun & Co. 1000 S. Fremont Ave Alhambra 91802

QUIDACHAY, RONALD EVANS, municipal court judge; b. Mar. 8, 1947, San Francisco; s. Antonio Taisipic and Edith Georgiagina (Evans) Q.; m. Katharine Swan, Aug. 1, 1976; chil2;ey; Evan Andrew b. 1978, Seth Ryan b. 1982; edn: BA, CSU San Francisco 1970; JD, UC Berkeley 1973; admitted to Calif. State Bar. Career: staff atty. San Francisco Neighborhood Legal Assistance Found., S.F. 1974-77; asst. dist. atty., S.F. District Atty's Office, 1977-80; ptnr. Lenvin Gesmer & Quidachay, 1980-81; traffic commnr. San Francisco Municipal Court 1981-81; judge S.F. Municipal Ct., Dept. 4 Civil Div., 1983--; awards: 1983

Outstanding Young Man; appreciation as founder, Filipino Bar Assn. of No. Calif.; mem: Calif. Judges Assn., Filipino Bar Assn. (hon.), San Francisco Bar Assn. (hon.), American Bar Assn., Asian Am. Judges Assn., Queen's Bench, Native Sons of Calif., Dimasalang House bd. dirs.; Catholic; rec: tennis, camping. Res: 1058 Rhode Island St San Francisco 94107 Ofc: S.F. Municipal Court, City Hall, San Francisco 94102

QUINN, JOHN JOSEPH, bank executive; b. Apr. 8, 1939, New Haven, Ct.; s. Frank X. and Celia A. (Kelley) Q.; first cousin, George M. Conway, Chief Justice Conn. Superior Ct.; m. Nancy Deick, 1968; children: Cara b. 1975 (Australian cit.); Marc, b. 1978; edn: BA, and BS, UC Berkeley 1963, MBA, 1968. Career: v.p. and general manager First International Bank, 1980--, v.p. and mgr. S.F. Internat. Div. 1978-80, v.p., corres., Bank and Trade Finance, S.F. Intl. Div. 1976-78; UCB rep. Sydney, Australia, 1973-76; mgr., dir. Euro Pacific Finance Corp., Melbourne, Aust., 1970-73; asst. v.p., UCB, L.A. Internat. Regional mgr., SEA, 1970; mng. dir. Multinatl. Bus. Corp., London, U.K. 1968-70; First Nat. City Bank, N.Y. and Repub. of Philippines. Honors: asst. cashier awards and honors, Beta Gamma Sigma, Business Sch. Hon. Soc.; mem: World Trade Club, Bankers Club (SF), Naval and Mil. Club (Melbourne), Phi Kappa Sigma frat.; mil: lt. cmdr. USN 1963-67, also 5 yrs. as reservist with Royal Australian Naval Res.; mem. Commonwealth Club of Calif.; dir. British Am. CofC (SF); Republican (contbg.); Catholic; rec: boating, skiing, gardening. Res: 5 Descanso Dr Orinda 94563 Ofc: First Internatl. Bank, 405 Montgomery St, 3d Flr, San Francisco 94104

QUINN, JOHN R., clergyman; b. March 28, 1929, Riverside; s. Ralph J. and Elizabeth (Carroll) Quinn; edn: St. Francis Sem. and Immaculate Heart Sem., S.D. 1947-8; N. Am. Coll.; S.T.B. 1953, S.T.B. 1954, Gregorian Univ., Rome. Career: ordained priest in Rome, 1953; assoc. pastor St. Georges Parish, Ontario, Ca. 1954; Theology faculty Immaculate Heart Sem., San Diego 1955-; apptd. Rector Sch. of Theol., 1964; apptd. pres. St. Francis Coll. Sem. 1962; bishop (2d Aux. Bishop, S.D.; 1st native of Diocese to hold ofc.)San Diego, 1967; provost/bd.trustees Univ. of San Diego, 1968; pastor St. Therese Parish 1969; apptd. by Pope Paul VI as consultor, Sacred Cong. for the Clergy in Rome, 1971; bishop Okla. City and Tulsa, 1972, 1st archbishop of Okla. City 1973; papal appt. rep. to 4th Synod of Bishops, Vatican City, 1974; pres. Okla Conf. of Chs. 1976-8; archbishop of San Francisco, 1977--; pres. Nat. Conf. Catholic Bishops, 1977-80; mem. Canon Law Soc. of Am., Catholic. Theol. Soc. of Am. Address: Archdiocese of San Francisco, 445 Church St., San Francisco 94114

QUINN, KAREN SUE, oncology social worker; b. July 22, 1954, Stockton; d. Douglas Charles and Sylvia Bernetta (Webb) Hanson; m. Michael Quinn, Oct. 8, 1983; edn: AA, Delta Comm. Coll. 1974; BA, CSU Fresno 1976, MSW, 1978; LCSW, Lic. Clin. Soc. Wkr. 1982. Career: medical social wkr. St. Joseph's Hosp., Stockton 1978-80, oncology social wkr., 1980--; orgnzr. and bd. mem. Hospice of San Joaquin (non-profit health care orgn.), co-authored grant proposals; bd. dirs. American Cancer Soc. 1980-, mem. var. Calif. Div. coms., chair Service and Rehab. Com.; honors: Volunteer of the Year 1981, Am. Cancer Soc.; mem. Nat. Assn. of Soc. Wkrs.; Democrat; Catholic; rec: gourmet cooking. Res: 125 E Pine St Stockton 95204 Ofc: St. Joseph's Hospital 1800 N California St Stockton 95204

QUINN, ROBERT DEAN, physician; b. June 3, 1926, Firth, Idaho; s. Robert Merril and Allein (Jensen) Q.; m. Linda Saufnauer, Oct. 4, 1975; children: Judy b. 1949, Robert b. 1953, Craig b. 1955, Tina b. 1956, Gale b. 1958, Brian b. 1959; edn: BS, biol. scis., Stanford Univ. 1950; MD, Cornell Medical Sch. 1954. Cert. Medical Examiner for FAA. Career: rotating internship Letterman Army Hosp., San Francisco 1954-55; pvt. practice family medicine, Hollister, 1955--, med. dir. Hollister Convalescent Hosp.; Asst. Prof. of Community Medicine, Stanford Univ.; Asst. Clin. Prof. of Family Practice, UC Davis; fmr. chief of staff Hazel Hawkins Meml. Hosp.; fmr. trustee Hollister Elem. Sch. Dist.; honors: Finalist National Radio contest for American Town Meeting of the Air 1944; mem: Am. Med. Assn.; Calif. Med. Assn. (del., pres. PRSO 1981-82); Am. Acad. of Family Practice; Diplomate Am. Bd. of Family Practice; Calif. Acad. of Family Practice (past pres. San Benito chpt.); San Benito County Med. Soc. (past pres.); active mem. Los Medicos Voladores (practicing and tchg. in state of Sonora, Mexico); mem. Kiwanis (past pres. 1968), Hollister Rotary (dir. Internat. Stu. Activities 1970-), Am. Field Service (pres. 1977-79), American Host Pgm., People to People, active participant Martin Luther King's march at Selma Ala. to Montgomery 1965; author: Gravity -A Mechanical Theory; resrch. grant for devel. of Flexible Endoscope, Rockefeller Inst. NYC 1952-54; mil: US Army 1944-46, 3 Battle Stars, Combat Inf. Badge ETO, Combat svc. in France and Ger., 1st lt. US Med. Corps 1954-55; rec: pvt. pilot, travel, fishing, astronomy. Res: 41 Eastview Rd Hollister 95023 Ofc: 930 Sunset Dr Hollister 95023

QUINN, TOM, communications co. executive; b. Mar. 14, 1944, Los Angeles; s. Joseph M. and Grace (Cooper) Q.; m. Amy Lynn, Nov. 25, 1982; children: Douglas b. 1967, Lori b. 1969; edn: BS, Northwestern Univ. 1965. Career: reporter City News Bureau of Chicago, 1964; reporter WLS Radio, Chgo. 1965; reporter, newswriter ABC Radio, Los Angeles 1965; reporter KXTV Ch. 10, Sacramento 1966; day editor City News Service of Los Angeles, 1966-68; pres. Radio News West, L.A. 1968-70; campaign mgr. Jerry Brown for Secretary of STate, L.A. 1970; Deputy Secty. of State of Calif., Sacto. 1971-74; campaign mgr. Jerry Brown for Gov., 1974; chmn. Calif. Air Resources Board and Secty. of Environmental Quality, State of Calif., Sacto. 1974-79; mem. Calif. Governor's Cabinet, 1975-79; chmn./ pres. City News Service, Los Angeles 1980--;

pres. December Group, Los Angeles 1981--; pres. K-Hits Radio, Reno, Nev. 1982--; bd. chmn. KBCR, Inc. Steamboat Springs, Colo.; dir. Parallel Communications Corp., L.A.; ptnr. MacArthur Square, L.A.; Democrat; rec: skiing. Ofc: City News Service, 304 S. Broadway, Ste 520, Los Angeles 90013

QURESHEY, SAFI U., electronics manufacturing co. president; b. Feb. 15, 1951, Karachi, Pakistan; s. Razi R. and Ishrat Qureshey; m. Anita Savory, Sept. 19, 1976; children: Uns, b. 1979, Zeshan, b. 1981; edn: BSC, Physics, Univ. of Karachin, Pakistan 1971; BS in Elec. Engring., Univ. of Texas 1975. Career: test splst., documentor Div. of A.M. International, Santa Ana 1975-77; test engr. Computer Automation Inc., Irvine 1977-78; design engr. Telefile Computer Products, Irvine 1978-80; pres. AST Research Inc., Irvine 1980--; mem. IEEE; mem. Islamic Soc. of Orange County; Islamic. Res: 21 Tidewater Irvine 92714 Ofc: AST Research, Inc. 2121 Alton Ave Irvine 92714

R

RABY, RICHARD ELLERY, safety consultant; b. Feb. 6, 1922, Phila.; s. Thomas, Jr. and Anna (Brown) R.; m. Ingrid Christine Moller, Dec. 1, 1981; children (by previous marriage) Richard Jr., b. 1946, Stephanie Jo, b. 1949; edn: BA bus. econ., Muhlenberg Coll. 1949; BS Mech. Engr., Univ. of Penna., 1955; MS Systems Mgmt., USC 1970; Reg. Calif. Profl. Engr.: Safety Engr., Quality Engr. Career: Chief of Quality Engring. Kaiser Metal Products, Inc./Aircraft, 1952-55; Down Range Base Mgr., Eastern Test Range, Pan Am Airways, Inc., Cape Canaveral 1955-56; Sr. Reliability Flt. Test Engr./Test, Thor Pgm., Douglas Aircraft Co., 1957-58, Navaho Pgm., No. Am. Aviation, Inc./Missile 1956-57; Lead System Safety Engr. Rockwell Internat./ Space-Shuttle, Apollo, other programs 1956-70, 1973-78; self employed Safety Cons. 1970-73, 1981--; System Safety Engr., FACC/Aeroneutronic, Div. Air Def. Weapon Sys. Program 1978-79, 1982-83; System Safety Cons., Ocean Thermal Energy Conversion (OTEC) Pgm., Global Marine Devel. Inc., 1979; System Safety Cons.: GD/Pomona, DIVAD, 1980; G&II Technology, Inc., MX 1981; Infotek, inc. Space Payloads, 1981, USN Weapon Systems, Hughes, currently. Recipient Tech. Utilization award 1974; var. achieve. certs., 1965-70, Apollo Achieve. awd. 1970, NASA. Mem: Am. Rocket Soc. 1957, Jr. CofC 1956-58, Soc. of Logistics Engrs. 1966, System Safety Soc. 1967-, ASQC 1978-, Reliability Club 1956, Foreman Assn. 1952-55, Assn. of the U.S. Army 1980-, publs: various tech. handbooks; mil: officer/pilot USAF 1943-46; Presbyterian; rec: scuba diving, body building. Res: 5219 Gatewood Ln Anaheim 92807

RACCIATO, TERRY JANE (HENSHUE), nursing service executive; b. July 27, 1952, Allentown, Pa.; d. Walter E., Jr. and Phyllis Jane (Hilberg) Henshue; m. Joseph S. Racciato, May 7, 1971; children: Christopher, b. 1971, Gregory, b. 1972; edn: BS Nursing, with high honors, San Diego St. Univ. 1977, Public Health Nurse Cert. Career: staff nurse VA Hospital 1977-78; dir. Nursing Svcs. Frost St. Conv. Hosp. 19787-79; staff nurse ICU -Nurse Finders, 1979-80; founder Specialty Nurses, Inc., San Diego 1980--; founder Special Health Care, Inc., S.D. 1983--; Dir. Calif. Assn. of Temp. Serv., First Med. Chpt. 1982-; mem: Am. Fedn. of Home Health Agcs., Nat. Assn. of Home Care, Calif. Assn. for Health Serv. at Home, Am. Assn. of Critical Care Nurses; Mesa Youth Soccer Assn.; Republican; rec: breeding St. Bernards. Res: 4522 Aroma Ave San Diego 92117 Ofc: Specialty Nurses, 8304 Clairemont Mesa Blvd, Ste. 109, San Diego 92111

RACOSKY, JANICE LEE, speech pathologist; b. Dec. 10, 1935, Wichita, Kans.; d. Ellis J. and Nina Belle (Anderson) Drake; m. Vincent B. Racosky, June 16, 1979; children: David Dunn, b. 1955, Daniel Dunn, b. 1957, Chris Dunn, b. 1960, Michael Racosky, b. 1964; edn: BA, Univ. of Houston 1966, MA, 1970; Cert. of Clin. Competency, Am. Speech & Hearing Assn. 1970; lic. Speech Pathol., Calif. 1971. Career: Humble Ind. Sch. Dist., Humble, Tx. 1966-70, devel. dist.'s 1st speech and lang. itinerant pgm.; Riverside Unif. Sch. Dist., Riverside, Ca. 1970-72; speech pathologist Sunshine Sch. for the Orthoped. Handic., and asst. prof. speech pathology/ dir. Speech Pathol. Services, Loma Linda Univ. 1972-76; language, speech, and hearing splst. Corona-Norco Unif. Sch. Dist., 1976--; awards: scholarship, Nat. Easter Seal Soc. for Crippled Children and Adults 1969; mem. Am. Speech and Hearing Assn. 1970-; Democrat; Catholic, church organist, St. Joseph the Worker Cath. Ch. Res: 25888 Juniper, Loma Linda 92354 Ofc: Corona-Norco Unif. Sch. Dist., 300 Buena Vista Corona 91720

RADUS, SIDNEY LOUIS, lawyer; b. Jan. 19, 1920, Dayton, Oh.; s. Louis Henry and Eugenia (Pollock) R.; m. Jacqueline Ulrich, Dec. 20, 1959; children: Steven Robert, b. 1946, Gwen Elizabeth, b. 1961, Pamela Lee, b. 1963; edn: Miami Univ. 1938-9, 1940-42, Univ. 4 Dayton 1939-40, Long Bch. City Coll. 1952-3; JD, Southwestern Univ. 1967; Calif. State Bar Board Cert. Family Law Splst. Career: elec. constrn. and engineering, 1945-51; Contractual Splst. (Procurement), USAF, Wright Patterson AFB, 1951-52; v.p. sales, Hallamore Mfg. Co., Long Beach 1952-56; mfr.'s rep. Aero-Space, 1956-59; contract administrn. & mgmt., Air Research, Inc., North Am. Aviation, Leach Corp. and TRW, Inc., 1959-68; pvt. practice law, Santa Ana 1968--; judge pro tem and court apptd. arbitrator Superior Ct., Co. of Orange; mem. Family Law sections of Am., Calif., and Orange County Bar Assns.; mem. Orange Co. Trial Lawyers Assn.; pres. Jewish Family Svc. of Orange Co.; dir. Jewish Fedn. of Orange Co.; dir., exec. com. Legal Aid Soc.; mem. Masons, Amicus Publico,

Nat. Rifle Assn., Am. Aviation Hist. Soc., 8th Air Force Assn., Santa Ana Air Base Wing of Costa Mesa Hist. Soc.; mil: 1st lt. US Army Air Corps, USAF 1942-45, Air Medal w/T Clusters; Democrat; Jewish; rec: sailing, US Power Squadron, flying. Res: 5212 Mt. View Ave Yorba Linda 92686 Ofc: Sidney L. Radus Law Corp., 611 Civic Center Drive W., Ste. 206, Santa Ana 92701

RADZIENDA, LEO EDWARD, insurance executive; b. Oct. 5, 1945, Chicago, Il.; s. Leo Francis and Helen Pearl (Schleichert) R.; m. Georgiann Inglese, Sep. 30, 1972; children: Jennifer, b. 1975; Leo, b. 1981; edn: BA in Sci, DePaul Univ. 1968; cert., Ins. Inst. of Am. 1974; cert. Calif. Sch. Insur. 1975; cert., Life Underwriters Training Council 1976; career: oper. mgr. Reserve Insur. Co., Chicago and Los Angeles, 1971-74; agent Sentry Insur. Co., Los Angeles 1974-81; agent Maren & Assoc., Los Angeles 1981--; spkr. Western Ins. Information Svc. 1973; adminstr. Calif. Machinists Assn. (ins. assn.); distinguished mil. grad., DePaul Univ., 1968; mem: Independent Ins. Agents Assn.; Prof. Ins. Agents Assn.; mil: capt. US Army, Inf. (Ranger) 1968-71; Vietnam Svc. Medal, Bronze Star (101 Airborne Div); rec: sailing; Res: 611 Hampshire Rd #532, Westlake 91361 Ofc: Maren & Assoc., 18321 Ventura Blvd. #500, Tarzana 91356

RAE, MATTHEW SANDERSON, JR., lawyer; b. Sept. 12, 1922, Pittsburgh, Pa.; s. Matthew S. and Olive (Waite) R.; m. Janet Hettman, May 2, 1953; children: Mary-Anna, b. 1959, Margaret, b. 1961, Janet, b. 1962; edn: AB, Duke Univ. 1946, LL.B, 1947; postgrad. Stanford Univ. 1951. Career: asst. to dean, Duke Law Sch. 1947-48; admitted to Md. bar 1948, Calif. bar, 1951, Supreme Ct. of US 1967; assoc. Karl F. Steinmann law firm, Baltimore, Md. 1948-49; nat. field rep. Phi Alpha Delta Law Frat. 1949-51; research atty. Calif. Supreme Ct. 1951-52; partner Darling, Hall & Rae and predecessor firms, 1953--; v.p. Los Angeles Co. Republican Assembly 1959-64; L.A. Co. Repub. Central Com. 1960-64, 1977-, mem. exec. com. 1977-, chmn. 27th Senatorial Dist. 1977-, v.chmn. 17th Cong. Dist. 1960-62, 28th Cong. Dis. 1962-64, hmn. 46th Assem. Dist. 1962-64; Repub. State Central Com. of Calif. 1966-, exec. com. 1966-67; pres. Calif. Repub. League 1966-67j; pres. Republican Assocs. 1983-; mem. A.F. Assn., Aircraft Owners and Pilots Assn.; Comdr. Allied Post, Am. Legion 1969-70; mem. So. Bay Bar Assn.; Fellow Am. Coll. of Probate Counsel; Internat. Acad. Estate and Trust Law (exec. council 1974-78); L.A. County Bar Assn. (chmn. probate and trust law com. 1964-66, chmn. Legislation Com. 1980-81, co-chmn. 1982-; chmn. Program com. 1981-2; bd. of trustees 1983-); Am. Bar Assn. (sect. probate, trust, and real prop. law and taxation); Calif. State Bar (bulletin chmn. 1970-72, chmn. Probate Com. 1974-5, exec. com. Estate Plnng. Trust and Probate Law Sect, 1977-83); mem. Probate Law Consulting Group, Calif Bd. of Legal Splzn. 1977 ; Lawyers Club of L.A. (first v.p. 1983); Supreme Justice, Phi Alpha Delta 1972-74, elected. to Distinguished Service Chpt. 1978; Legion Lex (pres. 1969-71); Stock Exchange Club; Chancery Club; World Affairs Council; IPA; Rotary Intl.; Commonwealth Club; St. Andrews Soc., Town Hall (pres. 1975); Los Angeles Com. of Fgn. Relations; mil: 2d lt. USAAF, WWII; United Presbyterian; rec: theatre, volleyball, swimming. Res: 600 John St Manhattan Beach 90266 Ofc: 523 W. Sixth St, Rm. 400, Los Angeles 90014

RAFFERTY, KEVIN ANTHONY, manufacturing co. executive; b. June 13, 1954, Kansas City, Kans.; s. Francis S. and Elizabeth R. (Murphy) R.; m. Billie R. Wright, Feb. 12, 1984; edn: BA in soc. sci., Cleveland ST. Univ. 1980; Exec. MBA, Claremont Grad. Sch. 1984. Career: gen. laborer, gen. foreman, plant supt. Daniel Radiator, Cleveland Oh. 1974-79, division mgr. 1979-81, gen. mgr. Daniel Radiator, San Bernardino, Calif. 1981--; bd. of consultants, Nat. Automotive Radiator Splsts. of Am.; honors: Founders Awd., Daniel Radiator 1981; Nat. Hon. Soc. 1972; mem. Am. Space Found., United Way vol., Warner Springs Ranch soc. com.; Republican; Catholic. REs: 3855 Skofstad, 41, Riverside 92505 Ofc: Daniel Radiator 1455 San Bernardino Ave San Bernardino 92408

RAFFETTO, ELWYN LULL, health insurance consultant; b. Apr. 21, 1935, San Francisco; s. Dr. Joseph James and Vivian Velma Veronica (Parnigoni) Raffetto; m. Nancy Elizabeth Law, Jan. 27, 1962; chil: Mary, b. 1965, Gregory, b. 1967; edn: BA, UCB 1962. Career: dir. mktg. SFO Helicopter, 1962-69; v.p. sales Cal-State Airlines, 1969-71; insurance sales agt. 1971--: for Penn Mutual (life & disability), Blue Cross (med.), group sales mgr. Family Hlth. Pgm. (prepd. HMO plans) 1973-75; estab. Raffetto & Assocs. Inc. (employee benefit sales spec. in hlth. ins.) 1975, pres./CEO Raffetto & Assocs., Inc., Huntington Bch. 1980--; lectr. on medical/dental cost containment 1978-; cons. to (Teamsters) Union Hlth & Welfare Trusts 1978-81, Off. & Profl. Employees Internat. Union, 1980-, Meml. Med. Ctr. of Long Beach 1983-. Mem: Internat. Found. of Employee Benefit Plans, Calif. Jaycees (pres. Berkeley 1966-7), life mem. UCB Alumni Club. Publs: art., Internat. Foundation Digest, 2/83. Mil: spl.svcs. USAF 1955-9; Democrat; Lutheran; rec: fish, garden, camp, hike. Ofc: Raffetto & Assocs. Inc. 15052 Springdale St., Ste. D, Huntington Bch 92649

RAHDERS, RICHARD RANDOLPH, architectural/development firm executive; b. Nov. 30, 1947, Mnpls.; s. James Richard (Sandberg) Rahders; edn: AB, Princeton Univ. 1969, JD, Univ. of Minn. 1973. Career: partner law firm Rahders & Cargill, Mnpls. 1974-76; partner/chief fin. ofcr./energy cons. Thacher & Thompson Architects & Builders, Santa Cruz, Ca. 1976--; mem. (chmn. 1982-4) city of Santa Cruz Planning Commn. 1981-, mem. city of S.C. Zoning Bd. 1981-; mem. Lighthouse Field Commn. 1981-; guest spkr. 5th Nat. Passive Solar Conf., Amherst, Mass. 1980. Awards: Top 20 Producers, Santa Cruz Co. Bd. of Realtors, 1983; Valedictorian of Golden Fifty Club, Princeton Univ., 1969; water-ski champion, Fair Hills Resort, 1959; Santa Cruz Independent League All-Star Softball Team, 1983. Mem: Minn. Bar Assn. 1974-, Calif./

Nat. Assn. of Realtors 1976-, No. Calif. Solar Energy Assn. 1978-. Publs: Your House Can Do It: The Passive Approach To Free Heating & Cooling, 170 pp., 1979, profl. papers. Rec: archtl. photog., disc golf, softball, poetry. Res: 104 Moore Creek Rd, Santa Cruz 95060 Ofc: Thacher & Thompson 819-1/2 Pacific Ave Santa Cruz 95060

RAINES, FRANCES ELIZABETH, real estate broker; b. Aug. 14, 1928, Norfolk, Va.; d. Ernest Chapman and Lula Elizabeth (Bibb) Clark; m. Horace Franklin Raines, Aug. 19, 1950; children: Sandra, b. 1952, John, b. 1955, Elizabeth, b. 1960, Rebecca, b. 1960, Joan, n. 1962; edn: stu. William and Mary, 1946-47, Converse Coll. 1947-48; BA, fgn. affairs, George Washington (D.C.) Univ. 1950; grad. wk. American Univ. (Wash DC) 1950-51, San Francisco St. Coll. 1955-57; postgrad. wk. UC Berkeley 1958-59; Calif. Teaching Cred. (Secondary) 1957. Career: resrch. clk. typist, Dept. Navy, Pentagon, Wash. 1950, Dept. Army, Pentagon 1951-53, Dept. Army, Presidio, San Francisco 1954-55; high sch. tchr./counselor Howard Union High Sch. Dist., San Lorenzo H. Sch., 1957-60; bus. owner, Figure Salon, Sacramento 1970-73; real estate sales spec. in resales, San Jose 1974-76, Orange Co. 1976-82; broker assoc., New Home Sales, The Ryness Co., Danville 1982--; awards: Ford Found. III Fellowship 1956-57; Highest Producer, Forest Olson Co. 1977; Million Dollar Sales, 1979, 80, 81; mem: San Jose Real Estate Bd. 1974-76, West Orange Co. R.E. Bd. 1976-77, Huntington Bch. Fountain Valley R.E. Bd. 1977-82 (PAC), Nat. Assn. of Realtors 1974-82, Calif. Assn. Realtors 1974-82, Sales & Mktg. Council of BIA 1983-; Republican; Prot.; rec: needlepoint, profl. seminars, travel. Res: 532 Marine World Pkwy, 6101, Redwood City 94065 Ofc: The Ryness Co. 801 San Ramon Valley Blvd Danville 94526

RAINEY, MICHAEL BRUCE, lawyer; b. Apr. 12, 1946, San Francisco; s. James Edward and Patricia Jean (Merrill) R.; m. Gaye Chapman, Mar. 25, 1979; children: Michael Sean, b. 1968, Katrina Leanne, b. 1972, Kathleen Ann, b. 1972, Suzanne Amy, b. 1976; edn: BA, Loyola Marymount Univ. 1974; JD, Loyola Univ. 1979. Career: staff atty. for Honda for product liability cases in Western USA, 1980-82; litigation attorney Kern & Wooley, Los Angeles 1982--; admitted to All Fed. Courts in Calif., Tax Court, Mil. Ct. of Appeals, Ct. of Internat. Affairs, Ct. of Customs and Patents; dir. Pacific Lodge Boys Home; honors: Alpha Sigma Nu (Jesuit hon. soc.); mil: capt. US Army (Armor), Bronze Star, Air Medal; Republican; rec: model aircraft, model R.R., skiing. Res: 6740 Faust Ave Canoga Pk 91307 Ofc: Kern & Wooley 10920 Wilshire, Ste. 1500, Los Angeles 90024

RAINS, MICHAEL DAVID, orthodontist; b. Nov. 21, 1946, Pomona; s. Jack Arthur and Mary Jo (Hill) R.; m. Liliane, July 24, 1977; 1 son, Laurent F., b. 1978; edn: AA, Chaffey Coll. 1967; BA, Humboldt St. Univ. 1969; DDS, UCLA Sch. of Dentistry 1977; cert. in orthodontics, Univ. Conn. Sch. of Dentistry 1981. Career: sr. asst. dental surgeon USPHS, 1977-79; pvt. practice, Orthodontist, Santa Ana, Ca. 1982--; clin. instr. Dept. Orthodontics, UC Los Angeles 1983-; awards: USPHS scholarship 1975,76, postdoc. resrch. fellowship, Univ. of Conn. 1979, 80; mem: Am. Assn. of Orthodontists, Pacific Coast Soc. of Orthodontists, Calif. State Soc. of Orthodontists; mem. Zool. Soc. of San Diego, The Smithsonian Assocs.; articles in profl. jours.; mil: lt. 03, USPHS 1977-79; Catholic; rec: computer, sailing, backpacking. Res: 6600 W. Warner Ave, 203, Huntington Bch 92647 Ofc: 3620 S. Bristol St, Ste. 208, Santa Ana 92704

RAISBECK, CLIFFORD CLINTON, JR., orthopaedic surgeon; b. May 13, 1928, Milwaukee, Wisc.; s. Clifford C. and Minnie (Hommersand) R.; m. Margaret L., June 14, 1952; children: Clifford C. III, b. 1956, Christopher J., b. 1963, Wendy A., b. 1966, Kimberly L., b. 1967; edn: BS, Northwestern Univ. 1950, MD, 1953; US Naval Sch. of Aviationl. Med., Pensacola, Fla. 1955; certified Am. Bd. of Orthopaedic Surgeons 1964, 1983. Career: active duty, US Naval flight surgeon, 1954-57; med. res. gen. surg., St. Vincent's Hosp., NY 1957-58; orthopaedic res. pgm., Northwestern Univ., 1959-62; pvt. practice orthopaedic surg., trauma and reconstrn., founder/pres. The Orthopaedic Group of San Francisco, Inc., in S.F. and Daly City, 1962--; Independent Med. Examiner, Calif. Dept. of Indsl. Relations, 1977-; Oral Examiner, Am. Bd. of Orthopaedic Surgeons, 1983-; staff mem. S.F. Orthopaedic Residency Tng. Pgm. 1962-; asst. clin. prof. UCSF, 1965-; chief Ortho. Div. VA Hosp., Livermore 1969-72; cons./ CARE Medico, Tunis, Tunisia, 1969, 71; cons., Joint Replace. Clinic, VA Hosp., Martinez 1972-; elected mem. Sausalito- Marin Sanitary Bd.; recipient AMA Phys. Recognition Awd.; Dip. Nat. Bd. of Med. Examiners 1955; mem: W. Orthopaedic Assn., Am. Acad. of Ortho. Surgeons, S.F. Med c., Calif. Med. Soc., AMA (1966-82); pres. Marin Ski Club; publs: arts. in me ours.; mil: USN 1954-57;capt. USNR, Navy Commendn. Medal, C.O. 4th M. Air Wing Med. MAG 42 (1982-84); Prot.; rec: antique auto restoration; v tner Domaine Raisbeck. res: 31 Girard Ave Sausalito 94965 Ofc: The Orthopaedic Group of S.F. Inc., 4141 Geary Blvd, Ste.304, San Francisco 94118

RAJADHYAKSHA, SADASHIV Y., psychiatrist; b. Aug. 17, 1950, Bombay, India; s. Yashawant S. and Suhasini Y. (Varde) R.; m. Amita, Aug. 11, 1978; children: Jui, b. 1981, Geeti, b. 1982; edn: MB., BS, Univ. of Bombay, India 1972; psychiat. res. Harlem Hosp./Columbia Univ. 1975-78, chief res. 1977-8; bd. cert. in psychiat., Am. Bd. of Psychiat. & Neurol. 1981. Career: registrar, Pub. Health, K.E.M. Hosp., Bombay 1974; lectr. Preventive Med., Univ. of Bombay, 1974-75; served to lt. cmdr. USN, 1978-81; assoc. dir. Inpatient Unit, dir. Sexual Dysfunc. Clin., liaison Sleep Resrch. Lab., in chg. dept. grandrounds; currently, consulting psychiatrist Stanislaus Co. Dept. of Mental Health, Modesto; cons. psychiat. to regional counseling centers; panel cons. psychiatrists to Superior Ct. of Calif.; honors: Merit. Svc. Cert. for refugee

relief wk. 1972, highest honors in Inter Sci., 1968, Univ. of Bombay; mem: Am. Psychiat. Assn., AMA, World Med. Assn., Am. Orthopsychiat. Assn., Indian Psychiat. Soc., Assn. of Mil. Surgeons of US, Nat. Assn. of Residents and Interns; Bombay Youth Ctr. (secty.); Maharashtra Mandal, NYC; sci. presentations, profl. confs. in Bombay (1974), Manila (1980); Liberal; Hindu; rec: philately. Res: 6614 Olive Tree Ln Riverbank 95367 Ofc: 800 Scenic Dr Modesto 95350

RAKOW, LYDIA D'FONSECA, executive; b. Jan. 7, 1930, Alameda; d. Marcus and Dominga (Lomba) D'Fonseca; children: Claude Durham b. 1952, Gerald Durham b. 1954, Leslie Barros b. 1959; edn: stu. (Quaker Fellowship) Mills College; spl. writing courses, Coll. of Alameda 1979-80. Career: pioneer trade unionist, Food Tobacco Agriculture Union, First Black Woman trade union leader -Calif., sec.treas. FTA-CIO Local So. Oakland, 1947-54; secty. Willie Brown, Jr. 1957; exec. secty. San Francisco Branch NAACP 1962; adminstrv. asst. poet-actor Oscar Brown Jr. 1969; coord. of volunteers, Cong. Ronald V. Dellums 1982--; builder Rainbow Coalition; dir. Third World Economic & Edn. Found.; mem. Platform Speakers Assn.; Writers Guild, Amsterdam, Holland; League of Women Voters; Black Women Organized for Political Action; Democrat; Quaker; rec: photog. Res: 1029 Oak St, 20, Oakland 94607 Ofc: R.V.Dellums, 201 13th St, Oakland 94617

RALEY, THOMAS PORTER, retail food & drug chain executive; b. Apr. 8, 1983, Lead Hill, Ark.; s. Reglus and Nancy (Parrish) R.; div.; 1 dau. Joyce Nadine (Teel). Career: owner/bd. chmn. Raley's Supermarkets and Drug Centers; estab. his first market in Placerville, 1935, chain now has 46 superstores op. in No. Calif. and W. Nev.; past chmn. United Grocers, Ltd.; past pres. United Seed Co.; pres. Insurance Buyers, Inc.; honors: First Charter Mem., Grocers Hall of Fame, Sales Mgrs. Club of San Francisco 1979; Paul Harris Fellow, Rotary Intl. 1973; mem: St. Francis Yacht Club, World Trade Club (SF), Del Paso Country Club, Sutter Club (Sacto.), Shriners, and Masons; mem. U.S. Bus. Adv. Bd.; rec: yachting. Res: 4100 Folsom Blvd, Sacramento 95819; 1200 California St San Francisco 94109 Ofc: Raley's, 1515 20th St Sacramento 95814

RALPH, RICHARD, investment co. president; b. July 23, 1933, Bakersfield; s. Ralph Louis and Marie (White) R.; m. Ursula E. Wehres, May 1968; 2 sons: Christopher, Jeffrey; edn: BS, Univ. Calif. 1955. Calif. lic. Real Estate Broker. Career: investment supr. Northwestern Mutual Life; asst. vice pres. Pacific States Mortgage (now First Interstate); pres. R. Ralph & Co. Inc., San Francisco; bd. chmn. National Wood Products Inc. 1983-; chmn. Pi Kappa Alpha Nat. Housing Commn. 1978-; past pres. Bay Area Mortgage Assn. 1968-69; mem./pres. UCB Alpha Sigma Building 1966-; mil: USN 1956-58; Republican; rec: travel, photog. Ofc: R. Ralph & Co. Inc. P.O.Box 18131, San Francisco 94118

RAMER, BRUCE M., lawyer; b. Aug. 2, 1933, Teaneck, NJ; s. Sidney and Anne (Strassman) R.; m. Ann Greenberg, Feb. 15, 1965; children: Gregg, b. 1967, Marc, b. 1969, Neal, b. 1972; edn: AB, Princeton Univ. 1955; JD, Harvard Law Sch. 1959. Career: assoc. law firm of Morrison, Lloyd and Griggs, Hackensack, NJ 1959-60; partner law firm of Gang, Tyre & Brown, Inc., Los Angeles, Ca. 1963--; dir. Entertainment Law Inst., USC Law Center, 1973-; bd. regents Loyola Marymount Univ., L.A. 1982-; mem: American Jewish Com. (past pres. L.A. Chpt.; mem. Nat. bd. of govs., bd. trustees), Am. Bar Assn., Calif. Bar Assn., L.A. County Bar Assn., Beverly Hills Bar Assn.; past pres. Calif. Copyright Conf. 1973-74, past pres. L.A. Copyright Soc. 1974-75; mem. bd. trustees, bd. govs. Am. Diabetes Assn.; Princeton Club (So. Calif. pres. 1975-78); past mem. United Way task force on human svcs.; mil: US Army 1958-59 (pvt.), 1961-62 (2d lt.). Res: 622 Alta Dr Beverly Hills 90210 Ofc: Gang, Tyre & Brown, Inc., 6400 Sunset Blvd Los Angeles 90028

RAMIREZ, AMERICO RALPH, manufacturing co. executive; b. Oct. 20, 1939, Vega Alta, P.R.; s. Antonio G. and Trinidad (Roses) R. de Arrellano; m. Christine C. Sprague, Sept. 15, 1962; children: Lisa, b. 1963, Douglas, b. 1965, Renee, b. 1967, Keith, b. 1976; edn: BA, C.U.N.Y., Hunter campus, 1965. Career: joined KoRecType Corp. in 1965, set up internat. div., mass market, govt. sales, 1965-69; estab. own bus., Arellano Industries (selling comml. office supplies), 1969-71; vice pres. mktg. KoRecType, 1971-, set up factory in Puerto Rico in 1976, set up current factory in Calif. in 1979, currently pres. KoRecType Corp. of Calif., serving 15 western states; mem. Westlake CofC, Conejo CofC, Conejo Ski Club; Catholic; rec: skiing, biking, hiking. REs: 3114 Sunset Ln. Channel Islands 93030 Ofc: KoRecType Corp. 2551 Azurite Cir. Newbury Park 91320

RAMIREZ, FRANK, community college administrator; b. May 6, 1938, Los Angeles; s. Frank Gomez and Helen (Rendon) R.; m. Eleanor I. Olivas, Feb. 5, 1966; children: Rochelle Lynn, b. 1967, Jaso Ross, b. 1968, Felicia Ann, b. 1972, Ryan Keith, b. 1976; edn: stu. East Los Angeles Coll. 1960-65; BA in hist., CSU Los Angeles 1967; MS in edn., USC 1972; PhD, edn., Claremont Grad. Sch. 1976; Calif. Life Teaching and Adminstrv. Cred., kindergarten thru comm. coll. Career: L.A. Unified Sch. Dist. tchr. Eastman Elem. Sch., 1968-71, acctng asst. prin., 10th St. Elem., 1971-72, tchr. advisor/personnel div. Central Ofc., 1972-74, asst. prin. Loma Vista, 1974-75, personnel splst./ North Field Service Ctr. 1975-77, prin. Magnolia Elem., Area F, 1977; asst. supt./Personnel Svcs., Montebello Unified Sch. Dist., 1977-80; dir. employeremployee rels., Cerritos Comm. Coll. Dist., 1980--; personnel cons. to Alhambra City Schs. 1977, 81, Whittier City Schs. 1980, Compton Comm. Coll. 1982-83, Rio Hondo Comm. Coll. 1984; honors: service awards, Bella Vista PTA 1982, Monterey Park Sports Club 1981, Dept. of Navy, Navy Recruiting

Dist. of L.A. 1982, Hispanics from IRS (HIRE orgn.) 1983; mem: PTA, Bella Vista, 1971-, Macy Intermediate 1977, Schurr High Sch. 1981-; PDK, USC chpt. 1976-; Cal State Alumni Assn. 1970-; USC Alumni Assn. 1972-; Claremont Grad. Alumni Assn. 1976-; Southern 30 Info. Exchange Consortium (chmn. 1984); So. San Gabriel Personnel Assn. 1977-80; Bella Vista Mens Optimist Club of Montebello (pres. elect 1984-5); Monterey Pk Sports Club Baseball Commnr. 1983, 84; mil: A/2c USAF, GCM; Democrat; Catholic; rec: sports. res: 206 W. Gleason St Monterey Pk 91754 Ofc: Cerritos Community college 11110 E. Alondra Blvd Norwalk 90650

RAMOS, ERNEST DAVID, optometrist; b. July 12, 1946, Cordon Isabella, Philippines, nat. 1956; s. Getulio Garcia and Froilana (Apostol) R.; edn: BA, psychol. Coll. of William and Mary, 1968; MS spl. edn., CSU Fullerton 1976; BS in optometry, So. Calif. Coll. of Optometry 1978, O.D., 1980. Career: optometrist Anaheim Eye Medical Group, 1980-83; private practice, Brea, 1983--. Awards: ROTC Scholar 1966-68; distinguished mil. student 1968; Younger Optics Awd. 1980; mem. Pi Lambda Phi frat. (pres. 1966); Yearbook ed. So. Calif. Coll. of Opt. 1978-9; mil: capt. MSC, US Army 1968-72; Democrat; Catholic; rec: black belt in karate, photog., sports coaching, travel. Res: 525 Blue Water Lane Fullerton 92635 Ofc: Ernest D. Ramos O.D., 100 Brea Mall, Brea 92621

RAMOS, JOSE LUIS, EPA administrator; b. Aug. 29, 1922, Wash. DC; s. Jose Cosme Ramos and Margaret Elizabeth Bruen; mat. gr. grandfather John Henry Walsh, Supt. NYC Public Sch., 1953; m. Grace Hardy, div. 1968; m. 2d. Meredith Littleton, 1973; children: Kathleen, b. 1947, Suzanne, b. 1948, Robert, b. 1950, Rosemary, b. 1953, Grace Marie, b. 1961; edn: Catholic Univ. of Am. 1940-1, Univ. of Md. 1941-2; Grad. US Army Engr. Sch. 1943; spl. stu. British Royal Engr. Sch. Ripon, Yorkshire, Eng. 1944; Grad. AUS Cmd. and Gen. Staff Coll. 1956; Grad. Vox Inst. of Languages 1961. Career: enlisted, served to col. US Army Corps Engrs. 1942-1971, ret.; with initial beach assault Normandy, France, June 6, 1944; served in five European campaigns WWII; comdr. Spec. Demolition Unit, Austria 1953, Regular Army Engr. Nat. Guard Instr. Pa. 1953-55, Engr. Combat Bn. Ops. Ofcr. 7th Infantry Div. Korea 1957-58; Chief of Engrs. Liaison Ofcr. 1959, Cmbt. Devel. Expt. Command 1960; US mil. mission in Paraguay 1962-63; Inter-Am. Peace Force Cmd. Engr. during revolution in Dominican Repub. 1965-66; cmdr. 43rd Engr. Constrn. Bn. 1966-67; Post Cmdr. Camp Roberts, Calif. 1970-71. Decorated Bronze Star, Legion of Merit w/Oak Leaf Cluster, Army Commendn. w/3 Oak Leaf Clusters, Disting. Unit Citation, French Croix de Guerre w/Silver Star, Paraguayan Order of Mil. Merit in grade of Cmdr., Paraguayan Mil. Engr., Brazilian Peacemaker, Tamandare Merit and service medals. Instr. US ARmy Engr. Sch. 1946-50, Cmdr. Non-Com Officers Acad., Linz, Austria 1951; Ofcr in Chg. US Forces Austria Demolition Sch. 1952. Recipient Spl. U.S. Environmental Protection Agcy. award 1981; mem. Am. Soc. of Mil. Engrs., Retired Officers Assn.; publs: tech. demolition manual; devel. mil. gap calibrator (1949); Republican; Catholic; rec: fishing, swimming, art. REs: 350 Beach Rd Belvedere 94920 Ofc: U.S. Environmental Protection Agency, 215 Fremont St San Francisco 94105

RAMSER, HAROLD CHARLES, business consultant; b. Feb. 2, 1908, Ashton, S.D.; s. Frank C. and Fredreika (Skibbe) R.; m. Elizabeth B. Eves, Feb. 3, 1928; 2 sons, Harold C., Jr. and Philip Scott; edn: stu. USC 1926-29. Career: current bd. chmn. Ramco Industries, City of Industry; dir. Plastic Employers Assn.; owner Upholstery Supply Co.; dir./pres. Cal-Sierra Corp.; owner Ramser Oil Co.; v.p./dir. Rancho Corta Madera; dir./v.p. Oak Tree Racing Assn.; dir. Masters of Foxhound Assn.; pres. Am. Foxhound Club; v.p./dir. Santa Barbara Polo Club; dir./commodore P.C.C. Yachting Fleet; mem. Sigma Chi Frat., Newport Harbor Yacht Club, L.A. Yacht Club; Republican (past chmn. fin. Repub. State Com. Calif. & mem. Repub. Nat. Fin. Com.); Episcopal; rec: polo, foxhunting. Res: 870 Stone Canyon Rd Los Angeles 90077 Ofc: Ramco Industries 18525 Railroad St City of Industry 91744

RAMSEY, CAROLE BROOKS, controller; b. Sept. 25, 1932, Oklahoma City, Okla.; d. Curtice Brooks and Julya Jeanne (Hansen) Robertson; children: Candace B. Oden, b. 1960, Kelly L. Oden, b. 1961; edn: Okla. Univ. 1951-2; Bus. Coll. Rutledge, Dallas, Tx. 1952-3; Brunswick Sch of Mgmt., Chgo. 1963. Career: hostess Braniff Airlines, 1954; sec./receptionist Carrier Bock Corp., Dallas, Tx. 1954-55; legal steno, Cooper, Pitman & Lawrence, Okla. City 1956-59; part owner Lincoln Lanes (bowling), Okla. City, Okla. (league orgnzr., bkkpr., bowling instr., mem. LPBA), 1959-66; sec. Public Warehouse Co., Okla. City 1966-69; gen. office, Western Std. Bred Harness Racing Assn., Inglewood, Ca. 1970-71; exec. sec./ controller/ office mgr. Ralph E. Phillips, Inc. Consulting Mech. and Elec. Engrs., Santa Monica 1971--; Republican; Methodist; rec: golf (Pala Mesa Resort, Fallbrook), tennis, bowling, Raiders fan. Res: 4120 Oak Island Ln Fallbrook 92028 Ofc: 2200 Michigan Ave Santa Monica 90404

RAMSEY, JACK, library director; b. June 12, 1922, Kansas City, Ks. s. Clay and Floy Ramsey; m. Sue Worsley, Apr. 4, 1946; edn: AB, Univ. Kans. 1945; MS, Univ. Ill. 1946, MLS, 1947. Career: librarian, NY Pub. Lib., 1947-48; adminstrv. asst. Lib. of Stockton and San Joaquin Co., 1948-49; county librn. Solano Co., 1949-52; lib. dir. City of Glendale, 1952-59, 1966--; chief of customer H.W. Wilson Co., NYC 1959-65; mem: Phi Kappa Psi frat., Beta Phi Mu hon. lib. sci. frat. (past pres), NY Lib. Club (past pres.); bd. trustees Billig Medical Found. 1983-; mil: AUS, 1942-43; Republican; Episcopal (Vestry); rec: music, travel. Res: 548 Mesa-Lila Rd Glendale 91208 Ofc: 222 E. Harvard St. Glendale 91205

RAND, JUDITH SEESE, interior designer; b. Mar. 18, 1937, Milwaukee, Wisc.; d. Austin Harland Seese and Mildred Evelyn (Silliman) Mercier; m. Douglas Harris Rand, Aug. 29, 1959; children: David b. 1962, Lynda b. 1964; edn: Indiana Univ. 1955-57; cert. of design, LaSalle Univ. 1975; AA, cert. interiors, Orange Coast Coll. 1984; desig: Assoc. ASID 1980; Profl. ISID 1982; Calif. Comm. Colls. Tchr. Cred. (Voc. Design) 1984. Career: interior designer Miller & Miller Interiors, Tustin 1969-70, W. Lee & Assoc. (int. design firm), Tustin 1975; design prin. Judith Rand Interiors (comml. and residential interiors), Santa Ana 1975--; voc. tchr. int. design Orange Coast Coll., ISID student advisor; recipient Orange Coast Coll. Award, ISID Pres. appreciation award; mem: Internat. Soc. of Int. Designers (mem. com., corres. sec.), profl. assoc. Am. Soc. of Int. Designers; mem. ISID Design House com.; Battered Children's Home design com.; PEO; Western Med. Ctr. aux.; Republican; Christian; rec: paint, needlework, golf. Res: 13831 Winthrope Santa Ana 92705 Ofc: Judith Rand Interiors, 222 Fashion Lane, 105, Tustin 92680

RANDALL, LESLIE DIANE, real estate broker; b. Mar. 6, 1953, Los Angeles; d. William and Phyllis Adele (Krasne) Axelrod; m. Ronald Randall, June 2, 1974; 1 child, Lindsey, b. 1982; edn: BA, UC Los Angeles 1976; paralegal, Univ. of W. Los Angeles Law Sch. 1977-78; broker, Anthony Sch. of Real Estate 1981; certs. in R.E. and Corp. Law, Univ. of W.L.A. Law Sch. 1978. Career: recept./ salespsn. AppleOne Employment Agcy., Los Angeles 1975-78; paralegal Youner & Hampar Law Firm, Century City 1978-79; recept./ salespsn. Warner Village Townhse. Subdiv. Woodland Hills, 1979-80; tract sales mgr. Warner Village, "The Woods", 1980-82; owner/broker Leslie Randall & Assocs., real estate co., Canga Park 1982--; cons. Jeri-Co Real Estate Co., Az. 1983-; area mktg. cons. for Builders Sales Corp. (new res. subdiv., Canoga Pk) 1984; awards: cert. of excellence, Nat. Forensic League 1969; heart princess, Am. Heart Assn. 1969; top sales of month, AppleOne Empl. Agcy. 1969, sales achieve. awd., Warner Vill. Twnhse Dev., Woodland Hills CofC 1980-82; mem. realty bds. of Beverly Hills, and San Fernando Valley; mem. United Hostesses Charity Gp., Variety Club Charity, City of Hope, Vista Del Mar, United Jewish Welfare; Democrat; Jewish; rec: tennis, golf, swimming. Res: 23681 Burton St Canoga Park 91304 Ofc: Leslie Randall & Associates, 23681 Burton St. Canoga Park 91304

RANGLAS, GERRY ATHAN, real estate management executive and syndicator; b. Oct. 25, 1948, Athens, Greece; came to USA at age 5; s. Tom and Marina (Famelis) R.; m. Jeannie Tina Dale, Mar. 12, 1978; 1 son, Athan, b. 1981; edn: bus. fin., San Diego St. Univ. 1973; Calif. lic. real estate broker 1979. Career: asst. property m;gr. Seltzer, Caplan, Wilkins, et al (law firm), San Diego 1971-73; regional dir. of prop. mgmt. for No. Calif., American Housing Guild, S.D. 1973-74; gen. partner num. R.E. syndications, 1974-; co-owner/ dir./ pres./ chief exec. R&V Mgmt. Corp (mng 1,000 apt. units and 100,000 sq.ft. comml. space, S.D. County), 1974--; mem. San Diego Bd. of Realtors 1974-; Am. Hellenic Ednl. Progressive Assn. (pres. El Cajon Heartland Chpt. 1980-81); Republican; Greek Orthodox; rec: bowling, fishing, golf. Res: 944 Vista Del Monte Way, El Cajon 92020 Ofc: R&V Management Corp. 2650 Camino Del Rio No., Ste. 104, San Diego 92108

RAPER, FRANK EUGENE, packaging products distbn. co. president; b. Jan. 18, 1946, Portsmouth, Va.; s. Frank Henry and Virginia Edith (Tigner) R.; m. Marla Joy, Mar. 8, 1975; children: Deborah Anne, b. 1964, Stephanie Joy, b. 1983; ed. pub. schs.; Comml. Rated Pilot. Career: sales mgr. Blake, Moffit, & Towne in Los Angeles; founder/pres. United Packaging Corp., 1971--; mem. Inner Circle, Calif. Film Extruders and Converters Assn. (pres. 1984, com. chmnships); Republican; rec: flying, snow skiing. Res: 12005 East Norino Drive Whittier 90601 Ofc: United Packaging Corporation, 1215 Bixby Drive Industry 91745

RAPSOMANIKIS, EVANS ALEX, researcher; b. May 2, 1916, Corfu, Greece; s. Alexander John and Olga Evans (Karvouni) R.; m. Fanny E., Mar. 10, 1940; children: John, b. 1942, Mary, b. 1946, Constantin, b. 1951; edn: BSME/EE, Univ. of Athens, Greece 1940; MSEE, Brit. Inst. of Engring. Tech., Cairo, Egypt 1951; postgrad. stu. bio-med. field, physics, McGill Univ. 1954-57; Calif. reg. profl. engr. Career: supr. eng. Pratt & Whitney Aircraft, 1952-55; gen. mgr. Montral Indsl. Designs Ltd. 1955-60; project systems engr. Curtiss-Wright Corp., NJ 1960-65; project systems engr. A.G. McKee & Co., 1965-68; research splst. senior, Lockheed California Co., 1968-80; mgr. Tri-County Technical Svcs. 1980-83; chief exec. ofcr. Electro-Bio-Morphic Research., 1983--; recipient var. profl. achievement awards, mil. awds. Mem: Sigma Xi, Sci. and Engineering Council of Santa Barbara, SW5 Community Council (civic), Masons, Am. Hellenic Ednl. Progressive Assn. (AHEPA); research: patent applications, tech. papers in bio-med. field; mil: lt.cmdr. Greek/British Royal Navy, 1942-45; Republican; Greek Orthodox; rec: boating, golf, tennis, swimming. Res: 4610 Eastbourne Bay Channel Ils, Oxnard 93030 Ofc: Electro-Bio-Morphic Research, 350N Lantana, Ste. 212, Camarillo 93010

RASCH-CHABOT, NANCY D., lawyer; b. Oct. 19, 1952, Schenectady, NY; d. Robert Allan and Sarah Doris (Evans) Rasch; m. Joseph E. Rasch-Chabot, July 31, 1976; 1 dau. Meagan, b. 1983; edn: stu. Univ. of Bordeaux, France 1972-73; BA, UC Santa Barbara 1974; JD, Univ. of Santa Clara 1980. Career: law clerk Consumer Fraud/ White Collar Crime Unit, S.F. District Atty's Ofc. 1979; law clk. to Hon. John A. Ertoca, S.F. Superior Court, 1979; law clk. 1980, staff atty., Legal Asst. To The Elderly, 1980--; Task Force on Elder Abuse, 1982-83; ch. steering com. Consortium for Elder Abuse Prev., 1983-; mem. San Francisco Bar Assn., Calif. and Federal Bar, Del. 1980; Democrat. Res: 280 Clipper San Francisco 94114 Ofc: Legal Assistance to the Elderly, 333 Valencia San Francisco 94103

RASMUS, DANIEL WAYNE, writer/manufacturing specialist; b. Oct. 28, 1961, Los Angeles; s. Arthur Lee and Shirley Ann (Ottosen) R.; stu. creative writing, Univ. Calif., Santa Cruz 1979-81. Career: data proc. supr. Christie Elec. Corp., 1981-83; supr. EDP Ops., Dataproducts Corp., 1983-84, mfg. systems specialist 1984--; ed. Oakes Literary Rev. 1981; honors: elected Ephebian, L.A. Unified Sch. Dist. 1979; Univ. Calif. Pres.'s. Undergrad. Fellowship grant 1981; mem. Am. Prodn. Inventory Control Soc., Mensa; publs: Song for Sandy, America Sings (1979), contbg. poet, Oakes Lit. Rev. (81), Poetry Mag. (Apr. 82, June 82), Harbor Lights (1982), Negative Capability (Spring 83), and Goblets (Summer 83); arts. in profl. journals; artist (portraits), So. Bay Art Assn. Gallery (1/83, 6/83); Democrat; strategic plnng. adv. to Carol Ann Bradford for Cong. cpgn.; congl. dist. coord. CD40, Hart for Pres. cpgn. Res: 3410 S. Main St, El, Santa Ana 92707 Ofc: Dataproducts Corp. 17426 Daimler Ave Irvine 92714

RASMUSSEN, WILLIAM MARTIN, local govt. special district administrator; b. Feb. 2, 1926, Modesto; s..Martin Wm. and Margret Mildred (Wight) R.; m. Annette Ruth Bright, June 5, 1960; children: James William, b. 1952, Eric Jon, b. 1956, Christopher Lynn, b. 1957; edn: cadet ofcr. US Maritime Acad.; AB, cum laude, CSC Chico 1953; MPA, magna cum laude, CSC Bakersfield, 1979; PhD, mgmt., Columbia Pacific Univ. 1983; Reg. Recreation (No. 131), Calif. Bd. of Park and Rec. Personnel; Credential Adult Edn., Calif. Career: seaman, lic. third ofcr. US Maritime Svc. and lt. jg USNR, 1943-48; asst. exec. dir. Chico Area Rec. and Park Dist., 1950-52; dir. of recreation, City of Turlock 1952-53; rec. dir. combined sch. and community pgm., Lemoore Union H.S. Dist., Avenal Kettleman City Reef Sunset Union Elem. Sch. Dist., 1953-57; gen. mgr. North Bakersfield Rec. and Park Dist., 1957--; instr., mgmt. and rec., Coalinga Coll., Fresno St. Coll., Bakersfield Coll., 1956-67; cons./ prin. Rasmussen and Assocs. (devel. & fin. feasibility of capital projects), var. cities, counties; instr. in pub. adminstrn., UCSB, var. wkshops. Mem. Am. Soc. for Pub. Adminstrn., Municipal Fin. Ofcrs. Assn., Nat. Rec. and Park Assn., Calif. Spl. Dist. Assn., Calif. Park and REc. Soc., W. Govtl. Resrch. Assn., Valley Regl. Tng. Ctr. (bd. dirs. 1975-81); num. service orgns.; recognition awards: TV-Radio Station KLYD (1965), Joshua Tree Girl Scout Council (1965), Calif. Park and REc. Soc. (1966), Am. Soc. for Pub. Adminstrn. (Doubenmier Awd. 1966), Bksfld. North Rotary Club (hon. mem. 1967). Res: 1025 Elizabeth Ct Bakersfield 93308 Ofc: North Bksfld. Rec & Park Dist. 405 Galaxy Ave Bakersfield 93308

RASSOULI, FRED FREYDOON, architectural designer; b. Nov. 18, 1943, Isfahan, Iran; s. Ahmad Haji and Nosrat (Haji) R.; m. Gitty Vaziri, Aug. 13, 1967; children: Neda, b. 197, Nima, b. 1978; edn: B.Arch., Univ. of N.M. 1969; M. Urban & Regl. Plnng., USC 1971. Career: arch. designer, Gruen Assocs., Los Angeles 1970-75; pres. F. Rassouli & Assoc. (arch. design firm), Tehran, Iran 1975-79; pres. Italin Interiors (design & remodeling of kitchens, baths), Sherman Oaks 1979--; awards: fellowship, Inst. of Internat. Edn. 1968-69; works: semi profl. artist (painting) 1962-; num. articles for Iranian papers. Res: 4642 Louise Ave Encino 91316 Ofc: Italin Interiors, 14301 Ventura Blvd Sherman Oaks 91423

RATCLIFF, THEODORE PERRY, real estate broker; b. Apr. 28, 1918, Bogalusa, La.; s. Peter and Bertha Ratcliff; m. Wilma, Oct. 23, 1951; children: Sheila, Gilda, Teddy, Wonzer, Kenya, and Sean; edn: BS, Alcorn Univ. 1939; MA, So. Univ., 1958; stu. Iowa State Univ. 1947-8, USC 1963, UCLA 1966; lic. edn. and suprvn. Career: public school tchr., El Centro 1959-64, Paramount Schs. 1965-83; real estate broker/prin. Ratcliff Realty, Hawthorne, currently; editor The Informer (newspaper), Bogalusa, La. 1951-54, The Builder (newspaper), L.A. 1966-68; awards: fed. student grants 1964, 68; trophy, Intercoll. Essay contest of 12 land-grant colls. 1983; mem: (fmr.) Internat. Student Council, Iowa State Univ., Calif. Tchrs. Assn., Nat. Assn. of Realtors, Alpha Phi Alpha Frat., Foster Parent Assn. of Calif.; inventor/mfr. of Ratchet Paint Roller; author, pub. book of poetry: Black Forever More; devel. copyrighted tchg. device: Letto (1958); Democrat; Methodist; rec: fishing, pool. Res: 14106 Maple Ave Los Angeles 90061 Ofc: Ratcliff Realty, 13407 Crenshaw Blvd Hawthorne 90250

RATTAZZI, GIANLUCA URBANO, computer co. executive; b. Oct. 18, 1952, Ascoli Piceno, Italy; s. Urbano and Maria Francesca (Crudeli); m. Chiara Filippone-Thaulero, Aug. 29, 1980; edn: Laurea, Univ. of Rome 1976; MS (C.S.), UC Berkeley 1980, PhD, physics. Career: research asst. Italian Research Labs., 1975-76, Lawrence Berkeley Lab., 1976-80; supr., mgr. advanced devels. Olivetti, Cupertino 1980--; tchg. asst. UCB, 1976-78; mem. ACM, IEEE, Am. Physics Soc.; num. publs. in major Am., European sci. journals; invited papers sev. nat. and internat. confs.; Catholic; rec: scuba diving. Res: 105 Via De Tesoros Los Gatos 95030 Ofc: Olivetti, 10430 S. De Anza, Cupertino 95014

RAUBOLT, JOHN STUART, data processing administrator; b. Apr. 6, 1950, Wyandotte, Mich.; s. Robert C. and Patricia A. (Price) R.; m. Hong Thi Le, Jan. 22, 1972; children: Min-Tam, b. 1972, Lee, b. 1976, Kim-Lan, b. 1978, Lien-Thi, b. 1979; edn: Santa Ana Coll. 1971-73, Fullerton Coll. 1973-75, Chaffey Coll. 1975-77; Comm. Coll. Instr. Credential 1981. Career: computer opr., offset printer, Products of Information Systems, Costa Mesa 1971-73; computer opr. North Orange Co. Comm. Coll. Dist., Fullerton 1973-77, computer ops. supr. 1977-79, computer systems supr. 1979--, adult edn. instr. (Intro. to Computers, Data Proc. Mgmt.), 1980-; recipient recognition, Cypress Coll. Assoc. Students 1983; mem: District Mgmt. Group (pres. 1983-4), Vietnam Veterans of Am.; advisor/ partner, Raubolts' Landscape Care, 1982-; mil: sgt.

US Army 1969-71, Bronze Star, Nat. Def. Svc., Vietnam svc., Vietnam Cmpgn. medals; Republican; Catholic; rec: boating, fishing, home garden. Res: 1039 Seashell Ct Ontario 92761 Ofc: N. Orange Co. Comm. College District, 1000 N. Lemon St Fullerton 92634

RAUH, ROBERT BRUCE, advertising agency executive; b. July 24, 1942, San Francisco; s. Rudolph Louis and Virginia Isabel (Vincelli) R.; m. Darlene A. Colose, Apr. 3, 1971; children: Joshua, b. 1977, Joanna, b. 1981; edn: AA, San Francisco City Coll. 1962; BA, San Jose St. Univ. 1964; grad. wk. in mktg., SFSU, 1965. Career: prodn. mgr., asst. account exec., market res. analyst, Allen & Dorward Advt., San Francisco 1964-66; acct. supr. ATD Advt., Palo Alto 1966-67; vice pres., creative dir. Markman Inc., Los Gatos 1968-69; owner Robert B. Rauh Advt., 1969-; pres. Rauh, Good & Darlo Advertising, Los Gatos 1979--; adj. prof. of advt. San Jose St. Univ.; guest lectr. Univ. of Santa Clara Grad. Sch. of Bus.; dir. Acc-u-Tune, Inc.; awards: Nat. Addy Award (1982), AAF Best in the West (1982), AAF Silver Medal Awd. (1982); mem: Am. Assn. of Advt. Agencies, Am. Advt. Fedn., San Jose Advt. Club (bd. dirs., past pres.), Monterey Advt. Club, Santa Clara Valley Advt. Agencies Assn. (founder, past pres.); mil: PO3, US Navy Air Corp 1964-70; Democrat (Century Club); Catholic; rec: photog., creative writing, woodworking, golf. Res: Summit Rd Los Gatos 95030 Ofc: Rauh, Good & Darlo Advt. Assocs. Inc. 142 S. Santa Cruz Ave Los Gatos 95030

RAVETCH, HERBERT, college president; b. Aug. 17, 1924, Newark, N.J.; s. I. Shalom and Sylvia (Shapiro) R.; m. Gloria Ahrens, June 19, 1955; chil: David Shalom, b. 1958; Joshua Aaron, b. 1959; Adam Benjamin, b. 1961; edn: BA in Eng., UCLA, 1948, MA in Eng., 1950, EdD, 1972. Career: instr./dept. chmn. L.A. Pierce Coll., 1958-68, asst. dean, 1968-70; dean instrn., L.A. Southwest Coll., 1970-72, pres. 1972-73; chmn. North Valley Task Force, 1973-75; founding pres. Los Angeles Mission Coll., 19775-79; pres. Los Angeles Pierce Coll. 1979--. Mem: Calif. Community Coll. Admin. Assn. 1973-; L.A. Comm. Coll. Admin. Assn. 1968-; Calif. Comm. & Jr. Coll. Assn. 1975-; Am. Assn. of Comm. & Jr. Colls. 1976-; Woodland Hills CofC (bd.dirs. 1980-3); pres. Valley Cultural Ctr., L.A. 1982-4. Rec: write, tennis, jog. Res: 19811 Dina Pl. Chatsworth 91311 Ofc: L.A. Pierce College 6201 Winnetka Ave Woodland Hills 91371

RAWISZER, STEVEN JAY, hearing conservation specialist; b. June 24, 1949, Jackson Heights, NY; s. Henry and Blanche (Epsenhart) R.; m. Charleen, June 7, 1975; edn: AA, early childhood edn., Am. Rivers Coll. 1975; BA, communicative disorders, CSU Fresno 1977, MA, 1979; lic. audiologist, 1980. Career: audiologist, Sacramento Hearing Services, 1979-80, Sutter Hearing & Speech, 1980-81; hearing conserv. splst. Maternal and Child Health Branch, State Dept. of Health Svcs., 1981--; audiology cons. to Calif. Children Svcs. and Child Health and Disability Prev. Pgm. 1981-; awards: Pres.'s Medallion, CSUF, Dean's Medal, CSUF, Nat. Student Speech and Hearing Assn., Am. River Coll. Faculty Assn. Scholarship; mem: Am. Speech Language Hearing Assn., Calif. Speech Language Hearing Assn., Maternal, Child and Adolescent Health Adv. Bd. for Sacto. County; mil: E4 USAF 1968-72; rec: bicycling (instr. class for beginners). Res: 3720 Station St Sacramento 95827 Ofc: St. Dept. Hlth Svcs, Maternal & Child Hlth, 714 P St, Rm 300, Sacramento 95814

RAWLINGS, CLAUDETTE, school counselor; b. Apr. 8, 1938, Phenix City, Ala.; d. Wilbur and Fannie (Foy) Turner; m. Preston A. Rawlings, Dec. 22, 1961 (dec.); children: Cathy, b. 1955, Mervin, b. 1958, Loretta, b. 1961, Preston, b. 1962; edn: AA in behav. sci., San Diego Comm. Coll. 1974; BA, soc. welfare, San Diego State Univ. 1976, MS, counseling, 1977; lic. counseling psychologist, MFCC Intern. Career: soc. wkr., counselor Community Crisis Ctr. 1975-76; guidance aide Baker Elem. Sch., 1977-78, district counselor, 1978--; instr. adult edn./parenting; awards: Community Friend Scholarship 1975; Black Comm. Ctr. Awd. for Acad. Achieve. 1976, 77; appreciation, Lincoln H.S. (1978), S.D. City Coll. (1975), Co. Mental Health (1983); Who's Who in Am. Colls. and Univs. 1977; mem: Urban League Adv. Bd.; Sch. Adv. Council Baker Elem. 1981-83; Nat. Assn. of Black Soc. Wkrs.; S.E.Assn. for Youth Svcs. 1974-; Concerned Black Americans; Mountainview Comm. Task Force; Comm. Med. Ctr. bd. dirs. 1981-83; Democrat; Baptist; rec: bowling, crafts, fishing. Res: 5110 Palin St San Diego 92114 Ofc: Baker Elem. Sch. 4041 T St San Diego 92113

RAY, BURTON ALBERT, certified public accountant; b. Mar. 22, 1952, Orange; s. Lester B. and Sylvia C. (Fredericks) R.; edn: BS, USC, 1974; MBT, USC, 1976; CPA, Calif. 1977. Career: acctg., mgmt., Arthur Young & Co., 1974-79; partner, Ray & Sweeney, 1980--; chief fin. ofcr., bd. dirs. Evalucom, Inc. 1983--; honors: Beta Alpha Psi, Blue Key, recipient John F. Forbes Award; mem: Am. Inst. of CPAs, Calif. Soc. of CPAs, Jonathan Club, Hollywood Heritage Assn.; Republican; Prot.; rec: travel, restoration of hist. properties. Res: 2031 Holly Hill Terrace Los Angeles 90068 Ofc: Ray & Sweeney, 1888 Century Park East, sTe. 621, Los Angeles 90067

RAY, GLENN JERRY, computer graphics executive; b. May 8, 1932, Indiansprings, Ala.; s. Roy Andy and Lydia Conella (Sanders) R.; m. Mary Claussen, Dec. 21, 1968; edn: Sarrland Ala. Murphy Sch., Mobile, Ala.; BAIA, CSU Long Beach 1973; Calif. Comm. Coll. Tchg. Credentials (arch., engrg., related tech.) 1972; Std. Sec. Tchg. Cred. 1973. Career: engring. assoc. design No. Am. Rockwell 1962-64 (designed Apollo instrument panel structure and air condtg. sys. welfare sys. for Apollo Trainer (for tng. astronauts); supvr., sr. design, Hughes Aircraft, Fullterton 1964-67; sr. designer, Lead design, TRW, Redondo Bch. 1967-70; proj. engr. Am. Meter, Fullerton, 1973-75; proj. engr., Scanbe, El Monte, 1975-77; mgr., design, Gen. Automation, Anaheim 1978-79; real estate sales, Allstate, 1979-80; mgr. design, Fairchild, Manhattan Beach, 1980--; instr. blueprint reading Fairchild pgm., 1981-; tchr. L.A. Trade Tech. Coll. (blueprint reading 1975; CAD/CAM 1982-84, computer automated design/computer automated mfg.); mem: ASCUS, CAD/CAM Users Grp.; publs: Design, Drafting, Mfg. Workbook (Glenn J. Ray and Fairchild Control Systems Co., 1982, 2d. ed. 1983); tchg. manual for adv. archit., mech. drafting; winner nat. poetry contest, Reformed Ch. (poem set to music and recorded) 1951; Poems and Memories (1970); mil: s/sgt. USAF, 1950-54, supvsd. drafting grp. Republican; Prot.; rec: woodworking, photog., writing poetry. Res: 2024 Ravenhill Ct Fullerton 92631 Ofc: Fairchild Control Systems Co., 1800 Rosecrans Ave Manhattan Bch 90266

RAY, JOSEPH SUNDERLAND, cable television co. president; b. Dec. 27, 1913, Anaheim; s. Maurice and Florence (Sunderland) R.; m. Marjorie Melczer, Sept. 12, 1970; edn: BA, hist., UC Los Angeles 1935. Career: pres. Redwood Empire Tel. Co., San Miguel 1960-75; exec. cons., Continental Tel. Co. of Ca. 1975-83; pres./ gen. mgr. Redwood Empire Cablevision, Inc. The Sea Ranch, Ca. 1976--; dir. Redwood Empire Tel. Co., Redwood Empire Cablevision, Inc.; mem: Calif. Cable TV Assn., U.S. Independent Tel. Assn. 1972-73, Lions, Wild Oak Saddle Club of Santa Rosa, The Sea Ranch Golf Club; mil: lt. USN-R 1942-46, served on Adm. Halsey's staff in comm.; Republican; Catholic; rec: flying, golf. Res: 114 Hares Tail Close, The Sea Ranch 95497 Ofc: Redwood Empire Cablevisio, Inc. 38951 So. Coast Hwy, Ste. 1, Gualala 95445

RAY, SANDRA SUE, clinical social worker; b. July 1, 1944, Lincoln, Nebr.; d. Francis Harlow and Ellene Sigrid (Melsted) Goldsmith; children: Dana Sue Lenhart, b. 1967; Brandon Garrett Lenhart, b. 1969; Nicole Sharron Ray, b. 1979; edn: BS, Univ. of Ore. 1964; MSW, UCLA 1966; LCSW, lic. clin. soc. wkr, Calif. 1975-. Career: deputy probation ofcr. L.A. County Probation Dept., 1970-78; guidance mgr. L.A. Job Corps, Hollywood 1978-79; clin. dir. Penny Lane, Sepulveda 1980--; psychiat. cons., I-ADARP, Inc. Reseda/Van Nuys 1981--; assoc. prof. Calif. Sch. of Profl. Psychol., 1975-78; honors: Alpha Kappa Delta (1964); Democrat; Methodist; rec: the theater, LA Civic Light Opera. Res: 7806 Rhea Ave Reseda 91335 Ofc: Penny Lane, 15302 Rayen St Sepulveda 91343

RAYL, CHARLES L., agricultural lending association executive; b. Nov. 7, 1938, Havana, Kans.; s. Arthur Leonard and Velda (Brooks) R.; m. Marilyn Kelly, Aug. 29, 1959; children: John, b. 1961, William, b. 1963, Kelly, b. 1967; edn: BS agri., Cal Poly, S.L.O. 1960, grad. wtu. in agri. edn., 1961-62; Calif. Comm. Coll. lmtd. svc. credential in Agri. Svcs. and Processing, Banking & Fin., and Indsl. Mgmt. 1976. Career: mill foreman, herdsman Kern River Land & Cattle Co. Bakersfield 1960-61; instr. Animal Sci. Dept., Calif. St. Polytech. Coll., San Luis Obispo 1962-63; agri. rep. Wells Fargo Bank, Sacto. 1963-70; loan analyst/asst. mgr. Woodland Prodn. Credit Assn., Woodland 1970-71; gen. mgr. Chico Prodn. Credit Assn. 1971-76; chief exec. ofcr. Woodland Prodn. Credit Assn. and Federal Land Bank Assn., Woodland 1976--; instr. Yuba Coll. 1976-78, guest lectr. agri-bus. classes, Sierra Coll., UCD; mem. Yolo Co. Agri. Round Table Steering Com. 1979-; mem. agri. adv. com. Woodland H. Sch. 1981-; mem. Heidrick Scholarship Selection Com. 1977-; livestock judging, Future Farmers of Am.; mem: Yolo Co. Farm Bur., Rotary, Yolo Co. Fair (F.F.A. Auction Com.), Calif. Thoroughbred Breeders Assn., No. Calif. Thoroughbred Assn., Am. Quarter Horse Assn., Elks, Woodland CofC (pres. 1984), Lions; past pres. Woodland Little League, past BSA scoutmaster, 4-H leader; Republican; Prot.; rec: raising thoroughbred horses, fish, hunt. Res: Rte 1, Box 1083, Woodland 95695 Ofc: Woodland Prodn. Credit Assn. 283 Main St, (Fed. Land Bank Assn., POB 269), Woodland 95695

RAMSEY, JACK, library director; b. June 12, 1922, Kansas City, KS; s. Clay and Floy Ramsey; AB, Univ. KS, 1945; MS, Univ. IL, 1946; MLS, 1947; m. Sue Worsley, Apr. 4, 1946; Career: librn., NY Pub. Lib., 1947-48; adminstry. asst., Lib. of Stockton and San Joaquin Co., 1948-49; Co. librn., Solano Co., 1949-52; lib. dir., City of Glendale 1952-59, 66---; chief of customer H.W. Wilson Co., NYC, 1959-65. Mil: AUS, 1942-43. Mem: Phi Kappa Psi frat.; Beta Phi Mu, hon. lib. sci. frat., past pres.; NY Lib. Club, 1947---; past pres. Republican; Episcopalian, vestryman. Rec: music, travel. Res: 548 Mesa-Lila Rd., Glendale 91208; Office: 222 E. Harvard St., Glendale 91205.

RAYMOND, FREDERICK MARTIN, ophthalmic surgeon; b. Oct. 1, 1949, Los Angeles; s. Alfred Larry and Lucille (Marillo) R.; m. Emily Louise Militzer, Sept. 2, 1979; 1 dau. Jessica Louise, b. 1981; edn: BA, UC Los Angeles 1971; MD, USC 1975; lic. physician LA Co./USC Med. Ctr. 1976, ophthalmic surg. 1977-79. Career: postgrad. tng. Ophthalmology, Childrens Hosp., L.A. and St. Johns Hosp., Santa Monica; certifications from IOPTEX Implant Co. and IOLAB Intraocular Co.; assoc. with Francis O'Neal Morris in practice of Ear, Nost, Throat, and Ophthal., Whittier 1979-81; currently, solo practitioner on staff at Presbyterian Intercomm. Hosp., Whittier, Beverly Hosp., Whittier Hosp.; teaching faculty Family Practice Residents, L.A. Co./USC Med. Ctr.; honors: achievement awds. from AMA, Childrens Hosp., Salvation Army, Rotary Club of Am.; mem: L.A. Med. Assn., Calif. Med. Assn., Am. Acad. of Ophthalmol., Intraocular Implant Soc., Found. Assoc. bd. dirs. Presbyn. Inter. Hosp.; Rotary Club of Am. (Comm. Affairs); public spkr., infor. on eye disease and treatment; Democrat; Catholic; rec: tropical salt water fishes, MEDICOS Fox Terriers with Am. Kennel Club, breed finches, computer studies. Res: 1893 N. Nueva Vista Dr La Habra Hts 90631 Ofc: Frederick M. Raymond MD, Inc. 7200 Greenleaf Ave, Ste. 250, Whittier 90602

RAYMOND, GENE, actor, producer, dir., composer; b. Aug. 13, 1908, New York City; s. LeRoy D. and Mary (Smith) Guion; student Profl. Children's Sch., N.Y.C.; m. Jeanette MacDonald, June 16, 1937 (dec. Jan. 14, 1965); m. former Mrs. Nel Bentley Hees, Sept. 7, 1974. Career: Broadway debut in The Piper, 1920, other Broadway appearances include: Eyvind of the Hills, 1921, Why Not?, 1922, The Potters, 1923, Cradle Snatchers. 1925, Take My Advice, 1927, Mirrors, 1928, Sherlock Homes, 1928, Say When, 1928, The War Song, 1928, Jonesy, 1929, Young Sinners, 1929, A Shadow of My Enemy, 1957; other theater appearances include: The Man in Possession, Dennis, Mass., 1946, The Guardsman, 1951, The Voice of the Turtle, 1952, Angel Street, Richmond, Va., 1952, Petrified Forest, 1952, Call Me Madam, 1952, Private Lives, 1953, The Moon is Blue, 1953, Be Quiet, My Love, 1953, Detective Story, 1954, The Devil's Disciple, 1954, The Fifth Season, 1955, Will Success Spoil Rock Hunter, Los Angeles, San Francisco, 1956, Romeo and Juliet, Pasadena Playhouse, 1956, The Seven Year Itch, 1948, Holiday for Lovers, Chgo., 1959; appeared as Joseph Cantwell in nat. touring co. The Best Man, 1960, Majority of One, 1962, Mr. Roberts, 1962, Kiss Me Kate, 1962; other roles include: Candida, 1961, The Moon is Blue, 1963, Madly in Love, 1963; film appearances include: Personal Maid, 1931, Stolen Heaven, 1931, Ladies of the Big House, 1932, The Night of June 13th, Forgotten Commandments, 1932, If I Had A Million, 1932, Red Dust, 1932, Ex-Lady, 1933, The House on 56th Street, 1933, Zoo in Budapest, 1933, Brief Moment, 1933, Ann Carver's Profession, 1933, Flying Down to Rio, 1933, Sadie McKee, 1934, I Am Suzanne Fox, 1934, Coming Out Party, 1934, Transatlantic Merry-Go-Round, 1934, Behold My Wife, 1935, The Woman in Red, 1935, Seven Keys to Baldpate, 1935, Hooray for Love, 1935, Love on a Bet, 1936, Walking on Air, 1936, There Goes My Girl, 1937, Life of the Party, 1938, Cross-Country Romance, 1940, Mr. and Mrs. Smith, 1941, The Locket, 1946, Assigned to Danger, 1948, Million-Dollar Weekend, 1948, Sofia, 1948, Hit the Deck, 1955, Plunder Road, 1957, The Best Man, 1964, I'd Rather Be Rich, 1964; TV appearances include: Ed Sullivan's Toast of the Town, Ken Murray Show, Robert Montgomery Presents, Tales of Tomorrow, Lux Video Theater, Pulitzer Prize Theater, Broadway TV Theatre, Schlitz Playhouse, Fireside Theater, TV Reader's Digest, Barbara Stanwyck Show, Sam Benedict, U.S. Steel Hour, Adamsburg, U.S.A., The Defenders, Outer Limits, Channing, The Loretta Young Show. Matinee Theater, Playhouse 90, Climax, Johnny Ringo, Ethel Barrymore Theater, F.B.I., Ironside, Apple's Way, Judd for the Def., Bold Ones, Name of the Game, The Interns, Mannix and others; author teleplay Prima Donna: compser songs Will You?, Let Me Always Sing, Release. Past v.p. Arthritis Found. So. Calif.; pres. Motion Picture and TV Fund, 1980. Served with USAAF, 1942-45; ETO; served to col. USAFR, 1945-68. Decorated Legion of Merit and others. Recipient Disting. Service award Arthritis Found.; Humanitarian award Air Force Assn.; Better World award VFW; Bronze Halo award So. Calif. Motion Picture Council. Mem. Screen Actors Guild (dir.), Acad. TV Arts and Scis. (trustee), Air Force Assn. (pres. Los Angeles chpt.). Clubs: Players (N.Y.C.); N.Y. Athletic; Bel Air Country (Los Angeles); Army and Navy (Washington); Order of Daedalians. Address: 9570 Wilshire Blvd., Beverly Hills 90212.

RAYMOND, JOHN CALVIN, investment co. president; b. Oct. 20, 1937, Greeley, Colo.; s. John Calvin and Gladys M. (Raymond) R.; m. Caroline McCourt, Jan. 2, 1966; 2 daus., Midge, b. 1969, Becky, b. 1972; edn: BS, Cornell Univ. 1960. Career: asst. gen. mgr. to exec. vice pres. Formulabs, Inc., Escondido 1960-76; pres. Terraton Corp. (pvt. capital investments), Escondido 1976--; dir./sec. Par Crest Inc. 1976-; co-founder/dir. North County Bank 1974-; honors: Outstanding Young Man of Year 1971, and Good Govt. Leadership Awd. 1982, J.C.s; service award, Assn. of Calif. Sch. Adminstrs. 1973; apptd. mem. bd. dirs. San Diego Economic Devel. Corp. (chmn. No. Co. Adv. Council) 1981-84; apptd. mem. Calif. Economic Devel. & New Technologies Adv. Com. 1983-; mem: Escondido CofC (pres. 1982/3), Escondido Rotary (pres. 1974/5), Palomar Family YMCA (chmn. Bd. of Mgmt. 1968/9), Escondido Boys &: Girls Club dir. 1980/1; elected to bd. of edn. Escondido Union Elem. Sch. Dist. 1969-73; bd. dirs. S.D. Building Contractors Assn., No. Co. Div.; mil: capt. USAR, ret., Qtrmaster Corps 1960-68; Republican; Prot.; rec: community svc., tennis. Res: POB 204, Escondido 92025 Ofc: Terraton Corp. 350 E. Grand Ave, Ste 201, Escondido 92025

RAYOR, FREDERICK G., mortgage banker; b. Dec. 3, 1954, Los Angeles; s. Franklin Nathan and Marion (Noe) R.; m. Randa Copeland, May 19, 1979; children: Rebecca, b. 1980, Richard, b 1982; edn: AA in real estate, El Camino Coll. 1974; Mortgage Brokers Inst. 1981; lic. Calif. real estate broker (1975), notary public (1975), personal property broker (1980). Career: asst. trainer los Angeles Lakers, 1968-72; quality control mgr. California Bankdata Corp., 1972-75; sales mgr. Rayor & Co. Realtors, 1975-78; weekly financial columnist Palos Verdes View Newspaper, 1978-81; owner Rayor Financial Services Escrow, 1981--; bd. chmn./dir. Rayor Fin. Services, Inc. (mortgage bankers), 1981--; dir. Spruce Investment Corp. Mem: Calif. Assn. of Realtors, Nat. Assn. of Realtors, Torrance-Lomita-Carson Bd. of Realtors, South Bay Bd. of Realtors; Active 20-30 Club, Palos Verdes cofC, Centinela Hosp. Aux., Long Beach State Booster Club; Democrat; Temple Menorah; rec: fishing, sports. Res: 1056 W. 187th Pl Gardena 90248 Ofc: Rayor Financial Services, Inc. 727 Silver Spur Rd, Ste 101, Rolling Hills Estates 90274

RAZIN, SHELDON, corporate president; b. Dec. 28, 1937, Everett, Mass.; s. Asher and Faye Razin; m. Janet Murrin, Apr. 2, 1963; children: David, b. 1963, Mark, b. 1965; edn: BS, math, Mass. Inst. of Tech. 1959. Career: engineer/ pgmmr. Northrop Corp., Van Nuys 1959-60; mathematician/ pgmmr./ analyst/ supr./ mgr. Rockwell Internat., Anaheim 1960-72; asst. to pres. Index Systems,

Cambridge, Mass. 1973-74; founder/ pres./ bd. chmn. Quality Systems Inc., Tustin 1974--; mem. Assn. for Computing Machinery, UCI Chancellors Club; works: Explicit (Non-Iterative) Loran Solution (Inst. of Navigation 1967); Republican; Jewish; rec: boating, tennis, racketball, backgammon. Res: 1940 Pinecrest Dr Corona 91720 Ofc: Quality Systems Inc. 17822 E. 17th St Tustin 92680

READER, ROBERT JAMES, college counselor, real estate broker; b. Mar. 9, 1949, Shreveport, La.; foster parents: Daniel and Cora Jordan; m. Ruscel Grimes, Nov. 29, 1969; 1 son, Robert J., Jr. b. 1970; edn: BS, phys. edn., Ore. State Univ. 1972, MS, counseling, 1973; Calif. lic. real estate broker 1976, notary public 1983. Career: salesman, Milgrays Clothes, Richmond Bros. Men's Store, Bakersfield 1969-70; roustabout Shell Oil Co., 1969-70; counselor./tchr Bakersfield Jr. Coll., 1972--, dir. Martin Luther King Jr. Center for Social Change/ coll. track and field coach; owner Olympic Sporting Gallery, 1974-80; broker/owner Property Mart Realtors, 1976--; honors: Track and field awards for triple jump, Metropolitan Champion (1968, 69), So. Calif. Champion (1969), State Champion (1969), National Champion and Record Holder (1969); Record Holder, Pacific Eight Conf. (1969-72), Ore. State Univ.; mem. Amateur Athletic Union Team, NCAA All American (1970, 71), Indoor All American, mem. of three internat. USA Teams against Russia; finalist in 1972 and 1976 Olympic Trials; alternate to 1975 Pan Am Games in Mex. City; recipient US Jaycees Outstanding Young Man of Am. awd. mem. Alpha Phi Alpha Frat., Lyons club, NAACP; designer: triple jump shoe mktd. by Blue Ribbon Sports/ Nike Shoe Co.; Democrat; Prot.; spl. interest: bus. consulting for those in low socio-econ. areas. Res: 5001 College Ave Bakersfield 93306 Ofc: Bakersfield College, 1801 Panorama Dr Bakersfield 93305

REARDAN, NANCY BRIGGS, lawyer; b. Aug. 14, 1928, New York, d. Mead Greacen and Ida Lee (Fleming) Briggs; m. John Reardan 1954; children: Susan (Dayton), b. 1955, Linda, b. 1956, John, b. 1958, Bradley, b. 1964; edn: BA, Wellesley Coll. 1949, JD, McGeorge Sch. of Law 1971. Career: atty. Law offices of Nancy B. Reardan, Sacramento 1972--; instr. Lincoln Law Sch. 1974-76; bd. dirs. Briggs Schaedle and Co., Inc.; honors: Class Pres. McGeorge Sch. of Law 1970-71; cert. appreciation for trial work done in San Diego Sch. Desegr. Case, Carlin Sch. Comm. 1977; mem: Sacramento County Bar Assn., Calif. Bar Assn., Am. Bar Assn., Calif. Women Lawyers, Sacramento Women Lawyers, NAACP; publs: articles in Pacific Law Jour., Crisis mag.; Democrat; Presbyterian (Elder); rec: Arabian Horse breeder. Res: 800 Columbia Dr sacramento 95828 Law offices of Nancy B. Reardan, 2018 19th St Sacramento 95818

REAVILL, DAVID WILLIAM, stockbroker; b. Sept. 18, 1948, Los Angeles; s. Wm. Arthur and Marian E. (Stocks) R.; edn: AA, Santa Barbara City Coll. 1968; BA, pol. sci., Westmont Coll. 1971, Calif. State Teaching Cred. (life), 1972; MA, ergonomics, UC Santa Barbara 1978; Financial and Ops. Principal, Gen. Securities Prin., Municipal Secs. Prin., Registered Options Prin., Reg. Representive, multi state registration. Career: vice pres. Charles Schwab & Co., Santa Barbara 1978-80; mgr. William Oneil & Co., L.A. 1980-81; founder/ pres./ chief exec. First Los Angkes Discount Securities, Encino; mem: Am. Mgmt. Assn., Finl. Mgrs. Soc., Securities Traders Assn., Better Bus. Bur., CofC, Gr. L.A. Zoo, L.A. County Art Museum; writer/prod. financial T.V. pgms. (seen twice daily in S.F. and L.A.); Democrat; Prot.; rec: swimming, sailing, scuba, hiking. Res: 18307 Burbank Blvd, 306, Tarzana 91356 Ofc: First Los Angeles Discount Securities, 16055 Ventura Blvd, Ste. 777, Encino 91436

RECSEI, ERIC JOHN, clinical social worker; b. June 28, 1943, Los Angeles; s. Andrew A. and Milica (Ivanovich) R.; edn: BA, UC Santa Barbara 1966; MSW, Washington Univ. (St. Louis, Mo.) 1970; Calif. Sch. of Profl. Psychol. 1974-76; LCSW, Lic. Clin. Soc. Wkr. 1978. Career: soc. wkr. Sacramento Comm. Mental Health Services, 1970-74, Project Phoenix (res. facility for young heroin addicts), Fresno 1976-77, Kings Co. Public Welfare Dept., Child Protection Div., Hanford 1977, Contra Costa County Med. Services, Psychiatric Crisis Unit, Martinez 1978-80, Nevada Mental Health Inst., Reno, Nev. 1980-83; clin. social wkr. in private practice, Truckee 1983--; mem. Nat. Assn. of Soc. Wkrs., Truckee Optimist Club; Democrat; Jewish; rec: ski instr., river raft guide. Res: 10276 Jeffrey Pine Rd Truckee 95737 Ofc: 10020 Church St, Ste. 9, Truckee 95734

REDD, CHARLES HENSLEY, lawyer; b. June 16, 1931, Santa Monica; s. John Charles and Freda Teresa (Stoeckl) R.; m. Mary Jean, Nov. 30, 1973; children: Michael William, b. 1966 (Top Amateur Tennis Player); Melissa Jean, b. 1974; edn: AA, St. Josephs Coll. 1951; BA, Univ. of San Francisco 1953; MA, ednl. admin., UC Berkeley 1960; JD, Western State Univ. Coll. of Law 1972; admitted to Calif. State Bar 1973; grad. Hastings Coll. of Law, Coll. of Appellate Advocacy 1977. Career: sole practitioner law, Cottonwood, Shasta Co., 1973-76; senior staff atty. The Hartford Ins. Co., Fresno 1976-78; plaintiff trial atty. Law Offices of Oren & McCartney, Fresno 1978-79; counsel in def. civil litigationj with Kinkle, Rodiger & Spriggs, Riverside, 1979-81; trial atty. with Falsetti, Crafts, Pritchard & Darling, Riverside 1981; deputy city atty., Civil Div., City of Anaheim 1981--: defense of City of Anaheim in First Amendment action filed by Iskcon, Laguna Beach Temple, and others, in Ninth US Circuit Ct. of Appeals actions (1983-4); mem. various local bar assns., (past) Elks, Kiwanis, Moose, mil. E5 US Army 1955-6, Arty., Guided Missiles, GCM, Republican; Catholic; rec: tournament bridge, civics. Res: 3133 Newell Dr Riverside 92507 Office of the City Atty., City of Anaheim, 200 S. Anaheim Blvd, 3d Flr. Anaheim 92805

REDDY, NERABETLA DAMODARA, electronic engineer; b. Aug. 11, 1938, Bhairapuram, A.P. India; s. Buchi N. and Ramulamma Reddy; m. Prameela, May 28, 1958; children: Venkateshwar, b. 1966, Anupama, b. 1967, Srikanth, b. 1971; edn: BSEE, Osmania Univ., India 1965; MSEE, N.Dak. State Univ. 1969; MBA, Univ. of Santa Clara 1975. Career: design engr. at Sylvania, Woburn, Boston 1969-70; sr. design engr. RCA Solid State Tech. Ctr., Summerville, NJ 1970-72; sr. design engr. Fairchild Semiconductor Div., Mt. View 1972-74; devel. mgr. Four Phase Systems (Motorola), Cupertino 1974-81; advanced engring. mgr. Synertek (Honeywell), Santa Clara 1981-83; founder/pres. Modular Semiconductor Inc., Santa Clara 1983--; mem. IEEE; rec: swimming, exercise. Res: 10756 Linda Vista Dr Cupertino 95014 Ofc: Modular Semiconductor Inc. 2334 Walsh Ave Santa Clara 95051

REED, CHARLES RAY, health care executive; b. Feb. 12, 1940, Carthage, Mo.; s. Steward M. and Neva M. (Owens) R.; m. Sally, Jan. 16, 1976; children: Tammi, b. 1962, Michele, b. 1964, Lorr, b. 1965, Kerri, b. 1967, Charles, b. 1968; edn: BA, Bethany Nazarene coll. 1965; MBA, Calif. Western Univ. 1977; Grad. Pgm. in Health Care Adminstrn., Western Reserve Univ. 1968; Grad. Pgm. for Nursing Home Adminstrs., Univ. of Okla. 1967. Career: asst. to V.P. Ops., Manor Care Inc., Wash DC 1967; ops. coordinator, Four Seasons Nursing Ctrs., Okla. City 1968; ops. asst., Beverly Ents., Pasadena 1969-71; cons. to Health Care Mgmt. Cos., Wash DC 1971-73; dir. of ops., Mid America Nursing Ctrs. Wichita, Ks. 1974-75; exec. v.p. Beverly Ents., Pasadena 1975-81; pres. Serra Medical Found., Sun Valley 1981--; taught health care adm. Univ. of Okla.; cons. to US Senate Com. of Health; chmn. Gov's Adv. Com. Long Term Care, State of Nev., 4 years; adv. to Gov. of Okla. on health issues; publs. in field; Republican; Nazarene; rec: tennis. Res: 146 Highland Pl Monrovia 91016 Ofc: Serra Medical Foundation, 9375 San Fernando Rd Sun Valley 91352

REED, HAROLD WILLIAM, marketing executive; b. Mar. 12, 1935, St. Cloud, Minn.; s. Dewey and Erma (Fromelt) R.; m. Leonore, Aug. 1, 1957; children: Robert, b. 1959, Jacqueline, b. 1961, Heidi, b. 1965; edn: BA and BS, St. Cloud Univ. 1960; MS/PhD indsl. adm. (cand.), Purdue Univ. 1962. Career: asst. store mgr. J.J. Newberry Co.; controller Harbert Constrn. Co.; dir. New Enterprises, dir. Mktg. General Mills, Mnpls.; v.p./gen. mgr. Consumer Products, Crown Zellerbach, San Francisco; currently v.p./gen. mgr. Crown Advanced Films (pkg. div.), S.F.; bd. dirs. FPA, MBOF, PMA; instr. Purdue Univ. 1958-60; awards: Distinguished Mil. Graduate, AFROTC 1958, Ford Found. Fellow 1958-60, grad. cum laude, St. Cloud Univ. 1958; Top 10 New Products SAMI, 1968; clubs: Olympic, Orinda CC, Commonwealth; served on Park Commn., on Wazeta Parochial Sch. Bd., 1964-70; dir. St. Bart's CCD, 1965-69; Alameda Recycling Council 1981-; mil: 1st. lt. USAF 1954-58, USAFR 1958-65; Catholic; rec: hunt,, fish, ski, golf. Res: 1216 Cambridge Dr Lafayette 94549 Ofc: Crown Zellerbach, One Bush St, Ste. 1700, San Francisco 94104

REED, JACK HARLEY, private investigation co. president; b. Apr. 13, 1933, Los Angeles; s. John B. and Nehoma (Newton) R.; m. Mary Rickerl Reed, Sept. 28, 1973; edn: LLB, Western State Univ. Coll. of Law, 1972; Calif. Lic. Private Investigator; career: nine years in personal finance mgmt.; owner/pres. J.H.R.I., INC. (one of 50 largest privately held pvt. investigation cos.); awards: Internat. Investigator of the Year 1983; 5 awards for outstanding svc.Calif. Assn. of Lic. Investigators; mem: CALI, dir. 1973-78, 81, v.p. 1979; pres. 1980; CII, dir. 1981; 3rd v.p. 1982; 2nd v.p. 1983; 1st v.p. 1984; NCISS, 1st v.p. 1981; v.p. legislation 1981-84; sev. arts. written for orgns. publs.; Republican; rec: computers, travel, horses; Ofc: J.H.R.I., INC., 3777 N. Harbor Blvd., Fullerton, 92635

REED, JACQUELINE ANN, real estate broker; b. June 7, 1947, Los Angeles; d. Milton and Carrie Lue (Towns) R.; 1 dau. Mondella, b 1972; edn: AA, West L.A. Coll. 1982; undergrad. CSULA 1982-; spl. courses, Anthony Sch. of R.E., W.L.A. Coll.; Calif. lic. real estate broker 1977. Career: real estate agt. Century 21, Signa Realty, L.A. 1975-76; real estate broker/mgr. Century 21 Houses, Etc., 1977-78; assoc. broker J.D.F. Properties, L.A. 1979, Forest Olson, Granada Hills 1980; real estate broker/prin., 1981--; awards: Winners' Circle 1975, 76, Million Dollar Club 1976; mem. Southwest L.A. bd. of Realtors 1975-76, San Fernando Valley Bd. of Realtors 1979-80; Democrat; Baptist; rec: horticulture, sewing, int. design, counseling. Address: Jacqueline Ann Reed, 116 East Fairview Blvd, Inglewood 909302

REED, JOHN FARLEY, lawyer; b. Apr. 12, 1917, Springfield, Ill.; s. John Noble and Theo (Nichols) R.; m. Emily R., Mar. 5, 1976; children: Christina, b. 1943, Craig, b. 1945 (dec.); edn: BA, UCLA, 1937; JD, Univ. of Okla. 1940; admitted to practice Supreme Courts, US, Calif. & Okla. 1940. Career: pres. John F. Reed, APC; dir./ofcr.: De Luxe Corp., Wahl Instruments, Inc., Wahl International, Ltd., Kirschner Corp., Alto United Corp., Toal Corp., Titan Corp., Avalon Foods, Inc., The Wassco Group, Wassco, Av-Ox, Inc., Chica Corp., Fire Protection Systems, Inc., Fisher Forging, Inc., Louis Walter Co., Inc., The Karosen Co., Selder Corp.; mem: Phi Delta Phi, Theta Xi, Marina City Club; mil: served in WWI 1940-45, Korean War 1951-53, cmdr. USNR; decorated Am. Defense w/star, Phil. Def. w/star, ETO w/3 stars, Bronze Star w/star, Korean theatre w/star, UN, Naval Reserve medals; 7 unit cits., 3 letters commdn.; Republican; rec: skiing, tennis. Res: 4309 Redwood Ave, 3, Marina del Rey 90292 Ofc: John F. Reed APC, 4676 Admiralty Way, Ste. 704, Marina del Rey 90292

REED, SHARON ANN, vocational school executive; b. Nov. 13, 1948, Little Rock, Ark.; d. Hugh Edgar and Doris Jean (Hogan) Daniels; m. Allen Reed, Apr. 25, 1968; children: Stacy, b. 1969, Billy, b. 1971, Alicia, b. 1977; edn: AA, Compton Comm. Coll. 1970; BA, CSU Dominguez Hills 1977; MS, Pepperdine Univ. 1978; Calif. Std. tchg. and administrv. credentials. Career: tchr. Compton

Unified Sch. Dist., 1970-, head tchr. 1973, staff asst. 1975-80; life ins. agt. The Equitable Life Ass. Soc. Calif., 1980; program dir. Technical Health Careers School, Inc. 1981-, executive dir. 1984--; cons./seminar leader Career Inst., Inc.; facilitator Future Woman Seminars; cons. CVS Computer Systems; honors: Outstanding Educator, Council Grove III Elem. Sch. 1980; spl. recognition Curriculum Devel., Chester Adult/Childrens Center. Mem: Nat. Assn. of Health Career Schools, Calif. Assn. of Adminstrs. (mem. ch.), Inglewood CofC, Compton Bus. and Profl. Womens Club, Assn. of Compton Unified School Adminstrs. (secty. 1978); City of L.A. Pub. Relations Com. 1983-84; v.ch. Compton Invitnl. Track Com., 1979-84; Democrat; Rel. Sci.; rec: public presentations, fashion show commentation. Res: 2712 W. 101st St Inglewood 90303 Ofc: Technical Health Careers School, Inc. 4656 W. Century Blvd Inglewood 90304

REEDER, WENDELL LEE, community college president-superintendent; b. Apr. 21, 1926, Silverton, Ore.; s. Timothy Louis and Viola Mae (Olsen) R.; m. E. Almeda, June 3, 1952; children: Terri Lee, b. 1955, Tamari Lynn, b. 1958; edn: bS, Linfield, 1948; MS, Univ. of Ore. 1956; EdD, Ore. State Univ. 1972; Calif. Gen. Secondary Tchg. Credential (K-12) 1959, Pupil Personnel Cred. 1962, Comm. Coll. Chief Adminstr. 1974. Career: tchr. McMinnville (Ore.) High Sch. 1948-50; tchr., vice prin. Oak Ridge, Ore. 1952-59; tchr. Pittsburg (Calif.) Unified Sch. Dist., 1959-64; asst. to pres./asst. prof. Central Ore. Coll. 1964-67; dean of academic affairs Clackamas Comm. Coll., Ore. 1967-75; pres./supt. West Kern Comm. Coll., 1975-80, Butte Community Coll., 1981--; adj. prof. Portland St. Univ. 1972-75; honors: Jr. Citizen of Year, Oakridge, Ore. 1955; recipient Oakridge H.Sch. annual dedication (1955); Outstanding Educators of Am. (1974); Citizen of Year 1976, Taft CofC; mem: Phi Dk Country Club; mil: maj. Inf. AUS-R (Merril's Marauders) WWII 1943-64; Republican; Presbyterian; rec: golf, travel. Res: 140 Estates Dr Chico 95926 Ofc: Butte College, 3536 Butte Campus Dr Chico 95965

REESE, CHARLES WOODROW, JR., lawyer; b. June 21, 1944, San Antonio, Tex.; s. Charles W. and Mary Ruth (Gott) R.; m. Jill Fritschi Olsen, 1979; children: Clarissa, b. 1972; Alexandra, b. 1982; edn: BA, cum laude, Washington and Lee Univ. 1966; JD, Boalt Hall Sch. of Law, UCB 1969. Career: atty., law firm McCutchen, Doyle, Brown and Enersen, San Francisco, 1970-75; atty., Kaiser Industries Corp. and Kaiser Cement Corp., 1975-78; asst. gen. counsel, Kaiser Cement Corp., 1978--; trustee Clotilde DeMartini Trusts, 1976-; mng. dir. Reese Interests, 1978-; hon. trustee Orinda Foundation, 1976-; bd. dirs. Planned Parenthood 1981-; honors: Omicron Delta Upsilon (1966), Robert E. Lee Research Scholar, 1965-66, Moot Court Board UC Berkeley 1969; mem: American, Calif. State, San Francisco, Alameda County bar assns., American Corporate Counsel Assn., The Pacific Union Club, Orinda Co. Club, Merchants Exchange Club, Sigma Chi frat., Phi Delta Phi legal frat.; Republican; Episcopal; rec: skiing, tennis, duck hunting. Res: 89 La Salle Ave Piedmont 94611 Ofc: Kaiser Cement Corp. 300 Lakeside Dr, Ste. 2459, Oakland 94612

REESE, DONALD MILLER, manufacturing co. executive; b. Dec. 28, 1932, Savannah, Ga.; s. George Anslem and Bessie (Miller) R.; m. Ida Louise Richards, Dec. 25, 1952; children: George, b. 1954, Burmah, b. 1956, Steven, b. 1958, David, b. 1960. Career: owner Suspension Eyewear Ent., Ltd.; patentee: Suspension Eyewear (design which suspends eyeglass lenses from earpieces without the customary temples; design is recommended for vigorous active wear). Res: 1805 Palos Verdes Drive West Palos Verdes Estates 90274 Ofc: Suspension Eyewear Ent., Ltd. 332 L Street, Newport Beach 92661

REESE, ROBERT SYDNEY, economist; b. Feb. 18, 1908, St. Paul, Minn.; s. George Richard Stanley and Effie Eugenie (Longfield) R.; m. Lydamar Hayward, Dec. 18, 1938 (dec. 1979); stu. Univ. of Ill. 1927-8, Univ. of Nebr. 1930-3, Geo. Washington Univ. 1936-7, Loyola Univ., L.A. 1937-8. Career: economist/ prop./ dir. Los Angeles Bureau of Municipal Research, Inc.; prepared local wage data used to set indsl. wage rates in Los Angeles and Long Beach area during WWII; devel. new property tax law for Arkansas, passed in 1955, which was the basis for the rapid growth of industry in Ark. 1955-60 (more new jobs per capita than were added in any other state during same period); pvt. practice as land economist; editor/pub. Tax Talk, semi-monthly pub. dealing with property tax matters; mem: L.A. CofC (research com.), Sunland-Tujunga Rotary Club, Paul Harris Fellow; trustee Assn. of Congregational Christian Churches of Calif. and Western States (past moderator); mil: AAF and Army Transp. Corps, 1943-46, Commndn.; Republican; Congregational. Address: Los Angeles Bureau of Municipal Research, Inc. POB 576, Tujunga 91042

REEVES, CLARENCE ALBERT, JR., physician; b. Jan. 13, 1946, Auburn; s. Clarence A., Sr. and Amy Jewel (Webb) R.; m. Adrienne Morales, June 14, 1969; children: Amanda, b. 1974, Ryan, b. 1978, Adam, b. 1979; edn: BA, UC Berkeley 1967; D.Pharm., UC San Francisco 1971; MD, UCLA, 1975. Career: residency in Family Practice, San Bernardino Co. Medical Ctr., 1975-78; pvt. practice family med., Las Posas Family Practice Group, 1978--; chief of med. Pleasant Valley Hosp., Camarillo; mem: AMA, CMA, Am. Acad. of Family Practice. Res: 607 Deseo Ave Camarillo 93010 Ofc: Las Posas Family Practice Grp. 2438 Ponderoso, Ste C101, Camarillo 93010

REEVES, EUGENIA GASTON, psychiatric social worker; b. Feb. 26, 1956, Fresno; d. Rutherford Boyd, Sr. and Willodyne Eugenia (Shields) Gaston; m. Sorlie Reeves, July 4, 1981; edn: BA in psych., CSU Long Beach 1978; MSW, USC 1980; LCSW, Lic. Clin. Soc. Wkr. Calif. 1982. Career: psychiatric social wkr. L.A. County Dept. Mental Health, Los Angeles 1980--; clin. soc. wkr. Daniel Freeman Hosp. Emergcy Rm., 1983--; oral examiner LCSW exam., State Bd. Behavioral Scis. 1983; mem: Nat. Assn. of Black Social Wkrs. (edn. com. ch.), Nat. Assn. of Soc. Wkrs., Delta Sigma Theta Sor. (hlth resources com.); profl. presentations; Democrat; Baptist; rec: church activities. Res: 5505 Ackerfield, 409, Long Beach 90805 Ofc: L.A. County Dept of Mental Health, 3751 Stocker ST Los Angeles 90008

REEVES, ROBERT LEE, lawyer; b. Jan. 31, 1942, New London, Conn.; s. Waldo Norwell and Mary (Dandona) R.; div.; children: Terry, b. 1959, Robert, b. 1961, Mary, b. 1962; edn: BA (cum laude), John Jay Coll. 1976; JD, Pepperdine Univ. Sch of Law 1980; admitted to Calif. Supreme Court 1980. Career: police ofcr. New London City Police Dept., 1964-67, NYC Police Dept., 1967-76 (assigned patrol, Undercover Investigns., teaching and adminstrv. duties; ret. 1976 due to line of duty injuries); pres. Robert L. Reeves, profl. law corp., Los Angeles 1980--, active in practice of immigration, personal injury, family and criminal law; awards: Highest award for Bravery, Conn., 1964; 13 awards for bravery and achievement, Police Commnr. NYC; full academic scholarship grantee to St. Johns Univ. Sch. of Law and NY Sch. of Law; mem: Am., Calif. State, Los Angeles County bar assns., L.A. Trial Lawyers Assn.; Pepperdine Univ. Assocs., and Century Club; life mem. NYC Police Dept. Honor Legion; recipient recognition for Atty. Rendering the Most Svcs. to Cambodian Refugees; mil: spl/c US ARmy 1959-62; Republican; Catholic; rec: sailing, photog. Res: 14010 Captains Row Marina Del Rey 90291 Ofc: Robert L. Reeves, APLC, 2500 Wilshire Blvd, PH-G, Los Angeles 90057

REGAN, J. THOMAS, actor/writer; b. Mar. 2, 1940, Jacksonville, Ill.; s. George M. and Kathryn M. (Pease) R.; edn: BA, chem./math., Univ. of Mo. 1963; stu. with Lee Strasberg (3 yrs), Al Morganstern (1 yr), Jeanne Robbins (singing), Robert Easton (dialectic). Career: with B.F. Goodrich Chem. Co. 1963-70: sales & tech. rep. plastic products, 13 countries in Europe, internat. sales office The Hague, Holland 1965-67, product engr., Cleveland, Oh. 1967-70; indsl. sales engr. Texaco Inc., Los Angeles area 1971-73; W. regl. mgr. Drew Chem. Corp., 1973; tech. writer/regional editor for chemical processing mag. 1982-; actor in ten movies, over 35 TV roles, over 40 commercials; stage appearances (20 credits), mem. Group Repertory Theatre, bd. mem. Newport Theatre Arts Ctr.; motion picture credits incl. All Night Long, Stone (NBC MOW); TV film credits incl. Crises Counselor (lead), General Hospital, McLain's Law, Freebe & The Bean, Flamingo Road (7 episodes), Knotts Landing (2), Dallas (3), Police Story, Police Woman, Hotel, others; frequent spkr. local schs. on acting as a profession; fmr. instr. TV comml. acting; mem. SAG, AFTRA, AEA; mil: USAR 1963-69; rec: photog. Res: 212 Marguerite St Corona Del Mar 92625 Ofc: 474 E. 17th St, Ste. 205, Costa Mesa 92627

REGNIER, VICTOR ALBERT, architect/ educator; b. Sept. 12, 1947, Kansas City, Ks.; s. Victor L. and Helen (Benning) R.; m. Judith Nancy Gonda, Aug. 11, 1980; edn: BS, Kansas St. Univ. 1971; B.Arch., 1971; M.Arch., USC 1973; lic. architect, Calif. 1977; mem. AIA 1977. Career: v.p. Gerontological Plng. Assocs., Santa Monica 1973-74; lab. chief Environmental Studios Lab., Andrus Gerontology Ctr., USC 1974-80; assoc. prof., Sch. of Architecture, Pgm. of Housing, Research & Devel., Univ. of Ill., Champaign- Urbana 1980-83; cons. to 23 corps., univs., municipalities on design, plng. & research in environments for the aged. honors: fellow, gerontological Soc. 1983; awd. in soc. plng., St. of Calif. chpt. Am. Plng. Assn. 1978; Meritorious Plng. Awd., L.A. chpt. Am. Plng. ASsn. 1978, 79; Tau Sigma Delta Arch. Hon.; mem: Am. Inst. of Arch.; Am. Inst. of Plnrs.; Gerontological Soc.; Western Gerontol. Soc.; Environmental Design Research Assn.; Los Angeles Community Design Ctr. (pres. 1978); publs: book, Planning for the Elderly, USC Press 1979; over 25 pub. papers & arts.; over 50 presentations profl., sci. meetings; prin. investigator 7 major research projs. 1974-83; Democrat; rec: photog. Res: 2635 Hollyridge Dr Los Angeles 90068 Ofc: USC, Whatt Hall, 210 D, Los Angeles 90089

REID, JACK H., real estate broker/developer; b. Nov. 10, 1913, Bandana, Ky.; s. James M. and Lula (Thomas) R.; m. Ina M. Byrd, July 9, 1939; children: James F., b. 1944; Harold H., b. 1946; edn: pilot, Navy Flight Sch. 1937-38; law, La Salle Ext. Univ. 1947-52; cert. in R.E., Univ. of Calif. 1961-66; FAA ground instr. cert. Career: naval pilot, capt. USN, 1937-1957, ret.; decorated D.F.C.; (Capt. Reid sighted Japanese Fleet 800 miles away from Midway in Battle of Midway; his picture, along with crew and plane, on permanent exhib. Nat. Air. & Space Mus., Smithonian Instn.; sighting described in four separate books on the Battle of Midway); airline transport capt. US Overseas Airline, Oakland 1957-61; real estate broker/ developer, Reid & O'Neil Realty, Hayward 1962-68; R.E. broker Pacific Realtors, Aptos 1979--; bd. dirs. Southern Alameda Co. Bd. Realtors; dir. Calif. Real Estate Assn.; mem: Ret. Ofcrs. Assn.; Monterey Bay Srs. Golf. Assn.; Calif. Alumni Assn.; Airline Pilots Assn.; Silver Eagles Assn.; Rep. Pres. Task Force; Hole-in-One Club; Republican; Protestant; rec: golf, hunting, fishing. Res: 110 Paseo Ballena Aptos 95003 Ofc: Pacific Realtors, 8037 Soquel Dr Aptos 95003

REILLY, PATRICK JOHN, chemical company executive; b. Oct. 10, 1925, Nutley, NJ; s. Philip and Anna (Cox) O'Reilly; edn; Bach., Civil Engring., NY Univ., 1950; practical constrn. law, Univ. of Santa Clara, Sch. of Law, 1977; m. Marcie Garcia Vasquez, July 27, 1957, chil: Ann, b. 1958; Patrick J. Jr., b. 1960; Thomas J., b. 1962; Francis P., b. 1964. Career: asst. equipment mgr., Brown-Raymond-Walsh, Madrid, Spain, 1954-55; proj. engr., Zaragoza Air Base, Spain, 1955-57; v.p., proj. mgr., Wastewater Treatment Plants, Shamley Constrn. Co., S.F., Calif., 1957-65; constrn. mgr., W.W. Kimmons & Sons, Buffalo, N.Y., highways utilities and underground constrn., 1965-70; dir. Municipal Wastewater Plants, Monsanto Environ. Chem. Systems Inc.,

Chicago, Ill., 1970-74; v.p., constrn. mgr., proj. mgr., Solid Waste Facilities, BSP Div. Envirotech., Belmont, Calif., 1974---; constrn. cons., Monsanto Enviro. Chem., 1979-81. Listed: Who's Who in West. Mem: Amer. Mgmt. Assn., 1978-81; Amer. Assn. of Individ. Investors, ---; Internatl. Platform Assn., ---. Mil: 1st Lt., USAFR; T/Sgt., US Army Air Force; DFC, Air Medal w/5 clusters. Rec: jogging, reading. Res: 20719 Woodward St., Saratoga 95070; Office: EBSP Envirotech., 1 Davis Dr., Belmont 94002.

REIMAN, THOMAS ANDREW, association executive; b. Sept. 17, 1951, Oakland; s. Martin and Eve (Morgan) R.; m. Cynthia Anne Dennis, Aug. 24, 1975; children: Joshua, b. 1979; Jeffrey,b. 1982; edn: BA, UC Berkeley 1973; MA, Univ. SF/Lone Mtn. Coll. 1976; Calif. Jr. Coll. Tchg. Cred. 1980. Career: Vista vol. Fulton Co. Probation Dept., Atlanta, Ga. 1973-4; personnel analyst Alameda Co. Civil Svce., Oakland 1974-6, administrv. intern to Cong. Leo J. Ryan 1974-5; sr. adminstr. Correctional Svcs. Div. Dept. of Social Welfare, Melbourne, Australia 1976-9; dir. comm. affairs and security Community of Harbor Bay Isle (Calif.) Owners Assn. 1979-81, exec. dir. 1981--, exec. dir. Harbor Bay Business Pk. Assn., bus. mgr. Bay Farm Is. Reclamation Dist. Mem: Am. Soc. for Indsl. Security, Community Assns. Inst., Australian and New Zealand Soc. of Criminology, Nat. Assn. Chiefs of Police, Rotarian, BSA. Pub. jour. arts. Democrat. Jewish. Rec: swim, racquetball. Res: 501 Ironwood Rd Alameda 94501 Ofc: Harbor Bay Isle, 885 Island Dr., 200, Alameda 94501

REIMANN, HANS, physicist; b. Mar. 29, 1943, Wald ZH, Switz.; s. Ernst and Marta (Suter) R.; m. Amy M. Quan, Nov. 23, 1980; edn: electro mech., Georg Fischer (by apprenticeship) 1963; Maturitat C, acad. in Zurich 1966; MSc, dip. exptl. physics, Univ. of Zurich 1973, PhD, 1978. Career: research asst./ postdoc. research assoc. Physics Dept., Univ. of Zurich 1973-79, Physics Dept., Ohio State Univ. 1979-81; staff engr. Nat. Semiconductor, Santa Clara 1981-82; staff scientist/ R&D mgr. Sensym, Inc., Sunnyvale 1982--; awards: postdoc. fellowship, Grad. Sch. Ohio State Univ. 1979-80; mem: Am. Physical Soc.; IEEE, Electron Device, Magnetics, & Engring. Mgmt. Socs.; Fellow British Interplanetary Soc.; 13 scientific publs.; rec: history of space flight. Res: 1526 Norland Dr Sunnyvale 94087 Ofc: Sensym, Inc., 1255 Reamwood Ave Sunnyvale 94089

REINBOLD, BUDDIE REX, financial consultant; b. Aug. 28, 1933, Chariton, Iowa; s. Zeno E. and Colleen May (Oliver) R.; m. Sylvia Rosina Horsnell, Nov. 21, 1959; edn: Air Univ., Maxwell AFB, Ala. 1961; (Outstanding Grad.) Air War Coll. 1972; (Honor Grad.) Indsl. Coll. at Armed Forces, Wash DC 1974; desig: CFP, Coll. of Finl. Plnng., Denver 1983. Career: served to lt. col. USAF 1952-76, commn. and aviation cadet pgm. 1954, sta. in eight fgn. countries 1954-76, flew 18 different types of fighters from F-86 thru F-4, served as instr., base commander and ops. staff ofcr. with 3 AF, 13AF and Tactical Air Command, combat in Vietnam F-105 Wild Weasel, ret. 1976; decorated Silver Star, Air Medal, Purple Heart, Legion of Merit, Merit. Svc. Medal, AF Commendn., var. other awards; gen. mgr. Nelbarden Mfg. Co., 1976; finl. cons. Shearson American Express, Palm Springs 1979--; mem: Finl. Professional Advisory Panel; awards: Presidents Council, Shearson Am. Express; mem: Desert Estate Planning Council, Nat. Assn. of Estate Plnng. Councils, Inst. of CFPs, Internat. Assn. for Finl. Plnng., Internat. Mgmt. Assn.; orgns: Aircraft Owners and Pilots Assn., Retired Officers Assn., AF Assn., Order of Daedaliens, Red River Valley Fighter Pilots Assn., Guide Dogs of the Desert; Indep.; Methodist; rec: flying, comml. pilot, photog. Res: 72-770 Somera Rd Palm Desert 92260 Ofc: Shearson American Express 707 Tahquitz McCallum Palm Springs 92262

REINER, WILLIAM GEORGE, pediatric urologist; b. Nov. 21, 1947, San Francisco; s. Ralph Everett, Sr. and Elizabeth Ann (Anderson) R.; m. Irene Murphy, Aug. 5, 1978; children: David, b. 1979; Matthew, b. 1981; edn: BA, UC San Diego 1969; MD, UC Irvine 1974; urology res., Johns Hopkins Hosp., 1980; Diplomate Am. Bd. of Urology 1982. Career: intern, UCLA Hosp., Los Angeles 1974-75; res., UC Irvine Hosp., Irvine 1975-76; urological res., Johns Hopkins Hosp., Baltimore, MD 1976-77; fellow, Dept. of Urology, Johns Hopkins Univ., Baltimore, MD 1977-78; chief res. pediatric urology/ chief res. adult urology, Johns Hopkins 1978-80; pediatric and adult urologist, William G. Reiner, MD, Inc., Visalia 1980--; urological advr. Tulare Co. Spina Bifida Clinic & Calif. Childrens Svcs.; lectr., UCSF Sch. of Med., Med. Edn. Pgm., Fresno Veterans Hosp. 1983--; honors: fellow, Am. Cancer Soc. 1977-78; Alpha Omega Alpha nat. med. hon. soc.; mem: AMA, CMA, Am. Urological Assn.; Visalia Unified Sch. Dist. Family Life Curriculum Adv. Bd.; Visalia Unified Schs. for Cancer Prevention & Detection Edn. Pgm.; Coll. of Sequoias Nursing Pgm. urology lectr.; num. arts. in med. journs. 1979; research; Republican; Presbyterian; rec: woodwork, gardening, fishing. Rex: 500 Gilmer Ct Visalia 93291 Ofc: William G. Reiner, MD, Inc., 2752 W Main Visalia 93291

REINHARDT, BENJAMIN M., lawyer; b. Dec. 29, 1917, NYC; s. Meyer and Miriam R.; m. Marlaena Chubey, May 23, 1971; 3 children: Dennis, Sara, Dixie; edn: undergrad. Harvard Univ. 1940; JD, magna cum laude, Southwestern Univ. Law Sch. 1956. Career: admitted to practice law in Calif. and Fed. Cts., 1956, US Supreme Ct. 1960; trial attorney, Van Nuys 1957--; fmr atty. Calif. State Psychol. Assn.; fmr instr. real estate law, bus. law, L.A. Bd. of Edn. Past pres. Welfare Planning Council, San Fernando Vly.; past pres. Northridge Hosp. Found. Mem: Calif. State Bar, Calif. Trial Lawyers Assn.; Pacific Corinthian Yacht Club (Commodore 1984), Republican; yachting, fishing, reading. Res: 4034 Romany Dr. Oxnard 93030 Ofc: 7100 Hayvenhurst Ave. Ste. 202 Van Nuys 91406

REINHARDT, CARL H., financial planner; b. May 20, 1943, Regensburg, Germany, nat. 1959; s. Karl and Josephine R.; m. Geraldine Caballo, Mar. 19, 1967; children: Erich, b. 1970, Matthew, b. 1979; edn: AA, Monterey Penin. Jr. Coll. 1967; BS, mktg. resrch, CSU Fresno 1969; Reg. Principal, NASD, CLU, ChFC. Career: financial planner, Fresno 1969--, Employee Benefit cons., Cincinnati, Oh. 1973-75; founder/owner Pacific Financial Services Ltd. (fmrly Reinhardt & Assocs.), in Campbell, Ca. 1975, now in San Jose; honors: 1969 S.M.E. Award most likely grad. to succeed, Pi Sigma Epsilon (pres. Fresno chpt.); mem: Internat. Assn. for Fin. Planners (pres. Santa Clara Chpt. 1984-85), Soc. of CLUs (dir. San Jose chpt.); adv. bd. Big Brother Big Sisters of Santa Clara Co.; publish Fin. Newsletter 1983-; frequent spkr. on fin. planning; mil: Calif. Nat. Guard 1962-68; Republican; Catholic; rec: painting, fishing. Res: 3480 Oakwood Ct Morgan Hill 95037 Ofc: Pacific Financial Services Ltd. 4030 Moorpark, San Jose 95117

REINSCH, HARRY ORVILLE, engineering/construction co. executive; b. Feb. 12, 1922, Los Angeles; s. Harry O., Sr. and Olive Gladys (Cooper) R.; m. Helen, Oct. 19, 1942; children: E. James, b. 1942; John, (dec.); Richard, b. 1946; Linda (Marsh), b. 1958; edn: engring., UC Davis 1940-42. Career: from gen. supt. to mgr. of bus. devel. Bechtel Power Corp. 1968-72; v.p./ dir. Bechtel Power Corp. 1972-73; exec. v.p./ dir. 1975; pres./ dir. 1975--; bd. dirs. Wells Fargo Bank; mem: ASCE, ASME, Am. Nat. Stds. Inst.; Atomic Indsl. Forum (dir. and exec. com.); US/Repub. of China Economic Council (dir. and exec. com.); bd. trustees, Univ. of Montana Found.; Korean-Am. CofC (bd.); Com. for Energy Awareness (dir.); Calif. Council for Environmental & Economic Balance (dir.); bd. dirs. No. Calif. Soc. to Prevent Blindness; bd. dirs., That Man May See; Republican; rec: golf, shooting. Res: 1940 Broadway, Apt 10, San Francisco 94109 Ofc: Bechtel Power Corp., 50 Beale St San Francisco 94105

REISER, RICHARD DAVID, electronic engineer; b. Jun. 3, 1937, Port Jervis, NY; s. Walter Henry and Mildred Olive (Allen) R.; m. Caroljean Gilman, Jul. 7, 1966; edn: BSEE, San Jose State Univ. 1976, MS C&IS, 1979; career: mgr. processors & adapters Singer Bus. Machines, San Leandro; sr. staff engr. Memorex, Santa Clara 1974-76; v.p./tech. officer Priam, San Jose 1976--; consultant process control, system architecture, storage control; mem: IEEE, Tau Beta Phi; Eta Kappa Nu; patentee (8); mil: cpl. USMC, GCM, Nat. Def.; rec: flying, scuba, skiing; Res: 11457 Lindy Pl Cupertino 95014 Ofc: Priam, 20 W Montague San Jose 95134

REISMAN, CARL, executive; b. June 11, 1920, Atlanta, Ga.; s. Joseph Nathaniel and Elsie (Kleiner) R.; m. Betty Scholer, Apr. 23, 1946; children: Aileen Ann, b. 1948; Richard, b. 1950; edn: BS, Georgia Inst. of Tech 1941. Career: partner Surgical Selling Co., Atlanta, GA 1946-60; v.p. Ipco Hosp. Supply Corp., NY, NY; sales mgr. Gentec Hosp. Supply Corp., NY, NY 1967-68; v.p. 1968-73; v.p., Gentec, San Francisco 1973-74; v.p. Daylin Med. Supply Corp., Los Angeles 1974-75; chmn. bd./ CEO/ pres. 1975--; pres. Abco Dealers, Inc. 1953-56, 1959, chmn. bd. 1960; mem: Verdugo Club, Glendale; mil: Lt. Cmdr., USNR 1941-46; rec: hunting, fishing, skiin. Res: 3609 Cananea Dr Encino 91436 Ofc: Tri-anim Health Services, Inc., 1630 Flower St Glendale 91436

REISS, BONNIE MICHELLE, lawyer/business manager; b. Aug. 24, 1955, NY, NY; d. Ben and Mildred (Goodman) Reiss; edn: JD, Antioch Coll. 1980; admitted to Calif. State Bar. Career: tax auditor Peat, Marwick & Mitchell, CPAs, Miami, Fla. 1976-77; staff of Sen. Edward M. Kennedy 1978-79, Antitrust Com. and Juciciary Com.; staff of Nat. Campaign Com. for Edward M. Kennedy 1979-80; investment advisor Kriegsman and Ader (tax and bus. mgmt. firm), Century City 1981-82; partner/founder law firm Lytle and Reiss (business, tax, real estate, entertainment firm), Century City 198200; bd. dirs. Homecoming Records; seminars on fin. and tax plng. to var. womens gps.; honors: Key to City of Miami 1975; mem: Am., Calif., L.A. County, Beverly Hills bar assns.; Women in the Law; Hollywood Womens Coalition; L.A. Womens Campaign Fund; Save Our Seniors; rec: water ski instr., equestrian, tennis. Res: 2910 Neilson Way Santa Monica 90405 Ofc: Lytle & Reiss, 2029 Century Park East, Ste 600, Los Angeles 90067

REISS, ROBERT JOSEPH, JR., company executive; b. Oct. 1, 1950, Red Bank, NJ; s. Robert Joseph Sr. and Veronica Mary (Stubbs) R.; edn: AA, Moorpark Coll. 1975. Career: engr. Vlier Engring., Burbank 1972-74; mktg. supvr. 1974-77; cust. svc. mgr. Bishop Graphic, Westlake 1977-79; owner Restoration, Valencia 1979-80; v.p. tech. ops. Sprague Magnetics, Van Nuys 1981--; cons. to recording ind. on profsl. care of magnetic tape hds.; mem: Nat. Assn. of Broadcasters; author: Causes & Cures, booklet on care & failures of tape hds.; mil: E5, USN 1970-72, Vietnam decorations; rec: fishing. Res: 27546 Esterbrook Canyon Country 91351 Ofc: Sprague Magnetics, 15904 Strathern, Ste 12, Van Nuys 91406

REITZ, RICHARD ELMER, physician-educator; b. Sept. 18, 1938, Buffalo, NY; s. Elmer and Edna Anne (Guenther) Reitz; edn: BS, Heidelberg Coll., Tiffin, Ohio, 1960; MD, State Univ of NY, Buffalo, 1964; m. Gail Pounds, Aug. 20, 1960; chil: Richard, b. 1963; Mark, b. 1966. Career: intern, resident in med., Hartford Hosp., Conn., 1964-67; resident in med., Yale Univ., West Haven, Va., Hosp., 1965-66; resrch assoc., Natl. Heart Inst., NIH, Bethesda, Md. 1967-68; research fellow in med., Harvard Med. Sch. and Clin. and Research Fellow in Med., Endocrine Unit, Mass. Gen. Hosp. 1968-69; asst. dir. Clin. Investigation Center, Naval Hosp., Oakland, 1969-73 (joint opn. w/

Dept. of Medicine, UC San Francisco); adj. instr., then adj. asst. prof. of medicine in residence, Dept. of Medicine, U.C.S.F., 1971-76; director, Endocrine-Metabolic Center, Oakland, 1976---. Mem: Endocrine Soc.; dip., Natl. Bd. of Med. Examiners; Amer. Heart Assn.; Amer. Fedn. for Clin. Research; Amer. Diabetes Assn.; Amer. Fertility Soc.; Internatl. Fedn. of Fertility Soc.; Amer. Soc. for Bone and Mineral Research. Num. articles in med. journs., profl. presentations. Mil: served to Lt. Cmdr., Med. Corps, USN, 1969-71. Res: 867 Stonehaven Dr., Walnut Creek 94598; Office: Endocrine-Metabolic Ctr., 3100 Summit St., Oakland 94623.

RELF, WILLIAM JAMES, engineer, business owner; b. Oct. 1, 1930, El Paso, TX; s. Percy B. and Corrine A. Relf; m. Patsy J. Loveall, Dec. 31, 1950; children: Russell C., b. 1958; Charles W., b. 1966; edn: Univ. of Nevada 1949-50; Vallejo J.C. 1954; BS, CalPoly, S.L.O. 1954-58; Calif. Reg. Profl. Engr. (mech. engring.) 1972. Career: engr. Pahl Harry Co. 1958-60; chief engr., J.H. Simpson Co. (mech. contractor/ engr.) 1960-, co-owner 1977--; mem: Stockton Builders Exchange (dir.); Htg. & Air Condtg. Contrs. Assn. (dir.); CofC (dir.); Stockton Engrs. Club (past pres.); ASHRAE; NSPE; CSPE (chpt. past pres.); SMANCA (v.p. chpt.); Rotary; Salvation Army adv.; Better Business Bureau com.; Little League; Protestant; rec: amateur radio, pilot, skiing. Res: 3131 Christina Ave Stockton 95204 Ofc: J.H. Simpson Co., 4025 Coronado Ave Stockton 95204

RELOVA-NEILSON, MERLYN, sales executive; b. May 26, 1947, Philippines, nat. 1977; d. Larry E. and Libertad S. (Ramos-Silvestre) Relova; m. Gary Grant Neilson, Nov. 18, 1972; children: Katherine Ann, b. 1974; Glen Wesley, b. 1977; edn: BA Stella Maris Coll. 1967; econ. (spl. scholarship), Wharton Sch. Bus., Univ. of Penn. 1969; R.E. salesman lic., Anthony Sch. 1981. Career: dir. sales & mktg. Berry & McCarthy Shipping 1981-82; acct. exec. Air Sea Fwdrs. 1983-84; dir. Philippine- Calif. CofC 1983-84; currentl: VIP Lounge Ground Hostees KLM Royal Dutch Airlines, gen. mgr. Merlyn's Collections; acct. rep. Varig Airlines; assoc. Konecki Internat.; realtor assoc. ERA Country Manor Realty; mem. Export Mgrs. Assn. of So. Calif.; certs: OJT's Varig Airlines 1973, 78; Export Seminar; Transportation of Restricted Articles; mem: Export Mgrs. Assn. of So. Calif., Philippine- Calif. CofC; Philippine Arts Council; personal wardrobe designs by Merlyn, 1981; rec: dancing, travel. Address: Merlyn's Collections, 2412 Santa Cruz Ct Torrance 90501

REMEDIOS, FRANCIS MATHIAS, chiropractor; b. July 13, 1942, Gatooma, Zimbabwe (Rhodesia); s. Cornelio Mathias and Luiza Especiosa (Fernandes) R.; m. Margaret Gaul, June 25, 1966; children: Barbara L., b. 1967; Gregory F., b. 1969; Douglas P., b. 1970; Stephanie L., b. 1973; edn: DC, Palmer Coll. Chiro. 1968; cert. clinical nutrition, Nat. Coll. Chiro 1978; cert. physical therapy, L.A. Coll. Chiro. 1978; cert. acupuncture, Nat. Acad. of Acupunct. 1977; currently, post grad. work, L.A. Coll. Chiro.; lic.: Alberta (Can.) Chiro. Assn. (1968), Calif. State Bd. of Chiro. Examiners (1979). Career: assoc. chiropractor, Koch Chiropractic Clinic, Edmonton, Alberta 1968-70; owner, Dr. Francis M. Remedios, Chiropractor, Edmonton 1970-79; owner Remedios Chiropractic Clinic, Redding, Calif. 1980--; pres. Edmonton Chiropractic Soc. 1971 (secty./ treas./ registrar/ exec. ofcr. 1971 77); tchr., Santavicca Cos. 1982-83; columnist, The Monitor, 1982-83; guest spkr./motivational cons., num. clubs, orgns. & businesses; mem: Am. Chiro. Assn. (Council on Nutrition); Canadian & Alberta Chiro. Assns.; Canadian Council of Chiro. Roentgenology; Diplomate Calif. St. Bd. of Chiro. Examiners; Internat. Arthritis Soc.; Soc. of Remedial Masseurs & Physical Therapists; Nat. Acad. of Acupuncture; Diplomate Nat. Bd. of Naturopathic Examiners; Business Leaders, Redding; Pvt. Indus. Council; Gr. Redding CofC; Toastmasters (distinguished toastmaster); Rotary; Catholic; Res: 4685 Saratoga Dr Redding 96002 Ofc: Remedios Chiropractic Clinic, 1800 Pine Street Redding 96001

REMITZ, TONY VICTOR, real estate broker; b. Apr. 29, 1917, Sublette, Wyo.; s. Tony and Josephine (Yes) R.; m. Constance Parino, May 11, 1947; children: Tony, b. 1948; Valerie, b. 1951; William, b. 1954; edn: pre standard cert., Am. Inst. Banking 1941; taxation & exch., USC Univ. Pgms. 1983; ethics, 1983. Career: from page to loan dept. asst., Bank of Am., Sacto. 1937-42; dist. mgr./ ofc. mgr./ circulation promotion mgr. McClatchy Newspapers, Sacto. 1947-58; broker Tony V. Remitz Realty, Sacto. 1959--; commnr. City of Sacto. Housing Code Adv. Bd. 1971; original Preserv. Bd. 1975; awards: Awd. of Merit, Am. Inst. of Plnrs. 1975; Outstanding Citizen Awd., Calif. PTA 1976; Man of the Yr. for Sacto., Davis & Stockton, Optimists 1972; Man of Yr. (baseball), Am. Legion 1969; past pres: Tahoe Sch. PTA; High 12 Club; Methodist Mens Club; Optimist Club; Southside Improvement Club; Am. Legion; past dir.: Jr. Mus. Sci. Ctr.; Sacto. Hist. Soc.; SPCA; BSA;; Tahoe Little League; mem: Masonic Order; Shrine; Jobs; DeMolay; mil: 2nd Lt., USAF 1943-46; Protestant; rec: stamps, coins, antique furniture. Address: Tony V. Remitz Realty, 6240 3rd Ave Sacramento 95817

REMLINGER, ROGER RIGGS, lawyer; b. Dec. 7, 1944, Fresno; s. Tadeusz and Dorothy Elizabeth (Garner) R.; m. Sandra Lois; 1 dau: Christina Marie; edn: BS, Cal Poly 1974; adv. cert., Peace Ofcrs. Standards & Tng., St. of Calif. 1974; team bldg. wrkshp., USC 1974; JD, Univ. of La Vern 1978; atty. at law, admitted to practice in all cts. in Calif., and the US Supreme Ct. 1983. Career: police ofcr./ investigator 1967-79; atty. at law 1979--; Plng. Commissioner, City of Upland; mem: Western San Bernardino Co. Bar Assn. (bd. dirs.; Resolution Com.); San Bernardino Co., Los Angeles Co. & Am. Bar Assns.; Supreme Ct. Hist. Soc.; Internat. Footprint Assn.; Calif. Trial Lawyers Assn. Ofc: Roger R. Remlinger, 99 C St, Ste 106, Upland 91786-6080

REMOS, S. NONA, artist; b. May 14, 1920, Queensland, Australia, nat. 1944; parents: Albino and Elvira Remus; edn: AA, Los Angeles Jr. Coll. 1941. Career: art dir. Technical Measurement Corp., No. Haven, Conn. 1964-65; artist Empire Graphics, Rochester, NY 1966-69; artist, Condenast, NY, NY 1970-71; free lance artist, San Diego 1971---; tchr. airbrush, San Diego City Coll.; Silver Sandi Awd., CAG 1983; Los Angeles Ad Show awd.; mem: Communicating Arts Club of San Diego; Unitarian; rec: sailing, reading. Address: 4053 8th Ave, No 9, San Diego 92103

RENARD, JOHN S., executive; b. Mar. 13, 1938, NY, NY; s. Henry H. and Ruth L. (Pasternack) R.; m. Judith Slaminsky, Aug. 13, 1961; children: Eric, b. 1965; Marc, b. 1967; edn: BA, Tufts 1960; MBA, C.C.N.Y. 1969; real estate lic.; indsl. realtor (S.I.R.). Career: pres. Cushman & Wakefield Western, Inc., San Francisco 1983--; adj. lectr. C.C.N.Y., Fairleigh Dickinson, NY Int. of Tech.; New York chpt. Soc. Indsl. Realtors (pres. 1977-78, dist. v.p. 1979-82, dir. 1983-84); past dir. Salvation Army Adv. Bd.; Mount Olive, NJ Indsl. Com. Adv. Bd.; Yonker, NY Indsl. Devel. Agcy.; mem: NY Real Estate Bd.; Am. Arbitration Assn.; Am. Economic Devel. Council; Metropolis Country Club, White Plains, NY; City Athletic Club; NYC; Bankers Club, S.F.; The Bd. Room, NYC; Balboa Bay Club, Newport Bch.; frequent contbr., num. real estate trade journals; mil: USAR; rec: skiing, tennis, golf. Res: 465 Pullman Rd Hillsborough 940101 Ofc: Cushman & Wakefield Western, Inc., Bank of Am., 555 California St, Ste 2700, San Francisco 94104

RENDELMAN, IRVING FORCMINK, company executive; b. Feb. 22, 1926, Phila., PA; s. Samuel F. and Jennie (Diamond) R.; m. Annette Garber, July 15, 1945; children: Mark, b. 1948; Roger, b. 1952; Bob, b. 1955; edn: BS, USC 1948, MS, 1950. Career: pres. Stone Electronics 1951-75; exec. v.p. Halving Ind., Inc., Los Angeles 1975--; pat. holder/ inventor Hi Voltage Chromatic Probe; instr. Los Angeles Electronics Tech.; awards: Man of the Yr., Calif. State Inventors Assn. 1972; Golden Gavel Awd., Inst. of Hi Fidelity 1978; mem: Calif. St. Inventors Assn.; Inst. of Hi Fidelity; Inst. of Electronic Engrs. (past pres.); Masons; Elks, Lions Club, author. book, The Transistor, Working Application and Theory, pub. 1966; mil: USN capt.; comdr. of destroyer William L. Bagley, hon. disch. 1945; Democrat; Jewish; rec: stunt pilot, avid sailor Res: 7022 Mammoth Ave Van Nuys 91405 Ofc: Halving Industries, Inc., 1088 So Fairfax Los Angeles 90019

RENFROW, LANCE L., chemical engineer; b. Oct. 25, 1942, Long Beach; s. Warren E. and Ruby C. (Stone) R.; m. Mary Susan Boyle, Nov. 4, 1967, children: Shunna Lynn, b. 1968; Nicole Christine, b. 1972; Traci Louise, b. 1979; edn: BS chem., Ariz. State Univ. 1966; MBA, CSU Long Beach. Career: sales rep. Stauffer Chemical, NY & L.A. 1966-69; asst. gen. mgr. Georgia Pacific, L.A. 1969 77; v.p. sales Western States Chem., L.A. 1977-79, v.p. sales Transmeridian, San Francisco 1979-81; western mgr. HCI Chemicals, L.A. 1981-82; v.p./ co-owner Flask Chemical, Lynwood 1982--; Chem. Mktg. Assn., So. Calif. pres. 1977-78; mem: AICE; CMA; DCAT; NACD; Am. Water Ski Assn.; Nat. Search Site Com.; builder of one of the first man made lakes for water skiing in US, current cons. on many projects. Republican; Catholic; rec: past profl. water skier, past U.S. National Champion. Res: 9905 Rutgers Cir Anaheim Hills 92807 Ofc: Flask Chemical Corp., 11642 Mona Blvd Lynwood 90262

RENSHAW, LOLITA BERNS, civic leader; b. Nov. 1, 1930, Oak Park, Ill.; d. George William and Libuse (Roubik) Berns; m. Alan Nichols, June 16, 1952, div. 1974; children: Sharon, b. 1957, Alan, Jr. b. 1958; m. 2d. John Paine Renshaw, Jan. 3, 1976; stepchil: Corinne, b. 1958, Allison Renshaw, b. 1960; edn: AB, Stanford 1952; MA, 1954; Calif. std. tchg. credential. Career: sch. tchr. in Palo Alto, San Francisco, and Ill., 1954-56; vol. work: Junior League, Red Cross bd., S.F. Conservatory of Music bd., Stanford Womens Club bd.; exec. com. S.F. Opera Assoc.; mem., past pres. (1972-4) S.F. Opera Guild; assoc. dir. of Boys Clubs of Amer.; bd. dirs. Archives of Amer. Art, Smithsonian Instn.; pres. Guthrie House, Stanford Univ.; mem. Mus. of Fine Arts; clubs: Franciscan, Metropolitan, Burlingame, Balboa; Republican; Episcopal; rec: swim, ski, opera. Res: 1808 Floribunda Hillsborough 94010

REPASKY, RICHARD LEE, company president; b. Jan. 19, 1943, Canton, OH; s. Matthew Lee and Elizabeth H. (Herner) R.; m. Marcia Elliott, div., m. 2d. Susan Mary Miller, Aug. 28, 1982; children: Nicole Repasky, Daniel Cassidy, Jeanine Cassidy, Timothy Cassidy, Kathy Cassidy, Jennifer Kabbany, Christine Kabbany; edn: BS, The Ohio State Univ. 1965; Spl. Agent US Secret Service, Apr. 1972. Career: tchr. math. & sci. 1970-72; spl. agent Defense Investigative Svc. 1978-82; pres. Buckeye Investigations, Inc. 1982--; owner Coast Guns & Police Supple; mem. Cardiff Town Council; awards: NROTC Scholarship 1961; Libby-Owens Ford Scholarship 1961; mem: Calif. Peace Ofcrs. Assn.; Assn. of Pvt. Investigators; Lions Club; Treasury Law Enforcement Assn.; Pop Warner JR. Football League; Cardiff Town Council; Parent Tchrs. Assn.; mil: lt. USN 1965-69, Navy Unit Cit., Navy Achievement medal; Republican; Presbyterian; rec: scuba diving, photog., shooting. Res: 2004 Bulrush Ln Cardiff by the Sea 92007 Ofc: Coast Guns & Police Supply, 2145 Newcastle Ave Cardiff by the Sea 92007

RESNICK, MICHAEL LAURENCE, physician; b. Mar. 27, 1947, Brooklyn, NY; s. Solomon and Evelyn (Dernis) R.; edn: BS, Northwestern Univ. 1969; MD, 1971; res., Cornell Univ. Med. Ctr. 1971-75; MD, 1975; TV News Medical Commentator; Career: externship Mayo Clinic, Rochester, Minn. 1970; chief res. Cornell Univ. Med. Ctr. 1975; instr. 1975; attdg. physician Cedars Sinai Med. Ctr. 1976; Ob/Gyn/Infertility practice, San Diego 1977; became The

Woman's Doctor, on Channel 39 TV News 1981-82; med. consultant on KGTV Channel 10 News, S.D. 1983-, and med. specialist on Newscope (nat. syndicated TV pgm.); conduct seminars on PMS and menopause, 1981-; founder/ dir. Menstrual Ctr., San Diego 1983--; ; honors: Phi Beta Kappa 1967; AMA Phys. Recognition Awd. 1983; mem: Alpha Epsilon Delta Soc.; March of Dimes; San Diego Co. Med. Soc.; mil: maj. USAF 1975-76; Jewish; rec: breeding thoroughbred horses, Rancho Mirage in Rancho Santa Fe. Res: 435 So Sierra Ave, No. 320, Solano 92075 Ofc: Menstrual Center, 4282 Genesee Ave, Ste. 304, San Diego 92117

REYBURN, STANLEY SHORTRIDGE, banker; b. May 28, 1930, Los Angeles; s. Wilbur Wm. and Margaret (Leslie) R.; m. Jeanette Smith, May 29, 1982; children: Valerie, b. 1953; Stephen, b. 1955; Stuart, b. 1959; Paul, b. 1971; edn: AA, El Camino Coll. 1956; BS, CSU Los Angeles 1959; MBA, USC 1961; grad. Sch. of Mortgage Banking, Northwestern Univ. 1964; postgrad. work, USC 1965-66; A.I.B. std. certs. 1967; life jr. coll. tchr. credential (bus. ad., econ.) 1968; cert. Sr. Loan Escrow Ofcr., Calif. Escrow Assn. 1970; cert. R.E. Instr. (cand.), Real Estate Educators Assn., 1984. Career: asst. secty./ asst. treas. Western Mortgage Corp. 1961-66; v.p./ mgr. Security Pacific Nat. Bank 1967-77; pres. Commonwealth Escrow Co. and Commonwealth Svc. Co., 1977-79; 1st v.p.; sr. v.p.- admin. Century Bank, Los Angeles 1979-82; exec. vice pres., corp. secty., loan adminstr. and dir. Wilshire State Bank, 1982--; coll. instr. UCLA Ext. 1964-68, CSU Long Bch. 1966-7, L.A. Valley Coll., 1968-; instr. Continuing Edn. for the Bar; mem. Calif. Escrow Assn. (dir. 1970-82), L.A. Escrow Assn. (pres. 1968), Am. Escrow Assn., Assn. of Corporate R.E. Execs., Calif. Assn. of R.E. Tchrs., R.E. Educators Assn.; author: Careers in Escrow (Calif. Escrow Assn. 1976); Calif. Escrow Procedures: A Blueprint for the Nation (coll. text) Prentice-Hall, 1980); monthly column in CEA News (Calif. Escrow Assn.); num. mag., newsletter articles; Republican; Presbyterian; rc: numismatics, preserving radio history, writing. Res: 7422 Hazeltine Ave, 3, Van Nuys 91405 Ofc: Wilshire State Bank, 3200 Wilshire Blvd, Los Angeles 90010

REYES, BENJAMIN LOPEZ, dentist, b. Aug. 30, 1933, Pangasinan, Philippines, nat. 1959; s. Manuel Baudsta and Olimpia (Lopez) R.; m. Eleanor, May 5, 1958; children: Benjamin, b. 1959; Victoria, b. 1960; Phillip, b. 1962; Jeffrey, b. 1967; edn: DMD, Centro Escolar Univ., Manila 1953; DDS, UC San Francisco 1969. Career: gen. dentistry, Philippines 1953-54; asst. to sr. dental ofcr. US Public Health Svc., US Coast Guard Base, Govt. Island 1955-60; Alameda, Calif. & US Coast Guard Recruiting Ctr., Cape May, NJ 1960-62; pres. B.L. Reyes, DDS, Inc. 1976--; mem: Am., Calif., Alameda Co. Dental Assns.; Alameda City Dental Soc.; Am. Soc. of Clinical Hypnosis; Am. Profl. Practice Assn.; Acad. of Internat. Dental Studies (fellow); Civic Orgn.; So. Alameda Kiwanis Club; Knights of Columbus; mil: asst. to sr. dental ofcr., chief dental tech., US Coast Guard 1955-62; Republican; Catholic; rec: piano, painting, collecting cars. Res: 1342 Bay St Alameda 94501 Ofc: Dr. B.L. Reyes, DDS, Inc., 2059 Clinton Ave Alameda 94501

REYES, BRUCE ALFRED, chiropractor; b. May 19, 1949, San Diego; s. Augustus and Hope (Caranzz) R.; edn: D.C., summa cum laude Palmer Coll. of Chiropractic 1975; lic. D.C. in Colo., Calif.; CCA, cert. in Disability Evaluation, Calif. Chiro. Assn. 1978. Career: pvt. practice, Reyes Chiropractic Offices, Santa Rosa; gov. appt. mem. 3rd Dist. Med. Quality Rev. Com., Bd. of Med. Quality Assurance, 1980-83; spkr. on wkrs. compensation and disability eval. with Gibson Mgmt. Pgm. nat.; seminar spkr.; trustee Statewide Safety Council, spons. by Santa Rosa CofC; involved with defense malpractice for chiropractors nat.; awards: Dr. Robert L. Botterman Awd., and Disting. Svc., No. Bay Chiro. Soc.; Outstanding Young Chiro. of Year 1978, Calif. Chiro. Assn.; mem. Calif. Chiro. Assn. (mem. chmn., dir. Key Doctor Pgm., PAC trustee); North Bay Chiro. Soc. (past pres.); rec: skiing, sailing. Reyes Chiropractic Ofcs. 2801 Yulupa Ave, Ste. C, Santa Rosa

REYES, EMERSON VINUYA, equal employment executive: b. Pampanga, Philippines, nat. 1969; s. Alfonso L. and Dominga (Vinuya) R.; m. Violeta Tabernilla, Nov. 3, 1966; children: Rossana, b. 1965; Normita, b. 1967; Jo Ann, b. 1971; edn: AA, Monterey Peninsula Coll. 1980; AS, 1980; BS, USF 1981. Career: woodworker 1958; floor wax salesman 1960; public opinion research interviewer 1962; computer operator 1964; med. lab. tech. 1965; surgical tech. 1966; chem. lab. tech. 1968; car salesman 1972; auto svc. mgr. 1973; mechanic, US Army 1974; career counselor, US Army 1975; admin. tech. 1977; Calif. Army Nat. Guard 1978; Veterans Affairs ofc. Monterey Peninsula Coll. 1980--; EEO spec. US Army 1982--; awards: Young Man of Yr., Jaycees 1979; First Honor, USF 1981; Meritorious Svc. Awd. US Army 1977; Vietnam Campaign Medal 1974; mem: Boys Club of Monterey Pen. (pres.); Am. Assn. of Minority Veterans Pgms. Admistr.; Assn. of Coll. Dirs. of Calif.; Disabled Am. Veterans; Knights of Columbus; Am. Legion; Calif. Assn. of Veterans Pgm. Adminstrn.; Catholic; rec: camping, fishing, travel. Res: 665 Harcourt Ave Seaside 93955 Ofc: US Army, EEO, Ft. Ord 93941

REYNOLDS, STEPHEN SCOTT, lawyer; b. Aug. 1, 1949, Ann Arbor, Mich.; s. Albert Gordon and Polly Rae (Staples) Reynolds; m. Cynthia J. Scritchfield, Dec. 10, 1977; children: Stephanie, b. 1978; Jessica, b. 1982; edn: BA, Stanford Univ. 1971; MBA, UC Berkeley 1973; JD, Univ. of Pacific McGeorge Sch of Law 1976. Career: tax acct. Arthur Andersen & Co., San Francisco 1976-79; atty., Welebir & Brunick, San Bernardino 1979-82; atty., Hanover, Reynolds, Reider & Bawden (and predecessor firm), Redlands 1982--; instr. (Legal Aspects of Human Resource Mgmt.) Univ. of Redlands; honors: Journey for

Perspective, UCB 1972; distinguished svc. award Redlands Jaycees 1982; mem. Redlands CofC (pres. 1983-84); Redlands Planning Commn. 1982-; trustee Redlands United Ch. of Christ 1979-82; United Way 1982-; dir. Redlands Local Economic Devel. Corp, 1981-; Republican; rec: skiing, racquetball, jogging. Res: 30589 Mirasol Dr Redlands 92373 Ofc: Hanover, Reynolds, Reider & Bawden, 300 E. State St, Ste. 450, Redlands 92373

REYNOLDS, W(YNETKA) ANN, university chancellor; b. Nov. 3, 1937, Coffeyville, Ks.; d. John Ethelbert, Jr. and Glennie (Beanland) King; m. Dr. Thomas Kirschbaum, M.D. Apr. 9, 1983; children: Rachel, b. 1967, Rex, b. 1971; edn: BS in biol./chem., Kans. State Tchrs Coll. 1958; MS, zool., Univ. of Iowa 1960, PhD in zool., 1962. Career: chancellor The California State Univ. (19 campuses, 314,000 students, 18,000 faculty), 1982--; prof. biology, CSU Dominguez Hills, 1982-, hon. prof. biol. scis., SFSU, 1982-; past: faculty, Ball State Univ. 1962-65, Univ. of Ill., 1965-79 (prof. of anatomy 1965-, research prof. of ob-gyn. 1973-, assoc. vice chancellor for research and dean of Grad. Coll. Med. Ctr. 1977-79); provost, Ohio State Univ. (prof.; dean Graduate Coll. U. of Ill. at the Medical Center and pres. Ohio State Univ. Research Found., 1979-82. Fellow, Calif. Acad. of Scis. (1983); Dr. of Science (hon.), Ind. State Univ., Evansville (1980); Assoc. Fellow, Am. Coll. of Obstets. and Gyns. (1977); recipient NSF Predoctl. Fellowship 1958-62; Woodrow Wilson Fellow (hon.) 1958; Distinguished Alumna, Kansas State Tchrs. Coll. (1972); mem: AAAS, Am. Assn. of Anatomists, Am. Diabetes Assn., Am. Soc. of Zoologists, Endocrine Soc., Perinatal Research Soc., Sigma Xi, Soc. for Exptl. Biology and Medicine, Soc. for Gynecologic Investigation; works: resrch. in developmental biology, spec. in studies of fetal devel., placental transfer and nutrition; over 100 publs. incl. med. book chapters, arts. in sci. and med. journals. Res: 620 Stone Canyon Rd. Los Angeles 90077 Ofc: Office of the Chancellor, The California State University, 400 Golden Shore, Ste. 324, Long Beach 90802

RHEAM, DEBORAH ANN, optometrist; b. Oct. 21, 1953, Selma, Ala.; d. Robert Edward and Rose Marie (Gallucci) R.; m. Donald Witt, May 21, 1983; edn: BS, Univ. of Santa Clara 1975; D.O., Ill. Coll. of Optometry 1979. Career: partnership practice optometry, 1979--; Calif. Optometry assoc. instr. 1982, 93; research assoc. Cooper Vision Labs., Alcon, Barnes- Hind, Hydrocurve, Vistakon 1980-83; awards: Young O.D. of the Yr., Santa Clara Co. 1983; mem: Santa Clara Co. Opt. Soc.; Soroptimist Internat.; Mtn. View CofC; publs: Evaluation of Contact Lens Solution, 1983; Catholic. Res: 255 So Rengstorff, No 130, Mountain View 94040 Ofc: 495 Castro Mtn. View 94040

RHEE, TAE RYANG, physician; b. Oct. 7, 1940, Taegu, Korea, nat. 1975; s. Myong Suk and Hee Kyong (Sung) R.; m. Choel Ja, May 5, 1968; children: Erina K., b. 1970; Emmy, b. 1971; Tony J., b. 1973; edn: BS, Kyungpook Nat. Univ. 1961; MD, Kyungpook Nat. Univ. Sch. of Med. 1965; MD lic. NY 1974, CA 1975, OH 1977. Career: intern, Surgery Dept. The Jewish Hosp. & Med. Ctr., NYC 1971; res. Surgery Dept. The Brookdale Hosp. & Med. Ctr., NYC 1972; chief res. Otolaryngology Dept. Downstate Univ. Kings Co. Hosp., NYC 1975; pvt. med. practice ENT spec., Flushing, NY 1977, Youngstown, Ohio 1981; currently, pres. T.R. Rhee, MD, Inc., Garden Grove; mem: The Korean CofC; Calif. CofC; art., Archives of Otolaryngology, 1975; mil: Capt., Korean Army Med. Corp. 1970; Republican; Protestant; rec: golf, travel. Res: 610 Frontier Ct Anaheim Hills 92807 Ofc: T.R. Rhee, MD, Inc., 12555 Garden Grove Blvd, Ste 408, Garden Grove 92643

RHINEHART, LARRY LEE, computer systems executive; b. Oct. 4, 1940, Los Angeles; s. Dale W. and Nellie M. (Caywood) R.; m. Judith A. Wortman, Sept. 2, 1960; children: Martin S., b. 1963, Richard A., b. 1965; edn: AA in engring., Mt. San Antonio Coll. 1970; BS in mgmt. sci., CSU Los Angeles 1975. Career: prodn. assembler, test driver, insp. Freightliner Corp., 1960-66; quality control analyst, project design engr., pgmmr/systems analyst, Ameron Corp. 1966-76; systems proj. ldr. Proto Tool Div. Ingersoll Rand Co., 1976-81; sr. systems analyst/group ldr. General Dynamics Corp., 1981-84; Information Systems Requirements and Planning mgr., Northrop Corp., 1984--; data proc. cons. Pomona 1st Baptist Ch. & Sch. 1977; data proc./computer sys. cons. Chaffey Joint Union High Sch. Dist., 1984; mem: Nat. Mgmt. Assn., Jaycees 1966-76, Data Proc. Mgmt. Assn. 1976-81; elected City Councilman, City of Montclair 1984-, Plng. Commnr. 1980-84, mem. Montclair Comm. Action Com. 1978-80; Republican; Baptist; rec: football, basketball, track. Res: 10221 Pradera Ave Montclair 91763 Ofc: Northrop Corp. 8900 E. Washington Blvd, S500/1K, Pico Rivera 90660

RHOADS, ISSAC ELDREDGE, educator, ret.; b. July 23, 1921, Cedarville, NM; s. Robert Moroe and Jeffie Ida (Denham) R.; m. Katrina Avyrilla Burdine, Oct. 2, 1942; children: Jerral E.; Michael I.; Patricia C.; Jonnette D.; edn: AB, San Jose State Coll. 1952; Sacto. State Coll.; Chico State Coll. Career: indsl. edn. tchr., dept. chmn., San Juan Unified Sch. Dist. 28 yrs.; coordinator taxshelter annuity pgms., Zahorik Co., Pasadena, 13 yrs.; honors: Cert. of Commdn., Calif. Indsl. Arts Exposition & Awd. Pgm.; mem: Calif. Tchrs. Assn.; Nat. Edn. Assn.; Masons; Scottish Rite; World War II Glider Pilots

Assn.; Ret. Ofcrs. Assn.; PTA; mil: flt. ofcr., USAF (disability ret.) Purple Heart, Air Medals (2); Campaign Battle Stars (6); Dutch (Holland) Orange Lanyard; Democrat; Protestant; rec: sports, cooking, photog. Res: 8168 Winding Way Fair Oaks 95628

RHOADS, J. MARK, lawyer; b. May 22, 1929, Indianapolis, Ind.; s. Mark Waugh and Mary Rebecca (Snodgrass) R.; m. Janice C. Belcher, Dec. 23, 1951; 1 son: Craig Manson, b. 1955; edn: BA, Wabash Coll. 1951; JD, Indiana Univ. 1960; admitted to practice Supreme Cts. of Calif. (1962), Ind. (1960). Career: contracts coord. Gen. Motors Corp., Allison Div., Indianapolis, Ind. 1955-60; atty. Gen. Dynamics Corp.- Gen. Atomic Div., San Diego 1960-64; assoc. atty. Luce, Forward, Hamilton & Scripps, San Diego 1964-68, partner, 1969-78, sr. partner, 1979--; chmn. State Bar of Calif. Cont. Edn. of the Bar, S.D. Co. (1968-72), v.chmn. San Diego-Imperial Cos. Adminstrv. Com. 1973-77; bd. Francis W. Parker Sch., San Diego 1971-76; honors: Order of the Coif 1960; mem: Am. Bar Assn.; San Diego Co. Bar Assn.; S.D. Zoological Soc.; S.D. Symphony Orch. Assn.; Principal Oboe, S.D. Co. Symphony; mil: sr. lt. USNR active duty 1951-54, ret., Nat. Defense. Korean Svc. w/ 2 Battle Stars, UN Svc. medals; Republican; Presbyterian; rec: model railroading, music. Res: 6520 Norman Ln San Diego 92120 Ofc: Luce, Forward, Hamilton & Scripps, 1700 The Bank of Calif. Plaza, 110 West A Street San Diego 92101

RICARDO-CAMPBELL, RITA, economist; b. Mar. 16, 1920, Boston, Mass.; d. David A. and Elizabeth (Jones) Ricardo; m. W. Glenn Campbell, Sept. 15, 1946; children: Barbara, b. 1954, Diane, b. 1956, Nancy, b. 1960; edn: BS, Simmons Coll. 1941; MA, Harvard Univ. 1945, PhD, 1946. Career: tchg. fellow, tutor, instr. Harvard Univ. 1946-48; asst. prof. Tufts Coll. 1948-51; economist, Nat. Wage Stab. Bd., 1951-53, Ways & Means Com., US House of Reps., 1953; cons. econ., 1957-61; archivist and research assoc., Hoover Instn. 1961-68, sr. fellow, 1968--; mem. bd. dirs., chmn. finance com. The Gillete Co., Boston; bd. Watkins-Johnson, Inc., Palo Alto; mem. Nat. Council on the Humanities, Nat. Endowment for the Humanities, Presidential Appt., 1982-; mem. Pres.'s Economic Policy Adv. Bd., 1981-; mem. Adv. Council SRI Internat. and Mont Pelerin Soc.; awards: senior fellowship Nat. Endowment for the Humanities (1975), Alumnae Achievement Awd., Simmons Coll., Boston (1972); Phi Beta Kappa, Radcliffe Coll., Harvard Univ., Cambridge (1946). Authority on the health care sector, the Soc. Sec. regulations, and drug indus. regs.; lectr. internat. on med. care in US; author: The Economics and Politics of Health (1982); Social Security: Promise and Reality; Drug Lag: Federal Government Decision Making; Food Safety Regulations; The Economics of Health and Public Policy; coauthor (with husband, Dr. Glenn Campbell) Economics of Mobilization and War. Res: 26915 Alejandra Dr Los Altos Hills 94022 Ofc: The Hoover Instn., Rm. 318, Stanford 94305

RICE, DONALD BLESSING, company executive; b. June 4, 1939, Frederick, Md.; s. Donald B., Sr. and Mary Celia (Santangelo); m. Susan Fitzgerald, Aug. 25, 1962; children: Donald, b. 1963, Joseph, b. 1965, Matthew, b. 1969; edn: BS, chem. engr., Univ. of Notre Dame, 1961; MS, indsl. adm., Purdue Univ., 1962, PhD, mgmt./ economics, Purdue Univ. 1965; Dr. Engring. (hon.), Univ. of Notre Dame, 1975. Career: acting deputy dir. for academics, 1966-67, asst. prof. of mgmt. US Naval Postgrad. Sch., 1965-67; dir. of cost analysis Ofc. of the Secty. of Defense, 1967-69, Deputy Asst. Secty. of Defense (resource analysis), 1969-70; asst. dir. Office of Mgmt. and Budget, Exec. Office of the President, 1970-72; pres./chief exec. ofcr. The Rand Corp., Santa Monica 1972--; dir. Wells Fargo Bank, Wells Fargo Co., 1980-; mem. Nat. Sci. Bd., NSF, 1974-; mem. Defense Sci. Bd., DOD, 1977-83, sr. cons. Def. Sci. Bd., 1984-; chmn. Nat. Commn. on Supplies and Shortages, 1975-77; mem. Nat. Adv. Com. on Oceans and Atmosphere, Dept. of Commerce, 1972-75; mem. Adv. Panel, Office of Technology Assessment, 1976-77; past pres. The Inst. of Mgmt. Scis.; mem. Adv. Council for the Coll. of Engring., Univ. of Notre Dame, 1974-77; dir. Defense Resource Mgmt. Study, 1977-79. Awards: Secty. of Defense Meritorious Civilian Service Medal (1970); Ford Found. Doctl. Fellow in Mgmt. and Econ., Purdue Univ. 1962-65; one of Ten Outstanding Young Men of Am., US Jaycees, 1975. Mem: Am. Economic Assn.; AAAS (Fellow); Council on Foreign Relations; Tau Beta Pi; publs: arts. in Management Sci. (1966), Internat. Jour. of Prodn. Research (1966), Behavioral Sci. (1965), and The Armed Forces Comptroller (1969); mil: capt. US Army 1965-67; rec: golf. Res: 518 Georgina Ave Santa Monica 90402 Ofc: The Rand Corporation, 1700 Main St Santa Monica 90406

RICE, GLENN RICHARD, telecommunications co. chief executive; b. Nov. 29, 1948, Odessa, Tx.; s. George Lorenzo and Valeta Grace (Riley) R.; m. Lori Stevens, Mar. 23, 1974; div. 1981; 2 daus., Chaurice, . 1976, Melissa, b. 1978; stu. aerospace engring., bus. mgmt. and fin., Calif. State Polytech. Univ., Pomona 1966-68, 1976-77; num. courses in real estate, options, finance, taxation, securities and econ.; registered with NYSE, AMSE, etc.; Reg. Representative, NASD (1976); lic. commodity broker, CFTC (1976); Gen. Securities Prin., NASD (1981); Reg. Option Prin., Chgo. Bd. of Options, Am. Options Exchange & NASD (1981). Career: musician/entertainer, 1964-71; quality control engineering analyst Mattel, Industry, Ca. 1968-70; sales mgr. Kirby Co., Ontario and Santa Barbara, Ca. 1972-74; branch rep. HFC Finance, Pomona 1973; prodn. foreman, Soundesign, Industry, Ca. 1974-75; plant mgr. Neward Enterprises, Cucamonga 1975-76; stock, bond & commodity broker Bache Halsey Stuart Shields, Claremont 1976-81; account exec.-in-charge/ broker Dean Witter Reynolds, Corona 1981; asst. mgr./ stockbroker, commodity broker & finl. planner Thomson McKinnon Securities, Newport Beach 1981; co-founder/ pres./ chief exec. ofcr., gen. securities prin., Rice Morgan Internat., Inc., Newport Beach & Upland, 1981--; founder/ chmn./ chief exec. ofcr. American Telenet, Inc., Ontario 1983--; dir. Penn Pacific Corp. 1983; awards: 5 Hon. Mentions, finalist in Am. Song Festival & Lyric competition; BSA Eagle Scout, and Scout of Year, 1961, letter of recognition from Pres. Kennedy (1961); mem. Internat. Assn. of Fin. Planners; charter mem. Exchange Club of Corona (pres. elect); Republican; Christian; rec: racquetball, scuba diving, golf. Res: Rancho Cucamonga 91730 Ofc: American Telenet, Inc., 337 N. Vineyard Avenue Ontario 91764

RICH, JOYCE BROMEIER, speech and language therapist; b. Sept. 16, 1939, Pittsburgh, Penna.; d. Charles Henry and Etta Lutricia (Gibbs) Bromeier; m. Donald Wyatt (dec. 1964, Good Friday Earthquake, Alaska); m. 2d. Jerald Warren Rich, Apr. 8, 1967; 1 son, Charles Warren, b. 1977; edn: AA, Orange Coast Jr. Coll. 1966; BA, CSC Fullerton 1970. Std. Teaching Credential, Speech and Lang. Therapy, Spl. Edn. 1971-; Sch. Audiometrist 1974-; Service Cred., Admin. 1981-; Pvt. Lic. Speech Pathol. 1974-. Career: radar station opr. (only woman to hold position) for Fairchild Aerial Surveys, Alaska, 1964 (survived an 80 foot tidal wave while trapped on beach during the Good Friday Earthquake, due to the heroism of late husband and sev. Indian villagers); grad. asst. Speech Clinic, CSCF 1969-70; group home house parent (with spouse, Jerald), LeRoy's Boys Home, LaVerne 1970-72; speech therapist Ontario-Montclair Sch. Dist., Ontario, Ca. 1971-72; speech therapist Klamath-Trinity Unified Schs., Hoopa (Ca.) Indian Reservation, 1972--; pvt. clin. practice, speech and lang. therapy, Redwood Coast Regional Ctr., Eureka 1980--; dist. apptd. rep. Comm. Adv. Com. for Master Plan for Spl. Edn., 1983/4; mem. North Coast Speech, Hearing, and Language Assn., Eureka (past pres.); active in PTA, Trinity Valley Gym. Orgn.; Republican; Prot. PTL Club; rec: writing (poetry, humor), crafts. Res: POB 685 Willow Creek 95573 Ofc: Klamath-Trinity Unified School District, POB 1308, Hoopa 95546

RICH, WILLIAM DEXTER, newspaper executive; b. May 18, 1928, Riverside; s. Percy and Beatrice Laura (Dexter) R.; m. Patricia Elizabeth Abraham, Feb. 8, 1948; children: Julie, b.; Victoria, b. 1954; edn: UC Riverside; career: with Press-Enterprise Co. 1942--; circulation supvr. 1947, asst. circ. mgr. 1949, circ. mgr. 1965, gen. mgr. 1981--; past pres. Cal-West Circulation Mgr. Assn. and Calif. Newspaperboy Found.; past pres. Riverside Sales & Mktg. Execs. Club; mem: Calif. Newspaper Pub. Assn.; Am. Newspaper Pub. Assn., orgns. bd. dir. Kiwanis Club Riverside; exec. com. economic devel. Riverside CofC; past pres. Riverside Area United Way; mil: M/Sgt. US Army 1951-52, Korea; Republican; Lutheran; Res: 4015 Sequoia Street Riverside 92503 Ofc: Press-Enterprise Co., 3512 14th Street Riverside 92501

RICHARDS, GERALD THOMAS, research laboratory executive; b. Mar. 17, 1933, Monrovia, s. Louis Jacquelyn and Vivian Inez (Richardson) R.; m. Marilyn Derry, Aug. 25, 1968; children: Patricia, 1956; Laura, b. 1958; Dag, b. 1963; edn: BS, magna cum laude, Lafayette Coll. 1957; Lehigh Univ. 1957-58; MS, Purdue Univ. 1963; UC Davis 1963-65; JD, Golden Gate Univ. 1976; admitted Calif. State Bar 1976; patent atty., US Patent & Trademark Ofc. 1981. Career: math. instr. Lafayette Coll., Easton, PA 1957-58; mgmt. sci. trainee Standard Oil of OH 1958-59; computational physicist Lawrence Livermore Nat. Lab., 1967-69, gp. leader, 1969-73, cons. 1973-74; atty. in pvt. practice Staley & Richards, Livermore 1976-78; assoc. dir. Computer Ctr. San Jose St. Univ., 1978-79; gp. leader Lawrence Livermore Nat. Lab., 1979; staff physicist, 1980, Tech. Transfer Ofcr., 1981, mgr. Ofc. of Research & Tech. Applications, 1981--; del., Nat. Conf. on Tech. & Aging, Wingspread Wisc. 1981; coord. Far West Region & Exec. Com. mem. Federal Lam. Consortium for Tech. Transfer 1980-83; panelist White House Conf. on Productivity 1983; honors: Phi Beta Kappa, Beta Pi, 1956, Sigma Pe Sigma 1963, G.E. Scholarship 1956, AAUP Grad. Study Grant 1957, Mitman Math. Prize 1957; mem: AAAS; Am., Contra Costa Co. & Livermore- Amador Valley Bar Assns.; Calif. State Bar; Tech. Transfer Soc.; Western Gerontological Soc.; Housing Choices, Inc. (pres. 1980-); Tomorrows Technology Inc.; Valley Volunteer Ctr.; commnr. Livermore Housing Authority; mil: maj. US Army, Armor 1959-67, enlisted svc. 1948-52, Commdn., Occ., Nat. Svc. medals; Republican; rec: sailing, novel in progress. Res: 2210 Caballo Ranchero Ct, POB 728 Diablo 94528 Ofc: Lawrence Livermore National Lab., POB 808, L-700, Livermore 94550

RICHARDS, M(ICHAEL) GREGORY, clergyman; b. Feb. 8, 1947, Torrance; s. Michael J. and Vera Marie (Fout) R.; m. Deborah E. Saville, Aug. 16, 1969; children: Michael, b. 1980, Matthew, b. 1981; edn: BA, CSU Fullertin 1968; M.Div., General Theological Sem., NY 1971. Career: assoc. rector St. Stephen's Episcopal Ch., Whittier 1971-73; asst. minister All Saints Episcopal Ch., Beverly Hills 1973-75, sr. assoc. rector 1975-82, rector 1982--; chaplain La Habra (Calif.) Police Dept. 1972-73; pres. Clergy Senate of Episcopal Diocese of L.A., 1977; chmn. Diocese Commn. on Scouting 1974-80; dir. Corp. of the Episcopal Diocese of Los Angeles, 1983-; Diocesan Council of Episcopal Ch. in L.A., 1984-. Honors: DAR Bicentennial Award (1976), St. George Award, Nat. Epis. Ch. (1982), La Habra Area PTA hon. service awd. (1974); mem: Beverly Hills Meals on Wheels (founding trustee, treas. 1978-81); Great Western Council BSA (exec. bd. 1975-81); Beverly Hills Comm. Adv. Com. 1976-77; Red Cross (bd. Rio Hondo chpt. 1972-73); Emmy TV Awards Blue Ribbon Panel (judge) 1975; resrch. cons. on religious subjects for film indus.; Morning Devotional pgm. for KTTV-TV (1978); writer on gardening, var. publs. 1980-; rec: gardening, camping, fishing. Ofc: All Saints Episcopal Church, 504 N. Camden Dr Beverly Hills 90210

RICHARDSON, BOB, executive; b. Mar. 16, 1949, Los Angeles; s. George Robert and Violette E. (Zobell) R.; edn: BS, Calif. State Coll., Dominguez Hills 1968; MS, incomplete, USC Inst. of Arch. 1974. Career: owner/ pres./

chief exec.: Bob Richards Design & Development, 1975--, Innovative Design and Systems, 1982--; sales engr. Automated Systems, Hobart Brothers Welding Div. (Troy, Ohio), Santa Fe Springs Br. 1975-79; resrch. chemist/ surg. asst. Harbor Gen. Hosp., Torrance; past chmn. Valley Chpt. Am. Welding Soc.; mem. Windjammers Yacht Club, Wilshire CofC (bd. dirs. 1983); steroid chem. research pub. Am. Med. Assn. Journal; mil: 2d lt. Army Nat. Guard; rec: sailing. Res: 11420 Decente Ct. Studio City 91604 Ofc: Bob Richardson Design & Devel. 3107 Wilshire Blvd Los Angeles 90010

RICHARDSON, JOHN FRANCIS, business executive/educator; b. Nov. 22, 1938, Newark, NJ; s. John Stanley and Helen Ana (Rathburn) R.; m. Monika Gatzweiler, Mar. 14, 1966; 1 son: Christopher J., b. 1966; edn: BA, Montclair St. Coll. 1960; MS, Polytech. Inst. of Brooklyn 1968; BSL, Calif. Coll. of Law 1978; JD, 1980; MBA, summa cum laude, Pepperdine Univ. 1982; IBM computer sys. schs., 1962-67; grad. courses, Purdue Univ., Rutgers Univ., Seton Hall Univ., Fairleigh Dickinson Univ. Career: high sch. tchr., NJ 1960-62; mktg. rep. IMB Corp., NYC 1962-68; pres. Universal Learning Corp., NYC 1968-70; acct. mgr. Realtronics, Inc., NYC 1970; acct. exec. Merrill Lynch, NYC 1970-71; Bache rep. Bache & Co., NYC 1971; v.p. John S. Studwell Assoc., NYC 1972-73; sales rep. Control Data Corp., NYC 1973; asst. prof. Purdue Univ., Fort Wayne, Indiana 1973-74; physics tchr., Kearney (NJ) High Sch. 1975-76; acct. exec. Dean Witter, Santa Monica 1976; lectr. USC, Los Angeles 1977-78; mktg. rep. National CSS, Inc., Newport Bch. 1977-80; realtor assoc. Forest E. Olson, Inc., Santa Ana 1980-81; mktg. rep. Informatics, Inc., L.A. 1981-82; exec. v.p. Computique, Santa Ana 1982-83; pres. New Venture Strategies, Newport Bch. 1983--; mem. New York CofC; computer sys. cons., num. firms; honors: Kappa Delta Pi 1958; Am. Jurisprudence Awd. 1978; mem: Pepperdine Univ. Assocs.; John Wayne Tennis Club; U.S. Tennis Assn.; U.S. Chess Fedn.; author 6 travel books/ tapes, and 12 courses/ tapes; num. tape lectrs.; Republican; Presbyterian; rec: travel, writing, tennis. Address: 334 Baywood Dr Newport Beach 92660

RICHARDSON, KEITH MERRITT, financial analyst; b. Oct. 2, 1948, Wilmington, Del.; s. Howard Clifton Jr. and Grace Elaine (Cunningham) R.; edn: BS, Wofford Coll. 1972; MBA, Georgia St. Univ. 1976; PhD, Univ. of Georgia 1978. Career: acct. Georgia Hwy. Express, Atlanta, Ga. 1972-75; sr. acct. Blue Cross & Blue Shield of Ga., Atlanta, Ga. 1975-77; acct. analyst Bechtel, Inc., San Francisco 1977-80; finl. consulting prin., San Francisco 1980-82; finl. analyst Bank of America, S.F. 1982--; prof. City Coll. of San Francisco, part- time, 1980--; treas. Jr. CofC 1974-77; publs: arts., Harvard Bus. Review 1977, 79, Forbes 1980, 81; rec: sailing, golf. Res: 249 Roosevelt Way San Francisco 94114 Ofc: Bank of America, Bank of Am. Ctr., Bax 3700 San Francisco 94137

RICHARDSON, MADISON FRANKLIN, physician-surgeon; b. Dec. 26, 1943, Prairie View, Tex.; s. William A. and Vivian A. (Perry) R.; m. Constance, Mar. 30, 1965; children: Kelly, b. 1969; Kimberly, b. 1974; Karen, b. 1977; edn: BS, Howard Univ. 1965; MD, 1969. Career: Walter Reed Med. Ctr. 1969-76; res. surgery 1969-73; fellow, head & neck surgery, 1974; asst. chief head & neck surgery 1976; chief head & neck surgery Martin Luther King Hosp. 1978; assoc. dean Charles Drew Med. Sch.; asst. prof. UCLA 1979; asst. prof. USC 1981; honors: Man of Tomorrow (1983), Man of Distn. (1982); mem: Am. Coll of Surgeons; Am. Med. Assn.; Soc. of Head & Neck Surgeons; Nat. Med. Assn.; Los Angeles Urban League; Charles Drew Med. Soc. (pres.); Inglewood Physicians Assn.; num. profl. papers & presentations; mil: Lt. Col., US Army 1968-78; Republican; rec: horseback riding, polo. Res: 314 So. Hudson Ave Los Angeles

RICHARDSON, VERSIE MAE, concert singer, real estate broker, ret.; b. Mar. 13, 1920, bkemah, Okla.; d. Frank and Octavia (Bryant) Miles; div.; children: Barbara Ann, b. 1943, Samuel Percy, b. 1946; edn: stu. Pasadena City Coll. 1950, USC 1959, Univ. of Pepperdine 1976. Calif. Real Estate lic. 1952-, broker 1962-. Career: dollmaker, self emp., 1949-; clin. lab. asst., Pasadena 1956-62; owner/broker Richardson Realty, Pas. 1962-1980, Century 21 Real Estate franchisee, 1970-80; certified mediator, City of Pasadena, 1984-; past mem. bd. of multiple listing, Pasadena Bd. of Realtors; past mem Urban Coalition bd. Pasadena Cultural Heritage Com.; concert singer, perf. in concert halls in US, solo concerts in Spain, Russia, Africa; singer, Pres. Jimmy Carter's Inauguration 1977. Honors: hon. mem. Phi Delta Kappa nat. sor. 1969; NAACP award 1971; recognition, Omega Psi Phi Frat. (1972), Nat. Council of Negro Women Inc. (1981); mem: Quota Club of Pasadena 1970-79; Women in Action in Pas. (chpsn. 1962-); The Womens Leadership Devel. Corp. (chpsn.); ACT; NAACP; The League of Allied Arts; Democrat; Methodist; rec: sewing, bridge. Res: 1115 Cordova St, 304, Pasadena 91106

RICHARDSON, WALLACE GENE, pilot; b. Oct. 19, 1923, Inglewood, CA; s. Frank Wallace and Alvinl Louise (Younge) Richardson (both dec.); attended US Naval Aviation Cadet Pgm., 1943-45; Sawyers Univ. of Commerce, 1947-48; m. Jenny Montandon, Mar. 14, 1958; chil: Linda, b. 1950; Deborah, b. 1954; Stanley, b. 1959; Susan, b. 1961. Career: Lt. Cmdr., USN, 1941-47, 1950-53; office mgr., Burroughs Add. Machine Co., 1949-50; Capt., United Air Lines, 1953---; also gen. partner, mgr., Real Estate Sundicator, 1956---; bd. dirs., Ocean Science Services, 1970-72; bd. Ceric Corp., 1971-73. Co-author: Path to Illumination; also Spiritual Value of Gemstones, 1980. Mil: Lt. Comdr., USNR, 1941-46, 1950-53; Air Medal; w/5 Stars. Republican. Protestant, Deacon. Rec: writing, stained glass, bonsai. Res: 35 Buckeye, Portola Valley 94025; Office: United Air Lines, San Francisco Internatl. Airport, Flt. Operations, San Francisco.

RICHMAN, VIVIAN, computer retailing executive; b. Mar. 7, 1939, Montreal, Canada, nat. 1960; d. Louis and Anne (Kunin) Freedman; m. Barry Richman, June 5, 1960 (dec. 1978); children: Viana, b. 1963; Stuart, b. 1965; edn: BS, McGill Univ. 1960; MLS, UCLA 1968. Career: librarian Biomed. Lib. UCLA 1968-70; research assoc. R-K Research & Sys. Design, Malibu 1970-76; assoc. librarian Brain Information Svc., UCLA 1976-79; bd. dirs./ v.p. Rainbow Computing, Inc., Northridge & Woodland Hills 1979--; num. tech. reports on sys. design & application; ed. bibliographies in the neuroscis.; pub. software catalogs, pub. newsletters; conducted seminars on content analysis, Naval Postgrad. Sch., Monterey.; tchr. Intro. Computing classes for women; cons. Futures Gp., Glastonbury, Conn.; mem: Am. Soc. for Info. Sci.; Calif. Library Assn.; UCLA Alumni Assn.; Mailbu Township Council; Concerned Citizens for Water Control; Hebrew. Res: 20755 Seaboard Rd Malibu 90265 Ofc: Rainbow Computing, Inc., 21038 Victory Blvd Woodland Hills 91367

RICHMOND, JOHN, lawyer, business executive; b. Dec. 10, 1907, Oakland, CA; s. Samuel and Sarah (Stein) Richmond; BS, UC Berkely, 1928; MS, 1934; LLB, Oakland Coll. of Law, 1942; PhD, hon., Hamilton State Univ., 1973. Career: pres., Richmond Enterprises, 1928---, and law counselor, 1946---; admitted to Calif. Bar, 1946; gen. pract., Berkeley, since; founder, mem., Natl. Lawyers Club, 1952; founder, mem., Supreme Ct. Hist. Soc., 1976; mem., Grand Lodge, F&AM of Calif. Sojourners Com., 1957; VFW of US natl. membership com., 1971. Mem: Calif. State, Alameda Co., Berkely-Albany, Amer., Fedl. Bar Assn.; VFW, comdr. Berkeley Post 1962; United Vets Council of Berkeley, pres. 1963; F&AM Henry Morse Stephens Lodge, Master, 1958; Scottish Rite; Aahmes Temple A.A.O.N.M.S.; Masters & Past Masters Assn., Masons; Pan Xenia frat.; Intercontinental Biographical Assn., Engl.; AAAU; IPA; Izaak Walton League of Amer.; Amer. Fisheries Soc.; Internatl. Oceanographic Found.; Natl. Hist. Soc.; UC Berkeley Alumni Assn. Mil: USAAF, 1942-45; stu. Balliol Coll., Oxford Univ., Engl., 1944, spnsored by USAAF. Rec: golf. Res: 1611 Bonita Ave., Apt. 2, Berkeley 94709; Office: Richmond Enterprises, 1611 Bonita Ave., Apt. 2, Berkeley 94709.

RICKERSHAUSER, CHARLES E., JR., stock exchange president; b. June 23, 1928, Los Angeles; s. Charles Edwin and Lila (Alameda) R.; m. Mary Faurot, June 25, 1955; 1 dau: Janet Mary; edn: AB, UCLA 1949; JD, 1957. Career: law clerk Justice Wm. O. Douglas, Wash. DC 1957-58; lawyer Gibson, Dunn & Crutcher, Los Angeles 1963; spl. advisor Div. of Corp. Fin., SEC 1964; commnr. of corps. State of Calif. 1964-65; partner Munger Tolles & Richershauser, Los Angeles 1965--; chmn. bd./ CEO Pacific Stock Exch. 1979--; frequent lectr. on legal subjects; honors: Order of Coif 1957; mem: Calif., Am. & Los Angeles Co. Bar Assns.; Calif. Club; Los Angeles Yacht Club; Stock Exch. Club of L.A.; mil: 1st lt. US Army 1950-53; Protestant; rec: sailing, tennis. Res: 381 Meadow Grove St Flintridge 91011 Ofc: Pacific Stock Exchange, 618 So Spring St Los Angeles 90014

RIDDER, DANIEL HICKEY, newspaper publisher; b. May 3, 1922, New York City; s. Bernard Herman and Nell (Hickey) Ridder; edn: BA, Princeton, 1943; m. Frani Cooper, Oct. 13, 1971; chil: Daniel H. Jr., b. 1949; Randy H., b. 1950; Richard J., b. 1952. Career: reporter, New York Journal of Commerce, Grand Forks (No. Dak.) Herald, St. Paul Dispatch and Pioneer-Press, 1952-58; co-publisher, Long Beach (Calif.) Independent, Press-Telegram, 1958-69; publisher, 1969---; former dir. Newspaper Adv. Bur.; v.p., Knight-Ridder Newspapers, Inc.; pres., Twin Coast Newspapers, Inc.; dir., Associated Press. Mem: bd. dir., St. Mary's Med. Center; bd. dir., United Way, Inc.; bd. dir., California Mus. Found. of Calif. Mus. of Science & Industry; bd. dir., Calif. Community Found.; former chmn. bd. trustees, Calif. State Univ. & Colls.; former bd. dir., Los Angeles County Mus. of Art. Mil: Lt. (j.g.), USN, 1942-46. Rec: golf, tennis, skiing. Res: 5531 Bryant Dr., Long Beach 90815; Office: Press-Telegram, 604 Pine Ave., Long Beach 90844.

RIDDER, P. ANTHONY, newspaper publisher; b. Sept. 22, 1940, Duluth, Minn.; s. Bernard H., Jr. and Jane (Delano) R.; m. Constance Meach, Nov. 6, 1960; children: Katherine Lee, b. 1961, Linda Jane, b. 1963, Susan Delano, b. 1965, Paul, Jr. b. 1968; edn: BA in econ., Univ. of Mich. 1962. Career: worked at Aberdeen American News (S.D.), Detroit News (Mich.), Duluth News-Tribune and Herald (Minn.), Pasadena Star-News (Calif.), and St. Paul Pioneer Press and Dispatch (Minn.); with San Jose Mercury News 1964--, bus. mgr. 1969-75, general mgr. 1975-77, publisher 1977--, pres. 1979--; v.p. Northwest Publs., Inc.; honors: San Jose's Outstanding Young Man of the Year (1970), BSA Santa Clara Co. Council distinguished citizen award (1976), brotherhood awd., NCCJ (1979), BSA Stanford Area Council, Good Scout (1982); mem: Calif. Newspaper Pubs. Assn. (bd. dirs., exec. com.), Young Pres.'s Orgn., Santa Clara Co. Mfg. Group (bd. dirs.), San Jose CofC (bd. chmn. 1975); past pres., campgn. chmn. United Way of Santa Clara Co.; chmn. Adv. Bd. Pres.'s Council, SJ State Univ. 1980-85; bd. regents Univ. of Santa Clara; mem. Stanford Univ. Center for Economic Policy Resrch. 1983-85; bd. dirs. Indsl. Relations Bur. (pres. 1983); bd. dirs. Bay Area Council; clubs: La Rinconada CC, Rotary, Sainte Claire, Cypress Point, Pebble Beach. Ofc: 750 Ridder Park Dr San Jose 95190

RIGGS, KATHLEEN TANSEY, customhouse broker; b. Sept. 23, 1953, Evergreen Park, Ill.; d. Frank William and Eleanor Margaret (Ramker) Tansey; m. Harbert Bryant Riggs II, Dec. 27, 1981; 1 dau: Jessica Eleanor, b. 1982; edn: BA, secondary tchrs. cert., No. Ill. Univ. 1975; customhouse broker lic. 1980; oert., US Dept. Commerce Export Admin. Regulations 1983. Career: supvr./ clerk/ mgr. Internat. Customs Svc., Inc., Chgo. 1976-78, import mgr. Los Angeles Import Dept., L.A. 1978-79; asst. mgr. airport ofc. Frank P. Dow Co.,

Inc. 1979-81; lic. freight forwarder/ cons./ mgr. MIT Shipping, Inc. 1981--; owner Kathleen Tansey Riggs Lic. Customhouse Broker, El Toro 1981--; secty./ treas. MIT Shipping Inc., El Toro and MIT Shipping Ltd., London, England; treas. Western Bay Forensic League 1980-81; speech & debate coach Miraleste H.S. 1979-81; mem: Nat. Assn. for Profl. Saleswomen; Foreign Trade Assn. of Los Angeles; Nat. Assn. Female Execs.; publs: art., League of Am. Wheelman 11/75; Catholic; rec: theatre, dance, voice. Res: 22872 Leo Lane El Toro 92630 Ofc: Kathleen Tansey Riggs/ MIT Shipping Inc., 22706 Aspan St, Ste 307, El Toro 92630

RILEY, JAMES FRANCIS, investor; b. Nov. 29, 1929, Johnsonburg, Penn.; s. Leon I. and Eleanor C. (Donnelley) R.; m. Elizabeth Weisbecker, Apr. 19, 1952; children: Michael, b. 1955; James, b. 1956; Kathleen, b. 1959; edn: BS, Lehigh Univ. 1955. Career: salesman, sales mgr. Corning 1957-64; pres. Signetics 1964-70; pres. Intersil 1970-72; self- empl. 1972-74, Dataquest 1974--; Dir: Zitec Inc., Valley Data Scis., Brag Systems, Vitelic, Calif. Devices; honors: Phi Beta Kappa, Beta Gamma Sigma, Phi Eta Sigma; mil: ATI 1947-51; Catholic. Res: 20011 Bella Vista Saratoga 95070

RILEY, JOHN HOMER, engineering executive; b. Aug. 28, 1950, Erie, Penn.; s. John Moris and Hazel Dolores (Sparkman) R.; m. Rebecca Langlois, Sep. 14, 1973; children: Christopher, b. 1981; Matthew, b. 1984; edn: BSEE w/distinction, Harvey Mudd Coll. 1972, MSEE w/distinc. 1973; career: MTS, ADAC, Sunnyvale 1973-76; section head Hughes Aircraft Co., Irvine 1976--; awards: full scholarship Harvey Mudd Coll. 1972-73; mem: Hughes MSD Mgmt. Club (secty. 1982-); works: Analysis of Fast Fourier Transforms with Applications to Tactical Air Navigation (TACAN) 1973; Noise Pollution in Petroleum Plants, a Design Tool for Fluor Inc. 1973; Republican; Catholic; rec: home remodeling, travel. fishing, family; Res: 489 Walnut Pl Costa Mesa 92627 Ofc: Hughes Aircraft Co., 2601 Campus Dr, Bld 711 M/S 1100, Irvine 92715

RINDE, JOSEPH, computer communications design executive; b. Mar. 24, 1947, Paris, France, nat. 1957; s. Maurice and Stella (Klein) R.; m. Sheila L. Levin, July 2, 1981; edn: BS, high honors, Stevens Inst. of Tech. 1968; MS, Carnegie- Mellon Univ. 1972. Career: math. pgmr. Lawrence Livermore Lab., 1972-73; mgr. network architecture Tymshare, Inc., Cupertino 1974-83; dir. future plng. & prod. dir. Amdahl Communications Sys. Div., Marina del Rey 1983--; mem: Assn. for Computing Machinery; num. publs.; Republican; Jewish; rec: skiing, sailing. Res: 9350 Oakmore Rd Los Angeles 90035 Ofc: Amdahl, 2500 Walnut Ave Marina del Rey 90291

RINEHART, NERL DAVID, gauge & instrumentation co. owner; b. Jan. 26, 1941, Bakersheld; s. Nerl D. and Dorothy L. (Bennett) R.; m. Beverly June Smith, Aug 3, 1979; children: Michael, b 1963, David, 1967, Bill, b 1975, Jeff, b. 1967; cdn: AA, Solano Coll. 1969; tech. schools: Am. Optical Heart Monitor Repair Sch., PG&E Power Distbn. Sch., PG&E Motor and Motor Controller Sch., Bksfld. Coll. Refrigeration Sch., and Welding, Arc and Gas; var. mil. schs. in field medicine, electrician; desig. Clin. Lab. Tech., USN, 1960; Lab. Tech., Am. Soc. of Clin. Pathols. 1966, Royal Soc. of Health, Eng. 1965. Career: lab. technologist Biological Research Ctr., San Francisco 1966-69; electrician. St. Joseph's Hosp., Stockton 1969-71; chief electrician Kern Valley Packing, Bksfld. 1971-73; chief electrician Consol. Fiberglass Prods., Bksfld. 1973-74; chief elec. & instrumentation, Camay, Sunmarine Drilling, Alaska 1974-76; Sunland Refining Corp., Bksfld. 1977-82; owner/ v.p.- Design & Engring., Par Industries (Alpha Gauge & Instrumentation Co.), Bakersfield 1982--; USNR instr. 1971-: Recon Team Tng. Sch., survival tng., mil. tactics, first aid, weaponry, electronics; awards: Sailor of the Year, 11th Naval Dist. (1979), Navy League (1979); mem: Sr. Mem. Instrumentation Soc. of Am.; Petroleum Club; Royal Soc. of Health in England; Am. Soc. of Med. Technologist; Royal Order of Moose, BSA, Demolay, Naval Reserve Assn. of Am.; works: tech. inventions incl. Oil Vapor Recovery Unit (1971), computerized combination gate opener for security devices (1980), computerized Oil-Gas Separator (in prog.); Patentee: Draft Controller (1982), Oil Sampler (1983); mil: petty ofcr. USN 1969-66; sgt. US Army 1970-72; USNR 1972-; Democrat; Prot.; rec: tennis, Karate Neidan (2d deg. Black Belt), square dancing. Res: 206 Dogwood Ln Bksfld 93308 Ofc: Par Industries 3051 Fairhaven Dr Bakersfield 93308

RINEHART, VINCENT RAYMOND, real estate executive; b. Apr. 1, 1950, Altadena; s. William Raymond and Florence Marie (Trotechaud) R.; m. Barbara, Sept. 16, 1972; children: Christine, b. 1979; Jacqueline, b. 1981; Theresa, b. 1983; edn: BA, CSU Long Beach 1972; lic. real estate broker, Calif. Career: acct. exec. Merrill Lynch, Pierce Fenner & Smith, Long Beach 1972-78; pres./ CEO Equity Loans, Inc., Long Beach 1978--; dir. R.E.O. Svcs., Inc.; dir. E.L.I. Svcs., Inc.; honors: Calif. Legislative Commdn. 1981; City of Long Beach Commdn. 1981; Long Beach Jaycees Distng. Svc. Awd. 1980; mem: Long Beach & Calif. Assns. of Realtors; Alpha Kappa Psi, nat. bus. frat.; Kiwanis Club, Long Beach (past pres.); Pacific Hosp. Found., Long Beach (past pres.); Long Beach Grand Prix Benevolent Assn. (past pres.); past bd. CSULB 49th Shops, Inc.; Republican; Catholic; rec: fishing, golf. Res: 1470 Bryant Dr E, Long Beach 90815 Ofc: Equity Loans, Inc., 647 E 4th St Long Beach 90802

RIORDAN, WILLIAM FRANCIS JOSEPH, investment banker; b. Jan. 18, 1924, NY, NY; s. Joseph Timothy and Sarah Agnes (Hughes) R.; m. Donna Marie Vladeff, Jan. 11, 1980; edn: BS, US Naval Acad., Annapolis 1944; MA, Catholic Univ. of AM. 1952; US Naval Aviator, USN 1947; comml. pilot, FAA 1947; life jr. coll. tchg. credential. Career: sales mgr. Sylvania Electronics Sys. 1956-59; sales mgr. Raytheon Electromagnetic Div. 1959-61; asst. to pres.

Emerson Electric Co. 1961-66, exec. v.p. Rantec Div., 1963-66; pres. Capabilities Devel. Corp. 1966-75; investment exec. Paine Weber 1975--; cons. Emerson Elec., Ratheon, EG&G & Gould Inc. 1966-75; mem: Sci. & Engring. Council of Santa Barbara; Gov. Reagan Commn. on Rehab. 1968-69; Coral Casino Beach Club, Santa Barbara; pres. New Vistas Charitable Corp., Santa Barbara 1980-82; coauthor: US Naval Sea Cadet Tng. Manual 1981-83; mil: lt. USN 1944-50 ret., Secty. of the Navy Combat Awd. 1944; Christian; rec: tchg. airmanship and seamanship to US Naval Cadets. Res: 614 Sunrise Vista Way Santa Barbara 93109 Ofc: Paine Weber, 22 East Carrillo Santa Barbara 93109

RIPPERTON, BETTY, securities broker; b. Oct. 4, 1916, Maquoketa, Iowa; d. H. Gale and Madge L. (Hainer) Buchner; m. John M. Ripperton, June 6, 1939 (dec.); 1 dau. Sandra (Landes); edn: AA, Maquoketa (Iowa) Jr. Coll. 1936; contg. edn. in securities and insurance; Reg. Sec. Representative, NASD, and State of Calif., 1975-; Life Ins./Annuities Agt., State of Calif. 1976-. Career: deputy county auditor Jackson Co., Iowa 1936-39; secty. to project mgr. Alcan Hwy, Alaska 1942; secty. to supt. of Scottsdale (Az.) Schs. 1957-58; exec. secty. Camelback Inn, Phoenix 1959-60; exec. secty. for Robt. E. Maytag (now dec.), founder of Ariz. Zoological Park, Phoenix 1961-62; wholesaler, Reg. Securities and Ins. Rep. (sales), and vice pres., Franklin Group of Mutual Funds, San Mateo, 1970-83; securities broker, self-emp. 1983--, reg. through Judy & Robinson Securities, Inc., Menlo Park; mem: Internat. Assn. of Fin. Planners; Stock & Bond Club, San Diego; Showcase of the Arts, Escondido; rec: acrylic and oil painting, parapsychology. Res: Rancho Bernardo Ofc: POB 271069, Escondido 92027

RIPPLE, BERTRAM JOHN, life insurance executive; b. Apr. 26, 1940, San Bernardino; s. Bertram William and Mary Catherine (McGuire) R.; m. Eileen Reilly, Aug. 25, 1962; children: Sharon, b. 1963; Stephen, b. 1966; Linda, b. 1970; Paul, b. 1972; Michelle, b. 1973; Christine, b. 1975; edn: BA, Univ. of San Francisco 1962; CLU, Am. Coll. of Life Underwriters 1970. Career: agent New York Life, 1965-, asst. mgr., San Franciso 1967-, gen. mgr. Vallejo Gen. Ofc. 1974-, assoc. mgr. Concord Gen. Ofc. 1984--; tchr. life ins. courses, Nat. Assn. Life Underwriters, Napa & Solano Cos.; bd. dirs. Solano/ Napa Assn. of Life Underwriters; Pub. Rels. Com. State Life Underwriters Assn.; mem. Solano Execs. Assn., Exec. Lions Club, Vallejo (past pres.), Justin/ Siena 200 Club, Napa; Republican; Catholic; rec: camping, travel. Res: 1514 Silver Trail Napa 94558 Ofc: New York Life Ins. Co., 235 Georgia Mall So., Vallejo 94590

RITCHIE, ZELBERT BROWN, chiropractor; b. Sept. 15, 1906, Oklahoma; s. Hiram Edward and Minnie May (Redford) R.; children: Hiram Roscoe, b. 1927; Zelbert Wallace, b. 1928; Bobby Donald, b. 1930; Alonzo Ray, b. 1936; edn: grad. Los Angeles Sch. of Auctioneering 1952; DC (Valedictorian), Cleveland Chiro. Coll 1960; tchr. cred. Central State Tchrs. Coll., Edmond, Okla. Career: tchr., Oklahoma 1925-30; opr. large farming & dairy op., Okla. 1931-48; asst. engr. Schlumberger Oil Well Surveying Corp., Casper, Wyo.; supt. L.C. Gordon Construction Co.; baseball pitcher 19 yrs.; DC; orgzr. Central Calif. Chiro. Research Soc.; pres. bd. dirs. Oklahaven (philanthropic orgn.); Grand Master, Order of Odd Fellows Of Okla. 1975; Okla. rep. Sovereign Grand Lodge Sem. 1976; founder and instr. Success & Happiness Seminars (Hanford); Lions Club; Kiwanis; arts. on chiro. health care, local papers; Republican; Protestant; rec: fishing, woodworking, gardening. Res: 9501 12th Ave Hanford 93230 Ofc: 609 N. Douty St Hanford 93230

RITHAPORN, RUTHACHAI, physician; b. Jan. 29, 1945, Thailand, nat. 1982; s. Virat and Montha (Ratana) R.; m. Yooppadee, Aug. 17, 1973; children: Sompop Tat, b. 1975; Tara, b. 1979; edn: MD, Chiangmai Med. Sch. 1970. Career: med. staff/clinical instr. Ob-Gyn. Svc., Perry Meml. Hosp., Princeton, Ill. 1975; med. staff Sharp Hosp, San Diego 1982; courtesy staff Paradise Valley Hosp., Hill Side Hosp., 1982; 1982; active staff Clairmont Comm. Hosp., National City 1983; pvt. practice Ob- Gyn., Fresno 1984--; Com. on Maternal Welfare, Ill. State Med. Soc.; mem: San Diego Co. Med. Soc.; Am. & Calif. Med. Assns.; fellow, Am. Coll. of Surgeons; fellow, ACOG; works: Stool Occult Blood Test 1971; Unilateral Tubo- Ovarian Abscess with IUD 1976; Republican; Buddist; rec: philately, golf, tennis. Address: Rithaporn Med. Gp., 3000 No Fresno St, Ste 2930, Fresno 93703

RITHAPORN, YOOPPADEE, physician; b. Sept. 11, 1948, Thailand; d. Kamhang and Kayoon (Soon Thorn) Morakran; m. Ruthachai Rithaporn, Aug. 17, 1973; children: Sompop Tat, b. 1975; Tara, b. 1979; edn: BSc, Chiangmai Univ. 1969; MD, Chiangmai Med. Sch. 1971. Career: courtesy med. staff Perry Meml. Hosp., Princeton, IL 1976; active med. staff Paradise Valley Hosp., 1982, Clairmont Comm. Hosp., 1983; pvt. practice, San Diego 1983, Fresno 1984-; secty. Rithaporn Med. Gp., Inc.; mem: San Diego Co. Med. Soc.; Calif. Med. Assn.; Ill. Physical Med. & Rehab. Soc.; Am. Women Med. Assn.; Buddist; rec: stained- glass. Address: Rithaporn Medical Group, 3000 No Fresno St, Ste 2930 Fresno 93703

RITTER, FRANCIS DUDLEY, private investigator; b. Oct. 13, 1943, San Ferando; s. John Joseph and Grace Dudley (Kirby) R.; m. Mary Fennell, Ap. 4, 1964, div.; children: Michael, b. 1965; Stephan, b. 1968; edn: BA, St. Edward's Univ. 1968; pvt. investigator; pvt. patrol opr. Career: ops. ofcr. 1st Western Bank, Lloyds, Los Angeles 1965-68; dir. personnel & ops. Walston & Co., Los Angeles 1969-72; syndicate coord. Mitchum, Jones & Templeton, Los Angeles 1972-73; sole owner Backtrack Unlimited Co., pres. Backtrack Unlimited, Tng. & Weapons Ctr., Inc., 1973--; asst. tnr. Women's Anti-Rape & Self-Defense, Garden Grove Unified Sch. Dist. adult edn. 1980-83; mem: Mensa; City of Hope, Newport chpt.; Civil Air Patrol 1964-70, comdr. svl. squadrons, rank Capt.; coauthor two novels; Republican; Catholic; rec: chess, swimming, writing. Address: Backtrack Unlmtd. Co. 18311 Patterson Ln, Ste 3, Huntington Beach 92646

RITTER, JAMES JOHN, real estate investor/developer, banker; b. Nov. 27, 1923, Los Angeles; s. Frederick and Anna M. (Lescoulie) R.; m. Margo G. Coppleman, Feb. 29, 1964; children: James F., b. 1960; Douglas A., b. 1962; Jennifer A., b. 1965; edn: spl. degree, Korean lang., Univ. of Wash. 1943-44; BA, Occidental Coll. 1947; cont. edn., Brookings Inst. 1965-66; exec. MBA pgm., UC 1963-64; lic. Calif. R.E. broker 1946. Career: asst. to pres. Land Title Ins. Co., Los Angeles 1946-50; dir. of fin. ops. IBM Corp., Harrison, NY 1952-68; pres. Transamerica Computer Co., San Francisco 1969-71; v.p. Hale Bros. Assoc., San Francisco 1972-74; chmn. Pacific Union Bank & Trust Co., Menlo Park 1975-80; v.p. The Imperial Gp., San Francisco 1981-83; v.p. N.A.I. Corp., San Francisco 1983--; pres. Pacific Basin Mortgage Co. (1983-), Pacific West Brokers, Inc. (1983-), Allied Diversified Svcs., Inc. (1983-); num. directorships; ex-officio pres. Holbrook Palmer Found., Atherton; honors: Citizen of the Yr., Atherton Civic Interest League 1981; mil: capt. US Signal Corps./ Army Security Svcs., Korean Pres. Unit Citation; Republican; Episcopal; rec: fishing. Res: 49 Patricia Dr Atherton San Francisco 94025 Ofc: NAI Corp., One Lombard St San Francisco 94111

RITTER, MARGO G., fund raiser/philanthropist; b. May 19, 1938, Kenora, Ontario, Canada; d. Coppleman and Shragge; m. James John Ritter, Feb. 29, 1960; children: James F., b. 1960; Douglas A., b. 1962; Jennifer A., b. 1965; edn; Crofton House Acad., Vancouver, BC 1950-56. Career: data processing div. IBM Corp., Los Angeles 1958-60; home maker, Harrison, NY & Atherton, CA 1960-69; fund raiser 1969--; past pres. Herbert Hoover Boys Club, Menlo Park; dir. The Cygnet Cp., San Bruno; dir. Anglo Pacfic Mgmt. Corp., San Francisco; honors: Citizen of the Yr., Atherton 1982; commnr. Park & Recreation Com.; mem: Atherton Civic Interest League; Atherton Dames; Atherlons (pres.); Peninsula Volunteers; Episcopal. Res: 49 Patricia Dr Atherton 94025 Ofc: Cygnet Group, 1001 Sneath Ln, Ste 201, San Bruno

RIZZA, JOSEPH PADULA, maritime academy president; b. Jan. 30, 1915, Johnstown, Pa.; s. Paul and Concetta Rizza; m. Marie Follin, Aug. 30, 1947; edn: Dip., Penna. Maritime Acad. 1936; BA, Univ. of Wash. 1950; MA, Boston Univ. 1958; Dip., Naval War Coll., Newport R.I. 1959, Nat. War Coll., Wash DC 1970; Master Mariner, lic. by USCG 1942-. Career: served to capt. USN, 1942-72, Pacific Fleet WWII 1943-45; held major command positions ashore and at sea: cmdg. ofcr. US Naval Adv. Group to Rep. of Korea, 1960-62; staff mem. Jt. Chiefs of Staff Wash DC 1964-66; cmdr. Destroyer Squadron 24, 1966-68; Chief of Staff US Naval Forces Vietnam 1968-68; dir. of instrn. and curriculum devel. National War Coll. Wash DC 1969-72; pres. California Maritime Academy 1972-84; Rear Admiral USMS 1972-84. Honors: Phi Beta Kappa 1950; Brass Hat Award 1981 (for svc. to the US Merchant Marine), Propeller Club of the Golden Gate; Person of the Year, Johnstown, Pa. 1983; US Dept. of Trans. highest award for exceptnl. public service 1983; distinguished alumni, Penna. Maritime Acad. 1980; Calif. Senate and Assembly Resolutions for outstanding leadership, 1983. Mem: Am. Soc. of Internat. Law, Nat. Assn. for Indsl. Technology, Council of Am. Master Mariners, (Lic. Master Mariner unlmtd. tonnage any ocean), Maritime Tng. Adv. Bd.; mem. Rotary Intl., dir. Vallejo CofC 1980-83, Propeller Club of the Golden Gate, Navy League, v.p. Silverado Council Boy Scouts 1979-82; mil. decorations: 2 Legions of Merit US, The Meritorious Service Medal, Joint Service Commendn. Medal, Navy Unit Commendn. Medal, Calif. Medal of Merit; rec: sailing, golf. Res: 1830 Avenida Del Mundo, 1605, Coronado Shores 92118

RO ANE, SUSAN, professional speaker, seminar leader; b. Dec. 8, 1945, Chgo.; edn: BA, Univ. Ill. 1967; MA, San Francisco State Univ. 1976; m. Griggs Ro Ane, July 25, 1970. Career: teacher Chgo. Public Schools 1967-70, San Francisco Unified Sch. District 1970-79; prin. The Ro Ane Group, 1979--, cons. on career transitions via keynote presentations, seminars, workshops; contbg. columnist S.F. Examiner weekly "Careers" series; contbg. writer, Executive Female; num. radio/t.v. guest appearances on career issues; guest lectr. USC, Univ. of S.F.; instr. SFSU, CSU Long Beach; mem: Commonwealth Club, Nat. Speakers Assn., Women Entrepreneurs, S.F. Chamber of Commerce, No. Calif. Soc. of Assn. Execs.; rec: writing, jogging. Ofc: The Ro Ane Group, 44 Monterey Blvd, Ste. 80, San Francisco 94131

ROBBINS, GRETCHEN MARY, real estate broker; b. July 28, 1938, New Orleans, La.; d. Allen Henry and Lucy Genevieve (Malone) Junker; m. James Leroy Robbins, Aug. 21, 1982; children: Michele Ann Shaw, b. 1960; Allen Robert Vogel, b. 1964; real estate broker lic. 1981. Career: bus. & ofc. mgr. Century Motor Sales, Alhambra 1959-65; self- empl. 1965-72; sales Ritterhouse Realty, San Gabriel 1972-74; sales Baldwin Realty, Arcadia 1974--; pgm. com. for Bd. Realtors; pres. Multi Million Dollar Club 1981; honors: Top Sales 1980; One of Eight for taped series, Superstar of Real Estate by Duane Gomer; Awd. of Achievement in acctg. proficiency, Arcadia Bd. Realtors 1964; Multi Millon Dollar Club, Baldwin Realty 1980-83; mem: View of Hope; Bradbury chpt. City of Hope; her home (blt. 1981) selected as one of four Arcadia homes for Holiday Home Tour; Republican; rec: skiing, hunting. Res: 375 Mt Olive Dr Bradbury 91010 Ofc: Baldwin Realty Co., 900 So 1st St Arcadia 91006

ROBBINS, JACK LOEHR, metallurgist/research lab. executive; b. May 14, 1938, Denver, CO; s. Luther Sigford and Lasetta (Loehr) R.; m. Patricia Sue Jones, June 26, 1960; children: Sheri, b. 1965; Craig, b. 1967; edn; BS, Stanford Univ. 1960, MS, 1961; Degree of Engr. 1064. Career: Lawrence Livermore National Laboratory, Livermore 1963--: staff metallurgist, plutonium, 1963-66; sect. leader plutonium metallurgy, 1966-73; assoc. div. leader plutonium metallurgy 1973-74; metallurgy div. leader 1974-76; metals & cermanics div. leader 1976-80; dept. of energy sr. metallurgist in op. Morning Light', US-Canadian joint task force (search & recovery of Russian Cosmos 954 reactor satellite) 1978; assoc. dept. hd. for weapons, chem. & materials sci. dept. (sr. mats. scientist for weapons pgm., LLNL) 1980--; co-founder Identra Inc. as small R&D corp., initially v.p. for tech. applications; chmn. bd. trustees, fin. dir. Brentwood Comm. Methodist Ch.; honors: fellow, Am. Iron & Steel Inst., Stanford 1960-62; 2nd in class, Internat. Metallographic Exhibit 1972, 79; Soc. of Sigma Xi 1965; mem: Livermore Rod & Gun Club; Nat. Rifle Assn.; Calif. Rifle & Pistol Assn.; co- inventor: Method and Apparatus to Detect Identify, Authenticate and Date and Article, pat. pend.; 16 publs. in sci. journs.; Republican; Methodist; rec: hunting, model railroading, four wheeling. Res: Rt 1 Box 41B Brentwood 94513 Ofc: Lawrence Livermore National Laboratory, POB 808 L-328, Livermore 94550

ROBERSON, JOE BOB, mechanical engineer, utility co. mgr.; b. Nov. 21, 1934, Dallas, Tex.; s. Arthur Wheatley Jr. and Thelma Jo (Merritt) R.; m. Donna Roa Schneidewind, Oct. 16, 1965; children: Laura, b. 1969; Robert, b. 1975; edn: BS, Texas A&M Univ. 1956; uMBA, USC 1972. Career: dist. prod. spec. Carrier Corp., Dallas, TX 1956-58;sales engr. valley Weathermakers, Inc., Harlingen, TX 1958-59; dealer engring. mgr. The Prentiss Corp., Los Angeles 1959-67; exec. rep. So. Calif. Edison Co., Rosemead 1982, latest of 9 So. Calif. Edison assignments since 1967; Calif. Energy Commn. adv. com. on Implementation of Energy Standards for New Res. Bldgs. 1980-82; mem: Pacific Coast Electrical Assn.; Nat. & Calif. Socs. of Profl. Engrs.; Am. Soc. of Mech. Engrs.; Am. Soc. of Heating, Refrigeration & Air Conditioning Engrs.; Assn. of Energy Engrs.; Am. Mktg. Assn.; Am. Assn. of Public Opinion Research; Town Hall of Calif., Whittier Lodge; F&AM; mil: Capt., USAR, Signal Corps, hon. discharge; Republican; Lutheran; rec: photog., theater, sports events. Res: 9606 Hidden Farm Rd Alta Loma 91701 Ofc: So. Calif. Edison Co., 2244 Walnut Grove Rosemead 91770

ROBERTS, CHARLES PEARSON, chemical engineer; b. Feb. 23, 1915, Freeman, MO; s. Fred Byron and Edna M. (Pearsan) R.; m. Melva Dean Farmer, Aug. 7, 1943; 2 sons: Charles F., b. 1944; Richard J., b. 1950; edn: BS, Kans. St. Univ. 1939; reg. chem. engr., Calif. Career: proj. engr., works maint. supt. Filtrol Corp., Los Angeles 1945-54; proj. engr. Macco Corp., Paramount 1954-58; proj. engr. Ralph M. Parsons Co., Los Angeles 1958-59; research enfr., asst. maint. supt. U S Borax & Chem. Corp., Boron 1959-69; supt. proj. admin. Kerr- McGee Chem. Corp., Trona 1969-82; ret.; prin. Roberts Cons. Svc., Lake Isabella 1982--; recipient: two nat. awds., AIchE; mem: Am. Inst. of Chem. Engrs.; CofC; Lyons Culb; Boy Scouts of Am. Council; Mutual Water Co. (pres.); mil: Maj., US Army, Med. Svc. Corps. 1941-45; Republican; Methodist; rec: fishing, bowling. Address: Rt 1 Box 249-C Lake Isabella 93240

ROBERTS, DOUGLAS WAYNE, chiropractor; b. Dec. 13, 1955, Modesto; s. John Jay and Aileen (Rasmussen) R.; m. Laurie Smith, Apr. 28, 1979; 1 dau: Jennifer Lynn, b. 1983; edn: DC, Cleveland Chiro. Coll. 1977. Career: owner Roberts Chiro. Ctr. & Roberts Health Club; nutritional counselor, sports tnr. Roberts Health Club; honors: Sacral Occuputal Technique, Sept. 1976; mem: Internat. Acad. of Preventive Med.; Council on Nutrition; Council on Sports Injury; Calif. Chiro. Assn.; Democrat; rec: body conditioning. Res: 904 Standiford Ave, No C, Modesto 95350 Ofc: Roberts Chiropractic Center, 1801 Tully Rd, Ste A-2, Modesto 95350

ROBERTS, JAMES FREDRICK, JR., manufacturing co. executive; b. Aug. 8, 1935, Hartshorn, MO; s. James Fredrick Sr. and Alice Ruth (Murfin) R.; m. Ruth Johnson, May 31, 1956; children: Janice, b. 1957; James, b. 1961; edn: bus. admin. undergrad., UCLA Cont.; adv. spec. in govt. contracts, UCLA 1982; profl. designation govt. contracts, UCLA 1969; cert. assoc. contracts mgr., Nat. Contract Mgmt. Assn. 1981. Career: with Hughes Aircraft 1956--; contract analyst 1956; buyer 1960; subcontract adminstr. 1962; proj. adminstr. 1966; hd. of procurement 1967; mgr. purchasing dept. 1970; mgr. material dept. 1978; also mgr. Material Indsl. Electronics Gp., Hughes Aircraft; bd. dirs. Moore Engring. Co., Torrance 1982--; mem: Nat. Contract Mgmt. Assn.; Torrance CofC; Westside Comm. for Independent Living; fund raising, YMCA Campaign 1983, BSA Explorer Scouts, 1984; mil: Yeoman 2/c, USN 1952-56, GCM, overseas svc.; Republican; Protestant; rec: sports enthusiast, golf. Res: 759 Marine Ave Manhattan Beach 90266 Ofc: Hughes Aircraft Co., 3100 W Lomita Blvd Torrance 90509

ROBERTS, LEE MACK, JR., security co. president; b. Sept 14, 1949, Gastonia, NC; s. Lee Mack Sr. and Bonnie Estelle (Smallwood) R.; m. Vernon Wooten, Nov 11, 1972; children: Paula, b. 1963; Paul, b. 1965; edn: AA, Golden West Coll. 1974; BA, Univ. of Redlands 1977; pvt. investigators & pvt. patrol lic. Career: detective Newport Beach Police Dept. 1970-81 (med. ret.); owner Roberts Protection & Investigation 1982--; instr. Newport Beach Police & Fire Depts.; instr./ tchr. Golden West Coll. & Criminal Justice Tng. Ctr.; awards: Outstanding Police Ofcr. of the Yr., Newport Bch. PD 1973; three time recipient of Newport Beach Police Awd. of Merit 1976, 77, 79; Orange Co. Honored Citizen Awd., O.C.. Bd. Supvrs., 1979; mem: Calif. Conf. & Internat. Assn. of Arson Investigators; Internat. Police Assn.; Calif. & Western US Confs. of Safe & Burglary Investigators; Internat. Assn. for Identification; Am. Fedn. of Police; Nat. Assn. Home Bldrs. of US; BSA Police Explorer Sect.; works: Procedural Crime Scene Investigators Handbook, Newport Bch. PD; proposal for creation of multi- jurisdictional burglary impact team; plan to create Orange

Co. Police Museum; mil: Corp., USMC 1965-68; Republican; Baptist; rec: police memorabilia collector. Res: 3218 So Center St Santa Ana 92704 Ofc: Roberts Protection & Investigations, 828 N. Bristol St, Ste 103, Santa Ana 92704

ROBERTS, MARY ELIZABETH, real estate broker; b. Jan. 19, 1925, Independence City, Ark.; d. Allen and Edna Ruth (Williams) Sullivan; m. Robert F. Luckel, Oct. 19, 1983; children: Carol R. Yocum, b. 1946; Sandra J. Ghormley, b. 1952; edn: acctg., Okla. Univ. Norman 1946; bookeeping/ comptomter, San Jose State 1950; San Luis Obispo Jr. Coll. 1952; Long Beach Jr. Coll. 1965. Career: gen. bookeeper Ford Motors 1953-56; real estate 1976--; Tarbell Realtors 1976-77; United Properties 1977-78; owner So. Calif. Realty 1978-80; Liz Roberts Realty 1980--; income taxes Liz Roberts 1980--; cons.; honors: eroiled agent, dir. of Golf Commn. City of Long Beach; pres. PTA; pres. Golf Orig.; mem: Am. AmVets; Condo Assn. (pres.); American Vets; Methodist; rec: golf, charities. Res: 21329 Norwalk Blvd, No 28, Hawaiian Gardens Ofc: Liz Roberts Realty/ Tax, 5897 Cerritos Cypress 90630

ROBERTS, TOM JOHN, architect; b. Dec. 8, 1944, NY, NY; s. Andrew John and Cecilia Frances R.; edn: B Arch., UC Berkeley 1967. Career: (past) designer William L. Pereira Assoc., Charles Kober Assocs., Maxwell Starkman Assocs., Daniel, Mann, Johnson & Mendenhall; pres. Tom Roberts Assoc., Los Angeles 1976--; mem. MOCA, LA County Mus. of Art; works incl: Crewe Building (1982), Three Residences - Coldwater Cyn. (1978), Dessau Apartments (1980), Reseda Apartments (1979). Res: 2439 Coldwater Canyon Dr Beverly Hills 90210 Ofc: 11009 1/2 Strathmore Dr Los Angeles 90024

ROBERTS, WILLIAM LOUIS, architect/ urban sociologist; b. Dec. 8, 1929, Los Angeles; s. William Louis and Marth Louise (Strahan) R.; m. Collette Ponsal, Sept. 6, 1952; edn: AA, L.A. City Coll. 1949; Bach., mil. sci., UCLA 1953; Bach., arch., USC 1960; M.Arch., MA sociology, USC 1973; PhD USC 1974. Career: instr. USC, L.A. 1970-75; asst. prof. CSU Northridge 1975; assoc. prof. architecture Calif. Polytech. St. Univ. Sch. of Arch. & Environ. Design, SLO 1975-78; pres. architect & property cons. William L. Roberts, a Calif. corp., Rancho Palos Verdes 1972--; The Salvation Army Adv. Bd., Mens Soc. Svc. Adult Redah. Ctr., Honolulu, HA 1954-70; guest critic Sch. of Arch. & Environ. Design, Cal Poly, SLO 1974; honors: Gold Key Hon. Soc., UCLA 1952; Scarab Design Hon., Sch. of Arch. & Fine Arts, USC 1960; fellow, Environ. Studies Lab., Adminstrn. on Aging 1971-73; Biomed. Scis. Support Grant, Nat. Inst. of Health 1973-74; Alpha Kappa Delta, USC 1974; Phi Kappa Phi, USC 1974; mem: Lambda Chi Alpha frat.; Pi Delta Epsilon (pres. 1953); Scarab Archit. Soc.; Tau Sigma Delta; Am. Inst. Arch.; Am. Sociological Assn.; num. publs. papers 1975--; 1st Lt., US Army 1953-55; Protestant; rec: mountain climbing, flying. Res: 28137 So Ridgecove Ct Rancho Palos Verdes 90274 Ofc: William L Roberts, A Calif. Corp., 30840 Hawthorne Blvd Rancho Palos Verdes 90274; PO Box 7000-8 Palos Verdes Peninsula 90274

ROBERTSON, ANDREW WELLS, lawyer; b. Mar. 29, 1949, Pasadena; s. Lilliam and Jane (Patterson) R.; edn: AB, Brown Univ. 1971; JD, UCLA Law Sch. 1974. Career: law clerk Judge William P Sray, US Dist. Ct., Los Angeles 1974-75; assoc. Lillick Inc Hose & Charles, Los Angeles 1975-80; partner 1980--; mem: Los Angeles Co., Calif. St. & Am. Bar Assns.; Los Angeles Jr. CofC (pres. 1980-81); Glen Campbell Los Angeles Open; rec: amateur golf. Res: 2764 Fleur Dr San Marino 91108 Ofc: Lillick Inc Hose & Charles, 707 Wilshire Blvd Los Angeles 90017

ROBERTSON, HARRY CARSON, insurance executive; b. Jan. 9, 1941, Covinon, Va.; s. Carl R. and Jane Virginia (Hicks) R.; children: Jody, b. 1968, Harry Jr., b. 1970. Career: chief petty officer US Navy 1959-79, decorated Combat Action, GCM (4 awds.), Vietnam Campaign (7 awds); agent, district mgr., agcy. supr., Raymond C. Ferro Insurance Agency, San Diego 1979-, assoc. general agent, 1983--; awards: San Diego Life Managers Assn. Agent of the Year 1981, 1982; qualifying mem. Million Dollar Round Table; pres.'s cabinet of Nat. Public Service Insur. Co.; mem: Nat. Assn. of Life Underwriters (PAC), MDRT Foundation (Knight), VFW, Vietnam Veterans of S.D.; YMCA; Methodist; rec: golf, fishing. Ofc: Raymond C. Ferro Insurance Agcy. 3455 Camino Del Rio South, San Diego 92108

ROBERTSON, FLORENCE EVA, real estate broker/accountant; b. Jan. 9, 1906, Alexandria, Ohio; d. Harry Joseph and Carrie Lucretia (Oyler) Buxton; m. Richard Robertson, Mar. 27, 1948; edn: att. Newark Bus. Coll. (Ohio) 1923, Univ. of Calif., Davis; AA, Sacto. City Coll. 1970. Calif. lic. Real Estate Broker 1956. Career: auditor/credit mgr. Ohio State Univ. Hosp. 1928-42; expediter Wright Field, Dayton 1942-45; night auditor Palace Hotel, San Francisco 1946-48; auditor/v.p. R R Construction Co. (R R Robertson, husband), 1948-55, acct., decorator, 1984-; real estate broker, Office on Arden Way, Sacramento 1956-84; mem. Calif. Real Estate Assn., Women's Aux. 1956-66; Tuesday Club (Sacto) 1955-83; works: writing history of the Buxton Family 1769-; Republican. Res: 3540 N. El Macero Dr El Macero 95618

ROBERTSON, PERMELIA, real estate broker; b. Feb. 9, 1933, Los Angeles; d. Felix Edward Sr. and Gladys Permelia Henderson; m. Arthur W. Robertson Sr., Nov. 14; children: Arthur Jr., b. 1956; Pamela Michele, b. 1958; edn: AA, L.A. Metro Jr. Coll. 1966; R.E. cert., Sacto. City Coll. 1973; R.E. broker, Anthony Real Estate Sch. 1982. Career: real estate broker; mem: Sacto. Bd. Realtors; Nat. Council of Negro Women; Democrat; Methodist; rec: travel, languages. Address: Pam Robertson-Calvados Realty, 6614 Fordham Way Sacramento 91831

ROBERTSON, SUSAN TERRY, corporate controller; b. Aug. 4, 1954, Orange; d. William Henry and Diane Eleanor (Comer) R.; m. Kim Z. Turtenwald, Nov. 6, 1982; edn: BA, Biola Univ. 1976; MBA, USC 1978; CPA, Calif. Career: staff acct. Arthur Young & Co. 1978-80; corp. controller Home Health Care of Am., Newport Beach 1980--; mem: Am. Inst. of CPAs; Calif. Soc. of CPAs; Womens Economic & Career Advancement Network; Women in Bus.; Orange Co. Profl. Womens Network; Weight Watchers; Evangelical; rec: racquetball, theater. Res: 400 So Flower, No 174, Orange 92668 Ofc: Home Health Care of Am., 4340 Von Karman Newport Beach 92660

ROBINSON, ARTHUR HOBART, writer, natural foods retailer; b. June 2, 1896, Glen Ellyn, Ill.; s. Arthur O. and Katherine Robinson; widower; ed. pub. schs. thru 8th gr., var. colls. Career: farming, well digger, logger, soldier, seaman, timekeeper; electronic engr. for IBM, Remington-Rand, Addressograph, Graphotype, Address-Elliot, ret. 1957; free lance writing, organic farming 1957--, owner 41.82 acres of woodlands in Scott Bar Mountains; wholesaler/retailer Natural Foods, Candy, and All Products, owner/pres. Robinson Supply Co.; founder Everybody's Friend Foundation; writer/pub. Robinson's Hobby Press; mem: Disabled Am. Veterans (life), Nat. Assn. of Retired People, Good Sam Club; author: Everybody's Friend - Unknown Famous; (book in prog.) The Unknown and Some Answers; mil: pvt. US Army M.C. 1917-18; Indep.; Mormon Ch./Universal; rec: walking, nature studies. Address: 20421 McAdams Creek Rd Fort Jones 96032

ROBINSON, DEL FRANK, real estate broker/farmer; b. Sept. 5, 1939, Albuquerque, NM; s. Frank and Docia Velma (Parker) R.; 1 son: Brent, b. 1966; edn: real estate, Delta 1974; CE, cert. exchangor, Interex 1981. Career: real estate broker/exchangor, 1968--, owner Robinson Realty dba Agri-Industries; hog farmer (large farrow to fat hog op.); listed, Who's Who in Creative Real Estate; mem: FLI/Sacto. Region; Lodi Bd. Realtors; Interex; Lions Club (pres.); Sacto. Exch. Club; mil: submarine svc. 1959-64; Republican; Baptist; rec: travel, hunting, fishing. Res: 19975 N. Elliott Rd Lockford 95237 Ofc: Robinson Realty, 23233 No Jack Tail Rd Lockford 95237

ROBINSON, HARRELL EDWARD, physician; b. July 9, 1952, Thomasville, Ala.; s. Sandy C. Jr. and Savannah Patricia (Atwood) R.; m. Jacqueline, Aug. 29, 1976; edn: BA, Oakwood Coll. 1974; MD, Loma Linda Univ. 1977, Splst. Hd. & Neck/ENT, 1981; Otorhinolaryngologist (ENT) Head & Neck Surgeon. Career: intern gen. surg., 1978, res. otorhinolaryngology White Memorial Med. Ctr. 1979-81; lab instr. Oakwood Coll.; NIH resrch. in biochem.; currently physician Head & Neck Surgeon, Ross Loos Med. Group, Orange; teaching staff White Meml. Med. Ctr. of Loma Linda Univ.; awards: research grants from public, pvt. orgns.; Am. Chem. Soc. award 1973; Outstanding Young Men of Am. 1972; mem: CHOMS, CMA, AMA, Am. Council Otolaryn.; Am. Acad. Otolaryn./ Head & Neck; NARI; sci. publs.; rec: painting, sketching. Res: 21187 Ambushers St Diamond Bar 91765 Ofc: Ross Loos Medical Gp., 2629 E Chapman Ave Orange 92669

ROBISON, JAMES TROY, JR., insurance agency executive; b. June 11, 1943, Alton, Ill.; s. James Troy and Edith Eleanor (Vick) R.; m. Sally Franklin, June 22, 1969; 1 dau: Amy, b. 1977; edn: BS, USAF Acad. 1965; MS, USC 1971; chartered fin. cons., The Am. Coll. 1983; CLU, The Am. Coll. 1979; lic. realtor, Calif. 1978. Career: v.p. Protech Investment Realty, West Germany 1972-75; agent Washington Nat. Ins. Co., Sacramento 1975-77; supvr./ tng. mgr. Bankers life Nebraska, Sacto. 1977-80; No. Calif. agcy. mgr. Woodmen Accident & Life, Sacto. 1980--; chmn. Agcy. Mgmt. Tng. Course 1983-84; awards: USAF Europe Well Done Awd.' 1971; Nat. Sales Achiev. Avd. 1975-77; Nat. Quality Awd. 1976; Health Ins. Quality Awd. 1976; Million Dollar Round Table 1976-80; mem: Gen. Agents & Mgrs. Assn.; Nat. Assn. Life Underwriters; Am. Soc. of CLUs; Nat. Assn. Realtors; Elks; mil: Capt., USAF 1961-72, Colorado, Sacto., W. Germany, Thailand, DFC, Air Medals (2); Republican; Assemblies of God. Res: 8550 Walden Woods Way Loomis 95650 Ofc: Woodmen Accident & Life, 1555 River Park Dr, Ste 203, Sacramento 95815

ROBLES, MAURO PACHECO, company president; b. Dec. 8, 1923, Zacatecaz, Mex., nat. 1965; s. Prudenciano and Celsa (Pacheco) R.; m. Estela Arellano, Sept. 11, 1954; children: Marisela, b. 1955; Ricardo, b. 1957; Pablo, b. 1961; Marina, b. 1963; Jacqueline, b. 1969. Career: owner La Reina, 1958--; pres., adminstrv. controller La Reina Inc., 1968--; Republican; Catholic. Res: 10 Halsted Cir Alhambra 91801 Ofc: La Reina, Inc., 316 N. Ford Blvd Los Angeles 90022

ROCHA, RAY FRANCIS, consulting firm executive; b. Apr.3, 1943, Eureka; s. Frank P. and Zelma M. (Cardoza) R.; m. Carole Lyons, Aug. 24, 1977; edn: BA, Univ. of Idaho 1965. Career: sales rep. Mobil Oil, Boise, Ida. 1965; gen. sales mgr. Nashua Homes/Conchemco Homes, Boise 1970-74; v.p. mktg. Shelterex, Boise 1974-77; gen. sales mgr. Fleetwood Ent. Lakeland, Fla. 1977-79; regional mktg. dir. Gustafson/Williams, Costa Mesa, Calif. 1980-81; dir. of sales/ptnr. Williams Associates Inc., Walnut Creek 1982--; co-dir. Tites Unlmtd. 1982; co-dir. Redibilt 1975-76; co-dir. Ebronix of Nompa, Ida. 1967-69; awards: Blue Key 1964; Super Pro Club, Conchemco Homes Group 1973-74; mem. Jaycees (sec. Capitol chpt. 1969-7); CofC; Beta Theta Pi; mil: E4 Army Nat. Guard; Republican; Sci. of Mind; rec: tenns, fishing; wt. lifting. Res: 1060 Arlington Way Martinez 94853 Ofc: Williams Assocs Inc. 2850 Shodelands Dr, Ste 215, Walnut Creek 95687

ROCHE, AUDREY LOUISE, educator; b. Mar. 7, 1936, Los Angeles; d. Paul Raymond and Myrtle A. (Swanson) Steele; m. Lowman B. Lyon, Dec. 27, 1981; children: Danielle K., b. 1965; Christine D., b. 1966; edn: AA, Coll. of the

Sequoias 1956; BS, UCLA 1958; MBA, 1959. Career: acct. Biophysical Research Inc. 1960-62; prof. acctg. Santa Monica Coll. 1963-82; chmn. bus. dept. Santa Monica Coll. 1982--; acct: Corel Electronics, Inc. 1972-83; Denmar Investment Co. 1969--; mem: Faculty Assn. of Calif. Comm. Colls. 1965-84; Santa Monica Coll. Faculty Assn. (pres.; leader Negotiations Council); Santa Monica Coll. Patrons Assn.; Republican; Christian. Res: 826 Oxford Ave Marina del Rey 90292 Ofc: Santa Monica Coll., 1900 Pico Blvd Santa Monica 90405

ROCKOWITZ, MURRAY, software engineering executive; b. Apr. 8, 1933, Brooklyn, NY; s. Herman and Frieda Rockowitz; m. Marcia Lachman, June 27, 1954; children: Neal, b. 1956; Bruce, b. 1958; Steve, b. 1963; edn: BS, Queens Coll. 1954; MS, cum laude, Xavier Univ., OH 1960. Career: navigator USAF, Tex. & Mass. 1954-57; engr. AVCO Corp., Cinninnati, Ohio 1957-60; staff scientist, AVCO, Wilmington, Mass. 1960-65; tech. staff Lincoln Lab., Mass. 1965-79; mgr., software intergration TRW 1979--; mem: IEEE; Sigma Xi; Operation Hedstart, Mass.; author/ coauthor over 50 tech. documents; devel. technique to detect voids in honey combed Apollo heat shield; mil: 1st Lt., USAF1954-57; Jewish; rec: piano, tennis, flying. Res: 27 Oak Tree Ln Rolling Hills Estates 90274 Ofc: TRW, One Space Park, 131/2105, Redondo Beach 90278

RODE, EDDIE, real estate broker; b. Aug. 21, 1920, No. Chicago, IL; s. Jacob and Mary (Kosir) R.; m. Marguerite Wagner, Nov. 15, 1947; children: Susan, b. 1949; Mark, b. 1951; Joanne, b. 1955; Patricia, b. 1957; edn: BS, Univ. of Md. 1954-59. Career: mil. ofcr. USAF 1942-63; mil. advr. Yugoslavia 1951-54; staff ofcr., Pentagon 1954-59; pilot WII SW Pacific 1942-44; owner/broker Eddie Rode Realty 1963--; founder/ pres. Pacific Tube & Containing 1971-72; mem: Santa Barbara Bd. Realtors; Lompoc Bd. Realtors; Channel City Club; Ret. Ofcrs. Culb; Santa Barbara Apt. Owners Assn.; Santa Barbara Bd. Realtors; mil: Lt. Col., USAF 1942-63, Air Medal, 7 Oak Leaf Clusters; Republican; Protestant; rec: golf, fishing, bridge. Res: 3360 Braemar Dr Santa Barbara 93105 Ofc: Rode Realty, 3114 State St Santa Barbara 93105

RODERICK, RICHARD DALE, distribution co. executive; b. Jan. 15, 1934, Springfield, Ill.; s. Raymond Earl and Lyda Ethel (Oakleaf) R.; m. Joy Schrader, Dec. 23, 1951; children: Roxanne Denise, b. 1958; Richard Dale, b. 1965; edn: Santa Monica City Coll. 1957-58; US Naval schs. 1952, 54. Career: regl. mgr. Solitron Devices, Tappan, NY 1966-68; pres./ founder Rical Assocs., Inc., Santa Ana 1968-76; v.p./ founder Emitter Electronics, Inc., Santa Anan 1976-80; pres./ founder VSI Military & Space Components, Santa Ana 1980-81; pres. Pacesetters Electronics, Santa Ana 1981--; past bd. dirs. Rical Elect., Emmiter Elec., VSI M&S; bd. dirs. Pacesetter Elec., Internat. Devices Inc.; mem: Irvine School Bond Com. 1972; mil: lt. 2/c, USN 9152-56; Republican; Protestant; rec: boating, fishing. Res: 15351 Nimes Cir Irvine 92714 Ofc: Pacesetter Electronics, 31378 W Warner Santa Ana 92704

RODGERS, PATRICIA ANN, real estate broker; b. June 15, 1947, Portola, CA; d. Donald George and Theresa M. (Stella) Smith; m. James William Rodgers, July 25, 1965; 1 dau: Theresa Nicole, b. 1974; edn: bus. admin., Yuba Coll. 1965-67; R.E., Butte Coll. 1977-78; realtor, 1977. Career: acct. clerk Butte Co. Housing Authority, Gridley, Calif. 1970-73; bookeeper Piret Tire Ctr., Chico 1975-77; real estate assoc. Red Carpet, Oroville 1978-79; real estate broker Realty World, Oroville 1980-81; broker/ owner Century 21 Rodgers Realty 1982--; mem: Oroville Bd. Realtors; Calif. Nat. Assns. Realtors; Eastern Star, Oroville Amapola chpt.; Oroville are CofC; Republican; Catholic; rec: fishing, water sports, travel. Res: Rt 2 Box 2788-A Oroville 95965 Ofc: Century 21 Rodgers Realty, 2295 Feather River Blvd, Ste D, Oroville 95965

RODRIGUEZ, CHRISTOPHER, commercial credit consultant; b. Jun. 4, 1954; s. Walter and Rosa R.; m. Lavena Rodriguez, May 9, 1974; children: Christopher, b. 1975; Aimee, b. 1978; edn: credit specialist, Control Data Inst. 1974; qualification cert. 1980. Career: collections to vice pres. Greater Financial Svcs., Pasadena 1974-79; CEO, P.U.S.H. Internat. Bus. Systems Inc., Arcadia 1979--; author annual comml. credit manual for corporations; Christian; rec: family, raquetball. Res: 2613 Brookdale Ln Duarte 91010 Ofc: P.U.S.H. Intl., 107 W. Huntington Dr, Ste. E, Arcadia 91006

RODRIGUEZ, ROMAN, physician; b. Jan. 21, 1951, NYC; s. Roman Rodriguez and Margarita (Castillo) Torres; edn: BS in biol., St. Mary's Coll., Calif. 1972; MD, UC San Francisco 1976; psychiatric externship, Menninger Found., 1973; pediatric externship, Univ. of Miami, 1974. Career: resident gen. psychiat. Menninger Sch. of Psychiatry, 1976-79; fellowship in child psychiat. 1978-80; res. physician Topeka VA Med. Ctr., 1976-79; dir. of psychiatric svcs. Youth Center at Topeka, 1979-80; assoc. med. dir., child psychiatrist Mission/ Southeast Adolescent Day Treatment Ctr., Children's Hosp. of San Francisco 1980-81; staff psychiatrist Youth Guidance Ctr., S.F. 1980-82; clin. dir. Growing Mind Corp., Bolinas 1980--; physician, child psychiatrist Monteagle Med. Ctr./ St. Luke's Hosp., S.F.; asst. clin. prof. of psychiatry UCSF Sch. of Med. 1981-; staff phys. Children's Hosp. (1980-), St. Luke's Hosp. (1981-), Univ. of Calif. Hosps. & Clinics (1983-), San Francisco; staff phys. Marin Gen. Hosp. (1983-); mem. UCSF Sch. of Med. admissions com. 1980-; mem: Am. Acad. of Child Psychiatry, No. Calif. Psychiatric Soc., Am. Psychiatric Assn., AMA; (past) Kansas Med. Soc. 1976-80, Fellows Assn. of the Menninger Sch. of Psychiat. 1976-80; Republican; Catholic; rec: keyboard music, walking, travel. Res: 275 Bahia Ln San Rafael 94901 Ofc: 1580 Valencia St, Ste. 210, San Francisco 94110

ROE, CLINTON HAROLD, real estate broker; b. July 20, 1952, Beaumont, Tex.; s. Harold Edwin and Dana Gwendolyn (Rogers) R.; m. Keiko Sakatani, Nov. 18, 1978; 1 son: Matthew, b. 1983; edn: AA, Pasadena City Coll. 1972; BS, USC 1977. Career: br. inventory mgr. Xerox Corp. 1973-78; Mulhearn Gallery of Homes 1978--; sales assoc. 1978-79; br. mgr./ v.p. 1980--; sales tng. instr. Homes Mgmt. Tng. Dir.; awards: Mgr. of the Yr. 1982; Million Dollar Sales Club 1978, 79; mem: Nat., Calif. & Rancho Los Cerritos Bds. Realtors; La Mirada Tennis Club; publs: in Financial Freedom Report 1981; Republican; rec: golf, tennis. Res: 11758 Broadfield La Mirada 90638 Ofc: Mulhearn Realtors, 5928 South St Lakewood 90713

ROESCHKE, DONALD FREDERICK, lawyer; b. Mar. 20, 1938, Pago Pago, Samoa; s. Charles Edward and Madeline (McCarty) R.; m. Suzann Hogue, July 12, 1969; 1 son: David, b. 1976; edn: BS, CSU Northridge 1961; LLD, Southwestern Univ. Sch. of Law 1965; admitted to practice US Supreme, US Dist. & 9th Circuit Ct. of Appeals; writs coordinator for State Atty. General, L.A. Office. Career: self- empl. atty. 1966-72; deputy attorney general (IV), Calif. Dept. of Justice, Ofc. of Atty. Gen. 1972--; author Deputy tng. manuals on state & fed. writ & state appellate procedures; lectr. on writs; prosecutor, Daniel Caudillo case (discussed in book Judging Judges by Preble Stolz); sev. cases in state Appellate, Fed., & Calif. Supreme courts; defender for people when Sirhan Sirhan filed for release, Fed. Ct.; mem: Calif. State Bar; US Supreme Ct. Bar; publs: Mastering the Art of the Great Writ, Los Angeles Lawyer, Feb. 1981; The Continuing Role of the Peace Officer After a Criminal Conviction, Police Officer Law Report, June 1981; Republican; Catholic; rec: model railroading, weight lifting. Ofc: Office of Atty. General, 3580 Wilshire Blvd, Rm 703, Los Angeles 90010

ROGERS, DONNA ALDEN, corporate accountant; b. Apr. 20, 1954, Somerville, NJ; d. Charles Ely, Jr. and Elizabeth Willson (Auerbacher) Rogers; m. Brooks Brown Ammerman, Jan. 20, 1978; two children: Jesse Galen b. 1978, Marie Christine b. 1979; m. 2d. Marc Anthony La France, 1983, div.; edn: stu. Coll. of Alameda 1976-7, UC Berkeley 1977-8. Career: bookkeeper King Books, 1975-78, Systemetrics Inc., 1980; full chg. bookkeeper California Appliances Inc., 1980-81, Sheraton Santa Barbara Hotel & Spa, 1981; farming financial analyst National Pacific Cos., 1981-82; acctg. mgr. Carpinteria Valley Lumber Co., 1982-83; owner The Paper Works, Ojai 1983--; honors: Internat. Rotary Exchange student to Brazil 1970-71; Who's Who in Junior Colls. 1977; tchr. 4th & 5th grades/Am. Lung Assn., Oakland 1976; Candy Striper, All Souls Hosp., Morristown, NJ 1969-70; mem: Am. Businesswomens Assn., Smithsonian, DAR; orgn: Morehelp 1969-70, Bernardsville NJ Student Panel seminars on drug abuse; works: art: three dimensional wall hangings, drawing, painting; unpub. poetry, short stories, essays; Republican; Prot.; rec: rowing, basketball, pianist. Address: 229 Arnaz (POB 1522) Ojai 93023

ROGERS, REBECCA SUSAN, telecommunications business executive; b. Nov. 14, 1952, Jackson, Miss.; d. John Milben and Jackie Sue (Newsom) R.; edn: BBA, Univ. of Miss. 1974; MBA, Stanford Univ. 1980; CPA, Calif. 1976. Career: auditor/ sr. tax acct. Deloltte, Haskins & Sells, San Francisco 1974-77; asst. to pres. Rogers Poultry Inc., Morton, Miss. 1977-78; cons. Boston Consulting Gp., Menlo Park 1980-82; dist. staff mgr. strategic plng. Pacific Telephone, San Francisco 1982--; honors: Arjay Miller Scholar (top 10 percent), Stanford Grad. Sch. of Bus.; Who's Who in Am. Colls. & Univs.; mem: Am. Inst. CPAs; S.F. Economic Round Table; Telegraph Hill Dwellers; S.F. Bay Club; Stanford Bus. Sch. Alumni Assn.; Univ. of Miss. Alumni Assn.; Republican; rec: cross country skiing, singing, art deco design. Res: 1360 Montgomery St, No 8, San Francisco 94133 Ofc: Pacific Telephone, 140 New Montgomery, Rm 722, San Francisco 94105

ROGERS, ROBERT REED, mfg. co. executive; b. Feb. 22, 1929, Oak Park, Ill.; s. Glen Charles and Lucile (Reed) R.; m. Barbara June Fain, Feb. 22, 1951; children: Robin, b. 1951, Janeen, b. 1952, Kevin, b. 1954; edn: BS in chem., Berea Coll. 1951; MBA, Ill. Inst. of Tech. 1958, postgrad. work in econ. 1959-62. Career: asst. mgr. Metallurgy Resrch Dept. Armour Research Found. 1955-56; faculty Ill. Inst. of Tech. Dept. of Bus. and Econ., 1956-62; cons. McKinsey & Co. Inc., 1962-64; mgr. Devel. Planning, Profl. Group, Litton Indus. Inc., 1964-67; pres. No. Am. Subsidiaries, Muirhead & Co. Ltd, Beckenham, Kent, UK, 1967-68; group v.p. American Elec. Inc. subs. City Investing Co., 1968-70; pres. Cleartight Corp., 1971-73; pres. NIMCO Inc. 1973-76; pres. Kensington Assocs. Inc., 1976-; pres. The Proteus Group Inc. (OTC), 1981-; pres. Comparator Systems Corp., 1983-; Dir. UCAP, Inc. (OTC) 1982-; dir. World Series Baseball Parks, Inc. (OTC) 1983-. Awards: Berea Coll. Study Grant 1951; MAPI Fellow 1956. Mem. Lido Isle Yacht Club, Ferrari Owners Club, Navy League, Internat. Platform Assn. Mil: lt. USNR 1951-55; Libertarian; Sci of Mind; rec: chamber music, theatre, ballet. Res: 819A W. 15th St. Newport Bch 92663 Ofc: 881 Dover Dr, Ste. 35, Newport Bch 92663

ROHDE, RUSSELL ALLAN, physician-surgeon; b. Dec. 7, 1930, Glendale; s. Ralph Wm. and Hazel Mae (House) R.; m. Maureen Ann Finn, Mar. 1, 1975; children: David Lynn, b. 1962, William Arthur, b. 1967, Jennifer Lynn, b. 1975; edn: BS, Univ. N.Dak. 1953; MD, Harvard Sch. of Med. 1956; Bd. Certified in Internal Med. 1967. Career: phys. solo practice, spec. in cardiology invasive cardiac procedures, pacemaker implantations (20 yrs), and assisting in major vascular surgery reconstrn. of arteries; chief of medicine, and chief of cardiology, Queen of Valley Hosp., West Covina; mem: Fellow Am. Coll. of Physicians; Los Angeles and Calif. Med. Assn.; sgt. L.A. Co. Sheriff's Dept. Spl. Enforcement Bur., Emerg. Svcs. Detail Reserve (1969-); works: Research papers (42), largely genetics, and cardiovascular disease; pres. Synoptic Systems (resrch computer oriented pgms. devel. co.); rec: micro and macrophotography of living organisms. REs: 2820 E. Cortez West Covina 91791 Ofc: Russell Rohde, MD, Inc., 1535 W. Merced, Ste. 202, West Covina 91790

ROMANO, DAVID JOHN, financial executive; b. April 1, 1959, San Jose; s. Benjamin John and Marie Rose Romano; m. Karen B. Ruiz, June 1, 1983; edn: West Valley Coll. 1977-8, John Hancock Inst. 1980-; Reg. rep. Nat. Assn. of Security Dealers, 1982. Career: asst. mgr. Sport Barn, Inc., Santa Clara 1975-6; founder/owner Nor Cal Tackle Co., and Yankee Bait Co. (mfg. & mktg. fishing lures), Santa Clara 1975-79; rep. John Hancock Cos. (youngest agt. in hist. of agcy), San Jose 1979--, sales supr. John Hancock Cos., Los Gatos 1983--; exec. dir. Randall E. Banta & Assocs. (finl. planning firm) Los Gatos 1983-; pres./stockhldr. Financial Mgmt. Concepts, Inc. (finl. plnng., consulting), Los Gatos 1984--; (bus. cons. emplyee benefits 1982-; instr. for ins. cos. 1982-; lectr. on careers, goals, local hi schs., colls. Honors: Bank of Am. Awd. 1977; Presidents Council, Allied Assocs. 1982, 83. Mem: Nat. Assn. of Life Underwriters, Internat. Assn. for Finl. Planners, Assn. for Finl. Planning Advis. Council. Designer fresh and salt water fishing lures 1975-78. Publs: sales visual aids for John Hancock Cos.; arts. on fishing tackle in local newspapers 1975-8; Democrat. Christian (Cath. of Faith, New Life Ministry). rec: golf, pianist. Res: 165 Blossom Hill Rd San Jose 95123 Ofc: Financial Management Concepts, Inc. 16795 Lark Ave, 260, Los Gatos 95030

ROMANO, MALCOLM JOSEPH, patent lawyer; b. Feb. 13, 1939, NY, NY; s. Joseph and Catherine (Tamburello) R.; m. Mary, Aug. 15, 1964; children: Matthew, b. 1968; Mark, b. 1972; edn: BEE, CCNY 1964; MS, UCLA 1969; JD, Western St. Univ. 1975. Career: sr. engr./ gp. leader Rockwell Internat.; patent atty. Christie, Parker & Halee; currently, chief patent counsel/ asst. secty. Lear Siegler, Inc., Santa Monica; mem: Los Angeles Co. Bar Assn.; Italian- Am. Lawyers; Assn. of Corp. Patent Counsels; Republican; Catholic; rec: skiing, sailing. Res: 116 So Citrus Los Angeles 90036 Ofc: Lear Siegler, 2850 Ocean Park Blvd Santa Monica 90405

RONAGHY, HOSSAIN ALI, physician, university professor; b. Mar. 21, Fassa, Iran, nat. 1977; s. Hashem and Batool Ronaghy; m. Sima, Oct. 16, 1966; children: Sara, b. 1967; Ali, b. 1969; edn: MD, Pahlavi Univ. 1954-60; MPH, Johns Hopkins Univ. 1971; adj. prof., UCSD. Career: med. instr./ chief res. Chicago Med. Sch., Chgo. 1965-66; prof. of med./ asst. dean Shiraz Univ. Sch. of Med., Shriaz, Iran 1966-79; dean Fassa Sch. of Med. 1972-77; internat. assoc. dept. internat. health, John Hopkins Univ. Sch. of Hygiene & Public Health 1977-81; adj. prof. dept. community & family med. UC San Diego Sch. of Med., La Jolla 1981--; visiting lectr. UCLA; cons./ advr. World Health Orgn.; World Health Expert Com. on Nutrition; honors: Internat. Migration; mem: CMA; AMA; San Diego Co. Med. Soc.; coauthor: four med. books; author; over 50 arts. pub. in internat. journs.; Unitarian; rec: research in health care. Res: 5431 Bahia Ln La Jolla 92037 Ofc: 3023 Bunker Hill St, Ste 106, San Diego 92109

RONDEAU, DORIS JEAN, entrepreneur; b. Nov. 25, 1941, Winston-Salem, NC; d. John Delbert and Eldora Virginia (Klutz) Robinson; m. Wilfrid D. Rondeau, June 3, 1971; edn: Syracuse Univ. 1959-62, Fullerton Jr. Coll. 1974-75, BA (philosophy) CSU Fullerton 1976; postgrad. wk. CSU Long Beach 1976-80; cert. minister, The Spirit of Divine Love (1974). Career: trust real estate clk. Security First Nat. Bank, Riverside Main Office, 1965-68; profl. entertainer, Hollywood 1969-72; co-founder, dir., minister The Spirit of Divine Love, Capistrano Beach, 1974--; publisher Passing Through, Inc. 1983-; instr. The Learning Activity, Anaheim 1984-; owner/bd. chmn. D J Rondeau, Entrepreneur, Inc., Capistrano Beach 1984--; corporate co-founder/dir.: The Spirit of Divine Love Inc., Spiritual Positive Attitude Inc., Passing Through Inc., Moon in Pisces Inc., Vibrations by Rondeau Inc., Divine Consciousness, Expressed Inc.; honors: Arista (acad. hon.), Permanent Roll, Curtis High (1958/9), VFW Award (1958), Boar's Head Soc. (drama hon.), USAF Talent Contest, 1st. Place Female Pop Vocalist (1964/65); Epsilon Delta Chi; mem. Hamel Bus. Graduate, Smithsonian Assocs., Am. Mgmt. Assn., Nat. Assn. of Female Execs.; orgns: Salesian Missions (Mamaroneck, NY), World Vision (Pasadena), North Shore Animal League (Port Wash., NY), Covenant House (NY, NY) Opportunities for the Blind; mil: A2C, USAF 1963-65, GCM; Metaphysician; rec: long dist. running, body fitness. Res: 34525 Camino Capistrano Capistrano Beach 92624 Ofc: D J Rondeau, Entrepreneur, Inc. POB 2607, Capo Beach 92624

RONKA, BOB, lawyer, businessman; b. Nov. 2, 1942, Mnpls.; s. Ilmari and Loraine Vera (Aalbu) R.; edn: AB, Stanford Univ. 19654; JD, Harvard Law Sch. 1967; postgrad. polit. sci., Exeter Coll., Oxford Univ., Eng. 1967. Career: professional musician (piano, trombone, vocal), recording artist with Capitol Records, 1959-60; atty., Century City law firm of Pacht, Ross, Warne, Bernhard & Sears, 1967-68; congl. intern, staff of rep. Edward Roybal (D-Calif.), Wash. D.C., 1963; legislative intern and speechwriter, staff of V.P. Hubert Humphrey, 1965; atty. and indsl. real estate developer in San Fernando Valle, 1971-75; finance dir. US Sen. John V. Tunney Election Campaign, 1976; elected city councilman, rep. 1st Council Dist., N.E. San Fernando Valley, Los Angeles City Council, 1977-81; businessman, Sun Valley, 1981--; bd. dirs. Century Thrift and Loan, 1982--; vis. prof. of law Comparative Am. & Vietnamese Law, Univ. of Saigon, Repub. of Vietnam 1969. Honors: Phi Beta Kappa (1964); 1st Place, Los Angeles City-Wide, Bank of America Achievement Awards competition (1960); mem: State Bar of Calif. 1968-; Musicians Union Local 47, 1959-; chmn. R.E. Law Section, San Fernando Valley Bar Assn. 1972-74; Alpha Sigma Phi. Authored Olympics cost-control amendment to L.A. City Charter, adopted by 72 percent of L.A. voters 11/78, shielding taxpayers from costs of 1984 Olympic Games; mil: 1st lt. US Army Intell., decorated Bronze Star and Jt. Service Commendn. medal; Democrat; Prot.; rec: music, cinema, swimming, travel. Res: 11029 Allegheny St Sun Valley 91352

RONNING, ANNE MARIE, real estate broker; b. July 31, 1931, San Bernardino; d. Ebenezer Fred and William Ammerette (Dolby) Mueller; edn: San Bernardino Valley Coll.; Calif. real estate lic. 1955, R.E. Broker, 1969; desig. expert witness for state courts. Career: real estate sales Belknap & Assoc., Lynwood 1955; assoc. Verne Miller Construction Co., San Bernardino 1955-70; owner/realtor office in San Bernardino 1970-, office now in Carlsbad 1983--; bldr. var. constrn. projects: two comml. buildings, six multi-apt. units, one residence; past pres. (1969) San Bernardino Bd. of Realtors (Million Dollar sales awd. 4 yrs.; named Realtor of the Year 1970; awarded life mem. 1979), orgnzr. S.B. Valley Council of Real Estate Bd. in 1975; bd. mem. Uptown YMCA, San Bernardino 1976-79; orgnzr. S.B. Valley Council of Women Realtors (1975); Republican; co-chair campaigns of St. Assemblyman Wm. R. Leonard and Co. Bd. of Supvrs. chmn. Robt. L. Hammock; worked on zoning legislation for San Bernardino City (SB 5) and Co. (SB 869); Catholic; rec: gardening, sewing, painting. Office: Anne M. Ronning, Realtor, POB 1845, Carlsbad 92008

ROOSEVELT, JAMES, business consultant; b. Dec. 23, 1907, NYC; s. President Franklin Delano and First Lady Eleanor Roosevelt, nephew of Pres. Theodore Roosevelt; m. Mary Lena Winskill, 1969; children: Kate; Sara; Jim Jr.; Michael; Anne; H. Delano; Rebecca; edn: Groton Sch. 1926; Harvard Univ. 1930; LLD, hon., Woodbury Univ.; PhD, hon., Calif. Western Univ.; LHD, hon., Salem Coll., W.Va. Career: ins. broker, founder, pres. Roosevelt & Sargent, Inc., Boston, 1930-37, resigned 1938; motion picture indus. 1938-40; reentered Roosevelt & Sargent as exec. v.p., estab. West Coast Ofc., 1946; elected US Congressman (84th-89th Congresses) from Calif. 1955-66; US Rep. to ECOSOC 1965-66; with L&S Mgmt. Co. 1966-70; bus. cons. James Roosevelt & Co., Newport Beach 1970--; lectr. UC Irvine, Woodbury Univ., Chapman Coll.; awards: Richard M. Nixon Chair, Whittier Coll.; former mem. Congress Guest Otterbein Coll. & Baylor Univ.; mem: March of Dimes Birth Defects Found.; Roosevelt Warm Springs Found.; Eleanor Roosevelt Cancer Inst.; Chapman Coll.; South Coast Repertory Theatre; NCCJ; del. Armand Hammer Peace & Human Rights Conf.; Orange Co. Transportation Commn. (commnr.); Nat. Com. for Research in Neurological & Communicative Diseases (pres.); author: Affectionately, F.D.R. (1959), My Parent, A Differing View (1976), A Family Matter (Simon & Shuster, 1980); mil: Brig. Gen., USMC, ret., Navy Cross, Silver Star; Democrat, (Nat. Com.; Dem. Cand. for Calif. Gov. 1950; US Congressman 1955-66); Episcopal; rec: sailing. Ofc: James Roosevelt & Co., 120 Newport Center Dr, Ste 206, Newport Beach 92660

ROOT, EDMOND M., gem and jewelry consultant/ appraiser; b. Aug. 24, 1928, Amsterdam, Holland; s. Alois J. and Phil. W. (Nieuwenhuis) Roothooft; m. Phyllis Roy, Sept. 18, 1950; edn: Univ. of Amsterdam 1947-48; bus. admin. Univ. of Chgo. 1957-58; grad. gemologist, G.I.A. 1979. Career: internat. mktg. exec., v.p. German subsidiary, Heidelberg, Borg- Warner Corp., Chgo. 1954-69; internat. mgr. Rohr. Ind., Chula Vista 1970-71; independant internat. cons. 1972-73; independant gem & jewelry cons./ appraiser/ broker 1979--; mem: Am. & Internat. Socs. of Appraisers; Accredited Gemologists Assn.; British Gemmological Assn.; San Diego World Trade Assn.; GIA Alumni Assn.; designer fine jewelry; author var. arts. in Gem pubs.; spkr. gem & jewelry appraisal topics; mil: Sgt., USAF 1952-56; rec: yachting, photog. Res: 1350 Virginia Way La Jolla 92037 Ofc: POB 3277 La Jolla 92038

ROSBERG, DAVID ADAM, antique store owner; b. Oct. 10, 1942, San Francisco; s. Bertram Richard and Elsie C. (Segal) R.; 2 sons: David, b. 1968, Shane, b. 1979; grad. Polytech H.S., S.F., 1960; lic. cosmetology, New Hampshire 1965. Career: hairstylist, beauty school instructor, 12 years; devel. garage sales into antique bus.; currently, owner Antique Freak (oak & brass shop with 3 stores), South Lake Tahoe; tightwire walker, freestyle skier, mogul champion; winner ski awards for freestyle skiing 1970, 71, 72; mem. Toastmasters Club, 1968-71; adv. com. Green Valley Childrens Center; mil: E4 USAF 1960-65; Jewish; rec: windsurfer, skiing, tennis. Res: POB 9794 South Lake Tahoe 95731 Ofc: Antique Freak, 1044 Emerald Bay Rd So. Lake Tahoe 95731

ROSE, ANTHONY CORNELL, real estate investor; b. Aug. 10, 1932, Utica, NY; s. Anthony A. and Louise E. (Cornell) R.; m. Sherry Davies, May 7, 1966; children: Andrew, b. 1968, Nicholas, b. 1972; edn: BA, Hamilton Coll. 1954; LLB, Albany Law Sch. 1957; JD, Union Univ. 1968. Career: assoc. atty. Garvey and Conway, NYC 1958; assoc. atty. John Balio (now Supreme Ct. Justice) Utica, NY 1959; chief clerk City Court of Utica, NY 1959; pvt. solo law practice, Utica, NY 1960-70; pres. Anthony Rose Real eState Investments, Inc. Santa Barbara, Ca. 1971--; seminar panelist NY State Bar Assn. 1960, Career Day Hamilton Coll. 1962; awards: two scholarships, Practicing Law Inst., 1957, 58; Montessori Center Sch. Man of the Year 1978; mem: NY State Bar Assn. 1958-, Am. Bar Assn. 1958-70, Am. Judicature Soc. 1960-63, Oneida County Bar Assn. 1959-70, Elks Club 1959-61, Univ. Club of Santa Barbara 1971-79; bd. trustees (pres. 1979) Montessori Center Sch. 1977-79; bd. dirs. Laguna Blanca Sch. 1980-82; bd. dirs. Santa Barbara Disaster Com.; mem. S.B. Blues Soc.; art., Am. Judicature Soc. Jour. 1962; life mem. Internat. Chili Soc.; mil: s/sgt. USAFR 1957-63; Democrat; Unitarian; rec: chess, jazz, baseball. Res: 345 Malaga Dr Santa Barbara 93108 Ofc: Anthony Rose R.E. Investments, Inc. 1224 Coast Village Circle Santa Barbara 93108

ROSE, FRANCES REBECCA, community relations executive; b. Jan. 27, 1912, Cambridge, Mass.; d. David and Ann (Rappoport) Levin; m. David Edward Rose, Jan. 1, 1936; children: Terry Roger, b. 1945, Bonnie Lee, b. 1945; edn: grad. Berkeley High Sch., num. spl. courses, Univ. Calif. Ext., CSU San

Jose. Career: community rels. experience, Santa Clara County, 1940--: lectr. on comm. rels., vocational edn., parent edn., human rels.; past mem.: San Jose Welfare Solicitation (21 yrs); S.J. City Council Steering Com. for Capital Improvement Pgm.; Mayor's Commn. on Human Rels., and Advis. Bd. (pres.); S.J. Commn. for Brotherhood Week; Youth Employment Service; exec. bd. (12 yrs), v.p. 6th Dist. Calif. Conf. of Parents and Teachers; S.J. Civil Def. 1942-44; originator/hd. Speakers Bur. (copied nat.), Pub. Rels. Dept., Information Ofc., Comm. Rels., and coordinated County First Aid Records; served on Calif. State CofC Panel during a State Conf. (only woman to be so honored); past chmn. Santa Clara UN Festival (two years); instituted num. spl. human relations film forums, confs., workshops for youth leaders to coordinate all segments of community: past chmn. (1 yr) S.J. Sr. Citizens Commn. (mem. 4 yrs.). Honors incl. San Jose Civic Medallion (2), hon. life mem. 6th Dist. PTA, hon. life UN Assn., ADL regl. and local awds.; pres. Temple Emanuel Sisterhood; chmn. A.D.L.; Republican; Brotherhood of Man, Fatherhood of God. Res: 3637 Snell Ave, No. 50, San Jose 95136; 13900-B39 Marquesas Way, Marina Del Rey 90291 Ofc: Instant Sealer, 13706 S. Normandie, Gardena 90249

ROSE-DUMAS, CECILLE JEANNE, real estate broker; b. Sept. 27, 1918, San Francisco; d. Maymillan and Jeannie (Lewis-Stuart) Brav; edn: Teachers Coll., SF, 1955; Univ. Calif. Ext. SF, 1957; m. Adrian W. Rose (dec.), Sept. 24, 1943; 1 son, Robert Ward, b. 1948 (audio engr. for Beach Boys, Screen Gems, etc.); m. 2d. Alvis N. (Jack) Dumas (electronics tchr. USN, ret.), May 25, 1980. Career: US Govt. wrkr. 1942-43; pilot, W.A.S.P., Sweetwater, Texas 1943; flew All Women's Transcontinent Air Races: 1957 (1st in class) San Carlos, Ca. to Phila.; 1958 (completed) San Diego to Charleston, S.C.; real estate broker/owner Rose Realty, 1962--. Awards: num. flying awards, golf trophies. Mem. 99 Club (for women pilots) 1940-; Presidio Golf Club; Harding Park (SF) Womens Golf Club. Mil: lt. (equiv), WASP (Womens AF Svc. Pilots) 1943; Democrat; Christian Sci. Rec: world travel, golf. Address: Rose Realty, 540 Ortega St. San Francisco 94122

ROSEN, MANUEL M., architect-designer; b. Dec. 2, 1926, Mexico City; US Resident 1978; s. Dan and Rose (Morrison) R.; m. Laura, Dec. 1, 1957; children: Ronald, b. 1959; Karen, b. 1962; Dana, b. 1964; edn: grad. Architecture Faculty, Mex. National Univ. 1953. Career: designer and decorator 1953--, prof. of design, Archit. Faculty of the Mexican Nat. Univ., 1959--; spkr. num. confs. 1960-; winner of contest for design of Olympic gymnasium and swimming pool for the Games of the XIX Olympiad, and recipient awards (for the Olympic gym. & pool), Internat. Amateur Swimming Fedn., Nat. Assn. of Mfrs. of Aluminum Products for the Constrn. Industry, Industrias Monterrey; Annual Prize, Tech. Council of Mex. Nat. Univ. Faculty of Arch.; award winning residences for Mr. Federico Patino (Acapulco), Mario Moreno, "Cantinflas" (Mexico City); mem. Soc. of Mexican Architects, Mex. Coll. of Architecs, Mex. Soc. of Decorators, Technion Mexican Soc. (pres. 1966), Nat. Soc. of Interior Designers Inc. USA, Central Soc. of Architects of Buenos Aires, Argen.; bd. dirs. Friends of the Jewish Univ. of Jerusalem; num. published works in US, Mex., Argentina; Republican; Jewish; rec: golf, tennis, jogging. Address: 7843 E. Roseland Dr La Jolla 92037

ROSENBAUM, JOHN ANTONE, construction executive; b. Sept. 27, 1926, Buffalo, NY; s. John and Elizabeth Helen (Wolf) R.; m. Audrey Collen, Nov. 22, 1947; children: Donna Marie, b. 1950; John Karl, b. 1952; Eric Francis, b. 1961. Career: chief designer Jacoby & Babinsky, Buffalo, NY 1955-59; gen. mgr. Paul Hardeman, Inc., Stanton 1959-65; pres. Divelcon, Inc., Brea 1965-73; exec. v.p. Dynalectric Corp., Los Angeles 1973-75; br. mgr. E C Ernst Co., Concord 1976-77; pres. Ericon Corp., Chino 1977--; mem: Soc. of Am. Mil. Engrs.; mil: CPO, USN 1944-47; Republican; Catholic; rec: fishing, golf. Res: 2657 Medford Pl Fullerton 92635 Ofc: Ericon Corp., 13735 Arapahoe Pl Chino 91710

ROSENBERG, DONALD DUANE, radio and television personality; b. July 5, 1939, Hasting, Nebr.; s. Virgil J. and Cecile L. (Morrison) R.; m. Mary K. McDermott, Nov. 8, 1958; children: David, b. 1959; Daniel & Kelly, x. 1960; Jay, b. 1964; John, b. 1966; edn: BS, Univ. of Nebr. 1956. Career: emcee The Dr. Don Rose Radio Pgm. (6-9 a.m. Mon.-Fri.), KFRC Radio, San Francisco 1973--; 11 radio stations since 1955, last three: WQXI, Atlanta 1966-68; WFIL, Phila. 1968-73; KFRC, San Francisco 1973--; since 1972: emcee cartoons (KBHK- TV, San Francisco; WFLD- TV, Chgo.; WKBD- TV, Detroit; WKBS-TV, Phila.); appearances an num. spl. pgms. KPIX- TV, KGO- TV, KRON- TV, San Francisco; featured in A First Class Miracle', Emmy- winning pgm; awards: Disc. Jockey of Yr., Billboard Mag. (2), The Pop Music Soc. (2), Nat. Music Report; Alumni Achievement awd., Univ. of Nebr.; honored by Mayor Feinstein who designated his 10th Anniversary of Bdcstg., Oct. 15, 1983, as Dr. Don Rose Day in San Francisco; mem: Bay Area March of Dimes (Walkathon chmn. 1975-); Big Brothers (bd. dirs.); Cerebral Palsy (bd. dirs.); Knights of Columbus; Catholic; rec: sailed sailboat, The Firz Claz, to Hawaii (bdcstg. on the way) 1980; scuba; golf. Res: 231 Vagabond Ct Danville 94526 Ofc: KFRC Radio, 415 Bush St San Francisco 94108

ROSENBERG, JERRY M., physician; b. Dec. 31, 1946; Wiesbaden, W.Ger., nat. 1956; s. Monty and Laurie (Abenstein) R.; edn: BA, New York Univ. 1968; MD, Univ. of Paris, 1975; cardiologist, 1980. Career; splst. in preventive medicine, internal medicine, cardio-vascular disease; dir. of clin. services Ocean Front Med. Group Pritikin Longevity Ctr., Santa Monica 1981-82; pvt. practice, Marina Del Rey, currently, with emphasis on optimal health through exercise, nutrition and stress reduction; staff Santa Monica Med. Center; clin. instr. of med. USC, 1979; mem. American Heart Assn., Toastmasters, Sierra Club; arts. in J. of Cardiac Rehabilitation; Jewish; rec: tennis, yoga, camera collectn. Address: 13816 Bora Bora Way Marina Del Rey 90291

ROSENBERG, STEVEN LEE, podiatrist; b. Sept. 22, 1953, Atlantic City, NJ; s. Seymour H. and Ethel (Biederman) R.; edn: BS, Univ. of Ariz. 1975; BMS, Calif. Coll. of Podiatric Medicine 1982, DPM, 1981. Career: podiatrist, Bresler Center Medical Group, Santa Monica; lectr.: Masters of Motion Aerobic Dance Sch., Santa Monica 1983, The Third Internat. Symposium on the Orthopedic and Med. Aspects of Dance, L.A. & London, 1984, The 1984 Olympic Sci. Congress, Univ. of Ore., Freedom from Pain a transdisciplinary approach, Seattle, Anaheim, San Francisco, 1984; clin. instr. Phila. Coll. of Podiat. Med. 1982; cons. Ballet Petit Dance Sch.; mem. Nat. Injury Prev. Found.; bd. mem. Profl. Dance Soc.; mem. Am. Coll. of Sports Medicine, Am. Fitness and Running Assn., Am. and Calif. Podiatric Assns., Am. Coll. of Podopediatrics; Patent: metatarsal abduction splint for infants (1983); Democrat; Jewish; rec: dance, art. Res: 1240 Yale St Santa Monica 90404 Ofc: Bresler Center Medical Group, 2901 Wilshire Blvd, Ste. 345, Santa Monica 90403

ROSENDAHL, ROGER W., lawyer; b. June 1, 1943, Bremerton, Wash.; s. Lester Stanley and Isabel (Martineau) R.; edn: JD, 1969, LLM, 1971, Georgetown Univ. Law Center and Goethe Univ. of Frankfurt, W.Ger.; AB, 1965, USC and Cambridge Univ., Eng. Career: US Treas. Dept. Internatl. SEct. of Gen. Counsel, Wash DC, 1968 summer; lectr., law, Goethe Univ. of Frankfurt, 1971; Mueller, Weitzel &: Weisner, Frankfurt, W. Ger. 1971-72; assoc. Curtis, Mallet-Prevost, Colt & Mosle, NYC 1972-74; gen counsel Star-Kist Foods, Inc., Terminal Island, Ca. 1974-79; partner Lawler, Felix & Hall, Los Angeles 1979--. Honors: USC Man of Troy award for outstanding achievement in Scholarship, Leadership, Community Service, Athletics; Crown-Zellerbach Found. grant 1965; scholarship to Cambridge Univ. 1964; USC Alumni scholarship (4 year full tuition). Mem: State Bar of Calif., NY Bar, Am. Bar Assn. (Internat. Law Sect.; vice chmn. Far Eastern Law Com. 1983-; co-chmn. ABA Nat. Inst. on Strategies for Trade and Investment in the Pacific Basin, 1983; chmn. subcom. on South Pacific Law 1980-;), Internat. Bar Assn. (exec. com. So. Calif. Chpt. 1981-), L.A. Co. Bar Assn., Harbor Bar Assn., USC Oceanographic Assocs. and Commerce Assocs., L.A. Athletic Club, Calif. Yacht Club, Kappa Alpha Order; author books on foreign investment in the USA (pub. in Eng., Ger., Jap.), law journal articles; Republican; Prot.; rec: music, sailing, athletics. Res: Six Eastwind, Marina del Rey 90291 Ofc: Lawler, Felix & Hall, 700 S. Flower St, 30th Flr. Los Angeles 90017

ROSENFELD, IRVING, lawyer; b. Oct. 2, 1927, Phila., Pa.; s. Benjamin and Ann (Goldberg) R.; children: Sandra Michele Rosenfeld- Cope, b. 1961; Steven Michael, b. 1968; edn: BA, UCLA 1953; LLB, Westminster Coll. of Law 1957; admitted to Colo. State Bar 1957, Calif. State Bar 1959; splst. cert., Worker's Comp. Law, Calif.; arbitrator, Am. Arbitration Assn. Career: asst. archivist Colo. State Hist. Soc. Mus., Denver, Colo. 1956-57; deputy corporation commnr. State of Calif. Corporations Commission, Los Angeles 1958-61; pvt. practice, law./ partner Katz & Rosenfeld 1961-75; pres. Irving Rosenfeld, A Profl. Corp., No. Hollywood 1975--; Judge Pro Tem, Workers Comp. Appeals Bd., State of Calif. 1982-; mem: Am. Arbitration Assn. (panel of arbitrators); US Supreme Ct. Hist. Soc.; Royce 270, UCLA; Chancellor's Circle, UCLA; mil: PFC, US Army 1945-46, WII Victory medal; Democrat; Jewish; rec: sailing, stamp collecting. Res: 29500 Heathercliff Rd, 183, Malibu 90265 Ofc: Irving Rosenfeld, A Profl. Corp., 6350 Laurel Canyon, No. Hollywood 91606

ROSENFELD, JOHN THOMAS, building contractor; b. Sept 27, 1944, Elizabethtown, Pa.; s. David and Tina (Becker) R.; m. Mary Unruh, Mar. 14, 1964; children: John, b. 1964; Michael, b. 1965; Julie, b. 1969; David, b. 1980. Career: designer/ architect/ builder 1964--; gen. contractor/pres. Rosenfeld Cons. Co., Inc. (blt. over 120,000 unique homes); architect/ builder of Fresno landmark home (the Castle) 1979;, Mennonite Brethren; rec: photog., organist. Res: 2817 W. Bluff Fresno 93711 Ofc: Rosenfeld Const. Co., Inc., 4055 W. Shaw, Ste 105, Fresno 93711

ROSENTHAL, JOSEPH A., university librarian; b. Aug. 11, 1929, Pittsburgh, Pa.; s. Joseph A. and Elizabeth K. Rosenthal; edn: BA, Dickinson Coll. 1949; MA, Penn. St. Univ. 1951; MS, Columbia Univ. 1957. Career: with N.Y. Pub. Lib., NYC: ref. librn. 1956-57, 58-60; documents librn. 1960-64; chief Preparation Svcs. 1964-70; lib. recruit Library of Congress, Wash. DC 1957-58; with UC Berkeley: assoc. univ. librn. tech. svcs. 1971-78; acting univ. librn. 1978-79; univ. librn. 1979--; cons: City Coll of N.Y.; Univ. Hawaii; Biblioteca Nacional, Venezuela; Conf. of Dirs. of Nat. Libs.; mem: Phi Beta Kappa; Phi Beta Mu; publs: Co-ed W/ James W. Henderson, Library Catalogs; Their Preservation and Maintenance by Photographic and Automated Techniques, Cambridge, Mass., MIT Press, 1968; arts. and reviews in var. profl. journs. Res: 51 Buena Vista Terrace San Francisco 94117 Ofc: Room 245, General Library, UC Berkeley, Berkeley 94720

ROSENTHAL, STEVEN S., lawyer; b. Aug. 26, Wash. DC; s. Jacob Wolfe and Miki Hanna (Brenner) R.; edn: BA, magna cum laude, Clark Univ. 1975; JD, Hastings Coll. of Law 1978; admitted to Calif. State Bar 1978, Wash. DC Bar 1979. Career: pvt. law practice 1979--; honors: Phi Beta Kappa, Clark Univ. 1975; Best Brief awd., David E. Snodgrass Moot Ct. Competition, Hastings Coll. of Law 1977; mem: State Bar of Calif.; Lawyers Club of San Francisco (chmn. Com. on Rels. w/ Judiciary, Municipal Ct.); Am. & Calif. Trial Lawyers Assns.; Hebrew Free Loan Soc. Assn., San Francisco; Jewish Affairs Forum; Clark Univ. & Hastings Coll. of Law Alumni Assns.; Jewish Community Fedn.; Democrat; Jewish; rec: photog., skiing, golf. Res: 2965 Sacramento St, 101, San Francisco 94115 Ofc: Law Ofc. of Steven S Rosenthal, 1255 Post Street, Ste 935-939, San Francisco

ROSENZWEIG, HERBERT STEPHEN, securities co. account executive; b.

Aug. 5, 1943, Phila., Pa.; s. Morton and Helen (Katzen) R.; m. Myra Pauline Saltzburg, June 7, 1964; children: Helene, b. 1969; Michael, b. 1972; Elisa, b. 1973; Jeffrey, b. 1976; edn: BS, Temple univ. 1964. Career: US Army, El Paso, Tex. & Vietnam 1965-67; acct. exec. Walston & Co., Inc. 1967-73; acct. exec. Reynolds Securities 1973-74; acct. exec., sr. acct. exec., asst. v.p. Merrill Lynch Pierce Fenner & Smith, Upland 1974--; mem. Pres.'s Club Merrill Lynch; mem: Kiwanis Club, Upland (pres. 1979; Kiwanian of Yr. 1982); mil: 1st lt. US Army 1965-67, Inf. Platoon Ldr. Central Highlands, Vietnam; Republican; Jewish. Res: 2109 N. San Antonio Ave Upland 91786 Ofc: Merrill Lynch Pierce Fenner & Smith, 876 N. Mountain Ave Upland 91786

ROSENZWEIG, SAUL LOUIS, communications co. executive, investor; b. Aug. 3, 1925, NY, NY; s. Maurice Lee and Laura (Widrevitz) R.; m. Carol Coppersmith, Feb. 11, 1961; children: Davy, b. 1954; Laurance, b. 1965; edn: BS, naval sci., Georgia Tech. 1945; BS, indsl. gmt. 1947. Career: broadcast pioneer, radio & TV ownership & mgmt. 1947--; sr. acct. exec. Batten, Barton, Durstine & Osborne, NYC; dir. of TV devel. Katz Broadcasting, NY; v.p. Skyway Broadcasting, Ashevill, NC; v.p. KPLR- TV, St. Louis, Mo.; partner, family diversified investments, Rosetree Partners real estate & broadcast properties; currently pres. Figgie Communications, Inc., Los Angeles; v.p. Rosebranch Corp., gen. partner Rosetree Partners; bd. dirs. Powerline Sales Co.; chmn. comm. dept. United Jewish Fund 1984; pres./ v.p. Palm Springs Conv. & Visitors Bureau 1966-75; bd. trustees Palm Springs Valley Sch. (pres. 1972-73) 1966-75; LACMA Contemporary Art Council 1973-84; mem: Broadcast Pioneers; Nat. Assn. of Broadcasters; Television Bureau of Advtg.; The Palm Springs Club; Mountain Gate Country Club; The Friars Club; mil: Ensign, USNR 1943-46; Republican; Jewish; rec: tennis, skiing, alto saxophone. Res: 1051 Angelo Dr Beverly Hills 90210 Ofc: Figgie Communications, Inc., 10889 Wilshire Blvd, Ste 906, Los Angeles 90024

ROSS, DEBORAH LYNN, speech pathologist; b. Feb. 19, 1950, Sacramento; d. Roy Albert and Marcella Marie (McKay) Green; m. Patrick Ross, Aug. 31, 1975; children: Lindsay, b. 1978, Aaron, b. 1980, Whitney, b. 1983; edn: BA, CSU Sacto 1972, MA 1974, postgrad. wk. Neuroanatomy, UC Davis; Cert. and Lic. Speech Pathologist. Career: staff speech pathologist Easter Seal Rehab. Ctr., Sacto 1973-76; chief speech pathologist, UC Davis Med. Ctr., Sacramento 1976--; clin. faculty UCD Med. Sch. 1977-; listed, Who's Who in West 1980; mem: Am. Speech & Hearing Assn., Cal. St. Speech & Hearing Assn., Am. Cong. of Rehab. Medicine; mem. Junior League of Sacramento Inc., Child Abuse Council, Child Abuse Speakers Bur.; Republican; Presbyterian; rec: dist. running, biking. Res: 4313 Palacio Wy Fair Oaks 95628 Ofc: UCDMC, 2315 Stockton Blvd, G512, Sacramento 95817

ROSS, DELORES MASON, clinical social worker; b. Dec. 15, 1943, Boissevain, Va.; d. Randolph and Pauline (Murrell) Mason; children: Kevin, b.1963; Kimberly, b. 1966; edn: AA, Solano Comm. Co8l. 1974; BA, UC Davis 1977; MSW, CSU, Sacto. 1980; lic. clinical soc. wkr., Calif. 1982. Career: supvr./ counselor youth tng. pgm. proj. MOVE, Yolo Co. Ofc. of Edn., W. Sacto. 1975-76; research assoc. Inst. for Human Svcs. Mgmt., CSU, Sacto. 1978-79; lic. clinical soc. wkr., Stanford Home for Children, Sacto. 1980--; dir./ coord. Adolescent Therapy Gp., Mental Health Assn., Yolo Co., Davis; Nat. Scholarship grantee 1974; mem: Soc. for Clinical Soc. Wkrs.; Smithsonian inst.; Cal Aggie Alumni Assn., UC Davis; CSU Alumni Assn., Sacto.; Democrat; Protestant; rec: classical literature. Res: 4515 San Sebastian Way Sacramento 95823 Ofc: Stanford Home for Children, 800 N Street, Sacramento 95814

ROSS, JAMES HARRY, real estate broker; b. June 11, 1939, Billings, Mont.; s. Cecil Hector and Doris May (Mann) R.; m. Grace Marcine Haskin, Mar. 10, 1957; children: Jeffrey, b. 1957, Deren, b. 1960, Theresa, b. 1963; edn: AA, Sierra Coll. 1961; BA, Sacto. State Coll. 1966. Career: clk., group supr., Section head, Dept. mgr., to Operation project mgr. Aerojet Liquid Rocket Co., 1957-75; realtor assoc. Harrigan & Assoc. Realtors, 1976-80; owner/ broker/ pres. The James Ross Co., 1981-83; broker/mem. Re/Max of Roseville, 1983--; guest lectr. R.E. Edn. Seminars (1978-84); pres. Oakmont High Sch. Parents Club 1972; pres. Placer Million Dollar Club, 1980; recipient num. sales awards; mem: Placer County Bd. of Realtors (pres. 1983, dir. 1978-84, pres./ life mem. Masters Club); Calif. Assn. of Realtors (dir. 1978-84); Re/Max Intl. Presidents Club 1983; mem., past pres. Lions Club; sponsor Roseville Bobby Sox Softball, Adult Softball & Basketball; troop counselor BSA 1974-76; Democrat; Lutheran; rec: golf, civic svc. Res: 7520 Dove Ct Roseville 95678 Ofc: Re/Max of Roseville, 720 Sunrise, Ste. 104, Roseville 95678

ROSS, PAULA JO, certified financial planner; b. Oct. 19, 1938, Denver, Colo.; d. Donald Lewis and Annie Ruth (Reeves) Wells; children: Randall, b. 1960; David, b. 1963; Michael, b. 1967; edn: Tex. Christian Univ., Ft. Worth, Tex. 1956-58; CFP, Coll. for Fin. Plng. 1981. Career: sales & admin. secty. Western State Life, Great Commonwealth Life & Republic Nat. Life, Dallas, Tex. 1966-68; broker supvr. Nat. Security Ins. Agcy., Los Angeles 1968; fin. plng. rep. United Profl. Plng., West Los Angeles 1971; fin. svcs. Life Fin. Svcs., Inc. 1975; owner/ opr. Independently Yours, Manhattan Beach 1978--; guest spkr. on fin. plng.; mem: Nat. Assn. of Security Dealers; Nat. Assn. of Life Underwriters; Internat. & Los Angeles Co. Assns. Fin. Plnrs.; Womens Life Underwriters Council; Gr. South Bay Life Underwriters Assn.; Inst. CFPs; Registry Fin. Plnrs. Practitioners; Pres.'s Adv. Council, Private Ledger Fin. Corp., Inc.; Am. Heart Assn. Plannned Giving Com., Los Angeles; Manhattan Beach CofC; works: Financial Independence Workshop/ Workbook 1977-, and Railshop, (wrkshp. on wheels) 1977-80; Republican; Christian. Res: 225 9th Street Manhattan Beach 90266 Ofc: Independently Yours, 901 Manhattan Ave, Manhattan Beach 980266

ROSS, RALPH, insurance agency owner; b. Mar. 17, 1923, D'Lo, Miss.; s. Joseph Thomas and Lillie Marie (Fails) R.; m. Madalene I. Warner, 1961; 1 dau: Pamela Renee, b. 1964; edn: BA, mgmt., St. Mary's Coll. 1977; CFP (cert. fin. plnnr.) in progress, USC; NASD lic., gen. casualty, life & disability lic.; pvt. pilots lic. 1948. Career: USN 1941-70; Seaman recruit to chief petty ofcr., 10 yrs. commnd. ofcr. (Deck ofcr., Supply ofcr., Tng. ofcr., Ofcr. in charge of physical tng., Naval Tng. Ctr. & exec. ofcr. of a ship (18 months); independent contr. Farmers Ins. Gp. 1970-, agency owner/mgr., San Ramon 1970--; plng. duties); honors: Outstanding American, 1976; mem: Nat. Assn. of Life Underwriters; Mt. Diablo Assn.; Crow Canyon Country Club; works: trainer two All Navy Champions in boxing; Am. Red Cross Water Safety instr./ trainer; mil: lt. USN 1941-70, ret., USN Commdn.; Democrat; Protestant; rec: swimming, tennis. Res: 1811 St Norbert Dr Danville 94526 Ofc: Farmers Insurance Group, 110 Ryan Industrial Ct, Ste 4, San Ramon 94583

ROSSELLI, JOHN SANGUINETTI, pharmacist; b. Apr. 14, 1912, Los Angeles; s. Antonio S. and Carla (Bacigalupi) R.; m. Mary Donvito; children: Faye, b. 1945, John, b. 1946; edn: AA, Los Angeles Jr. Coll. 1933; Ph.G., Univ. Calif. 1936; Calif. lic. Pharmacist 1936. Career: partner Lock Drug Co., Redwood City, devel. bus. into 7 pharmacy chain, 1939-75; pharmacy cons. Raleigh Hills Alcohol Hosp., 1975-82; cons. sev. nursing homes; past bd. chmn. Enzyme Products (now part of Data Diagnostics); elected Redwood City Council, 1958-70, mayor 1962-66; honors: Pharmacist of Month (1963), Award of Merit, Calif. Pharmacists Assn.; Calif. State Senate Resolution (state coll. site); mem: Am. Pharmacists Assn., Am. Soc. Consultant Pharmacists, Calif. Pharm. Assn. (dir. 3 yrs.), San Mateo County Pharm. Assn. (past pres.), UC Pharm. Alumni (past pres.); mem. Native Sons Golden West, Forestors of Am., Sirs, UC Alumni Assn. (life), Kiwanis Club, Italian America Fedn. (pres. elect 1983); Democrat (served as San Mateo Co. treas., Com. to Elect John F. Kennedy Pres. 1960); Catholic; rec: all sports. Res: 950 Nob Hill Rd Redwood City 94061

ROSSER, JAMES M., university president; b. Apr. 16, 1939, East St. Louis, Ill.; s. Wm. M. and Mary E. (Bass) R.; m. Carmen Rosita Colby, Ed.D., Dec. 27, 1962; 1 son, Terrence, b. 1965; edn: BA and MA, microbiol., So. Ill. Univ., Carbondale, 1962, 1963, PhD, health admin., 1969. Career: resrch. bacteriologist Eli Lilly & Co., Indnpls. 1963-66; tchg. asst./ asst. prof. health edn./ grad. faculty Coll. of Edn./ asst. to the Chancellor, So. Illinois Univ., Carbondale 1962-70; lectr./ assoc. prof. Edn. and Pharmacol. and Toxicol., Univ. of Kansas, Lawrence 1970-74; vice chancellor State of NJ Dept. of Higher Edn., Trenton, NJ 1974-79, vis. faculty Harvard Univ. Grad. Sch. of Edn., 8/79; pres. Calif. State Univ., Los Angeles 1979--, prof. of health care mgmt., 1979-; frequent spkr. profl. confs., workshops; mem. Am. Assn. of State Colls. & Univs. (com. on urban affairs 1979-); Western Assn. of Schs. & Colls. (accreditation teams); The Calif. St. Univ. (trustees long range fin. plng. com. 1982-; Am. Council on Education, Wash DC sub-coms. 1979-); honors: Kappa Delta Pi, Phi Kappa Phi, Omega Psi Phi Freshman Scholarship Award, Langston Univ. 1957-58, Coll. Student of Year 1958, E. St. Louis, Ill.; NSF Fellowship 1961; Beta Gamma Sigma; West Coast Father of the Year 1981; Brotherhood Crusade, Pioneer of Black Hist. Achievement Awd., L.A. 1981. Mem. bd. trustees, Orthopaedic Hosp.; bd. dirs.: L.A. Council for Internat. Visitors, Urban League, United Way of Gr. L.A., Community TV of So. Calif. (KCET), Boys Scouts L.A. Area Council, Hispanic Urban Ctr., Alhambra CofC; Rotarian; publs: arts. in Liberal Education, Catalyst, Trustee Quarterly, Cross Reference, Dialogue, State Budgeting for Higher Edn., others; Democrat; Catholic. Res: 225 El Cielo Lane Bradbury 91010 Ofc: CSULA, 5151 State University Dr Los Angeles 90032

ROSSI, MARIE JOSEPHINE, land developer; b. Sept. 10, 1949, Napa; d. Joseph Sr. and Elodia (Pascale) R.; m. Richard Flejstad, Feb. 8, 1969; children: William, b. 1969; Christina, b. 1971; edn: Napa Coll. 1967-69; R.E. agent lic., Anthony Schs. 1977; broker lic., 1981; Notary Public 1979. Career: realtor assoc. Century 21 1977; realtor assoc. Pacific Coast Properties 1977-78; sales mgr. Rossi's Sweet Antiques', Yountville 1980-81; owner Rossi Realty Co. (afil. broker Lewis C. On & Assoc.), Chinatown, S.F. 1981--; assoc. Rossi Development Co.; Internat. R.E. Conv. sponsor, participant, Hong Kong 1983; bd. dirs: Restoration of Calif. Hist. Landmarks (Napa Valley), Pvt. Landowners (S.F.), Samuel Springs Resort (Water Springs); honors: No. Calif. Winners Circle, Century 21 1978; mem: Napa Co. Bd. Realtors; Silverado Country Club; Napa Womens Political Caucus (Screening Com.); works: resrch. hist. mineral health resorts of Napa 1980-84 and devel. mineral spring water co. 1983; Republican; Catholic; rec: gardening, decorating, theater. Res: 899 Oak Leaf Way (Silverado Country Club), Napa Valley 94558 Ofc: Rossi Realty Co., 3040 Jefferson St, Alta Plaza, Napa 94558

ROSSKOPF, WALTER JOSEPH, JR., veterinarian; b. Mar. 3, 1945, Aliceville, Ala.; s. Walter, Sr. and June (Ethridge) R.; m. 3d. Christine Davis, Apr. 6, 1983; twin sons: Walter III, and William, b. 1969; edn: BS, honors, UC Davis 1967, DVM, 1969. Career: pvt. veterinary practice, pioneer in many exotic animal med. and surgical procedures, avian and reptilian splst; Lawndale Pet Hosp., 1969-74; co-owner Animal Medical Centre of Lawndale, 1974--; pres. Rosskopf-Woerpel, Inc.; seminar spkr. nat., state, and local vet. med. assns.; author over 70 med. articles and over 100 lay arts. on med. subjects, contbr. to four textbooks on exotic animal medicine; resrch. assoc. CSU Dominguez Hills, 1980-; instr. in exotic animal med., UC Riverside 1981-; editorial bd. Modern Veterinary Practice mag. 1981-, Avian/Exotic Practice Journ. 1983-; honors: Turtle Trust Award (1982), Sigma Phi Vet. Hon. Soc.; mem: Am. Calif., So. Calif. vet. med. assns.; Assn. of Avian Vets.; Am. Assn. of Avian

Pathols.; Am. Assn. of Zoo Vets.; Internat. Assn. of Aquatic Animal Vets.; U.S. Animal Health Assn.; World Poultry Health Assn.; Desert Tortoise Council, Wildlife Disease Assn.; Calif. Turtle & Tortoise Club; Republican; Prot.; rec: antiques, military collectibles, hist. Res: 28738 Golden Meadow Dr Rancho Palos Verdes 90274 Ofc: Animal Med. Ctr. of Lawndale, 4473 W. Rosecrans Ave, Hawthorne 90250

ROSSON, KENNETH RAY, karate expert/organization director; b. Mar. 26, 1942, Hatfield, Ark.; s. Artie Ray and Patsy Ruth (Dixon) R.; m. Melva Howard, June 24, 1963; children: Mitzi b. 1964, Karla b. 1; desig: PhD in Martial Arts, Fedn. All Japan Karate Organizations, Osaka, Japan, 1980. Career: asst. instr. and team capt. Goju-Kai Karate Team, Tokyo, Japan 1961-63; team capt. Karate University Osaka, 1966-67; chief instr. Bakersfield Karate Acad., Bakersfield, Calif. 1968-75; director of Japan Karate Organization Goju-Ryu, for USA 1976--, also dir. for Mexico and Panama, 1980--, currently dir. for Goju-Ryu USA, Mexico, & Panama; author/pub. community service newspaper on sel-defense 1983-84; participant and dir. World Games I, Santa Clara 1981; bd. dirs. World Karate Union; awards: Black Belt of Year 1974, 76, 81; gold medal in World Karate Championships, Japan and Korea, 1978, 79, 80; Who's Who in Karate 1984; mem: F.A.G.K.O. Osaka, Japan (USA bd. dirs. 1976-84); A.A.U. (chmn. Karate Com. Central Calif. 1981-84); G.K.F.A. (pres. 1975-84); Fedn. of All Japan Karate Orgns. (Osaka), World Union of Karate Orgns., Amateur Athletic Union Nat. Karate Com., Goju-Ryu Karate Fedn. of America and rep. of Panama; Democrat; Christian. Rec: 749 3rd St McFarland 93250 Ofc: Japanese Village 1213-1/2 Main St, Ste. 202, Delano 93215

ROSTEN, HOWARD, lawyer; b. May 13, 1943, Los Angeles; s. Mark and Ann (Relin) R.; m. Anne, Dec. 22, 1979; stepson, Jeremy, b. 1974; edn: BS in bus. adm., UC Berkeley 1965; JD, cum laude, Univ. of San Diego Sch. of Law 1968; admitted to Calif. State Bar 1969. Career: asst. to pres. Macrodyne-Chatillon Corp., 1968-70; city attorney, City of Inglewood 1971--; honors: 3 Am. Jurisprudence Prizes; Republican; rec: woodworking, skiing, boating. Res: 1384 Jonesbor Dr Los Angeles 90049 Office of the City Attorney, City of Inglewood, One Manchester Blvd, 8th Flr., Inglewood 90301

ROSTEN, MARTIN JAY, physician; b. Jan. 18, 1917, Brooklyn, NY; s. Jay and Hetty (Gould) R.; m. Estelle Janiger, May 29, 1941; children: Diane, b. 1943; Joan, b. 1944; edn: BS, N.Y.U. 1938; MD. Career: country doctor, Silver Creek, NY 1942-51; gen. practice, Burbank 1951-57; gen. practice, El Cajon 1957--; Citizens Anti-Smog Com. 1949-51; mem: fellow, Am. Acad. of Family Physicians; Am. Soc. of Bariatric Physicians; San Diego Co. Med. Soc.; San Diego Gem & Mineral Soc.; Exch. Club; mil: 1st Lt., US Army 1941; Republican; Unitarian; rec: gems & minerals. Res: 875 Wakefield St El Cajon 92020 Ofc: 596 N. Westwind Dr El Cajon 92020

ROSTON, QUDSIA, Montessori school owner; b. Calcutta, India, nat. 1978; d. Jalal-Udin and Rokeya Khatoune (Ali) Peerzada; m. Martin Roston, Feb. 7, 1959; children: Rokeya, b. 1960; Rehanna, b. 1962; Rezia, b. 1963; edn: AA, Univ. of Gaujhati 1954; BA, Cardinal Cushing Coll. 1960; M.Ed., Boston Coll. 1962; Montessori dip., Assn. Montessori Internat. 1952. Career: opened 1st Montessori class after WWII, USA, Dumbarton Coll., Wash. DC 1958; dir., exec. v.p., chief op. ofcr. Roston Montessori Schoolhouses, (chain of Montessori schs.); dean, prof. of Montessori edn. Roston Inst., Inc.; founded 1st Montessori Sch. in Orange Co. 1964; assoc. with 1st post- war Montessori sch. in Calif. 1962; only god- daughter of Mrio Montessori; Republican. Res: 12962 Villa Rose Ln Santa Ana 92705 Ofc: Roston Inst., Inc., 1929 S. Manchester Anaheim 92802

ROTH, KENNETH RAYMOND, orthopaedic surgeon; b. Oct. 1, 1935, Kankakee, Ill.; s. Dane Frederick and Ruby Rose (Nichols) R.; m. Patricia, June 13, 1964; children: Molly, b. 1969; Bradley, b. 1971; edn: BS, Florida Southern Coll. 1959; MD, Marquette Univ. Sch. of Med. 1963; orthopaedic surgery, Baylor Univ. affiliated hosps. 1971; Am. Bd. of Orthopaedic Surgery 1972. Career: pvt. practice orthopaedic surgery, Redlands 1971--; pres. Redlands Orthopaedic Med. Gp., Inc.; asst. clinical prof. orthopaedic surgery, Loma Linda Univ. Sch. of Med. 1972-; mem: San Bernardino Co. Med. Soc.; Calif. & Am. Med. Assns.; Inland Orthopaedic Assn.; Am. Bd. & Am. Acad. Orthopaedic Surgery; Scoliosis Research Soc. (Terminology Com. 1984); Friends of Redlands; City Council; Mayor, City of Redlands 1982-83; Med. Ofcr., USN 1964-67; Republican; Protestant; rec: wood working, making furniture. Res: 1720 Sarrita Redlands 92373 Ofc: Redlands Orthopaedic Medical Gp., Inc., 259 Terracina Blvd Redlands 92373

ROTHELL, GEORGE EDWIN, bank president; b. Dec. 17, 1930, Norfolk, NE; s. Frank Stephen and Margaret Anna (Howorth) Rothell; BSBA, Univ. Neb., 1952; m. Elaine Jones; chil: Leslie E. Career: v.p., Bank of Amer., L.A., 1960-72; mng. dir., Western Amer. Bank, Europe, Ltd., London, 1972-77; exec. v.p., First Interstate Bank of California, L.A., 1977-78; pres., First Interstate Bank of California, L.A., 1978-80; pres., First Interstate Bancorp., L.A., 1980--. Mil: USMCR, 1952-56. Office: First Interstate Bancorp, 707 Wilshire Blvd., Los Angeles 90017.

ROTHMAN, FRANK, studio executive; b. Dec. 24, 1926, Los Angeles; s. Leon and Rose (Gendel) R.; m. Loraine Edelstein, July 15, 1951; children: Steven, b. 1955; Robin, b. 1960; Susan, b. 1964; edn: BA, USC 1949; LLB, 1951; atty. Calif., Wash. DC. Career: chief trial deputy Office of City Atty., City of Los Angeles 1952-56; sr. partner Wyman, Bautzer, Rothman, Kuchel & Silbert

1956-82; chmn. bd./chief exec. MGM/UA Entertainment Co. 1982--; mem: fellow, Am. Coll. of Trial Lawyers; Chancery Club; Antitrust & Litigation Sects. of Am. Bar Assn.; Bar of the Dist. of Columbia; State Bar of Calif.; Continental Air Lines, Inc. (bd. dirs.); Norton Simon Mus. of Art. (bd. trustees); Democrat; Jewish. Res: 2377 Century Hill Los Angeles 90067 Ofc: 10202 W. Washington Blvd Culver City 90230

ROTHWELL, GEOFFREY SCOTT, consulting energy and legal economist; b. July 20, 1953, Longview, Wash.; s. Michael Olin and Dona B. (Adams) R.; edn: Baccalaureat, Lycee Francois Premier, Le Havre, France 1972; BA, Evergreen St. Coll. 1975; Univ. of Nice, France 1977-78; MA, UC Berkeley 1981; JSP pgm., Boalt Law Sch. UC Berkeley 1981-83; PhD, 1983. Career: tng. fellow Grand Valley St. Colls., Grand Rapids, Minn. 1975; research assoc. The Evergreen St. Coll., Olympia, Wash. 1976; research analyst Bank of Am., San Francisco 1978; research economist Calif. Pub. Utilities Commn., S.F. 1979; tng. assoc. dept. of economics, UC Berkeley 1980; pres. Energy Economics, Berkeley 1980--; antitrust cons. w/ fin. & statistical economists 1979--; honors: Newton Booth Fellowship, Dept. Economics, UC Berkeley 1978-79; mem: Western & Am. Economics Assns.; The Econometric Soc.; publs: Market Coordination in the Uranium Ore Industry, The Antitrust Bulletin, 1980; Power and the Corporation 1978; rec: micro- computing, Mediterranean cooking. Res: 739 Santa Ynez Stanford 94305 Ofc: Energy Economics, POB 4287 Berkeley 94704

ROUBINIAN, JIRAYR ROUBEN, physician; b. Sept. 11, 1939, Beirut, Lebanon, nat. 1966; s. Levon and Mary Roubinian; m. Meline Garabedian, Oct. 12, 1969; children: Raffi, b. 1971; Nareg, b. 1976; Garine & Nayiree, b. 1978; edn: MD, USC 1967; PhD, UC Berkeley 1980; JD, Univ. of S.F. Law Sch. 1984. Career: post-doctoral fellow NIH, UC Berkeley 1972-75; research asoc. V.A. Hosp., San Francisco 1975-77; asst. prof. med. U.C., San Francisco 1977-80; clinical investigator V.A. Hosp., S.F. 1980; currently chief emergency med. svcs.; mem: Am. Assn. of Immunologists; Am. Fedn. Clinical Research; Am. Rheumatism Assn.; Am. Soc. of Law & Med.; publs: 28 arts. on cancer & autoimmunity research in med. journs.; Armenian Apostolic Ch.; rec: music, jogging, travel. Res: 190 Porto Marino Tiburon 94920 Ofc: Kaiser Foundation Hosp., 1330 Cuffing Blvd Richmond

ROUMAN, THEODORE SAMUEL, insurance executive; b. Mar. 6, 1943, Escanaba, Mich.; s. Samuel G. and Helen R. (Keriazakos) R.; m. Ann A. Louskos, Sept. 8, 1962; children: Terry Theodore, b. 1966; Ellen Ann, b. 1968; edn: BA, Univ. of Mich. 1956; MBA, USC 1968; CLU, 1972, Chartered Fin. Cons., 1982 The Am. Coll.; CFP, The Coll. of Fin. Plng. 1983. Career: with Mutual of New York 1958-78; regl. claims mgr. 1958-68; mgr. gp. admin. 1968-70; gp. & pension adminstr. 1970-72; adv. underwriter 1972-78; principal/ owner T.S. Rouman & Assocs. 1978-82; regl. ins. mgr. Merrill Lynch Life Agcy., Inc., Pasadena 1982--; instr.: CSU, Los Angeles 1979-80; Pasadena City Coll. 1977-79; Valley Coll. 1978-79; honors: Beta Gamma Sigma, nat. bus. hon. 1968; mem: Estate Plng. Council, San Gabriel Valley (pres. 1980); Soc. of Life Underwriters, San Gabriel Valley (pres. 1983-84); Internat. Assn. Fin. Plnrs.; Inst. of Fin. Plnrs.; The Acad. of Magical Arts, Inc.; The Magic Castle; mil: Spec. 4/c, US Army 1956-58; Orthodox; rec: magic, baseball, jazz. Res: 2125 Bristow Dr La Canada 91011 Ofc: Merrill Lynch Life, 225 South Lake Ave Pasadena 91101

ROUSE, LILLIAN McPHERSON; publisher; b. Santa Cruz, CA; d. Frederick Duncan and Matye Eliza (Patton) McPherson; UC Berkeley, 1926-28; BA, Univ. Wash., Seattle, 1928-30; Tchrs. Cert., San Jose State Univ., 1930-31; grad. sch., Stanford Univ., 1931-32; m. Robert P. Rouse, June 30, 1933; chil: Mary Ellen, b. 1934; Robert, b. 1936; Ruth, b. 1941; James Charles, 1944, dec. 1978. Career: tchr., pub. schs., Watsonville, Calif., 1931-34; partner, Corner Drug Store, Watsonville, 1938-60; partner, McPherson Land Co., Santa Cruz, 1960-82; partner, Santa Cruz Sentinel-News, 1941-60; v.p., dir., Santa Cruz Sentinel Publrs. Inc., 1960-82. Listed in 1981-82 Marquis Who's Who of Amer. Women and 1982-83 Who's Who in the West; accepted for current edn., World's Who's Who of Women; Internatl. Who's Who of Intellectuals; Personalities in America; Directory of Distinguished Americans. Mem: AAUW; Calif. Press Assn.; Stanford Univ. Alumni Assn.; UC Berkeley Alumni Assn.; PEO Sisterhood; Watsonville Woman's Club; Travel Clubs; Historical Socs. and other local orgns. Republican. Congregationalist. Rec: gardening, swimming, stamps. Res: 32 Gonzales St., Watsonville 95077; Office: Santa Cruz Sentinel Co., 207 Church St., Santa Cruz 95060.

ROWELL, DAVID BENTON, investor; b. March 8, 1939, Hartford, Conn.; s. Harry George and Helen (Krech) Rowell; m. Joanna Fortune, Aug. 4, 1962; 1 son, Andrew, b. 1969; edn: BA, Amherst Coll. 1965; lic. real estate broker, Mass., Calif.; cert., Executive Broker Devel. Series, USC, 1981. Career: exec. dir. Amherst (Mass.) Chamber of Commerce, 1965-69; advt. sales/pub. rels. cons., Mass. & Calif., 1969-77; real estate broker/devel. and investor, 1978--; mem. Advt. Club of Gr. Santa Barbara, 1978-; pres. Santa Barbara/Puerto Vallarta Sister City Com.; dir. Old Spanish Days in Santa Barbara, Inc.; mem. Santa Barbara Uptown Lions, S.B. Jaguar Club. Publs: various non-fiction, poetry, jazz reviews/criticism. Mil: E5 USN 1959-63; GCM, Commendation letter. Republican. Episcopal. Rec: writer/photog; jazz prod./critic; classic car buff. Address: InterMedia, 2977 Hillcrest Rd., Niskayuna, NY 12309

ROWLEY, LARRY D., financial planner; b. Dec. 20, 1952, Ariz.; s. Jesse and Edna Rowley; m. Diane B., Aug. 14, 1976; children: Brian, b. 1977; Leland, b. 1979; Jared, b. 1983; edn: BS, Brigham Young Univ. 1977; Eastern Ariz. Coll.

1970-71. Career: assoc. United Calif. Bus. & Estate Plng., Inc., Riverside 1977-83; pres. Inland Fin. & Estate Plng., Sunnymead 1983--; spkr. var. svc. & profl. orgns.; honors: Million Dollar Roundtable (5 yrs.); mem: Riverside Co. Assn. of Life Underwriters; Nat. Assn. Life Underwriters; Internat. Assn. for Fin. Plng.; Boy Scouts of Am.; Republican; LDS; rec: hiking. Address: Inland Financial & Estate Planning, 12111 Zinnia Sunnymead 92388

ROZANSKI, STANLEY HOWARD, lawyer; b. July 1952, Brklyn., NY; s. Israel and Frida (Huber) R.; m. Ilene Newman, Dec. 31, 1975; edn: BA, Hunter Coll. 1974; JD, San Fernando Valley Coll. of Law 1977; admitted to Calif. State Bar 1978. Career: partner Law Offices Mackey & Rozanski with offices in Los Angeles,Encino, and San Jose 1980--; mem: Calif., American, Los Angeles trial lawyers assns., Los Angeles County and Beverly Hills bar assns. Res: 8160 Manitoba St, 318, Playa del Rey 90293 Ofc: Law Offices Mackey & Rozanski, 11330 Santa Monica Blvd, Los Angeles 90025

RUBENSTEIN, MICHAEL A., architect; b. July 18, 1944, St. Louis, Mo.; s. Melvin Paul and Miriam (Schwartz) R.; edn: BS in A.S., Wash. Univ. Sch. of Architecture, 1966; M.Arch., Wash. Univ. Grad. Sch. of Arch. 1968; Reg. Architect, Calif. 1974. Career: profl. experience with Skidmore, Owings, Merrill (NYC), Helmuth, Obata, Kassabaum (St. Louis, Mo.), Peckham/Guyton Assocs. (St. Louis, Mo.), B.A. Berkus (Los Angeles), Gruen Assocs. (L.A.), Design Consultants, Gruen Assocs. (NYC), Studio Works (L.A.), design cons. and staff, Experiments in ARt and Tech. (L.A.); current: principal, Michael A. Rubenstein Associates Architects; pres. Rubenstein Construction Inc.; pres. Plaza Street Cafe Inc., gen. ptnr. Plaza Street Cafe Limited Partnership; awards: PG&E Energy Efficient Housing (1978), Solar Cal Council, State of Calif. energy savings builder awd. (1982), Builder Mag. hon. mention Small House (1982), Energy Efficient House (1982, 1983), Architecture Mag. (AIA Journal) int. design competition winner, Truck 4 (1984); first local recipient Key to the City of Healdsburg (1982); mem. AIA (dir. Redwood Empire Chpt. 1984); publs: arts. in profl. jours., Bay Views Mag. (1979), Sunset Mag. (1980); Democrat; Jewish. Res: 110 First St Healdsburg 95448 Ofc: Michael A. Rubenstein Assocs. Architects, 327 East St Healdsburg 95448

RUBIN, ANDREA, graphic designer; b. Aug. 18, 1955, Los Angeles; d. Harold and Sylvia Ruth (Rose) R.; m. Jeffrey Gregg Kichaven, Esq. Sept. 7, 1981; edn: BA, CSU Northridge 1976; stu. graphic design/ advtg. George Washington Univ. 1976, Art Center 1977, UCLA 1973-74. Career: art dir. Loren Miles & Assoc., Los Angeles 1977-79; art dir. Grey Advtg., L.A. 1979, art dir. Delilofcli-Wilson, L.A. 1980-82; graphic designer ESQ Graphics (litigation visual aids), L.A. 1982--; lectr. on use of visual aids in the courtroom, 13th Annual Far West Conf. on Women in the Law, Mac George Sch. of Law, Sacto. Oct. 1983; mem: Am. Jewish Com.; Democrat; Jewish; rec: gourmet cooking. Address: ESQ Graphics, 1840 Camden Ave, 208, Los Angeles 90025

RUCH, WILLIAM VAUGHN, educator, author; b. Sept. 29, 1937, Allentown, Pa.; s. Weston Heylin, Sr. and Dorothy (Daubert) R.; edn: BA, Monrovian Coll. 1959; MA, Syracuse Univ. 1969; MBA, Fairleigh Dickinson Univ. 1972; PhD, Rennselaer Polytech. Inst. 1979; JD, Western State Univ. Coll. of Law 1983. Career: prof. Univ. of Maryland, European Div., 1984--; San Jose State Univ., 1979-83, CSU Sacto. 1977-79, Bloomsburg (Penn.) State Coll. 1975-76, Fairleigh Dickinson Univ. 1974-75; field rep., US Army Recruiting Command Acct., N.W. Ayer & Son, Inc., NYC 1972-73; asst. editor The Bell System Technical Jour., Bell Tel. Labs., Murray Hill, NJ 1969-71; tech. writer/ ed. Engineering Consultants & Publs., Phila. 1969; finl. ed. Penna. Power & Light Co., Allentown, Pa. 1965-69; asst. ed. Dixie News, Dixie Prods. Div. of American Can Co., Easton, Pa. 1964-65. Mem: Internat. Assn. of Bus. Communicators, Am. Bus. Comm. Assn., Acad. of Mgmt., Internat. Platform Assn.; author: Corporate Communication A Comparison of Japanese and Am. Practices (1983, Greenwood Press, Westport, Ct.); Republican; United Ch. of Christ. Address: Univ. of Md., European Div., APO New York 09102

RUCKER, RUFUS CAPERS, dermatologist; b. May 24, 1910, Jennings, LA; s. Maxwell Lee and Ruby (Bauknight) R.; m. Clara Victoria Marchus, Jan. 23, 1937; children: Marilyn Rae, b. 1942; Rufus Edward, b. 1944; Howard, b. 1946; edn: Texas A & M 1928-29; UC 1930-35; MB, Northwestern Med. 1941; MD, Northwestern Med. 1942; Fellow Am. Bd. of Dermatology Cert. 1951. Career: active practice dermatology, Los Angeles 1951-52, Chico 1952; Volunteer Clinical Faculty Dept. Dermatol., Stanford Univ. Med. Sch. clinical instr. 1955-56; asst. prof. 1966-72; clin. assoc. prof. 1972-75; clin. assoc. prof. emeritus 1975--; mem: Masons; Butte Creek Country Club; Calif. Med. Assn.; Butte- Glenn Med. Soc. (pres. 1960); AMA; Southern Med. Assn.; San Francisco Derm. Assn. (pres. 1978); Pacific Derm. Assn. (pres. elect 1982, pres. 1983); Masters Derm. Assn.; No. Am. Clinical Derm. ssn.; Am. Acad. of Derm.; Srs. Golf Assn. of No. Calif.; Calif. Srs. Golf Assn.; mil: Maj., Med. Corps. AUS 935th Engr. Aviation Regt., Okinawa 1942-46; Republican; Protestant; rec: photog., ham radio, golf. Res: 239 Estates Dr Chico 95926 Ofc: R.C. Rucker Dermatologist, 676 E 1st Ave, Ste 15, Chico 95926

RUDLOFF, JOSEPH STEPHEN, educator; b. Aug. 28, 1932, Brklyn., NY; s. John Andrew and Jane Barbara (Kucharski) R.; edn: BBA, City Coll. of NY, 1954; MA in spl. edn., S.F. State Coll. 1960; edn., S.D. St. Coll. 1960-62, admin., Calif. Western Univ. 1965; EdD, UCLA 1966. Career: acct. Chase Manhattan Bank Pension Trust, NY, NY 1952-55; auditor Proctor & Gamble, Cincinnati, Oh. 1957-59; tchr. of the deaf & hard of hearing, writer in field, 1960--; tchr. San Diego City Schs., 1960-66; cons. Deaf Edn., Kent (Oh.) City Schs., 1966-67; asst. prof. of Edn. (deaf edn.), Kent State Univ. 1966-67, USC,

1967-71; dir. Demonstrn. Sch., John Tracy Clin., L.A. 1967-71; tchg. L.A. County Schs., 1971-79; pvt. practice, 1979-; lectr. var. tchr. tng. instns., parent groups; awards: Crown Zellerback Awd. in Spl. Edn. 1960, Zeta O. Doyle Scholarship 1963, 64, UCLA Edn. Dept. Awd. 1965, 66; mem: Council for Exceptional Children, Hearing Handicapped Chil. Assn., Alexander G. Bell Assn., Nat. Bus. Edn. Assn., Nat. Edn. Assn., alif. Tchrs. Edn. Assn.; profl. revs., journal arts.; recL art, folk dance. Res: 8732 Rosewood Ave Los Angeles 90048; POB 69354, Los Angeles 90069

RUDOLPH, ROSS, plastic surgeon; b. Nov. 25, 1940, Reading, Pa.; s. Dr. Herman Louis and Esther (Soskin) R.; m. Nancy Taylor, June 25, 1967; children: Daniel, b. 1969, Rebecca, b. 1973, David, b. 1975, Susan, b. 1977; edn: BA phil., Yale Univ. 1962; MD, Columbia Coll. of Physicians and Surgeons 1966. Career: intern Hosp. of Univ. of Penna. 1966-67; USPHS surgeon, Gallup (NM) Indian Hosp., 1967-69; res. in plastic and gen. surg., Univ. Hosps. of Cleveland and Case Western Reserve Univ., 1969-74; asst. prof. plastic surg. Med. Coll. of Wisc. 1974-75; asst./assoc. prof. plastic surg. in residence, UC San Diego 1975-80, assoc. adj. prof. 1980--; chief Div. of Plas. Surg., VA Hosp., La Jolla 1975-80; pvt. practice of plastic surgery, San Diego 1980--; honors: Phi Beta Kappa (1961), Alpha Omega Alpha (1965), AMA Phys. Recognition Awds.; mem: Am. Soc. of Plastic Surgeons, Fellow Am. Coll. of Surgeons, Plastic Surgery Resrch. Council, Calif. Med. Assn., San Diego Co. Med. Soc., S.D. Internat. Plastic Surg. Assn., AAAS, Am. Assn. for Hand Surg., Am. Cleft Palate Assn., Phi Gamma Delta, Yale Club of San Diego (pres. 1981-84); author two books on plastic surgery (Skin Grafting, 1979, and Chronic Problem Wounds, 1983, Little Brown and Co.), 74 articles; Republican; Jewish; rec: writing, reading, surfing. Res: 8434 Sugarman Dr La Jolla 92037 Ofc: Ross Rudolph, M.D., Inc. 4060 4th Ave, Ste 120, San Diego 92103

RUDYNSKI, JOSEPH, aerospace consultant; b. Mar. 12, 1934, South Bend, Ind.; s. Joseph Richard and Clara Catharine (Larson) R.; m. Sandra Schneidewind, June 28, 1980; children by previous marriage: Joseph, b. 1967, Maria Theresa, b. 1969; edn: AA, L.A. Harbor Coll. 1954; AB, San Diego St. Coll. 1959; Naval Aviation Cadet, Pensacola, Fla. 1954-55. Career: with United Air Lines 1959-83; passenger agent, San Diego 1959; flight engr., NY 1960, First Ofcr., L.A. 1966; Airline Capt., L.A. 1979-83; mem: Airline Pilots Assn. 1961-; Am. Mensa, Ltd. 1982-; Palos Verdes Yacht Club 1972-81; nat. Model R.R. Assn. 1977-; Tailhook Assn. 1978; mil: Lt. J.G., USN 1954-57; Republican; rec: recording engr., model railroading. Res: 2229 Via Alamitos Palos Verdes Estates 90274 Ofc: 7910 Ivanhoe Ave, Ste 417, La Jolla 92037

RUECKERT, WILLIAM ALFRED, manufacturing co. executive; b. Jan. 23, 1932, Berwin, IL; s. Leo Andrew and Florence Albertha (Haslam) R.; m. Patricia Roy, Jan. 22, 1972; 1 dau. by previous marriage, April, b. 1963; edn: lib. arts., Kalamazoo Coll. 1950-51; chem., UCLA 1956; safety tng., Trade Tech. 1958. Career: trainee Person & Covey Inc., Glendale 1956-60; prodn. supvr. Leo Linden Labs, Culver City 1960-62; R&D, Teknol Labs, Burbank 1962-63; prodn. supvr. Boyle & Co., Bell Gardens 1963; prodn. mgr./ dosage forms Rachel Labs, Long Beach 1963-66; Manufacturing Packaging Equipt.-Millwright, Los Angeles 1966-70; plant mgr. Austra Chem., Fountain Valley 1970-71; prodn. mgr.- Tablets, Westpro Labs, Garden Grove 1971-72; v.p. mfg. Alacer Corp., Buena Park 1972-73; owner/ pres. Rajar Enterprises Inc., and Frendz O Mine, San Juan Capistrano 1973--; cons. Mfg. & Coating; mil: HM 1, USN 1952-56, GCM; Republican; metaphysical; rec: boating. Res: 26506 Ave Veronica Mission Viejo 92691 Ofc: Rajar Enterprises, Inc., 26081 Ave Aeropuerto San Juan Capistrano 92675

RUEPPEL, CHARLOTTE N., real estate broker; b. Oct. 15, 1937, NY, NY; children: Bruce E., Jr., b. 1958, Denise C., b. 1960; edn: prep, Lycee Francais de New York, The Lenox Sch.; BA, Univ. of Penna. 1956; GRI, Grad. Realtors Inst. of Calif.; Community Coll. tchr. credential 1976. Career: real estate broker Jones Brand and Hullin, 1969-79, Coldwell Banker (Top Prod. 1981), 1979-81, owner/broker The Nikki Rueppel Co., Sacramento 1981--; honors: Humanitarian of the Year Award 1967, Calif. Br., Humane Soc. of the U.S.; charter mem. Masters Club, Sacramento Bd. of Realtors (1973); mem. Nat. Assn. of Realtors, Calif. Assn. of Realtors, PEO Sisterhood, Sacto. Childrens Home Guild, bd. mem. Family Service League, Sacto. Sym. League, Opera Guild, World Affairs Council, Sierra Club, Smithsonian, SPCA; Episcopal; rec: animal welfare concerns. Ofc: The Nikki Rueppel Co. 1162 Seventh Ave Sacramento 95818

RUGH, RUTH L., antiques dealer; b. Sept. 15, 1897, Butler, Mo.; d. Amos and Anna Iva (Light) Lockridge; m. Frank James Rugh, June 15, 1917 (dec. 1966); children: June Blossom, b. 1918; Frank James Jr., b. 1924; ed. Douglas H.S., Okla. 1914-16, spl. courses Modesto Jr. Coll. Career: ship welder in Stockton, Calif. 1943-45; estab. first antique shop on family ranch near Escalon, Ca., expanded bus. 1966-78, traveled through 20 states on buying trips; currently buying/selling antiques throughout Calif.; owner Rugh's Copper Kettle, Modesto; mem. Home League, Salvation Army; works: restoration antiques (quilting, weaving, caneing, upholstery). Address: Rugh's Copper Kettle 1613 Pimlico Dr Modesto 95350

RUIZ, JAMES JOHN, architect, b. May 7, 1952, San Antonio, Tex.; s. Cecil John and Tomasa (Hinojosa) R.; edn: AS, Long Beach City Coll. 1972; BA, CSU Long Beach 1974; BS, Cal Poly S.L.O. 1976; Reg. Architect, Calif., 1984. Career: design team Long Beach Unified Sch. Dist. Arch. Div. 1970-72; design team (archtl. development, engring. and contracting) Integrated Inc, Paramount 1972-74; designer J.J. Ruiz & Assoc. San Luis Obispo 1974-75; project designer San Luis Obispo Co. Arch. Div. 1975-76; prin. designer in prodn. Ruiz, Mason, Orefice A.I.A, Pismo Bch., 1976-81; design team Morris Skenderian & Assoc. A.I.A., Laguna Bch., 1981-83; project designer Arch/West, Newport Bch. 1983--; continuing education seminars; free lance arch. design cons. Awards: Sunset House Beautiful award 1977; mem: AIA 1979-83; CSI 1983-84; works: Tri-Mod, a triangular modulated creative geometric puzzle, 1975; Democrat; Catholic; rec: photo., painting; Res: 32 Lakeshore Irvine 92714 Ofc: Arch/West 4665 MacArthur Ct, 100-C Newport Beach 92660

RUIZ, LOUIS FLORES, manufacturing co. executive; b. Oct. 30, 1918, Chihuahua, Chihuahua, Mex., nat. 1944; s. Luis Hermosillo and Lucy (Flores) R.; m. Rose Rivadenerya, June 11, 1941; children: Rose Margaret, b. 1942; Frederick, b. 1943; Arthur, b. 1945; Anna Marie, b. 1947; Carrie Ann, b. 1959; edn: McKay Bus. Coll., Los Angeles 1940-41. Career: ins. agent Unity Mutual Life Ins., Los Angeles 1943; Provost Marshal US Army 1945; owner Frederick's Shoe & Clothing Store, Los Angeles 1946-52; partner Ruiz Brother Food Distbr., Tulare 1964--; currently, pres./ bd. dirs. Ruiz Food Prods., Inc. (subject of ABC Night Line & var. other news shows); guest spkr. Loyola Marymount Univ., L.A. 1983 & Nat. Chamber Found., Wash. DC 1983; mem: Nat. Fedn. of Independent Bus.; Tulare CofC; Tulare Co. Economic Devel. Assn.; Calif. CofC; Tulare Co. Pvt. Indl. Council; US CofC; Moose Lodge, Tulare; design & devel. equip. used in pvt. plant; mil: US Army 1943-45; Democrat; Catholic; rec: landscaping home, inveting food machinery. Res: 1243 Kristen Cir. Tulare 93274 Ofc: Ruiz Food Products, Inc., 1025 E Bardsley Tulare 93274

RULE, ROGER COLLINS, builder/ developer/ publisher; b. Dec. 31, 1944, Kansas City, Mo.; s. Forrest Collins and Margaret Evelyn (Thompson) R.; m. Joyce Kindred, Dec. 26, 1965; children: Sean, b. 1971; Ryan, b. 1979; edn: BS, Univ. of Mo. 1966; US Army Quartermaster Ofcrs. Adv. Course, Fort Lee, Va. 1971; B-1 gen. contractors lic., Calif. 1971; Mo. Life Tchg. Cert.; R.E. broker lic., Calif. 1981. Career: gen. contractor Rule Devel., Modesto 1973-76; pres. Rule Enterprises, Modesto 1977--; pres. Alliance Books, Inc., Northridge 1982--; owner/ partner Sky- Trek Aviation, Modesto Airport, Modesto 1983--; tchr. probational & remedial students, N.K.C. Public Schs., summer 1968; honors: A.R.C. Pvt. Bus. Awd. 1983; Council of Bus. Mgrs. 1977; Commandant's List, QMC Adv. Course, Fort Lee' Va. 1971; mem: Nat. Edn. Assn.; Mo. Tchrs. Assn.; Principal's Adv. Com.; No. Coast & Fresno Bldrs. Exch.; ; San Joaquin Valley Exchs.; Nat. & Modesto Home Bldrs. Assns.; Nat. & Modesto Rifle Assns.; Winchester Coll. Arms Assn.; Winchestr Club of Am.; Mo. Univ. Alumni Assn.; author: book, The Rifleman's Rifle, 1982; book, Twetieth Century Winchester, 1984; art., The Rifleman's Rifle, Guns Mag. 3/84; mil: Capt., US Army (temp.); 1st Lt., US Army (perm) QMC Airborne, GCM, Meritorious Svc. Medal; Republican; Methodist; rec: parchutist, snow skiing, target shooting. Res: 2816 Eastridge Cir Modesto Ofc: Rule Enterprises, 2909 Coffee Rd, Ste 10, Modesto 95355

RUNEZ, ART FLORES, nursing home administrator; b. March 17, 1909, Caba, La Union, Philippines, nat. 1983; s. Matias and Margarita (Flores) Runez; m. Maria Dolores Reyes, Oct. 3, 1982; chil: Artemio Jr., b. 1936; Ricardo, b. 1937; Manuel, b. 1940; Malou, b. 1944; Antonio, b. 1946; Bonifacio, b. 1947; Dolores, b. 1968; Theresa, b. 1969; Maria, b. 1970; edn: MD, Univ. Santo Tomas, Phil. 1934; cert. Pub. Hlth, Univ. of Phil. 1936; leprologist, Dept. Hlth, Phil. 1939; spl. course George Wash. Univ. 1981; lic. Nursing Home Adminstr, Calif. 1982. Career: pres. Sanitary Div., Isabela, Phil. 1936-9; bacteriologist Dept. Hlth, Phil. 1939-41; chief Mindanao Central Sanitarium, Zamboanga City, Phil. 1946-51, chief Eversley Childs Sanitarium, Cebu, Phil. 1951-4, chief/sr. leprologist Central Luzon Sanitarium, MetroManila (3000 leprosy in-patients, 500 out-patients) 1954-76; ret. 40 yrs. govt. svc. 1976; pvt. transp. bus., Manila 1976-80; med. record supr. Mission Blvd. Convalescent Hosp., Fremont, Ca. 1980-84, hosp. adminstr. 1984--. Awards: Fellowship, World Hlth Orgn. 1958-9; honored by Boy Scouts of Phil. 1955, Phil. Women's Univ. 1958, Phil. Vets. Legion (Gold Medal) 1966, Pres. of Phil. 1965, Secty. Hlth, Phil. 1973, Quezon Times awd. 1975, Phil. Inst. of Awards 1976, Am. legion Phil. Dpt. 1980, num. others. Mem: Am. Assn. Nursing Home Adminstrs.; fellow Soc. Aesthetic Medicine; fellow Phil. Coll. Tropical Dermatol.; life mem. Phil. Leprosy Soc. (pres. 1969-76), Phil. Med. Assn., Manila Med. Soc; Zamboanga City Med. Assn. (pres. 1950-1); Nat. Assn. Med. Hlth Adminstrs. (bd. 1973-4); Dept. Hlth Phys. Assn. (bd. 1970-6); Phil. Army ADTC Assn. (vp 1963); num. civic orgns. Resrch: leprosy. Mil: 1st lt., M.C., USAFFE 1941-5; lt. col., M.C., Phil. Reserve. Democrat. Catholic. Rec: chess, table tennis. Res: 1324 Bonner Ave Fremont 94536 Ofc: Mission Blvd. Convalescent Hosp. 38650 Mission Bl. Fremont 94536

RUSCH, KENNETH ALLEN, real estate broker; b. Sept. 13, 1937, Seattle, Wash.; s. Max and Ruth Elenoir (Sickels) R.; m. Sharon, Jan. 24, 1970; 1 son: Kenneth Jr., b. 1971; edn: Seattle Univ. 1955-57, 59-60; Univ. of Wash. 1960; adv. R.E. certs., Masters Sales (1982), Lumbleau Sch. (1978), Am. Inst. of Cont. Edn. (1978). Career: owner Ken's Distributing Co., Kennewick, Wash. 1965-70; ofc. mgr. Blasi Constrn., Healdsburg 1971; real estate agent Lockwood Realty, Santa Rosa 1972-76; co- owner Fireside Realty, Santa Rosa 1976-81; owner/ broker/ dir. Kenneth A. Rusch, Inc., Santa Rosa 1981--; owner/ bldr./ dir. Oak Leaf Const., Inc., Santa Rosa 9181--; dir. Sonoma Co. Bd. Realtors 1982-82; awards: spl. recogn. for highest producer, Sonoma City Bd. Realtors 1978, 80; spl. recogn. 10 million in sales 1979, 15 million 1980; mem: Sonoma Co. Bd. Realtors; Sonoma Co. Multiple Listings Svc.; sponsor Little League Baseball, Rincon Valley Soccer and football teams; mil: cpl. USMC 1957-59; Democrat; Catholic; rec: golf, fishing. Res: 5530 Yerba Buena Rd Santa Rosa 95405 Ofc: 824 Mendocino Ave Santa Rosa 95401

RUSH, GERARD THOMAS, international business consultant; b. Oct. 10, 1933, New York City; s. Lewis William and Beatrice Lillian (Daily) Rush; m. Katherine King, June 26, 1953; chil: Maureen, b. 1955; Susan, b. 1956; Laurene, b. 1957; Gerard Jr., b. 1959; Lawrence, b. 1960; John, b. 1963; Steven, b. 1964; Christen, b. 1972. Career: chain supvr., Mayfair Inc., Plainfield, NJ, 1953-58; CEO, partner, Supermkt. Promotions Inc., Milford, Penn., 1958-64; with Black & Decker Mfg. Co., Towson, Md., 1964-81: gen. sales mgr., dir. mktg., dir. adv. planning, v.p. mktg., pres. McCulloch Corp. major subs. responsible for the mfg. and mktg. of 2-cycle engines worldwide, dir. 1979---; currently, pres., CEO, Pragmatic Strategies, Inc., internatl. cons. firm in bus. strategy devel. and software model devel. for exec. decision making; dir., L.R. Nelson, 1979; dir., Amagin, Inc., TV prodn. co., 1980---. Mem: Black & Decker World Corp. Adv. Council; past. chmn. Chain Saw Mfg. Assn., 1979; US Senate Bus. Adv. Bd.; Newcomen Soc. of No. Amer.; Town Hall of Calif.; Soc. Mfg. Engrs.; Natl. Assn. Mfgrs.; Platform Assn.; Publs: num. articles in business journals incl. Don't Clone Business Management in Enterprise mag., Oct. 1981; public speaker, various groups nationwide on free enterprise sys. and govt. impact on free soc. Republican. Catholic. Rec: sketching/painting, tennis, fishing. Res/Office: Pragmatic Strategies Inc., 11 Cayuse Lane, Rancho Palos Verdes 90274.

RUSH, JOHN A., insurance agent; b. Oct. 6, 1928, Toledo, Ohio; s. Arnold E. and Bessie A. Rush; m. Patricia Bush, Oct. 1977; children: Leslie, b. 1954; Kurt, b. 1957; Linda, b. 1958; Karl, b. 1960; edn: AA, Univ. of Toleda 1951. Career: mgr. Ventura Calif. Retail Credit Co. 1951-58; asst. mgr. customer svc. Sears-Roebuck 1958-59; ins. agent State Farm Ins. Co. 1960--; commnr. Calif. St. Coastal Commn. 1979-81; City of Camarillo city councilman 1976-80, mayor 1979-80; bd. dirs. Camarillo Hospice 1983; pres. Lima Bean Soc., Bean Hive No. 1, 1983; dir. Camarillo Sanitation Dist. 1976-80; dir. Ventura Regl. Co. Sanitation Dist. 1978-80; mem: Camarillo Kiwanis Club (charter pres. 1967; pres. 1982-83); life fellow, Kiwanis Internat.; mil: Sgt., US Army, 24th infantry Div., apan. 1946-47; Democrat; Unitarian; rec: gardening. Res: 1404 Calle Aurora Camarillo 93010 Ofc: John A. Rush, POB 156 Camarillo 93011

RUSHFIELD, LEONARD H., banker; b. May 31, 1941, NY, NY; s. Joseph and Shirley Rushfield; m. Karen Aurnou, Aug. 22, 1965; children: Richard, b. 1968; Alexandra, b. 1971; edn: BA, City Univ. of NY 1962; MA, Columbia Univ. 1963; Univ. of Ceylon 1966-67. Career: foreign svc. ofcr. US Dept. of State, Wash. DC 1867-68; asst. treas. Asia Div. Bankers Trust Co., NY 1968-73; v.p. Bankers Trust Internat. Corp., Los Angeles 1973-74; v.p./ mgr. Bankers Trust Co. Tokyo, Japan 1974-77; pres., Los Angeles 1977-80; currently: sr. v.p. Republic Nat. Bank of NY; pres. Republican Internat. Bank, Beverly Hills; sr. v.p. Republic Bullion Corp., Los Angeles; awards: New York Regents fellowship 1962-64, 1965-66; Fulbright fellowship 1966-67; mem: Am. CofC in Japan; Los Angeles Area CofC; Los Angeles World Affairs Council; Asia Soc. (New York); Los Angeles Internat. Visitors Assn.; L.A. Co., Mus. of Art; Democrat. Res: 1321 Avenida De Cortez Pacific Palisades 90272 Ofc: Republic Nat. Bank, 9808 Wilshire Blvd, Ste 200, Beverly Hills 90212

RUSSELL, CRYSTAL ANNE, lawyer; b. June 29, 1942, North Tonnawanda, NY; d. Clarence Leonard and Ruth Ione (Brayley) Krueger; m. Thomas Russell, June 28, 1960; 1 son, Thomas, b. 1961; edn: BA, summa cum laude, Ariz. St. Univ. 1970; JD, cum laude, Ariz. St. Univ. Coll. of Law 1973. Career: atty. assoc. Browder & Gillenwater 1973-74; asst. counsel Anchor Nat. Life Ins. 1974-75; partner/ atty. Horsack & Russell 1975-77; asst. counsel Beneficial Standard Life 1977-78; corp. counsel Ameron, Inc. 1978-81; general counsel Vidal Sassoon, Inc., Los Angeles 1981--; awards: Phelps Dodge Scholarship 1970; mem: Los Angeles Co. Bar Assn. (Corp. Counsel Sect.); Calif. State Bar (Bus. Law Sect., Corp. Counsel Subcom.); rec: running, swimming. Res: 1526 San Vicente Santa Monica 90402 Ofc: Vidal Sassoon, Inc., 2049 Century Park East, Ste 3800, Los Angeles 90067

RUSSELL, JOHN DUNCAN, electrical engineer, inventor; b. Nov. 11, 1913, Jamestown, Calif.; s. Daniel Palmer and Martha (Devoney) R.; m. Vera Miller, June 5, 1943; 1 son, John Michael, b. 1945; edn: BS in E.E., Stanford Univ. 1936; Profl. Engr., St. of Calif. 1970-. Career: elec. engr. Hawaiian Electric Co., Honolulu, 1940-42; test engr. Douglas Aircraft Co., Santa Monica 1942-48; pres./ chief engr./ owner, Micro-Test, Inc., Santa Monica 1948-60; research engr. Microdot Inc., So. Pasadena 1960-65, Pacific Missile Test Center, Point Mugu 1967-79; consulting engr. Eaton Corp., L.A. 1980--; honors: Phi Beta Kappa, Tau Beta Pi (1936); mem. Precision Measurements Assn. (SESA), Malibu Township Council; Patents (1960-) in the Weldable Strain Gage field (pd. royalties by Eaton Corp.); Democrat; Catholic; rec: travel. Res: 26878 Sea Vista Dr Malibu 90265 Ofc: Eaton Corp. 5340 Alla Rd Los Angeles

RUSSWORM, LARRY CLIFTON, manufacturing engineer; b. Nov. 23, 1954, Los Angeles; s. Kenneth and Lois Decema (Himes) R.; edn: BS, CalPoly San Luis Obispo 1979; AA, L.A. Harbor Coll. 1976. Career: design draftsman Rockwell Internat. L.A., Lax. summer 1972; Ralph M. Parsons Co., Pasadena, 1973-74; tool designer FMC Corp., San Jose 1977-78; mfg. engr. TRW, Redondo Beach 1979; TRW college recruiter for CalPoly, SLO; design drafting & blueprint reading instr., Los Angeles; curriculum advr. Los Angeles Harbor Coll.; TRW classroom tech. advr., Inglewood Bd. of Edn. Cooperative Ind., Academic Student Pgm. and steering com. mem.; blueprint reading instr. L.A. Harbor Coll. 1982; mem: Soc. of Mfg. Engrs. (edn. chmn. 1983-84; Engring. council rep. 1977-78; Engring. Tech. Rep. 1979); devel. model steam engine, CalPoly machine shop class; Democrat; Baptist; rec: music, recording, racquetball. Res: 1106 West 49th St Los Angeles 90037 Ofc: TRW, One Space Park Redondo Beach 90278

RUSSELL, ROBERT CHANDLER, photographer; b. Nov. 15, 1926, Battle Creek, Mich.; s. Dr. Edwin Phillips and Mary Creamer (Chandler) R.; m. Eleanor McGann, Aug. 8, 1960; children: Carol Anne, b. 1961; Jean Elizabeth, b. 1963; edn: BS, Loyola Univ. 1955; postgrad. work, CSU Northridge; undergrad. Northwestern Univ., UCLA, USC, UC Berkeley. Career: photographer/ pres. Russel Photo 1975--; awards: Sepulveda VAVS 1000- hr. awd. 1982; Am. Red Cross, 1.5 gallon awd.; mem: Alpha Delta Phi; The Library Assocs., LMU; works: Western Photographer, typewriter improvement, 1948; mil: Seaman 1/c, USNR 1945-46, WWII Victory Medal, Asia-Pac., Am. Theatre; Catholic; rec: travel, exercise, good books. Address: 17275 Lassen St Northridge 91325

RUTH, ROGER, insurance broker; b. Oct. 4, 1945, Los Altos; s. Leo William Jr. and Dorothy Helen (Davidson) R.; m. Nadine Atwood, Sept. 27, 1967; children: Kellie, b. 1968; Corinne, b. 1971; Shannon, b. 1976; edn: BA, Univ. of Santa Clara 1967; Cert. Ins. Counselor, CIC Soc. 1979. Career: supvr. trainee Allstate Ins. Co. 1970; div. mgr. 1974; independent broker 1974--, pres. Marx, Lewis & Ruth (and predecessor firms), San Jose 1975--; bd. dirs. Independent Ins. Agents of San Jose; Continental Ins. Cos. Producer Council; Indsl. Indemnity Producer Council; St. Paul Ins. Co. Nat. Producer Council; Distng. Achiev. awd., Safeco Ednl. Inst. 1975; mem: Profl. Ins. Agents of Am.; Independent Ins. Agents of Am.; Western Assn. of Ins. Brokers; Almaden Country Club; Metropolitan Univ. Club; Univ. of Santa Clara Bd. of Fellows; mil: 1st lt. US Army (ROTC Distng. Mil. Grad., Scabbard & Blade Hon. Soc.); Republican; Catholic; rec: golf. Res: 1055 Mountain Shadows Rd San Jose 95120 Ofc: Marx, Lewis & Ruth, 1655 Willow St, Ste 4, San Jose 95125

RUTHERFORD, KAREN MARIE, audiologist; b. Aug. 24, 1955, Knoxville, Tenn.; d. Johnnie Willard and Lois Marie (Minnich) Murphy; m. Philip Rutherford, Sept. 2, 1978; edn: BS, East Tenn. St. Univ. 1978; MS, 1980; audiology lic., Calif. 1981; lic. hearing aid dispenser, Calif. 1981; cert. CAOHC course dir. 1980. Career: grad. research asst. East Tenn. St. Univ. 1976-77; clinical audiologist Riverview Hearing, Speech & Language Ctrs., Long Beach 1980-82; clinical audioligist Kaiser Permanente Med. Gp., Harbor City 1982; clinical audiologist Bernard A. Landes & Assoc., Long Beach 1981, hearing aid dispenser/ audiologist AAA Hearing Aid Ctr., Hollywood 1982; clinical audiologist Rancho Los Amigos Hosp., Downey 1982--; dir. Karen M. Rutherford & Assocs.; cons. audiological svc., South Bay area 1983-; honors: cert. of clinical competence in audiology, Am. Speech- Language- Hearing Assn. 1981; mem: Am. & Calif. Speech- Language- Hearing Assns., United States Ski Assn.; rec: snow skiing, bicycling, tennis. Res: 7452 Brian Ln La Palma 90623 Ofc: Rancho Los Amigos Hosp., Dept. of Communication Disorders, 7601 E Imperial Hwy Downey 90242

RUTLAND, GEORGE PATRICK, banking executive; b. Sept. 4, 1932, Tifton, Ga.; s. George Patrick, Sr. and Peggy (Roberts) R.; m. Dawn Mary O'Neill, Jan. 2, 1954; children: Michael, b. 1954; Kathleen, b. 1955; Dawn, b. 1959; Mary, b. 1961; Thomas, b. 1968; edn: BA, Pace Univ. 1961; grad., Stonier Sch. of Banking, Rutgers St. Univ. 1962-64. Career: with Citicorp., NYC 1954-75; sr. v.p. corp. svcs. 1970-73; exec. v.p. adv. mortgage subs. 1973-75; with Crocker Nat. Bank, San Francisco 1975-82; sr. v.p. domestic br. admin. 1975-77; sr. v.p. ops. 1977-78; exec. v.p./ cashier 1978-80; sr. exec. v.p./ cashier 1981-82; with California Federal Savings & Loan Assn. 1982--: exec. v.p. admin./ dir. 1982, sr. exec. v.p. 1983, pres. & c.o.o. 1983, pres. & chief exec. 1984--; pres. & c.o.o. CalFed, Inc. 1984--; dir. Los Angeles Area CofC; mem: Nat. Council of Savings Instns.; US & Calif. Leagues of Savings Instns.; Los Angeles Area CofC; Calif. Club; Wilshire Country Club; Desert Horizons Country Club; mil: USN 1950-53; Republican; Catholic. Res: 7220 Avenida Altisima Rancho Palos Verdes 90724 Ofc: California Federal S&L Assn., 5670 Wilshire Blvd, 15th Flr, Los Angeles 90036

RUZI, HOWARD VINCENT, SR., chiropractor; b. Oct. 1, 1928, Detroit, Mich.; s. Stuart Joseph, Sr. and Catherine Lucretia (Draguiscu) R.; m. Mary Lou Hemmings, Feb. 14, 1953; children: Howard V., Jr., b. 1958; Elizabeth Lucretia, b. 1961; edn: Fullerton Jr. Coll. 1946-47; Pasadena City Coll. 1948-49; BS, Woodbury Coll. 1956; DC, Cleveland Chiro. Coll. 1976. Career: prop. Monterey Interiors, Paramount 1956-59; prop. Howmar Vinyls, Venice 1960-67; owner Howard V. Ruzi, A Chiropractic Corp. 1976--; apptd. mem. Calif. Board of Chiro. Examiners 1983; mem: South Bay Athletic Club, Redondo Beach; Internat. Chiro. Assn. of Calif.; mil: Cpl., US Army 1953; Republican; Protestant; rec: breeding & racing thoroughbred horses. Res: 5029 Rolling Meadows Rd Rolling Hills Estates 90274 Ofc: Howard V. Ruzi, D.C., 707 Silver Spur Rd, Ste 102, Rolling Hills Estates 90274

RUZICS, IVAN ZOLTAN, lawyer; b. Jan. 26, 1952, Budapest, Hungary, nat. 1962; s. Ivan Laszlo and Eva Ruzics; edn: Masters in public adm. & judicial adm., USC 1981; JD, Southwestern Univ. 1978; BSc., Univ. of Ore. 1974. Career: sr. contracts analyst Co. of L.A. 1979-82; v.p. ADP Contracts Security Pacific Nat. Bank 1982; computer contracts cons. 1980--; exec. v.p. Softsystems Tech. Corp. 1978-80; honors: Calif. St. Grad. Fellowship, Calif. 1976; Am. Jurisprudence Awd. in Adminstrv. 1978; mem: Pi Sigma Alpha nat. hon. soc. 1981; Calif. State Bar; Am. Bar Assn.; Computer Law Assn.; Fed. Bar Assn.; L.A. Co. Bar Assn.; admitted Central Dist. Ct. & Ninth Circuit Ct. of Appeals; rec: skiing, scuba diving, aviation. Ofc: POB 971 Glendale 90291

RYAN, DANIEL PAUL, vice president, director, Van Cleef & Arpels; b. June 18, 1927, St. Nazaire, France; s. Daniel P. and Andree (Charbonnier) Ryan; edn: Coll. de Combre, France, 1948; m. Patricia Keating, July 30, 1978; chil: Carolene, b. 1959; Daniel, b. 1962. Career: salesman, Van Cleef &

Arpels, NYC, 1957; dir. Palm Beach (Fla.) 1959-69, v.p., dir., Beverly Hills, 1969---. Honors: Societe d'Encouragement au Progress of France silver medal, 1982. Mem: Chevaliers du Tastevin, Societe d'Encouragement au Progress, Los Angeles World Affairs Council, Beverly Hills Chamber of Commerce, Rodeo Drive Assn., Indianhead Gun Club. Res./Office: 300 N. Rodeo Dr., Beverly Hills 90210.

RYAN, JOHN P., record producer; b. Oct. 26, 1948, Rochester, NY; s. Bernard and Dora; m. Diana Hubbard, Mar. 15, 1982; edn: BA, Univ. Chgo. 1970; PhD, Univ. Chgo. Grad. Sch. 1972-71. Career: admin. asst. Woodlawn Experimental Sch. Proj., Chgo. Inner City Parent Controlled Sch. Bd.; Wold- FM Radio, Chgo. 1970-71; bd. dirs. Chgo. Naras 1971; first prodn., STYX 1972, first gold album 1975; hit records with Santana, Climax Blue Bank, Allman Brothers, Billy Rankin, Patrick Simmons, Pure Prairie League; pres. Chicago Kid Productions; scientology counselor; awards: Top 20 Producers, Billboard Map. 1981; mem: Naras Bd. of Dir., Chgo. 1970-71; rec: travel, films. Res: Los Angeles & London Ofc: Chicago Kid Productions, 13251 Ventura, Ste 3, Studio City 91604

RYAN, LOUIS B., insurance agency president; b. Jan. 27, 1935, Lincoln, Nebr.; s. Paul V. and Dorethea (Trowbridge) R.; edn: BA, Univ. of Iowa 1959. Career: mgmt. trainee Wells Fargo Bank, San Francisco 1959-60; rehabilitation counselor State of Calif., Berkeley 1960-61; agt. Northern Life Insurance, S.F. 1961-75, general agt. Midlands Nat. Life, S.F. 1975-80, pres. Ryan Financial & Insurance Services 1980--; awards: Nat. Quality Award 1983, Nat. Sales Achievement Awd. 1983, President's Club 1983, Security Life of Denver; mem. San Francisco Life Underwriters Assn., Commonwealth Club of Calif.; mil: ensign USN 1955-57; Republican; Catholic; rec: tennis, backpacking. Res: 249 Rivoli St San Francisco 94117 Ofc: Ryan Financial & Insur. Services 249 Rivoli St San Francisco 94117

RYAN, SUSAN CORNWELL, publisher; b. July 26, 1946, South Gate; d. Ervin Richardson and Edith K. (Durand) Cornwell; children: Julie, b 1970; Steven, b. 1973; edn: BA, Ariz. St. Univ. 1968; tchg. cred., Ariz. Career: elem. sch. tchr. Scottsdale Sch. Dist., Scottsdale, Ariz. 1968-70; pub. rels. R & D Devel. Co., Phoenix, Ariz. 1975-76; co- owner Home Secretarial Svc., Huntington Beach 1977-79; owner Susan C. Ryan & Assoc. (property mgrs.), Huntington Beach 1977--; pres./ publisher Home Publications, Inc., Huntington Beach 1977--; asst. nat. dir. of alumnae, Kappa Kappa Gamma frat. 1982-; leader Publs. Workshops, Kappa Kappa Gamma, Regl. 1983, Nat. 1982, 84; mem: Women In Communications, Inc.; Nat. Fedn. of Presswomen, Inc.; Jr. League, Long Beach; KKG So. Calif. Area Council (past pres.); Long Beach Alumnae Assn. of KKG (past pres.); Scottsdale Alumnae Assn. of KKG (past pres.); Brownies; AYSO Soccer; ed. KKG Graphics Manual, nat. distbn. 1984; ed./ writer 2 monthly real estate newsletters: Homeowner's Digest, & The Courier, 1977-; Republican; Methodist; rec: aerobic dance, swimming. Res: 6161 Kelly Cir Huntington Beach 92647 Ofc: Home Publications, Inc., 8071 Slater, Ste 110, Huntington Beach 92647

RYLAND, W. BRADFORD, investment advisor; b. Aug. 3, 1939, Richmond, Va.; s. William Bradford I. and Mary Elizabeth (Neal) R.; m. Judith Dubben, May 5, 1973; edn: BA, Brown Univ. 1962; Masters, New York Univ. 1968. Career: Chemical Bank 1962-67; asst. v.p. Shearson Himmill 1967-72; v.p. Bear Stearns 1972-74; dir. E.F. Hutton 1974-82; v.p./ dir./ assets mgr. Prudential 1982--; dir. Kay Pro Corp.; mng. dir. Rancho Bernardo Partners; mng. dir. Seaview Assocs.; mem: La Jolla Beach & Tennis, Southampton, L.I., NY; Beach & Tennis & Meadow Club; dir. Old Globe Theatre; mil: airman 1/c USAF; Republican; Episcopal; rec: photo., skiing, sailing. Res: 6006 Avenida Cresta La Jolla Ofc: Prudential, 1200 Prospect, Ste 101, La Jolla 92037

S

SABELLA, JOSEPH D., physician/pathologist; b. July 25, 1929, San Francisco; s. Antonio and Katherine (Gelardi) Sabella; m. Iris, Dec. 21, 1951; children: Gianna, b. 1956, Frank, b. 1957, Matthew, b. 1965; edn: AB, UC Berkeley 1950; MD, UC Sch. Med., S.F. 1954; internship Kings County Hosp., Bklyn, NY 1954-55; asst. resident Gen. Surg., S.F. VA Hosp. 1955-56; clin. fellow Pathology, Mass. Gen. Hosp. 1956-57. Career: USAF Medical Corps, stationed in Wiesbaden, Ger. 1963-69; assoc. pathologist, three San Francisco hospitals, 1969--; dir. Lab., Brookside Hosp., San Pablo; pres./chmn. bd. of govs. The Doctors' Co. (doctor-owned interinsurance exchange) 1976--; bd. dirs. Alvarado Bank, San Pablo; asst. clinical prof., Health & Med. Sci., UC Berkeley; mem: Calif. Soc. Pathology (bd. 1978-82), Fellow Coll. of Amer. Pathologists, Amer. Assn. Blood Banks, Alameda-Contra Costa Med. Assn., Calif. Med. Assn.; mil: capt. USAF (M) 1956-63, commendn. medal; Republican; rec: cabinet making, gardening. Res: 15 Mark Terrace Tiburon 94920 Ofc: Pathology Consultants Medical Grp. 2000 Vale Rd San Pablo 94806; The Doctors' Co. 401 Wilshire Blvd Santa Monica 90401

SABHARWAL, RANJIT SINGH, mathematician, educator; b. Dec. 11, 1925, Dhudial, India; naturalized 1981; s. Krishan Chand and Devti (Anand) Sabharwal; Edn: BA, with honors, Punjab Univ. India 1944; MA, Punjab Univ. India 1948; MA, UC Berkeley 1962; PhD, Wash. St. Univ. 1966; m. Pritam Chadha 1948; child: Rajinderpal, b. 1949; Armarjit, b. 1951; Jasbir, b.

1955; Career: lecturer in math., Khalsa College, Bombay, India, 1951-58; teaching asst., UC Berkeley, 1958-62; instructor in mathematics, Portland St. Univ., 1962-63; instr. in math, Washington St. Univ., 1963-66; asst. prof., Kansas St. Univ., 1966-68; assoc. prof., CSU, Hayward, 1968-74; prof. of math., CSU Hayward, 1974—. Mem: Amer. Math Soc.; Math Assn. of America; Sigma Xi. Research in Non-Desarguesian Geometries. Res: 27892 Adobe Court, Hayward 94542; Office: California State Univ., Hayward 94542.

SACKS, ZACHARY HERMAN, lawyer; b. Aug. 10, 1935, NYC; s. Joseph A. and Florence (Oster) S.; m. V. Salley, Aug. 30, 1969; children: Benjamin, b. 1970, Alexander, b. 1978; edn: BA, Yale Univ. 1957; JD, Columbia Law Sch. 1960; admitted to California State Bar 1963; Cert. Splst. Workers' Compensation Law, Calif. Bd. of Legal Spec. Career: house counsel, spec. Wkrs. Comp. def., R. L. Kautz and Co., 1963-65; pvt. practice, 1965-73; dir.: Kendig, Stockwell & Gleason, all phases Workers Comp. def., 1973-78; law offices of Zachary H. Sacks & Associates, APC, practice ltd. to Workers Comp. defense, 1978--; lectr., moderator, frequent guest speaker on Wkrs. Comp., 1973-; mem: Calif. Bar Assn., Los Angeles Co. Bar Assn. (Workers Comp. Sects.), Calif. Workers Comp. Defense Attorneys Assn. (founding pres. 1982-83), Workers Comp. Defense Attys. Assn. (pres. 1980-82), Nat. Counsel of Self-Insured Insurers; mil: served in USMC; Republican; Jewish; rec: computers, video, films. Res: 6811 Zumirez Dr Malibu 90265 Ofc: Law Offices of Zachary H. Sacks & Assocs., APC, 2121 Cloverfield Blvd, Santa Monica 90404

SADLER, BRUCE PHILLIP, attorney; b. Aug. 11, 1928, Berkeley; s. Clarence Theodore and Doris Reba (Smoak) S.; m. Ruby Vidich, June 24, 1961; children: Stephen Paul, b. 1962, Susan Elaine, b. 1963; edn: BS, Univ. Calif. 1949, MBA, 1955; JD, UC Hastings Coll. of the Law 1954; admitted to Calif. State Bar 1955. Career: reader, Univ. of Calif., Berkeley 1948-51 & 1953-55; expediter Gilmore Steel & Supply Co., San Frnacisco 1944-50; adjuster/ claims investigator/ atty. Industrial Indemnity Co., S.F. 1955-58; atty./supr. Workers' Compensation Sect., Pacific Gas & Elec. Co. 1958-79; mgr. Safety, Health & Claims Dept., PG&E, S.F. 1979--; lectr. Calif. Continuing Edn. of the Bar 1962; awards: Gold Medal, Pacific Coast Gas Assn. 1960; mem: Pacific Coast Gas Assn., Pacific Coast Elec. Assn., Calif. State Bar Assn., Amer. Bar Assn., No. Calif. Council of Self-Insurers (past chmn.), S.F. Barristers Club (past chmn. Wkrs. Comp. Com.), Calif. CofC (Com. on Ins.), Calif. Self-Insurers Assn. (past chmn. Legislative Com., past Bd. Mgrs., past Exec. Com.), Amer. Gas Assn. (Claims Com.), Pacific Service Employees Assn.; mil: capt. US Army Qtrmaster Corps 1951-53, USAR 1949-64; Methodist. Res: 2736 Comstock Circle Belmont 94002 Ofc: Pacific Gas & Electric Co. 245 Market St, Rm. 814, San Francisco 94106

SADOWSKI, ROSE MARY, certified public accountant; b. May 3, 1955, Cleveland, OH; d. John Anthony and Rose Grace (Plute) Sadowski; edn: BS in bus. adminstrn., cum laude, USC 1977. CAreer: audit adminstr. National Broadcasting Co. Inc., Los Angeles; honors: SPOONE Award 1977; Acctg. Awd., USC; listed Who's Who Among Exec. Women in Business, Who's Who Among Amer. Coll. Students (1977), Who's Who Among Amer. H.S. Students (1973); mem: Amer. Inst. CPAs, Calif. Soc. CPAs, Amer. Film Inst., USC Accounting Circle, USC Gen. Alumni Assn., USC Sch. of Bus. Dean's Adv. Bd. 1976-77, Geta Gamma Sigma, Beta Alpha Psi, Smithsonian Assocs., Amer. Museum of Natural Hist., Town Hall of Calif., Internat. Platform Assn.; Democrat; Catholic; rec: racquetball, body building, cooking. Res: 717 Raymond Ave, Santa Monica 90405

SAFA, BAHRAM, civil engineer; b. May 15, 1941, Abadan, Iran, nat. 1978; s. Ghassem and Sekineh (Khaki) S.; m. Nahid Araji, 1966; children: Shari, b. 1967; Sarah, b. 1973; Susan, b. 1979; edn: BSc, Abadan Inst. of Tech., Iran 1965; MBA, State Univ. of NY, Albany, 1967; Cert. Engring. Mgmt. in Constrn., Univ. Calif. 1982; lic. Gen. Building Contractor 1982; Cert. in Constrn. Mgmt., ASCE 1982; Reg. Civil Engr., Calif. 1983. Career: civil engr. VTN Engineers, Los Angeles 1980--; constrn. coordinator Security Pacific Bank, L.A. 1979-80; asst. v.p. constrn., Internat. Housing Ltd., Westport, Conn. 1975-79; designer and field engr. Myrick and Chevalier, Albany, NY 1971-75; project engr. Rist-Frost Engring., Glens Falls, NY 1970-71; project engr. National Iranian Oil Co., Iran 1965-70; mng. dir./mem. bd. dirs. Internat. Housing Ltd., Iran Division; mem: Amer. Concrete Inst. 1979-81, Assn. of MBA Execs. (student mem. 1973-75); publs: sev. research papers on low-cost housing systems for use in other countries; Republican; rec: research, cultural activities. Res: 1694 Fair Ave Simi Valley 93063 Ofc: VTN Engineers, 5919 Van Nuys Blvd Van Nuys 91401

SAFARJAN, PAULA TINDER, psychologist; b. Sept. 7, 1946, Butte, Mont.; d. Layton Eugene and Sonya (Romantum) Tinder; m. William Safarjan, May 26, 1978; edn: AB in psychol., CSU San Diego 1972, MA in psychol., 1976; EdD in ednl. psychol., Rutgers Univ. 1980; Calif. lic. psychologist 1983. Career: branch locations analyst So. Calif. 1st Nat. Bank, San Diego 1967-69; economic analyst Fotomat Corp., S.D. 1969-72; teaching asst. CSUSD 1972/3 and Rutgers Univ. 1973/4; research asst., NIMH grantee, Trenton State Coll., NJ 1975-77; district psychometrist Woodbridge (NJ) Township School Dist., 1977-80; staff psychologist Porterville (Calif.) State Hosp., 1980--; awards: Phi Kappa Phi 1972, Grad. Sch. of Edn. Alumni Assn. Scholarship 1974/5, Charles Sumner Crow Award 1975/6; mem: Soc. for Research in Ch. Dev. 1974-80; Amer. Psychol. Assn. 1975-80; NY Acad. of Scis. 1975-80; AAMD 1983-; Calif. State Psych. Assn. 1983-; San Joaquin Psychol. Assn. 1984-; publs. in profl., med. journals; papers presented Eastern Psychol. Assn. 1976, Western Psychol. Assn. 1979; Democrat; Prot.; rec: calligraphy, cooking. Res: 1704 W. Olive Ave, No. 108, Porterville 93257 Ofc: Porterville State Hosp., Box 2000, Porterville 93258

SAFAVI-FARD, M. HOSSEIN, civil engineer; b. Feb. 4, 1941, Tehran, Iran; Calif. resident since 1982; s. Mohamad and Razieh Safavi-Fard; m. Parizad, Feb. 1, 1964; children: Kay, b. 1967, Yasi, b. 1970, Ali, b. 1975; edn: BSCE, CSU Los Angeles 1963; MS in C.E., CSU Northridge 1982. Career: constrn. mgr. Pan American Oil Co., Kharg Island, Iran 1963-64; chief of Structrl. Design Branch Iranian Air Force (engr. mgmt.) 1965-74, chief of Technical Ofc. (engr. mgmt.) 1975-77, chief of Airport & Spl. Project (engr. mgmt.) 1977-79; vice pres. of Ops., Maaps Constrn. & Dev. Inc., Beverly Hills, Calif. 1980--; asst. prof. CSUN 1981; civil engr. cons. to CEMACO Consultants Inc. (Iran), IMER Consultant Inc. (Iran), 1967-78; mem: ASCE, Calif. Soc. of Profl. Engrs., Masonry Inst. of Calif., Am. Concrete Inst., So. Calif. Chpt. ACI, Am. Inst. of Steel Constrn., Wood Preservers Inst., Nat. Assn. of Gen. Contrs., Structural Engrs. Assn. of So. Calif. (assoc. mem.); clubs: Family Fitness Ctr., Iranian Comm. Ctr.; rec: racquetball. Res: 922 Stanford St Santa Monica 90603 Ofc: Maaps Construction & Development Inc., 9460 Wilshire Bl, Ste. 710, Beverly Hills 90212

SAFIR, PAVITTAR S., financial executive; b. March 12, 1936, Amritsar, India, nat. 1980; s. Assa Singh and Jaswant (Kaur) Safir; m. Anne Marie Geffray, Apr. 3, 1971; 2 sons: Karan Edward, b. 1972, Philip Jeffrey, b. 1984; edn: BA, Univ. of Panjab 1956, MA, 1958, acad. dip., Univ. of London 1968. Career: chief operating ofcr. Nat. Cadet Corps (First Panjab Batt.) 1959-65; tchr. Inner London Ednl. Authority, 1967-71; sr. vice pres. adminstrn. Reinsurance Facilities Corp., Los Angeles 1972--, dir. 1979-; dir. RFC Intermediaries, Inc. 1979-. Mem: Fin. Execs. Inst., Planning Execs. Inst. Rec: photog. Res: 422 S. Lapeer Dr. Beverly Hills 90211 Ofc: Reinsurance Facilities Corp. 2020 Century Park E., Ste. 1610, Los Angeles 90067

SAGO, PAUL EDWARD, university president; b. July 5, 1932, Frankclay, Mo.; s. John and Mabel (White) S.; m. Audrey Dane, Aug. 23, 1952; children: Bruce Edward, b. 1955, Dane Bradford, b. 1959; edn: BS, Findlay Coll. 1953; MS, St. Francis Grad. Sch. 1964; PhD, Walden Univ. 1976. Career: pastor Bloom Center First Church of God, N. Baltimore, OH 1952-55, Anthony Wayne Ch. of God, Ft. Wayne, OH 1955-64; dir. of devel., Findlay (OH) Coll. 1964-67, Hiram (OH) Coll. 1967-68; v.p. Fin. Affairs/treas. Anderson (IND) Coll. 1968-76; pres. Azusa Pacific Univ., Azusa, CA 1976--; condr. seminars, frequent speaker; mem: Am. Assn. for Higher Edn., Assn. of Governing Boards of Colls. and Univs., Christian Coll. Coalition, Council for Advance. and Support of Edn., Council of Independent Colls., Internat. Platform Assn., Nat. Assn. of Coll. and Univ. Bus. Officers, Nat. Assn. of Fund Raiser, Nat. Assn. of Independent Colls. and Univs.; club: University (Pasadena); Ch. of God, Anderson, Ind. Res: 19749 E. Cameron Covina 91724, POB 4336 Ofc: Azusa Pacific University, Citrus and Alosta, Azusa 91702

SAHI, PARVESH KUMAR, restaurateur/real estate broker; b. May 22, 1943, Lahore, W. Pakistan; s. J. P. Singh and Indra (Rani) Sahi; m. Jeannette J., Nov. 17, 1973; chil: Savita, Sanya, Parvesh Jr.; edn: AA/cert., Hotel & Restaurant Sch., City Coll. of S.F. 1969; Anthonys Real Estate Sch. 1976; lic. real estate broker, Calif. Career: food service dir. ARA Food Services, Burlingame 1970-72; food service dir. Alameda County 1973; owner/mgr. North India Restaurant, San Francisco 1974--; realtor/owner Sahi Real Estate Co., S.F. 1976--; restaurant cons. Honors: rated best Indian restaurant in Bay Area (3 stars), S.F.Chronicle. Mem. S.F. Real Estate Board, S.F. Historical Soc. Works: estab. Meals on Wheels Pgm. in Santa Clara, 1970. Rec: golf, tennis, tching. Indian cuisine. Address: North India Restaurant Inc. 3131 Webster St. San Francisco 94123

SAINZ, GRETCHEN RUTHARA, corporation president; b. Dec. 18, 1942, Canton, Ohio; d. Dr Theodore J. and Ruthara (Artz) Dodd; m. Richard Climes, Jan. 14, 1961; children: Deborah, b. 1961; Tim, b. 1965; m. Ed Sainz, Dec. 10, 1978; edn: Bus. Coll. Canton Actual 1960. Career: sales Union Metal Mfg., Canton, 1961-66; purchasing Dynair Electronics and ELgar Corp. 1966-70; founder/prop. Ohm Spun (first woman mfr.'s rep. in electronics in US), 1970-78; distrbn. mgmt./ gen. mgr. Jaco, and gen. sales mgr. Arrow Electronics 1978-82; founder/ pres. Ohm Spun Electronics 1982--; rec: profl. musician (5 instruments), sing. write. Res: 10565 Arbor Park Pl San Diego 92131 Ofc: Ohm Spun Electronics Inc., 9560 Black Mountain Rd San Diego 92126

SAINZ, RON A., builder/development co. executive; b. Dec. 29, 1934, Lone Pine, Ca.; s. Albert L. and Thelma S. (Baker) S.; m. Charlene Brakebill, Apr. 21, 1956; children: Ronald Jr., b. 1953, Karen J., b. 1958, Libby A., b. 1961.; lic. real estate broker, Calif. 1963-. Career: salesman Pepsi Cola Bottling Co., Calif. 1952-55; salesman Coca Cola Bottling Co., Bakersfield 1955-60; sales mgr. Reed & Thompson Realty, Bakersfield 1960-65; exec. vice pres./mktg. dir. Reeder Corps. USA, 1965--, bd. dir. 7 Reeder Corps.; v.p. 15 Reeder Corps.; pres. 2 Sainz Corps.; rec: numismatics. Res: 48-630 Monroe Ave Indio 92201 Ofc: Reeder Corporations, 1830 Brundage Ln Bakersfield 93304

SALA, FRANCES MARIAN, real estate broker; b. Nov. 18, 1928, San Francisco; d. Roy Waldo and Anna Mae (Fitzgerald) Allen; m. Antone Sala, May 28, 1950; children: Shirley Ann Wehe, Richard C. Wehe; edn: LVN (voc. nurse), Hayward Coll.; spl. courses Chabot Coll., Olone Coll.; lic. real estate broker, Calif. Career: lic. vocational nurse 1950-70, Doctors Hosp. 1965-70; real estate broker Aramas Realtos 1980-82, Century 21 Aramas Realtors 1983--; instr. real estate seminars; mem: Calif. L.V.N. Assn., realty assns.; orgns: Crippled Chil., Girl Scouts; Republican; Catholic; rec: hiking, golf, skiing.

Res: 140 Teddy Dr. Union City 94587 Ofc: C21 Aramas, 7058 Thornton Ave Newark 94560

SALEH, RICHARD EDWARD, insurance agency owner; b. Aug. 25, 1935, Long Beach; s. Edward Fredrick and Viola (Savage) S.; m. Roberta L. Leach, Nov. 19, 1955; children: Edward, b. 1958, James, b. 1959; edn: pre-law/bus. law, Orange Coast Coll. 1973; grad. Allstate Sch. of Sales and Ins. (Menlo Park); grad. USN Submarine Sch., USN Instructors Sch. Career: semi-pro football fullback, Orange Co. Rhinos two yrs.; baseball and football coach, City of Carson 4 years; stereotyper apprentice Los Angeles Herald (daily newspaper) 1953-57; stereotyper R.W. Ernst Printing Co. 1957-62; prodn. supt. Stereotype Dept. Culver City Evening Star News, 1962-66; ins. agent Allstate Ins. Co., Wilmington 1966-69; district sales mgr. Neighbors of Woodcraft (L.A., San Bernardino, and Riverside Counties), 1969-71; ins. agt./ broker/ agcy. v.p., Mortimer-Saleh and Assocs. Inc., 1971-79; prin. Richard E. Saleh Insurance, Buena Park 1979--; past dir. pub. rels., Calif. Jaycees (3 yrs); past dir. internat. affairs City of Culver City; past mem. City of Carson Plnng. Commn.; awards: Western Regl. champion Kempo-Blackbelt (3 yrs); past pres. Harbor Aquarium Soc. (4 yrs); mil: E5 USN, USNR (8 yrs); rec: swimming, boatin, fishing, radio control models. Res: 13530 Semora Pl Cerritos 90701 Ofc: Richard E. Saleh Ins. 7342 Orangethorpe, A-103, Buena Park 90621

SALEHOMOUM, NADER, electronics engineer; b. Jan. 15, 1953, Tehran, Iran, nat. 1979; s. Mahmoud and Aghdass (Mozaffarian) S.; m. Soudabeh Hafezi, Aug. 25, 1975; children: Negar, b. 1981, Combiz, b. 1983; edn: BS, N.C. State Univ. 1976; MS, CSU San Jose 1978. Career: engr. Amdahl Corp., Sunnyvale 1978-79; senior design engr. Fairchild Systems, San Jose 1979-81; staff engineer/project mgr. Nicolet/Paratronics, Fremont 1981--; instr. Ohlone Coll., Mission Coll., 1982--; honors: Nicolet Jr. Fellow 1983; rec: skiing, fishing. Res: 1439 Torrington Ct San Jose 95120 Ofc: Nicolet/Paratronics, 201 Fourier Ave Fremont 94539

SALES, PHILIP DEL RIO, dentist; b. May 28, 1952, Los Angeles; s. Antonio and Juanita (Del Rio) S.; m. Kathleen Murry, June 22, 1974, children: Anthony, b. 1975, Dominick, b. 1978, Samantha, b. 1980; edn: BA in polit. sci., CSU San Bernardino 1977, BSDS dental scis., UCSF 1981, DDS, 1982. Career: employment devel. office, EDD Ontario, 1975-78; assoc. dentist in Riverside 1982--; dentist in pvt. practice, San Bernardino, 1982--; mem: Amer., Calif., Tri-County dental assns., San Bernardino CofC; mil: sgt. USAF 1971-74; Ind.; Catholic; rec: golf. Res: 6195 Oswego dr Riverside 92506 Ofc: Dr. Philip D. Sales Family Dentistry, 1298 North D Street San Bernardino 92405

SALFITY, CHARLES GEORGE, certified financial planner; b. Feb. 23, 1953, Amman, Jordan, nat. 1974; s. George Khalil and Muhjeh George (Amash) S.; m. Nagma Sheikh, July 14, 1982; edn: AA, El Camino Coll. 1974, BS in mktg. CSU Long Beach 1976; C.F.P. Denver Coll. for Fin. Plnn. 1982; L&D ins. lic., Calif., NASD Reg. Rep., stockbroker. Career: machinist Transequip, El Segundo 1974-75; retail sales K-Mart, Torrance 1975-76; sales rep. Internat. Products Co., Torrance 1977-78; L & D insurance agt. Certified Life of Calif., Sherman Oaks 1978, Ohio State Life, Torrance 1978-79; Reg. Representative, Independent Planning Corp., Torrance 1979--; adult edn. instr. finl. plnng., Cerritos Coll.; mem. Internat. Assn. for Finl. Planners; clubs: Torrance Jaycees, Hawthorne Jaycees (editor), Calif. Jaycees (Dist. Gov.); Catholic; rec: basketball, flying. Res: 14623 Bodger Ave Hawthorne 90250 Ofc: Independent Planning Corp. 21515 Hawthorne Blvd, Ste. 350, Torrance 90503

SALIH, KARIM HADI, manufacturing co. executive; b. Dec. 24, 1933, Sinjar, Iraq; s. Hadi and Nathera (Sulieman) S.; m. Suehayla Al-Naimi, Dec. 24, 1968; children: Reema, b. 1971, Laith, b. 1975, Rana, b. 1977; edn: BA, Univ. Ore. 1967; MA, Golden Gate Univ. 1968; CPA, 1973. Career: with Harold Shein & Co. CPA firm, San Francisco 1974; v.p. fin. & adminstrn. Denticator Co., Brisbane 1974-78; pres. Amera Inc., Novato 1978-80, bd. dirs. 1978-; finl. ofcr. Giltspur Exhibit, Burlingam 1980--; instr. Heald Coll. 1971-73; mem: Arab Amer. University Grad. S.F. Chpt. (bd. 1979-81); Arab Cultural Center (pres. 1982-); Moslem. Res: 737 Bolero Ct Novato 94947 Ofc: Giltspur Exhibit 826 Burlway Dr Burlingame 94010

SALINERO, JOHN HERNANDEZ, corporate executive; b. July 8, 1929, San Leandro; s. Valeriano Zaballos and Teresa (Hernandez) S.; m. Donna, Nov. 8, 1948; children: Richard John, b. 1950; Daniel James, b. 1960; real estate lic., Calif. 1955. Career: salesman De Coite Realty, San Leandro 1955-60; tract mgr. Bevit Enterprises, 1961-63; tract mgr. Perma Bilt Homes, 1964-66; sales mgr. Dame Homes, San Ramon 1966-68; regl. sales mgr. Wm. Lyon Dev., Santa Clara 1969-70; nat. dir. mktg. and sales El Dorado Homes (Kaiser/Aetna) Riverside, 1971-74; v.p. Kelly Snow and Assocs. Palm Springs, 1975-76; bd. chmn. S.F. Realty, Inc., Palm Desert 1977--; bd. chmn. Salinero Petroleum Co.; honors: young man of year 1960, City of San Leandro; mem: No. Calif. Builders Assn. 1969-70, So. Calif. Bldrs. Assn. (mktg. mem.) 1972-74; past chmn. bd. of zoning adjustments 1958-61, and past v.chmn. Planning Commn. 1960-61, City of San Leandro; mil: seaman USN 1947-48; Democrat; Catholic; rec: golf. Address: S.F. Realty, Inc. 74-614 Yucca Tree Dr Palm Desert 92260

SALRIN, ROBERT EUGENE, manufacturing co. president; b. Nov. 16, 1927, Elyria, Ohio; s. Raymond Augustus and Helen Marie (Brucken) S.; m. Mary Jean Kohl, Jan. 3, 1947; children: Robert Eugene, Michael Thomas, Shiela Marie; edn: Fenn Coll. 1950; Reg. Profl. Engr., Calif. Career: chief mfg. engr. Lear, Inc., Santa Monica, Ca. and Elyria, Ohio 1959; mfg. mgr. Litton Industries, Woodland Hills 1959-62; dir. Ops., Northrop Corp., Hawthorne 1962-68;

group vice pres. Internat. Rectifier Corp., El Segundo 1968-70; vice pres. A.C. & C., Inc., Torrance 1970; pres. Industrial Products group, Aeronca, Inc., Montebello 1971-73 and corp. group v.p., Environmental Controls Gp., Aeronca, Inc., Charlotte, N.C. 1973-76; pres. Western Methods Corp., Gardena 1976-77, Dir. 1976-78; gen. mgr. So. Calif. Signal Industries, Carlsbad 1976-77; staff v.p. Mfg., Bourns, Inc., Riverside 1977-78, pres. (subs.) Bourns Instruments, Inc., 1978--, sr. v.p. Technical Products Gp., Bourns, Inc. 1980--; Dir. Commuter Transp. Services, Inc., Los Angeles; mem: APICS, Am. Helicopter Soc., Instrument Soc. of Am., Internat. Electronics Pkg. Soc., Soc. of Mfg. Engrs.; clubs: Victoria, Canyon Crest Country, Elks; Republican; Catholic. Res: 6718 Rycroft Dr Riverside 92506 Ofc: Bourns Instruments, Inc., 6135 Magnolia Ave Riverside 92506

SAMBERG, HELEN CLEMONS, business owner; b. Jan. 13, 1933, NY, NY; d. Adrian J. and Marie Josephine (La Salle) La Grua; 1 son, John Mark Samberg, b. 1955; edn: BA, Atlanta So. Univ. 1963, MA, 1964; lic. private investigator, Calif. 1975. Career: past legal resrch. for Stephan P. Ladas, Atty. and Patent expert, NYC; staff of Nelson Rockefeller, NY 1963-66; owner Samberg Legal Service (finl. systems advisor and research for banks, ins. cos., brokers), Calif. 1969--; writer short stories (J. Azaria, Can.) 1963-65; accomplished pianist; instr. metaphysical teachings; Republican (Presdtl. Task Force 1980-, US Senatl. Club); Catholic. Address: Samberg Legal Service, 3901 Los Feliz Blvd Los Angeles 90027

SAMELSON, JEROME VICTOR, optometrist; b. Mar. 17, 1947, St. Ottilien, Ger.; s. William and Rosalie (Neiberg) S.; m. Barbara, June 9, 1974; children: Hannah Rose, b. 1981, Aaron Isaac, b. 1982; edn: BS in biol., honors, Univ. of Ill. 1969; OD, honors UC Berkeley 1974. Career: optometrist Law Vision Rehabilitation Clinic, VA Hosp., Palo Alto 1975; pvt. practice of optometry; San Jose, 1975, Susanville, Ca. 1976--; Fellow Am. Acad. of Optometry; mem. Kiwanis; rec: photog., equestrian, fishing. Res: 505 Wildwood Way Susanville 96130 Ofc: Dr. Jerome Samelson, 1825 Main St Susanville 96130

SAMMS, JAMES NEWELL, organizational effectiveness consultant, b. Oct. 5, 1946, Grand Junction, CO; s. Harry Newell and Virginia Lee (Miller) S., m. Linda Cassidy, Mar. 11, 1981; children: Matthew, b. 1967; Christine, b. 1969; Dawn, b. 1970; Christopher, b. 1973; Shiloh, b. 1979; edn: AA, Hawaii Pacific Coll. 1983; grad. consultant training program, US Army Organizational Effectiveness Ctr. & Sch. 1983; career: US Army 1965--; various med./nursing positions 1965-80; wardmaster, Tripler Army Med Ctr., Hawaii 1980-81, chief wardmaster, 1982-83; staff officer Organizational Effectiveness Ctr. & Sch., Fort Ord; pres. Samms Assoc. (consulting firm), Monterey Carmel 1983; orgns: Masonic Lodge #579, Ft. Benning, GA, Scottish Rite Bodies Honolulu; Timemasters, Honolulu; mil: 1st Sgt. US Army 1965--, meritorious svc., good conduct, humanitarian svc. medals; Republican; Mormon; rec: tennis, personal computing, fishing, hunting; Res: 811 Bayonet Cir Fort Ord 93941 Ofc: USA Organizational Effectiveness Ctr. & Sch., Attn: ATXW-RMA-TD, Ft Ord 93941

SAMUELS, S. S., real estate broker; b. Dec. 8, 1945, San Francisco; s. Louis Cornblith and Ida (Klebanoff) S.; edn: BA, UC Berkeley 1967; num. spl. courses in real estate, bus., law; Calif. lic. real estate agt. 1977, R.E. broker 1979. Career: involved in the Natural Foods movement, 1967-71, assoc. with Rock Island Line and You Are What You Eat; co-prod. musical festivals, 1970s; co-founder sev. Vajrayana Buddhist & ecclectic churches; real estate sales, Mill Valley 1977-78, independent broker dba S & S Rlty., 1978--; S.S.Samuels Rlty., 1979--; Dir. Four Corners Foundation; honors: BSA Eagle Scout 1958; mem: Marin Co. Bd. of Realtors, Calif. Assn. of Realtors, Nat. Assn. of Realtors; works: Four Corners Brochure (1983); Vajrayana tantric art (paintings); introduced methods for awakening the intuition through yoga, meditation and vision, 1966-, active in preservation of the Vajrayana classical traditions; mem. Vajrayana Ch. of Am. & Internat.; rec: sports, dance, yoga, art, philosophy. Res: 30 Juanita Way San Francisco 94127 Ofc: S.S.Samuels Rlty, POB 1940, San Anselmo 94960

SANCHEZ, ROBERT, fire protection co. president; b. May 23, 1953, Los Angeles; s. Ignacio B. and Amelia M. (Valcan) S.; m. Susan Viramontes, Nov. 2, 1975; edn: Rio Hondo Coll. 1971-72; cert. Fire Extinguisher Tech., CSULA 1977; lic. State Fire Marshal Office 1980, 84. Career: service tech. Fire Safety Industries, Anaheim 1975-76, All-Fire Control, Vernon 1976-78; mgr. J & M Fire Protection, Montebello 1978-80; pres. Fire Prevention Services, Commerce 1980 ; mem: Indsl. Council of Commerce, Small Minority Bus., Southern Regl. Council of L.A.; Christian; rec: photog., ennis. Res: 11574 East Beverly Blvd Whittier 90602 Ofc: Fire Prevention Services, 2202 So Atlantic Blvd Commerce 90040

SANDEL, DAVID JOHN, test applications engineer; b. Aug. 8, 1956, Oyster Bay, L.I., NY; s. David Arthur and Charlotte Bertha (Williams) S.; m. Carol Lynn Jolimay, July 26, 1980; children: David Wm., b. 1981, Daniel Arthur, b. 1984; edn: Bach. in Electronic Engrg., Ohio Inst. of Tech. 1977; var. spl. courses. Career: electronic tech. 1977-79, test engr. 1980-81, test engr. supr. 1981-82, sr. test applications engr., Fairchild, San Jose 1982--; mem. Heritage Found.; Republican (Presdtl. Task Force 1981, Nat. Repub. Congl. Com. 1981); Free Methodist (treas. 1973-); rec: bowling, softball, computers, wilderness backpacking. Res: 277 Watson Dr, No. 1, Campbell 95008 Ofc: Fairchild DTS, 1725 Technology Dr San Jose 95115

SANDERS, GARY ALAN, maintenance equipment co. president; b. July 12, 1936, Detroit, Mich.; s. Elmer Theodore and Christie Eugenia (Hamilton)

Lusty. Career: file clk., cost acct., asst. to the controller, Foote & Davies, Atlanta, Ga. 1953-63; office mgr. Curtis Equip. Co., San Francisco 1963-67; office mgr. San Francisco Equip. Co., S.F. 1967-75, gen. mgr. 1975-82, pres. S.F. Equip. Co., San Leandro 1982--; mem. San Leandro CofC; mil: sgt. Georgia Nat. Guard; Republican; rec: painting. Res: 767 J Street Lathrop 95330 Ofc: San Francisco Equipment Co., Inc. 14361 Catalia St San Leandro 94577

SANDERSON, GEORGE ROBERT, food scientist; b. Feb. 14, 1942, Galashiels, Scotland; s. George and Margaret Harkness (Outerson) S.; m. Sylvia Bell, Sept. 9, 1967; children: Alan, b. 1970, Richard, b. 1974; edn: BS (1st Class hons.), Edinburgh Univ. 1964, PhD, 1967; Chartered Chemist, Fellow Royal Soc. of Chem., London (C.Chem. FRSC) 1984. Career: postdoctoral fellow McGill Univ., Montreal, Can. 1967-69; research assoc. Inst. Ronzoni, Milan, Italy 1969-70; food scientist Unilever Research, Colworth House, Sharnbrook, Bedfordshire, Eng. 1970-79; tech. rep. Kelco/AIL Internat., London 1979-81, mgr. Food Dev. Section, Kelco, San Diego 1981--; awards: Edinburgh Pharmaceutical Industries Prize, 1964; works: 25 publs. (sci. papers and patents) 1965-; rec: music, golf, tennis. Res: 2813 El Rastro Ln Carlsbad 92008 Ofc: Kelco, 8355 Aero Dr San Diego 92123

SANDERSON, JOYCE ANN, author; b. June 19, 1936, Vandergrift, Pa.; d. Louis and Gilda Mildred (La Cava) Pugliese; m. Charles Sanderson, Feb. 2, 1958; children: Michele, b. 1959, Charles, b. 1960; edn: BA, San Jose St. Univ. 1958, grad. work inc.; real estate broker, Anthony's Sch. of R.E., 1967; profl. model J.J. of California 1981; minister Universal Life Ch. 1983; Writers Digest Fiction 1983. Career: administrv. asst. rocket research, Service Bureau Corp., San Jose 1960; realtor/owner Sanderson Realty, San Jose 1970-78; pres. Conner/Sanderson Publications, Los Gatos 1980--; author: Life Love Laugh (1980), Why Are You Here Now (1981), Rainbow Path (1982), Miracles to Share (1983), fiction novel in progress; honors: service award, Am. Cancer Soc. 1981; mem. AAUW, Cupertino Writers, Am. Cancer Soc., Miracles Group, Beyond War; Republican; Catholic; sci. of Mind; rec: tennis, bowling, skiing. Res: 191 Altura Vista Los Gatos 95030

SANDHU, IQBAL SINGH, real estate broker; b. Dec. 1, 1928, Patiala, Punjab, India; s. Beant Singh and Gurbachan Kaur (Birring) S.; m. Rajinder-Raj, July 1, 1978; children: Davinder, b. 1964, Ravinder, b. 1965, Baljinder, b. 1968; edn: civil engr. Thomson Engring. Sch. 1949; struc. engr., Batetersea Coll. 1959; real estate cert., Mt. San Antonio Coll. 1982; Calif. lic. R.E. Broker, R.E. Commnr.; R.E. Teaching Cert., UCLA. Career: civil engineer 1949-54; designer 1960-62; railway engr. 1962-65; senior site engr. 1965-68; prop. Telstar Sports 1968-72; hotelier and restaurateur 1972-78; mng. dir. A.I.Investments (broker/cons. in investments spec. in board & care) 1980--; honors: elected exec. vice pres. India - USA Olympic Reception Com. (1984); Best Top Site Controller 1966; field hockey team London Univ. 1956-58; assoc. mem. Inst. of Structural Engrs. 1960-65; Sikh; rec: field hockey. Res: 313 Banbridge Ave La Puente 91744 Ofc: A.I. Investments, 652 Sunset, Ste. 205, West Covina 91790

SANDHU, TEJINDER SINGH, gynecologist-obstetrician; b. June 9, 1943, Moshi, Tanzania; s. Mall Singh and Gurdial Kaur (Toor) S.; m. Devinder Dhami, Aug. 23, 1970; children: Abhi, b. 1972; Kamlesh, b. 1976; edn: MB, ChB, highest honors, Univ. of East Africa 1968; FRCS (C), McGill Univ., Canada 1978. Career: private medical practice, Kampala, Uganda 1969-72; internship, residency tng. McGill Univ., Montreal 1973-78; pvt. practice in ob.-gyn., Fresno, Calif. 1979--; chief of staff Sanger Hosp., active staff Fresno Comm. Hosp.; mem. Calif. Med. Soc., Fresno Madera Med. Soc.; rec: reading, jogging. Res: 6795 E. Lane, Fresno 93727 Ofc: 2570 Jensen, Ste. 103, Sanger 93657

SANDLER, ELISE BEVERLY ROSENTHAL, artist representative; b. May 29, 1946, NYC; d. Louis and Ruth B. (Dinerstein) Rosenthal; m. Neil Sandler, Nov. 24, 1979; edn: BA, Queens Coll. 1964; MA, Stanford Univ. 1971; postgrad. wk. New York Univ. 1974. Career: elem. school teacher NYC Public School 175, and splty. art tchr., PS 175 and PS 189, 1968-78; artist rep. and advt. sales dir. Push Pin Studio (art studio), NYC 1978-79; owner/ designer/ fabricator Bead-e (jewelry mfg. co.), 1974-80; prin. Rosenthal Represents (artist rep., and photographers), Los Angeles 1979--; co-owner with husband Business Connection (monthly cocktail party bus. to facilitate business contacts); honors: recipient Soc. of Illustrators of Calif. Awards, Soc. of Illustrators in NYC, Illustrators West Awards, Art Directors Club (1980-83); mem. Graphic Artist Guild (1979-), Executive Breakfast Club, So. Calif. Exec. Lunch Club; works: jewelry designs sold to major department stores and boutiques in NYC, Long Is., Maryland, Wash DC, and Pa.; rec: ballet, skiing, sailing. Address: Rosenthal Represents, 3443 Wade St Los Angeles 90066

SANDLIN, BILLIE JEAN, escrow co. executive; b. May 28, 1925, Olympia, Wash.; d. Clarence and Ann Marie (Runing) Pier; m. Donald Sandlin, Mar. 28, 1953; 1 dau., Sharon, b. 1954; edn: AA, Fullerton Jr. Coll. 1944; spl. courses, East L.A. Comm. Coll., 1970s, USC, 1982; Calif. Escrow Assn.: Certified Escrow Ofcr. 1976, Cert. Sr. Escrow Ofcr. 1980, Edn. Achievement Awd. 1982. Career: escrow mgr. Raif Realty Corp., Escrow Div., Montebello 1975-76; gen. mgr. VIP Escrow Svc., Inc. Alhambra 1976-77; escrow mgr. Safeco Title Ins. Co., Los Angeles 1977-81, Stewart Title, L.A. 1981-82, Commonwealth Land Title Co., L.A. 1982--; prior experience: sale escrow ofcr. ten yrs., loan ofcr. four yrs., loan processor three yrs., and four yrs. in sales; mem: Los Angeles Escrow Assn. (pres. elect 1984); Calif. Escrow Assn. (Exec. com. 1983; chmn. of Exhibitors, 1982, 83; chmn. Mktg. Prods. Com. 1983; Profl. Designations Com. 1981-83; Pres.'s Com. 1977; mem. Mazzie, Simmons, Swink

Edn. Fund 1983); Escrow Associates of San Gabriel Valley (pres. 1977); Assn. of Corporate Real Estate Execs.; Century City CofC; British Olympics Orgn.; rec: golf, travel. Res: 1880 Sierra Alta Way Monterey Park 91754 Ofc: Commonwealth Land Title Co. 2049 Century Park East, Ste. 1000, Los Angeles 90067

SANDOVAL, BERNARDO ROBLES, educator; b. Dec. 4, 1941, Juarez, Chihuahua, Mex.; nat. 1966; s. Abel and Rosa (Robles) S.; m. Cecilia Carrillo, Sept. 7, 1962; children: Bernadine, b. 1963, Irene, b. 1966; edn: BA, CSU Los Angeles 1966, MA, 1972; EdD, UCLA 1977; Calif. Educ. credentials: Gen. Adminstrn.; Sec. School Adminstrn.; Gen. Pupil Personnel Svcs.; General Secondary; Gen. Elem.; Comm. Coll. Instr.; Occupational Electronics; Std. Supvsn.; Spl. Secondary I.A. Career: instr. electronics Jordan High Sch. 1966-72, career advisor South Gate & Jordan H. Schs. 1972-73; instr. bilingual edn., Whittier Coll. 1972-3 (summer); cons. Voc. Ed. Programs for the Disadvantaged 1974-76; asst. principal Wilson/Lilncoln Adult Sch. 1976; cons. US Agcy. for Internat. Devel. 1976-77; currently dir. Manpower Program Devel., Los Angeles Unified Sch. District; asst. prof. CSU Long Beach 1978-, CSULA 1981-; awards: postdoc. fellowship Advanced Study Ctr. Ohio State Univ. 1978; 1983 Award for Excellence, Voc. Ed. Services to Students with Spl. Needs; mem: PDK, EPT, CMAA, AMAE (scholarship com. 1978); mem. community advis. com. ELA Occupational Center 1976-; advis. com. Bilingual Edn. Los Nietos Sch. 1979; Catholic; rec: photog. Res: 420 N. Electric Alhambra 91801 Ofc: Los Angeles Unified School District, 1320 W. 3rd St Los Angeles 90017

SANDOVAL, NOE M., manufacturing co. executive; b. Nov. 10, 1952, Durango, Mex.; nat. 1974; parents: Juan and Francisca (Sandoval) Macias; edn: AA, Los Angeles City Coll. 1978; lab. tech. Inst. Tecnol. Dgo. Mex. 1972. Career: var. positions Chuck's Steak House, Hollywood Films Co., Directors Life Ins. Co., 1973-77; salesman Mitchell/Man Inc., Los Angeles 1979-83; asst. mgr. Bruce Eichner Inc., L.A. 1983--; free lance buyer decorative items for the trade; clubs: Extended Opp. Pgm. to Students (LA regl. rep. 1977-78), Internat. Students Club (pres.), LACC Student Body Directors Bur., Latin Club; works: lead actor: Horizons (UCLA grad. student movie 1978), T.V. poetry interpretations; Democrat; Catholic; rec: poetry, music, writing, volleyball. Res: 3332 Hamilton Way Los Angeles 90026 Ofc: Bruce Eichner Inc. 7273 Santa Monica Blvd Los Angeles 90046

SANDS, MICHAEL, baked goods mfg. co. executive; b. Dec. 14, 1945, Boston, Mass.; s. Joseph and Frances (Ross) Shapiro; edn: Amer. Internat. Coll. 1964-65, Boston Univ. 1966-67. Career: started modeling, appearing in fashion mags. and T.V. commls., Boston area 1968-, acting role in motion picture The Boston Strangler (20th Century Fox) 1968; modeling wk., NYC 1968-72, and student, Neighborhood Playhouse 1968-70; actor, T.V. & films, at MGM, Universal, Los Angeles area 1978; founder/pres. C'est Cheese-cake Inc. (designer line of baked goods found in frozen food sections of all Ralphs, Vons, Hughes mkts.), 1978--; honors: Hon. Deputy Sheriff, Boston, Mass. 1973; mem: SAG 1968-, Actors Equity 1972-, Am. Fedn. of T.V. & Radio Artists; mil: pvt. US Army 1963; Democrat; Jewish; rec: skiing, ice hockey, sailing, tennis. Ofc: C'est Cheese-cake, Inc. 8422-1/2 West Third St Los Angeles 90048

SANDS, MONTY GAIL, real estate broker; b. Aug. 21, 1941, Tulare, Calif.; s. C. E. and Katherine Leadora (McDonald) S.; m. Beatrice Machado, Mar. 15, 1969; children: Lori, b. 1961, Kurt, b. 1963, Sheri, b. 1964, (stepdaus.) Susan and Sandra, b. 1960; edn: AA, Coll. of Sequoias 1971; Calif. lic. real estate broker. Career: sgt. Tulare Co. Sheriff's Office, 1965-74; real estate sales agt. 1974-, broker/owner Sands Realty, Visalia 1979--; part-time counselor with Tulare Co. Probation Dept.; recipient sev. awards, Tulare Co. 4-H Club; mem: Visalia Bd. of Realtors; Nat., Calif. Assn. of Realtors; Elks; mil: A/2c USAF 1961-64; Republican; Catholic; rec: politics. Address: Sands Realty, 926 S. Watson, Visalia 93277

SANFORD, DELORES A., computer software co. executive; b. Apr. 4, 1937, Birmingham, Ala.; d. Arnold W. and Nora Ophelia (Montgomery) S.; 1 son: Patrick Dana Carson, b. 1960; edn: BS, Univ. Alabama 1958; MBA, Pepperdine Univ. 1976; career: systems analyst US Dept. Agriculture, New Orleans and Wash. D.C. 1962-65; mgmt. analyst First Nat. City Bank, NYC 1965-68; mgr. fin. systems UC Berkeley Systemswide Offices 1968-73; acctg. officer UCLA, Westwood 1973-76; bus. mgr. Marin Comm. College Dist., Kentfield 1976-79; v.p. planning and adm. Integral Systems, Inc., 1979-83, v.p. profl. svcs. div., Walnut Creek 1983--; lectr. in mgmt. St. Mary's Coll. 1980--; cons. in finance, mgmt., and payroll to Federal Reserve Bd. 1965, Marin Muni. Water Dist. 1979-80, UCLA 1980-81; guest lectr. Sloam Sch. of Mgmt. MIT 1984; awards: chair Calif. Comm. Coll. Commn. on Plant and Facilities 1979; Comm. Adv. Com. for Aeronautical Programs, MCCD, Marin County Coll. Dist. 1979-80; Bd. Resolution of Outstanding Contbns., MCCD and Marin Muni. Water Dist. 1979-80. Mem: Math and Sci. Network 1979-; bd. mem. MIWOK Museum 1979; Women's Polit. Caucus; Commonwealth Club, 1977-83; publs: case study in increasing employee productivity, 1976; ICP 1984, Human Resource Systems: The Need for a Mgmt. Policy; Democrat; Protestant; rec: pilot (AOPA mem.), Skiing; Res: 710 LaFayette St Martinez 94553 Ofc: Integral Systems Inc., 165 Lennon Ln Walnut Creek 94598

SANFORD, WALTER SCOTT, real estate broker/consultant; b. Mar. 5, 1956, Pasadena; s. Harry Wm. and Nadine Helen (Grayson) S.; m. CathyLyn Rossi, July 12, 1980; edn: AA, Pasadena City Coll. 1977; BS, honors, USC 1979; lic. real estate broker, Calif. 1979; certified R.E. Cons., Nat. Inst. of R.E. Consultants 1980. Career: pres. Walter Sanford and Associates (oil & gas leases), El Monte 1976-79; pres. N & S Enterprises (R.E. contractor) 1977-80; assoc.

broker/cons. JTM Brokerage, Long Beach 1980--; lectr. Long Beach City Coll. 1984-; honors: investment counselor of year 1983, Long Beach Inv. & Exchg. Group 1983; Top Selling/ Top Listing Broker 1980, 81, 82, 83 JTM Brokerage; mem: Nat., Calif. Assn. of Realtors; Long Beach Dist. Bd. of Realtors; L.B. Inv. and Exchg. Group; Internat. R.E. Fedn.; L.B. Area CofC; Beta Gamma Sigma; Kappa Alpha Order; publs: columnist for local newspaper; Conservative; Prot.; rec: real estate. Res: 275 Park Ave Long beach 90803 Ofc: JTM Brokerage, 312 Redondo Ave 90814

SAN JUAN, JAVIER, company executive, b. Apr. 21, 1951, Manila Philippines; citizen of Spain, US Permanent Resident; s. Guillermo and Maria Del Carmen (Galatas) S.; m. Elaine Meyers, Aug. 23, 1974; 1 dau: Cristina, b. 1981; edn: CSU Long Beach 1971-72; BA, San Francisco State Univ. 1974; spl. courses US Brewing Acad. 1980, Stanford Univ. Grad. Sch. Bus. 1981,82, UC Berkeley Sch. Bus. 1984. Career: with Ansor Corp.: sales rep. Hawthorne 1971-72, statistician San Francisco 1973-75; exec. asst. 1975-77; v.p./gen. mgr. San Miguel Internat., Brisbane 1977-82, pres./treas., 1982--; bd. dir. San Miguel Internat. 1977--; officer Staats Internat., San Francisco 1982--; mem. bd. dirs. Philippine-Am. CofC, NY 1982-; mem. Adv. Council, San Francisco State Univ. 1983-; mem. Soc. of Graduates US Brewing Acad. 1980-; mem. San Francisco Advt. Club; mem. Round Hill CC, Presidio Officer's Club, Long Beach Police Officer's Assn, Casa De Espana (Los Angeles), Magic Island (Newport Bch); Catholic; rec: autos., audio/visual equip., sports. Res: 3147 Hambletonian Ln Walnut Creek 94598 Ofc: San Miguel Internat. (USA), 100 West Hill Dr Brisbane 94005

SANTILLAN, ANTONIO, real estate, motion picture finance executive; b. May 8, 1936, Buenos Aires, Argentina, nat. 1966; s. Gillermo Spika and Raphaella C. (Abaladejo) S.; children: Andrea, b. 1964, Miguel, b. 1967, Marcos, b. 1970; edn: grad. Morgan Park Mil. Acad., Chgo. 1954; Coll. of William & Mary, 1958; Calif. lic. Building Contr. 1973, Real Estate Broker 1975. Career: (past) actor in summer stock and the San Diego Old Globe Theatre; writer/prod./dir. The Glass Cage (motion picture); asst. in chg. of prodn., (responsible for Ford comml. prodn.) Wilding Studios, Chgo.; co-writer "Donner Party" with Jean Renoir; dir. west coast premiere of two one act plays by Ray Bradbury at Desilu Playhouse; co-writer "Dirty Mary/Crazy Harry" for 20th Century Fox (1973), "Viva Knievel" for Irwin Allen and Warners (1978); (current) pres. Adams Finl. Services, Los Angeles (co. is producing his screenplay "Khyber Passage" in Mex. & Ariz. 1984); designer/ bldr.: The Upstairs/Downstairs Gallerie (L.A.), The Gallerie in Westwood, Alandale's (Westwood), residences for Neil Diamond, Carroll Rosenbloom, Joe Barbera, others: contbg. writer to Apartment Times, Apartment Age, Apartment Owner/Builder on fin. and mkt. conditions; recipient awards as American rep. at San Francisco Film Festival and Cork Ireland Film Fest. 1961; film reviews in Playboy and Time Mag. (1973), building project rev. in Home Mag. Section, L.A. Times (1973); mem: Writer's Guid of Am., Beverly Hills Bd. of Realtors (Income/Inv. Div. steering com.), Westside Realty Bd. (bd. dirs.); mil: active duty, Spl. Svcs. USNR 1959; rec: tennis, skiing. Address: Adams Financial Svcs. 425 N. Alfred St Los Angeles 90048

SANTOS, ABELARDO BANGCO, JR., civil engineer, real estate broker; b. Jan. 21, 1946, Bataan, Philippines; s. Abelardo Canlas, Sr. and Constancia Zabala (Bangco) S.; m. Corazon Eugenio, Oct. 28, 1972; children: Alvin b. 1974, Bernard b. 1976, Brian b. 1982; edn: BSCE, Mapua Inst. of Technology 1967. Calif. lic. General Contractor, lic. Real Estate Broker, Registered Profl. Civil Engr. Career: civil engr. Philippine Rock Products Inc., Metro Manila 1967-69; civil engr. Giffels and Assocs., Toronto, Canada 1969-72; project engr. ACS Constrn. Co., Bataan, Phil. 1972-74; cost engr. So. California Edison, Los Angeles 1974--; R.E. broker/owner Key Realtors, Glendale 1982--; mem: Nat. Assn. of Realtors; Profl. Engineers EIT; Am. Assn. of Cost Engrs.; Republican; Catholic; rec: fishing, bowling, basketball. Res: 3217 Sagamore Way Los Angeles 90065 Ofc: Key Realtors 118 E. Glenoaks Blvd Glendale 91207

SANTOS, AQUILINO BOCOBO, realty co. owner; b. Dec. 26, 1907, San Nicolas, Ilocos Norte, Phil.; s. Valeriano S. and Margarita (Bocobo) S.; m. Juanita Peralta Cortina, Sept. 8, 1946; 1 son, Michael A., b. 1959; edn: AA, San Diego St. Coll. (now SDSU) 1930s; law stu. Cosmopolitan Coll. of Law, Manila 1948-51; BA, Calif. Western Univ. (now US Internat. Univ.) 1955, MA, 1957. Career: came to USA in 1927; counselor, contact rep., US Vets. Adm., 1946-52; real estate, life & disability ins. broker/owner, San Diego 1952-66, 1975--; empl. counselor, State of Calif. Employment Devel. Dept., S.D. 1965-74; mem: founder Philippine Am. Bus. & Profl. Soc. of S.D. Co. (achievement award 1977); US Internat. Univ. Alumni Assn. (bd.); co-founder The Phil. Am. Community of S.D. County, Inc.; mil: sgt. US Army 1943-45; mem. Filipino Am. Democratic Club; Catholic; rec: tennis, horticulture. Res: 827 26th St San Diego 92102 Ofc: A.B.Santos Realty, 3308 Midway Dr San Diego 92110

SAPIRO, JEROME (SR.), lawyer; b. July 15, 1915, San Francisco; s. Philip Herman and Belle (Jalumstein) S.; m. Mary E., July 22, 1940; chil: Jerome, Jr. b. 1942; Barbara E. (Collins), b. 1946; Denis, b. 1949; Stephan, b. 1951; Dolores M., b. 1954; edn: AB (highest hons. in hist.), UC Berkeley 1936; LLB (1st in class), Hastings Coll. of Law 1939; admitted to practice, Supreme Ct., Calif. 1939; admitted to practice in Fed. Cts., US Supreme Ct., Bd. of Immigration Appeals. Career: gen. practice of law with Judge Milton D. Sapiro (uncle), 1939-42; sole practitioner, spec. wills, probate, trusts, conservatorships, 1946--; past bd.dirs. French Hosp. Med. Ctr. Awards: John Bell Mhoon scholarship and Legal Bibliography prize, Hastings; Phi Beta Kappa; Legion of Honor (Argen), France; Audie Murphy Achievement Awd., Soc. of 3rd Inf. Div. AUS 1983; Silver Beaver, BSA; St. George Awd. for svc. to youth, S.F. Archdiocese. Mem: Calif. State Bar, S.F. Bar Assn.(Pub. Def., Juvenile Ct. coms.), Assn. of US Army, Am. Legion, Retired Ofcrs Assn., BSA; nat. pres. Soc. of 3rd Inf. Div. 1954-5; pres. Sunset Comm. Improvement Club; incorporated West of Twin Peaks Cub Softball League, Troop Service Assn., and a youth football team. mil: US Army 1942-46, col. USAR, ret. 1974, decorated 10 battle stars, 5 beachhead landing arrowhds., Bronze star w/cluster, merit. svc., presdtl. unit cit., Rhin et Danube, Croix le Guerre w/dbl. palm, Victory, Occupation, Am. Def. medals; Republican; Catholic; rec: gardening; res: 66 Sotelo Ave San Francisco 94116 ofc: 100 Bush St., Ste.520, San Francisco 94104.

SAPUTO, PETER T., lawyer; b. July 2, 1954, Walnut Creek; s. Peter and Magdalena (Paladino) S.; m. Nancy Southworth, June 4, 1983; edn: BS, UC Berkeley 1976; JD, Golden Gate Univ. 1979, MBA, 1979, LLM in taxation, 1980; admitted to practice Calif. State Bar 1979, US District Ct. 1979, US Tax Ct. 1980; Calif. lic. real estate broker 1983. Career: extern Calif. Supreme Court, San Francisco 1978-79; atty. law firm Van Voorhis & Skaggs, Walnut Creek 1979-83; partner law firm Little & Saputo, Walnut Creek 1983--; chmn. Tax Sect., Contra Costa County Bar Assn.; chmn. No. Calif. Bldg. Indus. Assn. Dept. of Real Estate Task Force; publs: art., Calif. Cont. Edn. of the Bar, 10/82; Republican; rec: skiing, tennis, racquetball. Res: 3181 Stanwood Ln Lafayette 94549 Ofc: Little & Saputo, 49 Quail Court, Ste. 311, Walnut Creek 94596

SARAFIAN, ARMEN, university president; b. Mar. 5, 1920, Van Nuys; s. Kevork and Lucy (Gazarian) S.; div.; children: Norman, Winston, Joy; edn: AB (magna cum laude) La Verne Coll. 1940; MA, Claremont Grad. Univ. 1947; PhD, USC 1967; LLD (hon), La Verne Coll. 1967. Career: tchr. in elementary and secondary edn., chmn. Banning High Sch. English Dept., five yrs.; tchr. Pasadena Jr. Coll. Dist., 1947-51; coordinator of sec. and jr. coll. edn., Pasadena City Schs., 1951-59; adminstrv. dean for instr., Pasadena City Coll. 1959-65, pres., and supt. of Pasa. Area Comm. Coll. Dist., 1965-76; pres. Univ. of La Verne, 1976--; cons. to bus., indus. and govt., adj. prof. Comm. Coll. Adminstrn., USC, 1968-78; summer faculty var. colls. and univs. incl. UCLA, Occidental, Claremont, CSCs, 30 yrs. Pres. Calif. Conservation Council, 1966-68; trustee La Verne Coll. 1969-76; mgmt. team Univ. Alaska Statewide System, 1977-78; founder, adult adviser Pasadena Area Youth Council; founder Am. Armenian Internat. Coll. Bd. 1972; founder, exec. com. Pasa. Hall of Sci. Project, 1965-76; mem. USC Educare. Honors incl. recognition awards, Calif. Conservation Council 1964, Omicron Mu Delta 1965, USC 1972, Salvation Army 1975, Arthur Noble Gold Medal, Pasadena City Bd. Dirs. 1976. Mem. Pasadena Area Sch. Trustees Assn. (founder), La Verne CofC (pres. 1978), Pasa. CofC (v.p. 1972, hon. life), Native Sons of Golden West, Pasa. Hist. Soc.; New Century Club of Pasa. (pres. 1975-76); clubs: Kiwanis (v.p., Pasa. 1971), Oneonta, University. Ch. of the Brethren. Res: POB 1624, Glendora 91740 Ofc: University of La Verne, 1950 Third St, La Verne 91750

SARAO, NORMA MAALA, physician; b. Apr. 19, Manila, Phil.; d. Cecilio M. and Vicenta M. (Monis) Maala; m. Fideliz Sarao, Apr. 22, 1973; edn: AB and MD, Univ. of the East. Career: intern/res. internal medicine, Mountainside Hosp. 1975, hematology & oncology, Irvine Univ.; physician specialist Internal Med., pvt. practice Hematology, Oncology; mem. AMA; Catholic. Address: Norma M. Sakao MD, Inc., 1923 Eleanor Pl. Lomita 90717

SARAYDARIAN, ARJUNA T., lawyer; b. Aug. 6, 1943, Amman, Jordan, nat. 1964; s. Torkom and Elizabeth (Bekarian) S.; m. Sandra Jean McBurney, b. 1970; children: Garo, b. 1976; Ani, b. 1978; edn: premed. stu., UCLA 1962-64; BA, CSU Northridge 1968; JD, UOP McGeorge Sch. of Law 1971; admitted to Calif. State Bar 1972. Career: research clk./atty., Sacramento Superior Ct. judges, 1971-72; deputy dist. atty. Sacto. County, 1972-75, supvsg. deputy of Writs, Appeals & Spl. Projects Sect., 1975-77; pvt. solo practice of law, Los Angeles 1977-81; deputy dist. atty. Riverside County, 1981-, deputy in chg. Three Lakes Judicial Dist. Ofc. in Perris, 1983--; instr. CSU Sacto. 1973-77; judge pro tem L.A. Municipal Ct. 1981; apptd. mem. Riverside Cô. Drug Abuse Commn. 1973-; counsel to Calif. Bus. & Transp. Bd. of Inquiry, 1977; founder/ dir. Armenian Gen. Benevolent Union Legal Aid Clinic., Hollywood 1977-81; mem. L.A. Lawyers Club Speakers Bur. 1977-79; honors: Am. Jurisprudence acad. awards in criminal procedure & legal research; staff law journal and first class pres. in law school; num. public speaking and comm. service awards, Kiwanis, Lions, 1977-81; mem: Am., Calif., Los Angeles, Hollywood (past), Riverside bar assns.; Calif. Dist. Attys. Assn.; Armenian Lawyers Assn. (past pres.); Armenian Alumni Assn. (past vp); Armenian Congress (past bd. dirs.); Armenian Bus. Alliance (founding bd.); US Power Squadrons; past pres. Washington Sch. PTA; clubs: Lions, YMCA (Y Guides tribal chief); publs: num. arts. on legal topics; Republican; Armenian Apostolic; rec: sailing, fencing, playing the oud (musical instrument). Res: 6946 Jody Ct. Riverside 92506 Ofc: District Attorney, 135 N. D St Perris 92370

SARGENT, WAYNE CUMMINGS, newspaper editor; b. Feb. 7, 1925, Brooklyn, NY; s. Arthur Harder and Myrtle (Rohr) Sargent; Edn: B.A. Journalism Stanford 1948; m. Marybeth Street 1955. Career: reporter, United Press Assn.; bus. mgr.-Southern CA, Ariz., Nev., UPA; div. mgr. 8 Southern St. United Press International; v.p. & gen. sales mgr., UPI, pres. & publisher, Nashville Banner, pres. Cajun Music Publishing Co.; editor, San Bernardino, Sun; dir., Southern Newspaper Publ. Assn.; dir. Tennessee Pres. Assn.; mem. Tech. & Telecomunications Committees ANPA & ASNE. Mil: 1942-46 USAF & Signal Corps. Rec: golf, music. Res: 1345 South Center, Redlands 92373; Office: Sun Co. (Gannett Corp.), 399 N. "D" St., San Bernardino 92401.

SARVER, SUSANN MARIE FERNANDEZ, company president; b. Jan. 18, 1958, Montebello; d. Wallace Merrill and Roberta Carrie (Fernandez) Sarver; edn: BS, USC 1982. Career: warranty clk. Longo Toyota, 1974-78; nat. sales mgr. H.J.R. Baretta of America, Inc. 1978-81, chief cons. of franchise moped dealerships re sales, advt., pub. rels., and interoffice comm.; pres. SMS Enterprises, Inc., Rosemead 1981--, dba Cycle Barn, dba SMS Lien Sales (cons. to Tow yards and repair shops re Calif. State Dept. Motor Vehicle regs.), dba Sarver/Langley Impound Yard; awards: Ramona Convent service award 1976; Toyota Inc. efficiency awd. 1978; Cycle Mag. (Cycle Barn) customer rels. for motorcycle drivers 1983; mem: Calif. Assn. of Motorcycle Dismantlers, Nat. Fedn. of Independent Businessmen, Nat. Fedn. of Female Execs.; clubs: Sailing Club (Commodore), Santa Anita Cath. Singles Club, Young Republicans; Repub.; Catholic; rec: sailing, scuba diving, windsurfing, water skiing. Res: 524 Anderson Way San Gabriel 91776 Ofc: SMS Ent. Inc. 9121 Garvey Ave Rosemead 91770

SASAKI, KATSUHISA, company president; b. Feb. 9, 1947; Sapporo, Japan.; s. Sadao and Ryoko (Miyauchi) Sasaki; Edn: B.A. Univ. of Waseda 1970; USC 1972-73; m. Kimiko Tanaka 1980. Career: chief cashier, Hokkaido Takushoku Bank, Yokohama Japan; pres., Tokyo Ryowa Corp. 1975; pres, Winbell Intern. Corp. (L.A.) 1976---; pres., Silverton Inc. (Tokyo) 1976---; pres., Hawaii Ryowa Corp. 1978---; pres., Cal Land Foods Inc. (L.A.), 1980; pres., Elk Fashion Inc. (L.A.) 1981; pres., Ryowa Enterprise Corp. (L.A.) 1981. Mem: Southern CA Japanese CofC 1975; Japanese Bus. Assn. of Southern CA, 1976; L.A. CofC 1976; Lions Club 1981. Rec: golf, antique collection, traveling, sailing. Res: 3480 Barham Blvd., Suite 304, Los Angeles 90068; Office: 123 Weller St., Suite 313, Los Angeles 90012.

SATIN, SCOTT ARTHUR, manufacturing co. executive; b. Mar. 9, 1958, Los Angeles; s. David D. and Miriam (Stern) S.; m. Yolanda Cantellops, July 25, 1981; 1 son, Drew, b. 1982; edn: BA, USC 1981. Career: sales mgr. Imperial Pallet Co., Inc., Los Angeles 1976-81, general mgr. 1981-82, vice pres. 1982--; tng. director Imperial Western Mfrs., Santa Fe Springs 1983-; finl. cons. Westwood Mgmt., Tulare 1983-; mem. American Film Inst.; Delta Sigma Phi (v.p. 1979-80); Bnai Brith; author 3 pub. screenplays: Tell Me When The Whistle Blows (1980), How To Write A Screenplay (1982), Spot (1983); Republican; Jewish; rec: writing, athletics. Res: 1 Rock Bluffj Road Phillips Ranch 91765 Ofc: Imperial Pallet Co. Inc. 840 S. Mission Road Los Angeles 90023

SATTERLEE, ROBERT LOUIS, transportation engineer; b. Oct. 1, 1919, Winnebago, Minn.; s. Levi Herbert and Genevieve (Westlake) S.; m. Mary Eliza Keetch, Apr. 19, 1949; children: Clara, b. 1951, Ruth, b. 1953, Donna, b. 1956; edn: AA, L.A. City Coll. 1940, AB, Coll. of the Pacific 1950, MA, CSC Chico 1955; M.T., Inst. of Psychostructural Balancing 1979; Calif. lic. psychologist 1967. Career: elementary sch. tchr. Toyon Sch. 1950-54; research educationist, UCLA, 1955-58; reading splst. Tehachapi Unified Schs. 1958-59; asst. prof. Calif. Western Univ. 1959-62; engineering tech. Caltrans, 1963-78, asst. transp. engr. Caltrans Air Quality and Noise Analysis Sects. (computer and math. analysis), 1978--; pvt. tutoring (ref. La Jolla Tutoring Clinic) 1978-; mem: Photographic Soc. of Am., Internat./Nat. Stereoscopic Assn., Assn. of Humanistic Psychol., Stereoscopic Photo Club of San Diego (pres. 1965-77); works: Inventor of the Year, S.D. Council of Engring. Socs. 1977; publs: num. tech. reports on air pollution and noise analysis along proposed freeway routes; mil: s/sgt. USAF 1941-45, N. Africa, Moroccan Cpgn.; rec: presentation of 3-Dimensional slide shows. Res: 4488 Rolfe Rd San Diego 92117 Ofc: Caltrans Lab., 7177 Opportunity Rd San Diego 92111

SAUER, ROBERT EUGENE, computer scientist; b. July 31, 1930, Humboldt, Kans.; s. Frederick John and Gladys Ella (Patch) S.; m. Lorraine King, Aug. 2, 1959; edn: San Diego Comm. Coll. 1977-; cert. Air Intercept Controller, USN Fleet Air Def. Tng. Ctr., San Diego 1955. Career: dairy wkr. Ottawa, Kans. 1946-48; served to master chief radarman, USN, 1948-69: combat duty in Korea incl. Inchon Landing 1950-57; chief radarman and instr. (air intercept control, radar, ships tactics, navigation and NTDS- Naval Tactical Data System computer complex), shipboard in both Atlantic and Pacific, 1957-65; Vietnam combat duty, sr. radarman in cruiser-destroyer flotilla, computer pgmmr. & system analyst, 1965-69; civil service computer pgmmr. analyst, Fleet Computer Pgmmg. Ctr. Pacific (FCPCP), San Diego 1969-72; civil service computer splst./mgr. Fleet Combat Direction Systems Support Activity (FCDSSA), and head Exec. Systems Software Devel. Div. FCDSSA, 1972-77; tech. dir./computer scientist Marine Corps Tactical Systems Support Activity (MCTSSA), Camp Pendleton 1977--; prin. R.E. Sauer Systems cons. firm, 1984-; mil. decorations: 23 USN medals, cmpgn. ribbons and naval service awards. Mem. ACM, IEEE, Fleet reserve Assn., Mensa; works: op. system software used in USN NTDS equipped aircraft carriers 1976-86; Republican; Prot.; rec: computer systems, billiards. Res: 3580 Jennings St San Diego 92106 Ofc: USMC MCTSSA, Camp Pendleton 92055

SAUL, STANLEY RICHARD, physician, surgeon; b. Mar. 18, 1941, Reading, Pa.; s. Charles David and Sara (Kemp) S.; m. Sandra Casselberry 1958; children: Brent, b. 1960, Scott, b. 1964; edn: BS, Albright Coll. 1963; DO, Phila. Coll. of Osteopathic Med. 1967; diplomate Am. Osteopathic Bd. of Surgery 1977. Career: asst. prof. of surgery Mich. State Univ. Coll. of Osteopathic Medicine, 1973-77; adj. faculty in surg. Coll. of Osteopathic Med. of the Pacific, 1977--, coordinator Renal System, 1983-84; elected bd. govs. Ontario Comm. Hosp. 1983-, v.chief of staff 1981, chmn. dept. of surg. 1982; mem: Masons, Shriners; Democrat; Ontario Brethren in Christ Ch. (secty bd.

dirs. 1980-81); rec: racquetball, tennis, swimming, skiing. Res: 5041 Via Verde, Alta Loma 91701 Ofc: Dr. Stanley R. Saul, 653 East E, Ste. 106, Ontario 91764

SAUNDERS, FRANK HENRY, expert police court witness; b. Dec. 6, 1934, Rochester, NY; s. Wm. H., Sr. and Frances E. (Lovejoy) S.; m. Michelle Anne Lamar, July 18, 1981; stepdau., Michelette R. Lamar, b. 1966; edn: Univ. of Ariz. (Tucson) 1954-6, 1958-9, UC Santa Cruz 1982; Calif. lic. Pvt. Investigator 1982; Qual. Police Ct. Expert, State Ct. 1981, Federal Ct. 1983. Career: investigator Continental Casualty Ins., 1964; ofcr. Santa Monica Police Dept. 1965-80; owner Frank Saunders Investigations (pvt. investigative firm), Pacific Grove, and expert police court witness, 1980--; recipient Medal of Valor, City of Santa Monica 1978; citations, Santa Monica City Council, State Sen. Paul Priolo, 1967; Chief of Police Commendn. 1967; mem: Santa Monica Police Assn. (founder/ed. newsmag. Soundoff 1970-79); Santa Monica Retired Police Assn.; Monterey Co. Peace Ofcrs Assn. Peace Ofcrs Resrch Assn. of Calif.; Pacific Grove CofC; club: Meadowbrook Swim & Tennis, Seaside; mil: A/2c USAF 1956-58; Republican; Prot.; rec: tennis, bicycling, creative writing. Res: 910 Del Monte Blvd Pacific Grove 93950 Ofc: Frank Saunders Investigations, POB 161, Pacific Grove 93950

SAUNDERS, JOHN WESLEY, real estate broker; b. June 9, 1942, Long Beach; s. David W. and Helen O. Saunders; edn: stu. CSULB, UCLA, Long Bch City Coll.; BS in BA, Calif. Coll. of Commerce 1963; spl. courses NY Univ. 1980. Career: with US Rubber Co., Los Angeles 1964; office mgmt. Sinclair Paint Co., L.A.; auditor, accountant, budget analyst Blue Chip Stamps, City of Commerce, 8 years; currently owner/broker John W. Saunders Realty, Huntington Beach; instr. R.E. seminars for Huntington Bch. F.V. Bd. of Realtors; honors: Top Producer of Year, Investment Prop. 1981, Huntington Bch. Fountain Valley Bd. of Realtors; mem. $12,000,000 Club 1976; one of Top Ten newsmakers, LA Magazine 1982; named one of 81 of O.C. Most Interesting People, Orange Coast Mag. 1981; Am. Legion Award for Outstanding Svc.; mem. Huntington Bch. Bd. of Realtors (past chmn. Inv. Div.); Nat., Calif. Assn. of Realtors; Internat. City Club Long Beach; adv. bd. Interval House Seal Beach; Rotary; (past) Jaycees; mil: s/sgt Calif. Army Nat. Guard, GC, 2 service medals; Republican; Presbyterian. Res: 25 Argonne, No. 3, Long Beach 90803 Ofc: John W. Saunders Realty, 8072 Warner Ave Huntington Beach 92647

SAUZA, JO BRITTAIN DE, commercial real estate broker; b. Nov. 10, 1938, Center, Tex.; d. Theron W. and Doris Norma (Ross) Brittain; edn: Univ. Houston, Univ. Md. 1959-61; profl. courses, Exchange Mktg. Seminars 1978, Anthony R.E. Sch. 1979; lic. R.E. broker, Tex. 1966, Calif. 1981. Career: secty. Mayor Lewis Cutrer, Houston, Tex. 1962-64; advt./pub. rels. dir. Divcon Inc., Houston 1964-66; comml. real estate broker/owner Sauza Realty, Houston 1966-77; prin., pres. TL Financial Inc., San Diego 1977-81; v.p./dir. Maturo Image Corp., S.D. (motion picture prodn. co.); v.p./dir. Sandpiper Point Homeowners Assn.; recipient of Film Advisory Board's award of excellence as assoc. prod. film, Bully, starring James Whitmore as Theodore Roosevelt, 1978; mem. World Vision, Women in Film, NOW; Republican (Nat. Com.); Prot.; rec: tennis, golf, travel. Address: Sauza Realty, 3218 Lone Jack Rd Olivenhain 92024

SAVAGE, VICTOR JAMES, dentist; b. Aug. 20, 1941, Berkeley; s. Victor Wesley and June (Hamilton) S.; m. Linda E., June 30, 1962; children: Claudia, b. 1963, Amber, b. 1964, Victor M., b. 1967, Matthew, b. 1969; edn: AA, Yuba Coll. 1972; BS, CSU Hayward 1974; DDS, Univ. of the Pacific 1977. Career: owner dental practice, Yuba City 1977--; advisor on dental issues to Assem. Wally Heryen, Yuba City Conv. Hosp.; recipient dental student achievement awards, Internat. Coll. of Dentists; mem: Butte Sierra Dist. Dental Soc. (pres. 1982), UOP Alumni Assn. Sch. of Dentistry (pres. 1983); Am. Heart Assn. CPR instr.; mem. adult com. Twin Citys Young Life; Republican; Christian; rec: backpacking, skiing, fishing. Res: 4950 Railroad Ave Yuba City 95991 Ofc: Victor J. Savage DDS, 664 Shasta St Yuba City 95991

SAVEDRA, MANUEL ANGEL, dentist; b. Oct. 22, 1943, Los Angeles; s. Manuel Diza and Evangeline (Vasquez) S.; m. Cheryl D. Silver, Sept. 11, 1982; 1 dau., Carli Dana, b. 1983; edn: AA, East L.A. Coll. 967; BA, UC Los Angeles 1969; DDS, UCLA Dental Sch. 1974; lic. Hawaii, Calif. Career: dental resident, Queens Med. Center, Honolulu 1974-75; dentist/asst. prof., UCLA, 1975-76; dental staff St. Joseph Med. Center, 1975-76; pvt. practice dentistry, West L.A. and Hawthorne, 1976--; mem. State Dental Bd. of Examiners 1981; honors: Omicron Kappa Epsilon, Alpha Gamma Sigma, Mosby Publ. Award 1970-74; mem: Am., Calif. dental assns.; Western Dental Soc.; Acad. of Gen. Dentistry; UCLA Dental Alumni Assn. (pres. 1982); Am. Legon; mil: E5 US Army dental corps 1963-66; Republican; Jewish; rec: languages, sports, travel. Res: 9645 Wendover Dr Beverly Hills 90210 Ofc: Manuel A. Savedra DDS, 11600 Wilshire Blvd, Ste. 308, Los Angeles 90025

SAWYER, ERNEST WALKER, JR., corporate executive; b. Harrow-on-the-Hill, Hove, Eng.; s. The Hon. Ernest Walker (exec. asst. Sec. of Interior, Hoover Cabinet, spl. assgmt. w/Sir Winston Churchill and Lord Beaverbrook, WWI, sent first wireless message across the Atlantic) and Florence Victoria (Davies) S.; grandneph. of Albert Finlayson (fmr Brit. Amb. to Argentina) m. Miriam Camille Patty (desc.Capt. James Cook, Ralph Waldo Emerson) 1949; children: Camille Agnes, Christian Emerson; ed. Colo. Sch. of Mines, Harvard Univ., Univ. of Calif. (Berkeley) 1948. Career: pres. Sawyer Petroleum Co. 1955-69; pres. Ore. Trail Land and Cattle Co.; pres. Sawyer Cattle Co.; exec. Frawley Corp.; pres. US Oil & Mineral Corp.; Dir. Sawyer Exploration Co.,

Sawyer Found.; Trustee United Found.; mem: USC Associates, Am. Nuclear Soc., Am. Assn. of Petroleum Geol., Am. Inst. of Mining, Metal, & Petrol. Engrs., Am. Inst. of Profl. Geologists, Geol. Soc. of P.I., Calif. Cattlemens Assn.; mil: capt. US Army Corps of Engrs., Disting. Unit Presdtl. Cit. (unit cmdr.), Merit Svc., Australian Govt. Cmpgn. Award, Austral. Pac. Star, battle hon.: New Guinea, Borneo, Bismark Archip. cmpgns.; clubs: Bel Air Bay Club, Alta Club (Salt Lake City). Ofc: 1801 Ave of the Stars, Ste 1025, Los Angeles 90067

SAWYER, FREDERIC ALLEN, lawyer; b. June 4, 1926, Oakland; s. Wm. Brewster, Jr. and Irma (Foveaux) S.; m. Diane Denault, June 26, 1948; children: Denise, b. 1954, Frederic Jr., b. 1957, William, b. 1961; edn: AB, UC Berkeley 1947; JD (valedictorian), UCB Boalt Hall 1951; admitted Calif. State Bar 1952. Career: legal asst. Kaiser Services, Oakland 1950-51; assoc. McCutcheon law firm, San Francisco 1951-65, partner 1965-80; owner Law Office of Frederic A. Sawyer, Orinda 1980--; State Bar Com. on Federal Cts. 1975-80 (chmn. 1978-79); mem. Parks & Rec. commn., Town of Moraga 1983-; mem. bd. govs. Moraga Elementary Sch. 1961-73 (twice pres.); mgr. Ato Found. of Berkeley (ednl. found.) 1981-; honors: asst. editor Calif. Law Rev. 1950 51; mem: ADA (litigation and antitrust sects.), Bar Assn. of S.F. (past chmn. pub. rels. com.), Contra Costa Bar Assn.; mem. Orinda CofC; past v.p. Orinda Assn. 1955-56; dir. Ato House Assn. 1955-; Bohemian Club; capt. Sheldrake Lodge; mil: ltjg USNR 1944-46, 1952-53, Korean Service medal; Republican; Episcopal; rec: gardening, biking, swimming, skiing. Res: 153 Ravenhill Rd Orinda 94563 Law Office of Frederic A. Sawyer, 23 Altamira Rd Orinda 94563

SAYLES, SUE ANN, temporary services co. owner; b. July 21, 1934, Fort Jones; d. Fredell DeForrest and Marie Elizabeth (Ball) Taber; children: Leonard, b. 1958, Clayton, b. 1960, Barbara, b. 1962; edn: Bus. Adm., Univ. of San Francisco 1977. Career: Justice Court, Selective Service Sys., Boeing Airplane Co., Pacific Tel., and Sears Roebuck & Co., mgr.; mgr. Div. Edn. Sys., San Jose 1970-72; mgr. Tempo-Uniforce, San Jose 1973-74; Ofcr. Personnel, COMPATWINGSPAC, Moffett Field, Calif. 1974-76; bd. dir./mgr. Roma Tile, Ltd., Los Gatos 1977-80; mgr. Western Temporary Service, Inc., Campbell 1980-84; founder/owner Diamond Temporary Services, San Jose 1984--; Spanish-speaking program coordinator, NAS, Moffett Field; honors: Girl of the Year, Valentine Sweetheart for Beta Sigma Phi; Top Performer (1981-82), and Public Relations awards (1982), Western Temporary Service. Mem: VFW Aux. (sec.treas.), Jaycettes (vp), CofC (comm. chmn. B.P.W.); secty. PTA; Beta Sigma Phi (vp); Republican; Episcopal; rec: genealogy, hunting, skiing, dancing. Res: 3896 Moss Hollow Dr San Jose 95121 Ofc: Diamond Temporary Services, 675 N. First St, Ste. 401, San Jose 95112-5111

SCAVO, GIOVANNI, cosmetology school president; b. Aug. 11, 1932, Bari, Italy; s. Nicola Antonio and Maria (DeGiulio) S.; m. Rita Guardi, June 3, 1956; children: Nickolas Anthony, b. 1957, Maryellen, b. 1959, John Lou, b. 1969; edn: UCLA 1976-77; Calif. State lic. cosmetologist 1960, Cosmetology instr. 1967, voc. edn. teaching credential (Class A, life) 1977. Career: pres. Coiffure Elegante Inc. (beauty salons div.) in La Mirada, Hacienda Hts., Rowland Hts., Fullerton, West Covina, 1963-69; dept. chmn. (cosmetology) Hacienda-La Puente School Dist., City of Industry; pres. Estetica Ltd. (skin care equip. & products); pres. Coiffure Elegante Inc. (beauty colls. div.); pvt. edn. rep.: RAVEC Council for Voc. Edn. Saddleback Coll., and Mt. San Antonio Coll., 1978-83; mem: Calif. Assn. Cosmetologists (pres. Mt. SAC afil. 1974-75); Calif. Assn. of Schools of Cosmetology (pres. 1979-81); Calif. Assn. School Finl. Administrators; CAROC; Sons of Italy, Kiwanis; patentee: Derma-Estetica skin care machine comprising four electrical modalities for skin application; mil: s/sgt. USAF, Japanese, Korean, Nat. Air Def., and UN medals; Catholic; rec: golf, swimming, travel. Res: 8390 Waverly Cr. Buena Park 90621 Ofc: Coiffure Elegante Inc., POB 42, 34052 La Plaza, Dana Point 92629

SCEPER, DUANE HAROLD, lawyer; b. Nov. 16, 1946, Norfolk, Va.; s. Robert G. and Marion E. (Hynes) S.; m. Sharon D., July 4, 1981; stepchil: Karin Stevenson, b. 1970, Diane Stevenson, b. 1973; edn: undergrad., San Diego St. Univ. 1964-65; BS, WSU Coll. of Law, 1979, JD, 1980; admitted to Calif. State Bar 1982. Career: field engr. Texas Instruments, 1969-70; field engr. Memorex Corp. 1970-71; var. sales and sales mgmt. positions (investments, real estate and ins.), 1971-80; commercial diver 1979-81; atty./ estate & bus. plnng. cons. AID Insurance Services, Allied Life Ins. Co. (home ofc. Des Moines, Iowa), San Diego 1982--; mem. Am. Bar Assn., Calif. Bar Assn., Am. Trial Lawyers Assn., Calif. Trial Lawyers Assn., Delta Theta Phi; works: computer devices, computer pgms., vapor recovery equip.; mil: E4 USAF 1965-68, Air Commando, Vietnam; rec: hist. restoration, scuba diving, computers, karate. Res: 2641 Massachusetts Ave Lemon Grove 92045 Ofc: AID Ins. Co. 7777 Alvarado Rd, Ste. 500, La Mesa 92041

SCHAEFER, IMELDA RUEL, senior citizens group president; b. Jan. 25, 1908, Lawrence, Mass.; d. Cyril and Exilia Alice (Houle) Ruel; m. Fred Crabtree, Apr. 28, 1925; children: Norma, Florence, Shirley; sixteen grandchildren; m. 2d. William Schaefer, Sept. 7, 1959; edn: Weatherby (Mass.) public schs.; cert. sewing machine opr., L.A. Adult Edn. Career: homemaker since age 12, caring for three brothers, then own 3 daus.; worked as a weaver, spinner, sewing machine opr. and assembly wkr.; president Placentia Senior Citizens Club, 1982-; bd. pres. Orange Co. Senior Citizens; honors: Placentia Advisory Council commendation for outstanding service, 1983, City of Placentia Community Service Award; dancing first prize ($2 Gold Piece), waltz, Polish Hall (Mass.); works: arts, crafts, needlework; Democrat; Episcopal; rec: family reunions. Res: 3320 Topaz Ln., B19, Fullerton 92631 Ofc: Placentia Senior Center, 143 So. Bradford, Placentia 92670

SCHAEFER, WERNER HELMUT, company president; b. Jan. 16, 1948, Arolsen, Hesse, West Germany; s. Heinrich and Elisabeth (Janson) S.; m. Dr. Barbara Klimkeit, Dec. 31, 1975; edn: MS in chem. Philipps Univ. (Marburg, Ger.) 1971, PhD in chem., 1975. Career: asst. tchr. Philipps Univ., Marburg, FRG 1971-75; research chemist, Behringwerke AG, Marburg, 1975-78; asst. R&D dir. Behringwerke AG, Marburg 1978-79; vice pres. Internat. Affairs, Calbiochem-Behring, La Jolla, Calif. 1980-82; dir. Corp. Mktg. & Planning/ Diagnostics, Behringwerke AG, Marburg, FRG 1982-83; pres. Calbiochem-Behring, La Jolla, 1983--; mem. Indsl. Advis. Com., UC San Diego; publs: 23 sci. publs., 1971-76; Prot.; rec: windsurfing, skiing, reading. Res: 319 Glenmont Dr Solana Beach 92075 Ofc: Calbiochem-Behring, 10933 N. Torrey Pines Rd La Jolla CA 92037

SCHAERRER, STEVEN RAY, health care administrator; b. Apr. 30, 1955, Payson, Utah; s. Russell J. and Marie (Bird) S.; m. Sherrie Lund, June 16, 1979; edn: AA, Pierce Coll. 1978; BS in hlth care adm., CSU Northridge 1981; MS in hlth care adm., CSU Los Angeles 1982; Calif. lic. Nursing Home Administrator 1983. Career: Outpatient Project coord. VA Medical Center, Brentwood 1979-83; asst. administr. Rancho Los Padres Convalescent Hosp., Norwalk 1982-83; adminstr. Rimrockrock Hosp., Barstow 1983-84; asst. adminstr. Riverside Medical Clinic, Riverside 1984--; chmn. Everhealth Found. -YMCA Golf Benefit, Whittier (1983, 84); honors: Outstanding Young Men of Am., 1982, 83; Alpha Mu Gamma (1978); mem. Medical Group Management Assn., Optimist Internat. Barstow (We Care Com. chmn.); Republican; L.D.S. Ch.; rec: golf, softball, fishing. Res: 5600 Falling Leaf Ln Riverside 92509 Ofc: Riverside Medical Clinic, 3660 Arlington Ave Riverside 92506

SCHAFER, HOWARD C., engineering consultant; b. July 31, 1932, Lincoln, Nebr.; s. Marion Howard and Ruby Alene (Thompson) S.; m. Bernice Larson, Aug. 29, 1953; children: Kathleen, b. 1956, Sharon, b. 1958, Thomas, b. 1960; edn: A.A., engr., L.A. City Coll. 1955; BS in M.E., CSU, 1959; Reg. Profl. Engr., Calif. 1979. Career: jr. engr. Crown Coach Corp. (bus & firetruck design), Los Angeles 1954-56; assoc. engr. Fluor Corp. (petroleum resrch. & cooling tower design, patent granted for flow nozzle), L.A. 1956-59; chem. engr. USN Ordnance Test Sta. (pilot escape rocket design, environ. test lab., explosive test facility design and constrn.), China Lake 1959-62; sr. engr. North American Aviation (wrote natural environ. criteria document for Saturn S-II moonrocket, instrumentation design - test lab liaison, invented Hypsometer for space use), Downey 1962-64; gen. engr. USN Weapons Center (head of environ. criteria determination pgm. for air-launched ordnance, conducted free worldwide coop. field measurement of ordnance thermal response, DOD cons. for mil. environ., frequent lectr.), China Lake 1964-84; engineering consultant/ entrepreneur, 1984--; awards incl. Calif. Federal Service medal, Navy Superior Civilian Service medal (1975), Naval Weapons Center Tech. Dirs. award (1973) and superior achievement award (1974); mem: Inst. Environ. Scis., Internat. Platform Assn., Naval Aviation Exec. Inst.; works: num. tech. papers, tech. R&D 1961-84; 4 patents 1957-80; mil: sgt. AUS 1950-52, Nat. Defense, Korean Service, Army Occ., UN Service medals, Korean Presdtl. Unit Cit.; Independent; Prot.; rec: orchardist, vinedresser, craftsman. Res: 1274 Palo Verde St Ridgecrest 93555 Ofc: 30340 Watts Valley Rd Tollhouse 93667

SCHAFFNER, GERALD, electronics engineer; b. May 14, 1927, Chgo.; s. Samuel and Rose (Cannon) S.; m. Arlene Ruth Ginsburg, Apr. 6, 1952; children: James, b. 1955, Sue, b. 1958, Ellen, b. 1960; edn: BSEE, Purdue Univ. 1949, MSEE, 1950; PhD, Northwestern Univ. 1956. Career: transformer design engr. Thordarson Electric, Chgo. 1950-51; RF Group mgr. Stewart-Warner, Chgo. 1951-57; senior scientist Motorola Aerospace, Scottsdale, Ariz. 1957-59; group leader Motorola Solid State Div., Phoenix 1959-63; ops. mgr. Motorola Semi-Conductor, 1963-69; Senior Group engr. (Microwave & Microelectronics) Teledyne-Ryan Electronics, San Diego 1969--; honors: Etta Kappa Nu 1948, Tau Beta Pi 1959, Sigma Xi 1955; Who's Who Men of Science; Sr. Mem. IEEE, Phoenix chmn. Microwave Group 1969, San Diego chmn. Microwave Gp. 1977, Tech. Pgm. chmn. Internat. Microwave Symp. 1977; publs: 17 papers on Microwave Diodes & Circuits, 1 paper, Computer Aided Design, 2 papers projecting Technology, editor of Two Microwave Magazine issues 1958-84, 3 patents; mil: Lt. JG USNR 1945-53; rec: duplicate bridge, tennis, computer pgmmg. Res: 10325 Caminito Cuervo, 193, San Diego 92108 Ofc: Teledyne-Ryan Electronics, 8650 Balboa Ave San Diego 92123

SCHAIN, RONALD BURTON, chiropractor, b. Dec. 13, 1934, Los Angeles; s. David and Ida Jeraldine (Hyman) S.; m. Kimberly Scott, Nov. 17, 1979; children: April, b. 1961, Mark, b. 1964; edn: elec. courses, L.A. Trade Tech. Jr. Coll. 1952-54; pre-engring., L.A. City Coll. 1956-58; med. splst. Brooke Army Med. Ce976. Career: journeyman wireman, field engr., elec. supt., elec. contractor, 1954-69, 1972-79; pres. Jack Frost Co. Inc. (four Army Navy Surplus stores), pres. Unified Wholesale Distbrs., 1969-72; instr. Cleveland Chiro. Coll. 1976; assoc. with Encino/Tarzana Chiro. Offices, 1976-79; pvt. practice, chiropractic, Canoga Park, 1979--; awards: Chiropractor of the Year, San Fernando Valley 1983; merit awd., 23 years, Intl. Brotherhood of Elec. Wkrs.; mem: Am. Chiro. Assn., Calif. Chiro. Assn. (cert. Disability Evaluator of Workers Comp. cases 1979), San Fernando Valley chiropractic Soc. (1st v.p. 1983), Am. Assn. of Nutrition & Dietary Consultants (profl. mem.); clubs: Masons (instr. of degrees 1970-72); contbg. writer local newspapers, 1976-, Valley Green Sheet, Century 21 Mag. SFV ed. 1981; mil: s/sgt. M.C. USAF 1958-64, GCM; rec: cultural interests. Res: 20301 Enadia Way Canoga Park 91306 Ofc: Ronald B. Schain, D.C., 8231 Canoga Ave Canoga Park 91304

SCHALLER, JAMES LEE, manufacturing co. executive; b. Oct. 19, 1942, Sioux City, Iowa; s. Donald Phillip and Ruth Sarah (Schuller) S.; children: Jeffrey, b. 1967, Angela, b. 1970; edn: BS in BA, Univ. of Nebr. 1967, BS in econ., 1968, MBA, 1969. Career: sales mgr. W/M Volker Co., San Diego 1970-79; branch mgr. G.A.F. Corp., 1979-81; general mgr. Tarkett, Inc. 1981-83, S.W. district mgr. 1983--; v.p./bd. dirs. S.A.S. Corp.; honors: San Diego County Man of Year 1977; winner Earl Falbrook Award for Excellence in Mktg. 1970; mem: S.D. County Floor Covg. Assoc. (pres. 1976/7, bd. dirs.); Golf Assn. S.C. (pres. 1983); clubs: Lions, Rotary, Floor Covering Club of S.D.; mil: capt. USAF 1965; Republican; Methodist; rec: golf, flying, racquetball. Res: 22662 Reinosa Mission Viejo 92692 Ofc: Tarkett, Inc. 2340 E. Artesia Blvd. Long Beach 90801

SCHANK, JOHN PATRICK, sales executive; b. Apr. 26, 1949, Allentown, Penna.; s. Joseph Ralph and Lillian (Jensen) S.; m. Linda Blalock, Nov. 23, 1967; children: JoAnn, b. 1968, Melissa, b. 1972; edn: grad. Venice High Sch. 1967. Career: service mgr. National Paper Co., New Orleans, La. 1972-74; owner/opr. Schank's Photocopy, Dallas, Tex. 1974-78; office mgr., salesman Petes Fence Co., Palmdale 1978-80; owner/opr. A-1 Copiers, Palmdale 1980--; mem: Nat. Office Machines Dealers 1977-78 (past pres. Dallas chpt. 1977); charter pres. High Desert Jaycees 1980, bd. chmn. 1983; charter dist. gov. Calif. Jaycees 1983 (Jaycee of the Year 1982, Dist. 22); Palmdale Optimist (bd. dirs. 1979-80); Palmdale CofC (Diplomat 1981); Republican; Prot.; rec: community svc. Res: 38628 Yucca Tree St Palmdale 93550 Ofc: A-1 Copiers, 1017 E. Palmdale Blvd Palmdale 93550

SCHANKMAN, ALAN ROBERT, physician; b. Jan. 1, 1947, Brooklyn, NY; s. Barnet and Sylvia (Barken) S.; m. Vicki Gellman, 1972; children: Dana, b. 1979; Lauren, b. 1979; Alison, b. 1981; Michael Alden, b. 1983; edn: BS, Brooklyn Coll. 1968; MD, Downstate Med. Coll. of SUNY 1972; Am. Bd. Certified Ophthalmology 1977. Career: Ophthalmology: solo practice, New York 1976-78, Los Angeles 1978--; investigator in Keratorefractive surgery; forerunner in laser treatments for eye diseases; Braille Inst. consultant. Mem. Calif. Med. Assn., L.A. County Med. Assn., Am. Acad. of Opthalmology, Calif. Assn. of Ophthalmology, Keratorefractive Soc. of Am.; rec: sailing. Ofc: 12840 Riverside Dr North Hollywood 91607

SCHARF, ROBERT LEE, lawyer; b. May 13, 1920, Chgo.; s. Charles A. and Ethel Virginia (McNabb) S.; m. Jacqueline Bauer, Nov. 2, 1940; children: Bonnie Lee, b. 1942, Mary Ellen, b. 1951, Robert Jr., b. 1954; edn: JD, Loyola Law Sch. 1948; Lifetime teaching credential, Police Sci. and Law, Calif. Comm. Colls.; admitted to State Bars of Calif., Ill., US Supreme Ct, US Ct. of Mil. Appeals, US Dist. Ct. Central District. Career: with Federal Bur. of Investigation 1940-73 in Chgo., Birmingham, Ala., Wash DC, Los Angeles; deputy city atty. Office of the City Atty. of Los Angeles, 1973--; mem. State Bar of Calif., L.A. County bar Assn., Lawyers' Club of L.A. Co. (bd. govs.); mil: 2d lt. AUS 1944-46; Republican; Presbyterian; rec: music (mem. ASCAP). Office of City Attorney, Rm. 1110, City Hall East, 200 N. Main St Los Angeles 90012

SCHAUER, FREDERICK HERBERT, real estate broker; b. July 5, 1934, Santa Barbara; s. Herbert F. and Ethel E. (Nemes) S.; m. Maxine Dexter, July 6, 1957; children: April Ann, b. 1954, Sharon Ann, b. 1955, Scott Frederick, b. 1958; edn: Pierce Coll. 1953, 60; desig: GRI, Calif. Real Estate Assn. 1971; Instr. Rating, Nat. Tan Soo Do Congress 1974; Profl. Hypnotherapist, HMI Inst. 1981. Career: real estate sales agt. Oakdale Realtors, Woodland Hills 1959-61; gen. mgr./corp. pres. Schauer Ent. dba Schauer Realty, Woodland Hills 1962-76, ret.; mem. San Fernando Board of Realtors (chmn. Profl. Stds. Com., bd. dirs., Adv. Com.) 1961-83; mil: sgt. (SP4) US Army 1955-57, GCM; Republican; Christian; rec: archery, scuba diving, backpacking, antiques, martial arts. Res: 23836 Crosson Dr Woodland Hills 91367

SCHAUER, JEAN, real estate property management co. owner/broker; b. May 1, 1939, Nogales, Ariz.; d. Loy Robert and Emma Mae (Conley) Wedderburn; edn: AA in Bus. Adm., Coll. of the Sequoias, Visalia 1963; Calif. lic. real estate broker, notary public; Calif. Comm. Coll. teaching credential. Career: exec. secty. Armstrong Rubber, Hanford until 1963; past exec. secty. Himovitz Constrn.; various real estate positions as sales agt., loan ofcr., escrow ofcr., office mgr. until 1981; broker/owner J & M Realtors, Lemoore 1981--; instr. West Hills Coll.; honors: recognition for wk. with Spl. Olympics Pgm.; mem: Nat., Calif. realtors assns.; Kings County Bd. of Realtors (bd. dirs., ethics com.); Lemoore CofC (legis. com.); Calif. Tchrs. Assn.; Calif. Assn. of R.E. Tchrs.; Calif. Escrow Assn.; Democrat; Methodist; rec: camping, fishing, needlepoint. Address: J & M Realtors, 1060 Fern Court Lemoore 93245

SCHEID, ALFRED G., biotechnology company president; b. Feb. 7, 1932, Wheeling, W.Va.; s. George Edward and Isabelle Adolphin (Jonard) S.; children: Scott b. 1960, Heidi b. 1963, Emily b. 1970, Tyler b. 1974; edn: BA in bus., Claremont Men's Coll. 1957; MBA, Harvard Grad. Sch. of Bus. Adm. 1959. Career: v.p./mgr./invest. banker EF Hutton & Company, Los Angeles 1960-68; senior v.p. Shareholders Capital Corp., L.A. 1968-70; pres./chmn. bd. HS Group Inc. (predecessor firm, A.G. Scheid Inc., 1970) 1971--; pres./chmn. bd. California Biotechnology Inc. 1982--; mem: Calif. Assn. of Winegrape Growers, bd. mem./past chmn. State Advis. Com. on wine indus. affairs; clubs: Riviera Tennis, Bel-Air Bay; mil: seaman 1/c USN 1952-54; Republican; Prot.; Res: 2227 Armada Way San Mateo 94404 Ofc: California Biotechnology Inc., 2450 Bayshore Frontage Rd Mt. View 94043; HS Group Inc., 2665 Main St, Ste 240, Santa Monica 90405

SCHEIDT, OMAR H., college district superintendent/president; b. Jan. 10, 1925, Biola, Calif.; s. August H. and Mollie (Grass) S.; m. Lorraine Richardson, Dec. 23, 1950; children: Suzanne, b. 1951, Lucinda, b. 1957, Patrick, b. 1959; edn: BS, Fresno State Coll. 1950; MS, USC 1955; EdD, UC Los Angeles 1966; Life Diploma, Calif. State Bd. of Edn.; Comm. Coll. Cert., Wash. St. Bd. for Community Colls.; Calif. Gen. Sch. Services Credential Sec. Sch. Adminstrn., Life. Career: spl. asst. chemist, Am. Crystal Sugar Co., Oxnard 1950-53; lab. asst. in chem., USC 1953-54; tchr. Phineas Banning High Sch., Wilmington 1955, North High Sch., Bksfld. 1955-56; tchr. Bakersfield Coll. 1956-61; dean Bakersfield Coll. Desert Div., Ridgecrest 1961-66; pres. Yakima (Wash.) Valley Coll., CEO Comm. Coll. District 16, 1966-70; prs. Cypress (Calif.) Coll., 1970-77; supt./pres. Palomar Comm. Coll. District, San Marcos 1977--; mem. Pepperdine Univ. Grad. Sch. Advisory Bd. 1977-; Western Assn. of Schs. and Colls. chmn./mem. Team: Yuba Coll. 1983, Butte Coll. 1980, Coll. of the Canyons 1980, Evergreen Valley Coll. 1977, Sierra Coll. 1974, Canada Coll. 1972, Coll. of the Desert 1971, Marymount Coll. 1970; honors: Omar H. Scheidt Annual Scholarship award presented by Cypress College Class of 1973; recipient USC Edn. Alumni Assn. annual honor award 1955; mem: Am. Chemical Soc., Am. Assn. Comm./Jr. Coll., Calif. Comm. Colls. (bd. dirs. 1981-), San Diego and Imperial Cos. Colls. (vp 1983/4), Assn. of Calif. Comm. Coll. Adminstrs., Calif. Comm./Jr. Coll. Assn., So. Calif. Comm. Colls. Chief Exec. Ofcrs. Assn. (bd. dirs. 1981-), Calif. Jr. Coll. Faculty Assn. (bd. govs. 1959-61); UCLA Doctor of Edn. Alumni Assn.; USC Edn. Alumni Assn.; Bksfld. Coll. Faculty Club (pres. 1958-59); Cypress Coll. Faculty Assn. 1970; Rotarian; v.p. Concerned Citizens of Escondido; CofC; United Way; Nat. Tchrs. Hall of Fame, Anaheim (nat. hon. bd. mem.); coauthor Bksfld. Coll. lab. manual; mil: s/sgt. USAF 1943-45; rec: farming. Res: 14237 Calle de Vista Valley Center 92082 Ofc: Palomar College, 1140 W. Mission Rd San Marcos 92069

SCHERZER, RICHARD, engineering program manager; b. Sept. 23, 1940, Brklyn., NY; s. David and Aranka (Gedaly) S.; m. Claire Edgar, June 19, 1965; 1 son, David, b. 1971; edn: BS math & phys. scis., Liceo Andres Bello, 1957; BSEE (electronic eng.), Pacific States Univ. 1962; ops. research/systems analysis, Polytech. Inst. of Brooklyn, 1967-69; Calif. lic. Profl. Engr. (Quality) 1978. Career: sr. engrg. technician Ampex Computer Products, Culver City 1962; supvy. test and eval. engr. McDonnell Aircraft Co., St. Louis, Mo. 1963-64; project engr. Barnes & Reinecke, Indpls. 1964; tech. staff US Post Office, Indpls. 1965; project engr./sr. proj. engr. US Govt. (Army, Picatinny Arsenal), Dover, NJ 1965-75; sr. project engr./program mgr. US Govt. (Naval Weapons Station), Seal Beach, Ca. 1975--; mem. IEEE, ISA, Soc. of Reliab. Engrs., B'nai B'rith, ARMDI. Res: 20452 Graystone Lane Huntington Beach 92646 Ofc: Naval Weapons Station (34) Seal Beach 90740

SCHIERN, LARRY ALLEN, manufacturing co. executive; b. May 2, 1945, Los Angeles; s. Hymand and Mary (Genstel) S.; m. Barbara Alice abrams, Dec. 31, 1966; children: Stephanie, b. 1970, Tamara, b. 1972; edn: AA, L.A. Valley Coll. 1965; UCLA Ext. 1967. Career: credit mgr. Carte Blanche Corp., Los Angeles 1970-74; W. Regl. credit mgr. Pharmavite Inc., Arleta 1978-80; dir. of credit, Cole of California, L.A. 1980--; cons. Calibri Co. 1978; mem: Credit Mgrs. of So. Calif. (Apparel Grp. chmn. 1981); Catalina Federal Credit Union (bd. dirs. 1983-); bd. Temple Beth Shalom, Newhall; bd. Bouquet Canyon Hills Homeowners Assn. (ed. monthly newsletter); Republican; Jewish; rec: writing, sports. Res: 27568 Caraway Lane Saugus 91350 Ofc: Cole of Calif. 2615 Fruitland Ave Los Angeles 90058

SCHIMEL, LUCILLE, pharmacist; b. Dec. 18, 1922, Loretto, Minn.; d. Herman and Julia Santer; m. Herbert Karl Schimel, Dec. 14, 1946; edn: lic., Moderne Beauty Sch. 1947; BS Pharm., honors, Univ. of Wash., Seattle 1952. Career: pharmacy intern (Sisters of Charity), Providence Hosp., Seattle; pharmacist Horton & Converse Professional Pharmacy, Los Angeles 1952-54, Stacy Drug, Anaheim 1954-60, Sav-On, Santa Ana 1960-62; honors: Lambda Kappa Sigma 1950, Dean's List 1951, Mortar Board 1952; mem: CPHA, APHA, CEPA; Republican; Catholic. Res: 18312 James Road Villa Park 92667

SCHINASI, LEO M., manufacturing co. executive; b. Sept. 20, 1926, NY, NY; s. Abraham and Elizabeth L. (Chaiken) S.; m. Georgianne Gerber, Feb. 12, 1950; children: Steven, b. 1953, Debra, b. 1956; edn: BS in chem., Coll. of the City of New York 1955; Fellow Am. Inst. of Chemists 1975. Career: chemist H. Kohnstamm, NY, NY 1950-55; asst. prodn. mgr. Harshaw Chemical, Louisville, Ky. 1956-68; prodn. mgr. Tenneco Chemicals, Pischtaway, NJ 1968-71; group leader Pilot Plant, 1972-78, plant mgr. 1978-82, plant mgr. Nuodex Inc., Pleasanton, Calif. 1982--; honors: Kentucky Colonel 1964; mem. NY Pigment Club 1955, Fedn. of Paint Technology 1959; club: Crow Canyon Country; Jewish; rec: latch hooking, woodworking, tennis. Res: 576 Rolling Hills Ln San Ramon 94583 Ofc: Nuodex Inc. 5555 Sunol Blvd Pleasanton 94566

SCHINDLER, ELISABETH HILMA, real estate broker; b. Sept. 9, 1924, Harnosand, Sweden; d. Arvid Carl and Hilma (Norberg) Lofroth; m. Frank Schindler, Mar. 23, 1957; 1 dau. Margaret Elizabeth; edn: bus., Palmans Handelsinstitut Business Sweden; Realtors Inst. of Calif. Career: broker/owner Schindler Real Estate, Torrance; mem. Calif. Assn. of Realtors, Torrance Lomita Carson Bd. of Realtors, Swedish Womens Ednl. Assn. Internat. Inc., Vasa Order of Am.; Rel. Sci.; rec: travel. Res: 2620 W. 226th St Torrance 90505 Ofc: Schindler Real Estate, 2244 W. Sepulveda Blvd Torrance 90501

SCHIRM, LOUIS, IV, manufacturing executive/engineer; b. Jan. 27, 1948, Burbank; s. Louis, III, and Henriette (Scribe) S.; m. Linda Nesbit, Aug. 4,

1973; 1 child, Kelli, b. 1982; edn: BSEE, CalPoly Pomona, 1971. Career: design engr. Rockwell Intl., Anaheim 1f1-78; applications engr./systems engr. TRW, El Segundo 1978-81; pres. DSP Systems Corp., Anaheim 1981--; periodic consulting for various firms on optimized architures for digital signal processing; honors: Eagle Scout 1965; mem. IEEE; publs: 23 tech. articles in engring. mags. 1981-83; designer DSP Systems line of array processors; Republican; Catholic; rec: radio control airplanes, skiing. Ofc: DSP Systems, 1081 North Shepard St, Ste. E, Anaheim 92806

SCHLEGEL, GARY LEE, podiatrist/foot surgeon; b. Apr. 8, 1953, Los Angeles; s. Forrest Martin and Ida Christina (Oberg) S.; m. Suzanne, Dec. 15, 1979; edn: AA, Cosumnes Riv. Coll. 1973; BA, UC Davis 1975; DPM, State Univ. of NY 1976; DPM, Penn. Coll. of Podiatric Med. 1979; res. in foot surg., Milwaukee, Wis. 1980; real estate lic., Calif. Career: deputy sheriff of Sacramento Co., 1973-75; currently: pvt. practice podiatry, foot and ankle surgery, Sacto. with offices in Carmichael and Folsom; assoc. prof. Calif. Coll. of Podiatric Medicine 1980-81; cons. for Dow Corning Medical Implants Div. 1980-81; mem. Founders Bd. Placer Bank of Commerce; awards: Orthopedics Awd., PCPM 1979; Who's Who in Am. Colls. and Univs. 1979-80; Am. Coll. of Foot Orthopedists Awd. 1979; pres. Pi Delta Nat. Podiatry Honor soc. 1978/9; mem. Fellow Am. Coll. of Foot Orthopedists, Assoc. Am. Coll. of Foot Surgeons, Am. Bd. of Podiatric Surg., Calif. Podiatry Assn.; mem. Sacto. Bd. of Realtors; mem. bd. Sacto. Ballet Theatre; works: creator Anatomical Mus. at Penn. Coll. of Podiat. Med. 1978; author num. research arts. on foot surgery and med. 1978-; Republican; rec: gardening, racquetball, flying. Res: 109 Coffee Berry Ct. Folsom 95630 Ofc: 6403 Coyle Ave, Ste. 390, Carmichael 95608

SCHLEGEL, MICHAEL GENE, insurance co. executive; b. Mar. 1, 1949, Albany, Ore.; s. Oscar Leland and Margaret Jean (Canning) S.; m. Marcella Kay Leaton, Aug. 12, 1976; children: Kaellen, b. 1972, Krystalynn, b. 1978; edn: BSBA, Ore. State Univ. 1971; Chartered Life Underwriter 1977, Chartered Financial Cons. 1983, American Coll. Career: special agent The Prudential Ins. Co., Eugene, Ore. 1971-74, development mgr., 1974-80; agency mgr. The Prudential Ins. Co., San Rafael, Ca. 1980-83; regional field cons. The Prudential Ins. Co., Westlake Village 1983--; awards: Devel. Mgr. Citation (1977, 79), Agency Cit. & Vice Pres.'s Awd. (1981), Prudential; Junior Rotarian, 1966; Jr. CofC Strawberry Festival Chmnn. 1975; mem: Nat. Assn. Life Underwriters, Am. Soc. of CLU, Jr. CofC, Elks, Rotary; Republican; Presbyterian; rec: golf, tennis. Res: 10 San Blas Ct. Novato 94947 Ofc: Prudential Ins., 111 Lakeview Cyn Rd Westlake Village 91362

SCHLEMMER, GEORGE STEPHEN, safety engineer; b. Jan. 10, 1910, Thomas, Okla.; s. George Wm. and Elizabeth R. Schlemmer; m. Helen Ehrler, Apr. 9, 1936; div. 1942; m. 2d, Juana Lee Franklin, Oct. 25, 1945; children: Nancy, b. 1937, Charles, b. 1941, Sandra, b. 1947; edn: grad. Brighton H.S., 1928; various serv. schs., courses; Reg. Profl. Engr. Calif. Career: served to Comdr., LDO Engin. USN, 1932-63: enlisted 1932, out of serv. 1937-39, commnd. Warrant Ofcr. 1942, and Ensing, 1944; chief engr. aircraft carrier USS Bon Homme Richard, 2 yrs.; chief engr. cruiser USS Helena, 2 yrs.; instr. Naval Engring. Line Sch., US Naval Post Grad. Sch., Monterey, Calif. 2 yrs.; chief engr. cruiser USS Quincy, 6 mos.; asst. tech. tng. ofcr. US Naval Electronics Material Sch., Treas. Is., Calif. 3 yrs.; ret. USN 1963; staff State of Calif. Div. of Indsl. Safety 1964-76: sr. safety engr. offices in L.A. and Long Beach, 1972, dist. mgr. Panorama City ofc. 1973, consulting staff 1973-; covered 8 So. Calif. Counties for OSHA, conducted tng. seminars, spkr. employer and assn. meetings, prepared safety surveys, reports for US Dept. Labor under Target Indus. Pgm. for state 1971; currently cons. engr. Ellkim Corp., Irvine; bd. dirs. G.S.P. Corp., Elkim Corp.; trustee Kim Rush Patent Trust; mem. Retired Officers Assn., Soc. of Auto. Engrs., Vets. of Safety; Republican. Res: 1006 Rossmoyne Ave Glendale 91207 Ofc: Ellkim Corp., 6 Emperor, Irvine 92714

SCHMIDT, JOHN ALEXANDER, insurance/banking industry executive; b. Nov. 29, 1930, Chgo.; s. Walter Henry and Aili Elaine (Hanka) S.; edn: BS, UC Berkeley 1956. Career: ofcr. USN, 1956-60; underwriter Industrial Indemnity, San Francisco 1960-65; vice pres. Mission Ins. Group, SF 1965-70; pres. Schmidt & Schmidt Ins. Assocs. Inc., SF 1970--; bd. chmn. Atlas Savings & Loan Assn., SF 1979--; chief exec. Gemini Mgmt. Corp., SF 1984--. Mem: Golden Gate Bus. Assn. (founder, pres., dir. 1971-81); SF Chamber Orch. (dir. 1983-); Independent Agents/ Brokers Assn. of San Francisco (founder, pres., dir. 1973-79); Pride Found. (dir. 1976-80); Profl. Ins. Assn.; Western Assn. of Ins. Brokers; Nat. Assn. of Bus. Councils; CofC (SF and Nat.); mil: ltjg USN 1956-60; cpl. USMC 1950-52; Republican; Catholic; rec: music, gardening. Res: 1182 Fulton San Francisco 94117 Ofc: 130 Bush, Ste. 7, San Francisco 94104

SCHMIDT, LYNDA WHEELWRIGHT, jungian analyst; b. July 29, 1931, Peking, China (US parents); d. Joseph Balch and Jane B. (Hollister) Wheelwright; m. Klaus Schmidt, June 28, 1950; children: Karen (Calley), b. 1953, Claudia (Lewis), b. 1955; edn: BA, UC Berkeley 1965, MSW, 1968; analytical psychologist of the C.G. Jung Inst., San Francisco. Career: clinical social wkr. Presbyterian Hosp. (Pacific Med. Center), San Francisco 1968-71; pvt. practice of analytical psychology, S.F. 1971--; teaching analyst/ chmn. Certifying Bd., C.G. Jung Inst., S.F.; mem: C.G.Jung Inst. (S.F. and Internat. Orgn.), Nat. Assn. of Social Wkrs., Soc. of Clin. Social Work; author: Time Out of Mind, Trekking the Hindu Kush (1978); arts. in psych. journals; Democrat; rec: horses, piano, wilderness. Address: 2021 Webster St San Francisco 94115; North Brooklin, Maine

SCHMIDT, WERNER ERICH, computer management executive; b. June 21, 1959, San Jose; s. Winfred P. and Asta W. (Ewaardt) S.; m. Deborah C. Matson, June 11, 1983; edn: AA in D.P., De Anza Coll. 1979; mgmt. courses, Mission Coll. 1981-82. Career: computer opr. Benson, Mountain View 1978-80; software engr. Versatec, Santa Clara 1980-83; mgr. computer systems, Scientific Calculations, San Jose 1983--; honors: Senate Resolution No. 777 for scholastic extracurricular activites, May 25, 1977; mem. Monta Vista Madrigals singing grp.; Prot.; rec: camping. Res: 7759 Lilac Way Cupertino 95014 Ofc: Scientific Calculations, 625 River Oaks Pkwy, San Jose 95134

SCHMITT, CAROLYN SUE, vocational counselor; b. Dec. 19, 1940, Charleston, W.V.; d. Charles Lee and Louise Mary (DeHainaut) Jarrett; m. Carveth J. R. Schmitt, May 14, 1954; edn: BS in bus. adm., Univ. Charleston, Morris Harvey Coll. 1962; BS, liberal studies, Univ. NY, Albany 1978; BA, soc. sci., Edison State Coll., Trenton, NJ 1979; MA, edn./manpower adm., Univ. Redlands 1974. Career: adminstrv. asst. TRW Inc., Def. & Space Sys., San Bernardino 1962-63; ins. dept. So. Calif. Mortgage & Loan Corp., San Bernardino 1963-66; empl. counselor Calif. State Empl. Devel. Dept., 1966-78; instr. Pacific Am. Inst./Whitehead Coll., Redlands 1979; sr. voc. supv. rehab. counselor Westside Counseling Center, San Berdo. 1979-80; voc. counselor pvt. practice, Rialto 1980--; honors: recognition, Westside Counseling Ctr. 1980; listed num. biographical dictionaries; mem: Calif. Personnel & Guidance Assn., Calif. Career Guidance Assn., Calif. Rehab. Counselor Assn., Internat. Assn. of Personnel Empls. (chpt. vp 1970); Univ. of Redlands Fellows; Valley Prospectors, Phi Kappa Kappa Sor., Nat. Travel Club, Fontana Tour Club, M & M Tour Club, Am. Philatelic Soc., Arrowhead Stamp Club, Am. Topical Assn. (life); mem. Rex, Edison State Coll., Univ. of Charleston, Univ. of Redlands alumni assns.; Republican; rec: philately, badminton, hiking. Address: 538 N. Pampas Ave Rialto 92376

SCHMITT, CARVETH JOSEPH RODNEY, internal auditor; b. Sept. 10, 1934, Manitowoc, Wisc.; s. Clarence Charles and Thelma June (White) S.; m. Carolyn Sue Jarrett, May 14, 1965; edn: dip. bus. adm. & acctg., Skadron Coll. of Bus., San Bernardino 1959; AA, bus. mgmt., San Bernardino Valley Coll. 1962; BS in bus. adm., Univ. riverside 1970; BS, liberal studies, Univ. of NY, Albany 1977; BA, soc. sci., Edison State Coll., Trenton, NJ 1978; MA, edn./ manpower adm., Univ. Redlands 1975; cert. tchr., community coll. counselor and personnel worker, Calif. Career: acct. Barnum & Flagg Co., San Bernardino, 1959-70; credit mgr. Stationers Corp., 1970-77, office mgr. 1977-83; registered rep., ins. agt. (part-time), Inland Amer. Securities, Inc., 1966-70, reg. rep. Parker Jackson & Co., 1970-73, LeBarron Securities, Inc., 1974; internal auditor Stockwell & Binney Office Products Centers, 1983--; honors: listed, Who's Who in the West, num. biog. dictionaries, mem: Colo., N.W., Nev. mining assns.; Gold Prospectors Assn. of Am. (charter), Valley Prospectors, Nat. Travel Club, Fontana Tour Club, M & M Tour Club, Univ. of Redlands Fellows, Am. Philatelic Soc., Arrowhead Stamp Club, Nat. Rifle Assn. (life), Nat. Geog. Soc., Masons; Rex, Edison State Coll., Univ. of Redlands alumni assns.; mil: personnel splst. USAF 1954-58, GCM, Nat. Def. medal; Republican; rec: collector first editions, rock collector. Res: 538 N. Pampas Ave Rialto 92376 Ofc: Stockwell & Binney Office Products Centers, 420 S. E St, POB 5219, San Bernardino 92412

SCHMITT, EDWARD GEORGE, II, microcomputer software c. executive; b. Feb. 4, 1946, Santa Rosa; s. Edward George and Mae (Hirschey) S.; m. Phyllis Kemp, Feb. 3, 1968; children: Edward b. 1971, Kelly b. 1974, Katherine b. 1979; edn: BS (cum laude), Syracuse Univ. 1968, MS, 1970; Calif. lic. Real Estate Broker 1982. Career: supt. Container Corp. of America, Phila., Pa. 1970-75; mill supt. Container Corp. of Am. Santa Clara, Ca. 1975-80; owner Bountiful Enterprises, San Jose 1980-84; pres. Trinity Solutions Inc., San Jose 1982--; mem. Paper Industry Mgmt. Assn./Southwest Div. 1972-83 (PIMA 2d v.p. 1977, 1st v.chmn. 1978, chmn. 1979, bd. trustee 1980-82); San Jose Real Estate Bd. 1980-; honors: Alpha Xi Sigma 1967, NSF research grant in biology 1968; mem. Los Gatos Christian Ch. 1982-, deacon, corp. ofcr. 1982-, Retirement Fund adminstrv. com., Capital Funding com., New Members com., Seminars spkr.; works: research Cellulose Consumption in the Powder Post Beetle (1968); designed, constructed a Long Tube Vertical Evaporator still in use for resrch. projects Syracuse Univ., 1969-70; tech. presentations Penn-Jer-Del Div., Paper Indus. Mgmt Assn. 1970, 73; Republican; Fundamental Christian; rec: racquetball. Res: 1144 Carla Dr San Jose 95120 Ofc: Trinity Solutions Inc. 5340 Thornwood Dr, Ste 102, San Jose 95123

SCHMITZ, EUGENE GERARD, consulting firm president; b. Sept. 17, 1929, Brackenridge, Pa.; s. Wienand Gerard and Florence Marie (Grimm) S.; m. Anna May Lee, May 3, 1952; children: Joyce, b. 1953, Michael, b. 1956, Carol, b. 1957, John, b. 1959, John, b. 1961; edn: BSME (equiv) Ariz. St. Univ. 1959-63, Phoenix Coll. 1947-48; Reg. Profl. Engr., Calif. Career: Field Enterprises Ednl. Corp., Phoenix 1955-59; dist. sales mgr., self empl. freelance design 1959-61; design engr. Motorola Inc., Govt. Electronics Div., Scottsdale, Az. 1961-67; project engr./supvr., methods engr. Philco-Ford Corp., Space &: Reentry Sys. Div., Palo Alto 1967-70; pgm. adminstr./sr. mfg. engr. Memorex Equip. Grp., Santa Clara 1970-71; res. plant mgr. Philco-Ford Corp., Western Dev. Labs., Palo Alto, Remote Assy Op. 1971-72; cons. engr. FMC Corp., Def. Tech. Lab, Santa Clara 1972-73 and Ordnance Engr. Div., San Jose 1973-75; deputy dir. engring. and sr. staff consulting engr. Stetter Assn. Inc., Palo Alto 1975-80; pres./chief engr. Schmitz Engr. Assocs., San Jose 1980--; project engr. FMC Corp. Ordnance Div. Engr. 1982-; mem: Nat. Soc. of Profl. Engrs. (sr. mem. 1979), Profl. Engrs. in Pvt. Practice, Soc. Mfg. Engrs. (sr. mem. 1970), Am. Inst. of Indsl. Engr. (sr. mem. 1981); publs: over 200 major proposals for US & fgn. corps.; Motorola Govt. Electr. Div. Drafting Manual

(1962 ed.); Philco-Ford, Space & Re-Entry Sys. Div. Mfg. and Process Stds.; mil: US Army 1948-55, Korean Service, GCM, Occup. Japan, Occup. Germany medals, Presdtl. and Korean Pres. Unit Citations; Republican; rec: gourmet cooking, camping, carpentry, automotive repair. Address: Schmitz Engr. Assocs. 3061 Vesuvius Ln. San Jose 95132

SCHMUNK, DONALD FRED, physicist; b. Mar. 9, 1937, Portland, Ore.; s. Fred and Arpa (Pfaff) S.; m. Peggy Rae Locke, Dec. 4, 1965; chil: Dennis Donald, b. 1966; m. 2d, Sara May Goldstein, Mar. 3, 1968; chil: Sara Lynn, b. 1969, Donna May, b. 1973, Angela Joy, b. 1978; edn: BS, Portland State Coll. 1959; MS, Ore. State Coll. 1960; postgrad. wk, USC 1962, UCLA 1967. Career: tech. staff Pacific Semiconductors, Inc., Lawndale 1961-64; tech. staff TRW Sys. (fmr. Space Tech. Labs.), Redondo Beach 1964-66; group mgr. research TRW Semiconductors, 1966-67; group sci./supr. solid state material studies Autonetics Div. No. American Rockwell (now Rockwell Intl. Corp., 1967-71; staff engr./mgmt. Microelectronics Div., Rockwell Intl. Corp., 1972-77, project mgr. Electronic Sys. Grp. 1977-80, proj. coord. focalplane prods. Strategic Sys. Grp. 1980-81; sr. sci. solid state Electronics Research Lab., Aerospace Corp., El Segundo 1981--; mem: IEEE (computer grp., electron devices grp., solid state circuits grp.); Amer. Vacuum Soc.; Soc. Photo-Optical Instrumentation Engrs.; Amer. Inst. Aero. and Astro.; Orange Co. Amateur Astronomers Assn.; Full Gospel Businessmens Fellowship Intl. (past chpt. dir., v.p.); Portland State Coll. Engrs. Club (past secty.); Intl. Platform Assn.; Smithsonian Instn.; Nat. Rifle Assn.; Calif. Rifle and Pistol Assn. (state marksman precision air pistol champ. 1974); recipient Human Resources of USA award, Amer. Heritage Research Assn. 1975. Res. 3245 Greenleaf Dr Brea 92621 Ofc: Aerospace Corp., 2350 E. El Segundo Blvd El Segundo 90245

SCHNAIDT MILLER, CLARA JULIA, real estate broker; b. June 6, 1912, Childstown, S.Dak.; d. Wm. Charlie and Christina Marie (Schindler) Unruh; m. John R. Schnaidt, June 13, 1931; m. 2d. Henry W. Miller, Dec. 25, 1977; edn: grad. Wasco Union H.S. 1931; Calif. lic. notary public 1945, real estate broker 1951, insurance agt. 1951. Career: fmr. teletype opr. Santa Fe Railway, beauty shop owner, real estate ofc. secty.; realtor/ insurance agent/ owner Schnaidt's Real Estate, Shafter 1951--; recognition awards from Shafter Potato & Cotton Festival 1972, Bus. & Profl. Womens Club 1977, Shafter CofC 1983; mem: Nat., Calif. assns. of realtors, Bakersfield Bd. of Realtors, Nat. Inst. of Farm & Land Brokers, Independent Ins. Agents, Nat. Assn. of Women Realtors, Shafter CofC & Agriculture, Shafter Hist. Soc., Shafter Potato & Cotton Festival Com., Shafter Womens Club, Bus. & Profl. Womens Club, Am. Legion Aux.; Democrat; Prot.; rec: coins & antiques, gardening, travel. Res: 17473 Scaroni Ave Shafter 93263 Ofc: Schnaidt's Real Estate, 317 Central Ave Shafter 93263

SCHNATHORST, WILLIAM CHARLES, plant pathologist; b. May 8, 1929, Fort Dodge, Iowa; s. Wm. T. and Elizabeth N. (Nelson) S.; m. Rosemarie Meyer, Dec. 29, 1951; children: Diana, b. 1956, William, b. 1957, Douglas, b. 1961; edn: BS, Univ. of Wyo. 1952, MS, 1953; PhD, Univ. Calif. 1957. Career: teaching asst. Univ. of Wyo. 1952-53; research asst., plant pathol., UC Davis 1953-56; research plant pathologist, US Dept. of Agriculture, Dept. of Plant Pathol. UC Davis 1956--; lectr. in plant pathol. UC Davis; USDA designated rep. Tropical and Subtropical Agriculture, regl., nat., internat. cons. on plant disease; honors: Sigma Xi (1952) (1956), Phi Kappa Phi (1956), Alpha Zeta(1951); secty./chmn. of the Cotton Disease Council, 1978-81; chmn. of the Conf. on Control of Soet Fungi 1979; mem: Am. Phytopathological Soc., Mycological Soc. of Am., Botanical Soc. of Am., Internat. Soc. for Plant Pathol., Am. Inst. of Biological Scis., Calif.- Wyo. Acad. of Sci., Am. Assn. of Arts and Scis., BSA, Fedn. of Fly Fishers; publs: 138 sci. papers on plant diseases and plant pathogens; Prot.; rec: fly fishing, conservation, camping. Res: 647 Cleveland St Davis 95616 Ofc: Dept. Plant Pathology, Univ. of Calif., Davis 95616

SCHNEIDER, BARRY LEE, contract furnishing co. president; b. June 5, 1954, Santa Cruz, Ca.; s. Monroe C. and Barbara L. Schneider; m. Ann Baumgartner, Sept. 24, 1977; children: Brandon, b. 1979, Blake, b. 1981, Kevin, b. 1982; edn: BA, honors, UC Los Angeles 1976. Career: asst. to the president, Monroe Schneider Assocs., San Francisco 1977, vice pres. 1979, senior v.p. 1982, pres. and chief op. ofcr. 1983--, founded MSA (Texas), Inc. in Dallas (1980), Houston (1981); founded MSA-LA in Los Angeles (1983); mem. Neo-Con Panel, Chgo. 1980; mem. Building Owners & Mgmt. Assn.; dir. Annual Am. Cancer Research Dinner, A.M.C. 1979, 80, 83; recipient pres.'s award San Francisco YMCA 1982, 83; publs: interview, Contract Mag. 1983; Republican; Jewish; rec: golf, outdoor sports. Res: 2586 Butternut Dr Hillsborough 94010 Ofc: Monroe Schneider Assocs. 274 Wattis Way South San Francisco 94083-2387

SCHNEIDER, JOHN FREDRICK, certified public accountant; b. Apr. 7, 1945, Berkeley; s. George Mathias and Virgiinia (Watson) S.; m. Roberta, Aug. 29, 1970; children: Janet, Julie, George, and James; edn: BS in B.A., Calif Poly State Univ. 1971; CPA, Calif. 1974. Career: staff acct. Arthur Andersen & Co., L.A. 1971-73; auditor Keith V. Lapp Acctcy Corp., Santa Maria 1973-74; acct. Felice & Jimenez Acctcy. Corp., Gilroy 1974-76; finl. vice pres. Bostons Pet Supply Inc., Buellton 1976-77; finance dir. City of Grover City, Calif. 1977-79; CPA/vice pres. De Pauw &: Schneider, Inc., Los Osos 1979--; honors: U.S. Presidential Award for V.I.T.A. Pgm.; mem: Nat. Assn. of Accts., AICPA, CSCPA, Chamber of Commerce; Republican; Christian; rec: hunting, fishing, bowling. Res: 941 Mesa St Morro Bay 93442 Ofc: De Pauw & Schneider Inc., 2115 10th St, Ste. B, Los Osos 93402

SCHNEIDERMAN, WILLIAM LEE, physician, obstetrician-gynecologist; b.

June 19, 1944, Brklyn., NY; s. Sol and Pearl S.; m. Michele, Aug. 27, 1972; children: Matthew, b. 1977, Jordan, b. 1983; edn: BA, Franklin & Marshall Coll. 1967; MD, NY Medical Coll. 1974. Career: intern and resident in obstets. & gyn., Kings County Hosp. Downstate Med. Center, Brklyn. 1974-77; pvt. practice in Ob-Gyn in New Hartford and Winsted, Conn., Kaiser Permanente Medical Group, Santa Clara, Ca. 1978--; clin. instr. State Univ. of NY 1976-77, Univ. of Conn. 1977-78; honors: All-American in Wrestling 1965-66; mem: AMA, Am. Coll. of Obstets. & Gyns., Schufelt Sco., Peninsula Gynecol. Soc.; Jewish; rec: swimming, hiking, numismatics. Res: 1068 Queensbridge Ct., San Jose 95120 Ofc: Permanente Medical Group, 900 Kiely Blvd Santa Clara 95051

SCHNIEPP, WALTER HERMAN, rancher, real estate broker; b. Oct. 6, 1913, Orange, Calif.; s. Fred G. and Rosa L. (Rosenthal) S.; m. Catherine L. Melton, Apr. 3, 1937; children: Gary David, b. 1942, Ann Louise, b. 1947; grad. Orange H.S. 1932. Career: orchard contractor, rancher, real estate broker; dir. Villa Park Orchards (1946), served 18 years; dir. Orange County Pest Control (1947), 12 years; dir. Orange Co. Mosquito Abatement, 10 years; served on first council, Villa Park City Council, councilman 3 terms 1962-72, mayor 1970; Republican; Lutheran; rec: fishing, travel. Res: 515 36th St. Newport Beach 92663

SCHNYDER, LINDSAY ANNE, radio station president; b. July 2, 1952, Bloomington, Ill.; d. Robert John and Constance (Sherbert) Schnyder; grad. Huntington Beach H.S. 1970. Career: gen. mgr. radio sta. KZZZ, Albuquerque, N.Mex. 1978-80; account exec. KVOR-AM, Colo. Spgs., Colo. 1980, KRDO T.V., Colo. Spgs., Colo. 1980-81; mktg. dir. Columbus (Ohio) Zoo, 1981-83; pres./gen. mgr. radio sta. KOTE-KKZZ, Lancaster, Calif. 1983--; dir. Antelope Valley Health Fund.; honors: Exec. of the Year 1979, Sunbelt Communications; One of 80 Women in N.Mex. to Watch in the 80s; mem: AAZPA, NOW, AWRT, Greenpeace, March of Dimes, Desert Haven, Salvation Army; rec: skiing, swimming. Res: 44200, No. 33, Kingtree, Lancaster 93534 Ofc: KOTE-KKZZ, 44748 Elm, Lancaster 93534

SCHOENFIELD, CONNIE HUNTER, inventor/consultant; b. Dec. 8, 1938, Indpls.; d. Robert C. and Inez Blanche (Hunter) Webber; m. Leslie J. Schoenfield, Oct. 26, 1975; children: David, Tiffany, Philip; edn: AA, Stephens Coll. for Women 1958; Harvard summer sch. 1958, Purdue Univ. 1959-60, UCLA Ext. 1982. Career: producer "Funny Money" (game show pilot) 1971; inventor for The Jack Ryan Group, 1972-75; invented "Planter People" (new way of growing seeds) and devel. it into a greeting card that "gets fat & grows hair"; current: internat. mktg. consultant (new products), dba Pennytower Prodns., Los Angeles; sales agt./cons. Lou Ehlers Cadillac, L.A.; mem. Cadillac Crest Club, Gen. Motors; arbitrator L.A. Better Business Bur.; mem. Doctors Wives Service League, Diabetics Unit of Cedars Sinai, Nat. Notary Assn., Loren Zachary Soc. for Young Operatic Singers, The Magic Castle (magicians club). Address: Pennytower Productions, 10122 Empyrean Way, No. 102, Los Angeles 90067; Lou Ehlers Cadillac, 5151 Wilshire Blvd, Los Angeles 90036

SCHORADT, FRED S., electric supply wholesaler; b. Mar. 29, 1931, Bishop; s. Richard B. and Onetta M. (Linge) S.; div.; two sons, Steven F., b. 1954, Michael W., b. 1956; grad. Bishop H.S. Career: with an elec. supply wholesaler, 1955-72; founder/pres. Norcal Electric Supplin Inc., Redding 1972--; mil: aviation electrician 2c USN 1951-5; Republican; rec: fishing, hunting. Res: 565 Terrace Dr Redding 96002 Ofc: Norcal Elec. Supply Inc. 935 Industrial St Redding 96002

SCHORKEN, DOROTHY LOUISE, inventor/co. president; B. Jan. 23, 1932, San Pedro; d. Dick Edward (poet laureate of San Pedro, Calif.) and Katherine Lorrine (Davidson) Wolfe; m. Carl Schorken, Dec. 24, 1960; children: Sheri, b. 1963, Carl, b. 1965; edn: AA, Harbor Jr. Coll. 1952; BA, CSU Long Beach 1958; Calif. gen. teaching credential 1983. Career: elem. sch. tchr. (sub.), Los Angeles Unified Sch. Dist., 1977-78; inventor/pres. Products Exceptionale, Thousand Oaks 1979--; inventions incl. Device for Supporting Infants (US Patent, 1970); honors: first woman inventor to appear on the Inventors' Mart TV Show (1973); mem: Inventors Club of Am., World Assn. of Inventors and Researchers, Am. Entrepreneurs Assn., Internat. Engrepreneurs Assn.; mem. The Statue of Liberty, Ellis Island Found.; mem. The Research Council of Scripps Clinic, and Research Found., La Jolla; mem. Nat. Humane Edn. Soc., Leesburg, Va.; mem. Am., So. Calif. Bouvier des Flandres Club; Republican; Methodist; rec: inventing. Address: Products Exceptionale, 2271 Northpark St Thousan Oaks 91362

SCHORR, MICHAEL SANDY, physician; b. July 9, 1951, Los Angeles; s. Richard Carl and Sara (Roth) S.; m. Phyllis, Dec. 21, 1976; 1 son, Joshua, b. 1981; edn: BA, UC Santa Barbara 1974; MD, Eastern VA. Medical 1977; Bd. Cert. Family Practice, Med. Coll. of VA. 1981. Career: medical dir. Skilled Nursing Facility, Ceres, Ca. 1982-83; current: phys., Gould Medical Group, Modesto/Patterson; chief of staff Del Puerto Hosp., Patterson 1984--; med. dir. Intercept Alcoholism Treatment Program, 1983--; teaching faculty UC Davis, Gen. Family Practice Center; mem: AMA, Am. Acad. of Family Practice, Calif. Med. Assn., Rotarian; publs: arts. in med. & sci. journals, nat. conf. presentations; Jewish. Res: 3612 Ganado Way Modesto 95356 Ofc: 325 W. Las Palmas, Patterson 95365

SCHOTT, ROBERT GENE, produce co. president; b. Nov. 22, 1946, Santa Cruz, Ca.; s. Nick and Ethel (Litchfield) S.; m. Robyn Adamina, July 27, 1968; 1 son, Nick, b. 1975; edn: BS, CalPoly St. Univ., S.L.O. 1968. Career: plant mgr. Spiegl Foods, Santa Maria 1974; plant mgr. Dalgety Foods, Salinas 1975, area mgr. 1977, regional mgr. 1979; pres. Nature Pak, Inc., 1981--, and pres.

Fresh Harvest, Inc., 1983--; mem: Am. Mgmt. Assn., Aircraft Owners and Pilots Assn.; Democrat; rec: hunting, fishing, automobiles. Res: 13000 Paseo Barranco, Salinas 93908 Ofc: Nature Pak, POB 143, Salinas 93902

SCHOUN, WILLIAM, dentist; b. Oct. 22, 1927, Brookfield, Ill.; s. Joseph and Mary (Barant) S.; div.; edn: BA, Andrews Univ. 1951; DDS, Loma Linda Univ. 1958. Career: dental practice partnership with Henry Chab, DDS, Hollywood 1958-60, sole owner 1960--, moved to Ventura, Calif. 1970--; lectr. on dental health in high schs.; joins other Seventh-Day Adventist doctors in trips to Mexico to provide free dental service for the poor; honors: Am. Coll. of Dentists Writing Award 1958; mem. Am. Dental Assn., Calif. Dental Assn., Lions Club, Philosda, Loma Linda Alumni Assn.; Republican; Seventh Day Adventist; rec: sailing, movie photog., travel, skiing. Res: 5562 Lewis Ln Agoura 91301 Ofc: 3400 Loma Vista Dr Ventura 93003

SCHRAMM, ARTHUR DANIEL, financial services co. executive; b. July 21, 1938, Cincinnati, Ohio; s. Arthur Daniel and Emma Laura (Clift) S.; m. Patricia M. Severi, Oct. 21, 1978; children: Pamela, b. 1962, Michael, b. 1965; edn: San Bernardino Valley Coll. 1976-78, Nat. Installment Banking Sch. Univ. of Colo. 1979, Pepperdine Univ. Key Executive Pgm. 1983. Career: branch rep. to mgr., Economy Savings & Loan, Cincinnati, Ohio 1959-64; mgr. Credithrift Financial Corp. offices in Napa and Carmichael, 1964-75; regl. vice pres. Morris Plan Co. of Calif., supvsg. branches in L.A., San Bernardino, and Riverside Counties, 1975-81; pres., CEO, founder and dir. Corona Thrift & Loan and Corona Credit Corp., 1982--; vice pres., secty. and dir. Corona Bancorp.; Dir. Southcoast Thrift & Loan, Southcoast Bancorp, and Southcoast Financial 1983-84; Dir. Palm Springs Bancorp, Palm Springs Thrift & Loan, Oasis Finance; Dir./secty. Thrift Association Bancorp; Dir./secty. Riverside Bancorp, Riverside Thrift & Loan; secty. Raincross Finance; cons. Intrastate Finl. Devel. Corp., Moreno Valley Thrift & Loan; mem: Rotary, Masons, past pres. Napa Active 20-30 Club; mil: sgt. USMC 1956-59; Republican; Prot.; rec: hunt, fish, rockhound. Res: PO Box 5639, San Bernardino 92412 Ofc: Corona Thrift & Loan, 505 S. Corona Mall, Corona 91720

SCHRAMM, SUSAN JONES, clinical social worker; b. Dec. 20, 1940, Charlotte, N.C.; d. William Charles Jones and Suzanne (Westbrook) Jones Holden; m. Gordon Luther Schramm, May 29, 1964; 2 daus: Natalie, b. 1970, Valerie, b. 1973; edn: BA in sociol, Univ. N.C. at Greensboro 1963; MSW, Univ. Tenn. 1965; lic. Clin. Social Worker, Calif. 1976; lifetime Tchg. Cred. (Sec., Jr. Coll.), Calif. 1974. Career: sr. child welfare wkr. San Diego Co. Adoption Svcs. 1965-7; psychiatric social wkr. Calif. State Dept. Mental Hlth, Santa Rosa 1967-74; clin. soc. wkr. Family Svc. Agcy. of Sonoma County, 1971-77; cons. Sonoma Co. Supt. of Schs. Child Devel. Ctrs., 1974-76; instr. CSU Sonoma Ext. 1981--; lic. clinical social worker, pvt. practice 1976--; cons. to convalescent hosps., resdtl. care facilities, retail cos., 1970--; instr. Santa Rosa Jr. Coll. 1974-77; bd. dirs. (pres. 1982-4) Summerfield-Waldorf Sch. of Santa Rosa. Mem: Calif. Soc. Clin. Social Wkrs. (bd.dirs. 1982-4); Nat. Registry of Hlth Care Providers in Clin. Social Work 1975-; Soroptomist; Sonoma Co. Forum. Helped estab. first crisis telephone service in Sonoma Co. (1968), devel. reg. manual and tng. pgm. for volunteers. Lutheran (Bd. of Youth). Rec: ringing handbells, jog, needle crafts. Address: Susan Schramm, LCSW, 2330 Cassidy Ct. W., Santa Rosa 95401

SCHREDL, MICHAEL GEORGE, educator, resource specialist for spl. edn./ German instr.; b. Aug. 23,1939, Sacramento; s. Michael and Renee (Weisel) Schredl; m. Judy Ann Schwarz, June 9, 1962; chil: Michael, b. 1963, Karen, b. 1965; edn: BS, engr., US Mil Acad., 1962; MS, math., Univ. of Santa Clara 1969 and MA, learning disabilities, 1975; PhD, edn., Walden Univ., 1976; grad. Air Command and Staff Coll., grad. Air War Coll.; grad. Indsl. Coll.of the Armed Forces. Career: USAF satellite control integrations ofcr. 1962-66; pgm. adminstr. IBM, 1966-68; educator 1968--; owner MMJK and Assocs., gen. contracting firm; dir. The Rohner Corp. (computer software); honors: elected to Mathematics Assn of Am. 1975; mem: Santa Clara Co. Math. Assn (pres. 1977), Calif.Teacher's Assn. (Faculty pres. 1972), Nat.Council of Math. Tchrs., Am. Assn. of Teachers of German, Reserve Ofcrs.Assn. (state del, com. mem.), Air Force Assn., Train Collectors Assn.; publs: A Collection of Original Proofs of Desargue's Theorem (1969), Metronome Paced Remediation (1976); mil: lt.col. USAF 1962-66, USAFR 1966-, 18 decorations incl. Meritorious Service Medal; Democrat; Roman Catholic; rec: clock repair, toy train collection res: 10315 Kenny Ln San Jose 95127 ofc: East Side Union High Sch District, 1776 Ed. Park Dr. San Jose 95133.

SCHRIEBMAN, JEFFREY ALAN, software co. president; b. Jan. 21, 1948, San Francisco; s. Harry and Annette Ethel (Sabel) S.; m. Judith Webb, Sept. 9, 1979; 1 son, David, b. 1982; edn: BS, 1970, and MS, 1971, Univ. of Calif. Career: computer system pgmmr. UC Berkeley, 1971-75, computer system mgr. 1975-78; computer consultant, self-empl. 1978-81; founder/pres. Unisoft Corp., Berkeley 1981--. Ofc: Unisoft Corporation, 739 Allston Way, Berkeley 94710

SCHROEDER, RITA MOLTHEN, chiropractor; b. Oct. 25, 1922, Savanna, Ill.; d. Frank Joseph and Ruth Jessie (McKenzie) Molthen; m. Richard H. Schroeder, D.C., Apr. 23, 1948; div. 1981; children: Richard, b. 1949, Andrew, b. 1952, Barbara, b. 1953, Thomas, b. 1956, Paul, b. 1960, Madeline, b. 1962; edn: DC, Palmer Sch. of Chiropractic 1949; DC, Cleveland Coll. of Chiro. 1960; Calif. lic. Dr. Chiro., 1961. Career: engring. tooling liaison, Douglas Aircraft Co. 1942-46; chiropractic practise in Brooklyn, NY 1949-59, Fresno, Ca. 1961--, pres. Schroeder Chiropractic, Inc.; bd. dirs. Pacific States Chiropractic Coll. 1978-79, pres. 1980-81; honors: Ambassador Awd., Palmer

Coll. of Chiro.; mem: Internat. Chiro. Assn., Internat. Chiro. Assn. of Calif., Fedn. of Chiropractors, Calif. Chiro. Assn., Internat. Platform Assn.; Republican; Catholic; rec: hunting, fishing, swimming, diving. Res: 9870 N. Millbrook Fresno 93710 Ofc: Schroeder Chiropractic Inc., 2535 N. Fresno, Fresno 93703

SCHUBERT, FREDERICK WILLIAM, JR., orthodontist; b. May 17, 1936, San Francisco; s. Frederick Wm. and Veronica Mary (Hyde) S.; m. Midge L. Conroy, Nov. 10, 1980; children: John Frederick, b. 1965, Robert Anthony, b. 1967, William Frederick, b. 1970; edn: BS, DDS, UCSF Sch. Dentistry 1964; num. postgrad. tng. courses 1964-. Career: currently staff orthodontist, Robert G. Oliver, 5600, No. 4, California, Bakersfield; orthodontic cons. Naval Regl. Med. Ctr. Oakland, 1973-83; awards: Internat. Coll. of Dentists Award 1964, Mosby Book Scholarship Award 1964, charter editor sr. dental students yearbook 1964, 1st nat. prize literary award Dental Students Mag. 1963; recipient 2 public health research fellowships 1962; mem: Am. Assn. of Orthodontists, Pacific Coast Soc. of Orthodontists (bd. dirs. 1970-72), Calif. Soc. of Orthodontists, E. Bay Orthodontic Study Club, Peter K. Thomas Orthognathic Study Club, Am. Cleft Palate Assn., Am./Calif. Soc. Dentistry for Children, Am./ Calif. Dental Assn., So. Alameda Co. Dental Soc. (past bd. dirs., ed.), Kern Co. Dental So., Alameda Co. Health Dept.; charter fellow Coll. of Dentistry internat. (exec. bd. 1975-78); dental adv. bd. Chabot Coll. 1968-9, Eden Voc. Ctr., San Lorenzo 1976-80; mem. Naval Reserve Assn. (life), Reserve Officers Assn. (life), US Naval Inst., Assn. of Mil. Surgeons (life); served to capt. USNR-R 1954-; Catholic; rec: psychology. Ofc: Robert G. Oliver, 5600 No. 4, California, Bakersfield

SCHUCK, LAWRENCE ANDREW, manufacturing co. executive, pharmacist; b. Aug. 23, 1915, Oxnard; s. John Frank and Anna Francis (Bryant) S.; m. Doris H. Altland, July 26, 1941; children: Lawrence B., b. 1943; Thomas B., b. 1946; Michael R., b. 1959; edn: AA, Ventura Coll. 1935; BS pharm., UC Berkeley 1938; Ensign USNR, Cornell Univ. 1943. Career: pharmacist, Owl Drug Co., 1939-, mgr. 1942; pharmacist Parke-Davis & Co., 1946-, dist. mgr. 1951-, gov. sales supr. P.D. Div. Warner Lambert 1965, ret. 1975; awards: nat. sales award (new Pontiac) 1947, nat. sales dist. mgr. award 1954, 58; mem: Fellow Am. College Pharmacists (1955), Bay Area Pharmacy Assn., DSA (past councilor), Elks, UC Berkeley life mem. & donor UC Coll. of Pharmacy (Blue & Gold Assn.); works: devel. clerk tng. program; mil: lt. USNR, 2 combat awards, Presdtl. Unit Cit. for Solomon Island Op.; Republican (Pres. Task Force); Catholic; rec: workshop, keeping current with pharm. devels. Res: 23 Tahquitz Ct Camarillo 93010

SCHUELE, WILLA C., musician, business owner; b. Nov. 27, 1927, Ada, Okla.; d. Andrew Jackson and Lena Laten (Gray) Clelland; m. Charles Wretling; children: Charles, b. 1945, Delayna, b. 1950, Mark, b. 1953; m. 2d. John Schuele, Oct. 12, 1979; edn: music maj., Bethany Coll. 1946-47; grad., Oklahoma City Bus. Coll. 1950; music courses, Kans. State Univ. 1970. Career: tchr. piano and voice, 1950-77; church choir dir., vocalist/pianist num. civic & comm. affairs (as minister's wife) 1949-75; profl. pianist var. resorts in the Catskills, NY 1956-59; owner/tng. supvsr. Willa's Janitorial Service, Carlsbad, Ca. 1983--; mem. Carlsbad CofC, Women's Information Network; Republican; Methodist; rec: oil painting, dancing, singing. Address: Willa's Janitorial Service, 6673-A Paseo Del Norte Carlsbad 92008

SCHUETZ, DAVID HAROLD, clinical hospital pharmacist; b. Mar. 24, 1943, Bakersfield; s. Harold Francis and June Ada (Draheim) S.; m. Victoria Kelso, June 14, 1969; children: Christopher, b. 1972, Heather, b. 1976; edn: BA, St. Mary's Coll., Calif. 1965; Dr. Pharm., Univ. of Pacific 1970, MSc, 1973. Career: comm. pharm., Rosse's Pharm., Stockton 1970-71; comm. pharm., Guy's Moraga (Calif.) Drugs, 1971-72; grad. stu. UOP Sch. of Pharm. 1972-73, instr. clinical pharm. unit 1973-75; hosp. pharm., Roseville Comm. Hosp., 1975-77, asst. dir./dir. of pharmacy services, 1977--; co-ordinator of Home Hickman Catheter Care, Home Intravenous Antibiotic Therapy, Home Parenteral Nutrition and Ambulatory Intravenous Chemotherapy, Pharmacist mem. Roseville Comm. Hosp. Hospice Team; honors: 1969 achievement award, Student chpt. APhA; Rho Chi pharm. soc.; Phi Kappa Phi; UOP Preceptor of Year in Clin. Pharm. 1979; mem: Kappa Psi Pharm. Frat. 1967- (past pres. Gamma Nu chpt.), Am. Soc. of Hosp. Pharm., Am. Soc. of Parenteral & Enteral Nutrition, Calif. Soc. of Hosp. Pharm., Central Valley Soc. of Hosp. Pharms. 1972-75; publs.: art., Am. Journ. of Hosp. Pharms., 1978; Democrat; Catholic; rec: sailing, running, flying. Res: 602 Wren Ct Roseville Ofc: Roseville Comm. Hosp. Pharmacy, 333 Sunrise Ave Roseville 95678

SCHULHOF, NATHAN MARC, software mfg. co. president; b. May 17, 1949, McKeesport, Pa.; s. Marvin and Sarah Helen (Schacter) S.; 1 son, Randi N., b. 1982. Career: past vice pres. of land devel. co., public co. ofcr.; behavioral scientist (10 yrs.), author/lectr. in field, and staff inst. psychologist San Francisco Gen. Hosp.; founder/pres./bd. chmn. Silicon Valley Systems, 1980--; trustee Lincoln Univ. & Law Sch.; instr. S.F. Comm. Coll.; cons. S.F. Gen. Hosp.; mem. Vista; publs: Survival Kit; initiated SVS ongoing vol. project helping disabled children in S.F. area learn about computers; initiated SVS software give-away pgm. for public schools 1983; Republican; Jewish; rec: boating, business. Res: 1623 Forrestview, Hillsboro Ofc: Silicon Valley Systems, 1625 El Camino Real Belmont 94002

SCHULKIN, RONALD MICHAEL, certified public accountant; b. Aug. 19, 1945, Chgo.; s. Harold David and Annette (Markowitz) S.; m. Michele M., Dec. 21, 1968; 2 sons, David M., b. 1974, Steven B., b. 1978; edn: AA, Milw. Inst. of Tech. 1965; BA in bus. adm. Univ. Milw. 1972; CPA, Calif. 1982.

Career: acct. Seidman & Seidman, Beverly Hills 1972-73, Miller & Co., Westwood 1973-75; sr. acct. Saul Ramin & Co. (and predecessor firm) L.A. 1975-82; self-empl. CPA, 1982--; mem: AICPA, Soc. of Calif. Accts., Assn. of Valley CPAs, Cong. Beth Kodesh Mens Club (vp), Alpha Epsilon Pi (life); mil: SP4 US Army 1968-70, Airborne Medal of Valor, GCM, Heroic/Merit Achmt., Viet Cross of Service Award, Expt. Marksman, Bronze Star, US & Viet. Service, Valor-Oak Leaf Cluster, Nat. Def.; Democrat; rec: stamp & coin collector. Address: Ronald M. Schulkin, CPA, 20727 Covello St Canoga Park 91306

SCHULMAN, ROBERT STUART, lawyer, b. July 9, 1941, NYC; s. Donald Benedict and Edythe (Coopersmith) S.; m. Susan Helbig, Sept. 18, 1974; children: Elizabeth, b. 1967, Jennifer, b. 1970; edn: BA, Rutgers Univ. 1963; JD, Rutgers Univ. Sch. of Law 1966; admitted to practice in New Jersey 1967, US Supreme Ct. 1970, Calif. State Bar 1976, and all federal trial and appellate cts. in Calif. 1977. Career: assoc. atty. Stevens & Mathias, Newark, NJ 1966-69; partner, Weintraub, Urato & Schulman, Hackensack, NJ 1970-72; 1st sr. deputy atty. gen./chief Spl. Litigation Section, office of the NJ Attorney Gen., Trenton, NJ 1973-74; assoc. atty. Pitney, Hardin & Kipp, Newark 1975; sr. partner Zobrist & Vienna, Los Angeles, Calif. 1976-82; sr. partner Stephens, Berg, Lasater & Schulman, L.A. 1982--; attorney, Fairview, NJ bd. of edn. 1970-72 and zoning bd. of adjustment 1971-72; panelist Nat. Safety Council annual cong., Chgo. 1981; mem. Nat. Panel of Arbitrators, Am. Arbitration Assn. 1970-. Honors: Myron S. Harkavy Prize as most promising trial lawyer, Rutgers 1966, Am. Jurisprudence awards for acad. excellence in 4 subjects, 1966. Mem: Phi Delta Phi, Los Angeles County Bar Assn. (Trial Lawyers Sect. 1976-); ins. pgms. com. 1981-), Assn. Bus. Trial Lawyers, Am. Bar Assn., Rutgers Univ. Law Sch. Alumni Assn. Publs: Icarus Again (play prod. Off-Broadway 1961); Reinsurance: A Primer for the Practitioner, The L.A. Lawyer (1981); Civil Liability of Safety Prof. Under OSHA, Nat. Safety Council Annual Cong. (Chgo. 1981). Republican. Presbyterian. Rec: creative writing. Res: 1627 E. Mendocino St Altadena 91001 Ofc: Stephens, Berg, Lasater & Schulman, 707 Wilshire Blvd, Ste. 4100, Los Angeles 90017

SCHULSTER, NATHAN, electrical advertising co. president, builder/ developer; b. Mar. 21, 1913, NYC; s. Philip and Mary Schulster; m. Rachel, Oct. 10, 1937; children: Marilyn, b. 1942, Lucille, b. 1947; edn: Julliard Sch., NY 1925-26, National Acad. of Design, NY 1926-27. Career: designer/artist electrical displays, owner Brady Sign Co., Bklyn. 1939-51, Continental Neon Sign Co., L.A. 1951--; owner/ builder/ developer Stewart Shopping Center (Downey), apartment bldgs. (Hollywood, Santa Monica, Torrance, Downey, Los Feliz area), single family homes (Woodland Hills), Strip Centers (Arcadia, Long Beach), 1951--; clubs: Knights of Phythias (NYC), Hollywood Los Feliz Center; Republican; rec: art, music, business. Res: 2302 Nella Vista Ave Los Angeles 90027 Ofc: Continental Neon Sign Co. 4508 Santa Monica Blvd Los Angeles 90029

SCHULTE, KRISTOPHER, insurance industry executive; b. Aug. 20, 1953, Long Is., NY; s. Francis J. and Lorraine (Wilbur) S.; m. Elizabeth Gettle, Sept. 12, 1981; 1 dau., Jessica, b. 1983; edn: bus. maj., Palomar Coll. 1974; LUTC, San Diego City Coll. 1964; Estate Plnng., 1978, Pension & HR-10, 1979, Mutual of Omaha; lic: Life & Disability, 1975, Fire & Casualty, 1979, NASD Securities, 1978. Career: estab. Schulte World Imports (import export co.), 1974; agent Mutual of Omaha, 1975--, founder/owner Schulte Ins. Agency, San Diego 1981--, general agent (9 sub-agents) United American Ins. Co.; NASD Securities broker 1978--; cons. Global Imports 1980; sales awards: Mutual of Omaha Honor Club (1975-), Chairmans Council (4 yrs.), Sales Masters Roundtable (4 yrs.); mem. Life Underwriters Tng. Council, Better Bus. Bur., Shadowridge Country Club; Republican; Catholic; rec: tennis, golf, family. Res: 344 Sylvia St Encinitas 92024 Ofc: Mutal of Omaha, 7380 Clairemont Mesa blvd, Ste. 103, San Diego 92111

SCHULTZ, ROLF JAMES, tour co. executive; b. Mar. 10, 1941, Czechoslovakia, nat. 1972; s. Franz Stefan and Frieda Anna Schultz; m. Latchmee Singh, Oct.22, 1972; children: Melanie, b. 1975, Debbie, b. 1978; edn: BCom., Dalhousie Univ., Halifax, Can. 1965; MBA, Univ. Ore. 1969. Career: tchr. business econ. Simon Fraser Univ., B.C., Can. 1969; bought travel agcy. in Salinas, Calif., devel. into wholesale tour co. spec. in Mexico and Hawaii travel, chief exec. Contelco Corp., 1970--; recipient profl. awards from var. airlines, hotels, and CofCs; mem: Lions Club Internatl., Liontamer Salinas Host Club, 1982; Republican; Catholic; rec: swimming, tennis, art collector. Res: 12800 Corte Cordillera Salinas 93908 Ofc: Contelco Corp., 120 Del Rey Gardens Dr. Monterey 93940

SCHUMACHER, STEPHEN JOSEPH, lawyer; b. Feb. 5, 1942, Los Angeles; s. Joseph Charles and Theresa (Flynn) S.; m. Paula, Aug. 20, 1982; children: W. Scott, b. 1967; Stacey E., b. 1970; edn: AB in econ., USC 1963; JD, UCB Hastings Coll. 1967; LL.M (taxation), NY Univ. 1969; Calif. lic. real estate broker, attorney at law. Career: atty. law firm Stephens, Jones, LaFever and Smith, 1967-68, Wenke, Taylor, Schumacher and Evans, 1970-79, partner law firm Schumacher and Evans, Costa Mesa 1979--; dir. J.C. Schumacher Co.; dir. Orange County Opportunities Indslzn. Control; instr. in real estate taxation, UCI, USC, Santa Ana Coll.; awards: NYU Schwed Meml. Scholarship; OIC Director of Year; Who's Who in Am. Law; Who's Who in Real Estate. Mem: Am., Calif., Los Angeles & Orange County Bar Assns.; Am., Calif. Assn. of Realtors; Newport-Costa Mesa Bd. of Realtors; Newcomen Soc.; clubs: Balboa Bay, Back Bay; publs: num. arts. on real estate taxation; coauthor: Real Estate Taxation (text mats.); rec: running. Res: 2031 Yacht Defender, Newport Beach 92660 Ofc: Schumacher and Evans, 3151 Airway Ave, Ste A1, Costa Mesa 92626

SCHUMACHER, WELDON DAVID, physician; b. Jan. 4, 1936, Tacoma, Wash.; s. Alden B. and Marie Kathryn (Harm) S.; m. Bonnie Joan, Aug. 15, 1957; 1 dau., Cindy Lou, b. 1970; edn: BA, Loma Linda Univ. 1958, MD, Loma Linda Sch. of Med. 1962; Diplomat Am. Board of Family Practice. Career: med. internship, residency, 1962-64; pvt. practice, Glendale 1964-66, solo pvt. practice, family phys., Lodi 1968--; farming cherries, walnuts, grapes, 1968--, devel. innovations in tree farming techniques; founding bd. dirs. Bank of Lodi 1981; chief of staff/ bd. dirs. (past chmn.) Lodi Community Hosp.; past pres./ mem. county chpt. Am. Acad. of Family Physicians; honors: Mosby Scholarship Award, Alpha Omega Alpha; mem: AMA, Calif. Med. Assn., San Joaquin Co. Med. Assn., Lodi Execs. Club; mil: capt. US Army 1966-68, Vietnam, Army Commendn., two Bronze Stars, Purple Heart; Republican; Seventh-day Adventist; rec: farming, tropical birds, travel, photog. Res: 1303 Rivergate Dr Lodi 95240 Ofc: 1240 W. Vine St Lodi 95240

SCHUMAKER, LAWRENCE FRANCIS, logistics specialist; b. Nov. 6, 1921, Aberdeen, SD; s. Frank and Regina (Biegler) Schumaker; BSEE, S.D. State, 1949, stu. S.D. State, 1950; m. Florence Schmitt, Sept. 1, 1945; chil: Gary, b. 1946; Kathy, b. 1947; Barbara, b. 1949; Phyllis, b. 1952; JoAnn, b. 1950; Patricia, b. 1957. Career: elec. engr., Ia.-Ill. Gas & Elec., Davenport, Ia., 1950-51; devel. engr., Northrop Aircraft, hawthorne, 1951-55; proj. engr., Resdel Engr. Corp., Pasadena, 1955-56; sr. res. engr., No. Amer. Aviation, L.A., 1956-57; sr. engr., Northrop Aircraft, Hawthorne, 1957-58; sr. research engr., No. Amer. Aviation, L.A., 1958-59; mgr. of European suppt. equip., Supv. of test equip. design/devel., pgm. mgmt., Litton, Woodland Hills, 1959-77; mem. tech. staff, logistics splst., TRW, Redondo Beach, 1977---. Honors: CHRIS Award, Knights of Columbus, 1975. Mem: L.A. Maintainability Assn.; Dist. Dep., Knights of Columbus, grand knight; coach, mgr. and pres., Little League. Author: Maintainability Pgm. & Methods Guide, TRW, 1977; Data Mgmt., Litton, 1973. Mil: Pfc., US Army Air Corps, 1941-45. Democrat. Catholic. Rec: painting, fishing, gardening. Res: 7801 ElManor, Los Angeles 90045; Office: TRW, One Space Park, Redondo Beach.

SCHUTZ, JOHN ADOLPH, historian, educator; b. Apr. 10, 1919, Los Angeles; s. Adolph John and Augusta K. (Glicker) S.; edn: AB, UCLA 1942, MA, 1943, PhD, 1945. Career: asst. prof. Calif. Inst. of Tech., 1945-53; assoc. prof./prof. Whittier College, 1953-65; prof. of history USC, 1965--, dean 1976-82; vis. prof. (summers) Univ. of Brit. Columbia 1960, Univ. of Waterloo, Ont. 1966, Boston Coll. 1969, CSCLA 1953-65; trustee Citizens Research Council, New England; awards: grantee Nat. Endowment for Humanities 1971-74, Danforth Fellow 1959. Mem: Am. Hist. Assn. (Pacific Coast Br. pres. 1973, sec.treas. 1951-); Historic Genealog. Soc.; Orgn. of Am. Historians; Southern Calif. Hist. soc.; author: The American Republic (1978), The Dawning of America (1981), William Shirley, King's governor of Massachusetts (1961), Spain's Colonial Outpost: California (Boyd & Fraser 1983); Democrat; Catholic; rec: philately, travel. Res: 1100 White Knoll Dr Los Angeles 90012 Ofc: Univ. of So. California, College Park, Los Angeles 90007

SCHWARTZ, DONALD BUTCHER, physician, pediatric hematologist/ oncologist; b. Nov. 1, 1942, Los Angeles; s. Victor M. and Roberta (Podoll) S.; m. Lois, June 17, 1965; children: Jonathan, b. 1971, Daniel, b. 1972; edn: AB, Dartmouth Coll. 1964; MD, USC 1968; intern/res. Children's Hosp. of L.A. 1968-70, fellow 1969-70. Career: co-director Div. of Hematology/Oncology, Children's Hospital, San Diego 1974--; honors: Leukemia Soc. of Am. for asst. in nat. edition of "Emotional Aspects of Childhood Leukemia: A Handbook for Parents"; mem: Am., Calif., San Diego Co. Med. Assns.; Nat. Hemophilia Soc.; L.A. Pediatric Soc.; AAAS; Salerni Collegium; Fellow Am. Acad. of Pediatrics (Oncol./Hematol. Sect.); Age Quod Agis; Am. Soc. of Hematology; World Hemophilia Fedn.; Assn. of Comm. Cancer Ctrs.; Am. Soc. of Clin. Oncology; resrch: Pediatric Hematology, Cancer Immunology; publs: coauthor var. handbooks for parents of patients, for health care profls.; paper, First Nat. Conf. for Parents of children with Cancer (1980); med. journal arts.; mil: lt. cmdr. Public Health Service; rec: guitar, bike, running, swimming. Res: 727 Hoska Dr Del Mar 92014 Ofc: Children's Hospital, 8001 Frost St San Diego 92123

SCHWARTZ, MICHAEL LOUIS, real estate and retail co. executive; b. July 15, 1948, NY, NY; s. Bernard Lee and Rosalyn S. (Ravitch) S.; edn: BA, Stanford Univ. 1970, MBA, Harvard Univ. 1974. Career: analyst US Treasury Dept., Wash DC 1970-72; finl. analyst Morgan Guaranty Trust Co., NY 1974-76; finl. analyst Sherman Clay & Co., Burlingame, Ca. 1977-78, vice pres. 1978-79, exec. v.p. Sherman Clay & Co., San Bruno 1979-83, pres. real estate div. 1983--; trustee Pomfret (Conn.) Sch. 1980-; mem. Internat. Council of Shopping Ctrs, Urban Land Inst.; club: St. Francis Yacht; Republican; rec: sailing. REs: 132 Locust St San Franisco 94118 Ofc: Sherman Clay & Co 851 Traeger Ave, Ste. 200, San Bruno 94066

SCHWARTZ, NORMAN HOWARD, financial planner; b. Oct. 13, 1947, Santa Monica; s. Isidore Schwartz and Louise Schwartz-Levine; m. Carol Tanner, June 19, 1971; children: Matthew, b. 1973, Davina, b. 1980; edn: BA, Long Beach St. Coll.; MBA, National Univ. 1980. Career: sales mgr. Prudential Ins., 1973-80, Mutual of New York, San Diego 1980-81; mgr. Provident Mutual Insurance, Orange Co., 1981-; owner South Co. Financial Group; instr. (personal and bus. ins.) Life Underwriter Tng. Council, 1978-80; awards: Agent of the Year 1981, S.D. Life Underwriters; num. co. awards incl. Prudential presdtl. citation, nat. quality awd., nat. sales achievement awd.; mem: Qual. mem. Million Dollar Round Table, Knight MDRT, Orange Co. Life Underwriters; mem. O.C. Bus. & Indsl. League, Saddleback CofC, General Agents & Mgrs. Assn.; mil: sgt. USAF 1967-71, Vietnam Vet.; rec: sailing, tennis. Res: 258

Skyridge Escondido 92026 Ofc: South County Financia Group, 23291 Mill Creek Dr, Ste. 100, Laguna Hills 92675

SCHWEBEL, PAUL ROBERT, pharmacist/manufacturing executive; b. Sept. 1938, Miami, Fla.; s. Arthur Norman and Sylvia Schwebel; m. Elsie Rose, Dec. 24, 1971; children: Gary, b. 1964, Dawn, b. 1967; edn: BS Pharm., Chem., Columbia Univ. 1959; JD, Univ. San Fernando Valley Coll. of Law 1978; Reg. Pharmacist, Calif. 1959; Atty. at Law, Indiana 1983. Career: community, medical center and chief hospital pharmacist: Sisters of Mercy Hosp. 1959-61, Thrifty Drug, 1965, self-emp., Clark Drug, then pharm./mgmt. for Gemco, and currently Palmdale Hospital Medical Center--; owner/pres. Applied Methods Inc. (prin. inventor developer of disposable jet medicant injector); patentee; past pres. Lake View Terrace Improvement Assn. 1967-8; mil: 1 lt. USAF 1961-65, Small arms expert; Democrat; Jewish; rec: photog., competitive marksmanship; res: 8414 Langdon Ave No. 22, Sepulveda 91343 Ofc: Palmdale Hosp. Med. Ctr. 1220 E Ave. S, Palmdale 93550

SCHWEITZER, FREDERICK VERNON, accountant/educator; b. May 19, 1907, Amarillo, Tex.; s. Fred R. and Olive (Smith) S.; edn: Kansas Wesleyan Univ., 1924-26; AB, USC 1928; postgrad. Univ. of Berlin, 1933; MA, Pub. Adm., Columbia Univ. 1943; m. Cora Henderson 1928, div. 1931; m. 2d. Ruth Twenhoefel 1935, div. 1941; m. 3d. Margaret Cunha 1942, div. 1949; m. 4th Mary Ann Hiatt 1949, div. 1972; children: Gordon Merle, b. 1928, Fred Karl, b. 1946 (dec.). Career: pub. acct. Arthur Anderson & Co., L.A. 1927-30; consul US Dept. of State, Brisbane, Queensland, Aus., 1930-33; field aud., US Dept. Agri., Wash DC 1933-36; sr. pub. acct. Peat Marwick Mitchell & Co., S.F. 1936; chief div., Research & Stat., Calif. Dept. of Soc. Welfare, 1936-37; chief acct. Marchant Calculators Inc., Oakland, Calif. 1938-42; dep. dir. Veterans Preference Div., War Assets Adminstrn., S.F. 1946-47; sr. adminstrv. analyst Calif. Joint Legis. Budget Comm., Sacramento 1948-52; agcy. mgr. Marchant Calculators Inc., Santa Rosa, Ca. 1952-53; S.W. div. dir. Olivetti Corp. of Am., Dallas, Tex. 1954-61; mgr. systems sales Friden Inc., Sacto. 1962-66; data proc. systems analyst Calif. Dept. of Water Res., Sacto. 1967-72, and internal aud. 1972-74; own bus., pub. acct., Sacto., 1974--; owner/opr. Walnut Orchard, Yuba City, 1966-79; instr. Palo Alto Adult Edn., 1948-49; instr. Sacto. City Coll., 1950-51; instr. Mgmt. Devel. Inst., Sacto. 1969; instr., auditing of computer systems, Calif. Internal Aud. Assn., 1972-74; instr., hunting safety, Calif. Dept. Fish and Game. Honors: varsity track team Kans. Wesleyan Univ. 1925-27; varsity tennis, Univ. of Berlin 1933; mem: Calif. State Empl. Assn. (pres. chpt. 165 1965/6, 66/7); Nat. Assn. of Accts.; Mgmt. Systems Assn.; Phi Mu Alpha, Shriners, VFW Post No. 85, Scottish Rite (Sacto.), AF&AM (Cambridge, Mass.); author: Unemployed Wkrs Insurance Plan of Queensland, Aus.; Monthly Labor Review, US Dept. Labor Jan. 1933; Public Assistance in Calif. (Dept. Soc. Wel. Jan. 1967); Acctg. Manual for Ship's Service Depts. Ashore (Bur. of Naval Pers. Apr. 1944); mil: lt.cmdr. USNR 1942-48; Republican (Sacto. Co. Rep. Cent. com. 1966-70; chmn. data proc. com. Calif. State Rep. Com., 1968-70); Presbyterian; rec: tennis, philately, gardening. Res: 3908 Heights Ct. Cameron Park 95682 Ofc: F.V.Schweitzer, Pub. Acct., 902 Del Paso Blvd, Rm 43, Sacramento 95815

SCHWEITZER, H. HOYLE, multi-national corporation executive; b. Apr. 8, 1933, Los Angeles; s. J. Henry and Phoebe Money (Hoyle) S.; m. Diane Pardue, June 23, 1956; children: Tara, b. 1957, Matthew, b. 1960, Ted, b. 1964; edn: BA in econ., Pomona Coll. 1955. World Council mem. Internat. Windsurfer Class Assn. 1971-. Career: senior systems analyst, General Tel. Corp., 1956-67; vice pres. Data Systems Continental, Orange, Calif. 1967-69; pres./CEO Windsurfing International, Inc. (and subsidiaries), Torrance 1969--; inventor of the Sailboard (1967), designer of the Windsurfer Sailboard (1968); honors: Inventor of the Year, 1983, So. Calif. Patent Attorneys Assn.; mem: Internat. Windsurfer Class Assn.; Lahaina Yacht Club (Maui, Hi.), Marina City Club (Marina del Rey); rec: boardsailing, tennis, bridge. Res: 621 Stone Canyon Rd Los Angeles 90077 Ofc: Windsurfing International, Inc., 1955 West 190th St Torrance 90509

SCHWEITZER, STEPHEN CARL, lawyer; b. Feb. , 1939, New York; s. Abraham and Mina Ruth (Smolocoitz) S.; m. Judith Bennett, Sept. 2, 1978; edn: JD, honors, Southwestern Univ. 1967; num. postgrad. seminars, courses 1968-; admitted Calif. State Bar 1967; Certified Splst. (Workers Compensation), Bd. of Legal Spec. 1973, 1978. Career: wkrs. comp. claims adjuster State Compensation Ins. Fund, 1958-59; wkrs. comp. claims supr. National Auto and Casualty Ins. Co., 1962-63; claims supr. Mission Ins. Co. and part time hearing rep. at Wkrs. Comp. Appeals Bd., 1963-64; sr. wkrs. comp. claims supr. Firemen's Fund Ins. Co., 1965-68, staff atty. 1968; assoc. law firm Chernow and Lieb, 1969-70; partner law firm Rowen and Schweitzer (spec. in defense of Wkrs. Comp.), 1971-73; sr. partner law firm Ghitterman, Schweitzer & Assocs., 1973-81; partner Sanford & Schweitzer (spec. in defense of Wkrs. Comp.), 1981-,-; instr., wkrs. comp., Ventura Coll. of Law, Santa Barbara Coll. of Law; guest lectr. San Fernando Valley Coll. of Law, State Employees Assn., Calif. Sch. Empls. Assn.; judge protem Workers Comp. Appeals Bd.; past mem. Los Angeles Co. elections commn.; bd. mem. Anacapa High Sch.; mem: Ventura Co., Santa Barbara Co. Bar Assns.; clubs: Pierpont Racquet, La Cumbre G&C; mil: US Army Active Reserve 1959. Address: 1114 State St, Ste. 295, Santa Barbara 93101

SCHWEIZER, KATHY ANN, school administrator; b. Oct. 11, 1947, Springville, NY; d. Jack Oatway and Dolores Violet (Whitmer) S.; edn: BA, Kent State Univ. 1965; exchange student, Univ. of Americas, Mexico City, Mex. 1967, Oxford Univ., Eng. 1967; Montessori Tchr. Cert., Santa Monica Montessori Tchrs. Coll. 1974. Career: customer services Air Indies Airlines, San Juan, Puerto Rico 1968, Pan Am. Airlines, NY, NY 1970; academic coordinator (prin.) Katrice Montessori Sch., Honolulu, Hi. 1974-75; Montessori tchr. Harbor Mesa (Calif.) Montessori Sch., 1975-76; owner/adminstr./dir. Casa Dei Bambini Montessori Sch., Mission Viejo 1977--, C.D.B. Montessori Sch. (2nd facility), Lake Forest 1980-; owner/adminstr./dir. Saddleback Valley Montessori Teachers College, Lake Forest 1981--; spkr. Parent/Tchr. Seminars on Montessori edn., Saddleback community; honors: recognition, Educational Dept. Saddleback Coll. 1979, Outstanding Women in Bus., Saddleback Comm.; mem. (1975-): N. Am. Montessori Teachers Assn., AMI- Am. Montessori Internatl., IMS- Internat. Montessori Soc., AMS- Am. Montessori Soc., IMA- Independent Montessori Assn.; writer editorials: The Register; New Dawn Mag. arts. on Montessori philosophy of edn., childrens aerobics pgm.; rec: aerobics, hair fashions and clothes modeling. Res: 21705 Superior Ln, El Toro 92630 Ofc: Casa Dei Bambini Montessori School, 25435 Trabuco Rd, Ste. C-5, El Toro 92630

SCHWINDT, ROBERT NEVIN, health products international distribution co. president; b. July 1957, Takoma Park, Md., s. Robert Frederick and Lynne (Kennedy) S.; m. Claudia Halstead, Jan. 3, 1982; 1 dau., Mallory Lynne, b. 1983; edn: BS, psychol. & bus. adm., Columbia Union Coll. 1981; grad. wk. Loyola of Md., 1981. Career: pres. Columbia Union Coll. Student Assn., 1978-79; pres. Adventist Intercollegiate Assn. (nat.), 1979-80, exec. dir. 1980-81; surgical support team Washington Adventist Hosp., Wash. DC 1976-80; mental health assoc. Lealand Hosp., Wash DC 1980-81; dir. of Clinic Devel., World Life Research Inst., Grand Terrace, Ca. 1981-82; pres./CEO/dir. Terrace Internat. Distbrs. Inc., Grand Terrace, Ca. 1982--; dir. Pure Products of New Zealand (Aukland, NZ); honors: Who's Who in Am. Colls. and Univs. 1981; Outstanding Young Men of Am. 1982; mem: Am. Acad. of Medical Preventics; N.W. Acad. of Preventive Med., S.E. Acad. of Preventive Med.; Colton CofC; works: Casa Da Vida (House of Health) conceptual research & devel. of a total care preventive health facility; devel. of "Imu-Stim" profl. immune stimulating products; Republican; Seventh Day Adventist; rec: camping, skiing, travel, photog., hang gliding. Res: 9361 Canyon Dr, Box 817, Forest Falls 92339 Ofc: Terrace Intl Dist. Inc., 1330 Cooley Dr Colton 92324

SCOTT, ETHEL MARIE, recycling co. executive; b. Oct. 28, 1947, Smithville, Tex.; d. Henry and Lullaby (Jones) Burleson; m. Thomas Scott, Sept. 17, 1979; 1 son, Keith, b. 1970; edn: BS, CSU Dominguez Hills, 1981. Career: secty. Los Angeles Job Corps, 1968-70; adminstrv. secty./asst. account exec. Edward Windsor Wright Corp., Hollywood 1971-76; vice pres., T & S Services, Pomona 1976--; mem. Assn. of Records Managers and Adminstrators, Inc., West End Toastmistress Club. Address: T & S Services, 2393 Carlton Ave Pomona 91768

SCOTT, KENNETH S., company president; b. Mar. 19, 1947, San Francisco; s. Laurence M. and Ida Jane (Erlanger) S.; m. Nancy Arnold, jan. 29, 1972; children: David, b. 1976, Jessica, b. 1979, Kristina, b. 1981; edn: AA, American Coll., Paris 1967; BS, Univ. Santa Clara 1969. Career: pres. Polo Microsystems, Mountain View; Dir: Radofin Far East, Radofin Ets.; international ops. cons.; bd. trustees Ford Country Day Sch. Ofc: Polo Microsystems, 2570 El Camino Real W Mountain View 94040

SCOTT, JACK ALAN, college president; b. Aug. 24, 1933, Sweetwater, Tex.; s. Wm. Hopkins (dec.) and Ethelda (Cravy) S.; m. Lacreta Isbell, Sept. 2, 1954; children: Sharon, b. 1955; Sheila, b. 1956; Amy, b. 1960; Gregory, b. 1963; Adam, b. 1966; edn: BA, Abilene Christian Univ. 1954; M.Div., Yale Univ. 1962; MA, Claremont Grad. Sch. 1967, PhD, 1970. Career: asst. to pres. Abilene Christian Univ., 1955-57; assoc. prof. of history and religion, Pepperdine Univ., Los Angeles 1962-71, Provost and Dean of the College, Los Angeles Campus, Pepperdine 1971-73; dean of instrn. Orange Coast College, Costa Mesa 1973-78; pres. Cypress College, 1978--; bd. of regents Pepperdine Univ.; chmn. bd. trustees Humana West Anaheim Hosp.; gov. apptd. mem. Empl. Services Bd. 1972-75; mem. Calif. Commn. on Crime Control and Violence Prev. 1980-82. Awards: Alumni award Claremont Grad. Sch. 1980; Danforth Teachers Grant 1966-68; Soc. of Colonial Dames Prize 1968; Who's Who in Am.; mem: Am. Assn. of Higher Edn., Assn. of Calif. Community Coll. Adminstrs. (chmn. bd. dirs. 1981-83); Am. Heart Assn. (chmn. Orange Co. Chpt. 1981-83); Calif. Heart Assn. (bd. dirs. 1983-); Rotarian; author: An Annotated Edition of Witherspoon's Lectures on Moral Philosophy (Univ. of Delaware Press 1982); Democrat; Ch. of Christ; rec: cycling, jogging, racquetball. Address: Cypress College, 9200 Valley View St, Cypress 90630

SCOTT, JAMES B., designer; b. Mar. 24, 1923, Jersey City, NJ; s. James and Alice (O'Brien) Basralian; edn: Baccalaureate, Univ. of Paris 1947; BA, Univ. of Princeton 1943; ISID, Internat. Soc. Int. Designers, London, Eng. 1961. Career: past treas. Fortnight Magazine, L.A. ten years; partner (24 yrs.), current owner Heather House Interiors, Ventura; honors: charter mem. Ventura Architectural Review Bd.; recipient Better Homes & Garden Award 1964; writer art column, Fortnight Mag.; mil: 1 sgt. US Army 1944-45. Res: 241 Dorothy Ave Ventura 93003 Ofc: Heather House Interiors, 566 E. Main St Ventura 93003

SCOTT, JAMES CARROLL, JR., clergyman; b. Dec. 5, 1953, Santa Cruz; s. James C., Sr. and Imogene Elizabeth (Kropp) S.; m. Melinda, June 19, 1976; edn: AA, Rio Hondo Coll. 1973; BS, Fresno State Univ. 1975; MA, Fuller Theological Sem. 1981; ordained minister Inter.Church - Foursquare Gospel 1981. Career: past police work, retail grocery clk.; youth pastor Orange Foursquare Ch., 1979-82; pastor Norwalk Foursquare Church, 1982--; adj. instr. in Biblical languages, Melodyland Sch. of Theol. 1981-82; district youth rep. S.W.

Dist. of Foursquare Chs., 1981-83; exec. asst. to S.W. Dist. Supr. 1981-83; mem. National Youth Council, 1983-84; chaplain Norwalk Sheriff's Sub-Station, LA County Sheriffs Dept. 1984; Republican; Prot.; rec: racquetball, softball. REs: 14508 S. Funston Norwalk 90650 Ofc: Norwalk Foursquare Ch. 12316 E. Rosecrans Ave Norwalk 90650

SCOTT, JOSEPH CHARLES, lawyer/legal publishing co. executive; b. May 10, 1953, Reseda; s. Dean Joseph and Georgia Louise (Emslie) S.; edn: BS, CSU Northridge 1976; JD, Pepperdine Univ. Law Sch. 1979; admitted to practice Calif. State Bar 1980. Career: pvt. practice of law, 1980-, afil. with Cavallo, Schaeffer and Greenberg in Beverly Hills, then partner Greenberg and Scott in Lakewood; pub. relations West Publishing, and sales, Westlaw computer, presenting it to judges, courts, and lawyers, currently regional mgr. Western Region, Westlaw Services Inc.; honors: Law Rev., Dean's List, Nat. finalist Moot Court, H. Wayne Gillies Awd., Moot Ct. Honor Bd. chmn.; mem. Calif. Bar, L.A. Bar Assn., Amicus Pepperdine; Republican; Baptist. Res: 20310 Anza Ave, Twnhse G, Torrance 90503 Ofc: Westlaw Services Inc. 1925 Century Park East, Ste. 295, Century City 90067

SCOTT, R(OBERT) CRAIG, lawyer; b. Jan. 23, 1953, Salt Lake City; s. Robert Darrell and Doris (Heward) Scott; m. Jackie Larson, March 18, 1975; chil: Megan, b. 1976; Cameron, b. 1977; Tyson, b. 1979; Brittany, b. 1982; edn: BS in mgmt, magna cum laude, Univ. of Utah 1975, JD, 1978. Career: atty. firm of Sheppard, Mullin, Richter & Hampton, Los Angeles, 1978--; honors: Order of the Coif 1978; articles ed. Utah Law Rev. 1977-8; Ch of Jesus Christ of L.D.S. (bishop). Res: 2630 Colinton Dr. Rowland Hts 91748 Ofc: Sheppard, Mullin, Richter & Hampton, 333 S. Hope St., 48th Flr. Los Angeles 90071

SCOTT, WALTER ROBERT, law enforcement ofcl., school administrator; b. July 19, 1902, Trinidad, Colo.; s. James Marion and Rosa Grace (Crandall) Scott; m. Hazel Warren, Feb. 24, 1933; edn: stu. Eastman Kodak Sch. of Photography 1924, Chgo. Acad. of Fine Arts 1925; BA, Hastings Coll., Hastings, Nebr. 1927; FBI/Dept. of Justice Tng. School 1940. Career: machinist Burlington R.R. 1923-27; high school manual training Trumbull, Nebr. 1927-29; recreation director, City of San Diego 1932-35; Lt. in Charge, San Diego Police Crime Laboratory, 1945 until retirement; author: Fingerprint Mechanics (Charles C. Thomas, Springfield, Ill. 1951) and rev. ed., Scott's Fingerprint Mechanics (1977); contbg. writer to police (pub. Charles C. Thomas) 1956-59; past editor Espinas Y Flores (garden club pub.) San Diego; rec: photog., gardening. Res: 3430 Wilshire Terrace, San Diego 92104

SCOULAR, ROBERT FRANK, lawyer; b. July 9, 1942, Del Norte, Colo.; s. Duane Wm. and Marie Josephine (Moloney) S.; m. Donna Votruba, June 3, 1967; children: Bryan, b. 1971; Dean, b. 1975; Bradley, b. 1980; edn: Carroll Coll. 1960-61; BS, Aero. Engring., St. Louis Univ. 1964; JD, St. Louis Univ. Sch. of Law 1968; admitted to Calif., Mo., Colo., N.Dak. and US Supreme Court Bars. Career: aerodynamics engr., contract adminstr. Emerson Electric Co., St. Louis, Mo. 1964-66; law clk. US Ct. of Appeals for the Eighth Circuit, St. Louis 1968-69; partner Bryan, Cave, McPheeters & McRoberts, St. Louis, 1969--; mng. partner, Los Angeles office, 1979--; dir. Corley Printing Co., St. Louis 1973-82. Awards: recognition, Missouri Bar Young Lawyers Section 1978; outstanding senior awd. St. Louis Univ. 1964; Nat. Outstanding Cadet & Internat. Air Cadet Exchange, Civil Air Patrol, 1960; mem: Am. Bar Assn. (national dir. Young Lawyers Div. 1977-78; chmn. Young Lawyers Div. Corp. Law Comm. 1973-74); Missouri Bar (dir. Mo. Lawyers Credit Union 19787-79, chmn. Credit Union Task Force 1977-78, chmn. Young Lawyers Sect. 1976-77); Bar Assn. of Metro. St. Louis (v.p. 1978-79, chmn. Young Lawyers Sect. 1975-76); St. Louis Bar Found. (dir. 1975-76, 79); Calif. Bar Assn.; Trial Lawyers of Am.; Am. Judicature Soc.; Conf. on Personal Finance; St. Louis Univ. Law Sch. Alumni Assn. (secty. 1970-72); St. Louis Univ. Alumni Council; Mo. Athletic Club; Univ. Club of L.A.; Town Hall of Calif.; L.A. CofC; publs: articles in law journals; Republican; Catholic; rec: golf, tennis, running. Res: 4 Horseshoe ln Rolling Hills Estates 90274 Ofc: Bryan, Cave, McPheeters & McRoberts, 3100 Crocker Center, 333 South Grand, Los Angeles 90071

SCRITSMIER, JEROME LORENZO, manufacturing co. executive; b. July 1, 1925, Eau Claire, Wisc.; s. Fredrick L. and Mary Alvera (Schwab) L.; m. Mildred Joan Lloyd, June 27, 1947; children: Dawn Marie, b. 1953; Lloyd Fredrick, b. 1958; Janet Alvera, b. 1960; edn: BS, Northwestern Univ. 1950; lic. real estate broker, Calif. 1968. Career: salesman Sylvania Elec. Products 1951-70; owner/opr. opr. Real Properties, 1958--; owner/chief exec. Environmental Lighting for Architecture Inc., City of Industry 1973--; owner/pres. Cameron Properties Inc. 1979--; dir. Independent National Bank, Covina 1983-; honors: Who's Who in the West, Who's Who in Fin. and Industry; mem: Apartment Assn. of Greater Los Angeles (dir. 1960-, twice pres.); Calif. Assn. of Realtors; club: Jonathan (L.A.); mil: s/sgt. USAF 1943-46, Air Medal, Presdtl. Unit Citation; Republican; Prot.; rec: flying, travel. Res: 2454 N. Cameron Ave Covina 91724 Ofc: Environmental Lighting for Architecture, 17891 Arenth St, Industry 91748

SCROGGINS, LLOYD RONALD, general contractor; b. Feb. 1, 1930, Holtville, Calif.; s. Leacle R. and Oneda Faye (Thompson) S.; m. Eva M. Smith, June 16, 1950; children: Faye, b. 1951, Shirley, b. 1953, Laura, b. 1957, William, b. 1962; edn: East Bakersfield H.S. 1949. Career: carpenter in Bakersfield, 1952-60; foreman McNauls, Bksfld. 1953-66; acoustical tile and insulation contractor, 1961-66; general contractor, 1967--; owner Lloyd Scroggins Custom Homes, Bksfld. mem: Tulare Kings Employers Council, Nat. Fedn. of Independent Bus.; Democrat; Baptist; rec: hunting, fishing, waterski-

ing. Address: Lloyd Scroggins Custom Homes, 8106 Lanora Ave Bakersfield 93306

SCUDERI, SAMUEL A., physician; b. Jan. 1, 1902, Italy; came to USA in 1908; s. Salvatore and Rosa (Vitale) S.; m. Leah Ciocca, Dec. 3, 1932; three sons: Robert, b. 1937, Thomas, b. 1942, Richard, b. 1944; edn: public schs., Tampa, Fla.; Univ. of Fla. 1921-23; Univ. of Chgo. 1923-25; Univ. of Chgo. Medical Sch. 1924-28. Career: estab. medical practice, Los Angeles 1928--; house staff attending staff, LA/USC Medical Center, 1928-49; instr. in med. Loma Linda Univ. Med. Sch., 1933-48; Los Angeles City physician (part time), 1937-48; honors: Star of Italian Solidarity, Ital. Govt.; mem: AMA, Calif. Med. Assn. (del.), Los Angeles Co. Med. Assn., Elks, Sons of Italy Garibaldina M.B. Soc., Alpha Kappa Kappa, Elks; Catholic; rec: golf, music, light opera. Res: 4627 Gainsborough Ave Los Angeles 90027

SEABORG, GLENN THEODORE, industry leader; b. Apr. 19, 1912, Ishpeming, Mich.; s. H. Theodore and Selma Olivia (Erickson) S.; m. Helen L. Griggs, June 6, 1942; children: Peter Glenn, b. 1946; Lynne Annette, b. 1947; David Michael, b. 1949; Stephen Keith, b. 1951; John Eric, b. 1954; Dianne Karole, b. 1959; edn: AB, UCLA 1934; PhD, UC Berkeley 1937; over 45 hon. degrees. Career: research assoc. w/Prof. Gilbert N. Lewis, Coll. of Chem. UCB, 1937-39; instr. Dept. of Chem., 1939-41, asst. prof. 1941-45, section chief Metallurgical Lab., Univ. of Chgo. 1942-46; prof. Dept. of Chem. UCB, 1945-71; dir. Nuclear Chem. Research, Lawrence Radiation Lab., 1946-58; assn. dir. 1954-61; chancellor, UCB, 1958-61; chmn. US Atomic Energy Commn., Wash DC 1961-71; univ. prof. of chemistry, UCB, 1971--, acting director Lawrence Hall of Science; assoc. dir. Lawrence Berkeley Lab., 1971--; pres., Science Service Inc.; pres., bd. dirs. Swedish Council of Am. Awards include Nobel Prize, Chem. (1951); Enrico Fermi Award (1959); Arches of Sci. Award, Pacific Sci. Ctr. (1968); US DOD Distinguished Honor Award (1971); Priestley Medal, ACS (1979). Mem. Bohemian Club (SF), Commonwealth Club (SF), Cosmos Club, Univ. Club (Wash DC), Chemists Club, Council on Fgn. Rels. (NYC); Pi Kappa Alpha, Alpha Chi Sigma; Contra Costa CC, Claremont CC; holder of 43 patents; Prot.; rec: hiking, golf. Res: 1154 Glen Rd Lafayette 94549 Ofc: Lawrence Berkeley Lab., Univ. of California, Berkeley 94720

SEAMAN, MARGARET MARY, buyer/cosmetician; b July 4, 1932, Thief River Falls, Minn.; d. George M. and Margaret Ann (Roark) Kotinek; m. Earl W. Seaman, May 2, 1953 (dec.); edn: undergrad. Wisc. State Univ., La Crosse; grad.: Physicians Formula, Bonne Bell, Helena Rubenstein, Revlon, Dorothy Gray, Elizabeth Arden and Fragrance Found. Cosmetic Schools. Career: buyer/cosmetician Millers Drug, 1953-71; buyer/cosmetician Lincoln Park Pharmacy, Alameda 1971--; cosmetic cons. skin care clinics in schools, other orgns.; honors: Woman of Year, Isle City Bus. and Profl. Women of Alameda 1978 (charter mem. 1959-; pres. 1961/2, 1972/3); mem.: City of Alameda Social Service Human Relations Bd. 1977-(pres. 1982-83); advisory bd. Historic Alameda High Sch. Found. Inc.; bd. dirs. Alameda Youth Sym. 1978-79; life mem. Alameda Hist. Soc. Inc.; mem. Alameda Animal Rescue Control; Bay Valley Dist. Bus. and Profl. Womens Clubs (num. chmnships 1975-); Calif. Fedn. Business & Profl. Women (state PAC coordinator and liaison to nat. fedn. PAC, 1983-84; state Legis. Screening Com. 1980-82); League of Women Voters; Quota Club; Democrat; Catholic. Res: 2416 Marti Rae Ct Alameda 94501 Ofc: Lincoln Park Pharmacy, 1433 High St, Alameda 94501

SEAY, ROBERT LAUDERDALE, investment co. president; b. June 5, 1946, Dallas, Tex.; s. Charles Eugene and Sarah Lee (Meadows) S.; edn: BBA, So. Methodist Univ. 1973; Calif. lic. real estate broker; stockbroker, NASD. Career: pres. Robert L. Seay Investments (real estate, securities, oil and gas, international investments), Marina del Rey 1967--; mem: L.A. Board Realtors, Internat. Council Shopping Centers, Internat. Real Estate Fedn., Merchant Brokers Exchange-London, Calif. Assn. Realtors, Internat. Assn. of Fin. Planning, Nat. Assn. Real Estate Investment Trusts; clubs: Metropolitan, Marina City, The Mayflower Soc., Who's Who Internat.; rec: cooking, travel. Res: 13900 Marquesas Way, B-57, Marina del Rey 90292 Ofc: Robert L. Seay Investments, 330 Washington St, Ste 400, Marina del Rey 90292

SECHRIST, JAMES RONALD, medical equipment manufacturing co. president; b. Apr. 13, 1943, Artesia; s. Dr. Clifford G. and Cumi Ann Sechrist; m. Christina Heaps; children: James Robert, b. 1969, James Richard, b. 1978, James Radford, b. 1981; 2 yrs. college. Career: mgmt. trainee, project mgr. Sechrist & Kelly Constrn. Co., 1964-65; design engr., project mgr. Fluor Corp., then with Mathews Steel; vice pres. United Systems Corp., 1967-72; founder/pres. Sechrist Industries, Inc. (high tech. co. involved in design and mfg. of med. equip., life support systems), Anaheim 1972--; bd. trustees. Northrup Univ.; mem. econ. devel. bd. Calif. Baptist Coll.; mem: ASME, NFPA, HIMA; mil: USN 1962-64; Republican. Res: 4010 Channel Pl Newport Beach 92660 Ofc: Sechrist Industries Inc. 2820 Greta Ln Anaheim 92806

SEEBERGER, ROBERT MONROE, audio-video co. owner; b. Dec. 19, 1937, San Francisco; s. Samuel Henry and Esther Marie (Nelson) S.; m. Sharon Anne Leach, June 4, 1977; children: Ginger, b. 1969, Benjamin, b. 1980; edn: BA, CSU San Francisco 1961. Career: soils engineer (civil) Dames & Moore, 1961-78, Harding & Lawson, 1978-82; founder/owner RMS Audio-Video, So. San Francisco 1982--; direct distbr. Amway Corp. 1979-; mem. Internat. Television Assn., San Mateo Co. Visitors & Conv. Bur.; mil: ROTC; Republican; Christian (chmn. church bd. edn. 1963-4); rec: still photog. Res/Ofc: RMS Audio-Video, 1204 Crestwood Dr. South San Francisco 94080

SEEGER, TWILA JEAN, real estate broker; b. Nov. 5, 1954, Auburn, Calif.; d. Lyman Samuel and Ruth Lenora (Hoskins) Irwin; m. Robert Seeger, Oct. 18, 1975; Calif. lic. real estate broker 1981. Career: real estate sales agent, George Schnarre Real Estate 1977-81; owner/broker T.J. Seeger & Assoc., San Bernardino 1981--; mem. San Bernardino Valley Board of Realtors, S.B. Chamber of Commerce, Trade Club; rec: tennis, deep sea sport fishing, boating. Res: 2945 Irvington St San Bernardino 92407 Ofc: T.J.Seeger & Assoc., 301 W. 40th St. San Bernardino 92407

SEGURA, SPENCER F., international lawyer; b. July 9, 1952, NY, NY; s. Pancho and Virginia Spencer (Smith) S.; edn: BA in hist., UCLA 1974; JD, Loyola Law Sch. 1979. Career: lawyer/ sole practitioner, pres. American Business Assocs., Inc., practice entertainment and internat. law: rep. South Am. refineries in purch. of crude oil; Mid East rep. of US cos. in sale of machinery; honors: 4 year Varsity Letterman, UCLA Tennis Team (capt. 1974), mem. UCLA History Dept. honor soc.; clubs: Beverly Hills Tennis, Marina City; Catholic; rec: tennis, languages. REs: 831 Gretna Green Way, Penthouse 301, Los Angeles 90049 Ofc: Spencer F. Segura, 2049 Century Park East, Ste. 1800, Los Angeles 90067

SEID, ALLAN BASIL, pediatric otolaryngologist; b. Dec. 26, 1942, Johannesburg, S.Africa, nat. 1981; s. Harry and Fanny Seid; m. Sheila, Dec. 16, 1965; children: Michael b. 1967, Hugh b. 1970, Cindy Lee b. 1971; edn: MBBCH(rand), Univ. of Witwatersrand Med. Sch., 1966; M.Med. Otology, Univ. of Cape Town 1971; Pediatric Otolaryngologist, Am. Acad. of Pediatrics. Career: full time cons. University Hosp., Cape Town 1971-72; assoc. prof. of otolaryngology, Univ. of Cincinnati 1972-80; asst. dir. Dept. of Pediatric Otol. Children's Hosp., Cinn. 1975-80; assoc. clin. prof. of otol., Univ. of Calif. 1980-83; attending phys. Children's Hosp. and Health Center, San Diego, 1980-83; pvt. practitioner Pediatric Otolaryngology, San Diego 1980--; Diplomate Am. Board of Otolaryngology; mem: Soc. for Ear, Nose and Throat Advances in Children (exec. bd. 1982); Fellow Am. Coll. of Surgeons; Fellow Am. Acad. of Pediatrics (exec. bd. Sect. of Otol. 1982); Am. Acad. of Otol. and Head and Neck Surgery; mem. Toastmasters Intl., San Diego Mission Bay Boat and Ski Club; publs: num. arts. med. journals; num. presentations profl. meetings; vis. prof., lectr., panelist nat. & internat.; Jewish; rec: sailing, skiing, scuba diving. Res: 1510 Rancho Serena Rancho Santa Fe 92067 Ofc: Allan B. Seid MD, 550 Washington St San Diego 92103

SEIDENWURM, RICHARD LEWIS, lawyer; b. Feb. 1, 1941, NY, NY; s. Jesse and Lillian (Epstein) S.; m. Carol Wender, Aug 14, 1965; children: Amy, b. 1967, Robert, b. 1971; edn: AB, Williams Coll. 1962; JD, Columbia Law Sch. 1965; admitted to practice NY State Bar 1966, Calif. State Bar 1973. Career: asst. gen. counsel, Office of Economic Opportunity, Wash. DC 1965-66; assoc., Davis Polk & Wardwell, NYC 1966-72; partner of Solomon, Ward, Seidenwurm & Smith and predecessor firms, San Diego 1973--; lectr. on corporations Calif. Continuing Edn. of the Bar 1981, 83; arbitrator Am. Arbitration Assn. 1978-; Jewish; rec: golf, theater. Res: 4543 Vista de la Tierra, Del Mar 92014 Ofc: Solomon, Ward, Seidenwurm & Smith, 600 B St, Ste. 2100, San Diego 92101

SEIFERT, DONALD EDWARD, international marketing executive; b. Sept. 26, 1937, Webster, Mass.; s. Richard and Maxyne (Emmons) S.; m. Cynthia, 1980; 2 daus: Shana, b. 1970, Heather, b. 1972; edn: BS, Mich. St. Univ. 1961; grad. sci. stu., Harvard, M.I.T., 1961-64; AMA courses, fgn. trade, acct., fin., time mgmt. Career: O.E.M. sales & mktg. mgr. Extracorporeal, 1965-70; dir. internat. mktg. American Bentley, 1970--; honors: Appreciation Award, Assn. of Thoracic & Cardiovascular Surgeons of Asia, 1983; E Award for Export, first Soviet-Am. Med. Symposium in Russia, 1979; mem: Am. Soc. of Extra Corporeal Tech. Inc., Fellow Royal Soc. of Health (London), Inst. of Mktg. London, Brazil Trade Assn., Internat. Mktg. Assn. Orange Co., World Affairs Council of Orange Co., World Trade Center Assn. O.C., Assn. of Renal Tech. (Eng.), Assn. of Thoracic & C.V. Surgeons of Asia (life patron), Nat. Notary Assn., So. Coast Rep. Theatre (Silver Circle), AAMI 32 Degree Mason, Aleppo Temple, Boston; mil: US Army Sch. pre comm. Ft. Benning 1962-67, E7, Army Nat. Guard 6 yrs., Distinguished Svc. Award; Republican; Methodist; rec: skiing, hunting, coins. Res: 31452 Holly Dr South Laguna 92677 Ofc: Bentley International (Div. AHSIS), 17502 Armstrong Ave Irvine 92714

SELBY, LARRY GLEN, computer systems div. executive; b. Feb. 19, 1944, Long Beach; s. Robert Dell and Ruby Myrtle (Bean) S.; m. Ann Marie Anthony, Jan. 8, 1966; children: David, Lori; edn: BS bus. adm., MIS, CSU Los Angeles 1973, MBA, 1975. Career: Douglas Aircraft Co., Long Beach 1966--, accountant clk. 1966, acct. 1968, MIS analyst Acctg. Systems 1971, project leader/MIS splst. Acctg. Systems 1976, branch mgr. Acctg. Systems 1977, mgr. Product Systems Mfg. Div. 1980--; speaker on user driven computing at var. computer symposia; career councilor CSU Fullerton; mem. Douglas Mgmt. Club 1971-; bd. mgrs. YMCA (nation chief YMCA Indian Guides); chpsn. Carmenita Jr. High Sch. Site Council; band booster Cerritos H.S.; works: devel. integration of Sperry and IBM Computer systems to provide user-driven, fourth generation, information services; mil: splst. 5/c US Army 1964-66; Republican; Ch. of Christ; rec: power boating, deep sea fishing, personal computers. Res: 13224 Palm Pl Cerritos 90701 Ofc: Douglas Aircraft Co, POB 200, 2-55, Long Beach 90846

SELFRIDGE, BENJAMIN DEXTER (JR.), clinical psychologist; b. Sept. 24, 1936, Garden City, Kans.; s. Benjamin Dexter and Gertrude (Parks) S.; m. Robin, Nov. 19, 1983; edn: AB in psychol., CSU San Diego 1966; LLB,

Blackstone Sch. of Law 1969; MA, 1973, and PhD, 1976, US Internat. Univ.; contg. edn. certs. Calif. State Psychol. Assn. 1976-; lic. psychologist, lic. marriage, family and child counselor. Career: indsl. engr. General Dynamics, San Diego 1961-69; finl. analyst/mgr. for County of S.D. and S.D. Co. Employee's Credit Union, 1970-71; child care counselor Boys & Girls Aid Soc. (resdtl. treatment facility), S.D. 1971-72; counselor YMCA projects, Grossmong and with Calif. Youth Authority parolees, 1973-75; clin. intern San Bernardino Co. Mental Health, 1975-76; grad. teaching asst. USIU, San Diego 1975-76; psychol. asst./clin. intern, Mission Psychol. Center, San Diego 1976-77; clin. psychologist in independent practice, 1977--, instr. USIA, cons. Calif. State Dept. of Rehabilitation and Dept. of Social Services, cons. Calif. Dept. of Edn., 1977-; mem.; Am. Psychol. Assn.; Calif. State Psychol. Assn. (Champus Peer Review Com.); Assn. for Advance. of Psych.; Soc. for Personality Assessment; Acad. of San Diego Psychologists; Calif. Assn. of Marriage and Family Counselors; W. Psychol. Assn.; Internat. Council of Psychologists; Am. Assn. for Marriage and Family Therapy; publs: articles in psychol. journals; mil: personnel splst. US Army 1958-60. Address: Benjamin D. Selfridge, Ph.D. 2356 Moore St, Ste. 101, San Diego 92110

SELLERS, ESTHER EDITH, psychotherapist, nurse, educator; b. June 15, 1933, Loma Linda; d. James Edwin (missionary nurse) and Hazel Ruth (Ard) (teacher, nurse) Boehne; m. Rev. Lloyd Harley Sellers, June 19, 1958; (husband 7th-Day Adventist pastor, chaplain 18 years, currently chaplain Hoag Memorial Hosp., Newport Bch.); children: Christine Esther (Christiansen), b. 1960; James Lloyd, b. 1961; Maelinda Ruth, b. 1965; edn: BS nursing, Columbia Union Coll. 1958; MA counseling and guidance, Andrews Univ. 1970; MS psychiat. nursing, Univ. of Mich. 1972, postgrad. work 1973; R.N. Md. 1958, Calif. 1973-; MFCC (lic. Marriage, Family & Child Counselor) 1977-. Career: team capt. nurse, Washington Adventist Hosp., Tacoma Park, Md. 1958-59, nursing registry pvt. duty, 1960; office nurse, 1960-61; summer camp nurse Mo. Conf. 7th Day Adventists, K.C., Mo. 1963; psychiatric mental hlth nursing instr. St. Mary's Hosp. Sch. Nursing, K.C., Mo. 1964-65; head nurse pediatrics, St. John's Med. Ctr., Joplin, Mo. 1967; instr. Holy Cross Sch. of Nursing, South Bend, Ind., 1968-69; VA Hosp. psychiat. charge nurse, 1971; psychiat. instr. St. Vincent's Hosp sch. of nursing, Toledo, Oh. 1972; asst. prof. (grad. adviser, dept. chmn. psychiat. mental hlth nursing) Loma Linda (Calif.) Sch. of Nursing, 1973-79; mental health nurse psychotherapist Orange Co. Health Care Agcy., Fullerton 1974--; num. workshops, comm. spkr., school consulting; awards: NIH grantee 1970-72, Univ. Mich. Fellowship 1973; cert. splst. Psychiat. Mental Health Nursing, Am. Nurses Assn. 1978, 83; mem. Internat. Transactnl. Analysis Assn., Am. Nurses Assn. (Psychiat. M.H. Nursing Council), Nat. League Nursing, Calif./Am. Assn. Marriage & Family Therapists (W.Covina chpt.), Assn. 7th Day Adv. Nurses; past PTA pres. Pomona Adventist Jr. acad. 1977; past church organist, Tacoma Pk., Md. and Claremont, Ca.; Seventh Day Adventist; rec: wilderness hiking, travel, photog., geneology. Res: 987 Val Vista St Pomona 91768 Ofc: Orange Co. Health Care Agcy, M.H., 211 W. Commonwealth Fullerton

SELLERS, GEORGE SPENCER, JR., stockbroker; b. Mar. 14, 1944, Berkeley; s. George S. and Flora Harmer (McLean) S.; edn: BA, UC Santa Barbara 1967; reg. rep. NYSE 1969, reg. rep. NY Commodity Exchange. Career: bus analyst Dun & Bradstreet, 1968; account exec. Glore Forgan Staats, Walnut Creek 1969-71; Mitchum Jones Templeton, 1971-73, Paine Webber, 1973--; dir. Doug. Gillespie & Assoc., Orinda; honors: Pacesetter, Paine Webber; mem. Rotary Intl., Phi Kappa Psi frat.; rec: racquetball, skiing. Res: 370 No. Civic Dr, No. 312, Walnut Creek 94596 Ofc: Paine Webber, 1990 No. Calif. Blvd, Ste. 18, Walnut Creek 94596

SELSMAN (Selden), MARLENE SIGNE, public relations executive; b. May 17, 1946, Miami, Fla.; d. Victor and Rose Goldstein (Benzer) Selsman; edn: BA, UC Los Angeles 1968. Career: teacher Los Angeles city schools, 1968-70; freelance actress, dancer, model, 1970-78; pres. Up In The Air, L.A. 1978-82; exec. v.p./ head Personality Dept., Public Relations Associates, Los Angeles 1982--; instr.: How to turn an idea into reality, L.A. Courses, 1982; honors: UCLA Dean's list, Best Director, 1968; listed, Foremost Women in Comm. 1980; mem: Nat. Assn. Female Execs., AAUW, Internat. Platform assn., SAG, AFTRA, Profl. Womens Club; works: created the Solar Powered Bikini (1980), and Beanie (1978); rec: stand-up comedienne. Res: 1155 Hacienda Pl Los Angeles 90069 Ofc: Public Relations Associates, 552 Norwich Dr Los Angeles 90048

SELVY, MARY ALICE, university administrator; b. Feb. 1, 1949, Galveston, Tex.; d. Felix and Alice Marie Brown; m. James Selvy, June 9, 1973; 1 dau., Carmen, b. 1975; edn: JD, 1983, BA in pol. sci. 1976, BS in legal sci., Golden Gate Univ. 1971. Career: full charge bookkeeper, Florence Crittenton Serv., San Francisco, 1975-76; office mgr. Law Faculty Center, Golden Gate Univ., 1976-79; Paralegal Legal Assistance for Seniors, Oakland, 1979; probate asst. Kaplan, Levy, Samrick and Bernard Law Corp., Oakland 1979-80; asst. dir. LL.M. (Tax) Pgm., Golden Gate Univ., 1980--, consulting, mng. and facilitating in academic pgm. designed to provide attys. with a thorough knowlege of the practical applications of fed. and state tax law; mem: 1984 Calif. Bar candidate, student mem. Am. Bar Assn. (1st, 2d yr. Bar Review rep. 1978-81); sec/treas. Black Amer. Law Student Assn. 1978-79; sec. Afro Amer. Soc. 1968-9 (cofounder); legal resrch: appellate brief on Wrongful Death on the High Seas (1979), The Allen Charge, Criminal Law (1981); Democrat; Catholic; rec: piano, chess, cooking. Res: 36648 Sugar Pine Ct Newark 94560

SENTER, ARNOLD J., insurance co. executive; b. Mar. 24, 1942, Los Angeles; s. Harold H. and Betty E. (Slater) S.; m. Linda M. Milburn, Jan. 17, 1978; 1 dau., Zoe, b. 1966; edn: BS, Ariz. State Univ. 1965; MBA, Pepperdine Univ. 1982; Calif. reg. profl. engineer. Career: senior engr. Travelers Ins. Cos., Phoenix, Dallas, Fresno, San Francisco 1965-69; asst. to airlines co. pres., Los Angeles, NY, 1969-70; regional loss control mgr. Hartford Ins. Group, Oakland, Pasadena, Norwalk, Houston, 1970-78; asst. v.p.-engring., Mission Ins. Group, L.A. 1978-81; v.p. underwriting/mktg., Zenith Insurance Co., Encino 1981--; honor: Outstanding Young Man of Year - Pacifica (S.F.) Jaycees, 1967; mem: Sales and Mktg. Execs. Assn., Nat. Assn. of MBA Execs., Soc. of Fire Protection Engrs., Am. Soc. of Safety Engrs., Nat. Safety Mgmt. Soc., Am. Mgmt. Assn., Masons; mil: E7, US Army, Reserve 1960-68; Republican; rec: sailing. REs: 17938 Mayerling St Granada Hills 91344 Ofc: The Zenith Insurancc Co. 15760 Ventura Blvd, 15th Flr. Encino 91436

SERAFINI, FULVIO GIORGIO, physician/surgeon; b. Aug. 18, 1921, Piombino, Italy, nat. 1969; s. Serafino and Evelina (Zucchelli) S.; m. Maria Louise Berritto, Dec. 3, 1966; children: Stefano, b. 1968, Evelina, b. 1969; edn: MD, Univ. of Bologna, 1951; Board certified in radiology, Univ. of Torino, Italy 1955; Bd. cert. in orthopedics, Univ. of Genova, Italy 1964. Career: orthopedic surgeon and joint implants (total hip replacements), pvt. practice, Burbank, Calif.; chief of surgery Burbank Community Hosp. 1976-78; staff mem. St. Joseph's Med. Ctr., Hollywood Presbyterian Med. Ctr., Glendale Adventist Med. Ctr., Burbank Comm. Hosp., No. Hollywood Med. Ctr., Henry May Hosp.; chmn. of medical com. for Italian Olympic Team 1984; mem: Fellow Internatl. Coll. of Surgeons, Hollywood Acad. of Medicine (entertainment com.), AMA, LACMA, LACC; club: Jonathan; Republican; Catholic; rec: equestrian, tennis, swimming, racquetball. Res: 5206 Los Bonitos Way, Los Angeles 90026 Ofc: Fulvio G. Serafini, MD, 500 E. Olive Ave Burbank 91501

SERGE, SALLY S., wholesale sales executive; b. May 29, 1956, Encino; d. John E. and Susan A. (Fredrickson) Boething; m. David J. Serge III, Jan. 20, 1979; edn: BS, Pepperdine Univ. 1979. Career: sales trainee to mktg. mgr. in (family owned business) Boething Treeland Farms, Inc. 1979-, bd. dir./vice pres. mktg., 1984--, top salespsn. 1979-, expanded bus. mkts. into Nev., Ariz., New Mex. and Texas; mem: Calif. Landscape Contractors Assn., Calif. Assn. of Nurserymen, Nat. Assn. of Female Executives, L.A. Beautiful; Republican; Presbyterian. Res: 28521 W. Conejo View Agoura 91301 Ofc: Boething Treeland Farms, 23475 Long Valley Rd, Woodland Hills 91367

SERRANO, OSCAR VILLEZA, civil engineer; b. Sept. 25, 1932, Pampanga, Philippines, nat. 1975; s. Pablo Soriano and Eusebia Morales (Villeza) S.; m. Andrea S., Apr. 1, 1961; children: Donna, b. 1962; Remy, b. 1963; Willie, b. 1965 (dec.; public sch. field, Willie Serrano Field, named in his honor); Francis, b. 1966; Kathy, b. 1972; edn: BS in C.E., Mapua Inst. of Tech. 1957; Calif. reg. profl. engr. 1975. Career: assoc. civil engr. BPW, Manila, Phil.; structural designer in Ghana, West Africa 1965; constrn. engr. in South Vietnam 1970; staff, City of Chula Vista (Calif.) Engring. Design Section, 1975; designer, Dhahran-Abqaiq Cloverleaf Interchange; prof. Angeles University; engineering consultant; honors: Engr.-Writer of the Year 1978, Phil. Engrs.; mem: Phil. Engring. Assn. of Civil Engrs., ASCE, Pampanguenos Assn., Batu Balani Club of San Diego Co.; publs: contbg. ed. MOD-Filipina; articles: Life in Saudi Arabia; Glimpse of Saudi Arabia; Peculiarities of Arabian Marriages; My Boy Died on Graduation Day; Republican; Catholic; rec: writing, sports. Res: 9206 Twin Mtn Circle, San Diego 92126 Ofc: San Marcos Engineering, 75 Rose Ranch, San Marcos, Calif.

SEVCIK, JOHN JOSEPH, new product development engineer; b. Feb. 1, 1952, Cleveland, Ohio; s. John George and Lillian Jean (Hrabak) S.; edn: BS (polymer sci./chem. engr.), Case Western Reserve Univ. 1974. Career: asst. engr. Borg-Warner Chem., Wash. W.Va. 1973; assoc. engr. Boeing Comml. Aircraft Co., Seattle 1974-75; engr. structural Composites Indus., Irwindale, 1975-77; engr. McGaw Lab., Irvine 1977-78, project engr., 1978-80; project engr./sr. project engr. IVAC Corp., San Diego 1980--; awards: John Huntington Fund Scholar 1970-74; alumni club service awards 1978-80; mem: Soc. of Plastics Engr., Theta Tau profl. engr. frat. 1972-4, Catholic Alumni Club 1977-82; patents pending (4): medical devices (1981-82); Catholic; rec: sailing, racquetball, biking, drums, swimming. Res: 9685 Genesee, San Diego 92121 Ofc: IVAC Corp., 10300 Campus Point Dr San Diego 92121

SEXTON, PHILLIP LEE, manufacturing co. executive; b. Feb. 17, 1943, Antioch, Ca.; s. Cecil Sherman and Mildred E. (Phillips) S.; m. Ruthie M. Roller, Aug. 25, 1962; children: Kevin, b. 1964, Jill, b. 1966. Career: currently pres. Kilpatrick's Bakeries, Inc. San Francisco 1981--, past v.p. San Francisco Plant, past v.p./gen. mgr. Oak Plant, 1979, route sales 1964, route supr. 1975, sales mgr. 1976, sales service 1978; fmr. jr. high sch. tchr. one term; mem. exec. com. No. Calif., City of Hope; Protestant; rec: golf. Res: 304 Camaritas Way Danville 94626 Ofc: Kilpatrick's Bakeries Inc. 2030 Folsom St San Francisco 94110

SHACKLEFORD, SAM G., insurance executive; b. Sept. 17, 1922, El Reno, Okla.; s. Samuel G. and Opal W. (Kelly) S.; m. Marcia Nation, Aug. 13, 1950; children: David, b. 1951; Jana, b. 1952; Gary, b. 1957; Linda, b. 1960; edn: BS, Univ. of Okla. 1947; grad. Inst. of Ins. Mktg., So. Methodist Univ. 1948; CLU, Am. Coll. of Life Underwriters 1951; agency mgmt. diploma, 1959; reg. principal, Nat. Assn. of Securities Dealers 1965. Career: sales John Hancock Ins. Co., El Reno, Okla. 1947-50; assoc. dir. Inst. of Ins. Mktg., So. Methodist Univ. 1950-53; sr. cons. Life Ins. Mgmt. Research Assn., Hartford, Conn. 1953-57; v.p. Lamar Life, Jackson, Miss. 1957-62; v.p. Texas Life Ins. Co., Waco, Tex. 1962-69; v.p. Lincoln Nat. Ins. Co., Atlanta, GA 1969-72; reg. dir. Am. Nat. Ins. Co., San Mateo 1972--; instr./bd. mem. Inst. of Ins. Mktg.; instr. Life Underwriters Council, Dallas, Tex. and Jackson, Miss.; bd. dirs. Nat. Coms., LIMRA (3); honors: pres. Miss. chpt. CLU 1959; pres. Waco, Tex. CLU 1968; pres. Peninsula Gen. Agents & Mgrs. Assn., San Mateo 1980; mem: Peninsula Life Underwriters Assn.; Peninsula Gen. Agents & Mgrs. Assn.; Peninsula Chpt. CLU; author: Delivering the Policy (1957), Mastering Your Rate Book (1956) and Agent Devel. Program (1958), LIMRA; mil: 1st Lt., US Army, Field Arty. 1943-46, Pacific Battle Star; Republican; Presbyterian (deacon, elder); rec: sports, music, travel. Res: 2740 St. James Rd Belmont 94002 Ofc: American National Insurance Co., 177 Bovet Rd, Ste 510, San Mateo 94403

SHAH, AMRUTLAL M., investment co. president; b. Mar. 11, 1931, Indian, nat. 1969; s. Maganlal F. and Ichchhaben M. Shah; m. Chandra, 1950; children: Shila A., b. 1952; Paresh A., b. 1962; edn: BS, L.M. Coll. of Pharmacy 1954; MS, Purdue Univ. 1955; D.Phil., State Univ. of Iowa 1957. Career: research chemist Block Drug Co., Jersey City, NJ 1960-65; research chemist Rexall Drug & Chem. Co., Los Angeles 1965-67; pharmacy Thrifty Drug Co., Calif. 1967-68; pres. Shah Investments, Inc., Fullerton 1968--; presently, lic. real estate broker and lic. gen. contractor in Calif.; honors: Sigma Xi 1957; charter mem. of Rho Chi 1960; mem: Am. Pharmaceutical Assn.; Am. Chem. Soc.; Am. Soc. of Engrs. & Arhitects; Republican; rec: travel, jogging, photog. Address: 2300 Calle Meleno, Fullerton 92633

SHAHRYAR, ISHAQ M., company president; b. Jan. 10, 1936, Kabul, Afghanistan, nat. 1967; s. Ahmad Ali and Zahra S. (Sarwar) S.; div.; edn: BS, UC Santa Barbara 1961; MA, 1968. Career: prodn. superintend. Continental Device Corp. 1961-66; sr. engr. Centralab Inc. 1968-71; mem. research team TRW Semi- Conductor Div. 1971-72; research engr. Spectrolab (div. Hughes Aircraft) 1972-76; founder/ pres. Solec Internat., Inc. 1976--; awards: 6 yr. academic scholarship to study in U.S., Afghanistan Govt.; developed low cost solar cell at Spectrolab; Republican; Moslem; rec: racquetball, swimming, health. Res: 1132 Tellem Dr Pacific Palisades 90272 Ofc: Solec International, Inc., 12533 Chadron Ave Hawthorne 90250

SHAFFER, J. ROBERT, stock broker, account executive; b. Dec. 11, 1915, Tyndall, So. Dakota; s. Charles A. and Dorothy B. (Elton) S.; m. Lorraine Fulton, Apr. 20, 1940; children: J. Robert, b. 1944; Susan, b. 1948; edn: AA, Oceanside- Carlsbad Jr. Coll. 1936; BA, UCLA 1939; reg. rep., New York Stock Exch. Career: supvr. Shell Oil Co. 1939-42; U.S. Army Air Corp 1942-45; pres. Shaffer and Son 1946-63; mgr. Oceanside- Carlsbad Ofc., Crowell, Weedon & Co. 1963-81; acct. exec. Crowell, Weedon & Co., Carlsbad 1981--; investments instr. Mira Costa Coll. 1965-70; awards: Outstanding Man of Yr., Oceanside 1949; U.S. Award for best sister- city in U.S. 1973-74; CofC Chmn. of Yr. 1973; mem: Stock & Bond Club; Oceanside- Carlsbad Jr. CofC (pres. 1948); St. of Calif. Jr. CofC; U.S. Jr. CofC; Oceanside Plng. Commn.; Oceanside Tourism Commn.; Sister City Chmn., Pago Pago, Samoa; Oceanside CofC (pres. 1963); Mira Costa Coll. Bd.; Alpha Sigma Phi Frat; BPOE Elks; Gr. San Luis Rey Plng. Council; Rotary; mil: Capt., U.S. Army Air Corps 1942, 93rd Heavy Bombardment Gp. B-24 Liberators, Bombardier, Navigator 1945; ETO, 5 Bronze Stars, Silver Star, DFC, five air medals, two Pres. Citations; Republican; rec: civic work. Res: 1916 Calle Buena Ventura St Oceanside 92056 Ofc: Crowell, Weedon & Co., 2584 El Camino Real Carlsbad 92008

SHAKARIAN, DEMOS DEE, association president/founder; b. July 21, 1913, Downey, CA; s. Isaac and Zarouhi (Yessayian) Shakarian; m. Rose Gabrielian, Aug. 6, 1933; chil: Geraldine (Mrs. Gene Scalf), b. 1939; Richard, b. 1936; Stephen, b. 1947. Career: dairyman-owner, Reliance, Dairy; land developer in comm. R.E., incl. shopping ctrs.; farmer-rancher, San Joaquin Valley; founder., internatl. pres., Full Gospel Business Men's Fellowship Internatl., orig. in L.A., Costa Mesa, 1979—; FGBMFI is a laymen's orgn. with over 2300 chpts. in 75 countries and the U.S.; more than 600,000 men gather monthly for chpt. meetings; the orgn. publishes VOICE mag. with over one million readers monthly; on behalf of the fellowship, have traveled as a delegate of Pres. Carter to Cairo, Egypt for Mt. Sinai transferral; have met with Prime Ministers and Presidents, and heads of state in many countries. Honors: recip., Religious Heritage of Amer. Special Award; The Unione Della Legion D'Oro Award, given by the Vatican. Mem: State of CA 48th Agri. Dist., 12 yrs.; apptd. under Gov. Edmond G. Brown and Ronald Reagan; trustee and v.-chmn., Bd. for Oral Roberts Evangelistic Assn.; mem. bd. dirs., Religious Heritage of Amer.; trustee, bd. mem., Downey Comm. Hosp., helped to fund. Author: book, The Happiest People On Earth, 1974, publ. by Chosen Books, over one million copies sold, translated into 20 languages. Republican. Protestant. Rec: various sports activities. Res: 8417 Lexington Rd., Downey 90241; Office: Full Gospel Business Men's Fellowship Internatl., 3150 Bear St., Costa Mesa 92626.

SHALES, SHIRLEY DIANE, corporate executive; b. Oct. 20, 1943, Highland Park, Ill.; d. David Gilbert and Ruth Marie (Bucher) Smith; m. James E. Shales, Jan. 25, 1963; children: Gordon Scott, b. 1964; Chad Brandon, b. 1969; Cary Lane, b. 1970; edn: No. Ill. Univ. 1961-62; Assoc., Elgin Comm. Coll. 1963; Univ. of Ill. 1965-66. Career: secty. to dir. of non-academic personnel, Univ. of Ill., Champaign, Ill. 1965-67; escrow secty. Lawyers Title & Trust, Scottsdale, Ariz. 1967-69; ed.- in- chief This Month In Taiwan, Taiwan 1978-80; interior decorator Sherwood Interiors, Taiwan, Hong Kong, Singapore 1979-81; pub. rels. mgr. Gen. Instument Corp., Hong Kong 1980-81;

domestic/ far east liaison ofcr. Bolnar Internat. Corp. 1983--; art instr. St. Charles, Ill. Rec. Dept. 1963; Cupertino Elementary Schs. 1974-75; co. dir. Dataswift Asia Ltd. 1983--; mem: Am. Legion Aux. of Taiwan; Am. Women's Assn. of Hong Kong 1980-81; Ariz., Calif., Taiwan, and Hong Kong PTA; Am. Club in China; Am. Club in Hong Kong; Decathlon Club, Santa Clara; art shows: No. Ill. Univ. 1962; Gallery in Geneva, Ill. 1965; Republican; Lutheran; rec: fashions; interior decorating, tennis. Address: Bolnar International Corp., 15780 Oakridge Ct Morgan Hill 95037

SHAMMA, JOANE AUDREY, environmental designer; b. Nov. 20, 1933, Glendale; d. Lennie Estell and Victoria Mary Margaret (Richuisa) Shain; m. Tariq Shamma, July 29, 1967; children: Cynthia, b. 1952; Randall, b. 1956; Nadia, b. 1956; Zaynea, b. 1957; Karima, b. 1958; edn: Calif. St. Polytechnic Inst. Career, current positions: chief environmental designer/ v.p. Shamma Enterprises, Inc., Anaheim; v.p./ secty. T.M. Shamma Internat., Inc., Anaheim; v.p./ secty. El Shamma & Co., Anaheim; v.p./ secty. Taj Corp., Corona; chwmn. of bd. Internat. Tours of Anaheim; instr. landscaping, UCR 1976, 77; How to Design Your Own Garden and Landscaping 1980; Masterplanning Your Own Landscape Devel. Plan 1983; awards: winning design, major water fountains and gardens, internat. competition for Internat. Airport, Abu Dhabia, U.A.E. 1981; publs: Pictorial Mag. (Cover) 1957; LA Times Home Mag. 1964-72; Designers West Mag.,t Chase Dr Corona 91720 Ofc: Shamma Enterprises, Inc., 2229 E Lincoln Ave Anaheim 92806

SHAMES, IRA ALLEN, business owner; b. May 26, 1931, Brooklyn, NY; s. Philip and Rose Lillian (Gertler) S.; m. Harriet Resnick, June 15, 1958; children: Michele Eileen, b. 1961; Gregory Brian, b. 1964; edn: BA, San Diego State Univ. 1955; LLB, Southwestern Univ. 1960; real estate broker, DRE, State of Calif. 1978. Career: lic. collection agent; entered liquor bus. 1958; opened own bus. 1967; also check cashing bus.; also lic. real estate broker; cons. bus. opportunities; currently: owner, Lucky 6 Liq; Check Casher Plus; Equity Exchange; mem: Bani Brith; mil: Airman 1/c, USAF, 1951-53; Republican; Jewish; rec: photog. Res: 5301 Rural Ridge Cir. Anaheim 92807 Ofc: Lucky 6 Liq, 112 No Tustin Ave Anaheim 92807

SHAMS, ZAKARIA AHMED, real estate broker; b. Jan. 25, 1942, Tanta, egypt, nat. 1972; s. Ahmed Soliman and Mona Mohammad (Shahab) S.; m. Faiza, July 19, 1969; children: Ameer, b. 1975, Laila, b. 1980; edn: dip. (top ten H.Sch. grads. in Egypt, 1958), Maadi High Sch. 1958; BS and MS, mech. engr. (First Deg. honors), Moscow Inst. of Tech., USSR, 1964, 1965 (Egyptian Govt. Scholar); Calif. lic real estate broker 1975. Career: currently, mgr. Nat. Consol. Invest., Pasadena 1982--; real estate consultant to local & fgn. investors; v.p. The Walden Co., Beverly Hills 1979-82; mgr. Century 21 Sierra Realty, Westwood 1975-79; piping design engr. & piping stress analyst: C.F. Braun, Alh.; Bechtel Corp., Norwalk, Ralph M. Parson, L.A.; & Fluor Corp., L.A., 1967-75; mech. engr. general Cable Corp., Bayone, NJ 1966; mem. ASME 1967-71, Nat. Real Estate Bd., BSA; Republican; Muslim; rec: travel, chess, photog., music. Res: 6842 N. San Gabriel Blvd San Gabriel 91775 Ofc: Nat'l. Consolidated Invest., 281 No. Altadena Dr, Pasadena 91107

SHANKS, JACK GILBERT, management consultant/co. president; b. Sept. 1, 1944, East Liverpool, Ohio; s. Austin Gilbert and Ila Mae (Wolfe) S.; m. Mary Jo Olmstead, May 15, 1965; children: Deana, . 1967, Todd, b. 1970; edn: BA, math., Walsh Coll. 1969; grad. work indsl. engring., Ariz. State, 1969-71; spl. GE mgmt. tng. pgm. 1964-68. Career: tchr. computer pgmmg. Walsh Coll. 1966-68; project mgr. for Gen. Elec. in Canton, Oh. and Phoenix, Az., 1964-71; mgr. World Wide Conversion Support Ctr. for Honewell, Inc., Phoenix 1971-76, mktg. support mgr. for states of Calif. and Nev., office in Sacramento, 1976-78; data proc. mgmt. cons., 1978--; owner Management Consultants and bd. chmn./pres. Management Information Software, Inc. (spec. in design, devel., support of proj. mgmt. software), 1984--; honors: num. awards for seminars and speeches to Calif. D.P. Mgmt. Assn. chapters 1979-; Who's Who in Am. Colls. and Univs. 1969; mem. Data Proc. Mgmt. Assn.; formed the San Juan Youth Competitive Soccer Club, 1979, coached the first girls team from Sacto. to be ranked in top 10 in W. USA Div. and won 3 consecutive Sacto. championships; works: devel. computer conversion mgmt. and software system for GE and Honeywell; devel. and released a D.P. mgmt. methodol. now used by over 30 cos.; author/pub. (book): Yes! Data Processing Projects Can be Successful; arts. in Data Proc. Mag.; Republican; Prot.; rec: golf, bass fishing. Address: Mgmt. Consultants/ Management Info. Software, Inc., 5857 Rich Hill Dr Orangevale 95662

SHANKS, RILEY HAMILTON, JR., corporate executive; b. Sept. 29, 1951, Blytheville, Ark.; s. Riley Hamilton and Janet Olene Shanks; m. Saudia Pawling, July 17, 1982; edn: BA, UC Santa Barbara 1975; MS, Univ. of LaVerne 1983; MS, USC 1984; cert. production inventory mgmt., APICS; cert. purchasing mgmt., NAPM. Career: materials plnr., jr. buyer Information Magnetics Corp., Goleta 1973-75; prodn. control coord., engring. tech. writer, long range materials plnr., master scheduler, mgr. of master scheduling and subcontract plng. Abex Corp., Oxnard 1976--; instr. Prodn. & Inventory Plng. Techniques, UC Ext. 1984; mem: Am. Prodn. and Inventory Control Soc.; Nat. Assn. of Purchasing Mgmt.; Republican; Lutheran; rec: reading, spelunking. Res: 2073 Pamela St Oxnard 93030 Ofc: Abex Corp., 3151 W Fifth Oxnard 93030

SHAPERY, SANDOR WAYNE, lawyer; b. May 15, 1944, Chicago, IL; s. Arthur Winner and Lillian (Goldberg) Shapery; BA, San Diego State Univ., 1958; JD, cum laude, Univ. of S.D. Sch. of Law, 1971; m. Judith Constanza, Oct. 2, 19178; chil: Stephen Wayne, b. 1973. Career: law clerk, Melvin Belli,

S.F., 1970; Shapery adn Assoc., Attys. at Law, 1972---, La Jolla and San Diego; Shapery Enterprises, a sole proprietorship, San Diego, 1978---; corp. dev. cons., Internatl. Comodities, 1975-77; partner, Presidio Devel. Co., 1973---, Del Mar; partner, Prospect Manor Limited, 1979---, La Jolla; partner, Chula Vista Med. Enterprises, 1980---. Honors: City of San Diego, Downtown Improvement Citation, 1976; Pac. Coast Bldrs. Conf., Gold Nugget Award, 1978; Bldg. Contractors Assn. Sales & Mkg. Council SAM Award Best Coml. Proj., 1978. Mem: Calif. State Bar, 1972; U.S. Dist. Ct., 1972; US Ct. of Appeals, 1974; US Supreme Ct., 1975; Phi Delta Phi legal frat., 1969; Coalition for Responsible Planning, 1979; Amer. Mensa Ltd., 1981; Friends of Arthritis; United Way; President's Council, La Jolla Cancer Research Found.; Diabetes Assn.; Publ: San Diego Law Review, 1970; R.E. Restoration, las Casitas, Del Mar, 1975; Victoria Square, San Diego, 1976; Victorian Property, Aspen, Colo., 1979; Columbia Profl. Bldg., San Diego, 1980; The Del Mar Castle, Del Mar, 1978. Jewish. Res: 5920 Camino de la Costa, La Jolla; Office: Shapery Enterprises, 443 W. C St., Ste. 201, San Diego.

SHARE, RICHARD HUDSON, lawyer; b. Sept. 6, 1938, Minneapolis, MN; s. Jerome and Millicent Share, m. Adrienne Pearlin, 1962; 1 son: Mark, b 1964; m. 2d. Carolee Martin, Dec. 1970; children: Gregory, b. 1974; Jennifer-Hillary, b. 1976; Ashley, b. 1980; edn: BS, UCLA 1960; JD, USC 1963. Career: sr. counsel/ asst. secty. law corp., Frandzel, Beverly Hills 1972-78; partner in charge of comml. litigation, Frandzel & Share, Beverly Hills 1979--; lectr. to bank personnel, collection of loans and related legal problems; lectr. Debt Collection Torts, Calif. Edn. of the Bar; mem: Calif. Bankers Assn.; Fin. Lawyers Assn.; publs: panelist, cassette tape, Seminar on Debt Collection Torts, Calif. Edn. of the Bar. Ofc: Frandzel & Share, 8383 Wilshire Blvd, Ste 400, Beverly Hills 90211

SHARMA, CHANDRA SHEKHAR, imports and consulting co. president; b. Nov. 11, 1953, Bikaner, India, nat. 1979; s. Hanumant Kumar Beher and Sushila Sharma; m. Kimi Agrawal, Oct. 9, 1981; edn: B.Tech., Indian Inst. of Tech., Kanpur, India 1975; MS, Univ. of Texas 1977. Career: EE research asst., Univ. of Tex., Arlington, Tex. 1975-77; sr. engr. Harvis Controls, Melbourne, Fla. 1977-79; ind. computer cons., Santa Clara 1979-82; pres., formed Vishall California, Inc., Santa Clara 1982--; bd. dirs. PEDCUG, computer user gp.; awards: gold medal, first rank Pre-Univ. Exam., India 1970; rec: reading. Res: POB 51117 Palo Alto 94303 Ofc: Vishall California, Inc., 2771 Newhall, Ste 32, Santa Clara 95050

SHARMA, KAUSHAL KUMAR, forensic psychiatrist; b. Sept. 19, 1949, Ajmer, India, nat. 1982; s. Vivak Anada and Sumitro (Mishra) S.; m. Vickie, May 6, 1978; children: Nicole, b. 1979; edn: MD, Univ. of Rajasthan 1970; asst. prof, of clinical psych , USC Sch. of Med. 1979. Career: sr. house ofcr. Sedgefield Hosp., England 1973; psych. intern, Highland Park Hosp., Highland Pk., MI 1973-74; res. psych. Sinai Hosp., Detroit, Mich., 1974-77; fellow, psych. & law, USC Sch. of Med. 1977-78; asst. dir. USC Int. w Psych. & Law 1978-81; pvt. practice, Newport Beach 1981--; sr. forensic psych. USC Inst. of Psych. & Law, Los Angeles; cons. Forensic Psych., Superior, Municipal and Mental Health Cts., L.A. and Orange Cos.; honors: diplomate, Am. Bd. of Forensic Psychiatry 1981; diplomate, Am. Bd. of Psych. & Neurology 1979; mem: Am. Psych. Assn.; Am. Acad. of Psych. & Law; Am. Soc. of Law & Med.; Forte Found., Encino; works: research on fire- setting behavior 1976; presentation of prof. papers on forensic psychiatrists 1979, 81, 82, 83; Republican; rec: tennis, gourmet food, travel. Res: Huntington Beach Ofc: 320 Superior, Ste 300, Newport Beach 92663

SHARP, MILDRED LOUISE "Pat", real estate broker; b. Dec. 30, 1927, Mabelville, Ark.; d. John Henry and Clara Allie (Smith) Patterson; m. Thomas Henry Sharp, Dec. 7, 1946; children: Patricia, b. 1947; Sherry, b. 1949; State of Calif. Div. of Real Estate 1960 & 1962. Career: real estate salesman Lancaster Ins. & Realty, Lancaster 1960-62; real estate broker Mildred L. Sharp Real Estate, Watsonville 1962-67, Watsonville 1967-73, Redding 1973--; real property listing, selling & mgmt.; awards: Statuette Awd., Girl Scouts of Am. 1960; mem: CSA #6; Democrat; Methodist; rec: sewing, ceramics, gardening. Address: Mildred L Sharp Real Estate, 7300 Bear Mountain Rd Redding 96003

SHARP, WILLIS EUGENE, electronic manufacturing co. executive; b. Apr. 3, 1933, Salem, Ore.; s. Earl and Opha Gertrude (MacNeil) S.; m. Elaine Belmarce, May 14, 1955; children: Phyllis, b. 1960; Christopher, b. 1963; edn: AAS, Capital Inst. of Tech. 1958; Univ. of New Mexico 1959-61; De Anza Coll. 1969; commercial pilot, FAA 1976. Career: staff asst. Sandia Corp., Albuquerque, NM 1958-61; with Ampex Corp., Redwood City 1961--, field svc. engr. 1961-65; field sales engr. 1965-67; Field Ofc. mgr. 1967-69; Nat. Field Ofc. mgr. 1969-72; mgr. Mktg. Comm. 1972-74; mgr. Corp. Mktg. Svcs. 1974-83; mgr. Corp. Adminstrv. Svcs. 1983--; mem: Am. Mgmt. Assn.; Printing Indus. of Am.; Printing Indus. of No. Calif.; IEEE (chpt. pres. 1958-60); Amateur Radio Relay League; works: estab. the German Friendship Prize, and the Norman F. Martin S.J. endowed scholarship fund for students from middle income families, Univ. of Santa Clara; mil: Radioman 1/c, USN 1961-56, GCM, UN, China Cpgn., Korea Cpgn. medals; rec: sailing. Res: 11280 Mellowood Saratoga 95070 Ofc: Ampex Corp., 401 Broadway, M.S. 14-01, Redwood City 94063

SHARPE, GWEN LANIER, executive secretary; b. Apr. 14, 1937, Dayton, Ohio; d. Mervin Walsh and Thelma K. (Breckner) Whitesell; div.; 1 dau., Teresa Kirsten Katz; edn: AA, bus. adm., Ind. Univ. 1958; bus. mktg. courses; CPR lic. Career: past secty. Bendix Aviation; with American Airlines (1959--)

as stewardess, passenger sales secty., passenger services rep., ticket agent, internat. vacation cons., secty. to regl. director, Govt. Affairs, currently secty. to mgr. Freight Sales & Services; prin./distbr. Success Motivation Casettes (div. SMI Intl. Inc.); awards: appreciation, Inglewood (Ca.) Hot Line, patron Ellis Island Centennial Commn. fund for restoration of the Statue of Liberty; 25 Year cert., Am. Air Lines; mem. L.A. Interline Cargo Secty. Assn. (bd.), Westchester CofC, Nat. Thespian Soc.; works: movie script in prog.; tributes to Liberace and his mgr. Seymour Heller, in Liberace Mus., Las Vegas; Republican (Presdtl. Task Force); Prot.; rec: writing, music, theatre. Res: 9440-C Airport Blvd Los Angeles 90045 Ofc: American Airlines, 5908 Avion Dr Los Angeles 90009

SHARPTON, THOMAS, physician; b. July 15, 1949, Augusta, GA; s. Thomas and Elizabeth (Dozier) S.; edn: BA, Northwestern Univ. 1971; MS, Stanford Univ. 1973; DM, 1977; spec. internal med., Am. Coll. of Physicians 1981. Career: internship and residency at Martinez Veterans Administration Medical Center; med. staff Oakland Kaiser Permanente Med. Gp.; cons. Berkeley Free Clinic; honors: Phi Beta Kappa 1971; mem. Am. Coll. of Physicians; rec: classical piano. Res: 2323 Arrowhead Dr Oakland 94611 Ofc: Kaiser Permanente, 280 W MacArthur Blvd Oakland 94611

SHARRAT, ROY VERNON, educator, civil service ofcr., ret.; b. Sept. 6, 1905, Green Valley, Minn.; s. John and Elfie (Tucker) S.; m. Daryl Wheeler, Sept. 18, 1953; edn: BA, Hamline Univ., St. Paul 1928; cert. transp. ofcr., Lowry AFB, Denver, Colo. Career: tchr (English), and principal Manila Central Sch., Philippine Is. Bur. of Edn., 1928-37; sr./prin. storekeeper, then traffic mgr. USAF (fmr. Army Air Corps) Nichols Field, Phil., McClellan Air Base, Calif., Hickam Air Base, Hawaii, 1937-70; honors: Merit. Civilian Service Award, USAF, 1955; mem: Masons (Master 1979), Order of Eastern Tar, Scottish Rites, Shriners, Carmel-By-the-Sea Hi-12 Club (pres. 1984); Republican; Methodist; rec: reading, travel. Res: 1136 Surf Ave Pacific Grove 93950

SHASKEY, NORMAN JOHN, certified public accountant; b. Sept. 6, 1947, Denver, Colo.; s. Eugene Norman and Betty Jean (Fry) S.; m. Elizabeth, June 26, 1971; 1 dau: Laura, b. 1981; edn: BA, UC Santa Barbara 1969; MA, economics, 1971; MA, geography, 1971; gen. securities, US Securities & Exch. Commn. 1969; lifetime comm. coll. instr. cred. 1971; real estate broker, Calif. 1974; IRS Spl. Enrollment, US IRS 1975; CPA, Calif. 1980. Career: fin. analyst McKay Mgmt. & Research Co., Santa Barbara 1969-72; instr. Ventura & Santa Barbara City Colls. 1972-73; auditor Bank of America, San Francisco 1973; controller A.T.C. Svc., Los Altos 1973-75; acctnt. Chas. H. Peterson & Co., CPAs, Mountain View 1975-76; mgr. Consolidations & Gen. Ledger, Fairchild Camera & Instrument, Mtn. View 1976-78; CPA Melton & Munniks, CPAs, Palo Alto 1978-80; controller Sausedo Metal Prods. Inc. & Advanced Metal Finishers, Inc., San Jose 1980--; owner Pacific Fin. Mgmt. Co. 1974--; honors: Phi Beta Kappa 1969; Kappa Delta Theta 1970; mem: Mtn. View Jaycess; Mtn. View Bd. of Realtors; Foothill De Anza Comm. Coll. Dist. Bd. of Trustees; Christian; rec: running, skiing, camping. Res: 600 Rainbow Dr, No. 166, Mountain View 94041 Ofc: Sausedo Metal Products, Inc., 1596 So. 7th St San Jose 95112

SHAVER, LLOYD FREDERICK, nursery and landscape co. president; b. Mar. 20, 1940, Santa Ana; s. Lloyd Pearl and Elizabeth Carol (Bullard) S.; m. June Ellen Terry, Mar. 1, 1959; children: Lloyd Alan, b. 1962; Veronica June, b. 1975; Calif. cert. nurseryman, Calif. Nurserymen Assn. 1972. Career: asst. foreman Shaw's Nursery, Garden Grove 1956-57; salesman Lee's Nursery, Anaheim 1957; salesman Evergreen Nursery, Costa Mesa 1957-60; founder Lloyd's Landscape Co., Costa Mesa 1960; founder Lloyd's Nursery and Landscape Co., Costa Mesa 1960; pres. Lloyd's Nursery and Landscape Co., Inc., Costa Mesa 1974--; convention chmn. Calif. Nurserymen Assn. 1973; awards; Best landscape in comml.- indsl., State of Calif., Calif. Landscape Contractors Assn. Inc. 1966; mem. Orange Co. chpt. Calif. Assn. of Nurserymen; Republican (Nat. Repub. Com. campaigner 1980); Protestant; rec: racquetball, fishing. Res: 153 Tulip Lane Costa Mesa 92627 Ofc: Lloyd's Nursery & Landscape Co., Inc., 2038 Newport Blvd Costa Mesa 92627

SHAVINSKY, STEWART WAYNE, certified public accountant; b. Mar. 12, 1956, Chgo.; s. Leon and Dina Frida (Lewin) S.; m. Brenda, Oct. 17, 1981; edn: BS, Univ. of Ill. 1977; CPA, State of Calif. 1980. Career: a 1978-79; sr. acct. Daniells, Phillips, Garner & Vaughan Accty. Corp., Bakersfield 1979-81; sr. acct. Henderson & Garner, CPAs, Bakersfield 1982--; bd. dirs. Bakersfield Lions Club 1983--; bd. dirs. Am. Commerce Corp., Bakersfield 1983--; mem: Am. Inst. CPAs; Calif. Soc. of CPAs; Bakersfield chpt. CPAs; Bakersfield Lions Club; Hebrew Christian; rec: sports, church. Res: 3605 Truman Bakersfield 93309 Ofc: Stewart W. Shavinsky, CPA, 3501 Bernard, No 35B, Bakersfield 93306

SHAW, HOMER ELI, corporate communications consulting co. president; b. Sept. 21, 1911, Bement, Ill.; s. Homer E. and Iva (Monson) S.; m. Morlais Householder, June 4, 1936; 1 son, Arthur Evans, b. 1943; edn: B.Ed., Ill. State Univ. 1933; MA, Columbia Univ. 1938. Career: sci. and math. editor (textbooks), Silver Burdett Co., 1938-41; research assoc. (exptl. sci. tching. materials) Bur. of Ednl. Research in Sci., Columbia Univ., 1941-42; lt. USNR, Bur. of Naval Personnel (in chg. Curriculum Section, Tng. Activity), 1942-46; high sch. editor (textbooks in sci., hist.) and later ed. of internat. publs., Silver Burdett Co., 1946-56 (prod. 15 textbks in Urdu for West Pakistan; 5 textbks in Bengali for E. Pakistan); publs. mgmt./suprvsn. Lockheed Missiles and Space Co. Inc., 1956-73, head of writing & editing in R&D div. 1957, then publications supvr. (staff up to 100) spec. in proposals, other new-business, and mktg. publs.;

currently pres./ CEO/ mng. dir. Homer E. Shaw, Inc. (cons. in corp. comm., mgmt. for high-tech. cos. in Bay Area) Palo Alto; corp. comm. cons. to Koltron Corp., Sage Ent., Modulation Assocs.; dir. Sentry Products Inc., Santa Clara; honors: Soc. for Technical Comm. (nat. v.p. 1961; past pres. Golden Gate chpt.), Am. Assn. of Physics Tchrs., Nat. Assn. of Sci. Tchrs., Kappa Delta Pi, Phi Delta Kappa, Kappa Phi Kappa, Kappa Mu Epsilon; club: Sirs; Calif. del. to congl. advis. com. on Peace through Strength; mil: lt. USNR 1942-46; Democrat; Prot.; rec: classical music, gourmet cooking. Address: Homer E. Shaw, Inc. 2029 Channing Ave Palo Alto 94303

SHAW, SUSAN LEE, psychometrist; b. Sept. 12, 1941, Los Angeles; d. Spencer Lorraine Sr. and Margret Ruth (Schofield) Shaw; edn: BS, UCLA 1963, Dental asst., UCLA, 1965, spl. courses, Caroline Leonetti Modeling Sch. 1962, Willis Bus. Coll. 1964, Lumbleau R.E. Sch. 1975; grad. wk. UCLA-Cambridge Exchg. 1981, law stu. No. Am. Coll. of Law. Career: var. positions Western Airlines, UCLA Med. Ctr., Leliah T. Pearson (real estate), Rand Inst., 1963-80; psychic con., clairvoyant, psychometrist (over 7000 clients); minister/ healer/ tchr./ ch. founder, New Age Fellowship; pres. Shawlee Ents., presenting psychic fairs throughout So. Calif., 1982--; v.p. Glen Mar Properties, Inc., Beverly Hills; author four books on past lives of the famous: Elvis, Another Time and Space; Comings and Goings in the Lives of Frank Lloyd Wright & J. Paul Getty; Thru Time in the Lives of Henry E. Huntington and Winston S. Churchill; Times Past; mem. Beverly Hills Spiritualist Soc. (bd. dirs. 1977-9), Calif. Realtors Assn., Am. Cong. on Real Estate, Dental Assts. Assn. of Calif., Philosophical Resrch. Soc., Assn. for Research & Enlightenment Inc., So. Calif. Genealogical Soc. Inc.; Amer. Fellowship Ch.; Univ. Christ Ch.; Nat. Spiritualist Assn.; Biblical Archaeology Soc.; Republican; Scientologist; rec: gourmet cook, needlewk., flying. Address: 1860 Idlewood Rd Glendale 91202

SHAW, WILLIAM VAUGHAN, architect; b. Mar. 12, 1924, Los Angeles; s. Norman Topler and Elizabeth Allison (Kennedy) S.; m. Mary Morse, Sept. 14, 1967; stepchildren: Susan (Mrs. Kenneth Schley), Charles, Mary, and Ellen Osborne; edn: BA, UC Berkeley 1950; Am. Inst. of Architects. Career: partner Burde, Shaw 7 Assocs., Carmel 1955-69; pres. Will Shaw & Assocs., Monterey 1969--; bd. dirs. Pebble Beach Corp. 1980-82; awards: Calif. Governor's Awd. of Excellence 1964; Urban Renewal Design Awd., Progressive Architecture 1973; mem: Am. Inst. of Architects (pres. Monterey chpt. 1964); Monterey Co. Citizens Plng. Assn. (pres.); Big Sur Found (pres.); Larkin House Preservation Com. (pres.); Monterey Peninsula Museum of Art; Old Capital Club; Pacific Biological Lab; honors: fellow, Am. Acad. in Rome 1968; mil: Lt., USNR 1944-47; Episcopalian. Res: 502 Pierce St Monterey 93940 Ofc: Will Shaw & Assocs., 225A Cannery Row Monterey 93940

SHAW, WILLIAM WAYNE, III, sales distribution co. executive; b. Apr. 3, 1957, Concord; s. William Wayne and Carol Jean (Peterson) S.; edn: BA, magna cum laude, San Francisco St. Univ. 1979; BA, acctg., 1979; CPA, State of Calif. 1982. Career: supvr. Coopers & Lybrand, San Francisco 1979-83; controller/corp. treas. Aesculap Instruments Corp., Burlingame 1983--; bd. dirs. Mercantile Bank of San Carlos, N.A. 1982--; honors: Western Reg. Undergrad. of the Yr., Delta Sigma Pi 1979; Beta Gamma Sigma, SFSU 1979; mem: Am. Inst. CPAs; Calif. Soc. of CPAs; Republican; Methodist; rec: music, sports. Res: 763 Ulloa St San Francisco 94127 Ofc: Aesculap Instruments Corp., 875 Stanton Rd Burlingame 94010

SHEAHAN, FRANK, insurance broker; b. Sept. 9, 1944, Jersey City, NJ; s. Frank E. and Gertrude M. (Boone) S.; m. Michelle Glick, Dec. 27, 1980; children: Francis, b. 1967; Timothy, b. 1973; edn: BA, San Francisco State Univ. 1971; CLU designation, Am. Coll. 1974. Career: dir. fin. svcs. Neal-Truesdale Ins., San Luis Obispo 1973-80; pres. Frank Sheahan Ins., San Luis Obispo 1980--; former pres. San Luis Obispo Co. Life Underwriters Assn.; awards: Man of Yr., Delta Sigma Pi 1970; Outstanding Young Man of Am. 1976; mem: Nat. Assn. of Life Underwriters; Mustang Booster Club of CalPoly; San Luis Obispo CofC (Co. Health Com.); Kiwanis Club; Santa Lucia Council of Boy Scouts of Am. (former); mil: Capt., US Army Spl. Forces, Green Berets 1963-73, Vietnam, Bronze Star, Air Medal, Vietnamese Cross of Gallantry, Army Commdn.; Republican; Presbyterian; rec: model railroads, military figurines. Res: 1720 FixLini St San Luis Obispo 93401 Ofc: Frank Sheahan Ins., 1325 Chorro St San Luis Obispo 93401

SHEETS, MARILOU JOYCE, manufacturing co. executive; b. Aug. 31, 1929, Los Angeles; d. Paul Andrew and Inez Loraine (Cheely) Calderwood; m. Edward E. Weiss Sr., Aug. 31, 1946, div. 1972; 2 sons: Edward E. Jr., b. 1950, Donald R., b. 1956; m. 2d. Volney Sheets, Mar. 9, 1974; edn: Riverside City Coll. 1968-69, 1973-74; Calif. lic. notary public 1972-. Career: secty. acctg., Inland Concrete Enterprises, Inc., Riverside 1969-, also Inland Concrete Constrn., Inc. 1972-, also Riverside Foundry (dba) 1975-, also Inland Masonry Material (dba) 1983-: currently controller/ office mgr. acctg. of above cos.; pension trustee Inland Concrete Constrn. 1970-; bd. treas. Inland Concrete Ent. Inc., 1970-; mem: Corona Firemans Aux. (pres. 1954-55), Corona Red Cross Plnng. Com. 1954-55, Rubidoux Firemens Aux. (pres. 1960-62); Democrat; Baptist; rec: travel, camping, photog. Res: 7187 Font Ave Riverside 92509 Ofc: Inland Concrete Ent. Inc., 2434 Rubidoux Blvd Riverside 92509

SHEK, TAK WAI, optometrist; b. Oct. 16, 1948, Hong Kong; s. Chun Tak and Lai Hoo (Wong) Shek; edn: BS, San Francisco St. Univ. 1971; MSc, chem., Univ. of Wisc. 1973; MSc, pharm., Univ. of Houston 1975; Dr. Optometry, Univ. of Houston 1980; lic. optometrist, Calif. 1981, Texas 1982. Career: tchg. asst., chem. Univ. of Wisc., Madison, Wisc. 1971-73; tchg. & research assoc.,

Pharmacy, Univ. of Houston 1974-75; tchg. asst. Optometry, 1979-80; clinic instr., Optometry, Univ. of Waterloo, Ont. 1980-81; optometrist, Los Angeles 1981--; awards: Nat. Sci. Found. Research, SDSU 1970; Better Vision Awd., Univ. of Houston; mem: Calif., Texas, Ontario, and Brit. Columbia Optometric Assns.; Wah Yan Old Student Assn.; SFSU Alumni Assn.; publs: art., Journal Med. Chem. 1977; rec: music, sports. Res: 4544 Delay Ave Covina 91723 Ofcs: 4001 Wishire Blvd Los Angeles, and 1516 Burnaby St, No 204, Vancouver, BC, Canada

SHELBY, MICHAEL J., writer; b. May 31, 1955, Long Beach; s. Ralph and Virginia (La Boon) S.; m. Renee, June 6, 1981; 1 son, Brandon, b. 1982; edn: AA, Long Beach City Coll. 1977; creative writing major, CSULB 1979-80. Career: writer/photog./ owner Professional Resume & Business Writing Service (afil. with Profl. Resume Service, Inc.), Long Beach 1978--; mktg./advt. cons. re scripts for presentations or commls. (radio, tv), brochures and proposals; comml. photog.; vocational counseling, cons., Resume Preparation Wkshops for students (high sch., coll.); mem. Long Beach Area CofC; rec: writing, photog., fishing. Res: 9080 Bloomfield, Sp. 41, Cypress 90630 Ofc: Professional Resume & Business Writing Service, 717 E. Artesia Blvd Long Beach 90805

SHELDON, KIRK ROY, financial executive; b. Aug. 17, 1958, San Diego; s. Gale W. and Ruth Charlotte (Krueger) S.; edn: AS, Grossmont Coll. 1983; fin. plnng. cert., SDSU Coll. of Extended Studies 1983; CFP, Cert. Finl. Plnnr., Coll. of Fin. Plng. 1983; RECI, Real Estate Cert. Inst., Calif. Assn. of Realtors 1979; Gen. Sec. Registered Rep. Series 7, NASD, lic. R.E. Broker; Life and Disability Ins. lic.; Career: v.p. Guardian Brokers 1977--; mem: San Diego Bd. Realtors; Calif. Assn. of Realtors; Nat. Assn. Realtors; Internat. Assn. of Fin. Planners.; Inst. of Cert. Finl. Plnnrs.; Methodist. Ofc: Guardian Brokers, 2565 Camino Del Rio So., Ste A, San Diego 92108

SHELDON, SANDRA LEE, marriage counselor; b. May 6, 1940, Mnpls.; d. Andrew C. and E. Muriel (Hoffmockel) Sloss; m. Frank E. Stan, 1962, div. 1974; 2 son, Michael b. 1962, Matthew b. 1966; m. 2d. Warren Sheldon, Oct. 18, 1975; edn: AA in journ., Mount San Antonio Coll. 1974; BA in sociol./psych. (honors) CUS Fullerton 1978; MA, marriage, family, child counseling, Chapman Coll. 1981; lic. MFCC Intern, BBSE 1981. Career: tchr. aide Charter Oak Unif. Sch. Dist., 1968-73; grad. asst. Chapman Coll. 1981; substitute tchr. Walnut Valley Sch. Dist. 1979-80; counselor Downey Area Counseling Ctr., Downey 1980-81, Western Youth Services, Fullerton 1981-82; counselor, co-dir, Sexual Abuse Unit, trainer Brea United Methodist Counseling Ctr., Brea 1982--, bd. chair BUMCC, awards: Beta Phi Gamma, Alpha Kappa Delta, journalism award USC Sch. of Journ. 1973; mem: Calif. Assn. of Marriage and Family Therapists, O.L.A.M., V.O.I.C.E., Center for Applications of Psychological Type Inc.; contbg. writer for Paragraphs and Themes (Canavan, 1974); Methodist; Ch. of the Magi (metaphysical); rec: ceramics, writing, hypnosis. Res: 7702 Southcliff Dr Fair Oaks 95628 Ofc: Brea United Methodist Counseling Ctr, 480 N. State Coll. Brea 92621

SHELDON, TERRY LEE, real estate developer; b. Sept. 20, 1947, Long Beach, Balicornia; s. Robert Eugene and Patricia Alice (Rogers) S.; m. Susan Elizabeth Carr, Nov. 3, 1973; children: Jonathan, Shannon; edn: stu. USC 1965-67, Lake Tahoe Coll. 1967-68; Calif. lic. real estate broker. Career: asst. food & beverage mgr. Heavenly Valley, S. Lake Tahoe, 1968-69; food & bev. mgr. Christiana Lodge, 1969-70; sales assoc. Landholders Inc., San Diego 1971-72; mgr./broker assoc. Beach N' Towne Realty, 1974-75, Grubb & Ellis Co., 1975-77; pres./CEO T. L. Sheldon Corp., San Diego 1977--; mem. Mayor Roger Hedgecock's Housing Advis. Bd.; awards: 1981 Shelter Award, City of San Diego Housing Com.; over 17 Sales & Managers awards, Grubb & Ellis; mem: Building Industry Assn. (Polit. Policies com.; advis. bd. 1984 Multi-Housing Nat. Conf.); Calif. Assn. of Realtors; San Diego Bd. of Realtors (chmn. PAC; County Council of Realtors for San Diego County); dir. USA Men's Volleyball 1984 Olympic Com.; mem. San Diego CofC, Zoological Soc. of S.D.; publs: arts. in Multi Housing News 6/83, BIA Mo. Publ. 9/79; Republican. Res: POB 329, Rancho Santa Fe 92067 Ofc: T.L. Sheldon Corp., 2254 Moore St. Ste. 202, San Diego 92110

SHELL, WILLIAM ELSON, physician; b. Sept. 8, 1942, Detroit, Mich.; s. Sam and Sydelle (Elson) S.; m. Susan, May 30, 1964; children: Jeffrey, b. 1965, Stephanie, b. 1967, Dana, b. 1970, Daniel, b. 1976; edn: BS, Univ. Mich. 1963, MD, Univ. Mich. Med. Sch. 1967. Career: Director of CICU, Cedars-Sinai Medical Ctr., Los Angeles 1975-76, Assoc. Cardiologist 1976-81, Dir. In Patient Cardiac Rehabilitation 1981--; physician pvt. practice, Beverly Hills; asst./ assoc./ Prof. of Medicine UCLA Sch. of Med. 1976--. Recipient 1981 American Heart Assn. Service Recognition Award; mem. Am. Fedn. of Clin. Resrch., Am. Heart Assn. (Dir. Program Com.); mil: major USAF, active duty 1973-75, Commendation Medal; Democrat; Jewish; rec: sports. Res: 956 Chantilly Rd Los Angeles 90077 Ofc: William E. Shell MD, APC, 435 No Roxbury, Ste 300, Beverly Hills 90210

SHELTON, GEORGE PERRY, III, financial executive; b. Aug. 9, 1952, St. Louis, Mo.; s. George Perry, Jr. and Janet Frances (Lutkehaus) S.; m. Breda Louise Bey, Nov. 21, 1981; 1 dau., Candace, b. 1982; edn: BBA, Univ. of Notre Dame, 1974; CPA, State of Texas, 1976. Career: internal auditor Zale Corp., Dallas, Tx. 1974-76; asst. controller of mfg. subs., NY, NY 1976-78; operations & finl. mgr. of subs., Barley Banks & Biddle, Washington DC 1978-81; controller Animated Playhouses Corp., Rockville, Md. 1982-84; controller, secty. & treas. Capt. Andy's River Towne Corp., Rolling Hills Estates, Ca. 1984--; cons. Bus. Systems Plnng., Zale Corp. 1981; charter mem. Statue of Liberty, Ellis

Island Centennial Commn. (1984); finl. sponsor to VFW yearly projects 1983-84, to Concept 7 (benefit pgm. for abused children, Orange Co.) 1983-84; mem. Tex. Soc. of CPAs, US Senatorial Club 1984, Tennessee Squire 1984; works: bus. plan for Critter Pizza Jamboree 2/84; Republican; Catholic; rec: photog., jogging. Res: 7762 La Casa Way Buena Park 90620 Ofc: Capt Andy's RiverTowne Corp., 27520 Hawthorne Blvd, Ste. 170, Rolling Hills Estates 90274

SHELTON, JOEL EDWARD, psychologist/county executive; b. Feb. 7, 1928, Havre, Mont.; s. John Granvil and Rose Fahy (Ervin) S.; m. Mae Platzek, Dec. 17, 1949; 1 dau., Sophia, b. 1964; edn: AB, Chico State Coll. 1951; MA, Ohio State Univ. 1958, PhD, 1960. Career: school psychologist Sutter County Schs., Yuba City 1952-53; tchr./vice prin., Lassen View Sch., Los Molinos 1953-55; tchr. S.W. Licking Schs., Pataskala, Oh. 1955-56; child psychologist Franklin Village, Grove City, Oh. 1957; clin. psychologist Marion (Oh.) Mental Health Clinic, 1958; intern Children's Mental Health Center, Columbus, Oh. 1958-59; acting chief research psychologist Children's Psychiat. Hosp., Columbus 1959-60; guidance and data proc. cons. to supt. schs. Sacramento County, Calif. 1960-63; faculty CSC Sacto., 1961-69; clin. psychologist DeWitt State Hosp., Auburn 1965; exec. dir. Children's Center of Sacto., Citrus Heights 1965-66; exec. dir. Gold Bar Ranch (now Mayaro Ranch Sch., Pulga), Garden Valley 1964-72, cons. 1972-74; clin. psychologist El Dorado County Mental Health, Placerville 1968-70, Butte County Mental Health, Chico 1970--, dept. dir. consultation, edn. and community services, 74--; exec. sec. Protaca Agrl. Research, 1974--; assoc. Ecology House, 1974--; mem. Am., Western psychol. assns.; works: orgnzr. 200 mem. Speakers Bur. and Pub. Edn. Pgm. for Sacto. Area Mental Health Assn.; frequent public speaker var. subjects, ednl. and comml. TV programs; editor/contbg. writer profl. newsletters; mil: T/3 US Army 1946-47; Republican; Prot.; rec: lapidary, philately, camping, travel. Res: 1845 Veatch St. Oroville 95965 Ofc: Butte County Mental Health, 18-C County Center Dr Oroville 95965

SHELTON, RICHARD LEE, real estate broker, b. Sept. 14, 1942, Upland; s. Orville Wm. and Harriet (Holt) S.; grandson of Pliny Eastman Holt, civil engr., devel. the Caterpillar Tractor in Stockton, Calif.; m. Alison Mary Tomlin, June 25, 1966; children: Laura, b. 1970, Susan, b. 1975; edn: BS in agri., CalPoly St. Univ. S.L.O., 1964; Calif. Std. Teaching Cred. (life) 1968, Voc. Tchg. Cred. (life) 1971; Calif. lic. real estate broker. Career: mgmt. trainee Wells Fargo Bank, W. Sacramento 1966-67; horticulture tchr. (dev. federally funded pgm.) Grant Joint Union High Sch. Dist., 1968-72; agent/mgr Lawrence Realty, Sacto. 1972-75; owner/ broker/ pres. Century 21 Shelton & Assocs., Fair Oaks 1975-78; partner/ broker/ pres. Cen. 21 American River Brokers Inc., Fair Oaks 1978-82; owner/broker Dick Shelton Investment Properties, Fair Oaks, 1982--; real estate instr. Consumnes River Coll. 1979-80, Sierra Coll. 1980-81; honors: elected pres. Century 21 Sacto. Valley Council (42 offices) 1977; elected pres. Sacto. Bd. of Realtors Masters Club 1980, Life mem. 1976; mem: Nat., Calif. assn. realtors; Sacto. Board of Realtors (golf chmn., past membershp chmn.); clubs: Carmichael Elks, Ducks Unlmtd., El Dorado Hills Mens Golf, US Golf Assn.; mil: capt. US Army, M.P., 1964-66, USAR 1966-69; Republican; Episcopal; rec: golf, tennis, hunting, fishing. Res: 8867 Nimbus Way Orangevale 95662 Ofc: Dick Shelton Inv. Properties, 9900 Fair Oaks Blvd, Fair Oaks 95628

SHEPARDSON, MARY LOUISE, magazine editor, city councilmember; b. July 13, 1945, Pasadena; d. David Runyan and Marion Louise (Glenn) Shepardson; edn: BA in Eng. lit., Calif. Western Univ. 1967. Career: feature editor Ranch & Coast Mag.; councilmember City of Poway (mayor 1982-83); dir. Pomerado County Water District (v.p., pres.); editor Sentinel Horseman; regl. ed./editor Calif. Horseman's News; regl. editor Calif. Horse Review; Republican; Episcopalian; rec: equestrian, gardening. Res: 12025 Poway Rd, No. 3, Poway 92064 Ofc: American Ranch & Coast Pub., Inc., POB 1349, Solana Beach 92075

SHEPHERD, MARY JO, veterinarian; b. Mar. 1, 1954, Shelby, Ohio; d. Dick Beelman and Eleanor Jean Shepherd; edn: BS, The Ohio State Univ. 1976, DVM, 1980. Career: practitioner, The Associated Veterinary Emergency Service, Tucson, Az. 1980-81; small animal practitioner, solo, Woodside Animal Hosp., Lakeside, Ca. 1981--; instr., veterinary assist. course, Regl. Occ. Pgm.; honors: Freshman Honors Scholar, Ohio St. Univ., Gamma Sigma Delta; mem: Am. Veterinary Med. Assn., San Diego Co. Vet. Med. Assn., Assn. for Women Veterinarians; clubs: Soroptimist Int., pianist for Kiwanis of Lakeside; Methodist; rec: running, aerobics, needlwork. Res: 12802 Mapleview, No. 33, Lakeside 92040 Ofc: Woodside Animal Hospital, 12149 Woodside Ave Lakeside 92040

SHEPHERD, STEPHEN ERIC, certified public accountant; b. Oct. 21, 1953, Los Angeles; s. Frederick Jackson, Jr. and Franklyn May (Ellis) S.; edn: BA, CSU Northridge 1976; MS (taxation), Golden Gate Univ. 1981; CFP (cert. finl. planner) provisional mem., Coll. of Finl. Planning, 1983-; CPA, State of Calif. 1980; AICPA, Am. Inst. of CPAs 1980. Career: tax service mgr. Beneficial Mgmt. Corp., Glendale 1973; statistician Shadur, LaVine & Assocs., Inc. Encino 1973-74; pension administr. Gallop & Price, Inc. Los Angeles 1974-76; senior tax splst. Peat, Marwick, Mitchell & Co., L.A. 1976-78; mgr. Laventhol & Horwath, L.A. 1978--; instr. USC masters of business pgm. in taxation, 1980-81; recipient appreciation certs., Los Angeles Dist. Dir. IRS; mem. Planned Giving Advis. Com., So. Calif. chpt. Nat. Multiple Sclerosis Soc.; Variety Club of So. Calif.; publs: coauthor art. in USC 40th Ann. Inst. on Federal Taxation (10/81, 10/82); arts. in The Tax Advisor; Republican; Christian; rec: photog., tennis. Res: 17161 Palisades Cir. Pacific Palisades 90272 Ofc: Laventhol & Horwath, 3699 Wilshire Blvd, Ste. 700, Los Angeles 90010

SHEPPARD, JOY MARILYN, real estate broker associate; b. Mar. 24, 1930, Mnpls.; d. Aaron Emanuel and Alma (Erickson) Swanberg; div.; 3 sons, Michael, Steven, David; grad. Murray H.S., St. Paul, Mn. 1947. Career: secty. Thompson Ramo-Wooldridge (TRW), Redondo Beach, 1960-65; real estate assoc. var. firms in Monterey and Carmel, 1965-79; real estate assoc./broker firms in Westlake Village 1979-, assoc. broker Fred Sands Realtors, 1973--; awards: outstanding salespsn. first year with co. (1983), Fred Sands Realtors; rec: tennis, stained glass art. Res: 574 Treetop Lane Thousand Oaks 91360 Ofc: Fred Sands Realtors, 699 Hampshire Rd, Ste. 100, Westlake Village 91361

SHERIF, MOSTAFA HASHEM, research consultant; b. Sept. 6, 1950, Cairo, Egypt; permanent res. USA; s. El Said Gabr and Fatia (Draz) S.; edn: BS, Cairo Univ. 1972, MS 1975; PhD, UCLA 1980. Career: resrch. engring. Texas Tech Univ., 1975-76; tchg. fellow UCLA, 1978-80; postdoctl. fellow Brain Resrch. Inst. UCLA 1981-82; sr. systems engring. Recognition Systems, Inc. 1981-82; cons. in engring. systems and bioengring., 1982--; mem. tech. staff Bell Labs., 1983--; instr. seminars UCLA (1981, 82), USC (1981), Jet Propulsion Lab (1982); participant in pgm. com. First Internat. Conf. on Islamic Information, L.A. 1983; pgm. com. 1984 Conf. Alliance of Engring. in Medicine and Biology, L.A.; honors: Sigma Xi, Alpha Pi Mu; mem: IEEE (Biomedical Engineering Soc.), Human Factors Soc., Am. Soc. of Biomechanics, AAAS, Soc. of Appropriate Technology (founding); mem. Sierra Club, Islamic Ctr. of So. Calif., So. Calif. Early Music Soc.; publs: contbr. IEEE Transactions on Biomed. Engring. & Jour. of Biomechanics, Internat. Jour. of Control, Am. Jour. of Physiol.; author book in Arabic on the Muslim Brotherhood; Moslem; rec: jazz, travel. Res: 3340 Gauntlet Dr West Covina 91011

SHERLOCK, ROBERT LAMONT, lawyer; b. July 17, 1943, Chelsea, Mass.; s. Wm. Henry and Eileen Julia (Sullivan) S.; m. Charla Knox, Aug. 23, 1981; edn: BS in fin., Boston Coll. Univ. 1965; JD cum laude, Southwestern Univ. Sch. of Law 1973; admitted to Calif. State Bar 1973. Career: 1st lt./ finance ofcr. US Army 1965-68; claims adjuster Liberty Mutual Ins. Co., 1968-73; assoc. Law Offices of Virgil R. Wells, 1973-81; sr. partner Law Offices of Wells, Barber & Sherlock, Los Angeles 1981-; owner/partner Sherlock and Neal, L.A. 1982--; guest speaker var. insurance cos. on litigation and legal aspects of ins., 1973-; guest lectr. Western Coll. of Ins., 1980; mem: Los Angeles Co. Bar Assn., Assn. of So. Calif. Defense Counsel (sustaining mem. 1974-), Am. Bd. of Trial Advocates (assoc. 1981-); rec: scuba diving, music. Res: 3414 Blair Dr Los Angeles 90068 Ofc: Sherlock & Neal, 520 So. Lafayette Park Place, Los Anges 90057

SHERMAN, DANA, lawyer; b. Apr. 1, 1953, Los Angeles; s. Harry P. and Lillie (Epstein) S.; edn: BA, math, UC Los Angeles 1975; JD, Loyola Univ. Law Sch., L.A. 1978; MBA, Claremont Grad. Sch. 1980; M.Bus. Taxation, USC 1984; admitted Calif. State Bar 1978; lic. real estate broker, Calif. 1980; reg. investment advisor, SEC 1981. Career: student clerk Los Angeles Superior Ct., 1976, and Calif. Ct. of Appeal, 1977; assoc. atty. Pachter, Gold & Schaffer, L.A. 1978-82; pvt. law practice, 1982--, investment advisor, and real estate broker; lectr. USC Sch. of Engring., 1979-; judge pro tem L.A. Municipal Ct. 1984; honors: recognition cert., State Bar of Calif. 1983; St. Thomas More Law Soc. 1978; mem: Am., Calif. State, L.A. County bar assns.; bd. trustees Calif. State Mental Health Assn.; bd. dirs. L.A. County Mental Health Assn.; UCLA Alumni Assn.; Mensa; publs: Class Actions and the Uniform Class Actions Act, Vol. 11, Loyola Law Rev. 1978; rec: travel, photog., outdoor sports. Res: Reseda 91335 Ofc: Dana Sherman, Esq., 611 W. Sixth St. Ste. 800, Los Angeles 90017-3109

SHERMAN, MARY PELLINO, dance studio owner; b. Dec. 8, 1950, San Jose; d. Michael Wm. and Ruth Margaret (Archibald) Pellino; m. Donald Sherman, Dec. 31, 1975; 1 dau., Deva, b. 1978; edn: grad. Saratoga H.S. 1969; pvt. study var. forms of dance in San Francisco, Santa Cruz, San Jose, Honolulu, Marrakech, Morocco and Paris, Fr.; pvt. study with physical therapists; dance therapy -health & fitness splst. Career: dancer, touring Western states and Canada, 10 yrs.; instr., movement re-education and devel., Physical Therapy Center, Mill Valley 1979-; worked with mentally and physically retarded and multiple sclerosis patients; developed a dance related, therapy oriented exercise pgm. for the general public; founder/owner Moving Arts Studio, Sausalito; instr. Adventist Health continuing edn. seminars: The Physiology of Exercise; mem. AFTRA, demonstrator on Morning Stretch with Joannie Greggains, KPIX, 1983; rec: jazz dance, painting, writing, singing. Res: 110 Inez Pl Mill Valley 94941 Ofc: Moving Arts, 1505 Bridgeway, Ste. 128, Sausalito 94965

SHIBUSAWA, YOSHIAKI, banker; b. Sept. 12, 1929, Kamakura, Japan; s. Tomo-o and Setsuko (Nakamura) S.; m. Kieko, May 9, 1960; children: Ken, b. 1961, Naoko, b. 1964, Tomoko, b. 1965; edn: BA, Tokyo Univ. of Fgn. Studies 1956. Career: with The Bank of Tokyo, Ltd., Tokyo, Japan 1956-68; asst. v.p. The Bank of Tokyo Trust Co., NY 1968-70; chief rep. Southern USA, The Bank of Tokyo, Ltd., Houston, Tx. 1970-76; dir./pres. Tokyo BanCorp Internat., Houston 1976-78; senior loan ofcr. The Bank of Tokyo, Ltd., Tokyo 1978-79; dir./sr. v.p. California First Bank, San Diego 1979-81; exec. vice pres./resident dir. in Los Angeles, California First Bank/The Bank of Tokyo Group, 1981--; dir./pres. CFB Venture Capital Corp. 1982-; dir. Calif. Bankers Assn. 1983; chmn. spl. com. on Unitary Tax, Japanese Bus. Assn. of So. Calif. 1982-; dir./ exec. com. mem. Japanese Chamber of Commerce, So. Calif. 1983-; mem: Nisuikai (Assn. of Japanese Banks in Calif.), Japan America Soc. (sr. advis. bd. 1983), L.A. CofC, L.A. World Affairs Council, Central City Assn. of Los Angeles, The Internat. Bankers Assn. in Calif., La Jolla Cancer Research Found. (trustee 1981-83, advis. bd. 1983-); publ: English Conversation for Bank

Personnel (1944); Christian; rec: music, golf. Res: 14975 Corona del Mar Pacific Palisades 90272 Ofc: California First Bank, Office of the President, 616 West 6th St Los Angeles 90017

SHIMIZU, AKIRA, bank executive; b. Jan. 2, 1933, Shanghai, China (Japanese subject); s. Kenji and Tazuko (Kobayashi) S.; m. Taeko Fujima, Oct. 23, 1958; children: Keiko, b. 1960, Yasuhisa, b. 1964; edn: BA in econ., Keio Univ. 1955; Internat. Banking School, Brown Univ. 1973; Art Student League of NY, 1972-76; JACI, Tokyo 1958. Career: raised in Shanghai until 1946, schooling mostly in Tokyo; banker with The Mitsui Bank, Ltd., Tokyo engaged in international banking at London Br., New York Br., Osaka Br. and later as gen. mgr. Head Office Foreign Banking Div., 1955-80; bd. dirs. Sony Corp., Tokyo 1980-82, as dir./senior deputy gen. mgr. Internat. Ops. Group, and then Consumer Products Group; currently general mgr. & agent The Mitsui Bank, Ltd., and dir./deputy chmn. Mitsui Manufacturers Bank, 1982--; awards: NIKA Exhib. (oil painting), Tokyo 1975; NIKA Nat. Circular Exhib. (Japan major cities) 1975; amateur finalist, U.S. Ballroom Dancing Championship, NY, 1976; amateur finalist, North American Ballroom Dancing Championship, Boston, 1976; mem: Japan Business Assn. of So. Calif. (bd. dirs.; advisory bd. mem. 1984); International Bankers Assn. In Calif. (dir.); Japan Chamber of Commerce of So. Calif. (hon. advisor); clubs: Riviera Country (Los Angeles), Foreign Correspondent Club of Japan (Tokyo); Buddist; rec: painting, sculpture, ballroom dancing, sports, photog. Res: 3505 Monterey Road San Marino 91108 Ofc: The Mitsui Bank, Ltd., Ste. 400, Mitsui Mfrs. Bank, Ste. 500, 515 South Figueroa St, Los Angeles 90071

SHIN, HUNG WOO, retail business owner; b. Feb. 22, 1941, Chung-Ju, Korea, nat. 1979; s. Seung Hyu and Sang Sook (Kim) S.; m. Min-S. Lee, Dec. 30, 1969; 1 child, Soo-Wan, b. 1978; edn: BA in pub. adminstrn., Korea Univ. Law Sch. 1964; grad. stu. Northeastern Coll., UCLA, 1972-73; MA in sociol., CSU Los Angeles 1977. Career: section chief Korea Fertilizer Co., 1968-71; prop. Rally Shops, and Numero Uno #23, Chatsworth 1977--; awards: full 4-year scholarship, Korea Univ.; mem. Korea Tennis Assn. in the USA (vice pres. 5 years); pres. Korea Univ. Alumni Tennis Club in L.A.; mil: 1st lt. Korean Air Force 1964-68; Democrat; rec: sports, reading. REs: 6727 Rudnick Ave Canoga Park 91303 Ofc: Numero Uno #23, 20926 Lassen St, Chatsworth 91311

SHINGLER, ARTHUR LEWIS, JR., savings & loan co. president; b. Mar. 8, 1941, Donalsonville, Ga.; s. A. Lewis and Bertha (Gunn) S.; m. Ginger Brady, July 28, 1961; children: Elizabeth, b. 1962, Art III, b. 1966, Brad, b. 1970, Jonathan, b. 1973; edn: BA, Pasadena Coll. 1962; MBA, USC 1965; CPA, State of Calif. 1967, Colo. 1969; lic. real estate broker, Colo. 1974. Career: audit & executive search Peat, Marwick, Mitchell in Los Angeles 1966-69, supvr., in Denver 1969-73; pres. Western Empire Financial, Denver 1973-75; personal venture, Denver 1975-76; chief fin. ofcr. Central Federal S & L, San Diego 1976-79; exec. vice pres. First Federal S & L, San Diego 1979; senior exec. vice pres./chief ops. ofcr., American S & L, Stockton 1980-84, president 1984--, dir. American Svgs & Loan and var. subs.; mem. Am. Inst. CPAs; dir. Eastern European Bible Mission; chmn. bd. stewards Delta Nazarene Church; bd. properties Sacto. Dist. Nazarene Ch.; Adult Bible tchr.; Republican; rec: hunting, skiing. Res: 10610 Thornton Rd Stockton 95209 Ofc: American Savings & Loan, 343 E. Main St, 10th Fl. Stockton 95201

SHIPOW, AARON, manufacturing co. technologist, executive; b. Mar. 26, 1938, Chgo.; s. Meyer and Jeanette (Fall) S.; edn: BS in EE, Ill. Inst. of Tech. 1963; m. Dee Stitt, June 18, 1961. Career: junior engr./sr. engr. Fairchild Microwave Products div. Fairchild Semiconductor (mem. design team that blt. first solid state microwave components for gen. sale on a std. product basis) 1963-67; chief engr./div. mgr. Pacific Microwave Div., Alpha Ind., Inc. (co. purchased by Spectra Electronics, Inc. in 1970), Mtn. View 1967-72; dir./pres./ CEO Solid State Technology, Inc. (mfr. microwave components for govt. & comml. application), Santa Clara 1972-82; marketing and mgmt. cons. high tech. cos.; recipient num. business media awards 1972-; mem. IEEE; num. publs. on tech. of Active Solid State Microwave Components; rec: audio equip., music appreciation, bodybuilding. Address: 3408 Ramstad Dr San Jose 95127

SHIPP, WILLIAM WELDON, certified public accountant; b. June 8, 1927, Los Angeles; s. Pat and Mae (Harris) Shipp; m. Dorothy Forse, Sept. 23, 1967; children: Karyn, b. 1971, William, b. 1973; edn: BS, Univ. of San Francisco 1962; MBA, Golden Gate Univ. 1963; CPA, State of Calif. 1966. Career: staff auditor Price Waterhouse &: Co., S.F. 1952-56; acctg. supr. C.C. Moore &: Co., S.F. 1956-63; chief acct. Westland Life Ins. Co. S.F. 1963-66; audit mgr. Soule Steel Co., S.F. 1966-67; system analyst, supvg. acct., senior acct. Bechtel Power Corp., S.F. 1967-82; CPA, Oakland 1983--; bd. dirs. Westland Life Ins. Co. 1963-66, Schiller Constrn. Co. 1969-, Optrans Inc. 1983-; instr. in accounting UC Berkeley 1983-, Golden Gate Univ. 1984-; mem. Am. Inst. of CPAs, Calif. Soc. of CPAs; club: The Hills Swim & Tennis (Oakland); mil: sgt. US Army 1945-46; Republican; rec: stamp collecting US Plate Blocks, golf, swimming. Res: 5068 Dublin Ave. Oakland 94602 Ofc: William W. Shipp, CPA, 1964 Mountain Blvd, Ste. 199, Oakland 94611

SHIRILLA, ROBERT M., bank executive; b. Mar. 21, 1949, Youngstown, Ohio; s. Michael and Jayne Shirilla; edn: BA in econ., magna cum laude, UCLA 1971; MBA with honors (Corning Fellow), Harvard Bus. Sch. 1975. Career: mktg. cons. Boston Consulting Group, Inc., summer 1974; asst. product mgr., Shake'n Bake, Gen. Foods Corp., White Plains, NY 1975-77; product mgr./sr. mktg. mgr., Hunt Wesson Foods, Inc., Fullerton, Ca. 1977-81; dir. strategic planning Citicorp/Citibank, N.Y. and L.A., 1981, v.p. planning & devel., 1982-3; vice pres. The Crocker Bank, San Francisco 1984--. Honors: mem. nine nat. honor socs.; past pres. Pershing Rifles, mil. hon. soc.; Army ROTC and Alpha Kappa Psi Scholarship Awards. Bd. dirs. (1977-): Hugh O'Brian Youth Found. (chmn.); Los Angeles Bus. Sch (chmn.); March of Dimes (chmn. adv. com., mem. exec. com.); Charity Found.; Golf Found. Mem: L.A. Jr. CofC (bd.dirs.); Am. Mgmt. Assn. (bd.dirs); World Affairs Council of L.A.; Acad. of Polit. Sci. (NYC); Harvard Club; Internat. Platform Assn.; Theta Chi frat. (past pres.). Mil: 1st lt. US Army 1971-3, maj. USAR 1975-, Army Commendation, Meritorious Svc. Medals, outstanding achievement awd., Reserve Ofcrs Assn. Rec: skiing, golf, tennis. Res: 2000 Broadway, Apt. 1002, San Francisco 94115 Ofc: Crocker Nat. Bank, 74 New Montgomery (6), San Francisco 94105

SHIVERDAKER, JAY DEE, manufacturing co. executive; b. Dec. 16, 1939, Enid, Okla.; s. Ivan J. and Oleta May (Polk) S.; m. Jan Simpson, Nov. 20, 1976; 1 son, Jeff, b. 1966; edn: BBA, West Texas St. Univ. 1966. Career: finance dept. City of Amarillo, Tx. 1958-66; IBM: senior mktg. and tech. support positions Data Proc. and Gen. Products Divs., incl. pres./bd. chmn. Dastek Corp., 1978-81; pres./bd. chmn. Encore International (energy, computers & resrch. corp.) USA, Canada, 1981--; Dir: VenTech Capital Corp., Tectonic Control Inc. (both USA & Can.); recipient sev. internatl IBM awards; rec: open water diving, skiing, boating, flying. Res: 1308 Crossgates Ln. San Jose 95120 Ofc: Encore International 170 Knowles Dr Los Gatos 95030

SCHOCKLEY, WILLIAM BRADFORD, inventor, scientist; b. Feb. 13, 1910, London, Eng. (Am. parentage); s. Wm. Hillman and Cora May (Bradford) S.; m. Emmy Lanning, Nov. 23, 1955; children: Alison (Iannelli) b. 1945, Wm. Alden, b. 1942, Richard Condit, b. 1947; edn: BS, Calif. Inst. of Tech. 1932; PhD, MIT, 1936; ScD (hon.), Univ. of Penna. 1955; Rutgers Univ. 1956, Gustavus Adolphus Coll. 1963. Career: tech. staff Bell Tel. Labs., 1936-42; research sp. physicist, 1945-64; sci. adv., Policy Council, Jt. R&D Bd., 1947-49; dir. Transistor Physics Research, 1954-55; dir. Schockley Semiconductor Lab. of Beckman Instruments Inc. 1955-58; dir. Research Weapons Sys. Evaluation Group, Dept. of Def., 1954-55; pres. Shockley Transistor Corp., 1958-60; dir. Schockley Transistor Unit of Clevite Transistor, 1960-63; sp. lectr. Stanford Univ. 1958-63; Alexander M. Poniatoff prof. of engring. and applied sci., 1964-75; exec. cons. Bell Tel. Labs., 1965-75. Inventor junction transistor, holder over 90 US patents; research dir. Anti-Sub Warfare Opns. Group, USN, 1942-44; expt. cons. Ofc. Secty. of War, 1944-45, WWII. Honors: Medal for Merit, Secty. of War, 1946; Air Force Assn. Cit. of Hon. 1951; Liebmann Prize, I.R.E., 1952; Army Cert. of Appreciation 1953; Buckley Prize, Am. Phys. Soc. 1953; Comstock Award, Nat. Acad. of Scis. 1954; The Nobel Prize (physics) 1956; Wilheim Exner Medal, Austria 1963; Holley Medal, ASME Medal, 1963; CalTech Alumni distinguished service award 1966, Nat. Aerons. & Space Adminstrn. Cert. (Apollo 8), 1969; NASA pub. service group achievement award 1969; IEEE gold medal, 25th anniversary of Transistor, 1972; Nat. Inventors Hall of Fame 1974; honored by SEMI Fellowship estab. at MIT; IEEE Medal of Honor 1980. Mem: fellow, IEEE, Am. Acad. Arts & Scis. Adv. Panel, 1951-63; Air Force Sci. Adv. Bd. 1959-63; Nat. Acad. of Scis.; fellow Am. Physical Soc.; fellow IRE; Am. Inst. of Physics; Sigma Xi; Taubeta Pi; clubs: Cosmos, University (Wash DC), Bohemian (S.F.); Res: 797 Esplanada Way Stanford 94305 Ofc: McC 202, Stanford University Stanford 94305

SHOEMAKER, LOREN RAYMOND, manufacturing co. president; b. June 22, 1913, Wilsonville, Nebr.; s. Fred Wm. and Clara L. (Vise) S.; m. Faye Blanchard, May 5, 1935; children: Sharon Lynn, b. 1936, Gary Loren, b. 1938, Randy Raymond, b. 1946; edn: dip. Monrovia H.S. 1931; Pasadena Police Acad. 1933-34; Calif. Acad. of Police Sci. 1936-37; police adminstrn., East Los Angeles Coll. 1945-46. Career: cowboy wk. on homestead in S.W. Nebr. (birthplace); police force, Sierra Madre, Calif. Police Dept. 1933-, apptd. Chief of Police, LaVerne, Calif. 1935-; joined Los Angeles County Sheriffs Dept. 1941 , robbery detail last 20 years, ret. 1966; founder/pres. Tex Shoemaker & Sons, Inc. (leather bus. making police equip.) 1936-, expanded business since ret., now shipping police leather worldwide 1966--; Adv. Bd. mem. Rancho Bank, San Dimas; honors: recognition, San Dimas CofC, City Council of LaVerne, num. commendations; mem. San Dimas CofC (dir. 1975); Trail Boss, Westerners (San Dimas, Calif. Corral); works: holster designer, patents in USA & Can.; co. creates the Artist's Award for the Am. Indian and Cowboy Artists Assn. of San Dimas; Republican; Baptist; rec: nature, hunting, fishing. Res: 664 Chaparro Rd Covina 91724 Ofc: Tex Shoemaker & Sons Inc. 714 W Cienega Ave San Dimas 91773

SHONK, ALBERT D., JR., publishers representative; b. May 23, 1932, Los Angeles; s. Albert D., Sr. and Jean (Stannard) S.; edn: BS in bus. adm., USC 1954. Career: field rep., mktg. div. Los Angeles Examiner, 1954-55, asst. mgr. 1955-56, mktg. div. mgr. 1956-57, account exec. Hearst Advt. Serv., 1957-59; acct. exec. Keith H. Evans & Assoc., 1959-63, San Francisco mgr. 1963-65; owner/pres. Albert D. Shonk Co., 1965--; founder, v.p., life dir. Inter-Greek Soc., USC, 1976-; USC Comm. Assoc.; hon. life dir. Signet Circle Corp. (pres. 1977-81); dir. Florence Crittendon Services (exec. v.p. 1979-81, pres. 1981-83; bd. chmn. 1983-); founding chmn. Crittendon Assoc., 197;8-80; hon. life mem. Junior Advt. Club of L.A. (past dir., treas., v.p.); Nat. Assn. of Publishers Reps. (West Coast v.p. 1981-83); Magazine Reps. Assn. of So. Calif. & No. Calif.; Bus./Profl. Advt. Assn.; mem. Phi Sigma Kappa (dist. gov. 1960-62, nat. v.p. 1962-70, Grand Council 1977-83, Grand Pres. 1979-83, Chancellor 1983-); Alpha Kappa Psi; Interfrat. Alumni Assn. of So. Calif. (v.p., pres. 1957-61). Presbyterian. Res: 3460 W. 7th St, Wilshire Towers, Los Angeles 90005 Ofc: 3156 Wilshire Blvd Los Angeles

SHONKA, PAUL RICHARD, podiatrist; b. Oct. 11, 1951, Chgo.; s. Francis R. and Louise M. (Cuchna) S.; edn: BA, Loyola Univ. of Chgo. 1973; DPM, Ill. Coll. of Podiatric Medicine, 1979. Diplomate Nat. Board of Podiat. Examiners 1979. Career: externships at Northlake (Ill.) Hosp., Hines VA Hosp., Westside Community Hosp. (Long Beach, Ca.); postgrad. work, Boulder Podiatric Sportsmed. Clinic; currently active staff Petaluma (Ca.) Valley Hosp. with private practice Rohnert Park; lectr. on Podiatric Sportsmed. and Biomechanics; mem: Am., Calif. Podiatric Med. Assns., Redwood Empire Podiatry Soc., Am. Acad. of Podiatric Sportsmed., Rohnert Park CofC; club: Philosophic Motorcycle; publs: Radiographic study of orthotic device therapy in Alpine Skiers, Profl. Ski Instr.'s Jour.; Republican; Catholic; rec: skiing, sailing, running. Res: 7444 Bridget Dr, Apt. 29, Rohnert Park 94928 Ofc: Paul R. Shonka DPM, 6950 Commerce Blvd, Ste. 2, Rohnert Park 94928

SHORE, I. DENNIS, lawyer; b. July 10, 1946, Pomona; s. Solomon A. and Lillian L. (Lustig) S.; m. Marilyn Shore, Mar. 30, 1969; children: Melinda, b. 1977, Stefanie, b. 1979; edn: BA, UC Davis 1969; JD, Univ. of Santa Clara 1974; admitted Calif. State Bar 1974. Career: deputy district atty., San Joaquin Co. Dist. Atty's Office, Stockton 1975-79; partner, Freeman, Rishwain & Hall, 1979--; prof. Humphreys Coll. Sch. of Law 1977-78; prof. San Joaquin Delta Coll. 1979; honors: assoc. ed. Santa Clara Law Rev.; mem: Stockton Delta Rotary Club (charter pres. 1979-80; Sustaining Paul Harris Fellow 1981); San Joaquin Co. Heart Assn. (dir. 1982-83); Better Bus. Bur. of Mid-Counties (dir.); works: sev. registered musical compositions (1979-); Republican; Jewish; rec: sports, music, woodcraft. Res: 4219 Fort Donelson Dr Stockton 95209 Ofc: Freeman, Rishwain & Hall, 1818 Grand Canal Blvd Stockton 95207

SHORENSTEIN, MICHAEL LEWIS, physician; b. Sept. 11, 1944, NY, NY; s. Joel and Marilyn (Kritzer) S.; m. Rosalind Greenberg (also MD), June 18, 1967; children: Anna, b. 1975, Claire, b. 1981; edn: ScB, Mass. Inst. of Tech. 1966, MS 1967, PhD 1971; MD, Stanford Univ. Sch. of Med. 1976; Bd. cert. Internal Med. 1977. Career: fmr. research scientist at MIT, Cambridge, Mass.; med. residency at UCLA Hosp. & Clinics, 1976-79; currently, co-partner with wife/ pvt practice of internal medicine, Santa Cruz, Ca.; full staff mem. Depts. of Internal Med. at Dominican Santa Cruz Hosp. and Community Hosp. of Santa Cruz; prin. partner/co-dir. Health Enhancement & Lifestyle Planning Systems (cons. firm spec. in health promotion for industry); honors: Xigma Xi and Sigma Gamma Tau (1966), Continuing Med. Edn. Award, Calif. Med. Assn. 1981. Mem: Am. Soc. of Internal Medicine, AMA, CMA, Santa Cruz Med. Soc.; bd. dirs. American Diabetes Soc. (S.C. chpt.); mem. (via H.E.L.P.S.) of Chambers of Commerce in Santa Cruz, Watsonville, Scotts Valley; art. (in press), Western Jour. of Med., 1984; Jewish; rec: photog. Ofc: Michael Shorenstein, M.D., 700 Frederick St, Ste. 103, Santa Cruz 95062

SHOTTON, FRANCIS THOMAS, opthalmologist; b. Aug. 23, 1938, Floyd, Va.; s. Frank T. and Catherine Emily (Booton) S.; edn: BS, US Naval Acad., Annapolis 1960; MD, Univ. of Va. 1969; res. Wilford Hall, USAF Medical Center, 1971-74; Fellowship, Ophthalmic Plastic and Reconstructive Surgery with Alston Callahan, M.D., 1977; Diplomate Am. Acad. of Ophthalmol. 1975. Career: private practice. Mem: AMA, Riverside Co. Med. Assn., Los Angeles Soc. of Ophthalmol., Soc. of AF Clinical Surg., Fellow Am. Coll. of Surgeons, Fellow Am. Soc. of Ophthalmic Plastic and Reconstrv. Surgery; mil: USAF ret. Res: 11430 Tiffany Ln, POB 202, Sunnymead 92388

SHOWERS, LINDA JACKSON, company president; b. Aug. 31, 1936, Altoona, Pa.; d. Frank B. and Lucia (Burton) Jackson; children: Susan, b. 1957, David, b. 1959, Frank, b. 1960, John, b. 1967; edn: Smith Coll. 1954-56, Ariz. State Univ. 1976-78. Career: director European Fine Arts, Scottsdale, Az. 1978; mktg. coordinator Andrew M. Toth, AIA, Scottsdale 1979; pres. Fiber-Seal/ San Diego Inc. (fabric protection sys.), San Diego 1979--; dir. Assn. of Fabric Services 1980-; steering com. Expo. 1981, 82, 83-; co.chair Industry Found. of ASID, San Diego Chpt. 1981, 82 (1983 Steering Com. ASID/IF); honors: Pres.'s Award, San. Diego Chpt. ASID 1981, 1982; mem: ASID/IF, Internat. Soc. of Int. Design/Trade, Women in Business, Soroptimist Internat. of La Jolla, Scripps Aux., Child Abuse Prev. Found., Phoenix Art Mus., Smith Coll. (Class of 1958, pres. 1978-83) Club of San Diego; Republican; Prot.; rec: art history. Res: 7145 Draper Ave La Jolla 92037 Ofc: Fiber Seal/San Diego Inc. 4250-A Morena Blvd San Diego 92117

SHREVE, CLYDE GAROLD, marketing executive; b. Aug. 18, 1925, Baker, Mont.; s. Wm. Hanna and Nellie Ann (Adams) S.; m. Dawn, Dec. 27, 1946; children: Louise, b. 1947, Lynn, b. 1948, Kathleen, b. 1950, Gary, b. 1952; edn: stu. Centenary Coll. 1943-44; BS, Ore. State Coll. 1949, grad. work 1952. Career: mgr. Standard Oil Co. of Calif., Portland, Ore. 1949-58; store mgr., dist. supvr. Firestone Tire & Rubber Co., Portland 1958-65, regional mgr., Los Angeles, 1965-69; nat. sales mgr. Kingsway Prodns., Hollywood 1969-72; vice pres. Coyle Advt. Inc., West Covina 1972-75; vice pres. J-2 Marketing, Whittier 1975-79; pres./owner Advance Mktg. Services, Fullerton 1979--; secty. bd. dirs. Town & Country Retirement Ctr./Hosp., 1978-; adv. bd. Beret Camps for Retarded and Crippled Children, 1973-75; regl. dir. Mens Work, Baptist Gen. Conf. Churches, 1969-83; honors: Nat. Award of Excellence - Graphic Arts, Potlatch Paper Co. 1979; mil: flyer USAAF 1943-46, two Presdtl. Cits., Army Commendn., Air Medal; Republican; Baptist. Res: 1051 Site Dr, No. 105, Brea 92621 Ofc: Advance Marketing Services, 3711-C No. Harbor Blvd Fullerton 92635

SHRIMPTON, WALLACE, company president; b. Nov. 29, 1913, Napier, NZ; s. Walter and Edith Maude (Forster) S.; m. Marian Bliss, Aug. 29, 1941; 1 dau.

Suzzanne Dworak Peck, b. 1943; edn: stu. animal sci., econ., Univ. of NZ, 1932; grad. Pan Am. Nav. Sch. 1941; photogrammetric engr. USC and Fairchild Aerial Surveys, 1941; cert. indsl. psych., UCLA 1944; A.F.M., UC and Am. Soc. of Mgrs. and Rural Appraisers, 1959. Career: rep. (contr. negotiation with Australian govt.) Fairchild Aerial Survey corp., 1938-39; tech. instr., navigator, command pilot, R.A.F., Pacific and N. Atlantic areas, 1941-43; project engr. Photogrammetric Instruments (Pasadena, Ca.) dev. geodetic camera for USN, 1943-45; Matapiro Agricultural Ops., NZ, mgmt. trainee to gen. mgr., 1933-54, tech. cons. 1952-64, trustee 1964--, devel. low profit orgn. into largest privately owned agri. op. in NZ; currently pres. Bio Genetics; pres. Internat. Agricultural Services Inc. (mgmt. counselling to indus. and govt.), 1954--; gen partner SRM Ltd.; Patentee; sev. new patents pending in biological sci.; over 100 research papers for clients; three fundamental devels. in agri. sci. (pub. in process); mem. Am. Soc. of Agri. Consultants, Am. Soc. of Farm Mgrs. and Rural Appraisers, Am. Inst. of Biol. Scis., Am. Inst. of Photogrammetry, Internat. Soil Sci. Soc.; rec: hiking, music. Res: 411 Roberts Rd Pacifica 94022 Ofc: Internat. Agricultural Service Inc. 1015 Grandview Dr. South San Francisco 94080

SHUKMAN, SOLOMON JOSEPH, artist; b. July 5, 1927, Bobr, Minsk, USSR; nat. 1980; s. Joseph and Eugenia (Golden) S.; m. Ludmila Berman, Nov. 14, 1954; children: Janna, b. 1955, Roman, b. 1959; edn: Coll. of Fine Arts and Theatre, Moscow 1946-49, Stroganov Inst. of Art, Moscow 1949-52. Career: artist, Artists Found. of USSR, 1952-74; internat. exhibs: NY (1956), Paris (1959), Brussels (1961), Ehrfurt (1962), Warsaw (1964), Prague (1967), Sokolnike (1968, 71, 73); vs. pers. exhibs. 1963-64, mem. Union of Soviet Artists; recipient 20 diplomas and awards, Artists Found. of USSR; pers. exhibns: Denver (1974), TransAm. Bldg., Loeb rhoades Mkt. Gall., S.F. (1975), Los Altos (1976), Nathan Gall., Union Sq., S.F. (1977), Pantheon Gall., Sutter St., S.F. (1978), Magnes Mus., Berkeley (1979), Los Altos (1981); mem: World Print Council, S.F.; Graphic Arts Counc.; Soc. of the Calif. Palace of the Legion of Honor, S.F.; Internat. Graphic Arts soc., NY; Democrat; Jewish. Res: 554 Beresford Ave Redwood City 94061

SHUMATE, VALERIE HELEN, real estate broker, journalist, educator; b. Mar. 29, 1933, Lameroo, S. Australia, nat. 1959; d. John Roy and Kathleen (Bowman) Dunn; m. Clyde K. Shumate, Oct. 12, 1957; children: Michael, b. 1958, Sandra, b. 1960, Pam, b. 1963, Wanda, b. 1966; edn: tchr. cert. Adelaide Teachers Coll., 1953; BA, honors, Cal Poly 1975, spec. edn. T.C., 1974, 75; Calif. lic. real estate sales 1978, broker 1981. Career: sch. tchr., Australia, 1953-55; world tour (tennis & tourist), 1956, 57; tchr. London County Council, Glasgow, Scotland, 1956-57, Augusta, Ga. 1960, prin. International (Brit.) Sch., Asmara, Eritrea, Ethiopia 1961-63, also Eng. instr. Univ. of Addis Ababba; tennis tchr., Calif. 1964-65; piano tchr., Landstuhl, Ger. 1966-68; tchr. jr. high sch. phys. edn, spl. edn. tchr., San Luis Obispo Co. 1975-78; tennis coach Paso Robles High Sch., 1975-80; real estate broker assoc. Century 21 Home & Land Realtors, Paso Robles, 1979--; tennis coach 1960--; writer weekly edn. column.: On Board, Country News (Paso Robles); travel articles "Wimbledon" 1983; mem: Paso Robles Bd. of Realtors (edn. pgm. chmn. 1979-); AAUW (internat. chair 1984); PTA, Red Cross (Water Safety Instr.), Order of Eastern Star; mem. Art Theatre site com.; Parks & Rec. tennis instr.; Republican; Prot.; rec: travel, piano, tennis, swimming. Res: 1704 Highland Park Drive Paso Robles 93446 OFc: Century 21 Home & Land Realtors, 521 Spring St Paso Robles 93446

SHUTTLEWORTH, CHARLES HOMER, III, real estate broker; b. May 24, 1942, San Rafael; s. Chas. H. and Doris M. Shuttleworth; m. Carol J. Hilbun, Apr. 23, 1960; children: Debra, b. 1962, Tammy, b. 1965, Jill, b. 1968; edn: AA in bus., Coll. of Marin, 1966; AA in real estate, Am. River Coll. 1981; BA in bus. adm., CSU 1975; MPA, honors, Univ. of San Francisco 1983; Calif. lic. real estate broker. Career: state tax auditor, 1966-80; real estate broker 1980--; v.p. Amador Resources, Inc.; treas. Fun N' Fashion Co.; honors: Alpha Gamma Sigma; mem. Sacto. Bd. of Realtors, Elks; mil: cpl. US Army Paratroopers 1960-63; Catholic; rec: skiing. Address: Amador Resources, Inc. 9245 Wausau Way Sacramento 95826

SICKLER, GERALD LLOYD, SR., corporate executive/newspaper publisher; b. Aug. 27, 1936, Hollywood; s. Gerald Eugene and Ruth Orby (Moore) S.; m. Laura Lynne O'Brien, Apr. 12, 1959; children: Gerald Jr., b. 1960, Brien Wm., b. 1965; edn: dip. Canoga Park H.S. 1954, stu. Pierce Coll. 1959-61, Coll. of the Canyons 1970-72; Calif. lic real estate broker. Career: deputy sheriff County of Los Angeles, 1959-82; pres. Rancho Valley Realty Inc., 1972--; pres. Juniper Devel. Corp., 1982--; pres./chief fin. ofcr./editor and pub. The Acton Rooster, 1983--; mem. L.A. County Planning Advisory Council 1981; mem: Acton CofC (bd. dirs., v.p. 1978-80); Soledad Cyn Property Owners Inc. (bd. dirs. 1978-80, pres. 1980-); mil: cpl. US Army 1954-57; rec: writing, civic affairs. Res: 5301 Soledad Cyn Rd Ravenna 93510 Ofc: The Acton Rooster, POB 147, Acton 93510

SIDHPURA, DILIP VALLABHDAS, structural engineer; b. Dec. 6, 1943, Mahuva, India; s. Vallabhdas B. and Sumanta V. (Mistry) S.; m. Rita, Jan. 24, 1970; 1 son, Rishiraj, b. 1980; edn: BE (civil engg.), M.S. Univ. of Baroda (India), 1964; MS (civil engg.) N. Mex. State Univ. 1966; Registered Civil Engr., Calif. Career: asst. structural engr. William Schmidt & Assoc., Chgo. 1966-67; assoc. struc. engr. The Austin Co., Des Plaines, Ill. 1967-68; struc. engr. The Ralph M. Parsons Co., Pasadena 1968-72; senior struc. engr. Daniel, Mann, Johnson, Mendenhall, L.A. 1972-73; principal struc. engr. Fluor Engineers, Inc. Irvine 1973--, assigned to Indonesia for technology transfer pgm., Oct.-Dec. 1981; mem. ASCE; trustee The Gujarati Cultural Soc. of So. Calif.; Democrat; Hindu; rec: travel, photog., swimming. Res: 5 Hawkridge Irvine 92714 Ofc: Fluor Engineers Inc. 3333 Michelson Dr. Irvine 92730

SIEBEN, RICHARD ERNEST, JR., control systems engineer; b. Nov. 11, 1983, Oak Park, Ill.; s. Richard Ernest and Florence Agnes (Gray) S.; m. Arline Louies, May 12, 1965; 1 son, Richard E., III; edn: elec. engg., Chgo. Tech. Coll. 1951; Brooklyn Polytech. 1952-53. Career: electrical job engr. Bechtel Corp. 1958-62; control systems engr. Aetron, Div. Aerojet General 1962-64, C.F. Braun Co. 1965-67, Ralph M. Parsons Co. 1967-72, Daniel Mann Johnson & Mendenhall 1973-76, North American Rockwell 1977-80; control sys. engr./supr. electrical & instrument design, Kaiser Steel Corp. 1980-83; control system engineer/cons. City of Anaheim 1983--; mem. Iron & Steel Engineers; devel. test equip. for testing Gemini & Apollo Rocket Engines 1962-63; assisted in devel. for fuel storage of spent nuclear fuel rods 1977-80; Presbyterian; rec: hunting, fishing, flying, camping. Res: 16375 Ladysmith St Hacienda Hts 91745 Ofc: City of Anaheim, 200 S. Anaheim Blvd Anaheim 92805

SIEGEL, HOWARD ALLEN, financier; b. Feb. 28, 1940, Detroit, Mich.; s. Sydney and Sylvia (Raskin) S.; m. Diane Marie Wesolowski, June 28, 1974; children: Scott, b. 1970, Lisa, b. 1967; edn: BS in ME, USC, 1961. Career: draftsman, designer, sr. designer for Vickers Inc., Amelco Corp., John Charles Co. prior to 1959; mech. engr. Hughes Aircraft, Culver City 1959-62; pres. Technical Services Engineering, Torrance 1962-64; exec. vice pres. Empire Savings & Loan, Van Nuys 1964-75; pres. State Mutual S&L (now Far West Savings), Newport Beach and bd. chmn. Far West Finl. Corp., Newport Bch., 1975-80; 1980--: bd. chmn. The West Companies (full service real estate firm) and subs. cos. Golden West Capital Group Inc., Sun West Brokerage Co. Inc., Sea West Construction Co. Inc.; bd. chmn./chief exec. Western Empire S&L Assn., and Western Empire Finl. Corp.; honors: Businessman of Year 1979, Trade Labor Union Council; King Neptune Man of Year 1980, United Cerebral Palsy Assn.; resolution, Orange County Bd. Supvrs. 1980; afils.: So. Coast Repertory Theatre (past pres. bd. trustees), Easter Seal Soc. (bd. dirs.), O.C. Bldg. Industry Assn. (bd. advisors), var. USC alumni, support groups; 552 club Hoag Meml. Hosp.; treas. Bus. and Profls. for Effective Representation; Democrat (arrangements com. Dem. Nat. Com. 1980; conv. arrangements ch. Calif. Dem. Party 1980). Res: 65 Belcourt Dr North Newport Beach 92660 Ofc: The West Companies, 4 Upper Newport Plaza, Newport Beach 92660

SIEGEL, ROBERT CHARLES, physician, medical scientist; b. Julyl 26, 1940, Brklyn.; s. Samuel and Selma (Cohen) S.; m. Judith Pickard, Sept. 8, 1963; children: David, b. 1968, Sandie, b. 1zwl, Marcia, b. 1977; edn: stu. Calif. Inst. of Tech. 1958-59; AB, Princeton Univ. 1962; MD, Harvard Med. Sch. 1966; Fellow American Coll. of Physicians 1977. Career: intern and resident, internal medicine, UC San Francisco 1967-68; research assoc. Nat. Inst. of Dental Research, Nat. Insts. of Health, 1968-70; chief res. Dept. of Medicine, UCSF, 1970-71; fellow, immunology, Stanford Univ. Med. Ctr. 1971-72; asst. prof. of medicine and orthopedics, UCSF, 1972-77, assoc. prof. 1977-78, assoc. clin. prof. of med. UCSF 1978--; cons. Collagen Corp. 1982--; vice chmn. Medical and Sci. Com., No. Calif. Rheumatism Assn. 1983-; awards: Research Career Devel. Award, Nat. Inst. of Arthritis Metabolic Disease 1975-78; mem: Am. Soc. of Clin. Investigation, W. Soc. Clin. Research, Am. Rheumatism Assn., No. Calif. Rheumatism Assn.; trustee Castle Art Mus. and Resrch. Lab. 1981-; dir. Hillsborough Schools Found. 1982-; orgnzr./dir. Credit Bank of San Mateo 1983-; publs: 50 sci. papers 1970-; patent pending: new method for generating native crosslinks in collagen helical domains; mil: surgeon PHS 1968-70; Jewish; rec: art collecting, wine tasting, tennis. Res: 1440 Southdown Rd Hillsborough 94010 Ofc: Robert C. Siegel, MD, Inc. 101 S. San Mateo Dr, Ste. 211, San Mateo 94401

SIEUX, GEOFFREY, pharmacist; b. Dec. 25, 1946, Hong Kong; s. Joseph Young and Kimmy (Au) S.; m. Lily Tom, Nov. 30, 1977; 1 child, Liane, b. 1982; edn: BS, Univ. of San Francisco 1973; D.Pharm., Univ. of the Pacific 1976; reg. pharmacist, Calif. 1976. Career: staff pharmacist Pay N' Save No. 51 in Oakland, head pharmacist No. 47 in San Francisco; currently head pharmacist Pay N' Save No. 43, S.F.; mem: Am., Calif., Alameda County Pharmacist Assns.; Kappa Psi Pharmaceutical Frat.; mil: sp5 US Army 1967-70, Viet Nam Combat Medal; pharm. ofcr./lst lt. Calif. Army Nat. Guard; Republican; Catholic; rec: pop and jazz pianist, gun collector, sports cars. Res: 4000 Plumas court Hayward 94542 Ofc: Pay N' Save Corp. 2030 Market St San Francisco 94114

SIGG, CLAY WALKER, real estate broker; b. Oct. 5, 1950, Los Angeles; s. Robert Wm. and Patricia (Davies) S.; m. Sandra Moldenhauer, Aug. 6, 1954; children: Nicole, b. 1980, Julia, b. 1981; edn: BA, UC Davis 1972. Career: realtor assoc. Donovan, Rauizza & Witzel Realtors, Carmichael 1976, Bohannon, Realtors, Fair Oaks 1976-81, Western National, Realtors, Citrus Hts. 1981-82; co-owner/broker Real estate Forum, Citrus Hts. 1982--; awards: life mem. Sacramento Bd. of Realtors Masters Club; Bohannon, Realtors Man of the Year 1978, Top Male Agt. 1978-79; mem: Nat./ Calif. Assn. of Realtors; Sacto. Bd. of Realtors (cons. SBOR Grievance Com. 1983-; MLS Svc. Com. 1982; contbr. Ednl. Seminars); Toastmasters Intl. (CTM desig.); mem. UC Davis Comm. Baseball Stadium Com.; Sierra Club; Ancil Hoffman Park Mens Golf Club; No. Calif. Golf Assn.; Republican; Congregational; rec: archtl. design, golf, skiing. Res: 5141 Molakini Ct. Fair Oaks 95628 Ofc: Real Estate Forum, 7919 Pebble Beach Dr, Ste. 103, Citrus Hts. 95610

SIGMAN, MELVIN MONROE, psychiatrist; b. Dec. 15, 1935, NY, NY; s. Irving and Lillian (Pearlman) S.; edn: BA, Columbia Univ. 1956; MD, State

Univ. of NY Downstate Med. Ctr., 1960; psychiatry residency tng. The Roosevelt Hosp., NYC 1963-66; psychoanalytic tng. Wm. Alanson White Psychoanalytic Inst. 1966-69; NY State Med. Lic. 1961, Calif. 1974. Career: pvt. practice, psychiatry, 1966--; Hawthorne Cedar-Knolls Residential Treatment Center for Children and Adolescents, Hawthorne, NY 1966-68; cons. Bellevue Hosp., NYC 1966-72; assoc. attending Roosevelt Hosp., NYC 1967-72; cons. NY Foundling Hosp. 1968-72; cons. Collegiate School, NYC 1969-72; staff psychiatrist Community Mental Health Div. Fresno (Calif.) County Dept. of Health, 1974--; asst. clin. prof. of psychiatry, UC San Francisco and mem. Core Faculty and Supervisors Coms., Fresno Campus UCSF; mem. Am. Psychiatric Assn. 1966-, Fellow Royal Soc. of Health 1970-, Fellow Am. Orthopsychiatric Assn. 1978-; mil: capt. USAF 1961-63; Democrat; Jewish; rec: piano. Res: 2351 W. Warner, Fresno 93711 Ofc: Fresno County Dept. of Health, POB 11867, Fresno 93775

SIGMUND, RICHARD D., lawyer; b. Nov. 9, 1948, Wilmington, Del.; s. Howard and Rosalie (Statnekoo) S.; m. Andrea, Aug. 22, 1971; children: Kevin, b. 1978, Cara, b. 1981; edn: stu. Rider Coll. 1966-69, Brandywine Coll. 1969; BA, CSU Long Beach 1971; JD, Calif. Western Sch. of Law 1974; admitted to Calif. State Bar 1974, US Supreme Court 1980. Career: assoc. atty. Uribe, Sorem & McNeil, San Diego 1975-77; deputy district atty. Tulare Co. Dist. Atty's Office, Visalia 1977-79; assoc. Mitchell & Sigmund Profl. Law Corp., Visalia 1979-82; partner Wilson, Altschule & Sigmund, Visalia 1982--; dir. Family Planning Program, Inc. 1983-; mem: Central Valley Orgn. of Social Sec. Claimants Reps. (pres. 1983-84); Am. Bar Assn.; Phi Alpha Delta Law Frat. 1972-; Rotary Intl. Democrat; Jewish; rec: photog., aerobics. Res: 2209 South Valley Ave Visalia 93277 Ofc: Wilson, Altschule & Sigmund, 5349 West Hillsdale Dr Visalia 93291

SILCOCK, MARY MARGARET, corporate executive; b. Mar. 11, 1944, Hayward; d. Francis Ellsworth and Ruth (Wightman) Case; m. Russell Dee Silcock, Sept. 2, 1972 (husband is senior cost acct. Novitiate Wines of Los Gatos); children: Russell, b. 1965, Jeffrey, b. 1970, Mandy Ruth, b. 1978; foster chil: Glenda, Donnie, rank, Michael, Kathy, Duane; edn: undergrad. bus., Clarke Coll. 1969-70, sci., Univ. of Ariz. 1975-76, sci., Brigham Young Univ. 962-63, bus., West Valley Coll. 1967; Masters deg., Stella Rae Acad. of Arts 1959; reg. psychiat. technician, Calif. 1962. Career: current gen. mgr. five corps.: De Anza Properties Inc., De Anza Properties Inc. Escrow Dept., Real Estate Management Co. Inc., Sunset Investors, and Sunset Capital (Los Gatos) 1983--; freelance writer; cons./in process of forming mgmt. and talent agcy. dba Mandy Enterprises; (past) mgmt. Caseys Chicken Inn 1958-60, Caseys Giant Hot Dog 1960-63; psychiat. tech. Agnews St. Hosp. 1961-65, 67-69, VA Hosp. 1969-70; var. positions with Western Electric 1970-71, Greyhound Intl. 1971-73, Biscayne Apt. 1973-74, Ky. Fried Chicken 1975-77, US Govt. in Germany 1977-80, in Wash. DC 1980-82, awards: Merit Award in Acctg., Military Dist. of Wash.; mem: Nat. Assn. Female Execs., Writers Connection (Cupertino), Nat. Thespian Soc. (life), Nat. Forensic League (life), Nat. Notary Assn.; editor Pattonville Pipeline, comm. newsletter, Stuttgart, Ger.; mem. Golden Gate Tip Toppers, Tall Clubs Internat., PTA; works: semi-profl. theatre perf.; num. pub. articles; books incl. sci-fi novel, action adventure novel, cookbook, and a teaching play for teenage drama students; mil. wife of non-commnd. ofcr. AUS active duty 11 years; Democrat, Ch. of Jesus Christ of LDS; rec: writing, dancing, theatre. Res: 4361 Jan Way San Jose 95124 Ofc: De Anza Properties Inc.2 259 University Ave Los Gatos 95030

SILVA, GERALD ROLAND, architect; b. July 19, 1950, Las Vegas, N.Mex.; s. Leo E. and Tillie Mary (Lucero) S.; edn: BS, Univ. of N.M. 1972, M.Arch. 1977; Calif. Lic. Architect. Career: job captain TBA/Dorman FAIA, Los Angeles 1977, Peter Lendrum Associates, San Diego 1979, PDAS Architects, San Diego 1981; architect Hope Consulting Group, S.D. 1981; prin. Jerry R. Silva, Architect AIA, S.D., arch./quality control rep. Testing Engineers, S.D. 1983, KDH Corp., Encinitas 1983; instr. of arch. Albuquerque Pub. Schools 1975-77; mem: Am. Inst. of Architects, US Navy League, Soc. for Mktg. Profl. Services, Coast Guard Aux.; works: plnng./design of Mid Valley Airpark; Catholic; rec: pvt. pilot, boating. Address: Jerry R. Silva, Architect AIA, 3731 Columbia St San Diego 92103

SILVA, RAYMOND ARNOLD, chartered life underwriter; b. June 29, 1930, San Jose; s. Henry Francisco and Emily Eleanor (Fields) S.; m. Carolyn Helms, July 16, 1953; children: Terrence (stepson) b. 1951, Jennifer, b. 1954, Jeffrey, b. 1955, Laurie, b. 1958, Erin, b. 1961, Shannon, b. 1972; edn: BA, San Jose State Univ. 1952, MA 1956; Chartered Life Underwriter (CLU) The Am. Coll. 1965. Career: physical educator, athletic coach Berkeley High Sch., 1955-59, Camden H.S., San Jose 1959-62; field rep. The Guardian Life Insurance Co. of Am., San Jose 1962---84; senior sales cons. The Guardian Life Ins. Co. of Am., NY, NY 1981--; adv. bd. Am. Bank & Trust Co., Walnut Creek/ San Jose; bd. trustees (pres. 1977-9) Campbell Union H.Sch. Dist. 1973-81; dir. San Jose St. Univ. Found. 1982-, mem. SJSU Pres.'s Council; dir. (pres. 1974-6) The Spartan Found., San Jose 1968-; Honors: agent of year, San Jose Life Underwriter Assn. 1978; nat. pres. Guardian Life Leaders Club, 1978, pres. Guardian Life CLU Assn. 1977-79; life & qualifying mem. Million Dollar Roundtable 1971-Mem: Am. Soc. of CLUs (W. regional v.p. 1981-2), Assn. for Advanced Underwriting, Santa Clara County Estate Plnng. Council (pres. 1982-3); mil: lt. USNR (ret.), active duty 1952-54; Republican; Presbyterian; rec: basketball, raquetball, ski. Res: 185 Surmont Court Los Gatos 95030 Ofc: Guardian Life, 1602 The Alameda, Ste. 200, San Jose 95126

SILVA, WILLIAM HEYWARD, real estate developer; b. Oct. 17, 1923, Cleveland, Oh.; s. Abbott Beecher and Gladys Loie (Heyard) S.; m. Marilyn Jean Elkouri, Dec. 9, 1968; children: June (Cornea), b. 1950, David Beecher, b. 1955, Janice Heyward, b. 1963, William Abbott, b. 1969; edn: BS in bus., Miami Univ. (Oxford, Oh.) 1947; Harvard Grad. Sch. of Bus., Naval Supply Corp Sch., 1944-45; cert. of real estate, UCLA; Calif. lic. general contractor, lic. real estate broker; CPM, Cert. Prop. Mgr. Career: founder/pres. Citizens' Realty & Development Inc., 1957--, acquisition and land devel., constr. homes, condominiums, apartments, office & indsl. bldgs., prop. mgmt.; awards: General Elec. Builder of the Month, 1970; mem: Nat. Assn. of Realtors, San Fernando Bd. of Realtors, Inst. of Real Estate Mgmt.; bd. dirs. Campbell Hall Sch. (pres. PTA); Dist. Atty's Comm. Adv. Council; v.p./dir. L.A. Tennis Club, mem. Beach & Tennis Club (Pebble Bch), Carmel Valley Ranch Tennis Club; mil: lt.jg. USN 1944-46; Prot. Res: 14587 Deervale Pl Sherman Oaks 91403 Ofc: Citizens Realty, 4331 Woodman Ave Sherman Oaks 91423

SILVEIRA, ANTHONY PERRY, real estate broker/consultant; b. Oct. 27, 1956, San Jose; s. Manuel F. and Carment Francise (Cardoza) S.; m. Kandie Lee Vandenburg, Dec. 2, 1978; edn: bus., Cabrillo Coll. 1974-77; Calif. lic. real estate sales 1976, R.E. broker 1978. Career: lot boy, car washer, dispatcher, job coordinator Santa Cruz GM Automotive Dealership, 1972-75; real estate agt. Merit McBride Realtors, Santa Cruz 1976; agt./branch ofc. mgr. Oak Ridge Realty 1977-80; broker/owner Time Realty, Santa Cruz 1980--; sales awards incl. 1978 Top Listing & Sales (13 offices), Oak Ridge Rlty; 1982 Top Producer, Santa Cruz Bd. of Realtors; mem. 2 Million Dollar Club 1979-84; Mem: Santa Cruz Exchangers, Mid-County Exchange Club (bd. dir. 1983), Santa Cruz Board of Realtors (MLS Memshp. Com. 1983, 84), National Exchange Club; club: Monterey Bay Classic Thunderbird (pres. elect 1984); participant Miss Calif. Parade 1980-81; art., Real Estate Mag.; Democrat; Catholic; rec: restoration antique and classic autos, skiing, renovation older homes. Res: 1310 Webster St Santa Cruz 95062 Ofc: Time Realty, 1980 Fifteenth Ave Santa Cruz 95062

SILVER, LAURENCE E., veterinarian; b. July 19, 1937, Los Angeles; s. Don and Tillie (Silver) Prager; m. Roberta Silver, Aug. 18, 1957; children: David, b. 1958, Mark, b. 1963, Stefanie, b. 1965; edn: DVM, UC Davis 1963; capt. lic., USCG 1978. Career: practice veterinary medicine, 1963-80, trust deed mortgage broker, 1968-; garment indus. 1969-; bd. dirs. six corporations in real estate, electronics, mfg., marine industry etc., 1970-; honors incl. Man of the Year 1982, Marine Electronic Assn.; mem. Veterinary Cardiology Soc., Mortgage Brokers Assn., Soc. of Aquatic Medicine, Marine Captains Assn., etc.; Patentee (10) in electronics and human hosp. medicine; Jewish; rec: scuba diving, celestial navigation. Address: 18939 Mayall St Northridge 91324

SILVER, LEE RICHARD, physician; b. Apr. 8, 1947, Prov., R.I.; s. Ben and Molly (Berman) S.; m. Helle Mikkelsen, June 29, 1980; edn: BS in E.E., Univ. of Rhode Is. 1970, Masters Work in biomed. engineering 1972-1974; MD, Geo. Washington Univ. 1978; Calif. Class A physician and surgeon. Career: project engr., estimator, purch. agt. Lera Electric, San Francisco 1970-72; tchg. asst. in biomed. engring. Univ. of R.I., 1972-74; NIH Cancer Resrch., imaging unit, Bethesda, Md. 1974-76; resident in clin. pathol., UC San Diego Univ. Hosp., 1978-79; med. dir. of Human Biologic Procurement, Westmar Biologics, San Diego 1979-80; phys. Gen. Practice, Family Practice, pres. Huntington Valley Med. Group Inc., 1980--; gen. practice Hollywood Free Clinic, 1980-81; mem. Optimist Club, Huntington Bch CofC; publs: Half Tone Images, Soc. of Information Display, Gordon, Silver and Rigel, 1976; professional pianist. Res: 21791 Windsong Cir Huntington Beach 92646 Ofc: Lee Silver MD Inc. 9131 Adams Ave, Ste. 3, Huntington Beach 92646

SILVER, MARK STEVEN, lawyer; b. Dec. 7, 1952, NYC; s. Samuel N. and Pauline (Meyer); m. Amanda Ferrari, May 27, 1979; 1 dau. Valerie, b. 1980; edn: AA, Nassau Comm. Coll. 1972; BS, Western State Univ. 1979, JD, WSU Coll. of Law 1980; admitted to practice: Calif. (1981), US Dist. Ct., Central and So. Districts of Ca., US Ninth Circuit Ct. of Appeals. Career: law clerk/ legal intern, 1979-81; atty., law firms of Marlin & Assocs., Tustin, 1981, Orange County Lawyers Group, 1981, Mackey & Sullivan, 1982, law offices of Mark S. Silver, Santa Ana 1982--; owner Scholarship Plus (student/athlete consultants) 1983--; dir. /v.p./ gen. counsel: Moran Noah Systems, Inc., Garfield's Night Spot, Inc. 1983-; dir./ pres./ gen. counsel: Cabaret Mgmt. Systems, Inc. 1984-; gen. counsel: Indian Internat. Airlines Inc., Columbia Beverages Internat. Inc., American Computer Terminals, Inc., Virgin Is. Airways, Inc., 1983-; honors: American Jurisprudence Awards, 1979; WSU Coll. of Law: Moot Ct. (bd. dirs.), Law Rev., Student Bar Assn. (exec. bd.); mem: Am. Bar Assn., Young Lawyers Div. of ABA (coms.), Calif. Bar Assn., Orange Co. Bar Assn. (Bridging the Gap Com.; spkr. 1983), Orange Co. Barristers, Assn. of Trial Lawyers of Am., Calif. Trial Lawyers Assn., Council of Better Bus. Bureaus (Nat. Panel of Consumer Arbitrators 1982-); rec: travel, baseball, softball, football. Res: Irvine Bus: Law Ofcs. Mark S. Silver, 444 W. 10th St Ste 200, Santa Ana 92701

SILVERMAN, SOL, real estate broker; b. July 15, 1905, Beltz, Rumania, nat. 1918; s. Benjamin and Sarah (Saltzman) Silberman; widower; children: Donald Sterling, b. 1929, Joan Grossman, b. 1935; edn: LLB, Brklyn. Law Sch. 1926; admitted NY State Bar 1927; Calif. lic. real estate broker. Career: law practice in New York 1927-56; joined Union Bank, Los Angeles, Calif. 1957-, head escrow dept. in Beverly Hills Ofc., asst. vice pres. 1962-; formed own escrow bus., Beverly Canon Escrow Co., sold bus. 1975; currently partner with son/ founder/ pres. Sterling-Silverman Realty Corp., Beverly Hills; instr. escrow procedure Santa Monica City Coll.; mem: L.A. Escrow Assn. (pres.), Calif.

Escrow Assn. (dir.), Bev. Hills Real Estate Board (Afil. of the Year), West Side Real Estate Assn. (pres.), Beverly Hills Bus. and Profl. Mens Assn. (pres.), Bnai Brith (pres. Bev. Hills Lodge, pres. L.A. Council), ADL (regl. bd.). Res: 441 N. Oakhurst Dr Bev. Hills 90210 Ofc: Sterling-Silverman Realty Corp. 211 So. Beverly Dr Beverly Hills 90212

SILVERSTON, RANDALL ABRAM, psychologist; b. Apr. 6, 1947, Detroit, Mich.; s. Harold Morton and Sara S.; m. Bess Ellesberg, May 24, 1970; 1 dau. Hallie, b. 1983; edn: BA, Univ. Mich. 1969; M.Ed, Wayne State Univ. 1972; PhD, So. Ill. Univ. 1974; Psychologist, BBSE, Calif. 1978. Career: adminstrv. asst. Nuclear Medicine, Univ. Hosp., Univ. of Mich., Ann Arbor, 1970-71; staff counselor Voc. Residential Ctr., Ann Arbor, Mi. 1971-72; spl. doctoral asst. So. Ill. Univ., Carbondale 1972-74; asst. prof. Univ. of Texas, Arlington 1974-76; dir. Skills and Assessment, CSU Dominguez Hills, Carson, Ca. 1976-79; dir. Psychological Health Services, Downey 1979--; cons./lectr., TMJ Facial Pain Ctr., 1983-; psychol. cons. Community Learning Ctr. 1982-; honors: Kappa Delta Pi 1973; Outstanding Young Men in Am. 1979; Who's Who in the West 1982; mem: Am. Ednl. Research Assn., Am. Psychol. Assn., Calif. State Psychol. Assn., So. Calif. Psychotherapy Affil. (bd. mem. 1980-81), Alliance for Survival; publs: 15 research and profl. articles; Democrat; Jewish; rec: olf, cetacean research, hist. of cinema. Res: 17147 Gunther Ave Granada Hills 91344 Ofc: Psychological Health Services 8320 E. Florence 90240

SILVERSTONE, PAUL CHARLES, consultant; b. Apr. 26, 1915, NY, NY; s. Charles and Rose (Horowitz) S.; m. Frances, Aug. 17, 1940; 2 sons, Steven, b. 1941, Kenneth, b. 1944; edn: BS in chem. eng., Univ. of Wash. 1937; MS in chem. eng., USC 1941; Reg. Profl. Chem. Engr./Cal. 1947. Career: chemical engr. Hall-Baker Co., Richfield; proc. & engr. non metal, North American Aviation (now Rockwell), 1941-46; head of Electroforming, R.C.A., 1948-50, then consultant 1950-69; pres. Electroforms, Inc. 1950-79; cons. 1979--, CDJ Co. (mfg. of contractometer & current density meters); Sole Licensee for Boeing Airplane Co.; mem. American Electroplaters Soc.; Lions Intl., Temecula CofC, Masons, Shriners; rec: travel, tennis. Res: 28828 Via Roja Murrieta Hot Springs 92362

SILVESTER, ROBERT BRIAN, sales executive; b. Sept. 23, 1925, Los Angeles; s. Oswald Alfred and Buelah Elizabeth (Dray) S.; m. Diana Guillent, June 22, 1950, div. 1968; children: Denise, b. 1951, Lance, b. 1953, Lisa, b. 1955, Michelle, b. 1956; m. 2d. Rose Morino 1979, div. 1983; edn: stu. Los Angeles City Coll. 1948, El Camino Coll. 1955-60; Reg. Investment Adviser, SEC 1981; Calif. Investment Adviser Cert. 1983. Career: able seaman US Merchant Marine, Overseas (WWII) 1943-46; comml. fisherman self-empl. San Pedro and Newport beach, 1946-49; foreman Pacific Ryolex Corp., L.A. 1949-50; with Vickers Inc. (hydraulics co.), El Segundo and Torrance, 1952--: hydraulic assem. 1952-55, sales coordinator 1955-57, estimator 1957-58, supvr. Planning Dept. 1958-59, application engr. 1959-69, dist. sales mgr. 1969-70, dist. and facility mgr. 1970-74, dist. mgr. and regl. distbr. mgr. 1974--; known throughout the hydraulics indus. as Mr. Hydraulics (32 yrs. in the trade in Calif.); instr. var. company pgms. in mgmt. skills; honors: Appreciation, Nat. Heart, Lung and Blood Inst., Dept. Hlth & Human Svcs USA; club: El Prado Mens Golf (Chino); prin., Robert Brian Silvester Co. (investment adv.) 1982-; writer monthly inv. adv. newsletter; mil: cpl. US Army Inf. 1950-52, Korea, Combat Inf. Award; Republican; Christian; rec: swim, fish, golf, cooking, wine tasting. Res: 1631 Shady Brook Dr Fullerton 92631 Ofc: Vickers Inc. 445 Maple Ave Torrance 90503

SIMMONS, EARL MELVIN, otolaryngologist and facial plastic surgeon; b. Feb. 20, 1931, Brklyn.; s. Isaac and Iris C. (Small) S.; m. Elena L., Sept. 7, 1956; children: Erin, b. 1960, Erlan, b. 1962, Elissa, b. 1964, Erik, b. 1968; edn: dip. Haaren H.S., NYC 1949; elec. eng. stu. Brklyn. Coll. 1949-53; BS chem., magna cum laude, Howard Univ. 1958; MD, Howard Univ. Med. Coll. 1962; intern. cert., Cook Co. Hosp., Chgo. 1963; surgical cert., Meadowbrook Hosp., NYC 1964; otolaryngol. cert., Mt. Sinai Hosp., NYC 1967. Med. lic. in state of NY, NJ, Calif. Career: clin. instr. Mt. Sinai Med. Sch. 1966; chief Dept. Otolaryngol. East Orange (NJ) Gen. Hosp., 1967-79; att. phys. Newark Eye and Ear Infirmary & NJ Med. Sch., 1967-79; att. phys. Orange (NJ) Meml. Hosp., 1967-80; E.N.T. pvt practice, two offices, East Orange, NJ, 1967-79; chief Dept. Otolaryngol. USAF Hosp., Vandenberg AFB, Calif. 1979-81; pvt. practice, Encinitas, Calif. 1981--; honors: Beta Kappa Chi 1957; AMA Phys. Recognition Awd. 1978-80; US Congl. Advis. Bd.; Far Eastern Talent Contest winner 1955. Mem: Council of Otolaryngology; Deafness Research Found.; Med. soc. of San Diego; AMA; NMA; Undersea Med. Soc.; Assn. of Military Plastic Surgeons; mem. YMCA, UNICEF, NAACP; mil: pfc US Army 1953-55; surgeon PHS 1963-79; lt. col. USAF 1979-81; spl. interests: grad. Mind Dynamic Tng. 1976; open water cert. scuba diver (art. on Bimini Road discovery); redesign scuba diving face mask; two books of poetry: Turn Hourglass (1977), Eagle Spree (1979), Vantage Press; solo concert singer (dramatic tenor) Carnegie Hall Debut, NYC 1956, lead perfs. with Lyric Opera Co. of NJ, 1976-79; 5 languages; parapsych. investgr.; Democrat; Presbyterian. Res: 319 Sierra Ridge Encinitas 92024 Ofc: Earl M. Simmons, MD, 317 N. El Camino Real, Ste. 406, Encinitas 92024

SIMMONS, HENRY, consulting electrical engineer; b. July 1, 1910, NYC; s. Max and Julia Eugenia (Brenner) S.; m. Frances Edith Sullivan, Feb. 25, 1938; 2 sons, Robert H., b. 1939, Wesley F., b. 1941; edn: indsl. elec., Pratt Inst. of Tech. 182; BS in E.E., Georgia Inst. of Tech. 1936; Reg. Profl. Engr. in Calif. 1947, Nev. 1964, Ariz. 1965. Career: cable splicer & tester, NY Tel. Co., 1928-32; elec. engr. Bethlehem Steel Co., Terminal Isle, Ca. 1940-43; elec. engr. Naval Operating Base, Port Hueneme, 1943-46; elec. contr. Simmons Electric Co., Long Beach 1946-50; cons. engr., H. Simmons, E.E., 1950--; cons. with profs. and dept. heads at CSULB and Comm. Coll. Dist.; awards: merit certs., City of Long Beach, County of Los Angeles, and State of Calif., 1980; awards, CSULB and Comm. Coll. Dist. Long Beach, 1980; certs. of excellence, So. Calif. Edison Co., 1967, 68, 71; voted Engineer of Year, Harbor Div. L.A. Chpt. NECA; mem: Internat. Assn. Elec. Inspectors, Assn. Consulting Elec. Engrs., Illum. Engr. Soc., Nat. Soc. Profl. Engrs.; publs: Standard Testing Procedure (manual) 1944, Electrical Spec-Data (manual) 1984, tech. articles in trade mags., 1960-81; Republican; Methodist; rec: sailing, football. Res: 3749 Cerritos Ave Long Beach 90807

SIMON, C. SHOSHANA, lawyer; b. July 28, 1944, NY, NY; d. Charles Westlake and Mally Irene (Carnegie) Mackenzie; m. Wm. J. Simon, Aug. 15, 1979; edn: BA, magna cum laude, Univ. Calif. 1967; JD, Univ. of La Verne 1978; admitted Calif. State Bar 1978. Career: social wkr./adminstr. Riverside County Dept. of Public Soc. Svcs., 1968-75; solo gen. practice law, San Bernardino Co., 1978-80; partner law firm Simon & Simon (insolvency splty.), San Bernardino 1980--; chpsn Task Force on Domestic Violence, S.B. County Commn. on Status of Women 1980-81; pro-bono counsel to Option House, Battered Womens Shelter 1980-82; vol. atty. S.B. County Legal Aid Clinic 1979-; honors: law rev. 1976; recognition, San Bernardino Co. Judiciary 1981. Mem: Calif. State Bar Assn. (bankruptcy study gp.); San Bernardino Co. Bar Assn. (judicial select. com.); Family law Council (sec. treas. 1981-3); ACLU; Am. Bar Assn. (Law Ofc. Econ. com.); Toastmasters 1977-9; coauthor art., Things Fall Apart: A Critical Approach to Chinua Achebe (1969, repub. in A Study of African Lit. 1978); Democrat; Jewish; rec: folk dancing, philately. REs: 5915 Newcomb St San Bernardino 92404 Ofc: Simon & Simon, 141 N. Arrowhead Ave, Ste. 12, San Bernardino 92408

SIMON, LESLIE MATTHIAS, manufacturing co. executive; b. Aug. 15, 1916, Budapest, Hungary, nat. 1960; s. Marton M. and Theresa (Nagy) S.; m. Muriel M., Jan. 1, 1982 (pub. rels. expt./vol. soc. wk. with abused children); children: Ilona, b. 1944, Peter, b. 1946; edn: BSME, Tech. Univ. of Budapest 1938; MSME, Higher Edn. Inst. 1939; doctoral pgm. US Internat. Univ.; Reg. Profl. Engr. Calif.; Lic. MTM Instrn. 1964. Career: indsl. engineering mgr. Burroughs Corp., Pasadena 1966-78; plant mgr. Control Data Corp., Anaheim 1978--; writer, lectr., instr. Burroughs Corp., MTM Assn., 1966-78; recipient Great Performers Awd., Control Data 1980; mem: MTM Assn. (bd. dirs. 1968), Profl. Engrs. Soc. Calif., Indsl. Engrg. Assn. (senior mem. 1967); Big Brothers, R.I. (1960); past pres. Toastmaster Intl. 1966-76; publs: tech. arts. in-house publs.; unpub. book: Manufacturing Operations (1973); mil: 1st lt. Hungarian ARmy 1942-44; Libertarian; rec: chess master, bridge, dog and horse breeder. Res: 1281 Cumberland Cross Santa Ana 92705 Ofc: Control Data Corp. 3285 E. Carpenter Ave Anaheim 92806

SIMONIAN, RICHARD JACK, manufacturing co. president; b. Dec. 27, 1931, Los Angeles; s. Harry P. and Nellie (Bozigian) S.; m. Gitte, July 21, 1946; children: David, b. 1961, Bianca, b. 1978; grad. Montebello H.S. Career: founder/pres. Eemus Mfg. Corp., El Monte, 1975--, built bus. to sales in excess of 2 mil. annually; devel. methods of photo chem. machining; Republican; Christian; rec: sailing. Res: 15428 Los Molinos St Hacienda Heights 91745 Ofc: Eemus Mfg., 11111 Rush St So. El Monte 91733

SIMONIAN, SIMON KRIKOR, physician, surgeon; b. Dec. 25, 1948, Beirut, Lebanon, US citizen 1983; s. Krikor Simon and Azadouhi Mardiros (Mihranian) S.; m. Lena Oknayan, June 26, 1977; 1 child, Shiraz, b. 1980; edn: BS in biol., Am. Univ. of Beirut 1970, MD, 1975; Otorhinolaryngology (splty.) Thomas Jefferson Med. Ctr., Phila. 1980; Am. Board (splty.) cert. 1981. Career: surgery res. Thomas Jefferson Med. Ctr., 1976-77, otolaryngol. res. 1977-80; assoc. physician Kaiser Permanente Med. Group, 1980-81; solo practice in otolaryngology and head & neck surgery, Simon K. Simonian MD Inc., 1981--; assoc. phys. Arcadia Medical Group, 1981--; awards: AMA Physician Recognition Awd.; mem: Am. Acad. of Otolaryngol. and Head & Neck Surg. 1983; Penna. Acad. of Otolaryngol. 1979; L.A. County Med. Assn.; Armenian Tekeyan Cultural Assn. (pres. LA chpt., Nat. Central Bd.); Armenian Gen. Benevolent Union; med. journal arts., sci. presentations; Christian; rec: tennis, swimming, philately. Res: 3795 Valley Lights Dr Pasadena 91107 Ofc: Simon K. Simonian MD, 7080 Hollywood Blvd, Ste. 1012, Los Angeles 90028

SIMPSON, WENDELL PHILLIPS, personal financial consultant; b. Dec. 1, 1927, New Orleans, La.; s. Wendell Howard and Margaret S. Patten (Scruggs) S.; m. Pamela L. Brown, July 28, 1956; children: Wendell, III b. 1958, James b. 1960, Richard b. 1963; edn: Air War Coll. (1974), Command and Staff Sch. (1963), Squadron Ofcrs. Sch. (1960), USAF Air Univ.; econ., mech. engr., Cornell Univ. 1945-50. ChFC, Chartered Finl. Cons. (1984), CLU, Chartered Life Underwriter (1978), The Am. Coll.; Career: Agency- Interline mgr., TACA Internat. Airlines, 1952-54; v.p., International, Raybestos-Manhattan Inc., NY 1954-69; v.p. Industria Americana, Los Angeles 1969-73; prin. Wendell P. Simpson and Assocs., L.A. 1973-78; pres. Deferred Benefits Inc., Pasadena 1978-81; pres. Personal Financial Planning Inc., San Marino 1981--; guest lectr. Pepperdine Univ. Malibu, and Calif. Soc. of CPAs; honors: The Distinguished Service Cross, NY State 1970; mem: Estate Planning Council; CLUs (dir); Western Pension Conf.; v.chmn. Am. Red Cross Pasadena chpt.; Pasa. Tournament of Roses; USAF Acad. Liaison Ofcr.; Christian Businessmens Com.; Civil Air Patrol; mil: col. USAFR, 1946-80, Disting. Unit Medal, WWII Victory Medal, USAF Reserve Medal, Small Arms Exp. Medal; Republican; Episcopal; rec: aviation, recreational vehicles, golf, tennis. Address: Personal Financial Planning, 1699 Lorain Rd San Marino 91108

SIMPSON, WILLIAM BRAND, economist, educator; b. Nov. 30, 1919, Portland, Ore.; s. John Alexander and Janet Christie (Brand) S.; m. Ruth Decker, June 12, 1957; edn: BA, Reed Coll. 1942; MA, Columbia Univ. 1943; PhD, Claremont Grad. Sch. 1971. Career: consultant Nat. Defense Mediation Bd., Portland 1941-43, US Dept. of Interior, Portland 1942, head Economic Sect. Counter-Intelligence Office, Manila, 1945; spl. representative Supreme Cmdr. of Allied Powers, Japan, 1945-46; asst. research dir./exec. dir. Cowles Commn. for Resrch in Econ., Chgo. 1948-53; co-founder and bd. mem. Inst. of Soc. and Personal Relations, Oakland 1955-61; prof. economics, CSU Los Angeles 1958--; mng. editor and co-ed. Econometrica, 1948-53; cons. to var. univs. and higher education agcs., 1954--; honors: Phi Beta Kappa, 1942; Fellow Nat. Soc. Sci. Research Council, 1946-48; mem: Econometric Soc. (internat. secty 1948-52); AAUP (state pres. 1975-76, Nat. Councl 1978-81, Com. on Govt. Rels. 1982-84); Am. Economic Assn. (ch. panel on polit. discrimination 1978-81); Am. Assn. for Higher Edn.; ACLU; Cong. of Faculty Assn.; Eagle Rock Hist. Soc.; profl. journal arts. incl. Socio-Economic Planning Scis. (Oxford) 1975, Jour. of Higher Edn. 1981; mil: spl. agt. counter-intell. US Army 1943-46; Democrat; Unitarian; rec: travel, Scottish postal history, pre Columbian sculpture. Res: POB 1456, South Pasadena 91030 Ofc: CSULA, 5151 State University Dr Los Angeles 90032

SIMS, WILLIAM EARL, real estate broker; b. Oct. 25, 1935, Dallas, Tex.; s. William and Geraldine (Rutherford) S.; m. Mirey, 1980; edn: BS, Wiley Coll. 1958; fin. courses, UCLA 1968-70; Calif. lic. real estate broker, personal prop. broker. Career: pres. William E. Sims and Assocs., Inc., Los Angeles 1973--; dir. National Housing Partnership, Wash DC; fmr. sales mgr. Nicholas L. Dyer, L.A.; mem. NAACP, Urban League; mil: pfc US ARmy; Republican; rec: travel, tennis. Res: 5729 S. La Cienega Blvd Los Angeles 90056 Ofc: William E. Sims & Assoc. 5757 W. Century Blvd, Ste. 700, Los Angeles 90045

SINCLAIR, LARRY, scientist/inventor/computer design engineer; b. May 13, 1950, Hollywood; s. Virgil Daniel and Rose Marie (Lance) S. Career: test engineer Autologic, 1973; logic design engr. Information International, 1975; project engr. Amperif, 1983; proj. engr. Megavault, 1983, sr. engr. Digital Productions, 1984-; pres.: Anti Grav Labs, Intellimatics, Trivec, Computer Design Engineering; mem. Alliance for Survival; research: Gravitation, Laser Imaging/ Projection Systems, 3-D. TV; inventions: Layout/ Pagination Sys., Color Vector Refresh Display Sys., 3D Computer Graphics Sys.; rec: music composition. Res: 8750 Topanga Canyon, No. 70, Canoga Park 91304 Ofc: Computer Design Engineering, 7831 Alabama Ave, Ste. 10, Canoga Park 91304

SINCLAIR, RICHARD CARROLL, lawyer; b. July 15, 1945, Modesto; s. Carroll burns and Katherine Louise (Miller) S.; m. Deborah Ann Romine, July 17, 1951; children: Brandon, b. 1978, Justin, b. 1r0, Megan, b. 1982; edn: BA in sociol., Univ. Calif. 1970, JD, McGeorge Sch. of Law UOP 1975; LLM, taxation, Univ. of Miami 1976; admitted to practice Calif. State Bar, Federal Courts, Tax Ct.; Calif. Comm. Colls. instr. credential 1976. Career: computer analyst 1966-70; realtor associate 1970--; judicial hearing officer 1972-75; cattle rancher 1978--; real estate developer 1977--; attorney pvt. practice spec. in taxation, real estate, business and corporate law, investment counseling, 1976--; lectr. Stanislaus State Coll. 1981; Comm. coll. instr. 1976-; listed Who's Who in Am. Law 1979, Who's Who in Real Estate 1983; mem: Am., Calif. Stanislaus County bar assns.; Nat., Calif. assns. of realtors; Modesto Bd. of Realtors; Republican; Mormon. Address: 8212 Oak View Dr Oakdale 95361

SINGLETON, JACK LEONARD, manufacturing co. executive; b. Aug. 14, 1935, Los Angeles; s. Jack Edwin and Irene Lois (Munger) S.; m. Nicole Kupinskas, Aug. 13, 1973; edn: BSEE, Ore. State Univ. 1977. Career: president Matrix System Corp., 1969--. Res: 24111 Malibu Rd Malibu 90265 Ofc: Matrix System Corp. 5177 N. Douglas Fir Rd Calabasas 91302

SINISCAL, ALBERT VINCENT, audio engineer; b. July 6, 1941, St. Louis, Mo.; s. Dr. Arthur A. and Janet (Pitman) S.; edn: BS in chem. engring., Washington Univ., St. Louis 1963, MBA, 1965; postgrad. stu. elec. engring., USC, UCLA, 1971; Reg. Profl. Electrical Engr., Calif. Career: audio engr./ mixer; owner/pres. A-1 Audio Systems, Hollywood, Las Vegas, Atlantic City, and Lake Tahoe; mem. Audio Engring. Soc.; publs: articles in Recording Engr./Producer mag.; mil: 1st lt. USAF 1966-69, Vietnam Svc, Expt. Marksman medals. Res: 1817 Hillcrest Rd, Penthouse, Hollywood 90068 Ofc: A-1 Audio Systems, 6322 Delongpre Ave Hollywood 90028

SINSHEIMER, ROBERT LOUIS, university chancellor; b. Feb. 5, 1920, Wash., D.C.; Edn: SB, MA Inst. of Tech., Quantitative Biology, 1941; SM, MA Inst. of Tech., biophysics, 1942; PhD, MA Inst. of Tech., biophysics; m. Karen B. Keeton; chil: Lois June (Wickstrom); Kathy Jean; Roger Allen. Career: MA Inst. of Tech, Radiation Lab staff mem., 1942-46; MA Inst. of Tech. Amer. Cancer Soc. Fellow, 1946-48; MA Inst. of Tech, research assoc., biology, 1948-49; IA State Coll., assoc. prof. of biophysics, 1949-55; IA State Coll., prof. of biophysics, 1955-57; CA Inst. of Tech, prof. of biophysics, 1957-77; CA Inst. of Tech., chmn., Div. of Biology, 1968-77; chancellor, UC Santa Cruz, 1977---; CA Scientist of Yr., 1968; Beijerinck Virology Medal of the Royal Netherlands Acad. of Scis. and Letters, Dec. 1969; D.Sc., St. Olaf Coll., 1974; D.Sc., Northwestern Univ., 1976. Mem: Natl. Acad. of Scis., USA; Edit. Bd., Proceedings of the Natl. Acad. of Scis.; bd. of Scientific Advs.; The Jane Coffin Childs Meml. Fund for Med. Research; Amer. Acad. of Arts and Scis. fellow; numerous articles in scholarly journs. in fields of phys. and chem. properties of nucleic acids, replication of nucleic acids, bacterial viruses, biological effects of ultraviolet radiation, and biological appls. of ultraviolet and infrared spectroscopy. Res: Univ. House, 1000 Heller Dr., Santa Cruz 95064; Office: Chancellor's Office, UC Santa Cruz, McHenry Library, Santa Cruz 95064.

SIPOS, SANDOR, manufacturing co. executive; b. June 26, 1931, Budapest, Hungary; s. Imre and Margit (Thetazs) S.; m. Lucy M., Jan. 30, 1976; children: Michael, b. 1978, Jessica, b. 1981; edn: tech. coll., UJ Pest (Hungary) 1947-49, industrial tech., 1952-54. Career: textile engineer, Budapest (Hungary, Sweden, USA); industrial mechanic (Sweden, USA); tool engr. 1980-83, pres. SA-SI Cutting Tool Mfg., Rialto, Calif. 1983--; inventor Lathe Universal Tool Assembly (1983); mil. service in Hungary 1949-52; Republican; Catholic. Res: 281 Fillmore Ave Rialto 92376 Ofc: SA-SI Cutting Tool Mfg. 755-D W. Rialto Ave, Rialto 92376

SIRIPOCANONT, CHUSAK, industrial engineer; b. May 7, 1953, Bangkok, Thailand; parents: Kwang and Lin Hoi Young; m. Chwen Siripocanont, Oct. 20, 1979; 1 dau. Sue Yee, b. 1983; edn: BSIE, Khon Kaen Univ., Thailand 1974; MSIE, CSU San Jose 1976, MBA 1979; reg. profl. engineer (indsl. engr.) Calif. 1983. Career: industrial engr. Bangkok Rubber Co., 1974-75; indsl. engr. Facility Engineering Inc., San Jose 1978-80; facilities engr., prodn. engr. Rolm Corp., Santa Clara 1980-83, logistics supt. 1983--; mem: Am. Inst. of Indsl. Engr., Am. Inst. of Plant Engr., Internat. Materials Mgmt. Soc.; rec: tennis, landscaping, music. REs: 586 Bella Vista, Fremont 94539 Ofc: Rolm Corporation, 4900 Old Ironsides Dr Santa Clara 95050

SIROIS, BYRON KENNETH, company president; b. Apr. 9, 1929, Kankakee, Ill.; s. Lester Xavier and Elda Mae (Goodknecht) S.; m. Rebecca Mieras, Nov. 8, 1963; children: Andrea Jane, b. 1964, Lisa Nannette, b. 1966, Charles Antoine, b. 1967; edn: BS, Univ. Ill. 1952. Career: vice pres., pres. (west coast), Aluminum and Chemical corp., Greenwich, Conn. 1956-62; district mgr. (west coast) Tandy Corp., Ft. Worth, Tx. 1962-66; gen. mgr. Leather Supply Co., Compton 1966-69; dist. mgr. (west coast) Pier 1 Imports, Ft. Worth, Tx. 1969-75; owner Del Cerro Distributers 1975--; pres. Sirois Land Co. (Ill.), 1966--; honors: First to fly a helicopter from Korea to Japan, 1955; mem. Alpha Delta Phi Alumni Assn., Univ. of Ill. Alumni Assn., US Senatorial Club, mil: capt. USMC 1952-56, helicopter pilot Korea, 5 Medals; Republican (Presdtl. Task Force); Presbyterian; rec: anthropology, gardening. REs: 6204 Del Paso Ave San Diego 92120 Ofc: Del Cerro Distributors, POB 849, Lemon Grove 92045

SISSON, JOSEPH EUGENE, builder/developer; b. Apr. 30, 1937, Oakland; s. Frank and Ruth Edna (Knowles) S.; m. Leila Mary, Feb. 24, 1963; 2 stepchildren: Shiela S. Providenza, Robert E. Smith; edn: Coll. of Pacific 1955-58. Career: foreman CT Lindsay Co., Las Vegas, Nev. 1963-64; gen. mgr. A & Dee Constrn. Co., 1964-68; gen. supt. Kaufman & Broad, 1968-72; gen. mgr. John B. Clark Co., 1972-75; pres. Joseph E. Sisson Inc., 1975-78; pres. Remington Co. Builders and Developers, Inc., 1978--; instr., class for supts., Stanford Univ.; profl. singer 1954-57; mem. The Senators, an Honest Barbershop Quartet; mem. Soc. for the Preservation and Encouragement of Barbershop Singing in Am. (v.p. Sacto. Chpt.); mil: E4 US Army 1960-62; Democrat; Prot.; rec: golf, hunting, fishing, bowling. Res: 6328 Fall River Way Sacramento 95824 Ofc: Remington Co. Builders and Dev. Inc., 3815 Marconi Ave Sacramento 95821

SIVE, EUGENE BELMONT, thoracic and vascular surgeon; b. Oct. 15, 1911, Cincinnati, OH; s. A. Websterand Annette (Fischer) Sive; B.S., U. Cin., 1933, M.B., 1936, M.D., 1937; C.M., Univ. Ark., 1941; postgrad. course in surgery Univ. Pa., 1958-59 (div. 1957); Chil: Eugene Belmont, Edith Angela; m. 2d, Joan Marie Van Sciver, Nov. 3, 1959; Chil: Jonathan, b. 1960, Geoffrey, b. 1963, Valerie, b. 1966, Barkley, b. 1970. Career: Intern Cin. Gen. Hosp., 1936-37; surgical residencies Univ. Ark. Med. Sch. and Univ. Hosp., 1937-41; chief surg. res. Kern County Gen. Hosp. Bakersfield, Calif., 1944; surg. res. Meml. Hosp., Houston, 1949; thoracic surgery res. Olive View Sanatorium, Olive View, Calif., 1950-52, sr. res. in thoracic and cardiovascular surgery VA Hosp., Martinsburg, W. V.A., 1952; pvt. practice of gen. surgery, Cin., 1941-44, Santa Monica, Calif., 1945-49, in thoracic surgery, Santa Ana, Calif., 1953-58, thoracic and vascular surgery, Santa Ana, 1961---' research fellow surgery Hahnemann Med. Coll. and Hosp., Phila., 1959-61. Com. chmn. Webelos leader Cub. Scouts also troop recruitment chmn. local Boy Scouts Amer. Bd. dirs. Big Brothers. Diplomate Amer. Bd. Surgery. Fellow Amer. Coll. Chest Physicians, Amer. Coll. Angiology; Mem. Amer. Assn. Ry. Surgeons, A.M.A., Amer. Med. Writers Assn., Amer. Thoracic Soc., Internat. Coll. Surgeons, Amer. Trauma Soc. (pres. Orange County chpt.). Republican. Episcopalian. Clubs: Jonathan, Santa Ana CC, Coral Casino Kiwanian (pres. N. Santa Ana 1956). Author articles med. jours. Res: 1616 La Loma Dr., Santa Ana 92705; Office: 309 Civic Center Dr. W., Santa Ana 92701.

SIVERTSEN, WIGGSY AIMEE, educator; b. Dec. 7, 1935, Hollywood; d. Ivar, Jr. and Aimee Christine (Rochester) S.; edn: AA, Stephens Coll. 1957; BA, San Jose State Univ. 1962; MSW, Tulane Univ. 1967; LCSW, lic. clin. soc. wkr. Calif. Career: program dir. Peninsula Childrens Center, Palo Alto 1963-69; prof. Counseling Services, San Jose State Univ., 1967--; also pvt. practice clin. social work, San Jose; adj. prof. St. Francis Coll. Sch. of Nursing 1981, 82; cons. Coastal Comm. Counseling Ctr., Santa Cruz 1980-; mem: Nat. Assn. of Social Wkrs., Soc. for Clin. Soc. Wk., United Professors of Calif. (chpt. pres.), AIDS/KS Found., San Jose (bd. dirs.), ACLU, NOW, Gay Rights Advocates, Nat. Womens Polit. Caucus; adv. bd. mem. South Bay Comm. Counseling Center; Democrat; rec: rowing single person shell. Res: 20820 Locust Dr Los Gatos 95050 Ofc: San Jose State Univ., Admin 223, Washington Sq. San Jose 95192

SIZEMORE, WILLIAM FLOYD, real estate broker/contractor; b. Mar. 18, 1936, Brookhaven, Ga.; s. Benjamin Floyd and Lorena Amelia (Hood) S.; m. Lynda McCloud, Mar. 21, 1959; children: Lynette Ruth, b. 1961, Eugene Floyd, b. 1962, Betsy Irene, b. 1964, Jean Edward, b. 1972; grad. Chamblec (Ga.) H.S. 1955, Fullerton Jr. Coll. 1959; Calif. lic. real estate broker, gen. contractor. Career: realtor, general contr.: area mgr. Western Hills Sales :& Investments, Yucca Valley 1966; owner/broker Sizemore Investment Co., Anaheim 1968; owner/partner Wizard Constrn. Co., Fullerton 1978; owner/broker/partner Dukes Country Real Estate, Hesperia 1979; instr. Real Estate Law; mem: Nat., Calif. assns. of realtors; North Orange County, Victor Valley bds. of realtors; mem. Masons, Scottish Rite, York Rite; mil: cpl. USMC 1953-57; Democrat; Baptist; rec: flying, gardening. REs: 5358 Rural Ridge Cir Anahehim Hills 92807 Ofc: Dukes Country Real Estate, 16057 Main St Hesperia 92345

SKAGGS, CHARLES EDWARD, fire department officer; b. July 15, 1939, Visalia; s. Charles E. and Irene F. (Tunnell) S.; m. Carole Samerin, Jan. 13, 1961; children: Robert, b. 1965, Jeff, b. 1975, Gregg, b. 1975; edn: AS, Rio Hondo Coll. 1971; bus. adm. maj., MA in prog., Calif. Coast Univ.; Calif. Comm. Colls. life teaching credential; lic. real estate sales. Career: income tax preparer, 1 yr.; real estate sales agt., 4 yrs.; fire equip. sales, service, cons. (state lic.), 14 years; engr./crew chief Crash Rescue, Fire Dept., USAF 1957-61; firefighter Oxnard (Ca.) Fire Dept., 1961-63; fireman, fire engr., fire capt. West Covina Fire Dept., 1961-80, battalion chief (chg. tng., personnel, comm., hazardous mats.) 1980--; mil: A/1c USAF 1957-61. Res: POB 1021, West Covina Ofc: West Covina Fire Dept. 1444 W. Garvey, West Covina 91790

SKARMAN, JOHN STANTON, manufacturing co. president and chairman, physicist; b. Nov. 13, 1937, Louisville, Ky.; s. Albin Ernest and Helen Marie (Adolphson) S.; m. Kristi Zanids, Aug. 19, 1972; children: David, b. 1962; Susanne, b. 1965; Ashley, b. 1974; edn: BS, Univ. of Louisville 1959. Career: sr. research scientist National Cash Register Corp. 1959-68; v.p. research & devel. Quantrol Electronics, Inc., El Paso, tex. 1968-73; v.p. Wellen Industries, Calif. 1973-81; pres./ chmn. Southwest Laboratories Inc., Costa Mesa 1981--; bd. dirs. National Peripheral Corp. 1983; bd. dirs. Right- Touch Camera, Inc.; mem: Soc. of the Sigma Xi; Inst. of Electronic and Electrical Engrs.; Nat. Fire Prevention Assn.; Rotary Internat. Newport- Balboa chpt.; author one tech. textbook, num. tech. papers, presentations; 23 patents (1963-); Republican; Presbyterian; rec: down hill skiing, tennis. Res: 920 Nottingham Rd Newport Beach 92660 Ofc: Southwest Labs., Inc., 3505 Cadillac Ave, Bldg F1, Costa Mesa 92626

SKIFF, RUSSELL ALTON, plastics co. president; b. Feb. 26, 1927, Waterford, PA; s. Albert Alton and Leah Gladys (Allen) S.; m. Dolores Molnar, June 25, 1950; children: Russell James, b. 1952; Sandra Lee, b. 1954; Eric Alan, b. 1960; Rebecca Lynn, b. 1971; edn: BS, Univ. of Pittsburgh,1950. Career: metallurgical chemist Jones & Laughlin Steel Co., Aliquippa, PA 1950-51; res. & devel. chem. General Electric Co., Eric, PA 1951-57; tech. sales & plant opr. Hysol Corp. of CA, El Monte 1957-60; sr. research engr., Autonetics Div., No. Am. Aviation Co., Downey 1960-62; pres., dir. Delta Plastics Co., Visalia 1962--; cons. in field of Epoxy resin tech.; mem. first US mfg. People- to- People Goodwill delegation to Europe and Russia, 1979, China 1980; mem: Exch. Club of Visalia (dist. dir.); Lions (past pres.); Soc. of Plastics Engrs.; Nat. Fedn. of Ind. Bus.; Calif. Fedn. of Ind. Bus.; US Senatorial Bus. Adv. Bd.; holder nine US patents; authored over 50 tech. publs.; mil: SSgt., USAAF, 1944-46; Republican, councilman 1954-57; Presbyterian; rec: antique furniture, hunting, fishing. Res: 5525 W Pershing Visalia 93291 Ofc: Delta Plastics Co., 7449 Ave 304 Visalia 93291

SKLAR, BERNIE, merchant; b. Apr. 9, 1924, Sioux Fall, So. Dakota; s. Robert and Ida (Nelson) S.; m. Norma Louise Schloker, Apr. 15, 1942; children: Marcia E., b. 1943; Terry E., b. 1947; Peggy A., b. 1951; edn: UCLA 1941-42; UC Berkeley 1942-43; UCLA 1946-48. Career: twice pres. Inglewood Retail Merchants Assn. 1956, 70; twice pres. Inglewood CofC 1972-74; pres. Los Angeles Co., City of Inglewood Civic Ctr. Joint powers Commn. 1974-80; bd. mem. Inglewoode Charities 1974--; adv. bd. Inglewood Salvation Army 1970--; pres./ owner Polka Dot Shops; chmn. bd. Daniel Freeman Meml. and Daniel Freeman Marina Hosps.; awards: Man of the Year, Inglewood Lion's Club; Dist. Awd. Man of the Yr. 1978; mem: Masons; Kiwanis; Inglewood Charities Corp.; mil: Sgt., US Army 11th Armored Div. 1943-46, European Theater, battle stars (3), Div. Commdn.; Democrat; Jewish; rec: golf, swimming. Res: 1813 Marcheeta Pl Los Angeles 90060 Ofc: Palka Dot Shop, 11 Del Amo Fashion Ctr Torrance 90503

SKOGLUND, ELIZABETH RUTH, counselor, author; b. June 17, 1937, Chgo.; d. Ragner Emmanuel and Elizabeth Alvira (Benson) Skoglund; edn: BA, UCLA 1959; MA, Pt. Loma (Pas. Coll.) 1969. Career: English tchr. Marlborough Sch., Los Angeles 1959-61; Eng. Tchr. Glendale High Sch., 1961-72; counselor Glendale Family Svc. 1971-73; pvt. practice, Burbank 1972--; supt. Drug Abuse Adv. Comm. for Glendale Unif. Sch. Dist.; asst. psychiatric cons. on Burbank Unif. Sch. Dist.; cons. Teze-Dru Nar (drug re-hab grp.); TV talk show appearances; recipient Beautiful Activist Award 1973, Germaine Monteil Cosmetics, The Broadway; author num. books, 1972-83; Republican; Protestant; rec: swim, shell collector, photog. Res: 619 E Providencia Ave, No F, Burbank 91501 Ofc: 303 So Glenoakes Blvd, Ste 14, Burbank 91502

SLATER, DORIS HALE (BRIGITTE), lawyer; b. Mar. 19, 1946, Steinbach, Hallenberg; d. William Francis and Irene Hildegard (Knoth) Hale; m. Russell Slater, Dec. 30, 1967; children: Stephen, b. 1968; Kristina, b. 1969; Sean, b. 1978; edn: BA, CSU Hayward 1967; MA, 1974; JD, Univ. of Santa Clara 1979.

Career: lectr. Chabot Coll. 1975-76; coordinator/ mental health advocate Alameda Co. Mental Health Assn.; law clerk, var. local law ofcs.; assoc., law ofcs. John H. Garvin 1980-81; currently sole prop. law ofcs. Doris Hale Slater, Pleasanton; honors: Outstanding Sr. Woman, Soc. Scis., CSUH 1968. Mem: secty. Amador- Livermore Bar Assn., Alameda Co. Bar Assn., Calif. Women Lawyers, Calif. Trial Lawyers, Ám. Bar Assn., Calif. State Bar; commnr. Pleasanton Human Services Commn.; Democrat. Res: 1987 Paseo Del Cajon Pleasanton 94566 Ofc: Law Offices Doris Hale Slater, 699 Peters Ave, Ste C, Pleasanton 94566

SLATER, JERRY GRANT, computer software co. president; b. July 22, 1946, Cleveland, Oh.; s. Peter Allen and Jeanne J. (Richards) S.; m. Lillian Dodson, Dec. 9, 1980; children: Shayna, b. 1981, Joshua, b. 1983; edn: BSEE, CSC Long Beach, 1969. Career: F.E., IBM Corp., Long Beach, 1965-68; M.T.S.E.E., Hughes Aircraft Co., Fullerton, 1969-71; M.T.S. Pgm., Hughes Aircraft, Fullerton, 1971-72; tech. opr./spec. sr., Century Data Systems, Anaheim, 1972-73; sys. pgm., City of Long Beach, 1973-75; pres./bd. chmn., Tone Software Corp., Anaheim 1974--. Mem. Aircraft Owners and Pilots Assn.; works: Hexadecimal Calculator; TONE 3, Intersystem Spool Processor, and TONE 4 (computer software pgms.); rec: flying, music. Address: Tone Software Corp., 1735 S. Brookhurst Anaheim 92804

SLAUGHTER, SUSAN ANN, educator; b. Mar. 13, 1934, Bluefield, VA; d. Reginald Fairfax and Beatrice Lyndell (Froe) Carter; m. Clarence Slaughter, June 29, 1959; children: Lynette, b. 1960; Ovette, b. 1962; edn: BS, cum laude, Bluefield State Coll. 1955; MS, Pepperdine Univ. 1975; American Studies and Julian Virtue Fellowships, Pepperdine 1980-81; courses, UCLA, Calif. State Univs., and Pacific Oaks Coll. 1984. Career: press opr. and typesetter Carter Printing Co., Inglewood 1960-67; (first woman to operate Web Rotary Newspaper Press); tchr. Compton Unified Sch. Dist., 1967--; co- owner Slaughter Vending Co.; printing instr. Tabloid Teen Newspaper, Carter Printing 1964-66; master tchr. for student tchrs. UCLA and CSU Long Beach 1970-74; Outstanding Tchr. of Yr., Compton Unif. Sch. Dist. 1979-80; PTA Awd., Washington Elem. 1981; mem: Phi Delta Kappa; Alpha Kappa Alpha; Calif. Tchrs. Assn.; Democrat; Protestant; rec: reading, photog., plate collecting. Res: 623 E Regent St Inglewood 90301

SLAYTON, THOMAS EUGENE, accountant; b. Dec. 2, 1950, Evansville, Indiana; s. James Robert and Mary Beatrice (Deeds) S.; edn: BS, Indiana State Univ. 1974. Career: currently: pres. Sassy Productions, Inc., Los Angeles; pres. Shamma Music, pub., Los Angeles; controller Davis, Johnson, Mogul & Colombatto Advtg., Inc., Los Angeles; bus. mgr. of rock star, Doug Phillips; mem: ASCAP; BMI; exec. producer, album Schizophrenic', by Doug Phillips, Sassy Prodns. label, 1984; mil: USAF; Baptist; rec: flying (pvt. pilot), swimming. Res: 1570 No Edgemont, No 601 Hollywood 90027 Ofc: DJMC Inc., 3435 Wilshire Blvd, 18th Flr, Los Angeles 90010

SLIGER, TERRY ALLEN, restaurant corporation executive; b. Sept. 5, 1956, Hanford; s. Glen Albert and Barbara Ann (Klein); m. Denise Reardon, Aug. 25, 1984; edn: AA, Ventura Coll. 1976. Career: from dishwasher to gen. mgr. Jeremiahs Restaurants, Northridge, Sacto., Huntington Bch., and Lubbock, Tex. 1974--, in charge all ops. 11-restaurant chain (with over 700 employees); bd. dirs. Sacramento Hotel & Restaurant Assn. (youngest dir. in chpt. history) 1978-79; mem: Am. Mgmt. Assn., Americans for Wine, Le Amis Du Vin; past mem. Optimist; Republican; Catholic. Res: 823 W. Valerio St Santa Barbara 93101 Ofc: Jeremiahs Restaurants, Inc., 800 Miramonte Dr. Santa Barbara 93109

SLIGH, WILLIAM FREDRICK, jewelry designer; b. Nov. 4, 1922, Long Beach; s. James Auther and Mable Lilian (Girard) S.; m. Anita Kili, July 10, 1947; children: Karen, b. 1950; Mark, b. 1952; edn: Gemological Inst. of Am. 1978. Career: clerical pos. Superior Oil Co., welry, Bakersfield 1977--; jewelry designer; awards: 1st awd. for Inlay, Texas Fedn. Mineral Soc. 1971; publs: Helpful Hints on Art Inlay, Lapidary Jorn., 5/68; Inlay, a Different Eye, Gems and Minerals, 7/71; mil: Cpl., US Army Air Corps, 1942-46; Republican; rec: jewelry inlay. Res: 1006 Castaic Oildale 93208 Ofc: Burning Bush Jewerly Mfg., 1727 19th Street Bakersfield 93301

SLIPOCK, PHILIP STEVEN, real estate investor- consultant; b. July 12, 1943, New York, NY; s. Louis Abraham and Ida (Heit) S.; edn: BSBA, Univ. of Fla. 1965; JD, Univ. of Miami Sch. of Law 1968; real estate broker lic., Calif. 1978. Career: atty. Securities & Exch. Commn., Wash. DC 1968-72; pres. Antique Wholesalers Inc., Kensington, MD 1970-78; ind. real estate broker Altemus, Warner & Co., Los Angeles 1979-80; pres. Antique Wholesalers West Inc., Los Angeles 1974--; real estate broker/ cons. Philip S. Slipock & Assocs., Los Angeles 1980--; cons./ dir. Thoren Corp., Miami, Fla. 1982--; honors: Wall Street Journ. Corp. Fin., Univ. of Miami Sch. of Law 1968; mem: Fla. Bar Assn.; Dist. of Columbia Bar Assn.; Los Angeles Bd. Realtors; Marina City Club; Univ. of Miami Alumni Assn.; Republican Nat. Com.; rec: handball, tennis, skiing. Res: 4200 Via Dolce #132 Marina Del Rey 90291 Ofc: Philip S. Slipock & Assocs., 702 Washington St, Ste 203, Marina Del Rey 90291

SLOAN, HIRAM COOPER, company president; b. Apr. 16, 1929, Amarillo, Texas; s. Hiram Cooper, Jr. and Mary Lou (Thomas) S.; div.; 1 son, Jeffrey Dean b. 1974; edn: BSEE, Texas A & M Univ. 1949; grad. wk., MBA, Univ. of Calif., Ohio State Univ.; Reg. Profl. Engr., Ohio 1954, Reg. Profl. Electrical Engr., Calif. 1977, Gen. Engring. Contractor, Calif. 1977. Career: test engr., sales engr. General Electric Co. 1949-53; 1st lt., proj. engr. USAF, Wright Patterson AFB, Oh. 1953-55; sales mgr. GE Co., Waynesboro, Va. 1955-61;

mgr. of sales GE Co., Phila., Pa. 1961-62; sales mgr. Internat. Rectifier Corp., El Segundo, Ca. 1962-64; sr. proj. adminstr. AiResearch Mfg. Co., Garrett Corp., Torrance 1965-72; pres./bd. chmn. UPS Company, Torrance 1972--; honors: Disting. Stu. and Disting. Military Student, Texas A&M 1948; Diamond Derby Award, GE Co. 1954; mem. IEEE, USAF rep. to Soc. of Automotive Engrs. 1954-55; North Orange Co. Computer Club (users gp.); patent: new concept of fluorescent light ballast (1982); Republican; rec: computers, camping. Address: UPS Co. 3726 W. 172nd St, Torrance 90504

SLOANE, BEVERLY LEBOV, author; b. May 26, 1936, NYC; d. Benjamin Samuel and Anne (Weinberg) LeBov; m. Robert Sloane, Sept. 27, 1959; l dau., Alison, b. 1965; edn: AB, Vassar Coll. 1958; MA, Claremont Grad. Sch. 1975, doctoral wk. 1975-76; grad. Coro Found. (Fellowship) Leadership Tng. in Pub. Affairs, Women's Pgm. 1979; grad. UCLA Grad. Sch. of Mgmt. Exec. Pgm. 1982; grad. Stanford Univ. publishing course 1982. Career: circulation librarian Harvard Med. Lib., Boston 1958-59; soc. wkr. Conn. State Welfare, New Haven 1960-61; English tchr. Hebrew Day Sch., New Haven 1961-64; instr./lectr. in creative writing and English lit., Monmouth Coll., NJ 1967-69; freelance writer, author in Arcadia, Calif. 1969--; author: (with R.M. Sloane) A Guide to Health Facilities - Personnel and Management (1971, 77); From Vassar to Kitchen (1967). Mem. Adv. Council for Tech. and Profl. Writing, English Dept. CSU Long Beach 1980-82; adv. bd. Calif. Health Rev. (mag.) 1982-3; bd. dirs. Los Angeles Commn. on Assaults Against Women 1983-; trustee The Ctr. for Improve. of Child Caring Inc. 1981-83. Honors: Claremont Grad. Sch. Student Body vice pres. 1971-72, mem. Claremont Coll. Faculty House 1983-; spl. recognition, L.A. Chpt. Women in Comm. Inc. 1983; listed, Who's Who of Am. Women, Who's Who in the West. Mem: Women in Communications, L.A. Chpt. (bd. dirs. 1980-82, ch. 1st Ann. Agnes Underwood Freedom of Info. Awards Banquet 1982); Am. Med. Writers Assn. (nat. boom awards com. ch. 1983, ch. nat. networking luncheon 1983), Pacific S.W. Chpt. (bd. dirs., nat. del.); AAUW, Arcadia Br. (past ofcr.); Calif. Press Women (L.A. Dist. bd. dirs. 1982-); AAUP; Inst. of Technology (past ch. creative writing); Soc. for Tech. Comm.; Internat. Comm. Assn.; Am. Pub. Health Assn.; Assn. of Western Hosps.; College English Assn., Coro Assocs.; Town Hall of Calif. (v.ch. Community Affairs Sect. 1982-); Ex-Rotary of Duarte; Vassar Club of So. Ca.; Womens Club Calif.; League for Crippled Children; L.A. Orthopaedic Hosp. Address: 1301 N. Santa Anita Ave Arcadia 91006

SLOCUMB, WILLIAM HENRY, JR., lawyer; b. Feb. 18, 1951, Oakland; s. William Henry and Susan Patricia (Ostrander) S.; m Rosemary K., Aug. 9, 1980; l dau. Susan Marie, b. 1983; edn: BA, UC Davis 1973, JD, Western St. Univ., San Diego 1980; Deputy Dist. Atty. Career: owner/ mgr. Slocumb Ins. Agcy., San Diego 1975-81; Deputy Dist Atty., Co. of Imperial, El Centro 1981-83; Deputy Dist. Atty. Co. of Kern., Bakersfield 1983--; awards: Am. Jurisprudence Awd., Real Property, Bancroft- Whitney Co. 1979; mem: Am. Bar Assn., Calif. Bar Assn., Imperial Co. Bar Assn.; Republican; Episcopal; rec: jogging, history. Res: 3400 Dovewood St Bakersfield 93309 Ofc: Co. of Kern, Criminal Justice Bldg., 1215 Truxton Ave Bakersfield 93301

SLOMAN, JAMES EARL, liability consultant; b. Sept. 12, 1945, San Francisco; s. John Robert and Alice Roberta (Wreath) S.; edn: AA, Ariz. 1968; BA hist. (cum laude) Brigham Young Univ. 1970; desig: Special Agent, Internat. Police Congress. Career: investigative splst. in profl. and products liability, owner/chief op. ofcr. James E. Sloman & Assocs., Investigators & Adjusters; profl. cons. to Farmers Ins. Agents of Am., et al; mem. Assistance to the Adoption of Spl. Kids (AASK), Mission Internat. (Christian aid to impoverished children); mil: E3 USMC, 1963-66, decorated; rec: travel, languages, basketball. Res: 13802 Northwest Passage, 313, Marina del Rey 90291 Ofc: James E. Sloman & Assoc. 330 Washington Blvd, 4th Fl, Marina del Rey 90291

SLOMICH, SIDNEY JEROME, real estate investment co. owner; b. July 15, 1921, Boston, Mass.; s. Harry and Bessie (Bartnowski) S.; m. Rosalyn Feinberg, Nov. 1, 1944; children: Michael b. 1945, Maxwell b. 1949, Elaine b. 1952; edn: AB, Harvard Univ. 1944; AM, 1948; PhD, 1951. Career: research assoc., foreign area studies, Yale Univ., New Haven, Conn. 1051-52; ops. ofcr. Central Intelligence Agcy. 1952-62; sr. scientist, Research Analysis Corp., Wash. DC 1962-64; dir. Arms Control & Disarmament Study Gp., Inst. of Technology/ Jet Propulsion Lab, Pasadena 1964-68; lectr. Political Theory & Internat. Rels., CSU, L.A. 1965-68q sr. scientist SRI Internat., Menlo Park 1968-71; writer 1971-72; owner Slomich & Co., real estate inv. and brokerage 1973--; awards: Boston -Old North Church Am. History Prize 1939 Washington- Franklin History Medal, Dorchester H.S. 1939 Harvard Coll. Scholarships 1940-43; author: American Nightmare, (Technology and Society), NY, MacMillan 1971; arts., Bulletin of Atomic Scientists, Astronautics and Aeronautics; Wash. Post, LA Times syndicate, 1969-71; Democrat; Jewish; hobby: San Francisco Res: 921 Elsinore Dr Palo Alto 94303 Ofc: Slomich & Co., 467 Hamilton Ave Palo Alto 94301

SMALL, GILPIN DONEVAN, III, sales executive; b. Mar. 31, 1940, Youngstown, Ohio; s. Gilpin D., Sr., and Vera Grace (Tobey) S.; m. Marjorie Christine Grey, Jan. 31, 1969; children: Gilpin, IV, b. 1972, Charlene Marie, b. 1969; edn: AS, Chaffey Coll. 1975. Career: sales/service rep. Independent Indsl. Supply and Welding Supply Houses, 1974-83, selling machine shop and welding shop equip. and supplies, cryogenic gases, field svc. repairs; rep. Rhoades Welding Supplies, Riverside, 1983--; awards: appreciation, State of Calif. 1980, 1981; empl. achievement, Douglas Aircraft 1969, Lockheed Aircraft 1974; sev. championship trophies as mgr. of Fontana Youth Sports; mem: State of Calif. Metal Trades Advis. Council (chmn.); Fontana Cable Club (vp,

dir.); bd. dirs./coach Little League Baseball, AYSO Soccer, Poney League Baseball; mem. Masons, Scottish Rite, Shriners; PTA orgns.; mil: E3, US Army 1957-60, GCM, Polish Army Service Medal, M.P. in Ingrandes, Fr., Baseball Championship 1959; rec: youth sports coach, fishing, camping. Res: 9107 Sierra Ave, 9, Fontana 92335 Ofc: Rhoades Welding Supply 3614 Chicago Ave Riverside 92507

SMALL, JOHN RICHARD, dentist; b. Oct. 18, 1931, Endicott, NY; s. John J. and Mary (Kushner) S.; m. Faye Anderson, July 1980; children: Michael, b. 1956; Allen, b. 1960; David, b. 1962; edn: Glendale Coll.; UCLA; DDS, Northwestern Univ. 1960. Career: owner/ opr. dental office; founder Dental Found. of Calif. 1967; secty. Western Study Club 1967-77; clinician, So. Calif. Dental Conv. 1972-76; awards: Outstanding Young Man Awd., Jr. CofC 1965; Distng. Svc. Awd., Kiwanis 1964; mem: Am. Dental Soc.; Dental Hypnosis Soc.; Acad. of Gen. Dentistry; Internat. Coll. of Applied Nutrition; Kiwanis; Oneonta Club; Magic Castle; mil: Dental Tech 2/c, USN 1951-54; Republican; Presbyterian; rec: magician. Res: 1013 Easy St Los Angeles 90042 Ofc: John R Small, DDS, 1016 Fair Oaks Ave, So. Pasadena 91030

SMALL, PORTER LEON, printing co. owner; b. July 14, 1944, Yazoo County, Miss.; s. Walter and Minerva (Farris) S.; m. Paula Randisi, Feb. 19, 1983; edn: AA, graphic arts, Laney Coll. 1969. Career: press opr. CSU Hayward, 1970-72; offset tech./instr. Laney Coll., 1972-76; offset printing instr. part-time, Oakland Boy's Club, 1975-76; press opr./prodn. mgr. Copy Mat, Berkeley 1976-79; owner/opr. P.S. Printing, Hayward 1979, in Berkeley 1981--; instr. Calif. Berkeley Youth Alternative, setting up printing bus. for youths, 1980-81. Sci. of Mind; Rec: camping. Res: 7721 Greenly Dr Oakland 94605 Ofc: P.S. Printing, 2445 San Pablo Ave Berkeley 94702

SMALL, RICHARD FRANCIS, engineering executive; b. July 2, 1936, Buffalo, ny; s. Frank and Rose (Cohn) S.; m. Marilyn Murphy, Jan. 14, 1984; edn: AAS, State Univ. of NY 1957; BSME, Tri-State Univ. 1959; MBA, UCLA 1974; reg. profl. engr., Calif. 1972, Ill. 1972. Career: proj. mgr. Bechtel Power Corp., Norwalk 1969-74; v.p. energy div. VTN Corp., Irvine 1974-76; dir. adv. energy proj. ofc., U.S. Dept. of Energy 1976-77; sr. cons./ co- founder Western Pacific Assocs., Costa Mesa 1977-83, cons. Rockwell Internat. Corp. 1980; cons. Airesearch Mfg. Co. 1980-83; mem: Am. Mgmt. Assn.; Am. Soc. of Profl. Engrs.; Am. Soc. for Mechanical Engrs.; Am. Nuclear Soc.; Nat. Soc. for Profl. Engrs.; Calif. Soc. for Profl. Engrs; Orange Co. CofC (Energy Task Force); publs: num. arts on adnv. energy sys., energy conversion, and conservation, patentee. (6) 1960, 62, 69; mil: Sgt., USAR 1958-64; rec: photog., art collecting, music. Res: 5200 389 Irvine Blvd Irvine 92714 Ofc. Western Pacific Assocs., 129 Cabrillo, Ste 103, Costa Mesa 92627

SMART, GEORGE SEVILLE, III, financial executive; b. Feb. 16, 1944, Louisville, Ky.; s. George Seville, Jr. and Mary Helen (Rouse) S.; m. Marita Ritter, Aug. 10, 1983; children: Gregory, b. 1975; Malerie, b. 1979; edn: BS, Indiana Univ. 1965; MBA, USC Fullerton 1968; law degree, LaSalle Ext., Chgo.; Calif. State Bar 1974. Career: with Carnation 1966--; fin. analyst 1966; asst. treas. 1973; asst. v.p. fin. 1977; v.p. fin. 1979; also active in real estate; dir: YMCA, Boy Scouts of Am., People for Playa Del Rey; mem. Calif. Yacht Club; YMCA; NY Roadrunners; Toastmasters; SAE Frat.; Republican; Christian; rec: marathon running, skiing, all sports. Res: 6927 Vista Del Mar Ln Playa Del Rey 90291 Ofc: Carnation Co. 5045 Wilshire Blvd Los Angeles 90036

SMELSER, DIANA VIRGINIA DANN, real estate broker; b. Jan. 23, 1935, Rahway, NJ; d. Charles Raymond and Mary Virginia (Bell) Dann; m. Donald G. Smelser, Feb. 1, 1976; children: Catherine, b. 1956; Christian, b. 1957; Cynthia, b. 1959; Sharon, b. 1961; Justin, b. 1966; edn: Syracuse Univ. 1952-55; realtor assoc., Anthony Real Estate Sch. 1976; broker,, USC 1982; broker, Calif. Dept. Real Estate 1982. Career: campaign mgr. Assemblyman Irwin, Union City, NJ 1967-68; legis. aid State of NJ, Trenton, NJ 1968-71; lab techn. Dr. Bernard Feldman, Westfield, NJ 1973-74; mktg. spec. Melitta, Inc., NY, NJ, Penn., Calif. 1974-76; comml. mgr. R.G. Real Estate, Walnut Creek 1977-80; owner The Property Line Real Estate, Walnut Creek 1980-82; pres. Diana D. Smelser, Inc., Walnut Creek 1982--; tchr. comml. real estate, R.G. Real Estate 1978-80; investment & property mgmt. cons. The Property Line 1980-82; awards: Outstanding Salesprsn. Awd. (3), R.G. Real Estate 1977; Mgr. of Yr. Awd., R.G. Real Estate 1979; mem: Constra Costa Bd. Realtors; Calif. Assn. Realtors; Nat. Assn. Realtors; Mountainside, NJ Newcomers Club (pres. 1966-67); Visiting Homemakers, Westfield, NJ; Overlook Hosp., Summit, NJ; Perth Amboy Performing Arts Ctr.; Community Players (asst. choreographer); works: research & draft NJ Legis. Bills 1968-71; Comml. Real Estate Manual 1978; Campaign Lit. 1968; Melitta Avdtg. 1975; Republican; Presbyterian; rec: skiing, riding, golf. Address: Diana D. Smelser, Inc., 2125 Danville Blvd Walnut Creek 94595

SMILEY, BRUCE M., real estate lawyer; b. Feb. 9, 1949; s. Bernard J. and Peggy E. Smiley; m. Wendy, Dec. 26, 1971; children: Stacie; Ryan; edn: BA, UCLA 1971; JD, Southwestern Univ. 1974. Career: assoc. atty. Mazirow, Schneider, Lawrence & Forer, Beverly Hills 1974-77; principal/ sr. partner Freeman, Freeman & Smiley, Los Angeles 1977--; assoc. staff mem. Southwestern Univ. Law Review 1972-73; instr. real estate law, UCLA 1978-81; mem: Calif. Bar Assn.; Los Angeles Co. Bar (real property sect.); Beverly Hills Bar Assn.; Internat. Council of Shopping Ctrs.; rec: running. Res: 12808 Malkirk St Studio City 91604 Ofc: Freeman, Freeman & Smiley, 9911 West Pico Blvd, Ste 950, Los Angeles 90035

SMILEY, STANLEY ROBERT, lawyer; b. Feb. 19, 1947, NYC, NY; s. Arthur and Rose Smiley; m. Anita Kape, June 28, 1970; children: Wayne, b. 1972; Lori, b. 1975; edn: BA, State Univ. of NY, Buffalo 1968; JD, St. John's Univ. Sch. of Law, NY 1971. Career: atty. ofc. of Chief Counsel, IRS, Newark, NJ 1971-72; Judge Advoc. (atty.) USAF, Madrid, Spain 1973-76; atty. ofc. of Chief Counsel, IRS, L.A. 1976-78; atty. McLaughlin & Irvin (attys.) Los Angeles, San Francisco, Newport Bch. 1978--; guest instr. Univ. of MD (European div.), Madrid, Spain 1974-76; dir. Courtside Comm. Assn., Orange 1976-78; commentator, var. legal subjects, Armed Forces Radio Network, Torrejon Air Base, Spain 1973-76; awards: Law Review Scholarship, St. John's Univ. Sch. of Law. 1969-71; USAF Commdn. Medal for Meritorious Svc. 1973; mem: Phi Delta Phi, legal frat.; Los Coyotes Country Club; Am. Bar Assn. (committeeman, Sub. chpt.'s com., sect. of taxation 1978; committeeman, Court Proceedure 1981-); New York State. of San Francisco; admitted to practice law: NY State 1971; Calif. 1977; U.S. Tax Ct. 1972; U.S. Mil. Ct. of Appeals 1972; publs: mem. and assoc. ed. St. John's Law Review 1969-71; mil: Capt., USAF (ofc. of Judge Advocate) 1972-76; rec: sailing, music. Res: 1224 Summersworth Pl Fullerton 92633 Ofc: McLaughlin & Irvin, 800 West Sixth St, Ste 300, Los Angeles 90017

SMITH, ALVIN MARION, real estate broker; b. Nov. 19, 1924, Jaroso, Colo.; s. Joseph Alvin and Florence Josephine (Watts) S.; m. Clara Edna Balantine, Apr. 3, 1079; 1 dau: Joyce Cozette, b. 1951; edn: BS, Univ. of Portland 1949; real estate broker, State of Calif. 1979. Career: product engr./ mgr. semi conductor mfg. cos.: Hughes Aircraft, Librascope, Internat. Rectifier, Texas Instruments, Motorola, Transitron 1951-74; real estate salesprsn. 1974--; broker 1979--; owner/broker Blue Ribbon Properties, Fresno (spec. exchange brokering); recipient award for patent devel., Motorola, Phoenix; mem: Fresno area Mktg. Exch. (pres. 1981); svl. patents; mil: Radioman 3/c, 1943-46; Republican; Protestant; rec: flying, electronics, computer sci. Res: 6567 No Orchard Fresno 93710 Ofc: Blue Ribbon Properties, 1239 No Chestnut Fresno 93703

SMITH, ANNETTE R., social worker; b. Apr. 3, 1936, Glen Cove, NY; d. Benjamin and Dorothy (Goldstein) Raymon; div.; children: Marjorie b. 1960, Laraine b. 1962, Andrew b. 1963 (surname Glickman); edn: BA, Barnard Coll. 1958; MSW, Univ. of Calif. 1964; MA, sociol., UC San Diego 1983; LCSW, Lic. Clin. Social Wkr., Calif. 1967. Career: caseworker State of Fla. Public Welfare, Gainesville 1959; casewkr. Alameda County DPW, Oakland, Ca. 1960; psychiatric soc. wkr. Calif. Dept. of Mental Hlth. Napa State Hosp., Imola 1964-69; dir. Summer Head Start, Napa County, Napa 1965; psychiatric soc. wkr. County of San Diego, Depts. Pub. Hlth. and Mental Hlth, 1969-75, chief Alcohol Pgm. Div., Dept. of Substance Abuse 1975-76; administr. Nouveau Vie Corp. (Alcoholism Recovery Pgms.) 1977-81; instr. UCSD Ext. Alcohol Studies 1971-; instr. National Univ., grad. student/tchg. asst. UCSD Dept. Sociol.; field instr. CSUSD Sch. of Social Wk. 1978-81; mem: Nat. Assn. of Social Wkrs. 1964- (pres. Napa-Solano Br. 1965, bd. dir. Golden Gate Ch. 1966); Am. Orthopsychiatric Assn. (Fellow) 1973-; Assn. of Labor/Mgmt. Adminstrs. and Consultants on alcoholism 1978-82; Am. Sociological Assn. (stu.) 1983-; mem. Calif. Womens Commn. on Alcoholism (1st pres. S.D./Imperial Ch. 1974); NOW; Nat. Council on Alcoholism (bd. dir. S.D. Area 1971-75); publs: arts. in profl. journals; Democrat; Jewish; rec: bridge, theater, bowling. Res: 4026 Mt. Acadia Blvd San Diego 92111

SMITH, AUDREY LISETTE, consultant; b. Apr. 6, 1936, El Centro; d. Edward and Charlesetta (Mason) Garmon; children: Deryl, b. 1954; Curve, b. 1955; Thomas, b. 1956. Career: Economic Opportunity Commn., Western Addition 1965-68; founder Audrey Smith, Developmental Ctr. 1968; coord. Infant Day Care Project, Mt. Zion Hosp., San Francisco 1969-71; admin. asst. Infant Day Care Proj., Family Svc. Agcy., San Francisco 1971; asst. dir. Sacto. Neighborhood Health Svc. Corp., Sacto. 1971-82; exec. dir. Economic Opportunity Commn. of Yolo Co. 1971-82; self- empl. cons.- trainer 1982--; bd. dirs: Nat. Mental Health Assn.; Sacto. Mental Health Assn.; Calif. Mental Health Assn.; Audrey L. Smith Devel. Ctr.; United Way Citizen Review Commn.; Gov.'s Adv. Commn. on Child Devel. Pgm.; awards: Cert. of Honor, San Francisco Bd. of Supvrs., Resolution Calif. State Legis., AIA Devel. Ctr.; mem: Nat. Commn. Negro & Bus. & Profl. Wkr.; Nat. Assn. Female Exec.; Cal- Nevada Exec. Dir. Assn.; Democrat; Baptist. Res: 7271 15th Street Sacramento 95822

SMITH, BARBARA L., sales training executive; b. Gibsonburg, OH; d. Albert Leo and Vivian L. (Rugh) Zeller; m. Robert F. Smith, Dec. 5, 1947; div. 1982; children: Craig L., b. 1955; Kirk L., b. 1957; edn: BS, Bowling Green Univ. 1971. Career: supvr. Pgm. for Developmentally Disabled, St. of Ohio 1964-74 (1st such pgm. in Ohio); dir. admissions Barbizon Schs., Toledo, OH and Fort Wayne, Ind. 1979-80; sales mgr. Borg- Warner Ednl. Sys., Arlington Hghts., Ill. 1974-80; mgr. sales tng. Microdata Corp., Newport Beach 1980--; honors: 1st runner up, Mrs. Ohio Contest 1960; mem: Profl. Buswmn., Irvine; AAUW; Women In Sales; Nat. Assn. of Profl. Saleswmn.; Am. Soc. Trainers & Developers. Res: 6907 Ellesmere Way Cypress 90630 Ofc: Microdata Corp., 4000 MacArthur Blvd Newport Beach 92660

SMITH, BERNARD JOSEPH, consulting engineer; b. Aug. 29, 1900, Liverpool, Eng., nat. 1930's; s. Thomas Joseph and Sarah Anne (Crum) S.; m. Julia Susan Connolly, June 4, 1929; children: Bernard; Sarah; Maureen; Una; Aislin; Thomas; Joan; John; edn: pvt. tutors, math, 1923-24; St. Edwards Coll.; Blackrock Coll., Dublin; Oxford Univ.; BE, honors, Univ. of Liverpool 1923; M.Engring; lic. profl. engr. Tex., NJ; reg. engr. CA, NJ, TK; Career: est. US res. 1912; res. engr. Underpinning & Found. Co., NYC, Phila. 1924; insp./ underground conduit engr. NY, NJ Tel. Co. and Ohio Bell Tel. Co. 1924-26; asst. engr. Alexander Potter, cons. engr. 1926-30; pvt. res. in hydrology & hydraulics 1930; des. engr. Humble Oil Refining Co. 1930-32; city engr. Baytown, Tex. 1931-33; city mgr. 1932-33; cons. engr. 1931-34; engring. insp. PWA, Ft. Worth 1934-35; engring. examiner 1935-37; pvt. cons. engr. 1937-38; dir., res. & personnel, Ft. Worth 1938-41; lectr. Tex. Christ. Univ.1940-43; state plng. engr./ state dir. Tex. Pub. Works Res., 1941-42; asst. reg. rep./ economist Nat. Housing Agcy., Dallas 1942-47; lectr. econs., bus. admin. and engring. So. Meth. Univ. 1947-53; cons. engr. Dallas 1947--; chief, S.F. Bay Devel. US Corps of Engrs., S.F. Dist. 1957-65; mem: Am. Econ. Assn.; Soc. of Evolutionary Econ.; Hist. of Econ. Soc.; Commr. Santa Cruz Co., CA, Water Adv. Commn.; spec. cons. S.F. Bay Conserv. and Devel. Commn. 1966--; lectr. on profl. subjects and radio conf. panelist; author: Town Bldg., 1939; El Paso Housing Mkt., 1945; Journey to Petra (1979 pvt. pub.); Odyssey (1982 pvt. pub.); mem: Fellow Am. Soc. of C.E.; S.F. Irish Lit. and Hist. Soc. (pres. 1961-63); Am. Waterworks Assn.; Dallas Fed. Rey. Exch.; Gov. Reagan's Task Force of Transp.; Am. Econ. Assn.; TX Soc. Profl. Engrs.; County Louth Arch. Soc.; Third Order of St. Francis Club Clogher Hist Soc.; Commonwealth Club; Serra Club (Dallas); pres. Holy Name Soc., Holy Trinity Ch.; rec: photog., painting, travel. Ofc: POB 663 Aptos 95003

SMITH, BOBY WARREN, real estate resort timesharing executive; b. Feb. 24, 1944, Hastings, Okla.; s. Cecil Blaine and Jewell E. (Burchett) S.; m. Barbara Ann Gooch, Feb. 24, 1979; children: Robert, b. 1961, Elizabeth, b. 1967, Heather, b. 1971; stu. Mt. San Antonio Coll. 1973-74, San Gabriel Valley Sch. of Law 1979; lic. Calif real estate broker, realtor, NAR, 1976. pres. Smith Trucking Inc., San Jose 1968-72; R.E. sales agt. Diamond Bar Realty, Diamond Bar 1972-74; vice pres. Century 21 Showcase, San Jose 1974-76; v.p. Estate Realty, Diamond Bar 1976-78; v.p. Alpha Escrows Inc., Diamond Bar 1977-81; owner Canyon View Realty & Financial, Diamond Bar 1978-84; mktg. & tng. mgr. Resort Marketing Internat., San Gabriel 1979-83, mktg. dir. 1984--; v.p. mktg. Park Station Mktg., San Gabriel 1982; v.p./broker LVJ Consulting, Diamond Bar 1983; cons. to timeshare developers; recipient num. bus. sales awards, fundraiser awd. Miss Diamond Bar Pageant 1977; mem: Nat./Calif. Assn. Realtors, Hacienda Rowland Diamond Bar Bd. of Realtors, Diamond Bar CofC (charter); clubs: Diamond Point, Lions (breakfast), Elks; publs: The Traditional Malfeasance of the Conventional Lender 1975; Republican; Assem. of God; rec: flying. Res: 21319 Tambo Pl Diamond Bar 91765 Ofc: Resort Marketing Int. 835 E. Las Tunas San Gabriel 91776

SMITH, CATHY HEYMANN, sales executive; b. Mar. 23, 1953, San Jose; d. Leland A. and Eleanore L. (Savullo) Heymann; edn: AA, West Valley Coll. 1972. Career: sec. Ultra Tec, Santa Clara 1972-73; purch. mgr. Monolithic Memories, Sunnyvale 1973-75; sales Internat. Matl. Research, Santa Clara 1975-76; sales eng. Nat. Semi Conductor, Sunnyvale 1976-77, sales mgr. 1977-78; sales eng. Micro Fab., Palo Alto 1978-79; nat. sales mgr. Bell Ind. (Photo Glass Div.), Sunnyvale 1979-80; gen. sales mgr. Bell Ind. (Elec. Div.), Sunnyvale 1980-81; sales eng. to gen. sales mgr. Hamilton/Avnet, Sunnyvale 1981--; profl. sales awards: outstanding performance 1981, spl. achievement 1981, two million dollar field sales club 1981, field salespsn of yr. 82; mem. Female Exec. Club; singer (Channel 36 award, Santa Clara Co.); rec: singing, skiing. Res: 4130 Holly Dr San Jose 95127 Ofc: Hamilton/Avnet 1175 Bordeaux Dr Sunnyvale 94086

SMITH, CHARLES ARTHUR, nuclear pharmacist; b. Feb. 11, 1953, San Diego; s. Charles Richard and Joan Betty (Shorter) S.; m. Sandra Kay, Aug. 14, 1974; edn: U.S. Internation Univ. 1971-74; BS, Drake Univ. Coll. of Pharmacy 1977; MS, Univ. of the Pacific 1979; reg. pharmacist, Calif. 1979; bd. cert. nuclear pharmacist, Am. Pharm. Assn. 1983. Career: instr. Univ. of the Pacific 1978; adj. prof. clinical pharm., Mercer Univ. 1981-84; staff pharm. Nuclear Pharmacy of Calif., San Diego 1979-80; mng. nuclear pharm. Nuclear Pharm. of Calif., Inc., Anaheim 1980-82; dist. mgr. Nuclear Pharm., Inc., Anaheim 1982-83; dist. mgr. Syncor Internat. Corp., So. Calif. 1983--; tchg. asst. Fluid and Electrolyte Therapy and Clinical Lab. Procedures and Physical Assessment, Univ. of the Pacific 1978; awards: scholarship awd., No. Calif. chpt. of the Achievement Awds. for Coll. Scientists; Calif. State Scholarship, Drake Univ. Coll. of Pharmacy; mem: Soc. of Nuclear Med.; Calif. Pharm. Assn.; Am. Pharm. Assn.; Acad. of Pharmacy Practice; Am. Soc. of Hosp. Pharm.; Drake Univ. Nat. Alumni Assn.; Kappa Psi Pharm. Frat.; Episcopalian; rec: racquetball, computers, stamp collecting. Res: 9 Misty Run Irvine 92714 Ofc: Syncor Internat. Corp., 1141 Air Way Glendale 91201

SMITH, CHARLES VINTON, electrical engineer; b. July 21, 1932, Frankfort, OH; s. Vinton Jay and Bernice Louetta (Blue) S.; m. Nancy Johnson, Apr. 9, 1960; children: Robin Jeffrey, b. 1961; Stacy, b. 1967; Scott, b. 1973; edn: B.EE., Ohio State Univ. 1959; grad. sch., UCLA 1961-63; lic. real estate broker, State of Calif. 1978. Career: mem. tech. staff Hughes Aircraft, Culver City 1959-61; research engr. No. Am. Aviation, Anaheim 1961-63; sr. research engr. 1963-65; engring. supvr. No. Am.- Rockwell, Anaheim 1964-76; proj. engr. Rockwell Internat., Anaheim 1976--; v.p./ treas. Merit Micro Software Corp., Okla. City, Okla. 1983--; v.p. SDS Land Corp., Chillicotle, OH 1966-70; pres. Charles Smith Realty & Investments 1978--; chmn Westminster Plng. Commn., City of Westminster 1978--; honors: hon. mem. Westminster Comm. Theatre for Outstanding Svc. 1979; mem: IEEE; Profl. Gp. on Microwave Theory & Techniques; West Orange Co. Bd. Realtors; Westminster Lions Club (past pres.); Westminster Comm. Theatre; Masonic Lodge, Frankfort, OH; mil: Tech. Sgt., USMC 1950-54, Korean Svc. Ribbon w/ 2 Battle Stars, Sigman Rhee Unit Citation; Republican; Protestant; rec: fishing, golf. Res: 8761 Tamarisk Cir Westminster 92683 Ofc: Rockwell International, 3311 E Miraloma, MCDC01, Anaheim 92801

SMITH, DANA PROM, psychotherapist, writer, theologian; b. Apr. 7, 1927, Glendale; d. Tom Nelson Miles and Hazel Marguerite (Prom) S.; div.; children: Timothy Rinck, b. 1955; Paul Prom, b. 1955; Elizabeth Marie, b. 1961; edn: AB, Princeton Univ. 1951; B.Div., Louisville Presbyn. Theol. Sem. 1955; Th.M., 1955; MA, Univ. of Ariz. 1958; MA, CSU Dominguez Hills 1978; MS, 1980; S.T.D., S.F. Theol. Sem. 1982. Career: pastor First Presbyterian Ch., Manchester, OH 1953-55, Ch. of The Covenant, Tucson, AZ 1955-58, Garden Plain Presbyn. Ch., Fulton, Ill. 1958-60 Fox Valley Presbyn. Ch., Geneva, Ill. 1960-68, Saint Lukes Presbyn. Ch., Rolling Hills. Estates, Calif. 1968-80; sr. assoc. St. Pauls Found., 1981--; lectr. Eng. Dept. CSUDH 1979-81; Arts editor Palos Verdes Peninsula News 1981; cons. L.A. Retarded Childrens Found. 1982; cons. Bd. of Christian Edn., United Presbyn. Ch. 1962-68; honors: Who's Who in Religion, 1978; named one of ten best ministers in So. Calif., L.A. Times 1976; mem: Calif. Assn. Marriage & Family Therapists; publs: The Educated Servant, The Debonair Disciple; An Old Creed for a New Day, Reflections on the Light of God; poems: Sacred, Profane; mil: Sgt./Maj. US Army 1945-47; Republican; Ind. Prot.; rec: fishing, hiking, gardening. Res: 6414 Via de Anzay Rancho Palos Verdes 90274

SMITH, DAVID ERNEST, manufacturing co. executive; b. Nov. 9, 1936, Woodbury, NJ; s. Ernest Browne and Evelyn Maud (McCarthy) S.; 1 son, David E., Jr., b. 1970; edn: BS in chem./biol., Muhlenberg Coll. 1959; MBA, Univ. of Scranton 1969; MS in intl. bus. (summa cum laude), West Coast Univ. 1978. Career: current dir. sales and mktg. ATI Div. of Warner Lambert (intro. 18 new products for co., 1983); bd. dirs. NBS Medical Inc.; owner/gen. mgr. Smith Arabians; (prior): western div. mgr. C.R. Bard Inc. (biomed. div.), Costa Mesa; internat. mkg. mgr. Cavitron Corp., Irvine (high tech. med. equip. for opthalmology mkt.); product mgr. Varian Assocs.; sales engr. Bechman Instruments Inc.; nat. sales mgr. Gulton Industries, Costa Mesa (med., indsl. and aerospace transducers and connectors); v.p. sales & mktg. Automated Screening Devices, Inc., Costa Mesa (med. prods.); mem: Internat. Assn. of Hospital Central Supply, Medical Mktg. Assn., South Coast Gun Club, Aircraft Owners and Pilots Assn.; publs: art., Europe and Oil 4/71, tech. papers; Republican; Lutheran; rec: ham radio opr., comml/instrument rated pilot and pilot examiner. Res: 28 Lonepine, Irvine 92714 Ofc: ATS, POB 9338 North Hollywood 91609

SMITH, EDWARD O., stock broker; b. June 16, 1934, Yelm, Wash.; s. Raymond Wentworth and Margaret (Eells) S.; m. Anne M. Hollowell, Aug. 22, 1959; 1 dau: Rebecca H., b. 1967; edn: BA, Univ. of Wash., Seattle 1956. Career: dept. mgr. Sears Roebuck, Pasadena 1959-62, stockbroker/asst. vice pres. Merrill Lynch Pierce Fenner & Smith, Inc., Pasadena 1962--; mem: pres. Pasadena Bond Club 1984-85; bd. govs. Univ. of Wash., Alumni Assn. 1983-86, Univ. Club of Pasadena (past pres.); Pasadena East Rotary Club (past pres.) Pasadena Quarterbacks Club (past pres.); Alaroma Club (past pres.); coms. and reg. mem. 17 yrs. Tournament of Roses; Glendora Country Club; mil: 1st Lt. US Army 1956-58; Republican; Protestant; rec: collector US stamp plate blocks, golf. Res: 3248 George Cir Pasadena 91107 Ofc: Merrill Lynch, 225 South Lake Ave Pasadena 91101

SMITH, ELIZABETH MARTINEZ, county librarian; b. Apr. 14, 1943, Upland, CA; d. Miguel Serrato and Venus (Espinoza) Martinez; Edn: Masters, Lib. Sci., UCLA, 1966; BA, UCLA, 1965; m. Michael W. Smith, June 29, 1968; chil: Nicolas Miguel, b. 1973; Maya Maria, b. 1977. Career: intern, Pomona Pub. Lib., 1965; children's librn., Rosemead Reg. Lib., 1966; coord., Way Out Proj., L.A. Co. Pub. Lib., 1968; regional adminstr., instns., L.A. Co. Pub. Lib., 1972; regional admin., L.A. Co. Pub. Lib., 1976-79; Co. librn., Orange Co., 1979; lectr., Sch. of Lib. Sci., CSU Fullerton, 1973-76. Honors: George I. Sanchez Award, 1976; Hispanic Women's Recognition Award, 1982, League of United Latin Amer. Citizens. Mem: CA Lib. Assn., 1966—; Amer. Lib. Assn., 1968—; REFORMA, Natl. Assn. of Spanish Speaking Librns.; Mex. Amer. Polit. Assn.; Amer. Assn. of Univ. Women. Author various arts. in lib. publs., 1972-80. Protestant. Res: Upland; Office: Orange Co. Public Library, 431 City Dr. South, Orange 92668.

SMITH, GARY CLEVELAND, lawyer; b. July 26, 1946, San Francisco; s. Harvey Cleveland and Geraldine Newlin (Brandt) S.; m. Pamela Allred, Oct. 18, 1981; children: Deke, b. 1965; Dawn, b. 1976; Summer, b. 1979; Derek, b. 1982; edn: Lincoln Univ.; BA, Sacto. State 1968. Career: trial lawyer sole practitioner 1975--; involved with Hells Angel case (largest criminal case in State of Calif.), San Francisco Fed. Dist. Ct.; atty. in O'Hara vs. Western Seven Trees, (changed Calif. laws requiring landlord to be responsible for the acts of criminals on his premises against tenants or third parties under certain circumstances); dir. Trilliam Computer Co.; instr. West Valley Jr. Coll.; cons. var. law firms in Santa Clara Co., and venture capitalists grps. involved with software; mem: State Bar of Calif.; Am. Bar Assn.; Santa Clara Co. Bar Assn.; Los Gatos Athletic Assn.; Sacto. State Alumni Assn.; Sacto. State Gold Card Assn.; Santa Clara Co. Trial Lawyers Assn.; Republican; Methodist; rec: hunting, fishinig, outdoor life. Res: 24868 Miller Hill Rd Los Gatos 95030 Ofc: Gary C. Smith, Esq., Inc., 3 High School Court Los Gatos

SMITH, GEORGE LEON, manufacturing co. executive; b. Aug. 27, 1944, Los Angeles; s. George Henry and Leonore (De Ville) S.; m. Graciela Guerrero, Nov. 15, 1982; children: Kenneth, b. 1967; Keith, b. 1969; edn: BA, Long Beach State 1968; APICS Cert., CSDH 1979; Indsl. Rels. Cert., Loyola- Marymount Univ. 1976. Career: quality control supvr. Max Factor & Co., Hawthorne 1962-67; quality control mgr. Packaging Corp. of Am., Los Angeles 1967-74; asst. plant mgr. K & M Co., Torrance 1974-83; plant mgr., Wesco, Gardena 1983--; mem: APICS; Lions Club (past pres.); Democrat; Catholic; rec: racquetball, woodworking. Res: 434 223rd St, No 226, Carson 90745; Ofc: Wesco, 510 E Airline Way Gardena 90248

SMITH, GLENN DAVISON, financial co. president; b. June 23, 1940, Niagara Falls, NY; s. Robert L. and Isabel D. (Davison) S.; m. Patricia Walsh, Sept. 17, 1983; children: Eric, b. 1964; Curtis, b. 1965; Shannon, b. 1970; Carey, b. 1975; edn: BS, Cornell Univ. 1962; MBA, Ohio Univ. 1970; CFP, Coll. of Fin. Plng. 1982. Career: v.p. Servomation Corp., NY, NY 1970-72; v.p./ div. mgr. Interstate United Corp., Seattle, Wash. 1972-74; v.p./ div. mgr. CFC, Los Angeles 1974-75; pres. Sequoia Financial Gp., Inc. 1980--; corp. dir. Associated Planners Securities; mem: AAII, IAFP, AAFP, ICFP, NALU, CMS; mil: Lt., USN 1963-66; Protestant. Res: 19660 Glen Una Dr Los Gatos 95030 Ofc: Sequoia Financial Group, Inc., 987 University Ave, Ste 6, Los Gatos 95030

SMITH, G(ODFREY) T(AYLOR), college president; b. Nov. 12, 1935, Newton, MS; Taylor and Edna (Blanton) S.; m. Joni Eaton, Sept 1, 1956; children: Paul Brian, b. 1959; Sherry Lynn, b. 1963; edn: BA, The Coll. of Wooster 1956; MPA, w/ distn., Cornell Univ. 1960; LLD, Bethany Coll. 1979. Career:assoc. dir. devel. Cornell Univ. 1960-62; dir. devel. The Coll. of Wooster 1962-66; v.p. 1966-77; pres. Chapman Coll. 1977--; lectr. Am. Council on Edn., Assn. of Am. Coll., Assn. of Governing Bds., Council for Adv. & Support of Edn., Council of Adv. of Small Colls.; awards: William A. Galpin Prize, The Coll. of Wooster 1956; Alfred P. Sloan Fellowship, Cornell Univ. 1959-60; Outstanding Young Men of Am.; Comm. Leaders of Am.; bd. dirs. Wayne Co., OH, Indl. Devel. Corp. 1966-72; World Affairs Council, Orange Co. 1978-; NCCJ, Orange Co. 1979-; Goodwill Ind., Orange Co. 1979-; Boy Scouts of Am., Orange Co. 1980-; Ind. Colls. of So. Cali. 1977- (pres. 1981-82); bd. dirs. United way, Orange Co. 1982-; dir. Christian Temporary Housing Facility 1981-; Assn. of Ind. Calif. Colls. & Univs. 1980-; Div. of Higher Edn., The Christian Ch. (Disciples of Christ) 1980-; mem: Pacific Club, Newport Beach; Balboa Bay Club, Newport Beach; Republican; Presbyterian; rec: family, horseback riding, farming. Res: 9631 Fleet Rd Villa Park 92667

SMITH, GORDON MICHAEL, television network executive; b. July 10, 1954, Chgo.; s. Leon L. and Blanche Smith; edn: BS, UC Berkeley 1976, MBA, Harvard Bus. Sch. 1978. Career: cons. Ofc. of Edn., Dept. DEW, Wash. 1976; mgr. plng. WBBM-TV, CBS, Chgo. 1978-79; dir. plng. 1979-81; controller CBS TV Network, Los Angeles 1981--; dir./ bd. dirs./ pres. Gordon M. Smith Prodns. 1984--; committee mem. CBS/Fox Studios Mgmt. Com. 1982-; dir. of bd. dirs. Trilogy Inc. 1981; honors: Corning Glass Fellowship; Wall Street Journ. Awd.; Claudius N. White Scholarship; Gov.'s Scholarship; mem: Acad. of TV Arts & Scis. (Blue Ribbon Emmy Panel); Harvard Bus. Sch. Club of So. Calif.; Beta Gamma Sigma, Livermore Peace Park Com.; Commonwealth Club of Calif.; MENSA; Order of the Golden Bear; Valley Ecology Ctr.; publs: Federal Student Aid Programs: A Comparison of Legislative Options, 1975, registered with ERIC; rec: painting, sculpture, racquetball. Res: 4444 Wishire Blvd, No 304, Los Angeles 90005 Ofc: CBS Television Network, 7800 Beverly Blvd Los Angeles 90036

SMITH, G. GREGORY, management consultant; b. Nov. 24, 1936, Teaneck, NJ; s. George G. and Gertrude Jean (O'Rourke) S.; m. Marilyn L. Roth, Apr. 28, 1961; children: Adrienne, b. 1963, Allison, b. 1966, Douglas,b. 1969; edn: BS in econ., Columbia Univ. 1966. Career: sr. systems analyst Gen. Motors Overseas Ops., NY 1954-65; pgm. dir. American Mgmt. Assn. Inc., NY 1966-68; vice pres. Advanced Mgmt. Research Inc., NY 1968-73; vice pres. Bell & Howell Co., Chgo. 1973-75; pres. Control Data Industry Education Inc., Baltimore 1975-76; gen. mgr. mktg. Control Data Corp., Mnpls. 1976-78; dir. mktg. Apple Computer Inc., Cupertino 1978-83; pres. G.G. Smith & Assocs. Inc, Saratoga 1983--; founder, chmn. Apple Foundation, Inc. 1978-82; Dir: Saga Systems Inc., Fremont, Ca., Reactive Systems Inc., Englewood, NJ, Prentice Assocs. Inc., Boston. Publs: ed. Computer & Software Security (AMR Int'l 1971); author: Operational Auditing (Am. Inst. of CPAs 1973); Microcomputers in University Networks (Lakeview Press 1980). Res: 12827 Ashley Ct. Saratoga

SMITH, HUEY PIERCE LONG, chiropractor; b. July 23, 1936, East Prairie, MO; s. Gilbert Sherman and Bessie Melissa (Laxton) S.; m. Jacqueline Lee Ross, Sept. 22, 1956; children: Bruce Wayne, b. 1957; Chad Ross, b. 1958; Michael Todd, b. 1962; Sherri Renae, b. 1965; Kari Jean, b. 1976; edn: BC, Palmer Coll. 1958. Career: chiropractor, Smith Chiropractic Ofcs. 1958--; Internat. Chiropractic Assoc., Calif. del. to Russian Med. Community 1977; mem: Internat. Chiropractors Assn.; Internat. Chiropractors Assn. of Calif.; Serve our Seniors, Orangevale; Masonic Lodge; Shriners; Square Dance Club; Republican; Protestant; rec: flying, skiing, ocean fishing. Res: 6508 Pecan Ave Orangevale 95662 Ofc: 6248 Main Ave Orangevale 95662

SMITH, JAY ARTHUR, insurance co. president; b. Aug. 3, 1932, Summit, NJ; s. Clark Howard and Evelyn Irene (Schmidt) S.; children: Preston, b. 1957; Wendy, b. 1959; Paul, b. 1961; Jay, Jr., b. 1963; edn: BS, Seton Hall Univ. 1957; Chartered Life Underwriter, CLU 1967. Career: stockbroker Bruns Nordeman & Co., NYC, 1953-62; dir. of agencies, Pension Life, Newark, NJ 1962-64; sales v.p. Consumers Life, Camden, NJ 1964-65; dir. of agencies Hanover Life 1965-69; v.p. Trust Securities Corp., Boston, Mass. 1965-69; pres. Meridian Ins. Co. of Calif. 1969-70; chmn./ CEO Life Inst. Rx Corp., Sausalito 1970--; awards: var. IAFP acclamations for svc.; mem: IAFP (founding bd. mem.; founding pres. North Bay Chpt.); NCFE (founding bd.); publs: Financial Plng. Guide; num. arts. and speeches on life ins.; mil: Regt. Sgt./Maj., M/Sgt., US Army 1951-53, Meritorious Svc., Purple Heart, Korea; rec: softball, golf. Res: 33 Wray Ave Sausalito 94965 Ofc: Life Insurance Rx Corp., PO Box 0', Ste 107, Sausalito 94966

SMITH, JOHN LLOYD, investment co. president; b. Aug. 26, 1943, Sterling, Ill.; s. Orville O. and Cecelia Althea (Barker) S.; m. Sherilyn M. Noon, Dec. 1, 1963; children: Kevin, b. 1969; Michelle, b. 1973; edn: BS, CalPoly, S.L.O. 1969; reg. principal, NASD; branch mgr. lic., NYSE; past lic. inv. counselor, Calif. R.E. Secs. broker. Career: stockbroker Dupont, Mitchum Jones, S.F. & Walnut Creek 1969-73; investment counselor John L. Smith & Co., Walnut Creek 1973-75; sales/ mgmt. Paine Weber, Walnut Creek 1975-78; pres./ owner Equivest Fin. Corp., San Ramon 1978--; past dir. Bank of Walnut Creek; honored by Contra Costa Co. Spl. Olympics; mem: Nat. Assn. of Securities Dealers; Rotary; Optomist Club (past pres.); Boy Scouts of Am.; Diablo Advocates; Contra Costa Winter Spl. Olympics Pgm.; works: founded two charities, a bank and personal investment corp.; mil: cpl. USMC 1961-64, Vietnam and Cuban Crisis; Republican; Methodist; rec: hunting, fishing, tennis. Res: 46 St. Teresa Ct Danville 94526 Ofc: Equivest Financial Corp., 2500 Old Crow Rd, Ste 413, San Ramon 94583

SMITH, JOHN PHILIP, cardiology consultant; b. Oct. 1, 1947, Dallas, TX; s. Bernard J. and Julia Susan (Connolly) S.; edn: BA, honors UC Berkeley 1970; MD, UC Davis 1974; res., Univ. of Mich., Ann Arbor 1974-77; pulmonary fellowship, Univ. of Ariz., Tucson 1977-78; cardiology fellowship, Univ. of Mich., Ann Arbor 1978-80; elective tng. in cardiol., London (Eng.) Hosp.; neurology and endocrine tng. at Mayo Clinic. Career: tchg. & research, Ann Arbor, Mich. and Tucson, Ariz.; pvt. practice, Los Angeles 1981; Cardiology Consultation practice, San Jose 1982--; chmn. Spkrs. Bureau, Am. Heart Assn.; cons. cardiologist local San Jose hosps.; honors: Phi Beta Kappa, UCB honors in Econ.; med. sch. honors in Cardiol., Pediatrics and Surgery. Active involvement in Phi Beta Kappa, the No. Am. Soc. for Pacing and Electrophysiology, and the Soc. of Nuclear Med.; mem: Am. Coll. of Cardiology; Am. Coll. of Physicians; Am. Heart Assn.; Am. Thoracic Soc.; Soc. of Nuclear Med.; Electrophysiology; Am. Soc. of Echocardiography; mem. Newman Club, Sierra Club of Calif.; publs: Effect of a Monopoly Upon a Developing Economy Coccidiodies Imitis and Diabetes Mellitus, Effect of Diabetes Upon Skin Testing of Fungal Infections; Catholic; rec: camping, hiking, racketball. Ofc: 1835 Park Ave San Jose 95126

SMITH, KELLY RUSSLEE, insurance broker; b. June 15, 1951, Kansas City, Mo.; s. Jesse Edward and Mable Alice (Shipman) S.; m. Kim Luree Du Bois, July 20, 1979; children: Heather b. 1981, Kelly Jr. b. 1983; edn: AA, El Camino Coll. 1972; BS, CSU Long Beach 1974; grad. Counselor Selling (I, II, III) Wilson Learning. Career: manager valet, Mermaid Restaurant 1966-73; mgr. Red. Eye Clothes Corp., 1973-74; v.p. marketing Synthelube Corp. of America, 1974-76; agent NY Life Ins. Co., Torrance 1976-77; agt. Northwestern Mutual Life, Santa Ana 1977-83; pres./ptnr. The Smith-Rhodes Co., Laguna Hills 1983--, also agent Connecticut Mutual Life, Beverly Hills 1983; Dist. mgr. for Conn. Mutual, General Agent Contracts with various life insurers; awards: Million Dollar Roundtable, 1976-84, National Quality Award (NALU) 1977-84, Nat. Sales Achiev. (NALU) 1977-84; Harold Baird Award (1978) and Mountain Top Award (1979), Leaders/Diamond Club (1978-82), Northwestern Mutual Life; Alumni of Year 1978, Kappa Sigma Frat. Theta Beta Chpt.; mem: MDRT, Century Club- Life Underwriters Pol.Action Com., Orange County Life Underwriters Assn., Calif. Life Und. Assn., Nat. Life Und. Assn., American Soc. CLU; mem. Dick Richards Breakfast Club, CSULB Alumni Assn., Kappa Sigma Alumni Assn.; editor: Trends -Quarterly Finl. Newsletter, Endorsement As Insurance; cons., Assn. of L.A. County Deputy Dist. Attys.; Republican; Christian; rec: art, sports. Res: 2 Lonepine, Irvine 92614 Ofc: The Smith-Rhodes Co. 22952 Alcalde Dr, Ste 140, Laguna Hills 92653

SMITH, LARRY T., mining-real estate development co. president; b. Jan. 4, 1938, Nashville, Tenn.; s. Frank M. and Clarice T. (Silay) S.; m. Margaret Linden, June 13, 1961; children: Gregory, b. 1964; Laurie, b. 1965; Kristen, b. 1969; Kelly, b. 1972; edn: BS; USC 1960; MBA, 1962; CPA, Calif. Career: CPA Price Waterhouse & Co., Los Angeles 1963-68; v.p. fin. Davis Mgmt. Corp., Beverly Hills 168-71; partner Smith & Linden, CPAs, Newport Beach 1972-80; partner Margaret Hills Land & Exploration Co., Newport Beach 1972--; pres. Margaret Hills, Inc., Newport Beach 1974--; chmn. bd. Marine Nat. Bank, Santa Ana 1981-; owner/ developer real estate projects; mem: Am. Inst. CPAs; Calif. Soc. of CPA's; Nevada Mining Assn.; mil: Lt., USNR; Republican; Presbyterian; rec: hunting. Res: 3 Oakmont Ln Newport Beach 92660 Ofc: 500 Newport Center Dr Newport Beach 92660

SMITH, LAUREN DWIGHT, graphic designer; b. Apr. 20, 1952, Eureka; s. Roger Dwight and Alice Patricia (Chegwidden) S.; m. Valerie Salerno, Sept. 28, 1975; 1 dau., Erin, b. 1982; edn: BS, Pacific Union Coll. 1974. Career: asst. art dir. Pacific Press Pub. Assn., Mt. View 1974-80; owner Lauren Smith Design, Mt. View 1980--; awards: num. art. and avtg.; mem: Western Art Dirs. Club; Am. Inst. of Graphic Arts, Artist in Print; Republican; 7th Day Adventist. Res: 1719A Springer Rd Mountain View 94040 Ofc: Lauren Smith Design, 2241 Charleston Rd, Ste 600, Mountain View 94043

SMITH, LA VERNE W., financial services co. president; b. Mar. 2, 1942, Los Angeles; s. Worthie L. and Alma L. (Washington) S.; m. Izetta Gray, Feb. 2, 1964; children: Sofiya, b. 1965; Pamela, b. 1968; Adimika 1973; edn: AA, Pasadena City Coll. 1968; CLU, American Coll. 1973; BS, Windsor Univ. 1974. Career: with Pacific Mutual Corp.: asst. to regl. v.p. Corporate Ofcs., Newport Beach 1968-70, asst. mgr. Wilshire Blvd Ofc. 1970-73; mgr. Burbank Ofc. 1973-78; owner Smith Financial Svcs. Co., Monrovia 1978--; former dir. Los Angeles Life Underwriters; Cont. Edn. Com. Am. Soc. of CLU; mem: Million Dollar Roundtable; Estate Plnnrs. Council; Nat. Assn. of Securities Dealers; Duarte Plnng. Commn.; Duarte CofC; Duarte Citizens Awareness Com.; Duarte Exec. Rotary Club; mil: Sgt. E5, US Army 1959-63; Democrat; Methodist; rec: tennis, golf, photog. Res: 2221 Rim Rd Duarte 91010 Ofc: 434 Foothill Blvd Monrovia 91016

SMITH, MARK LEE, architect; b. Nov. 16, 1957, Los Angeles; s. Selma (Moidel) S.; edn: stu. arch., UC Berkeley 1975-6; BA (hist. of arch.) summa cum laude, UC Los Angeles 1978, MA (arch.) 1980; Reg. Architect, Calif. 1983. Career: designer/drafter John B. Ferguson & Assoc., 1976-83, architect, 1983; architect/prin. Ferguson-Smith Offices, 1984--; awards: National Merit Scholar 1975, UC Regents Scholar 1975-78, Phi Beta Kappa 1978-, UCLA Grad. Sch. of Arch. Resrch. Fellowship 1979-80, Dean's Award-Best Thesis 1980; mem. Am. Inst. of Architects, L.A. Chpt.; publs: arts., L.A. Architect (9/79), UCLA (6/80). Res: 5272 Lindley Ave Encino 91316 Ofc: Mark L. Smith, AIA, Ferguson-Smith Offices, 18340 Ventura Blvd, Ste. 225, Tarzana 91356

SMITH, MYRON D, insurance executive; b. Oct. 29, 1954, Spokane, Wash.; s. Ben L. and Betty Jean (Decker) S.; edn: BA, Coll. of the Holy Names 1977. Career: ins. agent Conn. Mutual Lif. 1975-78; sales mgr. John Hancock Cos., Los Angeles 1980-81; owner Business & Estate Design Co. (personal bus. fin. and ins. planning co.) 1978--; v.p. mktg. West Coast Ins. Mktg. Corp., 1982--; bd. dirs. San Fernando Valley Life Underwriters Assn. 1982-, bd. dirs. Los Angeles Health Underwriter Assn. 1983-; awards: Harry S. Truman Scholarship 1977; Citizenship Awd., Wash. State House of Reps. 1971; Outstanding Student of Yr., Spokane Comm. Coll. 1976; mem: Council of Reps. & Pres., Wash. State; Assoc. Students, Spokane Comm. Coll. (EVP 1975); US Pacific Council (bd. 1983); SSGLC, Proj. Rainbow; num. arts. on health maintenance orgns.; ed. Valley View Mag.; mil: NG and US Army, Nat. Svc. Awd.; Republican (nom. for House of Reps., Wash. 1978); Catholic; rec: hobie cat sailing. Res: 7230 Kelvin Ave, 17, Canoga Park 91306 Ofc: West Coast Insurance Marketing Corp., 19510 Ventura Blvd, Ste 200, Tarzana 91356

SMITH, NEVA MINNETTE, real estate broker; b. Nov. 25, 1923, Douglas, Az.; d. James Stanley and Nina E. (Marken) Harris; m. Orville Wade Smith, Dec. 8, 1951; children: Knox M., b. 1953; E. Craig, b. 1956; edn: BA, Univ. of N.Mex. 1947; Calif. lic. real estate broker 1981. Career: executive secty. Phelps Dodge Corp., Douglas, Az. 1948; secty. US Army Ft. Huachuca, Az. 1950-51; R.E. agent assoc./ real estate broker assoc. Red Carpet Realty Kowalski, Sacto. 1977--; honors: Spurs (hon. soc.) 1945; Leaders Club, Red Carpet R.E. 1983; mem: Sacramento Bd. of Realtors, Bus. & Profl. Soc., Chi Omega Alumni Assn.; Republican; Christian Ch.; rec: bridge, alumni assn. work. Res: 2306 Knollwood Dr Shingle Springs 95682 Ofc: Red Carpet Realty-Kowalski, 3213 Julliard Dr Sacramento 95826

SMITH, NORMAN HENRY, insurance executive; b. Jan. 26, 1937, St. Louis, Mo.; s. Norman Joseh and Helen Ann (Wiedey) S.; m. Susan Sommerfeld, Oct. 5, 1968; children: Carson, b. 1977, William, b. 1979; edn: Bach. Gen. Eng., Univ. of Ill. 1960, MBA, honors, 1965; lic. Insurance Adminstr., Surplus Lines, Broker & Agent Calif. State Dept. of Ins. 1972-. Career: sales mgr. Uniroyal in NY, NY and Southbend, Ind., 1965-70; mgmt. cons. Craig, Cutten in Oakland, Ca. 1970-72; sales trainee Travelers Insurance, San Francisco 1972-75; current: pres./owner Capital Workshop Finl. & Ins. Services, S.F. and Los Angeles; pres./owner Capital Workshop Gen. Insurance Agency, S.F., 1975--; instr. Depts. of Engring. and Mgmt., Univ. Ill. 1963-65; honors: Monticello (Ill.) H.S. Valedictorian 1955; Ma-Wan-Da, 1957, Sachem, 1959 (activity honors); Western Regl. sales leader, Travelers 1975; mem: IIAA, 1975-80, PIA, 1975-83, WAIB, 1980-83; mem: Sierra Club, Snowmobilers (Bear Valley), Homeowners Assn.; author and underwriting mgr. Oxford Lawyers Profl. Liability Policy (1983); var. pub. articles on legal malpractice; mil: lt. jg USN 1960-63; Republican; rec: 2400 Paradise Dr Tiburon 94920 Ofc: Capital Workshop, 550 California St, Ste. 1130, San Francisco 94104

SMITH, ORVILLE WADE, insurance executive; b. July 30. 1924, Carrizozo, NM; s. Orville Vernon and Elsie Avisa (Townsend) S.; m. Neva Minnette Harris, Dec. 8, 1951; children: KnoxM., b. 1953; E. Craig, b. 1956; edn: BA, Univ. of NM 1947; CLU, Am. Coll. of Life Underwriters 1959. Career: dist. mgr., Salibury, MD 1955-62; regl. mgr., Sacto. 1962-72; life. mem. MDRT; life underwriter Jefferson Standard Life; pension cons. 1972--; honors: Man of Yr., Sacto. Agcy. 1972-82; Pres.'s Cabinet, Jefferson Standard Life 1977-82; mem: Salisbury Assn. Life Underwriters (pres. 1959); Sacto. Gen. Agents & Mgrs. Assan. (pres. 1967); Sacto. chpt. Am. Soc. of CLU (pres. 1971-72); Sacto. Estate Plng. Council; Lions; Kiwanis; Elks; AF&AM; San Juan Lodge; Aztec; Scottish Rite; mil: LCDR, USNR 1942-55, Navy Occupation, Asiatic Paacific, Korean Svc., United Nations Svc.; WWII Victory Medal; Am. Defense Medal; Nat. Defense Medal; Naval Reserve Medal; Republican; Protestant; rec: golf, art. res: 2306 Knollwood Dr Shingle Springs 95682 Ofc: Jefferson Standard Life, 350 University Ave, Ste 270, Sacramento 95825

SMITH, PATRICIA ALICE, administrator; b. July 29, 1935, Los Angeles; d. Gerrit Henry and Wanda Blanch (Henderson) Van Vliet; m. J. Harold Smith, Feb. 18, 1955; children: Clairlyn, b. 1956; Jolene, b.1961; Karleen, b. 1964; edn: Brigham Young Univ. 1954; Orange Coast Coll. 1967; State Dept. of Edn. authorization for svc.. Career: currently, administr./owner Electronic Assembly School of Orange Co.; instr./ counselor Ctr. for Employment Tng. 1979-80; mem: Southern Counties Rehabilitation Exch.; Reserve Deputy Sheriff, Co. of Orange; LDS Ch. Relief Soc. (pres.); rec: shooting, crafts, cooking. Res: 14152 Taft Street Garden Grove 92643 Ofc: Electronic Assembly School of O.C., 5027 W Edinger Ave, Santa Ana 92704

SMITH, R. MARIE FEGAN, educator; b. Sept. 14, 1925, Chandler, Okla.; d. John Josphus and Willia Candas (May) Fegan; div. 1966; children: Stephanie, b. 1958; Joshua A., Jr. b. 1955;; edn: RN, Meml. Hosp. Sch. of Nursing 1952; Los Angeles City Coll. 1947-49; UCLA 1969-71; BA, Pepperdine Univ. 1977; Career: hd. nurse Los Angeles Co. Med. Hosp. 1952-5; hd. nurse Homer G. Phillip Hosp., St. Louis, MO 1955-58; public health nurse, Detroit, Mich. 1960-67; clinical nurse out patient dept., surgical emergency room Kaiser Hosp., 1967-70; owner/ administr. Marie Fegan Schools, Inc. 1970--; Pre-school Adv., Southwest Coll. 1971-72; instr. Pre-school Tchr. Tng., Pepperdine Univ. 1975; awards: Alpha Kappa Alpha; Nat. Assn. for Univ. Women; Pre-school Assn., So. Calif.; So. Calif. Assn. of the Edn. of Young Children; 700 Club; YWCA; Democrat; Relig. Sci.; rec: discussion gps., gardening, remodeling. Res: 4131 Charlene Dr Los Angeles 92243 Ofc: Marie Fegan Scools, Inc., 2069 W Slauson Ave Los Angeles 90047

SMITH, ROBERT H., III, certified public accountant; b. Dec. 27, 1910, San Francisco; s. Robert H., II, and Kathryn M. (Treacy) S.; m. Mary Josehine Doran, Aug. 15, 1937; children: Kathleen P. (Gless), Maurine D., Robert H. IV; edn: St. Mary's Coll. 1927-29; AB, Univ. of Ore. 1929-41. Career: auditor Calif. State Bd. Equalization 1934-46; practicing accountant 1946-74, ret. from Anderson, Smith, Droast & Connolly, Accts., Inc. 1974; founding bd. dirs. Solano Co. Taxpayers; founding chmn. No. Coast CPAs; past bd. dirs. S.F. chpt. Calif. CPAs; first pres. No. Bay Estate Plng. Council; mem: AICPA, Calif. Soc. of CPAs; past pres. Vallejo Choral Soc.; Chetco Indian Tribe; past bd. YMCA, Vallejo and Fairfield CofC, United Crusade, March of Dimes, Cerebral Palsy Soc.; bd. dirs. Solano Workshop Svcs.; mem. Benicia Old Town Theatre Gp., Vallejo Musical Theatre; Green Valley Country Club (past pres.); BPOE; Calif. Native Sons; Vallejo Kiwanis (past pres.); Republican; Catholic. Res: 112 Bella Vista Way Vallejo 94590

SMITH, ROBYNE MARIA, pralegal consultant; b. Aug. 26, 1959, Gary, Ind.; d. John L. (stepfather) and Sylvia Maria (Hill) Johnson; m. Dennis L. Smith, June 5, 1982; edn: BA, cum laude, DePaul Univ., Chgo. 1981; Paralegal Certification (honors), cert. ABA Legal Asst., USC, 1982. Career: paralegal asst. Fields & Fields, Chgo. 1978-80; legal assoc. Walzer & Gabrielson, Beverly Hills 1981-82; legal asst. assoc. Northrop Corp., Los Angeles 1982--; paralegal cons. Telview Communications Gp., Inc. 1982--; corp. secty. Provisions, Inc. 1984; Outstanding Young Women of Am. 1982; mem: Los Angeles Paralegal Assn.; Nat. Fedn. of Legal Assistants.; Nat. Assn. of Female Execs.; Nat. Assn. of Legal Adminstrs.; Am. Bar Assn. (Legal Adminstr. Sect.); NAACP, Beverly Hills; Nat. Urban League; Wilshire CofC; Catholic; rec: research, writing. Res: 720 South Kingsley Dr Los Angeles 90005 Ofc: Northrop Corp., 1800 Century Park East, Los Angeles 90067

SMITH, ROGER T., financial planner; b. Aug. 16, 1953, Fort Worth, TX; s. Thomas Floyd and Rose O. (O'Neal) S.; m. Betty C. Nevling, Oct. 6, 1977; 1 son: Shawn Christopher; edn: Southwest Texas State 1974-75; BA, criminal justice, CSU Sacto. 1976; Coll. of Fin. Plnrs. 1981--; reg. principal, Nat. Assn. of Security Dealers. Career: salesman, asst. dept. mgr. Montgomery Ward, San Antonia, Tex. 1972-75; Sacto. 1975-78; fin. plnr. Lawrence E. McCarty & Assoc. 1978-81; pres. Smith, Robertson & Johnson, Inc. 1981--; chmn. bd. Planned Solutions, Inc.; mem: Internat. Assn. of Fin. Plnrs.; Coll. of Fin. Plnrs.; KVIE, public tv; Friend of the Sacto. Zoo; Republican; Baptist; rec: sailing. Res: 4811 Zube Ct Carmichael 95608 Ofc: Smith, Robertson & Johnson, 1111 Howe Ave, Ste 425, Sacramento 95825

SMITH, RUDOLPH WALTER, pharmacist; b. May 30, 1915, New Orleans, LA; s. Walter George and Ruth Cornelia (Baquie) S.; m. Blanche Black, July 8, 1940; children: Arnold, b. 1947; Rudolph, b. 1950; edn: BS, Univ. of Calif. Pharmacy 1940; reg. pharmacist, Calif. Bd. of Pharmacy 1942. Career: Red Cap with Southern Pacific, Oakland 1937; ship-fitter, Richmond 1942; army 1943-46; real estate salesman, Richmond 1976; real estate broker, Richmond 1981; ret. 1981; hd. pharmacist/ mgr. Rumford's Phmcy., Berkeley 1946-76; mem: UC Alumni Assn.; NC Med., Dental, Pharm. Assn.; Calif. Pharm. Assn.; Contra Costa Pharm. Assn.; Alpha Phi Alpha; Am. Bridge Assn.; Am. Contract Bridge League; mil: SSgt., US Army 518th Regt., Phil. Liberation Ribbon, Bronze Star, Am. Campaign, Asiatic Pac. Campaign, WWII Victory medals; Democrat; Methodist; rec: bridge, life master. Res: 1623 Arlington Blvd El Cerrito 94530

SMITH, SELMA MOIDEL, lawyer, composer; b. Apr. 3, 1919, Warren, Ohio; d. Louis and Mary (Oyer) Moidel; 1 son, Mark Lee b. 1957; edn: stu. L.A. City Coll. 1936-37, Univ. Calif. 1937-39, USC 1939-41; JD, Pacific Coast Univ. 1942; admitted to Calif. State Bar 1943, US Dist. Ct. 1943, US Supreme Ct. 1958. Career: general practice law; mem. firm Moidel, Moidel, Moidel & Smith. Field dir. civilian adv. com. WAC, 1943; mem. nat. bd. Med. Coll. Pa. (fmrly. Woman's Med. Coll. Pa.), 1953-, exec. bd., 1976-80, pres. 1980-82. Decorated La Order del Merito Juan Pablo Duarte (Dominican Republic); mem: ABA, Calif. Bar Assn. (servicemen's legal com.), Los Angeles Bar Assn. (psychopathic ct. com.), L.A. Lawyers Club (pub. defenders com.), Nat. Assn. Women Lawyers (chmn. com. unauthorized practice of law, social commn. UN, regional dir. western states, Hawaii 1949-50, mem. jud. adminstrn. com. 1960, nat. chmn. world peace through law com. 1966-67), League of Ams. (dir.), Inter-Am. Bar Assn. (dir.), So. Calif. Women Lawyers Assn. (pres. 1947, 48), Women Lawyers Assn. chmn. Law Day com. 1966), State Bar Conf. Com., Council Bar Assns. Los Angeles County (charter sec. 1950), Calif. Bus. Women's Council (dir. 1951), L.A. Bus. Women's Council (pres. 1952), Calif. Pres.'s Council (1st v.p.), Nat. Assn. Composers USA (dir. 1974-79, ann. luncheon chmn. 1975), Nat. Fedn. Music Clubs (state chmn. Am. Music

1971-75, state conv. chmn. 1972), Docents of L.A. Philharmonic (v.p. 1973-, chmn. Latin Am. comm. rels. 1972-75, press and pub. rels. 1972-75, cons. coordinator 1973-75), ASCAP, Euterpe Opera Club (v.p. 1974-75, chmn. auditions 1972, chmn. awards 1973-75), Plato Soc. of UCLA Iota Tau Tau (dean L.A., supreme treas.); composer: Espressivo-Four Piano Pieces. Res: 5272 Lindley Ave Encino 91316

SMITH, SHERRY LYNN, mortgage banker; b. Oct. 16, 1956, Huntington Park; d. Charles Dwight and Delores A. (Snyder) S.; edn: BSBA, CSU Long Beach 1979; JD, Western State Univ. Coll. of Law 1983-. Career: legal secty. Carlton B. Casjens, Bell 1974-79; fashion model, John Robert Powers 1977-79; real estate broker Delores Smith & Assocs., Bell 1980-84; mortgage banker, Smith Financial Corp., Garden Grove 1980-84; owner/ opr. Sucess Images, Inc., Huntington Beach 1983--; nat. gov. Womens Council of Realtors, liason to State of Calif. for Nat. Assn. of Realtors; honors: Omega Tah Roa (nat. R.E. hon.); mem: Womens Council of Realtors; Toastmistress Internat.; dir. Long Beach Fair Housing Found.; Republican; Protestant; rec: flying, tchg., public spkg. Res: 3347 Tempe Dr Huntington Beach 92649 Ofc: Smith Financial Corp., 12832 Valley View St, Ste F, Garden Grove 92645

SMITH, STANLEY DAVID, lawyer; b. Apr. 12, 1935, Los Angeles; s. Samuel Joseph and Edna (Bridge) S.; m. Natalie Cailingold, July 11, 1964; children: Samantha, b. 1968; Joshua b. 1971; edn: UCLA 1952-55; LLB, Southwestern Univ. 1964. Career: claims mgr. General Ins. Co. of Am. (now SAFECO) 1960-65; lawyer, sr. mng. partner, firm of Kinkle, Rodiger and Spriggs, San Diego Ofc. 1965--; prof. of law Southwestern Univ. 1965-70; instr. first law school course in med. malpractice in state of Calif. (Southwestern Univ. 1973); judge pro tem, Orange Co. Superior Ct 1977--; awards: Resolution of Cmmdn. for outstanding achievement as Judge Pro Tem, Orage Co. Bd. Supvrs. 1977; mem: State Bar of Calif.; Am., Orange Co., and San Diego Co. Bar Assns.; Town Hall; Am. Jurisprudence Soc.; mil: USNR 1952-60, active duty 1958-60; Democrat; rec: tennis, swimming, surfing. Res: 512 Santa Carina Solana Beach 92075 Ofc: Kinkle, Rodiger & Spriggs, 1200 Third Ave, Ste 1524, San Diego 92101

SMITH, WILLIAM FRENCH, attorney general of the United States; b. Wilton, NH; s. William French and Margaret (Dawson) Smith; Edn: AB, summa cum laude, Phi Beta Kappa, Univ. CA, 1939; LLB, Harvard Law Sch., 1942; m. Jean Webb; chil: William French, III; Stephanie Oakes; Scott Cameron; Gregory Hale. Career: admitted to CA Bar, 1942; sr. partner, Gibson, Dunn & Crutcher law firm; apptd. U.S. Atty. Gen., 1981---; directorships: Pacific Tel & Tel Co., S.F., 1969---; Crocker Natl. Bank, Crocker Natl. Corp., S.F., 1971---; Pac. Mutual Life Ins. Co., L.A., 1970---; Pac. Lighting Corp., L.A., 1967---; Jorgensen Steel Corp., L.A., 1974---; Pullman Inc., Chicago, 1979---. Regent, Univ. of CA, 1968---; chmn. bd. regents 1970-72, 74-75, 76; trustee, Henry E. Huntington Lib. and Art Gallery, 1971---; Claremont's Men's Coll., 1967---; The Cate Sch., 1971---; Northrop Inst. of Tech., 1973-75; UCLA Found., 1972---; Ind. Colls. of So. CA, 1969-74; Bds. of dir.: CA CofC, 1963, pres. 1974-75; L.A. World Affairs Council, 1970---, pres. 1975-78; mem. Adv. Council, Harvard Univ. Sch. of Govt., 1977---; adv. bd., The Center for Strategic and Internatl. Studies, Georgetown Univ., 1978---; U.S. Adv. Commn. on Internatl. Ednl. and Cultural Affairs, Wash., D.C., 1971-78; U.S. Del., The East-West Ctr. for Cultural and Tech. Interchange, Hawaii, 1975-77. Mem. bd. of trustees: Natl. Sym. Orch., 1975---; Ctr. Theatre Group, v.p., 1973---; Partnership for the Arts in CA, Inc., S.F., 1971---; Bd. Govs. Performing Arts Council, L.A. Music Ctr., 1978---. Mem: The CA Roundtable, exec. com., 1976---; L.A. Mayor's COms. on finances, labor mgmt.; CA Found. for Commerce and Edn., 1975---; Indus. Edn. Council of CA, 1973---; Fellow, Amer. Bar Found., Chicago. Mem: Amer. Law Inst., Philadelphia; Amer. Judicature Soc., Chicago; Amer. Bar Assn.; L.A. Co. Bar Assn.; State Bar of CA; Pi Gamma Mu; Pi Sigma Alpha. Republican, chmn. del. to natl. conv., 1968, v-chmn. 1972, 76. Res: San Marino; Office: Washington, D.C.

SMITH, WILLIAM FRENCH, III, lawyer, brokerage firm owner; b. Jan. 24, 1946, Los Angeles; s. William French and Marion (Hannah) Smith; Edn: BA, Occidental Coll.; JD, Western State Univ. Coll. of Law. Career: atty., Jennings, Campbell & Smith, La Jolla, 1975-77; William French Smith III, profl. law corp., La Jolla, 1977-79; SMith & Hickson, La Jolla, 1979-80; broker/ owner, La Jolla Land Brokers, real estate brokerage and exchange co., currently. Grad. mem., Real Property Securities and Syndication Inst.; frequent speaking appearances profl. groups; lectr., Retirement and Estate Planning Courses, various groups. Recipient US Army Achievement Award; profl. tennis, Second Round, 1978 US Open, Mxd. Mem: Amer. Bar Assn., Real Prop., Probate and Trust Law sect.; CA Bar Assn.; San Diego Co. Bar Assn., taxation and probate sections; La Jolla Probate Sect. Res: 5642 Dolphin Pl., La Jolla 92037; Office: La Jolla Land Brokers, 7855 Ivanhoe Ave., #200, La Jolla 92037.

SMITH, WILLIAM HOWARD, lawyer; b. Dec. 6, 1934, Wilmington; s. Bruce Edmond and Lorna Louine (Parrish) S.; m. Jolene C., Nov. 18, 1961; children: Renee, b. 1964; Kevin, b. 1968; Kimberly and Kristen, b. 1970; Dennis, b. 1977; edn: AA, Compton Coll. 1954; BA, UC Long Beach 1956; JD, Western State Univ. 1971; atty. at law, Calif. State Bar 1972. Career: acct., land/ lease spec. Richfield Oil 1964; Right of Way Agent 1966; mktg. atty. Atlantic Richfield Co. 1972; currently, sr. atty. mktg. Atlantic Richfield Co.; adv. Arco Travel Club Inc. 1972--; mem: Am. Bar Assn. ; Bus. & Banking Com. 1974-; State Bar of Calif.; mil: Airman 1/c, USAF 1957-61; GCM; Republican; Catholic; rec:

photog., gardening, recreational sports. Res: 5084 Melbourne Dr Cypress 90630 Ofc: Atlantic Richfield Co., 515 So Flower St, Ste 4569, Los Angeles 90017

SMITH, WILLIAM RAY, engineer; b. June 26, 1925, Lyman, Okla.; s. Harry Wait and Daisy Bell (Hull) S.; edn: BA, Bethany Nazarene Coll. 1948; MA, Wichita State Univ. 1950; Univ. of Kans. 1950-51; PhD, UCLA 1967. Career: structures engr. Beach Aircraft Corp., Wichita, KS 1951-53; sr. gp. engr. McDonnell Aircraft, St. Louis, MO 1953-60; sr. engr. Lockheed Aircraft, Burbank 1961-63; sr. engr. sci. McDonnell Douglas Corp., Long Beach 1966-71; mem. tech. staff Rockwell Internat., Los Angeles 1973--; tchr. Pasadena Coll., Pt. Loma 1960-62; Glendale Jr. Coll. 1972; Mt. St. mary's Coll. 1972-73; honors: Citation for Profl. Achievement, McDonnell Douglas Corp. 1968; Tech. Utilization Awd., Rockwell Internat. 1981; NASA Cert. of Recogn. 1982; mem: NY Acad. of Scis.; AAAS; Inst. of Aero. and Astro.; life mem. Yosemite Nat. Hist. Assn.; Sigma Xi; Pi Mu Epsilon; Delta Epsilon; tech. publs. 1969, 1981; Republican; Presbyterian; rec: sailing. Res: 2405 Roscomare Rd Los Angeles 90077 Ofc: Rockwell Internat. Corp., 201 No Douglas El Segundo 90245

SMITH, YVONNE SMART, advertising agency executive; b. June 25, 1947, Asheville, N.C.; d. Gardner Ford and Yvonne (Boyd) Smart; edn: BFA, Auburn Univ. 1969. Career: asst. art dir. Mademoiselle Mag., NY 1969-71; art dir. Cargill, Wilson & Acree Advtg., Charlotte, NC 1971-73; creative supvr. Tracy Locke Advtg., Dallas, TX 1973-76; v.p./ art dir. Chiat/Day Advtg., Los Angeles 1976--; guest lectr., instr. UCLA, Art. Ctr. Coll. of Design, Utah State Univ.; awards: num. one show, Beldings, Andy's, and Clio awards; mem: Los Angeles Creative Club, Communicating Arts, Am. Cancer Soc.; Episcopal; rec: fine arts. Res: 344 No Orange Grove Blvd Pasadena 91103 Ofc: Chiat/Day Advertising, 517 So Olive St Los Angeles 91103

SMITHAM, H. BRUCE, real estate broker; b. July 22, 1934, Los Angeles; s. Thomas and Emilie W. (Mac Kinnon) S.; m. Sandra Burke, Sept. 14, 1957; children: Hugh, b. 1961, Andrew, b. 1963, Jane, b. 1965, Bruce, b. 1967, Sarah, b. 1970; BA, UCLA 1961. Career: chmn., Aid to Families w/ Dependent Children, State of Calif. Welfare Dir.'s Assn. 1975-76; asst. dir. Kings Co. & Mendocino Co. 1969-77; owner/ opr. Stage Coach Realty, Ukiah, and Redwood Valley, Ca. 1977-83; currently realtor/owner Stage Coach Realty, Del Mar; chmn. Realtors Active in Politics; San Dieguito Bd. Realtors; chmn. profl. standards & ethics com., Mendocino Co. Bd. Realtors; mem: Farm & Land Inst.; Nat. Assn. Realtors; Downtown Ukiah Kiwanis Club; Optimists Club of Del Mar; Democrat; Episcopal; rec: aviation, computers, real estate. Res: 13953 Boquita Dr Del Mar 92014 Ofc: Stage Coach Realty, POB 2804 Del Mar 92014

SMITHER, LARRY MYRON, business owner; b. June 21, 1941, San Pedro; s. Hershel Clarence and Effie (Thompson) S.; m. Joyce, Feb. 12, 1960; children: Mark, b. 1960, Keri, b. 1964; edn: grad. Orosi H.S. 1959; Cabinet Sch. apprenticeship, Visalia 1962. Career: foreman Visalia Cabinet Shop 1962-64; co-partner Mid-Valley Cabinets 1965-67; pres./chief fin. exec. Kaweah Cabinet Shop, Inc. 1968--; Republican; Assem. of God; rec: golf, travel. Res: 10571 Ave 320 Visalia 93291 Ofc: Kaweah Cabinet Shop, Inc., 234 N.E. 2nd Visalia 93291

SMOLENSKI, MARIA, dentist; b. Sept. 18, 1948, Poland; d. Bernard and Barbara Bleja; m. Janusz Smolenski, Sept. 3, 1972; 2 daus: Eva, b. 1975, Anna, b. 1977; edn: DDS, Gdansk Sch. of Dentistry 1972. Career: dentist, Poland 1972-79; dentist, own dental ofc., Los Altos 1982--; adj. faculty, Univ. of the Pacific Sch. of Dentistry, San Francisco; cons. Inst. of America, Berkeley; mem: Calif. Dental Assn.; Am. Dental Assn.; Los Altos CofC. Res: 717 Edge ln Los Altos 94022 Ofc: Maria Smolenski, DDS, 827 Altos Oaks Dr, Ste 2, Los Altos 94022

SMOLKER, GARY STEVEN, lawyer; b. Nov. 5, 1945, Los Angeles; s. Paul and Shayndy (Charolette) (Sirott) S.; 1 child, Terra, b. 1071; edn: BS, Univ. Calif. 1967; MS, Cornell Univ. 1968; JD, cum laude, Loyola Univ. 1973. Career: mem. tech. staff Hughes Aircraft Co., Culver City 1968-70; Advanced Mktg. & Tech., TRW, Redondo Beach 1970-72; Law Ofcs. Gary Smolker, Beverly Hills 1973--; guest lectr. UCLA Ext. 1973, 74, Loyola Law Sch. 1979; contbg. editor Beverly Hills Bar Assn. Journ. 1980--, sr. ed. 1978; panelist & spkr. Innovative Financing Session, Calif. Escrow Assn. Annual Edn. Conf. 1981; speaker var. orgns. on Son of Rent Control, 1981; awards: Palm Springs Sci. Fair 1963; guest researcher Lawrence Radiation Lab, UC 1967; tchg. fellowship Sch. of Chem. Engring., Cornell Univ. 1968; US Patent, Self- Destruct Aluminum Tungstic Oxide Films, USN 1972; US Patent, Electrolytic Anticompromise Process, Hughes Aircraft 1973; Research Div. Invention Awd., Hughes Aircraft; mem: Calif. State, L.A. Co., Beverly Hills & Am. Bar Assns.; Assn. of Real Estate Attys.; Anti- Defamation League of B'nai B'rith; Guardian, Jewish Home for the Aged; Nat. Audubon Soc.; Advoc. Loyola Law Sch.; NY Metropolitan Mus. of Art. publs: Inclusionary Housing: A Wrong Approach (1981); The Govtl. Name Recall Pgm.; Model Affordable Living Ord.; Unenforceability of Balloon Payments (1980); Racial Ratios, A Further Dissention; Title Insurance v. Ownership of Realty (1979); Attys. Riddle. Republican; Jewish; rec: writing. Res: 15 63rd Ave Playa del Rey 90291 Law Ofcs. of Gary Smolker, 361 No Canon Dr Beverly Hills 90210

SMUCKLER, EDWARD AARON, pathologist, educator; b. Feb. 10, 1931, NY, NY; s. Abraham Franklin and Agnes Lydia (Jacobson); children: Cynthia L., B. 1955; Douglas E., b. 1956; Alison L., b. 1958; Elizabeth L., b. 1960; Daniel J., b. 1962; edn: AB, Dartmouth Coll. 1952; MD, Tufts Univ. 1956; PhD, Univ. of

Wash. 1963; Am. Bd. of Pathology (anatomical path.) 1963. Career: asst. prof. Univ. of Wash. 1963-66; assoc. prof. 1966-769; prof. 1969-76; dir. Joseph Gottstein Cancer Lab., Univ. of Wash. 1974-76; prof./ chmn., Dept. Pathology and Forensic Pathology, UC Sch. of Med. 1976--; honors: sr. mem., Nat. Sci. Found. 1965-66; fellow, Am. Assn. of Pathologists 1963; fellow, Am. Acad. for Adv. of Sci. 1983; mem: Internat. Acad. of Pathology; Am. Assn. of Pathologists; Am. Soc. of Biological Chemists; AAUP; Coll. of Am. Pathologists; Biochemical Soc., London; mil: sr. med. ofcr. USNS, Frederick Funston and USNS MM Patrick, MSTS, NORPAC Sub Area 1957-59. Res: 609 Wateree St Sausalito 94965 Ofc: Univ. of Calif., Dept. of Pathology, HSW-501, San Francisco 94143

SMUTKO, JOHN RICHARD, certified public accountant; b. Apr. 9, 1940, Somerville, NJ; s. John Anton and Maria Helen (Cichon) S.; m. Kumi, July 24, 1969; 1 son: Eric, b. 1978; edn: B. Chem. Engring., Cornell Univ. 1963; MBA, Harvard Bus. Sch. 1969; profl. acctg. pg., Northwestern Grad. Sch. Bus. 1970-71; CPA, State of Calif. 1972. Career: acctg., Twentieth Century Fox and Arthur Young & Co.; v.p. fin. Western Yarns, Inc., Commerce 1977-79; controller western area ARA Food Svcs. Co., El Segundo 1979-81; prin. John Smutko, CPA in Culver City 1981--; dir. Welborn Co., Inc. 1981-; Dir. Harvard Bus. Sch. Assn. of So. Calif. 1973-74; bd. govs. Cornell Club of So. Calif. 1973-74; awards: McMullen Regl. Scholar 1958; Navy Regular Appointee 1959; Nom. to Attend Naval War Coll., Monterey 1963; mem: Calif. Soc. CPAs; Harvard Bus. Sch. Assn. of So. Calif.; Culver City, Sunset Hills, Thousand Oaks CofCs; bd. advisors to State Assem. Thomas McClintock; mil: lt. USN 1963-67; Catholic; rec: golf. Res: 1610 Corte De Acero Thousand Oaks 91360 Ofc: John R. Smutko, CPA, 11262 Washington Blvd. Culver City 90230

SMYTH, DELTON RAY, mobile home park owner; b. May 13, 1929, Ada, Okla.; s. James M. and Lula Mae (Smith) S.; m. Norma Virginia Stanley, June 7, 1948; children: Steven Ray, b. 1949; Robert Allen, b. 1951; Catherine Lolita, b. 1955; Lic. plumbing contractor, Calif. 1964. Career: produce car loader 1948-51; boiler attdnt. Holly Sugar 1951-53; plumbing apprentice and journeyman 1954-65; plumbing controller/ owner Smyth Plumbing 1965-81; owner/ opr. Smyth Mobile Home Park, Brawley 1981--; pres. Brawley Co. Water Dist. 1960-82; mem. Thomas Budges Assn.; Republican; Baptist (deacon); rec: hunting, tarvel. Res: 260 East I Rd Brawley 92227 Ofc: Smyth Mobile Home Park, 263 East I Rd Brawley 92227

SNIPSTAD, MELINDA EILEEN, real estate broker; b. Jan. 17, 1949, Los Angeles; d. William Hartwell and Dorothy Mae (Irvin) Middleton; div.; 1 dau: Jennifer, b. 1969; edn: E.L.A. Coll. 1967-74; R.E. salesprsn., Lumbleau R.E. Sch. 1974; R.E. broker, 1980. Career: assoc. Frank Venti, Inc. 1974-75; sales assoc. Herbert Hawkins Realty 1975-80; owner Civic Employment Agency, Alhambra 1978-79; partner L & S Enterprises 1983--; owner/realtor M. Snipstad Realty, San Marino 1980--; mem: San Marino Bd. Realtors; So. Pasadena Bd. Realtors and Multiple Listing Svc.; West San. Gabriel Valley Bd. Realtors (past); Job's Daughters (parent vol.); publs: Reap a Bumper Crop of Sales, Saleman's Opportunity Mag.; Democrat; Protestant; rec: writing, oil painting. Res: 701 So 8th Street Alhambra 91801 Ofc: M. Snipstad, 1765 Los Robles Ave San Marino 91108

SNITOWSKY, HOWARD E., health inspector; b. Aug. 27, 1950, Los Angeles; s. Milton and Annette B. (Braveman) S.; edn: AA, zoology Santa Monica Coll. 1970; BS, zoology CSU, San Diego 1973; BS, environmental health 1974; Reg. Sanitarian, Calif. State 1975. Career: fire fighter, Bureau of Land Mgmt., Alaska 1974-79; L.A. Co. Health Dept. 1979; currently, environmental health sanitarian, Vietnamese community, Orange Co. Health Dept.; extensive job related travel throughout the Orient 1981-; awards: profl. commendations, Dept. Director (1983), Bur. of Land Mgmt. (1977); mem: Calif. Environmental Health Assn.; Apartment Assn. of Orange Co.; Republican; rec: real estate inv. Res: 17572 Santa Elena Cir Fountain Valley 92708 Ofc: Health Dept., 1725 W 17th Street Santa Ana 92702

SNOECK, YVES ETIENNE, engineering executive; b. Aug. 4, 1943, Brussels, Belgium, nat. 1970; s. Xavier Gustave and Simone (Minette) S.; m. Elaine Keiko Wada, Sept. 25, 1982; edn: AAS, electromech., Hartford Univ.1967. Career: field engr. General Electric, Wilburn, NJ 1967-73; design engr. Applied Data Research, Princeton, NJ 1973-75; reliability engr. ITT, Paris, France 1975-77, National Semiconductor, Santa Clara 1977-79; reliability engring. mgr. Racal Vadic, Sunnyvale 1979--; mem: Am. Quality Cir.; mil: Sp5 US Army 1968-70, GCM; Republican; rec: chess, racquetball. Res: 3106 Ryan Ave Santa Clara 95051 Ofc: Racal Vadic, 222 Caspian Dr Sunnyvale 94086

SNOG, COMMANDER, manufacturing conglomerate executive; b. Oct. 13, 1927, Wash. DC; s. John and P. Jane (Blaine) S.; m. Lula Lilacs, Oct. 31, 1953; children: Denny, b. 1954; Lum, b. 1956; Skipper, b. 1960; edn: BA, Bend Univ. 1949; MA, Stanford 1954. Career: v.p. Luke Hurdle Mfg. Co. 1955; v.p. Henderson Blotter Co. 1960; chmn. Capital Capgun, Inc. 1971; pres. Elmoco, Santa Monica 1978--; dir. Capital Capguns, Inc. 1978-80; recipient Polkinghorn Prize 1981; mem: Knights of Elvira (lodge master 1979); Merchant Marine purser, 1943-47; Republican; Baptist; rec: golf, lawn bowling. Res: POB 3073 Santa Monica 90403 Ofc: Elmoco, 6430 Seastar Dr, Ste 48, Malibu 90265

SNOW, BECKY (REBECCA) H., real estate broker; b. Nov. 20, Donalsonville, GA; d. John R. and Frances Jenelle (Linday) Hornsby (dec.); m. Gordon E. Snow, Aug. 29, 1958; children: Jenelle, b. 1959; Misty, b. 1964; Gordon, Jr., b. 1968; edn: Coll. of the Redwoods 1965; Ventura Coll. 1972; Oxnard Coll. 1981; GRI, Grad. Realtors Inst. 1976. Career: US Civil Svc. employee 1960-70;

broker/ pres. Snow Real Estate 1973--, real estate exchanger, cons.; sponsor tax seminars related to real estate 1978; guest spkr. coll. salesmanship classes; awards: Beneficial Suggestion Awd., US Civil Svc. 1967; Excellence Svc. Awd., Client Follow-up Pgm. 1980; mem: Nat. Bd. Realtors; Calif. Bd. Realtors; Oxnard Harbor Bd. of Realtors (past pres. Women's Council of Realtors); Oxnard Harbor & Camarillo Multiple Listing Svcs.; Central Coast Exchangers, Nat. Council of Exchangers Gold Card holder; Channel Islands Toastmistress Club (past); publs: contbr. Real Estate Today; author/ prod. The Golden Rule (a R.E. play 1977); Democrat; Baptist; rec: golf, football, baseball. Res: 1702 Ramona Dr Camarillo 93010 Ofc: Snow Ral Estate, POB 7206 Oxnard 93030

SNOWDEN, MARY LOUISE H., artist; b. Mar. 15, 1952, Los Angeles; d. George Holburn and Louise A. (Weider) Snowden; m. James A. Hagel, May 14, 1983; edn: BA, magna cum laude, Loyola Univ.; post grad. cert., Conservatoire dall'Abaco, Verona, Italy; post grad. study grants in Florence, Venice, Rome, and Paris. Career: sculptor/painter, dir. Snowden Studios; exhibs: Nat. Sculpture Soc., Ave of the Americas, NY; Showcase 21; lectr./ exhib., The Artist: Message and Medium, Mt. St. Mary's Coll.; Spencer's Huntington Sheraton Galleries; awards: achievement award, Loyola Univ. Depts. of Art and Art History; TRY Found. fine arts grantee; The Nat. Soc. of Arts of Letters Painting Awd.; Redken Fine Art Grantee. Mem: Alpha Sigma Nu; Kappa Gamma Pi; Los Angeles Patrons of Fine Arts; Art Historians Assn. of So. Calif.; Showcase 21; So. Calif. Early Music Soc.; Ambassador Found.; Long Beach Civic Light Opera; Cedar House Found. for Child Abuse; Nat. Sculpture Soc., NY; Nat. Acad. of Design, NY; works: marble setting & bronze sculpture, Albert Gersten Pavilion, Los Angeles; Ira Kaufman Meml.; marble lobby Centinela Hosp. Med. Ctr. 1983; Commn. of the Calif. Visual Arts Council, Sacto.; Frank Sullivan Commemorative sculpture, Von der Ahe Lib., Los Angeles; Episcopal; classical pianist, studied with Madame Ethel Leginska. Res: Snowden Studios, 444 Orlena Ave Long Beach 90814 (rep.) Bowater Galleries, POB 648 Los Angeles 90048

SNYDER, ARTHUR, JR., stockbroker; b. July 26, 1926, Boston, MA; s. Arthur and Frances (Duffum) S.; m. Jean Rogers, Sept. 20, 1950; children: Katherine, b. 1951; Barbara, b. 1953; Nancy, b. 1956; Arthur, b. 1960; edn: Noble & Greenough Sch., Dedham, Mass. 1938-44; BS, US Mil. Acad. 1948; MBA, USC 1961; reg. rep. NY Stock Exch. 1962; Commodity Futures Trading Commn. 1978. Career: USAF, Denver, Colo. 1948-57 (Capt. 1957); mem. tech. staff Hughes Aircraft Co., Culver City 1957-59; rep. Mutual Fund Assn., Los Angeles 1959-61; acct. exec. Merrill Lynch (and predecessor firms) 1961--; vice pres., research coord., L.A. Office, 1982-; honors: Win Smith Fellow (1984), Pres.'s Club (1979-), Merrill Lynch; mem: Soc. for the Investigation of Recurring Events; Westwood Gardens Civic Assn.; West Point Soc. of Los Angeles, USC/ MBA Alumni Assn.; Commerce Assocs. USC; mil: capt. USAF 1948-57; Republican; Episcopal; rec: biking, family activities. Res: 2804 Westwood Blvd Los Angeles 90064 Ofc: Merrill Lynch, 400 So Hope St, Ste 300, Los Angeles 90071

SNYDER, JOHN JOSEPH, optometrist; b. June 30, 1908, Wonewoc, Wisc.; s. Burt Frederick and Alta Lavinia (Hearn) S.; edn: AB, honors, UCLA 1931; postgrad, Univ. of Colo. 1936, 38, 40, 41; postgrad, USC (part time) 1945-47; BS, L.A. Coll. of Optometry 1948; OD, 1949; optometrist, Bd. of Optom., Calif. 1949. Career: tchr. rural schs. grades 1-8, La Plata Co., Colo. 1927-28; supintend. public schs./ h.s. tchr. Marvel, Colo. 1932-33; tchr. biology/ physics/ chem., Durango, Colo. 1933-41; optometrist pvt. practice, Los Angeles 1952-72, Torrance 1972-78; vacation (and other) relief optometrist, var. optometrists, L.A. County 1979--; honors: fellew, Internat. Biographical Assn.; mem: Calif. Opt. Assn.; Am. Opt. Assn.; L.A. Co. Opt. Soc.; AAAS; Nat. Eye Research Found.; Am. Inst. Biological Scis.; Exchange Club of So. L.A. (past pres.); Francia Boys Club, L.A.; Republican; S.D.A.; rec: fishing. Res: 735 Luring Dr Glendale 91206

SNYDER, RICHARD EUGENE, high technology electronics co. president; b. July 15, 1932, Ault, Colo.; s. Victor and Mary (Bakel) S.; m. Carol Lou Dunbar, Aug. 27, 1982; children: Victoria Ruth McLean, b. 1957, Brett Thomas Snyder, b. 1958; edn: Colo. State Tchrs. Coll. 1949-50;profl. deg. geophysics, Colo. Sch. of Mines, 1958; Adv. Mgmt. Pgm. Harvard Univ. 1974. Career: geophysicial engr. The California Co., 1958-61; systems software supr. General Dynamics 1961-63; engineering mgr., pgm. mgr., dir. of identification systems Rockwell International 1963-78; dir. advanced systems Hughes Helicopters Inc. 1978-81; pres. DeLaRue Printrak, Inc. Anaheim 1981--; honors: Theta Tau, Blue Key, Who's Who Among Students in Am. Colls. and Univs. 1958; Who's Who in Am. Bus. & Fin. 1978, 78; Who;s Who in Am. Law Enforcement 1983; mem: Internat. Assn. of Chiefs of Police, Internat. Assn. of Identification; San Diego JCs; Anaheim, Orange Co., and Los Angeles Chambers of Commerce; Western Hills G&C; publs: Seismic Exploration of Salt Domes (1959); Automation of "N-Body" Theory (1962); mil: s/sgt. USMC 1950-52; Republican; rec: gen. aviation pilot, tennis, golf, skiing. Res: 18031 Mariposa Ave Yorba Linda 92686 Ofc: De La Rue Printrak Inc. 2121 S. Manchester Ave Anaheim 92801

SNYDER, ROBERT L., clinical psychologist; b. Jan. 30, 1925, Los Angeles; s. Wm. L. and Lydia A. (Hurst) S.; m. Nelly Salgado de Snyder, Jan. 27, 1979; edn: BA human services, Gov's State Univ., Chgo. 1977; MS human svcs. Pepperdine Univ. 1979; PhD clin. psych., Columbia Pacific Univ. 1983; MFCC, Marriage Family and Child Counselor lic. 1982. Career: founder/owner Snyder & Son Men's Fashions (retail), Century Plaza Hotel, Los Angeles 1947-80; counselor/comm. pgms. devel. Inst. for Advancement in Human Svcs., L.A. 1978-80; psychotherapist Suicide Prev. Center, L.A. 1979--; psychologist, pvt. practice in Beverly Hills, currently; pvt. practice assoc. with Walter Ling, MD (neurologist/psychiatrist), Oxnard 1982--; pvt. practice assoc. with Harvey Ross, MD (orthomolecular psychiatrist), Hollywood 1981--; instr., drug abuse and the schs., Loyola Marymount Univ., L.A. 1980, num. seminars on drug abuse, UCLA Ext., USC, num. orgns.; Dir.: Calif. State Com. on Youth Suicide Prevention 1983-, Am. Assn. of Suicidology 1982-, Internat. Coll. of Applied Nutrition 1982-, Suicide Prev. Center 1979-; dir., chmn. LA Co. Narcotics and Dangerous Drugs Commn. 1979-82; chmn. Inst. for Advance. in Human Services 1978-80; chmn. Partners of the Americas, So. Calif. 1976-78; honors: Life Award for distinguished service to humanity, Inst. for Studies on Destructive Behaviors and Suicide Prev. Ctr., 1976; mil: sgt. USAAF 1943-46; Catholic; rec: flying, karate, tennis. Res: 2700 Neilson Way Santa Monica 90405 Ofc: Robert L. Snyder PhD 291 S. La Cienega Bl., Ste. 107, Beverly Hills 90211

SNYDER, WALTER MC CLELLAND, business owner; b. June 20, 1919, La Junta, Colo.; s. Walter Shirley and Ada (McClelland) S.; 2nd cousin to US Pres. Wm. McKinley; 1 son, Bruce C., b. 1946; edn: BBA, Woodbury Coll. 1941. Career: office mgr. Blue Diamond (Nev.) Corp., 1947-52; treas. Indsl. Steel Tank & Body Works, Berkeley, Calif. 1952-55; comptroller Iranian Air Lines, Tehran, Iran 1955-59; comptroller Tchitsazi Tehran, 1960 61; comptroller Meyers Jewelers, Vallejo, Calif. 1966-72; owner/partner Dal Porto Flowers, Vallejo 1972--; English instr. Iran-Amer. Soc., Tehran 1955-59; honors: Boss of Year, Am. Business Womens Assn. 1972; mem: Vallejo Rotary (bd. dirs. 1981-84), Elks, Vallejo Historic Mus., Navy League of the US, No. Calif. Unit of Teleflora (pres. 1980, bd. chmn. 1981-82); Republican; Catholic. Res: 103 Dyer Court Vallejo 94590 Ofc: Dal Porto Flowers 611 Floria St Vallejo 94590

SO, WAI KEUNG, dentist; b. Jan. 30, 1952, Canton, China; s. Kwan Yu and Tam Chun (Ho) So; m. Sui-Mui, Dec. 23, 1978; 1 son, Joseph, b. 1981; edn: B.D.S., Nat. Defence Med. Center, 1976; MS, Marquette Univ. Sch. of Dentistry 1978-796; DDS, USC Sch. of Dent. 1981; lic. dentist, R.O.C. 1977, Hong Kong 1978, Calif. 1980. Career: internship VA General Hosp., Taipei, Taiwan 1975-76; clin. instr. Marquette Univ. Dental Sch., Milwaukee, Wisc. 1978-79, instr./clin. asst. prof. USC Dental Sch. 1980--; dentist/pres. Wai-Keung So DDS, MS Inc., Cypress 1983--; honors: Omicron Kappa Upsilon, Zeta Chpt. 1981, achievement awd. USC Sch. of Dent. 1981; mem: Am., Calif. Dental Assn., Los ANgeles Dental Soc., Hong Kong Dental Council, Century Club; rec: swim, travel. Res: 2024 West Compass Lane Anaheim 92801 Ofc: Wai-Leung So DDS, MS Inc. 9907 Walker St Cypress 90630

SOARES, JAMES ENOS, electronic tech. engineer; b. Aug. 30, 1925, Newman, Calif.; s. Joseph Machado and Theresa A. (Luiz) Soares; m. Misako Itosh, Jan. 3, 1962; children: Jackie, b. 1963, David, b. 1967, James, b. 1968. Career: electronic tech. engr., Service Support Co., SSSC; mem: com. chmn. Boy Scouts Troop 1; mil: MSG 1950 75; Catholic. Res: 209 Rio Vista King City 93930 Ofc: SSSC, POB 898, Jolon 93928

SOCAL, LIVIO LEO, construction co. president; b. July 26, 1932, San Francisco; s. Giovanni Ivan and Maddalena M. (Scopel) S.; m. Maureen O'Donnell, Sept. 7, 1957; children: Kathleen, b. 1958, Debra, b. 1960, John, b. 1963; edn: AA, Skyline Coll.; cert. in real estate, Coll. of San Mateo. Career: pres. A&P Constrn. Inc., 1969 77; pres. Socal Constrn. Inc., 1978--; mem: ABCA (2nd v.p.); mil: SP3 US Army 1954-56; Democrat; Catholic; rec: lapidary. Address: Socal Construction Inc., 65 Turquoise Way San Francisco 94131

SODARO, ROBERT M., physician; b. 1924, Aurora, Ill.; s. Salvatore Francis and Marie (Borino) S.; m. Marie Stanaska, Apr. 12, 1947; children: robert F., b. 1952, David L., b. 1954, Marianne, b. 1957; edn: BS in EE, Ill. Inst. of Tech. 1945; A.E.C. Fellow in radiol. physics, Oak Ridge Nat. Labs. (Nat. Research Council fellowship) 1949-50; MD, USC Med. Sch. 1955. Career: radio and TV licensee appls. engr. Hazeltine Research of Calif., 1947-48; med. intern L.A. County Gen. Hosp., 1954-55, radiology resident, 1955-59; assoc. radiologist St. Jude Hosp., Fullerton 1959-60; att. staff (pres. 1972-3) Orange Co. General Hosp. 1963-76; vol. att. staff UCI Med. Center, 1976-; dir. Dept. of Radiol. and Nuclear Med., Santa Ana Comm. Hosp. 1960-75, vice dir. Dept. Radiol. and Nuclear Med. Santa Ana - Tustin Comm. Hosp. 1975-77; asst./assoc. clin. prof. in Radiology UCI 1969--; honors: Tau Beta Pi, Eta Kappa Nu; Diplomate Am. Bd. of Radiol. with medallion in Nuclear Med. 1959, Dip. Am. Bd. of Nuclear Med. 1972; mem: Fellow Am. Coll. of Radiol., Orange Co. Radiol. Soc. (pres. 1967), Radiol. Soc. of No. Am., Soc. of Nuclear Med.; bd. dirs. Found. for Medical Care, 1974-; tech. adv. gp. Orange Co. Health Plnng. Council 1970-; bd. dirs. O.C. Tuberculosis Assn. 1964-71; sci. papers, exhibits, profl. soc. meetings, 1973-; mil: lt. jg USNR 1942-46, res. 1946-54. Address: Dr. Robert M. Sodaro, 801 N. Tustin Ave Santa Ana 92705

SOGOMONIAN, HENRY TORCOM, company president; b. Aug. 22, 1937, NYC; s. Mesrob and Alice (Calfayan) S.; m. Carol Austin, Jan. 22, 1961; children: Cynthia, b. 1962, Laura, b. 1965, Steven, b. 1968; edn: stu. El Camino Coll. 1959; dip. cosmetology, Louis Corday Beauty Coll.; voc. edn., UC Los Angeles; Calif. lic. voc. educator, lic. cosmetologist. Career: hair stylist Clark Sevon Hair Salon, Beverly Hills 1959-60, Leading Lady Coiffures, Reseda 1960-61; hair stylist/owner International Set Coiffures, Encino 1961-76; hair stylist Hair Tecnique, Tarzana 1976-80; pres./lectr. and tchr. Sogo, Inc., Woodland Hills 198--; adv. bd. Corona Women's Penitentiary 1983; honors: Competition Hairstyling 1959-61; mem: Calif. Cosmetology Assn. (hon. bd. mem. 1982), Calif. Teachers of Cosmetology, Encino CofC; works: creator Sogo Nail Glass System (1982); Republican; Armenian Apostolic; rec: pvt. pilot, tennis. Address: 22635 Jameson Dr Woodland Hills 91364

SOKOLOFF, FRANCINE LANDIS, psychotherapist; b. Oct. 17, 1944, Phila.;

d. Martin and Mildred (Greenblatt) Landis; m. Tilden Sokoloff, June 20, 1965; children: Randy, b. 1971, Michelle, b. 1975; edn: BA, Temple Univ. 1966; MS, CSU Hayward 1980. Career: elementary sch. tchr., Phila. 1965-68, San Leandro, Calif. 1968-71; intern Hotline Clinic, Pleasant 1980; private practice Marriage & Family Counselor, Walnut Creek currently; community lectr.; devel. kindergarten, Jewish Comm. Center, Walnut Creek; mem: Calif. Psychotherapist Assn., Am. Personnel Guidance Assn., Am. Orthopsychiatry Assn., Berkeley Therapy Assn., AAUW, Womens Bd. Jewish Fedn., Hadassah, Ort; publs: papers on Jewish sterotypes, Intimate Women 1983; Jewish; rec: tennis, jogging. Res: 72 Mott Dr Alamo 94507 Ofc: 1844 San Miguel, Ste. 304A, Walnut Creek

SOKOLOW, LEWIS, automobile dealership owner; b. Jan. 20, 1916, NY, NY; s. Maurice and Sarah S.; m. Mildred Grace Goodlad, July 2, 1939; children: Kent Erle, b. 1953; Gale Louise Stead, b. 1955. Career: delivery man, all positions to service mgr., Howard Auto Co., Pasadena 1933 until WWII; sales mgr./gen. mgr. Silver Motors, Montebello 1946-53; owner/pres. Colonial Buick, Glendale 1953--, bought franchise for Honda, Volvo, and Mercedes; bd. dirs. Directors Life Ins. Co.; mem. G.M. Presidents Council; pres. Glendale Motor Car Dealers; pres. Auto Acceptance Corp.; honors: hon. PhD in Bus. Adminstrn., Calif. Western Univ., Santa Ana; mem. Rotary, Masonic Order, Verdugo Club, Oakmont CC; mil: lt. col. US Army WWII, Bronze Star, Medal of Merit, Ordnance; Methodist; rec: horses, boats, golf. Res: 2241 Via Saldivar Glendale 91208 Ofc: Colonial Buick, 144 So. Glendale Ave Glendale 91205

SOLEIMANY, ALI REZA, sales executive; b. Apr. 23, 1947, Tehran, Iran, nat. 1982; s. Mohamad R. and Azizeh (Vantankhah) S.; edn: MSc, mech. engring., Pahlavi, Shiraz, Iran 1970; MSc, material science 1973; MBA, Armstrong Coll., Berkeley 1978; postgrad., US Internat. Univ.. Career: material scientist General Motors Co., Tehran 1973; proj. engr., proj. mgr., engring. mgr. Iran electronics Indus., Tehran 1974-77; sales mgr. Rohrback Instruments, Santa Fe Springs 1979--; past instr. Pahlavi Univ. in Shiraz Iran; mem. Nat. Assn. of Corrosion Engrs. and ASTM; published papers in profl. journals; mil: 1st Lt. Spl. Industrial and Progress 55 Corps.; rec: piano, painting, tennis, golf, ski; Res: 3309 Florida Cir Costa Mesa 92626 Ofc: 11861 East Telegraph Rd. Santa Fe Springs 90670

SOLO, GAIL DIANNE, lawyer; b. Aug. 29, 1950, Sacramento; d. Myron B. and Betty (Codron) S.; edn: AB, UC Los Angeles 1972, JD, 1975; admitted to Calif. State Bar 1975. Career: aide to the Calif. State Senate, Sacto. 1975; assoc. atty. McKay & Byrne, L.A. 1976-78; assoc. atty. Joseph Shalant Law Corp., L.A. 1978-79; partner, Solo & Baron (emphasis, civil rights litigation and personal injury), Century City 1979--; honors: Outstanding Young Woman of Am. 1982, service awd. Women's Legal Clinic (1979, 83), num. scholastic awds.; mem: founder Women's Legal Clinic, Attorneys Against Discrimination, Women Lawyers Assn. of Los Angeles, Los Angeles Co. Bar Assn., Am. Judicature Soc.; mem. L.A. World Affairs Council, NOW, Affil. Network of Executive Women, United Jewish Welfare Fund; Democrat; Jewish; rec: biking theater, music, cooking. Res: 9733 Monte Mar Dr Los Angeles 90035 Ofc: Solo & Baron, 1875 Century Park East, Ste. 1450, Los Angeles 90067

SOMKOPULOS, SPEROS GEORGE, venture capitalist; b. Aug. 14, 1957, NY, NY; s. George S. and Adrienne (Alexio) S.; m. Margaret Sweeney, Apr. 13, 1979; children: Christopher, b. 1979, Aryanna, b. 1981, Stephanie, b. 1983; edn: BS in bus. adm./fin., San Francisco State Univ.; MBA, Golden Gate Univ.; lic. paralegal, Hastings UCSF; lic. gemologist and contract jeweler. Career: sr. vice pres. Mink Int., San Francisco, NY, Paris, Greece; pres. Specular Ent., S.F.; supvr. var. of task groups of splsts.; opr. third largest contract furrier business in USA with plants in NY, France, Greece; work improvement grad. advisor Am. Bankers Assn.; treas. Bay Area Latin Am. Cultural Orgn.; United Way coordinator; Republican (Nat. Com.); Greek Orthodox; rec: tennis, swimming, squash, soccer. Res: Hwy 1, No. 207 Off Ocean, Moss Beach Ofc: Paff-Williams Inc., 1255 Post, Ste. 1050, San Francisco 94109

SOMMER, SHIRLEY ANN, counselor, administrator; b. Apr. 7, 1932, Durham, N.C.; d. Leon H. and Alice J. (Fleagle) Gooch; m. Ervin Sommer, Dec. 25, 1958; edn: BS in edn. (honors), Miss. State Univ. 1954; dip. num. splties. incl. acctg., sectl., int. decor. & design, indsl. mgmt., ins. claim & adjustment, travel agt., law, real estate; lic: accred. accountant, US Treas. Dept. Enrolled Agt., Calif. Ins. Broker, Calif. real estate sales, Lifetime Tchg. Credential in Calif., Miss. Career: department store sales, 1948-49; Girl Scout Counselor 1950; public school tchr., Miss., Tex., Calif., 1954-59; self-empl. counselor administr. (taxation, real estate, acctg., fin.), Calif. 1956--, research, devel. profl. seminars and course material; honors: Phi Kappa Phi hon., university choir Miss. State; mem: Nat. Soc. of Public Accts. 1974-, Enrolled Agents Assn. 1973-76, Am. Mgmt. Assn.; Laubach Language Tchr.; Miss. State Univ. Alumni, Kappa Kappa Gamma sor.; publs. incl. mktg. brochures, illustrations 1965-, bus. forms 1970-, school courses 1953-60, devel. seminar lit. for adult courses in taxes and real estate 1980-; Republican; Prot.; rec: travel, cooking, research. Res: POB 2277, Escondido 92025

SOMMERFIELD, RONALD FREDRICK, construction administrator; b. Mar. 3, 1935, Chgo.; s. Ralph Fredrick and Evelyn Ann (Kellinger) S.; m. Helen Ann Ruppel, Apr. 15, 1955; children: Kenneth, b. 1956, Cynthia, b. 1960, Patricia, b. 1963; edn: indsl arts, 1956-59; eng., Orange Coast Jr. Coll. 1972-74; var. mil. schools; lic. Calif. state contr. (elec. signs), lic. ins. agt. Career: current project mgr. N.F.L. Constrn. Co., various locations incl. Altus (Okla.) AFB, Vandenberg AFB, Seymour Johnson AFB (N.C.); electrical advt. field, 25 years; concept design/ mktg./ suprvsn. contracts elec. advt. ornamental metals and

splty. products for hotels, casinos in Reno, and Las Vegas, Nev.; prin. own co., Huntington Beach 1978-80; past project mgr. for spl. elec. advt. pgms. for Ford Motor Co. (Western states), Gen. Motors Co. (Calif., Nev.), No. Am. Aviation merger with Rockwell (Ill., Wisc., Ind., Ohio, Pa.); civic vol. Little League, Boys Scouts (asst. scoutmaster Troop 226); Explorer Post 226 (founder, chmn., advisor, backpacking pgms.); Orange Co. Scout Council (chmn. No. Beach Dist. #41); Edison H.S. booster club; mem. Elks; St. Simon & Jude Ch.; mil. USMC 1953-55. Address: 8701 Knights Cir. Huntington Beach 92646

SOMMESE, DEAN M., sales executive; b. Oct. 21, 1956, South Amboy, NJ; s. Joseph Anthony and Mary A. (Selaberto) S.; geology maj., Fairleigh Dickinson Univ. 1978, Univ. of Las Vegas 1976. Career: salesman, sales mgr., vice pres. sales American Graphics Inc., San Diego 1978--; past bldg. svc., Prudential Ins., Newark, NJ 1975; salesman Regal Shoes, Las Vegas 1975-76; salesman, mgr. trainee, 50 States Distrbn. Co., Las Vegas 1976-78; Republican; Catholic; rec: motorcycling, drawing. Res: 9906 Backer Ct San Diego 92126 Ofc: American Graphics 11045 Roselle San Diego 92121

SONG, ALFRED H., lawyer; b. Feb. 16, 1919, Hawaii; s. Chin Koo and Chung Youn (Kim) S.; children: Leslie, Marsha, Mark, Frances; edn: BS, USC 1942, JD, 1949, LL.M., 1967; admitted to practice Calif. State Bar 1950; elected Councilman, City of Monterey Park, Calif. 1960-62, mem. Calif. State Assembly 1962-65, mem. Calif. State Senate 1966-78; chmn. Agricultural Labor Relations Bd., State of Calif. 1983; Democrat. Address: State capitol Bldg Rm 3070 Sacramento 95814

SONG, LEO CHUL, produce broker, grower, shipper, packer; b. Jan. 23, 1894, Kumsan Choongnam, Korea; s. Hockwoon and Yoon Song; m. Rose Lee, Aug. 5, 1939; children: Brenda (dec.), b. 1940; Leo C. Jr., b. 1941; Ugene, b. 1942; Gary, b. 1944; edn: BS, Univ. of Berkeley 1930, stu. UCLA, USC. Career: partner of K & S Jobbers, Los angeles 1927-75, sole owner 1975-79, pres. K & S Jobbers Inc., 1979--; dir. Calif. Korea Bank 1976-; hon. PhD, Chung Ang Univ., Seoul, Korea 1975; mem. Korean Dong Ji Hoi Soc., League of So. Calif. Koreans, Pusan Sister City Com.; Christian. Res: 1064 S. Grammercy Pl Los Angeles 90019 Ofc: K & S Jobbers Inc., 1057 S. San Pedro St, Ste. 217, Los Angeles 90015

SOOY, FRANCIS A., university chancellor; Edn: UC School of Med., 1941; Res. tr. in Otolaryngology, Univ. of Cal. & Wash. Univ., St. Louis; bd. cert. Amer. Bd. of Otolaryngology, 1944; faculty, Univ. of Cal., S.F. Sch. of Med., 1946---; chmn. Otolaryngology, 1958-72, chancellor, 1972---. Served numerous Sch. of Med. & Univ. Cal. Coms. Research contrib. to publs. in Otolaryngology, prob. of deaf. Mem: pres., Med. Alumni Assn., 1963-64; chmn., Acad. Senate Budget Com. & Acad. Senate Comm. on Coms.; chmn., Assembly of Acad. Senate, Cal.; chmn., Acad. Council of Cal.; Natl. Inst. of Health Adv. Neurological Diseases & Blindness council & subcoms., 1964-69; pres., Ot-Rhino-Laryngological Soc., 1979; pres., Collegium Oto-Rhino Laryngologicum Amicitiae Sacrum, 1980; Oto-Rhino Laryngologicum Amicitae Sacrum Lyon, France, 1965; pres., Soc. of Univ. Otolaryngologists, 1969-70; pres., Pac. Coast Oto-Ophthalmological Soc., 1973-74. Office: Univ. of Calif., San Francisco 94122.

SORENSEN, FERDINAND, wood carver; b. Feb. 26, 1900, Dannebrog, Nebr.; s. Louis Henry and Ellen Margrete (Jensen) S.; m. Gudrun Jorgensen, May 27, 1927; 1 son, Rikard, b. 1932; stu. Grand View Coll., Iowa. Career: summer school tchr., Danish language, in Luck, Wis.; building project equip. opr., Dubuque, Iowa 1927-33; var. bldg. trades (carpentry, plumbing, electrical) in Calif. 1933-, devel. special Danish provincial style decorative wood work for home interiors, decor, lamps, display cases, etc., still active in field 1933--; honors: Dane of the Year, So. Calif. 1975; Knighted by Queen of Denmark 1976; Hon. Mayor for a Day, Aalborg, Denmark 1971; pres. Solvang CofC 1974; pres. Dania Club 1958; pres. Rebild National Park Soc. (Br. of Denmark Soc. (1969-74; works: design/constrn. num. bldgs. and monuments; Democrat; Luthern. Address: Ferdinand Sorensensen, 1818 Old Mill Rd Solvang 93463

SORENSEN, RIKARD LOUIS, mortgage banker; b. Oct. 20, 1931, Chgo.; s. Ferdinand and Gudrun (Jorgensen) S.; m. Alyce Lewis, July 17, 1965; children: Tracy, b. 1956, Loree, b. 1958, David, b. 1959; edn: BS, agri., Cal. St. Poly. Univ., S.L.O. 1958; var. real estate schs.; Calif. Rural Appraisal Sch. 1973; Calif. lic. real estate broker 1968-. Career: land & water use analyst Calif. Dept. of Water Resources, Sacramento 1959-67; senior farm loan rep. Travelers Ins. Co., Mortgage Loan Dept., Sacto. 1959-67; partner/mgr. Agricultural Inv. Dept., Mason-McDuffie Co., Berkeley 1967-82; owner/pres. Mason-McDuffie Agricultural Investment Co., Orinda 1982--; mem: Mortgage Bankers Assn. of Am. (Agri. Credit Com. chmn. 1980-81); Am. (past legis. com. chmn.), Calif. (past pgm. chmn.) Soc. of Farm Mgrs. & Rural Appraisers; mem. Nat. Agri. Credit Com. 1979; mem. Walnut Creek Hist. Soc., Scottsdale and Tahoe-Donner homeowners assns., Boundary Oaks Racquet Club; mil: cpl. US Army 1952-54, GCM; Republican; Presbyterian; rec: skiing, tennis, travel. Res: 193 Dover Dr Walnut Creek 94598 Ofc: Mason-McDuffie Agricultural Investment Co. 4 Orinda Way, Ste. D-250, Orinda 95463

SORGATZ, ERIK KARL, computer analyst; b. June 24, 1952, Glendale; s. Robert D. and Jane (Kephart) S.; m. Linda D. Ludwick, Dec. 17, 1979; edn: L.A. Valley Jr. Coll. 1972-75; cert. pgmmg./analysis, ACS/ L.A. Pierce Jr. Coll. 1971; cert. 68000 System, Motorola 1984; Career: sr. computer opr., sr. math analyst/pgmr. Jet Propulsion Lab., Pasadena 1971-76; systems engr./cons. Lee Systems, Chatsworth 1976-77; R/AD electronics tech. Sigmatron-Nova

Research and Devel. Co., Chatsworth 1977-78; computer analyst, mem. tech. staff Transaction Technology Inc., Santa Monica 1978--; mem. New York Acad. of Sciences; research: invention- Free Energy Systems, 1980-; Republican; Christian; rec: music synthesis, motorcycling, Bonsai. Res: 11257 Covello St Sun Valley 91352 Ofc: TTI, 3100 Ocean Park Blvd Santa Monica 91405

SOUDER, C(HARLES) WILLIAM, engineer/executive; b. Jan. 27, 1945, Los Angeles; s. Charles Lee and Lillian Josephine (Bradbee) Souder; m. Ernestina Aragon, Aug. 27, 1966; chil: Patricia, b. 1969; Michael, b. 1972; edn: BSE, UCLA 1966; MSEE, USC 1971; MBA, CSU Long Beach 1982; cert. mfg. engr., SME, 1981. Career: engr. Northrop Corp., 1966-83: sr. engr. Electronics Div., Hawthorne 1966-76; pgm. mgr. of Indsl. Automation Tech., Palos Verdes1976-81; pgm. mgr. Factory of the Future pgm., Aircraft Div., El Segundo 1982; resrch engr. Adv. Devel. Gp., Electronics Div., Hawthorne 1983; vice pres. engring. Photonic Automation, Santa Ana 1984--; cons. Automated Insp. Products, 1982-3. Mem: IEEE, Internat. Soc. for Optical Engring., Robotics Internat. Publs: six tech. papers, SPIE. Republican; rec: astronomy, jog. Res: 28621 Mt. Rose Rd. Rancho Palos Verdes 90732 Ofc: Photonic Automation Inc. 3613 W. MacArthur Bl. Ste. 600 Santa Ana 92704

SOUTHWORTH, LEMONT ELWIN, computer co. executive; b. May 29, 1945, Pocatello, ID; s. Joseph Elwin and Virginia Lea (Holmes) S.; m. Darlene Dotson, Feb. 14, 1969; children: Michael, b. 1970; Jerry, b. 1972; m. 2d. Marilyn Baker, Aug. 9, 1975; children: Langdon, b. 1976; Kristen, b. 1978; Angela, b. 1980; edn: Univ. of Ore. 1964-66; Bach., LDS Inst. of Relig. 1964-66. Career: dir. of data processing Investment Data Corp., Santa Monica 1976-77; ofc. mgr. Advanced Systems Applications, Sherman Oaks 1977-78; dir. of data processing Vector Enterprises, Santa Monica 1978-81; exec. v.p. 1981--; bd. dirs. 1973--; cons. City Nat. Bank, on-line banking; devel. 1st operational nat. credit/ debit card computer switch 1979-83; works: design/ devel. 1st PATRIC (Pattern Recgn. and Info. Correlation sys.) for LAPD; design/ devel./ implementation of on-line med./ dental claims processing sys.; creator data processing facility for Consumer Shopping Guide & Consumer News (nat. cable TV data pgms.); author: Basics of EFT Network Switching, Data Communications, Sept. 1983; mil: Sgt., USAFR, 1968-72; Republican; Latter-day Saints; rec: guitar, camping, dirt bikes. Res: 745 Darmont Cir Simi Valley 93065 Ofc: Vector Enterprises, Inc., 1550 17th St Santa Monica 90404

SOWUNMI, EKUNDAYO AKIN, civil engineer/ businessman; b. Sept. 9, 1945, Calabar, Nigeria; s. Ebenezer Michael and Theodora Olubunmi (Adewakun) S.; m. Elina Randle, Dec. 19, 1970; children: Lisa, b. 1969; Jasmine, b. 1973; Kristina, b. 1981, edn: BSCE, UC Berkeley 1968, MSCE, 1970, PhD 1971; registered profl. civil engr., Calif. 1972. Career: asst. civil engr. City of Oakland 1971; asst. civil engr. Port of Oakland 1972; assoc. civil engr. 1973-74; suprvg. civil engr, 1974-79 civil engr / assoc. Jordan, Casper, Woodman, Dobson, Oakland 1979-81; suprvg. engr. Wilsey & Ham, Foster City 1980-82; pres. Ackland Internat., Hayward 1982--; chief exec. Ackland Engring. Construction Co., Ebute Metta, Lagos, Nigeria 1982--; mem: Am. Soc. of Civil Engrs; Protestant; rec: swimming, brainstorming. Address: Ackland Internat., Inc., 3620 Seabreeze Ct Hayward 94542

SOZINHO, MATTHEW GONSALVES, sales executive; b. Jan. 9, 1949, Tulare, Calif.; s. Mateus Gonsalves (dec.) and Lorraine J. (Bettencourt) S.; m. Luan Feleciano, Feb. 16, 1974; children: Matthew, b. 1975; David, b. 1977; Michael, b. 1981; edn: AA, Coll. of the Sequoias 1969; BS, Cal Poly, SLO 1973; Calif. Real Estate Brokers Lic. Career: dairy herdsman, family dairy 1967-74; dairy feed salesman Carnation- Albers, Fresno 1974-80; dairy feed salesman J.D. Heiskell & Co., Inc., Tulare 1980-82; dairy feed sales mgr. Coast Grain Co., Tulare 1982--; mem: Tulare Bd. Realtors; Tulare Multiple Listing Svc.; Tulare Town & Country Club; TDES Assn. (pres. 1980-82); Democrat; Catholic; rec: racquetball, raising holstein steers & heifers, travel. Res: 1210 West Prosperity Tulare 93274 Ofc: Coast Grain Co., 26301 Road 52 Tulare 93274

SPACKE, JAMES WILLIAM, manufacturing co. owner; b. June 25, 1939, San Diego; s. William F. and Mabel F. (Bowman) S.; m. Maureen, May 23, 1981; children: Theresa, b. 1959; Anthony, b. 1960; Timothy, b. 1962. Career: started as helper, ended as prodn. control mgr. Conseco, Inc., San Leandro 1957-70; Lox Equip. Co., Livermore 1970-73; inspector Rancho Seco Nuclear Power Plant; owner/ opr. Mariposa Custom Fabricators, Mariposa 1974--; Rec. Resolution #83-122 from Bd. Supvrs., (pos. pres. of Mariposa CofC), secured relocation of Blue Shield Ins. Co. to Mariposa; mem: Mariposa CofC (pres. 1982-); Catheys Valley Fire Dept. (fire fighter); rec: scuba, water skiing, hunting. Res: 3156 Hwy 140 Catheys Valley 95306 Ofc: Mariposa Custom Fabricators, POB 277 Catheys Valley 95306

SPALSBURY, JEFF R., designer educator/ training consultant, writer; b. Apr. 7, 1935, Mt. Pleasant, Mich.; s. Jeff R. and Majorie (Bell) S.; m. Diane de la Rosa, Aug. 30, 1964; children: Lisa E.; Sara M.; edn: BA, Univ. of San Jose 1967; MA, Univ. of Denver 1976. Career: instrl. designer Nat. Ind. Study Ctr., Denver, Colo. 1875-79; dir. sales tng. Raychem, Menlo Park 1980-81; nat. tng. mgr. Velo-Bind, Inc., Sunnyvale 1981-83; pres. JRS Enterprises & JRS Pub. Co., San Jose 1959--; mem: Am. Soc. for Tng. & Devel.; Assn. for Ednl. Communications & Tech.; Nat. Soc. for Performance & Instruction; works: num. profl. and popular publs.; motion picture & TV writer, dir., ed., make-up dir., musical score, and actor; mil: US Army 1956-58; Ofc: Box 53630 San Jose 95153

SPANGLER, DENICE IRENE, gerontologist, retirement home developer; b. Jan. 1, 1953, Los Angeles; d. Kenneth Arlo and Gertrude LaVerne (Wenquist) S.; m. Charles Henry Nicholson, MD, Apr. 10, 1976; edn: AA, Pierce Comm. Coll. 1971; World Campus Afloat, Chapman Coll.; BA, CSU Northridge 1973; BS, Ctr. for Studies in Aging, No. Texas State Univ. 1975; lic. nursing home adminstr, CA & LA. Career: recreational dir. Los Angeles City Sch. Dist. 1969-72; admin. San Francisco Convalescent Ctr. 1974; admin. Tulane Univ. Hosp. & Med. Sch. 1975-77; health plnr. Golden Empire Health Sys. Agcy. 1978-79; dir. plng. & devel. Retirement Housing Found. 1979--; v.p. Calif. Assn. Homes for the Aging; approved housing cons., Dept. of Housing and Urban Devel. (HUD); tax- exempt bond issues, Calif. Health Facilities Autherity, Calif. Mortgage Ins.; chprsn. Public Policy CAHA; dir. Friendly Visitor Pgm.; United Ch. fo Christ Health & Welfare Council Public Policy Com. (nat.); mem: Am. Health Plng. Assn.; Gerontological Soc.; UCC Health & Welfare Council; Am. & Cali. Assns. of Homes for the Aging; Nat. Orgn. for Women; Nat. Women's Political Caucus; Jr. League; Med. Auxillary; Bus. & Profl. Women; works: devel. nearly 1000 rental units for low to middle income srs.; devel. & plng. of 403 nursing home beds; rec: gardening, public advocacy, ethics. Res: 170 La Vista Grande Santa Barbara 93103 Ofc: Retirement Housing Found., 255 So Hill, Ste 407, Los Angeles 90012

SPANGLER, JAY FRANK, plant executive; b. Dec. 25, 1937, Okla. City, Okla.; s. James Nixon and Flossie Johnny (Brown) Sp; m. Betty Hill, June 14, 1969; 1 son: Eric, b. 1975; edn: Coe Coll., Cedar Rapids, Iowa 1956-57; BSBA, Univ. of Denver 1961; grad., Fafnir Bearing Sch. 1963; Morse MIT 1972; Diamond Chain 1966; TRW Bearings 1981; Morse Transmission Sem. 1980; Lubriplate Sch. 1976; GE triclad Tech 1967; GE Dist. Sales Sem. 1968; Stephens Adamson Sales Sem. 1974. Career: purchasing/ inventory control/ bookeeping Colorado Bearing, Denver, Colo. 1959-63; ofc. mgr. outside sales Valley Bearings & Power Trasmission, Sacto. 1963-67; div. mgr./ sales mgr. Van Alstyne Electric & Power Transmission, Sacto. 1967-78; pres. Calif. Bearing & Transmission, Sacto. 1978-83; br. mgr. Bearing, Inc., Sacto. 1983--; mem: Assoc. Bearing & Power Transmission Distbrs. (past pres.); Am. Inst. of Plant Engrs., Sacto.; Active 20-30 Internat., Sacto. (past); Democrat; Christian; rec: golf, swimming. Res: 6840 Oaklawn Way Fair Oaks 95628 Ofc: Bearings, Inc., 2130 20th Street Sacramento 95628

SPAULDING, KENNETH ERNEST, insurance agency owner; b. Dec. 31, 1917, Rome, NY; s. Forest Dayle and Corinne Gertrude (Bolten) S.; m. Lois Beightol, Jan. 8, 1950; children: Ernest Neil, b. 1946; Suzanne Elaine, b. 1948; edn: BRS, United Ch. of Relig. Sci. 1950; R.Sc.P., Glendale Ch, of Relig Sci 1964; R.S.Ms. 1965 Career: life sales Central Life of Illinois, Santa Ana 1939-41; tool engr. Douglas Aircraft, Long Beach 1941-46; life sales Pacific Mutual Life Ins. Co., Pasadena 1946-49; owner Spaulding Ins Agency, Glendale 1949--; honors: Top Star Mem., Pacific Mutual Lif, 1947, 48; Big Tree Mem , Pacific Mutual Lif. 1949, 51, 54; Nat. Quality Awd., Nat. Assn. of Life Underwriters 1955; mem: Profl. Ins. Agents; Ch. of Relig. Sci., Glendale; (pres. 1970-71); coauthor: Simple I Ching, 1978; poem, The Mystical Connection, 1982; Republican; Relig. Sci.; rec: writing. Res: 1900 Verdugo Loma Dr Glendale 91208 Ofc: Spaulding Insurance Agency, POB 889 Glendale 91209

SPEAKS, DENISE DIANE, lawyer; b. Nov. 21, 1953, Pittsburgh, Penn.; d. Herbert (dec.) and Juanita Wade (Waller) S.; edn: Sarbonne, Paris, France 1973-74; Baccalaureate, Lincoln Univ. 1975; JD, cum laude, Univ. of Pitts. 1978. Career: French tchr. Pittsburgh Public Schs. 1975-78; tax acct./ atty. Mellon Bank, Pitts., PA 1978-79; contracts atty. Bendik Corp., Sylmar 1979-82; staff atty. Northrop Corp., Hawthorne 1982--; chief counsel Celebrity Profl. Svcs., Hollywood 1982--; awards: Outstanding Scholastic Achievement in French; Volunteer Awd., Urban League; Pittsburgh Model of Yr. 1977; mem: Nat., Am., Calif., Penn., Century City, Beverly Hills, and Los Angeles Co. Bar Assns.; Black Women Lawyers Assn. of So. Calif.; Black Entertainment Lawyers Assn.; Women Entertainment Lawyers ; NAACP; Urban League; Black Exec. Exch. Pgm. (BEEP); Youth Motivation Task Force; Alpha Kappa Alpha; rec: entertainment & sports law, French, Aerobic Exercise. Res: 1131 No Alta Loma Rd, No 419, W Hollywood 90069 Ofc: Northrop Corp., One Northrop Ave, Hawthorne 90250

SPEAR, JOHN DAVID, real estate broker; b. Dec. 8, 1936, Wash. DC; s. Mont Clair and Mary Lou (Hill) S.; edn: BA, Univ. of Wash. 1958; grad. work, UCLA 1958-60; real estate cert., Long Beach Comm. Coll. 1975-79; real estate broker, State of Calif. 1979. Career: cons. Calif. State Assembly 1959-62; sales rep. Braniff Airways, Chgo., Miami 1962-68; So. Calif. rep. sch. dept. Rand, McNally 1968-74; real estate salesman Walker & Lee, Lakewood 1974-78; real estate broker/ assoc. Goldenwest Realtors, Lakewood 1978-84; self-empl. John D. Spear, Realtor 1984--; designer original new- agent tng. pgm., Goldenwest Realtors 1978; num. com. chmnshps., Long Beach Dist. Bd. Realtors; discussion leader annual conv., Calif. Assn. Realtors; honors: Pi Beta Alpha 1957; Ford Found. Grants (2) 1958, 59; Walker & Lee's Winner Circle 1976-77; Competant Toastmaster, Toastmasters Internat. 1983; mem: Phi Sigma Kappa, Univ. of Wash. (pres. 1957); Calif. Bookmens Assn.; Long Beach Dist. Bd. Realtors; Calif. Assn. Realtors; Nat. Assn. Realtors; (RECI) nat. Real Estate Cert. Inst.; Bd. Realtors Toastmaster Club, Long Beach; Nat. Geographic Soc.; Sierra Club; Metropolitan Opera Guild; The Cousteau Soc.; The Verdi Festival of San Diego Opera; Los Angeles Museum of Contemporary Art; mil: Sgt., USMCR 1954-66; Republican; rec: opera, art collector, gourmet. Res: 19121 Benfield Ave Cerritos 90701

SPEAR, J.W. EDWIN, college president; b. Jan. 28, 1937, Blackwell, OK; s. Arthur Louis and Eva Pearl (Revel) S.; m. Louise Eileen Schmidt, July 7, 1973; children: Kathleen, b. 1945; Jospeph, b. 1955; Thomas, b. 1956; Jimmy, b. 1958;

David, b. 1961; Susan, b. 1963; Valerie, b. 1966; David, b. 1968; John, b. 1974; edn: AA (Valedictorian) Riverside Coll. 1959; BA, UC Riverside 1961; MA, UCLA 1963; D.Phil., UC Riverside 1974; Supvr. and Mgmt. credentials, State of Calif. 1978. Career: riveter Rohr Aircraft 1954-56; tchr. (European and Am. hist., sociol., anthropol.) Barstow Coll. 1963, chmn. soc. sci. div., 1975-78; supt./pres. 1978--; guest lectr.; honors: Alpha Gamma Sigma, Life, 1959; Outstanding Tchrs. of Am. 1975; Outstanding Tchr., Barstow Coll. 1959; Nat. Hon. Soc., Hist. 1962; mem: Am. Hist. Soc.; Faculty Assn. of the Calif. Comm. Coll.; Assn. of Calif. Adminstrs.; Barstow Economic Devel. Corp.; mil: Pvt., US Army Air Corps.; A/2c, USAF 1951-53; WWII, Korean War; Republican; rec: building own home. Res: 27423 Crestview St Barstow 92311 Ofc: Barstow College, 2700 Barstow Rd Barstow 92311

SPECKERT, BRUCE LLEWELLYN, investment services co. president; b. June 20, 1955, Yuba City; s. Leo Joseph and Gertrude Louise (Cooper) S.; edn: AS, bus., Univ. Colo., Boulder 1975; BS, fin. CSU San Diego 1977, real estate cert. 1977; Calif. lic. Real Estate Broker 1977. Career: real estate sales agt. Century 21/La Mesa, 1976-77, broker assoc. 1977; project investigator Steinberg & Assocs., La Jolla; broker assoc. Stevenson Realty, Yuba City 1978; broker S.M.T. Corp., Yuba City 1979; loan cons. California Capital Loans, Yuba City 1980-82, v.p./branch mgr. Sacto., 1983--; broker/owner Speckert Realty, 1980--; broker/owner Speckert Investment Cos.: Speckert Realty, Speckert Mortgage Services; spkr. on equity lending var. brokerage firms, ASA, Soc. of Real Estate Appraisers; mem. Westcamp H.O. Assn. (pres.), Sacto. CofC, Rotary; Young Republicans; Episcopal (Acolyte, St. Johns); rec: skiing, theater. Res: 4717 Quail Meadow Way Fair Oaks 95628 Ofc: Speckert Investment Cos./California Capital Loans, Inc. 601 University Ave, Ste. 243, Sacramento 95825

SPECTOR, ANDREW LAWRENCE, biomedical engineer; b. Mar. 10, 1947, Brooklyn, NY; s. Wm. and Miriam (Jankelowitz) S.; edn: BA in math., Wash. Sq. Coll. NY Univ. 1969, BE in elec. engr., NY Univ. Sch. of Engring. 1969; grad. stu. in E.E., Univ. of Penna. 1969-72; MS, biomed. engring., USC 1974. Career: electrical engr. (computer systems R&D for aerospace med. and aeronautical simulation), US Naval Air Devel. Center, Warminster, Pa. 1969-72; research assoc. (devel. sys. to measure cardiac output non-invasively), Children's Hosp., Los Angeles 1973-74; chief biomedical engr. VA Medical Center, Palo Alto, 1974-83, systems mgr. 1983--; instr. Biomed. Engring. Tech. Pgm., Foothill Comm. Coll. 1976-78; part time cons. to industry and hosps.; honors: US Naval Air Devel. Ctr. graduate study award; Tau Beta Pi (engrg. hon.), Eta Kappa Nu (elec. engrg. hon.); NYU University Scholar, and NY State Regents Scholar; Under 21 National Saber Fencing Champion 1966. Mem: IEEE (chmn. Silicon Valley Section, Engrg. in Medicine Biology Soc. 1978-79); Profl. & Technical Consultants Assn. (assoc.); Sierra Club; rec: sailing, photog., travel. Res: POB 2484 Stanford 943405 Bus. Office of the Director (001C), VA Med Center, Palo Alto 94304

SPEIER, K. JACQUELINE, county supervisor; edn: BA, UC Davis; LLD, UC Hastings Coll. of Law. Career: caseworker 26th Assembly Dist. 1969-71; research cons. Calif. State Assembly 1971-72; legal counsel/ legis. asst. Congressman Leo J. Ryan 1973-78; honors: Outstanding Young Woman of Am.; mem: Assn. of Bay Area Govts.; Bay Area Air Quality Mgmt. Dist.; Chope Hosp. Joint Conf. Com.; CSA Public/ Pvt. Partnership Commn.; Exercise Trials Task Force; Housing Task Force; Interagency Com. on Aging; San Bruno Mountain Liaison; San Mateo Co. Adv. Council on Women; San Mateo Co. Conv. & Visitors Bureau; bd. dirs. Mercy H.S.; Peninsula YMCA; San Mateo Performing Arts Ctr. Capital Campaign; rec: running, gardening, reading. Ofc: County Government Center, Redwood City 94063

SPEIZER, MARK ADLER, insurance co. executive; b. July 30, 1943, Youngstown, OH; s. Alfred T. and Maxine Ruthe (Adler) S.; m. Linda S. Beasley, Aug. 23, 1979; children: Stephanie Loren, b. 1980; Stacey Michelle, b. 1982; edn: Santa Monica City Coll. 1962-64; ins. broker, State of Calif. Career: ins. agent Southland Co., Hollywood 1962-64; ins. broker Pacific Growth Corp., Concord 1964-66; pres. Bay Cos. Ins. Agency, Inc., San Francisco 1966-72; chmn. bd./ pres. Mark A. Speizer & Co., Inc., San Bruno 1972--; chmn. bd./ pres. Great Pacific Ins. Co., San Bruno 1977--; mil: Cpl., US Army; Republican; rec: water skiing, boating, swimming. Res: Hillsborough Ofc: Mark A. Speizer & Co., Inc. and Great Pacific Ins. Co., 1250 Bayhill Dr, Ste 212, San Bruno 94066

SPELBER, LEONARD GEORGE, manufacturing co. executive; b. Mar. 6, 1925, NYC; s. Harry and Mildred (Vigdor) S.; m. Mildred Silvering, July 19, 1949; children: Michael, b. 1950; Wendy, b. 1952; Erline, b. 1957; Layne, b. 1961; edn: BS, St. Louis Univ. 1951. Career: engr. draftsman NASA, Langley Field, VA 1942-44; USAF 1944-46; designer A Republic Aviation, Long Island, NY 1951-55; design engr. aerodynamicist Grumman Aircrayt, Beth Page, LI, NY 1955-57; sr. design Convair; sr. reliability engring. Gen. Dynamics/ Astronautics; sr. test engr. Gen. Dyn./ Astr.; gp. leader, exptl. aerodynamics Wagner Aircraft Co., Inc.; v.p./ secty./ treas. Sunrise Aircraft Corp. of Am.; bus. economist R.E. Rose & Assocs.; exec. v.p. Intratek, Inc.; exec. v.p. New Products Corp.; currently, pres. Wastemate Corp., San Diego; guest spkr. Nat. Univ.; mem: SAE; EAA; patents (4); Jewish; rec: home-built aircraft, sailing, model aircraft. Res: 4559 Mt Laplatta Pl San Diego 92117 Ofc: Wastemate Corp., 4380 Viewridge San Diego 92123

SPENCER, C(LARK) WILLIAM, hospital administrator; b. Mar. 26, 1945; s. Mr. & Mrs. R.L. Spencer; edn: grad., St. Vincent's Seminary, Orange Union H.S. 1962; Orange Coast Coll. 1965; Cypress Jr. Coll. 1967; Fullerton Jr. Coll. 1967-68; BA, St. Mary's Coll., San Jose 1979; lic. nursing home adminstr., Calif. Career: dept. supvr. Orange Co. Gen. Hosp., UC Irvine Med. Ctr. 1963-68; pres./ chmn. bd. APA, Inc. 1968-73; gen. partner Valley Med. Ctr. & adminstr. Perris Intercomm. Meml. Hosp. 1973-75; exec. v.p. Med. Care Mgmt., Inc. 1975-76; dir. New Health Facility Acquisitions, cons. Acute Hosp. Oprs. 1976-77; exec. dir. Fairway Convalescent Ctr., Fullerton, Heritage Convalescent Ctr., Torrance, No. Am. Health Ctrs. 1977-79; adminstr. Fountain Convalescent Hosp. 1979--; guest lectr. UC Berkeley 1980-81; awards: Arrowhead Honor 1977; Leaders Tng. Awd. 1977; Nat. Pres.'s Leader of Distinction Awd. 1976; Bronze Pelican 1978; Scouters Tng. Awd. 1979; St. George 1979; Fellow Am. Coll. of Nursing Home Adminstrs. (1983); mem: Am. Soc. for Hosp. Personnel Adminstrn.; Health Care Adminstrs. Assn. (pres.); Calif. Tchg. Hosp. Assn. (past pres.); Assn. of Bus. Mgrs. in Calif. Tchg. Hosps.; Hosp. Fin. Mgmt. Assn.; Nat. Assn. Accts.; Calif. Assn. of Health Facilities; Am. Health Care Assn.; Calif. Assn. of Employers; Orange CofC; Orange Jaycees; Oceanic Soc.; Knights of Columbus; Internat. Oceanographic Found.; Nat. Geographic Soc.: BSA (dist. & council coms.); BSA Golden Eagle Club; Confrat. of Christian Doctrine; Orange Suburbia Kiwanis. Address: 2383 No Bellbrook Orange 92665

SPENCER, LEE ANTHONY, psychologist; b. July 24, 1918, St. Louis, MO; s. Edward Samuel and Frances (Puleo) Spinaio; m. Vivian Dorgan, Feb. 20, 1943; children: Thomas, b. 1944, Susan, b. 1954, Stephen, b. 1963; edn: BS, Univ. of Mo. 1940; M.Edn., Univ. of Ariz. 1955; MA, 1956; PhD, St. Louis Univ. 1972; lic. psychologist, State of Calif. 1959-; Career: tchr. Sheridan Mil. Acad., Chgo. 1940-42; asst. personnel supr. Am. Steel Foundries, 1942-43; classification splst., pfc (detached enlistedman) US Army 1942-45; psychol. VA Regl. Offices, St. Louis, Milwaukee, Tucson, 1945-57; writer RCA, Tucson, Az. 1957-58; tchr. mentally retarded, Desert High Sch., Edwards, Ca. 1958-59; school psychologist King, Fresno, and Shasta Counties, 1959-64; psychologist (orgnznl.) Auto Club of S.F., Summer 1960, Vacaville State Prison, Summer 1962, (resrch.) Pac. Missile Range, Pt. Mugu, Summer 1963; field wk. Harcourt, Brace, & World, psychol. test dept., NY 1964-67; sch. psychol. Alton, Granite City, and Jacksonville, Ill. 1966-67, Coachella Valley (Ca.) Schs., 1977-82; psychol. pvt. practice, 1982--; instr. So. Ill. Univ. 1967-72; staff, Indio Comm. Hosp. 1981-; psychologist Riverside County courts, 1981-, State Voc. Rehab. and Soc. Sec. Disability Eval. Dept. (Az., Ill., Ca.) 1951-; recipient appreciation awards, Coachella Valley Uni. Sch. Dist., Hanford Lions Club; pres. Coachella Valley Big Brother Big Sister Orgn. Inc. 1978-83; bd. chmn. Jobs for the Handicapped Found., C.V. 1979-81; v.p. So. Ill. Psychol. Assn. 1969-70; charter mem. Nat. School Psychologist Assn. 1974, mem. Calif. Psych. Assn. 1978-79; publs: 20 research projects in ednl. and psychol. fields, 1959-74; six short stories 1945-46; Democrat; rec: sports coach/ofcl. Res: 36665 Donna Cir. Rancho Mirage 92270 Ofc: Lee A. Spencer, PhD, Lic. Psychologist, 471 E. Tahquitz-McCallum Wy Ste. 13, Palm Springs 92262

SPERRY, SHARON E., hospital finance administrator; b. July 29, 1938, Winona, Mo.; d. Delbert Franklin and Opal (Barnes) Norton; m. Donald Bell, June 8, 1956; div.; m. 2d. Clyde Sperry, Oct. 21, 1966; children: Michael Allen Bell, b. 1958, Janice Lee Bell, b. 1959; (step): Cynthia Renee, Pamela Mary (dec.), Curtis Clyde Sperry; stu. USC 1980-81, UC Los Angeles and Fullerton Coll., 1981-. Career: medical secty., Dr. Wennerman, St. Louis, Mo. 1954-57; exec. secty. Angelica Uniform Co., St. Louis 1957-60; chief copywriter Advt. Dept., Sears, Roebuck & Co., St. Louis 1966-68; med. coordinator Orthopaedic-Neurology Service, Rancho Los Amigos Hosp., Downey, Ca. 1970-75, Quality Assurance Pgm. coordinator 1975-77, Revenue Dir. 1977-83, assoc. hospital administrator, finance 1983--; works: authored AB 4431 (enacted into law 1977) designating rehabilitation as a Medi-Cal benefit throughout the state of Calif. (1977); estab. quality assurance pgms. leading to first Profl. Stds. Rev. Orgn. (PSRO) in a county hosp. in Los Angeles County; first woman to be apptd. Revenue Mgr. in the L.A. County health care delivery system. Mem: L.A. County Health Care Mgmt. Council, Calif. Assn. of Rehab. Facilities (long-range plnng. com.), Hospital Council of So. Calif. (bus. com.); Democrat; Quaker; rec: bowling, canoeing, macrame. Res: 2219 Heritage Way Fullerton 92633 Ofc: Rancho Los Amigos Hospital, 7601 E. Imperial Hwy Downey 92633

SPIERER, DIANE NANCY, pharmacist; b. June 5, 1956, Los Angeles; d. Dr. Eugene and Gloria (Dichner) Spierer; edn: BA in psychology, magna cum laude, UC Los Angeles 1977; D.Pharm., USC 1981. Career: intern pharmacist Cedars Sinai Medical Center, Los Angeles 1978-79; staff pharmacist Bay Harbor Hosp., Harbor City, 1981-83; staff pharmacist, UCLA Medical Center, 1983--; lectr. R.N. continuing edn.; lectr. poison prev. & drug abuse in elem. schs.; honors: Wash DC Govt. Intern, D.C. Lung Assn. 1977; 1977 UCLA Graduation Chancellor's Marshall, Banner Marshall, Nat. Hon. Soc. for Psychology Students, Nat. Hon. Soc. for Soc. Sci. Students, Alpha Lambda Delta (pres.), UCLA Honors Pgm.; mem: Am. Soc. of Hospital Pharmacists, Calif. Soc. of Hosp. Pharmacists (secty. South Bay Chpt. 1982-83); Calif. Pharmacist Assn.; Republican; rec: dance piano, theatre. Res: 23115 Samuel St Torrance 90505 Ofc: UCLA Medical Ctr, 10833 Le Conte Ave Los Angeles 90024

SPIES, JON LEWELL, employee relations executive; b. July 23, 1942, Marshalltown, Iowa; s. F. Lewell and Ruth E. Spies; m. Barbara Claypool, Mar. 25, 1967; children: Dianne, b. 1970, Wade, b. 1974; edn: cert. of sci., Kantonschule Aargau, Aarau, Switz. 1960-61; BA, Univ. of Kans. 1965; law, Univ. of Mo. 1965-67. Career: personnel mgr. Whirlpool Corp., Benton Harbor, MI 1971-75; dir. indsl. & community rels. Beatrice Foods Corp., Denver, Co. 1975-79; mgr. employee rels. western reg. Petro-Lewis Corp., Bakersfield 1979--; bd. dirs. Denver Opportunities Industrialization Council 1976-77; bd. dirs. Academic Bus. Sys., Santa Clara 1980-; co-op. adv. bd. Calif. State Bakersfield 1981-;

mem: Am. Soc. of Personnel Adminstrs.; Am. Soc. of Tng. & Devel.; Phi Alpha Delta; Employers Adv. Council; Laurelglen Tennis Club; Alpha Tau Omega; Boy Scouts of Am.; Couples Against Cancer; mil: Capt., USAF, 3 unit citations; Republican; Disciples of Christ; rec: baseball, golf, tennis. Res: 900 Camino Del Oeste Bakersfield 93309 Ofc: Petro- Lewis Corp., 5500 Ming Ave, Ste 300 Bakersfield 93309

SPILLMAN, NANCY ZOE, economics professor; b. Chgo.; d. Leo and Sarah Spillman; edn: BS, USC, 1963; MBA, magna cum laude, 1965; doctoral wk. in econ., UCLA 1969-73. Career: prof. of economics, Los Angeles Trade Technical Coll., 1969--, fmr. chair Bus. Adm. Dept.; mem. Federal Reserve Bd. Consumer Advisory Council; mem. State of Calif. Retail Credit Adv. Com.; mem. Calif. Beef Council, State Dept. of Agri.; frequent speaker for profl. assns. and media; editor Consumer Education Forum, Am. Council on Consumer Interests publ.; awards: Mabel Wilson Richards Scholarship, Theta Alpha Delta award for contbns. to business edn., Commerce Assoc. Fellow (MBA), Phi Kappa Phi, Freedoms Found. Awd. 1981. Mem: Town Hall of Calif. (tax and fin. sect. secty.); Am. Economic Assn.; Consumer Credit Counselors of Calif. (bd. dirs.); Calif. State Atty. Gen. Commn. on Consumer Edn.; L.A. Energy/Edn. Council; US Metric Assn. (past nat. secty.); Freedoms Found.; Internat. Consumer Credit Assn.; author of articles and books on economics, appears on TV and radio, presents seminars to Fed. Reserve Bd. of Govs. Office: Los Angeles Trade Technical College, 400 W. Washington Blvd Los Anges 90015

SPINHARNEY, STEPHEN JACOB, physician; b. Feb. 13, 1911, Cherokee, Iowa; s. Steven Albert and Sophia Josephine (Bush) S.; m. Mary Printy, June 5, 1950; children: Ann; James; Maura; Stephen; Mark; edn: BSc Creighton Univ. 1949; MD, 1950. Career: physician; mem: Calif. Med. Assn.; mil: C.Ph.M, USN; Republican; Catholic; rec: model railrods, african violets, gardening. Ofc: 20877 Muheli Rd, POB 449, Mi Wuk Village 95346

SPOHN, ORVILLE WILLIAM, marketing co. owner; b. May 2, 1929, Omaha, Nebr.; s. Frank Orville and June Ada (Galentin) S.; m. Louise Joan Dawson, Maay 10, 1950; children: Darla Louise Hodnett; Brenda Rachille Yavasile; Orville William Spohn, Jr.; Sherria Kay Smith; Nanette Aileen S.; Trudy Ellen S.; Adrian Eric S.; edn: station agent & acctg., Am. Railroad Sch. 1950; CLU, Am. Coll. 1983. Career: wire chief So. Pacific Railroad Co., Bakersfield & Fresno 1950-63; customer svc. rep. Transamerica Fin. Corp., Los Angeles 1963-65; rep. Uniplan, Los Angeles 1965-66; pres. Duval Co. & Duval Securities, Fresno 1966-69; v.p./ gen. mgr. Sensor Moisture Control Corp., Aubery, Calif. 1969-73; regl. v.p. Executive Life Ins. Co., Beverly Hills 1973-74; dir. spl. mktg. Sunset Life Ins. Co. of Am., Olympia, wash. 1974-75; gen. agent Exec. Life Ins. Co., Beverly Hills and Anchor Nat. Life Ins. Co., Phoenix, Ariz. 1969-73; gen. ins. agent; owner/ mgr. The Beerocks Factory (USDA Food Processing Plant w/ retail & wholesale outlets) 1978--; pioneered sale of new ins. prod. and devel. ins. & securities pkgs. for ins. replacement sales, Transamerica; devel. tax related ins. pgms. Executive & Sunset Lif.; mem: CLU Club; Evelle J. younger Atty. Gen.'s volunteer adv. council 1972, 75; mil: PFC, field artillery, US Army 1947-49, MP; Republican; Ch. of Jesus Christ LDS; rec: animals, outdoors. Res: 12657 E Heather Dr Clovis 93612 Ofc: The Beerocks Factory, 2055 Peach, Ste 105, Clovis 93612

SPRINGER, CLYDE HENDERSON, physician; b. June 28, 1952, Barbados, West Indies, nat. 1978; s. Milton DeCarlo and Esther Onetha (Todman) S.; edn: BS, Long Isl. Univ., NY 1975; MD, Meharry Med. Coll., Nashville, Tenn. 1979; obstetrician/ gynecologist. Career: res. tng. Lincoln Hosp., NY Med. Coll.; San Joaquin Hosp., Stockton; St. Luke's Hosp., CSWU, Cleveland, OH; pvt. practice in oby/gyn; cons. Clinica Sierra Vista Clinc, Lamont; honors: Med. Soc. at Long Island Univ.; Pharmacology hon. Meharry Med. Coll.; mem: AMA, SMNA; Am. Coll. of Obs/Gyn; Master Mason; Prince Hall Lodge; Mount Pisga, NY; Phi Beta Sigma; Baptist. Ofc: Clyde H. Springer, MD, 3733 San Dimas St, Ste 107A, Bakersfield 93301

SPROUSE, MARK RYAN, insurance/ financial planning executive; b. Aug. 9, 1949, Long Beach; s. Bennie G. and Wilma R. Sprouse; m. Dyana Lucretia Muse, July 2, 1971; 1 son: Jason Ryan, b. 1973; edn: BS, Univ. of the Redlands 1977; bus. mgmt., Redland, Calif.; CFP, in progress. Career: loan ofcr. Security Pacific Nat. Bank 1977-79; CIGNA/ Conn. Gen. Life Ins. Co. 1979-84; owner/ partner Resource Plng. & Mgmt., San Bernardino 1980--; honors: Million Dollar Roundtable 1981, 82, 83; mem: Estate Plng. Council of San Bernardino Co.; Internat. Assn. of Fin. Plnrs.; Rotary; mil: E-6, USN 1971-75; Republican; rec: golf, tennis, jogging. Res: 322 Brigette Ct Redlands 92373 Ofc: Resource Planning & Management, 1898 So Business Ctr Dr, Ste 203, San Bernardino 92408

SRAMEK, B. BO, medical electronics co. executive; b. Dec. 30, 1933, Prague, Czech., nat. 1970; s. Bohumir and Ruzena (Storcova) S.; m. Hevka Sevelova, Dec. 23, 1956; edn: MSEE, Tech. Univ. BRNO, Czech. 1957. Career: chmn. of bd., Bomed Medical Mfg., Ltd., Irvine, Ca. 1980--; pres. Powerex, Inc. Newport Bch. 1975-80; consulting mem. engineering staff Xerox Corp., El Segundo 1977-78; sr. staff mem. Nixdorf Computer, Costa Mesa 1981-83, also Internat. Peripherals & Computers Corp.; past staff mem. General Electric; respons. for R&D/new products devel. at Powerex and Bomed cos.; 10 patents; Rotarian; Republican; rec: tennis, skiing. Res: 19211 Edgehill Dr Irvine 92715 Ofc: Bomed Medical Mfg. Ltd. 5 Wrigley St. Irvine 92714

SRBICH, ALEXANDER LEKA, university professor; b. Sept. 16, 1914, Zajecar, Yugoslavia, nat. 1955; s. Zivko Djordje and Persida Leka (Valovich)

S.; m. Jeanette, Dec. 20, 1961; children: Leo, b. 1951, Eva, b. 1952, Victor, b. 1955; edn: MA, Cologne Univ., Germany 1949; BSE, Univ. of Mich. 1953; MBA, Univ. of Mich. 1955; PhD, Univ. of Minn. 1961; regis. profl. engr., State of Calif. Career: mgmt. trainee Timken, Detroit, Mich. 1955-56; instr. Univ. of Utah, Salt Lake City, Utah 1956-57; lectr. Univ. of Minn., Minneapolis, Minn. 1957-59; prof. of mgmt. sci. San Diego State Univ. 1959--; cons.: San Diego Zoological Soc. 1961-62; Mercy Hosp. 1963-65; USN, San Diego 1973; Superior Engring. & Electronics Co., Inc., San Diego 1983; visiting prof.: Tokyo, Manila, Hong Kong, London, Brussel (Belgium), Graz (Australia); awards: Ford Found. Scholarship 1957; Man of Yr., APICS 1973; Awd. of Merit, APICS 1974-75; Pres. Awd. of Merit 1975, 80; APICS Bibliography 5th & 6th eds.; mem: Am. Inst. Indsl. Engrs.; Am. Assn. Univ. Profs.; Am. Prodn. and Inventory Control Soc. (APICS); Operations Research Soc. of Am.; Serbia, Inc.; British Ofcrs. Mess; publs: Lumber as an Article of World Trade, 1961, Mfg. Management in Japan, 1961, Application of Modern Prodn. and Mgmt. Techniques to Large Metropolitan Zoo Ops., 1963, Recent Progress of Computer Aided Mfg. Mgmt. in the U.S. and Europe, 1982; mil: lt. Royal Yugoslav Army 1934-45, lt. Brit. Army 1945-46; Republican; Serbian Eastern Orthodox; rec: eqestrian, swimming, skiing. Res: 6465 Dwane Ave San Diego 92120 Ofc: San Diego State Univ., 5300 Campanile Dr San Diego 92182

STABBERT, FREDERICK JOSEPH, paper company president; b. Nov. 17, 1943, Seattle, Wash.; s. Wallace Roger and Eleanor Clarice (Joringdal) S.; m. Faith Edna Jordan, Nov. 22, 1963; children: Monica, b. 1966; Michael, b. 1968; edn: BA, Univ. of Puget Sound 1968. Career: Zellerbach Paper Co.: div. trainee 1969-70, sales rep. 1970-71, So. San Francisco, adm. mgr. 1971-75, Los Angeles, mgr. 1975-76, Sacramento, mgr. industrial bus. unit 1976-79, v.p./reg. mgr. 1979-80, exec. v.p. 1983, pres. 1983--; bd. dir. Nat. Paper Trade Assn.; Republican; Protestant; rec: skiing, golf, tennis; Res: 3550 Tripp Rd Woodside 94062 Ofc: Zellerbach Paper Co., 55 Hawthorne St San Francisco 94015

STACEY, KENNETH ERMES, contractor; b. Oct. 28, 1946, Los Angeles; s. George Talcott and Erminia (Rota) S.; m. Sherli, Aug. 12, 1972; 1 dau: Christine, b. 1967; edn: BS, Cal Poly, Pomona 1969; UCLA 1969-70. Career: tchr. Moreno Valley H.S. 1970-72; owner Stacey Refurbishing 1972--; partner D.K. Devel. 1981; mem: Nat. Trust for Hist. Preservation; Nat. Hist. Soc.; Cultural Heritage Bd., City of Riverside; Riverside Cultural Heritage Found.; Raincross Musicale (pres.); Internat. Arabian Horse Assn.; Arabian Horse Assn. of So. Calif.; owner Journeys End Reg. Arabian Horses. Res: 5620 Mt View Ave Riverside 92504 Ofc: Stacey Refurbishing, 2675 3rd, Ste H, Riverside 92507

STAFFORD, OLIVER MEAD, financial consultant; b. Jan. 17, 1936, Yonkers, NY; s. Frankland F. and Hermine J. (Jisa) S.; m. Joy Allen, June 21, 1982; children (prev. m.): Robert, b. 1964; Anne, b. 1962; edn: BA, Williams Coll. 1958; CFP 1979. Career: fin. cons.; mktg. trainee General Foods, White Plains, NY 1958-59; US Army Intelligence, US Army Adv. Corp., Trenton, NJ; gen. mgr., MA Mutual Lif. Ins. Co., Oakland 1961-70; exec. v.p. AIS Fin. Svcs., Oakland 1983--; faculty Golden Gate Univ. 1979--; adj. faculty Coll. for Fin. Plng., Denver, CO 1978--; adv. to the Coll. on Nat. Testing Pgms.; faculty USC Adult Edn. (devel. tng. material); devel. MBA pgm. in fin., Ctr. for Profl. Devel., Golden Gate Univ.; recipient Cert. of Commdn., AM. Coll. Fin. Plng. 1981-82; mem: Kappa Alpha Soc. 1955; Mt. Diablo Estate Plng. Council; Internat. Assn. Fin. Plnrs.; Inst. of CFPs; Rosicrucian Order; Big C Athletic Club, Concord; The Racquetball Club, Walnut Creek; publs: arts. on tax and ins. plng. in profl. journs.; mil: Spec. 4/c, E-4, US Army 1959-61, Commdn. Awd.; Republican; Protestant; rec: racquetball, classical piano, tennis. Res: 403 Lassen Dr Martinez 94553 Ofc: AIS Financial Services, 428 13th St, Ste 900, Oakland 94612

STAGG, CHARLES HOYT, marketing director; b. Aug. 1, 1926, La Habra; s. Hoyt and Julia Auvuergne (Wresche) S.; m. Debby, July 4, 1982; edn: BA, San Jose State 1954; UCLA Ext. 1958-62. Career: internat. mktg. dir. Astro Science Corp./ Bell & Howell, v.p. Wash. DC ops. 1970-78; v.p. American Nucleonics 1978-80; dir. internat. ops. Cincinnati Electronics Corp. 1980-82; gen. mgr. Ametek/ Sawyer Div. 1983--; pvt. cons. in mktg., data mgmt. & internat. mktg.; mil: USN 1942-46, 1950-52; Protestant; rec: golf, photog. Res: 27035 Rio Prado Valencia 91355 Ofc: Ametek/ Sawyer Division, 5649 Peck Rd Arcadia 91006

STAGNER, JAMES RAY, engineering executive, Federal Aviation Administration; b. Aug. 12, 1937, Wichita Falls, Texas; s. James Henry, Jr. and Wilma Elizabeth (Ray) Stagner; m. Barbara Rowland 1956-1968; m. 2d. Margaret Rex, Nov. 13, 1968; children: Elizabeth b. 1956, Anthony b. 1959, Melissa b. 1978; edn: electronics engrig., FAA Acad. (Oklahoma City, Okla.) 1960-73, mgmt., FAA Mgmt. Sch. (Lawton, Okla.) 1973-82; gen. engring. Ohlone Coll. 1973-76, Bakersfield Coll. 1955-56; Calif. Reg. Profl. Engr. 1977. Career: elect. tech. (Radar), FAA, var. Calif., 1960-72; supervisory electronics tech. (Automation), FAA, Fremont, Ca. 1972-77, supvsry. electronics engr. (Automation), 1977; chief enroute Radar/Automation Sect., (GS-14), FAA Regional Hdqtrs., Hawthorne 1978-79, supvr. Electronics Sect., 1979-84; mgr. Air Traffic Automation & Flight Info. Pgm. Sect. (GS-15), FAA Regl. Hdqtrs., Hawthorne 1984--; dir. FAA Mgmt. Assessment Lawton OK 1979; staff asst. to Secty. of Transp. San Francisco 1977; awards: HHIA Citizen of the Year 1982, 1983; FAA Outstanding Performance 1983, Quality Perf. 1979, 76, EEO Awd. 1976; mem: Mensa Internat. 1973-; County Sanitation Dists. of Los Angeles County Citizen's Adv. Com. 1981- (chmn. 1983); Hacienda Hts. Improvement Assn. (v.p. 1984), chmn. Landfill Com. 1981-83, Environ. Improvement 1983, Waste Mgmt. dir. 1982, 1984/5; US Chess Fedn.; publ: art., Flying Safety Mag.

USAF 1959; mil: A/1c USAF 1956-60; Democrat; Ch. of Christ; rec: philately, chess, computers. Res: 1530 Ameluxen Ave Hacienda Heights 91745 Ofc: FAA AWP 454 POB 90027 WWPC, Los Angeles 90009

STALLINGS, BETTY JEAN, military officer; b. Jan. 16, 1935, Champaign, Ill.; d. Harris Dean and Harriett Louise (Pillsbury) S.; edn: BS, Stanford Univ. 1957; dip. Army Command & Gen. Staff Coll. 1973; dip. Armed Forces Staff Coll. 1975; mem. Logistics Officer Pgm., DOA Hdqtrs 1972-. Career: served to lt. col. US Army, 1963--: tng. and supply ofcr., Vietnam 1969-70; developed subsistence policy AUS Qtrmaster Sch., Ft. Lee, Va. 1970-72; dir. of logistics, US WAC Center and Sch. (mng. 30 dormitories, 13 dining facilities) 1972-74; budget analyst major accts, DOA, 1975-79; supr. AUS Food Service policies and ops., Europe 1979-81; asst. insp. gen. DOD, W. Area, Alameda, Ca. 1981--; spkr. on women's legislative issues; chmn. UNICEF card/gift sales, Alameda 1982-3. Mil. awards: Merit. Svc., Bronze Star, Army Commend. w/2 Oak Leaf Clusters, VietNam Svc., Nat. Def. Svc. medals. Mem: Am. Soc. of Mil. Comptrollers (nat. secty. 1977-8), Qtrmaster Ofcrs Assn., Bus. and Profl. Women (recognition award 1984), Internat. Toastmistress Clubs (Council 4 Founder's Region secty. 1983-4), League of Women Voters; publs: mag. art. Int. Toastmistress Mag. 1983; Methodist; rec: fund-raising for non-profit orgns., knitting. Res: 2101 Shoreline Dr #478 Alameda 94501 Ofc: DOD Inspector General, 2155 Mariner Sq. Loop, Alameda 94501

STAMBLER-WOLFE, TERRY JOAN, community planning executive; b. May 3, 1946, Phila., PA; d. Dr. Ross N. and Mary Jane (Clark) S.; m. Lester E. Gene' Wolfe, Jan. 22, 1977; edn: BA, UC Berkeley 1967; MPA, w/ distn., CSU Fullerton 1978. Career: var. plng. pos. Cities of Fullerton, Claremont & Montebello; principal Terry Stambler-Wolfe & Assoc. 1975-78; city plnr. The Community Redevel. Agcy., City of Los Angeles 1978-82; dir. community devel. City of Manhattan Beach 1982--; owner cons. bus. 1975-78; guest spkr. comm. orgns. and univs.; honors: Phi Kappa Phi; first woman dept. hd., Manhattan Beach; only woman bldg. official L.A., Ventura & Orange Cos.; mem: Am. Plng. Assn.; Urban Land Inst.; Internat. Conf. of Bldg. Officials; rec: travel, wine tasting, property restoration. Res: 609 13th St Manhattan Beach 90266 Ofc; City of Manhattan Beach, 1400 Highland Ave Manhattan Beach 90266

STANEK, HERBERT STEVEN, lawyer; b. July 31, 1931, Spencer, NE; s. Joseph Anton and Gladys Louise (Weeks) S.; brother, Col. Robert G. Stanek, MD is surgical cons. to US Surgeon Gen.; m. Huali G. Chai, Dec. 30, 1978; children: James, b. 1956; Jane, b. 1962; Jennifer, b. 1964; Matthew, b. 1966; edn: BA, UC Berkeley 1958; JD, UCB Boalt Hall 1961; Cert. Worker's Comp. Splst., Calif. Bd. of Legal Specialization 1973; Cert. Civil Trial advoc., Nat. Bd. of Trial Advocacy 1982; admitted to practice US Supreme Ct. 1969. Career: partner Thorne, Clopton, Herz & Stanek, 1963-78; partner Stanek & Eddy 1978-79; partner Stanek & Boyle 1982; partner Santa Clara St. Profl. Bldg. 1980--; partner McDowell Ranch Co. 1973--; lectr. Univ. of Santa Clara Sch. of Law 1978; instr. San Jose Comm. Coll. 1973; mem: State Bar of Calif.; Santa Clara Co. Bar Assn. (Wkr.'s Comp. sect.); Calif. Applicants Attys. Assn.; Croation Fraternal Union; P&L Seminar Soc.; mil: SSgt., USAF 1950-55, Air Crew Badge; Democrat (Superior Ct. cand. 1972); rec: WWII history, bowling. Res: 38711 Greenwich Cir Fremont 94536 Ofc: Stanek & Boyle, 425 E Santa Clara St, Ste 220, San Jose 95113

STANFIELD, LARRY MARK, security systems co. president; b. Aug. 27, 1942, San Francisco; s. Norman Wesley and Evelyn Marie (Burns) S.; m. Peggy Anne McCaffrey, Dec. 22, 1962; children: Kerry Anne, b. 1963; Trish Kathleen, b. 1964; edn: AA, City Coll. of San Francisco 1963; instr. tng. cert., Dektor/ C.I.S. 1980; adv. cert. Peace Ofcrs. Standards, Tng. State of Calif. 1975; cert. of proficiency (criminology), City Coll. of S.F. 1963; adv. cert. Psychological Stress Evaluator, Dektor/ C.I.S. 1979. Career: police ofcr. Marin Co. Sheriff's Ofc. 1966-78; pres. Stanfield Security Systems, Inc., San Rafael 1978--; num. radio-TV appearances & newspaper interviews; mem: Bldg. Ind. Assn.; Calif. Assn. Lic. Investigators; Internat. Soc. of Stress Analysis; San Rafael Lions Club; Neighborhood Alert Pgm., San Anselmo; publs: copywrite book, Home Safety Survey Guide, 1982; mil: Sgt., USMC 1962-68, GCM; Democrat; Catholic; rec: sail boat racing, cruising. Res: 56 Jordan Ave San Anselmo 94960 Ofc: Stanfield Security Systems, Inc. 68 Paul Dr San Rafael 94903

STANFILL, DENNIS CAROTHERS, venture capitalist; b. Apr. 1, 1927, Centerville, Tenn.; s. Sam Broom and Hattie (Carothers) S.; m. Therese Olivieri, June 29, 1951; children: Francesca, b. 1953, Michaela, b. 1956, Dennis Jr., b. 1964; edn: BSc, US Naval Acad. 1949; MA (Rhodes Scholar), Oxford Univ., Eng. 1950-53. Career: served to lt. US Navy, 1949-59, last post, political mil. policy div., office of Chief of Naval Ops.; corporate finance splst Lehman Bros., NY 1959-65; vice pres. fin. Times Mirror Co., Los Angeles 1965-69; exec. vice pres. Twentieth Century-Fox Film Corp., L.A. 1969-71, chmn. bd. and chief exec. ofcr. 1971-81; founder/pres. Stanfill, Doig & Co. (investments and venture capital mgmt.), L.A. 1982--; dir. Greyhound Corp.; bd. chmn. Comm. TV of So. Calif. (public broadcasting); mem. bd. and exec. com. Rand Corp.; mem. bd., audit and exec. coms. Calif. Inst. of Tech.; honors: LHB (hon.), Univ. of S.C.; clubs: California (L.A.), Links (NY). Res: 908 Oak Grove Ave San Marino 91108 Ofc: Stanfill, Doig & Co., Inc., 444 So. Flower St, Ste.4650, Los Angeles 90017

STANFILL, THERESE OLIVIERI, civic leader; b. West Haven, Conn.; d. Salvatore and Maria Carmela (Rea) Olivieri; m. Dennis Carothers Stanfill, June 29, 1951; children: Francesca Rea (Tufo), b. 1953; Michaela Maria, b.

1956; Dennis C., Jr. b. 1964; edn: BA, Univ. of Conn. 1956. Career: bd. dirs. Norton Simon Mus.; Music Ctr. Opera Assn.; Ctr. Theatre Gp.; Save Venice, Inc.; Amazing Blue Ribbon 400; awards: Caveliere della Republica Italiana 1972; Commendatore della Republica Italiana 1982; Craft & Folk Art Mus. Honoree; mem: Los Angeles Co. Mus. Costume Council; Decorative Arts Council; Am. Friends of Covent Garden; organizer charity events, var. cultural orgns., incl. Am. Film Inst. 1971-81; rec: Venetian art history, opera. Address: Venetia and the Grand Tour, 908 Oak Grove Ave San Marino 91108

STANILOFF, HOWARD MEDA, cardiologist; b. Sept. 18, 1948, Saskadon, Saskatchewan, Canada; s. Sidney and Ethel (Epstein) S.; m. Robin, June 27, 1981; edn: BSc, Univ. of B.C. 1970; MD, 1973; MPH, UCLA 1980; cardiologist, epidemiologist. Career: med. res. Toronto Gen. Hosp. 1973-5; cardiology fellow, 1975-78; cardiology research fellow Cedars- Sinai Med. Ctr. 1978-80; cardiologist, dir. cardiac rehab., 1980--, epidemiologist, Sch. of Public health, UCLA 1981--; awards: Research Carrer Devel. Awd., Nat. Heart, Lung & Blood Inst. 1981; fellow, Am. Coll. of Cardiology 1980; fellow, Royal Coll. of Physicians & Surgeons, Canada 1978; mem: Am. Heart Assn. (Gr. L.A. affiliate); research in cardiology 1975--; Jewish. Res: 15825 Vose St Van Nuys 91406 Ofc: Cedars- Sinai Medical Ctr., Div. of Cardiology, 8700 Beverly Blvd Los Angeles 90048

STANLEY, EMERSON WARE, investor; b. June 7, 1906, Jacksonville, Fla.; s. Arthur Claudius and Lillian Agnes (Ware) S.; m. Allie Ylinen, June 11, 1949; 1 dau: Donna, b. 1953. grandfather, Edward G. Ware, prod. bus. in 1860's, became R.R. station agent, pioneer res. and landowner in Garden Grove 1876, later wrote num. arts. on walnut culture and poultry; sch. named for mother, L. Agnes Ware/ Stanley; family donated 2 acres from orig. homestead to Garden Grove Hist. Soc., now. Heritage Park, Stanley House Mus., Emerson Hall, etc.; edn: BA, Whittier Coll. 1934; grad. Sch. of Bus., Stanford Univ. 1936; O.C.C., Fullerton Coll. Career: bus. owner, Santa Monica 1936-40; rancher, Garden Grove area, prop. mgmt. investor 1946-71; prop. mgmt. ivests. 1971--; bd. trustees, Dana Point Ocean Inst. Found. (now Pacific Ocean Found.); bd. dirs. Garden Grove Hist. Soc.; past bd. dirs. Capo. Bch. CofC; bd. dirs. Garden Grove Hist. Soc.; past bd. dirs. United Way of Orange Co. No./So.; recip. cert. of merit, hon. cit., Orange Co. Bd. Supvrs. 1979; resolution of commdn., Orange Co. Bd. Supvrs.; Lib. Bell Awd., Or. Co. Bar 1978; hon. for outstanding & dedicated svc., Saddleback Reg. Lions, (pres. 1968-69); Niguel Capo. Valley Lions (pres. 1974-75); Garden Grove, San Clemente CofC; San Clemente Elks; Am. Leg.; Or. Co. Bird Club (past pres.); Tri-Cities Lapidary Soc.; La Cristianita Pag. Assn., San. Clem.; San Juan Capo. Hist. Soc.; UCI Friends of the Library; San Clem. Arts & Crafts; mil: Sgt.Maj., US Army 1942-46; Republican; Protestant; rec: world travel. Res: 24895 Doheny Pl, POB 2758 Capistrano Beach 92624

STANLEY, MAX RICHARD, experimental test pilot, ret.; b. Apr. 7, 1909, Santa Monica; s. Albert and Estelle (Michelson) Stanley; m. Jean R., Apr. 27, 1979; children: Dinah Jane, b. 1949, Paul Richard, b. 1954, Jeffrey Hamilton, b. 1957; edn: Santa Monica pub. schs., Stanford Univ. 1926-30. Career: solo flt. in 1934; co-pilot Lockheed Aircraft (ferrying Hudson bombers from Burbank, Ca. to East Coast for shipment to Eng.) 1939-40; capt. Pan Am. Airways (delivering airplanes from Miami across Atlantic to the Brit. in Africa under Lend Lease Act) 1940-41; capt. United Airlines, passenger/cargo flts., 1942-43; exptl. test pilot Northrop Aircraft, Inc. (now Northrop Corp.), 1943-71, (capt./ prin. pilot of the XB-35 and the YB-49 large Flying Wing airplanes, flew all models of the P-61 Black Widow, the F-15, the Tri-Motor Pioneer, the Tri-Motor C-125 Radar, the F-89 Scorpion, N-9M scale model Flying Wing, and flts. for the Snark intercontinental cruise missile devel. pgm.;). Co-inventor of take-off monitor system for Jet aircraft; founding mem., Fellow Soc. of Exptl. Test Pilots (chmn. Scholarship Found.); founding mem., past pres. Aviation Country Club of Calif.; mem. Quiet Birdmen; vice pres. So. Calif. Historical Aviation Found.; trustee emeritus Elliott-Pope Prep. Sch., Idyllwild; honors: Barnstormer Trophy for distinguished achievements in aviation; Calif. State Assembly Resolution; Caterpillar Club (two awds.); Republican; rec: woodworking, antique auto restoration. Res: 769 Bonhill Rd Los Angeles 90049

STANNARD, RAYMOND EDWARD, physician-surgeon, ret.; b. July 1, 1902, Laclede, MO; s. Edward Eugene and Margaret (Moore) S.; m. Marjorie Eugenia Smith, June 14, 1921, dec. 1980; children: Marjorie Jean, b. 1924; David Robertson, b. 1925; Dorothy Rae (Noyes), b. 1927; Elda Cecile, b. 1928 (dec. 1929); Raymond Edward, Jr., b. 1931; Marian Janet (Heidel), b. 1936; John Richard, b. 1937; edn: Univ. of Redlands 1919-1922; BA, Kansas St. Univ. 1923; MD, UC Med. Sch., S.F. 1930. Career: missionary phys.- surgeon Am. Baptist Fgn. Mission Soc., Hwa Mei Hosp., Ningpo, China 1930-38; supt. The Christian Hosp., Shaohing, China 1938-43, surgeon 1938-48; supt. The Pickford Meml. Hosp., Kinwha, China 1945-48; pvt. practice in Opportunity, Wn. 1944-56; phys.-surg. Roslyn- CleElum (Wn.) Beneficial Co., 1949-50; pvt. practice Morro Bay, Calif. 1951-56; chief of health div., (ICA) US Op. Mission to Nepal, Kathmandu, Nepal 1956-60; chief med. ofcr. Madera Co. Hosp. 1960-61; pvt. practice in Oakhurst, Ca. 1962-72, ret. Mem: Fellow Am. Acad. Family Phys.; AMA (Fifty Yr. Club); Bass Lake Lions Club; past mem. Kiwanis, Rotary; Internat. publs: Sulfanilamide, China Nat. Med. Journ.; Republican; Baptist; rec: fishing, back- packing, photog. Res: 53661 No Shore Rd Bass Lake 93604

STANSBERRY, RICHARD RANDALL, microlithography executive; b. Jan. 9, 1950, Burbank; s. Roy Randall and Rosemary Patten (Ohlson) S.; edn: AA, Pierce Coll. 1970; BS, USC 1972. Career: prod. supvr. Vero, Inc., Gardena 1970-72; prod. mgr. Electromask, Inc., Woodland Hills 1972-78; v.p./ co-owner Photo Sciences, Inc., Torrance 1978--; cons. Adv. Microlithography, self- empl. 1980--; mem: ISHM; SEMI; Torrance CofC; USC Alumni Assn.; Republican; Protestant; rec: tennis, travel., collecting sports memorabilia. Res: 2113 W 237 Street Torrance 90501 Ofc: Photo Sciences, Inc., 2542 W 237 Street Torrance 90505

STARBUCK, RANDY LEE, community development specialist;o b. Mar. 4, 1958, Whittier; s. Ernest Lee and Mary Evelyn (Branson) S.; m. ELizabeth Ann Grisham, Aug. 21, 1982; edn: BA, Westmont Coll. 1980; MAPA, Northern Ill. Univ. 1983. Career: research assoc. Northern Ill. Univ./Proj. SCOPE, De Kalb, IL 1980-81; dep. community dir. City of Geneva, IL 1981-83; redevelopment assoc. City of El Cerrito Redevelopment Agency 1983--; awards: academic participant in the Am. Studies Program, Christian Coll. Coalition 1979; appreciation, City of Geneva 1983; mem. Calif. Assn. for Local economic Development; co-author: Neighborhood Related Programs of the Federal Govt.- A HUD Publication, Wash. D.C. 1979; Republican; Christian; rec: cycling, volleyball, softball; Res: 1011 Ygancio Valley Rd, #10 Walnut Creek 94598 Ofc: El Cerrito Redevelopment Agency, 10890 San Pablo Ave El Cerrito 94530

STARK, WILBUR HOWARD, real estate developer; b. Apr 4, 1909, Vallejo; s. John and Isabello Marshall (Young) S.; m. Betty Ann Purser, Apr. 3, 1982; children: Mary Ann., b. 1944; Robert William, b. 1946; edn: Coll. of the Pacific 1929-31; courses 1 & 2, Oakland Realty Bd.; State of Calif. Engring. Contractors lic. 1974; State of Calif. Bldg. Contractors lic. 1974; State of Calif. Real Estate Broker lic. 1937. Career: estab. Accident Dept., Naval Test Stn., Inyokern, Calif. 1945; initiated Ridgecrest Co. Sanitation Dist. 1947; initiated concept of Ridgecrest Co. Water Dist. (later Indian Wells Water Dist.) 1953--; maintained Indian Wells Valley Realty, Ridgecrest 1953--; owner Triangle Mobile Homes, Ridgecrest; co- owner Whispering Winds Mobile Home Park; co- founder Monument Bank, Ridgecrest; pres. No. Mohave Lands, Inc., 1953--; Eastern Kern Co. Resource Dist. (twice pres., now secty./ dir.); pres. Ridgecrest Land & Water Co., Inc. 1969--; v.p. Calif. Realty Assn. 1971; pres. Golden Acres Estates, Inc.; mem: CofC; Sister Cities (Tepatitlan); Desert Empire Bd. of Realtors (charter mem.); Eastern Kern Co. Resource Conservation Dist.; Community Svc. Dist., Inyokern; AARP; Republican; Lutheran; rec: beach comber. Res: POB 463, 242 Lilac St Ridgecrest 93555 Ofc: Indian Wells Valley Realty, 501 Atkins St Ridgecrest

STECHER, MICHAEL JOSEPH, lawyer; b. Feb. 22, 1944, San Francisco; s. Frederick Ralph and Mary Agnes (Rheimers) S.; m. Marian, Nov. 23, 1968; children: Carole, b. 1969, Stacy, b. 1971, Christopher, b. 1973, Matthew, b. 1975, Jennifer, b. 1977; edn: BS, Univ. San Francisco 1966; JD, Golden Gate Univ. 1969. Career: law practice spec. in transp. litigation before Interstate Commerce Commn.; vice pres./secty. Silver, Rosen, Fischer & Stecher profl. law corp., San Francisco, transp. law instr. Golden Gate Univ. 1978-; mem. Assn. of Interstate Commerce Commn. Practitioners 1971-: exec. com. 1979-; pres. 1981; chmn. S.F. Region Chpt. 1977; chmn. Western Transp. Law Seminars 1978, 79); chmn. Motor Carrier Lawyers Assn. 1981 Ann. Conf. Res: 2900 Hillside Dr Burlingame 94010 Ofc: Silver, Rosen, Fischer & Stecher APLC, 100 Bush St, Ste. 410, San Francisco

STEELE, RUTH E. WILSON, real estate broker; b. Oct. 6, 1925, Blue Diamond, KY; d. Sim A. and Margaret Elizabeth (PetRey) Wilson; div.; 1 son: William Arnold; edn: B.Theol., Clarksvill Sch. of Theology 1968, M.Theol., 1976, D.Theol., 1978; ASc, Allan Hancock 1977; AA, 1980; life instr. cert., 1976; real estate broker, State of Calif. 1972. Career: minister 1953--; evangelist, missionary, & pastor, semminaries & lectrs.; pres. Santa Maria Ministeria Assn. 1979-80; chaplain Santa Maria Bd. Realtors 1979-82; state dir. Calif. Assn. of Realtors; instr. Allan Hancock Coll.; sr. pastor, councellor, adminstr. Calvary Temple; honors: 1st Lady Pres. Awd., Santa Maria Ministerial Assn.; mem: Ch. of God; Nat. Assn. Realtors; Calif. Assn. Realtors; Democrat; rec: swimming, biking, tennis. Res: 2633 Ocotillo Santa Maria 93454 Ofc: Linetta Realty, 302 E Chapel Santa Maria 93454 & Calvary Temple, 324 No Suey Rd Santa Maria 93454

STEELE-LANFRANCO, JUDITH LILLIAN, real estate broker; b. Mar. 7, 1940, Seattle, Wash.; d. Robert Eric and Helen Marguerite (McNeal) Heppenstall; div. 1965; m. 2d. Robert Lanfranco, Sept. 30, 1979; children: Michael Steele, b. 1963; Michelle S., b. 1964; Bobby Gene Lanfranco, b. 1980; stepchil: Debra L., b. 1961; Mark L., b. 1962; Scott L., b. 1965; edn; Univ. of Wash. 1958-62; GRI, CSU 1974; MIRM, CSU 1978; real estate salesman lic., Calif. Dept. R.E. 1969; real estate broker lic., Calif. Dept. R.E. 1976. Career: sales assoc. Time Real Estate, Inc., Orange 19469-74; sales assoc. Red Hill Realty, Tustin 1974-75; sales mgr. M.J. Brock & Sons (200 home subdiv.), Chino 1975-77; sales mgr. M.J. Brock & Sons (100 home subdiv.), Lake Forest 1077-79; sales mgr. Clayton, Clayton & Co., (39 condo subdiv.), Garden Grove 1978; sales mgr. Donald M. Bird Assoc. (3 condo developments), Costa Mesa 1979-80; sales mktg. dir. Starland Devel. Co. (102 ret. home subdiv.), Lakeport 1983--; 23rd Dist. Profl. Stannards Com., East Orange Co. Bd. 1974-; East Or. Co. Bd. Realtors (Multiple Listing Com. 1974; Young Realty Com. 1974-75); awards: Top Salesman & Top Lister of the Month awds., Time Real Estate, Inc. 1970-74; Semi-Annual Listings Awd., Red Hill Realty 1975; Million Dollar Circle Awd., Nat. Home Bldrs. Assn. (sales & mktg. council); Outstanding Recgn., Bldg. Ind. Assn. of Calif. (sales & mktg.); mem: E Orange Co., & Saddleback Valley Bds. Realtors; Nat. & Calif. Assn. Realtors; sales & mktg. council, Nat. Home Bldrs. Assn. & Bldg. Ind. Assn. of Calif. 1970-79; PTA; Lakeport & Lake Co. CofC; Lakeport Beautification Com.; US Defense Com.; Republican Nat. Com.; Lake Co. Women In Bus. Club; Lake Co. Hist. Soc.; Republican; Catholic; rec: interior decorating, gourmet cooking, law study. Res: 3645 Lakeshore Blvd Lakeport 95453 Ofc: Westlake Homes & Marina, 212 Marina Dr S, Lakeport 95453

STEFFENS, ARTHUR JOHN, JR., stockbroker; b. July 17, 1920, Cleveland, Oh.; s. Arthur John and Josephine (Paladino) S.; m. Doris Spies 1942, dec. 1965; m. 2d. H. Carol Beresford, Oct. 4, 1969; children: Laura, b. 1952, Gregory, b. 1955, Guy J., b. 1970; edn: BBA, Western Reserve Univ. 1948; Harvard Grad. Sch. of bus. 1949, 1966; Cleveland Coll. Grad. Sch. 1950. Career: regional sales mgr. Osborn Mfg., Charlotte, N.C. 1949-58; regl. sales mgr. Stanley Works, Atlanta, Ga., Dallas, Tx., San Francisco, Ca. 1958-68; account exec. Merrill Lynch, Pierce, Fenner & Smith, Inc. San Jose, 1968--; honors: Citizen of the Year 1982, Optimist Clubs of San Jose; Omicron Delta Kappa nat. hon. 1947; mem: Southeastern Travelers Club; S.F. Pot & Kettle Club 1966-68; Phi Soc., Delta Kappa Epsilon Frat.; Lambda Iota Delta engr. frat.; Project Business (tch. bus. on vol. basis to 8th graders); Am. Legion; Disabled Am. Vets; Elks; Optimists Intl. (past pres. San Jose Club 1981-2; lt. gov. Zone 9, 1983-4); secty. Optimist Volunteers for Youth (dir. Boysville Camp); v.p. Lincoln Glen Little League; orgnzr. annual No./So. Santa Clara Co. high schs. soccer tournament 1981; bus. cons. for Junior Achievement; Republican; Catholic; rec: youth coaching baseball, soccer, football. Res: 6142 Valley Glen Dr San Jose 95123 Ofc: Merrill Lynch, 95 So. Market St, Ste. 202, San Jose 95113

STEIGER, JOANN MC KENNA, financial services executive; b. May 24, 1943, Newark, NJ; d. John J. and Rae D. (Wolf) McKenna; m. Paul E. Steiger, Aug. 29, 1964; children: Erika Maven, b. 1967; Laura Arlene, b. 1970; edn: BA, Harvard (Radcliffe) 1965; M.Ed., UCLA, 1969; Ed.D., UCLA, 1973. Career: mgr. So. Calif. Group Field Office, Manufacturers Life Ins. Co., 1983--; dir. ops. Mgmt. Compensation Group, L.A. 1982-83; acct. exec. Merrill Lynch, Pierce, Fenner and Smith Inc., L.A. 1979-82; founder/pres. Steiger, Fink and Kosecoff Inc. (consulting firm in edn. and health pgm. evaluation), Los Angeles and McLean, Va. 1974-79; dir. Plnng. and Eval., Nat. Adv. Council on Vocational Edn., Wash DC 1972-74; Career Edn. Intern, US Ofc. of Edn., Wash DC 1971-72, elem. school tchr. Calif. and Conn., 1965-69; recipient grad. fellowship, Economic Edn. Council 1972; mem. Western Pension Conf., Harvard-Radcliff Club of So. Calif. (treas. 1982-3), Univ. Club, Stock Exchange Club; publs: contbr. US House of Rep. Hearings on elem. and voc. edn. (1975); film strip (NEA 1974); var. govt. agcy. publs.; rec: flute, tennis. Res: 1425 Brinkley Ave Los Angeles 90049 Ofc: Manufacturers Life, 3250 Wilshire Blvd, Ste. 1404, Los Angeles 90010

STEIGER, LEE, manufacturing co. controller; b. Jan. 26, 1947; s. Benjamin Franklin and Louise Ann (Samul) S.; edn: BA, Cornell 1971; MBA, Wharton 1975. Career: controller Sargent Industries, Kahr Bearing Div., Burbank; mil: 2nd Lt., USAR; LDS; rec: banjo, guitar, basketball, swimming. Res: 1347 Atchison Pasadena 91104 Ofc: Sargent Industries, 3010 No San Fernando Blvd Burbank 91503

STEIKUNAS, JONAS ALGIRDAS, architect; b. May 5, 1918, Lithuania; s. Jonas and Izabella (Czerwenka) S.; m. Birute, Aug. 17, 1946; children: Dalia, b. 1948; Daina, b. 1952; Dobilas, b. 1960; Laima, b. 1962; edn: dip., Univ. of Graz, Austria 1946; M. Urban Design & Town Plng., 1946; Univ. of Vytautas the Great, Kaunas, Lithuania 1935-38, 1941-44; lic. architect, Calif. State Bd. of Architectural Examiners 1978. Career: architect Co. Architect's Ofc., Southampton, Gr. Britian 1947-49; partner/ architect Struct. Engineer, Buenos Aires, Argentina, So. Am. 1949-59; proj. capt./ acting proj. architect Welton Becket Assocs., Architects & Engrs. 1961-73; practicing architect, self- empl.; sr. engr./ proj. architect C.F. Braun Engring. Co. 1974-79; sr. architect Parsons Co. 1980-82; awards: first prize, public competition, design of Cultural Exhibit stand, Lithuania 1943; hon. mention, public competition for design of monument for Lithuanian Martyrs 1942; mem: AIA (Pasadena & Foothill chptrs.); Am.- Lithuanian Engrs. & Architects Soc. (L.A. chpt.); Am.- Lithuanian Nat. Soc. (L.A.); mil: reserve ofcr. pilot, Ind. Lithuanian Air Force 1939-40; Republican; Catholic; rec: soaring, chess, music. Address: 1930 Canyon Dr Los Angeles 90068

STEIN, MARGUERITE BLACKWELL, lawyer; b. Oct. 16, 1924, Evanston, Ill.; d. George Robert and Marguerite Loyola (Keegan) Blackwell; m. Alfred Ferdinand Stein, Sept. 3, 1950, div. 1962; children: Janet Loyola (Spirer); Laur F.; Frederick T.; Karen E.; Christopher B.; edn: Hunter Coll. 1940-46; Fordham Univ. 1948-50; BS, Univ. of San Francisco 1960; JD, Univ. of San Diego 1966; admitted Calif. Bar 1967; US Dist. Ct. 1967; Career: secty. W.R. Grace Co., NYC 1942-44; ofcl. reporter war crimes trial & ct. martial, US Army, Italy, Austria, Germany 1946-48; secty. to atty. P. Zimet, NYC 1948-50; ct. reporter N.C., Ore., VA, DC, NY, NJ, & CA 1950-67; deputy dist. atty. San Diego Co. 1967-75; deptuy co. counsel, Napa Co. 1981--; instr. Southwestern Jr. Coll., Chula Vista 1968-79, San Diego Evening Coll. 1968-79; Calif. Western Univ. Sch. Law, San Diego 1974-75; pres. So. Bay Cities League of Women Voters, San Diego Co. 1973-74; bd. dirs. Family Svc. No. Co., San Diego 1958-59; Marian H.S. 1971-73; Adult Protective Svcs., San Diego 1971-79; Evening Coll. Found. 1973-76; mem: Am. Legion (post comdr.); Bus. & Profl. Women; AAUW; Soroptimist Internat.; Am. Bus. Womens Assn.; Calif. Ct. Reporters Assn.; San Diego Co., South Bay, Napa Co. Bar Assns.; Lawyers Club of San Diego; Calif. Trial Lawyers Assn.; Chula Vista CofC; Phi Alpha Delta; Phi Delta Delta; ed. San Diego Law Rev. 1965-66; mil: USNR 1944-46; Catholic Daus. Am. Res: 33 Belvedere Ct Napa 94559 Ofc: 1195 Third St Napa 94559

STEIN, STEVEN PAUL, lawyer; b. Nov. 5, 1952, Stockton; s. Leopold and Hilda (Thalheimer) S.; edn: BA, USC 1974; JD, Univ. of LaVerne 1977. Career:

practicing atty. Samuel Shore, Esq., Los Angeles 1981; currently, pvt. practice Steven Stein, Esq. (personal injury & landlord-tenant law), Stockton; awards: Stockton Police Dept. Awd. for Heroic Rescue 1983; mem: Calif. Trial Lawyers Assn.; San Joaquin Co. Bar Assn.; La Verne Law Review; LaVerne Law Student Body Assn. (v.p.); Yosemite Club, Stockton; Boys Club, Stockton; publs: art. on no-fault ins., CTLA Journ. 1973; Jewish; rec: reading, tennis, coin collection. Res: 3525 W Benjamin Holt Dr, No 1, Stockton 95209 Ofc: Steven Stein, Atty. at Law, 11 So San Joaquin St, Ste 911, Stockton 95202

STEINBERG, DAVE SOLOMON, electromechanical engineer; b. Oct. 6, 1923, Chgo.; s. Harry P. and Tillie (Solomon) S.; m. Annette Shapiro, June 29, 1958; children: Cori, b. 1959; Stacie, b. 1962; edn: BSME, Ill. Inst. of Tech. 1948; Ill. Inst. of Tech. 1948-49; reg. P.E., Mich. 1952, NY 1956, NJ 1973. Career: design engr. Pioneer Engring., Detroit, Mich. 1950-55; design engr. Lehigh Engring., NY 1955-60; design engr. Arde Engring., Newark, NJ 1960-69; gp. leader Singer Kearfott, Wayne, NJ 1969-79; mgr. M.E. dept. Litton GCS, Woodland Hills 1979--; pres. Steinberg & Assoc. 1975--; visiting prof. Univ. of Wisc., Wilwaukee Ext. 1977--; tchr. Cont. Edn. State of NJ 1971-79; chmn. Inst. of Environmental Scis. Sem. on Random Vibration 1982; chmn. McDonnel Douglas Automation Sem. on Finite Element Computer Modeling 1982; fellow, IES 1983; mem: Inst. on Environmental Scis.; Boys Club; Model Airplane Club; patent: electric lift truck author: Vibration Analysis for Electronic Equipment, John Wiley & Sons 1973; Cooling Techniques for Electronic Equipment, John Wiley & Sons 1980; 24 publs.; mil: Capt., bomber pilot, US Army Air Corps 1942-45, Air Medal w/ 2 Oak Clusters; Jewish; rec: model airplanes, weight lifting, jogging. Res: 3410 Ridgeford Dr Westlake Vill 91361 Ofc: Litton GCS, 5500 Canoga Ave Woodland Hills 91365

STEINHOFF, H(AROLD) RICHARD, real estate broker; b. Feb. 2, 1936, Cuba City, Wisc.; s. Harold Ludwig and Kathlyn Annette (Waterman) S.; children: Richard Robert, b. 1958; Nina Leone, b. 1964; edn: cert. in indsl. rels., UCLA 1970; BS, Mgmt. Sci., SCU Long Beach 1974. Career: asst. pgm. mgr. Aerojet Corp., Azusa 1969-72; mgr. pgm. admin. Collins Radio, Newport Beach 1972-76; dir. fin. & admin. Irvine Sensors Corp., Irvine 1976-78; dir. Digital Datacom, Irvine 1978-80; pres. & dir. The Business Group, Newport Beach 1978-80; broker/ owner ERA, Main Street Realty 1980--; v.chmn. ERA of Orange Co.; awards: top producer, Irvine CofC 1983; mem: Phi Eta Sigma, Internat. Entrepreneur Assn.; Irvine Bd. Realtors; Calif. Assn. Realtors; Nat. Assn. Realtors; Irvine CofC (membership com.); mil: USMCR 1958-64; Republican; rec: tennis, sailing, chess. Ofc: ERA- Main Street Realty, 4482 Barranca Pkwy Irvine 92714

STEINMAN, MORTON HARRY, editor, lawyer, educator, musician; b. Apr. 28, 1950, Boston, MA; s. Nathan and Rosa (Palenker) S.; m. Heddy Soski, Aug. 19, 1978; edn: BA, UCLA 1972; JD, Southwestern Univ. Sch. of Law 1975; Calif life. comm. coll. tchg. cred. (law) 1979; admitted to State Bar of Calif. 1976, US District Ct., Central Dist. of Calif. 1976, US Ct. of Appeals, Ninth Circuit 1971, US Supreme Ct. 1980. Career: profl. accordionist (live concerts, radio and t.v.) Boston, Mass. and Los Angeles, 1956--; pvt. practice law, Morton H. Steinman, Esq., Los Angeles 1976--; founder/ owner/ instr. Morton Steinman Seminars, 1981--; editor Weekly Law Digest, Daily Journal Company, L.A. 1982--, head Legal Publs. Dept., 1983--; settlement officer/ overseer of settlemt. ofcrs., L.A. Municipal Ct., 1977-78, judge pro tem, 1981-; law prof. Univ. of West Los Angeles Sch. of Law, 1976-80, Northrop Univ. Sch. of Law 1980-; guest lectr. in law, USC Law Ctr., Southwestern Univ. Sch. of Law, L.A. County Pub. Defender's Ofc., var. high schs.; awards: Am. Jurisprudence Awd., remedies, 1975; svc. awds., L.A. Municipal Ct./L.A. Co. Bar Assn., and Century City Bar Assn. Mem: Am., Los Angeles Co., Beverly Hills, Century City Bar Assns.; Calif., L.A. Trial Lawyers Assns.; US Supreme Ct. Hist. Soc.; publs: contbr. Northrop Univ. Law Jour. of Aerospace, Energy, and the Environment; Democrat; Jewish; rec: music, hiking, water sports, travel. Res: 6624 McLennnan Ave Van Nuys 91406 (POB 8092, V.N. 91409) Ofc: Morton H. Steinman, Legal Publs. Dept., Daily Journal Co., 210 S Spring St (POB 54026) Los Angeles 90054

STEINMETZ, ARTHUR FRANK, ophthalmologist; b. Oct. 25, 1903, Indian Falls, Ind.; s. Henry S. and Hattie (Hauser) S.; m. Kathleen Cunningham, Jan. 29, 1980; edn: MD, Indiana Univ. 1929; res. Univ. of Alabama 1950; post grad. tng. Munich, New Delhi, Chgo., Portland, Maine; MD, FACS. Career: practice ophthalmology 1950-69; tchr. Alameda Co. Hosps.; honors: John & Arthur Steinmetz Eye Clinic, Vespir Hosp., San Leandro; mil: Cmdr., USMC; Republican; Lutheran; rec: swimming, gardening. Res: 2585 Humbolt Dr San Leandro 94577

STEPHENS, DON RICHARDS, bank chairman of the board- chief executive officer; b. June 28, 1938, San Francisco; s. Donald Lewis and Anona Marie (O'Leary) S.; m. Christina Brinkman, Sept. 11, 1971; children: Lane Brinkman, b. 1975; Justin Hunnicutt, b. 1976; Nicholas Wathne, b. 1979; Adam Haworth, b. 1981; edn: BS, USC 1961; JD, Hasting Coll. of Law 1969. Career: pres. Campodonico & Stephens, comml. real estate brokerage 1963-65; pres. Union Investment Co., owner Cooperage Restaurant 1966-69; lawyer Law Ofcs. D.R. Stephens 1976-80; pres. Stephens & Co. 976--; chmn. bd./ CEO/ principal The Bank of S.F.; dir. WI Forest Prods. (formerly Pack River Co.); dir. Adv. Med. Concepts; dir. Skouras Pictures, Beverly Hills; mem. Young Pres. Orgn.; bd. mem./ dir. San Francisco CofC; mem: Bohemian Club; Calif. Tennis Club; Meadowood Country Club; Republican; Presbyterian; rec: skiing, tennis. Res: 220 Sansome St, 2nd Flr, San Francisco 94104 Ofc: The Bank of S.F., Pine & Sansome St, San Francisco 94104

STEPHENSON, GERALD LANE, dentist; b. Sept. 16, 1952, Alma, Nebr.; s. Gerald Dwayne and Lois Jean (Carpenter) S.; edn: Millsaps Coll. 1970-71; Northeast LA State Univ. 1971-73; DDS, L.S.U. Sch. of Densistry 1977. Career: gen. dentist Indian Health Council, Inc., Pauma Valley; gen. dentist, pvt., San Diego Co. 1981-82; asst. dental ofcr., USNR 1977-81; comdg. ofcr. NAS0194 Dental, No. Island, Coronado 1983--; VFW Citizenship Awd. 1967; C. Edmund Hon. Soc. 1977; Acad. of Gen Dentistry Awd. 1977; mem: Paul Revere Study Club; Ed Nutting Edodontic Seminar; San Diego Jr. CofC; Assn. of Mil. Surgeons of the US; Holiday Proj.; Jerry Cole- Whittaker Ministries; mil: Lcdr., USNR-R 1973-83, Expert Marksman, 10 Yr. Reserve duty; Relig. Sci.; rec: running, skiing, scuba. Res: 1841 Fleetwood St Escondido 92025 Ofc: Indian Health Council, POB 406 Pauma Valley 92061

STERLING, JOHN EWART WALLACE, university chancellor; b. Aug. 6, 1906, Linwood, Ontario, Canada; nat. U.S. cit., 1947; s. The Rev. William and Anna (Wallace) Sterling; Edn: BA, Univ. of Toronto, 1927; MA, Univ. of Alberta, 1930; PhD, Stanford Univ., 1938; LLD, hon., Pomona Coll., 1949; LLD hon., Occidental Coll., 1949; LLD, hon., Univ. of San Francisco, 1950; LLD, hon., Univ. of Toronto, Can., 1950; DCL, hon., Durham Univ., Engl., 1953; LLD, hon. Univ. of Caen, France, 1957; LLD, hon., Univ. of Brit. Columbia, Northwestern Univ. and Univ. of CA, 1958; hon. Litt.D, USC, 1960; hon LLD, Univ. of Denver, Loyola Univ. and McGill Univ., Can., 1961; Columbia Univ. 1962, St. Mary's Coll., 1962; Univ. of Santa Clara, 1963; McMaster Univ., 1966; m. Ann Marie Shaver, 1930; chil: William, b. 1939; Susan, b. 1941; Judith, b. 1944. Career: lectr. in history, Regina Coll., Saskatchewan, 1927-28; instr. in hist., ath. coach, Univ. of Alberta, 1928-30; research asst., Hoover Lib., Stanford Univ., 1932-37; instr. in hist., Stanford Univ., 1935-37; asst. prof. of Hist., CA Inst. of Tech., Pasadena, 1937-40; assoc. prof., 1940-42; secty of faculty, 1941-44; prof., 1942-45; chmn. of faculty, 1944-46; E.S. Harkness Prof. of Hist. and Govt., 1945-48; dir., Huntington Lib. and Art Gallery, San Marino, 1948-49; news analyst, CBS, 1942-48. Mem: resident civilian faculty, Natl. War Coll., Wash., D.C., 1947-48; 5th Pres., Stanford Univ., 1949-68; chancellor, 1968---; trustee, 1969-76; chmn., Amer. Rev. Bicent. Commn., Wash., D.C., 1969-70; chmn. bd. dirs., Stan. Research Inst., 1949-66; ret. former bd. dirs., Fireman's Fund Amer., Shell Oil Co., Dean Witter Reynolds, Kaiser Alum. & Chem. Corp. Co-editor, vol. in Hoover Instn. series, 1932-37. Honors: Hon. Knight Comdr., Order of Brit. Empire, 1976; Dist. Cit. Award by Palo Alto CofC, 1959; Comdr's Cross of Order of Merit Fed. Repub. of Germ., 1959; Chevalier de la Legion d'Honneur, France, 1960; 2nd Degree Imperial Order of Rising Sun, Japan, 1961; Grand Gold Badge of Honor for Merits to Repub. of Austria, 1965; Clark Kerr Award, Academic Senate, UC Berkeley, 1969; Uncommon Man Award, Stanford Assocs., 1978. Mem: Amer. Geog. Soc., fellow; Amer. H ist. Assn.; Pac. Coast Hist. Assn.; Canadian Hist. Assn.; Council on Foreign Rels., Inc.; World Affair Council of No. CA; Commonwealth; Bohemian; Pacific-Union; Burlingame Country; The Family; Univ. Clubs of Palo Alto, San Fran., NY, L.A., hon.; CA, Sunset, L.A. Res: 2220 Stockbridge Ave., Woodside 94062; Office: Office of the Chancellor, P.O. Box 5096, Stanford 94305.

STERN, ARTHUR P., engineer, business executive; b. July 20, 1925, Budapest, Hungary; s. Leon and Bertha (Frankfurter) Stern; Edn: dip., Swiss Fed. Inst. of Tech., 1948; MSEE, Syracuse Univ., NY, 1956; m. Edith Marguerite Samuel, 1952; chil: Daniel, b. 1954; Claude, b. 1955; Jacqueline, b. 1958. Career: research engr., Jaeger Inc., Basel, Switz., 1948-50; instr., Swiss Fed. Inst. of Tech., 1950-51; engr., Gen. Elec. Co., 1951-57; mgr., Electronic Devices Lab., 1957-61; dir., Engr. Electronics Div., Martin Marietta Corp., 1961-64; dir. opns., Def. Systems Div., Bunker-Ramo Corp., 1964-6; v.p., gen. mgr., adv. prod. div., Magnavox Co., 1966-79; pres., Magnavox Adv. Prods. and Sys. Co., 1980---. Mem: fellow, IEEE, 1962; fellow, Amer. Assn. for the Adv. of Sci., 1982. Author 20 tech. and sci. articles; co-author, 2 tech. books; 12 US and several foreign patents. Mem: chmn., engring. div., United Jewish Appeal, Syracuse, NY, 1955-57; gen. cmn., Internatl. Solid State Circuits Conf., 1960; dir., IEEE, 1970---, secty. 1972, treas. 1973, v.p. 1974, pres. 1975, served approx. 20 electronics engring. coms. Res: 606 N. Oakhurst Dr., Beverly Hills 90210; Office: 2829 Maricopa St., Torrance 90503.

STERN, TAMAS GEORGE, insurance co. executive; b. Aug. 24, 1945, Budapest, Hungary; nat. 1967; s. Bela and Veronica (Weisz) S.; m. Magdalena Mark, June 19, 1971; children: Adam, b. 1973, Jennifer, b. 1976; grad. No. Hollywood H.S. 1963. Career: mil. computer pgmmr. 1963-65, systems pgmmr. 1965-68; computer opr. Nat. Auto & Casualty Ins. Co., Los Angeles 1968-69, asst. data proc. mgr. 1969, systems pgmmr. 1971-76; sr. systems pgmmr. Certified Life Ins. Co., Sherman Oaks 1976-80; sr. systems pgmmr. Zenith Ins. Co., Encino 1980-82, asst. vice pres. 1982--; mem. Data Proc. Mgrs. Assn. 1983-, cubmaster BSA 1981-; mil: Sp6 US Army 1963-68, GCM, Presdtl. Unit Citation; Republican; Jewish; rec: soccer, football, tennis. Res: 6923 Burnet Ave Van Nuys 91405 Ofc: Zenith Insurance Co. 15760 Ventura Blvd Encino 91436

STERN, WOLF HARRY, lawyer, financial executive; b. May 28, 1923, Gelsenkirchen, Germany; nat. 1942; s. Morris and Johanna (Loeb) S.; Edn: BA, UCLA, 1947; LLB, JD, USC, 1950; m. 2d., Alban Ann Weiss, June 13, 1982; children: Lawrence Alan, b. 1952, Douglas Wayne, b. 1953, William Rodney, b. 1955. Career: senior partner law firm Stern & Goldstock, Newport Beach, 1950--; pres. Bellflower Investment Co., 1964--; partner S & S Properties, Newport Bch. 1965--; partner G & W Properties, Newport Bch. 1967--; partner Norwalk Law Center, Bellflower 1968--; partner Belco Rentals 1958--; partner Maier, Perlin & Stern, Los Angeles 1970--; v.chmn., adv. bd., Bellflower Natl. Bank, 1962-64, dir. 1964-65; dir. Calif. Pacific Bank, 1969-77; dir. Garden State Bank, 1973-76; v. chmn. Cerritos Valley Bank, 19747-80; chmn. Bellflower Svgs. & Loan, now Equitable Svgs. & Loan, 1977--. Honors: Young Man of Year, City of Bellflower 1954. Mem: Am., Calif., Orange County, Long Beach, Downey-Los Cerritos bar assns., Am. Trial Lawyers Assn., Bellflower Jr. CofC (pres. 1956), Bellflower Lions Club (pres. 1954, 58), Bellflower Elks Lodge, Bellflower CofC, VFW, Lions Internat. (Dist. Gov. 1965-66), Bellflower Coordinating Council (pres. 1953), Compton Bar Assn. (treas. 1956), Costa Mesa Newport Harbor Lions Club 1982-, Newport Irvine Profl. Assn. 1982-, Balboa Bay Club (Newport Beach); mil: sgt. AUS Signal Corps, 3 Battle Stars; Jewish, pres. Bellflower-Lakewood Jewish Community Ctr., 1952; rec: photog., travel. Res: 49 Southampton Ct Newport Beach 92660 Ofc: Stern & Goldstock, 500 Newport Center Dr Ste. 400, Newport Beach 92660

STERNBACH, HARVEY ALLEN, psychiatrist, b. Sept. 16, 1951, NY, NY; s. Sidney and Martha Sternbach; m. Laura, Jan. 6, 1980; edn: BA in psychobiology, NY Univ. 1973; MD, Rutgers Med. Sch.; Physician lic. Calif. 1978, NJ 1981. Career: med. intern, psychiat. residency, Wadsworth VA Hosp., UCLA Neuropsychiat. Inst., 1977-81; co-dir. Outpatient Dept., Fair Oaks Hosp., Summit, NJ 1981-82; adj. asst. prof. psychiat. UCLA 1982-; staff mem./psychiatrist St. Johns Hosp., Santa Monica; ms. reviewer, psychiatry research 1982, 83; mem: Am. Psychiatric Assn., So. Calif. Psychiatric Soc., Internat. Soc. of Psychoneuro- endocrinology, Am. Acad. Clin. Psychiatrists; num. med. journal articles; rec: collector antique med./psychiat. books, sports. Ofc: Harvey A. Sternbach, MD, 11645 Wilshire Blvd, Ste. 901, Los Angeles CA 90025

STEVENS, BERNARD RICHARD, heating and air conditioning business owner; b. Feb. 9, 1929, London, England; s. Archibald Richard and Florence Carolyn (Kemp) S.; div.; children: Dianne, b. 1958, Mark, b. 1956. Career: came to USA in 1963, empl. with Raychem Corp., Menlo Park 15 years, with Union Local 393 one year; estab. own htg. & air conditioning bus., Cupertino 1976--; honors: American and World Record Mile Relay 50-59 Division 1948; Coronation Medal Award 1953; mem. West Valley Track Club; mil: cpl. Brit. Army Tank Corps 1950-52; rec: track. Address: Stevens, 7610 Kirwin Lane, Cupertino 95014

STEVENS, PHILLIP JOSEPH, company president; b. Jan. 17, 1929, Los Angeles; s. Joseph Andrew and Mildred (Adler) S.; m. Joan Scudder, Dec. 6, 1952; children: Gregory, b. 1953, Kimberly, b. 1960, Sherri, b. 1962; edn: BS eng., UCLA 1951, MS, 1958; Calif. State lic. contractor. Career: head Rocket Engine Design Grp. Hughes Aircraft Co., 1951-57; pgm. dir. Minuteman III Pgm., TRW Systems Inc., located at Norton AFB, Ca. 1957-69; pres./bd. chmn. Ultrasystems Inc., Irvine 1969--; Patentee, advanced rocket engine design; awards: Conservation Service awd. US Dept. of Interior; Ballistic Missile Divs. Comdrs. awd., Outstanding Achievement awd., USAF; mem: Am. Inst. of Aero. and Astro., American Indian Sci. and Engring. Soc.; founder Orange Co. Perf. Arts Center; Prot.; rec: skiing, tennis. Ofc: Ultrasystems Inc. 16845 Von Karman Ave Irvine 92715

STEVENS, PHYLLIS ERNESTINE, educator; b. Mar. 8, 1915, Radville, Sask., Canada, nat. 1962; d. Ernest Wesley and Frances Ann (Crane) Hinkson; m. Edmund Guise Stevens, Oct. 21, 1949; children: Ernest Edmund b. 1951, Brian Frederick b. 1953; edn: BS, early childhood edn., Tchrs. Coll. Columbia Univ. 1947, MA, supvn. of edn., 1949; sectl. cert. Balfour Tech. Sch. (Regina, Sask.) 1932, First Class cert. Regina Normal Sch. 1933; Calif. (life dip.) Educator, Kindergarten Primary 1963. Career: tchr. Early Childhood Edn., Rural Schs., Sask. Can. 1933-35, Regina (Sask. Can.) Public Schs., 1935-44, Kensington, Md. and Rockville S.D., Md. 1947, Carpinteria (Calif.) Unif. School Dist., 1959-69, Santa Barbara City Schs., 1969-75, ret. 1975; dir. Art Contests, Carpinteria Schs. 1978-80, Performing Arts chpsn. 2 yrs.; mem. Calif. Retired Teachers Assn., Nat. Retired Tchrs. Assn., AARP, Santa Barbara Woman's Club, Carpinteria Woman's Club 1975-83; afiliate Pritikin Better Health Pgm. 1984; afil. UC Santa Barbara 1980-84, Teacher's Coll. Columbia Univ. N:YC 1950, International House NYC 1950; secty. Methodist Board of Missions, NYC 1949; mil: Leading Wren, Women's Royal Canadian Naval Service 1944-45; Democrat; Prot.; rec: health oriented pgms. Res: 1350 La Manida Carpinteria 93013

STEVENSON, BARRY JOSEPH, real estate broker; b. Sept. 14, 1940, Santa Rosa; s. Joseph Samuel and Helen Marie (Brady) S.; m. Alicia Cerda, Aug. 12, 1972; children: Darren, b. 1973, Sabrina, b. 1978; edn: AA, Santa Rosa Jr. Coll. 1961; BA, San Jose St. Univ. 1964; real estate cert. Pierce Coll. 1977; Calif. lic. R.E. Broker and Notary 1978. Career: broker assoc. Forrest E. Olson Realtors, Simi Valley 1978-80; broker/ mgr./ partner #1 Realty, Intl. Real Estate Network, 1981-82; owner/ broker/ pres. #1 Homes of California (real estate brokerage), Simi Valley 1983--; awards: pres. Santa Rosa Choral Group 1958, Arion Award for Music 1958; Million Dollar Club (R.E.) 1979-81, Multi-Million Club 1982-83; mem: Simi Valley Board of Realtors, Conejo Valley & San Fernando MLS; pres., chief photog. City Coll. of San Francisco 1965, San Jose State Alumnus 1965; winner SDSU 2d prize for photog. 1963; mil: Sp5, Calif. Army Nat. Guard 1964-70; Republican; Prot.; rec: writing, photog. Res: 1453 Branch Ave Simi Valley 93065 Ofc: #1 Homes of California, 5775 Los Angeles Ave Ste. 115 Simi Valley 93063

STEWART, JAMES ROCKWELL, architect; b. July 29, 1950, Los Angeles; s. Roscoe Orrin and Charlotte Ann (Redheffer) S.; edn: BS Arch., USC 1972, M.Arch., 1974; Architect, State of Calif. 1977. Career: during college empl. with Ralph M. Parsons, Pasadena 1969-70, Carl Day, AIA, Santa Monica 1971-76; arch./assoc. vice pres. Flood, Meyer, Sutton & Assoc., Santa Monica

1976--; ind. cons. residential design projects; designer/devel. single family residences spec. beachfront homes; awards: Builders Choice - Seascape 3 Redondo Beach, Merit Award; mem: Architectural Guild, Am. Inst. of Architects (Nat., Calif., L.A. Chpt.); club: Santa Monica Beach (bd. Bldg. Com.); publs: Sunset Mag., Metropolitan Home; Episcopal; rec: tennis, skiing, hiking. Ofc: Flood, Meyer, Sutton & Assoc. 1408 Santa Monica Mall Santa Monica 90401

STEWART, MARIANNE, traffic/distribution management exec.; b. Oct. 25, 1942, Stubenville, Ohio; d. James and Marcella A. (Kukulski) Marovich; m. James Stewart, May 1, 1964; children: Steven James, b. 1965, Cynthia Dawn, b. 1968; edn: Fullerton Coll. 1960-62. Career: credit, Hunt Wesson Foods, Fullerton 1961-66, Placentia Unified Sch. Dist. Fairmont Elem. Sch., Yorba Lina, 1975-79; traffic mgmt. Packers Cold Storage, Fullerton 1979; distribution mgr. Packers Cold Storage, La Habra 1979--; Republican; rec: swimming, gardening. Res: 19758 Segovia Ln Yorba Linda 92686 Ofc: Packers Cold Storage, 1111 Harbor Blvd La Habra 90631

STEWART, THOMAS LLOYD, county supervisor; b. Feb. 2, 1928, Los Angeles; s. Ernest John and Margaret Mary (Hein) S.; m. Brenda Yvonne Lamont, Jan. 31, 1948; children: Randall, b. 1949, Coleen, b. 1952, Jeffrey, b. 1966; edn: L.A. Harbor Coll. 1949-50; Calif. lic. real estate broker. Career: constrn. bus. in No. Calif. and Nev. 1950-53; real estate sales agt. Hughes Realty, South Lake Tahoe 1954-55; R.E. broker/prin. South Lake Tahoe 1956-69; elected county supr. 5th Dist., El Dorado County (now serving 4th four year term), 1970--; mem. (chmn. 1974) Calif. Tahoe Regl. Plnng. Agcy Govg. Bd. 1971-81; mem. (chmn. 1974-75)Tahoe Regl. Plnng. Agcy. Govg. Bd. 1971-; dir. S. Lake Tahoe Pub. Util. Dist. 1962-66; chmn. El Dorado Co. Echo Summit Tunnel Auth. 1971-; mem. El Dorado Co. Water Agcy 1971-; bd. dirs. Tahoe Transp. Dist. Bd. 1982-; Tahoe Resources Conservation Dist. Council 1982-; Gov. apptd. mem. to Cov's Advisory Council 1982-; mem. County Supervisors Assn. of Calif.; mem. Optimists, Elks, Am. Legion, Humane Soc., S. Lake Tahoe Hist. Soc.; mil: machinist mate 2c USN 1945-49; Republican; Catholic; rec: gardening, fishing. Res: POB 7275, South Lake Tahoe 95731 Ofc: El Dorado Co. Bd. of Supervisors, 330 Fair Lane, Placerville 95667

STEWART, WILFORD ROMNEY, retail sales executive; b. Dec. 22, 1946, White Plains, NY; s. Isaac Mitton and June (Woodruff) S.; m. Sonia Franklin, June 25, 1966; children: Patrick, b. 1967, James, b. 1968, Shannon, b. 1972, Somer, b. 1975; edn. BA, Univ. of Redlands, 1968; Calif. real estate sales lic., life/health ins. lic. 1974-. Career: dept. mgr. J.C. Penney Co. in Indio and Palm Springs, 1968-74; founder/chmn. bd. The Instep, Inc. (retail store), Palm Desert 1975--; pres. Stewart-Hoffman, Inc. Laguna Beach 1982--; pres. 4-Seasons, Inc. Palm Desert 1983--; real estate sales assoc. Tom Collins & Assoc., 1978-; sustaining mem. BSA 1982; Republican, Mormon. Res: 75-288 Palm Shadow Dr Indian Wells 92260 Ofc: The Instep, Inc. 73-370 El Paseo, Palm Desert 92260

STIEB, WILMA BEVERCOMBE, community worker; b. Oct. 28, Orient, Iowa; d. Alvin Lester and Ella Elmira (Reed) Bevercombe (both dec.); brother, Gale Reed Bevercombe (dec.); m. Clyde William Stieb, 1944 (dec.); 1 son, Jackson Wm. (dec.); edn: stu. Gregg Bus. Coll., Univ. of Ore., Univ. of Nebr.; BS in edn., Univ. of Idaho, 1931; MA in psychol. (fellowship), 1933. Career: spl. tchr. Bus. Adminstrn. Dept., Univ. of Ida.; secty. Standard Oil Co. of Calif.; secty. PEO Sisterhood, Chpt. NK; biographical listings in Who's Who of Calif. Exec. Women, The Idaho Digest and Blue Book, Who's Who in the World, American Women, Five Hundred First Families of Am.; Family archives record 21 ancestral Coats of Arms; mem. Sons and Daughters First Settlers of Newbury, Newburport, Mass.; mem. Daus. of Amer. Colonists, Daus. of the Amer. Revolution, Magna Charta Sureties (Achois Comihavit Chpt.), Panhellenic Club, Alpha Chi Omega (Xi Chpt.), PEO Sisterhood (NK Chpt.). Author: Occupations in the State of Idaho (1934); Democrat; Christian Ch.; rec: lectures; travel; collector Old Bibles, poetry, and thoughts for special occasions. Res: 15652 Woodvale Rd Encino 91436

STICKEL, JOHN FREDERICK, geologist; b. Aug. 23, 1922, Wash DC; s. John F., Sr. and Dorothy Raye (Keys) S.; m. Vee Henderson Oct. 1966; 1 dau. Jacqueline Elizabeth, b. 1968; edn: BS, West Va. Univ. 1947; MS, Wash. Univ. (St. Louis, Mo.) 1949; Cert. Consulting Geologist, Am. Inst. of Profl. Geol. 1963; Consulting Geologist and Geophysicist, State of Calif. 1965. Career: party chief Frost Geophys. Corp., Galveston, TEx. 1949; partner Wesley, Stickel & Co., Detroit, Mich. 1950-52; engr. in charge of geological and geophysical services, Dames & Moore, Los Angeles 1952-56, associate, 1956-63, chief geophysicist, 1963-67; cons. geologist Stickel & Associates, Inc., Tustin 1967--; mem: AAAS, Am. Geol. Inst., Am. Geophys. Union, Am. Inst. of Mining and Metallurg. Engrs., Am. Water Well Assn., Am. Water Works Assn., Am. Assn. Profl. Geol., Euro. Assn. Exploration Geophysicists, Northwest Mining Assn., Pacific Coast Gas Assn., Soc. Exploration Geophysicists; num. publications, presentations; mil: T/4 Sig. Corp., Inf. Para., Spec. Serv., 1943-46 ETO; Republican; Lutheran; rec: fishing, hunting, boating. Res: 1502 Sierra Alta Santa Ana Ofc: Stickel & Assocs Inc. POB 91, Tustin 92681

STICKELL, VANCE L., marketing executive; b. Feb. 15, 1925, Ong, Nebr.; s. Ora F. and Helen (Swanson) S.; m. Betty Lee Allen, July 11, 1953; edn: BA, DePauw Univ. 1948; Exec. Pgm., UCLA Grad. Sch. of Bus. 1960. Career: Los Angeles Times: mdsg. field trainee, 1948-49; nat. display sales trainee, 1942-55; nat. display sales rep. 1955-56; staff asst, Display, 1956-59; asst. to the advt. mgr., 1959-62; asst. display advt. mgr., 1956-62; display advt. mgr. 1962-68; advt. dir./vice pres. sales, 1968-; exec. vice pres. marketing, 1981--; hon. life mem. INAME, 1976; mem: AAF (chmn. 1983-84), The Advertising Council (bd. dirs.), NAB (chmn. Long Range Plans Com.); Los Angeles Advt. Club; bd. dirs: Crippled Childrens Soc., Skid Row Devel. Corp., Central City Assn., Better Business Bur.; trustee: Barlow Hospiatl, L.A. Times Fund, Am. Red Cross (past pres.); mem. bd. and exec. com. GLAVCB (Facilities com.; past pres.), The Pauma Valley CC, Wilshire CC, Frat. of Friends of the Music Center, Sigma Chi; Rotarian; served in USN; rec: flying, golf. Res: 211 S. Orange Grove Blvd, 8, Pasadena 91105 Ofc: Los Angeles Times, Times Mirror Square, Los ANgeles 90053

STILLMAN, A. WILLIAM, JR., engineer-executive; b. Sept. 11, 1942, Biloxi, Miss.; s. Alfred Wm. and Marie Ann (Hengen) S.; children: Shannon, b. 1975, Laura, b. 1977; edn: AA, American River Coll. 1966; BS in math, Cal Poly State Univ. 1-0, BS, electronic eng., 1970, MS, applied math., 1973; M.Eng., indsl. engring., Texas A&M Univ. 1976; Cert. Profl. Logistician, Soc. of Logistics Engrs. (SOLE), 1980. Career: engineering intern US Army, 1973-75; staff maint. engr. US Army Electronics Command 1975-77; ILS engr. OPM Artads, 1977-79; engrg. mgr. OPM Firefinder, 1979-80; prof. of systems acquisition mgmt., Defense Systems Mgmt. College, 1980-82; principle ILS engr., Northrop Corp., 1982-83; pgm. adminstr., Rockwell Space Group, 1983--; founder/pres. AWS Assocs., Inc. Woodbridge, Va. and AWS Assocs. of Calif., Inc. 1982; co-founder Dawstone, Inc. 1982; Div. pres./corp. v.p. Hope Assocs., Inc. 1983, co-founder/pres. Chicago Motor Works, Inc. 1983; honors: Tau Beta Pi; sr. mem. SOLE, sr. mem. AIE, sr. mem. IEEE, mem. Am. Mgmt. Assn., ADPA, Am. Security Council; num. sci., tech. publs.; mil: sgt. USAF 1962-66; Republican; Presbyterian. Address: AWS Associates, Inc., 16211 Parkside Ln, Ste. 177, Huntington Beach 92647

STINSON, JOHN W., real estate broker; b. May 7, 1929, Pittsburgh, Pa.; s. John W., Sr. and Bertha E. (Small) S.; m. Audrey W. Watt, Nov. 18, 1955; 2 sons, John, b. 1959, Scott, b. 1961; edn: Colby Coll. 1947-49; BA, Univ. of Pittsburgh 1951, MA, 1957; Calif. lic. real estate broker. Career: pres. J & L Investments, San Diego; fin. mgmt. var. firms; instr. real estate fin. seminars; honors: Outstanding Salesman of Year, and Top Listing Salesman; mem. Real Estate Inv. Club, Land Syndication Seminar, Elks, Exchangors Club, CofC; invention: Nodor Air Filter; mil: sgt. USMC 1951-54; Republican; Presbyterian; rec: sport fishing, auto restoration. Res: 4652 Cass St San Diego 92109 Ofc: J & L Investments, 2377 Beryl St San Diego 92109

STITT, CLYDE L(EROY), educator; b. Apr. 21, 1918, Pawnee City, Nebr.; s. Roy Samuel and Rose Alice (Nelson) S.; m. Inge Hess, Dec. 19, 1952 (dec. 1974); children: Gordon, b. 1956, Rene, b. 1960; edn: BS, Columbia Univ. 1949, MA, 1950, PhD, Stanford Univ. 1961; postdoc. wk. University Coll., London 1968, Edinburgh Univ. 1977; Calif. lic. Speech Pathologist 1974-. Career: radio announcer KTUS, Hot Springs, Ark. 1938-40; stage mgr./actor, Kennebunkport, Me. summers 1947, 48; recording supr. for Talking Books, Am. Found. for the Blind, NYC, 1950-51; prof. of speech Dept. Speech and Comm. Studies, San Francisco State Univ., 1952--, dept. chmn. 1965-69; speech cons. Job Corps Tng. Pgm. 1965-67; cons. speech pathology, 1978-82; awards: NIMH Fellowship 1959, Theta Alpha Phi (1942), Kappa Delta Pi (1950); mem: Am. Speech nd Hearing Assn., Calif. Speech & Hearing Assn. (pgm. chmn. 1963-4, Western Speech Comm. Assn. (pgm. chmn. 1964-5), AAUP; First Ch. of Christ, Scientist, San Mateo (First Reader 1979-82); advisor Christian Sci. Orgn. on Campus, 1974-; publs: devel. tests of Auditory Abilities: Phonetic Ability (inner language function) and Interphonemic Identification; research arts. in profl. journals; mil: pfc USMC 1942-45, So. Pac. (original landing on Bougainville); Democrat; rec: photog., travel, computing. Res: 2251 Cobblehill Pl San Mateo 94402 Ofc: San Francisco State Univ. 1600 Holloway Ave San Francisco 94132

ST. JOHN, RICHARD CLARKE, JR., computer systems equipment co. executive; b. Nov. 30, 1946, Mnpls., Minn.; s. Lt. Col. Richard Clarke, Sr., and Irene Ruth (France) St. J.; edn: AA, engr., Coll. of Marin 1966; BA, econ. internat., Sonoma State Univ. 1970; MBA mktg., San Francisco St. Univ. 1972. Career: var. entrepreneurial ventures incl. light mfg., indsl. ultra high pressure water systems dev., durable goods & technology export, crude oil import, 1972-78; prin./v.p. mktg. Support Systems Internat. Corp. (mfr. and worldwide marketer of computer and data comm. interconnect, switching, patching, and test equip.; currently rated 56th fastest growing pvt. co. in US), 1978--; cons. in areas of mktg. and gen. bus. orgn. to high tech. cos.; mem: Am. Electronics Assn., Am. Advt. Fedn.; bd. dirs. Marin Vocational Inst.; bd. dirs. Marin Co. Am. Red Cross; publs: EFT Electronic Funds Transfer for Small Banks (1981), Planning & Building a Local Network (1981) and Update 1984; frequent contbr. & interviewer, computer and bus. publs.; mil: ssgt. (co. 1st sgt.) USAR 1966-72; rec: Sports car road racing, SCCA, series championship titles holder, course record holder. Res: 17 Miramar Ave San Rafael 94901 Ofc: Support Systems International Corp., 150 S. Second St, Executive Bldg, Richmond 94804

STOLLER, MILLAN DANIEL, educator, research scientist; b. Mar. 25, 1903, Czech.; s. Michael and Anna (Sabovik) S.; m. Pauline Botto (dec.), Jan. 1, 1934; children: Janet (Glover), b. 1937; Harold, b. 1941; edn: BS, Grove City Coll. 1933; grad. study Univ. of Penna., W. Va. Univ., Univ. Del.; Sci. Teacher Cert., Penna. Career: acctg. clerk retail coal sales St. Clair (Pa.) Coal Co., 1933-42; asst. elec. engr. Signal Corps, Phila. 1942-48; assoc. prof. elec. engring. Davis & Elkins Coll., Elkins, WV 1948-53; research scientist Ballistic Resrch Labs., Aberdeen Proving Ground, Md. 1953-71; asst. prof. sci. (electronics) Harford Comm. Coll., 1957-63; past pres., chmn. bd. dirs., chief exec. Presbyterian

Beneficial Union (frat. insurance soc.); currently ret. Awards: recognition, Grove City Coll., Grove Presbyn. Ch., Aberdeen, Md.; mem. IEEE, Physical Soc.(past), Rotary, Lyons; pub. sci. papers; Republican; Presbyterian; rec: golf. REs: 3898 San Pablo Ave Oceanside 92056

STOLPE, JUDITH ANN (WILLS), consultant; b. Sept. 19, 1946, St. Paul, Minn.; d. Donald Robert and Anna (Simenuk) (Korolchuk) Wills; m. Richard Henry Stolpe II, July 30, 1971; children: Dawn Elsa, b. 1973, Richard Charles, b. 1974, Peter Kaal, b. 1974; edn: BS, Okla. State Univ. 1969, postgrad. 1971; lic. Secondary Teaching Cert., Okla. 1969, Calif. 1975. Career: math. tchr. Kerr Jr. High Sch., Midwest City, Okla. 1969-70; systems analyst, Okla. State Univ. 1970-72; girl friday, Dr. Bernard Lueck, 1972-75; dir. Math. Evening Sch., Coronado Unified Sch. Dist. 1975-83; owner/pres. End of the Line Race Consulting, 1978--; dir. 1983 Internat. Amateur Athletic Fedn. Women's World 10 KM Championship (Inaugural), Press Venue Chief for 1984 Olympics, dir. Levi-TAC U.S. Runner Ranking Service, 1983-; honors: The Circle of 100 Women (San Diego); mem: The Athletics Cong. of the U.S. 1976-; AAUW 1969-72; NEA 1969-72; publs: Geographical Locations of Minor Sports at the High Sch Level in the U.S., Rocky Mtn. Geograp. Soc. 1970; Republican; Methodist; rec: music. Res: 714 G Ave Coronado 92118 Ofc: End of the Line Race Consulting, 1013 Park Place Coronado 92118

STONE, FRED, artist; b. Apr. 13, 1930, St. Louis, Mo.; s. Sam and Dorothy (Chazen) S.; m. Norma Paley, 1951; children: Laura, b. 1954, Russell, b. 1956; edn: Art Center Sch. 1949-52, Chouinard Art Inst. 1946-48, L.A. City Coll. 1948-49, Otis Art Inst. 1945. Career: muralist (self-empl.) Kramer Stone, Los Angeles, 1959-60; dir. of sales and mktg. Monogram Industries, L.A. 1960-76; self-empl. as painter of Thoroughbred horses, 1976--: One-Two-Three (1978), Kentucky Derby - Seattle Slew (1979), Spectacular Bid (1979), Genuine Risk (1980), The Shoe, 8000 Wins (1981), John Henry, Bill Shoemaker up (1982), The Final Thunder -Man o'War (1983); mil: airman 1/c Air Nat. Guard 1948-58; Jewish. Res: 5911 Colodny Dr Agoura 91301

STONE, RICHARD ALAN, physician; b. Nov. 21, 1942, Cambridge, Mass.; s. Jack David and Gail (Polak) S.; m. Suanne Poteet, Dec. 5, 1982; 2 daus. Lisa, b. 1970, Caroline, b. 1973; edn: AB, Brown Univ. 1964; MD, Tufts Univ. 1970. Career: physician, nephrologist; asst./assoc. prof. of medicine UC San Diego, 1977-79; dir. Hemodialysis & Hypertension, VA Hosp., San Diego 1977-79; chmn. Nephrology Eisenhower Med. Ctr., Rancho Mirage 1979--, chmn. Medicine 1981--; honors: Alpha Omega Alpha 1969; Tufts Med. Alumni Prize Physiology, Anatomy, Pathology, Microbiology; mem. Am. Soc. of Nephrology, Am. Heart Assn., Am. Found. Clin. Res., Nat. Kidney Found.; publs: over 100 med. arts. on high blood pressure and kidney disease; mil: capt. USAR 1970-76; rec: tennis. Res: 45-605 Camino Del Rey Indian Wells 92770

STORY, CHRISTOPHER, VI, chartered life underwriter; b. Sept. 20, 1925, Plainfield, NJ; s. Christopher, V and Charlotte (Ballin) S.; m. Barbara Batt, May 7, 1965; children: Christopher VII, b. 1956, Dawn Michelle, b. 1962 (stepdau.), Tiffany Brooke, b. 1966, Cynthia Ballin, b. 1968, Sabrina Lynn, b. 1968, Heather Elaine, b. 1970; edn: UCLA 1949, Univ. of Mich. 1945-45; CLU, Am. Coll. 1972; Chartered Fin. Cons., Am. Coll. 1984. Career: guest rels. staff Nat. Bdcstg. Co., NY and Hollywood, 1947-49; communications, Metro Goldwyn Mayer, Culver City 1952; life and disability agt., Pacific Mutual Life Ins. Co., Newport Bch. 1956-; regis. rep. Southmark Financial, Long Bch. 1979--; tchr. LUTC Part I, Santa Barbara, 1983; tchr. symphony orch., Santa Barbara Adult Edn. Div.; honors: NQA, Nat. Assn. of Life Underwriters; Century Club (1982) Oppenheimer Mutual Funds; Fgn. Language Medal (1944), Valley Forge Mil. Acad.; mem: Am. Soc. of CLU, Santa Barbara Estate Plnng. Council, Santa Barbara Com. on Fgn. Rels. Channel City Club; past pres. Northside Bus. Assn.; mem. Santa Barbara Apt. Assn., Downtown Optimist Club; past bd. S.B. Ballet Theater; composer: RCA Columbia and MGM recordings; song for Lambda Chi Alpha nat. frat.; founder/condr. West Coast Sym. 1967-; Republican; Protestant. Res: 1812 La Coronilla Dr Santa Barbara 93109 Ofc: Andros & Story, Ste. 10, 1129 State St Santa Barbara

STOTT, KENHELM WELBURN, JR., zoologist, writer; b. Aug. 20, 1920, San Diego; s. Kenhelm W., Sr. and Dorothy Cranston (Hess) W.; div.; edn: BA in zoology, Pomona Coll. 1942; grad. work, San Diego State Univ. 1947-48. Career: curator of mammals and publications San Diego Zoo 1946-48, general curator 1948-54; research assoc. S.D. Natural History Museum 1957-74, Martin & Osa Johnson Safari Mus. 1974-, S.D. Zoological Gardens 1961-62; general curator emeritus San Diego Zoological Gardens, 1982--; life fellow Royal Geographical Soc. 1977; life fellow Calif. Acad. Scis. 1981; hon. trustee Martin & Osa Johnson Safari Mus. 1976; trustee Nat. Underwater & Marine Agcy. 1979; fellow Linnean Soc. of London 1980-; life fellow Explorers Club 1976-; ordinary fellow Zool. Soc. of London 1978; life scientific fellow Zool. Soc. London 1983; Smithsonian Resrch. Collaborator for Sci. Expeditions 1978; US Dept. State cons., West Pacific desk, 1980 (num. other fellowships). Honors: Pijoan Zool. Awd., Pomona Coll. 1941; S.D. Mayor's Commendn. 1954; Cit. of Merit, Explorers Club 1977; Personal Commendn. H.H. the 14th Dalai Lama 1978; Sweeney Medallist, Explorers Club 1980; Commendn. HM Queen Elizabeth II 1980; dedication Stott Explorers Library, Johnson Safari Mus. 1980; Gold Conservation Medal, SD Zool. Soc. 1981. Life memberships: Am. Soc. Mammalogists 1940, Am. Ornith. Union 1944, NY Acad. Scis. 1979, Nature Conservancy 1978, Fauna & Flora Preserv. Soc., London 1957, East Afr. Wildlife Soc. 1957, IUCN (Switz.) 1976, Bronte Soc. (GB) 1976, Bombay Nat. Hist. Soc. 1976, S.D. Nat. Hist. Soc. 1970. Life Endowment mem. Aero-Space Mus. 1978; Life mem. S.D. Mus. of Man. Author 2 books, 2 wildlife field guides, 1 wildlife booklet for city schs.; 3000 articles in sci. journals, popular mags., newspapers (1935-). Mil: Ph.M. 2/c USNR 1942-46, five service medals; Conservative; rec: natural hist., travel observing rare, endangered wildlife: 19 African exped. 1948-, 3 to India, 2 Australia, New Guinea, NZ, 1 to Phil., Madagascar, many to tropical America, 1956 trip down Amazon in dugout. Address: 2300 Front St., Apt. 402, San Diego 92101

STOUT, MARJORIE ANN, hospital administrator; b. Apr. 21, 1939, Oakland; d. Gustav Albert and Roberta Pauline (Leibe) Jergentz; m. Norman David Stout, Nov. 6, 1971; children: Pamela J. Talbot, b. 1960, Wm. A. Talbot, b. 1962; edn: BS, CSU Hayward 1973; dip. recreation therapy, CSUH 1973; lic. nursing home administrator 1982. Career: mgr., swim pools, Hayward Area Rec. Dept., Livermore Area Rec. Dept.; activity dir. Pleasanton Conv. Hosp.; rec. therapist Hacienda Conv. Hosp.; currently hosp. adminstr. Hacienda Conv. Hosp., Hillhaven Conv. Hosp.; Am. Red. Cross water safety instr. (14 yrs.); mem: Assn. of California Health Care Facilities, AAUW, Livermore Hist. Soc.; rec: photog., needlepoint, swimming. Res: 1776 Lomitas Ave Livermore 94550 Ofc: Flagg Industries, Hacienda Conv Hosp., 76 Felton St. Livermore 94550

STOVALL, DANNY FLOYD, developer/real estate broker; b. June 28, 1943, Poway; s. Lloyd G. and Laura Lorraine Stovall; children: Julie, b. 1967, Eric, b. 1971; edn: BA psy., Univ. of N.M. 1965; AA in crim. justice, AA in real estate, Miramar Coll., 1978, 79; Calif. lic. R.E. broker. Career: personal adminstrn. Dynalectron Corp., Land-Air Div., H.A.F.B., New Mex. 1969-71; FBI special agt., San Diego 1971-79; broker/devel. Realty Land, Poway 1979--; gen. partner Vista Sundowner 1977-81, Vista Santana 1979-; pres. Southcrest Dev. Corp. 1984-; honors: San Diego Board of Realtors Exchangor of Month 11/81; co. top sales awards 1981, 82; mem. San Diego Problem Solvers , S.D. Bd. of Realtors, Exchangors, Poway Problem Solvers, Poway CofC; publs: How to Buy Foreclosure Property (pamphlet 1982), How to Exchange, Poway R.E. Profls. 1982; mil: 1st lt. US Army Intell. Ofcr., 1966-69, Army Commendns.; Republican; Baptist; rec: hunting, camping, fishing. Res: 12302 Old Stone Rd Poway 92064 Ofc: Realty Land, 13507 Midland Rd Poway 92064

STRAIGHT, FORREST ALLEN, construction co. executive; b. Sept. 8, 1947, San Francisco; s. Forrest Allen and Virginia Claire (Simpson) S.; m. Cheryl Elaine Bader, Aug. 22, 1971; 1 dau. Shelly, b. 1977; edn: BS in C.E., San Jose St. Univ. 1971; MS in constrn. mgmt., Stanford Univ. 1972. Career: project mgr. Webcor Builders, Inc. San Mateo, 1971-81, constructed var. office bldgs. and office parks on the S.F. Peninsula; pres. Blazer Construction, Inc. San Mateo 1981--, constrn. comml. office bldgs. throughout Calif.; honors: Civil Eng. hon. soc. 1970; mem.AGC Collective Bargaining Com. 1980, Stanford Alumni Assn.; mil: capt. Army Corps of Engrs. 1969-75; Republican; Lutheran; rec: golf, fishing, backpacking. Res: 10250 Anthony Pl Cupertino 95014 Ofc: Blazer Construction, Inc. 1510 W. Cape Dr, Ste 104, San Mateo 94404

STRATOULY, BRIAN STEPHEN, mechanical engineer; b. May 16, 1956, Honolulu, HI; s. Dean Constantine and Elaine (DeClerico) S.; edn: BSME, Worcester Polytech. Inst. 1977, MSME, 1980; cert. German Goethe Inst. (Murnau, W.Ger.) 1977; reg. profl. engr. Calif. 1983. Career: teaching asst. Worcester (Mass.) Polytechnic Inst., 1978-79; research asst. Alden Research Lab., Holden Mass. 1979-80; mech. engr. Long Beach (Calif.) Naval Shipyard, 1980-81; design engr. Santa Fe/Braun, Orange 1981--; mem: student mem. ASME 1978-80; WPI Alumni Assn. (L.A. Region dir. 1983), Ski Club; Catholic; rec: bodybuilding, nutrition. Res: 2005 W. Culver Unit No. 20, Orange 92668 Ofc: S.F./Braun, 505 S. Main St Orange 92668

STRATTON, RICHARD JAMES, lawyer; b. May 17, 1946, Sandwich, Ill.; s. James L. and Dorothy (Olson) S.; m. Michele Disario, June 13, 1970; children: Matthew, b. 1977, Laura, b. 1980; edn: AB, Harvard Coll. 1968; MSc, London Sch. of Econ. 1969; JD, Harvard Law Sch. 1972; admitted to Calif. State Bar 1972. Career: atty. assoc. Bronson, Bronson & McKinnon, San Francisco 1972-, partner 1980--, spec. in civil trial practice, involving real estate litigation and defense of profl. liability claims; lectr./contbg. ed. real estate law publs., Continuing Edn. of the Bar, 1979-; dir. Bar Assn. of S.F., 1980; pres. Barristers Club of S.F., 1980; mem. Defense Research Inst., Northern Calif. Assn. of Def. Counsel, Am. Bar Assn., Bar Assn. of San Francisco; mem. Planning Assn. of The Richmond. Res: 546 11th Ave San Francisco 94118 Ofc: Bronson, Bronson & McKinnon, 555 California St, Ste. 3400, San Francisco 94104

STRAUGHAN, JERRY EUGENE, educator; b. July 2, 1933, Sebastopol; s. wm. Leslie and Alta Cordilla (Chapman) S.; m. Susan Hook, Sept. 13, 1963; children: Charles, b. 1958 (stepson), Carol, b. 1965, David, b. 1969; edn: BA, UC Los Angeles 1959; MA in edn., Calif. Lutheran Coll. 1974; num. spl. courses; teaching credentials: std. secondary/ comm. coll./ comm. coll. supvr.; real estate lic. 1959-. Career: full-time faculty Moorpark Coll., polit. sci., urban studies tchr., 1975--; prior tchg. in jr. high and high schs.; owner real estate brokerage, 1959--; mem. City Council of Moorpark; mem. (past chmn.) Calif. Comm. and Jr. Coll. Assn. Articulation Conf. Liaison Com. on Public Adm./Pub. Svc.; past mem. Ventura County Parks Adv. Commn.; past mem. Commn. of the Californias; Democrat. Res: 13130 Peach Hill Rd Moorpark 93021 Ofc: 7075 Campus Rd. Moorpark 93021

STRAUSS, MURRAY MILTON, real estate appraiser; b. July 17, 1916, Brklyn.; s. Charles and Tillie (Garfinkel) S.; m. Luceil Engel, Apr. 15, 1942 (dec. 1969); children: Louis Frank, b. 1944, Murray Daniel, b. 1946, Charles Alan, b. 1950; edn: stu. Ind. Univ. 1934-36, Univ. of Ill. 1936-37; ensign, Northwestern Univ. 1940; Lic. Gen. Contr.; Lic. R.E. Broker; VA Fee Appraiser; Sr. Mem. IREA, Intl. Real Estate Appraisers; ICA, Intl. Cert. Appraiser; CMHA, Cert. Mfd. Housing Appraiser; Nat. Register R.E. Appraisers Level III. Career: asst. purch. agt. Midwest Mfg. Co. Galesburg, Ill. 1937; asst. prod. mgr. Lennox Mfg. Co., St. Louis 1938-40; real estate appraising field 1945-: asst. supt./supt. Calif. Orange Bldg. Co., United Bldg. Co., Budlong Corp., Grandview Bldg. Co., Biltmore Homes, 1945-48; RME & purch. agt. Biltmore Homes, Inc. and Grandview Bldg. Co., 1948-52; pres. Murray M. Strauss & Assos., Inc. (subdivider/ bldr./ contr. num. tracts San Fernando Valley), 1952-81, subdiv., devel. of over 100 props., 25,000 homes & homesites (incl. Lakewood, Mount Olympus), also comml. & indsl. sites; real estate broker 1955-; real estate fee appraiser 1981--. Mem. IREA L.A. Chpt. (v.p., secty.); v.p. St. Louis County Jr. CofC 1938-40, mem. Calabasas CofC 1958-60, mem. L.A. Speakers Club 1983-; active in incorporating City of Hidden Hills; mil: lt. cmdr. USNR 1940-51, WWII Victory Medal, WWII Pacific Cpgn. 11 clasps, Am. Defense Medal, America Cpgn.; Republican; Christian Sci.; rec: pub. spkg., wood working, equestrian. Res: 1710, 15, Camino Palmero Hollywood 90046 Ofc: POB 1361, Studio City 91604-0361

STRIETER, MARTIN GERHARDT, acquisitions and mergers executive; b. July 23, 1927, Hindsale, Ill.; s. Theophilus Wm., D.D. and Martha (Henn) S.; m. Joan Grimm, Aug. 11, 1946; children: Steven M., b. 1951, Kurt H., b. 1953; edn: St. Johns Acad. and Coll. 1943-46; CLU, American Coll. of Life Underwriters 1962. Career: supt. group issue and adminstrn., Pacific Mutual Life, Los Angeles 1963-64; USAF Auditor Gen. spl. consultant under temporary appt. by Asst. Sec. of the Air Force (Material), 1964-71; asst. vice pres./ sr. cons./ mgr. internal support for employee benefit consulting dept., Johnson & Higgins, Los Angeles 1971-81; v.p./ sr. officer responsible HRM consulting ops. for 9 offices of Western Region, Alexander & Alexander, 1980--; pres./cons., merger and acquisition intermediary Corporate Growth Services, Van Nuys; instr. AMA Seminars, frequent spkr. co. sponsored seminars; mem: Los Angeles Club, Employee Benefit Planning Assn., Western Pension Conf. 1977-81; contbg. author, Corporate Controller's Manual (Warren, Gorham and Lamont 1981); mil: pfc USAF 1950-51; Republican; Lutheran; rec: travel, sports, continuing edn. Res: 9404 Haskell Ave Sepulveda 91343 Ofc: Corporate Growth Services, Inc. 15904 Strathern St, Ste 10, Van Nuys 91406

STRIFFLER, FRANK CHARLES, builder/developer; b. Jan. 23, 1942, NY, NY; s. Frank and Josephine (Troia) S.; m. Marsha, July 4, 1980; children: Lauren Michelle, b. 1965, Alison Dana, b. 1970; Calif. state lic. contractor 1977. Career: pres. Candella Construction Corp., Woodland Hills; developer and builder var. projects: shopping centers, apartment bldgs., mini-storage warehouses, mobile home pks., high rise condominiums and hotels; cons. on restoration of Victorian houses; Contractors Board mem.; rec: restoration classic autos. Address: Candella Constrn. Corp., 5031 San Feliciano Dr Woodland Hills 91364

STRINGER, JAMES DALE, JR., telecommunications executive; b. Jan. 25, 1938, West Point, Miss.; s. James Dale and Rachel Murl (Beaird) S.; m. Kathryn J. Merrill, May 30, 1963 (dir. desc. of C.P. Merrill, Adj., Mormon Battalion US Army 1847); children: Elizabeth, . 1964, Christopher, b. 1966, Donald, b. 1970, Joel, b. 1978, Matthew, b. 1980, Rebecca, b. 1981; edn: BS in math, Univ. of Ariz. 1963; MBA postgrad. work, Drexel Univ. 1976-77; Qual. Small Arms Instr. AUS 1966. Career: 27 years exp. in computers, pgmmg., comm., and real-time mil. & comml. systems; with RCA Missiles & Radar, Moorestown, NJ 1974-76, Raytheon Co. Equip. Div., Wayland, Mass. 1977-78, Computer Scis. Corp. Defense Systems Div., Moorestown, NJ 1978-79, Xerox Corp., Xten Services, Woodland Hills, Ca. 1979-80; mgr. Advanced Devel., Corp. Telecomms., Hughes Aircraft Co., 1981--; founder/pres. Exotel, Inc. (new venture estab. to design/devel. Universal Wireless Transceiver for use tel. & cable t.v. services) 1983-; independent mgmt. cons. 1976-; del. to Def. Sci. Bd. workshop (Specs. and Stds. Tailoring) 1977; guest lectr. Software Summit, London 1981 (DPMA); mem: IEEE, 1974- (Computer Soc., Comm. Soc., Aerospace Soc.); Nat. Security Indsl. Assn. (chmn. Software Com. 1976-9); fmr. Scoutmaster Post 606, Edison (NJ) Council, BSA; past Neighbor Council No. 1, City of Simi Valley; Patentee; pub. tech. papers, jour. articles; honors: cited in Datamation mag. (1971), Business Week mag. (4/4/83); mil: 1st lt. US Army Signal Corps 1959-66; Republican; Ch. of Jesus Christ of L.D.S. (tchr.); rec: astronomy, swimming, bowling. Res: 1444 Redpost Ct Diamond Bar 91765 Ofc: Hughes Aircraft Co., Comm. & D.P., POB 9399, Bldg C6/2031, Long Beach 90810-0465

STROM, RUSSELL LESTER, engineering executive; b. Feb. 2, 1917, Brooklyn, NY; s. Carl August and Florence Louise (Bird) S.; m. Rita Foshee, Sept. 25, 1943; children: Barbara, b. 1946, Stephen, b. 1948, Nancy, b. 1962; edn: BS, mech. engrg. Polytechnic Inst. of Bklyln. 1936; MS, eng. exec. pgm. UC Los Angeles 1960; PhD, computer scis., UCLA 1966. Career: electromechanical designer General Cable Corp., Rome, NY 1936-39; coordinator Navy Programs, Gibbs & Cox, NY, NY 1939-42; chief elec. engr. Kaiser Co., NYC 1942-45; section head Pacific Island Engrs., San Francisco 1945-50; chief elec. engr. Calif. Research & Devel., Livermore 1950-53; mgr. of engring. & sales, Gudeman Co., Sunnyvale 1953-55; supvr. Flight Control, North Amer. Aviation, Los angeles 1955-56, supvr. Electronic Lab., 1957-60, proj. engr. Corporate Ofc., 1960-63, chief of Sys. Anal. Autonetics, Anaheim, 1963-65, tech. dir. Sys. Engring. North Am. Rockwell, Downey 1965-68, asst. to sys. engring. mgr., L.A. 1968-69; asst. to sys. engring. mgr., Litton Ship Systems, Los Angeles 1969-72; sr. tech. splst. Northrop Aircraft, Hawthorne 1972-82; proj. mgr. Rockwell Internat., Aircraft Ops., Lakewood 1982--; honors: lectr. in engring./Ford Found. Fellow, UCLA 1960-63; mem. ASME, AIEE, IEEE,

AIAA, IES, Calif. Soc. Profl. Engrs.; orgns: Sunnyvale, CA CofC, pres. UCLA Exec. Engineering Alumni Assn., pres. Homeowners Assn., Pi Kappa Phi frat., pres. Republican Club of Playa Del Rey; class pres. Grad. Master's Deg. Class; rec: music. Res: 5 Meadowsweet Way Irvine 92715 Ofc: Rockwell Int'l., NAAO Div. Advanced Avionics, 2770 E. Carson St (Mail Code WA37) Lakewood 90712

STROMME, GARY L., law librarian; b. July 8, 1939, Willmar, Minn.; edn: BA, philo., Pacific Lutheran Univ. 1965; BLS, Univ. of Brit. Columbia Sch. of Librarianship, 1967; JD, Hastings Coll. of the Law 1973; admitted State Bar of Calif. 1973, US Supreme Ct. Bar, 1977. Career: serials librarian, Univ. of Minn., St. Paul Campus Lib. 1967-69; asst. librn. law firm McCutchen, Doyle, Brown, Enersen, San Francisco 1970-71; asst. librn. Graham & James, S.F. 1971-73; ind. contracting atty., 1973-74; law librn. Pacific Gas & Electric Co., S.F. 1974--; mem: Internat. Soc. Gen. Semantics (pres. S.F. Chpt. 1978-80; bd. dir. 1980-81); Am. Assn. Law Libraries; Am. Bar Assn. (Sect. of Economics of Law Practice, chmn. lib. com. 1978-82); author: An Intro. to the Use of the Law Library (1974); Basic Legal Research Tech. (rev. 4th ed. 1979); mil: elect. tech. USAF 1959-63. Res: 2589 LeConte Ave Berkeley 94709 Office: PG&E 77 Beale St, 31st Fl. San Francisco 94106

STROUD, FRANCES RUTH, psychologist; b. July 29, 1937, Dustin, Okla.; d. Robert Jess and Dot Lee (Stroud) Dexter; div.; 1 son, Scott Everett Taylor, b. 1965; edn: BS, Univ. Okla. 1959; MA, Ariz. St. Univ. 1968, PhD, 1972; clin. dir./psychologist Chronic Pain Mgmt. Pgm. Casa Colina Hosp., Pomona 1979--; postdoc. clinical psych. intern, VA Hosp., Long Bch. 1977-78; pvt. practice, Hartford, Conn. 1975-77; coordinator clin. svcs. Long Lane Sch. for adjudicated youth, Middletown, Conn. 1974-75; var. staff pos. to clin. dir. Community Orgn. for Drug Abuse Control, Phoenix, Az. 1971-74; psychotherapist Alcoholism Recovery Ctr., Az. Rehab. Ctrs., Phoenix 1969-70; counselor/tchr. Pacific Grove (Calif.) Unified Schs. 1968-69; tchr. Orangewood Sch., Phoenix 1966-67, Aztec Sch., Albuquerque, NM 1959-61; asst. buyer Macys Dept. Store, S.F. 1961-64; instr. Ariz. State Univ. 1970-73; awards: Az. State Univ. V.P.'s Award, Graduate Resrch. Fellowship, Kappa Delta Pi hon., NDEA Counseling Inst. stipend awd., Ten Outstanding Freshmen Women in Major Field. Res: 485 Stanford, Claremont 91711 Ofc: Casa Colina Hospital, 255 Bonita, Pomona, CA

STUART, SYLVIA WALPOLE, word processing co. owner; b. Apr. 10, 1930, Llanerch, Pa.; d. Charles Lloyd and Nora (Matthews) Whitney; niece of Janet Whitney, author; m. Glenn B. Stuart, Feb. 13, 1960 (dec. 1983); 1 son, Glenn Jr., b. 1966; edn: Santa Monica City Coll. 1954; UC Los Angeles 1965. Career: sec.treas. Microlectron, Inc. Santa Monica, 1964-; owner Stuart Assocs. Typing, Word Processing, 1964-82, pres. Stuart Word Processing Center, Inc., Los Angeles 1982--; mem: Internat. Word Processing Assn., City of Angels Chpt., Soroptimist Club of Redondo Beach (treas. 1967), Internat. Folk Dancers 1955-59, Santa Monica Comm. Chorus 1955-57, Womens Sym. Orch., Phila. 1950-51; Republican; Methodist; rec: nutrition, dancing, music. Res: 5127 Bluemound Rd Rolling Hills Estates 90274 Ofc: Stuart Word Processing Center, Inc. 624 S. Grand St, No. 1517, Los Angeles 90017

STUBBLEBINE, WILLIAM CRAIG, educator, college law structures director; b. July 1, 1936, USMA, West Point, NY; s. Albert Newton, Jr. and Mildred (Toland) S.; m. Carol Wiebe; children: Julia, b. 1967, Erik, b. 1969; edn: Ill. Inst. of Tech. 1953-56; BS, Univ. of Dela. 1958; PhD, Univ. of Va. 1963. Career: asst. prof. econ., Univ. of Va. 1961-63, Univ. of Dela. 1963-66; sci. faculty fellow MIT, 1965-66; Fulbright prof. of econ. Univ. of Turin, Italy 1967-68; vis. prof. of economics, So. Methodist Univ. 1971, and Va. Polytech. Inst. 1972; assoc. prof. econ. Claremont McKenna Coll. & Grad. Sch., 1966-77, Von Tobel prof. of political economy and dir. Center for the Study of Law Structures, 1977--; cons. federal, state and local govts., bus.; Voelker fellow, Nat.; Sci. Political Sci. Assn.; Pub. Choice Soc.; Western Tax Assn.; Laws at Work; Nat. Tax Limitation Comm. Publs: Externally (with J.M. Buchanan), Economica, 1962; Institutional Elements in the Fin. of Edn., So. Econ. Journ., 1965; On Property Right & Instns., Explorations in the Theory of Anarchy, 1972; editor (with T.D. Willett) and contbr. to Reaganomics: A Midterm Report, 1983; contbr. writer var. journals. Address: Bauer Center, Claremont McKenna Coll. Claremont 91711

STUCKEY, LLOYD C., university administrator; b. Sept. 27, 1915, Manteca; s. Britt Charles and Gladys May (Woodward) S.; m. Margaret Milwee, Jan. 19, 1941; 2 daus., Barbara, b. 1947, Sally, b. 1950; edn: AB, Univ. of the Pacific 1965; Public Acct., Calif. State Bd. Acctcy. 1950. Career: bus. mgr. Von Berg Motor Co., Manteca 1947-55; mgr. Elder Motor Co., Stockton 1955-59; controller Univ. of the Pacific, 1959-70; finl. vice pres. Univ. of Puget Sound, Tacoma, Wash. 1970-81, ret.; assoc. dir. WACUBO Business mgmt. Inst., Stanford, Ca. 1981--; Univ. of Puget Sound: Faculty Senate 1971-78, Presdtl. Search Com. 1973, Bd. Trustees Finance Com. 1970-78; honors: hon. Dr. of Humane Letters, Morningside Coll. 1978; mem. Western Assn. of Coll. & Univ. Bus. Ofcrs. (treas. & exec. com. 1974-5), Tacoma Urban League (bd. dirs. 1971-81, pres. bd. 1976-79, chmn. fin. com.), Nat. Urban League (del. assem. 1976, 77, 78; v.p. W. Region Council of Presidents 1978, 79), Tacoma Sym. (bd. dirs. 1975-81), Rotary; mil: s/sgt. AUS Corps of Engr. 1945-46; Republican; United Methodist; rec: travel, golf. Res: 683 Spindrift Way, Half Moon Bay 94019 Ofc: WACUBO Bus. Mgmt. Inst., 150 Encina Courtyard, Stanford Univ., POB 2349, Stanford 94305

STURGESS, ROBERT ALAN, real estate broker;b. Nov. 19, 1944, Los Alamos, N.M.; s. Robert Glen and Lorene L. (Lathrop) S.; m. Sharon Takahashi, Jan. 6, 1967; 1 dau. Shauna b. 1982; edn: BA, CSU Hayward 1970, MA, 1977. Career: sr. inside sales Westinghouse Appliance, San Lorenzo, Ca. 1966-69; real estate sales Valley Realty, Dublin 1972-74; mng. ptnr./ treas./ dir./ broker Vintage Realty Inc., Pleasanton 1974--; real estate consulting, expert testimony, var. lawyers, Civil Trials; mem: Nat. Assn. of Realtors, So. Alameda County Bd. of Realtors, Contra Costa Bd. of Realtors; Childrens Theater Workshop (1982), N.M. Mil. Inst. Alumni Assn.; Democrat; Prot.; rec: painting, photog., writing. Res: 6599 Arlington Dr Pleasanton 94566 Ofc: Vintage Realty Inc. 234 Main St, Ste B, Pleasanton 94566

STUTO, PHILIP JOHN, private investigator; b. Sept. 12, 1945, Sacramento; s. Frank Francis and Dorothy Mae (Cook) Stuto; m. Kathleen Ingrid Peterson, July 7, 1979; children: Shaun Philip, b. 1980, Nicole Kathleen, b. 1982; lic. pvt. investigator, Calif. 1974, Hawaii 1982. Career: claim agent So. Pacific R.R., 1967-72; investigator Dow Carter & Assocs., Glendale 1972-74; partner, Investigative Consultants Internat. (and predecessor firm Stuto-Wachtler), San Francisco 1974-78, sole owner/pres. 1978--, opened branch office in Hawaii 1982, br. office in London, Eng. 1983; investigative wk. for num. law firms nationwide; publs: International Consultant Directory (to be pub., Ziff Davis Pub. Co., NY); mil: E4 USN 1963-64; Democrat; Catholic; club: Round Hill Golf & Country (Alamo). Res: 2261 Shasta Ct. Martinez 94553 Ofc: Investigative Consultants Intl., Inc. 1657 California Blvd, Ste. 204, Walnut Creek 94596

SU, SHIH-TUN, engineer; b. Feb. 29, 1942, Peking, China, nat. 1975; s. Chin and Pei-Chang (Lu) Su; m. Vicky S., Apr. 4, 1970; 2 daus., Susun, b. 1975, Shaunin, b. 1980; edn: BS, Cheng-Kung Univ. (Taiwan) 1964; MS, Colo. State Univ. 1967; MBA, Univ. of Wisc. Milwaukee 1980; PhD, Colo. State Univ. 1970; reg. profl. engr. Calif. (1982), Conn., R.I., Mass. (1974-83), Wisc. 1978. Career: research leader Engring. Res. Center, Colo. State Univ., Fort Collins 1970-71; sr. engr./lead engr. Stone & Webster Engring. Corp., Boston, Mass. 1971-77; prin. engr./project mgr. Wisc. Electric Power Co., Milwaukee 1977-81; project mgr./supvg. engr. Tudor Engring. Co., San Francisco 1981--; faculty, Univ. of Wisc. 1980-81; honors: judge Internat. Sci. and Engineering Fair (1981); guest spkr. US Water Resources Council dam-break flood workshop (1977); mem: ASCE 1967-, US Com. on Large Dams 1983-; rep. Parents Club, Contra Costa Chinese Sch.; career counseling to Jr. High Sch. students; Dale Carnegie Course participant; publs: arts. in profl. journals; rec: music, basketball, travel. Res: 2108 Quiet Place Dr Walnut Creek 94598 Ofc: Tudor Engineering Co. 149 New Montgomery San Francisco 94105

SUBAR, JERRY ALLAN, clinical pharmacist; b. Apr. 12, 1954, Detroit, Mich.; s. Philip and Faye (Katz) S.; edn: Baccalaureate in Sci., UCLA 1976; D.Pharm., USC 1980; Pharm. lic., State of Calif. 1980. Career: pharmacy intern Barlow Hosp., L.A. 1977-79; sr. pharmacy intern Encino Hosp. 1979-80, staff clin. pharmacist 1980--; honors: Calif. Goldsealbearer, Calif. State Scholarship, UCLA Alumni Award of Merit, USC Sch. of Pharm. Faculty Scholarship Awd., San Fernando Valley Engrs. Council scholarship; mem. Rho Chi Hon. Soc., ASHP, APhA, CPhA, PPSSV, USC Sch. of Pharm. Alumni Assn., USC Pharm. QSAD Centurion; articles in profl. journals; Jewish; rec: model rocketry, chess, classical music. Res: 5825 Reseda Blvd Tarzana 91356 Ofc: Encino Hosp 16237 Ventura Blvd Encino 91436

SUBBIE, PAUL ANDREW, purchasing executive; b. Feb. 20, 1947, Los Angeles; s. Paul F. and Christine (Orvick) S.; m. Jacqueline Ochsner, Mar. 20, 1982; children: James Andrew, b. 1965; Andrea Marie, b. 1963; edn: West Los Angeles Coll. 1977-78; Los Angeles Valley Coll. 1979-80; pilots lic., High Performance Cert., FAA 1979. Career: lithographer Mobile Oil Corp., Los ANgeles 1963-71; purchasing mgr. Colony Chpt. Life Ins. Co., Los Angeles 1971-77; purch. mgr. 20th Century INs. Co., Woodland Hills 1977--; awards: creative writing awd., Dean of Languages, Los Angeles Coll. 1978; mem: Purchasing Mgmt. Assn.; Nat. Assn. of Purchasing Mgmt; Nat. Republican Congressional Com.; publs: art. on purchasing, The Office Mag. 1978; Republican; Catholic; rec: flying full size & radio control aircraft, target shooting. Res: 21801 Roscoe Ave, No 332, Canoga Park 91306 Ofc: 20th Century Ins. Co., 6301 Owensmouth Ave Woodland Hills 91367

SUBRAMANYA, SHIVA, engineer; b. Apr. 8, 1933, Hole-Narasipur, India; nat. 1970; s. Srikantaiah and Gundamma S.; m. Lee Silva, Mar. 3, 1967; two sons, Paul, b. 1968, Kevin, b. 1972; edn: BS, Mysore Univ. 1956; MS nuc. physics & electronics, Karnatak Univ. 1962; postgrad. work, Clark Univ. 1963-5; MBA (bus. mgt.) CSU Dom. Hills 1977. Career: project mgr., major USAF Contracts, TRW Defense Gp. 1979--; systems lead engr. on sev. DOD Projects, Space & Ground Systems, TRW 1973-79; electronics warfare cons. Gen. Instruments, NY 1972-73; prin. engr. DOD Projects, 1967-70, prin. engr. Tactical Comm. Gp., 1970-72, Gen. Dynamics/ Electronics; chief engr. DOD Contracts, TEI, 1964-67; lectr. various instns.; recipient Pres. of India awards & scholarships in nuclear physics research; mem: IEEE, Am. Inst. Physics, AOC, VISP, India Profl. Forum (nat. pres.); coordinator US West Coast, Viswa Hindu Parishad; publs: over 10,000 pages of tech. papers;. Res: 4133 Konya Dr. Torrance 90503 Ofc: 131-2115 TRW Defense Group, One Space Group, Redondo Beach 90278

SUBRAMANIAN, SUNDARAM, engineer; b. Sept. 7, 1934, Paramagudi, Madras, nat. 1973; s. Sundaram and Velammal Sappania; m. Hemavathy, Feb. 18, 1968; children: Anand Kuman, b. 1968; Malathy, b. 1973; edn: BE, Madras Univ., India 1959; PhD, Glasgow Univ., U.K. 1967; MBA, Roosevelt Univ., Chgo. 1977. Career: scientific ofcr., Govt. of India; asst. dept. hd. Zenith Radio Corp., Chgo.; staff engr. Motorola, Schaumburg, Ill.; asst. prof., Chapman Coll., Orange; proj. engr., Endevco, San Jaun Capo.; currently proj. mgr.

Burroughs, Mission Viejo 1984--; pres. So. India Cultural Assn. 1977-78; dir. Tamil Nadu Found. 1977-80; honors: Metropolitan Vickers Research fellow, Glasgow, Scottland, UK 1963-67; mem. IEEE; publs: 6 papers in internat. journs., ie. Journ. of Physics, Proceedings of the Royal Soc., IEEE Transactions; 4 US patents; Hindu; rec: internat. travel. Res: 17832 Morrow Circle Villa Park 92667 Ofc: Endevco, 30700 Rancho Viejo Rd San Jaun Capistrano 92675

SUDARICH, LUANN, hotel management executive; b. Sep. 9, 1958, McKeesport, Penn.; d. Leonard J. and Marie A. (Mazza) S.; edn: bus. adm., Robert Morris Coll. 1977-78; hotel mgmt. UNLU 1980-81. Career: account executive Flamingo Hilton Hotel and Towers, Las Vegas 1979-81; sales mgr. Hacienda Hotel Casino, Las Vegas 1981-82; western reg. dir. of sales USA Mandarin Singapore Internat. Hotels, Los Angeles 1982--; panel spkr. ASEAN-EATA 1984; honors: volunteer LA 1983; LAOOC 1984; mem: Pata 1982-; ASTA 1982-; EATA 1982-; ASEAN 1982-; NAFE (network dir.) 1983-; Res: 525 N Sycamore, #202 Los Angeles 90036 Ofc: Mandarin Singapore Int'l Hotels, 600 Wilshire Blvd, #870 Los Angeles 90017

SUGIONO, WENDY EKASUSANTI, dentist, b. May 13, 1950, Kudus, Indonesia; d. Imin and Kim Tjoe (Oei) Sugioni; m. Chuck S. Kon, June 12, 1977; 1 son: Ryan, b. 1981; edn: BS and R.D.H., Loma Linda Univ. 1975; DDS, 1978. Career: chief dental provider & cons. to the Sherman Indian High Sch., Riverside 1979--; gen. practitioner The Kon & Sugiono Profl. Dental Corp. 1980--, vice pres. 1981-; cons. for dental coronal polishing licensing to United Health Careers Inst., San Bernardino 1982-; vol. dentist, L.A. Chinese Community Free Clinic 1979-80; guest spkr. var. dental asst. graduating classes, and local service clubs; mem: Am., Calif., Tri- County Dental Assns.; Acad. of Gen. Dentistry; Am. Endodontic Soc.; Colton CofC; Colton Womens CofC; works: class artist 1973-75; research on dental need of L.A. Chinatown Community 1975; 7th Day Adventist; re: music (piano, organ, singing), oil painting; flower arrangements. Res: 2314 No Euclid Ave Upland 91786 Ofc: Kon & Sugiono Professional Dental Corp., 191 West H' Street Colton 92324

SUH, JEAN JUNG, musical academy director; b. Dec. 18, 1943, Seoul, Korea, nat. 1979; d. Sang Yul and Bok Yei (Kim) Suh, m. Sum Hunn, May 18, 1971; children: Nancy, b. 1973; Doris, b. 1975; edn: B.Law. Ewha Womens Univ. 1964; MA, Columbia Coll. 1967. Career: TV & voice actress 1959-64; pres. Korean Broadcasting of AM. 1970-74; prodn. mgr. 1979-79; pres. Internat. Music- Comml. Prodn. 1978--; pres. L.A. Art Acad 1981--; Jean Seung Trading 1981--; pres. Korean Broadcasters Assn. 1984; awards. Pres. Citation for 1st Korean radio station over seas, Republic of Korean 1970; Cert. of Merit, City of L.A. 1978; mem: Fedn. Internat. Des Orgns. de Festivals, Yugoslavia 1983, 84; founder, World Song Fest. in Am.; founder Korean Broadcasting of Am · Ch of LDS; rec: music. Ofc: Jean Seung Trading, 1212 No Vermont, Ste 102, Los Angeles 90029

SUKOENIG, MARK RICHARD, optometrist; b. June 16, 1948, NY, NY; s. Sidney and Shirley Hope (Eron) S.; m. Betsy Ann McNeill, June 20, 1982; edn: BA, Syracuse Univ. 1971; BS, cum laude, So. Calif. Coll of Optometry 1976, OD, 1978; lic. O.D. in Calif., Wash., NY. Career: optometrist empl. with Drs. Robert Collins, No. Hollywood, Larry Palikoff, Hollywood, Stanley Postar, Sherman Oaks; past solo pvt. practice in Montclair; currently, solo contact lens splty. (non- eyeglass dispensing) optometric practice, Encino; Amway dir. distbr.; school screening for San Fernando Valley Opt. Soc.; recipient Frederick W. Brock research award, So. Calif. Coll. Opt.; mem: Am., Calif., optometric assns.; San Fernando Valley Opt. Soc.; Aircraft Owners & Pilots Assn.; Amway Distbrs. Assn.; publs: articles in Optometric Weekly (7/77), and Optometric Monthly (4/78); rec: comml. pilot, photog., bluegrass guitarist. Res: 7300 Lennox Ave, No C3, Van Nuys 91405; Ofc: Mark R. Sukoenig, OD, 18075 Ventura Blvd, Ste 130, Encino 91316

SULLIVAN, HERLINDA PEREZ, sperm bank director; b. Mar. 10, 1928, Mexico; d. Eleuterio and Guadalupe (Gamboa) Perez; m. Joseph P. Sullivan, June 3, 1951; children: Brian, b. 1952; Eric, b. 1954; Laura, b. 1957; Kevin, b. 1959; edn: Escuela Nacional de Ciencias Biologicas; pharmacist, Inst. Politecnico Nacional. Career: pharmacist, Mexico City 1948-51; pharm. asst., El Monte 1953-55; restaurant hostess, San Gabriel 1955-59; real estate sales, El Hambra 1959-61; staff research assoc. UC Irvine, Irvine 1966-83; pres./ dir. Sperm Bank, Inc., Santa Ana 1983--; honors: outstanding performance award, UC Irvine 1975; commdn., Orange Co. Bd. Suprvs. 1981 and named L.U.L.A.C. Woman 1981; mem: Am. Assn. of Tissue Banks; Mexican Am. Womens Nat. Assn. (pres. 1981-83); Hispanic Bus. & Profl. Assn.; UCI Retiree & Emeritee Assn.; Minority Affairs Adv. Council; CSU Fullerton; Planned Parenthood; March of Dimes; Cancer Fund; Heart Fund; Leukemia Soc.; num. trade journs. arts.; Democrat; rec: music, theater, photog. Res: 1970 Windward Dr Anaheim 92801 Ofc: Sperm Bank, Inc., No Main St, Ste 108, Santa Ana 92701

SULLIVAN, JAMES EDWARD, company president; b. Sept 22, 1937, Indianapolis, Ind.; s. James E. and Rosemary Helen (Clark) S.; div.; 1 son: Scott, b. 1970; edn: AA, Long Beach City Coll. 1958; BA, Calif. St. Univ. 1960; grad. wk., Pepperdine Univ. 1980. Career: sales Bekins Van Lines, INc. 1960-62; sales Johnson & Johnson 1962-64; sales mgmt., Interpace Corp. 1964-75; v.p. Robertson Am. Corp., Morrisvill, Pa. 1976; v.p./ gen. mgr. Gail Internat. Corp. 1976-78; pres./ chief exec. Gail Internat. Corp., Tustin 1978--; dir. Ceramic Tile Mktg. Fedn.; mem: US Congl. Adv. Bd.; The Presidents Assn.; Bahia Corinthian Yacht Club, Corona Del Mar; Balboa Bay Culb, Newport Bch; Roosters Club, Chanteclair, Newport Bch.; mil: USMC, hon. dis. 1963;

Republican; Catholic; rec: sailing, deep sea fishing, skiing. Res: 3 Woodgrove Irvine 92714 Ofc: Gail Internat. Corp., 14791 Myford Rd Tustin 92681

SULLIVAN, MICHAEL EVAN, administrator, engineer, company executive; b. Dec. 30, 1940, Phila., PA; s. Albert and Ruth (Liebert) S.; div.; edn: BS, NM State Univ. 1966; MA, 1968; BS Univ. Tex. 1969; MBA, Univ. Houston 1974; BS, Univ. LaVerne 1981; MS, USC 1976; MPA, 1977; PhD 1982. Career: jr. engr. Physical Sci. Lab, N.M. State Univ. 1962-66; sr. analyst Houston, Tex. Lighting & Power Co. 1969-74; electronics engr. Software Support Activity, US Govt., Pt. Mugu, Calif. 1974-77; mem. tech. staff Hughes Aircraft Co., El Segundo 1977-78; staff pgm. adminstr. Northrop Corp., Newbury Park 1978-79; hd. engring. div. Navy Astronautics Gp., Pt. Magu 1979-82; pres./ bd. chmn. Diversified Mgmt. Sys., Inc., Camarillo 1978--; hd. offshore island div., Pacific Missile Test Ctr., Pt. Magu 1982--; awards: Ednl. Research Tng. Pgm. fellowship, NMSU 1967; Pi Gamma Mu, soc. sci. hon.; Phi Kappa Phi; mem: Assn. of MBA Execs.; Am. Math. Soc.; Am. Statistical Assn.; Math. Assn. of Am.; Am. Soc. of Pub. Admin.; Am. Personnel & Guidance Assn.; Am. Assn. of Ind. Investors; Fed. Mgr. Assn.; mil: Spl. E-5, US Army 1958-62; rec: tennis, fishing, back packing, chess. Res: POB 273 Point Hueneme 93041 Ofc: Diversified Mgmt. Systems, Inc., POB 447 Camarillo 93010

SULLIVAN, RALPH JAMES, research scientist; b. July 26, 1931, St. George, Utah; s. Victor and Clio (McArthur) S.; m. Lois Verena Peterson, Feb. 14, 1957; children: Vicki, b. 1957, Mark, b. 1959, Steven, b. 1961, Diane, b. 1962; edn: AA, Dixie Jr. Coll. 1955; BS Chem., Brigham Young Univ. 1957 MS in Physical -Inorganic Chem., BYU 1958; grad. stu. thermodynamics, UC Berkeley 1958-59, in radiochem., Univ. of Ida. 1962-63. Career: sr. chemist (nuclear reactor chemistry and on-line process control) Atomics Intl. Div. No. Am. Rockwell 1959-68; mgr. R&D6 (instrumentation and system design) Litton Environmental Systems 1968-72; mgr. engring., dir. R&D, Xonicx, Inc. 1972-81; dir. research & devel. XonTech, Inc., Van Nuys 1981--; awards: Gray Scholarship 1956-58, NSF Fellowship 1956-58, Teaching Fellowship, UCB 1958-59; mem. American Chemical Soc., Air Pollution Control Assn.; active BSA (25 yrs); publs: num. tech. papers, sci. jour. arts.; mil: cpl. US ARmy 1953-55, Nat. Def., Army Occ., GCM medals; Republican: Latter day Saints; rec: chess, bridge, hunting. Res: 5464 Laurel Ridge Ln Camarillo 93010 Ofc: XonTech, Inc. 6862 Hayvenhurst Ave Van Nuys 91406

SUN, ARTHUR HAI CHAU, acupuncturist, Oriental medical doctor; b. June 6, 1941, Monterey; s Nai Yeh and Wei Jen (Ho) S.; edn: BA, Taiwan Provincial Univ. 1968; MA, Lincoln Univ. 1972, OMD, Chi-Li Meml. Med. Sch. 1979; cert. acupuncturist, Calif. 1978. Career: dr. of acupunture, pain relief cons., Calif. 1978; chmn./ pres. Arthur Realty Co., Monterey Park; chmn. bd. dirs. United Nat. Bank, Monterey Park; chmn./ pres. San Ta Internat. Inc. ltd ofc Salt Lake City, Utah; also, sr. advr. Sun's Med. Gp., Los Angeles & Salt Lake City; sr. advr. US Congressional Adv. Bd., Wash. DC; delegate: rep. US, 11th World Chinese Traders Com., Taipei, Taiwan 1981; rep. US, 13th World Chinese Traders Com., Vienna, Austria 1982; 9th World Chinese Banking Amity Conf., Taipei, Taiwan 1981; 11th World Chinese Banking Amity Conf., Tokyo, Japan 1983; mem: ROC-USA & USA-ROC Economic Council; Oriental Med. Drs. Gp.; publs: Major Pain Relief in Human Life, Taipei 1970; mil: lt. US Army; rec: sailing, swimming, antique collection. Address: San Ta Internat., Inc., 224 East Aldergate St Monterey Park 91754

SUN, DAVID TAIWAI, computer co. president; b. Mar. 16, 1956, Shanghai, China, nat. 1984; s. Chieh Yeh and Kwai Wing (Ma) S.; m. Betty B. Lee, Jan. 2, 1977; children: Cynthia, b. 1981; Darren, b. 1982; edn: BA, UCLA 1978; MBA, CSU Long Beach 1980. Career: Sun Cons. 1979--; pres./ CEO Sun Computers (from 1 employee to 4 retail locations & a corp. hdqtrs.) 1980--; co-founder Profl. Computer Dealers Assn. 1983; awards: Annual Outstanding Supplier Awd., TRW's ADPE G Telecomm. Procurement 1983; mem: Omicron Delta Epsilon, UCLA 1977; rec: flying. Res: 5392 Valley View Rd Rancho Palos Verdes 90274 Ofc: Sun Computers, Inc., Corp. Hqtr., 20925 So Bonita St Carson 90746

SUN, HENRY HENG-YUAN, data processing, systems & programming exc-utive; b. May 5, 1932, Shanhai, China, nat. 1970; s. Ching Po and Den Ann (Huang) S.; m. Lily Chou, Nov. 19, 1965; children: Stella, b. 1970; Stacy, b. 1977; edn: BS, Taiwan Chung Hsing Univ.; sys. engring. tng., mktg. & mgmt. tng., IBM. Career: instr. Tam Kung Coll. of Bus., Taiwan; instr./ sys. engring./ mktg. rep. IBM, Taiwan; data processing mgr., Tobias Kotzen Co., Los Angeles; spl. projs. mgr. Ameron, Inc., L.A.; currently, sys. & pgm. mgr. ITT, Gilfillan, L.A.; pres. Sunny Computer Svc. (cons. computer software and hardware; leasing hardware/ software of micro- computers); honors: Top Performer, IBM 1969; mem: Am. Mgmt. Assns.; works: devel. computer software systems for supermarket (1980), garment indus. (1982); rec: stamp collecting, micro- computers. Res: 816 No Coffman Dr Montebello 90640 Ofc: ITT-Gilfillan, 7821 Orion Ave Van Nuys 91409

SURMANEK, JAMES, advertising executive; b. Dec. 9, 1941, NY, NY; s. Edward and Stephanie (Neciunskas) S.; m. Paula Diane Bostic, Jan. 22, 1983; children: Kimberly Jean, b. 1969; Keri Lin, b. 1965; edn: Queens Coll., NYC 1959-65. Career: Parade Mag., NY 1958-66; mail room clerk 1958-62; assoc. research dir. 1962-66; Ogilvy Mather, NY 1966-76, Chgo. 1976-79; US 1979-81, L.A. 1981--; media research supvr. 1966; media supvr. 1967; v.p. 1970; assoc. research dir. 1975; media dir. 1976; sr. v.p. 1978; mgmt. council 1979; exec. media dir. 1981; gen. mgr. 1983, currrently, sr. v.p., gen. mgr.; seminars & speeches: Chgo., L.A. & San Diego Ad Clubs; Avtg. Age Media Wrkshps.; Am. Assn. of Advtg. Wrkshps.; Mktg. & Media Decisions Wrkshps.; mem:

Chgo. Advtg. Club; Los Angeles Advtg. Club; MENSA; PTA; Floral Park Civic Assn; author: Media Plannig/ A Quick & Easy Guide, Crain Books 1980; coauthor: Advertising Media Planning, Crain Books 1982; var. arts. in Adtg. Age, Mktg. & Media Decisions, Mktg. Communications, the Chicago Tribune; rec: woodworking, painting. Res: 23625 Arminta Street Canoga Park 91304 Ofc: Ogilvy & Mather, 5757 Wilshire Blvd Los Angeles 90036

SUSKE, JOE EUGENE, life insurance co. executive; b. Oct. 8, 1931, Coffeyville, Ks.; s. Felix and Hazel Pearl (Crumrine) S.; m. Nancy Anderson, Oct. 19, 1957; children: Sharon, b. 1958; Bradley, b. 1959; Carol, b. 1962; edn: AA, Coffeyvill Coll. 1951; BS, Univ. of KS 1953; fellow, Life Mgmt. Inst., Life Mgmt. Assn. 1966. Career: underwriting dir. Inland Life, Chgo. 1964-65; underwriting dir. Guarantee Trust Life, Chgo. 1965-67; v.p. underwriting National Fidelity Life 1967-72; v.p. first Colony Life, Shawnee Mission, KS 1974-78; exec. v.p. Executive Life, Beverly Hills 1978--; dir. Executive Life 1978--; dir. Exec. Life of NY 1978--; dir. Reinsurance Subs. of Exec. Life; fellow, Life Mgmt. Inst.; mem. FLMI Soc.; contbr. sev. arts. for ins. publs.; mil: sgt. US Army 1953-55; Lutheran; rec: swimming, spectator sports. Res: 5900 Maury Ave Woodland Hills 91367 Ofc: Executive Life, 9777 Wilshire Blvd, 4th Flr, Beverly Hills 90212

SUSSMAN-PREJZA, DEBORAH, designer; b. May 26, 1931, Brklyn.; d. Irving and Ruth (Golomb) Sussman; m. Paul Prejza, June 28, 1972; edn: (scholarships) Bard Coll. 1948-50, Inst. of Design, Chgo. 1950-53, Black Mtn. Coll. 1950, (Fulbright scholar) Hochschule fur Gestaltung, Ulm, Ger. 1957-58. Career: art dir. Ofc. of Charles & Ray Eames, Venice, Ca. 1953-57; graphic designer Galeries Lafayette, Paris 1959-60; art. dir. Eames Ofc. and designer catalogs for Los Angeles County Mus. of Art, 1961-67; prin. Deborah Sussman & Co., in W.L.A. and Santa Monica, 1968-, founder/pres. Sussman/Prejza & Co. Inc. (current staff of 30) Santa Monica 1980--; teaching 1962-: USC, Cal Arts, Art Center Coll. of Design, UCLA Ext.; spl. guest Internat. Design Conf., Aspen 1967, 68; spkr./lectr. Aspen Conv., K.U., Art Directors Club of L.A., Art Center, and UCLA; awards: Fulbright Lectr. in India 1976; Graphic design awds., Am. Inst. of Graphic Arts, Art Dirs. Club of L.A., Communication Arts Soc.; Vesta Awd. from the Women's Bldg. of L.A.; appreciation, L.A. Chpt. of AIA; AIA awd. (1980) for contbns. to architecture. Mem: bd. dirs. Am. Inst. of Graphic Arts; edtl. adv. bd. Arts and Architecture Mag. 1981-; bd. Art Dirs. Club of L.A.; founder/ch. L.A. Chpt. Am. Inst. of Graphic Arts (1983-4); mem. Fulbright Alumni Assn., Adv. Bd. of Archs., Designers and Planners for Soc. Responsibility. Known as pioneers in recent art of Urban Decoration in US, Japan and Italy; works incl. graphics and color for Crocker Ctr. (largest ofc. complex dwntwn L.A.); the Look of the 1984 Olympic Games; new environmental image for City of Burbank; work pub. internat.; Democrat; Hebrew; rec: photog. Res: 8049 Selma Ave Los Angeles 90046 Ofc: Sussman/ Prejza & Co. Inc., 1651 18th St Santa Monica 90404

SUTLIFF, GERALD MERYL, labor arbitrator; b. Feb. 28, 1937, Bakersfield; s. Meryl Weryl and Marian Naomi (Triplett) S.; m. Joyce E. Kitchen, July 26, 1966; children: Alice, b. 1960, Lorna, b. 1961, Clyde, b. 1967; edn: BA, CSU Long Beach 1967; MA, Chapman Coll. 1970; Calif. tchr. credential (grievance hndlg & arbitration) 1973. Career: marine clerk, Pacific Maritime Assn., San Francisco 1966-67, labor rels., 1968-78; asst. v.p. West Gulf Maritime Assn., Houston, Tx. 1978-80; full-time labor arbitrator No. Calif. area (Internat. Longshoremen & Warehousemens Union/ Pac. Maritime Assn. contract) 1980--; cons. Assoc. Co. Employees Contra Costa Co., Pupil Personnel Svcs. L.R., Calif. Sch. Psychologists Assn., 1974-78; statewide tchg. & cons. C.P.S./ L.R. as per SB 190; mem: Fed. Mediation Conciliation Svc. (labor arbit.), Am. Arbitration Assn. (Labor Panel, Comml. Panel); fundraiser var. civic and arts orgns.; Vietnam Vets. Against the War (1965-69); mil: enlisted US Army, Okinawa & Vietnam; Democrat; Unitarian; rec: personal computing. Ofc: G M Sutliff Assoc., 51 Blade Way Walnut Creek 94596

SUTLIFF, LEO CURTIS, real estate broker; b. Dec. 16, 1924, Trinidad, Colo.; s. Allen Curtis and Clara Belle (Dooley) S.; m. Obra Elizabeth Kester, 1943; children: Obra, b. 1944; Robert, b. 1945. Career: farmer until 1946; constr. operating engr. mech. until 1960; worked Wyoming tunnels, dams, roads, in Calif., Oil Research, Alaska, real estate broker/ investor 1981--; mem: Bd. Realtors; Masonic Lodge, S.A.; Royal Arch Masons, S.A.; Knights Templar, S.A.; Santa Ana Scottish Rite Bodies; El Bekal Temple; AAONMS; El Bekal Motor Patrol (pres. 1983; asst. dir. Units on the Appointive Divan 1984); Democrat; Protestant; rec: camping, fishing, travel. Address: 135 Mt. View Tustin 92680

SUTTERBY, LARRY QUENTIN, physician; b. Sept. 11, 1950, North Kansas City, Mo.; s. John Albert and Wilma Elizabeth (Henry) S.; m. Luciana Magpuri, July 5, 1980; children: Leah, b. 1981, Liza, b. 1983; edn: BA, William Jewell Coll. 1972; MD, Univ. of MO, KS City 1976. Career: res. internal med. Mt. Sinai Hosp., Chgo. 1976-79; physician, Mojave Desert Health Svc., Inc., Wrightwood 1979-80, Barstow, 1980--; chief of staff Barstow Comm. Hosp. 1983; bd. dirs. Hospice of Mojave Valley 1983; awards: AMA Physicians Recogn. Awd. 1983; mem: AMA; Calif. Med. Assn.; San Bernardino Co. Med. Soc.; Desert Manna Food dist. pgm.; Instr. Marriage Prep. course, St. Joseph's Catholic Ch.; Catholic. Res: 1113 Bigger St Barstow 92311 Ofc: Family Health Ctr, 209 No 2nd Ave Barstow 92311

SUYAT, REGINALD JOHN, lawyer; b. June 13, 1946, Honolulu; s. Donald G. and Lauriana (Calangan) S.; m. Joan Thompson, May 11, 1979; edn: BS, Univ. Wash. 1968; MS, Stanford Univ. 1972; JD, Georgetown Univ. 1976. Career: US patent examiner, US Patent & Trademark Ofc., Wash. DC 1972-76; atty. Connolly, Bove & Lodge, Wilmington, Delaware 1976-78; atty. Chevron Research Co., San Francisco 1978-81; atty. Flehr, Hohbach, Test, Albritton & Herbert, S.F. 1981--; honors: Pres.'s Medal, Univ. of Wash. 1965; Phi Lambda Upsilon (chem. hon.) 1967; Phi Eta Sigma (academic hon.) 1965; Phi Beta Kappa, 1968; mem: San Francisco Patent & Trademark Law Assn.; Am. Bar Assn. (patent sect.); Am. Patent Law Assn.; Internat. Assn. for the Protection of Indsl. Property; Lawyers Club of San Francisco; Virginia State Bar; State Bar of Calif. (patent, trademark & copyrght sect.); Am. Chem. Soc. (No. Calif. sect.); Stanford Alumni Assn.; Georgetown Alumni Assn.; mil: Capt., USAR 1976. Res: 347 Flaming Oak Dr Pleasant Hill 94523 Ofc: Flehr, Hohbach, Test, Albritton & Herbert, 4 Embarcadero Ctr, Ste 3400, San Francisco 94111

SUZUKI, KAZUO, banker; b. July 14, 1939, Tokyo, Japan; s. Yukichi and Sawa (Thuthumi) S.; m. Keiko Thuru, Nov. 23, 1964; children: dau., Naoko, b. 1964; son, Yasuhiro, b. 1966; dau., Miho, b. 1972; edn: BA in commerce, Waseda Univ. 1962; cert. mgmt. cons., Japan Productivity Ctr. 1968. Career: Industrial Bank of Japan 1962-67; mgmt. cons. Japan Mgmt. System, Inc. 1967-71; asst. mgr./ bus. devel. Indsl. Bank of Japan 1971; mgr./ bus. devel. 1977-82; deputy gen. mgr. Los Angeles Agcy, Indsl. Bank of Japan 1982--; awards: 2d Prize for thesis: Modernization of Japanese Industry and Rationalization of Enterprise, Kawakami Meml. Found.; mem: Los Angeles Athletic Club; Rolling Hills Country Club; Yorba Linda Country Club; coauthor: Management System, Yuhikaku, 1970; Buddhist; rec: golf, travel. Res: 11983 Darlington Ave Los Angeles 90049 Ofc: The Industrial Bank of Japan, 800 W 6th St Los Angeles 90017

SVIDOR, RHONA BEVERLY, teacher, real estate broker; b. May 12, 1934, Boston, CA; d. Sydney and Bella Zonis; m. Leonard Svidor, May 23, 1957; children: Mark Allen, b. 1955; edn: AA, UCLA 1954; UC Berkeley; BA, CSU, L.A. 1959; MA, CSU, L.A. 1970; USC. Career: tchr., R.E. broker, part- time travel agent: Rivera Elem. Sch. 1957-59, Hermosa Bch. Sch. Dist. 1959-60, tchr. GK-4, L.A. City Schs., 20 yrs.; salesman/ broker, Heart Properties, 2 yrs.; broker Rhona Realty, currently, and travel agt., Valley Travel Store; instr. student tchrs. and parent volunteers, inservice tchg. asst.; mem: Am. Fedn. Tchrs.; United Tchr. of L.A.; Valley Univ. Women; SYVBR; Calif. Assn. Realtors; Nat. Assn. Realtors; author: poetry; Democrat; Jewish; rec: reading, tennis, travel. Address: S.O. Elem. Sch., Rhona Realty, 17760 Alonzo Pl Encino 91316

SWALLEY, CLINTON LAVON, electronic engineer/instructor; b. Nov. 12, 1937, Ponca City, Okla.; s. Fred Wesley and Mary Lena (Barber) S.; m. Donna Wood, July 5, 1983; children: Charles b. 1960, Lyle b. 1961, James b. 1962, Pamela b. 1958, Karen b. 1965, Sherlyn b. 1967, Patricia b. 1970, Christina b. 1977; edn: Allen Hancock Coll. 1970-72; USAF Inst. 1963; aircraft/ missile, missile checkout and launch Electronic Trade Schs., USAF, 1956-69. Career: served to staff sgt. (E5), US Air Force 1956-69: Master Missileman, electronic tech., missile checkout and launch equipment tech., missile launch data analyst; aircraft flt. test data analyst Ling-Tempco-Vaught (LTV Inc.), 1969-70; missile launch data quality control insp. Federal Electric Div. of ITT, 1970-72; electronic organ installation and maint. Baldwin Piano & Organ Co., 1972-73; design engr. Schrager Cue's, 1973-78; electronic test engr. Monolithic Memories Inc., Santa Clara 1979--, design engr., test fixturing and burn-in, 1984; instr. Am. Red Cross (First Aid and CPR, 1983-84); mem. AAAS, San Jose Symphonic Orchestra and Choir; Baptist deacon. Res: 19070 Barnhart Ave Cupertino 95014 Ofc: Monolothic Memories Inc. 2175 Mission College Blvd Santa Clara 95050

SWAN, STEPHEN MICHAEL, investor; b. Oct. 23, 1952, Oakland; s. Ernest Loyd and Alice Odella (Kling) S.; m. Gracelynn Marie Melenudo, Jan. 31, 1981; children: Christine, b. 1970; Stephanie, b. 1971; Stephen, b. 1981; edn: USAF Power Production Sch. 1971; Control Data Inst. 1976-77. Career: tech. instr. Four- Phase Sys., Cupertino 1977-79; co- founder Corvus Systems 1979; customer svc. mgr. 1980; mgr. ops. 1981; prod. mktg. mgr. 1983; currently self-empl. investor; tchr. computer related classes, Four- Phase Co., IBM, Tandy Corp., IMI, Corvus Sys. & Hurricane Labs; mem: Pasatiempo Mens Club; publs: arts. in Byte, P.C., 80-Microcomputing & TRS-80 Journ. 1980-82; mil: SSgt., USAF 1971-75; GCM, Nat. Svc.; Marksmanship; Republican; Baptist; rec: golf, creative writing. Res: 10510 Hwy 9 Ben Lomond 95005

SWANSON, GUNHILD ALBERTINA, educator; b. Oct. 17, 1935, Los Angeles; d. Ivar and Gudrun Maria (Stromsnes) S.; edn: BA, UC Santa Barbara 1957; Univ. Oslo 1959; Univ. Stockholm Internat. Grad. Sch. 1959-60; MA, UC Berkeley 1964; counseling cred., San Jose St. Univ. 1967. Career: girls physical edn. & gen. bus. instr. Ceres Union H.S., Ceres, CA 1957-59; visiting instr. Western Wash. State Coll., Bellingham, Wash. 1961; tchg. asst. UC Berkeley 1960-61; counselor Palos Verdes H.S., Palos Verdes 1967-68; instr./ counselor San Jose City Coll. 1961--; recreation svc. Am. Recreation Ctrs., Inc. 1981-83; res. camp dir. Campfire Girls, summer 1962, 64, 65; lang. camp dir. Sons of Norway Dist. 6, summer 1969, 70; cons./ coord./ interpreter Norwegian Olympic Track & Field Team trng. sessions, San Jose City Coll. 1984; honors: Campbell Scholarship, UCSB 1953; Grand Lodge Scholarship, Vasa Order of Am. 1958; listed, Who's Who in Am. Women, 1966; Royal Blue Book, Internat. Soc. and Geneol. Register of the Leaders of Contemp. Soc. 1966; Who's Who of Exec. Women in Calif., 1st ed. 1983; mem: Calif., Am. Alliances for Health, Phys. Edn., Recreation & Dance; Calif. Assn. of Women Deans and Counselors; Am. Camping Assn.; Calif. Fedn. of Tchrs. (pres. 1974-76); Women's Internat. Bowling Congress; Vasa Order of Am.; Sons of Norway Internat.; Lutheran Ch. of Am.; Internat. Platform Assn.; author: series of arts., Vasastjarnan, vasa Order of Am. 1959-60, & Wash. Assn. for Health, Phys. Edn., &

Recreation Journ. 1961; Democrat; Lutheran; rec: photog., music, travel. Res: 2151 Oakland Rd, No 490, San Jose 95131 Ofc: San Jose City Coll., 2100 Moorpark Ave San Jose 95128

SWANSON, OTTO FRANK, lawyer; b. Nov. 6, 1932, El Paso, Tx; s. Joseph Paul and Dorothy Elizabeth (Bryce) S.; div.; children: Steven, b. 1952; Karen, b. 1955; edn: JD, summa cum laude, Univ. of West L.A. 1970; atty., Calif. Supreme Ct. 1971. Career: US border patrol ofcr., US Immigration Svc., Calexico, Calif. 1954-57; border patrol ofcr., Stockton 1957-62; sr. patrol inspr., Harlingen, Tex. 1962-63; immigration law instr., Port Isabel, TX 1963; immigrant inspr., Los Angeles 1964-69; supvry. immigrant inspr., Los Angeles 1969-70; atty., Los Angeles 1971--; pres. Profl. Corp. 1973--; Outstanding Performance of Duty Awd., Dept. of Justice, 1964-69; mem: Am. Bar Assn.; Assn. of Immigration and Nationality Lawyers; Fraternal Order of Retired Border Patrol Ofcrs.; Democrat; Methodist; rec: cycling, travel, hiking. Res: 12530 Rosy Cir. Los Angeles 90066 Ofc: Otto Frank Swanson, Atty. at Law, APC, 4676 Admiralty Way, Ste 632, Marina del Rey 90292

SWANSON, ROBERT BOUDINOT, II, computer peripheral co. executive; b. Sept. 26, 1936, Crawfordshire, Ind.; s. Raymond Elias and Lucille Elaine (Runge) S.; children: Robert B., III and Lisa Gail (twins), b. 1961; edn: BSEE cum laude, Mich. State Univ. 1960, MBA (Outstanding Graduate), USC 1972. Career: pgmmr. (IBM 7090), Pentagon Computer Ctr., USAF, Wash. DC 1960; mktg. tng. rep. Gen. Elec. Co., 1961-63; sales mktg., mktg. mgmt., Divsnl. strategic plnng., Internat. Bus. Machines Corp., 1964-82; regl. mgr., S.W. Region Ofc. Data General Corp., Santa Ana 1982; dir. No. Am. Sales, QUME Corp. (ITT subs.), San Jose 1983--; honors: Wing Cmdr. USAF ROTC Wing, Blue Key, Excalibur, MSU Varsity Golf Team, EKN and TBP hons., MSU; 4.0 GPA, Phi Kappa Phi, Beta Gamma Sigma hons., two theses in perm. library, USC; pres. IBM Hundred Percent Club (IBM top salesman); mil: capt. USAF 1960-68; Republican; Lutheran; rec: golf, music, dancing. Res: 23 Curl Dr Corona Del Mar 92625

SWARTZLANDER, EARL EUGENE, JR., engineering executive; b. Feb. 1, 1945, San Antonio, TX; s. Earl Eugene and Jane (Nicholas) S.; m. Joan Vickery, June 9, 1968; edn: BS, Purdue Univ. 1967; MS, Univ. of CO 1969, PhD, USC 1972; reg. profl. engr. Calif. 1973, Colo. 1974; Ala. 1981. Career: devel. engr. Ball Bros. Research Corp., Boller, CO 1967-69; Howard Hughes doctoral fellow Hughes Aircraft Co., Culver City, CA 1969-73; mem. research staff Technology Svc. Corp., Santa Monica 1973-74; chief engr. Geophysical Sys. Corp., Pasadena 1974-75; sr. staff engr. TRW Defense & Space Sys. Gp., Redondo Beach 1975-79; asst. mgr. ballistic missile defense proj. TRW Huntsville Lab., Huntsville, AL 1980-81; mgr. advel. ofc. TRW Defense Sys. Gp., Redondo Bch. 1982--; UCLA, Univ. Maryland, Am. Univ. Univ Mich 1978--; sem. spkr. Auburn Univ., Univ. Minn., George Mason Univ. 1978--; awards: Howard Hughes Doctoral Fellow, Hughes Medical Found. 1969-72; Best Paper Awd., Hawaii Conf. on Sys. Sci., IEE & Univ. of Hawaii 1983; mem: IEEE (Computer Soc.); Tech. Com. on Real Time Sys.; Casiano Estates, Bel Air; ed. IEEE Trans. Computers, ACM 1982--; ed. books Computer Design Development, Hayden Book Co. 1976; Computer Arithmetic, Hutchinson Ross Pub. Co. 1980; author: 40 papers on signal processing, computer architecture and VLSI; rec: collecting 1st ed. mystery books. Res: 2847 Deep Canyon Dr Beverly Hills 90210 Ofc: TRW, MS: 02/2791, One Space Park Redondo Beach 90278

SWEENEY, STENDER EDWARD, communications co. executive; b. Mar. 5, 1939, Long Beach; s. Stender and Josephine (Branham) S.; m. Polly Gleason, Apr. 6, 1968; children: Stender, b. 1970; Alison, b. 1976; Ryan, b. 1979; edn: BA, Stanford Univ. 1961; MBA, Harvard Univ. 1964. Career: First Nat. City Bank, NYC 1964-68; asst. to v.p. fin. Times Mirror, Los Angeles 1968-69; dir. fin. Times Mirror, Los Angeles 1969-77; asst. treas. 1975-77; treas. 1977-82; v.p./ treas. 1982--; mem: L.A. Wholesale Prod. Mkt. Devel. Corp.; Republican Assocs.; Hoover Inst. on War, Revolution & Peace; Polytechnic Sch.; Town Hall of Calif.; Central City Assn.; Fin. Execs. Inst.; L.A. Treas. Club; Stock Exch. Club; Calif. Club; Flintridge Riding; Harvard of NY. Res: 1465 San Pasqual St Pasadena 91106 Ofc: Times Mirror Co., Times Mirror Square, Los Angeles 90053

SWEET, GEORGE ELLIOTT, geophysicist, author; b. Sept. 26, 1904, Denver, Colo.; s. Leroy Foydice and Bertie Belle (Cooper) S.; m. Mildred Thelma (dec.), Oct. 13, 1932; 1 son: J. Eric Flippin Sweet, b. 1943; edn: BS., Univ. of Okla. 1927; BS, 1928; law sch., Harvard Univ. 1940-41; reg. geophysicist, Calif. 1974. Career: party chief Geophysical Research Corp. 1928-32; party chief/ chmn. bd. American Seismograph Co., Okla. City, Okla. & Houston, Tx. 1933-39; ofcr.-in-chg. Boston Magnetic Ranges, 1942-45; party chief/ pres. Sweet Geophysical Co., Santa Monica 1945--; honors: Valedictorian, Univ. Okla. 1927; Phi Beta Kappa; Alpha Chi Sigma; Sigma Delta Psi (Blue Pencil, nat. pres.); mem: Soc. of Exploration Geophysicists; Am. Assn. Petroleum Geologists; Harvard- Radcliffe Club of So. Calif.; Santa Monica Pony League (pres. 1959-60); author: Shake-Speare, The Mystery (Stanford Univ. Press. 1956; enlarged London ed., 1963); Gentleman in Oil (1965); The History of Geophysical Prospecting (Vol. One 1966; Vol. Two 1969); The Petroleum Saga (1971); Seven Dramas From Seven Centuries (197)8; Beginning of the End (1982); mil: lt. s.g., USNR 1942-45. Address: Sweet Geophysical Co., 502 Georgina Ave Santa Monica 90402

SWEETLAND, KAREN ELIZABETH, editor; b. July 31, 1941, Portland, Ore.; d. Earle E. and Daisy E. (Cline) Sweetland; 1 son, Craig, b. 1976; edn: Stephens Coll. 1959-60, Centenary Coll. 1961. Career: news dir./memb. mgr. San Fran-

cisco Conv. & Visitors Bureau 1971-73; dir. pub. rels. Fairmont Corp., S.F. 1974; dir. Southwick Agency, 1975-76; polit. lobbying (social), major govt. contractor, 1976-79; pres. Creative Concepts Unltd., S.F. 1979-83; exec. editor Bohn & Bland Publ. Inc., Burlingame 1984--; cons. Emergency Relief Fund Int. 1981-82; fundraising mktg. cons. to var. small businesses; recipient recognition, Big Brothers, other orgns.; mem: Bay Area Big Bros/Sisters, Ad Club, C.I.R.F., E.R.F.I., Nat. Assn. Female Execs., Commonwealth Club, (vol. fundraising ch. sev. orgns.); num. articles, book in progress (SuperBowl By the By); rec: cooking, arts, crafts, travel. Res: 2570 14th Ave San Francisco 94127 Ofc: Bohn & Bland Publ. Inc. 1419 Burlingame Ave, Burlingame 94010

SWIFT, LYDIA ANN, computer sales representative; b. Mar. 10, 1957, Hollywood; d. Raymond and Aurora Rena (Baldelli) Zaffini; m. Michael Swift, Dec. 24, 1983; edn: BS, CSU, L.A. 1980. Career: with Four-Phase Systems, Inc., Los Angeles 1980--; assoc. mktg. rep. 1980-81; mktg. rep. 1981-83; nat. acct. mgr./ mktg. rep. 1983-84; adv. mktg. rep./ nat. acct. mgr. Four- Phase Sys., Inc., Los Angeles 1984--; awards: 150 percent Sales Achiever, Pacesetter 1983; 300 percent Sales Achiever, Feb.- Mar. sales contest 1984; mem: Nat. Assn. Female Execs.; rec: fitness, art. Res: 15144 La Maida Sherman Oaks 91403 Ofc: Four- Phase Systems/ Motorola, Inc., 6033 Century Blvd Los Angeles 90045

SWIGERT, C(HARLES) J(USTIN), engineer, educator; b. Sept. 18, 1939, Evanston, Ill.; s. Dr. Verne Wilson and Marjorie (Helm) S.; m. Karen Struebing, Apr. 28, 1974; children: Justin, b. 1977; Laurel, b. 1980; edn: BS, cum laude, Princeton Univ. 1961; MS, Univ. Mich. 1963; PhD, UC Berkeley 1967; certs: Microprocessor Design, 1978, and Synthetic Aperture Radar, 1979, Hughes Aircraft. Career: act. asst. prof. UC Berkeley 1967-68; MTS Gen. Research Corp., Santa Barbara 1968-70; MTS, TRW, Redondo Beach 1970-73; SMTS Hughes Research Labs., Malibu 1973-80; SMTS Hughes Aircraft Co., EDSG, Sys. & Controls Lab., Culver City 1980-81; SMTS, Pacific Sierra Rsearch, Los Angeles 1981--; organized and initiated computer curriculum, Pacific Palisades Sch., sponsored by Pacific Sierra Research 1982--; awards: Hon. Svc. Awd., Pacific Palisades Sch. PTA 1984; mem: IEEE; Palisades Enrichment Pgms. (pres.); PTA; publs: Applications of Shapes Torque Techniques, Journ. of Guidance & Control, Sept. 1980; patent: Electronic Cancelling of Acoustic Traveling Waves, June 1982, Republican; rec: sailing, hiking, computer projs. Res: 14827 Bestor Blvd Pacific Palisades 90272 Ofc: Pacific Sierra Research Corp., 12340 Santa Monica Blvd Los Angeles 90025

SWIMMER, ALAN ELLIS, computer software retailing chain president; b. July 18, 1958, San Francisco; s. Alan Jerome and Sara Wynette (Ellis) S.; edn: BA, UC Berkeley 1980; MBA, Golden Gate Univ. 1983. Career: buyer R.H. Macy's, San Francisco 1980-81; sales rep. Clairol, Inc., Oakland 1981-82; acct. exec. Richardson-Vicks, Walter Conn 1982-83; pres / founder Info Store, software retail outlet franchized chain, 1983--; num. spkg. engagements on personal computer software; mem: Alpha Tau Omega frat. (pres.); AISEC (treas.); Walnut Creek CofC; Republican; Episcopal; rec: coin and stamp collecting. Res: 190 Caldecott Ln Oakland 94618 Ofc: Info Store, 1666 Locust St Walnut Creek 94596

SWITZER, MARTHA MARY, real estate broker; b. May 10, 1922, Fort Worth, Tex.; d. Roland Lester and Margaret (Hornsby) Mellown; desc. of the original families of Texas, gr.gr.grandau. of Reuben Hornsby (donor of the land under the Tx. State Capitol); uncle, Roger Hornsby, mem. Baseball Hall of Fame; m. Wilfred Eugene Switzer, Oct. 7, 1944; children: Maida Lynn, b. 1945; Michael, b. 1946; edn: BA, Texas Christian Univ. 1943; GRI (Grad. Realtor Inst.). Career: airport traffic controller, Newark Airport, Newark, NJ 1943-45; fashion coord., Wash. DC & Pitts., PA 1947-50; regl. mgr. Slenderella, Inc., Phila., PA 1950-59; sales supvr./ tng. dir. Relaxacizor, Inc., Los Angeles 1960-70; v.p. sales Technicolor, Inc. 1970-72; nat. tng. dir./ v.p. Ovation, Inc. 1972-74; real estate broker/ pres. Martha Switzer Real Estate Co., No. Hollywood 1974--; sem. on sales & motivation (20 yrs.); tchg. & lectrg., TV and radio appearances; num. awds. for nat. sales records; mem: CofC, Womans Club; AAUW; CAR; NAR; San Fernando Bd. Realtors; Sales & Mktg. of Los Angeles; Chaparral Country Club; ed. Roadrunner 1982-83; Prot.; rec: golf, tennis, needlework. Address: 63 Camino Arroyo So., Palm Desert; Martha Switzer Real Estate Co., 11043 Kittridge St, No. Hollywood 91606

SY, VICTOR SANTOS, certified public accountant; b. Feb. 19, 1945, Philippines; s. Francisco S. and Juliana Nicolas (Santos) Sy; m. Bernadette, Jan. 21, 1981; children: Karen, b. 1973, Byron, b. 1982, Michael, b. 1983; edn: BSBA cum laude, Univ. of the East, Manila, 1966; MBA, Ind. State Univ. 1970; CPA, Calif. 1971. Career: auditor var. CPA firms incl. Ernst & Whinney, in Manila, Terre Haute, Inc., Los Angeles, Calif. 1966-77; partner Sy, Alas & Co., CPAs, Los Angeles 1977--, partner in chg. govtl. and comml. audits; lectr. Univ. of the East 1973; mem. Legal Service Advisory Council, State of Calif. 1982-; honors: Top Grad. Award, UE (1966), Outstanding CPA Awd., Phil. Inst. of CPAs (1978); mem: Calif. Soc. of CPAs, Mgmt. Advis. Services Com.(1976-77), Phil. Inst. of CPAs (bd. dirs. 1980-), Confedn. of Phil.- US Orgns. (bd. dirs. 1981-, umbrella orgn. of over 260 orgns.); publs: Tax Tips columnist, sev. local newspapers; editor Nat. Assn. of Accts., Coll. and H.S. publs.; Catholic; racquetball. Res: 2542 Armstrong Ave Los Angeles 90039 Ofc: Sy, Alas & Co, 4017 Ingraham St Los Angeles 90005

SYKES, ABEL BAXTON, JR., college president; b. June 1, 1934, Kansas City, Kans.; s. Abel B., Sr. and Grace Gladys (Buchannan) S.; m. Sylvia Thierry, Sept. 28, 1957; 3 daus.: Dawn, b. 1958, Daphane, b. 1964, Leslie, b. 1966; edn: BA, Univ. of Mo. 1959, MA, 1960; EdD, USC 1971; Inst. of Ednl. Mgmt., Harvard Bus. Sch., Grad. Sch. of Higher Edn., Cambridge, Mass. Career:

instr. O'Farrell Jr. High Sch., San Diego 1960-64; instr., US Hist., Grossmont Coll., El Cajon and San Diego Evening Coll., 1962-64; instr. Pol. Sci. & Hist., Grossmont Coll. 1964-68; Dean of Instrn. Compton Community Coll. 1968-69, pres./supt. Compton Community College Dist., 1969--; honors: 1972 Educator of the Year, Phi Delta Kappa. Mem: Am. Assn. of Comm. & Jr. Colls. (chmn. bd. dirs. 1975-76), Ednl. Pgms. Eval. Com. South Viet Nam, US. Dept. of Def./ AACJC; Am. Council on Edn. (bd. dirs.); Calif. Comm. & Jr. Coll. Assn. (Chancellor's Adv. Com.); AAUP, Phi Delta Kappa, Am. Hist. Assn., Sigma Pi Phi. Orgns: bd. govs. Dominguez Valley Hosp., Salvation Army Adv. Bd., United Crusade budget rev. com., City of Compton Local Govt. Adv. Bd., bd. dirs. Charles Drew Postgrad. Medical Sch. (L.A.), L.A. Regl. Family Planning Council; publs: contbr. Junior College Research Rev. 6/70; mil: airman l/c USAF 1952-56, Bandsman; Presbyterian Elder; rec: photog. Res: 1600 Tartar Ln Compton 90221 Ofc: Compton Community Coll, 1111 E. Artesia Blvd Compton 90221

SZOLOMAYER, MARTHA LORETTA, quality engineer; b. May 2, 1920, Erie, Penn.; d. Frank John and Anna Catherine (Haschalk) Mihalic; m. Ernest Levandoski, Sept. 5, 1942, div. 1960; m. 2d. Martin Szolomayer, May 27, 1961; children: John, b. 1940; Carol Ann, b. 1943; Martin, b. 1945; Alice, b. 1946; Robert, b. 1948; Elizabeth, b. 1948; Donald, b. 1950; Linda, b. 1952; edn: secty. & bus. mgmt., Academy Ext. Courses, Erie, Pa.; spl. courses, Pasadena City Coll., Milton Weiner Sch., USC ext.; var. profl. tng. courses. Career: line inspr. to quality control technician Burroughs Corp., Pasadena 1956-71; adminstrv. asst. Passport Agcy., Los Angeles 1971-72; adminstrv. asst. US Dept. of Agriculture, Pasadena 1972-73; quality control analyst Xerox, El Segundo 1973-77; mfg. methods analyst. 1977-80; quality engr. Xerox EDS, Pomona 1980-83; quality engr. Loral Electro Optical Sys., Pomona 1983--; mem: Nat. Mgmt. Assn.; Am. Assn. of Ret. Persons; ASQC; Motion, Time & Movement Assn. for Studies & Research; Republican; Catholic; rec: designing, int. decorating, gardening. Res: 1550 No Catalina Ave Pasadena 91104 Ofc: Loral Electro Optical Systems, 600 E Bonita Ave Pomona 91767

T

TAAKE, WILLIAM HOWARD, ophthalmologist; b. Aug. 14, 1930, Cleveland, Ohio; s. Howard Eames and Irene Margaret (Walsh) T.; m. Ann Hunnicutt, July 18, 1981; chil: Thomas H., b. 1956, Kathleen I., b. 1959; edn: BS, Case-Western Reserve Univ. 1952, MD, 1956. Career: eye surgery residency, Jules Stein Eye Inst., UCLA Med. Ctr., 1960-63; pvt. practice ophthalmology 1963--, pres. Ventura Eye Medical Group, Inc. mem: Fellow Am. Acad. of Ophthalmol., AMA, Calif. Med. Assn., Ventura Med. Soc., Am. Intra-Ocular Implant Soc.; arts. in Am. Jour. of Ophthalmology; mil: capt. USAF 1958-60; Republican; Catholic; rec: tennis, bicycling. res: 687-33 County Square Dr Ventura 93003 ofc: Ventura Eye Medical Gp Inc, 3085 Loma Vista Rd Ventura 93003.

TADEN, CLAUDIA ELIZABETH, speech and language pathologist; b. Aug. 4, 1942, Oak Park, Ill.; d. Claude and May (Youker) Schacht; m. Kenneth Taden, Nov. 27, 1970; edn: BS, Univ. of Iowa 1964; MA, Bradley Univ. 1966. Career: speech and language pathologist Family Guidance Ctr., St. Joseph, MO 1965-68; dir. speech pathology Easter Seal Soc., Ventura, CA 1968-76; dir. Dept. of Communicative Disorders/chief speech lang. path. St. John's Hosp., Oxnard 1976--; founder/cons. Compu Speech and Language Prods., 1981, 82; cons./lectr. to CA hosps. implem computers, 1982; honors: Phi Kappa Phi, Outstanding Young Women of the Year Award, Missouri 1967; listed Who's Who of Calif. Exec. Women, 1984; mem: Am. Speech-Lang.-Hearing Assoc 1966-; Calif. Speech and Hearing Assoc. 1970-; Ventura Co. Soroptimist Club 1973-77; Ventura Co. Apple Computer Users Group 1980-, (secty 1980-82); created and implemented the first computerized speech and language pathology hosp. treatment program in Calif. 1981; publs: Computer Assisted Speech and Language Pathology, Reflections, Jour. Speech-Lang. Path. 1981. Res: 593 Via Ondulando Ventura 93003 Ofc: St. John's Hospital, 333 North F Street Oxnard 93030

TAGGART, ROBERT BURDETT, communications co. president; b. Apr. 6, 1943, Paterson, NJ; s. Robt. B., Sr., and Marjorie Stewart (Wiley) T.; m. Donna Fay Bledsoe, Feb. 14, 1973; 1 son, David Robert, b. 1974; edn: BSME, Northwestern Univ. 1967, MSME, 1968; Degree of Engr., Stanford Univ. 1970. Career: engr. and product mgr. Advanced Products Div., & Gen. Systems Div., Hewlett-Packard, Palo Alto 1970-78; mech. engrg. mgr. Computer Printers Internat., Inc., Mtn. View 1978-80; sr. mem. technical staff Apple Computer, Cupertino 1980-82; founder/ pres./ bd. chmn. Chapparel Communications, Inc. (mfr. antenna feeds for satellite TV); San Jose 1980--; pioneer mem. Soc. for Pvt. and Comml. Earth Stations; Patentee: (5; two patents pend.), Particle Analyzer (4/74), Dish Reflector for High Gain Antenna (8/74), Miniature Rotable Shaft Coupler (2/75), Miniature Magnetic Card Reader/ Recorder (7/75), Low-Cost Parabolic Reflector (7/76); sci. arts. in tech. jours., NASA Tech. Brief, IEEE Internat. Conf. on Comm.; Republican; Presbyterian; rec: satellite TV, racketball. Res: 348 Ramona Rd Portola Valley 94025 Ofc: Chaparral Communications, 2360 Bering Dr San Jose 94025

TAGUCHI, TADAO, corporate president; b. Sept. 8, 1929, Tokoyo, Japan; s. Tatsuo and Kikuyo (Ohizumi) T.; m. Takako Kawano, Dec. 3, 1958; children: Masako, b. 1959; Junko, b. 1964; edn: BSc, Tohooku Univ., Japan 1953. Career:

with Toshiba Corp. 1953--; mgr. Info. System Dept. Fuchu Works 1971; gen. mgr. Computer Div. 1978; gen. mgr. Bus. Machines and Equip. 1980; pres. Toshiba America, Inc., 1982--; pres. Toshiba Bus. Computer, Inc., 1978-; recipient: Power Line Protection System Award of JEMA 1962; mem. JIEE; publs: Power Line Carrier Relaying 1965; Eletric Sequence Control 1967; num. engring. publs.; rec: classical music, golf, reading. Res: 26 Salzburg Newport Beach 92660 Ofc: Toshiba America, Inc., 2441 Michelle Dr Tustin 92680

TAHAN, BOBRA GENE, real estate broker; b. Jan. 30, 1946, Fresno; d. Robert Wilson and June J. (McKeever) Jones; div.; chil: Michael, b. 1965, Lisa, b. 1967, Carin, b. 1971; edn: stu. Fresno City Coll. 1976, CSUF 1977; lic. real estate sales 1978, lic. R.E. Broker 1980; designated tching. cred. 1980. Career: real estate sales 1978-, owner/broker Tahan Real Estate, Fresno 1980--; partner Valley Women (nat. mail order co.), 1983--; instr. real estate, Fresno Unified Sch. Dist. Adult Edn., 1980-; mem. Fresno City Civil Service Bd.; founding bd. mem. Meadow Lake Camp. Mem: Fresno Bd. of Realtors (ch. Grievance Com. 1980-2), Am. Inst. of Real Estate Appraisers (R. M. candidate), Calif. Real Estate Tchrs. Assn., Central Calif. Bus. & Profl. Assn. (a founder), Nat. Assn. of Business Councils (ch. Spkrs Bur.); mem. Sunshine Sch. Aux., PTA, NOW, Nat. Womens Political Caucus. Works: created two public svc. commercials re the physically handicapped (1973). Democrat; Prot. Res: 3363 W. Celeste Fresno 93711 Ofc: Tahan Real Estate 87 E. Olive, Ste. 2F, Fresno 93728

TAI, BOB LAI, restaurant executive; b. Oct. 31, 1948, Canton, China; s. Quon Poy and Nuey (Chan) Tai; m. Denise Nagai, Nov. 17, 1973; 3 sons: Gregory, b. 1976, Jeffrey, b. 1978, Michael, b. 1982; edn: AA, Coll. of Sequoias 1969, BA, Cal Poly 1972; Calif. Gen. Contractors lic. 1974. Career: owner/mgr. Sambo's Restaurant, Inc., Mt. Vernon, Wash. 1974-76; territory tng. stores supr., Sambo's Restaurant, Inc. Phoenix 1976-78, regional tng. dir., Sambo's Restaurant, Inc. Woodland, Ca. 1978-80; dir. ops. Zim's Restaurant, Inc., San Francisco 1980--; dir. Padre Town Station Restaurant Group, 1983--; dir. National Food Service Panel, 1982-. Awards: Mgr. of the Year 1975, and Restaurant of the Year 1976, Sambo's Restaurant, Inc. Mem. Nat. Restaurant Assn., Am. Soc. for Tng. & Devel. 1976-80; asst. chief YMCA Indian Guides; rec: travel, fish, camping. Res: 151 Picadilly Cir. Vallejo 94591 Ofc: Zim's Restaurant Inc. 2218 Lombard St. San Francisco 94123

TAKEDA, KENNETH KINGO, orthodontist; b. Dec. 24, 1929, Riverside, CA; s. Orisaburo and Umeko (Ando) T.; m. Mary Yamaguchi, Jan. 28, 1951; children: Matthew, b. 1955; Kristin, b. 1970; edn: AA, Riverside Coll. 1949; BSCE, UC Berkeley 1951; DDS, UC San Francisco 1965. Career: engr. draftsman US Bureau Reclamation, Boulder City, Nev. 1949; jr. engr. US Bur. Reclamation, Marble Canyon, Ariz. 1950; stress analyst Boeing Airplane Co., Seattle, Wash. 1951-53; structures engr. Douglas Aircraft, Long Beach 1953-60; research engr. The Boeing Co., Seattle, summers 1961-3; orthodontist pvt. practice, Stockton 1965--; bd. dir. UC Med. Ctr. 1964-65; v.p. UCSF Sch. Dentistry 1964-65; pres. UC Orthodontic Soc. 1964-65; pres. San Joaquin Dental Soc. 1972-73; rep. Calif. Dental Assn.; awards: Gabbs prize in Dentistry, UCSF 1965, Omicron Kappa Upsilon 1965, Delta Sigma Delta (Worthy Master 1963-64); mem: UC Dental Alumni Assn; UC Orthodontic Alumni Assn; Parnassus Club UCSF; Pacific Coast Soc. of Orthodontists; Calif. State Soc. of Orthodontists; Am. Assn. of Orthodontists; Am. Dental Assn.; Kiwanis Club of Metro. Stockton (pres. 1977-78); Japanese-Am. Citizen's League (Lodi chpt. pres. 1984); Presbyterian; rec: photog., hunting, skiing, travel. Res: 626 Birchwood Dr Lodi 95240 Ofc: Kenneth K. Takeda, DDS Inc., 532 W Harding Way Stockton 95204

TALAIE, MOHAMMAD ALI, lawyer; b. Feb. 1, 1950, Abadan, Iran, naturalized 1980; s. Abdul Karim and Ferdos (Riahi) T.; edn: BS in computer sci., CSU Northridge 1976; BS, law, Glendale Univ. 1979, JD, 1981; admitted to Calif. State Bar 1981. Career: pres. Talaie Corp., Los Angeles 1977; voluntary wk. for Amnesty International (L.A.), National Lawyers Guild (L.A.), Nat. Center for Immigrants Rights (L.A.), 1978-80; legal asst., atty. law firm Miller & Miller, Los Angeles 1981--; Moslem; rec: music, martial arts. Res: 5430 Manton Ave Woodland Hills 91367 Ofc: 3345 Wilshire Blvd, Ste 515, Los Angeles 90010

TALBERT, RICHARD CLARK, solar co. exec.; b. Oct. 27, 1950, Oak Park, Ill.; s. Austin Gertner and Kathryn Mary (Pokragac) T.; m. Patricia Parker, Mar. 16, 1974; 1 son, Jeffrey, b. 1977; edn: Univ. of Ill. 1968-71. Career: mgr. Rock Road Trailer (camper parts house), St. Louis, Mo. 1971-74; nat. director Narconon (drug rehabilitation pgm.), Los Angeles 1974-79; gen. partner/pres. Northland Environmental, Inc. One of Inc. 500 fastest growing US pvt. cos. (solar co., Sunland Solar distbr.), Burbank 1979--; mem: Calif., L.A., Orange Co. Solar Energy Industries Assn. & CAL-SEIA spokesman; Nat. Fedn. Independent Bus.; Calif. Chamber of Commerce, Burbank CofC; rec: pvt. pilot, skiing. Res: 352 W. Canyon Vista Dr, Los Angeles 90065 Ofc: Northland Environmental, Inc., 1115 Chestnut St Burbank 91506

TALBOT, ALAN MICHAEL, lawyer; b. Oct. 14, 1946, Phila.; s. Bernard and Ruth T.; m. Karen Talbot, Dec. 1, 1979; children: Matthew, b. 1981; Andrew, b. 1982; edn: BA, Penn. State Univ 1968; JD, Univ. San Francisco 1980. Career: pres./principal Whollyfoods, Berkeley 1970-71; assoc. atty. Sandvik & Martin, Oakland 1980-82; of counsel Brookman & Hoffman, Inc., Walnut Creek and Sacramento, 1982--; mem: Phi Alpha Delta Frat., Marshall 1978; Contra Costa, Alameda Co., Am., Calif. Bar Assns. Res: 6426 Ascot Dr Oakland 94611 Ofc: Brookman & Hoffman, Inc., 1990 N California Blvd, Ste. 740 Walnut Creek 94596

TALEGHANY, PARVIZ P., obstetrician-gynecologist; b. Jan. 11, 1928, Tabriz, Iran, nat. 1980; parents: Ali-Asghar and Esmat (Kiani) T.; children: Dean Darush, b. 1957; Jeffrey Jamshid, b. 1957; Noushafarin, b. 1963; edn: BA, biol., Am. Coll. of Tehran and Darolfunoun 1944; MD, Tehran Univ. 1951; sci. & gynecol., Paris Univ. 1951-2; surg. tng. for gyn. oncology, Meml. Hosp. and Meml. Ctr. for Cancer, Cornell Med. Sch. 1957-8. Career: clin. instr. Memorial Hosp., Cornell 1959; asst. prof. for Ob-Gyn., Tehran Univ. 1959-61; chmn. Dept. Ob-Gyn. Hedayat Hosp., Tehran 1961-77; clin. prof. of gyn., Nat. Univ. of Tehran Foc. Med. at Hedayat Hosp. 1971-7; pvt. practice ob-gyn. 1977--; expert family planning and pop. control World Health Orgn. 1970-75; elected secty. gen. Ob-Gyn. Assn. of Iran 1968-75; fellow Internat. Coll. of Surgeons, v.p. Iranian sect. 1977; mem: Soc. of Meml. Gynecol. Oncologists 1979; NY Acad. of Sci. 1958; fellow Internat. Coll. of Surgeons 1963; v. chmn. Qualifications Com. of Internat. Fdn. of Obstets. and Gyns. 1963; Iranian pres. of World Fdn. Internat. de Gynecol., Switz. 1965; Assn. of Gyn. Cancer Prevention 1965; adv. bd. Wilson Research Found. 1963; works: Fgn. ed. Aggiornamenti in Obstetricia Ginecologia (Rome), and Wilson Research Found. Bull. (NY), 1970-77; author: Feminity as a Permanent Virtue; Republican; rec: tennis, swim, ski, classical music. Res: 2705 Bottlebrush Drive Los Angeles 90077 Ofc: 10921 Wilshire Blvd, Ste. 811 Los Angeles 90024

TALLENT, STEPHEN EDISON, lawyer; b. Aug. 10, 1937, Columbus, Nebr.; s. Wm. Edward and Helen (Sappington) T.; m. Martha , Apr. 6, 1971; 1 dau: Jennifer, b. 1969; edn: BA, Stanford Univ. 1959; JD, Univ. Chgo. Law Sch. 1962. Career: assoc. Gibson, Dunn & Crutcher, Los Angeles 1962-68; partner, Gibson, Dunn & Crutcher, Los Angeles and Washington DC 1969--; mem. sections of labor and employment law, litigation and adminstrv. law; past mgmt. chmn., current liaison div. chmn. Com. on Equal Empl. Opportunity Law with Am. Bar Assn.; 1st v. chmn. Equal Opp. Law Com. of the Defense Research INst.; past adj. prof. Loyola Law Sch., L.A. 1978-80; mem: Am. Bar Assn.; Calif. Bar Assn.; Indsl. Rels. Assn; L.A. Co. Bar Assn.; D.C. Bar Assn.; University Club; Town Hall; World Affairs Council; mil: US Army 1959-67. Res: 7020 Glenbrook Rd Bethesda, Md 20814 Ofcs: Gibson, Dunn & Crutcher, 333 S Grand Ave Los Angeles 90071 and 1776 G Street NW Washington, DC 20006

TALLMAN, JOHANNA E., university library director; b. Aug. 18, 1914, Lubeck, Germany; d. Friedrich Franz and Johanna (Voget) Allerding; AB, Univ. of Calif., 1936; certificate in Librarianship, 1937; m. Lloyd Anthony Tallman, May 8, 1954, Laguna Beach. career: San Marino Pub. Lib., 1937-38; L.A. County Pub. Lib., 1938-42; Pacific Aeronautical Lib., 1942-44; Engrng. and Math. Sci. Lib., UCLA, 1945-73; Dir. of Lib., Calif. Inst. of Tech., 1973--; lectr., Sch. of Lib. Service, UCLA, 1961-73; Fulbright Lectr., Brazil, 1966-67; over fifty contbrs. profl. journs. Pres., Librarians Assn., Univ. of Calif., 1970-71; chmn. Sci. Tech. Div., Special Libraries Assn., 1969-70; pres., So. Calif. chpt. 1965-66; chmn. L.A. Regional Group of Catalogers, 1946-47; bd. dirs., Pasadena Hist. Soc. Mem. Zonta Internat., pres. Pasadena chpt. 1976-77; res: 4731 Deleridge Rd., La Canada Flintridge 91011 ofc: 1201 E. California Blvd. Pasadena 91125.

TAM, HARRY F., restaurateur, acupuncturist; b. Aug. 8, 1916, Canton, China; s. Shong Sing and Yee Yong T.; m. Kay Wong, Apr. 17, 1947; children: Calvin D., b. 1948; Margo, b. 1949; Alva, b. 1951; Delma, b. 1957; Collin, b. 1964; edn: AA, Hoy Ping Acad. 1930; AA, San Diego State Univ. 1940; DC, Los Angeles Chiropractic Coll. 1954; lic. D.C., 1954, C.A., Calif. Bd. of Med. Quality Ass. 1976. Career: capt. Trader Vics, Oakland 1939-40; mgr. Golden Pagoda Restaurant, Los Angeles, Chinatown 1949-54 pres. Chinaland Restaurant, San Diego 1971--; practicing acupuncturist 1976-82; practicing chiropractor, Mt. View 1954-82; owner Vint-Rich Co.; mem. of Chinese Am. Citizens Alliance; mem. Wah Ying Club, San Francisco; awards: Outstanding Service Award, Nat. Acupuncture Assn; Award of Honor, United Acupuncturist of Calif.; PhD Nat. Sch. of Acupuncture; Dr.Oriental Med., Samra Univ. of Health Sci.; mem: pres. UAC; AAUS. (pres); S.F. Democratic Club; CACA; Chinese YMCA; Self-Help for Elderly, Chinatown; Affirmative Action, SF; publs: ed. UAC Newsletter; contbr. UAC Spec. Journal; mil: m/sgt. US Army Air Corps. 1943-47, merit. svc. cit.; Democrat; Congregational; rec: basketball, tennis, 49ers Football fan. Res: 836 W El Camino Real Mt. View 94040 Ofc: Chinaland Restaurant, Inc., 3135 Midway Dr San Diego 92110

TAMAROFF, MARC ALLEN, physician; b. May 22, 1948, Phoenix, Ariz.; s. Sam Al and June Ann T.; m. Sybil Abelsky, Nov. 26, 1978; 1 son, David, b. 1980; edn: BS, Univ. of Ariz. 1970, MD, 1974. Career: intern St. Mary Med. Ctr., Long Beach 1974; resident internal med. 1975-7; post-doc. fellow Div. of Clin. Immunology & Allergy, UCLA Med. Ctr. 1977-79; pvt. practice, Allergy 1979--; assoc. dir. for Pgm. Developments, Ctr. for Interdisciplinary Research in Immunologic Diseases (CIRID) UCLA 1979--; assoc. dir. of Skin Test Svc. and spl. cons. Div. of Clin. Immunol. & Allergy UCLA Med. Ctr. 1979-80; chmn. Medical Edn. Com. Los Altos Hosp., Long Beach 1980--; Asst. Clin. Prof. of Med., UC Irvine 1982--; awards: Phi Kappa Phi 1970-; Physician Recognition Award, AMA 1977; Cert. Award Calif. Med. Assn. 1979; Nat. Research Svc. Award, NIH-PHS 1977-79; mem: Am. Coll. of Physicians; AMA; L.A. Soc. of Allergy and Clin. Immunol.; Immunol. Research Group. UCLA Sch. Med.; Am. Lung Assn.; Asthma & Allergy Found. of Am.; Am. Acad. of Allergy; AAAS; Am. Coll. of Allergists; research publs.; Democrat; Jewish; rec: tennis, softball. Res: 18171 Ivorycrest Ln Huntington Beach 92648 Ofc: Allergy & Clinical Immunology Consultants, 3325 Palo Verde, Ste. 107 Long Beach 90808

TAN, CHUNG C., orthopedic surgeon; b. Oct. 26, 1912, Canton China, nat. 1945; s. Shen G. and Ching-Ai W. Tan; m. Edna C. Tan, Aug. 1, 1939; children: Henry K. (MD), b. 1940; Sylvia M. (MS), b. 1947; Mary A. (Yen) (JD), b. 1949; John K. (BS), b. 1952; edn: BS, Yenchinf Univ., Peking, China 1933; MD, Peking Univ. Rockefeller Med. Sch. 1938; dip., Harvard Grad. Med. Sch. 1944; FAAOS, fellow Am. Acad. of Orthopedic Surgeons 1953; FACS, fellow Am. Coll. of Surgeons 1954; FICS, fellow Internat. Coll. of Surgeons 1955. Career: asstg. res. in gen. surgery Peking UMC Hosp. 1939-41; Rockefeller fellowship, physical med. and rehab. Columbia Presbyn. Med. Ctr. and Cornell Med. Ctr., NY 1941; orthopedic res. Mass. Gen. Hosp. and Boston Childrens Hosp. 1942-44; 1st lt. USMC active overseas 1945-6, major MC, AUS active reserve 1948-54; chief orthopedic svc. VA Hosp. Reno 1948-50, Fresno 1950-54; cons. orthopedics USVAH 1956--; pvt practice, orthopedic surgery, Fresno 1954-82; currently semi-ret., spl. cons.; med. lectr. 828 Station Hosps. 1948-54; awards: MD Boss of the Year 1976, Am. Assn. of Med. Assts., golf awd. (First Blind Bogey) Physicians, Lawyers, & Dentists 1959; mem: FACS 1954; FICS 1955; FAAOS 1953; FPPSA (Pan Pacific Surgical Assn.) 1968; WGA; AMA; CMA; FCMS; Optimist Club of Fresno 1954-76; Fay Wah Club of Fresno 1950-; San Joaquin Orthopedic Club 1955-; mil: 1st Lt. USMC 1945-46; major M.C. AUS 1948-54; Presbyterian; rec: hunting, fishing, trap & skeets. Res: 1230 E Swift Fresno 93704 Ofc: POB 5277 Fresno 93755

TAN, JIMMY CHIH-YU, hotelier/ trading co. executive; b. Feb. 10, 1936, Hunan, China, nat. 1982; s. Wen Sun and En Zen (Tung) T.; edn: Bach., Nat. Chung Hsing Univ., Taiwan, 1960; cert. assoc. prof., Dept. Edn. Taiwan 1972. Career: asst., Coll. of Commerce, Nat. Cheng Chi Univ. Taiwan 1960-64; instr. Nat. Cheng Chi Univ. 1964-68; auditor of Budget Commn. of Exec. Yuan, Taiwan 1968-69; assoc. prof. Nat. Cheng Chi Univ., Taiwan 1969-73; mgr. Sequoia Hotel, Los Angeles 1974-76; mgr./owner Grand Central Hotel, San Francisco 1978--; pres. General Union Trading Group Inc., SF 1981--; mem: Nat. Assn. of Exec. Sectys., Vir. 1978; SF Conv. & Visitor Bur.; author: Applied Mathematics of Management (World Books Co. Taipei, Taiwan 1969); Catholic; rec: draughts, travel, music. Address: Grand Central Hotel, 1412 Market St San Francisco 94102

TANA, ALICE M., business services co. president; b. Oct. 17, 1935, Freeland, PA; d. Adrian W. and Alice T. (Campbell) Carr; m. Yasuto Tana, Oct. 13, 1973; edn: US San Diego Univ. 1977-9; E. Mich. Univ. 1963-7; Univ. Mich. 1963-7; Georgetown Univ. and Catholic Univ. of Am. 1968-73; num. workshops, symps. Career: order dept. supvr. Gallant Inc., Wash. DC 1954-58; reg. dir. Mary Anne Baldwin Sch., Pittsburgh, Penn. 1958-60; dir. Sr. Citizens and Women, Ypsilanti, Mich. 1961-67; regl. dir. Nat. Council on Aging, Wash. DC 1967-70; dir. President's Task Force on Aging, Wash. DC 1972-73; tng. splst. Japanese Self Defense Force, Sumitomo Corp., Taura, Japan 1973-76; econ. devel. splst. County of San Diego 1977-80, transp. research and mktg. study dir. 1980; budget analyst 1981; founder/pres. (diversified bus. svcs. co.) Ask Alice 1982--; bd. dirs. GROW (women's bus. & profl. orgn.); bd. dirs. The Crime Victims Fund.; mem: Republicans Bus. and Profl. Women; Diversified Bus. Women (pres., founder); E. Mich. Univ. Alumni Assn.; Econ. Research Bur.; Calif. Women in Govt. (pres. 1980-81); Rutgers Univ. Women in Politics & Govt. 1980-81; adv. bd. women and mgmt, Georgetown Univ.; Republican; rec: skiing, travel. Address: 3114 East Fox Run Row San Diego 92111

TANENBAUM, ROBERT KARL, lawyer/author; b. Dec. 17, 1942, Brooklyn, NY; s. Julius and Ruth (Hitzig) T.; m. Patricia, June 24, 1967; children: Rachael, b. 1975; Roger, b. 1979; William, b. 1982; edn: BA, UC Berkeley 1965, JD, UCB Boalt Hall 1968. Career: asst. dist. atty. N.Y. County Dist. Atty's Ofc., bureau chief Criminal Courts and fellow trial bureau and deputy bureau chief Homicide Bureau 1968-76; deputy chief counsel of Investigation into Assassination of John F. Kennedy, House of Reps., US Cong. Assassinations Com. 1977; currently, pvt. practice law/ author; seminars USC, (labor, criminal justice); mem: Rotary; Beverly Hills Family YMCA (bd. dirs.); Beverly Hills CofC; author: Badge of the Assassin (pub. Dutton 1979, Fawcett 1982); Jewish. Address: 124 Lasky Dr Beverly Hills 90212

TANG, ALEXANDER P., dentist; b. Dec. 2, 1951, Manila, R.P.; s. Koo and Wui (Pang) T.; m. Elizabeth Wong, Sept. 13, 1980; 1 dau: Candice, b. 1981; edn: DDS, Univ. of the East, Coll. of Dentistry 1975; Univ. of Texas Dental Br. 179-80; UCLA Extension 1981; Calif. Lic. Dentist, Calif. State Bd. of Dental Exmainers. Career: private prcatice, dentist, Manilla 1976-78; dentist assoc., L.A. 1982; private practice 1983--; clinical dir. Santa Barbara Urban Indian Health Ctr. 1983; mem: Am. Dental Assn.; Calif. dental Assn.; Santa Barbara - Ventura Co. Dental Soc. 1983; Santa Barbara Filipino Comm.;publs: Tooth Peak, Dental Newletter 1983; Catholic. Res: 7551 San Cassino Way Goleta 93117 Ofcs: 422 N. Milpas, Ste. 5, Santa Barbara 93103; S.B. Urban Health Center, 614-616 N. Milpas, Santa Barbara 93103

TANIS, NORMAN EARL, librarian; b. Aug. 15, 1929, Grand Rapids, Mich.; s. Aaron Orrie and Gertrude (Medendorp) T.; m. Terese Tieman, Dec. 27, 1981; 2 daus: Kathy, b. 1962; Laura, b. 1964; edn: AB, Calvin Coll. 1951; AMLS, Univ. of Mich. 1951; MA, 1956. Career: library coord. Henry Ford Comm. Coll., Dearborn, Mich. 1956-66; lib. dir. Kans State Univ., Pittsburgh 1966-9; dir. of univ. libs. CSU, Northridge 1969--; ed./mgr. The Santa Susana Press 1973--; secty. & bd. trustees Univ. San Fernando Coll. of Law 1978-80; honors: Phi Kappa Phi, Beta Phi Mu, and D.H.L. (hon.) at Univ. San Fernando 1975; LLD (hon.), Mid-Valley Coll. of Law 1979; mem: Northirdge Draft Bd. (Selective Svc. no. 201); Marine Meml. Club of San Francisco 1976-; coauthor: Native Americans of North America. Scarecrow Press, Inc. 1975; Probemms in Developing Academic Library Functions, Jai Press, Inc. 1978; China in Books, Jai

Press, Inc. 1979; mil: Cpl., US Army 1952-4, Nat. Defense Medal.; Democrat; Protestant; rec: theatre, travel, horsemanship, art collector. Res: 9585 Reseda Blvd Northridge 91324 Ofc: Calif. State Univ., 18111 Nordhoff Northridge 91330

TANNER, ROBERT LEWIS, service company executive; b. Mar. 17, 1942, Rigby, Idaho; s. Lewis C. and Vivian D. (Driggens) T.; m. Judy Lee, July 28, 1979; children: Billy Joe, b. 1961; Ricky Todd, b. 1962; Debbie S., b. 1963; Pam S., b. 1967; edn: BS, Idaho State Univ. 1967. Career: ins. broker Am. National, Idaho Falls, Idaho 1969-72; sales mgr. Saxon Inds., Commerce 1972-75; regl. svc. mgr. Robertshaw Controls, Anahiem 1975-81; gen. mgr. Western Air & Refigerator Svc., Compton 1981--; instr., MBOR, Stanford Univ 1978; lectr., Saddleback Coll. 1983; mem: JJAC bd. apprenticeship 1982-; Agape Univ. Adv. Bd. 1983-; rec: wood working. Res: 24801 Via Princesa El Toro 92630 Ofc: Western Air & Refrigeration, 15914 So. Avalon Blvd Compton 90220

TANNER, SUSAN DIANE (Dede), marketing executive; b. Dec. 2, 1943, Pittsburgh, PA; d. Hal R. and Lucille Mela (Eberley) T.; edn: BSBA, Miami Univ.,, Oxford, Ohio 1967. Career: dist. sales mgr. Olan Mills, Inc., Springfield, OH 1967-70; acct. executive Hal Lawrence Advtg., Los Angeles 1970-2; acct. exec. Union Home Loans, Los Angeles 1972-4; editor nat. trade mag. Teleflora, Inc., Redondo Bch. 1974-7; pub. rels. mgr. Gibraltar Savings & Loan, Beverly Hills 1977-82; sales/mktg. mgr. Group W Cable, Inc. Buena Park 1982--; recognition for business leadership, YWCA 1980; 1st place, Nat. Cable T.V. Sales Contest 1983; mem: Publicity Club of L.A.; Women in Cable T.V.; So. Calif. T.V. Assn.; Internat. Assn. of Bus. Communicators; So. Calif. Assn. of Bus Communicators; Filmex Soc.; publs.: approx. 50 business related arts. in nat. trade mags. 1974-7; Republican; Catholic; rec: non-fiction and fiction writing. Res: 320 The Village, No. 306, Redondo Beach 90277 Ofc: Group W Cable, 7050 Village Dr, Ste E, Buena Park 90621

TAPERT, DONALD W., insurance agency owner; b. Sept. 2, 1932, Sault St. Marie, Mich.; s. Clarence William and Marjorie I. (Cowan) T.; m. Sally Ann Peapples, Sept. 7, 1957; children: Robert, b. 1958; Charles, b. 1961; Matthew, b. 1964; Tiffany, b. 1967; edn: BS, Western Mich. State 1954; Michigan State 1956-57; chartered life underwriter, CLU 1969. Career: spl. agent Northwestern Mutual Life Ins. 1962-78; founder Tapert Ins. Agency 1978, (developed to top 3 percent in gr. L.A.); pres./owner Tapert Ins. Agency, Pasadena, 1978--; awards: Man of Year, Northwestern Mutual Los Angeles Agency 1972; mem: Million Dollar Round Table (16 yrs.); pres., Upper Rancho Home Owners Assn 1976; mil: 1st Lt., Med. Svc. Corp., US Army, Austria and Germany 1954-6; Repubilcan; Protestant; rec: golf, travel, swimming. Res: 920 West Orange Grove Arcadia 91006 Ofc: Tapert Insurance Agency, Inc., 600 So. Lake Ave, Ste 510, Pasadena 91106

TAPPING, DAVID WILLIAM, engineer/executive; b. Aug. 4, 1928, Deal, U.K., nat. 1969; s. John Arthur and Kathleen (Oakridge); m. Patricia Roughton, 1954; children: Carol, b. 1956; Jonathan, b. 1960; edn: BS, Univ. Coll. London 1952; Reg. Profl. Engr., NY, Mo., Wash., Ore., Calif., and La.; Career: with Bechtel Corp. 1964--; responsible for structural design, including conformance to codes of Foothill Feeder water supply for L.A. and for complete design of fossil power generating stations in Centralia, Bowline Point, Rush Island, Creston and Boardman; honors: Fellow, Am. Soc. of Civil Engrs.; Fellow, Inst. of Civil Engrs., U.K. (for assisting in orig. design of comml. nuclear power); chmn. of panel for selection of USA residents seeking U.K. profl. engring. registration with Inst. of Civil Engrs.; mil: Lt. Royal Engrs., Brit. Army, Germany 1946; rec: backpacking, 10k, cross country, boating. Res: 160 Manor Dr Mill Valley CA 94941 Ofc: Bechtel Power Corp., POB 3965 San Francisco 94119

TARLETON, ERNESTINE ALVINA, educator, financial planner; b. Dec. 24, 1920, New Sharon, Iowa; d. Alvin Ernest and Mabel Evelyn (Mahan) Ehret; m. George Tarleton, Aug. 25, 1974; edn: AA, Central Coll. 1938-42; BA, Iowa State Teachers Coll. 1946; MA, CSU Sacto. 1972; Reg. Rep., NASD; Calif. State Life & Disability lic., Variable Contract lic. Career: teacher elem. public schools, Barnes City, Iowa 1940-42, Newton, 1943-46, Deep River, Iowa 1942-43; tchr. Jr. H.S., Pueblo (Colo.) Pub. Schs. 1946-7; exec. director Parkersburg (W.Va.) Girl Scout Council, 1947-50; dir. of camping, Girl Scouts of Greater St. Louis, Mo. 1950-52; exec. dir. Stanislaus Council of Girl Scouts, Modesto, Ca. 1952-55, 1958-64; dir. Christian Edn., Georgetown (Ky.) Christian Ch., 1955-6; exec. dir. Sadaquada Council of Girl Scouts, Utica, NY 1956-8; elem. tchr. Westport/ Ceres Unified Sch. Dist., Ceres, Ca. 1964-67, Sacramento City USD, 1967-82; finl. planner G.W. Story & Assocs. Inc., Sacto. 1982--; frequent seminars, lectrs. on finl. plnng.; honors: recognition Girl Scouts, 1952, United Crusade, 1963, Service to Youth Award, First Christian Ch., Modesto 1964; mem: Internat. Assn. of Fin. Plnnrs., Calif. Assn. of Fin. Plnnrs., NEA, Calif. Tchrs. Assn., Sacto. City Tchrs. Assn., Calif. Retired Tchrs. Assn., Girl Scout Council Sacto., Sacto. Metropolitan CofC, Sacto. Womens Network, Parent Support/ Kid Support Pgm.; fmrly active in AAUW, Sierra Club, Zonta Intl., Am. Camping Assn., Nat. Assn. Soc. Wkrs.; publs: mag. articles 1955, 83; oil paintings entered in art shows; trophy, Modesto Camellia Show 1969; Democrat; Presbyterian (elder); rec: oil painting, clay sculpture. Res: 69 Sandburg Dr. Sacramento 95819 Ofc: G.W. Story & Assoc. Inc. 1333 Howe Ave, Ste 103, Sacramento 95825

TASHEY, THOMAS ERNEST, JR., gemologist; b. Sept. 11, 1947, Highland Park, Mich.; s. Thomas E. and Doris Margaret (Hodgson) Tashey; m. Myriam Both, July 26, 1980; edn: stu. Kalamazoo Coll. 1965-7, 71-3; (GG),Grad. Gemologist, Gemological Inst. of Am. 1975; (FGA), Fellow, Gemmological Assn. (Gr. Brit.) 1978; (MGA), Master Gemologist Appraiser, Accred. Gemologists Assn. 1983. Career: staff gemologist Gemolog. Inst. of Am., Santa Monica 1975-8, supr. of grading, Gem Grade Lab., GIA 1976-8; dir. European Gemolog. Lab., Los Angeles 1978-9; salesman Luxor Diamond Co., Beverly Hills 1979-80; owner/dir. Independent Gemological Lab., L.A. 1980--. Mem: Accredited Gemologists Assn. (secty. 1981-, ed. AGA Cornerstone 1983-), GIA Alumni Assn., Gemmological Assn. of Gr.Brit.; author: Diamond Certificate of Quality Analysis (1981); mil: MM2, USN 1967-71; Democrat; Buddhist; rec: tennis, music; res: 641 Ocean Park Bl. #2, Santa Monica 90405 ofc: Independent Gem Lab, 608 S. Hill St. #1013, Los Angeles 90014.

TATE, ADOLPHUS, JR., life underwriter/district sales executive; b. Aug. 18, 1942, Turrel, Ark.; s. Adolphus and Rutha Lee (Johnson) T.; m. Patricia Levelle Dawson, Dec. 21, 1969; children: Adolphus III, b. 1971; Cherie Levelle, b. 1973; Faith Elizabeth Ann, b. 1981; edn: L.A. City Coll. 1963-4; grad. Life Underwriters Tng., 1981, Agcy. Mgmt. Tng. Council 1983. Career: agent Western So. Life Ins. Co. of Ohio, in Los Angeles 1967, million dollar producer 1968, assoc. sales mgr. 1968-, District Sales Mgr. 1975--; Policyholders' Merit Awards 1971, 77, 78, 79; mem: Nat. Assn. of Life Underwriters, Masons, Hollypark Homeowners Assn. (2d v.p. 1983); Gardena Interested Neighbors (past pres.); chmn. Gardena Neighborhood Improvement Assn.; mil: Sp4 US Army 1964-66; United Methodist (pres. U.M. Men 1969-77); rec: fish, hunt, camp, basketball. Res: 13204 So Wilkie Ave Gardena 90249 Ofc: Western Southern Life, 4300 So Crenshaw Blvd, Los Angeles 90008

TATHAM, LELAND L., real estate broker; b. Mar. 26, 1940, Bakersfield, CA; s. Leland L. and E Cornelia (Hines) T.; m. Bonnie Lynn Shubb, Dec. 25, 1978; edn: BA, CSU, L.A. 1968. Career: newscaster Armed Forces Radio/TV 1962-4; journalist US Navy Seabees 1964-6; human factors engr. Lockheed 1968-9; real estate 1969--, currently pres. C.M.S.T., Inc. dba Century 21 Dynasty Realty, Agoura --; mem: Coneyo Valley Bd. of Realtors, nom. com. 1983; Agoura - Las Virgenes CofC (5yrs.); mil: J05, USN 1962-6, Vietnam Cpgn, GCM; rec: flying, travel. Res: 29481 Trailway Lane Agoura Hills 91301 Ofc: Century 21 Dynasty Realty, 5823 Kanan Road Agoura 91301

TATSUNO, GEORGE THOMAS, chiropractor; b. Aug. 10, 1951, Bakersfield; s. George and Nellie Yuri (Murotani) T.; m. Jeanne Tatsuno, Sept. 11, 1976; children: Matthew, b. 1980; Shannon, b. 1983; edn: AA, Bakersfield Coll. 1971; BA, UCLA 1974; DC, Palmer Coll. Chiropractic 1978. Career: dr. of chiropractic private practice 1978--; pres. Kern Co. Chiro. Assn. 1983; v.p. Kern Co. Chiro. Soc. 1983; prgm. dir. KCCA 1981-2; mem: Nat. Fdn. of Independent Bus.; BBB; Am. Chiro. Assn.; Calif. Chiro. Assn.; Council on Diagnosis and Internal Disorders; Council on Roentgenology of the Am. Chiro.; N.Y. State Chiro. Assn.; Parker Chiro. Research Found.; Judo orgns: mem. Jr. Olympics 1968; UCLA Judo Team capt. 1973; UC Champ. 1973; bd. mem. Doryoku Judo Club 1983; delegate Ca Judo Inc.; Iowa State Champ. 1977; Nat. 189lb Master US Champ. 1983; team Doryoku Judo Chiropractor 1983; 3rd degree black belt; Methodist; rec: Judo. Res: 6508 Saddleback Dr Bakersfield 93301 Ofc: Dr. George T. Tatsuno, DC, 238 18th St Bakersfield 93301

TAVLIN, LINDA JEANNE, real estate broker; b. Feb. 7, 1950, Long Beach; d. Harry and Shirley Jeanne (White) T.; edn: BA, UC Irvine 1972; ins. solicitor, Dept. Ins. 1976; personal property broker, Dept. Corp., CA 1980; real estate broker, Dept. Real Estate, CA 1980. Career: mgr. Public Finance, Fullerton 1973-78; asst. mgr. Topa Thrift & Loan, Newport Beach 1978; ind. contractor Calif. Nova Financial, Huntington Beach 1978-80; owner/broker Independent Funding & Investments, Irvine 1980--; instr. Santa Ana Comm. Coll., Santa Ana 1980--; instr. Long Beach City Coll., Long Beach 1980--; guest lectr. Santa Ana Coll. 1980--; mem: Calif. Assn. of Real Estate Tchrs. 1980; Los Angeles Assn. of Profl. Mortgage Women 1982; Calif. Republican Party, assoc. 1983; Nat. Fdn. of Republican Women 1982-; Calif. Fdn. of Republican Women 1982-; Los Angeles Olympic Organization Comm.; Citizen's Long Beach GOP Jrs., Adv. Commission, fed. 1982; Los Angeles World Affairs Council, donor mem.; World Affairs Council of Orange Co.; Town Hall; UC Alumni Assn.; author Cont. Edn. Seminars 1982-; assoc. producer / co-host, Long Beach Republican Review, (talk show), Dimension Cablevision, Long Beach 3/84; Republican; rec: politics, world affairs, travel, theatre. Res: 19 Windwood Irvine 92714 Ofc: Independent Funding & Investments, POB 17754 Irvine 92713

TAVRIS, EUGENE DAVID, lawyer; b. Jan. 6, 1931, Chicago, Ill.; s. Hyman Victor and Miriam (Matelson) T.; m. Eleanor Susnow, Dec. 20, 1959; children: Holly Victoria, b. 1964; Melinda Lee, b. 1966; Leslie Roin, b. 1966; edn: BA, USC 1953; JD, Southwestern Univ. 1959; atty., Calif. State Bar 1959. Career: asst. inheritance tax atty. State of Calif. 1959-6u0; private practice 1960-4; dep. dist. atty. Co. of Los Angeles, 1964--; adj. prof. of law Southwestern Univ. 1960-70; awarded: Professor of the Year Award 1963; author: over 500 briefs submitted to the US and Calif. Supreme Cts., and Calif. Ct. of Appeal; Republican; Jewish; rec: astronomy, sailing. Ofc: Office of the District Atty., Appellate Div., 849 So. Broadway, 11th Flr. Los Angeles 90014

TAYLOR, B. DON, semiconductor equipment mfg. co. executive; b. Bay City, Texas; s. William Henry Jr. and Lena Mae (Walenta) T.; m. Mary Ann Jordan, Aug. 2, 1969; children: Tom, b. 1958; Kim, b. 1961; Deadra, b. 1961; Kevin, b. 1962; Patrick Andrew, b. 1970; Kathleen, b. 1964; Kimberly, b. 1964; Chellafon, b. 1966; edn: B. Theology, Bible Baptist Coll., Springfield, Mo. 1961; Univ. Texas, Austin 1968-9; BA, Univ. Texas, Arlington 1970. Career: Capt., Criminal Warrant Div., Tarrant Co., Texas Sheriffs Ofc. 1961-72; mgr. customer training Ofc. Prods. Div., Xerox Corp., Dallas, TX 1971-82; mgr. tech. publs. Wafer Systems Div. Eaton Corp., 1982--; devel. sales, svc., and customer training curricula for Ofc. Automation equip. for Xerox 1972-82; spkr. Word

Processing Ofc. Equip. Trade Show, San Jose 1982; awards: Outstanding Younng Man, Fort Worth Jr. CofC 1964; J.E. Hethington Meml. Awd., Texas State Jr. CofC 1965; var. awds. for contrb. to Nat. Dairy Assn. 1966; Texas 4-H clubs 1967; Texas State Tchrs. Assn. 1969; mem: Semiconductor Equip. and Materials Inst. 1982-4; founder Miss Texas Pageant Scholarship Found. 1965-6; Wendish Heritage Soc.; SAR; past dir. Heritage Hall, Ft. Worth; Episcopal Cursillo Secretariat for the dioceses of Dallas and El Camino Real; 32nd degree Scottish Rite Mason, Shriner; author: The IC Story, Eaton Corp. 1982; Anchors in the Storm and An Acolyte's Training Manual, Episcopal Diocese of Dallas 1981; Republican; Episcopal (lay minister); rec: hist. research, music & the arts. Res: 2341 Venn Ave San Jose 95124 Ofc: Eaton Corp., Microlithography System Div., 910 Benicia Sunnyvale 94086

TAYLOR, BURNARD NIELSON, building contractor, realtor; b. Sept. 1, 1920, Gridley, CA; s. Joseph Burnard and Hulda Agnes (Nielson) T.; m. Mellie Mae Burdick, Nov. 13, 1945; children: Sheryl, b. 1946; Celeste, b. 1949; Burnard, b. 1951; John, b. 1953; edn: Yuba Coll. 1939-40; East Central State Mission 1941-2. Career: Taylors Dept. Store, Yuba City; Gen. Bldg. Contractor 1947--; Real Estate Broker 1974--; missionary and pres. Tennessee West Dist. LDS Ch. (2 yrs.), scoutmaster (2 yrs.), mem. Yuba City Personnel Bd.; Republican Central Com.; Juvenile Justice Delinquency Commission; Sutter Co. Grand Jury; elected to Sutter Co. Bd. of Supvrs. (8 yrs.); Bishop Yuba City II Ward, LDS Ch. (7 yrs.); High Council, Gridley Stake, LDS Ch. (15 yrs.); Patriarch Yuba City Stake, LDS Ch.; twice chmn. Sutter Co. Bd. Supvrs.; past pres. Buttes Area Council 1974; founder Yuba City Builder Supply; awards: Silver Beaver 1974; cert. appreciation, Calif Supvrs. Assn. 1979; Gold Resolution Gilsizer Drainage Dist., Assembly Res. 133 1979, and Senate Res. 59 1979; disting. svc. awd., Veterans of Foreign Wars, 1976; Yuba City highest svc. awd.; Orgns: BSA Buttes Area Council (39 yrs. in scouting); Republican Central Com. co-chmn. for Richard Nixon 1968; Republican; Ch. Jesus Christ of L.D.S.; rec: gardening. Address: 177 Butte Ave Yuba City 95991

TAYLOR, CLIVE ROY, pathologist/consultant; b. July 24, 1944, Cambridge, England; s. Roy and Mildred (Harrison) T.; m. Susan Hoyland, July 29, 1967; children: Matthew, b. 1969; Jeremy, b. 1970; Benedict, b. 1975; Emma, b. 1979; edn: BA, Cambridge, U.K. 1966; MB.B.Chlr., (MD), 1969; D.Phil, (PhD), Oxford, U.K. 1973; MD, Cambridge, U.K. 1978; doctor, 1969; prof., 1979. Career: lectr. Univ. Oxford, England 1970-5; traveling research fellowship, USA 1976; assoc. prof. of pathology USC 1976; chief of immunology Los Angeles Co. Med. Ctr. 1976-82; prof./chmn. Dept. Pathology, USC 1983--; dir. of labs. L.A. Co. Med. Ctr. 1983--, cons., awarded: MacKenzie Scholar Emmanuel Coll. Bach. Scholar Kanger Research Prize; mem. sev. med. socs.; author: over 100 papers; 6 books; rec: soccer, books. Res: 1601 Marengo Ave So. Pasadena 91030 Ofc: Dept. of Pathology, Los Angeles Co. Medical Center, 1200 N. State St Los Angeles 90033

TAYLOR, HUBERT MORRIS, real estate investment counselor; b. May 3, 1947, Los Angeles; s. Morris Edward and Florence Loatha (Brigham) T.; m. Denese Taylor, Sept. 3, 1966; children: Nicole, b. 19649; Ryan, b. 1971; edn: El Camino Coll. 1969-71; L.A. Trade and Tech. Coll. 1971-2; Lumbleau Real Estate Sch. 1972, 74; Western Real Estate Sch 1976; real estate broker, State of Calif. 1978. Career: warehousepersn Max Factor & Co., Hawthorne 1969-70; rt. sales/driver United Parcel Svc., Los Angeles 1970-2; with Spring Realty Corp.: sales agt., Palos Verdes 1972-5; sales mgr., Carson 1975-6; v.p., Torrance 1976-8; corp. broker, 1st Choice Properties, Inc., Inglewood 1978-84; co-owner/mgr First Choice Prop. Mgmt. & Inv., Los Angeles 1984--; lectr. Ch. of Christian Fellowship 1977, 80; spkr. Carson Jaycees 1978; awards: Eagle Scout, BSA 1963; Million Dollar Club, Spring Realty Corp. 1977, 78; Outstanding Young Man of Am., US Jaycees 1980; Certs. of Appreciation: Torrance, Lomita, and Carson Bd. of Realtors 1982; mem: Torrance, Lomita, Carson and Inglewood Bd. of Realtors; Calif. Assn. of Realtors; Nat. Assn. of Realtors; orgns: Lockhaven Ch. Sch. PTF; Bakers Tennis Soc. (pres. 1973-); Cub Scouts of Am.; Ladera Heights Homeowners Assn.; US Jaycees; mil: s/sgt. E5, USAF 1965-9; rec: family. Res: 6115 Wooster Ave Los Angeles 90056 Ofc: First Choice Property Mgmt. & Inv., 3761 Stocker, Ste 100, Los Angeles 90008

TAYLOR, JOANNE STANLEY, real estate broker; b. Apr. 11, 1947, Sacramento; d. Everett N. and Mary A (Arriaga) Stanley; m. George R. Taylor Jr., Jan. 26, 1979; children: James Bowles, b. 1965; Andrea Taylor, b. 1980; edn: AA, Solano Jr. Coll. 1967; BA, Calif. State, Hayward 1968; JD in progress, JFK Univ., Orinda 1982-; life elementary tching. cred., CA 1969; realtor assoc., Dept. Real Estate 1979; broker, Dept. Real Estate 1980; notary public, Secty. of State, CA 1980. Career: elementary tchr. John Swett Unified Sch. Dist., Crockett 1969-83; realtor assoc. US Cities Realty, Vallejo 1980--; owner/mgr. Premium Prop. Realty, 1980--; Notary Public 1980--; honors: life mem. Alpha Gamma Sigma Honor Soc., Solano Coll. 1967; mem: v.p. John Swett Edn 1962; Robbins Awd. of Am. 1963; Leslie R. Groves Gold Medal Awd. 1974; Semmelweiss Medal Awd. 1977; Albert Einstein Awd., Technion Inst. of Israel 1977; Henry T. Heald Awd., Ill. Inst. Tech. 1978; Gold Medal AWd., Am. Coll. Nuclear Medicine 1980; named Disting. Scientist, Nat. Sci. Devel. Bd. 1981; Fellow Am. Phys. Soc.; Nat. Medal of Sci. 1983; mem: fellow, Am. Phys. Soc.; Am. Nuclear Soc.; Am. Acad. Arts. and Scis.; Am. Acad. of Achievement AAAS; Am. Geophys. Union; Am. Def. Preparedness Assn.; Soc. of Engring. Scientists (A.C. Eringen award 1980); Internat. Acad. Quantum Molecular Sci.; Nat. Acad. Scis.; Scientists and Engrs. for Secure Energy; Internat. Platform Assn;e Am. Ordnance Assn; author: (w/ Francis Owen Rice), The Structure of Matter 1949; (w/ Albert L. Latter) Our Nuclear Future 1958; (w/ Allen Brown) The Legacy of Hiroshima 1962; The Reluctant Revolutionary 1964; (w/ others) The Constructive Uses of Nuclear Explosives 1968; Great Assn.; CTA; NEA; MLS Com.; chprsn. Solano Bd. of Realtors; CAR, NAR, Nat. Notary Assn.; Solano Co. Nat. Orgn. for Women; Nat. Women's Polit. Caucus; Vallejo CofC; Solano Co. Apartment Owners Assn.; Democrat; Protestant; rec: reading, writing. Res: 438 Brentwood Dr Benicia 94510 Ofc: Premium Properties Realty, 631 Tennessee St Vallejo 94590

TAYLOR, LINDA TRACEH, information systems executive; b. Apr. 16, 1942, Cambridge, Mass.; d. Ferdinand and Hazel Irene (Towne) Karamanoukian; m. F. Jason Gaskell, Nov. 30, 1978; 1 son: John Robert Taylor, Jr., b. Jan. 21, 1961; edn: AA, West Los Angeles Coll. 1976; BS & MS, in bus. & info. scis., West Coast Univ. 1978-80. Career: admin. asst. Pittsburgh Plate Glass Co., Boston, Mass. 1960-1; admin. asst. to chief indsl. engr., Holtzer Cabot Corp., Boston 1962-4; admin. mgr. Financial Collection Agencies, Ltd., Boston 1964-7;: corp. secty./gen. mgr. Bankers Finl. Equity Corp., subs. of The Seaboard Corp., Boston and Los Angeles 1967-72; owner/opr. Tay-Kara Mgmt. & Systems (info. systems, mgmt. cons.), LA 1972-4; systems mgr. Transaction Technology, Inc., Santa Monica 1974-7; div. mgr. System Devel. Corp., 1977-81; .; dir. info. and mgmt. sys. Filmways, Inc., (Orion Pictures), LA 1981-2; v.p. Gaskell & Taylor Engring., Inc. (systems engrg., devel., cons. firm), 1982--; recipient Public Svc. Award, West Los Angeles CofC 1974; mem: Assn. for Women in Computing (pres. 1980-4, chpt. v.p. 1979-80); Nat. Computer Conf. (v. ch. 1980); Data Processing Mgmt. Assn. (chpt. v.p. 1979-80); IEEE Software Engr. Task Force 1980; spkr. Nat. Confs. of ACM, DPMA, AWC, and NCC; publs: profl. papers in field, 1979-82; Ofc: Gaskell & Taylor Engineering, 3572 Greenfield Ave Los Angeles 90034

TAYLOR, NEWELL EDWARD, clergyman; Oct. 4, 1916, Ennis, Texas; s. Roy and Bertha (Douglas) T.; m. Delight Murrell, July 22, 1941; children: Karen, b. 1956; Jeffery, b. 1956; edn: BA, Baylor Univ. 1940; M.Theol., Southern Baptist Theological Seminary 1943; D.Ministry, Golden Gate Baptist Theological Sem. 1983; ordained So. Baptist Ministe 1942. Career: pastor Markland Baptist Ch., Markland, Indiana 1942-3; Chaplain 1st Lt. to Col., US Army 1944-72; pastor Villa Baptist Ch., Clovis 1975-8; assoc. clerk Mid-Valley Southern Baptist Assn., Fresno 1980-3; interim pastor Calvary baptist Ch., Hanford 1982-3; Chaplain coord. Fresno Police Dept., Fresno 1983--; mem./exec. ofcr. US Army Chaplain Bd., Ft. Meade, Md. 1948-50; staff and fac., US Army Chaplain Ch., Ft. Slocum, N.Y. 1954-57; awards: Cert. of Achievement for Public Svc., Fresno Police Dept., 1981-2; mem: pres. Fresno So. Baptist Ministers Fellowship 1980-3; Am. Assn. of Marriage and Family Therapists, clinical; Military Chaplains Assn., life; Internat. Conference of Police Chaplains; author: Training Clerks and Using Computers to Keep Complete and Accurate Church Records, a ministry project report; mil: Col., Chaplains Br., US Army 1944-72, Legion of Merit, 3 Commendation Medals; So. Baptist; rec: sports, golf, physical exercise. Res: 6084 N Teilman Avenue Fresno 93711 Ofc: City of Fresno Police Dept., POB 1271 Fresno 93815

TAYLOR, ROSE (PERRIN), social worker; b. Feb. 11, 1916, Lander, Wyoming; d. Wilbur Rexford and Agatha Catherina (Hartman) errin; m. Louis Kugland, Sept. 10, 1942 (div.); m. Wilfred Taylor, Oct. 13, 1962; children: children: Mary Louise K., b. 1943; Carolyn Ann McE., b. 1946; edn: AB, Univ. Michigan 1937; Columbia Univ. 1936; MSW, Univ. Denver 1956; Santa Rosa Jr. Coll. 1974-83. Career: girl's gr. wkr. Dodge Christian Comm. House, Detroit, Mich. 1937-8; casewkr. Aid to Dependent Children, Detroit, Mich. 1938-40; child welfare wkr. Fremont Co., Lander, Wyoming 1940-2; children's svcs. wkr. Laramie Co. Welfare Dept., Cheyenne, Wyo.1951-4, 1956-7; dir. Laramie Co. Welfare Dept., Cheyenne 1957-8; supvr. Family and Children's Svcs., San Mateo Co. Welfare Dept. 1958-74; dir. Federal Day Care Proj. 1965-7; tchr. Univ. of Wyo. 1953-7, UC San Jose 1963-4; retired 1974-; wrkshp. prog. plannning mental health svcs., Ariz. Univ., Nat. Inst. Mental Health 1961; chmn. Day Care wrkshps. Pacific Coast Conf. Child Welfare League Am. 1969; Oregon State Family Day Care Wrkshp., Otter Crest, Oregon 1973; awards: commendation, Resolution of the Senate Rules Com., The Senate, Calif. Legislature 1974; KABL Citizen of the Day 5/18/74; Rose Taylor Awd. (annual), Child Care Coord. Council of San Mateo Co. 1982; mem: Co. Welfare Dir.'s Assn. (Wyo. ofcr. 1957-8); Nat. Assn. of Soc. Wkrs.; YWCA, Sonoma Co.; Gualala Arts; Native Plant Soc.; Pt. Arena Methodist Ch.; Am. Assn. Univ. Women; publs: papers, Ariz. Univ. 1962 and Nat. Inst. of Health 1961; art. Prevention 1978; watercolor painting sales 1975-82; Democrat; Protestant; rec: painting, writing, travel. Res: 137 Wild Moor Reach, Box 15 The Sea Ranch 95497

TAYLOR, STEPHEN CHARLES, lawyer; b. Aug. 17, 1943, New York, NY; s. Irving and Katherine Quayde (Snell) T.; m. Patricia Simmons, Feb. 14, 1969; twins: Marta and Jonathan, b. 1970; edn: BA, UCLA 1965; JD, Loyola Univ., L.A. 1970. Career: with Fishkin, Bilson & Taylor 1970--; associated 1970-3; partner 1973--; awarded: San Fernando Valley Legal Secties. Boss of Year 1979; mem: San Fernando Valley Bar Assn.; Los Angeles Co. Bar Assn.; Burbank Bar Assn.; Exec. Com., Conf. Delegates State Bar Calif.; Los Angeles Co. Democratic Central Com. 1976; coauthor: The Jury Game, Zenger Press, Los Angeles 1975; Democrat; Unitarian; rec: softball, model railroading. Res: No. Hollywood Ofc: 6350 Laurel Canyon Blvd, Ste 255, No. Hollywood 91606-3263

TAYLOR, TAMSIN, investment advisor; b. Aug. 26, 1943, Phila., PA; s. Thomas and Chorlott (Little) T.; edn: BA, Smith Coll. 1965; MA, New York Univ. 1968; MBA, Univ. Calif. 1978. Career: pres. Strategic Investment Advisors; mem: adv. bd. Working Assets Fund, S.F.; Governor's Public Invest. Task Force, past; bd. Council an Econ. Priorities, NY, NY, past; chair, Berkeley Citizens Com. on Responsible Invest., Berkeley, past; Commonwealth Club; Media Alliance; Friends of the Faith; Nat. Orgn. for Women; Citizen for a Better Environment; Campaign la Economic Democracy; Internat. Assn. of Financial Planners; chair, Public Pension Investment Proj., S.F.; econ. adv. bd., Cailf. Proj., S.F.; invest. com., Women's Found.; Res: 142 Lincoln, no. 781, Santa Fe, NM 97501 Ofc: Strategics Investment Advisors, Box 607 Star Route Muir Beach Sausalito 94965

TEARE, MARALYN L., marriage, family and child counselor; b. Sept. 2, 1937, NJ; d. Malcolm H. and Deleros T. (Griffin) T.; children: Cheryl, b. 1961; Shanna, b. 1967; edn: BS, Fla. State Univ. 1975; MS, 1978. Career: internship The Center for Behavior Therapy, Beverly Hls. 1977-8; Parent Trng. Clinic, Neuro-psychatric Inst., UCLA Med. Ctr. 1977-9; intern John M. Greener, Ed.D., M.F.C.C., Bev. Hls. 1978--; lic. family therapist spl. treatment of phobias 1977-; private Marriage, Family, Child Counselor, Bev. Hls. 1977--; lectr. num. gps. cons. w/ surgery, dent. on lowering patient anxieties; clinical inst. of psych. USC Med. Sch.; mem: Calif. Assn. of Marriage and Family Therap.; Kappa Alpha Theta Beta Nu chpt.1956--; partic. & adv., CBS TV 5-part series, Living Scared, NBC Hour Mag., and Mid-Morning L.A. Woman to Woman 1979; Republican; Episcopal; rec: sailing, skiing, riding. Res: POB 1386, 176 N. Alvarado Ojai 93023 Ofc: 383 S Robertson Blvd, Ste A, Beverly Hills 90211

TEHRANI, ALI MODARESSI, data processing executive; b. Apr. 21, 1955, Tehran, Iran; s. Mohsen Modaressi and Mery (Azghandi) T.; edn: grad. diploma, Leicester Polytechinc., U.K. 1979; post gard. dipl., 1980; M.Sc. Warwick Univ., U.K. 1981. Career: prgmmr./analyst General Systems Co., London 1978-80; prgmmr./anayst, Shiel Structured Systems, London 1981-2; data processing mgr. Alaska Land Leasing, Inc., Los Angeles 1983--; mem: Inst. of Mathematics and Its Applications, U.K. 1982; Data Processing Mgmt. Assn. 1984; developer: five computer packages 1979-84; rec: chess, flying (private pilot). Res: 174 Beloit Ave, Apt 305, Los Angeles 90025 Ofc: Alaska Land Leasing, Inc., 11726 San Vicente, 6th Flr, Los Angeles 90049

TELLER, EDWARD, physicist; b. Jan. 15, 1908, Budapest, Hungary, nat. 1941; s. Max and Ilona (Deutsch) T.; m. Agusta Harkanyi, 1934; children: Paul, b. 1943; Susan Wendy, b. 1946; edn: Karlsruhe Technical Inst., Germany 1926-8; Univ. of Munich 1928; PhD, Univ. of Leipzig 1930. Career: research assoc. U. Leipzig, 1929-31; U. Gottingen (Germany) 1931-3; Rockefeller fellow Inst. Theoretical Physics, Copenhagen 1934; lectr. U. London 1934-5; prof. Physics George Washington U. 1934-41; Columbia U. 1941-2; physicist U. Chgo. 1942-3; Manhattan Engring. Dist., Chgo. 1942-6; Los Alamitos (N.M.) Sci. Lab. 1943-6; asst. dir. 1949-52; prof. physics UC Berkely 1953-60; prof. physics-at-large 1960-70; dir. Lawrence Livermore Lab. 1958-60; assoc. dir. 1960-75; chmn. dept. applied sci. UC Davis- Livermore 1963-6; cons. Lawrence Livermore Nat. Lab. 1975--; sr. research fellow Hoover Instn. on War, Revolution and Peace, Stanford U. 1975--; vis. prof. Arthur Spitzer chair energy mgmt. Pepperdine U., Calif. 1976-7; adv. bd. Americans for More Power Sources 1979; sci. adv. bd. USAF 1951; bd. govs. American Friends of Tel Aviv 1973; mem. Coalition for Asian Peace and Security, Com. of Protectors and Andrei Sakharov 1980--, Com. on the Present Danger; bd. dirs. ThermoElectron Def. Intelligence Sch.; awards: Harrison Medal, Am. Ordnance Assn. 1955; Albert Einstein award 1958; Gen. Donovan Meml. Awd. 1959; Enrico Fermi Awd. Men of Physics 1969; The Miracle of Freedom 1972; Energy: A Plan for Action 1975; Nuclear Energy in the Developing World 1977; Energy from Heaven and Earth 1979; Pursuit of Simplicity 1980; editor: Fusion, Vol. I, Magnetic Confinement 1981; pioneer in thermonuclear reaction studies; contbr. to Spectroscopy of polyatomic molecules. Address: POB 808 Lawrence Livermore Laboratory, Livermore 94550, also Hoover Instn., Stanford 94305

TEMPLE, ROBERT WILLIAM, investigator; b. Mar. 21, 1943, Jersey City, NJ; s. Howard George and Rita Sonia (Coache) T.; m. Gail Davis-Ellis, Apr. 4, 1964; children: Jolie, b. 1966; Jed, b. 1974; edn: cert., Ventura Co. Sheriffs Acad. 1968; Ventura Coll. 1962-75; Moorpark Coll. 196876; lic. private investigator, 008574, 1981. Career: surveyor Ventura Co., Ventura 1962-8; deputy sheriff, Ventura Co., Ventura 1968-76; chief of police, Lamont, OK 1976-7; sr. private investigator, Russ Whitmeyer Private Investigations Inc., Ventura 1978--; Capitol Crime Defense Consulting, 17 Capitol cases, 54 counts of homicide 1978-84; coauthor w/ Richard H. Fox Sr. (cons. criminalist), a non-fiction book on the criminal justice system; mil: E-4, USAR 1960-6; Republican; Protestant; rec: hunting, fishing, aviation. Res: 5054 Primrose Dr Ventura 93001 Ofc: Whitmeyer Investigations, 478 E Santa Clara St Ventura 93001

TENNANT, FOREST S., JR., health services director; b. Jan. 23, 1941, Kan.; s. Forest S., Sr. and Vivian (White) Tennant; edn: BA, Univ. of MO, 1962; MD, Univ. of Kan., 1966; M.P.H., UCLA, 1973, Dr. P.H., 1974; m. Miriam Isaac, 1966; career: Res. internal med. Univ. of TX, Med Dept., 1967-68; Post-Doctoral Fellow, U.S. Publ. Health Serv., UCLA Sch. of Pub. Health, 1972-74; Assoc. Prof., 1980; prin. investigator, Public Health Found. of L.A. Co., 1974--; author, 90 sci. publs., 1968-77; Mem.: Amer. Public Health Assn.; L.A. Co. Med. Assn.; West Covina C. of C., pres. 1978; Rotary Internat., bd. mem.; Maj., US Army, Med. Ofcr., 1968-72; Republican; Methodist; rec: writing, gardening, golf, skiing, fishing; res: 1744 Aspen Village Way, West Covina 91791 ofc: 336½ S. Glendora Ave. West Covina 91790.

TENNER, MARK, manufacturing company executive; b. Sept. 16, 1948, Los Angeles; s. Harold and Cecily (Golden) T.; m. Jaclyn Ruth Dewey, Sept. 16, 1979; children: Alexis, b. 1982; edn: BA, cum laude, UCLA 1970; MA, 1971; MBA, 1973. Career: v.p. ops. School Days Equipment Co., Los Angeles 1971-4; pres. Orange County Construction Co., Fullerton 1974-5; v.p. sales Underwriters Auto Leasing, Beverly Hills 1975-6; chmn./ pres./ chief exec. ofcr. Relief Printing Corp., Boston and Los Angeles 1976--; tchg. cons. Jr. Achievement Proj. Bus. 1980; dir. Wings Travel, Beverly Hills 1982-3; intsr. UCLA Extension 1970-1; sr. partner J.K. Leasing Co. 1983--; honors: Phi Beta Kappa 1970; highest dept. honors UCLA 1970; O.F. Munson Fellow 1971; mem: Printing Inds. Assn.; Internat. Thermographers Assn.; L.A. CofC; mil: Sgt., USAR 1968-74, commdn. medal; Democrat; Jewish; rec: economic trends and cycles, art collecting, wines. Res: 10931 Oso Ave Chatsworth 91311 Ofc: Relief Printing Corp., 1737 Cordova St Los Angeles 90007

TEPPERMAN, MARGOT EVONNE, business consultant; b. Feb. 4, 1936, Chicago, Ill.; d. Frank Eastman and Irene Anne Grosse; m. David Tepperman, Mar. 26, 1967; children: Elliott Michael, b. 1969; Jonathan David, b. 1972; edn: BA, Univ. of Colorado 1957; MA, 1962; BSW, CSU, w/ dist., Fresno 1976. Career: elem./secondary sch. tchr., var. sch. dists. 1957-60; social wkr. Jewish Family and Children's Svcs. 1963-6; Jr. H.S. counselor Boulder Unified Sch. Dist. 1966-8; pgrm. coord., counselor/instr. Trinidad State Jr. Coll. 1970-4; clinical soc. wkr. Visalia Comm. Counseling Ctr. 1977-8; exec. dir. Fresno Co. Volunteer Bureau 1979-80; private cons., Transitions 1980--; pres. adv. bd. Lullaby Day Care Ctr.; awards: scholarship, grad. study, Univ. Colo.; Woman of Year, Midstate Bus. and Profl. Women 1982; 1st prize in Serigraphy, Colo. State Fair 1972; Cancer Prgm. 1979; Univ. Fellow 1961-2, Am. Assn. of Univ. Women; mem: Am. Assn. of Univ. Women; AAUW: v.p. 1972-3, public relations 1982-3; Bus. and Profl. Women; Am. Soc. for Trng. and Devel., secty. 1981-2; Nat. Assn. of Soc. Wkrs. 1975-83; Calif. Career Guidance Assn. 1983; Agriculture Personel Mgmt. Assn. 1982; Nat. Assn. of Profl. Women; contbr. Campus Poetry and Art Mag. 1961; rec: serigraphy, camping, travel. Res: 2004 S Karen Fresno 93727; Ofc: Transitions, 307 N Van Ness, Ste 103, Fresno 93701

TERAUDS, JURIS, professor of biomechanics; b. Oct. 15, 1937, Jelgava, Latvia, nat. 1963; s. Janis Hermanis and Tatijana (Odins) T.; m. Shirley Henry, Apr. 1, 1961; children: Jeffrey, b. 1964; Kelly, b. 1966; Kimberly, b. 1968; edn: BS, Univ. of Dubuque 1961; MS, L.A. State Univ. 1964; PhD, Univ. Maryland 1972. Career: dir. Biomechanics Cinematography of Olympic Games 1976,80, 84; prof. biomechanics San Diego State Coll. 1978--; pres. Internat. Soc. of Biomechanics in Sports 1981--; pres. Research Ctr. for Sports 1973--; pres. Xiser Inds. 1978--; cons. biomechanic research Olympic Games Bd. Dirs., Internat. Soc. of Photo Optical Instrumention Engrs.; honors: Sigma Delta Psi Nat. Honor Soc.; mem: Internat. Soc. of Biomechanics in Sports; wrkg. gp. NASA Space Shuttle Photography & Videography 1982-; dir. of biomech. research Olympic Games 1976, 80, 84; Internat. Soc. of Photo Optical Instrumentation Engrs. 1978-; wkg. gp. High Speed Photog., Videog. & Photonics (SPIE) 1982-; guest lectr. on biomech. at Univs. in Canada, USA, Finland, Denmark, Germany, USSR, S. Africa, India, Greece and Japan; editor: 9 research books on biomech.; publr: 63 papers; rec: photog., reading, travel. Rs: 2450 Lozana Road Del Mar 92014 Ofc: San Diego State Univ., San Diego

TERSHAKOWEC, MARKIAN GEORGE, plastic surgeon; b. Nov. 7, 1939, Peremysl, Ukraine; s. Andrew and Sophia (Pelenska) T.; edn: ARCT, Univ. of Toronto 1959; MD, 1965; fellow, Royal Coll. of Surgeons, Edinburgh 1970; fellow, Royal Coll. of Surgeons, Canada 1972; fellow, Am. Coll. of Surgeons 1980; med. spl., BMQA of Calif. 1976. Career: active staff mem.: Penisula Hosp., Burlingame; Mills Meml. Hosp., San Mateo; Harold D. Chope Comm. Hosp., San Mateo; courtesy staff mem.: Seton Med. Ctr., Daly City; Ralph K. Davies, San Francisco; Satnford Univ. Med. Ctr., Stanford; clinical instr. plastic surgery, Satnford Univ.; chmn. comm. realtions com. San Mateo Co. Med. Soc.; Internat. Abstracts Ed., Journal of the Am. Soc. of Plastic Surgeons; mem: Am. Soc. of Plastic Surgeons; Canadian Soc. of Plastic Surgeons, British Assn. of Plastic Surgeons; coauthor: Naked Face. Res: 1010 Parrott Dr. Hillsborough 94010 Ofc: 1828 El Camino Real, Ste 506, Burlingame 94010

TESHOME, MESRAK A., psychologist; b. Dec. 8, 1953, Ethiopia, nat. 1972; s. Adnew and Adey Gedle (Giorgis) T.; edn: BA, Wheaton Coll., Ill. 1976; grad stu. Azusa Pacific Coll. 1977-78; MA, Calif. Grad. Inst. 1981, PhD cand. 1981-; Calif. MFCC, Marriage, Family, Child Counselor, BBSE 1983. Career: counselor Pasadena Mental Health Ctr., Pasadena 1977-8; mental health asst. Metropolitan State Hosp., Norwalk 1978-9; therapist Schick Ctr., Cerritos 1979-81; psychotherapist, clinical intern Orange Co. Christian Psychiatric Ctr., Anaheim 1979-82; psychotherapist, psych. asst. Sunny Hills Psychological Ctr., Fullerton 1982-3; psychotherapist, diagnosis and treatment in biofeedback, private practice, Fullerton 1983--; psychological service, pvt. practice & neurological tng., Santa Ana 1984; pvt. practice in Orange, psychol. asst. in Santa Ana, 1984-85; instr./cons. behavior modification, County Regional Ctrs.; awards: Baush & Lomb Honorary Sci. Awd. 1972; two certs. of appreciation, Up-Ward-Bound tchg. orgn.; mem: Christian Assn. for Pschological Studies 1983; Ethiopian Comm. Ctr., L.A.; Melodyland Christian Ctr., Anaheim; creator: sculptured, Cera-Page, framed art work 1980-3; Christian; rec: tennis, arts & crafts, reading, writing. Res: 2712 W. Porter, No. 15, Fullerton 92633 Ofc: 1125 E. 17th St, Ste 127, Santa Ana 92701

TESSLER, DIANE J(ANE), psychotherapist, author; b. Nov. 21, 1947, NYC; d. Mitchell M. and Gail (Gunser) Tessler); edn: BSc, Long Is. Univ. 1968; MS, Pepperdine Univ. 1979; PhD in counseling psych., Columbia Pacific Univ. 1983; lic. M.F.T. (marriage family therapist), Calif. 1982. Career: educator Santa Monica Unified Sch. Dist., 1969-83, NYC Bd. of Edn.; univ. instr. (part time): Claremont Grad. Sch., UC Los Angeles, Loyola Marymount Univ., 1979-; psychotherapist/dir. Life Systems International, Los Angeles 1982--, individual & group psychotherapy, seminars to civic and business groups; frequent lectr. in USA and abroad; guest on num. TV and radio talk-shows; cons. to State Dept.

of Edn. of Calif., Los Angeles Co. Drug Abuse Program Ofc., BBC TV (London), The Disney Channel. Mem: Calif. Psychol. Assn., L.A. Co. Psychol. Assn., Calif. Assn. of Marriage & Family Therapists, Internat. Coll. of Applied Nutrition, Women's Referral Service, Century City CofC (Cultural Commn., Healthcare Com.), Beverly Hills Business Forum. Author: Drugs, Kids and Schools: Practical Strategies for Educators and Other Concerned Adults (1980, preface by Art Linkletter). Ind. Rec: painting, dance, poetry. Address: Life Systems International, (POB 6460, B.H. 90212) 291 S. La Cienega Blvd, Ste. 107, Beverly Hills 90211

THAGARD, SHIRLEY STAFFORD, marketing specialist; b. Nov. 29, 1940, Detroit, Mich.; d. Walter Jay and Marjorie G. Stafford; m. Charles W. Thagard, Sept. 21, 1963; children: Grayson, b. 1968, Devon, b. 1970; edn: AS in mdse., Webber Coll. 1961; spl. courses, Pierce Coll. Career: asst. buyer Burdines Dept. Stores, Miami, Fla. 1961-63; dir. pub. rels./classified advt. Miami Herald Newspaper, 1963-67; real estate investor, entrepreneur: orgnzr./opr. successful Rent-A-Santa business; bought, promoted on local, nat. media two tons of Spaghetti Squash from No. Calif.; mgr. real prop. investments in Fla. and Calif., 1967-81; owner Thagard Enterprises, editor/pub. Pediatric Network (newsletter), 1981--, creator of Medical Moppets (anatomically correct teaching puppets); v.p./bd. dir./mktg. dir. R.T. Durable Medical Products, Inc. (mfr. devices to enhance independent living for phys. handicapped), 1984--; distbr./rep. various materials & pgms. to assist psychosocial devel. of children, and reduce their trauma in health care settings; mem: Pilot Internat., Assn. for the Care of Children's Health, Am. Business Women's Assn., Nat. Alliance of Home Based Bus., Nat. Assn. for Edn. of Young Children, Calif. Assn. for the Phys. Handicapped Inc., Rehabilitation Internat. USA; various youth orgns. (BSA, Little League, PTAs); rec: family activities, travel, Old West memorabilia, Western films and art. Res: 5446 Lockhurst Dr Woodland Hills 91367 Ofc: POB 8396 Calabasas 91302

THATCHER, DICKINSON, lawyer; b. May 26, 1919, Huntington Beach; s. Charles Harold and Gladys T. (Dickinson) T.; m. Dale Nadine Mortensen, Feb. 2, 1952; children: Kirk Randolph, b. 1962; Jeffrey Lawrence, b. 1963; edn: BS, UCLA 1941; postgrad., New York Univ. 1943-4; Univ. of Paris 1945-6; JD, Stanford UNiv. 1948; LL.M. in Taxation, USC 1962. Career: admitted to Calif. State Bar 1948; Los Angeles Deputy City Atty. 1948-51; credit atty. Union Oil Co. of Calif. 1951-4; trial atty. Tax Div., Dept. Justice, Wash. DC 1954-6; asst. US Atty. Los Angeles 1956-7; practicing lawyer in No. Hollywood, Van Nuys 1957--; mem: St. Bar of Calif.; Disciplinary Bd. 1970-2; Client Security Fund Com. 1975-7; San Fernando Valley Bar Assn., pres. 1966; Am. Bar Assn; Los Angeles Co. Bar Assn., Commn. on Arbitration 1963-71, chmn. Council Affiliated Bar Pres. 1968-70; Kiwanian, pres Van Nuys Club 1975-6; mil. US Army 1942-6. Res: 15040 Hamlin St Van Nuys 91411 Ofc: Dicinson Thatcher, APLC, 14540 Haynes St, Ste 109, Van Nuys 91411

THILL, JOHN VAL, communications consultant/author; b. Dec. 27, 1953, Milwaukee, Wisconsin; s. Lewis Dominic and Carol Jean (Werner) T.; edn: BS, San Diego State Univ. 1977. Career: exec. ed. Banner Books Internat., Los Angeles 1979-80; pres. Roxbury Publishing Co., San Diego 1980-2; pres. Communication Specialists of Am., San Diego 1982--; awards: Outstanding Bus. Communicator, Am. Soc. of Journalists 1982; coauthor: Contemporary Business Communications, Addison-Wesley Publishing Co., Boston 1984; rec: racquetball, swimming. Ofc: Communication Specialists of America, 710 B Street, Ste 1300, San Diego 92101

THOM, DANIEL JOHN, management consultant; b. Oct. 17, 1953, San Diego; s. Major Joseph and Winona Estelle (Johnson) T.; edn: AA, Goldenwest Comm. Coll. 1976; BS, CSU Long Beach 1978; JD, Western State Univ. Coll. of Law, 1982; Calif. Comm. Colls. lmtd. svc. cred., Police Sci.; Calif. Basic Ednl. Skills Cred.; Calif. State Commn. on Peace Ofcr. Stds. & Tng. Career: comm. ofcr., police ofcr., sr. reserve ofcr./supr. Seal Beach (Calif.) Police Dept., 1973--; law clerk Glenn E. Stern Law Corp., West Covina 1981-82; accts. supr. Cablesystems Cable TV, Huntington Bch. 1980-83; cons. to nat. security dir. American Honda Motor Corp., 1983-; freelance mgmt. cons. various corps., 1983--; honors: Outstanding Young Man of Am. 1982, US Jaycees; mem: Calif. Peace Ofcrs. Assn., Calif. Reserve Peace Ofcrs. Assn.; pres./cofounder Bayside Amateur Radio Frat., Beach Area Gp.; mem. Am. Radio Relay League, Amateur Radio Emerg. Service, Long Beach Repeater Assocs., CSULB Alumni Assn., Masons (Master); Republican; Prot.; rec: electronics, photog., classic autos. Res: 712 Balboa Dr Seal Beach 90740

THOMAS, DEBRA DIANE, insurance agency owner; b. Nov. 1, 1954, Boise, Idaho; d. Steve M. and Barbara L. (Storie) Thomas; edn: bus. major, Long Beach City Coll., 1972-8. Career: adminstrv. asst. Penn Mutual Life Insurance Co., Long Beach 1976, dir. of recruiting and tng. 1978, asst. general agt. 1979; ptnr/owner Larry Lambert & Associates, and Financial Counseling Resources, 1980--; awards: Million Dollar Round Table 1982-, National Quality award 19820; mem: Nat. Assn. of Life Underwriters, Calif. Assn. of Life Und., Long Beach Assn. of Life Und. (bd. mem. 1981-, pres. 1984-5), Women Life Und. Assn.; Republican; Catholic; rec: travel, bike riding. Res: 5218 North Marina Pacific Long Beach 90803 Ofc: Larry Lambert & Associates, 3633 East Broadway, Long Beach 90803

THOMAS, GRACE FERN, psychiatrist; b. Sept. 23, 1897, Gothenburg, Nebr.; d. George Wm. and Martha C. (Johnson) T.; edn: BS, Univ. Nebr. 1924; MA, Creighton 1926; MD, USC 1935; postgrad., Univ. Colo. 1942-3; Inst. of Living 1943; USC 1946; UCLA 1947-50; Columbia Univ. 1953; MA, in religion, USC 1968; ordained to ministry United Methodist Ch. 1963; dip., Am. Bd. of Psychiatry and Neurology. Career: instr. chemistry, biology Duchesne Coll. 1924-7; lab. techn. var. hosps. 1927-32; intern los Angeles Co. Hosp. 1934-5; res. physician Riverside Co. Hosp. 1935-6; res. psychiatrist Los Angeles Co. Psychopathic Hosp. 1936-7; staff psych. Calif. State Hosp. System 1937-42; Glenside Sanitarium 1943-44; pvt. practice neuropschiatry, Long Beach 1946-51; organized and dir. Mental Health Clinics: Veterans Admin. Hosp., Albuquerque, NM (1951-53); Canton and Norwalk, Ohio (1955-61); and San Bernardino, Ukiah and Sonora, CA (1961-70); practice medicine, spl. psych., Turlock 1970-3, Modesto 1972--; honors: Commnd. Capt. Med. Corps. US Army, WWII 1944-6 (only 26 Am. Women w/ this distn.); Phi Beta Kappa; Sigma Xi; Phi Kappa Phi; Nu Sigma Phi; Phi Delta Gamma; listed: Who's Who in West; Who's Who of Am. Women; World Who's Who of Women; Dictionary of Internat. Biography and Internat. Who's Who of Intellectuals; mem: AMA; CMA; Am. Pschiat. Assn.; Am. Med. Women's Assn.; Central Calif. Psychiat. Soc.; Stanislaus Co. Med. Soc.; Am. Legion; Soroptimists; rec: cats. Res: 2001 La Jolla Ct Modesto 95350 Ofc: 1130 Coffee Rd, Ste 8-B, Modesto 95355

THOMAS, HOWARD WESLEY, association executive; Aug. 24, 1919, Los Angeles; s. Edward W. and Kathleen (Benedict) T.; m. Dawn Eldridge, Sept. 3, 1940; children: Baron, b. 1941; Drake, b. 1942; Lance, b. 1946; edn: Glendale Coll. 1938-9; Fresno State Univ. 1940; courses, UC San Diego 1960s. Career: dist. mgr. Automobile Club of So. Calif., 35 yrs.; bd. dirs. 200th Anniversary of San Diego 1968-9; pres., adv. bd. San Diego Hwy. Devel. Assn. 1972-; v.p. Sales and Mktg. Execs., San Diego, Inc. 1970; pres. San Diego Public Safety Com.; loan exec. United Way (CHAD), S.D, 1980; bd. dirs. Nat. Council of Alcoholism, S.D.; mem. Mayor's Bicycle Safety Com.; Cabrillo Festival, Inc. (pres. 1982), aquatic chmn. (11 yrs.); dir. S.D. Co. Safety Council (mid 1970's); commodore Rotary Internat. Yachting Fellowship, San Diego; awards: Loaned Exec. Awd., United Way/ Chad 1980; Spl. Awd Entitled, Don in Legion of Portola, City and Co. of San Diego for 200th Anniversary; appreciation, Calif. Hwy. Patrol, San Diego 1980; mem: Rotary Internat.; S.D. Public Safety Com.; Port Capt. of the Tallship, Californian, for training youth; Hwy. Users Fdn.; G.O.P. Conv. and Trans. Com. 1972; San Diego CofC; San Diego Conv. & Visitors Bureau; mil: Spl. A, 2nd class, combat swimming/ Judo instr. USN 1944-6; Republican; Protestant; rec: sailing. Res. 3111 Ibsen Street San Diego 92106 OFc: Automobile Club of So. Calif., 815 Date St San Diego 92101

THOMAS, JAMES DONALD, physician; b. Nov. 19, 1938, Gilmer, Texas; m. Sonia Thomas, June 20, 1973; children: Erin, b. 1959, Alison, b. 1960, Wendy, b. 1961, Mark, b. 1961, Tim, b. 1963, Elisabeth, b. 1968, Gilliam, b. 1974, Hilary, b. 1977, edn. BA, Arlington State Univ. 1962; MD, Univ. of Texas Medical Branch. Career: flight surgeon, US Naval Hosp., Rota, Spain 1968-71; general practice So. Calif. Permanente Medical Group, Pasadena 1971-72; med. dir. Alcohol Treatment and Rehab. Unit, Pasa. 1975; group psychotherapist Pasa. Guidance Clinic, 1974-75; pvt. practice Family Medicine, So. Pasa. 1974--; adj. prof. Graduate Sch. of Psychology, fuller Theol. Sem., Pasa. 1969--; clin. instr. USC Sch. of Medicine, 1977--; med. dir. Psychological Ctr., Fuller Sch. of Psychol., Pasa. 1977-; HMH Emergency Med. Gp., Huntington Mem. Hosp. 1974-, also med. dir. Ctr. for Occupational Health 1982-, and dir. Emergency Dept. 1976-; med. dir. Emmons Health Ctr., Occidental Coll. 1983-; mem: L.A. County Med. Assn., CMA, Am. Acad. of Family Practice, Am. Coll. of Emerg. Physicians, Am. Acad. of Psychosomatic Med., Am. Occuptnl. Med. Assn.; mil: lcdr. USN 1967-71; Democrat; Episcopal. Res: 1159 Huntington Dr South Pasadena Ofc: Huntington Memorial Hospital, 100 Congress St, Pasadena 91105

THOMAS, JAMES RANSDELLE, real estate/hotel executive; b. Aug. 7, 1944, Jacksonville, Fla.; s. Marion Ransdelle and Jessie Maude (Benefield) T.; m. Ellen Smith, July 7, 1978; children: Raeni, b. 1970; Shane, b. 1972; Rynan, b. 1974; Kyle, b. 1981; edn: BS, Flor. Atlantic Univ. 1969. Career: sr. research analyst Nat. Feasibility Corp., Miami, Fla. 1969-73; assoc. cons. Economic Studies of Am., Inc., Miami 1971-4; cons. AREEA, Inc., Miami 1974-8; mgr. of devel. Holiday Inns, Inc., Memphis, TN 1978-9; dir. of corp. devel. Calif. Inns. Mgmt., Inc., Los Angeles 1980-1; v.p. of real estate Vagabond Hotels, Inc., San Diego 1981--; mem: NACORE Internat.; Internat. Council of Shopping Ctrs.; Urban Land Inst.; Soc. of Real Estate Appraisers; author publs. in var. periodicals and newspapers; mil: RM2, US Coast Guard, Nat. Def. Ribbon; Republican; Baptist; rec: sailing. Res: 10611 Birch Bluff Ave San Diego 92131 Ofc: Vagabond Hotels, Inc., 10021 Willow Creek Rd San Diego 92131

THOMAS, JOHN RICHARD, petroleum research company president; b. Aug. 26, 1921, Anchorage, Kentucky; s. John R. and Mildred (Woods) T.; m. Beatrice Ann Davidson, Dec. 7, 1944; children; Jonnie Sue, b. 1945; Richard G., b. 1948; edn: BS, UC Berkeley 1943; PhD, 1947. Career: with Chevron Research Co., Richmond 1948-67, 1970- : research chemist 1948-9; sr. research assoc. 1951-60; sr. research sci. 1961-7; pres. 1970--; with Standard Oil Co. of Calif., S.F.: asst. secty. 1967-70, v.p. 1983--; fundraiser, permanent energy exhib. at Lawrence Hall of Sci. 1975-6; mem: Am. Chem. Soc.; Am. Assn. for Adv. of Sci.; Indl. Research Inst.; Sigma Xi; Soc. of Automotive Engrs; author: 32 research publs.; num. patents; Republican; Christian. Ofc: Chevron Research Co., 576 Standard Ave Richmond 94523

THOMAS, LEO H., financial-estate planner; b. July 5, 1947, Los Angeles, CA; s. Leo and Rose (Morris) T.; m. Bernice Roberts, Aug. 19, 1979; 1 son: Todd Pearl, b. 1967; edn: BA, Occidental Coll. 1969; Reg. Investment Adv., NASD. Career: public rels. adv. Democratic Party, 1968-9; ins. agent Prudential Life Ins. Co., 1969-78; finl. & estate planner/ securities broker Hansch Financial Gp. 1969--; cons. Financial Advisory Clinic, Los Angeles 1982-4; pres. Thomas Financial Ins. Svcs., Inc.; cons. First Profl. Bank of Santa Monica; bd. dirs.

Great Am. Inc., Los Angeles; bd. dirs. Employer Benefits Mktg.; awards: Agent of Year, Mutual Benefit 1983; Agent of Year of Los Angeles 1983; MDRT; Top of Table (300 leading life ins. salesman in world) 1982; Nat. Assocs. Mutual Benefit top 25 leaders 1983; mem: Internat. Assn. of Financial Planners; Am Soc. of CLU; Nat. Assn. of Life Underwriters; W. Los Angeles Life Underwriters Council; Life Ins. Leaders Round Table, L.A. 1982-4; Bev. Hills. Estate Planning Council (3 yrs.); AALU ; Independent Ins. Agents of Am. Assn.; Financial Digest 1983; Life Underwriters Political Action Com. (5 yrs.); Am. Assn. of Financial Profls.; NASD; orgns: Kiwanis; Simon Wiesenthal contrbg. mem.; Smithonian Inst.; Am. Film Inst.; So. Poverty Law Ctr.; Nat. Tax-Limitation Com.; annual sales presentations, Nat. Assocs. 1982-3; seminars, Hansch Financial Gp. 1981-4; Democrat (past pres. Young Democrats); Jewish. Res: 6216 W 6th St Los Angeles 90048 Ofc: Hansch Financial Group, 5900 Wilshire Blvd, Ste 17, Los Angeles 90036

THOMAS, MICHAEL EUGENE, electrical engineer; b. Oct. 4, 1949, Oakland; s. Lavern Junior and Louise Marie (Maldonado) T.; m. Aleta Rossi, Mar. 21, 1975; edn: AA, Chabot Jr. Coll. 1970; Chico State Univ. 1970-1; grad., Atomic Energy Sch. 1973. Career: assoc. engr. Memorex; assoc. engr. Nasa/Ames; engr. Varion; elec. engr. Allied Media; elec. engr. Memorex; cons./elec. engr. Kaiser Aero 1981; cons./ elec. engr. Commodore Computers, Santa Clara 1981; cons./ elec. engr. CA Computer System, Sunnyvale 1983; cons./elec. engr. Transpacific, San Jose 1984; cons./elec. engr. Memorex, Santa Clara 1984; elec. engr./ founder Evotex, Fremont 1981-3; cons./ elec. engr. Xebec, Santa Clara 1983; elec. design engr./ cons. IMC, Santa Clara 1983-4; currently: pres. Home Computer Systems Internat.; pres. Disk Star, Inc.; patentee micro/halt interface 1981 and 82, pat. pend., 3D recording w/ vert. plated media; mil: ETR3, US Navy 1971-5, honorable discharge; Republican; Catholic; rec: microprocessor devel. for robots. Address: Home Computer Systems Int'l, 3182 Napa Dr San Jose 95148

THOMAS, ROBERT CHARLES, physician; b. November 6, 1916, Vallejo, CA; s. Charles W. and Juanita N. (Young) Thomas; edn: Univ. of CA, 1935-39; MD, McGill Univ., 1943; m. Barbara Whiteley, June 17, 1939; chil: Sylvia, b. 1950, Dean, b. 1951, Amy, b. 1953; career: self-employed physician, private practice 1947--; Active on prof. staff of St. Francis Memorial Hosp. in San Francisco; Mem.: St. Francis Mem. Hosp., S.F., San Fran. Med. Society, Calif. Medical Assn.; works: publ. first book entitled "Drake at Olomp-ali", a historical work concerned with where Sir Francis Drake landed in California, May 1979; Mil: Captain, US Army, 1945-47; rec: writing; res: 18 Monte Vista Vallejo 94590 ofc: Robert C. Thomas, M.D., 1790 26th Ave. San Francisco 94122.

THOMAS, TIMOTHY WARREN, pest control co. executive; b. July 6, 1953, Los Angeles;s. Frank Harry and Dorothea Albertine (Kieffner) T.; edn: AA, El Camino Coll. 1976; oper. lic. br. II & III Calif. Structural Pest Control Bd. 1977. Career: book store clerk El Camino Coll., Gardena 1973; termite control techn. -gen. mgr. Lincoln Termite & Pest Control, Santa Monica 1974-6; mgr. termite div. Hydrex Pest Control, W. L.A., and subsidiaries Calif. Exterminator and Lincoln Termite and Pest Control, 1977--; svc. systems adv.; urban entomolgy cons.; tchr. Pest Control Ops. of Calif., L.A. Dist. 1980, 81; tchr. Cert. classes Calif. Dept. Agriculture and Structural Pest Control Bd. 1982; awards: 1st place Trophy, Rosamond Calif. Chili Cook-off 1981; finalist, Nevada State Chili Cook-off 1980; mem: Nat. Pest Control Assn.; Pest Control Ops. of Calif.; Termite Com.; Ednl. Com.; Pest Control Ops. of Calif., L.A. Dist., ednl. chmn.; Delta Phi Sigma Frat.; Internat. Chili Soc.; Harley Davidson Owners' Gp.; Harley Davidson Owners' Assn.; Democrat; Protestant/ Lutheran; rec: painting, cooking, gunsmith, silversmith. Res: 3612 W 117th Street Inglewood 90303 Ofc: Hydrex Pest Control, 12962 Washington Blvd W. Los Angeles 90066

THOMAS, WILLIAM F., newspaper editor; b. June 11, 1924, Bay City, Mich.; s. William F. and Marie T. (Billette) T.; m. Patricia Wendland, Dec. 28, 1948; children: Michael Wm., b. 1955; Peter Matthew, b. 1957; Scott Anthony, b. 1961; edn: BS, Northwestern Univ. 1950; MS, magna cum laude, 1951; LHD, (honorary), Pepperdine Univ., L.A. 1975. Career: copy ed. Buffalo Evening News 1950-2, asst. chief copy ed. 1953-5; ed. Sierra Madre News 1955-6; with Los Angeles Mirror- News, copy reader 1956-7; reporter 1957-59; asst. city ed. 1959 61; city ed. 1961-2; with the L.A. Times, asst. Metropolitan ed. 1962-5; Metropolitan ed. 1965-71; exec. ed. 1971; ed. 1971-2; ed./ exec. v.p. 1972--; awards: Harrington Awd., Medill Grad. Sch. of Journalism, Northwestern Univ. 1951; mem: Am. Soc. of Newspaper Editors (ASNE); mil: US Army 1943-6; Ofc: Los Angeles Times, Times Mirror Square, Los Angeles 90053

THOMAS, WILLIAM HENRY, manufacturing co. executive; b. Nov. 23, 1935, Pasadena; s. Daniel Waylette and Mary Elizabeth (Evans) T.; m. Eunice McAlisa, Dec. 20, 1959; 1 son: Kirk Henry, b. 1960; edn: BS, Univ. of Montana 1962. Career: adminstr. Dinklespied, Relavin, Steefel & Levitt, San Francisco; financial mgr. Vinnel Steel Corp., Oakland; acct./ ofc. mgr. Smyth Van & Storage, San Frncisco and Redwood City; secty./ treas. Utility Bedy Co., Berkeley; dir. Utility Body Co., Podl-lok Co., Pac Masher Co.; mil: E-5 USN 1954-9, Nat. Def. Medal; Republican; Disciples of Christ ; rec: antiques. Res 1209 Lafayette St Alameda 94501 Ofc: Utility Body Co., 901 Gilman St Berkeley 94701

THOMASHEFSKY, ALLEN JAN, physician; Aug. 8, 1944, Pittsburgh, PA; s. Norman and Charlotte (Weinberger) T.; children: Susan, b. 1968; Joshua, b. 1970; Eli, b. 1977; edn: BA, Case Western Reserve Univ 1965; MD, Case Western Reserve Sch. of Med. 1969. Career: physcian, US Public Health Svc., Wounded Knee, S.D. 1970-2; family practioner, Eugene, Ore. 1972-77; Santa Barbara 1978--; instr. UC Santa Barbara Extension courses; spkr. t.v., radio, and schs. in Santa Barbara; Calif. Spkg., Lung Assn., Heart Assn., ect.; mem. Am. Acad. of Family Practice; mil: Lt. Com., US Public Health Svc.; rec: completed World Champ. Iron Man Triathalon 1981, 82. Address: 200 N. La Cumbre Santa Barbara 93110

THOMPSON, ANTHONY WARREN, financial planning co. president; b. Jan. 8, 1947, Lyons, Kans.; s. Waldo W. and Sarah Elizabeth (Rogers) T.; m. Sharon D. Nelson, Apr. 18, 1975; children: Jessica, b. 1976; Ashley, b. 1979; edn: BS, Sterling Coll. 1969; Chartered Finl. Cons., Chartered Life Underwriter, American Coll. 1976/83. Career: insurance agt. Jefferson Standard Life, 1969-72, divisional mgr. 1972-75, regl. mgr. 1975-78; founder, pres. Creative Analysis, Inc., 1978--; general partner TMP Properties, 1978--; founder, chmn. bd. West Coast Pension Administrators, Inc. 1979--; founder, pres. West Coast Group Health Insurance SErvices, Inc. 1982--; mem. bd. advisors Frontier Bank; awards: Outstanding Young Men in Am., 1981; Leading Gen. Agent for Guardian Life for new agencies in 1983 for disability income sales; Nat. Mgmt. Award, Nat. Gen. Agents & Managers Assn. 1980-1; mem: Orange Co. Gen. Agents and Mgrs. Assn. (pres. 1983); Orange Co. Life Underwriters Assn. (bd. mem. 1980); Long Beach, Orange Co. CLU Soc. (bd. mem. 1980); past mem. bd. dirs. Community Devel. Counsel, 1981, Orange Co. Cancer Coping Center; mil: Airman 1st cl. USAF; USAF Nat. Guard 1969-75; Republican; Methodist; rec: bridge, computers, skiing. Res: 1962 La Questa, Santa Ana 92705 Ofc: 1072 S.E. Bristol, Ste 105, Santa Ana 92707

THOMPSON, BILL DEAN, certified public accountant; b. Sept. 12, 1944, Boise City, Okla.; s. James and Nora (Risely) T.; children: Deana, b. 1970; Lance, b. 1972; edn: BBA, Okla. Panhandle State Univ. 1970. Career: self empl. Thompson Acctg., Boise City, Okla. 1969-70; acct. Gaskill & Pharis, CPA, Dalhart, TX 1970-2; tax mgr. Arthur Andersen & Co., Okla. City 1972-7; v.p. tax & ins. Landmark Land Co., Carmel 1977--; mem: Am. Inst. of CPAs 1973; Texas State Soc. of CPAs 1973-; Okla. State Soc. of CPAs 1974-; Calif. State Soc of CPAs 1977-; Democrat; Methodist; rec: golf, tennis. Ofc: Landmark Land Co., 100 Clocktower Pl, Ste 200, Carmel 93923

THOMPSON, JACLYN MORELOCK, information systems executive; b. Oct. 21, 1942, Glendale; d. Howard Dean and Opal May (Thompson) Morelock; 2 sons: Jeffrey, b. 1963; Michael, b. 1964; edn: BBA, Eastern Nebr. Coll. 1974; A.A., computer sci., Coleman Coll., 1981; MBA in progress, Quantitative Analysis Nat. Univ. 1983-. Career: internal auditor Pacesetter Prods., Inc., Omaha, Nebr. 1970-4; bus. mgr. Day Care Svcs., Inc., Des Moines, IA 1974-8; bus. mgr. Linda Vista Health Care Ctr., San Diego 1978-81; systems cons. Univ. for Humanistic Studies, San Diego 1981; data systems mgr. McGraw- Hill Trng. Systems, Del Mar 1981--; awards: hon. admiral Nebraska Navy, Gov. of Nebr. 1974; KOIL Buswn. of Day 1974; Spkrs. Awd., Kiwanis 1973; mem: Exec. Forum, SDSU 1983; Data Processing Mgr. Assn.; Nat. Univ. Alumni Assn.; Nat. Mgmt. Assn.; Automation Inst. Assn.; secty. Nat. Bus. & Profl. Womens Assn.; Assn. for Female Execs.; orgns: fndg. mem./ v.p. Nebraska chpt. Nat. Orgn. for Women; bd. dirs., Eastern Nebr. Coll.; treas. Mayor's Commn. on the Status of Women; v.p., Planned Parenthood; bd. dirs. Nebr. Women's Polit. Caucus; publs: tech. paper, Mini-Computer Acquisition, San Diego Computer Confr. 1983; wrkshps. for Women's Day Conf. 1971-4: Women in Mgmt., The Executive Woman; Mng. the Small Business, and Investment Opps.; Democrat; Unitarian; rec: skiing, public spkg., writing, sewing. Res: 144 Candice Pl Vista 92083 Ofc: McGraw- Hill Training Systems, 674 Via de la Valle Solana Beach 92014

THOMPSON, JOSEPH A., producer/cameraman and film co. president; born and educated in Philadelphia. Career: began underwater filming in 1960, photog./ed. short film on life in the offshore northeast Atlantic Ocean; undersea engr./ filmmaker/ diver Underseas Div. Westinghouse Electric Corp., 1963, first Am. to train with diving pioneer Jacques Cousteau, prod. first film for Westinghouse on the cousteau diving saucer (won gold medal Nat. Underwater Film Festival); sr. pilot, Westinghouse Elec. Corp. for the Deep Diving Research Submarine Deep Star DS 4000 (commendn. from USN as pilot in chg. of Navy geological survey dive); prod. six films on ocean-oriented projects for var. cos., then worked as topside and underwater cameraman and dir. on ten Jacques Cousteau network television specials; founder/pres. Seavision Productions, 1973--: credits incl. The Undersea World of Jacques Cousteau, John Denver TV Variety Special (1975), Man From Atlantis, In Search of (tv series), Sharks, The Death Machines, Those Amazing Animals (NBC Spl.), and Nova (PBS Spl.); prod. one-hour documentary, Voyage of a Yankee Tuna Clipper, 1977 (won 4 Emmy awards, Nat. Assn. of TV Arts and Scis., San Diego Chpt.); prod. for DuPont Co. one-hour nat. TV spl. on the flight of the Gossamer Albatross, 1978-79, (awarded Nat. Emmy as prod.) and one-hour prodn. on the Solar Challenger, 1980,(won Grand Award, NY Internat. Film and TV Festival, and nat. Emmy); still photography pub. in Nat. Geographic Mag., Life Mag., Time, Newsweek, Jacques Cousteau Encyclopedias, US Naval Inst. Proceedings, others; Office: Seavision Productions, P.O. Box 82672, San Diego 92138

THOMPSON, LARRY ANGELO, entertainment lawyer/TV producer/personal manager; b. Aug. 1, 1944, Clarksdale, Miss.; s. Angelo and Annie (Tuminello) T.; m. Pamela Edwards; edn: BBA (bus. ad.), Univ. of Miss. 1966, JD, 1968; admitted Miss. State Bar 1968, Calif. State Bar 1970. Career: In-house counsel Capitol Records, Hollywood 1969-71; sr. partner in Entertainment Law firm of Thompson, Shankman, and Bond, Beverly Hills 1971-77; pres. Larry A. Thompson Organization, Inc. 1977--; frequent guest lectr. on Entertainment Bus., USC and UCLA; exec. prod. of Emmy nominated Jim Nabors Show 1968; exec. prod. TV movies: "Mickey Spillane's Margin for Murder" (TV Guide 1981 pick of top 10 movies) and "Mickey Spillane's Murder Me, Murder You"; exec. prod. CBS series "Bring 'Em Back Alive" 1982; author: (books) "How to Make a Record and Have Your Songs Recorded", "Four Dimensions of Stardom", "The Root to Sucess is always under Construction", and (TV thesis) The Prime Time Crime; honors: Law Jour., Moot Court Bd., Univ. of Miss. (1967), Show Business Attorney of the Year 1971, Capitol Records; Hon. Order of Kentucky Colonels 1978-; mem: Am., Miss., Calif., and Inter Am. Bar Assns.; Am. Film Inst.; Nat. Acad. of Recording Arts & Scis.; Aide de Camp Govs. Staff, Tenn. 1972; mil: Judge Advocate Gen's Corp. US Army 1966-72; Republican (Repub. Task Force; apptd. co-chmn. Nat. Repub. Entertainment Com. 1983); Catholic; rec: art coll., photog., tennis. Res: 1549 Lindacrest Dr Beverly Hills 90210 Ofc: 1888 Century Park East, Ste 622, Los Angeles 90067

THOMPSON, LA VOR COLE, tile roofing manufacturer; b. Feb. 13, 1926, Preston, Idaho; s. Thomas Vernon and Leona (Cole) T.; m. Dorothy W. Allan, Dec. 5, 1957; children: Vickie, b. 1947; LaJean, b. 1948; Cary, b. 1952; lic. contractor, Calif. 1973. Career: salesman Salt Lake Bartile Co., Salt Lake City, Utah 1947-48; sales mgr. Idaho Bartile, Pocatello, Idaho 1948-62; gen. mgr. Blue Mtn. RoTile, Walla Walla, Wash. 1962-66; sales mgr. Ro-Tile Mfg., Lodi, Calif. 1966-73; pres. Thompson Roofing, Lodi 1973--; pres. Ro-Tile Mfg. Co., Lodi 1975--; mem: Nat. Tile Roofing Mfg. Assn. (bd. dirs. 1975-82, pres. 1980-81); Elks (exalted ruler 1984-85); Lodi Dist. CofC; publs: Western Building Design 1981; The Profl. Designer News Letter 1981; Builder Developer West 1982; mil: Boatswain's Mate 2nd Class USN 1944-46, Asia-Pac. Campaign Medal, WW II Victory medal; LDS Ch.; Res: 1416 Midvale Rd Lodi 95240 Ofc: Ro-Tile Roof Mfg. Co., Inc., 310 Cluff Ave Lodi 95240

THOMPSON, OSCAR ALBEN, company owner; b. Feb. 24, 1931, Livingston, CA; s. Oscar Theodore and Emma (Forgnone) T.; m. Barbara Thompson, Apr. 9, 1961; children: Heather, b. 1962; Robert, b. 1963; edn: AA. Modesto Jr. Coll. 1951; BA, secondary edn., San Jose State Univ. 1956. Career: gas station mgr. 1949-52; Cpl., US Army Artillery Maint., Camp Chaffey, Ark. 1952-4; sch. tchr. metals shop, San Jose H.S. 1956-7; supvrg. equip. techn., San Jose State Univ. Sch. Engring. 1957-81; owner Laboratory Devices Co.; v.p. Calif. State Employees Assn., San Jose State Univ. 1964-5; pres. Support Staff Council, San Jose State Univ. 1969-71, 1975-6; pres. Wolfe Central Drug Store Corp. 1976-82, secty./ tres. Constillation Machinery Co., 1961-4; sec./ tres. Adminstr. Enterprises Corp. 1967-71; awards: outstanding employee awd., San Jose State Univ. 1971-2; bd. mem. Support Staff Council Adv. Gp., Calif. State Univs. & Coll. Trust; mem: Elks; Exchange Club of San Jose 1979-81; Calif. State Employees Assn., ret. div.; bd. dirs., treas. Auburn Fair Boosters Assn 1983--, mil: cpl. US Army 1952-4; Republican; Catholic; rec. skiing, woodworking, metalworking, wines. Address: 581 Stonehouse Rd Auburn 95603

THOMPSON, PAUL FRANCIS, library director; b. Nov. 6, 1926, Mount Etna Iowa; s. Forist and Tessie (Florence) Vern; grad., Modesto Jr. Coll., 1947, San Jose State Coll., 1958; m. Betty Jean Cover, Oct. 9, 1927, Modesto; chil: JoAnn (Abbas), b. 1949, Dennis Paul, b. 1953, Mark David, b. 1954, John Wayner, b.1956; career: Library director, Turlock Pub. Lib., 1957-58, Lompoc Pub. Lib., 1969--; AUS, 1945-46; Mem.: Turlock Lions Club, pres. 1968; pres., Black Gold Cooperative Lib. System, rec: fishing, chess, shuffleboard; res: 1412 W. Nectarine Ave., Lompoc 93436 ofc: 501 E. North Ave., Lompoc 93436.

THOMPSON, RICHARD MEREDITH, construction management consultant; b. Feb. 26, 1942, Cadiz, Ohio; s. Doyle Warney and Famie Victoria (Russell) T.; m. Jacquelyn Thompson, Dec. 27, 1978; children: Tamera, b. 1961; Russell, b. 1986; Jennifer, b. 1975; edn: journeyman surveyor, Ventura Jr. Coll. 1966. Career: surveyor to ofc. of mgr. Jensen - Thompson Assoc., Simi 1962-9; asst. proj. mgr./ sales coord. Bear Valley Springs, Tehachapi 1970-2; pres. W.T. Enterprises, Bakersfield 1973; const. supvr. W & B Builders, Santa Monica 1974-8; const. supvr. D & E Devel., Los Angeles 1978-9; pres. GTL Corp., Los Angeles 1979-80; const. mgr. Paul Moote co., Costa Mesa 1980-2; const. & mgmt. cons. SAVI Industrial Park, Yorba Linda 1982--; tchr. Electronic survey methods and equip., Moorpark Jr. Coll. 1967; recipient: performance award, SAVI Ranch Assoc., 1981; mem: Union; CofC; past v.p. Optimist Club; PTA; works: brochures for Tehachapi CofC and var. land devel. projs. 1973; Republican; Protestant; rec: water sports, mechanical pursuits, tracing Calif. history. Address: Thompson Consulting, 1372 E Palm Dr Covina 91724

THOMSETT, MICHAEL CHRISTOPHER, author; b. Mar. 31, 1948, Brighton, England; s. Ronald George and Rose Karen (Walbaum) T.; m. Linda Dinnocenzo, July 1, 1967; 2 sons: Michael, b. 1969; Eric, b. 1976; edn: accting. dip., LaSalle Extension Univ. 1969. Career: draftsman Tudor Engring. Co., San Francisco 1967; acctg. clerk Jordanos Inc., Santa Barbara 1968-9; jr. acct. Pacific Nat. Life Assurance, San Francisco 1969-70; owner acctg. practice, San Rafael 1970-4; chief acct. Utah Internat., San Francisco 1976-8; free lance writer, San Rafael 1978--, cons. Financial Planners Equity Corp. 1978-84, Unimarc Ltd. 1978-82, Fireman's Fund 1982; recipient: dramatics achievement award, Tamalpais H.S. 1966; author: Fundamentals of Bookkeeping and Accounting For The Successful Consultant (chosen for inclusion in Pres.'s Camp David Library); Builders Guide To Accounting; Builders Office Manual; Fundamentals of Bookkeeping and Accounting For The Sucessful Consultant, Bermont Books 1980; Contracters Year- Round Tax Guide; Computers For Contractors; num. bus. and sci. arts. 1978-; rec: music composition (two symphonies completed, chamber music). Address: 134 North San Pedro Road San Rafael 94903

THOMSON, RICHARD REID, insurance broker; b. June 22, 1933, Berkeley; s. George Reid and Theresa Agusta (Olson) T.; m. Jeanne Whitmore Kirkpatrick, Feb. 15, 1981; children: Richard Jr., Helen Theresa, Cynthia Lynn, George R. II; edn: AA, UC Davis 1951-53. Career: national sales mgr. Jacuzznal Assn. of Franchise Dist. Insurance Marketing, Dallas, Tx. 1968-69; dir. of mktg. Citation Mktg. Co., Siloam Springs, Ark. 1969-71; general agent/ owner Richard Thomson Ins. Brokers, So. Lake Tahoe 1971-84; awards: Leaders Club, Millionaires Club, Multimillion Dollar Club; mem. Profl. Insurance Agents Assn., Kiwanis Sunrisers (treas.), Alliance of Business & Lodging Lake Tahoe (v.p. 1982, sec. 1983, dir. 1984); mil: 2d lt. US Army 1953-55; Republican; Christian Sci. Res: 1707 Sherman Way So Lake Tahoe 95705 Ofc: Insurance Brokers, POB BQ, So Lake Tahoe 95705

THORDARSON, EYSTEIN G., manufacturing co. executive; b. Mar. 3, 1934, Iceland, nat. 1978; s. Thordur and Gurdrun (Sigurdardottir) Jonsson; m. Pamela Adams, Oct. 4, 1980; children: Gunner Thor, b. 1959; Leifur Egil; edn: mech. engring., Gothenburg Tech. Sch., Sweden 1956; cert. UC Berkely 1967; Alexander Hamilton Bus. Sch. 1964. Career: competitor 1960 Winter Olympics, Sqauw Valley, immigrated to U.S. following summer; design engr. Reytheon Co., So. San Francisco 1960-4; pres./founder Norwie Corp., Santa Clara 1967-70; dir. mfg. Vadie Corp., Mtn. View 1971-2; v.p. ops. Opties Tech., Palo Alto 1972-4; chief engr. Ampex Corp., Redwood City 1975-80, gen. mgr. 1980-2; gen. mgr. Tandon Corp., Westlake Vill. 1982-3; gen. mgr. mfg. ops., computer Prods. Div. Ampex Corp., Redwood City 1983--; pres. family firm in Iceland (1 yr.); recipient: award of distinction, Internat. Diecasting Competition 1964; Olympic Alpine Skier for Iceland 1956 and 1960 Olympics; rec: skiing, tennis. Res: 21863 Woodland Crest Dr Woodland hills 91364 Ofc: Ampex Corp., 200 No Nash St El Segundo 90245

THORMODSGAARD, GARY ERNEST, sales executive/consultant; b. Mar. 16, 1955, Huntington Park; s. Ernest L. and Rose Elaine T.; m. Elayn Ward, Oct. 9, 1983; 1 dau: Jennifer, b. 1973. Career:pressman Serigraphic Displays 1974; prod. asst. Hutton Roach Lithographers 1975; customer svc. coord. Rotary Offset Printers 1976; sales rep. Crown Printing 1977-81, sales dir. 1981-3; cons. and brokerage chmn. bd. Gary T. Inc. 1983--; publisher, Sun King Publishing; pres. Sun King Prods., spkr. Motivational & Sales Trng. for var. orgns. and commercial firms; awards: Eagle Scout, Boy Scouts of Am. 1972; mem: conference com., Printing Inds. of Am. 1982-3; past scout master, Boy Scouts of AM., Fullerton; Republican; Jewish. Address: Gary T. Inc., 5971 Jacaranda Lane Yorba Linda 92686

THORNBURY, WILLIAM MITCHELL, lawyer; b. Feb. 11, 1944, Kansas City, Mo.; s. Paul Cobb and Marguerite Madellaine (Schulz) T.; m. Joy Barrett, 1973; children: Barrett, b. 1979; Adele, b. 1981, edn: BA, UCLA 1964; JD, UCS Law Sch. 1967; USC Gard. Sch. 1967-9. Career: Los Angeles Co. Public Defender 1969--; lectr. Public Defender's Ofc. 1983--; legal asst. prof. CSU, L.A.; mem: Santa Monica Bar Assn (bd. trustees 1976-7, 1980-1, 1982-; Legislative com. 1974-, chmn. 1981-; chmn. Judicial Eval. Com. 1981-; chmn. Alternative Defense Counsel Com 1981-); Los Angeles Co. Bar Assn. (Criminal Indigent Defense com. 1982; vice- chmn. 1983); Del., Conf. of Dels., State Bar of Calif. 1974, 77, 80, 81, 82, 83; Public Defenders Assn. (bd. trustees 1982-); Navy League of U.S.; Santa Monica CofC; Republican: 44th A.D. Co. Central Com. (chmn. 1974-), S.M. Young Repubs.(exec. bd. 1967-72) S.M. Repub. Club (bd. dirs. 1968-) Santa Monicans Against Crime (bd. dirs. 1979-); L.A. Co. Repub. Party (legal chmn. 1977-81, 1983-) recipient One of Five Outstanding Repubs. Award 1978); L.A. Co. Young Repubs. (del. State Conv. 1969-72) La Follette for Congress (60th A.D. chmn. 1969-70); Repub. State Central Com. (mem. 1983); City of Santa Monica Commnr. 1981-; Fair Election Practices Com. (chmn. 1983). Res: 443 15th St Santa Monica 90402 Ofc: 1945 So Hill St, Ste. 200, Los Angeles 90007

THORNE, ROBERT, lawyer; b. Dec. 6, 1954, Los Angeles; s. Richard and Jacqueline Yvonne (Klowden) T.; edn: AB, w/ dist. & honors, UC Berkeley 1977; JD, UC Hasting Coll. of Law 1980. Career: civil litigator Long & Levit, Los Angeles 1980-2; entertainment litigator Lanely & Singer, Los Angeles 1982-3; entertainment atty. Mason & Sloane 1983--; honors: Phi Beta Kappa; spl. achievement award, Century City Bar Assn.; mem: Century City Bar Assn. (chief ed. Bar Jour. 1982-); Beverly Hills, American, and Los Angeles Co. Bar Assns.; publs: num. arts. in law revs., jours.; contbg. ed., Entertainment Law Reporter 1981-; note & comment ed., Hastings Constnl. Law Quarterly 1979-80; Jewish; rec: sailing, surfing, literature. Res: 1930 Ocean Ave, No. 109, Santa Monica 90405 Ofc: Mason & Sloane, 1299 Ocean Ave, Penthouse, Santa Monica 90401

THORNE, ROBERT WILLIAM, manufacturing co. executive; b. Jan. 5, 1923, San Francisco, dec. Nov. 26, 1981; s. William Edgar and Anna June (Canfield) T.; m. Patsy Parker, Feb 11, 1944; children: John, b. 1945; Mary Lou, b. 1950; Bonnie, b. 1954; William, b. 1957. Career: salesman: Winther Bros. Co., Fresno 1952-4; Premier Autoware Co., San Joaquin Valley 1954-5; Fullwell Motor Prods., San Joaquin Vlly. 1955-8; Rutter Armey Co., S.J.V. 1958-61; owner/ salesman Porta Flux Co., Western U.S. 1962-5; co-owner/ v.p. sales Porta Tool, Inc., Colvis 1965-79; retired 1979; developed Porta Flux Tool; mil: pvt. USMC 1942 (med. disch.); Republican; Presbyterian; rec: classic cars. Res: fmrly of Pebble Beach

THORNTON, SALLY BULLARD, civic leader; b. June 7, 1934, San Diego; d. Orlan Kellogg and Lucinda Catherine (Cairns) Bullard; m. John McBride Thornton, Aug. 20, 1955; children: Mark, b. 1957; Steven, b. 1960; edn: AA, Stephens Coll. 1953; BA in hist., Univ. San Diego 1981, MA in prog. Career: mem. community volunteer Bds., Chairmanships: S.D. Sym. Assn. (pres. 2 yrs.) 1961-74; Children's Hosp. and Health Ctr. 1962-66; Women's Com. for

Cerebral Palsy (founder) 1966-69; United Cerebral Palsy of S.D. County, 1966-76; Junior League of S.D., 1969-70; Civic Youth Orch. (pres. 9 yrs.) 1969-84; United Cerebral Palsy Assn. of Calif. 1970-72; Reuben H. Fleet Theatre & Sci. Ctr. (bd., chmn. Dedication Com.) 1971-73; Freedoms Found. at Valley Forge (pres., Advis. Council 10 yrs.) 1971-83; Family Service Assn. 1971-80; COMBO, 1973-79; Dana Jr. Hi Sch. (Citizens Advis. Com. 1973-5; PTA bd.); S.D. Co. Heart Assn., 1974-76; Am. Heart Assn. (Calif. Afil., bd.) 1975-6; S.D. Planetarium Authority (pres.) 1977-81; Young Audiences Inc., S.D. chpt. (pres.) 1977-81; Univ. of S.D. (Friends of Music, bd.) 1978-80; The John M. and Sally B. Thornton Found. (pres.) 1982-; S.D. Opera (bd. 1983-) 1965-; other chmnships incl: United Way 1966-75, S.D. Civic Light Opera Assn., Starlight, 1965, 71; S.D. Soc. for Crippled Children, 1967; Fine Arts Soc. of S.D., 1971, 74; Salvation Army Door of Hope Aux., 1972. Recipient num. vol. service awards; two Copley Awards for papers, S.D. Hist. Soc., 1982, 84; honors: Phi Alpha Theta, Delta Epsilon Sigma; Republican. Res: 2125 Evergreen St, San Diego 92106

THORNTON, SHANNON NEWELL, physician, surgeon; b. Sept. 15, 1923, Kimberely, Idaho; s. Alfred Shannon and Lenora E. (Humphrey) T.; m. Sally Long, Feb. 15, 973; children: Michael, b. 1951; Kathleen, b. 1953; Mark, b. 1956; edn: BS, Oregon State Coll. 1944; BSM, Creighton Univ. 1945; MD, Creighton Univ. Sch. of Med. 1948; lic. MD, Calif. 1949. Career: rotating intern, Sacramento Co. Hosp., Sacramento 1948-9; Capt. US Army Med. Corps., Korean War and Presidio of San Francisco 1951-4; gen. med. practice, Healdsburg 1954-74; gen. med. practice Happy Camp 1974-83; med. dir. Bigfoot Med. Ctr., Happy Camp 1983--; prepubl. reviewer, Patient Care, Communications, Inc.; editorial research bd. Sportsmedicine Med. Jour. 1982; awards: physicians recogn. awd., Am. Med. Assn. 1980-3; outstanding svc., Sonoma Co. Heart Assn.; mem: Sonoma Co. Heart Assn. (pres.); Am. Med. Assn.; Calif. Med. Assn. 1954-83; Am. Soc. of Abdominal Surgeons 1981-3; Siskiyou Co. Med. Soc. 1983; gov. Active 20-30 Clubs 1961-2; Lions Club; Grange; VFW; nat. adv. bd. Am. Security Council; author in med. field; Capt. US Army 1951-4, Far East Cmd., Korean War decorations; Republican; Assembly of God Ch.; rec: placer mining, editorial writing; sci-fi fan. Res: 61512 Highway 96 Happy Camp 96039 Ofc: Bigfoot Medical Center, 108 West Davis Road Happy Camp 96039

THORPE, JAMES, sr. research associate, Huntington Library-Art Gallery; b. Aug. 17, 1915, Aiken, S.C.; s. J. Ernest and RUby H. T.; m. Elizabeth Daniells, July 19, 1941; children: James, III, b. 1942; John D., b. 1944; Sarah M., b. 1947; edn: AB, The Citadel 1936; MA, UNiv. of N.C. 1938; PhD, Harvard Univ. 1941; Litt.D., Occidental Coll. 1968; LHD, Claremont Gard. Sch. 1968; Litt.D., The Citadel 1971; doctor of Humanities, Univ. of Toledo 1977. Career: prof. of English Princeton Univ. 1946-66, Master Gard. Coll. 1949-55; dir. Henry E. Huntington Library and Art Gallery 1966-83; mem: Aw. Philosophical Soc.; fellow, Am. Acad. of Arts and Scis.; fellow, Am. Antiquarian Soc.; Zamorano Club; author; (publ.) 14 books and var. arts. of literary scholarship; mil: Col., USAF 1941-6, WWII; Democrat; Episcopal; rec: horticulture. Res: 1199 Arden Rd Pasadena 91106 Ofc: Henry E. Huntington Libray and Art Gallery, San Marino 91108

THRAILKILL, JOSEPH ALLEN, lighting consultant/co. president; b. Apr. 16, 1955, Memphis, Tenn.; s. Allen Brown and Joan Margaret Thrailkill; m. Laury Ann Bergstrom, June 5, 1976; 1 son, David, b. 1983; edn: elec. engring., UC Berkeley 1974-5; desig: Assoc., Illuminating Engring. Soc., IES. Career: mechanic Sanderson Inc., San Francisco 1973; mech. draftsman Tempo Steel Inc., S.F. 1974-75; salesman/sales mgr. Lighting Distributors Inc., Irvine 1975-79; owner Sundown Lighting, San Diego 1980--; contract lighting cons. for City of San Diego, and SD Gas & Elec.; mem: Nat. Assn. of Indep. Lighting Distbrs., NAILD, IES (assoc.), S.D. Chamber of Commerce, BBB; splst. in Energy Efficient Lighting Products, first to devel. practical applications for low-pressure mercury discharge lamps in commercial lighting (1982); Democrat; Presbyterian; rec: all sports. Res: 14091 Davenport San Diego 92129 Ofc: Sundown Lighting 9535 Kearny Villa Rd. Ste 103, San Diego 92126

THUNSTROM, WILLIAM KEENAN, corporate executive; b. Mar. 31, 1945, NYC; s. Wilhelm Gustav and Katherine Thunstrom; m. Carol Platts, Aug. 13, 1966; children: Bryan b. 1975, Lisa b. 1975, Laura b. 1977, Brent b. 1979, Lorraine b. 1983; edn: BS in acctg., honors, CSU San Diego 1974; stu. econ., UCSD 1972-73; CPA cert. Calif. 1977. Career: audit staff, audit senior, tax staff, tax senior, tax dept. mgr. Arthur Young & Co., San Diego 1975-81; exec. IFM Group (restaurant, food distbrship, mining, computer leasing), S.D. 1981--: pres. IFM Properties (real estate holding corp., brokerage); dir./v.p. fin. IFM Services, Inc. dba Captain Kidd's Seafood Galley (chain of 16 S.D. restaurants); dir./CFO, Picnic N Chicken Inc. (chain of 33 S.D. and Sacto. restaurants); co-founder and dir./v.p. Pacific Dynasty Foods Inc. (food distbrship); dir./v.p. Sierra Properties Corp. (gold mining ops.); dir. Datronic Rental Corp. (computer leasing ops.); honors: Beta Alpha Psi; scholarship grant, Leaf and Cole, CPAs; mem: Am. Inst. of CPAs, Calif. Soc. of CPAs, Freeman Inst., Mormon Battalion, Inc., LDS Bus. & Profl. Assn., Boy Scouts of Am. (Troop 247) scouting coord.; mil: E5 USN 1968-72, Merit Unit Commendn., Nat. Defense Service, Vietnam Svc. with bronze star, Rep. of Vietnam Cpgn. medals; Republican; LDS Ch. (High Councillor, past Bishop); rec: sailing, tennis, golf. Res: 11699 Calamar Dr San Diego 92124 Ofc: IFM Group 8148 Mercury Ct San Diego 92111

THURSTON, THEODORE MARTIN, financial services executive; b. Jan. 12, 1942, Marion, Indiana; s. Donald Francis and Freda Mae (Howell) T.; edn: BA, Internat. Coll. 1963; CLU, Am. Coll. 1975; APA, Nat. Inst. of Pension Adminstr. 1983. Career : dir. spl. markets Mutual Security Life Ins. Co., Fort Wayne, Indiana 1963-79; dir. Pacific Mutual, Newport Beach 1979-81; v.p. PCC Financial Svcs. Co., Newport Beach 1979--; asst. v.p. ind. employee benefit plans, Pacific Mutual 1981--; pres. pension computer users gp., Mutual Security Life Ins. Co. 1977-8; awards: outstanding volunteer, Orange County 1982; mem: Orange Co. CLU 1979-; Orange Co. Forum 1982-3; Nat. Inst. Pension Adminstr. 1983-; Newport Harbor CofC 1982-; Newport Harbor Kiwanis (treas. 1981, v.p. 1982) 1979-82; Jr. Achievement Adv. and Coord. 1971-; works: cont. edn. seminars Los Angeles Co. CLU 1982; bus. lectures in High Schools; mil: Specialist 5th class, US Army, Commend. medal, Republican; Dutch Reformed Ch. in Am., Crystal Cathedral; rec: water sports. Res: 32 Blue Lagoon Laguna Beach 92651 Ofc: PCC Financial Services Co., Pacific Mutual Life Ins. Co., 700 Newport Center Dr Newport Beach 92660

TIBBITTS, SAMUEL JOHN, hospital society president; b. Oct. 7, 1924, Chicago, Ill.; s. Samuel John and Marion Charlotte (Swanson) T.; m. Audrey Slottelid, Aug. 28, 1949; children: Scott, b. 1953; Brett, b. 1955; edn: BS, UCLA 1949; MS, UC Berkeley 1950. Career: adminstrv. res. Calif. Hosp. Med. Ctr., Los Angeles 1950-1, asst. adminstr. 1951-3, assoc. adminstr. 1953-9; adminstr. 1959-66; chmn. mgmt. com./ asst. secty. Lutheran Hosp. Soc. of So. Calif. 1962-66, pres. 1966--; asst. supt. Santa Monica Hosp. 1952-4; pres. Commn. for Adminstrv. Svcs. in Hosps. 1963, 64, 67; pres. Calif. Health Data Corp. 1968-71; mem: Calif. Health Planning Council and Steering Com. 1968-; Los Angeles City Adv. Med. Council 1971, 73; Pres.'s Com. Health Svcs. Ind. (Adv. Health Council, CA 1973; adv. panel Pres.'s Cost of Living Council, Price Commn. and Pay Bd., Phase II); Calif. Hosp. Commn., State Calif. 1974--; bd. dirs. Calif. Hosp. Med. Ctr., Martin Luther Hosp., Henry Mayo Newhall Meml. Hosp.; trustee, exec. com. Blue Cross of So. Calif. 1966-75; honors: fellow, Am. Coll. of Hosp. Adminstr.; Delta Omega; Ritz E. Heerman Award, Calif. Hosp. Assn.; Svc. to Humanity Awd., Lutheran Mutual Life Ins. Co.; Outstanding Achievement Awd., Hosp. Council of So. Calif.; Most Venerable Order of the Hosp. of St. John, presented by Queen of England; Trustees Awd., Am. Hosp. Assn.; Freedom Awd., Wilshire Sertoma Club; Outstanding Svc. Awd., Blue Cross of So. Calif.; Individual of Year, Fdn. of Am. Hosps.; hon. mem. U. Minn. Alumni Assn.; author: Preferred Provider Organizations (1984), num. mag., journal arts.; mil: pfc US Army M.C. 1946-7; Republican; Lutheran; rec: golf, gardening. Res: 1224 Adair St San Marino 91108 Ofc: Lutheran Hosp. Soc. of So. Calif., 1423 So. Grand Ave Los Angeles 90015

TIDEMANIS, MODRIS ALEX, land developer; b. June 9, 1950, Memphis, Tenn.; s. Aleksandrs and Elsa V. (Liepins) T.; edn: BS, Ohio State Univ. 1972; MBA, UCLA 1976; MSc, Chapman Cell. 1982; lic. real estate broker, State Calif.; AICP 1980. Career: civil engr. Ohio Bell Telephone Co., Columbus, Ohio 1973; real estate mgr. Stern Realty, Brentwood, CA 1973-4; constrn. mgr. C.F. Brann Co., El Segundo 1974-5; proj. mgr. Am. Devel. Corp., Los Angeles 1975-6; mgr. adv. planning Anaheim Hills, Inc., Anaheim 1976-81; sr. proj. rep. Chevron Land & Devel. Corp. 1981--; guest spkr. UCLA Grad. Sch. of Mgmt. 1982; cons. to var. home bldrs. 1981; asst. womens volleyball coach, Chapman Coll.; awards: All-Amer. Volleyball player Ohio State 1971-2; Ohio State Scholar-Athlete 1972; Tau Beta Pi; Beta Sigma Gamma; mem: AICP; Chapman Coll. Athletic Found.; Riga (Latvian sports club); publs: art., Chapman College Women's Volleyball Conditioning Program, NCSA Journal, 1982; Lutheran; rec: sportsmed., volleyball, skiing, photog. Res: 244 Glenview Place Orange 92668 Ofc: Chevron Land & Dev. Co., 20031 Goldenwest Street Huntington Beach 92648

TIERNEY, THOMAS JAMES, business strategy consulting firm partner; b. Mar. 5, 1954, San Francisco; s. Ralph Thomas and Eleanor Fay (Walker) T.; edn: BA, highest honors, UC Davis 1976; MBA, w/ distinction, Harvard Bus. Sch. 1980. Career: Bechtel Internat., Arzew, Algeria 1976-8; field engr. 1976-7; supvr. cost and planning engrs. 1977-8; Bain & Co., Palo Alto 1980--; cons. 1980-1; mgr. 1982-3; partner 1983--; Pro-Bono Consulting 1983--; founder Fun Co. 1984; honors: Dean's List UC Davis 1972-6; Phi Kappa Phi; Internat. Economic Honor Soc.; appointed Student Asst. to Chancellor; Winslow Jr. Meml. Awd. (Most Outstanding Male Grad.) UC Davis 1976; mem: Sierra Club; Ducks Unlimited; Calif. Waterfowl Assn.; Nat. Rifle ASsn.; Harvard Bus. Sch. Alumni Assn.; UC Davis Sch. of Adminstr.; dir. UC Davis Alumni Assn.; Republican; Catholic; rec: photog., fishing, hunting. Res: 3645 Buchanan St, No. 102, San Francisco 94123 Ofc: Bain & Company, 660 Hansen Way Palo Alto 94304

TIMMERMAN, E. JOYCE, travel company president; b. Mar. 2, 1937, Twin Falls, Idaho; d. John Barney and Dorothea Leota (Diamond) Stephens; 1 son: Rallin Dale Black, b. 1959; edn: Loma Linda Univ. 1954-5; Southwestern Union Cell. 1955-6. Career: controller Eagle Mfg. Div. of Scott Paper Co. 1963-78; pres./ owner Travel With Joyce 1978--; Los Angeles Ofc. 1978--; Irvine Ofc. 1980--; awards: Most Valuable Past Pres. Orange Co. Chpt. NAA 1982; mem: NAA (1st woman pres. Orange Co. Chpt.; 1st woman pres. Wild West Council; Nat. Dir.); Financial Exec. Inst. (mem. sev. com., chmn, spl. functions); Newport CofC; ASTA; Republican; SDA; rec: singing, travel. Res: 222 So Figueroa St Los Angeles 90012 Ofc: Travel With Joyce, Inc., 800 s. Figueroa St, Ste 860, Los Angeles 90017

TINGLE, JAMES O'MALLEY, lawyer; b. June 12, 1928, NY, NY; s. Thomas Jefferson and Mercedes (O'Malley) T.; edn: BS, Univ. of Montana 1950; BA and LLB, 1952; LLM, Univ. of Mich. 1953; SJD, 1958; lawyer, Calif., Montana, and NY, and before var. fed. crts. Career: assoc. prof. of law Univ. of Montana Law Sch., Missoula, Mt. 1955-6; lawyer Shell Oil Co., Ny, Ny 1957-62; lawyer Pillsbury, Madison & Sutro, San Francisco 1962--; awards: William W. Cook

Fellowship, Univ. Mich. Law Sch. 1952-3; mem: Montana Bar Assn.; Calif. Bar Assn.; Am. Bar Assn.; Stack Exchange Club, San Francisco 1968-; author: The Stockholder's Remedy of Corporate Dissolution, 1959; editor: State Antitrust Laws, 1974; mil: 1st Lt. USAF 1953-5; Democrat; Agnostic; rec: tennis. Res: 1020 Union St, No. 28, San Francisco 94101 Ofc: Pillsbury, Madison & Sutro, 225 Bush, Rm 1956 San Francisco 94104

TINGLOF, BIRGER OLAF, JR., pediatrician; b. Apr. 1, 1932, Beverly Hills; s. Birger Olaf and Mary Ebba (Eister) T.; m. Marion Cross, 1955; children: Lisle, b. 1956; Eric, b. 1960; edn: BA, UCLA 1955; MD, 1958. Career: priv. practice physician 1966--; asst. prof. Pediatrics UCLA Med. Sch; pres. Med. Staff St. John's Hosp., Santa Monica 1982-3; honors: fellow Am. Acad. Pediatrics; mem: bd. dirs. Pacific Med. Review System; LA Pediatric Soc.; mil: Capt., USAR Med. Corps. 1959-62, Army Commendation Medal; Republican; Christian; rec: flyfishing, photography, backpacking. Res: 3342 Mandeville Canyon Rd Los Angeles 90049 Ofc: 2001 Santa Monica Blvd, Ste 690-W, Santa Monica 90404

TIPLER, JAMES HARVEY, lawyer; b. Jan. 13, 1951; s. Frank Jennings Jr. and Ann (Kearley) T.; edn: BA, summa cum laude, Yale Univ. 1973e; JD, Stanford Law Sch. 1977. Career: assoc. law firm of Kaplan, Livingston, Goodwin, Berkowitz & Selvin, Beverly Hills 1977-9; partner law firm of Tipler and Tipler, Malibu 1979--; partner Marathon Management, Malibu 1981-3; partner James Harvey Tipler & Assoc. 1983--; honors: Phi Beta Kappa 1973; mem: State Bar of Calif.; Am. Bar Assn.; Los Angeles Co. Bar Assn.; Beverly Hills Bar Assn. Res: 4267 Marina City Dr, Ste 1110, Marina Del Rey 90291 Ofc: 23410 Civic Center Way, Ste E9, Malibu 90265

TISON, LARRY GLENN, landscape architect; b. Jan. 14, 1952, Lodi; s. Charles Glen and Betty Ann (Rempfer) T.; m. Shiu-Zee Pow, Aug. 16, 1974; 1 dau: Lillian, b. 1979; edn: AA, Cosumnes River Coll. 1972; BS, honors, CalPoly, SLO 1976; Reg. Landscape Architect, Calif. Career: draftsman/ assoc./ principal Arthur G. Barton & Assoc. 1976-82; prin. Larry G. Tison & Assoc., Glendale 1982--; Student Jury chmn. UCLA 1984; instr. UCLA Ext. 1982; mem. Glendale Historical Dist. Task Force; mem: Am. Soc. of Landscape Architects, ASLA (So. Calif. Chpt., Northwest Sect. Chmn. 1984; var. chairs); Rotary Club of Glendale; Sigma Lambda Alpha- Theta Chpt.; Gledale Historical Soc.; Game Assoc.; Theodore Payne Found S.W.A.P.; works incl.: Ranney House, Pasadena 1984; Pilgrim Place, Claremont 1980; Hollenbeck Home, L.A. 1976-80; Republican; Presbyterian; rec: antique- classic car restoration. Res: 5112 Glenwood Ave La Crescenta 91214 Ofc: Larry G. Tison & Assoc., 312 E Mountain St Glendale 91207

TOALE, JOHN FRANCIS, securities co. president; b. Feb. 11, 1945, NY, NY; s. Peter Russell and Catherine Veronica (Mulligan) T.; m. Maryanne Vaz, Dec. 18, 1982; children: Jeffrey, b. 1967; Keri Ann, b. 1970; edn: BS, Mt. St. Mary's Coll. 1966; Gen. Securities Principal 1974; Financial and Ops. Principal 1974. Career: auditor Arthur Andersen & Co., NY 1966-71; var. positions to v.p. Damson Oil Corp., NY 1971-82; var. positions to sr. v.p./ secty./ dir. Damson Securities, Inc., NY 1971-82; v.p. finance Bennett Petroleum, Inc., Denver, Colo. v.p. 1982; Morgan Securities, Inc. 1982-3, pres./bd. chmn. 1983--; v.p. Morgan Petroleum, Inc., Monterey 1982-3, exec. v.p./ secty./v. chmn. 1983--, adv. com. Financial Planners Equity Corp.; Bus. Sch. adv. bd. Mt. St. Mary's Coll.; mem: Internat. Assn.of Financial Planners; Planning Execs. Inst.; Colo. Petroleum Accts. Soc.; Elks; KQED- Public TV; K.C.; actor var. little theater prods.; Republican; Catholic; rec: sports, acting, cooking. Res: 29147 Fern Canyon Rd Carmel 93923 Ofc: Morgan Securities, Inc., 700 Cass St Monterey 93940

TOBIN, SHARON LOUISE, psychotherapist; b. Aug. 19, 1940, Long Beach; d. Roy Nathan and Jean Carol (Tobin) Rorabough; edn: BS, Immaculate Heart 1962; MSW, USC 1968; Calif. Lic. Clinical Soc. Wkr. 1974. Career: psychotherapist in pvt. practice 1975--, full time since 1979; dir. Med. Social Svcs., St. John's Hosp. and Hlth Ctr. 1970-79; soc. wkr. Jewish Family Service, 1970-71, Holy Family Adoption Svcs., 1964-66, Extension Volunteers), 1962-64; chaired Incest Task Force, L.A. Commn. on Status of Women 1980; co-dev. incest project for Kuhner Inst., 1981-; instr. in grief therapy for Shanti Nilaya 1982-; cons. LaVina Respiratory Hosp. 1979-83; coordinator UCLA proj. on Cancer Care, 1980-; cons./lectr. various hosps., govt. agencies; clin. instr. USC 1973-4, 77-79, Univ. of Wash. 1975-77, CSU Fullerton 1978-82; mem: Am. Hospital Assn. Task Force on Discharge Plnng. (keynote spkr. 1978); mem: Am. Hosp. Social Wk. Directors (So. Calif. pres. 1975); Calif. Crippled Chil. Svcs.; Santa Monica Mayoral Commn. on Older Ams. 1973-9; Soc. for Clin. Soc. Wkrs.; past pres., bd. ch. S.M. Comm. Services Council; S.M. West Side Vol. Bur.; Soroptomists (past vp); So. Calif. Women for Understanding (bd.); New Age (bd.); rec: writing, painting. Address: North Hollywood 91601

TOBKIN, DAVID DEAN, certified public accountant; b. Apr. 12, 1951, Mahonomen, Minn.; s. Eugene E. and Elsie A. (Walz) T.; m. Donnajean Coon, 1984; children: Shannon, b. 1969; James, b. 1978; Erin, b. 1978; Jacqueline, b. 1980; edn: BS & C, Santa Clara Univ. 1973. Career: owner David D Tobkin, Inc., A Professional Accountancy Corp., San Jose; bd. dirs. Los Gatos Conv. Hosp.; Calif. Soc. of CPA; Affil. Mem. Bay Area Contract; Councilman Santa Clara City; bd. of Fellows, Univ. of Santa Clara; Democrat; Catholic; rec: tennis, water skiing. Res: 1776 Lexington St Santa Clara 95050 Ofc: 2007 W Hedding St, No. 205, San Jose 95128

TODD, DIANA RAYMOND, import-export food & beverage co. president; b. Jan. 10, 1943, Adelaide, So. Australia; d. Stanley Raymond and Margaret A. (Coates) Grosser; edn: BA in music (classical guitar), DePaul Univ., Chgo.; desig. Professeurs Chef de Cuisine, Confrerie de la Chaine des Rotisseurs. Career: (past) jobs incl. shearing sheep in New Zealand, picking tobacco, secty. to social editor Adelaide (Aust.) Advertiser; fmr. classical guitarist, TV apps., Adelaide, Aust., and USA; sales mgr. Hyatt Regency dwntwn Chgo., 1977; pres. Todd Internat. Assocs., 1977--; dir. Food & Wine Sch., Chalet Internationale 1979; pres. Australian Food & Wine Exchange, Inc. 1979--; pres. Australasia Ventures, Inc. 1981--; bd. dirs. Landorama Inc. (public co., parent corp. of A/V); sole US importer of Vegemite (condiment); frequent guest on radio and TV talk shows; honors: listed Internat. Whos Who in Music, Ky. Colonel; mem: Confrerie de la Chaine des Rotisseurs, Internat. Assn. of Cooking Schools, Newport Bch. CofC, Aust. Am. CofC; patron Orange Co. Perf. Arts Center, Laguna Bch Mus. of Art, mem. Laguna Cyn. Athletic Club; rec: tennis, fishing, contemplation. Address: 3941-B So. Bristol St Santa Ana 92704 Ofc: Australasia Ventures Inc. 3100 Airway Ave, Ste 106, Costa Mesa 92626

TODD, JOHN ALTON, corporate executive, restaurateur; b. Jan. 10, 1916, Murfreesboro, Tenn.; s. Gent and Mada J. (Wilson) T.; m. Natividad Garcia, July 4, 1942; children: John, Jr., b. 1943, Ray, b. 1946. Career: Todd Mgmt. Corp., San Diego (pres. 1963-84, dir. 1984--); Todd Purchasing Co., San Diego (pres. 1965-75, dir. 1975--); pres. Old Town Tamale Factory, Inc., San Diego 1947--; awarded: 1st place all svc. track- field meet, San Diego 1942; guest Art Linkletter, Garry Moore and Harold Keen T.V. Shows, World Title 24 inch mustache; mil: Cpl., US Army 1941-44, Five Battle Stars, GCM; Democrat; Catholic; rec: big game hunting, chess, sports. Address: Old Town Tamale Factory, Inc., 6034 Madra Ave San Diego 92120

TOFTNESS, CECIL GILMAN, lawyer; b. Sept. 13, 1920, Glasgow, Montana; d. Anton Bernard and Nettie (Pederson) Toftness; edn: A.A., S.D. Evening Jr. Coll., 1943; B.S., UCLA, 1949; J.D., Southwestern Univ., L.A. 1953; m. Chloe Vincent, 1951; career: priv. pract. of civ. law, 1954--; USN active duty 1938-46; USNR, Naval Officer, 1946--; Doctoral thesis: Historical Background to the 14th Amendment to the U.S. Constitution, 1953; class representative, Class 1953, Southwestern Law Sch; Masonic Lodge, Manhattan Beach-Redondo Beach #742 Blue Lodge, Royal Arch Mason, Knight Templar, LA Commander #9; Mem.: Kiwanis Club of Palos Verdes, 1955--; Phi Delta Legal Frat.; Democrat; Lutheran; rec: reading, gardening, golf; office: 2516 Via Tejon, Palos Verdes Estates 90274.

TOKUNAGA, ALLAN HIDEKI, manufacturing company executive; b. Feb. 3, 1943, Lonepine, CA; s. George Masato and Harue (Hanamoto) T.; edn: Los Angeles Valley Coll. 1967-71; Otis Art Inst. 1971. Career: salesman Foothill Pansy Gardens 1961-3; US Army 1964-6; svc. mgr. Valley Power Equipment 1967-71; owner/ pres. Tri-Arts, No. Hollywood 1971--; adv bd. West Valley Occupational Center; mem. VFW; mil: Specialist 4th Class, US Army 1964-66, Vietnam Svc.; Republican; Buddhist; rec: fishing, travel. Res: 10940 Laurel Canyon Blvd San Fernando 91340 Ofc: Tri-Ats, 7854 Lankershim Blvd No Hollywood 91605

TOLSON, CHESTER LOGAN, clergyman; b. Oct. 28, 1923, Los Angeles; s. Franklin James and Edith (Peters) T.; children: Stephen James, b. 1947; Kathleen June, b. 1951; edn: BA, Pasadena Coll. 1945; M. Div., San Francisco Tech. Seminary 1951; PhD, La Jolla Univ. 1980; Ordination, Presbyterian Ch. 1951. Career: pastor Comm. Presbyterian Ch., Lake Oswego, Ore. 1951-5; dir. of Missions Presbytery of Los Angeles 1955-7; pastor Village Presbyterian Ch., Rancho Santa Fe 1957-63; asst. v.p. pub. rels. Forest Lawn Meml. Parks 1963-6; area dir. Fifty Million Fund Presbyterian Ch. USA 1966-7; asst. to pres. Trinity Univ., San Antonio, TX 1967-8; dir./ fund raising cons. Ketchum, Inc., Pittsburgh, PA 1968-71; pres. C.L. Tolson & Assoc., fund raising cons., L.A. 1971--; minister of Stewardship, Geneva Presbyterian Ch., Laguna Hills; tchr. Lewis Clark Coll., Portland Ore.; pres. Chester L. Tolson Ministries Inc.; host Facing Life, TV and Radio Show; Calif. Real Estate Broker (Presbyterian Ch. Properties); honors: cum laude San Francisco Theological Sem. 1951; Who's Who- Am. Colls. and Univs.; mem: Presbytery of Los Ranchos CA; Kiwanis; pres. La Costa Fairways Homeowners Assn.; coauthor w/ C.W. Lieb, Peace and Power Through Prayer, Prentice- Hall Inc. 1962 (intro. by Norman Vincent Peale); Republican; Presbyterian; rec: golf, music, writing, lecturer. Res: 10 Sunstream Irvine 92715 Ofc: Geneva Presbyterian Church, 24301 El Toro Rd Laguna Hills 92653

TOM, JOSEPH, state employment executive; b. Sept. 1, 1930, Canton, China; s. Kwong Chang and Fung Chun (Wong) T.; m. Ivy Kwok Ying Choy, Nov. 29, 1955; children: Aland, b. 1958; Barnett, b. 1959; edn: AA, Coll. of San Mateo 1976; San Francisco State Univ. 1977; grad. 12 tech. schs. USAF; grad. Acad. Sch. of Pvt. Investign.; Calif. Real Estate Lic., Ins. Agt. Lic., NASD, Notary Public; Career: served to T/Sgt. USAF 1953-74 (11 decorations incl AF Commend., Navy Unit Cit.); currently dept. rep. State of Calif. Employment Devel. Dept.; real estate agt./ins. agt.; honored for work on behalf of Disabled Vets, Am. Legion, Calif. AmVets; mem: Calif. State Empl. Assn., DAV, Amvets (No. Area Calif. comdr.; charter comdr. S.F. Post 78), Disabled Vets Outreach Assn. (pres.), NCOA (counselor); Republican; Bud.; rec: sports, writing. Res: 936 Hillside Blvd Daly City 94014 Ofc: EDD, 211 Main St San Francisco 94111

TOMASSETTI, VICTOR JOHN, chiropractor; b. Aug. 13, 1955, Rochester, NY; s. Louis Phillip and Mary Rose (Delfino) T.; edn: BS, St. John Fisher Coll. 1977; Doctor of Chiro., Nat. Coll. of Chiropractic 1981; Dr. of Chiropractic, Dr. J. Janse 1981. Career: Dr. Stanley Wietzorek, Brockport, NYa 1981-2; coowner Courtyard Chiropractic Gp., Oceanside 1982--; mem: Calif. Chiropractic Assn.; Internat. Coll. of Applied Kinesiology; Oceanside CofC; Carlsbad

CofC; rec: water sports. Res: 666 Neptune Leucadia 92024 Ofc: Courtyard Chiropractic Group, 2741 Vita Way, Ste III, Oceanside 92054

TOMEI, JOEL ALAN, architect; b. May 11, 1941, San Mateo; s. Joseph Ambrose and Grace Leona (Nunes) T.; m. Patricia Hayden Brown, July 12, 1964; children: Amanda H., b. 1978; Elizabeth Y., b. 1983; edn: AA, Santa Rosa Jr. Coll. 1961; B.Arch., UC Berkeley 1966; M.Arch. 1967; M. City Plnng., Harvard Univ. 1973; Reg. Architect, Calif. 1970, Ill.; Mass.; Nat. Council of Registration Bds. (NCARB) Cert. Career: Skidmore, Owings & Merril, Architects/ Engineers, 1967-78; designer job captain, Chicago 1967-70; urban designer, Boston, Mass. 1971-4; urban designer, San Francisco, and Tehran 1974-8; Hope Cons. Gp., Arch./ Engrs., San Francisco 1979--; proj. mgr. 1979; v.p./ proj. mgr. 1980; v.p./ principal architect 1983--; steering com. chmn. Skidmore, Owings & Merrill 1976; design jury critic UC Berkeley 1975; awards: Mellon Scholarship, Harvard Univ. 1972; 28th annual Progressive Architecture Design Awd. 1981; AIP Awd., Republic Newspaper Plant, Columbus, Ind. 1980; mem: Harvard Club SF; Am. Inst. of Planners (AIP) 1974; San Francisco Planning and Urban Research; S.F. Market Street Proj.; design team mem: Sears Tower, Chgo. 1968; US Embassy in Moscow 1977; Bandai Shapour New Town, Iran 1975; Yanbu New Town in Saudi Arabia 1976; Saudi Arabian Naval Acad., Jeddah, 1981; Democrat; Episcopal; rec: photog., film making, gardening. Res: 167 20th Ave San Francisco 94121 Ofc: Hope Consulting Group, 562 Mission St San Francisco 94105

TOMEI, JOSEPH AMBROSE, investment planner-advisor; b. June 18, 1913, Princeton, CA; s. John and Filomena (Beffa) H.; b. Grace Leona Nunes, Jan. 12, 1936; children: Joyce, b. 1937; Joel, b. 1941; edn: San Mateo Jr. Coll. 1932-3. Career: in banking 13 yrs.; in business 24 yrs.; currently stock broker Merrill Lynch, Santa rosa; adv. bd. Bank of Am., Sebastopol 1963-7; economic devel. chmn. Sonoma Co. 1970; chmn. United Crusade; awards: Citizen of the Day, Sonoma Co., 1-19-71; mem: Rotary Club (Paul Harris Fellow) Sebastopol 36 yrs.; CofC bd. dirs.; pres. 20-30 Club; Salvation Army dir.; Mayor of the City of Sebastopol 1959-60; City Council mem. 1956; Planning Commission 1950; chmn. Taxpayers Assn. 1966; Republican; Catholic; rec: reading, golf, fishing, travel. Res: 468 Vine Ave Sebastopol 95472 Ofc: Merrill Lynch, 90 Santa Rosa Ave Santa Rosa 95472

TOMKE, TIM BRUCE, recording company executive; b. Nov. 22, 1940, Bay City, Mich.; s. Martin Emil and Laura Frances (Hoff) T.; children: Miles, b. 1981; Olivia, b. 1979; Tyrone, b. 1978; Bruce, b. 1962; edn: BA, Univ. of Mich. 1963; MD, 1968. Career: intern Highland Hosp., Oakland 1968; dir. emergency Fairmont Hosp., San Leandro 1969; emergency physician San Francisco area 1970-79; recording artist and record producer 1980--; owner Ocean Studio, Ocean Records, and Ocean TV; mastered at Warner Bros. Recording Studios and MCA Recording Studios, Hollywood; owner Wolfman's- On- The- Warf Nightclub, San Francisco 1969-70; exec. Wolfman Enterprises 1971-6; exec. dir. Tracks Mobile Recording, San Francisco 1977-80; honors: invitational performances at Northsea Jazz Festival Hague, Holland and The Montreaux Jazz Festival Montreaux, Switzerland 1981; mem: Am. Coll. of Emergency Physicians; Audio Engrs. Soc.; composer: over 100 musical works, jazz and pop; mil: Capt. Army Med. Corps.; rec: painting with oil and acrylics. Address: Ocean Studio, 9 Sacramento Patio Stinson Beach 94970

TOMS, ROBERT LEE, lawyer; b. May 12, 1935, Asheville, No. Carolina; s. Marion F. Sr. and Joy (Wellford) T.; m. Valeria Jean Franklin, May 8, 1957; children: Robert, Jr., b. 1958; Sandra Jean, b. 1959; Clayton Yandell, b. 1968; edn: BA, Bob Jones Univ. 1957; JD, Duke Univ. Law Sch. 1965; No. Carolina State Bar 1965; Calif. State Bar 1966. Career: sr. partner law firm of Caldwell & Toms; commissioner of corps., State of Calif. 1974-5; mem: Am. Bar Assn.; State Bar of Calif.; No. Carolina State Bar; Los Angeles Co. Bar Assn.; Lawyers' Club of Los Angeles; Trustee of Hollywood; Presbyterian Med. Ctr.; Republican; Presbyterian; rec: skiing, music, travel. Res: 1711 Bushnell Ave So. Pasadena 91030; Ofc: 700 So Flower St, 15th Flr., Los Angeles 90017

TONE, MARJORY FRANCIS, Arabian horse breeder; b. Feb. 19, 1915, Dos Palos, CA; d. Loren and Laura Pearl (Chapman) Woodworth; m. Jack Tone, Sept. 5, 1932; children: Jacqueline, b. 1933; Joanne, b. 1935; Kathleen, b. 1941; Susan, b. 1943; Patricia, b. 1945. Career: Arabian horse breeder 1952--; owner mgr. Fadjur prize stallion; dir./ 1st reg. dir. Internat. Arbian Horse Assn.; founder/ 1st pres. Arabian Riders & Breeders; 1st woman pres. Arabian Horse Assn. of No. Calif.; mem: World Arabian Horse Orgn.; Arabian Horse Registry of Am.; Internat. Arabian Horse Assn.; Arabian Riders & Breeders; Arabian Horse Assn. of No. Calif.; World Arabian Horse Orgn.; dir. Arabian Horse Trust; Am. Horse Shows Assn.; Republican; Catholic; rec: Address: Jacktone Ranch, 9749 No Jacktone Rd Stockton 95205

TONELLO-STUART, ENRICA M., political economist; b. Dec. 20, 1926, Monza, Italy, Nat. 1950; d. Alessandro P. and Maddalena Maria (Marangoni) Tonello; m. Charles L. Stuart, Feb. 14, 1975; edn: BA, UNiv. of Colo. 1961; MA, Claremont Grad. Sch. 1966; PhD, 1971; Dept. of Edn.; Dept. of Ins. Career: 1947-63: Ofcr. Wife USAF, Red Cross Gray Lady; base coord. Veteran Admin.; dir. Family Asst. Svc. Tactical Air Command, Langley ; sales mgr. Metropolitan Lifeu Ins. Co. 1974-79; pres. E.T.S. Research & Devel. Inc. 1977--; dir. Internat. Studies Prgm. Union Univ. WUM-KOSE Found. 1975--; L.A. and Tokoyo publisher and ed. Tomorrow Outline 1963--; tchr. UNION Univ.; research and sys. analyst Economical and Political Risk Mgmt. and Analysis; awards: Red Cross Svc. Awd.; VA volunteer and Air Force vol. svc. awds. 1950-55; Pi Sigma Alpha; WUM-KOSE Leadership and Svc. Awd.; mem: Corp. Planners Assn. (treas. 1974-9); World Future Soc. (pres. 1974-);

Planng. Exec. Inst. 1975-8; L.A. CofC 1978-; Zonta Internat. (ch. internat. com. South Bay Club); Investigative Reporters & Editors; S.F. Press Club; Italian Heritage Found. (pub. rels.); Palos Verdes Womens Club; Patrons of Ital. Culture; bd. dirs. Caesarea World Monument; Inland Empire, L.A. World Affairs Council; works: A Plan for a World Community 1963; Planning the World Community 1971; A Proposal for the Reorgn. of the U.N. 1966; The Role of the Multinationals in the Emerging Globalism 1977; Catholic; rec: travel, research, writing. Address: 80 Narcissa Dr Rancho Palos Verdes 90274

TONKIN, BERTRAM MELVIN, convention and trade show executive; b. June 29, 1926, Portland, Ore.; s. Samual and Kate (Arkin) T.; m. Mary Ann Brown, Apr. 6, 1956; children: Wendy, b. 1959, Jill, b. 1959; edn: BA, Univ. Ore. 1949; MBA, City Coll. of NY 1951. Career: buyer, furniture, Abraham & Straus, Brooklyn 1952-54; joined Western Exhibitors (conv. & trade show mgmt. firm), San Francisco 1954-, gen. mgr. of Western Merchandise Mart, S.F. 1967-70, pres. Western Exhibitors, Inc. 1971--; bd. dirs.: San Francisco Conv. & Visitors Bureau, Foreign Trade Mart, Gift Center, S.F.; honors: Eta Mu Pi (nat. retailing hon.); pres. No. Calif. Chpt., Nat. Assn. of Exposition Mgrs.; bd. dirs. Concordia Argonaut Club; mil: cpl. USAF; Republican; Jewish; rec: tennis, skiing, travel. REs: 268 Lombard, San Francisco 94133 Ofc: Western Exhibitors, Inc. 2181 Greenwich St San Francisco 94123

TONSICH, KATHLEEN SUE, real estate broker; b. Feb. 12, 1934, Gallup, NM; d. Wayne Emerson and Anna Marie (Kitchen) Ramage; m. Athony Nick Tonsich, Nov. 7, 1953; children: Anthony Marion, b. 1954; Nicholas Gerard, b. 1961; Suzanne Marie, b. 1965; edn: broker's lic., Anthony's Real Estate Sch. 1979; Calif. real estate broker, Dept. Real Estate, Sacramento 1979. Career: sales person Spring Realty and Carriage Realty 1974-79; mgr. Carriage Realty, San Pedro 1979-83; v.p. Re/Max Spring Realty, Rolling Hills Estates 1983-4; v.p. Re/Max Rolling Hills, Rolling Hills EStates 1984; CCD tchr. Mary Star of the Sea & St. Peter's Catholic Chs.; United Way Chmn. Mary Star of the Sea; past Cub Scout leader; num. realty bd. coms.; Spring Realty Million Dollar Club; Re/Max Top Twenty No.1 (8/83); Archdiocesan Council of Catholic Women; Spl. Recogn. Awd. United Way 1981; United Way Awd. 1980; Disting. Volunteer Catholic Soc. Svc., Mary Star of the Sea Parih 1983; mem: The Acctg. Circle USC 198; Pacific Coast Walking Horse Assn.; Nat. Pleasure Walking Horse Assn.; Brass Ring Handicap Found. sponser; Republican; Catholic; rec: skiing, sailing, horseback riding, travel. Res: 2251 Daladier Dr Rancho Palos Verdes 90274 Ofc: Re/Max Rolling Hills, 2483 Palos Verdes No., Rolling Hills 90274

TONSING, MICHAEL JOHN, lawyer; b. May 10, 1943, Los Angeles; s. John Maurice and Mary Ellen (McMahon) T.; m. Cecilia Degnan, Jan. 29, 1966; children: Catherine, b. 1969; Michael, Jr., b. 1976; edn: BA, Saint Mary's Coll. of CA 1965; MA, Claremont Grad. Sch. 1970; JD, Univ. of S.F. Sch. of Law 1975; lawyer, State Bar of Calif. 1976. Career: asst. dean Saint Mary's Coll. of Calif. 1968-76; ind. practice law, Walnut Creek 1976-7; Oakland 1977-80; hearing ofcr./ legal counsel Calif. Public Employment Relations Bd., San Francisco 1977-80; lectr. Law and Juris Prudence, Saint Mary's Coll. 1977--; co-founder Saint Mary's Coll. Paralegal Prgm. 1976; judical fellow US Supreme Court 1980-1; asst. US Atty., San Francisco 1981--; honors: judical fellow US Supreme Court 1980-1; Weaver fellow, Claremont Grad. Sch. 1965-6; mem: State Bar Calif. 1976-; pres. Calif. Admin. Law Coll. Bd. 1978-80; US Supreme Court Bar 1981-; S.F. Bar Assn.; Am. Bar Assn.; Am. Arbitration Assn.; Commonwealth Club of Calif.; US Supreme Court Hist. Soc.; Saint Mary's Coll. Alumni bd. dirs.; mil: maj. USAR 1967-, Army Commdn. medal; Catholic. Res: 911 Longridge Road Oakland 94610 Ofc: US Atty's Office, 450 Goldengate, 16th Flr, San Francisco 94102

TOOLE, MONTE, manufacturing company executive; b. Mar. 3, 1931, Winnipeg, Canada, nat. 1957; s. Harry and Esther (Siegel) T.; children: Esther, b. 1953; David, b. 1955; BSc, UCLA 1960. Career: systems analyst IBM Corp., Calif. 1960; mgr. quality control continental Device Inc., Calif. 1961-2; mgr1947-63 reliability and quality assurance Fairchild Semiconductor Corp. 1963-8; gen. mgr. Abogee Chemical 1968-9; pres. Monte Toole & Assoc., Inc., 1970-1; chmn./ pres./ CEO Atomel Products Corp. (dba Gasonics) 1971--; mem: Am. Soc. for Good Quality Control 1961--; patentee: 7 U.S. and Internat. patents for semiconductor equipment inventions and automation. Res: 1450 Oak Creek, No. 411, Palo Alto 94304 Ofc: Gasonics, 238 Caribbean Dr Sunnyvale 94089

TOPPEL, HALDIS RAUCHFUS, data processing executive; b. Aug. 27, 1942, Lueben, Germany; d. Harmanfried and Hildegard (Pogorzalek) Rauchfus; m. Kurt Toppel, Dec. 23, 1976; 1 son: Curt, b. 1980; edn: information system mgmt. student USF. Career: stewardess Continental Airlines, Los Angeles 1964-71; flight instr. Rose Aviation, Hawthorne 1973-75; pgmmr./d.p. mgr. Santa Anita Race Track, Arcadia 1972-75; sr. systems analyst EBM, Beverly Hills 1975-77; sr. systems analyst Wallace Berrie Co., Van Nuys 1977-78; sr. systems analyst/d.p. mgr. Commuter Computer, Los Angeles 1978--; spkr. workshops, APWA transportation application of microcomputers, Los Angeles, design and implementation of the nation's largest rideshare system; mem: Data Processing Mgmt. Assn., DPMA (dir. publs.) 1983--; publs. ed./ writer for DPMA newsletter, Diplomat; Catholic; rec: flying (2 Atlantic crossings in light craft); Res: 625 Enchanted Way Pacific Palisades 90272 Ofc: 3325 Wilshire Blvd, 9th Flr. Los Angeles 90010

TORNELL, RONALD C., real estate broker/farmer; b. Nov. 13, 1942, Santa Cruz; s. Carl E. and Helen E. (Dalander) T.; m. Jamalee A. Dunn, Aug. 21, 1971; children: Jannell (Trinidad), b. 1962; Ellen, b. 1978; Abigail, b. 1982; edn:

BA in acctg. CSC Stanislaus 1972; Calif. R.E. Broker lic. 1980; GRI, Grad., Realtors Inst. of Calif. 1979. Career: statistical acct., Allstate Ins. Co., Menlo Park regl. ofc. 1966-70; mgr. almond ranch (cultural methods resulted in 5 yr. av. yield increase of 53 percent), Manteca 1973-79; mgmt. Dunn Ranch (wine grape and walnut) Modesto, 1983--; real estate sales, Hill and Thomas Realtors, 1979-80, agt./gen. mgr. Homeowners Showroom, 1980-81; owner/broker Tornell Assocs. (spec. in agri. & comml. props.), Modesto 1981--; honors: Alpha Eta Sigma (pres. 1965); mem: Nat., Calif. (dir. 1982,3) Assn. of Realtors; Farm and Land Inst. (v.p. Calif. chpt. 1984); Modesto Bd. of Realtors (dir., ofcr.); Central Valley Mktg. and Exchg. Gp.; Stanislaus Area Farm and Land Brokers (pres. 1980-3); publs: Equity Sharing for the Single Family Home; Republican; Prot.; rec: music, books. REs: 1001 Edgebrook Dr Modesto 95354 Ofc: Tornell Associates, 1001 Edgebrook dr Modesto 95354

TORO-LIRA, GUILLERMO LUIS, mfg. co. executive; b. Dec. 3, 1954, Lima, Peru; s. Guillermo V. and Gertrude L. (Stahl) T.; m. Guadalupe, Jan. 19, 1978; children: Guillermo Jr., b. 1978; Martin, b. 1982; edn: BSEE, Nat. UNI Nat. Univ. of Engring. 1977, MSEE, 1978. Career: project mgr. Itintec, Lima 1978-81; electronic engr. Nanometrics, Sunnyvale 1981-2, dir. engrg. 1982-3, v.p./mgr. SEM Div., 1983--; instr. digital sys. courses, INI, 1978-81; mem. Planetary Soc. Patents (4) pending in field of scanning electron microscopes; Catholic; rec: soccer, music, astronomy. Res: 1061 Kerry Ave Sunnyvale 94087 Ofc: Nanometrics Inc. 930 W. Maude Ave. Sunnyvale 94086

TORPY, GARY BRYAN, lawyer; b. Apr. 16, 1951, Peekskill, NY; s. Joseph Thomas and Anne Marie (Pisani) T.; edn: AB, cum laude, Syracuse Univ. 1973; study, Syracuse Univ. Law Sch. 1973-5; JB, St. Louis Univ. Law Sch. 1976. Career: atty. Mazirow, Schneider, Forer & Lawrence 1977-80; partner Stone & Torpy, Los Angeles 1980--; instr. UCLA Extension Grad. Sch. of Mgmt. and Bus.; lectr. atty. gps. incl. CEB; mem: Am. Bar Assn.; Calif. Bar Assn.; Calif. Trial Lawyers' Assn.; Los Angeles Co. Bar Assn.; Republican; Catholic; rec: weight lifting, swimming, tennis. Res: 1916 Viso Dr Los Angeles 90068 Ofc: Stone & Torpy, 11440 San Vicente Blvd Los Angeles 90068

TOTO, MARK NICHOLAS, jewelry designer; b. May 5, 1954; NY, NY; s. Anthony Nicholas and Margaret Alice (Endicott) T.; m. Barbara Christopherson, July 24, 1980; 1 dau: Natasha, b. 1981; edn: BA, UC Irvine 1976; MA 1977. Career: Raciti Jewelers, Costa Mesa 1971-80; mgr. 1977-80; owner Moboco Newport Beach 1980--; lectr. on gems jewelry marmale; ring cons. Orange Coast Coll. 1981 ; mem: Nat. Assn. of Jewelry Appraisers 1982-; Jewelers Bd. of Trade 1978-; Jewelers Vigilance Com. 1983-; Calif. Jewelry Assn. 1983-; Jewelers Security Alliance 1983-; Newport Beach CofC; Gemological Inst. of Am.; MUFON, Mutual UFO Network; CUFOS, Center for UFO Studies; Magic Island; AOPA, Aircraft Owners and Pilots Assn.; Catholic; rec: aviation, psychic research, magic. Ofc: Moboco, Two Corporate Plaza, Ste 230 Newport Beach 92660

TOW, JEAN RUNYON, advertising agency president; b. Mar. 6, 1927, Concordia, Kans.; d. Brutus Kerr and Rowena (Thornburg) Hamilton; m. 2d Philip S. Tow, Mar. 5, 1980; children: Stephen Hamilton Runyon, b. 1950; Elizabeth Runyon (Mulligan), b. 1955; edn: BA, Univ. Calif. 1949. Career: (past) prin. Runyon, Inc., Dannenfelsor, Runyon, Craig, Inc.; current, pres. Runyon Saltzman, Inc. (advt., pub. rels.), Sacramento; recipient Business Woman of the Year, 1984, CofC; bd. mem.: Stanford Home, KXPR (pub. broadcast), Sacto Regional Theatre, Tree Foundation. Catholic; rec: tennis, piano. Res: 122 Tivoli Way, Sacramento 95819 Ofc: Runyon Saltzman 2503 K St Sacramento 95819

TOW, PHILIP SAMUEL, chemical engineer; b. Chicago, Ill.; s. James O. and Jeanne M. (Caburet) T.; m. Lois Rogers 1945-78; Jean Runyon, Mar. 5, 1980; children: Marjorie, b. 1948; Bruce, b. 1952; Douglas, b. 1954; Daniel, b. 1960; edn: BA, UCLA 1943; profl. engr. in chem. engring., State of Calif. 1959. Career: var. positions Los Angeles Co. Air Pollution Control Dist. 1948-60; Chief Air Pollution Control Sacramento Co. 1960-78; semi- retired; mem. Calif. Bd. of Registration for Profl. Engrs. 1981-; mem. Am. Chemical Soc.; AAAS, Air Pollution Control Assn.; Sacramento Opera Assn.; author: techl. arts. on air pollution control; var. free lance political arts.; mil: Col., USAR active 1945-6, meritorious svc. medal; Democrat; rec: travel. Address: 122 Tivoli Way Sacramento 95819

TOWNSEND, DANIEL THURSTON, consulting co. executive; b. Sept. 30, 1934, Covington, Tenn.; s. Jesse Edward and Lydia Ellen (Smith) T.; m. Dorothy Morgan, Aug. 7, 1954; 1 son, Daniel, b. 1956; edn: Univ. Tenn. 1952-4; BS physics, Henderson State Univ. 1960, grad. stu. Univ. Denver. Career: research engr. Gen. Dynamics Corp., Pomona 1960-62; sr systems engr. Martin Marietta Corp., Denver, Colo. 1962-68, staff engr. and project mgr. 1968-75; exec. staff, engring., Otis Elevator Co., Denver 1977-76, tech. dir. Transp., Comm. Redev. Agency, Los Angeles 1976-77; program dir. DPM, 1978-80, exec. dir. DPM Transit Authority, L.A. 1980-82; pres. Townsend Assn. Inc., a transp. consulting firm, 1982--; guest lectr. UCLA, USC; speaker (periodic) Town Hall; awards: commendation for contbns. to public mass transit, City of Los Angeles, 1982; Lions Club Awd. 1981. Mem. Am. Public Transit Assn., LA Area CofC; publs: num. tech. papers; devel. innovative public transit pgm. for Los Angeles (1980); Methodist; rec: golf, fish, woodworking, landscaping. Res: 18728 Bernardo Trails Dr Rancho Bernardo San Diego 92128 Ofc: Townsend Assoc. Inc. 611 W. Sixth St Ste 2300, Los Angeles 90017

TOWNSEND, DONALD educator/program specialist; b. Apr. 14, 1934, Frankfort, Kans.; s. Vincent Wade and Josie Bell (Ford) T.; m. Joyce Duncan, June 24, 1955; children: Lisa, b. 1956, Cheryl, b. 1958; edn: BA, CSC Stanislaus 1962; MSW, Univ. Utah 1965; D.Ed., Brigham Youn Univ. 1979; Lic. Clin. Social Worker 1968; Sch. Psychol. Credential 1975. Career: chief Div. Child Welfare Svcs, Stanislaus County Welfare Dept., Modesto 1958-68; school social worker and coordinator of community aides, Modesto City Schs., 1968-79; program splst. (Special Edn.), Ofc. of Merced County supt. of Schools, Merced 1979--; summer wk.: psychiat. social wkr Modesto St. Hosp. 1970, Stanislaus Co. Mental Health Clin. 1971, Emmanuel Mental Hlth Clin., Turlock 1972; instr. Chapman Coll. 1969-70, Modesto Jr. Coll. 1970-; honors: Phi Kappa Phi, 1965; recipient Child Welfare Scholarships, State Dept. of Edn. study grants; mem: Calif. Assn. of Compensatory Edn. (pres. 1983-4); Calif. Council on Children & Youth (pres. No. Reg. 1973); Calif. Assn. of Pgm. Splst. (exec. com. 1983-4); Citizens for Edn.; Calif. Curriculum Alliance (bd. 1981-2); mem. Christian Berets Adv. Com., Community Adv. Com. for Spl. Edn., Stanislaus Area Comm. Council (past pres.); publs: School Volunteers (booklet) 1975; Baptist; rec: hiking, camping, singing. Res: 3118 Mason Way Modesto 95355 Ofc of Merced County Supt. of Schools, 632 W. 13th St Merced 95340

TOY, BEN KERN, engineering operations executive; b. Feb. 10, 1948, Canton, China; nat. 1948; s. Doon Toy and Louise Y. (Lui) T.; m. Debi Lynn Aines, Aug. 18, 1973; children: Kelley, b. 1975, Brigitte, b. 1981; edn: Coll. of San Mateo 1966-68. Career: draftsman/designer Autek Systems Inc., 1967-75; partner Grandfood Market, 1975-79; supr. engring. services, Marathon Electronics Inc. 1979-83; deputy dir. hardware engring. Tak Automation Inc. 1983-, mgr. engrg. ops. 1984--; P.C. designer, pkging. designer, info./documentation cons. Res: 657 Edna Way San Mateo 94402 Ofc: Tak Automation, 868 Cowan Rd, Burlingame 94010

TOY, ROBERT CHUNG HOK, computer programmer; b. Nov. 13, 1949, San Francisco; s. Jum Yuen and Lang (Ting) T.; edn: AA, City Coll. of San Francisco 1970; BS, Calif. State Poly. Univ., Pomona 1978. Career: contract/EDP auditor, Bowen & McBeth 1980; contract/pgmmr. Clothestime, 1981; pgmmr. Data General 1980; sys. analyst Norwalk-La Mirada Unif. Sch. Dist. 1981; pgmmr./analyst Purex 1982; currently assoc. info system/analyst Southern California Edison Co.; mem. Data Processing Mgmt. Assn.; Democrat; Christian. Res: 111 S. Barranca St, 320, West Covina 91791 Ofc: Southern California Edison, Box 800, Rosemead 91770

TRAN QUAN THAI (John Washington), poet, educator, restaurateur, realtor, astrologer; b. Jan. 4, 1940, VietNam, nat. March 16, 1984; s. Tinh Van Tran and Luom Thi Nguyen, m. Tran Thu Thi, Dec. 6, 1960; children: Thu Dieu Hien, b. 1963; Thu Mailan, b. 1965; Thai Thu Minh, b. 1965; Thai Tuan Kiet, b. 1967; Thai Bao Chau (Qui), b. 1970; Thai Kimkhoi, b. 1971; Thai Long, b. 1960; edn: BA, Faculty of Letters, Saigon Univ., BA, Faculty of Sci.; lic. astrologer, var. bus. lic., city of Westminster. Career: past prof. of literature (Vietnamese) and sci. (biology), Vietnam; current: artist/writer (poems and prose); astrologer (I Ching); realtor with Century 21, 1979-, investment counselor/ million dollar club; owner Maxim Restaurant, Westminster 1980--; pres. Liberty World Inc. 1980--; elected pres. Petrus Truong Vinh-Ky High Sch. Assn., 1984. Author/ pub. book of poems: Nu Cuoi Tho Ngan Nam (1983), novel in progress; Republican; Deist; rec: tennis, soccer, health club. Res: 9041 Greenville Ave Westminster 92683 Ofc: Liberty World Inc., Thai-Thien Co., 9455 Bolsa Ave, Ste. B, C, D, Westminster 92683

TRAVES, JAMES GREGORY, naval officer, civil engineer; b. Oct. 27, 1948, Toronto, Can.; nat. 1966; s. James Norton and Doreen Patricia (Lovell) T.; m. Merle Janet Pierre-Viarruel, Dec. 27, 1972; children: James Gregory, b. 1977; Richard Benton, b. 1978; edn: AA, Orange Coast Coll. 1968; Calif. Maritime Acad. 1968-70; Orange Coast Coll. 1970-2; BSE (civil eng.), CSU Long Beach 1974; spl. courses, National Univ., various mil. schs.; Calif. lic. Profl. Engr. (Civil) 1977. Career: Lt., CEC, US Navy, 1975--; mil. assignments in San Francisco, 1976-78, San Diego 1978-80, Wash DC 1980-82, Adak, Alaska 1982-3; currently production ofcr. Public Works Dept. Naval Sta. Roosevelt Roads, Puerto Rico 1983--; instr. technical writing, Univ. of Alaska 1982-3, LA Metro. Coll. 1983-; wrote proposal for new museum; mem. Soc. of Am. Military Engrs. 1976-8; Adak Museum; mil. honors: Expert Pistol, Expert Rifle; rec: model railroading, writing, modelmaker. Res: 10057 Conejo Pl. Santee 92071 Ofc: Naval Sta. Roosevelt Roads Puerto Rico Box 3021 FPO Miami 34051

TRAYLOR, SONDRA LEE, chiropractor; b. June 22, 1951, San Francisco; d. Andrew Roger and Betty Bernice (Billingsley) Couthen; m. Charles Traylor, Jan. 9, 1982; edn: AA, Shasta Jr. Coll. 1971; DC, Life Chiropractic Coll. 1981. Career: intern postgrad. field training: Spinal Touch Clinic, Salt Lake City, Utah 1981; The McKay Clinic of Stuart, Fla. 1982; The Owner Clinic Rossville, Ga. 1982; Carnes Clinic Gainesville, Ga 1982; Housh Clinic Dalton, Ga 1982; owner Traylor Clinic of Chiropractic 1982--; lectr. Modern Health Symposium 1983; awards: commdn. for Outstanding Performance as Sr. Clinic Intern, Life Chiropractic Coll.; Diplomate of the Nat. Bd. of Chiropractic Examiners; mem: Calif. Chiropractic Assn.; Am. Chiro. Assn.; Am. Assn. of Nutrition and Dietary Cons.; Lombdfa Delta Epsilon; Delta Gamma; creator: nutritional and toxic elimination cleansing and health prgms.; rel. Eckankar; rec: sports cars, skiing, video equip. Res: 5181 N 4th Street, No. 108 Fresno 93710 Ofc: Traylor Clinic of Chiropractic, 1155 W Shaw Ave Fresno 93711

TREEN, WALTER FARRELL, JR., commercial deep sea diver; b. Apr. 30, 1940, Wilmington, Del.; s. Walter F. and Evelyn Nellie May (Holt) Treen, Sr.; m. Vickei Darlene Scruggs, Sept. 2, 1978; chil: Evelyn Ann, b. 1962; Walter F.,III, b. 1963; Jessica Victoria, b. 1980; Regina Denise, b. 1983; edn: BA, UCLA 1963; USN Submarine Sch., USN Diving Sch., 1957; Divers Tng. Acad., 1964-5. Career: comml. deep sea diver (oil pipelines/platforms installation, repairs): Subaqueous Engrg. Inc., Ft. Lauderdale, Fla. 1965-7, Internat. Diver's Inc., Santa Barbara, Ca. 1967-70, Active Diver's of Alaska, 1970-73, Oceaneering Internat. Inc., Anchorage, 1973-4, 76-8; Treen's Comml. Diving, Inc. 1970-, partner, v.p., treas. 1979-, v.p. West Coast & Alaska, 1983-; v.p. W.Coast & Alaska, Cal-Dive Int.; partner, dir. Internat. Marine Constructors Inc., 1975-. Mem. Elks, Masons, Eagles, Nat. Geographic Soc.; mil: 2d cl. diver US Naval Submarine Svc.; rec: flying, skiing; res: 355 N. Kellogg Ave. Santa Barbara 93111 ofc: Treen's Comml. Diving, Inc. 5760 Thornwood Dr. Goleta 93117.

TRENHAM, N. BRADFORD, taxpayers association executive; b. Oct. 3, 1889, Alexandria, MN; dec. Nov. 16, 1982; s. Newton Thompson and Ella (Sweet) T.; m. Lorain Noble, Aug. 29, 1929; children: Shari Lorain (Gillespie), b. 1932; Noble Bradford, b. 1934; edn: MA, Oxford, Eng. 1921; MA, USC 1926. Career: Calif. Taxpayers Assn., 30 years; exec. assoc. mgr., 15 yrs.; expt. in Govtl. Affairs, served on num. nat., state and co. coms.; mem: Town & Gown; English Speaking Union; So. Calif. Hist. Soc.; Oxford Soc.; University Club; Ebell Club; Sigma Chi; Alpha Kappa Delta; Phi Delta Kappa; Phi Kappa Phi; Chi Omega; Pi Lambda Theta; mil: Pvt., WWI; Republican; Congregationalist. Res: 4316 Marina City Dr, Apt. 733, Marina del Rey 90219

TRENT, RICHARD JAMES, newspaper publisher; b. Jan. 16, 1946, Logan, W. Va.; s. Herman Clarence and Lita (Mounts) T.; edn: BA, George Washington Univ. 1969; postgrad., Am. Univ. 1973-6. Career: advtg. mgr. The Washington Post, Wash. DC 1968-77; Seattle Post 1977-82; ad. dir. 1977-8; mktg. dir. 1978-9; gen. mgr. 1979-82; pres. Harte-Hanks Calif. Newspapers (La Jolla Light, Coronado Journal, Sentinel- San Diego, Mirror- Mira Mesa, Star News-Chula Vista, Publishers offset printing) 1982-4; instr. Am. Press Inst.; Vis. Com., Univ. of Wash. 1979-81; mem. Newspaper Mgmt. Council 1962-; awards: Newsmaker of the Future, Time Mag. 1978; Eagle Scout, Boy Scouts of Am.; silver medal awd., Am. Advtg. Fedn. 1980; mem: Govt. Rels. Com., Am. Advtg. Fdn. (chmn. 1983-4); former gov. of Wash., Ore., Id., Mont., and Alaska Advtg. Fdn.; Am. Newspaper Publishers Assn.; Calif. Newspapers Assn.; author: var. arts. in nat. trade mags.; inventor: Time and Territory Management for the Newspaper Industry (a training device); rec: flying, music, sailing. Res: No. 18 Kingston Ct Coronado Island 92118 Ofc: Harte-Hanks California Newspapers, 835 3rd Ave Chula Vista 92011

TRESMONTAN, OLYMPIA DAVIS, human relations consultant; b. Nov. 27, 1925, Boston, Mass.; d. Peter Konstantin and Mary (Hazimanolis) Davis; m. Dion Marc Tresmontan (dec.); Robert Baker Stitt, Mar. 21, 1974; edn: BS, Simmons Coll. 1946; MA, Wayne State Univ. 1960; PhD, UC Berkeley 1971. Career: inst. Chapman Coll. Ext., Travis Air Force Base 1971-4; priv. practice Marriage Family and Child Therapist, San Francisco 1971--; instr. UC Ext., San Francisco 1972-5; dir. Studio Ten Svcs. 1976-80; clinical cons. Childworth Learning Ctr., San Francisco 1976-80; dir. Promise for Children, San Francisco 1981--; bd. dirs. Childworth Learning Ctr 1976-80; cons. Queen's Bench Found. Proj. Rape Response 1977-8; awards: Wayne State Honors 1949-50, 1956-60; Pi Lambda Theta, UC Berkeley 1966-; Schaefer Found. Grantee, UC 1971; The Thomas Starr King Sch. for Religious Leadership, Honoring Women 1981; mem: Am. Psychological Assn. 1971-; Am. Orthopsychological Assn. 1976-; Calif. Assn. of Marriage and Family Therapists 1971-; Am. Assn. of Marriage and Family Therapists 1978-; Internat. Hosp. Com. of the Bay Area; Friends of the San Francisco Public Lib.; The Thoreau Lyceum; Am. Assn. of Univ. Women; author: The Science Curriculum Improvement Study in the Classroom, contained in What is Curriculum Improvement ? Six Answers, R. Karplus (editor) 1968; coauthor: with J. Morris, The Evaluation of a Compensatory Education Program, UC Berkeley 1967; rec: poetry, creative writing, antiques, gourmet cooking. Address: 2611 Lake Street San Francisco 94121

TRIBBLE, ROBIN ROY, consultant; b. Apr. 5, 1947, Lansing, Mich.; s. Roy Truitt and Betty Cloe (Hurd) T.; m. Geraldine A. Johnson, Jnue 16, 1969; children: Paul; Aaron; Christian; edn: BA, Univ. of Colo. 1969; MBA, Univ. of Chicago 1973. Career: principal/ dir. Technical Services, AMS, Arlington, VA 1977-9; with RAND Corp. 1979--; prod. mgr. 1979-80; gen. mgr. eastern reg. 1980-1; v.p. prod. devel. RAND 1981-2; v.p. cons. 1983--; bd. dirs. Dounis Systems Inc., NYC 1981--; Protestant. Res: 51 Hightree Ct Danville 94526 Ofc: RAND, 98 Batlery St San Francisco 94111

TRIFELETTI, CARMINE ANTHONY, land developer, engineer; b. Jan. 9, 1916, Denver, Colo.; s. Frank and Barbara (Dodero) T.; m. Jacqueline Belletti, June 27, 1942; children: Prank Peter, b. 1943; Sheila Marie, b. 1948. Career: U.S. Rubber Co., Los Angeles 1939; Consolidated Steel, Los Angeles 1940-2; Tech. Sgt. US Army 1942-47; gen. supt.. Howard Kelly 1948-53; v.p. Oddstad Homes Land Devel. 1953-64; engr./designer/dir. Mercury Mine Processing Plant (mined/opr. 3 yrs.) 1956-64; co-owner/ v.p. Challenge Devel. Inc., Redwood City 1964-74; co-owner/ v.p. Von-Jac Devel. Inc., Redwood City 1974--; honors: recognition, dedicated svc. to Kainos Home and Training Ctr. for Retarded Adults 1960-74; mem: Pacifica CofC 1968-74; var. Boys Clubs; Redwood City CofC; Redwood City Rotary Club; mil: Tech. Sgt., U.S. Army Engrs., 1942-7, U.S. & Europe, Cert. of Merit; Democrat; Catholic; rec: boating, water skiing, travel. Res: 1041 Twin Oaks Ct Redwood City 94061 Ofc: Von-Jac Development, Inc., 4th and Spring St Redwood City 94063

TRIGGS, ROBERT EDWIN, frozen food executive; b. Sept. 18, 1934, San Bernardino; s. Orville Charles and Elizabeth Blanche (Ballinger) T.; children: Diana, b. 1961; Robert, b. 1963; edn: John Burroughs Coll. 1952; Los Angeles City Coll. 1953-4. Career: buyer, frozen foods Quality Col-Pak, Los Angeles 1954-74; gen. mgr. Glen-Webb Co., Maywood 1974-8; mgr. frozen food div. S.E. Rykoff & Co., Los Angeles 1978--; P.A.C. No. Am. Food Svc., Chicago, Ill. 1979--; mem: past pres. So. Calif. Distbrs. Assn. 1975; past pres. Calif. Food Execs. Assn. 1980; Los Angeles Athletic Club; Republican; Catholic; rec: gourmet cook, reading. Res: 400 No Louise St Glendale 91206 Ofc: S.E. Rykoff & Co., 761 Terminal St Los Angeles 90021

TRINGALI, SALVATORE JOSEPH, manufacturing co. president; b. Aug. 12, 1916, Augusta, Sicily, nat. 1945; s. Salvatore and Rose (Bramanti) Tringali; m. Carmela, Mar. 27, 1948; children: Rose b. 1956, Joseph b. 1957, Salvatore b. 1958. Career: Conklins Bakery, San Diego 1953, Roma Bakery 1962, Holsom Bakery 1970; current owner Balboa Bakery; mem. Italian Catholic Fedn., Optimists; Democrat; Catholic. Res: 614 Cedar Ave Chula Vista 92010 Ofc: Balboa Bakery 4686 University Ave San Diego 92105

TROCHALAKIS, GEORGE, commercial photographer; b. Sept. 4, 1929, Canea, Crete, Greece, nat. Canada 1963; s. Terry and Evangelia (Franziskakis) T.; m. Betty Trochalakis, Apr. 29, 1961; children: Elsa, b. 1964; Linda, b. 1967; Tanya, b. 1974; edn: Finos Film Inc. 1951-3; color commercial photog., Profl. Photogs. Assn. of Canada. Career: mgr. Trochalakis Photo, Greece 1953-5; owner/ mgr. Park Town Photo, Montreal 1955-69; prop. Park's Photocolor, Montreal 1961-69, and in San Francisco, Calif. 1970--; awd. for photog. (for Microlab of Franklin Hosp.), Pan American Conv. 1976; Ofcl. photographer for Calif. State Treasurer the late Mrs. Ivie Baker Priest; mem: Photographer's Mktg. Assn. of U.S. 1981-; San Francisco Tourist Bureau 1982-; Pan Cretan Assn. of Am.; bd. dirs. Epimenides Chpt. S.F.; publs: photograph pub. in Greece for Prime Minister Karamanlis and the late King Pavlos 1951; fashion photog. in num. mags. and stores throughout the country for Lilli Ann Fashions,S.F.; mil: Pvt. A-2 Ofc., Greek Army, Greek Civil War; Orthodox; rec: hunting, fishing, trailer travel. Res: 659 Crane Ave Foster City 94404 Ofc: Park's Photocolor, 174 Valencia St San Francisco 94103

TRONO, RICHARD QUIRINO, hair salon company president; b. Jan. 2, 1954; s. Jose Lopez and Rolynda Irene (Vincente) T.; edn: AA, Indian Valley Coll. 1976; master barber, San Francisco Barber Sch. 1972; cosmetoloy/ tchg. Vidal Sassoon 1976-7; tricoanalysis degree, Redkin Labs. Career: style innovater/ instr. Markham, San Francisco 1974-77; instr./ trainee Vidal Sassoon, San Francisco 1977-8; owner Trono for Hair, Mill Valley 1978; formed PIPS Internat.(tchg. and touring. orgn.), Sao Paulo, So. Am. 1978; owner Just Cuts Hair Care and Action Wear Center, 1980; expanded and relocated Trono for Hair 1982; pres. Trono Enterprises; salon mgmt. cons.; test salon for Redkin Labs; awards: Master Stylist Awd. of So. Am. 1978; West Coast Beauty Supplies Top Salon Awd. 1983; mem: Marin Co. Styles (dir. 1981); bd. dirs. Muscular Dystrophy of Marin Co. 1981; Mill Valley CofC 1978-84; Campaigns for: Dist. Atty. Marin Co.; Jimmy Carter for Pres.; Al Curtis Bd. of Trustees of the Coll. of Marin; creator: cosmetic line for Brazil 1978; 1st hair care/ action wear center 1981; Kids Day, fund raising for Mill Valley Sch. Dist.; Democrat; Catholic; rec: tennis, running. Res: 27 Surrey Lane San Rafael 94903 Ofc: Trono, 655 Redwood Highway Mill Valley 94941

TROUT, BOBBI (EVELYN), aviatrix, real estate broker; b. Jan. 7, 1906, Greenup, Ill.; d. George Everett and Lola (Denman) Trout; edn: Roosevelt H. S., Los Angeles; archtl. stu. USC 1926; comml. photog. lic., Wiggins Trade Sch. 1938; Fuller's Flying Sch., 1928; Lic. Transport Pilot (5th woman in USA to obtain rating) 1928. Career: demonstration/test pilot Golden Eagle Aircraft Co., 1928-29, estab. Solo Endurance Flt. world record for women (12 hrs. 11 min.) 1/2/29; estab. 5 world records (incl. 1st woman to fly all night), Feb. 10-11, 1929; estab. new women's altitude record (15,200 ft.), 6/1/29; estab. world 1st refueling endurance record for women, 11/27-29/29; mem. Women's Air Reserve, 1931-41; inventor rivet sorting machines for defense indus., also estab. De Burring Service (2nd defense bus.) L.A. during WWII; real estate broker/ securities and life ins. bus., Palm Springs, 20 yrs.; flew in 1st (1929) Women's Air Derby, Santa Monica-Cleveland, dubbed The Powder Puff Derby by Will Rogers and flagged off Air Race Classic 1979 and the Angel Derby (50th ann. of 1st Women's Air Derby); currently, devel. num. inventions; book in progress. Honored as OX5 Woman of the Year 1976; charter mem. 99 Club; Republican; Rel. Sci.; rec: treas. hunting; travel; video taping old aviators for history. Res: 2517 Palmdale Ct., Santa Clara 95051; 7512 Vieja Castilla Wy. La Costa 92008

TROVER, DENIS WILLIAM, microcomputer company executive; b. Feb. 1, 1945, Columbus, Ohio; s. Kenneth Harold and Virginia June (Denis) T.; m. Ellen Lloyd, June 12, 1971; 1 dau: Florence Emma, b. 1977; edn: BS, physics, Mich. State Univ. 1967; MBA, Coll. of William and Mary 1972; MS, Vassar Coll. 1973. Career: optical physicist Internat. Business Machines, Fishkill, NY 1967-71; staff assoc. & sys. prgmr. Rockwell Int. Sci. Ctr., Thousand Oaks 1974-8; pres./ dir. Sonix Systems, Inc., Thousand Oaks 1978--; mem: Conejo Future Found. 1975- (chmn. Energy Task Force 1980-1); bd. dirs. Vassar Clib of So. Calif.; rec: astronomy, photog. Res: 11355 Presilla Rd Camarillo 93010 Ofc: Sonix Systems, Inc., 1107 East Thousand Oaks Blvd Thousand Oaks 91362

TROVER, ELLEN LLOYD, lawyer; b. Nov. 23, 1947, Richmond, Va.; d. Robert VanBuren and Hazel Pauline (Urban) Lloyd; m. Denis W. Trover, 1971; 1 dau: Florence, b. 1977; edn: AB, Vassar Coll. 1969; JD, Coll. of William and Mary 1972. Career: assoc. ed. Bancroft- Whitney 1973-4; sole practioner Ellen Lloyd Trover, Atty. at Law 1974-82; partner Trover & Fisher 1982--; Mem:

Com. Law Ofc. Lawout Design of Economics of Law Practice Section 1978-9, Word Processing Applications Com. 1981-4; Conejo Future Found. (trustee 1979-; secty. 1980-2, vice chair 1982-4); Hydro Help for the Hadicapped, trustee/ exec. com. 1980-; Zonta Club of Conejo Valley (pres. 1978-9); Phi Alpha Delta Legal Frat.; Am. Bar Assn.; Calif. State Bar (com. on Post-Mortem Planning, ed. Handbooks of State Chronologies 1972-3); Virginia State Bar Assn.; Sonejo- Simi Valley Bar Assn. (pres. 1979-80, dir. 1983-4); Ventura Co. Bar Assn. (client rels. com.); Democrat; Presbyterian. Res: 11355 Presilla Rd Camarillo 93010 Ofc: 1107 E Thousand Oaks Blvd 91362

TRUEBLOOD, JOHN PETER, stock broker; b. Apr. 27, 1934, Cincinnati, Ohio; s. Horace Dixon and Margaret (Bates) T.; 1 son: Jaimie John, b. 1971; edn: BA, Occidental Coll. 1955. Career: jet pilot, USAF, France 1955-8; bus. ofc. mgr. Pacific Tel & Tel, Pasadena 1959-61; v.p. sales F.I. du Pont, Los Angeles 1962-69; v.p. sales Lehman Bros., Los Angeles and Paris, France 1969-72; 1st v.p. sales Bateman Eichler, Los Angeles 1973-83; mng. dir. Morgan Olmstead, Kennedy G Gardner, Los Angeles 1983--; mem: Friends of the Music Center; Starlite Found.; Rivera Tennis Club; PIPS; Touch; mil: 1st Lt., USAF 1955-8; Republican; Episcopal; rec: skiing, flying, tennis. Res: 161 Greenfield Ave Los Angeles 90049 Ofc: Morgan Olmstead, Kennedy, & Gardner, 606 So Olive St, Ste 500, Los Angeles 90014

TRUGMAN, RONALD FRANCIS, educational technologist; b. May 13, 1943, Los Angeles; s. Ned J. and Ruth (Felder) T.; m. Ina Friedlander, July 12, 1981; BA CSU Long Beach 1970; MS, USC 1971; PhD, 1974; postdoctoral, 1978-80; Calif. Com. Coll. Admin. Ofcr., Calif. Com. Coll., Sacramento 1974. Career: prgm. assoc. Nat. Spl. Media Inst., Los Angeles 1971-3; dir. instrl. devel. Coll. of San Mateo, San Mateo 1973-7; faculty San Francisco State Univ. 1977; devel. dir. Nat. Iranian Radio and Television, Tehran, Iran 1976; dir. insl. television ops. KCSM-TV, San Mateo 1978-81; dir. insl. tech. Canada Coll., Redwood City 1981--; sr. cons. Coast Communications, Palo Alto 1978--; policy analyst Corp. for Public Broadcasting, Wash. DC 1979; honors: Profl. Development Fellow, USC 1973; Chataqua Fellow, AAAS/ Stanford Univ. 1979; mem: Assn. for Ednl. Comms. and Tech., Nat. Assn. of Ednl. Broadcasters; Am. Film Inst.; bd. dirs. San Mateo Co. Cancer Soc.; Am. Heart Assn.; Friends of Stanford Hosp.; author: Educational Media Yearbook 1981; Interactive Video: Computers and TV, 1983; TV and the Adult Learner 1980; mil: Lt. USN 1965-8, mil. sea transport svc.; rec: tennis, sail, ski, cycling. Res: 2469 Brewster Ave Redwood City 94062 Ofc: Canada College, 4200 Farmhill Blvd Redwood City 94061

TRUHER, JAMES WILDER, JR., telecommunications co. executive; b. Dec. 10, 1934, Seattle, Wash.; s. James Wilder and Helen Katherine (Burke) T.; m. Mary Louise, Feb. 14, 1982; children: James, b. 1957; Sarah, b. 1959; Julie, b. 1960; Mary, b. 1965; edn: BS, civil eng., Stanford Univ. 1957; Managerial Policy Inst., USC 1966. Career: various tech., mgmt. Am. Tel. & Tel and Pacific Tel. Cos., 1959-81, gen. mgr., Network Ops., Bell Tel. System (engring. & line mgmt. for 10 percent of US Long Distance Telephone Network) 1974-80, asst. v.p. (Calif., Nev.) 1981; founder/ pres./ CEO, Polaris Mgmt. Group, Inc., Costa Mesa 1981--; bd. dirs. Junior Achievement of So. Calif. 1972- (cmpgn. chmn. 1976, v.p. Personnel 1980); bd. dirs. L.A. County United Way 1966-70; pres. Soc. of TV Engrs. 1965; bd. dirs. St. Luke Hosp., Pasa. 1974-80; sr. mem. IEEE; mem. Citizens Advis. Commn., L.A. Olympic Org. Com.; mem. Stanford Univ. Alumnae Assn.; works: design of Blast Proof Microwave Antenna System (1960); mil: lt. USN 1957-59; Republican; rec: golf, camping. Res: 3090 C Mace, Costa Mesa 92626

TRUNK, GARY, physician; b. July 12, 1941, Detroit, Mich.; edn: BA, UCLA 1963; MD, UC Irvine 1967. Career: pres. Medical Staff Parkview Community Hosp., Riverside 1982; mem: Am. Coll. of Physicians; Assoc. Fellow Am. Coll. of Chest Physicians; Exchange Club of Riverside; mil: USAF, USMC. Ofc: 3838 Sherman Dr, Ste 3, Riverside 92503

TSOBANOUDIS, STAN ANTHONY, manufacturing co. owner; b. Feb. 20, 1931, Sovflion, Evru, Greece; s. Antonios and Palma (Papanastasiu) T.; m. Ellen Sotiropoulos, Apr. 16, 1975; children: Antonia, b. 1976; Tasia, b. 1979; Katherine, b. 1982; edn: Agriculture Colls., Lorisa, Gr.; Lodi Dairy Coll., Italy 1956-8. Career: food technologist, expert on dairy prodn., mgr. quality control, Greece: prodn. mgr. Peplo - Milk Producers Assn., prodn. mgr. Tsakiris Cheese Indus.; prodn. mgr., quality control, Calbarey Cheese Co., Milan, Italy 1958-67; came to USA in 1967, with Borden Co. Western Div.: Sonora (Calif.) Cheese Factory, Rock River Valley Creamery, Central Pt., Ore., Pleasanton (Calif.) Cheese Co., 1967-70; founder/ owner Stanislaus County Cheese Co., 1970--, and Real Natural Cheese Co., Inc. 1982--; awards: Fulbright Scholarship; Marshall Plan grant; Greek Orthodox. Res: 6426 First St Riverbank 95367 Ofc: Stanislaus County Cheese Co., 3141 Sierra Ave Riverbank 95367

TSUCHIYA, YUMA, piano/organ retail co. president; b. Feb. 12, 1932, Nagoya, Japan; s. Kiyoji and Fumi (Nagai) T.; m. Hisako, Apr. 29, 1956; children: Jayson, b. 1960, Howard, b. 1963, Bruno, b. 1966; edn: BA, Pacific Union Coll. 1961. Career: Seventh-Day Adventist Ch. work in Japan; owner music stores in Calif. 1960--, first Yamaha franchised piano/organ dealer (1960) in No. Calif. (2d. franchise in USA);founder/ pres. T. Yuma & Assocs. Inc., Palo Alto; adv. bd. Calif. 1st Bank 1970-; mem. Lions Club 1962-9; Seventh-Day Adventist (Central Calif. Conf. mem. 1976-83); rec: music, tennis, jogging. Res: 26025 Duval Way, Los Altos Hills 94022 Ofc: T. Yuma & Assocs., 3731 El Camino Real Palo Alto 94306

TSUJI, HAROLD K., thoracic cardiovascular surgeon; b. Apr. 5, 1926, Honolulu, HA; m. Anita Louise Tsuji, Mar. 26, 1957; children: Diana Tamiko, b. 1961; Mark Ichiro, b. 1963; edn: Univ. of Hawaii 1945-5; MD, Temple Univ. Sch. of Med. 1948-52. Career: chief cardiac surgery Los Robles Reg. Med. Ctr.; former assoc. prof. of Thoraic Surgery at USC Sch. of Med.; awards: Golden Apple Awd. for Excelence in Tchg., Class of 1965, 66 and 68, USC Sch. of Med.; mem: Am. Med. Assn.; Am. Thoracic Soc.; Am. Coll. of Chest Physicians; Am. Coll. of Surgeons; John Paul North Surgical Soc.; Fellow, Council on Clinical Cardiology; Fellow, Council on Cardiovascular Surgery; The Soc. for Vasculor Surgery; The Internat. Cardiovascular Soc.; Soc. of Thoracic Surgery; The Samson Thoracic Surgical Soc.; L.A. Surgical Soc.; L.A. Acad. of Med.; mil: Capt., USAF. Res: 1455 Chelsea Road San Marino 91108 Ofc: Harold K. Tsuji, MD, 227 W Janss Rd, Ste 300, Thousand Oaks 91360

TUBER, ARTHUR HARRY, corporate president; b. July 3, 1928, Phila., PA; s. Maurice Ralph and Jean Augusta (Shenkman) T.; m. Phyllis Rosenthal, Jan. 18, 1948; children: Barbara Elleen, b. 1949; Janice Lynn b. 1954; edn: Temple Univ. Tech. Sch. 1950-3; Los Angeles Co. Sheriff's Acad. 1970. Career: structural engr. Phila., Pa. 1951-3; sales, sales mgmt. Lempco Products, Cleveland, Ohio 1953-1964; pres./ CEO Armor Sales Co., Inc., Los Angeles 1964--; pres./ CEO Motive Engineered Products Corp., 1978--; 1st pres./ founding mem. Heavy-Duty Representatives Assn.; awarded num. sales record awds. from principal mfgrs. mem: HDRA (pres. 1973-5); Soc. of Automotive Engrs. 1970-; MANA 1966-; Automotive Svc. Inst. Assn. (1975); Shriners; Reserve Deputy, L.A. Co. Sheriff's Dept.; author: num. arts. for ind. trade publs.; Republican; rec: shooting, wood working, gardening, Police work. Res: 5813 Fairhaven Ave Woodland Hills 91367 Ofc: 23801 Calabasas Rd, Ste. 2033 Calabasas 91302

TUCKER, JAMES STEPHEN, clinical pyschologist/ college professor; b. Apr. 14, 1943, Detroit, Mich.; s. Joseph Michael and Mary (Perinovic) T.; edn: BA, St. John's Coll. 1965; MA, CSU Sacramento 1977; MS, Pacific Grad. Sch. of Psych. 1980; lic. psychologist, bd. med. quality assurance 1982; lic. marriage and family counselor, bd. behav. sci. examiners 1980. Career: ordination Roman Catholic Priesthood 1969; clinical dir. East Valley Family Services 1970-5; prof. of psych. St Mary's Univ. 1975-8, chair. dept. of psych./ dean of admissions, St. Joseph's Coll. 1978--; clinical dir. Pastoral Services Center 1980--; honors: diplomate clinical psych. 1982; fellowships: Masters & Johnson and Menninger Found. 1981; mem: Am. Assn. for Family Therapy; Christian Assn. for Psych. Studies; APA; author: Demographic, Clinical & Personality Variables of the Effective Roman Catholic Seminary Student, et al. 1983; Catholic; rec: Baroque music, overseas travel. Address: Pastoral Services Center, St. Joseph's College, Box 7009 Mountain View 94039

TUCKER, WANDA HALL, newspaper editor; b. Feb. 6, 1921, Los Angeles; d. Frank Walliston and Hazel Gladys (Smith) Hall; m. Frank R. Tucker, Apr. 16, 1943; children: Frank Jr., b. 1945, Nancy (Baker), b. 1949; edn: AA, Citrus Coll. 1939. Career: reporter San Marino Tribune, 1937; Society editor Azusa Herald, 1939-42, Editor 1942-43; City editor San Marino Tribune, 1943-44; Correspondent, Los Angeles Times, 1937-44; Corresp., San Gabriel valley Tribune, 1952, editor Canyon City News, 1952-53; reporter Pasadena Star-News, 1953-73, city editor 1973-75, day managing editor and mng. editor 1975-83, senior mng. editor Pasadena Star-News, 1983--; dir. internship pgm., Star-News, 1975-9, conductor Mini-Course in Journalism, 1983-4, mem. Star-News Spkrs. Bur. 1983-; mem. journalism advis. com. Pasadena Comm. Coll., 1979-81; mem. Associated Press Mng. Editors Profl. Standards Com. 1984; honors: Proclamations and Resolutions, various cities and L.A. County during career; named Woman of Year, Pasadena Womens Civic League 1974, and Pasa. Chpt. NAACP, 1977; Woman of Achievement, Pasadena Comm. Coll. 1984; mem: Greater LA Press Club, Sigma Delta Chi; active in Soroptimist Club, Azusa PTA Council, Azusa Little League in 1940s; Republican; Prot.; rec: travel, gardening. Res: 2515 Woodlyn Rd Pasadena 91104 Ofc: Pasadena Star-News, 525 E. Colorado Blvd Pasadena 91109

TUCKERMAN, RICHARD J., lawyer; b. Nov. 6, 1931, Long Beach, NY; s. Edward and Jeannette (Cohen) T.; m. Belle L., Apr. 7, 1963; children: Mark, b. 1964, Sara, b. 1968; edn: BS, NYU 1952, LLB, UC Hastings, 1958, LLD 1968; Edn. degree, Univ. Calif. 1969; admitted to Calif. State Bar 1960. Career: tax atty. State of Calif., Dept. of Personel, Sacramento 1962-64; Deputy Public Defender, San Bernardino Co. 1964-66; atty. law firm Evans, Taves & Tuckerman, Ontario 1966-68, law firm Jones & Tuckerman, 1968-70; sr. partner law firm, Richard J. Tuckerman, Atty. at Law, 1970--; prof. law & real estate course, Citrus Jr. Coll. 1969; vice pres. Bodymind Inc. (health retreat); mem: Am., Calif. Bar Assn., Calif. Trial Lawyers Assn.; mil: pfc US Army 1954-56, purch. agt. Presidio, SF; Republican; Jewish; rec: athletic & aerobic exercise, art collector, Mercedes Benz collector. Res: 25712 Paseo De La Paz, San Juan Capistrano 92675 Ofc: Richard J. Tuckerman, Atty. at Law, 1063 West Sixth St, Ste 101, Ontario 91762

TUCKNOTT, ROBERT ALLEN, construction/engineering co. president; b. Nov. 22, 1942, Oakland; s. James Andrew and Gladys Mary (Stickney) T.; m. Debra Lynn Middleton, Sept. 9, 1980; children: Rodney Allen, b. 1972; Robyn Ann, b. 1982; Ryan Andrew, b. 1983; edn: San Jose State Univ. 1960-1; Laney Coll. 1965-69; Arbitrator, Am. Arbitration Assn. Career: shop mgr. Active Electric Co., Hayward 1969-72; pres. Tucknott Electric Co., Inc., San Leandro 1972--; arbitrator Better Bus. Bureau and Am. Arbitration Assn.; bd. dirs.: Alameda County Taxpayers Assn.; Electrical Ind. Big Registry; San Leandro Mfgrs. Asn.; dir.: Alameda Co. Builder's Exchange; Nat. Elect. Contractors Assn.; Nat. Fdn. of Ind. Bus.; Electric & gas Inds. Assn.; Illuminating

Engring. Soc.; Assn. for Training and Devel.; Nat Assn. of Bus. Edn. Radio, Inc.; ofcr., Oakland East Bay Electric Club; awards: Nat. Exchange Club: Distg. Pres.'s Achievement Awd. 1976; Outstanding Area Governors Awd. 1977; Outstanding Dirs. Awd. 1978; Muscular Dystrophy Awd. for Svc.; 2 Rotary Club Merit Awds.; San Leandro CofC Awd.; 62 Trophies, Awds., and Plaques for sports car racing finishes; 6 awds. for Tropical Fish Breeding; Nat. Pilots Assns. Adv. Pilot Citation; mem: San Leandro area: Rotary; Exchange Club; Boys' Club; CofC, and Boys' Century Club; State of Calif. CofC; San Jose CofC; East Bay Municipal Water Dist. Water Adv. Com.; mil: Staff Sgt. E-6, US Army 1964-9; Repbulican; Methodist. Res: 5777 Jensen Road Castro Valley 94577 Ofc: Tucknott Electric Co., Inc., 295 Park St San Leandro 94577

TULLOCH, BRIAN LEE, real estate developer, marketing consultant; b. Aug. 10, 1945, Milwaukee, Wisc.; s. William Osborn and Anne Irma (Harvancheck) T.; edn: BBA, mktg., Univ. of Wisc. 1968. Career: commercial mgr. Wisc. Tel. Co. 1968-9; dir. sales/ mgr. Distinguished Resorts of Wisc.; v.p. ops. Sea Palms Resort, St. Simons Is., Ga.; real estate service New Dimension in Living, corporate relocation; internat. cons. pres. Vacation World Timeshare Resorts, Ltd.; v.p./ cons. Security Pacific Finance Corp.; honors: Who's Who Amongst Students in Am. Colls. & Univs. 1968; mem: Beta Theta Pi Frat.; CofC; author: The Art of Counseling & Sales For Time Share Resorts, num. arts. in real estate mags.; mil: USAR Med. Corps.; Republican; rec: all sports, skiing, golf, tennis. Res: 7314 Borla Place Rancho La Costa 92008 Ofc: Vacation World/ Relocation Systems, 731 So . Hwy 101 Solana Beach 92075

TULLOCH-REID, ELMA DEEN, consulting firm president; b. June 27, 1938, Erie, PA; d. Theodore and Roberta (Hicks) Carlisle; children: Robynne, b. 1969; Stacey, b. 1969; edn: BS, N.C. A&T State Univ. 1960; MA, CSU Long Beach 1977; EdD, Nova Univ. 1981. Career: staff nurse Michael Rees Hosp., Chgo. 1960-2; instr. Cook Co. Sch. of Nursing, Ill. 1962-3; tchr. St. Joseph Convent, Trinidad, West Indies 1964-6; instr. St. Vincent Coll. of Nursing, Los Angeles 1966-7; med.-surgical coord. 1967-9; charge nurse Coronary Care Unit, Century City Hosp., L.A. 1971-2; tchr. Los Angeles City Unified Schs. 1970-5; instr. St. Vincent Med. Ctr. 1975-7; dir. In Service Edn., Imperial Hosp., Inglewood 1977-9; pres. Elma Tulloch-Reid Assocs. 1979--; assoc. prof. CSU Long Beach; Approved Provider; Basic Life Support and Adv. Cardiac Life Support, Am. Heart Assn.; Calif. Bd. of Regis. Nursing; Continuing Edn. Provider; honors: Phi Kappa Phi 1977, appreciation, Los Angeles CPR Consortium 1982; listed, Who's Who of Am. Women, Who's Who in the West, Internat. Who's Who of Intellectuals; mem: Calif. Bus. Women's Network, AAUW, Nat. Assn. of Profl. Cons., Nat. Assn. of Female Execs., Nat. Orgn. Mothers of Twins Club, N.C. A&T Alumni Assn., Am. Nurses Found., Nova Univ. Alumni; publs: cassette pgms: How to Improve Your Leadership Skills, Assessing your Creativity, (1982); home study pgms incl.: How to Assess Your Leadership Skills (1982), What Time Is It? Time For Time Mgmt., others; rec: running, music, art, graphology. Res: 1056 Cochran Ave Los Angeles 90019 Ofc: Elma Tulloch- Reid Assocs., 5350 Wilshire Blvd, Ste. 36, Los Angeles 90036

TUNG, BETTY WONG, company president; b. Feb. 23, 1944, Shanghai, China, nat. 1972; d. Foo Yuan and Joanna Ming (Chen) Wong; m. Michael H. Tung, Dec. 23, 1967; children: Patricia, b. 1970; Eric, b. 1973; edn: BS, UC Berkeley 1966; MS, USC 1967. Career: research engr. NCR Crop., El Segundo 1967-73; engring. spl. Northrop Corp., Hawthorne 1973-8; pres. FERA Internat. Corp., Torrance 1978--; dir. Fy Garments, Singapore 1978--; dir. WT Investment Ltd. 1980--; tchg. fellow USC 1967; mem: Electrochemical Soc. 1967-78; Am. Chem. Soc. 1967-73; Ski Ind. of Am. 1979-; Am. Ski Fdn. 1980-; patentee: electroless plating bath 1973; Republican. Res: 5557 Seaside Heights Dr Rancho Palos Verdes 90274 Ofc: FERA International Corp., 20603 Earl St Torrance 90503

TUNISON, RICHARD EARL, solar company executive; b. May 17, 1929, Los Angeles; s. Wilbur Earl and Bernice MInnie (Wirick) T.; m. Marcia Marquering, Dec. 2, 1977; children: Gregg F., b. 1957; Brian W., b. 1958; Tracy N., b. 1960; edn: BA, Chapman Coll. 1951. Career: with Atlantic Richfield Co. 1957--; speech instr. 1957; inventory & appraisal supvr. 1966; mgr. compensation & benefits 1968; corp. mgr. compensation 1970; mgr. analytical svcs. 1972; mgr. orgn., compensation and presonnel sys. 1974; mgr. personnel policies 1976; v.p. ARCO Solar Ind. (div. of Atlantic Richfield) 1980--; dir: Community Food Resourches, Inc.; Airtron, Inc.; ARCO Seed Co.; Fahnstork, Inc.; ARCO Solar Electric Power, Inc.; ARCO Solar Internat., Inc.; Bogen, inc.; Pyradyne, Inc.; Valley Dehydrating Co., Inc.; George Smith, Inc.; ARCO Solar Technical Svc., Inc.; Gieske Sheet Metal Co., Inc.; awards: Am. Legion Awd. 1945; Awd. of Merit, BSA 1976; Republican of Year, 22nd Congl. Dist. 1968; Distg. Svc. Awd., Repub. Central Com., L.A. Co. 1968; mem: Am. Compensation Assn.; former L.A. Jr. CofC; Lyons Internat.; Civitan Internat.; mil: lt. USNR 1955, UN, Korean Svc.(w/Star) Victory, and Republic of Korea medals; Republican; Christian; rec: fiction writing, wood working, painting. Res: 1555 Knollwood Terrace Pasadena 91103 Ofc: Atlantic Richfield Co., 515 So. Flower St Los Angeles 90071

TUNNEY, JOHN VARICK, lawyer; b. June 26, 1934, NY, NY; s. Gene and Mary (Lauder) T.; m. Kathinka, 1977; children: Edward, b. 1961; Mark, b. 964; Arianne, b. 1967; edn: BA, Yale Univ. 1956; JD, Univ. of Virginia 1959; attended Acad. of Internat. Law, The Hague. Career: U.S. Rep., U.S. House of Rep. 1964-71; U.S. Senator, U.S. Senate 1971-77--; partner law firm Manatt, Phelps, Rothenberg and Tunney 1977--; chmn. bd. Cloverleaf, Inc.; mem: bd. of trustees, Westminster Sch.; bd. of visitors Loyola Law Sch.; Nat. Adv. Council, Multiple Sclerosis Soc.; Lawyers Adv. Council, Constitutional Rights Found.; bd. mem. Internat. Inst. of Kidney Diseas; author: The Changing Dream, Doubleday Publ., 1975; mil: Capt., USAF 1960-3; Democrat, US House of Reps. and US Senate; Catholic; Ofc: Manatt, Phelps, Rothenberg & Tunney, 1888 Century Park East, Ste. 1700, Los Angeles 90067

TUOMALA, MARVIN ARNOLD, aviation company executive; b. June 13, 1941, Perth, No. Dakota; s. William John and Minnie Emilia (Tapanila) T.; m. Glenna Erskine, Aug. 17, 1963; children: Liane, b. 1964; Ross, b. 1966; Scott, b. 1970; Kathy, b. 1973; edn: A&P, Area Vocational & Tech. Sch. 1965; BA, Melodyland Sch. of Theology 1982; airframe & powerplant lic. w/ inspector authorization, FAA 1965; commercial pilot lic., FAA 1971. Career: owner/ operatior Marv's Aero Repair, Rugby, N.D. 1966-76; pilot Rolla Flying Svc., Rolla, ND 1973-6; with Martin Aviation, Santa Ana 1976--; chief insp. 1976-7; mgr. 1976-81; v.p. 1981--; mem. Orange Coast Coll. Aviation Technolog Adv. Bd.; mem. Aviation Maintenance Found. 1972-; Republican; Assembly of God; rec: woodworking, camping, rock hounding. Res: 528 Cinda Street Anaheim 92806 Ofc: Martin Aviation, 19331 Airport Way So., Santa Ana 92707

TURKUS, BARRY ALLEN, real estate broker; b. Feb. 16, 1947, Rockville Centre, NY; s. Harlan B. and Evelyn K. (Kirsner) T.; m. Lynda Skinner, Feb. 6, 1972; children: Chad Austin, b. 1978; Carly Harlan, b. 1983; edn: BA, bus. mgmt., San Jose State Univ. 1969; Pepperdine Univ., 1973; Calif. lic. Real Estate Broker 1969. Career: partner/gen. mgr. Blickman Turkus, Inc. real estate brokerage firm spec. in comml. & indsl. props. in Santa Clara Co. and So. Almeda Co.; (past) sr. sales exec. Xerox Corp., salesman to gen. mgr. of San Jose Regl. Ofc., Ashwill-Burke, 1976-80; prin. comml. R.E. brokerage firm of Blickman, Turkus and Sakauye, 1980-81; dir. Silicon Valley Bancshares (holding co.); guest lectr. Univ. of Santa Clara 1984, real estate seminars: Office Condominium, 1983; mem: Assn. of South Bay Brokers (treas. 1978-80); San Jose Real Estate Bd. (R.E. Exchange Com. 1984); Nat., Calif. Assn. of Realtors; Rotary, San Jose CofC (dir. Indsl. R.E. Tour 1984); Milpitas CofC; publs: arts. in Western R.E. News, The Business Journal (San Jose), Santa Clara County Business; mil: E4 USAR 1969-75; Republican; rec: gardening, skiing, music. Res: 773 Raymundo Ave Los Altos 94022 Ofc: Blickman Turkus Inc. 2674 North First St San Jose 95131

TURNER, CARL JEANE, international business development executive, electronics engineer; b. July 27, 1933, Sevierville, Tenn.; s. Kenneth Albert and Lenna Faye (Christopher) T.; m. Flossie Ingram, Dec. 11, 1954; children: Marcia, b. 1956; Kenneth, b. 1958; Theresa, b. 1961; Christopher, b. 1962; Robin, b. 1965; edn: BS Edn./BSEE, Columbia Pacific Univ. 1980; MBA, 1982; PhD, 1983. Career: with Itek Corp. 1972-77, 1978-81; field svc. rep. Applied Tech. Div., Sunnyvale 1972-3; sr. field svc. rep./ gr. Iranian Field ops./ regl. mgr. Middle East Ops., Tehran, Iran 1973-6; sr. internat. mbtg. rep., Sunnyvale 1976-7; sr. engr./ analyst and chief instr. E-Systems, Inc., Greenville, TX 1977-8; prgm. devel. mgr. Optical Sys. Div., Athens, Greece 1978-9; Applied Tech. Div., res. mgr. German Prgm. Ofc. at AEG-Telefunken AG, Ulm, Ger. 1979-81; mgr. Internat. Prgms. Planning and Control, Sunnyvale 1981; mgr. export mktg. GTE Sylvania Sys. Gp. Western Div., Mt. View 1981-3; pres. Intermgmt. Tech., Sunnyvale 1983; internat. sales mgr. Probe Sys., Inc., Sunnyvale 1983-4; dir. internat. mktg. Govt. Sys. Div., General Instrument Corp., Hicksville, NY 1984--; awards: George Washington Honor Medal, Freedom Found. 1965; Presdtl. Medal of Merit, Pres. Ronald Reagan 1982; mem: IEEE; Air Force Assn.; Assn. of Old Crows; Armed Forces Comm. and Electronics Assn.; Internat. Biographical Assn.; Am. Entrepreneurs Assn.; Nat. Assn. of the Professions; Order of Seasoned Weasels; Internat. Platform Assn.; Smithsonian Assocs; publs: writer/ ed. mil. textbooks and course guides on electronics and mgmt subjects; internat. bus. guides and books: A Mktg. Guide to Iran; Estab. of a Branch Office in Greece; The Mgmt. Challenge in Coproducing High- Technology Systems in Germany; An Internat. Mktg. Plan for Defense Electronics; mil: Fla. Air NG 1948-50; USAF 1950-72; Republican (Nat. Com., Pres. Task Force); rec: coins, stamps, artifacts, languages (Ger., Thai, Persian, Japanese). Res: 51 Harbor Park Dr, Centerport, Long Island NY 11721

TURNER, CHRISTOPHER EDWARD, real estate finance company executive; b. Aug. 14, 1933, Lewiston, Mont.; s. Albert Maitland and Helena Johanna (Fopeano) T.; edn: AA, El Camino Coll. 1956; BS, Long Beach State Coll. 1958; MBA, UCLA 1960; Am. Soc. of Real Estate Counselors (CRE) 1983; Calif. lic. real estate broker. Career: grad. research economist, Urban Economics, UCLA 1960-3; Keystone Mortgage Co., Los Angeles 1963--, dir./ exec. v.p. 1971--; bd. dirs. Pinecrest Hosp. 1969-82; bd. govs. Am. Indsl. Real Estate Assn. 1974-5; instr. USC 8 yrs.; instr. Mt. St. Mary's Coll. 4 yrs.; lectr. Am. Continuing Edn. Pgm., Stanford Univ., Univ. of Houston, 1971-8; honors: Beta Gamma Sigma 1960; scholastic awards, Glenn D. Wellaman Found., and Am. Inst. of R.E. Appraisers, 1963; mem: Am. Soc. of Real Estate Counselors (CRE); Calif. Real Estate Assn.; Urban Land Inst.; Mortgage Bankers Assn. of Am. (MBA); Nat. Assn. of Realtors; Am. Indsl. Real Estate Assn.; CofC; publs: art., Journal of Am. Real Estate Assn. Vol. 13, Annual 1974-5; coauthor: w/ Jay Berger, PhD, Financing in 1984; Republican; Catholic; rec: jogging, golf. Res: 3255 Kelton Ave Los Angeles 90034 Ofc: Keystone Mortgage Co., 11340 W Olympic Blvd, Ste 300, Los Angeles 90064

TURNER, DALLAS RAY, real estate broker; b. Sept. 12, 1942, Gothenburg, Nebr.; s. Raymond E. and Erma E. (Schmeeckle) T.; m. Linda Olsen, Dec. 30, 1983; 1 son: Ryan, b. 1969; edn: BS, bus., Univ. of Nebraska 1964. Career: ins. mgmt. and sales, Lincoln, Nebr. 1964-6; plane Capt./ US Navy pilot 1966-71; real estate sales Merit- McBride Realtors, Sunnyvale 1971-9; broker lic. 1972; v.p. 1975; owner/ broker World Properties, Cupertino 1979--; owner/ dir.

Keystone Realty, Inc. dba World Properties; mem: var. real estate bds. San Jose, Sunnyvale, Saratoga/ Los Gatos, Los Altos, Palo Alto/ Mtn. View; Better Bus. Bureau; mil: Lt. USN, 2 air medals, 2 Vietnam Combat Campaign medals; rec: flying, fishing, sports, travel. Res: 955 Desert Isle Dr San Jose 95117 Ofc: World Properties, 20530 Stevens Creek Blvd Cupertino 95014

TURNER, DOUGLAS FREDERICK, real estate executive; b. Sept. 23, 1935, Honolulu, HA; s. Harvey W. and Phoebe (Perry) T.; m. Judith Ann Whitehouse, Jan. 6; children: Robert, b. 1964; Douglas, b. 1975; Christina, b. 1976; edn: BS, in BA, Univ. of Pheonix 1981; RECI, Real Estate Certificate Inst., Div. of C.A.R. 1978; GRI, Gard. Real Estate Inst., Nat. Assn. of Realtors 1978. Career: mgmt. Hewlett Packard, Palo Alto 1957-75; pres./ real estate exec. Nat. Finance Network, Inc., Santa Clara 1975--; State Calif. Life/ Disability Ins. Agent; awards: Cert. of Appreciation, San Jose Real Estate Bd. 1979; mem: San Jose Real Estate Bd. (adv., mem., MLS & PACs); Sunnyvale Real Estate Bd.; Nat. Assn. of Realtors; Tri-County Apartment Assn.; Rotary Club; Santa Clara CofC; mil: USAF 1954-8; Republican; Catholic; rec: golf, hiking, swimming, camping. Res: 1676 Betty Court Santa Clara 95051 Ofc: National Financial Network, Inc., 2470 El Camino Real Santa Clara 95051

TURPIN, BEN CRAMER, university counsellor; b. June 30, 1932, Richmond, Ky.; s. Russell George and Katie Mellen (Norris) T.; m. 2d. Phyllis Janssen, July 20, 1980; children: Lisa, b. 1956, Russell, b. 1957, Paul, b. 1969, William, b. 1974; edn: BS, Eastern Ky. Univ. 1954; Calif. lic. real estate broker; Blood Bank Splst., Reg. Med. Technologist, Am. Soc. of Clin. Pathologists. Career: blood bank director Macon (Ga.) Hosp. 1954-56; chief med. technologist Lexington (Ky.) Clinic 1956-66; supr. clin. tng. Univ. of Ky., Lexington 1962-66; sales mgr., US & Canada, Hyland Labs., Costa Mesa, Ca. 1966-74; western sales mgr. Upjohn Lab. Procedures, Woodland Hills, Ca. 1974-76; vice pres. Orange Crest Realty, Placentia 1976-81; counsellor Western State Univ. Coll. of Law, 1981--; ed. Am. Jour. of Med. Technol., 1959-67; real estate lectr., 1978-81; pres. Ky. Med. Technol. Soc., 1960-63; honors: Alpha Mu Tau 1960-, chmn. Nat. Advis. Council 1961, 62; named Med. Tech. of Year (Ky. 1963, 64), Nat. Male Med. Tech. of Year 1968; mem: Nat., Calif. Assn. of Realtors; Am. Assn. of Blood Banks (cons. 1958-66); clubs: Anaheim Exchange (v.p. 1976), Lexington Toastmasters (pres. 1964, 66), BSA Scoutmaster, Com. Chmn., Full Gospel Businessmens Fellowship Intl.; publs: photography, Eastman Internat Exhib. 1960-1, exhibs. 1962-3; Republican; Methodist; rec: hist., photog., gardening, bicycling. Res: 2851 Stonybrook Anaheim 92804 Ofc: Western State Univ. 1111 No. State College Blvd Fullerton 92631

TUSO, TONI KAY, magazine publisher; b. Apr. 24, 1954, Riverside; d. Joseph J. and Joyce A. Tuso; edn: BS, UC Berkeley 1975. Career: v.p. Hughes Ad House; owner/ publisher Orange Coast Mag.; awards: Miss Calif.; 3rd runner up Miss USA; mem: Western Publishers Assn; Maggie Award presentee. Ofc: Orange Coast Magazine, 1820 W McDurmott Irvine 92714

TVETEN, JOE ERIK, company president; b. Dec. 4, 1951, Yakima, Wash.; s. Hans Einar and Ana Mary Elizabeth (Shusta) T.; edn: BA, admin., Pacific Lutheran Univ. 1974. Career: pres. Tveten Corp., dba: Sierra Hi-Fi and Video; Tveten Oil Co.; Sierra Deli; Tveten Auto Sales; J & J Homes; mem: Q Club; PLU; CofC; Kiwanis; Republican Committee; Lutheran; rec: water- snow skiing, tennis, golf, hiking. Res: No. 55 Divot Court, POB 654 So Lake Tahoe 95705 Ofc: Tveten Corp., Hwy 50 and 89 So., Tahoe Paradise 95708

TYRRELL, JOAN ANGELA, educator; b. Dec. 3, 1938, Chgo.; d. Edward William and Shirley Mary (Perry) T.; edn: BA, Marymount Coll. 1958; postgrad. work, UCLA 1959-63, 1969-73, 1979-80. Career: elementary tchr. Los Angeles City Sch. Dist. 1958--; vol. J. Paul Getty Mus.; mem: Ednl. Adv. Council 1976-; honors: Outstanding Young Women of Am. 1967; mem: Coll. Alumnae Aux. of the Assistance 1963--; The Opera Assocs. 1966--; Metropolitan Opera Nat. Council (L.A. Dist. Treas. 2977-); Music Center Opera League; Metropolitan Assocs.; Las Angelitas Del Pueblo; Alumni Assn. of Loyola Marymount Univ.; life mem. UCLA Alumni; Assoc. Calif. Chamber Sym. Soc. Inc.; patron L.A. Co. Mus. of Art; Leakey Found.; Nat. History Mus. Alliance; So. calif. Hist. Soc.; San Diego Opera- Los Angeles Guild; nat. assoc. The Metropolitan Mus. of Art; Republican; Catholic; rec: tennis, music, UCLA football games. Res: 1463 Palisades Dr Pacific Palisades 90272 Ofc: Los Angeles Unified School Dist., 450 No Grand Ave Los Angeles

TYRELL, JOHN RIX, lawyer; b. May 6, 1921, Alhambra; s. John James and Ruth (Sands) T.; m. Marion Mallman, July 2, 1943; chidren: Sandra Sue, b. 1959; Jon Sands, b. 1960; Randy Rix, b. 1966; edn: AA, Pasadena Jr. Coll. 1941; AB, USC 1949; JD, USC Sch. of Law 1952. Career: life guard City of Alhambra, (summers) 1939-51, svc. U.S. Post Office, Alhambra 1940, 48, 49, 50; master router, Vega Aircraft Corp., Burbank 1941-2; welders helper to sales engr. C.E. Howard & Co., L.A. and South Gate 1945-8, atty. at law 1954-, partner Davidson, Tyrell & Davidson law firm, Alhambra 1956-70; pvt. practice law 1970--; Temple City Councilman 1960-84, Mayor five terms; past pres. Calif. Contracts Cities Assn.; bd. trustees Comm. Hosp. of San Gabriel 1973-; mem: Am., Calif., L.A. and San Gabriel Valley Bar Assns.; L.A. Trial Lawyers Assn.; Pasa. Tournament of Roses Assn. (patron); Temple City CofC; US Power Squadron; USC Alumni Assn.; San Gabriel Valley BSA (exec. bd.); Phi Alpha Delta; (past) bd. dirs. Alhambra CofC, exec. com. Alhambra Coord. Council, Alhambra Exchg. Club juvenile counselor com., juvenile div. Alhambra Police Res.; advisor Alhambra Youth Coord. Council; clubs: Am. Legion, Masons, Scottish Rite, Shriners, Alhambra Hi Twelve, Temple City Tennis, Arcadia Tennis; mil: lt., naval aviator, USN 1942-45, WWII; legal ofcr. Fleet Air Serv. Squadron Seven, adm. ofcr. Adm. Dept. Head, Composite

Squad. Eleven, 1953-54; rec: tennis, boating, fishing. Res: 5709 No. Allessandro Temple City Ofc: 9161 Las Tunas Dr Temple City 91780

TYSON, RUBY, psychologist; b. Apr. 8, 1929, Mira, La.; s. David and willie Lee (Hayes) T.; m. Mary Nicole Bucher, 1983; children: Kevin, b. 1951, Loren, b. 1955, Mark, b. 1959; edn: AA, L.A. City Coll. 1957; BA, CSU Los Angeles 1960; MA, psychol. 1962, PhD, psychol. Pacific Western Univ. 1981. Career: psychologist Los Angeles Unified School Dist. 1962--; Advisement Svc. 1962-8; spl. Voc. Guidance and Counseling 1968-72; head counselor/ dir. of counseling and guidance Abram Freidman Occupational Center 1972-7, West Valley Occ. Center 1977-83, East L.A. Occ. Center 1983--; pvt. practice Marriage Family Therapist 1977--; num. workshops in vocational counseling and guidance with emphasis on appropriate uses of testing for Calif. Personnel & Guidance Assn., Assn. of Calif. Sch. Adminstrs., Teacher and Counseling Assns., and for L.A.U.S.D.; recipient num. state and local profl. awards for workshops; mem: Assoc. Adminstrs. of Los Angeles (charter), Amer. and Calif. State Psychol. Assn., Calif. Personnel & Guidance Assn., Assn. of Calif. Sch. Adminstrs., Calif. Assn. of Marriage & Family Therapists, Calif. Assn. of Regl. Occ. Ctrs. & Pgms.; author: Standardized Testing for Adults (LAUSD 1978); mil: cpl. US Army 1950-52; Democrat; Jewish; rec: music. Res: 4939-B Laurel Cyn Blvd No Hollywood 91607 Ofc: West Valley Occup. Center, 20832 Roscoe Blvd, Ste 215, Canoga Park 91306

TZIKAS, GEORGE ARISTIDES, real estate broker; b. June 18, 1918, Ano Meros, Rethymnon, Crete, Greece; nat. 1954; s. Aristides Emmanuel and Eleni (Linoxilakis) T.; m. Margo P. Cooiures, June 17, 1968; children: Aristides, b. 1949; Emmanuel, b. 1951; Stanley, b. 1953; Mark, b. 1973; edn: dip. Hiram Johnson H.S. 1970. Career: meat dept. mgr. Van's Markets, Sacramento 1968-79; real estate salesman Century 21 Real Estate, Sacto. 1979-81; broker/ prin., Real Estate Forum, Citrus Heights 1981--; honors: Resolutions, Calif. State Assembly (1973), Senate (1975); mem: Am. Hellenic Profl. Soc.; Comstock Club (Sacto);Am. Hellenic Edn. Progressive Assn.; Pancretan Assn. of Am. (Dist. VI Gov. 1980), founding pres. PAA, Zeus Cretagenis Chpt., Sacto. 1972-5; mil: 1st lt. Inf., Greek Army 1939-46; decorated by Greek Govt. for mil. service 1941-45, Brit. Govt., 1939-45, UN Patriot; Democrat; Greek Orthodox. Res: 8360 Lake Forest Dr Sacramento 95826 Ofc: Real Estate Forum, 7919 Pebble Beach Dr, Ste 103, Citrus Hts 95610

U

UDWADIA, FIRDAUS ERACH, scientist, engineer; b. Aug. 28, 1947, Bombay, India; s. Dr. Erach R. and Perin E (Lentin) U.; m. Farida Gagrat, Jan. 6, 1977; 1 child: Shanaira F., b. 1978; edn: BA, Indian Inst. of Tech. 1968; MS, Calif. Inst. of Tech. 1969, PhD 1972. Career: research fellow, applied science Calif. Inst. of Tech.; asst. prof. Sch. Engring., USC, Los Angeles; prof. engring. USC; bd. dir. firm spec. in applied science, math. and biomechanics; resrch in geophysics, dynamics and biomechanics; permanent cons. Jet Propulsion Lab.; cons. Argonne Nat. Labs., Avery Internat., World Health Orgn.; awards: NSF research grantee, 1973-, spl. NSF adv. to Univ. Skopje 1974; mem: Seismological Soc. of Am.; Soc. for Indsl. and Applied Math.; Am. Acad. of Mechanics; Sigma Xi; ASCE; Earthquake Engring. Inst.; orgzr. confs. in areas of System I.D., and Dynamics; Publs: over 70 research papers in sci. jours. on earthquake engring., biomechanics, and physics; Zoroastrian; rec: piano, writing poetry, chess, computers. Res: 1708 No Roosevelt Ave Altadena 91001 Ofc: University of So California, Denny Research Bldg. Los Angeles 90007

UEBERROTH, PETER VICTOR, commissioner of baseball; b. Sept. 2, 1937, Chgo.; s. Victor C. and Laura (Larson) Ueberroth; m. Virginia Nicolaus; four children; edn: CSU San Jose. Career: founder Transportation Consultants International, 1963-, co. went public 1967, chmn. bd./chief exec. First Travel Corp. (2d-largest travel co. in US), 1967--; pres. Los Angeles Olympic Organizing Com., 1979-84; commnr. of baseball, 1984--; dir. Kaiser Cement Corp., Transam. Corp.; mem. Delta Upsilon, Bel Air CC; Christian; rec: water sports, golf, tennis; ofc: Los Angeles 90084

UEHLEIN, BETSY LOU, gourmet food co. president; b. Aug. 14, 1928, Whittier; d. Ernest C. and Helen M. (Jeske) Schuerman; m. George Uehlein, June 14, 1947; chil: Robert, Patricia, David,Kathryn, Gregory, Michael, Anthony. Career: began as part time Girl Friday, bookkeeper, salespsn., now pres./ gourmet splst./ sales mgr. Caviar & Fine Foods, Inc., Los Angeles 1979--; tng. new salesmen, distbrs., consulting, promotional shows. Co-vol. w/ husband Geo. estab. first blind Cub Scout Pack for Braille Inst. Res: 6624 Leland Way, Hollywood 90028 Ofc: Caviar & Fine Foods Inc. 6610 Melrose Ave Los Angeles 90038

UHLAND, KENNETH FRANCIS, software engineer; b. May 19, 1945, Baltimore, Md.; s. Austin Alexander and Lillian Cecile (Krymskl) U.; edn: Loyola Coll., 1963-5, R.E.T.S., 1965-7. Career: served in US Navy, 1968-77: data systems tech. aboard USS Wainwright (DLG-28), respons. for AN/SYA4 Display System; instr. Combat Systems Tech. Schs. Cmd.; hardware & software instr. Digital Equip. Corp., Santa Clara 1977-83; sr. software engr., system mgr. Xonics Imaging, Inc., Sunnyvale 1983-84; system pgmmr. Informatics General Corp., Palo Alto 1984--; cons. in field; mem. Mensa 1977-; author computer pgm: Catchall Task (for RSX-11M op. sys.); mil.: DS1, USN 1968-77,

Vietnam Svc, GCM (2); rec: woodwkg., philately, numismatics, sci-fi. Res: POB 390341 Mountain View 94039 Ofc: Informatics General Corp. 1121 San Antonio Rd Palo Alto 94303

ULLOM, GLENN TRUMAN, drafting supply co. owner; b. Dec. 3, 1927, Canon City, Colo.; s. Glenn Charles and Clara Mae (Hunter) U.; m. Harriet J. Burgett, June 13, 1953; chil: Dennis, b. 1954, James, b. 1955, Debra, b. 1956, Garrett, b. 1959, Robert, b. 1965; grad. Mission H.Sch., S.F. 1945. Career: buyer Westinghouse Corp. 1952-54; salesman Repco Products Co. 1954-64; owner J.G. Products Co., Oakland 1964--. Mem. Elks Club, S.F. Publs: J.G. Products Co. Catalog (1976). Mil: cpl. USMC 1950-2; Democrat; Catholic. Rec: sailing, photog. Res: 1008 Nimitz Dr. Daly City 94015 Ofc: J.G.Products Co. J226 13th Ave Oakland 94606

ULRICH, JOSEPH WILLARD, credit bureau executive; b. Oct. 17, 1929, Wewoka, OK; s. Everett Charles and Helen Elizabeth (Coley) U.; m. Lois Smith, Jan. 29, 1950; children: Steven, b. 1951; Dennis, b. 1952; Gregory, b. 1957; Lori, b. 1966; edn: Livingston H.S. Career: investigator chief insp. Retail Credit Co., Atlanta, Ga. 1950-55; owner/pres./gen. mgr. Credit Bureau of Turlock Inc. 1955; Dir. Assoc. Credit Bureaus Calif.; CRD Com. Assoc. Credit Bureaus of Am.; CSD instr.; honors: Exec. Achievement Award, Assoc. Credit Bureaus of Am. 1973; Charles Benson Mem. Award, Assoc. Credit Bureaus of Calif. 1982; mem: Rotary (pres. Turlock Club 1971-72); Am. Field Svc. Exchange Host Family; Turlock CofC (dir.); past pres. Turlock 20-30 Club; formed Denair Boosters Club; past pres. Livingston Alumni Assn.; pres. Assoc. Credit Bureaus of Calif. 1984-; past chmn. Turlock March of Dimes; past pres. chmn. United Crusade; past dir. Stanislaus Co. Grand Jury 1970; Republican; Lutheran, Mo. Synod; rec: poetry, fishing, racquetball, golf, travel. Res: 1937 No. Berkeley Turlock 95380 Ofc: Credit Bureau of Turlock, Inc., 321 South Thor St, Ste. B Turlock 95381

UMANA, HERNAN G., construction co. president; b. May 28, 1952, San Jose, Costa Rica, nat. 1974; s. Hernan and Naysla U.; m. Maureen, Feb. 20, 1972; children: Maureen, b. 1973; Carolyn, b. 1975; Stephanie, b. 1977; edn: postgrad., Central Am. Sch. of Banking 1975; BS, magna cum laude, USC 1979; MBA, Pepperdine Univ. 1981. Career: credit officer, internat. div. Bank of Am. 1974-75; pres. Cariari Corp., Beverly Hills 1976--; mem: Circle K Internat. v.p. 1972; Kiwanis 1974-75; pres. Nat. Hispanic Fellowship of the Christian Ch., US and Canada; author: Costa Rica, an economic analysis 1974; Christian Ch.; Res: Redondo Bch Ofc: Cariari Corp, 348 Tejon Place Palos Verdes Estates 90274

UNDERLY, THOMAS W., land development & management executive; b. Jul. 16, 1944, South Bend, Indiana; s. Joseph R. and Elennor L. (Skarpinski) U.; children: Dina, b. 1965; Tara, b. 1965; Marla, b. 1969; edn: BS, Arizona State 1966; MBA, UCLA. Career: partner Pocarello and Underly 1966-73; cons. City Ivesting Corp., NY 1974-75; cons. Kauffman Broad Home Systems/ Altamont Builderns, Los Angeles 1975-77; owner Thomas W. Underly Design & Mgmt. Inc.,(design and devel. more than 3 million sq. ft. of office and residtl. condo., exec. office space, med. facilities, since 1978) 1977--; tchr. suprvn. and orgznl. seminar to var. cos., including Broadmore Homese and Redman Ind. Sem. at State Real Estate Convention, San Francisco; awards: presidents cup Kauffman Broad Home Systems; constr. mgmt. award City Investing Corp.; mem: BSIA; ASTME Engring Soc.; Bldg. Ind. Assn.; Am. Inst. Bldg. Designers; Bldg. Designers Research In.◄.; Sacramento Yacht Club; Sacramento Childrens Guild; ref. Youth Soccer; Glen Oaks Tennis Club; Phi Gamma Delta; Republican (steering comm.); Catholic; rec: boating, skiing, dining; Res: 3140 Swallows Nest Dr Sacramento 95833 Ofc: Thomas W. Underly Design & Mgmt., Inc., 3550 Watt Ave. Sacramento 95821

UNDERWOOD, BARBARA LEE, fast food franchise co. executive; b. Feb. 27, 1958, Maywood, CA; d. Darold Lee and Nancy Lee (Dunn) U.; edn: Fullerton Coll. 1976-9, Adv. Instnl. Aide Cert. 1977. Career: tudor/aide Garden Grove Sch. Dist. (Aphasic, retarded and children with drug problems) 1974-79; mgmt. empl. various locations for McDonalds, (Okla. City, Okla. to Anaheim, Ca.); currently dist. mgr. 6 units Del Taco, Inc., Costa Mesa 1980--; cons. to tng. dept. Del Taco; awards: Sharon Topper Humanitarian Award, Fullerton Coll. 1978; Helping Hands Recognition Award 1975; mem: Nat. Assn. Female Executives; Irvine CofC; publs: vol. of poetry (used in Fullerton Coll. Eng. classes); Democrat; Baptist; rec: teaching, writing, horse riding, camping. Res: 1550-58 Rimpau Corona 91820 Ofc: 345 Baker St Costa Mesa 92626

UNG, JOHN KIN-FUN, product manager; b. Nov. 17, 1951, Hong Kong; US Res. 1980; s. Alberto and Chi Kin (Wong) Ung; m. Michele Leung, May 24, 1981; edn: BA in chem., math., Univ. of La Verne, 1975; MS in chem., Univ. of S.F., 1976, MBA mktg., 1979. Career: resrch asst./summer stu. NIH, Bethesda, Md. (work presented 1974 AMA Conf.); lab. asst. Dept. Chem. La Verne Coll. 1974-5; asst. chemist., Stauffer Chem. Co., Richmond, Ca. 1977; instr. Dept. Chem., Univ. of San Francisco 1975-8, and resrch. asst. Inst. of Chem. Biol. (cancer resrch funded by NASA, Ames Research Labs.); application chemist Dionex Corp., Sunnyvale 1979, tech. and sales support, 1980; sales engr., product splst. Kontron Analytical, Redwood City 1981-2, product mgr. 1982--; honors: track & field , cross country teams, Mackenzie Awd. for Sci. , Dorothy Brown Internat. Student, La Verne Coll. (1972), pres. Internat. Student Assn. (1973, 74); cert. Internat. Lab., Inc. 1975; Who's Who in Am. Univs. and Colls. 1975. Mem: Assn. of MBA Execs., Am. Chemist Soc. Works: profl. presentations; Catholic; rec: jog, swim, tennis. Res: 4866 Kenwood St. Union City 94587 ofc: Kontron Analytical, 630 Price Ave Redwood City 94063.

UNGAR, MICHAEL T., lawyer; b. Jul. 15, 1949, Hungary; s. Sandor A. and Katalin (Ornstein) U.; m. Paula, Jun. 29, 1980; children: Adam Horn, b. 1966; Lorraine Horn, b. 1965; edn: BA, CSU Northridge 1971; JD, Southwestern Univ. Sch. Law 1974; lawyer, admitted Calif., Fed., US Supreme Courts 1974; teaching cred. Calif. Comm. Colls. Career: constituent advocate for Calif. State 1975; atty Hamilton Supply Co., Inc. 1975; atty. Getty Oil Co. 1976-78; atty. self empl. 1978--; honors: recognition, Israel Consulate, var. Jewish orgns., Calif. State Senate, Shriners, Optimists, Rotarians, Lions, Pioneer Women, Torrance Nat. Little League. Mem: CofC., Bar Assns., Alumni Assns., The Acad. of Pol. Sci.; past chmn. Community Relations Com. of JFC; past chmn. Middle-East Task Force; 2nd v.p. bd. trustees Temple Beth-El, San Pedro; mem. Library Bd. Trustees, Palos Verdes; Jewish; rec: music and the arts, stamp, coin, and newspaper collecting, nature. Res: 3245 Barkentine Rd Rancho Palos Verdes 90274 Ofc: 715 Silver Spur Rd, Ste. 207, Rolling Hills Estates 90274

UNGER, SARITA HARRIET, psychotherapist; b. Mar. 30, 1927, Midland, Pa.; d. Myer and Frances (Freed) Silverman; m. Wm. Unger, M.D., Jan. 6, 1952; children: Joanne, b. 1953; Keren, . 1954; Marcy, b. 1958; edn: BS, Univ. Pittsburgh 1948; MSW, UCLA 1951; L.C.S.W., Lic. Clin. Social Worker, Calif. 1969, Approved Splst. for Developmentally Disabled, 1975; Cert. Sex Therapist, Sexual Dysfunction Clinic, UCLA 1976; Nat. Registry Health Care Providers, 1976. Career: social worker Vista Del Mar, 1951-52, Adoption Inst., 1960-62, LA Psychiatric Service, 1962-67, social work supr. Fernald School, UCLA 1968-70; clinical social worker Craniofacial Clinic, UCLA Hosp. 1972-79; current: psychotherapist pvt. practice; supr. Nat. Council Jewish Women; supr. Didi Hirsch Mental Health Ctr.; instr., marriage class, Univ. of Judaism; cons: Lincoln Ctr for Speech Pathol 1982-, Jeffrey Found. for Handicapped 1979, Cult Clinic Task Force, 1982-4. Awards: Cont. Edn. Awd., Soc. Clin. Social Work 1979; appreciation: Westchester Mental Hlth Clinic, 1974, Lions Club, 1977, VI World Cong. of Psychiatry, 1977. Mem: Fellow Soc. Clin. Social Wrkrs; LA County Counseling and Psychotherapy Referral Svc; LA Group Psychotherapy Soc.; Am. Group Psychotherapy Soc.; League of Women Voters, Hadassah, Anti Defam. League, Nat. Council Jewish Women. Publs: profl. conf. presentations. Democrat; rec: china painting, sewing. Res: 1909 Mandeville Cyn Rd Los Angeles 90049

UPTAIN, MICHAEL LARRY, certified public accountant; b. May 11, 1957, San Diego; s. Samuel Eugene and Arvilla May (Parkes) U.; m. Naomi Combs, May 1, 1983; edn: Porterville Coll. 1975-77; BS w/honors, CalPoly Tech., S.L.O. 1979. Career: mgr. Ted Brown's Auto Parts, Porterville 1974-77; shift mgr. Westside Auto Parts, San Luis Obispo 1977-78; staff acct. Rudolph Soukup, P.A., San Luis Obispo 1978-79; staff acct. Vollmer, Canfield, Daniel, Stout, Pine & Gaebe, Porterville 1979-80; semi-sr. acct. Carpenter, Kuhn & Williams, Bakersfield 1980-81; mng. partner Ainsworth & Uptain, Porterville 1981--, tax and mgmt. adv. svcs. partner 1982-;mem: Cal. Soc. CPA's 1982-83; Pres. Club-Olde Worlde, Inc.; Bakersfield Jaycees (charter pres.); Porterville Jaycees (mem. chmn.); Sierra Road Runners; 4 WD Club; Calif. Assn. Four Wheel Drive; Republican; rec: jeeping, camping. Res: 1681 Wall Lane Porterville 93257 Ofc: Ainsworth & Uptain, 639 No Main Street, Ste B, Porterville 93257

UREVICH, CONSTANTIN NICHOLAS, lawyer; b. Apr. 4, 1933, Shanghai, China, nat. 1957; s. Nicholas D. and Margaret (Kagan) U.; 1 dau., Robin Margaret, b. 1957; edn: Los Angeles City Coll.; BA, L. A. State Univ. 1959; LLB, Loyola Univ. 1961; MBA, USC 1971; admitted Calif State Bar 1976. Career: lawyer/prin., C.N. Urevich, gen. practice law firm, Los Angeles; dir. Didi Hirsch Mental Health Comm. Svc.; Vols. in Parole; lectr. Negotiation Techniques 1971; arbitrator Los Angeles County Bar/Los Angeles Superior Court; awarded Key to the City of Manila 1983; mem: Los Angeles County Bar Assn. (Customs Com.); Los Angeles Trial Lawyers Assn. (Adminstrv. Law); Jonathan Club; USC Assoc., life; sr. adv. US Congl. Adv. Bd. 1982; creative works: Feasibility Study Design-Allied Services Project 1973; How to Get the Most Out From Your Lawyer 1983; Operational Aspects of Trade with USSR 1974; mil: Crp., US Army 1953-55; Republican; Catholic; rec: flying, fishing, racquetball, art coll. Res: 545 S Figeroa St Los Angeles 90071 Law Ofcs of C.N. Urevich, 650 S Grand Ave, Ste. 914 Los Angeles 90017

URIDEL, LOREN HARRY, architect; b. Apr. 6, 1956, La Porte, Indiana; s. Loren George and Carol Joan (Powers) U.; edn: BS, and B.Arch., Ball State Univ. 1979; MBA, Loyola Marymount Univ. 1984; Architect (NCARB Reg. pending), AIA, Calif. BAE 1982. Career: co-pilot Lucky's Aircraft Svc., Valparaiso, Ind., 1975-78; asst. proj. mgr. Illinois Bank Bldg. Corp., Chgo. 1977; asst. proj. mgr. Froehlich & Kow, Beverly Hills 1979-80; proj. mgr./proj. architect Pearson & Wuesthoff AIA AICP, 1980--; pres. Collaborative Group, Los Angeles 1982--; dir. Andresen Design Assoc., Los Angeles 1983; cons. to LMU Coll. of Bus. bldg. com.; awards: Gold Palm-Eagle Scout 1971, Ad Altarie Dei; AIA Solar Housing Comp. finalist 1976; mem: AIA (Assocs. bd. dirs. 1981-); Aero Club of So. Calif.; San Diego Aero-Space Mus.; Nat. Council og Archtl. Regis. 1976; orgns: asst. Scoutmaster 1975-80; Ball State rep. to Ind., Newman Apostolate Conv. 1976; St. Francis of Assisi Parish Council 1974-79; LMU MBA Student Assn.; Ball State Univ. Alumni; Pres.'s Club LMU Coll. of Bus. Policy and Strategy Com.; profl. publs. Catholic; rec: private pilot, boating. Res: POB 9340 Marina del Rey 90295 Ofcs: Pearson & Wuesthoff, 4314 Marina City Dr, Ste. 166C Marina del Rey, 90292; Collaborative Group, POB 9340 Marina del Rey 90292

USINGER, RICHARD PUTNAM, dentist; b. Sep. 26, 1947, Oakland; s. Robert Leslie and Martha Boone (Putnam) U.; m. Lynne Journigan, Sep. 16,

1978; edn: BA, Univ. of Pacific 1969; DDS, USC 1973. Career: dentist private practice, Concord 1973--; mem: Am. Dental Assn.; Calif. Dental Assn.; Contra Costa Dental Soc.; So Calif. Acad. of Oral Pathology; Century Club; USC Sch. Dentistry; P and S Club; UOP Sch. Dentistry; Alumni Assns. USC, UOP; Los Medicos Volodores (The flying doctors); Academy of Sports Dentistry; SAR; publs: art., Dental Management Mag. 11/77; rec: photog., ski, sail. Address: 2991 Treat Blvd, Ste. G, Concord

UTZ, SARAH WINIFRED, nursing consultant, educator; b. Nov. 2, 1921, San Diego; d. Frederick Raymond and Margaret Mary (Gibbons) U.; edn: BS, Univ. of Portland 1943, EdM, 1958; MS, UCLA 1970; PhD, USC 1979. Career: asst. prof./prof. of nursing. Calif. St. Univ., Los Angeles 1969--; assoc. chmn. Dept. of Nsg., CSULA, 1984-; chmn. Liaison Com. on Nursing Edn.; Articulation Council of Calif.; past ed. the Oregon Nurse; honors: Who's Who in the West 1980-81; mem. research pgm. Western Interstate Commn. on Higher Edn. in Nsg. Mem: Am. Nurses Assn.; Calif. Nurses Assn.; Am. Ednl. Research Assn.; AAUP; Phi Delta Kappa; Town Hall of Calif.; publs.: 20 research publs. (HEW grant 1970-4, Kellogg Found. grant 1974-6); mil: Lt.jg USN Nurse Corps 1944-46. Res: 1409 Midvale Ave Los Angeles 90024 Ofc: Calif. State Univ. Los Angeles 5151 State Univ. Dr Los Angeles 90032

UY, STEPHEN SIONG, civil engineer; b. Mar. 15, 1932, Cotabato, Philippines; s. Cue Choc and Lim Biam; m. Juanita Tan, Sep. 13, 1957; children: Shirley, b. 1958; Doyna, b. 1962; edn: BSCE, National Univ., Manila 1955; postgrad., Univ. Wisconsin 1956-57; reg. profl. engr. Ill., Calif.; reg. structural engr. Ill.; lic. real estate broker Calif. Career: design engr. Hazelet & Erdal, Chicago, Ill. 1957-65; design supvr. Unitad Engineer & Constructors, Chiago 1965-67; chief bridge engr. DMJM, Los Angeles 1968-77; sr. engr. R.M. Parsons, Pasadena 1977-79; mgr. structural engring. B.A. Sinclair & Assoc., Los Angeles 1979-80; proj. structural engr. DMJM, Los Angeles 1980--; pres. Bee Kee Systems, Los Angeles 1980-; chmn./bd. dir. New Hall Comm. Hosp., New Hall 1981-; mem. ASCE; Catholic; rec: golf, swimming, bowling. Res: 8549 Aqueduct Ave Sepulveda 91343 Ofc: DMJM, 3250 Wilshire Blvd Los Angeles 90010

V

VADER, DONALD LEROY, power company executive; b. Sep. 6, 1944, Oakland; s. Arthur Leroy and Harriett Louise (Foglia) V.; m. Andree Louise, Aug. 31, 1965, children. Michael John, b. 1966; Amy Louise, b. 1968; edn: AA, Oakland City Coll. Career: salesman Westinghouse Electric Supply Co., Oakland 1964-70; purchasing agent Aladdin Elec. Inc., Oakland 1970-75; branch mgr. Tucknott Elec. Inc., San Leandro and San Jose 1975-81; owner Powercon Elec. Inc., Sunnyvale 1981--; com. mem. Nat. Electrical Contractors Assn., Santa Clara 1981-; Assoc. Bldrs. & Contractors Assn. 1981-; pres. San Jose Exchange Club; designer innovative energy mgmt. system design, over 300 systems installed; Republican, Christian; rec: flying, aircraft owner instrument rated, hunting, fishing. Res: 4972 Muirwood Dr Pleasanton 94566 Ofc: Powercon Elec, 1031 N Fairoaks Ave Sunnyvale 94089

VAIL, RONALD ALMON, financial planner; b. May 20, 1925, Chgo.; s. Almon John and Gertrude Jean Vail; m. Lois Mae Reeves, Mar. 27, 1948; children: Phyllis, b. 1949, Pamela, b. 1949, Cheron, b. 1951, David, b. 1953, Beckey, b. 1958, Bonnie, b. 1959; edn: BS, high honors, Univ. of Md. 1963; Calif. Comm Coll. tchr. credentials 1981; desig: CFP, Cert. Finl. Planner, Coll. for Finl. Plng. 1982; Reg. Financial Principal, NASD 1974. Career: registered representative Mutual Fund Associates, San Diego 1968-70; reg. rep. The Ralph S. Wilford Co., La Mesa 1970-73, v.p. sales 1973-79; reg. prin. American Pacific Securities Corp., S.D. 1979-80, regional mgr. 1980--; mng. ptnr. for eleven inv. gps. 1975-; honors: Phi Kappa Phi (1963), Admiral, Great Navy of the State of Nebr. (1967); mem: Navy Cryptologic Veterans Assn., Inst. of CFPs, Internat. Assn. for Finl. Plng., San Diego CofC; mil: cmdr. USN 1943-68, decorated Am. Service, Asia-Pacific Theater, China, Burma, India Theater, WWII Victory medals, Unit Commendn.; Republican. Res: 1301 Bobcat Ln Alpine 92001 Ofc: San Diego Regl. Ofc., American Pacific Securities Corp. 6150 Mission Gorge Rd, Ste 204, San Diego 92120

VALDES, HALCEA MAXINE, social worker; b. Dec. 13, 1928, Medford, Ore.; d. Chester Arthur and Orpha Dell (Stevenson) Moore; m. Victor Valdes, Mar. 27, 1948, div. 1966; children: Hayden, b. 1950; Victor, Jr., b. 1951; Chester, b. 1953; edn: BS, with honors, Texas Womens Univ. 1962; MSW, UC Berkeley 1967; lic. Marriage Family Child Counselor, lic. Clinical Soc. Wkr., Calif. Career: child welfare supr. for Alameda Co. 9yrs.; psychotherapist in pvt. practice 13 yrs.; child welfare adminstr. with Children's Home Soc. of Calif., 1975--, currently program mgr. Counseling & Adoptions; field work supvr., UCB Grad. Sch. of Soc. Work and SFSU; grantee Calif. State Dept. Grad. Soc. Wrk. edn. stipend 1965; mem: Nat. Assn. Soc. Wkrs.; Academy of Cert. Soc. Wkrs.; Bay Area Supervisers of Adoption; Democrat; rec: swimming, bicycling, travel, collecting minatures. Res: 2001 Francisco Berkeley 94709 Ofc: Children's Home Soc., 3200 Telegraph Ave Oakland 94609

VALDEZ, JOSE GABRIEL, clinical social worker; b. Feb. 9, 1941, Dixon, N.M.; s. Ross and Elsie (Espinoza) V.; edn: BA, Westminster Coll. 1972; MSW, Univ. of Utah 1974; post masters stu. Univ. of Denver 1978-80; LCSW (Lic.

Clin. Soc. Wkr) Calif.; Acad. of Cert. Soc. Workers, NASW; Utah Lic. Cert. Soc. Wkr./ LCSW. (1983-5). Career: psychiatric social wkr., Calif. Dept. of Health, CCSS, in Santa Monica Area 1974-78; clin. soc. wkr. Livermore VA Medical Center, 1980--; Expert Examiner, Calif. Bd. of Behav. Sci. Examiners 1983/4; honors: VA Administrator's Hands and Heart Award (1982); mem: Nat. Assn. of Social Workers, Reg. of Clin. Soc. Wkrs.; mil: SP4 US Army 1960-63, sgt. USAF 1963-68; Democrat; Catholic. Res: 3956 East Ave No. 27, Livermore 94550 Ofc: VA Med. Center at Livermore, 4951 Arroyo Road Livermore 94550

VALENTI, TERESA, author/lecturer, b. May 13, 1939, Bronx, NY; d. Guiseppe and Teresa (Ferrarese) Conticchio; m. Raf Dahlquist, Feb. 14, 1984; children: Jeanette, b. 1962, John, b. 1964; edn: AA, Pierce Coll. 1963. Career: cosmetologist/owner Michelangelo Salon; owner Personal Human Development, Unlmtd.; vice pres., mem. bd. dirs. Dahlquist Polestar; author bestseller: How To Kiss With Confidence. Res: 8333 Corbin Ave Canoga Park 91306

VALERDI, JORGE, electronics engineer; b. Dec. 21, 1944, Veracruz, Mex.; s. Molito H. and Zayde (Karam) V., m. Lucia Albarran, Sept. 12, 1974; children: Natalia, b. 1976, Ricardo, b. 1977; edn: BS, Inst. politecnico 1967; MS, Univ. of Houston, 1970, PhD, 1972. Career: asst. dir. for planning, Ministry of Commerce, Mexico 1972-76; head Telecomm. Dept., Acese Research Center, 1977-82; pres. Intelconsult Corp. in Calif., 1982--; honors: Sigma Xi, Eta Kappa Nu; mem. IEEE, Am. Mgmt. Assn., Toastmasters Internat. (past pres.); publs: over 20 tech. arts., engineering journals; rec: tennis. Res: 1682 Abalone Pt Ct, Chula Vista 92011 Ofc: Intelconsult Corp. 314 Fourth Ave, Ste. T, Chula Vista 92010

VALEU, JOHN WAYNE, computer operations executive; b. July 17, 1959, San Diego, CA; s. Bennie Joe and Mary Jean V.; m. Julia Ann Saunders, Feb. 23, 1979; 1 son: John, Jr., b. 1980. Career: keypuncher, opr./pgmmr. for USN, UNIVAC, IBM and Hewlett-Packard Systems; pgmmr./analyst, supvr. and system mgr. Hewlett-Packard 3000/40 computer, Staff Cmdr., Naval AF, Pacific Fleet; computer ops. splst./supvr. Pulse Engineering; mem.: HP Local Users Group, San Diego; Apple Corps. of S.D. users gp., active in BSA, Little League; mil: DP2 (E5), USN 1976-83; GCM, Navy Exped., Sea Svc. Medal, Unit Commend.; Christian; rec: home computers, music, sports, camping. Res: 151 East Olympia St Chula Vista 92011 Ofc: Pulse Engineering, 7250 Convoy Ct San Diego 92111

VALIERE, GARY MARK, business consultant; b. Feb. 24, 1931, Valley City, N.D.; s. Eugene Anthony and Doris Lois (Keeler) V.; m. Delores Elaine Leick, Jan. 2, 1950; children: Steven Mark, Michael Gordon, Thomas Paul, Gary James; edn: BS, N.D. State Coll., Valley City 1955; MBA, CSU Fullerton 1968; Nat. Security Mgmt., Indsl. Coll. of the Armed Forces 1968; PhD, US Internat. Univ. 1980; QC Cert., Iowa State Univ. 1957. Career: lab. foreman, research chemist Philips Chem. Co., Borger, Tex. 1955-58; research design engr. Boeing Co., Seattle 1958-61; sr. electronics engr., mgr. program mgmt. Raytheon Corp. Santa Barbara 1961-62; proj. dir. Mgmt. Systems Corp., Boston and Newport Beach 1962-65; dir. mgmt. analysis Douglas Aircraft, Santa Monica and Huntington Beach 1965-68; asst. v.p. dir. pgm. plnng and control, Mil. Aircraft Div. McDonnell Douglas Corp., Long Beach 1968-69; mgr. cons. Peat, Marwick, Mitchell, Los Angeles 1969-72; v.p./ dir. Rex Land & Assocs., Los Angeles 1972-77; pres./ chmn. bd. Gary Valiere & Assocs., Irvine 1977--, Office Word Processing, Irvine, 1982--; Satro Vista, Inc., Irvine 1982--; dir. Cypress Internat., Hovaly Inc., Garretson-Valiere & Assocs.; gen. partner, JWA Properties, Irvine; pres./ chmn. bd., Profl. Edn. Development (PED) Inc., Reno, Nev.; lectr. Am. Mgmt. Assn., Am. Inst. Indsl. Engrs., Nat. Contract Mgmt. Assn. UCLA, USC; active senatorial cpgns. 1960, 68; mem: AIAA, Univ. Doctoral Soc., Am. Def. Preparedness Assn., Assn. US Army, USAF Assn., Nat. Contract Mgmt. Assn., World Affairs Council, Nat. Security Council, Am. Legion; clubs: Congl., Senatorial, Elks; Author books, manuals, papers on orgn. and mgmt. Ofc: 2021 Business Center Dr, Ste. 211, Irvine 92715

VALSAMAKIS, HELEN, business owner; b. May 31, 1953, Hollywood; d. Christoper and Marina Valsamakis; edn: Orange Coast Coll. 1971-73. Career: owner Renaissance Bakery & Coffee House, Laguna Beach, 1976--, pres. Renaissance Bakeries Inc., 1981--; art patron, spons. of community special events and programs; collector: antiques, antique pottery; Greek Orthodox; hobby: interior design; rec: running, dance. Res: 31582 Monterey St, So. Laguna 92677 Ofc: 234 Forest Ave Laguna Beach 92651

VALVERDE, JOSEPH ARSENIO, construction co. president; b. Nov. 18, 1935, Santa Rosa, N.Mex.; s. Arsenio and Josephine (Padilla) V.; m. Rose, Sept. 19, 1955; children: Adele, b. 1956, Michael, b. 1957, Ahron, b. 1959, Edward, b. 1961, Christopher, b. 1963; ed. Fremont H.S.; Career: truck driver, Asbury Constrn. Co., eleven Western States 1959-64; svc. mgr., then sales rep. Shaw Sales and Service (heavy constrn. equip. firm), 1964-69; rental equip. mgr., sales mgr., gen. mgr. Herron, Richard, McCone Co., Norwalk 1969-72; pres./ gen. mgr. Valverde Constrn., Inc. (engring. and bldg. constrn. systems for public agencies and pvt. developers; emerg. repair for municipal water agcys.; equip. rentals), Santa Fe Springs 1972--; cons. land devel., constrn.; trustee Constrn. Indus. Advancement Fund of So. Calif. 1980-82; honors: legis. resolutions, Calif. State Senate (1975, 77, 81), Calif. State Assem. (1976); County of L.A. Commendation (1975); award, Contractors State Lic. Board, 1982; hon. Col., N.Mex. Gov. Bruce King, 1982; Pres. Reagan invitee to Small Bus. Sem., Wash DC, 1982; mem. Engring. Contrs. Assn. (pres. 1980, 1; Mem. of Yr.

1979); past pres. Tri-City USC Trojan Club, 1981-2; hd. coach La Mirada Colts football team, 1964-72; past pres. La Mirada Jaycees, 1969 (Jaycee of Yr. 1967); mil: sp4, US Army, 3 yrs., Korea; Republican (Calif. del. to nat. conv. 1980). Res: 1841 No Hills Dr La Habra 90631 Ofc: Valverde Construction, Inc. 8230 Sorenson Santa Fe Springs 90670

VAN BENSCHOTEN, MARK MATHEW, acupuncturist; b. Aug. 13, 1956, Los Angeles; s. Peter and Judith (Greenrock) V.; m. Celeste Tina Katz, Feb. 7, 1983; son, Noah Alexander, b. 1983; edn: UCLA, 1973-77; MA, Goddard Coll. 1980; grad. Calif. Acupuncture Coll. 1980, OMD, 1983. Career: pvt. practice in acupuncture, herbal medicine, orthomolecular nutrition, Tarzana, Ca. 1980--; clinical dir. Acupuncture Treatment and Research Center, Los Angeles 1982--; research assoc. instr. Oriental Healing Arts Inst., L.A. 1980--; prof./ chmn. dept. of herbal med., Calif. Acupuncture Coll. 1983--; honors: academic scholarship, Bunker-Ramo Corp. 1973; fellowship, Pharmacagnosy, Oriental Healing Arts Inst. 1979, hon. mbrship 1983; author: Treatment of Chi, Water, and Blood Disease by Chinese Herbal Medicine, 1981; contbg. writer Bull. of Oriental Arts Inst., nutrition column, The Transender Newspaper; rec: music, painting, martial arts. Res: 18620 Hatteras Ave, Ste. 237, Tarzana 91356 Ofc: Victory-Tampa Medical Square, 19231 Victory Blvd, Ste. 556, Reseda 91335

VAN BERGEN, HENRY WILLEM AUGUST, insurance broker; b. July 7, 1918, The Hague, Holland, nat. 1955; s. Charles Willem Adriaan and Henriette Wilhelmine (Baroness van den Heuvel tot Bijghelingen gezegd Bartolotti Rijnders) van B.; m. Emile Lydia Schmidt, Dec. 3, 1965 (dec. 1974); edn: BS, math & sci., Univ. of Harderwijk 1939; BS, bus. adm., Univ. of Leiden 1941; lic. agent, broker & life ins., Cal. Dept. of Ins. 1954. Career: editor Netherlands Pub. Co. 1941-47; mgmt. cons. 1947-60; pres. Transnorthern Ins. 1960--; tchr. ins. seminars, S.F. State Univ. 1962-3; mem: Ins. Brokers Assn. of Calif.; US Naval Inst.; US Chess Fedn.; No. Calif. Chess Assn.; Mechanics Inst.; Nat. Geographic Soc.; Royal Astronomical Soc.; Astron. Soc. of the Pacific; Olympic Club; mil: capt. Canadian Army (SIS), N.W. Europe 1945-6; Republican; Prot.; rec: sailing, astronomy, chess, computer sci. Address: 1844 Centro W., POB 946, Tiburon 94920

VAN BEURDEN, LEON ADRIANUS, real estate broker; b. July 4, 1951, Tilburg, Holland; s. Cornelius and Mary (Tuerlings) Van B.; m. Kathleen D. Barnes, Apr. 6, 1974; children: Adrion, b. 1975, Jennifer, b. 1977, Lanz, b. 1980; edn: bus. stu. Cuesta Coll. 1973, real estate broker prep., USC 1981. Career: mgr. Flying Dutchman Restaurant, Morro Bay 1970-74; constrn. framing, Los Osos 1974-75; restaurant owner/mgr. Friar Tucks Refectory, San Luis Obispo 1975-80; real estate sales agt. ERA Realty 4, Los Osos 1980-83, sales mgr. 1983-84, partner/broker 1984--. Awards: Million Dollar Club 1980, 81, 82, 83; ERA Nat. Winners Circle 1981, 82, 83, Top 100 Salesmen in US. Mem: Calif., Nat. Assn. Realtors, Kiwanis, Jaycees. Mil: E4 Army NG.; Catholic; rec: sailing, jog, baseball. Res: 1334 Fourth St. Los Osos 93402 Ofc: ERA Realty 4, 1398 Los Osos Valley Rd. Los Osos 93402

VAN BOXTEL, DIANE LYNN, financial planner/ training exec.; b. July 24, 1952, Green Bay, Wis.; d. Sylvester and Dolores Mae (Arnoldussen) Van B.; edn: finl. plnng., Golden Gate Univ. 1981-; spl. courses, Nat. Assn. Bank Women, Santa Rosa Jr. Coll., Wells Fargo Bank, N.E. Wis. Tech. Inst.; Cert. Fin. Planner. Career: adminstrv. asst. First Nat. Bank, Seymour, Wisc. 1970-72; with Wells Fargo Bank, 1973--: regional mktg. mgr., San Francisco 1980-82, asst. v.p./dir. tng. Retail Brokerage Svcs. (all Wells Fargo ofcs. statewide), S.F. 1982--; recipient 1982 Group Excellence Award, Nat. Assn. of Bank Women; Jr. Achievement Adv., 1973-78; mem: Calif. Bankers Assn. (legis. rels. com.), Nat. Assn. of Bank Women, Inc. (Calif. State Council 1981-; chmn. Redwood Empire Gp. Legislative and Pub. Affairs Rep. 1981-2; Pub. Affairs chmn. NABW, State of Ca. 1983-4); Democrat; Catholic; rec: writing, travel. res: 4938 Sunshine Ave,, Santa Rosa 95405 ofc: Wells Fargo Bank, N.A. 525 Market St, 17th Fl., San Francisco 94105

VAN BUSKIRK, LEWIS FRANKLIN, retail business executive; b. Aug. 13, 1937, Stockton; s. Harold J. and Wanetta Francis (Quile) Van Buskirk; m. Barbara J. Deicke, Aug. 23, 1959; children: Jeanne, b. 1961, Pamela, b. 1963, Lori, b. 1965; edn: BA, San Francisco St. Univ. 1960; Cert. Nurseryman, Calif. Assn. of Nurserymen 1969. Career: asst. credit mgr. McCormick, Schilling & Co. 1960-61; mgr. Van's Greenbriar Nursery, Inc. 1961-69, gen. mgr. 1969-73, pres./chmn. bd. 1973--; dir. Presidio Garden Centers; agri. adv. com. San Joaquin Delta Coll. Honors: Young Nurseryman of the Year 1971, Calif. Assn. of Nurserymen 1971, Superior Cpt CAN, 1970; Grand Cross of Colors, Internat. Order of the Rainbow for Girls in Calif., 1983-4. Mem: Calif. Assn. of Nurserymen (state pres. 1979-80, Superior Chpt. pres. 1969, 1972; chmn. Insurance Trustees); Stockton CofC (trustee); mem. Masons (Worshipful Master 1969), Scottish Rites, Shriners, Kiwanis, Rotary, De Molay Boys. Publs: garden columnist Stockton Peoples Mag.; TV teaching series for public broadcasting as The Galloping Gardner, TV appearances as the Galloping Gardener 1971-80. Republican. prot. Rec: golf, tennis, racquetball, music. Res: 5173 Solari Ranch Rd. Stockton 95205 Ofc: Van's Greenbriar Nursery, Inc. 646 W. Hammer Ln. Stockton 95207

VAN CAMP, BRIAN RALPH, lawyer; b. Aug. 23, 1940, Halstead, Kans.; s. Ralph A. and Mary Margaret (Bragg) V.; m. Mary Ann Gatewood, June 25, 1961; children: Marilyn Megan, b. 1962, Laurie E., b. 1963; edn: BA, UC Berkeley 1962, LLB, 1965; admitted to practice, State Bar Calif. 1966. Career: deputy atty. gen., State of Calif. 1965-7; agency atty. Redevel. Agcy, City of Sacramento 1967-70; asst./acting secty. Business and Transp. Agcy, State of Calif. 1970-71, Commnr. of Corps. 1971-4; partner, Diepenbrock, Wulff, Palnt

& Hannegan, Sacramento 1975-77; partner Van Camp & Johnson 1978-; lectr. and author Calif. Cont. Edn. Bar, Practicing Law Inst., CPA Soc. Calif.; dir. Original Sixteen to One Mine, Inc. 1982-; honors: Sumner- Mering Meml. Award, Sacto UC Alumni Assn. 1962; Outstanding Young Man of Year, Sacto Jaycees 1970; Internat. Young Man of Year, Active 20-30 Club, Internat. 1973; Who's Who in Am. 1982; mem: Am., Calif., Sacramento, LA County, Century City Bar Assns.; Mid-West Securities Commnrs. Assn. 1971-4 ; adv. bd. UCLA Securities Law Inst. 1978; Calif. CofC (dir. 1982-); Rotary; Lincoln Club of Sacramento Valley; The Comstock Club, Inc.; Sacto Area Commerce and Trade Orgn.; Sacto Sym. Assn.; Camellia Festival Assn.; Active 20-30 Club #1 1969-70; UC Men's Club of Sacto 1966-8; Wash. Neighborhood Ctr.; mem. Pres. Adv. Bd., CSUS 1978-; mem. Comm. on Program Plnng, Sutter Comm. Hospitals Inc. 1982-; Sacto Metro. CofC; United Cerebral Palsey Assn. of Sacto, Yolo Cos.; United Way; clubs: Sutter, El Rancho Racquet, Kandahar Ski, Tradewinds Sailing, Sacto Jaguar and Hobie Cat Fleet #17; publs: num. law rev., journal arts.; arts., fin. press, Cont. Edn. of the Bar; Republican; Presbyterian; rec: sailing, skiing. Res: 3614 Brockway Ct Sacto 95818 Ofc: Van Camp & Johnson, 555 Capitol Mall, Ste. 400, Sacto 95814

VANCE, JASPER, public relations consultant; b. July 11, 1946, East Chicago, Ind.; s. Stephen and Katherine (Garrett) V.; edn: BS, USC 1968, postgrad. 1968-71. Career: photo editor/copywriter Globe Photos, Inc., Los Angeles 1971-75; executive publicist/legit theatre div. Solters & Roskin, Inc., Los Angeles 1976-78; exec. pblicist/hd. TV dept. Hanson & Schwan, Los Angeles 1978-1980; pres. PR-II, Inc. Public Relations, Los Angeles 1980-81; pres. Jasper Vance Assocs., pub. rels./ mgmt., 1982--; tchr. consortium for t.v., adult edn., Los Angeles Sch. Dist. 1975; mem: Publicists Guild, Assn. of Independent Publicists (founding mem.), mem. Mens Aux. to Hywd. Womens Press Club; Rel. Sci.; rec: creative writing, kites, philately, recordings. Ofc: 1680 North Vine St. Ste. 1116, Hollywood 90028

VANDEGAER, SISTER PAULA, social worker; b. Feb. 14, 1939, Kansas City, Mo.; d. Thomas James and Lillian Loretta (Lynn) V.; edn: BA, psychol., Immaculate Heart Coll. 1962; MSW, Catholic Univ. of Am. 1965; Lic. Clin. Social Wkr., Calif. 1969; Acad. of Cert. Soc. Wkrs. (ACSW) 1970. Career: camp co-ordinator Camp Little Flower for Girls, K.C., Mo. 1961-65; branch dir. of Guadalupe Ctr. Settlement House, Canoga Pk., Ca. 1965-66, 68-70; casewkr. Catholic Welfare Bur., L.A. 1966-68; supr./casewkr. in Natural Parent Dept., Holy Family Svcs. (Adoption & Counseling), Los Angeles 1970-73; served alternately as dir. of postulants, dir. of novices, and vocation dir., Sisters of Social Service, 1973-77, comm. treas. 1976-82, served as first counselor 1978-82; occasional tchr. Mt. St. Mary's and Calif. Lutheran Colls.; director L.A. Branch, Alternatives to Abortion Internat. (orgn. dedicated to helping pregnant women), 1978--, and editor Heartbeat Mag.; vol., Right to Life League of So. Calif. 10 years; lectr. on pro-life counseling throughout USA, Australia, NZ; US Congl. and Calif. State Legis. testimony; appearances on Phil Donohue Show, Woman to Woman, num. other radio and TV pgms.; mem. Nat. Assn. of Soc. Wkrs., Right to Life League of So. Calif. (bd. dirs.), Alternatives to Abortion Internat. (trustee), Nat. Assn. of Christians in Soc. Wk.; publs: contbg. writer Heartbeat Mag. 1978-; tng. & counseling articles reprinted worldwide; Republican; Catholic; rec: music, art. Res: 1101 S. Arlington Ave, Los Angeles 90019 Ofc: Alt. to Abortion Intl. 2606 1/2 West 8th St Los Angeles 90057

VAN DENABEL, MICHAEL, department store executive; b. July 14, 1932, Tempe, Ariz.; s. Delbert Clyde and Goldie (Dexter) Lawrence; m. Linda Durbin, 1950; edn: BA in art, CSU Fullerton 1974; lic. in cosmetology 1952; lic. Real Estate Broker 1982. Career: cosmetologist for Toni King, Palm Springs, 1952, with Bullocks Wilshire 1959--, promo. to mgmt. beauty services, 1967-, opened Bullocks Del Amo 1967, Bullocks La Habra 1969, transf. to Pasadena store 1971, mgr. Beauty Services, Bullocks Wilshire, Los Angeles 1977--; works: restoration of (1900 period) Queen Anne cottages in hist. area of Long Beach; Democrat; Unity. Res: 230 W. 8th St. Long Beach 90813 Ofc: Bullocks Wilshire, 3050 Wilshire Blvd Los Angeles 90010

VANDENBERGHE, RONALD GUSTAVE, accountant; b. Oakland; s. Anselm Henri and Margaret B. (Bygum) V.; m. Patricia W. Dufour, Aug. 18, 1957; children: Camile, Mark, Matthew; edn: BA, honors, San Jose State Coll. 1959; postgrad., UC Berkeley Extension 1959-60; Golden Gate Coll. 1961-63; CPA Calif. State. Career: real estate investor, Plsanton, CA 1964-; instr. acctg. UC Berkeley, 1963-70; CPA, Pleasanton 1963--; mem: Calif. Soc. CPA's; Mason (Shriners); mil: USAF; Republican; Presbyterian. Res: POB 803 Danville 94526 Ofc: 24 Happy Valley Rd Pleasanton 94566

VAN DEN NOORT, STANLEY, medical college dean; b. Sept. 8, 1930, Lynn, MA; edn: AB, magna cum laude, Dartmouth Coll., 1951; MD, cum laude, Harvard Med. Sch., 1954; m. June LeClere, 1954; 5 children. Career: internship, 1954-55, and residencies: med. service, neurological unit, neuropathology unit, Boston City Hosp., 1958-60; research fellow in neurochemistry, Boston City Hosp., 1960-62; diplomate, Amer. Bd. of Neurology, 1963. Univ. Apptmts: sr. instr. to assoc. prof., Neurology, Case Western Reserve Univ., 1962-70; prof. of neurology, Calif. Coll. of Med., UC Irvine, 1970--; assoc. dean, 1972; acting dean, 1973; dean, Calif. Med., UCI, 1973---; Hosp. Apptmts: asst. neurologist, Cleveland, 1962-70; Univ. of Cleveland, Univ. Hosps. of Cleveland; cons., VA Hosp. of Cleveland; Highland View Hosp. of Cleveland; cons. VA Hosp., Long Beach, 1970; chief of neurology svcs., Orange Co. Med. Ctr., 1970-73; attndg. neurologist: St. Joseph Hosp. of Orange, 1972---; Meml. Hosp. Med. Ctr., L.B., 1975---, bd. dirs., 1975; mem. bd. dirs., Children's Hosp. of Orange Co., 1972---; v.p. bd. dirs., Amer.

Bechet's Found., 1978---; prn. invest., Alcohol Research Ctr., UCI; bd. dirs., Nelson Research and Devel. Co., 1973---; bd. dirs., Calif. chpt., Myasthenia Gravis, 1974---; Profl. Adv. Bd., A.L.S. Found., 1973---; Saddleback Coll. Nursing Adv. Com., 1973---; O.C. Coll. adv. com. Electro-Diagnostic Tech., 1973---; program devel. com., Calif. Com. on Regional Med. Program.; bd. dirs.: O.C. Heart Assn., O.C. Cancer Soc.; mem. Found. for Med. Care of O.C., 1973---; fellow, Amer. Coll. Phys., 1972---. Mem: O.C. Med. Assn.; Natl. Multiple Sclerosis Soc., 1974---, natl. med. adv. bd. 1974---, chmn. 1978, O.C. chpt. bd. dirs. 1973---, chmn. 1976-78; Pan Amer. Med. Assn., 1971---; O.C. Epilepsy Soc., chmn., 1978---; L.A. Soc. of Neurology and Psychiatry, Inc., pres., 1974; AUP of Neurology, 1971---; Soc. Clin. Neurologists, exec. com., 1968-70; AMA, 1965---; Sigma Xi; Assn. for Research in Nervous and Mental Diseases, Inc., 1965---; charter pres. No. Ohio Neurol. Soc., 1969; Fellow, Amer. Acad. of Neurology, 1968; exams com. Amer. Bd. of Psychiatry and Neurology, Inc., 1963---; Mass. Med. Soc., 1958---; Ohio Med. Assn., 1965-70. Mil: Lt. M.C., USNR and neurologist, US Naval Hosp., Chelsea, Mass., 1956-58. Publs: num. articles in med. journs.; book chapter, 1977. Address: UCI Coll. of Med., Dean's Office, Irvine 92717.

VAN DER MEULEN, JOSEPH PIERRE, university administrator; b. Aug. 22, 1929, Boston, Mass.; s. Edward Lawrence and Sarah Jane (Robertson)h V.; m. Ann Irene Yadeno, 1960; children: Elisabeth Ann, b. 1961; Suzanne Mari, b. 1965; Janet Christina, b. 1966; edn: AB in math, magna cum laude, Boston Coll. 1950; MD, cum laude, Boston Univ. Sch. of Med. 1954. Career: intern/ asst. res. in med. Bellevue Hosp., NYC 1954-6, res. neurol./ tchg. fellow Harvard Med. Sch., Boston City Hosp. 1958-60; instr. fellow. & dir. EEG Lab., 1962-67; asst./assoc. Case Western Reserve Univ. Sch. of Med. 1967-71; prof. neurology USC Sch. Med. 1971--, Dept. chmn. 1971-9, v.p. for Health Affairs, USC 1977--, dir. Dept. Neurology, L.A. Co.-USC Med. Ctr. 1971-9; phys. spec. 1979-; vis. prof. Autonomous Univ., Gadalajara, Mex., 1974; trustee, Eisenhower Med. Ctr. 1983; awards: Phi Kappa Phi, causo honoris; Humanitarian Awards, The Myasthenia Gravis Found. Inc., 1982, and USN League, 1978; Boston Coll. scholarship awd.; awards gen. excellence, Boston Univ., Alpha Omega Alpha Begg Soc., Mass. Med. Soc., student award; USC, grad. class, 1976; mem bd. trustees: Good Samaritan Hosp., Calif. Hosp. Med. Ctr., Good Hope Med. Found.; bd. dir. Children's Hosp., L.A.; med. adv. bd. Calif. chpt. Myasthenia Gravis Found. 1971-5 (chmn. 1974/5, 77/8); med. adv. bd. Amyotrophic Lateral Sclerosis Found., Calif. 1973-5 (chmn. 1974/5); Com. to Combat Huntingtons Disease, 1973-; trustee Eisenhower Med. Ctr. 1983-; Nobel Inst. Fellow Karolinska Inst. 1960-62; NIH grantee, 1968-71; Dip. Am. Bd. Psychology and Neurology; mem. Am. Neurol. Assn.; Am. Acad. Neurology; L.A. Soc. Neurol. & Psychiatry, pres. 1977-8; Mass., Ohio, Calif. Med. Socs.; L.A. Acad. Med.; Alpha Omega Alpha, councillor; Editl. bd. Archives of Neurol.; contrib. profl. journs.; mil: lt. MC, USNR, 1956-8; Democrat; Catholic; rec: golf, skiing. Res: 39 Club View Ln Rolling Hills Estates 90274 Ofc: USC, 1985 N Zonal Ave, PSC 100 Los Angeles 90033

VANDERPOOL, NANCY LEE, insurance executive; b. Aug. 19, 1948, Lynwood; d. Marty A. and Marie T. (Cody) Cubellis; m. Hoyt K. Vanderpool, Feb. 15, 1969; children: Hoyt, III, b. 1971; Brandan, b. 1975; edn: BS, Woodbury Coll., Los Angeles 1969; spl. courses, Santa Ana Coll. 1975-6; lic. Life & Disability Ins., Calif. 1974; reg. rep. NASD 1983. Career: agent life & health ins. Equitable Life, NY 1974-78; formed Vanderpool & Assoc. (group ins. sales) 1978-; co-estab./vice pres. (admin. & sales) Vanderpool & Vanderpool Ins. Svcs., Inc. 1983--; spkr., cons. Equitable Life Assur. 1976-; honors: pres.'s cabinet Equitable Life 1977-82; 2nd Nat. Leading Women's Agent 1982, 1st Nat. Small Group Agent, 3 time winner Nat. Sales Campaign for Equitable Life; leading group life & med. sales, United Pacific Life 1983; Bank of Am. award 1966; mem: Nat. Assn. Life Underwriters 1974-; Women Leader's Round Table; Equitable Life's Leading Women's Agcy. Council; Nat. Fedn. of Bus.; Canyon Hills Soccer Assn.; vol. tchr., Confrat. of Christian Doctrine; fundraising com. St. Catherine's Mil. Sch.; Peralta Hills Homeowners Assn.; Parents Against Chemical Abuse; Republican; Catholic; rec: needle work, decorating. Res: 119 S. Peralta Hills Dr Anaheim 92807 Ofc: Vanderpool and Vanderpool Ins. Svcs., 14751 Plaza Dr, Ste D, Tustin 92680

VANDERSTAY, OTTO RANDOLPH, hospital engineering director; b. Jan. 17, 1933, Houston, TX; s. Otto Randolph and Addie Byrd (Wallingford) Vanderstay; edn: engring., Univ. of Texas, Austin, 1950-51; engring., Univ. of Houston, Tex., 1956; m. Jacqueline Dochet, Oct. 9, 1968; chil: Natalie, b. 1974; Rachelle, b. 1976. Career: electronics supvr., CSU, Los Angeles, 1967-68; product specialist, Varian Assocs., Palo Alto 1966-67; president, owner, Van Ness Assocs., Glendale, 1968-74; service mgr., Honeywell, Inc., Los Angeles 1974-76; pres., Majority stockholder, Evaporation Apparatus, Inc., Los Angeles, 1976-79; dir., electronic engring., Children's Hosp. of L.A., 1980---; cons., Jet Propulsion Lab., Pasadena, 1972; cons., City of Hope, Duarte, 1982. Designed semi-portable hangar, USAF, 1956. Mem: Reserve Ofcrs. Assn. of Amer.; Natl. Guard Assn. of Calif.; A.F. Sgt's. Assn.; Assn. for the Adv. of Med. Instrumentation; Assn. of Field Service Mgrs.; Amer. Hosp. Assn. Acknowledged in 5 tech. publs. on nuclear magnetic resonance spectroscopy. Mil: Sgt., USAF, 1953-57; Capt., Calif. Natl. Guard, 1981---. Republican. Catholic. Rec: bowling, swimming, tennis. Res: 443 Edwards Pl., Glendale 91206; Office: Children's Hosp. of Los Angeles, 4650 Sunset Blvd., Los Angeles 90027.

VANDER TOP, ROGER DEAN, certified public accountant; b Nov. 28, 1953, Slayton, Minn.; s. John and Christina (Drooger) Vander Top; edn: Canby Area Vocational Tech. Inst. 1973; Modesto Jr. Coll. lic. Public Acct. 1975, So. Dak.; CPA cert., Calif. 1980. Career: staff acct. Bernell J. McGinnis CPA, Sious Falls, So.Dak., 1973-76; John A. Lane Acctcy. Corp., Modesto, Ca. 1976-81; prin. Roger D. Vander Top, CPA, Modesto 1981--; mem: Modesto CofC, Inland Soc. of Tax Consultants (treas. Modesto chpt. 1982), Calif. Soc. of CPAs; Democrat; rec: racquetball, music. Res: 2003 Coffee Rd Modesto 95355 Ofc: Roger D. Vander Top, CPA, 1500 J Street Modesto 95354

VAN DYKE, KORBIN S., electrical engineer; b. Nov. 4, 1958, Mesa, Ariz.; s. Donald M. and Kay F. (Stabenow) Van Dyke; m. Guineth E. Miller, June 24, 1978; edn: AA, Santa Rosa Jr. Coll. 1978; BS, EECS, UC Berkeley 1980, MS, EECS, 1982. Career: teaching asst., research asst., UC Berkeley, 1980-82; VLSI Systems engineer VLSI Technology Inc., San Jose 1982--; mem: IEE 1979-, ACM 1983-; publs: contbr. arts. VLSI Design (1981, 82). Res: 45770 Cayuga Ct Fremont 94539 Ofc: VLSI Technology Inc. 1101 McKay Dr San Jose 95131

VAN FLEET, RONALD NELSON, insurance agency president; b. July 20, 1931, Loma Linda; s. Nelson Merritt and Maude Alice (Poole) Van F.; m. Peggie L., June 20, 1956; children: Ronald, II, b. 1951; Sandra, b. 1952; Robyn, b. 1957; edn: BA, Antioch Univ. 1982, MA, 1984. Career: mktg. rep. Safeco Insurance Co. 1956-64; mgr. Wimmer Ins. Agency 1965-79; CEO/pres. Van Fleet Ins. Agency, Inc. 1979--; ordained minister Reorganized Ch. of Jesus Christ of Latter Day Saints 1956--; dir. Southeast Council on Alcholism and Drugs, Inc.; dir. Downey Comm. Hosp.; mem. (past pres.) Downey Kiwanis Club; past div. secty. Div. 13, Cal-Nev-Ha Dist. Kiwanis Internat.; mil: Petty Ofcr 3rd Class, USCGR 1950-56; Republican; rec: golf, R.V. travel. Res: 7901 E Harper Ave Downey 90241 Ofc: Van Fleet Ins. Agency Inc. 12027 Paramount Blvd, Ste 5 Downey 90242

VAN GORDER, GREGORY GENE, transportation co. president; b. May 10, 1954, St. Paul, Minn.; s. Lyman and Evelyn Van G.; m. Suzanne E., Sept. 13, 1980; edn: Univ. Calif. 1970-72; BS, Univ. of Wisc. 1974. Career: pres./ founder/ prin. owner Worldwide Services Inc. (limousine, sedan, bus, and air transp./delivery svc.), 1979--, cons. transp. field; area transp. cons. to 1984 Olympics Orgn. Com.; mem. CofC; Republican; Lutheran; rec: skiing, soccer, volleyball, piano, art. Ofc: Worldwide Limousine Inc. 303 No Indian Ave Palm Springs 92263

VAN HAMERSVELD, JOHN ALBERT, manufacturing co. executive; b. Sept. 13, 1915, Wilkensburg, Pa.; s. John Joseph and Anna (Dittman) Van H.; m. Betty Jane Merry, Nov. 23, 1939; children: John Walter, b. 1942, Cheryl, b. 1947; edn: BSME, Case Inst. of Tech. 1939; spl. courses, Univ. Calif., Rand Corp., Univ. Md., Johns Hopkins Univ. Career: 44 yrs. exp. in prodn. design, devel. aerospace vehicles: chief, materials engring. Engring. Div., Northrop Norair Div., 1951-64, hd. mfg. tech., engring., Engring. Labs., Hughes Aircraft Space Systems Div., 1964-68; staff scientist, Materials & Producibility Div. Lockheed-Calif. Co., 1968-81; pgm. mgr. composite technologies, DWA Composite Specialties Inc., Chatsworth 1981--. Mem. Aerospace Requirement Panel of Mats. Adv. Bd, Nat. Acad. of Scis.; SAE Mfg. Forum (exec. com.); AIAA (Nat. Aerospace Standards Com.); Soc. of Aerospace Mats. and Processes Engrs.; Soc. of Mfg. Engrs.; Am. Inst. Aero. and Astro.; Westlake Yacht Club. Publs: 27 sci. publs., presentations; Methodist; rec: profl. model bldr., sailing, photog. Res: 2826 N. Marietta Cir Thousand Oaks 91360 Ofc: DWA Composite Specialties Inc. 21119 Superior St. Chatsworth 91311

VAN HARREVELD, DONALD JOHANNES, oil company executive; b. Nov. 16, 1921, Avila, CA; s. Johannes Jacobus and Constance (Smith) Van H..; m. Gladys Hardisty, June 24, 1944; children: Donna, b. 1953; Lois, b. 1957; Lori, b. 1961; edn: US Navy V-12, Occidental Coll., 1944-5; BS, mech. engring., CalPoly, SLO 1950. Career with Union Oil Co. 1950--: pipeline engr. 1950-55; proj. engr. Oleum pipeline 1955-56; asst. supt. No. Div. Pipeline 1956-7; supt. So. Div. Pipeline 1957-60, 20" gasoline pipeline, Kenai, Alaska 1960-65, supt. No. Div. pipeline 1966--; awards: Eagle Scout, 1937, presented by James E. West, Wash DC; 1967 Alumnus of Year CalPoly, SLO; resolution, Calif. St. Assembly 1983; Calif. Parks & Rec. 15 Year Svc. Award, 1983; mem: Calif. Polytechnic Coll. Alumni Assn. (pres. 1960); Black and Gold Boosters of San Luis Obispo (pres. 1968); Pearl Harbor Survivors Assn.; Western Pipeliners (pres. 1980); Rotary, Toastmasters, Elks, Frat. Order Eagles; author: paper on Heat Transfer from Oil Storage Tanks 1950; mil: Chief Boatswain's Mate USN, 1940-46, Asia-Pac Area 3 Stars, Am. Area, Am. Defense Svc. 1 Star, Victory WWII, GCM w/ star; commend. for performance during 10/45 typhoon Okinawa; rec: skindiving, swimming, tennis. Res: 241 Westmont San Luis Obispo 93401 Ofc: Union Oil Co., POB 661, San Luis Obispo 93406

VAN HOOSE, JEFFERSON MITCHEL, manufacturing co. executive; b. May 24, 1918, Offutt, KY; s. Bert and Nancy Margaret (Ward) Van H.; m. Jacqueline Burt, May 14, 1942; children: Karen, b. 1943; Richard, b. 1948; edn: BA, L.A. Conservatory of Music & Arts 1951; Glendale Coll. 1952, 56, 64, 66; reg. Profl. Engr. (Indsl.), Calif. 1974. Career: supvr., mfg. engring. Bendix Aircraft, No. Hollywood 1951-56; supvr., mfg. engring. Librascope (Gen. Precision), Glendale 1958-67; sr. mfg. devel. engr. R.C.A., Van Nuys 1968-70; mgr./mfg. enging. Lipps, Inc., Santa Monica 1971-73; plant dir. Lipps, Inc., Tijuana, Mex. 1974-5; mgr. engring. (cons. re: DB Co.), Van Nuys 1975-6; mgr. mfg. engring. Data Products Corp., Van Nuys 1976-8, mgr. facilities 1979--; student tchr. L.A. Conservatory of Music & Arts 1949-51; awards: Zero Defects Award, Librascope 1966; mem: ASQC, Am. Instn. of Indsl. Engrs., Am. Assn. of Contamination Control; Masons (Worshipful Master 1974), Scottish Rite; prin. basoonist Inglewood Sym., San Fernando Valley Sym., Echo Park Sym., Highland Park Sym.; mil: sgt. US Army Combat Inf., 1943-6, Combat Inf. Badge, Phil. Lib. Ribbon w/ Bronze Star, Asiatic Pac. Cmpgn., WWII Victory medals; Republican; Christian; rec: golf, music, travel, teaching. Res: 1252 Highland Dr Glendale 91202 Ofc: Dataproducts Corp., 6200 Canoga Ave Woodland Hills 91365

VAN HOOSER, DAVID BARTON, manufacturing co. executive; b. July 13, 1939, Oakland; s. Cornelius Barton and Ruth David (Harrison) Van Hooser; m. JoAnn Southwick, July 2, 1979; children: David, b. 1960; Lance, b. 1963; Aaron, b. 1970; Billie, b. 1971; edn: BBA, Calif. State Coll. 1970; spl. courses in indsl. suprvn., purchasing, personnel & labor rels., 1957-69; La Salle Ext. Univ. of Law, 1966-9; Northwood Inst. of Mdsg. 1969. Career: adminstrv. asst. to the pres. Kaiser Jeep Corp., Oakland 1966-68, dist. sales mgr., So. San Francisco 1968-69; dist. mgr. Winnebago Industries, Concord, Ca. 1970, nat. bus. mgmt., Forrest City, Iowa 1970-71, nat. dealer devel. mgr., 1970-71; western regional mgr. Apollo Motor Homes, Reno, Nev. 1979, nat. sales mgr., Downey, Ca. 1980, v.p. Sales, 1981, v.p. Mktg/Sales, Carson, Ca. 1981--. Mem. Am. Mgmt. Assn.; charter mem. La Salle Univ. Alumni Assn. Republican. Ch. of Jesus Christ of Latter Day Saints. Rec: guns/desert survival. Res: Star Rte 1942, Lucerne Valley 92356 Ofc: Apollo Motor Homes, 1400 Watson Ctr Rd Carson 90745

VAN HORN, OTTO BENJAMIN, real estate broker; b. Jan. 19, 1906, Carmel; s. George Frederick and Emilie (Wyss) Van H.; m. Viola Hurd, Aug. 1927 (dec. 1981); two daus: Evalyn (Ellis), b. 1931, Joan (Heinsohn), b. 1936; m. 2d. Elgie Holman; edn: 1st grad. class, Paso Robles Union H.S. 1925; lic. real estate broker 1943-. Career: messenger boy to mgr. San Miguel branch, Bank of America (then Bank of Italy), 1925-43; real estate broker, income tax prep., 1944-84; bd. trustees Paso Robles Sch. Bd. 1942-53; honors: bronze medal for selling more than one million US war bonds, 1941; Marshall of Pioneer Day 1981; recognition 47 years of service, United Methodist Ch. Paso Robles; mem: Rotary 1942-(Paul Harris award), Masons (past Master), Scottish Rites, Al Malaikah, Eastern Star, Paso Robles Elks; Republican; Methodist; rec: golf, fishing & hunting. Res: 306 24th St, POB 1605, Paso Robles 93446

VANIAN, RUBEN ROY, clinical social worker; b. Dec. 15, 1939, Pasadena; s. Charles and Genieve (Teradian) Vanian; m. Sew Ping, Oct. 14, 1975; children: Aaron, b. 1977; Jonathan, b. 1983; edn: BA, Whitworth Coll. 1963; MSW, Univ. of Mich. 1970; PhD, Inst. for Clin. Soc. Work 1983; lic. Clin. Soc. Wkr., Calif. 1978. Career: clin. (psyc.) social wkr. Family Service Assn., Glendale 1970-72; staff psychiatric soc. wkr./instr. Univ. of Malaya Hosp., Kuala Lumpar, W. Malaysia 1972-75; clinical dir. Kern View Counseling Ctr., Delano 1976--; weekly mental health cons. local Juvenile Hall and gen. health clinic; Peer reviewer for CHAMPUS 1983. Mem: Fellow, Soc. of Clin. Soc. Work (1978); Nat. Assn. of Social Wkrs.; Delano Service Assn. (frequent spkr.); Republican; Protestant; rec: camping. Res: 711 Madison, Delano 93215 Ofc: Kern View Counseling Center, 1405 Main St. Delano 93215

VAN KIRK, JOHN ELLSWORTH, physician; b. Jan. 13, 1942, Dayton, Ohio; s. Herman Corwin and Dorothy Louise (Shafer) Van K.; m. Patricia Lynn Davis, June 19, 1966; 1 dau. Linnea, b. 1979; edn: BA, cum laude, De Pauw Univ. 1963; BS, Northwestern Univ. 1964; MD, with distinction, Northwestern Univ. Sch. Med. 1967. Career: med. intern Evanston Hosp., Northwestern Univ. 1967-68; USPHS staff assec. NIAID, sr. asst. surgeon, NIH 1968-70; res. in med./fellow in cardiology, Univ. Mich. 1970-74; instr. in intern med. 1973-74; staff cardiologist Mills Meml. Hosp., San Mateo 1974--, dir. of critical care, & dir. of The Pacemaker Clinic; Bd. Certified in Internal Medicine & Cardiovascular Disease; honors: Physician's Recognition Awards, Alpha Omega Alpha, recipient 1st prize in landscaping, State of Calif. 1977; listed Who's Who in the West 1980-81; mem: Fellow Am. Coll. of Cardiology; Am. Heart Assn.; San Mateo Co. Heart Assn., pres. 1977-79, bd. dirs. 1975-79; AMA; CMA; San Mateo Co. Med. Assn.; research: in devel. of live viral respiratory vaccines for human use; publs: arts. in med. journals; mil: USPHS 1968-70; Republican; United Brethren; rec: gardening, amateur radio, computer science. Res: 2200 Skyfarm Dr Hillsborough 94010 Ofc: 121 S San Mateo Dr San Mateo 94401

VAN MATRE, J.ED, mortician; b. May 7, 1937, Downey; s. John Stuart and Marjorie Dora (McDonald) Van Matre; m. Sherian Ann Heston, Feb. 26, 1966; edn: dipl. Calif. Coll. of Mortuary Sci., L.A. 1957; Pasadena City Coll. 1957-58, Chapman Coll., Orange 1968; Lic. Embalmer, Calif. 1958. Career: asst. mgr./Coroners rep., O'Donnall Funeral Home, Needles 1955-56; intern embalmer Ives & Warren Mort., Pasadena 9156-57; dir./embalmer Glasser & Miller Mort., Arcadia 1957-59; internat. embalmer, USN, 1959-77: 10th N.D. Caribbean Sea Frontier 1959-62, European & Mediterranean Area 1962-65, med. Adminstrv. Tech./Decedent Affairs rep. NAS Quonset Point, R.I., Mort. Insp. 1st N.D. 1965-66, Vietnam Svc. 1966-67, counselor/instr. NavHosp. Camp Pendleton, Ca. 1967-69, Med. Dept. rep. USS Fechtelor 1969-72, USS Passumpsic 1972-74, Patient Affairs chief/Decedent Affairs rep. NRMC Camp Pendleton 1974-75, Med. Dept. rep. USS Fox 1975-77; director/counselor/ embalmer El Camino Meml. Park and Mortuaries 1977--, Encinitas Mortuary, Encinitas; honors: Man of the Year 1975, Naval Regl. Med. Ctr. Camp Pendleton; Barbershopper of the Year 1980, Palomar-Pacific Chpt. SPEBSQSA; mem. San Diego Funeral Dirs. Assn.; charter mem. Toastmasters Int. de Napoli (Italy) 1964-5; mem. Soc. for the Preserv. and Encouragement of Barber Shop Quartet Singing in Am. (v.p.); Masons; Am. Legion; VFW; Loyal Order of Moose; Fleet Reserve Assn.; Indep. Order of Foresters; bd. dirs./orgnzr. Hospice of the North Coast 1979-80; mil: chief hosp. corpsman USN 1959-77, Purple Heart, Pres. Unit Cit., Navy Unit Cit., GCM (5), Navy Exped. Medal (Cuba), Armed Forces Exped. Medal (Korea), Am. Svc., Vietnam Svc., Vietnam Cpgn. medals; Republican; Episcopal; rec: travel, camping, fishing. Res:

527 Chinquapin Ave Carlsbad 92008 Ofc: Encinitas Mortuary 340 Melrose Ave Encinitas 92024

VANNUKUL, VIRACHAI, management consultant; b. Jul. 21, in Bangkok, Thailand; s. Oh Kyo Shiu and Mankong Vannukul; m. Bang-Orn, Apr. 30, 1971; edn: Dip. in higher acctg., The Sch. of Accounting, England 1959; MBA, Pepperdine Univ. 1979; MA, Claremont Grad. Sch. 1983, PhD cand. 1985; CMC, Cert. Mgmt. Cons. Career: fianacial controller Singer Sewing Machine Inc., Thailand 1960-61; v.p. adm. Thai Internat. Airline, Thailand 1962-71; pres. AIR SIAM Airline, thailand 1972-77; chief exec. Virachai Group Inc. 1978--; mgmt. cons. spec. in corp. turn-around; mem: FBIM, England; Fellow Inst. of Adm. mgmt., England; Lion Club; Bangkok Metropolitan; Thailand Royal Bangkok Sports Club; publ: Strategic Planning Development for Skybridge (1979); Buddhist; rec: pistol shooting, swimming, ping pong; Address: 400 Avenue E, Redondo Bch 90277

VAN RENSSELAER, EDWARD MAUNSELL, development co. executive; b. Sept. 23, 1937, Glendale; s. Thomas Haskins and Mary Ester (Eaton) Van R.; (family settled in Hudson Valley, NY in 1619; dir. desc. of first Patroon in New Amsterdam, now NY, Killian Killianson Van R.) children: Paige, b. 1964; Heidi, b. 1966; Ryan, b. 1972; edn: AA, Glendale City Coll. 1957; BA, CSU Los Angeles 1961; M. Bus. Tax., USC 1976; NASD Gen. Securities Principal. Career: dist. sales mgr. I.D.S., Pasadena 1963-68; regional v.p. Founders Mutual Depositor Corp., So. Calif., 1968-69; regl. v.p. May Petroleum Inc., West 11 States, 1970-76; exec. v.p. REB/PET Inc., Houston, Tex. 1976-77; exec. v.p. N.P. Energy Corp., 1977-79; pres./CEO/chmn. bd. Capital Energy and Op. Co., Calif. & Okla., 1979-82; dir. mktg./exec. v.p. World Services Group Inc., 1982-83; exec. v.p. Gibson, Reed & Kurtis Inc. and sr. mktg. dir. of parent co., Dover Devel. Corp., 1984--; recipient num. sales and mktg. awards; mem: Independent Petroleum Producers Assn.; Internat. Assn. Fin. Plnng. (Orange Co. chpt.); past v.p. Glendale Jr. CofC; W.Covina Kiwanis; Sigma Nu frat., Phi Kappa Psi (hon. forensic). Past mem. SAG, fmr. actor/singer: with The Life Guards (trio), The Statesmen (trio), and The New Christy Minstrels; mil: s/sgt. Calif. Air NG 1961-66; Republican; Prot.; rec: skiing, tennis, swimming. Res: 905 Emerald Bay, Laguna Beach 92651 Ofc: Gibson, Reed & Kurtis, 10760 Warner Ave Ste 201, Fountain Valley 92708

VAN VLECK, RICHARD WILLIAM, industrial engineering executive; b. Jan. 8, 1938, Placerville; s. Forest Allen and Mary Catherine (Revaz) Van V.; m. Barbara McKay, Nov. 4, 1961; children: Elaine, b. 1965; Crissa, b. 1967; edn: BS in indsl. engrg., Ore. State Univ. 1960. Career: officer (active duty) USN Civil Engr. Corps. in Hawthorne Nev., Puerto Rico, Vietnam 1960-67; var. positions at plant, div., and corp. levels General Foods Corp. in Ore., Minn., N.Y., and Ill. 1967-79; indsl. engring. mgr. C and H Sugar Co. 1979-83, ops. analysis mgr. 1983--; mem. Am. Inst. of Indsl. Engrs. (chap. v.p. 1982); mil: lt. USN 1960-67; Methodist (bd. trustees); rec: skiing, woodworking. Res: 3782 Argyle Street Napa 94558 Ofc: C and H Sugar Co., 830 Loring Ave Crockett 94525

VARGAS, RUDOLPH, artist; b. Apr. 20, 1904, Mexico; came to USA in 1926, nat. 1950; Gabriel and Maria (Vega) V.; m. Margaret Flotte, Aug. 8, 1931; children: Rudolph Jr., b. 1933, Christina, b. 1942; edn: Acad. of Fine Arts, Mex. Career: sculptor in wood, clay, bronze; teacher Monrovia High Sch.; commnd. to carve in wood a Madonna for the Vatican (1962); commnd. to create a large collection of contemporary and classical wood carvings, panels, large figures, and paintings for Santa Teresita Hospital in Duarte, Ca.; works incl. portraits in bronze, sculptures for film media, architl. and comml. displays; honors: recognition in print media, TV coverage, and a 30-min. film on his work; recognition from Gov. Brown Jr., Pres. Carter, City of Ontario, num. awards incl. Calif. Carvers Guild; listed in Who's Who in Am. Art, Internat. Ency. Degli Artisti (Acona, Italy), Who's Who in the West; mem: San Diego CofC (Xmas com.), Calif. Carvers Guild; rec: electronics, photog. Res: 1074 No Herbert Ave Los Angeles 90063 Ofc: 3661 Whittier Blvd Los Angeles 90023

VARRELMANN, ROBERT GALE, architect; b. Aug. 5, 1947, Los Angeles; s. Gale Lawrence and Jane E. (Weller) V.; m. Diane, Sep. 8, 1968; children: Erik, b. 1971; Sheri, b. 1975; Jason, b. 1979; edn: B.Arch., CalPoly, San Luis Obispo 1971; courses, Ft. Benjamin Harrison, Ind. 1971, 72; lic. architect, St. Calif. 1983. Career: draftsman/designer James Dodd & Assoc., 1973-4, Churchill-Zlatunich Architects., 1974, Hawley-Stowers and Assoc., 1975, Higgins and Root Architects, 1975-6, The Griffin/Joyce Assoc., 1976, Oscar E. Sohns Arch., 1976-9; owner/prin. Varrelmann Design, San Jose 1979--; awards: appreciation, Future Business Leaders Of Am. 1982; mem. AIA, 1984-; mem. Valle del Sur Art Guild 1976-81 (pres. 1980), Better Bus. Bur.; Little League, mgr. 1980-83; San Jose Girls Soccer coach 1982-83; Cub Scouts cubmaster 1982; profl. potter: 1st and 3rd awards Gilroy Art Show 1975, 80; merit award Santa Clara Valley AIA Art Show, Montalvo, Saratoga 1975; 2nd award Calif. Art Festival, Morgan Hill 1976; 1st award Calif. Art Show Pottery & Macrame, Morgan Hill 1977; artist of year, Morgan Hill Art Guild 1977; 1st award Calif. Art Festival, Morgan Hill 1978; mil: capt. USAR 1971-73; Republican; Methodist. Address: Varrelmann Design, 564 Jesse James Dr San Jose 95123

VARTERESSIAN, KEGHAM ARSHAVIR, chemical engineer (ret.); b. Jan. 25, 1908, Bahcecik, Izmit, Turkey, nat. 1941; s. Arshavir and Heranouche (Sinanian) V.; m. Araxy Ayrandjian, 1946; children: Armen, b. 1947; Astrid, b. 1951; edn: diploma, Am. Univ. in Cairo 1925; BS, Penn. State Coll. 1930, MS, 1931, PhD 1935. Career: research asst./instr. Penn. State Coll., 1930-38; chemical engr. Standard Oil Devel. Co., Linden, N.J. 1938-39; research assoc./instr.

Penn. State Coll. 1939-45; instr. and head Chem. Dept., American Univ., Cairo, Egypt 1945-49; assoc. to senior chem. engr. Argonne (Ill.) National Laboratory, 1949-73: sr. chem. engr. Chem. Engrg. Div. (1950-55, 65-68), Reactor Analysis and Safety Div. (1968-73), instr./chmn. Chem. Engrg. Dept., Internat. Sch. of Nuclear Sci. and Engrg. (1955-65), ret. 1973-; honors: Phi Lambda Upsilon, Honorary Chemical Fraternity 1928; Sigma Xi, Honarary Scientific Research Soc. 1935; mem: Am. Chem. Soc. 1929; Am. Inst. Chem. Engrs. 1943; fellow Am. Inst. of Chemists 1968; Nat. Geographic Soc. 1937; Beachcliff Homeowners' Assn. 1975; Seascape Improvement Assn. 1977; publs: num. sci. papers, book chapters, journal arts. rel. to petroleum and nuclear energy fields; Christian; rec: languages, math., sci. Res: 130 Paseo Farallon Aptos 95003

VASSILIADIS, ALKIVIADIS A., realtor; b. May 12, 1935, Athens, Greece, nat. 1968; s. Alkiviadis and Evangelia (Mouzas) V.; m. Carol Marie Hatounian, June 5, 1976; 1 son, Andrew, b. 1983; edn: BS, CSU San Diego 1968; lic. real estate sales, 1968, lic. broker 1971. Career: salesman Garris Realty 1969-74; broker/ realtor Laki Realty, San Diego 1974--; awards: best neighborhood bldg. improvement, Mid-City CofC 1976; mem: Bd. of Realtors; MLS; AHEPA; Mid-City CofC (v.p. 1978-); Kiwanis; Masons; Hellenic Cultural Soc.; Republican; Greek Orthodox; rec: soccer, swimming, bowling, dancing. Res: 4421 Yerba Santa Dr San Diego 92115 Ofc: Laki Realty, 2650 Camino Del Rio, Ste. 104, San Diego 92108

VASSTROM, LEIF WILHELM, company president; b. Dec. 11, 1951, Hango, Finland; s. Curt Eric and Peppina (Blomquist) V.; m. Alexis Christine 1983; edn: BA in mktg. Swedish Comml. Coll., Helsinki, Finland 1974; Lt. (Silver Cross Honours) Finnish Officers Sch., 1975. Career: vice pres. Silversand Ab, Hango, Finland 1975-76; mktg. mgr. Hot Spot Oy, Helsinki, Finland 1976-76, export mgr. Finnhot Oy (Hot Spot Co.), 1976-78; founder/pres., chief exec. The Silver Group Inc., San Francisco, CA 1979--; pres. Silver Solarium of NY, Inc., New York 1981--; pres. Silver Fountain Technology Inc., San Francisco 1984--; mem. San Francisco CofC, Danish/American CofC; publs: editor Veritas & Jocus 1973-74, ed. Finnish Officers Year Book 1974-75; mil: lt. Finnish Army 1974; rec: sailing, travel, music, wine. Res: 3953 Washington St San Francisco 94118 Ofc: 655 Montgomery, 17th Flr, San Francisco 94111

VAUGHN, MARY, nursing home administrator; b. Apr. 20, 1930, Trafford, Ala.; d. Grover Webster and Vivian Lenora (Dorman) V.; div. James T. Lovvorn, 1959; edn: Birmingham Bus. Co. 1952, Howard Coll. 1959, Univ. Ala. 1960-62; Calif. lic. nursing home adminstr., notary public. Career: loan mgr. Globe Fin. Co., 1950-63; partner/opr. Diplomat Printing & Letter Co., 1963-69; owner/adminstr. San Diego Intermediate Care Center, 1969--, pres. Balboa Manor, Inc. 1972-; sec./treas. Agusta Fraser Loan Fund 1983-4; recipient two safety awards, Indsl. Indemnity Ins. Co. 1973, 74; mem. adv. com. to US Cong. Rep. Jim Bates 1973-; mem. S.D. Com. on the Handicapped 1979-80; mem: Quota Club (charter pres. Birmingham, Ala. 1968); Calif., Am. Health Care Assns.; Am. Coll. Nursing Home Adminstrs.; Nat. Assn. Social Wkrs.; Am., Calif. Nursing Home Assns.; orgns: Bus. & Profl. Women's Club (pres. Birmingham chpt. 1967-9), S.D. Opera, S.D. Mus. Natural Hist., S.D. Mus. of Man, City Beautiful of S.D., The Mus./Klee Wyk Soc. (Com. of 100), S.D. Zool. Soc., Community Video Ctr., Nat. Notary Assn.; author: Exploring Mental Therapy (1978); Democrat; Methodist; rec: rare fruit grower, exercise, bridge. Res: 2804 C St. San Diego 92102 Ofc: S.D. Intermediate Care Center, 1119 28th St. San Diego 92102

VAUGHN, JOHN VERNON, industrialist - civic leader; b. June 24, 1909, Grand Junction, CO; s. John S. and Alice A. (Baylis) Vaughn; AB, UCLA, 1931; m. Dorothy M. Pickrell, Glendale, Calif., Oct. 12, 1934; chil: Mrs. Richard H. (Dorothy Dee) Stone, b. 1936; John Spencer, b. 1939. Career: asst. credit mgr., salesman, br. mgr., Natl. Lead Co., 1932-37; sales mgr., Sillers Paint & Varnish Co., 1937-46; pres., dir., 1946-60; merged with Benjamin Moore & Co., 1959; propr., pres., chmn. Dartell Labs., 1959-70; v. chmn. bd., Crocker Natl. Bank, 1970-74; cons., Coopers & Lybrand, 1974---; dir., Calif. Fed Svgs. & Loan Assn., Orthopedic Hosp. pres. 1973; chmn. 1974---; Awards: UCLA Disting. Serv. Award, 1956, Community Serv. Award, 1969; UCLA Alumnus of Yr., 1971; L.A. Realty Bd. Most Distinguished Citizen, 1972; LAACC Comm. Serv. Award, 1974, other honors. Mem: Jonathan Club, 1945-73; dir. 1961-64; pres. 1964; San Marino Lodge, F&AM 1945---; Scottish Rite, 1946---; charter Young Presidents' Orgn., 1951-56; dir. L.A. Better Bus. Bur., 1952---; chmn. bd. 1959-61; pres. L.A. Paint, Varnish & Lacquer Assn., 1952; v.p., Natl. Paint, Varnish & Lacquer Assn., 1953; San Gabriel Country Club, 1955---, dir., v.p. 1965-68; v.p. chmn., San Marino Rec. Com., 1956-58; pres. UCLA Alumni Assn., 1957-58; regent, Univ. of Calif. 1958-59; dir., L.A. CofC, 1961---, v.p. 1964, v.p. treas., 1966, pres. 1969, chmn. 1970; dir. YMCA, L.A. 1965---; chmn. Cits. Adv. Council on Pub. Transportation, 1965-67; dir., Natl. Conf. of Chrs. and Jews, Inc., 1966---; dir., Chancellor's Assocs., 1966---; Chmn. of bd., Recon/Optical Inc., dir., Forest Law, dr., Amer. Security; dir., United Way; CMSI Found.; trustee, Welfare Plannign Council, 1967---; dir., Calif. Mus. of Sci. and Indus., 1968---; Regent, Forest Lawn Meml. Park, 1968---; trustee, Natl. Safety Council, 1968---; dir., v.p., Mgmt. Council for Merit Employment, Trng. & Research, 1969---; v. chmn., Invest in Amer., 1970---; trustee, Claremont Men's Coll., 1970-71; regent, Pepperdine Univ., 1972---; World Bus. Council, 1972---; dir., Friends of Claremont Colls., 1973---; pres., Calif. Mus. Found., 1972---; pres. L.A. Clearing House Assn., 1973---; dir. So. Calif. Visitors Council, 1970---; v.p., treas., World Affairs Council, 1970---; Newcomen Soc., Town Hall, Lincoln Club, Calif. Club; pres., Beta Theta Pi and Beta Theta Pi Alumni Assn. of So. Calif. Republican. Presbyterian. Rec: hunting, stream fihsing, golf. Res: 1000 W. Sixth St., Los Angeles 90017.

VAWTER, HENRY MICHAEL, insurance brokerage executive; b. June 25, 1943, Oakland; s. Howard M. and Virginia Mae (Marvin) V.; m. Cheryl Gray, June 25, 1967; children: James, b. 1962; Michael, b. 1969; Diana, b. 1974; edn: BA, CSU Hayward 1967, M.Pub. Adm. 1968. Career: acct. mgr., salesman Hardware Mutual Ins. Co., San Francisco 1967-69; salesman Calif. Coastal Ins. 1969-71, partner 1971-, v.p. 1978-83, maj. stockhldr./ pres./ chief exec. 1983--; bd. dirs.: Foothill Sanitary Supply Co., Leisure Products, Inc.; adv. council United Pacific Ins. Co. 1983-84; profl. awards: agent of year 1968, Hardware Mutual; agent of the year 1974, Penn Mutual Life; achievement, Kempster Ins. Co. 1979, 80, 81, 82; mem: Profl. Ins. Agents, Ins. Svcs. Unlimited, Ins. Mktg. Svcs., Calif. Cast Metal Assn., Assoc. Bldrs. & Contractors, AHEPA, Lafayette CofC 1978-81; asst. coach Castro Valley Girls Softball League; vol. Cub and Boy Scouts of Am. 1973-; dev. group ins. pgms. for State of Calif., Calif. Cast Metals Assn., St. Calif. Auto Dismantlers Assn., and Assoc. Builders & Contractors; Republican; Orthodox; rec: fishing, camping, skiing, boating, travel. Res: 5787 Coldwater Dr Castro Valley 94546 Ofc: California Coastal Ins., 1020 Aileen St Lafayette 94549

VAZIRI, NOSRATOLA DADIR, physician; b. Oct. 13, 1939, Tehran, Iran; s. Abbas Dabir and Tahera V.; edn: MD, Tehran Univ. 1966; splst: Internist and Nephrologist. Career: chief Div. of Nephrology, UC Irvine Med. Ctr. 1978--, prof. Dept. Med. 1982-, v. chmn. Academic Affairs, Dept. Med. 1982-; cons. nephrology, Veterans Adm., Long Beach 1974-; dir. Hemodialysis Unit, UCIMC 1977--; edtl. bd. Internat. Journal of Artificial Organs and Critical Care Update; edtl. cons. num. med. journals; Scientific Adv. Com. Nat. Kidney Found.; honors: faculty mem. Alpha Omega Alpha; Golden Apple Award, UCI Coll. of Med. 1977, named Outstanding Tchr. (5); Kaiser Permanente, UCI Found. 1977; mem: Am. Bd. Internal Med. 1972; fellow Am. Coll. of Physicians; Am. Soc. Artificial Organs; Am. Soc. Nephrology; Am. Found. Clinical Research; author 22 book chapters, 146 sci. papers. Res: 66 Balboa Coves Newport Beach 92663 Ofc: UC Irvine Medical Ctr, 101 City Drive So. Orange 92668

VEGA, BENJAMIN URBIZO, municipal court judge; b. Jan. 18, 1916, La Ceiba, Honduras; s. Benjamin Urbizo and Catalina (Tablas) Vega; BA, USC, 1938, postgrad., 1939-40; LLB, Pacific Coast Univ. Law, 1941; admit. prac., Calif. 1947; US Dist. Ct. for So. Dist., 1947; Bd. Immigration Appeals, 1948; US Supreme Court, 1958. Career: legal practice, Anderson, McPharlin & Connors, L.A., 1947-48; Newman & Newman, L.A., 1948-51; Dep. D.A., Co. of L.A., 1951-66; judge, L.A. Co. Municipal Ct., East L.A. Judicial Dist., 1966---; Rec. award for oustanding service as judge, L.A. Mayor Sam Yorty 1973, Distinguished Pub. Serv. Award, 1973; past mem: Inglewood, E. L.A., Montebello, Amer., Inter-Amer., Bar Assns.; Amer. Judicature Soc.; L.A. Lawyers Club; past bd. dirs., Youth Opportunities Found. mem. Conf. Calif. Judges, Municipal Ct. Judges' Assn., L.A. Co. Mil: Cpl., USAF 1942-46. Democrat. Catholic. Rec: world travel, collects phonograph records, books. Office: 4837 E. 3rd St., Los Angeles 90022.

VEITCH, STEPHEN WILLIAM, investment counselor; b. Aug. 19, 1927, Albuquerque, NM; s. Kenneth Easton and Edna (Miller) V.; m. Nancy Baker, July 28, 1951; children: Christopher Oxnard, b. 1953; Julia Blair, b. 1958; edn: BA, Univ. New Mexico 1949; JD, Stanford Law Sch. 1957. Career: probate adminstr. Wells Fargo Bank 1957-59; sr. v.p. Vanstrum & Towne, Inc., 1959-82, pres./CEO 1982--; dir. Anza Pacific Corp. 1960-76; Advis. bd. Anza Shareholders' liquidating trust, 1976-; pres. Oxnard Found. 1979-; secty. William Knox Holt Found. 1978-; mem: Pacific Union Club (SF), Menlo Circus Club (Atherton), Commonwealth Club (SF); Sigma Chi Frat.; mil: USN 1945-6, 1st lt. USAF 1950-4; Republican; Episcopal. Res: 33 Spencer Ln Atherton 94025 Ofc: Van Strum & Towne, Inc., 505 Sansome St, Ste. 1001, San Francisco 94111

VELASCO, ANTONIO RAMIREZ, physician; b. Aug. 23, 1953, Colima, nat. 1975; s. Jose Dolores and Teresa (Ramirez) V.; m. Isabel Guzman, June 18, 1977; children: Anisvel, b. 1978, Beatriz, b. 1982; edn: BA, UC Santa Cruz 1975, MD, (Valedictorian, grad. spkr.) UC Davis 1979. Career: research asst. Minority Biomed. Support Pgm., UC Santa Cruz, 1972-4, coord. Crown Summer Pre-med. Pgm., 1973-5; mem. Bd. Admissions, UC Davis Med. Sch., 1975-7; dir. Clinica Tepati, Sacramento 1976-7; chief med. adv. US Bur. of Health Svcs., Pesticide Pgms. 1982-3; asst. clin. prof. UC San Francisco Sch. of Med. 1982-3; currently: pvt. practice (family medicine); cross cultural medicine pgm. director; vol. pesticide health related edn. and consulting; tchg. Family Practice Res. Pgm. Recipient outstanding med. student award, Clin. Tepati, 1977; diplomate Am. Bd. of Family Practice 1982; mem. bd. dirs. Migrant Student Pgm. Monterey Co. 1983, bd. dirs. TRUCHA Alcohol Rehab. Pgm., Salinas 1983; mem: Calif. Med. Assn., Fellow Am. Acad. of Family Practice, La Raza Med. Assn.; Cong. de Pueblos Unidos; Democrat; rec: photog., running (10K), mechanics, carpentry. Res: 1662 Cambrian Dr Salinas 93906 Ofc: A.R. Velasco, MD Inc., 1326 Natividad Rd, Ste D, Salinas 93906

VELASQUEZ, LENA, planning research analyst; b. May 20, 1955, South Gate; d. Gilbert V. and Dellas Velasquez; edn: BA, w/ honors, CSU Los Angeles 1978; MPL/MPA (M.Plng./M.Pub.Adm.), USC 1981. Career: economic plng. analyst Southern Calif. Assn. of Governments, L.A. 1982; research plnr. Highland Park Improvement Assn. 1981-82; training exec. Ashton-Tate, Culver City 1983--, tng. cons. for indus., bus., and govt.; honors: Young Careerist, Montebello-Sierra Mar Dist. Bus. & Profl. Women (1983), Scapa Praetor, USC (1981), Minorities in Plng. (1979), Las Rosas Debutantes, Montebello (1971); mem: American Plng. Assn., Am. Soc. for Public Adminstrn., The Planners Circle, Bus. and Profl. Women; works: research projects in govt. plng. areas; afil: Nat. Orgn. for Latino and Elected Ofcls.; rec:

skiing, aerobic dance, civic affairs. Res: 631 North 19th St Montebello 90640 Ofc: Ashton-Tate, 10150 W. Jefferson Blvd Culver City 90230

VERDUGO, SANDRA CARLEEN, university administrator; b. Sep. 28, 1941, Springerville, Ariz.; d. Sidney V. and Mildred (Rudd) Brown; m. George Verdugo, Oct. 4, 1961; children: George Jr., b. 1962; Shawna, b. 1965; edn: BA, psychol., CSU Fullerton 1974. Career: prodn. control coord./mgr. Jorgensen Steel Co., Lynwood 1964-71; fine arts asst., CSU Fullerton 1972-75; adm. asst., Youth Svcs. Program, Costa Mesa 1975-76; bus. mgr., Grad. Sch. Mgmt., UC IRvine 1976-79; gen. mgr. Sch. Biological Sciences, UC Irvine 1979--; system-wide rep. to Academic Bus. Officers 1980-82; v.p., Staff Assoc., UC Irvine 1978-79; honors: selected mgmt. consultant/assesor for UC systemwide mgmt. training; mem: v.p. Little League Assn 1973-74; consultant Women's Resources Ctr., UC; rec: dancing, racquet ball, writing, spectator sports. Res: 24552 Dardania Mission Viejo 92691 Ofc: UC Irvine, Sch. of Biological Sciences, Campus Dr Irvine 92717

VERGARA, MICHAEL PATRICK, computer programmer; b. Dec. 12, 1953, Tucson, Ariz.; s. Antonio Edward and Carolyn Pauline (Mulholland) V.; edn: BS, San Diego State Univ. 1979. Career: dir. info. systems Hartsons Ambulance Svc., San Diego 1980-83; systems devel. programmer Management Analysis Co., San Diego 1983--; computer related cons. to Hartsons Ambulance; mem: DPMA ; ACM; Mus. of Photographic Arts; Smithsonian Assoc.; Catholic; rec: photog., music. Res: 3075 51st St San Diego 92105 Ofc: Management Analysis Co., 11095 Torreyana Rd San Diego 92121

VERGARA, RODOLFO QUEMUEL, real estate broker, insurance executive; b. Dec. 3, 1937, Manila, Philippines, nat. 1973; s. Gonzalo G. and Susana B. (Quemuel) V.; m. Estrella De Vera, June 15, 1968; children: Vladimir, b. 1969; Faye, b. 1980; edn: BBA, Univ. of the East 1960; real estate salesman, Anthony Sch. 1976; real estate broker, Lumbleau Real Estate Sch. 1979; cont. edn., Exacta Sch. of Real Estate 1982; real estate broker 1980. Career: salesman Key Realty, San Francisco 1976-77; sales mgr. Regent Realty, San Francisco 1977-79; exec. v.p./treas. Homemakers Investment Corp., Daly City 1980-81; pres. Filam Inv. Corp., Daly City 1980-82; dist. mgr. Am. Bankers Life, Miami, Fla., 1981; broker/owner The Growers Realty, Daly City, 1980--; cooperating broker Roland Land Investment Co., Inc., 1982-; honors: Millionaires Club, Am. Bankers Life, 1982; Super Sales Starter Club, Am. Bankers Life 1981; SAM Briefcase Honor Club, Am. Bankers Life 1981; mem: S.F. Bd. of Realtors; Nat., Calif. Assn. Realtors; Notary Public; Univ. of the East Alumnae; Phil. Coll. of Commerce Assn.; United Pangasinanes of Am.; Homeowners Assn.; Republican; Catholic; rec: golf, bowling, swimming. Res: 30 Clayton Ct Daly City 94014 Ofc: The Growers Realty, 6069 Mission St Daly City 94014

VERMA, SANJIV, physician; b. Sept. 7, 1948, Mandalay (Burma); s. Shiv Lal and Yagya Vati (Marwaha) V.; m. Ila Verma, June 16, 1979; children: Prashant, b. 1980; Nishant, b. 1981; edn: pre med., DAV Coll., Chandigarh, India 1966; MB, BS, SMS Med. Coll., Jaipur, India 1971; MD, 1974. Career: resident physician, dept. Pediatrics, Mt Sinai Hosp., Chicago, Ill. 1974-76; postgrad fellow, dept. Pediatrics Allergy and Clinical Immunology, L.A.C. USC Med. Ctr., L.A., 1976-78; practicing physician, Ventura 1978--; clinical instr., Dept. Pediatrics, LAC USC Med. Ctr. 1976-78; top of class, MB, BS, 1st year (Anatomy) SMS Med. Coll., Jaipur, India; mem: Am. Acad. of Allergy; Sting, Allergy Com.; Los Angeles Allergy Soc.; Calif. Med. Council; Ventura Co. Med. Assn.; Gen. Medical Council, London, U.K.; author: num. publs. ain fields of asthma and allergies 1976-78; rec: tennis, photog., chess, scrabble. Res: 1297 Halifax Court Ventura 93004 Ofc: Sanjiv Verma, Inc., 3003 Loma Vista, Ste. A, Ventura 93003

VESELY, ERIC GARRIGUE, computer industry consultant; b. Feb. 26, 1935, Chgo.; s. Eric Jan and Gloria Mae (Rezebek) V.; m. Ruth Perls, 1956; children: Karen, b. 1963; Gloria, b. 1966; edn: BS, Univ. Ill. 1956; JD, De Paul Univ. 1958. Career: pgmmr. US Gymsum, Chgo. 1956-58; site mgr. RCA, Chgo. 1958-66; GE-600 proj. mgr. General Electric, Phoenix, Ariz. 195-66; pgmmmg. mgr. Mobility Systems, San Jose, 1966-67; USAF Mol Mission support mgr. Litton Ind., Sunnyvale 1967-69; pres. Applied Digital Systems, Palo Alto 1969-74; prin. The Analyst Workbench, San Francisco 1979--; lectr./cons. ADPAC Corp. and Peat, Marwick & Mitchell; mem: Phi Alpha Delta Legal Frat., Independent Computer Consultants Assn.; num. arts. in computer publs.; under contract to Prentice Hall; Republican; rec: chess, bridge. Address: 830 Urbana Circle San Francisco 94127

VESELY, LARRY JOE, architect; b. May 28, 1951, Laramie, Wyo.; s. Wayne Harold and Alice Nadine (Oder) V.; edn: BS, CalPoly, Pomona 1975; lic. architect, Calif. 1980. Career: sr. designer/draftsman Tozier & Assoc., Claremont 1973-79; proj. arch. E. Warren Bruce, AIA, Riverside 1979-83; chief arch. L A Wainscott & Assoc., Inc., Grand Terrace 1983--; Passive Solar Design Spkr.; recipient: Key Man Award, Riverside Jaycees, 1983; mem: Am. Inst. Architects; Soc. of Am. Mil. Engrs. 1982-83; Riverside Jaycees (pres. 1983-4); Kiwanis; mil: SFC, USAR 1970-; Republican; Presbyterian; rec: bicycling, golf, racquetball, woodworking. Res: 1935 Arroyo Dr Riverside 92506 Ofc: L A Wainscott & Assoc., Inc., 22400 Barton, Ste. 200, Grand Terrace 92324

· VICIAN, ELIZABETH OVERGAARD, psychologist; b. Aug. 15, 1934, Albert Lea, MN; d. Raymod O. ad Cora Marie (Ormseth) Overguard; Ph.D. Univ. Humanistic Studies 1979, M.A. San Jose St. Univ. 1965, B.A. Luther Coll. 1956; Postgrad. U.C. Santa Cruz/U.C.S.F. Med. Sch.; m. Thomas A.

Vician, Sr., 1957; Dir. Counseling Garey H.S., Pamona, Calif. 1964, Dir. Counseling Brownell Sch. Gilroy, Calif., 1966, Prof. of Psychology and Counseling Chabot Coll. Hayward, Calif. 1967---, Psychologist in priv. prac., Palo Alto, Calif. 1978---; Consul. with Dr. Ira Progoff in The Intensive Jour., lic. marriage, family, and child therapist; mem. A.A.U.P. World Future Of Soc. Sierra Club, Smithsonian Assoc., Center Study of Dem. Inst., Calif. Teac. Assn., San Andreas Health Council; Calif. Pers. & Guid. Assn.; Calif. Assn. of Marriage and Family Therapist. Republican. Lutheran. Rec: piano, swimming, jogging. Res: 3718 Redwood Cr., Palo Alto 94306; Office: 316 Town & Country Village, Palo Alto 94301.

VICKERS, DAVID LEROY, manufacturing company executive; b. Jan. 15, 1942, Detroit, Mich.; s. Vay Aldon Sr. and Vada Ann (Gaw) V.; m. Tomiye Tado, Apr. 22, 1961; children: David Jr., b. 1962; Steven T., b. 1965; edn: MBA, CSU Long Beach 1972; BS, ind. tech., Tenn. Tech. Univ. 1967. Career: chief indsl. engr. Pacific Tube Co., Commerce 1967-73; ops. auditor Ameron Inc., Monterey Park 1973-74; v.p. mfg. Ameron HC&D, Honolulu, Hi. 1974-81; dir. mfg. Ameron Inc., Monterey Park 1981-84; v.p./gen. mgr. H.G. Fenton Materials Co., San Diego 1984--; co. ofcr. H.G. Fenton Materials Co., Premixed Concrete Co., San Diego, Ameron HC&D, Honolulu; prof. bus. Univ. of Hawaii, 1978-81; lectr. Loyola Marymount Univ. 1970-74; mem: Am. Inst. Indsl. Engrs. 1969-; So. Calif. Work Simplification Assn. (pres. 1972); Greater L.A. Chpt. Quality Circles Inst. 1982; mil: E-5, USN 1959-63; Republican; Methodist; rec: jogging, racquetball, wine collecting. Res: 29177 Oceanridge Dr Rancho Palos Verdes 90274 Ofc: c/o H.G. Fenton Mat. Co., 702 Washington St San Diego 92112

VICKERY, BRIAN HENRY, physiologist/pharmaceutical co. executive; b. Jan. 25, 1941, Driffield, E. Yorkshire, England; s. Henry Charles and Olive Mary (Hyde) V.; m. Margaret, Mar. 28, 1964; children: Gillian, b. 1967; Alison, b. 1971; Christopher, b. 1972; edn: BSc., honors, London Univ. 1963, PhD 1970. Career: endocrinologist British Drug House Ltd., U.K. 1963-67; with Syntex Research, Palo Alto 68--, biologist/ sr. biologist 1968-70, staff researcher 1970-72, dept. hd. 1972--, sr. scientist, 1981--; recipient: 11th Hon. Gregory Pincus Lectureship, Wayne State Univ. Sch. Med. 1983; mem.: Soc. for the Study of Reproduction; Soc. for the Study of Fertility; Soc. for Endocrinol.; NY Acad. of Sciences; Endocrine Soc.; AAAS; Am. Soc. for Andrology (treas. 1984-); Soc. for the Adv. of Contraception (dir. 1982-); orgns: Santa Clara Valley Science and Engring. Fair Assn.; United Way Of Santa Clara County; publs: 160 profl. papers, book chpts.; 14 US patents; 17 (commercially avail.) audiovisual aids; rec: sculpture. Res: 20279 Carol Ln Saratoga 95070 Ofc: Syntex Research, 3401 Hillview Ave Palo Alto 94304

VIERHELLER, RALPH CHARLES, veterinarian/ hospital administrator; b. May 12, 1915, Fresno; s. Charles Emil and Clara May (Sloan) V.; m. Edna Helen Kettlewell, 1940, dec. 1975; children: Edward Charles, b. 1942; Denis Keith, b. 1944; Janet Lynn, b. 1954; edn: Fresno St. Coll. 1933-35; DVM, Colo. State Univ. 1939. Career: small animal veterinarian, Los Angeles 1939-42; owner/adminstr. Whittier Dog & Cat Hosp., Whittier 1946-75; pres. Drs. Vierheller-Clark, Inc., Pico Rivera 1961-75; owner/operator Animal Eye Clinic, La Habra 1976--; spkr., nat. and local vet. orgns.; awards: Distinguished Life Mem. SCVMA; Am. Vet Med Assn. Practitioner Research Award 1971; recognition award for research into eye anomalies of Collie dogs, Collie Club of Am.; mem: charter diplomat (1970) Am. Coll. Vet. Surgeons; Coll. Ophthal (pres. 1978-79); Am. Hosp. Assn.; So. Calif. Vet. Med. Assn (pres. S.E. chpt. 1961); Am. Vet. Med. Assn. (dir. 1961-63); Am. Soc. Vet. Ophthal (pres 1964-65); So. Calif. Vet. Golfers Assn. (pres. 1964-65); Calif. Vet. Med. Assn (pres. 1968-69); Rotary (dirc. Whittier Club 1960-62); publs: num. arts. on orthopedic and ophthalmic surg., vet. med. journals; Republican; Protestant; rec: private pilot, golf, travel. Res: 1651 El Portal Dr La Habra 90631 Ofc: The Animal Eye Clinic, 1301-F Beach Blvd La Habra 90631

VINYARD, JACK LEE, company owner; b. Dec. 25, 1929, St. Louis, Mo.; s. Ralph R. and Eva E. (Corder) V.; m. Ruth M., Nov. 14, 1953, div. 1977; children: Renee, b. 1956; Lisa, b. 1957; Jack, Jr., b. 1958; stu. Citrus Coll., 2 yrs. Career: Universal Equip. opr. Ace Pipeline Const. Co. Inc., Pomona, CA 1960-75; owner Vinyards Backhoe Svc. 1975--; contr. So. Calif. Gas Co. (Inland Div.), and So. Calif. Water Co. (Claremont); awards: Golden Rodent of Dugout 95, Azusa Nat. Order of Trench Rats; Best Dugout, in US, group two, Disabled Am. Veterans 1975-76; mem: Masonic Lodge 627; V.F.W. Post 8070 Azusa; D.A.V. chpt. 44, W. Covina; Loyal Order of Moose Lodge 650 Pomona; mil: pfc USMC 1948-52, Korean Medal 4 battle stars, pres. unit cit. two stars; Republican; Prot.; rec: travel, Am. hist. Address: Vinyards Backhoe Service, 2528 Kendall St La Verne 91750

VISCOTT, DAVID, psychiatrist, radio broadcaster/writer; b. May 24. 1938, Boston, Mass.; s. Hiram and Shirley (Levy) V.; m. Katherine Random, Dec. 31, 1982; children: Elizabeth, b. 1960; Penelope, b. 1963; Jonathan, b. 1965; Melanie, b. 1970; edn: BA, Dartmouth Coll. 1959; MD, Tufts Univ. 1963. Career: medical research St. Margarets Hosp., Dorchester, Mass. 1960-63; resident, intern, clinical assoc. in US hosps. 1963-67; sr. psychiatrist/consultant Boys Detention Ctr., Mass. Div. of Youth Svc. 1966-70; instr. psychiatry Boston Univ. Med. Sch. 1968-78; private practice 1968--; fellow in forensic psychiatry, Boston Univ. Law Medicine Inst. 1967-8; asst. clin. prof. psychiatry UCLA Med. Sch. 1980-; host Sat. Evening talk show on KABC radio; faculty, Cambridge (MA) Ctr. for Adult Edn.; awards: Mosby Book Prize, Tufts Univ. 1963; author: Making of a Psychiatrist (best seller, book of month, 1973), Risking (1977), Winning (1973), Language of Feelings (1975), How to Live with Another Person (1974); articles in Psychiatry Today, Advertising Age, Todays

Health, others; mem: fellow, N.Y. Acad. of Sci., Am. Psychiat. Assn., PEN Internat., Royal Soc. for Health, Mass. Med. Soc, Phi Sigma Delta; rec: clarinet, flute, piano, antiques. Address: 5717 W 2nd St Los Angeles 90036

VISITACION, MARCY, civil/structural engineer; b. Apr. 1, 1943, Bacarra, Ilocos Norte, Philippines, nat. 1963; s. Pedro Agustin and Pia Asuncion (Cadabuna) V.; m. Dolores Y. Locquiao, Dec. 27, 1969; children: Derek (adopted), b. 1966; Marc, b. 1970; Michael, b. 1972; Lisa, b. 1976; edn: dip. arch. drafting, Kauai Tech. Sch. 1963; BS, CalPoly 1968; reg. Civil Engr., Calif. 1975; Structural Engr., Hawaii 1977. Career: engring. asst./assoc. L.A. Dept. of Water & Power, Los Angeles 1968-76; prin. engr. M. Visitacion & Assoc., Inc., Lihue, Hawaii 1976-78; design engr. Steelform Contracting Co., Santa Fe Springs 1978-79; chief designer Don Perryman & Assoc., Inc., Walnut 1979-82; prin. engr. M. Visitacion & Assoc., Inc., West Covina 1983--; awards: Hartwood Award, All-State Drafting Contest-Hawaii 1962, DO., 1963; mem: Struc. Engrs. Assn. of So. Calif. 1979-; Aloha Softball League (dir. 1972); Menehune Golf Club (dir. 1973); Menehune Bowling Club (pres. 1974-75); Galaxie Little League (mgr. 1980-); Pacifica Golf Club, 1983-; rec: golf, Little League. Address: M. Visitacion and Assoc., Inc., 603 Sentous Ave W. Covina 91792

VISSERS, RICHARD HENRI, insurance agency president; b. June 12, 1941, Den Haag, Holland, nat. 1961; s. Jacobus and Lenie V.; children: Marisha, b. 1960; Merrick, b. 1962; edn: Fullerton Coll. 1969; Am. Coll. Bryn Mawr 1975; CLU, cert. life underwriter. Career: insurance agent/ mgr./ and tng. dir., ins. bus., Hollywood, Ca.; owner/pres. Vissers Ins. Agency, 1973--, opened 2d office in 1983; owner/pres. Vissers Express Travel (now w/ 14 agents), 1980--; awards: Nat. Ins. awards; mem: Nat. Orgn. of Life Underwriters; Assn. of Retail Travel Agents; World Affairs Council; So. African Trade Assn. (founder); rec: travel, swimming. Ofc: 1104 Buchanan Rd, Ste. 3 Antioch 94509

VITALE, DONALD EUGENE, publisher; b. Feb. 16, 1930, Oak Park, Ill.; s. Sylvester and Anne (Potenza) V.; m. Sarah Alice Brengle, June 9, 1956; children: Mark, b. 1957; John, b. 1958; Valerie, b. 1969; Paul, b. 1962; edn: Loyola Univ. 1948-51; NW Univ. 1952; UCLA 1956-57. Career: copy-boy, reporter, re-write City News Bur., Chgo. 1951-52; ed. L.A. Daily Journal (legal newspaper) 1954-59; asst. pub. rels. mgr., L.A. area CofC 1959-61, and ed. So. Calif. Business (weekly Chamber pub.) 1959-61, dir. pub. rels. 1961-65; assoc. dir. corp. comm. Dart-Kraft (then Rexall Drug & Chem.) 1965-67; Postal Instant Press franchisee, 1969-79; pub. Who's Who in Calif. 1978--; sr. lectr. USC Sch. of Journalism 1966-71; prod. radio show, Big Problems in Small Bus., L.A. 1966-67; playwright: The Aquarium (New Playwrights Found., Hollywood 1973), Bidding and Other Fables (Evergreen Stage Co., Hywd. 1976, 78); past chmn. Information Com. to Save Descanso Gardens; apptd. exec. secty., L.A. Mayor's Small Bus. Council 1967; advis. bd. Mt. St. Mary's Coll., L.A. 1963-65; pres. Catholic Press Council of So. Calif. 1966-67; mem: Greater L.A. Press Club, Pub. Rels. Soc. of Am. 1961-65, Town Hall of Calif, LA World Affairs Council, Am. Library Assn.; mil: cpl. US Army 1951-53, USAR 1954-6, Korea w/ 3 bronze stars, UN Svc., Korean Svc. medals; rec: theatre, travel. Res: POB 4240 San Clemente 92672

VITOLO, JOSEPH CARL, lithographic co. executive; b. Dec. 20, 1952, Queens, N.Y.; s. Gerard Ralph and Lucy Maria (Lentini) V.; m. Sue Ellen Tullar, Mar. 10, 1973; children: Anthony Joseph, b. 1977; Sandra Nicole, b. 1978; edn: AA, Fullerton Coll. 1972; UC Fullerton, 2 years. Career: apprentice bl. & white camera person/stripper, J and L Lithographers, Santa Ana 1972-, four color camera psn. and plant supvr. 1975-, owner/sec. treas. J n L Litho, 1981--; mem: Orange Co. Jaycees, Mens Christian Club of Calvary Chapel; innovator in spl. technique making four color separations w/o use of silver masks; rec: bowling, skiing, scuba. Res: 22145 Timberline Wy, Lake Forest 92630 Ofc: J n L Litho, 2403 S Broadway Santa Ana 92707

VITULLI, CLARK JOSEPH, automotive co. executive; b. Apr. 2, 1946, Bklyn.; s. William and Rosaria (Stallone) V.; m. Jacqueline Pain, June 22, 1968; edn: BSc, advt., Univ. Fla. 1968. Career: acct. exec. Rachesky Advtg., Palm Beach, Fla. 1968-69; Chrysler Corp. dist. mgr., Tampa and Miami, Fla. 1969-71, bus. mgmt. mgr., Orlando, Fla. 1971-74; asst. zone mgr., Wash. DC 1974-76; mgr. sales planning & analysis, Detroit, Mich. 1976, zone mgr., Orlando 1977-80; mgr. Imperial Mktg., Detroit, Mich. 1980, zone mgr. (direct sales & mktg. activities of 120 Dodge and Chrysler-Plymouth dealers in So. Calif. and HI) 1980--; ex-officio mem. Chrysler-Plymouth and Dodge Dealer Advt. Assns. 1980-, Chrysler-Plymouth and Dodge Dealer Advis. Councils 1980-; mem. Chrysler Calif. Mtkg. Project, 1981-; bd. mem. St. of Fla. Dept. of Motor Vehicles, Dealer Licensing Div. 1978-79; guest spkr. Rotary (1977); Fla. Newspaper Execs. Conv. (1978), Hawaiian Auto Dealers Conv. (1981); awards: 1st place, Inperial Announcement Meeting, Shows and Exhibs. N.Y., 1981; 2nd pl., Imperial Direct Mail, Direct Mktg. Assn. of Detroit 1981; patron-participant, Jack Benny Meml. Tennis Classic bene. Juvenile Diabetes Found., Houston 1980; mil: Army ROTC 1965-6; Democrat; Catholic; rec: photog., tennis. Res: 1331 Fawnridge Dr Brea 92621 Ofc: Chrysler Corp., 1600 E. Orangethorpe Ave Fullerton 92631

VO, SAM THI, dentist; b. Jan. 1, 1936, Hatinh, North Vietnam; s. Antony and Mary (Bui) V.; m. Diem Van Pham, May 8, 1961; children: Mary (Thien-Huong) b. 1962; John (Dam), b. 1963; Helen (Kim-Thu), b. 1964; edn: Bach. (philosophie) Couvent Des Oiseaux, 1955; DDS, Univ. Saigon, 1961; Hygienist, Calif. Bd. 1977; DDS, Calif. Bd. 1977. Career: assoc. dentist, Dr. Alwa Owyang 1978, opened San Francisco office 1978, opened San Jose office 1978, incorporated San Jose office (now with six operatories), 1980--; advis. mem. of USCC, 1979, advis. mem. of Health Ctr. Pgm. for Refugees, 1981-83; mem. Congl. Advis. Bd. (chmn. 1982-); Catholic; rec: cooking, sewing, embroidering. Res: 986 Live Oak Dr Santa Clara 95051 Ofc: 815 Van Ness Ave, Ste. 301 San Francisco 94109 Ofc: 2034 Forest Ave, Ste. 2B San Jose 95128

VOLK, HARRY J., financial institutions executive; b. July 20, 1905, Trenton, NJ; s. Michael Thomas and Susan (Harkins) Volk; Edn: A.B., Rutgers Univ., 1927, L.L.B., Rutgers Univ. Law Sch., 1930, L.H.D. (Hon.), Rutgers Univ., L.L.D. (Hon.), Pepperdine Univ., 1982; m. Marion Waters, Oct. 12, 1931; div. May 1972; m2d., Marjorie L. Hale, Aug. 11, 1976; chil: Robert, b. 1932; Richard, b. 1934; Carolyn, b. 1942. Career: senior v.p., Prudential Ins. Co. of Amer., Newark, N.J. and L.A., Calif., 1927-57, chmn. and CEO, Union Bank, 1957-80, chmn., Weingart Foundation, 1980---; Dir. Union Bank, 1955-81, Union Amer., 1969-75, Dir., Times Mirror, Co., 1952-76, Pacific Lighting Co., Western Air Lines, 1950-76, Pacific Indemnity Co. 1952-77, Redken Labs, 1978---; Trustee, Calif. Inst. of Tech., 1950-79, Hosp. of Good Samauten, 1965-79. Awards: founding pres., AID United Givers; Awarded Robert Milliken Medal by Cal Tech, Pres. Rutgers Alumni Assoc., 1940-45; Alumni Trustee, Rutgers Univ., 1942-47. Mem: Dir. L.A. CofC, 1949-52, mem. assoc. of Reserve City Bankers, 1957-80, L.A. Country Club; L.A. Club; Calif. Club; Bohemian Club; The Founders of the Music Center; the L.A. Museum of Art. Mil: Chief, US Strategic Bombing Survey, Statistics and Publications Branch, 1943-45. Rec: golf, travel. Res: 1110 Maytor Place, Beverly Hills 90210; Office: Union Bank, 1900 Ave. of the Stars, #200 Los Angeles 90067.

VON HECHT, JOHN CHARLES, postal system co. executive; b. June 27, 1930, Fresno; S. Frank Reinhaldt and Leda Frances (Charles) von H.; m. Barbara Anne Robertson, Nov. 6, 1976; children: Lorinda, b. 1951; Dorothy, b. 1953; John Jr., b. 1960; Shawn, b. 1951; Justin, b. 1980; edn: BA, UCLA 1952. Career: gen. sales mgr. Universal Publicizers, Inc., 1952-57; pres. Nat. Broadcasting Counselors 1957-65; dir. Nat. Anti-Litter Campaign 1965-70; pres. Nat. delivery Systems, Inc., 1970-82; chmn. bd./chief exec. Nat. Independent Postal System, Inc., 1982--; dir. Western Sampling Media Ltd.; pres. Multi Media Mktg., mem: Nat. Assn of Private Postal Systems (pres. 1982-4, bd. dirs. 1980-), Elks, Loyal Order of Moose; Pacific Corinthian Yacht Club; mil: US Navy; Republican; rec: boating, fishing. Res: 2240 Monaco Dr Oxnard 93030 Ofc: NIPS, 8306 Wilshire Blvd, Ste. 1017 Beverly Hills 90211

VOORHEES, GENE FRANK, healthcare company executive; b. Sep. 12, 1946, Austin, Minnesota; s. Frank Croll and Thelma Bernice (Prickett) V.; m. Betty Foley, Nov. 25, 1967; children: Shannon, b. 1970; Lexie, b. 1972, Anita, b. 1973; William, b. 1975; edn: BS, Univ. Arizona 1968, MA, 1969. Career: staff accountant audit prin. Arthur Young & Co., Los Angeles 1971-82; v.p. Lutheran Hop. Soc. of So. Calif., Los Angeles 1982--; mem: AICPA, CSCPA, Healthcare Fin. Mgmt. Assn.; EDP Auditors Assn. (pres. L.A. chpt. 1981-82); mil: 1st Lt., US Army 1969-71; Republican; Baptist; rec: golf, sport. Res: 5232 Somerset Westminster 92683; Ofc: Lutheran Hospital Society of So. Calif., 1423 So Grand Ave Los Angeles 90015

VORIES, DENNIS LYNN, consulting engineer; b. July 5, 1952, Walla Walla, Wash.; s. Eldon Lynn and Barbara Lou (Merklin) V.; m. Linda Shultz, MD, Feb. 25, 1979; edn: BSE, Walla Walla Coll. Sch. of Engrg. 1974; Engr. in Tng., Wash. State, 1974; Reg. Profl. Engr. (elec.), Nev. 1980, Calif. 1981. Career: mechanic, svc. mgr., Eldon Vories Motors, part time 1964-72; electronics engr. Naval Weapons Ctr., China Lake, Ca. 1974-79, dir. electronic design Terrain Denial Weapons Br. 1977-9; consulting engr. spec. in electronic and mech. R&D, 1979--; inventions in fields of air quality monitoring, solar energy, automotive applications, others; mem: IEEE, NSPE, CSPE; 7th-Day Adventist; rec: amateur radio, hiking, skiing. Address: Dennis L. Vories, P.E., 29142 Via Piedra Valley Center 92082

VORZIMER, KENNETH DOUGLAS, interior design co. president; b. Nov. 6, 1941, NYC, NY; s. Seymour and Roslyn Rosenblum (Lefkowitz) V.; m. Bonnie Marshall, Aug. 10, 1964, div. 1973; m. 2d. Janice Morein, Oct. 15, 1980, div. 1984; children: Jay, b. 1966; Adam, b. 1968; Jonas, b. 1972; Rachel, b. 1982; edn: BS, arch. engring., Univ. of Miami 1964; fallout shelter analyst, DOD, 1963. Career: engr. US Army Corps of Engrs., Jacksonville, Fla. & Phila. 1964-66; facilities planner Gen. Elec. Co., Phila. 1966-67; supvr. facilities planning Philco Ford, Phila. 1967-68; proj. dir. supvr. SLS Environetics, N.Y. and L.A., 1968-72; sr. partner Antonoff & Vorzimer, Century City 1972-73; pres. The Century Group Inc., Sherman Oaks 1973--; instr. L.A. Comm. Coll., L.A. 1978-79; awards: pub. in Design West, Interior/ Design/ Lighting, Melons 1981; service awards, Bnai Brith; architl. excellence/comml. interior, Beverly Hills CofC 1983; mem. Bnai Brith, 1970-75, Big Brothrs of Am. 1965-66, Alpha Epsilon Pi Frat.; Democrat; Jewish; rec: philatelist. Res: 10200 Bianca Ave Northridge 91325 Ofc: The Century Group, Inc., 14429 Ventura Blvd, Ste. 109 Sherman Oaks 91423

VOSGUANIAN, BRENDA KAREN, lawyer; b. Apr. 10, 1956, Yonkers, NY; d. Dr. Charles and Mary V.; edn: Pace Univ. 1973-75; BS, acctg., Fardham Univ. 1977; JD, Western State Sch. of Law 1980; stu. French cooking, Maxim's Restaurant, Paris 1983; restaurant mgmt., UCLA Grad. Ext. 1983-; admitted State Bar Calif. 1982. Career: staff acct. Keronix Inc., Orange 1978; internal auditor Global Van Lines, Anaheim 1978-79; sr. auditor McDonnell Douglas Corp., Huntington Beach 1979-82; partner Vosguanian & Vosguanian, Attys. and Counselors at Law, 1982--; mem: Am. Bar Assn.; Assn. of Trial Lawyers of Am.; Los Angeles Bar Assn.; Women Lawyers Assn. of Los Angeles; Armenian Profl. Soc.; rec: fitness, theatre and the arts, cooking. Res: 5924 Paseo

Canyon Dr Malibu 90265 Ofc: Vosguanian & Vosguanian, 2040 Ave of the Stars, Ste. 400 Los Angeles 90067

VOSGUANIAN, BRUCE CHARLES, lawyer/ certified public accountant; b. Oct. 28, 1951, NY, NY; s. Charles and Mary (Lordigyan) V.; edn: BS, Fordham Univ. 1973; JD, Pepperdine Univ. Sch. of Law 1980; CPA, NY 1980; admitted State Bar Calif. 1981, State Bar New Jersey 1981; lic. real estate broker, Calif. 1982. Career: acct. Charles Vosguanian CPA, Yonkers, NY 1973-74; acct. self-empl., Bruce C. Vosguanian, Yonkers, NY 1974-78; sr. partner Vosguanian & Vosguanian, Attys. and Counselors at Law, Los Angeles 1980--; awards: N.Y. State Regents Scholarship Award 1969-73; mem: Assn. of Trial Lawyers of Am.; Am. Assn. of Atty.-CPAs; Los Angeles Bar Assn.; Knights of Vartan Cultural and Civic Frat.; writer/lectr. on economic theories rel. to investment decisions; rec: bicycling, tennis, skiing, photog.. Res: 5924 Paseo Canyon Dr Malibu 90265 Ofc: Vosguanian & Vosguanian, 2040 Ave of the Stars, Ste. 400 Los Angeles 90067

VOSGUANIAN, RODNEY NERSES, lawyer/ certified public accountant; b. Apr. 1, 1950; NY, NY; s. Charles and Mary (Lordigyan) V.; edn: BS, Fordham Univ. 1972; JD, Pepperdine Univ. Sch. of Law 1979; CPA, NY State 1976, Calif. 1978; admitted State Bar Calif. 1980, State Bar Ariz. 1981, State Bar NJ.1981; lic. real estate broker, Calif. 1982. Career: acct. Charles Vosguanian CPA, Yonkers, NY 1972-74; self-empl.. Rodney N. Vosguanian CPA, Yonkers, NY 1974-77; sr. partner Vosguanian & Vosguanian, Attys. and Counselors at Law, Los Angeles 1980--; adjunct prof. of bus. adm. in accting. and fin. mgmt., Pepperdine Univ., Malibu 1981; awards: N.Y. State Regents Scholarship Award 1968-72; Fordham Univ. Scholar Incentive Award 1968-72; mem: Am. Bar Assn.; Assn. of Trial Lawyers of Am.; Am. Assn. of Atty.-CPAs; Los Angeles Bar Assn.; Beverly Hills Bar Assn.; Santa Monica Bar Assn.; Knights of Vartan Cultural and Civic Frat.; Alpha Kappa PSI Bus. Frat.; mil: USAR; rec: tennis, skiing, bicycling, photog. Res: 5924 Paseo Canyon Dr Malibu 90265 Ofc: Vosguanian & Vosguanian, 2040 Ave of the Stars, Ste. 400 Los Angeles 90067

VOYLES, ERNEST WILLIAM, clergyman/demographer; b. June 16, 1923, Sedalia, Mo.; s. Benjamin F. and Florence Eunice (Marquess) V.; m. Myldred M. Nowland, July 7, 1942; children: Vickie (McPherson) b. 1943, Howard Merle b. 1945; edn: BA, Union Coll. 1942-46, postgrad. wk. Loma Linda Univ., Pacific Union Coll., Calif. Graduate Sch.; cert. Modern Safety Mgmt. 1980, Risk Mgmt. 1982, Internat. Loss Control Inst. (ILCI). Career: pastor, Seventh-day Adventist Ch. in Minn. 1946-54, Wash. 1954-58, Mont. 1958, Calif. 1958--; assigned to S.E. Calif. Conference Office, 7th-Day Adventists, Riverside, as demographer/hd. Research Devel. Ofc., 1978--, also Loss Control Dir. (field safety insp. 112 churches and 33 parochial schs.) 1980--; att. num. U.S. Census Dept. Insts.,and var. insts., American Demographic Inst. of Ithaca, NY; fmr. Rotarian; works: specialized demographic profiles for Pacific Union Conference of Seventh-day Adventists; Republican. Res: 802 Ora Avo Dr Vista 92083 Ofc: 11330 Pierce St, POB 8050, Riverside 92515

VOZNICK, HENRY PETER, manufacturing company executive; b. Jan. 3, 1930, Sweet Hall, VA; s. Thomas Peter and Salomae Francis (Procko) Wozniak; Edn: M.S. in Chemical Engrg., Lehigh Univ, 1951 (1950-51), Bachelor in Chemical Engrg., Univ. of Virginia, 1950-1947-50, Virginia Military Institute, 1946-47; m. Jean Howard, Mar. 26, 1955; chil: Henry P., Jr., b. 1955, Daniel M., b. 1958, Steven C., b. 1962. Career: Exec. v.p. Wahl Instruments, Inc., Culver City, Calif. 1969--; Marketing Dir., Lockheed Propulsion Co., Redlands, Calif. 1964-69, Project Dir., Atlantic Research Corp., Alexandria, Vir., 1960-64, Project Engr., Rohm & Haas Co., Bristol, Penn., 1956-60, Sales Engr., Bethlehem Foundry & Machine Co., Bethlehem, Penn., 1955-56, Mem: Prof. Registration: Calif., Control Systems Engineer CS004046, mem. of Advisory Bd. of Measurement Sci. Conf., 1979-80, mem. of ISA and AIChE, present., Pres., Precision Measurement Assn. 1980-81,Pres., Levittown Civic Assn, 1957-59, (Pennsylvania), Trustee, Arcadia Presbyterian Church, 1968-71. Holds three (3) Patents in Temperature Measurement and Fire Control Systems, also numerous Publications. Republican. Presbyterian. Res: 565 Gloria Road, Arcadia 91006; Office: Wahl Instruments, Inc., 5750 Hannum Ave., Culver City, 90230.

VUKOV, JUDITH ANN, physician/ psychiatrist; b. Apr. 11, 1942, Seattle, Wash.; d. Dr. Silvio and Alice Margaret (Thorlin) V.; children: Jennifer - Abigayle Heathcock; edn: BA, Whitman Coll. 1964; MA in psych., tchg. cert., CSU Los Angeles 1971; MD, Univ. Autonoma de Guadalajara 1978; lic. Calif. and NY. Career: medical advt. NYC 1964-69; instr. in psych., CSULA, 1971-72; clin. psych. Orthopedic Hosp. 1974; intern Maimonides Med. Ctr., Brklyn. 1981-82; psychiatry res./ postgrad. phys. in psychiatry, Olive View Med. Ctr., Van Nuys, CA 1982--; W. regional rep. for Alumni Assn. of UAG (med. sch.); mem: UAG Alumni Assn.; AMA; Sigma Alpha Chi Omega; vol. mental health counselor, for Co. and free clinics early 1970s; Democrat; rec: health, ballet, swimming, Spanish. Res: 219 N Isabel, Unit 1 Glendale 91206 Ofc: Olive View Medical Center, 7533 Van Nuys Blvd Van Nuys

W

WADDELL, HARRIET M., real estate broker; b. May 30, 1928, Seattle; d. Wm. Clyde and Bertha Engeline (Jensen) Lamb; m. John Gibson, Dec. 24, 1946; m. 2d. Forrest Waddell, Jan. 16, 1958, div. 1979; chil: William, b. 1949,

Steven, b. 1950, Douglas, b. 1955, Leanne, b. 1958, Teresa, b. 1960, Leslie, b. 1962, Alan, b. 1967; edn: Solano Comm. Coll. 1967-83; GRI (Grad. Realtor Inst.), Calif. Assn. of Realtors 1979. Career: realtor associate Lippstreu Realty, Inc., Fairfield 1966--, mgr. Berryessa Highlands tract ofc. Honors: Associate of the Yr. 1972, Title Ins. & Trust Co. Mem. No. Solano County Bd. of Realtors (dir. 1973-6), charter mem. Women's Div. of CofC (dir. six yrs.); Little League ofcr. 1965-6; Republican; Prot.; rec: handcrafts, stitchery, travel. Res: 1105 Maryland St. Fairfield 94533 Ofc: Lippstreu Realty Inc. 1245 Travis Bl. Ste.A, Fairfield 94533

WADE, JOHN KENNETH, engineering executive; b. Apr. 15, 1933, Los Angeles; s. Jay Kenneth and Estella Lucille (Hanson) W.; m. Nancy Ann Gordon, Feb. 9, 1962; children: Tim, b. 1962; Chris, b. 1965; edn: BS, UCLA 1960; MS, 1964; exec. pgm., Univ. of VA Grad. Bus. Sch. 1975; profl. engr., State Calif. 1966. Career: with Pacific Bell 1961--; sr. engr., div. traffic supvr., Los Angeles 1961-5, 1968-9; dist. staff engr., San Francisco 1965-8, 1969-76, 1981--; dist. mgr., Reno, Nev. 1976-81; mng. partner Wade Assocs. 1973--; mem. IEEE; Kiwanis; mil: Lt., USNR 1954-8; Republican; Prot.; rec: sports, financial planning. Res: POB 9019, 881 Donna Dr Incline, NV 89450 Ofc: Pacific Bell, 666 Folsom, Rm 788, San Francisco 94107

WAGGONER, FLETCH A., real estate broker; b. Oct. 10, 1937, Bolivar, Mo.; s. William Aby and Hester Mae (Blacketer) W.; m. Moreane Hagar, July 10, 1959; children: Loretta M., b. 1960; Fletch, II, b. 1963; edn: dip. in broadcasting, Central Tech. Inst., Kansas City; lic. radio tel. opr.; spl. courses, Bakersfield Coll.; Calif. lic. R.E. salesman 1972, R.E. broker 1974; GRI, CRS, Nat. Assn. of Realtors. Career: currently, pres. Waggoner & Assoc., Inc., Bakersfield; pres. Central Calif. Escrow Co.; broker/pres. Real Estate 7, Inc.; fmrly. in real estate bus. with America West Realtors, 1972, BBR, 1973, Watson Co., 1974; transmitter engr., studio engr., tech. dir. KERO-TV, Bakersfield 1957-72; mem: Calif. Assn. of Realtors (regl. v.p. 1984); Bakersfield Bd. of Realtors (pres. 1981); Lions Club (pres. 1982-3); Exptl. Aircraft Assn. Chpt. 71; (past) vol., Camp Fire Girls, Cub Scouts, Explorer Scouts; Republican; Baptist; rec: pvt. pilot, bldg. RVA aircraft, skier. Res: 3605 Pinehurst Dr Bakersfield 93306 Ofc: Real Estate 7, 2222 E St, Bakersfield 93301

WAGNON, JOHN STUART, resort development- management company executive; .b Jan. 31, 1952, Covina; s. Jack Donald and Margaret Emiline (McRae) W.; m. Deborah Mangold, June 30, 1979; edn: Univ. of Santa Clara 1970-2; cert., Profl. Ski Instrs. of Am. 1973; examiner, Profl. Ski Instrs. of Am. 1974-82; divl. demonstration ski team mem., Profl. Ski Instrs. of Am. Western Div. 1975-6, 1979-80. Career: supvr. Bear Valley Ski Sch. 1970-6; asst. dir. Bear Valley Ski Sch. 1976-7; ski sch. dir. Kirkwood Assoc., Inc 1977-81; dir. of mktg., Kirkwood Assocs., Inc. 1981--; profl. ski racing: Sierra- Tahoe Pro Tour 1975-8; Peugeot Pro Tour 1978-9; Salomon Technl. Testing Team, Salomon No. Am., Inc. 1977--; awards: Tommi Tyndall Awd., Western Div. Profl. Ski Instrs. of Am. 1983; bd. dirs.: Profl. Ski Instrs. of Am. (Western Div. 1974-82, Ednl. v.p. 1977-82, exec. v.p. 1975-7, Nat. Edn. Com. 1977-81); Ski Lake Tahoe 1981--; mem: United States Coaches ASsn.; Am. Mktg. Assn.; San Francisco Advtg. Club; So. Lake Tahoe Visitors Bureau; author: book, Introduction to Ski Teaching, Profl. Ski Instrs. of Am. (3rd printing) 1983; arts., Ski Pointers, Ski Mag. Nov. 1980, Feb. 1981; art., The Advantages of Skiing Right, Any Mountain mag., vol. 7, 1983; manual, The Machine Teaching Manual, Skee Machine, Inc., Seattle, Wash. 1983; Republican; rec: amateur triathlete, cross country ski racing, bicycle racing. Res: POB 11, 34 Yarron St Kirkwood 95646 Ofc: Kirkwood Assocs., Inc., POB 1 Kirkwood 95646

WAHREN, PETER STURESSON, international education organization president; Dec. 9, 1937, Stockholm, Sweden; s. Sture Lindgren and Inga Wahren; m. Luz Pena, Apr. 21, 1970; edn: BA, UC Berkeley 1962; MA, Stockholm Univ. 1963; grad., Poppius Sch. of Journalism, Stockholm 1967. Career: tchr. Extramural Bd. of Stockholm Univ. 1963-8; asst. to dir. Am. Swedish Hist. Found., Phila., PA 1969-71; dir. western div. Student Internat. Svc. of Europe 1971-4; pres./ nat. dir. Am. Scandinavian Student Exch. 1975-81; pres. Am. Intercultural Student Exch. 1981--; v.p. San Diego Alcala Sister City Soc.; awards: scholarship J. Soderberg Found., Stockholm, Sweden 1963; mem: San Diego Alcala Sister City Soc.; Swedish Am. Soc.; Sallskapet, Stockholm; City Club of San Diego; World Affairs Council of S.D.; author: masters thesis, China Lobby 1963; mil: Code Spl., Swedish Armed Forces 1958-9; Republican; Lutheran; rec: yachting, travel, film theatre. Address: American Intercultural Student Exchange, 7728 Lookout Dr La Jolla 92037

WAKEFORD, GORDON COLEMAN, consultant, sales executive; b. Jan. 16, 1938, Toronto, Ontario, Canada; s. Norman and Doris Kathleen (Sinclair) W.; m. Marcia Alice Bailey, Oct. 30, 1982; children: Coleman, b. 1968; edn: journeyman machinist, ICS 19670-4; Riverside City Coll. 1971-3; coll. tchr. cert., State Arizona. Career: journeyman mach. Algoma Steel Corp., Sault Ste Marie, Ontario, Canada 1956-64; shop dir. Humko Prods. Div. Kraft Foods, Buena Park 1964-6; svc. engr. Signode Steel Corp., Chgo., Ill. 1966-9; maint. dir. Container Corp. of America, Corona 1969-71; maint. supvr. Inspiration Consolidated Copper Co., Globe, Ariz. and Riverside Cement Co., Riverside 1972-8; regl. tech. svc. mgr./ southwest regl. sales mgr D-A Lubricant Co. Div. Premier Corp., Cleveland, OH 1978--; coll. instr. Gila Pueblo Campus, Ext. Eastern Ariz. Coll. 2 yrs.; secty. Crestmore Fed. Credit Union, Riverside 1972-4; Appreciation awards, EMSA of Calif. 1982, So. Calif. Municipal Equip. Mgrs. 1983; mem: Soc. of Mining Engrs. of AIME; Smithsonian Assocs.; mil: active reserve Canada army RCEME 1956-64; Methodist; rec: tennis, water sports, collector pewter cars. Res: 603 No San Antonio Ave Ontario 91762 Ofc: D A Lubricant Co., 120 No Rebecca Ave Pomona 91766

WALDSTEIN, PETER SOMMERS, pediatrician; b. Nov. 5, 1947, NY, NY; s. Sinclair Z. and Shirley L. Waldstein; m. Laurie Slavin, Aug. 6, 1972; children: Matthew, b. 1978; Steven, b. 1980; edn: BS, Ohio Univ. 1969; MD, Univ. of Guadalajara 1973; MD, USC Sch. of Med. 1973. Career: pediatrics tng. Cedars Sinai Med. Ctr.; currently pediatrician, pvt. practice; awards: cert. of svc. UCLA; mem: L.A. Pediatrics Soc.; Children's Museum; Maple Center; Olympic Com.; Ctr. for Improvement of Child Caring; Democrat; Jewish; rec: sports, chess, karate. Res: 7220 Outpost Cove Dr Los Angeles 90068 Ofc: Beverly-Sunset Pediatrics, 9201 Sunset Blvd. Los Angeles 90069

WALEN, KIRSTEN H., geneticist; b. May 18, 1930, Vardo, Norway, perm. res.; d. Sigmund and Hjordis (Skui) W.; edn: AB, Tromso Gymnas 1949; BS, Univ. of Oslo 1952; PhD, UC Berkeley 1958; cert. cytologist, HEW 1976. Career: cancer research Norwegian Paduine Hosp. 1958-9; biology & cytogenetics Naval Biological Lab., Berkeley 1959-67; NIH fellowship, Canberra (Aust.) Med. Sch., 1967-8; assoc. prof. of Sydney Univ. 1968-74; cytologist Albert Bates Hosp., Berkeley 1974-6; dir. cytogenetic lab., Children's Hosp., Oakland 1976--; tchr. UC Ext. 1960s; awards: Bay Scholarship, Oslo 1952-3; Am. Women's scholarship 1952-3; Fulbright, 1952-4; NIH Spl. Fellow 1967-8; mem: Sigma Xi; Australian Soc. of Geneticists; Assn. of Cytogenetic Technologists; publs: 15 publs. in genetics; rec: backpacking, botany. Res: 763 Ocean Ave Richmond 94801 Ofc: Children's Hosp., 51st & Grove Streets Oakland 94609

WALKER, ANNE ELIZABETH, educator; b. Feb. 14, 1947, North Adams, Mass.; d. Edgar Eli and Beatrice Sarah (Vincelette) Remillard; edn: BS in mktg., CSU Fresno 1972, MBA 1974; lic. real estate broker, Calif. 1982. Career: instr./dept. hd. mktg., Fresno City College, 1978--; real estate broker, 1982--; conducts coll. seminars in mgmt., mktg., career goals. Honors: achievement awd., Fresno City Coll. Bd. of Trustees 1978, Calif. DECA Adviser 1978. Mem. Sales & Mktg. Assn. 1978-82. Rec: swim, travel, color analysis. Res: 2041 j. Laureen Fresno 93703 Ofc: Fresno City Coll. 1101 E. University Fresno 93741

WALKER, BRUCE JOHN, dentist; b. May 11, 1944, Youngstown, Ohio; s. Nelson William and Margaret Patricia (Hanley) W.; m. Toshie Walker, Mar. 1, 1975; children: Jeffrey, b. 1979; edn: AA, Santa Monica Coll. 1970; BA, Cal State Northridge 1972; DDS, Northwestern Univ. Dental Sch. 1977; DDS, Calif. Bd. Dental Examiners 1977. Career: oper. rm. tech. St. Vicents Hosp., Los Angeles 1967-71; eye bank supvr. Estelle Doheny Eye Found., Los Angeles 1972-3; hematology lab tech. Northwestern Meml. Hosp., Chgo., Ill. 1975-7; dentist, Douglas Oswell DDS, Santa Monica 1977-81, solo pvt. practice, Marina Del Rey 1981--; microscopic anatomy instr. Northwestern Univ. Dental & Med. Sch. 1975, awards: Northeastern Ohio Scholastic Art Awd., Golden Key 1962, mem: Am. Dental Assn.; Calif. Dental Assn.; Western Dental Soc.; Marina Dental Study Club; med. journal art.; mil: E-5, Army Med. Corps. 1965-7; Republican; Catholic; rec: snow skiing. Res: 3582 Military Ave Los Angeles 90066 Ofc: 12740 Culver Blvd Los Angeles 90066

WALKER, CLARENCE HOLLISTER, JR., wholesale flower distributor; b. May 28, 1912, San Mateo; s. Clarence H., Sr. (father 11th flyer in world) and Carolina Georgia (Biven) W.; m. Frances Lorriane Tremblay, May 29, 1936; children: Carol Lorriane, b. 1937; Clarence H. III, b. 1942; edn: San Mateo Jr. Coll. 1931-2. Career: partner, Floral Service Inc. (first to ship cut flowers by air in late 1930s), wholesale cut flowers shipping to USA & Canada; owner T&W Sales Co. (shipping dried flowers worldwide), San Mateo 1956--; mem: past pres. No. Calif. Wholesale Flower Shippers; Soc. of Am. Florist; Wholesale Florist and Florist Suppliers of Am.; created first Plastic Xmas Tree; rec: hunting, fishing, travel. Res: 927 W Hillsdale Blvd San Mateo 94403 Ofc: T & W Sales Co., POB 901, Sta. A, San Mateo 94403

WALKER, MARJORIE LOU, aerospace co. executive; b. Sept. 24, 1928, Columbus, Ohio; d. Austin Hamilton and Mabel Jean (Harkey) Brill; m. Bruce Walker, Jan. 20, 1952; children: Bruce, b. 1952; Steven, b 1954; Charles, b. 1955; Kathryn, b. 1957; Glenn, b. 1964; edn: BA/ BS, Ariz. State Univ. 1949; MA, Loma Linda Univ. 1979; sec. tchg. credential, Calif. 1978. Career: chem. engr. Beckman Instruments, So. Pasadena 1949-50; data analyst So. Calif. Coop Wind Tunnel, Pasadena 1950-3; chem. engr. Aerojet Corp., Azusa 1953-5; tech. editor Occidental Petroleum Corp., LaVerne 1967-9; sci. chmn., Eng. teacher Cath. Archdiocese of L.A. 1970-5; Mktg. Proposal Spec. & Sys., Integ. Engr. Honeywell Inc., W. Covina 1976-81; proposal spec. Aerojet Electro Systems Co., Azusa 1981-4; mfg. technology tech. svcs. mgr. Northrop Corp., Pico Rivera 1984--; set up pilot sci. pgm (Gr. 1-8) Cath. Archdiocese 1970; cons. E.G.& G. Reticon 1984; awards: tchg. fellowship, Ariz. State Univ. 1949; recognition, Huntington Hosp. (1958), Cong. Dreier 1983; mem: Am. Chem. Soc.; AAUW; Nat. Assn. Sec. School Principals; Techni. Mktg. Soc. of Am.; PTA; Cub Den Mother; Old Baldy Scout Council; St. Katherines Guild; Guadalupana Soc.; Huntington Hosp. Aux. ; OES, San Marino; United Way; Citrus Coll. bd. trustees; works: ecclesiastical embroidery 1970-5; founder/ pres. S.T.A.T.U.S., Inc. (Senior Tutoring Aid to Underachieving Students), 1983, pilot unit estab. in conjunction with Loma Linda Univ. in 1984; Republican; Catholic; rec: tennis, photog., computers. Res: 947 Fenn Court Claremont 91711 Ofc: Northrop Advanced Systems Div., 8900 E Washington Blvd Pico Rivera 90660

WALL, NANCY LEE, medical products co. executive; b. June 28, 1944, Chesnee, S.C.; d. Albert Lee and Sara Eleanor (Bush) W.; edn: Furman Univ. 1962-3; BS in med. tech./chem., Lander Coll. 1966; Reg. Med. Tech. (M.T.),

Am. Soc. of Clin. Pathol. (ASCP) 1966. Career: med. techn. Self Meml. Hosp., Greenwood, SC 1966-7; missionary med. techn. So. Baptist Conv., Ghana, W. Africa 1967-9; chem. techn. Alexandria (VA) Hosp. 1969-70; spl. chem. techn., chem. supvr. Baptist Hosp. System, Houston 1970-1, med. techn. tchg. coord. 1971-2; tech. sales rep Abbott Labs., Houston 1972-3, techn. laision 1973-5; intrnat. mktg. mgr. Abbott Diagnostics, So. Pasadena 1976-8; regulatory mgr., dir. Alpha Therapeutic Corp., Los Angeles 1978-83; pres. LeLynn Internat., San Dimas 1982--; exec. v.p. Pan Wal- LeLynn, 1984-; awards: Presidential Awd., Abbott Labs. 1975; Pres.'s Awd. Alpha Therapeutic 1981; listed: Who's Who of Am. Women 1983; mem: Nat. Assn. of Female Execs.; Nat. Orgn. Women; Am. Soc. of Clinical Pathologists; Am. Soc. Clinical Chemists; Via Verde Home Owners Assn.; Erwin Lake Homeowners Assn.; fundraising, Multiple Sclerosis; Christian; rec: golf, computers, real estate inv. Address: LeLynn Internat., 1640 Calle Miradero San Dimas 91773

WALLACE, ARLA STRASSBURG, clinical psychologist; b. June 21, 1933, Luverne, Minn.; d. Eldo Walter and Mary Genevieve (Ladd) Strassburg; children: Thomas, b. 1957; M. Kelly, b. 1960; edn: AA, Mankato State Coll., Mankato, Minn. 1953; BA, UCLA 1971; MA, CSU, L.A. 1973; PhD, Calif. Sch. of Profl. Psychology 1977. Career: psychologist Ctr. for Legal Psychiatry, Santa Monica, Child custody evaluations for the Superior Ct. sys. 1978--; psychologist Ctr. Legal Psychiatry, dir. Prostitute Therapy Pgm., Santa Monica 1976--; section on legal psychiatry, UCLA Neuropsychiatric Inst., asst. dir., Post Divorce Clinic 1977-8; Dependency Ct. Panel, Superior Ct., Los Angeles 1983--; Invitnl. Seminar with Dr. John Bowlby, London, Eng. 1982; pres. Dondalar Video Prodns., 1983--; TV apps., panel on prostitution, 1976, news pgm. 1978; awards: recognition, Airport Marina Couns. Ctr. 1973, UCLA Neuropsychiat. Inst. 1976-7; mem: Am. Pschological Assn.; Calif. Assn. of Marriage, Family, Child Counselors; Campfire Girls; Sierra Club; Republican; rec: raise Thoroughbred horses, hike, oil painter. Ofc: 1304 15th Street Santa Monica 90404

WALLACE, PAUL HARVEY, lawyer; b. Oct. 27, 1944, Fresno; s. Sam Dunn and Noami (Hickman) W.; m. Susan, Mar. 1, 1969; 1 dau: Christy, b. 1970; edn: BS, Fresno State Univ. 1966; JD, Calif. Western Sch. of Law, 1974; admitted to State Bar of Calif. 1974. Career: deputy dist. atty. County of San Diego 1975-9; assoc. Harrison and Watson, San Diego 1979-81; deputy county counsel, County of Butte, Oroville 1981--; lectr. Co. Counsel Assn. 1982; lectr. San Diego Bar Assn. 1979; faculty mem. Sixth Nat. Council of Juvenile and Family Ct. Judges 1979; awards: 1.H.C Man of Year, Fresno State Univ. 1966; Headnotes and Comments ed. Cal Western Sch. of Law Internat. Law Journ. 1974; listed: Who's Who in Colls. and Univs. 1974; mem: San Diego Dist. Atty.'s Assn. (pres. 1979); Butte Co. and Am. Bar Assns.; Masons; Scottish Rite; Shrine; arts. in law jours., mil. lt. col. USMCR 1966-, Silver Star, Purple Heart (2), Combat Action Ribbon; Cross of Gallantry w/ Palm; Democrat; rec: jogging, photog. Res: 1680 Flicker Lane Paradise 95969 Ofc: Butte County Counsel, 25 County Center Dr Oroville 95965

WALLER, ROBERT CARL, chiropractor; b. Aug. 1, 1931, Chgo.; s. Morton Sam and Linea (Anderson) Waller; div.; children: Wendy, b. 1959, Jeffrey, b. 1961; edn: undergrad. Youngstown Univ. 1950-2; BS in Pharm., Univ. of Ill. 1957; grad. stu. UCLA 1970-6; D.C., Los Angeles Coll. of Chiropractic 1979; Reg. Pharm. Fla., Ill., Calif.; D.C., Calif., HI. Career: pharmacist Thrifty Drugs, Granada Hills 1960-68, SavOn Drugs, Gran. Hills 1968-70; pharmacist/ mgr. HyLo Drugs, Sepulveda 1970-78; chiropractor/mgr. Chiropractic West, Santa Monica 1979-82; chiropractor/owner Wilshire - San Vicente Chiro. Center, Beverly Hills 1983, Alternative Care Chiropractic Ctr., Santa Monica 1984--; mem: Calif. Chiropractic Assn., LACC Alumni, UCLA Alumni, Mensa; publs: articles in Drug World Mag. 1970-73; Democrat; Jewish; rec: art collecting, phys. conditioning, running. Res: 3110 Barrington #203 Los Angeles 90066 Ofc: Alternative Care Chiropractic Ctr, 1530 Lincoln Bl Ste C, Santa Monica 90401

WALLS, MARION BENTON, property and governmental consultant; b. Sept. 24, 1916, West Frankfort, Ill.; s. Roscoe and Adele Lisetta (Voss) W.; m. Genevieve Sisney, 1942, dec. 1960. m. 2d. Dorothy Jane Lanier, Aug. 28, 1963; children: Barry, b. 1945; Susan, b. 1949; Deborah, b. 1952; Pamela, b. 1953; edn: BS, with honors, Univ. of Ill. 1944; BA, UCLA 1950s; Calif. lic. real estate broker. Career: machine repair Chicago, Wilmington & Franklin Coal Co., Orient, Ill. 1934-41; mining engr. Miami Copper Co. 1944-7; engr./ dir. prop., procurement, comm. & govtl. rels. Riverside Cement Co. & Amcord, Inc. 1947-74; cons. propert & govtl. rels. 1974--; travel cons. 1977-9; asst. secty. Amcord Inc.; dir. Spring St. Internat.; pres./ dir./ secty./ mgr. num. water cos. & canals 1952--; honors: Sigma Tau, Univ. of the Year; mem: AIME; Ill. Mining Inst.; Calif. Mfgrs. Assn.; Calif. Mining Assn.; County Water Resources Com.; County Flood Control Adv. Com.; Lions Club; Riverside CofC; Jurupa CofC (pres.); Press Club; County Economic Devel. Com.; works: co- designed Limestone Mine 1951-5; Republican; Baptist; rec: travel. Address: 1512 Bellefontaine Dr Riverside 92506

WALLSTROM, WESLEY DONALD, banker; b. Oct. 4, 1929, Turlock; s. Emil Reinhold and Edith Katherine (Lindberg) W.; m. Marilyn Hallmark, May 12, 1951; children: Marc, b. 1958; Wendy, b. 1960; edn: Modesto Jr. Coll. 1955-64; cert. Pacific Coast Banking Sch. Univ. of Wash. 1974. Career: bookkeeper, teller First Nat. Bank, Turlock 1947-50; v.p. Gordon Hallmark, Inc., Turlock 1950-3; asst. cashier, assn. mgr United Calif. Bank, Turlock 1953-68; regl. v.p. United Calif. Bank, Fresno 1968-72; v.p./ mgr. United Calif. Bank, Turlock 1972-6; founding pres./ CEO Golden Valley Bank, Turlock 1976--; dir. Independent Bankers of No. Calif. 1983; chmn. United Way 1971; chmn./ founding dir. Covenant Retirement Village 1973-; founding pres. Turlock Regl. Arts. Council; treas. Covenant Retirement Properties, Calif. 1980-; mem: Turlock Golf & Country Club (pres. 1975-6); commodore, Stanislaus Sailing Soc.; U.S. Yacht Racing Union; No. Calif. Golf Assn.; Nat. Soc. of Accts. for Cooperatives; Beulah Covenant Ch.; Rotary Club; Masons; author: thesis, The Turkey Industry - A Stabilized Industry ?, 1974; mil; 1st Sgt., Calif. Nat. Guard; Republican; Protestant; rec: sailing, golf. Res: 1720 Hammond Dr Turlock 95380 Ofc: Golden Valley Bank, 301 East Main St Turlock 95380

WALPER, MICHAEL CARY, wholesale distribution co. president; b. Aug. 8, 1951, Youngstown, Ohio; s. Bernard S. and Dorthey H. (McGuire) W.; m. Laura, June 24, 1978; 1 dau: Cassandra, b. 1982; edn: AA, Pierce Jr. Coll. 1975; Mid Valley Coll. of Law 1976-8. Career: with Century 21 Real Estate, Northridge 1973-4; sales Dillingham Construction Co., Los Angeles 1974-5; sales mgr. BBC Tennis Racket Co., Chatsworth 1976-8; pres. Omni Mktg. Co., Northridge 1978--; awards: top salesman, Cen. 21 R. E. 1973; mem: Northridge CofC; U.S. CofC; Republican; Catholic; rec: weight lifting, golf, tennis. Res: Encino 91316 Ofc: Omni Marketing Co. 19151 Parthenia St Northridge 91324

WALSH, DAVID WALTER, real estate broker; b. Nov. 20, 1954, Oshawa, Ontario, Canada; s. Lloyd Robert and Gladys Muriel (Audas) W.; b. Diana Strannigan, Mar. 3, 1979; edn: San Jose State Univ. 1972-4; De Anza Coll. 1974-5; Foothill Coll. 1975-7; San Jose Bible Coll. 1979; Calif. lic. real estate broker, 1982. Career: sales mgr. Tape Deck Corp., Los Altos 1972-6; dept. sales mgr. Matthews TV & Stereo, Daly City 1976-7, Soundworks C.B.S. Retail, Santa Clara 1977-9; realtor assoc. Red Carpet C.E.T.& T. 1979-81; broker assoc. Red Carpet, Santa Clara Valley Assocs. 1981--; sales awards: VIP Rep., No. Calif. and Top Ten national, Red Carpet Corp., 1983; mem: Nat./Calif. Assn. of Realtors; San Jose Real Estate Bd. (Mem. Com.); Republican; Christian; rec: Young Life (vol. leader, local high schools). Res: 1563 Ballantree Way San Jose 95118 Ofc: Red Carpet Santa Clara Valley Assocs., 234 E. Campbell Ave Campbell 95008

WALTERS, JAMES THOMAS, corporate president; b. Jan. 27, 1933, Canton, Ohio; s. George Cline and Myrtle Violet (Nelson) W.; m. Jane Margaret Finch, Sept 21, 1975; chilren: Stanton, b. 1956; Jay, b. 1962; edn: Univ. of Wisc. 1951-2, 1954-6; Univ. of Minn. Ext. 1956-9. Career: engr. Univac, St. Paul, Minn. 1956-62; diagnostic pgmr. Collins Radio Co., Cedar Rapids, Io. 1962-4; devel. pgmmr. Control Data, Mpls., Minn. 1964-9; staff cons. Data 100 Corp., Mpls. 1969-70; dir. of sys. Am. Totalizator Sys., Towson, Md. 1970-1; mgr. mktg. support Control Data, Mpls., 1970-79; pres./ dir. Internat. Totalizator Systems, San Diego 1979--; dir. W. R. Effinger & Co. 1983-; honors: Small Bus. Psn. of Yr., U.S. Small Bus. Admin. 1983; mem: Am. Inst. of Elec. Engrs., BSA (troop leader), San Diego CofC; works: design on Datamark Ticket Issuing Terminal; design num. software sys.; mil: IC3 (SS), USN 1952-4; Lutheran; rec: travel. Res: 1738 Hunsaker St Oceanside 92054 Ofc: I.T.S., 11095 Flintkote Ave San Diego 92121

WALTERSCHEID, RICHARD LEO, research scientist; b. Sept. 1, 1940, Phoenix, Ariz.; s. Leo Eugene and Etta Mae (Barnum) W.; m. Sherry Aug. 21, 1971; children: John, b. 1977; Amy, b. 1978; edn: BA, Univ. of Wisc. 1964; AB, UC Berkeley 1974; MS, UCLA 1969, PhD, 1978. Career: research assoc./ asst. adj. prof. UCLA 1978-9; research sci. Aerospace Corp., El Segundo 1979--; asst. prof., UCLA 1982--; honors: Phi Beta Kappa 1972; NSF Fellowship, NATO Adv. Studies Inst. 1977; mem: Am. Meteorol. Soc.; Am. Geophysical Union; AAAS; PTA; 11 publs. in sci. journals and books; mil: capt. USAF 1962-72, Merit. Svc. Medal; rec: travel, history, classical music. Res: 2928 Oakhurst Ave Los Angeles 90034 Ofc: Aerospace Corp., POB 92957 Los Angeles 90009

WALTHER, ROGER O., educational travel and real estate co. chief executive; b. Jan. 21, 1936, Plainfield, NJ; s. Clarence O. and Mary (Russo) W.; m. Anne Newton, Jan. 21, 1976; children: Wendy, b. 1962, Christine, b. 1965, Edward, b. 1967, John Dunning, b. 1968, Beau Dunning, b. 1971; edn: BS, USCG Acad. 1958; MBA, Wharton Sch. Univ. of Penna. 1961. Career: Brand mgmt., Procter & Gamble, Cincinnati 1961-65; exec. v.p./pres. Nat. Student Mktg. Corp., 1969-70 (when American Inst. for Foreign Study was a wholly owned subs.); owner/pub. San Francisco Mag. 1981-82; co-founder/pres./chief exec. and prin. shareholder, Queen's Gate Corp., op. in three basic areas: Educational Travel, Am. Inst. for Fgn. Study (the largest travel packager in the US); chief exec. major commercial real estate portfolio (incl. props. in London, Eng., Fairfield County, Conn., San Francisco) 1965-; co-founer/bd. chmn. San Francisco Bancorp., 1980--; Dir: Bank of San Francisco, SimuFlite Corp. (afil. Singer Co.), Dr. Meyer Friedman Inst.; trustee Richmond (Eng.) Coll.; lectr./ mem. Adv. Council, San Francisco State Univ. Graduate Sch. of Bus.; mem: Young Presidents Orgn., Commonwealth Club (SF), Wharton Alumni Club of SF, Lincoln Club of No. Calif., Calif. Tennis Club (SF), SF Golf Club, St. Francis Yacht Club (SF), Rye (Eng.) Golf Club, Annabel's (London); mil: USCG 1954-59; Republican; Episcopal; rec: golf, tennis, photog. Res: 2856 Vallejo St San Francisco 94123 Ofc: Queen's Gate Corp. 3661 Buchanan St San Francisco 94123

WALWYN, STEPHEN JOHN, lawyer; b. Nov. 8, 1947, Staffordshire, England; s. John and Lilian Mary (Baddeley) W.; edn: BA, Univ. of Santa Clara 1970; JD, cum laude, 1973; admitted Calif. State Bar 1973. Career: assoc. atty. Boccardo, Lull, Niland, Teerlink & Bell 1973-81; partner The Boccardo Law Firm 1981-, mem. mgmt. com. 1983-4, supvry. partner 1983--; prof. of law, Peninsula Univ. Sch. of Law 1997-9; Bar-L Club; recipient Bender Adminstrv. Law Awd. 1972, creative writing and graphic arts awds. 1965; Phi Alpha Theta (hist. hon.), Nat. Honor. Soc. 1965; Superior Ct. Judge Pro Tem., Santa Clara Co. 1977-83; mem: Calif. Trial Lawyers Assn.; Santa Clara Co. Bar Assn.; Santa Clara Univ. and Law Sch. Alumni Assns.; British- Am. Club; publs: Effects of Strategic Bombing European Theatre 1939-45, 1969-70; Safe Guarding the Mentally Ill Under Calif. Law 1972; Comparative Aspects of Guerilla Warfare Vietnam & Malaya 1967; mil: ofcr. cadet, British Army, Royal Corps of Transport, Royal Mil. Acad., Sandhurst 1966-7; rec: painting, sailing, history. Res: 663 Festivo Ct Fremont 94539 Ofc: Boccardo Law Firm, 111 W St. John Street, Ste 1100, San Jose 95115

WALZ, BETTY MARION, personnel service owner; b. July 23, 1934, Big Timber, Mont.; d. Milton Sureno and Donna Marion (Chapel) Willard; two children: Jemell b. 1955, Shawn b. 1958; Reg. Dental Asst., Calif. 1976. Career: (past) dental assistant 16 years, mgmt. in various dental offices, 7 yrs.; indep. bus. mgmt. cons. to dentists, 1979-, founder/owner/pres. Professional Fill-ins (personnel service for dental profls.), 1981--; mem. advis. bd. for dental assisting pgm. San Diego Comm. College Dist. 1982-; awards: Jr. Womens Club State Award for Youth Chmn. 1968; mem: Amer., Calif. Dental Asst.'s Assn.; San Diego County Dental Asst.'s Soc.; Amer. Women Bus. Owner's Assn.; Girl Scouts of Amer.; Flying Samaritans; Beta Sigma Phi; Republican; Relig. Sci.; rec: oil painting, fishing, travel. Res: 8619 Summerdale Rd San Diego 92126 Ofc: Professional Fill-ins, 3737 Camino Del Rio So., Ste 301, San Diego 92109

WANG, KUOCHUANG ANDY, educator, land developer; b. Oct. 11, 1942, China, nat. 1977; s. Yun Shen and Kuei Yin (Chien) W.; m. Agnes Liu Wang, Aug. 1, 1971; children: David, b. 1973; Calvin, b. 1978; edn: BE, Taiwan Christian Coll. 1968; MUP (urban plan), Univ. of Wash. 1971; M.S. (structure), Univ. of Wyo. 1977 PhD (structure), 1980; Reg. Profl. Engr., Wyoming & Calif.; lic. Gen. Contractor. Career: asst. campus planner Univ. of Wash., Seattle 1970; univ. engr. Univ. of Wyoming, Laramie, Wyo. 1971-80, asst. prof. 1980-1; assoc. prof. CSU Fullerton 1981--; pres. Diho Super Mkt., Los Angeles 1982--; pres. Diho Devel. & Constrn., 1982--; served on adv. bd. Parks and Rec., City of Laramie, Wyo., team chmn. Nat. Devel. Com., Rep. of China; honors: Phi Kappa Phi; Tau Beta Pi; mem: ASCE; Sigma Xi; Am. Inst. of Planners; publs: num. papers in area of solid mechanics in tech. journs.; mil: 2nd Lt., Engr. Corps. 1968; Republican; Christian; rec: fishing, hiking, remodeling houses. Res: 1544 Eagle Park Rd Hacienda Hghts 91754 Ofc: 15333 Gale Ave Industry 91745

WANG, JOSEPH KUO-HUA, engineer; b. Nov. 7, 1952, Taipei Taiwan; s. Jain-In and Yueh-Eng (Lin) W.; m. Wun-Chi Lee, Nov. 2, 1978; 1 son: Benjamin, b. 1979; edn: BS, Taipei Inst. of Tech. 1972; MS, Univ. of Alaska 1977; PhD pgm. Penn State Univ.; Reg. Profl. Engr., mech. engring., State Calif. Career: petroleum engr. Chinese Petroleum Corp. 1974-5; grad. research asst. Univ. of Alaska 1975-7, Penn State Univ. 1977-9; air resources engr. Calif. Air Resources Bd. 1979-80; energy splst. Calif. Energy Commn. 1981--; cons. to many pvt. industries; mem: Calif. State Employees Assn., Profl. Scientist; publs: num. sci. papers, reports; Christian; rec: fishing, ch. meeting. Res: 9199 Firelight Way Sacramento 95826 Ofc: California Energy Commission, 1516 9th Street Sacramento 95814

WANG, TZU-LI TOM, engineer; b. Apr. 9, 1948, China; s. Chi-Chang and Shu-Lan (Shao) W.; m. Sha-Li Chi, Jan. 29, 1984; edn: BSEE, National Cheng Kung Univ. 1969, MSEE, 1972; MSEE, highest honors, CSU San Jose 1976. Career: electrical engr. Sperry Univac, Cupertino 1974-77; development engr. Itel, Sunnyvale, 1978-80; staff engr. Lazor, Sunnyvale 1980-81; senior engr. Masstor, Sunnyvale 1981-83, cons. 1981; applications mgr. National Semiconductor, Santa Clara 1983--; tchg. asst. UC Berkeley 1977-78; recipient recogn. award, San Jose Sister City Pgm. com.; mem: IEEE (chmn. Student Assn.), Chinese Assn. (dir.), Pacific Neighbors, Sino-Amer. Assn.; publs: tech. paper, IEEE Jour. 1972, Handbook (pub. 1984); Catholic; rec: hikinig, fishing, swimming. Res: 1720 Halford Ave, 327, Santa Clara 95051 Ofc: National Semiconductor, 2900 Semiconductor Dr Santa Clara 95051

WANG, TZYY-CHENG, engineer/scientist; b. Aug. 8, 1949, Taipei, Taiwan; s. Sing-Sang and How-Chien (Chang) W.; m. Ye-Lian Liu, Aug. 12, 1973; children: Alice S., b. 1977; Emily L., b. 1982; edn: BS, Taipei Inst. of Tech. 1972; MSEE, Univ. of Miss., Rolla 1975; PhD pgm., Univ. of Houston 1975-7. Career: research asst. Univ. of Houston, Tex. 1975-7; elec. engr. Motorola Inc., Schaumburg, Ill. 1977-8; engr./ scientist splst. Douglas Aircraft Co., Long Beach 1978--; honors: Phi Kappa Phi; mem: AIAA; Aerospace Electrical Soc.; Chinese Culture Assn. of So. Calif. (pres. 1983-4, principal of Chinese School afil. 1982-3); publs: num. sci., tech. papers, reports; mil: ensign Chinese Navy, electronic ofcr. of destroyer escort; Republican; rec: jogging, tennis, reading. Res: 17334 So Maria Ave Cerritos 90701 Ofc: Douglas Aircraft Co., 3855 Lakewood Blvd, M/S 36-49, Long Beach 90846

WARD, DIANE KOROSY, lawyer; b. Oct. 17, 1939, Cleveland, Ohio; d. Theodore Louis and Edith C. (Bogar) Korosy; m. R. Michael Walters, Esq., June 30, 1979; children: Christopher LaBruce, b. 1965; Samantha Martha Thompson, b. 1968; edn: BA, Heidelberg Coll. 61; JD, Univ. of San Diego 1975. Career: partner law firm Ward & Howell 1978-80; Walters, Howell & Ward 1980-1; mng. partner Walters & Ward, San Diego 1981--; spkr. on estate plng. at num. seminars throughout state; v.p./ bd. dirs. Oak Broadcasting Systems, Inc., Glendale; honors: Phi Alpha Theta (history); Pi Delta Epsilon (journ.); Alpha Psi Omega (drama.); listed: Who's Who in Am. Colls. & Univs. 1961, 75; mem: Green Valley Civic Assn. (pres. 1980); Los Amados Aux., Children's Home Soc. (pres. 1969-70); Phi Delta Phi legal frat.; Am., Calif., San Diego and Rancho Bernardo Bar Assns.; Lawyers Club of San Diego; Profl. & Exec.

Women of the Ranch; Toastmasters of Rancho Bernardo; columnist, Univ. of S.D. Law Sch. newspaper Woolsack, De Minimus 1973-4; Espicopal; rec: philately, music: singing, guitar, flute. Res: 16503 Ave Florencia Poway 92064 Ofc: Walters & Ward, APC, 16776 Bernardo Ctr Dr, Ste 214, San Diego 92128

WARD, DOUGLAS WHITNEY, author/lecturer, labor executive, ret.; b. Oct. 10, 1910, Ft. Scott, Kansas; s. John Whitney and Pearl Ethel (Carver) W.; m. Clarissa Barish, July 30, 1939; children: Bruce, b. 1940; Erik, b. 1945. Career: author: China The Sick Dragon 1979; and Speak Common Language & Read Simplified Characters, Chinese; num. public lectures on the P.R. of China, Soviet, Siberia, Soviet Central Asia, etc.; telegrapher/ freelance writer 1926-34; editor ARTA, later ACA News, Am. Communications Assn., ACA-CIO, NYC 1935-6; 2nd internat. v.p. ACA-CIO, hdqtrs., NYC 1936-40; dist. chmn. Salt Lake Div., TCU-AFL/ CIO, transp.- comm. employees union, Ogden, Utah 1954-64; gen. chmn. TCU-AFL/ CIO, San Francisco 1964-70, ret.; mem: Brotherhood of Rwy. & Airline Clerks AFL/ CIO; Nat. Geographic Soc.; mil: Lt.jg, USMS in No. Atlantic, Mediterranean and S.W. Pacific war zones, (combat ribbons) 1943-5; Democrat; rec: study of Am. Indian life and lingual connections to N.E. Asia. Address: Sundowner Services, 2559 47th Ave San Francisco 94116

WARD, LINCOLN R., communications co. executive; b. Feb. 12, 1924, Rockville Centre, NY; s. James J. and Edith Ruth (Lerch) W.; m. Mary Sellinger, Oct. 20, 1951; children: James, b. 1952; Mary Beth, b. 1954; Ann, b. 1957; edn: BS, in bus. adm., Wayne Univ., mgmt. course, Stanford Univ. 1964; adv. studies, Brookings Inst. 1976. Career: New York Trust Co., NY, NY 1940; long lines commercial staff AT&T 1941-2; WWII 1942-5; techl. observer US War Dept., Frankfurt, Germany 1946-7; with AT&T 1947-62; network svcs., NY & Chgo. 1947-9; dist. mgr., Mnpls., Minn. 1949-50; plant staff mgr., Chgo. & Atlanta, Ga. 1950-2; commercial & traffic mgr., Detroit, Mich. 1953-5; div. mgr., Wash. DC 1955-7; NY major acct. and ind. sales mgr. 1957-62; Pacific Telephone, Los Angeles 1962--, gen. sales mgr. 1962-7, gen. commercial mgr. 1968, gen. mgr. Los Angeles, North, Central & West areas 1972-81, gen. mgr. San Diego, Imperial, Orange, Riverside, Inyo & San Bernardino Cos. 1982--; bd. dirs. Pvt. Indus. Council of S.D. 1983-4, S.D. Zoo Execs. 1981-4; exec. com./bd. dirs. Economic Devel. Corp.; S.D. Mayor's Adv. Com. 1983-4; L.A. Mayor's Adv. Com. on Water, City of L.A. Produce Mkt. Adv. Com. 1979-81; awards: 1984 Citizen of Yr., Gr. San Diego Indus.- Edn. Council; 1982 Headliner of Yr., S.D. Press Club.; Amigo de Distincion, Mexican & Am. Found. of S.D.; Distinguished Friend of the Univ., CSU Northridge 1982; Silver Beaver, BSA 1983; Citations from L.A. City Council and Calif. Assem. & Senate for civic leadership; 1984 Knights of the Holy Sepulchre; mem: Navy League; Telephone Pioneers of Am.; Jonathan Club, L.A.; University Club of L.A. & S.D.; bd. dirs.: San Diego CofC; United Way; San Diegans, Inc.; San Diego Symphony; S.D. POPS Orch.; BSA; bd. dirs. Noah Homes for Disabled; YMCA of S.D.; Gr. S.D. Sports Assn.; Univ. of S.D. Pres.'s Council; publs: Creativity in Business, used in courses San Jose State Univ. 1965-80; Men, Money and Markets, story of brokerage ind. 1961; contbr. arts. Bell Labs mag., AT&T mag., Mgmt. Journ; lectr. on Bus. Mgmt. AMA and State Bar Assn.; mil: Non-Com. WWII Signal Corps., ETO, Am. Def. Svc., WWII Victory medals; Republican; Catholic; rec: bridge, golf. Res: 10437 Sierra Vista Lance La Mesa 92041 Ofc: Pacific Bell, 525 B Street, Ste 1912 San Diego 92101

WARD, PHILLIP ALLEN, real estate executive; b. July 27, 1941, Wheeling, WV; s. Allen Loftus and Martha Evelyn (Ball) W.; m. Joan Cook, Mar. 31, 1961; children: Phillip, b. 1962; Dawn, b. 1967; edn: San Diego State Univ. 1959-64. Career: store mgr. Fed Mart Corp., San Diego 1959-68; sales rep. Kimberly Clark Corp., San Diego 1968-70; v.p. Cotton Companies, real estate brokerage, San Diego 1970-82; pres. Bignell- Ward- Bignell, Inc., real estate brokerage, San Diego 1972--; dir. real estate & fin. Big Bear Supermkts., San Diego 1976--; dir.: Great Western Ins. Co. 1981-; Golden Eagle Ins. Co. 196; Bignell- Ward-Bignell, Inc. 1972-; honors: Mayor for a day, San Diego 1958; Cmmndr. Sigma Nu Frat. 1961; Valedictorian, San Diego H.S. 1959; Master Counselor De Molay 1958; mem: Sigma Nu Alumni Assn. (pres. 1967); Masonic Lodge; Optimist; Stardust Country Club; Century Club of San Diego; Republican; Protestant; rec: golf, thoroughbred breeding. Res: 8986 Hillery Dr San Diego 92126 Ofc: Big Bear Supermarkets, 5075 Federal Blvd San Diego 92102

WARD, RODERIC CHARLES, architect; b. Apr. 17, 1935, Berkeley; s. Nairne Forsythe and Janet (Nundy) W.; m. Elizabeth Jean, June 18, 1957; children: Roderic, b. 1959; Gregory, b. 1960; Theodore, b. 1962; edn: Univ. of Colo. 1954-5; BA, Stanford Univ. 1957; B.Arch. 1958; reg. architect, Calif. 1966. Career: proj./ design/ maint. control ofcr. PWC, Guam 1958-62; draftsman Welton Becket & Assocs., San Francisco 1962; draftsman Claude Oakland, Arch. AIA, San Francisco 1962-3; ofc. mgr. Caywood & Nopp, Arch. AIA, Sacto. 1963-9; partner adminstr. Caywood, Nopp, Takata, Hansen & Ward, Architects, Sacto. 1969-72; treas. Caywood, Nopp, Ward, Arch., Sacto. & Placerville 1972-8; pres. Ward.Wolstenholm, AIA, Arch., Sacto. 1978--; dir. Ward. Walstonholm Pension & Profit Sharing Plan; partner, W.W. Devel. Co., Sacto. 1978-; recipient Bank of Am. Achievement Awd. 1952, Awd. for Excellence, WIC 1980; mem: AIA; Calif. Council AIA; CSI; Carmichael Kiwanis; Navy League Sacto. Council; Naval Reserve Assn., Fort Sutter Chpt.;Kappa Sigma, Beta Zeta Chpt.; Stanford Alumni Assn. of Sacto.; designed first Sacramento Atrium House (1965) and first Solar House (1976); mil: Cmdr., USNR-R, Civil Engring. Corps.; Republican; rec: photog., stained glass, boating. Res: 7630 Tobia Way Fair Oaks 95628 Ofc: Ward.Wolstenholm AIA, Inc., 1435 Alhambra Blvd, Ste 203, Sacramento 95816

WARD, VENCIL TERREL, SR., mortgage and real estate co. president; b. June 27, 1919, Everton, Mo.; s. Amos P. and Annie Mae (Terrel) W.; m. Frances Seneker, Oct. 14, 1940; children: Vencil Terrel, Jr., b. 1941; Steven Douglas, b. 1953; edn: dip. Joiner Bus. Coll., 1937-8; spl. courses, S.W. Baptist Coll., Am. Univ., Univ. of Kansas; sr. mem. Internat. Inst. of Valuers 1980. Career: fiscal acctg. Farm Credit Admin., US Dept. Agri. 1939-44; pvt. to lt. US Army 1944-46, USAR 1946-53, active State Mil. Reserves; pres. Mortgage and Real Estate Co.,1946-72; deputy chief adminstrv. ofcr. City of Fresno, Housing and Econ. Devel. 1972-9; exec. dir. Central Calif. Small Cities Econ. Devel. Com. 1979-81; sr. v.p./ sr. ed. U.S. Seniors monthly publ. 1981--; chmn. Ward Mortgage and Real Estate, Inc.; Sr. Senator, Calif. Senior Legislature 1981-; Fresno Co. Economic Devel. Com.; Soc. Dir. of Calif.; Dansforth Found. for Leadership; City of Fresno Fire Commnr., Water Commnr.; mem. Fresno Comprehensive Plng. Gp.; past pres. Central Valley Mortgage Lenders Assn.; past pres. Soc. of R.E. Appraisers of Fresno Metro Area; founding chmn. San Joaquin Valley Res. Senior Complex; founding chmn. First Am. Title Co. of Central Calif.; mem: Internat. Inst. of Valuers/ Appraisers (sr.); Fresno Bd. of Realtors; Nat. Assn. of Realtors; Am. Legion; Commonwealth Club (past); Calif. Legislative Council for Older Americans; Nat. Council of Sr. Americans, AARP, Fresno Co. and City CofC, works: innovative mobile home park design; Democrat; Friends; rec: fishing, boating, travel. Res: 2844 East Michigan Ave Fresno 93703 OFc: Ward Mortgage and Real Estate, Inc., 1900 Mariposa, Ste 303, Fresno 93721; U S Seniors, 3821 Blackstone Fresno 93703

WARDLAW, BRIAN T., lawyer; b. Mar. 11, 1945, Los Angeles; s. John R. and Margaret Ann (Thomson) W.; m. Margaret Calaba, Mar. 21, 1970; children: Jennifer, b. 1970; Margaret, b. 1970; Colin, b. 1972; edn: BA, UCLA 1970; JD, Loyola Law Sch. 1974; atty., State Bar of Calif. Career: atty. spec. in civil litigation 1974--; currently owner law firm; mem: bd. govs., Loyola Law School; Democrat; rec: guitar, tennis. Ofc: Wardlaw & Jones, 650 So Grand Ave, Ste 1000, Los Angeles 90017

WARING, DEREK ROBERT, counselor; b. May 7, 1948, Stockport, U.K., nat. 1968; s. Earl S. and Margaret Verna (Badham) W.; m. Ruth A., Jan. 30, 1971; children: Kristina Marie, b. 1971; Derek Owen, b. 1975; edn: AA, Modesto Jr. Coll. 1969; BA, Calif. St. Coll. 1974; MA, Univ. of San Francisco 1981; marriage, family, child counselor, State of Calif. 1983. Career: music dir., asst. pgm. dir., staff announcer KFIU Radio 1969-72; newsman, staff announcer KTRB Radio 1972-4; with Valley Mountain Regl. Ctr. 1974--; case mgr. 1974-9; case mgr./ supvr. of children's svcs. 1981-; currently intake/ assessment coord.; tchr. Positive Parenting; part- time practice MFCC; mem: adv. bd. Parents Helping Parents; Parenting Task Force Stanislaus Co.; adv. bd. Visiting Nurses Assn.; chmn. Children's Svcs. Task Force; Rose Ave Sch. PTA; La Loma Jr. High PTA; Modesto Youth Soccer Assn.; Modesto Little League; Modesto City Women's Softball; host: Sat. night radio pgm.: Solid Gold Saturday Night, KFIV Radio; Democrat; Prot.; rec: jogging, fishing, racquetball. Res: 2008 Ferrara Ct Modesto 95355 Ofc: Valley Mt. Regional Center, 2105 Lancey Dr, Ste 2, Modesto 95355

WARNE, WILLIAM ELMO, water resources consultant; b. Sept. 2, 1905, Seafield, IN; s. William R. and Nettie Jane (Williams) W.; m. Edith M. Peterson, 1929; children: Jane Ingrid (Beeder), b. 1934; William Robert, b. 1937; Margaret Edith (Monroe), b. 1944; edn: AB, Univ. of Calif. 1927; hon. LLD, Seoul Nat. Univ. 1959; hon. Dr. of Econ., Yonsie Univ., Korea 1959. Career: reporter S.F. Bulletin and Oakland Post-Inquirer 1925-27; news ed. Brawley News, Calif. 1927; news ed. Calexico Chronicle 1928; ed./staff writer Assoc. Press., L.A., San Diego, Wash DC 1928-35; ed. Bur. of Reclamation, US Dept. of Interior 1935-42; asst. commnr. 1943-47; asst. secty. Dept. of Interior 1947-51; chief of staff War Prodn. Dir., War Prodn. Bd. 1942; dir. AID, Iran 1951-55; Brazil 1956; Korea 1956-59; dir. Calif. Dept. of Fish & Game 1959-60; Agri. Dept. 1960-61; admr. Calif. Resources Agcy. 1961-3; Water Resources 1961-66; v.p. Devel. and Resources Corp. 1967-69; adj. prof. USC Sch. of Pub. Adminstrn., Sacto. 1976-79; water resources cons. 1969--; chmn. Pres.'s Com. on San Diego Water Supply 1944-6; chmn. Fed. Inter-Agcy. River Basin Com. 1948; Fed. Com. on Alaskan Dev. 1948; pres. Gp. Health Assn., Inc., Wash DC 1945-52; chmn. US Del., 2nd Inter-Am. Conf. on Indian Life, Cuzco, Peru 1949; US Del., 4th World Power Conf., London, Eng. 1950; bd. dirs. Near East Found. 1956-8, 1959-64; Calif. Water Polution Bd. 1959-66; adv. bd. Fed. Water Pollution Control 1962-5. Mem: Govs. Cabinet 1961; US Com., Internat. Commn. on Large Dams; dir. Nat. Water Supply Improvement Assn. 1971-81, pres. 1978-80; assoc. dir. CAREW 1973-7, 81; awards: Distng. Pub. Svc. Honor Awd., Foreign Ops. Adm. 1955; Ordier of Crown, Shah of Iran 1955; Outstanding Svc. Cit., UN Command 1959, Achievement Awd., Lambda Chi Alpha 1963; mem: Sigma Delta Chi; Lambda Chi Alpha; Nat. Press Club, Wash. DC; Sutter Club; Am. Acad. of Pub. Adminstrs.; NAPA Standing Co.m on Environ. and Resource Mgmt.; Explorers Club; author: Mission for Peace, Bobbs-Merrill 1956; the Bureau of Reclamations, Praeger Publs. 1973; How the Colorado River was Spent, NWSIA Journ. 1975; Mass Transfer of Water Over Long Distances, The California Experience, proceedings spl. session, Internat. Commn. on Irrig. and Drainage, Athens 1978; mil: 2nd lt. ORC 1927-37, Distng. Svc. Awd., Dept. of Interior 1951. Res: 2090 8th Ave Sacramento 95818

WARNER, RICKEY M., commercial real estate broker; b. Dec. 18, 1953, Auburn, NY; s. Leroy Morell and Patricia Ann (Stanley) W.; m. Diana Lu Johnson, Sept 8, 1979; children: Wesley, b. 1980; Charles, b. 1982; edn: AAS, Canton S.U.N.Y. 1974; BA, Mich. State Univ. 1977. Career: asst. mgr. Carrols Devel. Corp, Syracuse, NY 1974-5; assoc. v.p. Oneal Devel. Corp., Irvine 1978-79; partner Warner, Huston & Butts, Inc., Santa Ana 1980-82; Merrill Lynch Commercial Real Estate 1982--; mem: Santa Ana CofC, chmn. Devel.

Com. 1982; Rotary Club of Santa Ana, bd. dirs. 1982-3; Santa Ana/ Tustin YMCA, bd. dirs.; Republican; Christian; rec: sailing, tennis, golf. Res: 22751 So Canada St Lake Forest 92630 Ofc: Merrill Lynch Commercial Real Estate, 640 So Olive Los Angeles 90017

WARNER, SAM JOHN, office supply co. president b. Mar. 25, 1908, Medford, Wisc.; s. Louis Lawrence and Anna Amanda (Danielson) W.; m. Melissa Rudisell, Oct. 11, 1940; edn: grad. (Ephebian hons.) Lincoln H.S., Los Angeles. Career: mgr. wholesale & ednl. dept. Pioneer Stationers Corp., Los Angeles 1954-58, vice pres. 1958-70, pres./chief exec. 1970--; mem. San Marino Lodge; Scottish Rite; Malaikah Temple Shrine; Jonathan Club; Republican; Episcopal; rec: travel, photog., work. Res: 1325 Old Mill Rd San Marino 91108 Ofc: Pioneer Stationers, Inc., 4400 E Bandini Blvd Los Angeles 90023

WARREN, CAROL JOY, educator; b. Dec. 25, 1935, San Diego; d. Richard LeRoy and Jacqueline (Lema) Lindblad; m. William Warren, Feb. 14, 1975; edn: BA, San Diego State 1979, std. teaching credential, 1980; MA, 1981; spl. teaching cred., Nat. Univ. 1983; multiple subject cred. 1980, spl. edn. cred. 1983, Calif. Dept of Edn. Career: instr. MAAC, Lakeside 1980-81, 82; elem. tchr. Country Day Montessori 1981-82; high sch. spl. edn. tchr. Grossmont Sch. Dist. 1982--; pres. CJ Research (consulting); mem: Calif. Teachers Assn.; Grossmont Edn. Assn.; instr. wrkshps. on Clownology, confluent edn. techniques; Republican; Lutheran; rec: animals, auto racing. Address: CJ Research, 15175 Chad Rd El Cajon 92021

WARREN, ELIZABETH CORINE, film services co. officer; b. Mar. 7, 1923, Chicago, Ill.; d. Charles Edward and Lena Leora (Sumner) Miller; m. Peter Warren, 1942; children: Robert, b. 1943; Cynthia, b. 1944; Barbara, b. 1950; edn: L.A. Bus. Coll. 1948; num. night sch., corres. courses. Career: legal, bus. and tech. secty., 1948-60; with Technicolor, Inc. 1960--: exec. secty., var. Technicolor ofcs. and dir. 1960-75; overseas assignment, asst. to China Proj. mgr. 1975-76; exec. secty. to Gen. Counsel and secty. 1976-81; co. archivist, dir. corp. advtg. & pub. rels., asst. secty. 1981--; mem: Nat. Notary Assn.; Soroptimist; L.A. Civic Light Opera Assn.; Fair Ladies, Am. Airlines; Tujunga Civic Ballet; Ladies Comedy Club, show bus.; over 15 yrs. active involvement with dance troups perf. eves. and weekends for USO, L.A. Chamber of Music and var. lodges, schs. and clubs; Republican; Methodist; rec: photog., dancing, music. Ofc: Technicolor, Inc., 4050 Lankershim Blvd, No. Hollywood 91608

WARREN, FRAN GRACE, data processing executive; b. Aug. 29, 1946, San Francisco; d. Frank Sylvester and Clara Clare (Chotinsky) Caruso; m. Ira David Warren, June 17, 1967; children: Benjamin, b. 1982, Kayanna, b. 1982; edn: biol. major, UCLA 1964-67; Cert. Bus. Mgmt., Univ. Laverne 1979. Career: computer pgmmr./ analyst (self-taught) Harvard Univ. 1969-721, Avery Label Corp., 1972-74; computer system designer, and mktg. Data Corp., 1974-76; pgmmr./analyst Security Pacific Bank, 1976-78, Lockheed Calif. Co., 1978-79; data processing mgr. Intel Corp., Santa Clara 1979--. Honors: B'nai Brith awd., Fairfax H.S. 1964; mem. first Women's Intercollegiate Basketball Team at UCLA 1965. Mem: Productivity Info. Exchg. Roundtable (founder 1982); IEEE; Data Processing Mgmt. Assn. (past); Am. Mgmt. Assn. (past); Am. Contract Bridge League (life master 1966-); coach Girl's Bsktball for Catholic Youth Assn. 1981-82; host mother to fgn. exch. students from Brazil, Japan. Publs: profl. papers presented IBM Guide (11/82), APMA (Am. Productivity Mgmt. Assn. 10/83). Democrat. Jewish. Rec: bridge, gardening, travel, sports. Res: 275 Penn Way, Los Gatos 95030 Ofc: Intel, (ST3-2-460), 3065 Bowers Santa Clara 95051

WARREN, RICHARD WAYNE, obstetrician, gynecologist; b. Nov. 26, 1935, Puxico, Mo.; s. Martin Roscoe W. and Sarah Elizabeth (Crump) W. (1911-1983); m. Rosalie Franzoia, Aug. 16, 1959; children: Lani, b. 1961; Richard, Jr., b. 1963; Paul, b. 1965; edn: BA, UC Berkeley 1957; MD, Stanford 1961. Career: intern US Naval Hosp., Oakland 1961-62; gen. med. doctor USN 1962-64; resident Stanford Med. Ctr. 1964-67; pvt. practice 1967--; asst. clinical prof. Ob-Gyn Stanford Univ.; pres. Richard W. Warren, M.D., Inc.; mem: San Francisco Gynecological Soc. Royal Soc. of Med.; Am. Assn. of Gyn. Laparoscopists; Am. Med Assn.; Santa Clara Co. Med. Soc.; publs: sev. papers on effects of caffeine on humans 1959-62; mil: lt. USN M.C. 1961-4; Republican; Catholic. Res: 102 Atherton Ave Atherton 94025; Ofc: 2500 Hospital Dr, Bldg. 8, Mountain View 94040

WASHINGTON, KAYE, lawyer; b. Apr. 11, 1951, Detroit, Mich.; d. William Taft and Virginia (Hall) W.; div.; 1 son: Camilo Casey, b. 1972; edn: BA, Univ. of Mich. 1973; Hastings Coll. of Law 1978-9; JD, UCB Boalt Hall, 1981; admitted to Calif. State Bar 1981. Career: curriculum dir. Oakland (CA) Community Sch., 1973-77; assoc. atty. Fenwick, Stone, Davis & West, Palo Alto 1981--; honors: Tony Patino Finalist, Hastings Coll. of Law, S.F. 1978; Univ. of Mich Ctr. for Continuing Edn. for Women Award 1978; Most Outstanding Women in Am. 1979; mem: Am. Bar Assn.; Charles Houston Bar Assn.; NAACP; cofounder/ch. Breakfast and Tutorial Pgm. for Ann Arbor, Mich. school children 1970-72; Democrat; Baptist (hist. com. Allen Temple, Oakland); rec: scrabble, backgammon. Res: 5609 Evergreen Terrace Fremont 94538 Ofc: Fenwick, Stone, Davis & West, Two Palo Alto Square, Palo Alto 94306

WASSON, HAROLD TAYLOR, JR., real estate co. executive; b. Aug. 4, 1946, Los Angeles; s. Harold T. and Beatrice M. (Hansen) W.; 2 daus: Jennifer, b. 1968; Jill, b. 1970; edn: East L.A. Jr. Coll. 1966; Cerritos Coll. 1967-8; USC Taxation & Exch. 1982; lic Real Estate Broker, Calif. Career: with Walker & Lee 1970--: sales agent in Lakewood 1970-72 (top 10 in co. for sales, No. 1 in

listings); office mgr., Oxnard Ofc. 1972-74, Palos Verdes Ofc. 1974-7, Fullerton Ofc. 1975-78; regional v.p. (in chg. 16 ofcs.) 1978-80; v.p. sales for Resale Div. (92 ofcs.) 1980-82; senior v.p. 1982--; recipient num. sales and mgmt. awards, Walker & Lee; mem: Lakewood-Long Beach Bd. of Realtors (past); Whittier, Palos Verdes, Oxnard and No. Orange Co. Bds. of Realtors; Calif. and Nat. Assns. of Realtors; Republican; Protestant; rec: boating, fishing. Res: 1316 No Catalpa Anaheim 92801 Ofc: Walker & Lee, 1901 E 4th Street Santa Ana 92705

WATERS, CAROL ARTH, association executive; b. Aug. 20, 1922, Emmett, Idaho; d. Wm. Emmett and Marjorie Elizabeth (Alford) Renner; m. Daniel Carson Waters (dec.), Nov. 18, 1962; children: Nancy, b. 1942; Marie, b. 1944; edn: UCLA 1939-40; Riverside Jr. Coll. 1950; San Bernardino Jr. Coll. 1950. Career: spl. asst. to US Secty. of State/ pub. affairs ofcr. 1953-58; exec. secty. to the US Commn. on Civil Rights 1958-9; nat. dir. Women's Activities, Citizens for Nixon- Lodge 1960; state dir. spl. projects Nixon for Gov. 1962; asst. to exec. v.p. & dir. State & Fed. Liaison, Calif. World's Fair 1963-66; dir. pub. rels. Am. Heart Assn. and Gr. L.A. Affiliate 1966-7; dir. pub. policy/ pub. affairs Am. Heart Assn., Gr. L.A. Affiliate 1980--; lectr. in pub. rels. annual UCLA / PRSA Pgm.; instr. various orgns. on pub. policy, legislative process and campaign techniques; awards: Rome Betts Meml. Awd. for Excellence, Soc. of Heart Assn. Profls.; Mayoral Commdn. 1968; mem: Los Angeles Council of Nat. Voluntary Health Agencies; Women's Council CofC (pres. 1976; bd. dirs. Los Angeles Beautiful); L.A. City Human Rels. Commn. (pres. 1966-8); State Fair Polit. Practices Commn.; Town Hall; Colorado River Assn.; Women in Pub. Affairs; Los Angeles YWCA; Calif. Elected Womens Assn. for Edn. and Research; publs: Rone Betts papers on pub. policy in Heart Assn. Affils. 1983; Op. Telephone Manual for Getting Out The Votes 1962, 8; Republican; Prot.; rec: knitting, civil war hist., writing. Res: 421 So Van Ness Ave, Apt. 5, Los Angeles 90020 Ofc: American Heart Assn., 2405 W Eighth Street Los Angeles 90057

WATRING, WATSON GLENN, physician; b. June 2, 1936, St. Albans, WV; son H. Glenn and J. Louise (Johnson) W.; edn: BS, Washington & Lee Univ. 1958; MD, West Virginia Univ. 1962; diplomate, Am. Bd. of Obstets & Gyn. 1972, cert. of spl. competence in Gynecologic Onocology 1977. Career: intern The Toledo (OH) Hosp. 1963; res. (OB-Gyn) Ind. Univ., Indnpls. 1964-66; Tripler Gen. Hosp., Honolulu 1968-70; res. (gen. & oncologic surg.), City of Hope Nat. Med. Ctr., Duarte, Calif. 1970-71; (fellow) asst., acting dir. Gynecologic Oncology UCLA Med. Ctr., 1972-74, Junior Faculty Clinical Fellow, Am. Cancer Soc. 1974-77; assoc. prof./dir./sr. surgeon, Tufts New England Med. Ctr. Hosp., Ob-Gyn, 1977-80; clin. prof. Ob-Gyn, UC Irvine Coll. of Medicine, 1982--; regional dir. gynecologic oncol. So. Calif. Permanente Med. Group, L.A. 1982--; mem: AMA, fellow Am. Coll of Obstets & Gyn., fellow L.A. Obstet. & Gyn. Soc., W. Assn. of Gynecologic Oncologists (sec.treas. 1976-81), Am. Soc. of Clin. Oncol., Daniel Morton Soc., AAAS, Soc. of Gynecol. Oncologists, Sigma Xi, Internat. Soc. of Gynecol. Pathol., NY Acad. of Sci., Am. Radium Soc., Am. Coll. of Surgeons, other med. assns.; mem. Glendale CofC; past editorial cons., European Jour. of Med. 1976; mil: LTC US Army MC 1965-71, Commendn. Medal. Address: Kaiser Permanente Medical Group, 4950 Sunset Blvd Los Angeles 90027

WATSON, GLENN ROBERT, lawyer; b. May 2, 1917, Okla.; s. Albert Thomas and Ethel Amelia (Riddle) W.; m. Dorothy Mosiman, Feb. 25, 1945; 1 dau: Carol (Lynch), b. 1951; edn: East Central State Univ. 1933-6; LLB, Okla. Univ. 1939; admitted to Okla. State Bar 1939, Calif. State Bar 1946. Career: law practice, Okla. 1939-41; US Naval Reserve 1941-45, on Destroyer Duty, Atlantic & Pacific theatres; law practice Los Angeles 1946--, founder/sr. partner law firm Richards, Watson, Dreyfuss & Gershon, L.A. 1954--; city atty: Cerritos 1956-62; Industry 1958-65, 1979-83; Commerce 1961; Seal Beach 1972-80; Carson 1968--; Rosemead 1960-76; Victorville 1962-3; Artesia 1976--; Avalon 1976-80; So. El Monte 1976-9; honors: Phi Delta Phi, Coif (1939); mem: Los Angeles Co. Bar Assn.; Lawyers Club of L.A. (pres. 1958); Am. Bar Assn.; World Affairs Council of L.A.; L.A. CofC; Town Hall; Ducommen Soc.; La Canada CofC (pres.); mil: Lt. USNR, 1942-5; Democrat; Protestant; rec: breeding thoroughbred horses. Res: 800 West First St Los Angeles 90012 Ofc: Richards, Watson, Dreyfuss & Gershon, 333 So. Hope St, Ste 3800, Los Angeles 90071

WATSON, JAMES ROBERT, real estate developer; b. Jan. 25, 1940, Altus, Okla.; s. Robert Reginald and Ora Odella (Hammon) W.; m. Chyrl Ann Russell, July 17, 1977; children: Christopher Robert James, b. 1965; Thomas Scott, b. 1967; edn: BS, San Jose State Univ. 1961. Career: Real Estate appraiser, 1962-66; chief appraiser/dir. of real estate, Downey Savings and Loan Assn. 1966-71; owner Watson & Assocs., 1971--, devel. projects include shopping and retail-office centers (five completed pre-1971) in Sunnymead (1973), Ridgecrest (1973), Spokane, Wash. (1974), Oceanside (1976), Seal Beach (1976, 81), Riverside (1981), Southgate (1981), Cerritos (1982); city redevel. projects in South Gate (1981), Seal Beach (1981), Cerritos (1982), Perris, Huntington Park, and Oceanside (1984-); builder num. residential homes, units; mem: Soc. of R.E. Appraiser, Internat. Council of Shopping Centers, Comm. Redevel. Agencies Assn.; CofC, Seal Beach, Cerritos; recipient appreciation, South Gate City Council, YMCA; mil: s/sgt. USAF; Rel. Sci.; rec: skiing. Res: 96-A, Box 299, Surfside 90743 Ofc: Watson and Associates, 101 Main St, A, POB 610, Seal Beach 90740

WATSON, (FRANCES) "RUSTY" MARIE, management consultant; b. Feb. 12, 1949, Ventura, Calif.; d. John Francis and Bernice M. (Rickman) Bowler;

edn: BA, hist., UC Santa Barbara 1973; grad. School of Bank Mktg., Univ. of Colo. 1979; cert. Customer Rels. Tng., CSULA 1976, cert. Bank Mgmt., Internat. Corres. Sch. 1977, cert. Mgmt. and Suprvy. Devel., UCSB 1977. Career: adminstrv. asst. Bank of A. Levy, Oxnard 1975-78, mktg. ofcr. 19787-79, dir. of mktg. 1979-80, vice pres. 1980-81; prin./sole owner Watson and Assocs., Ventura 1981--; banking advisor American Bankers Assn. Wash. DC, 1979-81; mem. Docutel, Olivetti Corp. Advis. Bd., Dallas, Tx. 1982; honors: recogn., Multi Media Advt. Campaign, Advt. Club of Ventura Co. 1978; mem: Nat. Assn. of Bank Women (publicity ch. 1979-81), American Film Inst. (1980-), Am. Mgmt. Assn. (1981-82), Am. Soc. for Tng. and Devel. (1978-9), Bank Mktg. Assn. (1979-81), Advertising Club of Ventura Co. (1979-81), Nat. Geographic Soc.; publs: art., Bank Systems and Equipment Mag. (1983), num. interviews pub. in banking and finl. publs. (Wall Street Jour., Woman's Day, Money, Oui, others); rec: scuba diving, skiing, equestrian. Address: Watson and Associates 6657 Ralston St Ventura 93003

WATT, DONALD GIBBS, real estate developer; b. Nov. 29, 1911, Welda, Kans.; s. James Scott and Sarah Martha (Gibbs) W.; m. Florence Johnson, Dec. 7, 1970; stepson: Richard F. Landau, b. 1948; edn: Texas A & M College 1930-31. Lic. Real Estate Broker, Calif. 1947-. Career: dir. of mfg. (McDonnell) Douglas Aircraft Co., Santa Monica 1929-69; pres. American Mobilehome Corp., Santa Monica 1969-80; (AMH Corp. merged into Watt Indus. 1980); exec. vice pres. Watt Industries, Inc. (indsl. constrn. projs., residential home constrn., apt. complex projs.) 1980-81, vice chmn. of the bd., 1981--; (assoc./maj. prin. of the original R.A. Watt Co. 1947-); instr. adult courses, var. So. Calif. schools; mem: bd. dirs. Govt. Affairs Council of Building Indus. Assn. of So. Calif.; dir. Santa Monica Bay Shrine Club, dir. Ocean park Lodge Masonic Temple Assn., dir. Boys' Club of Santa Monica, dir. Great Western Council Inc. of Boy Scouts of Am.; mem. Riviera Country Club, MacDac Retirees Assn. Res: 500 Avondale Ave Los Angeles 90049 Ofc: Watt Industries 2716 Ocean Park Blvd Santa Monica 90405

WATTS, GARY LEE, investment counselor; b. Feb. 9, 1948, Santa Monica; s. John Wesley and Marcy May (Frost) W.; edn: CSU, Sacto. 1970; GRI, Grad. Realtors Inst. of Calif. 1982. Career: sales assoc. Coldwell Banker Co., El Toro 1972-73, asst. mgr. Mission Viejo Realty, Mission Viejo 1973-74; mgr./ dir. sales tng. Valley Realty, El Toro 1974-76; pres. Independent Investment Systems, Inc., El Toro 1976--; cons: First American Title Co., Santa Ana 1979-; instr. Saddleback Coll. 1976-, Nat. Relocation Assistance Corp. 1980-; awards: Realtor Associate of Year, Saddleback Valley Bd. of Realtors 1981; mem: Nat. Assn. of Realtors; Calif. Assn. of Realtors; AYSO; guest speaker to realty boards of Irvine, Newport Beach/ Costa Mesa, Saddleback Valley, Huntington Beach/ Fountain Valley, East Orange County, Laguna Beach, San Fernando Valley, and Nat. Council of Exchangers; publs. (5) on real estate financing and economic trends; arts. in For Sale mag. (Wash.), and LA Times; Republican; Radha Soami; rec: golf, diving, flying, travel. Address: Independent Investment Systems, Inc., 23220-2 Orange Ave El Toro 92630

WAUGH, RALPH B., oral and maxillo-facial surgeon; b. Apr. 27, 1924, Holdenville, Okla.; s. Gordon Beverly and Ellen Martha (Bucknoll) W.; m. Bonny Jean Haugen, Dec. 7, 1969; children: Janice Jean Waugh b. 1953, Wendy Jean Dixon b. 1965, Joseph Braddock Dixon, Jr. b. 1962, Ian Andrew Waugh b. 1973; edn: BS in chem. engring., UC Berkeley 1950; DDS, USC 1958; MD, UCLA 1966; Calif. lic. Dentist (1958), Physician, Surgeon (1967), Diplomate Am. Bd. of Oral Surgery (1970), Fellow Am. Bd. Oral & Maxillofacia Surg. (1978). Career: naval aviator WWII, 1943-63, served to lt., pilot torpedo bomber, pilot Anti Submarine warfare; residency and fellowship, oral & maxillofacial surgeon, USC-LA County Med. Ctr. 1959-62; med. intern. Orange County Med. Ctr. 1966-67; chief of staff Antelope Valley Hosp. Med. Ctr. 1975, 77; pres. LA County Medical Assn., Dist. 16, 1977-78; founding pres. Antelope Valley Dental Study Group 1984; mem. Com. on Rural Health, Calif. Med. Assn. 1980-84; Anesthesia Review, So. Calif. Soc. of Oral and Maxillofacial Surgeons 1981-84; mem. Antelope Valley RA (bd. dirs. 1984-5), LACCRA (pres. 1983-4), CRP (State Central Com. 1980-). Res: 40646 16th St West, Palmdale 93550 Ofc: 43713 20th St West, Lancaster 93534

WAXMAN, JACK, coin dealer; b. Nov. 19, 1941, NY, NY; s. Sam and Eva Waxman; edn: AA, Los Angeles City Coll. 1965; BA, CSU, L.A. 1968; MS, 1981. Career: fin. analyst Dun & Bradstreet, Inc., Los Angeles 1970-3; job developer United Way, Los Angeles 1976-7; job developer LA Urban League, Los Angeles 1977; employment spec. New Start, Inc., Santa Monica 1977-8; employment spec. Rosey Grier's Giant Step, Inc., Gardena 1978 80; pres. First Western Coin Corp., Hollywood 1980--; agent, investment analyst Global Land & Trade Corp. 1982; awards: Calif. State Svc. Ribbon, Calif. Air Nat. Guard 1965; v.p. Israel Coin Club of Los Angeles 1977-78; chmn. Law Day Seminar, CSULA 1967; bd. mem. Calif. State Univ. Hillel 1966-68; literary agent for film writers, screen plays 1979-; mil: sgt. USAR 1960-65, 1975-82, Expt. M-16 rifleman, GCM; Democrat; Jewish; rec: numismatics, philatelist, collectors plates. Res: 1006 No Sierra Bonita, Ste 8, Hollywood 90046

WAXMAN, SHELLY ROBERT, lawyer; b. Apr. 22, 1941, Chgo., s. Henri and Ann (Sokolsky) W.; m. Kathy McNally; children: Josiah, b. 1977; Zoe, b. 1981; edn: AB, Univ. of Ill. 1963; JD, DePaul Univ. Coll. of Law 1965. Career: staff atty. Argonne Nat. Laboratory 1968-71; asst. U.S. Atty. 1971-74; prin., Shelly Waxman & Assocs. 1976--; honors: 1978 Libertarian Party Candidate, Ill. Atty. Gen. Federal Defender, Panel mem. (Chgo.); mem: Libertarian Lawyers Alliance of Ill. (founder); People for a Simplified Tax Law; Nukes to the Sun; Am. Criminal Tax Bar; num. arts. in var. law journs.; Belanco Relig. Order; rec: running. Res: 504 Friant Ct Bakersfield 93309 Ofc: POB 665 Taft 93268

WAYNE, BRUCE FREDERICK, traffic and news reporter; b. Nov. 19, 1933, Manchester, NH; s. Frederick and Margaret (McCoo) Talford; m. Lois Garner, 1965; children: Linda, b. 1956; David, b. 1959; edn: comml. pilot, East Coast Aviation, Mass. 1960; 1st class engr., Mass. Radio Sch. 1951. Career: sports announcer Armed Forces Radio, Ser. NYC 1954-8; TV-News & Weather, WHDH, Boston 1958-61; traffic reporter, Boston 1961-5; pgm. dir., sales KEZY, Anaheim 1966-8; traffic reporter BRNO, San Bernardino 1968-70; KFI in the Sky, Traffic & News reporter, KFI 1970-81; M.C. Grand Opening of Spruce Goose, May 14, 1983; 25,000 hrs. as a comml. pilot, inst. rating, comm. helicopter, multi-eng. skaplane, has piloted Goodyear Blimp, flown w/ Blue Angels & wing-walked; awards: exceptional use of Aviation, A.F. Assoc. 1971; spot news awd., AP, 1974; Grand awd., L.A. Press Club 1976; 30 yrs. in broadcasting, May 15, 1982; listed: Jane's Who's Who in Aviation and Aerospace, US Edition; mem. Am. Fedn. of TV & Radio Artists; author, Bruce Wayne's Incredible Freeway Guide; mil: S/Sgt., USAF 1954-8; Prot.; rec: tennis, skiing, bike. Res: 1552 Yermo Pl Fullerton 92633 Ofc: 610 So Ardmore Los Angeles 90005

WEAVER, DORIS LEA, executive search firm owner; b. Jan. 22, 1933, Northport, NE; d. Benjamin Martin and Ione Myrtle (Cary) Jurgens; m. Dell Fullmer, Aug. 28, 1971; children: Deborah, b. 1951; Renee, b. 1953; Wayne, b. 1964; (step): Gary, b. 1959; Linda, b. 1961; Rebecca, b. 1964; edn: bus. & acctng., Columbia Basin Coll. 1967-8. Career: acct. Leirman Accountancy 1968-70; ofc. mgr. Wenatchee Valley Clinic 1971-73, Owl Companies 1973-75; cons. Robert Half 1975-76; co- owner: Accts. Associated Personnel Svc., Inc. 1977-84, Frederick/ Weaver & Co. 1981-84, Travel w/ Joyce 1978-83; owner: Doris Weaver Personnel Service, Doris Weaver Temporaries and D.L. Weaver & Assocs. Executive Search, 1983--; speaker various colls.; honors: Beckman NAA Award for Most Outstanding Dir.; NAA Most Valuable Mem.; NAA Most Valuable Past Pres.; Who's Who in State of Wash.; mem: Nat. Assn. of Accts. (pres.); Women in Mgmt.; Am. Acctg. Assn.; CSU Fullerton Pres.'s Council; Am. Employment Assn.; Calif. Employment Assn.; Orange Co. CofC; Irvine, Newport Beach, and Fullerton CofCs; Irvine Indsl. League; Republican; Methodist; rec: golf, hiking, tennis. Res: 570 Paseo Lucero Anaheim Hills 92807 Ofc: 550 Parkercenter Dr Fullerton 92705

WEAVER, WILLIAM JAMES, JR., corporate executive; b. Dec. 31, 1933, Vineland, NJ; s. William J., Sr. and Anne E (Morgan) W.; m. June Paetzell, June 20, 1936; children: James Paul, b. 1958; Thomas Morgan, b. 1960; Matthew Lawrence, b. 1968; edn: BSME, Lafayette Coll. 1956; MBA, Pepperdine Univ. 1978; Lehigh Univ. 1957-8. Career: mgr. equipt. div. F.J. Stokes 1958-61; v.p. CVI div. Pennwalt Chemicals Corp. 1961-66, pres./bd. chmn. Ohio Energy Systems, Inc., Columbus, OH 1967-74; pres./bd. chmn. & CEO Zia Corp., Long Beach 1974-8; pres./bd. chmn. & CEO Wentex Internat., Inc., Garden Grove 1978--; recipient num. awds. and honors; mem: SPE; AIAA; ASME; IES; Belmont Shore Optimist Club; Young Pres. Orgn.; Navy League; Brookside Golf & CC; Old Ranch Golf Club; Long Beach Petroleum Club; publs: The U.S. Today - A Nation of Energy, 1970; various tech. publs.; mil: 1st lt. US Army; Republican; Lutheran; rec: golf, sailing. Res: 5630 Las Lomas St Long Beach 90815 Ofc: Wentex Internat., Inc., 12842 Valley View St Garden Grove 92645

WEBB, JAMES MURPHY, architect; b. Apr. 5, 1939; s. James Ellis and Inez (Murphy) W.; div.; children: Jennifer, b. 1968; Justine, b 1972; Michael, b. 1974; edn: Univ. of Ark., BA 1963, and B.Arch., 1963; Lic. Architect, Calif., Ill.; Lic. Real Estate Broker, Calif. Career: project arch. Kaplan/McLaughlin/Diaz, S.F.; Democrat. Res: 89 Turquoise Way San Francisco 94131 Ofc: K/M/D, 222 Vallejo St San Francisco 94111

WEBER, CHARLES FREDERICK, III, real estate broker; b. Dec. 13, 1938, Lafayette, Ind.; s. Charles Frederick and Carolyn Lee (Melchoir) W.; b. Ann Marie Lamb, Oct. 11, 1975; 1 son: Randall Anthony, b. 1978; edn: bus. & mktg. courses, Purdue Univ., Drury Coll., Ariz. State Univ., San Jose City Coll., 1960-8; lic. real estate broker. Career: broker/owner C.F. Weber & Associates, Campbell 1970--; past electronics firm contract adminstr., San Jose; founding chmn. San Jose Core-area Re-devel. Task Force, 1969; mem. Green Peace, Internat. Motor Sports Assn., Historic Motor Sports Assn., Am. Chili Soc., Rolls Royce Owners Club, Ferrari Owners Club; honors: 1st place, San Jose Chili Cookoff Corp. Div. 1982; 2nd in class, Monterey Historic Races 1982; mil: Submarine Svc. USN; Republican (Nat. Com.); rec: auto racing. Res: 16136 Camino Del Sol Los Gatos 95030 Ofc: C.F. Weber & Assocs., The Weber Bldg., 1590 La Pradera Dr. Campbell 95008

WEBER, PETER, retail baker; b. Sept. 21, 1929, Denmark, nat. 1964; s. Asmus and Agnes (Andersen) W.; m. Ellen Skov, Dec. 15, 1956; children: Steen, b. 1961; Palle, b. 1963. Career: baker apprentice in Denmark; came to USA in 1957; baker, Petersen's Pastics, Solvang, Calif. 1957-59, bought bus. and changed name to Peter's Pastries, 1959--; mem: Retail Bakers of Amer., US Chamber of Commerce, Nat. Fedn. of Independent Bus., Solvang Bus. Assn. (bd. dirs. 1969-71), Danish Days chmn. 1972, Solvang Theaterfest (bd. dirs. 1974-76, campaign cabinet 1982), Santa Ynez Valley Advt. Counsel; mem. Rebuild National Park Soc.; mem. Danish Brotherhood in Amer. (v.p. 1984; nat. bd. 1975-), Dania Soc. Calif./ Nev. Dist. (past pres., bd. dirs.); mem. bd. dirs. Solvang Municipal Improvement Dist. 1972-76; Republican; Lutheran; rec: dancing, swimming. Res: 1820 Old Mill Rd Solvang 93463 Ofc: Peter's Pastries, 1665 Copenhagen Dr Solvang 93463

WEBSTER, JEAN-PIERRE, software manufacturing executive; b. April 30, 1949, Ft. Dix, NJ; s. Belton O. and Lucie (Dlugi) W.; m. Regina E. Davis, Apr.

30, 1971; children: Nichole Michelle, b. 1971, Malik Toussaint, b. 1975, Angelique Lucienne, b. 1979; edn: BSBA, CalPoly, Pomona 1975. Career: asst. mgr. Thrifty Drug and Discount Stores, L.A. 1975-77; sales rep. New York Life Ins. Co., W. Covina 1977-8; mgr. John English TV and Apps., Santa FE Springs 1978-9; retail ops. mgr. Olympic Sales Co., L.A. 1979-82; owner JP Distbg. (software distbn. co.), Claremont 1982-3; pres. SoftServ, Inc., Upland 1983-4; nat. sales dir., USA, Batteries Included, Costa Mesa 1984--; orgnzr. seminars on bus. uses of microcomputers, 1983; mem: Upland CofC, BBB, Claremont Computer Club (charter); mil: sgt USAF 1968-72, Vietnam Svc. Medal w/ cluster; Democrat; Catholic; rec: movie buff. Res: 328 W. Green St Claremont 91711 Ofc: Batteries Included, 3303 Harbor Blvd, Ste. C9, Costa Mesa 92626

WEDBUSH, EDWARD WILLIAM, securities co. president; b. Sept. 14, 1932, St. Louis, Mo.; s. Wm. H. and Edith Marie (Herman) Wedbush; m. Jean A. Lawrence, Dec. 18, 1960, Los Angeles; chil: Gary Lance, b. 1964, Eric Dean, b. 1967, Leigh Ann, b. 1969; edn: BA in mech. engring., Univ. Cincinnati 1955; MBA (Hughes Fellow), UCLA 1957; Regis. profl. engr., Calif. Career: stu. engr. Wagner Elec., 1949-55; engr. Hughes Aircraft Co., 1955-8; assoc. prof. in engring., UCLA, 1957-9; partner Wedbush, Noble, Cooke, Inc., Los Angeles 1957-67, pres. 1967--; pres./CEO Wedbush Corp.; chmn. bd. Pacific Stock Exchange 1976-7; dir. Pacific Securities Depository Trust Co., Nat. Securities Clearing Corp. Mem: Los Angeles Stock Exchange Club; Calif. Club; Triangle frat. Publs: arts. in engring. jours. Rec: tennis; res: 5441 Senford Ave., Los Angeles 90056 ofc: Wedbush, Noble, Cooke, Inc. 615 S. Flower St. Los Angeles 90017.

WEDEMEYER, LOWELL REMY, lawyer, farmer; b. June 27, 1941, Adair, Iowa; s. Lawrence Theodore and Loretta Agnes (Donohue) W.; edn: BS in chem. engrg., Iowa State Univ. 1963; JD, Harvard Law Sch. 1968; m. Linda Downie, June 23, 1979; children: Michelle, b. 1980, Rebecca, b. 1982. Career: aerospace engr. McDonnell Aircraft, St. Louis 1963; US Peace Corps, Bida, Nigera 1964-65; assoc. atty. law firm Wyman, Bautzer, Rothman & Kuchel, Beverly Hills y69-70; partner law firm Alexander, Inman, Tanzer & Wedemeyer, 1970-82; sole practitioner 1982--; active in election lawsuits; plaintiffs' lead counsel in investors' class action lawsuits; active in planning, zoning, land use and environmtl. quality litigation; honors: Tau Beta Pi, Pi Tau Sigma; mem: State Bar of Calif., Am. Bar Assn.; founder and first spkr. Santa Monica Citizens Congress (non-partisan local polit. orgn.); founding chmn. New Deal Democrats of Santa Monica (largest grassroots club in Calif.); works: lead counsel listed in various Calif. Appellate Ct. decisions; mil: 2d lt. USAFR; Democrat; rec: outdoor sports. Address: 3002 Catalina Dr Davis 95616

WEHR, RONALD DALE, manufacturing co. executive; b. Sept. 2, 1931, Youngstown, Ohio; s. Roy Cecil and Myrtle Elizabeth (Ripple) W.; m. Marcia Evans, Apr. 10, 1954; children: Patricia, b. 1954, Daniel, b. 1955, Richard, b. 1967; edn: grad. Fitch H.S. 1949. Career: overhead crane opr. US Steel, Youngstown, Oh. 1949-54; honeycomb wing panel assembler Boeing Aircraft, Seattle, Wash. 1954-55; installer West Coast Carpet and Linoleum, San Jose, Ca. 1955-57; assembler, Solar Aircraft, San Diego 1957-8; 100 ft. telescoping crane opr. Foster & Kleiser Outdoor Advt., San Diego 1958-64; fireman Gen. Dynamics/Convair, S.D. 1964; mgr. The Union Ice Co./Union Ice & Storage Co., 1964--; cold storage splst./cons. Sea World Penguin Encounter snow exhibit; dry ice uses/hazards; vegetable vacuum cooling; creator of Snow World at Sea World, 1973-83; created San Diego's first 300 lb. popsicle; pub. The Union Ice Co./Union Ice and Storage Co. Newsletter; honors: Manager of the Year 1978, The Union Ice Co., and Spl. Safety Award for 12 years accident free (all-time safety record in S.D.); mem. Masons; mil: USAF 1949; Republican; Prot.; rec: antique collector, model maker (wooden wagons). Res: 1803 Midvale Dr San Diego 92105 Ofc: The Union Ice Co, 1240 W. 28th St, Ste. 11, National City 92050

WEIKEL, NEIL S(TERLING), landscape architect; b. July 11, 1938, The Dalles, Ore.; s. Ivan Weller and Esther Jane (Chamberlin) Weikel; 1 dau., Tamara Leigh, b. 1976; edn: Bach. Landscape Arch., Univ. Ore. 1966; M.Landscape Arch., Cal Poly, Pomona 1984; spl. courses, UCLA; Reg. Landscape Architect, Calif. 1972; Comm. Coll. Tching. Cred.(life), Calif. 1976. Career: Master Street Pgm., City of Eugene, Ore. 1964-5; w/David E. Thompson, Lndscp Arch., Portland 1966; Wash. State Hwy Dept. 1968; planner, Consulting Svcs. Corp., Seattle, Wn. 1968-70; lndscp. arch. Keith French Assocs., E.S.I., Los Angeles 1971-3, Galper-Baldon Assocs., Venice 1974; prin., Neil S. Weikel, Lndscp. Arch., Santa Monica 1975--; faculty Santa Monica Coll. 1974-6, L.A. Pierce Coll. 1974-7, Cal Poly 1976, UCLA Ext. 1978-; recipient Outstanding Teacher Award, UCLA, 1983. Mem: Calif. Iris Soc., Pi Kappa Phi 1957-. Photog. exhib.: The Artist's I Gallery, Redondo Bch. 1978; sculpture exhibs: Univ. Ore. 1965, Seattle, Wn. 1970; author/pub. My 107 Plants in the Year. Mil: DM 2, USN 1962-4, GCM; Republican; Congregational; rec: photog., botany, wt. tng., travel. Address: Neil S. Weikel, Lndscp. Arch. 301 Ashland Ave. #8, Santa Monica 90405

WEIL, JOHN B., financial planner; b. Mar. 13, 1936, NY, NY; s. Hanford S. and Rosalind (Bornstein) W.; edn: BS, Univ. of Wisc. 1959; Reg. Investment Advisor, SEC, 1982. Career: owner National Counseling Centers; vice pres. Tourists International; cons./fin. planner/pres. John B. Weil & Assocs. Inc., San Diego; instr. community colls., lectr., writer; mem. Internat. Assn. Fin. Planners, Western Pension Conf., Sea Village Homeowners Assn.; mil: NG; rec: tennis, skiing, swimming. Res: 12921 Caminito En Flor, Del Mar 92014 Ofc: John B. Weil & Assocs Inc. 2650 Camino Del Rio North, Ste. 302, San Diego 92108

WEIL, ROBERT SCHEUER, real estate co. principal; b. July 16, 1919, Cincinnati, Ohio; s. Leopold and Irma (Scheuer) W., naturalized German immigrants (1891 & 1917); m. Rita Lauterstein, Apr. 27, 1956; children: Jim, b. 1946, Pamela (Matthews), b. 1947; edn: mech. engr., Univ. of Cincinnati 1942; lic. Profl. Engr., Ohio 1950; lic. Real Estate Broker, Calif. 1971. Career: 20 years experience in technical and tech. mgmt. incl. 4 yrs. at USNOTS, China Lake, Ca. in missile devel., 10 yrs. in Aerospace Ordnance Systems Devel. (Northrop, Lockheed), 5 yrs. in electronic instrumentation for missile systems (Aerojet Gen. Corp., Summers Gyroscope Co.); broker/pres. Robert Weil Assocs., Lakewood 1971--; cons. W.D. Industries Corp., Santa Monica; mem. Lakewood Country Club Golf Course Clubhouse Restoration Com. 1981; mem: Calif. Assn. of Realtors, Long Beach Dist. Bd. 1968-; Huntington Bch.- Fountain Valley Bd. of Realtors; US Naval Inst.; US Senatorial Club, Bus. Adv. Bd.; Heritage Found.; works: 3 inventions rel. to computer air-conditioning systems; arts. in profl. journals; Republican (Nat., Calif Party); rec: golf, contract bridge, boating. Res: 4131 Bouton Dr Lakewood 90712 Ofc: Robert Weil Assocs. 5230 Clark St Lakewood 90712

WEILAND, IRVIN HYMAN, psychiatrist; b. Sept. 17, 1921, Cincinnati, Oh.; s. Joseph and Goldie (Ginsburgh) W.; m. Sue Davis, Feb. 14, 1970; children: Sally, b. 1951, Ronald, b. 1953, Nancy, b. 1955, Elizabeth, b. 1961, Jonah, b. 1971, Sharon, b. 1973. Edn: BS, Univ. of Cincinnati 1943, MD, 1946; intern, So. Pacific Gen. Hosp. (now Harkness Hosp.), S.F. 1946-7; res. Univ. of Cincinnati 1947-9, sr. res./fellow Child Psychiatry, Cincinnati Child Guidance Home 1949-51; Phila. Psychoanalytic Inst. 1959-62; PhD, So. Calf. Psychoanalyt. Inst. 1964-71. Career: pvt. practice, Cincinnati 1949-51, Seattle, 1951-55, San Diego 1955-56, Phila. 1956-62, Los Angeles (part time) 1962-71, (full) 1971--; assoc. instr. So. Calif. Psychoanal. Inst.,1975--; clin. prof. UC Los Angeles 1979--; past faculty, Univ. Cincinnati, Univ. Wash., Univ. Penna., USC; dir. San Fernando Val. Child Guid. Clin. 1962-71, dir. San Fernando Val. Mntl. Hlth. Cntr. 1967-71; NIMH grantee (7); Diplomate, Am. Bd. of Psychiatry & Neurology 1953; mem: So. Calif. Psychiat. Soc., So. Calif. Soc. for Child Psychiat., So. Calif. Soc. for Adolesc. Psychiat., So. Calif. Psychoanalytic Soc., So. Calif. Psychoanalytic Inst.; fellow: Am. Psychiat. Assn., Am. Orthopsychiat. Assn. (life F.), Am. Acad. of Child Psychiatry; mem. Comm. Adv. Bd. Radio Sta. KOST; num. articles in sci., med. journals; mil: lcdr. USN 1955-56; rec: painting, golf, computer pgmg. Res: 9351 Shoshone Ave Northridge 91325 Ofc: Northridge Psychiat. Med. Grp. 18433 Roscoe Blvd, Ste. 203, Northridge 91325

WEIN, JOSEPH ALEXANDER, lawyer; b. June 4, 1931, Montreal, Canada, nat. 1952; s. Jacob and Eugenia (Szour) W.; m. Libby, June 20, 1957; children: Michele Georgeanne, b. 1959, Paul Frederick, b. 1960; edn: BA, UC Los Angeles 1952, JD, 1955. Admitted to Calif. State Bar 1956. Career: family importing bus., 1956-62; atty. law firm Buchalter Nemer Fields Chrystie & Younger, P.C., Los Angeles 1962-, pres./mng. partner, 1979--; panel moderator Calif. Contg. Edn. of Bar, 1977-79; panelist L.A. County Bar Bridging the Gap, 1978; panelist Calif. Conf. of Municipal Ct. Judges 1973; mem: Internat., Am., L.A. Co. Bar Assns., Fin. Lawyers Conf., Comml. Law League of Am., Town Hall of Calif., L.A. Co. Art Mus., Am. Film Inst., UCLA Law Sch. Founders, UCLA Chancellors Circle; listed Who's Who in American Law (1st ed.); rec: piano, photog. Res: 324 So Clark Dr Beverly Hills 90211 Ofc: Buchalter Nemer Fields Chrystie & Younger, 700 So Flower St, Ste. 700, Los Angeles 90017

WEINBERGER, CASPAR WILLARD, U.S. Secretary of Defense; b. Aug. 18, 1917, San Francisco, CA; s. Herman & Cerise Carpenter (Hampson) Weinberger; AB, magna cum laude, Harvard, 1938; LLB, 1941; m. Jane Dalton, 1942; chil: Arlin Cerise, Caspar Willard. Career: admitted to Claif. Bar, law clerk, U.S. Judge William E. Orr, 1945-47; with firm Heller, Ehrman, White & McAuliffe, 1947-69; partner, 1959-69; Mem: Calif. Legislature from 21st Dist., 1952-58; v.chmn. Com. Cal. Govt. Orgn. and ECons., 1967-68; dir. finl. Calif., 1968-69; chmn. FTC, 1970; dep. dir., Office Mgmt. and Budget, 1970-72; dir., 1972-73; counselor to the Pres., 1973; sec., HEW, 1973-75; gen. counsel, v.p., dir., Bechtel Group of Cos. 1975-81; former dir., Pepsi Co., Inc., Quaker Oats Co., sworn in as Secty. of Defense, Jan. 21, 1981; formerly staff book reviewer San Francisco Chronicle; moderator weekly TV pgm., Profile, Bay Area, Sta KQED, S.F., 1959-68; Frank Nelson Doubleday (Smithsonian) lecturer in 1974. Chmn., Pres. Com. on Mental Retardation, 1973-75; former mem. Trilateral Commn.; former mem., adv. council, Amer. Ditchley Found.; former mem., bd. trustees, St. Luke's Hosp., S.F.; former natl. trustee, Natl. Symphony, Wash. D.C. Mil: served from Pvt. to Capt., AUS Infantry, 1941-45; PTO decorated, Bronze Star. Mem: Amer. Bar Assn.; State Bar of Calif.; Phi Beta Kappa; Century, N.Y.; Bohemian and Pacific-Union, S.F.; Harvard, S.F. Wash. D.C.; Burlingame Country. Writer column on Calif. govt., 1959-68. Episcopalian, former treas. of Diocese of Calif. Office: Secty. of Defense, The Pentagon, Washington, D.C. 20301.

WEINER, JEFFREY CHARLES, design engineering and construction co. president; b. Oct. 13, 1958, Phila.; s. Raphael David and Shirley Faye (Litwin) W.; edn: BA, pol. sci., USC 1980. Career: pres. Systems Engineering and Constrn. Co., CA; exec. vice pres. Raphael Homes Corp., CA; guest lectr. USC, UCLA, CSU Fullerton; frequent guest spkr. various real estate orgns.; honors: cover story and feature art. in Automation in Housing (internat. mag. for factory built housing technologies), in Zinc (nat. mag. for the steel indus.); mem: Building Indus. Assn., Nat. Assn. of Home Mfrs., Nat./Calif. Assn. of Realtors; mem. US Congl. Advis. Bd.; Republican (Nat. Com.); rec: archtl. design, martial arts, music, metal sculptures. Res: 941 Paloma Pl Fullerton 92635 Ofc: Raphael Homes, 533 W. Central Park Ave Anaheim 92802

WEISENBERGER, THOMAS EUGENE, radio and communications engineer; b. Jan. 2 ,1941, Norwalk, Ohio; s. Gilbert F. and Marie E. (Culley) W.; m. Christy Price Ryan, Oct. 13, 1967; children: Katrina Marie, b. 1971; Ryan Thomas, b. 1973; AS in Tech., Univ. Dayton 1964; BS, Calif. State Coll., Long Beach 1969; MS, USC 1975. Career: computer pgmmr. Norwalk Truck Line, Norwalk, Ohio 1964-65; radio broadcast engr. WLKR and WRWR, No. Ohio 1964-65, for KABC and KNAC, Los Angeles 1966-68, for KENO, Las Vegas 1966-67; telemetry engr. Philco-Ford Telecomm., Menlo Park 1969-70; sr comm. engr. spl. svcs. Pacific Bell, San Diego 1970--; honors: Tau Alpha Pi; rec: video & sound recording, boating, home remodeling, auto repair; Res: 2114 Anaconda Ln Encinitas 92024 Ofc: 7337 Trade St San Diego 92121

WEINSTOCK, JAMES DAVID, real estate broker; b. July 6, 1948, Phila.; s. Robert Jeffrey and Lucille Lillian (Dorman) W.; edn: BS, Univ. Penna. Wharton Sch. 1974; undergrad. UCLA, UCB; realtor, Nat. Assn. of Realtors. Career: travelled thru Orient 1969-72, with rock group: Prophecy, 1970-71; sch. teacher, accountant in Phila., Pa. 1974-76; cab driver, chauffeur, driving instr., acct. in Los Angeles 1976-82; currently, realtor assoc. Century 21/Lightfoot, Van Nuys --; mem: Nat. Assn. Realtors; Calif. Assn. of Realtors (dir. 1984-, Equal Opp. Com.); San Fernando Valley Bd. of Realtors (chmn. Equal Opp. Com.); clubs: Aerobics and Nautilus Unlmtd., 20/20 Video Club, Video Express Club; publs: Realtor Report (1982, 83); perf., Comedy Store (1979); Republican; Jewish; rec: travel, guitar, sports. Res: 4137-1/2 No Cahuenga, N. Hollywood 91602 Ofc: C-21/Lightfoot, 15321 Roscoe Blvd Van Nuys 91402

WEISBAUM, EARL, law librarian, lawyer; b. May 18, 1930, Chicago, IL; s. Sam and Dolores (Rubin) Weisbaum; BA, L.A. State Coll., 1952; MS in L.S., USC, 1961; JD, Loyola Law Sch., 1970; m. Ahuva Saad, Sept. 1, 1965; chil: twin daughters, Deena and Elanit, b. 1969. Career: foreign law librn., L.A. Co. Law Library, 1966---; foreign law expert, 1970---; taught law, Loyola Law Sch.; legal bibliography at USC Library Sch., 1975-81. Honors: Achievement Award, 1982, Internatl. Law Sect., L.A. Co. Bar Assn. Mem: Calif. State Bar, 1971---; Amer. Bar Assn., 1978---; Foreign Law Assn. of So. Calif., 1975---; exec. com., Internatl. Law Sect., L.A. Co. Bar Assn., 1976---; chmn. symposium on Mexican law, 1975, Conv. of Amer. Assn. of Law Libraries. Regular column in The International Lawyer, 1981---; Mexican Law for Nor teamericanos, 68 Law Lib. Journ. 395 (1975). Democrat. Jewish. Rec: folk music. Res: 8316 W. 4th St., Los Angeles 90048; Office: L.A. County Law Library, 301 W. 1st St., Los Angeles 90012.

WEISER, ROBERTA ROOT, architect; b. Aug. 16, 1956, St. Petersburg, Fla.; d. Robert L. and Lela M. (Remington) Root; m. Stephen Weiser, Aug. 18, 1979; edn: Bach. Archit., Ariz. State Univ. Coll. of Arch. 1979; lic. Architect, Calif 1982. Career: drafter The Grad Partnership, NJ (summer) 1977, 78; job captain/drafter firm of Peters & Walling, Architects, Az. 1979-80; staff architect, Daniel L. Dworsky FAIA & Assocs., Los Angeles 1980--; projects incl: Angelus Plaza Garage for dwntwn L.A. Renewal, Hewlett-Packard Rcgl. Office for No. Hollywood Renewal; awards: Nat. AIA Scholarship 1978-9, New Jersey AIA Scholarship 1977, 78, Dougherty Found. Scholarship 1977-8; Outstanding grad. of Coll. of Arch. 1979; Sun Angel Awd. (archtl.) 1977; E. Blois du Bois Awd. (academic) 1978; Nat. Blue Key Hon. Soc.; mem. Am. Inst. of Architects, L.A. Chpt.; Girl Scouts of Am.; troop leader/mem. Orphan Voyage; Smithsonian Instn.; Az. State Univ. Alumni Assn.; works: restoration of 30 year old residence (w/ husband-architect) rec: raise hybrid tea roses, writing, sketching. Res: 6207 Satsuma Ave No. Hollywood 91606 Ofc: Daniel L. Dworsky, FAIA & Assoc., 2029 Century Park E., Ste. 350, Los Angeles 90067

WEISHAAR, ROSS WILLIAM, artist; b. Sept. 15, 1951, Santa Monica; s. Adrian Charles and Dorothy (Evans) W.; edn: BA, CSU Fullerton 1974. Career: artist, 1974--, work in painting incl. study of anatomy and dissection (18 mos.), devel. own paints and oils, extensive travel in Europe and US; owner Portraits in Oil, Garden Grove; pvt. instr. in painting and sculpture; writer for many t.v. and nightclub comics; rec: furniture making, golf, writing. Res: 146 Melody Lane, Costa Mesa 92627 Studio: Portraits in Oil, 11452 Pollard, Garden Grove 92641

WEISMAN, LYLE RONALD, financial specialist; b. June 17, 1957, Bridgeport, Conn.; s. David Samuel and Roslyn (Gomel) W.; m. Leah, May 1, 1983; children: Andrew b. 1981, Daniel b. 1981, Aaron b. 1984; edn: UC Los Angeles 1975-77; stu. West Coast Talmudical Sem., current. Career: pres./owner Lyle R. Weisman & Assocs. (finl. cons. num. clients in Entertainment, Arts and Sports field, pub. corps., local banks, museums, film indus. studios), 1975--; founding orgnzr. Wilshire Savings and Loan Assn., Los Angeles; dir. Western Secured Loan & Investment Inc.; finl. inv. advisor The Center for Individual and Family Counseling (non-profit orgn.); finl. cons. Friends of Lubavitch; exec. v.p. Yeshiva Ohr El Chonon; founder Valley Torah Center/Netzach; dir. Aleynu Aish Hatorah; founder Sephardic Study Center, Jerusalem; mem. Variety Club, Friars Club (Beverly Hills), volunteer Patients-UCLA; Republican; Jewish; collector/dealer of fine art; fund raising for charitable causes. Res: 619 North Rexford Dr Beverly Hills 90210 Ofc: Lyle R. Weisman & Assocs. 9033 Wilshire Blvd, Ste 201, Beverly Hills 90211

WEISS, JON ALEXANDER, telecommunication consulting firm president; b. Apr. 20, 1942, Budapest, Hungary, nat. 1972; s. Rudolf and Ilona (Wortman) Weiss; m. Harriet I., Jan. 22, 1964; 1 son, Jordan Daniel b. 1974; edn: BSEE, City Coll. of NY 1972; MSEE, 1974; grad. stu. Northeastern 1973-75, Polytech. Inst. of NY 1976. Career: customer engr. LMC Data Inc., NY, NY 1976-71; design engr. Hazeltine Corp., Greenlawn NY 1972-73; project engr. Com. Syst. Div. of GTE Sylvania, Needham, Mass. 1973-75; project ldr. RCA Americom, Piscataway, NJ 1975-77; program mgr. Fairchild Space & Electronics Corp., Germantown, Md. 1977-78; mgr. Xerox Telewm. Network Svcs. (Xten) Woodland Hills, Ca. 1978-80; pres. CNS Corp., 1980--; honors: Eta Kappa Nu 1970, Tau Beta Pi 1970, adj. prof. fellowship pgm. CCNY 1972; mem: IEEE, IEEE Commun. Soc., IEEE Comp. Soc.; publs: Low Cost Satellite Land Mobile Service for Nationwide Application (IEEE Vehicular Tech. Conf. 3/78), Local Distbn. Networks (Intellom 80 Conf. Proceedings 11/80); rec: computers, chess. Address: 24412 Martha St Woodland Hills 91367

WEISSMAN, ALAN MARSHALL, retail co. executive; b. April 11, 1944, Atlanta, Ga.; s. Jack and Sylvia R. (Efron) W.; m. Janice Urnstein, Dec. 20, 1970; 1 son, Justin, b. 1980; edn: BA, St. Louis Univ. 1966; MBA, Harvard Bus. Sch. 1969; JD, Harvard Law Sch. 1969. Career: director Internat. Ops., Intertherm, Inc. 1969-73; dir. real estate ops., Daylin, Inc. 1973-75; dir. of real estate, Handy Dan Home Improvement Centers, Inc. 1975-78; v.p. corporate devel. & real estate, Ole's Inc. 1978, group v.p. corp. plnng. & devel., Ole's, Inc. 1983--; cons. Profl. Health Services 1977-8; asst. prof., macro econ., Loyola Univ. Bus. Sch. 1980-81; honors: one of 10 outstanding young businessmen, Harvard Univ. Sch. of Bus. 1971; Nat. Board of United Jewish Appeal; mem, Nacore, Internat. Council of Shopping Centers (bd. dirs. PAC); orgns: Jaycee's (Intl. bd. 1970-3), Zeta Beta Tau frat., Order of Oriflamme, Alumni Assn. Harvard Univ. (bd. dirs. 1980-3), Temple Bethel (bd. dirs.); publs: art., Harvard Bus. Rev. 1967; Republican; Jewish; rec: tennis. Res: 1107 Via Sebastian San Pedro 90732 Ofc: Ole's, Inc. 3395 E. Foothill Blvd Pasadena 91107

WEISSMAN, I. DONALD, lawyer; b. Feb. 6, 1950, Maywood; s. Herbert and Esther D. Weissman; m. Bonnie Jill Burns, May 3, 1980; edn: BA in hist., CSU Northridge 1972; JD, Loyola Univ. 1975. Career: assoc. atty. for insurance defense firm, Mor gan, Wenzel & McNicholas, Los Angeles 1975-79; atty. with Simke, Chodos, Silberfeld & Soll, Inc., L.A. 1979-83; Pettler and Kantor, L.A. 1983--; splst. in negligence, product liability, legal and med. malpractice and aviation litigatio, active in litigation re asbestos exposure; vis. prof. Western State Univ. of Law, Fullerton 1979; lectr., Calif. law and litigation, Am. Assn. of Med. Assistance, 1978-; recipient Ben-Gurion Bnai Brith Award 1981; mem: Calif. State Bar, L.A. Co. Bar Assn., Am./L.A. Trial Lawyers Assn., San Fernando Valley Bar Assn.; Bnai Brith (past pres. David Ben-Gurion Lodge; advisor Youth Orgn. 1975-; chmn. San Fernando Val. Council of Lodges, BBYO 1980-82); Tau Epsilon Phi (pres.); Democrat; Jewish; rec: skiing, travel, local history. Res: 11934 Rexbon Rd Granada Hills 91344 Ofc: 8075 W. Third St, Ste. 407, Los Angeles 90048

WEISSMAN, ROBERT ALLEN, lawyer; b. May 26, 1950, Los Angeles; s. Joseph Jonas and Shirley Rhoda (Solitare) W.; m. Susan Renee Bashner, Apr. 5, 1975; children: Evan, b. 1979, Russell, b. 1982; edn: BA, UC Los Angeles 1972, JD, Southwestern Univ. 1975; lic. Calif. R.E. brokr, Notary Public; admitted Calif. State Bar; US District Ct., Central Dist. of Calif.; 9th Circuit Ct. of Appeals; Dist. of Columbia Ct. of Appeals; US Supreme Court, 1982. Career: partner Weissman & Weissman, L.A., 1975--; mem. adv. bd. West Coast Bank; honors: Outstanding Young Men in Am. 1980, US Jaycees; Who;s Who in Am. Law, 2d Ed.; mem: Am., Calif., Los Angeles, Hollywood, San Fernando Valley Bar Assns.; Bus. Trial Lawyers Assn.; Financial Lawyers Conf.; City of Hope (v.p. The PAC, 1983); Pres.'s Adv. Council; Massada Bnai Brith; Ionic Lodge No. 520; UCLA Alumni Assn. (life); UCLA Sportsmen of the South; The Acad. of Magical Arts Inc. (life); Democrat; Jewish; rec: art collecting, basketball, racquetball, volleyball. Res: 17150 Kinzie St Northridge 91325 Ofc: Weissman & Weissman, 6922 Hollywood Blvd, Ste. 506, Los Angeles 90028

WELCH, KENNETH WAYNE, JR., marketing executive; b. April 21, 1956, Glendale; s. Kenneth W., Sr., and Anna Jean (Atkins) W edn: grad. Antelope Valley H.S. 1974. Career: free-lance model, theatre experience, choregrapher & co-director, Galveston, Tex. 1976-79; owner/opr. Welch Landscaping, 1979; mgr. Pyramid Waterbeds, store design, interior designer, 1980-81, mgr. Water Wonderland, 1981; owner/opr. Ken Welch Co. (mail order sales corp.) 1981-82; vice pres. Whitmore & Assocs., and sales mktg. cons. for The Resort Center, Inc., 1982; owner The Resort Center, Inc., pres./gen. partner TRC Investments, 1983--; mem. Antelope Valley Pol. Action Com.; mil: pfc (A-1 Tank Driver, Capt.'s Driver/Gen.'s Driver) US Army 1974-76; Republican; Mormon; rec: building/designing. Res: 327 Chester, H, Glendale 91203 Ofc: The Resort Center, 858 W. Jackman, Ste. 207, Lancaster 93534

WELCH, WALTER ANDREW, JR., aeronautical lawyer/commercial pilot; b. Dec. 13, 1948, Melrose Park, Ill.; s. Walter Andrew Sr., and Myrtle Marie (Kunzmann) W.; edn: BSAS, So. Ill. Univ. 1974; grad. US Naval Justice Sch. Newport R.I. 1975; JD, Pepperdine Univ. Sch. of Law 1980; certs: lawyer, comml. pilot, teacher, real estate broker. Career: naval aviator 1974-77; legal officer USMC 1975-76; aircraft cmdr. USMC 1976-77; licensed comml. pilot, 1974--; aviation law practice, 1981--; admitted to practice: Calif. Supreme Ct., US Ct. of Internat. Trade, US Ct. of Customs & Patent Appeals, US Claims Ct., US Tax Ct., US Ct. of Mil. Appeals, US Ct. of Appeals for the Federal Circuit, and other state and fed. cts.; del. Calif. State Bar Conv.; mem: AIAA, Assn. of Naval Aviation, Lawyer/Pilots Bar Assn., Assn. of Trial Lawyers of Am., Christian Legal Soc., Phi Alpha Delta Internat. Law frat., Tau Kappa Epsilon; mem. Malibu Hist. Soc.; articles in law revs., law journals; Christian; rec: flying, skydiving, soaring, scuba diving. Address: POB 9606 Marina del Rey 90291

WELDON, BARBARA MALTBY, artist; b. Aug. 29, 1931, Yuma, Ariz.; d. John Perry and Johnnie Marie (Gammon) Maltby; div.; children: Laura (Toal), b. 1956, Scott Matthew, b. 1963; edn: CSU San Diego 1949-52, UCSD 1970-73.

Career: profl. artist, watercolorist, printmaker; solo exhibns. incl: San Diego Mus. of Art (1976, 79), Clark Gallery, Boston (1979, 80, 82), Allport Assocs. Gallery, S.F. (80), Thomas Babeor Gallery, La Jolla (1980, 81, 82, 83), Ivory/Kimpton Gallery, S.F. (82, 83), Laguna Bch Mus. of Art (1984); group exhibns. incl: Newport Harbor Art Mus. (81), Tortue Gallery, Santa Monica (81), Nat. acad. of Design, NYC (79), Yokohama (Japan) Citizens' Gallery (79), San Diego Mus. of Art (74, 75, 76, 79), Pelham-Von Stoffler Gallery, Houston (78), W. Assn. of Art Museums Traveling Exhibn. (78-9), Nat. Watercolor Soc., Laguna Bch. Mus. (71, 74, 76), CSU Northridge (77), Calif. State Fair, Sacto. (75), Virginia Mus. Traveling Exhibn. (75-6). Works in num. public, pvt. collections. Awards: Nat. Acad. of Design, NY, largest award for watercolor 1979; 2d prize, 1975 Artist Guild Exhbn., S.D. Mus. of Art; S.D. Watercolor Soc., 1st awd. 1975, 80; So. Calif. Expo., 1st awd., printmaking, 1974; Nat. Watercolor Soc. Drawing Exhbn., 1st awd., 1974. Mem: Nat. Watercolor Soc.; Artist Guild, S.D. Mus. of Art; La Jolla Mus. of Contemp. Art. Reviews incl. L.A. Times, S.D. Union and Eve. Tribune, Women's Opportunities Week (82, cover and feature), Artweek, Art New England, Applause Mag.; work repro. in textbook: The Art of Collage (Gerald Brommer, 1978); rec: music, theatre, ski, travel. Address: 6131 Romany Dr San Diego 92120

WELK, ROBERT EDWARD, transportation co. executive; b. Oct. 11, 1925, San Diego; s. Edward Wm. and Iva Marie (Stokes) W. Career: employed in mktg. dept. Santa Fe Railway Co., Calif. 1945-60; spl. assignment (re Western Pac. merger case) in Exec. Dept., San Francisco 1960-61; adminstrv. asst. to Calif. Law Dept. 1962, asst. to v.p./exec. rep., Los Angeles 1967; asst. to pres. and chmn., Chgo. 1977; western vice pres./pres. Calif. rail subsidiaries, 1979--; permanent mem. Gov. Deukmejian's Transition Com. on Apptmts.; dir. Calif. State R.R. Mus.; mem. Calif. State World Trade Commn.; corp. mem. Blue Shield of Calif.; mem. Bd. of Councillors USC; mem. Pres.'s Club, Univ. of San Diego; dir: Merchants & Mfr's Assn., Calif. CofC, Bay Area Council; clubs: California (LA), Pacific-Union (SF), World Trade (SF); honors: Outstandin Young Man, City of Berkeley 1957, US Jr. CofC; Calif. Senate Resolution 1977. Ofc: The Atchison, Topeka & Santa Fe Railway Co., 114 Sansome St, Ste 1407, San Francisco 94104

WELLER, NELSON SANFORD, security analyst, financial executive; b. Feb. 20, 1932, Pasadena; s. Edward Patton and Elizabeth Katharine (Gamble) W.; m. Jane Hammond, Sept. 8, 1967; edn: BA, Univ. of Mont. 1958; Chartered Fin. Analyst 1971. Career: security analyst Union Bank & Trust Co., Helena, MT 1958-62; security analyst Schwabacher & Co., San Francisco 1963-67, partner in charge of research, 1967-70; currently pres. Rowe & Pitman, Inc., San Francisco; mem: Security Analysts of San Francisco, Fedn. of Chartered fin. Analysts, Olympic Club, Commonwealth Club of Calif. (pres. 1983); mil: USCG 1949-54; rec: fishing, tennis, hiking. Res: 94 King Ave Piedmont 94611 Ofc: Rowe & Pitman, Inc. 24 California, 6th Flr, San Francisco 94111

WELLS, H(ERBERT) CLARKE, housing executive; b. May 17, 1934, Glens Falls, NY; s. Kenneth Herbert and Constance Elaine (Hayes) W.; children: Adria b. 1961, Stacia b. 1964; edn: BA, Oberlin Coll. 1956; desig: CAM (Certified Apartment Mgr.), Nat. Apt. Assn. 1975. Career: assoc. editor Book of Knowledge, Grolier Incc, NY 1956-57; asst. mng. ed. Printers' Ink mag., Vision Inc., NY 1957-62; asst. mng. ed. American Builder mag., Simmons-Boardman Co., NY 1962-64; senior ed. House & Home mag., Time Inc. and McGraw-Hill Inc., NY 1964-69; vice pres. L.B. Nelson Corp., Menlo Park, Calif. 1969--; dir. National Apartment Assn. Accreditation Bd., 1973-74; recipient G.M. Loeb Award for distinguished bus. and finl. journalism, Univ. of Conn. 1964; mem: Nat. Apt. Assn. 1971-74, Nat. Assn. of Home Bldrs. 1972--; author: Managing Apartments for Profits (McGraw-Hill 1972); rec: dist. running, bicycling. Res: 128 17th Ave San Francisco 94121 Ofc: L.B.Nelson Corp. 64 Willow Place Menlo Park 94025

WELLS, LAWRENCE LELAND, electronics engineer; b. Sept. 16, 1938, Onida, S.Dak.; s. Lewis Graham and Mary Magdeline (Geraths) W.; m. Mary Ann Stoll, Aug. 22, 1964; children: Cynthia, b. 1965, Lisa, b. 1967, Melilnda, b. 1971; edn: BS engrg., CSU Fullerton 1976. Career: technician, engr., project engr. Electrac Inc., Anaheim 1963-73; project engr. Automated Marine, Int'l, Irvine 1973-74; senior engr., staff engr., prin. engr. Interstate Electronics Corp., Anaheim 1974--; cons: the Ednl. Service Corps, Video Tape on Satellite Navigation Concepts for Orange Co. Sch. Dist., 1982; mem: IEEE, Inst. of Navigation; patent: Doppler Shift Computer (1975); sci. articles 1981, 83; mil: E4 USAF 1959-63; Republican; Catholic; rec: pvt. pilot (SEL). Res: 225 Breting Way Placentia 92670 Ofc: Interstate Electronics Corp. 707 E. Vermont Ave Anaheim 92803

WELLS, RICHARD VINCENT, real estate broker/property manager; b. May 5, 1946, Bakersfield; s. William Vincent and Helen (Sullivan) W.; m. Lynn Parker, Oct. 14, 1972; children: Courtney, b. 1974, Lindsay, b. 1977; edn: Bs, San Diego State Univ. 1969; desig. CSM, Intl. Council of Shopping Centers. Career: property mgr. Coldwell Banker, 1969-73; property mgr. Development, Ernest W. Hahn, 1973-77; prop. mgmt., Birtcher Pacific, 1978-81; pres. Wells Properties, Irvine 1981--; independent lease cons., So. Calif. Retail Stores; honors: Boss of the Year, Orange Co. JCs; mem. Sigma Alpha Epsilon, SDSU Alumni Assn.; mil: E4 CNG; Episcopal (Vestry); rec: sports coach. Res: 27401 Via Garcia Mission Viejo 92692 Ofc: Wells Properties, 10005 Muirlands Blvd, Ste. B, Irvine 92692

WELSH, GREGG, oral-maxillo facial surgeon; b. Jan. 4, 1945, San Leandro; s. Vincent and Pearl (Garcia) W.; m. Juli, Nov. 13, 1976; children: Suzanne Kimberly, b. 1978, James David, b. 1980; edn: BS, UC Santa Barbara 1967; DDS, Georgetown Univ. 1971; oral-maxillo facial surgeon, Highland General, 1975-79. Career: pvt. practice oral & maxillo facial surgery; owner/pres. GW Investments; mem. Am. Soc. of Oral &: Maxillo Facial Surgeons, Am./ Calif. Dental Assns., Santa Barbara Dental Soc. Res: 145 Pomar Ln, Montecito 93108 Ofc: 1515 State St, Ste. 9, Santa Barbara 93108

WELSH, WILLIAM DANIEL, physician; b. May 18, 1950, Baltimore, MD.; s. Joseph Leo and Bessie Mary (Tangiers) W.; edn: BS in biol., cum laude, Fairleigh Dickinson Univ. 1972; D.O. Coll. of Osteopathic Med. and Surg. 1975; stu. Russian lang., Johns Hopkins Univ. 1971; lic. Calif., Mich.; Diplomate Nat. Bds. 1976. Career: tng. clerkships, Mercy Hosp., Baltimore, COMS Coll. Clinics, Des Moines, Haight Ashbury (S.F.) Free Clinic; intern, resident Martin Place Hosp., Madison Htgs., Mich. 1975-77; physician in partnership Family Practice Assocs., Whittier 1979--; A.C.L.S. instr./med. dir. Family Asthma Forum 1978-; clin. instr. Coll. of Osteopathic Med. of the Pacific 1980-; v.chief of staff, bd. dirs., med. dir. alcohol treatment pgm., Whittier Hosp. Medical Ctr.; med. dir. Mirada Hills Rehab. Hosp. 1980-; honors: Phi Zeta Kappa, Recognition Awards Pathology 1973, 74; mem: osteopathic assns. of Am., Mich., Calif., Los Angeles Co.; Am. Coll. of Osteopathic Emergency Physicians; Am. Coll. of Emerg. Physicians; Am. Heart Assn.; contbr. Coll. of Osteo. Med. & Surg. Alumni, UCLA Alumni, Loyola H.S., Coll. of Osteo. Med. of the Pacific; mem. La Habra Hts. Comm. Assn., Surfside IV Homeowners; publs: edtl. NY Times; Ind.; Christian. Rec: 607 West Rd La Habra Hts 90631 Ofc: 16315 E. Whittier Blvd, Ste. 105, Whittier 90631

WELTS, TOMMIE ELIZABETH, real estate broker; b. Sept. 1, 1917, Irdell, Tex.; d. Franklin Virgine and Nannie (Jay) Anderson; m. Allen Welts, Sept. 30, 1940; children: Salley (Jones), b. 1943, Thomas, b 1951; edn: undergrad. Pasadena City Coll., Sacto. City Coll.; spl. courses USC; Calif. lic. R.E. Broker 1975. Career: assoc. real estate broker, afil. McBride Realty (founded by Frank McBride, 1934), Sacramento 1971--; recipient num. sales awards; mem. Sac. Bd. of Realtors, FIABCI (Internat. R.E. Fedn. Amer. Chpt.), Solano Co. Historical Soc., Westerners Internat.; Republican: mem. Presdtl. Task Force, Nat. Repub. Com., Am. Security Counsel, Citizens for the Republic; Prot.; rec: travel. Res: 5860 Sun Valley Way, Sacramento 95823 Ofc: McBride Realty, 2100 Capitol Mall, Sacramento

WENDELL, PETER C., venture capitalist; b. May 16, 1950, Englewood, NJ; s. Eugene O. and Virginia M. (Robiolio) W.; m. Lynn Mellen, June 14, 1980; children: Christopher, b. 1981, Brian, b. 1982; edn: AB, magna cum laude, Princeton Univ. 1972; MBA, w/high distinction, Harvard Univ. 1976. Career: served as corp. exec. in Data Processing Civ., holding 5 positions, IBM Corp., NYC, White Plains and Chgo., 1972-81; served as asst. to Dr. Geo. Gallup Poll, Inc., Princeton, NJ 1971-772; v.p. Wood River Capital, $20 million venture capital fund, Menlo Park, Calif. and NYC; pres. Sierra Ventures, $16 million venture capital fund, Menlo Park and NYC; corp. dir.: Unicon Internat., Berkeley; Bengal, Inc., Sepulveda; Energy Labs., Inc., Santa Fe Springs; CGX, Inc., Acton, Mass.; Environmental Testing Corp., Edison, NJ. Mem: bd. dirs., Ill. Soc. for the Prevention of Blindness; exec. com., Princeton Univ. Annual Giving Cpgn.; NY Athletic Club; Harvard Club of NYC; Princeton Club of NYC; Univ. Cottage Club (Princeton), Hasty Pudding Club (Cambridge); publs: Journal of Higher Edn. (1980, Ohio State Univ. Press); Catholic; rec: squash, running, lacrosse. Res: 3550 Washington St, San Francisco 94118 Ofc: Sierra Ventures, 3000 Sand Hill Rd, Bldg. One, Ste. 280, Menlo Park 94025

WENTWORTH, THEODORE SUMNER, personal injury lawyer; b. July 18, 1938, Brooklyn, NY; s. Theodore S., Sr., and Alice Ruth (Wortmann) W.; m. Sharon Arkush, Mar. 26, 1965; children: Christina Lind, b. 1968; Kathryn Allison, b. 1969; edn: JD, UC Hastings Coll. of Law 1962. Career: assoc. atty. Adams, Hunt & Martin, Santa Ana 1963-66; partner Hunt Lillestrom & Wentworth 1967-77; owner Law Offices of Theodore S. Wentworth, 1978--; pres. InterProfessional Leasing Inc. 1970-78; dir. Don Burns Inc. and Don Burns Prestige Porsche Audi (Garden Grove), 1970-76; owner Rancho Oro Verde, Pauma Valley 1970-78; pres. Santa Ana -Tustin Community Chest 1972; mem. bd. dirs./v.p. So. Orange Co. United Way 1973-4; pres. O.C. Fedn. of Funds 1972-3; bd. dirs. O.C. Mental Hlth Assn. 1971-4; mem: State Bar, O.C. Bar (bd. dirs. 1972-6), Amer. Trial Lawyers Assn., Calif. Trial Lawyers Assn. (bd. govs. 1968-70), O.C. Trial Lawyers Assn. (pres. 1967-8); Judge pro tem, Attys. Panel 1968-; Diplomate Nat. Bd. of Trial Advocates; Lawyer Pilot Bar Assn.; Aircraft Owners & Pilots Assn.; clubs: Balboa Bay (Newport Bch), Bahia Corinthian Yacht (Newport Bch), Club 33 (Anaheim); works: Vedic researcher synthesizing Eastern & Western laws of living in conjunction with num. Vedic scholars in India; Republican; Christian - Vedic. Res: 3 Malibu Circle, Corona del Mar 92625 Law Ofcs. of Theodore S. Wentworth, 2112 Business Center Dr, Irvine 92715

WENTZ, LEWIS EUGENE, lawyer; b. June 20, 1955, Lincoln, Nebr.; s. Laurence Eugene and Erma Jean (Bickel) W.; m. Nina Freeman, Oct. 23, 1982; edn: BS in bus./fin., CSU Chico 1977; JD, Western State Univ. Coll. of Law 1980; admitted to Calif. State Bar 1981. Career: solo law practice in Placerville 1981--, incl. family law, criminal law, general civil practice; judge pro tem, El Dorado Co. Justice Ct.; mem: El Dorado Dounty Lawyer Referral Svc. (bd. dirs.), El Dorado Co. Bar Assn., Kiwanis Club, Toastmasters Intl.; Democrat; Baptist; rec: landscape painting, travel, swimming. Res: 3006 53rd St Sacramento 95820 Ofc: Lewis Wentz, Atty., 78 Main St Placerville 95667

WERNING, JOSEPH ROBERT, computer co. executive; b. Nov. 9, 1928, Kansas City, Mo.; s. Joseph and Hester Clair (Casebeer) W.; m. Lucia Diller,

Oct. 1960; children: Cathy, b. 1959, Gryf, b. 1962, Dirk, b. 1969, Cort, b. 1971; edn: BS, math., Ore. State Univ. 1952, BS, chem. engr., 1953; PhD, phys. chem., UC Berkeley 1958. Career: mgr. Advanced Tech., IBM, San Jose 1958-69; dir. of engineering, Memorex, Santa Clara 1969-75; dir. ops. Silonics, Sunnyvale 1975-80; dir. engring. Andeson Jacobson, San Jose 1980-82; pres. WD Assocs., Santa Clarra 1983-84; pres. On Target Technology, Inc. Santa Clara 1984--; sev. publs., patents; mil: pfc USMC 1945-46; Republican; Christian; rec: philately, horticulture. Res: 6435 Montego Ct San Jose 95120 Ofc: On Target Tech. Inc. 3080 Olcott St, Ste. 125A, Santa Clara 95054

WESER, CAROL RUTH, psychotherapist; b. May 20, 1940, NYC; d. Erwin and Dorothy Anna (Ley) Lindeman; m. John Bernard Weser, 1971; 1 son, Garth, b. 1974 edn: BS, City Coll. of N.Y. 1961; MA, Univ. of San Francisco 1979; PhD, Internat. Coll. 1979; lic. marriage family counselor, cert. massage therapist, dip. in Reichian therapy, lic. realtor, credentialed primary school teacher, credentialed comm. coll. psychology instr. and counselor. Career: school teacher, NYC 1961-63; Peace Corps volunteer, Bolivia 1963-65; tech. cons. in comm. devel. to the Dominican Republic, U.S. AID, 1966; area supr. Am. Field Service 1966-7; chpt. dir. ACLU of No. Calif. 1968-71; pvt. practice in psychotherapy, 1979--; instr. Santa Rosa Jr. Coll. 1979-, lect. in field, various civic groups; mem. Calif. Assn. of Marriage and Family Therapists; rec: travel, food, crafts. Res: 16873 Lauri Ln, Occidental 95465 Ofc: 2525 Cleveland Ave, Santa Rosa 95401

WESLEY, PHILLIP, librarian; b. June 3, 1930, Los Angeles; s. Gregor and Olive (Barnette) Wesley; AA, Glendale COll., 1950; BA, UCLA, 1956; MSLS, USC, 1959. Career: Dean, Ednl. Resources, CSU Dominguez Hills, Carson, 1969---; Calif. of Tech. Services, CSU Northridge, 1967-69; acting coll. librn., 1969; head Catalog Librarian, CSU Northridge, 1966-67; L.A. Co. Law Library, Acquisitions Librn., 1960-61; reference librn., 1961-62; head catalog librn., 1961-66; Calif. State Univ., L.A., Limited Loan& Serials Librn., 1959-60; L.A. Co. Law Library, Bindery Clerk, acquisitions librn., 1958-59; chmn., Libr. Sec., L.A. Bicentennial Comm. Mem: Amer. Libr. Assn.; Calif. Libr. Assn.; Amer. Assn. of Law Libr.; So. Calif. Assn. of Law Libr.; Spec. Libr. Assn.; So. Calif. Tech. Process Group; Calif. State Employee Assn. Res: 2287 Panorama Terrace, Los Angeles 90039; Office: 1000 E. Victoria, Carson 90747.

WEST, JAMES GREGORY, real estate executive/investor; b. Mar. 20, 1940, Los Angeles; s. Arthur Benton and Isabel (Combs) W.; m. Ruth Berk, June 13, 1961; children: Cynthia, b. 1966, John, b. 1/2; edn: BS, USC 1962, MS, 1966; spl. courses, Orange Coast Comm. Coll. Dist. 1971-8; Calif. Life Teaching Cred., 1966, Gen. Supvsry. Cred. 1973. Career: educator/work exp. coordinator Los Angeles City Schs. and Huntington Bch. Union H.S. Dist., 1963-73; adult edn. instr. L.A. City Schs., 1963-79; asst. supt. Coastline ROP (regl. occ. pgm), 1973-79; instr. R.E. Principles, Coastline Comm. Coll. 1976-82; real estate broker/owner Newport Beach Realty, 1979--; 50' partner Westlee Finl. Group, Alta Vista Associates; mem: Nat. Assn. of R.E. Bds., Calif. R.E. Assn., Newport Harbor/Costa Mesa Bd. of Realtors, Orange Co. Apt. House Assn., Calif. Assn. Work Exp. Educators (life). Ofc: Westlee Financial Gp. 188 E. 17th St., Ste. 2A, Costa Mesa 92627

WEST, JULIAN RALPH, certified public accountant; b. Dec. 12, 1915, Hot Springs, S.Dak.; s. Joseph C. and Helen E. (Nason) W.; m. Marvel E. Knorr, May 1, 1937, Alliance, Nebr.; children: Stuart J., b. 1938; R. Bruce, b. 1940; Judy (Mrs. Jerome H. Hagedorn), b. 1943; edn: BA, Univ. Okla. 1969; CPA (Calif.), Certified Internal Auditor, Cert. Profl. Contracts Mgr. Career: public accounting, 1946-49; with Office of Auditor General, USAF, 1949-62; audit policy div. Ofc. of Secty. of Defense, Pentagon, 1962-67, chief Procurement Review Div. 1967-73; teacher UCLA Ext. Univ. 1977-81; freelance photog. and audio/visual presentations, 1979-; mem: Am. Inst. of CPAs, Nat. Contract Mgmt. Assn. (fellow, past nat. dir.), Internat. Platform Assn., Assoc. Photographers Internat., Friends of Photog.; mem. UN Assn. of USA, Town Hall of Calif., Gr. L.A. Zoo Assn., Earthwatch, Nat. Wildlife Fedn., Wilderness Soc., Christian Businessmen's Com. of USA, Hollywood YMCA (bd. govs.); sev. travel clubs; Presbyterian (deacon). Res: 1955 No Tamarind Ave, No. 14, Hollywood 90068

WETTLESON, JAMES JOSEPH, human resources & communications executive; b. Jan. 13, 1938, Fergus Fall, Minn.; s. Joseph E. and Mabel H. (Holmberg) W.; m. Shirley Zimmerman, July 27, 1971; children: Jeffrey, b. 1959; Jennifer, b. 1973; edn: BS, Pepperdine 1977; MBA pgm. 1979-81. Career: with Rockwell Science Center, Thousand Oaks 1962--; var. of non- mgmt. positions 1962-72; mgr. employment Space Shuttle Pgm. 1973-5; dir. staffing, B-1 div. 1975-7; dir. Human Resources & Communications 1978--; mil: USN 1956-60; Republican; rec: running. Res: 10 Carob Dr Newbury Park 91320 Ofc: Rockwell Science Center, 1049 Camino Dos Rios Thousand Oaks 91320

WEXLER, STEPHEN CHARLES, construction consulting co. president; b. Sept. 9, 1942, Boston, Mass.; s. Irving and Leona (Hurwitz) W.; m. Bette Cole, Nov. 5, 1983; children: Peter b. 1967, Jeffrey b. 1970; edn: BSCE Univ. of Mass. 1964; MBA, Univ. of Mich. 1967; Reg. Profl. Engr., Comm. of Mass.; CPE (Cert. Profl. Estimator), ASPE; CCE (Cert. Cost Engr.), AACE; CCS(Cert. Constrn. Specifier) CSI. Career: pres. Wexco International Corp., Santa Monica 1981--; pres. Stephen C. Wexler & Assoc., Wellesley, Mass. 1978-81; pres. Systematic Assocs. Inc. Needham, Mass. 1973-78; v.p. of constrn. Walden Constrn. Co. Inc., Acton, Mass. 19717-73; pres. Computer Corp., Needham 1969-71; proj. mgr. Jackson Const. Co. Inc., Needham 1967-69; proj. engr. Wexler Constrn. Co. Inc., Newton, Mass. 1960-65; instr. of constrn. mgmt.

UCLA Ext. currently; honors: Tau Beta Pi (eng. hon. soc.); mem: ABC, Assoc. Builders & Contrs.; AGC, Assoc. Gen. Contrs.; BIA, Bldg. Indus. Assn.; AAA, Am. Arbitration Assn., ASPE, Am. Soc. of Profl. Estimators; PMI, Project Mgmt. Inst.; SMPS, Soc. for Mktg. Profl. Svcs.; AACE, Am. Assn. of Cost Engrs.; CSI, Constrn. Spec. Inst.; publs: author, inventor Advanced Computer Pgm. for Constrn. Mgmt.; humorous arts.; rec: pvt. pilot, scuba diver. Res: 4335 Marina City Dr, 632, Marina del Rey 90291 Ofc: Stephen C. Wexler & Assocs., 506 Santa Monica Blvd, Ste 224, Santa Monica 90401

WHALEY, KENNETH JOSEPH, polygraphist/educator; b. Feb. 8, 1935, Everson, Pa.; s. Albert F. and Frances M. (Logston) W.; m. Luella J. Newman, July 25, 1954; children: Kenneth, b. 1956, Linda, b. 1958, James, b. 1960, Darlene, b. 1961, Deborah, b. 1965; edn: AA, Temple Univ. 1955-8; spl. tng., Nat. Tng. Ctr. of Polygraph, NYC, Nat. Tng. Ctr. of Lie Detection, NYC, num. seminars; full mem. Polygraph Examiners of NY State; lic. detective NY (1958-71), NJ, Conn., Penna. (1958-65), Calif. 1979-; lic. pvt. investigator, Calif. 1981-. Career: chief polygraph examiner, Hammer Security System, Buffalo, NY 1971-75, Merit Protective Service, L.A. 1974-79; part owner/opr. Hickman & Whaley Polygraph Splsts., Sherman Oaks, 1979-81, owner Whaley's Polygraph and Investigative Svcs., Sherman Oaks and Milano, Italy 1981--; director/owner Los Angeles Inst. of Polygraph (post sec. edn. polygraph school), 1979--, tng. polygraph examiners for pvt. cos., police depts., sheriff depts., and pvt. investigation cos. in US and internat.; school accred. by Am. Polygraph Assn., VA, Calif. State Dept. Edn.; owner, Inst. of Polygraph of Milano Italy. Mem. Am. Soc. of Indsl. Security, Studio Security Chief's Assn.; works: 12 TV shows in Italy: The Moment of Truth (1983); Republican; Prot. Res: 11878 Paso Robles, Granada Hills 91344 Ofc: Whaley's Polygraph and Investigative Svcs, 4419 Van Nuys Blvd, Ste. 406, Sherman Oaks 91403

WHARTON, DONALD EDWARD, lawyer; b. Oct. 26, 1953, London, Eng.; s. Donald Edgar and Donyne E. (Chapin) W.; m. Pamela Port, Dec. 20, 1980; child, Sara Dawn, b. Nov. 2, 1982; edn: JD, Golden Gate Univ. Sch. of Law 1977, MDA in Taxation, Golden Gate Univ. 1978, BA in psychology & econ., UC Davis, 1974; admitted Calif. State Bar Career: assoc. Law Offices of Clark and Wharton, Sacramento 1977--; honors. Second Prize, 1977 I.H. Prinzmetal Writing Competition for art. on Fifth Amendment; assoc. editor Golden Gate Law Rev. 1975-77; mem: State Bar of Calif. (Bus. Law Section, Estate Planning Sect., Probate Law Sect.), Am., Sacramento County Bar Assns., Sacto. Apartment Assn. Products Service Council; bd. dirs. Big Brothers/ Sisters of Greater Sacto.; publs: The Fifth Amendment and Property Value Diminution Resulting from a Rezoning: The Calif. Approach, Beverly Hills Bar Assn. Jour. 1978; Republican; Mormon; rec: golf, tennis, basketball. Res: 7905 Cottonleaf Way, Sacramento 95828 Ofc: Donald E. Wharton Inc., 1330 21st St, Ste. 200, Sacramento 95814

WHEELAND, DAVID EARL, stockbroker; b. Oct. 19, 1951, Patterson, Calif.; s. Gene Earl and June Alice (Alberti) W.; edn: Fresno State 1969-71; BA, CSC Stanislaus 1976; stockbrokers lic., SEC 1979; life & disability ins. agents lic., 1983, variable contract ins. agents lic., 1983, Calif. Insurance Commn. Career: acct. exec. Bateman Eichler, Hill Richards, Modesto 1979-80; acct. exec. Merrill Lynch Pierce Fenner & Smith, Modesto 1980--; broker/advisor Stanislaus Co. Mutual Investment Club; honors: Merrill Lynch Exec. Club 1983, 84; mem. Modesto City CofC; Democrat; Catholic; rec: golf (M.V.P. Stanislaus State 1973, 74, 75), basketball (All-League, Tourney M.V.P. 1969), baseball. Res: 317 N. 3rd St Patterson 95363 Ofc: Merrill Lynch, 3501 Tully Rd Modesto 95356

WHEELER, B(RYON) THOMAS, dentist; b. July 2, 1950, Salt Lake City, Utah; s. Bryon Coulam (b. Salt Lake City) and Maria (Acevedo) W. (b. San Juan, Puerto Rico); m. Ginger Kaye; children: Lindsay, Kevin, Amy, Megan; edn: BS, Brigham Young Univ. 1975; DDS, USC Sch of Dentistry 1979; lic. Nat. Boards, 1978, Calif. State Bd., 1979, Dental X-ray, 1976. Career: residency in gen. practice LAC/USC Med. Ctr., res. in pediatric dentistry Childrens Hosp. of L.A., 1979-80; pvt. practice, Boron, assoc. Dr. Bob Lackey, 1980-81, solo practice 1981--; instr. univ. courses USC; awards: Cancer Tng. Fellowship, Oral Pathol. 1978, TEAM (Teaching Effective Aux. Mgmt.) 1978, sr. honors pgm. Oral Surg. 1979, USC; mem: Am., Calif. Dental Assns., Am. Assn. of Hosp. Dentists, Kern Co. Dental Soc., So. Calif. Acad. of Oral Pathol., USC Dental Alumni Assn.; vol. USC Mobile Dental Clinics 1977-79, Nat. Ski Patrol 1978-80; L.D.S. Inst. Student Govt., USC (ofcr. 1975-6, pres. Young Adult Pgm. 1976-7); active mem. LDS Ch. (missionary to Brit. Isles 1969-71, teacher Early Morning Sem., No. Edwards, Calif., currently asst. Scoutmaster). Res: 24475 Joshua Ave. Boron 93516 Ofc: 12560 Boron Ave Boron 93516

WHEELER, HOWARD WILLIAM, certified public accountant; b. Apr. 28, 1957, Alhambra; s. Howard Woodrow and Jean Louise (Tate) W.; m. Heide Jensen, June 16, 1979; edn: AA, Coll. of the Sequoias 1977; BS, magna cum laude, CSU Fresno 1979. Career: supvr. Wheeler Trucking, Tulare 1975-9; audit supvr. Fox & Co., Fresno 1979--; volunteer income tax asst. (V.I.T.A.) Pgm. 1979, assisting. elderly, low income, minority people; mem: Calif. Soc. of CPAs; Am. Inst. of CPAs; Nat. Assn. Accts. (vice pers. 1981-83); CSU Fresno Alumni Assn.; Sigma Nu Alumni Assn.; Beta Alpha Psi; Beta Gamma Sigma (life); Organized, directed seminar qualifying as Continuing Profl. Edn. on pension plans; Democrat; rec: model railroad, furniture refinishing, gardening. Res: 1260 W Dyer Fresno 93711 Ofc: Fox and Company, 2455 W Shaw, Ste 102 Fresno 93711

WHEELER, JOHN VERNON, logging co. owner; b. Aug. 23, 1918, Caldwell, Idaho; s. John Vest and Ethel (Budden) W.; m. Pamela E., July 3, 1982;

children: Daryl, b. 1938; Gayle, b. 1939; John, Jr., b. 1963; Carolyn, b. 1941; Warren, b. 1960; Debra, b. 1952; ed. Medford, Ore. parochial schs. Career: owner John Wheeler Logging; honors: Bus. Man of the Yr., Red Bluff CofC 1981; mem: Internat. Arabian Horse Assn. (pres. 1983); Elks Lodge; Red Bluff CofC; Tehama Co. Cattlemens Assn.; Prot.; rec: hunting, fishing, raising Arbian horses. Res: Rt 1 Box 290 (Stice Road) Red Bluff 96080 Ofc: John Wheeler Logging, Junction Hwy 99E and Hwy 36E, POB 339, Red Bluff 96080

WHETTER, MARVIN EDWARD, manufacturing co. executive; b. Nov. 3, 1931, Chgo.; s. Harry H. and Margaret M. (Smith) W.; m. Janet L. Weinstein, June 7, 1952; children: Diane, b. 1956; Doreen, b. 1957; David, b. 1960; Denise, b. 1964; edn: AA, Wright Jr. Coll. 1958. Career: territory mgr. Columbus Parts, 1963-6, nat. accts. mgr. 1966-7, regl. mgr. 1967-70, sales mgr. 1970-3; sales mgr. Valley Industries, Lodi 1973-8, dir. of sales 1978-9, v.p. mktg. & sales 1979--; mem: WDA (Mfg. Div., pres. 1981-2); AWDA (Ednl. chmn, mktg. com., 1983-4); Woodbridge Golf and Country Club; mil: sgt. US Army 1952-4; Republican; Catholic; rec: golf, racquetball, boating. Res: 1180 W Ham Lane Lodi 95240 Ofc: Valley Industries, Inc., 1313 So Stockton St Lodi 95240

WHIPPLE, INMAN CHARLES, independent sales engineer; b. Sept. 8, 1916, Portage County, Wisc.; s. Harry Raymond and Lucena (Kauffman) W.; m. Irma D. Wiese, Nov. 24, 1938; children: Lucena Ann b. 1939, Rodger Earl b. 1947; edn: Bach. Eng., Univ. of Wisc. Stevens Point 1938. Life Tchg. Cert., Wisc. 1940; NASD Reg. Representative, SEC 1964; SCORE Business Councilor, US Small Bus. Adm. 1980. Career: athletic coach Viroque High Sch., Wis. 1938-42; owner sheet metal bus., Stevens Point, Wis. 1934-43; prodn. mgr. Lullabye Corp., 1942-3; indep. sales rep. N.Y. Furniture Exchange, 1948-75; owner/pres. Home Town Furniture Inc. 1950-52, East Central Sales Inc. Edison, NJ 1952-74; dir./v.p. Metuchen Svgs. Bank, NJ 1962-75; owner/pres. Johnsons Sewing Center, Ukiah, Calif. 1977-79; public spkr. genealogy, publishing, Americanism, history, and business; awards: Jack London Writers Award, Calif. Writers Club (1983), Spl. Commendn. Heroic Effort in Saving a Human Life, City of Rohnert Park (1982), Spl. Svc. Award, SBA (1982); Boxing, Wisc. State Colleges Champion 1937 (4 letter winner, team capt.); mem: Calif. Writers Club (pres. 1978); Conn. Genealogy Soc. (1955-); TROA Retired Ofcrs. Assn. Santa Rosa; Marin Self Publishing Assn.; Infant Furniture Mfrs. Reps. Assn.; Masons, Scottish Rite. (Sovrn. Grand Insps. Gen., 33 degree), Nat. Sojourners Inc. (past pres., columnist for Nat. Soujourners Mag.); Order of Saint John, Royal Order of Scotland, Knights Templar, Soc. of Mayflower Descendants (past State Gov. 1974), SAR, Jr. CofC, NJ Huguenot Soc., Phi Sigma Epsilon; mil: lt. USN 1943-47; Republican; Prot.; rec: travel, genealogy, hist. Address: 8650 Lords Manor Way Rohnert Park 94928

WHIPPS, PAT JONES, real estate broker; b. April 1, 1939, Rockdale, Texas; d. Cecil K. and Effie M. (Edwards) Jones; m. Eugene L. Whipps, Sept. 23, 1979; chil: Danny, b. 1956, Renee, b. 1957, Kimberley, b. 1959; edn: grad. num. real estate courses, Anthony Schools, 1972-; lic. real estate broker, Calif. 1976; GRI (Grad. Realtors Inst. of Calif.), Calif. Assn. of Realtors 1979; ICA (Internat. Cert. Appraiser), Internat. Orgn. R.E. Appraisers. Career: promoter live theatre Variety Internat. Prodns., Houston 1959-61; sales rep. Peel-O-Matique Cosmetics U.S., 1968-70; R.E. sales, Walker & Lee, Quail Place Properties, Select Properties, 1973-76; owner/realtor The Real Estate Connection, Fallbrook 1976--; pres. The Calif. Real Estate Connection Inc. Mem. Fallbrook Bd. of Realtors (Profl. Standards Com. 1981-); Sr. mem. Internat. Orgn. of R.E. Appraisers; Los Arrieros 4-wheel drive Club; Republican; Christian; rec: exploring Baja and Mex. for Indian sites. Address: The Real Estate Connection, 830 So Live Oak Park Rd Fallbrook 92028

WHITAKER, FRED MAYNARD, life underwriter; b. July 29, 1925, Cambridge, Mass.; s. Sidney and Alva Gertrude (Maynard) W.; m. Jane Manning, Dec. 31, 1960; 2 sons: Fred, b. 1965; Charles, b. 1966; edn: AB, Stanford Univ. 1953; Reg. Rep., NASD 1969. Career: gp. supvr. Travelers Ins. Co., San Francisco and Los Angeles 1953-62; agent, broker, Reg. rep. 1962--; guest lectr. USC Grad. Sch. of Bus., entrepreneurship pgm. 1979; honors: Ray Lyman Wilbur Awd., Stanford Univ. 1953; Public Svc., Inst. of Life Ins. 1974; Nat. Sales Achievement Awd., Nat. Assn. of Life Underwriters (5 yrs.); citation, Los Angeles Co. Bd. of Supvrs. 1982; Phi Eta Sigma 1947, Delta Sigma Rho 1953, Scabbard and Blade 1953; mem: Life Underwriters Assn. of L.A. (dir. 1980-4; chmn. legis. com. 1981-2); Calif. Assn. of Life Underwriters (legis. com. 1981-3); Nat. Assn. of Life Underwriters; Parents Assn. Syracuse Univ. (bd.); Stanford Alumni Assn. (life); mil: cpl. U.S. Army Inf. 1943-6, Purple Heart, ETO (3 stars), Combat Inf. Badge; Republican (treas. Repub. Party 41st. Calif. A.D. 1977-81; pres. Repub. Buck & Ballot Brigade 1981-2); Episcopal (vestryman, nat. pres. Young Laymen 1958-61). Res: 863 Matilija Rd Glendale 91202 Ofc: The Bankers Life of Iowa, 3807 Wilshire Blvd, Ste 800, Los Angeles 90010

WHITAKER, JANE MANNING, school board president; b. Aug. 9, 1929, Syracuse, NY; d. Wm. Francis and Florence Deborah (Gordon) Manning; m. Fred M. Whitaker, Dec. 31, 1960; children: Fred b. 1965, Charles b. 1966; edn: BA, Syracuse Univ. 1950. Career: customer service Bell Tele. Co., 1950-57; dist. dir. (profl. staff) Glendale Campfire Girls, 1957-60; case worker County of Los Angeles, 1961-64; mem./pres. bd. of edn. Glendale Unified School District, 1981--; bd. dirs. Foothill Youth Services Proj.; chmn. youth activities, bd. dirs., Glendale YWCA; awards: Finalist- Civic Affairs, San Fernando Hilltoppers (1983), honorary & service awards, PTA/Mortar Bd. (Syracuse Univ.); mem: L.A. County Sch. Trustees Assn., Calif. Sch. Boards Assn., Nat. Sch. Boards Assn.; past pres. Glendale Council PTA (1980-2), past pres. Glendale Republican Womens' Workshop, Fed. (1978), corres. sec. Pres.'s Adv. Council of Glendale (1984), past pres. Episcopal Churchwomen (L.A., 1975-79), v.p. Zonta Club of Glendale (1984), chair of furnishing YWCA Phoenix House (1978-9); mem. Roger Wagner Chorale (L.A. Philharmonic) 1955-64; Republican; Episcopal. Res: 863 Matilija Rd Glendale 91202 Ofc: Glendale Unif. School District 223 N. Jackson Glendale 91206

WHITAKER, ROBERT EDWIN, investigator/security consultant; b. July 28, 1944, Pontotoc, Miss.; s. Richard Ward and Irene Ripple (Busby) W.; m. Marcia Diane Keeley, Nov. 18, 1978; children: John, b. 1965; June, b. 1971; Matthew, b. 1980; edn: Univ. of Maryland 1968-9; Chabot Coll. 1971-6; Univ. of San Francisco 1976-8; pvt. investigators lic., Calif. Dept. of Consumer Affairs 1982. Career: U.S. Army Mil. Intell. 1961-9; sr. tech. assoc. Am. Insts. for Research 1969-71; police ofcr. Hayward Calif. Police Dept. 1971-82; owner/ dir. Whitaker & Assocs., Inc., Hayward, Calif., branch offices in Sacto. and Wash DC, 1982--; womens defense instr. San Lorenzo, Hayward Adult Schs.; cons., indsl. and high-tech. corps.; mem: Am. Soc. for Indsl. Security; Assn. of Former Intell. Ofcrs.; Calif. Assn. of Background Investigators; Union City CofC; Hayward Police Activities League (past pres.); publs: Coping With Cops (1971), Cold War In Korea (1968); num. arts., Neighborhood Alert Bull. 1979-81; mil: sgt. US Army 1961-9, Vietnam, Korea, Combat Inf. Badge, Purple Heart, Bronze Star/V; Prot.; rec: writing, Korean karate, skydiving. Ofc: Whitaker & Assocs., Inc., POB 4894 Hayward 94540

WHITE, ALLEN ARNOLD, engineering co. executive; b. Apr. 25, 1940, Murphysboro, Ill.; s. Kenneth A. and Irene E. (Arnold) W.; m. A. Valerie Powell, Oct. 14, 1967; 1 dau: Vanessa A., b. 1971; edn: Univ. of Mo. 1963; MBA, Pepperdine Univ. 1985. Career: senior vice pres. CDI Corp., Encino 1964--; pres. VIP Engineering Co.; mem: Nat. Tech. Svcs. Assn. (dir., past pres.); Ofc: CDI Corporation, 15760 Ventura Blvd Encino 91436

WHITE, BENJAMIN SCOTT, optician; b. July 7, 1935, Milledgeville, GA; s. James Elbert and Rosa Lee (Wray) W.; m. Rosalie Hunter, July 29, 1969; edn: Morehouse Coll. 1959-61; Wright State Univ. 1968-69; Univ. of Alburquerque, N.M. 1975-8; dip., Ophthal. Surgical Technician Sch., USAF 1971; Reg. Dispensing Optician, Consumer Affairs 1980. Career: orderly, Binion Hosp., Milledgeville, GA 1949-53; psychiatric med. attendant Melledgeville State Hosp. 1953-4, 1957-9; ward & optometry techn. U.S. Army 1954-7; ophthalmic asst., USAF 1961-79, and non com. ofcr. in charge EENT Clinic 1967-77; dispensing optician/ owner Cordova Optical, Rancho Cordova 1979--; mem: Joint Com. DN Allied Health Personnel in Opthalm. (Cert. Ophthalmic Asst.); Henry N. Wall Jr. Lodge; Marion Rhoton Consistory; Oro Temple; Shrine; NAACP; Internat. Black Network; mil: m/sgt. US Army & USAF decorated AF Commend., Merit Svc., Longevity Svc. Awd., GCM, Nat. Def. Svc. Medal, Repub. of Vietnam Galantry Cross w/ Palm; Democrat; Baptist; rec: fishing, dancing, music. Res: 2130 Danbury Way Rancho Cordova 95670 Ofc: Cordova Optical, 10259 Folsom Blvd, Ste G, Rancho Cordova 95670

WHITE, C(HARLES) BERNARD, consulting engineer; b. May 5, 1904, Truckee; s. Charles B. and Belle (Sullivan) W.; m. Thelma Wachhorst, June 12, 1937; 1 dau: Marilee, b. 1942; edn: Univ. of Nev. 1933-7; reg. profl. engr., Calif., Nev. Career: surveyor King & Malone Engineers 1926; hydrographer Nevada State Engr., Calif. Bd. of Equalization 1934-47; chief valuation engr. & cons. Nevada Tax Commn. 1947-51; cons. engr. and appraiser Sacramento 1951--; mem. Sacramento Co. Tax Appeals Bd. 1968-81; awards: Blue Key, Univ. of Nev.; mem: ASCE (fellow, life); Placer Co. Real Estate Bd.; Am. Inst. of Real Estate Appraisers; E Clampus Vitus; Sigma Alpha Epsilon; Del Paso Country Club; Masons; Scottish Rite; Shriner; Sutter Club; Grandfathers of Am.; Republican; rec: Sacto Banjo Band, past. pres., musical dir. Res: 4510 Capri Way Sacramento 95822

WHITE, DORIS JEAN, real estate broker; b. May 14, 1939, Taylor, Tx.; d. Odell and Dorothy Marie (Nevels) Johnson; m. Earl White, Feb. 19, 1960, div.; 2 sons: Jean Pierre b. 1960, Jacques Marcel b. 1963; edn: AA bus., Comm. Coll. S.F. 1974; BS, urban studies, S.F. State Univ. 1977; Calif. lic. Real Estate Broker, lic. Notary. Career: loan interviewer Calif. State Employees Credit Union No. 2, San Francisco 1979--; real estate agent Scandia Realty Inc., S.F. 1977-79; real estate agt./ofc. mgr. Haitsuka & Assocs. 1975-77; real estate agt. Weiner & Assoc. 1975-67; cons./sec. treas., E.H. White & Co. 1976, seminars on real estate 1978; honors: Sigma Sweetheart (1958), Miss San Francisco contestant (1960), Iota Phi Lambda Sor. (Outstanding Sor. 1981), charter mem. Anthony's Brokers Club; mem: United Negro Coll. Fund, NAACP, Am. Cancer Soc. (bd. mem. 1972-76, Vol. of the Year Award 1978), League of Women Voters (fmr.), Voter Registrar, var. PTAs; works: participant w/son in film for desegregation, KQEO (1972); Democrat; Methodist; rec: dancing, walking, swimming. Res: 429 Hazelwood Ave San Francisco 94127 Ofc: California State Employees Credit Union-2, 41 Van Ness Ave San Francisco 94102

WHITE, DOUGLAS BRUCE, educator, business manager; b. Dec. 25, 1950, Clinton, Iowa; s. Dwight Webster and Ruth Ann (Nilsen) W.; m. Kay Chetkovich, July 2, 1972; 1 son: Brandon Douglas, b. 1979; edn: AA, Coll. of the Redwoods 1971; BA, Humboldt State Univ. 1973; Std. Calif. teaching credential 1974, adminstrv. cred. 1976. Career: jr. high math tchr. Stewart Sch. 1974-6; tchr. Sunny Brae Middle Sch. 1976-82, also wrkshp. presenter for Humboldt Co. Schools and cons./pgm. reviewer for State Dept. of Edn.; mgr. Reliable Equipment Co. (tractor dealership), Arcata 1978--; mem: Calif. Tchrs. Assn.; Arcata CofC; commnr. Arcata Parks & Recreation Dept.; publs: arts. in County Professional mag., Simpson Timber Mag.; Democrat; Methodist; rec: water skiing, basketball, baseball. Res: 90 Whittier Lane Arcata 95521 Ofc: Reliable Equipment Co., 1219 11th Street Arcata 95521

WHITE, JESSE WILLIAM, real estate developer, corporate executive; b. May 2, 1935, Coffee Co., Ala.; s. Gary Lloyd and Blondell (Cotter) W.; m. Sylvia Tofi, Nov. 17, 1962; edn: BSME, Auburn Univ. 1956; lic. real estate broker, Calif. 1974; pvt. pilot, FAA 1981. Career: research & devel. engr. Dorsey Trailers, Elba, Ala. 1956-9; field engr. Aerojet General, Sacramento 1959-61; field engr. Boeing Co., Seattle, Wash. 1961-5; sr. field engr. Eastman Kodak, Santa Maria 1965-70; real estate sales R. Chesley Co., Sunnyvale 1970-2;

owner/ pres./CEO, Jud Perkins-Northern, Inc. 1973--; owner (one-third)/ pres./CEO, Millennium-New World, Inc. 1981--; independent cons. on medical bldg. projs.; honors: Tau Beta Pi, Pi Tau Sigma; recipient sev. CofC archtl. design awards; mem; Associated Builders & Contractors, Inc.; Aircraft Owners & Pilots Assn.; Full Gospel Businessmens' Fellowship Internat.; CofC of U.S.; Hayward CofC; Bethel Temple; Nat. Trust for Historic Preservation; mil: 1st lt. CNG 1959-61; Republican (Calif. Repub. Party); Assem. of God; rec: history, geog., pol. and religious study. Res: 5701 Greenridge Road Castro Valley 94546 Ofc: Millennium - New World, Inc., 1780 Whipple Road, Ste 201, Union City 94587

WHITE, PATRICIA MEADE, writer; b. Fremont, Nebr., July 17, 1902, dec. Nov. 22, 1983; d. Lloyd B. and Maria Wilhelmina (Schumann) W.; m. Everett H. Adams, 1923; m. 2d. Raymond W. White 1945; 1 son, Russell S., b. 1924 (changed surname to White by Court order, 1948); edn: Midland Coll., Fremont, Nebr. 1920-2; Art Inst. of Chgo. 1922-4; Univ. of Nebr., Lincoln 1930-2; UC Berkeley 1948. Career: publicity dir. American Inst. of the City of New York (the oldest sci. orgn. in USA); mem: Santa Barbara Co. Genealogical Soc.; author: How To Make Fragrances at Homes (New York 1938); New York Times Mag. and Travel features on Amazing Am. 1935-45; freelance writer for mags.; The Invincible Irish, Ronald Wilson Reagan, Irish Ancestry and Amer. Emigration (Santa Barbara 1981); Instruct My Sorrows to Be Proud, The Life and Times of Grace O Neill, Ireland: 1603-18, Virginia: 1618-1682 (1983; author was desc. of Grace O Neill, the first of 100 Irish children to be kidnapped and sold in Bermuda, but escaped to Virginia aided by an Irish priest disguised as a seaman); Republican; Protestant; rec: gardening, genealogy. Res: 637 Pilgrim Terrace Dr Santa Barbara 93101 Ofc: Portola Press, POB 1225 Santa Barbara 93102

WHITE, ROBERT MARK, insurance agent, real estate broker; b. Aug. 11, 1956, King City; s. Robert Leon and Ethel Mae (Wilson) W.; edn: AA, Harnell Coll. 1976; lic. R.E. broker, ins. agent, State of Calif. Career: real estate agent Century 21 Reavis & Williams, 1978-9; assoc. broker Henry Doyle Agcy., Greenfield 1979-80; owner/ agent Bob White Insurance Agcy. and owner/ broker Bod White Agcy., Greenfield 1981--; mem: Rotary (past pres., dir.); Republican; Protestant; rec: water skiing. Res: 305 10th Greenfield 93927 Ofc: Bob White Agency, 805 Oak Ave Greenfield 93927

WHITE, WILLIAM E., administrator/educator; b. Jan. 17, 1929, Cleveland, Oh.; s. Leo and Alma Frances (O'Connor) W.; m. Grace Mary Bisulca, June 4, 1952; children: Maureen, b. 1953, Thomas, b. 1954, Michael, b. 1955, Kathleen, b. 1957, Rosemary, b. 1959, Kevin, b. 1960; edn: AB, CSU Sacto. 1957; MPA, Golden Gate Univ. 1975; MA, consortium of Calif. State Univ. and Colls. 1979; EdD (cand.), Univ. of S.F. 1984; certs. in pgm. mgmt. and pub. sector labor rels., Univ. Calif.; CAM (cert. adminstrv. mgr.), Adminstrv. Mgmt. Soc. 1981. Career: adminstrv., staff, mgmt. with State of Calif. in Dept. Motor Vehicles, Bd. of Equalization, St. Water Pollution Control Bd., Mil. Dept. and Dept. of Justice, 1955--, currently asst. chief Mgmt. Svcs., St. Dept. of Justice; gen. mgr. The Catholic Book Store, Cleveland, 1948-51; mng. partner Berliner, Petersen and White, Printers and Publs., Nev. City, Ca. 1953-55; adjunct faculties: Univ. of S.F., National Univ., Chapman Coll., Sacto. City Coll., and Adv. Tng. Ctr., Calif. Dept. of Justice; chmn. Manpower Plnng. Adv. Council, Sacto-Yolo Employment and Tng. Agcy.; chmn. Sacto. Human Rights/Fair Housing Commn.; chmn. Sacto. Co. Dist. Atty's Adv. Com.; co-ch. orgn./mem. com. Private Indus. Council of Sacto., Inc.; recipient Spl. Service Award, CSU Sacto. 1978; mem: Assn. of the US Army (past pres. No. Calif.), CSU Sacto. Alumni (past pres.); community fund raising activities rep. for Calf. Atty. Gen., 1961-73; author curricula, video course for state tng. ctrs.; mil: served to maj. US Army (active, reserve, nat. guard) 1951-70; Democrat (Sacto. Co. Central Com.; treas. Mayor Anne Rudin cpgn.); Catholic. Res: 2160 Murieta Way Sacramento 95822 Ofc: Dept. of Justice, 1515 K St, Rm. 223, Sacramento 95814

WHITEAKER, LINDA JOYCE, minister, real estate broker; b. May 5, 1942, Cookeville, Tenn.; d. Beecher and Thelma Lee (Roberson) W.; edn: Univ. of Hawaii 1965; stu. Hancock Jr. Coll. 1970-; B.Theol., Clarksville Sch. of Theology 1980; M.Theol., 1983; lic. R.E. broker; GRI, Grad. Realtors Inst. Career: pastor Lahaina, Maui, Hawaii 1962-4; dir. of Youth & Christian Edn., Hawaii 1964-5; pastor Santa Maria, Calif. 1965--; real estate broker/ owner LinEtta Realty, 1972--; founder Accelerated Christian Schs. (Pre-Sch., K-6, H.S., and Bible Inst.) 1976-; founder Lady Minister's Fellowship Internat. 1981-; real estate developer/ bldr.; honors: Hawaii Pastor of Yr. 1964; mem: Santa Maria Bd. Realtors (dir. 1976-81; pres. 1978-9); Calif. Assn. of Realtors (dir. 19777-81); Nat. Assn. Realtors (dir. 1978-81); Santa Maria CofC (Spkrs. Club); LMFI; commnnr. Santa Maria/ Orcutt General Plan Adv. Com.; Republican; Ch. of God; rec: walking, collect Bibles. Res: 2633 Ocotillo Santa Maria 93455 Ofc: Calvary Temple of God, 324 No Suey Rd Santa Maria; LinEtta Realty, 302 E Chapel Santa Maria 93454

WHITEHEAD, DAVID BARRY, lawyer; b. Oct. 14, 1946, San Francisco; s. Samuel Barry and Fritzi Beth (Bowman) W.; m. Diana Goss, Sept. 12, 1971, div. 1982; edn: AB, Stanford Univ. 1968; JD, 1971; honor grad. US Southeastern Signal Sch. 1972; admitted to practice Calif. State Supreme Ct. 1972, US District Ct. N. and Central Dists. Calif., US Ct. of Appeals, Ninth Circuit. Career: assoc. atty. Cullinan Hancock Rothert & Burns 1972-4; assoc. atty., partner Cullinan Burns & Helmer 1975-78; mng. partner Burns & Whitehead 1979--; Dir: National Wood Prods. 1980-, Enterprise for H.S. Students 1982-, Profl. Electric X-Ray 1979-, ITP, Inc. 1979-; awards: Ira S. Lillian Scholarship 1968, Calif. Scholarship Fedn. (life); mem: Am. Bar Assn.; State Bar of Calif.; San Francisco Bar Assn.; Barristers Club; ABA Com. of Corp., Banking & Bus. Law; Family Club; Olympic Club; San Francisco Sym. Assn.; S.F. Opera; Am. Irish Found.; Stanford Alumni Assn.; publs: pgm. material for Legal Edn. Inst. Seminars on New Calif. Corp. Code, 1977; guest lectr. Paralegal Courses, Golden Gate Univ. 1979-81; mil: 1st lt. USAR, Signal Corps. 1968-72; Catholic; rec: actor, singer, writer. Res: 251 Urbano Dr San Francisco 94127 Ofc: Burns & Whitehead, 100 Bush San Francisco 94104

WHITEHILL, WAYNE WILLIAM, manufacturing co. executive; b. Nov. 9, 1936, Shenandoah, Iowa; s. Charles Delbert and Dorothy Adeline (Ryan) W.; m. Karen Davis, July 23, 1960; children: Brenda, b. 1961; Pamela, b. 1963; Sandra, b. 1965; edn: AA, Pasadena City Coll. 1960; USC 1961-2. Career: salesman Frieden Inc., Los Angeles 1962-3; with Unitek Corp., Monrovia 1963--: salesman 1963-5; mgr. research & devel. 1965-8; dir. R&D mfg. 1968-72; v.p. ops. Unitek Corp. (Div. Bristol- Myers) 1972-82, exec. v.p. 1982--; pres./ dir. Unitek Japan 1968-82; dir. Inter-Unitek Europe 1968-82; recipient Pres.'s Awd. for Excellence in Mgmt. 1982; mem. Internat. Assn. Dental Research; patentee: Endodontic Dowel & Sleeve, 1971; mil: s/sgt. Army Security Agcy. 1955-7; Methodist; rec. tennis, skiing, reading. Res: 1031 Don Alvarado Arcadia 91006 Ofc: Unitek Corp., 2724 So Peck Road Monrovia 91016

WHITEHOUSE, TESS M. NICGORSKI, social worker; b. Jan. 15, 1929, Milwaukee, Wisc.; d. John and Anna (Sima) Nicgorski (aka Morgan); m. Lt. Col. (USAF, ret.)John F. Whitehouse, Dec. 15, 1951, div. 1962; children: John, b. 1952, Victoria, b. 1954, Christopher, b. 1958; edn: Bach. (PhB), Marquette Univ. 1950; Postgrad. Sch. of Soc. Svc. St. Louis (Mo.) Univ. 1951-2; postgrad. Sch. of Librarianship UC Berkeley 1959-60; Reg. Social Wkr., Calif. 1962-; homemaker cert., Cuesta Coll. 1977-. Career: various jobs with Wisc. Telephone Co., 1946-50; social wkr. 1950-72: Wisc. Div. of Children and Youth, Milwaukee and Madison; Ill. Public Aid Commn., E. St. Louis, Ill.; Travelers Aid St. Louis, Mo.; Family and Childrens Svc. Clayton, Mo.; Contra Costa Co. (Ca) Public Welfare; Catholic Welfare Bur., Archdio. of Los Angeles; Childrens Bur. of L.A.; Rosemary Cottage (resdtl. treatment ctr. for adolescent girls), Pasadena; L. A. Co. DPSS (Juvenile Ct., Protective Svcs.); companion/ homemaker in Wisc., Ill., Ariz., Wash., and No. Calif. 1973-76, in San Luis Obispo Co. and Santa Barbara 1977--; past cons. to various social agcs., schools, Catholic parishes, public ofcls.; awards: academic incl. full postgrad. scholarship, US Childrens Bur. and Wisc. Div. for Chil. & Youth, 1950; Alpha Kappa Delta (sociol. hon. frat.) 1947, honors in journalism, forensics, drama; num. civic awards; mem: Catholic Conf. of Social Wk. 1962-6; (past) League of Women Voters, USAF Wives Clubs, Sociol. Club Marquette U., Parents Support Young Musicians (San Gabriel Mission H.S.), vol. for interracial justice efforts; Catholic; rec: culinary arts, folk/cultural presentations, wildlife. Res: POB 4279 Milpas, Santa Barbara 93103

WHITEMAN, H(ARVELLA) ANNE, real estate executive; b. Nov. 22, 1937, Little Rock, Ark.; d. Harvey and Anna Mae Elizabeth (Rundell) Elrod; m. Marvin Kirk Whiteman, June 25, 1955; children: Dave Kirk, b. 1956; Thomas James, b. 1959; Jamie Dianne, b.1962; edn: Mission Coll.; Lumbleau Sch. of Real Estate 1976; GRI, Graduate Realtors Inst. 1980. Career: with Household Finance, San Fernando Valley 1955-76; Golden Rule Real Estate, San Fernando Valley 1976-82; owner/broker Genesis II Real Estate, Mission Hills 1982-4; instr. Women's Workshop, Northridge: real estate, 3 yrs., oil painting, 1979-80, instr. oil painting, Mano Studios 1976-9; mem: Mission Hills CofC (dir.; legis. chair United Chambers, SFV 82-84); San Fernando Valley Bd. Realtors (coms.); Granada Hills Community Ch.; rec: geneologist, family historian, artist. Res: 17159 Tuba St Northridge 91324 Ofc: Genesis II Real Estate, 10328 Sepulveda Blvd Mission Hills 91345

WHITEMAN, MARVIN KIRK, real estate co. president; b. May 10, 1936, Wichita, Kansas; s. Ivan Phillip and Gladys May (Kirk) W.; m. H. Ann. Elrod, June 25, 1955; children: Dave Kirk, b. 1956; Thomas James, b. 1959; Jamie Dianne, b. 1962; edn: AA, Mission Coll. 1982; Pierce Coll.; Lumbleau Sch. of Real Estate 1976; Calif. lic. R.E. Broker 1982. Career: insp. General Motors, Van Nuys 1955-84; owner Genesis II Real Estate, Mission Hills 1982--; sales agent, Golden Rule Real Estate, 5 yrs.; mem: San Fernando Valley Bd. Realtors; Nat. Assn. of Realtors; Calif. Assn. Realtors; Mission Hills CofC; tax specialist; Granada Hills Comm. Ch.; rec: numismatist, phraseologist. Res: 17159 Tuba St Northridge 91324 Ofc: Genesis II Real Estate, 10328 Sepulveda Blvd Mission Hills 91345

WHITING, SANFORD DAVIS, II, precious metals trader; b. Apr. 30, 1956, Pasadena; s. Sanford Davis and Sue (Coggeshall) W.; edn: bus. mktg., USC 1974-8; bus. computers, Nat. Univ. 1980-3. Career: exec. in charge of advtg./ pub. rels., Cambridge Resources (investment bankers), W. Los Angeles; sr. acct. exec. La Jolla Trading Gp., Inc., 1984--; mem: Jonathan Club; USC Gen. Alumni Assn.; Inter-Greek Soc. (life); Navy League of the U.S. (life); Delta Tau Delta Frat.; mil: AMS-2, USN 1979-83, Aircrew Wings, Navy Achievement medal, GC; Republican; Christian; rec: chess, numismatics, books. Res: 8504 El Paseo Grande La Jolla 92037 Ofc: La Jolla Trading Group, Inc., 7777 Girard, Ste 204, La Jolla 92037

WHITLEY, FRANK KNAUFT, financial executive; b. Jan. 6, 1923, Sacramento; s. Herschell Orval and Edith (Dahlstrom) W.; m. Arleen Lehman, Sept. 12, 1948; children: Kevin, b. 1952, Leslie (Ausmus), b. 1954: edn: USC 1946-49; CLU (chartered life underwriter) The American Coll., Bryn Mawr, Pa. 1967. Career: payroll auditor, California Casualty, Los Angeles 1948-53; self-empl. casualty insurance broker, 1953-59; finl. splst. (lic. in all forms of ins.: life, disability, fire and casualty, NASD, and variable annuities), lifetime contract with Mutual Life Ins. Co. of New York, 1959--; profl. awards incl. Agent of the Year for MONY Orange Co. Agency, 1980, 81; MONY Hall of Fame, 1982; qualified Million Dollar Round Table 1980, 81; mem: Nat. Assn. Life Underwriters, O.C.-Long Bch. Chpt. (past dir.); Am. Soc. of CLU; past dir. Anaheim YMCA; Rotarian (Paul Harris Fellow; pres. Orange North 1984-5); mil: 2d lt. USAAF 1942-45, WWII Single Engine fighter pilot; Republican; Prot. (bd. dirs. Lake Hills Comm. Ch.); rec: handball, tennis, golf, bridge. Res: 1983 Keokuk St Orange 92665 Ofc: Mutual Life Ins. Co. of NY, 1240 So. State College Blvd, Ste. 275, Anaheim 92806

WHITLOCK, CHARLES RICHARD, alternative energy co. president; b. July 23, 1943, Chgo.; s. Edward Wayne and Helen Virginia (Bartholf) W.; m. Patricia Szempruch, July 20, 1960; children: Daniel, b. 1962; David, b. 1967; Denise, b. 1968; edn: BS in commerce, LaSalle Univ. 1978. Career: sales mgr. Honeywell 1966-72; pres. Hospital Silver Corp. 1972-9; pres. Whitlock Investigators Corp. 1979-82; pres. Airtricity Corp., Northridge 1982--; awards: Economic Leadership Medal, Pres. Monge, Costa Rica 1981; Internat. Alternativo Energy Awd. for wind energy 1983; mem: Internat. Assn. of Fin. Planners; Knights of Columbus; Optimist; author: Medical Repair Manual, and The Real Money Digest; mil: USMC; Republican; Catholic; rec: golf, flying. Res: 10454 Gloria Ave Granada Hills 91344 Ofc: Airtricity, 11145 Tampa St., Ste 19B, Northridge 91326

WHITMORE, FREDERIC LUTHER, stockbroker; b. Sept. 10, 1918, Montague, Mass.; s. Ralph Delano and Harriet A. (Ayer) W.; m. Eileen M. Elliott, Apr. 21, 1957; children: Holly A., b. 1958, Heather A., b. 1960, Brooks E., b. 1962; edn: BS, Arnold Coll. 1940; Reg. Representative, NYSE; Reg. Investment Adviser, SEC. Career: past v.p./trust inv. ofcr. San Diego based nat. bank (now branch Crocker Nat. Bank); current branch mgr. Duane Remsnyder & Co. (brokerage firm), San Diego; bd. dirs. Ensystec Corp., Fullerton; honors: listed as one of 125 exceptional stockbrokers in USA, 1982, (The Hirsch Orgn. Inc.); mem: Financial Analysts Soc., San Diego Stock and Bond Club, Kiwanis, Rancho Bernardo CofC (dir.), Boys Colt League Baseball (pres.); publs: columnist weekly investment column, San Diego Daily Transcript (9 years), San Diego Business Journal (1 yr); author chapter in Encyclopedia of Stock Market Techniques; finl. arts. in nat. publs.; founder/ed./pub. inv. advisory service, Investment Quality Trends; mil: ret. comdr. USNR, WWII, Korea; Republican; Presbyterian; rec: writing, jazz, sports. Res: 3121 Larga Ct San Diego 92110 Ofc: Duane Remsnyder & Co. 16776 Bernardo Center Dr Ste 104A, San Diego 92128

WHITMORE, KRISTENE E., physician/urologist; b. Oct. 29, 1952, Albany, CA; d. Robert E. and Marlene D. (Jorgensen) Emmerich; edn: BS, Millersville State Coll. 1975; MD, Hahnemann Med. Coll. 1979. Career: urology res. UCLA Med. Ctr. 1979-; medical advisor St. Elsewhere, MTM Prodns., NBC; honors: All State Gymnastics Team 1969-72; Middle Eastern Synchronized Swimming Champion 1968-70; mem: AMA; Calif. Med. Assn.; Santa Monica Scuba Club; research in bladder cancer monoclonal antibody , UCLA; arts. in Journ. of Urology; rec: sky diving, scuba, windsurfing. Res: 1122 6th Street, No. 203, Santa Monica 90403 Ofc: UCLA Medical Center, 10833 Le Conte Ave Los Angeles 90024

WHITNEY, DAVID, lawyer; b. April 25, 1942, Alamosa, Colo.; s. Robert F. and Clarissa I. (Wilson) Whitney; m. Marcie Green, April 20, 1980; chil. (by prev. marriage): LeAnn, b. 1968, Christopher, b. 1970; edn: AA, Santa Ana Coll. 1966, AB, UCLA Sch of Philos. 1968, JD, UCLA Sch of Law, 1971, postgrad. stu. 1971-2; career: law clerk Lawler, Felix and Hall, Attorneys, Los Angeles 1970-72; Deputy Public Defender, Los Angeles 1972-74; attorney, pvt. practice spec. in def. criminal cases, Brodey, Whitney & Price, Los Angeles 1974-77; atty. pvt. practice, spec. in def. criminal cases, emphasis on felonies and federal cases, offices in Los Angeles, San Bernardino, Riverside Cos.; spkr. govtl. and profl. seminars, confs., relating to defense of criminal cases. Listed Outstanding Young Men of Am., 1971. mem: Criminal Def. Attys. Assn. of San Bernardino Co. (bd.dirs.1978-); Court St. West Bar Assn., S.B. (pres.1979); Calif. Attys. for Criminal Justice; mem. criminal def. bar assns. of Los Angeles, Riverside Cos. 1972-. mil: USN 1959-63. rec: breeding, tng., showing Regis. Quarter Horses. res: 41000 Valley of the Falls Dr. Forest Falls 92339 ofc: 444 No. Arrowhead, #204, San Bernardino 92401.

WHITT, MICHAEL CARTER, physician; b. Sept. 12, 1936, LittleRock, Ark.; s. Carter and Ruth Mae (Sturgeon) W.; m. Barbara Benson, July 25, 1959; children: Garrett, b. 1969; Lazuli, b. 1973; edn: Univ. of Tex., Austin 1954-6; Univ. of Okla. 1956-9; BA, UC Berkeley 1961; MD, Univ. of Tex., Galveston 1968. Career: internship, Presbyterian Hosp., San Francisco; opened gen. practice in Pt. Reyes Sta., 1970--, pioneer in field of home obstetrics on west coast; gave num. lectures on home birth; work contbd. to attitude changes which led to father participation in childbirth, and to alternate birth centers; current spl. interest in gerontology and oncology; clin. instr. Family Practice, UC Davis 1977-82; preceptor UCSF Med. Sch.; honors: AAFR Recognition Award, Teacher Family Practice 1977, 78, 80; Phi Eta Sigma (scholastic); mem: Kappa Sigma frat., Calif. Acad. of Sciences, Pt. Reyes Bird Observ. (life), Pt. Reyes Businessmens Assn., Ducks Unlmtd., Calif. Waterfowl Assn., Nat. Audobon Soc., Inverness Assoc. environ. action com., Marin Conserv. League; author: La Ventana (book of poems), Saws (book of aphorisms); mil: sp4, US Army,1961-63; Republican; rec: ornithology, naturalist. Res: 106 Portola (Box 434), Inverness 94937 Ofc: West Marin Med Ctr, (Box 240) 11150 State Rt 1, Pt Reyes Sta. 94956

WHITTED, BRADLEY GENE, financial planner; b. July 27, 1947, Visalia; s. Bob Gene and Elfreda June (Smith) W.; m. Susan Welbrock, May 19, 1967; children: Sean, b. 1972, Marci, b. 1976, Sarah, b. 1979; edn: Orange Coast Jr. Coll., Santa Ana Jr. Coll., Univ. of So. Calif.,Coll. for Finl. Planning, American Coll. Career: route sales Arrowhead Water (Man of the Year 1974), 1970-74; finl. planning Huston & Assocs. (Man of Yr. 1975, 79), 1975-79; pres./CEO Associated Financial Group, 1981--; founder Associated Investment Planners, Inc.; regional dir. of agencies, American Mutual Life 1983.; Profl. awards incl. Million Dollar Round Table 1979, 80, 83; Golden Eagle, Am. Mutual Life 1980, 81, 82. Mem: Nat. Assn. Life Underwriters, Internat. Assn. Finl. Planners, Am. Assn. of Finl. Profls.; University Athletic Club. Mil: sgt USMC 1965-69; Democrat; rec: racquetball, running. Res: 3077 Johnson Ave. Costa Mesa 92626 Ofc: Assoc. Financial Group 3151 Airway Ave #C1 Costa Mesa 92626

WIATER, EDWARD JOSEPH, orthopedic surgeon; b. Dec. 15, 1915, Davenport, Iowa; s. Joseph S. and Anna T. (Wyroba) W.; m. Eleanor, July 15, 1944; children: Judith Ann, b. 1946, Edward, b. 1950, James, b. 1952; edn: BS, Albright Coll. 1937; MD, Temple Univ. Med. Sch. 1941. Career: internship Reading (Pa.) Gen. Hosp., 1941-2; general duty med. ofcr./flt. surgeon, USAAF 1942-46; orthopedic residency, Kennedy Hosp., Memphis, Tenn. and Crippled Children's Hosp., Little Rock, Ark. 1946-50; pvt. practice orthopedic surgery, Long Beach, Calif. 1950--; assoc. clin. prof. UCLA; resident tchg. pgm. in orthopedic surg., Harbor UCLA Med. Ctr., Torrance; mem. AMA and affil. assns.; Long Bch. Med. Assn. (pres. 1961); L.A. Med. Assn. (pres. 1972-3; del. to CMA 1962-77; del. to AMA 1974-78; past chmn. bd. trustees); So. Calif. Phys. Insurance Exchange (bd. govs. 1976-); mem. W. Orthopedic Assn., Am. Acad. of Orthopedic Surgeons (Councilor 1979-85), Pan Am. Surg. Assn., Pan Pac. Surg. Soc.; fellow Amer., Internat. Coll. of Surgeons; publs: contbr. arts. in LACMA and Long Beach Med. Assn. bulletins; mil: USAAF 1942-46; Republican; Catholic; rec: fishing, golf, gardening. Ofc: Orthopedic Surgery Med Gp of Long Beach, Inc. 1045 Atlantic Ave Long Beach 90813

WIEDEMAN, GARY DOYLE, educator; b. Nov. 9, 1941, Pasadena; s. Herbert and Edith May (Miller) W.; m. Alice Long, Jan. 29, 1965; children: Christopher, b. 1966; Mark, b. 1970; edn: BA, CSU, Long Beach 1964, MA, 1966; EdD, Laurence Univ. 1976; Std. Life & Adminstrv. Teaching Credentials. Career: arts instr. Fountain Valley Sch. Dist. 1964-6; music instr. Seal Beach Sch. Dist. 1966-72; instrumental music, fine arts, reading, math., adminstrv. intern (1975), and master tchr., Placentia Unified Sch. Dist. 1972--; lectr. CSU Fullerton; honors: Nat. Tchrs. Hall of Fame 1974; Outstanding Sec. Educators of Am. 1975; Mu Omicron Delta Men of Distinction 1961; mem: Phi Kappa Phi; CTA-NEA; Music Educators Nat. Conf.; Phi Mu Alpha Sinfonia; orgns: BSA; Lancer Soccer Club (coach); Orange Lions Soccer Team (father); Luther League (pres.); Republican; Lutheran; rec: real estate, philately, aviculture. Res: 2835 E Quincy Ave Orange 92667

WIEDMANN, ELEANORE AGNES, business executive, civic leader, investor; b. Apr. 17, 1923, Los Angeles; d. Robert E. and Ann E. (Thornton) Ibbeston; m. Clark Vronman Wiedmann; children: Louise Monroe, b. 1947; Clark Allen, b. 1948; Cheryl Ann, b. 1950; Darryl Lee, b. 1965; edn: BA, Mt. Holyoke Coll. 1944. Career: Naval Intelligence Wave Ofcr., USNR, Wash. DC 1944-6; jr. exec. Union Devel. Corp., Inc. 1952-61; treas. dir. 1961-78; treas. dir. Dutch Village Bowling Center, Inc. 1965-79; dir. Valley Prop., Inc. and Union Farms, Inc. 1966-78; owner, supvr. Buffalo Creek Cattle Ranch, Orovada, Nev. 1976-8; pres. Portugese Bend Nursery Sch. 1955-6; mem. bd. of edn. Palos Verdes Unified Sch. Dist. 1961-9; v.p. 1964-6; pres. 1966-7; PTA Council rep to Community Ctr. Com. 1979; awards: P.V. Rolling Hills, 1969; P.V. Fac. Assn. Hon. 1969; P.V. Penin. PTA Council Dist. Ser. 1969; P.V. Unified Sch. Dist. 1969; mem: Palos Verdes Women's Club (bd. 1982-3); Peninsula Seniors Steering Com.; P.V. Penin. Republican Women Federated (bd.); The Circle P.V. Community Arts Assn.; Los Serranos de P.V. (treas. 1980-3); Penin. Edn. Found. (bd. 1981-4); P.V. Penin. Sr. Bd. 1981-; Mt. Holyoke Coll. Alumnae Assn.; Cornerstone Club (So. Calif. Area ch. 1979-81) AAUW; P.V.H.S. PTA Bd.; Steering Com. Save Our Coastline 1969-70; div. com. L.A. Reg. Planning Commn.; Harbor Welfare Planning Council 1962; Harbor Coll. adv. bd. 1961-5; League Women Voters; P.V. Penin. Plan. Council 1960; chmn. P.V. Penin. Coord. Council 1959; BSA Cub Scout den mother 1957-8; Catholic; rec: world travel. Res: 30032 Palos Verdes Dr W., Palos Verdes Peninsula 90274

WIEDOW, CARL PAUL, research engineer/educator; b. Dec. 3, 1907, Pasadena; s. Carl and Clara Minna (Matthes) W.; m. Mary Louise Montesano, Nov. 27, 1947; edn: AB (math), Occidental Coll. 1933; MS (physics) Calif. Inst. of Tech. 1945, MS in E.E., 1946; PhD (elec. engr.) Ore. State Univ. 1956. Reg. Profl. Engr., Calif. 1950-. Career: assoc. prof. electronics US Naval Postgrad. Sch., Monterey 1956-59; design splst. Gen. Dynamics Astronautics, San Diego 1959-61, Ryan Aerospace Div., San Diego 1961-62; prof./chmn. Physics Dept., Calif. Western Univ., S.D. 1962-66; staff engr. Marine Advisors, La Jolla 1966-67; chief of research Humphrey Inc., San Diego 1967--; cons. to Elgin Nat. Watch Co., West Coast Micronics Div. 1959-60, Gen. Dynamics Astronautics 1963-64, Havens Indus. 1962-64, Solar (Div. of Internat. Harvester) 1964-66, Anka Indus. 1979-; honors: Sigma Xi, Sigma Tau, Sigma Pi Sigma, Pi Mu Epsilon; mem: Optical Soc. of San Diego 1962-, AAUP 1957-67; mem. Soc. of Wireless Pioneers, Quarter Century Wireless Assn., Old Time Communicators, San Diego Science Fair (1962-); research: Ionization and Tracking over solic dielectrics 1954-56; patent resrch: Prevention of breakdown in high voltage x-ray unit 1956; Transmission of very low frequency radio thru the earth near the surface for geophysical data telemtery 1972-; mil: 1st lt. USAR 1924-41;

Prot.; rec: radio comm., swimming. Res: 3023 Alcott St San Diego 92106 Ofc: Humphrey Inc. 9212 Balboa Ave San Diego 92123

WIENCLAW, RUTH A., industrial psychologist; b. Jan. 1, 1952, Chgo.; d. Walter A. and Dorothy K. (Reichenbauch) W.; edn: BA, cum laude, Northwestern Univ. 1973; MA, Marquette Univ. 1978; PhD, Memphis State Univ. 1979. Career: research assoc. Frye/ Joure & Assocs., Memphis, Tenn. 1976-7; cons. Memphis Police Dept., 1978; cons. Memphis Police Assn., 1979; asst. prof. Univ. of Central Florida, Orlando 1979-81; cons. Naval Tng. Equipment Ctr., Orlando, 1979-81; staff scientist Honeywell, Inc., W. Covina 1981--; independent cons. in indsl./ organizational psych. 1980--; mem. pgm. com. interservice Industry Tng. Equipment Conf. 1980-2; found. mem., ed. bd. Training Technology Today; resrch./spkr. in fields of tng., leadership, team bldg., career devel., and women in the work place; grantee: Florida State 1980-1; mem: Big Sisters, Memphis; Am. Psychological Assn.; Human Factors Soc.; Soc. for Applied Learning Technology; Acad. of Mgmt.; Ofc: Honeywell, Inc., 1200 E San Bernardino Rd West Covina 91790

WIESE, LOWELL M., physician; b. March 23, 1927, Chgo.; s. Ervin Albert and Edna Louise (Becker) Wiese; chil: David, b. 1954, Paul, b. 1956, Valerie, b. 1958, Victoria, b. 1960, James, b. 1965; edn: BA, Valparaiso Univ. 1948, MA, Univ. of Wyo. 1951, MPH, Univ. Hawaii 1970, MD, Univ. Tenn. 1959. Career: active military svc. 1945-46, 1951-53, 1960-65, 1977-81; County and State Public Health Ofcr., Mich. 1973-75, American Samoa 1970-72, N.H. 1972-73, Kans. 1975-77; physician, Calif. Youth Authority 1981-83, currently Chief, Med. Svcs. Calif. Dept. of Corrections; Assoc. Prof. Pediatrics Univ. of Hawaii Sch of Medicine 1967-70, Clin. Prof. Public Hlth. 1970-72; Adj. Prof. Pediatrics Univ. of Kans. 1975-77. honors: Outstanding Physician of USAFR, 1983; mem. exec. bd. Assn. State and Provincial Hlth Authorities of No. Am. (afil. Am. Pub. Hlth. Assn.) 1976; Diplomate Am. Bd. of Preventive Med. in Aerospace Med. and Gen. Preventive Med., Am. Bd. of Pediatrics, Am. Bd. of Family Practice. mem: Fellow Am. Coll. Preventive Med., Fellow Am. Acad. Family Physicians, Aerospace Med. Assn., Soc. USAF Flight Surgeons, Am. Correctnl Hlth Ofcr's Assn. Mil: Col. USAF, 14 years active, USAFR 9 yrs., Merit. Svc. Medal. Republican. Catholic. rec: jog, backpack. res. 6450 Hillspire Ct. Citrus Hts. 95610. ofc: Calif. Dept. of Corrections, 630 K St. Rm.306, Sacramento 95610.

WIGGETT, JAMES FREDERICK, human resource executive; b. Apr. 21, 1950, Red Bluff; s H. Frederick and Elizabeth (Sibert) W., m. Margaret Ann Bedell, Sept. 14, 1974, children: Lauren Christine, b. 1981; Courtney Ann, b. 1984; edn: BA, Ore. State Univ. 1975; Labor Law cert., Antioch Sch. of Law 1981. Career: exec. employment mgr., personnel mgr. R.H. Macy's 1975-8; Itel Corp., San Francisco 1979-81; mgr. of employment 1979; corp personnel mgr. 1979-81; Cambridge Plan Internat , Monterey 1981-3; dir. of personnel 1981-2; v.p. human resources/ admin. 1982-3; principal Unicon Management Services, Monterey 1983--; cons. Digital Research, Inc., and Serupro Industries, Inc.; mem: ASPA, Monterey Chpt; NCHRC; Employment Mgmt. Assn.; Interim, Inc.; Bayview Tng. Svc.; Monterey Co. Housing Council; mil: Spl. 4, US Army, Mil. Intell., 1972-4, GCM, Army Commdn. Medal; Republican; Catholic; rec; community svc., microcomputers. Res: 5 Forest Vale Monterey 93940 Ofc: Unicon, POB 2411 Monterey 93940

WIGGINTON, RON, landscape architect; b. Oct. 1, 1944, Oakland; s. Leslie George and Lola Sophia (Kaufman) W.; edn: BFA, Univ. of Mont. 1966, MFA, Univ. of Ore. 1968; Calif. Reg. Landscape Arch. 1982. Career: teaching fellow Mont. State Univ.,Bozeman 1966-7; instr. Mt. Hood Coll., Gresham, Ore. 1969-72, Cornish Sch. of Allied Arts, Seattle 1974-6; draftsman Wimmer, Yamada and Assocs., San Diego 1979; designer/draftsman Gillespie and Assocs. Inc., San Diego 1979-80; founder/principal Land Studio, San Diego 1981--; dir: Controlled Environment Design, Space Habitat Design Assocs., L.A. 1982-. Awards: McClung Undergrad. Awd. 1964, Pennell Grad. Awd. 1967, Univ. of Ore.; Resident Fellowshp., Nature Conservancy 1981; Awd. of Merit, San Diego/Am. Inst. of Archs. 1982; Nat. Merit Award, Am. Soc. of Landscape Architects 1984. Mem. Am. Soc. of Landscape Architects. Frequent lectr. various colls., civic orgns.; exhibiting visual artist, approx. 40 solo and group shows on West Coast and in Japan and France, 1964--; num. publs., TV documentaries. Democrat; Prot.; rec: swimming, computer graphics; address: Land Studio, 1047 Robinson Ave San Diego 92103

WIKTOROWICZ, ANDREW CHARLES, control systems co. president; b. Nov. 25, 1945, Kohalaphur, India; nat. 1956; s. Janusz Stanislaus and Kristina (Dziedzic) W.; m. Annajean Kessel, 1968; children: Tanya, b. 1970, Daniel, b. 1975; edn: BS in physics, Ill. Inst. of Tech. 1967; MBA in progress, UC Long Beach; Cert. Expert Exam. in Control Systems; reg. Profl. Engr. Control Systems (1975), Mfg. (1978), Calif.; reg. Calif. State Bd. of Profls. Career: instru. physicist CPC International, Argo, Ill. 1967-70; project engr. Fluor Corp., Irvine 1970-73; engrg. group leader Bechtel Power Corp., Norwalk 1973-74; chief controls engr. Ameron Process Systems Div., Santa Ana 1974-76; v.p./CEO, JPW Industries, Orange 1976-78; pres. Automated Dynamics Corp. (applications engrg. co.), 1978--. Awards: NSF Undergrad Research Grantee 1966; 1st Place 1980 Best Application of Programmable Controller, Texas Instruments distbrs. Mem: Instruments Soc. of Am. (v.p. internat. exec. bd. 1981-3; pres. Los Angeles chpt. 1975); SCMA; IAE; IBEW (trustee Welfare Fund 1976-80); pres. student sect. Am. Inst. of Physics 1966. Publs: num. profl. symposium presentations. Republican. Catholic. Rec: racquetball, golf, tennis. Res: 13102 Malena Dr. Santa Ana 92705 Ofc: Automated Dynamics Corp. 23170 Del Lago, Laguna Hills 92653

WILBURN, RUTH GERALDINE, corporate executive; b. Apr. 27, 1926, Dothat, Mo.; d. Elkin Viles and Myrtle (Gilliam) Courter; m. James E. Wilburn, Feb. 23, 1944; children: Darlene, b. 1945; James E., b. 1951. Career: secty. Orlando Homes, Inc. 1957--; secty. Wilburn Enterprises 1958--; mem: 100 Club of Alameda Co.; Republican; Protestant; rec: sewing. Res: 4628 Emily Court Castro Valley 94546 Ofc: Orlando Homes, Inc., 20861 Castro Valley Blvd, No 6, Castro Valley 94546

WILCOX, COLIN ROGER, real estate broker; b. Nov. 25, 1938; s. Roger Nelson and Irene Maud (Ennis) W.; edn: bus. admin., St. Andrews Coll., Dublin, Ire. 1958. Career: owner/ broker Wilcox Real Estate, 1979--, spec. in new home sales; Republican; Protestant. Res: 559 Wayland Court Claremont 91711 Ofc: Wilcox Real Estate, 2905 Colonial Ave Ontario 91761

WILDER, ERNEST WALTER, JR., realty co. president/general contractor; b. Feb. 27, 1942, Cumberland, Ky.; s. Ernest Walter and Dorcas Lee (Wilder) W.; m. Jacqueline Berry, July 6, 1965; children: Toni, b. 1966, James, b. 1968, Amy, b. 1969, Troy, b. 1972; edn: BS in adm. mgmt., Univ. of Cincinnati 1970; MPA, Consortium of Calif. State Univs. and Colls. 1976, Calif. lic. R.E. Broker 1979, lic. Gen. Contractor 1979; Comm. Coll. Instr. credential 1983. Career: medical administrator, Univ. of Cincinnati Med. Ctr., 1965-73, concurrently office supr. Blue Cross of Southwest Ohio, 1968-70; asst. adminstr. Saint Agnes Med. Ctr., Fresno, Calif. 1973-75; asst. adminstr. Hospital Corp. of America 1975-79; pres. Ernest W. Wilder, Inc. (fin. plnng. corp.), Fresno 1979--; cons. to Gary L. McDonald Constrn./Realty, 1979-82; honors: National Hon. Soc., Nat. Beta Club; mem: Nat./Calif. Assn. of Realtors, Building Indus. Assn. of the San Joaquin Valley; Masons; publs: arts. in indus. journals; mil: E5 US Army 1961-64, 1st lt. USAR; Republican; So. Baptist; rec: walking, piano, singing. Address: Ernest W. Wilder, Inc., 567 E. Richmond Ave Fresno 93710

WILHELM, MARGARET LENORE, financial analyst/accountant; b. Mar. 5, 1951, Walla Walla, Wash.; d. Joseph Valentine and Eulela Jeanne (Jorstad) W.; edn: Walla Walla Coll. 1969-70; BS, Pacific Union Coll. 1973; Loma Linda Univ. 1980-82. Career: sr. acct. Porter Meml Hosp., Denver 1974-76; sec. bus. edn. tchr. Gem State Acad. 1976-79; asst. to dean (finance) Loma Linda Univ. 1979--, and asst. dir. ext. pgms. Sch. Health 1983--; mem. Am. Mgmt. Assn.; Loma Linda Women's Club; Inland Empire Embroiderers Guild; Democrat; 7th Day Adventist; rec: needlework. Res: 1077-63 Santa Antonio Dr Colton 92354 Ofc: Loma Linda Univ. Loma Linda 92350

WILKE, MARGUERITE FAYE, lawyer; b. Mar 6, 1922, Chgo.; d. Adolph Christian and Margaret Lucille (Monahan) Mayer; m. Warren E. Wilke, Aug. 11, 1973; children: Laurie, b. 1944; Richard, b. 1947; David, b. 1950; Keith, b. 1959; Lita, b. 1973, edn: BBS, cum laude, Univ. of Miami 1963; JD, Univ. of Miami Law Sch. 1970; atty. at law, State Bar of Calif. 1974. Career: auditor U.S. Govt., Los Angeles and Miami, Fla., five yrs -1972; staff atty. in chg. west coast ofc., Mead Corp., Dayton, Oh. 1974-6; deputy dist. atty. County of Los Angeles, 1977-79, deputy public defender 1979-80; industrial labor relations officer, Dept. of Defense, 1980--; honors: grad. w/ highest scholastic average, Fla. Bd. of CPAs; mem: var. honor socs.; Fla., Calif. Bar Assns; Fla., Calif. Women Lawyers; Christian Sci.; rec: rock climbing, gardening, ballet dancing. Res: 15736 Hartsook St Encino 91436 Ofc: Defense Contract Administration, 11099 So La Cienega Blvd Los angeles 90045

WILKEN, CLAUDIA, U.S. magistrate; b. Aug. 17, 1949, Mnpls. Minn.; d. Claudius W. and Dolores Ann (Grass) W.; edn: BA, Stanford Univ. 1971; JD, Boalt Hall, UC 1975; atty. at law, Calif. State Bar 1975. Career: atty. Fed. Public Defenders, San Francisco 1975-8; partner Wilken & Leverett, Berkeley 1978--; magistrate U.S. Dist. Ct., San Francisco 1983--; lectr. Criminal Trial Practice, Boalt Hall, UC Berkeley 1978--; tchr. Criminal Proceedure, New Coll. Sch. of Law, San Francisco 1980--; honors: Phi Beta Kappa 1971; Order of the Coif 1975; mem: Calif. State Bar; Alameda Co. Bar Assn.; Women Lawyers of Alameda Co.; Ofc: Wilken & Leverett, 1919 Addison St, Ste 210, Berkeley 94704

WILKES, ARTHUR EDMOND, company chief executive; b. May 9, 1939, Sth. Norwalk, CT; s. Howard Ranki and Helen (Edmond) W.; m. Dallis Elizabeth Nelson- Banki, Dec. 24, 1981; edn: Prepartory Choate Sch., CT 1957; BA, Middlebury, Vermont 1961. Career: asst. dean of admissions Middlebury Coll. 1961-2; Lt. U.S. Army 1962-4; with Xerox 1964-82; sales rep. 1964-6; dist. mgr. 1966-7; br. mgr. 1967-9; mktg. support mgr., Xerox H.Q. 1969-71; regl. sales dir., U.S. mktg. 1975-7; dir. internat. mktg. Rank Xerox, London 1977-9; dir. far eastern ops., Rank Xerox 1979-8; chief exec. ofcr. Computers Internat. 1983; chief exec. ofcr. Advanced Cellular Phone Co. 1983--; cons. partner w/ Pacific Telesis in selected overseas mkts.; honors: pres. Mens Undergrad. Body, Middlebury; Most Valuable Athlete, Middlebury Coll., Distg. Mil. Grad., U.S. Army; mem: The Lakeside Golf Club, NTH. Hollywood; Los Angeles Tennis Club; Big Brothers; NAACP; sponsor of Traffic Safety Week & the Police Celebrity Golf Tourn. with LAPD, 1984; mil: 1st lt. US Army, DMG; Republican; Christian; rec: racquetball, tennis, golf. Res: 4055 Kraft Ave Studio City 91604 Ofc: Advanced Cellular Phone Co., 8885 Venice Blvd Los Angeles 90034

WILKINSON, DON FRANKLIN, investment marketing executive; b. Apr. 24, 1945, Charleston, WV; s. Donald Marion and Eunice Anna (Derrick) W.; m. Marie K. Pittman, 1969; 1 dau: Jennifer Nicole, b. 1973; edn: BS, FL State Univ. 1967; AA, Manatee Coll. 1965. Career: Vick Chem. Co., 1971-8; div. sales mgr., Phila., PA 1971-2; dist. sales mgr., Los Angeles 1972-4; area sales & mktg. mgr., W. Coast 1974-6; Western regl. sales mgr. 1976-8; v.p. mktg. South

County Devel. Co., Anaheim 1978-9; pres. R.H. Dev; K.S. DevCo, Santa Ana 1979-80; pres. Financial Freedom, Inc., Tustin 1980--; awards: Regl. Sales Mgr. 1973; Nat. Mktg. Rep. of the Yr., Vick Chem. Co. 1971; Lowry Nickerson Invest. Achiev. 1977; mem: Am. Soc. Profl. Cons.; Internat. Assn. for Fin. Plnrs., Inc.; Am. Mktg. Assn.; Republican; Prot.; rec: antique autos, reading. Ofc: 17852 E 17th St, Ste 207, Tustin 92680

WILKINSON, DUANE LAMAR, gold assayer; b. Aug. 27, 1933, Downey; s. Clifford Lamar and Beulah Marie (Zulie) W.; m. Mable Enriguez, June 25, 1960; children: Sherry, b. 1961; Mark, b. 1962; Bruce, b. 1964. Career: gold assayer Wilkinson Assays, Fontana 1967--; Rock Shop owner, mgr.; assayer, chemist, metallurgist, refiner; geologist, and mine cons. asst. geology inst. Adult Edn., High Sch ; awards: world's hard rock champion gold panner 1979; 3rd awd. in 1980; recipient 10 ribbons for 1st, 2d. & 3rd first in gold and silver ore county foir awds.; 5 newspaper writeups; mem: G.P.A.A. Gold Prospectors Assn. of Am. (14 yrs. chem. research on gold and silver assays); author two books: Sucessful Miner (1982), Pegleg Gold (1979); rec: worlds largest pvt. collection of gold, silver, coppper and lead ore, and largest gold nugget collection. Address: Wilkinson Assays, 8849 Sierra Ave Fontana 92335

WILKINSON, LAWRENCE HAMLETT, II, television production executive; b. Jan. 2, 1950, Greensboro, NC; s. William Cook, II, and Joy (Morgan) W.; edn: BA, summa cum laude, Davidson Coll. 1972; B.Phil., Oxford Univ. Magdalen Coll. 1974; MBA, honors, Harvard Bus. Sch. 1976. Career: assoc. prod. Maysles Films, New York 1969-70; prod. WBTV, Charlotte, NC 1971-2; dir. of plng. and mktg. WNET-TV, New York 1976-8; dir. devel., plng. and pgm. prod. KQEO TV & FM, San Francisco 1979-81; pres. Wilkinson & Assoc and v.p. Varitel Communications, Inc., S.F. 1982--; cons: SRI Internat., Sony Corp. of Am., Eastern Television Network, Small World Commns. 1982-; World Bank of Gulf Oil 1976; frequent pub. speaker; awards: PBS Devel. Awds. 1979, 80; mem: Nat. Cable TV Assn.; Nat. Assn. of TV Pgm. Execs.; Friends of KQED, Inc. (pres. 1982-); Commonwealth Club; co- editor: The Cambridge Milton, Vol. 5 (Cambridge Univ. Press 1974); author: Public Broadcasting in the U.S. (Harvard Univ. 1976); prod./exec. prod. num. t.v. programs; Democrat; rec: book and art collection. Res: Varitel Communications, 350 Townsend St San Francisco 94107

WILLEMS, JAMES EZRA, shopping center developer; b. Oct. 8, 1926, Tsachien, China; s. George K. and Mary (Koop) W., American missionaries; m. Betty Lou, Sept. 5, 1957; children: Steve Douglas, b. 1953; (stepchil.) Laurence J. (b. 1947), Lynne Marie (b. 1949), Dale Anne (b. 1953) Severance; edn: BA, CSC Fresno 1952; grad. work, USC 1958-62; Std. Calif. Teaching, Ednl. Adminstrv. Credential. Career: teacher public schools, Torrance Sch. Dist. 1953-56, Pasadena Sch. Dist. 1956-68; real estate devel., So. Calif. 1968-72; founder/pres. Maranatha Village, Inc. (Christian shopping ctr.), Santa Ana 1973--; dir. Pasadena Edn. Assn. 1960-64; bd. dirs. Calvary Chapel, Costa Mesa 1973-76; bd. dirs. Gospel Music Assn. 1983-; honors: Pasadena Teacher of the Year 1965, PTA life membership 1963; mem. PTA, CTA, NEA (1955-72); various rel. orgns.; Religion in Media 1976-9; founding publisher: Contemporary Christian (1978), Acts (1978, a Christian newspaper); mil: sgt. US Army 1945-6, GCM; Republican; Calvary Chapel, Costa Mesa; rec: travel, gardening. Res: 1119 Sunflower St Costa Mesa 92626 Ofc: Maranatha Village, 2400 Sunflower St Santa Ana 92704

WILLETT, JOHN GARY, real estate/financial planning consultant; b. May 27, 1948, Alameda; s. Wilbur Lewis and Evelyn Ann (White) W.; m. Sandra Michelle Hensley, Apr. 22, 1972; children; Caryn, b. 1964; Bryan, b. 1974; Robyn, b. 1978; edn: BS, CSU Hayward 1969; grad. sch. UC 1970; grad. sch. of banking, Univ. of Colo. 1975-7; lic. real estate broker, 1983. Career: National Bank examiner, U.S. Treasury 1971-7; exec. v.p./ dir. Nat. Bank of Whittier 1977-80; pres./ dir. Western Nat. Bank 1980-2; chmn./ prin. Executive Capital Corp., Upland 1982--; asst. prof. Whittier Coll. 1979; honors: Pres.'s Council, CSU Fullerton 1981; mem: Rotarian; Independent Bankers Assn.; Sunnyhills Racquet Club; Sunrise Country Club; Nat. Assn. of Eagle Scouts; leader, Christian Svc. Brigade Youth Pgm.; guest lectr. Pacific Christian Univ., various fin. plnng. seminars; mil: E-5, Calif. Nat. Guard, 1973; Republican (Presdtl. Task Force); Protestant; rec: tennis, gold, swimming. Res: 3106 Sunnywood Dr Fullerton 92635 Ofc: Executive Capital Corp., 1317 W Foothill Blvd Upland 91786

WILLETTE, JESSE FREDERICK, lawyer, businessman; b. Aug. 17, 1944, Chgo.; s. Francis Arthur and Margaret Mary (Rasor) W.; m. Susan Chamberlain, Dec. 24, 1966; children: Lesley Susan, b. 1967; Jesse David, b. 1970; edn: AA, El Camino Coll. 1965; BA, Calif. State Coll., Long Beach 1967; Jr. Coll. Tchg. cert., UCLA 1973; JD, BSL, So. Bay Univ. Coll. of Law 1973; admitted to Calif. State Bar 1973. Career: social wkr. 1968-71; criminal investigator Los Angeles Co. Supr. Ct. 1971-3; Los Angeles Co. Public Defender 1973-9; pvt. practice spec. bus., tax, real estate, and trial practice 1979--; bd. dirs. So. Central Bar Assn.; Judge Pro Tempore, Los Angeles Co. Municipal Ct.; awards: Corpus Juris Secondum Awd., West Publ. Co.; Hornbook Awd., Bancroft/ Whitney top student 1st yr.; Academic Scholarship; mem: Am. Bar Assn., Economics Sect.; So. Central Bar Assn.; Calif. State Bar; So. Bay Criminal Bar; lectr., writer on Jury summation and argument and Civil Discovery before trial, SCBA; mil: OCS, USMCR 1966; Protestant; rec: music composition (classical, jazz), computer research. Res: 2351 W 249th Street Lomita 90717 Ofc: Law Offices, 21707 Hawthorne Blvd, Ste 101, Torrance 90503

WILLIAMS, CHARLES JUDSON, lawyer; b. Nov. 23, 1930, San Mateo; s. John Augustus and Edith (Babcock) W.; children: Patrick, b. 1957, Victoria, b. 1958, Apphia, b. 1981; edn: AB, UC Berkeley 1952, LLB 1955; admitted to Calif. State Bar, US Dist. Ct., US Ct. of Appeal, 1955, US Supreme Ct. 1970. Career: assoc. atty. with Kirkbride, Wilson, Harzfeld & Wallace, San Mateo 1956-59 (spl. counsel to cities and districts throughout state for financing pub. improvements); with John A. Bohn and Assocs., Benicia 1959-64; solo law practice, 1964-76, assoc. w/ Fred Caploe, 1976-; public offices: asst. city atty. City of Benicia, 1959-64; assoc. counsel Central Contra Costa Sanitary Dist., 1959-64; legal advisor Alaska State Legislature, 1959-61, AK State Supreme Ct., 1959-60; city atty. for Lafayette (1968-), Moraga (1974-), and Danville (1982-); city atty. Benicia, 1980-82; gen. counsel Contra Costa Co. Municipal Risk Mgmt. Authority, 1977-; lectr. Cont. Edn. of the Bar 1964-5. 1977; instr. John F. Kennedy Univ. Sch. of Law 1965-8; lectr. UC Ext. Div. 1974-6; num. presentations on land use law and plnng., League of Calif. Cities confs. 1964-; bd. dirs. County Fair Bd. 1966-8. Publs: Municipal Code of Cities of Pleasant Hill, Benicia, Lafayette, Moraga, Danville; author Calif. Zoning Practice (CEB, 1977, 79, 80, 82, 3, 4); author law texts on Calif. Code, Calif. Comml. Code Forms, Calif. Govt. Code Forms (West Pub. Co. 1964, 65, 71). Res: 929 Janet Ln Lafayette 94549 Ofc: Williams & Caploe, APC, 1060 Grant St, Ste. 201, Benicia 94510

WILLIAMS, DARRELL JAY, investment advisor; b. Mar. 7, 1951, Chgo.; s. John Edward and Betty Lou (Cater) W.; edn: BA, No. Ill. Univ. 1973; cert. psychiat. tech., West Valley Coll. 1976-7; stu. Coll. for Fin. Planning 1983-4. Career: psychiatric therapist Good Samaritan Hosp., San Jose 1977-84; investment advisor University Securities Corp., 1982-4 currently Southmark Fin. Svcs.; fin. plng. instr., Sawyer Bus. Coll., San Jose City Coll., Palmer West Coll. of Chiropractic; honors: Eagle Scout, BSA 1968, Nat. Honor Soc. 1967-9; mem: Inst. of Cert. Fin. Plnrs.; The Holiday Project; pres. Employees Assn. Com. of Good Samaritan Hosp.; co-editor, Planning Matters; contbr., Pulsebeat; Libertarian; rec: massage, human potential. Res: 4951 Cherry Ave, Apt 18, San Jose 95118 Ofc: Southmark Financial Services, 4340 Stevens Creek Blvd, Ste 102, San Jose 95129

WILLIAMS, DONALD FREEMAN, urologist; b. Oct. 4, 1934, Butte, Montana; s. Freeman R. and Vonna L. (Olsen) W.; m. Nancy Russell, June 6, 1982; children: Scot, b. 1960; Bret, b. 1962; Jolene, b. 1963; Ryan, b. 1975; edn: BA, Univ. of Kansas 1956, MD, 1960; FACS, Fellow Am. Coll. of Surgeons 1972. Career: intern, res. Johns Hopkins Hosp., Baltimore, MD 1960-2; res. UCLA Med. Sch., Los Angeles 1964-8; pvt. practice urology, Newport Beach 1968--; pres. Williams- Brinton Medical Corp. and Orange Coast Urology Surgical Medical Group; asst. clinical prof. surgery/ urology UCLA & UCI Med. Schs.; honors: Phi Beta Kappa 1951; Alpha Omega Alpha 1959; mem: Orange Co., Calif., and Am. Med. Assns.; Am. and Orange Co. Urological Assns.; fellow, Am. Coll. of Surgeons; fellowship Inst. of Cardiology, London, Eng. 1959-60; publs: Journ. of Urology, British Jorn. of Med., New England Journ. Med; mil: Capt., USAF Med. Corp. 1962-4; Republican; rec: boating, skiing, tennis. Res: 40 Sycamore Creek Irvine 92715 Ofc: Orange Coast Urology Surgical Medical Group, 320 Superior Newport Beach 92663

WILLIAMS, DWIGHT DAVID, irrigation district executive; b. Nov. 18, 1936, San Diego; s. Stafford Miller and Mildred Monzell (Standridge) W.; m. Charlene Rae Alder, Nov. 21, 1982; 2 daus.: Michelle and Kristin, b. 1969; edn: AA, Los Angeles City Coll. 1966; BS, Univ. of San Francisco 1980; 1st Class Fed. Comm. Radio/ Telephone lic. Career: field engr. General Elec. Co., Los Angeles 1966-72; elec. div. supt. Turlock Irrigation Dist., Turlock 1972--; Adv. Bd., Modesto Jr. Coll. 1974-6; tchr. electronics Modesto Jr. Coll. 1976-9; awards: Royal Order of Lobster 1970, Safety Awd., 1972, G.E. Co.; mem. Instrument Soc. of Am.; Turlock Masonic Lodge; works: devel. message distr. sys., Army Hdqtrs., Wash. DC, letter of commdn. 1961; mil: E-5, Army Security Agcy. 1957-62, GCM; Republican; Protestant; rec: sports (baseball, volleyball, tennis, swimming). Res: 1115 No Quincy Road Turlock 95380 Ofc: Turlock Irrigation Dist., 333 E Canal Dr Turlock 95380

WILLIAMS, GEORGE, III, author, publisher; b. Mar. 3, 1949, Springfield, Mass.; s. George, Jr. and Millie W.; m. Edie; 2 children: Sarah, Michael; edn: BA, creative writing, music comp., UC Riverside. Career: pres. Tree By The River Publishing; cons. book publishing cos.; recipient John Stone Award in Music, Riverside City Coll.; nominated Nobel Prize in Literature 1984; mem. Publishers Assn. of So. Calif., COSMEP; author: Rosa May: The Search for a Mining Camp Legend (1980), The Guide to Bodie and Eastern Sierra Historic Sites (1981), The Murders at Convict Lake, The Redlight Ladies of Virginia City, Nevada (1984), The Songwriter's Demo Manual and Success Guide (1984); Born Again Christian; rec: music. Address: Tree By The River Pub., POB 413, Riverside 92502

WILLIAMS, HAL W., JR., lawyer; b. Apr. 25, 1935, Salt Lake City, Utah; s. Harold W., Sr. and Helen B. (Blaney) W.; m. Janis R., May 3, 1970; children: Jennifer; Michelle; David; Danny; Amy; Rachael; edn: BS, Univ. of Ore. 1959; JD, Southwestern Univ. 1965. Career: trial atty. Farmers Ins. 1971-3; pvt. practice spec. in civil trials or major products liability, med. malpractice and pers. injury cases for Plaintiff, 1973--; guest spkr. legal sems.; honors: selected by Medical Economics as one of ten best trial lawyers; mem: ATLA, LATLA, CTLA, ABOTA; mil: QM3, USN 1956-7; rec: fishing, golf, boating. Res: 10356 Claire Ave Northridge 91326 Ofc: Pollack Lintz Williams, 10880 Wilshire Blvd, Ste 300, Los Angeles 90024

WILLIAMS, HAZEL PEARSON, handicrafts manufacturer/author; b. Jan. 22, 1914, Kingsburg; d. Albert John and Nellie Ethel (Haskell) Kaiser; m. Jack K. Williams, Aug. 25, 1954; children: Sharon Raye Pearson Wiborg, Gagle Lorraine Pearson Merten; stu. UCLA, USC. Career: gen. elem. sch. tchr. 1932-49; crafts instr. Pasadena City Coll., Extended Day, 1945-49; founded small craft mfg. business, 1944-, built to multimillion dollar sales, sold in 1983; currently CEO, Hazel Pearson Handicrafts; bd. dirs. Hobby Industry of Am.; honors incl. Meritorious Award 1978, Hobby Indus. of Am., Good Egg award Craft Div., num. others; charter mem. The Committee of 200; author/publisher over 200 craft instrn. books, printed in Eng., Spanish, French, German, distbd. worldwide; Republican; Presbyterian (mem. Seniors Orgn.); rec: handicraft displays, local libraries. Address: Hazel Pearson Handicrafts, 300 West Norman Ave, Arcadia 91006

WILLIAMS, JAMES EDWARD, state executive; b. Feb. 23, 1939, Bastrop, LA; s. Woodrow and Armelia (Wanzo) W.; m. Azelia Darrington, July 3, 1961; children: Terrell, b. 1963; Heith, b. 1972; edn: acctg. dip., Healds Bus. Colls., Oakland, San Francisco, 1968; BS in acctg., Armstrong Coll., Berkeley 1976; Anthony Sch. of Real Estate 1983; real estate broker lic., Calif 1983. Career: asst. acct., Univ. of Calif., Berkeley, 1969-, acct. 1972-, sr. acct. 1976-, prin. acct. 1980--, hd. Capital Outlay Sect., University Controllers Ofc.; real estate broker, 1983--; mem. Nat./Calif. Assn. of Realtors; Oakland Bd. of Realtors; Democrat; Catholic. Res: 8101 Surrey Lane Oakland 94605 Ofc: Univ. of Calif., 2199 Addison St, Rm 441, Berkeley 94720

WILLIAMS, JAMES RICHARD, insurance co. president; b. Feb. 1, 1933, Van, Texas; s. Glen Jefferson and Goldie Almeda (Richard) W.; m. Dorothy Richey, Aug. 6, 1952; children: Glen, b. 1953; Danny, b. 1954; Donna, b. 1956; Debbie, b. 1959; edn: BS in acctg., Abilene Christian Univ. 1960; Gen. Agent, General Am. Life Ins. Co. Career: agent Business Men's Assurance 1961-6; assoc. gen. agent American National 1966-8; gen. agent, founder, pres. Coast Pacific Broker's Assurance, Inc., L.A. 1968--; pres. Los Angeles Life Underwriters Southwest Br. 1975-6, honors: Conf. of Champions for General Am. Life Ins. Co.; mem. Million Dollar Round Table (1984); Nat. Assn. Life Underwriters; Profl. Ins. Assn.; NASD; Lions Club, So. Torrance; publs: one of his poems on permanent display, Pepperdine Univ., Malibu Campus; Republican; Ch. of Christ; rec: poetry, voice. Res: 4222 Mesa Street Torrance 90505 Ofc: Coast-Pacific Broker's Assurance, Inc., 3055 Wilshire Blvd, Ste 510, Los Angeles 90010

WILLIAMS, JOHN HENRY, energy consultant executive; b. Jan. 6, 1930, Hazleton, PA; s. Stephen Charles and Helen Dorothy (Snyder) W.; m. Ruth Stoll, July 22, 1950; children: Curtis, b. 1952; Eric, b. 1953; Dale, b. 1955; Russell, b. 1957; Stephen, b. 1969; edn: BSME, summa cum laude, N.J. Inst. of Tech 1959; AA, Modeto Jr. Coll. 1964; incomplete MBA, Pepperdine Univ. 1972-4. Career: jr. proces engr. Schering Corp., Union, NJ 1956-9; nuclear engr. Atomics Internat., Canoga Park 1959-60; sales engr. VEECO Instruments, L.A. 1961-2; regl. mgr. 1963-4; mgr. of energy sys. So. Calif. Gas Co., L.A. 1964-72; new ventures mgr. Pacific Lighting Corp., L.A. 1972-4; founder/ pres. Insights West, Inc., L.A. 1974--; bus. cons. Nat. Fuel Cell Users Gp. 1982; chmn. Nat. Gp. to Adv. Total Energy 1968-70; honors: Outstanding Achiev., Am. Gas Assn. Hall of Fame 1971; mem: ASME (v.chmn. NJIT, 1958-9, nat. mem. 1958-70); Am. Rocket Soc., 1958-65 (pres.; founded first coll. student chpt. in US at N.J. Inst. of Tech., 1958); Soc. for Adv. of Mgmt. 1959-70; Am. Vacuum Soc. 1960-66; ASHRAE 1964-74; Am. Gas Assn. 1964-74; Assn. of Energy Engrs. 1980-; past mem. Jr. CofC, Northridge, Jr. CofC, Chatsworth (founding dir.); bd. dirs. Chatsworth Jr. Baseball League 1958-66; publs: num. articles in tech. journs. 1964-74; mil: s/sgt. USAF 1951-5; Methodist; rec: tennis, golf, reading. Res: 10633 Atlanta Ave Northridge 91326 Ofc: Insights West, Inc., 900 Wilshire Blvd, Ste 1100, Los Angeles 90017

WILLIAMS, JOHN SCOTT, mortgage loan officer; b. June 30, 1940, Los Angeles; s. George Wilkes and June Irene (Combs) W.; edn: Santa Monica City Coll. 1958-60; La Verne Coll. 1961-3; cert. real estate, UCLA 1963-7; Golden West Law Sch. 1974; lic. R.E. Negotiator, Hawaii, lic. R.E. Broker, Calif., 1967-. Career: real estate brokerage, John S. Williams Realty, West L.A. 1967-71; mortgage loan ofcr. Los Angeles Federal Savings, L.A. 1971-2; real estate brokerage John S. Williams Realty, West L.A. 1873-8; mortgage loan ofcr. Calif. First Bank, West L.A. 1977-8; mortgage loan ofcr. John S. Williams Realty, W. L.A. 1978-83; pres. Intex Internat., internat. exports, Torrance 1984--; mortgage loan ofcr. First Federal Savings Bank, Torrance 1983--; mem: UCLA Writers Block; UCLA Business Alumni (charter); publs: art., Discover Mexico mag., June 1979; mil: Sp4, US Army 1961; Republican; rec: travel, body surfing, philanthropic wk. in Mexico. Res: 23035 Madison, No. 10, Torrance 90505 Ofc: First Federal Savings Bank, 2824 Sepulveda Blvd Torrance 90505

WILLIAMS, JUDY ANN, real estate brokerage/construction co. owner; b. Mar. 14, 1944, Berkeley; d. Harry Robert and Eleanore Jane (Pfister) Butterfield; m. Gene Charles Smith 1963-74; m. 2d. Clifford McKinley Williams, Apr. 12, 1981; children: Jeffery Charles S., b. 1964; Steven Michael S., b. 1967; Valerie Christine S., b. 1969; Cathryn Yvonne W., b. 1983; (step) Susan Marie W., b. 1974; edn: Palo Alto Beauty Coll. 1962; R.E. courses, Am. River Coll. 1967; GRI, Grad. Realtor Inst. of Calif. 1976. Career: owner Berkeley Style Center, Berkeley 1963-9; decorator cons. Home Interiors, Sacramento area 1971-3; real estate agent Red Carpet Realtors, Sacto. Co. 1973-6, Prospector Realty, El Dorado Co. 1976, Red Carpet Realtors, Sacto. Co. 1976-8; assoc. broker River City Realty, Sacto. Co. 1978-9; owner/broker Gold Nugget Realty

1980-81, Sunset Oaks Real Estate, Investments & Construction, Sacto. Co. 1981--; mem: Nat./Calif. Assn. of Realtors 1973-; Sacramento, El Dorado Board of Realtors; (AGC) Assoc. Gen. Contractors; Parents Without Partners (moderator; grad. EST; Republican; Prot.; stu. metaphysics. Address: Sunset Oaks Real Estate, Investments & Construction, 2524 Knightwood Way Rancho Cordova 95670

WILLIAMS, LYTTON ADE-KUNLE, physician; b. Dec. 11, 1945, Freetown, Sierra Leone; s. Bedford and Patricia E. (McCormack) W.; m. Antonia Ruiz, Sept. 2, 1978; children: Ade-Kunle Alvin, b. 1979; Tungie Winston, b. 1982; edn: BA in chem., math., Hampton Inst. 1970; MD, Cornell Univ. 1974; postgrad., gen. surg.; North Shore University Hosp. 1974-76, orthopaedic surg. splty. res. 1976-79; res., Meml. Hosp. for Cancer and Allied Disease, 1974; lic. MD, Calif., NY, 1980. Career: phys./pres. Bellevue Orthopedic Group, Inglewood; assoc. asst. prof. of orthopedics, USC Med. Sch.; cons. staff phys., spinal deformity svcs., Rancho Los Amigos Hosp., Downey 1980-; honors: Nat. Sci. Honor Soc. 1969; Diplomate Amer. Bd. of Orthopaedic Surgeons 1981; mem: Orange Co. Med. Assn.; Inglewood CofC; rec: tennis, squash, fishing, construn. Res: 72 Dapplegray Ln Rolling Hills Estates 90274 Ofc: Bellevue Orthopedic Group, 501 E. Hardy ST, Ste. 315, Inglewood 90301

WILLIAMS, MAC, retailer; b. Mar. 19, 1921, Mowequa, Ill.; s. Clarence R. and Florence C. (Crowder) W.; m. Virginia M. Schultz, Mar. 10, 1944; 1 dau., Susan (Bengard); edn: No. Ill. Univ., DeKalb, 1939-41; grad. Elgin (Ill.) Nat. Wchmkrs Coll. 1941; AGS, R.J.; Horol. Inst. of Am., C.W. Wchmkr., Elgin Nat. Watch Co., Elgin, Ill., 1942-43; watch and chronograph repairs, Orville R. Hagens, Denver, Colo. 1943-44; owner Williams Jewelers, Porterville, Cal., 1944--; mem: Calif. Jlrs. Assn. (past pres.); Jlrs. 24K Club of So. Calif.; AGS; honors: Man of the Year, Porterville H.S. Student Body 1961; Man of Year, Porterville CofC 1974; past mem. Porterville City Parks Commn. (5 years), Porterville Plnng. Commn. (7 yrs.), Porterville City Council (6 yrs.); mem: Masons, Royal Arch Masons, Knights Templar, Shrine, Rotary, Porterville CofC (dir.), 20-30 Club (past pres.), Jaycees (past pres.), Executive Club (past pres.), Quarterback Club (past pres.), Breakfast Lions (past dir.), Comm. Concerts Assn. (past dir.), Porterville Coll. Patrons Found. (past pres.); Episcopal (past dir. St. John's Ch.); Republican; rec: golf, hunting, fishing. Res: 644 Village Green, Porterville 93257 Ofc: Williams Jewelers, 175 N. Main St Porterville 93257

WILLIAMS, MICHAEL JAMES, health consulting co. president; b. Sept. 23, 1951, Royal Oak, Mich.; s. Robert Burgett and Elizabeth (McGuire) W.; m. Karyn Wade, July 15, 1978; edn: BA, psych., Wayne State Univ. 1974, and BS, police adm., 1974; MPA, pub. adm., CSU Fullerton 1979; Nat. Reg. EMT (Emergency Med. Tech.), charter mem.; American Heart Assn. instr./trainer ACLS (Adv. Cardiac Life Support) 1978, and CPR, 1971. Career: supr. Suburban Ambulance Service, Royal Oak, Mich. 1970-74; dir. emergency medical systems, EMS Pgm., County of Imperial, El Centro, Ca. 1975-76, County of Orange, Santa Ana 1976-80; pres. EMS Systems Design (health consulting spec. in emergency med. pgms.), Irvine 1980--; instr. Paramedic Tng. Div., UC San Diego 1975, North Orange County Comm. Coll. Dist. 1976-79, Imperial Valley Coll. 1974-76; honors: recognition awards, Orange Co. Emergency Med. Care Commn. 1980, Orange Co. Fire Chiefs Assn. 1980, UCI Paramedic Tng. Pgm. 1980, Am. Heart Assn. Orange Co. Chpt. awd. 1982, Orange Co. Trauma Soc. Awd. 1984; mem: Am. Heart Assn. (O.C. bd. dirs. 1977-82), Soc. of EMS Administrators (ch. So. Calif. Soc. 1977-80), So. Calif. Health Care Execs., Orange Co. Trauma Soc. (bd. dirs. 1981-), Am. Trauma Soc. (LA County Trauma Task Force 1980-81); publs: contbg. writer on emergency care systems in med. textbooks, num. articles in field, editor: Contemporary Concepts in Emergency Medical Service Delivery (Aspen, 1985); Christian; rec: racquetball, running, fishing. Ofc: EMS Systems Design, 2691 Richter Ave, Ste. 111, Irvine 92714

WILLIAMS, OSCAR LEE, real estate broker; b. Nov. 22, 1934, Sallis, Miss.; s. Charlie and Ora D. (Suggs) W.; m. Sophia Thompson, June 28, 1975; children: Jayne W. (Boyd), b. 1956; Brenda, b. 1969; edn: L.A. City Coll. 1975; lic. real estate broker Calif.; GRI, Realtors Inst. of Calif. Career: broker/owner Big O' Realty, Pacoima; mem: San Fernando Valley Bd. Realtors (Mktg., Equal Opp. Coms.); Calif. Assn. of Realtors (By Laws Com.) honors: (past) Hon. Mayor of Pacoima; mem. Pacoima CofC Bd., NAACP (Bd.), Boys Club of A.S.F.V.; mil: pfc, US Army; Democrat; rel: U.MC. rec: skating, bowling. Res: 11614 Biltmore Ave Lakeview Terrace 91342 Ofc: 12501 Van Nuys Blvd Pacoima 91331

WILLIAMS, PEARL ESTHER, convalescent hospital administrator; b. Mar. 20, 1927, Terre Haute, Ind.; d. Edmond Alan and Pearl Thelma (Rogers) Laney; m. Edward Leroy Williams, June 20, 1947; children: Edward Alan, b. 1948, Daniel Arthur, b. 1950; edn: dip. Redondo Bch. Union H.S. 1944; cert. health care adminstrn., UCLA Ext. 1974; Calif. Nursing Home Adminstr. Lic. Career: personnel dir., then asst. adminstr. Bon Air Hosp., Los Angeles 1964-72; adminstr. Athens Park Hosp. 1972-3, City Center Hosp. Surgicenter 1973, Extended Care of Long Bch. 1973-4, Victory Conv. Hosp., No. Hollywood 1974-5, Hillhaven Conv. Hosp., L.A. 1975-6; dir. of ops./adminstr. of two conv. hosps., and a retirement hotel, D & E Hosp. Mgmt. Consultants, Marina Del Rey 1976-79; adminstr. Inglewood Convalarium 1979-81, Hawthorne Conv. Center, 1981--; mem Adv. Com., UCLA Extended Health Care Adminstrn.; field work instr. USC Gerontol. Ctr.; project adminstr. voc. nursing pgms. Santa Monica Coll., Valley Voc. Ctr., Mt. San Antonio Coll., Inglewood Adult Sch.; chmn. So. Bay Pvt. Industry Council; mem: Long Beach - South Bay

Health Care Assn. (pres.), L.A. Co. ROP (nursing adv. com.), Soroptomist. Address: 153 E. 231 St Wilmington 90745

WILLIAMS, RICHARD DESSERT, lawyer; b. Aug. 30, 1946, Los Angeles; s. Alfred Curry and Josephine Anne (Dessert) W.; m. Brenda, July 25, 1983; children: Alison, b. 1974, Christine, b. 1976; edn: BA in bus. adm., Wash. State Univ. 1969; JD, UC Los Angeles 1973; admitted Calif. State Bar 1973. Career: accountant Shell Oil Co., Los Angeles 1969-70; atty. Adams, Duque & Hazeltine, L.A. 1973-74; atty./partner Manatt, Phelps, Rothenberg & Tunney, L.A. 1974--; honors: Beta Gamma Sigma 1969; bd. editors UCLA Law Rev. 1972-3; speaker/author various law institutes, spec. in corporate, comml. litigation, 1979-; mem: Am. Bar Assn., State Bar of Calif., Los Angeles Co. Bar Assn., Assn. of Bus. Trial Lawyers, Wash. State Univ. Cougar Club; author: Attacking Barriers to Entry: An Alternative to Divestiture in Antitrust Enforcement (UCLA Law Rev. 1972); Republican; Presbyterian; rec: pvt. pilot. Res: 18408 Wakecrest Dr Malibu 90265 Ofc: Manatt, Phelps, Rothenberg & Tunney, 1888 Century Park East, Ste. 2100, Los Angeles 90067

WILLIAMS, ROBERT LOUIS, executive, entertainment artist; b. Nov. 12, 1950, Maybeury, W. Va.; s. Charlie James and Lucy (Vaughn) W.; edn: BS, elem. edn., Bluefield State Coll. 1976; lic. 3rd class radio/tel., FCC 1979; Notary Public, Calif. 1983; Indsl. Elec. cert. 1972. Career: founder/pres. B.W. Enterprises, Inc., Hollywood 1981--, incl. Kraft Photographics, B.W. Productions, Sonrise Records, B.W. Public Relations, and Jilord Productions; drama coach, Undiscovered Artists Guild; provider finl. and income tax prep. svcs.; past mgr. trainee, C.I.T. Fin. Svcs., Columbus, Oh.; mem. Internat. Alliance of Stage and Theatrical Employees, Local No. 44 (shop steward, sr. exec. bd. rep., del.), 1979-; awards: commendation, L.A. Co. Sheriff Dept., 1981, 82; hon. mention, Music City Song Festival; mem. Fishermans' Players West; Hollywood CofC; W. Hollywood Community Alliance; works: Hold On To Your Dream (recording artist), By-Word Newsletter, composer songs, Personal I.D. Check; Democrat; Baptist; rec: hike, jog, basketball, swim. Res: 1119 N. Poinsettia Dr, No. 1, Los Angeles 90046 Ofc: B.W.Ent. Inc, 7117-1/2 Santa Monica Blvd, Ste.A, Hollywood 90046

WILLIAMS, ROY RICHARD, JR., lawyer; b. Oct. 10, 1939, Chgo.; s. Roy Richard and Jeanne (Hamilton) W.; div.; children: Shannon, b. 1966; Nathan, b. 1969; Megan, b. 1973; edn: DePauw Univ. 1957-9; BS, Indiana Univ. 1962; postgrad., San Diego State Univ. 1965-6; JD, Cum Laude, Univ. of Minn. Law Sch. 1969. Career: assoc. atty. law firm Pillsbury, Madison & Sutro, San Francisco 1969-72; assoc. atty. Skornia, Roseblum & Geymant, S.F. 1972-73; assoc. atty., partner Meserve, Mumper & Hughes, Los Angeles 1973-78; sole practitioner, Lakeport 1978--; past dir. num. corp. bds. 1973-78; S.F. Bar Assn. chmn. for Bridging the Gap, 1970-71; pres. Lake Co. Bar Assn. 1982; contbr. law rev., Univ. of Minn. Law Sch.; mil: commnd. ofcr. USN 1962-65; lt. USNR 1965-70; rec: tennis, snow skiing. Res: 2565 Beach Ln Lakeport 95453 Ofcs: 301 No. Forbes St Lakeport 95493; 821 Mendocino Ave Santa Rosa 95401

WILLIAMS, RUSSELL LOUIS, executive; b. Jan. 6, 1943, Visalia; s. A. Clayton and Mildred J. (Russell) W.; m. Sarah Coburn, June 23, 1968; 2 daus: Kelly, b. 1969; Kimberly, b. 1972; edn: AA, Coll. of the Sequoias 1963; BS, Fresno State 1966. Career: field rep. for Agricultural Producers 1970-75; mgr., Citrus Ins. Trust Fund and Citrus-Avocado Pension Trust. 1975-77; elected pres., Agricultural Producers, 1977--; mem: Nat. Council of Agricultural Employers; Farm Labor Alliance; Agricultural Personnel Mgmt. Assn.; mil: petty ofcr. USN 1967-68; Republican; Episcopal; rec: skiing, jogging, gardening. Res: 400 Powell Terrace Visalia 93291 Ofc: Agricultural Producers, 25600 Rye Canyon Road, Ste 100, Valencia 91355

WILLIAMS, STANLEY DEHART, JR., physician, administrator; b. June 22, 1949, Elkhart, Indiana; s. Stanley DeHart and Gloria Elaine (Miller) W.; edn: BS, Wayne State Univ. 1970; MD, 1974; intern/ res., USC Sch. of Med. 1974-7; Univ. of West L.A. Sch. of Law 1979, 82; biomed. engring. stu., USC 1983-; physician and surgeon, Bd. Med. Examiners 1975. Career: tchg. staff USC Med. Ctr., Dept. of Emergency Med. 1975-6; pvt. med. practice, Los Angeles, 1979-82; chief med. staff, Plaza Ofc. Family Health Plan Med. Gp., 1982-83; malpractice risk analyst supvr., and Family Practitioner, Family Health Plan Med. Gp. 1983--; recipient AMA Phsician's Recognition Awd. 1980, 81, 82; mem: Am./Calif. Acads. of Family Physicians; Mensa (Am., USC); Nat. Med. Fellowships; NAACP; Charles Drew Med. Soc.; Bi-Plex Corp. (past bd. mem.); George Washington H.S. Mentor Pgm.; Nat. Rifle Assn.; Boy Scout, USC Sch. of Med., and Wayne State Univ. Sch. of Med. Alumni Assns.; Democrat; Christian; rec: biomedical engring., travel, racquetball. Res: 4572 Via Marina, No 303, Marina del Rey 90292 Ofc: Family Health Program, 2925 No Palo Verde Ave Long Beach 90815

WILLIAMS, VERLE ALVIN, energy control co. president; b. Apr. 8, 1933, New Virginia, IA; s. Donal Oliver and Josephine Emily (Read) W.; m. Mary Sue Earley, June 2, 1957; children: Steven Lee, b. 1960, Randall Joe, b. 1961, LeAnne Sue, b. 1965; edn: AA, Pueblo Jr. Coll., Colo. 1957; BS, bus., Colo. Univ. 1960, BSME, 1969; Reg. Profl. Engr., Calif.; CEM, Cert. Energy Mgr., AEE 1982. Career: sales engr. Johnson Service Co., Portland, Ore. 1960-67, Los Angeles 1967-68; sales engr. Johnson Controls, San Diego 1968-69, branch mgr. 1970-79; assoc. Dunn Lee Smith Klein & Assocs. (Profl. Engrs.), San Diego 1979-81; pres./owner Verle A. Williams & Assocs., Inc., San Diego 1981--; teacher UCSD Engring. Ext. Coll. 1983; awards: Energy Conservation Project of the Year, ASHRAE (Chapter, 1983; Region X, 1983); San Diego Chapter Energy Engr. of Year, Assn. of Energy Engrs. (AEE) 1982; mem: AEE (pres. 1979); ASHRAE (chmn. TC1.4); Am. Cons. Engrs. Council;

Energy Monitoring and Control Soc.; Internat. Cogeneration Soc.; Independent Energy Producers; Calif. Soc. for Hospital Engr.; Consulting Engrs. Assn. of Calif.; charter mem. Rancho Bernardo Bowleros; speaker re energy systems & conservation, various civic orgns.; publs: 2 tech. journal arts.; Baptist (founding, charter, treas., chmn. Rancho Bernardo Baptist Ch.); rec: bowling, golf. Res: 12561 Perla Ct. Rancho Bernardo 92128 Ofc: Verle A. Williams & Assoc., Inc., 8369 Vickers St, Ste. M, San Diego 92111

WILLIAMS, WILLA ETTA M., educator; b. Apr. 17, 1934, Steubenville, Ohio; d. Alex and Ida Lucille (Marbury) Mitchell; div.; edn: AA, L.A. City Coll. 1954; BA, CSU Los Angeles 1958; MA, Azusa Pacific Univ. 1979. Career: teacher public schools, Los Angeles Unified Sch. Dist., 1958--: spl. edn. 1965-67; training, 1968-71; Hoffman Reading Lab., 1972-76; tchr./coordinator 1977-80; bilingual tchr./coord., 1981-; Acad. for Adminstrv. Leadership Devel., LAUSD, 1981; service awards: United Way 1983, Nat. Sor. of Phi Delta Kappas 1982, Las Comunicadores Speech Contest, 1982, Marvin Ave. PTA, 1982; mem: Nat. Edn. Assn., Calif. Teachers Assn., United Teachers of L.A., Alpha Kappa Alpha Sor., Nat. Assn. of Coll. Women, L.A. Music Assn., Intl. Toastmistress of Am., Nat. Assn. of Supervision and Curriculum, Marvin Ave. Sch. Advis. Council, PTA; works: poetry and poetry readings; Democrat; Methodist; rec: handcraft jewelry (silver/gold), jazz, poetry. Res: 7900 Crenshaw Blvd, Apt. D, Inglewood 90305 Ofc: Marvin Ave Sch. 2411 Marvin Ave Los Angeles 90016

WILLIAMSON, ADELIA MAKAR, educator; b. July 6, 1920, Camrose, Alberta, Canada; d. Onofry and Katherine Margaret (Starchki) Makar; m. Ernest Williamson, Jan. 15, 1943; edn: Duffus Bus. Coll., Vancouver; MA, CSU L.A.; Calif. State Teaching Credential, life, sec. & jr. coll.; lic. real estate broker, Calif. and Hawaii. Career: admin. asst./ clerk Dept. of Defense USAF, Morocco, Eur. Cmd. 1954-57, Hickam AB, Hon., HI 1957-63; secty./ admin. asst. DOD, USAF, Los Angeles 1963-66; arts & crafts dr., recreation, Tripler Army Hosp., Hon., HI 1969-71; art tchr. secondary sch., Honolulu Bd. of Edn., Hon., HI 1974-77; instr. (part time): art lessons, painting, history 1946--; instr. travel seminars, art recreation mil. bases; mem: Beta Sigma Phi; CSU L.A. Arts & Crafts Club; Am. Bus Women's Assn.; recipient first, 2nd, 3d prizes art exhbns.; Republican; Protestant; rec: travel, photog., cooking. Res: 123 E Escalones San Clemente 92672

WILLIAMSON, DREW AUSTIN, manufacturing co. executive; b. Dec. 10, 1947, Phila., Penn.; s. George Austin and Helen Purvis Williamson; m. Cynthia, Dec. 29, 1971; children: Ian, b. 1973; Ryan, b. 1982; edn: BS, Colo. State Univ. Career: pilot, USMC, Santa Ana & El Toro 1971-6; real estate agent and broker/ developer, mgr. Regal Realty 1976-81; v.p. Eppco, Inc., Clearwater, Fla. 1980--; owner Eppco West, West Coast Distbr. 1981--; mem: Western World Pet Supply Assn., Inc.; works: Lightning Organic Pet Products; mil: Capt., USMC; Republican; Christian; rec: skiing, sailing, skin diving. Res: 15711 Pacific St Tustin 92680 Ofc: EPPCO West, 14661 Myford Rd, Ste B-2, Tustin 92680

WILLIAMSON, LYLE ROGER, realty co. president; b. June 24, 1937, Bristol, S.Dak.; s. Gilbert Clayton and Serene Margaret (Sigdestad) W.; m. Julie Berton, June 11, 1966; children: Diane, b. 1967; Karen, b. 1968. Career: data processing ops. Lockheed Corp. 1956; data processing mgr. Northrop Corp. 1957-65; v.p. data processing Electronic Specialty 1966-69; sr. v.p. data processing Computer Microfilm Systems 1969-70; sr. v.p. sales mgmt. Coldwell Banker 1971-78; sr. v.p./ partner Macelhenny Levy, sales brokerage 1978-81; Merrill Lynch Realty/ Vent. gen. mgr. 1981-82; Merrill Lynch Realty/ NLA pres./CEO 1982--; mil: Sgt., US Army 1952-4; Republican; Lutheran; rec: golf. Res: 5860 Fitzpatrick Rd Hidden Hills 91302 Ofc: Merrill Lynch, 5959 Topanga Cyn., Ste 150, Woodland Hills 91367

WILLIG, LEONARD, investment co. executive; b. Dec. 1, 1928, Brklyn.; s. Jacob and Rose (Weber) W.; edn: BS in bus. ad., Long Island Univ. 1952; BS in E.E., RCA Inst. 1953; lic: First Cl. Radiotelephone, FCC; SEC Series 7 lic.; NASD lic.; Calif. lic. Life Ins., Variable Annuity. Career: senior field engr. Ampex Corp., Redwood City 1959-75; investment exec. Bateman Eichler, Hill Richards Inc., Woodland Hills 1975-78, assoc. v.p. 1984--; 2d v.p. investments, Shearson/Am. Express, Woodland Hills 1978-81; consultant/prin., tax avoidance, fin. plnng., 1981-82; investment exec. (municipal bond, govt. secs. splst) Morgan, Olmstead, Kennedy & Gardner Inc., Woodland Hills 1982-84; conducts investment seminars. Awards: mktg. man of year, Ampex Corp. 1971; United Airlines 100,000 mile club 1961; Century Club 1980; recognition, Principles of Videotape Engrg. 1959; Bnai Brith Century Club 1977. Mem: Internat. Assn. of Fin. Plnng., Soc. of Motion Picture & TV Engrs., Bnai Brith, Tarzana Lodge; various tech. publs., Ampex; mem. tech. team videotape recorded Adolf Eichmann trial, Israel, 1961. rec: hiking, riding, music, theater. Res: 37564 Rondell St. Agoura Hills 91301 Ofc: Bateman Eichler Hill Richards Inc. 6355 Topanga Cyn Blvd Woodland Hills 91367

WILLINGHAM, ELIZABETH ELLEN, paralegal; b. Sept. 6, 1951, Houston, Tex.; d. Clarence and Jeanne Ellen (Clark) Schultz; m. Andrew Calvin Willingham, Jr. Dec. 29, 1979; edn: stu. Southwest Tex. State Univ. 1969-70; BA, psych., Univ. of Houston 1976, grad. wk. soc. psy., 1976; Paralegal Cert., Texas Paralegal Sch. 1978. Career: research asst. in a smoking proj. for Dr. Michael DeBakey and Baylor Coll. of Med., summer 1976; coord./counselor for Drug Abuse Rehab. Ctr., United Fund proj. 1976; temp. legal asst. law firm Bracewell and Patterson, also substitute tchr. Houston Indep. Sch. Dist., 1976-77; paralegal, adminstrv. asst. Superior Oil Co. 1977-79; legal asst. McCutchen, Black, Verleger & Shea, Los Angeles 1979--; spkr. var. colls. on career opportunities as a paralegal; honors: Nat. Thespian Drama Soc., Chi Phi Frat. (U.Tx.) Sweetheart 1970; mem. Desk and Derrick Club of L.A. (pgm. com.); Girl Scouts of Am., St. Joseph's Hosp. Alumni Club, Univ. of Houston Alumni Assn.; Democrat; Catholic; rec: fishing, bicycling. Res: 12345 Hillslope St Studio City 91604 Ofc: McCutchen, Black, Verleger & Shea, 600 Wilshire Blvd, Ste 1200, Los Angeles 90017

WILLIS, LEE FRANK, certified public accountant; b. Aug. 30, 1922, Rockwood, TN; s. John William and Cora May (Lee) Willis; AA, BA, Bakersfield Coll., 1947; Higher Acctg., Knoxville Coll., 1948; m. Janet Hirsch, 1973; chil: Phyllis, b. 1947; Erwin, b. 1949. Career: controller, Rocky Hill, Inc., Visalia, 1952-58; controller, Donald Shanedling, Inc., Beverly Hills, 1960-62; CPA practice, Salinas, 1963-71; CPA, Wain, Samuel & Co., San Mateo, 1972-73; tax mgr., Clow Acct. Corp., S.F., 1974-75; CPA, San Rafael, 1976---; profl. expert witness in Fed. Ct. and various Calif. Supr. Cts. relating to com. prop. valuations & alloc. and valuations of businesses and corps. Awards: Alpha Gamma Sigma, 1947. Mem: Calif. Soc. of CPA, 1961---; Kiwanis Club, 1958-59; Rotary Club, 1960-61; Lions Club, 1963-70. Mil: Airman 2/C, USN, 1942-45; Good Conduct, Asiatic/Pacific & Atlantic Medals. Republican. Protestant. Rec: golfing, skiing. Res: 50 Hampton Lane, Novato (Blackpoint) 94947; Office: 1010 B St., Suite 329, San Rafael 94901.

WILSON, ANDY IRWIN, manufacturing co. president; b. Jan. 18, 1922, Hazel, Minn.; s. Isaac Erwin and Anna May (Bergen) W.; m. Alexandria Beenkins, Sept. 3, 1949; children: Andrew, b. 1952; Peter, b. 1954; Carey, b. 1957; edn: West Point PS 1942; Tulane Univ. 1946; N.A.C.E., Nat. Assn. Corrosion Engrs. 1980. Career: rep. Philip Carey Mfg. Co., Ohio; founder, pres./ CEO Calpico, Inc., (mfg. finished prods. for cathodic protection pipelines & elec. grounding equip.), So. San Francisco 1957--; mem: Nat. Assn. of Corrosion Engrs.; San Mateo Elks Club; sev. tennis clubs, Penn. Country Club; patentee in field; mil: Major, (ret.), Africa, India, Japan, & Korea, WWI & Korean War decorations; Republican; Lutheran; rec: tennis. Res: 50 Mounds Rd San Mateo 94402 Ofc: Calpico, Inc., 185 Harbor Way, So. San Francisco 94080

WILSON, ARLYN MARIE, real estate broker; b. Sept 25, 1932, Oakland; d. Walter R. and Marie A (Clarlo) Retzlaff; m. Kurt Edward Wilson, May 12, 1956; children: Kurt E., Jr., b. 1959; Marc W., b. 1961; Thomas C., b. 1961; edn: BA, Univ. of the Pacific 1954 (first UOP woman to graduate with deg. in bus. adm.); Calif. lic. real estate broker. Career: real estate broker Century 21- Allen & Assoc., Los Gatos 1978-83; real estate broker, self employed 1983--; lectr. Dept. of R.E. approved Continuing Edn. courses, CSU San Jose and various cruise ships; co-owner World Wide Seminars (lectrs. and seminars for cont. edn. for attys. and real estate brokers); num. sales awards incl. C21 Two Million Dollar Club, SC Council Top Salespsn trophy; mem: Los Gatos and San Jose Bds. of Realtors; Assn. of Am. Univ. Women; Delta Gamma Sorority Alumni; Democrat; Catholic; rec: cooking, biking, camping. Address: Arlyn Wilson, Real Estate Broker, 150 Longmeadow Dr Los Gatos 95030

WILSON, CARTER EDWARD, businessman, b. Oct. 3, 1928, Birmingham, Ala.; s. Carter E., Sr. and Katherine Hope (Crump); children: Kelley, b. 1952, Edward, b. 1953, Sherry, b. 1957, John, b. 1959. Professional: lic. real estate broker (2 corporate, 1 personal lic.), Calif. 1968-, Realtor, GRI, Grad. Realtors Inst.; Calif. Teaching Credential, Jr. Coll. (life) 1974; Life and Disability Agt., Calif. 1968; Enrolled Agt., US Treas. Dept. 1974-; lic. securities broker/dealer, mem. NASD, 1968-75. Career: mgmt. and senior staff Lockheed Missiles & Space Co. Inc., 1951-84 (ret.); self-empl. real estate developer and tax practitioner; pres./dir. Wilson Tax Service Inc. 1968--; pres./dir. Spoerri-Wilson Realtors, Inc. 1973--; bd. dirs: WTS, Inc. 1968-, S-W Realtors, Inc. 1973-, LMSC Federal Employees Credit Union 1977-; instr., tax acctg., DeAnza Jr. Coll. 1974-75; frequent spkr. on income tax preparation; past dir., treas., v.p. Lockheed Mgmt. Assn.; honors: Junior Achievement Bus. Advisor, 1st Place Nat. 1956, nat. hon. mention 1957; loaned exec. United Fund of Santa Clara Co.; mem: Tri Co. Apartment Assn., Better Bus. Bur. of Santa Clara Co. (dir. 1972-75), LMSCFECU, Mgmt. Assn., Toastmasters of Ga. 1954-58; Reserve Police Ofcr. Santa Clara Co. 1960-64; publs: Financial Planning Newsletter (quarterly 1963-); rec: writing, speaking. Address: Wilson Tax Co. Inc. 891 Saratoga Ave San Jose 95129

WILSON, CHERYL ANN, hospital administrator; b. Oct. 17, 1948, Adelaide, Australia; d. Harry Penno and Patricia June (Seuline) Williams; m. Richard Wilson, Dec. 23, 1970; children: Richard, b. 1971; Troy, b. 1975; edn: dip. nursing, Prince Henry Hosp. Nursing Sch. 1969; BA, Univ. of Redlands 1976; M.Mgmt. in progress; Calif. R.N., lic. Nursing Home Adminstr. 1982; Career: R.N./ op. rm. & intensive care supvr., Rabaul Hosp., Papua, New Guinea 1969-70; nurse /clinic supvr. Expo 70 Worlds Fair, Osaka, Japan 1970; nurse/ ofc. mgr. Dr. F.A. Carlin, Jr., Pediatrician, Chula Vista 1971-73; nurse/ clinic supvr. Fredericica Manor, Chula Vista 1974-81; asst. adminstr. 1981--; nursing educator, Rabaul, Papua, New Guinea; com. mem. Wage & Benefit Com., Pacific Homes Corp.; spkr. civic gps. and schs.; recipient ANZAC spl. svc. awd., Consul-Gen. for TV show promo.; mem: Calif. Assn. of Homes for the Aging; Chula Vista CofC; Citizens Action Gp. of Imperial Beach; Australia, New Zealand, & Am. Club mem., past bd. BSA; rec: youth orgns., little league, boys club. Res: 237 Evergreen Ave Imperial Beach 92032 Ofc: Frederica Manor, 183 3rd Ave Chula Vista 92010

WILSON, DARLENE JOY, marriage family and child counselor; b. July 14, 1937, Los Angeles; d. Dr. Walter L. and Borgie (Knutsen) Holberg;; m. Sanford H. Anzel, Aug. 26, 1981; 1 dau: Julie Wilson, b. 1955; edn: BA, CSU Long BEach 1964; MS, 1978; MFCC, Calif., 1979. Career: baton twirling instr., City of Paramount 1956-63; dance instr. Paramount Elem. Sch. 1957-8; recept. secty. Macco Corp., Paramount 1958-64; elem. school teacher, 1964-81; cons. L.A. County Supt. of Schs., Tchg. Strategies Ctr. 1973-81; marriage, family and child counselor, Human Growth and Devel. Ctr., Long Beach 1979-83; marriage, family and child counselor, pvt. practice, Santa Ana 1983--; co- leader, Carkhuff Human Rels. Skills, Paramount USD 1973-74; mem: Calif. Assn. Marriage & Family Therapists; Calif. Personnel & Guidance Assn.; Calif. Assn. of Mental Health Counselors; Calif. Soc. for Hypnosis in Family Therapy; Las Amigas Guild of St. Joseph Hosp.; Childrens Home Soc.; Orange Co. Med. Assn. Aux.; Alla Gitana Guild of O.C. Perf. Arts Ctr.; Republican; Protestant; rec: tennis, cooking. Res: 1066 Regis Way Tustin 92680 Ofc: 1441 E 17th Street, Ste C, Santa Ana 92701

WILSON, FRANK, psychiatrist; b. Nov. 22, 1932, Marlin, Tex.; s. Frank Sr. and Mary Rodgers (James) W.; m. Rachel Sara McCague, 1984; children: Frank J., b. 1957; Allison G., b. 1958; Darryl J., b. 1962; Deborah Simone, b. 1974; edn: BS, summa cum laude, Wiley Coll. 1952; MS, Univ. Calif. 1960, MD, 1966; physician & surgeon, State of Calif. 1967. Career: fighter pilot & research proj. ofcr., USAF 1952-62; corp. physician, Family Doctor Med. Gp., Vallejo 1973 5; med. dir. Comm. Ambulatory Health Care Facility, Hunter's Point, San Francisco 1976-80; psychiatric res. Pacific Med. Ctr., S.F. 1977-80; staff psychiatrist Contra Costa Med. Svcs., Richmond 1980-2; pvt. practice, gen. psychiatry, San Bruno, San Francisco, and Richmond 1982--; cons. psychiatrist Ingleside Boys Home, and Putnam Home, S.F.; cons. Rubicon Day Treatment Ctr., Richmond; awards: Physician's Recgn. Awd., AMA 1981; Distinguished Aviation Cadet grad., USAF Pilot Tng. 1953; mem: Am. Psychiatric Assn.; Flying Phys.'s Assn.; Am. Assn. of Abdominal Surgeons, Emerg. Phys. and Family Practitioners; East Bay Peer Systems Review Orgn. (PSRO); publs: tech. reports re chem. of rocket propulsion for USAF; mil: capt. USAF 1951-62; rec: research on marginal stimuli. Res: 23 Baldwin Ct Walnut Creek 94596 Ofcs: 370 West San Bruno Ave, Ste B, San Bruno 95066; 237 25th Street Richmond 94804

WILSON, JOHN ROBERT, lawyer; b. Apr. 18, 1940, Santa Monica; s. Robert Lintrathen and (Anne) Marjorie Wilson; m. Maria-Gloria Montoya, Aug 17, 1967; 2 sons: Ian, b. 1971; Brian, b. 1972; edn: BS, Calif. State Polytechnic, Pomona 1964; standard tchg. cred., UCLA 1966; JD, Southwestern Univ. 1970. Career: tchr. Santa Monica Coll. 1966-75; Deputy Los Angeles City Atty., (sr. trial atty.) 1971--; pres./ chmn. bd. dirs. Lintrathen Corp., Pacific Palisadfes 1977--; tchr. bus. law.; lectr. LAPD Acad., So. Calif. Fire Fighters Assn.; awards: Boy Scouts of Am. Awd. of Merit 1968; Silver Beaver, BSA 1976; AYSO soccer referee 1978-; mem: Los Angeles Co. Bar Assn.; So. Calif. Fraud Investigators; Footprinters; BSA mem. 1948-, scoutmaster 1962-7, dist. commnr. 1978, dist. chmn. 1982, cubmaster 1977-, mem. exec. bd. Great Western Council; fund raiser, BSA, YMCA, ch., publs: Flora & Fauna of Santa Monica Mountains (1965); Republican; Episcopal (Sun. sch. tchr.); rec: numismatics. Res: 16800 Edgar St Pacific Palisades 90272 Ofc: L.A. City Attorney, 1700 City Hall East, 200 North Grand Ave Los Angeles 90012

WILSON, LIONEL JOSEPH, mayor of Oakland; b. New Orleans; BA in econ. UC Berkeley 1939; JD, UC Hastings Coll. Law 1949; m. Dorothy; children: Robin, Lionel, and Steven; admitted Calif. State Bar 1950. Career: presiding judge Oakland-Piedmont Municipal Ct. 1964, Alameda Co. Superior Cts. 1973; presiding judge criminal div. Alameda Co. Supr. Cts., Oakland 1969, 72, 75, Apellate Dept., 1976; mayor City of Oakland, 1977--; prin., Sta. KJAZ, Alameda 1980-; mem. adv. com. Alameda Co. Council Alcoholism, Alameda Co. Mental Health Assn.; cons. Far West Sch.; chmn., pres. Oakland Econ. Devel. Council, INc. 1964-69; chmn., pres. Oakland Men of Tomorrow, Charles Houston Law Club; chmn. Oakland's Anti- Poverty Bd., Oakland Bail Proj, 1964-65; awards: NAACP west coast region merit award 1960; outstanding profl. svc., No. Calif. Med., Dental, and Pharm. Assn. 1975; Man of Year 1978 Oakland Lodge Bnai Brith; leadership awd., Chinese- Am. Citizens Alliance 1979; mem: NAACP (dir.); Nat. League of Cities; League of Calif. Cities (dir.); U.S. Conf. of Mayors; Democrat. Ofc: Room 302, City Hall, Oakland 94612

WILSON, MARK STEPHEN, SR., quality assurance executive; b. Jan. 3, 1952, Pasadena; s. Francis Eugene and Billie Gene (Cosby) W.; m. Christina Parker, June 25, 1972; children: Mark Stephen Jr., b. 1973; Jason Eugene, b. 1975u; Trevor Aaron, b. 1978; Tonya Adele, b. 1982; edn: Laramie Co. Comm. Coll., Los Angeles Comm. Coll. Overseas, 1973-7; Pasadena Comm. Coll. 1983-. Career: inspector, inspn. supvr., quality assurance auditor Sargent Industries, Huntington Park 1978--; honors: BSA Order of the Arrow 1966, Life boy scout 1967; mem: Soc. Mfg. Engrs. nominee; voting mem. Cherokee Nation of Northeastern Oklahoma; mil: s/sgt. USAF 1973-78; Democrat; Protestant; rec: camping, scouting. Res: 4541 Livia Rosemead 91770 Ofc: Sargent Industries, 2533 E 56th Huntington Park 90255

WILSON, MARVIN LEON, artist, gemologist; b. Mar. 25, 1916, Chillicothe, Mo.; s. Virgil N. and Letitia Marie (McClallen) W.; m. Verna Ruth Bland, Mar. 29, 1937; 1 son, Michael, b. 1940; edn: GIA (grad. gemologist), Gemological Inst. of Am. 1970. Career: past merchant seaman, sales; currently carver in gemstone by commission; works commnd. by Kazanjian of Beverly Hills (carved world's largest known ruby, 9 lbs, 22,500 cts., designed by James Lincoln Borglum, Mt. Rushmore), and pvt. clients; pvt. instr. in gemstone carving; mem. Gem Carver Guild of Am., Masons, Shriners, Optimists, Eastern Star; Democrat; Baptist; rec: art, encouraging others. Res/studio: 14602 Norwalk Bl, Norwalk 90650

WILSON, PATRICIA GRAHAM, organization consultant; b. Jan. 4, 1946,

Detroit, Mich.; d. Lloyd George and Virginia Francis (Boswell) W.; edn: BA, Mich. State Univ. 1968; PhD in orgnl. behavior, Union Grad. Sch. 1979. Career: co- founder Wash. Area Feminist Theatre and Edn. dir. 1971-75; pres. Themis (network of independent organization cons. and trainers wkg. in over 80 orgns.) 1975--; partner Iris Partnership, spec. in custom designed interactive video for tng. 1981--; co-chair Bay Area Orgn. Devel. Network 1983-4; independent consultant/tnr.; profl. presentations, workshops; mem: Orgn. Devel. Network; Bay Area Orgn. Devel. Network; Am. Soc. for Tng. and Devel.; publs: Toward a Symbolic Approach to Systems, Vision/ Action 1983; Gnostic; rec: gardening. Res: 851 Loma Vista, POB 857, Moss Beach 94038

WILSON, PHOEBE SUE, accountant, consultant; b. May 14, 1946, Refugio, Tex.; d. William Hughes and Doris Marie (Linney) Moore; div.; 1 dau: Christina, b. 1970; edn: BS, CSU Sacto. 1977; CPA, Calif. 1979. Career: treas. El Dorado Sch. Employees Credit Union, Placerville 1974-76; audit mgr. Touche Ross & Co., Sacramento 1977-83; acct. & cons., exec. v.p. Diversified Mgmt. Gp., Sacto. 1983--; spkr. Grand Jury Seminars 8/83; mem: Am. Inst. CPAs; Calif. Soc. CPAs; Govtl. Acctg. and Auditing Com.; Healthcare Fin. Mgmt. Assn.; Democrat; Catholic; rec: photog., reading. Res: 6250 Holly Springs Ct Citrus Heights 95610 Ofc: Diversified Management Group, 2410 K Street, Ste C, Sacramento 95816

WILSON, ROBERT LINTRATHEN McBAIN, architect - builder; b. Oct. 6, 1898, Dundee, Scotland, nat. 1925; s. John Knox and Helen (Hunter) Wilson; edn: USC Ext., Archit., 1927-31; USC in Europe, Hist. of Archit., 1929; UCLA night sch., structural engr., 1973; Central YMCA, USC Ext. Strength of Materials, 1922; m. Annie Marjorie Terrill, June 4, 1937; chil: Donald George, b. 1938; John Robert, b. 1940; seven grandchildren. Career: partner in Wilson (John) Constrn. Co., 1921-24; partner w/brother George, 1924-68; owner, Wilson Bros. Bldrs., 1968-81; ret. Jan. 1, 1981; pres., Bay Bldrs Exchange, Santa Monica, 1930; chmn. Successful drive to secure 3 new schs. for Pac. Palisades and Brentwood, 1951-52; dir. Santa Monica Bank, 1960-75; designed and/or built 2000 structures in Bay Area during 60 yrs.; pres., Santa Monica Mens Club, 1925; installed Jr. CofC in Santa Monica, first pres., charter pres. 1931; Citizen of Year in Santa Monica, 1934; v.p., Optimist Internatl., Santa Monica, 1932; leader in Boy Scout and Sea Scouts, Santa Monica Bay Area, 1932-45; helped estab. Presby. Ch. of Pac. Palisades, elected elder; charter mem., Rotary Club of Pac. Palisades, 1951; pres., Palisades Rotary, 1969-70; estab. Rotary Man of Year in perpetuity in my honor after 30 yrs. continuous attendance and charter mem. Amer. Inst. Archits. Award for bldg. St. Matthews Episcopal Ch., Pac. Palisades. Mem: Rotary Club Internatl. of Pac. Palisades; elder, trustee, Presby. Ch. of Pac. Palisades. Republican. Presbyterian. Rec: reading, writing, gardening. Res: 654 Alma Real Dr., Pacific Palisades 90272; Office: Wilson Bros. Bldrs., 734 Twelfth St., Santa Monica 90402.

WILSON, WAYNE P., college administrator; b. Sept. 3, 1931, Loveland, Colo.; s. Tom J. and Mable C. (Crook) W.; m. Cecelia cond, June 1, 1956; children: Wayne b. 1957, Nannette b. 1959, Mitchell b. 1964, Connie b. 1968, Charles b. 1970, Mtthew b. 1979; edn: BS, Brigham Young Univ. 1959; MA, Univ. of Pacific 1967. Career: high school tchr., counselor, administrator, 1959-68; vice pres./director Condie Jr. College, San Jose 1968--; bd. dirs: Condie College, and Phillips Colleges, Inc.; honors: Phi Delta Kappa; mil: US Army 1950-53; Republican; Ch. of Jesus Christ of L.D.S. (Bishop). Res: 1249 Chateau Dr San Jose 95120 Ofc: Condie Jr. College, One W. Campbell Ave Campbell 95008

WINCHELL, ROBERT ALLEN, auditor; b. Oct. 28, 1945, Ft. Monmouth, NJ; s. Robert Winslow and Mary M. (Allen) W.; edn: BA, UC Santa Barbara 1967; MBA, Wharton Grad. Div., Univ. of Penn. 1969; CPA, State Calif. 1979. Career: finl. analyst, treas. Div., S.C. Gas Co., Los Angeles 1975-76; sr. auditor Defense Cont. Audit Agency, res. ofcr. Rockwell Internat. B-1 Div., El Segundo 1976-79; sr. auditor Defense Cont. Agcy., res. ofcr. Hughes Aircraft Co., El Segundo 1979--; mem: AICPA; Assn. of Govt. Accts.; L.A. Country Club; mil: 1st lt. US Army 1969-71, Bronze Star; Republican; Presbyterian; rec: golf, hiking, travel. Res: 2008 California Ave, Santa Monica 90403 Ofc: 200 N. Sepulveda Blvd El Segundo 90245

WIND, DONALD EDWARD, company executive; b. Aug. 27, 1927, Winfield, Kansas; s. Henry Charles and Laura Lillian (Anderson) W.; m. Deborah Ruel, May 28, 1983; children: Sandra Lee, b. 1951; Stephanie Sue, b. 1962; edn: BS, Wash. Univ., St. Louis 1967; CDP, DPMA 1962. Career: v.p. On-Line Computer Systems, Newport Beach 1969-74; pres. Bancord Svcs., Newport Bch. 1974-77; asst. gen. mgr. Boeing Computer Svcs., Seattle, Wash. 1977-78; nat. sales mgr. Ericson, Inc., Santa Ana 1978-83; pres. The Wind-Chambers Group, Inc., Houston, Tex. & Indian Wells, CA 1983--; mem: ADAPSO; AIM; Fin. Mgrs. Assn.; Nat. Assn. of Bank Svcs.; Indian Wells Country Club; mil: USNR 1945-46; Republican; Episcopalian; rec: golf, tennis. Res: 44017 Erie Ct Indian Wells 92260 Ofcs: The Wind-Chambers Group, Inc., Indian Wells, CA and 3346 E T.C. Jester Houston, Tex. 77202

WIDERGREN, ROBERT DEL, company president; b. Oct. 18, 1938, Hastings, Nev.; s. Arnold Vivian and Della Sophia (Anderson) W.; m. Evelyn Mae Hill, Jan. 28, 1961; children: Jeffrey Brook, Michael Craig; edn: BS, aero engrg., Univ. of Colo. 1960. Career: tech. staff Lockheed Missiles & Space, 1963-66; mgr. Telemetry Pgms., General Electric, 1966-70; mgr. Imagery Dept., Philco-Ford Corp., 1970-76; founder/exec. v.p. Compression Lavs, Inc. 1976-79; pres./CEO Widcom, Inc., 1979--; honors: Electronic Mail and Message Systems Award of distinction for wk. in video digital codecs 1983; patents: facsimile and television compression technology; mil: lt. jg, USN; Republican;

Rel. Scis.; rec: golf. Res: 19397 Zinfandel, Saratoga 95070 Ofc: Widcom, Inc. 1500 E. Hamilton Ave, Ste. 217, Campbell 95008

WINDES, JOHN A., manufacturing co. executive; b. Feb. 21, 1926, Phoenix, Ariz.; s. Dudley G. and Hope G. (Anderson) W.; m. Mary Lin, Apr. 2, 1950; children: Colby Lin., b. 1952; Craig Allen, b. 1956; edn: BS, agri. engr., Univ. of Ariz. 1950; BS, mech. engr., Univ. of Ariz. 1964. Career: rancher, cotton and cattle, Tucson, Ariz. 1952-60; tech. svc. Celanese Corp. & Amerian Can Co. 1964-69; chmn. bd./ CEO Colby Plastics, Anaheim 1969--; mil: Petty Ofcr. USN 1943-46; Republican; Presbyterian. Res: 24656 Eloisa Mission Viejo 92691 Ofc: Colby Plastics, 1335 Alles Anaheim 92805

WINDHAM, MARILYN ANN, real estate boker; b. Apr. 3, 1950, San Francisco; d. Charles Edward and Ann Laura (Carstensen) W.; m. Edward Windham, Mar. 27, 1973; 1 son: Ian, b. 1982; edn: stu. Cabrillo Coll., UCSB, UCSD, 1969-74; BA, San Diego State Univ. 1976; cert. profcy. acctg., Cabrillo 1983; real estate broker lic., Calif. 1981. Career: owner Tobacco Rd. Cattery 1971--; real estate sales agt. Bonanza Properties, Tustin 1976; escrow techn. Western Title Co., Santa Cruz 1977; real estate agt. Real Estate World, Santa Cruz 1978; realtor self empl., Santa Cruz 1981-82; independent real estate broker 1982--; pres., mng. partner Winn Leasing Co. (resdtl. prop. mgmt.) 1984--; honors: owner/ breeder best Havana Brown in Southwest region 1976, 1977; mem: Nat. and Calif. Assns. of Realtors; Cat Fanciers Assn.; Internat. Havana Brown Soc.; Mensa; Nat. Assn. for Gifted Children; Forum on Gifted Children; Early Childhood Edn. Gp.; Refunders- by- the-Sea; Parenthesis; Santa Cruz Exch. Club; Am. Contract Bridge League; research: inheritance of the brown gene in agouti and no-agouti cats, discovered new gene as reported to the geneticist Todd 1976; Democrat; rec: cat breeding, early childhood learning, genetics. Address: Marilyn Windham, Broker, 3907 Adar Lane Soquel 95073

WINELAND, ROSEMARY, real estate broker-developer; b. Mar. 1, 1931, Elkhart, Indiana; d. Wilbur D. and Helen Amy (Bryant) Anglin; m. Richard D. Wineland, June 27, 1953; children: Thomas, b. 1954; Robert, b. 1956; Jennifer, b. 1958; J'Amy, b. 1960; edn: B.Music Edn., w/ hon., Ind. Univ. 1952; BS summ cum laude, int. design, Woodbury Univ. 1974; AA, real estate 1980; real estate broker lic., Calif. & Indiana. Career: secty. Better Bus. Bureau, Elkhart, Ind. 1952-53; asst. to dean of women/ alumnae advisor to Alpha Chi Omega, USC 1953-54; staff designer EJM Devel. Corp., Los Angeles 1974; prin. Rosemary Wineland Interiors, Burbank 1971--; real estate sales, Burbank 1975--; real estate developer, 1981--; Bldg. & Fire Code Appeals Bd., chmn. 1979; Design Review Bd., chmn. 1974; awards: Top Real Estate Salesman of Yrs. 1975-76; Million Dollar Club 1976--; Hon. Mayor, City of Burbank; Mayor's Com. on Redevel.; Pi Kappa Lambda; Sigma Alpha Iota; mem: Burbank Bd. Realtors; Calif. Bd. Realtors; YMCA; Burbank Comm. Hosp. Health Care Gound.; Nat. Charity League; Presbyterian Ch.; Burbank Women's Golf Club; profl. photographer (that devel. from a hobby and her interest in antiques) and owner: Some Other Time (antique shop) 1980-); Republican; Presbyterian; rec: restoring antiques, bridge, water skiing, travel. Res: 1199 E Verdugo Ave Burbank 91501 Ofc: Chase Realty, 610 No Glenoaks Blvd Burbank 91502

WINETSKY, CAROL SCHUTZ, clinical psycchologist; b. Dec. 24, 1945, NY, NY; d. Nathan R. and Ruth (Goldsholl) Schutz; m. Henry P. Winetsky, May 15, 1977; 2 sons: Michael, b. 1978; Daniel, b. 1981; edn: BA, Univ. of Wisc. 1967; MA, Wash. Univ. 1969; PhD, Stanford Univ. 1977; lic. clinical psychologist, State Calif. 1981. Career: tchr. St. Louis Pub. Schs. 1969-72, Discovery Center, San Francisco 1974; research asst. Dr. Bruno Bettelheim 1974-75; research asst. Stanford Univ. Med. Sch. 1976; lectr. San Francisco State Univ. 1974-77; asst. prof. 1977-78; post doctoral fellow in psychology Childrens Hosp., S.F, Kaiser Permanente Med. Gp., So. S.F. 1979-80; staff psychologist, Child and Family Treatment Ctr., Children's Hosp., S.F. 1980-81; clinical psychologist, pvt. practice and lectr. 1981--; cons. San Francisco Council Parent Participatory Nursery Schs.; awards: chief trainee, Children's Hosp., S.F. 1978-79; Stanford Univ. Research Grant 1976; Phi Delta Kappa 1975, 76, 77; Outstanding Elem. Tchrs. of Am. 1975; mem: Am., Western, Calif. State, and San Francisco Bay Area Psychological Assns.; Temple Emanu-El and Temple Emanu-El Sisterhood, S.F; publs: Comparisons of the Expectations of Parents and Teachers for the Behavior of PreSchool Children, Child Development 1978; Sputnik and Its Aftermath, The Elementary School Journ. 1977; When the U.S. Paid for Day Care: The Kaiser Center, Day Care and Early Education 1975. Address: 1291 Bosworth St San Francisco 94131

WINFREY, DENNIS WAYNE, financial planner/writer; b. Oct. 14, 1947, Mexico, Mo.; s. Jess O. and Betty Jo (Moore) Winfrey; edn: stu. Orange Coast, Golden West, and Riverside City Colls., UCLA, num. finl. seminars. Career: branch mgr. two stores, Custom Furniture (chain of 30 stores), Riverside 1969-71; part-time advtg. sales and pvt. study in orgnzl. mgmt. and cons. techniques, 1971-75; estab. Priority Financial Group (finl. planning practice w/ clients in 5 states), Los Angeles 1975--; assoc. cons. Future Focus, mgmt. cons.co., Los Angeles 1975--; lectr. self-improvement, finl. planning seminars 1973--, assoc. lectr. Patrick McVay of Tom Hopkins Seminars; real estate investor in Calif., Ind., Fla.; mem: Authors Guild; author/pub. books on finl. planning subjects 1977--; num. mag. feature arts. in Orange Coast, Today's Professionals, Prosperity, Florida Central Scene, Black Hills Monthly, Sunday Woman mags., Survival Bks, etc. Rec: karate, skiing, Stephen King novels. res: 3032 Valevista Trail Hollywood Hills 90068 ofc: Priority Financial Group, 1000 Central Ave, 4th Flr., Glendale 91202

WINKLER, PIROSKA, real estate broker; b. June 26, 1918, Nagyhalasz,

Hungary, nat. 1956; d. Ignacz and Liona (Lichtman) Fenyes; m. Miklo Winkler, Dec. 7, 1937; children: (twins) Vera and Linda, b. 1958; lic. real estate, State of Calif. 1966. Career: concentration camp survivor; displaced person camp 1948-50; immigrant, U.S. 1950; farmed turkey, chicken, and beef cattle, Cotati 1950-71; real estate, Cotati 1966-71; assoc. broker Saxe Realty, San Francisco 1971--; Democrat; Jewish. Res: 17 Marvel Ct San Francisco 94121 Ofc: Saxe Realty Co., 1390 Noriega St San Francisco 94122

WINKLER, RALPH EUGENE, real estate investor, air force officer, ret.; b. Feb. 3, 1927, Elkville, Ill.; s. Hugh Stelle and Vesta M. (Schimpf); W.; m. Margaret Novaria, Dec. 30, 1981; 1 dau: Esther, b. 1960; edn: BS, mgmt., Univ. of Ill. 1950; DePaul Univ. Law Sch. 1957-8. Career: asst. base adj, Feamcom AFB, Japan 1952-55; commdr. Ofc. of Spl. Investigations, Edwards AFB 1963-66; agent-in-charge OSI Investigations Unit, NYC 1967; OSI cmdr. isl. of Greenland 1968; staff responsibility for Air Force counterintell. in 5-state area in midwest 1969-70; maj. investor in apt. bldgs. 1956--; Calif. R.E. Broker; honors: AF Meritorious Svc. Medal 1970; Sr. Class Hon., Coll. of Commerce, Univ. of Ill. 1950; mem. NOSI (Not One Sq. Inch) 1977-79, orgn. founded to oppose the Panama Canal Treaties; recipient resolution for efforts to save Panama Canal, Calif. State Senate Rules Comm. 1979; mem. Republican Central Com., Orange Co.; following landslide election 6/8/76, had total of 20 comm. election opponents in 7 yrs. and was never out polled; Repub. Party chmn., City of Los Alamitos; Am. Legion; Americanism Comm., Cypress VFW Post; delegate, state and nat. VFW convs.; depty. senatorial dist. dir. Calif. Republ. Assy.; Los Alamitos Museum Assn.; El Cajon Area Ret. Ofcrs. Assn.; Santee Methodist Ch.; rec: hiking, photog., political writing. Res; 10332 Escadera Dr Lakeside 92040

WINNICK, HELENE ANN, lawyer; b. Sept. 21, 1956, Sacramento; d. Byron Monroe and Estelle (Feinberg) W.; edn: AA, Am. River Coll. 1975; BA, UCLA 1977; JD, Southwestern Univ. Sch. of Law 1980; admitted to practice Calif., U.S. Dist. Cts., U.S. Tax Ct. 1981 Career: congl. staff mem. Los Angeles Dist. Ofc. (Waxman) 1976; Los Angeles Dept. of Consumer Affairs 1977; law clerk Rosenstock & Rosenstock 1977; Goller, Gillin & Menes, 1979-80; v.p. Winn's Sales, Inc., Sacramento 1977 ; assoc. atty. Wohl, Cinnamon & Hagedorn, Inc., Sacto. 1982--; atty. solo practice, Sacto. 1982--; prof. Pacific Coll. of Legal Careers 1983; dir. Quantum Ednl. Devel., Inc. 1981-2; Nat. Task Force mem. ABLE TV, Council of Jewish Fdns. 1982-; panelist Far West Conf. on Women & The Law- Media Law, Entertainment Law 1983; honors: articles ed. Law Rev., Southwestern 1979 80; Outstanding Women of Am. 1980; mem; Calif. State Sacramento Co., and Am. Bar Assns.; Women Lawyers of Sacto., sect. patent, copyright & trademarks; ABA coms. Media and the Law, Patent Copyright & Trademark; Religious Coalition for Cable TV; Sacto. Jewish Bus. & Profl. Women; publs: Palimony-A Trial Run, Community Property Law Journ. 1982; Democrat; Jewish. Res: 1100 Howe Ave, No 200, Sacramento 95825 Ofc: 1001 G Street, Ste 300, Sacramento 95814

WINSLOW, DENNIS MAURICE, inventory systems executive; b. Dec. 23, 1947, Denver, Colo.; s. Maurice Reece and Dorothy (Leonard) W.; m. Linda Pursel, Aug. 8, 1979; 1 son: John Dennis, b. 1981; Certified in prodn. and inventory control, APICS 1981. Career: supvr. Standard Brands, Oakland 1975-76; inventory systems mgr. Shaklee Corp., Oakland 1977--; spkr. APICS Nat. Conf., New Orleans 1983; mem: Am. Production and Inventory Control Soc.; Comserv Corp. User Gp.; Shaklee Runners; Jr. Achievement; San Francisco Bay Area Supply Corps. Assn.; Sierra Club River Touring Soc.; publs: Guidelines for Piloting a Material Requirements Planning System Conversion, Auerbach, Inc. 1982; mil: LCDR, USN 1970-74, Meritorious Unit Citation; Republican; Methodist; rec: whitewater kayaking. Res: 938 Rose Ave Piedmont 94611 Ofc: Shaklee Corp., 456 22nd St Oakland 94612

WINSTON, SCOTT THOMAS, reconstruction co. chief executive; b. Dec. 11, 1953, Long Beach; s. Wm. Henry, Jr., and Nancy Ann (Davies) W. (family res. in Long Beach since 1910); edn: BA, Occidental Coll. 1975; Grad. Theological Union, 1975-77. Career: began renovating historic properties, Long Beach 1977--, worked for estab. of Drake Park Historic (preservation) District, 1979; founder/owner/CEO, Seaside Land Co., and Roughstone (redev. co.); candidate Long Beach City Council 1980; apptd. mem., elected chmn. Cultural Heritage Com. for L.B., 1979; mem. Nat. Trust, L.B. Hist. Soc. (life), Sierra Club (life); L.B. CofC; lectr. local civic groups; publs. in local mags. and newspapers, L.A. Mag. 7/79; Republican; Congregational; rec: yachting, flying, travel, antiques. Res: 2505 E. 2nd St Long Beach 90803 Ofc: Roughstone, 3400 E 7th St Long Beach 90804

WINTERSTEIN, DAVID ALAN, computer consultant; b. June 13, 1947, San Luis Obispo; s. Carl John and Lola Evelyn W.; m. Blanca Ramirez Abad, Jan. 18, 1975; 1 dau. Lydia Elsie Rose, b. 1980; edn: pgmmg., Condie Coll. 1971. Career: USAF telecommunications splst. 1965-69; test tech. Teledyne Microwave 1969-73, (supr.) Aertech Indus. 1971-2, Cushman Elect. 1973-4; ins. agt. Washington Nat. 1972, Lutheran Mutual 1973; test tech. Fairchild Systems 1974, (test mgr.) Nutting Assoc. 1974-76, Memorex 1976; chief technician Zilog Inc. 1977-79; tech. staff Rolm Corp. 1979, Summit Systems. 1979-80; TeleVideo Systems 1980 82; tech. support mgr./cons. for hardware & software: instr. computer repair, TeleVideo Systems 1980-2, cons. Graphon Corp. 1983-4; product engring. mgr. TicketVision (TV peripheral co.), 1984--; Mil: E5 USAF 1965-9, Air Nat. Guard 1973, USCGR 1974; Lutheran; rec: photog., numismatics; res: 646 No White Rd San Jose 95127

WIRTHLIN, MILTON ROBERT, JR., dentist; b. July 13, 1932, Little Rock, Ark.; s. Milton R. and Margaret Frances (Clark) W.; m. Joan Krieger, Aug. 1, 1954; children: Michael, b. 1956, Steven, b. 1957, Laurie, b. 1959, David, b. 1960, Aina, b. 1966; edn: undergrad., UCB 1950-52; DDS, UC San Francisco 1956, MS, 1968; Diplomate Am. Bd. Periodontology 1974. Career: served to capt., Dental Corps, US Navy, 1955--; exec. ofcr., 1st Dental Co., Vietnam 1968-69; head Periodontol., Naval Dental Clin., Long Beach, Ca. 1969-73; exec. ofcr. 3rd Dental Co. FMF, Okinawa, 1973-74; chief Epidemiol., Naval Dental Research Inst., Great Lakes, Ill. 1974-76, cmdg. ofcr. 1976-81; cmdg. ofcr. Naval Regl. Dental Ctr., San Francisco 1981-83; asst. chief of staff Naval Med. Command S.W. Region, San Diego 1983--; clin. asst. prof. Periodontics, USC 1970-73, Univ. Ill. ;1977-81; honors: Gabbs Prize in Dentistry, UC 1956; Am. Acad. Dental Med. Award 1956; C.O.'s Award Excellence in Operative Dentistry, also Annual Award for Research Methods, Naval Dental Sch. 1966; Fellow Internat. Coll. of Dentistry 1980; mem: Omicron Kappa Upsilon, Am. Dental Assn., Internat. Assn. for Dental Resrch, Am. Acad. Periodontol., Western/MidWest Soc. Periodontol.; active in BSA (1968), ARC, Nat. Model R.R. Assn. (past trainmaster Midwest Reg. Fox Valley Div.); publs: 28 articles on dental research; mil: decorated: Merit. Svc. with Gold Star, Navy Commendn. with Combat V; Prot.; rec: model R.R., trout fly tying, archery. Res: 4460 Caminito Pedernal, San Diego 92117 Ofc: Naval Medical Command Southwest Region, San Diego 92134

WISDOM, DARWIN DALE, FBI special agent; b. Oct. 16, 1941, Wenatchee, Wash.; s. Glen Raymond and Enid Muriel (Gallaher) W.; m. Karen Nelson, Oct. 3, 1964; children: Elizabeth, b. 1968; Cherlyn, b. 1972; Christopher, b. 1974; edn: BA econ., bus. adm., Seattle Pacific Coll. 1963; grad. work, Univ. of W.Vir. 1965, Univ. of Wash. 1967. Career: underwriter and mgmt. trainee Farmers Insurance Group, Mercer Is., Wash. 1966; cost acct. Kenworth Motor Truck Co., Seattle 1977; spl. agent, FBI, Phoenix, Ariz. 1968-69, Financial Crimes Unit, San Diego, 1969--; bd. chmn. Cabrillo Federal Credit Union, S.D. 1980-; honors: Centurians (Service hon.) 1962; mem: Federal Criminal Investigators Assn. 1976-82 (bd. dirs. 1976), FBI Spl. Agents Assn.; Calif. Peace Ofcrs Assn. 1982-3; Nat. Assn. of Credit Union Presidents; mem. Green Valley Civic Assn , S.D. Zoological Assn., Silver Saddle Homeowners Assn. (bd. 1977-81), various PTAs; mil: US Army Inf. 1964-66, 1st lt. USAR 1966-68; Republican; Presbyterian; rec: gardening, sports. Res: 13310 Bronco Way Poway 92064 Ofc: FBI, Suite 6S31, 880 Front St San Diego 92188

WISHON, JOHN ALBERT, lawyer, hotel executive, b. Jan. 17, 1945, Los Angeles; s. Frank Rowntree and Dorothy (Woodhouse) W.; edn: AB, acctg., psychol., San Diego State Univ , 1968; JD, Univ. San Diego, 1971. Career: private law practice, sr. partner, real estate law, Lieb, Wishon, Catterlin, Gay, 1972 76; sr. v.p. gen. counsel, Hotel del Coronado, 1976-1982; sr. v.p., mgr. Hotel del Coronado (constrd. 1887, national and state hist. landmark), 1982--; mem: Coronado CofC (bd. dirs.), San Diego Conv. and Visitors Bur. (adv. com.), S.D. CofC (pres. council 1978), Am./S.D. Bar Assns., Navy League, Coronado Hist. Assn., Coronado Residential Assn., S.D. Marlin Club (jud. adv. 1976), West Atwood Yacht Club (v. admiral 1972), Rotarian, bd. dirs. Am. Red Cross; Sigma Alpha Epsilon (bd. dirs. alumni 1976-), Phi Delta Phi law frat. (pres. 1970). Office: Hotel del Coronado, Coronado 92118

WITHAM, PEGGY JUNE, real estate broker; b. Jan. 23, 1937, Springfield, Mo.; d. Howard Madison and Gertrude (Sims) Buckner; m. Edward Jackson Witham, Sr. Oct. 23, 1954; children: Edward J., Jr., b. 1955; Diane Louise (Nusz), b. 1957; Richard Gallup, b. 1960; Suellen, b. 1965; edn: real estate, Anthony Schools; Calif. real estate sales lic. 1974, R.E. broker lic. 1981. Career: sales agent Witham Woodland Real Estate, 1974-78; broker, Witham Kelsey W. Hatcher Real Estate, 1981-83; broker/owner Witham Realty in Woodland, 1983--; honors: Realtor Assoc. of Year 1981; mem: Nat./Calif. Assn. of Realtors; Yolo Co. Bd. of Realtors (dir. 1979-, chmn. mem. com.); Yolo Co. Farm Bureau 1960-; spons. car show benefit for Special Olympics Yolo Co.; spons. (painting maint.) historical bldg. for pvt. property week; Democrat; Baptist; rec: gardening, cooking, hist. of Yolo Co. real estate. Res: POB 57 (RD 97B), Yolo 95697 Ofc: Witham Realty, 405 Lincoln Ave Woodland 95695

WITT, CHARLES BENJAMIN, JR., thoracic surgeon; b. Mar. 17, 1929, Wash DC; s. Charles Benjamin Sr. and Hattie Iona (Simmons) W.; m. Colette Beach, June 10, 1956; children: Charles III, b. 1952 (by previous marriage); Alexandra, b. 1961; Walter, b. 1962; edn: So. Missionary Coll., Collegedale, Tenn. 1945-47; Columbia Union Coll., Takoma Park, Md., 1947-748; MD, Univ. Tenn. Coll. of Med. 1951. Diplomate Am. Bd. of Surg. 1963, Dip. Am. Bd. of Thoracic Surg. 1964. Career: practice of thoracic surg., Los Angeles 1961--; pres. Hollywood West Hosp. Med. Staff, 1975; chmn. Dept. of Surg., Hollywood Presbyn. Med. Ctr. 1977-78, bd. dirs. 1981-; v.regent, So. Calif. Div. Internat. Coll. of Surgs. 1980-; clin. instr. in surg. UCI Sch. of Medicine (fmr. Calif. Coll. of Med.), 1964-70; apptd. by Pres. Reagan to Central District Appeal Bd. of Calif. for Selective Service System, 11/82; pres. National Soc. of Wash. Family Descendants 1982-84; mem. Jamestowne Soc., Calif. Soc. SAR; listed Los Angeles Blue Book, Southwest Blue Book; mem: Fellow Am. Coll. of Surgeons, L.A. Surg. Soc., Hollywood Acad. of Med.; Alumni Council, Pres.'s Club, Univ. of Tenn.; Nat. Gavel Soc.; Masons; Los Angeles Club (bd. dirs. 1983); works: piano soloist (Tchaikovsky B minor Piano Concerto) with L.A. Doctors Sym. Orch., Ambassador Coll., Pasa. 1975; mil: capt. AUS M.C. 1953-55; Republican; Seventh-day Adventist; rec: music, skiing. Res: 450 S. Lucerne Blvd Los Angeles 90020 Ofc: 6634 Sunset Blvd Los Angeles 90028

WITT, NORMAN ERNEST, airline pilot, educator; b. May 2, 1927, Nebraska City, Nebr.; s. Ernie H. and Anna M. (Pruessing) W.; m. Alice thompson, Nov. 1, 1952; children: Norman E. Jr., b. 1953; Nancy Lynn, b. 1955; edn: BS in edn., Univ. of Nebr. 1949, MS, 1955; EdD, UC Los Angeles 1969; grad. (Distinguished Aviation Cadet) USAF Pilot School, Lubbock, Tx. 1951; cert. Indsl. Coll. of Armed Forces 1967. Career: aviation machinist mate, USNR (active 1945-46, Res. 1946-50, Teacher 1949-50); pilot & adminstrv. officer USAF (active 1950-56; Res. 1956-69); flight engr., co-pilot & captain United Air Lines, 1956--; teacher Los Angeles City Schools, 1956-73; research educationist, UCLA 19664-65; instr. Long Beach City Coll. 1974; account exec. municipal bonds, R.H. Moulton & Co., L.A. 1980--; Aviation Merit Badge counselor, BSA; honors: Phi Delta Kappa, UCLA Dean's Council, UCLA Doctoral Alumni Assn.; mem: Palos Verdes Breakfast Club 1968-, PV Rotary 1974-9, Airline Pilots Assn. 1967-, PV Estates City Plnng. Commn. 1976-81, PV Penin. Tax Advis. Com. 1976-7; Republican (pres. PV Repub. Club 1971); Lutheran; rec: music (sax, clarinet). Res: 4013 Via Campesina Palos Verdes Estates 90274 Ofc: R.H. Moulton Co., 523 W. 6th St Los Angeles 90014

WITTER, JAMES FREDERICK, purchasing co. president; b. July 5, 1930, Akron, Ohio; s. Victor F. and Margaret (Topper) W. Career: owner/ pres. JFW Enterprises, Los Angeles; owner/pres., counselor, Specialized Personnel, L.A.; real estate investor; Republican; Catholic. Res: 8110 Lesner Ave Van Nuys 91406 Ofc: JFW Enterprises, 5900 Wilshire Blvd, 1770, Los Angeles 90036

WITTIG, DALE LAVERNE, manufacturing co. executive; b. Aug. 29, 1935, Larned, Kans.; w. Wm. Frederick and Ruby Estelle (Salmans) W.; m. Yvonne Rose Peterson, Apr. 1, 1956; children: Ricky Dale, b. 1956; Randy Dale, b. 1957; Rhonda Gayle, b. 1959; edn: grad. Burdett (Kans.) H.S. 1953. Career: assem. line, lead, foreman Marlett Mobile Homes, Great Bend, Kans. 1958-66, foreman, transferred to Hermiston, Ore. 1966-68; asst. prodn. Fleetwood-Terry Industries, La Grande, Ore. 1968-71; mgr. Fleetwood-Wilderness Indus., Merced, Ca. 1971-73; prodn. mgr. Motor Homes Div. Fleetwood Ent. Inc., Riverside 1973-, product mgr. 1974-, Div. prodn. mgr. Travel Trailer Div., 1976--; Republican; Prot.; rec: hunting, fishing, wood working. Res: 6053 Cathcart Pl Riverside 92506 Ofc: Fleetwood Ent. Inc. 3050 Myers St Riverside 92523

WITZMAN, JOSEPH E., educator, publisher; b. Oct. 5, 1929, Minneapolis, MN; s. Melvin King and Anita (Shephard) Witzman; BA, law, Univ. of Minn., 1951, BSc. edn. 1953; m. Joyce Wolfson, Jan. 25, 1953; chil: Cindy, b. 1955; Scott, b. 1958. Career: hotel mgr., gen. prop., Midland Hotel Chain, Mpls., Minn., 1958-63; motel owner/operator, Travelodges, San Diego, Calif., 1964-68; educator, San Diego Sch. Sys., 1964-68; pres., Hiway Host Motor Inns, chain, 1969--; educator, San Diego Comm. Coll. Dist., 1970--, dir. Sch. of Hotel Adminstrn. Mesa Coll. San Diego; publshr., Apartment Guide of San Diego, 1974---; R.E. investor, 1968---; finl. adv., 1978---; pres. Hiway Host Motels, 1969---; dir., San Diego Golf Acad. Honors: Golden Egg Award, Travelodge Corp., Most Outstanidng Travelodge Operator, 1966. Mem: S.D. CofC; Council on Hotel, Restaurant and Instnl. Edn., Inc.; adv. bd., San Diego Comm. Coll. Dist. Developed first travel trailer co-op park in U.S., Yuma, Ariz. Author: Up-Front, guide to front office hotel procedure, college text in process of publ. for Prentice Hall Publshrs.; Apartment Guide of San Diego, publ., 1974---. Mil: Cpl., US Army, 1953-55. Republican. Rec: stamp collecting, gardening (roses). Res: 5946 Soledad Mtn. Rd., La Jolla 92037; Office: Apt. Guide of San Diego, 1585 Rosecrans, San Diego 92106.

WOFFINDEN, FRANKLIN BRAMWELL, mechanical engineer; b. June 24, 1925, Provo, Utah; s. Franklin B. and Vaneese (Harris) W.; m. Ella Doreen Jackson, Aug. 22, 1959; children: Gary, b. 1960, Todd, b. 1962, Brent, b. 1964, Catherine, b. 1967; edn: BSME, Univ. of Utah 1948; MSME, CSU San Jose 1970; lic. Profl. Engr. Calif. 1971. Career: mathematician North Am. Aviation, Inglewood 1948-49; grad. asst. Brigham Young Univ., 1949-51; dynamics engr. Convair/Gen. Dynamics, San Diego 1951-55, senior dynamics engr. 1958-65; missionary to Brazil, 1955-58; assoc. staff engr. FMC Corp., San Jose 1965-69; methods engr. General Electric Co., San Jose 1970--; mem. Instrument Soc. of Am. (sec. Power Plant Dynamics com. 1982-4); publs: paper presented ISA symposium, Pittsburgh, Pa. 1981; Republican: LDS Ch.; rec: youth activities, Boy Scouting. Res: 324 Pennsylvania Ave Los Gatos 95030 Ofc: Gen. Elec. Co. 175 Curtner Ave, M/C 186, San Jose 95125

WOLD, NANA BEHA, social worker; b. Nov. 4, 1943, NY, NY; d. Wm. John and Margaret (Robinson) Beha; edn: BA, Texas Womans Univ. 1965; MSW, UC Berkeley 1967; LCSW, lic. clin. soc. wkr., Calif. 1980. Career: psychiat. soc. wkr. Mendocino State Hosp., Talmage 1967-70; psychiat. soc. wkr. State Dept. Mental Health, San Diego 1972-74; suprvg. psychiat. soc. wkr. St. Dept. Developmental Svcs, S.D. 1974-81; asst. chief Case Mgmt. Svcs., S.D. Regl. Ctr. for Devel. Disabilities, 1981--; instr. in soc. wkr. Chapman Coll. 1972; honors: Kiwanis award (acad.) 1965, Who's Who in Am. Colls. and Univs. 1965, recognition as Army Comm. Service Vol., Ft. Wolters, Tx. 1969; mem. Am. Assn. of Mental Deficiency; Comm. Living Project adv. com. 1973-76; Sr. Citizens Day Care Ctr. adv. com. 1976-7; coauthor Sex Edn. for the Mentally Retarded (1975), num. pamphlets, brochures in field of devel. disabilities; Catholic; rec: music, needlework. Res: 10327 Centinela Dr La Mesa 92041 Ofc: S.D. Regl. Ctr. for Developmental Disabilities, 4355 Ruffin Rd, Ste. 306, San Diego 92123

WOLFE, DICKHAUT EDWARD, poet laureate of San Pedro; b. Feb. 20,.1910, Evansville, Inc.; s. Walter Von Geotz and Emma Marie (Dickhaut) W.; div.; 1

dau. Dorothy Louise Schorken, b. 1932; grad. (commencement spkr.) San Pedro H.S. 1929. Career: electric contractor, Wolfe Electric, San Pedro, now ret. (said to hold oldest elec. contr. lic. in City of L.A. in 1937 by the City Clerk); founder/chmn. Point Fermin Nature Trail, 1975-83; apptd. Poet Laureate of San Pedro, Los Angeles City Council May 12, 1978; mem: Friends of San Pedro Lib. (bd. dirs.), San Pedro Bay Hist. Soc. (named the orgn.; mem. bd. dirs.), founding com. Los Angeles Maritime Mus.; poetic works: Rubaiyat of Dick Edward Wolfe (1981); Republican; rec: athletics, nature study, hiking. Res: 934 N. Grand Ave San Pedro 90731

WOLFE, ELLIOTT SIDNEY, private investigation agency president; b. Dec. 8, 1933, Salt Lake City, Utah; s. Abraham B. and Minnie (Albert) W.; m. Phillene Lehrman, Feb. 16, 1958; div.; children: Steven, b. 1959, Dayna, b. 1961, Staci, b. 1967; edn: BS, USC, 1956; LLB, USFV Coll. of Law 1968; Calif. lic. owner pvt. investg. agency 1958. Career: deputy sheriff County of Los Angeles, 1955-56; free lance pvt. investigator, 1956-58; owner/pres. pvt. investigation agcy., 1958-82; investigator and civil procedures cons. to various law firms, 1982--; lectr. in field, state, nat., internat. assns., L.A. City Coll., 1970-82; recipient num. merit awards, profl. assns.; past mem: World Assn. of Detectives, Calif. Assn. Licensed Invstgtrs. (past pres., editor), Calif. Assn. Profl. Process Servers (past bd. chmn., editor), Nat. Council of Investigator & Security Svcs.; Republican; rec: wood carving, pottery. Res: 4655 Natick Ave Sherman Oaks 91403 Ofc: E.S. Wolfe & Assoc., POB 5534, Sherman Oaks 91413

WOLFE, JONATHAN SCOTT, lawyer; b. Feb. 28, 1950, San Francisco; s. Lawrence I. and Charlotte (Avrick) W.; m. Constance Jarvis, Sept. 14, 1974; edn: AB with distinction, Stanford Univ. 1972; JD, Harvard Univ. 1976; LLB, honors, Univ. of Cambridge, 1976; admitted State Bar of Calif. 1976. Career: assoc. atty. Davis, STafford, Kellman & Fenwick, Palo Alto 1976-78; assoc. Dinkelspiel, Pelavin, Steefel & Levitt, San Francisco 1978-79; assoc. atty. Steefel, Levitt & Weiss, 1980-82, partner 1983--; lectr. Am. Mgmt. Assns. and World Trade Inst.; honors: Phi Beta Kappa 1972; Evan Lewis-Thomas Law Studentship, Cambridge Univ., Eng. 1974; mem: Econ. Roundtable of S.F., Am. and Calif. Bar Assns., American Lives Endowment (Gen. Counsel); mem. Planning Group, Subcom. on Intell. and Security, Policy Council, Democratic Nat. Com., 1971-72; publs: law review arts.; coauthor, two books for UN Social Def. Resrch Inst. (re drug control) 1972, 73; coauthor (with R.H. Blum): Surveillance and Espionage in a Free Soc. (Praeger Pub., 1972), The Dream Sellers (Jossey-Bass Pub. 1972); rec: art, travel. Res: POB 887, Ross 94957 Ofc: Steefel, Levitt & Weiss, One Embarcadero Ctr, 28th Flr, San Francisco 94111

WOLFF, JEAN-PIERRE, power systems engineer/executive; b. June 1, 1949, Brussels, Belgium; nat. 1981; s. Freddy and Lisette (Gorremans) W.; m. Bridget Conneely, Oct. 5, 1974; 1 son, Mark, b. 1978; edn: BSEE, Heald Eng. Coll. 1974; M.Ed., UC Berkeley 1979; licenses: elec., gen. engring., solar engring. contr.; elec. insp. & energy auditor; std. teaching credential, univ. level, Calif. Career: v.p. A&D Engineering, Belmont, Calif.; chief designer Darmsted Parenti & Assocs., San Francisco; power system engr. Westinghouse Corp., Emeryville; currently, mgr. regl. & internat. ops., Electro-Test Inc., San Ramon; adj. prof. San Francisco St. Univ., mem. adv. bd. SFSU Power Engring. Dept.; recipient IEEE Engineering Award 1983; mem: IEEE (section chmn. 1984, chmn. Power Engring. Soc. 1982, v.chmn. Wescon 1983), AEE, IEIA, NFPA; publs: tech. papers in field, Elec. Apparatus Maint. & Testing Manual (copyright 1982); Republican; Catholic; rec: sports. Res: 320 Madatera Ct Danville 94583 Ofc: Electro-Test Inc. 3470 Fostoria Way San Ramon 94583

WOLFINGTON, VINCENT A., company executive; b. Apr. 17, 1940, Phila., Pa.; s. James Eustace and Mary Margaret (Kelly Tegler) W.; m. Alicia Usera; children: Christopher, b. 1968, Joan, b. 1969, Mark, b. 1970, Jonathan, b. 1974, Lindsay, b. 1979; edn: BA, Georgetown Univ.; MBA, N.Y. Univ. 1965. Career: A.V.P./ comml. lending ofcr. Chase Manhattan Bank, NY 1962-68; chmn. Tetra Devel. Corp., NY 1968-72; exec. v.p. Genway Corp., Chgo. 1969-71; pres./ chmn. bd. Carey Corp., Wash DC 1971--; pres. Carey Limousine Cos., Beverly Hills 1971--; chmn. bd. Pioneer Airlines 1972-73; bd. advisors Transp. Resrch. Bd. Acad. of Scis. 1975-78; pres. Nat. Para-Transit Assn. 1974-78; awards: Kroft Medal, Georgetown Univ. 1962; Georgetown Univ. trustee (1974-80), chmn. Devel. Com. and mem. Exec. and Fin. Com. (1976-80); trustee (chmn. 1975, 78) George F. Baker Trust-Scholarship Com. Wash DC, 1975-; bd. advisors Ctr. for Strategic & Internat. Studies, Wash DC 1976-80; dir. Greater Washington Bd. of Trade 1982; dir. Nat. Com., Arts for the Handicapped, JFK Ctr. for Perf. Arts, 1979-; publs: Regs. & Para-Transit Spl. Report Transp. Resrch Bd., Nat. Acad. Sci.; mil: USCG 1963-66; Republican; Catholic; rec: tennis, golf, sailing, investments. Res: 4949 Lowell Street, N.W. Washington, DC 20016 Ofc: Carey Corp. 4545 42nd St, Ste. 300, Wash DC 20016

WOLFSOHN, BERTRAM LIONEL, endodontist, educator; b. Aug. 29, 1905, San Francisco; s. Morris Leslie and Kathryn (Gutstadt) W.; m. Rachel Snyder, Nov. 27, 1952; edn: DDS, Univ. of Calif. 1927; instr. Operative Dentistry, Univ. of Calif. 1927-34; asst. clin. prof. Univ. of Pacific 1953, assoc. prof. 1956, clinical prof. 1959-79, Prof. Emeritus 1980--; assoc. prof. endodontics Univ. Calif. 1981-, vis. prof. nat. and internat.; author, lectr., clinician; contbr. to textbooks and encyclopedic vols.; pioneered clin. endodontic practice since 1938 with original research in basic, clin. endodontics; honors: Edgar D. Coolidge endodontic award 1974; Maimonides Award 1980; Sigma Xi, Omicron Kappa Upsilon, Alpha Omega FACD (1954), FICD (1959, FAIOB, FIDR, FADI; mem: Am., Calif. Dental Assns.; San Francisco (pres. 1959), San Mateo

Dent. Socs.; Am. Inst. Oral Biol. (fellow); Internat., Am. Assns. Dent. Research; Medical Dental Study Guild (pres. 1955); Rotary Club, Masons, Scottish Rite, Shriners; mil: USAR (dental corps) 1932-43; Republican; Jewish; rec: lecturing, writing, musician (orchestral & modern music). Res: 818 Northampton Dr Palo Alto 94303

WOLNY, LIDIA KRYSTYNA, chiropractor; b. July 10, 1953, Poland, naturalized Am. 1972; d. Aloszy Jan and Krystyna Anna (Roman) Wolny; edn: AA, Ohlone Coll. 1973; BS in biol., CSU Hayward 1976; DC, Palmer Coll. of Chiropractic West, 1982. Career: tchr. asst. handicapped children, Irvington High Sch., Fremont 1970; lab. tech. Western Laboratories, Oakland 1976-78; instr. (clin. chem.) Life Chiropractic Coll. West, 1980-83, faculty mem. 1983--; pvt. practice chiropractic, Hayward 1983--; mem. Nat., Amer., Calif. Chiropractic Assns.; Democrat; Catholic; rec: literature, symphony, ballet, skiing. Res: 34800 Daisy St Union City 94587 Ofc: Lidia K. Wolny D.C., 381 Jackson St Hayward 94544

WONG, ANNE TUNGLAU, chiropractor, acupuncturist, Chinese herbalist; b. Nov. 1, 1939, Mauea, China; nat. 1977; d. Youngchong and Mingfong Wong; edn: Chinese Med. Dr., Canton Chinese Med. Coll. 1956-62; RN & midwife, Kwongwah Nursing Sch. 1963-67; Reg. Psychiat. Nurse, Long Grove Nursing Sch. 1970-72; DC, Logan Chiropractic Coll. 1976-79. Career: traditional Chinese doctor Lam Clinic, HongKong 1963-70; R.N., Columbus Hosp., NYC 1973-76; Dr. of Chiro./Cert. Acupuncturist, Pack Chiropractic Clinc, Fresno 1980-82, Wong Acupuncture & Chiropractic, 1983--; frequent lectr. on herbs, natural healing arts, CSU Fresno, High Point Found., 1980-; mem. Am. Chiropractic Assn., Logan Alumni Assn.; rec: music, calligraphy, painting. REs: 4012 E. Farrin, Fresno 93726 Wong Chiropractic & Acupuncture Office: 440 E. Shield, Fresno 93705

WONG, HING CHUNG, physician; b. Sept. 29, 1941, Hong Kong; nat. US citizen 1978; parents: Chui Y. and Shui Man (Tang) Wong; m. King Y. Wong, Apr. 2, 1962; edn: B.Medicine, Nat. Taiwan Univ. 1965; MD, USA, 1976, Career: Family Practice (solo), Chinatown, Los Angeles 1978--; chief cons. Chaus Jou Assn. in USA; med. advisor for am. Vietnam Chinese Friendship Assn., Eng Family Ben Assn., Chinese Garment Assn., Elderly Indochinese Assn.; med. staff French Hosp. (pres. elect 1983); bd. dirs. Chinatown Service Center 1983-86; honors: good citizenship awd, City of Los Angeles; awards, Paralyzed Veterans Assn. (1977); mem. AMA, L.A. Co. Med. assn.; Christian; rec: golf. Res: 1117 Alpine St Los Angeles 90012 Ofc: H.C. Wong, MD, 709 N. Hill St, Ste. 19, Los Angeles 90012

WONG, KENNETH LEE, engineer; b. Aug. 15, 1947, Los Angeles; s. George Yut and Yue Sam (Lee) W.; m. Betty Louie, Jun 29, 1975; children: Bradford Keith, b. 1977, Karen Beth, b. 1980; edn: BS, in engrg., UCLA 1969, MS, 1972, postgrad. work; Calif. Comm. Coll. Instr. Cred. 1972. Career: engineering aide Singer Librascope, Glendale 1972-73; computer systems design engr. AF Avionics Lab, Wright-Pattersn AFB, Oh. 1973-75; mem. tech. staff TRW Defense & Space Systems Gp., Redondo Bch 1975-76, 1978-79, Hughes Aircraft Co. Culver City, 1976-78, El Segundo 1979-81; engrg. splst. Northrop Aircraft Co., Hawthorne 1981-84; mem. tech. staff Jet Propulsion Lab., Pasadena 1984--. Honors: AFROTC Disting. Mil. Grad. 1962, Upsilon Pi Epsilon 1976; Hughes Aircraft Co. Staff Engr. fellowship ;1977-78; Who's Who in Aviation & Aerospace 1983; mem: Assn. for Computing Machinery, IEEE, Am. Inst. Aero & Astro, UCLA Alumni Assn., Westside Family YMCA; publs: profl. papers; mil: 1st lt. USAF 1972-75, AF Commend.; Republican; rec: photog., basketball. Res: 3385 McLaughlin Ave Los Angeles 90066 Ofc: JPL, 4800 Oak Grove Dr Pasadena 91109

WONG, KING YUE, optometrist; b. July 29, 1948, Los Angeles; parents: George Yut and Yue Sam (Lee) Wong; edn: AA, L.A. City Coll. 1969; BA, UC Los Angeles 1971; OD, So. Coll. of Optometry 1983. Career: accounting clerk Ralph C. Sutro Co., Los Angeles 1971-72; statistical clerk Kaiser Found. Health Plan Inc, L.A. 1973-75, rates coordinator 1975-79, cons. 1980-81; First Aid Instr., Am. Red Cross 1979-81; honors: Tau Alpha Epsilon (1968); mem: Am. Optometric Assn. 1979-, Math. Assn. of Am. 1971-, UCLA Alumni Assn.; Republican; rec: magic, philately. Res: 947 So. Normandie Ave, Apt. 1, Los Angeles 90006

WONG, OTTO, epidemiologist; b. Nov. 14, 1947, China, nat. 1976; s. Kui and Foon (Chow) Wong; m. Betty Yeung, 1970; children: Elaine, b. 1978; Jonathan, b. 1983. edn: BS in physics and math., magna cum laude, Univ. of Ariz. 1970; MS, physics, Carnegie-Mellon Univ. 1972; MS. biostatistics, Univ. of Pittsburgh 1973, and ScD, biostat., 1975; acctg. courses UCB 1982. Career: public health service fellow Univ. of Pittsburgh, 1972-75; asst. prof. epidemiol. Georgetown Univ. Sch. of Med., 1975-78; mgr. Epid., Equitable Environmental Health, Inc., Rockville, Md. 1977-78; dir. of epid., Tabershaw Occupational Med. Assocs., Rockville, Md., 1978-80; dir. occup. research, Biometric Research Inst., Wash DC 1980-81; v.p./sr. epid., Environmental Health Assocs., Inc., Berkeley, Calif. 1981--; cons. to Nat. Cancer Inst., Fairfax Hosp., Motor Vehicle Mfrs. Assn., Western Elec. Corp., Organization Resources Counselors, Inc., Nat. Inst. for Occup. Safety and Health, Centers for Disease Control, Union Carbide Corp., Health Indus. Mfrs. Assn. Honors: Phi Beta Kappa, Pi Mu Epsilon, Univ. Scholar, Univ. of Ariz.; Fellow Am. Coll. of Epidemiology; mem: Am. Pub. Health Assn., Am. Statistal Assn., Biometric Soc., Soc. for Epidemiol. Research, Soc. for Occup. and Environ. Health; publs: over 40 arts. in profl. journals; Democrat. Res: 111 Clyde Dr Walnut Creek 94598 Ofc: Environmental Health Assoc., Inc., 2150 Shattuck Ave, Ste. 414, Berkeley 94704

WONG, SHERMAN K., quality control laboratory manager; b. July 1, 1951, San Francisco; s. Sydney S. and Dora Y. (Yee) Wong; m. Deborah Woo, July 8, 1978; edn: BA in biology, San Francisco State Univ. 1978; A.S., City Coll. S.F, 1973; A.S. Quality Control, Laney Coll. 1982; Calif. lic. Cert. Comml. Applicator of Restricted Material. Career: mgr. Quality Control Lab., Carnation Co. Pet Food Div., Oakland 1979--; environment control, City of Oakland, Joaquin Miller Park Ranger Station, 1978-79; dental lab. tech. US Public Health Services, San Francisco 1972-75; Quality Control Advisory Com., Laney Coll. Adv. Bd. mem. 1981-; recipient two Dale Carnegie Course awards in effective spkg. and human relations, 1980; mem: ASQC; Dunsmuir House, Norton/Simon Mus.; United Way Cmpgn. coordinator 1982; Democrat; Prot.; rec: photog., wood working. Res: 45 Van Cleave Way Oakland 94619 Ofc: Carnation Co., 2700 W. 7th St, Oakland 94607

WONG, WING SUN, restaurateur; b. Jan. 28, 1929, Canton, China, nat. 1973; s. Paul Man Chew and Mei Ping (Fong) Wong; m. Janet Quan, Apr. 2, 1958; chil: Daniel Y., b. 1963; Evan W., b. 1965; edn: B.Econ., Chu Hai Univ. 1953. Career: math. instr. Tak Ming High Sch., Hong Kong 1953 59; asst. prof. Chu Hai Univ., Hong Kong 1959-62; tchr. Chinese Community Sch., Oakland 1963-65; cook Senor Pico Mexican Restaurant, San Francisco 1965-67; chef Chinese Hosp., San Francisco 1967--; owner: Wong's Restaurant, S.F. 1979-81, Gourmet Kitchen, S.F. 1981--; community leader, S.F. Chinatown. Honors: cert. of honor, San Francisco City & Co. Bd. of Suprs., 1982; resolution, Calif. State Senate, 1982. Mem: Chinese General Peace Assn. (pres.), Wong's Family Benevolent Assn. in USA (pres.), Chinese Consol. Benevolent Assn. (Chinese Six Cos.) (pres.). Author: Inflation (1953, pub. in Hong Kong). Republican. Rec: community vol. work; cooking for family, friends. Res: 547 26th Ave. San Francisco 94121 Ofc: Gourmet Kitchen 1051 Stockton St. San Francisco 94108

WOO, DAVID, financial executive; b. Oct. 15, 1948, Oakland; s. Thomas Y. and Lucy Sik-Fun (Lui) W.; m. Linda Lum, Aug. 7, 1977; 1 dau. Valerie b. 1982; edn: BA, UC Berkeley 1970, MBA, 1972. Career: financial analyst Kaiser Aluminum & Chem. Corp., 1973-77, mgr. Lease Financing 1978-82, mgr. Corporate Treasury Services, 1982-82; treas. Televideo Systems, Inc., Sunnyvale 1983--; treas. Televideo Found.; mem. Peninsula Cash Mgmt. Assn.; Calif. Alumni Assn., Calif. Business Sch. Alumni Assn.; Democrat; Episcopal (Resolutions Com. of Epis. Diocese of Calif.); rec: tennis, photog. Res: 4207 Ridgemont Court Oakland 94619 Ofc: Televideo Systems Inc. 550 E. Brokaw Rd San Jose 95112

WOO, DEAN, real estate broker/developer; b. April 12, 1918, Canton, China, naturalized 1970; s. J. Sam and Yat Oy (Seto) W.; m. Jean Dei, Nov. 29, 1939; children: John, b. 1940, Franklin, b. 1948, Wilson, b 1949, Helen, b. 1952, Evelyn, b. 1954; ed. Univ. of Calif.; lic. real estate broker, Calif. Career: came to USA in youth; engaged in farming and real estate brokerage and development; currently, pres. Royal Pacific Motor Inn and mng. dir. Miriwa Center (office and comml. complex), San Francisco; Bank of Trade Advisory Council; apptd. to State of Calif. Atty. General's Volunteer Advisory Council 1968; Council for the Small Bus. Administrn., S.F. Regl. Office, Golden Gate Univ. Real Estate Program Pgm. Adv. Council; mem. Nat. Assn. of Realtors; clubs: Lions Club, Sportsman Club, Golden Gate Univ. Assocs.; (past) comdr. Am. Legion, Calexico, Calif., Council for the Public Library in Calexico; mil: tech. sgt. US Army 1942-45, WWI ETO; Democrat; Congregational; rec: fishing, reading. Res: 1541 Taylor St San Francisco 94133 Ofc: Golden Hills Realty, 838 Grant Ave, Ste. 402, San Francisco 94108

WOOD, DIANA ELAINE, realtor; b. Aug. 13, 1932; d. Kenneth and Elsie (Bancroft) Hoyle; m. Derrick Arnold Wood, Mar. 12; children: Nigel Mark, b. 1955, Gayle Elaine, b. 1957, Michael Derek, b. 1962, Roger Lindsay, b. 1961; edn: edn: Withington Girls Pvt. Sch., Eng.; bus. deg. Box Bus. Coll., Eng.; AA, Interior Designers Guild 1976; desig. V.I.P. Relocation Splst., Century 21, 1984. Career: secty. St. Matthews United Methodist Ch. 1971-78; int. design prin., Diana E. Wood Interiors, 1978--; realtor, Century 21 Emery R.E., 1978--; recipient spl. recognition, Top 100 Sales, (1983), One Million Dollar Club, Two Million Dollar Club (1979, 80, 81, 82, 83), Century 21 orgn.; mem: Colima Hacienda Republican Womens Club (pres. 1981-83); Whittier Tennis Club (1974-78); Hacienda Hts. Improvement Assn.; Whittier Coll., Womens Aux. (v.p. 1977); PTA (past v.p.); Republican (sustaining mem., Repub. Nat. Com.); Episcopal; rec: tennis, literature. Res: 3214 Montellano Ave Hacienda Hts 91745 Ofc: Century 21 Emery R.E. Inc., 16413 Colima Road, Hacienda Heights 91745

WOOD, DORA D., real estate developer, rancher; b. July 27, 1925, San Francisco; d. William Daryl and Lucile G. (Reardon) DeJarnah; m. Patrick Mills Wood, Jan. 10, 1947; edn: H.S. Dominican Convent 1940-43, Univ. of Ore. 1943-44. Career: organizer and leader, Girl Scouts, Boy Scouts of Am., 1944-56; owner/opr. D.D. Wood Ranches, 1957--; real estate devel./owner, Mulsford Devel. Co., 1978--; owner/opr. Sutter Buttes Wildlife art gallery and feed store, 1983--; dir. Meridian Farms Water Co. 1958-62; works: mfr. fine dish and glassware, 1978-; Republican; Christian; rec: hunting, fishing, travel. Res: 352 Second, Yuba City 95991 Ofc: Sutter Buttes Wildlife Gallery, POB 447, Yuba City 95991

WOOD, LARRY (MARYLAIRD), journalist, university educator; b. Sandpoint, ID; d. Edward Hayes and Alice (McNeel) Small; children: Mary, Marcia, Barry; edn: BA magna cum laude, Univ. Wash., Seattle 1938, MA, 1940; postgrad. stu. Stanford Univ. 1941/2, UCB 1943/4, cert. in photog. 1971; journ. stu. Univ. Wisc. 1971/2, Univ. Minn. 1971/2, Univ. Ga. 1972/3; art, archt., biol.,

UC Santa Cruz 1974-6, 77-80, Stanford Univ. 1979/80. Career: by-line columnist Oakland Tribune, San Francisco Chronicle, 1946--; feature writer Western region Christian Sci. Monitor, CSM Radio Syndicate and Internat. News, 1973--, Register and Tribune Syndicate, Des Moines, 1975--, also Times-Mirror Syndicate, Chevron USA, Calif. Today mag.; stringer Travelday mag., 1976--; contbg. editor Calif. Travel Guides, Fodor (NY and London, David McKay Pubs.), 1981--, collaborating with photojournalist son, Barry Wood, on 1984 ed., San Francisco and Nearby Destinations; feature writer for Lingupress (internat. newsmag., Paris, Fr.); cons./reviewer, Principles of Science Series and contbg. author, Focus on Science Series (pub. by Charles E. Merrill Co.); prof. journalism San Diego State Univ. 1975-, San Jose State Univ. 1976, CSU Hayward, Univ. Calif. Ext., 1979, Univ. of Pacific, 1979, 82; frequent speaker profl., ednl. confs.; dir. pub. rels./ cons. in field of sci., environ. affairs and recreation to num. orgns.; dir. pub. rels. No. Calif. Assn. Phi Beta Kappa, 1969-; selected by US & Brit. govts. to cover the 1983 visit of Queen Elizabeth II and Prince Philip to Calif.; features syndicated by USIA in all work from mags., books; trustee Calif. State Parks Found., 1976-. Honors: recognition, US Forest Service 1975, Nat. Park Service 1976, Oakland Mus. Assn. 1979, 81, Port Directors Assn. 1979; named in Top Ten Environ Writers in US today; Calif. Woman of Achievement (3). Citations: award winning (6th year) features in Sea Frontiers (pub. in Miami, Fla.) 1983; Pacific Crest Trail, Centennial Bike Trail, B.C. Totem Pole Series, 1982; Calif. Underwater Parks features, 1982; Ebey's Landing, Nat. Hist. Reserve series, 1982; her works in permanent archives: Univ. of Wash., Oakland Pub. Library. Mem: Public Rels. Soc. Am. (Consultants Acad., 1983-); Women in Communications, Inc. (v.p. Far West and Nat. bd. 1968-73, Nat. resolutions com. 1983-); Nat. Acad. of TV Arts and Scis.; Nat. Sch. Pub. Rels. Assn.; Environ. Cons. N. Am.; Am. Mgmt. Assn.; Internat. Environ. Cons.; Oceanic Soc.; Internat. Oceanagraphic Soc.; World Internat. Environ. Cons.; World Wildlife Fun; Am. ASsn. Edn. in Journalism (exec. bd. nat. mag. div. 1978-); Investigative Reporters and Editors; Soc. Travel Writers Am. (exec. bd. 1980-82); Soc. Profl. Journalists; Council for Advance. of Sci. Writing; Calif. Acad. Environ. News Writers; Nat. Press Photogs. Assn.; clubs: Nat. Press, S.F. Press, Eastbay Womens' Press, Calif. Writers; Sigma Delta Chi, Theta Sigma Phi. Res: 6161 Castle Dr. Oakland 94611

WOOD, RICHARD EARLE, manufacturing co. executive; b. Oct. 20, 1930, Ventura; s. Francis Bowman and Hertha Georgina (Hahn) W.; m. Norma Haworth, Mar. 3, 1951; children: Kathleen, b. 1953, Linda, b. 1956, Sharon, b. 1961; edn: AA, soc. sci. Long Beach City Coll. 1957; BA, psych., CSU Long Beach 1960. Career: pres. Wood's Enterprises, Laguna Beach 1970-75; pres. Wood's Ents., Lakeside 1980-82; mgr. quality control, Chem-tronics, El Cajon 1978-80; dir. quality control, Teledyne Case Products, Pomona 1975-78; mgr. qual. control, Southcom Internat., Inc. Escondido 1983--; sr. mem. Soc. of Mfg. Engrs. 1979-; Past Master Councilor, Order of DeMolay; mil: seaman USNR 1947-51, A/1c USAF 1951-55; rec: rare wine collector, chess, writing. Res: 28346 Glenmeade Way Escondido 92026 Ofc: Southcom Internat. Inc. 2210 Meyers Ave Escondido 92025

WOOD, WAYNE BARRY, photojournalist; b. June 23, 1958, Oakland; s. Byron and Marylaird (Small) W.; edn: cert. photog., Univ. Calif. 1975; BS, transp., CSU Hayward and S.F.; MBA, CSUH 1982. Career: bylined photojournalist, 1971-, with CSM News Syndicate (25 mil. readers worldwide; syndicated on 200 radio stations in US and Can.) 1973--, spec. in travel, sci., transp., urban renewal, people profiles, edn.; contbg. photojournalist: Sea Frontiers, Internat. Oceanographic Soc., Popular Mechanics, Focus On Science textbook series (Charles Merrill Co.), Fodor's San Francisco (guidebook); awards: Close Scholarship for outstanding jr. in econ. and business; R.R. Soc. photog. awards; mem: Soc. of Profl. Journalists, Nat. Press Photogs. Assn.; Presbyterian; rec: natural science, magic. Res: 6161 Castle Dr Oakland 94611

WOODMANSEE, GEORGE CLAY, administrative law judge; b. May 15, 1903, Los Angeles; s. Clay Goit and Jessie Viola (Anderson) Woodmansee; Edn: stu. USC, 1922-23; A.B., UCLA, 1927; m. Ruth Craig, Sept. 14, 1932; Chil: Craig, b. 1934, George, Jr., b. 1936. Career: secty./bookkeeper/asst. mgr. of ins. dept., A.Z. Taft Jr. and Taft Realty Co., Hollywood 1921-27; dept. mgr. Contract Dept., Guaranty Bldg. and Loan Assn. and successor, Hollywood 1928-37; office mgr., Marlow-Burns and Co., Los Angeles 1938-40; self-employed Real Estate Broker, Hollywood 1937-38, Culver City 1940-48; interviewer/office mgr., State of Calif. Dept. of Employment, Los Angeles 1941-45; Appeals Referee and Adminstrv. Law Judge, Calif. Unemployment Insurance Appeals Board, variously in Los Angeles, Sacramento, Long Beach 1945-68, retired 1968, recalled on temporary assignments 1968---. Mem: Hollywood High School Alumni Assn. (exec. bd. 3 yrs.; distinguished achievement award); Theta Psi frat. 1922-23; Kappa Upsilon frat. 1924-27; Town Hall of Calif.; United States Power Squadron; works: helped develop magnetic recording on steel wire, American Talking Wire Co., 1932-33; Republican, mem. Presdtl. Task Force. Christian Sci. Rec: gardening, woodworking, handball, swimming. Res: 27737 Calle Valdes, Mission Viejo 92692.

WOODMANSEE, RAYMOND KURTH, aircraft service owner; b. Dec. 18, 1928, Chgo.; s. Elmer O. and Corrine A. (Kurth) W.; children: Karen, b. 1954, Paul, b. 1958, Kennith, b. 1963, Diana, b. 1966; edn: grad. pub. schs., two yrs. jr. coll.; all pilot ratings, A&E, I.A., FAA. Career: mgr. Grants Airservice, Inc., Grants, N.M. 1960-61; owner Rays Aircraft Service, Porterville 1961--; chief pilot/partner Fliteline Ag Spraying Co.; cons. on old aircraft, mfr. outdated aircraft parts; mem. Aircraft Owners & Pilots Assn.; pres. Tulare Co. Sheriff Aero Sq.; past pres. Porterville Area Pilots Assn.; firechief Porterville Vol. Fire Dept.; mil: T5 US Army 1946-48; Democrat; rec: restoring old aircraft and autos. Res: 22251 Ave 168, Porterville 93257 Ofc: Rays Aircraft Service 1893 S. Newcomb Porterville 93257

WOODS, BARRIE JAMES, chiropractor, convention bureau executive; b. Dec. 23, 1931, Louisville, Ky.; s. James Hedden and Mary Jane (Franklin) W.; m. Wanda Mae Smith, May 14, 1955 (dec. 1975); two sons, Bradley, b. 1957, Rodger, b. 1960; edn: DC (valedictorian), Cleveland Coll., Los Angeles 1966; BS, Fullerton Coll.; teaching cred., UCLA 1968; . Career: doctor of chiropractic; asst. to exec. dir. Palm Springs Conv. and Visitors Bureau, 1980--; pres. Woods-Maeschen Investments Co.; past: administr. Marr-Stone & Assocs. (land devel.), Temecula 1978-80; administr. West Ball Radiology-Nuclear Group, Anaheim 1973-78; adminstrv. asst. Anaheim Gen. Hosp. 1969-73; store mgr. and dir. Design Dept., C.S. Wo & Sons (mfg. & retail furniture co.), Honolulu, 1967-69; asst. dir. community rels. Disneyland, Inc., Anaheim 1961-67; developed & taught first course for Calif. licensure (Radiologic Tech.) of non-reg. office people operating radiologic equip. 1971-75; author: Syllabus for Radiologic Technology (1971); Disneyland Dictionary; Handbook for Orthopaedic Radiology; Text of Radiologic Procedures For New And Sr. Technologists; frequent lectr. various subjects; honors: Legion of Honor & Order of Chevalier De Molay 1973; num. recognition awards for work in edn.; mem: Masons, Calif. Teachers Assn., Sr. De Molay, ARRT, ASRT, CSRT, SNMT, CCA, AURT; Republican; served in AUS M.C.; Prot.; rec: oil painting, skiing, tennis. Res: 44-775 Deep Canyon RD PALM Desert 92260 Ofc: Airport Park Plaza, 255 No El Cielo Rd, Ste. 315, Palm Springs 92262

WOODS, GERALDINE PITTMAN, scientist/National Institutes of Health consultant; b. W. Palm Beach, FL; d. Oscar and Susie (King) Pittman; edn: Talladega Coll., 1938-40; BS, zoology, Howard Univ., 1942; MA, Radcliffe Coll., Harvrd Biol. Lab., 1943; PhD, neuro-embryology, 1945; DSc., hon., Benedict Coll., 1977; DSc., hon., Talladega Coll., 1980; m. Robert I. Woods, Jan. 30, 1945; chil: Jan; Jerri; Robert I. Career: instr., Howard Univ., 1945-46; pres., Aux. to Med., Dental and Pharm. Assn. of So. Calif., 1951-55, state pres. 1955; pres., L.A. chpt., Jack and Jill, 1954-56; served on exec. bds.: YMCA and Family Services of L.A.; bd. dirs., Ctr. for Ednl. Opportunity at Claremont Colls., Calif. Dept. of Employment Personel Bd. interviewing panelist, two terms; natl. pres., Delta Sigma Theta, women's interracial pub. svc. orgn. with 85,000 mems., 1963-67;; invited by Mrs. Lyndon Johnson to White House to launch Project Head Start, 1965; mem. Natl. Adv. Council of Natl. Inst. of Gen. Med. Sciences, NIH, 1964-68; apptd. as spl. cons. to Dir and Staff in devel. of research, trng., and fellowship pgms. in biomedical areas for minorities in colls. and univs., 1969---; has helped in devel. of two pgms for minorities at Natl. Insts. of Health, MBS, Minority Biomed. Support Pgm. and MARC Minority Access to Research Careers Prgm.; mem. Gen. Research Support Pgm. Adv. Com., Div. of Research Resources, NIH, 1970-73, 1977-78; bd. dirs., Natl. Center for Higher Edn. Mgmt. Sys., 1977-78; chmn. bd., trustees, Howard Univ., 1975, mem. 1968---; mem. natl. bd. Girl Scouts, USA, 1975-78; bd. trustees, Atlanta Univ., 1974---; mem. Inst. of Med., Natl. Acad. of Scis., elected 1974; bd. dirs., Natl. Commn. for Certification of Phys. Assts., 1974---; apptd. mem., v.chmn., Calif. Postsec. Edn. Commn., 1974-78; EPA Air Pollution Manpower Devel. Adv. commn., 1973-75; bd. trustees, Calif. Mus. of Sci. & Indus. Found., 1971-79; Awards presented by Pres. L.B. Johnson, Council on Youth Opportunity, Natl. Council of Negro Women, Iota Phi Lambda sor.; Natl. Panhellenic Council, Howard Univ. Alumni Assn., Urban League, Natl. Assn. of Colored Women; Delta Sigma Theta, many chpts.; Friends at the NIH, and num. spl. tributes; fellowship estab. in her name at Howard Univ., by Delta Simga Theta for students in biol., 1981; selected as one of 20 Famous Amer. Black Scientists, 1981; scholarship given in her name, Atlanta Univ., 1980; Howard Univ. Achievement Award, Los Angeles, tribute by L.A. City Council; Mayor, and L.A. Co. Bd. Supvrs., Calif. Assy. & Senate, 1980. Congregationalist. Res: 12065 Rose Marie Lane, Los Angeles 90049.

WOODS, MICHAEL DENNIS, lawyer; b. Nov. 24, 1941, San Francisco; s. John Michael and Mary Monica (Regan) W.; m. Maureen Duggan, June 17, 1977; 1 son, Kevin, b. 1978; edn: BS, Univ. of San Francisco 1964; JD, UC Hastings Law Sch. 1968; admitted to Calif. State Bar 1969. Career: tax specialist Price Waterhouse, 1969-70; assoc. attorney W. J. Murphy, 1971-74; atty./ptnr. Woods, Woods & Woods, 1975-81; law practice Michael Woods, Atty., San Francisco 1981--; honors: winner Snodgrass Moot Ct. 1967; mem: Calif. Trial Lawyers, San Francisco Bar Assn., USF Law Soc., Olympic Club, Calif. Alumni Assn.; mil: USAR 1964-70; Democrat (Young Democrats); Catholic; rec: sailing, tennis. Res: 515 John Muir San Francisco 94132 Ofc: 333 West Portal San Francisco 94127

WOODS, THOMAS L., industrial psychologist; b. Oct. 2, 1943, Elgin, Ill.; s. Thomas H. and B. R. (Forbes-Martin) W.; engaged: Mystrada Legasse; children: Courtney, Whitney; edn: BA, CSU Fullerton 1967, MA, Univ. of Chgo. 1969, PhD, Northwestern Univ. 1977; lic: Psychologist, Ill.; Clin. Psychologist, Clin. Soc. Wkr., Calif. Career: adminstrv. staff coordinator Univ. of Chgo., 1969-74; pvt. practice, Glencoe, Ill. 1974-79; supvr. Orange County Human Services Agency, 1979-81; consultant, writer, therapist pvt. practice, 1981--; pres./TLW Dir., Thomas L. Woods, PhD and Assocs.; asst. prof. Calif. Graduate Inst.; honors: Nat. Assn. of Social Wkrs. Award for best clinical paper, 1973, Chgo. NASW Chpt.; mem: Internat. Platform Assn., Am. Psychological Assn., Applied Psychoanalysis Assn., NASW (chmn. Mental Health Council); works: designed/devel. Computerized Psychological Assessment System used in major corps. nat., internat.; founder American Growth Movement; Christian; rec: writing, public spkg. Res: 1330 S. Van Ness Santa Ana 92707 Ofc: 2121 E. Catalina Ave Santa Ana 92701

WOODWARD, DANIEL HOLT, librarian; b. Oct. 17, 1931, Ft. Worth, TX; s. Enos Paul and Jessie (Butts) Woodward; B.A. Univ. Col., 1951; M.A. 1955; Ph.D. Yale Univ., 1958; M.S.L.S., Catholic Univ. of America, 1969; m. Mary Jane, 1954; Chil: Jeffrey, b. 1958; Peter, b. 1960. Career: asst., assoc. prof. Mary Washington Coll., of the Univ. VA., 1957-72, Librn. 1969-72; Librn., Huntington Library, 1972---; Mil: AUS. Res: 1540 San Pasqual St., Pasadena 91106; Office: 1151 Oxford Rd., San Marino, 911008.

WOODWARD, RODNEY MADISON, human factors engineer; b. June 7, 1928, Bellingham, Wash.; s. Rodney Madison and Olive Lenore (Stewart) W.; m. Betty Jean Condon, Apr. 23, 1955; children: Elizabeth Ann, b. 1958, Rodney M. III, b. 1959, Roy Douglas, b. 1961; edn: BA, honors, San Diego St. Univ. 1956; grad. courses in edn., psych., mgmt.; cert. in Nat. Security Mgmt., Indsl. Coll. Armed Forces 1972. Career: field engr. Raytheon Co., Waltham, Mass. 1957-60; human factors engr. General Dynamics, San Diego, Ft. Worth 1960-66; sr. human factors engr. Rockwell Int'l. Los Angeles 1966-77; engineering splst. Rohr Marine Div. Chula Vista 1978; cons. human factors. Man Factors, Inc. San Diego 1979; design splst. General Dynamics, Pomona 1980--; lectr. National Safcty Council, L.A. 1972-76; Electronic Industries Assn. Com. on Human Factors 1964-66; honors: Alpha Mu Gamma, Psy Chi; mem: Human Factors Soc. (pres. L.A. chpt. 1978), IEEE, Nat. Mgmt. Assn., Soc. for Information Display, Internat. Platform Assn., Naval Reserve Assn., Sigma Pi Frat.; publs: Human Factors Journal vol. 14, 1972; Proceedings of Human Factors Soc. & Southwestern Psychol. Assn. 1963, 64, 66, 70; mil: cmdr. USNR 1945-76; Democrat. Res: 2868 West Rowland Cir Anaheim 92804 Ofc; General Dynamics, POB 2507, Pomona 91766

WOODWARD, ROY AYRES, real estate broker, city councilman; b. July 31, 1929, Bellingham, Wash.; s. Rodney M. and Olive Lenore (Stewart); m. Joy Louise Crotts, Aug. 29, 1959, div. 1973; 1 dau. Renee; edn: BA, San Diego St. Univ. 1958; lic. real estate broker, Calif. Career: owner/broker Woodward & Associates, Santee 1961--; elected Santee City Councilman, 1980-84; founder Cuyamaca Bank 1984; mem. Bd. Realtors (pres. 1967, Realtor of Year 1970), Rotary, Chamber of Commerce (pres. 1963, 79), Lions (pres. 1967); mil: CT2 USNR 1946-54; Democrat; rec: retired race car driver (porsche). Res: 9222 Inverness, Santee 92071 Ofc: Woodward & Associates, 8606 Cuyamaca, POB B, Santee 92071

WOOLSEY, EDWARD HYDE, songwriter, businessman; b. May 4, 1925, Galena, Kans., s. Ed and Dovie (Hyde) W.; m Dorothy Uvodich, Aug. 22, 1948; children: Mary, b.1950, Edward (M.D.), b. 1952; edn: BA, Univ. of Ariz. 1963; grad. language stu., McNeese Coll., Washburn Coll.; various mil. tech. schs. incl. radar computer sys., radar maint., jet nav., electronics; Lic. Comml. Pilot, FAA; Lic. Real Estate Broker, Calif. (1969). Career: mill. ofcr. USAF 1958-66; owner Ed H. Woolsey Enterprises, San Diego 1966--; owner Crest Chateau Apt. Devel., S.D., Crown Chateau Beach Apts., Pacific Bch., 1967-77; owner Sir George Smorgasbord Restaurant, La Mesa 1969-73; v.p. Aksym Corp. Beachfront Condo Devels., 1969-72; owner Air San Diego, Montgomery Fld., 1970-74; owner/broker Ridge View Props. Real Estate Co., S.D. 1969--; assoc. cons. partner Finova (Tijuana, Guadalajara) and COMSA (Tijuana), Mex. 1974-78; assoc. cons. broker D.I.M.E. of Dominica, Import, Mgmt., and Finl. Corp., 1971-73; bd. chmn. S.D. Unity Power Systems, and pres. Texas Power Sys., 1977-8; prin. (90) Classic Marble Inc., Santee 1976-82; owner Ed Woolsey Prods. (music), S.D. 1979--; honors: num. athletic awards: boxing lt. hvywt. champion, U.of Az.; coll. football star qtrback; handball singles champion 322nd Bomb Sq. Speaker, entertainer, M.C., num. charity benefits. Publs: Theme Song of Xmas TV pgm. 1982; 4 vols. pop. & gospel songs; num. recordings. Mil: major ret., USAF 1948-66; Democrat; Prot.; rec: boating, hunting, sports, travel, radio control model planes. Res: 4401 Topa Topa Dr, La Mesa 92041 Ofc: Ed H. Woolsey Ent. 13065 Aurora, El Cajon 92021

WOROTKO, WLADIMIR A., real estate/construction co. president; b. Oct. 30, 1950, Los Angeles; s. Alexander J. and Anna A. (Owerchenko) W.; m. Deborah Jean Andrews, Jan. 23, 1977; children: Alana Carlice, b. 79, Tatiana, b. 1981; edn: BA, UC Los Angeles 1975. Career: real estate sales agt. Forest E. Olson Realtors (Coldwell Banker), 1975; owner/pres. Dewor Properties (R.E. devel. co.) 1976--; owner/pres. Dewor Construction, Inc. 1982--; mem. San Fernando Valley, Burbank/Glendale, Los Angeles, Newport Harbor Boards of Realtors; Lions Club; co-founder Holy Note Press (music pub. co. spec. in Eastern Orthodox music); mil: sgt. USAF 1969-73; Republican; Eastern Orthodox; rec: yachting. Res: 1510 Thompson Ave Glendale 91201 Ofc: Dewor Properties, 1946 W. Glenoaks Blvd Glendale 91201

WORTHGE, WALTER JACOB, stockbroker; b. June 17, 1933, New Brunswick, NJ; s. Walter J. and Elizabeth J. Worthge; m. Ingrid Krueger, Jan. 14, 1956; children: Mark, b. 1957; Scott, b. 1958; Walter III, b. 1960; edn: BA, Rutgers Univ. 1955; desig: Principal, Options Prin., Mgmt. Credential. Career: v.p. Birr Wilson & Co.; 1966-79, v.p. Smith Barney Harris Upham & Co., 1979--; Dir. Koltron Corp. 1972-; civic: councilman City of Belmont, 1976-80, v.mayor 1977, mayor 1978; pres. Belmont Fire Protection Dist. 1978; honors: Outstanding Young Men of Am. 1967, Life mem. PTA, Scouters Key, Scout Award of Merit, Jaycee Distinguished Service Award, Outstanding Citizen of Belmont 1982. Mem. Peninsula Stock & Bond Club; pres. San Mateo County Arts Council 1983/4; dir. Center for Independence of the Disabled 1979-; dir. San Mateo Co. Mosquito Abatement; BSA cubmaster, scoutmaster; mil: capt. USAF 1956-59; Democrat; Methodist; rec: tennis. Res: 808 Miramar Terr. Belmont 94002 Ofc: Smith Barney Harris Upham & Co., 3000 Sand Hill Rd Menlo Park 94025

WRIGHT, DONALD LEE, construction co. president; b. Oct. 20, 1943, Los Angeles; s. Teddy Lee and Betty (Masterson) W.; m. Glenda Jean, Mar. 31, 1962; children: Melinda, b. 1962, Melessia, b. 1964; edn: AA, Cerritos Coll. 1972. Career: pres./owner South Coast Builders, Whittier 1970-76, Golden Crest Builders, La Habra 1976--; Republican; Baptist; rec: fishing, trap and skeet, camping. res: 1421 Oak Tree Ct La Habra 90631 Ofc: Golden Crest Builders, Inc. 11832 Pounds Whittier 90604

WRIGHT, GREGORY WALTER, sales/service co. president; b. June 6, 1955, Palo Alto; s. Virgil A. and Evaline Craven (Black) W., Jr.; m. Margaret Campbell, June 5, 1977; stepchil: Laura McMaster Welsh, b. 1959; Craig McMaster, b. 1960; grad. Homestead H.S. 1973. Career: stockrm. mgr. Television Research Internat., Palo Alto 1975-77; broker/appraiser The Source, Santa Clara 1977-83; pres. Catalyst Equip. Corp. (predecessor co. Capital Equip. Co., Santa Clara) Campbell 1983--; Calif. Scholarship Fedn. semifinalist 1981-2; mem. Entrepreneurs Alliance; booster Boulder Creek Vol. Fire Dept., San Lorenzo Valley Wrestling Club; Democrat; Episcopal; rec: jazz, R&B musician/vocalist, watercolorist. Res: 450 Redwood Dr Boulder Creek 95006 Ofc: Catalyst Equip. Corp. 1610 Dell Ave Ste D, Campbell 95008

WRIGHT, JOHN HAMILTON, computer co. president; b. Feb. 15, 1933, Torrance; s. Hamilton Wm. and Bernice Irene (Downing) W.; m. Carolyn ann Lantz, June 20, 1976; children: Jerien, b. 1955, John, . 1957, Jana, b. 1959, Michael, b. 1968, (step): Caren, b. 1960, James, b. 1965, Joseph, b. 1967; edn: BSAE, Northrop Univ. 1960; Calif. Reg. Profl. Engr. 1978. Career: supvr. System Analysis, North American Aviation, Los Angeles 1954-63; pres. United Computing Corp., Carson 1963-79 (privately owned 1963-72, publicly owned 1972-76, subs. McDonnell Douglas Corp. 1976-); pres. Automated Design Centers, Inc. Torrance 1979--; chmn. of bd. United Computing Corp., Automated Design Ctrs.; awards: 1972 SME Mfg. Technology Award, 1973 Calif. Soc. Profl. Engrs. Indsl. Achievement Award, 1973 IEEE Fellows Award, 1974 Tau Beta Pi Eminent Engineers Award, 1975 Numerical Control Soc. LA Chapter Man of Year awd.; sr. mem. Soc. Mfg. Engrs.; trustee Northrop Univ. 1970-; publs: num. papers on computer aided design and mfg.; mil: USNR 1950-57; Republican; Catholic; rec: running, bridge, tennis. Res: 30259 Palos Verdes Dr East, Rancho Palos Verdes 90274 Ofc: Automated Design Centers, Inc. 19401 S. Vermont Ave Torrance 90502

WRIGHT, KENNETH LYLE, psychologist; b. Sept. III, American Falls, Ida ; s. Jesse Joshua and Martha Sophia (Dickenson) W.; children: Anne Collins, Corrella Carmelette Brown, Sandra Lynne Sutherland; edn: BA, Univ. Wash. 1941; MA, USC, 1957, PhD, San Gabriel Coll. 1958. Career: coach State Tng. School for Boys, Chehalis, Wash 1941; dep. probation officcr, Los Angeles County, 1955-56; vis. Lectr. Whittier (Cal.) Coll. 1956; dist. sch. psychologist Anaheim Union High Sch. Dist.; edn. splst. Dept. Army, Orleans (France) Am. High Sch., psychol. services and spl. edn. coordinator Dependent Edn. Group Hdqrs., Karlsruhe, Germany 1959-62; edn. specialist USN, San Diego 1962-63; pvt. practice as psychologist, San Diego 1963-64, 1969--; psychol. cons. Clin. Bd. Speech Therapy, Children's Hosp., San Diego 1962-63; vis. prof. U. Western Ont. and lectr., sch psychologist London (Ont.) Bd. Edn., 1964-66; dir. psychol. services Niagara Falls (NY) Dist. Bd. Edn. 1966-69; tchr. Syracuse (NY) Univ. 1966-69. Pres. Coordinating Council, Whittier, Cal.; founder Niagara Inst Human Devel.; honors: Outstanding Award, San Diego Co. Assn. Retarded Children; Fellow San Diego Bio Med. Research Inst.; mem: Assn. Children with Learning Disabilities, Council Exceptional Children, Royal Soc. Medicine, Am., San Diego Co. psychol. assns., San Diego Assn. Clin. Psychologists; Mason; club: Koua Kai; mil: USNR 1942-46. Res: 751 Amiford Dr San Diego 92107 Ofc: 126 W. Maple St San Diego 92103

WRIGHT, LYLE ALLAN, manufacturing co. executive; b. Nov. 18, 1926, Lincoln, Nebr.; s. James Albert and Sarah Myrtle (Shaner) W.; m. Dorothy Fay McClymonds, Jan. 28, 1951; children: Kathleen, b. 1951; Jolene, b. 1954; Jon, b. 1962; edn: BSME, Univ. Nebr. 1951; USC Managerial Policy Inst. 1973-4; desig. Engring. Rep., FAA 1963-81. Career: power plant design engineer 1951-58; power plant design supr. 1958-65; deputy dir. Power Plant Engring. 1965-72; chief design engr. Commercial Aircraft 1972-77; dir. Aircraft Performance 1977-81; vice pres. Quality Assurance, Douglas Aircraft Co. 1981--; mem. Advisory Council CSU Long Beach; AIA/FAA Liaison Panel mem.; mem: ASME (vice pres. 1949-50); treas. Seal Beach Lions Club 1966-68; pres. PTA Garden Grove Mitchell Sch. 1958; Calif. for Nebr. Alumni Assn.; Nat. Coalition for Marine Preservation; Patentee: A Unique Target Type Thrust Reverser Concept Used on the DC-8 62 & 63 Series Aircraft; contbr. profl. conf. proceedings; mil: pfc US Army Parachute Inf.; Republican; Prot.; rec: boating, fishing. Res: 1540 Crestview Ave Seal Beach 90740 Ofc: Douglas Aircraft Co 3855 Lakewood Blvd, 18A-23, Long Beach 90846

WRIGHT, WALTER CLYDE, JR., electronics instructor, ret.; b. June 21, 1918, Cement, Calif.; s. Walter C. and Pearl Mae (Lambert) W.; m. Viva Downer, July 10, 1947, div. 1980; 2 sons: Timothy Clyde b. 1953, Thomas Michael b. 1956; grad. Armijo H.S., Fairfield; Life Adult Tchr. Credential (Electronics); 1st Cl. Radio & Tel. FCC Comml. Lic. Career: signalman for Southern Pacific R.R., 1937-79; electronics instr., Calif. Adult Edn. Pgm. 1961-78, home maint. instr. 1968-73; electronics instr. Napa Coll. 1976; author: Gravity Is A Push (book), 34 copyrighted booklets on gravity, over 3,000 sci. papers; devel. original sci. theories (magnetic-push gravity theory opposed to Newton's pull-theory), 1968--; blt. over 100 models depicting var. actions in the universe, planetary orbits, astronomical forces; mil: sgt. (radio) US Army 1941-45; rec: sports, dancing. Res: 732 Ohio St Fairfield 94533

WRIGHT, WILBUR E., clinical social work administrator; b. Redwood City, Calif.; s. Wilbur Samuel and Marie Ernestine (Clarke) W.; m. Mary J. Lavelle, June 1, 1963; div. 1982; children: Diane, b. 1964, Stephen, b. 1967, Jeanine, b. 1970, Brian, b. 1972; edn: BS in sociol., St. Peter's Coll., N.J. 1955; MSS in psychiat. social work, Fordham Univ. 1958; postgrad stu. US Army Med. Svc. Sch., US Army Spec. Warfare Sch., Univ. of Okla. Grad. Coll. Pub. Health Adminstrn. 1964-5. Career: field work: Catholic Charities, Archdiocese of NY, St. Michael's Home, Staten Is., NY, US VA Hosp., East Orange, NJ; family counselor United Family and Children's Soc., Plainfield, NJ 1958-59; Medical Svc. Corps officer US Army, Wash DC 1959-62; USPH Health Svc. officer/cons. Commnd. Ofcr. Corps, Wash DC 1962-65; sr. med. social wkr. UC San Diego Co. Hosp., 1965-66; dir. of social wk. Scripps Meml. Hosp., La Jolla 1966-68; dir. Service and Rehab., Calif. Div. Am. Cancer Soc., San Francisco, 1968-72; cons./dir. of Resource Devel., Orgn. for Business, Edn. and Community Advance., Catholic Charities, Archdio. of San Francisco, 1972-73; dep. head Dept. of Social Wk. Alfred-Monash Univ. Hosp., Prahran, Victoria, Australia 1973-74; hd. Dept. of Social Wk. Royal Perth Hosp., W. Austral. 1974-75; exec. dir. Community Mental Hlth Bd of Central Fla., Inc., Orlando 1975-78; secty.gen. Council of Internat. Pgms. US State Dept. Edn. and Cultural Affairs 1978-80; adminstr. Mental Health Pgms., San Francisco Council of Churches, 1980-81; Pub. Health Social Work cons. Calif. Dept. of Health Svcs., 1981-82; dir. Clin. Soc. Wk. Stanford Univ. Med. Ctr., Stanford 1982--; cons. Ministry of Hlth & Welfare, Rep. of Korea 1961-62; instr. Univ. of Md. Far East Ext. Div. 1961, Univ. of Okla. 1964; lectr. W. Australia Inst. of Tech. 1975, Stanford Univ. 1982-; U.S. rep. various Fulbright Panels, Eur., Scan.; mem: Fellow Am. Public Health Assn.; Fellow Royal Soc. for Health (UK); ACSW, Acad. of Cert. Social Wkrs.; Nat. Assn. of Soc. Wkrs.; US Com. Internat. Conf. of Soc. Welfare; Assn. of Mental Hlth Adminstrs.; Nat. Soc. of Fund Raisers; publs: articles in profl. journals. REs: 1405 Marshall St, 310, Redwood City 94063 Ofc: Stanford Univ Med Ctr, Ste. C-136, Stanford 94305

WU, ALBERT KING, real estate broker/developer; edn: BS, San Jose State Univ. 1973. Career: broker/developer dba Albert King Wu, Santa Clara; mem: Internat. Council of Shopping Center, Internat. Exchangors Assn., Nat. Assn. of Realtors, Calif. Assn. of Realtors. Res: POB 3286, San Jose 95156 Ofc: Albert King Wu, 1601 Civic Center Dr, Box 3286, Santa Clara 95156

WU, JONATHAN J., computer systems co. president; b. Nov. 6, 1942, Tainan, Taiwan; s. Ching Hsian and Chen Yin Wu; m. Cicy Wei-Wey, Mar. 25, 1976; children: Jane, b. 1979, Lisa, b. 1981; edn: BA in bus. adm., Nat. Chung Hsing Univ. 1965; MS in mgmt. sci., USC 1971. Career: sales rep. IBM Taiwan Corp., Taiwan 1967-68; data processing mgr. Facom Computer Co., Ltd. 1968-69; D.P. mgr. General Valve Co., Inc. (Calif.), 1970-73; mgmt. cons. Tatung Engineering Corp., 1974-75; assoc. prof. (part-time) Tatung Inst. of Tech., and Tam Kang Univ., 1974-75; mgmt. & computer cons. Olivet Computer Corp., 1976-79; computer cons. Kiddy Klad Co., Inc. (Calif.), 1979--; pres./owner National Systems Service, El Monte 1979--; computer cons. various cos.; mem: USC Taipei Alumni Club (pres. 1975); Lions Club, Downtown; dir. Santa Barbara YMCA and Y-Mens Club 1973; past mem. Taipei Y-Mens' Alpha Club 1968; dir. Chinese Computer Assn. 1968; author: Introduction to Data Processing (1969), Computer Principles (1969), num. articles on computer apps. in profl. journals; mil: 2d lt. Army; Christian; rec: Kung Fu, swimming, stamp & coin collection. Res: 1831 Paseo Azul Rowland Hts 91748 Ofc: National Systems Service, 11100 Valley Blvd, Ste. 340, El Monte 91731

WU, LY PING, hotel executive; b. Jan. 24, 1950, Taipei, Taiwan; parents: Yen and Wei-Fong (Wong) Wu; edn: BS, Univ. of Houston, Hilton Sch. of Hotel & Restaurant Mgmt. 1975; travel indus. mgmt. courses, Univ. of Hawaii 1970-72. Career: reservations mgr. Shamrock Hilton (780 rooms), Houston, Tex. 1975-78; asst. front office mgr. Washington (DC) Hilton (1165 rooms), 1978-79; field rep. Rooms & Guest Services, Hilton Hotels Corp., Dallas, Tex. 1979-81; exec. asst. mgr./dir. Front Office Ops., Oakland (Calif.) Airport Hilton (365 rooms), 1981-83; resident mgr. Los Angeles Airport Hilton & Towers (1300 rooms), 1984--; instr. hotel mgmt. course, Univ. of Lincoln, S.F. 1981; mem. American Harp Soc.; bd. dir. Oakland Chinese Community Council; com. mem. East Bay Culinary Show (1981, 82), Oakland (culinary exhibs. benefiting Childrens' Hosp.); rec: harp, opera, cooking, travel. Res: 941 West Carson Blvd, 306, Torrance 90502 Ofc: Los Angeles Airport Hilton & Towers, 5711 W. Century Blvd, Los Angeles 90045

WU, YI-TZE SETH, lawyer; b. June 14, 1950, Bangkok, Thailand; nat. 1980; s. Ta-yeh and Shu-hsien (Teng) Wu; edn: BA, Univ. of Denver 1973; JD, Univ. of Santa Clara 1979; LL.M. in taxation, Golden Gate Univ. 1983. Career: tax atty. Varian Assoc., Inc., Palo Alto 1979--; Dir. Santa Clara Pub. Interest Law Found. 1979; mem: Calif. State Bar Assn., Santa Clara Bar Assn., Am. Bar Assn., Phi Alpha Delta legal frat., Mensa, ARE. Res: 2758 Randers Ct. Palo Alto 94303 Ofc: Corporate Tax Dept., Varian Assoc., Inc., 611 Hansen Way, Mail Stop E-029, Palo Alto 94303

WUERFEL, ERIC STEVEN, chiropractor; b. June 6, 1949, Bay Shore, Long Is., NY; s. Frank Pierce and Penny Wuerfel; edn: BA, pol. sci., Univ. of Wyo. 1972; DC summa cum laude, Palmer Coll. of Chiropractic 1981. Career: naval aviator (combat search and rescue pilot), USN 1972-78; chiropractor Smith Chiropractic Office, 1981-82, Wuerfel Chiropractic Offices, Coronado 1983--; lectr. holistic health classes, Evening Coll. 1982; asst. instr. for Motion Palpation of the Spine, 1980-83; designer Sports Injury rehabilitation exercises; honors: Pi Tau Delta 1981; mem. Kiwanis Club of Coronado; exec. com. Freeway Drug Counseling of Coronado; mil: lt. USN 1972-8; Presbyterian; rec: tennis, sailing, running, scuba diving. Res: 8446-93 Via Sonoma La Jolla 92037 Wuerfel Chiropractic Ofcs: 575 Orange Ave Coronado 92118

WUNDRAM, ERNST PAUL, chiropractor; b. May 17, 1902, Ladysmith, Natal, Rep. of S. Africa, nat. 1942; s. Adolf Karl and Martha Louise (Prozesky) W.; m. Ruth A. Hoecker, Sept. 19, 1942; 1 son, Wayne, b. 1951; edn: pub. schools, S. Africa; DC, Los Angeles Coll. of Chiropractic 1948. Career: doctor of chiropractic, 1948--; mem. Calif. Chiropractic Assn., Elks Club; mil: pvt. USAF 1943; Democrat; Rel. Sci.; rec: writing prose, repairing old clocks. Res: 1416 West Main St Visalia 93291 Wundram Chiropractic Offices, 1414 W. Main Visalia 93291

WURZEL, MARK R., sales consultant; b. July 9, 1943, NY, NY; s. Sidney and Ruth (Fishberg) W.; m. Ruthanne Schwartz, Nov. 13, 1965; children: Stephanie, b. 1967, Alicia, b. 1971, Seth, b. 1976; edn: BS, NY Univ. 1965; Cert. Practitioner, Inventory Mgmt., APICS, 1984. Career: salesman, systems analyst IBM, NY 1965-72; systems mgr., national systems mgr., dir. Field Support, Itel Corp., 1972-80; sales rep., district sales mgr. Comserv, Corp., Torrance 1980--, currently sr. sales/mfg. consultant; awards: Million Dollar Award (1982, 83), Internat. Computer Programs Assoc.; No. 1 Sales Rep. (1981) Comserv Corp.; mem. Am. Prodn. and Inventory Control Soc.; dir. North Valley Jewish Comm. Ctr.; rec: sailing, flying, comm. service. Res: Granada Hills Ofc: Comserv Corp. 18411 S. Crenshaw, Ste. 370, Torrance 90504

WYATT, MICHAEL LEE, physician; b. Feb. 20, 1945, Kansas City, Mo.; s. Ernest Owen and Mary Jane (Guynn) W.; m. Karen, Mar. 29, 1969; children: Kent, b. 1975, Kelly, b. 1978; edn: BS, Central Mo. State Univ. 1967; MD, Univ. of Mo. 1971. Career: rotating internship, residency (OB-Gyn), San Bernardino Co. Hosp., 1971-75; served to maj. US Army Med. Corps, Okinawa, Japan 1975-78; pvt. practice, Santa Maria, Calif. 1978--, chief of staff Valley Comm. Hosp., Santa Maria 1982. Ofc: Santa Maria Medical Ofc. OB-Gyn, 1430 E. Main, Ste. 102, Santa Maria 93454

WYATT, PHILIP WARDER, marketing executive; b. Apr. 9, 1943, Crawfordsville, Ind.; s. John Burt and Catherine Louise (Willis) W.; m. Cynthia Mares, June 6, 1981; edn: BA, Denison Univ. 1965; stu. Sorbonne Univ. (Paris) 1965-6, Butler Univ. 1964, var. USN Schs. (flight tng., intell.) 1967-77, hosp. supply corp. mgm. pgms. 1971-84. Career: adminstrv. mgr. IBM 1969; sales rep., sales mgr., dir. of sales/mktg. Pharmaseal Indsl. AHSC, 1971-76; dir. of mktg. American Pharmaseal (AHSC) 1979-, vice pres. mktg. Am. Pharmaseal (AHSC) Medical/Surgical Div., Glendale 1982--; instr., mktg., USC 1981-; advis. bd./cons. Am. Assn. of Critical Care Nurses, 1979-; pvt. cons. var. medical mfrs. 1975-; awards: Pres.'s Award (1974, 76, 77, 79, 80, 81, 82) Am. Pharmaseal; mem: AMA, Medical Mktg., AACN (advis. bd.), AST, EAE Frat., La Canada/Flintridge YMCA; inventor: Closed Loop Thermodilution System for Cardiac Output Measurement; publs: var. mil. and tech. manuals; mil: served lt. to cmdr. US Navy (cmdr. in chief Pacific Fleet Staff) 1967-83, Vietnam and Expeditionary medals; Republican: Prot.; rec: antiques - cloisonne, numismatics, travel. Res: 741 Starlight Hts. La Canada 91011 Ofc: American Pharmaseal, 1015 Cranview Ave Glendale 91201

WYCOFF, CHARLES COLEMAN, physician; b. Sept. 2, 1918, Glazier, Tex.; s. James Garfield and Ada Sharpe (Braden) W.; m. Gene Marie Henry, May 16, 1942; children: Michelle, Geoffrey, Brian, Roger, Daniel, Norman, Irene, Teresa; edn: AB, UC Berkeley 1941; MD, UC San Francisco 1943. Career: estab. the Wycoff Group of anesthesiologists, San Francisco 1947-53; chief of anesthesia St. Joseph's Hosp. 1947-52, San Francisco County Hosp. 1952-54; teaching staff Presbyterian Hosp. NYC (asst. prof. anesthesiol. Columbia Univ.) 1955-63; clin. practice of anesthesiology St. Francis Meml. Hosp., S.F. 1963--; mem: S.F. County Med. Soc., Calif. Med. Soc., Am., Calif. Soc. of Anesthesiologists; works: twelve papers on anesthesiology; six 20-minute motion pictures on anesthesiology (distbd. by Astra Pharmaceutical Co. & Winthrop P.C.); mil: capt. AMC 1945-1947; rec: doing new things. Res: 870 Joost Ave San Francisco 94127 Ofc: Anesthesiologist's Medical Group of S.F., Inc., Ste. 311, 1375 Sutter St San Francisco 94109

WYGANT, JONATHAN HADLEY, manufacturing co. president; b. Nov. 23, 1948, Los Angeles; s. Benyaurd Bourne and Edith Edwards (Pinkham) W.; m. Michele Tornabene, Mar. 24, 1984; edn: BA, Hamilton Coll. 1970. Career: office mgr. San Ysidro Ranch, Santa Barbara 1970; various jobs in Europe, 1971-72; assembler Burroughs Corp., Santa Barbara 1973; social worker State of Calif. (Sonoma State Hosp.) 1974; chef Bo Tree Restaurant, St. Petersburg, Fla. 1975; founder/ pres. Iris Arc Crystal (mfr. giftware products), Santa Barbara 1976--; awards: President's Volunteer Action Award, 1982; Iris Arc selected as one (no. 281) of 1983 "INC. 500"; rec: tennis, gardening, self awareness seminars. Res: 1737 Paterna Rd Santa Barbara 93103 Ofc: Iris Arc Crystal, 114 E. Haley St Santa Barbara 93103, 614 Santa Barbara St, Santa Barbara 93101

WYMAN, BETH, grants coordinator; b. May 13, 1933, Hutchinson, Kans.; d. John Hart and Faye Belle (Newell) Dunham; m. Donald Wyman, Aug. 30, 1953; children: Jeffrey Hart, b. 1958, Barbara Ellan, b. 1959; edn: BA soc. sci., San Diego St. Univ. 1954, MA hist., San Jose St. Univ. 1982; Calif. teaching credentials pre-sch. through community coll. Career: coordinator San Benito Co. Child Care Programs, 1982-; history instr., Calif. Comm. Colls. 1975-; comm. svcs. asst. Gavilan Coll. 1974-77; owner History Associates of Morgan Hill, 1976-; co-owner Custom Software Products, 1982-; currently, grants coordinator of County of Santa Clara; vice-chair Intergovtl. Council (Santa Clara County Mayors) 1981/2; mem. Morgan Hill City Council, 1978-82 (mayor 1981/2; created Heritage Park housing project); commnr. Central Coast Regl. Coastal Commn. 1978-82; commnr. Santa Clara Co. Historic Heritage Commn. 1977-, major restoration and preservation projects incl. Machado Sch., Malaguerra Winery, Morgan Hill House, WelchHurst, and Alamaden Quicksilver

Park Master Plan; honors: Calif. Elected Women China Delegation 1979; nominated Woman of Achievement, Status of Women Commn. 1980, 81; mem: Calif. Child Passenger Safety Assn. (vp 1983-); Morgan Hill Hist. Soc. (pres. 1980, 82); United Way South Co. chpt. (Morgan Hill chmn. 1982/3); AAUW (legis. ch. 1982/3); People for Open Space (exec. bd. 1982-); Californians for Preservation Action 197;8-; Nat. Women's Polit. Caucus 1978-; publs: Hiram Morgan Hill (1983); History of Morgan Hill, CA: Indians to Incorporation (1982); Democrat; Prot.; rec: photog., nature expeditions. REs: 1095 Llagas Rd Morgan Hill 95037 Office of the County Executive, 70 West Hedding St, San Jose 95110

WYMAN, PHILLIP DAVID, state assemblyman; b. Feb. 21, 1945, Hollywood; s. Elliott and Rosalie Jane (Mauzy) W.; m. Lynn Larson, May 21, 1977; children: Andrea Dee, b. 1978, Elizabeth Frances, b. 1982; edn: BA, UC Davis 1967; JD, McGeorge Sch. of Law 1973; Atencio de Manila (Phil.) Univ. 1970. Career: active rancher in mgmt. of family owned Antelope Cyn. Ranch and recreational complex in Tehachapi; attorney; gen. mgr. Antelope Valley Bd. of Trade; elected assemblyman Calif. Legislature 1978-; named Assembly Republican Minority Whip 1980, chmn. Assem. Com. on Constnl. Amendments, 1981-2; mem. Assem. coms. on Judiciary, Transp. Ways & Means; mem. Commn. for Economic Devel.; Liggle Hoover Commn. (Commn. on Calif. State Govt. & Econ.), Spl. Legislative Investigation Com. on the State Bar; honors: Outstanding Young Men of Am. 1977, 79; mem: Am. Legion; Philippine Astronomical Soc. (founder); Astronomical Soc. of the Pacific; Tehachapi Mountain Observatory Assn. (cofounder); mem. Lancaster-West Rotary Desert Tortoise Preserve Commn., Kern Co. Farm Bur., and Federal and Calif. BAr Assns.; mil: sgt. USAF 1969, AF Commendn. Medal for service in US Emb., Manila; Republican; Christian; rec: astronomy (telescope making). Res: 110 Walnut, Tehachapi 93561 Ofc. of Assem. Phil Wyman, 5405 Stockdale Hwy, Ste. 112, Bakersfield 93309

XENOS, STEVE JR., psychological center clinical director; b. Jan. 20, 1931, Canton, Ohio; s. Steve and Antromahi (Zazopoulos) X.; m. Sheila T., July 31, 1952; children: Steve III, b. 1954, Mary Anne, b. 1956; Jane, b. 1958; edn: BA in vocational psych., Wayne State Univ. 1957; MA, psych., CSU Long Beach 1975; PhD, clin. psych., US Internat. Univ. 1978; lic. Marriage, Family, Child, Therapist (1977), Cert. Sex Therapist (1980). Career: (current) clinical director Human Resources Center (pvt. practice psychol. ctr), Santa Ana; vice chmn. Psychol. Services Dept., Brea Hosp. Neuropsychiatric Ctr., Brea; vocational expert witness, Bur. Hearing and Appeals, 9th Fed. Dist. Court; assoc. clin. prof., medical psych., Coll. Osteopathic Medicine, Pomona; assoc. prof. Calif. Graduate Inst., Orange Co. Campus; Diplomate, Am. Acad. Behavioral Med. 1981; mem: Am. Psychol. Assn.; Calif. Assn. Marriage, Family, Therapists; Am. Assn. Sex Therapists, Counselors, Educators; Calif. State Psychol. Assn.; mil: s/sgt. USAF 1950-53; Democrat; Catholic; rec: golf, woodworking, music. Res: 15291 Nimes Cir. Irvine 92714 Ofc: Human Resources Center, 1125 E. 17th St. E-201, Santa Ana 92701

XENOS, SHEILA ANNE, marriage, family, child therapist; b. July 20, 1932, Ann Arbor, MI; d. John Edward and Mary Estelle (VanRiper) Tomshack; PhD, in progress, Profl. Sch. for Humanistic Studies, 1980-82; MA, US Internatl. Univ., 1977-79; BA, CSU Dominguez Hills, 1977; m. Steve Xenos Jr., Ph.D., July 31, 1952; chil: Steve III, b. 1954; Mary Anne, b. 1955; Jane, b. 1958. Career: library asst., Miraleste H.S., 1969-79; co-dir., Human Resources Center, 1978---; asst. prof., Coll. of Osteo. of the Pacific, 1980-82; cert. sex therapist, 1981---; lic. clinical hypnotist, 1981; assoc. diplomate, Amer. Acad. of Behavioral Med. 1982; pres. PTA, 1960-65; lic. casualty ins. agent, 1965-67; Co. Bd. of Supvrs., Mt. Clemens, Mich., 1960-65; past secty., Mich. Assn. of Retarded Children, 1965. Mem: Amer. Psy. Assn.; student mem., Calif. State Psy. Assn.; student mem., Calif. Assn. Marriage, Family Therapy; Natl. Rehabilitation Assn.; Natl. Assn. of Rehabilitation Profls. in the Private Sector; Amer. Personnel & Guidance Assn.; Assn. Amer. Diplomate, Behavioral Med.; So. Calif. Assn. for Battered Women; Amer. Assn. of Sex Educators, Counselors & Therapists. Democrat. Catholic. Rec: golf. Res: 15291 Nimes Circle, Irvine 92714; Office: Human Resources Center, 1125 E. 17th St., #E-201, Santa Ana 92701.

YAMAMOTO, GARY TOKUYUKI, financial consultant; b. Sep. 11, 1945, Cleveland, Ohio; s. Tok and Anna (Yamada) Y.; m. June Oba, Oct. 30, 1971; children: Jennifer, b. 1976; Gina, b. 1978; edn: BS, CSU Fresno 1968; lic. life & health ins., Dept. of Corp. 1974, lic. investment advisor, SEC, 1975. Career: farming in Clovis -1968; ops. Merrill Lynch, Fresno 1968; English tchr. (self-empl.), Japan 1969-70; acct. exec. Merrill Lynch, Fresno 1970-73; San Joaquin Rep. for Lionel D. Edie, investment advisor, 1974; life & health ins. agt. Bankers Life Co. of Iowa, 1974-78; ind. investment advisor, 1975--, ind. life & health broker, 1978--, pres. GTY & Assocs., Inc., Fresno 1979-; pres. Tricon-

sultants, Inc., Fresno 1980-; pres. F & Y Mgmt. Inc., Fresno 1983-; mem: IAFP Nat. 1977-; IAFP Fresno Chpt. 1981- (bd. dir. 1983-); Fresno Life Underwriters (bd. dir.) 1981-; orgns: Rotary Club; CofC; Fresno Metropolitian Flood Control Dist. (bd. dir.) 1981-; Clovis Comm. Orgn. Fin. Adv.; Fresno Buddhist Ch. Retirement Chmn., 1981-; publish fin. planning workbook, monthly fin. newsletter; mil: Petty Ofcr. USN 1968-71, sec. communication; Republican; Buddhist; Ofc: GTY & Associates, Inc., 5477 N Fresno, Ste. 104 Fresno 93710

YAMANE, GLEN M., financial executive; b. Dec. 17, 1957, Burbank; s. Teddy M. and Midori (Suzuki) Y.; m. Cindy S. Louie, Oct. 9, 1982; Lic: Series 7, NASD 1980, Insurance lic. Calif. 1982. Career: police student Los Angeles Police Dept., 1975-79; acct. exec. M.S. Wien, Los Angeles 1980-81; acct. exec. Merrill Lynch, Glendale 1981-83; acct. executive E.F. Hutton, Universal City 1983--; mem: Stockbrokers Soc. 1980-; San Fernando Valley Japanese Am. Comm. Ctr.; Republican; Christian; rec: bowling, shooting. Res: 4049 Via Marisol, 316 Los Angeles 90042 Ofc: E.F. Hutton, 100 Universal City Plaza, Universal City 91608

YAMASAKI, MITSUNORI JOHN, manufacturing co. chief executive; b. Nov 9, 1941, Kobe, Japan; s. Yoshihide and Ayako Y.; m. Kay Hashimoto, May 5, 1967; 1 son: Jun Peter, b. 1970; edn: BS, Kwansei Gakuin Univ. 1964. Career: finance dept. Nichimen Co., Ltd., Osaka, Japan (export credit splst.) 1964-67; asst. mgr. mkt. research and devel. Nichimen Co., Inc., NYC 1967-74; mgr. prod. devel. & mktg., Nichimen, Osaka, Japan; gen. mgr. A.F. Seal, Inc., Anaheim 1975-, vice pres./chief exec. ofcr., 1980--; mem: Am. Mgmt. Assn.; Soc. of Glass Decorators; author: Handbook of Export Fgn. Exchange 1967; Protestant; rec: tennis. Res: 5171 Cavendish Ln Anaheim 92807 Ofc: American Fuji Seal, Inc., 1251 N. Blue Gum St Anaheim 92806

YANG, KUO LIANG, pharmacist; b. Apr. 29, 1947, Chungking Szechuan, China; s. William and Grace (Chung) Y.; m. Elaine Y. Yang, Mar. 28, 1978; 1 dau., Eileen, b. 1984; edn: BS, biology, Fu Jen Univ., Taiwan 1970; BS, pharm., Univ. Utah 1976. Career: chief pharm. Brookvale Med. Ctr. Pharmacy, San Pablo 1981; staff pharm. Central Pharmacy, Richmond 1981; owner/pharmacist Abreu's Drug Store, Oakland 1981--; drug consultant Random House; mem: Alameda Co. Pharmacists Assn.; Calif. Pharmacists Assn.; Am. Pharmacists Assn.; publs: The Mechanism and Pathway off Picotoxin in Cardiac Arrhythmia, 1972; Republican; rec: horseback riding, swim., music, reading. Res: 1129 Delta Way Danville 94526 Ofc: Abreu's Drug Store, 2286 E 14th St Oakland 94606

YANG, STEVE LIANG-YUAN, architect; b. Jan. 19, 1945, Peking, China, nat. 1981; s. Jen-Ling and Sih-Feng (Yen) Y.; m. Barbara, Jul. 17, 1971; children: Brian, b. 1973; Stephine, b. 1977; Solena, b. 1977; edn. D3, Tunghal Univ., Taichung, Taiwan 1968; M.Arch., Ohio State Univ. 1972; reg. profl. engr., State Ohio 1976; reg. arch., Ohio 1977, Calif. 1977. Career: proj. arch./designer Tully, Ames, Elzy & Thomas, Columbus, Ohio 1972-76; proj. arch. Karlsberger & Assoc., Columbus 1976-78; proj. arch. Winston & May Architects, Santa Clara 1978-80; principal Steve Yang & Assoc. AIA, San Jose 1980--; awards: design, preservation of historic landmark, Hotel St. Claire, San Jose Fine Arts Commn. 1982; mem: AIA; Nat. Council Arch. Record Bd. 1977; Nat. Soc. Profl. Engrs.; Nat. Historic Preservation Com.; mil: 2nd Lt., Corps. of Engrs., ROC; rec: painting, sporting. Res: 6978 El Marcero Ct San Jose 95119 Ofc: Steve Yang & Assoc., AIA, 12 South First St Ste. 817, San Jose 95113

YANG, WILLIAM TZYY-DAR, computer co. executive; b. Aug. 7, 1944, Qua-Cho, China, nat. 1984; s. Cha-Yue and Shi-Yen (Tu) Yang; m. Kitty Chou, Dec. 18, 1971; chil: Eric, b. 1974, Ellen, b. 1980; edn: BS, Nat. Taiwan Univ. 1967; MS, Cal Poly Univ., S.L.O. 1972. Career: system analyst Computer Machinery Corp. 1972-74, Planning Research Corp., 1974-75; mgr. Gen. Systems Internat., 1975-77; cons. Siemens Ag., 1977-80; sr. mgr. Sperry Corp., Irvine 1980--; dir. Inst. of Chinese Computer and Information Science, 1982-3; cons. Siemens Ag., Munich, W.Ger. 1977-80. Awards: 1969 Luce Found. Scholarship for international student. Mem: South Coast Chinese Cultural Assn. (dir.), Chinese Assn. of So. Calif.; Catholic; rec: personal computer, basketball. res: 3 Tidewater Irvine 92714 ofc: Sperry Corp. 16842 Von Karman, Irvine 92714

YANKEE, HELEN MARIE AUBERLIN, manufacturing co. executive; b. July 31, 1925, Detroit, Mich.; d. Lester G. and Irene (McGinniss) Auberlin; m. J. R. Yankee, June 1, 1956; children: Michael b. 1945, David b. 1948, Stephen b. 1952, Jennifer b. 1957; edn: Montessori Dipl., Montessori Inst. of Am. 1968; MS, Southeastern Univ. 1980, PhD, 1981; desig: Montessori Grad., Dr. C. Claremont, 1965. Career: founder/pres. The Fernhaven Studio 1966-; founder/pres. Montessori Educational Environments, Montessori Research Assocs., 1974-; pres. Yankee Montessori Mfg., 1980--; pres. Institute Montessori International (IMI), 1980--; CEO, Jemar Boat Ltd., 1980; tchr. IMI, seminar conductor, cons. public sch. districts and pvt. schs.; mem: Am. Montessori Soc. - Nat. Center for Montessori Studies, Montessori Internat. Assn., AAAS; author: How To Teach The Montessori Reading Method (1978), Montessori Math: The Basics (1979), Montessori Geography Curriculum (1980), Montessori Science Curriculum (1981), Montessori Curriculum (4 vols. 1982); Indep. Res: 22333 PCH Malibu 90265 Ofc: Yankee Mfg. 8655 S. Main St Los Angeles 90003

YAP, EDGAR OQUENDO, development co. executive; b. Oct. 10, 1939, Philippines; nat. 1973; s. Dr. Miguel U. and Adoracion Legaspi (Oquendo) Y.; m. Joselyn Vergara Geaga, Aug. 26, 1972; 2 sons: Edgar Jonathan b. 1977, Earl Jason b. 1981; edn: BS in chem. eng., Univ. of Sto. Tomas 1963; grad. wk. in petroleum & chem. engring., USC, 1965-67. Career: currently: pres./exec. ofcr. Filipinas Assoc., Ltd., Filipinas Development, Ltd., The Filipino American Service Group, Inc. (non-profit corp.); involved in commercial and residential devel.; low cost housing under the City Redevel. Program; real estate investor; dir. Greenhills Construction; cons. GLM Associates Consultants; past: sr. project engr. Barnard & Burk Inc., Pasadena , Robert Brown Engrs., Carson, process engr. Fluor Engrs. & Contractors Inc., Irvine, jr. engr. Hewitt & Robins Engrs. Inc., Santa Fe Springs, 1979-82; fmr. ptnr., Joy of Flowers; mem. Am. Inst. of Chemical Engrs.; Thomasian Engrs. (alumni assn.), Aklan Assn. of Los Angeles, Filipino Am. Community of L.A.; publs: tech. paper, AIChE Annual Meeting, S.F. 1971; Catholic; rec: basketball, camping, bowling. Res: 3162 Durand Dr Los Angeles 90068 Ofc: Filipinas Assoc. Ltd. 2422 W Temple St Los Angeles 90026

YAP, JOSELYN GEAGA, clinical social worker; b. Mar. 1, 1947, Baguio City, Phil., nat. 1970; d. Jose Vargas and Remedios Flores (Vergara) Geaga; m. Edgar O. Yap, Aug. 26, 1972; children: Jonathan Edgar, b. 1977; Jason Earl, b. 1980; edn: BS, UC Los Angeles 1969; MSW, USC, 1971; doctoral work in prog.; LCSW (lic. clin. social wkr.). Career: research clerk UCLA Neuropsychiat. Inst., 1968-69; sr. med. social wkr. Rancho Los Amigos Hosp., Downey 1971-76; field instr., psychiatric soc. wkr., asst. adminstr. Asian Pacific Counseling and Treatment Ctr., Los Angeles 1977-81, supvg. psychiat. soc. wkr., 1981--, asst. director, 1982--; pvt. practice psychotherapy, L.A. 1977--; mem. adv. bd./ vol. cons. to Ctr. for Pacific-Asian Families (non-prof. orgn.), 1980-; frequent panelist, presenter num. profl. confs.; offcl. del. White House Conf. on Aging, 1971. Mem: Nat. Assn. of Social Wkrs., Group Psychotherapy Assn. of So. Calif., Pacific/Asian Am. Mental Hlth Resrch Ctr., Los Angeles CofC; publs: arts., The American Journey (4/82), Asian Am. News (5/83); pub. papers internat. profl. confs.; orgnzr./ partner Joy of Flowers (flower shop); rec: floral designer. Res: 3162 Durand Dr. Los Angeles 90068 Ofc: Asian Pacific Counseling, 3407 W. 6th St Ste 510, Los Angeles 90020

YARNALL, CELESTE, real estate broker, actress; b. Jul. 26, 1944, Long Beach; d. Forest Elwood and Helene Jeanne (Colombel) Y.; m. Robert Colman, Feb. 8, 1979; 1 dau: Camilla Jeanne, b. 1970; lic. real estate broker, Calif. Dept. R.E. Career: Miss Rheingold 1964, spkswmn./goodwill amb. Rheingold Beer, (TV, radio commls, print ads); leading roles in TV and feature films; appeared in num. TV commls.; R.E. sales agt. Grubb & Ellis, Los Angeles; co-founder Greenwood & Co. 1974, v.p., then pres. Greenwood/ Yarnall (div. Greenwood & Co.); founder/ pres. Celeste Yarnall & Assoc., Los Angeles 1979--; mem. Appraisers Inst.; mem. Westside Leasing Assn.; Awards: Miss Rheingold 1964; Deb Star 1968; Most Promising New Star of 1968; mem: L.A. Bd. Realtors, Beverly Hills. CofC; Western. Reg. CofC; patron LA County Mus. of Art (Amazing Blue Ribbon 400; Inner Circle Childrens Mus., Founders II, Pres. Circle); publs: arts. for Century City News, num. R.E. publs.; rec: fitness, nutrition, jewelry design. Ofc: Celeste Yarnall & Assoc., 9200 Sunset Blvd Pent. 20 Los Angeles 90069

YATES, VIRGINIA LIEBNER, financial co. executive; b. Oct. 18, 1952, Los Angeles; d. Robert Wm. Liebner and Rebecca Peck (Ivans) Liebner Lewellyn; m. Donald Yates, Sr., Ph.D., Aug. 22, 1982; 1 son, Jason Nathaniel, b. 1983; edn: BSBA, cum laude, San Diego State Univ. 1976; cert. loan adminstr., Mortgage Bankers Assn. 1976; lic. real estate broker, Calif. 1976. Career: property mgr. (700 units), West American Mgmt. Co., 1975-76; broker/owner North County Properties, San Diego 1976-78; adminstrv. asst. United First Mortgage Corp., S.D. 1976-77; corp. broker/closing supr. Sunset Mtg. Corp., S.D. 1977-78; regional comml. & resdtl. loan ofcr. First Service Mtg. Corp., Arcs Mtg., Inc., San Diego 1978-81; v.p./broker Home Counseling Lending Services, 1979-82; exec. vice pres. La Jolla Newport Financial, 1981--; dir. Yates & Liebner, Inc. 1981--. Awards: State Champion ski racer 1974-5; highest producer as loan ofcr. 1978-80. Mem: Assn. of Profl. Mortgage Women 1981-, Gr. San Diego CofC, La Jolla Town Council, Gamma Phi Beta Alumnae, S.D. Ski Club; Republican; Presbyterian; rec: ski (racing), sailing, tennis, youth director. Ofc: La Jolla Newport Financial 1135 Torrey Pines Rd La Jolla 92037

YAW, ELBERT M., sales executive, b. May 5, 1940, Kansas City, Mo.; s. Elbert F. and Juanita F. (Black) Y.; m. Holly H. Chilson, May 16, 1982; children: Kimberly M., b. 1962; Sandi M., b. 1969; edn: pol. sci., Fullerton Coll. 1958-60; L.A. Trade Tech. Coll. 1962-3; BSME, Northrop Univ. 1966; Grad. Sch. Bus., CSU Los Angeles 1968; wholesale mgmt., Stanford Univ. 1980. Career: engr. So. Calif. Gas & Elec. Co., Los Angeles 1966-67; systems and territory sales Paul-Munroe Co., Pico Rivera 1967-69; western reg. mgr. Fluid Power Systems Div., Ambac Inc., Burligame 1969-74; area mgr. Paul-Munroe Co., Santa Clara 1974-79, v.p. mktg. and ops./dir. sales, Whittier 1979--; consultant, engr. and bus. 1969-74; honor soc. Northrop Univ. 1965; mem. Fluid Power Distbr. Assn.; Republican; Christian; rec: hunting, fishing, writing. Res: 17321 Bonner Dr Tustin 92680 Ofc: Paul-Munroe Co., 9999 E Rose Hills Rd Whittier 90601

YEAGER, PHILIP J., real estate executive; b. Mar. 1, 1930, Columbus, Ohio; s. William P. and Anna C. (Meidl) Y.; m. Peggy Wetzler, Nov. 1, 1952; children: Melissa, b. 1954; Susan, b. 1955; Kurt, b. 1956 (dec.); Stephen, b. 1959; Christine, b. 1961; Jennifer, b. 1966; edn: Claremont Mens Coll. 1951; grad. work, Ohio State Univ. 1956; life teaching cred. adult edn. (R.E. subjects). Career: 3d gen. Calif. realtor; pres./CEO: Century 21 Region 105 (w/ 152 Century 21 offices, adminstrv. ofc. Covina), Century 21 Region 113 (w/ 160 offices, adminstrv. ofc. Seattle, Wn.), Covina Realto Co. Inc. dba Mr. Build of the Northwest (Ore., Wn., Ida., Alaska), Resorts Mktg. Inc. (Seattle, Wn.), Estate Escrow Corp. (Covina); chmn. exec. com. Fifth Season (devel., mktg. timeshare condo., US & Mex.). Honors: Eagle Scout. Mem: past pres. Covina Valley Bd. of Realtors; past dir. Nat. Assn. of Realtors; past Scoutmaster and Dist. chmn. BSA; past pres. two Toastmaster Clubs. Num. R.E. articles in nat.

publs.; mil: 1st lt. USAF 1952-56; Republican; rec: flying, tennis. Res: 2808 Monte Verde Covina 91724 Ofc: Century 21, Region Five, 100 No. Citrus, W. Covina 91791

YEAMAN, BLAKE WILLIAM, graphic designer; b. Dec. 4, 1956, Van Nuys; s. Robert Dwight and Bette Marilyn (Kellum) Y.; m. Susan Lynne Richardson, June 23, 1979; children: Robert Blake, b. 1981, David Scott, b. 1984; edn: BS, sociol., UC Berkeley 1981. Career: owner Blake Yeaman Graphics, Albany 1976-80; mktg. dir. Redo Corp., Berkeley 1980-81; owner AFAB, Berkeley 1980-81; bd. chmn./v.p. California Capital Exports, Inc., Oakland 1981-84; pres./mng. ptnr. Williamson & Yeaman, Inc., Oakland 1984--; honors: Harvard Book, UC Honor Stu. Soc.; mem. San Francisco Rugby Club, Phi Kappa Psi; Republican; rec: music, sports, backpacking. Res: 962 Kains Ave, Albany 94706 Ofc: Williamson & Yeaman, Inc. 1630 Webster St Oakland 94612

YEE, GILBERT YEUNG, real estate insurance industry executive, ret.; b. May 23, 1907, Taishan, Kwangtung, China; s. Ying-Chung and Ngu-Gee (Ng) Y.; m. Mabel Kao Yee, MD, Mar. 24, 1949; children: Robert, b. 1940; Shubert, b. 1941; Fay, b. 1943; Herbert, b. 1950; Kay, b. 1952; Gay, b. 1956; grad., Duquesne Univ., 1934-7; Univ. Pittsburgh, 1937-9. Career: editor Chinese Nationalist Daily, 1939; mgr. Chinese Hosp. 1939-40; mgr. Grandview Film Co., 1941-45; independent ins. mgr. & agcy owner Permanent Security Agency 1946-76; owner/mgr. Hang On Investment Co. 1977-79; owner Golden Gate Residence 1971-79; adv. Overseas Chinese Affairs Commn., Taiwan, Rep. China; adv. to Bank of Trade of San Francisco; adv. US Congl. Adv. Bd. Chmn.; mem: Hop Wo Ben. Assn. Calif. (pres.) 1966-68; Chinese Con. Ben. Assn. (pres.) 1966-68; Chinese Am. Republican Club (sr. adv.) 1974-; Yee's Assn. of USA (elder/grand pres.) 1982-. Address: 751 Clay St San Francisco 94108

YEE, PETER MICHAEL, interior designer; b. Dec. 18, 1947, Tsingtao, China; s. Young Chin and Lai (Kuan) Yee; m. Glenda Wong, Sept. 10, 1977; edn: CSU 1967-9, BA, Art Center, 1972. Career: design director Mario Zamparelli & Co., 1971-76; project designer Setmakers, Inc., 1977-78; Fred Schmid Associates, 1978-80; design director Setmakers, Inc., Glendale 1980--, currently in chg. of devel. corp. identity for nat. major restaurant/entertainment chain; hotel clients incl. Desert Inn, Frontier Hotel, Maxim Hotel, Sundance Hotel (Las Vegas). Mem. Chamber of Commerce. Res: 11000 Ruffner Ave, Granada Hills 91344 Ofc: Setmakers Inc. 526 Commercial St. Glendale 91203

YEE, RAYMOND, physician; b. Apr. 7, 1952, San Francisco; s. Frank Yuen and May Kui (Soo Hoo) Y.; m. Lulu Yee, MD, Apr. 9, 1983; edn: AA, City Coll. San Francisco 1973; UC Berkeley 1974; MD, Autonomous Univ. Guadalajara 1979; lic. MD, State GA, 1981, Calif. 1981, Wyo. 1982. Career: vol. family physician, Tecate, Mexico 1981; family phys. in Martin and Phillip, So. Dak. 1981-82; psychiatry resident King/Drew Med. Ctr. 1982; affiliating resident USC, Los Angeles 1982-83; staff mem. Los Angeles Dept. of Mental Health; chief res. psychiatry, King/Drew Med. Ctr., Los Angeles 1983--; family physician Bennett Comm. Hosp., 1981-82; mem: Am. Med. Assn.; So. Calif. Psychiat. Soc.; Am. Psychiat. Assn.; mil: PFC USAR 1972-78; Democrat; rec: chess, bowling, hiking, travel. Res: 5488 Dobbs St, 99, Los Angeles 90032

YEGIAN, SHAHEN, civil engineer; b. Jan. 23, 1927, Tehran, Iran, nat. 1958; s. Aram and Anna (Petrossian) Y.; m. Isa Bella Avakian, Dec. 28, 1961; children: Richard, b. 1962; Suzanne, b. 1963; edn: BS in C.E., Univ. Tehran 1950; MS in C.E., 1952, PhD 1957, Univ. Ill.; Lic. Profl. Engr., Mass. 1973. Career: research asst. & assoc. Univ. Ill., Urbana 1951-57; proj. mgr. Jackson & Moreland Consult Eng., Boston 1957-60; chief engr. Frederic R. Harris Consult Eng., Stamford, Conn. 1970-72; mng. dir. Infotech Consult Eng. Tehran, Iran 1972-82; real estate broker Y & A Real Estate Co., Los Angeles 1982--; awards: Moisseiff Award, for research pub., Am. Soc. Civil Engrs. 1958; mem: ASCE, Am. Concrete Inst., Am. Inst. Steel Const.; publs: Lateral Buckling of Elastically End-Restrained I-Beams, ASCE 1958; rec: music. Address: Y & A Real Estate Co., 1721 Golf Club Dr Clendale 91206

YEH, BESSIE PEICHI, international economist; b. May 25, 1945, Shanghai, China, nat. 1971; d. Mot-Teh and Nee Chinn Yeh; m. Elliott McGinnies, Jan. 1967; children: Michelle b. 1968, Lisa b. 1969, Amy b. 1971; edn: BA, econ., Taiwan Provincial ChunHsin Univ. 1966; MA, internat. rels., The American Univ. 1970; PhD, econ., The Am. Univ. (ABD); credentials: SEC, NASD, SIPC. Career: program analyst National Science Foundation, 1972-74; economist Mitre Corp. 1974-75, US Dept. of Agric. 1975-77; internat. training adminstr. Agency for Int'l. Development, 1977-79; economist EconoTech Inc., Wash DC 1980-82; senior economist Wharton Econoetrics Assocs., 1982-83; current: vis. scholar Hoover Instn.; pres. First Investment of California Asian International 1984--; mem. American Economist Assn., Western Economic Assn., San Francisco CofC; num. publs. in field; Republican. Res: 1790 Arrowhead Dr Oakland 94611 Ofc: 221 Pine St, Ste 500, San Francisco 94104

YEH, CHAN-JONG, company president; b. July 5, 1941, Amoy, China; US citizen; s. Kuo-Koing and Jin-Jen (Lin) Y.; m. Jean Yeh, Dec. 24, 1972; 1 child, Yung-Ping, b. 1975; edn: BS, National Cheng Kung Univ. 1964; MS, Univ. of R.I. 1967, PhD, 1970; Calif. lic. real estate broker (1983), mechanical engineer. Career: resrch asst. Univ. of R. I., 1965-70; resrch engr. Chung Shan Inst. of Sci. & Tech., Taiwan 1971-73; vice pres. Ideographix, Inc. Sunnyvale, Ca. 1973-82; pres. Morningbell Enterprises Co., Mtn. View 1982--, engring. cons., real estate broker; honors: Tau Beta Pi, Pi Tau Sigma; mem: ASME, ASTE, Chinese Engr. Assn., Chinese Culture Assn., past pres. NCKUAA (Nat. Cheng Kung Univ. Alumni Assn., SF Bay area, 1981); patentee (No.

265,264) 1982; Republican; Confucius; rec: real estate inv., creative invention. Address: Morningbell Ent. Co., 3358 Tryna Dr Mountain View 94040

YEH, PAUL PAO, electrical/electronics engineer/educator; b. Mar. 25, 1927, Sun-yang, Chekiang, China, nat. 1963; s. Tsung-San and Sui-Wen (Mao) Y.; m. Beverley Pamela Eng, May 15, 1952; children: J. Elaine, b. 1953; Paul E., b. 1954; Richard, b. 1956; Ronald, b. 1960; edn: Natl. Central Univ. 1946-49; BASc, Univ. Toronto, 1951; MSEE, Univ. Penn., Philadelphia 1960, PhD, 1966. Career: design engr. Canadian Gen. Elec. Co., Toronto, Canada 1951-56; asst. prof. State Univ. of N.Y., Binghamton 1956-57; sr. design engr. H.K. Porter Co., Philadelphia 1957-58; transformer engr. I-T-E, Kuhlman and Fed. Pacific Electric 1958-61; chief engr. Eisler Transformer Co., Dover, NJ 1961; assoc. prof. EE, Newark Coll. of Engring., NJ 1961-66; supvr. Performance Analysis, Autonetics, No. Am. Rockwell, Anaheim, CA 1966-70; advanced sys. engr. Lockheed-Calif. Co. 1970-72; sr. scientist/grp. leader McDonnell Douglass, Huntington Bch. 1972-73; MTS Aerospace Corp., El Segundo 1973-78; sr. staff engr., ADP Lockheed-Calif. Co., Burbank 1978--; lectr. CSU Long Beach 1967-73; honors: achievement award, Lockheed-Calif. Co.; 1971; mem: Chinese Engrs. and Scientists Assn. of So. Calif. (pres. 1970-72); IEEE; Nat. Mgmt. Assn.; Assn. of Profl. Engrs. of Ontario, Canada; Am. Defense Preparedness Assn.; AF Assn.; AAAS; AAUP; Am. Inst. of Aero and Astro; Inst. of Navigation; Chinese Inst. of Engrs. of NY; Town Hall of Calif.; over 50 pub. sci. papers; Republican; Presbyterian; rec: computer operation, photog., travel. Res: 15461 Vassar St Westminster 92683 Ofc: Lockheed-Calif. Co., POB 551, Burbank 91520

YEH, THAIMOS EN-TEE, real estate co. president; b. Dec. 24, 1942, Laos, nat. 1977; s. Van Diep and Ngoc (Nhan) Y.; edn: MS, Univ. of Pacific 1973; cred. in edn., CSU Los Angeles 1973; MA, Calif. Lutheran Coll. 1977, MS, 1979; Calif. lic. realtor 1979. Career: R.E. sales agt. Century-21 May Wah Realty, Los Angeles 1978-79; dir. Grandway Realty, Los Angeles 1979; mgr. Osemand Realty & Mgmt. Co., Inc., Los Angeles 1979-82; dept. chmn. English as 2nd Language, King Jr. High Sch., LAUSD, Los Angeles 1980-82; owner/pres. Handfore Realty & Investment Co., Inc., Monterey Park 1982--; dir. 1983-;owner/pres. Osemand Realty & Co. (spec. in industrial props., Chinatown), Los Angeles 1983--; mem: West San Gabriel Bd. Realtors; Chinese Commerce Assn., Chinatown, L.A.; So. Chinese Merchants Assn.; Chinatown; Democrat; Baptist; rec: fishing, tennis. Res: 2228 S Fulton Ave Monterey Park 91754 Ofc: Osemand Realty & Co., 837 No Spring St, Ste. 205, Los Angeles 90012

YEN, JOHN K. H., physician/neurosurgeon; b. Jul. 7, 1942, Honolulu, Hawaii; s. John T.L. and Blanche L. (Wong) Y.; m. Joan P. Yen, Apr. 1, 1977; children: Gregory, b. 1977; Jeffrey, b. 1979; Stacey, b. 1981; edn: BS, UC Berkeley 1965; MD, Albany Med. Coll. 1969. Career: att. staff neurosurgeon: Methodist Hosp. of Sacramento, Sutter Davis Hosp., Woodland Memorial Hosp.; clinical instr. in neurosurgery UC Davis Med. Sch.; mem: Am. Assn. Neurol. Surgeons; Sacramento Neurol. Soc.; Am. Medical Assn.; publs: med. jour. arts., book chapters; rec: fishing. Res: 1408 Rosario St Davis 95616 Ofc: John K. H. Yen, Inc., 8110 Stockton Blvd Sacramento 95823

YERANIAN, ARTHUR S., electrical engineer, b. Feb. 22, 1910, Marash, Arm.-Turkey, nat. 1938; s. Avedis and Nazender (Charhudian) Y.; m. Rebecca Shamlian, Jan. 5, 1944; 1 dau. Lily, b. 1955; edn: BSEE, w/honors, Northeastern Univ. 1935; elec. engrg., music courses, sev. colls.; Reg. Profl. Elec. Engr., State Calif. Career: radio tester RCA Mfg. Co., Camden, NJ 1935-36; tchr./text writer Mass. TV Inst., Boston 1937-39; US War Dept. & Air Tech. Svc. Command, Los Angeles & San Bernadino 1942-45; designer/proj. engr. Hydro-electric Power Plants and High Tension and Extra High Tension Substations 1945-75; consultant engr. Kaiser Engrs., Internat. Engrs.1975-82; semiret. writer, engring. cons. currently; lectr. engring. Heald Coll., 1954-55, instr., PG&E Co. courses; awards: 1st prize essay on Freedom 1960; Man of Year, 1981, Knights of Vartan (Darin Lodge No. 16); mem. IEEE; Knights of Vartan; F&AM Mason (3d deg.); author: The Civilized (1980); composer: From The Hye-Land (for voice and piano) 1969; Protestant; rec: music composition, writing, gardening. Address: 825 Avalon Ave Lafayette 94549

YINGLING, H. JOHN, television administrator; b. July 3, 1939, Los Angeles; s. Harold John and Elizabeth Y.; m. Peggy Everett, Nov. 3, 1973; 2 children; edn: BA in mktg., USC 1961, MA in comm., 1964. Career: supvr network. ops. Columbia Broadcasting Systems 1964-68; dir. prod. KCET, Los Angeles 1968-76; labor relations consultant 1976-78; dir. bus. mgmt. & asst. to v.p. admin. American Broadcasting Cos., Inc., Los Angeles 1978--; bd. dir. Commuter Computer; mem: Acad. of Television Arts and Sciences; Hollywood Radio and Television Soc.; Nat. Assn. of Broadcasters; mil: Naval Air Observer, Ltjg, USN Air, 1961-64. Res: 975 Winston Ave San Marino 91108 Ofc: ABC-TV, 2040 Ave of The Stars, Ste 200, Los Angeles 90067

YOCK, SALLY, real estate broker; b. Mar. 23, 1953, Stockton; d. Howard and Mon Heung (Kong) Low; m. George Davis, Mar. 31, 1983; 1 dau. Athena Elizabeth, b. 1984; edn: BA, hist. and psych., CSU San Francisco 1975; MA, Lone Mountain Coll. 1978. Calif. lic. Real Estate Broker 1983. Career: prin./ president Seven Seas Enterprises (import, export), 1976-82; owner/broker Sally Yock-Davis Realty, 1983--; lectr. For Sale By Owner seminars; awards: California State Scholarship 1971-74, American Legion Scholarship 1971, PG&E Semifinalist Scholarship 1971, Graduate Province Scholarship 1977; recipient appreciation cert., UN Children's Fund 1978-9; mem: AAUW (life), Chinese Women in Action (co-chair 1977), S.F. YWCA (Downtown Mgmt. v.chair 1976), World Affairs Council, Calif. Hist. Soc.; del., UN Internat.

Women's Year Conf. Mexico City 1975; del., Nat. YWCA Conf., Univ. of Notre Dame 1976; del. YWCA Women's Forum; publ: article on Housing; Democrat; rec: classical music, travel, anthropology. Res: San Francisco 94133 Ofc: Yock-Davis Realty, 12480 Woodridge Rte. One, POB 450, White Water 92282

YOCUM, GEORGIA DOROTHEA, financial planner; b. Dec. 23, 1937, Tucson, Ariz.; d. Stanley Nicklaus and Minnie Hazel (Manues) Moore; m. Wyett Monroe Yocum, Jan. 25, 1969; : children: Richard, b. 1968; Deborah, b. 1961; Barbara, b. 1962; (stepchil.) Philip, b. 1943; Stephen, b. 1945; edn: grad., Life Underwriters Tng. Counsel 1974; grad., Adv. LUTC, 1975. Career: with Allstate Regional Legal Office, 1969-71, Massachusetts Mutual, 1971-73; agcy. owner/life agent Foothill Adminstrators, Grass Valley 1975--; num. sales awards incl. Allstate Allstar 1973, Top 25 Club 1976-, Continental Club 1976-; mem: Internat. Assn. Fin. Planners; Profl. Insurance Agents of Calif. & Nev.; Calif. Life Underwriters; mem. Soroptomist, Nevada Co. CofC, Nevada Co. Bus. Assn.; Republican; avocation: dev./restore historic bldgs.; rec: golf, fishing, travel, gardening. Res: 116 Dennis Way Grass Valley 95945 Ofc: Foothill Ahministrators, 131 So. Auburn St Grass Valley 95945

YODER, DORIS ELAINE, controller; b. Sept. 23, 1931, Los Angeles; d. John Charles and Bertha (Koenig) Allen; m. Willard Yoder, Feb. 12, 1966; 1 son, Paul, b. 1967; edn: stu. E.L.A. Coll. 1960-62, Woodbury Coll. 1965-66; BS in acctg., Beverly Hills Univ. 1981, MS in acctg., 1982. Career: gen. office, Northington Inc., W.I.A. 1950-55; one-girl ofc., Bonded Products Co., L.A. 1955-60; bus. owner, C & D Products, Monterey Park 1960-64; controller/ corp. secty./ bd. dirs. Kold Kist Foods, Inc., Los Angeles 1964 ; 1st chair violinist Huntington Park Sym. Orch. 1950-53, 2d chair, San Gabriel Sym. Orch. 1953-56, 3d chair, All Cities Orch. 1947-50; mem. American Management Assn.; Maranatha Band Booster Club (secty. 1983-4); Republican Nat. State Elections Com., 1984; Lutheran; rec: music. Res: 353 De La Fuente Monterey Park 91754 Ofc: Kold Kist Foods Inc., 5359 E. Washington Blvd Los Angeles 90022

YOUNG, DOUGLAS REA, lawyer; b. July 21, 1948, Los Angeles; s. James Douglas and Dorothy Belle (Rea) Y.; m. Terry Forrest, Jan. 19, 1974; 1 dau. Megann Forrest, b. 1979; edn: BA, cum laude, Yale Univ. 1971; JD, UC Berkeley 1976; cert., Nat. Inst. Trial Advocacy (adv.) 1983; admitted Calif. State Bar, 1976. Career: law clerk to US Dist. Judge Alfonso J. Zirpoli 1976-77; assoc. atty. Farella, Braun & Martel 1977-82, partner 1982--; twice apptd. spl. master in fed. antitrust litigation; faculty Calif. Cont. Edn. of the Bar, co-founder Berkeley Law Foundation; bd. dir. Legal Aid Soc. of San Francisco 1981-; awards: appreciation, Berkeley Law Found., exec. ed. Calif. Law Review 1975-76; mem: Calif. St. Bar; US Supreme Ct., 6th and 9th Circuit Cts. of Appeal; Fed. Dist. Cts. for No. and Central Dists. of Calif.; Berkeley Law Fdn.; ACLU; Environmental Defense Fund; Litigation and Criminal Law Sects. of Am. Bar Assn.; Lawyers Club of San Francisco; Bar Assn. of S. F.; Am., Calif. Bar Assns.; publs: Cal. L. Rev. 1975; mil: Sgt., USMC 1971-73; Democrat; Protestant; rec: skiing, mountaineering, running. Res: 67 Weybridge Ct Oakland 94611 Ofc: Farella, Braun & Martel, 235 Montgomery St, Ste 3000, San Francisco 94104

YOUNG, HENRY R., manufacturing co. executive; b. Oct. 13, 1940, Havana, Cuba, nat. 1966; s. Jaime and Eva (Cheruoni) Yudeleuski; m. Valerie M. Josephson, Dec. 30, 1961; children: David H.; Michael E.; Heidi J.; edn: BA, Univ. Havana 1959. Career: v.p./gen. mgr. Marine Swimming Pool Equip., 1962-74; Blue Haven Pools 1968-74; Sunset Pools 1969-74; Royal Pools 1969-74; v.p./gen. mgr. Premier Pump & Pool Products, Inc., 1974-80, v.p. chief financial ofcr. 1980-83; bd. dirs.: Blue Haven Pools, Sunset Pools, Royal Pools, Premier Pump & Pool Products 1983--; mem: Bnai Brith; Boy Scouts of Am.; Nat. Swimming Pool Inst.; Calif. Contractors Assn.; ISTE; SPEC.; patents: filtration & water treatment equip.; Democrat; Jewish; rec: 11Swimming, arts & crafts, numismatics. Res: 5063 Stern Ave Sherman Oaks 91403 Ofc: Premier Pump & Pool Products Inc., 3347 San Fernando Rd Los Angeles 90065

YOUNG, MATT NORVEL, JR., university chancellor; b. Oct. 5, 1915, Nashville, TN; s. Matt Norvel and Ruby (Morrow) Y.; m. Helen Mattox, 1939; children: Emily; Matt III; Marilyn; Sara; edn: BA, Abilene Christian Coll. 1936; MA, Vanderbilt Univ. 1937; PhD, Peabody Coll. of Vanderbilt Univ. 1943; LHD, Calif. Coll. Med. 1964; LLD, Lubbock Christian Coll. 1982. Career: minister Coll. Ch. of Christ, David Lipscomb Coll. 1941-43; Broadway Ch. of Christ, Lubbock, TX 1944-57; pres. Pepperdine Univ. 1957-71, chancellor 1971--; regent, Pepperdine Univ.; dir.: Forest Lawn Meml. Park, Pub. Savings Life Ins. Co., Imperial Bank; sr. editor 20th Century Christian Mag. (1945-), Power for Today Mag. (1955-); author num. publs.; mem: L.A. CofC, Phi Delta Kappa, Rotarian; clubs: California, Bohemian. Res: 24420 Tiner Ct Malibu 90265 Ofc: Pepperdine Univ., Malibu 90265

YOUNG, PATRICIA JANEAN, speech-language pathologist; b. Nov. 30, 1953, San Diego; d. Bernarr E. and Janean Elizabeth (Romig) Y.; edn: AA, Palomar Comm. Coll. 1974; MA, CSU Chico 1976; MA, CSU Long Beach 1971; Calif. Clin. Rehabilitative Svcs. Cred. Language, Speech and Hearing Spec. 1981; Calif. St. Lic. Speech-Lang. Pathology. 1982. Career: mgmt. trainee J.W. Robinson's 1977-8; speech-lang. pathologist/ screening coord./ adminstr. Riverview Hearing, Speech and Language Ctrs, Long Beach 1978--; profl. presentations w/ Dr. JoAnn Yates at W. Orange Co. Consortium of Spec. Edn. 1981; honors: recognition, CSULB Dept. Comm. Disorders, 1981, 2; Outstanding Young Women of Am. 1983; mem: Am., Calif. Speech-Lang. Hearing Assns., Nat. Assn. for Hearing and Speech (ch. pub. info. for NAHSA benefit w/ Disney TV Studios, 1983); Calif. Speech Pathologists and Audiologists in Pvt. Practice; Phi Delta Gama (Phi Chpt. 1st v.p. 1983-4); Kappa Delta Pi hon.; Zeta Tau Alpha, nat. women's frat.; Long Beach CofC Assn.; Calif. Scholastic Fedn. 1972; works: prod. two TV shows on communicative disorders for cable TV, 1983; pub. poetry, Phi Delta Gamma 1984 Nat. Journal; Republican; Protestant; rec: theatre, travel, writing, fashion. Res: 955 N. Beech St, Escondido 11484 Ofc: Riverview Hearing, Speech, Lang. Centers, 1165 E San Antonio, Ste. A Long Beach 90807

YOUNG, RONALD SAI WO, medical technologist, real estate broker; b. Sep. 22, 1945, San Francisco; s. Jack G.H. and Ruby (Lai) Y.; m. Jo Ann Cho (lic. D.Pharm.), Aug. 2, 1981; edn: AA, San Francisco CIty Coll. 1966; BA, UC Berkley 1967; medical tech., M.T. (ASCP) Calif. St. Dept. Health 1972; lic. real estate broker 1983. Career: med. tchnologist/supr. UC Med. Ctr., San Francisco 1972--; realtor/principal, 1983--; awards: 10-year service, UCSF 1983; Chinese Student Club scholarship, CCSF 1965; Alpha Gamma Sigma, Calif. Coll. Honor Soc. 1965; mem: Am. Soc. of Clinical Pathologists; San Francisco Bd. Realtors; Calif. Assn. of Realtors; Nat. Assn. Realtors; Com. for the Relief of Guatemala 1976; works: portfolio photos. of Guatemala; mil: spec. 5th class, US Army, GCM, Defense Svc. Medal; Democrat; Christian; rec: photog., tennis, jog, ski, numismatics. Address: 115 Anza Vista Ave San Francisco 94115

YOUNG, SALLY S., purchasing executive; b. Feb. 14, 1940, Detroit, Mich.; d. Philip C. and Pauline G. (Glidewell) Satterthwaite; m. Edsel Young, Sept. 7, 1978; children (by prev. m.): Lori, b. 1958; Kevin, b. 1964; edn: BBA, cum laude, Nat. Univ. 1980, MBA, 1981. Career: buyer Navy Exchg., Guam 1967-70, 1976-77; pub. rels./soc. dir. Guam Reef Hotel, Guam 1974; mktg. mgr. Global Marketing, Inc., Honolulu, Hawaii; buyer Navy Exchange, Mare Island 1977-78; assec. registrar National Univ., Vista 1979-82; buyer Marine Corps. Exchange, Santa Ana 1982--; honors: Ancient Order of Chamorri, Govt. Guam 1977; appreciation, Vista CofC 1980; mem: Women's Internat. Center; PEO Sisterhood; Nat. Mgmt. Assn.; Nat. Notary Assn.; Guam Press Club; Republican; Episcopalian; rec: reading, piano, grandchildren. Res: 852 Willow Tree Ln Fallbrook 92028 Ofc: Marine Corps Exchange, MCAS El Toro Santa Ana 92709

YOUNG, TYRUS CHARLES, certified public accountant; b. Aug. 6, 1957, Shreveport, La.; s. Thomas Creighton and Carol June (Skimerton) Y.; m. Louise Schmelka, Apr. 7, 1979; edn: BS, (Seaver Coll.) Pepperdine Univ. 1978; CPA, State Calif. 1982. Career: auditor Travelers Ins. Co., Orange Co., 1978-80; staff acct. Gregory A. Morrison Acctcy. Corp., Riverside 1980, sr. acct./v.p. ops. 1983--; staff auditor Eadie and Payne, CPAs, San Bernadino 1981; advisor to bd. dirs. My Family, Inc. (non-profit drug rehab. ctr.); mem: Am. Inst. of CPAs, Calif. Soc. of CPAs; Jaycees (mem. com. for Winston Western 500 Invitnl. Parade, Riverside); Republican; Protestant; rec: guitar, music composition. Res: 3565 Temescal Ave Norco 91760 Ofc: Gregory A. Morrison Acctcy. Corp., 3576 Arlington, Ste. 200, Riverside 92506

YOUNG, W. BRUCE, airline pilot; b. Feb. 28, 1941, Sargent, Nebr.; s. Ralph Ford and Irene Viola (Shively) Y.; m. Gaylene Louise Johnson, Jun. 11, 1961; children: Voni, b. 1963; Jeffery, b. 1964; edn: BS in B.A., Univ. Nebraska 1964; lic. pvt./comml./airline transport pilot. Career: combat pilot B-52 SAC March AFB, Riverside 1965-69; pilot Boing 737 1st ofcr. Western Airlines, Los Angeles 1969--; handicrafter of (collector, heirloom) full size walnut or oak cradles & rocking horses; awarded Regents Scholarship, Univ. Nebr.; mem Airline Pilots Assn.; mil: capt. USAF 1965-69, US Air Med. 5 Clusters, Vietnam Svc.; Methodist; rec: woodcraftsman. Res: 1021 Loma Vista Dr Napa 94558

YOUNGDAHL, PAUL FREDERICK, mechanical engineer; b. Oct. 8, 1921, Brockway, PA; s. Harry Ludwig and Esther Marie (Carlson) Y.; m. Elinor Louise Jensen, Nov. 27, 1943; children: Mark Erik, b. 1949; Marcia Linnea, b. 1952; Melinda Louise, b. 1954; edn: BSE (ME), Univ. Mich. 1942, MSE (ME), 1949; PhD, 1961. Career: indsl. and devel. engring., E. I. duPont deNemours, Bridgeport, Conn, 1942-43; Carney's Point, NJ 1946-48; dir. research Mechanical Handling Systems, Detroit, Mich, 1953-62; prof. mechn. engring. Univ. Michigan, Ann Arbor 1962-74; ind. mechn. engr.; Palo Alto 1974--; dir. Liquid Drive Corp., Holly, Mich.; guest lectr., vis. prof. sev. univs.; honors: Tau Beta Pi, Phi Kappa Phi, Pi Tau Sigma, Sigma Xi; mem: Am. Soc. of Mech. Engrs., Mich. Soc. of Profl. Engrs., Nat. Soc. of Profl. Engrs., Am. Soc. for Engring. Edn.; publs: Tool Engineers Handbook, Mat. Handling chpt. 1959, contbr. to profl. confs., journals, and engring. standards; mil: lt. USNR 1943-46; Republican; Methodist. Address: 501 Forest Ave Ste. 1002, Palo Alto 94301

YOUNGER, EVELLE JANSEN, lawyer, former state attorney general; b. June 19, 1918, NE; s. Harry C. and Maebel (Jansen) Younger; edn: AB and LLB, Nebr. Univ., 1940; grad. work in criminology, Northwestern Univ. Law ch.; m. ildred Eberhard, July 3, 1942; chil: Eric, Los Angeles Superior Ct. Judge. Career: special agent, FBI, 1940-46; admitted to Calif. Bar, 1946; dep. city atty., Criminal div., Los Angeles, 1946-47; city prosecutor, 1947-50; pvt. practice law, Los Angeles, 1950-53; judge L.A. Municipal Ct., 1953-58; elected Judge of Superior Ct., 1958-64; elected dist. atty., Los Angeles Co., 1964-71; elected Calif. Atty. General, 1970, 1st Republican Atty. Gen. since 1947; re-elected 1974; Repub. nominee for Gov. of Calif., 1978; pvt. practice law with Buchalter, Nemer, Fields, Chrystie &Younger, Los Angeles, 1979--; fellow, Amer. Coll. of Trial Lawyers. Mem: Amer. Bar assn., chmn. Crminal Law Sect. 1962-63; chmn., Pres. Reagan's Task Force on the Adminstrn. of Justice, 1980; State Bar of Calif.; Natl. Dist. Attys. Assn.; L.A. Lawyers Club

L.A. Peace Officers Assn., past pres.; Soc. Former FBI Agents, past chmn.; Masons; Shriners; Amer. Legion; Elks; Alpha Tau Omega frat.; Air Force Assn.; British United Services Club; Trojan Club, dir. Mil: Pvt. to Maj., US Army, 1942-46; Lt. Col., USAF, 1951-52; MajGen., USAFR; served in China, Burma, India Theatres WWII, Korean Conflict. Episcopalian. Office: Buchalter Nemer Fields Chyrstie & Younger, 7th Flr., 700 S. Flower St., Los Angeles 90017.

YOUNT, LUCY BARRINGER, writer, interior/industrial designer; b. Jul. 4, 1925, Columbia, SC; d. Victor Clay and Gertrude Ruffini (Hampton) Barringer; m. Barton Kyle Yount, Jr., Apr. 25, 1944; children: Bartin Kyle III, b. 1945; Victor Clay, b. 1947; edn: Stephens Coll. 1941-43. Career: exporter of Spanish antiques, Madrid, Spain 1966-75; women's ed. Iberian Daily Sun (sole Eng. lang. daily newsp. in Spain), 1968, soc. ed. 1969-70; fashion designer for Elizabeth Arden boutique, Madrid 1970-72; tobacco agent in Spain, Dickerson Leaf Tobacco Co. of Richmond, Vir., 1970-75; interior decorator, Marbella, Spain 1973-75, Los Angeles 1975-82; partner/indsl. designer Patric Interiors 1980--; honors: Nat. 1st prize in Dress Design, Butterick Pattern Co., 1942; mem: John Tracey Clinic Womens Aux. (bd. dir. 1976-8, 82); Footlighters, Inc. (prodn. com. 1981-82); Sunset Repub. Club, Sierra Club; Republican; Episcopal; rec: skiing, hiking, tennis. Res: 2812 Bottlebrush Dr Los Angeles 90024 Ofc: Patric Interiors, 1413 Cloverfield Blvd Santa Monica 90404

YOUNT, STUART, manufacturing company executive; b. Mar. 4, 1949, San Marino; s. Stanley G. and Agnes (Pratt) Yount; edn: Univ. of Nev., Reno, 1968; UCLA, 1972; m. Geraldine Silvio, July 18, 1970; chil: Trisha, b. 1974; Chirsopher, b. 1977. Career: salesman, Silverwoods, 1968; with Fortifiber Corp., Los Angeles, 1969---; mgmt. trainee 1969, asst. to v.p. for sales 1969-72, asst. to v.p./asst. treas. 1972, currently v.p./adminstrn./secty./treas./dir. 1974---; pres., Holister Ranch Cooperative, 1979-81, treas. 1977-79. Mem: Rotary Club of Los Angeles; Jonathan Club; San Marino City Club. Republican. Protestant. Res: 684 Winston Ave., San Marino 91108; Office: Fortifiber Corp., 4489 Bandini Blvd., Los Angeles 90023.

YSLAS, HENRY, city wastewater management exec.; b. Nov. 12, 1931, Los Angeles; s. Pedro Velasco and Carmen Gonzalez (Mesa) Y.; m. Emily Alcarcon Sanchez, Nov. 30, 1956; children: Henry Jr., b. 1954; Sylvia, b. 1957; Stephen, b. 1958; edn: Ventura Coll. 1953-54; spl. courses, Internat. Corresp. Sch. 1969, Internat. City Mgmt. Assn. 1972, San Marcos Tng. Ctr. 1975, CSU Sacramento 1976, UC. Ext. 1980, Wastewater Internat. 1982, UCSB 1983. Career: w/ City of Oxnard, 1956-: wastewater collection empl. 1956-58, sewer maint. II 1958-64, foreman 1964-81, supvr. 1981--; awards: City of Oxnard 25 Years Svc. Pin; mem: Calif. Water Palution Control Assn. 1971; Latin Am. Veteran Club; mil: Staff Sgt., US Army 1950-53, Korean Vet.; rec: sports, camp, fish. Res: 1030 Poplar Oxnard 93030 Ofc: City of Oxnard, 305 W 3rd Street Oxnard 93030

YUAN, TAI-AN, engineer; b. July 10, 1950, Taiwan, ROC, nat. 1980; s. Yiehjen and Feng-lin (Li) Yuan; m. ElaineChan, July 2, 1981; edn: BSME, Fengchia Univ. 1976; MSME, Univ. Tex., Arlington 1979; Reg. Mech. Engr., Calif. 1982; Reg. Control System Engr., Calif. 1984. Career: mech. engr. Yandell &: Hiller Consulting Engrs Inc., Ft. Worth, Tex. 1979-81; engr. Bechtel Power Corp., San Francisco 1981-83, sr. engr. Bechtel Civil & Mineral Inc., S.F. 1983--. Mem. Am. Soc. Htg., Refrig., and Air Conditioning Engrs.; sr. mem. Instrument Soc. of Am. Publs: resrch art., sci. jour. 1979. Res: 801 Franklin St. #620 Oakland 94607 Ofc: Bechtel Civil & Mineral Inc, 185 Berry St, San Francisco 94107

YUE, ALFRED SHUI-CHOH, materials scientist-engineer; b. Nov. 12, 1920, Canton, China, nat. 1961; s. Noon W. and Sze K. (Tom) Y.; m. Virginia C., May 23, 1944; children: Mary W. Yuan (PhD), b. 1945, John T. (PhD), b. 1946, David T. (MD and PhD), b. 1957; edn: BS, Chiao-Tung Univ. (China) 1942; MS, Ill. Inst. of Tech. 1950; PhD, Purdue Univ. 1956. Career: metallurgist Pettibone & Mulliken Corp., Chgo. 1950-51; instr. Purdue Univ., 1952-56; research engr. The Dow Chem. Co., Midland, Mich. 1956-62; research scientist, staff scientist, senior mem. Lockheed Palo Alto Research Labs., 1962-69; prof. engring. and applied sci., UC Los Angeles 1969--; cons. Lockheed Research Labs 1969-70, LTV 1971, ARCO 1982-83, Textron, 1975; honors: NASA Skylab Achievement Award 1975, NASA Apollo-Soyuz Achievement Awd. 1976, Hon. Professor of Xian Chiao-Tung Univ. 1980, chair-prof. National Tsing Hwa Univ., Taiwan, ROC 1975; mem: NY Acad. Scis. 1972-78, Am. Soc. for Metals, AIAA 1972-76, Am. Inst. of Mining & Metallurg. Engrs., AAAS, Inst. of Metals (Eng.) 1954-74, Am. Soc. of Crystal Growth, Materials Research Soc., Scholastic Soc. of Am. (pres. 1979-83); dir. United Chinese Am. League; dir. Chinese Culture Assn.; 3 Patents; Republican; Prot.; rec: swimming, gardening. Res: 2583 Cordelia Rd Los Angeles 90049 Ofc: Univ. of California 405 Hilgard Ave, Los Angeles 90024

YUEN, RAY, purchasing executive; b. Apr. 10, 1934, Honolulu, Hawaii; s. Robert and Ivy (Ching) Y.; m. Marilyn Liu, Jul. 6, 1957; children: Doug, b. 1959; Annette, b. 1961; John, b. 1964; edn: BBA, Univ. Hawaii 1956; JD, Golden West Univ. Sch. of Law 1980; spl. courses, Pasadena City Coll.; postgrad., UCLA 1982-; Cert. Profl. Contract Mgr. (CPCM), Nat Contract Mgmt. Assn. (NCMA); Cert. Purch. Mgr. (CPM), Nat. Assn. Purch. Mgmt. (NAPM). Career: in chg. US Army Edn. Ctr., 1956-58; lead buyer new bus. research proposals, The Boeing Co., Aerospace Div., Seattle, Wn. 1958-63; buyer, Gen. Dynamics/Pomona, Pomona 1963-64; paralegal, Law Ofc. L.E. Kellogg, Glendale 1975; intern Wkrs. Comp. Appeals Bd. 1976; mgr. purch./subcontracts Calif. Inst. Tech., Pasadena 1964--; instr. bus./ indsl. mgmt. Calif Comm.

Colls.; adv. bd. Northrop Univ. Sch of Law; mem. adv. coms. Pasadena City Coll.; honors: NCMA Council of Fellows. Mem: Asian Bus. Assn., Calif. Higher Edn. Assn. Purchasers, Caltech Mgmt. Club, Delta Theta Phi, Jt. Conf. for Increased Use of Minority Bus., Nat. Assn. of Ednl. Buyers, NAPM, NCMA, Purch. Mgmt. Assn. of LA, So. Cal. Regl. Purch. Council; arts. in profl. journals; mil: US Army, 1956-58; Republican; Congregational; rec: tennis, swimming, guitar. Res: 235 S. Parkwood Ave Pasadena 91107 Ofc: CalTech, 1201 E California Blvd Pasadena 91125

YUH, LUNDAR YEOU-YU, chemical engineer; b. Dec. 30, 1946, Shanghai, China, nat. 1973; s. Ding. Hsuan and Yung Yu (Koo) Y.; m. Elizabeth Pascual, Jan. 20, 1974; children: Jia-Ann, b. 1974; Jia-Lynn, b. 1976; Jia-Juh, b. 1983; edn: BS, Feng-Jia Univ. 1970; MS, Columbia Univ., 1972; MS, N.E. Mo. State Univ. 1973. Career: piping engr. Fluor Corp., 1975-78; owner/pres. United Investment Group (R.E. inv., land devel.), Los Angeles 1978--; chmn. So. Calif. Chinese Engring. Assn. 1978; dir. Far East Real Estate Investment and Syndication; awards: top producer, Kashu Realty Co., 1979, 80, 81; author: Spoken American Slang; Bassic English Grammar; Modern English Dialog. Res: 142 N Ardmore Los Angeles 90004 Ofc: United Investment Group, 1350 Wilshire Blvd Los Angeles 90057

YURMAN, HERMAN WALTER, financial services executive; b. Feb. 4, 1920, Brklyn.; s. Samuel J. and Fannie (Margolis) Y.; m. Phyllis L. Corino, June 9, 1945; children: Lynda (Pite), b. 1946, Bruce, b. 1950; edn: BS in B.A., National Univ., Wash DC, MS in fin. plg.; PhD, Internat. Univ., K.C., Mo.; hon. PhD, fin. adm., Univ. of Sarasota, Fla.; Cert. Fin. Planner, Coll. Fin. Plg., 1973. Career: Reg. prin. firm Raymond James, St. Petersburg, Fla. 1966-70; v.p. Delta Plng. Corp. of Am., St. Pete., 1968-70, pres. 1970-71; v.p. Petro-Lewis Securities Corp., Denver, Co. 1970-73; pres. Alpha/Omega Planning Corp., St. Petersburg, Fla. & Solana Bch., Ca. 1973-83; pres. Incap Advisory, Inc., Salt Lake City, Utah 1983--; pres. First Capital Fin. Services Inc., Newport Bch. 1983--. Mem: Internat. Assn. for Fin. Plg. (chmn. bd. College for Fin. Plg., bd. regents, v.chmn. of academics); fmr. mem. Kiwanis, CofC, Optimist, Jr. CofC. Author three books in fin. plg. (1972, 76, 78); mil: 1st sgt. Army Aircorps, US Inf. 1941-45, Africa, Italy, Combat Inf. Badge, Bronze Star; Republican; Jewish. Res. 930 Via Mi Cumbres, 201C, Solana Bch 92075 Ofc: First Capital Fin. Svcs Corp. 4000 MacArthur Bl Newport Bch

Z

ZACKS, HYMAN JOSEPH, certified public accountant/lawyer; b. March 22, 1938, Brklyn; s. Archie B. and Fannie Zacks; div.; chil: Michelle, b. 1975; Michael, b. 1978; Steven, b. 1978; edn: BS in B.A., Denver Univ. 1959; JD, N.Y. Univ. 1963, LLM in taxation, 1966. C.P.A., Calif. 1974, N.M. 1982, Tex. 1983. Career: partner, Levitz, Zacks & Ciceric, Inc., San Diego 1972--; admitted to Tax Court of US, 1967, NY State Supreme Ct., 1967, US Supreme Ct., 1970. Instr. in Fed. Income Tax Acctg., Univ. Calif. Ext. 1975-81; instr. Acctg. for Lawyers, Calif. Cont. Edn. of the Bar, 1982. Mem: Am. Assn. of Atty.-CPAs Inc.; Am. Inst. of CPAs; Calif. Soc. of CPAs. ofc: Levitz, Zacks & Ciceric Inc. 701 B St, 4th Flr. San Diego 92101

ZAIDI, SYED G., company president; b. June 10, 1945, Jaipur India; s. Hakeem M. and Asalat (Khan) Z.; m. Olga Moya, Jan. 5. 1971; children: Sara, b. 1972; Alia, b. 1975; Neal (adopted), b. 1968; Aysha, b. 1983; edn: BSEE; Oklahoma State Univ., 1971. Career: research engr. Victor Comptometer, Chicago, Ill., 1971-73; mgr. logic design, Bunker Ramo Corp., Trumbull, Conn., 1973-75; mgr. electronics design, Olivetti Corp., Harrisburg, Penn., 1975-78; mgr. prods./bus. planning, Olivetti, Cupertino, 1979; pres./CEO, Alphacom Inc., Campbell 1980; dir. Alphacom Inc.; awards: dean honor roll, OSU; Redskin (yearbook) Congratulate OSU; mem: pres. Internat. Student Assn. OSU 1970-71; pres. Pakistan Student Assn. OSU 1970-71; Muslim. Res: 895 Highland Cir Los Altos 94022 Ofc: Alphacom Inc., 2323 So. Bascom Ave Campbell 95008

ZALE, STEVEN JEFFREY, company executive; b. Oct. 12, 1955, Sioux City, Iowa; s. Isaac and Florence J. (Leviton) Z.; m. Cynthia Anne, Oct. 24, 1981; edn: AA, Santa Monica Coll., 1979. Career: salesperson Zales Jewelers, N. Hollywood, 1979-81; mgr. Zales Jewelers, Panorama City, 1981-83; founder, xchmn. bd. S.J. Zale & Co. Fine Jewelers (3 store chain), Los Angeles, 1983--; awards: Zales Top Architect of year; Zales Mgmt. Supr. of year; Debeers Diamond Salesman of year 1983; Designer of year 1984; mem: founder/pres. Essex Limousines; CofC; Democrat; Jewish; rec: boating. Res: Los Angeles Ofc: S.J. Zale & Co. Fine Jewelers, 15014 Ventura Blvd Sherman Oaks 91403

ZALOUMIS, CHARLES PETER, financial services co. executive; b. Dec. 1, 1936, New London, Conn.; s. Peter Charles and Viola V. (Fortinalis) Z.; m. Sarah Josephine Purdy, May 24, 1975; children: Dawn, b. 1957; Peter, b. 1959; Christopher, b. 1976; Nicole, b. 1980; edn: BS, Univ. Nebr. 1963; MBA, American Univ. 1968; Nat. Assn. of Securities Dealers, SEC Reg. Investment Adviser; Ins. lic. Career: enforcement ofcr. Securities and Exchange Commn., Wash DC 1963-68; v.p./financial prin. Travelers Equity Sales, Inc., Hartford, CT. 1968-71; pres./dir. Computech Fund Svc., Inc., Atlanta, GA 1971-72; v.p. Central Banking Systems, Inc. 1972-77; pres./dir. Cenval Agency, Inc. 1972-77; v.p./sr. trust officer Central Bank, Oakland 1972-77; pres./chmn. bd. The

Centrecorp Cos. 1977--; mem./chmn. Diablo West Finance Com.; mil: E-5 USAF, GCM; Democrat; Greek Othodox; rec: tennis, Little League coach. Res: 693 Contada Cir Danville 94526 Ofc: Centrecorp, 2001 Franklin St, Ste 200 Oakland 94612

ZAMPARELLI, MARIO ARMOND, artist-designer; b. June 4, 1927, NYC; s. Levcio and Giovanina (Ianiri) Z.; chil: Regina Neliya, b. 1959, Marisa Nina, b. 1964, Andrea Laura, b. 1967; edn: Pratt Inst. Career: artist, designer, N.Y.: contbr. Cosmopolitan, Esquire, Coronet, Colliers mags.; artist/designer, excl. contract, cons. to Howard R. Hughes and design cons. to Summa Corp. and multi-divs.; currently pres. Mario Armond Zamparelli and Co.; pres. Art Index, Inc. 1971-; pres. Orients Agcy. 1982-; prof. communication design Otis Parson Art Inst.; W.Coast editl. advisor Interiors Mag., NY. Awards: Haskell Travel Fellowship, Pratt Inst., J.W. Alexander Medal 1942, Paul Hoffman Gold Medal 1938. Mem. Art Directors Club, Los Angeles. Works: Office of the Future Project, Interiors Mag. 1981-2; Home of the Future, G.E., Epcot, corporate identity projects: Summa Corp., Hughes Airwest, Hughes Helicopters, Hughes Airwest Midway Airlines. Mil: served in US Third Army, ETO; Republican; Catholic; rec: art collector. Res. 555 Mesa Lila Rd. Glendale 91108 Ofc: Mario Armond Zamparelli & Co. POB 264 Verdugo Hills

ZAMZOW, CLAUDIA GOOCH, needle art designer; b. Aug.2, 1936, Day, Calif.; d. Rush Potter and Lila Adeline (Marvin) Gooch; m. Dale Zamzow, Dec. 15, 1962; edn: BA in costume design, Shasta Coll. 1956; BA in costume design, Calif. Coll. of Arts & Crafts, 1957; BA, design, CSU San Jose, 1962. career: profl. doll designer, developing original designs for lmtd. edition collections and licensed mfr., 1968--; curator, Bear Force Mus., San Jose 1982--; tchr., lectr., workshop leader in needle arts and lacemaking, 1978-; needlework appraiser, 1976-83; textbk. reviewer, Peninsula Lace Mavericks, 1980, 81; honors: commnd. to design teddy bear for HRH Prince William of Wales, 1982; awarded Master Bear Artist certification, 1982. mem: United Fedn. of Doll Clubs, Internat. Old Lacers, Nat. Assn. of Miniature Enthusiasts, Embroiderers Guild of Am. (charter mem.) Peninsula Lace Mavericks, (founder) Contemporary Doll Artists Guild, (founder) Santa Clara Doll Collectors, (founder, charter) The Lace Mus., (founder, charter) Doll Fashion Study Club of No. Calif. works: solo shows: Tapestry in Talent, San Jose 1979, 80; devel. trademarks: Needlemaid, U.S. Bear Force, P.W.Bear; Christian; rec: costume collections, hist. of costume research; ofc: POB 4610, Santa Clara 95054.

ZAMZOW, DENNIS ROBERT, podiatrist; b. Apr. 30, 1944, Ripon, WI; s. Arthur Robert and Charlotte Gwendolyn (Deibert) Z.; Electronics Techn. Sch., Great Lakes, Ill. 1962-63; Submarine Sch., New London, Conn. 1963; Inertial Navigation Computer Sch., Virginia Bch, VA 1963-64; Adv. Electronics Tchn. Sch., Treasure Island, San Francisco 1966-76; Coll. San Mateo, 1971-73; Doctor of Podiatric Medicine, Coll. Calif. Podiatric Medicine, 1973-76; svc. man on Nuclear Powered Polaris Missile Submarines, 1962-70; med. staff. Valley West Hosp., Mt. View and El Camino Hosp., Los Gatos 1970-76; private practise Doctor of Padiatric Medicine, Mt. View 1976--; founder/pres./dir Calif. Road Runners Running Club, 1978; past instr.(marathon training) De Anza Coll , Cupertino 1980-81; adv. Calif. Governor's Council on Wellness & Physical Fitness; vice chn. The Athletics Congress (TAC) Pacific Assn.; Lectr.; marathoner, ultramarathoner; pbls: for Runners World Mag., Runners Knee May 1980, Surgery and the Runner Nov. 1981, Orthotics Jun. 1982, Sciatica Aug. 1982, and Plantar Fasciitis, Feb. 1983; Runners World Foot Care Book, Anderson Pbls. Co., 1982; arts. in Sports Unlimited Newspaper, San Jose; arts. in Decathlon Club monthly newsletter, Santa Clara; mil: USN 1962-70; rec: private pilot, running, weightlifting, guitar. Res:11700 Upland Way Cupertino 95014 Ofc: 2500 Hospital Dr, #9 Mtn View 94040

ZANDBERG, CHARLES MARTIN, executive vice president; b. Dec. 19, 1936, Chicago, Ill.; s. Paul I. and Rena Z.; m. Kyra, Dec. 25, 1971; cihldren: Lisa Anne, b. 1974; Morgana, B. 1967; edn: D.Pharm., USC 1961; lic.pharmacist, 46 states. Career: pharm., 3 locations, 1961-; restaurant owner 1974-, Sizzler Rest. prin. 1979-, v.p. franchise ops. A&W Rest. Inc. 1982--; mem: CofC; Optimist Club (v.p.). Res: 11840 Babbitt Ave Granada Hills 91344

ZARUBICA, MLADIN, company president; b. Jan. 4, 1917, Long Beach; s. Sako and Lubjica (Rapovac) Z.; chil: Karyn, b. 1951, Shawne, b. 1953, Tadd, b. 1955, Darryl, b. 1958, Fionn, b. 1962; edn: BA eng., UCLA 1940, MBA eng., 1945; Dartmouth Grad. Sch., and Princeton Grad. Sch., 1942; lic: Constrn. Engr. 1948, Engring. lic. 1951. Career: credit ofcr/S.Am. Dist., First Nat. City Bank, NYC; European Div. dir. Coca-Cola Co., NYC; current: founder/pres. Zarubica Co., Los Angeles; pres. Zarubica Co. Internat., L.A.; cons: Consol. Coal Co., Coca-Cola Co., Du Pont, Conico, Beatrice Food. Dir. Metropolitan Water Dist. (5 yrs); mem. President's Adv. Council (1983), Blue Shield (dir. 1982-3), Underground Engineering (dir. 1955-70). Awards: Freedoms Found Awd., 1953-Electric Cos. Public Info. Pgm.; National Football Hall of Fame (1980); Engineer of the Yr. 1982, UCLA. Author: The Year of the Rat (Harcourt & Brace) best seller 1967; Voice From Another Season (Pier) 1970; Scutari (Farrar-Straus) 1969. Mil: lt.cdr. USN 1942-6; Republican; rec: art, ship models. Address: Los Angeles, Calif.; London, Eng

ZAVALA, ROXANNE MARIE, financial consultant; b. Sep. 7, 1952, Mexico City, Mexico; s. Salvador A. and Doris M. (Lynch) Z.; edn: BBA, UC Fullerton 1975; MBA, USC 1977. Career: accnt./computer coordinator VSI Recreational Products 1972-75; staff accnt. So. Calif. Rapid Transit 1975-76; planning analyst Dart Ind. 1977-78; sr. planning analyst, AM Internat. Inc. 1978-79; mgr.

bus. planning and dir. mgmt. info. systems AM Internat. Jacquad Systems Div. 1980-82; pres. Epic Systems 1982--; financial adv. Anoroc Co. 1978-; honors: Consortium for Grad. Study in Mgmt. 1976; Nat. Honor Soc. 1966-70; Class Valedictorian 1970; Student Body Pres.; mem: Commerce Assocs.; Consortium; CSUF Alumni Assn.; Gardena Valley CofC; Democrat; Catholic; rec: sports, scuba, reading. Res: 5781 Parkhurst Pl Yorba Linda 92686 Ofc: Epic Systems, 431 E Redondo Beach Blvd, Ste. 1A Gardena 90248

ZEE, FRANK WILLIAM, food co. executive; b. Dec. 22, 1927, Shanghai, China, nat. 1956; s. David T.Y. and Lucille S.F. (Lee) Z.; m. Maimie Louie, Dec. 17, 1955; children: Roland, b. 1957; Ramona, b.1960; edn: BA, UC Berkeley 1952; BS, UC Davis 1954; inst. food technologists. Career: jr research chem. Gerber Products Inc., Oakland 1952-53; quality control spvr. Gallo Wincry, Modesto 1954 55; quality assurance mgr. Hunt Wesson Foods (NSI), Hayward and Davis, 1955-67; dir. QA Kern Foods Inc, Industry 1967-79; v.p. Kern Foods Inc., R&D and Govt. Contracts, Industry 1979--; mem. Inst. of Food Technologists; Republican. Res: 1713 Longwood Ave Claremont 91711 Ofc: Kern Foods Inc., 1300 E Temple Ave Industry 91749

ZEICHNER-DAVID, MARGARITA, biochemist; b. July 20, 1946, Hungary; Mexican cit., permanent res. USA; d. Luis and Laura (Gancz) Zeichner; m. Michael M. David, Jan. 2, 1979; 1 son, Jason William, b. 1982; edn: Profl. Degree (cum laude) Iberoamericana Univ., Mexico City 1968; PhD in cell biol., Inst. Politecnico Nac., 1974; postdoctoral fellow, NIH Nat. Inst. of Dental Resrch., Lab. of Devel. Biology and Anomalies, 1974-77. Career: research asst./assoc. prof. USC Sch. of Dentistry, 1977--, and faculty Graduate Pgm. in Craniofacial Biology, USC Graduate School, 1977--; honors: CONACYT Fellowship, Mexico City (1970-74), Fogarty Fellowship, NIH (1974-77); mem: AAAS, Am. Assn. for Dental Research, Am. Soc. for Cell Biology, Am. Soc. for Zoology, Sigma Xi; publs: contbr. num. book chapters, contbr. sci. & med. journals, profl. presentations. Res: Santa Monica 90403 Ofc: USC Ethel Andrus Gerontology Center, University Park, Rm 325, Los Angeles 90078

ZEIGLER, LORRI YAKOWICZ, clinical social worker; b. Aug. 31, 1939, New Castle, Penn.; d. William Vincent and Anna (Kahocka) Yakowicz; m. Roland R. Zeigler, Mar. 4, 1978; 1 dau: Maria, b. 1964 dec. 1983; edn: BA, cum laude, Youngstown State Univ. 1963; MSW magna cum laude, Univ. Pittsburgh 1969; PhD cand., UCLA Sch of Soc. Welfare 1983--; Calif. lic. clinical. soc. wkr. 1980. Career: unit supr. St. Peter's Child Devel. Ctrs. Inc., Pittsburgh, Penn., 1969-74; mental retardation coordinator Allegheny County, Pittsburgh 1974-75; regional coord. Title I, ESEA Projects, State Penn., 1975-76; chief soc. wkr. McGuire Memorial, Rochester, Penn. 1976-78; psychiatric soc. wkr. State Calif., Continuing Care Svcs. Branch, El Monte 1979-80, Lanterman State Hosp., Pomona 1980--; founder/chmn. bd. Found. for Continued Care and Learning, Inc., Pasdena 1983; field instr., CSU Long Beach 1982--; profl. cons. Calif. Dept. Developmental Svcs. 1981--; awards: NIMH fellowship 1977-79; mem: NASW 1970-; AAMD 1971-; Soc. Wkr. Profl. Group, Lanterman Hosp., chprsn. 1983; orgns: Casa Pasadena Homeowners Assn.; Assn. for Retarded Citizens (life); Children's Hosp. of San Diego (contbg. mem. assoc.); publs: arts. re Geroge Tarjan Research Ctr.; Republican; Catholic; rec: water sports, music, dance, travel, dining. Res: 1127 E Del Mar Blvd Pasadena 91106 Ofcs: Lanterman State Hospital, 3530 W Pomona Blvd, Program 3 Pomona 91769. Foundation for Continued Care and Learning, Inc., 1127 East Del Mar Blvd Pasadena 91106

ZEITLER, EDDIE LORENZ, information systems security executive; b. Aug. 24, 1943, Hollywood; s. Bill L. and Betty Eileen (Thomas) Z.; children: Viena, b. 1969, Erin, b. 1974; edn: BS, univ. of Ariz. 1968, MS 1970, postgrad. work 1971-73. Career: radar systems analyst ITT Gilfillan, Van Nuys 1970-71; computer performance analyst Rockwell Internat., Downey 1973-75; mgr. computer capacity mgmt. Transam. Info. Svcs., Los Angeles 1975-76; dir. Tech. Svcs., 1976-78, dir. Computer Ops., 1978-79, Federated Dept. Stores, Cincinnati; v.p./mgr. info. systems security Security Pac. Nat. Bank, Glendale 1979--; mem. Theta Tau, ACM, IEEE, L.A. County Computer Crimer Task Force, Am. Nat. Standards Inst.; vol. SecuriTeam, mem. Alpha Sigma Phi; NSF grantee (design file structures and info. retrieval system for arid lands studies) 1970; mil: A3C, USAF 1963-67; Baptist; rec: pilot, LA Zoo guide. Res: 520 So Sixth St. #R, Burbank 91501 Ofc: Security Pacific Nat. Bank, 701 No Brand, Glendale 91203

ZELLER, DAVID JAY, airport operator; b. May 18, 1951, Glendale, CA; s. Phillip Monroe and Eleanor (Gabriel) Z.; edn: BA, in pyschol., Phi Betta Kappa, Univ. of Hawaii 1973; pre-med, Idaho State Univ. 1973-74; San Fernando Valley Coll. of Law 1975-76; piano technician; tax counselor; lic. (airport) fixed base operator. Career: owner three post office box rentals, West Hollywood 1979--; acct. Wonder Bread, Beverly Hills 1976; piano tuner/techn. (clients incl. Neil Simon, Johnny Mathis, Johnny Ray, J.P. Morgan) 1976-; FBO/leasee 29 Palms Airport 1982--; tchr. piano; owner piano store, Maui, Hawaii; mem: Diamond Aviation Flying Club; Cauu Flying Club; counselor self realization/awareness 1979-; Republican; rec: flying, sailing. Res: P.O. Box 15 Joshua Tree 92252 Ofc: Diamond Aviation, Star Rt. 2, Box 688 29 Palms 92277

ZELLMER, NEALE ALBERT, electronic engineer; b. Oct. 17, 1921, Atlantic, Iowa; s. Albert Frank and Nellie Laura (Hansen) Z.; m. Arlene Hogueisson, Jun. 21, 1953; children: Alan, b. 1956; Scott, b. 1960; edn: chem./math, Upper Iowa Univ. 1938-42; BSEE, Iowa State Univ. 1947; MSEE, Stanford Univ. 1973. Career: engr. aide SPE, Signal Corp. Labs, Fort Mammoth, NJ 1942; radio and radar maint., AUS Signal Corp., Central Pac. Theater 1942-45; observer Cities

Svc. Seismograph Dept., W. Okla. and W. Texas 1947-51; electronic engr. Convair Corp., San Diego 1951-53; electronic engr., proj. engr., dept. mgr., sr. staff engr. in mfg. engring., devel. engr., and adv. devel. Lankurt Electric Co., San Carlos 1953-79; dept. engr., prin. engr., and FDM devel. Farinon Electric (Harris Corp.), San Carlos 1979--; honors: Phi Kappa Phi 1947; Eta Kappa Nu 1947; sr. mem. IEEE 1960; mem: IEEE 1946-; Presbyn. Marine Corvettes; Am. Legion 1978-; Belmont 4-H (sheep leader), asst. scout leader BSA 1971-3, Little League vol. 1972; works: 17 patents; 7 pub conf. papers and arts.; mil: I/5 US Army 1943-5, GCM; Republican; Presbyterian; rec: wood working, walking, history. Res: 1588 Harbor Blvd Belmont 94002 Ofc: Harris Corp., Farinon Div., 1620 Bayport San Carlos 94070

ZEMP, KERRY LLOYD, petroleum engineer; b. May 1, 1954, Oxford, England; s. Lloyd Joseph and Betty (Marshall) Z.; edn: BS, chem. engring., Univ. Oklahoma 1977; reg. profl. engr. 1982. Career: petroleum engr. Amoco Prod. Co., Liberal, Kansas 1977-80; petroleum engr. Ogle Petroleum, Santa Barbara 1980--; mem. planning comm. Univ. Kansas Gas Compressor Inst. 1979-80; awarded National Science Foundation Contest, team award SCORE- Student Competitions On Relevant Engring.; mem. Soc. of Petroleum Engrs.; rec: handball, swimming, reading. Res: 3146 Channel Dr Ventura 93003 Ofc: P.O. Drawer 30740 Santa Barbara 93130

ZIAS, ELINOR RHODA, realtor; b. May 4, 1938, NY, NY; d. John and Cecelia (Gross) Bibaz; m. Arthur Zias, Jan. 5, 1958; children: Jeff Alan, b. 1959, Sheryl Alison, b. 1962; edn: AA, Foothill Coll. 1981; lic. real estate broker, Calif. 1981. Career: secty. Sears Roebuck NYC 1956-60; office mgr. Cytopath Labs, Palo Alto 1969-77; realtor Coldwell Banker, Los Altos 1977--; num. sales/ achievement awards, Los Altos Bd. of Realtors, 1983, Coldwell Banker, 1978-, Million Dollar Club 1978, 100 Club, 1983. Mem. Los Altos Board of Realtors, Gourmet Club, Winetasting Club; rec: gourmet cooking. Res: 941 Oxford Dr Los Altos 94022 Ofc: Coldwell Banker, 301 So San Antonio Rd Los Altos 94022

ZIEGLER, REINHOLD PETER, industrial designer; b. May 21, 1947, Ansbach, W. Germany; s. Fritz Friederich and Marianne (Schuster) Z.; edn: stu. CalPoly Univ. 1965-67; BA in design, Calif. Inst. of the Arts, 1972; Calif. Comm. College Tchr. Credential (life) 1983. Career: involved with study of renewable energy systems 1972-, wk. on early solar concentrating collectors and wind-energy systems, resrch. & devel. team of Aero-Power Systems Inc. 1976, founder/pres., designer, dir. Earth Lab Institute (R&D appropriate technology hardware and solar demonstration projects) 1979--; cons. wind-energy systems to major energy developers; instr. university courses; tng. designer (CETA Tng. Pgm.) Farallones Inst., 1980; co-designer, proj. architect (Dept. of Energy grant) the first Wind-Energy Pavilion in world, Fort Funston, S.F. (1980); producer wind-energy documentary: The Windcatchers (Rockefeller Found. and Corp. for Public Bdcstg. grant) 1979; other video prodns: Quick City (1972), Seeds of the 60's (1974), Surviving in the 80's (1981); publs: Village One (1972), The Instant Theater (1974), The Wind-Energy Pavilion (pub. US DOE), Siting Water Pumping Windmills (pub. Action Peace Corps); Democrat; Lutheran; rec: computers, flying, sailing. Address: Earth Labs Inc. 1523 Fourth St, 2000, Berkeley 94710

ZIFFREN, LESTER, lawyer; b. Apr. 13, 1925, Davenport, IA; s. Jacob and Belle (Rosenberg) Z.; m. Paulette C. Rolando; chidren: Teri, b. 1955; Mimi, b. 1959; edn: BA, UCLA 1949; JD, UCLA Law Sch 1952. Career: dep. atty. gen. Calif. Dept. Justice, Atty. Gen. Office 1953-59; partner Greenberg, Ziffren & Slhafton 1959-61; partner Ziffren & Ziffren 1961-79; partner Gibson, Dunn & Crutcher 1979--; bd. dir. Far West Financial Corp. (NYSE) 1979-; bd. dir. Far West Savings & Loan Assn. (fmr. State Mutual S&L) 1979-; mem: State Bar Calif.; Los Angeles Co. Bar Assn.; Beverly Hills Bar Assn. (Law Found. bd. trustees); UCLA Found. (bd. visitors); UCLA Sch. Med. (pres. council); Brandeis Univ. (bd. dir.); Cedars-Sinai Med. Ctr. (exec. com., chmn. profl. programs com.); rec: tennis. Res: 623 North Hillcrest Rd Beverly Hills 90210 Ofc: Gibson, Dunn & Crutcher, 2029 Century Park E, 41st Flr Los Angeles 90067

ZIMMERMAN, REA, singer, vocal/speech teacher; b. Feb. 23, 1906, Phila.; d. Charles King and Reba Brice (Whitecar) Z.; edn: music stu., N.Y. Univ., pvt. instrn.: vocal, piano, harmony, singers' languages, stage, 1925-41. Career: soprano soloist in church, oratorio, concert and radio, NY area, 1927-41; soloist/ ensemble singer (in over 30 languages), tchr./dir. /actress, tour mem. cultural missions worldwide, 1941-64; instr. Up With People (prev. Sing-Out) casts 1965-72, pvt. vocal and speech tchr. home studio, Los Angeles 1973--; recipient top Vocal Summer Juilliard Scholarship 1931. Mem. Nat. Assn. of Teachers of Singing, Inc. (ofcr. L.A. chpt. 1971-5); publs: Sing Out Like Never Before (62 pg. voice prodn. handbk., pub. Up With People, 1968, 9th printing 1983; and companion cassette tape of same name, 1971, 9th ed. 1983); Republican; Episcopal. Address: 222 So Mariposa Ave Los Angeles 90004

ZINI, GILBERT Y., emergency physician: b. Sept. 27, 1943, Fes, Morocco, nat. 1975; s. Jacob and Fortunee (Assouline) Zini; Edn: Lycee Gouraux Rabat Morocco/Baccalaureat. Uiv. of Grenoble, 1964-67. Premed. Brussels med. sch. Belgium, 1968-73, MD. Med. Center Altoona Pa. 1973-74, Internship Jackson Med. School, Mess Res. Family Practice Bd. Certified E.D., 1981. named fellow ABEM; m. Camela Rosson, Apr. 8, 1967; chil: Miriam, b. 1968, Shannon, b. 1970, Lara, b. 1971. Career: Emergency Dept., physician Camp Pendleton, Calif., 1975-77, San Antonio Community Hosp. 1976-82 and presently Senior Physician ED Assist. Dir. ED, Instructor ACLS. advanced Cardiac Life Support Insttructor ATLS Advanced Trauma Life Support. Assist. Dir. Emergency department chmn. child abuse committee. Awards: physician recognition Award. 1977-80, Letter of Commendation/Navy, 1976. Mem: AAFP Amer. Academy Family Practice, ACEP Amer. Coll. of Emergency Physicaian, C.M.A., Calif. Med. Assn. San Bernardino County Medical Soc. J.C.E.M.A. Inland County Emerg. Med. Authority. Mil: Navy Lt. Cdr, 1975-77. Republican. Jewish. Rec: gardening. Res: 715 S. Quail Circle, Anaheim Hills 92807; Office: San Antonio Co. Hosp., Upland 91786.

ZOBRIST, DUANE HERMAN, lawyer; b. Sep. 11, 1940, Salt Lake City, Utah; s. Herman A. and Virginia (Rasmussen) Z.; m. Sharon, Jun. 26, 1964; children: Duane, b. 1967; Melinda, b. 1970; Darren, b. 1971; Brooke, b. 1974; Lindsay, b. 1977; edn: AB, Univ. Utah 1965; JD, USC 1968; atty. at law, Calif. Career: atty. Hill, Farrer & Burrill, 7 years; managing partner Sobrist, Vienna & McCullough; former pres./trustee Brazil Calif. Trade Assn.; USC Law Alumni (past pres.); pres. US-Mexico CofC; mem: Calif Stak Bar Assn.; Am. Bar Assn.; Foreign Law Assn. of So. Calif.; orgns: Boy Scouts of Am. (bd. dir./council v.p.), San Gabriel Valley Council; Pasadena Boys Choir (hd. major gifts); L.A. CofC; Town Hall; Foriegn Trade Assn.; Jonathan Club; Republican; Ch. LDS; rec: Marlin fishing, traveling. Res: 2101 Midlothian Dr Altadena 91001 Ofc: Zobrist, Vienna & McCullough, 515 S Figueroa St, 9th Flr Los Angeles 90071

ZOLG, ROBERT JOSEPH, stockbroker; b. Jan. 20, 1911, Dayton, Ohio; s. Joseph Clemens and Beulah Marie (Furnas) Z.; m. Jane Scott (div. 1948), Sep. 9, 1942; 1 dau: Roberta Carpenter, b. 1944; edn: BS, Univ. Dayton 1933; Reg. Rep., NYSE 1956. Career: loan officer various small loan cos. 1933-39; v.p. Valley Nat. Bank of Phoenix 1939-54; Dean Witter & Co. 1955-60; investments adv./sr. stock broker Paine, Webber, Jackson & Curtis; mem: Knights of Columbus; Elks; Oxnard Pioneer Cert.; author: Financing the Frontier (hist. of Valley Nat. Bank of Phoenix) 1953; mil: capt. US Army 1942-46, purple heart; rec: wood carving, hist. research. Res: 121 South F St Oxnard 93030 Ofc: Paine, Weber, Jackson & Curtis, 400 Esplanade Dr, Ste. 301 Oxnard 93030

ZONTELLI, BOYD ARTHUR, industrial real estate broker, company president; b. May 5, 1933, Brainard, Minn.; s. Henry Andrew and Clara (Boyd) Z.; m. Karyne Ventris, Jan. 20, 1967; children: Landi, b. 1968, Cheyenne, b. 1971; edn: St. Thomas Coll. 1951-2, Univ. of Vienna 1952-3, Mexico City Coll. 1953-4, USC 1954-55; Calif. lic. R.E. sales 1974, R.E. Broker 1980. Career: study in Germany (govt. study grant) of the Krupp Renn Process for transforming low grade iron ore into high grade iron, 1962; bd. chmn. Zontelli Western Mining Co., Page, Ariz. 1953-54; mgr. Zontelli Bros., Crosby, Minn. 1966-70; self-empl. research, mktg. feasibility study of the snowmobile market (for franchises) in Sweden and the Alpine Mountain Region, Sweden & Italy, 1971; ranching, 1972-73; real estate sales, 1974--; Century 21, Agoura, Calif. 1974-76, Cen. 21, Davies Oakleaf, 1977-81, self empl. R.E. Development, 1978 81, indsl. real estate broker 1982--; pres. Pet Health, Inc. 1982--; honors: traveled to Indonesia as personal guest of Pres. Sukarno; Top Producer, Top Lister sales awards, Cen. 21 (1974, 75, 76, 77); mem: San Fernando Valley Bd. of Realtors 1974-82, Conejo Valley Bd. of Realtors 1974-; pres./founder Endurance Horse Registry of Am., 1974-; bd. dirs. Am. Endurance Ride Conv. 1981-82; bd. dirs. Santa Monica Trails Council 1982-84; Agoura CofC; works: twice winner of the Tevis Cup 1979, 1981 (world's most challenging 100 mile endurance horserace; record-holder for fastest riding time on this course); mil: pvt. US Army 1957; Republican; Christian; rec: breeding Arabian horses for endurance racing. Res: 29474 Lake Vista Dr Agoura 91301 Ofc: Pet Health Inc. 28914 Roadside Dr, Ste F-4, Agoura 91301

ZUCKER, HAROLD GENE, computer software co. owner; b. Jun. 10, 1950, New York, NY; s. Leon William and Arline (Davidson) Z.; m. Lisa M. Zucker, Oct. 10, 1982; edn: AB in anthropology, Cornell Univ. 1972; MA (anth), SUNY at Buffalo, 1975; PhD, UC IRvine 1978. Career: public opinion analyst CBS News, New York 1978; dir. news research CBS owned television stations, NY 1978-80; research dir. ERA Research (later Audience Research & Development), San Francisco 1980-82; owner Creative Research Systems, San Francisco 1982--; guest Lectr. San Francisco State Univ. 1981; awards: student award Mass Communication Div., Internat. Comm. Assn. 1978; distinguished scholar fellowship, UC Irvine 1975; univ. fellowship SUNY at Buffalo 1974; mem: Am. Assn. for Public Opinion Research; Am. Mktg. Assn.; Internat. Comm. Assn.; Bay Chpt. Oceanic Soc.; creator: The Survey System -for using a Microcomputer to do market research; rec: stained glass, photo., tropical fish. Res: 1864 Larkin St San Francisco 94109 Ofc: Creative Research Systems, 1864 Larkin St San Francisco 94109

ZUKIN, JAMES HENRY, financial consultant; b. June 29, 1948, s. Dr. Paul and Mary Jane (Goldbloom) Z.; m. Sheri L. Saloff, Sept. 2, 1979; edn: BA in econ., UC Berkeley 1970; MBA, fin., Harvard Univ. 1972. Career: vice pres. Niederhoffer, Cross & Zeckhauser, NYC 1972-74; senior cons. Marshall & Stevens, Inc. Los Angeles 1975-76; prin., chmn. Exec. Com., Pick & Associates, Inc. Irvine, 1976--; founder, prin., Chief Licensing Ofcr., Pick Computer Works, Inc. Irvine 1976--; prin. Houlihan, Lokey, Howard & Zukin, Inc. Los Angeles 1976--; dir. Health Mgmt. Group, Inc. Piedmont; pres. Zukin Orgn., Los Angeles; mem: IEEE, University Assoc. Pepperdine Univ. 1980; mem. Employee Stock Ownership Plan Assn. of Amer. (founder/chmn. Valuation Adv. Com., chmn. Valuation Study Gp.); Jewish. Res: 1745 Correa Way Los Angeles 90049 Ofc: Houlihan, Lokey, Howard & Zukin Inc., 1930 Century Park West, 2nd Floor, Los Angeles 90067

ZUMBERGE, JAMES HERBERT, university president; b. Dec. 27, 1923, Mnpls.; s. Herbert Samuel and Helen (Reich) Z.; m. Marilyn Edwards, June 21, 1947; children: John Edward, b. 1948; JoEllen, b. 1951; James Frederick, b. 1953; Mark Andrew, b. 1954; edn: BA, Univ. Minn 1946, PhD, 1950. Career:

instr. Duke Univ. 1946-47; mem. faculty Univ. Mich. 1950-62, prof. geology 1960-62; pres. Grand Valley State Coll., Allendale, Mich. 1962-68; prof. geology/dir. Univ. Arizona Sch. Earth Sci., Tucson 1968-72; chancellor Univ. Nebraska at Lincoln 1971-75; pres. So. Methodist Univ., Dallas 1975-80; pres. Univ. of So. Calif., Los Angeles 1980--; bd. dirs. Pac. Lighting Corp., Security Pac. Corp., Sec. Pac. Nat. Bank, Litton Ind., and Nat. Merit Scholarship Corp.; mem. bd. overseers of Hoover Instn., and mem. The Conference Bd. Grand Valley State Colls. 1970; L.H.D., Nebr. Wesleyan Univ. 1972; LL.D., Kwansei-Gakuin Univ., Japan 1979; and D.Sc., Chapman Coll., 1982. Mem: Cons. Geologist ground water and nonmetallic minerals, 1950-62; chief glaciologist Ross Ice Shelf Proj., IGY 1957-58; Chmn. Ross Ice Shelf Proj. 1970-73; Nat. Sci. Bd. 1974-80; Sigma Xi (nat. lectr. 1978-80); Am. Geophysical Union; AAAS; Geological Soc. of Am. (fellow); Soc. of Economic Geologists; Internat. Glaciological Soc., Arctic Inst. No. Am.; Internat. Council of Scientific Unions (pres./ofcl. del. to Sci. Com. on Antarctic Research); Antarctic Adv. Com. to US State Dept.; clubs: Cosmos (Wash DC), University (NYC), California, Bohemian; author: 10 books incl. widely used text: The Elements of Geology, over 100 journal arts. and papers given at nat. and internat. meetings; mil: 2nd Lt., USMC 1943-45; Methodist; rec: woodworking, skiing, hiking. Res: 1550 Oak Grove Ave San Marino 91108 Ofc: USC, Office of the President, University Park, ADM 153 Los Angeles 90089

ZURAEK, MARIA ELNORA, real estate broker; b. Nov. 12 ,1939, Manila, Philippines; d. Angel Ignacio and Juanita (Ricacho) Covita; m. Claude Zuraek, Nov. 5, 1961; children: Ingrid, b. 1962; Lester, b. 1967; Zaida, b. 1973; edn: BA, civil engring., St. Mary's Coll. 1960; MA, Ateneo Univ. 1969. Career: coll. instr. St. Mary's Coll. and Univ. of the East, Philippines 1960-68; accnt. spvr. Army and Airforce Exchange Svc. 1968-78; personal investments 1978-80; real estate broker/mgr. Zuraek Properties, Hillsborough 1980--; mem. Mensa Internat.; publs: A Season of Grace, a critical study of N.V.M. Gonzales (Philippine studies) 1980; Democrat; Catholic; rec: reading financial and business literature. Address: Zuraek Properties, 15 Lohama Ct Hillsborough 94010

ZVONICEK, JAROSLAV, architect, b. Dec. 2, 1939, Stitna, Czechoslovakia; s. Jarozlav and Marie (Kruzelova) Z.; m. Dagmar Zvonicek, Aug. 4, 1965; children: Robert, b 1966; Daniel, b. 1973; Philip, b. 1975; edrn: MA, Tech. Univ., Brno, Czech. 1956-62; reconstruction and restoratioan Swedish heritage, AMU Sch. 1975; profl. engr. arch. Alexa, Dean 1962. Career: hd. arch. prod. Stavoproject, Ostrava, Czech. 1962-68; proj. arch. Noos Co., Norrkoping, Sweden 1969-71; proj. arch. Uddenburg-Hjelm Inc., Stackholm, Sweden 1971-72; proj. arch. MK Architects Inc, Stockholm 1972 74; dir. arch./owner Zak Architect Inc., Stockholm 1974-80; arch. designer Jacobs Engring. Group, Pasadena 1982--; arch./owner Z-Architectural Design, 1982--; prof. Djursholm Jr. Coll., Sweden; awarded 2d prize Internat Architl. Competition, Restoration of downtown Banska Bystrica, Czech. 1965; mem: Nat. Assn. of Swedish Architects 1973-; profl. architect in State Calif. lic. 13369; creative works: Boarding Sch. for disabled student, Karvina, Czech.; Kista Ch., Stockholm, Sweden; brewery plants, Nigeria, Africa; shopping center, Salhia, Kuwait; motel complex and coffee shop, Los Angeles. Address: Z-Architectural Design, 6744 Limerick Ave Canoga Park 91306

ZWEBEN, IRWIN WILLIAM, financial consultant; b. April 6, 1915, Poland; nat. 1940; s. Abraham and Leah Z.; m. Ida Lorman, March 15, 1947; 1 dau. Lois Jean, b. 1955; edn: BBA, City Coll. of NY, 1938; Certified Pub. Acct., NY, Calif., Wash. Career: self-empl. CPA, Los Angeles 1940-41; dir./ treas. West Coast Fast Freight, L.A. and Seattle, Wn., 1947-51; founder/ gen. partner Atlas Factors, L.A. 1952-65; adv. bd. City Nat. Bank, Beverly Hills 1966; vice pres. United California Bank (LA) 1965-66; founder/ pres. Washington Acceptance Corp., L.A. 1966--; honors: Man of Year 1982, City of Hope; listed Who's Who in The West (1950-); mem: Childrens Art Guild, Bnai Brith, Fund For Democratic Majority, United Jewish Welfare Fund, Coll. of City of N.Y. Alumni Assn., Univ. of Coll. of L.A. Alumni, Common Cause, City of Hope; clubs: Friars (Bev. Hills), Caballero CC, The Guardians; mil: pvt. to warrant ofcr. USAF 1942-46; Democrat; Hebrew; rec: fishing, golf. Res: 2800 Anchor Ave Los Angeles 90064 Ofc: Washington Acceptance Corp., 1180 So Beverly Dr Ste 508, Los Angeles 90035